MAGAZINES
FOR
LIBRARIES

This edition of
Magazines for Libraries 16th edition
was prepared by ProQuest's Serials Editorial Department

Editorial
Laurie Kaplan, Director, Serials
Nancy Bucenec, Ewa Kowalska, Valerie Mahon, Managing Editors
Christopher King, Senior Editor
Martha David, Quality Control/Technical Manager
Shawn Chen, Senior Associate Editor
Alayne Mundt and Pappaparvathi Partham, Associate Editors
Halyna Testerman, Filippo Valli, Michael Weingardner, and Jennifer Williams, Assistant Editors
O'Sheila Delgado, Editorial Coordinator
Elizabeth McKeigue, Enrique Diaz, and Christine Oka,
Assistant Editors, Content and Development

Production and Manufacturing Services
Doreen Gravesande, Director
Ralph Coviello, Manager, Manufacturing Services
Gunther Stegmann II, Project Manager, Production
Myriam Nunez, Project Manager, Content Integrity

Editorial Systems Group
Mark Heinzelman, Chief Information Officer
Frank Morris, Director
Youliang Zhou, Programmer Analyst

MAGAZINES
FOR
LIBRARIES™

SIXTEENTH EDITION

Edited by Cheryl LaGuardia

created by

Bill Katz

For the general reader and
school, junior college, college, university
and public libraries

Reviewing the best publications
for all serials collections
since 1969

Published by ProQuest LLC
Copyright © 2007 by ProQuest LLC
All rights reserved
Printed and bound in the United States of America

International Standard Book Numbers ISBN 10: 1-60030-105-3
ISBN 13: 978-1-60030-105-6
International Standard Serial Number 0000-0914
Library of Congress Catalog Card Number 86-640971

ISBN 13: 978-1-60030-105-6

CONTENTS

CONTENTS

PREFACE

Where Have All the Abstracts, Indexes, and Aggregators Gone?

As you will see, we don't have separate Abstracts and Indexes or Aggregators sections any longer in *MFL*. The reason? Over the years, we'd lost track of the chapter's reason for being, which was, logically, listing the Abstracts and Indexes named by chapter authors as basic indexes for their subjects. But that chapter grew and grew to include (arbitrarily) A&I that were never named in an *MFL* chapter, and then Aggregators were added – which made the chapter even larger and less connected to *MFL* actual content. So this year, we've gone back to the "roots" established by Bill Katz when *MFL* began, and we're listing in the front matter of the volume the Abstracts and Indexes (with web addresses) that are referenced within the book by the chapter authors. From reader, and author, feedback, this seems to make better sense – but please let me know if you want something different! (claguard@fas.harvard.edu)

That said, here is my list of the top 20 "big names" in journal delivery services that you will certainly want to be aware of:

Blackwell Synergy Online Journals
http://www.blackwell-synergy.com

Cambridge Journals Online
http://journals.cambridge.org

CSA Journals
http://www.csa.com/e_products/journals.php

EBSCOhost Electronic Journals Service
http://ejournals.ebsco.com

Emerald's Management Journals
http://www.emeraldinsight.com

HighWire Press
http://highwire.stanford.edu

IEEE Journals
http://www.ieee.org/web/publications/journmag/index.html

IGI Full-Text Online Journal Collection
http://fulltext.igi-online.com

IngentaConnect
http://www.ingentaconnect.com

JournalsOvid
http://www.ovid.com/site/catalog/journals_landing.jsp

JSTOR: The Scholarly Journal Archive
www.jstor.org

OCLC's Electronic Collections Online
http://www.oclc.org/ electroniccollections

Oxford Journals
http://www.oxfordjournals.org
(from Oxford University Press)

Project Muse: Scholarly Journals Online
http://muse.jhu.edu

SAGE Publications' SAGE Journals Online
http://online.sagepub.com

ScienceDirect Journals
http://www.sciencedirect.com

SpringerLink Journals
http://www.springerlink.com/home/main.mpx

Taylor and Francis Journals Online
http://www.tandf.co.uk/journals/online. asp

Thomson Scientific Journals
http://scientific.thomson.com/mjl

Wiley InterScience
http://www3.interscience.wiley.com

Transdisciplinarity and "Transproduct-Detachment" – New Wave Research

In the past several years or so, it has been irksome to see individual brands overwhelming content to the extent that, if a journal is being delivered by a certain publisher or platform-provider, their brand name overshadows completely the actual source being referenced online. Well folks, that is starting to change, as files merge and content is repackaged and delivered by different services – because with some systems, it had gotten to the point where nobody could tell where an article was coming from. Both in looking at e-journal delivery, and at databases I review, I'm seeing clearer provenance emerging online, either through automatic citing features (bless their hearts!) or clearer citation presentation. More and more online files are being developed to address the emerging "transdisciplinarity" of modern research (http://en.wikipedia.org/wiki/Trans disciplinary). I think that's because publishers are realizing that the more varied electronic conduits of delivery they can send their products through (aka, "transproduct-detachment"), the better their bottom lines will be – so long as they retain clear provenance of the material for authority.

The World of Open Access

. . . seems to be leveling off, at least in terms of overall numbers. As of this writing, the number of journals listed in the *Directory of Open Access Journals* (http://www.doaj.org/) is 2,868, up from 2,436 (as compared to last year's rise from 1,730 the year before). Of the 2,868 listed at DOAJ, 918 are searchable at the article level.

Meanwhile, the Public Library of Science (PLoS) once again is delivering the new open-access content they promised last year. Later this year they'll officially launch *PLoS Neglected Tropical Diseases* (see preview articles at http://www.plosntds.org) and they've already launched *PLoS ONE* (e-ISSN: 1932-6203), featuring pre-publication peer-reviewed reports of primary research from all disciplines within science and medicine, which, upon publication, are available for further community-based online review (guidelines for post-publication review are particularly of note; go to: www.plosone.org/static/commentGuidelines.action). There is a publication charge for articles here of USD 1,250 (discounts and fee waivers are available based on an author's ability to pay). For detailed information see: www.plosone.org/static/about.action.

If It Ain't Electronic – Don't Bother

Yes, we're there. Retrospective digitization of back issues of journals is in high gear among publishers of all sorts (professional, university, and society presses), since the demand for online access to full runs of journals among researchers is through the roof. Unfortunately, this continues to be a hit-or-miss proposition; some publishers are going full steam ahead with retrospective digitization, others seem to take the attitude, "let them eat cak . . . print!" And some do very good jobs with creating online archives, while others create rather clunky electronic products that don't deliver their content well. The only thing that seems certain is that the drive for digitization-in-full will continue, especially as technologies for both creating the digital copy and delivering it improve. And they will.

Some Things Don't Change – and I'm So Grateful

At this point in the Preface (and year), I do feel just a bit like Bing Crosby and Rosemary Clooney in *White Christmas* . . . counting my publishing blessings. And foremost among these are the chapter authors. I urge readers to take good note of the folks who create the chapters in *MFL* – their hard work, caring, and expertise make this unique volume the contribution to the profession, and to research, that it continues to be. Right up there with the chapter authors on my list are Nancy Bucenec at ProQuest (the best managing editor and *such* a good person), Laurie Kaplan, Director, Serials Editorial, and Yvette Diven, Director, Serials Product Management (excellent ProQuest folks who also bowl extremely well . . . but that's another story), and the assistant editors on my end: Enrique Diaz, Elizabeth McKeigue, and Christine Oka. Many thanks to all of you for bringing another volume of *MFL* into being. And as ever, thanks to the late, and sorely missed, Bill Katz for his teaching, support, vision, and dedication.

STATISTICS FROM THE SIXTEENTH EDITION

Statistical information on the content of *Magazines for Libraries* continues a feature first introduced in the twelfth edition. The presentation of this information on recommended titles and their publishers is provided as the basis for further analysis - not only of the titles included in or excluded from the current edition of *Magazines for Libraries*, but of trends in the serials publishing industry.

All data in the charts and tables should be evaluated by the individual reader within the context of his or her own collection decision-making.

A Closer Look at Publishers and Their Titles

This sixteenth edition includes 6,205 titles produced by publishers of all types and sizes - from large commercial publishers, society and association publishers and university presses, to publishing start-ups and newsletter self-publishers. Overall, 3,243 publishers and imprints are represented. While the vast majority of publishers are those with 4 or fewer titles in *MFL*, there are 130 publishers with 5 or more titles selected for this edition.

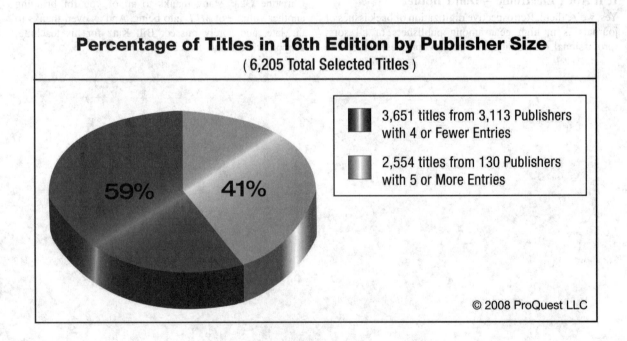

Percentage of Titles in 16th Edition by Publisher Size
(6,205 Total Selected Titles)

59%   41%

3,651 titles from 3,113 Publishers with 4 or Fewer Entries

2,554 titles from 130 Publishers with 5 or More Entries

© 2008 ProQuest LLC

The three columnar charts below illustrate the overall characteristics of the titles selected for this edition, noting the following key features: electronic format availability, refereed/peer-reviewed status, and inclusion in abstracting and indexing sources. The continued rise of online editions and the decline of CD-ROM as a delivery medium are evidenced across all publishing sectors.

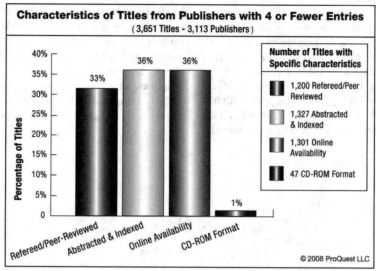

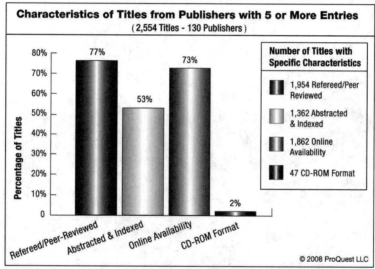

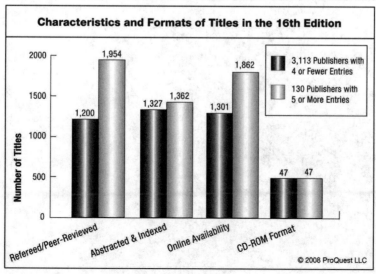

A focused analysis of the 130 publishers with 5 or more entries is provided in **Table 1**, which includes the number of selected titles by feature and format availability. **Table 1** also includes aggregate information on the titles from publishers with 4 or fewer entries.

Table 2 includes a report on the number of publishers in each *MFL* subject chapter. As a benchmark of journal availability and the specific recommendations of the subject section contributors, **Table 3** and **Table 4** contain lists of each of the titles deleted since the last edition of *MFL*, sorted by publisher and by *MFL* subject. The prior edition's record sequence number is provided in both tables to allow the reader to reference the complete listing for a specific title in the older edition.

Commercial Publishers of Scholarly Journals

It is not surprising to see the names and imprints of prominent commercial publishers among the companies with 5 or more entries in *Magazines for Libraries*. (See **Table 1**.) These names represent publishers in the professional publishing market with large portfolios of titles available for consideration - scientific/technical, legal, business, and medical journals utilized by university and college students, professionals in specific research disciplines, and consumers seeking authoritative sources of scholarly information. Many of these companies and their imprints are among the top journal publishers overall.

Table 2 / No. of Publishers by MFL Subject (cont.)

Section	No. of Publishers
NEWSPAPERS	13
NUMISMATICS	6
NURSING	6
OCCUPATIONS AND CAREERS	12
PALEONTOLOGY	19
PARAPSYCHOLOGY	10
PARENTING	22
PEACE AND CONFLICT STUDIES	18
PETS	24
PHILATELY	11
PHILOSOPHY	47
PHOTOGRAPHY	18
PHYSICS	18
PHYSIOLOGY	6
POLITICAL SCIENCE	33
POPULATION STUDIES	13
PREGNANCY	10
PRINTING AND GRAPHIC ARTS	25
PSYCHOLOGY	47
PUBLIC HEALTH	13
REAL ESTATE	12
RELIGION	57
ROBOTICS	21
SAFETY	9
SCIENCE AND TECHNOLOGY	29
SEXUALITY	24
SLAVIC STUDIES	26
SOCIOLOGY AND SOCIAL WORK	34
SPIRITUALITY AND WELL-BEING	16
SPORTS	76
STATISTICS	21
TEENAGERS	19
TELEVISION, VIDEO, AND RADIO	26
THEATER	42
TRANSPORTATION	71
TRAVEL AND TOURISM	17
URBAN STUDIES	28
VETERINARY SCIENCE	22
WEDDINGS	17
WORLD WIDE WEB	18
ZOOLOGY	15

Table 3 / Titles Deleted Since the Last Edition, by Publishers

Publisher	Title	ISSN	15th Ed. Sequence No.
A J Press	Animation Journal	1061-0308	2880
A M I - Weider Publications	Men's Fitness	0893-4460	3664
A Ross Eckler, Ed & Pub	Word Ways	0043-7980	4365
A S M E International	American Society of Mechanical Engineers. Transactions	0097-6822	2532
Academia Press	B E L L	1376-2958	4303
Academic Press	Computer Vision and Image Understanding	1077-3142	1672
Academic Press	Graphical Models	1077-3169	1680
Academic Press	International Journal of Human-Computer Studies	1071-5819	1692
Active Interest Media	Vegetarian Times	0164-8497	3135
Acumen Publishing Ltd	Critical Horizons	1440-9917	5909
African Studies Association	African Issues	0047-1607	362
American Chamber of Commerce of Mexico A.C.	Business Mexico	0187-1455	1270
American Chemical Society	Biotechnology Progress	8756-7938	2472
American Express Publishing Corp.	Travel & Leisure Family		6364
American Federation of Labor - Congress of Industrial Organizations Public Affairs Department	Work in Progress		4058
American Institute of Aeronautics and Astronautics, Inc.	A I A A Bulletin		328
American Institute of Chemical Engineers	Chemical Engineering Progress	0360-7275	2480
American Labor Conference on International Affairs, Inc.	The New Leader	0028-6044	4958
American Nuclear Society, Inc.	Fusion Science and Technology	0748-1896	2426
American Nuclear Society, Inc.	Nuclear News	0029-5574	2546
American Psychological Association	Monitor on Psychology	0001-2114	5573
American Public Human Services Association	Policy & Practice	0033-3816	5991
American Sociological Association	Journal of Health and Social Behavior	0022-1465	5929
America's Job Bank	America's Job Bank		5031
Arizona State University College of Education	Current Issues in Education	1099-839X	2360
Association for Supervision and Curriculum Development	Journal of Curriculum and Supervision	0882-1232	2227
Association for the Scientific Study of Consciousness	Psyche (Greenville, Online Edition)	1039-723X	5618
Association of Teachers of Mathematics	Micromath	0267-5501	1570
Athletic Insight, Inc.	Athletic Insight	1536-0431	5604
B M J Publishing Group	Injury Prevention	1353-8047	5750
Bahri Publications	Indian Journal of Applied Linguistics	0379-0037	4318
Begell House Inc.	Critical Reviews in Biomedical Engineering	0278-940X	2473
Beirut University College Institute for Women's Studies in the Arab World	Al-Raida	0259-9953	4768
Biblical Archaeology Society	B R	8755-6316	5654
BioMed Central Ltd.	B M C Psychiatry	1471-244X	5605

Publisher	Journal Title	ISSN	
BioMed Central Ltd.	Behavioral and Brain Functions		5607
BioMed Central Ltd.	Clinical Practice and Epidemiology in Mental Health		5609
Blackwell Publishing Ltd.	Bulletin of Economic Research	0307-3378	2098
Blackwell Publishing Ltd.	Expert Systems	0266-4720	1679
Blackwell Publishing Ltd.	Journal of Computer Assisted Learning	0266-4909	1694
Blackwell Publishing Ltd.	Social Policy and Administration	0144-5596	5951
Blackwell Publishing Ltd.	World Englishes	0883-2919	4366
Blackwell Publishing, Inc.	Language Learning	0023-8333	4343
Brill	Comparative Sociology	1569-1322	5907
Brill	Nin	1567-8474	3356
Brown University Division of Applied Mathematics	Quarterly of Applied Mathematics	0033-569X	4700
C K Media LLC	Quilter's Newsletter Magazine	0274-712X	1756
C K Media LLC	Quiltmaker	1047-1634	1757
Cambridge Center for Behavioral Studies	Behavioral Parenting Abstracts		5608
Cambridge University Press	Applied Psycholinguistics	0142-7164	4301
Cambridge University Press	English Language and Linguistics	1360-6743	4312
Cambridge University Press	English Today	0266-0784	4314
Cambridge University Press	International Phonetic Association. Journal	0025-1003	4323
Cambridge University Press	Journal of Child Language	0305-0009	4325
Cambridge University Press	Journal of French Language Studies	0959-2695	4328
Cambridge University Press	Journal of Social Policy	0047-2794	5939
Cambridge University Press	Nordic Journal of Linguistics		4354
Cambridge University Press	Phonology	0952-6757	4356
Catholics for a Free Choice	Conscience	0740-6835	1823
Center for Health, Environment, and Justice	Everyone's Backyard	0749-3940	2574
Center for Iranian Research and Analysis	Journal of Iranian Research and Analysis	1525-9307	4755
Christianity Today International	Christian Parenting Today	1065-7215	5080
Circuit Cellar, Inc.	Circuit Cellar	0896-8985	1665
Colegio Oficial de Psicologos	Psychology in Spain	1137-9685	5621
Conde Nast Publications, Inc.	Cargo	1547-8432	2767
Conde Nast Publications, Inc.	Gourmet	0017-2553	3132
Council of State Governments	Spectrum (Lexington)	1067-8530	3615
Crafts Council	Crafts	0306-610X	1727
Dictionary Society of North America	Dictionaries		4309
Dow Jones & Company	CareerJournal.com		5032
Eaglemoss Publications Ltd.	Real Robots		5740
Eating Well, Inc.	Eating Well	1046-1639	3130
Edicoes Colibri	Journal of Portuguese Linguistics		4336
Elsevier BV	Safety Science	0925-7535	5758
Elsevier BV North-Holland	Computer Networks	1389-1286	1669

Table 3 / Titles Deleted Since the Last Edition, by Publishers (cont.)

Publisher	Title	ISSN	15th Ed. Sequence No.
Elsevier BV North-Holland	Computer Standards & Interfaces	0920-5489	1671
Elsevier Inc.	Information Sciences	0020-0255	1689
Elsevier Inc.	Journal of Systems and Software	0164-1212	1698
Embry-Riddle Aeronautical University	Avion Online Newspaper		332
Emerald Group Publishing Limited	Disaster Prevention and Management	0965-3562	5748
Emerald Group Publishing Limited	Information Technology and People	0959-3845	1691
Euromoney Institutional Investor Plc.	Corporate Finance	0958-2053	2936
Euromoney Institutional Investor Plc.	P D I	0267-4823	6321
Evolutionary Psychology	Evolutionary Psychology	1474-7049	5611
Fairchild Publications, Inc.	Vitals Man	i551-1863	2815
Family Career and Community Leaders of America	Teen Times	0735-6986	6185
Film Music Network	Film Music	1520-3891	2901
400 Group	I S Analyzer Case Studies	0896-3231	1688
FreshAngles	FreshAngles		6188
G.V.R. Public Relations Agency	M A E S	1051-2616	2468
Gallup Organization	The Gallup Poll Briefing	1525-3120	4949
George Mason University Department of English	Enculturation	1091-1766	1869
Gestalt Global Corporation	Gestalt!	0894-9263	5613
Hachette Filipacchi Media U.S., Inc.	Premiere (Print Edition)		2915
Harrassowitz Verlag	Turkic Languages	0098-1389	4364
Haworth Social Work Practice Press	Social Work in Health Care	0040-2001	5998
Hearst Magazines	Teen	1072-7345	6183
Heart and Soul Enterprises	Heart & Soul	1206-940X	3660
Heron Publishing	Natural SCIENCE	0022-152X	5788
HeteroCorporation	Journal of Heterocyclic Chemistry	1476-1084	1414
Human Nature	The Human Nature Review	0926-227X	5614
I O S Press	Journal of Computer Security	0924-8625	1695
I O S Press	Space Communications	0307-6679	322
I P C Country & Leisure Media Ltd.	Stamp Magazine	1093-0736	5160
Independent Newspapers, Inc.	Delaware Capitol Review	1079-6622	3627
Independent Women's Forum	The Women's Quarterly	0008-1205	3370
Information for Public Affairs, Inc.	California Journal	1521-9917	3600
Institute for Local Self-Reliance	New Rules	0263-8762	3609
Institution of Chemical Engineers	Chemical Engineering Research & Design	1053-2838	2481
Insurance Publications Inc.	Financial Services Advisor	0731-9371	2946
International Insight, Inc.	Middle East Insight	0020-8442	4760
International Railway Congress Association	Rail International		6327

Table 3 / Titles Deleted Since the Last Edition, by Publishers (cont.)

Publisher	Title	ISSN	15th Ed. Sequence No.
National Center for Fathering	Today's Father	1081-1540	5091
National Center for Small Communities	Small Community Quarterly		3641
NetEc	NetEc		2195
Nielsen Business Publications	Amusement Business	0003-2344	1312
Nielsen Business Publications	Architecture	0746-0554	631
Oxford University Press	Annals of Occupational Hygiene	0003-4878	5746
Oxford University Press	International Journal of Lexicography	0950-3846	4321
Peabody Essex Museum of Salem	The American Neptune	0003-0155	3732
Pegasus Press	General Linguistics	0016-6553	4317
Pergamon	Accident Analysis & Prevention	0001-4575	5744
Pergamon	Applied Ergonomics	0003-6870	5747
Pergamon	Automatica	0005-1098	1664
Pergamon	Computer Languages, Systems and Structures	0096-0551	1668
Pergamon	Computers & Graphics	0097-8493	1673
Pergamon	Computers & Operations Research	0305-0548	1674
Pergamon	Control Engineering Practice	0967-0661	1676
Pergamon	Engineering Structures	0141-0296	2497
Pergamon	Information Systems	0306-4379	1690
Pergamon	International Journal of Multiphase Flow	0301-9322	2486
Pergamon	International Journal of Plasticity	0749-6419	2538
Pergamon	Linguistics and Education	0898-5898	4351
Presses Universitaires de France	Cahiers Internationaux de Sociologie	0008-0276	5899
Primedia Consumer Media & Magazine Group	Your Prom	1067-005X	6187
Priory Lodge Education Ltd.	Psychiatry On-Line		5619
Professional Engineering Publishing Ltd.	Institution of Mechanical Engineers. Proceedings		2535
Professional Surveyors Publishing Co., Inc.	Earth Observation Magazine (Online Edition)	1076-3430	3522
Psychnology	PsychNology	1720-7525	5620
Psychology Press	Language and Cognitive Processes		4338
Razor Magazine LLC	Razor (Scottsdale)		2803
Real Estate News Corp	Inland Architect	0020-1472	639
Reed Business Information	Electronic Business	1097-4881	1320
Reysen Group	Journal of Articles in Support of the Null Hypothesis	1539-8714	5615
Rogers Media Ventures	Government West	1520-8273	3605
Routledge	Australian Journal of Linguistics	0726-8602	4302
Routledge	Education, Communications & Information	1463-631X	2331
Routledge	English Studies	0013-838X	4313
Routledge	European Journal of Social Work	1369-1457	5984

Publisher	Title	ISSN	
Routledge	Research in Science & Technological Education	0263-5143	5776
Routledge	Sexualities, Evolution & Gender (Print Edition)	1461-6661	3361
S. Karger AG	Phonetica	0031-8388	4355
Sage Publications Ltd.	New Media & Society	1461-4448	5940
Sage Publications Ltd.	Second Language Research	0267-6583	4357
Sage Publications, Inc.	Sociological Methods & Research	0049-1241	5960
SatNews Publishers	SatNews OnLine Magazine		337
SCG, Inc.	Tycoon		2813
Science Reviews Ltd.	Journal of Chemical Research (Print Edition)	0308-2342	1399
Shardco, Inc.	B B W (Online Edition)	0192-5938	2764
Simmons College	Abafazi		3315
Southern Progress Corp.	Cooking Light	0886-4446	3127
Springer	Acta Informatica	0001-5903	1661
Springer Japan KK	New Generation Computing	0288-3635	1699
Springer Netherlands	Journal of East Asian Linguistics	0925-8558	4326
Springer Netherlands	Journal of Grid Computing	1570-7873	1696
Springer Netherlands	Journal of Paleolimnology	0921-2728	5044
Springer New York LLC	Algorithmica	0178-4617	1662
Springer New York LLC	International Journal of Parallel Programming	0885-7458	1693
Springer New York LLC	World Wide Web	1386-145X	1704
Stackpole Magazines	Rug Hooking	1045-4373	1733
State University of West Georgia Richards College of Business	B Quest	1084-3981	2190
Suomen Kielitieteellinen Yhdistys	SKY Journal of Linguistics	1456-8438	4358
Taylor & Francis A S	Fossils and Strata	0300-9491	5040
Taylor & Francis Ltd.	Ergonomics	0014-0139	5749
Teen Scene Magazine	Teen Scene Magazine		6190
Tennessee Technological University College of Arts and Sciences	Restoration: Studies in English Literary Culture, 1660-1700	0162-9905	4469
Thaddeus Computing, Inc.	Smartphone & Pocket P C		1714
The Behavior Analyst Today	The Behavior Analyst Today	1539-4352	5606
The Weekly Standard	The Weekly Standard	1083-3013	4972
ThomasTelford Ltd.	Institution of Civil Engineers. Proceedings. Civil Engineering	0965-089X	2499
Time, Inc.	Teen People	1096-2832	6184
Time, Inc.	Time for Kids News Scoop	1084-0168	1563
U.S. Department of Commerce International Trade Administration	Export America	1534-3588	1287
U.S. Department of Transportation Bureau of Transportation Statistics	Journal of Transportation and Statistics		6310
U.S. Fish and Wildlife Service Division of Endangered Species	Endangered Species Bulletin (Online Edition)	1091-7314	3586
Ububik New Media Research	Spank! Youth Culture Online		6189
Universitat Autonoma de Barcelona Servei de Publicacions	Catalan Journal of Linguistics	1695-6885	4305

Table 3 / Titles Deleted Since the Last Edition, by Publishers (cont.)

Publisher	Title	ISSN	15th Ed. Sequence No.
Universiteit Utrecht Faculty of Arts, Department of Arabic, Persian and Turkic Languages and Cultures	Electronic Journal of Oriental Studies	0928-6802	823
University of California at Berkeley Department of Mathematics	Pacific Journal of Mathematics	0030-8730	4699
University of California Press Journals Division	Journal of Linguistic Anthropology	1055-1360	4330
University of Chicago Press	The Journal of Business (Chicago)	0021-9398	1230
University of Florida	PsyArt	1088-5870	5616
University of Goettingen Department of Psychiatry	German Journal of Psychiatry	1433-1055	5612
University of Iowa Department of English	Philological Quarterly	0031-7977	4467
University of Iowa Libraries	Electronic Journal of Africana Bibliography		411
University of Michigan Press	Text	0736-3974	985
Wally Boyko Productions, Inc.	Ms. Fitness	1078-0661	3666
Weekly Reader Corp.	Teen Newsweek	1527-6775	1562
Weekly Reader Corp.	Weekly Reader. Grade 4 Edition	0890-3190	1564
Wenner Media, Inc.	Us Weekly	0147-510X	4970
Werner Publishing Corporation	Private Pilot	0032-8901	319
X R X, Inc.	Knitter's Magazine	0747-9026	1748
York Publishing	Smart T V & Sound	1094-6500	6219
Ziff Davis Media Inc.	Sync	1549-7305	2810

Note: A few sections have been removed from MFL 16 in their entirety, and the entries that were listed in those sections in MFL 15 do not appear in this table. Those sections are: Abstracts and Indexes, Singles, and Zines.

Table 4/Titles Deleted Since the Last Edition, by MFL Subject

Section	Title	ISSN	Publisher	15th Ed. Sequence No.
AERONAUTICS AND SPACE SCIENCE	A I A A Bulletin		American Institute of Aeronautics and Astronautics, Inc.	328
AERONAUTICS AND SPACE SCIENCE	Avion Online Newspaper		Embry-Riddle Aeronautical University	332
AERONAUTICS AND SPACE SCIENCE	Private Pilot	0032-8901	Werner Publishing Corporation	319
AERONAUTICS AND SPACE SCIENCE	SatNews OnLine Magazine		SatNews Publishers	337
AERONAUTICS AND SPACE SCIENCE	Space Communications	0924-8625	I O S Press	322
AFRICA	African Issues	0047-1607	African Studies Association	362
AFRICA	Electronic Journal of Africana Bibliography		University of Iowa Libraries	411
AFRICA	The East African Medical Journal	0012-835X	Kenya Medical Association	380
ANTIQUES	Antique Review	0883-833X	Krause Publications, Inc.	564
ANTIQUES	Barbie Bazaar	1040-094X	Murat Caviale Inc.	579
ANTIQUES	Collector Magazine & Price Guide	1077-2774	Krause Publications, Inc.	571
ANTIQUES	Collector's Mart	1066-551X	Krause Publications, Inc.	572
ARCHITECTURE	Architecture	0746-0554	Nielsen Business Publications	631
ARCHITECTURE	Inland Architect	0020-1472	Real Estate News Corp	639
ART	American Art Journal	0002-7359	Kennedy Galleries, Inc.	667
ASIA AND THE PACIFIC	Electronic Journal of Oriental Studies	0928-6802	Universiteit Utrecht Faculty of Arts, Department of Arabic, Persian and Turkic Languages and Cultures	823
BIBLIOGRAPHY	Text	0736-3974	University of Michigan Press	985
BUSINESS	Amusement Business	0003-2344	Nielsen Business Publications	1312
BUSINESS	Business Mexico	0187-1455	American Chamber of Commerce of Mexico A.C.	1270
BUSINESS	Electronic Business	1097-4881	Reed Business Information	1320
BUSINESS	Export America	1534-3588	U.S. Department of Commerce International Trade Administration	1287
BUSINESS	The Journal of Business (Chicago)	0021-9398	University of Chicago Press	1230
CHEMISTRY	Journal of Chemical Research (Print Edition)	0308-2342	Science Reviews Ltd.	1399
CHEMISTRY	Journal of Heterocyclic Chemistry	0022-152X	HeteroCorporation	1414
CLASSROOM MAGAZINES	Micromath	0267-5501	Association of Teachers of Mathematics	1570
CLASSROOM MAGAZINES	Teen Newsweek	1527-6775	Weekly Reader Corp.	1562
CLASSROOM MAGAZINES	Time for Kids News Scoop	1084-0168	Time, Inc.	1563
CLASSROOM MAGAZINES	Weekly Reader. Grade 4 Edition	0890-3190	Weekly Reader Corp.	1564
COMPUTERS AND INFORMATION TECHNOLOGY	Acta Informatica	0001-5903	Springer	1661
COMPUTERS AND INFORMATION TECHNOLOGY	Algorithmica	0178-4617	Springer New York LLC	4768
COMPUTERS AND INFORMATION TECHNOLOGY	Automatica	0005-1098	Pergamon	1664

Table 4 / Titles Deleted Since the Last Edition, by MFL Subject (cont.)

Section	Title	ISSN	Publisher	15th Ed. Sequence No.
COMPUTERS AND INFORMATION TECHNOLOGY	Circuit Cellar	0896-8985	Circuit Cellar, Inc.	1665
COMPUTERS AND INFORMATION TECHNOLOGY	Computer Languages, Systems and Structures	0096-0551	Pergamon	1668
COMPUTERS AND INFORMATION TECHNOLOGY	Computer Networks	1389-1286	Elsevier BV North-Holland	1669
COMPUTERS AND INFORMATION TECHNOLOGY	Computer Standards & Interfaces	0920-5489	Elsevier BV North-Holland	1671
COMPUTERS AND INFORMATION TECHNOLOGY	Computer Vision and Image Understanding	1077-3142	Academic Press	1672
COMPUTERS AND INFORMATION TECHNOLOGY	Computers & Graphics	0097-8493	Pergamon	1673
COMPUTERS AND INFORMATION TECHNOLOGY	Computers & Operations Research	0305-0548	Pergamon	1674
COMPUTERS AND INFORMATION TECHNOLOGY	Control Engineering Practice	0967-0661	Pergamon	1676
COMPUTERS AND INFORMATION TECHNOLOGY	Evolutionary Computation	1063-6560	M I T Press	1678
COMPUTERS AND INFORMATION TECHNOLOGY	Expert Systems	0266-4720	Blackwell Publishing Ltd.	1679
COMPUTERS AND INFORMATION TECHNOLOGY	Graphical Models	1077-3169	Academic Press	1680
COMPUTERS AND INFORMATION TECHNOLOGY	I S Analyzer Case Studies	0896-3231	400 Group	1688
COMPUTERS AND INFORMATION TECHNOLOGY	Information Sciences	0020-0255	Elsevier Inc.	1689
COMPUTERS AND INFORMATION TECHNOLOGY	Information Systems	0306-4379	Pergamon	1690
COMPUTERS AND INFORMATION TECHNOLOGY	Information Technology and People	0959-3845	Emerald Group Publishing Limited	1691
COMPUTERS AND INFORMATION TECHNOLOGY	International Journal of Human-Computer Studies	1071-5819	Academic Press	1692
COMPUTERS AND INFORMATION TECHNOLOGY	International Journal of Parallel Programming	0885-7458	Springer New York LLC	1693
COMPUTERS AND INFORMATION TECHNOLOGY	Journal of Computer Assisted Learning	0266-4909	Blackwell Publishing Ltd.	1694
COMPUTERS AND INFORMATION TECHNOLOGY	Journal of Computer Security	0926-227X	I O S Press	1695
COMPUTERS AND INFORMATION TECHNOLOGY	Journal of Grid Computing	1570-7873	Springer Netherlands	1696
COMPUTERS AND INFORMATION TECHNOLOGY	Journal of Machine Learning Research	1533-7928	M I T Press	1697
COMPUTERS AND INFORMATION TECHNOLOGY	Journal of Systems and Software	0164-1212	Elsevier Inc.	1698

Table 4 / Titles Deleted Since the Last Edition, by MFL Subject (cont.)

Section	Title	ISSN	Publisher	15th Ed. Sequence No.
ENGINEERING AND TECHNOLOGY	Critical Reviews in Biomedical Engineering	0278-940X	Begell House Inc.	2473
ENGINEERING AND TECHNOLOGY	Engineering Structures	0141-0296	Pergamon	2497
ENGINEERING AND TECHNOLOGY	Institution of Civil Engineers. Proceedings. Civil Engineering	0965-089X	Thomas Telford Ltd.	2499
ENGINEERING AND TECHNOLOGY	Institution of Mechanical Engineers. Proceedings		Professional Engineering Publishing Ltd.	2535
ENGINEERING AND TECHNOLOGY	International Journal of Multiphase Flow	0301-9322	Pergamon	2486
ENGINEERING AND TECHNOLOGY	International Journal of Plasticity	0749-6419	Pergamon	2538
ENGINEERING AND TECHNOLOGY	M A E S		G.V.R. Public Relations Agency	2468
ENGINEERING AND TECHNOLOGY	Nuclear News	0029-5574	American Nuclear Society, Inc.	2546
ENVIRONMENT AND CONSERVATION	Everyone's Backyard	0749-3940	Center for Health, Environment, and Justice	2574
FASHION AND LIFESTYLE	B B W (Online Edition)	0192-5938	Shardco, Inc.	2764
FASHION AND LIFESTYLE	Cargo	1547-8432	Conde Nast Publications, Inc.	2767
FASHION AND LIFESTYLE	Razor (Scottsdale)		Razor Magazine LLC	2803
FASHION AND LIFESTYLE	shuz		Magnolia Media Group	2806
FASHION AND LIFESTYLE	Sync	1549-7305	Ziff Davis Media Inc.	2810
FASHION AND LIFESTYLE	Tycoon		SCG, Inc.	2813
FASHION AND LIFESTYLE	Vitals Man	i551-1863	Fairchild Publications, Inc.	2815
FILMS	Animation Journal	1061-0308	A J Press	2880
FILMS	Film Music	1520-3891	Film Music Network	2901
FILMS	Premiere (Print Edition)	0894-9263	Hachette Filipacchi Media U.S., Inc.	2915
FINANCE	Corporate Finance	0958-2053	Euromoney Institutional Investor Plc.	2936
FINANCE	Financial Services Advisor	1053-2838	Insurance Publications Inc.	2946
GENDER STUDIES	Abafazi	1567-8474	Simmons College	3315
GENDER STUDIES	Nin	1461-6661	Brill	3356
GENDER STUDIES	Sexualities, Evolution & Gender (Print Edition)	1079-6622	Routledge	3361
GENDER STUDIES	The Women's Quarterly		Independent Women's Forum	3370
GEOGRAPHY	Earth Observation Magazine (Online Edition)	1076-3430	Professional Surveyors Publishing Co., Inc.	3522
GOVERNMENT PERIODICALS;b1FEDERAL	Endangered Species Bulletin (Online Edition)	1091-7314	U.S. Fish and Wildlife Service Division of Endangered Species	3586
GOVERNMENT PERIODICALS;b1STATE AND LOCAL	California Journal	0008-1205	Information for Public Affairs, Inc.	3600
GOVERNMENT PERIODICALS;b1STATE AND LOCAL	Delaware Capitol Review	1093-0736	Independent Newspapers, Inc.	3627
GOVERNMENT PERIODICALS;b1STATE AND LOCAL	Government West	1520-8273	Rogers Media Ventures	3605
GOVERNMENT PERIODICALS;b1STATE AND LOCAL	New Rules	1521-9917	Institute for Local Self-Reliance	3609

Category	Title	ISSN	Publisher	Number
GOVERNMENT PERIODICALS;b1STATE AND LOCAL	Small Community Quarterly		National Center for Small Communities	3641
GOVERNMENT PERIODICALS;b1STATE AND LOCAL	Spectrum (Lexington)	1067-8530	Council of State Governments	3615
HEALTH AND FITNESS	Energy for Women		Muscle Media, Inc.	3648
HEALTH AND FITNESS	Heart & Soul	1072-7345	Heart and Soul Enterprises	3660
HEALTH AND FITNESS	Men's Fitness	0893-4460	A M I - Weider Publications	3664
HEALTH AND FITNESS	Ms. Fitness	1078-0661	Wally Boyko Productions, Inc.	3666
HISTORY	Ohio History (Online Edition)	0030-0934	Kent State University Press	3808
HISTORY	The American Neptune	0003-0155	Peabody Essex Museum of Salem	3732
LABOR AND INDUSTRIAL RELATIONS	Work in Progress		American Federation of Labor - Congress of Industrial Organizations Public Affairs Department	4058
LINGUISTICS	Applied Psycholinguistics	0142-7164	Cambridge University Press	4301
LINGUISTICS	Australian Journal of Linguistics	0726-8602	Routledge	4302
LINGUISTICS	B E L L	1376-2958	Academia Press	4303
LINGUISTICS	Catalan Journal of Linguistics	1695-6885	Universitat Autonoma de Barcelona Servei de Publicacions	4305
LINGUISTICS	Computational Linguistics	0891-2017	M I T Press	4307
LINGUISTICS	Diachronica	0176-4225	John Benjamins Publishing Co.	4308
LINGUISTICS	Dictionaries		Dictionary Society of North America	4309
LINGUISTICS	Discourse Processes	0163-853X	Lawrence Erlbaum Associates, Inc.	4310
LINGUISTICS	English Language and Linguistics	1360-6743	Cambridge University Press	4312
LINGUISTICS	English Studies	0013-838x	Routledge	4313
LINGUISTICS	English Today	0266-0784	Cambridge University Press	4314
LINGUISTICS	General Linguistics	0016-6553	Pegasus Press	4317
LINGUISTICS	Indian Journal of Applied Linguistics	0379-0037	Bahri Publications	4318
LINGUISTICS	International Journal of Lexicography	0950-3846	Oxford University Press	4321
LINGUISTICS	International Journal of the Sociology of Language	0165-2516	Mouton de Gruyter	4322
LINGUISTICS	International Phonetic Association. Journal	0025-1003	Cambridge University Press	4323
LINGUISTICS	Journal of African Languages and Linguistics	0167-6164	Mouton de Gruyter	4324
LINGUISTICS	Journal of Child Language	0305-0009	Cambridge University Press	4325
LINGUISTICS	Journal of East Asian Linguistics	0925-8558	Springer Netherlands	4326
LINGUISTICS	Journal of French Language Studies	0959-2695	Cambridge University Press	4328
LINGUISTICS	Journal of Linguistic Anthropology	1055-1360: online 1548-1395	University of California Press Journals Division	4330
LINGUISTICS	Journal of Literary Semantics	0341-7638	Mouton de Gruyter	4332
LINGUISTICS	Journal of Multilingual & Multicultural Development	0143-4632	Multilingual Matters Ltd.	4333
LINGUISTICS	Journal of Pidgin and Creole Languages	0920-9034	John Benjamins Publishing Co.	4335
LINGUISTICS	Journal of Portuguese Linguistics		Edicoes Colibri	4336
LINGUISTICS	Language and Cognitive Processes		Psychology Press	4338

Table 4 / Titles Deleted Since the Last Edition, by MFL Subject (cont.)

Section	Title	ISSN	Publisher	15th Ed. Sequence No.
LINGUISTICS	Language and Speech	0023-8309	Kingston Press Services Ltd.	4341
LINGUISTICS	Language Learning	0023-8333	Blackwell Publishing, Inc.	4343
LINGUISTICS	Linguistic Typology	1430-0532	Mouton de Gruyter	4349
LINGUISTICS	Linguistics and Education	0898-5898	Pergamon	4351
LINGUISTICS	Nordic Journal of Linguistics		Cambridge University Press	4354
LINGUISTICS	Phonetica	0031-8388	S. Karger AG	4355
LINGUISTICS	Phonology	0952-6757	Cambridge University Press	4356
LINGUISTICS	Second Language Research	0267-6583	Sage Publications Ltd.	4357
LINGUISTICS	SKY Journal of Linguistics	1456-8438	Suomen Kielitieteellinen Yhdistys	4358
LINGUISTICS	Southwest Journal of Linguistics	0737-4143	Linguistic Association of the Southwest	4359
LINGUISTICS	Studies in Language	0378-4177	John Benjamins Publishing Co.	4360
LINGUISTICS	Theoretical Linguistics	0301-4428	Mouton de Gruyter	4363
LINGUISTICS	Turkic Languages		Harrassowitz Verlag	4364
LINGUISTICS	Word Ways	0043-7980	A Ross Eckler, Ed & Pub	4365
LINGUISTICS	World Englishes	0883-2919	Blackwell Publishing Ltd.	4366
LITERATURE	Philological Quarterly	0031-7977	University of Iowa Department of English	4467
LITERATURE	Restoration: Studies in English Literary Culture, 1660-1700	0162-9905	Tennessee Technological University College of Arts and Sciences	4469
MATHEMATICS	Pacific Journal of Mathematics	0030-8730	University of California at Berkeley Department of Mathematics	4699
MATHEMATICS	Quarterly of Applied Mathematics	0033-569X	Brown University Division of Applied Mathematics	4700
MIDDLE EAST	Al-Raida	0259-9953	Beirut University College Institute for Women's Studies in the Arab World	1662
MIDDLE EAST	Journal of Iranian Research and Analysis	1525-9307	Center for Iranian Research and Analysis	4755
MIDDLE EAST	Middle East Insight	0731-9371	International Insight, Inc.	4760
MIDDLE EAST	Middle East Report	0899-2851	Middle East Research & Information Project	4763
NEWS AND OPINION	The Gallup Poll Briefing	1051-2616	Gallup Organization	4949
NEWS AND OPINION	The New Leader	0028-6044	American Labor Conference on International Affairs, Inc.	4958
NEWS AND OPINION	The Weekly Standard	1083-3013	The\Weekly Standard	4972
NEWS AND OPINION	Us Weekly	0147-510X	Wenner Media, Inc.	4970
OCCUPATIONS AND CAREERS	America's Job Bank		America's Job Bank	5031
OCCUPATIONS AND CAREERS	CareerJournal.com		Dow Jones & Company	5032
OCCUPATIONS AND CAREERS	JobWeb		National Association of Colleges and Employers	5033
PALEONTOLOGY	Fossils and Strata	0300-9491	Taylor & Francis A S	5040
PALEONTOLOGY	Journal of Paleolimnology	0921-2728	Springer Netherlands	5044
PARENTING	Child	0894-7988	Meredith Corp.	5079
PARENTING	Christian Parenting Today	1065-7215	Christianity Today International	5080

Table 4 / Titles Deleted Since the Last Edition, by MFL Subject (cont.)

Section	Title	ISSN	Publisher	15th Ed. Sequence No.
SOCIOLOGY AND SOCIAL WORK	New Media & Society	1461-4448	Sage Publications Ltd.	5940
SOCIOLOGY AND SOCIAL WORK	Policy & Practice	0033-3816	American Public Human Services Association	5991
SOCIOLOGY AND SOCIAL WORK	Social Policy and Administration	0144-5596	Blackwell Publishing Ltd.	5951
SOCIOLOGY AND SOCIAL WORK	Social Work in Health Care	0098-1389	Haworth Social Work Practice Press	5998
SOCIOLOGY AND SOCIAL WORK	Sociological Methods & Research	0049-1241	Sage Publications, Inc.	5960
TEENAGERS	American Cheerleader	1079-9885	Macfadden Performing Arts Media, LLC.	6168
TEENAGERS	FreshAngles		FreshAngles	6188
TEENAGERS	Spank! Youth Culture Online		Ububik New Media Research	6189
TEENAGERS	Teen	0040-2001	Hearst Magazines	6183
TEENAGERS	Teen People	1096-2832	Time, Inc.	6184
TEENAGERS	Teen Scene Magazine		Teen Scene Magazine	6190
TEENAGERS	Teen Times	0735-6986	Family Career and Community Leaders of America	6185
TEENAGERS	Your Prom	1067-005X	Primedia Consumer Media & Magazine Group	6187
TELEVISION, VIDEO, AND RADIO	M Street Daily		M Street Publications	6201
TELEVISION, VIDEO, AND RADIO	Smart T V & Sound	1094-6500	York Publishing	6219
TELEVISION, VIDEO, AND RADIO	The M Street Journal	1052-7109	M Street Publications	6202
TRANSPORTATION	Journal of Transportation and Statistics		U.S. Department of Transportation Bureau of Transportation Statistics	6310
TRANSPORTATION	P D I	0267-4823	Euromoney Institutional Investor Plc.	6321
TRANSPORTATION	Rail International	0020-8442	International Railway Congress Association	6327
TRAVEL AND TOURISM	Marco Polo		Marco Polo Publishing Inc.	6369
TRAVEL AND TOURISM	Travel & Leisure Family		American Express Publishing Corp.	6364

Note: A few sections have been removed from MFL 16 in their entirety, and the entries that were listed in those sections in MFL 15 do not appear in this table. Those sections are: Abstracts and Indexes, Singles, and Zines.

HOW TO USE THIS BOOK

*Title. *ISSN. Date Founded. *Frequency. *Price.
Editor. Publisher and Address, *Internet-WWW.
lllustrations, Index, Advertising. *Sample. *Refereed.
Circulation. *Date Volume Ends. *CD-ROM.
Microform. Reprint. *Online. *Indexed.
*Book Reviews. *Audience. * Annotation.

The bibliographic data in the entries contain the items shown in the box above. Items preceded by an asterisk are fully explained in the paragraphs that follow. The Abbreviations section lists the general abbreviations found in the bibliographic information in the numbered entries.

The detailed Subject Index enables the user to access the enormous amount of information that may not be readily retrievable from the alphabetically arranged Title Index. All subject classifications used, as well as variations in wording of subject headings, and as many additional subject cross-references as the editors expected would be useful, are listed in the Subject Index. The numbers that appear in the indexes refer to the magazine entry numbers, not page numbers.

Title

The periodicals in this book are listed alphabetically, by title, under the subjects given in the Contents. They are numbered sequentially, beginning with 1 on page 1 and ending with 6,205, the last magazine entry in the book, on page 967.

ISSN Numbers

This international standard, which is used all over the world by serial publishers to distinguish similar titles from each other, directly follows the title. *Ulrich's Periodicals Directory* was used to verify this information.

Frequency and Price

The frequency is given immediately after the founding date, and the symbols used are explained in the General Abbreviations section. The price quoted is the annual subscription rate given by the publisher, usually as of 2007. A large

number are prices for 2008. Prices are relative and, of course, subject to change—probably upward. Furthermore, the fluctuation of the dollar makes the prices of foreign magazines even more relative. The phrase "Controlled Circ." is found after some titles. This means the magazine has a controlled circulation and is sent free to certain individuals whom the advertisers are trying to reach. Such a magazine is financed solely by advertisements, and the controlled circulation indicates the publisher has targeted a certain audience or audiences for the advertisers. For a listing of controlled circulation serials, with full addresses, see the index volume of *Ulrich's Periodicals Directory*. "Others" means those who are outside that select audience and must pay for the title. Often the publisher is willing to send the magazine free to libraries, but in any case an inquiry should be made.

World Wide Web

The web address (URL) represents the address at the time of the compilation. As anyone knows who uses the Internet, the address may change frequently. In a case where the address does not prove correct, try shortening the address back to the "root" or entering the name of the magazine in the search engine box. Normally this works.

Sample

Publishers were asked whether or not they would send a free copy of the magazine to a library if requested. Those who replied favorably are indicated by the single word "sample". The request should be made by the head of the library, or by the head of the serials department, and written on official stationery. The indication that publishers are willing to send samples to institutions does not mean they are necessarily interested in sending them to individual subscribers. And one additional note: Several publishers would not supply review copies of their publications. So, if there are a couple of titles not in the list that you might otherwise expect to see here, that is why. *MFL* does depend upon publisher cooperation to be able to access titles for possible inclusion.

Refereed

This term is used to indicate that manuscripts published in the journal have been reviewed by experts and specialists in the field before being accepted for publication. Sometimes refereed journals are characterized as "peer-reviewed." This process tends to make scholars trust the reliability of the content of an article more than a non-refereed article.

Date Volume Ends

Librarians find it helpful to know when a publisher ends a volume—obviously for purposes of binding. The information provided is from the publisher.

CD-ROM

Like the online designation, this includes the basic sources of CD-ROM access to a particular title. Again, this is in reference to an index where the periodical is accessed, or the name of the CD-ROM publisher, not the periodical itself. *Ulrich's* listings include information on indexes in CD-ROM format for some titles. For additional information, see the *Gale Directory of Databases* (Detroit: Gale Research) and the annual *CD-ROMs in Print* (Detroit: Gale Research).

Online

This includes the basic sources of online access to a particular title. This may be in reference to an index, or it may be in reference to the full-text of articles in the journal.

Indexed

Information on where titles are indexed or abstracted is given—in abbreviated format—following the bibliographic data. Also indicated are major subject indexes in which the periodicals are indexed. Major must be emphasized. The list of the A&Is recommended by *MFL* subject specialist, with publishers'/providers' web sites, can be found on page xxxix. Here one finds, too, whether that index is available online and/or on CD-ROM. The term index in the bibliographic description indicates that the publisher has an index to the periodical.

Book Reviews

Information given refers to the approximate number of reviews that appear in a typical issue of the periodical and the average length.

Audience

Ems (elementary and middle school students); Hs (high school students); Ga (General Adult); Ac (Academic audience); Sa (Special Adult). Each magazine has an indication of audience or type of library for which it is suited. The scale is specific, but as most magazines are for more than one audience, several audience levels are usually given for each title. Periodicals for elementary and middle school students (Ems) are not separated because it is often difficult to draw the line between these two age groups. The titles and descriptive annotations leave little doubt as to the level of maturity for which the magazine is intended. Generally, elementary and middle school means the age group from 4 to 14 years and/or those in elementary or middle school. The high school level (Hs) overlaps and may include middle school, but for the most part, these are titles suitable for those from 14 years up to 18 years and/or in high school. Magazines suitable for public libraries and college and university library reading rooms are rated General Adult (Ga). Publications designated Academic audience (Ac) should be considered for junior colleges, colleges, and universities. Magazines rated Special Adult (Sa) are for specialized audiences and will be read by few people other than professionals or students of a particular subject. It is assumed that the audience symbols are only guides, not designations for type of library—which is to say that the symbol Ga does not mean the magazine is only limited to public libraries any more than Ac means a magazine is only for academic libraries. Obviously the choice should be made by the librarian, and this will depend on his or her assessment of the audience to be served. Public libraries will often include many of the same magazines found in all other libraries.

Annotation

The annotations are generally short summaries describing the scope, purpose, and intent of each magazine, bias (if any), and target audience as described above. In making their recommendations chapter authors are assessing the usefulness and readability of articles in each journal for various audiences. The fact that a journal is listed in *Magazines for Libraries* indicates that it is considered to be a core title for the listed audience and recommended to the libraries serving them.

ABBREVIATIONS

■ GENERAL ABBREVIATIONS

a.	Annual	Irreg.	Irregular
Ac	Academic (Junior Colleges, Colleges, Universities)	ISSN	International Standard Serial Number
adv.	advertising	ITL	Italian Lira
Aud.	Audience	m.	Monthly
bi-m.	Every two months	N.S.	New Series
bi-w.	Every two weeks	NLG	Dutch Guilder
Bk. rev	Book reviews	no., #, nos.	number(s)
Circ.	circulation	q.	Quarterly
CND	Canadian Dollar	rev.	reviews
d.	Daily	Sa	Special Adult
DEM	Deutsche Mark	s-a.	Twice annually
Ed., Eds.	Editor(s)	s-m.	Twice monthly
Ems	Elementary and Middle School	s-w.	Twice weekly
EUR	Euro	3/m.	Three times a month
fortn.	Fortnightly	3/w	Three times a week
FRF	French Franc	3/yr.	Three times per year
Ga	General Adult	USD	U.S. Dollars
GBP	British Pound	vol., vols.	volume(s)
Hs	High School	w.	Weekly
illus.	illustrations	yr., yrs.	year(s)

Controlled Circ. Controlled circulation (free to certain groups)

ABSTRACTS AND INDEXES

This is a list of the abstracting and indexing tools recommended by *MFL* chapter authors in this edition. The basic information is provided to enable readers to access full product content at the publishers'/providers' web sites.

ABI/INFORM
http://www.proquest.com/products_pq/descriptions /abi_inform.shtml

Abstracts in Anthropology
http://www.baywood.com/Journals/ PreviewJournals.asp?Id=0001-3455

Abstracts in Social Gerontology
http://www.sagepub.com/journalsProdDesc.nav? prodId=Journal200770

Academic ASAP
http://www.gale.com/servlet/ItemDetailServlet? region=9&imprint=000&cf=n&titleCode=INFO2& type=4&id=F3615

Academic Search Premier
http://www.ebscohost.com/thisTopic.php?market ID=1&topicID=1

Aerospace & High Technology Database
http://www.csa.com/factsheets/aerospace-set-c.php

African Studies Abstracts Online
http://www.ascleiden.nl/Library/ Abstracts/ASA-Online/

AGELINE
http://www.aarp.org/research/ageline/

Agricola
http://agricola.nal.usda.gov/

Air University Library Index to Military Periodicals
http://www.dtic.mil/dtic/aulimp/

Alternative Press Index
http://www.altpress.org/

Alt HealthWatch
http://www.ebscohost.com/thisTopic.php?market ID=1&topicID=25

America: History and Life
http://www.ebscohost.com/thisTopic.php?market ID=1&topicID=838

American Bibliography of Slavic and Eastern European Studies (ABSEES)
http://www.ebscohost.com/thisTopic.php?market ID=1&topicID=27

ATLA (American Theological Libraries Association) Religion Database
http://www.atla.com/products/catalogs/catalogs _rdb.html

Annual Bibliography of English Language and Literature (ABELL)
http://www.mhra.org.uk/Publications/Journals /abell.html

Anthropological Index
http://www.oclc.org/services/ brochures/12447anthropological_ index_ database.pdf

Anthropological Literature
http://www.rlg.org/en/page.php?Page_ID=162

Applied Science and Technology Abstracts
http://www.hwwilson.com/Databases/applieds.htm #Abstracts

Applied Science and Technology Index
http://www.hwwilson.com/Databases/applieds.htm #Index

Aquatic Biology, Aquaculture and Fisheries Resources
http://www.nisc.co.za/databases?id=45

Aquatic Sciences and Fisheries Abstracts
http://www.fao.org/fi/website/ FIRetrieveAction.do?dom=org&xml=asfa_prog.x ml&xp_nav=1

Architectural Index
http://www.archindex.com/

Architectural Publications Index
http://library.rpi.edu/architecture/update.do? artcenterkey=38

ABSTRACTS AND INDEXES

Art and Archaeology Technical Abstracts
http://www.getty.edu/conservation/publications
/newsletters/17_2/news_in_ cons2.html

Art Index
http://www.hwwilson.com/Databases/artindex.htm
#Index0

ARTbibliographies Modern
http://www.csa.com/factsheets/artbm-set-c.php

Arts & Humanities Citation Index. *see also* **Web of Science**
http://scientific.thomson.com/products/ahci/

ASSIA: Applied Social Sciences Index and Abstract
http://www.csa.com/factsheets/assia-set-c.php

ATLA (American Theological Libraries Association) Database
http://www.atla.com/products/catalogs/catalogs
_rdb.html

Avery Index to Architectural Periodicals
http://www.getty.edu/research/
conducting_research/avery_index/

Bibliography of Asian Studies Online
http://www.aasianst.org/aboutbas.htm

Bibliography of the History of Art (BHA)
http://www.getty.edu/research/
conducting_research/bha/

BIOBASE
http://www.biobase-international.com/pages/

Biological Abstracts
http://scientific.thomson.com/products/ba/

Biological Abstracts/RRM
http://scientific.thomson.com/products/barrm/

Biological and Agricultural Index Plus
http://www.hwwilson.com/Databases/bioag.htm

Biology Digest
http://www.csa.com/factsheets/biodig-set-c.php

BioOne http://www.csa.com/factsheets/bioone-set-
c.php

BIOSIS
http://scientific.thomson.com/media/scpdf/bp_ovid
_qrc.pdf

BIOSIS Previews
http://www.ovid.com/site/catalog/
DataBase/26.jsp?top=2&mid=3&bott

Black Studies on Disc
http://www.gale.com/servlet/ItemDetailServlet?
region=9&imprint=000&
titleCode=M49&cf=n&type=4&id=194876

Book Review Digest
http://www.hwwilson.com/NewDDs/wn.htm

Book Review Index
http://www.gale.com/servlet/BrowseSeriesServlet?
region=9&imprint=000&cf=ps&titleCode=BRI&d
c=null&dewey=null&edition=

**British and Irish Archaeological Bibliography
(BIAB Online)**
http://www.biab.ac.uk/about.asp

British Humanities Index (BHI)
http://www.csa.com/factsheets/bhi-set-c.php

Business and Company ProFile ASAP
http://www.gale.com/pdf/facts/bcprof.pdf

Business and Company Resource Center
http://www.gale.com/BusinessRC/

Business and Industry
http://www.gale.com/pdf/facts/busind.pdf

Business Index
http://www.hwwilson.com/

Business Periodicals Index
http://www.hwwilson.com/

Business Source Elite
http://www.ebscohost.com/thisTopic.php?marketI
D=1&topicID=4

Business Source Premier
http://www.ebscohost.com/thisTopic.php?marketI
D=1&topicID=2

CAB Abstracts
http://www.cabi.org/datapage.asp?iDocID=165

**Canadian Business & Current Affairs Complete
(CBCA)**
http://www.il.proquest.com/products_pq/descriptio
ns/cbca.shtml

Catholic Periodical and Literature Index
http://www.epnet.com/thisTopic.php?marketID=1
&topicID=52

Chemical Abstracts (print)
http://www.cas.org/products/print/ca/ index.html

Chicano Database
http://www.rlg.org/en/page.php?Page_ID=176

Children's Book Review Index (CBRI)
http://www.gale.com/servlet/BrowseSeriesServlet?
region=9&imprint=k12&browseBy=series&titleCo
de=CBRI

Children's Magazine Guide
http://www.childrensmag.com/index.html

CINAHL
http://www.cinahl.com/prodsvcs/cinahldb.htm

Communication & Mass Media Complete
http://www.ebscohost.com/thisTopic.php?market
ID=1&topicID=56

Communication Abstracts
http://www.csa.com/factsheets/commabs-set-c.php

Computer & Control Abstracts
http://www.theiet.org/

Computer Science Index (CSI)
http://www.epnet.com/thisTopic.php?marketID=1
&topicID=60

Computing Reviews
http://www.reviews.com/masthead/
masthead_masthead.cfm

Contemporary Women's Issues (CWI)
http://www.oclc.org/support/documentation/first
search/databases/dbdetails/ details/CWI.htm

CPI.Q
http://www.gale.com/pdf/facts/ cpiq.pdf

Criminal Justice Abstracts
http://www.csa.com/factsheets/cja-set-c.php

CSA Worldwide Political Science Abstracts
http://www.csa.com/factsheets/polsci-set-c.php

**Cumulative Index to Nursing and Allied Health
Literature (CINAHL)**
http://www.cinahl.com/prodsvcs/cinahldb.htm

Current Bibliography on African Affairs (print)
http://www.baywood.com/journals/
previewjournals.asp?id=0011-3255

Current Contents Connect
http://scientific.thomson.com/products/ccc/

**Current Contents: Physical, Chemical and
Earth Sciences (CC: PC&ES)**
http://scientific.thomson.com/mjl/
scope/scope_ccpces.html

Current Index to Journals in Education (CIJE):
see **ERIC**

Current Law Index (print)
http://www.gale.com/servlet/BrowseSeriesServlet?
region=9&imprint=000&titleCode=CLI&edition

Design and Applied Arts Index (DAAI)
http://www.csa.com/factsheets/daai-set-c.php

EconLit
http://www.csa.com/factsheets/econlit-set-c.php

Education Abstracts
http://www.hwwilson.com/databases/educat.htm#
Abstracts

Education Index
http://www.hwwilson.com/databases/
educat.htm#Index

Education Full Text
http://www.hwwilson.com/Databases/educat.htm

EI Compendex
http://www.ei.org/databases/compendex.html

Ekistic Index of Periodicals
http://www.ekistics.org/Eindex.htm

EMBASE http://www.ovid.com/site/catalog/
DataBase/62.jsp

Engineering Index
http://www.elsevier.com/wps/find/journaldescripti
on.cws_home/622280/description#description

Environment Index
http://www.epnet.com/thisTopic.php?
topicID=61&marketID=1

**Environmental Sciences and Pollution
Management**
http://www.csa.com/factsheets/ envclust-set-c.php

ERIC
http://www.eric.ed.gov/

Ethnic NewsWatch
http://www.proquest.com/products_pq/descriptions
/ethnic_newswatch.shtml

Exceptional Child Education Resources
http://www.cec.sped.org

Exceptional Human Experience
http://www.ehe.org

Excerpta Medica
http://www.elsevier.com/locate/emset

ABSTRACTS AND INDEXES

Expanded Academic ASAP
http://www.gale.com/servlet/ItemDetailServlet?reg
ion=9&imprint=000&
titleCode=INFO9&cf=n&type=4&id=172032

Factiva
http://factiva.com

Family & Society Studies Worldwide
http://www.nisc.com/Frame/NISC_ products-f.htm

Family Index
http://fid.familyscholar.com/

Feminist Periodicals
http://womenst.library.wisc.edu/
publications/feminist-peri.html

Film Literature Index
http://webapp1.dlib.indiana.edu/fli/ index.jsp

Focus On: Veterinary Science and Medicine
http://scientific.thomson.com/products/fovsm/

Food Science and Technology Abstracts
http://www.foodsciencecentral.com

Forest Products Abstracts
http://www.cabi.org/Abstract
Databases.asp?PID=37

Forest Science Database
http://www.cabi.org/Abstract
Databases.asp?PID=114

Forestry Abstracts
http://www.cabi.org/Abstract
Databases.asp?PID=38

FRANCIS
http://international.inist.fr/article59. html

Garden Literature Index
http://www.epnet.com/thisTopic.php?
topicID=173&marketID=1

Gender Studies Database
http://www.nisc.com/factsheets/qgsd. asp

GenderWatch
http://www.il.proquest.com/products_pq/
descriptions/genderwatch.shtml

General Science Index
http://www.hwwilson.com/Databases/gensci.htm

GeoBase
http://www.ovid.com/site/catalog/
DataBase/94.jsp?top=2&mid=3&bottom=7&subse
ction=10

Geographical Abstracts: Human Geography
http://www.elsevier.com/wps/find/
journaldescription.cws_home/405885/description#
description

Geographical Abstracts: Physical Geography
http://www.elsevier.com/wps/find/journaldescrip
tion.cws_home/405886/description#description

GeoRef
http://www.agiweb.org/georef/index. html

Health and Safety Science Abstracts
http://www.csa.com/factsheets/health-safety-set-
c.php

Hispanic American Periodicals Index
http://hapi.gseis.ucla.edu/

Historical Abstracts
http://www.abc-clio.com/products/serials_ha.aspx

Horticultural Science Abstracts
http://www.cabi.org/Abstract
Databases.asp?PID=40

Hospitality and Tourism Index
http://www.ebscohost.com/thisTopic.php?market
ID=1&topicID=418

Humanities Index
http://www.hwwilson.com/Databases/humani.htm

Humanities International Index
http://www.epnet.com/thisTopic.php?marketID=1
&topicID=174

IBZ
http://www.saur.de/index.cfm?lang=
DE&ID=0000010140

ICONDA
http://www.ovid.com/site/catalog/DataBase/102.js
p?top=2&mid=3&bottom=7&subsection=10

IEEE Explore
http://ieeexplore.ieee.org/Xplore/guesthome.jsp

Imaging Abstracts
http://www.intertechpira.com

Index Islamicus
http://www.indexislamicus.com

Index of American Periodical Verse
http://www.scarecrowpress.com

Index to Black Periodicals
http://www.chadwyck.com/products_pq/
descriptions/iibp_ft.shtml

Index to Current Urban Documents
http://www.urbdocs.com

Index to How to Do It Information
http://www.nleindex.com/index.php?pID=HTDI

Index to Jewish Periodicals
http://www.jewishperiodicals.com/

Index to Legal Periodicals
http://www.hwwilson.com/Databases/legal.htm

Index Veterinarius
http://www.cabi.org/AbstractDatabases.asp?PID=87

Information Science and Technology Abstracts
http://www.ebscohost.com/thisTopic.php?marketID=1&topicID=91

InfoTrac
http://infotrac.thomsonlearning.com/

IngentaConnect
http://www.ingentaconnect.com/

INSPEC
http://www.theiet.org/publishing/inspec/index.cfm

International African Bibliography
http://www.saur.de/index.cfm?lang=DE&ID=0000008367

International Bibliography of the Social Sciences
http://www.lse.ac.uk/collections/IBSS

International Index to Black Periodicals Full Text http://www.chadwyck.com/products_pq/descriptions/iibp_ft.shtml

International Index to Film Periodicals
http://www.fiafnet.org/uk/publications/iifp.cfm

International Index to Music Periodicals
http://music.chadwyck.com/

International Index to the Performing Arts
http://iipa.chadwyck.com/

International Philosophical Bibliography
http://pob.peeters-leuven.be/content.php?bib=IPBfull

Internet & Personal Computing Abstracts
http://www.ebscohost.com/thisTopic.php?marketID=1&topicID=95

Journal of Economic Literature
http://www.aeaweb.org/journal.html

Language Teaching
http://journals.cambridge.org/action/displayJournal?jid=LTA

L'Annee Philologique
http://www.annee-philologique.com/aph/

LegalTrac
http://www.gale.com

Leisure, Recreation and Tourism Abstracts
http://www.cabi.org/AbstractDatabases.asp?PID=5

LexisNexis
http://www.lexisnexis.com/

LexisNexis Environmental
http://www.lexisnexis.com/academic/environmental/

LGBT Life
http://www.epnet.com/thisTopic.php?marketID=1&topicID=76

Library, Information Science, and Technology Abstracts
http://www.ebscohost.com/thisTopic.php?marketID=1&topicID=98

Library Literature & Information Science
http://www.ebscohost.com/thisTopic.php?marketID=1&topicID=98

Linguistics Abstracts
http://www.linguisticsabstracts.com

Linguistics and Language Behavior Abstracts (LLBA)
http://www.csa.com/factsheets/llba-set-c.php

LISTA
http://www.ebscohost.com/thisTopic.php?marketID=1&topicID=513

Magazine Article Summaries (MAS) Ultra-School Edition
http://www.epnet.com/thisTopic.php?marketID=7&topicID=156

MasterFILE Elite
http://www.epnet.com/thisTopic.php?marketID=6&topicID=104

MathSciNet
http://www.ams.org/mathscinet/

MEDLINE. *see also* **PubMed**
http://www.nlm.nih.gov/portals/librarians.html

ABSTRACTS AND INDEXES

METADEX
http://www.csa.com/factsheets/ metadex-set-c.php

Meteorological and Geoastrophysical Abstracts
http://www.csa.com/factsheets/mga-set-c.php

Microcomputer Index. *see* **Internet & Personal Computing Abstracts**

Middle East: Abstracts and Index (print only)
Pittsburgh: Northumberland Press, 1978 –

Middle Search
http://www.epnet.com/thisTopic.php?marketID=8
&topicID=110

MLA International Bibliography
http://www.mla.org/bibliography

Music Index
http://www.harmonieparkpress.com/MusicIndex.
asp

Mystery Short Fiction
http://www.philsp.com/homeville/msf/0start.htm

NASA Astrophysics Data System (ADS)
http://adsabs.harvard.edu/

New Testament Abstracts
http://members.aol.com/ntaweston/ nta.html

N T I S Data Base
http://grc.ntis.gov/ntisdb.htm

Numismatic Literature
http://www.numismatics.org/numlit/
index.html

**Nutrition Abstracts and Reviews Series A,
Human and Experimental**
http://www.cabi.org/Abstract
Databases.asp?SubjectArea=&PID= 79

**Nutrition Abstracts and Reviews Series B,
Livestock Feeds and Feeding**
http://www.cabi.org/Abstract
Databases.asp?SubjectArea=&PID= 80

Old Testament Abstracts
http://www.atla.com/products/catalogs/catalogs_
ota.html#online

Online Geographical Bibliography (GEOBIB)
http://geobib.lib.uwm.edu/cgi-
bin/Pwebrecon.cgi?DB=local&PAGE=First

PAIS International
http://www.csa.com/factsheets/pais-set-c.php

Peace Research Abstracts Journal
http://www.sagepub.com/journalsProdDesc.nav?
prodId=Journal200745

Philosopher's Index
http://www.philinfo.org/

Physical Education Index
http://www.csa.com/factsheets/pei-set-c.php

Pollution Abstracts
http://www.csa.com/factsheets/ pollution-set-c.php

Population Index
http://popindex.princeton.edu/

Primary Search
http://www.epnet.com/thisTopic.php?marketID=9
&topicID=122

Project MUSE
http://muse.jhu.edu/

ProQuest Accounting & Tax
http://www.proquest.com/products_pq/descriptions
/pq_accounting_tax.shtml

ProQuest Criminal Justice Periodicals Index
http://www.proquest.co.uk/products_
pq/descriptions/pq_criminal_justice. shtml

ProQuest Research Library
http://www.proquest.com/products_pq/descriptions
/pq_research_library. shtml

PsycArticles
http://www.apa.org/psycarticles/

PsycINFO
http://www.apa.org/psycinfo/

PubMed
http://www.ncbi.nlm.nih.gov/sites/
entrez?db=pubmed

**Quarterly Index to Africana Periodical
Literature**
http://lcweb2.loc.gov/misc/qsihtml/

Readers' Guide to Periodical Literature
http://www.hwwilson.com/Databases/Readersg.
htm

RePEc (Research Papers in Economics)
http://repec.org/

Repertoire Bibliographique de la Philosophie.
see **International Philosophical Bibliography
Resources in Education**
http://www.eric.ed.gov/

RILM Abstracts of Music Literature
http://www.rilm.org/

Risk Abstracts
http://www.csa.com/factsheets/risk-set-c.php

Sage Family Studies Abstracts
http://www.sagepub.com/journalsProdDesc.nav?
prodId=Journal200889

Sage Urban Studies Abstracts
http://www.sagepub.com/journalsProdDesc.nav?pr
odId=Journal200909

Science Citation Index. *see also* **Web of Science**
http://scientific.thomson.com/products/sci/

Scientific and Technical Aerospace Reports (STAR)
http://www.sti.nasa.gov/STI-public-homepage.html

SciSearch
http://support.dialog.com/searchaids/
dialog/f34_cited_ref.shtml

SCOPUS
http://info.scopus.com/

Social Sciences Full Text
http://www.hwwilson.com/Databases/socsci.htm

Social Sciences Citation Index.
see also **Web of Science**
http://scientific.thomson.com/products/ssci/

Social Work Abstracts
http://www.naswpress.org/
publications/journals/abstracts/ swabintro.html

SocINDEX http://www.epnet.com/thisTopic.php?
topicID=138&marketID=1

Sociological Abstracts
http://www.csa.com/factsheets/ socioabs-set-c.php

SPIE Digital Library
http://spiedl.org/

SPORTDiscus
http://www.sirc.ca/products/ sportdiscus.cfm

SSRN Management Research Network
http://www.ssrn.com/mrn/index.html

Studies on Women and Gender Abstracts
http://www.tandf.co.uk/journals/titles/1467596x.
asp

TOCS-IN
http://www.chass.utoronto.ca/ amphoras/tocs.html

TOXNET
http://toxnet.nlm.nih.gov/

TRANSPORT
http://www.ovid.com/site/catalog/
DataBase/157.jsp?top=2&mid=3&bottom=7&subs
ection=10

TRANweb
http://tran.library.northwestern.edu/

TreeSearch
http://www.treesearch.fs.fed.us/

TRIS Online
http://ntlsearch.bts.gov/tris/index.do

Vertical File Index
http://www.hwwilson.com/print/ vfi.html

Veterinary Bulletin
http://www.cabi.org/AbstractDatabases.asp?PID=
86

Violence & Abuse Abstracts
http://www.sagepub.com/journalsProdDesc.nav?
prodId=Journal200798

Web of Science. *see* **Arts and Humanities
Citation Index, Social Science Citation Index,**
and **Science Citation Index**

Wilson Business Full Text
http://www.hwwilson.com/Databases/business.htm

Wilson Omnifile Full Text
http://www.hwwilson.com/Databases/omnifile.htm

Women's Studies International
http://www.nisc.com/Frame/NISC_ products-f.htm

**World Agricultural Economics and Rural
Sociology**
http://www.cabi.org/Abstract
Databases.asp?PID=83

Zoological Record
http://scientific.thomson.com/media/
scpdf/zr_fs_0705.pdf

CONSULTANTS

Full names and addresses are given for the consultants at the head of each section.

Adams, Roger C. (Comic Books)

Altschiller, Donald (Middle East)

Angelini, Mary Frances (Craft)

Arendt, Julie (Animal Welfare)

Armstrong, Anne R. (Little Magazines)

Ashmun, Julia D. (Boats and Boating)

Aude, Stephanie (Medicine)

Avery, Bonnie E. (Forestry)

Bachmann, Todd (Beer, Wine, and Spirits)

Ball, Heather (Landscape Architecture)

Bartley, Drew (Genealogy)

Baughman, Pauline (Hiking, Climbing, and Outdoor Recreation)

Benedicto, Juanita (Physiology)

Becker, Nancy J. (Political Science)

Berard, G. Lynn (Engineering and Technology)

Blake, Laura Farwell (Literary Reviews)

Blake, Michael R. (Fish, Fisheries, and Aquaculture)

Bliss, Laurel (Photography)

Bourneuf, Joe (Philately)

Bobal, Alison (Public Health)

Boyd, C. Trenton (Veterinary Science)

Braxton, Susan M. (Chemistry; Science and Technology)

Bruno, Thomas (Anime, Graphic Novels, and Manga; Archaeology)

Burchsted, Fred (Geography)

Burkhart, Laura (Nursing)

Burnham, Erica (Canada)

Burton, Donna (Humor)

Burton, Jean Piper (Folklore)

Butler, Barbara A. (Marine Science and Technology)

Campbell, Nancy F. (Communication)

Casper, Christianne L. (Astrology; Parapsychology)

Ciaburri, Sara (Medicine)

Clack, Mary Beth (Literary Reviews)

Clark, George E. (Environment and Conservation; Television, Video, and Radio)

Coe, Erica L. (Music Reviews)

Collins, Linda (Horses)

Conley, Kathleen M. (Military)

Crane, Rachel (Fishing)

Crowley, Gwyneth H. (Economics)

Cushing, Lincoln (Labor and Industrial Relations)

Dalrymple, Connie (Physiology)

Dankert, Holly Stec (Art; Interior Design and Decoration)

Davis, Marta A. (Fiction: General/Mystery and Detective)

Dawson, Patrick Jose (Games)

Deemer, Kevin (Family Planning; Real Estate)

DeHart, Brian (Business)

Demetriou, Laura Burkhart (Nursing)

Diaz, Enrique (General Interest: Non-English Language; Management, Administration, and Human Resources)

Diaz, Joseph (Bob) (Latin America and Spain)

Dolan, Meghan (Informatics; Population Studies)

Donovan, Carrie (Fiction: Science Fiction, Fantasy, and Horror)

Dratch, Gladys I. (Education)

Duhon, Lucy (Children)

Dulin, Kim (Law)

Dunn, Donald J. (Law)

Duranceau, Ellen Finnie (Computers and Information Technology)

Ellis, Allen (Comic Books)

Elsen, Carol J. (Finance)

Esty, Barbara (Finance)

Feis, Nathaniel (Art)

Firpo, Andy (Computers and Information Technology)

Fladger, Ellen (History)

Flood, Beth (Music: Popular)

Fusich, Monica (Fashion and Lifestyle)

Futral, Meredith (Management, Administration, and Human Resources)

Garrison, Anne (Literature)

Garson, Deborah S. (Education)

Gauder, Heidi (Weddings)

Geary, Mary Kathleen (Transportation)

Giglierano, Joan (Marriage and Divorce)

Gillie, Esther (Music: General)

Greene, Brian C. (Model Making; Paleontology)

Groves, Adam (Fire Protection)

Hallman, Clark N. (Criminology and Law Enforcement)

Hammill, Sarah J. (Sociology and Social Work)

Harnsberger, R. Scott (Philosophy)

Hierl, Sebastian (Europe)

Highsmith, Doug (Comic Books)

Hodgson, Jim (Forensics)

Hoeppner, Christopher (Accounting and Taxation)

Hutton, Jane (Spirituality and Well-Being)

Huwe, Terence K. (Labor and Industrial Relations)

Imre, Andrea (Ethnic Studies)

Jackson, Amy (Library and Information Science)

Jenkins, Fred W. (Classical Studies)

Jerabek, Alexander (Canada)

Johns-Masten, Kathryn (Birds; Globalization)

Johnston, Robert C. (Native Americans)

Jones, Marie F. (Civil Liberties)

Kautzman, Amy (Automobiles and Motorcycles)

Kaye, Catherine (Civil Liberties)

Kendall, Susan K. (Biotechnology)

Kent, Caroline M. (Films; Journalism and Writing; Parenting)

Kilcullen, Maureen (Antiques)

Kilpatrick, Thomas L. (Fashion and Lifestyle; Gender Studies)

Kline, Hilary (Computers and Information Technology; Consumer Education; Safety)

Klink, Sara (Biology)

Kooistra, Judith Ohles (Gay, Lesbian, Bisexual, and Transgender)

Kosokoff, Jeff (Physiology)

Krajewski, Rex J. (Gardening)

Kraljic, Mary (Criminology and Law Enforcement)

Kumar, Suhasini L. (Peace and Conflict Studies)

Kunkel, Lilith R. (Gender Studies)

LaBonte, Kristen (Ecology)

Ladwig, J. Parker (Mathematics)

Leigh, Miriam (Menopause/ Andropause)

Lemay, V. Blue (Literature)

Lener, Edward F. (Earth Sciences and Geology)

Lenkowski, Patricia A. (Anthropology)

Lowrie, Reed (Zoology)

Maas, Jan A. (Occupations and Careers)

Macfarlane, Carrie M. (Do-It -Yourself)

Marshall, Jerilyn (Alternatives; Spirituality and Well Being)

Matz, Pamela (Home; Religion)

Mayfield, Tracey (Geriatrics and Gerontological Studies)

McCaffrey, Erin K. (Family)

McClusky, Duncan (Agriculture)

McCutcheon, Camille (Blind and Visually Impaired; Pets)

McGee, Lori L. (Gay, Lesbian, Bisexual, and Transgender)

McKeigue, Elizabeth (International Magazines; Theater)

McMinn, Howard Stephen (Aeronautics and Space Science)

Meszaros, Rosemary L. (Government Periodicals-Federal; Government Periodicals-State and Local)

Metcalf, Susan (Literature)

Molendyke, Joseph A. (Hunting and Guns)

Montilio, Ralph (Music: General)

Moore, Susan (Atmospheric Sciences)

Naylor, Sharon (Disabilities)

Newland, Patricia (Death and Dying)

Oakley, Alissa (Asia and the Pacific)

Oftedahl, Lenora A. (Fish, Fisheries, and Aquaculture)

Ohles, Janet (Elder Issues)

Oka, Christine K. (Asian American; Cartography, GIS, and Imagery; Computers and Information Technology)

Oka, Susan (Films)

Olivares, Olivia (Latin America and Spain)

Palmer, Pamela (Food Industry)

Park, Betsy (Sports)

Phillips, Margaret (Pregnancy)

Phillips, Sarah (Bibliography)

Piroli, Vivienne B. (Health Care Administration)

Pollock, Jennifer (Health and Fitness)

Popadak, John E., II (Hunting and Guns)

Power, Margaret (Africa)

Providenti, Michael J. (Communication)

Randall, Eleanor P. (Health Professions)

Reyes, Veronica (Latin America and Spain)

Reyes, Awilda (Latino Studies)

Richardson, Diane (Fire Protection)

Ronningen, Jim (Newspapers)

Roughneen, Mari (Botany)

Ruan, Lian (Fire Protection)

Rudisell, Carol A. (African American)

Ruppel, Margie (Linguistics)

Schaffner, Bradley L. (Slavic Studies)

Schwartz, Vanette M. (Cultural Studies)

Sheehan, Kathleen (Political Science; Travel and Tourism)

Shrode, Flora G. (Earth Sciences and Geology)

Siegler, Sharon L. (Energy; Robotics)

Silveria, Janie B. (Books and Book Reviews)

Skewis, Charles A. (Fashion and Lifestyle; Gender Studies)

CONSULTANTS

Smith, Donna B. (Printing and Graphic Arts)

Sommer, Deborah (Urban Studies)

Sprung, Amy (Teenagers)

Stam, Julian (Building and Construction)

Storm, Paula M. (Electronics)

Sugrue, Edward Creighton, Jr. (Astronomy)

Sullivan, Laura A. (Communication)

Taylor, Terry (Classroom Magazines)

Thomas, Mary Augusta (Dance)

Threlkeld, Robert (Food and Nutrition; Informatics)

Toth, Joe (General Interest)

Trendler, Amy E. (Architecture)

Tsang, Daniel C. (Sexuality)

Tyckoson, David A. (Physics)

Tyler, Peggy (Management, Administration, and Human Resources)

Van de Streek, David (Numismatics)

Vang, Vang (Fashion and Lifestyle)

Vick, Liza (Music)

Watson, Amy (Cooking And Cookery; Hospitality/Restaurant)

Webster, Janet G. (Marine Science and Technology)

Weir, Katherine M. (Statistics)

Wharton, Nicholas (Building and Construction)

Whitesell, David R. (Bibliography)

Wies, Lorraine (History)

Williams, Clay (Advertising Marketing, and Public Relations)

Williams, Helene (Computers and Information Technology)

Wilson, Holly A. (News and Opinion)

Wisner, Melanie (Archives and Manuscripts)

Wood, Wendy (Printing and Graphic Arts)

Woolums, Jill L. (Psychology)

Wylie, Roslyn E. (Children)

Young, Courtney L. (Interdisciplinary Studies)

Yu, Xiaochang (Media and AV; World Wide Web)

ONLINE SERVICES

African Journals Online
19 Worcester St, PO Box 377, Grahamstown 6140, South
Africa
TEL 27-46-6229698, FAX 27-46-6229550
E-mail info@ajol.info
URL http://www.ajol.info

Allen Press Inc.
PO Box 368, Lawrence, KS 66044
810 E 10th St, Lawrence, KS 66044-3018
TEL 785-843-1234, 800-627-0326, FAX 785-843-1244
E-mail OnlineJournals@allenpress.com
URL http://www.allenpress.com

American Chemical Society
PO 3337, Columbus, OH 43210
TEL 614-447-3776, 888-338-0012, FAX 614-447-3671
E-mail help@acs.org
URL http://pubs.acs.org

American Institute of Physics, Scitation
Ste 1NO1, 2 Huntington Quadrangle, Melville, NY
11747-4502
TEL 516-576-2664, 800-874-6383, FAX 516-576-2604
E-mail subs@aip.org
URL http://scitation.aip.org/

American Psychological Association
PsycARTICLES, 750 First St, NE, Washington, DC
20002-4242
TEL 202-336-5650, 800-374-2722, FAX 202-336-5633
E-mail psycinfo@apa.org
URL http://www.apa.org/psycarticles

American Theological Library Association
300 South Wacker Dr, Ste 2100, Chicago, IL 60606-6701
TEL 312-454-5100, 888-665-2852, FAX 312-454-5505
E-mail atla@atla.com
URL http://www.atla.com

Annual Reviews
4139 El Camino Way, PO Box 10139, Palo Alto, CA
94303-0139
TEL 650-493-4400, 800-523-8635, FAX 650-855-9815,
650-424-0910
E-mail service@annualreviews.org
URL http://www.annualreviews.org/

Ashley Publications Ltd.
Unitec House 3rd Fl, 2 Albert Pl, Finchley Central, London
N3 1QB, United Kingdom
TEL 44-20-83433883, FAX 44-20-83432313E-mail
info@ashley-pub.com
URL http://www.ashley-pub.com

Association For Computing Machinery, Inc., A C M D
igital Library
2 Penn Plaza, Ste 701, New York, NY 10121-0701
TEL 212 626-0500, 800 342-6626, FAX 212 944-1318
E-mail acm@helpacm.org
URL http://portal.acm.org/dl.cfm

Bioline International
E-mail Bioline.International@utoronto.ca
URL http://www.bioline.org.br

BioOne
21 Dupont Circle, Ste 800, Washington, DC 20036
TEL 202-296-2296, 800-843-8482, FAX 202-872-0884
URL http://www.bioone.org/

Blackwell Synergy
9600 Garsington Rd, Oxford OX4 2DQ, United Kingdom
TEL 44-1865-776868, FAX 44-1865-714591
URL http://www.blackwell-synergy.com

The Bureau of National Affairs, Inc.
1231 25th St, NW, Washington, DC 20037
TEL 202-452-4200, 800-372-1033, FAX 202-452-4226
E-mail customercare@bna.com
URL http://www.bna.com/

C S A
7200 Wisconsin Ave, Ste 601, Bethesda, MD 20814
TEL 301-961-6700, FAX 301-961-6720
URL http://www.csa.com

Cambridge University Press
The Edinburgh Bldg, Shaftesbury Rd, Cambridge CB2 2RU,
United Kingdom
TEL 44-1223-326070, FAX 44-1223-325150
E-mail journals@cambridge.org
URL http://journals.cambridge.org/

CanWest Interactive Inc., FPInfomart
1450 Don Mills Rd, Toronto, ON M3B 2X7, Canada
TEL 416-442-2121, 800-661-7678, FAX 416-442-2968
E-mail Helpdesk@canwest.com
URL http://www.fpinfomart.ca

CEDOCAR
9 Boulevard Liedot, Angouleme 16021, France
TEL 33-5-45371963, FAX 33-5-45371916
E-mail clt08@cedocar.dga.defense.gouv.fr
URL http://www.cedocar.defense.gouv.fr

ONLINE SERVICES

Chadwyck-Healey Inc.
789 E Eisenhower Pkwy, Ann Arbor, MI 48106-1346
TEL 800-521-0600
E-mail info@il.proquest.com
URL http://www.chadwyck.com

D I M D I
Weisshausstrasse 36-38a, Cologne D-50676, Germany
TEL 49-221-47241, FAX 49-221-4724444
URL http://www.dimdi.de

DataStar
11000 Regency Pkwy, Ste 10, Cary, NC 27511
TEL 919-462-8600, 800-334-2564, FAX 919-468-9890
Data Center, Laupenstrasse 18a, Berne 38008, Switzerland
TEL 41-31-3849511, FAX 43-31-3849675
E-mail customer@dialog.com
URL http://www.datastarweb.com/

The Dialog Corporation
11000 Regency Pkwy, Ste 10, Cary, NC 27518
TEL 919-462-8600, 800-334-2564, FAX 919-468-9890
E-mail customer@dialog.com
URL http://www.dialog.com

East View Information Services
10601 Wayzata Blvd, Minneapolis, MN 55305
TEL 952-252-1201, 800-477-1005, FAX 952-252-1202
E-mail info@eastview.com
URL http://www.eastview.com

EBSCO Publishing, EBSCO Host
10 Estes St, PO Box 682, Ipswich, MA 01938-0682
TEL 978-356-6500, 800-653-2726, FAX 978-356-6565
E-mail information@ebscohost.com
URL http://www.epnet.com

Emerald Group Publishing Limited
Howard House, Wagon Ln, Bingley BD16 1WA, United
Kingdom
TEL 44-1274-777700, FAX 44-1274-785201
URL http://www.emeraldinsight.com/

Factiva, Inc.
PO Box 300, Princeton, NJ 08543-0300
4300 Rt 1 N, Bldg 5, 2nd Fl, Monmouth Junction, NJ 08852
TEL 800-369-0166
URL http://www.factiva.com

FIZ Technik e.V.
Hanauer Landstr. 151-153, Frankfurt a.M. D-60314,
Germany
TEL 49-69-4308111
E-mail customer-service@fiz-technik.de
URL http://www.fiz-technik.de

Florida Center for Library Automation
5830 NW 39th Ave, Gainesville, FL 32606
TEL 352-392-9020, FAX 352-392-9185
E-mail fclecp@nersp.nerdu.ufl.edu
URL http://www.fcla.edu/index.html

G B I - Genios Deutsche Wirtschaftsdatenbank GmbH
Freischuetzstr 96, Munich 81927, Germany
TEL 49-89-9928790, FAX 49-89-99287999
E-mail info@genios.de
URL http://www.genios.de/

Gale
27500 Drake Rd, Farmington Hills, MI 48331-3535
TEL 248-699-4253, 800-877-4253, 800-347-4253, FAX
248-699-8035, 800-414-5043
27500 Drake Rd, Farmington Hills, MI 48331-3535
TEL 248-699-4253, 800-877-4253, 800-347-4253, FAX
248-699-8035, 800-414-5043
E-mail international@gale.com, galeord@gale.com,
gale.galeord@thomson.com
URL http://gale.cengage.com, http://www.galegroup.com

William S. Hein & Co., Inc.
1285 Main St, Buffalo, NY 14209-1987
TEL 716-882-2600, 800-828-7571, FAX 716-883-8100
E-mail mail@wshein.com
URL http://www.wshein.com

HighWire Press
1454 Page Mill Rd, Palo Alto, CA 94304-1124
TEL 650-723-2019, FAX 650-723-9335
E-mail contact@highwire.stanford.edu
URL http://www.highwire.org

I E E E
3 Park Ave, 17th Fl, New York, NY 10016-5997
TEL 212-419-7900, FAX 212-752-4929
445 Hoes Ln, Box 1331, Piscataway, NJ 08855-1331
TEL 732-981-0600, 800-678-4333, FAX 732-981-9667

IngentaConnect
1 Riverside Court, Lower Bristol Rd., Bath BA2 3DZ,
United Kingdom
TEL 44-1225-361000, FAX 44-1225-361155
875 Massachusetts Ave., 7th Fl., Cambridge, MA 02139
TEL 617-497-6514, FAX 617-354-6875
E-mail info@ingenta.com
URL http://www.ingentaconnect.com/

J S T
5-3, Yonbancho, Chiyoda-ku, Tokyo 102-8666, Japan
TEL 81-3-52148401, FAX 81-3-52148400
E-mail overseas@mr.jst.go.jp
URL http://www.jst.go.jp

J-Stage
Japan Science and Technology Agency, Department of
Advanced Databases, 5-3, Yonbancho, Chiyoda-ku, Tokyo
102-8666, Japan
TEL 81-3-5214-8455
E-mail contact@jstage.jst.go.jp
URL http://www.jstage.jst.go.jp/ja/index.html

JSTOR (Web-based Journal Archive)
149 Fifth Ave, 8th Fl, New York, NY 10010
TEL 212-358-6400, FAX 212-358-6499
E-mail support@jstor.org
URL http://www.jstor.org

Justis Publishing Ltd.
Grand Union House, 20 Kentish Town Rd., London NW1
9NR, United Kingdom
TEL 44-20-72848080, FAX 44-20-72671133
E-mail customerservices@justis.com
URL http://www.justis.com

LexisNexis
9443 Springboro Pike, Miamisburg, OH 45342
TEL 937-865-6800, 800-227-9597, FAX 937-865-1666
URL http://www.lexisnexis.com, http://www.lexisnexis.com/

LexisNexis Canada Inc., QuickLaw
Ste 700, 112 Kent St, Ottawa, ON K1P 5P2, Canada
TEL 613-238-3499, FAX 613-238-7597
URL http://www.lexisnexis.ca/ql/index.php

M D Consult
11830 Westline Industrial Dr, St Louis, MO 63146
TEL 314-997-1176, 800-401-9962, FAX 314-997-5080
E-mail mdc.customerservice@elsevier.com
URL http://www.mdconsult.com

Micromedia ProQuest
789 E Eisenhower Pkwy, Ann Arbor, MI 48106-1346
TEL 734-761-4700 ext 3333, 800-521-0600
E-mail info@il.proquest.com
URL http://il.proquest.com/brand/micromedia.shtml

N I S C International, Inc.
Wyman Towers, 3100 St Paul St, Baltimore, MD 21218
TEL 410-243-0797, FAX 410-243-0892
E-mail sales@nisc.com
URL http://www.nisc.com

National Library of Medicine
8600 Rockville Pike, Bethesda, MD 20209
TEL 301-594-5983, 888-346-3656, FAX 301-496-4000
8600 Rockville Pike, Bethesda, MD 20209
TEL 301-594-5983, 888-346-3656, FAX 301-496-4000
E-mail custserv@nlm.nih.gov
URL http://www.nlm.nih.gov

Newsbank, Inc.
4501 Tamiami Trail N., Ste. 316, Naples, FL 34103
TEL 802-875-2910, 800-762-8182, FAX 239-263-3004
E-mail CustService@newsbank.com
URL http://www.newsbank.com

Northern Light Technology, Inc.
Ten Canal Park, Cambridge, MA 02141
TEL 617-674-2074, FAX 617-674-2076
URL http://www.northernlight.com

O C L C Online Computer Library Center, Inc.
6565 Kilgour Pl, Dublin, OH 43017
TEL 614-764-6000, 800-848-5878, FAX 614-764-6096
E-mail oclc@oclc.org
URL http://www.oclc.org

OhioLINK
Ste 300, 2455 North Star Rd, Columbus, OH 43221
TEL 614-728-3600, FAX 614-728-3610
E-mail info@ohiolink.edu
URL http://www.ohiolink.edu/

Ovid Technologies, Inc.
333 Seventh Ave, New York, NY 10001
TEL 646-674-6300, 800-950-2035, FAX 646-674-6301
E-mail sales@ovid.com
URL http://www.ovid.com

Oxford Journals
Great Clarendon St, Oxford OX2 6DP, United Kingdom
TEL 44-1865-267907, FAX 44-1865-267485

Project MUSE
2715 N Charles St, Baltimore, MD 21218-4319
TEL 410-516-6989, FAX 410-516-6968
E-mail muse@muse.jhu.edu
URL http://muse.jhu.edu

ProQuest K-12 Learning Solutions
789 E Eisenhower Pkwy, PO Box 1346, Ann Arbor, MI 48106
TEL 734-761-4700, 800-521-0600
E-mail info@il.proquest.com
URL http://www.proquestk12.com/

ProQuest LLC (Ann Arbor)
300 N Zeeb Rd, PO Box 1346, Ann Arbor, MI 48106-1346
TEL 734-761-4700, 800-521-0600, FAX 734-997-4040, 800-864-0019
789 E Eisenhower Pkwy, PO Box 1346, Ann Arbor, MI 48106-1346
TEL 800-521-0600
E-mail info@il.proquest.com, info@proquest.com
URL http://www.umi.com, http://www.proquest.com

R M I T Publishing
A'Beckett St, PO Box 12058, Melbourne, VIC 8006, Australia
TEL 61-3-99258100, FAX 61-3-99258134
E-mail info@rmitpublishing.com.au
URL http://www.rmitpublishing.com.au/

SAGE Publications, Inc., SAGE Journals Online
2455 Teller Rd, Thousand Oaks, CA 91320
TEL 800-818-7243
URL http://online.sagepub.com/

SciELO
CONICYT, Canada 308 Providencia, Santiago de Chile, Chile
TEL 56-2-3654400, FAX 56-2-3654451
INFOMED, Calle 27 No 110 M y N, Vedado, Havana, Cuba
TEL 537-55-3375, FAX 537-33-3063
FAPESP - BIREME, Rue Botucatu 862, Sao Paulo SP 04023-901, Brazil
TEL 55-11-55769863, FAX 55-11-55758868
E-mail scielo@bireme.br
URL http://www.scielo.org, http://www.scielo.br

ScienceDirect
360 Park Ave S, PO Box 945, New York, NY 10010-1710
TEL 212-633-3730, 888-437-4636, FAX 212-462-1974
E-mail usinfo@scidirect.com
URL http://www.sciencedirect.com/

SilverPlatter Information, Incorporated
333 Seventh Ave, 20th Fl, New York, NY 10001
TEL 646-674-6300, 800-950-2035, FAX 646-674-6301
E-mail sales@ovid.com
URL http://www.ovid.com

Springer LINK
Tiergartenstr.17, Heidelberg 69121, Germany
TEL 49-6221-4870, FAX 49-6221-4878366
175 Fifth Ave., New York, NY 10010
TEL 212-460-1501, FAX 212-460-1595
URL http://www.springerlink.com/home/main.mpx

ONLINE SERVICES

SwetsWise Online Content
Heereweg 347 B, Lisse 2161 CA, Netherlands
TEL 31-252-435111, FAX 31-252-415888
160 Ninth Ave, PO Box 1459, Runnemede, NJ 08078
TEL 856-312-2690, 800-645-6595, FAX 856-312-2000
E-mail info@nl.swets.com
URL https://www.swetswise.com/

Thomson West
610 Opperman Dr, Eagan, MN 55123-1396
TEL 651-687-8000, 651-687-7000, 800-344-5008,
800-328-4880, FAX 651-687-7302, 651-687-6674
E-mail customer.service@westgroup.com
URL http://west.thomson.com

WanFang Data Corp.
Rm 432, 15 Fu Xing Lu, Beijing 100038, China
TEL 86-10-58882496, FAX 86-10-58882434
E-mail zjx@wanfangdata.com.cn
URL http://www.periodicals.net.cn/

Wiley InterScience
111 River St, Hoboken, NJ 07030
TEL 201-748-6000, FAX 201-748-6088
URL http://www3.interscience.wiley.com/cgi-bin/home

H.W. Wilson
950 University Ave, Bronx, NY 10452-4224
TEL 718-588-8400, 800-367-6770, FAX 718-681-1511
E-mail custserv@hwwilson.com
URL http://www.hwwilson.com

MAGAZINES FOR LIBRARIES

■ ACCOUNTING AND TAXATION

Professional/Scholarly/Taxation

Christopher Hoeppner, Associate Director of Libraries, DePaul University, 2350 North Kenmore Ave., Chicago, IL 60614; choeppne@depaul.edu

Introduction

Corporate malfeasance continues to be reported in the business press on a regular basis, and accounting issues are most often at the center of the wrongdoing. The Sarbanes-Oxley legislation enacted in 2002 ushered in a new era in corporate accountability, and boards and top executives are still grappling with the implications of the changed environment. Compliance with this new regulatory regime has placed a significant burden on public companies, and the relationship between the costs and benefits of the law has inevitably been a source of continuing controversy. On the taxation front, the federal tax legislation enacted between 2001 and 2004 included many provisions that are slated to expire in 2010 unless Congress acts to extend them, and this is creating considerable uncertainty as the deadline approaches.

In contrast to many academic disciplines, accounting and taxation lie at the intersection of the highly quantitative methods of economics, the behavioral approaches of the social sciences, and the precedent-driven methodology of legal research. Legal or regulatory authority can take the form not only of statutes and court decisions but also of the rulings of various governmental (e.g., the Securities and Exchange Commission) and non-governmental bodies (e.g., the Financial Accounting Standards Board and the Public Company Accounting Oversight Board). The interpretation and application of authoritative pronouncements from each of these sources comprise a topic of much ongoing discussion for both practitioners and academicians.

Periodicals in accounting (as opposed to taxation) have been classified below as either professional or scholarly in their orientation. While academicians occasionally write for professional publications, their research appears first and in greatest depth in the scholarly titles, which are little read by practitioners, given that the papers appearing there tend toward the theoretical, technical, and often highly quantitative. In cases where scholarly research has clear implications for accounting practice, the work is later presented in less technical form in the professional journals. The field of taxation is an exception to this pattern. Here there is much more dialogue between practitioners and academicians, with accounting and law professors on the one hand, and tax attorneys and accountants on the other, often publishing their work in the same journals. It is difficult to draw a distinction between professional and scholarly titles here and no attempt has been made to do so.

Basic Periodicals

Ac: *Accounting Review, The CPA Journal, Journal of Accountancy, Journal of Accounting Research, Journal of Taxation.*

Basic Abstracts and Indexes

ABI/INFORM, Accounting and Tax Index, Business & Company ASAP, Business Periodicals Index, EBSCO Business Source Elite.

Professional

1. **Accountancy.** [ISSN: 0001-4664] 1889. m. USD 100 United States; GBP 5.10 newsstand/cover per issue domestic; USD 10 newsstand/cover per issue foreign. Ed(s): Brian Singleton Green. Institute of Chartered Accountants in England and Wales, Chartered Accountants' Hall, PO Box 433, London, EC2P 2BJ, United Kingdom; http://www.accountancymag.co.uk. Illus., index, adv. Circ: 70000. Vol. ends: Jun/Dec. Microform: PQC. Online: EBSCO Publishing, EBSCO Host; Factiva, Inc.; Northern Light Technology, Inc.; OCLC Online Computer Library Center, Inc.; ProQuest LLC (Ann Arbor). Reprint: PSC. *Indexed:* ABIn, ATI, BPI, ExcerpMed. *Bk. rev.:* 0-2, 500-750 words, signed. *Aud.:* Sa.

Published on behalf of the Institute of Chartered Accountants in England and Wales, the British professional association for public accountants, this magazine offers a mix of news, opinion pieces, and feature articles. The focus is on the practical, with articles on taxation, management issues in accounting practice, and the implementation of new standards. Frequently, summaries or the full text of official releases, such as exposure drafts or new pronouncements, are included.

2. **The Accountant.** [ISSN: 0001-4710] 1874. m. GBP 867; EUR 1207; USD 1447. Ed(s): Marc Barber. Lafferty Publications Ltd., The Colonnades, 82 Bishops Bridge Rd, London, W2 6BB, United Kingdom; cuserv@lafferty.com; http://www.lafferty.com. Illus., index, adv. Online: Factiva, Inc.; Florida Center for Library Automation; Gale; LexisNexis; Northern Light Technology, Inc.; OCLC Online Computer Library Center, Inc.; ProQuest LLC (Ann Arbor). Reprint: PSC. *Indexed:* ATI, CWI, LRI. *Aud.:* Sa.

This monthly newsletter, typically 20 pages in length, contains news articles that describe trends and developments in accounting practice worldwide. Articles announce new standards, report news from accounting firms and associations, or survey the accounting profession within a particular country.

3. **Accounting & Business.** Former titles (until 1998): *Certified Accountant;* (until 1972): *Certified Accountants Journal.* [ISSN: 1460-406X] 1905. m. Free to members. Ed(s): John Prosser. Association of Chartered Certified Accountants, 29 Lincoln's Inn Fields, London, WC2A 3EE, United Kingdom; info@accaglobal.com; http://www.accaglobal.com/publications. Illus., index, adv. Circ: 59450. Vol. ends: Dec. *Indexed:* ATI. *Bk. rev.:* 3, 150-400 words, signed. *Aud.:* Sa.

This professional journal for British accountants is a publication of the Association of Chartered Certified Accountants. It offers news on accounting and auditing trends and developments, information about association activities, and feature articles that frequently focus on business topics outside of accounting. It also presents information on official pronouncements of the association. An archive (from 2003 on) of the full text of many articles is available at the journal's web site.

4. **Accounting Horizons.** [ISSN: 0888-7993] 1987. q. USD 225. Ed(s): Eugene Imhoff. American Accounting Association, 5717 Bessie Dr, Sarasota, FL 34233-2399; http://aaahq.org. Illus., index, adv. Refereed. Vol. ends: Dec. Reprint: PSC. *Indexed:* ABIn, ATI, BPI, IBSS. *Aud.:* Ac, Sa.

A product of the American Accounting Association, this publication features articles with a broader intended audience than accounting academics, including practicing accountants, educators, regulators, and students. Material tends to be presented in a less technical and quantitative manner than in most scholarly journals, including the association's own *Accounting Review.* Commentaries on current issues and reviews of authoritative pronouncements are also offered. The result is a journal that ties accounting theory to practice.

5. *Accounting Today: the business newspaper for the tax and accounting community.* [ISSN: 1044-5714] 1987. bi-w. except Apr., Aug. USD 99 domestic; USD 113 foreign. Ed(s): Bill Carlino. SourceMedia, Inc., One State St Plaza, 27th Fl, New York, NY 10004; custserv@ sourcemedia.com; http://www.sourcemedia.com. Illus., adv. Circ: 32000. Online: EBSCO Publishing, EBSCO Host; Factiva, Inc.; Florida Center for Library Automation; Gale; LexisNexis; Northern Light Technology, Inc.; OCLC Online Computer Library Center, Inc.; ProQuest K-12 Learning Solutions; ProQuest LLC (Ann Arbor). *Indexed:* ATI, LRI. *Aud.:* Sa.

This tabloid-size newspaper for accountants makes effective use of color, layout, and graphics. It reports on the activities of firms, individuals, and agencies in the tax and accounting community. Its annual surveys of regional accounting firms, of the top 100 firms nationally, and of the top 100 accounting software products are of particular interest. A web site produced by the publisher, www.webcpa.com, offers some of the print publication's content free.

6. *Business Valuation Review.* Formerly (until 1987): *Business Valuation News.* [ISSN: 0897-1781] 1982. q. Members, USD 50; Non-members, USD 60. Ed(s): James H Schilt. American Society of Appraisers, Business Valuation Committee, 555 Herndon Parkway, Ste 125, Herndon, VA 20170; asainfo@appraisers.org; http://www.appraisers.org/. Circ: 2500. *Aud.:* Ac, Sa.

Business valuation—the study of a privately held business with the purpose of assigning to it a dollar value—is a specialty that draws upon elements of accounting, finance, and taxation. Published under the auspices of the Business Valuation Committee of the American Society of Appraisers, this journal offers articles on business valuation topics that are authored by practitioners.

7. *C A Magazine.* Incorporates (1969-1996): *C I C A Dialogue;* Former titles (until 1974): *C A. Chartered Accountant;* (until 1971): *Canadian Chartered Accountant.* [ISSN: 0317-6878] 1911. 10x/yr. Ed(s): Christian Bellavance. Canadian Institute of Chartered Accountants, 277 Wellington St W, Toronto, ON M5V 3H2, Canada; camagazine@cica.ca; http://www.cica.ca. Illus., adv. Circ: 76635 Paid. Microform: PQC. Online: EBSCO Publishing, EBSCO Host; Factiva, Inc.; Gale; Micromedia ProQuest; OCLC Online Computer Library Center, Inc.; ProQuest LLC (Ann Arbor); H.W. Wilson. *Indexed:* ABIn, ATI, BPI, CBCARef, CPerI, LRI, PAIS. *Aud.:* Sa.

This is the publication of the Canadian Institute of Chartered Accountants, the association of public accountants in Canada. As such, it includes articles on a broad range of topics of interest to accounting practitioners, including taxes, technology, and practice development and management. Many articles are available in full text on the magazine's web site.

8. *The C P A Journal.* Former titles (until 1975): *The C P A;* (until 1975): *C P A Journal;* (until 1972): *Certified Public Accountant; New York Certified Public Accountant: C P A.* [ISSN: 0732-8435] 1930. m. USD 42 domestic (Students, USD 21). Ed(s): Mary Jo Kranacher, Thomas Morris. New York State Society of Certified Public Accountants, 3 Park Ave, 18th Fl, New York, NY 10016-5991. Illus., adv. Circ: 32000 Paid. Vol. ends: Dec. *Indexed:* ABIn, ATI, BPI. *Bk. rev.:* 0-1, 250-350 words, signed. *Aud.:* Sa.

Although this magazine is published by a state accounting society, its scope is national, and it has long been among the most important publications directed to accounting practitioners in the United States. Pronouncements of the American Institute of Certified Public Accountants, Financial Accounting Standards Board, and other regulatory bodies are covered, as are developments in tax law, technology, and other topics of interest to the practicing professional. The full text of each issue since 1989 is available at the journal's web site.

9. *Financial Management.* Former titles: *Management Accounting;* (until 1965): *Cost Accountant.* [ISSN: 1471-9185] 1921. m. GBP 40; GBP 3 newsstand/cover per issue. Ed(s): Gemma Townley. Chartered Institute of Management Accountants, 63 Portland Pl, London, W1N 4AB, United Kingdom; journal@cima.org.uk; http://www.cima.org.uk. Illus., index, adv. Circ: 55000. Vol. ends: Dec. Online: EBSCO Publishing, EBSCO Host; Florida Center for Library Automation; Gale; OCLC Online Computer Library Center, Inc.; ProQuest LLC (Ann Arbor). Reprint: SCH. *Indexed:* ABIn, ATI, JEL. *Aud.:* Sa.

This magazine is an official publication of the Chartered Institute of Management Accountants. It contains practical articles and columns on management accounting, as well as reports on activities of the institute. Although most articles are primarily concerned with practical aspects of management accounting in the United Kingdom, many may also be of value to readers elsewhere.

10. *Internal Auditing.* [ISSN: 0897-0378] 1986. bi-m. USD 240. Ed(s): Andrea Kingston. W G & L Financial Reporting & Management Research, 395 Hudson St, New York, NY 10014; ria.customerservices@ thomson.com; http://ria.thomson.com. Adv. Circ: 3500 Paid. *Indexed:* ABIn, ATI. *Aud.:* Ac, Sa.

This magazine publishes articles by practitioners and academics that focus on compliance issues, risk assessment, fraud prevention, corporate governance, information technology auditing, and many other topics. Also included are summaries of current audit research, case studies, and feedback on new initiatives and standards from the Institute of Internal Auditors and other organizations.

11. *Internal Auditing & Business Risk.* Formerly: *Internal Auditing.* 1978. m. EUR 120. Ed(s): Neil Baker. Institute of Internal Auditors (UK and Ireland), 13 Abbeville Mews, 88 Clapham Park Rd, London, SW4 7BX, United Kingdom; info@iia.org.uk; http://www.iia.org.uk/. Illus., adv. Circ: 6000 Paid. *Bk. rev.:* 1-2, 500-1,000 words, signed. *Aud.:* Sa.

This is the official journal of the Institute of Internal Auditors–United Kingdom and Ireland. It includes articles that focus on the internal auditing function, written for practitioners. In addition to auditing techniques, articles discuss such areas as recruitment and retention of staff, e-commerce, and professional ethics. Association news and events are also covered. A free archive (from 2001 on) of full-image articles is available at the association's web site.

12. *Internal Auditor.* Formerly: *I I A Research Reports.* [ISSN: 0020-5745] 1944. bi-m. USD 60 in North America; USD 84 elsewhere. Ed(s): Anne Scott. Institute of Internal Auditors, Inc., 247 Maitland Ave, Altamonte Springs, FL 32701-4201; custserv@theiia.org; http://www.theiia.org. Illus., index, adv. Refereed. Circ: 82000. Vol. ends: Dec. Microform: PQC. Online: EBSCO Publishing, EBSCO Host; Florida Center for Library Automation; Gale; Northern Light Technology, Inc.; OCLC Online Computer Library Center, Inc.; ProQuest LLC (Ann Arbor); H.W. Wilson. Reprint: SCH. *Indexed:* ABIn, ATI, BPI, CWI, ExcerpMed. *Bk. rev.:* 1-2, 500-1,000 words, signed. *Aud.:* Sa.

The magazine of the Institute of Internal Auditors offers articles of interest to the institute's membership of internal auditors and professionals in related fields. Topics include current auditing techniques and applications, information systems auditing, internal controls and quality assurance, corporate governance, and professional standards. Use of color graphics and sidebars makes the magazine appealing and easy to read.

13. *Journal of Accountancy.* [ISSN: 0021-8448] 1905. m. Non-members, USD 69. Ed(s): Colleen Katz. American Institute of Certified Public Accountants, Harborside Financial Ctr, 201 Plaza Three, 3rd Fl, Jersey City, NJ 07311-9801; journal@aicpa.org; http://www.aicpa.org. Illus., index, adv. Circ: 376691 Paid. Vol. ends: Jun/Dec. Microform: MIM; PQC. Online: EBSCO Publishing, EBSCO Host; Florida Center for Library Automation; Gale; LexisNexis; Northern Light Technology, Inc.; OCLC Online Computer Library Center, Inc.; ProQuest K-12 Learning Solutions; ProQuest LLC (Ann Arbor); H.W. Wilson. *Indexed:* ABIn, ATI, AgeL, BPI, BRI, CBRI, CLI, LRI, PAIS, SSCI. *Aud.:* Ac, Sa.

The official magazine of the American Institute of Certified Public Accountants (AICPA) contains feature articles on such topics as financial reporting, auditing, taxation, and electronic commerce; news reports on the AICPA's activities, regulatory matters, and business trends; and columns on such subjects as taxation, practice management, and technology. A list of outstanding exposure drafts from various accounting organizations, such as the Financial Accounting Standards Board, is presented in each issue. The full texts of new official releases are presented, as space permits. If a U.S. library subscribes to only one accounting magazine, this should be it. Selected articles from recent issues, as well as an index and archive (from 1997 on), are available at the AICPA's web site.

14. *Journal of Cost Management.* Formerly (until 1992): *Journal of Cost Management for the Manufacturing Industry.* [ISSN: 1092-8057] 1987. bi-m. USD 250. Ed(s): Joe Stenzel, Catherine Stenzel. W G & L Financial Reporting & Management Research, 395 Hudson St, New York, NY 10014; ria.customerservices@thomson.com; http://ria.thomson.com. Adv. Circ: 2649. Microform: PQC. Online: ProQuest LLC (Ann Arbor). Reprint: PSC. *Indexed:* ABIn, ATI, IBSS. *Aud.:* Sa.

This professional journal publishes articles written by academics and accounting professionals. Articles are practical in their orientation, with an emphasis on aiding professionals in improving their systems and procedures, and each includes a brief executive summary. Topics include performance measurement, costing systems, activity-based management, and the implications of e-business.

15. *The Journal of Government Financial Management.* Former titles: *Government Accountants Journal;* (until vol.25, 1976): *Federal Accountant.* [ISSN: 1533-1385] 1950. q. USD 95 domestic; USD 115 foreign. Ed(s): Marie S. Force. Association of Government Accountants, 2208 Mount Vernon Ave, Alexandria, VA 22301-1314; JCurtin@ agacgfm.org; http://www.agacgfm.org. Illus., index. Refereed. Circ: 18000 Paid. Vol. ends: Winter. Microform: PQC. Online: EBSCO Publishing, EBSCO Host; Northern Light Technology, Inc.; OCLC Online Computer Library Center, Inc.; ProQuest LLC (Ann Arbor). *Indexed:* ABIn, ATI, PAIS. *Aud.:* Ac, Sa.

This publication of the Association of Government Accountants publishes peer-reviewed articles that address all areas of accounting and financial management at all levels of government: federal, state, and local. The emphasis is on articles that provide practical insights. News and activities of the association are reported as well.

16. *N P A.* Formerly (until 2005): *National Public Accountant.* 1949. 6x/yr. Non-members, USD 25. Ed(s): Arleen Richman. National Society of Accountants, 1010 N Fairfax St, Alexandria, VA 22314; http://www.nsacct.org. Illus., index, adv. Circ: 20000 Paid. Vol. ends: Dec. Microform: PQC. Online: EBSCO Publishing, EBSCO Host; Florida Center for Library Automation; Gale; OCLC Online Computer Library Center, Inc.; ProQuest LLC (Ann Arbor); H.W. Wilson. *Indexed:* ABIn, ATI, BPI, PAIS. *Aud.:* Sa.

Although, as a matter of law, some public accounting services can be provided only by certified public accountants, this is not the case for many services. The National Society of Accountants is a professional association for public accountants who may or may not be CPAs, and this is the society's official publication. Articles focus on topics of interest to solo practitioners and those in smaller firms. Topics include issues in managing and marketing one's practice as well as tax, financial reporting, and other substantive practice areas. Information about the events and activities of the society is also included.

17. *Practical Accountant: providing the competitive edge.* Formerly: *Practical Accounting.* [ISSN: 0032-6321] 1967. m. USD 89 domestic; USD 109 foreign. SourceMedia, Inc., One State St Plaza, 27th Fl, New York, NY 10004; custserv@sourcemedia.com; http://www.sourcemedia.com. Illus., adv. Circ: 40000 Paid and controlled. Vol. ends: Dec. Microform: PQC. Online: EBSCO Publishing,

EBSCO Host; Factiva, Inc.; Florida Center for Library Automation; Gale; LexisNexis; Northern Light Technology, Inc.; OCLC Online Computer Library Center, Inc.; ProQuest LLC (Ann Arbor); H.W. Wilson. *Indexed:* ABIn, ATI, AgeL, BPI. *Aud.:* Sa.

This magazine appears to be targeted to the public accounting practitioner in a small to medium-sized firm. A broad range of topics in accounting, auditing, financial planning, taxation, and accounting practice management are discussed. As the name suggests, the focus is on providing readily useful advice, in a very accessible way; the level of technical complexity is not as high as in many of the more specialized journals.

18. *Public Accounting Report: competitive intelligence for accounting firms.* Incorporates (2000-2004): *C P A Financial Services Advisor.* [ISSN: 0161-309X] 1978. bi-w. USD 360. C C H Tax and Accounting, 2700 Lake Cook Rd, Riverwoods, IL 60015; http://tax.cchgroup.com. *Indexed:* ATI. *Aud.:* Sa.

This newsletter bills itself as a provider of competitive intelligence for the accounting profession, and it does just that. It includes news of which firms are gaining and losing which clients, and why; which are expanding—or closing—offices or practice areas; profiles of firms and key individuals; mergers and acquisitions: it's all here, and much of it is either absent or covered only in lesser depth elsewhere. This title is an indispensable source for keeping up with developments in mid-sized and larger CPA firms. Also included are periodic special reports and extras, including a ranking of the top 100 accounting firms.

19. *S E C Accounting Report.* [ISSN: 0146-485X] 1974. m. USD 450. Ed(s): Paul J Wendell. W G & L Financial Reporting & Management Research, 395 Hudson St, New York, NY 10014; ria.customerservices@ thomson.com; http://ria.thomson.com. Illus., index. Vol. ends: Nov. *Indexed:* ATI. *Aud.:* Sa.

This newsletter reports on rulings and official releases of the Securities and Exchange Commission. Articles are brief, summarizing key provisions and offering commentary directed to practitioners, including interpretations and suggestions for planning and compliance. Also included are reports on relevant court decisions and on pronouncements of other accounting standards-setting bodies, such as the Financial Accounting Standards Board and Public Company Accounting Oversight Board.

20. *Strategic Finance.* Former titles (until 1999): *Management Accounting Quarterly; N A A Bulletin - Management Accounting.* [ISSN: 1524-833X] 1919. m. USD 175, Libraries, USD 88. Ed(s): Kathy Williams. Institute of Management Accountants, 10 Paragon Dr, Montvale, NJ 07645-1760; ma@imanet.org; http://www.imanet.org. Illus., index, adv. Refereed. Circ: 68000. Vol. ends: Jun. Microform: PQC. Online: EBSCO Publishing, EBSCO Host; Florida Center for Library Automation; Gale; OCLC Online Computer Library Center, Inc.; ProQuest LLC (Ann Arbor); H.W. Wilson. Reprint: SCH. *Indexed:* ABIn, ATI, AgeL, BPI, JEL, PAIS. *Aud.:* Sa.

This magazine was formerly known as *Management Accounting.* It is a publication of the Institute of Management Accountants, a professional association for U.S. accountants and financial managers who practice in industry as opposed to public accounting. Thus, the range of topics discussed is broad and encompasses not only accounting standards and practices but also information technology, e-business, and methods of reporting business performance beyond the financial statements. Also provided are information on association activities and a useful annual career and salary guide.

Scholarly

21. *Abacus: a journal of accounting, finance and business studies.* [ISSN: 0001-3072] 1964. 3x/yr. GBP 286 print & online eds. Ed(s): G W Dean. Blackwell Publishing Asia, 550 Swanston St, Carlton South, VIC 3053, Australia; subs@blackwellpublishingasia.com; http://www.blackwellpublishing.com. Illus., adv. Refereed. Circ: 1200. Online: Blackwell Synergy; EBSCO Publishing, EBSCO Host; Gale; IngentaConnect; OCLC Online Computer Library Center, Inc.; OhioLINK; SwetsWise Online Content. Reprint: PSC. *Indexed:* ABIn, ATI, AmHI, IBSS, PAIS, RiskAb, SSCI. *Aud.:* Ac.

ACCOUNTING AND TAXATION

Published on behalf of the Accounting Foundation, University of Sydney, this scholarly journal is international in scope. It reports current research, critically evaluates current developments in theory and practice, and analyzes the effects of the regulatory framework of accounting, finance, and business. It also explores alternatives to, and explanations of, past and current practices.

22. *Accounting and Business Research.* Formerly (until 1970): *Accounting Research.* [ISSN: 0001-4788] 1970. q. Ed(s): J A Darnill. Institute of Chartered Accountants in England and Wales, Chartered Accountants' Hall, PO Box 433, London, EC2P 2BJ, United Kingdom; http://www.icaew.co.uk/. Illus., index. Refereed. Circ: 1500. Microform: PQC; WMP. Online: EBSCO Publishing, EBSCO Host; OCLC Online Computer Library Center, Inc. *Indexed:* ABIn, ATI, BPI, ExcerpMed, IBSS, PAIS. *Bk. rev.:* 0-4, 750-1,250 words, signed. *Aud.:* Ac.

This is the research journal of the Institute of Chartered Accountants in England and Wales, as opposed to the monthly news and practice-oriented magazine *Accountancy*. It presents empirical or analytical research in the fields of accounting and finance. Articles tend to be technical and may be international in scope. Sample topics include the effect of accounting information on investor and market behavior, international transfer pricing, and the market for audit services.

23. *Accounting Auditing and Accountability Journal.* Formerly (until 1989): *Accounting Auditing and Accountability.* [ISSN: 1368-0668] 1987. 8x/yr. EUR 5939 combined subscription in Europe print & online eds.; USD 5699 combined subscription in North America print & online eds.; AUD 5689 combined subscription in Australasia print & online eds. Ed(s): Lee D Parker, James E Guthrie. Emerald Group Publishing Limited, Howard House, Wagon Ln, Bingley, BD16 1WA, United Kingdom; information@emeraldinsight.com; http://www.emeraldinsight.com. Illus., index. Refereed. Vol. ends: No. 5. Reprint: PSC. *Indexed:* ABIn, ATI, CJA, IBSS. *Bk. rev.:* 1-2, 500-1,500 words, signed. *Aud.:* Ac.

This is a scholarly journal that focuses on the interaction between accounting and auditing and their socioeconomic and political environments. Articles emphasize critical and historical perspectives on current issues. Articles' topics are often international in scope; they may cover accounting practices in particular countries or do cross-country comparisons. Most issues include articles on a variety of topics, but occasional special issues have focused on subjects as diverse as online reporting, accounting research and the public interest, and theological perspectives on accounting.

24. *Accounting Education.* [ISSN: 0963-9284] 1992. q. GBP 548 print & online eds. Ed(s): Richard M S Wilson. Routledge, 4 Park Sq, Milton Park, Abingdon, OX14 4RN, United Kingdom; info@routledge.co.uk; http://www.routledge.co.uk. Illus., index. Refereed. Vol. ends: Dec. Online: EBSCO Publishing, EBSCO Host; Gale; IngentaConnect; OCLC Online Computer Library Center, Inc.; SwetsWise Online Content. Reprint: PSC. *Indexed:* ABIn, ATI, BrEdI, SWA. *Bk. rev.:* 0-2, 500-750 words, signed. *Aud.:* Ac.

This journal addresses all aspects of accounting education. The scope is international, and coverage includes curriculum issues, computing matters, teaching methods, and research pertinent to accounting education.

25. *Accounting Historians Journal.* Formerly (until 1977): *Accounting Historian.* [ISSN: 0148-4184] 1974. s-a. USD 55 (Individuals, USD 45). Ed(s): Stephen P Walker. Academy of Accounting Historians, c/o Culverhouse School of Accountancy, University of Alabama, Tuscaloosa, AL 35487; WalkerS2@cardiff.ac.uk; http://accounting.rutgers.edu/raw/aah/. Illus. Refereed. Circ: 900. Vol. ends: Dec. Online: Florida Center for Library Automation; Northern Light Technology, Inc.; ProQuest LLC (Ann Arbor). *Indexed:* ATI, AmH&L, HistAb. *Bk. rev.:* 4-5, 750-1,500 words, signed. *Aud.:* Ac, Sa.

Published by the Academy of Accounting Historians, this journal is unique in that it focuses on intellectual history and business history from the perspective of accountants and their profession. The journal presents scholarly articles on the history and development of accounting thought and practice. Citations and remarks from the annual inductions to the Accounting Hall of Fame are also reported here.

26. *Accounting, Organizations and Society.* [ISSN: 0361-3682] 1976. 8x/yr. EUR 1818. Ed(s): Anthony G. Hopwood. Pergamon, The Boulevard, Langford Ln, East Park, Kidlington, OX5 1GB, United Kingdom. Illus., adv. Refereed. Vol. ends: Nov. Microform: PQC. Online: EBSCO Publishing, EBSCO Host; Gale; IngentaConnect; OhioLINK; ScienceDirect; SwetsWise Online Content. *Indexed:* ABIn, ATI, AgeL, AmH&L, ArtHuCI, CJA, HistAb, IBSS, RI-1, SSCI. *Aud.:* Ac.

This international scholarly journal focuses on the behavioral, organizational, and social aspects of accounting. Articles have addressed such topics as the social dimensions of international accounting standards, organizational behavior as it impacts management accounting, auditor/client relationships, and historical studies of the accountant's role in business and society at a particular time and place.

27. *Accounting Review.* [ISSN: 0001-4826] 1926. q. Non-members, USD 275. American Accounting Association, 5717 Bessie Dr, Sarasota, FL 34233-2399; office@aaahq.org; http://aaahq.org. Illus., index, adv. Refereed. Circ: 18000 Paid. Vol. ends: Oct. Microform: PQC. Online: Chadwyck-Healey Inc.; EBSCO Publishing, EBSCO Host; Gale; JSTOR (Web-based Journal Archive); OCLC Online Computer Library Center, Inc.; ProQuest LLC (Ann Arbor); H.W. Wilson. Reprint: PSC. *Indexed:* ABIn, ATI, BPI, BRI, CBRI, IBR, IBSS, IBZ, JEL, SSCI. *Bk. rev.:* 2-3, 350-1,500 words, signed. *Aud.:* Ac.

The American Accounting Association is the principal professional association in the United States for college and university faculty in all areas of accounting. The association's Publications Committee has stated that the *Accounting Review* should be "the premier journal for publishing articles reporting the results of accounting research and explaining and illustrating related research methodology." It also says the journal's primary audience is academicians, graduate students, and others interested in accounting research. Scholarly articles are accompanied by book reviews and placement ads for college and university accounting educators. This is among the most important core titles for academic libraries that support accounting programs.

28. *Asia - Pacific Journal of Accounting & Economics.* Formerly (until 2000): *Asia - Pacific Journal of Accounting.* [ISSN: 1608-1625] 1993. s-a. HKD 390 (Individuals, HKD 273). Ed(s): Eden Yu. City University of Hong Kong, Department of Economics & Finance, c/o Leila Germano, 83 Tat Chee Ave., Kowloon, Hong Kong; http://fbweb.cityu.edu.hk/efweb/. Refereed. *Indexed:* JEL. *Aud.:* Ac.

Now published jointly by the City University of Hong Kong and National Taiwan University, this journal features empirical and theoretical research in all areas of accounting and economics. Although there is a focus on issues important to the Asia–Pacific region, papers are also published on global topics in such areas as corporate governance, capital markets, and financial institutions.

29. *Auditing: a journal of practice and theory.* [ISSN: 0278-0380] 1981. s-a. Non-members, USD 120. American Accounting Association, 5717 Bessie Dr, Sarasota, FL 34233-2399; office@aaahq.org; http://aaahq.org. Illus., adv. Refereed. Circ: 2000. Reprint: PSC. *Indexed:* ABIn, ATI, SSCI. *Aud.:* Ac, Sa.

This journal is published by the Auditing Section of the American Accounting Association, and its stated purpose is to contribute to the improvement of both the practice and theory of auditing. Several substantive research articles on auditing topics, as well as shorter research notes, are featured in each issue.

30. *The British Accounting Review.* [ISSN: 0890-8389] 4x/yr. EUR 669. Ed(s): C. Emmanuel, V. Beattie. Academic Press, 24-28 Oval Rd, London, NW1 7DX, United Kingdom; apsubs@acad.com; http://www.elsevier.com/. Adv. Online: EBSCO Publishing, EBSCO

Host; Gale; IngentaConnect; OCLC Online Computer Library Center, Inc.; OhioLINK; ScienceDirect; SwetsWise Online Content. Reprint: SCH. *Indexed:* ABIn, ATI, IBSS. *Aud.:* Ac.

The official journal of the British Accounting Association publishes scholarly papers on subjects across the whole spectrum of accounting and finance. Contributions are welcomed across a wide range of research methodologies (e.g., analytical, archival, experimental, survey, and qualitative case methods). Topic areas also include financial accounting, management accounting, finance and financial management, auditing, public sector accounting, social and environmental accounting, and accounting education and accounting history.

31. *Contemporary Accounting Research.* [ISSN: 0823-9150] 1984. q. USD 275 (Individuals, USD 125). Ed(s): Dr. Gordon Richardson. Canadian Academic Accounting Association, 3997 Chesswood Dr, Toronto, ON M3J 2R8, Canada; admin@caaa.ca; http://www.caaa.ca. Illus., adv. Refereed. Circ: 1400 Paid. Vol. ends: Winter. Online: EBSCO Publishing, EBSCO Host; Micromedia ProQuest; Northern Light Technology, Inc.; OCLC Online Computer Library Center, Inc.; ProQuest LLC (Ann Arbor); SwetsWise Online Content. Reprint: PSC. *Indexed:* ABIn, ATI, IBSS, JEL, SSCI. *Aud.:* Ac.

This journal presents scholarly and practical research in all areas of accounting, auditing, and taxation. Articles from other disciplines (such as economics or psychology) that have implications for accounting are also accepted. Although the journal is published in Canada, many articles are authored by academics from the United States or other countries. Articles may be in French or English, although most are in English, and abstracts are provided in both languages. The abstract in the language of the article is a standard brief synopsis, while the abstract in the other language is much more extensive, typically one to two pages in length.

32. *Critical Perspectives on Accounting.* [ISSN: 1045-2354] 1990. 8x/yr. EUR 729. Ed(s): David Cooper, C. Carter. Academic Press, Harcourt Pl, 32 Jamestown Rd, London, NW1 7BY, United Kingdom; apsubs@acad.com; http://www.elsevier.com/. Illus., adv. Refereed. Vol. ends: Dec. Online: EBSCO Publishing, EBSCO Host; Gale; IngentaConnect; OCLC Online Computer Library Center, Inc.; OhioLINK; ScienceDirect; SwetsWise Online Content. *Indexed:* ABIn, ATI, CJA, IBSS. *Aud.:* Ac.

This journal provides a forum for scholarly articles that attempt to go beyond "conventional theory and practice" in examining accounting practices and corporate behavior in relation to the "many allocative, distributive, social, and ecological problems of our era." An aptly titled journal, *Critical Perspectives* publishes papers that very often take a contrarian view of established practices and institutions in the world of accounting and business.

33. *The European Accounting Review.* Supersedes (1989-1992): *European Accounting Association. Newsletter.* [ISSN: 0963-8180] 1992. q. GBP 359 print & online eds. Ed(s): Kari Lukka. Routledge, 4 Park Square, Milton Park, Abingdon, OX14 4RN, United Kingdom; info@routledge.co.uk; http://www.routledge.co.uk. Adv. Refereed. Online: EBSCO Publishing, EBSCO Host; Gale; IngentaConnect; OCLC Online Computer Library Center, Inc.; SwetsWise Online Content. Reprint: PSC. *Indexed:* ABIn, ATI, IBR, IBSS, IBZ, SSCI. *Bk. rev.:* Number and length vary. *Aud.:* Ac.

This is a publication of the European Accounting Association. Given the development of the single European market and the increased harmonization of accounting standards across borders, the journal seeks to serve as a forum for research in accounting that is of international interest. Book reviews are also included.

Financial Accountability & Management. See Finance/Scholarly section.

Government Finance Review. See Finance/Scholarly section.

34. *The International Journal of Accounting.* Formerly (until 1989): *The International Journal of Accounting Education and Research.* [ISSN: 1094-4060] 1965. 4x/yr. EUR 375. Ed(s): A. R. Abdel-Khalik. Pergamon, The Boulevard, Langford Ln, East Park, Kidlington, OX5 1GB, United Kingdom. Illus., index. Refereed. Online: EBSCO Publishing, EBSCO Host; Gale; IngentaConnect; OhioLINK; ScienceDirect; SwetsWise Online Content. *Indexed:* ABIn, ATI, IBSS, PAIS. *Bk. rev.:* 5-6, 1,000-1,500 words, signed. *Aud.:* Ac.

A publication of the Vernon K. Zimmerman Center for International Education and Research in Accounting at the University of Illinois at Urbana–Champaign, this journal publishes scholarly articles that explore international aspects of accounting theory and practice. This may include the examination of accounting practices in a particular country or comparisons across countries. Articles that focus on the impact of cultural, political, and economic factors on accounting are encouraged, and the not-for-profit as well as the for-profit context is considered. The research tends to be empirical, with an emphasis on practical application.

35. *International Journal of Auditing.* [ISSN: 1090-6738] 1997. 3x/yr. GBP 399 print & online eds. Ed(s): Tom Lee, Stuart Turley. Blackwell Publishing Ltd., 9600 Garsington Rd, Oxford, OX4 2ZG, United Kingdom; customerservices@blackwellpublishing.com; http://www.blackwellpublishing.com. Sample. Refereed. Online: Blackwell Synergy; EBSCO Publishing, EBSCO Host; Gale; IngentaConnect; OCLC Online Computer Library Center, Inc.; OhioLINK; SwetsWise Online Content; Wiley InterScience. Reprint: PSC. *Indexed:* ABIn, ATI, IBSS, RiskAb. *Aud.:* Ac.

This journal provides an international forum for academics, professionals, and policy makers with research interests in new ideas, techniques, and approaches within all aspects of auditing.

36. *Issues in Accounting Education.* [ISSN: 0739-3172] 1983. s-a. USD 225. Ed(s): David E Stout. American Accounting Association, 5717 Bessie Dr, Sarasota, FL 34233-2399; http://aaahq.org. Illus., adv. Refereed. Vol. ends: No. 4. Reprint: PSC. *Indexed:* ABIn, ATI. *Bk. rev.:* 2-20, 500-1,500 words, signed. *Aud.:* Ac.

A publication of the American Accounting Association, this journal contains empirical research, commentaries, and literature reviews that pertain to accounting education. Instructional materials (such as case studies for classroom use) and reviews of accounting texts and other books are also included.

37. *Journal of Accounting and Economics.* [ISSN: 0165-4101] 1979. 6x/yr. EUR 1104. Ed(s): S. P. Kothari, Jerold L Zimmerman. Elsevier BV, North-Holland, Sara Burgerhartstraat 25, Amsterdam, 1055 KV, Netherlands; nlinfo-f@elsevier.nl; http://www.elsevier.nl. Illus., index, adv. Refereed. Vol. ends: Jun/Dec. Microform: PQC. Online: EBSCO Publishing, EBSCO Host; Gale; IngentaConnect; OhioLINK; ScienceDirect; SwetsWise Online Content. *Indexed:* ABIn, ATI, IBSS, JEL, RiskAb, SSCI. *Aud.:* Ac.

Scholarly papers published here apply economic analysis to such accounting issues as the determination of accounting standards, government regulation of corporate disclosure and of the accounting profession, the information content and role of accounting numbers in the capital markets, and the role of accounting in contracts and agency relationships.

38. *Journal of Accounting and Public Policy.* [ISSN: 0278-4254] 1982. 6x/yr. EUR 654. Ed(s): Lawrence A Gordon. Elsevier Inc., 360 Park Ave S, New York, NY 10010-1710; usinfo-f@elsevier.com; http://www.elsevier.com. Illus., index, adv. Refereed. Vol. ends: Winter. Microform: PQC. Online: EBSCO Publishing, EBSCO Host; Gale; IngentaConnect; OhioLINK; ScienceDirect; SwetsWise Online Content. *Indexed:* ABIn, ATI, AgeL, EAA, IBSS, PAIS, RiskAb, SSCI. *Aud.:* Ac, Sa.

This journal publishes scholarly articles on the relationship between accounting and public policy, including public administration, political science, sociology, law, and economics. Interdisciplinary review papers are also encouraged. The "Accounting Letters" section publishes short papers (up to 3,000 words) after an expedited review process.

39. Journal of Accounting, Auditing & Finance. [ISSN: 0148-558X] 1977. q. USD 225 (Individuals, USD 90; USD 60 newsstand/cover). Ed(s): Kashi Balachandran. Greenwood Publishing Group Inc., 88 Post Rd W, PO Box 5007, Westport, CT 06881; webmaster@greenwood.com; http://www.greenwood.com. Illus. Refereed. Circ: 1000. Vol. ends: Fall. *Indexed:* ABIn, ATI, BLI, BPI, CLI, ILP, JEL. *Aud.:* Ac.

This journal is sponsored by the Vincent C. Ross Institute of Accounting Research at the Leonard N. Stern School of Business, New York University. The journal seeks to serve as a forum that brings together academics and practitioners. Each issue contains three to six articles, which frequently are highly quantitative in their methodology.

40. Journal of Accounting Education. [ISSN: 0748-5751] 1982. 4x/yr. EUR 628. Ed(s): James E Rebele. Pergamon, The Boulevard, Langford Ln, East Park, Kidlington, OX5 1GB, United Kingdom. Illus., index, adv. Refereed. Circ: 1500. Vol. ends: Fall. Microform: PQC. Online: EBSCO Publishing, EBSCO Host; Gale; IngentaConnect; OhioLINK; ScienceDirect; SwetsWise Online Content. *Indexed:* ABIn, ATI. *Aud.:* Ac.

Articles published here are typically empirical in nature and often deal with issues of instructional design. Cases for use in accounting classes are also published, as are shorter papers on topics of interest to educators.

41. Journal of Accounting Literature. [ISSN: 0737-4607] 1982. a. USD 29 (Individuals, USD 25; Students, USD 15). Ed(s): Stephen Kwaka Asare, Bipin B Ajinkya. University of Florida, Fisher School of Accounting, College of Business Administration, PO Box 117166, Gainesville, FL 32611-7166; kathy.murphy@cba.ufl.edu; http://www.cba.ufl.edu. Illus. Refereed. Online: Northern Light Technology, Inc.; ProQuest LLC (Ann Arbor). Reprint: PSC. *Indexed:* ABIn, ATI. *Aud.:* Ac.

Publishes in-depth articles that review the scholarly literature on various topics in accounting. Papers presented at conferences held at the Fisher School of Accounting, University of Florida, also appear here. Articles typically conclude with a brief annotated bibliography and a comprehensive list of references.

42. Journal of Accounting Research. [ISSN: 0021-8456] 1963. 5x/yr. GBP 476 print & online eds. Ed(s): Lisa Johnson, Abbie Smith. Blackwell Publishing, Inc., Commerce Place, 350 Main St, Malden, MA 02148; customerservices@blackwellpublishing.com; http://www.blackwellpublishing.com. Illus. Refereed. Circ: 2800 Paid. Microform: MIM; PQC. Online: Blackwell Synergy; EBSCO Publishing, EBSCO Host; Gale; IngentaConnect; JSTOR (Web-based Journal Archive); Northern Light Technology, Inc.; OCLC Online Computer Library Center, Inc.; OhioLINK; SwetsWise Online Content. Reprint: PSC. *Indexed:* ABIn, ATI, BPI, IBR, IBSS, IBZ, JEL, RiskAb, SSCI. *Aud.:* Ac.

Published by the Institute of Professional Accounting at the University of Chicago's Graduate School of Business, this is among the most important scholarly journals in accounting. This journal publishes academic research on a broad range of topics. Papers generally are highly quantitative and often address the impact of accounting standards on investors and the capital markets. Subscribers also receive an annual compilation of papers presented at a conference held at the University of Chicago.

Journal of Business Finance & Accounting. See Finance/Trade Journals section.

43. Journal of Emerging Technologies in Accounting. [ISSN: 1554-1908] 2004. a. USD 100 per issue. American Accounting Association, 5717 Bessie Dr, Sarasota, FL 34233-2399; office@aaahq.org; http://aaahq.org. *Aud.:* Ac, Sa.

This is the academic journal of the Artificial Intelligence/Emerging Technologies Section of the American Accounting Association. The section's stated purpose is to improve and facilitate research, education, and practice involving advanced information systems, cutting-edge technologies, and artificial intelligence in the fields of accounting, information technology, and management advisory systems.

44. Journal of Forensic Accounting: auditing, fraud, and taxation. [ISSN: 1524-5586] 2000. s-a. USD 239 (Individuals, USD 119; Students, USD 49). Ed(s): D Larry Crumbley, Todd DeZoort. R. T. Edwards, Inc., P.O. Box 27388, Philadelphia, PA 19118; info@edwardspub.com; http://www.rtedwards.com. Index, adv. Sample. Refereed. Circ: 325 Paid. *Indexed:* ATI. *Aud.:* Ac, Sa.

Forensic accounting is the subfield that focuses on the evidentiary basis of economic transactions and accounting data. Issues such as fraud, risk assessment, and violations of accounting principles, auditing standards, and government regulations are among the topics treated. This journal publishes research dealing with models and methodologies of investigative and forensic accounting. It seeks to establish a balance between theoretical and empirical studies and to foster dialogue and collaboration among academicians and practitioners.

45. Journal of International Accounting, Auditing and Taxation. [ISSN: 1061-9518] 1992. 2x/yr. EUR 353. Ed(s): Kathleen E. Sinning, H. J. Dykxhoorn. Pergamon, The Boulevard, Langford Ln, East Park, Kidlington, OX5 1GB, United Kingdom. Illus., index. Refereed. Vol. ends: No. 2. Microform: PQC. Online: EBSCO Publishing, EBSCO Host; Gale; IngentaConnect; OhioLINK; ScienceDirect; SwetsWise Online Content. *Indexed:* ABIn, ATI, IBSS. *Aud.:* Ac, Sa.

This journal's goal is to "bridge the gap between academic researchers and practitioners," addressing all areas of international accounting. Applied research findings and critiques of current practices and their impact on management decisions are among the areas covered. Many articles are internationally comparative.

46. Journal of International Accounting Research. [ISSN: 1542-6297] 2002. a. Ed(s): R.S. Olusegun Wallace. American Accounting Association, 5717 Bessie Dr, Sarasota, FL 34233-2399; office@aaahq.org; http://aaahq.org. *Indexed:* ABIn, ATI. *Bk. rev.:* Number and length vary. *Aud.:* Ac, Sa.

The journal of the American Accounting Association's International Accounting Section publishes research that concerns accounting phenomena with an explicit global aspect. The editors are open to a wide variety of research methods, and international accounting is broadly defined. Book reviews are also included.

Journal of International Financial Management and Accounting. See Finance/Scholarly section.

47. Journal of Management Accounting Research. [ISSN: 1049-2127] 1989. a. USD 15. Ed(s): Anthony A Atkinson. American Accounting Association, 5717 Bessie Dr, Sarasota, FL 34233-2399; http://aaahq.org. Illus. Refereed. Online: EBSCO Publishing, EBSCO Host; Florida Center for Library Automation; Gale; Northern Light Technology, Inc.; OCLC Online Computer Library Center, Inc.; ProQuest LLC (Ann Arbor). Reprint: PSC. *Indexed:* ABIn, ATI, JEL. *Aud.:* Ac, Sa.

This journal is an official publication of the Management Accounting Section of the American Accounting Association, the principal professional association in the United States for college and university faculty in accounting. Articles cover a variety of topics within the broad area of management accounting, such as budgeting, costing systems, and internal reporting. Also covered is the relationship between internal and external reporting, performance measurement, and behavioral aspects of accounting.

48. Management Accounting Research. Supersedes: *I C M A Abstracts Bulletin.* [ISSN: 1044-5005] 1983. 4x/yr. EUR 448. Ed(s): R W Scapens, M Bromwich. Academic Press, 24-28 Oval Rd, London, NW1 7DX, United Kingdom; apsubs@acad.com; http://www.elsevier.com/. Illus., adv. Refereed. Circ: 400. Vol. ends: Dec. Online: EBSCO Publishing, EBSCO Host; Gale; IngentaConnect; OCLC Online Computer Library Center, Inc.; OhioLINK; ScienceDirect; SwetsWise Online Content. *Indexed:* ABIn, ATI, IBSS. *Aud.:* Ac.

This journal aims to serve as a vehicle for publishing original research in the field of management accounting. It includes case studies, field work, and other empirical studies, as well as scholarly papers, review articles, comments, and notes.

49. *Review of Accounting Studies.* [ISSN: 1380-6653] 1996. q. EUR 530 print & online eds. Ed(s): Stephen Penman. Springer New York LLC, 233 Spring St, New York, NY 10013-1578; service-ny@springer.com; http://www.springer.com/. Illus., adv. Sample. Refereed. Vol. ends: No. 4. Online: EBSCO Publishing, EBSCO Host; Gale; IngentaConnect; OCLC Online Computer Library Center, Inc.; OhioLINK; ProQuest LLC (Ann Arbor); Springer LINK; SwetsWise Online Content. Reprint: PSC. *Indexed:* ABIn, JEL, RiskAb, SSCI. *Aud.:* Ac.

This journal presents academic research in accounting. Articles may be theoretical models or empirical studies. Contributors are welcome to draw from related disciplines, such as economics or finance, but all articles must contribute to the discipline of accounting.

Taxation

50. *A T A Journal of Legal Tax Research.* [ISSN: 1543-866X] 2003. irreg. USD 125. American Accounting Association, 5717 Bessie Dr, Sarasota, FL 34233-2399; office@aaahq.org; http://aaahq.org. *Aud.:* Ac, Sa.

A more recently initiated publication of the American Taxation Association, this journal focuses on legal research in taxation, as opposed to the more theoretical and quantitative papers that often appear in the association's eponymous journal. The editors seek articles that treat current tax issues, including the history, development, and congressional intent of specific provisions. It also includes articles that propose improvements in tax systems and unique solutions to problems; and articles that critically analyze proposed or recent tax rule changes from both technical and policy perspectives.

51. *American Taxation Association. Journal.* [ISSN: 0198-9073] 1979. s-a. USD 30. Ed(s): Terrence J Shevlin. American Accounting Association, 5717 Bessie Dr, Sarasota, FL 34233-2399; http://aaahq.org. Illus., adv. Reprint: PSC. *Indexed:* ABIn, ATI. *Bk. rev.:* 5-10, 500-1,000 words, signed. *Aud.:* Ac, Sa.

Published by the American Taxation Association (the Tax Section of the American Accounting Association), this journal presents several types of articles on tax topics. Articles and research notes, most often authored by academicians, may be quantitative, theoretical, or primarily legal research. Reviews of books and of tax software and research on the teaching of taxation are also presented. In addition, abstracts of recent doctoral dissertations on taxation are included. The third issue of the volume is a Conference Supplement that contains papers presented at the conference held by the journal in conjunction with the American Taxation Association's mid-year meeting.

52. *Corporate Taxation.* Formerly (until Jan. 2001): *Journal of Corporate Taxation.* [ISSN: 1534-715X] 1973. bi-m. USD 335; USD 505 combined subscription (print & online eds.). R I A, 395 Hudson St, New York, NY 10014; ria.customerservices@thomson.com; http://ria.thomson.com/. Illus., adv. Vol. ends: Winter. Microform: MIM; PQC. Online: ProQuest LLC (Ann Arbor). *Indexed:* ABIn, ATI, BLI, BPI, CLI, ILP, LRI, PAIS, SSCI. *Aud.:* Sa.

This is a more specialized title from the publisher of the *Journal of Taxation.* Compared to those in its sister publication, articles in this journal are fewer in number and treat their subjects in greater depth. In addition to the feature articles, there are regular departments that discuss recent rulings and new developments.

53. *International Tax Journal.* [ISSN: 0097-7314] 1974. q. USD 270. C C H Inc., 2700 Lake Cook Rd, Riverwoods, IL 60015; cust_serv@cch.com; http://www.cch.com. Illus., adv. Vol. ends: Fall. Microform: WSH; PQC. Online: EBSCO Publishing, EBSCO Host; Gale; ProQuest LLC (Ann Arbor). *Indexed:* ABIn, ATI, BPI, CLI, IBR, ILP, LRI, PAIS. *Aud.:* Ac, Sa.

This journal publishes articles, often lengthy, that address a broad range of international tax topics. Foreign tax credit planning, business restructurings, and transfer pricing are examples of topics treated. Some issues focus on a particular country or region. This title will be of interest to both academics and practitioners.

54. *Journal of International Taxation.* [ISSN: 1049-6378] 1990. 1 Base Vol(s) m. USD 400; USD 610 combined subscription (print & online eds.). Ed(s): Peter M Daub. W G & L Financial Reporting & Management Research, 395 Hudson St, New York, NY 10014; ria.customerservices@thomson.com; http://ria.thomson.com. Adv. Circ: 2500. Microform: PQC. Online: ProQuest LLC (Ann Arbor). *Indexed:* ABIn, ABS&EES, ATI. *Aud.:* Sa.

Articles by practitioners as well as academics offer practical analysis of current tax issues. Some of the topics typically covered include: expatriation and inversion; transfer pricing policies and developments; tax treaties; financial products and currency strategies; and tax shelters. In addition to the articles, several regular columns and editorial features highlight new developments in the international tax scene.

55. *Journal of Taxation: a national journal of current developments, analysis, and commentary for tax professionals.* [ISSN: 0022-4863] 1954. m. USD 315; USD 470 combined subscription (print & online eds.). Ed(s): Joseph I Graf. R I A, 395 Hudson St, New York, NY 10014; ria@thomson.com; http://ria.thomson.com/. Illus., index, adv. Circ: 14000. Vol. ends: Jun/Dec. Microform: PQC. Online: ProQuest LLC (Ann Arbor); Thomson West. *Indexed:* ABIn, ATI, AgeL, BLI, BPI, CLI, ILP, JEL, LRI, PAIS, SSCI. *Aud.:* Sa.

Articles written by accountants, tax attorneys, and accounting and law professors seek to help practitioners reduce their time spent on research by summarizing, analyzing, and applying the law in specific areas. Issues are discussed in a practical but technical manner. This journal includes, in addition to feature articles, regular items that update readers on the latest tax law changes, court decisions, revenue rulings, and administrative actions.

56. *Journal of Taxation of Investments.* [ISSN: 0747-9115] 1983. q. USD 203 domestic; USD 233 foreign. Ed(s): Kevin M Keyes. Civic Research Insitute, 4478 US Route 27, PO Box 585, Kingston, NJ 08528; order@civicresearchinstitute.com; http://www.civicresearchinstitute.com. *Indexed:* ABIn, ATI, CLI, ILP, LRI. *Aud.:* Ac, Sa.

This journal covers tax issues surrounding the full range of investments (equity and debt securities, mutual funds and hedge funds, derivatives, real estate and other types), both domestically and internationally. Articles are authored most frequently by attorneys in tax practice but also in some cases by academics, and they are technical but practical in their orientation.

57. *National Tax Journal.* Formerly (until 1947): *National Tax Association. Bulletin.* [ISSN: 0028-0283] 1916. q. USD 170 (Individuals, USD 100). Ed(s): Therese J McGuire, Rosanne Altshuler. National Tax Association, 725 15th St, NW, Ste 600, Washington, DC 20005-2109; natltax@aol.com; http://www.ntanet.org. Illus., index. Refereed. Circ: 3300. Vol. ends: Dec. Microform: WSH; PQC. Online: EBSCO Publishing, EBSCO Host; Florida Center for Library Automation; Gale; Northern Light Technology, Inc.; OCLC Online Computer Library Center, Inc.; ProQuest LLC (Ann Arbor); H.W. Wilson. *Indexed:* ABIn, ATI, AgeL, BLI, BPI, CJA, CLI, IBR, IBSS, IBZ, ILP, IPSA, JEL, LRI, PAIS, SSCI. *Aud.:* Ac, Sa.

Published by the National Tax Association, this journal presents refereed papers that represent original research in government finance, that evaluate particular policies, or that report administrative developments. Papers from selected symposia are also included. The editors encourage authors to present their material in a manner that can be understood by all members of the association, including accountants, lawyers, tax administrators, and academicians. Technical and methodological discussions are kept to a minimum or placed in an appendix.

58. Practical Tax Strategies. Formed by the merger of (1966-1998): *Taxation for Accountants;* (1972-1998): *Taxation for Lawyers.* [ISSN: 1523-6250] 1998. m. USD 215. Ed(s): Sandra K Lewis. W G & L Financial Reporting & Management Research, 395 Hudson St, New York, NY 10014; ria.customerservices@thomson.com; http://ria.thomson.com. Illus., index, adv. Circ: 8544. Microform: PQC. Online: OCLC Online Computer Library Center, Inc. *Indexed:* ABIn, ATI, BPI, CLI, LRI, PAIS. *Aud.:* Sa.

Although its articles and columns, written by tax practitioners and professors, regularly cover technical tax topics, this journal seeks to be accessible to accountants and attorneys who are not tax specialists. Accordingly, many articles stress the broader business perspective relevant to tax planning. In each issue, about five feature articles are accompanied by regular departments that provide updates on recent developments.

59. The Tax Adviser: a magazine of tax planning, trends and techniques. [ISSN: 0039-9957] 1970. m. Membership, USD 165. Ed(s): Nick Fiore. CPA2Biz, Inc., 100 Broadway 6th Fl, New York, NY 10005; contactus.copy@cpa2biz.com; https://www.cpa2biz.com. Illus., index, adv. Circ: 30000. Microform: WSH; PQC. Online: EBSCO Publishing, EBSCO Host; Florida Center for Library Automation; Gale; OCLC Online Computer Library Center, Inc.; ProQuest LLC (Ann Arbor); H.W. Wilson. *Indexed:* ABIn, ATI, BPI, CLI, ILP, LRI. *Aud.:* Sa.

This journal of the American Institute of Certified Public Accountants covers a broad range of tax information. It focuses on the technical aspects of federal (and some state and local) taxation, providing practical commentary through feature articles and regular departments.

60. The Tax Executive. [ISSN: 0040-0025] 1944. bi-m. USD 120 in US & Canada; USD 144 foreign. Ed(s): Fred F Murray. Tax Executives Institute, Inc., 1200 G St NW, 300, Washington, DC 20005-3814. Illus., adv. Circ: 5500. Vol. ends: Nov/Dec. Microform: PQC. Online: EBSCO Publishing, EBSCO Host; Florida Center for Library Automation; Gale; Northern Light Technology, Inc.; OCLC Online Computer Library Center, Inc.; ProQuest LLC (Ann Arbor). Reprint: WSH. *Indexed:* ABIn, ATI, CLI, IBR, IBZ, ILP, LRI, PAIS. *Aud.:* Sa.

Each issue of this journal of the Tax Executives Institute includes articles on current issues of tax policy, administration, and management. The institute's position papers and testimony appear here, as do the minutes of official liaison meetings with federal, state, and provincial government officials.

Tax Law Review. See Law section.

Tax Lawyer. See Law section.

61. Tax Notes: the weekly tax service. [ISSN: 0270-5494] 1972. w. USD 1999. Ed(s): Christopher Bergin. Tax Analysts, 400 S Maple Ave, Ste 400, Falls Church, VA 22046; cservice@tax.org; http://www.taxanalysts.com/. Circ: Controlled. Online: The Dialog Corporation; LexisNexis. *Indexed:* ATI, CLI, LRI. *Aud.:* Ac, Sa.

Tax Notes offers a weekly review of news and commentary from the publisher's staff of analysts, concerning proposed and enacted tax legislation, court decisions, regulations, and other administrative guidance. Also included are frequent in-depth special reports, often authored by law professors.

62. Taxes - The Tax Magazine. Former titles: *Taxes (Riverwoods);* (until 1939): *Tax Magazine;* (until 1931): *National Tax Magazine;* (until 1930): *National Income Tax Magazine.* 1923. m. USD 279; USD 410 combined subscription print & online eds. C C H Inc., 2700 Lake Cook Rd, Riverwoods, IL 60015; cust_serv@cch.com; http://www.cch.com. Illus. Vol. ends: Dec. Microform: PQC. Online: ProQuest K-12 Learning Solutions; ProQuest LLC (Ann Arbor). *Indexed:* ATI, AgeL, BPI, CLI, ILP, LRI, PAIS, SSCI. *Aud.:* Ac, Sa.

This magazine is aimed primarily at practitioners working in all areas of the tax law—state, federal, and international—though academics will also find it of interest. Written by tax attorneys, professors, and the publisher's in-house analysts, articles are technical in nature and focus on current issues and trends as well as legislative developments. Regular columns provide information on tax trends, international issues, and other topics.

■ ADVERTISING, MARKETING, AND PUBLIC RELATIONS

See also Business; Communication; and Journalism and Writing sections.

Clay Williams, Coordinator for Bibliographic Instruction, Hunter College Library, Hunter College, New York, NY 10021

Introduction

In choosing the journals for inclusion here, one must recognize the profound influence that the online environment has upon both scholarship and business. As predicted, the Internet as the medium of the journals themselves has become the medium and the message. The web as a topic of intellectual discussion is not up for discussion, but the online world has become more transparent and a part of everyone's day-to-day life and is now taken for granted in many ways. The journals directed at practitioners describe uses of the web in the various manifestations of advertising, while the academic journals explore the effects the Internet is having on advertising, marketing, and public relations and what effects the authors think it could or should have.

Practitioners continue to discover ways to use the media to succeed, and the Internet is certainly the major game in town. However, comprehending the online world in its many manifestations and sometimes hidden agendas, if you will, makes things difficult to pin down for more than a moment. Many articles appear on these topics in journals focusing ostensibly on business and marketing. No one questions the importance of advertising, and certainly no one can avoid the role spin doctors or public relations practitioners are playing in the world today in business.

The inherent pitfalls of the Internet become problematic for a work such as *Magazines for Libraries* because some electronic journals (not to mention companies) do not stay around long enough for their importance to even register, particularly in the academic world. Where are these journals archived and for how long and in what format? Will they be archived somewhere? If not by the vendors, then where? Consider, as well, that the full-text versions of some journals are best reached via such databases as Lexis-Nexis Academic Universe and EBSCO's various indexes, now ubiquitous in colleges and public libraries and available at home to subscribers. However, occasional lags in the promptness of recent articles in the promised full-text format speak of other forces at work. The inconsistency only frustrates users, as they see excellent articles abstracted and unavailable because of costs. The variety of formats we see are representative of the transitional period we are now in, and the scholarship reflects that as well.

Basic Periodicals

Ga: *Advertising Age, Adweek, B to B, Brandweek, Public Relations Quarterly;* Ac: *Advertising Age, B to B, Journal of Advertising, Journal of Advertising Research, The Journal of Consumer Marketing, Journal of Consumer Research, Journal of Macromarketing, Journal of Marketing, Journal of Marketing Research, Marketing News, Marketing Research, O'Dwyer's P R Services Report, Public Relations Review, Sales & Marketing Management.*

Basic Abstracts and Indexes

ABI/INFORM, Academic Index ASAP, Business Index, Business Periodicals Index, Lexis-Nexis. Business Elite, EBSCO.

63. Academy of Marketing Science. Journal. [ISSN: 0092-0703] 1973. q. EUR 458 print & online eds. Springer Netherlands, Van Godewijckstraat 30, Dordrecht, 3311 GX, Netherlands; http://www.springeronline.com. Illus., adv. Refereed. Circ: 3000. Vol. ends: Oct (No. 4). Online: CSA;

The Dialog Corporation; EBSCO Publishing, EBSCO Host; HighWire Press; OCLC Online Computer Library Center, Inc.; ProQuest LLC (Ann Arbor); SAGE Publications, Inc., SAGE Journals Online; SwetsWise Online Content. Reprint: PSC. *Indexed:* ABIn, ATI, CommAb, HRA, PAIS, PsycInfo, SSCI. *Bk. rev.:* 2-6, 300-1,000 words. *Aud.:* Ac.

This is the official journal of the Academy of Marketing Science. Articles intended for theoreticians disseminate research results related to the international impact of economics, ethics, and social forces. A regular section concerns marketing and the law. Recent issues contain articles including a study that examines the effects of downsizing on organizational buying behavior, the concept of culture, the definition of organizational memory, and the dimensions of decision-making context. A reasonable price for an important journal dealing largely with theory.

64. *Advertising Age: Crain's international newspaper of marketing.* Incorporates (1979-2004): *American Demographics;* (198?-200?): *Focus;* Which was formerly (1982-198?): *Advertising Age's Focus;* (1953-1974): *Promotion;* Which was formerly: *Advertising & Sales Promotion;* (until 1961): *Advertising Requirements;* (in 1958): *Advertising Agency.* [ISSN: 0001-8899] 1930. w. USD 99 domestic; USD 229 in Canada & Mexico; USD 349 in Europe. Ed(s): Rance Crain, David Klein. Crain Communications, Inc., 711 Third Ave, New York, NY 10017-4036; info@crain.com; http://www.crain.com. Illus., index, adv. Sample. Circ: 34649 Paid. Vol. ends: Dec. Microform: CIS; PQC. Online: EBSCO Publishing, EBSCO Host; Factiva, Inc.; Florida Center for Library Automation; Gale; LexisNexis; Northern Light Technology, Inc.; OCLC Online Computer Library Center, Inc.; ProQuest LLC (Ann Arbor); H.W. Wilson. *Indexed:* ABIn, BLI, BPI, CWI, LRI, MASUSE, SD. *Aud.:* Ga, Ac, Sa.

For the student and the practitioner, this tabloid contains enormous amounts of fascinating and useful data. The coverage is thorough yet succinct and touches on all aspects of advertising. Because it is a weekly, the information is current and topical. It covers important campaigns with text and graphics. The "Annual Agency Report" is a statistical issue covering the top agencies worldwide. The publication has feature articles on people, on issues such as tobacco and alcohol advertising, and on forthcoming campaigns and spots to watch for, such as those during the Super Bowl. Advertising on the web is not ignored. The title is one of the best for the price in this field. Highly recommended for college, public, and special collections.

65. *Advertising & Society Review.* [ISSN: 1534-7311] 2000. irreg. Ed(s): William M. O'Barr. Advertising Educational Foundation, 220 E. 42nd St., Ste. 3300, New York, NY 10017-5806; sk@aef.com; http://www.aef.com. Refereed. *Aud.:* Ac.

This twenty-first-century addition to scholarship attempts to approach advertising as a cultural phenomenon and to look at it as an academic pursuit. The articles are extensive, and the topics covered are far from narrow. Recent articles discuss "Spirituality that Sells: Religious Imagery in Magazine Advertising," while others concern advertising during World War I. These are not just historical treatises or opinion pieces, but are empirical studies as well.

66. *Adweek: Eastern Edition.* Formerly: *A N N Y (Advertising News of New York).* [ISSN: 0199-2864] 1960. w. 51/yr. USD 149 domestic (Students, USD 85.20). Ed(s): Sidney Holt, Alison Fahey. Nielsen Business Publications, 770 Broadway, 7th Fl, New York, NY 10003; bmcomm@vnuinc.com; http://www.nielsenbusinessmedia.com. Illus., adv. Circ: 35940. Vol. ends: Dec. *Indexed:* ABIn, BPI, CWI, LRI, PAIS. *Bk. rev.:* short. *Aud.:* Ga, Ac, Sa.

This title is published in seven regional editions including Asia, with the Western U.S. edition being actually now larger than the Eastern U.S. edition, and the others having far less circulation than these two. They all have national and international articles, nonetheless. This is a trade publication, and the substance of the articles reflects that; the personalities and news in the industry are closely followed. Campaigns are covered graphically and in depth, and the regional aspects of the title allow in-depth reporting on aspects of the field that would not otherwise be covered. An excellent choice for agency and public libraries, although it is often carried by academic libraries as well because of its availability in popular databases.

67. *Art Direction: the magazine of visual communication.* [ISSN: 0004-3109] 1949. m. USD 29.97. Advertising Trade Publications, Inc., c/o Dan Barron, Ed, 456 Glenbrook Rd, Stamford, CT 06906-1800. Illus., adv. Sample. Circ: 7854. *Indexed:* ABS&EES, ArtInd, BRI, CBRI, DAAI. *Bk. rev.:* 3, 125-200 words. *Aud.:* Ga, Ac, Sa.

This title's circulation has fallen off a bit, but it still retains its attractions—namely, its coverage of graphic design, television, and print advertising. It is hoped that the smaller circulation does not reflect a lack of these skills in the computer industry. This magazine is written for the art design professional, but its glossy presentation would be attractive to lay readers as well. The regular features include news of people, a calendar, letters to the editor, and columns. Its reasonable price allows many kinds of libraries to subscribe, although it is directed at commercial artists and those in training for the profession.

68. *B to B: the magazine for marketing and e-commerce strategists.* Former titles (until 1999): *Advertising Age's Business Marketing;* (until 1993): *Business Marketing;* (until 1983): *Industrial Marketing.* [ISSN: 1530-2369] 1935. 26x/yr. USD 59 domestic; USD 69 Canada; USD 89 elsewhere. Ed(s): John Obrecht, Ellis Booker. Crain Communications, Inc., 360 N Michigan Ave, Chicago, IL 60601-3806; info@crain.com; http://www.crain.com. Illus., index, adv. Circ: 47853 Controlled. Vol. ends: Dec. Microform: MIM; PQC. Online: EBSCO Publishing, EBSCO Host; Florida Center for Library Automation; Gale; OCLC Online Computer Library Center, Inc.; ProQuest LLC (Ann Arbor); H.W. Wilson. *Indexed:* ABIn, ATI, BLI, BPI, CWI, LRI, LogistBibl, MicrocompInd, PAIS. *Aud.:* Ga, Ac, Sa.

Also known as *Advertising Age's B to B,* this Crain publication contains articles that discuss e-commerce, publishing, business-to-business marketing, and a variety of face-to-face encounters including trade shows. Case studies provide the foundation for suggestions on creating and expanding a presence in existing and emerging international markets. News, statistics, software reviews, technology reports, analysis of research aids, and company market share information are regularly included. The magazine's web presence is less extensive since the dot-com meltdown. There is certainly an effort to consider that the best customers will want their data quickly, and the web site provides e-mail updates to subscribers. Topics reflect changes in the information industry of interest to many librarians, and this title should be available in public, academic, and special libraries.

69. *Brandweek: the newsweekly of marketing communications.* Incorporates (in 2003): *Adweek Magazines' Technology Marketing;* Which had former titles (until 1997): *Marketing Computers;* (until 1987): *Adweek's Computer and Electronics Marketing;* (until 1985): *Computer and Electronics Marketing;* Which incorporated (1983-1985): *Computer Advertising News;* Former titles (until 1992): *Adweek's Marketing Week;* (until 1986): *Adweek (National Marketing Edition);* Which superseded (in 1985): *Ad Forum.* [ISSN: 1064-4318] 1980. w. 46/yr. USD 149 domestic; USD 342 Canada; USD 319 foreign. Ed(s): Karen Benezra. Nielsen Business Publications, 770 Broadway, New York, NY 10003-9595; bmcomm@vnuinc.com; http://www.nielsenbusinessmedia.com. Illus., adv. Circ: 24103 Paid. Vol. ends: Dec. Microform: PQC. Online: EBSCO Publishing, EBSCO Host; Factiva, Inc.; Florida Center for Library Automation; Gale; Northern Light Technology, Inc.; OCLC Online Computer Library Center, Inc.; ProQuest K-12 Learning Solutions; ProQuest LLC (Ann Arbor); H.W. Wilson. *Indexed:* ABIn, BPI, CWI, LRI. *Aud.:* Ga, Ac, Sa.

This title has a surprising amount of text, and it features major industries such as automobile companies. It does reflect the types of media as well: A major section, "From the Box," features various aspects of television advertising, with reports on the actions of a product or the actions of industry players in Hollywood. Extensive statistical information is made available, either presented according to the product and or the company behind it. The magazine is particularly good at keeping up with the various personalities in the marketing field. There is a news update column as well, which can include the effect of politics and current events on advertising. An important element of all marketing collections.

70. *Campaign (London, 1968): the national weekly of the communications business, embracing advertising, marketing, newspapers and magazines, television, radios and posters.* [ISSN: 0008-2309] 1968. w. GBP 140 domestic; USD 477 outside EU. Ed(s): Claire Beale. Haymarket Publishing Ltd., 174 Hammersmith Rd, London, W6 7JP, United Kingdom; hpg@haymarketgroup.com; http://www.haymarketgroup.co.uk. Illus., adv. Circ: 16452 Paid. Vol. ends: Dec. Online: EBSCO Publishing, EBSCO Host; Florida Center for Library Automation; Gale; LexisNexis; Northern Light Technology, Inc.; OCLC Online Computer Library Center, Inc.; ProQuest LLC (Ann Arbor). *Indexed:* ABIn, DAAI, PhotoAb. *Aud.:* Sa.

This title is included because of its prominence in Britain and the European Union. Political articles affecting American companies are available in the online version, *Campaignlive*, which also provides regular international news feeds. Full text is now available in mainstream databases as well, which certainly raises the publication's profile. The articles are generally short, 150–500 words.

71. *Direct Marketing (Online Edition): using direct response advertising to enhance marketing database.* Former titles (until 2004): *Direct Marketing (Print Edition);* (until 1968): *Reporter of Direct Mail Advertising.* 1938. m. Ed(s): Joseph Gatti. Hoke Communications, Inc., 224 Seventh St, Garden City, NY 11530; 71410.2423@compuserve.com. Illus., index, adv. Circ: 11000. Vol. ends: Apr. Microform: PQC. Online: EBSCO Publishing, EBSCO Host; Gale; OCLC Online Computer Library Center, Inc.; ProQuest LLC (Ann Arbor). *Indexed:* ABIn, BLI, BPI. *Aud.:* Ga, Sa.

This title is an up-to-date, easy-to-read online magazine dealing with all the major media and their needs regarding direct marketing. A recent article investigates the problems with rising postal costs; another discusses web-based marketing research, but the magazine certainly does not ignore catalog marketing. It has inclusive columns and a calendar of events. Essential for large public libraries, special libraries, and academic libraries.

72. *ICIS Chemical Business. Americas.* Former titles (until 2007): *Chemical Market Reporter;* (until 1996): *Chemical Marketing Reporter;* (until 1972): *Oil, Paint and Drug Reporter.* [ISSN: 1936-458X] 1871. w. USD 195 domestic; USD 421 United Kingdom; USD 351 elsewhere. ICIS Publications, 360 Park Ave. S., New York, NY 10010; http://www.icis.com/. Illus., adv. Circ: 20000 Paid and controlled. Vol. ends: Dec. Microform: PMC; PQC. Online: The Dialog Corporation; EBSCO Publishing, EBSCO Host; Factiva, Inc.; Florida Center for Library Automation; Gale; Northern Light Technology, Inc.; OCLC Online Computer Library Center, Inc.; ProQuest LLC (Ann Arbor); H.W. Wilson. *Indexed:* ABIn, BPI, ChemAb, EnvAb, EnvInd. *Aud.:* Sa.

With this reasonably priced title, marketing professionals involved in the chemical industry can obtain company information, reports of industry and market activities and conditions, government regulations, and international and U.S. news and trends. Each issue contains information on chemical imports, a chemical profile, and special reports on chemical manufacturing, as well as current reports of significant news on such topics as chemical spills or fines related to price fixing of vitamins. Information is grouped by categories, such as detergents, fats and waxes, and personal care products. Issues also provide information on jobs, a meetings calendar, and industry statistics, including a long list of the latest chemical prices.

73. *Industrial Marketing Management.* [ISSN: 0019-8501] 1971. 8x/yr. EUR 914. Ed(s): Peter J. LaPlaca. Elsevier Inc., 360 Park Ave S, New York, NY 10010-1710; usinfo-f@elsevier.com; http://www.elsevier.com. Illus., adv. Refereed. Circ: 1060 Paid and free. Vol. ends: Nov. Microform: PQC. Online: EBSCO Publishing, EBSCO Host; Gale; IngentaConnect; OhioLINK; ScienceDirect; SwetsWise Online Content. *Indexed:* ABIn, BPI, IBSS, PAIS, PsycInfo, SSCI. *Aud.:* Ac.

This very important scholarly journal provides eight to ten clear, well-written articles on topics such as product development, production presentation, advertising, sales, and pricing. Articles often focus on statistical analysis techniques, such as a recent one titled "A Conceptual Model for Building and

Maintaining Relationships between Manufacturers' Representatives and their Principals." There is diversity, however; for example, other recent topics include modeling of business-to-business partnerships and the impact of antitrust guidelines on competition.

74. *International Journal of Advertising: the quarterly review of marketing communications.* Formerly: *Journal of Advertising;* Which superseded (1978-1980): *Advertising Magazine;* Which was formerly: *Advertising;* (1964-1978): *Advertising Quarterly.* [ISSN: 0265-0487] 1982. q. USD 304 (Individuals, USD 160). Ed(s): Douglas West. N T C Publications Ltd., Farm Rd, Henley-on-Thames, RG9 1EJ, United Kingdom; orders@warc.com; http://www.warc.com. Illus., index, adv. Sample. Refereed. Circ: 800. *Indexed:* ABIn, BAS, BPI, LRI, PAIS, PsycInfo, RiskAb, SSCI. *Aud.:* Ac.

This refereed scholarly journal is devoted to publishing authoritative studies for practitioners and academics in the fields of marketing, advertising, and public relations. Articles average about ten pages each. Recent articles include such topics as beer brand advertising and market share in the United States between 1977 and 1998, and a study of the response to banner ads on the web. This title is imperative for research libraries that support programs in advertising and marketing.

75. *International Journal of Research in Marketing.* [ISSN: 0167-8116] 1984. 4x/yr. EUR 663. Ed(s): H Gatignon. Elsevier BV, North-Holland, Sara Burgerhartstraat 25, Amsterdam, 1055 KV, Netherlands; nlinfo-f@elsevier.nl; http://www.elsevier.nl. Illus., index, adv. Refereed. Circ: 800. Vol. ends: Nov. Microform: PQC. Online: EBSCO Publishing, EBSCO Host; Gale; IngentaConnect; OhioLINK; ScienceDirect; SwetsWise Online Content. *Indexed:* ABIn, PsycInfo, SSCI. *Bk. rev.:* 0-1. *Aud.:* Ac, Sa.

This title is intended to communicate developments in marketing theory and results of empirical research from all countries and a variety of disciplinary approaches. Coverage includes for-profit as well as nonprofit marketing, consumer behavior, products, pricing, marketing communication, marketing channels, strategic marketing planning, industrial marketing, and international marketing. Recent issues include five or six articles on such topics as consumer choice behavior in online and traditional supermarkets and the effects of brand name, price, and other search attributes; and homeostasis and consumer behavior across cultures. Although expensive for a quarterly, it does cover areas that other journals do not.

76. *International Marketing Review.* Incorporates: *Industrial Marketing and Purchasing.* [ISSN: 0265-1335] 1983. bi-m. EUR 9009 combined subscription in Europe print & online eds.; USD 10529 combined subscription in North America print & online eds.; AUD 12259 combined subscription in Australasia print & online eds. Ed(s): Robert E Morgan, Jeryl Whitelock. Emerald Group Publishing Limited, Howard House, Wagon Ln, Bingley, BD16 1WA, United Kingdom; information@emeraldinsight.com; http://www.emeraldinsight.com. Illus., index, adv. Refereed. Circ: 900. Vol. ends: No. 5. Online: Pub.; EBSCO Publishing, EBSCO Host; Gale; IngentaConnect; OCLC Online Computer Library Center, Inc.; OhioLINK; ProQuest LLC (Ann Arbor); SwetsWise Online Content. Reprint: PSC. *Indexed:* ABIn, CWI, PsycInfo, SSCI. *Bk. rev.:* 2, 1,000 words. *Aud.:* Ac.

International marketing management is a complex and interesting area of marketing research. This expensive journal is part of an expensive group of marketing journals from MCB. Despite its small subscriber base and high cost, it does have an international readership among academicians because of its excellent articles, research reports, literature reviews, and occasional book reviews. Issues are often devoted to a single topic, recently, for example, retailing. Despite its being indexed prominently, the subscription price makes this journal impossible for many libraries. Naturally, this makes document delivery problematic.

77. *Journal of Advertising.* [ISSN: 0091-3367] 1972. q. USD 209 print & online eds. Ed(s): Russell N Laczniak. M.E. Sharpe, Inc., 80 Business Park Dr, Armonk, NY 10504; custserv@mesharpe.com; http://www.mesharpe.com. Illus., index, adv. Refereed. Circ: 1850 Paid. Vol. ends: Dec. Microform: PQC. Online: EBSCO Publishing, EBSCO

Host; Gale; Northern Light Technology, Inc.; OCLC Online Computer Library Center, Inc.; ProQuest LLC (Ann Arbor); SwetsWise Online Content; H.W. Wilson. Reprint: PSC. *Indexed:* ABIn, AgeL, ArtHuCI, BLI, BPI, CWI, CommAb, HistAb, IBSS, L&LBA, PAIS, PsycInfo, RILM, SFSA, SSCI, V&AA. *Bk. rev.:* 0-1, 1,000-2,000 words. *Aud.:* Ac. This journal cleaves closely to the classic academic model: The articles are all well footnoted and abstracted. They are very theoretical, with extensive use of statistics and well-defined methodologies. A recent issue includes an article titled "The Role of Myth in Creative Advertising Design," and another article explores managers' perceptions of the impact of sponsorship on brand equity. The review process is a blind one, but unfortunately, a call for papers does not come through when reached only through the indexes.

78. *Journal of Advertising Research.* [ISSN: 0021-8499] 1960. q. USD 295 print & online eds. (Individuals, USD 165 print & online eds.; USD 78 combined subscription academic institutions). Ed(s): Courtney Wolf. Advertising Research Foundation, Inc., 432 Park Ave S, New York, NY 10016; subscriptions@warc.com. Illus., index. Sample. Circ: 2700 Paid. Microform: PQC. Online: Cambridge University Press; EBSCO Publishing, EBSCO Host; Florida Center for Library Automation; Gale; Northern Light Technology, Inc.; OCLC Online Computer Library Center, Inc.; OhioLINK; ProQuest K-12 Learning Solutions; SwetsWise Online Content. *Indexed:* ABIn, AgeL, BPI, CommAb, PsycInfo, RiskAb, SSCI, SUSA. *Aud.:* Ac, Sa.

This trade publication published by the Advertising Research Foundation consists of well-researched and footnoted articles that are easier to read than those found in most academic journals. The charts and illustrations will not intimidate undergraduates with complicated explanations of methodology. A recent issue presents an article titled "Brain-Imaging Detection of Visual Scene Encoding in Long-Term Memory for TV Commercials." The editorial board is a blend of academics and professionals in the field. There is a calendar of foundation events in each issue.

79. *The Journal of Business and Industrial Marketing.* [ISSN: 0885-8624] 1985. 8x/yr. EUR 7939 combined subscription in Europe print & online eds.; USD 3079 combined subscription in North America print & online eds.; AUD 10849 combined subscription in Australasia print & online eds. Ed(s): Wesley J Johnston. Emerald Group Publishing Limited, Howard House, Wagon Ln, Bingley, BD16 1WA, United Kingdom; information@emeraldinsight.com; http://www.emeraldinsight.com. Illus., index, adv. Refereed. Circ: 3000. Vol. ends: No. 4. Online: Pub.; EBSCO Publishing, EBSCO Host; Florida Center for Library Automation; Gale; IngentaConnect; OCLC Online Computer Library Center, Inc.; OhioLINK; ProQuest LLC (Ann Arbor); SwetsWise Online Content. Reprint: PSC. *Indexed:* ABIn, BPI, DSA, FS&TA. *Bk. rev.:* 1-4, 750-1,000 words. *Aud.:* Sa.

Academicians provide practical applications and new ideas based on marketing research to demonstrate the relationship of research to practice in each issue. This is another of MCB University Press's (Emerald Group) products. Recent articles explore sales force automation usage, effectiveness, and cost-benefit in Germany, England, and the United Kingdom; and studying distance learning for Malaysian sales forces. Marketing educators and practitioners are the intended audience.

80. *The Journal of Consumer Marketing.* [ISSN: 0736-3761] 1983. 7x/yr. EUR 7939 combined subscription in Europe print & online eds.; USD 3239 combined subscription in North America print & online eds.; AUD 11219 combined subscription in Australasia print & online eds. Ed(s): Richard C Leventhal. Emerald Group Publishing Limited, Howard House, Wagon Ln, Bingley, BD16 1WA, United Kingdom; information@emeraldinsight.com; http://www.emeraldinsight.com. Illus., index, adv. Refereed. Circ: 4000. Vol. ends: Nov. Microform: PQC. Online: Pub.; EBSCO Publishing, EBSCO Host; Florida Center for Library Automation; Gale; IngentaConnect; OCLC Online Computer Library Center, Inc.; OhioLINK; ProQuest LLC (Ann Arbor); SwetsWise Online Content. Reprint: PSC. *Indexed:* ABIn, BLI, BPI, CommAb, H&TI, PsycInfo. *Bk. rev.:* 2, 500-1,000 words. *Aud.:* Ac, Sa.

Articles in this expensive title report on a wide range of research related to all aspects of consumer marketing. Book reviews are extensive and well written. It is indexed in mainstream databases, and students will appreciate that the articles are on current topics of interest. For example, a recent article reports on "Baby Boomers and Busters: An Exploratory Investigation of Attitudes toward Marketing, Advertising and Consumerism." A regular feature on franchising adds to the mix.

81. *Journal of Consumer Psychology.* [ISSN: 1057-7408] 1992. q. USD 550. Ed(s): Durairaj Maheswaran. Lawrence Erlbaum Associates, Inc., 325 Chestnut St, Ste. 800, Philadelphia, PA 19106; journals@erlbaum.com; http://www.leaonline.com. Adv. Refereed. Reprint: PSC. *Indexed:* ABIn, H&TI, PsycInfo, RILM, SSCI. *Aud.:* Ac, Sa.

This title is very much directed toward academics in the field. Articles can include collaborations between faculty in management and psychology. There are peer-reviewed articles in the field of consumer psychology that include topics such as the role of advertising, consumer attitudes, decision-making processes, and direct brand experience. Other topics covered include the development and change of consumer attitudes; judgment, choice, and decision processes; and social cognition research. A recent article is titled "Consumers' Responses to Negative Word-of-Mouth Communication: An Attribution Theory Perspective."

82. *Journal of Consumer Research.* [ISSN: 0093-5301] 1974. bi-m. USD 260 domestic; USD 284.60 Canada; USD 280 elsewhere. Ed(s): John Deighton. University of Chicago Press, Journals Division, PO Box 37005, Chicago, IL 60637; subscriptions@press.uchicago.edu; http://www.journals.uchicago.edu. Illus., index, adv. Refereed. Circ: 2800 Paid. Vol. ends: Apr. Microform: PQC. Online: The Dialog Corporation; EBSCO Publishing, EBSCO Host; Florida Center for Library Automation; Gale; JSTOR (Web-based Journal Archive); ProQuest K-12 Learning Solutions; ProQuest LLC (Ann Arbor). Reprint: PSC. *Indexed:* ABIn, AgeL, Agr, ArtHuCI, BPI, CommAb, ErgAb, FS&TA, H&TI, HRIS, JEL, L&LBA, PsycInfo, RILM, SFSA, SSCI, SWA. *Aud.:* Ac, Sa.

A dozen associations co-sponsor this journal, which reports on the research results from numerous disciplines in a dozen articles in each issue. Culture swapping, price perception, consumer choice deferral, and the role of gifts in the reformulation of interpersonal relationships serve to represent the diversity of the contents. This title covers the latest hot topics in consumer research, and it is a good choice for both large public and academic libraries.

83. *Journal of Global Marketing.* [ISSN: 0891-1762] 1987. q. USD 615 print & online eds. Ed(s): Erdener Kaynak. International Business Press, 10 Alice St, Binghamton, NY 13904; getinfo@haworthpress.com; http://www.haworthpress.com/. Illus., adv. Sample. Refereed. Circ: 425 Paid. Vol. ends: Winter (No. 4). Microform: PQC. Online: EBSCO Publishing, EBSCO Host; OCLC Online Computer Library Center, Inc.; SwetsWise Online Content. Reprint: HAW. *Indexed:* ABIn, BPI, CommAb, HRA, IBR, IBZ, IPSA, PAIS, PsycInfo, RiskAb. *Bk. rev.:* 3-4, 500-1,000 words. *Aud.:* Ac, Sa.

Under the auspices of the International Business Press, this journal provides relatively inexpensive access to practical, and sometimes comparative, information on specific aspects of marketing in various countries and geographic regions. Topics address transborder information flow, intellectual property issues, counterfeit goods, market penetration strategies, and personal communication. Recent articles include "The Relationship Between Consumer Ethnocentrism and Human Values, On the Marketing of Nations: A Gap Analysis of Managers' Perceptions, Linking Product Evaluations and Purchase Intention for Country-of-Origin Effects" and "Increasing the Effectiveness of Export Assistance Programs: The Case of the California Environmental Technology Industry." A highly selective journal with about half international subscribers. Only information of interest to nonspecialists is considered for inclusion in this title.

84. *Journal of Hospitality Marketing and Management: the international forum for research, theory & practice.* Formerly (until 2008): *Journal of Hospitality & Leisure Marketing.* [ISSN: 1936-8623] 1992. q. USD 425 print & online eds. Ed(s): Bonnie Knutson. Haworth Hospitality Press, 10 Alice St, Binghamton, NY 13904-1580; getinfo@haworthpress.com;

http://www.haworthpress.com/. Illus., index, adv. Sample. Refereed. Circ: 269 Paid. Vol. ends: Winter. Microform: PQC. Online: EBSCO Publishing, EBSCO Host; OCLC Online Computer Library Center, Inc.; SwetsWise Online Content. Reprint: HAW. *Indexed:* CABA, CommAb, H&TI, HRA, IBR, IBZ, PEI, RRTA, S&F, SD, WAE&RSA. *Bk. rev.:* 1, 1,200-3,000 words. *Aud.:* Ac, Sa.

Edited by Michigan State's outstanding School of Hotel, Restaurant, and Institutional Management, this journal cannot be ignored by schools with hospitality programs. The articles are applicable beyond hospitality marketing. Several in-depth articles are included in each issue, along with selected abstracts and a lengthy, signed book review. Issues are often thematic; for example, a recent volume deals with the mature market, an important issue as baby-boomers age. The focus of the contents is understanding how consumer demographics, psychographics, and geographic location can be used to develop and enhance marketing strategies. This work is reasonably priced and invaluable for students in this area.

85. *Journal of Macromarketing.* [ISSN: 0276-1467] 1981. q. GBP 234. Ed(s): Clifford J Shultz, II. Sage Publications, Inc., 2455 Teller Rd, Thousand Oaks, CA 91320; info@sagepub.com; http://www.sagepub.com. Illus., adv. Refereed. Vol. ends: Fall (No. 2). Online: CSA; EBSCO Publishing, EBSCO Host; HighWire Press; Northern Light Technology, Inc.; OCLC Online Computer Library Center, Inc.; SAGE Publications, Inc., SAGE Journals Online; SwetsWise Online Content. Reprint: PSC. *Indexed:* ABIn, CommAb, HRA, PRA. *Bk. rev.:* 2-6, 1,000-3,000 words. *Aud.:* Ac.

The scholarly articles in this journal address a wide range of social issues, international and domestic, and the impact of marketing upon them. The authors approach topics from many perspectives: historical, analytical, theoretical, and general. Articles in recent issues discuss marketing and the natural environment and the role for morality, and a study that examines the marketing literature within the publications of the American Economic Association. Each issue has several extensive book reviews that are signed. This work is worth the price for a program concerned with business ethics.

86. *Journal of Marketing.* [ISSN: 0022-2429] 1934. q. USD 235 (Individuals, USD 95; Members, USD 53). Ed(s): Francesca Cooley, Ruth N Bolton. American Marketing Association, 311 S Wacker Dr, Ste 5800, Chicago, IL 60606; info@ama.org; http://www.ama.org. Illus., index, adv. Refereed. Circ: 10000 Paid. Vol. ends: No. 4. Microform: PQC. Online: Chadwyck-Healey Inc.; EBSCO Publishing, EBSCO Host; Gale; JSTOR (Web-based Journal Archive); Northern Light Technology, Inc.; OCLC Online Computer Library Center, Inc.; ProQuest LLC (Ann Arbor); H.W. Wilson. Reprint: PSC. *Indexed:* ABIn, ATI, BAS, BLI, BPI, BRI, CBRI, CommAb, H&TI, IBR, IBZ, JEL, LogistBibl, PAIS, PsycInfo, RILM, SSCI. *Bk. rev.:* 3, 1,000-4,000 words. *Aud.:* Ac.

This official publication of the American Marketing Association includes research articles that must provide a practical link to an application. Articles must be theoretically sound, provide new information or a fresh insight into an unsolved problem, and benefit both practitioners and academicians. Articles tend to be thoughtful, well researched, and interesting. This is a core title for any academic library that supports business programs, especially marketing education programs. There are regular, lengthy book reviews. Recent articles discuss the acquisition and utilization of information in new product alliances and two aspects of brand loyalty: purchase loyalty and attitudinal loyalty. Online subscriptions are available directly from the publisher.

87. *Journal of Marketing Education.* [ISSN: 0273-4753] 1979. 3x/yr. GBP 273. Ed(s): Douglas J Lincoln. Sage Publications, Inc., 2455 Teller Rd, Thousand Oaks, CA 91320; info@sagepub.com; http://www.sagepub.com. Illus., index, adv. Sample. Refereed. Circ: 400. Vol. ends: Fall (No. 3). Reprint: PSC. *Indexed:* ABIn, PsycInfo. *Aud.:* Ac.

This journal is cosponsored by the Western Marketing Educators Association and the publisher. Each issue includes several papers of about ten pages in length on various aspects of marketing education. Recent articles discuss analyzing the perceptions and preferences of master of business administration (MBA) students regarding face-to-face versus distance-education methods for

delivering a course in marketing management, and familiarizing marketing educators with the process of creative problem-solving. A wise investment as the makeup of marketing departments evolves.

88. *Journal of Marketing Research.* [ISSN: 0022-2437] 1964. q. USD 235 (Members, USD 53; Non-members, USD 95). Ed(s): Francesca Cooley, Wagner A. Kamakura. American Marketing Association, 311 S Wacker Dr, Ste 5800, Chicago, IL 60606; info@ama.org. Illus., index, adv. Refereed. Circ: 9000. Vol. ends: Nov. Microform: PQC. Online: Chadwyck-Healey Inc.; EBSCO Publishing, EBSCO Host; Gale; JSTOR (Web-based Journal Archive); OCLC Online Computer Library Center, Inc.; ProQuest LLC (Ann Arbor); H.W. Wilson. Reprint: PSC. *Indexed:* ABIn, ATI, AgeL, BPI, CommAb, FS&TA, IBR, IBZ, JEL, PAIS, PsycInfo, RiskAb, SSCI. *Bk. rev.:* Number and length vary. *Aud.:* Ac.

This core journal presents the results of scholarly and empirical research without the restriction (which accompanies the *Journal of Marketing*) of linking it to practical applications. Mathematical marketing research included in this journal requires that readers possess a strong background in quantitative methods. Papers in recent issues examine negative customer feedback and consumer reactions to corporate social responsibility. Each issue includes a section of research notes on topics such as an empirical analysis of the growth stage of the product life cycle or the design of research studies for maximum impact, and a section of book reviews.

89. *Journal of Public Relations Research.* Formerly (until 1992): *Public Relations Research Annual.* [ISSN: 1062-726X] 1989. q. GBP 387 print & online eds. Ed(s): Linda Aldoory. Lawrence Erlbaum Associates, Inc., 325 Chestnut St, Ste. 800, Philadelphia, PA 19106; journals@ erlbaum.com; http://www.leaonline.com. Adv. Refereed. Reprint: PSC. *Indexed:* ABIn, CommAb, PsycInfo, V&AA. *Bk. rev.:* Number and length vary. *Aud.:* Ac, Sa.

This academic journal contains long articles aimed at the advanced student or scholar. A recent article is on "Expansion of Ethics as the Tenth Generic Principle of Public Relations Excellence: A Kantian Theory and Model for Managing Ethical Issues," which demonstrates the journal's focus.

90. *The Journal of Services Marketing.* [ISSN: 0887-6045] 1986. 7x/yr. EUR 7939 combined subscription in Europe print & online eds.; USD 3239 combined subscription in North America print & online eds.; AUD 11219 combined subscription in Australasia print & online eds. Ed(s): Charles Martin. Emerald Group Publishing Limited, Howard House, Wagon Ln, Bingley, BD16 1WA, United Kingdom; information@ emeraldinsight.com; http://www.emeraldinsight.com. Illus., adv. Refereed. Circ: 1000. Vol. ends: Nov (No. 4). Online: Pub.; EBSCO Publishing, EBSCO Host; IngentaConnect; OCLC Online Computer Library Center, Inc.; OhioLINK; ProQuest LLC (Ann Arbor); SwetsWise Online Content. Reprint: PSC. *Indexed:* ABIn. *Bk. rev.:* Number and length vary. *Aud.:* Ac, Sa.

This international marketing journal for practitioners provides research reports on a variety of topics related to all aspects of the service economy including benchmarking, customer perception, customer satisfaction, quality and performance, marketing operations, and marketing management. A recent article concerns perceived managerial sincerity, feedback-seeking orientation, and motivation among front-line employees of a service organization. Each issue contains five to seven articles, 10–15 pages in length, abstracts of current research literature, and book reviews. This important journal is overpriced for many academic programs that could benefit from a subscription.

91. *Marketing.* [ISSN: 0025-3650] 1980. w. GBP 140 domestic. Ed(s): Craig Smith. Haymarket Publishing Ltd., 174 Hammersmith Rd, London, W6 7JP, United Kingdom; hpg@haymarketgroup.com; http://www.haymarketgroup.co.uk. Illus., adv. Circ: 40291. Vol. ends: Dec. Microform: PQC. Online: EBSCO Publishing, EBSCO Host; Gale; LexisNexis; Northern Light Technology, Inc.; OCLC Online Computer Library Center, Inc.; ProQuest LLC (Ann Arbor). *Indexed:* ABIn, CPerI, LRI. *Aud.:* Ga, Sa.

This publication is the newspaper of marketing. Functioning much like a trade magazine, it focuses on international marketing news regarding companies, individuals, brands, legal wrangles, technology, and general areas of market research, advertising, use of emerging technologies, image, and market positioning through dozens of short articles. Survey results and awards are reported, such as a recent report on awards for the best direct marketing campaigns.

92. *Marketing News: reporting on marketing and its association.* [ISSN: 0025-3790] 1967. bi-w. USD 130 (Non-members, USD 100). Ed(s): Lisa Keefer. American Marketing Association, 311 S Wacker Dr, Ste 5800, Chicago, IL 60606; info@ama.org; http://www.ama.org/pubs/mn/pub2.html. Illus., adv. Circ: 38000. Vol. ends: No. 26. Microform: MIM; PQC. Online: EBSCO Publishing, EBSCO Host; Gale; LexisNexis; Northern Light Technology, Inc.; OCLC Online Computer Library Center, Inc.; ProQuest LLC (Ann Arbor); H.W. Wilson. *Indexed:* ABIn, BPI. *Aud.:* Ac, Sa.

The American Marketing Association produces this core trade and industry newspaper to provide timely information to practitioners about the most recent innovations and practices of today's leading companies. A calendar of events, association activities, and a variety of methods and techniques for achieving marketing goals in a company, for a product, or within the industry as a whole are presented in short articles. An annual directory of consultants is published each June. Sample articles include one on digital yellow-pages and another on the actual profile of baby-boomers in marketing terms and marketing to them since the dot-com crash.

93. *Marketing Research: a magazine of management and applications.* [ISSN: 1040-8460] 1989. bi-m. USD 90 (Members, USD 53; Non-members, USD 75). Ed(s): Mary Egan Leader, Chuck Chakrapani. American Marketing Association, 311 S Wacker Dr, Ste 5800, Chicago, IL 60606; info@ama.org; http://www.ama.org/pubs/mr/index.html. Illus., index, adv. Sample. Refereed. Circ: 3500 Paid. Vol. ends: No. 4. Online: EBSCO Publishing, EBSCO Host; Gale; LexisNexis; OCLC Online Computer Library Center, Inc.; ProQuest LLC (Ann Arbor); H.W. Wilson. Reprint: PSC. *Indexed:* ABIn, BLI, BPI. *Aud.:* Ac, Sa.

In this core title, the American Marketing Association seeks to emphasize the advancement of the theoretical base of marketing science. Aimed at market research academicians and practitioners, each issue contains several well-written articles on the practical aspects of marketing research. Feature articles often examine cyber-research, including techniques, software, methods, and models for data collecting. Regular departments focus on software reviews, legislative and regulatory issues, secondary research, research methods, and data collections. A recent article is titled "Safe Harbor Principles for the European Privacy Directive Are Finalized." The editorial board includes representatives of research firms and academicians.

94. *Marketing Science: the marketing journal of INFORMS.* [ISSN: 0732-2399] 1982. q. Non-members, USD 146. Ed(s): Steven M. Shugan. I N F O R M S, 7240 Parkway Dr, Ste 310, Hanover, MD 21076-1344; informs@informs.org; http://www.informs.org. Illus., index, adv. Refereed. Circ: 1800. Online: EBSCO Publishing, EBSCO Host; Gale; HighWire Press; JSTOR (Web-based Journal Archive); OCLC Online Computer Library Center, Inc.; ProQuest LLC (Ann Arbor); SwetsWise Online Content. *Indexed:* ABIn, BPI, IBSS, JEL, PsycInfo, SSCI. *Aud.:* Ac, Sa.

The Operational Research Society of America and the Institute of Marketing Science produce this journal in which authors use mathematics and statistics to evaluate marketing science. It presents papers offering significant new marketing insights and implications for academics and quantitatively oriented practitioners. One example is a paper on "Direct Competitive Pricing Behavior in the Auto Market: A Structural Analysis." The wide variety of methodologies provides researchers with ideas for approaching research as well as reports on current concerns. Recent topics include "Patterns in Parameters of Buyer Behavior Models: Generalizing from Sparse Replication. A Model for the Analysis of Asymmetric Data in Marketing Research"; "Application, Predictive Test, and Strategy Implications for a Dynamic Model of Consumer Response"; and "Modeling Retail Customer Behavior at Merrill Lynch."

95. *Media Industry Newsletter.* Incorporates in part (in 2002): *m i n's New Media Report;* Which incorporated (1994-1997): *Interactive Video News;* Which was formed by the merger of (1993-1994): *Video Services News;* (1990-1994): *Video Marketing Newsletter;* Formerly: *Magazine Industry Newsletter.* [ISSN: 0024-9793] 1948. w. USD 895. Ed(s): Steven Cohn. Access Intelligence, LLC, 4 Choke Cherry Rd, 2nd Fl, Rockville, MD 20850; clientservices@accessintel.com; http://www.accessintel.com. Illus., index, adv. Circ: 2143. Vol. ends: Dec. Online: Gale; OCLC Online Computer Library Center, Inc.; ProQuest LLC (Ann Arbor). *Indexed:* ABIn. *Aud.:* Sa.

This loose-leaf title is devoted to the media industry, especially magazine and newspaper publications. Its eight to ten pages are filled with statistics regarding advertising in the consumer-magazine publishing industry. There is an opinion article in each issue and many short pieces on the various industries. This title describes itself as "the first source for magazine advertising data (boxscores)," and it does keep its readers up-to-date on what is happening in the field. Despite the importance of the data, it is a bit pricey for what it might bring to an academic library, but fortunately it is indexed in Lexis-Nexis Academic Universe.

96. *MediaWeek: the news magazine of the media.* Former titles (until 1990): *Marketing and Media Decisions;* (until 1979): *Media Decisions.* [ISSN: 1055-176X] 1966. w. Mon. USD 149 domestic; USD 319 elsewhere; USD 3.95 newsstand/cover per issue. Ed(s): Jim Cooper, Michael Burgi. Nielsen Business Publications, 770 Broadway, New York, NY 10003-9595; bmcomm@vnuinc.com; http://www.nielsenbusinessmedia.com. Illus., index, adv. Circ: 21978 Paid. Vol. ends: Dec. Microform: CIS; PQC. Online: The Dialog Corporation; EBSCO Publishing, EBSCO Host; Florida Center for Library Automation; Gale; Northern Light Technology, Inc.; OCLC Online Computer Library Center, Inc.; ProQuest LLC (Ann Arbor); H.W. Wilson. *Indexed:* ABIn, BPI, CWI, LRI. *Aud.:* Ga, Ac, Sa.

A core newsmagazine designed for the practitioner, this relatively short title presents pieces monitoring the several media it considers important. It naturally expends much effort and space on the world of television. It regularly reports on such matters as the ratings of the cable networks. The format is divided according to cable, magazines, new media, and media elite. The talk show competition is a good example of the kind of topics covered. The editors devote a lot of space to "Services and Resources," which includes listings of available jobs in the field. A good, breezy journal for practitioners that must be acknowledged by students of the field.

97. *O'Dwyer's P R Newsletter.* Former titles: *Jack O'Dwyer's Newsletter; Jack O'Dwyer's P R Newsletter.* 1968. w. USD 295. Ed(s): Jack O'Dwyer. J.R. O'Dwyer Co., Inc., 271 Madison Ave, Ste 600, New York, NY 10016; john@odwyerpr.com; http://www.odwyerpr.com. Circ: 20000 Paid. Online: LexisNexis. *Aud.:* Sa.

This indispensable weekly provides the latest news and information on public relations firms and professionals. It subdivides the news rather casually in the "PR Opinion/Items" and "Media News" sections. Under each are several stories that the editors have deemed important for professionals to read. The former gives editorial opinions on politics as they affect this field. In the latter, recently, CCNY Communications Hall of Fame inductees are found next to the announcement of the winner of the McDonald's account. Recommended for all professionals and large public libraries.

98. *O'Dwyer's P R Report.* Formerly (until 2006?): *O'Dwyer's P R Services Report.* [ISSN: 1931-8316] 1987. m. USD 60. J.R. O'Dwyer Co., Inc., 271 Madison Ave, Ste 600, New York, NY 10016; john@odwyerpr.com; http://www.odwyerpr.com. Adv. Circ: 4000. Online: LexisNexis. *Aud.:* Sa.

This newsletter publishes articles on current topics and trends of interest to PR professionals, including profiles of firms and discussions of legal and financial issues. It includes such columns as "Web Sitings," which reports on recent developments in the field on the web. This work differs from *O'Dwyer's PR Newsletter* in that it contains more news and less opinion. The columns are informational in intent without any particular political slant. Issues include a PR job market section.

99. *Potentials: ideas and products that motivate.* Formerly (until 1998): *Potentials in Marketing;* Which incorporated (1976-1989): *Marketing Communications.* [ISSN: 1522-9564] 1968. m. USD 59 domestic (Free to qualified personnel). Ed(s): Melinda Ligos. Nielsen Business Publications, 770 Broadway, New York, NY 10003-9595; bmcomm@vnuinc.com; http://www.nielsenbusinessmedia.com. Illus., adv. Sample. Circ: 50450 Controlled. Vol. ends: Dec. Online: EBSCO Publishing, EBSCO Host; Florida Center for Library Automation; Gale; OCLC Online Computer Library Center, Inc.; ProQuest LLC (Ann Arbor). *Indexed:* ABIn, AgeL, BPI. *Aud.:* Sa.

This title reports case studies, methods and trends in marketing, and sales promotions that are intended to help practitioners boost a company's competitive advantage. The primary function is to provide advertising and notice of available premiums and promotional items to potential buyers. Libraries will find this interesting for their own uses, as would some corporate special libraries. The title is available in full text via EBSCO.

100. *Psychology & Marketing.* [ISSN: 0742-6046] 1984. m. USD 1395. Ed(s): Dr. Ronald J Cohen. John Wiley & Sons, Inc., 111 River St, Hoboken, NJ 07030-5774; uscs-wis@wiley.com; http://www.wiley.com. Illus., index, adv. Refereed. Circ: 800. Vol. ends: No. 6. Microform: PQC. Online: Chadwyck-Healey Inc.; EBSCO Publishing, EBSCO Host; OhioLINK; ProQuest LLC (Ann Arbor); SwetsWise Online Content; Wiley InterScience. *Indexed:* ABIn, ASG, AgeL, BPI, CJA, CommAb, PsycInfo, SSCI, V&AA. *Aud.:* Ac, Sa.

This title presents research that bridges academic and practical interests in marketing and advertising through the application of psychological principles to marketing strategy. Research reports are based on "fundamental factors that affect buying, social and cultural trends, psychological profiles of potential customers, and changes in customer behavior." Recent papers discuss the dangers of using deceptive practices in the mail-order business, using deception to measure service performance, and "Romancing the Past: Heritage Visiting and the Nostalgic Consumer." The journal is widely indexed, and the in-depth articles are well written. An important, although expensive, addition for academic and special libraries.

101. *Public Relations Quarterly.* Incorporates: *International Public Relations Review.* [ISSN: 0033-3700] 1955. q. USD 65 domestic; USD 70 in Canada & Mexico; USD 77 elsewhere. Ed(s): Elaine Newman. Hudson Associates, 44 W Market St, Box 311, Rhinebeck, NY 12572-0311; hphudson@aol.com; http://www.newsletter-clearinghse.com. Illus., index. Circ: 5000 Paid. Vol. ends: Dec. Microform: PQC. Online: EBSCO Publishing, EBSCO Host; Florida Center for Library Automation; Gale; Northern Light Technology, Inc.; OCLC Online Computer Library Center, Inc.; ProQuest K-12 Learning Solutions; ProQuest LLC (Ann Arbor); H.W. Wilson. *Indexed:* ABIn, ATI, BPI, CommAb. *Bk. rev.:* 4, 300-600 words. *Aud.:* Ga, Ac, Sa.

This title is primarily directed at the practitioner, but its articles would be of interest to students as well. A recent article claims that *The Wizard of Oz* by L. Frank Baum was part of the movement that officially established the field of public relations in the twentieth century. Another featured article describes the vital role that public relations can play in attracting investors and licensing partners. The assumptions characterizing litigation public relations is the subject of another article. For the professor, there is a piece describing how poetry can help people improve their prose. Recommended for large public and academic libraries.

102. *Public Relations Review.* [ISSN: 0363-8111] 1975. 5x/yr. EUR 431. Ed(s): Ray E Hiebert. Elsevier Ltd., The Boulevard, Langford Ln, Oxford, OX5 1GB, United Kingdom. Illus., adv. Sample. Circ: 2500. Vol. ends: Dec. Microform: PQC. Online: EBSCO Publishing, EBSCO Host; Florida Center for Library Automation; Gale; IngentaConnect; Northern Light Technology, Inc.; OCLC Online Computer Library Center, Inc.; OhioLINK; ScienceDirect; SwetsWise Online Content; H.W. Wilson. *Indexed:* ABIn, AgeL, ArtHuCI, BPI, CommAb, HRA, PAIS, PRA, PSA, SSCI. *Bk. rev.:* 5-6, 500-1,000 words. *Aud.:* Ga, Ac, Sa.

This journal considers its title an important guide to its content: There are pieces that could be called research, although some might question the format of the methodology section in the articles. There are pieces that comment on how government policy directly affects aspects of a public relations officer's life. The book reviews alone are worth the cover price. They are extensive and could be considered articles in themselves, perhaps thus fulfilling the "review" promise in the title. A fifth issue published midyear is an extensive bibliography that will interest librarians.

103. *Public Relations Strategist.* [ISSN: 1082-9113] 1995. q. USD 100 domestic; USD 110 Canada; USD 120 elsewhere. Ed(s): John Elsasser, Alison Stateman. The Public Relations Society of America, Inc., 33 Maiden Ln, 11th Fl, New York, NY 10038-5150; http://www.prsa.org. Adv. *Aud.:* Sa.

This journal is included in the price of Public Relations Society membership dues. It contains about ten articles of interest to the trade. The editors wish to emphasize the regular interviews with CEOs of the leading firms in the field. Recent articles include one on the "Ethical Challenge of Global Public Relations."

104. *Public Relations Tactics.* [ISSN: 1080-6792] 1994. m. Non-members, USD 75; Students, USD 24. Ed(s): John Elsasser, Alison Stateman. The Public Relations Society of America, Inc., 33 Maiden Ln, 11th Fl, New York, NY 10038-5150; john.elsasser@prsa.org; http://www.prsa.org. Adv. Circ: 25000. *Aud.:* Sa.

This tabloid directs its articles toward professionals, and they are written by their peers. The articles can concern independent practitioners or employees of big firms. Each issue has a listing of upcoming events such as trade shows. Polls are included that are of interest and importance to the audience, but with little analysis. The articles also keep readers abreast of recent court rulings that have an impact upon the field. This paper is an important mouthpiece for the profession.

105. *Sales and Marketing Management.* Formerly (until 1975): *Sales Management.* [ISSN: 0163-7517] 1918. m. USD 48 domestic; USD 67 Canada; USD 146 elsewhere. Ed(s): Christopher Hosford, Christine Galea. Nielsen Business Publications, 770 Broadway, 7th Fl, New York, NY 10003; bmcomm@vnuinc.com; http://www.nielsenbusinessmedia.com. Illus., adv. Circ: 60000. Microform: CIS; PQC. Online: EBSCO Publishing, EBSCO Host; Factiva, Inc.; Florida Center for Library Automation; Gale; OCLC Online Computer Library Center, Inc.; ProQuest K-12 Learning Solutions; ProQuest LLC (Ann Arbor); H.W. Wilson. *Indexed:* ABIn, BLI, BPI, LRI, PAIS. *Aud.:* Sa.

This valuable trade magazine is aimed at executives who manage sales and marketing functions. Its annual surveys provide readers with "retail sales, effective buying income, and population data for both metro markets and media markets (DMAs), making comparisons between market types simpler." Regional and state-by-state tables are presented for market totals, five-year market summaries and projections, and merchandising line sales. A glossary and an alphabetical listing of hundreds of metro markets and their component communities are also included in this issue. Most issues contain numerous articles on all aspects of marketing. A core title for both public and academic libraries.

■ AERONAUTICS AND SPACE SCIENCE

Howard Stephen McMinn, Science and Technology Librarian, 152 Parks Library, Iowa State University, Ames, IA 50011; hsmcminn@iastate.edu

Introduction

The terms *aeronautics, astronautics,* and *space science* do not conjure up the romantic images of early aviators and aviation pioneers or the excitement of space exploration, but they are the basic elements of these inspiring endeavors. This romantic concept of flying and space exploration is displayed by the popular journals that capitalize on the adventure, excitement, and sport of all types of aviation, aircraft, and flight, from ballooning to spaceflight. The practical reality is that the science and technology that support aviation and spaceflight—i.e., aeronautics, astronautics, and space science—are highly technical fields that require very specialized, technical information created by experts. This section tries to take into account these differences by presenting the best aviation and spaceflight magazines, along with the most significant technical journals in these fields.

Some aspects of these fields, aspects connected with military aviation or the commercial aspects of aviation industry—that is, those dealing with airlines, airports, manufacturing, maintenance, and travel—can be found covered in the Military and Transportation sections. The journals included in this section comprise the important scientific and technical journals required by researchers, scientists, and engineers along with the leading general-interest publications covering the various areas of aviation and flight.

From a library perspective, the fields of aeronautics, astronautics, and space science have not seen the explosive growth in new technical journals that some disciplines have experienced in the past few years, but there are exciting new research-level journals focused on very specific research areas such as aeroacoustics, human factors, and communications. Some of these important new titles seem to be struggling to find an audience in a way that probably has more to do with the economic pressures faced by scientific and technical libraries (due to journal price inflation) than with the state of the industry or the quantity or quality of research conducted. It should be noted that most of the established journals are growing in size in that the number of published papers continues to rise.

Similarly, there hasn't been much change in terms of the number of general-interest flight and aviation magazines published. Most of these general-interest publications have some sort of Internet presence, but the amount of information available electronically varies greatly from title to title. Most of the electronic journals included in this section are either trade publications, focusing on news and business, or sites of interest to the general aviation and space enthusiast.

Most of the electronic publications are beginning to enhance their sites with multimedia, primarily videos and podcasts. The content of the journals in the space sciences (both print and electronic) tends to overlap with the field of astronomy; therefore, those interested in space sciences should also consult the Astronomy section for relevant titles. The list of journals that follows should provide enough information to develop a core collection for the researcher in aeronautics and space sciences or for those interested in general aviation and flying publications. Additionally, here are two notable web sites to consider logging on to:

Spaceflight Now: the leading source for online space news. d. Spaceflight Now Ltd, PO Box 175, Tonbridge, Kent TN10 4ZY, UK. wendy@spaceflightnow.com; http://spaceflightnow.com. *Aud:* Hs, Ga, Sa. Overall, a good comprehensive site covering space news and events.

Spacetoday.net: space news from around the web. 2001. d. info@spacetoday.net; http://spacetoday.net. *Aud:* Ga, Ac, Sa. A good site that gathers space-related news from a variety of sources for space news and technology.

Basic Periodicals

Hs: *Air & Space—Smithsonian, Aviation Week & Space Technology, Flying;* Ga: *Air & Space—Smithsonian, A O P A Pilot, Aviation Week & Space Technology, Flying, Plane and Pilot, FlyPast, Soaring;* Ac (Nontechnical): *Aerospace America, Aviation Week & Space Technology, Flight International, Interavia, Space Policy, Vertiflite;* Ac (Technical): *Acta Astronautica, The Aeronautical Journal, A I A A Journal, Journal of Aircraft, Journal of Astronautical Sciences, Journal of Spacecraft and Rockets, Progress in Aerospace Sciences.*

Basic Abstracts and Indexes

Engineering Index, International Aerospace Abstracts, Scientific and Technical Aerospace Reports.

106. *A A H S Journal.* Formerly (until 1980): *American Aviation Historical Society Journal.* [ISSN: 0882-9365] 1956. q. USD 49; USD 64 foreign. Ed(s): Albert Hansen. American Aviation Historical Society, 2333 Otis St, Santa Ana, CA 92704; http://cwalton.jovanet.com/aahs/. Illus., adv. Vol. ends: No. 4. *Indexed:* AUNI, AmH&L, HistAb. *Aud:* Ac, Sa.

Produced by the American Aviation Historical Society (AAHS), this journal consists of well-researched scholarly articles on all areas of aviation history. The primary emphasis is on the history of general aviation and commercial flight

technology, not on military or space history and events, as is the case with most general-interest aviation history magazines. However, all areas of aviation history are included, from famous aviators and engineers to aircraft design and manufacture to the history of aerospace advancements and technical achievements. The journal contains primarily black-and-white photographs (appropriate for the time periods covered) and illustrations. Articles are usually written by historians, military personnel, and scholars, and are produced by society members; and most have an American flavor. There are two ongoing departments: "Forum of Flight" (consisting of interesting or unusual black-and-white photographs of aircraft submitted by members) and "News and Comments from Members" (including items of interest, news, and conference activities). AAHS also publishes a newsletter that provides all of the society's membership-related information. This scholarly and informative journal is appropriate for academic and public libraries.

107. *A I A A Journal: devoted to aerospace research and development.* Formed by the merger of (1934-1963): *Journal of the Aerospace Sciences;* Which was formerly (until 1958): *Journal of the Aeronautical Sciences;* (1945-1963): *A R S Journal;* Which was formerly (until 1959): *Jet Propulsion;* (until 1954): *American Rocket Society. Journal.* [ISSN: 0001-1452] 1963. m. Non-members, USD 1385. Ed(s): Elaine S Oran, Luke McCabe. American Institute of Aeronautics and Astronautics, Inc., 1801 Alexander Bell Dr, Ste 500, Reston, VA 20191; custserv@aiaa.org; http://www.aiaa.org. Illus., index. Refereed. Circ: 3400 Paid. Vol. ends: No. 12. Microform: PMC; PQC. Online: EBSCO Publishing, EBSCO Host; IngentaConnect. Reprint: PSC. *Indexed:* AS&TI, ApMecR, C&ISA, CerAb, ChemAb, EngInd, ExcerpMed, H&SSA, IAA, MathR, SCI. *Bk. rev.:* 1-2, 300-500 words. *Aud.:* Ac.

This is the leading research-oriented journal of the American Institute of Aeronautics and Astronautics and covers all topics of broad interest to the membership as opposed to the more narrowly focused scope of the organization's other journals. This journal is designed to disseminate original research papers that discuss new theoretical developments or experimental results for the advancement of astronautics and aeronautics. The areas covered include aerodynamics, aeroacoustics, fluid mechanics, reacting flows, hydrodynamics, research instrumentation and facilities, structural mechanics and materials, propulsion, aircraft technology, STOL/VTOL, fluid dynamics, thermophysics and thermochemistry, and interdisciplinary topics. The journal is divided into sections arranged by broad subject classification: "Aircraft Technology, Conventional, STOL/VTOL," "Fluid Dynamics," "Interdisciplinary Topics," and "Structural Mechanics and Materials." Additional sections are added when appropriate, such as "Propulsion" and "Energy." Periodically, special sections or issues devoted to a specific topic are published, such as recent special issues on measurement techniques, combustion modeling, and flapped wing flight. The journal recently added a letters section to facilitate the rapid communication of new and potentially important results or ideas of interest to the journal's readership. Appropriate for all academic, technical, and larger public libraries.

108. *A O P A Pilot.* [ISSN: 0001-2084] 1958. m. USD 21 to qualified organizations (Members, USD 39). Ed(s): Thomas B Haines, Mike Collins. Aircraft Owners and Pilots Association (A O P A), 421 Aviation Way, Frederick, MD 21701; http://www.aopa.org. Illus., index, adv. Circ: 340000 Paid and controlled. Vol. ends: Dec. *Indexed:* HRIS. *Bk. rev.:* 1-2, 300-500 words. *Aud.:* Ga, Sa.

The journal is the primary vehicle of the Aircraft Owners and Pilots Association, which is the world's largest aviation organization that meets the needs of all pilots—from student pilots to space shuttle pilots. It is geared specifically toward the private pilot and aircraft owner. Articles include information on safety; flying tips and techniques; airports, nearby accommodations, and attractions; newly certified aircraft along with specifications; and, of course, general-interest pieces on aircraft and flying. The journal contains information pertinent to association members, such as regulatory news, information on new aircraft and equipment, a calendar of events, and meeting and organizational notes. The journal provides many photographs, as well as illustrations for aviation buffs that highlight the text. A companion publication, *AOPA Flight Training*, provides in-depth information for pilots and pilots-in-training. One of the best general-interest aviation publications and a good addition to general-aviation collections.

109. *Acta Astronautica.* Supersedes (in 1974): *Astronautica Acta.* [ISSN: 0094-5765] 1955. 24x/yr. EUR 3872. Ed(s): Jean-Pierre Marec. Pergamon, The Boulevard, Langford Ln, East Park, Kidlington, OX5 1GB, United Kingdom. Illus., index, adv. Sample. Refereed. Vol. ends: Dec. Microform: PQC. Online: EBSCO Publishing, EBSCO Host; Gale; IngentaConnect; OhioLINK; ScienceDirect; SwetsWise Online Content. *Indexed:* ApMecR, C&ISA, CerAb, ChemAb, EngInd, H&SSA, IAA, M&GPA, RiskAb, SCI, SSCI. *Aud.:* Ac.

This research-level publication covering the field of astronautics, with contributions and readership on a global scale, is the journal of the International Academy of Astronautics. It presents peer-reviewed papers in the areas of life sciences, astronautics, space sciences, and space technology to promote the peaceful scientific exploration of space to aid humanity. In addition, it covers the design, development, research, and technological advances necessary to accomplish this goal. Articles cover microgravity, space station technology, power and propulsion, satellite technology, and space economics, along with traditional areas of research such as materials science, guidance and control, etc. The journal periodically devotes an entire issue to, or publishes a special issue devoted to, a specific topic or a collection of selected conference papers from the International Academy of Astronautics and the International Astronautical Federation. The journal also publishes "Academy Transaction Notes" and other items of interest to academy members when appropriate. Overall, it is a broad-coverage publication with an international scope. Appropriate for academic and other research libraries.

Ad Astra. See Astronomy section.

110. *Advances in Space Research.* Formed by the merger of (1978-1980): *Advances in Space Exploration;* (1963-1980): *Life Sciences and Space Research;* (1960-1980): *Space Research.* [ISSN: 0273-1177] 1981. 27x/yr. EUR 3831. Ed(s): M A Shea. Pergamon, The Boulevard, Langford Ln, East Park, Kidlington, OX5 1GB, United Kingdom; http://www.elsevier.nl. Illus., index. Refereed. Vol. ends: No. 24. Microform: PQC. Online: EBSCO Publishing, EBSCO Host; Gale; IngentaConnect; OhioLINK; ScienceDirect; SwetsWise Online Content. *Indexed:* C&ISA, CerAb, ChemAb, EngInd, IAA, M&GPA, PollutAb, SCI. *Aud.:* Ac, Sa.

As the official journal of the Committee on Space Research (COSPAR), a scientific committee of the International Council of Scientific Unions, *Advances in Space Research* covers all areas of fundamental research obtained with the use of balloons, rockets, rocket-propelled vehicles, or other aerospace vehicles regardless of political considerations. A sampling of the topics covered includes planets and small bodies of the solar system, studies of the upper atmosphere, research in astrophysics from space, materials sciences research, life sciences as related to space, and space studies of Earth's surface. Much of the information contained in the journal has been taken from various meetings and symposia sponsored by COSPAR. Therefore, most issues contain papers on a similar theme in a single area of interest. Even though papers are taken from various conferences, they are thoroughly reviewed before inclusion in the journal. Readers who cannot justify the expense of a subscription to this specialized international journal can purchase the issues individually. This journal presents information on fundamental research obtained by utilizing aerospace vehicles and is primarily of interest to physicists, astronomers, and the general field of space science.

111. *Aero - News Network.* [ISSN: 1530-9339] 1999. d. Free. Ed(s): Jim Campbell. Aero - News Network, PO Box 9132, Winter Haven, FL 33883-9132; editor@aero-news.net; http://www.aero-news.net/. *Aud.:* Hs, Ga.

This site caters to the entire aviation community with articles and news from the now-defunct *US Aviator* print magazine. The web site has the advantage of being fresh and timely in its reporting. It is accurate and entertaining, with a commitment to making flying safer through reporting on consumer activism and education. Lots of columns, lots of color photographs, news, and editorials make this a worthwhile stop in the search for aviation information. This is similar to commercial newsstand publications but in an electronic format, and it is a good place to get a fresh view of the aviation industry. The majority of the information is on general and sport aviation, but commercial aviation, space news, and political news are included. It is refreshing that the site doesn't seem

to be bought and sold by its advertisers; you can actually distinguish the content from the ads. The site is segmented into categories such as aerospace, commercial airline, commercial biz-av, feature stories, general aviation, military aviation, and sport aviation. No matter what type of aviation you are interested in, this site will keep you up-to-date and informed. The site uses all of the latest technology to present information to aviators including RSS feeds, podcasts, and Internet radio.

112. *The Aeronautical Journal.* Incorporates: *Aeronautical Quarterly.* [ISSN: 0001-9240] 1897. 12x/yr. GBP 299. Ed(s): Mr. C S Male, J L Stollery. Royal Aeronautical Society, 4 Hamilton Pl, London, W1J 7BQ, United Kingdom; raes@raes.org.uk; http://www.aerosociety.com. Illus., index. Refereed. Circ: 1500. Vol. ends: Dec. Microform: PMC; PQC. *Indexed:* AS&TI, ApMecR, ChemAb, EngInd, ExcerpMed, H&SSA, IAA, MathR, SCI. *Bk. rev.:* 2-3, 300-500 words. *Aud.:* Ac.

The purpose of this long-standing monthly aeronautical engineering research journal, produced by the Royal Aeronautical Society, is to foster the advancement of all aspects of aeronautical, aerospace, and space sciences. It includes papers on the research, design, development, construction, and operation of aircraft and space vehicles. Topics of the papers include fluid mechanics and aerodynamics, propulsion, structures and materials, rotorcraft, astronautics, dynamics and control, noise and vibration, guided flight, air transport, test flying and flight simulation, and the history of aviation and flight. Also included are the sections "Technical Notes" and "Engineering Notes," to encourage rapid dissemination of information and to foster discussion on current research. The journal has moved away from information that is geared solely to society members, and includes strictly technical articles on aeronautics and astronautics. Occasional special issues are published that are focused on a single topic or theme or comprised of selected technical papers presented at major U.K. aeronautical conferences. Membership and related society information is available in the society's companion publication, *The Aerospace Professional.*

113. *AeroSafety World.* Formerly: *Aviation Safety World;* Formed by the merger of (1987-2006): *Accident Prevention;* Which was formerly (until 1987): *F S F Accident Prevention Bulletin;* (1987-2006): *Airport Operations;* Which was formerly (until 1987): *F S F Airport Operations Safety Bulletin;* (1954-2006): *Aviation Mechanics Bulletin;* (1987-2006): *Cabin Crew Safety;* Which was formerly (until 1987): *F S F Cabin Crew Safety Bulletin;* (until 1975): *Cabin Crew Safety Exchange;* (1988-2006): *Flight Safety Digest;* Which was formerly (until 1988): *F S F Flight Safety Digest;* (until 1984): *Flight Safety Digest (1982);* (until 1982): *Flight Safety Facts and Reports;* (until 1974): *Flight Safety Facts and Analysis;* (1987-2006): *Helicopter Safety;* Which was formerly (until 1987): *F S F Helicopter Safety Bulletin;* (until 1985): *Helicopter Safety Bulletin;* (1988-2006): *Human Factors & Aviation Medicine;* Which was formerly (until 1988): *F S F Human Factors Bulletin & Aviation Medicine.* [ISSN: 1934-4015] 2006. m. USD 350 (Members, USD 35; Non-members, USD 50). Ed(s): J A Donoghue. Flight Safety Foundation, Inc., 601 Madison St, Ste 300, Alexandria, VA 22314-1756; http://www.flightsafety.org. *Indexed:* HRIS. *Aud.:* Ga, Ac, Sa.

This journal is published by the Flight Safety Foundation and provides information and in-depth analysis of important safety issues facing the industry, along with standard departments. Since its creation, which meant merging seven newsletters produced by the society, the journal has been devoted to providing a greater emphasis on timely news coverage. The newsletters that were merged to form this new journal are *Accident Prevention, Airport Operations, Aviation Mechanics Bulletin, Crew Safety, Flight Safety Digest, Helicopter Safety,* and *Human Factors & Aviation Medicine.* The feature articles deal with all areas of safety within all sectors of the aviation industry. The departments contain news items, editorials, letters to the editor, a calendar of events, information on the foundation and its members, etc. The DataLink section provides information and statistics relevant to aviation and safety. The journal is an important timely publication for those working in the industry or interested in aviation safety.

114. *Aerospace America.* Former titles (until 1983): *Astronautics and Aeronautics;* (until 1963): *Astronautics and Aerospace Engineering;* Which was formed by the 1963 merger of (1957-1963): *Astronautics;* (1958-1963): *Aesrospace Engineering;* Which was formerly (until 1958): *Aeronautical Engineering Review.* [ISSN: 0740-722X] 1932. m. Free to members; Non-members, USD 163. Ed(s): Elaine J Camhi. American Institute of Aeronautics and Astronautics, Inc., 1801 Alexander Bell Dr, Ste 500, Reston, VA 20191; custserv@aiaa.org; http://www.aiaa.org. Illus., index, adv. Refereed. Circ: 41000 Controlled. Vol. ends: No. 12. Microform: PQC. Online: LexisNexis. *Indexed:* ABS&EES, AS&TI, ApMecR, C&ISA, CerAb, ChemAb, EngInd, ExcerpMed, IAA, SCI, SSCI. *Aud.:* Hs, Ga, Ac.

This society-focused journal is the general-interest publication produced for the membership of the American Institute of Aeronautics and Astronautics (AIAA). It contains informative feature articles of interest to those within the field of aeronautics and space science rather than the more technical articles and papers that are presented in the other AIAA publications. The articles are still quite sophisticated and comprehensive, utilizing many color photographs and illustrations. The journal is devoted to keeping AIAA members up-to-date on major events and issues in their field, and serves as the prime vehicle for relaying information on the association's activities. It contains valuable news of upcoming conferences and events, along with sections such as "International Beat" and "Washington Watch," with recent industry news, and "Conversations," which comprises interviews with important people in the industry or people who impact the industry (such as lawmakers). Other sections provide information on new systems, software, materials, or products of note; an almanac of past aerospace milestones of interest; and career-related information. The two or three feature articles in each issue cover all aspects of the industry—economic issues, aircraft, materials, space transportation, spacecraft, and defense. The articles primarily interpret or review new research, engineering issues, program developments, and future trends in aeronautics or space sciences. The December issue is a special issue devoted to reviewing the previous year in aerospace. There are over 40 short articles in this special issue, each devoted to the progress made during the past year in various categories. Overall, a valuable addition to all types of libraries, from high school to academic.

115. *Aerospace Engineering & Manufacturing.* Former titles (until 2008): *Aerospace Engineering Magazine;* (until 1982): *S A E in Aerospace Engineering.* [ISSN: 1937-5212] 1981. 10x/yr. Free to members; Non-members, USD 75. Ed(s): Jean Broge. Society of Automotive Engineers, 400 Commonwealth Dr, Warrendale, PA 15096-0001; advertising@sae.org; http://www.sae.org. Illus., index, adv. Circ: 24177. Vol. ends: Dec. *Indexed:* C&ISA, CerAb, IAA. *Bk. rev.:* 1-2. *Aud.:* Ac, Sa.

This journal, produced by the Society of Automotive Engineers (SAE), is designed to provide technical assistance and state-of-the-art technology information of interest to designers, manufacturers, and project managers of aerospace systems and components. Unlike most trade-oriented magazines, its emphasis is more on applications, testing, and reliability of aerospace components than on theoretical or experimental results. There is very little information on people and events or on the business side of the industry. The journal covers all areas of interest to aerospace engineers, including propulsion systems, system and component design and maintainability, avionics, structural design, and related engineering topics. It is important as a vehicle for new-product information, product literature, computer products, and other technical information, and it is mainly utilized to convey practical information to those working in the field. The more theoretical and technical research information and papers presented at the various SAE conferences and symposia are included in *SAE Transactions. Aerospace Engineering* is an appropriate publication for technical and academic libraries.

116. *Aerospace Science and Technology.* Formed by the merger of (1963-1997): *Recherche Aerospaciale;* Which was formerly (1948-1963): *La Recherche Aeronautique;* (1974-1997): *Recherche Aerospatiale (English Edition);* (1977-1997): *Zeitschrift fuer Flugwissenschaften und Weltraumforschung;* Which was formed by the merger of (1953-1977): *Zeitschrift fuer Flugwissenschaften;* (1964-1977): *Raumfahrtforschung;* Which was formerly (1957-1964): *Raketentechnik und*

Raumfahrtforschung. [ISSN: 1270-9638] 1997. 8x/yr. EUR 341. Ed(s): M. de Gliniasty, Fred Thomas. Elsevier France, Editions Scientifiques et Medicales, 23 Rue Linois, Paris, 75724, France; academic@elsevier-fr.com. Illus., index. Sample. Refereed. Vol. ends: No. 8. *Indexed:* ApMecR, C&ISA, CerAb, ChemAb, EngInd, ExcerpMed, IAA, MathR, SCI. *Aud.:* Ac, Sa.

This journal originated by combining two of the leading aerospace journals from France and Germany. *Aerospace Science and Technology* boasts a binational editorial team consisting of important members of the European aerospace community. The recent addition of research organizations from Italy, Spain, the Netherlands, and Sweden has solidified its position as one of the leading European journals in the discipline. It is international in scope, presenting articles on original research, review articles, and condensed versions of recently completed doctoral theses. Topics covered include all issues related to aerospace research, from fundamental research to industrial applications for the design and manufacture of aircraft, helicopters, missiles, launch vehicles, and satellites. Included are articles on fluid dynamics, materials and structures, flight mechanics, guidance and control, automatic systems, and propulsion systems. Occasionally, special issues are published comprising selected papers from European aerospace conferences. Recommended for a research-level collection.

117. *Aerospace Testing International.* [ISSN: 1478-2774] 2002. q. Free. U K & International Press, Abinger House, Church St, Dorking, RH4 1DF, United Kingdom; info@ukintpress.com; http://www.ukintpress.com/. Adv. *Aud.:* Ac, Sa.

This quarterly trade journal is specifically focused on the testing of aerospace systems and components. The publisher also produces other aerospace specialty niche publications such as *Aircraft Interiors International, Air Traffic Technology International,* and *Business Jet Interiors International.* This journal provides a wealth of information for those professionals within any of the areas associated with aerospace testing, evaluation, and inspection. The journal contains most of the elements of a typical trade publication—that is, news, feature articles, industry interviews, technical profiles of new equipment and technologies, and information on services available for the aerospace testing industry. The journal is also organized into sections similar to those of other trade journals, with regular columns presenting news, new-product and service information, and current information on the people and companies in the industry, along with announcements and newsworthy events. All areas of aviation and aerospace manufacturing are covered, including civil and military aerospace, airborne defense systems, launch vehicles, satellites, and space systems. Since the journal is published quarterly, it does not focus as much on breaking news and day-to-day activities as do other trade journals. However, the journal makes up for it by providing much greater depth and analysis of issues and trends within this section of the aerospace industry. Given the importance that safety plays in the industry, this is an important publication to address not only basic safety issues but performance issues, reliability issues, and quality issues that are critical to the aerospace community.

118. *Aerotech News and Review.* 1997. w. Ed(s): Stuart Ibberson. Aerotech News and Review, 456 East Ave, K-4, Ste 8, Lancaster, CA 93535; http://www.aerotechnews.com. Adv. *Aud.:* Ga.

This web site is primarily a weekly news bulletin for the aerospace and defense industries. The news is divided into sections, including main news (top stories), business news, defense news, space news, technology news, and international news. In addition, there are sections on mergers and acquisitions, financial news, people, and places, as well as an area titled "Commentary." These are editorials, speeches, or other commentary related to the aerospace industry from politicians, the military, NASA, or others in the industry. Some of the supplemental information available includes notices of upcoming air shows, events, a listing of other relevant aviation web sites organized by category, and a job fair section. The strength of the site is its in-depth coverage of the business aspects of the aviation and defense industries. URL: www.aerotechnews.com.

119. *Air & Space Law.* Formerly (until 1992): *Air Law.* [ISSN: 0927-3379] 1974. bi-m. EUR 439 print & online eds. Ed(s): Berend J H Crans. Kluwer Law International, PO Box 316, Alphen aan den Rijn, 2400 AH, Netherlands; sales@kluwerlaw.com; http://www.kluwerlaw.com. Illus., index. Refereed. Vol. ends: No. 6. Online: EBSCO Publishing, EBSCO Host; Gale; OCLC Online Computer Library Center, Inc.; OhioLINK; SwetsWise Online Content. Reprint: PSC. *Indexed:* CLI, IAA, ILP, LRI, PAIS. *Bk. rev.:* 1-5, 100-300 words. *Aud.:* Ac, Sa.

This journal provides current topical articles and research-level scholarly publications that primarily cover the civil, commercial, administrative, and penal aspects of air and space law from an international perspective. It also covers related societal, technical, and business topics, such as civil and military-aviation issues and policies, space transportation, trends in air transportation, regulatory and territorial issues, accident investigations and airworthiness, market access, environmental issues, and regulation and deregulation matters. Journal sections include "Case Law and Comment"; "Case Law Digest"; "Book Reviews"; and "EC Aviation Scene," which includes news from the International Aviation Organization and other international organizations. There is a wealth of information for policy makers and scientists. An additional feature is the annual bibliography of air law. Appropriate for specialized collections in law, aeronautics, and space sciences.

120. *Air & Space - Smithsonian.* Formerly (until 1986): *Air & Space.* [ISSN: 0886-2257] 1986. bi-m. USD 24 domestic; USD 30 foreign. Ed(s): George C Larson. Smithsonian Institution, Air & Space Magazine, Victor Bldg., 7100 MRC 951, P O Box 37012, Washington, DC 20013-7012. Illus., adv. Circ: 222305 Paid. Vol. ends: No. 6. *Indexed:* ASIP, AmH&L, BRI, C&ISA, CBRI, CerAb, HRIS, HistAb, IAA, MASUSE. *Bk. rev.:* 4-5, 800-1,000 words. *Aud.:* Ems, Hs, Ga, Ac.

This magazine is the best overall journal for general-aviation and space enthusiasts, as every area of aerospace and aviation is covered in a comprehensive and entertaining fashion, with outstanding photographs and illustrations. It provides current topical information, historical information, future trends, and scientific advancements in all areas of aviation, including military, general, and commercial, as well as space flight and exploration. It profiles people—both aviation pioneers and present-day decision-makers and innovators—as well as technological and scientific advancements. The articles provide a great deal of scientific and technical information in an informative, educational, and entertaining format. The range of topics is so broad that it is almost a disservice to mention only a few of them. This magazine is the closest thing to actually visiting the Air and Space Museum in Washington, D.C., and marveling at the history of aviation while imagining its future possibilities. Two interesting, informative departments are "Sightings" (which provides photographs of aircraft) and "Reviews and Previews" (which includes reviews of books, videos, CD-ROMs, and software). This is one of those rare magazines that should be mandatory for any type of library.

Air International. See Military section.

121. *Air Letter On-Line.* d. GBP 935 domestic; GBP 935 in Europe; USD 1980 United States. The Air Letter, 50-52 Upper Village Rd, Sunninghill, SL5 7AQ, United Kingdom; info@airletter.com; http://www.airletter.com. *Aud.:* Sa.

This web site advertises itself as a daily newsletter that reports on international news, business, politics, technology, and economics in the aerospace industry for those working in the industry. The site provides daily updates, Monday through Friday, on the industry from a worldwide perspective. Sections include "Headlines," "Air Transport," "Military," and "Industry." It includes a search engine, and also archives previous editions and the latest week's articles. The newsletter also contains a searchable calendar of aerospace events and a searchable index of more than 600 web sites, with hyperlinks to these sites. It is available by subscription only, by airmail, fax, and the Internet. URL: www.airletter.com.

122. *Air Power History: the journal of air and space history.* Former titles (until 1989): *Aerospace Historian; Airpower History.* [ISSN: 1044-016X] 1954. q. USD 45 (Individuals, USD 35; Students, USD 25). Ed(s): Jacob Neufeld. Air Force Historical Foundation, 1535 Command Drive, Ste A122, Andrews AFB, MD 20762-7002; bausumh@vmi.edu. Illus., adv. Refereed. Circ: 7000 Paid. Vol. ends: Dec. Microform: PQC. Online: EBSCO Publishing, EBSCO Host; Florida Center for Library

Automation; Gale; Northern Light Technology, Inc.; OCLC Online Computer Library Center, Inc.; ProQuest K-12 Learning Solutions; ProQuest LLC (Ann Arbor). *Indexed:* AUNI, AmH&L, BAS, BRI, CBRI, HistAb. *Bk. rev.:* 5-10, 500-750 words. *Aud.:* Ac, Sa.

This periodical is the premier scholarly journal for aerospace, aviation, and space science history. The journal chronicles historic events in all fields of aviation, including general aviation, space missions, and primarily military aviation. All time periods are covered, from the earliest use of aviation to current topics such as the Stealth bomber. Articles are good reading and solid history, with extensive bibliographies, and are written by historians, military personnel, museum curators, and others who possess both a strong academic foundation in history and a background in aviation. Numerous photographs and illustrations bring the text alive, but most of them are in black-and-white due to the time periods covered by most articles. The magazine also includes Air Force Historical Foundation symposium notices, book reviews, letters, news, notices, calendar, and reunions. This journal is highly recommended for aviation buffs, military history enthusiasts, and a general readership. It would be appropriate for all types of libraries based on its content, but its limited focus will not appeal to some general libraries.

123. *Air Transport World.* [ISSN: 0002-2543] 1964. m. USD 70 domestic (Free to qualified personnel). Ed(s): Perry Flint, Perry Flint. A T W Media Group, 8380 Colesville Rd, Ste 700, Silver Spring, MD 20910. Illus., index, adv. Circ: 1611 Paid. Vol. ends: No. 12. Microform: PQC. Online: The Dialog Corporation; EBSCO Publishing, EBSCO Host; Factiva, Inc.; Florida Center for Library Automation; Gale; Northern Light Technology, Inc.; OCLC Online Computer Library Center, Inc.; ProQuest K-12 Learning Solutions; ProQuest LLC (Ann Arbor); H.W. Wilson. *Indexed:* ABIn, ABS&EES, BPI, C&ISA, CerAb, EnvAb, HRIS, IAA, PAIS. *Aud.:* Sa.

This magazine of world airline management covers all aspects of commercial aviation and the surrounding industries, primarily airport management and related issues. It is a business-oriented journal that covers an important segment of the aeronautics field. The industry aspects of commercial aviation are a major topic, with several informative segments that include data and statistics on commuter traffic, airport usage, fuel prices, and foreign exchange rates. Broad article categories include technology, airways, airlines, safety, marketing, maintenance, cargo, and passenger service. Articles on the people involved with this side of the aviation spectrum are informative and enlightening. A recent addition is the "Trends" section on the first page, where industry snapshots are presented simply in graphical format and impart important industry data quickly. Another section is "Facts and Figures." Periodically, the journal includes directory information on specific topics that provides practical, factual information for industry insiders. The journal recently started to publish supplements that provide valuable information to those within the industry on recent trends such as security. Although the journal is primarily a trade publication for the commercial aviation segment of the industry, it provides valuable information on all aspects of aviation.

124. *Aircraft Engineering and Aerospace Technology: an international journal.* Formerly (until 1986): *Aircraft Engineering.* [ISSN: 1748-8842] 1929. 6x/yr. EUR 4009 combined subscription in Europe print & online eds.; USD 4319 combined subscription in North America print & online eds.; AUD 4899 combined subscription in Australasia print & online eds. Ed(s): Terry Savage. Emerald Group Publishing Limited, Howard House, Wagon Ln, Bingley, BD16 1WA, United Kingdom; information@ emeraldinsight.com; http://www.emeraldinsight.com. Illus., index, adv. Refereed. Vol. ends: No. 6. Online: Pub.; EBSCO Publishing, EBSCO Host; Gale; IngentaConnect; OCLC Online Computer Library Center, Inc.; OhioLINK; ProQuest K-12 Learning Solutions; ProQuest LLC (Ann Arbor); SwetsWise Online Content. Reprint: PSC. *Indexed:* ABIn, BrTechI, C&ISA, CerAb, ChemAb, EngInd, ExcerpMed, H&SSA, IAA, SCI. *Bk. rev.:* 1-3, 100-250 words. *Aud.:* Ac, Sa.

Although this is primarily a trade publication for the European aerospace industry, it contains a unique blend of scholarly articles on practical topics and features on all aspects of aircraft and aerospace technology. The trade journal portion of this title is divided into various departments: "News & Views," "Diary," "New Materials and Equipment," "Aerospace World," "Book Reviews," etc. These sections provide information on the business side of the industry, including news of recent and current activities, blurbs, industry highlights, profiles of equipment and tools, items on people in the industry, and a calendar of events. The main section contains six to eight research-level papers. The journal's strength is in getting leading practitioners in the field to contribute articles of interest to both researchers and fellow practitioners. The research articles are categorized as to their content via such categories as research paper, technical paper, general review, case study, conceptual paper, and viewpoint. The majority are either research or technical papers. This journal is appropriate for both academic and public libraries.

125. *American Helicopter Society. Journal.* [ISSN: 0002-8711] 1956. q. USD 95 domestic; USD 115 foreign; USD 20 per issue domestic. Ed(s): Gopal Gaonkar. American Helicopter Society, Inc., 217 N Washington St, Alexandria, VA 22314; http://www.vtol.org. Illus. Sample. Circ: 3000 Paid. Vol. ends: No. 4. *Indexed:* ApMecR, C&ISA, CerAb, EngInd, IAA, SCI. *Aud.:* Ac.

Original technical papers that deal with all aspects of the design, theory, and practice of vertical flight make up this journal, which is published by the American Helicopter Society. The papers cover three main areas: research and engineering, design and manufacturing, and operations. They are designed to foster the exchange of significant new ideas, information, and research about helicopters and V/STOL aircraft. The emphasis is on dynamics, structures, aerodynamics (both basic and applied), handling qualities, and acoustics. Additional areas include vehicle and component design, manufacture, and testing; operational aspects including support, noise and vibration, control and control failure, safety and reliability, materials, and design criteria; and historical information. In addition to full articles, the "Technical Notes" section provides a forum for brief, timely updates on current research topics. This journal focuses on the more technical aspects of vertical flight, with the general-interest and membership information included in the organization's companion publication *Vertiflite* (also in this section). Valuable to any academic collection that supports aeronautics and engineering.

126. *Aviation, Space, and Environmental Medicine.* Former titles (until 1975): *Aerospace Medicine;* (until 1959): *Journal of Aviation Medicine.* [ISSN: 0095-6562] 1930. m. USD 205 (Individuals, USD 185). Ed(s): Sarah A Nunneley, Pamela Day. Aerospace Medical Association, 320 S Henry St, Alexandria, VA 22314-3579; pday@asma.org; http://www.asma.org. Illus., index, adv. Refereed. Circ: 4000 Paid. Vol. ends: No. 12. Microform: PQC. Online: EBSCO Publishing, EBSCO Host; Gale; IngentaConnect. *Indexed:* AUNI, BiolAb, C&ISA, CABA, CINAHL, CerAb, ChemAb, ErgAb, ExcerpMed, H&SSA, HortAb, IAA, PEI, PsycInfo, RRTA, SCI, SSCI. *Bk. rev.:* 1-2, 500 words. *Aud.:* Ac, Sa.

This scholarly journal is concerned with the medical aspects of humans in spaceflight, aviation, and other environmentally and physically hostile environments. It is produced by the Aerospace Medical Association and contains original articles, clinical investigations, and applied medical studies related to humans as a result of aerospace travel, flight, and the factors that impact on humans in these extreme environments. Additional features include technical notes, news items, and other information of interest to members. The journal occasionally publishes review articles and papers drawn from major conferences in these areas. Most articles deal with the effects of physical exertions on human bodies during flight and their reaction to the environmental changes during spaceflight. Occasional special issues or supplements are published that cover specific topics such as advances in clinical space medicine, performance enhancement techniques, etc. The journal provides free electronic access to articles over one year old back to 2003. The wide variety of articles and research topics, combined with information on conferences and symposia, makes this a valuable information source for both medical specialists and engineers concerned with aircraft, space vehicles, or human factors.

127. *Aviation Week & Space Technology.* Former titles (until 1960): *Aviation Week, Including Space Technology;* (until 1958): *Aviation Week;* Which was formed by the merger of (1943-1947): *Aviation News;* (1922-1947): *Aviation.* [ISSN: 0005-2175] 1916. w. USD 103 domestic; USD 109 in Canada & Mexico; USD 160 in Europe. Ed(s): Anthony Velocci, Jr., James Asher. Aviation Week Group, 2 Penn Plaza, 25th Fl, New York, NY 10121-2298; AWNord@cdsfulfillment.com; http://www.aviationweek.com. Illus., adv. Circ: 95672 Paid. Vol. ends:

No. 26. Microform: PQC. Online: EBSCO Publishing, EBSCO Host; LexisNexis; OCLC Online Computer Library Center, Inc.; ProQuest K-12 Learning Solutions; ProQuest LLC (Ann Arbor). *Indexed:* ABIn, ABS&EES, AS&TI, ApMecR, BPI, BiolDig, BrTechI, C&ISA, CerAb, ChemAb, EngInd, EnvAb, ExcerpMed, HRIS, IAA, LRI, MASUSE, PRA, RGPR. *Aud.:* Ga, Ac.

This is the premier trade magazine covering aviation, aerospace, and aeronautics. All segments of the aerospace industry are featured and detailed, along with many short but insightful articles. The regular sections include "World News & Analysis" and "News Breaks," which contain news items of note and other industry happenings; "Air Transport," which covers commercial and general aviation; and "Business Aviation," which profiles commercial- and business-focused information. The magazine then segments the rest of its articles into topical sections such as "Space Technology," "Aerospace Business," "Aeronautical Engineering," "Avionics," and "Defense." Also provided is valuable, up-to-date information on the respective subject area. Special reports on important topics or issues, such as terrorism, are included when appropriate. In addition, the magazine contains industry outlooks and profiles, features on people within the industry, a calendar of events, and news and information from government and other regulatory agencies. The special issue "Aerospace Source Book," usually published the second week of the year, provides outlook/specification tables for all areas of the aerospace industry. Major sections include a world military aircraft inventory, prime contractor and major manufacturer profiles, major airline profiles, leading regional airline profiles, and leading all-cargo airlines. Other special issues are produced for the major air shows, Farnborough and Paris, each year. The combination of trade publication and general-interest articles makes this a valuable resource for all types of libraries, from high school to academic.

Aviation Week's Business & Commercial Aviation. See Transportation section.

128. *AVWeb.* 1995. w. Ed(s): Glenn Pew. AVWeb, 800 Connecticut Ave, Norwalk, CT 06854. *Aud.:* Ga.

This premier aeronautics web site offers a broad view of current aviation. The articles, usually by professionals (including the editor), highlight what is going on in every area of interest to general aviation pilots and enthusiasts from legislation to technology. The site provides valuable articles and columns as opposed to other aviation and aeronautics sites that are primarily news-reporting services. Also valuable are the numerous links to related web sites and to experts and others interested in various aspects of aviation. The site generally covers general-aviation topics as opposed to the commercial aviation industry, space industry, or the defense industry. The general aviation columns include articles on such topics as aeromedical, airmanship, aviation law, avionics, careers, insurance, maintenance, new and used aircraft, and safety and training. News is divided up into sections such as top news, more news, columns, features, and bizav news. The podcast and video section provides podcasts and other multimedia. The other tabs, community, resources, and services provide much of the information you would typically find in print aviation magazines such as classifieds, reader mail, calendars of events, photographs, and new product information. A good deal of the cost of this seems to be borne by advertisements for products and by classified ads. A clean, well-organized, authoritative site for aviation-related news and information. URL: www.avweb.com.

129. *Ballooning.* [ISSN: 0194-6854] 1977. bi-m. USD 45; USD 50 in Canada & Mexico; USD 85 elsewhere. Ballooning Magazine, PO Box 400, Indianola, IA 50125; ballon-fed@bfa.ycg.org; http://www.bfa.net/publications.htm. Illus., adv. Sample. Circ: 5100. Vol. ends: No. 6. *Indexed:* SD. *Bk. rev.:* 1-4, 300-500 words. *Aud.:* Ga, Sa.

This is the best of the very limited number of general-interest magazines for the ballooning enthusiast. Major articles cover a wide range of topics, including safety issues, equipment, profiles of members, descriptions of balloon trips, noteworthy events in ballooning, and other general-interest items. The magazine includes excellent color and black-and-white photographs, results from rallies, information on new products, reviews of products and literature, and a directory of the federation's officers. Although the journal is produced by the Ballooning Federation of America, it covers the sport from an international perspective. The federation's web site has recently been enhanced with content from the journal and podcasts of news and events. It provides quality content enhanced by a good layout and organization scheme, and is suitable for all ages.

130. *British Interplanetary Society Journal.* [ISSN: 0007-084X] 1934. bi-m. GBP 290; USD 536. Ed(s): A R Martin. British Interplanetary Society, 27-29 S Lambeth Rd, London, SW8 1SZ, United Kingdom; mail@bis-spaceflight.com; http://bis-spaceflight.com. Illus., index. Refereed. Circ: 1500. Vol. ends: No. 12. Microform: PQC. Reprint: PSC. *Indexed:* ExcerpMed, IAA, SCI. *Aud.:* Ac, Sa.

This monthly publication of the British Interplanetary Society contains original papers that cover all aspects of space exploration, with each issue dedicated to one or two specific subjects, topics, or themes. Emphasis is solely on space and space-based applications. Sample topics include the history of rocket development, hibernation in relation to space travel, solar sail technology, interstellar travel, orbital mechanics, the Earth–space environment, space missions and astrodynamics, new space concepts, and related areas of aeronautics, astronautics, and space sciences. Samples of current issue themes or conference topics that are included in the publication are: space tourism, space elevator, small remoter-sensing technology, and Cold War military space history. Most issues contain four to eight articles per issue. Additionally, the journal contains brief information on the society's activities and announce-ments. It incorporates photographs and illustrations to supplement the text. Appropriate for major research libraries.

131. *Canadian Aeronautics and Space Journal.* [ISSN: 0008-2821] 1955. q. CND 90 domestic; USD 80 foreign. Ed(s): Stewart W Baillie. Canadian Aeronautics and Space Institute, 1750 Courtwood Crescent, Suite 105, Ottawa, ON K2C 2B5, Canada; casi@casi.ca; http://www.casi.ca. Illus., index. Circ: 2000. Vol. ends: No. 4. Microform: MML; PQC. *Indexed:* ApMecR, C&ISA, CABA, CBCARef, CerAb, EngInd, ForAb, H&SSA, IAA, IBR. *Bk. rev.:* 2-3, 300-400 words. *Aud.:* Ac.

This official publication of the Canadian Aeronautics and Space Institute (CASI) disseminates technical and research information in the areas of aeronautical and aerospace sciences to the international community. The journal includes articles on recent research and technical discoveries in all areas of aeronautics, including aerospace materials, spacecraft thermal design, aerodynamics, aircraft design and analysis, aircraft component design, and wind tunnel investigations. Original articles cover such topics as flight testing, astronautics, structures and materials, simulation and training, aerospace operations, and aircraft design and development. The journal recently began to publish occasional special issues in which all articles are focused on a single topic, such as material problems that face aging aircraft. The journal also periodically includes book reviews. This research-oriented magazine belongs in academic, technical, and major public libraries.

132. *FAA Aviation News.* Former titles: *FAA General Aviation News; FAA Aviation News.* [ISSN: 1057-9648] 1962. 6x/yr. USD 21 domestic; USD 29.40 foreign. Ed(s): Dean Chamberlain. U.S. Federal Aviation Administration, 800 Independence Ave SW, Washington, DC 20591; http://www.faa.gov. Illus. Circ: 50000 Paid and controlled. Microform: MIM; PQC. *Indexed:* HRIS, IUSGP. *Aud.:* Ga.

This is the electronic version of *FAA Aviation News,* and it includes all the information found in the print magazine. The journal promotes aviation safety from cover to cover, with safety-related news from the Federal Aviation Administration (FAA) and much information on safety issues faced by pilots. Articles cover regulations, people within the aviation safety arena, FAA facilities, weather, night flying, and any aspect of aircraft, pilots, or equipment relating to safety. Major departments include "FlightFORUM," a feedback section with responses from the FAA; "AvNEWS," which provides aviation facts and figures, news, and safety tips; and "Medical Stuff," the latest information on aviation medicine. Other departments include editorials, runway safety issues, tales from the field, and maintenance alerts. The archive of back issues, at present, extends back to 2005. Regrettably, the archival issues, back to 2001, are no longer available due to changes in the FAA web sites. URL: www.faa.gov/news/aviation_news.

133. *Flight International.* [ISSN: 0015-3710] 1909. w. GBP 97 domestic; EUR 143 in Europe; USD 162 United States. Ed(s): Murdo Morrison. Reed Business Information Ltd., Quadrant House, The Quadrant, Brighton Rd, Sutton, SM2 5AS, United Kingdom; http://www.reedbusiness.co.uk/. Illus., index, adv. Circ: 50500. Vol. ends: Dec. Microform: PQC. Online: DataStar; EBSCO Publishing, EBSCO Host; Florida Center for Library Automation; Gale; LexisNexis; OCLC Online Computer Library Center, Inc.; ProQuest LLC (Ann Arbor); H.W. Wilson. *Indexed:* ABIn, AS&TI, AUNI, BrTechI, C&ISA, CerAb, ChemAb, HRIS, IAA. *Aud.:* Ga, Ac.

This trade publication provides a global perspective on the aerospace industry and covers every aspect—airframe systems and components, support equipment, air transport, general aviation, defense, spaceflight, and regulatory agencies and authorities worldwide. The journal is comprised of three main sections. The news section contains subsections such as "News Analysis," "Technology," "Business Aviation," "Defence," "General Aviation," and "Spaceflight." The articles section usually contains two or three feature articles on topics of interest such as industry forecasts for the upcoming year; market trends; military aircraft; new aircraft; and special or arising markets for implementation of new safety ideas or methods. The "Regulars" section contains letters, jobs, classifieds, commentary, aerospace awards, newsmakers, and similar topical sections. Occasionally, there are directories of world aircraft, maintenance facilities, turbine engine manufacturers, and world airlines, as well as useful ranking information such as the top 100 aerospace companies, airline safety statistics, and space launch calendars. There are also occasional supplements or special issues on hot topics or industry trends. The magazine is similar to *Aviation Week & Space Technology* (above in this section), with a greater international flavor. Recommended for both academic libraries and larger public libraries.

134. *Flying.* [ISSN: 0015-4806] 1927. m. USD 14 domestic; USD 22.97 foreign; USD 4.50 newsstand/cover per issue. Ed(s): Elizabeth Murray, J Mac McClellan. Hachette Filipacchi Media U.S., Inc., 1633 Broadway, New York, NY 10019; http://www.hfmus.com. Illus., index, adv. Circ: 305763 Paid. Vol. ends: No. 12. Microform: MIM; PQC. Online: The Dialog Corporation; OCLC Online Computer Library Center, Inc.; H.W. Wilson. *Indexed:* BRI, CBRI, ConsI, HRIS, IAA, RGPR. *Aud.:* Hs, Ga, Ac, Sa.

Flying has the broadest scope of the numerous magazines geared toward the private pilot and flying enthusiast. Most of the feature articles concern the various aspects of flying such as safety issues, historical aspects, airports, rules and regulations, aircraft, and aircraft instruments. Every aspect of general aviation is covered; however, the emphasis is on flying and contemporary aircraft. The feature articles are written primarily to enthuse the reader and instill or convey the love of flying. Other articles are designed to impart practical advice and cover items of interest to the flying public. The magazine includes the sections "Flying News and Notes," which is news for pilots and new product information; "Training," which provides information ranging from FAA examinations to job and student statistics; "Flying Opinion," which informs and aids readers with information imparted in a personal manner through anecdotes and stories; "Flying Safely"; and letters to the editor, a calendar of flying rallies and events, and other aviation news. The major articles fall into the "Pilot Reports" section. There are occasional special issues, such as one devoted to learning how to fly. Overall, the magazine is informative and interesting, with excellent photography. It deserves a place in most libraries, from high school to academic.

135. *FlyPast: the UK's top selling aviation monthly.* [ISSN: 0262-6950] 1980. m. GBP 35 domestic; EUR 63.98 in Europe; USD 68.97 United States. Ed(s): Ken Ellis. Key Publishing Ltd., PO Box 300, Stamford, PE9 1NA, United Kingdom; ann.saundry@keypublishing.com; http://www.keypublishing.com. Illus., index, adv. Circ: 44081. Vol. ends: No. 12. *Bk. rev.:* Number and length vary. *Aud.:* Ga, Sa.

This publication is advertised as Britain's top-selling aviation monthly and is essentially a general-interest, history-focused aviation journal. Although the primary focus is historical, with a particular emphasis on military history, there is an additional focus on restoration and preservation of aircraft. Unlike other historical aviation magazines, this journal is geared toward a general readership. The magazine is heavily illustrated with numerous photographs (in both color and black-and-white), which is expected given the historical focus of the journal. The articles are informative and interesting and cover many of the same topics as the general-interest aviation magazines, including events and news. The product review sections include memorabilia, books, videos, and art prints. Numerous advertisements for memorabilia and related items are found throughout. This magazine should appeal to military-history or general-history enthusiasts, and to those interested in military aviation, aviation history, and aircraft restoration and preservation.

136. *I C A O Journal.* Former titles (until 1990): *I C A O Bulletin;* (until 1952): *I C A O Monthly Bulletin;* (until 1948): *P I C A O Monthly Bulletin.* [ISSN: 1014-8876] 1946. m. 10/yr. USD 25 domestic; GBP 25 foreign; USD 3 newsstand/cover per issue. Ed(s): Eric MacBurnie. International Civil Aviation Organization, External Relations and Public Information Office, 999 University St, Montreal, PQ H3C 5H7, Canada; icaohq@icao.int; http://www.icao.int. Illus., adv. Vol. ends: Dec. Microform: CIS. *Indexed:* C&ISA, CerAb, EnvInd, H&SSA, HRIS, IAA, M&GPA, RiskAb. *Aud.:* Ac, Sa.

The primary mission of this journal is the dissemination of the accounts, activities, and progress of the International Civil Aviation Organization (ICAO) to the ICAO membership and the global aerospace community, primarily the international civil aviation community. It is published in English, French, and Spanish. Although the stated mission of the magazine is to relate the organization's activities to its members, it provides articles that would be of interest to anyone involved with civil aviation and air transport. Articles include such topics as airports and airport management; regulations; air traffic control and air traffic management; environmental issues; airport and aircraft safety issues and methodologies; new guidance, control, and monitoring equipment; aerodynamics and vehicle control; and related civil aviation issues. Beginning in 2007, the journal started an exciting new section, entitled "Performance Indicators," in which interesting and useful statistics related to civil aviation are provided. The "ICAO Update" section contains news of interest to members. The journal also includes an annual review on the state of civil aviation. This journal provides valuable insight into and information on the civil and commercial aviation industry, and is appropriate for research libraries.

137. *IEEE Aerospace and Electronic Systems Magazine.* Formerly (until 1986): *IEEE Aerospace and Electronic Systems Society Newsletter.* [ISSN: 0885-8985] 1961. m. USD 415. Ed(s): Harry Oman. IEEE, 445 Hoes Ln, Piscataway, NJ 08854-1331; subscription-service@ieee.org; http://www.ieee.org. Illus., index. Refereed. Vol. ends: No. 12. Online: Pub.; EBSCO Publishing, EBSCO Host. *Indexed:* C&ISA, CerAb, EngInd, IAA, SCI. *Bk. rev.:* 1, 500-1,500 words. *Aud.:* Ac, Sa.

This publication is the main avenue for the dissemination of information to the members of the Aerospace and Electronics Systems Society of the Institute of Electrical and Electronics Engineers (IEEE). The society consists of those members of the IEEE who are interested in the fields of navigation, avionics, spacecraft, aerospace power, radar, sonar, telemetry, defense, transportation, automated testing, and command and control. The three to six short articles in each issue cover those areas in which the fields of computer and electrical engineering overlap with the areas of aeronautical and astronautical engineering. These articles deal primarily with the organization, design, development, integration, and operation of complex systems for air, space, and ground environments in the above areas. The journal's objective is to provide timely, useful, and readable systems information for engineers. The journal also includes information of interest to the membership such as conference reports, columns (editorials), notices of upcoming meetings and conferences, book reviews, and other membership-related information. Primarily of importance to academic libraries and technical libraries.

138. *IEEE Transactions on Aerospace and Electronic Systems.* Formed by the 1965 merger of (1963-1965): *IEEE Transactions on Aerospace;* (1963-1965): *IEEE Transactions on Military Electronics;* (1963-1965): *IEEE Transactions on Space Electronics and Telemetry;* (1963-1965): *IEEE Transactions on Aerospace and Navigational Electronics.* [ISSN: 0018-9251] 1965. q. USD 1045. Ed(s): Dr. W Dale Blair. IEEE, 445 Hoes Ln, Piscataway, NJ 08854-1331; subscription-service@ieee.org;

http://www.ieee.org. Illus., index. Refereed. Vol. ends: No. 4. Online: Pub.; EBSCO Publishing, EBSCO Host. *Indexed:* AS&TI, ApMecR, C&ISA, CerAb, ChemAb, EngInd, ExcerpMed, IAA, MathR, SCI. *Aud.:* Ac.

This journal is primarily geared toward those individuals working or studying in the areas of aerospace electronic systems, which includes command, control, and communications systems; avionics; systems engineering; aircraft control; aircraft navigation; missile guidance; multisensor systems; electronic warfare systems; energy conversion systems; intelligent systems; radar systems; robotics systems; space systems; and support systems. The 20–30 articles per issue range from specific papers on individual systems to those that cover general research, design, and testing of systems and subsystems. The journal prides itself on being one of the top five most often cited scholarly journals in the areas of aerospace engineering, which demonstrates the importance computers, communications, and electronics play in the field. Included with the full papers is a correspondence section for brief discussions of new research. This research publication contains little or no membership-related information, just the reviewed technical articles in the same areas of coverage as the *IEEE Aerospace and Electronic Systems Magazine* (above in this section). Recommended for all types of academic and technical libraries.

139. *Institution of Mechanical Engineers. Proceedings. Part G: Journal of Aerospace Engineering.* Supersedes in part (in 1989): *Institution of Mechanical Engineers. Proceedings. Part D: Transport Engineering;* Which superseded in part (1847-1982): *Institution of Mechanical Engineers. Proceedings.* [ISSN: 0954-4100] 1989. 8x/yr. USD 2095 in the Americas; GBP 1123 elsewhere. Ed(s): Rodrigo Martinez-Val. Professional Engineering Publishing Ltd., 1 Birdcage Walk, London, SW1H 9JJ , United Kingdom; journals@pepublishing.com; http://www.pepublishing.com. Illus. Sample. Refereed. Circ: 800. Vol. ends: No. 6. Online: EBSCO Publishing, EBSCO Host; Gale; IngentaConnect; OCLC Online Computer Library Center, Inc.; ProQuest LLC (Ann Arbor); SwetsWise Online Content. *Indexed:* AS&TI, ApMecR, BrTechI, C&ISA, CerAb, EngInd, H&SSA, IAA, SCI. *Bk. rev.:* 1-2, 500-750 words. *Aud.:* Ac.

The *Journal of Aerospace Engineering,* produced by the United Kingdom's mechanical engineering society, publishes papers in the field of aeronautical engineering that are of interest to mechanical engineers. The publication provides both practical and theoretical articles that are designed to further the advancement of the field of aeronautical engineering, especially the areas of civil and military aircraft, along with space systems and their components. Topics cover research, design, development, testing, operation, and service and repair of vehicles and their components. Fields covered include aerodynamics, fluid mechanics, propulsion and fuel systems, avionics and flight control systems, structural and mechanical design, materials science, testing and performance, and airports and spaceports. The journal publishes 5–15 articles per issue that cover international aerospace engineering topics that are closely aligned with those generally associated with mechanical engineering. Occasionally, a volume may be devoted to a special topic or theme, such as computational fluid dynamics. These are often taken from conferences or symposia on the topic. Appropriate for academic and technical libraries.

140. *Interavia: business & technology.* Formerly (until 1994): *Interavia, Aerospace World;* Which was formed by the merger of (1946-1992): *Interavia;* (1987-1992): *Aerospace World.* [ISSN: 1423-3215] 1992. m. USD 150 in Europe; USD 175 rest of world. Ed(s): Oliver Sutton. Aerospace Media Publishing SA, 33 Route de l'Aeroport, PO Box 56, Geneva, 1215, Switzerland; interavia@swissonline.ch; http://www.aerospacemedia.com. Illus., index, adv. Sample. Circ: 21000 Paid. Vol. ends: Dec. Microform: PQC. Online: The Dialog Corporation; EBSCO Publishing, EBSCO Host; Florida Center for Library Automation; Gale; OCLC Online Computer Library Center, Inc.; ProQuest LLC (Ann Arbor); H.W. Wilson. *Indexed:* ABIn, AUNI, BPI, C&ISA, CerAb, HRIS, IAA. *Aud.:* Ga, Ac.

This trade journal covers the aerospace industry from a global perspective. It covers all aspects of the aerospace industry in such sections as "Finance, Markets, and Industry," "Air Transport and General Aviation," "Defence," and "Space." The journal also occasionally produces one or two "Special Reports," which cover important topics concerning the aerospace industry, such as analysis of regional markets, airline pilot training, or airline maintenance strategies. Each section details relevant news items and profiles people within the industry. Important dates are found in a calendar section. The journal covers the entire range of issues that face the commercial aviation and aerospace industries, including regulations, safety issues, defense issues, civil aviation issues and news, and new products and developments. The strength of this publication is its depth of analysis and thoroughness in reporting the news and events that affect the aerospace industry. Although the coverage is global in scope and not as timely as that of other trade publications that cover the aerospace industry, this journal is appropriate for most academic and major public libraries.

141. *International Journal of Aeroacoustics.* [ISSN: 1475-472X] 2002. q. GBP 209; GBP 233 combined subscription print & online eds. Ed(s): Dr. Ganesh Raman. Multi-Science Publishing Co. Ltd., 5 Wates Way, Brentwood, CM15 9TB, United Kingdom; sciencem@hotmail.com; http://www.multi-science.co.uk. Refereed. *Indexed:* C&ISA, CerAb, IAA. *Aud.:* Ac, Sa.

The subject of aeroacoustics has always been important in the overall aerospace and aeronautical engineering field. This importance has increased as of late due to advances in air, space, and high-speed ground transportation and their effects on people and the environment. The issue of noise and its impact on people, structures (both vehicle and ground-based support structures), vehicle components, and the overall environment comprise much of the focus of this research journal. The journal focuses on all areas of aeroacoustics (basic and applied), publishing both research articles and occasionally survey or review articles on the topics associated with fundamental and applied aeroacoustics. A sampling of the topics covered includes aeroacoustics, fluid flow, noise, computational fluid mechanics, aerodynamics, turbulence, and shock. The articles associate these topics with all aspects of civil and military aircraft, automobile, and high-speed train aeroacoustics and related phenomena. The journal makes exceptional use of illustrations (color and black-and-white) to enhance the technical information. Some issues are composed of selected papers from workshops and conferences related to aeroacoustics. Recommended for academic and research libraries.

142. *Jonathan's Space Report.* 1989. w. Free. Ed(s): Jonathan McDowell. Harvard-Smithsonian Center for Astrophysics, 60 Garden St, MS 6, Cambridge, MA 02138; http://hea-www.harvard.edu/QEDT/jcm/space/jsr/jsr.html. *Aud.:* Ac.

This electronic newsletter is designed to provide information on all space launches, including manned missions and automated satellites. The newsletter is fully archived and available back to its original issue in January 1989. It can also be received via e-mail. A recent issue contains information about the space shuttle and the Mir space station, several tables about recent launches, and current shuttle processing status. A recent addition is a link to Jonathan's Space Home Page, which provides links to image files, historical articles, and other information and sites related to space exploration. Not very fancy, but if you are looking for space vehicle launch information and need it from a reliable source, this is the place. URL: www.planet4589.org/space/jsr/jsr.html.

143. *Journal of Aerospace Computing, Information, and Communication.* [ISSN: 1940-3151] 2004. irreg. Members, USD 40; Non-members, USD 380. Ed(s): Michael Hinchey, Meredith Cawley. American Institute of Aeronautics and Astronautics, Inc., 1801 Alexander Bell Dr, Ste 500, Reston, VA 20191; custserv@aiaa.org; http://www.aiaa.org. *Indexed:* C&ISA, CerAb, EngInd, IAA. *Bk. rev.:* Number and length vary. *Aud.:* Ac, Sa.

This new electronic-only journal from AIAA is primarily geared toward those individuals who work or study in the areas of aerospace computing, information, and communication, which includes computational techniques, information technology, knowledge management, real-time systems, embedded systems, software engineering and reliability, systems engineering and integration, communication systems, signal processing, data fusion, high-performance computing systems and software, expert systems, robotics, intelligent and autonomous systems, and human–computer interfaces. The articles are designed to highlight current research from the three main areas of coverage—computing, information, and communications—and this research concerns the design of aerospace components, systems, and vehicles. The

journal aims to take full advantage of its online-only status by strongly encouraging the inclusion of multimedia, allowing for the use of over a dozen different file formats to not only convey information but to aid in the transfer of knowledge. Along with the full papers, the journal includes letters for the brief discussion of new research, as well as book reviews and invited papers. The journal occasionally publishes an issue devoted to a specific topic or theme, such as the recent issue on self-stabilization of systems. Given the increasingly greater role that electronics, communication, control, and information systems have in the design and operation of aerospace systems and vehicles, this journal should play an important role in transfer of information and technology from aerospace engineering to other engineering disciplines. Recommended for academic and technical libraries. URL: www.aiaa.org/jacic/index.cfm.

144. *Journal of Aerospace Engineering.* [ISSN: 0893-1321] 1988. q. USD 333. Ed(s): Firdaus P Udwadia. American Society of Civil Engineers, 1801 Alexander Bell Dr, Reston, VA 20191-4400; http://www.asce.org. Illus., index. Refereed. Circ: 1300. Vol. ends: No. 4. Microform: PQC. Online: American Institute of Physics, Scitation; EBSCO Publishing, EBSCO Host; SwetsWise Online Content. *Indexed:* AS&TI, ApMecR, C&ISA, CJA, CerAb, EngInd, EnvAb, H&SSA, HRIS, IAA, M&GPA, SCI. *Aud.:* Ac.

The main emphasis of this journal, produced by the American Society of Civil Engineers, is on the practical application and development of civil engineering concepts, designs, and methodologies for space and the transfer of these technologies to other civil engineering applications. This international publication provides information related to the civil engineering aspects of aerospace engineering, primarily structural aspects of space engineering, applied mechanics, aeronautics, and astronautics. Sample topics include MEMS, composite materials, lunar soil mechanics, environmental factors in inhabited space facilities, aerodynamics of structures, extraterrestrial construction, aerospace materials, advanced energy systems, remote sensing, and robotics as related to aeronautics and aerospace engineering. Both full papers (five to ten per issue) and technical notes are included, with the emphasis being on fully refereed papers that are designed to share information (developed through space applications and concepts) between civil engineers and related engineering disciplines. A valuable addition to academic and technical libraries.

145. *Journal of Aircraft: devoted to aeronautical science and technology.* [ISSN: 0021-8669] 1963. bi-m. Non-members, USD 760. American Institute of Aeronautics and Astronautics, Inc., 1801 Alexander Bell Dr, Ste 500, Reston, VA 20191; custserv@aiaa.org; http://www.aiaa.org. Illus., index. Refereed. Circ: 30000 Paid. Vol. ends: No. 6. Microform: PQC. *Indexed:* AS&TI, ApMecR, C&ISA, CerAb, EngInd, H&SSA, IAA, M&GPA, SCI. *Aud.:* Ac.

This journal, published by AIAA, is devoted primarily to the dissemination of original papers for the advancement of airborne flight. The focus is on the promotion of applied science and technology related to airborne flight, including articles on significant advances in the operation of aircraft, advances in aircraft themselves, and the application of aircraft technologies to other disciplines. All types of vehicles related to airborne flight are covered, including commercial and military aircraft, STOL and V/STOL aircraft, and subsonic, supersonic, transonic, and hypersonic aircraft. Areas covered include aircraft and aircraft systems design and operation, flight mechanics, flight and ground testing, computational fluid dynamics, aerodynamics, and structural dynamics. Related areas—such as application of computer technology to aircraft and aircraft systems, artificial intelligence, production methods, engineering economic analysis, and logistics support—are also covered. Accompanying the full-length papers (30–40 per issue) are "Technical Comments" and "Engineering Notes," the latter designed to further communication within the field. The journal occasionally produces special issues on a single topic. This highly technical journal is recommended for academic, technical, and research libraries.

146. *Journal of Guidance, Control, and Dynamics: devoted to the technology of dynamics and control.* Formerly: *Journal of Guidance and Control.* [ISSN: 0731-5090] 1978. bi-m. USD 775. Ed(s): Amanda Maguire. American Institute of Aeronautics and Astronautics, Inc., 1801

Alexander Bell Dr, Ste 500, Reston, VA 20191; custserv@aiaa.org; http://www.aiaa.org. Illus., index. Sample. Refereed. Circ: 2200 Paid. Vol. ends: No. 6. *Indexed:* AS&TI, ApMecR, C&ISA, CerAb, EngInd, H&SSA, IAA, SCI. *Bk. rev.:* 1, 750-1,000 words. *Aud.:* Ac.

This journal's primary focus is the advancement of guidance, control, and dynamics through the publishing of original peer-reviewed papers that highlight the development, design, and application of new technology in aeronautics, astronautics, celestial mechanics, and related fields. Topics of articles include astrodynamics, control systems design, control theory, dynamics, stability, guidance, control, navigation, systems optimization, avionics, and information processing. There are also articles that highlight advances in the guidance and control of new aircraft, spacecraft, and related systems. In addition to the 20–25 full-length papers, the journal includes engineering notes, survey papers, technical comments, and book reviews. It occasionally publishes special issues on a single topic. Although the journal is published by AIAA, the various topics covered by the fields of guidance, control, and dynamics are important to other engineering fields than aeronautics, making this journal a valuable addition to research collections in engineering.

147. *Journal of Propulsion and Power: devoted to aerospace propulsion and power.* [ISSN: 0748-4658] 1985. bi-m. Non-members, USD 840. Ed(s): Amanda Maguire. American Institute of Aeronautics and Astronautics, Inc., 1801 Alexander Bell Dr, Ste 500, Reston, VA 20191; custserv@aiaa.org; http://www.aiaa.org. Illus., index. Refereed. Circ: 1600 Paid. Vol. ends: No. 6. Online: EBSCO Publishing, EBSCO Host; Gale. *Indexed:* ApMecR, C&ISA, CerAb, ChemAb, EngInd, H&SSA, IAA, SCI. *Aud.:* Ac.

This journal focuses on the segment of aerospace that deals specifically with an engineer's interest in working on aerospace propulsion and power systems. It is the primary journal that covers combustion, power generation and use, and overall propulsion systems and/or individual propulsion system components as they relate to the fields of aeronautics, astronautics, and space sciences. Topics include air-breathing propulsion systems (from turbine engines to scramjets), electric propulsion systems, solid and liquid rocket systems, hybrid propulsion systems, and other advanced propulsion systems and components. Original papers are presented to highlight recent advances in the areas of research, development, design, and applications. Subjects include fuel and propellants; power generation and transmission in aerospace systems; combustion of fuels; fluid mechanics; and solid mechanics. Accompanying the full-length technical papers (20–30 per issue) are "Technical Notes" and "Technical Comments." These sections are designed for rapid dissemination of research results. The journal recently started publishing occasional special issues devoted to a single topic or subject, such as turbine science and technology, detonations in propulsion, or aircraft particulate emissions. An excellent addition to any research-oriented library.

148. *Journal of Spacecraft and Rockets: devoted to astronautical science and technology.* [ISSN: 0022-4650] 1964. bi-m. USD 720. Ed(s): Amanda Maguire, E Vincent Zoby. American Institute of Aeronautics and Astronautics, Inc., 1801 Alexander Bell Dr, Ste 500, Reston, VA 20191; custserv@aiaa.org; http://www.aiaa.org. Illus., index. Refereed. Circ: 2200 Paid. Vol. ends: No. 6. Microform: PQC. Online: EBSCO Publishing, EBSCO Host; Gale; IngentaConnect. *Indexed:* AS&TI, ApMecR, C&ISA, CerAb, ChemAb, EngInd, H&SSA, IAA, SCI. *Aud.:* Ac.

This journal covers recent research, design, and current developments in the broad area of spacecraft and rockets and their accompanying systems, subsystems, and components. Articles focus on space sciences, including spacecraft, space vehicles, tactical and strategic missile systems and subsystems, applications, missions, and environmental interactions. Information is given on spacecraft and missile systems configurations, launch and reentry vehicles, transatmospheric vehicles, system and subsystem design, application and testing, mission design and analysis, applied and computational fluid dynamics, applied aerothermodynamics, and structures and materials as related to vehicle design and analysis. In addition, the journal covers such topics as space processing and manufacturing, operations in space, interactions between space vehicles, design of sensors, ground support systems design, and the transfer of space technologies to other fields. All areas of aeronautics are covered, including propulsion, guidance and control, aircraft technology (conventional and STOL/VTOL), structural systems of spacecraft and missiles,

missile design, and performance of space vehicles. Occasionally, issues include engineering notes, technical notes, and special issues on specific topics. Recommended for all types of research libraries or collections.

149. *Journal of the Astronautical Sciences.* [ISSN: 0021-9142] 1954. q. USD 170 domestic; USD 190 foreign. Ed(s): Kathleen Howell. American Astronautical Society (Springfield), 6352 Rolling Mill Place, Ste 102, Springfield, VA 22152-2354; aas@astronautical.org; http://www.astronautical.org. Illus., index. Refereed. Circ: 1800. Vol. ends: No. 4. *Indexed:* AS&TI, C&ISA, CCMJ, CerAb, EngInd, H&SSA, IAA, M&GPA, MSN, MathR, SCI. *Aud.:* Ac.

This journal provides topical information, research, and reviews on state-of-the-art technologies in all areas of astronautics, including astrodynamics, celestial mechanics, flight mechanics, navigation and guidance, and space sciences. Topics of articles include such areas as altitude dynamics, orbit determination, altitude stability, orbital mechanics/dynamics, propulsion systems (both conventional and electric), trajectory optimization, space mission analysis, numerical methods, maneuvering of flight vehicles, dynamics and control, and new astronautical systems and their applications. The journal occasionally includes technical notes to speed up communication of new technological and scientific advances. Likewise, the journal occasionally consists of papers taken from important conferences or symposia sponsored by the American Astronautical Society. Most appropriate for academic and technical libraries.

150. *Journal of Thermophysics and Heat Transfer: devoted to thermophysics and heat transfer.* [ISSN: 0887-8722] 1987. q. USD 610. Ed(s): Luke McCabe. American Institute of Aeronautics and Astronautics, Inc., 1801 Alexander Bell Dr, Ste 500, Reston, VA 20191; custserv@aiaa.org; http://www.aiaa.org. Illus., index, adv. Sample. Refereed. Circ: 1000. Vol. ends: No. 4. Online: EBSCO Publishing, EBSCO Host; Gale. *Indexed:* ApMecR, C&ISA, CerAb, ChemAb, EngInd, IAA, SCI. *Aud.:* Ac.

This AIAA publication provides a forum for technical papers in areas utilized by designers of aerospace systems and components, including all methods of heat transfer—radiative, conductive, convective, and combinations of these methods. In addition, the effects of these heat transfer methods are also included. Topics of interest in the corresponding area of thermophysics include mechanisms and properties involved with thermal energy transfer and storage in liquids, gases, solids, and systems that compose one or more of the physical states. Articles cover such topics as aerothermodynamics, conduction, radiative heat transfer, thermophysical properties, vibrational kinetics, thermal control systems, convective heat transfer, and other areas of thermophysics, thermodynamics, and heat transfer. These issues are of primary importance to many aerospace-related areas of study, from the obvious propulsion and space vehicle areas to computational fluid dynamics, which could be affected by extreme temperatures and energy transfer. The journal also includes survey papers and technical notes. The use of color illustrations and photographs greatly aid in enhancing the technical information provided by this publication. Recommended for major research collections, whether academic or technical.

151. *Kitplanes: the independent voice for homebuilt aviation.* [ISSN: 0891-1851] 1984. m. USD 29.95 domestic; USD 41.95 foreign. Ed(s): Marc Cook. Aviation Publishing Group, 531 Encinitas Blvd 105, Encinitas, CA 92024. Illus., adv. Circ: 70000 Paid. Vol. ends: No. 12. *Indexed:* IHTDI. *Aud.:* Ga, Sa.

This magazine covers the specialized areas of hobbyists and enthusiasts who wish to design, build, and fly their own aircraft. Articles cover all aspects of flying, training, safety, and maintenance as well as theory and other technical issues related to aircraft design, construction, and flying. However, most articles center on construction and flying of personal aircraft. Along with feature articles, the magazine includes departments such as "Builder Spotlight," "Shop Talk," "Designers Notebook," "Exploring," and "Kit Bits." These sections provide information on new products and tools, news, a calendar of events, editorial and readers' comments, classifieds, and information on competitions and events. There are many color and black-and-white photographs and illustrations, plus information on products and services, in-flight reports, and information on new aircraft. Emphasis is placed on providing useful how-to tips and other practical information. Geared to the flying public, hobbyists, and enthusiasts.

152. *Landings.com.* 1994. d. Landings.com, 6280 S. Valley View Blvd., Ste. 314, Las Vegas, NV 89118; landings-ops@landings.com; http://www.landings.com/. Adv. *Aud.:* Ga, Sa.

Landings.com is one site that everyone associated with aviation should visit as a central meeting place as well as a jump-off to other specialized sites. The site is primarily devoted to general aviation, but it also covers military aspects. The news is timely and in focus, and the feature articles are brief but comparable to those of commercial aviation publications. The site is divided into various sections such as "airNews," "Highlight," "Flying," "airForums," "Connections," and "airStories." There are numerous other resources such as flight planning guides, links to weather sources, pilot and aircraft supplies, regulations, and reports. There are also links to information on airports and airlines as well as on specific types of general aviation and military aircraft. The strength of the site is its ability to locate all type of aviation-related information along with current news and feature articles.

153. *Plane and Pilot.* Incorporates (in 1987): *Homebuilt Aircraft; Airways.* [ISSN: 0032-0617] 1965. m. USD 11.97 domestic; USD 21.97 foreign; USD 4.99 newsstand/cover. Ed(s): Lyn Freeman, Steve Werner. Werner Publishing Corporation, 12121 Wilshire Blvd., Ste 1220, Los Angeles, CA 90025; editors@planeandpilotmag.com. Illus., adv. Circ: 134000. Vol. ends: No. 12. Microform: PQC. Online: ProQuest LLC (Ann Arbor). *Indexed:* IHTDI. *Aud.:* Hs, Ga, Sa.

This "magazine for active piston-engine pilots" is an official membership publication of the Pilots International Association and is devoted primarily to the interests of recreational flyers or pilots. It includes articles on flying, aircraft, new products and aircraft, pilot aids, safety information, flying events, information on rules and regulations, and other general-interest items for pilots and aviation buffs. There are classifieds, editorials, and letters to the editor. Regular columns and departments include a sections on aircraft, safety, and training such as "Pilot Reports," which highlights and evaluates new aircraft; "NTSB Debriefer," which covers safety issues; and "In Training," which provides practical advice and tips. One of the distinctive features of this journal that makes it more attractive for public libraries is a special issue devoted to the various careers available in the aviation industry, with a review of the present industry situation and a discussion of future trends, needs, and opportunities. There are usually features on topics of interest, from purchasing aircraft to tips on better piloting, as well as new planes and equipment.

154. *Progress in Aerospace Sciences.* Formerly: *Progress in Aeronautical Sciences.* [ISSN: 0376-0421] 1961. 8x/yr. EUR 1707. Ed(s): A B Haines. Pergamon, The Boulevard, Langford Ln, East Park, Kidlington, OX5 1GB, United Kingdom. Illus., index. Sample. Refereed. Vol. ends: No. 12. Microform: PQC. Online: EBSCO Publishing, EBSCO Host; Gale; IngentaConnect; OhioLINK; ScienceDirect; SwetsWise Online Content. *Indexed:* ApMecR, C&ISA, CerAb, EngInd, IAA, SCI. *Aud.:* Ac.

This review journal is designed to bring together current advances in the field of aerospace sciences for those involved with research and development and for other researchers who have a need for technical information. The review articles, which contain extensive bibliographies, provide a concise and orderly summary of topics with enough detail that even nonspecialists can gain insight into the most recent and advanced research available. All aspects of aeronautical engineering are covered, including aerodynamics and fluid dynamics; aircraft design and performance; avionics; vehicle dynamics; guidance and control; fracture mechanics; combustion and propulsion systems; composite materials; wind tunnel design and testing; wind shear; and flight safety. Each issue usually contains two or three in-depth articles that are usually broken down into the typical sections of review articles: extensive background into the subject, a state-of-the-art review, and recommendations for further research. Color illustrations add to the clarity and understanding of the research presented. Highly recommended for research collections, whether in the research sector or in academe.

155. *Science at N A S A.* d. Free. N A S A Headquarters, Code FEO-2, 300 E. St. SW., Washington, DC 20546; phillips@spacesciences.com. *Aud.:* Hs, Ga, Ac.

Science@NASA is a source for informative scientific and research-level articles based on the activities of the National Aeronautics and Space Administration (NASA). It serves as a gathering place for all NASA scientific and technical information and news releases on space events and phenomena. The main page lists a number of headline stories and recent stories. The stories are presented with a graphic (photograph or illustration), the article title, a brief description, and links to either read or listen to the story (both in English and Spanish). Podcasts are now available. Topics covered include space weather, planetary science, microgravity, science highlights, and technology transfer. There is a listing of further articles by subject—space sciences, astronomy, living in space, earth science, biological and physical sciences, and beyond rocketry. All of these sections provide a half-dozen or so stories that highlight NASA activities and discoveries. The site provides a wealth of searchable information that covers all areas of science and presents it in a readable, concise format, highlighted with illustrations and color photographs. This is a good starting point for scientific information from NASA for all educational levels. For teachers and students, the NASA Education site (education.nasa.gov) provides information for "Kids" (www.nasa.gov/forkids), "Students" (by grade range), and "Educators." For an alternative look at NASA's activities, check out the NASA Watch site (www.nasawatch.com). Suitable for almost any age and recommended for anyone interested in the space program. URL: http://science.nasa.gov.

156. *Soaring.* [ISSN: 0037-7503] 1937. m. Free to membership. Soaring Society of America, Inc, PO Box 2100, Hobbs, NM 88241-2100; info@ssa.org; http://www.ssa.org. Illus., adv. Circ: 14881. Vol. ends: No. 12. *Indexed:* BAS, SD. *Bk. rev.:* Number and length vary. *Aud.:* Ga, Sa.

This journal is analogous to *Ballooning* (see above in this section), except its primary emphasis is on propulsionless-aircraft flight or glided flight. The publication is the main communication vehicle for the Soaring Society of America, and it includes articles, photographs, news, and other items of interest for enthusiasts of gliding or soaring. The journal's feature articles include contest reports, information on safety issues, and product reviews of aircraft and systems. Topics of the general-interest articles include historical perspectives on gliding, pioneers, and aerial photography. There are additional regular features on soaring and gliding events, conferences and competitions, general news of the society, book reviews, tips on safety, reader mail, and classified ads. A good general-interest magazine for hobbyists and other interested readers, and appropriate for all types of libraries.

157. *Space Daily: your portal to space.* d. Mon. - Fri. Ed(s): Simon Mansfield. Space Daily, PO Box A447, Sydney South, NSW 2000, Australia; simon@spacer.com; http://www.spacedaily.com. *Aud.:* Ga, Ac, Sa.

Space Daily: Your Portal to Space is another good web site that deals with space-related news. The site is interconnected with a number of scientifically related sites such as *Terra Daily* (which deals with earth science), *Energy Daily, GPS Daily, Space War, Mars Daily,* and *Space Travel.* Most of *Space Daily's* articles are from a business or scientific or technical standpoint and cover space exploration, space science, and the overlap between these and the subjects of the companion sites. The news is on target and authoritative. The articles are provided with categories such as outer planets, solar science, tech page, space art, telescopes, stellar chemistry, and rocket science—all of which provide an idea of the scope of coverage of the site. The top stories from the companion web sites are also displayed on this site. Overall, a good place to keep up with developments, news, and technologies relevant to space science and exploration. URL: www.spacedaily.com.

158. *Space Policy.* [ISSN: 0265-9646] 1985. 4x/yr. EUR 1387. Ed(s): Frances Brown. Pergamon, The Boulevard, Langford Ln, East Park, Kidlington, OX5 1GB, United Kingdom. Illus., index, adv. Sample. Refereed. Vol. ends: No. 4. Microform: PQC. Online: EBSCO Publishing, EBSCO Host; Gale; IngentaConnect; OhioLINK; ScienceDirect; SwetsWise Online Content. *Indexed:* C&ISA, CerAb, CommAb, EAA, IAA, PAIS, PSA, SSCI. *Bk. rev.:* 4-5, 500-1,000 words. *Aud.:* Ac, Sa.

This journal is one of the few interdisciplinary journals in the field of aeronautics and space science and is designed to provide a forum for the discussion of how space policies will shape the future of space exploration, utilization, and related issues. The issues discussed include the impact of scientific discoveries obtained through space applications and research, space activities and discoveries that impact industry and society, and the resulting economic, political, social, legal, and moral issues raised. The exchange of ideas and opinions is as much a part of this journal as the exchange of scientific and technical information on space activities and developments. Many of the five to ten articles per issue center on the topics associated with the use of space and the overall implications of this use. Topics range from space law and space commercialization to the history and current status of space programs, to space exploration and lunar development, to satellite systems and global positioning systems. The journal also provides editorials and comments, along with information on new international developments in space, book reviews, and news of upcoming conferences and meetings. This unique approach of blending political, philosophical, business, and societal issues with scientific and engineering issues makes this a worthwhile addition for academic libraries.

159. *Space Science Reviews.* [ISSN: 0038-6308] 1962. 24x/yr. EUR 3008 print & online eds. Ed(s): Hans Bloemen. Springer Netherlands, Van Godewijckstraat 30, Dordrecht, 3311 GX, Netherlands; http://www.springeronline.com. Illus., adv. Sample. Refereed. Vol. ends: No. 4. Microform: PMC; PQC. Online: EBSCO Publishing, EBSCO Host; Gale; IngentaConnect; OCLC Online Computer Library Center, Inc.; OhioLINK; Springer LINK; SwetsWise Online Content. Reprint: PSC. *Indexed:* C&ISA, CerAb, ChemAb, EngInd, IAA, IBR, IBZ, M&GPA, SCI. *Bk. rev.:* 10-12, 100-300 words. *Aud.:* Ac.

This international review journal is comprised of papers on the various topics related directly to space sciences. The magazine defines space science as scientific research carried out by means of rockets, rocket-propelled vehicles, stratospheric balloons, and observatories on the Earth and the Moon. The journal is primarily oriented toward the advancement of pure science, with limited coverage of the technical aspects of space science. The papers, some of which are very lengthy and comprise an entire volume, provide a synthesis of the current research and developments in the numerous branches of space science. The journal covers all areas of space science, including, but not limited to, the Big Bang theory, supernovae, cosmic rays, solar variability and climate, infrared space observation, airborne observatories, solar-wind phenomena, and characteristics of interstellar matter. In addition, the journal includes book reviews along with a listing of books received. Appropriate for academic libraries.

160. *SPACE.com.* Incorporates (1989-200?): *SpaceViews.* 1999. d. SPACE.com, 120 W 45th St, New York, NY 10036; info@space.com; http://www.space.com. Adv. *Aud.:* Hs, Ga, Sa.

This is one of the premier web sites for space information. Space.com has incorporated several features that make it attractive to those interested in spaceflight and space science, including in-depth articles and special reports, along with basic headline and business news. The site's look and feel are so much fun that it is almost hard to take the information provided seriously, but the content is up-to-date and from credible sources. The information is also available by RSS feed or podcast, and the site is enhanced with videos and other multimedia. The main site is divided into major sections, which include "News," "SpaceFlight," "Science," "Technology," "SpaceViews," and "SETI" (Search for Extraterrestrial Intelligence Institute). Each section contains an area for top stories as well as related information including links, special reports, and recent news. The exception is the "SpaceViews" section, which provides access to stunning illustrations and art related to space. The site has links to *Ad Astra Online* and *Space News,* a weekly newspaper. These sources provide much of the current news content. However, in-depth information from *Space News* requires a subscription to the print publication. The heavily illustrated content and broad focus make this site worthwhile for anyone interested in space. Space enthusiasts will find plenty of interesting and informative content.

Spaceflight. See Astronomy section.

161. *Sport Aviation.* [ISSN: 0038-7835] 1953. m. Membership, USD 40. Ed(s): Scott M Spangler, Julie Russo. Experimental Aircraft Association, Inc., 3000 Poberezny Rd, Oshgosh, WI 54901; http://www.eaa.org/. Illus., adv. Circ: 170000 Paid. Vol. ends: Dec. *Indexed:* IHTDI. *Aud.:* Ga, Sa.

Sport Aviation, billed as the magazine of recreational aviation, is a cross between magazines geared for pilots and aviation enthusiasts and those aimed at specific areas of aviation, such as ultralights and ballooning. The magazine promotes general aviation and covers all types of aircraft, from military and private aircraft, helicopters, and rotocraft to purely sport aircraft. The primary emphasis is on the sport of aviation and sport planes. There are numerous feature articles and other information on all types of aircraft. Highlights include the technical aspects of customizing aircraft, and building and restoring aircraft, as well as articles on classic aircraft, whether military or commercial aircraft, or seaplanes. In addition, the magazine contains the major sections "Commentary," "News and Info.," "EAAers in Action," "Nuts & Bolts," and "Stick & Rudder." These sections provide the bulk of the information of interest to the members of the journal's parent organization, the Experimental Aircraft Association (EAA). "Commentary" consists of columns and editorials. "EAA in Action" provides information and news of interest to members of EAA, such as a calendar of events, association news, a memorial section, and member services. The other sections provide practical information for those restoring aircraft, along with training- and safety-related information. There are periodic special sections included that are primarily focused on EAA's educational, preservation, and legacy-building activities and youth initiatives. A worthwhile addition to general-interest collections and public libraries.

162. *Ultralight Flying!: international magazine of ultralight aviation.* Formerly: *Glider Rider.* [ISSN: 0883-7937] 1976. m. USD 36.95 domestic; USD 41.95 in Canada & Mexico; USD 44.95 elsewhere. Ed(s): Scott Wilcox, Sharon Wilcox. Glider Rider, Inc., Dept N, PO Box 6009, Chattanooga, TN 37401; http://www.ultralightflying.com. Illus., adv. Circ: 15500 Paid. Vol. ends: Dec. *Aud.:* Ga, Sa.

This magazine in newspaper format covers the ultralight and light sport segment of the aviation community and contains feature articles, columns, and departments. The feature articles cover the various issues related to owning and flying ultralight and light sport aircraft. There are articles on aircraft, flying, safety, and training, as well as reports from rallies and contests. There are also numerous advertisements and photographs. The standard departments and columns contain news, reports from events, information on competitions, new-product announcements and reviews, safety items, and a calendar of events. The journal provides an abundance of information on products, equipment, and safety. The articles are well written, and the magazine provides much practical information for ultralight enthusiasts. The January issue contains a "Buyer's Guide" section. Appropriate for general libraries.

163. *Vertiflite.* [ISSN: 0042-4455] 1955. q. Members, USD 90. Ed(s): Mike Hirschberg, L. Kim Smith. American Helicopter Society, Inc., 217 N Washington St, Alexandria, VA 22314; http://www.vtol.org. Illus., index, adv. Circ: 6000 Paid and controlled. Vol. ends: No. 5. *Indexed:* C&ISA, CerAb, EngInd, HRIS, IAA. *Bk. rev.:* 1-2, 700-1,000 words. *Aud.:* Ga, Ac.

The basic membership publication of the American Helicopter Society (AHS), *Vertiflite* aims at providing information on the advances being made in the areas of vertical flight and promoting the wider use of helicopters and vertical-flight aircraft. Research articles on rotocraft technology can be found in the *Journal of the American Helicopter Society* (above in this section). *Vertiflite* provides feature articles on helicopters and rotocraft technology and other issues relevant to the membership, such as new aircraft, new technologies, safety issues, and military technology. Along with these feature articles are book reviews, a calendar of events, departments on conference activities and industry briefs, a member update section, and related news items. Articles' range includes the value of helicopters as demonstrated by cruise ship rescues; reviews of civilian helicopters; addressing community concerns about vertical flight; and the problems of the helicopter industry's dependency on defense spending. The *AHS Annual International Directory,* a special issue, contains a wealth of practical information on members, sponsors, awards, the annual index, and surveys of engines and aircraft. Recommended for academic and technical libraries.

∎ AFRICA

Margaret Power, Coordinator of Reference Services, John T. Richardson Library, DePaul University Libraries, 2350 N. Kenmore, Chicago IL 60614; 773-325-7835; mpower@depaul.edu

Introduction

Because the study of Africa is generally multidisciplinary, many of the titles selected for inclusion in this section cannot be classified by a specific discipline, topic, or geography; therefore, the presentation here is in a straightforward alphabetical list. This section aims to provide representation in subjects and in geography at the regional level. Coverage includes subject areas such as literature, philosophy, ecology, basic science, and art as well as issue areas such as development, gender studies, and democratization. Increasingly, scholarship in African Studies also includes the African diaspora, and many titles will be of interest to those building a collection on African Americans. A selection of consumer magazines and newsmagazines is also included. Most publications are in English. However, some titles in French are important for covering former francophone African regions as well as providing significant contributions to African Studies. Daily newspapers are not included, as it is not possible to include a truly representative sampling of the most prominent newspapers. However, there is a major news service, *allAfrica* (allAfrica.com), whose stories come from newspapers, news agencies, and publications from all over the African continent. The site provides links to major African newspapers' web sites as well. Another Oslo-based news agency, Afrol News (www.afrol.com), provides up-to-date news stories and links to newspapers and other media. Except for comprehensive collections, access to electronic news and newspapers is probably a more realistic strategy than subscription to printed newspapers.

The selections overall represent a mix of titles published in the United States, Britain, and Europe, as well as a healthy representation of magazines and journals from Africa. The publishing industry in Africa is not strong outside of South Africa and perhaps Nigeria, having been greatly affected by the economic crises of the past decades and weak technological infrastructure. Industrialized countries have dominated the production of knowledge about Africa. Despite delays in production or receipt of materials published on the continent, the selected titles reflect the importance of including the African point of view. Publications are included that communicate African heritage and culture, provide commentary on current events, and present African scholarship. Scholarly journals in Africa have been particularly affected by socioeconomic issues as well as the "brain drain" to the North.

A significant development is the increasing presence on the Internet of African Studies journals and African publications. Electronic access to contents information and full text has mushroomed along with the appearance of many new all-electronic journals. Many journals from the United States and Europe are now available in part or in full on the web or through aggregators. Even when full text is available only to subscribers, many offer tables of contents and current-awareness services. Two projects of note bring greater visibility for African-published scholarship, including many journals too specialized for this section. *African Journals Online* (www.ajol.info), a project of International Network for the Availability of Scientific Publications, brings African scholarship to a world audience, offering current contents and abstracts on the web of 230 journals from 21 countries, along with a document delivery service. The *African E-Journals Project* (http://africa.msu.edu/AEJP), sponsored by Michigan State University, the Association of African Universities, and others, seeks to increase access to scholarly journals of Africa by providing access through Project Muse and by a digitization project that will offer free access through MSU to several more titles. To assess the totally expanded electronic presence, one can examine the web site of electronic journal links at Stanford University Library for the Electronic Technology Group, U.S. African Studies Association (www-sul.stanford.edu/depts/ssrg/africa/journal.html) or the journals list at Columbia University's African Studies pages (www.columbia.edu/cu/lweb/indiv/africa/ejournals.html) or the H-Africa list-serv (www.h-net.org/~africa). Heartening news for collections wishing to include print or online subscriptions to scholarly journals from the continent is the recent announcement by Routledge that it is strengthening its African Studies journal offerings with several new African titles.

Basic Periodicals

Hs: *Focus on Africa;* Ga: *Africa Research Bulletin. Economic, Financial and Technical Series; Africa Research Bulletin. Political, Social and Cultural Series, African Business, Journal of Modern African Studies, New African, Transition.* Ac: *Africa, Africa Confidential, Africa Today, African Affairs, African Studies Review, History in Africa, L'Intelligent, Presence Africaine, Research in African Literatures.*

Basic Abstracts and Indexes

African Studies, African Studies Abstracts, Current Bibliography on African Affairs, International African Bibliography, PAIS, Quarterly Index to Africana Periodical Literature.

164. *A S A News: a quarterly newsletter for African Studies Association members.* Former titles (until vol.13): *African Studies Newsletter; African Studies Association. Newsletter.* [ISSN: 0278-2219] 1968. 4x/yr. Ed(s): Carol L Martin. African Studies Association, Rutgers, The State University of New Jersey, 132 George St, New Brunswick, NJ 08901-1400; ckoch@emory.edu. Illus. Circ: 3600. Vol. ends: Oct/Dec (No. 4). *Aud.:* Ac, Sa.

Publications from the African Studies Association (ASA), now in its 50th year, are highly recommended for academic libraries and any libraries that support interest in African Studies. Members receive *ASA News* and two other publications, *African Studies Review* (in this section) and *African Issues* with their membership. *ASA News* is the association's communication organ for news and information for Africanists. The newsletter provides listings of grants and fellowships; news of awards, papers presented, and employment and research opportunities; ASA calls for papers; meeting schedules and minutes; other meeting calendars; letters; information on new members and donors; and a list of recent Africa-related dissertations. Issues viewable online at www.african-studies.org.

165. *Africa: journal of the International African Institute/revue de l'Institute Africain International.* [ISSN: 0001-9720] 1928. q. plus a. bibliography. GBP 247. Ed(s): Richard Fardon. Edinburgh University Press, 22 George Sq, Edinburgh, EH8 9LF, United Kingdom; http://www.eup.ed.ac.uk. Illus., index. Sample. Refereed. Circ: 1250. Vol. ends: No. 4. *Indexed:* AmH&L, AmHI, AnthLit, CABA, FR, ForAb, HistAb, IBR, IBSS, IBZ, IIBP, IPSA, IndIslam, MLA-IB, PAIS, RI-1, RILM, RRTA, S&F, SSCI, SWA, WAE&RSA. *Bk. rev.:* 10-15, 750-2,500 words. *Aud.:* Ac, Sa.

The International African Institute in London has played a seminal role in the development of African Studies. Its publication *Africa* is one of the oldest scholarly journals focusing on the continent, in publication for almost 80 years. It has an interdisciplinary approach, presenting topics in social sciences, history, the environment, and life sciences with strong emphasis on issues of development, links between local and national levels of society, and cultural studies. Each issue usually contains six major articles, which are well footnoted with extensive bibliographies. A recent issue has the theme of nature as local heritage in Africa. Articles are accompanied by abstracts in English and French. Book reviews and review essays are substantial. *Africa Bibliography* (see below in this section), a comprehensive, categorized, and indexed annual listing of published work in African Studies from the previous year, is included with the full subscription in every fourth issue, or it can be purchased separately. *Africa* is a basic African Studies periodical, highly recommended for all academic collections and large general collections.

166. *Africa Analysis: fortnightly bulletin on financial and political trends.* Incorporates: *Southern Africa Business Intelligence.* [ISSN: 0950-902X] 1986. fortn. GBP 210 to academics (Corporations, GBP 300). Ed(s): Ahmed Rajab. Africa Analysis Ltd., Diamond House, Ste 2F, 36-38 Hatton Garden, London, EC1N 8EB, United Kingdom; aa@africaanalysis.com; http://www.africaanalysis.com. Illus., adv. Sample. Circ: 1000. Online: Florida Center for Library Automation; ProQuest LLC (Ann Arbor). *Indexed:* ENW, IIBP. *Bk. rev.:* 3-4. *Aud.:* Ac, Sa.

Africa Analysis offers timely information on the African business and financial climate and political trends. It is published biweekly and subscribers may access the stories on the web site (www.africaanalysis.com) or by e-mail on the day of publication or by first-class or airmail post. Back issues are archived on the web site, available to subscribers via password. Billing itself as "information for decision makers," this journal offers analysis of current business conditions and also practical advice on doing business in various African countries. Regular features include diplomatic briefings, corporate updates, guest columns, African currency checklists, and market/industry sector reviews. Columns featuring "names in the news" with political and business gossip provide information similar to *Africa Confidential* (below). Now incorporated is *Gulf Analysis,* which reports on the dynamics of the Gulf States' economies and news of that region. Timely, informative, and expensive, this bulletin is recommended for business, economics, graduate schools of management, research, and corporate libraries. Other libraries may want to choose one or two other business and political news sources (see also *African Business* and *Africa Research Bulletin,* both below in this section).

167. *Africa Bibliography.* [ISSN: 0266-6731] 1985. a. GBP 80. Ed(s): T A Barringer. Edinburgh University Press, 22 George Sq, Edinburgh, EH8 9LF, United Kingdom; http://www.eup.ed.ac.uk. Illus. *Indexed:* FR, IBR, IBZ. *Aud.:* Ga, Ac, Sa.

Begun anew in 1984 in conjunction with the International African Institute's journal *Africa,* this annual review reports on African publications (books, periodical articles, pamphlets, book chapters) primarily in the social sciences, humanities, and arts, with selected coverage of the medical, biological, and physical sciences as they are relevant to readers from a social sciences/arts background. The entire African continent and its associated islands are included. It is arranged by region and country and preceded by a section for the continent as a whole. The sections are divided by subject classes with author and subject indexes. This recommended reference is an easy-to-use resource for locating current, popular, and scholarly African materials. It is useful both for those developing comprehensive collections and for libraries that can afford to select a few items for geographic coverage of current literature. Some libraries may opt to acquire the *Bibliography* with a subscription to *Africa* (see above in this section).

168. *Africa Confidential.* [ISSN: 0044-6483] 1960. fortn. 25/yr. GBP 710 combined subscription in the European Union print & online eds.; USD 1579 combined subscription elsewhere print & online eds. Ed(s): Clare Tauben, Patrick Smith. Asempa Ltd., 73 Farringdon Rd., London, ECIM 3JQ, United Kingdom. Illus., index. Sample. Circ: 3500. Vol. ends: Dec. Online: Blackwell Synergy; EBSCO Publishing, EBSCO Host; Gale; IngentaConnect; OCLC Online Computer Library Center, Inc.; OhioLINK; SwetsWise Online Content. *Indexed:* PAIS. *Aud.:* Ga, Ac, Sa.

A wealth of current information can be found in the eight pages of this widely read newsletter, and for over 45 years it has been a source of current political, military, and economic intelligence reporting and analysis. Biweekly issues provide "inside track" information on African leaders and analysis of general trends and specific events in Africa, written by a network of correspondents in every country. The articles have no bylines—the contributors write on the basis of anonymity. In 2006, *Africa Confidential* was purchased from Blackwell by the British company Asempa. Pricey, provocative, and current, this newsletter remains in heavy demand and is highly recommended for both general and academic collections.

169. *Africa Development.* [ISSN: 0850-3907] 1976. q. USD 32 (Individuals, USD 30). Ed(s): Felicia Oyekanmi. Council for the Development of Social Science Research in Africa, BP 3304, Dakar, Senegal; codesria@ sentoo.sn; http://www.codesria.org. Illus., adv. Refereed. Circ: 600. Online: African Journals Online. *Indexed:* AbAn, CABA, DSA, HortAb, IBR, IBSS, IBZ, PSA, RRTA, RiskAb, SociolAb, WAE&RSA. *Bk. rev.:* 2-5, 1,000-1,500 words. *Aud.:* Ac, Sa.

This quarterly bilingual journal (parallel title: *Afrique et Developpement*) is published by the Council for the Development of Social Science Research in Africa (CODESRIA). It supports CODESRIA's principal objectives of "exchange of ideas among African scholars from a variety of intellectual persuasions and various disciplines." African authors contribute articles on cultural, social, political, and economic issues of society in Africa. The focus

may be on an issue in a specific country, such as child labor in urban Nigeria, land tenure reform in Uganda, or on continent-wide issues. Many articles cut across disciplinary boundaries. Abstracts in French and English precede the articles, which may be in either language. The two-page book reviews are in French or English. *Africa Development* is the oldest regularly published social science journal in Africa. It sometimes lags in publication but is still highly recommended for academic and special audiences and institutions interested in including social science analysis from African scholars. Tables of contents and means of ordering articles are available through African Journals Online (www.ajol.info) and contents are also posted on the CODESRIA web site, along with abstracts from other organization journals, including *African Sociological Review* (see below) and *Afrika Zamani*.

170. *Africa Insight.* Formerly (until 1979): *South African Journal of African Affairs.* [ISSN: 0256-2804] 1971. q. ZAR 500 (Individuals, ZAR 250). Ed(s): Elizabeth Le Roux. Africa Institute of South Africa, PO Box 630, Pretoria, 0001, South Africa; ai@ai.org.za. Illus., index, adv. Sample. Refereed. Circ: 5000. Microform: PQC. Online: African Journals Online; H.W. Wilson. *Indexed:* AbAn, CABA, HortAb, IBR, IBSS, IBZ, IIBP, PAIS, PSA, RILM, RRTA, S&F, SociolAb, WAE&RSA. *Bk. rev.:* 3-5, 500-700 words. *Aud.:* Ga, Ac, Sa.

Africa Insight is a publication of the Africa Institute of South Africa, a think tank devoted to production of knowledge on Africa. The journal is a forum for diverse topics focusing on the process of change in Africa. Topics are wide ranging: political trends and events, democratization, economic issues, regional cooperation, international relations, conflict resolution, aspects of education and training, health, community development, food security, and institutional capacity building. While many articles focus on southern Africa, the whole continent is within this journal's scope. A recent issue contains essays on conflict management in Africa, privatization in Malawi, and malaria prevention in Zimbabwe. The articles are scholarly, well researched, and frequently illustrated. Of interest to educators, institutions, and decision makers in business and the public sector, but also to a wider audience interested in Africa, this publication is well recommended and suitable for academic and large public libraries as well as special audiences.

171. *Africa Quarterly: a journal of African affairs.* [ISSN: 0001-9828] 1961. q. USD 40. Ed(s): K Matthews. Indian Council for Cultural Relations, Azad Bhavan, Indraprastha Estate, New Delhi, 110 002, India; pdpub@iccrindia.org; http://www.iccrindia.org. Illus., index, adv. Circ: 1900. Vol. ends: Oct. Microform: PQC. *Indexed:* ABCPolSci, AmH&L, HistAb, IBR, IBSS, IBZ, IPSA, IndIslam, PAIS. *Bk. rev.:* Number and length vary. *Aud.:* Ac, Sa.

This publication of the Indian Council for Cultural Relations promotes understanding between India and Africa, with articles that examine important themes affecting both areas, e.g., justice and human rights, Asian–African relations, globalization, etc. Issues may have a country focus. Scholars from around the word contribute the six to eight well-researched and accessible articles in each issue. There are also three or four substantive book reviews. Africa-related activities in India and conference notes may also be included. Significant in the context of the growing importance of non-Western interregional cooperation, *Africa Quarterly* is a good addition to larger Africana collections.

172. *Africa Research Bulletin. Economic, Financial and Technical Series.* [ISSN: 0001-9852] 1964. m. GBP 741 print & online eds. Ed(s): Pita Adams. Blackwell Publishing Ltd., 9600 Garsington Rd, Oxford, OX4 2ZG, United Kingdom; customerservices@blackwellpublishing.com; http://www.blackwellpublishing.com. Illus., index, adv. Sample. Online: Blackwell Synergy; EBSCO Publishing, EBSCO Host; Gale; IngentaConnect; OCLC Online Computer Library Center, Inc.; OhioLINK; SwetsWise Online Content. *Indexed:* ABIn, ApEcolAb, RiskAb. *Aud.:* Ac, Sa.

In-depth coverage as well as comment and analysis drawn from Africa and around the world add value to this monthly economic news digest from *Africa Research Bulletin.* In both print and web formats, the *Bulletin* extracts text and summaries from media sources, including African newspapers, news agencies, radio broadcasts, and United Nations agency publications, as well as information from government gazettes, international organizations, and selected European newspapers and journals. After a lead article, six sections cover, for specific countries and entities, issues related to cooperation, trade, economic policies, infrastructure, commodities, industry, and economic aid. Charts, graphs, and maps accompany articles. The web format (www.blackwellpublishing.com/journals/ARBE) is available to subscribers. The publisher issues a companion series, *Africa Research Bulletin: political, social, and cultural series*. Both are highly recommended for specialized and large public and academic libraries for the extensive (but expensive) coverage.

173. *Africa Research Bulletin. Political, Social and Cultural Series.* [ISSN: 0001-9844] 1964. 12x/yr. GBP 741 print & online eds. Ed(s): Pita Adams. Blackwell Publishing Ltd., 9600 Garsington Rd, Oxford, OX4 2ZG, United Kingdom; customerservices@ blackwellpublishing.com; http://www.blackwellpublishing.com. Illus., index. Sample. Online: Blackwell Synergy; EBSCO Publishing, EBSCO Host; Gale; IngentaConnect; OCLC Online Computer Library Center, Inc.; OhioLINK; SwetsWise Online Content. *Indexed:* ApEcolAb. *Aud.:* Ga, Ac, Sa.

A companion to the *African Research Bulletin: Economic Series* (see above), this analysis service draws from hundreds of acknowledged sources including local press, web sites, and radio to provide news and commentary on politics and society. Sources from Africa are complemented by information from government gazettes, international agencies, and the European and American press. Coverage includes major conference reports; government changes, with lists of new officials; internal security; the military; international relations; and cultural and social information. A lead article (such as a recent one on elections in various countries) is followed by principal content sections that are geographically arranged by country with a geographic/subject index. Major political/military events often appear in chronological, tabular outlines; and charts, graphs, and maps illustrate the articles. The online format follows that of the print. In addition to providing a detailed index, the web allows full-text searching. Expensive, like the economic series, but essential for specialized and academic libraries, especially large research institutions.

174. *Africa Today.* [ISSN: 0001-9887] 1954. q. USD 110 (Individuals, USD 42.50). Ed(s): Gracia Clark, Ruth Stone. Indiana University Press, 601 N Morton St, Bloomington, IN 47404; journals@indiana.edu; http://iupjournals.org. Illus., index, adv. Sample. Refereed. Circ: 1300 Paid. Vol. ends: Fall. Microform: PQC. Online: Chadwyck-Healey Inc.; EBSCO Publishing, EBSCO Host; Florida Center for Library Automation; Gale; OCLC Online Computer Library Center, Inc.; OhioLINK; Project MUSE; ProQuest LLC (Ann Arbor); SwetsWise Online Content; H.W. Wilson. Reprint: PSC. *Indexed:* ABCPolSci, AbAn, AmH&L, ArtHuCI, BRI, CABA, CBRI, FPA, ForAb, HistAb, IBR, IBSS, IIBP, IPSA, IndIslam, L&LBA, PAIS, PRA, PSA, PollutAb, RILM, RRTA, RiskAb, S&F, SSCI, SociolAb, WAE&RSA. *Bk. rev.:* 5-15, 750 words. *Aud.:* Ga, Ac, Sa.

Articles in *Africa Today* examine a wide variety of current social, political, and economic issues. Originally the bulletin of the anti-apartheid American Committee on Africa, *Africa Today* is now an academic journal. With its move to Indiana University, its focus has broadened, making it more interdisciplinary, including occasional articles in the arts and humanities as well as reform-minded research in the social sciences. Many issues are on specific themes. A recent special issue features papers on "Creating the Kenya Post-Colony." The range of the journal can be seen in a recent issue that covers East African poetry, Ethiopian economy, and Zimbabwe's relations with China. Several well-written and incisive book reviews are included in each issue. A list of books received ends the issue. This is an affordable, well-recommended publication for both general audiences and academic collections. Available also through Project Muse (muse.jhu.edu/journals/at). Document delivery of articles and single issues can be had at the Indiana University Press site (iupjournals.org/africatoday).

175. *Africa Today: voice of the continent.* [ISSN: 1357-311X] 1995. m. USD 45; USD 94.99 combined subscription print & online eds. Ed(s): Kayode Soyinka. Africa Today, Suite 6, Third Floor, AMC House, 12 Cumberland Ave, London, NW10 7QL, United Kingdom; editor@africatoday-uk.com; http://africatoday.com. Adv. *Aud.:* Ga.

Not to be confused with the academic journal of the same title published by Indiana University, *Africa Today, Voice of the Continent* is a monthly consumer newsmagazine published, like many others, with a Nigerian editorial staff and an actual publication address in London. It aims to be a market leader in newsmagazine format for Pan-Africa news and current affairs, and its cover stories range from such topics as Nigeria's oil industry to the negotiations of Starbucks in Ethiopia. Features on business, sport, tourism, etc., complement regular coverage of developments in countries around the continent. Selected stories from current and back issues are featured on the web site (africatoday-.com). The editors pride themselves on the consistency of publication; it has not missed an issue in its 12 years of existence. Libraries with an African Studies or international focus may consider this title, as may public libraries that serve an African Diaspora community.

176. *Africa Update (New Britain).* [ISSN: 1526-7822] 1993. q. USD 25 (Individuals, USD 5). Ed(s): Gloria T Emeagwali. Central Connecticut State University, African Studies Program, PO Box 4010, New Britain, CT 06050-4010; emeagwali@ccsu.edu; http://www.ccsu.edu/afstudy/archive.html. Adv. *Bk. rev.:* Number and length vary. *Aud.:* Ga, Ac.

Students and scholars are contributors to this electronic newsletter of the Central Connecticut State University African Studies program. It presents a wide variety of interdisciplinary research and reports on social, political, and cultural issues in African Studies. Each issue has a thematic and/or geographic focus, e.g., "The Amistad Legacy" and "Nigerian Politics and Society." Available by subscription in print, the archive of issues is free on the web (www.ccsu.edu/afstudy/archive.html). Each issue is introduced by an editorial and followed by papers, interviews, or other pieces. Some are summaries or even reprints of articles published elsewhere. Some are footnoted, others are not. The brief, unfootnoted style of many of the articles allows for opinion pieces, conference reports, and other more topical reports. This is not a typical academic journal, but it is a fine magazine for students and others interested in Africa and African Studies. Recommended for both general and undergraduate collections.

177. *Africa Week: networking intelligence.* [ISSN: 1744-0734] 2004. w. USD 100; GBP 64. Ed(s): Desmond Davies. Trans Africa Publishing Company Limited, 19 Hatherley Mews, London, E17 4QP, United Kingdom; info@africaweekmagazine.com. *Aud.:* Hs, Ga, Ac, Sa.

The former editors of the now-ceased newsweekly *West Africa* launched this successor to cover news and politics of the African continent. Its publishing schedule at present is weekly online, with a monthly print edition. Articles cover politics, business news, and general interest stories on the continent. International and global issues with impact on Africa are also a focus. The web site is generally restricted to subscribers, but features a jobs section and also a Guest Opinion forum. It is hoped this new venture will carry on the tradition of *West Africa*, which was long a basic choice for most collections.

178. *African Affairs.* Formerly (until 1944): *Royal African Society. Journal.* [ISSN: 0001-9909] 1901. q. EUR 311 print or online ed. Ed(s): Tim Kelsall. Oxford University Press, Great Clarendon St, Oxford, OX2 6DP, United Kingdom; jnl.orders@oup.co.uk; http://www.oxfordjournals.org. Illus., adv. Refereed. Circ: 2350. Vol. ends: Sep. Online: EBSCO Publishing, EBSCO Host; Florida Center for Library Automation; Gale; HighWire Press; IngentaConnect; JSTOR (Web-based Journal Archive); Northern Light Technology, Inc.; OCLC Online Computer Library Center, Inc.; OhioLINK; Oxford Journals; ProQuest K-12 Learning Solutions; ProQuest LLC (Ann Arbor); SwetsWise Online Content. Reprint: PSC. *Indexed:* ABCPolSci, AICP, AbAn, AmH&L, AmHI, ArtHuCI, BrHumI, CABA, CJA, HistAb, HumInd, IBR, IBSS, IBZ, IIBP, IPSA, IndIslam, PAIS, PRA, PSA, RILM, RRTA, SSA, SSCI, SociolAb, WAE&RSA. *Bk. rev.:* 5-15, 500-1,500 words. *Aud.:* Ac, Sa.

Published on behalf of the Royal African Society (United Kingdom), this scholarly journal has a long tradition of covering Africa from a broad range of social science and cultural perspectives. Each issue includes several scholarly articles that focus on recent political, social, and economic developments in sub-Saharan countries. Historical studies relevant to current events on the continent are also featured. The journal regularly posts news of meetings of the Royal African Society and includes the society's annual meeting minutes, announcements, and annual report. Very useful to scholars, students, and librarians is the large bibliographic section with its review articles, book reviews, a bibliography of current publications by region, and a bibliography of Africa-related articles that appear in non-African periodicals. The full text of each issue is available online to print subscribers (http://afraf.oupjournals.org). Oxford University Press provides abstracts of major articles online and a facility to search the online tables of contents and abstracts. A valuable resource for a wide audience including researchers, students, scholars, librarians, and anyone interested in recent and historical literature on sub-Saharan Africa, *African Affairs* remains a basic choice for all collections.

179. *African and Black Diaspora: an international journal.* [ISSN: 1752-8631] 2008. s-a. GBP 152 print & online eds. Ed(s): Dr. Fassil Demissie, Abebe Zegeye. Routledge, 325 Chestnut St, Ste 800, Philadelphia, PA 19106; journals@routledge.com; http://www.routledge.com. Refereed. *Aud.:* Ga, Ac, Sa.

This new peer-reviewed journal publishes articles, commentaries, and book reviews on the interdisciplinary field of African Diaspora Studies. In a global context, it looks to consider the geographical, cultural, social, political, and psychological movements of peoples of African descent. The first issue addresses the theme "Navigating African Diaspora: Crossing, Belonging and Presence." This new journal should prove useful in libraries supporting African Studies and African American collections. Tables of contents and information about the journal at www.tandf.co.uk/journals/titles/17528631.asp.

180. *African Archaeological Review.* [ISSN: 0263-0338] 1983. s-a. EUR 343 print & online eds. Ed(s): Fekri A Hassan. Springer New York LLC, 233 Spring St, New York, NY 10013-1578; service-ny@springer.com; http://www.springer.com/. Illus., adv. Sample. Refereed. Microform: PQC. Online: EBSCO Publishing, EBSCO Host; Gale; IngentaConnect; OCLC Online Computer Library Center, Inc.; OhioLINK; Springer LINK; SwetsWise Online Content. Reprint: PSC. *Indexed:* AICP, AbAn, AmHI, AnthLit, FR, HumInd, IBR, IBZ, IIBP, IndIslam. *Bk. rev.:* 1-2, 1,000-1,500 words. *Aud.:* Ac, Sa.

This scholarly journal published in collaboration with the Society of Africanist Archaeologists features international scholarship on aspects of African archaeology. Each issue contains one or two authoritative, substantial, and detailed articles on archaeological research and activities in all parts of Africa, with emphasis on issues dealing with cultural continuities or discontinuities, interregional processes, biocultural evolution, the role of cultural materials in politics and ideology, and the application of ethno-historical techniques. Field data from key sites or localities are reported. A recent example of the research and analysis published here is "The Bab al Mandab vs the Nile-Levant: An Appraisal of the Two Dispersal Routes for Early Modern Humans Out of Africa." Usually one long book review is included in each issue. This publication is an important one in the field and is recommended for institutions with anthropology and archaeology interests.

181. *African Arts.* [ISSN: 0001-9933] 1967. q. USD 154 print & online eds. (Individuals, USD 78 print & online eds.). M I T Press, 238 Main St., Ste. 500, Cambridge, MA 02142; journals-info@mit.edu; http://mitpress.mit.edu. Illus., index, adv. Sample. Refereed. Circ: 5000. Microform: PQC. Online: Chadwyck-Healey Inc.; EBSCO Publishing, EBSCO Host; Florida Center for Library Automation; Gale; Northern Light Technology, Inc.; OCLC Online Computer Library Center, Inc.; ProQuest K-12 Learning Solutions; ProQuest LLC (Ann Arbor); H.W. Wilson. *Indexed:* ABM, AICP, AmHI, AnthLit, ArtHuCI, ArtInd, FR, HumInd, IBR, IBSS, IBZ, IIBP, IndIslam, MASUSE, MLA-IB, RILM, SSCI. *Bk. rev.:* 3-4, 200-700 words. *Aud.:* Hs, Ga, Ac, Sa.

African Arts celebrates its 40th year of publication with a special issue on ceramic arts in Africa. This is an attractive, glossy journal devoted to the plastic and graphic arts of Africa and its diaspora. Architecture, arts of personal adornment, and contemporary and popular arts are a focus, as well as music, film, theater, and other forms of expressive culture. Each issue usually includes four to eight articles with beautiful black-and-white and color illustrations and photos. Topical reviews and discussions are often featured. Recent issues feature articles on nineteenth-century Ghanaian weaving, an Ethiopian painting and essays on Dak'Art: Biennial of African Contemporary Art in Africa. Exhibit announcements, descriptive reviews of major exhibits, and book, video, and/or theater reviews appear in each issue. The presentation, subject matter, and

accessible writing make this a good choice for all audiences. This journal is published by the African Studies program at UCLA, and the full text is available in J-Store and through aggregators such as EBSCOHost and *International Index to Black Periodicals.*

182. *The African Book Publishing Record.* [ISSN: 0306-0322] 1975. q. EUR 348; EUR 93 newsstand/cover. Ed(s): Cecile Lomer. K.G. Saur Verlag GmbH, Ortlerstr 8, Munchen, 81373, Germany; info@saur.de; http://www.saur.de. Illus., adv. Circ: 500 Controlled. Vol. ends: No. 4. *Indexed:* IBR, IIBP, MLA-IB. *Bk. rev.:* 35-55, 200-400 words. *Aud.:* Ac, Sa.

ABPR provides comprehensive bibliographic and acquisitions data on new and forthcoming publications from the African continent. It includes books published in English or French and also lists significant titles in African languages. Bibliographic lists arranged by subject, author, and country supplement large book review sections. Features include reviews of new periodicals, an annual annotated review of African reference books, articles, news relating to the African book trade or African publishing, and listings of book awards and prizes. *ABPR* is recommended for academic, large public, and special libraries interested in acquiring specialized African materials.

183. *African Business.* [ISSN: 0141-3929] 1966. 11x/yr. GBP 40 domestic; EUR 80 in Europe Eurozone; USD 90 United States. Ed(s): Anver Versi. I C Publications Ltd., 7 Coldbath Sq, London, EC1R 4LQ, United Kingdom; http://www.africasia.com/. Illus., index. Sample. Circ: 18961. Microform: PQC. Online: Chadwyck-Healey Inc.; EBSCO Publishing, EBSCO Host; Florida Center for Library Automation; Gale; Northern Light Technology, Inc.; OCLC Online Computer Library Center, Inc.; ProQuest K-12 Learning Solutions; ProQuest LLC (Ann Arbor); H.W. Wilson. *Indexed:* ABIn, BPI, IIBP, PAIS, RRTA. *Bk. rev.:* 1-5, 100-500 words. *Aud.:* Hs, Ga, Ac, Sa.

In a familiar newsmagazine format, *African Business* provides information on business trends, risks, and opportunities in Africa. The focus is Pan-African. Each issue usually has three or four "cover stories" and longer articles on current business and economic issues. Surveys of major market sectors—energy, commodities, freight and transport, construction, technology—are included each month. The "Countryfile" section features several specific-country analyses of economic developments and trends. Shorter stories on "products and processes," an editorial page, and regular columnists with opinions and advice round out this newsy, upbeat review of Africa's business climate. The magazine also includes news of conferences, trade exhibition dates, African currency tables, and book reviews. *AB* has won awards for business reporting in Africa. With colorful production and a lively, readable style, it is recommended for general, academic, and special library collections. The web site includes some sections of current and past issues (www.africasia.com/africanbusiness). The London-based publisher IC Publications also produces *New African,* listed below. For in-depth country analysis, see *Country Reports* (below in this section).

184. *African Communist.* [ISSN: 0001-9976] 1959. q. ZAR 35; USD 30. South African Communist Party, PO Box 1027, Johannesburg, 2000, South Africa; sacp1@wn.apc.org; http://www.arc.org.za. Illus., adv. Circ: 10000. Microform: PQC. *Indexed:* IBR, IBZ, LeftInd. *Bk. rev.:* 1, 1,000-2,000 words. *Aud.:* Ac, Sa.

A forum for Marxist-Leninist thought, this is the journal of the South African Communist Party (SACP), which played a significant role in ending Apartheid and shaping South African politics and, perhaps, the political future of the country. Published furtively in Johannesburg at first and then produced abroad and smuggled into the country with false covers (as gardening magazines or antiques guides) throughout the 1970s and 1980s, the title finally came home in 1990. The major focus of the journal is now the South African transition. Issues may be devoted to a specific theme, such as HIV/AIDS and development or socialism and gender equality. Included are articles of opinion and debate, SACP documents and addresses, international political reports on socialism and communism in other countries, interviews, letters to the editor, and editorial notes. As with many continental journals, the publication schedule is sometimes behind. Useful for watching South Africa's development as a multiparty state from the leftist perspective, the *African Communist* provides insight into African opinion and debates. An appropriate selection for research centers, for libraries and institutions with an African Studies program or graduate political science program.

185. *African Development Review.* [ISSN: 1017-6772] 1989. 3x/yr. GBP 153 print & online eds. Ed(s): Kupukile Mlambo, John C Anyanwu. Blackwell Publishing Ltd., 9600 Garsington Rd, Oxford, OX4 2ZG, United Kingdom; customerservices@blackwellpublishing.com; http://www.blackwellpublishing.com. Illus. Sample. Refereed. Online: Blackwell Synergy; EBSCO Publishing, EBSCO Host; Gale; IngentaConnect; OCLC Online Computer Library Center, Inc.; OhioLINK; SwetsWise Online Content. *Indexed:* ABIn, ASSIA, ApEcolAb, CABA, ForAb, HortAb, IBSS, JEL, PAIS, PSA, RiskAb, S&F, SSCI, SociolAb, WAE&RSA. *Bk. rev.:* Number and length vary. *Aud.:* Ac, Sa.

The African Development Bank is a regional, multilateral development-finance institution. The *Review*, published by Blackwell on behalf of the bank, is a "professional journal devoted to the study and analysis of development policy in Africa." Emphasis is on the relevance of research findings to policy rather than purely theoretical or quantitative contributions. The journal is published usually three times a year, and each issue includes about six scholarly, technical articles on developmental economics, policy, and planning issues such as macroeconomic policies, private sector development, and income distribution and poverty alleviation. The focus may be on recent critical issues or empirical analyses and case studies, either comparative or of single countries. Articles are generally in English, and very occasionally in French. All articles have both English and French abstracts. There are book reviews, conference reports, and comments on review articles. Online access is provided for subscribers and through a variety of third-party service providers, and individual articles may be purchased through Blackwell Synergy. Free online access to institutions in the developing world is provided through United Nations initiatives (AGORA and OARE). More technical and more focused on economics than *Africa Development* (see above), this journal is recommended for academic and special audiences.

186. *African Economic History.* Formerly (until 1976): *African Economic History Review.* [ISSN: 0145-2258] 1974. a. USD 36 (Individuals, USD 18). Ed(s): Paul Lovejoy, Toyin Falola. University of Wisconsin at Madison, African Studies Program, 205 Ingraham Hall, 1155 Observatory Dr, Madison, WI 53706; publications@africa.wisc.edu; http://www.africa/wisc.edu. Illus., adv. Sample. Refereed. Circ: 250. Reprint: PSC. *Indexed:* AbAn, AmH&L, ArtHuCI, HistAb, IBSS, IIBP, JEL, PAIS, SSCI. *Bk. rev.:* 8-10, 600-1,000 words. *Aud.:* Ga, Ac, Sa.

Covering economic history from the pre-colonial era to the twentieth century, articles in this annual aim to contribute to historical knowledge and provide insights into contemporary economic and political issues on the continent. Scholarly, well-researched articles document historical topics such as cotton textile production in pre-colonial West Africa or the history of timber trade in Gabon. The focus makes this an important addition to collections with an interest in both African history and economics. The book review section is substantial. Although the publication schedule is very slow, usually a few years behind, this journal is recommended for specialized collections, academic libraries, and large public libraries.

187. *African Historical Review.* Formerly (until 2008): *Kleio.* [ISSN: 1753-2523] 1969. s-a. GBP 104 print & online eds. Ed(s): Muchaparara Musemwa. Unisa Press, PO Box 392, Pretoria, 0003, South Africa; unisa-press@unisa.ac.za; http://www.unisa.ac.za/press. Illus., adv. Refereed. Circ: 3200. *Indexed:* AmH&L, HistAb, IBR, IBZ. *Aud.:* Ac.

Published in South Africa for 35 years as *Kleio: A Journal of Historical Studies from Africa*, this journal was originally a research and teaching forum for histories taught in the History Department of the University of South Africa, evolving into a recognized academic journal known for the quality of its articles. It is being relaunched as *African Historical Review* aiming for a wider audience and contributors. While regional scholarship may be an emphasis, the intent is to include writing and research on an array of historical topics regarding Africa with diverse theoretical frameworks. Suitable for collections supporting African Studies, and valuable for bringing African scholarship to readers internationally.

188. *African Identities.* [ISSN: 1472-5843] 2003. s-a. GBP 305 print & online eds. Ed(s): Abebe Zegeye, Pal Ahluwalia. Routledge, 4 Park Sq, Milton Park, Abingdon, OX14 4RN, United Kingdom; info@routledge-ny.com; http://www.routledge.com. Online: EBSCO Publishing, EBSCO Host; Gale; IngentaConnect; OCLC Online Computer Library Center, Inc.; SwetsWise Online Content. Reprint: PSC. *Indexed:* IBSS, IIBP, IPSA. *Bk. rev.:* Number and length vary. *Aud.:* Ga, Ac, Sa.

In a new interdisciplinary venue for critical examinations of African and diasporic cultural production, including popular culture, this title is available in print and online. Five to eight articles in each issue examine film, drama, literature, popular music, and culture in the context of African identity. The meanings of Africanness, post-coloniality, and syncreticism are themes with an emphasis on gender, class, nation, marginalization, and "otherness." A recent special issue entitled "Re-imagining Africa" features articles exploring identity and establishing the meaning of life. The cultural studies approach and sometimes abstruse theoretical language of the articles means that this journal will be most useful in academic settings, but it is of high value for collections supporting cultural studies of Africa and its diaspora.

189. *African Journal of Ecology.* Formerly: *East African Wildlife Journal.* [ISSN: 0141-6707] 1962. q. GBP 618 print & online eds. Ed(s): F I B Kayanja. Blackwell Publishing Ltd., 9600 Garsington Rd, Oxford, OX4 2ZG, United Kingdom; customerservices@blackwellpublishing.com; http://www.blackwellpublishing.com. Illus., index, adv. Sample. Refereed. Circ: 380. Vol. ends: Dec. Microform: PQC. Online: Blackwell Synergy; EBSCO Publishing, EBSCO Host; Gale; IngentaConnect; OCLC Online Computer Library Center, Inc.; OhioLINK; SwetsWise Online Content. Reprint: PSC. *Indexed:* AbAn, ApEcolAb, BiolAb, CABA, DSA, FPA, ForAb, HortAb, IndVet, PollutAb, RRTA, S&F, SCI, SWRA, VB, WAE&RSA, ZooRec. *Bk. rev.:* 1-3, 250-800 words. *Aud.:* Ga, Ac, Sa.

While published on behalf of the East African Wild Life Society, this important journal publishes original research on the plant and animal ecology of the entire continent. Six to eight scholarly scientific articles are included in each issue. Recent articles include a policy paper on biofuels and ecology, a study of changes in large herbivore populations in Tanzania, and a review article on Nile perch in Lake Victoria. Graphs, tables, and high-quality illustrations accompany the articles on wildlife and plant ecology, with all of Africa as the geographic scope. Although articles are in English, a brief summary in French is included for each. Regularly featured book reviews and brief communications round out each issue. Comprehensive reviews on topical subjects are also sometimes featured. The editors see the readership as wildlife biologists, academics in biological sciences, undergraduates, and schoolteachers. It is published for the East African Wildlife Society. Tables of contents and reprint services are available at www.blackwellpublishing.com. The journal itself is also online through Blackwell's Synergy journals service for subscribers. Highly recommended for general science, biology, and botany collections and for research and academic libraries with an environment or ecology program.

190. *African Research and Documentation.* Supersedes: *African Studies Association of the United Kingdom. Bulletin; Library Materials on Africa.* [ISSN: 0305-862X] 1973. 3x/yr. GBP 20 domestic; USD 48 domestic; GBP 27 foreign. Ed(s): J McIlwaine. Standing Conference on Library Materials on Africa, University College London, School of Library, Archive and Information Studies, London, WC1E 6BT, United Kingdom; n.matthews@bradford.ac.uk; http://www.soas.ac.uk/scolma/. Illus., index, adv. Circ: 300. *Indexed:* AICP, AmH&L, BAS, HistAb, IBR, IBZ. *Bk. rev.:* 4-6, 250-1,000 words. *Aud.:* Ac, Sa.

Publishing articles on all aspects of libraries, archives, and bibliographical matters relating to Africa and African Studies, this journal is a good tool for building Africana collections and for keeping up with current African publishing trends, African bibliographic research projects, reference sources, book reviews, major scholarly writings, and announcements relating to African research sources. Articles focus on current topics (e.g., copyright and literary piracy in Ghana) or research resources (e.g., the SOAS Swahili Manuscripts Project). Issues also include information on Africa-related conferences and meetings, especially in Great Britain. Periodically, the journal provides an updated listing of African Studies resources on the Internet. In "Notes and News" one can find a summary of activities in various institutions with Africana collections. Book reviews by librarians cover a wide variety of scholarly works, including some very specialized items. Tables of contents for recent issues are available on the association web site (www.lse.ac.uk/library/scolma/ard.htm). Recommended as a very useful tool for Africana librarians and scholars.

191. *African Sociological Review.* Incorporates (in 1995): *South African Sociological Review;* Which was formerly (until 1988): *A S S A Proceedings (Association for Sociology in South Africa).* [ISSN: 1027-4332] 1973. s-a. ZAR 70 (Individuals, ZAR 40). Ed(s): Fred Hendricks. Council for the Development of Social Science Research in Africa, BP 3304, Dakar, Senegal; codesria@sonatel.senet.net; http://www.codesria.org. Illus., adv. Refereed. Circ: 600. Online: African Journals Online. *Indexed:* IBSS, PSA, SSA, SociolAb. *Bk. rev.:* 1,200-1,500 words. *Aud.:* Ac, Sa.

As with other publications sponsored by CODESRIA (Council for the Development of Social Science Research in Africa), *African Sociological Review* is a venue for research-based publishing by African scholars, in this case in sociology and anthropology. Each issue generally contains four or five articles, usually in English but with occasional French-language essays. Recent articles include one on gender and family life in Angola and a report on ethnographic aspects of land use controversies in Nigeria. Research reports, important addresses or speeches, review essays, or argument pieces ("Debates") are selectively included. A few critical book reviews appear in each issue. This journal is important for academic institutions with advanced degrees in sociology as well as Africana collections. The table of contents is available through African Journals OnLine (www.ajol.info). Although the publication schedule is semi-annual, there are often significant lags.

192. *African Studies.* Formerly (until 1938): *Bantu Studies.* [ISSN: 0002-0184] 1923. s-a. GBP 307 print & online eds. Ed(s): Clive Glaser, Charles Mather. Routledge, 4 Park Sq, Milton Park, Abingdon, OX14 4RN, United Kingdom; info@routledge.co.uk; http://www.routledge.com. Illus., adv. Refereed. Circ: 600. Reprint: PSC. *Indexed:* AICP, ASSIA, AbAn, AmH&L, AmHI, AnthLit, CABA, CJA, HistAb, IBR, IBSS, IBZ, IIBP, IPSA, IndIslam, MLA-IB, PSA, S&F, SSCI, SociolAb, WAE&RSA. *Aud.:* Ac, Sa.

This scholarly South African journal is based at the University of the Witwatersrand, an English-speaking institution with a progressive climate. The journal hopes to reflect local issues and also to contribute to a broader, more international debate. It encourages dialogue between scholars writing in and about various countries in the South, drawing on South African academics and those in other parts of Africa and abroad. Each issue includes six to nine articles. Originally focused on anthropology and linguistics, the scope is now much broader—including history, sociology, politics, geography, and literary and cultural studies, primarily in southern Africa, but also treating other countries and regions. A recent issue has articles on colonial Zimbabwe and on villagisation in Tanzania. This journal is published by Routledge, part of the Taylor & Francis Group, and at the publisher's web site (www.tandf.co.uk/journals) one can browse the contents pages of the issues, with full text available to subscribers. Recommended for larger collections.

193. *African Studies Quarterly: the online journal of African studies.* [ISSN: 1093-2658] 1997. q. Free. Ed(s): Leonardo Villalon. University of Florida, Center for African Studies, 427 Grinter Hall, PO Box 115560, Gainesville, FL 32611-5560; asq@africa.ufl.edu; http://www.africa.ufl.edu/asq/index.htm. Illus., adv. Refereed. Online: Gale. *Indexed:* AmHI, HumInd, IBSS, PSA, SociolAb. *Bk. rev.:* 5-15, 500-1,000 words. *Aud.:* Ac.

The Center for African Studies at the University of Florida publishes this interdisciplinary, refereed, online academic journal. Research and opinion in all disciplines are represented, with a focus on contemporary Africa. Each issue features three to five articles, several books reviews, and frequent review essays. Articles are in English and occasionally in French. A recent issue contains pieces on Africa's emerging security architecture, sweet potato preservation in Zimbabwe, and land tenure decisions in Kenya. The journal is available free on the web (www.africa.ufl.edu/asq), making available current research on Africa to a worldwide audience inside and outside academia.

194. *African Studies Review: the journal of the African Studies Association.* Formerly (until 1970): *African Studies Bulletin;* Incorporates (1975-1980): *A S A Review of Books.* [ISSN: 0002-0206] 1958. 3x/yr. Ed(s): Ralph Faulkingham, Mitzi Goheen. African Studies Association, Rutgers, The State University of New Jersey, 132 George St, New Brunswick, NJ 08901-1400. Illus., adv. Refereed. Circ: 3600. Vol. ends: Dec (No. 3). *Indexed:* ABCPolSci, AICP, AbAn, AmH&L, FR, HistAb, IBR, IBSS, IBZ, IIBP, IPSA, MLA-IB, PAIS, PRA, PSA, RILM, RRTA, SociolAb, WAE&RSA. *Bk. rev.:* Number and length vary. *Aud.:* Ga, Ac.

Published by the African Studies Association, this multidisciplinary journal includes peer-reviewed articles by international scholars along with numerous, extensive book and film reviews. The journal aims to encourage scholarly debates across disciplines. Readers are drawn into the issues of Africa and its diaspora from a discussion of sociological, political, and historical viewpoints. Articles in recent issues show the range of contributions: on popular culture and public space in Africa, open economy in Cote d'Ivoire, and a comparison of reparations claims by African and Jewish social movements. Highly recommended for academic and research libraries.

195. *Africana Libraries Newsletter.* Former titles: *Boston University Africana Libraries. Newsletter; Africana Libraries Newsletter.* 1975. q. Free. Ed(s): Marion J Frank-Wilson. Africana Libraries Newsletter, c/o Marion Frank Wilson, Ed, Librarian for African Studies, Main Library E660, Indiana University, Bloomington, IN 47405-3907; mfrankwi@indiana.edu; http://www.indiana.edu/~libsalc/african/aln/fall09.html. Illus. Sample. Circ: 480 Controlled. *Bk. rev.:* 400-500 words. *Aud.:* Ac, Sa.

This 8- to 12-page newsletter supports the work and activities of the Africana Librarians Council (ALC) of the African Studies Association and provides a forum for the exchange of ideas and opinions about issues in Africana librarianship. Issues contain news of the council's activities, including meeting minutes and information about the ALC, Cooperative Africana Microform Project (CAMP), meeting schedules, agendas, and news from relevant groups. The content is of particular benefit to Africana librarians and collection developers, as it routinely includes items dealing with information resources in and about Africa, as well as vendor news, acquisitions, trip reports, book awards, serial title changes, new and ceased serials, and electronic resources for Africana. Published by the Office of the Librarian for African Studies at Indiana University, it is also available free online at www.indiana.edu/~libsalc/african/aln.

196. *Afrique Contemporaine: Afrique et developpement.* [ISSN: 0002-0478] 1962. q. EUR 60 domestic; EUR 60 Belgium; EUR 70 elsewhere. Agence Francaise de Developpement, 5 Rue Roland-Barthes, Paris, 75598 cedex 12, France. Illus., index, adv. Circ: 2000. *Indexed:* IBR, IBSS, IBZ, IPSA, IndIslam, PAIS, PdeR. *Bk. rev.:* 95, 50-100 words. *Aud.:* Ac, Sa.

This French-language journal focuses on development and trends and issues in politics, economics, and country-to-country and international relations in contemporary Africa. Each number provides a chronology of major political events listed by country and brief biographies of principal personages. Articles are usually footnoted. *Afrique Contemporaine* includes numerous brief book annotations classed by country and topic. Recommended for larger collections.

197. *Afrique Magazine.* Former titles (until 1989): *Jeune Afrique Magazine;* (until 1986): *J A Magazine;* (until 1985): *Jeune Afrique Magazine.* [ISSN: 0998-9307] 1981. m. EUR 25. Ed(s): Zyad Liman. Groupe Jeune Afrique, 57 bis, rue d'Auteuil, Paris, 75016, France; redaction@jeuneafrique.com; http://www.jeuneafrique.com. Adv. *Bk. rev.:* Occasional. *Aud.:* Hs, Ga, Ac.

One of several glossy publications from Le Groupe Jeune Afrique, this is a consumer magazine, in French, aimed at a youthful, upwardly mobile African or African diasporic audience. Monthly issues contain lifestyle articles and features on international figures, food, health, sports, fashion, travel, and music. This journal is mostly info-tainment, but more serious subjects are treated—for example, in recent issues, a consideration of the role newly elected French president Sarkozy might play on the African continent and an essay on the anniversary of independence for Ghana. Lively and upbeat, it is a good purchase for French and African Studies undergraduate collections. Summaries of contents in the current issue can be seen on the web site at www.afriquemagazine.com.

198. *allAfrica.com.* 2000. d. Free. AllAfrica Global Media, 920 M St SE, Washington, DC 20003. *Aud.:* Hs, Ga, Ac, Sa.

allAfrica.com is the successor to *Africa News Online*. Like its predecessor the Africa News Service, the publisher AllAfrica Global Media is a content provider through partnership with media organizations in Africa. The news web site *allAfrica.com* provides news stories, analysis, and comment on a wide range of topics, drawing from newspapers, news agencies, and publications from all over the continent. Selected documents—key speeches, reports, and announcements—from governments, nongovernmental organizations, and other newsmakers are also posted. More than 800 new stories in English and French appear daily from over 100 African media organizations, as well as reporting and analysis from *allAfrica.com*'s own news staff. Links are also provided to newspapers and other media organizations such as *The Mail & Guardian* of Johannesburg and Nairobi's *The Nation*. The web site is keyword searchable, and stories can be viewed by region, topic, or country. The organization claims to be the "largest electronic distributor of African news and information worldwide." This is an invaluable source for news of Africa at all levels.

199. *Arts d'Afrique Noire.* [ISSN: 0337-1603] 1972. q. Ed(s): Eric Lehuard. Arts d'Afrique Noire, B.P. 24, Arnouville-les-Gonesse, 95400, France. Illus., index, adv. Sample. *Indexed:* AICP, AnthLit, ArtInd, FR, RILM. *Bk. rev.:* 6-10, 200-1,000 words. *Aud.:* Ac, Sa.

While it is actually more of a monographic series, this French publication on African art includes well-illustrated articles on aspects of the arts of black Africa and reviews of exhibitions. It also includes information on museums, exhibitions, private collections, public auctions, and recent art prices. For larger art collections and Africana libraries.

200. *Azania.* [ISSN: 0067-270X] 1966. a. GBP 22 per vol. Ed(s): P J Lane. British Institute in Eastern Africa, PO Box 30710, Nairobi, 00100, Kenya; office@biea.ac.uk; http://www.biea.ac.uk/. Illus., index. Refereed. *Indexed:* AICP, AnthLit, FR, IBSS, PLESA. *Aud.:* Ac, Sa.

Azania is the ancient name for East Africa. This annual journal of the British Institute in Eastern Africa (sponsored by the British Academy) is devoted to Eastern African precolonial history and archaeology. It reports on diverse research undertaken by staff, students, associated scholars, and grant recipients of the institute, but it also publishes relevant research on East Africa's precolonial past from other scholars, both local and international. Articles are technical and accompanied by photos, graphs, and data. More geographically focused than *African Archeological Review* (see above), but East Africa is broadly defined, with coverage from the Horn of Africa to Zimbabwe. Suitable for larger archaeology and Africana collections. The institute has also launched *Journal of Eastern African Studies,* a new title with a broader scope in the social sciences and humanities.

201. *C O D E S R I A Bulletin.* Formerly: *Africana Newsletter.* [ISSN: 0850-8712] 1987. q. Free to qualified personnel. Ed(s): Francis B Nyamnjoh. Council for the Development of Social Science Research in Africa, BP 3304, Dakar, Senegal; codesria@sonatel.senet.net. *Aud.:* Ac, Sa.

Based in Senegal, CODESRIA is an important Pan-African research organization with a primary focus on the social sciences. The *Bulletin* aims to stimulate discussion, encourage cooperation among African researchers, facilitate an exchange of information on projects, and report on conferences and seminars. Short, accessible articles are grouped as "Debates" on a theme or topical issue, or "Perspectives" on current issues. Recent themes include African women and rethinking African development issues. The organization publishes several other journals including *Africa Development* (see above), the longest-standing Africa-based social science journal; *Afrika Zamani,* a journal of history; the *African Sociological Review* (see above); and others such as the *African Journal of International Affairs.* Tables of contents, abstracts, and often the full text of articles are available at the CODESRIA web site, and the journals are part of the African Journals Online project (www.ajol.info).

202. *Cahiers d'Etudes Africaines.* [ISSN: 0008-0055] 1960. q. EUR 30.50 newsstand/cover per issue. Ed(s): J L Amselle. College de France, Ecole des Hautes Etudes en Sciences Sociales (E H E S S), 54 Boulevard Raspail, Paris, 75006, France; editions@ehess.fr; http://www.ehess.fr. Illus., adv. Sample. Circ: 760. Microform: IDC. *Indexed:* ABCPolSci, AICP, AmH&L, AnthLit, ArtHuCI, FR, HistAb, IBR, IBSS, IPSA, IndIslam, L&LBA, MLA-IB, PAIS, PSA, SSA, SSCI, SociolAb, WAE&RSA. *Bk. rev.:* 9-14, 100-1,400 words. *Aud.:* Sa.

International and interdisciplinary, this important French bilingual journal publishes scholarly articles on Africa and the diaspora (in the Caribbean, the Americas, and Europe). Focus is primarily in the social sciences, but the journal also features scholarship in history, popular culture, archaeology, communication, and literature. One or two articles of the five or six in each issue are in English. Each article has an abstract in either French or English. There are frequent thematic numbers with essays on a region or a problem or issue. Issues include review essays, critical book reviews, and a list of publications received. For specialized audiences, larger academic collections, and those with interest in francophone Africa.

203. *Canadian Journal of African Studies.* Formerly (until 1966): *Bulletin of African Studies in Canada.* [ISSN: 0008-3968] 1963. 3x/yr. Individuals, CND 70; Students, CND 35. Canadian Association of African Studies, c/o Concordia University, 1455 de Maisonneuve O., Montreal, PQ H3G 1M8, Canada; caas@concordia.ca; http://caas.concordia.ca. Illus., adv. Sample. Refereed. Circ: 1000. *Indexed:* ABCPolSci, AICP, AbAn, AmH&L, ArtHuCI, CABA, HistAb, HortAb, IBR, IBSS, IIBP, IPSA, MLA-IB, PAIS, PdeR, RI-1, RILM, RRTA, SSCI, WAE&RSA. *Bk. rev.:* 30-40, 500-1,000 words. *Aud.:* Ac, Sa.

Articles, research notes, book review essays, and book reviews in each issue of this bilingual journal of the Canadian Association of African Studies appear in English or French. Most articles are in English unless the theme of an issue is a francophone country. Articles carry an abstract in French if the article is in English and vice versa. There is broad coverage of the social sciences and humanities, with a focus on anthropology, political economy, history, geography, and development, especially assessment of development strategies. A section of "Debates and Commentaries" presents divergent viewpoints on current issues. Review essays and book reviews (in either language) are quite substantial. The extensive reviews and essays make this a bibliographic resource for librarians and researchers to keep up with research, debates, and publications in the field of African Studies.

204. *Country Reports.* Formerly: *Quarterly Economic Reviews.* 1952. q. USD 525; USD 245 per issue. Economist Intelligence Unit, 111 W 57th St, New York, NY 10019; newyork@eiu.com; http://www.eiu.com. Circ: 40000. *Aud.:* Ga, Ac, Sa.

Published by the Economic Intelligence Unit, this series of analyst reports aims to assist executive business decisions by providing timely and impartial analysis on worldwide market trends and business strategies for close to 200 countries. The quarterly reports (with free monthly updates on the Internet) monitor and analyze developments and trends in politics, policy, and economy. Putting recent events in context, the reports provide a two-year outlook for each country. Graphs and charts illustrate the economic trends and data. Subscriptions per country for print or web access include quarterly main reports and a Country Profile, an annual reference tool analyzing political, infrastructural, and economic trends over the longer term. From the same group that publishes *The Economist* and *EIU ViewsWire* (a daily intelligence service covering the same countries), the *Country Reports* are a long-standing source of data and country intelligence; formats are accessible and information is timely, especially with the Internet access and updates. At over $500 per country, this is an expensive publication; however, specialized collections may want to consider reports on countries of interest.

205. *Current Writing: text and reception in southern Africa.* [ISSN: 1013-929X] 1989. s-a. USD 20 (Individuals, USD 15). Ed(s): J U Jacobs. University of KwaZulu-Natal, Department of English, King George V Ave, Durban, 4001, South Africa; http://www.und.ac.za/und/english/curwrit/. Illus., index. Refereed. Vol. ends: Oct. *Bk. rev.:* 15-20, 300-1,200 words. *Aud.:* Ac, Sa.

Current Writing carries essays on contemporary and republished texts in southern Africa and on the reading of world texts from a southern African perspective. Scholars from southern Africa are the primary contributors. The review section, an important part of the journal, evaluates new publications that relate to the region. The journal is of interest to those studying developments in writing and literature in southern Africa, a region in which tremendous political and social changes have had an effect on writing style and content. While there is sometimes a delay in printing and distribution of the annual issues, this specialized journal appears to be still in publication. Suitable for large academic and special collections.

206. *Discovery and Innovation.* [ISSN: 1015-079X] 1989. q. KES 3000 (Individuals, KES 1500). Ed(s): S Akatch. Academy Science Publishers, PO Box 14798, Nairobi, Kenya; asp@africaonline.co.ke; http://www.aasciences.org. Illus., adv. Refereed. *Indexed:* AbAn, BiolAb, CABA, ChemAb, DSA, FPA, ForAb, HortAb, IIBP, IndVet, PAIS, PLESA, RRTA, S&F, SCI, SSCI, VB, WAE&RSA, ZooRec. *Aud.:* Ac, Sa.

A joint publication of the African Academy of Sciences (AAS) and the Third World Academy of Sciences (TWAS), this international journal aimed at academic and specialized audiences features peer-reviewed articles on science and technology in Africa. A wide range of subject areas is represented: the basic sciences, applied sciences, environment, traditional African sciences, and social and human sciences. Emphasis is on scientific research and development and policy, especially as the sciences, technology, and social sciences relate to concerns in Africa. Third World research is considered as it applies to the African situation. Each issue also includes an editorial essay, letters, review articles with extensive bibliographies, research reports, and conference announcements. Recent issues contain an editorial on building scientific capacity in Africa, reports on PCBS in the aquatic environment of the Niger Delta, Nigeria, and edible mushrooms in Tanzania. Up-to-date listings of contents appear in FirstSearch Article First. Tables of contents and the means to order photocopies are also available from African Journals Online, which is a project of the International Network for the Availability of Scientific Publications that offers the tables of content and abstracts from journals published in Africa in agricultural sciences, science and technology, and health and social sciences. URL: www.inasp.org.uk/ajol/journals/dai/about.html.

207. *Drum: Africa's leading magazine beating to the pulse of the times.* [ISSN: 0419-7674] 1951. m. ZAR 349.13 domestic; ZAR 725.29 Namibia; ZAR 1219.61 Zimbabwe. Ed(s): Esmare Weideman. Media24 Ltd., Naspers Centre, 40 Heerengracht St, PO Box 1802, Cape Town, 8000, South Africa; http://www.media24.com. Illus., adv. Circ: 59664. *Bk. rev.:* Number and length vary. *Aud.:* Hs, Ga, Ac.

Since the early 1950s *Drum* (South Africa) has been a very popular, consumer-oriented magazine, the sixth largest in Africa. Sports heroes, models, political figures, and entertainment personalities are featured on the covers of each weekly issue, along with headers of the stories on music, fashion, food, health, and features on popular figures, as well as some sensational stories. Sections for children and women appear in most issues in addition to regular columns offering advice, horoscopes, puzzles, etc. It has a bit of the flavor of both *People* and *The National Enquirer*. *Drum* reflects the multicultural, middle-class, youth-oriented new South Africa. A short history of *Drum* and its unique place as a vehicle for black expression in South Africa can be found on the *Afribeat* web site at http://home.worldonline.co.za/~afribeat/archiveafrica.html. Highly recommended as a colorful and appealing popular source that offers insight on the values and aspirations of South Africans.

208. *Eastern Africa Social Science Research Review.* [ISSN: 1027-1775] 1985. 2x/yr. USD 23 in Africa; USD 35 elsewhere. Ed(s): Mohamed Salih, Bahru Zewde. Organization for Social Science Research in Eastern Africa, PO Box 31971, Addis Ababa, Ethiopia; pub.ossrea@ telecom.net.et; http://www.ossrea.net. Refereed. Circ: 500. Online: African Journals Online; EBSCO Publishing, EBSCO Host; OCLC Online Computer Library Center, Inc.; OhioLINK; Project MUSE; SwetsWise Online Content. *Indexed:* IBSS, PLESA, PSA, SociolAb, WAE&RSA. *Bk. rev.:* Number and length vary. *Aud.:* Ac, Sa.

The Organization for Social Science Research in Eastern Africa (OSSREA), based in Ethiopia, publishes this twice-yearly forum for articles on economic, political, and social and development issues of the countries and sub-regions within Eastern and Southern Africa. It is a major African-published journal. The social sciences are broadly represented, and treatment of policies and issues in scholarly articles, book reviews, and shorter communications are presumed to be of interest to development planners and policy makers as well as academics. Recent issues contain substantial essays on such topics as HIV/AIDS on college campuses, Chinese imports in Zimbabwe, and development planning in Tanzania. A solid and consistent venue for African scholars, it is a good addition to libraries that support African Studies. There is online access to tables of contents through the African Journals OnLine program at www.ajol.info. Also, since 2002, full text is available via Project Muse at http://muse.jhu.edu.

209. *English in Africa.* [ISSN: 0376-8902] 1974. 2x/yr. ZAR 100 (Individuals, ZAR 90; USD 25 foreign). Ed(s): Mark Marais. Rhodes University, Institute for the Study of English in Africa, PO Box 94, Grahamstown, 6140, South Africa; http://www.ru.ac.za/affiliates/isea/. Illus., index, adv. Refereed. Circ: 500. Vol. ends: May/Oct (No. 2). Online: EBSCO Publishing, EBSCO Host; Florida Center for Library Automation; Gale. *Indexed:* AmHI, ArtHuCI, BEL&L, IBR, IBSS, IBZ, MLA-IB. *Bk. rev.:* Number and length vary. *Aud.:* Ac, Sa.

A scholarly journal devoted to the study of African literature and English as a language of Africa, *English in Africa* is published by the Institute for the Study of English in Africa, a research institute within Rhodes University. Contributors are generally established writers or academics from South Africa, England, and the United States. *English in Africa* specializes in publishing previously unpublished or out-of-print primary material, including articles and letters by writers of Africa as well as scholarly articles on African writing in English, especially African literature. The former editor described the range well: "Archival research; bibliographical work; charting emerging talent; looking afresh at well-known works; exploring the potential in exciting new writing." Most articles are historical or cultural studies rather than theoretical enquiries. Reviews, review articles, or discussions between writers regularly conclude each issue. More literary and broader in scope than *Current Writing* (see above), *English in Africa* is suitable for academic institutions with a strong English, cultural studies, or African Studies emphasis. As full-text articles are now available through EBSCO's Academic Search Premier, readers outside South Africa will become more familiar with the publication. URL: www.ru.ac.za/institutes/isea/EiA.

210. *Focus on Africa.* [ISSN: 0959-9576] 1990. q. GBP 23 (Individuals, GBP 14). Ed(s): Damian Zane. B B C, African Service, Bush House, Strand, London, WC2B 4PH, United Kingdom; worldservice@bbc.co.uk; http://www.bbc.co.uk/worldservice/. Illus., adv. Circ: 32000 Paid. *Indexed:* IIBP. *Bk. rev.:* Number and length vary. *Aud.:* Hs, Ga, Ac, Sa.

This colorful, well-produced newsmagazine from the BBC World Service is published in London, with content from journalists in the BBC's African Service programs. Each issue features news reports, feature articles, and color pictures covering the political, social, cultural, and sporting developments in the countries of Africa. A recent issue has a special feature on Africa's cities. Besides the feature stories and regular columns, each quarterly issue has an update on the previous three months of developments, sections on business and sports, and an entire section devoted to reader contributions showcasing short stories, poetry, letters, and articles. BBC programming schedules are also included. The BBC World Service has a web site on Africa with a link to the page containing the current issue of *BBC Focus on Africa* and an archive of selections of current affairs and business articles from back issues of the magazine. Highly recommended for all collections. URL: www.bbc.co.uk/worldservice/africa/features/focus_magazine/index.shtml.

211. *G E F A M E: journal of African studies.* [ISSN: 1558-7274] 2004. 2x/yr. Free. University of Michigan, Scholarly Publishing Office, Shapiro Library Bldg, 919 South University Ave, Ann Arbor, MI 48109-1185, MI 48109-1185; gefame.editors@umich.edu; http://www.hti.umich.edu/g/gefame. *Bk. rev.:* Number and length vary. *Aud.:* Ga, Ac.

Freely available through the joint efforts of the University Library and the Center for Afro-American and African Studies at the University of Michigan, *GEFAME* aims to "facilitate exchange of ideas between Africa-based scholars and scholars outside the continent of Africa." Articles and reprints of relevant speeches and delivered papers comprise the content. Recent contributions indicate the wide scope: articles on Spanish colonial policy in Equatorial Guinea, the use of visual arts in contemporary African novels, and the role of remittances on education in Eritrea. The web site also contains as a separate section a revival of a former print journal published at Northwestern University, *Passages: A Chronicle of the African Humanities*, intended to publish diverse contributions—readings, interpretations, reviews, essays, and debates. There is also a section to report events in Africa, announcing conferences on the continent. Frequency is stated as twice yearly for *GEFAME*, but each volume so far has only had one issue. *Passages* has had no new contributions since 2005.

212. **History in Africa: an annual journal of method.** [ISSN: 0361-5413] 1974. a. USD 35. Ed(s): David Henige. African Studies Association, Rutgers, The State University of New Jersey, 132 George St, New Brunswick, NJ 08901-1400; callasa@rci.rutgers.edu; http://www.africanstudies.org. Illus., adv. Refereed. Circ: 550. *Indexed:* AICP, AmH&L, ArtHuCI, HistAb, IBR, IBSS, IBZ, RILM. *Aud.:* Ac, Sa.

This annual publication of the African Studies Association contains 20–30 articles on aspects of African history and culture. Essays on historiography, historical methodology, and archival research within Africa make this a valuable resource for historians, researchers, and advanced graduate students. History teaching programs will find it an important resource because the essays often reflect new trends in African historical research. An essential journal for institutions that support African history programs and highly recommended as a basic journal for academic libraries.

213. **International Journal of African Historical Studies.** Formerly: *African Historical Studies*. [ISSN: 0361-7882] 1968. 3x/yr. USD 125 (Individuals, USD 50). Ed(s): Michael DiBlasi. Boston University, African Studies Center, 270 Bay State Rd, Boston, MA 02215; http://www.bu.edu/africa/publications/index.html. Illus., index, adv. Circ: 700. Vol. ends: No. 3. *Indexed:* ABS&EES, AICP, AbAn, AmH&L, AmHI, ArtHuCI, FR, HistAb, HumInd, IBR, IBSS, IBZ, IIBP, IndIslam, LRI, SSCI. *Bk. rev.:* 65-80, 500-800 words. *Aud.:* Ac, Sa.

The African Studies Center at Boston University publishes this scholarly periodical and reviewing source covering all aspects of African history with a "focus on the history of African communities through time, in Africa or elsewhere." Each issue contains three to five substantial articles. Recent articles include a study of taxation, a report on social conditions in early colonial Uganda, and an essay on the creation of Kanga, the elaborately patterned cloth of East Africa. The very extensive book review section in each issue and the frequent review essays make this journal a significant tool for collection development. For a similar journal, see *Journal of African History* (below in this section). Recommended for academic collections and large public libraries. URL: www.bu.edu/africa/publications/ijahs/current/index.html.

214. **Jenda: a journal of culture and African women studies.** [ISSN: 1530-5686] 2000. 3x/yr. Free. Ed(s): Nkiru Nzegwu, Oyeronke Oyewumi. Africa Resource Center, Inc., Binghamton University, Dept of Africana Studies, Binghamton, NY 13902-6000; http://www.jendajournal.com/jenda/. *Indexed:* SociolAb. *Aud.:* Ac, Sa.

This free e-journal promotes research and scholarship on and by African women to the global African community and friends of Africa. Articles are centered on women's history and studies in African social, cultural, political, and economic systems. It creates a forum for African women scholars, analysts, and activists to participate with their contemporaries worldwide in debates, exchanges of ideas, and the creation and documentation of knowledge. Issues feature lengthy articles on topics related to gender. Two recent issues feature articles on transglobal families, sex trade in Nigeria, historical women rulers in Botswana, and feminism in Kenya. Generally, a review essay and shorter pieces on current debates are also offered, as well as links to relevant articles in other online sources. Frequent pieces or reprinted research on public policy are also featured. While the web site indicates the schedule to be three issues a year, in reality so far, only one has appeared per year. The publisher Africa Resource Center is an educational portal that develops and distributes content on Africa and the African Diaspora.

215. **Jeune Afrique.** Former titles (until 2006): *L' Intelligent;* (until 2000): *Jeune Afrique.* [ISSN: 1950-1285] 1960. w. EUR 109 domestic; EUR 139 in Europe; EUR 149 in North Africa. Ed(s): Bechir Ben Yahmed. Groupe Jeune Afrique, 57 bis, rue d'Auteuil, Paris, 75016, France; redaction@jeuneafrique.com; http://www.jeuneafrique.com. Illus., adv. Circ: 100000. Microform: PQC. Online: East View Information Services. *Indexed:* MLA-IB, PAIS, PdeR. *Aud.:* Ga, Ac, Sa.

Jeune Afrique l'Intelligent is the principal French-language newsweekly on Africa. Published in Paris with a format similar to U.S. weekly newsmagazines, it has very good coverage of North Africa and formerly francophone sub-Saharan African countries, but it reports also on all countries of the continent. Each issue has news and interpretative and editorial commentary on Africa and includes feature articles on political, cultural, and economic developments. The corresponding web site is www.jeuneafrique.com. Recommended for collections with francophone-area interest and for general academic collections. See also *Focus on Africa* (above in this section).

216. **Journal of African Cultural Studies.** Formerly (until 1997): *African Languages and Cultures.* [ISSN: 1369-6815] 1988. s-a. GBP 162 print & online eds. Ed(s): Akin Oyetade. Routledge, 4 Park Sq, Milton Park, Abingdon, OX14 4RN, United Kingdom; info@routledge.co.uk; http://www.routledge.co.uk. Illus., index, adv. Sample. Circ: 300. Vol. ends: Dec. Online: EBSCO Publishing, EBSCO Host; Gale; IngentaConnect; JSTOR (Web-based Journal Archive); OCLC Online Computer Library Center, Inc.; SwetsWise Online Content. Reprint: PSC. *Indexed:* AICP, AmHI, CABA, IBSS, IIBP, L&LBA, MLA-IB, PSA, RILM, RRTA, SociolAb, WAE&RSA. *Aud.:* Ac, Sa.

The focus of *JACS* is not on technical linguistic descriptions of African languages, but rather on languages of Africa as channels for the expression of culture. Articles address literature (particularly African-language literature) performance, art, music, and media studies, as well as issues within fields such as popular culture in Africa, sociolinguistic topics of cultural interest, and culture and gender. Many articles have a historical focus. The content remains very scholarly, providing a venue for essays on African culture from inside and outside Africa. Tables of contents are free on the Taylor & Francis web site, as well as full text of articles to subscribers (www.tandf.co.uk/journals). Recommended for academic and general libraries with a large audience in Africana, cultural studies, literature, and linguistics interests.

217. **Journal of African Economies.** [ISSN: 0963-8024] 1992. 5x/m. EUR 447 print or online ed. Ed(s): Marcel Fafchamps. Oxford University Press, Great Clarendon St, Oxford, OX2 6DP, United Kingdom; jnl.orders@oup.co.uk; http://www.oxfordjournals.org. Illus., adv. Sample. Refereed. Circ: 700. Online: EBSCO Publishing, EBSCO Host; Gale; HighWire Press; IngentaConnect; OCLC Online Computer Library Center, Inc.; OhioLINK; Oxford Journals; ProQuest LLC (Ann Arbor); SwetsWise Online Content. Reprint: PSC. *Indexed:* ABIn, CABA, CJA, HortAb, IBSS, IIBP, IndVet, JEL, RRTA, S&F, SSCI, VB, WAE&RSA. *Bk. rev.:* 1-5, 800-1,200 words. *Aud.:* Ac, Sa.

This scholarly journal offers "rigorous economic analysis, focused entirely on Africa, for Africans and anyone interested in the continent." The audience is presumed to be not just academics, but consultants, policymakers, traders, financiers, development agents, and aid workers. The articles are accompanied by tabular data and graphs to illustrate trends and theories on African fiscal and monetary policies, trade, agricultural labor, and production issues. Recent issues offer articles on economic mobility in Rwanda, Morocco's trade options, and globalization and gender inequality in Africa. Book reviews and annotated listings of recent working papers in developmental economics are featured in some issues. An annual supplement provides text of ongoing research presented at the plenary sessions of the African Economic Research Consortium (AERC). The full text of each issue and archives back to 1996 are available online in pdf format to users with a print subscription (jae.oxfordjournals.org). Free or reduced-cost online access is offered to institutions in developing countries. Highly recommended for large libraries and economics collections.

218. **The Journal of African History.** [ISSN: 0021-8537] 1960. 3x/yr. GBP 178. Ed(s): Anne Majer, Justin Willis. Cambridge University Press, The Edinburgh Bldg, Shaftesbury Rd, Cambridge, CB2 2RU, United Kingdom; journals@cambridge.org; http://www.journals.cambridge.org.

Illus., index, adv. Sample. Refereed. Microform: PQC. Online: Pub.; EBSCO Publishing, EBSCO Host; Florida Center for Library Automation; Gale; JSTOR (Web-based Journal Archive); OCLC Online Computer Library Center, Inc.; OhioLINK; SwetsWise Online Content. Reprint: PSC. *Indexed:* AICP, AbAn, AmH&L, AmHI, AnthLit, ArtHuCI, BrHumI, FR, HistAb, HumInd, IBR, IBSS, IBZ, IIBP, IndIslam, NumL, PSA, RI-1, SSA, SSCI, SociolAb. *Bk. rev.:* 20-35, 500-1,400 words. *Aud.:* Ac, Sa.

While articles in this excellent journal cover all aspects and periods of African history from the late Stone Age to the present, there has been increasing emphasis on economic, cultural, and social history. It is published three times a year, and each issue includes five or six long scholarly research articles. Major essay topics have included slavery, resistance movements, African population history, medical and labor history, colonial trade, gender roles, the construction of ethnicity, Islam in Africa, and environmental history. Extensive and substantial book reviews assist in selection. For a similar journal in quality and scope, see *International Journal of African Historical Studies* (above in this section). Tables of contents and abstracts are available free on the journal's web site (journals.cambridge.org), but full texts of journal articles are available only to subscribers or for individual purchase. Highly recommended for collections supporting the study of African history.

Journal of African Languages and Linguistics. See Linguistics section.

219. *Journal of African Law.* [ISSN: 0021-8553] 1956. s-a. GBP 106. Ed(s): Fareda Banda, Tunde Ogowewo. Cambridge University Press, The Edinburgh Bldg, Shaftesbury Rd, Cambridge, CB2 2RU, United Kingdom; journals@cambridge.org; http://www.journals.cambridge.org. Adv. Circ: 550. Microform: WSH; PMC. Online: Pub.; EBSCO Publishing, EBSCO Host; JSTOR (Web-based Journal Archive); OCLC Online Computer Library Center, Inc.; OhioLINK; SwetsWise Online Content. Reprint: PSC; WSH. *Indexed:* AICP, CLI, IBR, IBSS, IBZ, IIBP, ILP, IPSA, IndIslam, LRI, PAIS. *Bk. rev.:* Number and length vary. *Aud.:* Ga, Ac, Sa.

For 50 years, the *Journal of African Law* has addressed the laws and legal issues of the entire sub-Saharan continent. Published by Cambridge University Press for the School of Oriental and African Studies of University of London, the journal highlights comparative legal issues and those of international significance. A separate section covers recent legislation, case law, law reform proposals, and international developments affecting Africa. The scope includes crime, family law, human rights, and nationality and constitutional law. Articles are on such topics as the legal framework for internally displaced persons, access to medical care in South African prisons, and historical treatments such as a consideration of equity in colonial West Africa. The aim of the journal is to reach development workers and policymakers, as well as academics and professional lawyers, with a focus on African institutions—laws, enforcement mechanisms and organizations—so that better understanding of the institutions and their histories will promote development on the continent. An obvious choice for law and Africana collections.

220. *Journal of Contemporary African Studies.* [ISSN: 0258-9001] 1981. 3x/yr. GBP 547 print & online eds. Ed(s): Roger Southall. Routledge, 4 Park Sq, Milton Park, Abingdon, OX14 4RN, United Kingdom; info@routledge.co.uk; http://www.routledge.co.uk. Illus., adv. Sample. Refereed. Circ: 2000. Vol. ends: No. 2. Online: EBSCO Publishing, EBSCO Host; Gale; IngentaConnect; OCLC Online Computer Library Center, Inc.; SwetsWise Online Content. Reprint: PSC. *Indexed:* ASSIA, AmH&L, CABA, CJA, FPA, ForAb, HistAb, IBR, IBSS, IBZ, IIBP, IPSA, PSA, S&F, SSA, SociolAb, WAE&RSA. *Bk. rev.:* 5-15, 500-1,000 words. *Aud.:* Ac, Sa.

This interdisciplinary journal aims to provide a scholarly understanding of developments and change in Africa through the publication of research and writing in the social sciences and humanities, with the social sciences predominating. This journal includes sociology, urban studies, modern history, education, literature, and development studies, and the wide scope of its research makes it an important journal for contemporary African Studies. While the editors are based in South Africa at Rhodes University, the scope is the whole sub-Saharan continent and the contributors are wide-ranging. Recent issues include articles on Ghana's slave forts, academic freedom in Botswana,

opposition parties in sub-Saharan Africa, and women's representation in the government of Mauritius. Book reviews appear in each semi-annual issue. Articles are available online to subscribers at www.tandf.co.uk/journals. Recommended for academic collections and those with strong interest in contemporary Africa.

221. *Journal of Eastern African Studies.* [ISSN: 1753-1055] 2007. 3x/yr. GBP 315 print & online eds. Ed(s): David M Anderson, Paul Tiyambe Zeleza. Routledge, 4 Park Sq, Milton Park, Abingdon, OX14 4RN, United Kingdom; info@routledge.co.uk; http://www.routledge.co.uk. *Aud.:* Ac, Sa.

Based in Kenya, The British Institute in Eastern Africa works to promote a better understanding of East Africa's pre-colonial past, through its mission to "undertake, promote, and facilitate research of international significance on the history and archaeology of peoples, cultures, and languages in eastern Africa." Newly launched by the institute and published by Routledge, this scholarly journal plans to feature broad enquiry on the region from academic disciplines within the humanities and the social sciences, especially encouraging interdisciplinary analysis, comparative perspectives, and research using significant theoretical or methodological approaches for the region. Some examples of the topics covered in the first issue include the South Asian diaspora of East Africa, missionary medicine in colonial Zambia, and Masai land struggles in Kenya. The institute also produces the annual journal *Azania*, focused on the archaeology and history of East Africa.

222. *Journal of Modern African Studies.* [ISSN: 0022-278X] 1963. q. GBP 185. Ed(s): Christopher Clapham. Cambridge University Press, The Edinburgh Bldg, Shaftesbury Rd, Cambridge, CB2 2RU, United Kingdom; journals@cambridge.org; http://www.journals.cambridge.org. Illus., index, adv. Sample. Refereed. Circ: 1700. Vol. ends: Dec. Microform: PQC. Online: Pub.; EBSCO Publishing, EBSCO Host; JSTOR (Web-based Journal Archive); OCLC Online Computer Library Center, Inc.; OhioLINK; SwetsWise Online Content. Reprint: PSC. *Indexed:* ABCPolSci, ABIn, AbAn, AmH&L, AmHI, ArtHuCI, BAS, BrHumI, CABA, CJA, FPA, ForAb, HistAb, HortAb, IBR, IBSS, IBZ, IIBP, IPSA, IndIslam, L&LBA, MLA-IB, NumL, PAIS, PRA, PSA, RILM, RRTA, S&F, SFSA, SSA, SSCI, SociolAb, WAE&RSA. *Bk. rev.:* 0-25, 500-2,000 words. *Aud.:* Ac, Sa.

Considering an audience of academics, students, practitioners as well as general readers, this scholarly but accessible journal aims to present fair and balanced views of "controversial issues," focusing on contemporary Africa, with an emphasis on current issues in African politics, economies, societies, and international relations. Specialists and scholars in the field contribute articles on political, economic, and social policies that affect people and progress on the continent. Recent articles treat such topics as language choice in education, revitalising African agriculture, and democracy in Cape Verde. Shorter pieces on literature, culture, and aspects of social history also appear. Issues also include critical book reviews. Available electronically to institutions via Cambridge Journals Online (uk.cambridge.org/journals). Guests can view abstracts of articles. Intended and suitable for students, academics, and general readers, it is highly recommended for academic libraries and general collections.

223. *The Journal of North African Studies.* [ISSN: 1362-9387] 1996. q. GBP 267 print & online eds. Ed(s): George Joffe, John P Entelis. Routledge, 4 Park Sq, Milton Park, Abingdon, OX14 4RN, United Kingdom; info@routledge.co.uk; http://www.routledge.co.uk. Adv. Sample. Refereed. Vol. ends: Winter. Reprint: PSC. *Indexed:* AmHI, BrHumI, IBSS, IIBP, IPSA, IndIslam, PSA, SSA, SociolAb. *Bk. rev.:* Number and length vary. *Aud.:* Ac, Sa.

This journal is one of a few that treat this region with its links to both sub-Saharan Africa and the Middle East. It provides a forum for scholars of and from North Africa. The peer-reviewed articles cover country-based and regional themes in historical topics and in the social sciences. There are five to eight articles per issue, featuring both contemporary analysis and historical treatments as well as book reviews. Special issues also available as books appear regularly, such as a recent one devoted to the Tuareg in Algeria. This journal is a positive addition to scholarship of Africa, covering a region rarely treated as coherent. Book reviews provide current awareness for this area of study. Recommended for academic and special libraries. Members of the American Institute of Maghrib Studies receive a subscription as part of their membership. There is online access for subscribers, and tables of contents and a contents alerting service are available at the publisher's web site (www.tandf.co.uk/journals).

224. *Journal of Religion in Africa.* Incorporates (1971-1975): *African Religious Research.* [ISSN: 0022-4200] 1967. q. EUR 245 print & online eds. (Individuals, EUR 118). Ed(s): Brad Weiss. Brill, PO Box 9000, Leiden, 2300 PA, Netherlands; cs@brill.nl; http://www.brill.nl. Illus., adv. Refereed. Vol. ends: No. 4. Reprint: PSC. *Indexed:* AmH&L, AmHI, ArtHuCI, FR, HistAb, IBR, IBSS, IBZ, IIBP, IndIslam, R&TA, RI-1, RILM, SSA, SociolAb. *Bk. rev.:* 4-6, 750+ words. *Aud.:* Ac, Sa.

As the only English-language journal to focus on the forms and history of religion within the African continent, particularly in sub-Saharan Africa, this is an important publication. Scholars from a variety of disciplines and countries contribute to each issue, which is frequently on a particular topic introduced by editorial comment. For example, a recent issue centers on faith and AIDS in East Africa. The journal occasionally publishes religious texts in their original African language. There are book reviews and longer review articles. This is a leading international journal in religious studies but is also of interest to a humanities and social science readership. For academic and larger collections.

225. *Journal of Southern African Studies.* [ISSN: 0305-7070] 1975. q. GBP 388 print & online eds. Ed(s): David Simon, JoAnn McGregor. Routledge, 4 Park Sq, Milton Park, Abingdon, OX14 4RN, United Kingdom; info@routledge.co.uk; http://www.routledge.co.uk. Illus., adv. Sample. Refereed. Circ: 900. Microform: PQC. Online: Chadwyck-Healey Inc.; EBSCO Publishing, EBSCO Host; Gale; IngentaConnect; JSTOR (Web-based Journal Archive); Northern Light Technology, Inc.; OCLC Online Computer Library Center, Inc.; ProQuest LLC (Ann Arbor); SwetsWise Online Content. Reprint: PSC. *Indexed:* ABCPolSci, AICP, AmH&L, AmHI, ArtHuCI, BrHumI, CABA, CJA, FPA, ForAb, HistAb, HortAb, IBR, IBSS, IBZ, IIBP, IPSA, IndVet, L&LBA, PSA, RILM, RRTA, S&F, SSA, SSCI, SWA, SociolAb, VB, WAE&RSA. *Bk. rev.:* 4-6, 200-1,000 words. *Aud.:* Ac, Sa.

Academic scholarship that presents new perspectives from various disciplines in social sciences and humanities is featured in this international journal. New theoretical approaches and scholarly inquiry are applied to issues and social problems in the region of southern Africa. Issues include six to ten extensive articles, excellent review essays, and signed book reviews. The range of topics is broad: recent issues contain articles on urban stratification in Angola, cultural representation of Zulus in America, and architecture in Zimbabwe. One or two of each year's four issues are devoted to broad themes such as "Women and the politics of gender in southern Africa." This journal is now published by Routledge, and its contents and full text to institutional subscribers are available at www.tandf.co.uk/journals. Highly recommended for academic and specialized collections.

226. *Journal of Sustainable Development in Africa.* [ISSN: 1520-5509] 1999. s-a. Ed(s): Valentine Udoh James. Fayetteville State University, 1200 Murchison Rd, Fayetteville, NC 28301; http://www.uncfsu.edu. *Bk. rev.:* 2 per issue. *Aud.:* Ac, Sa.

The sustainability issues in African development are the focus of this electronic-only refereed journal. Four to five articles and a book review in each issue bring a multidisciplinary perspective to the economic, socio-political, cultural, and environmental issues surrounding development and planning on the continent. The present focus emphasizes policy components of Africa's development issues. Articles address both broad and local topics, seeking contributions of both theoretical and applied discussions of the debates on sustainable development in Africa. Recent issues contain articles on wetlands in Tanzania and Zimbabwe, the human development crisis in Liberia, and the impact of public deficit on private savings. URL: www.jsd-africa.com.

227. *The Maghreb Review: a quarterly journal on all aspects of North Africa, the Middle East, Sub-Saharan Africa and Islamic studies from earliest times to the present day.* [ISSN: 0309-457X] 1976. q. GBP 240.

Ed(s): Mohamed Ben-Madani. Maghreb Review, 45 Burton St, London, WC1H 9AL, United Kingdom. Illus., adv. Refereed. Circ: 10000. *Indexed:* AmH&L, HistAb, IBR, IBSS, IPSA, IndIslam. *Bk. rev.:* 4-6, 2,000-4,000 words. *Aud.:* Ac, Sa.

Independent, interdisciplinary, and bilingual, this journal is one of the oldest English/French publications devoted to the study of North Africa and Islamic culture and religion. The specific focus is the region of the Maghreb: Algeria, Tunisia, Libya, Morocco, and Mauritania. International scholars contribute studies in archaeology, anthropology, politics, history, religion, and literature—the spectrum of the social sciences and humanities as they relate to the Berber, Arab, and Islamic heritage of this crossroads region and its interaction with sub-Saharan Africa, the Mediterranean, and the Middle East. Six to eight articles appear in each issue, some in both languages and some with translated abstracts. There are frequent special issues on topic such as migration or literacy. Abstracts of relevant theses or dissertations and conference papers are featured. Recommended for larger collections.

228. *Matatu: journal for African culture and society.* [ISSN: 0932-9714] 1987. s-a. Ed(s): Holger G Ehling. Editions Rodopi B.V., Tijnmuiden 7, Amsterdam, 1046 AK, Netherlands; orders-queries@rodopi.nl; http://www.rodopi.nl. Illus., adv. Refereed. Circ: 500. *Indexed:* IBR, IBZ, L&LBA, MLA-IB, PSA, SociolAb. *Aud.:* Ga, Ac, Sa.

Matatu, named for the crowded mini-buses used for public transport in East Africa, is a semi-annual refereed journal devoted to African literatures and societies that "promote interdisciplinary dialogue between literary and cultural studies, historiography, the social sciences and cultural anthropology." The focus is on African (including Afro-Caribbean) culture and literature, providing a forum for critical debates and exploration of African modernities. While *Matatu* is a journal, each volume is on a specific theme and is priced to also be purchased separately. Recent issues include a tribute to Nigerian writer Ezenwa-Ohaeto, consideration of how literary and oral forms of expression interrelate, creolization in the Caribbean, and sexuality and gender. Online access is included with print subscriptions. Considering Africa in the global context, this journal makes a nice addition to arts and cultural studies for academic libraries.

229. *N K A: journal of contemporary African art.* [ISSN: 1075-7163] 1994. s-a. USD 43 (Individuals, USD 27). Ed(s): Salah Hassan, Olu Oguibe. Mario Einaudi Center for International Studies, 170 Uris Hall, Africana Studies and Research Center, Ithaca, NY 14853-7601; http://www.einaudi.cornell.edu. Illus. Refereed. *Indexed:* ABM, ArtInd, IIBP. *Bk. rev.:* Number and length vary. *Aud.:* Ga, Ac, Sa.

Published in conjunction with the Africana Studies and Research Center at Cornell, this beautifully produced magazine is focused not primarily on the ethnographic and traditional art forms, but on contemporary art from Africa and the diaspora. Arts from film to poetry to sculpture are treated. The editors are art critics and curators who aim to make "significant contributions to the intellectual dialogue on world art and the discourse on internationalism and multiculturalism in the arts" and to bring an awareness of contemporary African and diasporic art and culture to the world. A good choice for both public and academic libraries. Tables of contents are available at www.nkajournal.org. While there have been recent delays in publication, a new number is out, treating the theme of lynching as represented in the arts and linking the historical to modern issues of torture such as Abu Ghraib.

230. *New African.* Former titles (until 1978): *New African Development;* (until 1977): *African Development.* [ISSN: 0142-9345] 1966. 11x/yr. GBP 40 domestic; EUR 80 in Europe eurozone; USD 90 United States. Ed(s): Baffour Ankomah. I C Publications Ltd., 7 Coldbath Sq, London, EC1R 4LQ, United Kingdom; http://www.africasia.com/. Illus., adv. Sample. Circ: 28853. Microform: PQC. Online: Chadwyck-Healey Inc.; EBSCO Publishing, EBSCO Host; Florida Center for Library Automation; Gale; Northern Light Technology, Inc.; ProQuest LLC (Ann Arbor). *Indexed:* IIBP, PAIS, RRTA, WAE&RSA. *Aud.:* Hs, Ga, Ac.

A glossy consumer newsmagazine from the same publishers as *African Business* (see above), *New African* covers the entire spectrum of contemporary African life: political reporting, economic and financial analysis, and articles on culture and social affairs including art, music, fashion, and sport. Each issue includes more than one cover story dealing with a major social or political issue or personality. Many of the articles take a muckraking stance. The scope is Pan-African and the diaspora, although most features focus on sub-Saharan Africa. Each issue has a section called "Around Africa," which reports news of specific countries and presents longer special reports on a featured country. The online version (www.africasia.com/newafrican) offers summaries of the cover stories and the table of contents of issues, as well as text of some special reports. The same publisher releases the *New African Yearbook* with facts and figures on each of the 53 countries. As one of the oldest monthly magazines, *New African* is recommended for all collections with an interest in Africa.

231. *Newswatch: Nigeria's weekly newsmagazine.* [ISSN: 0189-8892] 1985. w. NGN 70 per issue. Ed(s): Dan Ochima Agbese. Newswatch Communications Ltd., Oregun, 3 Billingsway, PMB 21499, Ikeja, Nigeria. Illus., index, adv. Circ: 150084. *Aud.:* Hs, Ga, Ac.

This Nigerian newsmagazine is Africa's largest-selling weekly outside of South Africa. It includes politically oriented news, primarily about Nigeria, but also African and international news, as well as news on business and the economy. Regular articles cover news in science, technology, politics, business and finance, the stock market, arts and society, and environment reports. Cheeky, muckraking, and critical of the government, it has sometimes been banned in Nigeria. This important, critical, and risk-taking newsmagazine is recommended for all audiences. A new web site offers online subscriptions, and there are also some feature stories available for free (www.newswatchngr.com).

232. *Philosophia Africana (Print Edition): analysis of philosophy and issues in Africa and the Black Diaspora.* Former titles (until 2001): *African Philosophy (Print Edition); (until 1998): SAPINA Newsletter.* [ISSN: 1539-8250] s-a. USD 590 (Individuals, USD 205). Ed(s): Emmanuel Chukwudi Eze. DePaul University, Department of Philosophy, 2352 N Clifton Ave, Ste 150, Chicago, IL 60614. Index, adv. Refereed. *Indexed:* AmHI, ArtHuCI, IBR, IBZ, IPB, IndIslam, L&LBA, PSA, PhilInd, SSA, SociolAb. *Bk. rev.:* Number and length vary. *Aud.:* Ac, Sa.

As African philosophy emerges with distinctive content and methodology, this academic journal publishes "philosophical or philosophically interdisciplinary works that explore pluralistic experiences of Africa and the Black Diaspora from both universal and comparative points of view." Articles also may represent original or critical interpretations of creative and artistic works relevant to Africa and the diaspora. Recent issues include a selection of essays on Chinua Achebe, a consideration of the Yoruba-language conception of human personality, and an essay on philosophical analysis and the definition of racism. Book reviews and occasional conference reports are included. In addition to the interest for Africana collections, academic libraries that support philosophy programs will want to acquire this title.

233. *Politique Africaine.* [ISSN: 0244-7827] 1981. q. EUR 60 domestic; EUR 70 in Europe; EUR 70 in Africa. Ed(s): Richard Banegas. Editions Karthala, 22-24 Boulevard Arago, Paris, 75013, France; karthala@wanadoo.fr; http://www.karthala.com. Illus., adv. Refereed. Circ: 3500. *Indexed:* FR, IBR, IBSS, IPSA, IndIslam, PAIS, PSA, RILM, SociolAb, WAE&RSA. *Bk. rev.:* 20-25, 50-200 words. *Aud.:* Ac, Sa.

Published in France, this quarterly political science journal includes contributed articles that usually relate to a thematic topic, or focus on a country. Recent issues, for example, centered on political parties in Africa and post-Apartheid South Africa, and another issue was devoted to the colonial past. While some focus is on francophone countries, the scope is really the entire continent, especially sub-Saharan Africa. The remainder of each issue includes briefer articles, speeches, and recent political developments. It also includes major meeting and conference announcements, book reviews, and lists of books received. Tables of contents and abstracts in English are available at www.politique-africaine.com. Older issues, generally after five years, have the full text of the articles available for free in pdf format, while newer issues have abstracts only for major articles. For larger collections and those with francophonic interests.

234. *Presence Africaine: revue culturelle du monde noir.* [ISSN: 0032-7638] 1947. s-a. Societe Africaine de Culture, 25 bis rue des Ecoles, Paris, 75005, France. Illus. Refereed. Circ: 3000 Controlled. *Indexed:* AmH&L, AmHI, HistAb, IBR, IBSS, IBZ, MLA-IB, PAIS, RILM, RRTA, WAE&RSA. *Bk. rev.:* Number and length vary. *Aud.:* Ga, Ac, Sa.

Presence Africaine has a long, illustrious history and remains the most influential French-language journal on Africa. It was founded in 1947 by Alioune Diop, a Senegalese intellectual and seminal figure in the discourse on Africa. Its early years coincided with the struggles against colonialism as well as the development of the "Negritude" movement. *PA* was the leading journal of anticolonial intellectuals in France and Africa and a major publisher of African writers. Now bilingual (in French and English), *PA* remains a leading cultural journal of the African diaspora and is indispensable for academic collections, especially those supporting African Studies and literature. Issues feature critical and historical articles, book reviews and discussions, and creative writing. Unfortunately, it presently seems to be interrupted in publication, although there has not been an announcement. Hopefully it will resume or be relaunched, as it remains important for all libraries with serious interest in Africa.

235. *Research in African Literatures.* [ISSN: 0034-5210] 1970. q. USD 115 (Individuals, USD 42.50). Ed(s): John Conteh-Morgan. Indiana University Press, 601 N Morton St, Bloomington, IN 47404. Illus., index, adv. Sample. Refereed. Circ: 900. Microform: PQC. Online: Chadwyck-Healey Inc.; EBSCO Publishing, EBSCO Host; Gale; OCLC Online Computer Library Center, Inc.; OhioLINK; Project MUSE; ProQuest K-12 Learning Solutions; ProQuest LLC (Ann Arbor); SwetsWise Online Content; H.W. Wilson. Reprint: PSC. *Indexed:* AbAn, AmHI, AnthLit, ArtHuCI, BEL&L, ENW, FLI, FR, HumInd, IBR, IBSS, IBZ, IIBP, L&LBA, MLA-IB, RILM, SSCI. *Bk. rev.:* 5-21, 1,000-2,000 words. *Aud.:* Ac, Sa.

The official journal of both the African Literature Association and the African Literatures Division of the Modern Language Association, *RAL* is an important source for research on the literatures of Africa. Included are scholarly essays; extensive, useful bibliographies; and long reviews of all aspects of oral and written literatures, music, film, and theater of Africa. Articles are in English, but literature in English, French, or African languages is treated. The scope also extends to literature of the black diaspora and other arts as well. Each issue contains up to 20 contributions including discussions of short and long fiction, poetry, drama, important new writers, music, film, and theater, as well as literary developments. Book reviews and often review essays are featured. Information is included on African publishing and announcements of importance to Africanists. Special issues or groupings of articles explore themes such as psychoanalysis and African literature, and literary movements in Lusophone literature in Africa. A standard and highly recommended source for academic and large public libraries and anyone interested in African literatures and literary criticism. Available electronically through Project Muse (muse.jhu.edu). Tables of contents for issues are available on the Indiana University Press web site (iupjournals.org).

236. *Review of African Political Economy.* [ISSN: 0305-6244] 1973. q. GBP 391 print & online eds. Ed(s): Janet Bujra, Jan Burgess. Routledge, 4 Park Sq, Milton Park, Abingdon, OX14 4RN, United Kingdom; info@routledge.co.uk; http://www.routledge.co.uk. Illus., adv. Sample. Refereed. Circ: 1500. Online: Chadwyck-Healey Inc.; EBSCO Publishing, EBSCO Host; Gale; IngentaConnect; OCLC Online Computer Library Center, Inc.; ProQuest K-12 Learning Solutions; ProQuest LLC (Ann Arbor); SwetsWise Online Content. Reprint: PSC. *Indexed:* ABIn, AltPI, CABA, DSA, FPA, ForAb, HortAb, IBR, IBSS, IBZ, IIBP, IPSA, JEL, LeftInd, PAIS, PSA, RiskAb, S&F, SSA, SWA, SociolAb, WAE&RSA. *Bk. rev.:* 4-7, 900-3,000 words. *Aud.:* Ac, Sa.

For over 30 years, this journal has had a focus on Africa's underdevelopment with a leftist analysis that examines imperialism, capitalism, and the social and political forces in the global economy. The editorial policy of *ROAPE* proudly reaffirms its definite political stance and an agenda that includes addressing globalized capitalism, U.S. militarism, patterns of social reproduction, state failures and conflict, and resistance and solidarity. Each themed issue begins with an editorial and contains five to nine articles dealing with such issues as

South Africa's first decade of democracy or the new "African Scramble" characterized by trade issues, petro-violence, and militarization. Shorter news articles and book reviews and announcements are also featured. Contributions by African scholars and activists are encouraged and published. The web site (www.roape.org/index.html) provides abstracts of articles from current and past issues. Highly recommended for academic and special audience categories.

237. Transition: an international review. Former titles (until 1977): *Ch'indaba;* (until no.50, 1975): *Transition.* [ISSN: 0041-1191] 1961. q. USD 80 (Individuals, USD 27; Students, USD 19). Ed(s): Michael C Vazquez, Nicole Lamy. Soft Skull Press, Inc., 55 Washington St., Ste. 804, Brooklyn, NY 11201-1066; http://www.softskull.com. Illus., adv. Sample. Circ: 1100 Paid and controlled. Vol. ends: Aug. *Indexed:* ABS&EES, AltPI, AmHI, FLI, IBR, IBZ, MLA-IB, PAIS, PSA, SSA, SociolAb. *Bk. rev.:* 2-3. *Aud.:* Ga, Ac, Sa.

Transition was originally published in Uganda, with a reputation as a forum for intellectual debate in the time of decolonization until 1976. Brought back as a new series by Henry Louis Gates in 1991, this journal takes a critical look at culture, cultural icons, literature, visual imagery, and the arts. There have been difficulties in publishing over the past few years, and only two issues appeared between 2003 and the end of 2006, but with a new publisher, Soft Skull Press, the magazine still hopes to appear quarterly. The scope of *Transition* is not just Africa but the entire postcolonial world with a multicultural perspective; the journal bills itself as "an international review of politics, culture, and ethnicity from Beijing to Bujumbura." It is edited by Harvard scholars Gates and Kwame Appiah, and its editorial board is equally star-studded, headed by Wole Soyinka and featuring Carlos Fuentes, Jamaica Kincaid, and other leading intellectuals and literati as board members. The essays are clearly written, provocative, and engaging. A recent issue features a story and interview with Zimbabwean author Tsitsi Dangarembga, a story about Guyana illustrated with art of Guyanese painter Stanley Greaves, and an essay on black players in Canadian hockey. Issues are well illustrated with high production values. While text is available in JSTOR, it is no longer current in Project Muse or other aggregators. The striking illustrations and photographs are not as well reproduced in JSTOR, so there is no substitute for the print journal. A three-time winner of the Alternative Press Award, this venue for cultural criticism is very highly recommended for both general and academic institutions, with hopes for its future vigor.

238. Ufahamu: journal of the African activist association. [ISSN: 0041-5715] 1970. 3x/yr. USD 28 (Individuals, USD 20). Ed(s): Shobana Shankar. University of California at Los Angeles, James S. Coleman African Studies Center, 10244 Bunche Hall, 405 Hilgard Ave, Los Angeles, CA 90095-1310; isacasc@international.ucla.edu; http://www.international.ucla.edu/africa. Illus., adv. Sample. Circ: 350. *Indexed:* AmH&L, HistAb, IBR, IBSS, IBZ, IndIslam, MLA-IB. *Bk. rev.:* 1-2, 1,000-2,500 words. *Aud.:* Ga, Ac.

From the Swahili word meaning "understanding, comprehension or being and remaining aware," *Ufahamu,* is published by the African Activist Association, a graduate student organization at the University of California at Los Angeles. *Ufahamu* presents articles from established writers and academics as well as graduate students and nonacademic researchers. Founded as a journal of opinion on social issues, it continues to provide an interdisciplinary forum for those whose approach is both scholarly and activist. It includes articles on history, politics, economics, sociology, anthropology, law, planning and development, and literature and the arts in the African continent and diaspora. Creative writing is occasionally included. An upcoming issue will be devoted to the theme of soccer and nationalism. Addressing an audience of both scholars and general readers, it is recommended for academic institutions and larger general libraries.

239. West Africa Review. [ISSN: 1525-4488] 1999. s-a. Free. Ed(s): Nkiru Nzegwu. Africa Resource Center, Inc., Binghamton University, Dept of Africana Studies, Binghamton, NY 13902-6000; http://www.westafricareview.com/war/right.htm. Refereed. *Indexed:* AmHI, HumInd, PAIS. *Bk. rev.:* Number and length vary. *Aud.:* Ga, Ac, Sa.

A relative newcomer in the African Studies field, this e-journal is one of several free titles published by the Africa Resource Center (see *African Philosophy* and *Jenda,* the latter above in this section). According to editorial statements, *West*

Africa Review is devoted to the promotion of research and scholarship of importance to the global African community, and also accepts technical and scientific papers that further the understanding of the geography and life in the region, research findings, analyses, and interpretations of scholars in West African Studies. While the publication schedule is supposed to be twice a year, publication times vary, as does the volume of material included. Issues contain generally four to six articles not solely on West Africa, book reviews, and research reports. It sometimes makes available works that have been published elsewhere but are deemed to deserve wider circulation. For example, the most recent issue features several articles celebrating African literary critic Biodun Jeyifo, including reprints of essays originally appearing in *The Guardian* (Nigeria) earlier in the year.

■ AFRICAN AMERICAN

See also Africa; and Ethnic Interests sections.

Carol A. Rudisell, Librarian, Reference Dept., University of Delaware Library, Newark, DE 19717-5267; rudisell@udel.edu

Introduction

Today's motivation for publishing African American magazines and journals does not differ significantly from that of yesteryear. John Brown Russwurm and Samuel E. Cornish wrote in their opening editorial of *Freedom's Journal* (1827), the first weekly edited by and for African Americans:

"We wish to plead our own cause. Too long have others spoken for us. Too long has the publick been deceived by misrepresentations, in things which concern us dearly, though in the estimation of some mere trifles." ["To Our Patrons," *Freedom's Journal* (16 March 1827): 1.]

The desire to set the record straight, to provide an authentic voice, and to define and interpret one's own reality can still be seen in the mission statements and editorials of contemporary African American periodicals.

The titles described in this section fall primarily into two categories: popular magazines whose target audiences are African American readers, and academic journals that seek to further scholarship in the interdisciplinary field of African American Studies. The readers of the two types of publications are not mutually exclusive; they intersect and overlap in interesting ways. Scholars studying African American popular culture use popular magazines as source material. African Americans outside of academe read scholarly journals in pursuit of a greater understanding of their history and culture. African American scholars, through writing or interview, appear in both popular magazines and academic journals. When making selections for their collections, librarians should be mindful of the interconnectedness of scholarly and popular publications and analyze the informational content that each can provide.

A topic addressed in all of the African American magazines issued during the past year was Hurricane Katrina and the devastating loss of African American lives, educational institutions, communities, and culture. While the tragedy affected both blacks and whites in the Gulf region, the aftermath of Katrina highlighted the gross disparities between the two communities and revealed America's continuing inability to come to terms with "the race question." While coverage of the disaster was featured throughout all the popular magazines, because of the lengthy maturation process of academic writing, Katrina was largely relegated to the editorial and comments sections of academic journals. A familiar adage reminds us that "today's news is tomorrow's history." Therefore, we can expect to see in future African American scholarly journals articles based on historical and empirical evidence that delve into the sociological, psychological, political, and economic aspects of Hurricane Katrina. We can expect to learn more about what the disaster has revealed about the nature of life in America for black people.

The readership of African American consumer magazines remains strong. Recent surveys have shown that the percentage of African Americans who regularly read magazines is greater than that of the mainstream population. The "digital divide" is in part responsible for this trend, as mainstream America has moved in greater numbers to the Internet as a primary source of information and entertainment. Publishers and advertisers have recognized the strength of the African American market, and new publications have been produced to meet the demand. Trends within the new offerings can be characterized as "aspirational" or lifestyle magazines targeted to middle-class and upper middle-class readers, hip-hop magazines designed for urban youth, and gospel magazines directed at African American Christians. Many of the new magazines are local or regional in scope and have not been included here; however, those that have acquired a national readership, such as *Homes of Color,* are described in this section. Librarians seeking to learn of local or regional titles should consult *Ulrich's Periodicals Directory.* Also, local bookstores can be a good source of new local publications.

The older popular magazines seem fairly well established, with loyal readerships. With respect to sales, the five top-selling African American magazines remain well ahead of the rest; they are *Ebony, Essence, Jet, Vibe* and *Black Enterprise.* Newer titles that are challenging their position in the market are the hip-hop magazines *XXL, Vibe Vixen* and *The Source,* and the lifestyle magazine *Upscale.* Representing a diversified body of literature, African American popular magazines cover news and opinion, fashion, lifestyle, personal finance and business management, popular history and culture, religion, and music. Some titles have modified their publishing schedules, and others have made slight changes in their format, but overall they have been very stable. *Essence* has been purchased by Time Warner, a move that is making some readers skittish. *Black Issues Book Review* has merged with *QBR (Quarterly Black Review of Books).* Titles that have suspended publication are *HealthQuest* and *The Messenger,* and *Savoy* is on hiatus.

Scholarly African American journals reviewed in this section are primarily interdisciplinary in scope. Cross-references are included for those journals that focus on a single discipline, for example the *Review of Black Political Economy.* Disciplines represented within the interdisciplinary publications include anthropology, art, art history, communications, creative writing, economics, education, gender studies, history, law, literature, music, political science, public policy, psychology, religion, sociology, and theater and the performing arts.

While all of the scholarly publications reviewed here have significant African American content, some have broadened their scope to include Africana Studies, Black Studies, Pan-African Studies, or the African diaspora. The first three terms are applied interchangeably to the study of people of African descent, regardless of where they live, whereas "the African diaspora" refers to people of African descent living outside of Africa. There has been a growing trend within academia to examine African American issues within a broader international context, and this trend is reflected in the journals under review. Also, some journals have adopted a multicultural or "ethnic" approach and feature topics on other people of color living in the United States.

Because of their small revenue streams and circulation, scholarly journals have a tougher time staying afloat. This is also true for African American journals, despite the support they receive from their host universities and professional associations. The demand for intellectually stimulating work about African Americans remains high, and scholarly publishers attempt to supply it, although it is not always economically feasible to do so. *Contours: A Journal of the African Diaspora* (University of Illinois Press) discontinued publication after only three volumes. On a brighter note, the *Journal of Pan-African Studies* has made an impressive online reappearance after a long hiatus. A new title that has met with much initial praise is the *Du Bois Review: Social Science Research on Race* published by the Du Bois Institute for African and African American Research at Harvard University. Another new entrant to the field is the *Journal of Race and Policy,* an annual publication from the Institute for the Study of Race and Ethnicity at Old Dominion University. And finally, a title change to note: the *Journal of African American Men* is now the *Journal of African American Studies.*

Basic Periodicals

Ems: *American Legacy, Black History Bulletin, Crisis, Right On!;* Hs: *American Legacy, Black Collegian, Black Enterprise, Black History Bulletin, Black Scholar, Blackgirl Magazine, Crisis, Ebony, Journal of African American History, Vibe;* Ga: *African American Review, American Legacy, Black Enterprise, Black History Bulletin, Black Issues Book Review, Black Scholar, Callaloo, Crisis, Ebony, Essence (New York), Jet, Journal of Black Studies, Journal of African American History, Souls, Vibe;* Ac: *African American Review, Black Collegian, Black Enterprise, Black History Bulletin, Black Issues Book Review, Black Music Research Journal, Black Scholar, Callaloo, Crisis, Diverse Issues in Higher Education, Du Bois Review, Ebony, Essence, International Review of African American Art, Jet, Journal of African American*

History, Journal of Black Psychology, Journal of Black Studies, Journal of Blacks in Higher Education, Journal of Negro Education, National Black Law Journal, Race & Class, The Review of Black Political Economy, Souls, Transition, Vibe, The Western Journal of Black Studies.

Basic Abstracts and Indexes

America: History and Life, Arts & Humanities Citation Index, Black Studies on Disc, EBSCOHost Masterfile, Ethnic NewsWatch, Expanded Academic ASAP, Humanities International Index, Index to Black Periodicals, International Index to Black Periodicals Full Text, Modern Language Association International Bibliography, Social Sciences Citation Index, Sociological Abstracts.

Abafazi. See Gender Studies section.

240. *About Time.* [ISSN: 1060-3905] 1972. m. USD 15; USD 3 newsstand/cover per issue. Ed(s): Carolyne S Blount. About...Time Magazine Inc., 283 Genesee St, Rochester, NY 14611. Illus., adv. Sample. Circ: 28000. Vol. ends: Dec. *Indexed:* ENW. *Bk. rev.:* 1-2, 500-1,500 words. *Aud.:* Hs, Ga, Ac.

This magazine is an independent publication based in Rochester, New York, that has continuously published stories of interest to African Americans since 1972. Although it has a strong focus on the local Rochester area, it also provides excellent coverage of issues of national or international significance. Through personal stories, reports, images, and analysis, its double issue on Hurricane Katrina yielded a critical perspective differing from that of more mainstream magazines. Its feature stories cover a wide variety of topics including history, politics, literature, education, and family issues. Insightful commentary from political analyst and journalist Earl Ofari Hutchinson frequently appears. The magazine includes poetry and reviews of books, music, theatrical productions, feature films, and television documentaries. Recommended for all public libraries and high school libraries serving African American communities. A highly recommended title for public, academic, and high school libraries in the New York State area.

African-American Career World. See Ethnic Studies section.

241. *African American Pulpit.* [ISSN: 1094-0111] 1997. q. USD 54 USD 40 domestic. African American Pulpit, PO Box 381587, Germantown, TN 38183; info@theafricanamericanpulpit.com. Adv. Circ: 2450 Paid. *Indexed:* IIBP. *Bk. rev.:* 1, 500 words. *Aud.:* Ga, Ac, Sa.

Through sermons, essays, interviews, and other types of articles, *African American Pulpit* seeks to provide ministers with quality materials to assist them with sermon preparation. This quarterly journal also aims to preserve "the genius of the primarily oral African American preaching tradition" and highlight sermons written by outstanding African American preachers. Unlike the *Journal of Religious Thought,* which is academic in focus, this journal takes a more practical approach. Its attractive design and presentation have earned it an expanded readership, as well as an APEX Award for publication excellence. Issues are often thematic and are sometimes accompanied by a CD-ROM disc, since an audio format can present the art of black preaching in a way that the printed page cannot. This publication would be a welcome addition to public and academic library collections and is essential to theological libraries and church collections.

242. *African American Review.* Former titles (until 1992): *Black American Literature Forum;* (until 1976): *Negro American Literature Forum.* [ISSN: 1062-4783] 1967. q. USD 80 (Individuals, USD 40). Ed(s): Miss Aileen M Keenan, Dr. Jocelyn Moody. African American Review, Saint Louis University, Humanities 317, 3800 Lindell Blvd, St Louis, MO 63108. Illus., index. Sample. Refereed. Circ: 3770 Paid. Microform: PQC. Online: Chadwyck-Healey Inc.; EBSCO Publishing, EBSCO Host; Florida Center for Library Automation; Gale; JSTOR (Web-based Journal Archive); Northern Light Technology, Inc.; OCLC Online Computer Library Center, Inc.; ProQuest K-12 Learning Solutions; ProQuest LLC (Ann Arbor). *Indexed:* ABS&EES, AmH&L, AmHI, ArtHuCI, BEL&L, BRI, CBRI, FLI, HistAb, HumInd, IAPV, IBR, IBZ, IIBP, MASUSE, MLA-IB, RILM. *Bk. rev.:* Number and length vary. *Aud.:* Ga, Ac.

Published quarterly, *African American Review* is a peer-reviewed journal that features literary and cultural criticism, interviews, poetry, short fiction, and book reviews. As the official publication of the Modern Language Association's Division of Black American Literature and Culture, this well-established journal provides a venue for scholars and practitioners of the arts and humanities to engage in intellectual discourse. The topics and time periods covered are wide ranging and include the works of lesser-known writers (e.g., slave narratives) in addition to the works of literary giants such as Toni Morrison and James Baldwin. While the primary focus is on the work of African American writers, the journal also includes pieces on African and Caribbean literature. "Back Talk," an occasional column that was recently added, offers guest editorials designed to provoke and challenge readers. This is an important publication for libraries that support undergraduate or graduate programs in American literature, creative writing, or dramatic arts. General readers will also appreciate the literary and cultural analysis that the journal provides, so libraries serving African American communities will also want to have this in their collections.

African Americans on Wheels. See Automobiles and Motorcycles section.

Africana. See Ethnic Studies section.

Afro-American Historical and Genealogical Society. Journal. See Genealogy/International section.

Afro-Americans in New York Life and History. See Ethnic Studies section.

Afro-Hispanic Review. See Ethnic Studies section.

243. *American Legacy: celebrating African-American history and culture.* Formerly (until 1996): *Legacy (New York).* [ISSN: 1086-7201] 1995. q. USD 9.95 domestic; USD 15.95 foreign; USD 2.95 newsstand/cover. Ed(s): Audrey Peterson. American Heritage, 90 Fifth Ave, New York, NY 10011; http://www.americanheritage.com/amlegacy. Illus., adv. Sample. Circ: 86184 Paid. Vol. ends: Winter. *Indexed:* AmH&L, HistAb, IIBP, RILM. *Aud.:* Ems, Hs, Ga, Ac.

American Legacy is an attractive, beautifully illustrated quarterly devoted to African American history and culture. Jointly published by RJR Communications and *American Heritage,* the popular history magazine affiliated with Forbes, Inc., *American Legacy* offers photographs, artwork, historical essays, stories, and folklore about black life and culture in the United States. It also looks beyond American borders at black societies in other parts of the world, as illustrated by a recent issue whose cover story delved into African customs found in Bahia, Brazil. This magazine is a required title for all school and public libraries, and all African American collections.

Black Beat. See Music/Popular section.

244. *The Black Collegian.* [ISSN: 0192-3757] 1970. s-a. Individuals, USD 8; Students, USD 4. Ed(s): James Perry. Black Collegian, 140 Carondelet St., New Orleans, LA 70130; scott@black-collegian.com; http://www.black-collegian.com/. Illus., adv. Sample. Circ: 122000 Controlled. Microform: PQC. *Indexed:* IIBP, MASUSE. *Aud.:* Hs, Ac.

The Black Collegian magazine and its companion web site provide black college students and others with information on career planning, self-development, and job opportunities. Founded in 1970, the magazine publishes two issues per year: a first semester and second semester issue. Often a third, somewhat larger, special "graduation" issue is also released. *The Black Collegian* has developed a reputation for providing quality information on study programs abroad, graduate and professional schools, resume writing, career overviews, employer profiles, and other topics designed to assist students with their transition from college to work life. The second semester issue also includes several brief articles on African American historical topics. Its web site has a searchable job bank that students will appreciate. Recommended for college libraries. High schools serving African American communities might also consider purchasing this title.

245. *Black Enterprise.* [ISSN: 0006-4165] 1970. m. USD 22; USD 3.99 newsstand/cover. Ed(s): Alfred A Edmond, Derek Dingle. Earl G. Graves Publishing Co., Inc., 130 Fifth Ave, 10th Fl, New York, NY 10011-4399; hanks@blackenterprise.com. Illus., adv. Sample. Circ: 500000 Paid. Vol. ends: Jul. Microform: PQC. Online: Chadwyck-Healey Inc.; EBSCO Publishing, EBSCO Host; Florida Center for Library Automation; Gale; LexisNexis; Northern Light Technology, Inc.; OCLC Online Computer Library Center, Inc.; ProQuest K-12 Learning Solutions; ProQuest LLC (Ann Arbor); H.W. Wilson. *Indexed:* ABIn, ATI, BLI, BPI, BRI, CBRI, CWI, ENW, IIBP, LRI, MASUSE, PAIS, RGPR. *Bk. rev.:* 2-3, 250-500 words. *Aud.:* Hs, Ga, Ac.

A magazine "whose mission has always centered on closing the black wealth gap and financially empowering African Americans," *Black Enterprise* was established in 1970. A glossy magazine with abundant corporate advertising, it addresses the financial and business concerns of the African American community, especially consumers, employees, professionals, and entrepreneurs. Each issue includes several feature articles that fall into recurring categories, some of which are "Black Wealth Initiative," which presents a biographical profile, "Family Finances," "Money Management," "Business Opportunities," "Homeownership," "Consumer Life," and "Career Management." The magazine also offers shorter columns on news, health, technology, popular psychology, and travel and leisure. While *BE* is rich with information on personal finance and corporate success, you won't find much critical analysis of capitalism or discussion of alternative economic systems. The magazine's annual polls, surveys, interviews, and company profiles will interest high school and academic audiences. Highly recommended for public and academic libraries. High school libraries serving African American students will also want to consider this title.

246. *Black History Bulletin: a publication of the Association for the Study of African-American Life and History.* Formerly (until Jun. 2001): *Negro History Bulletin.* [ISSN: 1938-6656] 1937. s-a. USD 40 (Individuals, USD 16; USD 45 foreign). Ed(s): Tamara Brown, Ida Jones. Association for the Study of African-American Life and History, Inc., 7961 Eastern Ave, Ste 301, Silver Spring, MD 20910; asalh@earthlink.net; http://www.asalh.org. Illus., index, adv. Sample. Refereed. Circ: 22000. Microform: PMC; PQC. Online: Chadwyck-Healey Inc.; EBSCO Publishing, EBSCO Host; Gale; Northern Light Technology, Inc.; ProQuest K-12 Learning Solutions. *Indexed:* AmH&L, ArtHuCI, BRI, CBRI, FLI, HistAb, IIBP, LRI, MASUSE, NumL, RGPR, RILM. *Bk. rev.:* 2-3, 250-500 words. *Aud.:* Ems, Hs, Ga, Ac.

Established in 1937 at the urging of Mary McLeod Bethune, *Black History Bulletin* (formerly *Negro History Bulletin*) traditionally served two major purposes: It addressed the needs of primary and secondary educators, and it presented news of its parent organization, the Association for the Study of African-American Life and History. The *Bulletin* recently unveiled a significantly reformatted publication that sports an attractively redesigned cover and logo. The magazine also has streamlined its publication schedule and tightened its mission. Now a semi-annual, peer-reviewed journal, it focuses solely on "serving primary and secondary teachers charged with educating African American youth" and aims to publish articles that "reflect the pedagogical and theoretical trends in the field of education." It also intends to help students understand the relevance of history to their lives. The magazine continues to offer teacher reflections, lesson plans that address national social studies standards, and reproductions of primary documents that may be incorporated into the curriculum. Subscribers will welcome the attractive presentation and content of the new format. Recommended for school libraries of all levels, but it is a must for middle and high school libraries serving African American youth. Also recommended for libraries supporting college and university teacher training programs and public libraries serving African American communities.

Black Issues Book Review. See Books and Book Reviews section.

247. *Black Masks: spotlight on Black art.* [ISSN: 0887-7580] 1984. bi-m. USD 22. Ed(s): Beth Turner. Black Masks, 302A W. 12th St. #231, New York, NY 10014; blackmasksmagazine@yahoo.com; http://www.blackmasks.com/. Illus., adv. Sample. Circ: 1500 Paid. Vol. ends: May/Jun. *Indexed:* ENW. *Bk. rev.:* Various number and length. *Aud.:* Ga, Ac.

For more than 20 years, *Black Masks* has celebrated black theater by publishing "articles and papers on performing, literary or visual arts and artists of African descent." Initially this slender magazine of 16 pages focused primarily on the performing arts in the New York area, but throughout the years its coverage has extended to other states as well. Each issue includes several feature articles and an "Arts Hotline" section that contains notices of new books, televised events, and upcoming performances and exhibitions throughout the United States. The "Arts Hotline" is available online and may be dropped from future editions of the magazine. Recommended for libraries with strong theater and/or African American Studies collections.

248. *Black Music Research Journal.* [ISSN: 0276-3605] 1980. s-a. USD 50 combined subscription domestic print & online eds.; USD 60 combined subscription foreign print & online eds. Ed(s): Christopher Wilkinson. University of Illinois Press, 1325 S Oak St, Champaign, IL 61820-6903; journals@uillinois.edu; http://www.press.uillinois.edu. Illus., index, adv. Sample. Refereed. Circ: 808. *Indexed:* AmHI, ArtHuCI, HumInd, IBR, IBZ, IIBP, IIMP, MusicInd, RILM. *Aud.:* Ga, Ac.

This journal began in 1980 at Fisk University's Institute for Research in Black American Music. Since 1983, the journal has formed part of the Center for Black Music Research at Columbia College in Chicago. A scholarly journal published semi-annually, it includes articles about the philosophy, aesthetics, history, and criticism of black music. The journal seeks to promote an understanding of "the common roots of the music, musicians, and composers of the global African diaspora," and supports interdisciplinary scholarship on all genres of black music. In addition to articles on blues, jazz, gospel, rhythm and blues, and hip-hop, there are also pieces on opera and concert music, ring shouts, reggae, meringue, salsa, and other forms of traditional and contemporary Caribbean and African music. Many issues are devoted to a single theme, such as African American music of Appalachia. A required journal for college and research library collections supporting music or African American Studies programs. Public libraries serving black communities will also want to consider this title.

249. *Black Renaissance.* [ISSN: 1089-3148] 1996. 3x/yr. USD 75 (Individuals, USD 40). Ed(s): Quincy Troupe. New York University, Africana Studies Program, 269 Mercer St, Ste 601, New York, NY 10003-6687; http://www.nyu.edu/gsas/program/africana/index.html. Illus., adv. Vol. ends: Spring. Online: Chadwyck-Healey Inc.; Florida Center for Library Automation; Gale; ProQuest LLC (Ann Arbor). Reprint: PSC. *Indexed:* AltPI, AmHI, ENW, IIBP, RILM. *Bk. rev.:* Various number and length. *Aud.:* Ga, Ac.

Edited by the accomplished writer Quincy Troupe, *Black Renaissance/ Renaissance Noire* "invites Black genius to apply itself to the realities of the twenty-first century with uncompromised thought, generous and readable analysis, and commentary." It publishes essays, poetry, fiction, interviews, letters, book reviews, photography, and art that critically address contemporary issues facing black people throughout the world. Its large format is well suited for the photographs and other pieces of visual art that contribute to the richness of this publication. It has published some of the most important black thinkers, writers, and artists; a single recent issue features interviews with Derek Walcott, John Edgar Wideman, and Chinua Achebe; poetry by Ntozake Shange and Sapphire; letters of John A. Williams and Chester Himes; a photographic essay by Deborah Willis; and a portfolio by Jean-Michel Basquiat. Recommended for academic collections and larger public libraries.

250. *Black Scholar: journal of Black studies and research.* [ISSN: 0006-4246] 1969. q. USD 85 (Individuals, USD 30). Ed(s): Robert Chrisman. Black World Foundation, PO Box 2869, Oakland, CA 94609. Illus., index, adv. Sample. Refereed. Circ: 10000 Paid. Microform: MIM; PQC. Online: Chadwyck-Healey Inc.; EBSCO Publishing, EBSCO Host; Factiva, Inc.; Northern Light Technology, Inc.; OCLC Online

Computer Library Center, Inc.; ProQuest K-12 Learning Solutions; ProQuest LLC (Ann Arbor); H.W. Wilson. *Indexed:* AgeL, AltPI, AmH&L, AmHI, ArtHuCI, BRI, CBRI, HistAb, IIBP, LeftInd, MASUSE, PAIS, PSA, RI-1, RILM, SSCI, SWA, SWR&A, SociolAb. *Bk. rev.:* 2-3, 500-1,000 words. *Aud.:* Hs, Ga, Ac.

Founded in 1969 during the Black Studies movement, *Black Scholar* continues to serve as a place where "college intellectuals, street academicians, and movement leaders come to grips with the basic issues of black America." Each issue is thematic, and although African American concerns feature prominently, *Black Scholar* regularly publishes articles on black culture outside the United States. The breadth of the journal's coverage can be illustrated by recent issue topics that have included the faces of Cuban culture, the Bill Cosby debate, black politics and the lessons of Fannie Lou Hamer, and multicultural issues in the Americas. While it regularly publishes the works of senior scholars and well-known activists, *Black Scholar* also encourages "young, newly developing black writers and black students" to submit their work. Each issue includes several feature articles, book reviews, current book announcements, and a classified ad section listing employment opportunities in higher education. Recommended for academic and public library collections. High schools with a sizable African American student body will also want to consider this title.

251. *Blackgirl Magazine.* [ISSN: 1546-4504] 2002. q. USD 24. Blackgirl Magazine, PO Box 90729, Atlanta, GA 30364; editor@blackgirlmagazine.com; http://www.blackgirlmagazine.com/. *Aud.:* Ems, Hs, Ga.

Founded in 2002 by 13-year-old Kenya Jordana James, *Blackgirl Magazine* "focuses on promoting positive messages and imagery among African American teens, while offering insightful coverage of history, culture, lifestyle, and entertainment news from a unique perspective." James, who was named Black Enterprise's 2003 Teenpreneur of the Year, wanted to create a magazine that was both entertaining and empowering. Now issued as a quarterly, the magazine includes feature articles about music, culture, and history, short stories, poetry, and interviews with people such as Venus and Serena Williams and Kyla Pratt, as well as commentary from "elders" like Attorney Alton Maddox and Dr. Asa Hilliard. Recommended for public libraries, in addition to middle and high school libraries.

252. *C L A Journal.* [ISSN: 0007-8549] 1957. q. USD 40 domestic; USD 41.50 Canada; USD 45.50 elsewhere. Ed(s): Cason L Hill. College Language Association, 12138 Central Ave, Ste 576, Mitchellville, MD 20721-1932; http://www.clascholars.org/. Illus., index, adv. Sample. Refereed. Circ: 2500 Paid. *Indexed:* ABS&EES, AmHI, ArtHuCI, HumInd, IBR, IBZ, IIBP, MLA-IB. *Bk. rev.:* 3-6, 500-1,500 words. *Aud.:* Ac.

The College Language Association (CLA), founded in 1937 by a group of black scholars and educators, is an organization of college teachers of English and foreign languages. Since 1957, the association has published the *CLA Journal*, featuring scholarly research and reviews of books in the areas of language, literature, literary criticism, linguistics, and pedagogy. Since only those articles written by CLA members and subscribers are considered for publication, the journal reflects the research interests of the association. While most articles focus on African American literature, West Indian, Afro-Hispanic, and African literatures are also covered. Criticism of black francophone literature is also represented in *CLA Journal*. Although English is the predominant language, articles written in other languages have been published. The journal also includes association news, such as membership lists, publications by members, committee rosters, and conference announcements. Additionally, the journal includes job announcements. Recommended for academic library collections.

253. *Callaloo: a journal of African diaspora arts and letters.* [ISSN: 0161-2492] 1976. q. USD 140. Ed(s): Charles H Rowell. The Johns Hopkins University Press, 2715 N Charles St, Baltimore, MD 21218-4363; http://www.press.jhu.edu. Illus., index, adv. Refereed. Circ: 938. Vol. ends: Fall. Online: Chadwyck-Healey Inc.; EBSCO Publishing, EBSCO Host; Florida Center for Library Automation; Gale; JSTOR (Web-based Journal Archive); OCLC Online Computer Library Center, Inc.; OhioLINK; Project MUSE; ProQuest K-12 Learning Solutions;

ProQuest LLC (Ann Arbor); SwetsWise Online Content. Reprint: PSC. *Indexed:* AmH&L, AmHI, ArtHuCI, BRI, CBRI, HistAb, HumInd, IAPV, IBR, IBZ, IIBP, MLA-IB, RILM. *Aud.:* Ga, Ac.

Although it began in 1976 as a venue for Southern African American writers lacking publishing outlets, *Callaloo* now ranks among the premier black literary journals. In keeping with its name—callaloo is a stew served in Louisiana, Brazil, and the Caribbean—it offers an array of cultures and genres; issues include fiction, poetry, plays, critical essays, cultural studies, interviews, annotated bibliographies, visual art, and photography. The journal regularly features new and emerging writers, including participants of the Callaloo Creative Writing Workshops, a national retreat of fiction writers and poets. Operating on the principle that there is "infinite variety in Black Art," the journal is international in scope and publishes in French and Spanish in addition to English. Special thematic issues focusing on individual authors, regions, or genres, such as the one on "Jazz Poetics," have earned awards from major publishing associations. Required for academic libraries and recommended for public libraries.

254. ***Challenge (Atlanta): a journal of research on African American men.*** [ISSN: 1077-193X] 1990. s-a. USD 25 (Individuals, USD 10). Ed(s): Ida Rousseau Mukenge. Morehouse Research Institute, 830 Westview Dr, SW, Atlanta, GA 30314; http://www.morehouse.edu/. Illus. Sample. Refereed. Vol. ends: Dec. Online: Chadwyck-Healey Inc. *Indexed:* IIBP, SSA, SociolAb. *Aud.:* Ga, Ac.

An official publication of the interdisciplinary Morehouse Research Institute at Morehouse College, *Challenge* publishes scholarly articles "on any aspect of issues germane to African American life with particular emphasis on African American men." The journal recently revised both its editorial board and its format, and now publishes thematic issues that are devoted to a social, health, or political issue that disproportionately affects African American men. All articles, solicited and unsolicited, are subjected to a blind review process. Recommended for academic libraries supporting African American and/or public policy collections. Large urban public libraries may also want to acquire this title.

255. ***The Crisis.*** Former titles (until May-June 2003): *New Crisis;* (until 1996): *The Crisis.* [ISSN: 1559-1573] 1910. bi-m. USD 12. Ed(s): Victoria L. Valentine. Crisis Publishing Co., 7600 Georgia Ave NW, Ste 405, Washington, DC 20012. Illus., adv. Sample. Circ: 250000 Paid. Vol. ends: Nov/Dec. Microform: BHP; PQC. Online: Chadwyck-Healey Inc.; EBSCO Publishing, EBSCO Host; OCLC Online Computer Library Center, Inc.; ProQuest K-12 Learning Solutions. *Indexed:* AmH&L, AmHI, HistAb, IIBP, MASUSE, PAIS, RILM. *Bk. rev.:* 2-3, 200-500 words. *Aud.:* Ems, Hs, Ga, Ac.

Founded in 1910 by W.E.B. Du Bois, the eminent scholar and founding father of the National Association for the Advancement of Colored People (NAACP), *The Crisis* is one of the oldest continuously published African American periodicals in print. Through the years it has been a "crusading voice for civil rights" and a respected source of thought, opinion, and analysis on issues pertaining to African Americans. Although the magazine is legally a separate entity, it serves as the official publication of the NAACP; news of the organization, both national and local, can be found in the "NAACP Today" section. All other sections of the magazine, including feature stories, current news, music reviews, theater reviews, book reviews, and interviews, reflect the opinion of the individual authors and not the NAACP. Although its issues are slender (each issue is about 70 pages), the magazine's sparse advertising and concentrated focus on the educational, economic, political, and social aspects of race make it a very substantial publication. The magazine states that it is committed to "an integrated, nonviolent society that rejects all forms of racism, anti-Semitism, sexism, and homophobia." *The Crisis* is highly recommended for academic, school, and public libraries.

256. ***Diverse Issues in Higher Education.*** Formerly (until Aug. 2005): *Black Issues in Higher Education.* [ISSN: 1557-5411] 1984. bi-w. USD 20 domestic; USD 40 Canada; USD 50 elsewhere. Ed(s): Hilary Hurd Anyaso. Cox, Matthews & Associates, Inc., 10520 Warwick Ave, Ste B 8, Fairfax, VA 22030. Illus., index, adv. Sample. Circ: 200000. Vol. ends: Feb. *Indexed:* ABIn, ENW, ERIC, EduInd, HEA, IIBP. *Aud.:* Ac.

Since its founding in 1984 as *Black Issues in Higher Education, Diverse* has been the premier news magazine covering issues concerning people of color in higher education. As its variant titles suggest, initially its focus was primarily on African Americans, but in recent years it has expanded its scope to include Latino, Asian American, Native American, and other interests. Its coverage of African American concerns remains quite strong, however. Its attractive design, liberal use of color photographs, and clear writing make it a very readable publication. Each issue includes feature stories that run the gamut from general educational trends (e.g., podcasting) to issues affecting people of color, such as the fate of African American faculty displaced by Hurricane Katrina. The magazine also carries news of recent appointments, grant awards, upcoming conferences, and a very substantial section devoted to academic employment opportunities. Its special report on the top 100 institutions that graduate the most students of color is a welcome annual feature. This is a required title for academic libraries and is highly recommended for public and secondary school libraries serving diverse communities.

257. ***Drumvoices Revue: a confluence of literary, cultural and vision arts.*** [ISSN: 1080-0522] 1992. a. USD 10. Ed(s): Eugene B Redmond. Southern Illinois University at Edwardsville, English Department, PO Box 1431, Edwardsville, IL 62026; http://www.siue.edu/ENGLISH/about.html#drumvoice. Illus., adv. Sample. *Indexed:* AmHI, IAPV. *Aud.:* Ga, Ac.

Drumvoices Revue is a literary review produced and published by poet/playwright Eugene Redmond of the English Department at Southern Illinois University at Edwardsville. The magazine, published in collaboration with the Eugene B. Redmond Writers Club of East St. Louis, includes the poetry, prose, interviews, photographs, and commentary of young artists and scholars, as well as that of established writers. It pays tribute to the Black Arts Movement of the 1960s, and recent issues feature a unique African American poetic form, the "kwansaba," which relates to Kwanzaa and to the Arabic numeral seven ("saba" in Swahili). Academic libraries seeking to build comprehensive, multicultural literary collections will want to acquire this title. Large public libraries, especially those in the Midwest, may also want to consider it.

258. ***Du Bois Review: social science research on race.*** [ISSN: 1742-058X] 2003. 2x/yr. GBP 102. Ed(s): Michael Dawson, Lawrence Bobo. Cambridge University Press, The Edinburgh Bldg, Shaftesbury Rd, Cambridge, CB2 2RU, United Kingdom; journals@cambridge.org; http://www.journals.cambridge.org. Refereed. *Indexed:* IIBP, PAIS, PRA, PSA, SociolAb. *Bk. rev.:* Number and length vary. *Aud.:* Ga, Ac.

Bearing the name of the gifted scholar W.E.B. Du Bois, this new journal seeks to present "the best cutting-edge research on race" from the social sciences. The journal is edited by professors Lawrence D. Bobo (Stanford University) and Michael C. Dawson (University of Chicago) and is published by Cambridge University Press for the W.E.B. Du Bois Institute for African and African American Research at Harvard University. Its editorial board is comprised of eminent scholars drawn from many disciplines. *DBR* also intends to provide a forum for discussion of race issues from a range of disciplines, including economics, political science, sociology, anthropology, law, communications, public policy, psychology, and history. Each issue of *DBR* opens with introductory remarks from the editors that set the stage for three subsequent sections: "State of the Discipline," where invited essays and provocative think-pieces appear; "State of the Art," which features articles based on empirical research; and "State of the Discourse," which includes review essays on current scholarly books, controversies, and research threads. With exceptionally well-written articles, the *Du Bois Review* has made an impressive debut. Highly recommended for academic and large public libraries.

259. ***Ebony.*** Incorporates (1985-1998): *E M: Ebony Man;* (1970-1976): *Black World;* Which superseded (1950-1970): *Negro Digest.* [ISSN: 0012-9011] 1945. m. USD 22; USD 2.99 newsstand/cover. Ed(s): Lerone Bennett, Jr., Aldore Collier. Johnson Publishing Co., Inc., 820 S Michigan Ave, Chicago, IL 60605. Illus., adv. Sample. Circ: 1937000 Paid. Vol. ends: Oct. CD-ROM: ProQuest LLC (Ann Arbor). Microform: NBI; PQC. Online: EBSCO Publishing, EBSCO Host; Florida Center for Library Automation; Gale; LexisNexis; Northern Light Technology, Inc.;

OCLC Online Computer Library Center, Inc.; ProQuest K-12 Learning Solutions; ProQuest LLC (Ann Arbor); H.W. Wilson. *Indexed:* AmHI, BRI, CPerI, FLI, IBR, MASUSE, MLA-IB, MRD, RGPR, RILM. *Bk. rev.:* 9-12, 25-50 words. *Aud.:* Ems, Hs, Ga, Ac.

Founded by the late John H. Johnson in 1945, *Ebony* continues to be the most widely circulated magazine targeted to African American readers. Committed to publishing positive, uplifting images of black people, the magazine includes articles on successful individuals in entertainment, sports, politics, and religion. It also has regular features on relationships, parenting, personal finance, fashion, beauty, travel, cooking, and medical advice. It also has a section on new books and memorable photographs drawn from its extensive photo archives. In recent years, *Ebony* has made an effort to boost its appeal to younger readers who might be drawn to *Vibe, Upscale,* or one of the other relatively recent entries in the magazine market. A popular title that has been credited with "helping promote and record African-American culture and providing important outlets for a community that for too long was neglected by the mainstream media," *Ebony* is highly recommended for all high school, academic, and public libraries.

Essence. See Fashion and Lifestyle section.

Ethnic and Racial Studies. See Ethnic Studies section.

260. *Griot.* [ISSN: 0737-0873] 1981. s-a. USD 40 domestic; USD 50 foreign. Ed(s): Andrew Baskin. Southern Conference on African-American Studies, Inc., c/o Howard Jones, PO Box 330163, Houston, TX 77233-0163; http://www.scaasi.org. Illus., adv. Circ: 250. *Indexed:* IIBP, MLA-IB, RILM. *Bk. rev.:* 1-4, 500-1,000 words. *Aud.:* Ac.

The Griot is the official journal of the Southern Conference on African American Studies, an organization that, in 1979, brought together "all interested minds, regardless of color or creed, who were interested in interpreting and preserving African American history and culture, especially that which had originated in and/or affected the south." The journal publishes articles in the humanities that "further enhance knowledge of the African's (African, African-American, Caribbean) experience." Essays, criticism, poetry, and book reviews are also featured in the journal. Recommended for academic libraries seeking to build comprehensive Africana collections.

261. *Harvard Journal of African American Public Policy.* [ISSN: 1081-0463] 1989. a. USD 40 (Individuals, USD 20; Students, USD 10). Ed(s): Cynthia Martinez. Harvard University, John F. Kennedy School of Government, 79 John F Kennedy St, Cambridge, MA 02138; webmaster@ksgwww.harvard.edu; http://www.ksg.harvard.edu. Adv. Refereed. *Indexed:* PAIS. *Aud.:* Ac, Sa.

Published by graduate students at the John F. Kennedy School of Government at Harvard University, this journal examines the relationship between policy making and the African American experience. Founded in 1989, the scholarly journal aims to "educate and provide leadership that improves the quality of public policies affecting the African American community." With an executive editorial board comprised of distinguished scholars in the field of African American Studies, the journal has published works by leading policy makers, scholars, and political analysts. Its 2006 volume, titled "A Nation Exposed: Rebuilding African American Communities," centers on the redevelopment of the Gulf Coast area, and addresses general strategies of urban revitalization and rural development. This excellent title is highly recommended for academic libraries and public policy collections.

Heart & Soul. See Health and Fitness section.

262. *Homes of Color: the magazine of African-American living & style.* [ISSN: 1540-0034] 2002. bi-m. USD 22.50. Ed(s): Corriece Perkins Gwynn. Gwynn Group, 12138 Central Ave #303, Mitchellville, MD 20721. *Aud.:* Ga, Ac.

This attractive bimonthly magazine showcases upscale African American homes and highlights home furnishings and interior design, including art and collectibles that can be used to add an "ethnic touch" to home decor. The magazine also covers architecture, new home construction, home renovation, and do-it-yourself projects, as well as landscape architecture and gardening tips.

Named one of the Top 30 magazine launches for 2002, *Homes of Color* is highly recommended for public libraries serving African American communities. The generously illustrated feature stories on African American art and artists will make this glossy magazine a welcome addition to any library supporting African American art, art history, or interior design.

263. *Howard Journal of Communications.* [ISSN: 1064-6175] 1988. q. GBP 186 print & online eds. Ed(s): Carolyn A. Stroman. Taylor & Francis Inc., 325 Chestnut St, Ste 800, Philadelphia, PA 19016; orders@taylorandfrancis.com; http://www.taylorandfrancis.com. Illus., index, adv. Refereed. Vol. ends: Dec. Online: EBSCO Publishing, EBSCO Host; Gale; IngentaConnect; OCLC Online Computer Library Center, Inc.; SwetsWise Online Content. Reprint: PSC. *Indexed:* ABS&EES, BAS, CINAHL, CJA, CommAb, FLI, HRA, IIBP, IPSA, L&LBA, PRA, PSA, PsycInfo, SFSA, SSA, SWA, SociolAb, V&AA. *Aud.:* Ac.

The *Howard Journal of Communications* is a scholarly journal that examines the influence of ethnicity, gender, and culture on communication issues. The majority of the editorial staff is located at Howard University, a historically black college; the editorial board is highly diverse and located at major research institutions in the United States and abroad. While many of the articles focus on African Americans, the scope of this quarterly is highly multicultural. Recent articles include "An Examination of Acculturative Stress, Interpersonal Social Support, and Use of Online Ethnic Social Groups among Chinese International Students" and "Television and Perceived Peer Expectations of Body Size among African American Adolescent Girls." This title is highly recommended for academic libraries that support programs in communications, journalism, speech, gender studies, and multicultural studies.

Howard Law Journal. See Law section.

International Review of African American Art. See Art/Museum Publications section.

264. *Jet.* [ISSN: 0021-5996] 1951. w. USD 26 domestic; USD 41 foreign; USD 1.25 newsstand/cover domestic. Ed(s): Malcolm R West. Johnson Publishing Co., Inc., 820 S Michigan Ave, Chicago, IL 60605. Illus., adv. Sample. Circ: 952342 Paid. CD-ROM: ProQuest LLC (Ann Arbor). Microform: NBI; PQC. Online: EBSCO Publishing, EBSCO Host; Factiva, Inc.; Florida Center for Library Automation; Gale; LexisNexis; Northern Light Technology, Inc.; OCLC Online Computer Library Center, Inc.; ProQuest K-12 Learning Solutions; ProQuest LLC (Ann Arbor); H.W. Wilson. *Indexed:* LRI, MASUSE, RGPR. *Aud.:* Hs, Ga, Ac.

Founded in 1951 by the legendary African American publisher John H. Johnson, *Jet* remains the leading weekly African American newsmagazine. A sister publication to *Ebony, Jet* provides a cover story; national and international news items pertaining to black people living in the United States, Africa, and the Caribbean; sports and entertainment news; regular columns on health, education, labor, parenting, and fashion; "This Week in Black History"; the "Week's Best Photos"; obituaries and wedding announcements; and the "Jet Beauty of the Week." It also includes film and music reviews, top music sales, and a television schedule. Its small, portable format and short items make *Jet* a quick, easy way to keep up with what's happening in "the Black community." Although it is receiving stiff competition from web sites such as blackamericaweb.com and magazines such as *Sister 2 Sister, Jet* continues to be a required title for all libraries serving African Americans.

265. *Journal of African American History.* Formerly (until Jun. 2001): *Journal of Negro History.* [ISSN: 1548-1867] 1916. q. USD 75 (Individuals, USD 35; USD 15 newsstand/cover per issue). Ed(s): V. P. Franklin. Association for the Study of African-American Life and History, Inc., 7961 Eastern Ave, Ste 301, Silver Spring, MD 20910; asalh@earthlink.net. Illus., adv. Refereed. Microform: PQC. Online: Chadwyck-Healey Inc.; EBSCO Publishing, EBSCO Host; Gale; JSTOR (Web-based Journal Archive). *Indexed:* AmH&L, AmHI, ArtHuCI, BRD, BRI, CBRI, HistAb, HumInd, IBR, IIBP, MLA-IB, NumL, RI-1. *Bk. rev.:* Number and length vary. *Aud.:* Hs, Ac, Sa.

Founded in 1916 as the *Journal of Negro History* by Carter G. Woodson, this is the premier journal in the field of African American history. Published by the Association for the Study of African American Life and History, the founders of Black History Month, this peer-reviewed quarterly includes scholarly articles on all aspects of African American history. The journal often releases special thematic issues; recent ones include "African Americans and the History of Sport," "Brown v. Board of Education, 1954–2004," and "Hip Hop in History." Also included are book reviews, memorial tributes, announcements, and publishers' advertisements. This is an essential title for libraries supporting black history programs, and is highly recommended for all academic and research libraries.

266. *Journal of African American Studies.* Former titles (until 2003): *Journal of African American Men;* (until 1995): *Journal of African American Male Studies.* [ISSN: 1559-1646] 1993. q. EUR 277 print & online eds. Springer New York LLC, 233 Spring St, New York, NY 10013-1578; journals@springer-ny.com; http://www.springer.com. Illus., adv. Sample. Refereed. Circ: 400. Vol. ends: Aug. Online: Chadwyck-Healey Inc.; EBSCO Publishing, EBSCO Host; Florida Center for Library Automation; Gale; OCLC Online Computer Library Center, Inc. Reprint: PSC. *Indexed:* AmHI, CJA, HEA, IIBP, SSA, SociolAb. *Bk. rev.:* Number and length vary. *Aud.:* Ac.

Formerly the *Journal of African American Men,* the *Journal of African American Studies* is a peer-reviewed quarterly that publishes theoretical and empirical articles on issues affecting persons, both male and female, of African descent. Although multidisciplinary in scope, the journal's content is largely sociological, and research dealing with gender or identity is especially strong. Published by Transaction Periodicals Consortium and edited at the University of Wisconsin–Milwaukee, the journal also includes scholarly book reviews. An important title for academic libraries, especially those supporting strong sociology and gender studies programs.

Journal of Black Psychology. See Ethnic Studies section.

Journal of Black Studies. See Ethnic Studies section.

267. *Journal of Blacks in Higher Education.* [ISSN: 1077-3711] 1993. q. USD 36. Ed(s): Robert Slater, Theodore Cross. The J B H E Foundation, Inc., 200 W 57th St, 15th Fl, New York, NY 10019. Illus., adv. Sample. Circ: 2500 Paid. Online: Chadwyck-Healey Inc.; JSTOR (Web-based Journal Archive); Northern Light Technology, Inc.; ProQuest LLC (Ann Arbor). *Indexed:* ArtHuCI, ENW, HEA, IIBP, PAIS, SSCI. *Bk. rev.:* Number and length vary. *Aud.:* Ac.

The *Journal of Blacks in Higher Education* is a scholarly publication whose purpose is "simply to show major racial imbalances and leave competitive markets and other nonlegislative forces to operate on the information provided." While the journal regularly runs feature articles addressing the history and current state of African Americans in higher education, the real strength of this publication lies in the wealth of statistical data that it regularly presents. Data from myriad sources—federal and state governments, colleges and universities, and other private institutions—grace each issue of the journal. Rankings, charts, and graphs covering everything from enrollments and educational attainment, to academic success in the professions, to most-frequently cited authors can be found here. Its "Vital Signs" feature reports statistics on the relative standing of blacks to whites in American society. The journal also regularly includes letters, news and views, book reviews, abstracts of new research, race relations on campus, appointments, tenure decisions and promotions, minority-related grants, and notable honors and awards. Highly recommended for academic libraries.

Journal of Health Care for the Poor and Underserved. See Medicine section.

268. *Journal of Multicultural Counseling and Development.* Formerly (until 1985): *Journal of Non-White Concerns in Personnel and Guidance.* [ISSN: 0883-8534] 1972. q. USD 80. Ed(s): Gargi Roysircar. American Counseling Association, 5999 Stevenson Ave, Alexandria, VA 22304-3300; http://www.counseling.org. Illus., adv. Refereed. Circ: 2900.

Vol. ends: Oct. Microform: PQC. Online: Chadwyck-Healey Inc.; EBSCO Publishing, EBSCO Host; Florida Center for Library Automation; Gale; OCLC Online Computer Library Center, Inc.; ProQuest LLC (Ann Arbor); H.W. Wilson. Reprint: PSC. *Indexed:* ABIn, ERIC, EduInd, HEA, IIBP, PsycInfo, SFSA, SSCI, SWR&A. *Bk. rev.:* Occasional. *Aud.:* Ac.

This journal is published by the Association for Multicultural Counseling and Development, a division of the American Counseling Association. Each issue includes four or five articles, and occasionally a book review, pertaining to multicultural and ethnic minority interests in all areas of counseling and human development. With a special focus on racial and ethnic issues in the United States, the journal accepts articles based on research, theoretical works, and reports on practical applications. Native American, Latino/a, Asian American, and African American concerns seem to get equal attention in this publication. Academic libraries supporting counseling, human resource management, psychology, social work, or ethnic studies programs will want to consider acquiring this title.

269. *Journal of Negro Education: a Howard University quarterly review of issues incident to the education of black people.* [ISSN: 0022-2984] 1932. q. USD 125 (Individuals, USD 65). Ed(s): Frederick D Harper, R C Saravanabhavan. Howard University Press, Marketing Department, 2600 Sixth St, NW, Washington, DC 20059. Illus., index, adv. Sample. Refereed. Circ: 2300 Paid. Vol. ends: Fall. Microform: MIM; PMC; PQC. Online: Chadwyck-Healey Inc.; JSTOR (Web-based Journal Archive); Northern Light Technology, Inc.; OCLC Online Computer Library Center, Inc.; ProQuest K-12 Learning Solutions; ProQuest LLC (Ann Arbor). Reprint: PSC. *Indexed:* ABIn, AgeL, AmH&L, BRI, CBRI, EAA, ECER, ERIC, EduInd, HEA, HistAb, IBR, IIBP, IMFL, L&LBA, PAIS, PhilInd, PsycInfo, RILM, SFSA, SSA, SSCI, SWR&A, SociolAb. *Bk. rev.:* 4-6, 1,000-2,500 words. *Aud.:* Ac.

The *Journal of Negro Education,* now celebrating its 75th year of publication, has long been a major source of scholarship on every aspect of black education. In addition to publishing on professional education, this peer-reviewed journal also encompasses the social sciences, the physical and natural sciences, the arts, and technology. JNE has published an interesting array of special issues on topics as diverse as "Black Women in the Academy," "African American Children with Special Needs," and "Juvenile Justice: Children of Color in the U.S." Although the journal aims to address educational issues pertaining to black people throughout the world, its contents focus primarily on African Americans. Special features include book and media reviews, news, and announcements. A core title for academic libraries, especially those supporting education programs.

270. *Journal of Pan African Studies: an international medium of African culture and consciousness.* [ISSN: 0888-6601] 1987. q. Ed(s): Itibari M Zulu. Journal of Pan African Studies, 10920 Wilshire Blvd, Ste 150-9132, Los Angeles, CA 90024-9132. Adv. Refereed. *Bk. rev.:* Number and length vary. *Aud.:* Ga, Ac.

The online, scholarly *Journal of Pan African Studies* publishes interdisciplinary, peer-reviewed articles and creative work on a wide range of topics pertaining to African peoples throughout the world. Resurrected after a long hiatus, the journal aims to include works that "ask questions and seek answers to critical contemporary issues, based on an affirmative African centered logic and language of liberation." JPAS is a unit of the Amen-Ra Theological Seminary Press and a subsidiary of the nonprofit Amen-Ra Community Assembly of California; it maintains an association with its first organizational publisher, the California Institute of Pan African Studies. Sporting an attractively designed interface and strong academic content, the journal has an impressive editorial board comprised of librarians, university faculty, independent scholars, and publishers. Recommended for academic libraries supporting Africana programs and public libraries serving black communities. URL: www.jpanafrican.com.

271. *The Journal of Race and Policy.* [ISSN: 1540-8450] 2005. a. Ed(s): Michael L. Clemons. Old Dominion University, Institute for the Study of Race and Ethnicity, 317 Batten Arts and Letters Bldg., Norfolk, VA 23529. *Aud.:* Ac, Sa.

Founded in 2005 by the Institute for the Study of Race and Ethnicity at Old Dominion University, the *Journal of Race and Policy* is an interdisciplinary journal published annually that includes research focusing on the interplay of race, ethnicity, and public policy. Although the inaugural issue focused on African Americans and had as its theme "Evolving Considerations of Race: African Americans in the Post-Brown Era," future issues will address other ethnic groups. *JRP* also publishes articles pertaining to race in the Commonwealth of Virginia, especially the Hampton Roads region. The journal's initial offering displays a commitment to presenting a variety of disciplines, approaches, and methodologies, and includes an excellent, commissioned article by Adolph Reed Jr. (University of Pennsylvania) on "Making Sense of Race, I: The Ideology of Race, the Biology of Human Variation, and the Problem of Medical and Public Health Research." Recommended for academic libraries supporting African American Studies, ethnic studies, and public policy programs. Collections documenting the South will also want to consider this title.

272. The Journal of Religious Thought. [ISSN: 0022-4235] 1943. s-a. USD 20 (Individuals, USD 18). Ed(s): Cain Hope Felder. Howard University, School of Divinity, 1400 Shepherd St, NE, Washington, DC 20017; cjnewsome@howard.edu; http://www.howard.edu/divinity/. Illus., adv. Refereed. Circ: 1500. Microform: PQC. Online: Chadwyck-Healey Inc.; EBSCO Publishing, EBSCO Host; Northern Light Technology, Inc.; OCLC Online Computer Library Center, Inc.; ProQuest LLC (Ann Arbor). *Indexed:* AbAn, AmH&L, AmHI, BAS, FR, HistAb, HumInd, IBR, IBZ, IIBP, NTA, PhilInd, R&TA, RI-1, RILM. *Bk. rev.:* 2-3, 250-1,500 words. *Aud.:* Ac, Sa.

The *Journal of Religious Thought* was established in 1943 by the faculty of the Howard University School of Divinity. This academic journal's mission is to "advance knowledge and share the results of scholarship in the field of religion generally, with special attention to the issues that variously pertain to ministry of the black church and related aspects of the black religious experience." In addition to feature articles, the journal includes book reviews, review essays, and a listing of books received for review. A special feature of the journal is its "Pastor's Corner," which is comprised of shorter pieces—poems, speeches, sermons, and other inspirational writings—that are aimed at people working in local religious settings. Libraries supporting seminaries, religious studies, African Studies, and Africana Studies programs will want to acquire this journal, as will black church libraries.

Just for Black Men. See Fashion and Lifestyle section.

273. Literary Griot: international journal of Black expressive culture studies. [ISSN: 1053-9344] 1988. s-a. USD 20 (Individuals, USD 15). Ed(s): Ousseynou B. Traore. Literary Griot, 300 Pompton Rd., Wayne, NJ 07470. Illus. Refereed. *Indexed:* MLA-IB, RILM. *Bk. rev.:* 2-3, 500-1,000 words. *Aud.:* Ac.

The *Literary Griot* is a scholarly journal associated with the African, African-American and Caribbean Studies Department of the William Paterson University. Edited by Dr. Ousseynou B. Traore, the journal has traditionally published critical and theoretical articles on the literatures, oral traditions, and other expressive arts of Africa, the Americas, the Caribbean, and elsewhere. Written primarily in English but also in French and various African languages, the *Literary Griot* publishes essays, scholarly articles, and book reviews. Initially a semi-annual publication, the journal appears to be on hiatus and its future is uncertain. Academic libraries seeking to build comprehensive black literary collections will want to consider this title.

Living Blues. See Music/Popular section.

Meridians. See Gender Studies section.

National Black Law Journal. See Law section.

National Medical Association. Journal. See Medicine section.

274. Negro Educational Review: a forum for discussion of Afro-American issues. [ISSN: 0548-1457] 1950. q. USD 30. Ed(s): Mac A Stewart. Negro Educational Review, Inc., School of Education, North Carolina A & T State University, Greensboro, NC 27411. Illus., index, adv. Sample. Refereed. Circ: 1000. Vol. ends: Oct. *Indexed:* ABIn, EduInd, HEA, IIBP. *Bk. rev.:* 1-2, 500-1,500 words. *Aud.:* Ac.

For more than 55 years, the *Negro Educational Review* has been a premier journal for faculty at historically black colleges and universities (HBCUs). This refereed quarterly, which recently relocated from Florida A & M University to North Carolina A & T University, publishes articles pertaining to issues related to "Black experiences throughout the African Diaspora." While its title suggests that its focus is solely on education, it actually covers the full spectrum of scholarship and includes articles on the social and behavioral sciences, the biological and physical sciences, and the humanities, as well as on professional education. For example, a recent issue includes articles on "The Impact of Cultural Behaviours, Local Beliefs, and Practices on Emerging Parasitic Diseases in Tropical Africa," "Investigating Environmental Concerns and Health Issues in Clarksville, Tennessee," and "Social Orientations at Home and at School: Gender Differences in Black Children's Perceptions and Preferences." In addition to scholarly articles, the journal also features book reviews, news reports, and announcements. Recommended for academic libraries and large public libraries serving black communities.

275. The Network Journal: black professional and small business magazine. [ISSN: 1094-1908] 1993. m. USD 15; USD 2.95 newsstand/cover per issue. Ed(s): Rosalind McLymont. Network Journal, 39 Braodway Ste 2120, New York, NY 10006; http://www.tnj.com. Illus., adv. Circ: 35000. Online: ProQuest LLC (Ann Arbor). *Indexed:* ENW. *Bk. rev.:* Various number and length. *Aud.:* Ga, Sa.

Beginning as a black-and-white tabloid newspaper in 1993, *The Network Journal* is now a full-color, glossy trade magazine with a robust readership. Targeted to African American professionals, business owners, and "upwardly mobile individuals," the monthly magazine presents feature articles designed to provide readers with innovative business ideas and techniques, inspirational stories, and information regarding legal matters, marketing, office technology, and taxation. While *The Network Journal* occasionally prints items regarding personal finance and consumer news, this type of information is far more abundant in *Black Enterprise*. Other features include book reviews and announcements of upcoming seminars and events. The magazine also sponsors the annual "40-Under-Forty Awards," which highlights 40 people for career excellence, and the "25 Influential Black Women in Business Awards." A useful publication for most public libraries and business collections.

276. The North Star (Poughkeepsie): a journal of African American religious history. [ISSN: 1094-902X] 1997. s-a. Free. Ed(s): Yolanda Pierce, Anthea Butler. North Star (Poughkeepsie), c/o Vassar College, Dept. of Religion, 124 Raymond Ave, Poughkeepsie, NY 12604; northstar@vassar.edu. Illus. Refereed. *Indexed:* AmH&L, HistAb. *Bk. rev.:* Various number and length. *Aud.:* Ga, Ac.

Published exclusively online, *North Star* is supported by the University of Kentucky in association with the Afro-American Religious History group of the American Academy of Religion. The journal publishes peer-reviewed articles based on historical research that explore the religious cultures of African Americans, although work from other disciplines is also considered. *North Star* also includes comparative studies of religious cultures in Africa and elsewhere in the African diaspora. Work from junior scholars and graduate students is encouraged. In addition to featured articles, each issue includes book reviews, events, and new publications, research collections, and Internet resources. URL: http://northstar.as.uky.edu.

277. Obsidian 3: Literature in the African Diaspora. Former titles (until 1999): *Obsidian 2: Black Literature in Review;* (until 1982): *Obsidian: Black Literature in Review.* [ISSN: 1542-1619] 1975. s-a. USD 28 (Individuals, USD 22). Ed(s): Thomas Lisk. North Carolina State University, English Department, PO Box 8105, Raleigh, NC 27695-8105; krsassan@unity.ncsu.edu; http://www2.ncsu.edu/ncsu/chass/obsidian.html.

Illus., adv. Refereed. Circ: 500 Paid. Microform: PQC. Online: Chadwyck-Healey Inc.; EBSCO Publishing, EBSCO Host. *Indexed:* AmHI, ArtHuCI, IAPV, IIBP, MLA-IB. *Bk. rev.:* Various number and length. *Aud.:* Ga, Ac.

This semi-annual literary review publishes contemporary poetry, fiction, drama, and nonfiction prose "from within and concerning the African Diaspora." Hosted for many years by the English Department of North Carolina State University, *Obsidian III* is currently being edited by Thomas Lisk. The journal seeks to support both new and established writers and displays an appreciation of the range and quality of writing by black authors. Scholarly critical studies have been added to the journal and often contribute to an issue's special theme, e.g., a celebration of the life and works of Jay Wright. Book reviews are also included. *Obsidian III* is recommended for academic libraries, especially those supporting creative writing and Black Studies programs. Large public libraries will also want to consider acquiring this excellent literary journal.

278. *Race & Class: a journal of racism, empire and globalisation.*
Formerly (until 1974): *Race.* [ISSN: 0306-3968] 1959. q. GBP 210. Ed(s): Hazel Waters, A Sivanandan. Sage Publications Ltd., 1 Oliver's Yard, 55 City Rd, London, EC1 1SP, United Kingdom; info@sagepub.co.uk; http://www.sagepub.co.uk. Adv. Refereed. Circ: 5000. Online: CSA; EBSCO Publishing, EBSCO Host; Florida Center for Library Automation; Gale; HighWire Press; OCLC Online Computer Library Center, Inc.; OhioLINK; SAGE Publications, Inc., SAGE Journals Online; SwetsWise Online Content; H.W. Wilson. Reprint: PSC. *Indexed:* AICP, AbAn, AltPI, AmH&L, AmHI, BAS, BrHumI, CJA, FR, ForAb, HistAb, IBR, IBSS, IBZ, IIBP, IPSA, LeftInd, PAIS, PRA, PSA, RI-1, RiskAb, SSA, SSCI, SUSA, SociolAb. *Bk. rev.:* Various number and length. *Aud.:* Ac.

Race & Class is a quarterly British journal that is international in scope and examines racism, class bias, and imperialism in contemporary society and historically. Formerly titled *Race*, the journal was established in 1959 by the Institute of Race Relations, a nonprofit organization known for cutting-edge "research and analysis that informs the struggle for racial justice in Britain and internationally." It has an international editorial board that includes African American scholars, and it regularly publishes articles about African American history and life. Its research articles, commentaries, and book reviews are scholarly, incisive, and usually far left of center. Contributors include academics, scientists, artists, novelists, journalists, and politicians. A recent special issue titled "Cedric Robinson and the Philosophy of Black Resistance" focuses on Robinson's studies of black Marxism. This title is highly recommended for academic libraries.

Race, Gender & Class. See Interdisciplinary Studies section.

The Review of Black Political Economy. See Labor and Industrial Relations section.

Right On! See Teenagers section.

279. *Sister 2 Sister: giving it to ya' straight, no chaser!* [ISSN: 1071-5053] 1988. m. USD 14.99; USD 2.99 newsstand/cover. Ed(s): Lorenzo Brown. Sister 2 Sister, Inc., PO Box 41148, Washington, DC 20018-0548. Illus., adv. Sample. Circ: 85000 Paid. Vol. ends: Dec. *Bk. rev.:* 1, 250 words. *Aud.:* Ga.

Begun in 1988 as an eight-page newsletter targeted at prominent black women in the entertainment and music industries, *Sister 2 Sister* has become a popular source of black celebrity news. Jamie Foster Brown, the magazine's founder and publisher, begins each issue with "Meow: Warm Whispers and Hot Secrets," a lengthy log of her latest findings written in a breezy, conversational style. In addition to the hottest news on African American movie, music, sports, and entertainment stars, the magazine also has regular columns on health and fitness, fashion and beauty, popular psychology, home improvement, and automobiles. Readers will also appreciate the biographical profiles of successful women in the entertainment industry, as well as the lengthy transcripts of interviews published in each issue. Each issue also includes music, television, and film reviews. Highly recommended for public libraries serving African American communities.

280. *Slavery and Abolition: a journal of slave and post-slave studies.*
[ISSN: 0144-039X] 1980. 3x/yr. GBP 323 print & online eds. Ed(s): Gad Heuman. Routledge, 4 Park Sq, Milton Park, Abingdon, OX14 4RN, United Kingdom; journals@routledge.com; http://www.routledge.co.uk. Illus., index, adv. Sample. Refereed. Vol. ends: Dec. Microform: PQC. Online: EBSCO Publishing, EBSCO Host; Gale; IngentaConnect; SwetsWise Online Content. Reprint: PSC. *Indexed:* AmH&L, AmHI, BrHumI, HistAb, IBR, IBZ, IIBP, PSA, SSA, SociolAb. *Bk. rev.:* 9-15+, 500-1,000 words. *Aud.:* Ac.

Slavery and Abolition is a refereed journal devoted to the study of slavery from the ancient period to the present; it also examines issues relating to the dismantling of slavery and to slavery's legacy. The journal provides perspectives on this sensitive and often controversial topic from a variety of disciplines including history, anthropology, sociology, and literature. Although readers will encounter articles on bondage in ancient Greece or in early Asian history, the bulk of the scholarship focuses on the transatlantic slave trade that brought enslaved Africans to Latin America, the Caribbean, and North America. In addition to special thematic issues, the journal provides an important bibliographical supplement on slavery compiled by Joseph C. Miller and Fred K. Drogula that updates their published bibliography, "Slavery and Slaving in World History." Book reviews and review articles are also included. *Slavery and Abolition* is highly recommended for academic libraries.

281. *Souls: a critical journal of Black politics, culture, and society.*
[ISSN: 1099-9949] 1999. q. GBP 120 print & online eds. Ed(s): Dr. Manning Marable. Taylor & Francis Inc., 325 Chestnut St, Ste 800, Philadelphia, PA 19016; orders@taylorandfrancis.com; http://www.taylorandfrancis.com. Online: EBSCO Publishing, EBSCO Host; Gale; IngentaConnect; OCLC Online Computer Library Center, Inc.; SwetsWise Online Content. Reprint: PSC. *Indexed:* AltPI, AmH&L, HistAb, IIBP, PSA, SociolAb. *Bk. rev.:* 1, 1,000-2,000 words. *Aud.:* Ga, Ac.

Souls is an interdisciplinary quarterly journal that is "produced in the spirit of the intellectual activism of W. E. B. Du Bois" and seeks to present "creative and challenging interpretations of the key issues now being confronted by scholars of modern Black America, Africa, and the Caribbean." Established in 1999, the journal is edited by activist scholar Manning Marable and is sponsored by the Center for Contemporary Black History, the research unit of the Institute for Research in African-American Studies at Columbia University. *Souls* brings together intellectual thought from within and without academe to critically examine black history, politics, socioeconomic research, social theory, and culture. It concentrates on the post-1945 period that witnessed anticolonial movements throughout Africa and the Caribbean, and the civil rights and Black Power movements within the United States. Beginning with a substantive quotation from Du Bois that sets the stage for the following pages, each issue focuses on a central theme that links the six or more feature articles. Most issues also include a "First Person" section that consists of an in-depth interview. Readers will appreciate both the attractive presentation and the hard-hitting analysis provided by this journal. Highly recommended for academic libraries and for large public libraries, especially those with Black Studies collections.

282. *The Source (New York, 1988): the magazine of hip-hop music, culture & politics.* [ISSN: 1063-2085] 1988. m. USD 19.95 domestic; USD 65.95 foreign. Ed(s): Carlito Rodriguez. Source Publications, 28 W. 23rd St., New York, NY 10010-5204. Illus. Circ: 370700 Paid. *Indexed:* IIMP, IIPA. *Aud.:* Ga, Ac.

Founded initially as a newsletter in 1988 by two Harvard University students, *The Source* is now one of the leading hip-hop magazines on the market. Once considered the "hip-hop bible," the magazine covers all aspects of the hip-hop music industry and includes musician interviews, feature stories, and concert and recording reviews. Although music is the heart of this publication, it also includes general news and current events, political commentary, and sports items. Recommended for urban public libraries serving 18- to 24-year-old populations. Also recommended for libraries with strong popular music collections.

Today's Black Woman. See Fashion and Lifestyle section.

283. Trotter Review. Formerly (until 1992): *Trotter Institute Review.* [ISSN: 1070-695X] 1987. a. USD 30 (Individuals, USD 15). Ed(s): Dr. Barbara Lewis. William Monroe Trotter Institute, 10th Fl, Healey Library, University of Massachusetts Boston, Boston, MA 02125-3393. Adv. Circ: 2500. *Aud.:* Ac, Sa.

An annual publication of the William Monroe Trotter Institute of the University of Massachusetts–Boston, the *Trotter Review* publishes articles addressing race and race relations in the United States and abroad. The journal's strong public policy content reflects the service orientation of its parent institution, the Trotter Institute, which was founded in 1984 to provide research, technical assistance, and public service to the black community and other communities of color in Boston and Massachusetts. Published since 1987, the journal's issues have a thematic approach; recent issues cover "Homosexuality and the Black Community," "Religion and Civil Society," and "Affirmative Action." Academic libraries supporting urban affairs, public policy, and African American Studies programs will want to consider this title.

284. Upscale: for the affluent lifestyle. [ISSN: 1047-2592] 1989. 9x/yr. USD 20.25. Ed(s): Sheila Bronner. Upscale Communications, Inc., 2141 Powers Ferry Rd, Marietta, GA 30067. Illus., adv. Sample. Circ: 250000 Paid. *Bk. rev.:* Various number and length. *Aud.:* Ga, Ac.

Upscale, a glossy, full-color publication, describes itself as "the ultimate lifestyle magazine that addresses the needs of the most stylish and educated African-American." It aims to keep "savvy, trendy and successful African-Americans" informed and entertained as well as enlightened and encouraged. Somewhat similar in scope to *Ebony,* the magazine regularly presents feature articles on up-and-coming people in entertainment and business; current events; fashion, beauty and style; relationships; health and fitness; interior design and the arts; and travel. *Upscale* also includes reviews of books, films, music, and restaurants. Although it reflects a Southern orientation, the magazine clearly has a national reach. Recommended for public libraries serving African American communities, especially those located in urban and suburban areas.

Venus Magazine. See Gay, Lesbian, Bisexual, and Transgender section.

285. Vibe. [ISSN: 1070-4701] 1993. m. USD 11.95 domestic; USD 24 Canada; USD 40 elsewhere. Vibe / Spin Ventures, 205 Lexington Ave, 6th Fl, New York, NY 10016; http://www.vibe.com. Illus., adv. Sample. Circ: 862933 Paid. *Indexed:* ASIP, IIMP, IIPA, MusicInd, RGPR. *Aud.:* Ga, Ac.

Founded in 1993 by famed record producer Quincy Jones, *Vibe* is one of the most popular African American magazines currently on the market. A lifestyle magazine that conveys the contemporary urban scene, *Vibe* highlights hip-hop culture, including not only the music and musicians but also the fashion industry that has grown up around rap and hip-hop. The magazine features celebrity interviews, and it covers *and creates* trends and events in music, fashion, and art. It is a well-photographed, well-designed publication that attracts considerable advertising. Urban public libraries serving an 18- to 24-year-old population will want to have this title. Also, libraries with strong fashion and/or popular music collections should consider it.

286. Vibe Vixen. [ISSN: 1556-2581] 2005. q. USD 9.95 domestic; USD 20 foreign; USD 3.99 newsstand/cover per issue. Vibe / Spin Ventures, 205 Lexington Ave, 6th Fl, New York, NY 10016. Illus., adv. Circ: 380000. *Indexed:* ASIP, IIMP, IIPA, MusicInd, RGPR. *Aud.:* Hs, Ga.

Begun in 2005 as a spin-off of *Vibe,* the highly popular urban magazine, *Vibe Vixen* is a beauty and fashion magazine targeted at the urban woman, or as one newspaper declared, "for fashionistas who worship hip-hop chic." A sleek, quarterly magazine, *Vibe Vixen* features interviews with women in the entertainment and fashion industry, and provides extensive coverage of cutting-edge fashion and the latest trends in beauty, makeup, and hair. The magazine also includes commentary and profiles new technologies available for purchase. Targeted to twenty-something women, this magazine is recommended for urban public libraries, especially those serving African American and Latino communities.

287. Vital Issues: the journal of African American speeches. [ISSN: 1056-6368] 1950. q. USD 49. Ed(s): Teta V Banks. Bethune - DuBois Institute, 8484 Georgia Ave, Ste 420, Silver Spring, MD 20910; info@bethune-dubois.org; http://www.bethune-dubois.org. Illus., index, adv. Sample. Circ: 5000. *Indexed:* IIBP, PAIS. *Aud.:* Ga, Ac, Sa.

Vital Issues is a unique journal whose mission is to document the strong oratorical tradition of African Americans. Published by the Bethune-DuBois Institute, which was founded by the late Pennsylvania Secretary of State C. Delores Tucker, the journal aims to achieve its objective by publishing "major speeches of African American professional leaders" so as "to preserve their spirit and voices for all generations to come." During the past decade, it has published the complete text of nearly 400 speeches by African Americans working in politics, civil and human rights, education, labor, law, health care, and religion. Occasionally, speeches addressing African Americans but not written or delivered by African Americans are included, such as one by Senator Hillary Rodham Clinton. The journal provides valuable primary source material for students, scholars, and policy makers as well as general readers. Recommended for academic and public libraries, and for special libraries and information bureaus serving federal and state legislative bodies.

288. The Western Journal of Black Studies. [ISSN: 0197-4327] 1977. q. USD 90 (Individuals, USD 30). Ed(s): Lincoln James. Washington State University Press, PO Box 645910, Pullman, WA 99164-5910; grunewan@wsu.edu; http://www.wsu.edu/~wjbs/. Illus., index. Refereed. Circ: 650. Vol. ends: Winter. Online: Chadwyck-Healey Inc.; EBSCO Publishing, EBSCO Host; Florida Center for Library Automation; Gale; Northern Light Technology, Inc.; ProQuest K-12 Learning Solutions; ProQuest LLC (Ann Arbor). *Indexed:* AmH&L, AmHI, CJA, HistAb, IIBP, L&LBA, PSA, PsycInfo, RILM, SSA, SWR&A, SociolAb. *Bk. rev.:* 1, 1,000-2,500 words. *Aud.:* Ac.

Founded in 1977, the *Western Journal of Black Studies* is an interdisciplinary journal that publishes scholarly articles on "issues related to the African Diaspora and experiences of African/African Americans in the United States." Sponsored by Washington State University, the journal has an editorial board comprised of distinguished scholars from throughout the United States who are working primarily in the social sciences and humanities. All articles are subjected to blind peer review. Each issue includes about five feature articles and several scholarly book reviews. The journal has received the C. L. R. James Award for scholarly publication in the field of Black Studies. Highly recommended for academic libraries and large public libraries serving African American populations.

289. X X L: hip-hop on a higher level. [ISSN: 1093-0647] 1997. m. USD 12 domestic; USD 15.60 Canada; USD 24 elsewhere. Ed(s): Elliott Wilson, Juleyka Lantigua. Harris Publications, Inc., 800 Kennesaw Ave, Ste 220, Marietta, GA 30060; http://www.harris-pub.com. Illus., adv. *Aud.:* Ga.

XXL, an urban lifestyle magazine, is regarded as one of the best hip-hop insider magazines. Somewhat similar to its rival, *The Source,* it covers all aspects of hip-hop music and culture, including the business side of the music industry. Published since 1997, the magazine includes feature articles, interviews, commentaries, and reviews. While its primary focus is on musicians, producers, and others affiliated with the industry, the magazine also features actors, filmmakers, comedians, and other entertainment industry personalities, as well as athletes. *XXL* also includes news, current events, upcoming music releases, and the "Eye Candy" section, which consists of photographs of scantily clad women. As with the music that it covers, the language of the magazine is "adult" in nature, and although its title suggests otherwise, this is a magazine that's all about music. Recommended for urban public libraries serving older teens and adults.

AGRICULTURE

■ AGRICULTURE

Duncan McClusky, Branch Librarian, College of Agricultural and Environmental Sciences Tifton Campus, University of Georgia, Tifton, GA 31793

Introduction

The agricultural sector has faced many changes and concerns in the last few years. Mad cow disease and avian flu are drawing the attention of animal farmers. Tomato spotted wilt disease and soybean rust are problems for plant farmers. There is competition from foreign nations on producing food for the United States, and quota systems for various crops have been stopped. Precision agriculture methods are allowing farmers to target specific problem areas in their fields. The market for organically grown produce seems to be growing as well. Some people want to spend their vacation on a farm, and agri-tourism is another way for farmers to make a profit.

Basic Periodicals

Hs, Ga: *Amber Waves, Farm Journal, Progressive Farmer, Successful Farming;* Ac: *American Journal of Alternative Agriculture, Crop Science, Journal of Animal Science, Journal of Dairy Science, Poultry Science.*

Basic Abstracts and Indexes

Agricola, Biological and Agricultural Index, CAB Abstract Journals.

290. *Acres U S A: the voice of eco-agriculture.* [ISSN: 1076-4968] 1971. m. USD 27 domestic; USD 32 foreign. Acres U S A, PO Box 91299, Austin, TX 78709-1299; info@acresusa.com; http://www.acresusa.com. Illus., adv. Circ: 11000 Paid. *Aud.:* Hs, Ga.

This trade journal recently changed from a folio sized to a smaller sized publication. It covers organic and sustainable farming. There are approximately eight feature articles in each issue, along with a number of columns such as "Eco-Update," "Foundations of Eco-Agriculture," "The Natural Vet," and "Eco-Resources." There is a reviving interest in organic gardening, and this publication would be a useful tool for those libraries serving populations interested in farming or gardening.

291. *Agri-Pulse Newsletter.* Incorporates (1981-2007): *The Webster Agricultural Letter.* 2005. w. USD 275. Ed(s): Sara Wyant. Agri-Pulse Communications Inc., 5 N 985 Rt #31, St. Charles, IL 60175. *Aud.:* Hs, Ga.

This electronic newsletter provides a quick way to review political activities related to agriculture. The "Names in the News" section includes news on political figures as well as reports from various agricultural associations and companies. This publication would be valuable to libraries serving an agricultural population.

292. *The Agricultural Education Magazine.* Formerly (until 1980): *Agricultural Education.* [ISSN: 0732-4677] 1929. bi-m. USD 10 domestic; USD 20 foreign. Ed(s): Jamie Cano. Agricultural Education Magazine, Inc., Department of Agricultural Education and Studies, Iowa State University, Ames, IA 50011; http://www.ageds.iastate.edu. Illus., index, adv. Sample. Circ: 4500 Paid. Vol. ends: No. 6. Microform: PQC. Online: OCLC Online Computer Library Center, Inc.; ProQuest LLC (Ann Arbor); H.W. Wilson. *Indexed:* ABIn, Agr, EduInd. *Aud.:* Hs, Ac.

This is a journal written for persons involved in teaching agriculture. Articles may be centered on a theme, and there are five or six articles on each theme. Other papers may be divided into categories such as "Professional Development," "Leadership," "Webmaster," and "Go to the Head of the Class."

293. *Agricultural History.* [ISSN: 0002-1482] 1927. q. USD 47 to indviduals for membership; USD 158 to institutions for membership. Agricultural History Society, Department of History, UALR, 2801 S University Ave, Little Rock, AR 72324-1099. Illus., index, adv. Sample. Refereed. Circ: 1200 Paid. Vol. ends: Fall. Microform: PQC. Online: Chadwyck-Healey Inc.; EBSCO Publishing, EBSCO Host; Florida Center for Library Automation; Northern Light Technology, Inc.; OCLC Online Computer Library Center, Inc.; ProQuest LLC (Ann Arbor); SwetsWise Online Content; H.W. Wilson. *Indexed:* ABS&EES, Agr, AmH&L, AmHI, ArtHuCI, B&AI, BAS, BrArAb, CABA, CJA, DSA, EnvAb, FR, ForAb, GardL, HistAb, HortAb, HumInd, IBR, IBSS, IBZ, NumL, RILM, RRTA, S&F, SCI, SSCI, VB, WAE&RSA. *Bk. rev.:* 15-30, 150-600 words. *Aud.:* Ac, Sa.

This journal focuses on all aspects of agricultural history in all countries, and there are about four articles in each issue, in addition to several book reviews. It would be of interest to agricultural as well as historical researchers.

294. *Agricultural Research: solving problems for the growing world.* [ISSN: 0002-161X] 1953. m. USD 50 domestic; USD 70 foreign. Ed(s): Robert Sowers. U.S. Department of Agriculture, Agricultural Research Service, Jamie L Whitten Bldg, 1400 Independence Ave, SW, Washington, DC 20250-9410; Marcia.Wood@ars.usda.gov; http://www.ars.usda.gov/is/AR. Illus. Circ: 39000. Vol. ends: Dec. Microform: PQC. Online: EBSCO Publishing, EBSCO Host; Florida Center for Library Automation; Gale; Northern Light Technology, Inc.; OCLC Online Computer Library Center, Inc.; ProQuest K-12 Learning Solutions; ProQuest LLC (Ann Arbor). *Indexed:* ABIn, Agr, BiolDig, C&ISA, CABA, CerAb, ChemAb, DSA, EnvAb, EnvInd, ExcerpMed, ForAb, GardL, HortAb, IAA, IndVet, PollutAb, S&F, VB, WAE&RSA. *Aud.:* Hs, Ga, Ac.

This publication reports on research by United States Department of Agriculture (USDA) scientists that benefits farmers or prevents an outbreak of disease. Most articles are less than two pages long and written so that a nonscientist can understand them. The journal is available online back to 1996, and there is an online index by title back to 1978. This publication is useful for those wanting to monitor current USDA research. "Complimentary one-year subscriptions are available directly from ARS to public libraries, schools, USDA employees and the news media. Call (301) 504-1660 or e-mail armag@ars.usda.gov."

295. *Agriculture, Ecosystems & Environment.* Incorporates (1979-1985): *Protection Ecology;* Formed by the merger of (1974-1982): *Agriculture and Environment;* (1974-1982): *Agro-Ecosystems.* [ISSN: 0167-8809] 1982. 24x/yr. EUR 2402. Ed(s): M R Carter. Elsevier BV, Radarweg 29, Amsterdam, 1043 NX, Netherlands; nlinfo-f@elsevier.nl; http://www.elsevier.nl. Illus., adv. Sample. Refereed. Vol. ends: Dec. Microform: PQC. Online: EBSCO Publishing, EBSCO Host; Gale; IngentaConnect; OhioLINK; ScienceDirect; SwetsWise Online Content. *Indexed:* Agr, ApEcolAb, B&AI, BiolAb, CABA, ChemAb, DSA, EnvAb, EnvInd, ExcerpMed, FPA, FS&TA, ForAb, HortAb, IndVet, M&GPA, PollutAb, RRTA, S&F, SCI, SSCI, SWRA, VB, WAE&RSA, ZooRec. *Bk. rev.:* 750-1,000 words. *Aud.:* Ac, Sa.

The four categories of papers in this journal are original articles, review articles, short communications, and views and ideas. The journal covers the interaction of agriculture and the environment. Special theme issues are occasionally published, and a recent one covers sub-Saharan African agriculture. This publication would be valuable to researchers interested in environmental issues.

296. *Agronomy Journal: an international journal of agriculture and natural resource sciences.* Incorporates (1988-1999): *Journal of Production Agriculture;* Formerly: *American Society of Agronomy. Journal.* [ISSN: 0002-1962] 1907. bi-m. Members, USD 50; Non-members, USD 625. Ed(s): Calvin H Pearson. American Society of Agronomy, Inc., 677 S Segoe Rd, Madison, WI 53711; journals@agronomy.org; http://www.agronomy.org. Illus., index, adv. Sample. Refereed. Circ: 3200 Paid. Vol. ends: Nov/Dec. Microform: PMC. Online: EBSCO Publishing, EBSCO Host; HighWire Press; OCLC Online Computer Library Center, Inc.; OhioLINK; ProQuest K-12 Learning Solutions; ProQuest LLC (Ann Arbor); H.W. Wilson. *Indexed:* Agr, B&AI, BiolAb, CABA, ChemAb, DSA, EngInd, EnvAb, EnvInd, ExcerpMed, FPA, FS&TA, ForAb, HortAb, IndVet, M&GPA, RRTA, S&F, SCI, SWRA, VB, WAE&RSA. *Aud.:* Ac, Sa.

This is a society publication that "publishes articles reporting research findings in soil-plant relationships; crop science; soil science; biometry; crop, soil, pasture, and range management; crop, forage, and pasture production and utilization; turfgrass; acroclimatology, agronomic models; integrated pest

48

management; integrated agricultural systems; and various aspects of entomology, weed science, animal science, plant pathology, and agricultural economics as applied to production agriculture." Other writings accepted include notes, observations, review and interpretation papers, and a forum section. This journal would be useful to an academic or research facility working in agronomy.

297. *Amber Waves: the economics of food, farming, natural resources and rural America.* Formed by the 2003 merger of: *Agricultural Outlook; Food Review; Rural America.* [ISSN: 1545-8741] 2003. 5x/yr. USD 49.95 domestic; USD 99.90 foreign. Ed(s): Sheila Sankaran. U.S. Department of Agriculture, Economic Research Service, 1800 M St, NW, Rm 3100, Washington, DC 20036; ersinfo@ers.usda.gov; http://www.ers.usda.gov. Illus. *Indexed:* ABIn, Agr, CABA, DSA, HortAb, IndVet, PAIS, RGPR, RRTA, VB. *Aud.:* Hs, Ga.

Three former USDA Economic Research Service journals were merged into this one to report on research and activities in the department. The electronic version will have additional articles that aren't included in the print version, and will also be updated more frequently. This journal would be valuable to people interested in the economics of agriculture.

American Journal of Agricultural Economics. See Economics section.

298. *American Society of Agricultural and Biological Engineers. Transactions.* Formerly (until 2006): *American Society of Agricultural Engineers. Transactions.* 1958. bi-m. Non-members, USD 386. Ed(s): Glenn Laing. American Society of Agricultural and Biological Engineers, 2950 Niles Rd, St. Joseph, MI 49085-9659; hq@asabe.org; http://www.asabe.org. Illus., index. Sample. Refereed. Circ: 900 Paid and controlled. Vol. ends: Nov/Dec. *Indexed:* Agr, B&AI, C&ISA, CABA, CerAb, ChemAb, DSA, EngInd, EnvAb, EnvInd, ExcerpMed, FPA, FS&TA, ForAb, HortAb, IAA, IndVet, M&GPA, PollutAb, RRTA, S&F, SCI, SWRA, VB, WAE&RSA. *Aud.:* Ac, Sa.

This journal is written for engineers. It publishes approximately 2,000 pages each year of peer-reviewed articles on engineering that addresses agricultural problems. This publication should be in any academic library providing support for agricultural or engineering programs.

299. *Computers and Electronics in Agriculture.* Incorporates (in 1998): *A I Applications;* Which superseded (1987-1990): *A I Applications in Natural Resource Management.* [ISSN: 0168-1699] 1984. 10x/yr. EUR 1391. Ed(s): R. E. Plant, J. W. Hummel. Elsevier BV, Radarweg 29, Amsterdam, 1043 NX, Netherlands; nlinfo-f@elsevier.nl; http://www.elsevier.nl. Illus. Sample. Refereed. Vol. ends: Dec. Microform: PQC. Online: EBSCO Publishing, EBSCO Host; Gale; IngentaConnect; OhioLINK; ScienceDirect; SwetsWise Online Content. *Indexed:* Agr, BiolAb, C&ISA, CABA, CerAb, CompLI, DSA, EngInd, FPA, FS&TA, ForAb, HortAb, IAA, IndVet, RRTA, S&F, SCI, SWRA, VB, WAE&RSA. *Aud.:* Ac, Sa.

This international journal contains seven to nine articles per issue covering the use of computers, software, and electronic instrumentation in the fields of agriculture, forestry, horticulture, aquaculture, veterinary medicine, and food processing. Color images may be included in the online version whether they appear in the print edition or not. This journal is valuable in any agricultural collection, especially where researchers are working on precision agriculture.

Country Woman. See Fashion and Lifestyle section.

300. *Crop Management.* [ISSN: 1543-7833] irreg. USD 500 non doctoral. Ed(s): Robert L Kallenbach. Plant Management Network, 3340 Pilot Knob Rd, St Paul, MN 55121-2097; http://www.plantmanagementnetwork.org. Refereed. *Indexed:* CABA, ForAb, HortAb, S&F, WAE&RSA. *Aud.:* Ac, Sa.

This is one of five serial titles received when subscribing to the online Plant Management Network. The journal focuses on "all aspects of applied crop management." Articles are published as they are approved by the peer reviewers, and there were approximately 70 "science-based, practitioner-oriented articles" published in this journal in 2005. Articles published fall into one of the following categories: briefs, guides, news, research, and reviews. Academic facilities and scientists will enjoy these Plant Management Network journals.

301. *Crop Science: a journal serving the international community of crop scientists.* [ISSN: 0011-183X] 1961. bi-m. Non-members, USD 255. Ed(s): Craig A Roberts, Nicholas H Rhodehamel. Crop Science Society of America, 677 S Segoe Rd, Madison, WI 53711; http://www.crops.org. Illus., index, adv. Refereed. Circ: 5000 Paid. Vol. ends: Nov/Dec. Online: EBSCO Publishing, EBSCO Host; Florida Center for Library Automation; Gale; HighWire Press; Northern Light Technology, Inc.; OhioLINK; ProQuest K-12 Learning Solutions; ProQuest LLC (Ann Arbor). *Indexed:* Agr, B&AI, BioEngAb, BiolAb, BiolDig, CABA, ChemAb, DSA, ExcerpMed, FS&TA, ForAb, HortAb, IndVet, RRTA, S&F, SCI, SWRA, VB, WAE&RSA. *Aud.:* Ac.

Papers are separated into the broad subject areas of crop breeding, genetics, and cytology; crop physiology and metabolism; crop ecology, production, and management; forages and grazing lands; genomics, molecular genetics, and biotechnology; seed physiology, production, and technology; turfgrass science; plant genetic resources; and registrations of new plant cultivars, germplasms, or parental lines. The journal will also consider review, interpretation, and perspective papers. This publication would be useful to a scientist or university student in the field of crop science.

302. *Experimental Agriculture.* [ISSN: 0014-4797] 1965. q. GBP 295. Ed(s): M K Carr. Cambridge University Press, The Edinburgh Bldg, Shaftesbury Rd, Cambridge, CB2 2RU, United Kingdom; journals@cambridge.org; http://www.journals.cambridge.org. Illus., adv. Refereed. Vol. ends: Nov/Dec. Microform: PQC. Online: Pub.; EBSCO Publishing, EBSCO Host; OCLC Online Computer Library Center, Inc.; OhioLINK; SwetsWise Online Content. Reprint: PSC. *Indexed:* Agr, B&AI, BiolAb, CABA, ChemAb, DSA, FPA, FS&TA, ForAb, HortAb, IndVet, PollutAb, RRTA, S&F, SCI, SWRA, VB, WAE&RSA. *Bk. rev.:* 5-10, 200 words. *Aud.:* Ac, Sa.

This scientific publication concentrates on crop field research projects in tropical or warm regions of the world. The journal also publishes reports on new experimental techniques and methods. Recent articles cover a tool for harvesting tea, barley trials in Syria, and sorghum in Nigeria. A valuable journal for libraries with an interest in tropical agronomy research.

303. *Farm Bureau News.* Formerly: *American Farm Bureau Federations Official News Letter.* [ISSN: 0197-5617] 1921. 23x/yr. USD 30 domestic; USD 63 foreign. Ed(s): Lynne Finnerty. American Farm Bureau Federation, 600 Maryland Ave, SW, Ste 800, Washington, DC 20024; fbnews@fb.com; http://www.fb.com/. Illus. Circ: 50000 Paid. *Aud.:* Ga.

This electronic publication from the American Farm Bureau Federation, with 23 issues per year, covers political and economic issues related to farming. The regular sections include "Top Stories," "Viewpoint," "Capital Update," "Grassroots," and "For the Record." "The Corner Post" provides various statistical facts, and there is a link to a Farm Facts publication with statistics on farming. This publication is easy to read and would be useful to anyone wanting to stay up-to-date on farming issues.

304. *Farm Journal: the magazine of American agriculture.* [ISSN: 0014-8008] 1877. 12x/yr. USD 25.95 domestic; USD 55 foreign. Ed(s): Sonja Hillgren, Charlene K Finck. Farm Journal Media, 1818 Market St., 31st Fl, Philadelphia, PA 19103-3654; http://www.agweb.com. Illus., adv. Circ: 443000 Paid and controlled. Vol. ends: Dec. Microform: PQC. Online: Factiva, Inc.; Gale; LexisNexis; OCLC Online Computer Library Center, Inc.; ProQuest LLC (Ann Arbor). *Aud.:* Hs, Ga.

This journal provides business information to people who own farms or ranches. There are five or six articles in each issue. Regular features include "Machinery Journal," "$100 Ideas," "Shop Journal," "Production Journal," "Outlook," and "Viewpoint." The publishers have started a web search engine called agwebsearch.com. This publication is available free on the web and has links to other journals such as *Dairy Today, Beef Today, Top Producer,* and *Ag Day.*

305. *Farmer's Market Online.* [ISSN: 1521-6802] 1994. w. Ed(s): Michael Hofferber. Hofferber, P.O. Box 441, Baker City, OR 97814-0441; http://www.farmersmarketonline.com/. *Aud.:* Ga.

This electronic shopping site is set up to "resemble an open air market" where producers can sell directly to the consumer. There are also helpful "booths" set up to provide advice for web surfers. Subscribers can sign up to receive a weekly newsletter that may include information on dates for a farmer's market, recipes, notes from readers, or information about people on the site. This is an interesting site for those wanting to explore available products.

306. *Feedstuffs: the weekly newspaper for agribusiness.* [ISSN: 0014-9624] 1929. w. USD 144 domestic; USD 150 Canada; USD 210 in the Americas. Ed(s): Sarah Muirhead. Miller Publishing Co., 12400 Whitewater Dr., Ste. 160, Minnetonka, MN 55343-2524. Illus., adv. Sample. Circ: 15650. Vol. ends: Dec. Microform: PQC. Online: EBSCO Publishing, EBSCO Host; Florida Center for Library Automation; Gale; OCLC Online Computer Library Center, Inc. *Indexed:* Agr, CABA, ChemAb, DSA, IndVet, LRI, RRTA, S&F, VB, WAE&RSA. *Aud.:* Ga, Ac, Sa.

This tabloid-format publication rotates sections such as dairy nutrition and health, beef nutrition and health, and specialty nutrition and health. Regular features include business markets, hog market insider, mill technology, bottom line of nutrition/beef, mill market, ingredient market, grains and ingredients, and livestock and poultry. The three special issues during the year are the Feed Additive Compendium, the Feedstuffs Reference Issue, and the Direct-Fed Microbial, Enzyme and Forage Additive Compendium. It is possible to purchase Internet access to this publication. Many articles are short, and it would be useful to anyone working with or interested in animal feeds.

307. *Food Outlook.* [ISSN: 0251-1959] 1975. m. Food and Agriculture Organization of the United Nations (F A O), Via delle Terme di Caracalla, Rome, 00100, Italy; FAO-HQ@fao.org; http://www.fao.org. Illus. *Aud.:* Ga, Ac.

This electronic journal is published in Chinese, English, French, and Spanish. It is available in print to 4,600 institutions and individuals. There may be special reports on such topics as food emergencies around the world. Statistical information is presented in tables and graphs. This publication would be useful to those interested in agricultural economics and to those concerned with food shortages.

308. *Hoard's Dairyman: the national dairy farm magazine.* [ISSN: 0018-2885] 1885. s-m. 20/yr. USD 16 domestic; USD 40 foreign. Ed(s): Steven A Larson, W D Knox. W.D. Hoard and Sons Co., PO Box 801, Fort Atkinson, WI 53538; hoards@hoards.com; http://www.hoards.com/. Illus., index, adv. Circ: 63023 Paid. Vol. ends: Dec. Microform: PQC. *Indexed:* B&AI, DSA, FS&TA, RRTA, WAE&RSA. *Aud.:* Ga, Ac, Sa.

This folio-sized publication provides brief articles on subjects of interest to dairy farmers. Regular sections include business; feeding, breeding, and herd health; crops, soils, and fertilizers; and people, places, and events. Departments include artificial breeding, cowside practice, farm flashes, handy hints, and "Washington Dairy Grams." This journal would be valuable for a library near dairy cattle farms.

309. *Horticulture and Home Pest News.* 1996. 30x/yr. USD 20. Iowa State University Entomology Extension Service, Iowa State University, Ames, IA 50011. *Aud.:* Ga, Ac, Sa.

This publication contains two or three brief, timely articles from Iowa State University extension agents from the entomology, horticulture, and plant pathology departments. Recent articles report on growing bee balms, underappreciated fungi, and bacterial wilt diseases of the geranium. The articles are easily understood by the general public. URL: www.ipm.iastate.edu/ipm/hortnews/

310. *International Journal of Fruit Science.* Formed by the merger of (1996-2005): *Journal of Tree Fruit Production;* (2000-2005): *Small Fruits Review;* Which was formerly (1992-2000): *Journal of Small Fruit & Viticulture.* [ISSN: 1553-8362] 2005. q. USD 290 print & online eds.

Ed(s): Amarjit Basra. Haworth Food & Agricultural Products Press, 10 Alice St, Binghamton, NY 13904-1580; getinfo@haworthpress.com; http://www.haworthpress.com/. Reprint: HAW. *Indexed:* CABA, FS&TA, GardL, HortAb, S&F. *Aud.:* Ga, Ac.

Two journals have been merged to cover international fruit culture scientific research in order to provide basic information to the farmer, extension agent, and researcher. One issue published articles that were generated from the "European COST Action 836 Towards an Organization of the Integrated Research in Berries: Model for a Strawberry of Quality in Respect with the Environment Rules and Consumers' Requirements." This journal would be valuable to libraries in areas where fruits are grown or studied.

311. *Journal of Agricultural and Food Chemistry.* [ISSN: 0021-8561] 1953. 24x/yr. USD 1425 print & online eds. Ed(s): James N Seiber. American Chemical Society, 1155 16th St, NW, Washington, DC 20036; service@acs.org; https://portal.chemistry.org/. Illus., adv. Refereed. Circ: 4735 Paid. Vol. ends: Dec. Online: Pub.; EBSCO Publishing, EBSCO Host; OhioLINK; SwetsWise Online Content. *Indexed:* Agr, B&AI, BioEngAb, BiolAb, CABA, ChemAb, DSA, EnvInd, ExcerpMed, FPA, FS&TA, ForAb, H&SSA, HortAb, IndVet, OceAb, PollutAb, S&F, SCI, VB. *Aud.:* Ac, Sa.

This journal publishes approximately 50 articles per issue on analytical methods, bioactive constituents, bio-based products, biotechnology, chemical and physical changes induced by processing or storage, composition of foods or feeds, crop and animal protection, flavors and aromas, food chemistry or biochemistry, and safety or toxicology. This journal is important for any food science or agricultural research library.

312. *Journal of Agricultural Safety and Health.* [ISSN: 1074-7583] 1995. q. Non-members, USD 118.75. Ed(s): Dennis Murphy. American Society of Agricultural and Biological Engineers, 2950 Niles Rd, St. Joseph, MI 49085-9659; hq@asabe.org; http://www.asabe.org. Illus., index. Refereed. Circ: 400. Vol. ends: Nov. *Indexed:* Agr, CABA, DSA, ErgAb, FPA, ForAb, H&SSA, HortAb, IndVet, RRTA, RiskAb, S&F, VB, WAE&RSA. *Aud.:* Ga, Ac.

This journal covers all areas related to agricultural safety and health, with approximately ten articles in each issue. There is a concern for safety on the farm and preventing accidents. This journal would be valuable in any rural library.

313. *Journal of Animal Science: leading source of new knowledge and perspectives in animal science.* [ISSN: 0021-8812] 1942. m. 1 vol./yr. USD 450 (Members, USD 160). Ed(s): Jean Rice, Lawrence P Reynolds. American Society of Animal Science, 1111 N Dunlap Ave, Savoy, IL 61874; johne@assochq.org; http://www.asas.org. Illus., index. Refereed. Circ: 5000. Vol. ends: Dec. Microform: PMC; PQC. Online: EBSCO Publishing, EBSCO Host; HighWire Press; Northern Light Technology, Inc.; OCLC Online Computer Library Center, Inc.; ProQuest K-12 Learning Solutions; ProQuest LLC (Ann Arbor). *Indexed:* Agr, B&AI, BiolAb, CABA, ChemAb, DSA, ExcerpMed, FPA, FS&TA, FoVS&M, ForAb, HortAb, IndVet, RRTA, S&F, SCI, SSCI, VB, WAE&RSA. *Bk. rev.:* 1-5, 35-100 words. *Aud.:* Ac, Sa.

This journal of the American Society of Animal Science covers all aspects of the subject, including applied animal science; breeding and genetics; contemporary issues; environment and behavior; growth and developmental biology; meat science; nonruminant nutrition; pharmacology and toxicology; physiology and endocrinology; rangeland, pasture, and forage utilization; ruminant nutrition; teaching; and a rapid communications section for molecular genetics articles. Some news about the society is also published. A supplement volume contains meeting abstracts. This journal should be in any collection providing support to animal researchers.

314. *Journal of Dairy Science.* [ISSN: 0022-0302] 1917. m. USD 450 in North America; USD 500 elsewhere. Ed(s): Gary W Rogers, Susan Pollock. American Dairy Science Association, 1111 N Dunlap Ave, Savoy, IL 61874; adsa@assochq.org; http://www.adsa.org. Illus., index, adv. Refereed. Circ: 5062 Paid and free. Vol. ends: Dec. Microform:

PMC; PQC. Online: EBSCO Publishing, EBSCO Host; HighWire Press; ProQuest LLC (Ann Arbor). *Indexed:* Agr, B&AI, BiolAb, CABA, ChemAb, DSA, EnvAb, ExcerpMed, FPA, FS&TA, FoVS&M, HortAb, IndVet, RRTA, S&F, SCI, SSCI, VB, WAE&RSA. *Aud.:* Ac, Sa.

The American Dairy Association publishes approximately 4,400 pages per year in this journal, covering all aspects of dairy cattle research including dairy foods; genetics and breeding; nutrition, feeding and calves; extension and teaching; and physiology and management. The announcements section may contain employment information. The annual proceedings of the association are published jointly with the *Journal of Animal Science.* This publication is a must for any library supporting a cattle research program.

315. *Poultry Science.* [ISSN: 0032-5791] 1908. m. USD 450 print & online eds. (Members, USD 170 print & online eds.). Ed(s): Colin Scanes, Susan Pollock. Poultry Science Association Inc., 1111 N Dunlap Ave, Savoy, IL 61874; psa@assochq.org; http://www.poultryscience.org. Illus., index, adv. Refereed. Circ: 3500 Paid. Vol. ends: Dec. Microform: PQC. Online: EBSCO Publishing, EBSCO Host; ProQuest LLC (Ann Arbor). *Indexed:* Agr, B&AI, BiolAb, CABA, ChemAb, DSA, ExcerpMed, FPA, FS&TA, FoVS&M, ForAb, HortAb, IndVet, RRTA, S&F, SCI, VB, WAE&RSA. *Bk. rev.:* 2-4, 200-500 words. *Aud.:* Ac, Sa.

This professional association journal separates papers into the sections "Environment, Well-Being and Behavior," "Genetics," "Immunology, Health and Disease," "Metabolism and Nutrition," "Physiology, Endocrinology and Reproduction," "Processing, Products and Food Safety," and "Production, Modeling and Education," plus "Association Notes." This journal would be valuable in any collection providing support to poultry farmers or researchers.

316. *Progressive Farmer (Southwest).* [ISSN: 0033-0760] 1886. 10x/yr. USD 20 domestic; USD 28 foreign. Ed(s): Joe Link, Victoria G Myers. Progressive Farmer, Inc., 2100 Lakeshore Drive, Birmingham, AL 35209; progressivefarmer@timeinc.com. Illus., adv. Circ: 630000. Vol. ends: Dec. Microform: PQC. *Indexed:* ABIn. *Aud.:* Hs, Ga, Ac.

This journal is written for those living on farms or involved in agriculture. There are two versions of the magazine, one subtitled "Helping You Make Money and Enjoy Your Lifestyle," directed to commercial farmers, and the other subtitled "Farm and Country Living at Its Best," aimed at everyone else who owns land in the country. There are also regional editions (such as Southeast, Southwest, Upper South, and Midwest) that contain advertisements specific to those geographic areas. A library in a farming area would find this journal valuable.

317. *Renewable Agriculture and Food Systems (Print Edition).* Formerly (until 2004): *American Journal of Alternative Agriculture (Print Edition).* [ISSN: 1742-1705] 1986. 3x/yr. GBP 155. Ed(s): J Doran. Cambridge University Press, The Edinburgh Bldg, Shaftesbury Rd, Cambridge, CB2 2RU, United Kingdom; journals@cambridge.org; http://www.journals.cambridge.org. Illus., adv. Sample. Refereed. Circ: 1000. Reprint: PSC. *Indexed:* Agr, B&AI, CABA, DSA, EnvAb, FPA, FS&TA, ForAb, GardL, HortAb, M&GPA, PollutAb, RRTA, S&F, SCI, SSCI, VB, WAE&RSA. *Bk. rev.:* 2-4, 400-600 words. *Aud.:* Ga, Ac.

In 2004, the name of the *American Journal of Alternative Agriculture* was changed to *Renewable Agriculture and Food Systems.* The aim of this journal is "to publish good science that underpins the diverse ideas and approaches to agricultural and food production that are economically, environmentally, and socially sustainable." Original research, review articles, preliminary research articles on interesting new advances, book reviews, and a forum section to promote discussions are found in this journal. It is easily understood by a wide range of readers and would be useful in any agricultural library.

318. *Resource (Niles): engineering & technology for a sustainable world.* Formed by the merger of (1920-1994): *Agricultural Engineering;* (1983-1994): *Within A S A E.* [ISSN: 1076-3333] 1994. m. 10/yr. Non-members, USD 86. Ed(s): Pam Bakken, Sue Mitrovich. American Society of Agricultural and Biological Engineers, 2950 Niles Rd, St. Joseph, MI 49085-9659; hq@asabe.org; http://www.asabe.org. Illus., adv. Circ: 10000 Paid. Vol. ends: Dec. Microform: PQC. Online: Florida

Center for Library Automation; Gale; OCLC Online Computer Library Center, Inc.; ProQuest LLC (Ann Arbor). *Indexed:* B&AI, CABA, ChemAb, DSA, EngInd, EnvAb, ExcerpMed, FPA, ForAb, HortAb, IndVet, PollutAb, S&F, SSCI, WAE&RSA, WRCInf. *Aud.:* Ac.

This society magazine is much smaller than the research publication *American Society of Agricultural and Biological Engineers. Transactions* (above in this section). It contains society news, member news, employment opportunities, student chapter news, an events calendar, and typically four short articles. Most appropriate for academic libraries.

319. *Soil Science Society of America. Journal.* Formerly (until 1976): *Soil Science Society of America. Proceedings.* [ISSN: 0361-5995] 1936. bi-m. USD 615 domestic; USD 653 foreign. Ed(s): Warren A Dick, Nicholas Rhodehamel. Soil Science Society of America, 677 S Segoe Rd, Madison, WI 53711; http://www.soils.org/. Illus., index, adv. Refereed. Circ: 5600 Paid. Vol. ends: Nov/Dec. Microform: PMC. Online: EBSCO Publishing, EBSCO Host; HighWire Press; ProQuest K-12 Learning Solutions; ProQuest LLC (Ann Arbor). *Indexed:* Agr, B&AI, BiolAb, C&ISA, CABA, CerAb, ChemAb, DSA, EngInd, EnvAb, EnvInd, ExcerpMed, FPA, ForAb, GSI, HortAb, IAA, PetrolAb, PollutAb, S&F, SCI, SWRA, WAE&RSA, WRCInf. *Aud.:* Ac, Sa.

Articles are grouped by the various sections of the Soil Science Society of America. Sections include soil physics; soil chemistry; soil biology and biochemistry; soil fertility and plant nutrition; pedology; soil and water management and conservation; forest, range, and wildland soils; nutrient management and soil and plant analysis; and wetland soils. Articles present original research for scientists or researchers in the field.

320. *Successful Farming: for families that make farming their business.* [ISSN: 0039-4432] 1902. m. USD 15.95 domestic; USD 27.95 foreign. Ed(s): Loren Kruse, Gene Johnston. Meredith Corp., 1716 Locust St, Des Moines, IA 50309-3023; http://www.meredith.com. Illus., adv. Circ: 485000 Paid. Vol. ends: Dec. Microform: NBI. Online: Florida Center for Library Automation; Northern Light Technology, Inc.; OCLC Online Computer Library Center, Inc.; ProQuest LLC (Ann Arbor). *Indexed:* ABIn, RGPR. *Aud.:* Hs, Ga.

This trade publication covers farms and farm life and includes many advertisements. The print version divides articles into business, production, family, personal, and feature sections. The electronic version has such sections as rural health, all around the farm, safe and secure, and women in agriculture. This journal would be valuable for any library in an agricultural area.

321. *Weekly Weather and Crop Bulletin.* Formerly (until 1924): *Weekly Weather Chronicle.* [ISSN: 0043-1974] 1872. w. USD 60 domestic. Ed(s): David Miskus. The Joint Agricultural Weather Facility, USDA S Bldg, Rm 4443B, Washington, DC 20250; http://www.usda.gov/oce/waob/jawf. Illus., index. Vol. ends: Dec. *Indexed:* AmStI, IUSGP. *Aud.:* Ga, Ac.

This electronic weekly is posted by 5:00 p.m. on Wednesday unless there has been a federal holiday earlier in the work week. It provides meteorological information for farmers and information on the status of various crops. Many charts of the United States are used to illustrate information such as temperature and precipitation data. International weather and crop information are also provided. This is a valuable resource for libraries that have patrons interested in meteorology and its relation to agriculture.

■ ALTERNATIVES

General/Reviews and Bibliographies

Jerilyn Marshall, Head of Reference & Instructional Services, Rod Library, University of Northern Iowa, 1227 W. 27th St., Cedar Falls, IA 50613-3675, jerilyn.marshall@uni.edu

Introduction

In a world characterized by increasing diversification and fragmentation, identifying alternative magazines has become both easier and more difficult than it was even ten years ago. The alternative press continues to do what it has always done best: provide alternative points of view and to report on issues from different perspectives than those of the mainstream media.

In recent years, the irony is that the alternative perspectives are just as easy to locate as the mainstream perspectives are. The Internet provides access to almost everybody, and it is fairly easy to find a huge variety of viewpoints on almost any topic through popular search engines. Some of the web sites represent self-proclaimed "magazines," while some others may be weblogs, and some are neither. So, although the alternative viewpoints are easy to find, locating the ones published in bona fide magazines is a bit trickier.

Another identification problem relates to the concept of alternative magazines in general. Alternatives can be classified under almost any subject, and the reader will find many publications that express alternative viewpoints interspersed within chapters throughout *Magazines for Libraries.*

The "Alternatives" chapter is focused on magazines that publish articles with alternative perspectives on social (and some political) issues. Many of these magazines promote social responsibility and social activism. There is one publication, *Rain Taxi,* that is mainly a review source, but book and media reviews are part of many of the magazines in this chapter.

Several alternatives from the previous edition have had to be eliminated due to lack of response to a request for a sample. These included *Alternative Press Review, The Baffler, Car Busters, Counterpoise,* and *Fuse Magazine.* Others have been removed because they have ceased or did not fit in with the new definition of "Alternatives" for this edition.

A good identification source for magazines of the alternative and independent press is *Annotations,* a publication of the Alternative Press Center. The third edition of this annotated directory of periodicals was published in 2004.

Basic Periodicals

Hs: *Adbusters, Utne;* Ga: *Adbusters, AlterNet, Briarpatch, Communities, Freezerbox, HopeDance Magazine, In Motion Magazine, OnEarth, Rain Taxi, The Sun (Chapel Hill), Utne;* Ac: *Rain Taxi.*

Basic Abstracts and Indexes

Alternative Press Index.

General

322. Adbusters: journal of the mental environment. [ISSN: 0847-9097] 1989. 6x/yr. CND 35 in US & Canada; CND 40 elsewhere. Ed(s): Kalle Lasn. Adbusters Media Foundation, 1243 W Seventh Ave, Vancouver, BC V6H 1B7, Canada; info@adbusters.org; http://www.adbusters.org. Illus., adv. Circ: 120000. Online: Gale. *Indexed:* AltPI, CBCARef, CPerI. *Bk. rev.:* Number and length vary. *Aud.:* Ga.

"Based in Vancouver, British Columbia, Canada, *Adbusters* is a not-for-profit, reader-supported, 120,000-circulation magazine concerned about the erosion of our physical and cultural environments by commercial forces. . . . *Adbusters* offers incisive philosophical articles as well as activist commentary from around the world addressing issues ranging from genetically modified foods to media concentration. . . . Ultimately, though, *Adbusters* is an ecological magazine, dedicated to examining the relationship between human beings and their physical and mental environment." This journal's articles are informed and literate, and the tone in which they are written advocates for activism. The magazine's web site offers links to articles, spoof ads, and videos. The Adbusters Media Foundation is an important advocacy group that created the social marketing campaigns called TV Turnoff Week and Buy Nothing Day. Thus, the magazine would be appreciated in libraries that collect materials related to social and media activism.

323. AlterNet: the mix is the message. irreg. Free. AlterNet, 77 Federal St, San Francisco, CA 94107. *Aud.:* Ga.

AlterNet "is an award-winning news magazine and online community that creates original journalism and amplifies the best of dozens of other independent media sources." As such, this journal displays a variety of elements. It carries online news stories written by *AlterNet* staff or culled from other sources. It also includes blogs and regular columnists. Readers of *AlterNet* can get their news in many ways: through RSS or XML feeds, via the AvantGo channel for PDAs, through a Mobile Edition for web-enabled mobile devices, or through a more traditional e-mail newsletter version. The aim of this site is "to inspire citizen action and advocacy on the environment, human rights and civil liberties, social justice, media, and health care issues." Although the main page is crowded with headlines, it is very attractively and efficiently formatted so that locating recent stories is easy. Readers of this site are likely to be interested in discussing mainstream media coverage of recent events.

324. Briarpatch. [ISSN: 0703-8968] 1973. 8x/yr. CND 35.31 (Individuals, CND 24.61; CND 3.99 newsstand/cover per issue). Ed(s): David Oswald Mitchell. Briarpatch Society, 2138 McIntyre St, Regina, SK S4P 2R7, Canada; http://www.cmpa.ca. Illus., adv. Sample. Circ: 2300 Paid. Microform: MML. Online: Gale; Micromedia ProQuest. *Indexed:* AltPI, CBCARef, CPerI. *Bk. rev.:* Number and length vary. *Aud.:* Ga.

Briarpatch: Fighting the War on Error is "Saskatchewan's independent alternative news magazine committed to building a socialist democratic society." Although it aspires to high ideals and is politically active, it never comes across as harsh or shrill. Articles are well reasoned and intelligently written in an informative, matter-of-fact tone. As are many magazines in this section, each issue of *Briarpatch* is organized around a theme. Two recent themes included Canadian foreign policy and the "Looming Energy Crunch." Labor issues are a strong focus of each issue, and several of the magazine's few advertments relate to labor unions. The editors have been working on improving layout, and recent issues are very attractive and easy to read. The web site at briarpatchmagazine.com includes tables of contents and selected articles back to early 2004. Recommended for libraries in and near Canada, and for comprehensive collections of current alternative or labor literature.

325. Communities: journal of cooperative living. Supersedes: *Modern Utopian; Alternatives Newsmagazine; Communitarian; Communitas.* [ISSN: 0199-9346] 1972. q. USD 20 domestic; USD 24 Canada; USD 26 elsewhere. Ed(s): Diana Christian. Fellowship for Intentional Community, Rt 1, Box 156, Rutledge, MO 63563; fic-missouri@ic.org; http://www.ic.org. Illus., adv. Circ: 5000. Microform: PQC. Online: EBSCO Publishing, EBSCO Host; Northern Light Technology, Inc.; ProQuest LLC (Ann Arbor). *Indexed:* AltPI. *Bk. rev.:* 1-2, 200 words. *Aud.:* Ga.

Communities is written for those who practice cooperative living in intentional communities or cohousing. This title belongs in this section for a different reason than some of the others listed here. Many of the others are members of the alternative press, meant to express a different political point of view than the mainstream. *Communities,* on the other hand, presents information on an alternative way of living. This journal's articles are not intentionally inciting people to change their political or social worldview. Instead, they seem to be written for people who have already chosen to live in intentional or cooperative communities. Each issue of *Communities* is based on a theme. Recent issues focused on themes such as "Resolving Conflicts" and "Urban Community." Most articles are based on the personal experiences of the authors, who offer advice and examples for others. Each issue also includes interviews and book reviews. The covers are glossy and in color, and contents are printed in black-and-white. The minimal amount of advertising in each issue is all directly related to the interests of its target audience of people who live in intentional communities. This title will be of interest to libraries located near intentional communities, or libraries that collect material about alternative lifestyles.

326. Freezerbox. [ISSN: 1936-0657] 1998. d. Free. Freezerbox, Speridakis Terrace, Cambridge, MA 02139; submissions@freezerbox.com; http://www.freezerbox.com. *Aud.:* Ga.

Freezerbox, an online news magazine, "aspires to create a forum for good thinking and good writing." They seek contributions advocating activism that include alternative views about current events. They recognize that there are many important issues to discuss, but also don't want contributions to consist merely of writers on their soapboxes, rousing the masses. *Freezerbox* has a more general aim, to provide "a forum for good thinking and good writing." Although most of the headlines on the main page are political in nature, the site also offers articles on Culture, Science, Media, and Technology, among other categories. Articles in the Archive are categorized under four labels: Criticism, Kulture, Power, and Sci-Tech. These categories help in site navigation.

Home Education Magazine. See Education/Home Schooling section.

327. HopeDance: radical solutions inspiring hope. [ISSN: 1533-8401] 1996. bi-m. USD 20. Ed(s): Bob Banner. HopeDance, PO Box 15609, San Luis Obispo, CA 93406; hopedanceaol.com; http://www.hopedance.org. Adv. Sample. *Bk. rev.:* Number and length vary. *Aud.:* Ga.

The purpose of *HopeDance* is twofold. The first and main focus is "to report on the outrageous, pioneering and inspiring activities of outstanding individuals and organizations who are creating a new world" in order to inspire hope in its readers. The second purpose is to inform people in central coastal counties of California of events, individuals, and projects that may be of interest. *HopeDance* is published every two months, in a small tabloid newspaper format. The writing style throughout is informed and accessible. Article topics are organized around a simple, broad theme for each issue. Recent themes have included "Shelter: Affordable AND Sustainable?," "Energy," and "Food." Although there is some local focus, most *HopeDance* articles cover basic human issues that everyone will recognize. *HopeDance* is highly recommended to libraries whose patrons are interested in alternative solutions to human social issues. The web site includes articles from recent issues and also links to flyers advertising current events in the area of San Luis Obispo, California.

328. In Motion Magazine: a multicultural US publication about democracy. 1996. d. Ed(s): Nic Paget-Clarke. N P C Productions, PO Box 927482, San Diego, CA 92192; publish@cts.com; http://www.inmotionmagazine.com. Adv. *Aud.:* Ga.

In Motion Magazine, established in 1995, "is a multicultural online U.S. publication about democracy." The diverse articles are in many forms: book excerpts, texts of speeches, original interviews, opinion pieces, film reviews, press releases, and blog extracts. This magazine succeeds in raising awareness about a wide range of social issues. Most articles are in English, and some in Spanish. The entry page for *In Motion Magazine* is categorized into broad topics such as Affirmative Action, Rural America, Healthcare, and Human and Civil Rights. This first page is very simple, with a button for each category. After entering a category the reader can select individual articles from a list. Features and interviews are at the top, followed by a listing of other articles in reverse chronological order. The format is easy to follow and to use. One problem with some parts of this site is a lack of updating. For example, the Links Around the World page lists over 130 links to organizations and other pages of interest to readers. A quick check of about ten of the links showed that more than half of them were no longer valid or that their URLs had been taken over by other sites or had expired. That caveat aside, *In Motion Magazine* is an important source of information on grassroots advocacy activities and issues.

The Next American City. See Urban Studies section.

329. OnEarth. Former titles: *The Amicus Journal; Amicus;* Which incorporated (in 1992): *N R D C Newsline.* [ISSN: 1537-4246] 1979. q. USD 8. Ed(s): Douglas S. Barasch. Natural Resources Defense Council, Inc., 40 W 20th St, 11th Fl, New York, NY 10011; nrdcinfo@nrdc.org nrdcinfo@nrdc.org; http://www.nrdc.org. Illus., index. Sample. Circ: 175000. Vol. ends: Winter. Microform: PQC. Online: Florida Center for Library Automation; Gale; Northern Light Technology, Inc.; OCLC Online Computer Library Center, Inc.; ProQuest K-12 Learning Solutions; ProQuest LLC (Ann Arbor). *Indexed:* AltPI, B&AI, BiolDig, CLI, EnvAb, IAPV, ILP, PAIS. *Aud.:* Ga.

OnEarth is published by the National Resources Defense Council, a national nonprofit organization with 650,000 members. The magazine is dedicated to discussion of environmental issues. It is open to diverse points of view; for example, a recent issue included a message from the president of the NRDC that discussed a controversial article they had run about making coal energy cleaner, and why the ensuing controversy had a positive effect. Articles in *OnEarth* are written in a journalistic style, and each quarterly issue is attractively presented in full color on glossy paper, with about 48 pages per issue. It is recommended

for all libraries for its informational and balanced coverage of environmental issues. *OnEarth* received an Independent Press Award for 2005 from *Utne* in the category "General Excellence: Magazines."

330. Sojourners Magazine. Former titles (until 2001): *Sojourners;* (until 1976): *Post American.* [ISSN: 1550-1140] 1971. m. 11/yr. USD 39.95 domestic (Students, USD 15). Ed(s): Jim Wallis. Sojourners, 3333 14th St, NW, Washington, DC 20010; sojourners@sojo.net; http://www.sojourners.com. Illus., adv. Circ: 25000. Online: Florida Center for Library Automation; Gale; Northern Light Technology, Inc.; OCLC Online Computer Library Center, Inc.; ProQuest K-12 Learning Solutions; H.W. Wilson. *Indexed:* AltPI, AmHI, ChrPI, HumInd, MRD, NTA, PRA, RI-1. *Bk. rev.:* Number and length vary. *Aud.:* Ga.

Sojourners informs its readers about and comments on national and world issues related to the concerns of its Christian constituency. The masthead says that "*Sojourners* is a Christian ministry whose mission is to proclaim and practice the biblical call to integrate spiritual renewal and social justice." It provides a reasonable voice advocating for peace and justice in a fragmented and harsh world. Advertising in each issue is mostly for Christian organizations or books. Each 50-page issue appears in a colorful, attractive, glossy format. Access to the magazine's web site is free, but requires registration. This magazine would be of most interest to Christian readers and others committed to social justice.

331. The Sun (Chapel Hill). [ISSN: 0744-9666] 1974. m. USD 36 domestic; USD 51 in Canada & Mexico; USD 56 elsewhere. Ed(s): Sy Safransky. Sun Publishing Company, 107 N Roberson St, Chapel Hill, NC 27516; http://www.thesunmagazine.org. Illus., adv. Circ: 50000 Paid. Microform: PQC. *Indexed:* AltPI, AmHI, IAPV. *Aud.:* Ga.

Recent issues of *The Sun* describe the magazine as "a non-profit, ad-free monthly magazine that publishes an eclectic mix of personal essays, fiction, interviews, poetry, and photographs." As one might expect from this description, *The Sun* is primarily a literary magazine. It is included in the "Alternatives" section because of its focus on self-expression of personal viewpoints that may be outside of the mainstream. Each issue features essays, fiction, poetry, and photographs by a variety of freelancers. This journal's readers are invited to actively participate in several ways. Every issue includes a theme-based column titled "Readers Write," which includes anecdotes and comments connected with the pre-chosen theme. Recent themes for this column included "Playing With Fire" and "In the Middle of the Night." Many readers of *The Sun* have formed discussion groups that get together to talk about each issue. The magazine's web site lists groups in 44 U.S. states along with six groups outside the U.S. *The Sun* is an attractive magazine, printed mostly in black-and-white. It would be a valuable addition for most libraries.

332. Utne Reader: understanding the next evolution. Former titles (until 2006): *Utne (2002);* (until Nov. 2002): *Utne Reader (1983).* 1984. bi-m. USD 19.97 domestic; USD 24.97 Canada; USD 30 elsewhere. Ed(s): David Schimke. Ogden Publications, 1624 Harmon Place, Ste 330, Minneapolis, MN 55403; http://www.ogdenpubs.com. Illus., adv. Circ: 282433. Microform: PQC. Online: OCLC Online Computer Library Center, Inc.; ProQuest K-12 Learning Solutions. *Indexed:* ABS&EES, AltPI, BRI, CBRI, IIMP, IIPA, MASUSE, RGPR, RI-1. *Bk. rev.:* Number and length vary. *Aud.:* Hs, Ga.

Utne Reader may be the most recognizable title in the "Alternatives" category. Since beginning publication over 20 years ago as *Utne Reader,* before changing its title briefly to *Utne,* it has distinguished itself for its mix of articles that include reprints and digests of stories from other media along with some well-written pieces by staff reporters. Each issue of *Utne Reader* has a theme, and many of the articles in each issue are organized around the subject of the month. The digests and reprints cover articles on topics of interest to the readers of this magazine, or those who are interested in social change. The magazine features many reviews of books, music, film, and works of art. One column lists "niche" magazines, covering a different subject area each time. A recent list included magazines about "permaculture and self-reliance." *Utne Reader* carries advertising from socially responsible companies that would be of interest to its readers, and also seems to include a "special advertising section" in each issue. One of the best-known features of *Utne Reader* is its annual Independent Press Awards. The winners are announced in the January/February issue each year. There were awards in 15 categories for 2006, with three General Excellence categories (Magazines, Newsletters, and Zines). Some content from back issues is available through www.utne.com. The site also includes updated news digests, unique articles that haven't appeared in the print version, and information on how to purchase back issues. Recommended for all libraries.

Reviews and Bibliographies

333. *Rain Taxi: review of books.* 1996. q. USD 12 domestic; USD 24 foreign. Ed(s): Eric Lorberer. Rain Taxi, Inc., P O Box 3840, Minneapolis, MN 55403. Illus. Circ: 180000. *Bk. rev.:* Number and length vary. *Aud.:* Ga, Ac.

Rain Taxi "is a quarterly publication that publishes reviews of literary fiction, poetry, and nonfiction with an emphasis on works that push the boundaries of language, narrative, and genre." Most of the books reviewed have been published by small or independent presses. There are also reviews of books from large publishers if they meet the description quoted above. They aim to feature books that would not otherwise get much media attention. Besides the usual fiction and nonfiction, there are reviews of poetry, drama, and graphic novels. Author interviews are a strong feature. The magazine's web site includes an online edition that has different material from the print version. *Rain Taxi* recently celebrated its tenth anniversary with a look back at its founding by two independent booksellers in Minneapolis. The anniversary issue features background articles on some regular journal features such as the comic strip "The New Life" and a series of public readings sponsored by the magazine. This magazine is recommended for all libraries.

■ ANIMAL WELFARE

See also Birds; Horses; Pets; and Veterinary Science sections.

Julie Arendt, Reference Librarian, Sciences; Library Affairs, Morris Library; Mail code 6632; Southern Illinois University, Carbondale; Carbondale, IL 62901-6632; jarendt@lib.siu.edu; FAX: 618-453-3440

Introduction

Animal welfare publications promote the humane treatment of animals. Despite sharing this broad goal, these periodicals encompass a variety of content. Publications on operating animal shelters, rescuing abused circus animals, protecting wildlife, and becoming vegetarian all fit under the broad animal welfare umbrella. Magazines that promote better treatment of laboratory and farm animals share the animal welfare category with magazines that promote an end to the use of animals in laboratories and for food.

In 2005, it seemed like the animal welfare magazines for general audiences all discussed abuse of circus animals and the effects of Hurricane Katrina on animals. Despite this similarity, these magazines are diverse. Various magazines emphasize pets, laboratory animals, wild animals, farm animals, and more. Nonprofit organizations produce many of these magazines, and the goals of a nonprofit influence its magazine. Animal protection organizations such as the Humane Society of the United States produce mild publications like *AllAnimals*. Animal rights organizations such as People for the Ethical Treatment of Animals produce more strident publications like PETA's *Animal Times*. This section includes magazines from national and international organizations. It does not include smaller local newsletters and magazines. Public libraries should also consider the local animal welfare periodicals from the regions they serve.

For academic and special libraries, several new publications about the legal aspects of animal welfare have emerged. Previously, *Animal Law* was the first and only law review on animal issues. *Journal of Animal Law* has joined the field of animal law reviews, and volume 1 of *Journal of Animal Law and Ethics* was released in April 2006.

From children's newsletters to specialized academic journals, from mild animal shelter magazines to strident animal rights activist tracts, animal welfare magazines cover a range of perspectives. The following magazines provide a glimpse of this range.

Basic Periodicals

Ems: *KIND News*; Hs: *AllAnimals, PETA's Animal Times*; Ga: *Act'ion Line, AllAnimals, The A V Magazine, PETA's Animal Times*; Ac: *Animal Law, ILAR Journal, Journal of Applied Animal Welfare Science*; Sa: *Animal Law, Animal Sheltering*.

Basic Abstracts and Indexes

Agricola, Humans & Other Species, UnCover.

334. *A S P C A Animaland.* [ISSN: 1526-9779] bi-m. American Society for the Prevention of Cruelty to Animals, 424 E 92nd St, New York, NY 10128-6804; publications@aspca.org; http://www.aspca.org. *Aud.:* Ems.

ASPCA Animaland is a highly interactive web site for children. It includes games and cartoons that are educational and fun. The site provides sections for educating about animals, including an "Animal Encyclopedia" and "Ask Azula," a question-and-answer section. Animal welfare concerns get coverage in the "Humane Education" and the "Real Issues" sections. Updates are not dated, so it is difficult to tell how much or how often new material is added.

335. *The A V Magazine.* Formerly: *A-V.* [ISSN: 0274-7774] 1892. q. Membership, USD 25. Ed(s): Crystal Schaeffer. American Anti-Vivisection Society, 801 Old York Rd. Suite 204, Jenkintown, PA 19046; aavsonline@aol.com; http://www.aavs.org/. Illus. Sample. Circ: 11000. *Aud.:* Hs, Ga.

Published by the American Anti-Vivisection Society, *The AV Magazine* opposes the use of animals in laboratory research. Articles in the magazine advocate for the three R's: refinement, reduction, and replacement. The magazine also includes articles on animal rights in general. Articles tend to be longer and more detailed than those in similar animal rights magazines. Most issues have a theme that spans the entire issue, such as women in animal advocacy or elephants under siege.

336. *A W I Quarterly.* Former titles (until 1992): *Animal Welfare Institute Quarterly;* (until 1981): *Animal Welfare Institute Information Report.* [ISSN: 1071-1384] 1951. q. USD 25 (Free to qualified personnel). Ed(s): Christine Stevens. Animal Welfare Institute, PO Box 3650, Washington, DC 20007; awi@awionline.org. Illus. Sample. Circ: 4000 Paid. Vol. ends: Winter. *Indexed:* Agr. *Bk. rev.:* 2, 500-700. *Aud.:* Hs, Ga.

AWI Quarterly is a colorful, glossy animal welfare magazine. While many animal welfare magazines have a heavy emphasis on pets, *AWI Quarterly* emphasizes wild animals, agricultural animals, and laboratory animals. Unlike animal rights magazines that advocate for a complete end to the use of animals in agriculture and in laboratories, *AWI Quarterly* instead advocates for the improved treatment of these animals. In addition to discussing issues of animal welfare in general, the magazine also highlights the activities of the Animal Welfare Institute (AWI) to uncover and fight animal mistreatment. A recent issue includes articles on marine mammals and on the threat of ozone depletion to wild animals. The AWI web site includes much of the magazine's content.

337. *Act'ionLine.* Former titles: *Friends of Animals Reports; Animals (New York); Actionline.* [ISSN: 1072-2068] 1977. q. USD 25. Ed(s): Priscilla Feral. Friends of Animals, Inc., 777 Post Rd, Ste 205, Darien, CT 06820-4721; http://www.friendsofanimals.org. Illus., index, adv. Sample. Circ: 200000. Vol. ends: Winter. *Bk. rev.:* Occasional. *Aud.:* Hs, Ga.

Essays written from an animal rights perspective are a large part of *Act'ion Line*. The magazine's rights-based reasoning sometimes leads to conclusions that are different from those of mainstream society or even other animal welfare organizations. Articles advocate for an end to exploitation of animals and often promote a reduction in human interference in animals' lives. *Act'ion Line* covers a wide range of animal rights issues, and it is especially strong in its coverage of farm animals and wildlife. Each issue also includes a "Cheers and Jeers" section and restaurant reviews. Much of the content is available for free at the magazine's web site.

338. *AllAnimals.* Former titles (until 1999): *H S U S News; Humane Society News; Humane Society of the United States. News.* 1954. q. USD 25 membership. Time, Inc., Time & Life Bldg, Rockefeller Center, 29th Fl, New York, NY 10020-1393; http://www.timeinc.com. Illus. Circ: 450000. *Aud.:* Hs, Ga.

AllAnimals is a colorful magazine from the Humane Society of the United States. Attractive photographs of animals accompany short articles about the welfare of both wild and domesticated animals. Topics in a recent issue include how to make your backyard an oasis for wildlife and the myths about mutts. In addition to covering animal welfare issues, it regularly includes tips to help pet owners care for their animals.

339. *Alternatives to Laboratory Animals.* Formerly (until 1983): *A T L A Abstracts.* [ISSN: 0261-1929] 1973. bi-m. Individuals, USD 240. Ed(s): Michael Balls. Fund for the Replacement of Animals in Medical Experiments, Russell & Burch House, 96-98 N Sherwood St, Nottingham, NG1 4EE, United Kingdom; http://www.frame.org.uk. Illus., index, adv. Sample. Refereed. Circ: 850. Vol. ends: Dec. *Indexed:* Agr, BiolAb, CABA, ChemAb, DSA, ExcerpMed, FoVS&M, HortAb, IndVet, S&F, SCI, SSCI, VB. *Bk. rev.:* 4, 575 words. *Aud.:* Ac, Sa.

This journal covers the development, validation, introduction, and use of alternatives to laboratory animals. Many articles describe research to validate and evaluate non-animal research techniques. The techniques evaluated range from computer models to media for growing cell lines. *Alternatives to Laboratory Animals* also includes a conference reports section and large comment section. This journal is appropriate for larger academic libraries or special libraries in organizations where laboratory animals are used.

340. *Animal Action.* Former titles (until 1994): *Animal World;* (until 1981): *Animal Ways.* [ISSN: 1354-7437] 1975. bi-m. GBP 8 domestic; GBP 11 foreign; GBP 1.70 newsstand/cover per issue. Ed(s): Sarah Evans. Royal Society for the Prevention of Cruelty to Animals (R S P C A), Wilberforce Way, Oakhurst Business Park, Southwater, Horsham, RH13 7WN, United Kingdom. Illus., adv. Sample. Circ: 75000. Vol. ends: Dec. *Aud.:* Ems, Hs.

Animal Action is a United Kingdom-based publication for children ages roughly eight to twelve. Colorful photographs and graphics accompany articles on topics such as pet care and backyard wildlife. Numerous contests and drawings give readers opportunities to win stuffed animals, clay, books, and electronic games. Readers' photographs and artwork regularly appear. Despite its colorful, dynamic format, *Animal Action* is not completely cheery; it includes reports on topics such as puppy mills, bird flu, and animal hoarding.

341. *Animal Defender & Campaigner.* Formed by the merger of (1986-2004): *Animals' Defender;* (1986-2004): *Campaigner (London);* Both of which superseded in part (in 1990): *Campaigner and Animal's Defender;* Which was formed by the merger of (19??-1986): *Campaigner (Ruislip);* (1983-1986): *Animals Defender and Anti-vivisection News;* Which was formerly (1962-1983): *Animals Defender;* (1957-1962): *Animal's Defender and Anti-vivisection News.* [ISSN: 1748-5452] 2004. q. Ed(s): Jan Creamer. National Anti-Vivisection Society, 261 Goldhawk Rd, London, W12 8EU, United Kingdom; info@navs.org.uk; http://www.navs.org.uk. Adv. *Aud.:* Hs, Ga.

Much of *Animal Defender & Campaigner* is devoted to emotional articles that expose the suffering of laboratory animals and of animals in the entertainment industry. Color photographs of distressed animals often accompany the articles. Other articles publicize the work of the magazine's publishing organizations, Animal Defenders International (ADI) and the National Anti-Vivisection Society (NAVS). A recent series on chemical testing in the European Union is impressively deep in its coverage of the proposed regulations and of ADI and NAVS efforts to influence those regulations.

342. *Animal Guardian.* [ISSN: 1061-4141] 1988. q. Free to members. Ed(s): Linda Dozoretz. Doris Day Animal League, 227 Massachusetts Ave NE, Ste 100, Washington, DC 20002; info@ddal.org; http://www.ddal.org. Illus. *Bk. rev.:* Number and length vary. *Aud.:* Hs, Ga.

Published by the Doris Day Animal League (DDAL), *Animal Guardian* covers a wide variety of animal welfare issues. Recent topics include pet trusts, apes in the entertainment industry, and neutering and spaying pets. It also includes many short articles about legislation pending in the United Sates that could affect animal welfare. Concerns on which the DDAL lobbies receive special emphasis. *Animal Guardian* includes book reviews in every issue.

343. *Animal Issues.* Formerly: *Mainstream (Sacramento).* 1969. q. USD 35. Ed(s): Michelle Thew, Karen Hirsch. Animal Protection Institute, PO Box 22505, Sacramento, CA 95822; info@api4animals.org; http://www.api4animals.org. Illus., adv. Sample. Refereed. Circ: 50000 Controlled. Vol. ends: Dec. *Aud.:* Ga.

The Animal Protection Institute (API) produces this magazine. API campaigns to end animal suffering in places such as fur farms, circuses, slaughterhouses, pet stores, and product testing labs. *Animal Issues* contains descriptions of both animal welfare issues and how these issues affect readers in their daily lives. Many articles focus on concerns that the API works to address and describe API activities. Also included are practical topics such as how to distinguish real fur from fake fur and how to find genuinely cruelty-free products. Most articles include color photographs and suggest ways that readers can take action.

344. *Animal Law.* [ISSN: 1088-8802] 1995. a. USD 32 (Individuals, USD 22). Ed(s): Liz Pifke. Lewis & Clark College, Northwestern School of Law, 10015 SW Terwilliger Blvd, Portland, OR 97219; lclr@lclark.edu; http://www.lclark.edu. Illus. Reprint: WSH. *Indexed:* CLI, LRI. *Bk. rev.:* 2, 3,000 words. *Aud.:* Ac, Sa.

Animal Law describes itself as the first law review devoted exclusively to animal issues. At one time it was the only law review devoted to animal law, but publications such as *Journal of Animal Law* and *Journal of Animal Law and Ethics* are removing that distinction. In-depth articles discuss legal and policy issues of animal welfare. The journal is international in scope, and recent articles have examined topics in animal law in the United States, New Zealand, China, and Germany. In addition to studying legal protections for animals, articles often examine how the law is implemented through enforcement or practice. *Animal Law* is appropriate for academic and law libraries.

345. *Animal Life.* Formerly (until 1990): *R S P C A Today.* [ISSN: 0964-4628] 1971. q. GBP 6 domestic (Membership, GBP 17.50). Ed(s): Amanda Bailey. Royal Society for the Prevention of Cruelty to Animals (R S P C A), Wilberforce Way, Oakhurst Business Park, Southwater, Horsham, RH13 7WN, United Kingdom. Illus., adv. Circ: 60000. *Aud.:* Hs, Ga.

Animal Life is the membership publication of the Royal Society for the Prevention of Cruelty to Animals (RSPCA). This full-color magazine emphasizes animal protection in the United Kingdom. Dogs, cats, and other pets get a great deal of coverage, but the magazine also touches on issues related to farm animals and wildlife. Recent issues have included such topics as animal hoarding, the special care needs of rabbits, and an interview with humane slaughter expert Temple Grandin. A "Court Reports" section highlights the RSPCA's involvement in protecting animals from cruelty in recent cases.

346. *Animal Sheltering: the community animal care, control, and protection resource.* Formerly (until 1996): *Shelter Sense.* 1978. bi-m. Ed(s): Nancy Lawson. Humane Society of the United States, 2100 L St, NW, Washington, DC 20037; asm@ix.netcom.com; http://www.hsus.org/. Illus., adv. Sample. Circ: 3000. Vol. ends: Nov/Dec. *Bk. rev.:* Number and length vary. *Aud.:* Sa.

Animal Sheltering, from The Humane Society of the United States, gives practical information for shelter operators. In addition to covering the animal care aspects of shelter operation, the journal discusses concerns such as fundraising, publicity and program operation. It also profiles successful programs at different shelters and humane societies. This magazine is appropriate for veterinary libraries and essential for animal shelter libraries. Back issues are available free online.

347. *Animal Welfare.* [ISSN: 0962-7286] 1992. q. GBP 200 print & online eds. (Individuals, GBP 75 print & online eds.). Ed(s): James Kirkwood. Universities Federation for Animal Welfare, The Old School, Brewhouse

Hill, Wheathampstead, St Albans, AL4 8AN, United Kingdom; ufaw@ufaw.org.uk; http://www.ufaw.org.uk/. Illus., index. Sample. Refereed. *Indexed:* Agr, AnBeAb, BiolAb, CABA, ChemAb, DSA, ExcerpMed, FS&TA, FoVS&M, IndVet, PsycInfo, RRTA, S&F, SCI, SSCI, VB, WAE&RSA, ZooRec. *Bk. rev.:* 9, 750 words. *Aud.:* Ac, Sa.

Universities Federation for Animal Welfare produces this journal. Scholarly articles in *Animal Welfare* discuss the care of companion animals, laboratory animals, farm animals, and zoo animals. Although scholarly in tone, many articles have practical implications. For example, recent articles compare the stress animals experience in two different types of housing environments. Other articles examine methods of handling and slaughtering animals. *Animal Welfare* also includes a commentary section and book reviews. This publication is appropriate for academic libraries at institutions with veterinary schools, agricultural research, or laboratory animals.

Anthrozoos. See Pets section.

Best Friends. See Pets section.

348. *Grrr!: kids bite back.* [ISSN: 1078-6244] 1994. 2x/yr. Free to members. Ed(s): Ingrid Newkirk. People for the Ethical Treatment of Animals, Inc., 501 Front St, Norfolk, VA 23510. Illus. Sample. Circ: 30000 Free. *Aud.:* Ems, Hs.

Grrr! is a publication for young people from People for the Ethical Treatment of Animals (PETA). *Grrr!* discusses many of the same issues covered in PETA's *Animal Times*, but it does so with less stridency. *Grrr!* encourages its readers to go vegetarian, to wear animal-friendly fashions, and to avoid entertainment that exploits animals. Some articles provide ways for kids to "Bite Back" by writing letters or boycotting businesses that mistreat animals. Like *Animal Times*, celebrity photos and interviews are prominent. Much of the content is available free at the magazine's web site.

349. *International Wolf: the quarterly publication of the International Wolf Center.* [ISSN: 1089-683X] 1990. q. USD 35; USD 6 newsstand/ cover. Ed(s): Mary Ortiz. International Wolf Center, 12615 County Rd 9, Ste 200, Minneapolis, MN 55441-1248; mortiz@wolf.org; http://www.wolf.org. Illus., adv. Circ: 10000 Paid and controlled. *Aud.:* Ga.

International Wolf covers the challenges and controversies in wolf recovery. It is produced by the International Wolf Center, but the magazine is not exclusively pro-wolf. Exuberant articles about wolf behavior share space with articles by ranchers frustrated by cattle lost to wolves, giving insight into the role of wolves in the ecosystem as well as the social and political dimensions of wolf re-introduction.

350. *Journal of Animal Law.* 2006. a. USD 23 (Individuals, USD 18). Ed(s): Brooke Jaye Bearup. Michigan State University, College of Law, 368 Law College Bldg, East Lansing, MI 48824-1300; law@law.msu.edu; http://law.msu.edu. Refereed. *Bk. rev.:* 1. *Aud.:* Ac, Sa.

Journal of Animal Law is a law review that seeks to explore legal and policy issues surrounding animals. This journal issued its first annual publication in 2005, so only the first volume was examined for this review. *Journal of Animal Law* is similar in scope to the law review *Animal Law*. Both journals include heavily footnoted articles on international issues regarding animal legislation and policy. In the first volume of *Journal of Animal Law*, the articles seem to advocate for legislative changes more than those in *Animal Law*.

351. *Journal of Applied Animal Welfare Science.* Supersedes (in 1995): *Humane Innovations and Alternatives;* Which was formerly (until 1991): *Humane Innovations and Alternatives in Animal Experimentation.* [ISSN: 1088-8705] 1989. q. GBP 274 print & online eds. Ed(s): Kenneth Shapiro, Stephen Zawistowski. Lawrence Erlbaum Associates, Inc., 325 Chestnut St, Ste. 800, Philadelphia, PA 19106; journals@erlbaum.com; http://www.leaonline.com. Illus., index, adv. Sample. Refereed. Reprint: PSC. *Indexed:* Agr, BiolAb, CABA, ChemAb, DSA, ExcerpMed, ForAb, IndVet, PhilInd, PsycInfo, RRTA, VB, WAE&RSA, ZooRec. *Bk. rev.:* Number and length vary. *Aud.:* Ac, Sa.

The Society and Animals Forum and the American Society for the Prevention of Cruelty to Animals jointly produce this journal. It publishes reports about methods of experimentation, husbandry, and care that enhance the welfare of animals. Included are research reports and essays on zoo animals, farm animals, laboratory animals, and pets. One recent article examines college students' behaviors toward pets. Another looks at the effects of various feedlot conditions on cattle. The research reports usually discuss the practical implications of their results. Most of the articles are well written, making this academic journal accessible to a nonscholarly audience.

352. *K I N D News.* 1983. m. USD 30 domestic; USD 50 foreign. Ed(s): Catherine Vincenti. National Association for Humane and Environmental Education, 67 Norwich Essex Turnpike, East Haddam, CT 06423-1736; nahee@nahee.org; http://www.nahee.org. Circ: 1126400 Paid. *Aud.:* Ems.

KIND News is a four-page children's publication that encourages good character, including kindness to people and animals and respect for natural habitats. It has three editions: Primary for kindergarten to grade two, Junior for grades three and four, and Senior for grades five and six. Short articles about animals, comic strips, and puzzles are regular features. The Junior and Senior editions include short stories that pose moral dilemmas. Classroom activities and materials are available for teachers to use with *KIND News*. The articles and activities are interesting and entertaining, so children would enjoy *KIND News* outside the classroom as well.

Our Animals. See Pets section.

353. *PETA's Animal Times (English Edition).* Formerly (until 1994): *PETA News.* 1980. q. Membership, USD 16. Ed(s): Ingrid Newkirk. People for the Ethical Treatment of Animals, Inc., 501 Front St, Norfolk, VA 23510; peta@peta.org; http://www.peta.org. Illus. Sample. Circ: 350000 Paid and controlled. Vol. ends: Winter. *Aud.:* Hs, Ga.

People for the Ethical Treatment of Animals (PETA) produces *PETA's Animal Times*. It promotes a vegan diet, an end to the wearing of fur, and an end to animal testing. It also encourages readers to speak up for animals. Photo-packed issues have numerous pictures of celebrities and stories about celebrities' activities to promote animal rights. Articles also highlight the animal rights advertising campaigns produced by PETA, such as a campaign that drew parallels between the struggle against slavery and the struggle for the rights of animals.

354. *Satya: vegetarianism, environmentalism, animal advocacy, social justice.* 1993. m. USD 20. Ed(s): Catherine Clyne. Stealth Technologies, Inc., 539 1st St, Brooklyn, NY 11215-2305. Illus., adv. Circ: 20000. *Bk. rev.:* Number and length vary. *Aud.:* Hs, Ga.

New York City–based *Satya* encompasses vegetarianism, environmentalism, animal advocacy, and social justice. *Sayta* is not strictly an animal advocacy magazine, and articles are roughly equally divided between animal concerns and social justice issues. *Satya* presents many perspectives from the social justice, animal welfare, and animal rights communities, so the content is eclectic. Most articles are well written and provocative. Each issue of the magazine emphasizes a particular topic, such as activism in the workplace, veganism, or chicken. Interviews with activists are regular features. Vegan recipes, restaurant reviews, and book reviews appear frequently.

■ ANIME, GRAPHIC NOVELS, AND MANGA

Thomas Bruno, Phillips Reading Room Supervisor, Widener Library Access Services, Harvard College Library, Harvard University

Introduction

There may have been a time when anime, graphic novels, and manga were unfamiliar terms to a librarian, but in recent years the market in North America for all three has exploded dramatically. Bookstores and public libraries now stock entire sections with the latest manga series, anime films have moved from special screenings at college fan clubs and art house theaters to the suburban multiplex, and graphic novelists have been National Book Award finalists and even won the Pulitzer Prize. Having long been relegated to the stuff of juvenile fiction or esoteric enthusiasts, these three art forms are beginning to gain mainstream respect among critics and the general public alike.

Anime and manga are terms that refer to animated (anime) and printed (manga) comics originating from Japan, although in Japan they can refer to any animated film or cartoon respectively—Japanese or otherwise. Unlike in the United States, where animation and print comics charted separate courses of production, distribution, and consumption until only very recently, anime and manga have always had a complementary relationship. Typically a comic will begin in printed serialization as manga, offered as part of large, telephone book–sized, weekly compilations and later collected into their own bound volumes or "tankobon." Particularly successful manga series will be translated into animated feature films or television programs, which can then spawn additional printed stories in the form of sequels, prequels, or spin-offs. Manga and anime have enjoyed widespread public acceptance in Japan since the 1980s, and are considered to be legitimate forms of art and entertainment suitable for all ages. While their influence on North American comics and animation can be traced back several decades, anime and manga remained somewhat obscure in the West until the 1990s. Over the past few years, however, manga and anime have experienced a surge in popularity in the United States and Canada, driven by a youth market enamored with Japanese popular culture ("J-pop") and adults who grew up reading comic books and watching early "Japanimation" exports such as *Astro Boy*, *Star Blazers*, and *Speed Racer* on television.

Graphic novels, on the other hand, are still a little more difficult to define, beginning with the seemingly basic question of what exactly constitutes a "graphic novel," as the term is used loosely by both industry insiders and outside observers to describe a broad spectrum of materials. At its most inclusive definition, graphic novels can be collections of individual comic book issues, such as Frank Miller's *The Dark Knight Returns*, and *Watchmen* by Alan Moore and Dave Gibbons, similar to the manga "tankobon" in Japan. In contrast, comics that are conceived as stand-alone works from start to finish are sometimes referred to as "original graphic novels" so as to disambiguate them from the former category. Many writers and artists within the genre consider the stand-alone graphic novel as its own unique medium, drawing its inspiration not only from within the comics milieu but seeking inspiration from the fine and graphic arts as well. Noteworthy graphic novel writers/artists include Marjane Satrapi (*Persepolis, Chicken With Plums*), Craig Thompson (*Goodbye Chunky Rice*), Seth (*Wimbledon Green*), and Chris Ware (*Jimmy Corrigan, the Smartest Kid on Earth*), although some of these individuals actually reject the term "graphic novel" to describe their work, further confusing the matter. For the sake of taxonomy, this section will restrict itself to magazines and periodicals that cover original graphic novels; related periodicals covering collections of limited series or anthologies can be found either in the cross-references or by consulting the Comic Books section.

Clearly, anime, graphic novels, and manga are art forms that resist easy categorization, and as these modes of expression gain a more secure foothold in popular culture, the more they are blurred into one all-encompassing genre. A fantastic example of this is the work of Bryan Lee O'Malley, a Canadian cartoonist whose award-winning *Scott Pilgrim* series of graphic novels is directly inspired by the manga tradition. At the same time, anime and manga are borrowing increasingly from North American comic books, graphic novels, feature films, and even literature—recent Japanese anime releases include a sequel to the American *Highlander* film franchise, a new animated television series adapted from the *Witchblade* comic book, and a film by Goro Miyazaki based upon Ursula K. Le Guin's *Earthsea* novels.

It is perhaps not surprising, then, that such a fluid and dynamic body of multimedia does not yet have many periodicals that cover it exclusively. While anime and manga do have slick and glossy magazines devoted to the latest news, reviews, and previews in the genre, these are often published by the same companies that create the content they are covering in the first place, and it is only in the past decade that attempts to approach anime and manga with a more critical or broader cultural perspective have taken root. Graphic novels, on the other hand, have maintained a stronger tradition of critical coverage in zines and other limited-readership publications of artists and fans, but bias against graphic novels as "serious" literature has hampered broader cultural appreciation or peer-reviewed study in academic circles. Thankfully, the recent launch of several new periodicals seems to address such shortcomings and may point to the beginning of a sea-change in the reception of these increasingly popular forms of art.

Basic Periodicals

None. See above.

355. *Anime Insider.* Formerly (until 200?): *Anime Invasion.* 2001. m. USD 18 domestic; USD 31.50 Canada; USD 44 elsewhere. Wizard Entertainment, 151 Wells Ave, Congers, NY 10920; customerservice@WizardUniverse.com; http://www.wizarduniverse.com. Illus., adv. *Bk. rev.:* 2-4 pages of manga reviews; movie, television, DVD reviews. *Aud.:* Hs, Ga.

Originally launched as *Anime Invasion* in 2001, *Anime Insider* is an 88-page monthly publication covering the latest anime and manga releases both in Japan and the United States. Each issue features roundups from the latest conventions and movie releases, in-depth reviews of recent anime films, an overview of current anime series on Japanese television, extended feature articles highlighting a particular film and director, and comprehensive (2-4 pages) previews of upcoming DVD, television, manga, and anime-related music, games, and toys including collectible card games. Every month a chapter from an upcoming manga release is also previewed, and a lengthy letters section solicits fan engagement with the editorial staff and encourages critical feedback. Recent spotlights include the hit anime film "Beck Mongolian Chop Squad" and the work of director Makoto Shinkai. A particularly endearing aspect of *Anime Insider* is its inclusion of whimsical features such as "Last Man Standing," a regular column that pits characters from different anime films against one another, as well as encyclopedia-like entries about anime monsters and mythology that help ground readers in the rich and complicated continuity of the anime/manga tradition. Also noteworthy are informative sections on modern Japanese culture, including a feature called "JPN101" that presents some basic vocabulary words and a lexicon of current slang popular among Japanese youth, as well as humorous short pieces playing on the cultural differences between the United States and Japan. More serious offerings explore such topics as the role of Japanese religion in anime and manga and highlight certain historical events and geographical locations that figure prominently in the medium. Relatively affordable when compared to other publications similar in scope, *Anime Insider* is an excellent resource for existing anime and manga fans, as well as a good introduction for newcomers to the genre.

356. *Comic Art.* [ISSN: 1542-7447] 2002. q. USD 36; USD 9 newsstand/cover per issue. Ed(s): Todd Hignite. Buenoventura Press, P O Box 23661, Oakland, CA 94623; comicartmagazine@buenoventurapress.com; http://www.buenoventurapress.com. Illus., adv. *Aud.:* Ga, Ac, Sa.

Nominated for both the Eisner and Harvey Awards, *Comic Art* is "the only beautifully produced, full-color art magazine focusing on the comic medium." Founded by Todd Hignite, renowned comics scholar and author, the magazine courts a broad audience of fans, collectors, scholars, and critics with insightful content and superb production values. Having recently moved from a quarterly to an annual format, *Comic Art* now boasts 176 full-color pages with illustrations shot directly from both new artwork and rare old comic prints and includes 10–15 essays, interviews, and reviews both written about and written by past and present comic artists, including the leading voices in the graphic novel genre such as Art Spiegelman, Seth (author of *Wimbledon Green*), and Chris Ware. Topics in *Comic Art* range from serious retrospectives of past comic art luminaries and meditations on the craft of graphic novel storytelling to whimsical flights of fancy and humorous short works featuring original art. Recent articles explore the pulp art of Edd Cartier, ponder the connection between Jay Gatsby and Charlie Brown, and offer a history of the speech balloon in comic art. The graphic novel has always been a very self-aware medium, and *Comic Art* does not shy away from this truth but revels in it, giving artists, writers, and their circle of readers a sumptuous forum in which they can not only interact but play with ideas of inspiration and influence. While this annual magazine would be useful to academic libraries and those specializing in fine and graphic arts collections, it would also be a great addition to public libraries. In the words of the editors, the readership of *Comic Art* "spans generations, from high school and college students passionate about our focus to working professionals and older fans attracted to a magazine that covers comics and cartoonists they loved as young readers." *Comic Art* is a wonderful companion piece to any library's existing graphic novel and comic art collection.

Comics Journal. See Comic Books section.

International Journal of Comic Art (IJOCA). See Comic Books section.

357. *Mechademia: an annual forum for anime, manga and the fan arts.*
[ISSN: 1934-2489] 2006. a. USD 19.95. Ed(s): Frenchy Lunning.
University of Minnesota Press, 111 Third Ave S, Ste 290, Minneapolis,
MN 55401-2520; ump@umn.edu; http://www.upress.umn.edu. Illus., adv.
Bk. rev.: 5-10 reviews, signed. *Aud.:* Ga, Ac.

A publication of the University of Minnesota Press, *Mechademia* is the first
academic journal for anime and manga in the United States. "[W]e see these not
as objects but as arts whose production, distribution, and reception generate
networks of connections. Thus our subject area extends from manga and anime
to game design, fashion, graphics, packaging, and toy industries as well as a
broad range of fan practices related to popular culture in Japan, including
gaming, cosplay, fan artwork, anime music videos, anime improvisations, etc."
In acknowledgment of this broad spectrum of interconnected content, criticism,
and cultural reception, the editors of *Mechademia* have cast their net wide,
soliciting submissions from not only traditional academics but from
filmmakers, writers, artists, and critics at large. The senior advisory board is
similarly diverse, with professors of Eastern Asian languages and literature,
communications, film studies, and fine arts and design, as well as independent
scholars and writers.

Each illustrated issue is 184 pages and contains 10–15 scholarly essays and
5–10 signed reviews of books, films, and other related media organized around
a central theme—the theme for the inaugural issue was "The Emerging Worlds
of Anime and Manga" and future themes will be "Networks of Desire," "Limits
of the Human," and "War/Time." *Mechademia* is ambitious in scope, a
delightful exploration of what its editors have dubbed the "Art Mecho"
movement that embraces the global J-Pop phenomenon from a critical distance,
and the journal would make a fine addition to both public and academic library
collections treating the subjects of contemporary Japanese culture and its
reception abroad.

358. *Newtype U S A: the moving pictures magazine.* [ISSN: 1541-4817]
2002. m. USD 89.95 domestic; USD 145 in Canada & Mexico; USD
165 elsewhere. Ed(s): Kimberly Guerre. Newtype USA, Inc., 10114 W
Sam Houston Pkwy S, Houston, TX 77099; info@newtype-usa.com.
Illus., adv. *Bk. rev.:* 15-20 manga reviews, 10-15 anime previews, 10-15
DVD reviews, 10-15 video game reviews, 10-15 music reviews. *Aud.:*
Hs, Ga.

The American version of the popular Japanese monthly *Newtype*, *Newtype USA*
is the Cadillac of anime and manga magazines. This glossy, 160-page periodical
is lush with color photographs, artwork, and screen captures from the latest
anime films and related video games, and contains myriad previews and reviews
of the latest anime and manga releases both in the United States and Japan, as
well as reviews of anime on Japanese television, video games, and J-Pop bands.
The "Newtype Press" section features columns and commentary from artists,
writers, voice actors, and other professionals working inside the anime/manga
industry; anime voice actors also get a special section providing interviews and
profiles. *Newtype* also extensively showcases the art of anime and manga, with
10–15 pages devoted to interviews with illustrators and exclusive sketches from
the latest movies and series, such as Yoshiyuki Tomino's *The Wings of Rean*, an
instructional section on how to draw, and a forum at the end of each issue that
celebrates fan artwork inspired by the genre. Anime and manga convention
coverage is interspersed throughout each issue, and is accompanied by color
photographs from each event of both featured guests and convention attendees.
As with many other periodicals covering Japanese animation, *Newtype USA* is
printed from right to left. It also offers a center insert with a preview chapter of
an ongoing manga title, as well as six glossy color "centerfold" posters
depicting characters from selected titles and a DVD containing three full-length
anime episodes, trailers of several upcoming anime films, music videos from
Japanese bands and American popular singers such as Avril Lavigne, and
playable demos of the latest anime/manga-related video games. Considerable
attention is also paid to the new video game/anime hybrid genre of "visual
novels," a popular format in Japan that is gaining ground here in the United
States as well. With a somewhat hefty cover price and annual subscription fees
that can be as much as twice that of similar magazines, it can be easy to pass up
Newtype USA in favor of competing titles. But this is a magazine that is easily

worth the extra investment, since it delivers a truly impressive amount of
material in each issue. It takes advantage of its oversized format to deliver
cinematic-quality "splash" pages of its featured previews and still have ample
room for short articles, blurbs, and factoids offering additional perspective in the
genre as well as modern Japanese culture at large. *Newtype USA* is a rare print
resource that feels like a multimedia composition, and as such is an indispensable part of any serious anime or manga collection.

359. *Otaku U S A.* [ISSN: 1939-3318] 2007. bi-m. USD 29.95. Ed(s):
Patrick Macias. Sovereign Media, 453B Carlisle Dr, Herndon, VA 20170;
sovmedia@erols.com; http://www.scifi.com. Illus., adv. *Bk. rev.:* 20-25
manga reviews, 5-10 anime reviews, 5-10 video game reviews, 3-5
music CD reviews. *Aud.:* Hs, Ga.

A new arrival to the field of anime and manga magazines, *Otaku USA* takes its
name from the Japanese word "otaku," which translates roughly as "nerd" or
"geek" or, better yet, the more colloquial slang word "fanboy." *Otaku USA*
offers a distinctly American fanboy take on the phenomenon of Japanese pop
culture, positioning itself as an "independent" alternative to the other glossy,
mass-media anime and manga magazines published by the Japanese entertainment industry jointly in North America and Japan (*Otaku USA* is published by
Sovereign Media, which also produces *Sci-fi: the official magazine of the Sci-Fi
Channel* and *Realms of Fantasy*). Only one issue was available for review, but
its glossy, colorful, 158-page debut makes it clear that *Otaku USA* has grand
ambitions for the future. Not only does the magazine offer the standard fare of
anime/magna previews and reviews, coverage of the latest video games, toy
releases, anime television reviews, Japanese and J-Pop-inspired music, anime
and manga conventions, but *Otaku USA* also devotes a significant amount of
attention to toys—including the emerging subgenre of gunpla (based on the
Gundam plastic models kits sold worldwide by Bandai), as well as cosplay
(a.k.a. dressing as your favorite anime/manga characters, a convention favorite).
Each issue is also accompanied by a manga preview insert, color centerfold
posters, and a DVD containing anime short features, trailers of upcoming
releases, and playable demos of the latest video games.

Although it is hard for a newcomer to compete with the established anime
and manga titles, *Otaku USA* carves out a niche for itself by emphasizing the
American perspective on the genre and the reaction in the United States to the
J-Pop invasion. Articles may not be as lavishly illustrated as the established
competition, but the editors of *Otaku USA* compensate with feature articles that
are specifically geared toward the American reader and that are written with a
fan's enthusiasm for the genre tempered with a broader introspection as to the
deeper meanings of Japanese pop culture and its two-way creative relationship
with the United States and the West. A good example of this cross-fertilization
and synthesis across cultural lines can be seen in the magazine's coverage of the
current *Transformers* film, originally inspired by a line of Japanese toys that
became an American comic and animation sensation as well as a popular anime
series in Japan, or the new anime incarnation of the American *Highlander* film
franchise. As such a hybrid creation itself, *Otaku USA* is a worthwhile addition
to any library collection and a great resource for both young and old would-be
American otaku.

360. *Protoculture Addicts.* Incorporates (in 2005): *Anime News Network.*
[ISSN: 0835-9563] 1987. bi-m. USD 30. Ed(s): Claude J Pelletier.
Protoculture, Inc., PO Box 507, Montreal, PQ H3B 3J5, Canada. Illus.,
adv. *Bk. rev.:* 10-15 manga reviews and one featured preview; movie,
television, and DVD reviews. *Aud.:* Hs, Ga.

"The longest running anime and manga-related magazine," *Protoculture
Addicts* began in 1987 as a fanzine dedicated to the popular *Robotech* anime
series. The publication later expanded its coverage to other anime and manga
offerings, and in 2005 merged with *Anime News Network* to form a joint
publication. Although billed as a bimonthly magazine, *Protoculture Addicts* has
a somewhat irregular publication schedule and therefore sells its subscriptions
in units of six issues instead of on an annual basis. Each color issue is 100 pages
in length and features news from the world of anime and manga, extended
spotlights on selected films and television series, interviews with voice actors
and artists, as well as convention notes, short reviews, a letters section on the
back page, and a complete listing of upcoming releases on DVD. A relatively
new feature of *Protoculture Addicts* is a 10- to 15-page preview excerpt from an
upcoming manga title that is presented as a black-and-white insert. Recent

issues have showcased the debut film by Goro Miyazaki, son of celebrated anime director Hayao Miyazaki, the recent Japanese television adaptation of the *Witchblade* comic book series, and an interview with musician and composer Susumu Hirasawa.

Aside from its fanzine origins, another thing that sets *Protoculture Addicts* apart from similar titles is its coverage of the genre in Francophone Quebec (Protoculture, Inc. is based in Montreal) and France, where anime and manga are considerably more mainstream in popular culture than they are in the United States. As a result *Protoculture Addicts* is geared to a slightly more educated lay reader and has a more "adult" feel than many anime and manga magazines published in the United States; it also contains less advertising than its American counterparts, although like all anime and manga publications it covers the extensive market for related games, toys, and other collectibles such as card games. *Protoculture Addicts* also offers an immersive introduction to a particular anime series that is either ongoing in Japan or slated for release on DVD, devoting 10–20 pages to a crash course introduction to the material in the form of a feature article and several related short features and interviews. While not by any means a scholarly periodical, *Protoculture Addicts* strikes a refreshing balance between gushing fandom and a more critical connoisseurship, which makes it a welcome addition to any library.

361. *Shojo Beat: manga from the heart.* [ISSN: 1932-1600] 2004. m. USD 29.95; USD 5.99 newsstand/cover per issue. Ed(s): Yumi Hoashi. VIZ Media, Llc, P O Box 77064, San Francisco, CA 94107; advertising@viz.com. Illus., adv. *Bk. rev.:* 10-15 manga chapter previews. *Aud.:* Hs, Ga.

The companion publication to *Shonen Jump*, VIZ Media's *Shojo Beat* is a monthly anthology dedicated to shojo ("girl") manga, which is less action oriented and more focused on romance and teen relationships. Each 384-page issue consists of 10–15 serialized shojo manga stories printed in black and white, with several color and a few glossy pages at both the beginning and the end of each book containing manga news and reviews, fashion and beauty tips, short articles about Japanese culture and the latest youth trends in J-Pop, as well as a fan-oriented section titled "SB & You" featuring fan art, design contests, letters, photographic submissions, and a monthly horoscope. *Shojo Beat* also highlights current popular Japanese bands and reports on the influence of Japanese culture abroad in America and elsewhere. Each serial chapter installment includes a useful introduction for first-time readers, including a summary of essential plot elements and a description of the dramatis personae. Recent issues of *Shojo Beat* feature Bisco Hatori's *Millennium Snow*, Yuu Watase's *Absolute Boyfriend*, and the surreal fantasy saga *Yuma Kira Dream Shoppe* by Aqua Mizuto. Although primarily marketed toward teenage girls, the creators of *Shojo Beat* have gone out of their way recently to cultivate a broader audience, capitalizing on the growing market for more adult-themed graphic noves in the United States: "[S]hojo manga are by no means just for girls. Shojo stories are about aspects of life that concern everyone—boys and girls, old and young." For collection development purposes, this is an essential addition to any library whose collection contains manga, but *Shojo Beat* is also a tangible introduction to Japanese culture for young readers—not only is each issue printed right-to-left, but the panels also read in this fashion, so as to preserve the original graphic aesthetics of the manga.

362. *Shonen Jump.* [ISSN: 1545-7818] 2003. m. USD 29.95 domestic; USD 41.95 Canada; USD 4.95 newsstand/cover per issue. Viz Communications, Inc., PO Box 77010, San Francisco, CA 94107; media@viz.com; http://www.viz.com. Illus., adv. *Bk. rev.:* 10-15 manga chapter previews. *Aud.:* Hs, Ga.

From the Japanese "shonen" meaning boy, *Shonen Jump* is a monthly American counterpart to Shueisha's *Weekly Shonen Jump*, published in partnership with VIZ Media since 2003. "Made of the characters meaning few and years," reads the editorial statement, "shonen is Japanese for boy but can also mean pure of heart. Manga and anime created for shonen are among the most popular in the world with fans of all ages and genders." Each 384-page issue contains 10–15 serialized manga chapters printed in black and white, with several color and a few glossy pages at both the beginning and the end of each book containing manga news, reviews of anime, video games, toys, and collectible card games. *Shonen Jump* also contains extensive coverage of video game and collective card gaming strategy, as well as interviews with developers and previews of new gaming products (some issues also contain free collectible trading cards from

such popular lines as Yu-Gi-Oh). Each serial chapter installment includes a useful introduction for first-time readers, including a summary of plot elements and a description of the major characters. Recent issues of *Shonen Jump* have featured Masashi Kishimoto's *Naruto*, Hiroyuki Takei's *Shaman King*, and of course several iterations of the anime/manga phenomenon *Yu-Gi-Oh!*. Like its companion publication *Shojo Beat*, *Shonen Jump* is printed right-to-left to preserve the aesthetics of the original manga. *Shonen Jump* is also an excellent overview of the field of available manga publications and a good indicator of what is currently popular among younger readers, and as such is an important part of any library manga collection.

Wizard. See Comic Books section.

■ ANTHROPOLOGY

Patricia A. Lenkowski, Instructional Media Librarian, F.H. Green Library, West Chester University of Pennsylvania, West Chester, PA 19383; plenkowski@wcupa.edu; FAX: 610-436-2251

Introduction

The study of humankind and the description and interpretation of the peoples of the world, past and present, define anthropology. All aspects of culture and society are studied, including social structures, traditions, group relationships, tools, language, economics, music, and art. The four major branches of anthropology are physical anthropology, cultural or social anthropology, archaeology, and linguistics. Each branch is further split into many subdivisions. Titles that represent cultural and social anthropology and physical anthropology were selected for inclusion and were chosen for breadth rather than depth in both subject material and geographic coverage. Although archaeology and linguistics fall under the broad discipline of anthropology, they are in separate sections in this volume.

The professional organization for anthropology is the American Anthropological Association (AAA). The AAA is a major publisher of anthropology serials, and several of its titles are included here. A library's core journal collection should contain some of the association's titles. Because there are several major branches as well as many subdivisions of the branches of anthropology, there are many journals published to cover the wide range of the discipline. This selection of anthropological journals provides information for building a core periodical collection and enhancing weak collections.

Basic Periodicals

Ga: *American Anthropologist, Annual Review of Anthropology, Current Anthropology, Reviews in Anthropology;* Ac: *American Anthropologist, American Ethnologist, American Journal of Physical Anthropology, Current Anthropology, Royal Anthropological Institute. Journal.*

Basic Abstracts and Indexes

Abstracts in Anthropology, Anthropological Index, Anthropological Literature.

363. *American Anthropologist.* Supersedes (in 1985): *Transactions of the Anthropological Society of Washington.* [ISSN: 0002-7294] 1888. q. USD 232 USD 62 newsstand/cover. Ed(s): Frances Macia-Lees, Susan H Lees. University of California Press, Journals Division, 2000 Center St, Ste 303, Berkeley, CA 94704-1223; journals@ucpress.edu; http://www.ucpress.edu/journals. Illus., index, adv. Refereed. Circ: 13000. Vol. ends: Dec. Microform: PQC. Online: JSTOR (Web-based Journal Archive); OCLC Online Computer Library Center, Inc.; ProQuest K-12 Learning Solutions; ProQuest LLC (Ann Arbor); H.W. Wilson. *Indexed:* ABS&EES, AICP, AbAn, AgeL, AmH&L, AnthLit, ArtHuCI, B&AI, BAS, BEL&L, BRD, BRI, BrArAb, CBRI, CJA, CommAb, EI, ExcerpMed, FLI, FR, GSI, HistAb, IBR, IBSS, IBZ, IPSA, IndIslam, L&LBA, MLA-IB, MRD, NumL, PRA, PSA, PsycInfo, RI-1, RILM, RRTA, SFSA, SSA, SSCI, SWA, SociolAb, WAE&RSA, ZooRec. *Bk. rev.:* 50-60, 250-300 words. *Aud.:* Ga, Ac.

As the flagship journal of the American Anthropological Association, this is the most general and most comprehensive of all the association's publications. Articles, essays, commentaries, and research reports covering the four major areas of the field—archaeology, biology, ethnology, and linguistics—are published, as well as many reviews of books, audiovisual materials, and exhibits. Issues average six or more major articles of 10 to 15 pages in length. A core title in anthropology.

364. *American Ethnologist.* [ISSN: 0094-0496] 1974. q. USD 138 USD 37 newsstand/cover. Ed(s): Virginia R Dominguez. University of California Press, Journals Division, 2000 Center St, Ste 303, Berkeley, CA 94704-1223; journals@ucpress.edu; http://www.ucpress.edu/journals. Illus., index, adv. Refereed. Circ: 3500. Vol. ends: Nov. Microform: PQC. Online: JSTOR (Web-based Journal Archive); OCLC Online Computer Library Center, Inc.; H.W. Wilson. *Indexed:* ABS&EES, AICP, AbAn, AmHI, AnthLit, ArtHuCI, BAS, BRI, CBRI, CJA, CommAb, EI, FR, IBR, IBSS, IBZ, IndIslam, LRI, PRA, PsycInfo, RI-1, RILM, SSA, SSCI, SociolAb. *Bk. rev.:* 40, length varies. *Aud.:* Ac.

Articles concerning any human group or society are the focus of this journal. Major areas addressed include social organization, ecology, politics, ethnicity, ritual, and economy. This title would be a good basic journal in most academic collections. The book review section is substantial, averaging 40 reviews per issue, although a recent issue has only a few reviews and a lengthy review article. Most issues contain six to eight articles of 20 or more pages each.

American Indian Quarterly. See Native Americans section.

365. *American Journal of Physical Anthropology.* [ISSN: 0002-9483] 1918. 14x/yr. USD 2423. Ed(s): Clark S Larsen. John Wiley & Sons, Inc., 111 River St, Hoboken, NJ 07030-5774; uscs-wis@wiley.com; http://www.wiley.com. Illus., index, adv. Refereed. Circ: 2550. Vol. ends: Dec. Microform: PQC. Online: EBSCO Publishing, EBSCO Host; OhioLINK; SwetsWise Online Content; Wiley InterScience. *Indexed:* AICP, AbAn, AmH&L, AnthLit, ArtHuCI, BAS, BiolAb, CABA, DSA, ExcerpMed, FR, ForAb, HortAb, IBSS, IndIslam, IndVet, RRTA, S&F, SCI, SSCI, SWA, VB, WAE&RSA, ZooRec. *Bk. rev.:* 5-10, 1,200 words. *Aud.:* Ac.

This is a major scholarly journal in the area of physical anthropology. It is issued 14 times a year and publishes articles on human evolution, behavior, genetics, and primate physiology, among other topics. "Brief Communication" articles, technical reports, letters, book reviews, and a list of books received are in many issues. The proceedings of the American Association of Physical Anthropologists annual meeting are published as a supplement. Articles are 7–15 pages long, and there are about eight per issue. This is one of the most expensive journals in anthropology, and that alone may factor into subscription decisions. It is also available in an online version.

366. *Annual Review of Anthropology.* Formerly (until 1971): *Biennial Review of Anthropology.* [ISSN: 0084-6570] 1959. a. USD 189 (Individuals, USD 78 print & online eds.). Ed(s): William Durham. Annual Reviews, 4139 El Camino Way, Palo Alto, CA 94303-0139; service@annualreviews.org; http://www.annualreviews.org. Illus., index, adv. Refereed. Microform: PQC. Online: HighWire Press. Reprint: PSC. *Indexed:* AICP, AnthLit, BAS, BrArAb, CJA, ChemAb, FR, IBR, IBSS, IBZ, IPSA, L&LBA, MRD, NumL, PSA, PsycInfo, RILM, SSA, SSCI, SociolAb. *Aud.:* Ga, Ac.

Like most annual reviews, the *Annual Review of Anthropology* is used to keep current with recent trends and research in the discipline. The articles are written for a general readership and for anthropologists, to make them aware of significant literature and current developments. Each article includes an abstract and keywords. A current subscription to an *Annual Review* series includes both print and online editions.

Anthropological Linguistics. See Linguistics section.

367. *Anthropological Quarterly.* Formerly (until 1953): *Primitive Man.* [ISSN: 0003-5491] 1928. q. USD 89 (Individuals, USD 46). Ed(s): Roy Richard Grinker. Institute for Ethnographic Research, George Washington University, 2110 G St, NW, Washington, DC 20052; ifer@gwu.edu. Illus., index, adv. Refereed. Circ: 913. Vol. ends: Oct. Microform: MIM; PQC. Online: Chadwyck-Healey Inc.; EBSCO Publishing, EBSCO Host; Northern Light Technology, Inc.; OCLC Online Computer Library Center, Inc.; OhioLINK; Project MUSE; ProQuest K-12 Learning Solutions; ProQuest LLC (Ann Arbor); SwetsWise Online Content; H.W. Wilson. *Indexed:* ABS&EES, AICP, AbAn, AgeL, AmH&L, AnthLit, ArtHuCI, BAS, CPL, CommAb, EI, EIP, FR, IBR, IBSS, IBZ, IMFL, IndIslam, L&LBA, MLA-IB, PRA, PSA, PhilInd, RI-1, RILM, SFSA, SSA, SSCI, SWA, SociolAb, WAE&RSA. *Bk. rev.:* Number and length vary. *Aud.:* Ga, Ac.

Focusing on social and cultural anthropology, *Anthropological Quarterly* is cross-disciplinary and therefore of interest to many other disciplines in the social sciences. Both scholarly and review articles are featured. The journal averages three articles (15 pages) per issue, a section on thought and commentary, and some book reviews, as well as a lengthy list of books received.

368. *Anthropology & Education Quarterly.* Former titles (until 1976): *Council on Anthropology and Education Quarterly;* (until 1974): *Council on Anthropology and Education Newsletter.* [ISSN: 0161-7761] 1970. q. USD 101 USD 27 newsstand/cover. Ed(s): Douglas Foley, Sofia Villenas. University of California Press, Journals Division, 2000 Center St, Ste 303, Berkeley, CA 94704-1223; journals@ucpress.edu; http://www.ucpress.edu/journals. Illus., index, adv. Refereed. Circ: 1500. Vol. ends: Dec. Microform: PQC. Online: JSTOR (Web-based Journal Archive); OCLC Online Computer Library Center, Inc.; ProQuest K-12 Learning Solutions; ProQuest LLC (Ann Arbor); H.W. Wilson. *Indexed:* ABIn, ABS&EES, AICP, AnthLit, ArtHuCI, EAA, ERIC, EduInd, FR, IBR, IBSS, IBZ, L&LBA, PsycInfo, RI-1, RILM, SSA, SSCI, SWA. *Bk. rev.:* Number and length vary. *Aud.:* Ga, Ac.

This journal, the official publication of the Council on Anthropology and Education, publishes four or five articles per issue on human learning inside and outside of formal schools, on schooling in cultural or social contexts, and on the teaching of anthropology. Articles are about 20 pages in length and would interest educators, sociologists, and social workers in addition to anthropologists. Book reviews are available only online. The list is cumulative from 1996 and arranged alphabetically by book author.

369. *Anthropology and Humanism.* Formerly (until 1992): *Anthropology and Humanism Quarterly.* [ISSN: 1559-9167] 1974. s-a. USD 62 USD 33 newsstand/cover. Ed(s): Edith Turner. University of California Press, Journals Division, 2000 Center St, Ste 303, Berkeley, CA 94704-1223; journals@ucpress.edu; http://www.ucpress.edu/journals. Illus., adv. Circ: 600. Vol. ends: Dec. *Indexed:* AICP, AbAn, AnthLit, EI, IBR, IBSS, IBZ, RILM. *Bk. rev.:* 3-5, 1,200 words. *Aud.:* Ga, Ac.

A publication of the Society for Humanistic Anthropology, this title celebrates human reality and promotes multicultural understanding. Recent issues contain about seven scholarly articles as well as poetry and fiction. There are also a few book reviews in some issues.

370. *Anthropos: revue internationale d'ethnologie et de linguistique.* [ISSN: 0257-9774] 1906. 2x/yr. CHF 180. Ed(s): Othmar Gaechter. Editions Saint-Paul Fribourg, Perolles 42, Fribourg, 1700, Switzerland; info@paulusedition.ch; http://www.paulusedition.ch. Illus., index. Refereed. Circ: 1000. *Indexed:* AICP, AbAn, AnthLit, BAS, IBR, IBSS, IBZ, L&LBA, MLA-IB, PSA, RI-1, RILM, SSA, SSCI, SociolAb. *Bk. rev.:* 30, length varies. *Aud.:* Ac.

2006 mark4ed the 100th anniversary of this publication. Its international character and its pluralistic approach are distinguishing marks of this journal. Articles on the anthropology of religion, economic and social anthropology, culture history, and linguistics are included in this publication. Every issue has about 700 pages, with roughly 125 authors typically contributing. Each issue contains over ten articles of 15–20 pages, as well as reports and comments. Article abstracts are available on the web. Half of each issue is devoted to about 30 book reviews of a page or two in length.

371. *Arctic Anthropology.* [ISSN: 0066-6939] 1962. s-a. USD 190 print & online eds. (Individuals, USD 65 print & online eds.). Ed(s): Susan Kaplan. University of Wisconsin Press, Journal Division, 1930 Monroe St, 3rd Fl, Madison, WI 53711-2059; journals@uwpress.wisc.edu; http://www.wisc.edu/wisconsinpress/journals. Illus., index, adv. Refereed. Circ: 500. Microform: PQC. Online: EBSCO Publishing, EBSCO Host. Reprint: PSC. *Indexed:* ABS&EES, AICP, AbAn, AmH&L, AnthLit, ArtHuCI, BAS, FR, HistAb, RILM, SSCI, SWA. *Bk. rev.:* Number and length vary. *Aud.:* Ga, Ac.

Scholarly, yet engaging and accessible, this journal focuses on arctic and subarctic cultures and peoples. Issues contain articles from international contributors writing on interdisciplinary Northern research and cultures of the circumpolar zone. Recent issues average eight articles, 15 pages in length, most with illustrations, photos, maps, or charts.

372. *The Australian Journal of Anthropology.* Formerly (until 1990): *Mankind.* [ISSN: 1035-8811] 1931. 3x/yr. AUD 110 (Individuals, AUD 60). Ed(s): Michael Allen. Australian Anthropological Society, LPO Box 8099 ANU, Canberra, ACT 2601, Australia; aas@anu.edu.au; http://www.aas.asn.au/. Illus., index, adv. Refereed. Circ: 450 Paid. Online: Chadwyck-Healey Inc.; EBSCO Publishing, EBSCO Host; Florida Center for Library Automation; Gale; Northern Light Technology, Inc.; OCLC Online Computer Library Center, Inc.; ProQuest K-12 Learning Solutions; ProQuest LLC (Ann Arbor); RMIT Publishing; H.W. Wilson. *Indexed:* AICP, AbAn, AnthLit, BAS, BrArAb, EI, FR, IBR, IBSS, MLA-IB, PSA, RILM, SSA, SSCI, SociolAb. *Bk. rev.:* Number varies, 800-1,000 words. *Aud.:* Ga, Ac.

This refereed scholarly journal of anthropology and related disciplines continues the journal *Mankind*. It publishes "theoretically focused analyses and fieldwork-based reports on research carried out in Australia and neighboring countries in the Pacific and Asian regions." One of the three annual issues is devoted to a special topic. Although intended for a scholarly audience, this journal, relatively jargon free, may be of interest to a wider audience, including undergraduates and an educated public.

373. *Cultural Anthropology.* [ISSN: 0886-7356] 1986. q. USD 95 USD 25 newsstand/cover. Ed(s): Ann Anagnost. University of California Press, Journals Division, 2000 Center St, Ste 303, Berkeley, CA 94704-1223; journals@ucpress.edu; http://www.ucpress.edu/journals. Illus., adv. Refereed. Circ: 2100. Vol. ends: Nov. *Indexed:* ABS&EES, AICP, ASSIA, AbAn, AmH&L, AnthLit, ArtHuCI, BAS, CABA, CJA, ForAb, HistAb, IBR, IBSS, IBZ, L&LBA, PRA, RI-1, RILM, RRTA, S&F, SSA, SSCI, SociolAb, WAE&RSA. *Aud.:* Ac.

This journal publishes articles on a broad array of cultural issues in many cultures. Recent issues contain articles on women in India, ethnography in the forest, and activist research versus cultural critique. Each issue contains four or five lengthy articles of 20 to 35 pages each.

374. *Current Anthropology.* Formerly (until 1956): *Yearbook of Anthropology.* [ISSN: 0011-3204] 1955. bi-m. USD 239 domestic; USD 262.34 Canada; USD 259 elsewhere. Ed(s): Benjamin S Orlove. University of Chicago Press, Journals Division, PO Box 37005, Chicago, IL 60637; subscriptions@press.uchicago.edu; http://www.journals.uchicago.edu. Illus., index, adv. Refereed. Circ: 4000. Microform: PQC. Online: EBSCO Publishing, EBSCO Host; Florida Center for Library Automation; Gale; JSTOR (Web-based Journal Archive); ProQuest K-12 Learning Solutions; ProQuest LLC (Ann Arbor). Reprint: PSC. *Indexed:* ABS&EES, AICP, AbAn, AgeL, AmH&L, AnthLit, ArtHuCI, BAS, BiolAb, BrArAb, CommAb, EI, FR, HistAb, IBR, IBSS, IBZ, IPSA, IndIslam, L&LBA, MASUSE, MLA-IB, NumL, PSA, PsycInfo, RI-1, RILM, SCI, SSA, SSCI, SWA, SociolAb, ZooRec. *Bk. rev.:* 3-5, 2,000 words. *Aud.:* Ga, Ac.

A transnational journal devoted to research in a wide variety of areas, including social, cultural, and physical anthropology, as well as ethnology, archaeology, folklore, and linguistics. Each issue is comprised of two to four major articles with several comments and the authors' replies to the comments. Issues also include reports on research, professional news, a few book reviews, and a list of books received. "Anthropological Currents" summarizes empirical research in other publications. For professional and general readership.

375. *Dialectical Anthropology: an independent international journal in the critical tradition committed to the transformation of our society and the humane union of theory and practice.* [ISSN: 0304-4092] 1975. q. EUR 430 print & online eds. Springer New York LLC, 233 Spring St, New York, NY 10013-1578; journals@springer-ny.com; http://www.springer.com. Illus., index, adv. Vol. ends: Dec. Microform: PQC. Online: EBSCO Publishing, EBSCO Host; Gale; IngentaConnect; OCLC Online Computer Library Center, Inc.; OhioLINK; Springer LINK; SwetsWise Online Content. Reprint: PSC. *Indexed:* AICP, AbAn, AltPI, AmHI, AnthLit, ArtHuCI, BAS, FR, IBSS, LeftInd, PRA, PSA, PhilInd, SSA, SSCI, SociolAb. *Aud.:* Ac.

"An independent international journal in the critical tradition committed to the transformation of our society and the humane union of theory and practice." This journal publishes social critiques of every aspect of contemporary civilization, comparative and historical essays, case studies of crisis and transition, and professional or personal memoirs. The journal is a contributor to the radical literature of our time. Issues average four or five essays of 20 to 30 pages in length. Available in print or electronic format.

Ethnohistory. See Ethnic Studies section.

376. *Ethnology: an international journal of cultural and social anthropology.* [ISSN: 0014-1828] 1962. q. USD 40 (Individuals, USD 21). Ed(s): Leonard Plotnicov, Richard Scaglion. University of Pittsburgh, Department of Anthropology, 3302 WWPH, Pittsburgh, PA 15260; ethnolog@pitt.edu. Illus., index, adv. Refereed. Circ: 2000 Paid. Vol. ends: Oct. Microform: PQC. Online: Chadwyck-Healey Inc.; EBSCO Publishing, EBSCO Host; Florida Center for Library Automation; Gale; Northern Light Technology, Inc.; OCLC Online Computer Library Center, Inc.; ProQuest K-12 Learning Solutions; ProQuest LLC (Ann Arbor). *Indexed:* ABS&EES, AICP, AbAn, AmH&L, AnthLit, ArtHuCI, BAS, BrArAb, EI, FR, HistAb, IBR, IBSS, IBZ, IPSA, IndIslam, MLA-IB, PSA, RI-1, RILM, SSA, SSCI, SUSA, SWR&A, SociolAb, WAE&RSA. *Aud.:* Ga, Ac.

This journal offers a broad range of articles on cultural and social anthropology. It is highly readable and reflects a cross section of specializations, making it useful for teaching, reference, and general readership. There are on average five articles per issue, each about 15 pages long.

377. *Ethnos: journal of anthropology.* [ISSN: 0014-1844] 1936. q. GBP 244 print & online eds. Ed(s): Wilhelm Oestberg, Don Kulick. Routledge, 4 Park Square, Milton Park, Abingdon, OX14 4RN, United Kingdom; info@routledge.co.uk; http://www.routledge.co.uk. Illus., index, adv. Refereed. Circ: 1000. Online: EBSCO Publishing, EBSCO Host; Gale; IngentaConnect; OCLC Online Computer Library Center, Inc.; SwetsWise Online Content. Reprint: PSC. *Indexed:* AICP, ASSIA, AbAn, AmH&L, AnthLit, BAS, BiolDig, EI, FR, HAPI, HistAb, IBR, IBSS, IBZ, IndIslam, L&LBA, PSA, RI-1, RILM, SSA, SSCI, SociolAb. *Bk. rev.:* Number varies, 1,000 words. *Aud.:* Ac.

Original papers on theoretical, methodological, and empirical developments in the discipline of sociocultural anthropology are featured in this publication. Contributors are international, and the scope is global. Each issue averages five articles of 25 pages each, with book reviews and correspondence. Available in print or electronic format.

378. *Ethos (Berkeley).* [ISSN: 0091-2131] 1973. q. USD 77 USD 21 newsstand/cover. Ed(s): Janet Dixon Keller. University of California Press, Journals Division, 2000 Center St, Ste 303, Berkeley, CA 94704-1223; journals@ucpress.edu; http://www.ucpress.edu/journals. Illus., adv. Refereed. Circ: 1100. Vol. ends: Dec. Microform: PQC. Online: JSTOR (Web-based Journal Archive); ProQuest LLC (Ann Arbor). *Indexed:* AbAn, AnthLit, IBR, IBSS, IBZ, L&LBA, PsycInfo, SSA, SSCI. *Aud.:* Ac.

This journal is the publication of the Society for Psychological Anthropology. It features the relationship between the individual and society. The editors "intend the journal to be instrumental in fostering the growth of an international, interdisciplinary community of scholars in psychocultural research and theory." Topics include psychodynamics, psychoanalysis, child development and socialization, interpersonal interaction, emotion, perception, motivation, self and identity, and religion. Most issues contain four to six articles approximately 30 pages in length, with occasional commentary. There are often theme issues.

379. Evolutionary Anthropology: issues, news, and reviews. [ISSN: 1060-1538] 1992. bi-m. USD 595. Ed(s): John Fleagle. John Wiley & Sons, Inc., 111 River St, Hoboken, NJ 07030-5774; uscs-wis@wiley.com; http://www.wiley.com. Illus., adv. Refereed. Microform: PQC. Online: EBSCO Publishing, EBSCO Host; OhioLINK; SwetsWise Online Content; Wiley InterScience. *Indexed:* AICP, AbAn, AnthLit, IBSS, SSCI, ZooRec. *Bk. rev.:* Number and length vary. *Aud.:* Ac.

This is a review journal that publishes four or five scholarly articles on contemporary research in paleoanthropology and biological anthropology. In addition, the journal has articles on social biology, bone biology, and human biology. Book reviews, professional news, letters to the editor, and a calendar are included. Available in print or electronic format.

Human Ecology. See Environment and Conservation section.

380. Human Evolution: international journal. [ISSN: 0393-9375] 1986. q. EUR 138 print & online eds. Springer Netherlands, Van Godewijckstraat 30, Dordrecht, 3311 GX, Netherlands; http://www.springeronline.com. Illus., index, adv. Circ: 700. Vol. ends: Dec. Reprint: PSC. *Indexed:* AICP, AnthLit, BAS, ExcerpMed, FR, ZooRec. *Bk. rev.:* Number and length vary. *Aud.:* Ac.

Published in Italy with text in English and summaries in French, this journal is international in coverage and is devoted to the arena of primates and human evolution. Average issues contain five articles of varying length. Of interest to scholars and professionals.

381. Human Organization. Formerly: *Applied Anthropology.* [ISSN: 0018-7259] 1941. q. USD 75. Ed(s): Donald D Stull. Society for Applied Anthropology, PO Box 2436, Oklahoma City, OK 73101; info@sfaa.net; http://www.sfaa.net. Illus., index, adv. Refereed. Circ: 4700. Vol. ends: Winter. Online: EBSCO Publishing, EBSCO Host; Northern Light Technology, Inc.; OCLC Online Computer Library Center, Inc.; ProQuest LLC (Ann Arbor). *Indexed:* ABIn, AICP, ASG, AbAn, AgeL, AmH&L, AnthLit, BAS, CABA, CJA, CommAb, DSA, EI, FPA, FR, ForAb, HRA, HistAb, HortAb, IBR, IBSS, IBZ, IPSA, IndVet, MCR, PRA, PSA, PsycInfo, RILM, RRTA, S&F, SFSA, SSA, SSCI, SUSA, SWA, SWR&A, SociolAb, V&AA, VB, WAE&RSA. *Aud.:* Ac.

This journal, a publication of the Society for Applied Anthropology, covers all areas of applied social science. Each issue contains eight to ten articles of ten pages each focusing on case studies, comparative studies, and fieldwork with an international approach. Meeting and conference notes, comments on previously published pieces, and commentaries are also included.

382. International Journal of Anthropology. [ISSN: 0393-9383] 1986. q. EUR 100 print & online eds. Springer Netherlands, Van Godewijckstraat 30, Dordrecht, 3311 GX, Netherlands; http://www.springeronline.com. Illus., index, adv. Circ: 500. Vol. ends: Dec. Reprint: PSC. *Indexed:* AICP, AnthLit, ExcerpMed. *Bk. rev.:* Number and length vary. *Aud.:* Ac.

As the official organ of the European Anthropological Association, this journal is a good source for current research in the international anthropological community. Issues cover biological anthropology. Subjects include studies on paleoanthropology, primate ethology, paleopathology, and biosocial anthropology. The articles vary in number and length from issue to issue.

383. Journal of Anthropological Archaeology. [ISSN: 0278-4165] 1982. 4x/yr. EUR 456. Ed(s): John M O'Shea. Academic Press, 525 B St, Ste 1900, San Diego, CA 92101-4495; apsubs@acad.com; http://www.elsevier.com/. Illus. Refereed. Vol. ends: Dec. Online: EBSCO Publishing, EBSCO Host; Gale; IngentaConnect; OCLC Online Computer Library Center, Inc.; OhioLINK; ScienceDirect; SwetsWise Online Content. *Indexed:* AICP, AbAn, AmHI, AnthLit, ArtHuCI, BAS, BrArAb, FR, HumInd, IBSS, NumL, SSCI. *Aud.:* Ac.

This journal publishes articles on the theory and methodology of archaeology as it relates to human societies, covering the broadest scope of time. Issues typically contain three or four scholarly articles ranging in length from 15 to 40 pages, with most being 30 pages long. An occasional special-topics issue will have shorter contributions. Available in print and electronic format. The online version posts the articles as they are finally accepted.

384. Journal of Anthropological Research. Former titles (until 1972): *Southwestern Journal of Anthropology;* (until 1945): *New Mexico Anthropology.* [ISSN: 0091-7710] 1937. q. USD 50 (Individuals, USD 30). Ed(s): Lawrence G Straus. University of New Mexico, Department of Anthropology, 1 University of New Mexico, MSC01 1040, Albuquerque, NM 87131-0001. Illus., index. Refereed. Circ: 1200 Paid. Vol. ends: Winter. Microform: PQC. *Indexed:* ABS&EES, AICP, AbAn, AmH&L, AnthLit, ArtHuCI, BAS, BrArAb, CommAb, EI, FR, HistAb, IBR, IBSS, IBZ, L&LBA, LRI, MLA-IB, NumL, PRA, RI-1, RILM, SSA, SSCI, SociolAb, WAE&RSA. *Bk. rev.:* Number and length vary. *Aud.:* Ga, Ac.

Publishes recent research from all areas of anthropology, primarily on the Americas but with an occasional international piece. Most issues have four articles, 20 pages in length, and approximately 15 current, critical book reviews.

385. Journal of Human Evolution. [ISSN: 0047-2484] 1972. 12x/yr. EUR 1566. Ed(s): William H. Kimbel, Susan Anton. Academic Press, Harcourt Pl, 32 Jamestown Rd, London, NW1 7BY, United Kingdom; apsubs@acad.com; http://www.elsevier.com/. Illus., adv. Refereed. Vol. ends: Dec. Online: EBSCO Publishing, EBSCO Host; Gale; IngentaConnect; OCLC Online Computer Library Center, Inc.; OhioLINK; ScienceDirect; SwetsWise Online Content. *Indexed:* AICP, AbAn, AnBeAb, AnthLit, ArtHuCI, BiolAb, BrArAb, ExcerpMed, FR, GSI, IBSS, SCI, SSCI, ZooRec. *Bk. rev.:* Number and length vary. *Aud.:* Ac.

This journal is devoted to publishing research papers on all aspects of human evolution, especially paleoanthropological work on human and primate fossils. Three to six articles per issue is typical, and most are 15–20 pages long. Additional features that may be included are communications on new discoveries, reports of meetings, and review papers. Also included are abstracts for the Paleoanthropology Society meeting. Available in print and electronic format.

386. Journal of Latin American and Caribbean Anthropology. Former titles (until 2007): *Journal of Latin American Anthropology;* (until 1994): *The Latin American Anthropology Review.* [ISSN: 1935-4932] 1989. s-a. USD 59 USD 31 newsstand/cover. Ed(s): Jean Rahier. University of California Press, Journals Division, 2000 Center St, Ste 303, Berkeley, CA 94704-1223; journals@ucpress.edu; http://www.ucpress.edu/journals. Adv. Refereed. *Indexed:* AICP, AbAn, AnthLit, HAPI, IBR, IBSS, IBZ, PSA, SSA, SociolAb. *Aud.:* Ac.

The official publication of the Latin American Anthropology Section of the American Anthropological Association, this journal is devoted to publishing articles on anthropological research in Mexico, Central and South America, and the Caribbean. Articles may be published in Spanish or English. Each issue has five to seven articles, and theme issues are common.

Journal of Linguistic Anthropology. See Linguistics section.

387. Medical Anthropology Quarterly: international journal for the cultural and social analysis of health. Former titles: *Medical Anthropology Newsletter; Medical Anthropology.* [ISSN: 0745-5194] 1970. q. USD 52 USD 28 newsstand/cover. Ed(s): Pamela Erickson. University of California Press, Journals Division, 2000 Center St, Ste 303, Berkeley, CA 94704-1223; journals@ucpress.edu; http://www.ucpress.edu/journals. Illus., adv. Refereed. Circ: 2000. Vol. ends: Dec. *Indexed:* ABS&EES, AICP, AbAn, AgeL, AnthLit, ArtHuCI, BRI, EI, HortAb, IBR, IBSS, IBZ, SSA, SSCI, SociolAb. *Bk. rev.:* Number and length vary. *Aud.:* Ac.

The range of subjects in this journal include illness, disease, and health of individuals and groups, using an anthropological focus. The cultural, linguistic, and biological aspects of health issues are addressed. This scholarly journal is cross-cultural and multidisciplinary and addresses topics of interest in public health, health policy, nutrition, and maternal-child health. Each issue includes articles, research reports, and book reviews of varying length. There are occasionally theme issues.

388. *Oceania: devoted to the study of the indigenous peoples of Australia, Melanesia, Micronesia, Indonesia, Polynesia and Insular Southeast Asia.* [ISSN: 0029-8077] 1930. q. AUD 84 (Individuals, AUD 72). Ed(s): Neil Maclean. Oceania Publications, University of Sydney (H42), 116 Darlington Rd, Sydney, NSW 2006, Australia; oceania@arts.usyd.edu.au; http://www.arts.usyd.edu.au/publications/oceania/. Illus., index. Refereed. Circ: 800. Microform: PQC. Online: Chadwyck-Healey Inc.; EBSCO Publishing, EBSCO Host; Florida Center for Library Automation; Gale; Northern Light Technology, Inc.; OCLC Online Computer Library Center, Inc.; ProQuest K-12 Learning Solutions; ProQuest LLC (Ann Arbor); RMIT Publishing; H.W. Wilson. *Indexed:* AICP, ASSIA, AbAn, AmHI, AnthLit, ArtHuCI, BAS, EI, FR, IBR, IBSS, IBZ, MLA-IB, PAIS, RI-1, RILM, SSCI. *Bk. rev.:* 7, length varies. *Aud.:* Ac.

This refereed scholarly journal publishes research in social and cultural anthropology on the "indigenous peoples of Australia, Melanesia, Polynesia, Micronesia, and Southeast Asia." It is an important source for Australia and Pacific Studies. It covers past and present customs, ceremonies, folklore, and belief systems of the region. Guest-edited thematic issues also appear. It includes maps and graphs, some illustrations, and an abstract for each article. This journal is recommended for academic libraries that serve anthropology or Asian, Pacific, or Australian Studies faculty. (ChD)

389. *Practicing Anthropology.* [ISSN: 0888-4552] q. USD 35 domestic; USD 40 foreign. Ed(s): Alexander Ervin. Society for Applied Anthropology, PO Box 24083, Oklahoma City, OK 73124-0083; info@sfaa.net; http://www.sfaa.net. Illus., index, adv. Vol. ends: Fall. Reprint: PSC. *Indexed:* AICP, AbAn, AnthLit, FR, RILM. *Bk. rev.:* Number and length vary. *Aud.:* Ac.

This journal publishes short, readable articles focused on a single topic. Applied or practicing anthropology is the focus. Some of the stated goals of the publication are to provide career information for anthropologists who work outside academia; to explore the use of anthropology in policy research and implementation; and to serve as a forum for inquiry into the present state and future of anthropology in general. In a typical issue, there is an introduction to the theme, six to ten articles of three to five pages each, and the feature "Teaching Practice."

390. *Reviews in Anthropology.* [ISSN: 0093-8157] 1974. q. GBP 463 print & online eds. Ed(s): Roger Ivar Lohmann, Megan Cotton-Kinch. Taylor & Francis Inc., 325 Chestnut St, Ste 800, Philadelphia, PA 19016; orders@taylorandfrancis.com; http://www.taylorandfrancis.com. Illus. Refereed. Vol. ends: Fall. Microform: PQC. Online: EBSCO Publishing, EBSCO Host; IngentaConnect; OCLC Online Computer Library Center, Inc.; SwetsWise Online Content. Reprint: PSC. *Indexed:* ABS&EES, AbAn, AnthLit, BRI, CBRI, IBR, IBSS, IBZ, RILM. *Bk. rev.:* 3-5, essay length. *Aud.:* Ga, Ac.

An international quarterly publication devoted to review commentary on recently published books in anthropology, including the subdisciplines of cultural anthropology, human biology, comparative linguistics, and archaeology. The papers, which are submitted by invitation only, are few (three to five) but lengthy (over 20 pages) and appeal to both generalists and specialists. A useful collection development resource.

391. *Royal Anthropological Institute. Journal.* Formerly (until 1995): *Man;* Incorporates (1871-1965): *Royal Anthropological Institute of Great Britain and Ireland. Journal;* Which was formerly (until 1906): *Anthropological Institute of Great Britain and Ireland. Journal;* Which was formed by the merger of (1848-1871): *Ethnological Society of London. Journal;* Which was formerly (until 1869): *Ethnological Society of London. Transactions;* (until 1861): *Ethnological Society of London. Journal;* (1863-1871): *Journal of Anthropology;* Which was formerly (until 1870): *Anthropological Review.* [ISSN: 1359-0987] 1901. q. GBP 379 print & online eds. Ed(s): Glenn Bowman. Blackwell Publishing Ltd., 9600 Garsington Rd, Oxford, OX4 2ZG, United Kingdom;

customerservices@blackwellpublishing.com; http://www.blackwellpublishing.com. Illus., index, adv. Refereed. Circ: 3200. Vol. ends: Dec. Microform: BHP; PQC. Online: Blackwell Synergy; Chadwyck-Healey Inc.; EBSCO Publishing, EBSCO Host; Florida Center for Library Automation; Gale; IngentaConnect; JSTOR (Web-based Journal Archive); OCLC Online Computer Library Center, Inc.; OhioLINK; ProQuest K-12 Learning Solutions; SwetsWise Online Content; H.W. Wilson. Reprint: PSC. *Indexed:* AICP, AbAn, AgeL, AmH&L, AnthLit, ApEcolAb, BAS, BRI, BrArAb, EI, ExcerpMed, FR, HistAb, IBR, IBSS, IBZ, IndIslam, L&LBA, MLA-IB, PSA, PhilInd, RI-1, RILM, SSA, SSCI, SWA, SociolAb. *Bk. rev.:* 40, 350 words. *Aud.:* Ac.

This publication is international in both contributors and content. It covers all the subfields of anthropology. Abstracts are in English and French, and text is in English. Each issue is comprised of eight or so articles and numerous book reviews divided into subject areas such as anthropology and history, religion, social anthropology, and theory and methodology. Beginning in 2006, the Royal Anthropological Institute published the first in a special issues series that is included with a subscription to *JRAI*. The theme of the inaugural isssue is "Ethnobiology and the Science of Humankind."

392. *Urban Anthropology and Studies of Cultural Systems and World Economic Development.* Formerly (until 1984): *Urban Anthropology.* [ISSN: 0894-6019] 1972. q. USD 75. Institute for the Study of Man, 1133 13th St, NW, No C 2, Washington, DC 20005. Illus. Refereed. Circ: 500. *Indexed:* ABS&EES, AICP, AbAn, AmH&L, AnthLit, BAS, CABA, DSA, FPA, ForAb, IBR, IBSS, IBZ, PRA, RILM, RRTA, SSA, SSCI, SUSA, SWA, SociolAb, WAE&RSA. *Aud.:* Ac.

As the title suggests, this journal is devoted to urban anthropology and global economic development in the world's cultural systems. Articles focus on urbanization, development and underdevelopment, and colonialism and neocolonialism. A typical issue has two or three lengthy articles of 30 to 50 pages each. There are often theme issues.

393. *Visual Anthropology.* [ISSN: 0894-9468] 1987. 5x/yr. GBP 654 print & online eds. Ed(s): Paul Hockings. Taylor & Francis Inc., 325 Chestnut St, Ste 800, Philadelphia, PA 19016; orders@taylorandfrancis.com; http://www.taylorandfrancis.com. Illus. Refereed. Online: EBSCO Publishing, EBSCO Host; Gale; IngentaConnect; OCLC Online Computer Library Center, Inc.; SwetsWise Online Content. Reprint: PSC. *Indexed:* AICP, AbAn, AmHI, AnthLit, FLI, IBR, IBSS, IBZ, RILM. *Bk. rev.:* Number and length vary. *Aud.:* Ac.

Published in cooperation with the Commission on Visual Anthropology, this international journal aims to present articles, comments, discussions, and film and book reviews that contribute to the study, use, and production of anthropological and ethnographic films, videos, and photographs for research and teaching. The journal also is concerned with the analysis of visual symbolic forms and the study of human behavior through visual means.

■ ANTIQUES

General/Doll Collecting

Maureen Kilcullen, Reference Librarian, Kent State University Stark Campus Library, 6000 Frank Ave., Canton, OH 44720; mkilcullen@ stark.kent.edu; FAX: 330-494-6212

Introduction

There is still a market for antiques and collectibles; however, the impact of eBay and the consolidation of some of the antiques trade publishers have impacted the number of publications. Unfortunately, these factors have eliminated at least two more collectibles magazines—*Collector's Mart* and *Collector Magazine & Price Guide*. There are far fewer collectibles magazines. This is regrettable because the antiques magazines limit coverage of the more modern collectibles.

The biggest population in the United States is that of the baby boomers, who are especially interested in collectibles from their childhood. These collectibles are not considered antiques, which by definition are at least 100 years old.

Examples of this type of collectible are Depression glass, PEZ candy dispensers, celebrity memorabilia, board games, Hallmark ornaments, and sports, cartoon, and movie memorabilia. These items are often found on eBay, but eBay does not provide much guidance or expert opinion on what these items are really worth. Fortunately, the *Antiques Roadshow Insider* and the Kovels are filling the gap. The experts who write for these magazines fill the need for tips on evaluating, restoring, cleaning, and displaying antiques and collectibles.

America's fascination with antiques and collecting continues. As mentioned above, this is reflected in the continued growth of eBay and the Internet. A few years ago, most of the antique and collectibles magazine web sites would offer full text of older issues and other incentives. Many of them are now limiting information on their web sites to actual subscribers. Few offer access to any of the full text of their magazines.

Interest in fine antiques remains high, and auction prices indicate that the most popular pieces are antique American furniture. Many of the editors of the magazines reviewed herein stated that prices for antique American furniture were soaring and they did not see an end to that trend. The art market, as well as estate and antique jewelry, continues to attract buyers. Many standard titles remain, and the trends increasingly indicate that interest in fine antiques will remain high. Once again, the Jacqueline Kennedy Onassis estate "Sale of the Century" in 1996 can help define the differences between collecting antiques and collecting memorabilia. If one defines an antique as an object from the past that has artistic or historical value and is more than 100 years old, then the small Louis XV gilt-tooled, red Morocco leather casket (trunk), once owned by Marie Antoinette and then by Mrs. Onassis, is definitely an antique. At the auction, this trunk sold for $105,000. The walnut humidor that Milton Berle presented to John F. Kennedy in 1961 is not considered an antique, but because it was in the possession of both Kennedy and Berle, it is considered a collectible. At the auction, it sold for $574,000.

Basic Periodicals

FINE ANTIQUES/OBJETS D'ART. Ga: *Antique Collecting, The Magazine Antiques.*

POPULAR ANTIQUES/COLLECTIBLES. Ga: *Antique Trader Weekly, Collector Editions, Collector Magazine & Price Guide, Maine Antique Digest.*

DOLL COLLECTING. Ga: *Contemporary Doll Collector, Doll Reader, Dolls: the collector's magazine.*

Basic Abstracts and Indexes

Readers' Guide to Periodical Literature.

General

394. Antique & Collectibles Showcase. Formed by the merger of (1965-2003): *Antique Showcase;* Which was formerly (until vol.17, Nov. 1981): *Ontario Showcase;* (1982-2003): *Collectibles Canada;* Which superseded in part (in 1993): *Insight on Collectables;* Which was formerly (until 1987): *Insight;* (until 1986): *Insight on Collectables.* [ISSN: 1708-6469] 2003. 6x/yr. CND 27 domestic; USD 28 United States. Ed(s): Judy Penz Sheluk. Trajan Publishing Corp., 103 Lakeshore Rd, Ste 202, St Catharines, ON L2N 2T6, Canada; office@trajan.com; http://www.trajan.com. Illus., adv. Sample. Vol. ends: Jun. *Bk. rev.:* 5, length varies. *Aud.:* Ga.

Antique & Collectibles Showcase advertises itself as Canada's national collectors magazine, but don't let that fool you, because the coverage is international. This journal aims for diversity of content, and it is laid out in an attractive format. The factual and informative articles offer valuable information to the novice as well as the experienced collector. Regular columns such as "Fakes & Forgeries," "Collector's College," and "Travelling Collector" keep the reader up to date. Features include museum exhibitions, book reviews, and an antique show calendar. Many antiques publications concentrate on antiques and collectibles in a specific market, whether it be fine art or collectible Americana. This journal's focus is for the generalist, and it is

an excellent magazine. Its web site is www.antiqueandcollectiblesshowcase.ca, and this offers editorials and partial articles from the current issue and archives. Recommended for those libraries searching for a general title about antiques and collectibles.

395. Antique Collecting. Incorporates: *Antique Finder.* [ISSN: 0003-584X] 1965. m. except Aug. & Jan. GBP 25 domestic; GBP 30 foreign. Ed(s): Susan Wilson. Antique Collectors Club, 5 Church St, Woodbridge, IP12 1DS, United Kingdom; http://www.antiquecc.com/. Illus., adv. Sample. Circ: 20000. Vol. ends: Apr. *Indexed:* RILM. *Bk. rev.:* 2-6, 100-500 words. *Aud.:* Ga, Sa.

This fine British magazine is tastefully done and does not include the annoying "every-other-page" advertising found in other magazines. It is the journal of the Antique Collector's Club, and the topics of the signed articles range from American antiques to French clocks and Irish art. The articles are interesting and informative, and are written by dealers or collectors with firsthand knowledge of their subject. Photographs are mostly in color and large enough to show details. The information found in this magazine, written "for collectors, by collectors about collecting," focuses on European, British, and American antiques and collectibles from the sixteenth through the eighteenth century. Most of the articles offer advice on evaluating a piece and provide a list of recommended books. Regular features include an auction calendar, entertaining editorials, auction news, and a fairs preview calendar. Several article extracts from past issues can be found at the magazine's web site at www.antiquecollectorsclub.com. Highly recommended for public libraries with an interest in British, American, and European antiques.

396. Antique Trader: America's weekly antiques and collectibles marketplace. Former titles (until 2000): *The Antique Trader Weekly; Antique Trader.* 1957. w. USD 35 domestic; USD 106 Canada; USD 156 elsewhere. Ed(s): Catherine Saunders-Watson. Krause Publications, Inc., 700 E State St, Iola, WI 54990-0001; info@krause.com; http://www.krause.com. Illus. Sample. Circ: 28559 Paid and free. Vol. ends: Dec. *Bk. rev.:* 30, length varies. *Aud.:* Ga.

Antique Trader offers weekly antiques news coverage, collector profiles, articles on general antiques topics, auction reviews, and antique show reports. The publication features classified ads, a question-and-answer section, a national shopping directory, an Internet shopping directory, and show and auction calendars. These are combined with expert advice and in-depth articles on anything to do with antiques. It is one of the most comprehensive newspapers available on the antique trade and is popular in libraries if holdings are a consideration. *Antique Trader Online* at www.antiquetrader.com does not provide the complete print publication, but it offers feature articles from past issues and weekly news stories. A free e-newsletter debuted October 2006 that offers late-breaking news and features. The e-newsletter can be accessed at the magazine's web site, and subscription simply requires an e-mail address.

397. Antiques & Auction News. Formerly: *Joel Sater's Antiques and Auction News.* 1969. w. Fri. USD 80. Ed(s): Denise M. Sater. Circ: 38000 Paid and free. *Aud.:* Ga.

This weekly newspaper focuses on the geographic area east of and including Pennsylvania and is advertised as "the most widely read collector's newspaper in the East." A few articles are included with tips for taking care of antiques as well as news from the field, but the real value lies in its extensive coverage of auctions, exhibitions, and shows. Regular departments such as the "Auction Calendar," "Shows and Markets," "Shops and Centers," and the "Auction Sale Bills" provide detailed information for collectors in the eastern United States. The web site is located at www.antiquesandauctionnews.net and offers the full text of weekly articles and archives back to 2005. If your library does not carry *Antique Trader* (above), this title should be considered for public libraries in the geographic region with patrons interested in antique shows and auctions.

398. Antiques & Collecting Magazine. Former titles (until Oct. 1993): *Antiques and Collecting Hobbies;* (until 1985): *Hobbies, the Magazine for Collectors.* [ISSN: 1084-0818] 1931. m. USD 38 domestic; USD 50 foreign. Ed(s): M Therese Nolan. Lightner Publishing Corporation, 1006 S Michigan Ave, Chicago, IL 60605. Illus., adv. Sample. Circ: 20000

Paid. Vol. ends: Feb. Microform: PQC. Online: EBSCO Publishing, EBSCO Host; Northern Light Technology, Inc.; OCLC Online Computer Library Center, Inc.; ProQuest LLC (Ann Arbor); H.W. Wilson. *Indexed:* BRI, CBRI, MusicInd, RGPR. *Bk. rev.:* 4-6, 30-100 words. *Aud.:* Ga.

Antiques and Collecting Magazine has several feature articles per issue. The focus of this magazine is eclectic, ranging from Americana to international antiques and collectibles. Articles are brief, and the photographs are in both color and black-and-white. The magazine features regular columns such as "A Passionate Collector," "The Celebrity Collector," and "Rinker on Collectibles," in which experts answer questions about antiques and collectibles, provide restoration tips, and discuss their passion for collecting. "Ken's Korner," by Ken Hall, has an absolute wealth of information about all things collectible and/or antique. The web site at www.acmagazine.com offers just the table of contents for some past issues. As evidenced by their letters, subscribers love this magazine. Recommended for public libraries where there is an interest in collectibles and antiques.

399. *Antiques Roadshow Insider.* [ISSN: 1544-2659] 2001. m. USD 45 domestic; USD 55 Canada. Ed(s): Larry Canale. Antiques Insider LLC, 800 Connecticut Ave, Norwalk, CT 06854-1631. *Aud.:* Ga.

This full color monthly magazine tracks antiques' and collectibles' news and trends and is becoming as popular as the television show that inspired it. The issues take you behind the scenes where you learn from dealers, appraisers, auctioneers, and collectors. You will learn how to discover the value of your antiques and collectibles as well as determine whether they really are collectible or merely reproductions. Articles in reviewed issues were written by "Antiques Roadshow" appraisers and collectors and were entertaining and informative. Topics ranged from Betty Crocker cookbooks to establishing the best way to determine the value of your antique furniture. Collectibles reviewed in recent issues include lunch boxes, antique maps, vintage cookbooks, movie posters, and vintage purses. Tips for collecting are also offered. The web site at www.antiquesroadshowinsider.com includes subscription information and a few full-text articles. This would be a popular addition to any public library.

400. *AntiqueWeek: weekly antique, auction and collectors' newspaper.* Former titles (until 1986): *Antique Week - Tri-State Trader;* (until 1983): *Tri-State Trader.* [ISSN: 0888-5451] 1968. w. Mon. USD 38.95 for Central or Eastern ed.; USD 67.97 combined subscription for Central & Eastern eds. Ed(s): Connie Swain. D M G World Media, Inc., 27 N Jefferson St, PO Box 90, Knightstown, IN 46148-0120. Illus., adv. Sample. Circ: 64000 Paid. Vol. ends: Mar. *Bk. rev.:* 16, length varies. *Aud.:* Ga.

The Central and Eastern U.S. editions of this newspaper cover antique auctions, shows, and flea markets in their geographic areas and are very similar. Topics of articles, which focus on the United States, currently range from American Indian collectibles to cowboy spurs. The articles are interesting and informative, and there is a lot of Internet coverage. Regular columns offer great advice from the experts and include "The Jewelry Box," "Wood Works," and "Political Parade." *AntiqueWeek* includes helpful articles about identifying antiques. The publication's web site at www.antiqueweek.com not only includes a discussion forum, classified ads, and auction and shows calendars, but it also offers links to current articles, news archives, and a very useful glossary. Recommended for public libraries in the geographic region (depending on the edition) with an interest in popular collectibles.

401. *Art & Antiques.* Incorporates (1967-Jan. 1994): *Antique Monthly;* Formerly (until 1980): *American Art and Antiques.* [ISSN: 0195-8208] 1978. m. USD 24.95 domestic; USD 44.95 Canada; USD 54.95 elsewhere. Ed(s): Barbara Tapp, Patti Verbanas. CurtCo Robb Media LLC, 29160 Heathercliff Rd, Ste 200, Malibu, CA 90265; http://www.curtco.com. Illus., adv. Sample. Circ: 105000 Paid. *Indexed:* ABM, ABS&EES, ASIP, AmH&L, AmHI, ArtInd, HistAb, RILM. *Bk. rev.:* 6, length varies. *Aud.:* Ga.

This magazine presents beautiful photography and finely written articles on antique furniture and interesting but brief sketches of emerging artists. Regular departments include "Art Crimes" (art thefts), "Objects of Desire," "Critic's Notebook," "A Closer Look," and "Traveling Collector." The publication focuses on antiques, regularly showcases a wide variety of art exhibitions, and

provides the collector with news and trends in art and auction reports. Of value are the articles that offer practical advice about the world of antiques, such as what qualifications to look for in an antique consultant. The web site at www.artantiques.net offers many feature articles as well as access to free e-news. Recommended for libraries that want a title covering both art and antiques.

Blade. See Hunting and Guns section.

402. *Collector Editions.* Former titles (until 1981): *Collector Editions Quarterly;* (until 1977): *Acquire.* [ISSN: 0733-2130] 1973. q. USD 14.95; USD 4.99 newsstand/cover per issue. Ed(s): Linda Kruger. Pioneer Communications, Inc., 506 Second St, Grundy Center, IA 50638. Illus., adv. Circ: 100000 Paid. Microform: PQC. *Bk. rev.:* 4, 75-200 words. *Aud.:* Ga.

Collector Editions features brief but fascinating articles on contemporary collectibles such as plates, figurines, prints, ornaments, and other limited-edition collectors' pieces. It also covers fine and decorative art and introduces new product selections, covers new club events, and profiles artists. It features very useful tips on decorating with contemporary collectibles. The web site at www.collector-editions.com offers tables of contents for the current issue and archived issues. This magazine is popular in many libraries. Public libraries with a clientele interested in limited-edition contemporary collectibles would be safe in adding this title to their holdings.

403. *Kovels on Antiques and Collectibles: the newsletter for collectors, dealers and investors.* [ISSN: 0741-6091] 1974. m. USD 36 in US & Canada. Ed(s): Terry Kovel, Ralph Kovel. Antiques, Inc. Illus. Circ: 100000 Paid. *Bk. rev.:* Number and length vary. *Aud.:* Hs, Ga.

What distinguishes this newsletter from many of the others is not only the Kovels' 40-plus years of experience but also the lack of advertising. This simple, full-color, 12-page monthly publication is filled with the most recent news affecting prices of antiques and collectibles. It includes information about fakes, sale reports, prices, and book reviews. Advice is given on what's hot, which items are rising in value, and where to find the best prices. The Kovels teach you how to distinguish originals from reproductions and how restoration affects value. The chatty newsletter provides information on what's selling in flea markets and at auctions, and the Kovels answer questions about readers' antiques and collectibles. An annual index is provided with a subscription. The web site at www.kovels.com features excerpts from articles and answers to collectors' questions. If you register at the web site, you can freely search the price guide.

404. *The Magazine Antiques.* Formerly: *Antiques.* [ISSN: 0161-9284] 1922. m. USD 39.95; USD 5 newsstand/cover per issue. Ed(s): Alfred Mayor, Allison Ledes. Brant Publications, Inc., 575 Broadway, 5th Fl, New York, NY 10012. Illus., index, adv. Circ: 63969. Vol. ends: Dec. Microform: PQC. Online: EBSCO Publishing, EBSCO Host; Gale; Northern Light Technology, Inc.; OCLC Online Computer Library Center, Inc.; ProQuest K-12 Learning Solutions; ProQuest LLC (Ann Arbor); H.W. Wilson. *Indexed:* ABM, AmH&L, ArtHuCI, ArtInd, BAS, BRI, CBRI, HistAb, RGPR, RILM. *Bk. rev.:* 1-9, length varies. *Aud.:* Ga, Ac, Sa.

There is no doubt that this American periodical is one of the finest offered on the topic of antiques. The articles are well written by experts. Although the focus is on antique furnishings, topics also include folk furniture, paintings, architecture, and silver and art shows. Regular departments include a "Calendar of Exhibitions," "Symposiums and Lectures," "Report from Europe," and "Museum Accessions." Beautifully illustrated feature articles focus not only on the antique or historical piece but also on the person who created it. The magazine's new web site is at www.themagazineantiques.com. International in coverage, this journal should be in all public libraries.

405. *Maine Antique Digest: the marketplace for Americana.* [ISSN: 0147-0639] 1973. m. USD 43 domestic; USD 55 foreign. Ed(s): Samuel C Pennington. Maine Antique Digest, Inc., PO Box 1429, Waldoboro, ME 04572; mad@maine.com; http://www.maineantiquedigest.com. Illus. Sample. Circ: 30000. Vol. ends: Dec. Microform: PQC. *Bk. rev.:* 2-3, 500-2,000 words. *Aud.:* Ga, Sa.

This 300-page tabloid newspaper covers most of the information you need to know if you collect antiques or art either in Maine or across America. Regular features include auctions and shows and articles on all kinds of collectibles. The coverage is extensive and includes everything from estate sales to understanding furniture finishes. New features are profiles of dealers or shops each month, a new medals column, and "Real Deals: $2500 or less." This journal is intended for dealers and collectors on the East Coast, but its focus is on fine antiques and Americana. Although it has traditionally concentrated on the East, it has always covered the United States in general, and it continues to be a basic title that all libraries should consider. After visiting the web site at www.maineantiquedigest.com, you will understand both the online and print popularity of this title. It is the best web site previewed in this category. Market concentration has been expanded to include the world. Included in the searchable, full-text database are hundreds of book reviews, a selection of recent articles, hot news items, and shareware and demo programs for antiquers. Subscribers have access to a searchable price database (with descriptions).

406. *Teddy Bear Review.* [ISSN: 0890-4162] 1986. bi-m. USD 27.95 domestic; USD 39.95 foreign. Ed(s): Sara Peterson. Jones Publishing, Inc., N 7450 Aanstad Rd, PO Box 5000, Iola, WI 54945; jonespub@jonespublishing.com; http://www.jonespublishing.com. Illus., adv. Circ: 60000 Paid. *Bk. rev.:* 2, 250-300 words. *Aud.:* Ga.

Cuddly stuffed animals, mainly teddy bears, have been the most popular gifts for children over the years. Collecting teddy bears has gained even more popularity in the past few years, especially for adults. This publication covers antique, contemporary, and miniature teddy bears. Teddy bear experts contribute well-written articles profiling bear manufacturers, interviewing bear artists, and showcasing the latest bear creations. An auction report is included. Columns include "Tracking the Market" and "Bear Essentials." The web site at www.teddybearreview.com leads to the tables of contents of current and earlier issues and allows one to subscribe to the magazine, shop its bookstore, and view a show calendar. Recommended for public libraries with clientele interested in the subject.

407. *Yesteryear: your monthly guide to antiques and collectibles.* [ISSN: 0194-9349] 1975. m. USD 19. Ed(s): Michael Jacobi. Yesteryear Publications, Inc., PO Box 2, Princeton, WI 54968. Illus., adv. Circ: 6500 Paid. *Bk. rev.:* 2-10, 200-300 words. *Aud.:* Ga.

Yesteryear focuses on Wisconsin and neighboring Midwestern states. It offers valuable information in a variety of question-and-answer columns. There are hundreds of listings for upcoming antique shows, flea markets, auctions, and arts-and-crafts shows. New columns include a "Calendar of Events," "Antique or Junque," "Know Your Antiques," "Yesterday's Collectibles," and "Contemporary Collectibles." Although the focus is Midwestern, the information is priceless. The web site at www.yesteryearpublications.com features a "Calendar of Events" and "A Selection of Shops." Recommended wherever there is a gap in information about antiques and collectibles.

Doll Collecting

Doll collecting is skyrocketing. This is reflected in the growth of the number of doll collecting magazines and the fact that it is one of the top three collecting hobbies in America. Much of doll collecting stems from nostalgia. What you played with when you were a child becomes a collectible when you become an adult. This is evidenced in the enormous array of doll clubs and associations, ranging from the Doll Artisan Guild, the Madame Alexander Doll Club, and the Chatty Cathy Club to the National Organization of Miniaturists and Dollers.

The hottest trend in doll collecting today appears to be in collecting fashion dolls. These are part of the group of contemporary or modern dolls, but they are defined by their higher prices ($50 or more) and their extensive wardrobes. An example of the fashion doll is Ashton-Drake's Gene. New magazines in this field are *Art Doll Quarterly*, *FDQ: Fashion Doll Quarterly*, and *Haute Doll*. High prices are also reflected in the new fashion doll magazines that reach $10

per issue. Despite the expense, these dolls are gorgeous and the magazines that feature them are becoming famous for their beautiful photographs. Trends indicate that despite the often high prices, fashion dolls are being collected due to their quality in relation to the mass production of other dolls. Another trend reflected in the doll collecting magazines is the growth of costuming and accessorizing.

Speaking of fashion dolls, the field has lost *Barbie Bazaar*, which ceased publication as of the April/May 2006 issue.

Despite the popularity of the fashion doll, interest in collectible and antique dolls remains high. There are three distinct categories of dolls: antique dolls (those produced 75 years ago or earlier), collectible dolls (those produced between 25 and 75 years ago), and modern or contemporary dolls (those produced within the last 25 years). The magazines included here range in coverage from how to make dolls and dollhouses to collecting and accessorizing antique, vintage, contemporary, and art and fashion dolls.

408. *Antique Doll Collector.* Formerly (until 1997): *Antique Doll World.* [ISSN: 1096-8474] 1993. m. USD 39.95; USD 5.95 newsstand/cover domestic; USD 6.95 newsstand/cover Canada. Ed(s): Donna C. Kaonis. Puffin Co., LLC, 6 Woodside Ave., Ste. 300, Northport, NY 11768. Adv. Circ: 7000 Paid. *Aud.:* Ga.

If you are interested in antique dolls (of every kind) and their accessories, this magazine is for you. *Antique Doll Collector* truthfully advertises itself as "the magazine for antique doll lovers." Coverage includes antique and vintage dolls and teddy bears, doll houses, miniature furniture, and doll clothing and accessories. Color photographs are extraordinarily detailed, and the article contributors are experts in the field. The magazine regularly features columns (such as "News" and "Auction Gallery") and a calendar of shows, conventions, and auctions. There is a web site for this magazine at www.antiquedollcollector.com that has been updated and includes links and a calendar of events. The web site still features abstracts of information (with pictures) from the current issue and subscription information. Of value is an extensive list of doll links. This magazine would be of value to museums and public libraries that have an interest in this area.

409. *Art Doll Quarterly.* [ISSN: 1939-5027] q. USD 34.95 domestic; USD 44.95 Canada; USD 59.95 elsewhere. Ed(s): Sharilyn Miller. Stampington & Company, LLC, 22992 Mill Creek, Ste B, Laguna Hills, CA 92653; http://www.stampington.com. *Bk. rev.:* Number and length vary. *Aud.:* Ga.

This magazine is the epitome of doll-making techniques. It features artist dolls of all sizes, shapes, and mediums from clay to wire. Issues are full of photographs of stunning artist creations, interviews with the artists, and articles that discuss the historical and cultural significance of different dolls. Information on doll puppets, crocheted dolls, and sculpted fabric dolls is also included. Patterns for making some of the dolls can be found as well as information on doll shows. Practical advice can be found on how to use dyes, paints, and glazes; tips on costume decoration; embroidery techniques; and sewing, gluing, and other dollmaking techniques. Featured departments include "Doll Artist Profile," "Odd Doll," and product, video, and book reviews. The web site at www.artdollquarterly.com offers previews of upcoming issues and subscription information. Recommended for libraries that serve art doll enthusiasts.

410. *Contemporary Doll Collector: for the love of dolls.* Formerly (until 1994): *Contemporary Doll Magazine.* [ISSN: 1075-8674] 1990. bi-m. USD 21.95 domestic; USD 33.95 foreign. Ed(s): Ruth M Keessen, Laurel Bowen. Scott Publications, 30595 Eight Mile, Livonia, MI 48152-1798; contactus@scottpublications.com; http://www.scottpublications.com. Illus., index, adv. Sample. Vol. ends: Oct/Nov. *Aud.:* Ga, Sa.

The focus of this magazine is on contemporary and modern dolls, but it also offers advice on collecting, identifying, and preserving antique dolls. The importance of *Contemporary Doll Collector* lies in its clear advice and tips on how to collect, restore, and display dolls. It offers coverage of the doll industry's newest attractions such as fabric, felt, vinyl, plastic, and composition dolls. Regular departments include "Auction Report," "Doll Supplies and Accessories," "Doll Talk," "Doll Shop Profiles," and "Doll Artists." As do other doll magazines, this one also offers a show calendar and auction report. The web site at www.contemporarydollcollector.com is an advertisement. Recommended for public libraries where patrons have an interest in collecting dolls.

411. *Doll Castle News: the doll collector's magazine.* [ISSN: 0363-7972] 1961. 6x/yr. USD 19.95 domestic; USD 24 Canada; USD 39 elsewhere. Ed(s): Dorita M Mortenson. Castle Press Publications, Inc., PO Box 247, Washington, NJ 07882. Illus., adv. Sample. Circ: 4000. Vol. ends: Jan/Feb. *Bk. rev.:* 3-4, 100-150 words. *Aud.:* Ga, Sa.

This magazine is now in color and features articles about dolls ranging from vintage through contemporary. Here you will find many projects and patterns for dolls, and each issue includes a doll craft project. The instructions are very clear and well written. Feature articles are signed, well researched, and written in a familiar style, and the illustrations and photographs are excellent. Highly recommended for public libraries whose clientele has an interest in the subject. The web site at www.dollcastlemagazine.com offers a wealth of practical and fun information and an online newsletter.

412. *Doll Crafter and Costumer: published for creators and collectors.* Formerly (until 2006): *Doll Crafter;* Which incorporated (in 2003): *Doll Artisan;* (1994-2003): *Dollmaking;* Which was formerly (until 1996): *Dollmaking Crafts & Designs;* Which was formed by the merger of (1985-1994): *Dollmaking Projects & Plans;* (198?-1994): *Doll Designs;* Which was formerly (1979-198?): *National Doll World Omnibook.* 1983. m. USD 39.95 domestic; USD 54.95 foreign; USD 4.95 newsstand/cover. Ed(s): Pat Duchene. Jones Publishing, Inc., N 7450 Aanstad Rd, PO Box 5000, Iola, WI 54945; http://www.jonespublishing.com. Illus., adv. Circ: 42000 Paid. Vol. ends: Apr. *Indexed:* IHTDI. *Aud.:* Ga, Sa.

Doll Crafter and Costumer is an invaluable publication for the doll creator and collector and is even more so since it incorporated two other fine doll magazines, *Doll Artisan* and *Dollmaking*. Feature articles provide very clear instructions and illustrations not only for creating or sculpting dolls but also for doll costuming and accessorizing. The brief articles include specific materials and color guides that are extremely useful to the doll crafter, plus beautifully photographed examples of the finished doll or accessory. Costuming accessories and artist profiles along with casting dolls and a pullout pattern are also included. In this magazine, doll crafters recreate antique and vintage dolls and create modern original dolls. Issues include a "Pullout Pattern" and the sections "Studio Scene," and "Doll Events." The web site (www.dollccmag.com) offers a snapshot of what is in the current issue, and some older articles are available. Highly recommended wherever there is interest.

413. *Doll Magazine: the international doll collector's magazine.* [ISSN: 1358-3506] 1992. bi-m. GBP 21 domestic; GBP 38.50 in Europe; USD 69.50 United States. Ed(s): Alison Sibley. Ashdown Publishing Ltd., Avalon Ct, Star Rd, Partridge Green, RH13 8RY, United Kingdom; esther.forder@btinternet.com; http://www.ashdown.co.uk. Adv. *Bk. rev.:* 1, 300-400 words. *Aud.:* Ga, Sa.

Doll Magazine offers more feature articles than any of the other doll magazines in this section. The articles offer in-depth research, are well written, and cover what the editors consider the finest dolls in the world today. The magazine features artists' limited editions, fashion dolls, current collections, profiles, competitions, doll artists, and fantasy and art dolls. Instructions for making dolls and their accessories are clear and easy to follow. The web site at www.dollmagazine.com offers subscription information, shopping online, news, and auction and show reports, as well as the complete digital edition of a previous issue. Another fine British publication, this should be in every public library that has a clientele interested in the subject.

414. *Doll Reader: the ultimate doll authority.* [ISSN: 0744-0901] 1972. 9x/yr. USD 24.97 domestic; USD 25 Canada; USD 49 elsewhere. Ed(s): Kathryn Peck, Jill Jackson. Madavor Media, Llc., 420 Boylston St, 5th Fl, Boston, MA 02116; info@madavor.com; http://www.madavor.com. Illus., adv. Circ: 72999 Paid. Vol. ends: Nov. *Aud.:* Ga, Sa.

One of the top doll-collecting magazines, *Doll Reader* deals with every facet of doll collecting. Eight to ten signed feature articles are offered in each issue, covering everything from antique, modern, artist, and play dolls to profiles of

doll designers and artists. Regular departments include "Antique Q & A" and "Curious Collector." The articles are well written, beautifully photographed, and informative, and include information on hairstyles, costumes, and paper dolls. The web site at www.dollreader.com offers information about the current issue, doll doctor information, tutorials, fun doll projects, crafts, and patterns. This magazine is essential for any library serving patrons interested in the subject.

415. *Dolls: the collector's magazine.* Incorporates (in 2003): *Doll World.* [ISSN: 0733-2238] 1982. 10x/yr. USD 32.95. Ed(s): Nadya Rondon. Jones Publishing, Inc., N 7450 Aanstad Rd, PO Box 5000, Iola, WI 54945; jonespub@jonespublishing.com; http://www.jonespublishing.com. Illus., adv. Circ: 95000 Paid. Vol. ends: Dec. *Bk. rev.:* 2-4, 100-150 words. *Aud.:* Ga, Sa.

Most of the feature articles in this magazine are about contemporary, antique, and reproduction dolls, doll artisans and their dolls, and fashion accessories. The photographs are beautiful, and the articles are often first-person accounts in which the artists discuss how and when the inspiration to create dolls struck them. Coverage appears to have expanded to include more costuming, cloth dolls, and even dolls made of natural materials such as gourds. Regular departments cover auction reports, the identification and valuation of dolls, and a calendar of doll events. The web site located at www.dollsmagazine.com offers some limited information such as tables of contents for current and older issues and a list of shows and events. Subscribers can view the online editorials. *Dolls* is recommended for public libraries where there is an interest in doll collecting and doll artists.

416. *Dolls House World.* [ISSN: 0961-0928] 1990. m. GBP 42 domestic; GBP 73 in Europe; USD 74.50 United States. Ed(s): Joyce Dean. Ashdown Publishing Ltd., Avalon Ct, Star Rd, Partridge Green, RH13 8RY, United Kingdom; esther.forder@btinternet.com; http://www.ashdown.co.uk. Illus., index, adv. Circ: 30000. *Aud.:* Ga, Sa.

This British publication has beautiful photographs and will hold your interest. The several monthly articles are well written and humorous, and feature favorite doll houses as well as doll-house craftspeople and miniaturists. Very practical projects from creating frosted glass windows to furniture making are offered and have clear, easy-to-follow instructions. In fact, there is a wealth of how-to projects for miniaturists in this magazine, and it includes the latest news in the hobby. Advice is also given on decorating doll houses in different styles such as Art Deco or Victorian. You must be a club member to enter the web site, located at www.dollhouseworld.com. *Dolls House World* is a delightful complement to the other doll magazines and should be considered by public libraries where there is an interest in the subject.

417. *FDQ Fashion Doll Quarterly.* 2006. q. EUR 36. Ed(s): Pat Henry. FDQ Media LLC, 610W 110th St, Ste 5C, New York, NY 10025-2106. *Aud.:* Ga.

This pricey fashion doll magazine is not for children. It is for adult collectors and doll artists. The photography is spectacular and the articles are informative and entertaining. Interviews of doll costume designers, reports on the latest events in the doll universe, crafting dolls and accessories, and shopping for doll accessories are all highlighted here. The dolls featured are not just the new fashion dolls; Barbie and her history were included in one of the issues reviewed. If your clientele is interested in the fashion doll and how it is created and dressed and accessorized, this is a good addition. The web site at www.fashiondollquarterly.com features the table of contents of the newest issue, international fashion doll news, what's new, and downloads for your personal computer.

418. *Haute Doll: the magazine for dolls who love to shop.* [ISSN: 1544-4775] 2003. bi-m. USD 30.95 domestic; USD 43 Canada; USD 64.95 elsewhere. Ed(s): Karen F Caviale. Murat Caviale Inc., 5711 8th Ave, Kenosha, WI 53140. Adv. Circ: 27000 Paid. *Aud.:* Ga.

Geared to the adult collector, this highly fashionable magazine features vintage and contemporary dolls, especially fashion dolls. Some of the dolls portrayed here are artist dolls, celebrity dolls, Barbie, Ginny, Cissy, and Gene. Articles showcase fashion doll clothes, accessories, furnishings, artists, and events. *Haute Doll* includes well-written articles, beautiful photography, and interesting projects. The web site at www.hautedoll.com includes a featured article, information about becoming a *Haute Doll* club member, and a shopping boutique. If you are not going to add *FDQ: Fashion Doll Quarterly* (above) to your collection, you should consider this title.

■ ARCHAEOLOGY

Thomas Bruno, Phillips Reading Room Supervisor, Access Services, Widener Library, Harvard University, Cambridge, MA 02138

Introduction

Archaeological publications fall into three distinct subdivisions: general, regional, and scientific. While most general and some regional magazines may be of interest to high school and public libraries, scientific archaeology journals tend to appeal primarily to an academic audience. As the field of archaeology evolves, however, its relationship with the physical, biological, and material sciences will only continue to grow. Scientific journals of interest to general audiences therefore will be noted herein when appropriate.

For various historical reasons, regional archaeological journals have aligned themselves with related disciplines in a manner that is peculiar to each region. For example, the archaeology of ancient Greece and Rome is studied in close association with the fields of classical philology, the fine arts, and history; while New World archaeology is strongly influenced by trends in anthropology, ethnology, and linguistics. As a result, many regional publications will not only be of interest to readers outside of the traditional sphere of archaeology but may also be considered indispensable parts of other scholarly collections.

Periodicals that are truly local in scope are not included in this section, but can be found among the listings of magazines for specific geographical regions.

Basic Periodicals

Hs: *American Archaeology, Archaeology, Expedition;* Ga: *American Archaeology, Archaeology, Biblical Archaeology Review, Egyptian Archaeology, Expedition;* Ac: *American Antiquity, American Journal of Archaeology, Antiquity, Archaeology, Archaeometry, Expedition, Journal of Roman Archaeology, Near Eastern Archaeology, North American Archaeologist, World Archaeology.*

Basic Abstracts and Indexes

Abstracts in Anthropology, Anthropological Index Online, Art and Archaeology Technical Abstracts, British and Irish Archaeological Bibliography.

419. *Acta Archaeologica.* [ISSN: 0065-101X] 1930. a. USD 132 print & online eds. Ed(s): Klavs Randsborg. Blackwell Munksgaard, Rosenoerns Alle 1, PO Box 227, Copenhagen V, 1502, Denmark; customerservice@ munksgaard.dk; http://www.blackwellmunksgaard.com. Illus., adv. Refereed. Circ: 650. Reprint: PSC. *Indexed:* AICP, AbAn, AmHI, AnthLit, ArtHuCI, BrArAb, FR, IndIslam, NumL, SSCI. *Aud.:* Ac.

This annual publication of the Institute of Archaeology in Copenhagen is a scholarly journal with editors and contributors of international renown. Although its primary focus is the archaeology of Scandinavia and the North Atlantic until 1500 AD, *Acta Archaeologica* also explores the relationship of the Nordic world to that of Continental Europe, the Mediterranean, and beyond (contributions from arctic and maritime archaeology are specifically solicited by the editorial board). Articles are written mostly in English, with occasional offerings in French, German, and Italian. Each volume is published in two issues: the first is often devoted to a single theme, such as archaeology in architecture or the excavation of a Copper Age settlement in Bulgaria; the second issue contains a series of four to ten articles on various topics. Both issues of each volume contain numerous illustrations and line drawings. The rising prominence of "Atlantic Studies" and other such cross-disciplinary modes of research make this journal an indispensable part of any academic research collection.

African Archaeological Review. See Africa section.

420. *American Antiquity.* [ISSN: 0002-7316] 1935. q. Free to members. Ed(s): Timothy Kohler. Society for American Archaeology, 900 Second St, NW, 12, Washington, DC 20002-3557; publications@saa.org; http://www.saa.org/Publications/AmAntiq/amantiq.html. Illus., index, adv. Refereed. Circ: 6400. Vol. ends: Oct. Online: Florida Center for Library Automation; Gale; JSTOR (Web-based Journal Archive); Northern Light Technology, Inc. *Indexed:* ABS&EES, AICP, AbAn, AmH&L, AmHI, AnthLit, ArtHuCI, ArtInd, BRI, BrArAb, CBRI, ChemAb, FR, HAPI, HistAb, HumInd, IBR, NumL, SSCI. *Bk. rev.:* Varies per issue, 500-700 words, signed. *Aud.:* Ac, Sa.

One of several journals published by the Society for American Archaeology, *American Antiquity* is a quarterly review of New World archaeology, with a focus on the prehistory of the United States and Canada (since 1990 articles on the archaeology of Latin America have appeared in *Latin American Antiquity*, also a publication of the Society for American Archaeology and reviewed in this section). Each issue features four to six original scholarly papers, field reports from archaeological sites throughout the Americas, and a varying number of book reviews, as well as a "Comments" section permitting society members to address at length and debate the merits of the work presented in previous issues. Although the primary focus of the journal is prehistoric, recent issues cover such topics as a nineteenth-century shipwreck off the coast of Bermuda and a case of cannibalism in 1870s southern Colorado. Special attention is also paid to scholarship in the fields of linguistics and anthropology. Articles are accompanied by high-quality illustrations and maps. *American Antiquity* is a free publication for members of the Society for American Archaeology.

421. *American Archaeology: a quarterly publication of the Archaeological Conservancy.* Formerly (until 1997): *Archaeological Conservancy Newsletter.* [ISSN: 1093-8400] 1980. q. Free to members; USD 3.95 newsstand/cover. Ed(s): Michael Bawaya. Archaeological Conservancy, 5301 Central Ave, NE, Ste 902, Albuquerque, NM 87108-1517; tacinfo@ nm.net; http://www.americanarchaeology.org. Illus., adv. Sample. Refereed. Circ: 35000 Paid. *Indexed:* AbAn, AnthLit, BiolDig. *Bk. rev.:* 2-4, 200-300 words, signed. *Aud.:* Ga.

A quarterly publication of The Archaeological Conservancy, located in Albuquerque, New Mexico, *American Archaeology* "is the only consumer magazine devoted to the excitement and mystery of archaeology in the United States, with additional coverage of Canada and Latin America." Each issue contains several articles with color photographs, maps, and other illustrative material highlighting recent developments in the field. Recent articles have covered such topics as the historical archaeology of Colonial America, genetic research, and prehistoric migration to the New World, as well as features about the role and responsibilities of archaeological conservators. *American Archaeology* also contains information of interest to members of The Archaeological Conservancy and lists the acquisition of new sites under its aegis, field reports from current conservancy projects, and opportunities for field school and volunteer work. Book reviews are concise but informative, and include recently published multimedia offerings as well.

422. *American Journal of Archaeology.* Formerly (until 1896): *American Journal of Archaeology and of the History of the Fine Arts.* [ISSN: 0002-9114] 1885. q. USD 250 (Individuals, USD 75; Students, USD 47). Ed(s): Naomi Norman. Archaeological Institute of America (Boston), c/o Mark Kurtz, 656 Beacon St, Boston, MA 02215-2006; aia@aia.bu.edu; http://www.archaeological.org. Illus., index, adv. Refereed. Circ: 3600. Vol. ends: Oct. Microform: PMC; PQC. Online: JSTOR (Web-based Journal Archive). *Indexed:* ABS&EES, AICP, AbAn, AmHI, AnthLit, ArtHuCI, ArtInd, BAS, BRD, BRI, BrArAb, CBRI, ChemAb, FR, HumInd, IBR, IBZ, IndIslam, NTA, NumL, OTA, RI-1, SSCI. *Bk. rev.:* 15-25, 1-2 columns, signed. *Aud.:* Ac, Sa.

Published by The Archaeological Institute of America, located at Boston University, the *American Journal of Archaeology* is a quarterly review of current scholarship in the field of Mediterranean, Near Eastern, and Egyptian archaeology. Each issue includes articles, field reports, "necrologies" of recently deceased archaeologists of note, proceedings and awards of The Archaeological Institute, and museum and book reviews, as well as longer thematic review articles two or three pages in length. Materials reviewed in the journal range from technical scholarly monographs to Eric Shanower's *Age of*

Bronze, an award-winning graphic novel series dramatizing the Trojan War. The fourth issue contains a cumulative contents listing for the entire volume, arranged by section.

423. *Ancient Mesoamerica.* [ISSN: 0956-5361] 1990. s-a. GBP 186. Ed(s): William R Fowler, Jr. Cambridge University Press, The Edinburgh Bldg, Shaftesbury Rd, Cambridge, CB2 2RU, United Kingdom; journals@ cambridge.org; http://www.journals.cambridge.org. Adv. Refereed. Reprint: PSC. *Indexed:* AICP, AbAn, AnthLit, HAPI. *Aud.:* Ac, Sa.

An international publication, *Ancient Mesoamerica* is a scholarly journal covering the study of pre-Columbian Mesoamerican archaeology and its intersection with the allied disciplines of art history, ethnohistory, linguistics, and cultural anthropology. Each issue contains approximately 8–12 articles written in English and (to a lesser extent) Spanish, accompanied by maps, line drawings, and other illustrative matter. The subject matter reflects the interdisciplinary ethos of the periodical, with special attention paid to the historical linguistics of indigenous Mesoamerican languages. *Ancient Mesoamerica* also has a strong anthropological focus, reflecting the New World affinity between the fields of archaeology and anthropology. Recent issues explore such topics as Maya astronomical practices, agricultural methods in the Yucatan, the transmission of loan words from highland to lowland Mexico and Guatemala, and the political organization of the Early Formative Olmec in southern Veracruz. This is an excellent review of the state of Mesoamerican research that is as accessible to laypersons as it is useful to scholars.

424. *The Antiquaries Journal.* Formerly (until 1921): *Society of Antiquaries of London. Proceedings.* [ISSN: 0003-5815] 1843. a. USD 185 in North America; GBP 85 elsewhere. Ed(s): David Morgan Evans. Society of Antiquaries of London, Burlington House, Piccadilly, London, W1V 0BE, United Kingdom; admin@sal.org.uk; http://www.sal.org.uk. Illus., index. Refereed. Microform: IDC; PQC. *Indexed:* A&ATA, AICP, API, AbAn, AmH&L, AmHI, AnthLit, BRI, BrArAb, BrHumI, FR, HistAb, IBR, IBZ, IndIslam, NumL, RILM, SSCI. *Bk. rev.:* 40-50, 1-2 columns, signed; 1-2 review articles. *Aud.:* Ac, Sa.

The Society of Antiquaries of London publishes this annual journal, an international review "concerned with all matters of interest to antiquarians—including all aspects of archaeology, architectural and art history, conservation, heraldry, anthropological, ecclesiastical, documentary, musical and linguistic study." Each volume offers five to ten submissions of 20–80 pages in length, a dozen or more "shorter" contributions that are as substantial as feature articles in other magazines, review articles, and 40–50 book reviews offering a comprehensive survey of recent publications in the field. Articles are lavishly illustrated both in color and black-and-white. While *The Antiquaries Journal* solicits original research from around the globe, the majority of work focuses on the United Kingdom and continental Europe. Recent volumes present findings from an excavation of a Viking barrow cemetery in Derbyshire, a reconstruction of the Jesus Chapel in St. Paul's Cathedral in London, and an economic analysis of an Iron Age salt-mining operation in the Austrian alps. This is a first-rate publication that will appeal to scholars not only in archaeology but many other related fields.

425. *Antiquity: a quarterly review of archaeology.* [ISSN: 0003-598X] 1927. q. EUR 170. Ed(s): Martin Carver. Antiquity Publications Ltd., Bidder Bldg, 140 Cowley Rd, Cambridge, CB4 4DL, United Kingdom; sales@biologists.com; http://www.biologists.com. Illus., index, adv. Refereed. Vol. ends: Dec. Microform: MIM; IDC; PQC. Online: EBSCO Publishing, EBSCO Host; Florida Center for Library Automation; Gale; Northern Light Technology, Inc.; OCLC Online Computer Library Center, Inc.; ProQuest K-12 Learning Solutions; ProQuest LLC (Ann Arbor); H.W. Wilson. *Indexed:* A&ATA, AICP, AbAn, AmH&L, AmHI, AnthLit, ArtHuCI, ArtInd, BAS, BrArAb, BrHumI, CABA, FR, ForAb, HortAb, HumInd, IBR, IBSS, IBZ, IndIslam, MLA-IB, NTA, NumL, RI-1, RILM, S&F, SSCI. *Bk. rev.:* 12-15, 1-3 pages, signed; 4-6 book review articles, 3-5 pages, signed. *Aud.:* Ac, Sa.

A quarterly publication of the Antiquity Trust edited by the Department of Archaeology at the University of York in the United Kingdom, *Antiquity* "is an international peer-reviewed journal of archaeological research that aims to communicate the most significant new discoveries, theory, and method and cultural resource issues rapidly and in plain language to the academy and the

profession." Each issue features 8–12 articles focused on research, three to six concerning method, several "debate" articles in which authors respond to each other's recent work, and book reviews as well as more substantial, thematic book-review articles. The scope of *Antiquity* is truly international and diachronic—recent topics range from the use of World War I aerial photography in archaeology to the cultural reinvention of the Postclassic Maya goddess Ix Chel as a modern feminist pop icon. Both color and black-and-white illustrations accompany each article, as well as maps, charts, and photographs. This journal is an indispensable part of any archaeological research collection.

426. *Archaeology.* [ISSN: 0003-8113] 1948. bi-m. USD 21.95; USD 4.99 per issue. Ed(s): Peter Young, Mark Rose. Archaeological Institute of America, 36-36 33d St, Long Island City, NY 11106; peter@archaeology.org; http://www.he.net/~archaeol/. Illus., index, adv. Refereed. Circ: 215000 Paid. Vol. ends: Nov/Dec. Microform: PQC. Online: EBSCO Publishing, EBSCO Host. *Indexed:* A&ATA, ABS&EES, AICP, AbAn, AmH&L, AmHI, ArtHuCI, ArtInd, BAS, BRD, BRI, BiolDig, BrArAb, CBRI, FR, HistAb, HumInd, IBR, IndIslam, MASUSE, NTA, NumL, OTA, RGPR, RI-1, RILM, SSCI. *Bk. rev.:* 5-10, 1-2 columns, signed. *Aud.:* Hs, Ga, Ac, Sa.

While the Archaeological Institute of America, located at Boston University, also publishes the more scholarly *American Journal of Archaeology* for a professional archaeological audience, its bimonthly title *Archaeology* is a general-interest magazine intended for wider circulation. Each issue contains several feature articles with glossy color photos, a "World Roundup" of archaeology news, interviews with prominent archaeologists, and five to ten reviews of books, movies, multimedia products, and museums. The scope of *Archaeology* is global and ranges from prehistoric archaeology to the present, with a special emphasis on the growing role of science and technology in the field. Recent issues cover topics in deep-sea underwater archaeology, Nazi misuse of the Paleolithic archaeological record during the 1930s, and the discovery of a possible Olmec outpost in southern Mexico. This informative and entertaining magazine is useful not only to general audiences but to college and university libraries as well.

427. *Archaeology in Oceania.* Formerly: *Archaeology and Physical Anthropology in Oceania.* [ISSN: 0003-8121] 1966. 3x/yr. AUD 60.50 domestic; USD 55 foreign. Ed(s): J Peter White. Oceania Publications, University of Sydney (H42), 116 Darlington Rd, Sydney, NSW 2006, Australia; oceania@arts.usyd.edu.au; http://www.arts.usyd.edu.au/ publications/oceania/. Illus., index, adv. Refereed. Circ: 500. Vol. ends: Oct. Online: EBSCO Publishing, EBSCO Host; Gale. *Indexed:* AICP, AbAn, AnthLit, ArtHuCI, BAS, BiolAb, FR, IBR, IBSS, IBZ. *Bk. rev.:* 1-10, 1-3 columns, signed. *Aud.:* Ac, Sa.

Oceania Publications, a department within the Faculty of Arts at the University of Sydney in Australia, produces this journal three times a year, covering the archaeology of "the lands of the western Pacific rim and all the islands of the Pacific Ocean, including Australia." Each issue contains one to three articles refereed by scholars in the field, research reports from the field, and several book reviews. Accompanying illustrations are in black-and-white and include maps, line drawings, and photographs. Recent issues feature articles about the transport of prehistoric megaliths by sea in Micronesia, pottery finds in the Western Solomon Islands, and a *Homo erectus* find in Ngandong. *Archaeology in Oceania* also welcomes research in the field of human biological studies, with a strong emphasis on anthropology.

428. *Archaeology Ireland.* [ISSN: 0790-892X] 1987. q. USD 50. Ed(s): Tom Condit. Archaeology Ireland, PO Box 69, Bray, Ireland. Illus., adv. *Indexed:* BrArAb, FR, NumL. *Bk. rev.:* 0-1, 1 page, signed; 5-10 mini-reviews. *Aud.:* Ga.

This glossy color periodical has been published four times a year since 1987 by a group of archaeology enthusiasts. Although the magazine is primarily focused on the archaeology of Ireland and the British Isles, *Archaeology Ireland* trumpets a strong interdisciplinary philosophy and also explores issues of interest to archaeologists and the lay reader alike, including the transformative impact of technology on the theory and practice of archaeology in the twenty-first century. The book review section is supplemented by "Book News," which offers shorter mini-reviews of recent publications in the field. This magazine is targeted to professional and amateur archaeologists, but is written in an accessible and informative manner with dozen of illustrations and color photographs. Each issue concludes with a "Hindsight" feature that aims to illuminate topical issues in an ancient light and demonstrate the ongoing relevance of archaeology in the modern era.

429. Archaeology of Eastern North America. [ISSN: 0360-1021] 1973. a. USD 30 domestic; USD 40 foreign. Ed(s): Arthur Spiess. Eastern States Archeological Federation, PO Box 386, Bethlehem, CT 06751. Illus. Circ: 500. *Indexed:* AICP, AbAn, AnthLit. *Aud.:* Ac.

An annual publication of the Eastern States Archaeological Federation, *Archaeology of Eastern North America* is a forum for the latest fieldwork and research by archaeologists and state archaeological societies in the Eastern United States. Each issue contains five to ten articles ranging from site reports to ethnohistorical research and "applied archaeology." Recent articles cover such topics as Nanticoke Indian burial practices, the suitability of instrumental neutron activation analysis (INAA) for identifying Hathaway Formation Chert from the Northern Champlain Valley of Vermont, and a possible Paleoindian settlement in present-day Atlantic City. Illustrations are in black-and-white, and include photographs, charts, maps, and line drawings. Subscription to this journal is a benefit of membership in the Eastern States Archaeological Federation.

430. Archaeometry. [ISSN: 0003-813X] 1958. q. GBP 178 print & online eds. Ed(s): James Burton, Marco Martini. Blackwell Publishing Ltd., 9600 Garsington Rd, Oxford, OX4 2ZG, United Kingdom; customerservices@blackwellpublishing.com; http://www.blackwellpublishing.com. Illus., adv. Refereed. Circ: 1500. Vol. ends: Aug. Reprint: PSC. *Indexed:* A&ATA, AICP, AbAn, AnthLit, ArtHuCI, BAS, BrArAb, ChemAb, FR, IBR, IBZ, NumL, SCI, SSCI. *Aud.:* Ac, Sa.

Published for the University of Oxford in association with the Gesellschaft fur Naturwissenschaftliche Archaologie, ARCHAEOMETRIE, the Society for Archaeological Sciences, and the Associazione Italiana di Archeometria, *Archaeometry* is "an international research journal covering the application of the physical and biological sciences to archaeology and the history of art." Each issue contains 8–12 articles from scholars in the fields of archaeology and intersecting scientific disciplines, with a strong emphasis on materials science research. High-quality color and black-and-white illustrations accompany each article. The geographical and temporal scope of *Archaeometry* is wide-ranging, and recent articles cover such topics as bronze metallurgy in Machu Picchu, Peru, prehistoric spinning technology, and the geometrical patterns of Late Bronze Age wall paintings in Akrotiri, Thera.

431. Australasian Historical Archaeology. Formerly: *Australian Journal of Historical Archaeology;* Supersedes (in 1983): *Australian Society for Historical Archeology. (Annual Publication);* Which was formerly (until 1973): *Studies in Historical Archeology.* [ISSN: 1322-9214] a. AUD 50 for membership to individuals; AUD 60 for membership to institutions. Australasian Society for Historical Archaeology, University of Sydney, PO Box 220, Sydney, NSW 2006, Australia; http://www.asha.org.au. Refereed. Circ: 400. *Indexed:* AbAn, AmH&L, AnthLit, HistAb. *Bk. rev.:* 2-5, 1-3 pages, signed. *Aud.:* Ac, Sa.

This annual publication of the Australasian Society for Historical Archaeology (ASHA) represents the expanded scope of the ASHA beyond the borders of Australia to cover research in the field of historical archaeology in New Zealand and throughout the Asia-Pacific region in general. Each volume is comprised of eight to ten articles that are often organized around a central theme, such as the archaeology of the overseas Chinese; articles are amply illustrated in black-and-white. Several book reviews are included in each volume as well. *Australasian Historical Archaeology* also includes informational articles on significant archaeological sites, artifact repositories, and archives germane to the field.

432. Biblical Archaeology Review. Incorporates (1998-2006): *Archaeology Odyssey.* [ISSN: 0098-9444] 1975. bi-m. USD 13.97 domestic; USD 19.97 foreign. Ed(s): Steven Feldman, Hershel Shanks. Biblical Archaeology Society, 4710 41st St, NW, Washington, DC 20016;

bas@bib-arch.org; http://www.bib-arch.org/. Illus., adv. Circ: 180000. Vol. ends: Nov/Dec. *Indexed:* AbAn, AmHI, ArtInd, ChrPI, FR, HumInd, IJP, NTA, OTA, R&TA, RI-1, RILM. *Bk. rev.:* 3-4, length 2-3 columns, signed. *Aud.:* Ga, Ac, Sa.

Biblical Archaeology Review, a bimonthly publication of the Biblical Archaeology Society, describes itself as "the only nonsectarian forum for the discussion of Biblical archaeology." Recently consolidated (as of January/February 2006) with the society's secular general-interest archaeology magazine *Archaeology Odyssey*, *BAR* promises an expanded periodical that will offer articles of interest both to biblical archaeology enthusiasts and those with a broader interest in the field. Each glossy color issue offers several feature articles and regular departmental columns presenting news, reviews, and editorials, as well as thoughtful and intelligent debate on current controversial subjects. Recent topics explored include Islam on the Temple Mount, copper mining in the biblical state of Edom, and a short history of the practice of circumcision.

433. Cambridge Archaeological Journal. [ISSN: 0959-7743] 1991. 3x/yr. GBP 128 print & online eds. Ed(s): John Robb. Cambridge University Press, The Edinburgh Bldg, Shaftesbury Rd, Cambridge, CB2 2RU, United Kingdom; journals@cambridge.org; http://www.journals.cambridge.org. Illus., index, adv. Refereed. Vol. ends: Oct. *Indexed:* AICP, AmHI, AnthLit, ArtHuCI, ArtInd, BrArAb, BrHumI, IBSS, NumL. *Bk. rev.:* Varied, 1-3 pages, signed. *Aud.:* Ac, Sa.

Although this journal, published by Cambridge University Press on behalf of the McDonald Institute for Archaeological Research, has recently undergone some minor changes in format, its new editor John Robb promises that "*CAJ* will continue to be defined by its core area, the archaeology of human symbolic capabilities and practices—whether in potlaches or pyramids, hand-axes or henges, rock carvings or castles—and as studies in all approaches from evolutionary archaeology to interpretive archaeology, from human evolution to hermeneutics." This formerly biannual publication will now offer three issues per year, in February, June, and October, and will add to its combination of feature articles, research notes, and reviews of occasional "conversations" with members of the international archaeology community on various topics of current interest to the field. The first issue of this new format offers scholarly articles on the evolution of language and on Maya sculpture, and a larger review feature about music among the Neanderthals.

434. Canadian Journal of Archaeology. [ISSN: 0705-2006] 1977. a. CND 100 (Individuals, CND 75; Students, CND 35). Ed(s): George Nicholas. Canadian Archaeological Association, c/o Butch Amundson, Sec -Treas, Dept of Anthropology and Archeology, Saskatoon, SK S7N 5B1, Canada; nicholas@sfu.ca; http://www.canadianarchaeology.com. Illus., adv. Refereed. Circ: 500. *Indexed:* AICP, AmH&L, AnthLit, BrArAb, CBCARef, FR, HistAb, IBSS. *Bk. rev.:* 8-15, 3 pages, signed. *Aud.:* Ac, Sa.

A biannual publication of the Canadian Archaeological Association, this journal functions both as a comprehensive review of ongoing field projects and research in Canada and as a scholarly forum for the broader issues of theory and praxis in the archaeological discipline. Articles are in either English or French and are illustrated with black-and-white photographs, line drawings, maps, graphs, and charts. Each issue contains a feature article approximately 20–30 pages in length, followed by several shorter research and field reports, and reviews of recent monographs in archaeology and anthropology from Canadian authors. Although the principal contributors to the *Canadian Journal of Archaeology* are college and university faculty in Canada, other cultural institutions from both the public and private sectors are also represented. Recent articles focus on issues such as the repatriation of Native American/First Nations artifacts and hunting technologies in the Paleolithic Era.

435. Egyptian Archaeology. [ISSN: 0962-2837] 1991. s-a. GBP 4.95 per issue. Ed(s): Patricia Spencer. Egypt Exploration Society, 3 Doughty Mews, London, WC1N 2PG, United Kingdom; http://www.ees.ac.uk. Illus., index, adv. Circ: 5000. Vol. ends: Spring. *Indexed:* IndIslam, NTA. *Bk. rev.:* 4-7, 1-2 columns, signed. *Aud.:* Ac, Ga.

The Egypt Exploration Society, founded in 1882, has published this biannual magazine for its membership since 1991. Each issue has approximately 12–14 articles varying from one to three pages in length on a variety of topics in ancient Egyptian archaeology, art, and papyrology, accompanied by glossy color photographs, drawings, and computer recreations. The "Digging Diary" offers a roundup of field reports from ongoing excavations and highlights expeditions headed by the society, and a "Notice Board" details upcoming events for members in both Egypt and the United Kingdom. Recent issues present new research in the field of ancient Egyptian literature, recent attempts in Alexandria to locate a temple dedicated to Cleopatra VII, and the creation of a new digital resource, The Giza Archives Project. Although this periodical is chiefly targeted toward members of the Egypt Exploration Society, its accessible articles and rich visual content make it a fine resource for amateur archaeologists and Egyptophiles alike.

436. *Expedition.* Formerly (until 1958): *University Museum Bulletin.* [ISSN: 0014-4738] 1930. 3x/yr. USD 27 domestic; USD 31 foreign; USD 9.95 newsstand/cover per issue. Ed(s): James R Mathieu. University of Pennsylvania Museum, 3260 South St, Philadelphia, PA 19104-6324; http://www.museum.upenn.edu. Illus., index. Refereed. Circ: 4250. Vol. ends: Winter. Microform: PQC. Online: EBSCO Publishing, EBSCO Host. *Indexed:* A&ATA, AICP, AbAn, AnthLit, ArtInd, BAS, FR, NumL, RILM. *Bk. rev.:* Varied, 1-2 columns, signed. *Aud.:* Hs, Ga, Ac.

Published three times a year by the University of Pennsylvania's Museum of Archaeology and Anthropology, *Expedition* "offers direct access to the latest findings of archaeologists and anthropologists around the world." Each issue contains several feature articles, a special feature that often takes a closer look at the museum's own members and component academic departments, field and research notes, book reviews, and an "exhibit notes" section detailing the latest traveling and permanent museum exhibitions of note. The glossy color format allows for ample and lavish illustrations, including photographs and topographical maps of featured archaeological sites. Recent issues of *Expedition* cover such topics as anthropology in the movies, reed boats, and a special issue devoted entirely to caves. This lively magazine is an interesting synthesis of scholarly topics with a more accessible general-interest format, and as such is a useful resource for both academic and public libraries.

437. *Geoarchaeology: an international journal.* [ISSN: 0883-6353] 1986. 8x/yr. USD 1650. Ed(s): Rolfe D Mandel, Paul Goldberg. John Wiley & Sons, Inc., 111 River St, Hoboken, NJ 07030-5774; uscs-wis@wiley.com; http://www.wiley.com. Refereed. Microform: PQC. Online: EBSCO Publishing, EBSCO Host; OhioLINK; SwetsWise Online Content; Wiley InterScience. *Indexed:* AbAn, AnthLit, ArtHuCI, BrArAb, NumL, SCI. *Bk. rev.:* 0-3, 1-2 pages, signed. *Aud.:* Ac, Sa.

This journal, published eight times a year, presents cutting-edge interdisciplinary scholarship between the fields of archaeology and the earth sciences, "focusing on understanding archaeological sites, their natural context, and particularly the aspects of site formation processes." While the primary focus of *Geoarchaeology* is on the relationship of archaeology to dynamic physical processes, the editorial board also solicits articles concerning faunal and botanical remains, as well as the material analysis of man-made artifacts. Each issue contains several features of 20–40 pages in length, covering topics as diverse as Pleistocene archaeology sites in North America, ancient Egyptian waterways, and the effect of fire on phytoloth coloration. Most issues also contain book reviews and "short contributions" that allow scholars to promulgate interim findings with fewer editorial restrictions. Black-and-white illustrations accompany each article in the form of photographs, charts and graphs, and line drawings. Although seemingly esoteric in its appeal, *Geoarchaeology* highlights the fundamental scientific processes that underlie all branches of archaeology. This journal is an invaluable asset to any research collection.

438. *Hesperia.* [ISSN: 0018-098X] 1932. q. USD 130 (Individuals, USD 70). Ed(s): Dr. Tracey Cullen. American School of Classical Studies at Athens, ascsa@ascsa.org; http://www.ascsa.edu.gr. Illus. Refereed. Circ: 1100. *Indexed:* AbAn, AmHI, ArtHuCI, ArtInd, FR, IBR, IBZ, IndIslam, MLA-IB, NTA, NumL, SSCI. *Aud.:* Ac, Sa.

An impressive quarterly publication of the American School of Classical Studies at Athens, *Hesperia* "welcomes submissions from all scholars working in the fields of Greek archaeology, art, epigraphy, history, materials science, ethnography, and literature. Geographical boundaries are broadly defined as those of the entire Greek world, and no chronological restrictions are imposed."

Each attractively composed issue contains several articles of substantial length (20–80 pages) and includes lavish illustrations both in color and black-and-white, ample footnotes, and comprehensive scholarly bibliographies. Recent issues cover Venetian archaeology in the Pylos region, the synagogue at Delos, and a theme issue about feasting in Mycenaean society. This flagship journal of Greek archaeology is an indispensable part of any research collection, and by virtue of its diachronic and interdisciplinary approach, will be of interest to anyone interested in Greek history and culture in general.

439. *Historical Archaeology.* [ISSN: 0440-9213] 1967. q. Free to members. Ed(s): Rebecca Allen. Society for Historical Archaeology, PO Box 30446, Tucson, AZ 85751; the_sha@mindspring.com; http://www.sha.org. Illus., index, adv. Sample. Refereed. Circ: 2500 Paid. Vol. ends: Dec. *Indexed:* A&ATA, AbAn, AmH&L, AmHI, AnthLit, ArtHuCI, BrArAb, HistAb, HumInd, IBR, IBSS, IBZ, NumL. *Bk. rev.:* 20-40, 1-2 columns, signed. *Aud.:* Ac, Sa.

This quarterly publication of the Society for Historical Archaeology focuses on the archaeology of past societies that are also part of the historical record, a multidisciplinary field that draws upon the allied disciplines of anthropology, history, geography, and folklore to help reconstruct the past. Each issue contains several feature articles that are submitted primarily by members of the society (with occasional offerings from other scholars as well) and are illustrated with black-and-white photographs, maps, and line drawings, covering an international range of topics such as Irish country landscapes, early tourism at Yellowstone National Park, and the archaeology of the African diaspora. "Theme" issues devoted entirely to one topic are common and have recently covered utopian communities and the presidios of North American colonial Spain. The journal also reviews a substantial number of recent publications (20–40 books) in the burgeoning field of historical archaeology. Subscription is free to society members.

440. *International Journal of Osteoarchaeology.* [ISSN: 1047-482X] 1991. bi-m. USD 1161 print or online ed. Ed(s): Terry O'Connor, Shelley R Saunders. John Wiley & Sons Ltd., The Atrium, Southern Gate, Chichester, PO19 8SQ, United Kingdom; customer@wiley.co.uk; http://www.wiley.co.uk. Adv. Refereed. Circ: 500. Microform: PQC. Online: EBSCO Publishing, EBSCO Host; OhioLINK; SwetsWise Online Content; Wiley InterScience. Reprint: PSC. *Indexed:* AnthLit, ArtHuCI, BrArAb, NumL, SSCI, ZooRec. *Bk. rev.:* 2-4, 1-2 pages, signed. *Aud.:* Ac, Sa.

This bimonthly scholarly publication deals with "all aspects of the study of human and animal bones from archaeological contexts." As with most scientific archaeological journals, the *International Journal of Osteoarchaeology* is both global and diachronic in scope, covering such diverse topics as the Great Auk in the Netherlands during the Roman Period, adult fracture patterns in prehistoric Thailand, and a case of metastatic carcinoma from eighteenth-century London. Each issue contains between five and ten research articles, occasional short reports, and two to four book reviews of recently published monographs in the field. Although this is a highly specialized journal, its subject matter is of critical importance to the modern archaeologist, and its usefulness to historians and other social scientists makes it a fascinating addition to any academic collection.

441. *Journal of Archaeological Method and Theory.* Former titles (until 1994): *Archaeological Method and Theory;* (until 1988): *Advances in Archaeological Method and Theory.* [ISSN: 1072-5369] 1978. q. EUR 468 print & online eds. Ed(s): James M Skibo, Catherine M Cameron. Springer New York LLC, 233 Spring St, New York, NY 10013-1578; service-ny@springer.com; http://www.springer.com. Adv. Refereed. Online: EBSCO Publishing, EBSCO Host; Gale; IngentaConnect; OCLC Online Computer Library Center, Inc.; OhioLINK; Springer LINK; SwetsWise Online Content. Reprint: PSC. *Indexed:* AICP, AnthLit, ArtHuCI, BrArAb, IBSS, NumL, ZooRec. *Aud.:* Ac, Sa.

A quarterly international scholarly journal, the *Journal of Archaeological Method and Theory* "furnishes timely and authoritative topical syntheses, substantial original articles that critically assess and integrate research on a specific subject in archaeological method or theory." Special attention is given to scholarship about the method and theory of archaeological method and theory, allowing practitioners of the field an interesting opportunity for self-criticism and a meta-critique of archaeology. Each issue contains two to six articles with black-and-white illustrations covering such topics as zooarchaeology and historical archaeology, pottery designs from southwest New Mexico, and the phenomenon of self-citation in archaeology.

442. *Journal of Archaeological Science.* [ISSN: 0305-4403] 1974. 12x/yr. EUR 1317. Ed(s): Thilo Rehren, J. Grattan. Academic Press, Harcourt Pl, 32 Jamestown Rd, London, NW1 7BY, United Kingdom; apsubs@acad.com; http://www.elsevier.com/. Illus., index, adv. Refereed. Vol. ends: Nov. Online: EBSCO Publishing, EBSCO Host; Gale; IngentaConnect; OCLC Online Computer Library Center, Inc.; OhioLINK; ScienceDirect; SwetsWise Online Content. *Indexed:* A&ATA, AICP, AbAn, AnthLit, ArtHuCI, BiolAb, BrArAb, FR, FS&TA, NumL, SCI, SSCI, ZooRec. *Bk. rev.:* Review articles of varying number and length, signed. *Aud.:* Ac, Sa.

Published monthly in association with the Society for Archaeological Sciences, the *Journal of Archaeological Science* is "aimed at archaeologists and scientists with particular interests in advances in the application of scientific techniques and methodologies to all areas of archaeology." Every issue includes approximately 12–15 articles from an international group of scholars covering a truly interdisciplinary range of topics, including the production of ancient Nasca ceramics, use of radar in mapping subsurface archaeological features, paleoparasitological techniques, statical methods in bioarchaeology, and the origins of banana cultivation in Africa. Review articles are also occasionally featured. Each article is amply illustrated in black-and-white and includes substantial charts, graphs, and other ancillary materials, as well as an extensive bibliography.

443. *Journal of Field Archaeology.* [ISSN: 0093-4690] 1974. q. USD 75 (Individuals, USD 60). Ed(s): Curtis Runnels. Boston University, Journal of Field Archaeology, 675 Commonwealth Ave, Boston, MA 02215; jfa@bu.edu; http://jfa-www.bu.edu. Illus., adv. Sample. Refereed. Circ: 1200 Paid. Vol. ends: Winter. Microform: PQC. Online: JSTOR (Web-based Journal Archive). *Indexed:* A&ATA, ABS&EES, AICP, AbAn, AmHI, AnthLit, ArtHuCI, ArtInd, BAS, BrArAb, FR, HumInd, IBR, IBZ, NumL, OTA, RILM, SSCI. *Bk. rev.:* 3-12, 2-4 pages, signed. *Aud.:* Ac, Sa.

Boston University publishes the *Journal of Field Archaeology* four times a year as both a global survey of current archaeological excavations and as a forum for methodological and theoretical discussion. Each issue contains field reports from around the world, "special studies" of selected topics or archaeological sites, review articles, and a varying amount of shorter book reviews covering new publications in the field. Illustrations are in black-and-white and include photographs, maps, charts, and graphs, as well as line drawings. Recent special study topics examine flintknapping among Eastern Canadian Arctic Palaeo-Eskimos, seventeenth-century Pueblo settlements, and the modern illegal antiquities market.

444. *Journal of Mediterranean Archaeology.* [ISSN: 0952-7648] 1988. s-a. USD 240 print & online eds. Ed(s): John F Cherry, A Bernard Knapp. Equinox Publishing Ltd., Unit Six, The Village, 101 Amies St, London, SW11 2JW, United Kingdom; jjoyce@equinoxpub.com; http://www.equinoxpub.com/. Adv. Online: EBSCO Publishing, EBSCO Host; SwetsWise Online Content. *Indexed:* AnthLit, IBR, IBZ, L&LBA, RI-1. *Aud.:* Ac.

A semi-annual publication with a truly regional focus, the *Journal of Mediterranean Archaeology* is "the only journal currently published that deals with the entire multicultural world of Mediterranean archaeology." Each issue presents several scholarly articles from a host of international contributors, with special emphasis on social interaction and change, as well as broader contemporary theoretical approaches to Mediterranean archaeology with respect to "gender, agency, identity and landscape." Illustrations are in black-and-white, and include photographs, maps, and line drawings. As the archaeology of the Mediterranean has historically been attracted to somewhat insular modes of inquiry, the *Journal of Mediterranean Archaeology* brings a much-needed interdisciplinary philosophy and methodology, and as such it is a welcome addition to any academic research collection.

445. *Journal of Roman Archaeology.* [ISSN: 1047-7594] 1988. a. Individuals, USD 62.75. Ed(s): John H Humphrey. Journal of Roman Archaeology L.L.C., The Editor, JRA, 95 Peleg Rd, Portsmouth, RI 02871; jra@journalofromanarch.com; http://JournalofRomanArch.com. Illus. Refereed. Circ: 1050. *Indexed:* ArtInd, BrArAb, IBR, IBZ, NTA, NumL. *Bk. rev.:* 50-70, 4 pages, signed. *Aud.:* Ac, Sa.

This international journal, published annually in two fascicules, covers not only the latest developments in Roman archaeology, but topics in ancient Roman art, history, classical philology, and Greco-Roman culture. The first fascicule of each volume contains 10–15 scholarly articles of varying lengths (5–30 pages), followed by 10–15 archaeological reports and notes from the field; the second fascicule contains either a "Review Discussions" or "Debates and Response" section, followed by 50–70 book reviews averaging four pages each. Occasionally articles and book reviews will be clustered around a particular theme: for example, the 2005 volume featured five scholarly papers about Roman slavery. Although submissions are welcomed in English, Spanish, French, Italian, and German, the majority of material is written in English. Illustrations and photographs are mostly in black-and-white, with a rare color plate. Drawing submissions from the most respected academic institutions around the world, the *Journal of Roman Archaeology* is an indispensable resource for scholars of Greco-Roman civilization.

446. *Kiva: the journal of Southwestern anthropology and history.* [ISSN: 0023-1940] 1935. q. USD 80 (Individuals, USD 40). Ed(s): Stephen H Lekson. AltaMira Press, 1630 N Main St, Ste 367, Walnut Creek, CA 94596; http://www.altamirapress.com. Illus., adv. Sample. Refereed. Circ: 1100. Vol. ends: Jun. *Indexed:* AICP, AbAn, AmH&L, AnthLit, HistAb, IBR, RILM. *Bk. rev.:* Variable number and length, signed. *Aud.:* Ac, Sa.

A quarterly publication of the Arizona Archaeological and Historical Society, *Kiva* covers the archaeology of the American Southwest, publishing "the best voices in southwest archaeology" while incorporating the related fields of history, ethnology and anthropology, and linguistics. Each issue contains three to five feature articles and includes black-and-white illustrations, exploring such topics as Native American perceptions of the past, Zuni demographic structures, and Cliff polychrome pottery. A recent theme issue focuses on the Chaco world. Each volume also features several book reviews.

447. *Latin American Antiquity.* [ISSN: 1045-6635] 1990. q. Free to members. Ed(s): Jose Luis Lanata, Mark Aldenderfer. Society for American Archaeology, 900 Second St, NW, 12, Washington, DC 20002-3557; publications@saa.org; http://www.saa.org/Publications/LatAmAnt/latamant.html. Illus., index, adv. Refereed. Circ: 1500. Vol. ends: Dec. *Indexed:* AICP, AbAn, AmHI, AnthLit, ArtHuCI, BRI, CBRI, HAPI. *Bk. rev.:* 4-5, 300-700 words, signed. *Aud.:* Ac, Sa.

A sister publication of *American Antiquity* (above in this section), this quarterly journal is the Society for American Archaeology's clearinghouse for scholarly research in "archaeology, prehistory, and ethnohistory in Mesoamerica, Central America, and South America, and culturally related areas." Each issue presents two to four feature articles written in either English or Spanish (with an English abstract), preliminary reports, comments, and book reviews. Illustrative matter is sparse and in black-and-white. Recent topics explored include Early Formative Mesoamerican ceramics, the sacred political landscape of the highland Andean Wari people, and prehistoric salt production in Veracruz, Mexico. *Latin American Quarterly* regularly features some of the most preeminent scholars and archaeologists in the field today, and as such is an essential component in any New World archaeological research collection.

448. *Medieval Archaeology.* [ISSN: 0076-6097] 1957. a. USD 161. Ed(s): Dr. Sally M Foster. Maney Publishing, Ste. 1C, Joseph's Well, Hanover Walk, Leeds, LS3 1AB, United Kingdom; maney@maney.co.uk; http://www.maney.co.uk. Illus., adv. Refereed. Circ: 1500. Reprint: PSC. *Indexed:* A&ATA, AbAn, AmHI, BEL&L, BrArAb, HumInd, IBR, IBZ, NumL, RILM. *Bk. rev.:* 30-50, 500-1,000 words, signed. *Aud.:* Ac, Sa.

The Society for Medieval Archaeology publishes this annual scholarly journal of international standing. *Medieval Archaeology* primarily covers the archaeology of Britain and Ireland from the fifth to the sixteenth century A.D., although articles about contemporaneous developments in continental Europe and elsewhere are welcomed by the editors. For example, the 2005 volume featured an archaeological project in Iceland and a review of Byzantine influences on medieval English cultural identity. More general articles focusing on theory and methodology are also featured, especially those concerned with the impact of new technologies on the discipline of archaeology. Each issue has approximately eight feature articles, notes and news, and 30–50 reviews of monographs in archaeology and related disciplines in the humanities and social sciences, as well as a directory of current archaeological fieldwork in Britain and Ireland. Illustrations are primarily black-and-white drawings, with the occasional photograph and color plate.

449. Midcontinental Journal of Archaeology. [ISSN: 0146-1109] 1976. 2x/yr. USD 80 (Individuals, USD 35). Ed(s): Dr. Janet G Brashler. AltaMira Press, 1630 N Main St, Ste 367, Walnut Creek, CA 94596; explore@altamirapress.com; http://www.altamirapress.com. Illus., index, adv. Refereed. Circ: 600. Vol. ends: Oct. *Indexed:* AICP, AbAn, AmH&L, AnthLit, BrArAb, FR, HistAb, IBR. *Aud.:* Ac, Sa.

Under new editorship as of 2006, *MCJA* is the semi-annual publication of the Midwest Archaeological Conference, whose purview encompasses "the region between the Appalachian Mountains and the Great Plains, from the Boreal Forests to the Gulf of Mexico, and on closely related subjects." Each issue contains five to eight articles on topics ranging from archaeology to anthropology, history, and linguistics, spanning from the prehistoric period to the nineteenth century. Illustrations are sparse and in black-and-white. *MCJA* will occasionally offer an issue dedicated to a single theme, such as the archaeology of the Potawatomi during the Removal Period or the Mississippian occupation of Cahokia. This journal has widened its scope significantly in recent years to become the preeminent forum for archaeological research in the Midwestern United States and Canada, and is therefore an important component in any research collection specializing in North American archaeology.

450. Near Eastern Archaeology. Formerly (until 1998): *Biblical Archaeologist.* [ISSN: 1094-2076] 1938. q. USD 100 (Individuals, USD 35). Ed(s): Sandra Scham. American Schools of Oriental Research, 825 Houston Mill Rd, Atlanta, GA 30329; asorpubs@asor.org; http://www.asor.org. Illus., index, adv. Refereed. Circ: 4500 Paid. Vol. ends: Dec. Microform: PQC. Online: American Theological Library Association; EBSCO Publishing, EBSCO Host; JSTOR (Web-based Journal Archive); OCLC Online Computer Library Center, Inc.; Ovid Technologies, Inc.; ProQuest K-12 Learning Solutions; ProQuest LLC (Ann Arbor); H.W. Wilson. *Indexed:* A&ATA, AICP, AbAn, AmHI, AnthLit, ArtHuCI, ArtInd, CPL, ChrPI, FR, HumInd, IBR, IBSS, IBZ, IJP, MLA-IB, NTA, NumL, OTA, R&TA, RI-1, RILM, SSCI. *Bk. rev.:* 1-4, 500-1,000 words, signed. *Aud.:* Ac, Sa.

This glossy color magazine, published four times a year by the American Schools of Oriental Research, "brings to life the ancient world from Mesopotamia to the Mediterranean with vibrant images and authoritative analyses." Each issue offers four to six lavishly illustrated feature articles detailing recent archaeological research in the Middle East, with special emphasis on new and alternative approaches to traditional methodologies, while shorter "Arch-facts" provide a forum for preliminary findings and quick reports from the field. Several book reviews are also included in each issue. Recent topics explored range from the archaeology of Paphlagonia (in north-central Anatolia) to brewing and beer drinking in the ancient Near East, to the unsung professional contributions of several prominent archaeologists' wives.

451. North American Archaeologist. [ISSN: 0197-6931] 1979. q. USD 324. Ed(s): Roger W Moeller. Baywood Publishing Co., Inc., 26 Austin Ave, PO Box 337, Amityville, NY 11701-0337; info@baywood.com; http://www.baywood.com. Illus., adv. Sample. Refereed. Vol. ends: No. 4. *Indexed:* AICP, AbAn, AmH&L, AmHI, AnthLit, ArtHuCI, BrArAb, HistAb, IBR, IBZ. *Bk. rev.:* 2-6 per volume, 2 pages, signed. *Aud.:* Ac, Sa.

This quarterly publication describes itself as "the only general journal dedicated solely to North America—with total coverage of archaeological activity in the United States, Canada, and Northern Mexico (excluding Mesoamerica)," with particular interest in exploring archaeology in an evolutionary perspective and addressing issues in the growing fields of Resource Management and Contract Archaeology. Each issue offers several feature articles, with occasional book reviews; the fourth issue of each volume contains an annual directory of National, Regional, State, and Provincial Archaeological Associations in North

America. Illustrations are sparse and in black-and-white. Recent topics include Navajo tree ring dates, women in the Iroquoian economic system, and a shell midden in prehistoric California. With such offerings as special issues dedicated to "Ethics and the Hyperreality of the Archaeological Thought World," *North American Archaeologist* offers readers a thought-provoking mix of theory and methodology that makes it a welcome addition to an academic research library.

452. Oxford Journal of Archaeology. [ISSN: 0262-5253] 1982. q. GBP 389 print & online eds. Ed(s): Andrew Sherratt, Helena Hamerow. Blackwell Publishing Ltd., 9600 Garsington Rd, Oxford, OX4 2ZG, United Kingdom; customerservices@blackwellpublishing.com; http://www.blackwellpublishing.com. Illus., adv. Sample. Refereed. Circ: 550. Online: Blackwell Synergy; EBSCO Publishing, EBSCO Host; Gale; IngentaConnect; OCLC Online Computer Library Center, Inc.; OhioLINK; SwetsWise Online Content. Reprint: PSC. *Indexed:* A&ATA, AnthLit, ApEcolAb, BrArAb, FR, IBSS, L&LBA, NumL. *Aud.:* Ac, Sa.

A quarterly journal published in association with the Institute of Archaeology at the University of Oxford, the *Oxford Journal of Archaeology* provides an unparalleled comprehensive review of the latest scholarship in European and Mediterranean archaeology. Each issue consists of four to eight articles solicited from some of the most respected scholars in the field, ranging in subject matter from wealth and status in Iron Age Knossos to Etruscan house urns and tomb paintings to the sociology of the Roman frontier in northern Britain. Special emphasis is also given to the latest technological developments in the field. Illustrations are in black-and-white, and include photographs, maps, charts and graphs, and fine line drawings. This journal is an essential part of any archaeological research collection, and required reading for any practitioner of European or Mediterranean archaeology.

453. Post-Medieval Archaeology. [ISSN: 0079-4236] 1967. s-a. USD 278. Ed(s): John Allan, Hugo Blake. Maney Publishing, Ste. 1C, Joseph's Well, Hanover Walk, Leeds, LS3 1AB, United Kingdom; maney@maney.co.uk; http://www.maney.co.uk. Adv. Refereed. Circ: 650. Reprint: PSC. *Indexed:* AbAn, AmH&L, BrArAb, HistAb, NumL. *Bk. rev.:* 15-20, 1-2 pages, signed. *Aud.:* Ac, Sa.

This semi-annual publication of the Society for Post-Medieval Archaeology is "devoted to the study of the material evidence of European society wherever it is found in the world," documenting the archaeology and ethnohistory of the transition from the medieval era to modern industrial society. The first issue of each volume contains several scholarly articles on a diverse range of topics, such as sixteenth- and seventeenth-century castles in the Scottish highlands, colonial-era pottery in Virginia and Maryland, and the management of battlefields as cultural resources; the second issue offers feature articles, society notes, a comprehensive roundup of archaeological fieldwork in Great Britain and Ireland, and a subject index to the volume. Articles are amply illustrated in black-and-white, and include photographs, maps, charts, graphs, and line drawings. While *Post-Medieval Archaeology* has traditionally focused on the archaeology of the British Isles and to a lesser extent that of Ireland and continental Europe, recent issues have broadened this scope to include the Western Hemisphere and elsewhere. The archaeology of this period is of critical importance not just to practitioners of the field but to anyone with an interest in modern history.

454. World Archaeology. [ISSN: 0043-8243] 1969. q. GBP 325 print & online eds. Ed(s): Peter Rowley-Conwy. Routledge, 4 Park Sq, Milton Park, Abingdon, OX14 4RN, United Kingdom; info@routledge.co.uk; http://www.routledge.co.uk. Illus., index, adv. Refereed. Vol. ends: Feb. Microform: PQC. Online: EBSCO Publishing, EBSCO Host; Gale; IngentaConnect; JSTOR (Web-based Journal Archive); OCLC Online Computer Library Center, Inc.; ProQuest K-12 Learning Solutions; SwetsWise Online Content. Reprint: PSC. *Indexed:* A&ATA, AICP, AbAn, AmH&L, AmHI, AnthLit, ArtHuCI, ArtInd, BAS, BiolDig, BrArAb, BrHumI, FR, HistAb, HumInd, IBR, IBSS, IBZ, IndIslam, NTA, NumL, RI-1, SSCI. *Aud.:* Ac, Sa.

A quarterly scholarly publication, *World Archaeology* "is the only journal established specifically to deal with archaeology on a world-wide multiperiod basis." Each issue contains six to ten articles organized around a particular theme by a different editor; articles are accompanied by photographs, maps, charts, graphs, and line drawings in black-and-white. Past themes have included sedentism, race and racism in archaeology, "alternative" archaeologies, seascapes, and the archaeology of epidemic and infection disease. Since 2004, each fourth issue of *World Archaeology* has been published in a special format under the title "Debates in World Archaeology" as a forum for less formal scholarly debate on topics of interest to the archaeological community. Both the thematic emphasis and the dedicated space for regular discussion make this journal an indispensable resource for any archaeological collection.

■ ARCHITECTURE

Amy Trendler, Architecture Librarian, Ball State University, Muncie, IN 47306; aetrendler@bsu.edu

Introduction

Collectively, the titles in this section might form a list of core periodicals for an architecture library. However, many of the titles would also be at home in an academic or public library. More than a field of study, more than simply a practice, architecture is a subject of cultural studies and history, aesthetics and popular interest. There is at least one journal targeted to every segment of the architecture audience, from architect to student to academic to layperson.

Many of the titles here are well illustrated with spectacular images of newly completed buildings, proposed designs, and archival photographs. Some titles go a step farther and seek to more fully document works through plans, drawings, sections, elevations, and site plans. The text, too, is rich and varied, from simple descriptions to detailed analysis and thoughtful critiques of buildings and designers or the theory, history, and aesthetics of architecture.

While some titles have a narrow focus on a particular geographic region, a great many present buildings and designs from around the world. Beyond the work of well-known American or European architects overseas in places like China or Dubai, the international scene is represented by the designs of local and lesser-known or up-and-coming designers. In addition to the international aspect, architecture has an interdisciplinary aspect. Journals devoted to theory and academic subjects as well as those that focus on popular culture and general interest often acknowledge that architecture is not an isolated practice or field of study through their choice of topics and authors. Many "architecture" titles feature articles on other aspects of art, design, or culture, from food and fashion to the fine arts, and contributors are not limited to practicing architects or architectural faculty.

There are an increasing number of architecture titles available electronically, but print remains the primary method of delivery. Those journals that are text-heavy and include few illustrations are more likely to provide full text online and usually through the publisher. While there are more and better images available online today, few journals reproduce the full extent of the printed magazine on the web. As a title available only online, *Architecture Week* is one of the few exceptions. Other titles have made a variety of information and features available on their web sites, but these sites often exist independently or in addition to the printed magazine and not as complete electronic reproductions of the print version. In the annotations that follow, I have made note of the titles that currently provide significant online content.

Basic Periodicals

Ga: *Architectural Record, Architecture, Architecture Week, Fine Homebuilding, Metropolis, Preservation;* Ac: *A & U, L'Architecture d'Aujourd'hui, Architectural Design, Architectural Review, Architecture, Built Environment, El Croquis, Domus, GA Document, Journal of the Society of Architectural Historians, Places, RIBA Journal.*

Basic Abstracts and Indexes

Architectural Index, Architectural Publications Index, Art Index, Avery Index to Architectural Periodicals.

455. A A Files: annals of the Architectural Association School of Architecture. Formerly: *A A Quarterly.* [ISSN: 0261-6823] 1981. 3x/yr. GBP 15 per issue. Ed(s): Mark Rappolt. Architectural Association, 36

Bedford Sq, London, WC1B 3ES, United Kingdom; publications@aaschool.ac.uk; http://www.aaschool.ac.uk. Illus., index. Circ: 2500. *Indexed:* API, ArtInd. *Bk. rev.:* 6-8, 1,500 words. *Aud.:* Ac.
Wide-ranging articles on contemporary architects and their projects, essays on architectural history or theory, and thorough exhibition and book reviews can be found in the richly illustrated, advertisement-free pages of the *AA Files*. Architects, architectural and art historians, academics, and the occasional poet, composer, or sound artist make up the list of contributors to this journal, which is published by the Architectural Association School of Architecture in London. The journal's web site offers tables of contents for published volumes. Recommended for academic and architecture libraries.

456. A & U. [ISSN: 0389-9160] 1971. m. JPY 30000 domestic. Ed(s): Nobuyuki Yoshida. Japan Architects Co., Ltd., 2-31-2 Yushima, Bunkyo-ku, Tokyo, 113-0034, Japan; ja-business@japan-architect.co.jp; http://www.japan-architect.co.jp/. Illus., index, adv. Circ: 25000. Vol. ends: Dec. *Indexed:* API, ArtHuCI, ArtInd. *Bk. rev.:* Various number and length. *Aud.:* Ac, Sa.
A brief section of news and current events precedes the articles in this profusely illustrated Japanese periodical. A selected theme characterizes each issue; the firm MVRDV, architects' homes, and theaters and halls were featured recently. A page or two of text and many illustrations, details, plans, elevations, and conceptual drawings make up the articles, which are mostly building studies international in scope. Brief biographies of the architects whose work appears in the issue are always included in the last few pages of the journal. Text is in both Japanese and English. Tables of contents beginning with issues published in 1999 and selected text, with the occasional page view, from more recent issues are freely available online. Recommended for architecture libraries.

457. A R Q: Architectural Research Quarterly. [ISSN: 1359-1355] 1995. q. GBP 168. Ed(s): Richard Weston. Cambridge University Press, The Edinburgh Bldg, Shaftesbury Rd, Cambridge, CB2 2RU, United Kingdom; journals@cambridge.org; http://www.journals.cambridge.org. Refereed. Online: Pub.; EBSCO Publishing, EBSCO Host; OCLC Online Computer Library Center, Inc.; OhioLINK; SwetsWise Online Content; H.W. Wilson. Reprint: PSC. *Indexed:* API, ArtInd. *Bk. rev.:* Number and length vary. *Aud.:* Ac.
A quarterly published in Great Britain, *ARQ* is meant to act "as an international forum for practitioners and academics by publishing cutting-edge work covering all aspects of architectural endeavour." The lengthy, well-illustrated articles in an issue are grouped into the broad categories of design, theory, and history. Topics range from the historical to the contemporary. Detailed building studies and book reviews, editorials, and thought pieces complete each issue. Organizations have the option of subscribing to online only or to online and print versions of the journal. Abstracts for issues beginning with volume 5, 2001, are freely accessible. Recommended for architecture libraries.

458. Abitare: home, town and environmental living. Formerly (until 1962): *Casa Novita.* [ISSN: 0001-3218] 1961. 11x/yr. EUR 55 domestic; EUR 117 in Europe; EUR 247 elsewhere. Ed(s): Italo Lupi. Editrice Abitare Segesta SpA, Corso Monforte 15, Milan, 20122, Italy; abitaremag@abitare.it; http://www.abitare.it. Illus. *Indexed:* ArtInd, DAAI. *Bk. rev.:* Various number and length. *Aud.:* Ga, Sa.
This glossy Italian monthly covers the international architecture and design scene with, not surprisingly, a somewhat higher concentration of Italian subjects. The numerous feature articles are grouped in recurring categories of architecture, design, interiors, and art. An issue of *Abitare* may also include a topical category such as children's environments or parks and urban space. Each feature and section is well illustrated with beautiful photographs and often several plans, sections, and elevations. Text in all sections, including features, exhibition and book reviews, and product information, is in both Italian and English. The product information section is edited and every issue highlights a different theme. Italian content from the magazine is available online along with the current issue's table of contents. Recommended for architecture and large public libraries.

459. Architect. Former titles (until 2006): *Architecture;* (until 1983): *A I A Journal;* (until 1957): *American Institute of Architects. Journal;* Architecture Incorporated (1992-1995): *Building Renovation;* (1920-1995): *Progressive Architecture;* Which was formerly (until 1945): *Pencil Points (East Stroudsburg, 1944);* (until 1943): *New Pencil Points;* (until 1942): *Pencil Points (East Stroud, 1920);* Which incorporated: *Monograph Series (New York, 1929);* (1983-1986): *Architectural Technology.* [ISSN: 1935-7001] 2006. m. USD 59 domestic (Free to qualified personnel). Ed(s): Ned Cramer. Hanley Wood, LLC, One Thomas Circle, NW, Ste 600, Washington, DC 20005-5701; http://www.hanleywood.com. *Indexed:* AmHI. *Aud.:* Sa.

Architect is a new magazine that replaces the now defunct title *Architecture* (at one time the monthly trade magazine of the American Institute of Architects until it was sold by the AIA in 1989). In the premier issue, editor-in-chief Ned Cramer wrote, "*Architect* will portray architecture from multiple perspectives, not just as a succession of high-profile projects, but as a technical and creative process, and as a community." The focus is on the business of architecture, including marketing and market data as well as case studies, news and events, architect interviews, and book, product, and exhibition reviews. This is a good resource on the practice of architecture in the United States. The online component of this title includes job reviews, blogs, additional sections, and full text from current and past issue of the print magazine. Some, but not all, of the images and graphics found in the print magazine are online. Recommended for architecture libraries.

460. Architects' Journal. [ISSN: 0003-8466] 1895. w. GBP 152.75 domestic. Ed(s): Kieran Long. Emap Construct Ltd., 151 Rosebery Ave, London, EC1R 4GB, United Kingdom; http://www.constructionplus.co.uk. Illus., adv. Circ: 17180. *Indexed:* A&ATA, API, AmHI, ArtInd, BrHumI, BrTechI, C&ISA, CerAb, HRIS. *Aud.:* Ac, Sa.

Numerous news briefs, thought pieces, book and exhibition reviews, recruitment notices, as well as classified advertising appear in each issue of this weekly British trade publication. An excellent resource for those working or contemplating working in Great Britain, the *Architect's Journal* also showcases lengthy, well-illustrated building studies. The building study topics are not limited to British subjects; recent studies highlight OSh House by the firm of Toh Shimazaki, Oscar Niemeyer's Palacio da Alvorada, and the building by Lars Gitz Architects for the Copenhagen offices of the World Health Organization. Subscribers have access online to *AJ Plus,* which includes updated news and articles from the past six years of the journal. Recommended for architecture libraries.

461. Architectural Design. [ISSN: 0003-8504] 1930. bi-m. USD 335 print or online ed. John Wiley & Sons Ltd., The Atrium, Southern Gate, Chichester, PO19 8SQ, United Kingdom; customer@wiley.co.uk; http://www.wiley.co.uk. Illus., index, adv. Circ: 6500 Paid. Vol. ends: Nov/Dec. Reprint: PSC. *Indexed:* API, ArtHuCI, ArtInd, C&ISA, CerAb, EIP, IAA, IBR, IBZ, SSCI. *Bk. rev.:* 8, 250 words. *Aud.:* Ac, Sa.

Each issue of *Architectural Design* is devoted to the chosen theme of a guest editor or editors. Recent issues of this bimonthly journal focus on landscape architecture, architextiles, and "art and architecture in the age of software." Twelve or more pieces on the selected topic, with a wealth of accompanying illustrations, make up the bulk of the journal, but the recurring departments are also of interest. An in-depth look at an architectural firm, a building profile, an interior profile, and a section devoted to housing complete each issue. The subjects of the recurring departments in this British publication are frequently in the United Kingdom, but they are just as likely to be buildings and architects from farther afield. Beginning with issues published in 2006, full text of this title in pdf is available through subscription to Wiley InterScience. Recommended for architecture and large academic libraries.

Architectural Digest. See Interior Design and Decoration section.

462. Architectural Record. [ISSN: 0003-858X] 1891. m. USD 49 domestic; USD 59 Canada; USD 79 Mexico. McGraw-Hill Construction Dodge, 2 Penn Plz, 9th Fl, New York, NY 10121-2298; http://www.fwdodge.com. Illus., index, adv. Circ: 90000 Paid. Vol. ends: Dec. Microform: IDC;

PQC. Online: EBSCO Publishing, EBSCO Host; LexisNexis; Northern Light Technology, Inc.; ProQuest LLC (Ann Arbor). *Indexed:* ABS&EES, API, AmHI, ArchI, ArtHuCI, ArtInd, GardL, IBR, IBZ, LRI, MASUSE, RGPR, RI-1, RILM, SSCI. *Bk. rev.:* 6, 50-250 words. *Aud.:* Ga, Ac, Sa.

A glossy trade magazine that contains information on all aspects of contemporary American architecture, *Architectural Record* is essential reading for architects, students, and anyone interested in architecture. Although the focus is on the United States and Canada, issues often include information on projects and architects from all over the world. Sections devoted to selected building types, product information, architectural technology, and current projects are regularly published alongside feature articles, architect interviews, book reviews, and exhibition and lecture notices. All of the sections and articles are well illustrated. American Institute of Architects (AIA) members receive this title as a benefit of membership. Excerpts from the print magazine, including images, are available online, but full content is reserved for those who subscribe to the print or digital versions of this title. Recommended for all library types.

463. Architectural Review. [ISSN: 0003-861X] 1897. m. GBP 79 domestic; GBP 70 United States; GBP 89 in Europe. Ed(s): Catherine Slessor, Paul Finch. Emap Construct Ltd., 151 Rosebery Ave, London, EC1R 4GB, United Kingdom. Illus., adv. Circ: 18500. Vol. ends: Jun/Dec. Microform: IDC. Online: Florida Center for Library Automation; Gale; Northern Light Technology, Inc.; OCLC Online Computer Library Center, Inc.; ProQuest LLC (Ann Arbor). *Indexed:* A&ATA, API, AmHI, ArchI, ArtHuCI, ArtInd, BAS, BrHumI, BrTechI, C&ISA, CerAb, DAAI, GardL, IAA. *Bk. rev.:* 4-6, 500 words. *Aud.:* Ac,Sa, Ga.

Covering some of the same ground as *Architectural Record,* this journal offers the British perspective and a focus on European architecture. Feature articles in *Architectural Review* revolve around a different theme in each issue; recent themes include conserving Modernist buildings, structure, and office buildings. Numerous illustrations, plans, and details appear in each issue. Departments devoted to interiors, houses, and product reviews occasionally join those that make a more regular appearance including book reviews, news and events, and opinion pieces. Tables of contents and one or two articles in pdf are freely available online. Recommended for architecture and large public libraries.

464. L'Architecture d'Aujourd'hui. Formerly: *Architecture Francaise.* [ISSN: 0003-8695] 1930. bi-m. EUR 25 per issue. Ed(s): Jean Michel Place. Editions Jean-Michel Place, 3 rue Lhomond, Paris, 75005, France; place@jmplace.com; http://www.jmplace.com. Illus., adv. Circ: 19275. *Indexed:* API, ArtHuCI, ArtInd, BAS, IBR, IBZ, SSCI. *Bk. rev.:* Number and length vary. *Aud.:* Ac, Sa.

Issues of the elegant French journal *L'Architecture d'Aujourd'hui* feature articles on a chosen theme. The recent themes of temporary architecture, Portugal, and London illustrate the scope of the journal, which ranges from historical to contemporary topics and is international in focus. Recurring departments include news and events, brief building studies, and sections on materials and built works. Although most departments are published in French only, the text of the articles and longer building studies is in both French and English. A well-illustrated journal with many full-color photographs, plans, sections, and details. Recommended for architecture libraries.

465. Architecture Week: the new magazine of design and building. w. Free. Ed(s): Kevin Matthews. Artifice, Inc., PO Box 1588, Eugene, OR 97440. Adv. *Aud.:* Ga, Sa.

This online weekly offers readers a good way of keeping current, and especially if they opt to have the week's headlines delivered via e-mail. The e-mailed newsletters and the text and thumbnail images of the magazine are available free; paid subscribers have access to the full-size images. Each issue highlights several of the new articles and provides links to the current content in the magazine's categories of news, design, building, design tools, environment, culture, people and places, and products. Building studies and architect interviews are the subject of some articles; news and events, profiles of well-known architects, and hot topics are also featured. The intended audience includes practicing architects, students and faculty, and builders, as well as "everyone who appreciates good buildings and places, great design, quality craftsmanship, and the thoughts that make them real." The site also maintains sections on competitions, conferences, events and exhibits, architecture books, a web directory, and a forum for posting comments. Recommended for architecture libraries and larger public libraries.

466. *Architektur Aktuell.* [ISSN: 0570-6602] 1967. m. EUR 108. Ed(s): Matthias Boeckl. Springer Wien, Sachsenplatz 4-6, Vienna, A-1201, Austria; journals@springer.at; http://www.springer.at. Adv. Sample. Refereed. Circ: 7500. *Indexed:* IBR, IBZ. *Aud.:* Ac, Sa.

Buildings and projects in Europe, with some subjects from farther afield, are the focus of each issue of this well-designed Austrian monthly. The occasional interview or a handful of essays may also be included. Advertisements are printed on the front and back pages of the journal, which serves to further highlight the thoughtful, well-documented features. Illustrations are lavish and include photographs, elevations, sections, and plans. While the text of news, reviews, product information, and other recurring departments are in German, the text of feature articles appears in both German and English. The first paragraphs of articles in current and previous issues starting with number 211–212 are available online in German and English. Recommended for architecture libraries.

467. *Canadian Architect.* [ISSN: 0008-2872] 1956. m. CND 50.95 domestic; USD 99.95 foreign. Business Information Group, 12 Concorde Pl, Ste 800, Toronto, ON M3C 4J2, Canada; http://www.businessinformationgroup.ca. Illus., adv. Circ: 10770. Microform: MML. Online: EBSCO Publishing, EBSCO Host; Micromedia ProQuest; Northern Light Technology, Inc.; ProQuest LLC (Ann Arbor). *Indexed:* API, ArtInd, CBCARef, CPerI. *Aud.:* Ga, Sa.

The monthly magazine of the Royal Architectural Institute of Canada, *Canadian Architect* offers articles, building studies, news and events, and product reviews related to the practice of architecture in Canada. The two or three feature articles highlighted in an issue focus on a chosen topic such as architecture for aboriginal Canada, empowering community, or sustainability. Although slim (about 50 pages), *Canadian Architect* is well illustrated and a great resource for those interested in Canadian architecture. Full text and all images from the print magazine are available online starting with the January 2001 issue. However, the images seem to have been scanned at a low resolution and the images in the magazine are superior. Recommended for architecture and public libraries.

468. *Casabella: rivista internazionale di architettura.* Former titles (until 1964): *Casabella Continuita;* (until 1954): *Costruzioni Casabella;* (until 1939): *Casabella;* (until 1932): *La Casa Bella.* [ISSN: 0008-7181] 1928. m. 10/yr. EUR 88.20. Arnoldo Mondadori Editore SpA, Via Mondadori 1, Segrate, 20090, Italy; http://www.mondadori.com. Illus., index, adv. Circ: 46000. *Indexed:* API, ArtHuCI, ArtInd. *Bk. rev.:* 8, 150 words. *Aud.:* Ac, Sa.

Gorgeous color and black-and-white photographs fill the pages of this large-format Italian journal. The scope is international contemporary architecture with the occasional historical subject. A theme or themes tie feature articles together in each issue. A roll call of contemporary architects was the topic of one recent issue; cars, industry, and museums the eclectic topic of another. English translations are included in the captions for the illustrations, and English text for most, but not all, of the articles is printed in the back of the journal. Book reviews, shorter articles, and the extensive product review section are in Italian only. Recommended for architecture libraries.

469. *Competitions (Louisville).* [ISSN: 1058-6539] 1991. q. USD 38 domestic (Students, USD 25). Ed(s): Dr. G Stanley Collyer. Competition Project, Inc., PO Box 20445, Louisville, KY 40250; hotline@ competitions.org; http://www.competitions.org. Circ: 1700 Paid and controlled. *Aud.:* Sa.

This quarterly journal is devoted to the subject of "major competitions in architecture, landscape architecture and public art around the world." The five feature articles in an issue profile recent competitions and present the winning design and finalists and discuss their solutions for the program. Articles detailing participants' experiences in competitions, interviews, and related topical articles may also be included. The hotline section calls for entries for

5–10 competitions worldwide. The journal's web site posts lists of competitions after the journal has been published but stresses that the full list appears in the journal itself. Recommended for architecture libraries.

470. *Crit.* Formerly (until 1977): *Telesis (Washington).* [ISSN: 0277-6863] 1976. q. USD 25 Free to members. Ed(s): R. Todd Gabbard. American Institute of Architecture Students, 1735 New York Ave, NW, Washington, DC 20006; aiasnatl@aol.com. Illus., adv. Circ: 10000. *Aud.:* Ac.

The journal of the American Institute of Architecture Students (AIAS), *Crit* is a "celebration of student work" published twice a year. Contents are usually made up of projects, essays and opinion pieces in the "comments" section, book reviews, and interviews. Most articles are two to four pages in length, and many are one page of text and a facing page of black-and-white or monochrome photographs, drawings, or a featured quote. Although recent issues include a listing of current exhibitions, volunteer or fellowship opportunities, and competitions, the AIAS web site contains more extensive and updated information on these topics, conferences, and other events. A useful snapshot of student projects and interests in the United States and Canada. Recommended for architecture libraries.

471. *El Croquis: de arquitectura y diseno.* [ISSN: 0212-5633] 1982. bi-m. EUR 190 domestic; EUR 248 in Europe; EUR 248 in US & Canada. Ed(s): Paloma Poveda. El Croquis Editorial, Av. Reyes Catolicos 9, El Escorial, Madrid, 28280, Spain; elcroquis@elcroquis.es; http://www.elcroquis.es/. Adv. Circ: 30000. *Indexed:* API, RILM. *Aud.:* Ac, Sa.

The advertisements one expects in a journal are present in the first several dozen pages of *El Croquis*, but there are no recurring departments. Instead the entire issue is devoted to an international architect, firm, or the occasional theme. Essays, interviews, or biographies may appear, but it is the exhaustive documentation of built works and projects that is the true subject. Each work is accompanied by numerous illustrations, plans, details, conceptual drawings, sections, and elevations. The illustrative matter far outweighs the textual descriptions, which are usually supplied by the architect. An excellent source for information on international architects and their work. Readers will find a summary of the journal's contents and representative images on the *El Croquis* web site, but not the full content. Recommended for architecture libraries.

472. *Detail (English Edition).* [ISSN: 1614-4600] 2004. 6x/yr. EUR 89 (Students, EUR 67). *Aud.:* Ac, Sa.

Like other titles listed here, *Detail* is a journal with a focus on contemporary international architecture and an impressive array of color photographs of recent works. What sets the journal apart is that each article on a building in its documentation section is accompanied by a detailed section drawing in addition to the photographs, plans, and small-scale sections that may be found in other journals. Buildings featured in the documentation section and the articles of the shorter discussion and technology sections focus on a selected theme. Eco-refurbishment and climatic design, glass, timber, and lightweight construction and systems are recent themes. Brief news pieces, book and exhibition reviews and a products section complete each issue. The original German-language bimonthly is available in a bilingual German/English edition with a translation supplement, the English edition (reviewed here), and four other language editions. Online users have access to the text of the articles from the documentation section of the journal, one of the photographs from the article, and a list of the details that appeared in print. The entire article in pdf may be downloaded for a fee. Recommended for architecture libraries.

473. *Domus: architettura arredamento arte.* [ISSN: 0012-5377] 1928. m. 11/yr. EUR 93.50 domestic; EUR 125 foreign. Ed(s): Maria Bordone. Editoriale Domus, Via Gianni Mazzocchi 1/3, Rozzano, 20089, Italy; editorialedomus@edidomus.it; http://www.edidomus.it. Illus. *Indexed:* API, ArtHuCI, ArtInd, DAAI, RILM. *Bk. rev.:* 7, 750 words. *Aud.:* Ac, Sa.

An excellent source for information on the international architecture and design scene, *Domus* is a large-format Italian monthly magazine. All the text, from the extensive exhibition calendar to the feature articles and building studies to the interviews and book and product reviews, is in both English and Italian. Color photographs often fill the pages and extend to double spreads, but there are also many plans, sections, and details. The focus is truly international in scope; articles in a recent issue range from Italy and Europe to Great Britain, the United States, and the Middle East. Within the last year Brazil, South America, Scandinavia, China, and Japan were also featured. Through a separate subscription, the online Domus Archive offers access to articles published in the journal from 1998 up to the present but excluding the most recent two issues. Recommended for architecture and large public libraries.

474. Fine Homebuilding. Formerly (until 1991): *Fine Homebuilding.* [ISSN: 1096-360X] 1981. bi-m. USD 37.95 in US & Canada; USD 45.95 elsewhere; USD 7.99 newsstand/cover domestic. Ed(s): Roe Osborn, Kevin Ireton. Taunton Press, Inc., 63 South Main St, Newtown, CT 06470-5506; publicrelations@taunton.com; http://www.taunton.com. Illus., adv. Circ: 300000 Paid. *Indexed:* API, AS&TI, ASIP, BRI, CBRI, IHTDI. *Bk. rev.:* 3, 500 words. *Aud.:* Ga, Ac, Sa.

A popular bimonthly magazine for the homebuilder, this journal also makes good reading for those interested in building or remodeling a home. Departments and articles cover topics related to construction and home improvement projects, tools and methods, materials and best practices. The focus is on houses that are average or small size and affordable building projects that most do-it-yourself amateurs could successfully complete. More than simply a publication devoted to technique, *Fine Homebuilding* pays equal attention to the finished products. Many color photographs accompany the feature articles, and the annual houses and kitchen and bath special issues showcase stunning, well-crafted designs. Online members have access to full text of articles; excerpts and some images are available to all. Recommended for public libraries and architecture libraries where there is interest.

475. G A Document. [ISSN: 0389-0066] q. JPY 11392. A.D.A. Edita Tokyo Co. Ltd., 3-12-14 Sendagaya, Shibuya-ku, Tokyo, 151-0051, Japan. *Indexed:* ArtInd. *Aud.:* Ac, Sa.

Like *El Croquis*, this large-format journal has no recurring departments, news updates, or book reviews. Instead issues focus on six or more recently completed buildings designed by a variety of architects and firms from all over the world. Special issues may be devoted to the work of a single architect or firm. A page of text in both English and Japanese prefaces a rich collection of photographs, plans, sections, and details of the chosen works. *GA Houses* is a similar title offered by the same Tokyo publisher, A.D.A. Edita. Both are great resources for recent, international architecture. Recommended for architecture libraries.

476. Grey Room. [ISSN: 1526-3819] 2000. q. USD 245 print & online eds. (Individuals, USD 68 print & online eds.). Ed(s): Reinhold Martin, Branden W Joseph. M I T Press, 238 Main St., Ste. 500, Cambridge, MA 02142; journals-info@mit.edu; http://mitpress.mit.edu. Refereed. *Indexed:* ABM, ArtInd, IBR, IBZ. *Aud.:* Ac.

A handful of lengthy articles are the main feature of this quarterly, which seeks to "[bring] together scholarly and theoretical articles from the fields of architecture, art, media, and politics to forge a cross-disciplinary discourse uniquely relevant to contemporary concerns." Theory plays a significant role in most articles. Recent topics included advertising posters, Bauhaus textiles, Situationism, and Buckminster Fuller. Contributors are largely academics from North America, but Great Britain and Europe are also represented. Articles are available in JSTOR with a moving wall of five years. Recommended for architecture and academic libraries.

477. Harvard Design Magazine. Former titles (until 1997): *G S D News;* (until 1983): *H G S D News.* [ISSN: 1093-4421] 1977. 2x/yr. USD 75 (Individuals, USD 35; Students, USD 28). Ed(s): Nancy Levinson, William S Saunders. Harvard University, Graduate School of Design, 48 Quincy St, Cambridge, MA 02138; hdm@gsd.harvard.edu; http://www.harvard.edu/hdm. Illus., adv. Refereed. Circ: 16000 Paid. *Indexed:* ABM, ArtInd. *Aud.:* Ac.

The magazine of Harvard University's Graduate School of Design, this title covers current topics in architecture, landscape architecture, and urban design and planning with a critical eye. A theme serves as the touchstone for an issue; "new skyscrapers in megacities on a warming globe," urban design now, and regeneration have been recently featured. Within the boundaries of the selected theme, articles focus on culture, theory, design, history, technology, and materials. Article authors are academics, practicing architects and designers, architectural historians and critics, and the occasional graduate student. Book reviews and an editorial or discussion from the magazine's practitioners advisory board may also appear. The last 15 or so pages are given over to notes on faculty books and projects, events and programs, and other news of Harvard's Graduate School of Design. Text-only of selected articles is available on the magazine's web site. Recommended for architecture libraries.

478. J A. Formerly (until 1991): *Japan Architect.* [ISSN: 1342-6478] 1956. q. JPY 10000 domestic; USD 100 in North America. Ed(s): Yutaka Shikata. Shinkenchiku-sha Co. Ltd., 2-31-2 Yushima, Bunkyo-ku, Tokyo, 113-0034, Japan; http://www.japan-architect.co.jp. Illus., adv. Circ: 18000 Paid. *Indexed:* API, ArtHuCI, ArtInd, BAS. *Aud.:* Ac, Sa.

A year's worth of this Japanese quarterly is made up of a yearbook issue, an issue featuring detailed drawings of recent buildings ("Space in Detail"), a topical issue, and an issue on a Japanese architect or firm. Virtually advertisement-free, the large format pages are given over to the numerous color photographs, detailed drawings, plans, sections, and elevations that accompany a short description of each building. The "Space in Detail" issue features a higher concentration of detailed drawings; the yearbook issue is made up of two-page spreads of photographs and plans of recently completed works. An excellent resource for Japanese architecture. Some content is freely available online including a photograph and a plan for most of the works featured in an issue, but these represent only a fraction of the images and plans that appear in print. Recommended for architecture libraries.

Journal of Architectural and Planning Research. See Urban Studies section.

479. Journal of Architectural Education. Former titles (until 1983): *J A E;* (until 1974): *Journal of Architectural Education.* [ISSN: 1046-4883] 1947. q. GBP 182 print & online eds. Ed(s): Barbara L Allen. Blackwell Publishing, Inc., Commerce Place, 350 Main St, Malden, MA 02148; http://www.blackwellpublishing.com. Illus., index, adv. Refereed. Vol. ends: Aug. Microform: PQC. Online: Blackwell Synergy; EBSCO Publishing, EBSCO Host; Gale; IngentaConnect; JSTOR (Web-based Journal Archive); OCLC Online Computer Library Center, Inc.; SwetsWise Online Content. Reprint: PSC. *Indexed:* API, AgeL, AmHI, ArchI, ArtHuCI, ArtInd, IBR, IBZ. *Bk. rev.:* 5-6, 1,500 words. *Aud.:* Ac.

Articles in this scholarly, refereed quarterly published by the Association of Collegiate Schools of Architecture cover the broad categories of "criticism, design, history, technology, pedagogy, practice." Feature articles in an issue often revolve around a theme such as sustainability, recycling, and the recently featured "1966: forty years after." Five or six book reviews appear in an issue; illustrations throughout are in black and white. Good for discovering those topics of interest in North American architectural education and current scholarship in the field. Full text of articles published from 1999 to the present is available via subscription to Blackwell Synergy; articles published 1947–1974 are available in JSTOR. Recommended for architecture libraries.

480. The Journal of Architecture. [ISSN: 1360-2365] 1996. 5x/yr. GBP 588 print & online eds. Ed(s): Allen Cunningham. Routledge, 4 Park Sq, Milton Park, Abingdon, OX14 4RN, United Kingdom; info@routledge.co.uk; http://www.routledge.co.uk. Illus., adv. Sample. Refereed. Online: EBSCO Publishing, EBSCO Host; Gale; IngentaConnect; OCLC Online Computer Library Center, Inc.; SwetsWise Online Content. Reprint: PSC. *Indexed:* API, C&ISA, CerAb, IAA, IBR, IBZ, SUSA. *Aud.:* Ac.

Published by Routledge for the Royal Institute of British Architects, this scholarly, peer-reviewed journal has an international scope and an editorial board that includes regional editors from 20 countries. Students, academics, and practitioners contribute articles on contemporary and historical topics in architectural theory, methodology, or the intersections between architecture and technology or architecture and culture. Recent issues include articles on architecture and cultural identity in Kuwait, the relationship between photography and architecture, and organic architecture. Most issues include book reviews and a detailed, critical review of a building or group of buildings. Subscribers may choose a print only, online only, or combined subscription. Recommended for architecture and large academic libraries.

481. *Journal of Green Building.* [ISSN: 1552-6100] 2006. q. USD 389 (Individuals, USD 139). Ed(s): Annie Pearce, Michael Horman. College Publishing, 12309 Lynwood Dr, Glen Allen, VA 23059; collegepub@ mindspring.com; http://www.collegepublishing.us. Refereed. *Aud.:* Ac, Sa.

Two sections, the industry corner and research articles, make up each issue of this new quarterly journal devoted to topics in green building. The scholarly research articles are peer reviewed while the industry corner is written by practicing architects, engineers, and others for an audience of practitioners. Small black-and-white photographs and diagrams accompany the articles, but the focus here is on the research and textual information. The relationships between green building and materials, techniques, building and case studies, and education have been the focus of articles published to date. A strong mix of practical information, theory, and research, this title is a great resource on a timely topic. Institutions may subscribe to the print journal or the combination of print and online access via the publisher's web site. Recommended for architecture libraries.

Landscape Architecture. See Landscape Architecture section.

Landscape Journal. See Landscape Architecture section.

482. *Metropolis: architecture design.* [ISSN: 0279-4977] 1981. 10x/yr. USD 32.95 domestic; USD 52.95 Canada; USD 72.95 elsewhere. Ed(s): Susan S Szenasy. Bellerophon Publications, Inc., 61 W 23rd St, 4th fl, New York, NY 10010; http://www.metropolismag.com. Illus., adv. Circ: 47000 Paid. Vol. ends: Jun. *Indexed:* ASIP, DAAI. *Bk. rev.:* 2. *Aud.:* Ga, Ac, Sa.

This suave design magazine covers the urban international scene in recent architecture, restorations, product and furniture design, and planning. Alongside news and events, interviews, book reviews, and short essays, the "Metropolis Observed" section contains eight to ten short articles labeled under headings such as architecture, planning, textiles, education, products and materials, and preservation. The somewhat longer feature articles may cover similar topics in greater detail or focus on broader themes. Of interest to those working in design fields, *Metropolis* also makes for good reading for the design-conscious and the urban dweller. Subscribers have access to the full text of articles on the magazine's web site. Recommended for architecture, academic, and large public libraries.

483. *Places: a forum of environmental design.* [ISSN: 0731-0455] 1983. 3x/yr. USD 55. Ed(s): Donlyn Lyndon. Design History Foundation, 201B Higgins Hall, Pratt Institute, Brooklyn, NY 11205; places@allenpress.com; http://www.places-journal.org. Illus., adv. Refereed. Circ: 4200. *Indexed:* API, ArtHuCI, ArtInd, GardL, PRA, SUSA, V&AA. *Bk. rev.:* Various number and length. *Aud.:* Ac, Sa.

A refereed, scholarly journal published three times a year for the Design History Foundation, *Places* is meant to be a "forum of design for the public realm." Two issues per year focus on a theme and a third issue presents winners of the annual Environmental Design Research Association and *Places* Awards for design and research projects. Subjects of the themed issues are the focus of five or more articles by practitioners and academics. Book reviews, photo essays, and a handful of shorter articles complete this journal. Except for the current issue, articles from all issues (beginning with volume one in 1984) are freely available in pdf on the journal's web site. Recommended for architecture and academic libraries.

484. *Praxis (Cambridge): a journal of writing and building.* [ISSN: 1526-2065] 1999. 2x/yr. USD 96 (Individuals, USD 52; Students, USD 40). Ed(s): Ashley Schafer, Amanda Reeser. Praxis, Inc., P O Box 380225, Cambridge, MA 02238-0225. *Aud.:* Ac.

Design, theory, and practice in North America are the emphasis of the articles published under the overarching themes of each issue of *Praxis, the journal of writing and building.* "Untitled Number Seven" is the coy title of an issue

devoted to considering the museum in terms of both space and discourse. Issue 8 examines the topic of architectural programming and issue 9 is set to explore surface. The dozen or more thoughtful articles and thought-provoking essays that make up an issue are joined by few, if any, recurring departments or advertisements. *Praxis* is published approximately two times a year by an all-volunteer staff. Recommended for architecture libraries.

485. *Preservation.* Former titles (until vol.48, no.4, 1996): *Historic Preservation;* (until 1951): *National Council for Historic Sites and Buildings Quarterly Report;* Which incorporated (1961-1995): *Historic Preservation News;* Which was formerly (until 1990): *Preservation News.* [ISSN: 1090-9931] 1949. bi-m. USD 20 membership; USD 5 newsstand/cover. National Trust for Historic Preservation, 1785 Massachusetts Ave, NW, Washington, DC 20036; law@nthp.org; http://www.nationaltrust.org. Illus., adv. Circ: 215000 Paid and controlled. Vol. ends: Nov. Microform: PQC. *Indexed:* A&ATA, ABS&EES, API, AbAn, AmH&L, ArtHuCI, ArtInd, GardL, HistAb, RILM, SSCI. *Bk. rev.:* 4, 300-500 words. *Aud.:* Ga, Ac, Sa.

A bimonthly snapshot of preservation activities in the United States, *Preservation* is a glossy magazine that is circulated to National Trust members. Buildings, towns, main streets, and the natural world are all candidates for preservation and subjects for the journal's articles and departments. Issues include book reviews and short pieces on news and events. A recurring travel feature highlights historic buildings and sites in the United States and abroad and promotes National Trust tours. The recurring "transitions" section keeps tabs on that which has been "lost, threatened, saved, [or] restored." Those in the historic preservation field should be aware of this title; members of the general public interested in the topic will consider it essential reading. Excerpts from the printed magazine are available on the National Trust web site. Recommended for all libraries.

486. *R I B A Journal.* Incorporates (1986-2003): *R I B A Interiors;* Former titles (until 1993): *Royal Institute of British Architects. Journal;* (until 1987): *Architect; R I B A Journal.* [ISSN: 1463-9505] 1893. m. GBP 70 domestic; EUR 196 in Europe; USD 201 elsewhere. Ed(s): Amanda Baillieu. Builder Group plc., Exchange Tower, 2 Harbour Exchange Sq, London, E14 9GE, United Kingdom; http://www.riba.org/riba/ advice2.htm. Illus., index, adv. Sample. Circ: 24180. Vol. ends: Dec. Microform: PQC. Online: Gale; IngentaConnect. *Indexed:* API, AmHI, ArtHuCI, ArtInd, BAS, BrHumI, BrTechI, DAAI, EIP. *Bk. rev.:* 3, 200 words. *Aud.:* Ac, Sa.

A rich source of information for practicing architects in Great Britain, the Royal Institute of British Architects' monthly trade journal is also notable for its coverage of British architecture. Although shorter news articles may report on international architecture, the three to four building studies that appear in each issue are usually devoted to British works. A couple of brief essays on materials, technological applications, restoration, or other topics join with sections on news and events, book and exhibition reviews, and opinion pieces to complete the public portion of the journal. The RIBA members' section contains updates on the organization's news and events and a number of short pieces on architectural practice that range from drawing up health and safety policies to establishing and maintaining a web presence for an architectural firm. Classified and display advertisements and recruitment postings complete the journal. Another good resource for those considering work in Great Britain. This title's web site offers a free, searchable archive of articles from past issues; articles are accompanied by images and updated monthly. Recommended for architecture libraries.

487. *Society of Architectural Historians. Journal.* Formerly: *American Society of Architectural Historians. Journal.* [ISSN: 0037-9808] 1940. q. Free to members. Ed(s): Zeynep Celik. Society of Architectural Historians, 1365 North Astor St, Chicago, IL 60610-2144; http://www.sah.org. Illus., index, adv. Refereed. Circ: 4000. Vol. ends: Dec. Microform: PQC. Online: JSTOR (Web-based Journal Archive); OCLC Online Computer Library Center, Inc.; H.W. Wilson. *Indexed:* ABS&EES, API, AmH&L, ArtHuCI, ArtInd, BAS, BrArAb, GardL, HistAb, NumL, RILM. *Bk. rev.:* 20, 1,500 words. *Aud.:* Ac.

A scholarly, refereed quarterly composed of lengthy essays and thoughtful, informative exhibition and book reviews. Black-and-white illustrations accompany essays on a wide range of topics in the history of architecture from ancient to modern. The many book reviews are grouped in broad thematic categories such as urbanism, Baroque Rome, Medieval Venice, and theory and modernity. Reviews of videos, films, and web sites are also included. An indispensable resource for architectural history. Articles are included in JSTOR with a moving wall of three years. Recommended for architecture libraries.

488. *Techniques et Architecture.* [ISSN: 0373-0719] 1942. bi-m. EUR 25 per issue. Ed(s): Jean-Francois Pousse, Marie Christine Loriers. Editions Jean-Michel Place, 3 rue Lhomond, Paris, 75005, France; place@jmplace.com; http://www.jmplace.com. Adv. Circ: 16800. *Indexed:* IBR, RILM. *Bk. rev.:* Number and length vary. *Aud.:* Ac, Sa.

Young architects in Europe, stage design, and landscape architecture are the common themes that recently tied together feature articles in this French bimonthly journal. Public buildings and European architecture, with some examples from farther afield, are the focus of the building studies and essays on the chosen theme. Feature articles are accompanied by English translations of the text, but the shorter articles, news and events, book reviews, projects, furniture and design section, and product reviews are only in French. The layout of the text and translations interspersed with photographs and illustrations (many of them small) makes this journal less visually appealing than others in the genre. Nonetheless, *Techniques et Architecture* is a good source of information on European architecture. Recommended for architecture libraries.

489. *Wallpaper.* [ISSN: 1364-4475] 1996. 10x/yr. GBP 72.80 domestic; GBP 105 in Europe; USD 112 in US & Canada. Ed(s): Tyler Brule. Time Inc., Brettenham House, Lancaster Pl, London, WC2E 7TL, United Kingdom. Adv. Circ: 134402 Paid. *Indexed:* DAAI. *Aud.:* Ga, Ac, Sa.

The focus of this British magazine is international design, interiors, fashion, and travel. Issues include sections on architecture, design, features, food, grooming and beauty, interiors, media and resources, style, and travel. In addition to its own section, architecture may appear in the feature articles, the book reviews in media and resources, and elsewhere. Recently completed international buildings, future projects, materials, and well-known or up-and-coming architects are highlighted. The "newspaper" series of short pieces in the first half of the magazine presents "*Wallpaper*'s pick of the latest global goings-on" in a range of fields including architecture. This title is well-suited to architecture audiences and those interested in all forms of trendy world design. The magazine's web site includes brief summaries and some images, but full content is reserved for the printed magazine, which is published eleven times a year. Readers can sign up to receive a free weekly newsletter via e-mail. Recommended for architecture libraries, academic, and large public libraries.

490. *Werk - Bauen & Wohnen.* Formed by the merger of (1946-1982): *Bauen und Wohnen;* (1914-1982): *Werk.* [ISSN: 0257-9332] 10x/yr. CHF 200 domestic (Students, CHF 140). Zollikofer AG, Fuerstenlandstr 122, Postfach 2362, St. Gallen, 9001, Switzerland; leserservice@zollikofer.ch; http://www.zollikofer.ch. Adv. Circ: 9000. *Indexed:* API, ArtInd, BAS, IBR, IBZ. *Aud.:* Ac, Sa.

Werk - Bauen & Wohnen is a German-language, Swiss publication that is published ten times a year. While Switzerland is the primary focus, international buildings and projects may also be featured in the articles devoted to the issue's theme or the shorter articles that complete the issue. Architecture around 1970, steel and space, and a collection of buildings that "communicate in an intensive way" are recent themes. Feature articles are accompanied by an impressive collection of color photographs, plans, site plans, sections, and details, as well as English and French summaries. Profiles of new buildings and interiors, book and exhibition reviews, news and events, and shorter articles on architectural practice, and other topical subjects are in German only. Recommended for architecture libraries.

■ ARCHIVES AND MANUSCRIPTS

General/National, Regional, and State Newsletters/National, Regional, and State Newsletters—Canada/National, Regional, and State Newsletters—United States/Special-Interest Newsletters

See also Bibliography; History; and Library and Information Science sections.

Melanie Wisner, Technical Services—Manuscript Section, Houghton Library, Harvard University, Cambridge, MA 02138; mmwisner@ fas.harvard.edu; FAX: 617-495-1376

Introduction

The periodical literature of archives and manuscripts treats all aspects of the fundamental archival mission. Summarized by the Society of American Archivists (SAA), this is "to establish and maintain control, both physical and intellectual, over records of enduring value." Records encompass a huge range of cultural heritage materials in all physical and electronic formats. The literature reviews current professional trends and practices; it also celebrates the use of original archival materials in increasingly innovative ways.

Archival practice encompasses appraising, accessioning, arranging, describing, preserving, and providing access to the materials entrusted to public and private institutions. The archivist, manuscript curator, and records manager must keep current with and reconcile legal, ethical, and technological requirements. The range of magazines and newsletters available in the field serves both the individual collector and the largest research institutions.

Standards for describing and preserving collections in archives, libraries, and museums are evolving quickly, sometimes converging, sometimes diverging toward more specialized tools. Journals present fresh reports and updates on these developments. There are reports from larger, well-funded institutions on cutting-edge practices alongside articles from small, slimly staffed repositories about subject-focused collections available publicly for the first time or regional efforts to document local history.

Archives users are learning to expect instantly available digital content without necessarily understanding the cost to the general archival enterprise. For all the ways it has revolutionized access to original documents, digitization has a way of blocking out the sun when it hits an institution; money and staff energy must be spent on deadline. Repositories that lack basic systems and staff to catalog and house their material adequately may seek or be pressured into a digital project, good in itself but nonetheless distracting from longer-term access and preservation goals. Project management and the technology of digital media are heavily covered in archival journals and newsletters.

Simultaneously and ironically, from within the larger library profession has come the call to face our collective backlog of "uncataloged and unprocessed archival, manuscript, and rare book materials" (Association of Research Libraries conference, "Exposing Hidden Collections," 2003). This, too, is an expensive proposition, long known to archivists but not as attractive to funders; it requires commitment to material of unknown "value" to future researchers and to the marketplace. Suggested strategies for meeting this mandate will likely appear in the journals for some time.

If there can be silver linings to natural and manmade disasters suffered globally, one has been awareness of the danger of losing cultural memory when cultural records are lost. To quote its current president, "the Society of American Archivists is encouraging every archivist to take some personal responsibility for emergency preparedness." Archival leaders and workers in the trenches alike have contributed to salvage efforts in the United States and globally; these firsthand stories have appeared in many archival publications along with prescriptions for response to future crises.

The literature of archives and manuscripts is predominantly scholarly in the larger journals, often quite theoretical, and very practical in the newsletters. It aims to discover and illuminate best practices and to build community among and between the custodians and the users of original cultural materials.

Basic Periodicals

Ga: *Archivist, Prologue;* Ac: *American Archivist, Archival Issues, Archivaria, Comma, The Information Management Journal.*

Basic Abstracts and Indexes

America: History and Life, Historical Abstracts, Library and Information Science Abstracts, Library Literature.

General

491. American Archivist. [ISSN: 0360-9081] 1938. s-a. USD 85 domestic; USD 100 foreign. Ed(s): Philip B Eppard. Society of American Archivists, 527 S Wells St, 5th Fl, Chicago, IL 60607; info@archivists.org; http://www.archivists.org/publications.html. Illus., index, adv. Refereed. Circ: 4900 Paid. Vol. ends: Fall. Microform: PMC. *Indexed:* A&ATA, ABS&EES, AgeL, AmH&L, ArtHuCI, BRI, CBRI, FR, HistAb, IBR, IBZ, ISTA, IndIslam, LISA, LibLit, PAIS, SSCI. *Bk. rev.:* 9-11, 400-1,500 words. *Aud.:* Ac, Sa.

American Archivist is the premier journal of archival history, theory, and practice in the United States and the official forum for the national professional association, the Society of American Archivists (SAA). The nearly book-length semi-annual volumes often examine an issue, organization, or practice in depth in a special section or, occasionally, in a special issue. The journal composes an archival curriculum by itself, offering the literature that most often supports coursework in archival training programs across the nation; SAA has recently committed to republishing basic archival texts, and substantive reviews appear in the journal. Regular content includes research articles, case studies, commentary and opinion, coverage of international issues, practical bibliographies and other professional tools, reviews of archival literature and end products, and letters to the editor. *American Archivist* is a vital part of the American archival profession and consistently representative of the trends in the field.

492. Archival Issues. Formerly (until 1992): *Midwestern Archivist*. [ISSN: 1067-4993] 1976. s-a. USD 60 (Individuals, USD 30). Ed(s): Todd Daniels-Howell, Mark Greene. Midwest Archives Conference, Menzi Behrnd-Klodt, 7422 Longmeadow Rd, Madison, WI 53717; http://www.midwestarchives.org. Illus., index, adv. Refereed. Circ: 1100. Vol. ends: No. 2. *Indexed:* AmH&L, HistAb, ISTA, LibLit. *Bk. rev.:* 6-8, 400-1,200 words. *Aud.:* Ac, Sa.

Archival Issues is a refereed journal whose scope extends well beyond the boundaries of the Midwest. Its articles are interesting geographically and topically, providing wide-ranging current awareness, often from refreshing viewpoints. The journal reviews publications in basic archival areas, extends the range of the *American Archivist*, and is equally well-edited. It particularly invites archivists who have never published to submit work and awards an annual prize to a first-time author. Every two years, the journal awards the Margaret Cross Norton Award to the author of what is judged to be the best article in the previous two years.

493. Archival Science: international journal on recorded information. Incorporates (in 2000): *Archives & Museum Informatics;* Which was formerly (1987-1989): *Archival Informatics Newsletter.* [ISSN: 1389-0166] 2000. q. EUR 318 print & online eds. Ed(s): Eric Ketelaar, Karen Anderson. Springer Netherlands, Van Godewijckstraat 30, Dordrecht, 3311 GX, Netherlands; http://www.springeronline.com. Adv. Refereed. Online: EBSCO Publishing, EBSCO Host; Gale; IngentaConnect; OCLC Online Computer Library Center, Inc.; OhioLINK; ProQuest LLC (Ann Arbor); Springer LINK; SwetsWise Online Content. Reprint: PSC. *Indexed:* ABIn, ISTA, LISA. *Aud.:* Ac, Sa.

Archival Science is an "integrated, interdisciplinary, and intercultural" journal on "the whole field of recorded process-related information, analysed in terms of form, structure and context." Its jargon can be an obstacle to the uninitiated, but it works for its target audience, researchers and educators in archival science. In seeking to develop "archival science as an autonomous scientific discipline," the journal presents theoretical articles, some by practitioners who also frequent more mainstream archival journals, but the theory is offered in the service of very current, practical issues facing the profession. Recent issues include "Macroappraisal in the Netherlands," "Create Once, Use Many Times: The Clever Use of Recordkeeping Metadata for Multiple Archival Purposes,"

and "A Tower of Babel: Standardizing Archival Terminology." Attention is given to work in the non-English-speaking world. Online tables of contents and abstracts, as well as an online version, are available.

494. Archivaria. Supersedes: *Canadian Archivist.* [ISSN: 0318-6954] 1975. s-a. CND 278.20 (Individuals, CND 117.70). Ed(s): Robert McIntosh. Association of Canadian Archivists, P O Box 2596, Ottawa, ON K1P 5W6, Canada. Illus., index. Refereed. Circ: 1300. *Indexed:* A&ATA, AmH&L, BRI, CBCARef, CBRI, CPerI, HistAb, LISA, LibLit. *Bk. rev.:* 10-20, 750-2,500 words. *Aud.:* Ac, Sa.

Archivaria is the journal of the Association of Canadian Archivists, "devoted to the scholarly investigation of archives in Canada and internationally." The journal "aims to be a bridge of communication among archivists, and between archivists and users of archives." National archival policy, practice, and new areas of research are generally found in every issue. Article abstracts are given in both French and English; a few book reviews are in French. The journal reviews books and exhibits and exchanges tables of contents with the journal *Archives* (published by the Association des archivistes du Quebec). The range of regular features, including "Counterpoint" ("argumentative pieces, longer rejoinders..."), "Studies in Documents," and "Pot-pourri" ("documents related to archives, having amusing, poignant, or piquant appeal"), offers a lively whole. *Archivaria* should be considered required reading alongside *American Archivist*.

495. Archives. [ISSN: 0003-9535] 1949. s-a. Institutional members, GBP 55; Individual members, GBP 25; Non-members, GBP 50. British Records Association, 40 Northampton Rd, London, EC1R 0HB, United Kingdom; http://www.hmc.gov.uk/bra. Illus., index. Circ: 1300. Vol. ends: Oct. *Indexed:* AmH&L, AmHI, ArtHuCI, BrArAb, BrHumI, HistAb, IndIslam, LISA, LibLit, NumL. *Bk. rev.:* 25-30, 300-800 words. *Aud.:* Ac, Sa.

The British Records Association, parent of *Archives,* "co-ordinates and encourages the work of owners, individual scholars, archivists and librarians, institutions and societies interested in the preservation and use of archives." The journal is elegant and scholarly, sometimes densely so, perhaps austere, but it demonstrates fervent devotion to British heritage and its preservation. Its six or so articles and numerous book reviews are generally slanted toward the British user, rather than administrator, of collections, often publishing historical scholarship derived from hours spent in archives. The "Report and Comment" section offers a detailed picture of the health and activities of British archival agencies.

496. Archives and Manuscripts. [ISSN: 0157-6895] 1955. s-a. AUD 165 domestic; AUD 150 foreign. Ed(s): Maggie Shapley. Australian Society of Archivists Inc., PO Box 83, O'Connor, ACT 2602, Australia; asa@asap.unimelb.edu.au; http://www.archivists.org.au. Illus., adv. Refereed. Circ: 850. Vol. ends: Nov. Online: RMIT Publishing. *Indexed:* AmH&L, HistAb, LISA. *Bk. rev.:* 15-20, 500-2,000 words. *Aud.:* Ac, Sa.

Archives and Manuscripts, the journal of the Australian Society of Archivists, covers issues of the South Pacific and Pacific Islands region, but it also offers the rest of the English-speaking world a refreshing viewpoint from a diverse and culturally aware part of the archival world. The journal is fully refereed, describing itself as a "professional and scholarly journal about the theory and practice of archives and recordkeeping." The "International Notes" section, organized geographically, describes regional activities in detail; extensive reviews and a review article are of interest to archivists beyond the region.

497. Archivist: magazine of the National Archives of Canada. [ISSN: 0705-2855] 1973. 2x/yr. Free. Ed(s): Rebecca Grace. National Archives of Canada, 395 Wellington St, Ottawa, ON K1A 0N3, Canada; publications@archives.ca; http://www.archives.ca/. Illus. Circ: 14000. *Indexed:* ABS&EES, AmH&L, CBCARef, CPerI, HistAb, IBSS. *Aud.:* Ga, Ac, Sa.

The Archivist is the Canadian archival magazine produced by the National Archives of Canada, a component of the recently merged Library and Archives Canada. The merger has resulted in a reevaluation of the organization's publication program, and, as of this writing, publication of *The Archivist* has been suspended and readers are encouraged to check its web site for updates. In the meantime, its past issues are of enduring value, for which reason it is included here; it is fully expected that a publication will fill the void. A counterpart to *Prologue* (below in this section), its glossy back-to-back bilingual format offers an easy, continuous flow for readers in both languages. Black-and-white photographs accompany feature articles often written by archives division heads, highlighting particular collections. *The Archivist* is an excellent guide to the issues and collections native to the Canadian archival and records management environment.

498. *Comma: international journal on archives.* Formed by the merger of (1951-2000): *Archivum;* (1983-2000): *Janus;* (1958-2000): *Conseil International des Archives. Table Ronde Internationale des Archives. Actes.* [ISSN: 1680-1865] 2000. 3x/yr. EUR 158; EUR 58 newsstand/cover. Ed(s): Nancy Bartlett. K.G. Saur Verlag GmbH, Ortlerstr 8, Munchen, 81373, Germany; info@saur.de; http://www.saur.de. Index. *Indexed:* HistAb, IBR, IBZ. *Aud.:* Ac, Sa.

Comma is the journal of the International Council on Archives (ICA). The title is meant to suggest "the pause in the continuum, the realization of change." The focus of the only internationally focused and produced journal is "the research, administration, and development of archives and the archival profession worldwide." It includes reports and studies from ICA bodies. Abstracts appear in Arabic, Chinese, and Russian, as well as English, French, German, and Spanish (articles appear in English, French, and Spanish); translation and dissemination in other languages is encouraged. Topics from recent issues include indigenous people's archives, Nordic archives, and human rights and archives. The multilingual format requires extra effort to navigate, and the journal cannot reflect quickly shifting events, but *Comma*'s work is impressive, and crucial to understanding the directions of the field globally. In 2003, ICA began publication of a newsletter, *Flash*, to "communicate news on ICA activities and highlight current issues in archives." Published three times a year, it is a benefit of membership.

History News. See History section.

499. *The Information Management Journal: the journal for the information management professionals.* Former titles (until 1999): *Records Management Quarterly;* (until Jan. 1986): *A R M A Records Management Quarterly;* (until 1976): *Records Management Quarterly;* (until 1967): *Records Review.* [ISSN: 1535-2897] 1967. bi-m. USD 53 (Non-members, USD 95). Ed(s): Cynthia Launchbaugh, Mike Pemberton. A R M A International, 13725 W 109th St, Ste 101, Lenexa, KS 66215; hq@arma.org; http://www.arma.org. Illus., index, adv. Circ: 10500 Paid. Vol. ends: Dec. Microform: PQC. Online: EBSCO Publishing, EBSCO Host; Gale; OCLC Online Computer Library Center, Inc.; H.W. Wilson. *Indexed:* ABIn, BPI, CompLI, ISTA, LISA, LRI. *Bk. rev.:* 1-4, 1,000-2,500 words. *Aud.:* Ac, Sa.

The Association of Records Managers and Administrators International is the professional not-for-profit association for records and information managers worldwide. Its journal, *IMJ*, focuses on "records, information, and knowledge as corporate assets and as contributors to organizational success," in all settings and all formats. From their origins in the New Deal era as processors of new paper mountains of governmental records, records and information managers now face an onslaught of legal, technological, preservation, privacy, security, and commercial issues inherent in the digital environment. Recent journal articles concern legislation proposed to prevent security breaches, uses of medical records in healthcare fraud, and FBI electronic record-keeping practices. The journal is glossy and highly professional, with regular columns on legislation and the international scene. The current table of contents is available online.

500. *Journal of Archival Organization.* [ISSN: 1533-2748] 2002. q. USD 290 print & online eds. Ed(s): Thomas J Frusciano, Ruth C Carter. Haworth Press, Inc., 10 Alice St, Binghamton, NY 13904-1580; getinfo@haworthpress.com; http://www.haworthpress.com. Adv. Circ: 42 Paid. Reprint: HAW. *Indexed:* IBR, IBZ, ISTA, LISA. *Bk. rev.:* Number and length vary. *Aud.:* Ac, Sa.

The *Journal of Archival Organization* is offered by Haworth Press, publishers of scores of academic journals and an established presence in library training. *JAO* focuses on primary archival functions, selecting articles that sample a variety of institutional experiences pointing toward best practices. International topics are covered to a limited degree, offering, for instance, recent pieces on archives in Pakistan and Vietnamese culture in California. A recent double issue published the "Proceedings of the European Conference on Encoded Archival Description and Context (EAD and EAC)," a major effort to review the application of these standards globally. Regular features include web site reviews, coverage of standards, interviews, and book and resource reviews. Tables of contents and abstracts are available online.

501. *Manuscripts.* [ISSN: 0025-262X] 1948. q. Membership, USD 45. Ed(s): David R Chesnutt. Manuscript Society, 1960 E Fairmont Dr, Tempe, AZ 85282-2844; manuscrip@home.com; http://www.manuscript.org. Illus., index, adv. Circ: 1500. Vol. ends: No. 4. Microform: PQC. *Indexed:* AmH&L, AmHI, HistAb, MLA-IB. *Aud.:* Ga.

Manuscripts is the quarterly journal of the Manuscript Society, founded in 1948 as the National Society of Autograph Collectors. The journal provides community to its somewhat independent constituency of private historians, amateur antiquarians, and private and institutional collectors of literary and historical materials. "Excellent scholarly and collector articles" educate readers in the sometimes arcane, sometimes culturally hot culture of the document, from Sotheby's to flea markets, promoting ethical practices and preservation along the way. Regular features include "Auction Trends," a very detailed survey of prices paid for specific items at auction, and a hefty section of advertising directing member-collectors to member-sellers. A news section covers events not necessarily discussed elsewhere in the archival literature: discoveries, acquisitions, upcoming sales, legal questions, thefts, forgeries, and replevin actions. While harking back to a private-society tradition, the journal is well worth pointing out to users of archives, and archivists should take note of this community's viewpoints.

502. *Prologue (College Park): quarterly of the National Archives and Records Administration.* Formerly (until 1967): *National Archives Accessions.* [ISSN: 0033-1031] 1969. q. USD 20 domestic; USD 25 foreign. Ed(s): Mary C Ryan. National Archives and Records Administration, PO Box 100684, College Park, MD 30384-0684; http://www.archives.gov. Illus., index. Circ: 3000 Paid. Vol. ends: Winter. *Indexed:* ABS&EES, AmH&L, AmHI, ArtHuCI, HistAb, HumInd, IUSGP, RGPR, SSCI. *Aud.:* Ga.

Prologue celebrates the remarkable holdings and programs of the National Archives and Records Administration (NARA), the regional archives, and the presidential libraries. This handsomely produced pictorial quarterly in the Smithsonian style offers essays in American history based on original documents, photographs and illustrations from the collections, and news of numerous outreach and education programs of interest to historians, students, and other archivists. Recent issues include articles on baseball records, "The Frozen Sucker War" (popsicles in pre-air-conditioned America), and NARA's role in the wake of Hurricanes Katrina and Rita salvaging the region's cultural records. Articles are particularly suited to middle and high school teachers and students (for whom NARA also created the suite of resources called the Digital Classroom). NARA's valuable publications are noted, many of which will aid genealogical researchers.

503. *Provenance.* Formerly (until 1983): *Georgia Archive.* [ISSN: 0739-4241] 1972. a. Individuals, USD 25; Students, USD 10. Ed(s): Susan Broome. Society of Georgia Archivists, PO Box 133085, Atlanta, GA 30333-3085; admin@soga.org; http://www.soga.org. Illus., index, adv. Refereed. Circ: 300 Paid. Vol. ends: No. 2. *Indexed:* AmH&L, HistAb. *Bk. rev.:* 3-4, 750-1,250 words. *Aud.:* Ac, Sa.

The first (1972) professional archival journal published by a state or regional organization, *Provenance* naturally covers regional issues for its parent, the Society of Georgia Archivists, but it also prints articles from archivists around the country in somewhat thematic issues. Its stated primary focus is the archival profession in the theory and practice of archival management. *Provenance* samples American archival concerns in a format especially appealing to archival students, new professionals, and archivists in local and subject-oriented collections. Every year it awards a prize for a superior contribution, and the journal especially encourages first-time authors.

504. ***The Public Historian: a journal of public history.*** [ISSN: 0272-3433] 1978. q. USD 161 print & online eds. USD 44 newsstand/cover. Ed(s): Anne Marie Plane, Mary E. Hancock. University of California Press, Journals Division, 2000 Center St, Ste 303, Berkeley, CA 94704-1223; journals@ucpress.edu; http://www.ucpress.edu/journals. Illus., index, adv. Refereed. Circ: 1514. Microform: PQC. Online: EBSCO Publishing, EBSCO Host; Florida Center for Library Automation; Gale; OCLC Online Computer Library Center, Inc.; ProQuest LLC (Ann Arbor); SwetsWise Online Content. *Indexed:* AmH&L, AmHI, ArtHuCI, BRI, CBRI, HistAb, IBR, IBZ, PAIS, SSCI. *Bk. rev.:* 30-60, 1,000-2,800 words. *Aud.:* Ac, Sa.

Published by the University of California Press for the National Council on Public History, *The Public Historian* is a multidisciplinary journal, the "voice of the public history movement." Its territory includes but is not limited to oral history, corporate information services, grassroots efforts in local history at all levels, historic preservation, museum and archives administration, cultural resources management, litigation support and expert witnessing, editing, publishing, and media. The journal pays particular attention to public land and cultural artifact issues. Each issue offers over 25 pieces sometimes gathered loosely around a theme; a recent issue is a self-reflection on the enterprise and ethics of public history itself. The diversity of approaches to defining public history makes for a provocative mix of articles but with an academic underpinning. Reviews cover books, museum exhibits, film, video, and electronic media. The journal may offer particular inspiration to the student fan of history who is facing school and career choices, especially if he or she has never heard of public history.

505. ***R B M: A Journal of Rare Books, Manuscripts and Cultural Heritage.*** Formerly (until 2000): *Rare Books and Manuscripts Librarianship.* [ISSN: 1529-6407] 1986. s-a. USD 42 domestic; USD 47 in Canada & Mexico; USD 58 elsewhere. Ed(s): Marvin Je Taylor, Lisa Brower. Association of College and Research Libraries, 50 E Huron St, Chicago, IL 60611; acrl@ala.org; http://www.ala.org/acrl. Illus., index, adv. Refereed. Circ: 450. Vol. ends: No. 2. *Indexed:* LISA, LibLit, MLA-IB. *Aud.:* Ac, Sa.

RBM: A Journal of Rare Books, Manuscripts, and Cultural Heritage is the Association of College and Research Libraries' (ACRL) independent journal, "covering issues pertaining to the world inhabited by special collections libraries and cultural heritage institutions" (ACRL is a division of the American Library Association). Noting that "rare book and manuscript libraries have metamorphosed into special collections libraries," the journal embraces the broader range of institutions that care for a broader range of types of cultural heritage materials. Content appeals chiefly to the rare book librarian who may carry responsibility for manuscripts and archives, but articles are also relevant to purely book or manuscript professionals, dealers, private collectors, auction houses, museums, practitioners of copyright and intellectual property law, and students. One of ACRL's very notable contributions to the special collections world nationally and worldwide lately has been the "hidden collections agenda," a call to deal with our collective backlog of undocumented library and archival material; core documents and commentary appeared in *RBM.*

506. ***Society of Archivists. Journal.*** [ISSN: 0037-9816] 1955. s-a. GBP 211 print & online eds. Ed(s): Cressida Annesley, Kate Manning. Routledge, 4 Park Sq, Milton Park, Abingdon, OX14 4RN, United Kingdom; info@routledge.co.uk; http://www.routledge.co.uk. Illus., index, adv. Refereed. Circ: 1600. Microform: PQC. Online: EBSCO Publishing, EBSCO Host; Gale; IngentaConnect; OCLC Online Computer Library Center, Inc.; ProQuest LLC (Ann Arbor); SwetsWise Online Content. Reprint: PSC. *Indexed:* AmH&L, AmHI, ArtHuCI, BrArAb, BrHumI, FR, HistAb, LISA, NumL, SSCI. *Bk. rev.:* 15-25, 600-1,400 words. *Aud.:* Ac, Sa.

The *Journal of the Society of Archivists* offers a balanced picture of the well-developed archival profession in the United Kingdom and Ireland with occasional forays into other English-speaking lands. It is oriented to British and Irish archivists, records managers, and conservation professionals. The tone is professional but can range from reflective and personal to fairly technically scientific; conservation issues, in particular, are covered in some depth. Issues often suggest, by clusters of articles, a focus. Recent issues offer articles ranging from a reexamination of Jacques Derrida to international criminal justice archives to the management of music manuscripts in the United Kingdom. Numerous book reviews, notices of publications by the society and by the Royal Commission on Historical Manuscripts, and obituaries primarily serve the British archival community, but reviews of reference works and guides to collections will interest American researchers traveling to the United Kingdom.

National, Regional, and State Newsletters

State, provincial, and regional associations provide archivists in the field with current awareness of challenges and opportunities, a sense of community, and a forum for professional development. Newsletters issued at the local level track state and provincial legal trends, list professional and public workshops, announce and report on local meetings, describe funding opportunites, and publish job announcements, as well as gather news from member repositories. The larger or most active associations may publish articles on a par with the national journals, but they generally focus on shorter-range issues and resources to support the daily work of their members.

Publication can be irregular due to changes in activity levels and editorship within local associations. Many newsletters, following the lead of the Society of American Archivists, publish online only; others send paper to members and also make issues available online; a few still print newsletters that are a benefit of membership.

The following publications of national, regional, state, and provincial archival associations are arranged geographically.

National, Regional, and State Newsletters—Canada

ACA Bulletin. [ISSN: 0709-4604] 6/yr. Larry Dohey. ACA Bulletin, Roman Catholic Archdiocese, P.O. Box 1363, St. John's, NL Canada A1C 5M3 (http://archivists.ca/publications/bulletin.aspx).

ALBERTA

ASA Newsletter. q. Archives Soc. of Alberta, P.O. Box 4067, South Edmonton Post Office Edmonton, Alberta T6E 4S8 (http://www.archivesalberta.org/newsl.htm).

BRITISH COLUMBIA

AABC Newsletter. [ISSN: 1183-3165] q. Archives Assn. of British Columbia, P.O. Box 78530, Univ. Post Office, Vancouver, BC V6T 1Z4 (http://aabc.bc.ca/aabc/newsletter/default.htm).

MANITOBA

ArchiNews/ArchiNouvelles. [ISSN: 1193-9958] q. Assn. for Manitoba Archives, Box 26005 Maryland P.O., Winnipeg, MB R3G 3R3 (http://www.mbarchives.mb.ca/communique.htm).

NEWFOUNDLAND AND LABRADOR

ANLA Bulletin. [ISSN: 0821-7157] q. $25. Association of Newfoundland and Labrador Archives, P.O. Box 23155, RPO Churchill Sq., St. John's, NL A1B 4J9 (http://www.anla.nf.ca/).

NOVA SCOTIA

The Council of Nova Scotia Archives Newsletter. [ISSN: 0829-7142] s-a. Newsletter, Council of Nova Scotia Archives, 6016 University Ave., Halifax, NS B3H 1W4 (http://www.councilofnsarchives.ca/news/newsletter.htm).

ONTARIO

Off the Record. q. Archives Association of Ontario, Archives Association of Ontario, 258 Adelaide Street East, Suite #301, Toronto, Ontario, M5A 1N1 (http://aao.fis.utoronto.ca/aa/otr.html).

QUEBEC

La Chronique. L'Association des archivistes du Quebec, C. P. 423, succ. Sillery, Sainte-Foy (Quebec) G1T 2R8 (http://www.archivistes.qc.ca/publication/chronique.html).

SASKATCHEWAN

SCAA Newsletter. Saskatchewan Council for Archives and Archivists, Kathlyn Szalasznyj, Outreach, 2506 Woodward Avenue, Saskatoon, SK S7J 2E5 (http://scaa.usask.ca/newsletter.html).

YUKON

YCA Newsletter. Yukon Council of Archives, Publications Committee, Box 31089, Whitehorse, Yukon Y1A 5P7 (http://www.whitehorse.microage.ca/yca/sections/newsletter/newsletter.html).

National, Regional, and State Newsletters—United States

Archival Outlook. [ISSN: 1520-3379] 6/yr. Teresa M. Brinati. Soc. of Amer. Archivists, 527 S. Wells, 5th Floor, Chicago, IL 60607 (www.archivists.org/periodicals/ao.asp).

ALABAMA

The Alabama Archivist. s-a. $10. Carol Ellis. Soc. of Alabama Archivists, Society of Alabama Archivists, P.O. Box 300100, Montgomery, AL 36130-0100 (http://www.auburn.edu/sala/publications.html).

CALIFORNIA

SCA Newsletter. q. $45. Josh Schneider and Jessica Lemieux. Soc. of California Archivists, The Bancroft Library, Univ. of California Berkeley, Berkeley, CA 94720-6000 (http://www.calarchivists.org/newsletter.html).

DELAWARE VALLEY

Archival Arranger. 3/yr. $7.50 Joanne Seitter. Delaware Valley Archivists Group, New Jersey Division of Archives and Records Management, 2300 Stuyvesant Ave., P.O. Box 307, Trenton, NJ 08625 (http://www.dvarchivists.org/).

FLORIDA

The Florida Archivist. q. Michael Zaidman. Society of Florida Archivists, P.O. Box 2746, Lakeland, FL 33806-2746 (http://www.florida-archivists.org/).

GEORGIA

SGA Newsletter. q. $25. Miriam Hudgins. Soc. of Georgia Archivists, P.O. Box 133085, Atlanta, GA 30333 (http://soga.org/pubs/nltr/newsletter.html).

INTERMOUNTAIN

CIMA Newsletter. q. Roy Webb. Conference of Inter-Mountain Archivists, P.O. Box 2048, Salt Lake City, UT 84110-2048 (http://www.lib.utah.edu/spc/cima/news.html).

KENTUCKY

The Kentucky Archivist. s-a. Jim Cundy. Kentucky Department for Libraries and Archives, 300 Coffee Tree Road, P.O. Box 537, Frankfort, KY 40602-0537 (http://kyarchivists.org/kyarch.htm).

LOUISIANA

LAMA Newsletter. [ISSN: 1073-1008] s-a. Phyllis Kinnison. Louisiana Archives and Manuscripts Assn., P.O. Box 17203, Baton Rouge, LA 70893-7203 (http://www.nutrias.org/lama/lama.htm).

LOUISIANA, NEW ORLEANS

Greater New Orleans Archivists Newsletter. 3/yr. $10. Barbara Vaughn. Greater New Orleans Archivists, Nunez Community College Archives, 3710 Paris Rd., Chalmette, LA 70043 (http://nutrias.org/gnoa/gnoa.htm).

MICHIGAN

Open Entry. s-a. $15. Leslie Gowan Armbuster. Michigan Archival Assn., Ford Motor Co., 1338 Hollywood St., Dearborn, MI 48124 (http://www.maasn.org/).

MID-ATLANTIC

Mid-Atlantic Archivist. [ISSN: 0738-9396] q. $35. Katy Rawdon-Faucett. Mid-Atlantic Regional Archives Conference, 8233 Old Courthouse Road, Suite 200, Vienna, VA 22182 (http://www.lib.umd.edu/MARAC/committees/marac-pubs.html#back).

MIDWEST

MAC Newsletter. [ISSN: 0741-0379] q. $30. Janet Carleton. Ohio University Libraries, Alden 235A, Athens, OH 45701 (http://www.midwestarchives.org/macnewsletter.htm).

MISSISSIPPI

The Primary Source. [ISSN: 0741-6563] q. $10. Soc. of Mississippi Archivists, Society of Mississippi Archivists, P.O. Box 1151, Jackson, MS 39215-1151 (http://www.lib.usm.edu/~smainfo/pubs.html).

MISSOURI, KANSAS CITY

The Dusty Shelf. q. Kara Kelly. Kansas City Area Archivists, University of Missouri-Kansas City, 5100 Rockhill Road, Kansas City, MO 64110-2499 (http://www.umkc.edu/KCAA/DUSTYSHELF/DUSTY.HTM).

MISSOURI, ST. LOUIS

The Acid Free Press. $7.50. Mike Everman. Assn. of St. Louis Area Archivists, Missouri Historical Soc., P.O. Box 11940, St. Louis, MO 63112 (library.wustl.edu/units/spec/archives/aslaa/).

NEW ENGLAND

NEA Newsletter. q. $30. New England Archivists, George C. Gordon Library, Worcester Polytechnic Institute, 100 Institute Road, Worcester, MA 01609 (http://newenglandarchivists.org/newsletter/index.html).

NEW YORK, CAPITAL DISTRICT

CAA Newsletter. $5. Rachel Donaldson. Capital Area Archivists of New York, New York State Archives and Records Admin., Rm. 9C71-CEC, Albany, NY 12230 (http://library.albany.edu/speccoll/caa/Newsletters/index.htm).

NEW YORK, NEW YORK

Metropolitan Archivist. s-a. $25. Joseph M Ciccone. Archivists Round Table of Metropolitan New York, Inc., P.O. Box 5070, Somerset, NJ 08875-5070 (http://www.nycarchivists.org/main.html).

NORTH CAROLINA

North Carolina Archivist. s-a. Paula Brown. Soc. of North Carolina Archivists, P.O. Box 20448, Raleigh, NC 27619 (http://www.ncarchivists.org/pubs/newslet.html).

NORTHWEST

Easy Access. q. $15. John Bolcer. Northwest Archivists, Inc., Univ. Washington, UW Libraries, Box 352900, Seattle, WA 98195-2900 (http://www.lib.washington.edu/nwa/EasyAccess.html).

OHIO

The Ohio Archivist. [ISSN: 1047-5400] s-a. Beth Kattelman. Soc. of Ohio Archivists, Wright State Univ., Special Collections and Archives, Dunbar Library, 3640 Colonel Glenn Highway, Dayton, OH 45435-0001 (http://www.ohiojunction.net/soa/newsletter.html).

ROCKY MOUNTAINS

The Rocky Mountain Archivist. [ISSN: 1098-7711] q. Kent Jaehnig. Soc. of Rocky Mountain Archivists, Douglas County History Research Center, Philip S. Miller Library, 100 South Wilcox, Castle Rock, CO 80104-1911 (http://www.srmarchivists.org/newsletter/default.htm).

SOUTHWEST

The Southwestern Archivist. [ISSN: 1056-1021] q. $10. Amanda York Focke. Soc. of Southwest Archivists, P.O. Box 700761, San Antonio, TX 78270 (http://southwestarchivists.org/HTML/Publications.htm).

TENNESSEE

Tennessee Archivist. q. Steven P. Cox. Tennessee Archivists, Lupton Library, Univ. of Tennessee at Chattanooga, 615 McCallie Ave., Chattanooga, TN 37403-2598 (http://www.geocities.com/tennarchivists/newsletter.html).

Special-Interest Newsletters

Archivists caring for the same types of records, performing the same functions, working in similar specialized institutions, or collecting in the same areas benefit from sharing knowledge and news in special-interest newsletters. Many of these newsletters are published by sections and roundtables of the Society of American Archivists; these groups meet at the SAA annual conference, and many print or post online meeting notes as well as periodic news, reviews, outside resources, and sometimes fuller articles.

The list below offers selected special interest publications, many of which are available online. Newsletters from the allied fields of preservation and conservation are included; individual repositories' publications are not included. Newsletters published by sections of the Society of American Archivists are listed under the section's name unless it forms part of the title. Editors change frequently, so readers are advised to contact SAA directly for current information: Society of American Archivists, 527 S. Wells St., 5th Floor, Chicago, IL 60607 (archivists.org).

BUSINESS

Business Archives Current News. Business Archives Section, Soc. of Amer. Archivists (http://www.archivists.org/saagroups/bas/newsletter.asp).

COLLEGE AND UNIVERSITY ARCHIVES

The Academic Archivist. College and Univ. Archives Section, Soc. of Amer. Archivists (http://www.archivists.org/saagroups/cnu/index.asp).

CONGRESSIONAL PAPERS

Congressional Papers Roundtable Newsletter. Chris Burns. Soc. of Amer. Archivists (http://www.archivists.org/saagroups/cpr/newsletters.asp).

DESCRIPTION

Descriptive Notes. John Rees. Description Section, Soc. of Amer. Archivists (http://www.archivists.org/saagroups/descr/index.asp).

ELECTRONIC RECORDS

Crossroads: developments in electronic records management and information technology. 4/yr. Membership benefit; table of contents available online. National Association of Government Archives and Records Administrators, 90 State Street, Suite 1009, Albany, NY 12207 (http://www.nagara.org/index.html).

FILM

AMIA Newsletter. [ISSN: 1075-6477] q. $50. David Lemieux. Assn. of Moving Image Archivists, 1313 North Vine Street, Hollywood, CA 90028 (http://www.amianet.org/publication/publications/newsletter/submissions.html).

Film Technology News. Irreg. Free. Alan Stark. Film Technology Co., 726 North Cole Avenue, Los Angeles, CA 90038.

GOVERNMENT RECORDS

Official Word: The Government Records Section Newsletter. Paul R. Bergeron. Government Records Section, Soc. of Amer. Archivists (http://www.archivists.org/saagroups/gov/newsletters/index.asp).

NAGARA Clearinghouse: news and reports on government records. 4/yr. $75. Membership benefit; table of contents available online. Roy H Tryon. National Association of Government Archives and Records Administrators, 90 State Street, Suite 1009, Albany, NY 12207 (http://www.nagara.org/index.html).

LESBIAN AND GAY

LAGAR. Irreg. Maggi Gonsalves. Lesbian and Gay Archives Roundtable, Soc. of Amer. Archivists (http://www.archivists.org/saagroups/lagar/newsletters/index.html).

MANUSCRIPTS

The Manuscript Society News. 4/yr. $60. The Manuscript Society, 1960 East Fairmont Drive, Tempe, AZ 85282-2844 (http://manuscript.org/publications.html).

RBMS Newsletter. 2/yr. Assn. of College and Research Libs., Amer. Library Assn., 50 E. Huron St., Chicago, IL 60611 (http://www.rbms.nd.edu/publications/index.shtml).

Manuscript Repositories Section Newsletter. 3/yr. Beth Bensman. Soc. of Amer. Archivists (http://www.archivists.org/saagroups/mss/newsletter.asp).

MULTICULTURAL

Archivists and Archives of Color Newsletter. Paul Sevilla. Archivists and Archives of Color Roundtable. Soc. of Amer. Archivists (http://www.archivists.org/saagroups/aac/Activities.htm).

MUSEUMS

Museum Archivist. s-a. Museum Archives Section, Soc. of Amer. Archivists (http://www.archivists.org/saagroups/museum/index.htm).

ORAL HISTORY

Oral History Section Newsletter. s-a. Rebecca Hankins. Oral History Section, Soc. of Amer. Archivists (http://www.archivists.org/saagroups/oralhistory/newsletters.asp)

PERFORMING ARTS AND RECORDED SOUND

Performance!. 3/yr. Performing Arts and Recorded Sound Roundtable, Soc. of Amer. Archivists (http://www.archivists.org/saagroups/performart/newsletter/index.html).

PRESERVATION/CONSERVATION

AIC News. [ISSN: 0887-705X] 6/yr. $105. The Amer. Inst. for Conservation of Historic & Artistic Works, 1717 K St. N.W., Suite 200, Washington, DC 20006 (http://aic.stanford.edu/library/print/index.html).

Conservation, the Getty Conservation Institute Newsletter. [ISSN: 0898-4808] 3/yr. Free. Jeffrey Levin. Getty Conservation Inst., 1200 Getty Center Dr., Suite 700, Los Angeles, CA 90049-1684 (http://www.getty.edu/conservation/publications/newsletters/).

Guild of Book Workers Newsletter. [ISSN: 0730-3203] 6/yr. $60. Jody Beenk. Guild of Book Workers, 521 Fifth Ave., New York, NY 10175 (http://palimpsest.stanford.edu/byorg/gbw/news.shtml).

Infinity. Preservation Section, Soc. of Amer. Archivists (http://www.archivists.org/saagroups/preserv/text/news.htm).

International Preservation News: a newsletter of the IFLA Core Activity for Preservation and Conservation. 3/yr. Library of Congress, 101 Independence Avenue, S. E. Washington, D. C. 20540-4500 USA (http://www.ifla.org/VI/4/ipn.html).

WAAC Newsletter. [ISSN: 1052-0066] 3/yr. $30. Western Assn. for Art Conservation, 5905 Wilshire Blvd., Los Angeles, CA 90036 (http://palimpsest.stanford.edu/waac/wn/).

RECORDS MANAGEMENT

Records & Information Management Report: issues in information technology. [ISSN: 1096-9624] 10/yr. $182. Richard J. Cox. M. E. Sharpe, Inc., 80 Business Park Drive, Armonk, NY 10504 (http://www.mesharpe.com/journals.asp).

REFERENCE

RAO News. Irreg. Sharon Pullen. Reference, Access, and Outreach Section, Soc. of Amer. Archivists (http://www.archivists.org/saagroups/rao/index.asp).

RELIGIOUS

The Archival Spirit. Wesley W. Wilson. Archivists of Religious Collections Section, Soc. of Amer. Archivists (http://www.saa-arcs.org/).

NEARI Newsletter. $10. New England Archivists of Religious Institutions, Boston CSJ Archives, 637 Cambridge St., Brighton, MA 02135-2801 (http://www.csjboston.org/neari.htm).

SCIENCE, TECHNOLOGY, AND HEALTH CARE

Archival Elements. Science, Technology, and Health Care Roundtable, Soc. of Amer. Archivists (http://www.archivists.org/saagroups/sthc/publications.html).

VISUAL MATERIALS

Views. Visual Materials Section, Soc. of Amer. Archivists (http://www.lib.lsu.edu/SAA/views.html).

■ ART

General/Museum Publications

See also Craft section.

Holly Stec Dankert, Head of Readers' Services, The School of the Art Institute of Chicago, John M. Flaxman Library, 37 S. Wabash, Chicago, IL 60603, hdankert@saic.edu, FAX: 312-899-1851

Nathaniel Feis, Serials-Cataloging Librarian, John M. Flaxman Library, The School of the Art Institute of Chicago, 37 S. Wabash, Chicago, IL 60603; nfeis@saic.edu; FAX: 312-899-1851

Introduction

Though the primary readers of art publications continue to be artists, art dealers, art collectors, museum curators, art historians, and scholars, many of the titles in this section will be of interest to members of the general public and, especially, students. The terms *art* and *arts* as used in this section can be defined as two- or three-dimensional visual arts of all media including, but not limited to, paint, pencil, ink, found objects, clay, bronze, other metals, video, film, new media, photography, decorative arts, and performance art. However, as museums, scholars, and the artists themselves continue to redefine what art is, many other types of work are up for discussion in these publications, including sound art and art of who can say which of the senses an artist might attempt to reach next.

The "General" subsection below features core titles for art collections or libraries where there is an interest in artistic work and culture, including general-interest magazines, scholarly and professional journals, and instructional magazines for artists. Also, attempts have been made to include journals that focus on art from various parts of the globe and on specific areas in the art world. Bulletins from major museums highlighting their own collections are divided into a separate category following the "General" subsection.

Most titles exist in some online version; but, partially due to the fact that full-color imagery is still largely dependent on print media for the best-quality reproduction, the print journals are still the primary venue for art scholarship and information. Many of these magazine web sites provide only subscription and general information. Core titles with additional web content are indicated usually within the description of the apropos titles; however, due to the ever-changing nature of the web, a title that lacks a noteworthy web site at the time of publication may, in fact, have a significant Internet presence by the time one is consulting this resource. The contributors hope that the entries in this section will give librarians a reasonable perspective on the sorts of journals that are available concerning art in all its diverse forms.

Basic Periodicals

GENERAL. Ems: *The Artist's Magazine;* Hs: *American Artist, Art in America, The Artist's Magazine;* Ga: *American Artist, Art & Antiques, Art in America, Artforum International, The Artist's Magazine;* Ac: *Art Bulletin, Art History, Art in America, Art Journal, Artforum International, Artnews.*

MUSEUM PUBLICATIONS. The *Metropolitan Museum of Art Bulletin* is the best multipurpose museum publication for all ages. A local museum publication should also be chosen for regional representation.

Basic Abstracts and Indexes

Art Index, Artbibliographies Modern; the *Bibliography of the History of Art* (*BHA*) succeeded RILA.

General

507. *2wice.* Formerly (until 1996): *Dance Ink.* 1990. s-a. USD 50. Ed(s): Patsy Tarr. 2wice Arts Foundation, Inc., P O Box 980, East Hampton, NY 11937. Adv. *Aud.:* Ga, Ac, Sa.

2wice is a very special publication. Each issue has a unique theme and all of the contents within the issue, which are selected from all corners of the art world, are geared toward exemplifying that theme. Some themes are intangible, like "formal" or "glow," while others are more visceral, like "animal" or "car," and while still others are quite specific, like "Cunningham-Rauschenberg" —a retrospective of the two artists. The journal describes itself on its web site, which includes excerpts and images from the journal, as "popular and academic, serious and humorous." It is beautifully constructed and printed, and artfully made. Though the dimensions of the journal remain consistent (30 x 21 in.), each issue is structured in a different manner—sometimes horizontal; sometimes vertical; sometimes with extensive text; sometimes with almost no text at all; sometimes printed on very thin paper. And sometimes it is a collection of booklets inside a box that is the size of the other issues. Each issue is a bit of a surprise.

African Arts. See Africa section.

508. *Afterall: a journal of art, context and enquiry.* [ISSN: 1465-4253] 1999. s-a. GBP 25 (Individuals, GBP 12). Ed(s): Mark Lewis, Charles Esche. Central Saint Martins College of Art & Design, 107-109 Charing Cross Rd, London, WC2H 0DU, United Kingdom; info@csm.linst.ac.uk; http://www.csm.linst.ac.uk. Indexed: ABM. *Aud.:* Ga, Ac, Sa.

According to its web site, *Afterall* "provides a forum for the quiet consideration of contemporary art practice." Each issue provides the reader with lengthy, well-researched articles—including notes and bibliographies—about a few select contemporary artists; and it often includes several different writers discussing the same artists' work from varying perspectives. These articles are also accompanied by numerous illustrations. Adding to the information in the print journal, the web site includes many other articles not included in the print version, among other information.

Afterimage. See Photography section.

509. *American Art: the journal of the Smithsonian American Art Museum.* Formerly (until 1991): *Smithsonian Studies in American Art.* [ISSN: 1073-9300] 1987. 3x/yr. USD 155 domestic; USD 170.30 Canada; USD 163 elsewhere. Ed(s): Cynthia Mills. University of Chicago Press, Journals Division, PO Box 37005, Chicago, IL 60637;

subscriptions@press.uchicago.edu; http://www.journals.uchicago.edu. Illus., adv. Refereed. Vol. ends: Fall. Online: EBSCO Publishing, EBSCO Host; JSTOR (Web-based Journal Archive). *Indexed:* ABM, AmH&L, AmHI, ArtInd, HistAb, IBR, IBZ, MASUSE, RILM. *Aud.:* Ga, Ac.

Produced by the Smithsonian American Art Museum, *American Art* encompasses the visual heritage of the United States from its beginning in the colonial era to the present. Interdisciplinary articles range from history to archaeology, anthropology, and cultural studies, all with a focus on visual arts. While the editorial statement indicates that the scope is primarily fine arts, *American Art* includes works of popular culture, public art, film, photography, electronic multimedia, and decorative arts and crafts. Each issue offers a mix of scholarly feature articles and a commentary that focuses on an issue or artist of importance to the Smithsonian or to the American art world at large. Articles are written in accessible language, and the mix of color and black-and-white photographs makes this well suited to public libraries and colleges and universities.

510. *American Artist.* [ISSN: 0002-7375] 1937. m. 11/yr. USD 29.95 domestic. Ed(s): Stephen Doherty. Nielsen Business Publications, 770 Broadway, New York, NY 10003-9595; bmcomm@vnuinc.com; http://www.nielsenbusinessmedia.com. Illus., index, adv. Circ: 123300 Paid. Vol. ends: Dec. Microform: NBI. Online: EBSCO Publishing, EBSCO Host; Factiva, Inc.; Florida Center for Library Automation; Gale; OCLC Online Computer Library Center, Inc.; ProQuest K-12 Learning Solutions; ProQuest LLC (Ann Arbor); H.W. Wilson. *Indexed:* A&ATA, ABM, ABS&EES, ArtInd, BEL&L, BRI, CBRI, IBR, IBZ, MASUSE, RGPR, RILM. *Bk. rev.:* 2-3, 500 words. *Aud.:* Hs, Ga.

This is a consumer publication that covers how-to information on oil painting, watercolor, acrylics, drawing, sculpture, and printmaking. Geared to aspiring and commercial artists, the subject matter tends to be traditional representational art, with landscapes, still lifes, and portraiture predominating. Interviews with contemporary artists provide insights into the technical aspects of their work. Current news on societies and organizations of special interest to painters, notices on business and commercial opportunities, and advertising for supplies and materials are useful. A subscription to *American Artist* includes the *Annual Directory of Art Schools & Workshops*. Not to be missed is the web site at www.myamericanartist.com, which has full-text articles and many other resources for artists. This periodical is suited for public libraries and institutions with fine arts programs.

511. *Apollo: the international magazine of the arts.* [ISSN: 0003-6536] 1925. m. GBP 98 domestic; GBP 114 in Europe; GBP 100 United States. Ed(s): Dr. David Euserdjian. Apollo Magazine Ltd., 20 Theobald's Rd, London, WC1X 8PF, United Kingdom; editorial@apollomag.com. Illus., index, adv. Sample. Vol. ends: Dec. Microform: PQC. Online: Gale. Reprint: PSC. *Indexed:* ABM, API, ArtHuCI, ArtInd, BAS, BRI, BrHumI, CBRI, DAAI, IBR, IBZ, IndIslam, RILM. *Bk. rev.:* 6-7, 800-1,000 words. *Aud.:* Ga, Ac.

Tastefully illustrated and international in scope, *Apollo*'s themed issues revolve around broad categories (decorative arts, Asian arts, etc.), with six or seven articles aimed at an educated audience and written by curators, professors, and other art experts. The December issue reviews the year with feature articles on acquisitions, exhibitions, and a personality of the year. Each issue includes a diary of museum shows, book reviews, and loads of Paris, London, and New York gallery ads. It is geared toward collectors and curators but is also relevant to academicians. Appropriate for large public libraries and academic libraries that serve art programs.

512. *Archives of Asian Art.* Formerly (until 1966): *Chinese Art Society of America. Archives.* [ISSN: 0066-6637] 1945. a. EUR 58.40 in the European Union; EUR 62.40 elsewhere. Ed(s): Naomi Noble Richard. Asia Society, 725 Park Ave, New York, NY 10021. Illus., index. Refereed. Circ: 600. *Indexed:* ArtHuCI, ArtInd, BAS, FR, IBR, IBZ. *Aud.:* Ac, Sa.

Published biennially by the Asia Society, a nonprofit, nonpolitical educational organization, *Archives of Asian Art* provides a forum for research by scholars on numerous topics concerning Asian art history. Four to six lengthy articles are generously illustrated and feature East Asian art. The journal also documents significant acquisitions of Asian art by North American museums and other institutions, covering a two-year period. This publication serves as one of the few English-language resources for serious students and scholars. It is highly recommended for research collections in academic libraries.

Art & Antiques. See Antiques section.

513. *The Art Book.* Formerly: *International Publishing Review (Fine Arts Edition).* [ISSN: 1368-6267] 1993. q. GBP 102 print & online eds. Ed(s): Sue Ward. Blackwell Publishing Ltd., 9600 Garsington Rd, Oxford, OX4 2ZG, United Kingdom; customerservices@blackwellpublishing.com; http://www.blackwellpublishing.com. Illus., adv. Online: Blackwell Synergy; EBSCO Publishing, EBSCO Host; Gale; IngentaConnect; OCLC Online Computer Library Center, Inc.; OhioLINK; SwetsWise Online Content. Reprint: PSC. *Indexed:* ABM, AmHI, ArtInd. *Bk. rev.:* 45-60. *Aud.:* Ga, Ac, Sa.

Different from the other art titles listed in this section, *The Art Book* is devoted exclusively to reviews of art books and articles related to the art book publishing industry. The Association of Art Historians in the United Kingdom provides authoritative and independent critical oversight of the contents, in conjunction with Blackwell staff. Three feature-length reviews, frequently thematic, are included in each issue. There are also interviews; exhibition, museum, and gallery publication reviews; and commentary segments. Book reviews in general art, photography, and architecture genres and a bestseller list round out each issue. Librarians will find this a useful collection development tool. Highly recommended for academic and special collection libraries.

514. *Art Bulletin.* Former titles (until 1918): *College Art Association of America. Bulletin;* (until 1913): *College Art Association. Bulletin.* [ISSN: 0004-3079] 1913. q. 0 membership. Ed(s): H. Perry Chapman. College Art Association, 275 Seventh Ave, New York, NY 10001; nyoffice@collegeart.org; http://www.collegeart.org. Illus., index, adv. Refereed. Circ: 9500. Vol. ends: No. 4. Microform: IDC; PQC. Online: Chadwyck-Healey Inc.; EBSCO Publishing, EBSCO Host; Florida Center for Library Automation; Gale; JSTOR (Web-based Journal Archive); Northern Light Technology, Inc.; OCLC Online Computer Library Center, Inc.; ProQuest LLC (Ann Arbor); H.W. Wilson. *Indexed:* ABM, ABS&EES, API, AmHI, ArtHuCI, ArtInd, BAS, BRD, BRI, BrArAb, CBRI, HumInd, IBR, IBZ, IndIslam, MASUSE, NumL, RI-1, RILM. *Bk. rev.:* Numerous, essay length. *Aud.:* Ac.

Published quarterly by the College Art Association (CAA), *Art Bulletin* serves as a forum for leading scholarship and debate in contemporary art-historical practice. In this slightly oversized, glossy journal, research articles cover all periods, many in Western art, and are usually accompanied by some color but mostly black-and-white photos. Abstracts of each article are provided in the table of contents. See www.collegeart.org, CAA's portal for table of contents archives back to 1996, plus job listings in the arts and other benefits to members. *Art Bulletin* is considered essential for all research collections and academic libraries.

515. *Art Criticism.* [ISSN: 0195-4148] 1979. a. USD 20 (Individuals, USD 15). Ed(s): Donald B Kuspit. State University of New York at Stony Brook, Department of Art, Staller Center, Stony Brook, NY 11794-5400; artcriticism@hotmail.com. Refereed. Circ: 300. *Indexed:* ABM, ABS&EES, ArtHuCI, ArtInd. *Aud.:* Ac.

Published twice yearly, *Art Criticism* focuses on psychoanalytic, philosophical, and popular-culture theories and criticism of Modern through contemporary visual arts. A half-dozen articles in each issue cover individual artists and/or works, and the history of criticism. Recent issues are thematic and authored by one scholar, e.g., "Administrativism and Its Discontents" or "Ritual and the Creative Process: The Psychoanalysis of Transformation." Recommended for academic libraries.

Art Education. See Education/Specific Subjects and Teaching Methods/ The Arts section.

516. Art History: journal of the Association of Art Historians. [ISSN: 0141-6790] 1978. 5x/yr. GBP 450 print & online eds. Ed(s): Fintan Cullen, Deborah Cherry. Blackwell Publishing Ltd., 9600 Garsington Rd, Oxford, OX4 2ZG, United Kingdom; customerservices@ blackwellpublishing.com; http://www.blackwellpublishing.com. Illus., index, adv. Refereed. Circ: 2500. Vol. ends: Dec. Microform: PQC. Online: Blackwell Synergy; EBSCO Publishing, EBSCO Host; Gale; IngentaConnect; OCLC Online Computer Library Center, Inc.; OhioLINK; SwetsWise Online Content. Reprint: PSC. *Indexed:* ABM, API, AmH&L, AmHI, ArtHuCI, ArtInd, BAS, BrHumI, DAAI, HistAb, HumInd, IBR, IBZ, NTA, RILM. *Bk. rev.:* 9-11, essay length. *Aud.:* Ac.

The U.K.-based Association of Art Historians publishes *Art History* to provide research in the historical and theoretical aspects of traditional visual arts—primarily two-dimensional works on paper and canvas, with occasional forays into three-dimensional art—from both Western and Eastern hemispheres. Articles that explore the arts in their interdisciplinary context are encouraged. Targeted to art and design professionals and others concerned with the advancement of the history of art, *Art History* seeks to consider related cultural, economic, and social issues as well. Illustrations are minimal and appropriate to the theses posited in the four papers that are presented in each issue. Librarians will especially appreciate the extensive scholarly book reviews written by experts in the field. Recommended for all academic libraries.

517. Art in America. Former titles (until 1939): *Art in America and Elsewhere;* (until 1921): *Art in America.* [ISSN: 0004-3214] 1913. m. USD 34.95 domestic; USD 64.95 Canada; USD 69.95 elsewhere. Ed(s): Richard Vine, Elizabeth C. Baker. Brant Publications, Inc., 575 Broadway, 5th Fl, New York, NY 10012. Illus., adv. Circ: 65000. Microform: PQC. Online: EBSCO Publishing, EBSCO Host; Florida Center for Library Automation; Gale; Northern Light Technology, Inc.; OCLC Online Computer Library Center, Inc.; ProQuest LLC (Ann Arbor); H.W. Wilson. *Indexed:* ABM, ABS&EES, AmH&L, AmHI, ArtHuCI, ArtInd, BRD, BRI, CBRI, DAAI, FLI, HistAb, HumInd, IBR, IBZ, IndIslam, MASUSE, RGPR, RI-1, RILM, SSCI. *Bk. rev.:* 2-3, 1,000 words. *Aud.:* Ga, Ac.

A standard in the field, *Art in America* strives to bring big-name artists, exhibitions, and performances to the American art world. Brief articles cover both U.S. and international news items, issues, commentary, exhibitions, and occasional regional pieces. A handful of feature articles focuses primarily on contemporary artists, while including one on past masters of the nineteenth and twentieth centuries. Written for an educated audience of art collectors, dealers, and curators, *Art in America* nevertheless is suitable for large public and academic libraries whose users will find the many gallery and exhibition advertisements and show listings useful.

518. Art India: the art news magazine of India. [ISSN: 0972-2947] 1996. q. USD 34. Ed(s): Abhay Sardesai. Art India Publishing Co. Pvt. Ltd., Jindal Mansion, 5-A Dr G Deshmukh Marg, Mumbai, 400 026, India. *Aud.:* Ac, Sa.

For over a decade, *Art India* has been showcasing the contemporary Indian art world and promoting a critical platform for exploring new media art, painting, sculpture, photography, and architecture. There is substantial reporting in English covering cultural and societal issues in the visual arts; profiles and interviews of current visual artists; many reviews of Indian artists—local and international; and book reviews and gallery listings. Much current content and access to archives are available at www.artindiamag.com. Appropriate for museum, academic, and public libraries that serve visual artists and collectors.

519. Art Journal. Former titles (until 1960): *College Art Journal;* (until 1941): *Parnassus.* [ISSN: 0004-3249] q. USD 50 domestic to non-member individuals; USD 60 foreign to non-member individuals; USD 75 domestic to non-member institutions. Ed(s): Joe Hannon. College Art Association, 275 Seventh Ave, New York, NY 10001. Illus., adv. Refereed. Circ: 11000. Microform: PQC. Online: Chadwyck-Healey Inc.; EBSCO Publishing, EBSCO Host; Gale; JSTOR (Web-based Journal Archive); OCLC Online Computer Library Center, Inc.;

ProQuest LLC (Ann Arbor); H.W. Wilson. *Indexed:* A&ATA, ABM, ABS&EES, API, AmHI, ArtHuCI, ArtInd, BAS, BRI, CBRI, DAAI, HumInd, IBR, IBZ, MASUSE, RILM, SSCI. *Bk. rev.:* 6, length varies. *Aud.:* Ac.

Art Journal is an academic periodical published by the College Art Association. It is a visionary work; the editorial board seeks to create a dialogue among educators teaching art, design, criticism and theory, art history, and visual culture. Articles are of a scholarly nature and focus on cultural change reflected in the visual arts, selecting "vital, intellectually compelling, and visually engaging" subjects of the twentieth and twenty-first centuries. Contemporary works and artists are featured, with black-and-white and color illustrations. This journal is highly recommended for all academic libraries.

520. Art Monthly. [ISSN: 0142-6702] 1976. 10x/yr. GBP 47 (Individuals, GBP 39; Students, GBP 28). Ed(s): Patricia Bickers. Britannia Art Publications Ltd., 4th Fl., 28 Charing Cross Rd, London, WC2H 0DB, United Kingdom. Adv. Sample. Circ: 5500. Online: EBSCO Publishing, EBSCO Host; OCLC Online Computer Library Center, Inc.; H.W. Wilson. *Indexed:* ABM, AmHI, ArtInd, BrHumI, IBR, IBZ. *Bk. rev.:* 1-3, 1,000 words. *Aud.:* Ga, Ac.

This journal is primarily concerned with the contemporary art world as it manifests itself in the United Kingdom. Each issue of *Art monthly* includes interviews with, and profiles of, leading figures in the art world, as well as up-and-coming artists and critics' explorations of germane trends in art and the art world. It also contains art news, book reviews, reports from other parts of the globe, and a lengthy section of exhibition listings and reviews from throughout the United Kingdom.

521. Art New England: a resource for the visual arts. [ISSN: 0274-7073] 1979. 6x/yr. USD 28 domestic; USD 33 Canada; USD 40 elsewhere. Ed(s): Barbara O'Brien. Art New England, Inc., 425 Washington St, Brighton, MA 02135. Illus., adv. Circ: 30000. Vol. ends: Dec. *Indexed:* ArtInd. *Aud.:* Ga, Ac.

This tabloid-format magazine offers regional art news for the New England area, focusing on artists, exhibitions, performances, and installations from that region. Also useful to local artists are the guides to schools and artists' directories found in each issue, plus advertising for classes, workshops, degrees, and programs in the area. Recommended for public and academic libraries that serve studio arts programs in the Northeast.

522. The Art Newspaper (International Edition). Incorporated (1988-1989): *Journal of Art.* [ISSN: 0960-6556] 1990. 11x/yr. EUR 110 in Europe; EUR 130 elsewhere. Umberto Allemandi & C., Via Mancini 8, Turin, 10131, Italy; http://www.allemandi.com. Adv. Sample. Circ: 14000 Paid. *Indexed:* ABM, ArtInd, RILM. *Aud.:* Ga, Ac, Sa.

The Art Newspaper is a true newspaper in its format and content. Its focus is commentary and news of the international art world. It is divided into two sections. The first is devoted to what's going on in private, national, and international museums; legislation/regulation in the arts; financial crises and funding issues; the effects of world events on art collections; and scandals from all areas. Columnists and op/ed writers turn a critical eye on governments around the world and the effects that their policies have on the arts; plus there are other regular commentaries. The second section lists "What's On," exhibitions around the globe, divided into New York; the rest of the United States; London; the rest of the United Kingdom; France; Germany; and the rest of the world. There is also an auction listing. The web site offers some free content and is worth bookmarking. An excellent source for keeping up with world art news and people. Highly recommended for all libraries.

523. Art Nexus (Spanish Edition). Formerly (until 1991): *Arte en Colombia Internacional.* [ISSN: 0121-5639] 1976. q. USD 32. Ed(s): Celia Sredni de Birbragher. Arte en Colombia Ltda., 12955 Biscayne Blvd., Ste. 410, North Miami, FL 33181-2023; info@artnexus.com. Illus., adv. Refereed. Circ: 16000. *Indexed:* ABM, ArtInd, HAPI, RILM. *Bk. rev.:* 1-3, 1,000 words. *Aud.:* Ga, Ac, Sa.

Art Nexus offers an opportunity to explore many aspects of Latin American visual arts. Issues include interviews, profiles, discussion, and criticism focusing on individual artists or groups of artists. These inspections of art at the individual level are augmented by features on international festivals, fairs and conferences, and reviews and discussions of exhibitions by Latin American artists or concentrating on Latin American art held all over the world. There are also book and catalog reviews as well an extensive gallery guide. Online, the reader is provided with further information about news, exhibitions, and events throughout the Latin American art world, visual galleries, and an astounding database of contemporary Latin American artists, along with other relevant information.

524. *Art Now Gallery Guide: Collector's Edition.* Former titles: *Art Now Gallery Guide: International Edition; Art Now Gallery Guide: National Edition; Art Now: U S A - National Art Museum and Gallery Guide.* 1982. 10x/yr. USD 45 domestic; USD 52 foreign. Ed(s): Patricia Yannotta. Art Now, Inc., 111 8th Ave, Ste 302, New York, NY 10011-5204. Illus., adv. Circ: 6000. *Aud.:* Ga, Ac, Sa.

Art Now Gallery Guide informs readers about exhibitions at art galleries and museums across the United States, serving as a current-awareness resource in the contemporary art world. Divided into regional publications—New York, Boston/New England, Philadelphia, Southeast, Chicago/Midwest, Southwest, and West Coast editions—this pocket-size monthly reference book offers events, highlights, and listings of private art dealers and services in each region. Area maps provide a special feature in these regional editions. A great value for the price, this title is useful for all types of libraries.

525. *Art Papers Magazine.* Formerly (until 1999): *Art Papers;* Formed by the 1980 merger of: *Contemporary Art - Southeast; Atlanta Art Papers;* Formerly (until 1978): *Atlanta Art Workers Coalition Newspaper.* [ISSN: 1524-9581] 1976. bi-m. USD 40 in Canada & Mexico (Members, USD 30; Non-members, USD 35). Ed(s): Sylvie Fortin. Art Papers, Inc., PO Box 5748, Atlanta, GA 31107. Illus., adv. Circ: 162000. Vol. ends: Nov/Dec. Microform: PQC. Online: OCLC Online Computer Library Center, Inc.; H.W. Wilson. *Indexed:* ABM, ABS&EES, ArtInd, RILM. *Bk. rev.:* 1, 1,000 words. *Aud.:* Ga, Ac, Sa.

Art Papers defines itself as "the critical voice covering more regions of the U.S." and is dedicated to providing advocacy and a forum for the examination and exchange of diverse and independent perspectives on the role of art. Controversial topics and criticism cover cultural, social, and philosophical issues related to all visual arts, including photography, mixed media, and film. The excellent web site, www.artpapers.org, plus departments that feature studio visits, interviews, collecting and art resources, regional artists' gallery shows, and reviews make this resource valuable for artists and all those interested in contemporary art. Appropriate for public, college, and university libraries.

526. *Art Press: la revue de l'art contemporain.* [ISSN: 0245-5676] 1972. m. EUR 6.20 per issue. Ed(s): Catherine Millet. ArtPublications, 8 rue Francois Villon, Paris, 75015, France. Circ: 48000. *Indexed:* ABM, ArtInd, IBR, IBZ. *Aud.:* Ac, Sa.

Published bilingually, with French and English integrated side by side, this international monthly explores visual arts, literature, video, film, performance, electronic arts, music, theater, new media—a broad array of global cultural phenomena. Feature-length articles are sometimes thematic, covering important events, philosophies, and trends in contemporary art and society. Editorials, interviews (with artists, curators, dealers), book and exhibition reviews, and thematic columns (art market, literature) complete each issue. Recommended for research collections in the arts.

527. *Art Review (London): international art and style.* Former titles (until 1993): *Arts Review (London); Art News & Review.* [ISSN: 1745-9303] 1949. m. GBP 38 domestic; GBP 93 in Europe; USD 99 in US & Canada. Ed(s): Rebecca Wilson, David Lee. Art Review Ltd., Hereford House, 23-24 Smithfield St, London, EC1A 9LF, United Kingdom. Illus., index, adv. Circ: 15000. Microform: BNB; PQC. Online: OCLC Online Computer Library Center, Inc. *Indexed:* ABM, ArtInd. *Bk. rev.:* Number and length vary. *Aud.:* Ga, Ac.

A consumer publication reporting on the current international art scene, *Art Review* features five articles on contemporary visual arts, photography, design, or the artists themselves. The United Kingdom is primarily covered, but there are also segments devoted to international art, style, objects, collectors, and

critics. Regional reviews and exhibition guides attempt a more inclusive overview of contemporary art. The magazine's glitzy, insider presentation of art news will appeal to all audiences. Useful for research collections that are trying to provide comprehensive coverage of the art world.

528. *Art Therapy: journal of the American Art Therapy Association.* Supersedes in part: *American Journal of Art Therapy.* [ISSN: 0742-1656] 1983. q. USD 200 (Individuals, USD 125). Ed(s): Lynn Kaplan. American Art Therapy Association, Inc., 5999 Stevenson Ave., Alexandria, VA 22304; info@arttherapy.org; http://www.arttherapy.org. Adv. Circ: 5000. *Indexed:* ABM, CINAHL, ECER, ERIC, PsycInfo. *Bk. rev.:* 3-5, 1,000 words. *Aud.:* Ac, Sa.

This is the official journal of the professional association of art therapists, and its stated purpose is to "advance the understanding of how visual art functions in the treatment, education, development and enrichment of people." Each issue contains three articles written by art therapy professionals; viewpoints and commentary on issues of concern to the profession; and book reviews and news briefs in the field. One of the few scholarly publications devoted exclusively to this profession, *Art Therapy* is appropriate for academic libraries.

529. *Art U S.* [ISSN: 1546-7082] 2003. bi-m. USD 30 in US & Canada; USD 55 elsewhere; USD 6 newsstand/cover per issue. Ed(s): Malik Gaines. Art U S, 530 Molino St., Ste 21, Los Angeles, CA 90013; http://www.arttext.org. *Indexed:* ABM, ArtInd. *Aud.:* Ga.

Art US, as its title suggests, is primarily concerned with art and artists in the United States, though it does stray beyond this scope to look at the arts internationally as well. Specifically, it focuses on art and artists at work or exhibiting within the present incarnation of the art world. In addition to artist profiles and studies of particular art movements and concepts, each issue includes an extensive section of current gallery and museum reviews from around the world. Recommended for academic and public libraries where there is an interest in contemporary art.

530. *ArtAsiaPacific: today's art from the tomorrow's world.* [ISSN: 1039-3625] 1993. 6x/yr. USD 72. Ed(s): Elaine E Ng. Art Asia Pacific Publishing, Llc., 245 Eighth Ave #247, New York, NY 10027. Illus., adv. Circ: 7000. *Indexed:* ABM, AmHI, ArtInd. *Aud.:* Ac, Sa.

Relaunched in 2003, *Art AsiaPacific* covers leading figures and trends in Asian contemporary art. Several feature-length articles cover artists from Korea, China, Japan, Taiwan, Thailand, and Pacific islands in this glossy and minimally stylized magazine. Full-color imagery predominates in both features and international gallery ads. Regular departments showcase happenings (Events, State of the Arts, News, Profile, Hot Spots, One-on-One) and exhibition reviews in Asia and major U.S. cities. Subscriber information and tables of contents for the current and the previous issue are available at www.aapmag.com. Written in straightforward language to appeal to a wide audience, *Art AsiaPacific* is recommended for academic and large public libraries.

531. *Artes de Mexico.* [ISSN: 0300-4953] 1953. q. MXN 900 domestic; USD 90 foreign. Ed(s): Ana Maria Perez Rocha. Artes de Mexico y del Mundo S.A., Plaza Rio de Janeiro 52, Col Roma, Mexico City, 06700, Mexico; artesdemexico@artesdemexico.com; http://www.artesdemexico.com/. Illus., adv. Refereed. Circ: 20000 Paid. *Indexed:* ABM, AICP, ArtInd, HAPI, RILM. *Aud.:* Ac, Sa.

Artes de Mexico is reminiscent of coffee-table art books with its large format and lavishly illustrated blend of vibrantly photographed arts, crafts, and cultural phenomena of Mexico. Each thematic issue offers divergent viewpoints on a single subject, as seen most recently in "Art & Poetry of the Circus" and "The Jesuits & Science." This journal usually contains at least some feature-length articles, and the variety and length of essays, interviews, or poetry make each issue distinctive. All are written in Spanish with English translations at the back of the issue. Recommended for libraries with strong art and/or multicultural collections.

532. *Artforum International.* Formerly (until 1982): *Artforum.* [ISSN: 1086-7058] 1962. m. 10/yr. USD 46 domestic; USD 72 elsewhere; USD 8 newsstand/cover. Ed(s): Tim Griffin, Jack Bankowsky. Artforum International Magazine, Inc., 350 Seventh Ave, New York, NY 10001;

http://www.artforum.com. Illus., adv. Circ: 32000. Vol. ends: Sep/Jun. Microform: PQC. Online: Florida Center for Library Automation; Gale; Northern Light Technology, Inc.; ProQuest K-12 Learning Solutions; ProQuest LLC (Ann Arbor). *Indexed:* ABM, ABS&EES, AmHI, ArtHuCI, ArtInd, BAS, DAAI, FLI, HumInd, RILM. *Bk. rev.:* 1, length varies. *Aud.:* Ga, Ac.

The primary magazine for reporting on international contemporary art, *ArtForum* is accessible to a wide audience. Critical articles on all media—sculpture, painting, installation, architecture, video and music art, mixed media, and popular culture—frequently include artist interviews. Glossy ads proliferate, featuring the latest shows at galleries around the world. Regular reviews cover individual artists, gallery exhibits, film, music, books, top-ten lists, and other art world happenings. Included three times a year are previews of 50 upcoming exhibitions. A calendar of international art events is provided in every issue. The web site, www.artforum.com, offers worthwhile extras beyond tables of contents and samples of the current print issue: an international museum finder, blogs, festivals/biennials, free art resources, art zines, news briefs, etc. Essential for all art libraries, collectors, and curators of contemporary art. Highly recommended for all academic and large public libraries.

533. *The Artist: inspiration, instruction & practical udeas for all artists.* Incorporates: *Art and Artists.* [ISSN: 0004-3877] 1931. m. GBP 25.50 domestic; USD 37 foreign. Ed(s): Sally Bulgin. The Artists' Publishing Company Limited, Caxton House, 62-65 High St, Tenterden, TN30 6BD, United Kingdom. Illus., index, adv. Sample. Circ: 19000. *Indexed:* ArtInd. *Bk. rev.:* Number and length vary. *Aud.:* Ga, Ac.

The British equivalent to *American Artist, The Artist* provides many instructional articles for professional and amateur artists. A dozen articles offer practical advice on technique, materials, and other helpful technical information, and are illustrated with lots of easy-to-follow color illustrations. The focus is generally representational art, landscapes, and figurative and still-life portrayals. Exhibition reviews, profiles of contemporary artists, interviews, and other current news in the United Kingdom make up the rest of the contents. This periodical is recommended for public libraries and schools with fine arts programs.

534. *The Artist's Magazine.* [ISSN: 0741-3351] 1984. m. USD 36 domestic; USD 46 Canada; USD 4.99 newsstand/cover. Ed(s): Joanne Moore. F + W Publications, Inc., 4700 E Galbraith Rd, Cincinnati, OH 45236; http://www.fwpublications.com. Illus., adv. Circ: 175000 Paid. Vol. ends: Dec. *Indexed:* ABIn, IHTDI. *Bk. rev.:* 50, 200 words. *Aud.:* Hs, Ga.

The Artist's Magazine is a monthly publication designed for artists of all levels of accomplishment from beginner to professional. Most of the articles instruct and present various working methods, materials, tools, and techniques. Marketing information is provided, plus announcements of study opportunities and art competitions. The accompanying web site, www.artistsmagazine.com, is most useful to artists, providing business tips, technical questions and answers, clinics, and much more. This is an educational and instructive publication that would be most useful for school art programs or public libraries.

535. *Artlink: Australian contemporary art quarterly.* [ISSN: 0727-1239] 1981. q. AUD 72 (Individuals, AUD 40). Ed(s): Stephanie Britton. Artlink Australia, 363 Esplanade, Henley Beach, SA 5022, Australia; artlinkmag@webmedia.com.au. Illus., adv. Circ: 3400. *Indexed:* ABM. *Aud.:* Ac, Sa.

An Australian contemporary art magazine, *Artlink*'s scope includes all sorts of visual-culture expression by the cutting-edge artists of Australia and the Asia–Pacific area. Articles on new media, Internet art, video, electronic arts, performance pieces, photography, mixed media, and outsider and aboriginal art are presented with analyses of "legal issues, artist's rights, [and] funding and employment issues." Each richly illustrated issue examines a broad theme such as "Biennales/Biennials," "Ecology," or "The Word as Art," with a wide range of viewpoints and media presented. Also included are a dozen or more short articles; "Artrave"—news for the region; and a dozen exhibition reviews. Recommended for libraries where there is an interest in contemporary art.

536. *ArtNet Magazine.* 1996. d. Free. Ed(s): Walter Robinson. ArtNet Worldwide Inc., 61 Broadway 23 Fl, New York, NY 10006-2701; artnet@artnet.com. Illus. *Bk. rev.:* Number and length vary. *Aud.:* Ga, Ac, Sa.

This web zine—which is part of artnet.com, an online resource for researching, buying, and selling fine art—is designed as a selling tool aimed at buyers and dealers. That said, it is useful to the artist and layperson because it includes a wide variety of information about the visual arts: color images of artworks, book reviews, exhibition reviews, and other news of the art world. Additionally, it is a good resource for finding images of contemporary artists' works. Artists, art dealers, critics, curators, and a handful of staff writers frequently post articles, dated accordingly. Heavily geared toward New York City, *ArtNet*'s coverage also includes the U.S. art world, but it mentions international artists and shows. Additional services (e.g., auction prices database) are available for subscription, but much of the content is free. URL: www.artnet.com.

537. *Artnews.* [ISSN: 0004-3273] 1902. 11x/yr. USD 39.95 domestic; USD 59.95 Canada; USD 99.95 elsewhere. Ed(s): Robin Cembalest, Jamie Reynolds. Artnews LLC, 48 W 38th St, New York, NY 10018. Illus., adv. Circ: 81585 Paid. Vol. ends: Dec. Microform: MIM; PQC. Online: OCLC Online Computer Library Center, Inc. *Indexed:* A&ATA, ABM, ABS&EES, AmHI, ArtHuCI, ArtInd, BRI, CBRI, DAAI, IIPA, MASUSE, RGPR, RILM. *Bk. rev.:* 3-4, 300-500 words. *Aud.:* Hs, Ga, Ac.

As the name implies, *ARTnews* is a primary news source for keeping current with American and international contemporary art. Many feature-length articles cover new genres, plus cover pieces for collectors and those who maintain collections. Regular departments explore personalities, national and international art news, new talent, the art market, book reviews, exhibition and competition listings, classifieds, and a smattering of regional, national, and international exhibition reviews. The web site, www.artnews.com, mirrors the print edition and offers some free content along with tables of content to back issues since 1996. A biweekly report on the art market, *ARTnewsletter,* can be delivered via e-mail and is targeted toward art professionals and serious collectors who wish to follow art treads globally. This standard art magazine is highly recommended for all libraries.

538. *Artweek: the national voice of West Coast contemporary art.* [ISSN: 0004-4121] 1970. m. USD 34 domestic; USD 60 foreign. Ed(s): Laura Richard-Janku. Artweek, PO Box 52100, Palo Alto, CA 94303-0751. Illus., index, adv. Circ: 14500. Vol. ends: Dec. Microform: MIM; PQC. Online: OCLC Online Computer Library Center, Inc.; H.W. Wilson. *Indexed:* ArtInd. *Bk. rev.:* 2, 500 words. *Aud.:* Ga, Ac, Sa.

A monthly tabloid-style publication, *Artweek* is a standard source of information for contemporary fine arts on the West Coast. Arranged by state and region, it includes gallery and museum exhibition listings and reviews of artists in California, the Pacific Northwest, and Hawaii, and gives the most comprehensive reviews of gallery shows in the western United States. Additional content includes regional and international competitions, exhibition calendars, previews of upcoming events, and news updates geared toward art professionals and collectors. It is well suited for public, academic, and museum collections on the West Coast and large public and academic libraries with comprehensive art holdings. The web site, www.artweek.com, includes a table of contents for the current month plus the full gallery listings and subscriber information.

539. *Audio Arts Magazine (CD-ROM Edition).* Formerly (until 2003): *Audio Arts Magazine (Audio Cassette Edition).* 1973. q. Audio Arts Magazine, 6 Briarwood Road, London, SW4 9PX, United Kingdom. *Aud.:* Ga, Ac, Sa.

Originally issued on cassette and now on compact disc, *Audio Arts Magazine* grants the rare opportunity to interact with different aspects of the art world with one's ears rather than the eyes. This journal is called a "recorded space for contemporary art," and each disc or pair of discs includes a collection of contemporary interviews, discussions with artists, artists commenting on their own works, artistic collaborations, sound art, and archival recordings. Some issues correspond with specific biennials or performances, while others collect pieces from a variety of places and venues. Each issue is accompanied by a booklet that includes further information about the artists involved.

540. *Beaux Arts Magazine: actualite des arts.* [ISSN: 0757-2271] 1983. irreg. Editions Flammarion, 87 Quai Panhard et Levassor, Paris, 75647 Cedex 13, France; http://www.flammarion.com. Illus., index, adv. Sample. Circ: 49000. *Indexed:* ABM, ArtInd, IBR, RILM. *Bk. rev.:* Number and length vary. *Aud.:* Ga.

Published in France, *Beaux Arts Magazine* is a beautifully illustrated periodical aimed at the art collector. Articles are written for a general audience, and the scope covers all of Europe. Included are auction news and sales, exhibition announcements, museum events, interviews, a calendar of events, book reviews, and occasional performance and movie reviews. Written in French, the American edition includes abstracts of the articles in English, which increases the utility of this attractive publication. Recommended for libraries with extensive art holdings.

541. *Bidoun: a quarterly forum for middle eastern talent.* [ISSN: 1551-4048] 2004. 4x/yr. USD 36 in Middle East & US; USD 38 Canada; USD 42 in Europe. Ed(s): Lisa Farjam, Brian Ackley. Bidoun, 130 W 15th St, Ste 1, New York, NY 10011-5702. Illus., adv. Circ: 8000 Paid and controlled. *Bk. rev.:* 1-5, 1,000+ words. *Aud.:* Ga, Ac, Sa.

This journal is a forum for spreading information and creating a dialogue about arts and culture in the Middle East and its "Diaspora." Its cross-cultural and multidisciplinary approach allows it to cover any and all aspects of culture and art created by Middle Easterners, those of Middle Eastern descent, and/or those who relate to the Middle East as a region or as a concept. Issues are composed of artist interviews and profiles, and articles about specific arts, cultural ideas, or events. Subjects include art, music, literature, and architecture, among others. The web site includes selected full-text articles and general information. Recommended for public and academic libraries, especially those with an interest in the arts and/or Middle Eastern or cross-cultural studies.

542. *Burlington Magazine.* Formerly (until 1947): *Burlington Magazine for Connoisseurs.* [ISSN: 0007-6287] 1903. m. GBP 189 domestic; USD 494 in North America; GBP 215 elsewhere. Ed(s): Richard Shone. Burlington Magazine Publications Ltd., 14 Dukes Rd, London, WC1H 9AD, United Kingdom; burlington@burlington.org.uk. Illus., index, adv. Refereed. Vol. ends: Dec. Microform: IDC. Online: JSTOR (Web-based Journal Archive). Reprint: PSC. *Indexed:* A&ATA, ABM, API, ArtHuCI, ArtInd, BAS, BEL&L, BRI, BrArAb, BrHumI, CBRI, DAAI, IBR, IBZ, IndIslam, RILM, SSCI. *Bk. rev.:* 10-15, 1,000 words. *Aud.:* Ac.

Begun in 1903 to lavishly illustrate, attribute, discover, and document western European art for connoisseurs, *Burlington Magazine* has long maintained a well-respected reputation among art historians and other scholars. Its aim and scope today cover all historical periods from prehistoric art to modern Western art, including works and artists outside of Europe. Its design is elegant and gracious, and it has lots of full-color images. Articles by experts in the field focus on new developments, historical documents, conservation practices, and the history of collecting art. Book reviews, shorter notices, obituaries, exhibition information, and a calendar of events round out this important journal. Recommended for all research collections in academic and special libraries.

Calyx. See Literature section.

543. *Canadian Art.* Formed by the merger of (1940-1984): *Arts Canada;* Which was formerly (until 1967): *Canadian Art;* (until 1943): *Maritime Art;* (19??-1984): *Artsmagazine;* Which was formerly (until 1974): *Art;* (until 1969): *Society of Canadian Artists. Journal.* [ISSN: 0825-3854] 1984. q. CND 24 domestic; USD 32 United States; USD 40 elsewhere. Ed(s): Richard Rhodes. Canadian Art Foundation, 51 Front St E, Ste 210, Toronto, ON M5E 1B3, Canada. Illus., adv. Circ: 20000 Paid. Vol. ends: Winter. Microform: MML. Online: Micromedia ProQuest. *Indexed:* ABM, ArtInd, CBCARef, CPerI. *Bk. rev.:* 1-3, 500 words. *Aud.:* Ga, Ac, Sa.

Published in part by the Canadian government, Canada Council, and the Ontario Arts Council, *Canadian Art* is a quarterly that is devoted to the visual arts of that country. It is beautifully designed, with lots of full-color images, and the subject matter covers painting, sculpture, illustration, design, architecture, photography, and film. Articles are not limited to any particular time period; however,

profiles of individual contemporary artists with reproductions of their works or group shows predominate, making this an invaluable resource for contemporary Canadian art. Also worth bookmarking is the web site, www.canadianart.ca. This magazine is aimed toward a general audience that includes art collectors and regular guests of art galleries.

Comic Art. See Anime, Graphic Novels, and Manga section.

544. *Contemporary.* Incorporates (1994-2002): *World Art;* Former titles (until 2001): *Contemporary Visual Arts;* (until 1997): *Contemporary Art.* [ISSN: 1475-9853] 1995. m. GBP 59 (Individuals, GBP 49; GBP 5.95 newsstand/cover per issue). Ed(s): Brian Muller. Gordon & Breach Magazines Unlimited, Tower Bridge Business Complex, 100 Clements Rd, Ste. K101, London, SE16 4DG, United Kingdom; cva@gbhap.com; http://www.contemporary-magazine.com. Illus., adv. Circ: 45000. *Indexed:* ABM. *Bk. rev.:* 1-2, 1,000 words. *Aud.:* Ac, Sa.

Boasting a readership of 75,000, the international art journal *Contemporary* has contributors from the United Kingdom, North America, Africa, New Zealand, and Australia. Bimonthly issues are devoted to special themes. These special issues, titled *Contemporary 21,* offer critical analysis of broad categories, e.g., art and architecture, performance, digital art, and photography, including profiles of 21 artists in that field. The remaining issues throughout the year present regular observations on "visual arts, news, books, trivia, architecture, houses, design, fashion, film, music, new media, photography, dance, [and] sport," offering a very wide range of every media utilized by visual artists worldwide. Important for libraries with collections that address contemporary art.

Critical Inquiry. See Cultural Studies section.

545. *F M R (English Edition).* [ISSN: 0394-0462] 1984. bi-m. EUR 159.50. Illus., adv. Circ: 43000. Vol. ends: Nov/Dec. *Indexed:* ArtInd, IBR, IBZ. *Aud.:* Ga, Ac.

FMR, published by Italian fine arts book publisher Franco Maria Ricci, strives to create a magazine covering the arts that is itself a work of art. Lavishly illustrated with vibrant color images that regularly play across both pages, *FMR* highlights traditional, representational European paintings; places of architectural significance; and objects elevated to the status of art. Its international coverage provides exhibition information arranged by country, indicating the museum, exhibition title, dates, and a short description, plus an international calendar of events. Recommended for general audiences in either public or academic libraries.

546. *Flash Art International.* [ISSN: 0394-1493] 1980. bi-m. EUR 50 in Europe; EUR 90 Oceania; EUR 70 elsewhere. Ed(s): Helena Kontova, Giancarlo Politi. Giancarlo Politi Editore, PO Box 95, Borgo Trevi, 06032, Italy; subscription@flashartonline.com; http://www.flashartonline.com. Illus., adv. Circ: 55000. *Indexed:* ABM, ArtInd, IBR, IBZ. *Bk. rev.:* 2-3, 600-900 words. *Aud.:* Ga, Ac.

This self-proclaimed world's leading art magazine is filled with glossy ads from galleries as widely disparate as McLean, Virginia, and Milan to the Netherlands and New York. *Flash Art* has long used its journalistic tone to bring the North American and European contemporary art world into its readership, and it continues as a strong voice in current news and criticism in the visual arts. Each issue contains news updates, gallery reviews, interviews, and feature articles on two- and three-dimensional and performance art, video, and mixed media works and their creators. Recommended as an important basic international source for all libraries with an interest in art and art criticism.

547. *Frieze: contemporary art and culture.* [ISSN: 0962-0672] 1991. 8x/yr. GBP 40 (Individuals, GBP 29). Ed(s): James Roberts. Durian Publications, 5-9 Hatton Wall, London, EC1N 8HX, United Kingdom; admin@frieze.com. Adv. *Indexed:* ABM, DAAI. *Bk. rev.:* 3-4, 500-1,000 words. *Aud.:* Ac, Sa.

London-based *Frieze* is the self-proclaimed "leading contemporary art and culture publication" in Europe. This claim is supported not only by a half-dozen feature articles on the current European art scene and numerous gallery/exhibition reviews, but also by extensive coverage of film, performance, music, and all visual arts. The editors give exposure to established but also very new artists in reviews, feature articles, and hundreds of full-color gallery ads in each packed issue. *Frieze* sponsors the annual Frieze Art Fair in London every October, showcasing 150 galleries and their artists. The web site offers full-text magazine content, art world news, and Frieze Art Fair updates. Recommended for all libraries that wish to provide access to international contemporary art.

548. *I F A R Journal.* Formerly (until 1998): *I F A R Reports;* Which was formed by the merger of (1981-1984): *Art Research News;* (1979-1984): *Stolen Art Alert;* Which was formerly (until 1980): *Art Theft Archive Newsletter.* [ISSN: 1098-1195] 1984. q. USD 65 domestic; USD 85 foreign; USD 100 domestic associate (active subscriber). Ed(s): Sharon Flescher. International Foundation for Art Research, Inc., 500 Fifth Ave, New York, NY 10110; http://www.ifar.org. Illus., index, adv. Circ: 1500. *Indexed:* ABM, ArtInd. *Aud.:* Sa.

IFAR Journal, the mouthpiece of the International Foundation for Art Research (IFAR), informs the art community about recent art theft, authentication, fraud, and art laws through feature articles. From its founding, IFAR has been a resource for scholarship in authentication research, maintaining a list of stolen art plus authenticating problematic works of art and providing a clearinghouse for legal issues. With its recent shift away from maintaining a stolen-art database (now the purview of the Art Loss Register), IFAR is able to publish new depths of scholarship in authentication research. Featured in each issue are four or five well-researched articles, plus brief discussions of art and the law, updates, and news items. Selections from the Art Loss Register, consisting of art theft reports and recent items stolen, plus a recovery list, are printed in each issue. As an advocate for the entire art community, *IFAR Journal* provides important research about provenance and attribution not found in other art journals. Appropriate for research and municipal libraries.

Journal of Aesthetic Education. See Cultural Studies section.

Journal of Aesthetics and Art Criticism. See Cultural Studies section.

549. *The Journal of Canadian Art History.* [ISSN: 0315-4297] 1974. s-a. CND 25; CND 30 foreign. Ed(s): Sandra Paikowsky. Journal of Canadian Art History, 9 Campus Dr, Saskatoon, SK S7N 5A5, Canada. Illus., index, adv. Refereed. Circ: 700. Vol. ends: No. 2. Microform: MML. Online: OCLC Online Computer Library Center, Inc.; H.W. Wilson. *Indexed:* AmH&L, ArtHuCI, ArtInd, CBCARef, CPerI, HistAb, IBR, IBZ, PdeR. *Bk. rev.:* 4-5, lengthy. *Aud.:* Ac, Sa.

The national art history journal in Canada, *JCAH* is a scholarly periodical devoted to the research of Canadian art, architecture, decorative arts, and photography. It includes all historical and contemporary periods with articles that are sparingly illustrated in black-and-white. Both English- and French-language submissions are accepted, and three- or four-page summaries are translated into the other appropriate language. Also included on a regular basis are bibliographies, such as individual artists and architects; theses and dissertations in Canadian art and architecture; and book reviews and reviews of exhibition catalogs specific to Canadian art. Appropriate for research collections in academic libraries.

550. *Journal of Pre-Raphaelite Studies.* Former titles (until 1992): *Journal of Pre-Raphaelite and Aesthetic Studies;* (until 1987): *Journal of Pre-Raphaelite Studies;* (until 1980): *Pre-Raphaelite Review.* [ISSN: 1060-149X] 1977. 2x/yr. CND 40 (Individuals, CND 24). Ed(s): David Latham. Journal of Pre-Raphaelite Studies, 208 Stong College, York University, Toronto, ON M3J 1P3, Canada; dlatham@yorku.ca. Illus. Sample. Refereed. Circ: 450 Paid. *Indexed:* AmHI, ArtHuCI, HumInd, MLA-IB, RILM, SSCI. *Aud.:* Ac.

Founded to create a forum for the study of Pre-Raphaelite, Aesthetic, and Decadent art, culture, and literature of the nineteenth century, *JPRS* publishes research on such renowned artists as Dante Gabriel Rosetti, Christina Rosetti, Edward Burne-Jones, William Morris, and the cult of Pre-Raphaelites worldwide and its interaction with Victorian literary figures (Edith Wharton, Oscar Wilde) and Victorian culture and mores. A dozen papers, sparsely illustrated with black-and-white images, are printed in this small-scale

semi-annual journal. Articles include historical examinations and interdisciplinary studies on the creation of sexual knowledge, Victorian masculinities, and consumerism and industrial art. Although targeting a fairly narrow topic, *JPRS* is important for academic libraries with studies in nineteenth-century literary and art history programs.

551. *Journal of the Warburg and Courtauld Institutes.* Formerly (until 1939): *Warburg Institute. Journal.* [ISSN: 0075-4390] 1937. a. GBP 75 per vol. Warburg Institute, University of London, Woburn Sq, London, WC1H 0AB, United Kingdom; warburg.books@sas.ac.uk; http://www.sas.ac.uk/warburg/. Illus., index. Refereed. Circ: 1500. Reprint: PSC. *Indexed:* AmHI, ArtHuCI, ArtInd, BEL&L, BrHumI, CCMJ, FR, IBR, IBZ, IndIslam, MLA-IB, MSN, MathR, RILM. *Aud.:* Ac.

Published in a single volume, *JWCI* provides an outlet for scholarly research in art history and classical studies, especially as reflected in European art and letters. It is the scholarly journal for the University of London, School of Advanced Study, The Warburg Institute, and the University of London's Courtauld Institute of Art. Although plagued by a lagging publication cycle, the half-dozen lengthy scholarly articles in each edition are important not only to art historians but to scholars in religion, science, literature, sociology, philosophy, and anthropology. Recommended for all academic libraries that support significant art history programs and other special research collections.

552. *Journal of Visual Culture.* [ISSN: 1470-4129] 2002. 3x/yr. GBP 274. Ed(s): Marquard Smith, Joanne Morra. Sage Publications Ltd., 1 Oliver's Yard, 55 City Rd, London, EC1 1SP, United Kingdom; info@sagepub.co.uk; http://www.sagepub.co.uk. Adv. Refereed. Online: EBSCO Publishing, EBSCO Host; HighWire Press; OCLC Online Computer Library Center, Inc.; SAGE Publications, Inc., SAGE Journals Online; SwetsWise Online Content. Reprint: PSC. *Indexed:* ABM, AICP, ArtHuCI, ArtInd, CommAb, IBR, IBSS, IBZ. *Bk. rev.:* Number and length vary. *Aud.:* Ac, Sa.

This is an international and interdisciplinary scholarly journal, with editors from the United Kingdom, the United States, and France. The *Journal of Visual Culture* "promotes research, scholarship and critical engagement with visual cultures." Authored by professors, scholars, and critics in the humanities and social sciences, each issue features six to eight thought-provoking articles that examine ideas, concepts, metaphors, and philosophies in international visual and cultural practices. A variety of methodologies broaden the debate in topics that include blackness and whiteness; appearances; surfaces; voyeurism; the public sphere; image; imagination; censorship; copy; reproduction; aesthetics; mimesis; tropes; spectacle and simulation; and many other critical theories studied in academe today. Appropriate for academic libraries.

553. *Koreana: Korean art and culture.* [ISSN: 1016-0744] 1987. q. KRW 18000 domestic; USD 33 in Japan, Hong Kong, Taiwan & China; USD 37 elsewhere. Ed(s): Jeong-yeop Park. Korea Foundation, Publication & Reference Materials Team, 1376-1, Seocho-2-dong, Seocho-gu, Seoul, 137072, Korea, Republic of. Adv. Circ: 9000. Online: EBSCO Publishing, EBSCO Host; OCLC Online Computer Library Center, Inc.; H.W. Wilson. *Indexed:* AmHI, ArtInd, BAS, MLA-IB, RILM. *Aud.:* Ga, Ac, Sa.

This beautifully illustrated quarterly magazine in English is devoted to traditional and contemporary Korean art and culture. Four to six feature articles typically revolve around a theme such as weddings, traditional and contemporary; Korean perceptions of life and death; or national treasures such as the Gyujanggak archives. Regular departments include interviews with architects and artists, cuisine and arts of living, discovering Korea, a featured masterpiece, an art review, and a small section devoted to Korean literature. Much full-text content from current and archived issues can be found for free at www.koreana.or.kr. Recommended for academic libraries and large public libraries.

554. *Leonardo: Art Science and Technology: journal of the International Society for Arts, Sciences and Technology.* Formerly: *Leonardo/Isast.* [ISSN: 0024-094X] 1968. 6x/yr. USD 568 print & online eds. (Individuals, USD 80 print & online eds.). Ed(s): Dr. Roger F Malina. M I T Press, 238 Main St., Ste. 500, Cambridge, MA 02142; journals-info@

mit.edu; http://mitpress.mit.edu. Illus., adv. Refereed. Circ: 1155 Paid. Microform: PQC. Online: EBSCO Publishing, EBSCO Host; Gale; IngentaConnect; JSTOR (Web-based Journal Archive); OCLC Online Computer Library Center, Inc.; OhioLINK; Project MUSE; SwetsWise Online Content; H.W. Wilson. *Indexed:* A&ATA, ABM, ABS&EES, ArtHuCI, ArtInd, EIP, IBR, IBZ, PhilInd, RILM. *Bk. rev.:* 10-15, 2,000+ words. *Aud.:* Ac, Sa.

Leonardo focuses on the arts as they intersect with the scientific disciplines and developing technologies, within an international scope and from an academic perspective. It attempts to foster communication between technology-minded artists by providing information on current, emerging, and historical trends in the use of science in the arts. Issues contain artists' statements, interviews, general articles, and special sections all related to the journal's mission. The web site includes sample articles, cumulative indexing, and general information about the journal, the society, and relevant news and events. Recommended for academic libraries.

555. Master Drawings: devoted exclusively to the study and illustration of drawings. [ISSN: 0025-5025] 1963. q. USD 95 domestic; USD 105 foreign. Ed(s): Anne Marie Logan. Master Drawings Association, Inc., 29 E 36th St, New York, NY 10016; administrator@masterdrawings.org . Illus., index, adv. Refereed. Circ: 1250 Paid and free. Vol. ends: No. 4. *Indexed:* ArtHuCI, ArtInd, IBR, IBZ. *Bk. rev.:* Number varies, essay length. *Aud.:* Ac, Sa.

This journal is published by the Master Drawings Association of New York, and its audience is primarily art historians, collectors, and dealers. An academic quarterly, it provides a venue for the exclusive study of drawings and occasionally other works on paper, e.g., engraving and watercolor since the Renaissance. Thematic issues concentrate mainly on the old masters up to 1900, and are written for scholars. Authors tend to be art history fellows, professors, and museum curators, and focus on new developments and reattributions of specific drawings. Appropriate for academic libraries that support art history programs.

556. Mediamatic Off-Line. Formerly (until 2001): *Mediamatic.* [ISSN: 1571-2559] 1986. irreg. Mediamatic Foundation, Postbus 17490, Amsterdam, 1001 JL, Netherlands; mail@mediamatic.nl; http://www.mediamatic.nl. Illus., adv. Circ: 4000. *Indexed:* ABM. *Bk. rev.:* 6, 200 words. *Aud.:* Ac, Sa.

Mediamatic provides international coverage of new media, art, culture, and theory, and is published in Dutch and English. The journal specializes in electronic media and hardware design, with a particular emphasis on video. Each issue is filled with a variety of material, including theoretical and historical articles, interviews with artists, technical pieces, and announcements about upcoming events. The web site is www.mediamatic.net.

557. Modern Painters. [ISSN: 0953-6698] 1988. m. GBP 35.90 domestic; GBP 45 in Europe; EUR 64.50 in Europe. Ed(s): Roger Tatley. L T B Media, 111 8th Ave, Ste 302, New York, NY 10011; http://www.ltbholding.com/. Adv. Circ: 20726. *Indexed:* ABM, ArtInd, DAAI, RILM. *Bk. rev.:* 5-8, 500 words. *Aud.:* Ac, Sa.

Not devoted exclusively to painting as the name implies, *Modern Painters* brings together leading voices in visual arts criticism and analysis—academics, writers, and artists—to provide stimulating discussions of current practices in international art. Stating a mission to "not only report...but define and shape important events and trends in the art and cultural worlds," *Modern Painters* succeeds admirably. Feature articles are devoted to politics and art, reviews of current practices, introduction of new artists, and examination of important movements and media. Full-page color gallery and exhibition ads predominate in this oversize monthly. One artist's studio practice is featured in each issue, as well as book and exhibition reviews. An important international title for all comprehensive art collections in any library.

558. New American Paintings. [ISSN: 1066-2235] 1993. bi-m. USD 89 in North America; USD 119 elsewhere; USD 20 newsstand/cover domestic. Ed(s): Steven T Zevitas. The Open Studios Press, 450 Harrison Ave., #304, Boston, MA 02118; szevitas@newamericanpaintings.com; http://www.newamericanpaintings.com. Illus. *Aud.:* Ga, Ac, Sa.

New American Paintings is a unique publication in the art world. Rather than including a number of interviews, critical essays, or artist profiles, each well-constructed, lushly illustrated issue features page after page of paintings (one per page), broken up only by a brief biography, artist statement, and contact information for each of the painters presented. The painters in each issue are usually culled from a specific regional juried exhibition, so a variety of lesser-known artists are brought to light in each issue.

559. New Criterion. [ISSN: 0734-0222] 1982. m. 10/yr. USD 48 domestic; USD 55 in the Americas; USD 62 elsewhere. Ed(s): Hilton Kramer. Foundation for Cultural Review, 850 Seventh Ave, New York, NY 10019. Illus., adv. Circ: 8000. Microform: PQC. Online: EBSCO Publishing, EBSCO Host; Florida Center for Library Automation; Gale; OCLC Online Computer Library Center, Inc.; H.W. Wilson. *Indexed:* ABM, AmHI, ArtInd, IBR, IBZ, MLA-IB, RILM. *Bk. rev.:* 3, lengthy. *Aud.:* Ga, Ac.

New Criterion is published by the Foundation for Cultural Review, which gives the magazine a much wider scope than strictly visual arts. Poets, authors, public policy scholars, humanities lecturers, and critics all contribute to create a vehicle for poetry, arts criticism, and commentary on cultural life in America. Departments in theater, art, music, and the media provide substantial reviews, and exhibition listings and book reviews make regular appearances in this periodical. Engaging and interesting to the informed reader, *New Criterion* is recommended for both public and academic libraries.

560. n.paradoxa: international feminist art journal. [ISSN: 1461-0434] 1998. s-a. GBP 32 including the UK (Individuals, GBP 18 including the UK; GBP 7.95 newsstand/cover per issue in Europe including the UK). Ed(s): Katy Deepwell. K T Press, 38 Bellot St, East Greenwich, London, SE10 OAQ, United Kingdom. Adv. Refereed. Circ: 1000. *Indexed:* ABM, ArtInd, FemPer, IBR, IBZ. *Aud.:* Ga, Sa.

This international feminist journal focuses on the visual arts. It publishes in-depth analyses of contemporary women's art and interviews with women artists, as well as articles on feminist art theory. It also provides information on women's art organizations and exhibitions; chronicles the contemporary women's art movement; and includes reviews of publications about contemporary women artists. Some issues are thematic. It is a valuable resource for students, artists, and academics and is available in online and print editions.

561. October. [ISSN: 0162-2870] 1976. q. USD 190 print & online eds. (Individuals, USD 49 print & online eds.). M I T Press, 238 Main St., Ste. 500, Cambridge, MA 02142; journals-info@mit.edu; http://mitpress.mit.edu. Illus. Refereed. Circ: 4000. Vol. ends: Spring. Microform: PQC. Online: EBSCO Publishing, EBSCO Host; Gale; IngentaConnect; JSTOR (Web-based Journal Archive); OCLC Online Computer Library Center, Inc.; SwetsWise Online Content; H.W. Wilson. *Indexed:* ABM, ABS&EES, AltPI, AmHI, ArtHuCI, ArtInd, FLI, IBR, IBZ, MLA-IB, RILM. *Aud.:* Ac.

For the last quarter-century, *October* has stood at the leading edge of art criticism and theory. Founded in New York by a group of theoreticians, it has focused on themes of postmodernism and poststructuralist discourse in America. Frequently monothematic, issues offer approximately a half-dozen lengthy scholarly discourses of the societal or cultural impact of the visual arts. Contributors are scholars, critics, and artists from a variety of academic disciplines, with the arts, film, and literature predominating. Intellectually rigorous, *October* will appeal to many scholars in the humanities. Recommended for academic research collections.

562. Oriental Art: devoted to the study of all forms of Oriental art. [ISSN: 0030-5278] 1948. 5x/yr. USD 80; GBP 60. Oriental Art Magazine, 47 Hill St, #06-06, Singapore, 179365, Singapore. Illus., index, adv. Vol. ends: Winter. *Indexed:* A&ATA, ArtHuCI, ArtInd, FR, IBR, IBZ, IndIslam, RI-1, RILM. *Bk. rev.:* 4-5, length varies. *Aud.:* Ac, Sa.

Lavishly illustrated with glossy, full-color reproductions, *Oriental Art* is an inclusive publication that extends coverage to art in India, the Islamic world, and all of Southeast Asia, beyond the traditional China and Japan focus. Five or six scholarly, in-depth articles written by international experts in the field are featured. Similarly, book reviews are quite lengthy and written for scholars.

Departments include the sales and auction reports from London and New York, plus exhibition reviews and reports. This is one of the best publications on historical Asian art and is well suited to research collections in academic and special libraries.

563. *Oxford Art Journal.* [ISSN: 0142-6540] 1978. 3x/yr. EUR 198. Ed(s): Jon Bird. Oxford University Press, Great Clarendon St, Oxford, OX2 6DP, United Kingdom; jnl.orders@oup.co.uk; http://www.oxfordjournals.org. Illus., adv. Sample. Refereed. Circ: 900. Vol. ends: No. 2. Online: Chadwyck-Healey Inc.; EBSCO Publishing, EBSCO Host; Gale; HighWire Press; IngentaConnect; JSTOR (Web-based Journal Archive); OCLC Online Computer Library Center, Inc.; Oxford Journals; ProQuest LLC (Ann Arbor); SwetsWise Online Content; H.W. Wilson. Reprint: PSC. *Indexed:* ABM, AltPI, AmH&L, ArtHuCI, ArtInd, BrHumI, DAAI, HistAb, RILM. *Bk. rev.:* 8, essay length. *Aud.:* Ac.

A venue for critical analysis of the visual arts, primarily Western, the *Oxford Art Journal* has contributed to the reexamination of art history through social context and political interpretations. Seven to ten scholarly, peer-reviewed papers represent research in the visual arts and related historical and philosophical issues from antiquity to contemporary art practice. It is well illustrated with black-and-white photos. Six or seven signed book reviews and the focus on the historical, social commentary of art make this appropriate for college and university libraries.

564. *Print Quarterly.* [ISSN: 0265-8305] 1984. q. GBP 43 domestic; EUR 79 in Europe eurozone; USD 96 in US & Canada. Ed(s): David Landau. Print Quarterly Publications, 52 Kelso Pl, London, W8 5QQ, United Kingdom. Illus., adv. Refereed. Circ: 1300. Vol. ends: Dec. *Indexed:* ABM, AmH&L, ArtHuCI, ArtInd, HistAb, RILM. *Bk. rev.:* Number and length vary. *Aud.:* Ac, Sa.

Print Quarterly is the leading publication in its field. Devoted to the art of the printed image, whether engraving, intaglio, woodprint, lithograph, drypoint, or zincograph, it covers the history of printmaking from the fifteenth century to the present. Features include three to four peer-reviewed articles and in-depth book reviews. The publication is well illustrated, and the articles are written for such academicians as art historians, although collectors would also find this a very useful source of information. It includes unique sections devoted to news items in the print and graphic arts world (new attributions, the latest serial publications, brief articles on societies) that go beyond the ordinary current events news. This journal is recommended for academic art libraries, museums, and other special collections.

565. *Public Art Review.* [ISSN: 1040-211X] 1989. s-a. USD 24 domestic; USD 31 in Canada & Mexico; USD 37 elsewhere. Forecast Public Artworks, 2324 University Ave W, St. Paul, MN 55114-1802; melinda@ForecastART.org; http://www.forecastpublicart.org. Refereed. Circ: 2500 Paid. *Indexed:* ABM, ArtInd. *Aud.:* Ga, Ac, Sa.

Public Art Review is produced by Forecast Public Artworks, a Minneapolis-based consulting group that also administers grants to emerging Minnesota artists. The magazine's scope includes not only local public artworks but regional and national as well. Striving to encourage public art and artists, *PAR* features articles on maintaining and conserving public art; consulting and managing projects—often of city-wide plans; and exploring critically contemporary public art in America, whether smaller-scale individual pieces or large-scale, big-name projects. Occasional pieces cover international public art constructions. Recommended for art, architecture, and urban planning collections in large public and academic libraries.

566. *R A C A R.* [ISSN: 0315-9906] 1974. s-a. CND 35 domestic; USD 35 foreign. Ed(s): Barbara Winters. Association d'Art des Universites du Canada, Department of History in Art, University of Victoria, Box 1700, Victoria, BC V8W 2Y2, Canada; bwinters@finearts.uvic.ca. Illus. Circ: 900. Vol. ends: No. 2. *Indexed:* ABM, AmH&L, ArtHuCI, ArtInd, CBCARef, CPerI, HistAb. *Bk. rev.:* 6, essay length. *Aud.:* Ac.

RACAR is published by the Universities Art Association of Canada with the assistance of the Social Sciences and Humanities Research Council of Canada, and it is the leading scholarly Canadian art journal. It continues to suffer from delays in the publication cycle; current issues are running at approximately a two-year lag. Peer-reviewed articles feature lengthy treatments of Western art history written in either French or English and illustrated with black-and-white photos. The latest issues focus on art of nineteenth- and twentieth-century Europe. Appropriate for academic and research collections.

567. *Raw Vision: international journal of intuitive and visionary art, outsider art and contemporary folk art.* [ISSN: 0955-1182] 1989. 4x/yr. GBP 33 (Individuals, GBP 23). Ed(s): John Maizels. Raw Vision Ltd., 42 Llanvanor Rd, London, NW2 2AP, United Kingdom. Adv. Refereed. Circ: 9000 Paid and controlled. *Indexed:* ABM, ArtInd, IBR, IBZ. *Bk. rev.:* 5-10, 1,000+ words. *Aud.:* Ga, Ac.

Self-described as "the world's leading journal of outsider art, art brut and contemporary folk art," this journal covers art, artists, and art forms that are usually not included in traditional art histories or studied in art journals. Each heavily illustrated issue contains features on individual artists, movements within the above areas, and other "intuitive" and "marginal" arts. There are also news and reviews of contemporary exhibitions and events. The web site includes news, excerpts from current and past issues, links to associated galleries and museums, and other relevant information. Recommended for academic, museum, and public libraries where there is an interest in non-traditional arts and culture.

568. *Revue de l'Art.* [ISSN: 0035-1326] 1968. q. Ophrys, 27 rue Ginoux, Paris, 75015, France; editions.ophrys@ophrys.fr; http://www.ophrys.fr. Illus. *Indexed:* A&ATA, ArtHuCI, ArtInd, IBR, IBZ, RILM. *Bk. rev.:* 4-5, essay length. *Aud.:* Ac.

Emphasizing French art of the Neoclassic through Impressionist eras, this journal provides international scholarship. Abstracts occasionally summarize the contents of the French-language articles in English and German. Each issue includes book reviews, biographical essays, a calendar of museum exhibitions, and critical bibliographies. Appropriate for research collections in academic libraries that serve art history programs.

569. *Sculpture.* Incorporates (1993-1995): *Maquette;* Former titles (until Jan. 1987): *International Sculpture;* (until Apr. 1985): *Sculptors International;* (until 1981): *International Sculpture Center Bulletin; National Sculpture Center Bulletin.* [ISSN: 0889-728X] 1982. 10x/yr. Free to members. Ed(s): Laura Dillon. International Sculpture Center, 1529 18th St NW, Washington, DC 20036; isc@sculpture.org; http://www.sculpture.org/. Illus., adv. Circ: 22000. Vol. ends: Dec. *Indexed:* ABM, ArtInd. *Bk. rev.:* 10-12, 150 words. *Aud.:* Ga, Ac, Sa.

Published by the International Sculpture Center, this is the only international publication of its kind devoted exclusively to all forms of contemporary sculpture. Richly illustrated with full-color photography, the feature articles concentrate on traditional forms of three-dimensional arts. With gallery ads, news briefs, exhibition announcements, interviews with sculptors, a column devoted to commissions (a major source of revenue), and reviews of installations, this a useful title to artists, collectors, and scholars. It is recommended for all academic libraries with significant art programs and for larger public libraries.

570. *Studies in the Decorative Arts.* [ISSN: 1069-8825] 1993. s-a. USD 30 domestic; USD 35 in Canada & Mexico; USD 37 elsewhere. Ed(s): Sarah B Sherrill. Bard Graduate Center for Studies in the Decorative Arts, 18 W 86th St, New York, NY 10024. Illus. Refereed. Circ: 1000 Paid. *Indexed:* ABM, AmH&L, ArtInd, BRI, CBRI, HistAb. *Bk. rev.:* Number varies, essay length. *Aud.:* Ga, Ac.

According to its mission, *Studies in the Decorative Arts* emphasizes analytical and interpretative scholarly research of the decorative arts regardless of media, culture, era, or geographic location. However, recent issues have a decided preference for western European and American objects from the nineteenth and twentieth centuries. The journal focuses on the decorative arts as documents of material culture and placing them within their social and political contexts, and its four to six peer-reviewed articles are sparsely illustrated with black-and-white photographs. Each issue includes signed reviews of important new books, exhibitions, and discussions of developments in conservation and restoration. Recommended for larger public libraries and college and university libraries.

571. Tribal. Formerly (until 2001): *The World of Tribal Arts.* [ISSN: 1549-4691] 1994. q. USD 60 in US & Canada; EUR 50 in Europe; USD 95 elsewhere. Ed(s): Jonathan Fogel. Primedia, Inc., 2261 Market St. #644, San Francisco, CA 94114. Illus., adv. Sample. Refereed. Circ: 5000. *Indexed:* ArtInd. *Bk. rev.:* 8-12, 1,000+ words. *Aud.:* Ga, Ac, Sa.

According to this journal's web site, *Tribal* is the "only magazine dedicated to fine and antique traditional art from the Americas, Africa, Asia, Indonesia, Polynesia, Melanesia and Micronesia." Each extensively illustrated issue features articles and information on art and antiques from specific tribes, geographic areas, and time periods. It also includes features on collectors, collecting, and exhibitions and auctions. *Tribal,* sometimes called "Tribal Art," provides a unique perspective on some of the non-canonical histories of art. Recommended for museum, academic, and public libraries with an interest in indigenous arts and antiques.

572. Woman's Art Journal. [ISSN: 0270-7993] 1980. s-a. USD 58 (Individuals, USD 26). Ed(s): Joan Marter, Margaret Barlow. Old City Publishing, Inc., 628 N 2nd St, Philadelphia, PA 19123; info@oldcitypublishing.com; http://www.oldcitypublishing.com. Illus., index, adv. Refereed. Circ: 4000. Vol. ends: No. 2. Microform: PQC. Online: JSTOR (Web-based Journal Archive); OCLC Online Computer Library Center, Inc.; H.W. Wilson. *Indexed:* ABM, ABS&EES, ArtHuCI, ArtInd, DAAI, FemPer. *Bk. rev.:* 5-13, 400-3,500 words, signed. *Aud.:* Hs, Ga, Ac, Sa.

This publication covers women and issues relating to women in the visual arts from antiquity to the present. Each 50-page issue includes a "Portraits" section, about individual women artists, and a "Reviews" section, which covers exhibitions and publications by and about women artists. An "Issues and Insights" section addresses topics relating to women in the visual arts, and shorter notes and reviews. Contributors include artists, critics, art professionals, and academics. Issues include high-quality black-and-white and color illustrations. Of interest for art and women's studies collections.

573. Word & Image: a journal of verbal/visual enquiry. [ISSN: 0266-6286] 1985. q. GBP 497. Ed(s): John Dixon Hunt. Taylor & Francis Ltd., 4 Park Sq, Milton Park, Abingdon, OX14 4RN, United Kingdom; info@tandf.co.uk; http://www.tandf.co.uk/journals. Illus., adv. Refereed. Circ: 750. Vol. ends: Dec. Reprint: PSC. *Indexed:* ABM, AmH&L, AmHI, ArtHuCI, ArtInd, BEL&L, CommAb, FR, HistAb, L&LBA, MLA-IB, NTA, RILM. *Bk. rev.:* Number varies, 1 page. *Aud.:* Ac, Sa.

Word & Image is an interdisciplinary journal that focuses on the "study of the encounters, dialogues and mutual collaboration (or hostility) between verbal and visual languages," regardless of media. As such, it is important to literary critics, art historians, linguisticians, social historians, philosophers, and psychologists alike. Scholarly articles examine the many complicated relationships between words and images. Issues sometimes revolve around a central theme, with guest editors invited to participate, but most cover a variety of subjects. Articles are primarily in English, but French and German occasionally appear. Strictly a scholar's resource, it is recommended for academic libraries. Universities that support programs in linguistics and literature, art history, and communications will find this journal indispensable.

574. Zeitschrift fuer Kunstgeschichte. Formed by the merger of (1876-1932): *Repertorium fuer Kunstwissenschaft;* (1866-1932): *Zeitschrift fuer Bildende Kunst;* (1905-1932): *Jahrbuch fuer Kunstwissenschaft;* Which was formerly (until 1923): *Monatshefte fuer Kunstwissenschaft;* (until 1908): *Monatshefte der Kunstwissenschaftlichen Literatur.* [ISSN: 0044-2992] 1932. 4x/yr. EUR 92; EUR 28 newsstand/cover. Ed(s): Andreas Toennesmann, Andreas Beyer. Deutscher Kunstverlag GmbH, Nymphenburger Str 84, Munich, 80636, Germany; info@deutscherkunstverlag.de; http://www.kunstbuecher-online.de. Illus., index, adv. Circ: 900. Vol. ends: No. 4. Reprint: PSC. *Indexed:* AmH&L, AmHI, ArtHuCI, ArtInd, HistAb, IBR, IBZ, IndIslam, NTA, RILM. *Bk. rev.:* 3-4, lengthy. *Aud.:* Ac.

This leading German publication has been a standard in the field of art history since the 1930s. Black-and-white and occasionally color photography illustrate the five or six peer-reviewed articles that represent international research in the history of Western art. The focus is scholarly research in traditional Western visual arts, from the ancient Greeks through twentieth-century European artists. Articles appear in German, English, French, or Italian. Lengthy book reviews provide extensive treatment of three or four books in each issue. Appropriate for all academic libraries, but especially for those with art history programs.

Museum Publications

575. Archives of American Art Journal. Formerly (until 1964): *Archives of American Art. Quarterly Bulletin.* [ISSN: 0003-9853] 1960. q. USD 35; USD 15 newsstand/cover per issue. Smithsonian Institution, Archives of American Art, 750 9th St, NW, Washington, DC 20560-0937; http://www.aaa.si.edu. Illus. Circ: 1700. *Indexed:* ABM, AmH&L, ArtHuCI, ArtInd, HistAb, IBR, IBZ. *Bk. rev.:* Number and length vary. *Aud.:* Ac, Sa.

This journal publishes cultural and social research about the permanent collections of the Archives of American Art. Housed in the Smithsonian Institution, the Archives of American Art provide researchers with access to the largest collection of documents on the history of the visual arts in the United States from the eighteenth century to the recent past. Three or four articles in each issue feature papers of artists, collectors, art historians, and other art world figures, and records of dealers, museums, and other institutions. Book reviews and regional reports that cover new acquisitions to the archives round out this important resource of historical documentation. Highly recommended for research collections.

576. Art Institute of Chicago. Museum Studies. [ISSN: 0069-3235] 1966. s-a. USD 50 (Individuals, USD 30; Members, USD 25). Ed(s): Gregory Nosan, Susan F Rossen. Art Institute of Chicago, 111 S Michigan Ave, Chicago, IL 60603-6110; pubsmus@artic.edu; http://www.artic.edu/aic/books. Illus., index. Circ: 1500 Paid. Vol. ends: No. 2. *Indexed:* ABM, AmH&L, ArtHuCI, ArtInd, HistAb, RILM. *Aud.:* Ac, Sa.

Museum Studies is published semi-annually, and more often than not it is monothematic, covering such subjects as decorative arts, European painting, American art, architecture, or individual collectors. Anywhere from three to six articles, lavishly illustrated in color and black-and-white, feature the permanent collection and history of the Art Institute of Chicago. Presenting recent scholarship, contributors include museum curators, art historians, and lecturers, in addition to museum personnel. Recommended for all museum collections and academic libraries.

577. Folk Art: magazine of the American Folk Art Museum. Formerly (until 1992): *Clarion.* [ISSN: 1067-3067] 1971. q. Individual members, USD 65; Students, USD 50 member; USD 8 newsstand/cover per issue. Ed(s): Tanya Heinrich. American Folk Art Museum, 45 W 53rd St, New York, NY 10019; info@folkartmuseum.org; http://www.folkartmuseum.org. Illus., index, adv. Circ: 10000. Vol. ends: No. 4. *Indexed:* ArtInd. *Bk. rev.:* 1-2, 300-500 words. *Aud.:* Hs, Ga, Ac, Sa.

Folk Art is the magazine of the American Folk Art Museum in New York, which is devoted to traditional and contemporary American folk art and self-taught art. Articles, essays, and reviews treat subjects such as ceramics, pottery, textiles, quilts, furniture, sculpture, painting, and prints. Regular departments briefly treat traveling exhibitions, museum shows, American antique shows, outsider art, seasonal programs, books, and museum news. There are a variety of contributors, including scholars, curators, freelance writers, and collectors. Recommended for academic, museum, and public libraries.

578. International Review of African American Art: an international publication. Formerly: *Black Art.* [ISSN: 1045-0920] 1976. q. USD 36 domestic; USD 44 foreign. International Review of African American Art, Hampton University Museum, Hampton, VA 23668-0101; jbowles@hamptona.edu. Illus., adv. Refereed. Circ: 5000. Vol. ends: No. 4. *Indexed:* ABM, AmHI, ArtHuCI, ArtInd, IIBP. *Bk. rev.:* Number and length vary. *Aud.:* Hs, Ga, Ac, Sa.

This monthly magazine published by the Hampton University Museum features interviews, biographical essays, and articles about visual and performing artists of African American heritage. While stating that it is "international," *IRAAA* primarily covers African American artists in the United States and occasionally Caribbean and South American artists as well. This full-color, well-illustrated journal frequently chooses one aspect of African American art for the subject of an issue. It includes a handful of book or exhibition reviews and noteworthy news on rising artists or new acquisitions. Cultural history and social themes related to the experience of the African American artist make this of interest to anyone conducting research in African American culture or American Studies. Recommended for all academic and large public libraries.

579. *Metropolitan Museum Journal.* [ISSN: 0077-8958] 1968. a. EUR 83.10 in the European Union; EUR 90.10 elsewhere; EUR 100.20 combined subscription in the European Union print & online eds. Ed(s): Barbara Burn. Brepols Publishers, Begijnhof 67, Turnhout, 2300, Belgium; periodicals@brepols.net; http://www.brepols.net. Illus. Refereed. *Indexed:* ArtHuCI, ArtInd, BAS, RILM. *Aud.:* Ac, Sa.

This journal publishes new scholarly research that examines works of art in the permanent collection of the Metropolitan Museum of Art and related matters. Articles investigate the cultural context of these art objects and cover archival research and technical analyses. Contributors are usually specialists, researchers, or museum staff. Because the Metropolitan Museum is one of the premier museums in the United States, this publication is highly recommended for all research collections in academic, museum, and special libraries.

580. *Metropolitan Museum of Art Bulletin.* [ISSN: 0026-1521] 1905. q. USD 25. Ed(s): Joan Holt. Metropolitan Museum of Art, 1000 Fifth Ave, New York, NY 10028; http://www.metmuseum.org. Illus., index. Sample. Circ: 112000. Vol. ends: No. 4. *Indexed:* A&ATA, AmH&L, AmHI, ArtHuCI, ArtInd, BAS, FR, HistAb, NumL, RILM. *Aud.:* Ga, Ac, Sa.

One of the two Metropolitan Museum of Art publications, the *Bulletin* focuses on one artist, theme, historical period, or item from the permanent collection in one lengthy article. Most contributions are written by museum personnel, but occasionally outside scholars may compose an article. Recent acquisitions are noted in the fall issue. The primary audience for this publication is museum members and art historians, but it is highly recommended for all academic libraries.

581. *The Outsider.* 1996. s-a. Ed(s): Janet Franz. Intuit. The Center for Intuitive and Outsider Art, 756 N Milwaukee Ave, Chicago, IL 60622; intuit@art.org; http://www.art.org. *Bk. rev.:* 2-5, 1,000+ words. *Aud.:* Ga, Ac, Sa.

This journal from Intuit: the Center for Intuitive and Outsider Art focuses on outsider art, folk art, intuitive art, and art brut, which are all featured at this unique museum and within the unique niche of the art world that it serves. *The Outsider* includes features on artists and surveys and studies of aspects of outsider art, among other articles. It also functions as a newsletter for the center that provides information on upcoming events, exhibitions, recent acquisitions, and other pertinent information. Recommended to museum and academic libraries with an interest in outsider art.

582. *La Revue du Louvre et des Musees de France.* [ISSN: 0035-2608] 1951. bi-m. EUR 15 per issue. Ed(s): Danielle Gaborit Chopin, Jean Pierre Cuzin. Editions de la Reunion des Musees Nationaux, 49 Rue Etienne Marcel, Paris, 75001, France; http://www.rmn.fr. Illus., adv. Refereed. *Indexed:* A&ATA, ArtHuCI, ArtInd, BAS, FR, IBR, IBZ, RILM. *Aud.:* Ac, Sa.

This beautiful publication with lavish illustrations provides coverage of the special collections and works of art in the Louvre. It also includes scholarly articles on the collections of other national art museums in France. Information on new acquisitions, temporary exhibitions, and restoration work is regularly featured. Exhibition reviews, subject bibliographies, and calendars of events are also included. Recommended for all academic and museum libraries.

583. *Studies in Modern Art.* [ISSN: 1058-997X] 1991. a. USD 25. Ed(s): John Elderfield. Museum of Modern Art, 11 W 53rd St, New York, NY 10019. Illus. *Indexed:* ArtInd. *Aud.:* Ga, Ac, Sa.

Issued by the Museum of Modern Art in New York, *Studies in Modern Art* might be more appropriately categorized as a monograph published serially. It showcases important collections, important works of art, and special programs

at the museum. The journal maintains high standards of scholarship and makes a significant contribution to the serious study of contemporary art. Issues are frequently monothematic. Appropriate for academic, museum, and large public libraries.

584. *Studies in the History of Art.* Formerly: *Report and Studies in the History of Art.* [ISSN: 0091-7338] 1971. irreg. National Gallery of Art, 2000B South Club Dr, Door #7, Landover, MD 20785; cl-messineo@ nga.gov. Illus. Circ: 6000. *Indexed:* ArtHuCI, ArtInd. *Aud.:* Ga, Ac, Sa.

Designed to document scholarly symposia, this series-as-a-book is sponsored in part by the National Gallery of Art's Center for Advanced Study of the Visual Arts. Each monothematic volume presents a dozen or so research papers from a single symposium, and they foster study of the history, theory, and criticism of art, architecture, and urbanism. Recent topics cover Renaissance bronzes, paintings of Hans Holbein, and Olmec art and archaeology. An important resource for research art collections in all institutions.

585. *Tate Etc.* Formerly (until 2004): *Tate (London).* [ISSN: 1743-8853] 1993. 3x/yr. Ed(s): Simon Grant. Tate Etc., 20 John Islip St, London, SW1P 4G, United Kingdom; http://www.tate.org.uk. *Indexed:* ABM. *Aud.:* Ga, Ac, Sa.

The Tate Gallery's contribution to museum literature is refreshing in its presentation of its collections in a contemporary art-magazine format. *Tate Etc.* features essays, artist interviews, briefs, artistic collaborations, and updates about the Tate's vast holdings that range from 1500 through contemporary art. A significant portion of the magazine is devoted to modern and contemporary international art in all media. In a change from most publishers, every past issue is available free at tate.org.uk/tateetc, with many images. Recommended for large public libraries and academic and special collections.

586. *Winterthur Portfolio: a journal of American material culture.* Incorporates: *Winterthur Conference Report.* [ISSN: 0084-0416] 1964. 3x/yr. USD 149 domestic; USD 162.94 Canada; USD 157 elsewhere. Ed(s): Katherine C. Grier. University of Chicago Press, Journals Division, PO Box 37005, Chicago, IL 60637; subscriptions@ press.uchicago.edu; http://www.journals.uchicago.edu. Illus., index, adv. Refereed. Circ: 1000 Paid. Reprint: PSC. *Indexed:* ABM, API, AmH&L, AmHI, ArtHuCI, ArtInd, HistAb, IBR, IBZ, MLA-IB, RI-1, SSA, SSCI. *Aud.:* Ac.

Winterthur Portfolio provides an outlet for scholarship at the confluence of the visual arts and material culture in the historic United States. Interdisciplinary in nature, *WP*'s scope presents American art within its cultural context. This journal is currently published with a one-year lag time. The articles are sparsely illustrated with black-and-white photos and give in-depth treatment to subjects as diverse as the commercialization of nineteenth-century weddings to domestic habitations of American slaves. Appropriate for academic research libraries.

587. *Women in the Arts.* Formerly (until 1991): *National Museum of Women in the Arts News.* [ISSN: 1058-7217] 1983. q. Free to members. Ed(s): Laureen Schipsi. National Museum of Women in the Arts, 1250 New York Ave NW, Washington, DC 20005-3920; http://www.nmwa.org. Adv. Circ: 43000 Controlled. *Aud.:* Ac, Sa.

This is a glossy magazine, produced by the National Museum of Women in the Arts (NMWA), that recognizes the achievements of women artists, musicians, authors, and other contributors to world culture. The museum exists to promote women in all the arts throughout the world. This broad mission allows for a wide variety of topics to be featured in each issue, articles that run the gamut from contemporary feminist writers and innovators in TV and film to Italian Renaissance artists and aboriginal women painters. This eclectic title regularly reports on new acquisitions, regional updates, and other NMWA news; plus it contains a calendar of events and exhibitions. Available with an annual museum membership, *Women in the Arts* is recommended for museum, academic, and large public libraries.

■ ASIA AND THE PACIFIC

Online Newspaper Resources

See also Slavic Studies section.

Alissa Oakley, Librarian, Evans Library, Fulton Montgomery Community College, Johnstown, NY 12095; alissao@gmail.com

Introduction

In this section you will find journals (print and online) published about Asia—the world's largest and most diverse continent—as well as the Pacific Islands. Asia consists of the eastern four-fifths of the Eurasian land mass, and can be considered more of a "geographic term than a homogeneous continent"—with a very diverse population, including varied languages, cultures, and geographies. Its size and great diversity are reflected in the varied titles of this section (*Encyclopaedia Britannica*, 2007).

The United Nations recently estimated that the population of Asia will be more than five billion by the year 2050—an increase of over two-fifths from its estimated population in 2000. In addition, Asia contains many of the world's developing economies as well as one of the world's most economically developed countries—Japan. As both the populations and economies of Asia continue to grow and change, Asia will continue to have great impact on global politics and be an important area of study (*Encyclopaedia Britannica*, 2007).

All of the print journals in this section are refereed and abstracted and/or indexed in at least one source.

Basic Periodicals

Ga: *Modern Asian Studies;* Ac: *Journal of Japanese Studies, Asia Institute. Bulletin.*

Basic Abstracts and Indexes

Bibliography of Asian Studies.

588. American Schools of Oriental Research. Bulletin. Formerly (until 1921): *American School of Oriental Research in Jerusalem. Bulletin.* [ISSN: 0003-097X] 1919. q. USD 150 (Individuals, USD 60). Ed(s): James Weinstein. American Schools of Oriental Research, 825 Houston Mill Rd, Atlanta, GA 30329; asorpubs@asor.org; http://www.asor.org. Illus., adv. Refereed. Circ: 2100 Paid. Vol. ends: Nov. Microform: PQC. Online: EBSCO Publishing, EBSCO Host; JSTOR (Web-based Journal Archive); OCLC Online Computer Library Center, Inc.; ProQuest LLC (Ann Arbor); H.W. Wilson. *Indexed:* AICP, AnthLit, ArtInd, FR, IBR, IBSS, IBZ, IndIslam, L&LBA, NTA, NumL, OTA, R&TA, RI-1, RILM. *Bk. rev.:* Number and length vary. *Aud.:* Ac.

This ancient Near Eastern Studies journal includes the subject areas of history, anthropology, archaeology, literature, and epigraphy, predominantly of Southwest Asia. The American Schools of Oriental Research (ASOR) is a consortium of educational and research institutions. This quarterly publication contains preliminary excavation reports, research notes, technical reports of original research, and book reviews. Examples of recent articles are "Landscape and Settlement in the Neo-Assyrian Empire" and "Scribal Education in Ancient Israel: The Old Hebrew Epigraphic Evidence."

Archives of Asian Art. See Art/General section.

589. Ars Orientalis: the arts of Asia, Southeast Asia and Islam. Supersedes: *Ars Islamica.* [ISSN: 0571-1371] 1954. a. USD 40. Ed(s): Margaret A Lourie. Department of History of Art, Tappan Hall, University of Michigan, Ann Arbor, MI 48109-1357; http://www-personal.umich.edu/~plourie. Illus. Refereed. Circ: 500. Online: OCLC Online Computer Library Center, Inc.; H.W. Wilson. *Indexed:* ArtInd, BAS, BrHumI. *Bk. rev.:* Number and length vary. *Aud.:* Ac, Sa.

Published for over 50 years, this peer-reviewed journal is cosponsored by the Department of the History of Art at the University of Michigan, and the Freer Gallery of Art of the Smithsonian Institution. Appearing annually, it includes scholarly articles and book reviews on archaeology and art of Asia, including

the Islamic world and the ancient Near East. Occasionally the volumes are thematic; recent themes have included Indian Ocean societies, and the Median and Persian empires. Recent article titles include "Auspicious Motifs in Ninth to Thirteenth-Century Chinese Tombs," "From Textbook to Testimonial: *The Emperor's Mirror, An Illustrated Discussion* in China and Japan," and "Origins of Daoist Iconography." Intended for scholars in various fields, including art, history, archaeology, and architecture.

590. Asia Institute. Bulletin. [ISSN: 0890-4464] 1987. a. USD 65. Carol Altman Bromberg, Ed. & Pub., 3287 Bradway Blvd, Bloomfield Hills, MI 48301; BAI34@aol.com; http://www.bulletinasiainstitute.org. Illus., index, adv. Sample. Refereed. Circ: 300 Paid. *Indexed:* BAS, FR. *Bk. rev.:* Number and length vary. *Aud.:* Ac, Sa.

This nicely clothbound journal covers the literature, art, archaeology, history, coins, etc., of much of Asia. There is an emphasis on West and Central Asia, but East Asia is also included. Recent articles have included "Cultural Riddles: Stylized Deer and Deer Stones of the Mongolian Altai" and "The Late Neo-Elamite Glyptic Style: A Perspective from Fars." Photographs and illustrations are frequently included with the articles. An index of previous editions can be found on the web site by both volume and by subject area. Book reviews cover works in English, French, and German. Appropriate for academic libraries and institutions with strong programs in Asian Studies and archaeology.

Asian Folklore Studies. See Folklore section.

The Australian Journal of Anthropology. See Anthropology section.

591. Electronic Journal of Contemporary Japanese Studies. [ISSN: 1476-9158] 2001. irreg. Free. Ed(s): Peter Matanle. University of Sheffield, School of East Asian Studies, Fl 5, The Arts Tower, Western Bank, Sheffield, S10 2TN, United Kingdom. Index. Refereed. *Indexed:* IBSS. *Bk. rev.:* 6 per year. *Aud.:* Ga, Ac.

This social science journal is devoted to scholarly writing and academic research on all topics connected to contemporary Japanese culture, economy, politics, and society. This journal is totally published online; its web site, www.japanesestudies.org.uk, provides the full content for free. Recent articles include "Deprofessionalisation of Buddhist Priests in Contemporary Japan: A Socio-Industrial Study of a Religious Profession" and "Desperate Housewives in Modern Japanese Fiction: Three Novels by Sawako Ariyoshi." Highly recommended for academic libraries and interested generalists.

Europe-Asia Studies. See Slavic Studies section.

592. Graduate Journal of Asia - Pacific Studies. [ISSN: 1176-2152] 2002. s-a. Free. University of Auckland, Department of History, Private Bag 92019, Auckland, New Zealand. Illus. Refereed. *Bk. rev.:* 1 per issue. *Aud.:* Ac, Sa.

This peer-reviewed electronic journal publishes the work of graduate students from a variety of disciplines. It publishes "thought-provoking interdisciplinary articles, reviews, commentary and visual works that engage critical issues, themes and debates related to the Asia-Pacific region and its peoples." For this title, the region includes Southeast, Northeast, and East Asia; the Pacific Islands; Australia; New Zealand; and the American West Coast. Each volume has an overlying theme that provides the focus. Recent themes include "Global Convergence, Local Divergence" and "Imagining the Asia-Pacific." Recent articles have included "E-Democracy in the Information Age: The Internet and the 2002 Presidential Election in South Korea" and "China Comparisons: Images of China in Japanese Popular Non-Fiction." The web site, www.arts.auckland.ac.nz/sites/index.cfm?P=5687, provides the entire journal in full text. Reviews include film and manga as well as book titles.

593. Harvard Journal of Asiatic Studies. [ISSN: 0073-0548] 1936. s-a. USD 45 (Individuals, USD 30). Ed(s): Joanna Handlin Smith, Wilt Idema. Harvard-Yenching Institute, 2 Divinity Ave, Cambridge, MA 02138; http://www-hcl.harvard.edu/hyl/hylhome.html. Illus., index. Sample. Refereed. Circ: 1200. Vol. ends: Dec. Microform: MIM; PQC.

Online: Factiva, Inc.; JSTOR (Web-based Journal Archive); H.W. Wilson. Reprint: SCH. *Indexed:* AmH&L, AmHI, AnthLit, ArtHuCI, BAS, BRI, CBRI, FR, HistAb, HumInd, IBR, IBSS, IBZ, IndIslam, MLA-IB, RILM. *Bk. rev.:* 8-12 pages. *Aud.:* Ac, Sa.

This highly respected journal is published twice a year, and it covers research on art, literature, history, and philosophy of all parts of Asia, with a recent emphasis on China and Japan. The Harvard-Yenching Institute has published this scholarly journal since 1936. Recent article topics have included "The Physician as Philosopher of the Way: Zhu Zhenheng (1282-1358)," "The Principles are Many: Wang Tingxiang and Intellectual Transition in Mid-Mind China," and "Remembering When: The Uses of Nostalgia in the Poetry of Bai Juyi and Yuan Zhen." The journal also includes detailed reviews; recently reviewed titles include "The Other Side of Zen: A Social History of Soto Zen Buddhism in Tokugawa Japan" and "China Marches West: The Qing Conquest of Central Eurasia." This journal is most likely to interest specialists, but it provides enough information that high-level general readers and students may find it of use as well. Highly recommended.

594. *Indonesia.* [ISSN: 0019-7289] 1966. s-a. USD 32 domestic; USD 34 foreign. Ed(s): Deborah Homsher. Cornell University, Southeast Asia Program, 180 Uris Hall, Ithaca, NY 14857-7601; SEAP-Pubs@ cornell.edu; http://www.einaudi.cornell.edu/SoutheastAsia/. Illus., index, adv. Sample. Refereed. Circ: 900. Vol. ends: Oct. Microform: PQC. Online: Northern Light Technology, Inc.; ProQuest K-12 Learning Solutions; ProQuest LLC (Ann Arbor). *Indexed:* AmH&L, BAS, EI, HistAb, IBR, IBSS, IPSA, IndIslam, MLA-IB, RILM. *Bk. rev.:* 0-4, 1,000-2,500 words. *Aud.:* Ac, Sa.

This semi-annual journal has been published by Cornell University's Southeast Asia Program since 1966. It is devoted to studying the culture, government, history, economy, and society of Indonesia. Issues include articles, book reviews, and interviews. Article titles have included "Local Civil–Military Relations during the First Phase of Democratic Transition, 1999-2004: A Comparison of West, Central, and East Java," "Colonizing Borneo: State-building and Ethnicity in Central Kalimantan," and "Playing the Game: Ethnicity and Politics in Indonesian Badminton." The web site, www.einaudi.cornell.edu/southeastasia/publications/indonesia.asp, offers free access to the content of volumes 1–68 (1966–2000); newer articles are available for a fee.

Japanese Journal of Religious Studies. See Religion section.

Journal of Asian Martial Arts. See Sports/Specific Sports section.

595. *Journal of Japanese Studies.* [ISSN: 0095-6848] 1974. s-a. USD 42 domestic; USD 47 foreign. Ed(s): John Whitter Treat, Susan B Hanley. Society for Japanese Studies, University of Washington, Box 353650, Seattle, WA 98195-3650; jjs@u.washington.edu; http://depts.washington.edu/jjs. Illus., adv. Refereed. Circ: 1900. Vol. ends: Summer. Reprint: PSC. *Indexed:* AmH&L, AmHI, ArtHuCI, BAS, HistAb, HumInd, IBSS, IPSA, MLA-IB, RILM, SSCI. *Bk. rev.:* 10-40, 1,500-3,000 words. *Aud.:* Ac, Sa.

This multidisciplinary journal is published twice a year with the goal of providing new interpretations, new information, and recent research on Japan to the English-speaking world. Also included are detailed book reviews and translations of published Japanese articles. The journal's focus on modern Japanese literature and history makes it very complimentary to other more general Japanese journals. Examples of recent articles are "The Political Economy of Postwar Family Policy in Japan: Economic Imperatives and Electoral Incentives," "Japan in the Life of Early Ryukyu," and "Matter Out of Place: Carnival, Containment, and Cultural Recovery in Miyazaki's *Spirited Away.*"

596. *Modern Asian Studies.* [ISSN: 0026-749X] 1967. bi-m. GBP 246. Ed(s): Gordon Johnson. Cambridge University Press, The Edinburgh Bldg, Shaftesbury Rd, Cambridge, CB2 2RU, United Kingdom; journals@cambridge.org; http://www.journals.cambridge.org. Illus., index, adv. Sample. Refereed. Vol. ends: Oct. Microform: PQC. Online: Pub.; EBSCO Publishing, EBSCO Host; JSTOR (Web-based Journal Archive);

OCLC Online Computer Library Center, Inc.; OhioLINK; SwetsWise Online Content. Reprint: PSC. *Indexed:* ABCPolSci, AmH&L, AmHI, ArtHuCI, BAS, CABA, EI, FPA, ForAb, HistAb, HumInd, IBR, IBSS, IBZ, IPSA, IndIslam, JEL, L&LBA, PSA, RI-1, RILM, RRTA, S&F, SSA, SSCI, SociolAb, WAE&RSA. *Bk. rev.:* 0-12, 1,500-3,500 words. *Aud.:* Ac, Sa.

This journal covers China, Japan, South Asia, and Southeast Asia; research articles cover the area's history, geography, sociology, literature, politics, social anthropology, culture, and economics. Issues include longer monographic essays taken from both new field work and archival materials, and can include book reviews of recent literature. Recent articles have included "Emerging Trends in Youth Sex Culture in Contemporary Urban Vietnam," "Terribly Severe Though Mercifully Short: The Episode of the 1918 Influenza in British Malaya," and "Information Technology Professionals and the New-Rich Middle Class in Chennai (Madras)." This journal is recommended for academic and research libraries, as it is best suited to scholars.

597. *Nichibunken Japan Review.* [ISSN: 0915-0986] 1990. a. Free to qualified personnel; JPY 2500 newsstand/cover. Ed(s): James C. Baxter. International Research Center for Japanese Studies (Nichibunken), 3-2 Oeyama-cho, Goryo, Nishikyo-ku, Kyoto-shi, 610-1192, Japan; shuppan@nichibun.ac.jp; http://www.nichibun.ac.jp. Index. Refereed. *Indexed:* BAS. *Bk. rev.:* Number and length vary. *Aud.:* Ac, Sa.

Japan Review is the refereed English-language journal of the The International Research Center for Japanese Studies. Published annually, it is a compilation of technical reports, book reviews, research notes and materials, and original or translated articles, all covering Japanese civilization and culture. The journal is distributed free to approximately 1,000 institutions in over 40 countries that study Japan. Copies are also available for sale to individuals and institutions for 2,500 yen per copy. Recent articles include the topics "'So That We Can Study Letter-Writing': The Concept of Epistolary Etiquette in Premodern Japan" and "*Sagoromo* and *Hamamatsu* on *Genji*: Eleventh-Century Tales as Commentary on *Genji Monogatari*." The full-text contents of all previous issues is available at www.nichibun.ac.jp/graphicversion/dbase/review_e.html. Suitable for academic and research libraries.

Oceania. See Anthropology section.

598. *Oriental Society of Australia. Journal.* [ISSN: 0030-5340] 1961. a. Membership, AUD 30. Ed(s): Leith D Morton. Oriental Society of Australia, The University of Sydney, School of Languages & Cultures, Sydney, NSW 2006, Australia; yasuko.claremont@arts.usyd.edu.au; http://www.arts.usyd.edu.au/publications/JOSA/index.htm. Illus., index, adv. Sample. Refereed. Circ: 500. *Indexed:* AmH&L, BAS, EI, HistAb, IBR. *Bk. rev.:* Number and length vary. *Aud.:* Ac, Sa.

Published annually since 1960, the *Journal of the Oriental Society of Australia* (*JOSA*) is the oldest Asian journal currently published in Australia. An index of the initial 42-year run of *JOSA* was published in 2002 and is also available on the journal's web site, www.arts.usyd.edu.au/publications/JOSA/journals.htm. Over the years, its most common topic has been China, followed by Japan. Articles have also covered Southeast Asia, South Asia, and other related areas. Topics frequently pertain to Asian literature and the arts, although not exclusively so. Recent article topics have included "Translating Shakespeare: The Case of Tsubouchi Shoyo" from 2003 and "Brushes and Booze in the Poetry of Yi Kyubo (1168-1241)" from 2004–2005. Book reviews are also included.

Pacific Historical Review. See History section.

Pacific Philosophical Quarterly. See Philosophy section.

Philosophy East and West. See Philosophy section.

599. *positions: east asia cultures critique.* [ISSN: 1067-9847] 1993. 3x/yr. USD 155 (Individuals, USD 33). Ed(s): Tani Barlow. Duke University Press, 905 W Main St, Ste 18 B, Durham, NC 27701; subscriptions@ dukeupress.edu; http://www.dukeupress.edu. Adv. Refereed. Circ: 660 Paid and controlled. Online: EBSCO Publishing, EBSCO Host; Gale;

HighWire Press; OCLC Online Computer Library Center, Inc.; OhioLINK; Project MUSE; SwetsWise Online Content. Reprint: PSC. *Indexed:* AmH&L, ArtHuCI, BAS, HistAb, MLA-IB, PSA, SSA, SociolAb. *Bk. rev.:* Number and length vary. *Aud.:* Ga, Ac.

This independent refereed journal contains criticism, commentary, essays, scholarly articles, and detailed book reviews on the political, intellectual, and economic cultures and histories of East Asia and Asian America. The direction of the journal is determined by its editorial collective and its readers and writers. Recent articles have included "Talking, Linking, Clicking: The Politics of AIDS and SARS in Urban China," "Contagion of Laughter: The Rise of the Humor Phenomenon in Shanghai in the 1930s," "Beauty Queens: Gender, Ethnicity, and Transnational Modernities at the Miss India USA Pageant," and "Revolutionary Flesh: Nakamoto Takako's Early Fiction and the Representation of the Body in Japanese Modernist and Proletarian Literature."

600. *Royal Asiatic Society. Journal.* Former titles (until 1991): *Royal Asiatic Society of Great Britain and Ireland. Journal;* Formerly (until 1835): *Royal Asiatic Society of Great Britain and Ireland. Transactions;* Incorporates: *Society of Biblical Archaeology. Proceedings.* [ISSN: 1356-1863] 1827. q. GBP 121. Ed(s): Sarah Ansari. Cambridge University Press, The Edinburgh Bldg, Shaftesbury Rd, Cambridge, CB2 2RU, United Kingdom; journals@cambridge.org; http://www.cup.cam.ac.uk/. Illus., index, adv. Sample. Refereed. Microform: BHP; IDC. Online: Pub.; EBSCO Publishing, EBSCO Host; OCLC Online Computer Library Center, Inc.; OhioLINK; SwetsWise Online Content. Reprint: SCH. *Indexed:* AICP, AmH&L, AmHI, ArtHuCI, BAS, BrHumI, FR, HistAb, IBR, IBSS, IBZ, IndIslam, MLA-IB, NumL, RI-1. *Bk. rev.:* Number varies; 500-750 words. *Aud.:* Ac, Sa.

Published for the Royal Asiatic Society of Great Britain and Ireland, this journal has been published since 1834. Its articles provide information on South Asia, the Middle East (including North Africa and Ethiopia), Central Asia, East Asia, and South-East Asia. It covers the topics of archaeology, literature, history, language, religion, and art; it also has book reviews. Recent article titles include "The establishment of Calcutta Botanic Garden: plant transfer, science and the East India Company, 1786-1806," "Further evidence for intercity co-operation among neo-Babylonian temples," and "The bear yawns? Russian and Soviet relations with Macao." This excellent resource is recommended for both specialists and general readers.

601. *Studies on Asia (Online).* Formerly (until 2004): *Studies on Asia (Print).* [ISSN: 1554-3749] 1960. s-a. Free. Michigan State University, Asian Studies Center, 301 International Center, East Lansing, MI 48824; asiansc@msu.edu; http://www.isp.msu.edu. Illus. Refereed. *Indexed:* AmH&L, HistAb. *Aud.:* Ga, Ac, Sa.

The Asian Studies Center at Michigan State University publishes this online journal twice a year. The journal covers "any and all aspects of Asia, past and present, such as culture, history, education, and literature." A recent special issue is themed "Baseball and Besuboru in Japan and the U.S." Recent articles include "The Samurai Way of Baseball and the National Character Debate," "Urban Chinese Perspectives on the U.S. Occupation of Japan, 1945-1947," and "Surviving the National Revolution: Chinese Women's Press Writings." The web site, www.isp.msu.edu/studiesonasia, provides the full content in pdf format. Highly recommended for academic libraries and public libraries that serve patrons with an interest in Asian culture.

Online Newspaper Resources

In this digital era, more and more regional, national, and local newspapers in English or with English versions are available online. Many are free of charge. These online daily, weekly, or monthly newspapers cover such topics as current world news, historical events, business, culture, politics, economics, finance, employment, sports, entertainment, art, and performance. Some have archives of back issues. These online publications are great resources for keeping up-to-date with information about the countries within each area. They are especially valuable sources for studying countries not sufficiently covered by print publications. Compared with print newpapers, online newspapers are usually more interactive and often provide a method for quick feedback. Readers can ask questions or make comments easily via the newspapers' web sites, which often include useful links to other, related online resources.

Several excellent guides found online are useful tools for searching and accessing online newspapers published in and about Asia and the Pacific area. These online guides are free, easy to use, and recommended for all types of libraries.

ASIA

Mondo Times. www.mondotimes.com/world/index.html. This excellent, free, worldwide media guide was launched in December 2001, and now covers 15,017 media outlets in 211 countries. It provides a single point of access to all kinds of mass media (newspapers, magazines, radio, television, and news agencies). It allows searching local media by country (countries are grouped into regions such as Asia, Europe, etc.) and major media by topics such as news, business, science, society, entertainment, and sports. Conveniently, it also indicates the type and the language of the media, making it a very useful tool. It is updated frequently, and allows users to rate the media and to report broken links online.

ABYZ Web Links. www.abyznewslinks.com/asia.htm. This is a guide to local, national, and foreign broadcast news, Internet news, newspapers, magazines, and press agencies in individual countries in Asia, as well as a comprehensive Asian regional category. The guide includes the title, publication location, and media type and language. Australia and New Zealand are included in an "Oceania" section.

Worldpress.org. World Newspapers. Asia. www.worldpress.org/newspapers/ASIA/index.htm. This guide is owned by Worldpress, whose mission is to foster the international exchange of perspectives and information. The guide provides lists of newspapers published in Asia, both in English and in the local language, in print or online. Titles and the publication point of origin are provided. If the newspaper is available online, the title is hyperlinked to its web site. Newspapers are first categorized by broad regions such as Southeast Asia and South Asia, and then by individual countries.

AllYouCanRead.com. Asia Newspapers. www.allyoucanread.com/newspapers.asp?id=R8. This web page dedicated to Asian newspapers is part of AllYouCanRead.com, a large database of magazines and newspapers on the Internet. AllYouCanRead.com provides listings for some 26,500 magazines and newspapers from all over the world. It is an excellent guide to world media sources, with more than 200 countries represented on the web site. The magazine and newspaper listings are not only categorized by their country of origin, but also subcategorized by topics such as art, business, or travel. Basic and advanced search engines can be used to search publications by name, keyword, category, or location. Another available feature for registered users is a personalized news collection service, free of charge, that allows users to create their own page listing favorite publications without having to bookmark them on individual computers. The guide provides the title and occasionally a brief introduction to each newspaper, but the language of the paper is not indicated.

PACIFIC/OCEANIA

ABYZ Web Links. www.abyznewslinks.com/pacif.htm. This is a guide to national, local, and foreign broadcast news, Internet news, newspapers, magazines, and press agencies in individual Pacific Islands, as well as a regional Oceania category. The guide includes the title, publication point of origin, and media type and language. Titles are hyperlinked. Australia and New Zealand are included in this section.

Escapeartist.com. Newspapers and media, Pacific Islands. www.escapeartist.com/media12/media12.htm. This is a good guide to newspapers and media of the Pacific Islands. The newspapers and media are grouped by individual islands. Titles are listed and hyperlinked to the newspaper's and the media's web sites. There is occasionally a brief introduction to the media listed.

AllYouCanRead.com. Australia and Pacific Newspapers. www.allyoucanread.com/newspapers.asp?id=R11. This web page, dedicated to newspapers in Australia and the Pacific area, is part of AllYouCanRead.com, a large database of magazines and newspapers on the Internet. AllYouCanRead.com provides listings for some 26,500 magazines and newspapers from all over the world. It is an excellent guide to world media sources, with more than 200 countries represented on the web site. The magazine and newspaper listings are not only categorized by their country of origin, but also subcategorized by topics such as art, business, or travel. Basic and advanced search engines can be used to search publications by name, keyword, category, or location. There is also a free, personalized news collection service for registered users. The guide provides the title and occasionally a brief introduction to each newspaper, but the language of the paper is not indicated.

ASIAN AMERICAN

Christine K. Oka, Library Instruction Coordinator, 270 Snell Library, Northeastern University, Boston, MA 02115; c.oka@neu.edu; FAX: 617-373-5409

Introduction

Asian Americans are an incredibly diverse ethnic, religious, and socioeconomic group that defies (and sometimes denies) the single descriptor. This presents a challenge to libraries when it comes to providing Asian American magazines and journals for their users. The official U.S. Census description "Asian" refers to those having origins in any of the original peoples of the Far East, Southeast Asia, or the Indian subcontinent—including, for example, Cambodia, China, India, Japan, Korea, Malaysia, Pakistan, the Philippine Islands, Thailand, and Vietnam. "'Pacific Islander' refers to those having origins in any of the original peoples of Hawaii, Guam, Samoa, or other Pacific Islands" (Reeves, 2003). These definitions give only the tip of the iceberg of how this population self-identifies. Organizations with the "Asian Pacific American" descriptor were criticized by Pacific Islanders, who pointed out, "We're from the Pacific Islands, not the Pacific Ocean!" When the Asian or Pacific Islander racial category was separated into two distinct groups—"Asian" and "Native Hawaiian and Other Pacific Islander"—per an Office of Management and Budget directive, there was discussion within the AAAS (Association for Asian American Studies) about changing the name of the association to include the new category.

Most standard periodical directories do not use "Asian American" or "Pacific Islander" as subject headings. For example, *The Standard Periodical Directory* and *Ulrich's Periodicals Directory* both use the heading "Ethnic Interests." Even when "Asian American" appears in a subject index, such as that of the *International Directory of Little Magazines and Small Presses*, some of the titles appear to be more "Asian" than "Asian American." Lack of that subject heading puts *Amerasia Journal*, the oldest scholarly journal in the field of Asian American studies, under the subject heading of "History" in *The Standard Periodical Directory* and under "Sociology" in *Ulrich's Periodicals Directory*. To be fair, when *Amerasia Journal* began publication in 1971, the field of Asian American studies was just developing as an area of research.

What is new today is how individuals who match the U.S. Census description view themselves. Sandra Oh, an actress of Asian descent from Canada, working in the U.S., described her reaction to the institutional racism in Hollywood, something she did not encounter in Canada. "I was told you can't audition for this because you're not white. . . . That was very significant. I remember that. You remember when your heart breaks" (Knoll, 2005). In a survey about Asian American studies, some participants, students matching the U.S. Census Asian American description, asked *not* be identified as Asian Americans. But assimilation is not always easy. Shawn Wong noted, "Sixty percent of the Asians in America are foreign born, which makes me the exception rather than rule in the country of my birth. People in Asia know I'm foreign and people in America assume that I am foreign born" (Wong, 1998). Of course, Asian American ethnic self-identification also can be very specific. B.S. Prakash, India's Consul General in San Francisco, responded to the question "Am I a Punjabi?" with "No, I am not, I am a Kannadiga. . . . No. I am not a Madrasi, though Karnataka is in the South, too" (Prakash, 2005). While admitting the answer is "quite a mouthful," he pointed out the question didn't ask if he was an Indian, which was evident to the questioner.

Finally, there's the bottom line. While the Asian American market is perceived as a prosperous demographic for advertisers, the magazines must move carefully to capture enough readers to justify the advertising investment. Jeff Yang, cofounder of the late *a.Magazine,* described the tightrope magazines have to walk in order to appeal to "Asians who want hard news and coverage of political and social issues, and . . . the ones who bought it because Lucy Liu was on the cover. . . ." He hopes there will be another "independent, community-

owned general interest title that strives to reach a broad base of Asian Americans" (Chansanchai, 2003). Indeed, many promising titles have come in and out of existence since the last edition of *Magazines for Libraries,* while other titles are published infrequently or irregularly or are of interest only to geographically focused groups. Therefore, covered here are those titles likely to be longer-term, continued publications that libraries can reasonably expect to obtain (or link to), and that are of interest to a broad spectrum of library readers throughout the country.

In the interest of "truth in advertising," I have concentrated on those magazines and e-zines in English that I have had the opportunity to examine. However, I have found libraries could meet the periodical reading needs of their users by exploring newspapers as an option. Two English-language newspapers examining Asian American issues nationally are *Asian Week* (http://www.asianweek.com) and the *International Examiner* (http://www.iexaminer.org/). Bilingual newspapers for transnational Asians include *Sampan,* Boston Chinatown's only Chinese English newspaper since 1971 (http://sampan.org/), or *Rafu Shimpo,* the Los Angeles Japanese Daily News, published in Los Angeles for over 100 years (http://www.rafu.com/).

Also, the full text of a number of Asian American publications are available on the web by subscription; most notably, in *Ethnic NewsWatch,* a database published by ProQuest (www.proquest.com).

REFERENCES

Chansanchai, Athima. "Struggle to Survive on the Newsstands." *DateLine AAJA: Quarterly Newsletter of the Asian American Journalists Association.* Spring 2003; vol. 10, no. 1; pp. 1–4. Retrieved June 11, 2006, from http://www.aaja.org/resources/publications/dateline/dateline_spring_03.pdf.

Knoll, Corina (2005). "In the Moment with Sandra Oh." *KoreAm.* August 2005; vol. 16, no. 8; pp. 76–82.

Prakash, B.S. "Second Opinion: Am I a Punjabi?" *Indian Life & Style.* September-October 2005; vol. 2, no. 7; pp. 62–64.

Reeves, Terrance, and Claudette Bennett. *The Asian and Pacific Islander Population in the United States: March 2002.* Current Population Reports, P20-540, U.S. Census Bureau, Washington, D.C., 2003. Retrieved June 13, 2006, from http://www.census.gov/prod/2003pubs/p20-540.pdf.

Wong, Shawn. "The Chinese Man Has My Ticket." In: Susan Richards Shreve and Porter Shreve, eds. *How We Want to Live: Narrative on Progress.* Boston: Beacon Press, 1998; pp. 142–149.

Basic Periodicals

Hs: *Filipinas, India Currents, KoreAm Journal;* Ga: *Amerasia Journal, Audrey, Filipinas, Hyphen, India Currents, KoreAm Journal, Monolid Magazine;* Ac: *AAPI Nexus, Amerasia Journal, Asian American Movement Ezine, Asian American Policy Review, Journal of Asian American Studies, Korean and Korean-American Studies Bulletin.*

Basic Abstracts and Indexes

America: History and Life, Sage Race Relations Abstracts, Ethnic NewsWatch.

602. *A A P I Nexus: Asian Americans and Pacific Islanders - policy practice and community.* [ISSN: 1545-0317] 2003. s-a. USD 55 (Individuals, USD 25). Ed(s): Julia Heintz-Mackoff. University of California at Los Angeles, Asian American Studies Center, 3230 Campbell Hall, PO Box 951546, Los Angeles, CA 90095-1546; apa@aasc.ucla.edu; http://www.sscnet.ucla.edu/aasc/. *Indexed:* PSA, SSA, SociolAb. *Aud.:* Hs, Ga, Ac, Sa.

Published by the UCLA Asian American Studies Center Press, *AAPI Nexus* connects peer-reviewed articles "from professional schools, applied social science scholars and practitioners with the explicit goal of reinvigorating Asian American Studies' traditional mission of serving communities and generating practical research." Each thematic issue contains a "Message from the Editors," along with articles categorized under "Practitioners' Essays" and "AAPI Almanac," or statistical studies. Two recent issues examined the model minority perception and its effect in "Special Focus on Health" and "Special Focus on Employment." An intriguing range of topics is covered, including "From Pedestrian Safety to Environmental Justice: The Evolution of a Chinatown Community Campaign," "Preferred Language and Asthma among Asian Americans," and "Screening Names Instead of Qualifications: Testing with

Emailed Resumes Reveals Racial Preferences." Highly recommended for academic libraries that support sociology, anthropology, public policy, health sciences, and ethnic studies. Also recommended for large public libraries that serve Asian American communities.

603. *Amerasia Journal: the national interdisciplinary journal of scholarship, criticism, and literature on Asian and Pacific American.* [ISSN: 0044-7471] 1971. 3x/yr. USD 295 (Individuals, USD 35). Ed(s): Ku Charles. University of California at Los Angeles, Asian American Studies Center, 3230 Campbell Hall, PO Box 951546, Los Angeles, CA 90095-1546; rleong@ucla.edu; http://www.sscnet.ucla.edu/aasc/. Illus., index, adv. Sample. Refereed. Circ: 1500 Paid. Vol. ends: No. 3. Microform: PQC. *Indexed:* AmH&L, AmHI, ArtHuCI, BAS, BRI, CBRI, FLI, HistAb, HumInd, IBR, IBZ, MLA-IB, PSA, RI-1, RILM, SSA, SSCI, SociolAb. *Bk. rev.:* Number varies, 3-4 pages. *Aud.:* Ga, Ac.

Amerasia Journal is the oldest continuously published academic journal in the interdisciplinary field of Asian American studies, and it appears three times a year—winter, spring, and fall. In addition to lengthy book and film reviews, each thematic issue contains articles by writers of all ethnicities and disciplines. In the volume titled "30 Years AfterWARd: Vietnamese Americans & U.S. Empire," articles include discussions of culture and the literature of displacement, mixed-race Vietnamese identities, and examination of memories (and representations of the memories) of the war—"My Mother's War" and "What's Going On with the Oakland Museum's 'California and the Vietnam Era' Exhibit?" The articles also look at the lessons of the Vietnam War, such as "A Tale of Two Cities: Saigon, Fallujah, and the Ethical Boundaries of Empire" and "On the Unredressability of U.S. War Crimes: Vietnam and Japan." The thought-provoking articles and in-depth reviews make this journal essential for all academic libraries and highly recommended for large public libraries that serve Asian American and other ethnic communities.

604. *Asian American Movement Ezine: progressive radical and revolutionary Asian American perspectives.* 1999. m. Asian American Movement Ezine, yellowpower@aamovement.net; http://www.aamovement.net/. *Bk. rev.:* Number and length vary. *Aud.:* Hs, Ga, Ac, Sa.

Started in 1999 by a group of Asian Americans in the Boston area, this online publication has the stated goal of providing "a forum for exchanging ideas on how to better organize for contemporary conditions, a vehicle through which to organize mass social change, and a place for social and artistic expression." This is a tall order for an e-zine run by volunteers with donated funds (no advertising dollars are accepted). *Azine* meets the challenge, with articles and updates under the main categories of Art & Culture, Community, Current Events, Features, and Viewpoints. Each subject category has a dropdown list. For example, Art & Culture contains the expected book, film, music, game, and visual arts reviews, but there also are articles and editorials. Among the book reviews is "Why *The Joy Luck Club* Brings Me Misery," an article about media stereotyping of Asian American women. Each review or article has the link, "Comments on this article? Go to our forums." Some articles are three or four years old; but this web site is a nonprofit run by volunteers, and there are many recent responses in the forums. The history of the Asian American Movement is documented with reprints of notable articles from the past, as well as new articles that reflect the perspective of the present. This informative and accessible e-zine is recommended for students, researchers, and activists.

605. *Asian American Policy Review.* [ISSN: 1062-1830] 1989. a. USD 40 (Individuals, USD 20; Students, USD 10). Ed(s): Sharon Chae, Samuel Lee. Harvard University, John F. Kennedy School of Government, 79 John F Kennedy St, Cambridge, MA 02138; webmaster@ ksgwww.harvard.edu; http://www.ksg.harvard.edu. Illus., adv. Refereed. Circ: 500 Paid and controlled. *Indexed:* BAS, PAIS, PSA. *Bk. rev.:* Number and length vary. *Aud.:* Ga, Ac.

This independent, student-run journal is funded by donations and published annually by students at the John F. Kennedy School of Government at Harvard University. It has a respected academic advisory board for every issue and publishes in-depth, scholarly articles by researchers in Asian American Studies. Predictably, it concentrates on the political science and public policy issues facing the Asian Pacific American community. Recent article topics included "The Global Enclave Model: Economic Segregation, Intra-ethnic Conflict, and the Impact of Globalization on Chinese Immigrant Communities" and "The Asian American as Victim and Success Story: A Discursive Analysis of the Brian Ho v. SFUSD Lawsuit." In addition to interviews with prominent Asian American politicians at local and national levels, such as U.S. Congressman Mike Honda and New York City Councilman John Lui, *APR* contains book and film reviews. Recommended for special libraries and academic libraries that support Asian American and ethnic studies, political science, or public policy programs.

606. *Audrey Magazine.* [ISSN: 1936-3362] 2003. bi-m. USD 14; USD 3.95 newsstand/cover. Ed(s): Anne H. Kim. Audrey Magazine, 17000 S Vermont Ave., Ste A, Gardena, CA 90247. Adv. Circ: 10000. *Aud.:* Hs, Ga, Sa.

In *Audrey* magazine's third anniversary issue, the publisher and editor-in-chief, James Ryu, "aware of the life span of most Asian American magazines," stated his ambition for this one to "become the definitive publication for Asian American women." There are the usual glossy photos showing fashion and beauty trends, and articles about women's health issues: heart disease, cancer, etc. What makes *Audrey* stand out is seeing Asian faces and Asian names profiled in articles. Recent issues included what at first glance would look like "the usual" topics in women's magazines, but there is a dedicated approach to presenting the Asian/Asian American perspective. For example, issues covered in "The Top Five Myths of Interviewing" addressed some of the cultural biases that may sabotage job applicants with an Asian/Asian American upbringing; the myths included "assertiveness is immodest," "academic performance is paramount," and "rejection means failure." Other cultural links include a "News/Gossip" section, with regular columns about "Upstarts: Asian Americans making noise" and "The Red Thread: News and tidbits to keep you connected with your fellow AAs." The "red thread" alludes to a Chinese proverb about an invisible red thread connecting people who are destined to meet—this column is such a connection. *Audrey* doesn't shy away from tough issues either—with articles discussing the "Asian fetish," the pitfalls of raising achieving children "the Asian American way," and adoption ("The Korean word for 'adoptee' is *ibjang,* which simply means 'a very bad person'"). Recommended for high school and college libraries and public libraries that serve large Asian/Asian American populations.

607. *Chinese America, History and Perspectives.* [ISSN: 1051-7642] 1987. a. USD 60 (Individuals, USD 17.50). Ed(s): Madeline Hsu. Chinese Historical Society of America, 965 Clay St, San Francisco, CA 94108; http://www.chsa.org. Illus., index. Refereed. Online: EBSCO Publishing, EBSCO Host; Florida Center for Library Automation. *Indexed:* AmH&L, HistAb, MASUSE. *Aud.:* Ga, Ac, Sa.

The Chinese Historical Society of America was established in 1963, for those interested in studying and preserving manuscripts, books, and other artifacts that have a bearing on the history and contributions of Chinese in America. *Chinese America, History and Perspectives* is a peer-reviewed annual published by the Chinese Historical Society of America, and sponsored by Asian American Studies at San Francisco State University. Each annual contains six or seven essays. The 2006 volume covered a broad range of topics, beginning with an article comparing "Gold Mountain" exhibitions at Chinese American museums in San Francisco, New York, and Los Angeles, three cities with the largest Chinese American populations in the United States. Another essay presented historical notes about Chinese restaurants in Portland, Maine, a city not known for its Asian—let alone Chinese—population. A more global perspective was presented in a study comparing the rural Chinese of New South Wales and California. Highly recommended for special and academic libraries that support research in history and Asian American studies.

608. *Filipinas: the magazine for Filipinos worldwide.* [ISSN: 1063-4630] 1992. m. USD 18; USD 2.95 per issue. Ed(s): Mona Lisa Yuchengco. Filipinas Publishing, Inc., 1580 Bryant St, Daly City, CA 94015-1926. Illus., adv. Sample. Circ: 30000 Paid. Vol. ends: Dec. *Indexed:* BAS, ENW. *Aud.:* Hs, Ga, Ac.

This Filipino American monthly now sports the subtitle *the Magazine for Filipinos Worldwide.* In either case, *Filipinas* continues to appeal to a wide range of readers, featuring historical, current-events, and general-interest articles, along with stories about achievers, role models, and politics in the United States and the Philippines. There is something for both immigrant and

American-born Filipinos as well as those interested in Filipino culture. One enthusiastic non-Filipino reader said of himself that he "must have been Pinoy in a past life." Cover stories in recent issues have ranged from Filipino roots in New Orleans, the story of a Louisiana native of Cajun-Filipino descent, to a human interest story about Christina Bugayong, a little girl in the Philippines with an inspiring story of hope. There is also an interview with Allan Pineda, a member of the hip-hop group, the Black-Eyed Peas. Regular columns include "Mediawatch," "Community Beat," "We Mean Business" (business and personal financial planning tips), "Buhay Pinoy Abroad" (humorous stories contributed by the readers), and "Expat's Kitchen" (recipes and culinary interviews). *Filipinas* also contains a section about the care of the elderly called "AARP Corner" and produced in a partnership between AARP California, the Stanford Geriatric Education Center, and *Filipinas Magazine*. This is an essential title for public libraries that serve the Filipino and Filipino American community, and is highly recommended for academic libraries that support Asian American or ethnic studies programs.

609. *Hyphen.* 2003. 3x/yr. USD 18 domestic for 4 issues; USD 28 Canada for 4 issues. Ed(s): Melissa Hung. Hyphen, PO Box 192002, San Francisco, CA 94119-2002. *Aud.:* Hs, Ga, Ac, Sa.

A glossy magazine funded by grants and with articles contributed by volunteers, *Hyphen* is an edgy, new publication for young Asian Americans covering news, culture, profiles of Asian American leaders, politics, and commentary. A recent thematic issue had a sex survey of readers (ranging from ages 15 to 58); an article examining the relationship between obesity and the changing Asian American diet; pictures and interviews with Asian American athletes who challenge stereotypes, such as a 6'3" pole-vaulter; and a 58-year-old sharpshooter. Regular sections in the magazine include "Redux: Another Look at Media," with articles about Asian Americans on prime-time TV or on the Internet; "Gifted and Talented: The Arts"; and "Take Out: Stuff to Take Home." The latter showcases trendy new products such as clothing for yoga, Real Kidz multiracial dolls, and handmade gourmet chocolates. Judging by the great cover photos on recent issues—you have to have a sense of humor as well—this publication is written by, and directed towards, hip, young Asian Americans. Recommended for public libraries and college libraries.

610. *India Currents: North America's magazine of Indian arts, entertainment & dining.* [ISSN: 0896-095X] 1987. m. Free. Ed(s): Ashok Jethanandani. India Currents, PO Box 21285, San Jose, CA 95151. Illus., adv. Sample. Circ: 30200 Paid and free. *Indexed:* ENW, RILM. *Bk. rev.:* Number varies, 300 words. *Aud.:* Ems, Hs, Ga, Ac.

India Currents says it is "the nation's leading Indian-American monthly with features, reviews, opinion, analysis, and a detailed calendar of Indian events nationwide." The newsprint-quality paper is surprising, but on the plus side it is printed using soy ink and is fully indexed by *Ethnic NewsWatch*. The magazine is "devoted to the exploration of the heritage and culture of India as it exists in the United States," with recipes, book and film reviews, and a "What's Current" section, with a Cultural Calendar and a Spiritual Calendar. Each issue has fascinating feature articles, such as one about the information-services boom in India and an interview with Russell Peters, a rising Indian Canadian comedian. There's also a feature on the top ten South Asian Americans, or Desis, of 2005, with biographical profiles including a film producer, a constitutional attorney, an author, and the 13-year-old winner of the 78th Annual National Scripps Spelling Bee. While insightful editorials and letters appear in "Perspectives," the articles appearing in the "Lifestyle" section provide a close look at Indian and American culture from a variety of perspectives. Articles range from a description and comparison of Indian and American cultural taboos to a story about a Westerner's assimilation into Indian culture. The latter concludes the "Through Blue Eyes" series, which also is archived in its entirety on the magazine's web site. Recommended for libraries that serve Indian American communities and readers of all ages who have an interest in India and Indian American culture.

611. *Indian Life & Style.* [ISSN: 1549-1838] 2003. bi-m. USD 1 newsstand/cover per issue. Ed(s): Ms. Bina A Murarka, Bala Murali Krishna. India - West Publications Inc., 933 MacArthur Blvd, San Leandro, CA 94577-3062. *Indexed:* ENW. *Aud.:* Hs, Ga.

This sumptuous, glossy magazine publishes news, views, interviews, and articles on a wide variety of topics to reach Indians in America, including "The Color of Religion: Why It's Safe to Stick to Your Own Kind If You Are A

Religious Person," "Melting Pot or Salad Bowl: Examining the Multicultural Challenges on American Campuses," and "Home Box Office: New Technologies are Helping Hindi Films Go Global." Many articles highlight the contributions of notable Indians in the public eye—such as Neal Katyal, a Georgetown University law professor who was recently named "one of the top 40 lawyers under 40 by the National Law Journal"; "The Khan of Our Times: A Conversation with Cricket Legend Imran Khan"; and in the same issue, "A 'Con' Among Us: The Neoconservative Ideology of *National Review*'s Ramesh Ponnuru." Regular columns reach out to a wide demographic, and include the provocative "Second Opinion," the fun "Bollywood Bloopers," the views of "20-Something" writers, and "Sophomore Speak," written by a sophomore at Piedmont High School in California. Writers and subjects of articles are from a variety of regional, ethnic, and religious backgrounds. *Indian Life & Style* provides a diverse picture of India and Indians in America and abroad, with something to appeal to a broad demographic. Recommended for public, academic, and special libraries that serve an Indian population, or users interested in learning more about India and Indian culture and Indian Americans.

612. *Journal of Asian American Studies.* [ISSN: 1097-2129] 1998. 3x/yr. USD 100. Ed(s): George Anthony Peffer, Kandice Chuh. The Johns Hopkins University Press, 2715 N Charles St, Baltimore, MD 21218-4363; http://www.press.jhu.edu. Illus., adv. Sample. Refereed. Circ: 891. Vol. ends: Oct. Online: EBSCO Publishing, EBSCO Host; OCLC Online Computer Library Center, Inc.; OhioLINK; Project MUSE; ProQuest K-12 Learning Solutions; ProQuest LLC (Ann Arbor); SwetsWise Online Content. Reprint: PSC. *Indexed:* AmH&L, BAS, HistAb, IBR, IBZ, SSA, SociolAb. *Bk. rev.:* Number varies, 2-3 pages. *Aud.:* Ga, Ac.

The Association for Asian American Studies was founded in 1979 with the mission of advancing excellence in teaching and research in the field and promoting closer ties and understanding among the various groups within it—Chinese, Japanese, Korean, Filipino, Hawaiian, Southeast Asian, South Asian, and Pacific Islander, among others. The association's official journal, *Journal of Asian American Studies,* publishes articles that explore the historical, social, and cultural aspects of the Asian American experience along with book, media, and exhibition reviews. In a recent issue, articles examine the self-identity and empowerment of Asian Americans in "Between the Personal and the Universal: Asian American Solo Performance from the 1970s to the 1990s" and "To Be, or Not to Be South Asian: Contemporary Indian American Politics." The online version of this journal is available in the Johns Hopkins University collection, *Project Muse*. Essential for academic libraries that support Asian American and other ethnic studies programs.

613. *KoreAm Journal: Korean American Experience.* [ISSN: 1541-1931] 1990. m. USD 28 domestic; USD 118 Canada; USD 3.95 newsstand/ cover domestic. Ed(s): James Ryu. Korean American Publications, 17000 S. Vermont Ave., Ste. A, Gardena, CA 90247-5854. Illus., adv. Circ: 33723 Paid. *Bk. rev.:* Number and length vary. *Aud.:* Hs, Ga, Ac, Sa.

Originally a tabloid-format publication, *KoreAm Journal* has burst onto the glossy magazine market. Established "to provide a forum nationwide for English-speaking Korean Americans," each issue has a Cover Story, Feature Stories, Korean Culture, and Community Network. The Departments section includes "Dear Clara," an advice column; recipes from "The KoreAm Kitchen"; and "Spotlight" news. Articles in recent issues cover a wide range of interests and achieve a balance between informing and entertaining. The covers of two of the 15-year anniversary issues reflect this diversity: one had a photo of actress Sandra Oh, "sitting pretty" in a blue chiffon dress; the other cover showed Irene Crews, an Orange County, California, police officer, "on the beat, patrolling the community." *KoreAm* also reflects this diversity in its content. One article, "Greetings from Kyrgyzstan," looked at the history of the 5.1 million Koreans in this Central Asian country. Another issue published a series of articles titled "Remembering the Riots." Then there are the chatty first-person interviews in each issue: "How'd Ya End Up in Montana" or Maryland. *KoreAm* also includes general interest articles focusing on entertainment, gossip, and celebrities. Recommended for public libraries that serve Korean American populations and for academic libraries that support Asian American and ethnic studies programs.

614. *Korean and Korean-American Studies Bulletin.* [ISSN: 0749-7970] 1984. s-a. USD 26. East Rock Institute, 251 Dwight St, New Haven, CT 06511; Eri3@pantheon.yale.edu; http://www.eastrockinstitute.org/eastrock/. *Aud.:* Ga, Ac, Sa.

Aptly named, the *Korean & Korean American Studies Bulletin* is published by the East Rock Institute, or ERI, a nonprofit research, educational, and cultural organization dedicated to the study of Korean culture and the Korean Diaspora throughout the world. It is the only journal dedicated to covering Koreans in America, along with Korean culture in Korea and around the world. The major focus of the institute's research is on major Korean communities in Japan, the United States, China, and the former Soviet Union, which make up more than 90 percent of the Korean population outside of Korea. The journal's editorial staff is drawn from a highly diverse range of academic disciplines and from universities worldwide, with specialist guess editors for some issues. Recent thematic issues demonstrating this interdisciplinary and global research include: "Korean Religion and Cultural Values," "Korean American Cancer Control and Awareness," "Koryuo Saram: Koreans in the Former U.S.S.R.," and "Korean Diaspora in the U.S.A.: Challenges and Evolution." Each issue thoroughly explores the topic. For example, articles in the "Korean Religion and Cultural Values" issue cover Korean Taoism, Buddhism, Confucianism, Christianity, and twentieth-century religious movements in Korea. Recommended for academic libraries that support anthropology and ethnic studies research and for public libraries that serve an Asian American, especially Korean American, community.

615. *Theme: Asian culture quarterly.* [ISSN: 1554-1770] 2005. q. USD 19. Ed(s): N rain Noe. Theme Publishing, Inc., 203 Rivington St, 1D, New York, NY 10002-2570. *Aud.:* Ga.

Theme is a beautifully photographed, artistic magazine, each issue focusing on an idea or concept, such as "I Live Here," "Skin," and "Siblings." Art transcends borders, so while *Theme* interviews Asian Americans, or Asians in America, there also are articles and profiles of Asian artists, designers, musicians, writers, and photographers overseas. In fact, many of the subjects have multinational backgrounds. There's the profile of jazz singer Yukimi Nagano, whose hometown is in Gothenburg, Sweden. She describes it as "a great place if you want to be creative; it's peaceful and down to earth, and there's a lot of music going on, from classical, to jazz, to house, to Gothenburg death metal." Artist O-Sang Gwan describes the art in Korea as "a confluence of artists that draw influences from having studies and worked abroad." And there is a heartbreaking but inspirational profile of Liao Yiwu, the most censored contemporary writer and poet in China, who "continues to write and publish, despite continued police harassment and censorship." In the "Siblings" issue, artist and designer David Choong Lee is interviewed "in his hometown of San Francisco" and his older brother, Choon San Lee, in Seoul, Korea. Some articles have been translated into English. Highly recommended for academic and large public libraries. *Theme* publishes articles you won't see anywhere else!

■ ASTROLOGY

Christianne Casper, Instruction Coordinator, Broward Community College, South Campus, 7200 Pines Blvd., Pembroke Pines, FL 33024; a012724t@bc.seflin.org

Introduction

Interest in astrology remains strong, and access to the Internet has only increased astrologists' ability to share their studies and predictions with amateurs and professionals from around the world. Do a Google search on astrology and you will receive over 166 million results, and this number continues to grow. People turn to astrology as a way to gain greater insight into their lives and themselves. There are various types of astrology, including horary and natal; horary astrologists study questions based on the exact moment they arise and then make predictions, and natal astrologists analyze people based on their place and time of birth. The study of astrology involves observations, measurements, and calculations about the stars and planets to produce a framework for symbolic patterns according to their positions and aspects. Analyzing these patterns, astrologists attempt to explain and predict social, political, emotional, and other important aspects of life. Some popular astrology journals include *American Astrology, Dell Horoscope, Mountain Astrologer*, and *Welcome to Planet Earth.* These journals provide information on personal horoscopes and guides to world events. Other journals, *Considerations, Mercury Hour*, and *Today's Astrologer*, focus on a more scholarly, research-oriented approach. The following list includes publications for all levels of interest.

Basic Periodicals

Hs: *American Astrology, Dell Horoscope;* Ga: *American Astrology, Dell Horoscope, The Mountain Astrologer, Welcome to Planet Earth;* Ac: *American Astrology, Considerations, The Mountain Astrologer, Today's Astrologer;* Sa: *Considerations, Mercury Hour, The Mountain Astrologer, Today's Astrologer.*

616. *American Astrology.* [ISSN: 0002-7529] 1933. m. USD 23. Ed(s): Lee Chapman, Ken Irving. Starlog Group, Inc., 1372 Broadway, 2nd Fl, New York, NY 10018; http://www.starlog.com. Illus., index, adv. Circ: 185000. Vol. ends: Feb. Microform: PQC. *Bk. rev.:* 2. *Aud.:* Hs, Ga.

American Astrology is one of the oldest and most popular astrology magazines. Its focus is on the practical application of astrology to everyday life. Each issue is divided into three sections. "Features" contains articles that cover topics from astrology for a new age to astrological aspects of celebrities. "Popular Astrology" includes book reviews, astrology for ages 50-plus, birthday forecasts, and astro-crosswords. The final section, "Forecasts," includes monthly, weekly, and daily horoscopes.

617. *Dell Horoscope.* Formerly (until 199?): *Horoscope.* [ISSN: 1080-1421] 1935. 13x/yr. USD 39.87 domestic. Ed(s): Ronnie Grishman. Dell Magazines, 475 Park Ave S, 11 Fl, New York, NY 10016-6901; juliamcevoy@dellmagazines.com. Illus., adv. Circ: 240000 Paid. Vol. ends: Dec. *Indexed:* BRI, CBRI. *Bk. rev.:* 3 signed. *Aud.:* Hs, Ga.

Dell Horoscope is one of the most popular astrology magazines. The articles cover general-interest topics ranging from world and national affairs to personal problems. Also included are yearly, monthly, and daily guides. The regular features include letters to the editor, lucky numbers, a monthly planetary data table, and book and product reviews. *Dell* is written with both professional astrologers and amateurs in mind. The online version includes daily horoscopes, a readers' forum, and links to other astrology web sites. Also of interest is "Cosmic Connections," which lists astrological activities in the United States and Canada.

618. *Mercury Hour: the astrologer's astrology magazine.* 1974. q. Ed(s): Jewel Cook Fahey. Mercury Hour, 283 Gardenpark Ave., Lynchburg, VA 24502-2397. Illus., adv. *Bk. rev.:* 3. *Aud.:* Sa.

Mercury Hour is a unique publication, providing an international forum for discussing anything and everything astrological. The letters, opinions, and articles are all contributed by astrologers for astrologers. Research is presented, and questions are posed seeking answers from other readers. All branches of astrology are discussed. The online version at www.starflash.com/mercury-hour includes previously published articles, a bulletin board, chat rooms, conference listings, and links to other web sites.

619. *The Mountain Astrologer.* [ISSN: 1079-1345] 1987. 6x/yr. USD 36 in US & Canada; USD 54 elsewhere in the Americas; USD 64 in Europe. Ed(s): Nan Geary. Mountain Astrologer, PO Box 970, Cedar Ridge, CA 95924-0970; subs@mountainastrologer.com; http://www.mountainastrologer.com. Illus., adv. Sample. Circ: 20000 Paid. Vol. ends: Nov/Dec. *Bk. rev.:* 3-5. *Aud.:* Ga, Sa.

The Mountain Astrologer provides a wealth of information for professional and amateur astrologers alike. Standard features include a "Forecast Calendar," "New and Full Moon Reports," "Where's That Moon?," "Astrology News," letters to the editor, a professional directory, and signed book and astrological web site reviews. The web site reviews and the abundance of charts are extremely helpful. The online version lists the table of contents of the current issue, provides an index of articles from 1990 to the present, and offers an article archive. Web site recommendations are also available. In addition there is a "Beginner Information" section, which provides an overview of basic concepts of astrology.

620. *Today's Astrologer.* Formerly: *American Federation of Astrologers Bulletin.* [ISSN: 1067-1439] 1938. m. USD 45. Ed(s): Kris Brandt Riske. American Federation of Astrologers, Inc., 6535 S Rural Rd, Box 22040, Tempe, AZ 85283-9760. Illus., index. Sample. Circ: 2700 Controlled. *Aud.:* Sa.

Today's Astrologer, the bulletin of the American Federation of Astrologers, was established as a forum to promote astrology through research and education. There is an average of five articles per issue. Regular departments include "Data Exchange," "The Question Box," and "The Communication Center." This last department is a calendar of activities of member organizations and other astrology affiliates. Finally, a "Lunation/Full Moon" chart is provided.

621. *Welcome to Planet Earth: journal of new astrology in the contemporary world.* Former titles: *Pass the Word; Great Bear.* [ISSN: 0747-8968] 1979. m. USD 45. Ed(s): Mark Lerner. Great Bear Press, PO Box 5164, Eugene, OR 97405. Illus., adv. Sample. Circ: 2100. *Aud.:* Ga.

Welcome to Planet Earth includes astrology articles on individuals and information on current and historical events. The articles are written for a general audience in order to provide a deeper understanding of contemporary astrology. The monthly features include letters to the editor, "Your Cosmic Kalendar," and "Astro-Shamanic Perspectives." The online journal at www.mcn.org/greatbear includes current articles covering world events, astro-software, computer reports, articles from back issues, celebrity profiles, and educational materials.

■ ASTRONOMY

See also Aeronautics and Space Science; and Atmospheric Sciences sections.

Edward Creighton Sugrue, Jr., Wolbach Library, Harvard-Smithsonian Center for Astrophysics, 60 Garden St., Cambridge, MA 02138; edsugrue@hotmail.com

Introduction

We are only seven years into the twenty-first century, and already astronomy has progressed more than in most other centuries in human history. The search for planets beyond our solar system, the quest to understand the origin of our universe, and even the drive to protect our home planet from dangerous asteroids have all advanced with incredible speed. But as swiftly as these advances are being made, they are all quite dependent upon ease of communication amongst astronomers, and on astronomers' ability to share their findings with the rest of humanity. Modern astronomers' jobs are made vastly easier by staying well informed about recent developments in their field, and one of the best ways to do this is by means of the journals discussed in this section. Similarly, the interested public is well served to be enabled to follow these astronomers as they work, as their research is published.

The selections put forward here include titles of interest to a diverse range of readers, ranging from Spanish-speaking children, to the average intelligent adult, to hobbyists with a specific astronomical interest, to professional astronomers.

There is a wide range of astronomical periodicals available, many of which are indeed quite democratic in spirit, and aim at a wider audience. However, librarians need to take extra care concerning which periodicals they select in this area of study for their institutions. Although many of the following periodicals are aimed at the general public, other periodicals are so esoteric that even undergraduate astronomy students have trouble wading through them.

Take care, also, not to assume that the periodicals listed under Basic Periodicals below are "basic" in the sense of being simple. Many of them are overflowing with high-level equations, and are only basic in that they are invaluable components of any serious academic astronomy library. Also note that "basic" periodicals are distinct from "core" periodicals. Core periodicals are chosen and agreed upon by specialized science libraries. They can be identified by consulting PAMNET and/or ASTROWEB, which are each described three paragraphs below in this introduction. In general, in determining

a periodical's prospective value to your library, pay attention to the audience codes that periodicals have been assigned, and take time to examine their annotations and their web sites.

That said, a lot of these periodicals do provide terrific information to committed amateur astronomers, of whom there are many. Amateur astronomers, after all, make major contributions to the field on a regular basis. The general-audience periodicals serve a role that is at least as valuable as the specialized journals, because many thoughtful people, including children, harbor a great love of astronomy yet simply don't have the time to study it in any great depth. Many periodicals listed here fall somewhere between the abstruse journals and the nontechnical ones. Quite a few of these tend to specialize in a particular area of astronomical research, such as meteors, cosmology, or the planets of our solar system.

Most of these publications, although not all, can be found on the Internet. Several excellent periodicals are available free of charge on the web. This section includes a couple of journals that are designed entirely to translate research being done in Russia. For journals with a similar function, seek out *Ulrich's Periodicals Directory.*

A word to the wise: If you are new to this field, do not confuse *Astronomy and Astrophysics Abstracts* with *Astronomy and Astrophysics.* They sound like they should be connected somehow, but they are completely unrelated publications, and the similarity in their titles is merely an annoying coincidence.

Special mention in this category goes to a publication that is technically not a serial, but that needs to be mentioned in this context. A valuable, beautifully illustrated, eye-catching resource, *Astronomical Calendar* by Guy Ottewell, published by Furman University in Greenville, South Carolina, is generally considered to be the most beautiful, and one of the most treasured, of all the annual sky atlases.

Academic librarians who are new to the field also need to be aware of *PAMNET* and *ASTROWEB. PAMNET* is a valuable, professional online forum, useful for discussing astronomy periodicals and other information sources with fellow information professionals and librarians. *PAMNET* can easily be found online at http://pantheon.yale.edu/~dstern/astro.html. *ASTROWEB* is maintained by an international group of astronomers, and provides easy access to a host of astronomical databases and other resources that are just outside the scope of this section. *ASTROWEB* can be located at http://www.stsci.edu/science/net-resources.html. *Astronomy and Astrophysics Abstracts,* NASA's *ADS,* which is at http://adswww.harvard.edu, and *INSPEC* are excellent indexing services.

Basic Periodicals

Ems: *Abrams Planetarium Sky Calendar, Odyssey, SkyWatch;* Hs, Ga: *Astronomy, Griffith Observer, Mercury, Sky & Telescope, SkyWatch;* Ac: *Astronomical Journal, Astronomy, Astronomy & Astrophysics, The Astrophysical Journal, Royal Astronomical Society. Monthly Notices.*

Basic Abstracts and Indexes

INSPEC, NASA Astrophysics Data System (ADS).

622. *A A V S O Journal.* [ISSN: 0271-9053] 1972. s-a. USD 40 (Individuals, USD 25). Ed(s): Charles A Whitney. American Association of Variable Star Observers, 25 Birch St, Cambridge, MA 02138; aavso@aavso.org; http://www.aavso.org/journal.html. Illus., index. Refereed. Circ: 1500. Vol. ends: No. 2. *Bk. rev.:* 1-2, 400-600 words. *Aud.:* Ac, Sa.

The American Association of Variable Star Observers (AAVSO) has members in more than 40 countries and is the largest organization of variable-star observers in the world. Its members include both amateur and professional astronomers, and they watch and track variable stars (those whose luminosity changes over time), and then submit their observations to the AAVSO. Amateur astronomers play a very important role in the tracking of variable stars, as there are far too many for only professionals to follow. The AAVSO web site has such features as a search engine designed to locate variable stars in the AAVSO charts; a variety of online tools to assist observers in processing their information; and even a "variable star of the month." The journal publishes scientific papers on variable-star research, activities of the AAVSO, letters to the editor, and the Annual Report of the Director. Both are valued, valuable sources of information within the astronomical community.

623. *Abrams Planetarium Sky Calendar: an aid to enjoying the changing sky.* [ISSN: 0733-6314] 1969. q. USD 10 domestic; USD 14 in Canada & Mexico. Ed(s): Robert C Victor. Michigan State University, Talbert & Leota Abrams Planetarium, 113 Angell Bldg, East Lansing, MI 48824-1234; ladiski@pilot.msu.edu; http://www.pa.msu.edu/abrams/ SkyCalendar. Illus. Circ: 15000. *Aud.:* Ems, Hs, Ga, Ac.

Sky Calendar, as the name suggests, presents a page for each month that is laid out like a calendar. The reverse side of each page presents a simplified sky map for that month, printed for use at mid-evening and approximately 43 degrees north latitude. Diagrams in the boxes invite the reader to track the moon's rapid motion past the planets and bright stars of the zodiac, as well as to follow the more leisurely pace of the planets in their conjunctions with bright stars and other planets. This is a very specialized publication that serves only the purpose described here. You will not find, for example, articles, book reviews, or evaluations of software; you will just find the charts. The highly illustrated format and easy-to-follow guide make the loose-leaf calendar popular. Information presented in the calendar can be used (with permission) as a teaching tool by members of astronomical societies, teachers, and park interpreters.

624. *Ad Astra: to the stars: the magazine of the National Space Society.* [ISSN: 1041-102X] 1989. 6x/yr. USD 60 (Individuals, USD 45; Students, USD 20). Ed(s): Anthony Duignan-Cabrera. National Space Society, 1620 I St., N.W., Ste 615, Washington, DC 20003-4316; nsshq@nss.org; http://www.nss.org. Illus., adv. Circ: 26800 Paid and free. Vol. ends: No. 6. *Indexed:* ABS&EES, GSI, IAA, RGPR. *Aud.:* Hs, Ga, Ac, Sa.

Ad Astra contains articles and news stories concerning U.S. and international space programs, federal space policy formation, commercial space endeavors, new technologies, and recent scientific achievements pertaining to astronomy. It is the membership publication of the National Space Society, and its articles can be read by space and astronomy enthusiasts and by those with extensive education in the field. Regular departments in the publication include "Launch Pad," "Mission Control," "Countdown," "Space Community," and "Lifting Off." Obviously, the primary focus is on the space program, but often there are articles dealing with broader astronomical issues such as cosmology, or wholly speculative articles about possible future space-related ventures. This popular journal has numerous beautiful illustrations and photographs, and has helped spark an early interest in space in many people. A valuable addition to any library, whether it specializes in astronomy or not.

625. *American Astronomical Society. Bulletin.* [ISSN: 0002-7537] 1969. q. USD 30 in North America; USD 55 elsewhere. Ed(s): P B Boyce. American Astronomical Society, 2000 Florida Ave, NW, Ste 400, Washington, DC 20009; http://www.aas.org. Illus. Vol. ends: No. 4. *Aud.:* Ac, Sa.

The function of the *Bulletin* is to give the American Astronomical Society (AAS) a forum to present the abstracts of papers from conferences and meetings, and to present notices of the society that are likely to be of interest to the astronomical community. Annual observatory reports and reports of the society itself are also published here. The observatory reports are particularly useful to people wanting to determine the observational capabilities and major research programs of various observatories. The *Bulletin* sometimes includes such interesting papers as "The Most Frequently-Cited Astronomical Papers Published during the Past Decade," Alvin Toffler-esque discussions of likely cultural changes in the twenty-first century and their impact on astronomy, and the real value of a Ph.D. The AAS reserves its *Astronomical Journal* and *Astrophysical Journal* (both below in this section) for original research papers.

626. *Annual Review of Astronomy and Astrophysics.* [ISSN: 0066-4146] 1963. a. USD 205 (Individuals, USD 84 print & online eds.). Ed(s): Samuel Gubins, Geoffrey Burbidge. Annual Reviews, 4139 El Camino Way, Palo Alto, CA 94303-0139; service@annualreviews.org; http://www.annualreviews.org. Adv. Refereed. Microform: PQC. Online:

Pub.; EBSCO Publishing, EBSCO Host; HighWire Press; OCLC Online Computer Library Center, Inc.; ProQuest K-12 Learning Solutions; ProQuest LLC (Ann Arbor); SwetsWise Online Content; H.W. Wilson. Reprint: PSC. *Indexed:* C&ISA, CerAb, ChemAb, GSI, IAA, M&GPA, MRD, SCI. *Aud.:* Ac, Sa.

This is a valuable synthesis of the current state of research in a wide range of astronomical fields. Each volume contains about 15–20 articles, each dealing with a currently "hot" topic in astronomy. The articles give the reader a detailed overview of what kind of research is being done, and upon what specific problems and issues researchers are striving to focus more energy. Each article is followed up by a select bibliography of several dozen of the most important published papers in the particular area of inquiry for the year, chosen by some of the top people in the world in that specific field. Be aware that the articles assume a certain scientific sophistication and awareness on the part of the reader. *ARAA* is a tremendously useful volume for librarians and astronomers, and is often kept behind the circulation desk in science libraries to keep it safe.

627. *Association of Lunar and Planetary Observers. Journal.* [ISSN: 0039-2502] 1947. q. USD 26 in North America; USD 33 elsewhere. Ed(s): John E Westfall. Association of Lunar and Planetary Observers, P O Box 13456, Springfield, IL 62791-3456; poshedly@bellsouth.nt; http://www.LPL.Arizona.edu/~rhill/alpo/member.html. Illus., adv. Sample. Refereed. Circ: 410 Paid. Vol. ends: No. 4. *Bk. rev.:* 1-2, 300-500 words. *Aud.:* Ac, Sa.

Sometimes known by its alternate title, *The Strolling Astronomer,* this journal is a publication of the Association of Lunar and Planetary Observers (ALPO), and it is regularly mailed to members of this international organization of amateur and professional astronomers. Not an easy magazine to leaf through, it is definitely designed for the reader who really knows physics and astronomy. ALPO has many subdivisions, each with its own publication, and subscriptions to these other publications need to be handled directly with each division. The ALPO web site can help settle questions concerning which publications might be best for you. This specific journal is considered to be the means of coordinating all the various areas of ALPO research under a single cover. Reports and observations from readers and staff are always welcome for all publications, provided they have not been published elsewhere.

628. *The Astronomical Almanac.* Supersedes (1960-1981): *Astronomical Ephemeris;* (1852-1980): *American Ephemeris and Nautical Almanac;* (1766-1852): *Nautical Almanac and Astronomical Ephemeris.* [ISSN: 0737-6421] 1766. a. USD 55. U.S. Naval Observatory, c/o Dr D D McCarthy, Department of the Navy, Washington, DC 20392-5100; http://www.usno.navy.mil. *Aud.:* Hs, Ga, Ac, Sa.

The *Astronomical Almanac* contains precise ephemerides of the Sun, Moon, planets, and satellites, data for eclipses, and information on other astronomical phenomena for a given year. Most data are tabulated at one-day intervals. This journal includes geocentric positions of the Sun, Moon, planets, and bright stars; heliocentric positions of the planets and their orbital elements; universal and sidereal times; daily polynomials for the Moon's position; physical ephemerides of the Sun, Moon, and planets; elongation times and differential coordinates of selected satellites of the planets; rise, set, and transit times of the Sun and Moon; eclipse data and maps; tables of reference data for various celestial objects; useful formulas; and other information. Don't miss the "Explanatory Supplement" to this publication. The supplement is an authoritative source on astronomical phenomena and calendars, and offers detailed directions for performing practical astronomy. All in all, this is a very valuable, esteemed resource—generally given pride of place in any serious astronomy collection.

629. *The Astronomical Journal.* [ISSN: 0004-6256] 1849. m. USD 600 combined subscription print & online eds. Ed(s): John S. Gallagher, III. Institute of Physics Publishing, Inc, The Public Ledger Bldg, Ste 929, 150 S Independence Mall W, Philadelphia, PA 19106; info@ioppubusa.com; http://www.iop.org/. Illus., index. Refereed. Vol. ends: No. 6. Online: EBSCO Publishing, EBSCO Host. Reprint: PSC. *Indexed:* ApMecR, CPI, ChemAb, CompR, MathR, SCI. *Aud.:* Ac, Sa.

A vehicle for publishing original observations and research with a fairly short publication time, the journal publishes many seminal papers. Coverage includes the traditional areas of astronomy and expanded topics, including such topical areas as detection of new planets; large-scale structure of the universe; asteroids that are likely to strike the Earth; and every imaginable other topic pertaining to astronomy. This journal and *Astrophysical Journal* (below in this section) comprise the main U.S. publications of new research in the fields of astronomy and astrophysics, similar to the European *Astronomy and Astrophysics* (below in this section). Considered to be one of the five or six "core" journals in any serious astronomy collection, *AJ* is essential for any academic institute with an astronomy program and indispensable to serious astronomers.

630. Astronomy. [ISSN: 0091-6358] 1973. m. USD 42.95 domestic; USD 58 Canada. Ed(s): Dick McNally, David Eicher. Kalmbach Publishing Co., 21027 Crossroads Circle, PO Box 1612, Waukesha, WI 53187-1612; http://www.kalmbach.com. Illus., index, adv. Sample. Circ: 152821 Paid. Vol. ends: Dec. Online: EBSCO Publishing, EBSCO Host; Florida Center for Library Automation; Gale; Northern Light Technology, Inc.; OCLC Online Computer Library Center, Inc.; ProQuest K-12 Learning Solutions; ProQuest LLC (Ann Arbor); H.W. Wilson. *Indexed:* BRI, CBRI, CPerI, FLI, GSI, IHTDI, MASUSE, RGPR. *Bk. rev.:* 5-6, 50-500 words. *Aud.:* Hs, Ga, Ac.

As indicated by its circulation, this is one of the most popular astronomy publications among casual sky watchers. Insightful, well-written articles, aimed at a popular audience, are brought together here with some truly spectacular photographs of some of the most "stellar" sights in the heavens. *Astronomy* provides readers with news reports, hobby information, copious reviews of astronomy equipment, and the latest news on space exploration. A very helpful sky chart, as well as observing tips for locating specific objects in the sky, are to be found here in a visually appealing format that is both pleasant and stimulating to read. This would be a welcome addition to virtually any library.

631. Astronomy & Astrophysics: a European journal. Superseded in part (in 1968): *Zeitschrift fuer Astrophysik;* Incorporated (1947-1992): *Astronomical Institutes of Czechoslovakia. Bulletin;* (1966-2000): *Astronomy & Astrophysics. Supplement Series;* Which was formerly (until 1970): *Astronomical Institutes of the Netherlands. Bulletin. Supplement Series;* Which incorporated (1900-1960): *Kapteyn Astronomical Laboratory at Groningen. Publications;* Which was formerly (until 1924): *Astronomical Laboratory at Groningen. Publications.* [ISSN: 0004-6361] 1930. 48x/yr. EUR 3559 print & online eds. (Individuals, EUR 3486 print & online eds.). E D P Sciences, 17 Ave du Hoggar, Parc d'Activites de Courtaboeuf, BP 112, Les Ulis, F-91944, France; subscribers@edpsciences.org; http://www.edpsciences.org. Illus., index, adv. Sample. Refereed. Vol. ends: No. 3. Microform: PQC. Online: EBSCO Publishing, EBSCO Host; SwetsWise Online Content. *Indexed:* ApMecR, C&ISA, CerAb, ChemAb, EngInd, IAA, M&GPA, MathR, SCI. *Aud.:* Ac, Sa.

Sponsored by the European Southern Observatory, this publication represents scientific organizations in 17 European countries. The journal is a cooperative effort that grew out of the merger of the publications of several of the represented organizations. It once had a supplement, published separately, but today the main journal and the supplement are published under a single cover. Papers present all aspects of astronomy and astrophysics, regardless of the techniques used to obtain the results. Some items that will *not* be found in this journal include observatory reports, review papers, and conference proceedings. Especially since the merging of this title with its supplement, coverage includes all areas of astronomy and astrophysics, including connected fields. Therefore, for example, this journal might include articles on such subjects as computational techniques that might have applications in astronomy, atomic or molecular physics, or even statistical mathematics. The journal intends to review all important fields relevant to the study of astronomy and astrophysics from time to time, while frequency of review is dictated by the amount of activity in an area. This research publication is comparable to *The Astronomical Journal* and *The Astrophysical Journal*.

632. Astronomy & Geophysics. Formerly (until 1997): *Royal Astronomical Society. Quarterly Journal.* [ISSN: 1366-8781] 1960. bi-m. GBP 208 print & online eds. Ed(s): Sue Bowler. Blackwell Publishing Ltd., 9600 Garsington Rd, Oxford, OX4 2ZG, United Kingdom; customerservices@ blackwellpublishing.com; http://www.blackwellpublishing.com. Illus., index, adv. Sample. Refereed. Circ: 3700. Vol. ends: No. 6. Microform:

PQC. Online: Blackwell Synergy; EBSCO Publishing, EBSCO Host; Gale; IngentaConnect; OCLC Online Computer Library Center, Inc.; OhioLINK; SwetsWise Online Content. Reprint: PSC. *Indexed:* ChemAb, M&GPA, MathR, SCI. *Bk. rev.:* Number and length vary. *Aud.:* Ac, Sa.

After a redesign in 1996, *Astronomy & Geophysics* replaced the *Quarterly Journal of the Royal Astronomical Society* as its topical publication. One objective of the journal is to promote communication among general astronomers and planetary scientists. Therefore, it often has exceptionally strong coverage of planetary sciences, yet it also has excellent coverage of cosmology, black holes, astrophotography, etc. Articles are written in accessible language, without many equations or formulae, and include related topics such as interdisciplinary research, information about upcoming international conferences, science policy, social issues within the astronomical community, news, and book and software reviews. Many of the traditions from the *Quarterly Journal* remain, such as the journal being a forum for discussion of fundamental and controversial scientific issues.

633. Astronomy Education Review: a lively electronic compendium of research, news, resources and opinion. [ISSN: 1539-1515] 2002. q. Free. Ed(s): Sydney C Wolff, Andrew Fraknoi. National Optical Astronomy Observatory, 950 N Cherry Ave, Tucson, AZ 85719; aer@noao.edu. *Indexed:* EduInd. *Bk. rev.:* Number and length vary. *Aud.:* Hs, Ac.

An innovative new online journal, this unassuming little venture can really be of great assistance to astronomy educators. The mission of this journal is shaped as much by the philosophy of education as it is by the spirit of astronomy. Subscribers will find articles on applying educational methodologies to astronomy; pointers on salient educational journals of which the educator may have been unaware; and postings concerning symposia, workshops, funding sources, and job openings. There are also book reviews and the opportunity to participate in online discussions on issues pertaining to astronomical education.

634. Astronomy Reports. Former titles (until 1993): *Soviet Astronomy;* (until 1974): *Soviet Astronomy A.J.* [ISSN: 1063-7729] 1924. m. EUR 2688 print & online eds. Ed(s): Alexander A Boyarchuk. M A I K Nauka - Interperiodica, Profsoyuznaya ul 90, Moscow, 117997, Russian Federation; compmg@maik.ru; http://www.maik.ru. Illus., index. Sample. Refereed. Vol. ends: No. 6. Online: American Institute of Physics, Scitation; EBSCO Publishing, EBSCO Host; IngentaConnect; OhioLINK; Springer LINK; SwetsWise Online Content. *Indexed:* CPI, IAA, MathR, SCI. *Bk. rev.:* Number and length vary. *Aud.:* Ac, Sa.

Astronomy Reports is a cover-to-cover translation of the principal Russian astronomy journal, *Astronomicheskii Zhurnal*, and is available simultaneously with the Russian edition from Maik Nauka/Interperiodica Publishing. Russia has a long and proud tradition of producing great astrophysicists, and a lot of cutting-edge science is first reported in the Russian journals. This journal is displayed prominently at any serious astronomy library. Issues consist of about 10–20 articles in many areas of astronomy, including radio astronomy, physics of the sun, planetary science, and issues having to do with cosmological large-scale structure. Proceedings of international conferences and book reviews are also included.

635. The Astrophysical Journal: an international review of astronomy and astronomical physics. [ISSN: 0004-637X] 1895. 36x/yr. USD 2050 combined subscription domestic print & online eds.; USD 2313 combined subscription Canada print & online eds.; USD 2190 combined subscription Mexico print & online eds. Ed(s): Ethan T. Vishniac. University of Chicago Press, Journals Division, PO Box 37005, Chicago, IL 60637; subscriptions@press.uchicago.edu; http://www.press.uchicago.edu/. Illus., index. Refereed. Circ: 2900 Paid. Microform: PMC; PQC. Online: EBSCO Publishing, EBSCO Host. Reprint: PSC. *Indexed:* ChemAb, M&GPA, MathR, SCI. *Aud.:* Ac, Sa.

Many astronomy and astrophysics discoveries of the twentieth century were first reported in this peer-reviewed official publication of the American Astronomical Society. Any major astronomy library considers this to be part of its "core" collection. The astrophysics presented here is as esoteric as it ever gets, with many equations and graphs in every article. A supplement series accompanies it, its main purpose being to present substantial and extensive support for material found in the main journal. Access to a full-text electronic version is free with a paid print subscription.

636. *Astrophysics.* [ISSN: 0571-7256] 1965. q. EUR 2714 print & online eds. Ed(s): D M Sedrakyan. Consultants Bureau, 233 Spring St, New York, NY 10013; service@springer-ny.com; http://www.springeronline.com. Illus., index, adv. Sample. Refereed. Vol. ends: No. 4. Microform: PQC. Online: EBSCO Publishing, EBSCO Host; Gale; IngentaConnect; OCLC Online Computer Library Center, Inc.; OhioLINK; Springer LINK; SwetsWise Online Content. Reprint: PSC. *Indexed:* ApMecR, C&ISA, CerAb, ChemAb, IAA, M&GPA, MathR, SCI. *Aud.:* Ac, Sa.

Data obtained at all principal observatories in Russia, along with recent theoretical and experimental advances in astrophysics, are published in this journal. Fortunately for those of us who do not read Russian, much of the scientific literature from this part of the world is translated into English in a timely fashion. Like *Astronomy Reports,* this is full of cutting-edge Russian science and is geared toward a higher-level audience. It contains data obtained at the Sternberg Astronomical Institute and all principal Russian observatories—data that deals with the entire range of astronomical and astrophysical phenomena. The Consultants Bureau, a subsidiary of Plenum Publishing, is responsible for publishing dozens of English translations of Russian journals, including *Astrophysics,* which is a cover-to-cover translation of *Astrofizika.* Topics of papers include planetary atmospheres, interstellar matter, solar physics, and space astrophysics, along with a broad range of related topics.

637. *Astrophysics and Space Science: an international journal of astronomy, astrophysics and space science.* Incorporates (1970-1972): *Cosmic Electrodynamics;* (1975-1981): *Space Science Instrumentation.* [ISSN: 0004-640X] 1968. s-m. EUR 3859 print & online eds. Ed(s): Willem Wamsteker, John E Dyson. Springer Netherlands, Van Godewijckstraat 30, Dordrecht, 3311 GX, Netherlands; http://www.springeronline.com. Illus., index, adv. Sample. Refereed. Vol. ends: No. 2. Microform: PQC. Online: EBSCO Publishing, EBSCO Host; Gale; IngentaConnect; OCLC Online Computer Library Center, Inc.; OhioLINK; Springer LINK; SwetsWise Online Content. Reprint: PSC. *Indexed:* C&ISA, CCMJ, CerAb, ChemAb, IAA, M&GPA, MathR, SCI. *Aud.:* Ac, Sa.

This journal publishes original contributions, invited reviews, and conference proceedings over the entire range of astronomy and astrophysics. It includes observational and theoretical papers as well as those concerned with the techniques of instrumentation. Observational papers can include data from ground-based, space, and atmospheric facilities. *Astrophysics and Space Science* has published, and continues to publish, landmark papers in its field. It is widely considered an indispensable source of information for professional astronomers, astrophysicists, and space scientists. The supplemental publication *Experimental Astronomy* (below in this section) is included with the subscription at no extra cost.

638. *Astrophysics and Space Sciences Transactions (Online).* [ISSN: 1810-6536] 2004. irreg. Free. Copernicus GmbH, Max-Planck Str 13, Katlenburg-Lindau, 37191, Germany; info@copernicus.org; http://www.copernicus.org. *Aud.:* Ac.

ASTRA is a wide-ranging, international scientific publication, dealing with all areas of astronomy. Papers dealing with the technology and instrumentation accompanying various areas of inquiry are also included. A (free) article alert system is included, for enthusiasts with a particular research interest. Articles are double-blind peer-reviewed. Although the journal is published in Germany, articles are in English. Back issues of articles are available in print, if so desired.

639. *Astrum.* [ISSN: 0210-4105] 1960. bi-m. Membership, EUR 78. Agrupacio Astronomica de Sabadell, Apdo de Correos 50, Sabadell, 08200, Spain; secretaria@astrosabadell.org; http://www.astrosabadell.org. Illus., adv. Circ: 2000. *Aud.:* Hs, Ga.

Astrum is a colorful astronomy magazine in Spanish, aimed at a popular audience. Bowker chose this year to survey some astronomy periodicals in Spanish, so that librarians serving constituencies with a growing Spanish-speaking population can accommodate the needs of those patrons. *Astrum* serves this role quite well. It is not a commercial magazine—it is mailed free to members of the Agrupacio Astronomica de Sabadell, and to astronomical centers and libraries. However, if your library seeks to foster an interest in science in Hispanic children, you might consider e-mailing the publishing part of the Agrupacio. *Astrum* includes articles, sky charts, ephemerides, and even surveys of Spanish-language Internet resources having to do with astronomy. Furthermore, it is full of very colorful, high-resolution photographs of many of the more beautiful areas in the sky.

640. *British Astronomical Association. Journal.* [ISSN: 0007-0297] 1890. bi-m. GBP 35.10. Ed(s): H McGee. British Astronomical Association, Burlington House, Piccadilly, London, W1J 0DU, United Kingdom; 100257.735@compuserve.com; http://www.britastro.org. Illus., index, adv. Sample. Refereed. Circ: 3500. Vol. ends: No. 6. *Bk. rev.:* 6-20, 500-1,000 words. *Aud.:* Ac, Sa.

Since its founding in 1890, this journal has published the observations and work of British Astronomical Association (BAA) members, and members receive the journal free. However, nonmembers are eligible to receive the journal if they contact the publisher. Many articles and items of interest to all amateur astronomers are published, along with the observations and work of BAA members. The letters to the editor are often lively, with discussions on any subject having to do with astronomy, especially at the amateur level. Subscribers are offered special deals on astronomy-related products from time to time, such as CD-ROMs or software. Although this publication is geared to amateur astronomers and professionals who focus on observational techniques, it does not include the star charts and viewing guides that are published by equivalent American publications, such as *Astronomy* and *Sky & Telescope.*

641. *Celestial Mechanics and Dynamical Astronomy: an international journal of space dynamics.* Formerly: *Celestial Mechanics.* [ISSN: 0923-2958] 1969. m. EUR 2073 print & online eds. Ed(s): Sylvio Ferraz-Mello. Springer Netherlands, Van Godewijckstraat 30, Dordrecht, 3311 GX, Netherlands; http://www.springeronline.com. Illus., index, adv. Sample. Refereed. Vol. ends: No. 4. Microform: PQC. Online: EBSCO Publishing, EBSCO Host; Gale; IngentaConnect; OCLC Online Computer Library Center, Inc.; OhioLINK; Springer LINK; SwetsWise Online Content. Reprint: PSC. *Indexed:* ApMecR, C&ISA, CCMJ, CerAb, IAA, M&GPA, MSN, MathR, SCI. *Aud.:* Ac, Sa.

This international publication is concerned with the broadest range of dynamical astronomy and its applications, as well as with peripheral fields. It is heavily math- and physics-oriented, which can make reading difficult for those not well versed in these fields. Articles cover all aspects of celestial mechanics: mathematical, physics-related, and computational, including computer languages for analytical developments. The majority of the articles are in English. This noteworthy publication is considered in the astronomical community to be the journal of record in its area, and it belongs in any complete astronomical library. URL: http://www.springerlink.com/content/1572-9478/

642. *Earth, Moon, and Planets: an international journal of comparative planetology.* Former titles: *Moon and the Planets; Moon.* [ISSN: 0167-9295] 1969. 8x/yr. EUR 1069 print & online eds. Ed(s): Giovanni B Valsecchi, Mark E Bailey. Springer Netherlands, Van Godewijckstraat 30, Dordrecht, 3311 GX, Netherlands; http://www.springeronline.com. Illus., index, adv. Sample. Refereed. Vol. ends: Dec. Microform: PQC. Online: EBSCO Publishing, EBSCO Host; Gale; IngentaConnect; OCLC Online Computer Library Center, Inc.; OhioLINK; Ovid Technologies, Inc.; Springer LINK; SwetsWise Online Content. Reprint: PSC. *Indexed:* C&ISA, CerAb, ChemAb, IAA, M&GPA, SCI. *Bk. rev.:* Number and length vary. *Aud.:* Ac, Sa.

Earth, Moon, and Planets, an international journal of solar system science, publishes original contributions on subjects ranging from star and planet formation and the origin and evolution of the solar and extra-solar planetary systems, to asteroids, comets, meteoroids, and near-Earth objects. The research done in this journal on near-Earth objects (NEOs) includes studies on asteroids that are considered likely candidates to one day strike Earth. The journal also publishes relevant special issues and topical conference proceedings, review articles on problems of current interest, and book reviews. The editor welcomes proposals from guest editors for special thematic issues.

643. *Experimental Astronomy: an international journal on astronomical instrumentation and data analysis.* [ISSN: 0922-6435] 1989. bi-m. EUR 693 print & online eds. Ed(s): A Boksenberg. Springer Netherlands, Van Godewijckstraat 30, Dordrecht, 3311 GX, Netherlands; http://www.springeronline.com. Illus. Sample. Refereed. Vol. ends: No. 4. Microform: PQC. Online: EBSCO Publishing, EBSCO Host; Gale; IngentaConnect; OCLC Online Computer Library Center, Inc.; OhioLINK; Springer LINK; SwetsWise Online Content. Reprint: PSC. *Indexed:* C&ISA, CerAb, IAA, M&GPA, SCI. *Aud.:* Ac, Sa.

Experimental Astronomy acts as a medium for the publication of papers on the instrumentation and data handling necessary for the conduct of astronomy at all wavelength fields. *Experimental Astronomy* publishes full-length articles, research letters, and reviews on developments in detection techniques, instruments, and data analysis and image-processing techniques. Occasionally, special issues are published to provide in-depth coverage on the instrumentation or analysis connected with a particular project, such as satellite experiments. Subscribers to *Astrophysics and Space Science* (above in this section) receive this publication as a supplement, but it can also be purchased alone.

644. *Griffith Observer.* [ISSN: 0195-3982] 1937. m. USD 23 domestic; USD 30 Canada; USD 35 Mexico. Ed(s): E C Krupp. Griffith Observatory, 2800 E Observatory Rd, Los Angeles, CA 90027; info@GriffithObs.org; http://www.griffithobs.org/Observer.html. Illus., index. Sample. Circ: 5000 Paid. Vol. ends: Dec. *Aud.:* Hs, Ga.

Published monthly by the observatory, this journal provides information about the activities at the Griffith Observatory as well as popular articles about astronomy. This journal is comparable in aims and scope to the Spanish-language journal *Astrum*. Sky charts, illustrations, guides to useful Internet links, and photographs enhance this publication, which strives to create a lifelong interest in science in its readers. For its efforts at popularizing astronomy, the *Griffith Observer* has been characterized as "the Carl Sagan of astronomy periodicals."

645. *Icarus.* [ISSN: 0019-1035] 1962. 12x/yr. EUR 4759. Ed(s): P. D. Nicholson. Academic Press, 525 B St, Ste 1900, San Diego, CA 92101-4495; apsubs@acad.com; http://www.elsevier.com/. Illus., index, adv. Refereed. Vol. ends: No. 2. Online: EBSCO Publishing, EBSCO Host; Gale; IngentaConnect; OCLC Online Computer Library Center, Inc.; OhioLINK; ScienceDirect; SwetsWise Online Content. *Indexed:* C&ISA, CerAb, ChemAb, GSI, IAA, M&GPA, SCI. *Bk. rev.:* 2-3, 150-2,000 words. *Aud.:* Ac, Sa.

Devoted to publishing original contributions in planetary science and the science of solar systems, this is another very prominent journal for academic libraries. Librarians should note that these fields are focused primarily on relatively local astronomy. Articles are generally about planets, moons, the Sun, or asteroids within our solar system. Coverage of cosmology, black holes, quasars, or theoretical physics is very rarely included. The main exception to this general rule is the appearance of articles concerning extrasolar planets, that is, planets revolving around stars other than the Sun. This field is quite new, but it is increasingly important. All aspects of planetary system research are included, such as results of new research and observations. Special sections or issues are also a feature. All articles appear in English, but occasional abstracts are in German, French, or Russian.

646. *International Astronomical Union. Minor Planet Center. Minor Planet Circulars - Minor Planets and Comets.* Former titles (until 1978): *Cincinnati Observatory. Minor Planet Circulars; Smithsonian Institution. Astrophysical Observatory. Minor Planet Circulars - Minor Planets and Comets.* [ISSN: 0736-6884] 1947. irreg. approx. m. Ed(s): Brian G Marsden. Smithsonian Institution Astrophysical Observatory, 60 Garden St, Cambridge, MA 02138; iausubs@cfa.harvard.edu; http://cfa-www.harvard.edu/cfa/ps/services/MPC.html. Illus. Circ: 250. *Aud.:* Ac, Sa.

Generally published on the date of the full moon (hence, the approximately monthly frequency), *Minor Planet Circulars* are available in both print and electronically as the *Minor Planets Electronic Circulars.* Astrometric observations on comets and minor planets are included, although some information is summarized in observatory code. For those who may not be aware of this, "minor planets" is another accepted term for "asteroids." These circulars are published by the agency in charge of keeping an eye out for asteroids that may one day strike Earth. The circulars were once sent out as telegrams, and retain the pithiness of the telegram. No space is wasted, and there is seldom anything resembling actual articles. New numberings and namings of asteroids/minor planets are also announced in the *Circulars.*

647. *International Comet Quarterly.* [ISSN: 0736-6922] 1979. q. plus a. handbook. USD 31 domestic; USD 46 foreign. Ed(s): Daniel W.E. Green. International Comet Quarterly, Smithsonian Astrophysical Observatory, M S 18, 60 Garden St, Cambridge, MA 02138; icq@cfa.harvard.edu; http://cfa-www.harvard.edu/cfa/ps/icq.html. Illus., index, adv. Refereed. Circ: 500. Vol. ends: No. 4. *Aud.:* Ac, Sa.

The *International Comet Quarterly* (*ICQ*) is the primary location for information about comets and observing comets, and it serves as a link between professional and serious amateur astronomers. Observations, discoveries, and research related to comets can be found in this publication. Also published are announcements concerning international conferences that have to do with the extremely important work of detecting comets and asteroids that are likely to someday strike Earth. The annual subscription cost includes a copy of the annual *Comet Handbook,* which contains ephemerides and orbital elements for comets observable in the coming year. This journal is not geared to a general readership; only professionals and serious amateurs who focus on comets will need this publication for their research.

648. *International Journal of Astrobiology.* [ISSN: 1473-5504] 2002. q. GBP 200. Ed(s): Simon Mitton. Cambridge University Press, The Edinburgh Bldg, Shaftesbury Rd, Cambridge, CB2 2RU, United Kingdom; journals@cambridge.org; http://www.cup.cam.ac.uk/. Online: Pub.; EBSCO Publishing, EBSCO Host; OCLC Online Computer Library Center, Inc.; OhioLINK; SwetsWise Online Content. Reprint: PSC. *Indexed:* M&GPA. *Bk. rev.:* Number and length vary. *Aud.:* Ga, Ac, Sa.

A new publication, this fascinating journal provides an introduction to the burgeoning world of "astrobiology." This topic includes not only the search for extraterrestrial life, but also related inquiries into such issues as adaptations made by lifeforms to extreme environments on Earth. The journal includes peer-reviewed research papers, book reviews, and overviews of this fast-evolving discipline. This journal is intended primarily as a forum for biochemists, astronomers, and other professionals in allied fields, but the inherently fascinating nature of the topic could make some readers choose to put in the extra effort required to wade through an issue.

649. *Journal for the History of Astronomy.* Incorporates (1979-2002): *Archaeoastronomy.* [ISSN: 0021-8286] 1970. 4x/yr. USD 240 in the Americas & Japan. Ed(s): M A Hoskin. Science History Publications Ltd., 16 Rutherford Rd, Cambridge, CB2 2HH, United Kingdom; http://www.shpltd.co.uk. Illus., index. Sample. Refereed. Circ: 650. Vol. ends: No. 4. *Indexed:* AICP, AbAn, AmH&L, ArtHuCI, BrArAb, CCMJ, FR, GSI, HistAb, IBR, IBZ, IndIslam, MathR, NumL, PhilInd, SCI. *Bk. rev.:* 6-16, 300-1,000 words. *Aud.:* Ac, Sa.

The only journal of its type, this covers the history of astronomy from its earliest times. The research presented is a pleasant, fascinating change of pace from the heavily math- and science-oriented publications so common (and so important) in astronomy. Few journals capture more successfully the spirit of astronomy, in the sense of the important role it has played throughout the historical struggle between reason and superstition. This journal's subject matter is not rigidly restricted to the history of astronomy per se. For example, sometimes intellectual forays are made into relevant topics in the study of the history of mathematics or physics. A supplemental publication, *Archaeoastronomy,* is included with a subscription. This supplement is dedicated to investigating astronomical practice and celestial lore in ancient societies from all over the world. Sample articles might include, for example, discussion of ancient Mayan, Inca, Greek, or Egyptian astronomical traditions and edifices, by experts who are learned in the field.

650. *Journal of Cosmology and Astroparticle Physics.* [ISSN: 1475-7516] 2003. irreg. USD 1245. Institute of Physics Publishing, Dirac House, Temple Back, Bristol, BS1 6BE, United Kingdom; custserv@iop.org; http://www.iop.org. Refereed. *Indexed:* CCMJ, MSN, MathR, SCI. *Aud.:* Ac, Sa.

A new journal, *JCAP* is an ambitious, selective online periodical focusing on the interrelationships beween the smallest subatomic particles and the nature of the universe "in the large." Common topics include string theory, gravitational waves, black holes, large-scale structure of the universe, and other cosmological issues. Criteria for article acceptance are "scientific quality, originality and relevance." This journal is probably too advanced for most amateur hobbyists, but it has been placed on many "core" reading lists for academic science libraries, even in these financially strapped times. URL: http://www.iop.org/EJ/journal/JCAP

651. *Living Reviews in Solar Physics.* [ISSN: 1614-4961] 2004. irreg. Free. Ed(s): S K Solanki. Max-Planck-Institut fuer Sonnensystemforschung, Max-Planck-Str 2, Katlenburg-Lindau, 37191, Germany; presseinfo@mps.mpg.de; http://www.mps.mpg.de. Refereed. *Aud.:* Ac, Sa.

This is a peer-reviewed, online forum for cutting-edge research and discussion of solar and heliospheric physics. The word "living" is built into this journal's title because authors keep their articles "alive" by means of frequent online updates. *Living Reviews* also wishes to be known for its up-to-date, critical reviews of the particular subfield of solar research covered by a given article. Bibliographic subject guides, to assist in further research, are always appended. These guides are updated often by the authors, and include links to helpful web sites. This journal aims to become an online starting point for graduate students; and for professionals in the field, it aims to open the most significant doors of online research as they emerge. URL: http://solarphysics.livingreviews.org/

652. *Lunar and Planetary Information Bulletin.* [ISSN: 1534-6587] 1970. q. Free. Ed(s): D Brian Anderson. Lunar and Planetary Institute, 3600 Bay Area Blvd, Houston, TX 77058-1113; http://www.lpi.usra.edu. Illus. Circ: 5500. *Indexed:* IAA. *Bk. rev.:* Number and length vary. *Aud.:* Ac, Ga.

Here is a real treat for the layperson who has the background and command of vocabulary. This publication covers astronomical topics that are likely to be of interest to the average, involved reader, such as potential fossils on Mars, or the adaptation of hydroponic plant cultures to possible long-term space missions for life-support purposes. There is a "New in Print" section that takes the reader on a tour of recently published books in the field. Often, one of these titles is singled out for an in-depth review, which sometimes includes an interview with the author. Also, the "News from Space" section is excellent, containing six or seven short articles about exciting goings-on in astronomy. Intelligent, well-written discussions can be found dealing with such questions as the origin of the solar system or of the asteroid belt. An objective and scientific approach, written in a delightfully accessible style. URL: http://www.lpi.usra.edu/publications/newsletters/lpib/

653. *Mercury (San Francisco).* [ISSN: 0047-6773] 1972. bi-m. USD 48. Ed(s): James White. Astronomical Society of the Pacific, 390 Ashton Ave, San Francisco, CA 94112; editor@astrosociety.org; http://www.astrosociety.org. Illus., index, adv. Sample. Circ: 7000. Vol. ends: No. 6. Online: EBSCO Publishing, EBSCO Host; Florida Center for Library Automation; OCLC Online Computer Library Center, Inc.; H.W. Wilson. *Indexed:* GSI, MASUSE. *Bk. rev.:* 2-6, 50-200 words. *Aud.:* Hs, Ga, Sa.

The purpose of *Mercury* is to provide the necessary perspective for understanding astronomy. This nonspecialist magazine features articles on topics ranging from astronomy research and education to archaeoastronomy, history, and public policy. It is the most widely read publication of the Astronomical Society of the Pacific (ASP), a nonprofit organization whose goal is to promote public interest and awareness of astronomy through education and outreach programs. As the membership magazine of the ASP, it has made a name for itself as *the* resource for teachers to follow innovations in astronomy education. Frequently there are articles dealing with the role of education in science, and the role of

science in society. The magazine includes sky calendars and sky maps for use in the Northern Hemisphere. Book reviews are included, as are regular sections on current observing prospects, "armchair astrophysics," and news highlights from the world of astronomy.

654. *The Messenger.* [ISSN: 0722-6691] 1974. q. Free. Ed(s): M H Ulrich. European Southern Observatory, Karl Schwarzschild Str 2, Garching, 85748, Germany; ips@eso.org; http://www.eso.org. Illus., index. Sample. Vol. ends: Dec. *Aud.:* Ac, Sa.

Published by the European Southern Observatory (ESO) in La Silla, Chile, this magazine presents the activities of the ESO to the public. It is roughly comparable to the *Griffith Observer*, in that it acts as a window into the activities of a major observatory, but it adds an international flavor. The primary significance of this journal is that it emphasizes the astronomy of the Southern Hemisphere, which is often given short shrift in many astronomy journals. As the audience codes indicate, many of the articles are quite high-level, full of equations, graphs, etc. However, the photographs of the ESO staff happily toiling away at their astro-projects make the reader feel like a guest in the home of an interesting extended family. The ESO observatory is supported by eight countries—Belgium, Denmark, France, Germany, Italy, Sweden, Switzerland, and the Netherlands—and it receives 800 proposals a year for research that would require use of the facility.

655. *Meteorite!* [ISSN: 1173-2245] 1995. q. USD 35. Ed(s): Larry Lebovski, Nancy Lebovski. University of Arkansas, Center for Space and Planetary Sciences, 202 Old Museum Bldg, Fayetteville, AR 72701; metpub@uark.edu; http://meteoritemag.uark.edu/index.htm. *Aud.:* Ga, Ac, Sa.

Some past articles from this publication are available at the publisher's web site, but the only way to get the full articles and the photos is to subscribe. It is a forum for publishing information and research on collecting, new falls and finds, asteroids, craters, and historical meteorite events. Of the several journals described in this section that focus on meteors, this is perhaps the best suited for the amateur enthusiast.

656. *Meteoritics and Planetary Science.* Formerly (until 1996): *Meteoritics.* [ISSN: 1086-9379] 1953. m. USD 900 Free to members. Ed(s): Dr. A J Timothy Jull. Meteoritical Society, Dept. of Geosciences, University of Arizona, Tucson, AZ 85712-1201; meteor@uark.edu; http://www.meteorite.ch/metsoc2.htm. Illus., index, adv. Sample. Refereed. Circ: 1200 Paid. Vol. ends: No. 6. Microform: PQC. Online: EBSCO Publishing, EBSCO Host; Gale; IngentaConnect. *Indexed:* ChemAb, IAA, MinerAb, SCI. *Aud.:* Ac, Sa.

This scholarly journal is published by the Meteoritical Society, an international organization that studies the smallest bodies in the solar system. It is free to society members. It provides a forum for discussing the study of extraterrestrial matter and history, including asteroids, impact craters, and interplanetary dust—uniting professionals from a variety of backgrounds, including geology, physics, astronomy, and chemistry. Of the several journals dealing with meteors and asteroids, this is the one that deals most directly with what we can *learn* from meteors, especially about the origins of our solar system. This journal is different from, for example, the *Minor Planet Circulars*, in that it includes articles as well as raw data.

657. *New Astronomy.* [ISSN: 1384-1076] 1996. 8x/yr. EUR 702. Ed(s): W. D. Cochran. Elsevier BV, North-Holland, Sara Burgerhartstraat 25, Amsterdam, 1055 KV, Netherlands; nlinfo-f@elsevier.nl; http://www.elsevier.nl. Illus. Sample. Refereed. Vol. ends: No. 8. Online: EBSCO Publishing, EBSCO Host; Gale; IngentaConnect; OhioLINK; ScienceDirect; SwetsWise Online Content. *Indexed:* C&ISA, CerAb, EngInd, IAA, SCI. *Aud.:* Ac, Sa.

An institutional subscription provides web access for everyone at a subscribing institute, an archival paper edition, and an electronic copy for LAN distribution. Slightly lower prices for smaller institutions and for individuals are available upon request, and a two-month free trial is available for individuals. This journal includes full-length research articles and letter articles. It aims to have a very short publication time, which keeps it very close to the cutting edge of astronomy. It prides itself on sending personal e-mails to astronomers about upcoming articles in their specialties. It covers solar, planetary, stellar, galactic, and extragalactic astronomy and astrophysics, and reports on original research in all wavelength bands, ranging from radio to gamma-ray. Topics include all fields of astronomy and astrophysics: theoretical, observational, and instrumental. URL: http://www.elsevier.com/locate/newast

658. *New Astronomy Reviews.* Formerly: *Vistas in Astronomy;* Incorporates (1977-1991): *Astronomy Quarterly.* [ISSN: 1387-6473] 1958. 12x/yr. EUR 1027. Ed(s): J. Audouze. Elsevier BV, North-Holland, Sara Burgerhartstraat 25, Amsterdam, 1055 KV, Netherlands; nlinfo-f@elsevier.nl; http://www.elsevier.nl. Illus., index, adv. Sample. Refereed. Vol. ends: No. 45. Microform: PQC. Online: EBSCO Publishing, EBSCO Host; Gale; IngentaConnect; OhioLINK; ScienceDirect; SwetsWise Online Content. *Indexed:* BAS, ChemAb, IAA, MathR, SCI. *Aud.:* Ac, Sa.

Although the name of this journal has changed, there has been no significant content change. The journal still includes historical perspectives and in-depth reports, review articles, and surveys of findings on major activities in astronomical research. Contributions include reprints in specific areas and in-depth review articles surveying major areas of astronomy. The journal covers solar, planetary, stellar, galactic, and extragalactic astronomy and astrophysics. It reports on original research in all wavelength bands, ranging from radio to gamma-ray. This journal might be seen as taking the broad-based coverage of *Mercury* to a higher level, for reading by professional scientists. Written for astronomers, astrophysicists, and space scientists.

659. *Night Sky.* [ISSN: 1546-9743] 2004. bi-m. USD 17.99 domestic; USD 24.99 Canada; USD 29.99 elsewhere. Sky Publishing Corp., 90 Sherman St., Cambridge, MA 02140. Illus., adv. Circ: 50000. *Aud.:* Hs, Ga.

Designed to introduce novice stargazers to the wonder of the heavens, this new journal has already garnered wide praise from readers. Published by the folks who brought us the esteemed *Sky and Telescope,* this journal also seeks to introduce backyard astronomers to the *fun* that astronomy can be. Without being condescending, this publication elucidates the basics, such as buying one's first telescope, getting it to work, and providing a straightforward guide to some of the most popular regions of the skies for viewing. Equipped with this information, it is hoped a novice astronomer will get a lot more out of this pursuit.

660. *North American Skies.* 1996. m. Ed(s): Larry Sessions. Final Copy, 6874 E Harvard Ave., Denver, CO 80224; starman@usa.net; http://webcom.com/safezone/NAS/. *Aud.:* Ems, Hs, Ga.

This is a layperson's guide to the stars and planets, suitable for both young people and adults. *North American Skies* provides information on stars, planets, eclipses, meteor showers, and other events visible in the sky. Times are given for the Mountain Time Zone, and some information, such as the Sun and moon rise-and-set tables, is specific to Denver. However, most information is applicable throughout North America, given the appropriate time-zone change. Each issue provides a feature article (with past articles also available online) and a sky chart and instructions for its use. Another regular feature is a monthly sky calendar that lists only events that can be seen in North America with the unaided eye. Other helpful features include links about sighting satellites or shuttlecraft, telescope-related questions, and forms to facilitate reporting meteor sightings.

661. *The Observatory: a review of astronomy.* [ISSN: 0029-7704] 1877. bi-m. GBP 48 GBP 10 newsstand/cover per issue. Observatory, c/o Dr. D.J. Stickland, Ed, Space and Astrophysics Div., Rutherford Appleton Laboratory, Didcot, OX11 0QX, United Kingdom. Illus., index, adv. Refereed. Circ: 1000 Paid. Vol. ends: No. 6. *Indexed:* ChemAb, MathR, SCI. *Aud.:* Ga.

This journal is sent free to members of the Royal Astronomical Society (RAS), and it is owned and managed by the editors. Meetings of the RAS are reported, but information does not generally overlap with what appears in the official RAS publications *Monthly Notices* and *Astronomy and Geophysics*. Those two are considered the most important publications of this society, while *The Observatory* is more of a supplement. Papers and correspondence tend to be short but scholarly, with few illustrations.

Odyssey. See Children section.

662. *Planetarian.* [ISSN: 0090-3213] 1972. q. USD 36. Ed(s): John E Mosley. International Planetarium Society, Griffith Observatory, 2800 E Observatory Rd, Los Angeles, CA 90027; jmosley@griffithObs.org; http://www.griffithobs.org/IPSPlanetarian.html. Illus., index, adv. Circ: 750. Vol. ends: No. 4. Microform: PQC. *Aud.:* Hs, Ac, Sa.

Planetarian is free with membership in the International Planetarium Society, but there is also the option for libraries to purchase the journal separately. The majority of the publication is devoted to astronomy education, with special emphasis on the role planetariums can play. For example, an article may discuss the value of planetariums as teaching aids to help students develop a three-dimensional vision of the structure of our galaxy. Another topic is planetariums acting as aids in helping students visualize actual or potential space voyages. This is a fairly specialized journal, but certainly a very interesting and very readable one. It includes much information of interest to astronomers, academic libraries, school libraries, and science teachers.

663. *Planetary and Space Science.* [ISSN: 0032-0633] 1959. 15x/yr. EUR 3359. Ed(s): T. Encrenaz. Pergamon, The Boulevard, Langford Ln, East Park, Kidlington, OX5 1GB, United Kingdom. Illus., index, adv. Sample. Refereed. Circ: 1250. Vol. ends: No. 12. Microform: PQC. Online: EBSCO Publishing, EBSCO Host; Gale; IngentaConnect; OhioLINK; ScienceDirect; SwetsWise Online Content. *Indexed:* ApMecR, C&ISA, CerAb, ChemAb, EngInd, ExcerpMed, IAA, M&GPA, SCI, SSCI. *Aud.:* Ac, Sa.

Significant reorganization during 1998 changed some aspects of this official journal of the European Geophysical Society, Planetary and Solar Systems Sciences Section. While this journal still focuses primarily upon coverage of planetary and solar system research, its scope has broadened to include extra-solar systems and astrobiology, comprehensive review articles, and meetings papers. Articles still tend to be focused upon planetary systems—but with recent advances in astronomy, some of the planets studied lie outside of our solar system. Ground-based and space-borne instrumentation and laboratory simulation of solar system processes are included. This journal has a fairly similar mission and audience to *Icarus,* and libraries may want to compare these two excellent journals to consider which best meets their needs. The intended audience includes professional astronomers, astrophysicists, atmospheric physicists, geologists, and planetologists.

664. *Popular Astronomy.* Formerly: *Hermes.* [ISSN: 0261-0892] 1953. q. GBP 12; GBP 16 in Europe; GBP 20 elsewhere. Society for Popular Astronomy, c/o Tom Hosking, Ed, 6 Queensberry Pl, Richmond, TW9 1NW, United Kingdom. Illus., adv. Circ: Controlled. *Aud.:* Hs, Ga, Ac.

This highly readable publication covers all aspects of astronomy. Each issue is packed with articles and photographs, many in color. Regular features include a review of developments in astronomy and space science; methods, advice, and ideas for the practical amateur astronomer; and a sky diary of what's upcoming in the next week. There is an unusual section called "Amateur Scene," which provides interviews and surveys dealing with the very active amateur astronomy scene—astronomy clubs, "open sky nights" at college observatories, and the like. The clear, readable style will appeal to beginners and more experienced amateurs alike. This journal is roughly comparable in scope and approach to *Astronomy* and *Sky & Telescope.*

665. *Publications of the Astronomical Society of the Pacific.* [ISSN: 0004-6280] 1889. m. USD 395 combined subscription domestic print & online eds.; USD 445 combined subscription Canada print & online eds.; USD 435 combined subscription elsewhere print & online eds. Ed(s): Paula Szkody. University of Chicago Press, Journals Division, PO Box 37005, Chicago, IL 60637; subscriptions@press.uchicago.edu; http://www.journals.uchicago.edu. Illus., index. Refereed. Circ: 3000. Online: EBSCO Publishing, EBSCO Host. Reprint: PSC. *Indexed:* ChemAb, MathR, SCI. *Aud.:* Ac, Sa.

The Astronomical Society of the Pacific (ASP) publishes several titles, among them *Mercury* (above in this section), *Publications of the ASP,* and *Selectory,* a catalog of equipment for astronomy. The ASP's mission is "to advance the science of astronomy and disseminate astronomical information," and it uses some of its publications to this end. Be aware that *Publications* is an actual title—it does not simply refer to a group of publications, but rather constitutes an actual periodical in and of itself. *Publications* is the ASP's technical journal, which includes refereed reports on current research, Ph.D. thesis abstracts, and review articles on astronomy and astrophysics. It prides itself on giving equal coverage to "all wavelengths and distance scales" of astronometric data.

666. *Royal Astronomical Society. Monthly Notices.* [ISSN: 0035-8711] 1827. 36x/yr. GBP 3483 print & online eds. Ed(s): A C Fabian. Blackwell Publishing Ltd., 9600 Garsington Rd, Oxford, OX4 2ZG, United Kingdom; customerservices@blackwellpublishing.com; http://www.blackwellpublishing.com. Illus., adv. Refereed. Circ: 1130. Microform: PQC. Online: Blackwell Synergy; EBSCO Publishing, EBSCO Host; Gale; IngentaConnect; OCLC Online Computer Library Center, Inc.; OhioLINK; SwetsWise Online Content. Reprint: PSC. *Indexed:* C&ISA, CerAb, ChemAb, IAA, M&GPA, MathR, SCI. *Aud.:* Ac, Sa.

This journal is considered to be a "core" publication for any high-level astronomy library. Since 1827, it has published timely articles on all areas of astronomy, including positional and dynamical astronomy, astrophysics, radio astronomy, cosmology, space research, instrument design, and more. Replete with equations, this periodical is indispensable for the serious astronomer, but rather slow going for anyone but the most committed amateur. Note that *The Observatory: A Review of Astronomy* (above in this section) is an optional companion to this journal.

667. *Royal Astronomical Society of Canada. Observer's Handbook.* [ISSN: 0080-4193] 1908. a. USD 25.95. Ed(s): Dr. Rajiv Gupta. Royal Astronomical Society of Canada, 136 Dupont St, Toronto, ON M5R 1V2, Canada; nationaloffice@rasc.ca; http://www.rasc.ca. Illus., index. Circ: 12000. Microform: PQC. *Aud.:* Ems, Hs, Ga, Ac, Sa.

The *Observer's Handbook* is a guide published annually since 1907 by The Royal Astronomical Society of Canada. Through its long tradition and the highly respected expertise of its contributors, it has come to be regarded as the standard North American reference for data concerning the sky. The material in it is of interest to professional and amateur astronomers, scientists, teachers at all levels, students, science writers, campers, scout and guide leaders, and others. The guide is an integral part of many astronomy courses at the secondary and university levels, and it is on the reference shelf of many libraries of various kinds. This useful annual volume is comparable in aims and scope to the *Annual Review of Astronomy and Astrophysics*.

Science. See Science and Technology section.

668. *The Science Teacher.* Formerly (until 1937): *Illinois Chemistry Teacher.* [ISSN: 0036-8555] 1934. 9x/yr. USD 75 (Members, USD 72). Ed(s): Michelle Chovan, Janet Gerking. National Science Teachers Association, 1840 Wilson Blvd, Arlington, VA 22201; membership@ nsta.org; http://www.nsta.org/. Illus., index, adv. Circ: 27000 Paid. Vol. ends: May. Microform: PQC. Online: EBSCO Publishing, EBSCO Host; Gale; OCLC Online Computer Library Center, Inc.; ProQuest LLC (Ann Arbor); H.W. Wilson. *Indexed:* ABIn, BRI, BiolDig, ERIC, EduInd, MRD, PhilInd. *Aud.:* Ems, Hs.

Science Teacher is not exclusively an astronomy periodical, but it frequently devotes a lot of coverage to astronomy. This is one of the publications of the National Science Teachers Association (NSTA), and is aimed at secondary school teachers. *Science and Children* is a parallel journal published by the same association, directed at teachers of a younger age bracket. Both of these are highly respected journals that take a hands-on approach to education. They are each constantly brimming over with specific ideas for age-appropriate activities, as opposed to the jargon of educational theory. If your library includes teachers among its patrons, you should be aware of these journals for their utility in the communication of the wonder of astronomy to young minds. NSTA journals are a member benefit and are not available by subscription.

669. *Sky & Telescope: the essential magazine of astronomy.* Former titles: *Telescope: Drama of the Skies; Sky.* [ISSN: 0037-6604] 1941. m. USD 42.95 domestic; USD 49.95 Canada; USD 61.95 elsewhere. Sky

Publishing Corp., 90 Sherman St., Cambridge, MA 02140. Illus., index, adv. Circ: 111528 Paid. Vol. ends: Jun/Dec. Microform: PQC. Online: EBSCO Publishing, EBSCO Host; Gale; Northern Light Technology, Inc.; OCLC Online Computer Library Center, Inc.; ProQuest K-12 Learning Solutions; ProQuest LLC (Ann Arbor); H.W. Wilson. *Indexed:* BRI, BiolDig, CBRI, GSI, IAA, IHTDI, LRI, RGPR. *Bk. rev.:* 4-5, 350-1,000 words. *Aud.:* Hs, Ga, Ac.

Since it began publication in 1941, *Sky & Telescope* has been a leader in providing accurate and up-to-date information on astronomy and space science. The magazine chose its subtitle of "the essential magazine of astronomy" itself, but it is able to get away with it. It is written so that it appeals to all astronomy enthusiasts, from the youngest novice to the most seasoned professional; its articles are painstakingly edited to be easily understood by both technically savvy readers and those who benefit from clear descriptive language and graphics. Regular features include book reviews, a sky calendar, news notes, and tips on imaging the sky. Annually, the journal prints a directory of organizations, institutions, and businesses related to astronomy.

670. *SkyNews: the Canadian magazine of astronomy and stargazing.* [ISSN: 0840-8939] bi-m. CND 28.72 domestic; USD 26 United States. Ed(s): Terence Dickinson. Canada Science and Technology Museum Corp, P O Box 9724, Ottawa, ON K1G 5A3, Canada; cmgroup@ interlog.com. Illus. Vol. ends: No. 6. *Indexed:* CBCARef, CPerI. *Aud.:* Hs, Ga, Ac.

A useful, very popular publication for novice stargazers. Each colorful issue contains news, columns, features, an excellent sky chart, and equipment reviews. Articles are directed primarily, but not exclusively, to a Canadian audience. What this may mean to an American library is simply that some of the tables presented will have been calibrated with more northerly latitudes in mind. This may have a certain impact on the utility of *some* of the information provided, but the articles and equipment reviews, of course, will still be quite useful, enjoyable, and engrossing.

671. *SkyWatch: tour guide for stargazing and space exploration.* [ISSN: 1089-4888] 1996. a. USD 6.99 newsstand/cover per issue domestic; USD 7.99 newsstand/cover per issue foreign. Sky Publishing Corp., 90 Sherman St., Cambridge, MA 02140. Adv. Circ: 85000 Paid and controlled. *Aud.:* Ems, Hs, Ga.

Published by the people who bring us *Sky & Telescope,* this annual listing of sky events is meant for beginners or serious amateurs. A portable, uncomplicated guide to the night sky, *SkyWatch* is a useful observing tool. Included are star charts from September of one year through December of the following year; a map of the lunar surface; a gallery of state-of-the-art astrophotography; and articles on choosing telescopes, binoculars, and other astronomy gear. Also helpful is the featured how-to article on finding 16 of the most popular objects for viewing in the night sky. This publication can be compared to the *Observer's Handbook* (see *Royal Astronomical Society of Canada. Observer's Handbook* above in this section).

672. *Solar Physics: a journal for solar and solar-stellar research and the study of solar terrestrial physics.* [ISSN: 0038-0938] 1967. 14x/yr. EUR 4213 print & online eds. Ed(s): Zdenek Svestka, Jack W Harvey. Springer Netherlands, Van Godewijckstraat 30, Dordrecht, 3311 GX, Netherlands; http://www.springeronline.com. Illus., index, adv. Sample. Refereed. Vol. ends: No. 14. Microform: PQC. Online: EBSCO Publishing, EBSCO Host; Gale; IngentaConnect; OCLC Online Computer Library Center, Inc.; OhioLINK; Springer LINK; SwetsWise Online Content. Reprint: PSC. *Indexed:* ChemAb, IAA, IBR, IBZ, M&GPA, SCI. *Aud.:* Ac, Sa.

Solar Physics was founded in 1967 and is the principal journal for the publication of the results of fundamental research on the Sun. The journal treats all aspects of solar physics, ranging from the internal structure of the Sun and its evolution, to the outer corona and solar wind in interplanetary space. Papers on solar-terrestrial physics and on stellar research are also published when their results have a direct bearing on our understanding of the Sun.

673. Solar System Research. [ISSN: 0038-0946] 1967. bi-m. EUR 3050 print & online eds. Ed(s): M Ya Marov. M A I K Nauka - Interperiodica, Profsoyuznaya ul 90, Moscow, 117997, Russian Federation; compmg@maik.ru; http://www.maik.ru. Illus. Sample. Refereed. Vol. ends: No. 6. Online: EBSCO Publishing, EBSCO Host; Gale; IngentaConnect; OCLC Online Computer Library Center, Inc.; OhioLINK; Springer LINK; SwetsWise Online Content. *Indexed:* M&GPA, SCI. *Aud.:* Ac, Sa.

This journal is translated into English by MAIK Nauka/Interperiodica Publishing and is published simultaneously with the Russian edition. Review papers appear regularly, along with notes on observational results and communications on scientific meetings and colloquiums. *Solar System Research* is the only journal from Russia dealing with the topics of planetary exploration, including the results of original study obtained through ground-based and/or space-borne observations and theoretical/computer modeling. In recent years the journal has significantly expanded the scope of its interest through the involvement of new research fields, such as planetary geology and cosmophysics, planetary plasma physics and heliosphere, atmospheric sciences, and general problems in comparative planetology.

Space Daily. See Aeronautics and Space Science section.

674. Spaceflight: the magazine of astronautics and outer space. Incorporates: *Space Education.* [ISSN: 0038-6340] 1956. m. Membership, GBP 43; Students, GBP 15 (under 22 years); Senior citizens, GBP 29 (over 65 years). Ed(s): Clive Simpson. British Interplanetary Society, 27-29 S Lambeth Rd, London, SW8 1SZ, United Kingdom; mail@bis-spaceflight.com; http://bis-spaceflight.com. Illus., index, adv. Circ: 8000. Vol. ends: No. 12. Microform: PQC. Online: OCLC Online Computer Library Center, Inc.; H.W. Wilson. *Indexed:* AS&TI, ApMecR, BrArAb, BrTechI, C&ISA, CerAb, ChemAb, IAA, IBR. *Aud.:* Hs, Ga, Ac, Sa.

Published since 1956, this is considered to be a core journal by most astronomy libraries. Regarded as an authoritative periodical, *Spaceflight* focuses primarily upon national, international, and commercial efforts to explore space. Articles cover such topics as ongoing space shuttle missions, details of space station life, and educational efforts aimed at popularizing these initiatives. In general, articles are aimed at a presumably intelligent audience that may or may not be professionally involved in space exploration.

675. StarDate. Formerly: *McDonald Observatory News.* [ISSN: 0889-3098] 1972. bi-m. USD 21 domestic; USD 25 in Canada & Mexico; USD 36 elsewhere. Ed(s): Damond Beeningfield, Gary Harrison. University of Texas, Austin, McDonald Observatory, PO Box 1337, Fort Davis, TX 79734-1337; http://stardate.org. Illus. Sample. Circ: 11000 Paid. *Indexed:* BiolDig. *Aud.:* Ems, Hs, Ga.

StarDate is known to many as a radio show, but you can find the same information and more in the online edition, *StarDate Online*, at http://stardate.org, or by purchasing a paper copy. The magazine is perfect for amateur astronomers and anyone interested in celestial events and space exploration. It is updated daily, and includes such helpful features as an astronomical "Tip of the Day," which concerns interesting things to observe in the sky; a section called "Today on Stardate," which presents articles on all kinds of topics from astronomy and the history of astronomy, including archaeo-astronomy; and daily astronomical questions to ponder. There are also Internet links about astronomy and an astronomical search engine for online research.

676. Universo Online. 1997. m. Ed(s): Gary Harrison. University of Texas, Austin, McDonald Observatory, PO Box 1337, Fort Davis, TX 79734-1337; http://universo.utexas.edu/. *Aud.:* Ems, Hs, Ga.

A valuable online Spanish-language resource for astronomy. There is much variety in the coverage, which is updated daily. Interesting features include an observer's tip of the day, or "Aviso del dia para mirar las estrellas"; a daily interesting fact in the "Hoy en Universo" section; and a daily question of cosmic import, such as "Will we ever visit the stars?" This popular web site can be viewed at http://radiouniverso.org/. The site is searchable by keyword in Spanish.

■ ATMOSPHERIC SCIENCES

See also Marine Science and Technology section.

Susan Moore, Catalog Librarian and Bibliographer, Rod Library, University of Northern Iowa, Cedar Falls, IA 50613; susan.moore@uni.edu

Introduction

The term *atmospheric sciences* covers a wide variety of disciplines including meteorology, climatology, atmospheric chemistry, and weather forecasting, as well as other disciplines concerned with weather and the study of the atmosphere. The advances in satellite technology, computer modeling, and data gathering have greatly increased the knowledge and understanding that atmospheric scientists can bring to their subject. With satellites providing data about atmospheres of other planets, atmospheric scientists can begin to explore what processes are unique to Earth and what processes exist wherever there is an atmosphere. One response to the last few hurricane seasons and the number and severity of the storms that struck the United States has been an increase of interest in the atmospheric sciences.

The publications listed in this section include important journals and general-interest periodicals devoted to the study of weather and atmospheric sciences. The list provides information on titles for libraries in North America that primarily publish articles concerning meteorology, climatology, atmospheric chemistry, atmospheric physics, weather forecasting, and related areas.

Journals in languages other than English have not been included; however, some journals from countries other than the United States and Canada that are published in English are included because researchers are interested in weather phenomena wherever they occur.

As the federal government moves increasingly to electronic publishing, many of the titles formerly printed are now available chiefly via the World Wide Web. Additionally, government sites provide access to additional information. These sites include:

National Weather Service, Internet Weather Source. http://weather.noaa.gov/index.html. This is a very useful web site of weather and forecasting data from the National Weather Service and includes links to areas covered by watches and warnings. Other links included are: *United States Weather, Radar Graphics, Weather Maps, International Weather Conditions, Aviation Weather,* and *Marine Weather.* Conditions at each National Weather Service observing station are available by following the United States Weather link. Specific conditions provided for each station are: wind, visibility, sky conditions, temperature, dew point, relative humidity, and barometric pressure. Summaries of the previous 24 hours for each station are also included. Conditions for areas not covered by a NWS station are given in the section "Forecasts, Watches and Warnings," though the National Weather Service does indicate that the weather conditions given for non-official sites may not meet Weather Service quality-control standards.

National Climatic Data Center. http://www.ncdc.noaa.gov/oa/about/about.html. This web site is the homepage for the National Climatic Data Center. Information about weather in the United States is available either for free or by subscription through this site. Free titles include: *Monthly Precipitation Probabilities 1971–2000, Annual Degree Days to Selected Bases 1971–2000, Monthly Divisional Normals/Standard Deviations 1971–2000, Frost/Freeze Data 1951–1980, Snow Normals 1971–2000, Extreme Weather and Climate Events,* and *State of the Climate,* as well as many other informative publications.

Weather and Climate. http://www.usda.gov/oce/weather/index.htm. This web site is a joint project of the World Agricultural Outlook Board of the U.S. Department of Agriculture and the National Oceanic and Atmospheric Administration and includes links to publications that provide important meteorological information to those engaged in agriculture and related fields. Titles included are: *U.S. Agricultural Weather Highlights, Weekly Weather and Crop Bulletin,* and *Major World Crop Areas and Climatic Profiles.* These publications include specific information for farmers, such as current agricultural weather highlights and crop production reviews.

Basic Periodicals

Hs: *Weatherwise;* Ga: *Bulletin of the American Meteorological Society; Local Climatological Data; Weather; Weatherwise; WMO Bulletin;* Ac: *Bulletin of the American Meteorological Society; Climate Dynamics; Journal of Applied Meteorology; Journal of Climate; JGR: Journal of Geophysical Research: Section D: Atmosphere; Journal of the Atmospheric Sciences; Monthly Weather Review; Royal Meteorological Society. Quarterly Journal; Weather; Weather and Forecasting; Weatherwise; WMO Bulletin.*

Basic Abstracts and Indexes

Geo Abstracts B: Biogeography and Climatology, Meteorological and Geoastrophysical Abstracts, Chemical Abstracts, INSPEC, Science Citation Index.

677. *Acta Meteorologica Sinica.* [ISSN: 0894-0525] 1987. 4x/yr. USD 300. Ed(s): Zhou Xiuji. China Meteorological Press, 46 Zhongguancun Nandajie, Haidian District, Beijing, 100081, China; ams@rays.cma.gov.cn. Illus., index, adv. Refereed. Circ: 300 Paid. Microform: PQC. Online: ProQuest LLC (Ann Arbor). *Indexed:* ChemAb, IAA, M&GPA. *Aud.:* Ac, Sa.

This title publishes papers translated from the Chinese edition of this journal, along with papers submitted in English from other countries. Areas of emphasis include climatology, marine meteorology, atmospheric physics and chemistry, pure and applied meteorology, cloud physics, atmospheric sounding and remote sensing, and air pollution meteorology. The title accepts review articles as well as original research. Recommended for research collections.

Agricultural and Forest Meteorology. See Forestry section.

678. *American Meteorological Society. Bulletin.* [ISSN: 0003-0007] 1920. m. Free to members. Ed(s): Ronald McPherson. American Meteorological Society, 45 Beacon St, Boston, MA 02108; amsinfo@ametsoc.org; http://ams.allenpress.com. Illus., index, adv. Refereed. Circ: 11528. Vol. ends: Dec. Microform: PMC. Online: Allen Press Inc.; EBSCO Publishing, EBSCO Host; OCLC Online Computer Library Center, Inc.; ProQuest K-12 Learning Solutions; ProQuest LLC (Ann Arbor); H.W. Wilson. *Indexed:* ABS&EES, AS&TI, ApMecR, BiolDig, CABA, ChemAb, EngInd, EnvAb, EnvInd, ExcerpMed, ForAb, GSI, IAA, M&GPA, OceAb, PollutAb, RRTA, S&F, SCI, SSCI, SWRA, WAE&RSA. *Bk. rev.:* Occasional, 200-500 words. *Aud.:* Ga, Ac.

This publication is the official organ of the American Meteorological Society and as such is "devoted to editorials, articles of interest to a large segment of the membership, professional and membership news, announcements, and Society activities." In each issue is a calendar of professional meetings. Particularly helpful for librarians is the regular supplement that lists current publications available from the society. The society's annual report is also a regular supplement. This title should be in the collection of any library in the United States that supports teaching and research in atmospheric science, meteorology, climatology, and related fields. It is also available for free on the web at www.ametsoc.org/pubs/bams/index.html.

679. *Atmosfera.* [ISSN: 0187-6236] 1988. q. MXN 70. Ed(s): Carlos Gay. Universidad Nacional Autonoma de Mexico, Centro de Ciencias de la Atmosfera, Circuito Exterior, Ciudad Universitaria, Mexico City, 04510, Mexico. Illus., index. Refereed. Vol. ends: Dec. *Indexed:* M&GPA, PollutAb, SCI. *Aud.:* Ac.

Articles published cover "theoretical, empirical and applied research on all aspects of the atmospheric sciences." Articles are in English, with abstracts in English and Spanish. While publishing articles on atmospheric science in general, this journal is particularly good at covering Latin America and neighboring oceans.

680. *Atmosphere - Ocean.* Supersedes (with vol.16, 1978): *Atmosphere.* [ISSN: 0705-5900] 1963. q. CND 125 (Individuals, CND 45). Ed(s): Patrick Cummins, Steven Lambert. Canadian Meteorological and Oceanographic Society, Station D, PO Box 3211, Ottawa, ON K1P 6H7,

Canada; Pubs@meds-sdmm.dfo-mpo.gc.ca; http://www.cmos.ca. Illus., index. Refereed. Circ: 600 Paid. Online: EBSCO Publishing, EBSCO Host. *Indexed:* ApMecR, CABA, ForAb, M&GPA, OceAb, PollutAb, S&F, SCI, SWRA, WAE&RSA. *Bk. rev.:* Occasional, 750-1,000 words. *Aud.:* Ac, Sa.

This journal reports on original research as well as publishing survey articles. It is the principle scientific journal of the Canadian Meteorological and Oceanographic Society, and it is very good at reporting results of studies done in Canada. Many of the researchers are Canadian, although studies and contributors from outside Canada are also published. The journal publishes occasional special issues on topics of interest in meteorology and related fields. Articles may be in English or French, although most are in English. Abstracts are in both languages.

681. *Atmospheric Environment.* Formed by the merger of (1961-1994): *Atmospheric Environment. Part A, General Topics;* (1961-1994): *Atmospheric Environment. Part B, Urban Atmosphere;* Both of which superseded in part (in 1990): *Atmospheric Environment;* Which superseded in part (in 1966): *Air and Water Pollution.* [ISSN: 1352-2310] 1994. 40x/yr. EUR 5888. Ed(s): H. B. Singh, P Brimblecombe. Pergamon, The Boulevard, Langford Ln, East Park, Kidlington, OX5 1GB, United Kingdom. Illus., index, adv. Refereed. Circ: 2600. Microform: MIM; PQC. Online: EBSCO Publishing, EBSCO Host; Gale; IngentaConnect; OhioLINK; ScienceDirect; SwetsWise Online Content. *Indexed:* AS&TI, ApMecR, B&AI, BiolAb, C&ISA, CABA, CEA, ChemAb, DSA, EngInd, EnvAb, EnvInd, ExcerpMed, FPA, ForAb, H&SSA, HortAb, IAA, IndVet, M&GPA, OceAb, PollutAb, RRTA, RiskAb, S&F, SCI, SSCI, SWRA, VB, WAE&RSA, WRCInf. *Aud.:* Ac.

Atmospheric Environment puts an emphasis on "air pollution research and its application." The journal publishes original research and review articles that extend scientific understanding of air pollution and its effects.

682. *Atmospheric Research.* Formerly (until 1986): *Journal de Recherches Atmospheriques.* [ISSN: 0169-8095] 1963. 16x/yr. EUR 1888. Ed(s): Dr. Clive P.R. Saunders, A. Flossmann. Elsevier BV, Radarweg 29, Amsterdam, 1043 NX, Netherlands; nlinfo-f@elsevier.nl; http://www.elsevier.nl. Illus., index. Refereed. Circ: 350. Online: EBSCO Publishing, EBSCO Host; Gale; IngentaConnect; OhioLINK; ScienceDirect; SwetsWise Online Content. *Indexed:* C&ISA, CABA, CerAb, ChemAb, EngInd, EnvAb, EnvInd, ForAb, IAA, M&GPA, OceAb, PollutAb, S&F, SCI, SWRA. *Aud.:* Ac.

This journal publishes articles concerning the meteorological processes that occur in the troposphere, which is the part of the atmosphere where meteorological events occur. Of particular interest is the physics of clouds and precipitation. Special issues are published occasionally. Articles are primarily in English.

683. *Australian Meteorological Magazine.* [ISSN: 0004-9743] 1952. q. AUD 43. Ed(s): Michael Manton. Bureau of Meteorology, 150 Lonsdale St, Melbourne, VIC 3000, Australia; http://www.bom.gov.au. Illus., index. Refereed. *Indexed:* ChemAb, M&GPA, OceAb, SCI, SWRA. *Bk. rev.:* 300-400 words, signed. *Aud.:* Ac.

Since this title is an official publication of the Australian Bureau of Meteorology, Australia's and the Southern Hemisphere's meteorology are featured. Most of the contributors are Australian as well. This journal publishes research articles that deal with the meteorology of Australia, the South Pacific Ocean, and the Indian Ocean. These are areas not well served by other titles in the field.

684. *Boundary-Layer Meteorology: an international journal of physical and biological processes in the atmospheric boundary layer.* [ISSN: 0006-8314] 1970. m. EUR 2954 print & online eds. Ed(s): P A Taylor, John R Garratt. Springer Netherlands, Van Godewijckstraat 30, Dordrecht, 3311 GX, Netherlands; http://www.springeronline.com. Illus., index, adv. Refereed. Vol. ends: Dec. Microform: PQC. Online: EBSCO Publishing, EBSCO Host; Gale; IngentaConnect; OCLC Online

Computer Library Center, Inc.; OhioLINK; Ovid Technologies, Inc.; Springer LINK; SwetsWise Online Content. Reprint: PSC. *Indexed:* ApMecR, C&ISA, CABA, CerAb, EngInd, ExcerpMed, ForAb, HortAb, IAA, M&GPA, OceAb, S&F, SCI, SWRA. *Bk. rev.:* Occasional, 350-500 words. *Aud.:* Ac.

This journal focuses on "the physical, chemical and biological processes occurring in the lowest few kilometres of the Earth's atmosphere." Articles are intended for professionals in atmospheric science. The subject areas included are forest meteorology, air pollution, hydrology, micrometeorology, planetary boundary layer, surface boundary layer, mesometeorology, numerical modeling of boundary layers, and urban meteorology.

685. *Climate Dynamics: observational, theoretical and computational research on the climate system.* [ISSN: 0930-7575] 1986. 16x/yr. EUR 3115 print & online eds. Ed(s): Dr. Jean-Claude Duplessy, Edwin K Schneider. Springer, Tiergartenstr 17, Heidelberg, 69121, Germany. Adv. Refereed. Online: EBSCO Publishing, EBSCO Host; OhioLINK; Springer LINK; SwetsWise Online Content. Reprint: PSC. *Indexed:* ForAb, M&GPA, OceAb, PollutAb, S&F, SCI, SWRA. *Aud.:* Ac.

This title covers all aspects of the dynamics of the global climate system. The articles and the editorial board are international in scope. The journal especially welcomes "papers containing original paleoclimatic, diagnostic, analytical or numerical modeling research on the structure and behavior of the atmosphere, oceans, cryosphere, biomass and land surface as interacting components of the dynamics of global climate." Recommended for academic libraries.

686. *Climatic Change: an interdisciplinary, international journal devoted to the description, causes and implications of climatic change.* [ISSN: 0165-0009] 1977. 18x/yr. EUR 2850 print & online eds. Ed(s): Stephen H Schneider. Springer Netherlands, Van Godewijckstraat 30, Dordrecht, 3311 GX, Netherlands; http://www.springeronline.com. Illus., index, adv. Refereed. Microform: PQC. Online: EBSCO Publishing, EBSCO Host; Gale; IngentaConnect; OCLC Online Computer Library Center, Inc.; OhioLINK; Springer LINK; SwetsWise Online Content. Reprint: PSC. *Indexed:* ArtHuCI, BiolAb, CABA, ChemAb, EngInd, EnvInd, ExcerpMed, FPA, ForAb, HortAb, IBR, IBZ, IndVet, M&GPA, OceAb, PollutAb, RRTA, S&F, SCI, SSCI, SWRA, VB, WAE&RSA. *Aud.:* Ac.

As an interdisciplinary journal "dedicated to the totality of the problem of climatic variability and change," this title publishes articles from a variety of disciplines in the sciences, social sciences, and other fields. Occasional special issues focus on topics of particular interest. Given the wide range of disciplines covered and the increasing interest in interdisciplinary research, this journal should be of interest to academic libraries in general.

687. *Dynamics of Atmospheres and Oceans.* [ISSN: 0377-0265] 1977. 8x/yr. EUR 1224. Ed(s): A Moore. Elsevier BV, Radarweg 29, Amsterdam, 1043 NX, Netherlands; nlinfo-f@elsevier.nl; http://www.elsevier.nl. Illus., index, adv. Sample. Refereed. Vol. ends: Jan. Microform: PQC. Online: EBSCO Publishing, EBSCO Host; Gale; IngentaConnect; OhioLINK; ScienceDirect; SwetsWise Online Content. *Indexed:* ApMecR, C&ISA, CerAb, EngInd, EnvAb, IAA, M&GPA, OceAb, SCI, SWRA. *Aud.:* Ac, Sa.

This journal focuses on research into atmospheres and oceans as fluid dynamic systems, especially the interaction of atmospheres and oceans. Most articles are technical in nature and assume familiarity with mathematical modeling. Fields represented by the authors include earth science, oceanography, atmospheric science, and other fields. Occasionally, an issue will be devoted to a specific topic.

688. *Earth Interactions.* [ISSN: 1087-3562] 1996. d. USD 115 1-100 workstations. Ed(s): Jon Foley. American Geophysical Union, 2000 Florida Ave, NW, Washington, DC 20009-1277; http://www.agu.org. Illus. Refereed. *Indexed:* M&GPA, SCI, SWRA. *Aud.:* Ac.

This journal publishes articles that "explore the interactions among the biological, physical, and human components of the Earth system." *Earth Interactions* is a joint publication of the American Geophysical Union, the American Meteorological Society, and the Association of American Geographers. The journal aims to be a "comprehensive source of information

for Earth system science researchers focused on human interactions with the natural world." The URL is http://earthinteractions.org, and a subscription is required to view the published articles.

689. *International Journal of Biometeorology: the description, causes, and implications of climatic change.* [ISSN: 0020-7128] 1957. bi-m. EUR 698 print & online eds. Ed(s): Masaaki Shibata. Springer, Tiergartenstr 17, Heidelberg, 69121, Germany. Illus., index, adv. Refereed. Circ: 1300. Vol. ends: Mar. Online: EBSCO Publishing, EBSCO Host; OhioLINK; Springer LINK; SwetsWise Online Content. Reprint: PSC. *Indexed:* Agr, BiolAb, CABA, ChemAb, DSA, ExcerpMed, FR, ForAb, HortAb, IndVet, M&GPA, PollutAb, RRTA, S&F, SCI, SSCI, SWRA, VB, ZooRec. *Aud.:* Ac.

This title publishes "studies concerning the interactions between living organisms and factors of the natural and artificial physical environment." Articles cover the impact that the environment has on humans, animals, and plants. Recent topics include the influence of weather on strokes in Japan, cooling system effects on dairy cattle, pollen transport in a region of Argentina, and the effect of physical activity on temperature perception in humans. This title is of interest to biologists and medical professionals as well as earth and atmospheric scientists.

690. *International Journal of Climatology.* Formerly: *Journal of Climatology.* [ISSN: 0899-8418] 1981. 15x/yr. USD 2750 print or online ed. Ed(s): G. R. McGregor. John Wiley & Sons Ltd., The Atrium, Southern Gate, Chichester, PO19 8SQ, United Kingdom; customer@wiley.co.uk; http://www.wiley.co.uk. Illus., index, adv. Refereed. Circ: 578. Vol. ends: Dec. Microform: PQC. Online: EBSCO Publishing, EBSCO Host; OhioLINK; SwetsWise Online Content; Wiley InterScience. Reprint: PSC. *Indexed:* CABA, EngInd, EnvAb, FR, ForAb, HortAb, IBR, IBZ, M&GPA, OceAb, PollutAb, RRTA, S&F, SCI, SSCI, SWRA, WAE&RSA. *Bk. rev.:* 300-500 words. *Aud.:* Ac, Sa.

The title "aims to span the well-established but rapidly growing field of climatology." Thus, it covers climate system science, climatic variability and climate change, seasonal to interannual climate prediction, and climate and society interactions, as well as other topics. The journal is international in scope. Book reviews are also included.

691. *The International Journal of Meteorology.* Formerly (until Sep. 2005): *Journal of Meteorology.* [ISSN: 1748-2992] 1975. 10x/yr. GBP 99 (Individuals, GBP 38). Ed(s): Robert K Doe. Artetech Publishing Co., Editorial Office, PO 5161, Bournemouth, BH10 4WT, United Kingdom; advertise@journalofmeteorology.com; http://www.journalofmeteorology.com/advertise.htm. Illus., index, adv. Sample. Refereed. Vol. ends: Dec. *Indexed:* CABA, ForAb, M&GPA, S&F. *Bk. rev.:* 750-1,000 words. *Aud.:* Ga, Ac.

Published in association with the Tornado and Storm Research Organisation, this title specializes in weather extremes. It also covers atmospheric phenomena in the United Kingdom, Ireland, and the European continent. Well-illustrated, the journal is of interest to meteorologists as well as to weather enthusiasts. The editorial board's membership is international, but half are from the United Kingdom and Ireland.

692. *J G R: Journal of Geophysical Research: Atmospheres.* 1896. s-m. USD 5192. American Geophysical Union, 2000 Florida Ave, NW, Washington, DC 20009-1277; http://www.agu.org. Illus. *Indexed:* EnvAb, SCI. *Aud.:* Ac, Sa.

This journal publishes articles about the physics and chemistry of the atmosphere, including "the atmospheric-biospheric, lithospheric, or hydrospheric interface." Articles can include reports of findings or cover methodology and instrumentation, or be brief reports or comments and replies. Geared to professionals and graduate students.

693. *Journal of Applied Meteorology and Climatology.* Formerly (until Jan. 2006): *Journal of Applied Meteorology;* Which supersedes in part (in 1988): *Journal of Climate and Applied Meteorology;* Which was formerly (until 1983): *Journal of Applied Meteorology.* [ISSN: 1558-8424] 1962. m. USD 555 (Individuals, USD 490; Members, USD

75). Ed(s): Robert M Rauber. American Meteorological Society, 45 Beacon St, Boston, MA 02108; amsinfo@ametsoc.org; http://www.ametsoc.org. Illus., index, adv. Refereed. Circ: 1978. Vol. ends: Dec. Online: Allen Press Inc.; EBSCO Publishing, EBSCO Host; Northern Light Technology, Inc.; OCLC Online Computer Library Center, Inc.; ProQuest K-12 Learning Solutions; ProQuest LLC (Ann Arbor); H.W. Wilson. *Indexed:* AS&TI, ApMecR, B&AI, BiolDig, C&ISA, CABA, CerAb, ChemAb, EngInd, ExcerpMed, ForAb, HortAb, IAA, M&GPA, OceAb, PollutAb, S&F, SCI, SWRA, WAE&RSA. *Aud.:* Ac, Sa.

A publication of the American Meteorological Society, the journal "covers applied research related to physical meteorology, weather modification, satellite meteorology, radar meteorology, boundary layer processes, air pollution meteorology (including dispersion and chemical processes), agricultural and forest meteorology, and applied meteorological numerical models." The articles can be technical and are scholarly in nature. Given its wide scope, this journal is of interest to more than just atmospheric scientists.

694. *Journal of Atmospheric and Oceanic Technology.* [ISSN: 0739-0572] 1984. m. USD 278. Ed(s): Edward V Browell, Kevin Leaman. American Meteorological Society, 45 Beacon St, Boston, MA 02108. Illus., index, adv. Refereed. Circ: 798. Vol. ends: Dec. Online: Allen Press Inc.; EBSCO Publishing, EBSCO Host; OCLC Online Computer Library Center, Inc.; ProQuest K-12 Learning Solutions; ProQuest LLC (Ann Arbor); H.W. Wilson. *Indexed:* AS&TI, C&ISA, CABA, CerAb, ChemAb, EngInd, ForAb, IAA, M&GPA, OceAb, SCI, SWRA. *Aud.:* Ac.

This journal concerns itself with descriptions of the instrumentation and methodology for atmospheric and oceanic research. Not surprisingly, the articles can be very detailed and technical. A section for brief articles on works in progress is occasionally included. Given its focus, the title is primarily of interest to those in the atmospheric sciences.

695. *Journal of Atmospheric Chemistry.* [ISSN: 0167-7764] 1983. 9x/yr. EUR 1328 print & online eds. Ed(s): Andreas Wahner, Elliot L Atlas. Springer Netherlands, Van Godewijckstraat 30, Dordrecht, 3311 GX, Netherlands; http://www.springeronline.com. Illus., adv. Refereed. Microform: PQC. Online: EBSCO Publishing, EBSCO Host; Gale; IngentaConnect; OCLC Online Computer Library Center, Inc.; OhioLINK; Ovid Technologies, Inc.; Springer LINK; SwetsWise Online Content. Reprint: PSC. *Indexed:* CABA, ChemAb, EnvInd, ExcerpMed, FPA, ForAb, HortAb, IAA, IBR, IBZ, M&GPA, OceAb, PollutAb, S&F, SCI, SWRA. *Aud.:* Ac.

Publishes research on the chemistry of the earth's atmosphere, especially the region below 100 km. Topics covered include observational, interpretive, and modeling studies of the composition of air and precipitation (excluding air pollution problems of local importance only). Other topics include the role of the atmosphere in biogeochemical cycles; laboratory studies of the mechanics of transformation processes in the atmosphere; and descriptions of major advances in instrumentation. As might be assumed by the topics covered, the articles are meant for scientists and researchers.

696. *Journal of Climate.* Supersedes in part (in 1988): *Journal of Climate and Applied Meteorology;* Formerly (until 1983): *Journal of Applied Meteorology.* [ISSN: 0894-8755] 1986. s-m. USD 495. Ed(s): Dave Randall. American Meteorological Society, 45 Beacon St, Boston, MA 02108; amsinfo@ametsoc.org; http://ams.allenpress.com. Illus., index, adv. Refereed. Circ: 1689. Vol. ends: Dec. Online: Allen Press Inc.; EBSCO Publishing, EBSCO Host; Northern Light Technology, Inc.; OCLC Online Computer Library Center, Inc.; ProQuest K-12 Learning Solutions; ProQuest LLC (Ann Arbor); H.W. Wilson. *Indexed:* Agr, CABA, EngInd, ForAb, GSI, M&GPA, OceAb, PollutAb, S&F, SCI, SSCI, SWRA, WAE&RSA. *Aud.:* Ac, Sa.

Focuses on articles concerned with research in such areas as large-scale variability of the atmosphere, oceans, and land surface; changes in the climate system (including those caused by human activities); and climate simulation and prediction. Brief reports and comments are also published. The journal will occasionally publish review articles, but they must be approved by the editor prior to submission.

697. *Journal of Hydrometeorology.* [ISSN: 1525-755X] 1999. bi-m. USD 154. Ed(s): Dennis P Lettenmaier, Efi Fouroula-Georgiou. American Meteorological Society, 45 Beacon St, Boston, MA 02108; amsinfo@ametsoc.org; http://ams.allenpress.com. Refereed. Online: Allen Press Inc.; EBSCO Publishing, EBSCO Host; OCLC Online Computer Library Center, Inc. *Indexed:* CABA, ForAb, M&GPA, PollutAb, S&F, SCI, SWRA, WAE&RSA. *Aud.:* Ac, Sa.

This journal covers "research related to the modeling, observing, and forecasting of processes related to water and energy fluxes and storage terms, including interactions with the boundary layer and lower atmosphere, and including processes related to precipitation, radiation, and other meteorological inputs." As with most American Meteorological Society publications, it also publishes brief reports and comments.

698. *Journal of the Atmospheric Sciences.* Formerly (until 1962): *Journal of Meteorology.* [ISSN: 0022-4928] 1944. s-m. USD 499. Ed(s): Theodore G Shepherd. American Meteorological Society, 45 Beacon St, Boston, MA 02108; amsinfo@ametsoc.org; http://ams.allenpress.com. Illus., index, adv. Refereed. Circ: 2136. Online: Allen Press Inc.; EBSCO Publishing, EBSCO Host; Northern Light Technology, Inc.; OCLC Online Computer Library Center, Inc.; ProQuest K-12 Learning Solutions; ProQuest LLC (Ann Arbor); H.W. Wilson. *Indexed:* AS&TI, ApMecR, C&ISA, CCMJ, CerAb, ChemAb, EngInd, ExcerpMed, GSI, IAA, M&GPA, MSN, MathR, OceAb, PollutAb, SCI, SWRA. *Aud.:* Ac, Sa.

This journal publishes "basic research related to the physics, dynamics, and chemistry of the atmosphere of Earth and other planets, with emphasis on the quantitative and deductive aspects of the subject." Some brief articles are published, but most are longer and quantitative in nature.

699. *Meteorological Applications.* [ISSN: 1350-4827] 1994. q. USD 455 print or online ed. Ed(s): John Thornes. John Wiley & Sons Ltd., The Atrium, Southern Gate, Chichester, PO19 8SQ, United Kingdom; cs-journals@wiley.co.uk; http://www.wiley.co.uk. Adv. Online: Cambridge University Press; EBSCO Publishing, EBSCO Host; OCLC Online Computer Library Center, Inc.; OhioLINK; SwetsWise Online Content. *Indexed:* CABA, ForAb, HortAb, M&GPA, PollutAb, RRTA, S&F, SCI, SWRA, WAE&RSA. *Aud.:* Ac.

Meant for applied meteorologists, forecasters, and other users of meteorological services, this journal covers a range of topics, including applications of meteorological information and their benefits, analysis and prediction of weather hazards, performance and verification of numerical models and forecasting aids, and training techniques. Brief news items on applications of meteorology are also published.

700. *Meteorological Society of Japan. Journal.* [ISSN: 0026-1165] 1882. bi-m. JPY 10200 (Individuals, JPY 6600). Ed(s): Dr. Hiroshi L Tanaka. Meteorological Society of Japan, c/o Japan Meteorological Agency, 3-4 Ote-Machi 1-chome, Tokyo, 100-0004, Japan; http://www-cmpo.mit.edu/met_links/full/imsjap.full.html. Illus. Refereed. Circ: 2000. Vol. ends: Dec. *Indexed:* CABA, ChemAb, ForAb, M&GPA, S&F, SCI. *Aud.:* Ac.

The journal serves as "a medium for the publication of research papers in the science of pure and applied meteorology and related studies of atmospheric physics/chemistry, climate system and geophysical/planetary fluid." All articles are in English. Many cover East Asia and the western Pacific Ocean, but articles concerning other parts of the world are published as well.

701. *Meteorology and Atmospheric Physics.* Formerly (until 1986): *Archives for Meteorology, Geophysics, and Bioclimatology. Series A: Meteorology and Geophysics - Archiv fuer Meteorologie, Geophysik und Bioklimatologie. Series A.* [ISSN: 0177-7971] 1948. m. EUR 2398 print & online eds. Ed(s): Reinhold Steinacker. Springer Wien, Sachsenplatz 4-6, Vienna, A-1201, Austria; journals@springer.at; http://www.springer.at. Illus., adv. Sample. Refereed. Vol. ends: Dec. Microform: PQC. Online: EBSCO Publishing, EBSCO Host; OhioLINK; ProQuest LLC (Ann Arbor); Springer LINK; SwetsWise Online Content. Reprint: PSC. *Indexed:* C&ISA, CABA, CerAb, ForAb, IAA, M&GPA, S&F, SCI. *Bk. rev.:* 200-500 words. *Aud.:* Ac, Sa.

Publishes articles reporting on original research in the areas of physical and chemical processes in the atmosphere, including radiation, optical effects, electricity, atmospheric turbulence, and transport processes. Atmospheric dynamics, general circulation in the atmosphere, synoptic meteorology, and analyses of weather systems in specific regions are also covered. The journal is international in scope, and authors and research are from around the world.

702. Monthly Weather Review. [ISSN: 0027-0644] 1872. m. USD 461. Ed(s): David Jorgensen, Ying Hwa Kuo. American Meteorological Society, 45 Beacon St, Boston, MA 02108; amsinfo@ametsoc.org; http://ams.allenpress.com. Illus., index, adv. Circ: 2327. Vol. ends: Dec. Microform: PMC. Online: Allen Press Inc.; EBSCO Publishing, EBSCO Host; Northern Light Technology, Inc.; OCLC Online Computer Library Center, Inc.; OhioLINK; ProQuest K-12 Learning Solutions; ProQuest LLC (Ann Arbor); H.W. Wilson. *Indexed:* AS&TI, ApMecR, C&ISA, CABA, CerAb, ChemAb, EngInd, ExcerpMed, IAA, M&GPA, PollutAb, S&F, SCI, SSCI, SWRA. *Aud.:* Ac, Sa.

Focusing on phenomena that have seasonal or subseasonal time scales, this journal publishes research related to the analysiis and prediction of observed atmospheric physics and circulations.

703. National Weather Digest. [ISSN: 0271-1052] 1976. q. USD 29 (Free to members). Ed(s): Kenneth Mielke, Patrick S Market. National Weather Association, 1697 Capri Way, Charlottesville, VA 22911-3534; natweaasoc@aol.com; http://www.nwas.org. Illus., index, adv. Circ: 3100. Vol. ends: Nov. *Indexed:* M&GPA. *Bk. rev.:* 1-2, 500-700 words. *Aud.:* Ga, Ac.

This official publication of the National Weather Association focuses on specific meteorological incidents that have occurred in the United States. It also includes correspondence and information for the members of the association. Technical papers published in the section labeled "Articles" are fully refereed, while those published in "Technical Note" are not.

704. Royal Meteorological Society. Quarterly Journal: a journal of the atmospheric sciences, applied meteorology, and physical oceanography. [ISSN: 0035-9009] 1871. 8x/yr. USD 860 print or online ed. Ed(s): I Roulstone, P L Read. John Wiley & Sons Ltd., The Atrium, Southern Gate, Chichester, PO19 8SQ, United Kingdom; cs-journals@wiley.co.uk; http://www.wiley.co.uk. Illus., index, adv. Refereed. Circ: 1100. Vol. ends: Oct. *Indexed:* C&ISA, CABA, CerAb, EngInd, ExcerpMed, ForAb, HortAb, IAA, M&GPA, OceAb, S&F, SCI. *Bk. rev.:* Number and length vary. *Aud.:* Ac, Sa.

This publication is considered one of the major research journals in the atmospheric sciences. It covers all aspects of meteorology, climatology, atmospheric chemistry, and physical oceanography. The papers are scholarly and technical. Although the editorial board is primarily British, the journal publishes articles from scholars around the world. Book reviews appear in some issues. Recommended for libraries that support atmospheric and Earth science programs.

705. Russian Academy of Sciences. Izvestiya. Atmospheric and Oceanic Physics. Formerly: *Academy of Sciences of the U S S R. Izvestiya. Atmospheric and Oceanic Physics;* Which superseded in part (in 1965): *Academy of Sciences of the U S S R. Bulletin. Geophysics Series.* [ISSN: 0001-4338] 1959. bi-m. EUR 1278 print & online eds. Ed(s): Greorgii S Golitsyn. M A I K Nauka - Interperiodica, Profsoyuznaya ul 90, Moscow, 117997, Russian Federation; compmg@maik.ru; http://www.maik.ru. *Indexed:* CABA, CCMJ, ForAb, M&GPA, MSN, MathR, S&F, SCI. *Aud.:* Ac, Sa.

This is the English translation of *Izvestiya Rossiiskoi Akademii Nauk—Fizika Atmosfery i Okeana,* and it "publishes original scientific research and review articles on vital issues in the physics of the Earth's atmosphere and hydrosphere and climate theory." Also it occasionally publishes brief communications. Articles are technical in nature and written primarily by scientists from Russia and the CIS.

706. Tellus. Series A: Dynamic Meteorology and Oceanography. Supersedes in part: *Tellus.* [ISSN: 0280-6495] 1949. bi-m. GBP 185 print & online eds. Ed(s): Harald Lejenas. Blackwell Munksgaard, Rosenoerns Alle 1, PO Box 227, Copenhagen V, 1502, Denmark; info@mks.blackwellpublishing.com; http://www.munksgaard.dk/chemica/toc.html. Illus., index, adv. Refereed. Circ: 1470. Vol. ends: Oct. Reprint: PSC. *Indexed:* ApMecR, C&ISA, CABA, CerAb, ChemAb, EnvAb, EnvInd, ExcerpMed, IAA, IBR, IBZ, M&GPA, MathR, OceAb, S&F, SCI, SWRA. *Aud.:* Ac, Sa.

When *Tellus* split into two parts, this section's focus became dynamic meteorology, climatology, and oceanography, which includes synoptic meteorology, weather forecasting, numerical modelling, and climate analysis. The journal publishes both original research and review articles. Recommended for libraries that serve atmospheric scientists and oceanographers.

707. Tellus. Series B: Chemical and Physical Meteorology. Supersedes in part: *Tellus.* [ISSN: 0280-6509] 1949. bi-m. GBP 185 print & online eds. Ed(s): H Rodhe. Blackwell Munksgaard, Rosenoerns Alle 1, PO Box 227, Copenhagen V, 1502, Denmark; info@mks.blackwellpublishing.com; http://www.munksgaard.dk/. Illus., index, adv. Refereed. Circ: 1000. Vol. ends: Nov. Reprint: PSC. *Indexed:* ApMecR, BiolAb, CABA, ChemAb, EnvAb, EnvInd, ExcerpMed, FPA, ForAb, HortAb, IAA, IBR, IBZ, M&GPA, OceAb, PollutAb, S&F, SCI, SWRA. *Aud.:* Ac, Sa.

When *Tellus* was split, this section's focus became biogeochemical cycles, air chemistry, long-range and global transport, aerosol science, and cloud physics. The journal publishes both original research and review articles. Recommended for libraries that serve those studying hydrology, geography, atmospheric sciences, and oceanography.

708. Theoretical and Applied Climatology. Formerly (until 1985): *Archives for Meteorology, Geophysics, and Bioclimatology. Series B: Climatology, Environmental Meteorology, Radiation Research - Archiv fuer Meteorologie, Geophysik und Bioklimatologie. Series B.* [ISSN: 0177-798X] 1948. m. EUR 2398 print & online eds. Ed(s): H Grassl. Springer Wien, Sachsenplatz 4-6, Vienna, A-1201, Austria; journals@springer.at; http://www.springer.at. Adv. Sample. Refereed. Microform: PQC. Online: EBSCO Publishing, EBSCO Host; OhioLINK; ProQuest LLC (Ann Arbor); Springer LINK; SwetsWise Online Content. Reprint: PSC. *Indexed:* BiolAb, CABA, FR, ForAb, HortAb, IBR, IBZ, M&GPA, S&F, SCI. *Aud.:* Ac, Sa.

This journal's focus includes "climate modeling, climate changes and climate forecasting, micro- to mesoclimate, applied meteorology, effects of anthropogenic and natural aerosols and gaseous trace constituents, and hardware and software elements of meteorological measurements, including techniques of remote sensing." Articles are technical and scholarly in nature.

709. W M O Bulletin. [ISSN: 0042-9767] 1952. q. CHF 85. Ed(s): Hong Yan. World Meteorological Organization, 7 bis Avenue de la Paix, Case postale 2300, Geneva, 1211, Switzerland; pubsales@gateway.wmo.ch; http://www.wmo.int. Illus., index, adv. Circ: 6500. Vol. ends: Oct. *Indexed:* CABA, ForAb, HortAb, M&GPA, OceAb, RRTA, S&F, SWRA, WAE&RSA. *Bk. rev.:* 2-5, 300-500 words. *Aud.:* Ga, Ac.

The World Meteorological Organization is a specialized agency of the United Nations, and this is its official journal. It is therefore both a serious meteorological journal and a medium for reporting on the meetings and programs of the organization. It publishes scholarly articles and descriptions of recent weather events. Each issue includes a calendar of coming events. Recommended.

710. Weather. [ISSN: 0043-1656] 1946. m. GBP 90 print or online d. John Wiley & Sons Ltd., The Atrium, Southern Gate, Chichester, PO19 8SQ, United Kingdom; cs-journals@wiley.co.uk; http://www.wiley.co.uk. Illus., index, adv. Refereed. Circ: 5300. Vol. ends: Dec. *Indexed:* ChemAb, ForAb, HortAb, IAA, IndVet, M&GPA, PollutAb, S&F, SWRA. *Aud.:* Hs, Ga, Ac.

This journal is geared to the educated layperson, although the articles remain scholarly. It covers weather around the world, but since it is a publication of the Royal Meteorological Society, there is a slight emphasis on the United Kingdom. Also included is information about the activities of the society. Recommended for both academic and public libraries.

711. **Weather and Forecasting.** [ISSN: 0882-8156] 1986. bi-m. USD 180 (Members, USD 40). Ed(s): David J Stensrud, Harold E Brooks. American Meteorological Society, 45 Beacon St, Boston, MA 02108; amsinfo@ametsoc.org; http://ams.allenpress.com. Illus., index, adv. Refereed. Circ: 1640. Online: Allen Press Inc.; EBSCO Publishing, EBSCO Host; OCLC Online Computer Library Center, Inc.; ProQuest K-12 Learning Solutions; ProQuest LLC (Ann Arbor). *Indexed:* EngInd, M&GPA, SCI. *Aud.:* Ac.

Publishes "research on forecasting and analysis techniques, forecast verification studies, and case studies useful to forecasters." As with most American Meteorological Society publications, a section for brief reports and comments is part of many issues. Geared to forecasters, it may also be of interest to atmospheric scientists in general.

712. **Weatherwise.** [ISSN: 0043-1672] 1948. bi-m. USD 111 (Individuals, USD 40). Ed(s): Lynn Elsey. Heldref Publications, 1319 18th St, NW, Washington, DC 20036-1802; subscribe@heldref.org; http://www.heldref.org. Illus., index, adv. Circ: 9050 Paid. CD-ROM: ProQuest LLC (Ann Arbor). Microform: PQC. Online: EBSCO Publishing, EBSCO Host; Florida Center for Library Automation; Gale; Northern Light Technology, Inc.; OCLC Online Computer Library Center, Inc.; ProQuest K-12 Learning Solutions; ProQuest LLC (Ann Arbor); H.W. Wilson. *Indexed:* BiolDig, ChemAb, EnvAb, EnvInd, GSI, IAA, M&GPA, MASUSE, RGPR. *Aud.:* Ga, Ac, Sa.

This popular magazine has as its target audience the intelligent layperson interested in weather. It publishes articles on weather, particularly on weather anomalies. A regular feature is a review of weather over North America during the preceding two months. The March/April issue includes a summary of weather events from the previous year. Recommended for all libraries that serve users with an interest in weather.

Weekly Weather and Crop Bulletin. See Agriculture section.

■ AUTOMOBILES AND MOTORCYCLES

Amy Kautzman, Head, Research, Reference, and Collections, Doe/Moffitt Libraries, 212 Doe Library, #6000; University of California, Berkeley, CA 94720-6000; akautzma@library.berkeley.edu

Introduction

Automobiles and motorcycles are economic, political, aesthetic, and sometimes race and gender signifiers. In the United States and other first-world nations our lives are built around the ability to commute to work from our suburbs and exurbs. Without our cars most of us could not shop for groceries, visit the doctor, or go to the movies. Our entire infrastructure is built on the promise of affordable gasoline and free flowing traffic.

Today, as I write this introduction, the price of crude oil has reached a record $75 a barrel, sending people into a tail spin of public transportation, mopeds, bicycles, and compact cars. The debate over why our troops are fighting in Iraq is played out on our city streets as people choose sides in the Hummer vs. Prius argument. It is, however, becoming a somewhat false debate as smaller versions of Hummers are introduced and hybrid technology is placed in SUVs. The bottom line is that very few people are willing to give up their automobile.

Our egos complicate our relationship with the cars we drive. While many of us use our vehicles for mundane commuting, popular culture continues to support the reign of the automobile as expression of personality or fantasy. The car culture continues to grow as tricked-out rides rule our fantasy automotive world. East L.A. brought us the lowrider, the films *The Fast and the Furious* and *2 Fast 2 Furious* brought us the nitro-burning joyride, and MTV's *Pimp My*

Ride is bringing souped-up Hondas and Daihatsus to a family room near you. Baby boomers refuse to give up the ghost of market influence, thus we have redesigns of muscle cars now flooding the market. Hello Mustangs, Camaros, and gas-guzzling Challengers!

On the two-wheel front, the Discovery Channel's *American Chopper* features the dysfunctional Teutul family of Orange County Choppers. Each week a bike springs from the fertile imagination of Paul Sr. and his sons as they design and manufacture an elongated motorcycle from the ground up. Here the motorcycle is seen as an engineering problem masking as art. The producers seldom if ever show the bikes on the road except for a test drive that proves the bike can move under its own power.

The concept of the motorcycle as macho incarnate is ignored by the largest new group of riders—women. According to the Motorcycle Industry Council, more than 4.3 million women are riding bikes, up 34 percent from 1998. This growing audience is gaining representation in the media, and female faces and bylines are beginning to appear in the glossy two-stroke magazines. When perusing titles for your collection, look for full gender, race, and class representation in the content.

It makes sense that automotive and motorcycle tribal affiliations are reinforced via magazines. We subscribe to titles that support our version of the Autobahn as a lifestyle. As the average sale price of a used car hits $12,500 and a new car is roughly $25,600, we use car reviews and motorcycle magazines to assist us in justifying a purchase that has become emotionally and politically loaded.

A quick perusal of the titles below (despite the fact that hundreds of magazines have not been included in the list) show that Christians, African Americans, Latinos, truck drivers, and those boisterous motorcycle aficionados all have print materials representing their clans and their passions. When choosing titles for your library, it is important to understand the demographics of your local audience. NASCAR is popular in the South in a way it will likely never be in the West. And while motocross isn't huge in large urban centers, there are regions where it is extremely important. And honestly, almost everybody wants to read the general automobile titles that display and critique the newest offerings.

Automotive and motorcycle magazines are colorful and full of technical detail, and pander to our fantasies. However superficial the content looks, we cannot undercut the importance of transportation to our library users. Good luck in choosing the titles that best represent their interests.

Basic Periodicals

Automobile, Car and Driver, Cycle World, Motor Trend, Motorcyclist, Roadbike.

Basic Abstracts and Indexes

Consumer's Index, Readers' Guide to Periodical Literature.

713. **African Americans on Wheels.** [ISSN: 1931-4949] 1995. 6x/yr. Free to qualified personnel. Ed(s): Lyndon Conrad Bell. On Wheels, Inc., 585 E Larned St, Ste 100, Detroit, MI 48226; http://www.onwheelsinc.com. Illus., adv. Circ: 720000 Paid and controlled. *Aud.:* Hs, Ga, Ac.

This is a slight magazine, written and published by and for an African American audience. The main strength of the title is its reportage in the "Around Town" section. Here is where you'll find celebratory vignettes and name dropping (in the tradition of *Jet* magazine) of African Americans in the automotive world. Titles are broad, from "African-American Men in the Executive Suite: Brothers with Clout" to "Maximum Economy," about fuel efficiency. Interestingly enough, an article about segregationist policies and auto racing is followed by a NASCAR ad with the tagline, "There's Room for Everyone." The same publisher also puts out the partially bilingual *Latinos on Wheels*, one of the nation's 35 leading Latino publications. Sample articles focus on visiting the Miami Hispanic Heritage Festival or teaching your teenager to drive. Text is available on the web site. These two titles represent important ethnic groups and should be considered for public libraries supporting a diverse audience, especially in communities with auto workers.

714. *American Iron Magazine: for people who love Harley-Davidsons.* [ISSN: 1059-7891] 1989. m. USD 23.95 domestic; USD 36.95 foreign; USD 4.99 newsstand/cover. Ed(s): Buzz Kanter, Chris Maida. T A M Communications Inc., 1010 Summer St, Stamford, CT 06905-5503. Adv. Circ: 174261 Paid. *Aud.:* Hs, Ga.

American Iron Magazine is exactly what its subtitle claims: *for people who love Harley-Davidsons.* Dream-inducing and instructional, this title features glossy photographs of bikes throughout each issue. Harley fans can read about both new and historic models, from the featured hog on the cover to hundreds of bikes within (including Buell, H-D's sport bike). This is a participatory magazine, and most of the letters to the editor include photos of readers' bikes. Travel information, reviews (detailed if not highly critical), and wrenching advice abound. Chock-full of text and photos, this magazine is a true joy to read and drool over. Also, kudos to the editors for their baby steps toward including women reviewers and riders. Suggested for all public libraries with a large wrenching and cruising population.

715. *American Motorcyclist: journal of the American Motorcyclist Association.* Former titles (until Sep. 1977): *A M A News; American Motorcycling.* [ISSN: 0277-9358] 1947. m. Free to members. Ed(s): Grant Parsons. American Motorcyclist Association, 13515 Yarmouth Dr, Pickerington, OK 43147-8214; http://www.ama-cycle.org/magazine/index.html. Illus., adv. Circ: 247588 Paid. Vol. ends: Dec. *Bk. rev.:* 1-5, 500-2,000 words. *Aud.:* Ga, Sa.

Available to the more than 250,000 members of the American Motorcyclist Association (AMA), this magazine covers every facet of motorcycling. Each monthly issue details the people, places, and events—from road rallies to road races—that make up the American motorcycling experience. The AMA is the world's largest motorsports sanctioning body, and here is where you'll find the officially sanctioned rules and events. The AMA also acts as a political lobby for motorcyclists, and there is excellent reporting on legislation and activities, state-by-state and nationally. The social lives of bikers are also described, with Daytona, Sturgis, and other rallies covered in a family-friendly format (i.e., no naked babes). For responsible riders who consider their bikes an extension of their personality, this title is absolutely necessary. Recommended for large public libraries.

716. *Antique Automobile.* [ISSN: 0003-5831] 1937. bi-m. Members, USD 30. Ed(s): West Peterson. Antique Automobile Club of America, 501 W Governor Rd, Hershey, PA 17033. Illus., adv. Circ: 40000 Paid. Microform: PQC. *Aud.:* Ga.

According to the Antique Automobile Club of America web site, "The aim of the AACA is the perpetuation of the pioneer days of automobiling by furthering the interest in and preserving of antique automobiles, and the promotion of sportsmanship and of good fellowship among all AACA members. The AACA uses the term 'automobile' in a comprehensive sense to include all self-propelled vehicles intended for passenger use (cars, race vehicles, trucks, fire vehicles, motorcycles, powered bicycles, etc.). Similarly, the term includes various power sources, such as gasoline, diesel, steam and electric." As you would expect, this is a serious title for people who wish to commune with like-minded collectors at meets and social events. As the first historical automotive society publication, this title features articles and photos of prime vehicles—lots of history, some fabrication info, but not much on the mechanical transformation. Many of the articles are first-person narratives about the finding and subsequent revitalization of their prized machine; staid but fascinating. A good title for high-income communities with a strong public library.

717. *Automobile.* Former titles (until 1988): *Automobile;* (until 1987): *Automobile Magazine.* 1986. m. USD 10 domestic; USD 23 Canada; USD 48 elsewhere. Ed(s): Gavin Conway. Source Interlink Companies, 261 Madison Ave, 6th Fl, New York, NY 10016; edisupport@sourceinterlink.com; http://www.sourceinterlink.com. Illus., adv. Sample. Circ: 642953 Paid. Vol. ends: Dec. *Indexed:* ASIP. *Aud.:* Hs, Ga, Ac.

Automobile is your average generic car title. Highlighting the most recent models from Detroit, Germany, Japan, and the rest of the world, it is a fanzine with shiny metal objects in lieu of Hollywood superstars. That said, it is a fun, worshipful read. A recent story on the newly redesigned Chevy Camaro is supported by good text and amazing photographs celebrating the car's lines. Part of the huge Primedia publishing empire, the magazine has a professional design on glossy paper with lots of photos, and text that is never too critical of the automotive industry. The writing is interesting but not in-depth. Reviews appreciate size and speed while rarely commenting on gasoline mileage. If you can only buy one general automobile title for a public library collection, either *Car and Driver* or *Road and Track* would be a better choice.

718. *Automotive Engineering International.* Former titles (until Dec. 1997): *Automotive Engineering;* (until 1972): *S A E Journal of Automotive Engineering;* Which supersedes in part (until 1970): *S A E Journal;* Which was formerly (until 1928): *Society of Automotive Engineers. Journal.* [ISSN: 1543-849X] 1905. m. Free to members; Non-members, USD 130. Society of Automotive Engineers, 400 Commonwealth Dr, Warrendale, PA 15096-0001; advertising@sae.org; http://www.sae.org/automag. Illus., adv. Circ: 85300. Vol. ends: Dec. Microform: PMC. *Indexed:* AS&TI, C&ISA, CerAb, ErgAb, ExcerpMed, H&SSA, HRIS, IAA, RRTA. *Aud.:* Ac, Sa.

The Society of Automotive Engineers has been around just over 100 years. *Automotive Engineering International* is a combination trade journal and academic resource that features editorials, technical briefs, and many in-depth articles on computers, material innovations, and product briefs. It is very much a technical title, and the casual reader may not find it accessible, but for gearheads and automotive engineers it is a must read. Complimentary subscriptions are available to engineering management, engineers, corporate officials, and purchasing and other qualified industry personnel. If you don't qualify for a free subscription, consider this title a necessary purchase for academic and special engineering and design libraries.

719. *Automotive Industries.* Former titles (until 1994): *Chilton's Automotive Industries (Radnor);* (until 1976): *Automotive Industries (Philadelphia);* (until 1972): *Chilton's Automotive Industries;* (until 1970): *Automotive Industries;* (until 1947): *Automotive and Aviation Industries;* (until 1942): *Automotive Industries;* (until 1917): *Automobile and Automotive Industries.* [ISSN: 1099-4130] 1895. m. Free. Ed(s): Edward Richardson. Diesel & Gas Turbine Publications, 20855 Watertown Rd, Ste 220, Waukesha, WI 53186-1873; mosenga@dieselpub.com; http://www.dieselpub.com. Illus., adv. Circ: 100834 Paid and controlled. Microform: CIS; PMC; PQC. Online: The Dialog Corporation; EBSCO Publishing, EBSCO Host; Factiva, Inc.; Florida Center for Library Automation; Gale; OCLC Online Computer Library Center, Inc.; ProQuest LLC (Ann Arbor); H.W. Wilson. *Indexed:* ABIn, AS&TI, BPI, C&ISA, CWI, CerAb, EngInd, EnvAb, ExcerpMed, HRIS, IAA. *Aud.:* Ga, Ac, Sa.

According to its web site, "*Automotive Industries* is a monthly publication devoted to providing global coverage of all aspects of the automobile marketplace, with an emphasis on the people, products and processes that shape the industry." Founded in 1895 as *The Horseless Age*, this title puts a strong emphasis on news that affects automotive manufacturing. For example, a current article is titled, "Our readers determine their favorite suppliers in 50 product categories." If you truly care about production scheduling, inventory control, materials development, personnel management techniques, robotics and automation applications, and European manufacturing, you will find a little bit of nirvana in this read. Highly recommended for public libraries with constituents in the automotive industry, and for academic libraries supporting programs in automotive design, engineering, business, and other affiliated studies.

720. *Automotive News: engineering, financial, manufacturing, sales, marketing, servicing.* [ISSN: 0005-1551] 1925. w. Mon. USD 155 domestic; USD 239 Canada; USD 395 elsewhere. Ed(s): David Sedgwick. Crain Communications, Inc., 1155 Gratiot Ave, Detroit, MI 48207-2997; http://www.crain.com. Illus., adv. Circ: 80000 Paid. Vol. ends: Dec. Microform: CIS; PMC; PQC. Online: EBSCO Publishing, EBSCO Host; Florida Center for Library Automation; Gale; LexisNexis; Northern Light Technology, Inc.; OCLC Online Computer Library Center, Inc.; ProQuest K-12 Learning Solutions; ProQuest LLC (Ann Arbor); H.W. Wilson. *Indexed:* ABIn, BPI, C&ISA, CWI, CerAb, HRIS, IAA. *Aud.:* Ac, Sa.

As stated on their web site, "for more than 80 years *Automotive News* has been the leading source of news for the North American automotive industry. *Automotive News* covers the manufacturing side of the automotive industry, including engineering, design, production and suppliers, with equal emphasis on the retail side of the industry, including the marketing, sales, service and resale of vehicles." It's actually more of a newspaper, and a necessary read for all involved in any aspect of the automotive business. It has a strong online presence as well as a chock-full print edition. Statistics, new models, CEO biographies, and more are found in its rich pages. Recommended for libraries with automotive research collections or public libraries in automotive factory towns.

721. Car and Driver. [ISSN: 0008-6002] 1956. m. USD 12; USD 3.99 newsstand/cover. Ed(s): Csaba Csere. Hachette Filipacchi Media U.S., Inc., 1633 Broadway, New York, NY 10019; http://www.hfmus.com. Illus., adv. Sample. Circ: 1381909 Paid. Vol. ends: Jun. Microform: NBI; PQC. Online: The Dialog Corporation; OCLC Online Computer Library Center, Inc.; H.W. Wilson. *Indexed:* CPerI, ConsI, HRIS, LRI, MASUSE, RGPR. *Aud.:* Hs, Ga.

In publication since 1956, *Car and Driver* reviews and tests domestic and foreign automobiles. It is slickly designed and full of photographs, well-written reviews, and interesting articles. I love reading this title even when I'm not in the market for a car. The magazine excels in comparative reviews of a particular vehicle genre, such as German sedans or the five best trucks. Featured articles cover the gamut from a NASA 25-hour classic to how best to test drive a car. The rich history of car porn continues as each month's publication features dream cars few of us will ever own. That aside, most of the magazine is devoted to educating buyers and enthralling enthusiasts. *Car and Driver* does this competently and with a bit of elan. Recommended for high school and public libraries.

722. Car Craft: do-it-yourself street performance. [ISSN: 0008-6010] 1953. m. USD 10 domestic; USD 22 Canada; USD 34 elsewhere. Ed(s): Douglas Glad. Source Interlink Companies, 6420 Wilshire Blvd, Los Angeles, CA 90048; edisupport@sourceinterlink.com; http://www.sourceinterlink.com. Illus., adv. Circ: 375186 Paid. Microform: PQC. Online: Gale. *Aud.:* Hs, Ga.

Car Craft is the entry-level title for the weekend "rebuilt" warrior. Supporting all aspects of owning, maintaining, and customizing high-performance street cars, this title is a must for any wrenching fool who likes to do it her/himself. Technical articles give the basics on nitrous fuel and diagnosing used engines. After reading each issue I feel the urge to replace my transmission or some other nonsense. The featured articles show amazing cars (at least five to seven of them). The columns are funny, irreverent, and actually pretty enjoyable, with *Cosmo*–like titles such as "25 Carb Tech Tips and Tricks for Under 25 Bucks." With more than 375,000 paid subscribers, this magazine obviously fulfills some basic American need. Suggested for high school and public libraries.

723. Christian Motorsports Illustrated. Incorporates (in 1999): *Chrysler Power.* [ISSN: 1099-9396] 1996. q. USD 19.96; USD 4.99 newsstand/cover. Ed(s): Tom Winfield. C P O, PO Box 929, Bristow, OK 74010-0929; http://www.christianmotorsports.com. Illus., adv. Circ: 15000 Paid and controlled. *Aud.:* Hs, Ga.

Along with Christian Rock and Christian Skateboard Ministries, the born-again influence in the United States continues to expand and grow in the most interesting ways. *Christian Motorsports* recently procured 501C3 status with the IRS, which means that instead of subscribing to this title, one now "donates" to the cause and receives the magazine as a gift. According to the blurb, it is "a colorful, exciting motorsports magazine reporting on God's invasion of the world of motorsports." Muscular Christianity indeed! This magazine is an incongruent combination of technical information, NASCAR worship, and proselytizing. As the editor's note says, "Unlike other magazines, we wait on the Holy Spirit to give us a theme which translates into an explosive cover." Although the audience for this title is limited, it is a vocal one. The publication might be considered for libraries with car-focused, conservative Christian patrons. However, I'm not convinced that giving to causes is an appropriate action for public libraries.

724. Collectible Automobile. Formerly: *Consumer Guide Elite Cars.* [ISSN: 0742-812X] 1984. bi-m. USD 37.95; USD 6.65 newsstand/cover per issue. Ed(s): John Biel. Publications International Ltd., 7373 N Cicero Ave, Lincolnwood, IL 60646. Illus., adv. Circ: 100000. *Bk. rev.:* 1-5, 500-2,000. *Aud.:* Ga, Sa.

Imagine, if you will, the automotive equivalent of *National Geographic*, a magazine on high-gloss paper with amazing photography and writing that incorporates automobile history with mechanical talk and places it in its proper place in the historical/sociological continuum. That magazine exists, and it is *Collectible Automobile*. This is the premier title on automotive restoration—not muscle-car wrenching but the careful reconstitution of older vehicles. Four cars are featured in each issue, with magnificent photos and great supporting text. Sections are titled "Expert Advice," "Trends," and "Hot Models," with much more practical and fanciful content for the auto enthusiast. If a public library can purchase only one auto-restoration/old-car-buff title, *Collectible Automobile* should be it. Also of interest to academic libraries that collect in automotive history.

725. Consumer Reports New Car Preview. Former titles (until 2000): *Consumer Reports Preview;* (until 1999): *Consumer Reports New Car Yearbook.* [ISSN: 1551-3009] 1994. a. USD 5.95. Consumers Union of the United States, Inc., 101 Truman Ave, Yonkers, NY 10703-1057; http://www.consumerreports.org. *Aud.:* Ga, Ac, Sa.

Any reference librarian will tell you that *Consumer Reports* automobile reviews are an amazingly popular resource. While many car magazines present a fair and nuanced opinion, nobody has the respect, the history, and the firewall separating them from the industry like *Consumer Reports*. Consumers Union was founded in 1936 as an independent, nonprofit testing and information organization, with the motto "Test, Inform, Protect." The annual *New Car Preview*, a great value for the price, has two sections. The first includes articles on how to shop for a new car, overviews on new models and trends, and hints for haggling on price. The second is filled with detailed model reviews. Lacking the lyrical content of most auto appraisals, there is a short chapter of text and then information on safety, specs, reliability history, forecasts, and "From the Test Track." These nitpicky facts are more useful than the perceptions and specifications that fill most automotive reviews, and they can be implicitly trusted as unbiased. Highly recommended for public and academic libraries.

726. Cycle World. Incorporated (in Oct. 1991): *Cycle (New York, 1952).* [ISSN: 0011-4286] 1961. m. USD 21.94 domestic; USD 29.94 foreign. Ed(s): David Edwards, Mark Hoyer. Hachette Filipacchi Media U.S., Inc., 1633 Broadway, New York, NY 10019; http://www.hfmus.com. Illus., adv. Sample. Circ: 325000 Paid. Vol. ends: Dec. Microform: NBI; PQC. Online: Factiva, Inc.; OCLC Online Computer Library Center, Inc.; H.W. Wilson. *Indexed:* ConsI, LRI, MASUSE, RGPR. *Bk. rev.:* Various number and length. *Aud.:* Hs, Ga.

Cycle World goes toe-to-toe with *Motorcyclist* for the best generalist (mostly metric) bike title. Although *Motorcyclist* is older, *Cycle World* has a healthy 100,000-plus subscribers. *Cycle World* has the same combination of reviews, side-by-side comparisons, and worshipful praise that are staples of all motorcycling publications. The bikes on the cover appear to fly off the page, and it only gets more intense between the covers. In addition, there are lifestyle articles, reporting on races and rallies, video game reviews, book reviews, and more. If it came to a tie-breaker I'd chose *Motorcyclist*, if only for its informative, text-rich web site. Otherwise, it's up to you to decide which of these two should be added to your public library collection.

727. Hot Rod. [ISSN: 0018-6031] 1948. m. USD 18 for 2 yrs. domestic; USD 42 for 2 yrs. Canada; USD 66 for 2 yrs. elsewhere. Ed(s): Rob Kinnan. Source Interlink Companies, 6420 Wilshire Blvd, Los Angeles, CA 90048; edisupport@sourceinterlink.com; http://www.sourceinterlink.com. Illus., adv. Sample. Circ: 709257 Paid. Vol. ends: Dec. Microform: PQC. Online: The Dialog Corporation; Gale; Micromedia ProQuest; OCLC Online Computer Library Center, Inc.; ProQuest LLC (Ann Arbor); H.W. Wilson. *Indexed:* ASIP, CBCARef, CPerI, ConsI, MASUSE, RGPR. *Bk. rev.:* 1-3, 200-500 words. *Aud.:* Hs, Ga.

Hot Rod is a prime example of car porn. Directed toward men and visually oriented, with hundreds of photographs of cars, this hugely popular title takes most of its readers into a gasoline-powered fantasyland. Focusing on high-performance vehicles, the technical (chassis, drive train, engine) and how-to (painting, oiling, installing, etc.) articles take up much of the magazine's real estate. With over 800,000 subscribers (double that of *The Atlantic Monthly* and equivalent to *The New Yorker*), it is *Car Craft*'s uptown sibling. If your readers want articles such as "Best Hot Rodder Ever," "Hottest Car Show On TV," or "Fastest LT1 Camaro," this is a title your library should own. Public libraries should seriously consider this magazine for their popular periodicals collection.

728. Hybrid & Electric Vehicle Progress: industry news and technical developments in elctric, hybrid and fuel cell vehicles. Formerly: *Electric Vehicle Progress.* [ISSN: 1548-7997] 1979. bi-m. USD 590. Ed(s): Layne Holley. Alexander Communications Group, Inc., 712 Main St Ste 187B, Boonton, NJ 07005; info@alexcommgrp.com; http://www.alexcommgrp.com. Illus. Sample. *Aud.:* Ga, Ac, Sa.

More than ever, automobile customers are considering the importance of alternative technologies. For close to 30 years, *Hybrid & Electric Vehicle Progress* has provided worldwide news concerning research, development, and commercialization of battery-electric, hybrid, and fuel cell vehicles. From this long-range perspective, it distills important information and market intelligence to bring you a clear, concise picture of the industry. It is published twice each month, and short articles focus on research and development, alternative power sources, real-world applications, marketing strategies, and more. OK, full disclosure, it is really more newsletter than magazine, but with today's emphasis on alternative fuels, this is a necessary purchase for large public, academic, and special engineering and design libraries.

729. Import Tuner. [ISSN: 1528-0845] 1998. m. USD 19.97 domestic; USD 44.97 foreign; USD 4.99 newsstand/cover per issue. Source Interlink Companies, 27500 Riverview Center Blvd, Bonita Springs, FL 34134; edisupport@sourceinterlink.com; http://www.sourceinterlink.com. Adv. *Aud.:* Hs, Ga.

Sometimes I find myself listing titles that are more than a little sexist and foolish. The web site for this title claims that "*Import Tuner* is a must-have for enthusiasts looking to enhance the performance and appearance of their import! You'll get new information each month on the hottest cars, GIRLS, and events in the import industry along with accurate dyno-proven technical information." OK, did you get the subtext? You'll get girls if you have a hot car. If you don't believe the web site, you'll see this same attitude embedded throughout the magazine. This is *The Fast and the Furious* on paper, with amazing photos, wonkish mechanical guides—oh, and girls. Lots of girls. Perfect for communities with populations who trick out their cars. Recommended for public libraries.

Lowrider. See Latino Studies section.

730. Moto Kids. [ISSN: 1933-9712] 2002. bi-m. USD 9.95 domestic; USD 21.95 foreign. Ed(s): Paul Carruthers. Cycle News, Inc., 3503-M Cadillac Ave, Costa Mesa, CA 92626; advertising@moto-kids.com. Adv. Circ: 70000. *Aud.:* Hs, Ga, Sa.

Looking at *Moto Kids*, with its high-gloss paper and full-color, full-page photos, makes me more than a bit jealous of its target audience. I love the family and safety focus, with its busily designed pages, product evaluations, personality profiles, riding tips, and motorcycle maintenance help. Kudos to the editors and advertisers, who are taking baby steps toward including girls here and there. The text is written to be accessible and youthful in style, which is not to say that it is dumbed down. In fact, the magazine is an excellent access point for reluctant readers. The focus is on the "future of our sport," and lest we forget, the parents are paying for an inexpensive magazine but a very expensive hobby. The web site calls *Moto Kids* "Not your Daddy's Motorcycle Magazine!" Recommended for public libraries where there is a strong motocross community.

731. Motor Trend. Incorporates: *Car Life; Sports Car Graphic; Wheels Afield.* [ISSN: 0027-2094] 1949. m. USD 10 domestic; USD 23 Canada; USD 25 elsewhere. Ed(s): Angus MacKenzie. Source Interlink

Companies, 261 Madison Ave, 6th Fl, New York, NY 10016; edisupport@sourceinterlink.com; http://www.sourceinterlink.com. Illus., index, adv. Circ: 1285178 Paid. Vol. ends: Dec. CD-ROM: ProQuest LLC (Ann Arbor). Microform: PQC. Online: The Dialog Corporation; Gale; Micromedia ProQuest; OCLC Online Computer Library Center, Inc.; ProQuest LLC (Ann Arbor); H.W. Wilson. *Indexed:* CBCARef, ConsI, MASUSE, RGPR. *Aud.:* Hs, Ga, Ac.

Even if you've never picked up a copy of *Motor Trend*, you've more than likely heard of the "Motor Trend Car of the Year Award." Around since 1949, *Motor Trend* competes with *Car and Driver* and *Road & Track* for your subscription money. It covers news and trends in the worldwide auto market along with excellent road tests and reviews. The writing is breezy, funny, and critical when it needs to be. Unlike some car reviews, those in *Motor Trend* tend to take into account what sort of driver is drawn to a car and why. This mix of the sociological with the automotive makes for a fuller read. A recent issue features "Hydrogen, Fuel Cells, and Reality." Articles on car care, auto shows, and race results round out a fun and often useful title. Recommended for public libraries and specialized academic collections.

732. Motorcyclist. Incorporates (1970-1988): *Motorcycle Buyer's Guide.* [ISSN: 0027-2205] 1912. m. USD 10 domestic; USD 22 Canada; USD 34 elsewhere. Ed(s): Mitch Boehm. Source Interlink Companies, 6420 Wilshire Blvd, Los Angeles, CA 90048; edisupport@sourceinterlink.com; http://www.sourceinterlink.com. Illus., adv. Circ: 255456 Paid. Microform: PQC. Online: Gale. *Indexed:* ConsI, IHTDI. *Aud.:* Hs, Ga.

If you can only afford one motorcycle magazine for your library, *Motorcyclist* should be it. In existence since 1912, it covers a bit of everything: racing bikes, cruisers, American motorcycles vs. others, reviews, and more. The cover story is generally some new bike that simply screams for attention, or so it would seem when the tilted bike is photographed being driven at full speed and surrounded by text in a huge yellow font ending with exclamation points. There are really enjoyable non-feature articles, columns, and departments written by experienced writers/bikers. Sections include "First Rides," "Road Tests," "Flashback," "Gearbox," and "Motorcycle Escapes." Safety is given a priority throughout the magazine. Unlike most Harley magazines, there are no riders without helmets on these pages. *Motorcyclist* is akin to the older sister or brother biker that every youth should learn from. Highly recommended for public libraries.

733. Racer X Illustrated. [ISSN: 1099-6729] 1998. bi-m. USD 24; USD 4.95 newsstand/cover per issue. Ed(s): Davey Coombs. Racer X Illustrated, 122 Vista Del Rio Dr., Morgantown, WV 26508-8832; davey@racerxill.com; http://www.racerxill.com. Illus., adv. *Bk. rev.:* Various number and length. *Aud.:* Hs, Ga.

If *Moto Kids* is the entry-level title for motocross racing, *Racer X Illustrated* is the next logical step up as the motocross racer reaches young adulthood. This title just keeps growing and getting better. Covering all aspects of motocross racing and recreation, this kinetically designed magazine seeps testosterone through its text, ads, and photographs. Each month a number of events, stars in the field, and instructional articles are featured along with multiple photos on almost every page. This monthly extravaganza of 250-plus pages constantly features terms like "broken clavicle" and "mild concussion." For public libraries that support motocross enthusiasts.

734. Racing Milestones: America's race fan magazine. [ISSN: 1931-5082] 1996. m. USD 19.95 domestic; USD 29.95 Canada; USD 42.95 elsewhere. Ed(s): Mary Scully. Racing Milestones, 100 West Plume St, Norfolk, VA 23510; bwalton@traderonline.com; http://www.racingmilestones.com/. *Aud.:* Hs, Ga.

Racing Milestones claims to be "America's Race Fan Magazine, with the best coverage of NASCAR available!" I can't vouch for the truth of that statement, but I can say that this lively fanzine is as NASCAR as they come. Filled with full-color photographs on glossy paper and supported by knowledgeable text, this title could be the go-to guide for the racing season's stats, background stories, and (nice) gossip. Articles include race reports from Atlanta, Texas, Phoenix, etc. Winners are celebrated, but the also-rans get their own stories full of facts and stats. Like baseball, you never know who is going to jump into fame after one fantastic day. Fan photos, letters to the editor, and the advertisements (all NASCAR, all the time) show how both the racers and viewers are equal partners in one of the fastest growing attractions in the United States. Suggested for public libraries who support sports and automobile collections.

735. Road & Track. [ISSN: 0035-7189] 1947. m. USD 10 domestic; USD 20 foreign; USD 3.99 newsstand/cover per issue. Ed(s): Thomas L Bryant, Douglas Kott. Hachette Filipacchi Media U.S., Inc., 1633 Broadway, New York, NY 10019; http://www.hfmus.com. Illus., index, adv. Sample. Circ: 740000 Paid. Vol. ends: Dec. Microform: NBI; PQC. Online: OCLC Online Computer Library Center, Inc.; H.W. Wilson. *Indexed:* ASIP, ConsI, MASUSE, RGPR. *Bk. rev.:* 1-2, 2,000 words. *Aud.:* Hs, Ga.

Started in 1947, *Road & Track* is the original automotive enthusiast magazine. In the same genre as *Car and Driver* and *Motor Trend*, it focuses on automotive design, engineering, driving reports, road tests, racing coverage, and in-depth technical discussions. The magazine's road tests are detailed and fun to read, the technical articles truly interesting (for example, all-wheel drive is explained with a few cars reviewed), and the photographs ensure car lust. The news features cover industry insiders, automotive shows, and trends. One of my personal favorites, it is a strong contender for collections in public and academic libraries, especially those supporting an automotive industry audience.

736. RoadBike. Former titles (until 2002): *Motorcycle Tour & Cruiser; Motorcycle Tour and Travel.* [ISSN: 1538-4748] 1993. m. USD 19.94 domestic; USD 30.94 foreign; USD 3.99 newsstand/cover per issue domestic. Ed(s): Buzz Kanter, Jessica Prokup. T A M Communications Inc., 1010 Summer St, Stamford, CT 06905-5503. Illus., adv. Sample. Circ: 55000 Paid. Vol. ends: Nov. *Aud.:* Hs, Ga.

There are two reasons why libraries should consider *RoadBike* (formerly *Motorcycle Tour & Cruiser*). To this reviewer, the first and most important is that it features a good number of female authors and focuses on regular folks. The second reason is specialization; its subtitle is *Ride Metric*, meaning that it specializes in non-American bikes. If your library can afford to buy more than one motorcycle magazine, it should consider a touring/travel title, and this is a superior example. There are bike reviews, articles on paint jobs and customizations, up to seven mechanical/tech articles, and a bunch of gear write-ups. What makes this title different, other than its respect for women riders, are the roadtrip articles included each month. Be it the heart of the Ozarks or a two-part trip along the Mexican coast and into Belize, these articles include history, maps, events, and contact information. With roadbike cruising growing in popularity, this would be a superb addition to any public library travel or motorcycle collection.

737. Scoot! Quarterly. [ISSN: 1545-1356] 199?. q. USD 19.95 domestic; USD 26.80 in Canada & Mexico; USD 31.86 elsewhere. Scoot!, 9605, San Jose, CA 95157-0605; casey@scooter.com; http://www.scooter.com. *Aud.:* Hs, Ga.

Scoot! calls itself "North America's #1 Magazine for Vintage and Modern Motorscooters." I agree. No other title features, celebrates, and has as much fun with the motorscooter as this one does. Colorful, glossy, and well designed, this is the magazine one should turn to when shopping for a new scooter, revitalizing the rusty old one in the shed, or simply dreaming about the Vespa lifestyle. In addition to the many excellent new-product reviews, there are articles such as "Navigating the Maze of Chinese Scooters" and "Winterizing Your Scooter," as well as wonderful regular features. "Scootin' News," "Music Review," and "Readers' Rides" spread the scooting lifestyle—cute, tatooed, and adventurous. Think of it as Harley lite, in the best possible way. Recommended for public libraries that support cities with alternative scenes and those that wish they did.

738. Stock Car Racing. [ISSN: 0734-7340] 1964. m. USD 12 domestic; USD 24 Canada; USD 36 elsewhere. Ed(s): Larry Cothren. Source Interlink Companies, 9036 Brittany Way, Tampa, FL 33619. Illus., adv. Circ: 257296 Paid. *Aud.:* Hs, Ga.

Published since 1964, *Stock Car Racing* has been along for the ride as NASCAR has risen in popularity. The editors appear to be coming to terms with their growing readership and continue to put out a product that isn't dumbed down. Recognizing its core audience, it continues to cover all aspects of the racing lifestyle, profiling drivers, reporting on events, and reviewing equipment.

According to the literature, the title has "renewed its emphasis to develop grassroots entry-level racing." This magazine accurately reflects a sport that is all about noise, hero worship, safety (barely), and the quick reflexes of men (and a few women) willing to risk their lives for riches. Recommended for public libraries with racing fans.

739. Truckin': world's leading sport truck publication. [ISSN: 0277-5743] 1975. m. USD 20 domestic; USD 33 Canada; USD 46 elsewhere. Ed(s): Steve Warner. Source Interlink Companies, 2400 E Katella Ave, Ste 1100, Anaheim, CA 92806; edisupport@sourceinterlink.com; http://www.sourceinterlink.com. Illus., adv. Circ: 206000 Paid and free. Vol. ends: Dec. *Aud.:* Hs, Ga.

A record 54.3 percent of all new vehicles sold in the country last year were classified as "light trucks," as opposed to passenger cars. This wacko statistic shows what happens when Congress allows trucks to go incognito as SUVs, sans gas-mileage restrictions. That said, I have to admit I love trucks (although not SUVs). *Truckin'* is an example of the genre specialization that exists in the automotive publishing world. Tilted toward the enthusiast, this title emphasizes all things truck. Customization, new model reviews (domestic and imported), tech tips, and lots of interaction between readers and the publisher fill the pages for those who can't get enough from more generalist magazines. Recommended only for specialized collections.

740. V-Twin. Incorporates (1994-2001): *V Q.* [ISSN: 1042-5365] 1989. m. USD 29.95 domestic; USD 4.99 newsstand/cover per issue; USD 6.99 newsstand/cover per issue Canada. Ed(s): Sandie Nilsen, Keith Ball. Paisano Publications, Inc., PO Box 3075, Agoura Hills, CA 91301. Illus., adv. *Aud.:* Hs, Ga.

The other bike magazines, *Motorcyclist*, *RoadBike*, etc., lean a bit heavily toward touring bikes and racebikes. Our popular imagination and that of West Coast Choppers and Arlen Ness lean more toward the perfect form of the V-Twin. This title is a celebration of freedom and customization. Glossy and in full color, this title is chock-full of articles on the mechanics of upgrading your bike or just dreamy examples of different paint schemes. This is the perfect title for those riders who want to appear more "outlaw" than they'll ever really be. Great for a public library bent on representing all motorcycle enthusiasts.

741. Vintage Motorsport: the journal of motor racing history. [ISSN: 1052-8067] 1982. bi-m. USD 35 domestic; USD 45 in Canada & Mexico; USD 65 in Europe. Ed(s): Randy Riggs. Vintage Motorsport Inc., PO Box 7200, Lakeland, FL 33807. Adv. Circ: 9350. *Bk. rev.:* Various number and length. *Aud.:* Hs, Ga, Ac.

This title is a celebration of the history of automotive racing. According to its web site, "*Vintage Motorsport, the Journal of Motor Racing History*, celebrates the heroes of motorsport, the people, cars, and venues that have given the sport its rich heritage. In addition, the magazine covers current vintage racing, which continues to reach new levels in participation and attendance." While NASCAR and drag racing are huge, the magazines that support them seldom look deeply into the past. This title views racing history through an international lens. Examples of content include midget racing after World War II and a celebration of "George Follmer: The Racer's Racer." For the public library that fully supports the racing enthusiast.

742. Ward's AutoWorld. Formerly: *Ward's Quarterly.* [ISSN: 0043-0315] 1964. m. USD 63 domestic (Free to qualified personnel). Ed(s): Barbara L McClellan. Ward's Automotive Group, 3000 Town Center, Ste 2750, Southfield, MI 48075-1212; wards@prismb2b.com; http://www.wardsauto.com. Illus., index, adv. Circ: 68200 Controlled. Online: EBSCO Publishing, EBSCO Host; Florida Center for Library Automation; Gale; Northern Light Technology, Inc.; OCLC Online Computer Library Center, Inc.; ProQuest K-12 Learning Solutions; ProQuest LLC (Ann Arbor); H.W. Wilson. *Indexed:* ABIn, BPI, C&ISA, CerAb, HRIS, IAA. *Aud.:* Ac, Sa.

An insider's publication, *Ward's AutoWorld* reports on industry news, trends, and technology. According to their web site, "Content includes information on vehicle technology, global industry trends, labor and management issues, supplier technology and business trends, automaker-supplier relationships, the latest in manufacturing and materials, and economic, political and legal issues."

Articles are interesting even to non-industry readers. Gas prices and exterior airbags that protect pedestrians are recent features. Recommended for specialized academic collections and public libraries with industry connections.

■ BEER, WINE, AND SPIRITS

Todd Bachmann, Associate Head of Imaging Services, Harvard College Library, Harvard University, Cambridge, MA 02138

Introduction

In the same way that high cuisine and celebrity chefs led to an ever-increasing number of publications in food and cooking, more and more magazines are now dedicated to the appreciation of beer, wine, and spirits. Magazines covering wine have been available to consumers for three decades, but the industry and ensuing publications continue to expand. At the same time, beer, which has received nominal attention in the past, has recently experienced a resurgence in the marketplace due to the popularity of microbreweries, artisan ales, and homebrewing enthusiasts. Distilled spirits are also being featured more prominently in publications.

Basic Periodicals

Wine Spectator, Wine & Spirits, Imbibe.

Basic Abstracts and Indexes

Hospitality and Tourism Index.

743. *All About Beer.* [ISSN: 0898-9001] 1980. bi-m. USD 19.99 domestic; USD 29.99 in Canada & Mexico; USD 39.99 elsewhere. Ed(s): Julie Johnson Bradford. Chautauqua Press, 501-H Washington Street, Durham, NC 27701; publisher@allaboutbeer.com. Illus., adv. Circ: 26000 Paid. *Bk. rev.:* Occasional. *Aud.:* Ga, Sa.

With few publications in the marketplace dedicated exclusively to beer, *All About Beer* has become the standard magazine for beer enthusiasts over the past few decades. While *Beer Advocate* magazine attempts to reshape the image of beer as a serious, respectable beverage, *All About Beer* is not shy about embracing the more down-to-earth view of beer. In many cases, the publication tries to bridge the distance between the high-end, small-scale artisanal approach to beer-making and the mass-production beer giants. In trying to appeal to all, however, it may be unsatisfying for many, because it is too broad and basic in coverage. After all, few beer consumers are interested in both the craft brew and the conventional domestic brew. In general, the publication does provide some interesting articles on beer-making, travelogues, marketplace products, events, and book and beer reviews, but it does suffer from the occasional insertion of frivolous topics. Where it succeeds is with well-written pieces by columnists like Michael Jackson, perhaps the most well-known of the beer gurus. The design is unadventurous: a traditional glossy magazine with gimmicky covers that perpetuate the established "good times" aspect of beer. Ultimately, these cover designs tend to detract from the quality content contained inside. Overall, the core of this publication has much to offer, but a redesign and re-examination of current features may be necessary if it is to remain relevant.

744. *BeerAdvocate.* 2007. m. USD 19.95. Ed(s): Joe Keohane. BeerAdvocate, PO Box 534, Boston, MA 02128. Illus., adv. Circ: 10000. *Aud.:* Ga, Sa.

BeerAdvocate magazine is the newest beer-oriented publication to arrive in the marketplace. The magazine comes from the same people who created and continue to manage the BeerAdvocate web site. As expected, it has a lot in common with that site, including current news, feature articles, and of course numerous beer reviews and ratings (the foundation of this popular site). It is true that while the craft brew phenomenon is now well established in the United States, there has never been a comprehensive and comparable monthly periodical to focus on the specialty beer/ale obsession. Clearly, the editors are hoping to simultaneously elevate both the image of beer as a respectable beverage and the beer enthusiast as a true taste-setter, in the same way that fine wine and high cuisine magazines are now commonplace. Paralleling the web

membership, the target audience for this publication is mostly the younger "X-treme" beer crowd. Will this be enough to sustain the production of a high-end glossy publication every month? At some point, in order to sustain and develop their publication, the editors may need to decide whether to appeal only to their own hardcore artisan ale quaffers or attempt to draw in casual, recreational imbibers. Judging from the initial issues, they appear to be off to a promising start, with lots of quality photos and slick experimental layout. However, while the design is very appealing, the content may need a little development in order to differentiate the magazine from the free and easy access to content on the web site and other Internet forums. Nevertheless, the editors have gone from a fledgling web site in ten years to the standard source for beer aficionados; it would not be a stretch to believe that they can produce the equivalent in magazine format.

745. *Brew Your Own: the how-to homebrew beer magazine.* [ISSN: 1081-826X] 1995. 8x/yr. USD 24.95 domestic; USD 29.95 in Canada & Mexico; USD 39.95 elsewhere. Ed(s): Chris Colby. Brew Your Own, 5053 Main St, Ste A, Manchester Center, VT 05255. Illus., adv. Circ: 105000 Paid. *Aud.:* Ga, Sa.

With a focus on the recreational homebrewer, this magazine will appeal to amateurs planning to embark on brewing as a hobby. While oriented to the novice, it is not superficial in content and is realistic about what resources its readers must be willing to commit to this pursuit. While much of this information may also be available in numerous introductory books on homebrewing, this magazine can provide additional information to encourage the new homebrewer to experiment as well. Each issue often features more in-depth information of a particular aspect of the brewing process than commonly found in introductory books. As a community building forum, "Ask Mr. Wizard" columns are dedicated to solving problems and answering questions.

746. *Drinks: the magazine of fine wine, spirits and living.* 2003. q. USD 9.95. Greenspring Media Group, 600 U.S. Trust Bldg, 730 Second Ave. S, Minneapolis, MN 55402; http://www.greenspring.com. Illus., adv. Circ: 354786 Paid. *Aud.:* Ga, Sa.

Drinks is not as all-encompassing, creative, or as inventive as the newer magazine *Imbibe*. *Drinks*, a publication of the Greenspring Media Group, may be more of a trendy party companion than a magazine with journalistic insight or content. With a focus mostly on lifestyle, the magazine appears to take itself a little less seriously than many of the more prominent wine publications. It is well illustrated, with an emphasis on entertainment and social gatherings, along with a copious selection of mixed drink recipes. However, while the enjoyment of wine and spirits can revolve around entertainment and social events, this publication does not appear to provide much more than that for consumers.

747. *Imbibe.* [ISSN: 1557-7082] 2006. bi-m. USD 15.95 domestic; USD 25.95 Canada. Imbibe Media Inc, 1028 SE Water Ave Ste 285, Portland, OR 97214. Illus., adv. *Aud.:* Ga, Sa.

One of the more creative, exciting, and enjoyable magazines to arrive on the scene, *Imbibe* is a stylish, in-depth exploration of the world of drinks and drink culture. The editors of this fledgling publication have clearly picked up on the growing consumer trend toward specialty drinks and artisan ales. However, *Imbibe* is also meant for the caffeine-oriented crowd as well. The publisher is gambling that the same people who seek creative drinks also want flavorful coffees and teas. The publication is well designed and very accessible, full of the latest news, interviews, reviews, and innovative recipes. There is a positive buzz growing about this publication, and it appears poised to make inroads with the younger hip crowd. The only question remains whether the editors can continue to find enough quality content to fill the pages and keep their audience's attention.

748. *Malt Advocate: beer and whisky magazine.* [ISSN: 1086-4199] 1994. q. USD 18 domestic; USD 24 Canada; USD 40 elsewhere. Ed(s): Lew Bryson, John Hansell. Malt Advocate, Inc., PO Box 158, Emmaus, PA 18049-0158; info@maltadvocate.com; http://www.whiskeypages.com. Illus., adv. Circ: 40000. *Aud.:* Ga, Sa.

Although *Malt Advocate* magazine is dedicated to all malt beverages, it is mostly dominated by whisky-related information. Like beer, single-malt whisky is undergoing a renaissance in both appreciation and consumption. While this magazine tries to tie the two beverages together, beer seems to be an afterthought in most of the issues. Each issue includes a short synopsis of new products in the marketplace, whisky news, articles from current and historical perspectives, as well as the obligatory reviews, recipes, and a buyers' guide. Its strength remains with its lively columns by such experts as Michael Jackson and Stephen Beaumont. The publisher is also the host of WhiskyFest, an annual sampling and educational event, which it heavily advertises. Overall, the magazine struggles to balance serious, sophisticated content with banal advertising and design cliches.

749. Quarterly Review of Wines. [ISSN: 0740-1248] 1977. q. USD 17.95 domestic; USD 22.95 Canada; USD 39.95 in Europe. Ed(s): Randolph G Sheahan. Q R W, Inc., 24 Garfield Ave, Winchester, MA 01890; qrwine@qrw.com; http://www.qrw.com. Illus., adv. Sample. Circ: 25000 Free. *Bk. rev.:* Occasional. *Aud.:* Ga, Sa.

With 30 years in the industry, the *QRW* is one of the founding magazines in the marketplace and still going strong. Often listed among the top three periodicals covering wine, the *QRW* has knowledgeable contributors and a classic, tabloid design format. Each issue contains a sought-after buying guide, along with wine ratings and reviews, plenty of comprehensive articles, society and celebrity pieces, restaurant and book reviews, and occasional features on spirits and cigars. Uniquely, the *QRW* uses a five-point rating system rather than the more accepted 100-point system. Implicit in its title, this magazine is published quarterly and thus contains more content and in-depth articles per issue than many of its competitors. Libraries may want to consider the *QRW* as a perfectly acceptable alternative to *Wine Spectator*, providing expert information without the high cost commitment.

750. Wine & Spirits: the practical guide to wine. Formerly: *Wine and Spirits Buying Guide.* [ISSN: 0890-0299] 1981. 8x/yr. USD 29.95 domestic; USD 39.95 Canada; USD 59.95 elsewhere. Ed(s): Tara Q Thomas, Joshua Greene. Wine & Spirits Magazine, Inc., 2 W. 32nd St., Ste. 601, New York, NY 10001. Illus., adv. Circ: 70000 Paid. *Indexed:* H&TI. *Aud.:* Ga, Sa.

W&S readership has grown significantly in recent years, and the publication can be viewed as a respectable alternative to the more-upscale wine consumer magazines. In fact, *W&S* prides itself on providing more fundamental and pragmatic information for judging and enjoying wine and other spirits than other publications. Echoing this sensible approach to meaningful content, the publication is designed in a conventional magazine format. Among its most notable features is the annual issue dedicated to wine education, recognizing that not all wine consumers automatically fall into the expert class. Like many of its competitors, *W&S* embraces the 100-point system for wine reviews. While the magazine has received awards for its fine wine journalism, it is truly targeted to more than just the wine enthusiast, with extensive articles on premium distilled spirits. Overall, *W&S* is a fine publication to consider when trying to reach and satisfy a greater audience of readers for wine and spirits topics.

751. Wine Enthusiast. Formerly (until 1990): *Wine Times.* [ISSN: 1078-3318] 1988. 14x/yr. USD 29.95 domestic; USD 49.95 Canada; USD 79.95 elsewhere. Ed(s): Mary Hunt. Wine Enthusiast, 103 Fairview Pk Dr, Elmsford, NY 10523-1553; custserv@wineenthusiast.net. Illus., adv. Circ: 95000 Paid and free. *Aud.:* Ga, Sa.

Although lacking the household name recognition of *Wine Spectator, Wine Enthusiast* remains an equally revered publication in the industry and provides authoritative content and stylish tabloid design and layout. Only a short time ago, *Wine Enthusiast* was exclusively a catalog service for wine accessories. In 1988, the publishers created a consumer-based magazine to reach a wider audience. Like *Wine Spectator*, it is mostly focused on the sophisticated palette; however, it does try to cater to the novice, and provides numerous reviews of affordable wines. The publisher hosts an annual tasting event to promote and provide access to many fine wines. In addition, unlike most of its competitors, *Wine Enthusiast* provides significant coverage of distilled spirits and beer.

752. The Wine News. [ISSN: 1065-4895] 1985. bi-m. USD 25 domestic; USD 60 foreign; USD 5 newsstand/cover. Ed(s): Kathy Sinnes. T.E. Smith, Ed. & Pub., PO Box 142096, Coral Gables, FL 33114; http://www.thewinenews.com. Illus., adv. Circ: 60000 Paid and controlled. Vol. ends: Dec/Jan. *Aud.:* Ga, Sa.

Published bimonthly, *The Wine News* is an upscale wine appreciation magazine and yet another alternative to the *Quarterly Review of Wines* (*QRW*) and *Wine Spectator*. It does differ slightly in that it is more oriented toward the American landscape with a focus on California/West Coast wines rather than those found on the international scene. On the whole, *The Wine News* still covers much of the same subject matter as its competitors, including the 100-point rating system and evaluating wines for the best value. The overall content is a blend of cuisine, features, history, and commentary to provide comprehensive coverage of the wine industry from a consumer standpoint. Among its panel of experts are those have also been contributors to other publications like *Wine Spectator* and the *QRW*.

753. Wine Spectator. [ISSN: 0193-497X] 1976. s-m. 18/yr. USD 45 domestic; USD 58.85 Canada; USD 135 elsewhere. Ed(s): Kim Marcus, Marvin R Shanken. Marvin R. Shanken Communications, Inc., 387 Park Ave S, New York, NY 10016. Illus., adv. Vol. ends: Dec. *Indexed:* H&TI. *Aud.:* Ga, Sa.

With the largest circulation, *Wine Spectator* may be the most influential and commonly referenced wine consumer magazine in the industry, and thus the standard to which other magazines are compared. Its lofty reputation has been built upon regular contributions from noted viticulturalists and wine critics as well as its fashionable art direction and design. Over the years, the publication has become synonymous with the 100-point scoring system. Wine retailers frequently reference such reviews for consumers. Unlike other publications in the field, *Wine Spectator* does not retain a steady panel of expert tasters. Instead, the magazine engages a number of critics who only critique wines in their own area of expertise. Of course, *Wine Spectator* provides more than just expert reviews and scores to educate one about wine selection; there are features on travel and celebrities, collecting advice, in-depth articles, culinary advice, recipes, and restaurant reviews. The oversized glossy format lends itself perfectly to the lavish layout of images and articles. *Wine Spectator* does cater heavily to the celebrity social scene, which can become distracting and tiresome. Nonetheless, the magazine richly deserves the distinguished reputation it has garnered since 1976.

754. Zymurgy. [ISSN: 0196-5921] 1978. q. USD 38. Ed(s): Jill Redding. American Homebrewers Association Inc., PO Bos 1679, Boulder, CO 80306; dena@aob.org; http://www.beertown.org. Illus., adv. Circ: 24000 Paid. *Aud.:* Ga, Sa.

Published by the American Homebrewers Association for almost 30 years and slanted toward the serious homebrewer, this magazine provides exciting recipes, comprehensive technical information, and the latest trends. Some novice homebrewers may find this magazine somewhat inaccessible or intimidating since it seems to be oriented to the "experienced insider," with extremely technical content and advanced expert advice. On the other hand, the publication expects its readers to be serious and knowledgeable about the field, and it provides valuable behind-the-scenes information from and interviews with brewmasters. In addition, advertising from specialized manufacturers and distributors of homebrew products and supplies provides a great resource for the reader. Most notably, the recipes are from award winners in competitions and not just the usual recycled fare. Of special interest is the annual survey of brewers and the annual theme issue focusing on a particular aspect of the brewing process.

■ BIBLIOGRAPHY

See also Books and Book Reviews; Library and Information Science; and Printing and Graphic Arts sections.

David R. Whitesell, Curator of Books, American Antiquarian Society, 185 Salisbury Street, Worcester, Massachusetts 01609; dwhitesell@mwa.org

Sarah Phillips, Research Librarian, Widener Library, Harvard University, Cambridge, MA 02138; sphillip@fas.harvard.edu

Introduction

Bibliography refers to books, and, more specifically in this section, to rare books—often grouped with archives and manuscripts in special collections. An excellent summary of the state of these libraries can be found in "Special Collections in the Twenty-First Century," the Summer 2003 issue of *Library Trends* (52, 1), edited by Barbara M. Jones. Among its hot topics: bringing rare books to a broader audience, particularly in the classroom; the complex intellectual property and conservation issues of digital projects; war booty; and the crippling grip of uncataloged backlogs.

Bibliographical periodicals fall into three distinct categories. The most important are those published by bibliographical societies, many of which are national in scope. Only the leading journals of American and English bibliographical societies are included here, although librarians should not overlook the excellent journals published by societies in Canada, Australia and New Zealand, and Western Europe. Another category is comprised of periodicals published by leading research libraries. While these house organs tend to publish articles based on research in their own rare book and manuscript collections, the quality of their holdings and the high level of scholarship make these important contributions to the field. A final category is more diversified, containing various and sundry specialist periodicals in manuscript studies, textual bibliography, book collecting, and the lively field of the history of the book within its social and cultural matrix.

Basic Periodicals

Ac, Sa: *Bibliographical Society of America. Papers (New York); The Library (Oxford); Studies in Bibliography (U. Virginia).*

Basic Abstracts and Indexes

America: History and Life, Historical Abstracts, Library Literature & Information Science, MLA International Bibliography.

755. *American Antiquarian Society. Proceedings: journal of American history and culture through 1876.* [ISSN: 0044-751X] 1812. s-a. USD 45 domestic; USD 53 foreign. Ed(s): Caroline F Sloat. American Antiquarian Society, 185 Salisbury St, Worcester, MA 01609; jkeenum@mwa.org; http://www.americanantiquarian.org. Illus., index, adv. Refereed. Circ: 1000. Microform: PQC. *Indexed:* A&ATA, AmH&L, ArtHuCI, HistAb, MLA-IB, RILM. *Aud.:* Ac, Sa.

Now approaching its 200th anniversary, this venerable periodical has lost none of its relevance. Indeed, it has carved out a niche as the primary scholarly journal in the history of the book in the United States and British North America through 1876. Of the three to five articles in each substantial issue, most treat the printing or publishing history of American books, magazines, newspapers, music, and prints. Book illustration and the history of reading are also regular topics. Other articles may include edited transcriptions of important manuscripts in the American Antiquarian Society Library and topical bibliographies of primary source materials. Some examples: "Scribal [handwritten] Publication in 17th Century New England," "Davy Crockett Is Dead, but How He Died Lives On," and "Jesuits, Huguenots, and the Apocalypse: the Origins of America's First French Book." Each article is briefly abstracted in the table of contents. Supplementing the articles are the "proceedings" of the society: minutes of its meetings, reports of the council and treasurer, news of the library and the research undertaken by its fellowship recipients, obituaries of former members, full lists of present members and staff, and a detailed index. Highly recommended for special collections as well as academic and larger public libraries.

756. *La Bibliofilia: rivista di storia del libro e di bibliografia.* [ISSN: 0006-0941] 1899. 3x/yr. EUR 72 domestic; EUR 95 foreign. Ed(s): Luigi Balsamo. Casa Editrice Leo S. Olschki, Viuzzo del Pozzetto 8, Florence, 50126, Italy; celso@olschki.it; http://www.olschki.it. Illus., adv. Circ: 1000. Vol. ends: Sep/Dec. *Indexed:* AmH&L, HistAb, IBR, IBZ, LibLit, LingAb, MLA-IB, RILM. *Bk. rev.:* 6-10, 300-3,000 words. *Aud.:* Ac, Sa.

This elegantly designed, large-format periodical printed on coated paper is the leading scholarly journal on Italian printing and publishing history. Each issue contains three or four longer and two or three shorter articles. Many concern the fifteenth and sixteenth centuries, when Italian printers were arguably the best and certainly the most prolific in Europe, although more recent times are also covered, as are Italian medieval and Renaissance manuscript production and book culture. Recent articles discuss the Venetian printing of Castiglione's *Book of the Courtier,* bindings stamped with the coat of arms of the Prince Cardinal of Savoy, and an article on Giovanni Giacomo Hertz, a German bookseller in Venice. Although most articles are in Italian, short English abstracts are also provided. Each issue also includes a number of lengthy book reviews by leading scholars, notices of important upcoming conferences and exhibitions worldwide, and a useful "green paper" section of advertisements for new Italian bibliographical publications. For large academic and special collections libraries.

757. *Bibliographical Society of America. Papers.* [ISSN: 0006-128X] 1904. q. USD 80 (Individuals, USD 65). Ed(s): Trevor Howard-Hill. Bibliographical Society of America, PO Box 1537, New York, NY 10021; bsa@bibsocamer.org; http://www.bibsocamer.org. Illus., index, adv. Refereed. Circ: 1200. Vol. ends: Dec. Reprint: PSC. *Indexed:* AmH&L, AmHI, ArtHuCI, BEL&L, BRI, CBRI, HistAb, HumInd, IBR, LibLit, MLA-IB, RILM, SSCI. *Bk. rev.:* 7-10 of 500-2,500 words; plus 4-6 more of 200-500 words. *Aud.:* Ac, Sa.

The *Papers of the Bibliographical Society of America* is the leading bibliographical journal in the United States. According to its editorial policy, contributions "should involve consideration of the book or manuscript (the physical object) as historical evidence, whether for establishing a text or illuminating the history of book production, publication, distribution, or collecting, or for other purposes. Studies of the printing, publishing, and allied trades are welcome." Hence, articles may touch upon virtually any aspect of bibliography, although American and English subjects predominate. Recent contributions include "Books as History: Changing Values in a Digital Age," "Sylvia Plath, Ted Hughes, and the Myth of Textual Betrayal," "Inigo Jones and Early Printed Books," and "The Reputation of the 1932 Odyssey Press Edition of *Ulysses.*" Each issue typically contains four articles and one or two shorter bibliographical notes, along with a substantial section of book reviews and occasional review essays. Each annual volume concludes with minutes of the society's annual meeting and other news notes, and a full index. An essential addition for most academic library collections, special collections, and major public libraries.

758. *Bodleian Library Record.* Formerly (until 1938): *Bodleian Quarterly Record.* [ISSN: 0067-9488] 1917. s-a. GBP 18 in the European Union; GBP 20 elsewhere. Ed(s): Jack Flavell. Bodleian Library, Broad St, Oxford, OX1 3BG, United Kingdom; mrk@bodley.ox.ac.uk. Illus., index. Refereed. Circ: 1500 Paid. Vol. ends: Oct. Microform: PQC. *Indexed:* AmH&L, AmHI, BrHumI, HistAb, IBR, IBZ, IndIslam, LISA, MLA-IB. *Aud.:* Ac, Sa.

Although focused on its own collections and activities, the *Bodleian Library Record* is well written and international in appeal. The three or four articles in each issue deal primarily with English literature and history of all periods, as revealed through research in the Bodleian's holdings, while other articles concern aspects of its fascinating 400-year history. Recent examples include "'Motheaten, Mouldye, and Rotten': The Early Custodial History and Dissemination of John Leland's Manuscript Remains" and "The Bodleian Library and its Readers, 1602–1652." Shorter "Notes and Documents" present research on individual rare books and manuscripts. Each issue also contains several regular features, such as reports of "Notable Accessions," news of Bodleian Library friends groups, and "Notes and News" concerning staff arrivals and departures, exhibitions, and obituaries of prominent staff and donors. For larger academic libraries and special collections.

759. *Book Collector.* [ISSN: 0006-7237] 1952. q. EUR 42 domestic; GBP 45 foreign. Ed(s): Nicolas Barker. Collector Ltd., PO Box 12426, London, W11 3GW, United Kingdom; http://www./ thebookcollector.co.uk. Illus., index, adv. Vol. ends: Winter. Microform: PQC. Reprint: PSC. *Indexed:* AmHI, ArtHuCI, BEL&L, BRI, BrHumI, CBRI, IBR, IBZ, LibLit, LingAb, MLA-IB, RI-1, RILM. *Bk. rev.:* 4-8, 500-3,000 words. *Aud.:* Ac, Sa.

An erudite and essential journal for serious book collectors, antiquarian booksellers, bibliographers, and special collections librarians. Each issue contains three or four articles on such wide-ranging topics as famous book collectors and libraries, the history of the book trade, noted bookbinders and bindings, and more traditional bibliographical subjects; e.g., the decline and fall of the English country house library, the first U.S. impression of *The Portrait of a Lady,* and Cambridge illuminated manuscripts. Most readers, however, turn first to other features: the long opening editorial essay that reviews significant new books or takes a stand on important issues; news of notable "Exhibitions and [Exhibition] Catalogues"; obituaries of prominent booksellers, collectors, and librarians; and the indispensable "News and Comment" section with its insightful look at recent book and manuscript auctions, booksellers' catalogues, and anything else of note in the antiquarian book world. Each issue concludes with a traditional book review section. Every other year, the journal publishes its famous "Christmas Catalogue" of humorous errors spotted in booksellers' catalogues. Belongs in large academic and public libraries, as well as special collections.

760. *Book History.* [ISSN: 1098-7371] 1998. a. USD 57. Ed(s): Jonathan Rose, Ezra Greenspan. Pennsylvania State University Press, 820 N University Dr, USB-1, Ste C, University Park, PA 16802-1003; pspjournals@psu.edu; http://www.psupress.org. Illus. Refereed. Circ: 1000. Online: EBSCO Publishing, EBSCO Host; OCLC Online Computer Library Center, Inc.; OhioLINK; Project MUSE; SwetsWise Online Content. *Indexed:* AmH&L, AmHI, HistAb, MLA-IB. *Aud.:* Ac, Sa.

Interdisciplinary, cutting-edge, readable, and only nine years old, *Book History* successfully embodies much of the dynamism of its slightly older parent, SHARP (Society for the History of Authorship, Reading, and Publishing). Each 300-page annual volume contains a dozen scholarly essays, all in English. Most are selected from among the best presented at SHARP's annual conference, which is perhaps the world's leading forum for interdisciplinary studies in the "history of the book." Contributions are diverse in subject matter and tone, their sometimes uneven quality mirroring the present difficulties in defining what constitutes "book history," with its interest in capturing the cultural matrix surrounding a work. Yet many are very readable and quite fascinating, including such articles as "'Jane Eyre Fever': Deciphering the Astonishing Popular Success of Charlotte Bronte in Antebellum America," "Canadian Pulp Magazines," and "Publishing French Translations of Mark Twain's Novels *Tom Sawyer* and *Huckleberry Finn.*" Each volume closes with an important literature review article, such as "Empirical Approaches to Studying Literary Readers." This is an important history/literature journal for special collections as well as academic and larger public libraries.

761. *Cambridge Bibliographical Society. Transactions.* [ISSN: 0068-6611] 1949. a. GBP 12; USD 27. Ed(s): Elisabeth Leedham-Green. Cambridge Bibliographical Society, c/o Cambridge University Library, West Rd, Cambridge, CB3 9DR, United Kingdom. Illus. Circ: 500. *Indexed:* AmH&L, HistAb, IBR, IBZ, MLA-IB. *Aud.:* Ac, Sa.

Although seemingly modest in scope and appearance, the *Transactions* has earned an international reputation for distinguished scholarship. Most of the four to seven articles in each issue have a Cambridge theme, such as studies of important books and manuscripts in Cambridge University libraries, or histories of Cambridge libraries, or Cambridge printers, stationers, and bookbinders. Other emphases are medieval manuscripts and English book culture of the fifteenth, sixteenth, and seventeenth centuries. Recent articles include "The Birth of Literary Property in England," "Caxton's printings of *The Horse, the Sheep and the Goose,*" and "John Siberch, the First Cambridge Printer." Each issue generally includes one or two brief bibliographical notes and a summary of the Cambridge Bibliographical Society's recent activities. For large academic and special collections libraries.

762. *Gutenberg - Jahrbuch.* [ISSN: 0072-9094] 1926. a. EUR 75. Ed(s): Stephan Fuessel. Gutenberg-Gesellschaft e.V., Liebfrauenplatz 5, Mainz, 55116, Germany; gutenberg-gesellschaft@freenet.de; http://www.gutenberg-gesellschaft.uni-mainz.de. Illus., adv. Circ: 2200. Reprint: PSC. *Indexed:* AmH&L, FR, HistAb, IBR, IBZ, IndIslam, MLA-IB, RILM. *Aud.:* Ac, Sa.

This attractively produced, well-illustrated, large-format annual has long been one of the world's foremost journals on printing history. Its central focus has traditionally been scholarly research on Johann Gutenberg and fifteenth-century printing, although the two dozen articles in each 300-page volume typically span six centuries of printing history, book illustration, bookbinding, the book trade, and library history. Articles may be in German, English, French, Spanish, and Italian—even Latin!—although only occasionally will abstracts be provided in other languages. Some recent articles focus on "Gems in Book Illustrations," an incunable edition of the legend of Saint Brendan's voyage, and a xylographic image of St. Thomas Aquinas. A well-respected addition to general academic library collections.

763. *Harvard Library Bulletin.* Former titles (until 1942): *Harvard University Library Notes;* (until 1940): *Harvard Library Notes.* [ISSN: 0017-8136] 1920. q. USD 35 domestic; USD 41 foreign; USD 15 newsstand/cover. Ed(s): William P. Stoneman. Harvard University Library, Houghton Library, Cambridge, MA 02138; libraries@harvard.edu; http://www.harvard.edu/. Illus. Refereed. Circ: 1500. Vol. ends: Winter. Microform: MIM; PQC. *Indexed:* ABS&EES, AmH&L, ArtHuCI, BAS, HistAb, IBR, IBZ, IndIslam, LISA, LibLit, MLA-IB, RILM, SSCI. *Aud.:* Ac, Sa.

The *Harvard Library Bulletin* continues to offer a varied perspective on the history, collections, and activities of the library. Each issue, now reduced in size, ranges from 50 to 100 pages. Some issues may contain three or four traditional, scholarly articles based on research in Harvard's rare book and manuscript collections. Recent contributions include "The 'Dry-Lighted Soul' Ignites: Emerson and His Soul-Mate Caroline Sturgis as Seen in Her Houghton Manuscripts" and "The 'Head Quarters of Balladry': Harvard, Child, Kittredge, and *The English and Scottish Popular Ballads.*" Other issues may publish papers presented at Harvard library symposia, author bibliographies, collection catalogs or Harvard library exhibition catalogs ("Benjamin Franklin: a How-To Guide"). Some issues also include "Among Harvard's Libraries," a section of library news and short articles on notable acquisitions. Recommended for special collections and larger academic libraries.

764. *Huntington Library Quarterly: studies in English and American history and literature.* Formerly (until 1937): *The Huntington Library Bulletin.* [ISSN: 0018-7895] 1931. q. USD 159 print & online eds. USD 44 newsstand/cover. Ed(s): Susan Green. University of California Press, Journals Division, 2000 Center St, Ste 303, Berkeley, CA 94704-1223; journals@ucpress.edu; http://www.ucpress.edu/journals. Illus., index, adv. Sample. Refereed. Circ: 740. Microform: PQC. Online: Chadwyck-Healey Inc.; EBSCO Publishing, EBSCO Host; Northern Light Technology, Inc.; OCLC Online Computer Library Center, Inc.; ProQuest LLC (Ann Arbor); SwetsWise Online Content. *Indexed:* AmH&L, AmHI, FR, HistAb, HumInd, IBR, MLA-IB, RI-1, RILM, SSCI. *Bk. rev.:* 1-4, 2,000-7,500 words. *Aud.:* Ac, Sa.

A leading scholarly journal issued by a distinguished private library. It focuses on sixteenth- to eighteenth-century Britain and America, and includes articles not necessarily based on Huntington Library collections. Each issue of 120–200 pages contains four to ten thoroughly documented articles, often organized around a specific theme such as "Travel Writing in the Early Modern World" or "The Uses of History in Early Modern England." Also included in some issues are shorter "Notes and Documents" that publish manuscripts owned by the Huntington Library or offer bibliographical notes on selected rare books. Of particular value are the occasional review essays, each discussing from one to five recent books. The long-standing "Intramuralia" feature has been revamped: It now includes a comprehensive annual list of notable Huntington Library acquisitions in addition to articles on specific acquisitions. A popular choice for academic libraries and special collections.

765. *John Rylands University Library of Manchester. Bulletin.* Formerly: *John Rylands Library. Bulletin.* [ISSN: 0301-102X] 1903. 3x/yr. GBP 65. Ed(s): Dorothy Clayton. John Rylands University Library, John Rylands University, Oxford Rd, Manchester, M13 9PP, United Kingdom; d.clayton@man.ac.uk; http://rylibweb.man.ac.uk. Illus., index, adv. Refereed. Circ: 700. Microform: IDC. *Indexed:* AmH&L, AmHI, ArtHuCI, BAS, BEL&L, BrArAb, BrHumI, FR, HistAb, IBR, IBZ, MLA-IB, NTA, NumL, OTA, R&TA, RI-1. *Aud.:* Ac, Sa.

Serious scholarly articles comprise this impressive, substantial publication, in which each issue contains up to a dozen imaginative and well-researched (often at this library) interdisciplinary articles. Issues are often organized around a theme, such as Walter de la Mare or Anglo-Saxon England, and include such articles as "English Knighthood in Decline," "Anglo-Saxon and Norman Methods of Tithe-Payments Before and After the Conquest," and "Jean-Baptiste de Secondat's Marginalia in Boulainvilliers's 'Etat de la France.'" Recommended for special collections and larger academic libraries.

766. *The Library: the transactions of the Bibliographical Society.* [ISSN: 0024-2160] 1899. q. EUR 204 print or online ed. Ed(s): Dr. Oliver Pickering. Oxford University Press, Great Clarendon St, Oxford, OX2 6DP, United Kingdom; jnl.orders@oup.co.uk; http://www.oxfordjournals.org. Illus., index, adv. Refereed. Circ: 1200. Vol. ends: Dec. Microform: PQC. Online: EBSCO Publishing, EBSCO Host; HighWire Press; Oxford Journals. Reprint: PSC. *Indexed:* AmH&L, AmHI, ArtHuCI, BRI, BrArAb, CBRI, HistAb, IBR, LibLit, LingAb, MLA-IB, NumL. *Bk. rev.:* 10-13, 1,000-2,000 words. *Aud.:* Ac Sa.

A standard-bearer of the field, which, like its peer publication *Papers of the Bibliographical Society of America*, ranks as one of the world's foremost bibliographical journals. The four or five articles in each issue cover "all aspects of descriptive and historical bibliography . . . including the general and economic history of the production and distribution of books [and manuscripts], paper, printing types, illustration, and binding, as well as the transmission of texts and their authenticity." The majority of articles dwell on English themes. Recent ones include "George Parker, Defoe, and the Whitefriars Trade," "Edmund Spenser's Irish Papers," a discussion of the library owned by the exceptionally well-educated daughter of King Edward VI's tutor (her name is Mildred Cooke Cecil, Lady Burghley) and a timely review of the online English Short Title Catalogue. Perhaps the journal's most valuable component, however, is the superb reviews section that provides thorough coverage to bibliographical publications in many languages, including those from Russia and Eastern Europe. Scholarly reviews and review essays are supplemented by a "Recent Books" section containing brief reviews or abstracts in English, with helpful English translations of titles in Slavic languages, together with a "Recent Periodicals" section listing relevant articles published in dozens of journals worldwide. *The Library* also publishes news of the Bibliographical Society and its annual report. Essential for all academic and special collections libraries, and for major public libraries.

767. *Matrix (Herefordshire): a review for printers and bibliophiles.* [ISSN: 0261-3093] 1981. a. GBP 90. Ed(s): John Randle. Whittington Press, Lower Marston Farm, Near Risbury, HR6 0NJ, United Kingdom; http://www.whittingtonpress.com. Illus. Circ: 800 Paid. *Indexed:* ABM, IndIslam. *Bk. rev.:* 12-25, 100-2,500 words. *Aud.:* Ac, Sa.

A browsable feast, *Matrix* has a well-earned reputation as one of the world's foremost publications on the arts of the book. Edited, designed, and produced at the highly regarded Whittington Press, *Matrix* is a stunning 200-page annual printed letterpress to the highest standards. Each issue contains approximately 20 articles, ranging from short reminiscences to lengthy scholarly studies on typography, type design, typefounding, printing, papermaking, book illustration, private presses, and the people who produce fine books, with an emphasis on English and American fine printing of the past two centuries. Also included are an annual survey of new private press books and a substantial book review section, along with numerous tipped-in color illustrations, type specimens, broadsides, and printed ephemera contributed by some of the world's leading private presses. Recent articles include a charming story about exhuming books owned by Edith Wharton from Sir Kenneth Clark's library, paper-making by hand in the twenty-first century, "Early Days at Penguin," and "*Typomania* in

Germany." *Matrix* is an excellent value for the price for large academic, public, and special collections libraries. Keep it in the library's noncirculating collection or special collections department: It's a work of art.

768. *Princeton University Library Chronicle.* [ISSN: 0032-8456] 1939. 3x/yr. USD 65 (Membership, USD 75). Ed(s): Gretchen M Oberfrane. Friends of Princeton University Library, 1 Washington Rd, Princeton, NJ 08544; principi@princeton.edu; http://www.princeton.edu/~rbsc/Friends. Illus., index. Refereed. Circ: 1250 Paid. Vol. ends: Spring. Microform: PQC. *Indexed:* AmH&L, BAS, HistAb, LibLit, MLA-IB. *Aud.:* Ac, Sa.

Published by the Friends of the Princeton University Library, the *Princeton University Library Chronicle* "is an interdisciplinary journal whose mission is to publish articles of scholarly importance and general interest based on research in the rare book and manuscript collections of the Princeton University Library," with some emphasis on work based on Princeton's holdings of twentieth-century literary manuscripts and historical archives. Examples include "Of Memory and Massacre: A Soldier's Firsthand Account of the 'Affair on Wounded Knee,'" "Mortimer and Company: Virginia Woolf, Nancy Mitford, and Other Moderns," and "George Anson's *Voyage Round the World*: The Making of a Best-Seller." These have been supplemented by obituaries of prominent library staff and donors, news of the Friends of the Princeton University Library, extensive notes on recent rare book and manuscript acquisitions, and an annual index. For special collections and larger academic libraries.

Printing Historical Society. Journal. See Printing and Graphic Arts section.

Printing History. See Printing and Graphic Arts section.

769. *The Private Library.* [ISSN: 0032-8898] 1957. q. Membership, GBP 25. Ed(s): Paul Nash, David Chambers. Private Libraries Association, Ravelston, South View Rd, Pinner, HA5 3YD, United Kingdom. Illus., adv. Sample. Refereed. Circ: 800. Vol. ends: Winter. *Indexed:* LISA, LibLit. *Bk. rev.:* 1-3, 500-3,000 words. *Aud.:* Sa.

Intimate in size and scope, quintessentially British in idiom, *The Private Library* offers a refreshing counterpoint to many of the journals listed in this section. It is published by the Private Libraries Association, "an international society of book collectors—collectors of rare books, fine books, single authors, special subjects, and, above all, collectors of books for the simple pleasures of reading and ownership." Each 50-page issue contains three or four articles on "books that can be collected today," concentrating on English illustrated and private press books of the nineteenth and twentieth centuries. A liberal use of illustrations (some in color) add to the charm of this work. Some topics include "Richard Doyle's *In Fairyland*," "The Electronic Book: Some Thoughts on the Present and the Future," "Rare Architectural Books," "Bird Books," and "In Search of Edward Gorey." Many articles include checklists of books as an aid to collecting. Also included are occasional reviews and a useful section on "Recent Private Press Books" (primarily from the United Kingdom) with brief descriptions and ordering information, and personal notes on the press and printing world by the editor. *The Private Library* will appeal not only to collectors, but to specialist scholars and special collections librarians. Highly recommended for larger public libraries as well.

770. *Publishing History: the social, economic and literary history of book, newspaper, and magazine publishing.* [ISSN: 0309-2445] 1977. s-a. Ed(s): Simon Eliot. ProQuest LLC, The Quorum, Barnwell Rd, Cambridge, CB5 8SW, United Kingdom; http://www.proquest.co.uk/. Illus., adv. Circ: 500. Online: Chadwyck-Healey Inc. *Indexed:* AmH&L, AmHI, ArtHuCI, BEL&L, BrHumI, HistAb, IBR, IndIslam, MLA-IB. *Aud.:* Ac, Sa.

Nearly thirty years ago, *Publishing History* was a pioneering periodical in the new field of "book history" as a window into social history. It remains a leading journal, with each 100-page issue containing three or four articles representative of the most distinguished current scholarship. Its primary emphasis is on the publishing history—broadly defined—of England and the British Commonwealth, with occasional articles on European or American themes. Of particular note are its diverse coverage and interdisciplinary approach. Recent articles include "Edith Wharton and the House of Macmillan," "The Book Trade in English Provincial Towns, 1700–1849," "*Lady Chatterley's Lover* Uncovered," and imperial and post-colonial book history in India and Africa. Book reviews are no longer included. A valuable addition to academic and special collections libraries.

Quaerendo: a quarterly journal from the Low Countries devoted to manuscripts and printed books. See Printing and Graphic Arts section.

Rare Book Review. See Books and Book Reviews section.

RBM: a journal of rare books, manuscripts, and cultural heritage see Books and Book Reviews section.

771. *Scriptorium: international review of manuscript studies and bulletin codicologique (book reviews).* [ISSN: 0036-9772] 1947. s-a. Ed(s): O Legendre, P Cockshaw. Centre d'Etude des Manuscrits, Bd de l'Empereur 4, Brussels, 1000, Belgium. Illus., adv. Refereed. Circ: 900. Vol. ends: No. 2. *Indexed:* ArtHuCI, BEL&L, FR, IBR, IPB, IndIslam, MLA-IB, NTA, RILM. *Bk. rev.:* 300-350, 50-1,500 words. *Aud.:* Ac, Sa.
Scholarly work of the highest order appears in *Scriptorium,* the leading international journal in medieval manuscript studies and an indispensable addition to any medieval studies collection. Each semi-annual issue is 250–350 pages in length, divided into two sections. The first consists of eight to ten thoroughly documented articles and shorter "notes," illustrated by up to 20 plates (some in color), followed by several review essays. The second section, "Bulletin codicologique," is an exceptionally valuable collection of reviews ranging from 50-word abstracts to full 1,500-word reviews. Each issue reviews approximately 350 publications, including books, journal articles, and even booksellers' catalogs, with lists of the manuscripts offered for sale therein. Concluding each volume are comprehensive indexes, including indexes of manuscript dates and identifying numbers. Articles are often in English; reviews appear in French, German, English, Italian, and Spanish. Articles cover all aspects of manuscript production, codicology, palaeography, illumination, medieval libraries, collectors and collections, etc. Some recent articles include "Observations on the Habits of 12th and 13th Century Music Scribes," "Celestial Transmissions: Constellation Cycles in Manuscripts," and "A Breton Book of Hours for M. de Fontenay." Recommended for special collections and larger academic libraries.

772. *Studies in Bibliography.* [ISSN: 0081-7600] 1948. a. USD 55 per issue domestic. Ed(s): Dr. David L Vander Meulen. University Press of Virginia, PO Box 400318, Charlottesville, VA 22904-4318; upressva@ virginia.edu; http://www.upress.virginia.edu. Illus. Refereed. Circ: 1000. *Indexed:* ArtHuCI, IBR, IBZ, MLA-IB. *Aud.:* Ac, Sa.
One of the most highly respected journals in the field, *Studies in Bibliography* has been, and remains, profoundly influential in shaping the disciplines of descriptive, analytical, and textual bibliography. *Studies* has been stewarded by several of America's best-known bibliographers, including founding editor Fredson Bowers, current editor David L. Vander Meulen, and frequent contributor G. Thomas Tanselle. The long-standing editorial policy is straightforward: "The editor invites articles and notes on analytical bibliography, textual criticism, manuscript study, the history of printing and publishing, as well as related matters of method and evidence." Each annual volume of 250–350 pages contains 10–15 thoroughly documented articles. A few articles now include illustrations, some in color, and the journal's web site has begun to offer supplementary images. Volumes usually begin with another in Tanselle's magisterial series of articles defining some aspect of bibliography, such as "Dust-Jackets, Dealers, and Documentation." Other recent, eclectic contributions include "Historiographical Problems and Possibilities in Book History and National Histories of the Book," "The Dissemination of Shakespeare's Plays circa 1714," and "The Bibliographical Description of Italian Printed Music of the 16th and 17th centuries." A recent innovation has been articles outlining the careers and contributions of noted bibliographers, such as "David Foxon, Humanist Bibliographer" and "Charlton Hinman and the Roots of Mechanical Collation." Each volume closes with brief notes on Bibliographical Society of

the University of Virginia activities. The first 54 volumes are now available online at etext.lib.virginia.edu/bsuva/sb. Essential reading at academic and special collections, and major public libraries.

773. *Textual Cultures: texts, contexts, interpretation.* [ISSN: 1559-2936] 2006. 3x/yr. USD 91 print & online eds. (Individuals, USD 43.45 print & online eds.). Ed(s): Edward Burns, H Wayne Storey. Indiana University Press, 601 N Morton St, Bloomington, IN 47404; journals@ indiana.edu; http://iupress.indiana.edu. *Indexed:* AmHI, HumInd, MLA-IB. *Bk. rev.:* 4-12, 800-2400 words. *Aud.:* Ac, Sa.
"God is in the details" is the motto of this journal, which views all texts as fluid, and takes a close look at manuscripts as they wend their way through the editorial process, from the authors' hands to those of their readers. Articles comment on the behind-the-scenes "power of readers to coerce revision and actually rewrite an author's text" and the cultural matrices that drive editors. Articles are often beautifully written and thought provoking, with such titles as "The Diary May Be From Dixie But The Editor Is Not," "The Human Touch: Software of the Highest Order," and "The Genealogy of Scribal Versions: a 'Fourth Way' in Medieval Editorial Theory." Other topics have included Boccaccio on Dante's *Divine Comedy,* Shakespeare's "good" vs. "bad" quartos of Hamlet, and Emily Dickinson in interactive electronic format. Of special interest is the Spring 2007 issue, which explores the "messy" influences of race, class, gender, and sexuality; it tells such compelling stories as that of the "incommensurate public notice" given to women editors of 19th century poetry and religious periodicals, compared to that of their male relatives. This journal is the official voice of the Society for Textual Scholarship, and some of its articles are drawn from its biennial conference. When its co-founding editor retired in 2005, the journal changed title and publisher, and acquired a new editor-in-chief, but its mission, to pay attention to the significance of invisible hands, remains intact. Book reviews, both Anglo-American and Continental, appear in the back. Meaty reading, recommended for all academic libraries, special collections, and those interested in the history of the book.

774. *Yale University Library Gazette.* [ISSN: 0044-0175] 1926. s-a. USD 20. Ed(s): Stephen Parks. Yale University Library, PO Box 208240, New Haven, CT 06520-8240; stephen.parks@yale.edu; http://www.library.yale.edu/. Illus., index. Circ: 1500. Vol. ends: Apr. Online: EBSCO Publishing, EBSCO Host. *Indexed:* AmH&L, BEL&L, HistAb, IBR, IBZ, LibLit, MLA-IB, RILM. *Aud.:* Ac, Sa.
The *Yale University Library Gazette* capably upholds a long tradition of publishing substantive scholarly articles based on the library's superb collections. Each 100-page semi-annual issue contains three or four articles, authored by faculty, graduate students, and visiting library fellows, on a wide range of topics from medieval manuscripts to modernism. Among recent articles are "Mark Twain's Birthday Letter to Walt Whitman," "The Music of Ezra Pound," and "'The Case of the Suffering Clergy of France': A Short Study in Bibliography, History and Textual Criticism." Other features include detailed listings of recent rare book and manuscript acquisitions; obituaries of prominent library donors and staff; a "Gazette" providing a comprehensive summary of the library's many exhibitions, lectures, symposia, and other activities; and an annual index. A new editor came on board in 2005. Suitable for large academic libraries and special collections.

■ BIOLOGY

General/Biochemistry and Biophysics/Cell and Molecular Biology/Developmental Biology/Genetics/Microbiology

See also Agriculture; Biotechnology; Birds; Environment, Conservation, and Outdoor Recreation; Marine Science and Technology; and Science and Technology sections.

Sara Klink, Librarian, Stark County District Library, Canton, OH 44702-1080

Introduction

Biology is the science of life. It is concerned with the characteristics and behaviors of organisms, how species and individuals come into existence, and the interactions they have with each other and with their environment. Biology encompasses a broad spectrum of academic fields that are often viewed as independent disciplines. Since the field of biological science is so encompassing and covers so many disciplines, it becomes necessary to create a number of subsections to organize this section. In keeping with the previous edition, these subsections are: general biology, genetics and microbiology, developmental biology, biochemistry and molecular biology, and cell and molecular biology, with much crossover in the genetics, biochemistry, and molecular biology disciplines. The majority of these titles are geared toward a very specific audience such as subject-specific biologists, researchers, professors and educators, college-level students, and occasionally the general biologist. Since much of today's research involves timely access to information, it becomes imperative that journals within these disciplines maintain an online presence. Each of the journals selected for this section do have easy-to-find, accessible web sites. Many titles offer some level of access for free to nonsubscribers, with a few offering open access. To readers, open access means that anyone is free to copy, distribute, and display the work; to make derivative works; and to make commercial use of the work, as long as the original author is given credit and the license terms of the work are made clear. Another important feature found with many of these titles is full-text online access to entire issues six months to one year after an issue's publication date. With so many journals offering special online features including early publication and free access, the online resources are becoming an invaluable tool for users.

Basic Periodicals

Ac: *Biochemistry; Cell; Genetics; Microbiology and Molecular Biology Reviews; National Academy of Sciences. Proceedings; Quarterly Review of Biology.*

Basic Abstracts and Indexes

Biological Abstracts, Biological Abstracts/RRM, Biological and Agricultural Index, Biology Digest, Current Contents/Agriculture, Current Contents/Life Sciences.

General

The Auk. See Birds section.

775. Biological Reviews. Former titles (until 1997): *Cambridge Philosophical Society. Biological Reviews;* (until 1937): *Cambridge Philosophical Society. Biological Reviews and Biological Proceedings;* (until 1926): *Cambridge Philosophical Society. Proceedings. Biological Sciences.* [ISSN: 1464-7931] 1923. q. GBP 210 print & online eds. Ed(s): W Foster. Blackwell Publishing Ltd., 9600 Garsington Rd, Oxford, OX4 2ZG, United Kingdom; customerservices@blackwellpublishing.com; http://www.blackwellpublishing.com. Illus., index. Refereed. Vol. ends: Nov. Microform: IDC; PQC. Online: Cambridge University Press; EBSCO Publishing, EBSCO Host; OCLC Online Computer Library Center, Inc.; OhioLINK; SwetsWise Online Content. Reprint: PSC. *Indexed:* Agr, AnBeAb, ApEcolAb, B&AI, CABA, ChemAb, ExcerpMed, FPA, ForAb, GSI, HortAb, IndVet, S&F, SCI, SSCI, VB, ZooRec. *Aud.:* Ac, Sa.

Covering the entire range of the biological sciences, *Biological Reviews* presents review articles aimed at general biologists as well as specialists in the field. Each issue contains about five articles, each having a detailed table of contents, an introduction, a summary, and a substantial bibliography. Online access is available through Cambridge Journals Online. The basic subscription is for the online journal. With a small additional fee, one can have the print subscription as well. Individuals interested in biology are likely to find at least one article of interest in every issue. Document delivery is available from BLDSC, CASDDS, EMDOCS, The Genuine Article, UMI, and UnCover. This journal is appropriate for experts, researchers, and scholars. An excellent resource for general academic as well as research collections supporting biology programs.

776. BioScience. Formerly (until 1963): *A I B S Bulletin.* [ISSN: 0006-3568] 1951. m. USD 294 print & online eds. (Individuals, USD 70; USD 55 K-12 institutions). Ed(s): Timothy M Beardsley, Rebecca Saxer. American Institute of Biological Sciences, 1313 Dolley Madison Blvd, Ste 402, McLean, VA 22101; admin@aibs.org; http://www.aibs.org. Illus., index, adv. Refereed. Circ: 6100 Paid. Vol. ends: Dec. Microform: PQC. Online: BioOne; CSA; EBSCO Publishing, EBSCO Host; Florida Center for Library Automation; Gale; IngentaConnect; JSTOR (Web-based Journal Archive); Northern Light Technology, Inc.; OCLC Online Computer Library Center, Inc.; OhioLINK; ProQuest K-12 Learning Solutions; ProQuest LLC (Ann Arbor); SwetsWise Online Content; H.W. Wilson. *Indexed:* Agr, AnBeAb, ApEcolAb, B&AI, BRI, BiolAb, BiolDig, CABA, CBRI, ChemAb, DSA, EnvInd, FPA, ForAb, FutSurv, GSI, GardL, HortAb, IndVet, MASUSE, PollutAb, RGPR, RRTA, S&F, SCI, SSCI, SWRA, VB, WAE&RSA, ZooRec. *Bk. rev.:* 2-7, 600-2,000 words. *Aud.:* Ga, Ac, Sa.

BioScience is geared toward "a broad readership including professional biologists, biology teachers/professors, and advanced students." Content includes authoritative overviews of current research in biology, accompanied by essays and discussion sections on education, public policy, history, and basic concepts of the biological sciences. Published by the American Institute of Biological Sciences (AIBS), selected sections are available for free access online each month. Full text is available with a subscription. All AIBS members receive free subscriptions to print and online issues. Recommended for special, academic, and large public libraries.

Chickadee. See Children section.

777. Current Biology. [ISSN: 0960-9822] 1991. 24x/yr. EUR 1544. Ed(s): Geoffrey North. Cell Press, 600 Technology Sq, 5th Fl., Cambridge, MA 02139; http://www.cellpress.com/. Illus., adv. Sample. Refereed. Circ: 1908 Paid. Vol. ends: Dec. *Indexed:* AnBeAb, ApEcolAb, BiolAb, BiolDig, CABA, ChemAb, DSA, ForAb, HortAb, IndVet, PsycInfo, S&F, SCI, SSCI, VB, ZooRec. *Aud.:* Ga, Ac, Sa.

Current Biology's primary goal is to foster communication across fields of biology by publishing important findings of general interest from diverse fields and by providing highly accessible editorial articles that aim to inform nonspecialists. The journal includes articles that present conceptual advances of unusual significance regarding a biological question of high interest, concise reports concerning findings of broad biological interest, and news. Online coverage is available through the Cell Press web site, and papers are free 12 months after publication. Appropriate for special and academic libraries, especially those supporting biology programs, and large public libraries.

778. Evolution: international journal of organic evolution. [ISSN: 0014-3820] 1947. m. GBP 425. Ed(s): Mark D Rausher. Blackwell Publishing Ltd., 9600 Garsington Rd, Oxford, OX4 2ZG, United Kingdom; customerservices@blackwellpublishing.com; http://www.blackwellpublishing.com. Illus., index, adv. Refereed. Circ: 4500. Vol. ends: Dec. Microform: PQC. Online: Allen Press Inc.; BioOne; CSA; EBSCO Publishing, EBSCO Host; Gale; JSTOR (Web-based Journal Archive); Northern Light Technology, Inc.; OCLC Online Computer Library Center, Inc.; OhioLINK; H.W. Wilson. Reprint:

PSC. *Indexed:* AbAn, Agr, AnBeAb, ApEcolAb, B&AI, BiolAb, BiolDig, CABA, ChemAb, DSA, ExcerpMed, FPA, FS&TA, ForAb, GSI, HortAb, IAA, IndVet, OceAb, PhilInd, S&F, SCI, SSCI, VB, ZooRec. *Bk. rev.:* 0-2, 1,000-3,000 words. *Aud.:* Ac, Sa.

The main objectives of this journal are the promotion of the study of organic evolution and the integration of the various fields of science concerned with evolution. Contents include regular papers, perspectives, brief communications, and comments, as well as book reviews. *Evolution* is online for subscribers through JSTOR from 1943 on and through Allen Press for more recent issues, with full text from 2000 on. This title is highly recommended for all academic libraries and some special libraries.

779. *The F A S E B Journal.* Supersedes (in 1987): *Federation of American Societies for Experimental Biology. Federation Proceedings.* [ISSN: 0892-6638] 1987. 14x/yr. USD 798 print & online eds. (Individuals, USD 182 print & online eds.; Members, USD 106 print & online eds.). Ed(s): Vincent T Marchesi. Federation of American Societies for Experimental Biology, 9650 Rockville Pike, Rm L-2407A, Bethesda, MD 20814-3998; staff@faseb.org; http://www.faseb.org. Illus., index, adv. Refereed. Circ: 6000 Paid. Vol. ends: Dec. Online: EBSCO Publishing, EBSCO Host; HighWire Press. *Indexed:* Agr, B&AI, BiolAb, BiolDig, CABA, ChemAb, DSA, ExcerpMed, FPA, FS&TA, ForAb, HortAb, IndVet, S&F, SCI, SSCI, VB. *Bk. rev.:* Number and length vary. *Aud.:* Ac, Sa.

The FASEB Journal (Federation of American Societies for Experimental Biology) publishes papers that have integrated one or more of the member disciplines. These member societies are American Physiological Society, American Society for Biochemistry and Molecular Biology, American Society for Pharmacology and Experimental Therapeutics, American Society for Investigative Pathology, American Society for Nutritional Sciences, American Association of Immunologists, Biophysical Society, American Association of Anatomists, Protein Society, American Society for Bone and Mineral Research, American Society for Clinical Investigation, Endocrine Society, American Society of Human Genetics, Society for Developmental Biology, American Peptide Society, Association of Biomolecular Resource Facilities, Society for the Study of Reproduction, Teratology Society, Radiation Research Society, Society for Gynecologic Investigation, and Environmental Mutagen Society. Contents include editorials, essays, review articles, research communications, and book reviews. Online full-text access is provided by Stanford's HighWire Press from July 1987 to the present, with some free access to hot-topic editorials. Recommended for most biology collections in special and academic libraries.

780. *Journal of Neuroscience.* [ISSN: 0270-6474] 1981. w. USD 2608 (print & online eds.) Members, USD 377 (print & online eds.); USD 197 domestic student members (print & online eds.). Ed(s): David C Van Essen. Society for Neuroscience, 11 Dupont Circle, NW, Ste 500, Washington, DC 20036; http://www.sfn.org/. Illus., index, adv. Refereed. Circ: 4100. Vol. ends: Dec. Microform: PQC. Online: EBSCO Publishing, EBSCO Host; HighWire Press. *Indexed:* AnBeAb, B&AI, BiolAb, CABA, ChemAb, DSA, ExcerpMed, IndVet, PsycInfo, RILM, S&F, SCI, SSCI, VB, ZooRec. *Aud.:* Ac, Sa.

This is the official journal of the Society for Neuroscience. It publishes papers on a broad range of topics for those working on the nervous system. Contents include brief communications intended for fast publication of exciting and timely findings and regular articles; these range from cellular and molecular research to developmental and behaviorial studies. Full text is available online with print subscriptions. Free access is provided to tables of contents, abstracts, and searching. This journal is appropriate for academic and special libraries, and will be useful in biology and medical collections.

781. *National Academy of Sciences. Proceedings.* [ISSN: 0027-8424] 1914. w. Individuals, USD 290 print & online eds. Ed(s): Nicholas R Cozzarelli. National Academy of Sciences, 500 Fifth St, NW, Washington, DC 20001; subspnas@nas.edu. Illus., index, adv. Sample. Refereed. Circ: 10132. Vol. ends: Dec. Microform: PQC. Online: EBSCO Publishing, EBSCO Host; HighWire Press; JSTOR (Web-based Journal Archive); National Library of Medicine; SwetsWise Online Content.

Indexed: Agr, AnBeAb, ApEcolAb, ArtHuCI, B&AI, BiolAb, CABA, ChemAb, DSA, ExcerpMed, FPA, FS&TA, ForAb, GSI, HortAb, IndVet, M&GPA, MathR, OceAb, PollutAb, PsycInfo, RRTA, S&F, SCI, SSCI, VB, WAE&RSA, ZooRec. *Aud.:* Ac, Sa.

Covering the physical sciences, biological sciences, and social sciences, this journal includes papers in the categories of research reports, commentaries, reviews, colloquium papers, perspectives, and reports on the National Academy of Sciences. As one of the world's most-cited multidisciplinary scientific serials, it covers all areas of the biological sciences, with the heaviest focus on cell biology and biochemistry. It is published weekly in print and daily online. Full text is available online with a subscription. There is free access to tables of contents and abstracts, and to all content older than six months. Individual and institutional subscriptions are available. Appropriate for academic and special libraries, and essential for most science collections.

Natural History. See Science and Technology section.

Nature. See Science and Technology section.

Owl. See Children section.

782. *Perspectives in Biology and Medicine.* [ISSN: 0031-5982] 1957. q. USD 135. Ed(s): Robert L Perlman, Richard L Landau. The Johns Hopkins University Press, 2715 N Charles St, Baltimore, MD 21218-4363; http://muse.jhu.edu. Illus., index, adv. Sample. Refereed. Circ: 1135 Paid. Vol. ends: Summer. Microform: PQC. Online: EBSCO Publishing, EBSCO Host; Florida Center for Library Automation; Gale; OCLC Online Computer Library Center, Inc.; OhioLINK; Project MUSE; ProQuest K-12 Learning Solutions; ProQuest LLC (Ann Arbor); SwetsWise Online Content. Reprint: PSC. *Indexed:* AmH&L, B&AI, BiolAb, BiolDig, CABA, ChemAb, ExcerpMed, GSI, HistAb, IBR, IBZ, IndVet, PhilInd, RRTA, SCI, SSA, SSCI, VB, WAE&RSA. *Bk. rev.:* 2-9, 300-1,200 words. *Aud.:* Ac, Sa.

Perspectives in Biology and Medicine is an "interdisciplinary journal that publishes articles on a wide range of biomedical topics such as neurobiology, biomedical ethics and history to genetics, evolution, and ecology." Contents include "essays that place biological and medical topics in broader scientific, social, or humanistic contexts." Also included are book reviews, essay reviews, and letters to the editors. Most essays range from 4,000 to 7,000 words in addition to an abstract. Although many essays are invited, voluntary contributions are welcomed. Authors are encouraged to adopt individualized writing styles. Print and online subscriptions are available for individuals and institutions. Full text is provided online by The Johns Hopkins University Press Project Muse from 2000 to the present with a subscription. This journal is appropriate for academic, special, and medical libraries.

783. *The Quarterly Review of Biology.* [ISSN: 0033-5770] 1926. q. USD 260 domestic; USD 279.60 Canada; USD 267 elsewhere. Ed(s): Albert D Carlson, Massimo Pigliucci. University of Chicago Press, Journals Division, PO Box 37005, Chicago, IL 60637; subscriptions@press.uchicago.edu; http://www.journals.uchicago.edu. Illus., index, adv. Refereed. Circ: 1700 Paid. Vol. ends: Dec. Microform: PQC. Online: EBSCO Publishing, EBSCO Host; Florida Center for Library Automation; Gale; JSTOR (Web-based Journal Archive). Reprint: PSC. *Indexed:* AbAn, AnBeAb, ApEcolAb, B&AI, BRI, BiolAb, BiolDig, CABA, CBRI, ChemAb, DSA, ExcerpMed, ForAb, GSI, HortAb, IndVet, S&F, SCI, SWRA, VB, ZooRec. *Bk. rev.:* 100 or more, 200-1,500 words. *Aud.:* Ga, Ac, Sa.

The Quarterly Review of Biology presents "insightful historical, philosophical, and technical treatments of important biological topics." Contents include concise, authoritative articles, theoretical papers, comprehensive book reviews arranged by subject, and timely assessments of the life sciences. Online full text is available from March 2002 to the present. Back issues are made available online from JSTOR from 1926 to 2001. Individual and institutional subscriptions are available. Appropriate for general biology collections and special, academic, and large public libraries.

Ranger Rick. See Children section.

Science. See Science and Technology section.

784. Systematic Biology. Formerly (until 1991): *Systematic Zoology.* [ISSN: 1063-5157] 1952. bi-m. GBP 144 print & online eds. Ed(s): Chris Simon. Taylor & Francis Inc., 325 Chestnut St, Ste 800, Philadelphia, PA 19016; orders@taylorandfrancis.com; http://www.taylorandfrancis.com. Illus., index. Refereed. Circ: 2800. Vol. ends: Dec. Microform: PQC. Online: EBSCO Publishing, EBSCO Host; Gale; IngentaConnect; JSTOR (Web-based Journal Archive); OCLC Online Computer Library Center, Inc.; ProQuest K-12 Learning Solutions; ProQuest LLC (Ann Arbor); SwetsWise Online Content. Reprint: PSC. *Indexed:* Agr, B&AI, BiolAb, BiolDig, CABA, ChemAb, ForAb, HortAb, IndVet, OceAb, PhilInd, S&F, SCI, SSCI, VB, ZooRec. *Bk. rev.:* 0-2, 800-2,000 words. *Aud.:* Ac, Sa.

Systematic Biology is a bimonthly publication of the Society of Systematic Biologists. The goal of this journal is the "advancement of systematic biology in all its aspects of theory, principles, methodology, and practice, for both living and fossil organisms." Contents include original research papers on methods of systematics as well as phylogeny, evolution, morphology, biogeography, paleontology, genetics, and the classification of all living things. There is a viewpoint section that offers discussion, book reviews, and news. Full text from 1998 to the present is available online through Ingenta with a print subscription. Recommended for special and academic libraries.

Biochemistry and Biophysics

785. Analytical Biochemistry. [ISSN: 0003-2697] 1960. 24x/yr. EUR 6665. Ed(s): William B Jakoby. Academic Press, 525 B St, Ste 1900, San Diego, CA 92101-4495; apsubs@acad.com; http://www.elsevier.com/. Illus., index, adv. Refereed. Online: EBSCO Publishing, EBSCO Host; Gale; IngentaConnect; OCLC Online Computer Library Center, Inc.; OhioLINK; ScienceDirect; SwetsWise Online Content. *Indexed:* BiolAb, CABA, ChemAb, DSA, ExcerpMed, FS&TA, ForAb, HortAb, IndVet, S&F, SCI, VB. *Bk. rev.:* 0-2, 240-500 words. *Aud.:* Ac, Sa.

Analytical Biochemistry places an emphasis on methods in the biological and biochemical sciences. More specifically, it publishes methods in analytical techniques, membranes and membrane proteins, molecular genetics, protein purification, immunological techniques, cell biology, general cell and organ culture, and pharmacological and toxicological research. Contents include original research articles, review articles on methods for biological and biochemical sciences, and notes and tips, which include methods summarized in a short format. Full-text articles are available online for the entire run of the publication through Elsevier's ScienceDirect. Sample issues are available online for free. This journal is geared specifically toward biochemists and would be a useful source for academic and research libraries.

786. Biochemical and Biophysical Research Communications. [ISSN: 0006-291X] 1959. 52x/yr. EUR 7532. Ed(s): W. Baumeister. Academic Press, 525 B St, Ste 1900, San Diego, CA 92101-4495; apsubs@acad.com; http://www.elsevier.com/. Illus., index, adv. Refereed. Online: EBSCO Publishing, EBSCO Host; Gale; IngentaConnect; OCLC Online Computer Library Center, Inc.; OhioLINK; ScienceDirect; SwetsWise Online Content. *Indexed:* Agr, BiolAb, CABA, ChemAb, DSA, ExcerpMed, FPA, FS&TA, ForAb, HortAb, IndVet, S&F, SCI, VB. *Aud.:* Ac, Sa.

Biochemical and Biophysical Research Communications is known as the "premier international journal devoted to the very rapid dissemination of timely and significant experimental results in diverse fields of biological research." Contents include the "Breakthroughs" and "Views" sections, which contain minireviews as well as collections of special-interest manuscripts. The broad range of research areas includes biochemistry, biophysics, cell biology, developmental biology, immunology, molecular biology, neurology, plant biology, and proteomics. Print and online subscriptions are available to individuals and institutions. Full text is available online from 1993 to the present via Elsevier's ScienceDirect. Free online sample issues are available. This journal is useful for biochemists and biophysicists as well as academic and research libraries.

787. Biochemical Journal. Formed by the merger of (1906-1984): *Biochemical Journal. Part 1: Cellular Aspects;* (1906-1984): *Biochemical Journal. Part 2: Molecular Aspects;* Both of which superseded in part (in 1973): *Biochemical Journal.* [ISSN: 0264-6021] 1984. s-m. EUR 3087 print & online eds. Portland Press Ltd., 3rd Fl, Eagle House, 16 Procter St, London, WC1V 6NX, United Kingdom; editorial@portlandpress.com; http://www.portlandpress.com. Illus., index, adv. Sample. Refereed. Circ: 2300. Microform: PMC; PQC. Online: EBSCO Publishing, EBSCO Host; National Library of Medicine; SwetsWise Online Content. *Indexed:* Agr, BiolAb, CABA, ChemAb, DSA, EngInd, ExcerpMed, FS&TA, ForAb, HortAb, IndVet, RRTA, S&F, SCI, VB. *Aud.:* Ac, Sa.

Biochemical Journal publishes research "papers on all aspects of biochemistry and cellular and molecular biology." Theoretical contributions will be considered equally with papers dealing with experimental work. Contents include research papers that make a significant contribution to biochemical knowledge, including new results obtained experimentally, descriptions of new experimental methods or new interrpretations of existing results, research communications, and reviews. Published by Biochemical Society's Portland Press, the journal provides free online access to its entire archive in full text from 1906 to the present. Recommended for special and academic libraries.

788. Biochemistry. [ISSN: 0006-2960] 1962. 51x/yr. USD 4177 print & online eds. Ed(s): Richard N Armstrong. American Chemical Society, 1155 16th St, NW, Washington, DC 20036; service@acs.org; http://pubs.acs.org. Illus., index, adv. Refereed. Circ: 4787. Vol. ends: Dec. Online: Pub.; EBSCO Publishing, EBSCO Host; OCLC Online Computer Library Center, Inc.; OhioLINK; SwetsWise Online Content. *Indexed:* Agr, B&AI, BiolAb, CABA, ChemAb, DSA, EngInd, EnvAb, ExcerpMed, FPA, FS&TA, ForAb, GSI, HortAb, IndVet, S&F, SCI, VB. *Aud.:* Ac, Sa.

Published weekly by the American Chemical Society (ACS), *Biochemistry* "presents the latest discoveries from around the world, to deepen your understanding of biological phenomena." Contents include developments in which chemistry, biochemistry, and molecular and cell biology meet. Articles cover structure, functions, and regulation of biologically active molecules; gene structure and expression; biochemical mchanisms; protein biosynthesis; membrane structure function relationships; and immunochemistry. There is free access to sample issues online. Full text is provided online with institutional subscriptions to ACS Web Editions, covering content from 1996 to the present, and ACS Legacy Archives contains articles from 1879 to 1995 in pdf format. Appropriate for special and academic libraries.

789. Biochemistry and Cell Biology. Former titles (until 1986): *Canadian Journal of Biochemistry and Cell Biology/Revue Canadien de Biochimie et Biologie Cellulaire;* (until 1983): *Canadian Journal of Biochemistry;* Which supersedes in part (in 1963): *Canadian Journal of Biochemistry and Physiology;* Which was formerly (until 1954): *Canadian Journal of Medical Sciences;* (until 1950): *Canadian Journal of Research. Section E: Medical Sciences.* [ISSN: 0829-8211] 1929. bi-m. CND 556 (Individuals, CND 185 print & online eds.). N R C Research Press, National Research Council of Canada, Ottawa, ON K1A 0R6, Canada; pubs@nrc-cnrc.gc.ca; http://pubs.nrc-cnrc.gc.ca. Illus., index, adv. Sample. Refereed. Circ: 913. Vol. ends: Nov/Dec. Microform: MML; PMC; PQC. Online: EBSCO Publishing, EBSCO Host; Gale; IngentaConnect; Micromedia ProQuest; OCLC Online Computer Library Center, Inc.; Ovid Technologies, Inc.; ProQuest K-12 Learning Solutions; ProQuest LLC (Ann Arbor); SwetsWise Online Content; H.W. Wilson. *Indexed:* Agr, B&AI, BiolAb, CABA, CBCARef, ChemAb, DSA, EngInd, ExcerpMed, FS&TA, HortAb, IndVet, S&F, SCI, VB, ZooRec. *Aud.:* Ac, Sa.

Published bimonthly, *Biochemistry and Cell Biology* "explores every aspect of general biochemistry, and includes up-to-date coverage of experimental research into cellular and molecular biology." Contents include review topics of current interest and notes contributed by international experts. Special issues are dedicated each year to expanding new areas of research in biochemistry and cell biology. First published in 1929, this Canadian journal presents papers in both

French and English, although the majority are in English. Online sample issues are available in full text with a separate subscription. Recommended for special and academic libraries.

790. Biochimica et Biophysica Acta: international journal of biochemistry and biophysics. [ISSN: 0006-3002] 1947. 100x/yr. EUR 14677 in Europe; Japan; USD 16418 elsewhere. Elsevier BV, Radarweg 29, Amsterdam, 1043 NX, Netherlands; nlinfo-f@elsevier.nl; http://www.elsevier.nl. Illus., index, adv. Refereed. Circ: 4500. Microform: PQC. Online: EBSCO Publishing, EBSCO Host; ScienceDirect. *Indexed:* Agr, ChemAb, ExcerpMed, FS&TA, VB. *Aud.:* Ac, Sa.

This journal publishes content within the areas of "Bioenergetics, Biomembranes, General Subjects, Gene Structure and Expression, Molecular and Cell Biology of Lipids, Molecular Cell Research, Proteins and Proteomics, Molecular Basis of Disease, and Reviews on Cancer." Contents include "Regular papers, Rapid Reports, Short Sequence papers, Promoter papers, Reviews, and Mini-Reviews." Online access is provided through Elsevier's ScienceDirect. Full text from 1967 to the present is available for subscribers. The table of contents for this journal is now available pre-publication via e-mail, as part of the free ContentsDirect service from Elsevier. Further information can be found on Elsevier's web site. This journal is appropriate for special and academic libraries.

791. Biophysical Journal. [ISSN: 0006-3495] 1960. m. USD 1007 combined subscription domestic print & online eds.; USD 1137 combined subscription Canada print & online eds.; USD 1063 combined subscription elsewhere print & online eds. Ed(s): Robert Callender. Biophysical Society, 9650 Rockville Pike, Bethesda, MD 20814; ckenney@biophysics.org; http://www.biophysics.org/. Illus., index, adv. Refereed. Microform: PQC. Online: EBSCO Publishing, EBSCO Host; HighWire Press; National Library of Medicine; Northern Light Technology, Inc.; ProQuest K-12 Learning Solutions; ProQuest LLC (Ann Arbor). *Indexed:* Agr, ApMecR, BiolAb, CABA, ChemAb, DSA, ExcerpMed, FPA, FS&TA, ForAb, HortAb, IndVet, S&F, SCI, VB. *Aud.:* Ac, Sa.

Information published in *Biophysical Journal* includes "original articles, letters and reviews on biophysical topics" that emphasize molecular and cellular aspects of biology. There are original research articles, biophysical letters for the rapid publication of short and important articles, comments to the editor, reviews of current interest in biophysics, and new and notable commentaries that highlight papers found in the same issue. The journal is published by the Biophysical Society, and all programs and abstracts for annual meetings are included with a subscription. Online access provided by Stanford's HighWire Press is a separate subscription from the print version. Online content from 1976 to the present varies from tables of contents to full text. This journal is appropriate for academic and research libraries.

792. The F E B S Journal (Print Edition). Former titles (until 2004): *European Journal of Biochemistry (Print Edition); (until 1967): Biochemische Zeitschrift.* [ISSN: 1742-464X] 1906. fortn. GBP 2348 print & online eds. Ed(s): Richard Perham. Blackwell Publishing Ltd., 9600 Garsington Rd, Oxford, OX4 2ZG, United Kingdom; customerservices@blackwellpublishing.com; http://www.blackwellpublishing.com. Illus., index, adv. Refereed. Circ: 1950. Microform: PQC. Online: Blackwell Synergy; EBSCO Publishing, EBSCO Host; Gale; HighWire Press; IngentaConnect; OCLC Online Computer Library Center, Inc.; OhioLINK; Ovid Technologies, Inc.; SwetsWise Online Content. *Indexed:* Agr, B&AI, BiolAb, CABA, ChemAb, DSA, ExcerpMed, FPA, FS&TA, ForAb, HortAb, IndVet, S&F, SCI, VB. *Aud.:* Ac, Sa.

The FEBS Journal is "devoted to the rapid publication of full-length papers describing original research in all areas of the molecular life sciences." Publishing preference is given to research that advances new concepts or develops new experimental techniques. Contents include research papers, reviews, minireviews, and meeting reports. Article topics cover a variety of subdisciplines including but not limited to immunology, molecular genetics, nucleic acids, protein synthesis, developmental biology, bioenergetics, systems biology, and molecular evolution. The journal is published by Blackwell on behalf of the Federation of European Biochemical Societies. There is free access to all review articles published to date, and there are some free sample issues. Online full text is provided through Blackwell Synergy and Stanford's HighWire Press. Recommended for special and academic libraries.

793. F E B S Letters. [ISSN: 0014-5793] 1968. 30x/yr. EUR 4821. Ed(s): F. Wieland. Elsevier BV, Radarweg 29, Amsterdam, 1043 NX, Netherlands; nlinfo-f@elsevier.nl; http://www.elsevier.nl. Illus., index, adv. Refereed. Circ: Controlled. Microform: PQC. Online: EBSCO Publishing, EBSCO Host; Gale; IngentaConnect; OhioLINK; ScienceDirect; SwetsWise Online Content. *Indexed:* BiolAb, CABA, ChemAb, DSA, EnvAb, EnvInd, ExcerpMed, FPA, FS&TA, ForAb, HortAb, IndVet, S&F, SCI, VB. *Aud.:* Ac, Sa.

FEBS Letters, published by the Federation of European Biochemical Societies, is an "international journal established for its rapid publication of essentially final short reports in the fields of molecular biosciences." Contents cover biochemistry, structural biology, biophysics, computational biology, molecular genetics, molecular biology, and molecular cell biology. Studies may be on microbes, plants, or animals. Found within each issue are minireviews, hypotheses, and research letters, all on an international level. Online full-text access is available through Elsevier's ScienceDirect and at www.FEBSLetters.com Appropriate for special and academic libraries.

794. Journal of Biochemistry. [ISSN: 0021-924X] 1922. m. EUR 329 print or online ed. Ed(s): Naoyuki Taniguchi. Oxford University Press, Great Clarendon St, Oxford, OX2 6DP, United Kingdom; jnl.orders@oup.co.uk; http://www.oxfordjournals.org. Illus., index, adv. Refereed. Circ: 2650. Microform: PMC. Online: EBSCO Publishing, EBSCO Host; Gale; HighWire Press; IngentaConnect; Oxford Journals; SwetsWise Online Content. Reprint: PSC. *Indexed:* Agr, BiolAb, CABA, ChemAb, DSA, ExcerpMed, FS&TA, ForAb, HortAb, IndVet, S&F, SCI, VB. *Aud.:* Ac, Sa.

This journal publishes articles on biochemistry, biotechnology, molecular biology, and cell biology. Contents include reviews, regular research articles, and brief communications in English. Published by Oxford University Press on behalf of the Japanese Biochemical Society, online full text is available with a subscription. Additional online features include e-mail alerts with CiteTrack. The journal is recommended for special and academic libraries that support chemists, biologists, physicians, and physiologists.

795. Journal of Biological Chemistry. [ISSN: 0021-9258] 1905. w. USD 2625 domestic; USD 3493 Canada; USD 3335 elsewhere. Ed(s): Herbert Tabor. American Society for Biochemistry and Molecular Biology, Inc., 9650 Rockville Pike, Bethesda, MD 20814-3996; asbmb@asbmb.faseb.org; http://www.asbmb.org. Illus., index, adv. Refereed. Circ: 6000. Vol. ends: Dec. Microform: PMC; PQC. Online: EBSCO Publishing, EBSCO Host; HighWire Press. *Indexed:* Agr, B&AI, BiolAb, CABA, ChemAb, DSA, EngInd, ExcerpMed, FPA, FS&TA, ForAb, HortAb, IndVet, S&F, SCI, VB, ZooRec. *Aud.:* Ac, Sa.

This weekly journal focuses on original research reports in biochemistry and molecular biology, and includes such topics as developmental biology, computational biology, metabolism, protein chemistry, and nucleic acids. Contents include original research papers that make novel and important contributions to the understanding of any area of biochemistry or molecular biology. Accelerated publication that presents new information of high importance and interest to the broad readership is by invitation only. Both print and online subscriptions are available. Online full text is available in pdf format from 1905 to the present, and is free for issues published before the current year via Stanford's HighWire Press. This journal is highly recommended for special libraries and academic libraries that support biology programs.

Cell and Molecular Biology

796. BioEssays: advances in molecular, cellular and developmental biology. [ISSN: 0265-9247] 1984. m. USD 1331. Ed(s): Adam S Wilkins. John Wiley & Sons Ltd., The Atrium, Southern Gate,

Chichester, PO19 8SQ, United Kingdom; customer@wiley.co.uk; http://www.wiley.co.uk. Adv. Refereed. *Indexed:* CABA, ChemAb, DSA, ExcerpMed, ForAb, HortAb, IndVet, S&F, SCI, VB, ZooRec. *Bk. rev.:* 0-3, 500-600 words. *Aud.:* Ac, Sa.

As one of the leading review journals in biology, *BioEssays* publishes "short news-and-views articles plus broad reviews and insightful discussion articles on the latest findings and ideas in molecular cell biology, developmental biology, plant science and neurobiology." Contents are divided into two main sections, "Reviews" and "Features." "Reviews" consists of short articles that highlight issues of interest as well as broader review articles with a wider scope; "Features" focuses on subjects of special interest, including novel hypotheses, discussions of various issues, presentations of molecular or cellular model systems, firsthand accounts of discoveries, or subjects in applied biological science, particularly medicine. Also included are "What's New" articles, commentaries, meeting reports, and book reviews. Online subscriptions are available at Wiley InterScience. This is a good source for all biology collections as well as special and academic libraries.

797. Cell. [ISSN: 0092-8674] 1974. 26x/yr. EUR 1599. Ed(s): Emilie Marcus. Cell Press, 1100 Massachusetts Ave, Cambridge, MA 02138; http://www.cellpress.com/. Illus., index, adv. Refereed. Circ: 12000 Paid. Online: EBSCO Publishing, EBSCO Host; Gale; IngentaConnect; OhioLINK; ScienceDirect; SwetsWise Online Content. *Indexed:* B&AI, BiolAb, BiolDig, CABA, ChemAb, DSA, ExcerpMed, FS&TA, GSI, HortAb, IndVet, S&F, SCI, SSCI, VB, ZooRec. *Aud.:* Ac, Sa.

Launched in 1974, *Cell* publishes novel results within all areas of experimental biology including human genetics, cancer, immunology, systems biology, neuroscience, signaling, and disease. Papers considered for publication must provide significant conceptual advances or raise provocative questions regarding an interesting biological issue. In December 2005, *Cell* was relaunched, and contents now include reviews and minireviews that provide in-depth analysis on scientific policy and economic, political, and social trends. There are also commentaries, viewpoints, essays, point-counterpoint discussions of controversial findings, and letters to the editor. Online and print access can be purchased separately or in a combined package. *Cell* is recommended for academic and special libraries.

798. The E M B O Journal. [ISSN: 0261-4189] 1982. s-m. EUR 2665. Ed(s): Iain Mattaj. Nature Publishing Group, The MacMillan Building, 4 Crinan St, London, N1 9XW, United Kingdom; NatureReviews@nature.com; http://www.nature.com. Illus., index, adv. Sample. Refereed. Circ: 4200. Vol. ends: Dec. Online: EBSCO Publishing, EBSCO Host; HighWire Press; National Library of Medicine; OCLC Online Computer Library Center, Inc.; OhioLINK; ProQuest LLC (Ann Arbor); SwetsWise Online Content. *Indexed:* Agr, B&AI, BiolAb, CABA, ChemAb, DSA, ExcerpMed, FS&TA, ForAb, HortAb, IndVet, S&F, SCI, VB, ZooRec. *Aud.:* Ac, Sa.

The EMBO Journal (European Molecular Biology Organization) provides "rapid publication of full-length papers describing original research of general rather than specialist interest in molecular biology and related areas." Articles report novel findings of wide biological significance in such areas as structural biology, immunology, plant biology, RNA, proteins, cellular metabolism, and molecular biology of disease. The journal is published 24 times a year by the Nature Publishing Group, and full text is available free online. Established as one of the most influential molecular biology journals, it is recommended for academic and research libraries.

799. Experimental Cell Research. [ISSN: 0014-4827] 1950. 20x/yr. EUR 6390. Ed(s): U. Lendahl. Academic Press, 525 B St, Ste 1900, San Diego, CA 92101-4495; apsubs@acad.com; http://www.elsevier.com/. Illus., index, adv. Refereed. Online: EBSCO Publishing, EBSCO Host; Gale; IngentaConnect; OCLC Online Computer Library Center, Inc.; OhioLINK; ScienceDirect; SwetsWise Online Content. *Indexed:* Agr, B&AI, BiolAb, CABA, ChemAb, DSA, ExcerpMed, IndVet, S&F, SCI, VB. *Aud.:* Ac, Sa.

Experimental Cell Research "promotes the understanding of cell biology by publishing experimental studies on the general organization and activity of cells." Research is published on all aspects of cell biology from the molecular level to cell interaction and differentiation. Contents include papers that provide

novel and significant insights into important problems within these areas. Specific topics include cancer research, developmental biology, meiosis and mitosis, RNA processing, and stem cell biology. Online full-text access is provided by Elsevier's ScienceDirect, and sample issues are available free. This journal is recommended for molecular and cell biologists and cancer researchers, and for academic and research libraries, especially those supporting research in cell or molecular biology or cancer.

800. The Journal of Cell Biology. Formerly (until 1961): *Journal of Biophysical and Biochemical Cytology.* [ISSN: 0021-9525] 1955. bi-w. USD 1735 (Individuals, USD 325). Ed(s): Ira Mellman. Rockefeller University Press, 1114 First Ave, New York, NY 10021-8325; rupress@rockefeller.edu; http://www.rupress.org. Illus., index, adv. Sample. Refereed. Circ: 3931. Microform: PQC. Online: EBSCO Publishing, EBSCO Host; HighWire Press; JSTOR (Web-based Journal Archive); OhioLINK. *Indexed:* Agr, B&AI, BiolAb, CABA, ChemAb, DSA, ExcerpMed, ForAb, GSI, HortAb, IndVet, S&F, SCI, VB, ZooRec. *Aud.:* Ac, Sa.

The Journal of Cell Biology publishes papers on all aspects of cellular structure and function. Articles must provide novel and significant mechanistic insight into a cellular function that will be of interest to a general readership. Published materials are limited in size but may include concise articles and reports that have the potential to open new avenues of research. The biweekly journal is published by The Rockefeller University Press with the assistance of Stanford University Libraries, a nonprofit organization. Editors are scientists who review articles only within their chosen field. Online content is available through Stanford's HighWire Press with a print subscription. All articles are available in full text online after six months in print. Free archives date back to 1955. Additional online features include supplemental material such as videos, charts, and graphs that correlate to print articles, and advanced publication notices. This journal provides news and short reviews that are useful to students, researchers, and professionals. It is appropriate for academic and special libraries. Document delivery is available from BLDSC, CASDDS, CISTI, The Genuine Article, LHLDS, UMI, and UnCover.

801. Journal of Cell Science. Formerly (until 1966): *Quarterly Journal of Microscopical Science.* [ISSN: 0021-9533] 1852. s-m. USD 2295 (Individuals, USD 475). Ed(s): Dr. Fiona M Watt. The Company of Biologists Ltd., Bidder Building, 140 Cowley Rd, Cambridge, CB4 0DL, United Kingdom; sales@thecob.demon.co.uk; http://www.biologists.com. Illus., index, adv. Sample. Refereed. Circ: 1550. Vol. ends: Dec. Microform: BHP. Online: EBSCO Publishing, EBSCO Host; HighWire Press. *Indexed:* Agr, B&AI, BiolAb, CABA, ChemAb, DSA, ExcerpMed, ForAb, HortAb, IndVet, S&F, SCI, VB, ZooRec. *Aud.:* Ac, Sa.

Covering the complete range of topics in cell biology, *Journal of Cell Science* is also of key interest to developmental biologists, molecular biologists, and geneticists. Contents include research articles, review articles, brief syntheses of important areas, and topical comments. The journal is published twice a month by the Company of Biologists, a nonprofit organization determined to promote research and knowledge in the study of biology. Early released articles are available through JCS ePress. Recommended for special and academic libraries.

802. Journal of Molecular Biology. [ISSN: 0022-2836] 1959. 50x/yr. EUR 7757. Ed(s): P Wright. Academic Press, Harcourt Pl, 32 Jamestown Rd, London, NW1 7BY, United Kingdom; apsubs@acad.com; http://www.elsevier.com/. Illus., index, adv. Sample. Refereed. Online: EBSCO Publishing, EBSCO Host; Gale; IngentaConnect; OCLC Online Computer Library Center, Inc.; OhioLINK; ScienceDirect; SwetsWise Online Content. *Indexed:* Agr, B&AI, BiolAb, CABA, ChemAb, DSA, ExcerpMed, FPA, FS&TA, ForAb, HortAb, IndVet, S&F, SCI, VB. *Aud.:* Ac, Sa.

Published weekly, the *Journal of Molecular Biology* contains "original scientific research concerning studies of organisms or their components at the molecular level." Specific research areas include gene structure, expression, replication, and recombination in eukaryotic and prokaryotic organisms; the structure, function, and chemistry of proteins, nucleic acids, and other macromolecules; cellular and developmental biology; and the genetics, structure, and growth cycles of viruses and bacteriophages. Online full-text access is provided by Elsevier's ScienceDirect from 1966 to the present. This journal is appropriate for any academic library or research institution that supports biologists.

803. *Molecular and Cellular Biology.* [ISSN: 0270-7306] 1981. s-m. USD 1560. Ed(s): Dafna Bar-Sagi. American Society for Microbiology, 1752 N St, NW, Washington, DC 20036-2904; asmjournals@asm.org; http://www.asm.org. Illus., index, adv. Sample. Refereed. Circ: 10668 Paid. Vol. ends: Dec. Microform: PQC. Online: EBSCO Publishing, EBSCO Host; HighWire Press; National Library of Medicine. *Indexed:* B&AI, BiolAb, CABA, ChemAb, DSA, ExcerpMed, HortAb, IndVet, S&F, SCI, VB, ZooRec. *Aud.:* Ac, Sa.

Molecular and Cellular Biology is an "authoritative source of fundamental knowledge and new developments in all aspects of the molecular biology of eukaryotic cells." Topics emphasized include gene expression, transcriptional regulation, cell growth and development, nucleocytoplasmic communication, cell and organelle structure and assembly, and mammalian genetic models. Full text is available free online six months after an issue's publication. The ISI 2004 Journal Citation Reports ranked *Molecular and Cellular Biology* No. 18 out of 155 journals in the cell biology field and No. 22 out of 261 journals in the biochemistry and molecular biology field. Recommended for undergraduates and researchers in special and academic libraries.

804. *Molecular Biology and Evolution.* [ISSN: 0737-4038] 1983. m. USD 644. Ed(s): William Martin. Oxford University Press, 2001 Evans Rd, Cary, NC 27513; jnlorders@oup-usa.org; http://www.us.oup.com. Illus., index, adv. Refereed. Circ: 918 Paid. Vol. ends: Nov. Microform: PMC; PQC. Online: EBSCO Publishing, EBSCO Host; Gale; HighWire Press; IngentaConnect; OCLC Online Computer Library Center, Inc.; OhioLINK; Ovid Technologies, Inc.; Oxford Journals; SwetsWise Online Content. Reprint: PSC. *Indexed:* AbAn, BiolAb, CABA, ChemAb, DSA, ExcerpMed, ForAb, HortAb, IndVet, S&F, SCI, VB, ZooRec. *Aud.:* Ac, Sa.

Publishing research at the interface between molecular and evolutionary biology, *Molecular Biology and Evolution* "publishes investigations of molecular evolutionary patterns and processes, tests of evolutionary hypotheses that use molecular data and studies that use molecular evolutionary information to address questions about biological function at all levels of organization." Contents include two types of categories: research articles, which are conventional in form without strict length limitations; and letters, which are short communications that contain findings of outstanding interest to a broad readership. Full text is available online from 1983 to the present. Appropriate for academic and research libraries.

805. *Molecular Cell.* [ISSN: 1097-2765] 1997. 24x/yr. EUR 1599. Ed(s): Dorit Zuk. Cell Press, 1100 Massachusetts Ave, Cambridge, MA 02138; editor@cell.com; http://www.cellpress.com/. Adv. Refereed. Circ: 2301 Paid. Online: EBSCO Publishing, EBSCO Host; Gale; IngentaConnect; OhioLINK; ScienceDirect; SwetsWise Online Content. *Indexed:* BiolAb, CABA, ChemAb, ExcerpMed, IndVet, SCI, VB, ZooRec. *Aud.:* Ac, Sa.

Molecular Cell publishes reports of unusual significance to researchers in the field. Topics focus on "analyses at the molecular level in any area of biology, particularly that of molecular biology (including replication, recombination, repair, gene expression, RNA processing, translation, and protein folding, modification and degradation)." Papers considered for publication must provide significant insights or raise provocative questions and hypotheses. The majority of each issue consists of research articles, and shorter papers make up a small section. Free online full text is available 12 months after publication. Appropriate for special and academic libraries.

806. *Nucleic Acids Research.* [ISSN: 0305-1048] 1974. 22x/yr. EUR 3279. Ed(s): Richard J Roberts, Michael Gait. Oxford University Press, Great Clarendon St, Oxford, OX2 6DP, United Kingdom; jnl.orders@ oup.co.uk; http://www.oxfordjournals.org. Illus., index, adv. Sample. Refereed. Circ: 1730. Vol. ends: Dec. Online: EBSCO Publishing, EBSCO Host; Gale; HighWire Press; IngentaConnect; National Library of Medicine; OCLC Online Computer Library Center, Inc.; OhioLINK; Ovid Technologies, Inc.; Oxford Journals; ProQuest LLC (Ann Arbor); SwetsWise Online Content. Reprint: PSC. *Indexed:* Agr, BioEngAb, BiolAb, CABA, ChemAb, DSA, ExcerpMed, FS&TA, ForAb, HortAb, IndVet, S&F, SCI, VB. *Aud.:* Ac, Sa.

Nucleic Acids Research is an open access journal that provides for rapid publication of cutting-edge research into nucleic acids within chemistry, computational biology, genomics, molecular biology, nucleic acid enzymes, RNA, and structural biology. Print contents include standard papers, surveys, and summaries that present brief, formal reviews relevant to nucleic acid chemistry and biology. Online contents include all articles and methods papers that describe novel techniques or advances in existing techniques that are highly significant, and supplemental materials. Published by Oxford University Press, issues are freely available online under an open access model. This journal is recommended for academic and research libraries with biology, medical, and chemistry collections.

Developmental Biology

807. *Development (Cambridge).* Formerly (until 1986): *Journal of Embryology and Experimental Morphology.* [ISSN: 0950-1991] 1953. s-m. USD 2695 (Individuals, USD 555). Ed(s): Dr. Jim Smith. The Company of Biologists Ltd., Bidder Building, 140 Cowley Rd, Cambridge, CB4 0DL, United Kingdom; http://www.biologists.com/ development. Illus., index, adv. Refereed. Circ: 2700. Vol. ends: Dec. Online: EBSCO Publishing, EBSCO Host; HighWire Press. *Indexed:* B&AI, BiolAb, CABA, ChemAb, DSA, ExcerpMed, ForAb, HortAb, IndVet, S&F, SCI, VB, ZooRec. *Aud.:* Ac, Sa.

Known as a primary research journal, *Development* provides "insight into mechanisms of plant and animal development covering all aspects from molecular and cellular to tissue levels." It acts as a forum for all research that offers genuine insight into developmental mechanisms, and experimental papers are given top priority. Published by the Company of Biologists, the journal includes research articles and meeting reviews. Full text is available online, and all content becomes free at year's end. Additional online services include e-mail alerts to citations and corrections. Recommended for academic and special libraries.

808. *Developmental Biology.* [ISSN: 0012-1606] 1959. 24x/yr. EUR 8679. Ed(s): Dr. Eric N Olson. Academic Press, 525 B St, Ste 1900, San Diego, CA 92101-4495; apsubs@acad.com; http://www.elsevier.com/. Illus., index, adv. Refereed. Online: EBSCO Publishing, EBSCO Host; Gale; IngentaConnect; OCLC Online Computer Library Center, Inc.; OhioLINK; ScienceDirect; SwetsWise Online Content. *Indexed:* Agr, B&AI, BiolAb, CABA, ChemAb, DSA, ExcerpMed, GSI, HortAb, IndVet, S&F, SCI, VB, ZooRec. *Aud.:* Ac, Sa.

Developmental Biology publishes "research on the mechanisms of development, differentiation, and growth in animals and plants at the molecular, cellular, and genetic levels." Research areas of particular interest include molecular genetics of development, cell interactions, growth factors and oncogenes, regulation of stem cell populations, and fertilization. Contents include original research papers that contribute new information to the understanding of developmental mechanisms, review articles intended to reach a broad readership, and a new section called "Genomes and Developmental Control," dedicated to papers that address the analysis of developmental processes and systems involving animals and plants. Online full-text access is provided through Elsevier's ScienceDirect. Although expensive, *Developmental Biology* is considered the best in its field. Recommended for academic and special libraries.

809. *Genes & Development.* [ISSN: 0890-9369] 1987. s-m. USD 1058 (Individuals, USD 140; Students, USD 196). Ed(s): T Grodzicker. Cold Spring Harbor Laboratory Press, Publications Department, 500 Sunnyside Blvd., Woodbury, NY 11797-2924; cshpress@cshl.edu; http://www.cshl.org. Illus., index, adv. Sample. Refereed. Vol. ends: Dec. Online: EBSCO Publishing, EBSCO Host; HighWire Press; National Library of Medicine. Reprint: PSC. *Indexed:* AbAn, B&AI, BiolAb, BiolDig, CABA, ChemAb, DSA, ExcerpMed, FPA, ForAb, GSI, HortAb, IndVet, S&F, SCI, SSCI, VB. *Aud.:* Ac, Sa.

Genes & Development publishes "high quality research papers of broad general interest and biological significance in the areas of molecular biology, molecular genetics and related fields." Contents include two main formats: research papers that occupy up to 12 journal pages and short research communications that provide compelling, novel, and important conclusions. Also included are review articles and perspectives. Online and print subscriptions are available separately. Free samples issues are found online, as well as access to tables of contents and abstracts. Recommended for special and academic libraries.

Genetics

810. American Journal of Human Genetics. [ISSN: 0002-9297] 1948. m. USD 1150. Ed(s): Katherine M. DyReyes, Cynthia C. Morton. University of Chicago Press, Journals Division, PO Box 37005, Chicago, IL 60637; subscriptions@press.uchicago.edu; http://www.journals.uchicago.edu. Illus., index, adv. Refereed. Circ: 3000 Paid. Vol. ends: Dec. Microform: MIM; PQC. Online: EBSCO Publishing, EBSCO Host; Florida Center for Library Automation; Gale; National Library of Medicine; ProQuest LLC (Ann Arbor). Reprint: PSC. *Indexed:* AICP, AbAn, B&AI, BAS, BiolAb, CABA, CINAHL, ChemAb, DSA, ExcerpMed, GSI, SCI. *Bk. rev.:* 0-3, 200-1,200 words. *Aud.:* Ac, Sa.

Published for the American Society of Human Genetics, which is the primary professional membership organization for human geneticists in the Americas, this journal is a "record of research and review relating to heredity in man and to the application of genetic principles in medicine, psychology, anthropology, and social services, as well as in related areas of molecular and cell biology." Papers appear on such topics as behavioral, biochemical, or clinical genetics; immunogenetics; genetic counseling; and epidemiology. Also included are review articles, reports, conference announcements, employment notices, and letters to the editors. Online access is provided by the University of Chicago Press. Access to full text of the past six month's issues is restricted to subscribers. Prior issues are freely accessible to all users. A good source for special and academic libraries.

811. Genetics: a periodical record of investigations bearing on heredity and variation. [ISSN: 0016-6731] 1916. m. USD 900 print & online eds. Ed(s): Elizabeth W Jones. Genetics Society of America, 9650 Rockville Pike, Rm L-3503A, Bethesda, MD 20814; staff@dues.faseb.org; http://www.genetics.org. Illus., index, adv. Refereed. Circ: 5000. Microform: MIM; PMC; PQC. Online: EBSCO Publishing, EBSCO Host; HighWire Press; ProQuest LLC (Ann Arbor). *Indexed:* AbAn, Agr, B&AI, BiolAb, BiolDig, CABA, ChemAb, DSA, ExcerpMed, FPA, FS&TA, ForAb, GSI, HortAb, IndVet, OceAb, S&F, SCI, VB, ZooRec. *Aud.:* Ac, Sa.

Published by the Genetics Society of America, *Genetics* promotes the communication of advances in genetics and related fields. Contents include concise research articles, perspectives, and essays that outline the history of an event paying tribute to an important figure within the field. There are also articles on genetics and education, which provide a scholarly forum for persons having created new teaching instruments in their role as educator. Online access is provided through Stanford's HighWire Press. Online and print subscriptions are available to society members, individuals, and institutions. Full text is available online from 1998 to the present. Appropriate for special and academic libraries.

812. Genome Research. Formerly (until Aug 1995): *P C R Methods and Applications (Polymerase Chain Reaction)*. [ISSN: 1088-9051] 1991. m. USD 1010 (Individuals, USD 123; Students, USD 98). Ed(s): L Goodman. Cold Spring Harbor Laboratory Press, Publications Department, 500 Sunnyside Blvd., Woodbury, NY 11797-2924; cshpress@cshl.edu; http://www.cshl.org. Illus., adv. Refereed. Online: EBSCO Publishing, EBSCO Host; HighWire Press; National Library of Medicine; H.W. Wilson. Reprint: PSC. *Indexed:* BiolAb, CABA, ChemAb, DSA, ExcerpMed, FS&TA, ForAb, GSI, HortAb, IndVet, S&F, SCI, VB. *Aud.:* Ac, Sa.

Articles published in *Genome Research* focus on gene discovery, comparative genome analysis, proteomics, evolution studies, informatics, genome structure and function, technological innovations and applications, statistical and mathematical methods, cutting-edge genetic and physical mapping, and DNA sequencing. This journal presents new data published in the form of articles and letters, review articles, perspectives, and insight/outlook articles that provide commentary on recent advances. Submitted articles selected by the editor are peer reviewed, and all accepted papers must present original research; researchers should be prepared to make available all materials needed to duplicate their work. *Genome Research* follows the guidelines for fair use of community resource data. Print and online subscriptions are available for both individuals and institutions. Nonsubscribers have free access to one sample issue as well as tables of contents and abstracts. A new online feature for subscribers is CiteTrack, which offers personal e-mail alerts on topics, authors, and articles. This journal is appropriate for academic and special libraries.

813. Heredity. [ISSN: 0018-067X] 1947. m. EUR 753. Ed(s): Richard A Nichols. Nature Publishing Group, The MacMillan Building, 4 Crinan St, London, N1 9XW, United Kingdom; NatureReviews@nature.com; http://www.nature.com. Illus., index, adv. Sample. Refereed. Circ: 1075. Microform: PQC. Online: Blackwell Synergy; EBSCO Publishing, EBSCO Host; IngentaConnect; OCLC Online Computer Library Center, Inc.; OhioLINK; ProQuest LLC (Ann Arbor); SwetsWise Online Content. *Indexed:* AbAn, Agr, ApEcolAb, B&AI, BiolAb, CABA, ChemAb, DSA, ExcerpMed, FPA, FS&TA, ForAb, GSI, HortAb, IndVet, S&F, SCI, VB, ZooRec. *Bk. rev.:* 4-5, 400-2,000 words. *Aud.:* Ac, Sa.

Heredity, published for The Genetics Society, presents "high-quality articles that describe original research and theoretical insights in all areas of genetics." Contents include original research articles, short reviews, book reviews, and news and commentaries that keep researchers and students updated about advances in the field. Subscriptions can be print-only, online-only, or combined. There is full-text access from 1996 to the present online. Appropriate for special and academic libraries.

814. Human Biology (Detroit): the international journal of population biology and genetics. [ISSN: 0018-7143] 1929. bi-m. USD 190 (Individuals, USD 66; Students, USD 35 & seniors). Ed(s): Sarah Williams-Blangers. Wayne State University Press, The Leonard N Simons Bldg, 4809 Woodward Ave, Detroit, MI 48201-1309; http://wsupress.wayne.edu/. Illus., index, adv. Refereed. Circ: 1654. Vol. ends: Dec. Microform: PQC. Online: Chadwyck-Healey Inc.; EBSCO Publishing, EBSCO Host; Florida Center for Library Automation; Gale; OCLC Online Computer Library Center, Inc.; OhioLINK; Project MUSE; ProQuest K-12 Learning Solutions; ProQuest LLC (Ann Arbor); SwetsWise Online Content; H.W. Wilson. *Indexed:* A&ATA, ABS&EES, AICP, AbAn, AgeL, AnthLit, B&AI, BAS, BiolAb, BiolDig, CABA, ChemAb, DSA, ExcerpMed, GSI, IndIslam, SCI, SSA, SSCI, SociolAb. *Bk. rev.:* 1-3, 500-1,400 words. *Aud.:* Ac, Sa.

This journal publishes ideas, methods, and techniques in the human biology field. Topics include evolutionary and genetic demography, behavioral genetics, population genetics, quantitative genetics, genetic epidemiology, molecular genetics, and growth physiology focusing on genetic/environmental interactions. There is online access to full text from 2001 to the present. Subscriptions are available to individuals and institutions, and student/senior discounts are offered. Appropriate for academic and special libraries with collections in anthropology, biology, and medicine.

815. Journal of Heredity. [ISSN: 0022-1503] 1910. bi-m. EUR 322 print or online ed. Ed(s): Stephen O'Brien. Oxford University Press, Great Clarendon St, Oxford, OX2 6DP, United Kingdom; jnl.orders@oup.co.uk; http://www.oxfordjournals.org. Illus., index, adv. Refereed. Circ: 1600. Vol. ends: Nov/Dec. Microform: IDC; PMC; PQC. Online: EBSCO Publishing, EBSCO Host; Gale; HighWire Press; IngentaConnect; OCLC Online Computer Library Center, Inc.; OhioLINK; Oxford Journals; ProQuest LLC (Ann Arbor); SwetsWise Online Content. Reprint: PSC. *Indexed:* AbAn, Agr, AnBeAb, ApEcolAb, B&AI, BiolAb, CABA, ChemAb, DSA, ExcerpMed, FPA, FS&TA, ForAb, GSI, HortAb, IndVet, S&F, SCI, VB, WAE&RSA, ZooRec. *Bk. rev.:* 0-5, 300-900 words. *Aud.:* Ac, Sa.

This journal contains articles on organismal genetics such as "gene action, regulation, and transmission in both plant and animal species, including the genetic aspects of botany, cytogenetics and evolution, zoology, and molecular and developmental biology." Contents include research papers, brief communications, announcements, and review articles. Also included are papers on rapidly advancing fields such as genome organization, comparative gene mapping, animal models of human disease, and molecular genetics of resistance to infectious disease in plants and animals. Full text is available online from 2001 to the present with a subscription. Articles prior to 1996 require an additional subscription to the digital archive. Recommended for a wide range of biologists as well as special and academic libraries.

816. *Molecular Genetics and Genomics: an international journal.* Former titles (until 2001): *Molecular and General Genetics;* (until 1966): *Zeitschrift fuer Vererbungslehre;* (until 1957): *Zeitschrift fuer Induktive Abstammungs- und Vererbungslehre.* [ISSN: 1617-4615] 1908. m. EUR 3760 print & online eds. Ed(s): Dr. Cornelis P Hollenberg. Springer, Tiergartenstr 17, Heidelberg, 69121, Germany. Illus., index, adv. Refereed. Microform: PQC. Online: EBSCO Publishing, EBSCO Host; OhioLINK; Springer LINK; SwetsWise Online Content. Reprint: PSC. *Indexed:* Agr, B&AI, BiolAb, CABA, ChemAb, DSA, ExcerpMed, FPA, FS&TA, ForAb, HortAb, IndVet, S&F, SCI, VB, ZooRec. *Aud.:* Ac, Sa.

Molecular Genetics and Genomics publishes research in all areas of genetics and genomics as well as encompassing experimental and theoretical approaches in all organisms. The journal is intended for biologists, and contents include review articles and original research articles in areas including genetic engineering, molecular genetics, developmental genetics, and somatic cell genetics. Full text is available online from 1996 to the present. Some articles are offered free online through Springer Open Choice. Recommended for special and academic libraries.

817. *Nature Genetics.* [ISSN: 1061-4036] 1992. m. EUR 2170. Ed(s): Myles Axton. Nature Publishing Group, 75 Varick St, 9th Fl., New York, NY 10013. Illus., index, adv. Refereed. Circ: 3000. Online: EBSCO Publishing, EBSCO Host; ProQuest LLC (Ann Arbor); SwetsWise Online Content. *Indexed:* Agr, ArtHuCI, B&AI, BiolAb, BiolDig, CABA, ChemAb, DSA, ExcerpMed, HortAb, IndVet, S&F, SCI, SSCI, VB. *Bk. rev.:* 1, 700-1,000 words. *Aud.:* Ac, Sa.

Nature Genetics publishes genetic and functional genomic studies on human traits and other organisms including the mouse, fly, nematode, and yeast. It focuses on the genetic basis for common and complex diseases as well as the mechanism, architecture, and evolution of gene networks. Contents include editorials, research articles, letters, news and views, and meeting reports. Online access comes in a package with a print subscription. Online full text is available from 1997 to the present. According to the ISI Journal Citation Reports, *Nature Genetics* took first place out of 120 journals in the field of genetics and heredity. Appropriate for special and academic libraries supporting biology programs.

818. *R N A.* [ISSN: 1355-8382] 1995. m. USD 760 (Individuals, USD 260). Ed(s): Dr. Timothy W Nilsen. Cold Spring Harbor Laboratory Press, Publications Department, 500 Sunnyside Blvd., Woodbury, NY 11797-2924; cshpress@cshl.edu; http://www.cshl.org. Adv. Refereed. Online: EBSCO Publishing, EBSCO Host; HighWire Press; National Library of Medicine; OCLC Online Computer Library Center, Inc.; OhioLINK; SwetsWise Online Content. *Indexed:* BiolAb, CABA, ExcerpMed, HortAb, IndVet, S&F, SCI, VB. *Aud.:* Ac, Sa.

RNA serves as an international forum. It is a monthly publication that "provides rapid publication of significant original research in all areas of RNA structure and function in eukaryotic, prokaryotic, and viral systems." Topics covered include structural analysis; rRNA, mRNA, and tRNA structure, function, and biogenesis; alternative processing; ribosome structure and function; translational control; RNA catalysis; RNA editing; RNA transport and localization; regulatory RNAs; large and small RNP structure, function, and biogenesis; viral RNA metabolism; RNA stability and turnover; in vitro evolution; and RNA chemistry. Contents include reports, articles, bioinformatics that describe computer-based analysis of sequence data, hypotheses, methods, letters to the editor, prespectives, minireviews, and meeting summaries. Subscriptions to the print journal include full online access; online-only subscriptions are available to institutions. Full text from 1995 to the present is provided by Stanford's HighWire Press. Appropriate for special and academic libraries.

Microbiology

819. *Canadian Journal of Microbiology.* [ISSN: 0008-4166] 1954. m. CND 659 (Individuals, CND 195). Ed(s): Dr. Jim J Germida, H G Deneer. N R C Research Press, National Research Council of Canada, Ottawa, ON K1A 0R6, Canada; pubs@nrc-cnrc.gc.ca; http://pubs.nrc-cnrc.gc.ca. Illus., index, adv. Sample. Refereed. Circ: 1341. Vol. ends: Dec. Microform: MML; PMC; PQC. Online: EBSCO Publishing, EBSCO Host; Gale; IngentaConnect; Micromedia ProQuest; OCLC Online Computer Library Center, Inc.; Ovid Technologies, Inc.; ProQuest K-12 Learning Solutions; ProQuest LLC (Ann Arbor); SwetsWise Online Content; H.W. Wilson. *Indexed:* Agr, B&AI, BiolAb, CABA, CBCARef, CPerI, ChemAb, DSA, EngInd, EnvAb, EnvInd, ExcerpMed, FPA, FS&TA, ForAb, HortAb, IAA, IndVet, PollutAb, RRTA, S&F, SCI, SWRA, VB. *Aud.:* Ac, Sa.

Published since 1954, *Canadian Journal of Microbiology* presents "contributions by recognized scientists worldwide." Topics include "applied microbiology and biotechnology; microbial structure and function; fungi and other eucaryotic protists; infection and immunity; microbial ecology; physiology, metabolism, and enzymology; and virology, genetics, and molecular biology." Contents include articles, notes, minireviews, reviews, and letters. Although papers in French are accepted, the majority of the journal is in English. Sample issues are available online in full text from 1998 to the present. A recommended source for academic and special libraries.

820. *International Journal of Systematic and Evolutionary Microbiology.* Former titles (until 1999): *International Journal of Systematic Bacteriology;* (until 1966): *International Bulletin of Bacteriological Nomenclature and Taxonomy.* [ISSN: 1466-5026] 1951. m. GBP 650 print & online. Ed(s): Dr. Peter Kaempfer. Society for General Microbiology, Marlborough House, Basingstoke Rd, Spencers Wood, Reading, RG7 1AG, United Kingdom; http://www.sgm.ac.uk. Illus., index, adv. Refereed. Circ: 1100. Vol. ends: Oct/Dec. Microform: PQC. Online: EBSCO Publishing, EBSCO Host; HighWire Press. *Indexed:* Agr, BiolAb, BiolDig, CABA, ChemAb, DSA, ExcerpMed, FPA, FS&TA, ForAb, IndVet, S&F, SCI, VB, ZooRec. *Bk. rev.:* 1, 1,000-1,200 words. *Aud.:* Ac, Sa.

This journal publishes papers dealing with "all phases of the systematics of bacteria, including taxonomy, nomenclature, identification, characterization and culture preservation." Online access is provided by Stanford's HighWire Press to print subscribers, and free sample issues are available online. Now in its 56th year, this journal is a cornerstone in the field of microbial systematics. Appropriate for special and academic libraries.

821. *Journal of Bacteriology.* [ISSN: 0021-9193] 1916. fortn. USD 1440. Ed(s): Philip Matsumura. American Society for Microbiology, 1752 N St, NW, Washington, DC 20036-2904; asmjournals@asm.org; http://www.asm.org. Illus., index. Refereed. Circ: 10839 Paid. Vol. ends: Dec. Microform: PQC. Online: EBSCO Publishing, EBSCO Host; HighWire Press; National Library of Medicine. *Indexed:* Agr, B&AI, BiolAb, BiolDig, CABA, ChemAb, DSA, ExcerpMed, FPA, FS&TA, ForAb, GSI, HortAb, IAA, IndVet, S&F, SCI, VB, WRCInf. *Aud.:* Ac, Sa.

This journal is ranked number 13 out of 84 journals in the microbiology category by ISI's Journal Citation Reports. It publishes new knowledge of bacteria and other microorganisms. Topics include structural biology, molecular biology and pathogens, microbial communities and interactions, gene replication, and plant microbiology, physiology, and metabolism. Contents include guest commentaries, minireviews, meeting reviews and presentations, and research articles on genetics and molecular biology. There is online access to articles from 1916 to the present, and access is free six months after an issue is published. Highly recommended for biology collections in special and academic libraries.

822. *The Journal of Eukaryotic Microbiology.* Formerly (until 1993): *Journal of Protozoology.* [ISSN: 1066-5234] 1954. bi-m. GBP 208 print & online eds. Ed(s): Denis H Lynn, Portia A Holt. Blackwell Publishing, Inc., Commerce Place, 350 Main St, Malden, MA 02148;

http://www.blackwellpublishing.com. Illus., index, adv. Refereed. Circ: 1800. Vol. ends: Nov/Dec. Reprint: PSC. *Indexed:* Agr, B&AI, BiolAb, BiolDig, CABA, ChemAb, DSA, ExcerpMed, ForAb, HortAb, IndVet, S&F, SCI, VB, ZooRec. *Aud.:* Ac, Sa.

The Journal of Eukaryotic Microbiology publishes "original research on protists, including lower algae and fungi." Topics cover all aspects of these organisms, including behavior, biochemistry, cell biology, chemotherapy, development, ecology, parasitology, and systematics. Journal contents include research articles, communications, and reviews by invitation only. Occasionally, special reports make up supplements. Online access from 2000 to the present is available with a subscription. Additonal online features include free e-mail alerts and free sample issues.

823. *Journal of Virology.* [ISSN: 0022-538X] 1967. fortn. USD 1800. Ed(s): Lynn W Enquist. American Society for Microbiology, 1752 N St, NW, Washington, DC 20036-2904; asmjournals@asm.org; http://www.asm.org. Illus., index, adv. Refereed. Circ: 10225 Paid. Vol. ends: Dec. Microform: PQC. Online: EBSCO Publishing, EBSCO Host; HighWire Press; National Library of Medicine. *Indexed:* Agr, B&AI, BiolAb, CABA, ChemAb, DSA, ExcerpMed, FPA, FS&TA, ForAb, HortAb, IndVet, SCI, VB. *Aud.:* Ac, Sa.

Known as a premier source concerning viruses, the *Journal of Virology* "provides fundamental new information obtained in studies using cross disciplinary approaches." Topics included are structure and assembly, replication, recombination and evolution, virus-cell interaction, transformation and oncogenisis, gene therapy, vaccines and antiviral agents, and pathogenesis and immunity. Much content is focused on viruses impacting humans, through guest commentaries, minireviews, and spotlight features. There is online access from 1967 to the present. This highly regarded title is recommended for academic and special libraries.

824. *Microbiology.* Formerly (until 1993): *Journal of General Microbiology.* [ISSN: 1350-0872] 1947. m. GBP 935 print & online eds. Ed(s): C J Dorman. Society for General Microbiology, Marlborough House, Basingstoke Rd, Spencers Wood, Reading, RG7 1AG, United Kingdom; http://www.sgm.ac.uk. Illus., index, adv. Refereed. Circ: 2440. Vol. ends: Dec. Microform: PMC. Online: EBSCO Publishing, EBSCO Host; HighWire Press. *Indexed:* Agr, B&AI, BiolAb, BiolDig, CABA, ChemAb, DSA, ExcerpMed, FPA, FS&TA, ForAb, GSI, HortAb, IndVet, S&F, SCI, VB. *Aud.:* Ac, Sa.

Microbiology is one of the world's leading microbiological journals, with more than 3,000 pages per issue. It is published by the Society for General Microbiology. Contents include research papers, reviews, minireviews, a microbiology comment section for readers' responses, and the occasional special issue. Sections include "biochemistry and molecular biology, biodiversity and evolution, cell and developmental biology, environmental microbiology, genes and genomes, pathogens and pathogenicity, physiology, plant-microbe interactions, and theoretical microbiology." Full text is available online from 1994 to the present via Stanford's HighWire Press. This source is appropriate for academic and special libraries.

825. *Microbiology and Molecular Biology Reviews.* Former titles (until 1997): *Microbiological Reviews;* (until 1978): *Bacteriological Reviews.* [ISSN: 1092-2172] 1937. q. USD 840. Ed(s): John E. Cronan, Jr. American Society for Microbiology, 1752 N St, NW, Washington, DC 20036-2904; asmjournals@asm.org; http://www.asm.org. Illus., index, adv. Refereed. Circ: 11694 Paid. Vol. ends: Dec. Microform: PQC. Online: EBSCO Publishing, EBSCO Host; HighWire Press; National Library of Medicine. *Indexed:* Agr, B&AI, BiolDig, CABA, ChemAb, DSA, ExcerpMed, FS&TA, GSI, HortAb, IndVet, S&F, SCI, VB, WRCInf, ZooRec. *Aud.:* Ac, Sa.

This is recognized as the "definitive broad-based review journal in the disciplines of microbiology, immunology, and molecular and cellular biology." It is published by the American Society of Microbiology. Articles provide the lastest findings about bacteria, viruses, parasites, fungi, and other eukaryotes. Contents include mostly review articles on the following topics: cellular biology, ecology, genetics, host-parasite relationships leading to disease, molecular biology, physiology and enzymology, and virology. Subscriptions are available as print and online only with various online subscription options.

Online access is provided via Stanford's HighWire Press, with full text from 1998 to the present. Nonsubscribers have access to tables of contents, abstracts, and search features. There is free access six months after an issue's publication. This journal is a good source for special libraries and academic biology collections.

826. *Virology.* [ISSN: 0042-6822] 1955. 26x/yr. EUR 7272. Ed(s): Robert Lamb. Academic Press, 525 B St, Ste 1900, San Diego, CA 92101-4495; http://www.elsevier.com/. Illus., index, adv. Refereed. Online: EBSCO Publishing, EBSCO Host; Gale; IngentaConnect; OCLC Online Computer Library Center, Inc.; OhioLINK; ScienceDirect; SwetsWise Online Content. *Indexed:* Agr, B&AI, BiolAb, CABA, ChemAb, DSA, ExcerpMed, FS&TA, ForAb, GSI, HortAb, IndVet, SCI, VB. *Aud.:* Ac, Sa.

Virology publishes results of basic research in all areas of virology, including the viruses of vertebrates and invertebrates such as plants, bacteria, yeasts, and fungi. Contents include regular articles presenting results of basic research that breaks new ground; rapid communications, which are brief, definitive reports of high significance; and minireviews, which discuss cutting-edge developments and themes in virology. Topics include virus replication, virus structure and function, virus-cell biology, gene therapy, viral pathogenesis and immunity, and emerging viruses. Elsevier's ScienceDirect provides online access to full text for subscribers. This journal is recognized as a leading resource for current information in this field. Recommended for academic and special libraries, and appropriate for undergraduates as well as researchers.

■ BIOTECHNOLOGY

See also Biology section.

Susan K. Kendall, Ph.D., Health Sciences Coordinator and Liaison and Bibliographer for the Basic Biomedical Sciences, Michigan State University Libraries, East Lansing, MI 48824-1048

Introduction

Biotechnology is an emerging and growing field with exciting potential. Knowledge from the basic biological sciences—particularly from genetics, molecular biology, or cell biology—is applied to practical purposes in medicine, agriculture, food science, or environmental studies. In some cases biological sciences are combined with other areas such as engineering, material science, or chemistry in interdisciplinary ways.

Areas of biotechnology that have received a lot of attention lately include stem cell research and regenerative medicine, which have the promise of healing diseases by creating new tissues or regenerating tissues that are damaged or diseased. Gene therapy promises to correct diseases by replacing faulty genes with good ones. Customized drugs for individuals based on their genetic makeup is another hope for the future. The use of transgenic plants in agriculture is a controversial and current issue, and many companies have invested a lot of money to research how biotechnology can improve their crops. Probably less high-profile but just as promising are the latest developments from environmental scientists in creating transgenic organisms that degrade pollutants or produce biodegradable plastics.

Scientists publish biotechnology research and discoveries in many different journals, ranging from basic biology journals to medical, chemical, or engineering journals, depending on their focus. There is a growing number of journals devoted specifically to biotechnology and all its subfields, such as drug discovery, regenerative medicine, genomics and proteomics, agricultural biotechnology, gene therapy, bioinformatics, and the like. Many of the best ones in these areas are listed in this section. However, none of these journals quite reaches the high level of some of the most prestigious journals that publish biological or medical sciences. The librarian collecting in this area should be aware that, depending on the topic, the very best biotechnology papers will probably be published in top journals such as *Nature, Science, Nature Genetics, Cell,* and *The New England Journal of Medicine.*

As in the other sciences, electronic formats of journals have greatly increased and printed formats have declined in importance to the professional researcher or academic. All of the journals mentioned here are available in electronic format, and, increasingly, there is extra information (video or large data sets, for example) available in the electronic journal that is not available in the printed version. Rapid publication online ahead of print is advertised by many of these journals to keep up with demand for the newest information in this rapidly changing field. Any library that subscribes only to the printed version of any of these journals will not be keeping up.

Open access publishing is a trend in all of the life sciences, and biotechnology is no exception. The open access philosophy says that information should be freely available electronically to everyone, and the publishing costs of editing, peer review, and putting the papers online should be covered by something other than a personal or library subscription. The funding source could be a granting agency or the authors themselves. While the majority of important journals in biotechnology are still traditional, subscription-based journals, a growing number of open access journals are taking their place alongside the traditional journals in importance. One such journal is noted here.

Like the rest of the life science areas, the number of publications in biotechnology is already quite large and continues to grow. The journals or magazines listed here were chosen from that large number for several reasons. Impact factor, as calculated by Thomson Scientific (formerly the Institute for Scientific Information, or ISI), and which is based on numbers of citations to journals, is very important for the life sciences, so professional journals with higher impact factors were usually picked over journals with lower impact factors.

General biotechnology journals that are are top for either original research or reviews were chosen, as were specialized journals that represent the many different subfields of biotechnology. The newness and emerging quality of the field can be noted from some of the information about the journals included in this section. Many are less than 20 years old, while some have only been around for a few years; still others have undergone recent name changes to reflect a new trend or focus. Some of the journals publish only original primary research; others publish only review articles; and still others publish a combination of these, along with other types of articles commenting on the ethical, legal, or regulatory issues surrounding biotechnology. A good academic or corporate research and development library that serves scientists in biotechnology will want to have a mix of these journals, because all of these kinds of articles are important for that user group.

A library serving non-scientists interested in biotechnology from a business or other angle will want to focus only on the journals that contain a news section or articles that have a business, legal, or regulatory focus. These are the ones noted as appropriate for a general audience. Only a couple of the most general journals or magazines listed would be appropriate for a public library.

Basic Periodicals

Ga: *Scientific American;* Ac, Sa: *Nature Biotechnology, Trends in Biotechnology.*

Basic Abstracts and Indexes

Biological Abstracts, Medline, Science Citation Index (Web of Science).

827. *Applied and Environmental Microbiology.* Formerly (until 1976): *Applied Microbiology.* [ISSN: 0099-2240] 1953. m. USD 1260. Ed(s): L Nicholson Ornston. American Society for Microbiology, 1752 N St, NW, Washington, DC 20036-2904; asmjournals@asm.org; http://www.asm.org. Illus., index, adv. Refereed. Circ: 12658 Paid. Vol. ends: Dec. Online: EBSCO Publishing, EBSCO Host; HighWire Press; National Library of Medicine. *Indexed:* Agr, ApEcolAb, B&AI, BioEngAb, BiolAb, CABA, ChemAb, DSA, EngInd, EnvInd, ExcerpMed, FPA, FS&TA, ForAb, GSI, H&SSA, HortAb, IBR, IndVet, OceAb, PetrolAb, PollutAb, RRTA, S&F, SCI, SWRA, VB, WRCInf, ZooRec. *Aud.:* Ac, Sa.

Published by the American Society for Microbiology, this journal, while not solely focused on biotechnology, contains a significant number of articles devoted to research in biotechnology; industrial, environmental, and food microbiology; and applied areas in which new products or practical benefits are the results of microbial research. Each issue is divided into anywhere from 12 to 15 subject sections, so researchers can easily skip to the sections that interest them the most—for instance, food microbiology or biodegradation or

physiology and biotechnology. Almost all of the articles are peer-reviewed research articles, but occasional issues will contain a minireview, guest commentary, or meeting review article at the beginning. A methods section publishes peer-reviewed articles on new methods that can demonstrate a practical application. Research scientists in many different applied microbiology fields would be interested in this journal.

828. *Applied Microbiology and Biotechnology.* Former titles (until 1984): *European Journal of Applied Microbiology and Biotechnology; European Journal of Applied Microbiology.* [ISSN: 0175-7598] 1975. 18x/yr. EUR 5698 print & online eds. Ed(s): Alexander Steinbuechel. Springer, Tiergartenstr 17, Heidelberg, 69121, Germany. Refereed. Microform: PQC. Online: EBSCO Publishing, EBSCO Host; OhioLINK; Springer LINK; SwetsWise Online Content; H.W. Wilson. Reprint: PSC. *Indexed:* AS&TI, Agr, B&AI, BioEngAb, BiolAb, CABA, ChemAb, DSA, EngInd, ExcerpMed, FPA, FS&TA, ForAb, HortAb, IndVet, OceAb, PollutAb, S&F, SCI, SWRA, VB, WAE&RSA, WRCInf. *Aud.:* Ac, Sa.

This journal covers a wide range of topics that qualify as applied microbiology and biotechnology, including molecular biotechnology, genomics, proteomics, applied microbial physiology, bioprocess engineering, and environmental biotechnology. Most of the papers are original, peer-reviewed research articles; however, minireviews are an important component of this journal. Every recent issue contained at least one, and usually several, of these short, 5- to 6-page review articles, which summarize and provide perspective on a research area or trend. A recently added methods section publishes short articles that describe the development of a novel method and its potential impact on the field. As with many of these biotechnology journals, the focus is on the science rather than other issues, and so the journal would be of interest to scientists in the field.

829. *B M C Bioinformatics.* [ISSN: 1471-2105] 2000. m. Free. Ed(s): Dr. Melissa Norton. BioMed Central Ltd., Middlesex House, 34-42 Cleveland St, London, W1T 4LB, United Kingdom; info@biomedcentral.com; http://www.biomedcentral.com. Adv. Refereed. *Indexed:* BioEngAb, BiolAb, CABA, ExcerpMed, HortAb, IndVet, SCI, VB. *Aud.:* Ac, Sa.

This is an open access journal, meaning that it is freely available online to everyone without subscription costs. Funding to support the journal comes from other sources, such as author payment to publish. BioMed Central, the publisher, focuses primarily on publishing such open access journals in biomedical areas. Because they are freely available, usage and citation of some of their journals can be fairly high, making them rank by impact factor fairly well against some traditional journals. This journal was chosen to list here because it is the highest ranking BioMed Central journal by impact factor, presumably meaning it is one of their most cited journals. Bioinformatics combines biology with computer science to create a new field in which genetic and protein sequence information is processed and analyzed using computers and computer algorithms. Computer scientists tend to be less traditional than biologists in their publication venue choices, and scientists coming from that background may be more open to online-only and open access journals, especially since there are very few traditional journals that exist in the rather new field of bioinformatics. Also, because this is an online-only journal, articles are published immediately on acceptance, and there are no discrete issues. Volumes of the journal correspond to different years of publication. The online format allows authors to publish large data sets that readers can download and manipulate themselves. The journal publishes original peer-reviewed research articles and also methodology articles and articles that describe databases or software. A supplement section reports proceedings of workshops or conferences. Of interest to researchers in the bioinformatics field. URL: http://www.biomedcentral.com/bmcbioinformatics/

830. *Bioinformatics (Print Edition).* Formerly (until 1998): *Computer Applications in the Biosciences (Print).* [ISSN: 1367-4803] 1985. 24x/yr. Corporations, EUR 2216. Ed(s): Alfonso Valencia, Alex Bateman. Oxford University Press, Great Clarendon St, Oxford, OX2 6DP, United Kingdom; jnl.orders@oup.co.uk; http://www.oxfordjournals.org. Illus., adv. Refereed. Circ: 1200. Online: EBSCO Publishing, EBSCO Host; Gale; HighWire Press; IngentaConnect; OCLC Online Computer

Library Center, Inc.; OhioLINK; Ovid Technologies, Inc.; Oxford Journals; ProQuest LLC (Ann Arbor); SwetsWise Online Content. Reprint: PSC. *Indexed:* Agr, B&AI, BioEngAb, BiolAb, CABA, ChemAb, CompLI, ExcerpMed, HortAb, IndVet, OceAb, S&F, SCI, VB. *Aud.:* Ac, Sa.

This is the leading and one of the oldest journals in the field of bioinformatics, which is defined as the collection, processing, and analysis of genetic and protein sequence information using computers and computer algorithms. Much of the information and data generated today in biotechnology is on a large scale (see subsection on large-scale biology), making manipulation by computers essential. While bioinformatics started out as a combination of biology and computer science, in the last ten years, bioinformatics has become highly visible and has evolved to become a scientific discipline in its own right. The journal publishes both original research and review articles about new developments in the field. Two sections within the journal, "Discovery Notes" and "Application Notes," publish shorter papers—respectively, one describes biologically interesting discoveries made using computational techniques, and the other describes novel software, algorithm implementations, databases, or the like.

831. *Biosensors and Bioelectronics.* Formerly (until 1989): *Biosensors.* [ISSN: 0956-5663] 1985. 12x/yr. EUR 1725. Ed(s): Anthony P.F. Turner. Elsevier BV, Radarweg 29, Amsterdam, 1043 NX, Netherlands; nlinfo-f@elsevier.nl; http://www.elsevier.nl. Illus., adv. Refereed. Online: EBSCO Publishing, EBSCO Host; Gale; IngentaConnect; OhioLINK; ScienceDirect; SwetsWise Online Content. *Indexed:* Agr, BioEngAb, BiolAb, C&ISA, CABA, ChemAb, DSA, EngInd, EnvAb, ExcerpMed, FPA, ForAb, HortAb, IndVet, S&F, SCI, VB, WAE&RSA. *Aud.:* Ac, Sa.

This is a journal that covers an emerging interdisciplinary field. In general, bioelectronics integrates biological molecules with electronics to make functional devices. Some of those devices are biosensors, which are analytic or detection devices that couple biological or biologically-derived material with a transducer to transmit a digital electronic signal for the presence of a specific substance. Biosensors and bioelectronics have been applied to problems in medicine, pharmaceuticals, the environment, food processing, and security. This journal publishes primarily original, peer-reviewed research articles either as full papers or as short communications. Most issues also contain one or two review articles. A separate "Synthetic Receptors" section in each issue is dedicated to research papers "focusing on the complementary intersection between synthetic receptors, nanotechnology, molecular recognition, molecular imprinting and supramolecular chemistry." Some issues have also contained other special topic sections. This journal would be of interest to research scientists.

832. *Current Opinion in Biotechnology.* [ISSN: 0958-1669] 1990. 6x/yr. EUR 1889. Ed(s): Martin Rosenberg, Kenneth Timmis. Elsevier Ltd., Current Opinion Journals, 84 Theobald's Rd., London, WC1X 8RR, United Kingdom; http://www.current-opinion.com. Illus., adv. Refereed. Circ: 1000. Vol. ends: No. 12. Online: EBSCO Publishing, EBSCO Host; Gale; IngentaConnect; OCLC Online Computer Library Center, Inc.; OhioLINK; ScienceDirect; SwetsWise Online Content. *Indexed:* BioEngAb, CABA, ChemAb, DSA, EngInd, ExcerpMed, FPA, ForAb, HortAb, IndVet, PollutAb, S&F, SCI, SWRA, VB, WAE&RSA. *Aud.:* Ac, Sa.

The Current Opinion series of journals is geared toward helping researchers keep up with the large amount of information published in their fields. *Current Opinion in Biotechnology* covers all areas of biotechnology by dividing the subject into topics, each of which is covered once a year. Each of the six issues per year covers only one or two of these topics, and the journal has expert section editors for each: analytical biotechnology, plant biotechnology, food biotechnology, environmental biotechnology, systems biology, protein technologies and commercial enzymes, biochemical engineering, tissue and cell engineering, chemical biotechnology, and pharmaceutical biotechnology. Each topical issue contains commissioned reviews of recent advances by authorities in that field. Experts also annotate and evaluate the most interesting primary research articles recently published. The journal is geared toward scientists and focuses on scientific advances rather than business or regulatory issues.

833. *Drug Discovery Today.* Incorporates (in 2005): *Drug Discovery Today: Targets;* (1998-2001): *Pharmaceutical Science and Technology Today.* [ISSN: 1359-6446] 1996. 24x/yr. EUR 2701. Ed(s): S L. Carney. Elsevier Ltd., Trends Journals, 84 Theobald's Rd, London, WC1X 8RR, United Kingdom; http://www.trends.com/. Adv. Online: EBSCO Publishing, EBSCO Host; Gale; IngentaConnect; OhioLINK; ScienceDirect; SwetsWise Online Content. *Indexed:* BioEngAb, BiolAb, CABA, ChemAb, ExcerpMed, HortAb, IndVet, SCI, VB, WAE&RSA. *Aud.:* Ac, Sa.

Similar to Elsevier's Trends series, this journal publishes current news and reviews for scientists to help them maintain currency in their research area. The format was recently changed to include a shorter "Perspective" section at the front, with comments from international experts on future directions and important developments. An editorial at the front also comments on current topics. These are the only sections of the journal that comment on the pharmaceutical industry. The majority of the journal is the "Reviews" section, focused on scientific discoveries and divided into sections: "Gene to Screen," "Informatics," and "Postscreen." Geared toward a research scientist audience.

834. *Gene Therapy (Basingstoke).* [ISSN: 0969-7128] 1994. 24x/yr. EUR 1451. Ed(s): Nick Lemoine, Joseph Glorioso. Nature Publishing Group, The MacMillan Building, 4 Crinan St, London, N1 9XW, United Kingdom; http://www.nature.com. Illus., adv. Sample. Refereed. *Indexed:* BioEngAb, BiolAb, CABA, ChemAb, ExcerpMed, IndVet, SCI, VB. *Aud.:* Ac, Sa.

This journal is from Nature Publishing, which will also, by January 2007, be publishing *Molecular Therapy,* a competing journal for papers in this subject area. *Gene Therapy* is devoted to peer-reviewed papers on both the basic research and clinical applications of gene therapy, which involves the correction of diseases by replacing abnormal or faulty genes with normal ones. The bulk of the journal is research articles, but each issue might also contain a couple news and commentary or review articles. One recent special issue contained all review articles. New articles are published weekly in the online version of this journal and are later published in the archived print version. Of interest to scientific researchers and clinicians in this area.

Genome Research. See Biology section.

835. *Genomics.* [ISSN: 0888-7543] 1987. 12x/yr. EUR 2822. Ed(s): Dr. N A Jenkins, Dr. V A McKusick. Academic Press, 525 B St, Ste 1900, San Diego, CA 92101-4495; apsubs@acad.com; http://www.elsevier.com/. Refereed. Online: EBSCO Publishing, EBSCO Host; Gale; IngentaConnect; OCLC Online Computer Library Center, Inc.; OhioLINK; ScienceDirect; SwetsWise Online Content. *Indexed:* AbAn, Agr, BiolAb, CABA, ChemAb, DSA, ExcerpMed, IndVet, S&F, SCI, SSCI, VB, ZooRec. *Aud.:* Ac, Sa.

Focusing on the genome sciences, which study all the genes of any given organism, this journal has both a basic science and a more applied biotechnology bent. It is primarily a forum for the publication of original, peer-reviewed research in such areas as comparative or functional genomics, proteomics, bioinformatics, computational biology, and other genome technologies. Each issue usually also contains one or more articles that focus on methods. While the instructions for authors suggest that review articles might also be published, no recent issues contained review articles. Of interest to scientific researchers.

836. *Human Gene Therapy.* [ISSN: 1043-0342] 1990. m. USD 3480. Ed(s): James M Wilson. Mary Ann Liebert, Inc. Publishers, 140 Huguenot St, 3rd Fl, New Rochelle, NY 10801-5215; info@liebertpub.com; http://www.liebertpub.com. Adv. Sample. Refereed. Circ: 24450. Vol. ends: Dec. Online: EBSCO Publishing, EBSCO Host; Gale; OCLC Online Computer Library Center, Inc.; SwetsWise Online Content. Reprint: PSC. *Indexed:* BioEngAb, BiolAb, CABA, ChemAb, ExcerpMed, IndVet, SCI, VB. *Aud.:* Ac, Sa.

Like two other journals listed in this section, *Molecular Therapy* and *Gene Therapy,* this journal also publishes peer-reviewed scientific papers on all aspects of gene therapy, which involves the correction of diseases by replacing abnormal genes with normal ones. All three journals were included here because they were all ranked fairly similarly in impact factor and seem to have similar value to researchers. Besides the research articles, recent issues tend to include a review article. There are also "Brief Reports," which discuss new methodologies in gene transfer. While the editors state that they welcome articles on ethical, legal, or regulatory issues, any articles of this type could not be found in any of the recent issues viewed. Because the field of gene therapy is so dynamic, this journal has a policy of rapid publication, publishing articles within three to four weeks of their acceptance. Of interest to scientific researchers or clinicians in this area.

837. *Journal of Biotechnology.* [ISSN: 0168-1656] 1984. 24x/yr. EUR 3688. Ed(s): A. Puehler. Elsevier BV, Radarweg 29, Amsterdam, 1043 NX, Netherlands; nlinfo-f@elsevier.nl; http://www.elsevier.nl. Adv. Refereed. Microform: PQC. Online: EBSCO Publishing, EBSCO Host; Gale; IngentaConnect; OhioLINK; ScienceDirect; SwetsWise Online Content. *Indexed:* Agr, B&AI, BioEngAb, BiolAb, CABA, ChemAb, DSA, EngInd, ExcerpMed, FPA, FS&TA, ForAb, HortAb, IndVet, RRTA, S&F, SCI, VB, WAE&RSA. *Aud.:* Ac, Sa.

This is a multidisciplinary journal covering all aspects of biotechnology from medical to plant and agricultural to bioprocess engineering. It provides for rapid publication of peer-reviewed research articles, both long and short. It particularly seeks to publish interdisciplinary articles that are not suitable for publication in a journal for a more specific discipline. The focus is on primary research articles rather than reviews or other types of articles. Of interest to researchers in many areas of biotechnology.

838. *Metabolic Engineering.* [ISSN: 1096-7176] 1998. 6x/yr. EUR 477. Ed(s): G N Stephanopoulos. Academic Press, 525 B St, Ste 1900, San Diego, CA 92101-4495; apsubs@acad.com; http://www.elsevier.com/. Adv. Online: EBSCO Publishing, EBSCO Host; Gale; IngentaConnect; OCLC Online Computer Library Center, Inc.; OhioLINK; ScienceDirect; SwetsWise Online Content. *Indexed:* BioEngAb, ChemAb, EngInd, ExcerpMed, FS&TA, SCI. *Aud.:* Ac, Sa.

Metabolic engineering involves the alteration or manipulation of the metabolic pathways of organisms (often by genetic engineering) for commercial objectives, whether these are environmental, agricultural, or medical. The research in this area is interdisciplinary, drawing on ideas and techniques from molecular biology and biochemistry as well as engineering and bioinformatics. This journal is devoted to publishing only original peer-reviewed research and would be useful for research scientists.

839. *Molecular Therapy.* [ISSN: 1525-0016] 2000. 12x/yr. EUR 1342 in Europe except the UK. Nature Publishing Group, The MacMillan Building, 4 Crinan St, London, N1 9XW, United Kingdom; NatureReviews@nature.com; http://www.nature.com. *Indexed:* BioEngAb, CABA, ChemAb, ExcerpMed, IndVet, SCI, VB. *Aud.:* Ac, Sa.

Currently published by Elsevier but moving to Nature Publishing in January 2007, this is the official publication of the American Society of Gene Therapy. However, this journal has an international scope and publishes original, peer-reviewed scientific papers on molecular and cellular therapy. This coverage includes gene therapy, which involves the correction of diseases by replacing abnormal or faulty genes with normal ones. These primary articles can report basic or preclinical studies, define new methods, or report the results of clinical trials. Besides these papers, each issue may also contain one or two review articles, commentaries, or a meeting report. Of interest to scientists or clinicians working in this field.

840. *Nature Biotechnology.* Formerly (until vol.14, no.3, Mar. 1996): *Bio-Technology.* [ISSN: 1087-0156] 1983. m. EUR 2170 (academic) Corporations, EUR 3488). Ed(s): Andrew Marshall. Nature Publishing Group, 75 Varick St, 9th Fl., New York, NY 10013; http://www.nature.com. Illus. Refereed. Circ: 15000 Paid. Microform: PQC. Online: EBSCO Publishing, EBSCO Host; ProQuest LLC (Ann Arbor); SwetsWise Online Content. *Indexed:* Agr, B&AI, BioEngAb, BiolAb, BiolDig, CABA, ChemAb, DSA, EngInd, ExcerpMed, FPA, FS&TA, ForAb, HortAb, IndVet, S&F, SCI, SSCI, VB, WAE&RSA, WRCInf. *Aud.:* Ga, Ac, Sa.

If a library wanted to buy only one journal in the field of biotechnology, this should be it, because it has something for everyone. This journal has the highest impact factor among biotechnology journals ranked by Thomson Scientific. The scope of the journal includes all of biotechnology, from the agricultural and environmental to the biomedical. The latter part of the journal is devoted to peer-reviewed research papers, both shorter and longer, on new developments in these areas. The beginning section of the journal is devoted to news from both the business and research communities as well as essays, comments, and articles that cover the current political, ethical, legal, and societal issues surrounding biotechnology. Regular columns include the "Bioentrepreneur" (with advice on building a business), "Investor's Lab" (with biotechnology company investing advice), and a patents section, with advice for those seeking patents and lists of recent patent applications in different areas. There are usually a careers section and information about new CEOs of different companies. A section is regularly included that covers the latest developments in computational biology. While the research article section and some other sections will be of most use to scientific academic and special libraries, the essays and news sections will be valuable to business libraries and public libraries as well.

841. *Nature Reviews. Drug Discovery.* [ISSN: 1474-1776] 2002. m. EUR 2170 (academic) Corporations, EUR 3488). Ed(s): Adam Smith. Nature Publishing Group, The MacMillan Building, 4 Crinan St, London, N1 9XW, United Kingdom; NatureReviews@nature.com; http://www.nature.com. Adv. *Indexed:* BioEngAb, ChemAb, ExcerpMed, SCI. *Aud.:* Ga, Ac, Sa.

This journal is part of the Nature Reviews series of journals that contain three main sections and are geared toward keeping researchers informed and up-to-date. "Research Highlights" provides short updates on recently published research papers. The online version of the journal may contain more of these than the print version because highlights are added continuously to the online journal. The larger "Reviews" section contains commissioned review articles by leading researchers in their field, and these have some added features. Certain specialized words in this section are explained in a glossary, and some of the references are annotated. There is usually one article published in each issue in the "Perspectives" section, which covers broader issues: opinions, implications of science on society, new developments, future directions, and business outlooks. At the beginning of each issue is a fourth smaller section for "News and Analysis," which contains current stories on the scientific or business aspects of drug discovery, information on patents, and the latest drugs, as well as interviews. The journal is geared toward scientists in the field but also non-scientists such as those working in the pharmaceutical industry.

842. *Oligonucleotides.* Former titles (until Aug.2003): *Antisense and Nucleic Acid Drug Development;* (until 1997): *Antisense Research and Development.* [ISSN: 1545-4576] 1991. q. USD 746. Ed(s): C. Frank Bennett, C A Stein. Mary Ann Liebert, Inc. Publishers, 140 Huguenot St, 3rd Fl, New Rochelle, NY 10801-5215; info@liebertpub.com; http://www.liebertpub.com. Adv. Sample. Refereed. Circ: 1245 Paid. Vol. ends: Dec. Online: EBSCO Publishing, EBSCO Host; Gale; OCLC Online Computer Library Center, Inc.; ProQuest LLC (Ann Arbor); SwetsWise Online Content. Reprint: PSC. *Indexed:* BioEngAb, BiolAb, CABA, ChemAb, ExcerpMed, IndVet, SCI, VB. *Aud.:* Ac, Sa.

This journal changed its name in 2004 from *Antisense and Nucleic Acid Drug Development* and has become the official journal of the very newly formed (in 2005) Oligonucleotide Therapeutics Society. This journal's scope is the development of therapeutics that modulate gene expression using oligonucleotides, RNA, ribozymes, or other synthesized nucleic acid molecules. Almost all of the articles are original, peer-reviewed research articles from scientists who develop and design these technologies. One 2007 issue contains seven original papers. Of interest to researchers in the field.

843. *Pharmacogenetics and Genomics (Print Edition).* Formerly (until 2005): *Pharmacogenetics.* [ISSN: 1744-6872] 1991. m. USD 1595 (Individuals, USD 382). Ed(s): M Eichelbaum, W E Evans. Lippincott Williams & Wilkins, 530 Walnut St, Philadelphia, PA 19106-3621; http://www.lww.com. Index, adv. Refereed. Circ: 180. Online: EBSCO Publishing, EBSCO Host; OCLC Online Computer Library Center, Inc.; Ovid Technologies, Inc.; SwetsWise Online Content. *Indexed:* BiolAb, ChemAb, ExcerpMed, SCI, SSCI. *Aud.:* Ac, Sa.

This journal falls into the "drug discovery" group of biotechnology journals. Pharmacogenetics (or pharmacogenomics) is the study of how genetics affects people's and animals' responses to drugs. The ultimate goal is to use these genetic insights to improve drug delivery and therapy by tailoring drugs to individuals. This journal publishes primarily original research articles in this subject area, but also occasional mini-reviews. This journal is not very large—recent issues contained less than ten articles. However, a high impact factor indicates that at least some of these articles are being cited frequently. Only of interest to scientific researchers.

844. *Pharmacogenomics.* [ISSN: 1462-2416] 2000. 8x/yr. EUR 1251. Future Medicine Ltd., Unitec House, 3rd Fl, 2 Albert Pl, Finchley Central, London, N3 1QB, United Kingdom; http://www.futuremedicine.com/. Illus. Sample. Refereed. *Indexed:* ExcerpMed, SCI. *Aud.:* Ac, Sa.

The terms pharmacogenomics and pharmacogenetics are often used interchangeably to describe the study of genes that influence response to drugs and ways to use this knowledge to develop better drugs tailored to individuals' genetic variations. This flagship journal of the publisher Future Medicine aims to comment on and analyze the field, publishing both original research and review articles, as well as company profiles, opinion or perspective articles, editorials, and technology reports. This journal is geared toward research scientists as well as other non-scientists involved or interested in the pharmaceutical industry, and authors are asked to keep this multidisciplinary audience in mind.

845. *Plant Biotechnology Journal.* [ISSN: 1467-7644] 2000. bi-m. GBP 576 print & online eds. Ed(s): Keith J Edwards. Blackwell Publishing Ltd., 9600 Garsington Rd, Oxford, OX4 2ZG, United Kingdom; customerservices@blackwellpublishing.com; http://www.blackwellpublishing.com. *Indexed:* BioEngAb, CABA, ForAb, HortAb, S&F, SCI. *Aud.:* Ac, Sa.

This journal is published in association with two societies, the Society for Experimental Biology and the Association of Applied Biologists, and its focus is on research articles in the applied plant sciences. Applications of plant studies can be for such wide-ranging industries as agriculture, food sciences, forestry, pharmaceuticals, medicine, and bioremediation. A large number of the papers in the journal are devoted to genomics, functional genomics, and transgenic technologies. Most articles are primary peer-reviewed research articles, although some issues may also contain a review or news-and-views article. Of interest to researchers in the field.

Scientific American. See Science and Technology section.

846. *Stem Cells and Development.* Former titles (until 2004): *Journal of Hematotherapy & Stem Cell Research;* (until 2000): *Journal of Hematotherapy.* [ISSN: 1547-3287] 1993. bi-m. USD 747. Ed(s): Dr. Denis English. Mary Ann Liebert, Inc. Publishers, 140 Huguenot St, 3rd Fl, New Rochelle, NY 10801-5215; info@liebertpub.com; http://www.liebertpub.com. Adv. Sample. Refereed. Circ: 1700 Paid. Online: EBSCO Publishing, EBSCO Host; Gale; OCLC Online Computer Library Center, Inc.; SwetsWise Online Content. Reprint: PSC. *Indexed:* ExcerpMed, SCI. *Aud.:* Ac, Sa.

Mary Ann Liebert publishes a great many journals in biotechnology subject areas, and this is their highest-ranked journal by impact factor. The journal is primarily a forum for the publication of original peer-reviewed research articles on human or animal stem cell research and its potential therapeutic applications. Besides the original research, which takes up most of each issue, there are occasionally other types of articles: editorials, "Issues in Development," "Comprehensive Reviews," or "Technology Reports." The issues and editorial articles are focused on scientific issues and controversies, not on societal or ethical concerns, so this journal would be of interest only to research scientists in the field.

847. *Tissue Engineering. Part A. Tissue Engineering.* Supersedes in part: *Tissue Engineering.* [ISSN: 1937-3341] 1993. m. USD 1026. Mary Ann Liebert, Inc. Publishers, 140 Huguenot St, 3rd Fl, New Rochelle, NY 10801-5215; info@liebertpub.com; http://www.liebertpub.com. Adv. Sample. Refereed. Circ: 1400 Paid. Vol. ends: Dec. Reprint: PSC. *Indexed:* BioEngAb, BiolAb, ChemAb, EngInd, ExcerpMed, SCI. *Aud.:* Ac, Sa.

This is the official journal of the Tissue Engineering and Regenerative Medicine International Society. The goal of this emerging field is eventually to be able to regenerate tissues or create new tissues and artificial organs using biological cells and biomaterials, along with biotechnology techniques. Much of this is still in the experimental rather than the clinical stage. Such current topics of research as nanobiotechnology, gene therapy, and stem cells are included. This journal publishes primarily peer-reviewed research articles. Occasional issues may contain a review article or an article commenting on a recent issue. Research scientists in the field would be interested in this journal.

848. *Trends in Biotechnology.* [ISSN: 0167-7799] 1983. 12x/yr. EUR 1450. Ed(s): S Berry. Elsevier Ltd., Trends Journals, 84 Theobald's Rd, London, WC1X 8RR, United Kingdom; http://www.trends.com/. Illus., adv. Refereed. Vol. ends: No. 19. Online: EBSCO Publishing, EBSCO Host; Gale; IngentaConnect; OhioLINK; ScienceDirect; SwetsWise Online Content. *Indexed:* AS&TI, Agr, BioEngAb, BiolAb, CABA, ChemAb, DSA, EngInd, ExcerpMed, FPA, FS&TA, ForAb, HortAb, IndVet, RRTA, S&F, SCI, VB, WAE&RSA. *Aud.:* Ac, Sa.

Part of the *Trends* journal series from Elsevier, this serial publishes review articles by leading researchers rather than original research articles. The reviews summarize and discuss recent scientific developments in all areas of biotechnology, from agricultural and environmental to biomedical. Opinion articles form the other largest section of this journal, providing commentary or debate and focusing more on political, ethical, and regulatory concerns. An update section at the front of this journal provides short, two-page articles surveying a specific field or advancement. This journal is geared primarily to a scientific and academic research audience. However, non-scientists would probably be able to understand the opinion articles.

■ BIRDS

See also Environment and Conservation; and Pets sections.

Kathryn Johns-Masten, Assistant Librarian, Standish Library, Siena College, Albany, NY 12211; kjohns-masten@siena.edu

Introduction

"I never for a day gave up listening to the songs of our birds, or watching their peculiar habits, or delineating them in the best way I could."—John James Audubon

As Audubon indicates, we have always had an interest in the birding world. The titles listed here will appeal to amateur birders, students of ornithology, and professional ornithologists. From around the world, the titles provide insight into a wide range of geographic areas. Some titles focus on a specific area while others focus on specific types of birds, for example waterbirds or predators. The titles appropriate for a general audience or for those new to birding provide color photographs and articles from ornithologists as well as fellow amateur birders. The professional academic journals contain in-depth articles including scientific studies and field research. Web sites provide birders with the ability to interact with each other over great distances, submit bird counts, listen to birdsongs, and communicate with researchers on current projects. The majority of the electronic journals provide feature articles and multiple links to other sources. These print and electronic publications were selected based on their appeal to a range of readers from amateur to professional.

Basic Periodicals

Hs: *Bird Watcher's Digest, Living Bird, Wildbird;* Ga: *Birder's World, Living Bird, North American Birds, Virtual Birder;* Ac: *The Auk, Condor, Ibis, Journal of Field Ornithology.*

BIRDS

Basic Abstracts and Indexes

Biological Abstracts.

●

Audubon See Environment and Conservation section.

849. *The Auk: a quarterly journal of ornithology.* Supersedes (1876-1883): *Nuttall Ornithological Club. Bulletin.* [ISSN: 0004-8038] 1884. q. USD 255 print & online eds. USD 47 newsstand/cover. Ed(s): Spencer Sealy. University of California Press, Journals Division, 2000 Center St, Ste 303, Berkeley, CA 94704-1223; journals@ucpress.edu; http://www.ucpress.edu/journals. Illus., index, adv. Refereed. Circ: 4500. Vol. ends: Oct (No. 4). Microform: IDC; PQC. Online: BioOne; CSA; EBSCO Publishing, EBSCO Host; Factiva, Inc.; Northern Light Technology, Inc.; OCLC Online Computer Library Center, Inc.; OhioLINK; ProQuest K-12 Learning Solutions; ProQuest LLC (Ann Arbor). *Indexed:* AnBeAb, ApEcolAb, B&AI, BiolAb, CABA, ChemAb, ForAb, GSI, HortAb, IBR, IndVet, OceAb, PsycInfo, S&F, SCI, VB, ZooRec. *Bk. rev.:* 10, 500 words. *Aud.:* Ac, Sa.

The Auk is a well-regarded journal that publishes original reports on the biology of birds. Research articles are well documented and topics include documentation, analysis, and interpretation of laboratory and field studies, and theoretical or methodological developments. Commentary, letters, and reviews provide additional information. North American customers receive the bimonthly *Ornithological Newsletter* with their subscription. Recommended for academic and special libraries that support ornithology, zoology, and ecology.

850. *Bird Study: the science of pure and applied orinthology.* Incorporates: *Bird Migration;* Formerly: *Bulletin.* [ISSN: 0006-3657] 1954. 3x/yr. GBP 85 in Europe; USD 155 in US & Canada; GBP 95 elsewhere. Ed(s): Mary Fox, GrahamJohn Martin. British Trust for Ornithology, The Nunnery, Nunnery Pl, Thetford, IP24 2PU, United Kingdom; info@bto.org; http://www.bto.org/. Illus., index, adv. Refereed. Circ: 2400. Vol. ends: No. 3. Microform: PQC. Online: EBSCO Publishing, EBSCO Host; Gale; IngentaConnect; OCLC Online Computer Library Center, Inc.; ProQuest LLC (Ann Arbor); SwetsWise Online Content. *Indexed:* AnBeAb, ApEcolAb, BiolAb, CABA, EnvAb, FPA, ForAb, IndVet, S&F, SCI, VB, ZooRec. *Bk. rev.:* 1, 50 words. *Aud.:* Ac, Sa.

This international journal from the British Trust for Ornithology publishes high-quality papers in field ornithology, especially covering patterns of distribution and abundance, movements, habitat preferences, developing field census methods, and ringing and other techniques for marking and tracking. The journal focuses on birds in the Western Palearctic, which includes Europe, North Africa, and the Middle East, although papers are accepted from any part of the world. Critical book reviews are included. Recommended for the professional and for serious students of bird life.

Bird Talk. See Pets section.

851. *Bird Watcher's Digest.* [ISSN: 0164-3037] 1978. bi-m. USD 18.95 domestic; USD 23.95 in Canada & Mexico; USD 28.95 elsewhere. Ed(s): W.H. Thompson, III. Pardson, Inc., 149 Acme St, PO Box 110, Marietta, OH 45750; editor@birdwatchersdigest.com. Illus., adv. Circ: 90000. Vol. ends: Jul/Aug. Microform: PQC. *Indexed:* BiolDig. *Bk. rev.:* 8, 50 words. *Aud.:* Hs, Ga.

Bird Watcher's Digest is a popular magazine that offers articles for the amateur birder written by ornithologists. Regular columns cover attracting birds, bird behavior, backyard birdwatching, and helpful hints to new birders. Other regular features include letters from readers, gardening tips, humor, cartoons, and color photographs. Recommended for general audiences.

852. *Birder's World: exploring birds in the field and backyard.* [ISSN: 0895-495X] 1987. bi-m. USD 24.95 domestic; USD 31.50 foreign; USD 4.95 newsstand/cover. Ed(s): Chuck Hagner. Kalmbach Publishing Co., 21027 Crossroads Circle, PO Box 1612, Waukesha, WI 53187-1612; customerservice@kalmbach.com; http://www.kalmbach.com. Adv. Circ: 60689 Paid. *Indexed:* BiolDig. *Bk. rev.:* Number and length vary. *Aud.:* Hs, Ga.

Birder's World is geared toward enthusiasts new to birding as well as experienced birders, and offers readers superb color photography. Feature articles and regular columns cover identification tips, photography pointers, attracting birds, worldwide bird movement, and travel tips for birders. Highly recommended for the beginning birder.

853. *Birding.* [ISSN: 0161-1836] 1969. bi-m. Free to members; Non-members, USD 45. Ed(s): Ted Floyd. American Birding Association, 4945 N 30th St, Ste 200, PO Box 6599, Colorado Springs, CO 80919; beview@aba.org; http://www.americanbirding.org. Illus., index, adv. Refereed. Circ: 19000. Vol. ends: Dec (No. 6). *Indexed:* ZooRec. *Bk. rev.:* 3, 200 words. *Aud.:* Ga, Ac.

The magazine of the American Birding Association, with a mission to educate the general public in the appreciation of birds and their relationship to the environment. It focuses on North American birds both native and exotic. Topics include conservation, monitoring, behavior, identification techniques, and habitats. Association membership includes the monthly newsletter *Winging It*. An online archive covering 2001 to the present is available on the association's web site. Recommended for scholars and ornithologists in the field.

854. *BirdSource: birding with a purpose.* irreg. Free. National Audubon Society, 700 Broadway, New York, NY 10003; http://www.audubon.org. *Aud.:* Ga.

BirdSource is an electronic journal formed by a partnership between scientists and the general public. Enthusiasm for birds is combined with state-of-the-art technology to promote conservation and environmental learning on this interactive web site. Readers are invited to record and share their counts of birds online, and the site includes an extensive list of projects. The data is used to track and display the density and movement of birds in North America. *BirdSource's* interactive information system hopes to become the long-term record of North American bird populations. URL: www.birdsource.org

855. *British Birds.* [ISSN: 0007-0335] 1907. m. GBP 83 (Individuals, GBP 45). Ed(s): Dr. R Riddington. British Birds, The Banks, Mountfield, Roberts Bridge, TN32 5JY, United Kingdom. Illus., index, adv. Sample. Refereed. Circ: 9000. Vol. ends: Dec. Microform: IDC; PQC. *Indexed:* BiolAb, IBR, SCI, ZooRec. *Bk. rev.:* 2, 200 words. *Aud.:* Ga, Ac.

British Birds is considered "*the* journal of record in Britain," and it publishes original research from the Western Palearctic, which includes Europe, North Africa, and the Middle East. Emphasis is given to areas of behavior, conservation, distribution, ecology, identification, movement, status, and taxonomy. Regular features include book reviews, news and comments, recent reports of rarities, and information on equipment and travel for birders. It is important to note that while many reports are scientific in nature, they are written for the nonscientist who is interested in birds.

856. *The Condor: an international journal of avian biology.* Formerly (until 1900): *Cooper Ornithological Club. Bulletin.* [ISSN: 0010-5422] 1899. q. USD 180. Cooper Ornithological Society, Inc., c/o David S. Dobkin, High Desert Ecological Research Institute, Bend, OR 97702; http://www.cooper.org. Illus., index, adv. Refereed. Circ: 3300. Vol. ends: Nov. Microform: PQC. Online: BioOne; CSA; JSTOR (Web-based Journal Archive); OCLC Online Computer Library Center, Inc.; OhioLINK; ProQuest K-12 Learning Solutions; ProQuest LLC (Ann Arbor). *Indexed:* AnBeAb, ApEcolAb, B&AI, BiolAb, CABA, ChemAb, FPA, ForAb, HortAb, IndVet, OceAb, RRTA, S&F, SCI, VB, ZooRec. *Bk. rev.:* 1, 2,000 words. *Aud.:* Ac, Sa.

Includes original articles that focus on biology of wild species of birds from anywhere in the world. Research reports contain substantial references, and many include detailed discussions of fieldwork and habitat. Other features include book reviews, news, and society announcements and notes. Tables of contents and abstracts for issues from Februrary 2001 to the present can be found at the Cooper Ornithological Society's web site (www.cooper.org). Recommended for institutions that support advanced ornithological research.

857. *Emu: Austral Ornithology.* [ISSN: 0158-4197] 1901. q. AUD 390 print & online eds. Free to individual members. Ed(s): Camilla Myers. C S I R O Publishing, 150 Oxford St, PO Box 1139, Collingwood, VIC

140

3066, Australia; publishing@csiro.au; http://www.publish.csiro.au/. Illus., index, adv. Refereed. Circ: 1500. Vol. ends: Dec. Microform: IDC; PQC. Online: EBSCO Publishing, EBSCO Host; Gale; OCLC Online Computer Library Center, Inc.; SwetsWise Online Content. *Indexed:* AnBeAb, ApEcolAb, BiolAb, CABA, FPA, ForAb, IBR, S&F, SCI, ZooRec. *Bk. rev.:* 2, 1,000 words. *Aud.:* Ac, Sa.

Emu publishes original papers and reviews in all areas of ornithology in the Australasian region (Australia, New Zealand, New Guinea, Pacific Islands, and Antarctica). While scholarly articles are the main feature, book reviews are also included. This is one of the standard journals in the field of ornithology in the Southern Hemisphere. The variety of species covered by this geographic area makes it a recommended title for research libraries that serve ornithologists.

858. Ibis: the international journal of avian science. [ISSN: 0019-1019] 1859. q. GBP 318 print & online eds. Ed(s): Andrew G Gosler. Blackwell Publishing Ltd., 9600 Garsington Rd, Oxford, OX4 2ZG, United Kingdom; customerservices@blackwellpublishing.com; http://www.blackwellpublishing.com. Illus., index, adv. Refereed. Circ: 2650. Vol. ends: Oct. Reprint: PSC. *Indexed:* AnBeAb, ApEcolAb, B&AI, BiolAb, CABA, EnvAb, ForAb, IndVet, OceAb, RRTA, S&F, SCI, VB, WAE&RSA, ZooRec. *Bk. rev.:* 25, 300 words. *Aud.:* Ac, Sa.

The British Ornithologists' Union encourages active research and the publication of that research in its journal. *Ibis* presents well-documented articles on the cutting edge of ornithology with an emphasis on bird behavior, biology, ethology, and systematics of birds throughout the world. Abstracts of papers from 2002 to the present are available online at the union's web site. Recommended for academic and research libraries that support ornithological research.

859. InterBirdNet Online. 1997. m. InterBirdNet Online, P O Box 1, Studley, B80 7JG, United Kingdom; http://www.birder.co.uk/indexmain.htm. *Bk. rev.:* Number and length vary. *Aud.:* Ga, Sa.

Originating in the United Kingdom and regularly updated, this web site is now called *Free-Living Birder.* It offers a bird-of-the-month feature, book reviews, and a birding for beginners section. The focus is very much on birding in the United Kingdom, but the links will be of interest to a North American audience. A "New Horizons" feature highlights birding trips from U.K. tour companies. Written by bird enthusiasts for bird enthusiasts.

860. Journal of Field Ornithology. Formerly: *Bird-Banding.* [ISSN: 0273-8570] 1930. q. GBP 173 print & online eds. Ed(s): Gary Ritchison. Blackwell Publishing, Inc., Commerce Place, 350 Main St, Malden, MA 02148; customerservices@blackwellpublishing.com; http://www.blackwellpublishing.com. Illus., index. Refereed. Circ: 2200. Vol. ends: No. 4. Microform: PQC. Online: BioOne; Blackwell Synergy; CSA; EBSCO Publishing, EBSCO Host; OCLC Online Computer Library Center, Inc.; OhioLINK. Reprint: PSC. *Indexed:* AnBeAb, ApEcolAb, BiolAb, CABA, FPA, ForAb, HortAb, IndVet, S&F, SCI, VB, ZooRec. *Bk. rev.:* 4, 200 words. *Aud.:* Ac, Sa.

Journal of Field Ornithology publishes original articles with a focus on the descriptive or experimental study of birds in their natural habitats. Bird banding, conservation, habitat, and fieldwork are emphasized. Technology used to perform or aid in the study of birds is discussed in detail, such as solar-powered transmitters and audio-video systems. Articles are written in English, with Spanish translation of the titles and abstracts. Recommended for academic and research collections.

861. Journal of Raptor Research. Formerly (until vol.20, 1987): *Raptor Research.* [ISSN: 0892-1016] 1967. q. USD 65 (Individuals, USD 40). Ed(s): James C Bednarz. Raptor Research Foundation, Inc., Allen Press Box 1897, Lawrence, KS 66044-8897; osna@allenpress.com; http://www.biology.boisestate.edu/raptor/. Illus., index, adv. Sample. Refereed. Circ: 1200 Paid. Vol. ends: No. 4. *Indexed:* BiolAb, CABA, EnvAb, ForAb, IndVet, S&F, SCI, VB, WAE&RSA, ZooRec. *Bk. rev.:* 3, 800 words. *Aud.:* Ac, Sa.

Journal of Raptor Research publishes original research reports and review articles focused on all aspects of predatory birds throughout the world. Features include book reviews, letters, short communications, and articles with extensive

references. Raptor Research Foundation members receive the newsletter *Wingspan,* which contains current news, job postings, and meeting information. Recommended for academic and research libraries.

862. Living Bird. Former titles (until 1991): *Living Bird Quarterly;* (until 1982): *Living Bird.* [ISSN: 1059-521X] 1962. q. Members, USD 35. Ed(s): Tim Gallagher. Cornell University, Laboratory of Ornithology, c/o Communications, 159 Sapsucker Woods Rd, Ithaca, NY 14850; http://www.birds.cornell.edu/. Illus., index, adv. Circ: 22000. Microform: PQC. *Indexed:* BiolDig. *Aud.:* Hs, Ga, Ac.

Living Bird is published by the Cornell Laboratory of Ornithology and provides readable articles on all aspects of bird life, including biology, behavior, and environmental concerns. It reviews current research and activities related to ornithology. Included are birders' guides to various countries and travel opportunites. The journal contains high-quality color photos and paintings. The "Great Backyard Bird Count" can be found on its web site. Recommended for amateur birders.

863. The Loon. Formerly (until 1964): *Flicker.* [ISSN: 0024-645X] 1929. q. USD 35 (Individual members, USD 25; Students, USD 15). Ed(s): Anthony Hertzel. Minnesota Ornithologists' Union, James Ford Bell Museum of Natural History, University of Minnesota, Minneapolis, MN 55455-0104; mou@biosci.cbs.umn.edu; http://moumn.org. Illus., index. Circ: 1400. Vol. ends: Winter. *Indexed:* ZooRec. *Bk. rev.:* 1, 200 words. *Aud.:* Ga, Ac.

The Minnesota Ornithologists' Union (MOU) has a goal of promoting conservation and natural history study of birds in the Minnesota area. *The Loon* provides a way to meet those goals by publishing articles with extensive references that focus on all aspects of birding. Field studies, observation of birds, a seasonal report on bird migration, and book reviews are included. All members receive the MOU newsletter *Minnesota Birding.* The journal concentrates on birds in the Minnesota area, but it is one of the best regional bird journals available.

864. North American Bird Bander. Incorporates (in 1986): *Inland Bird Banding Newsletter;* Formed by the 1976 merger of: *Western Bird Bander;* (until vol.39): *E B B A News.* [ISSN: 0363-8979] 1976. q. Membership, USD 15. Ed(s): Robert Pantle. North American Bird Bander, 35 Logan Hill Rd, Candor, NY 13743; rjpl@cornell.edu. Illus., index, adv. Sample. Circ: 2000. Vol. ends: Oct/Dec. Microform: PQC. *Indexed:* ZooRec. *Bk. rev.:* 1,250 words. *Aud.:* Ac, Sa.

This essential journal for the serious bird bander includes research from the Eastern, Inland, and Western Bird Banding Associations. Bird banding equipment, capture techniques, and marked birds and plumages are some of the topics covered. Recent literature and books on banding, annual reports of the associations, regional news, and notes and comments are included. Recommended for professional ornithologists in the field.

865. North American Birds: a quarterly journal of ornithological record. Former titles (until 1999): *National Audubon Society Field Notes;* (until 1994): *American Birds;* (until 1971): *Audubon Field Notes.* [ISSN: 1525-3708] 1947. q. USD 60 (Members, USD 30; Non-members, USD 32). Ed(s): Edward S Brinkley. American Birding Association, 4945 N 30th St, Ste 200, PO Box 6599, Colorado Springs, CO 80919; beview@aba.org; http://www.americanbirding.org. Illus., index, adv. Circ: 6000. Vol. ends: Winter. Microform: PQC. Online: ProQuest LLC (Ann Arbor). *Indexed:* B&AI, BiolDig, ZooRec. *Aud.:* Ga, Ac, Sp.

North American Birds publishes reports that encompass the continent's bird life, including range extensions and contractions, migration patterns, and seasonal occurrences of birds. Regional reports contained in each issue provide the reader with articles that cover migration sightings, and effects of climate and weather patterns on bird movement specific to that region. Color photos and information on tours are included. Recommended for academic libraries and special libraries that serve ornitholgists.

Owl. See Children section.

866. *Pacific Seabirds: a publication of the Pacific Seabird Group.*
Formerly: *Pacific Seabird Group Bulletin.* [ISSN: 1089-6317] 1974.
2x/yr. Individuals, USD 25. Ed(s): Steven Speich. Pacific Seabird Group,
c/o Ron LeValley, Treasurer, 920 Samoa Blvd. Ste 210, Arcata, CA
95521; info@pacificseabirdgroup.org; http://www.pacificseabirdgroup.org.
Illus., adv. Sample. Circ: 400. Vol. ends: Fall (No. 2). *Indexed:* ZooRec.
Bk. rev.: 2,500 words. *Aud.:* Ac, Sa.

Pacific Seabirds is published by the Pacific Seabird Group to improve
communication among Pacific seabird researchers. Topics relating to the
conservation of seabirds in the Pacific Ocean, regional seabird research, and
news keep members and the general public informed. The journal covers the
entire Pacific region (including Russia, Alaska, Canada, Southeast Asia, the
west coast of the United States, and all Pacific Islands). It contains forums,
articles, news, reports, and book reviews.

867. *The Virtual Birder: the internet magazine for birders.* 1996. m.
Ed(s): Don Crockett. Great Blue Publications, TVB@greatblue.com;
http://www.virtualbirder.com. *Aud.:* Ga.

The Virtual Birder is an electronic journal with a goal of bringing content to
birders via the web. In addition to standard articles about birds, the site also
incorporates interactivity. A photo and sound gallery is included and
information on birding tours and "hot spots" in the United States and Canada is
highlighted. The site maintains links to other bird web sites and several
discussion groups.

868. *Waterbirds: the international journal of waterbird biology.* Former
titles (until 1998): *Colonial Waterbirds;* (until 1980): *Colonial Waterbird
Group Conference. Proceedings.* [ISSN: 1524-4695] 1977. 3x/yr.
Members, USD 90 per page; Non-members, USD 100 per page. Ed(s):
David Duffy. Waterbird Society, Pacific Cooperative Studies Unit,
Department of Botany, Honolulu, HI 96822-2279; membership@
osnabirds.org; http://www.nmnh.si.edu. Refereed. Circ: 900. Online:
BioOne; CSA; JSTOR (Web-based Journal Archive); OhioLINK.
Indexed: AnBeAb, ApEcolAb, BiolAb, CABA, ForAb, IndVet, OceAb,
S&F, SCI, VB, ZooRec. *Bk. rev.:* Number and length vary. *Aud.:* Ga, Ac.

Waterbirds publishes original research about all types of waterbird species
living in marine, estuarine, and freshwater habitats internationally. It has been
published by the Waterbird Society for nearly 30 years with a goal of promoting
and encouraging communication about the world's waterbird population.
Topics include conservation and techniques used to study the world's
waterbirds, which include seabirds, wading birds, shorebirds, and waterfowl.
Tables of contents for all issues since 1998 are available on the society's web
site.

869. *Western Birds: quarterly journal of Western Field Ornithologists.*
Formerly (until 1973): *California Birds.* [ISSN: 0160-1121] 1973. q.
USD 25 domestic; USD 35 foreign. Ed(s): Philip Unitt. Western Field
Ornithologists, c/o Robbie Fischer, Treasurer, 1359 Solano Dr, Pacifica,
CA 94044-4258; robbie22@pacbell.net; http://www.wfo-cbrc.org/. Illus.,
index, adv. Sample. Refereed. Circ: 1000 Paid. *Indexed:* BiolAb,
ZooRec. *Bk. rev.:* 1, 1,000 words. *Aud.:* Ga, Ac.

A quarterly journal that provides articles for both amateur and professional field
ornithologists while maintaining a high level of scientific literature. Lengthy
articles, reports, book reviews, and shorter articles found in the notes section
cover topics on identification, conservation, behavior, population dynamics,
migration status, effects of pollution, and techniques for censusing. Sound
recording and photographing birds in the field are discussed. Reports and
studies focus on birds from the Rocky Mountain and Pacific states and
provinces, including Hawaii and Alaska, northwestern Mexico, and the
northeastern Pacific ocean.

870. *Wildbird.* [ISSN: 0892-5534] 1987. bi-m. USD 19.97 domestic; USD
21.99 elsewhere. Ed(s): Amy Hooper, Marylou Zarbock. BowTie, Inc.,
2401 Beverly Blvd, PO Box 57900, Los Angeles, CA 90057;
http://www.animalnetwork.com/. Illus., index, adv. Circ: 65523 Paid. Vol.
ends: Dec. *Indexed:* BRI. *Aud.:* Hs, Ga.

In its 20th year *Wildbird* continues a tradition of educating and entertaining
readers. Focusing on North American birds and birding, it provides readers with
information on backyard bird identification, feeding, and habitat conservation.
A feature titled "Birding America" provides travel locations and tips for birders.
Excellent color photographs are included. Highly recommended for a general
audience.

871. *The Wilson Journal of Ornithology.* Formerly (until 2005): *Wilson
Bulletin.* [ISSN: 1559-4491] 1889. q. USD 40. Wilson Ornithological
Society, c/o Robert C Beason, Ed, Biology Dept, State University of
New York, Geneseo, NY 14454; http://www.ummz.lsa.umich.edu/birds/
wos.html. Illus., index. Refereed. Circ: 3500 Paid. Vol. ends: Dec.
Microform: PQC. Online: BioOne; CSA; Florida Center for Library
Automation; Gale; Northern Light Technology, Inc.; OCLC Online
Computer Library Center, Inc.; OhioLINK; ProQuest K-12 Learning
Solutions; ProQuest LLC (Ann Arbor). *Indexed:* AnBeAb, ApEcolAb,
BiolAb, CABA, FPA, ForAb, GSI, IndVet, OceAb, S&F, SCI, VB,
ZooRec. *Bk. rev.:* 3, lengthy. *Aud.:* Ac, Sa.

Wilson Bulletin contains scholarly research from around the world on all aspects
of ornithology. It is a major journal in the field, containing articles with
extensive references, footnotes, charts and maps, and shorter articles focused on
bird behavior. Lengthy book reviews are found in the section titled
"Ornithological Literature." Recommended for research libraries that serve
ornithologists.

**872. *Winging It: the monthly newsletter of the American Birding
Association.*** [ISSN: 1042-511X] 1989. m. USD 41 (Individuals, USD
36; Students, USD 18). Ed(s): Jennie Duberstein. American Birding
Association, 4945 N 30th St, Ste 200, PO Box 6599, Colorado Springs,
CO 80919; beview@aba.org; http://www.americanbirding.org. Illus., adv.
Sample. Vol. ends: Dec. *Aud.:* Ga.

Winging It is published by the American Birding Association. It has recently
expanded in size and substance. Members provide much of the information in
the newsletter, including bird-finding articles, letters, and field notes. It includes
a monthly summary of the previous month's rare-bird reports, current events,
and site guides for birders in North America.

■ BLIND AND VISUALLY IMPAIRED

See also Disabilities section.

*Camille McCutcheon, Coordinator of Library Instruction/Associate
Librarian, University of South Carolina Upstate, 800 University Way,
Spartanburg, SC 29303, CMcCutcheon@uscupstate.edu, FAX:
864-503-5601*

Introduction

The title of this section has been changed from "Visually Impaired" to "Blind
and Visually Impaired" to better reflect the intended audiences of the periodicals
and the diversity of publication formats that are noted in this section.

There are many print and electronic periodicals available to address the
needs of blind and visually impaired individuals and their support networks.
The intended audiences of these publications include individuals with low
vision, parents of blind children, diabetics who have vision-related diseases, and
blinded veterans of the U.S. Armed Forces. The subject matter of some of these
periodicals varies widely, from tips on day-to-day living with blindness or a
visual impairment, to poetry or prose submitted by blind and visually impaired
individuals, to ways in which to adjust to vision loss late in life, to
improvements in adaptive technology. Other publications contain reprints and
compilations of articles from mainstream newspapers and magazines.

All of the publishers of the periodicals featured in this section have web sites,
and almost of all them can be contacted via e-mail. Aside from the electronic
journals, there are several other magazine titles that have current and back issues
accessible online. Most of the publications included here are in the large-print

format, which is 14-point type or higher. In addition to large print and online, other available formats for these titles include Braille, two- or four-track cassette, e-mail, computer disk, digital text, electronic Braille, press Braille, CD, and ASCII via e-mail or diskette.

Basic Periodicals

FOR THE BLIND AND VISUALLY IMPAIRED. *Braille Book Review, Guideposts, The New York Times Large Type Weekly, Reader's Digest Large Print for Easier Reading, Syndicated Columnists Weekly, Talking Book Topics.* Many of the organizations listed below also have catalogs of mainstream magazines that are reprinted for the visually impaired.

ABOUT THE BLIND AND VISUALLY IMPAIRED. *Journal of Visual Impairment and Blindness, Review.*

BASIC REFERENCE MATERIALS. *Library of Congress. National Library Service for the Blind and Physically Handicapped.*

Organizations

American Council of the Blind, 1155 15th St., N.W., Suite 1004, Washington, DC 20005, www.acb.org, info@afb.org.

American Association of the Deaf-Blind, 814 Thayer Ave., Suite 302, Silver Spring, MD 20910-4500, www.aadb.org, AADB-Info@aadb.org.

American Foundation for the Blind, 11 Penn Plaza, Suite 300, New York, NY 10001-2017, www.afb.org, afbinfo@afb.net.

American Printing House for the Blind, Inc., P.O. Box 6085, Louisville, KY 40206-0085, www.aph.org, info@aph.org.

Clovernook Center for the Blind and Visually Impaired, 7000 Hamilton Ave., Cincinnati, OH 45321-5297, www.clovernook.org.

Helen Keller National Center for Deaf-Blind Youths and Adults, 141 Middle Neck Rd., Sands Point, NY 11050, hkncinfo@hknc.org.

Library of Congress, National Library Service for the Blind and Physically Handicapped, 1291 Taylor St., N.W., Washington, DC 20011, www.loc.gov/nls, nls@loc.gov.

Lighthouse International, 111 E. 59th St., New York, NY 10022, www.lighthouse.org, info@lighthouse.org.

National Association for Visually Handicapped, 22 W. 21st St., 6th Floor, New York, NY 10010, www.navh.org, navh@navh.org.

National Federation of the Blind, 1800 Johnson St., Baltimore, MD 21230, www.nfb.org, nfb@nfb.org.

Basic Abstracts and Indexes

The only index specific to this subject, *Rehabilitation Literature*, ceased publication in 1986. General indexes provide some guidance.

873. *A F B Directory of Services for Blind and Visually Impaired Persons in the United States and Canada.* Former titles: *A F B Directory of Services for Blind and Visually Impaired Persons in the United States; A F B Directory of Agencies Serving the Visually Handicapped in the U S.* [ISSN: 1067-5833] biennial. USD 79.95 combined subscription print & online eds. American Foundation for the Blind, 11 Penn Plaza, Suite 300, New York, NY 10001; afbinfo@afb.net; http://www.afb.org. *Aud.:* Ga, Sa.

Provides information on organizations and agencies in the United States and Canada that serve the needs of blind and visually impaired individuals. Section one consists of federal agencies, national organizations, national membership organizations, types of organizations, types of services, computer training, and products. Section two includes U.S. organizations; section three, Canadian organizations; section four, U.S./Canadian publishers of Braille, audio, and other nonprint formats; section five, U.S./Canadian sources of adapted products for persons with visual impairments; and section six, an alphabetical index. This publication is available in standard print. With the purchase of the print directory, a one-year access to the online version is included. An excellent reference source.

874. *AccessWorld (Online Edition): technology and people who are blind or visually impaired.* [ISSN: 1526-9574] 2000. bi-m. Free. Ed(s): Jay Leventhal. American Foundation for the Blind, 11 Penn Plaza, Suite 300, New York, NY 10001; afbinfo@afb.net; http://www.afb.org. Illus. Sample. *Aud.:* Ga, Sa.

AccessWorld has news and articles concerning technology for the blind and visually impaired. It also includes product reviews and information on accessibility issues. *AccessWorld Extra* is an e-mail newsletter that includes additional content. The *AccessWorld* archives contain issues dating back to 2000 and are accessible via the AFB web site.

875. *Aging & Vision (Online).* s-a. Free. Ed(s): Cynthia Stuen. Lighthouse International, 111 E 59th St, New York, NY 10022; info@lighthouse.org; http://www.lighthouse.org. *Aud.:* Sa.

Lighthouse International is a "leading resource worldwide on vision impairment and vision rehabilitation." *Aging & Vision* provides information for practitioners, researchers, and educators who work with individuals who are blind or visually impaired. Articles range from news about Lighthouse International to health issues related to aging and vision, to assistive technology, to living with and adjusting to vision loss late in life. The archives of this newsletter contain issues dating back to 2004. Individuals who do not have computer access can contact Lighthouse International to receive a print copy of the newsletter.

876. *The B V A Bulletin.* [ISSN: 0005-3430] 1946. q. Free to members. Ed(s): Stuart Nelson. Blinded Veterans Association, National Board of Directors, 477 H St, NW, Washington, DC 20001; bva@bva.org; http://www.bva.org. Illus. Circ: 13700 Controlled. Online: ProQuest LLC (Ann Arbor). *Aud.:* Sa.

Information in *The BVA Bulletin* is written by blinded veterans for blinded veterans. This publication contains legislation, news, feature articles, information from the president of the Blinded Veterans Association, recent and upcoming activities of the association, letters to the editor, and an "in remembrance" section for blinded veterans who have recently died. The current issue, along with issues dating back to 2003, are accessible via the BVA web site. *The BVA Bulletin* also is available in 14-point type and on cassette.

877. *Blind World Magazine.* 2003. irreg. Free. Ed(s): George Cassell. Blind World Magazine, http://www.blindworld.net. *Aud.:* Sa.

Blind World Magazine is a wonderful online publication for the blind and visually impaired. Newspapers and magazines in both print and electronic formats, scientific and medical journals, and newsletters are just some of the sources for the blindness-related articles found in this magazine. Topics vary, from national and international news to human-interest stories, to guide-dog news, to medical news and blindness research, to a listing of national and international events of interest to the blind and visually impaired. There are also links to additional web sites that offer information on topics such as eye-care associations, low-vision resources, mobility canes, and guide-dog schools.

878. *Braille Book Review.* [ISSN: 0006-873X] 1932. bi-m. Free to blind and physically handicapped. Ed(s): Edmund O'Reilly. U.S. Library of Congress, National Library Service for the Blind and Physically Handicapped, 1291 Taylor St, NW, Washington, DC 20011; nls@loc.gov; http://www.loc.gov/nls. Illus., index. Sample. Circ: 10389. Vol. ends: Nov/Dec. *Aud.:* Ems, Hs, Ga, Sa.

Braille Book Review contains annotated lists of the most recent nonfiction and fiction titles produced in Braille for adults and children that are available through the National Library Service for the Blind and Physically Handicapped (NLS) and its network of cooperating libraries. It includes one-line annotations from *Talking Book Topics* and a Braille order form. Genres represented include mysteries, classics, biographies, gothics, and how-to and self-help guides. *BBR* also lists Braille magazines that are available through the network of cooperating libraries. The Braille edition of *BBR* includes recorded books, with abbreviated annotations. The current issue of *BBR*, along with back issues to 1994, can be accessed via the NLS web site. *BBR* is also available in the following formats: 14-point type, digital Braille, press Braille, and digital text.

879. *The Braille Forum.* [ISSN: 0006-8772] 1962. m. USD 25 Free to members. Ed(s): Sharon Lovering. American Council of the Blind, 1155 15th St, NW, Ste 1004, Washington, DC 20005; editor@acb.org; http://www.acb.org. Illus., adv. Sample. Circ: 25000. Vol. ends: Jun. Online: EBSCO Publishing, EBSCO Host. *Aud.:* Sa.

The Braille Forum is a resource for blind and visually impaired individuals. It contains poetry, news, and human interest stories, along with information about legislation, employment, health, new products and services, and sports and leisure activities. Information and updates about the American Council of the Blind (ACB) are also featured. The current issue, along with issues dating back to 1990, is accessible via the ACB web site. *The Braille Forum* is also available in the following formats: Braille, 16-point type, half-speed four-track cassette, and e-mail.

880. *Braille Mirror.* [ISSN: 0006-8810] 1926. 6x/yr. USD 15. Ed(s): Douglas Menville. Braille Institute of America, Inc, 741 N Vermont Ave, Los Angeles, CA 90029; http://www.brailleinstitute.org. Circ: 250 Paid. *Aud.:* Sa.

The Braille Mirror contains reprints of articles from magazines such as *People, Time, Newsweek,* and *Entertainment Weekly* and from newspapers such as *The New York Times, The Wall Street Journal,* and *The Christian Science Monitor.* Topics vary, from profiles of famous people to articles on science, health, language, and history. Recipes, humor, stories submitted by blind readers, and announcements of interest to the blind and visually impaired are also featured. *The Braille Mirror* is available in Braille and on four-track cassette. The cassette version of *The Braille Mirror* is free.

881. *Braille Monitor: voice of the nation's blind.* [ISSN: 0006-8829] 1956. 11x/yr. Non-members, USD 25. Ed(s): Barbara Pierce. National Federation of the Blind, 1800 Johnson St, Baltimore, MD 21230; nfb@nfb.org; http://www.nfb.org. Illus., index, adv. Sample. Circ: 25000. Vol. ends: Dec. *Indexed:* ECER. *Aud.:* Sa.

The leading publication of the National Federation of the Blind (NFB), *Braille Monitor* is read by the blind, their families, and the professionals who serve them. *Braille Monitor* contains recipes, human interest stories, profiles of blind individuals, and highlights of NFB activities and programs. It also addresses concerns of the blind, such as civil rights, social issues, legislation, employment, and education, and provides information on technology and aids/appliances used by the blind. The current issue, along with issues dating back to 1987, is accessible via the NFB web site. Other available formats of *Braille Monitor* include 14-point type, Braille, two- or four-track cassette, and e-mail.

882. *The Complete Directory of Large Print Books and Serials.* Formerly (until 1988): *Large Type Books in Print.* [ISSN: 0000-1120] 1970. a. USD 360. R.R. Bowker LLC, 630 Central Ave, New Providence, NJ 07974; info@bowker.com; http://www.bowker.com/. *Aud.:* Sa.

This resource is an excellent tool for determining the availability of large-print newspapers and periodicals. It lists all active large-print books, newspapers, and periodical titles included in Bowker's *Books In Print* and *Ulrich's* databases. The directory contains two indexes for looking up newspaper and periodical titles. One index is arranged alphabetically by subject, the other alphabetically by title.

883. *The Deaf - Blind American.* 1962. q. USD 50 (Individuals, USD 20). Ed(s): Elizabeth Spiers. American Association of the Deaf-Blind, 8630 Fenton St., Ste 121, Silver Spring, MD 20910-3803; info@aadb.org; http://www.aadb.org. Circ: 700. *Bk. rev.:* Number and length vary. *Aud.:* Sa.

The Deaf-Blind American is the official publication of the American Association of the Deaf-Blind (AADB). Topics vary, from activities and news about the AADB to articles about people living successfully with deaf-blindness, to poetry and essays written by deaf-blind people about deaf-blindness, to information on the latest technology including computers and telecommunication assistive devices. Other regular features include information on legislation, medical research, book reviews, services, products, and programs for deaf-blind people. The publication is available in 18-point type, Braille, CD, and disk formats.

884. *Deaf - Blind Perspectives.* [ISSN: 1526-9841] 1993. 3x/yr. Free. Ed(s): Peggy Malloy, John Reiman. Western Oregon University, Teaching Research Institute, 345 N Monmouth Ave, Monmouth, OR 97361; kenyond@wou.edu; http://www.tr.wou.edu/. Illus. Sample. Circ: 4000. *Bk. rev.:* Number and length vary. *Aud.:* Sa.

This publication provides information on issues of interest to deaf-blind individuals and has announcements, articles, and essays about the deaf-blind, their family members, and the professionals who serve them. Persons affiliated with DB-LINK (National Information Clearinghouse on Children Who Are Deaf-Blind) and NTAC (National Technical Assistance Consortium for Children and Young Adults Who Are Deaf-Blind) regularly contribute to this publication. The current issue of *Deaf-Blind Perspectives* and issues dating back to 1993 are accessible via the *Deaf-Blind Perspectives* web site. This publication is also available in grade 2 Braille, 16-point type, standard print, and ASCII via e-mail or diskette.

885. *Dialogue (Salem): a world of ideas for the visually impaired of all ages.* Incorporates (1983-1995): *Lifeprints.* [ISSN: 1069-6857] 1961. bi-m. USD 42 for cassette, email , disk, braille ed. Ed(s): Karen L Thomas. Blindskills, Inc., PO Box 5181, Salem, OR 97304-0181; info@blindskills.com; http://www.blindskills.com. Illus., adv. Sample. Circ: 1200 Paid. Vol. ends: Winter. *Bk. rev.:* Number and length vary. *Aud.:* Ga, Sa.

Dialogue contains informative articles written by people who are blind or visually impaired. Technology, spotlights on families of visually impaired individuals, sports and recreation, travel destinations, cooking, gardening, and health are just some of the topics covered. News and information on ways to obtain new products and services, computer-related and otherwise, are also included. This publication is available in the following formats: 18-point type, four-track cassette, Braille, e-mail, and diskette.

886. *EnVision: a publication for parents and educators of children with impaired vision.* 1993. s-a. Free. Ed(s): Cynthia Stuen. Lighthouse International, 111 E 59th St, New York, NY 10022; info@lighthouse.org; http://www.lighthouse.org. Illus. *Aud.:* Sa.

EnVision is a newsletter that contains information for both educators and parents of children with impaired vision. Issues dating back to 2004 are accessible via Lighthouse International's web site.

887. *Future Reflections.* [ISSN: 0883-3419] 1981. q. Free. Ed(s): Barbara A Cheadle. National Federation of the Blind, 1800 Johnson St, Baltimore, MD 21230; nfb@nfb.org; http://www.nfb.org. Sample. Circ: 20000. *Aud.:* Sa.

Future Reflections is a resource for parents and educators of blind children. It contains profiles of blind children and their parents and educators as well as information on the NFB. Also included are articles on issues concerning blind children, educational programs for blind students, and resources for parents and teachers. The current issue of *Future Reflections* and issues dating back to 1991 are accessible via the NFB web site. This journal is also available in the following formats: two-track cassette, 14-point type, and e-mail.

888. *Guideposts: true stories of hope and inspiration.* [ISSN: 0017-5331] 1945. m. 11/yr. USD 16.97 domestic; USD 19.97 Canada; USD 28.97 elsewhere. Ed(s): Edward Grinnan. Guideposts, 39 Seminary Hill Rd, Carmel, NY 10512; http://www.guideposts.org. Illus., index, adv. Sample. Circ: 680000. Vol. ends: Mar. *Aud.:* Ga, Sa.

Guideposts is an inspirational, interfaith publication that presents first-person narratives that encourage readers to achieve their "maximum personal and spiritual potential." Selected departments and stories from the current issue of the magazine are accessible from the *Guideposts* web site. This publication is available on four-track cassette, in 15-point type, and in Braille.

Journal of Visual Impairment & Blindness. See Disabilities section.

889. *Library Resources for the Blind and Physically Handicapped.* Formerly: *Directory of Library Resources for the Blind and Physically Handicapped.* [ISSN: 0364-1236] 1968. a. Free to blind and physically handicapped. Ed(s): Edmund O'Reilly. U.S. Library of Congress,

National Library Service for the Blind and Physically Handicapped, 1291 Taylor St, NW, Washington, DC 20011; nls@loc.gov; http://www.loc.gov/nls. Illus. Sample. Circ: 4608. *Aud.*: Sa.

This is an annual directory with budget, staff, and collections information and fiscal year statistics on readership and circulation of the libraries within the National Library Service for the Blind and Physically Handicapped, Library of Congress's "talking book" program. Libraries affiliated with the program are listed by state. Appendixes include readership and circulation for the fiscal year, along with budget, staff, and collections within each network library. Available in 14-point type and digital text. An excellent reference source.

890. *Musical Mainstream (Large Print Edition).* Former titles (until Dec.1976): *New Braille Musician; Braille Musician.* [ISSN: 0364-7501] 1942. q. Free to blind and physically handicapped. Ed(s): Edmund O'Reilly. U.S. Library of Congress, National Library Service for the Blind and Physically Handicapped, 1291 Taylor St, NW, Washington, DC 20011; nls@loc.gov; http://www.loc.gov/nls. Sample. Circ: 2082. *Bk. rev.:* Number and length vary. *Aud.*: Ga, Sa.

Published by the Music Section of the National Library Service for the Blind and Physically Handicapped, *Musical Mainstream* contains reprints of articles on classical music, music criticism, and music education from national publications such as *Opera News, Billboard, Piano Today,* and *American Record Guide.* This publication is available in 16-point type, cassette, digital Braille, and press Braille.

891. *N A V H Update.* 1997. q. Free. Ed(s): Dr. Lorraine H Marchi. National Association for Visually Handicapped, 22 W 21st St, 6th Fl, New York, NY 10010; staff@navh.org; http://www.navh.org. Circ: 12000. *Aud.*: Ga, Sa.

NAVH Update contains brief articles on technological advances and on nutrition and health. Also featured are recent additions to NAVH's Large Print loan library, news, gift ideas, and many other tips and items of interest. This newsletter is available in 16-point type and via e-mail upon request.

892. *Nat-Cent News.* 1970. 3x/yr. Free for physically disabled & librarians. Ed(s): Robert J Smithdas. Helen Keller National Center for Deaf - Blind Youths and Adults, 141 Middle Neck Rd, Sands Point, NY 11050; hkncinfo@hknc.org; http://www.hknc.org. Circ: 2000. *Aud.*: Sa.

This publication includes poetry submitted by and profiles of deaf-blind persons, announcements of new products, technological advances, and news and feature articles that are of interest to deaf-blind individuals. *Nat-Cent News* is available in 24-point type and in Braille.

893. *New York Times Large Type Weekly.* [ISSN: 0028-7814] 1967. w. Mon. USD 78. Ed(s): Tom Brady. New York Times Company, 229 W 43rd St, New York, NY 10036; 1-800@nytimes.com; http://www.nytimes.com. Illus. Sample. Circ: 15000. Vol. ends: Feb. *Aud.*: Ga, Sa.

This publication contains selected articles that have appeared throughout the past week in *The New York Times.* Graphics and color photographs enhance stories on national and international news, science and health, business, the arts, sports, and editorials. A crossword puzzle is also included. This publication is available in 16-point type and in Braille.

894. *Our Special: magazine devoted to matters of interest to blind women.* [ISSN: 0030-6959] 1927. bi-m. USD 15. Ed(s): Dana Nichols. National Braille Press, 88 St Stephen St, Boston, MA 02115; orders@nbp.org; http://www.nbp.org. Circ: 700. *Aud.*: Sa.

Our Special is a resource especially for blind women. It contains original articles along with ones reprinted from women's magazines such as *Good Housekeeping* and *Redbook* and from newspapers such as *The New York Times, The Christian Science Monitor,* and *The Wall Street Journal.* Topics featured in *Our Special* include career issues, family life, health, dating, cooking, travel, and fashion. This publication is available only in Braille.

895. *Reader's Digest Large Print for Easier Reading.* Formerly: *Reader's Digest Large Type Edition.* [ISSN: 1094-5857] 1964. m. USD 27.96 domestic. Ed(s): Jacquelia Leo. Reader's Digest Association, Inc, Reader's Digest Rd, Pleasantville, NY 10570-7000; http://www.rd.com. Adv. Circ: 603157 Paid. *Aud.*: Ga, Sa.

Reader's Digest Large Print for Easier Reading contains in-depth feature articles, departments such as "Word Power," "Humor in Uniform," "Life in these United States," and "Laughter, the Best Medicine," a crossword puzzle, and a book-length feature. It is available in 21-point type from Reader's Digest. This periodical is also available from the American Printing House for the Blind (APH) on four-track cassette and in Braille. The advertising has been removed from the editions produced by the APH.

RE:view. See Disabilities section.

896. *Sharing Solutions: a newsletter for people with imparied vision and their support networks.* 1993. s-a. Free. Ed(s): Cynthia Stuen. Lighthouse International, 111 E 59th St, New York, NY 10022; info@lighthouse.org; http://www.lighthouse.org. Circ: 30000. *Aud.*: Ga, Sa.

Sharing Solutions is a resource for individuals with impaired vision and their support networks. Topics vary from news, legislation, Medicare, exercise, health, eye diseases, and adaptive computer technology to articles of interest on solutions to life's everyday problems. The current issue, along with selected issues dating back to 2004, is accessible via Lighthouse International's web site. This newsletter is available in 16-point type and on cassette. Upon request, it is also available in Braille.

897. *Syndicated Columnists Weekly.* 1984. w. USD 24. Ed(s): Diane Croft. National Braille Press, 88 St Stephen St, Boston, MA 02115; orders@nbp.org; http://www.nbp.org. Circ: 300. *Aud.*: Sa.

Syndicated Columnists Weekly contains the best editorials written by syndicated columnists that have appeared that week in major U.S. newspapers such as *The Wall Street Journal, The New York Times, The Washington Post,* and *The Boston Globe.* Available only in Braille.

898. *Talking Book Topics.* [ISSN: 0039-9183] 1935. bi-m. Free to blind and physically handicapped. Ed(s): Edmund O'Reilly. U.S. Library of Congress, National Library Service for the Blind and Physically Handicapped, 1291 Taylor St, NW, Washington, DC 20011; nls@loc.gov; http://www.loc.gov/nls. Index. Sample. Circ: 380506. *Aud.*: Ems, Hs, Ga, Sa.

Talking Book Topics contains an annotated list of recent additions of "talking books" that are available through the National Library Service for the Blind and Physically Handicapped (NLS) and its network of cooperating libraries. Genres represented include gothics, mysteries, biographies, classics, and how-to and self-help guides. *TBT* also includes announcements from the NLS, recent additions of "talking books" available in Spanish, and a listing of magazines on cassette. The current issue of *TBT,* along with issues dating back to 1997, is accessible via the NLS web site. This publication is also available in the following formats: cassette, 14-point type, press Braille, and digital text.

899. *Voice of the Diabetic.* [ISSN: 1041-8490] 1986. q. Non-members, USD 20. Ed(s): Ed Bryant. National Federation of the Blind, Diabetes Action Network, 1200 W Worley, Columbia, MO 65203; http://www.nfb.org. Adv. Circ: 345000. *Aud.*: Ga, Sa.

Voice of the Diabetic contains articles about diabetes and blindness and promotes "good diabetes control, diet, and independence." Included are profiles of diabetics, recipes, a resource column, and informational articles on topics ranging from diabetes education and physical exercise to Social Security disability. There is also a question-and-answer section where readers can pose diabetes-related questions to a physician. The current issue and issues dating back to 1995 are accessible via the NFB web site. This publication is available in the following formats: four-track cassette, e-mail, and standard print.

■ BOATS AND BOATING

See also Fishing; Hunting and Guns; and Sports sections.

Julia D. Ashmun, Senior Software Engineer, Information Technology Services, Widener Library, Harvard University, Cambridge, MA 02138; ashmun@fas.harvard.edu

Introduction

Titles in this section will appeal to a wide range of boating enthusiasts, from the person on the street thinking about buying a first boat to expert yachtsmen and -women to old salts. There is something for every boater here, covering topics from boating safety to personal watercraft to oceangoing vessels, and the boats are powered variously by sail, motors, or muscles. Although some titles are general in approach, others focus on specific types of crafts (i.e., sailboats or powerboats) or address particular aspects of boating (i.e., navigation or competition).

Publications have been chosen for their generally interesting coverage or to address specialized boating interests.

There are many boating magazines out there on the web, but most titles listed here also have established print versions. Most sites that call themselves online magazines are not magazines in the traditional sense, but rather are newsletters or a collection of links to directories of products or services; these are almost always lacking feature material. *By-the-Sea* (www.by-the-sea.com) has some articles and stories online, and is the best of this style of online publication.

Basic Periodicals

Ems: *BoatSafe and BoatSafeKids, Personal Watercraft Illustrated;* Hs: *Boating World, Personal Watercraft Illustrated;* Ga: *Boating, Boating World, Boatworks, Canoe & Kayak, Cruising World, Personal Watercraft Illustrated, Practical Sailor, Sail, The Woodenboat;* Ac: *Boating World, Boatworks, Canoe & Kayak, Sail, The Woodenboat.*

Basic Abstracts and Indexes

Readers' Guide to Periodical Literature.

900. *Blue Water Sailing: the magazine of cruising and offshore sailing.* [ISSN: 1091-1979] 1996. m. USD 29.95 domestic; USD 39.95 Canada; USD 44.95 elsewhere. Ed(s): Quentin Warren. Blue Water Sailing, 747 Aquidneck Ave, Ste 201, Middletown, RI 02842. Adv. *Aud.:* Ga, Sa.

Focused on various aspects of offshore sailing, *Blue Water Sailing* gives practical tips for offshore seamanship, safety, design, boat reviews, offshore events (including racing), news, live-on-board suggestions, and special sections on aspects of offshore navigation, including articles on electronic navigation, electronic charts, raster versus vector charts, radar, GPS, etc. Departments include a Captain's Log (editorial), Readers' Forum, Blue Water Dispatches, World Sailing Adventures, and Blue Horizons—stories of ideal regional destinations. Recommended for public libraries serving offshore boaters.

901. *Boating.* Incorporates (1973-1980): *Motorboat;* Which incorporated (in 1975): *Family Houseboating;* Formerly: *Popular Boating.* [ISSN: 0006-5374] 1956. m. USD 14 domestic; USD 24 Canada; USD 4.99 newsstand/cover per issue. Ed(s): Randy Steele. Hachette Filipacchi Media U.S., Inc., 1633 Broadway, New York, NY 10019; http://www.hfmus.com. Illus., index, adv. Sample. Circ: 198818 Paid. Vol. ends: Dec. Microform: MIM; PQC. Online: The Dialog Corporation; OCLC Online Computer Library Center, Inc. *Indexed:* ASIP, ConsI. *Aud.:* Ga.

The magazine with the highest circulation in the genre, *Boating* offers a wide range of information for power boaters. Most material is aimed at increasing boaters' knowledge, with regular features on seamanship, navigation, equipment, maintenance, and safety. A significant portion of the coverage is new-boat testing and evaluation. Other material includes articles on trips, recreational activities, and boating industry news. This is a highly polished, visually satisfying journal with extensive use of color and graphics, along with a substantial amount of advertising (generally integrated well with the text). The emphasis is on midsized to large boats, but there's also a broader perspective for power boaters, and it can be useful as part of a basic collection.

902. *Boating World.* Former titles: *Boat Journal; Small Boat Journal.* [ISSN: 1059-5155] 1979. 10x/yr. USD 18 domestic; USD 38 foreign; USD 3.95 newsstand/cover per issue. Ed(s): Ryan McNally. Trans World Publishing, Inc., 2100 Powers Ferry Rd, Ste 300, Atlanta, GA 30339; editor@artandantiques.net. Illus., index, adv. Sample. Circ: 100000. *Indexed:* IHTDI, RGPR. *Aud.:* Hs, Ga.

The focus here is on powered boats of 35 feet or less, a popular size for short trips, water-sports activities, and fishing. There's a very wide range of material on boats and equipment, activities on and off the water, and the general boating environment. Each issue contains a lengthy feature article on a special topic and an article focusing on a boat of the month. Articles offer practical advice for hands-on upkeep and maintenance, as well as consumer tips (such as buying a used boat or insuring boats). A colorful production, with good graphics and broad coverage. Because it focuses on boats of such a popular size, this publication merits strong consideration as part of a library's core collection.

903. *BoatSafe and BoatSafeKids: boating courses, boating tips, boating safety, boating contests.* m. Nautical Know How, Inc., 5102 S E Nassau Terrace, Stuart, FL 34997; http://Boatsafe.com. *Aud.:* Ems, Hs, Ga.

This comprehensive web magazine, sponsored by International Marine Educators, Inc., is dedicated to promoting boating knowledge and safety. Its archive is full of articles on safety issues for boats and people, along with instructional material and narratives about navigation, equipment, boat maintenance, and boat handling. Other articles here deal with the same topics—but they're written specifically for children. The magazine has a state-by-state listing of boating regulations and online boating courses designed to satisfy most boating-education requirements. A very useful site for boaters, and one that will be helpful to public libraries for reference service. It is free at www.boatsafe.com.

904. *Boatworks: how to rewire your boat.* Formerly: *Boatworks for the Hands-On Sailor.* 2004. q. USD 12 domestic; USD 17 Canada; USD 18 elsewhere. Ed(s): Peter Nielsen. Source Interlink Companies, 98 NWashington St, Boston, MA 02114; edisupport@sourceinterlink.com; http://www.sourceinterlink.com. Adv. Circ: 75000. *Aud.:* Hs, Ga, Sa.

An outstanding publication, useful to boat owners and soon-to-be boat owners. There is excellent advice on what to look for in purchasing a boat and then how to go about maintaining it. Do-it-yourself articles are practical, informative, and—most importantly—accurate. They provide very hands-on information about maintenance and upgrading of sailboats, with lots of instructive illustrations including step-by-step guides to carrying out specific repairs and upgrades. This title will appeal to all types of boating enthusiasts; you don't need to have a yacht to get a lot out of it. Highly recommended for all public libraries with boating journal collections.

905. *By-the-Sea: the online boating magazine.* 1998. d. By-the-Sea, 1315 Samoset Rd, Eastham, MA 02642; http://www.by-the-sea.com. *Aud.:* Ga.

This web-based smorgasbord for boaters includes feature articles and stories, posts message boards, and lists boats for sale as well as boat builders and boat dealers. There's a huge amount of readily available, useful information—this is a title all those interested in boating will want to know about. Find it at www.by-the-sea.com.

906. *Canoe & Kayak: the #1 paddlesports resource.* Formerly: *Canoe;* Supersedes (in 1978): *American Canoeist.* [ISSN: 1077-3258] 1973. 7x/yr. USD 17.95 domestic; USD 30.95 Canada; USD 32.95 elsewhere. Ed(s): Ross Prather. Source Interlink Companies, 27500 Riverview Center Blvd, Bonita Springs, FL 34134; edisupport@sourceinterlink.com; http://www.sourceinterlink.com. Illus., adv. Sample. Circ: 60000 Paid. Vol. ends: Dec. *Indexed:* PEI, SD. *Aud.:* Ga, Ac.

An excellent offering with information for canoe and kayak enthusiasts in all kinds of paddling environments. Primary emphasis is on descriptions of paddling trips, ranging from casual day outings to rigorous white-water excursions. There is also considerable coverage of paddling techniques, skills, safety, and health. This is topped off by material on boat design and construction and new products and accessories. Articles often voice environmental concerns and are usually very thorough and well written. Tastefully done, the magazine is both informative and enjoyable to read. *Canoe & Kayak* will be appreciated by a wide audience.

907. *Cruising World.* [ISSN: 0098-3519] 1974. m. USD 28 domestic; USD 40 Canada; USD 64 elsewhere. Ed(s): Herb McCormick. World Publications LLC, 460 N Orlando Ave, Ste 200, Winter Park, FL 32789; info@worldpub.net; http://www.worldpub.net. Illus., adv. Sample. Circ: 151000 Paid. Vol. ends: Dec. Microform: PQC. Online: EBSCO Publishing, EBSCO Host; Gale. *Indexed:* SD. *Bk. rev.:* 3, 50 words. *Aud.:* Ga.

A popular magazine dedicated to open-water sailing and enjoying the sailing life, most of *Cruising World*'s content centers on descriptive narratives of cruising trips or on practical solutions and techniques for long-term cruising. Trip narratives convey a good sense of the open-water experience and provide interesting glimpses of the character, history, and culture of international areas visited. Practical material covers such topics as navigational techniques, fishing, and boat maintenance. Supporting material includes news items and reviews of new equipment and new boats. The writing is sound, the graphics are pleasing, and the overall quality of the magazine is good. This title is useful and informative, and with its emphasis on living on the water, it offers a different approach than most other boating magazines.

908. *D I Y Boat Owner: the marine maintenance magazine.* [ISSN: 1201-5598] 1995. q. USD 18; CND 16.60; CND 39 foreign. Ed(s): Jan Mundy. D I Y Boat Owner, PO Box 167000, Dallas, TX 75261-9652. Adv. *Aud.:* Ga, Sa.

A technical, how-to title for powerboat and sailboat owners aimed at increasing knowledge of boat maintenance, upgrade, and repair, *DIY* offers articles on engine maintenance, building projects, electrical problems, installing accessories, troubleshooting engines and electronics, rigging, hull and deck maintenance, and more. Also included are reviews and articles on equipment, tools, parts, and products. A solid title for any boating collection.

909. *Good Old Boat.* [ISSN: 1099-6354] 1998. bi-m. USD 39.95 in US & Canada; USD 49.95 elsewhere. Ed(s): Karen Larson. Partnership for Excellence, Inc., 7340 Niagara Lane N, Maple Grove, MN 55311-2655; http://www.goodoldboat.com. *Bk. rev.:* Number and length vary. *Aud.:* Ga, Sa.

A good ol' magazine aimed at average, do-it-yourself sailors who are not sailing the latest and greatest new yachts but are instead "celebrating older-model sailboats." Like *The WoodenBoat*, it has in-depth reviews about models of boats that include the history, design, biography of the designer(s), and articles about the owner(s) of that model, along with photos of the boat—inside and out—in an attractive, glossy format. Most material is focused on furthering a sailor's knowledge of boat maintenance, seamanship, and safety, and do-it-yourself improvement projects are routinely included. Issues include design lessons, book reviews, equipment reviews, and features about fellow sailors relating their experiences and favorite weekend or extended cruise spots.

910. *Houseboat Magazine: the family magazine for American houseboaters.* 1990. 10x/yr. USD 29.95 United States; USD 44.95 elsewhere; USD 3.95 newsstand/cover per issue. Ed(s): Steve Smede. Harris Publishing, Inc. (Idaho Falls), 360 B St, Idaho Falls, ID 83402; hbsubscriptions@houseboatmagazine.com; http://www.harrispublishing.com. Illus., adv. Circ: 25000. *Aud.:* Ga.

A publication focusing exclusively, and extensively, on houseboats, this title covers all facets of boat ownership and maintenance, interesting boating locales, and activities and lifestyles of houseboaters. One of the defining features of this magazine is its focus on a different destination in each issue, including some of the history, scenic qualities, and services found there. This is a thin but attractively packaged publication that fills a need for a unique group of boaters. Houseboats are seen most frequently on large lakes and rivers, especially in the Western and Midwestern regions, so libraries in those areas would be the most likely to consider this title.

911. *Maritime Life and Traditions.* [ISSN: 1467-1611] 1998. q. USD 35 United States; USD 41 Canada; USD 51 elsewhere. Ed(s): Bernard Cadoret. WoodenBoat Publications, Inc., Naskeag Rd, PO Box 78, Brooklin, ME 04616-0078; subscriptions@woodenboat.com. Illus., adv. Online: EBSCO Publishing, EBSCO Host. *Aud.:* Ga, Sa.

Jointly published by the publishers of *Le Chasse-Maree* and *The WoodenBoat* and produced in France, this magazine elegantly describes international maritime culture in superb detail combined with glossy photos. Each issue covers naval history, nautical archaeology, boat building and restoration, naval architecture, yachting history, maritime art, merchant maritime history, maritime trades and crafts, social and cultural issues, model making, exploration, and/or contemporary maritime industries. A beautifully designed magazine, recommended for libraries serving true boating enthusiasts who may not be able to afford a subscription themselves.

912. *Motor Boating.* Former titles (until 2000): *Motor Boating & Sailing;* (until 1970): *Motor Boating.* [ISSN: 1531-2623] 1907. m. USD 10 domestic; USD 21.97 foreign; USD 3.99 newsstand/cover domestic. Time4 Media, Inc., 2 Park Ave, New York, NY 10016. Illus., adv. Sample. Circ: 121670 Paid. Vol. ends: Jun/Dec. Microform: NBI; PQC. Online: EBSCO Publishing, EBSCO Host; Gale; Northern Light Technology, Inc.; OCLC Online Computer Library Center, Inc.; ProQuest K-12 Learning Solutions; H.W. Wilson. *Indexed:* ConsI, MASUSE, RGPR. *Aud.:* Ga.

One of the oldest boating magazines currently published, this popular title is for powerboaters only. Its scope includes powerboats of all sizes; its emphasis is on reviews of new boats, with supporting material covering both the pleasure and the practical aspects of boating. A particularly useful feature is the "Boatkeeper" section, designed as a cut-out section for hands-on boaters and containing a number of practical ideas and applications for boat maintenance, upkeep, and problem solving. Like several other high-circulation boating magazines, this has abundant advertising plus classified and brokerage sections that take up close to half of each issue. This effectively obscures some of the informational content that has been relegated to the latter part of the magazine. Its web site has the table of contents for the current issue, but no material is available in full text; prior issues are not archived, but material from the "Boatkeeper" section is, along with keyword search capability.

913. *Multihulls.* [ISSN: 0749-4122] 1975. bi-m. USD 29 domestic; USD 39 foreign. Ed(s): Charles K Chiodi. Chiodi Advertising & Publishing, Inc., 421 Hancock St, PO Box 7, N Quincy, MA 02171. Illus., adv. Sample. Circ: 56000 Paid and controlled. Vol. ends: Nov/Dec. *Bk. rev.:* 1-3, 100-600 words. *Aud.:* Ga.

Devoted to sailing craft with two hulls (catamarans) or three (trimarans), this title offers insightful knowledge about the "buying, building, racing, cruising, and safety of multihulls." Most articles cover cruising or racing activities, but these are supplemented nicely by material on boat design, construction, navigation, seamanship, and safety. Most articles are written by multihull sailors rather than magazine staff, and they are lengthy and detailed, almost always relating personal sailing experiences. Some material is geared toward boaters who do their own maintenance and repair work. Not as flashy as most publications in this field, but tastefully done, and it has considerably less distracting advertising than many others.

914. *Ocean Navigator: marine navigation and ocean voyaging.* Formerly (until Dec. 1985): *Navigator.* [ISSN: 0886-0149] 1985. bi-m. USD 27.95 domestic; USD 31.95 Canada; USD 33.95 elsewhere. Ed(s): Tim Queeney. Navigator Publishing LLC., 58 Fore St, Portland, ME 04101-4842. Illus., adv. Sample. Circ: 44000 Paid and controlled. *Indexed:* RiskAb. *Bk. rev.:* 2-4, 75-200 words. *Aud.:* Ga.

Ocean boating requires considerable navigational skills and knowledge, and this is the only magazine we know of whose major focus is on these. While primary content concerns the art, tools, and techniques of navigation and seamanship, there is also a good sampling of articles on other aspects of ocean voyaging, such as boat maintenance or inviting cruise destinations. Some articles give accounts of voyages in which navigational skills or equipment have been a significant or crucial factor in the trip's outcome. Most topics offer detailed, in-depth coverage and are interesting, informative, and sometimes instructional. Although most of the material applies to sailing craft, the navigational features can be valuable for all boaters.

915. *Paddler.* Formerly: *River Runner.* [ISSN: 1058-5710] 1981. 6x/yr. USD 18 domestic; USD 31 Canada; USD 34 elsewhere. Ed(s): Eugene Buchanan, Mike Kord. Paddlesport Publishing, Inc., 7432 Alban Station Blvd, Ste B-226, Springfield, VA 22150. Illus., adv. Sample. Circ: 100000. Vol. ends: Nov/Dec. *Indexed:* SD. *Bk. rev.:* 1-2, 400 words. *Aud.:* Ga, Sa.

This is intended for canoe, kayak, and raft enthusiasts on both white water and flat water. Much of its material, however, is about white-water kayaking, which gives the magazine its allure and probably much of its readership. Featured articles are predominantly about paddling destinations or narratives of paddling experiences, balanced by news items and material on boat and gear evaluations and paddling skills and techniques. There is an emphasis throughout on paddlers' health and safety and on environmental concerns. The quality of the publication is good, and it is enhanced by many action photos. A good choice for libraries needing a title focused on white-water paddle sports.

916. *PassageMaker: the trawler and ocean motorboat magazine.* [ISSN: 1095-7286] 1996. q. USD 25 domestic; CND 37 Canada; USD 49 elsewhere. Ed(s): Bill Parlatore. PassageMaker Magazine, Inc., 105 Eastern Ave, Ste 103, Annapolis, MD 21403. Adv. *Aud.:* Ga, Sa.

Trawlers are an up-and-coming area of interest in boating, and this title is a good contribution to the literature. It includes recommended travel locations, human interest stories about cruisers and their boats, technical aspects of this type of boating (electronics, engine maintenance, anticipating and coping with weather, etc.). Each issue includes boat and equipment reviews, an editorial feature called "From the Pilothouse," a food section (called "The Galley"), and an update highlighting upcoming events of interest to trawler fans. This will be both a practical help and a cosy read for a growing segment of library readers: Aging baby-boomers who don't relish the rigors of other kinds of boating are fast becoming trawler enthusiasts.

917. *Powerboat: the world's leading performance boating magazine.* [ISSN: 0032-6089] 1968. 11x/yr. USD 29 domestic; USD 32 Canada; USD 40 elsewhere. Ed(s): Gregg Mansfield, Doug Thompson. Nordskog Publishing, Inc., 2575 Vista Del Mar Dr., Ventura, CA 93001-3920; edit-dept@powerboatmag.com. Illus., adv. Sample. Circ: 50000 Paid and controlled. Vol. ends: Dec. *Aud.:* Ga.

An artfully done magazine targeted at high-performance powerboat enthusiasts, the main focus here is on evaluations of new boats, with an emphasis on performance features. Reviews are thorough and detailed, testing a boat's speed and handling characteristics, its construction and workmanship, and its interior design and overall impact. Many of these boats are also tested for their qualities as water-skiing boats. The magazine also features powerboat racing coverage, with commentary and results of racing events plus articles about significant figures in powerboat racing. Additional material includes information on products, accessories, and various watersports activities. The magazine has excellent photography and graphics, complemented by intelligent and informative writing. *Powerboat* is a very complete magazine for performance-minded boaters and would be a good complement to a basic collection.

918. *Practical Sailor.* [ISSN: 0161-8059] 1974. 26x/yr. USD 84 in US & Canada; USD 120 elsewhere. Ed(s): Darrell Nicholson. Belvoir Media Group, LLC, 800 Connecticut Ave, Norwalk, CT 06854-1631; customer_service@belvoir.com; http://www.belvoir.com. Circ: 50000 Paid. *Indexed:* SD. *Aud.:* Ga, Sa.

Practical Sailor is the *Consumer Reports* of sailing. The focus is on reviewing equipment and supplies with a review of one sailboat (both new and old are covered in various issues). Most of the magazine is dedicated to reviewing equipment and supplies, such as the best bottom paint by region, testing of hand-held radios, ladders, radar, autopilots, etc. The publication recently underwent a makeover, and now includes color photographs and appears in a glossier format. Sailboat reviews contain quotes from previous or existing customers about items they like or don't like; value/price graphs over the years starting with original cost; interior, exterior, hull, and manufacturing quality information; and how the boat handles under sail.

919. *Sail.* [ISSN: 0036-2700] 1970. m. USD 10 domestic; USD 15 Canada; USD 20 elsewhere. Ed(s): Peter Nielsen. Source Interlink Companies, 98 NWashington St, Boston, MA 02114; edisupport@sourceinterlink.com; http://www.sourceinterlink.com. Illus., adv. Sample. Circ: 170000 Paid. Vol. ends: Dec. Microform: PQC. *Indexed:* ConsI. *Bk. rev.:* 1-2, 200 words. *Aud.:* Ga, Ac.

A very popular magazine that provides a balanced selection of material, with an emphasis on boating knowledge and skills as applied to equipment, maintenance, navigation, and seamanship. Articles address these issues in very practical terms. Another focus is on cruising and racing activities. These are usually narratives describing interesting cruise destinations or situations that demonstrate sailing skills and experiences. The magazine's content applies to both small and large boats and to both novice and expert sailors. The consistent focus is on the enhancement of sailing skills. One of the boating periodicals with the highest circulation, this title contains a great deal of advertising that sometimes overwhelms the text. However, it is well done overall, and should be a core holding for most boating collections.

920. *Sailing: the beauty of sail.* Formerly: *Lake Michigan Sailing.* [ISSN: 0036-2719] 1966. m. USD 28 domestic; USD 39 Canada; USD 54 elsewhere. Ed(s): William F. Schanen, III. Port Publications, Inc., 125 E Main St, Port Washington, WI 53074. Illus., adv. Sample. Circ: 43802 Paid and free. Vol. ends: Aug. Microform: PQC. *Indexed:* BRI. *Bk. rev.:* 2-4, 200-400 words. *Aud.:* Ga.

An oversized magazine combining lengthy feature articles with pictorial beauty. Its primary content is balanced between cruising locales and thorough reviews of boats and equipment. Additional material covers maintenance skills, sailing techniques, and racing news. What separates this magazine from others is its sense of artistry. Not only is it tastefully done, but the photography is often stunning. The large format allows full-page photos to convey the panorama of certain places or the sensation of skimming through the water. An interesting, enjoyable, and often instructive magazine that does a very good job of portraying the sailing experience.

921. *Sailing World: the authority on performance sailing.* Former titles: *Yacht Racing and Cruising; Yacht Racing; One-Design and Offshore Yachtsman.* [ISSN: 0889-4094] 1962. 10x/yr. USD 28 domestic; USD 38 Canada; USD 48 elsewhere. Ed(s): John Burnham. The Sailing Company, 55 Hammarlund Way, Middletown, RI 02842. Illus., adv. Sample. Circ: 51376 Paid. Vol. ends: Dec/Jan. Microform: PQC. Online: EBSCO Publishing, EBSCO Host; Gale. *Indexed:* MASUSE. *Aud.:* Ga.

The definitive periodical for performance- and competition-oriented sailors. Its coverage includes narratives about competitive events and articles focusing on sailing techniques, boat technology, and racing tactics and strategies. The material is primarily oriented toward larger boats, but it is also applicable to smaller ones. Most articles are thorough and informative, with the intent of enhancing sailing skills and performance. The magazine also includes boat reviews and evaluations of high-performance equipment and gear. Racing news and results are included for many levels of competition. This is a visually appealing publication, with good photography, graphics, and layout design. The web site largely links to racing news and events, but it does provide an index for all magazine issues since 1991 and an archive of selected published articles. Intended for serious sailors involved in competitions, this is an excellent choice for libraries near sailing centers.

922. *Sea Kayaker.* [ISSN: 0829-3279] 1984. bi-m. USD 23.95; USD 4.95 newsstand/cover. Ed(s): Chris Cunningham. Sea Kayaker Inc., 7001 Seaview Ave, NW, Ste 135, Seattle, WA 98117; mail@seakayakermag.com; http://www.seakayakermag.com. Illus., adv. Sample. Circ: 28000 Paid and controlled. Vol. ends: Dec. *Indexed:* SD. *Bk. rev.:* 1-2, 500 words. *Aud.:* Ga, Sa.

The only publication dedicated specifically to the sport of sea kayaking. Interesting and informative, its primary content is lengthy first-person narratives of paddling adventures and related aspects, such as conditioning and health, food, safety, and camping. Additional feature material is usually instructional, dealing with techniques such as navigation or paddling. Coverage is rounded out with reviews of new kayaks, equipment, and products. There are occasional articles on environmental issues or wildlife. This publication is recommended for libraries located in coastal regions or near large, open bodies of water.

923. *ShowBoats International.* [ISSN: 0749-2952] 1982. m. USD 23.95 domestic; USD 38.95 Canada; USD 63.95 elsewhere. Ed(s): Jill Bobrow. CurtCo Robb Media LLC., 29160 Heathercliff Rd, Ste 200, Malibu, CA 90265; http://www.curtco.com. Adv. Circ: 50000. *Indexed:* ABIn. *Aud.:* Ga, Sa.

A fantasyland for boating enthusiasts, this title reviews showboats—and we're not talking the kind that used to run on the Mississippi. Reviews include boat specs, interior and exterior photos, biographical material on the wealthy individual and corporate owners, and the manufacturers of these beauties. Advertising is glossy, extensive, and targeted at the well-heeled—think Maserati, AIG Private Client Group, and Hublot watches. These showboats are the highest of the high-end, high-concept vessels typically costing in the millions of dollars. Your readership will probably not be buying these boats, but true boating enthusiasts can always dream.

924. *Trailer Boats: guiding avid boaters since 1971.* [ISSN: 0300-6557] 1971. 11x/yr. USD 16.97 domestic; USD 27.97 foreign; USD 4.99 newsstand/cover domestic. Ed(s): Ron Eldridge. Ehlert Publishing Group, Inc., 6420 N Sycamore Ln, Ste 100, Maple Grove, MN 55369-6003. Illus., adv. Sample. Circ: 102000 Paid. Vol. ends: Nov/Dec. Microform: PQC. Online: Gale; Northern Light Technology, Inc.; OCLC Online Computer Library Center, Inc.; ProQuest LLC (Ann Arbor). *Indexed:* ConsI. *Aud.:* Ga.

This magazine is dedicated to boats small enough to be towed on a trailer (generally powerboats less than 30 feet long). Content consists of thorough evaluations of new boats and engines and towing equipment and vehicles. It is the only boating resource that regularly features articles on towing vehicles and techniques and regulatory issues involved with towing. Additional material covers gear and accessories, seamanship, and boating activities. Much of the material has enough detail and technical description to make it very useful for boaters who do their own maintenance. The magazine is well written, has pleasing graphics, and is enjoyable to read. With its emphasis on those smaller, portable boats that are owned by a sizable segment of the boating community, this publication will appeal to a wide readership.

925. *The Woodenboat: the magazine for wooden boat owners, builders and designers.* [ISSN: 0095-067X] 1974. bi-m. USD 29.95 domestic; USD 34.95 in Canada & Mexico; USD 42.95 elsewhere. Ed(s): Jonathan A. Wilson, Matthew P Murphy. WoodenBoat Publications, Inc., Naskeag Rd, PO Box 78, Brooklin, ME 04616-0078; subscriptions@ woodenboat.com. Illus., adv. Sample. Circ: 106000 Paid. Vol. ends: Nov/Dec. *Indexed:* IHTDI. *Bk. rev.:* 2, 500-1,000 words. *Aud.:* Ga, Ac.

Modern boats are usually made of synthetic materials, but the tradition of building boats of wood still has a devoted following. This magazine is dedicated to preserving that tradition, and it is one of the finest and most informative of all boating periodicals. It covers the history, design, building, and preservation of wooden boats of any size or style. Feature articles range from highly detailed descriptions and plans for building or restoring a boat to historical pieces on a style of boat or a boat-building operation. Articles often include substantive biographical profiles of individuals prominent in some area of the wooden-boat industry. There is also material on wood technology and tools and techniques for working with wood. Detailed feature articles provide more depth than is usually found in boating periodicals. The color photography, illustrations, and design all lend a sense of artistry to the magazine. This stylish publication is a pleasure to read and should be in a core collection.

926. *Yachting: power and sail.* [ISSN: 0043-9940] 1907. m. USD 19.97; USD 5 newsstand/cover per issue domestic; USD 6 newsstand/cover per issue Canada. Time4 Media, Inc., 2 Park Ave, New York, NY 10016. Illus., adv. Sample. Circ: 133016 Paid. Vol. ends: Jun/Dec. Microform:

PQC. Online: EBSCO Publishing, EBSCO Host; Gale; Northern Light Technology, Inc.; ProQuest K-12 Learning Solutions; ProQuest LLC (Ann Arbor). *Indexed:* ASIP, BRI, CBRI, ConsI, MASUSE, SD. *Aud.:* Ga.

This title's coverage emphasizes large, upscale yachts plus activities and lifestyles associated with those boats. It is intended for experienced, knowledgeable yachtsmen of both powerboats and sailboats and contains lengthy, well-written articles on a variety of boating topics. Evaluations of new boats are numerous, as are cruise narratives describing interesting, exotic, or out-of-the-way places to visit. There are a number of informational articles on boating know-how, especially relating to equipment. The magazine has high production values and a very good sense of style. There is an appreciable amount of advertising, with the latter half of each issue given over to ads for boat brokerages and chartering services. This is a sound, stylish, and useful magazine that represents the high end of boating very well.

■ BOOKS AND BOOK REVIEWS

See also Archives and Manuscripts; Bibliography; Library and Information Science; and Printing and Graphic Arts sections. Book reviews in subject areas are located within their specific subject areas (e.g., *Science Books and Films* in the Science and Technology section).

Janie B. Silveria, Coordinator of Reference Services, California State University Monterey Bay Library, 100 Campus Center, Seaside, CA 93955, janie_silveria@csumb.edu

Introduction

In an 1873 poem, Emily Dickinson expressed it well: "There is no frigate like a book / To take us lands away." Children of today may puzzle over the meaning of "frigate," but they will still understand what a book is, thankfully. Despite predictions of a paperless world, books of all types and formats—from hardback and paperback to audiobook and e-book, from scholarly treatise to picture book and cookbook—are still the heart of most libraries' collections. Computers and the Internet have, of course, brought fundamental changes to both publishing and librarianship; one simultaneous benefit and challenge is the plethora of information now available about new and forthcoming titles. Most of the resources listed below have been used by generations of librarians seeking reliable, critical information on book publishing and selection. In many cases, the print versions of these magazines have been augmented by electronic editions, which may include enhanced features such as searchable archives, e-newsletters, or RSS feeds.

Basic Periodicals

Ems: *Booklist, Center for Children's Books. Bulletin, The Horn Book Magazine;* Hs: *Booklist, Kirkus Reviews;* Ga: *Booklist, Kirkus Reviews, New York Review of Books, New York Times Book Review, Publishers Weekly;* Ac: *Choice, London Review of Books, New York Review of Books, New York Times Book Review, Publishers Weekly, T L S.*

Basic Abstracts and Indexes

Book Review Digest, Book Review Index, Children's Book Review Index, Library Literature.

927. *American Book Review.* [ISSN: 0149-9408] 1977. bi-m. USD 30 (Individuals, USD 24; USD 35 foreign). Ed(s): Joe Amato. Writers Review, Inc., c/o Unit for Contemporary Literature, Campus Box 4241, Normal, IL 61790-4241; rakaise@ilstu.edu; http://www.litline.org. Illus., adv. Sample. Circ: 5000. Vol. ends: Sep/Oct. Online: EBSCO Publishing, EBSCO Host; OCLC Online Computer Library Center, Inc.; H.W. Wilson. *Indexed:* AmHI, ArtHuCI, BRD, BRI, CBRI, HumInd, SSCI. *Bk. rev.:* 25-30, 500-2,500 words. *Aud.:* Ac, Sa.

Edited and produced by writers for other writers and for the general public, *ABR* provides informed and informative literary criticism. Its reviews focus on "frequently neglected" published works of fiction, poetry, and literary criticism from small, regional, university, ethnic, avant-garde, and women's presses. Well-known authors such as Rudolfo Anaya, Andrei Codrescu, Joyce Carol Oates, and Ishmael Reed serve as contributing and associate editors. In recent issues, highlights include a survey of prizewinning poetry books, reviews of debut fiction, and opinions on the 100 best opening lines from novels. Academic libraries with strong collections in modern American literature will appreciate this bimonthly resource. Excerpts from issues back to 1997 are available on the web site, along with *ABR* lists of notable first novels, literary sports fiction, and feminist children's books.

928. *Black Issues Book Review.* [ISSN: 1522-0524] 1999. bi-m. USD 14.95 domestic; USD 21.95 Canada; USD 28 elsewhere. Ed(s): Clarence V Reynolds. Target Market News, Empire State Bldg, 350 Fifth Ave, Ste 1522, New York, NY 10118-0165. Illus., adv. Sample. Vol. ends: Nov/Dec. *Indexed:* AmHI, BRI, CBRI, ENW, IIBP, RGPR, RILM. *Bk. rev.:* 15-20 (100-250 words). *Aud.:* Ga.

Billed as the "African-American book publishing authority," this glossy bimonthly combines reviews of current fiction and nonfiction by black authors with broader articles on "the arts and culture of the African Diaspora." Along with illustrated reviews of popular fiction, nonfiction, and children's books, each issue contains such regular features as "Between the Lines" (news of the publishing industry), "Book Bytes" (the Internet and publishing), "Eye" (coffee-table and art books), and "Tribute" (black writers who have made a significant contribution to society and culture). Many news articles and review excerpts are available on the web site. Most public libraries will want to subscribe, both for selection purposes and to offer to their clientele.

929. *Book Links: connecting books, libraries, and classrooms.* [ISSN: 1055-4742] 1991. 6x/yr. USD 39.95 domestic; USD 46 foreign; USD 8 per issue. Ed(s): Laura Tillotson. American Library Association, 50 E Huron St, Chicago, IL 60611-2795; http://www.ala.org. Illus., index, adv. Circ: 30000. Vol. ends: Aug. *Indexed:* AmHI, MASUSE. *Bk. rev.:* 50-75, 50-150 words. *Aud.:* Ems, Ga.

An offshoot of *Booklist*, this readable, attractive magazine is aimed at teachers, librarians, library media specialists, booksellers, parents, and other adults interested in connecting children with high-quality books. Packed with ideas for using books in the classroom and fostering children's interest in reading, each issue of *Book Links* focuses on a core curriculum area, including science, social studies, language arts, history, geography, and multicultural literature. Arranged by grade level, useful annotated bibliographies identify best books on a variety of popular topics (e.g., baseball, adoption, money, family history, etc., in a recent issue on social studies), and include ideas for discussion questions and related activities. Author biographies and interviews are also regular features, as are how-to articles written by educators. Engaging yet practical, this periodical would be welcome in any public or school library.

930. *BookEnds: the book pl@ce magazine.* 1997. m. Free. Ed(s): Chris Martin. Book Data, Globe House, 1 Chertsey Rd, Twickenham, TW1 1LR, United Kingdom; editor@thebookplace.com; http://www.bookends.co.uk/. *Aud.:* Ems, Hs, Ga.

This online publication is an adjunct to the British equivalent of Amazon.com, the BookPl@ce web site. This useful site is packed with news, reviews, competitions, short stories, author interviews, and top ten lists from the world of books. The editors clearly enjoy their work in providing "over eighty pages every month of good reading and irreverent humour." There is a "Reviewers Reviewed" section that summarizes recent criticism from the British press. Readers can browse by subject, from art and antiques to travel, to get overviews of new releases. Extracts of selected books are provided, along with lists of literary awards and special features such as a guide to television and movie tie-ins.

931. *Booklist.* Formerly (until 1969): *Booklist and Subscription Books Bulletin.* [ISSN: 0006-7385] 1905. bi-m. 22/yr. USD 89.95 domestic; USD 105 foreign; USD 6 per issue. Ed(s): Bill Ott. American Library Association, 50 E Huron St, Chicago, IL 60611-2795; http://www.ala.org. Illus., index, adv. Circ: 30000 Paid. Vol. ends: Sep. CD-ROM: SilverPlatter Information, Incorporated. Microform: PQC. Online: EBSCO Publishing, EBSCO Host; Florida Center for Library Automation; Gale; Northern Light Technology, Inc.; OCLC Online

Computer Library Center, Inc.; ProQuest K-12 Learning Solutions; ProQuest LLC (Ann Arbor). *Indexed:* ABS&EES, AmHI, BRD, BRI, CBRI, ConsI, GardL, ISTA, LibLit, MASUSE, MRD, MicrocompInd. *Bk. rev.:* 200-250, 75-150 words. *Aud.:* Ems, Hs, Ga, Ac.

Now available in an augmented online edition at www.booklistonline.com, this venerable ALA publication has passed its 100th anniversary. *Booklist* is primarily intended as a guide to current library materials in many formats appropriate for public libraries and school library media centers, with small- and medium-sized libraries receiving particular consideration. According to its long-established selection policy, all materials reviewed in the Adult Books, Books for Youth, and Media sections are recommended for purchase; both quality and anticipated demand are considerations for inclusion. Starred reviews indicate outstanding works. Many articles are thematic (e.g., mysteries, poetry, black history), providing "best of" lists in particular subject areas. Other regular features include the Read-alikes section, which gives readers' advisory recommendations, and the He Reads/She Reads comparative reviews. The Reference Books Bulletin section, edited by a separate editorial board, contains longer reviews of reference sources in any format. For over a century and into the foreseeable future, *Booklist* remains a vital source for collection development, particularly in public libraries.

932. *Bookmarks: for everyone who hasn't read everything.* [ISSN: 1546-0657] 2002. bi-m. USD 29.95 domestic; USD 39.95 Canada; USD 59.95 elsewhere. Ed(s): Jon Phillips. Bookmarks Publishing LLC, 1818 MLK Blvd #181, Chapel Hill, NC 27514. Illus. *Bk. rev.:* 55-65, 500 words. *Aud.:* Ga, Ac.

The subtitle says it all: *Bookmarks* is for avid readers, for anyone for whom the "So many books, so little time" T-shirt resonates. Glossy and graphically appealing, this bimonthly focuses on new books, but also spotlights classic authors and their masterworks. The unique aspect of this magazine is its rating system and summary of critical response from the national media. Using a scale of one to five stars, the editors summarize other critics' reviews of new books, then add their own evaluation. This "clearinghouse" function is indeed a timesaver for library selectors and potential book buyers, presenting a quick visual representation of critical reception from national newspapers and other review sources. Each issue also features a topical overview—cookbooks, graphic novels, travel, wine—and contains a Readers Recommend section. A fine addition for public libraries.

933. *Books in Canada: the Canadian review of books.* [ISSN: 0045-2564] 1971. m. 9/yr. CND 53 (Individuals, CND 37.50). Ed(s): Olga Stein. Canadian Review of Books Ltd., 427 Mount Pleasant Rd, Toronto, ON M4S 2L8, Canada. Illus., index, adv. Circ: 10000. Vol. ends: Dec. Microform: MMP; MML. Online: EBSCO Publishing, EBSCO Host; Micromedia ProQuest. *Indexed:* BRD, BRI, CBCARef, CBRI, CPerI. *Bk. rev.:* 20-30, 500-2,000 words. *Aud.:* Ga, Ac, Sa.

As its title implies, *Books in Canada* provides a review and discussion forum for contemporary Canadian literature. Signed reviews are in-depth and evaluative. The accompanying web site (www.booksincanada.com) provides an opportunity for readers to present feedback. A partnership with Amazon.ca is evident in special features on the site. Amazon now co-sponsors the annual Books in Canada First Novel Award, and there are links to Amazon from individual online reviews. Back issues of the magazine are available online in full text from 1971 (some issues in pdf). Another unique feature on the web site is called Timescroll; enter a date (from 4241 BCE to the present) to view summaries of historical events, literature, music, art, etc., for that date. Within these accounts, keyword links lead to lists of books related to that word or name (the booklists, in turn, link to—you guessed it—Amazon). Commercial ties aside, this publication and its web site are interesting and definitely worth investigating.

934. *The Bookseller.* [ISSN: 0006-7539] 1858. w. GBP 175 domestic; GBP 189 in Europe; GBP 231 elsewhere. Ed(s): Neill Denny. Nielsen Entertainment Media UK Ltd, 5th Fl, Endeavour House, 189 Shaffeday Ave, London, WC2H 8TJ, United Kingdom. Illus., adv. Circ: 11250. Vol. ends: Dec. Online: EBSCO Publishing, EBSCO Host; Gale. *Indexed:* AmHI, BrHumI, IBR, LISA. *Bk. rev.:* 30-40, 100-150 words. *Aud.:* Ga, Ac, Sa.

This publication is the British counterpart to *Publishers Weekly*, providing ongoing coverage of events and trends in publishing and the book trade in the United Kingdom. In addition to weekly print issues, there are numerous monthly supplements (e.g., "Travel Bookseller"). Comprehensive Buyer's Guides and Children's Buyer's Guides listing forthcoming titles are issued twice annually. The Bookseller.com web site provides daily news and commentary plus a mix of author interviews, career advice, job opportunities, bestseller charts, and searchable archives. Special features include a searchable directory of trade-related organizations and an interactive forum for debate on current issues. For any library with interest or collection strengths in British publishing.

935. *BookWire.* [ISSN: 0000-1759] 1999. irreg. approx. m. Free. R.R. Bowker LLC, 630 Central Ave, New Providence, NJ 07974; info@bowker.com; http://www.bowker.com/. Adv. *Aud.:* Ga, Ac, Sa.

Although more a portal than a periodical, *BookWire* is a useful one-stop shop for information about the book industry. The site contains reviews "not found anywhere else," author interviews and biographies, trade news, statistical information on the book industry, and monthly themed booklists on currently popular topics. There are also sets of links to authors' and publishers' web sites, libraries, booksellers, editors and agents, trade organizations, book groups on the web, and more.

936. *Boston Review: a political and literary forum.* Formerly (until 1982): *New Boston Review.* [ISSN: 0734-2306] 1975. bi-m. USD 40 (Individuals, USD 20). Ed(s): Joshua J Friedman, Joshua Cohen. Boston Critic, Inc., 30 Wadsworth St, E53 407 MIT, Cambridge, MA 02139-4307. Illus., index, adv. Sample. Circ: 170000 Paid and controlled. Vol. ends: Dec/Jan. Microform: LIB; PQC. Online: EBSCO Publishing, EBSCO Host; LexisNexis. *Indexed:* AltPI, AmHI, BRI, CBRI, HumInd, IAPV, IBR, IBZ, LeftInd, MLA-IB. *Bk. rev.:* 20-25, 250-2,000 words. *Aud.:* Ga, Ac, Sa.

Boston Review is self-described as "a left-center of gravity magazine of ideas," putting poetry and political commentary on the same page and thereby transcending the scope of either a literary review or political journal. Each issue is an intriguing blend of poetry, short fiction, essays on current events, and book reviews. Regular features are the New Democracy Forum, which probes sociopolitical issues from the Iraq War to "Caregiving in Crisis," and the New Fiction Forum, which seeks to identify original, creative writing and discuss emerging trends and innovations in fiction. The magazine's web site provides free full text of articles and reviews, both current and archival, and also contains a bookstore locator, writing contests, and a list of "literary links" to other sites. This highly regarded publication is recommended for both academic and public libraries.

C M Magazine. See Canada section.

937. *Center for Children's Books. Bulletin.* [ISSN: 0008-9036] 1947. m. except combined issue July/Aug. USD 85 USD 9 per issue. Ed(s): Deborah Stevenson. The Johns Hopkins University Press, 2715 N Charles St, Baltimore, MD 21218-4363; http://muse.jhu.edu. Illus., index, adv. Circ: 3000 Paid. Vol. ends: Jul/Aug. Microform: PQC. Online: EBSCO Publishing, EBSCO Host; OCLC Online Computer Library Center, Inc.; Project MUSE; ProQuest LLC (Ann Arbor); SwetsWise Online Content; H.W. Wilson. Reprint: PSC. *Indexed:* BRD, BRI, CBRI. *Bk. rev.:* 70, 50-100 words. *Aud.:* Ems, Hs, Ga, Ac.

The *Bulletin* rightly calls itself "one of the nation's leading children's review journals for school and public librarians." Signed evaluative reviews are thorough, and include complete bibliographic information and intended grade level. There is a ratings code ranging from NR (not recommended) to starred R (recommended book of special distinction). Annually, a list of Blue Ribbon Books is provided. The magazine's web site (http://bccb.lis.uiuc.edu) includes summaries of the monthly features, a listing of the starred titles, and access to a subject index. Full text of the reviews themselves, in a searchable database, is available only to print subscribers. An essential source for children's librarians, or for academic librarians selecting for children's literature collections.

938. *Choice Magazine: current reviews for academic libraries.* [ISSN: 0009-4978] 1963. m. USD 300 in North America; USD 350 elsewhere. Ed(s): Francine Graf. Association of College and Research Libraries, 100 Riverview Center, Middletown, CT 06457; acrl@ala.org. Illus., index, adv. Refereed. Circ: 3500 Paid. Vol. ends: Jul/Aug. CD-ROM: SilverPlatter Information, Incorporated. Microform: PQC. Online: EBSCO Publishing, EBSCO Host; Gale; ProQuest LLC (Ann Arbor). *Indexed:* BAS, BRD, BRI, CBRI, IBR, IBZ, ISTA, LibLit, MRD. *Bk. rev.:* 600, 100-250 words. *Aud.:* Ga, Ac.

Choice has long been the selection tool of, well, choice for thousands of academic libraries. A publication of ALA's Association of College and Research Libraries (ACRL), the journal reviews scholarly books, electronic media, and Internet resources of interest to those in higher education. Reviews, grouped by discipline, are concise and authoritative, and give suggested LC class numbers, audience/academic level, and a final "Summing Up" recommendation regarding purchase. Also included in each issue are a longer bibliographic essay on selected topics or trends, and a list of significant forthcoming titles. An annual list of Outstanding Academic Titles is published in January, and a special issue devoted to best-of-the-web reviews is also issued annually. For an additional fee, subscribers can receive reviews on cards or online. Summing up: highly recommended for all libraries, particularly undergraduate collections.

939. *Criticas (Online Edition): an English speaker's guide to the latest Spanish language titles.* 2005. m. Free. Reed Business Information, 360 Park Ave South, New York, NY 10010; http://www.reedbusiness.com. *Bk. rev.:* 100, 75-200 words. *Aud.:* Ga, Sa.

Formerly a bimonthly print publication, *Criticas* is now a free monthly e-newsletter that provides comprehensive coverage of the international Spanish-language publishing market. The online edition (www.criticasmagazine.com) is complemented by two print issues a year, one published in May to coincide with BookExpo America and the other in November for distribution at the Guadalajara Book Fair. *Criticas* presents reviews of adult and children's books, interviews with major authors, profiles of Spanish-language imprints and programs, and coverage of Spanish-language audios, videos, web sites, and backlist titles. Special resources on the magazine's web site include a directory of the Spanish-language publishing marketplace, lists of Spanish-language literary awards, and collection development guides such as a list of the top 100 Spanish-language fiction titles. A valuable resource for public libraries, or for any library serving Spanish-speaking clientele.

940. *E-Streams: electronic reviews of science and technology references covering engineering, agriculture, medicine and science.* [ISSN: 1098-4399] 1998. m. Free. Ed(s): H Robert Malinowsky. Yankee Book Peddler, Inc., 999 Maple St, Contoocook, NH 03229; estreams@ybp.com; http://www.e-streams.com. *Indexed:* BRI, CBRI. *Bk. rev.:* 30-50, 100-250 words. *Aud.:* Ga, Ac.

A collaborative venture between an academic librarian and the well-known book jobber YBP Book Services, *E-Streams* provides online reviews of new titles in science, technology, and medicine. Subject librarians and professors contribute signed reviews, which include tables of contents and bibliographic information. Archival issues are available free on the web site in html or pdf formats, and are searchable by keyword. Though publication became less frequent during 2005–06, *E-Streams* continues to be a valuable selection tool for academic libraries and public libraries with substantial science collections.

941. *Horn Book Guide to Children's and Young Adult Books.* [ISSN: 1044-405X] 1989. s-a. USD 35 domestic introductry rate; USD 49.50 renewals domestic. Ed(s): Kitty Flynn. Horn Book, Inc., 56 Roland St, Ste 200, Boston, MA 02129-1235; info@hbook.com; http://www.hbook.com. Illus., index, adv. Sample. Circ: 5000 Paid and free. Vol. ends: Jan/Jun. Online: ProQuest K-12 Learning Solutions; ProQuest LLC (Ann Arbor). *Indexed:* BRD, BRI, CBRI. *Bk. rev.:* 2,000, 40-50 words. *Aud.:* Ems, Hs, Ga.

Published twice annually, this offshoot of *The Horn Book Magazine* reviews and rates virtually every children's and young adult hardcover book published in the United States. Fiction entries are arranged by genre or grade level, from preschool to young adult. Nonfiction is categorized by subject, according to the divisions of the Dewey Decimal System. Brief, critical annotations are signed and include a numerical rating, with notable titles indicated by a symbol. There are useful, comprehensive indexes by author/illustrator, title, series, and subject. An electronic version of the *Horn Book Guide* is available by separate subscription. Sample content is available on the www.hbook.com web site; subscribers to the print *Horn Book* publications may also preview many of the reviews in advance. An essential resource for all children's literature collections.

942. *The Horn Book Magazine: recommending books for children and young adults.* [ISSN: 0018-5078] 1924. bi-m. USD 34.95 domestic introductory rate 1st yr.; USD 49 renewals domestic. Ed(s): Roger Sutton. Horn Book, Inc., 56 Roland St, Ste 200, Boston, MA 02129-1235; info@hbook.com; http://www.hbook.com. Illus., index, adv. Sample. Circ: 16000 Paid and free. Vol. ends: Nov/Dec. Microform: NBI; PQC. Online: EBSCO Publishing, EBSCO Host; Florida Center for Library Automation; Gale; Northern Light Technology, Inc.; OCLC Online Computer Library Center, Inc.; ProQuest K-12 Learning Solutions; ProQuest LLC (Ann Arbor); H.W. Wilson. *Indexed:* ABS&EES, ASIP, BRD, BRI, CBRI, LISA, LibLit, MRD. *Bk. rev.:* 70-120, 100-300 words. *Aud.:* Ems, Hs, Ga, Ac.

Immediately identifiable by its artistic covers, *The Horn Book Magazine* has long been an insightful source of critical information on contemporary children's literature. Each issue includes lengthy signed and illustrated reviews of picture books, fiction, poetry, nonfiction, and audiobooks. Most titles are recommended; starred items indicate outstanding works. In addition to reviews themselves, readers will find editorials and feature articles on authors, issues, and trends. A perennial feature called "The Hunt Breakfast" gives information on current literary awards, conferences, and other announcements. On the magazine's web site are selected articles and reviews from current and past issues, plus lists of recommended reading for parents and teachers, an interactive forum, news, award lists, and more. A "Virtual History Exhibit" provides an interesting glimpse into *The Horn Book*'s first 75 years, incorporating artifacts and memorabilia, notable correspondence and articles, recordings, and anecdotes. Highly recommended for school and public libraries, and for academic libraries with children's literature collections.

943. *January Magazine.* 1997. d. Free. Ed(s): Linda Richards. January Publishing Inc., 101-1001 W Broadway, Ste 192, Vancouver, BC V6H 4E4, Canada; scribe@mindlink.bc.ca; http://www.januarymagazine.com. *Aud.:* Ga.

Launched in 1997 in the early days of electronic-only publications, *January Magazine* has become one of the most popular and respected book-related sites on the web. The site presents reviews of contemporary fiction, nonfiction, and children's books, plus interviews with authors worldwide. Signed reviews are lengthy and readable, and reflect the contributors' insight into the writing process and their own passion for books. Special sections include the "Blue Coupe," which reviews music and DVDs. Subscriptions to free e-mail updates and/or the "Rap Sheet," an e-newsletter about crime fiction, are available via registration.

944. *The Journal of Electronic Publishing.* [ISSN: 1080-2711] 1995. q. Free. Ed(s): Eve Trager, Judith Axler Turner. University of Michigan Press, 839 Greene St., Ann Arbor, MI 48104-3209; um.press@umich.edu; http://www.press.umich.edu. Refereed. *Indexed:* CommAb, ISTA, LISA, LibLit, PAIS. *Aud.:* Ac, Sa.

It's back! After a hiatus of more than three years (a long time in the online universe), *JEP* resumed publication in early 2006. Devoted to examining the range of issues affecting publishing in an electronic environment, this peer-reviewed e-journal is intended for "the thoughtful forward-thinking publisher, librarian, scholar, or author." The comeback issue has provocative articles on Google Scholar, intellectual property on the Internet, electronic poetry, and the economics of e-publishing. Full text of back issues is available on the journal's web site. Required reading for anyone interested in the current and future state of scholarly electronic publishing.

945. *Journal of Scholarly Publishing.* Formerly: *Scholarly Publishing.* [ISSN: 1198-9742] 1969. q. CND 100 domestic; USD 100 United States; USD 120 elsewhere. Ed(s): Tom Radko. University of Toronto Press, Journals Division, 5201 Dufferin St, Toronto, ON M3H 5T8, Canada; journals@utpress.utoronto.ca; http://www.utpjournals.com. Illus., index, adv. Sample. Refereed. Circ: 1200. Vol. ends: Jul. Microform: MML;

PQC. Online: EBSCO Publishing, EBSCO Host; OCLC Online Computer Library Center, Inc.; OhioLINK; Project MUSE; SwetsWise Online Content. Reprint: PSC. *Indexed:* AmH&L, ArtHuCI, BAS, CBCARef, CLI, FR, HEA, HistAb, IBR, IBZ, ILP, ISTA, LISA, LibLit, MLA-IB, SSCI. *Bk. rev.:* 1-2, 400-500 words. *Aud.:* Ac, Sa.

As its title implies, this peer-reviewed journal concerns all aspects of the scholarly publishing world, from authoring and editing to marketing and production. Combining philosophical analysis with practical advice, the journal addresses such topics as the future of scholarly communication, scholarship on the web, digitalization, copyrights, editorial policies, computer applications, marketing, and pricing models. Regular features include an editorial column titled "The Transom" and a small section of book reviews. A vital resource for college and university libraries that are interested in following trends in academic publishing and effects of new technology on the transmission of scholarly ideas.

946. *Kirkus Reviews: adult, young adult and children's book reviews.* [ISSN: 0042-6598] 1933. m. USD 450 combined subscription domestic print & online eds.; USD 505 combined subscription foreign print & online eds. Ed(s): Anne Larsen. Nielsen Business Publications, 770 Broadway, New York, NY 10003-9595; bmcomm@vnuinc.com; http://www.nielsenbusinessmedia.com. Illus., index. Circ: 5000 Paid and controlled. Microform: PQC. Online: EBSCO Publishing, EBSCO Host; Florida Center for Library Automation; Gale; LexisNexis. *Indexed:* BRD, BRI, CBRI, MASUSE. *Bk. rev.:* 320 words. *Aud.:* Ems, Hs, Ga, Ac.

This long-standing review service, now augmented by an online database and e-newsletter, provides 500 pre-publication book reviews each month. Written by subject specialists, *Kirkus Reviews* is intended for libraries, bookstores, the media, and others who want to be informed about new books before they go on sale. Unsigned reviews are arranged by genre: fiction, mystery, science fiction, nonfiction, and children's and young adult. Full bibliographic information and expected publication date are included; starred titles are judged to be "of remarkable merit." Several special editions are published annually, such as "The Best Books for Reading Groups." The web site includes searchable indexes to current and archival content; full text for most reviews is accessible only by subscribers. A highly useful selection tool for public libraries.

947. *Kliatt: reviews of selected current paperbacks, hardcover fiction, audiobooks, and educational software.* Former titles: *Kliatt Young Adult Paperback Book Guide; Kliatt Paperback Book Guide.* [ISSN: 1065-8602] 1967. 6x/yr. USD 39 domestic; USD 41 foreign. Ed(s): Claire Rosser. Kliatt, 33 Bay State Rd, Wellesley, MA 02481-3244; kliatt@aol.com. Illus., index, adv. Sample. Circ: 2300. Vol. ends: Nov. Microform: PQC. Online: Gale. *Indexed:* BRI, CBRI, MRD. *Bk. rev.:* 150-200, 150-200 words. *Aud.:* Hs, Ga.

Kliatt, a bimonthly magazine, publishes reviews of paperback books, hardcover fiction for adolescents, audiobooks, and educational software recommended for libraries and classrooms serving young adults. Signed reviews by educators and librarians are arranged by broad subject area and are coded by reading level and difficulty (junior high, senior high, advanced students/adults). Starred reviews highlight exceptional books. Each issue includes a lead article of interest to librarians and teachers (e.g., "To Blog or Not to Blog?") and a title index. There is an annual compilation of Editor's Choice titles for hardcover YA fiction and audiobooks. An invaluable resource for school or public librarians serving young adults.

The Literary Review. See Literary Reviews section.

948. *London Review of Books.* [ISSN: 0260-9592] 1979. s-m. GBP 63.72 domestic; GBP 76.50 in Europe; USD 42 United States. Ed(s): Mary-Kay Wilmers. L R B Ltd., 28 Little Russell St, London, WC1A 2HN, United Kingdom; subs@lrb.co.uk. Illus., index, adv. Circ: 42525. Vol. ends: Dec. Microform: PQC. *Indexed:* AmHI, BEL&L, BRD, BRI, BrHumI, CBRI, MLA-IB, RI-1, RILM. *Bk. rev.:* 15-20, 1,500-2,500 words. *Aud.:* Ga, Ac.

Established in 1979 when the *Times Literary Supplement* was on hiatus due to a lock-out, the *London Review of Books* has since flourished as a twice-monthly independent literary review. Content and format are similar to that of the venerable *TLS* and the *New York Review of Books* (see entries below). Signed critical commentaries on contemporary British literature contributed by notable writers, critics, and thinkers are essay-length and scholarly in tone. Some poetry is included, and there is an active Letters to the Editor section and a multi-page classified section. On the *LRB* web site are thorough indexes to the archives by subject and contributor, plus full text of selected articles. Primarily of interest to academic libraries, but will also find readership in larger public libraries.

MultiCultural Review. See Ethnic Studies section.

949. *New York Review of Books.* [ISSN: 0028-7504] 1963. 20x/yr. USD 69 combined subscription domestic; USD 89 combined subscription Canada; USD 105 combined subscription elsewhere. Ed(s): Robert Silvers, Robert Silvers. N Y R E V, Inc., 1755 Broadway, 5th Fl, New York, NY 10019-3780; nyrb@nybooks.com. Illus., adv. Circ: 130000 Paid. Vol. ends: Jan. Microform: PQC. Online: EBSCO Publishing, EBSCO Host; Northern Light Technology, Inc.; OCLC Online Computer Library Center, Inc.; H.W. Wilson. *Indexed:* A&ATA, ABS&EES, AltPI, AmHI, AnthLit, ArtHuCI, BRD, BRI, CBRI, FLI, FutSurv, IAPV, LRI, MASUSE, MLA-IB, MusicInd, NTA, PRA, RGPR, RI-1, RILM, SSCI. *Bk. rev.:* 15-20, 2,000-3,500 words. *Aud.:* Ga, Ac, Sa.

To browse the archives of the *New York Review of Books* is to view a Who's Who of contemporary American literature and culture; its inaugural issue, for example, included contributions from Susan Sontag, Norman Mailer, Gore Vidal, John Berryman, Robert Lowell, Adrienne Rich, and William Styron. Stimulating essays on current topics, lengthy reviews by and about major authors, and original poetry comprise the core of this highly regarded publication. Full text of many articles is available on the *NYRB* web site (www.nybooks.com), with some content restricted to subscribers. The online archives are fully indexed and cross-linked, and are searchable by date, author, keyword, and other specific fields. The clever caricatures by artist David Levine that illustrate the print issues have become famous in their own right; the web site provides a gallery of classic Levines for browsing or purchase. An essential source for academic libraries, and for most public libraries.

950. *New York Times Book Review.* [ISSN: 0028-7806] 1896. w. USD 54.60 domestic; USD 74.36 foreign. Ed(s): Sam Tanenhaus. New York Times Company, 229 W 43rd St, New York, NY 10036; http://www.nytimes.com/books/home/. Illus., index, adv. Circ: 1638908. Vol. ends: Dec. Microform: PQC. Online: Gale; Newsbank, Inc.; ProQuest LLC (Ann Arbor). *Indexed:* ABS&EES, AmHI, ArtHuCI, BEL&L, BRD, BRI, CBRI, GardL, LRI, MLA-IB, MusicInd, NTA, NewsAb, RGPR, RI-1, RILM. *Bk. rev.:* 45-50, 250-2,500 words. *Aud.:* Ga, Ac, Sa.

As a supplement to the huge Sunday edition of *The New York Times*, the *NYTBR* has the widest circulation and potential readership of any American review source. Its evaluations of noteworthy and/or newsworthy publications have influenced bookselling for over a century. New fiction and nonfiction, both scholarly and popular, are the focus of longer reviews, with regular coverage of mysteries, children's books, first novels, and pop culture. The *Review*'s bestseller lists, themselves a key indicator and selection tool for librarians, have expanded over the years to include multiple categories: hardcover fiction, nonfiction, and "advice" books; paperback fiction, nonfiction, and advice; and children's books. Online access to a searchable archive of reviews dating from 1981 is free, but requires one-time registration. Another online feature is "First Chapters," which tantalizes readers by providing the opening chapters of selected books. Every library, large or small, should utilize this core resource.

951. *Publishers Weekly: the international news magazine of book publishing.* [ISSN: 0000-0019] 1872. w. USD 239.99 domestic; USD 299.99 in Canada & Mexico; USD 399.99 elsewhere. Ed(s): Sara Nelson, Robin Lenz. Reed Business Information, 360 Park Ave South, New York, NY 10010; http://www.reedbusiness.com. Illus., index, adv. Circ: 38500 Paid. Vol. ends: Dec. Microform: CIS; PQC. Online: EBSCO Publishing, EBSCO Host; Factiva, Inc.; Florida Center for Library Automation; Gale; LexisNexis; OCLC Online Computer

Library Center, Inc.; ProQuest K-12 Learning Solutions; ProQuest LLC (Ann Arbor); H.W. Wilson. *Indexed:* ABIn, ABS&EES, BAS, BPI, BRD, BRI, CBRI, CWI, GardL, IBR, LISA, LRI, LibLit, MASUSE, PAIS, RGPR, RI-1, RILM. *Bk. rev.:* 70, 50-150 words. *Aud.:* Ga, Ac, Sa.

Another core title for book selectors, particularly in public libraries, *PW* covers news and trends of interest in the contemporary publishing and bookselling trade. Though the subtitle reflects an international scope, most information has a U.S. focus. Useful features include advance reviews of forthcoming titles, and bestseller lists in a variety of categories, such as "books most borrowed in U.S. public libraries." Each issue also has special feature articles, author interviews, regular columns, calendars of events, and classifieds. The web version provides access to reviews from 1987 on, with most of the content restricted to subscribers. Other web enhancements include a daily e-newsletter, a "Talk Back Tuesday" discussion forum, and interactive calendars and job listings.

952. *Publishing Research Quarterly.* Formerly (until 1991): *Book Research Quarterly.* [ISSN: 1053-8801] 1986. q. EUR 225 print & online eds. Ed(s): Robert Baensch. Springer New York LLC, 233 Spring St, New York, NY 10013-1578; journals-ny@springer.com; http://www.springer.com/. Illus., index, adv. Refereed. Circ: 800. Vol. ends: Winter. Online: EBSCO Publishing, EBSCO Host; Florida Center for Library Automation; Gale; OCLC Online Computer Library Center, Inc.; OhioLINK; ProQuest LLC (Ann Arbor); SwetsWise Online Content. Reprint: PSC. *Indexed:* ABIn, AbAn, AgeL, AmHI, FR, IBR, IBZ, ISTA, LISA, MLA-IB, PAIS, SSCI. *Bk. rev.:* 2-3, 1,000 words. *Aud.:* Ac, Sa.

This refereed journal covers the publishing environment writ large. It provides "analysis of the content development, production, distribution, and marketing of books, magazines, journals, and online information services in relation to the social, political, economic, and technological conditions that shape the publishing process, extending from editorial decision-making to order processing." Recent issues include articles on such diverse subjects as gray literature, religious publishing, the book industry in China, and Oprah's book club. A short book review section complements the in-depth scholarly articles. Recommended primarily for academic libraries.

953. *Rare Book Review.* Former titles (until 2004): *Antiquarian Book Review;* (until 2002): *Antiquarian Book Monthly.* [ISSN: 1746-7101] 1974. bi-m. GBP 27 domestic; GBP 35 in Europe; USD 60 United States. Countrywide Editions Ltd., 24 Maddox St., London, W1S 1PP, United Kingdom; subs@abmr.demon.co.uk. Illus., index, adv. Sample. Circ: 5000. Vol. ends: Dec. *Indexed:* DAAI. *Bk. rev.:* 2-5, 300-500 words. *Aud.:* Ac, Sa.

Formerly *Antiquarian Book Review*, this niche publication is newsy, readable, and attractively illustrated. Published in London, the magazine has a U.K. focus, but it will be appreciated by anyone with interest in the collecting or selling of fine books. Each issue features articles on various aspects of book dealing and collecting—interviews with collectors, surveys of important collections, and profiles of major authors, illustrators, and publishers—and regular columns by leading dealers from both Britain and America. The "Essentials" section provides detailed information on the rare book scene, including listings of major auctions, fairs, and catalogues, and previews and reviews of important sales. Text from the current issue is available on the www.rarebookreview.com web site; back issues may be purchased. One particularly useful online feature is the directory of links to book dealers, auction houses, and other book-related resources.

954. *Reference and Research Book News: annotations and reviews of new books for libraries.* Incorporates (1989-1992): *University Press Book News.* [ISSN: 0887-3763] 1986. q. USD 175 (Individuals, USD 130). Ed(s): Jane Erskine. Book News, Inc. (Portland), 5739 N E Sumner St, Portland, OR 97218; BookNews@BookNews.com. Illus., adv. Circ: 1700. Vol. ends: Nov. *Indexed:* BRI, CBCARef, CBRI. *Bk. rev.:* 2,500, 25-75 words. *Aud.:* Ga, Ac.

A quarterly annotated bibliography of new scholarly books, this publication is intended for acquisitions librarians in academic, special, and large public libraries. As its title implies, the periodical primarily covers general reference works and titles in the humanities and social sciences. (A sister bibliography by the same publisher, *SciTech Book News*, provides reviews of high-level science, technology, and medical titles.) Arranged by LC classification, unsigned reviews are concise and descriptive rather than evaluative. The editors have flagged with four stars any reissue or new edition of titles that appeared in the classic resources *Books for College Libraries* and *Guide to Reference Books*. Current issues are downloadable in pdf format on the www.booknews.com web site. Libraries wanting access to the full database of current and past reviews may subscribe to Book News Online (www.paratext.com/booknews.htm), which is updated monthly and may be linked to local holdings.

955. Small Press Review. Formerly (until Feb. 1994): *Small Press Review;* Incorporates (1993-1994): *Small Magazine Review.* 1967. bi-m. USD 35 (Individuals, USD 25). Ed(s): Len Fulton. Dustbooks, PO Box 100, Paradise, CA 95967; publisher@dustbooks.com; http://www.dustbooks.com. Illus., adv. Circ: 3500. *Indexed:* ASIP, AmHI, BRI, CBRI. *Bk. rev.:* 10-15, 200-500 words. *Aud.:* Ac, Sa.

Small Press Review, a bimonthly newsprint publication, provides news, practical information, and reviews focusing on the often-overlooked small press and small magazine industry. Since the incorporation of *Small Magazine Review*, the publication has included two sections, one for books and one for magazines. Regular articles and columns discuss trade news, editorial needs, and contests, and often supply how-to-get-published advice for potential authors. Each issue includes a review section, a "picks" column, guest editorials, and letters. Particularly useful are the descriptions of new publishers and their editorial slants, and the "Free Sample Mart" offering samples of 30 magazines and books. Although the evaluations of new books and magazines cover material not often reviewed elsewhere, library selectors should be aware that reviews are usually favorable. For a more critical analysis of similar titles, compare the content of *Small Press Review* to *American Book Review* (see entry above).

956. T L S: the Times literary supplement. Formerly (until 1969): *Times Literary Supplement.* [ISSN: 0307-661X] 1902. w. GBP 92 domestic; GBP 119 in Europe; USD 135 United States. Ed(s): Peter Stothard. T S L Education Ltd., Admiral House, 66-68 E Smithfield, London, E1 1BX, United Kingdom; webmaster@the-tls.co.uk; http://www.tlseducation.co.uk. Illus., index, adv. Circ: 34000. Vol. ends: Dec. Microform: RPI. Online: EBSCO Publishing, EBSCO Host. *Indexed:* AmH&L, AmHI, ArtHuCI, BRD, BRI, BrHumI, CBRI, FLI, HistAb, HumInd, LRI, MLA-IB, NTA, RI-1, RILM, SSCI. *Bk. rev.:* Various number and length. *Aud.:* Ga, Ac.

TLS, The Times Literary Supplement quite rightfully describes itself as "the leading paper in the world for literary culture." Since 1902, it has scrutinized, dissected, applauded, and occasionally disparaged the work of leading writers and thinkers. (Many of those same writers and thinkers have been notable contributors to *TLS*, from T.S. Eliot and Virginia Woolf in the 1920s to Gore Vidal and Seamus Heaney today.) Its signed, essay-length commentaries have set the standard for authoritative literary review. In addition to reviewing the "books that matter" from many countries on a variety of subjects, *TLS* also covers current theater, opera, exhibitions, and film. On its web site (tls.timeson-line.co.uk) readers may explore the current issue, or use the index to archival issues from 1994 forward. Full text of back issues, as well as access to a special Centenary Index spanning the twentieth century, is limited to subscribers. Other features on the web site include blogs, a weekly e-newsletter, and the online Times Book Group. An essential resource.

957. The Women's Review of Books. [ISSN: 0738-1433] 1983. m. USD 63 (print & online eds.) Individuals, USD 35). Ed(s): Amy Hoffman. Old City Publishing, Inc., 628 N 2nd St, Philadelphia, PA 19123; info@oldcitypublishing.com; http://www.oldcitypublishing.com. Illus., index, adv. Circ: 16000 Paid. Vol. ends: Sep. Microform: PQC. Online: EBSCO Publishing, EBSCO Host; Gale; Northern Light Technology, Inc.; OCLC Online Computer Library Center, Inc.; H.W. Wilson. *Indexed:* ABS&EES, AltPI, AmHI, BRD, BRI, CBRI, CWI, FemPer, IBZ, LeftInd, MASUSE, RI-1, RILM, SWA, WSA. *Bk. rev.:* 15-20, 1,000-1,500 words. *Aud.:* Ac, Sa.

Since 1983, *The Women's Review of Books* has provided "a unique forum for serious, informed discussion of new writing by and about women." Suspended in 2004 due to financial woes, the magazine was re-launched in 2006 with a new look, a bimonthly format, and a new publishing partner. *WRB*'s ambitious goal

is to bridge the split between theory and action that has often divided the feminist movement, through its role as "the only publication that offers in-depth, feminist discussion of current information, ideas, experiences, and trends in our movement." Signed, essay-length reviews provide literate, insightful commentary on new fiction and poetry by women authors, biographies of prominent women, and nonfiction titles on a range of current topics (e.g., feminism in the Third World, pornography, balancing parenting and worklife). Each issue also highlights original poetry, photography and other artwork by women. The web site, (www.wcwonline.org/womensreview) includes an index to all past reviews, searchable by author, title, or reviewer. Recent tables of contents, with links to full text for selected articles, are also available online. Highly recommended, particularly for academic libraries. Welcome back!

■ BOTANY

See also Biology; and Ecology sections.

Mari Roughneen, Manager, Richmond Green Library, Richmond Hill Public Library, 1 William F. Bell Pkwy, Richmond Hill, Ontario, L4S 2T9, Canada

Introduction

The journals in this section will be of interest to botanists, ecologists, plant industry professionals, and, in some instances, general researchers interested in plant properties, growth, and propagation. Important scientific journals from the United States, Canada, and the United Kingdom are represented, the sum of which covers content from the wide spectrum of research within plant sciences, including new and experimental areas of study.

Basic Periodicals

Ac: *American Journal of Botany, Annals of Botany, International Journal of Plant Sciences.*

Basic Abstracts and Indexes

AGRICOLA, Biological Abstracts, Biological & Agricultural Index, Horticultural Science Abstracts.

958. American Journal of Botany: the journal for all plant biologists. [ISSN: 0002-9122] 1914. m. USD 470 combined subscription domestic print & online eds.; USD 485 combined subscription in Canada & Mexico print & online eds.; USD 510 combined subscription elsewhere print & online eds. Ed(s): Karl V Niklas. Botanical Society of America, Inc. (Columbus), Business Office, PO Box 299, St. Louis, MO 63166-0299; orders@allenpress.com; http://www.allenpress.com. Illus., adv. Refereed. Circ: 5000. Microform: IDC; PMC. Online: EBSCO Publishing, EBSCO Host; HighWire Press; JSTOR (Web-based Journal Archive); OCLC Online Computer Library Center, Inc.; H.W. Wilson. *Indexed:* Agr, ApEcolAb, B&AI, BiolAb, BiolDig, CABA, ChemAb, ExcerpMed, FPA, ForAb, GSI, HortAb, OceAb, PollutAb, RRTA, S&F, SCI, SWRA, ZooRec. *Bk. rev.:* Number and length vary. *Aud.:* Ac, Sa.

This journal publishes original research in the following areas of plant biology: "structure, function, development, diversity, genetics, evolution, reproduction, systematics, all levels of organization (molecular to ecosystem), and all plant groups and allied organisms (cyanobacteria, algae, fungi, and lichens)." The journal also contains "Brief Communications, and Special Papers, which include reviews, critiques and analyses of controversial subjects." The print journal is published by the Botanical Society of America (BSA), and the online version is published by BSA in association with Stanford University's HighWire Press. Tables of contents, subject listings, and abstracts are available on the journal's web site. Future tables of contents are available online one month before publication. Searches are also available free of charge. Coverage is available through JSTOR for Vols. 1–87 (1914–2000), with a moving wall of five years. For academic biology and botany collections and special botany collections.

959. *American Society for Horticultural Science. Journal.* Formerly (until 1968): *American Society for Horticultural Science. Proceedings.* [ISSN: 0003-1062] 1903. bi-m. USD 400 in North America; USD 450 elsewhere. Ed(s): Neal E DeVos. American Society for Horticultural Science, 113 S West St, Ste 200, Alexandria, VA 22314-2851; ashs@ashs.org; http://www.ashs.org. Illus., index, adv. Sample. Refereed. Circ: 2500 Paid. Vol. ends: Nov. *Indexed:* Agr, B&AI, BiolAb, BiolDig, CABA, ChemAb, DSA, ExcerpMed, FPA, FS&TA, ForAb, GardL, HortAb, S&F, SCI, WAE&RSA. *Aud.:* Ac ,Sa.

This journal publishes "results of original research on horticultural plants and their products or directly related research areas." It covers such content areas as developmental physiology, environmental stress physiology, genetics and breeding, photosynthesis, source-sink physiology, postharvest physiology, soil-plant-water relationships, molecular biology-biotechnology, and seed physiology. A listserv for advance notice of the journal's table of contents is available. This journal is suitable for academic or special botany collections.

960. *Annals of Botany.* [ISSN: 0305-7364] 1887. 13x/yr. EUR 879. Ed(s): Michael Jackson. Oxford University Press, Great Clarendon St, Oxford, OX2 6DP, United Kingdom; jnl.orders@oup.co.uk; http://www.oxfordjournals.org. Illus., index, adv. Refereed. Circ: 830. Microform: IDC; PMC. Online: EBSCO Publishing, EBSCO Host; Gale; HighWire Press; IngentaConnect; OCLC Online Computer Library Center, Inc.; OhioLINK; Ovid Technologies, Inc.; Oxford Journals; ProQuest LLC (Ann Arbor); ScienceDirect; SwetsWise Online Content. Reprint: PSC. *Indexed:* Agr, ApEcolAb, B&AI, BiolAb, CABA, ChemAb, ExcerpMed, FPA, FS&TA, ForAb, HortAb, OceAb, RRTA, S&F, SCI, SWRA. *Bk. rev.:* Number and length vary. *Aud.:* Ac, Sa.

Annals of Botany is a monthly journal with an annual special issue. The journal covers papers in "all areas of plant science. These include those applying molecular, analytical, mathematical and statistical techniques to examine topical questions at any level of biological organization ranging from cell to community, from tissue culture to crop production, and from microclimate to ecosystem. Its scope extends to all flowering and non-flowering taxa, and to taxonomic and evolutionary questions particularly when these are addressed using molecular tools." The journal content includes full-length research papers, short communications, review articles, and book reviews. Special features include "Botanical Briefings" ("short commissioned reviews that appear in both printed and electronic forms and that are accessible electronically free of charge"). "Content Snapshots" are also published, which provide briefings of articles contained in the issue along with color images, as well as "Content Select," which provides short summaries and highlights of articles of note in the issue along with color images. Back issues are available on the web site (http://aob.oxfordjournals.org). Tables of contents are available via e-mail, and current and archived issues are available via Oxford Journals Online. Pay-per-article access is available. This journal belongs in academic or special botany collections.

961. *B M C Plant Biology.* [ISSN: 1471-2229] 2001. m. Free. Ed(s): Dr. Melissa Norton. BioMed Central Ltd., Middlesex House, 34-42 Cleveland St, London, W1T 4LB, United Kingdom; info@biomedcentral.com; http://www.biomedcentral.com. Adv. Refereed. *Indexed:* BiolAb, CABA, FS&TA, ForAb, HortAb, S&F, SCI. *Aud.:* Ac, Sa.

This is an open-access, peer-reviewed electronic journal that covers "all aspects of cellular, tissue-level, organismal, functional and developmental aspects of plants." A full-text archive back to 2001 is available on the site, as are article alerts. Provisional pdfs of new articles are posted upon acceptance, pre-publication. All content is free. Suitable for academic or special botany or biology collections.

962. *The Botanical Review.* [ISSN: 0006-8101] 1935. q. EUR 142 print & online eds. Springer New York LLC, 233 Spring St, New York, NY 10013-1578; journals@springer-ny.com; http://www.springer.com. Illus., adv. Sample. Refereed. Circ: 2000. Vol. ends: Oct/Dec. Microform: IDC; PMC; PQC. Online: BioOne; CSA; Florida Center for Library Automation; Gale; Northern Light Technology, Inc.; OCLC Online

Computer Library Center, Inc.; OhioLINK; H.W. Wilson. *Indexed:* Agr, B&AI, BiolAb, CABA, ChemAb, EnvAb, EnvInd, FPA, ForAb, GSI, HortAb, RRTA, S&F, SCI, SSCI. *Aud.:* Ac, Sa.

This is an international journal that covers the following areas of plant science: systematics, phytogeography, cladistics, evolution, physiology, ecology, morphology, paleobotany, and anatomy. As stated in the journal, "the function of TBR is to present syntheses of the state of knowledge and understanding of individual segments of botany." The reviews in each journal are substantial, with detailed contents preceding each review. "Articles are obtained primarily by invitation, but unsolicited manuscripts are also considered." Contents and abstracts from previous issues are available on the web site (http://sciweb.nybg.org/science2/BotanicalReview.asp). Back issues are available from the New York Botanical Garden Press. This journal is suitable for academic and special botany collections.

963. *Canadian Journal of Botany.* Formerly (until 1950): *Canadian Journal of Research. Section C: Botanical Sciences;* Which superseded in part (in 1935): *Canadian Journal of Research.* [ISSN: 0008-4026] 1929. m. USD 295 (Individuals, CND 295). Ed(s): Barry J Shelp, Larry R Peterson. N R C Research Press, National Research Council of Canada, Ottawa, ON K1A 0R6, Canada; pubs@nrc-cnrc.gc.ca; http://pubs.nrc-cnrc.gc.ca. Illus., index, adv. Refereed. Circ: 1506. Vol. ends: Dec. Microform: MML; PMC; PQC. Online: EBSCO Publishing, EBSCO Host; Gale; IngentaConnect; LexisNexis; Micromedia ProQuest; OCLC Online Computer Library Center, Inc.; ProQuest K-12 Learning Solutions; ProQuest LLC (Ann Arbor); SwetsWise Online Content; H.W. Wilson. *Indexed:* ABS&EES, Agr, ApEcolAb, B&AI, BiolAb, CABA, CBCARef, CPerI, ChemAb, EngInd, EnvAb, EnvInd, ExcerpMed, FPA, FS&TA, ForAb, HortAb, IndVet, M&GPA, PollutAb, RRTA, S&F, SCI, SWRA, WAE&RSA, ZooRec. *Aud.:* Ac, Sa.

Canadian Journal of Botany, published by National Research Council of Canada (NRC), "the Government of Canada's premier organization for research and development . . . active since 1916," "publishes comprehensive research by internationally recognized botanists in all segments of plant science, including cell and molecular biology, ecology, mycology and plant pathology, phycology, physiology and biochemistry, structure and development, systematics, phytogeography, and paleobotany." Articles are published in either English or French (most are in English), and abstracts are published in both English and French. Notification of recent NRC publications is available by e-mail. Issues are available via the web site from 1998 forward (http://pubs.nrc-cnrc.gc.ca/cgi-bin/rp/rp2_desc_e?cjb). A journal for academic or special botany collections.

964. *Canadian Journal of Plant Pathology.* [ISSN: 0706-0661] 1979. q. CND 75 domestic; USD 85 foreign. Ed(s): Dr. Zamir K Punja. Canadian Phytopathological Society, Dept of Environmental Biology, University of Guelph, Guelph, ON N1G 2W1, Canada. Illus., adv. Refereed. Circ: 900. *Indexed:* Agr, B&AI, BiolAb, CABA, ChemAb, EnvAb, FPA, ForAb, HortAb, RRTA, S&F, SCI, WAE&RSA. *Aud.:* Ac, Sa.

This journal "contains the results of scientific research and other information relevant to plant pathology, as articles, notes, disease reports, and special topics, including reviews." It is published by the National Research Council of Canada, "the Government of Canada's premier organization for research and development." A research news highlights section is compiled by the editor. Abstracts are provided in English and French. The majority of articles appear in English. This journal is suitable for academic or special botany collections.

965. *International Journal of Plant Sciences.* Former titles (until Mar. 1992): *Botanical Gazette;* (until 1876): *Botanical Bulletin.* [ISSN: 1058-5893] 1875. 9x/yr. USD 640 domestic; USD 701.40 Canada; USD 668 elsewhere. Ed(s): Manfred Ruddat. University of Chicago Press, Journals Division, PO Box 37005, Chicago, IL 60637; subscriptions@press.uchicago.edu; http://www.journals.uchicago.edu. Illus., index, adv. Sample. Refereed. Circ: 1000. Vol. ends: Nov. Microform: IDC. Online: EBSCO Publishing, EBSCO Host; Florida Center for Library Automation; Gale; JSTOR (Web-based Journal Archive); OCLC Online Computer Library Center, Inc.; ProQuest K-12 Learning

Solutions; ProQuest LLC (Ann Arbor). Reprint: PSC. *Indexed:* Agr, ApEcolAb, B&AI, BiolAb, BiolDig, CABA, ChemAb, ExcerpMed, FPA, FS&TA, ForAb, GSI, HortAb, S&F, SCI, SWRA. *Aud.:* Ac, Sa.

This journal covers "plant-microbe interactions, development, structure and systematics, molecular biology, genetics and evolution, ecology, paleobotany, and physiology and ecophysiology." Subscriptions to the journal include electronic access. Back issues are available via the publisher's web site from 1998 forward. Access is also available via JSTOR for Vols. 153–159, 1992–1998, and for the journal's precursors, *Botanical Gazette* (Vols. 2–152, 1876–1991) and *Botanical Bulletin* (Vol. 1, 1875–1876). A distribution list for tables of contents is available. Symposia and supplements are available on the journal's web site (www.journals.uchicago.edu/IJPS/home.html). A journal that should be held in academic or special botany collections.

966. *Journal of Experimental Botany.* [ISSN: 0022-0957] 1950. m. plus six special issues. EUR 1469 print or online ed. Ed(s): Jerry J Roberts. Oxford University Press, Great Clarendon St, Oxford, OX2 6DP, United Kingdom; jnl.orders@oup.co.uk; http://www.oxfordjournals.org. Illus., index, adv. Sample. Refereed. Circ: 1100. Vol. ends: Dec. Microform: PQC. Online: EBSCO Publishing, EBSCO Host; Gale; HighWire Press; IngentaConnect; OCLC Online Computer Library Center, Inc.; OhioLINK; Ovid Technologies, Inc.; Oxford Journals; ProQuest LLC (Ann Arbor); SwetsWise Online Content. Reprint: PSC. *Indexed:* Agr, B&AI, BiolAb, CABA, ChemAb, DSA, EngInd, ExcerpMed, FPA, FS&TA, ForAb, HortAb, PollutAb, RRTA, S&F, SCI, SWRA. *Aud.:* Ac, Sa.

This journal is published on behalf of the Society for Experimental Botany, and is an offical publication of the Federation of European Societies of Plant Physiology. The journal covers content from "molecular and cellular physiology and biochemistry through whole plant physiology to community physiology." Content includes review articles, focus papers, and research papers in addition to "Perspective" articles, which are "reviews of research areas that are particularly exciting and important, topical or controversial." Free access is available to articles older than one year. Abstracts are available via the web site from 1996 forward; full text from 1997 forward (http://jxb.oxfordjournals.org). Registration for electronic tables of contents is available. Full 24-hour access to all articles on the site is available for purchase. There is free access to themed collections of articles. This journal is appropriate for academic or special botany collections.

967. *Journal of Herbs, Spices & Medicinal Plants.* [ISSN: 1049-6475] 1991. q. USD 365 print & online eds. Ed(s): Lyle E Craker. The Haworth Herbal Press, 10 Alice St, Binghamton, NY 13904; getinfo@haworthpress.com; http://www.haworthpress.com/. Illus., index, adv. Sample. Refereed. Circ: 313 Paid. Vol. ends: No. 4. Microform: PQC. Online: EBSCO Publishing, EBSCO Host; OCLC Online Computer Library Center, Inc.; SwetsWise Online Content. Reprint: HAW. *Indexed:* Agr, BiolDig, CABA, CINAHL, DSA, ExcerpMed, FPA, FS&TA, ForAb, GardL, H&SSA, HortAb, IndVet, S&F, VB, WAE&RSA. *Bk. rev.:* Number and length vary. *Aud.:* Ga, Ac, Sa.

A journal with scholarly content that will serve the interests of a wide readership, from industry to a broad spectrum of scientific disciplines. Some of the more readable content will also be relevant to the general researcher interested in plant history, folklore, medicinal properties, propagation, and cultivation. The journal covers content on herbs, spices, and medicinal plants in the following areas: growth development, horticulture, ecology, genetics, chemistry and economics. The journal "serves as a focus point through which investigators and others may publish material of importance to the production, marketing, and utilization of these plants and associated extracts." Document delivery is available through Haworth Document Delivery Service. Electronic access is available with library print subscriptions. There is free table of contents service via e-mail. Suitable for academic and specialized botany collections as well as those collections supporting relevant industry and health subject areas.

968. *Journal of Phycology: an international journal of algal research.* [ISSN: 0022-3646] 1965. bi-m. GBP 466 print & online eds. Ed(s): Patricia A Wheeler. Blackwell Publishing, Inc., Commerce Place, 350 Main St, Malden, MA 02148; customerservices@

blackwellpublishing.com; http://www.blackwellpublishing.com. Illus., index, adv. Sample. Refereed. Circ: 2000. Reprint: PSC. *Indexed:* BiolAb, CABA, ChemAb, ForAb, HortAb, IndVet, OceAb, PollutAb, S&F, SCI, VB, ZooRec. *Bk. rev.:* Number and length vary. *Aud.:* Ac, Sa.

This is "an international journal of algal research," published on behalf of the Phycological Society of America. It covers content relevant to the "ecologist, physiologist, cell biologist, molecular biologist, morphologist, oceanographer, aquaculturist, systematist, geneticist, and biochemist." The journal also focuses on the functioning of algae within natural ecosystems. It is available online through Blackwell Synergy (www.blackwell-synergy.com/loi/jpy). Via this web site, e-mail updates including tables of contents and abtracts are available free. This journal represents research important to a number of academic disciplines and should be part of academic algology, biology, oceanography, and botany collections as well as in special collections in the aforementioned areas.

969. *Linnean Society. Botanical Journal.* Formerly: *Linnean Society of London. Journal.* [ISSN: 0024-4074] 1855. m. GBP 1501 print & online eds. Ed(s): Stephen L Jury. Blackwell Publishing Ltd., 9600 Garsington Rd, Oxford, OX4 2ZG, United Kingdom; customerservices@blackwellpublishing.com; http://www.blackwellpublishing.com. Illus., adv. Refereed. Microform: BHP. Online: Blackwell Synergy; EBSCO Publishing, EBSCO Host; Gale; IngentaConnect; OCLC Online Computer Library Center, Inc.; OhioLINK; ScienceDirect; SwetsWise Online Content. Reprint: PSC. *Indexed:* Agr, ApEcolAb, BiolAb, CABA, ChemAb, FPA, ForAb, HortAb, OceAb, S&F, SCI, SWRA, ZooRec. *Aud.:* Ac, Sa.

This journal "publishes papers of relevance to, and reviews of, the taxonomy of all plant groups and fungi, including anatomy, biosystematics, cytology, ecology, ethnobotany, electron microscopy, morphogenesis, palaeobotany, palynology and phytochemistry." It is available to institutions in the developing world at no cost through the AGORA initiative (http://aginternetwork.org). The *Botanical Journal* is one of four publications by the Linnean Society (founded in 1788 and named after Carl Linnaeus), which has as its aim "the cultivation of the science of Natural History in all its branches." A journal suitable for academic and special botany collections.

970. *Native Plants Journal.* [ISSN: 1522-8339] 2000. 3x/yr. USD 82.50 (Individuals, USD 42.50). Ed(s): R Kasten Dumroese. Indiana University Press, 601 N Morton St, Bloomington, IN 47404. Illus., adv. Sample. Refereed. *Indexed:* Agr, B&AI, CABA, FPA, ForAb, GardL, HortAb, RRTA, S&F, WAE&RSA. *Bk. rev.:* Number and length vary. *Aud.:* Ga, Ac, Sa.

This journal is an "eclectic forum for dispersing practical information about planting and growing North American native plants for conservation, restoration, reforestation, landscaping, highway corridors, and so on." It is a publication of the USDA Forest Service, the USDA Agricultural Research Service, and the Natural Resources Conservation Service. *Native Plants Journal* accepts general technical articles, refereed research articles, and "propagation protocols," which are short articles detailing propagation methods for a particular plant. Accepted refereed research articles are designated as such in the journal. All manuscripts are double-blind peer-reviewed. This journal is suitable for academic and special botany collections as well as public collections where there is interest in growing native plants.

971. *New Disease Reports.* 2000. irreg. Free. Ed(s): Rick Mumford. British Society for Plant Pathology, membership@bspp.org.uk; http://www.bspp.org.uk. Refereed. *Aud.:* Ac, Sa.

This is an international, electronic reporting service, published by the British Society for Plant Pathology for global plant disease situations for the following categories: fungi, bacteria, phytoplasmas, viruses, and viroids. The journal publishes reports on plant pathogens with respect to "new naturally infected hosts, new races for known pathogens, new symptoms and damage for known pathogens, new geographical locations for known pathogens, and new disease symptoms for as-yet-undescribed or partly described plant pathogens." Access is free. Suitable for academic or special botany collections.

972. *The Plant Cell.* [ISSN: 1040-4651] 1989. m. Members, USD 185; Non-members, USD 400 print & online eds. Ed(s): Richard Jorgensen, John Long. American Society of Plant Biologists, 15501 Monona Dr, Rockville, MD 20855-2768; beths@aspp.org; http://www.aspb.org. Illus., index, adv. Sample. Refereed. Circ: 1992 Paid. Online: EBSCO Publishing, EBSCO Host; Gale; HighWire Press; National Library of Medicine; ProQuest K-12 Learning Solutions; ProQuest LLC (Ann Arbor). *Indexed:* Agr, B&AI, BioEngAb, BiolAb, CABA, ChemAb, DSA, EngInd, FPA, FS&TA, ForAb, HortAb, S&F, SCI. *Aud.:* Ac, Sa.

This journal covers research in the following areas of plant biology: cellular biology, molecular biology, genetics, development, and evolution. "The primary criterion for publication is new insight that is of broad interest to plant biologists, not only to specialists." Included in issues are "Current Perspective" essays and/or "Historical Perspective" essays along with research articles. Stanford University Libraries' HighWire Press assists in the publication of the online journal (www.plantcell.org). Access to research articles is free after 12 months. Tables of contents and abstracts are free. The free full archive of the journal (from Vol. 1, 1989) is available at both HighWire Press and PubMed Central. Open-access articles can be viewed online without a subscription. A journal suitable for academic or special botany collections.

973. *Plant Health Progress.* [ISSN: 1535-1025] irreg. USD 750. Ed(s): Timothy Murray. Plant Management Network, 3340 Pilot Knob Rd, St Paul, MN 55121-2097; http://www.plantmanagementnetwork.org. Adv. Refereed. *Indexed:* CABA, FPA, ForAb, HortAb, S&F, WAE&RSA. *Aud.:* Ac, Sa.

This is "a multidisciplinary science-based journal covering all aspects of applied plant health management." This electronic journal contains peer-reviewed articles. Categories of content include plant health research, plant health reviews, plant health management, diagnostic guides, plant health briefs, industry news, and perspectives. The site provides access to a five-year public archive with full text back to 2000. New articles and articles for the past 18 months are noted, with public summaries available free. Subscriptions provide access to the Plant Management Network, which includes access to the PMN Plant Science Database PMN Image Collections, access to Applied Turfgrass Science, Crop Management, Forage and Grazinglands, and tests and proceedings. Suitable for academic and special botany collections.

974. *The Plant Journal.* [ISSN: 0960-7412] 1991. s-m. GBP 2161 print & online eds. Ed(s): Harry Klee. Blackwell Publishing Ltd., 9600 Garsington Rd, Oxford, OX4 2ZG, United Kingdom; customerservices@blackwellpublishing.com; http://www.blackwellpublishing.com. Illus., adv. Refereed. Circ: 1220. Microform: PQC. Online: Blackwell Synergy; EBSCO Publishing, EBSCO Host; Gale; IngentaConnect; OCLC Online Computer Library Center, Inc.; OhioLINK; Ovid Technologies, Inc.; SwetsWise Online Content. Reprint: PSC. *Indexed:* Agr, BioEngAb, BiolAb, CABA, ChemAb, DSA, EngInd, FPA, FS&TA, ForAb, HortAb, S&F, SCI, WAE&RSA. *Aud.:* Ac, Sa.

This is an international journal published in association with the Society for Experimental Botany. The research published in this journal "must provide a highly significant new contribution to our understanding of plants and be of general interest to the plant science community. All areas of plant biology are welcome and the experimental approaches used can be wide-ranging." Primary research articles and technical advances are included. Blackwell Publishing's OnlineEarly service provides articles online in advance of their print publication. Table of contents and e-mail alerts are available through Blackwell Synergy. A journal suitable for academic or special botany collections.

975. *Plant Physiology.* [ISSN: 0032-0889] 1926. m. Members, USD 185; Non-members, USD 350 print & online eds. Ed(s): Donald R Ort, John Long. American Society of Plant Biologists, 15501 Monona Dr, Rockville, MD 20855-2768; mjunior@aspp.org; http://www.aspb.org. Illus., index, adv. Sample. Refereed. Circ: 1997 Paid. Microform: MIM; PMC; PQC. Online: EBSCO Publishing, EBSCO Host; Gale; HighWire Press; National Library of Medicine; ProQuest K-12 Learning Solutions; ProQuest LLC (Ann Arbor). *Indexed:* Agr, B&AI, BioEngAb, BiolAb, CABA, ChemAb, DSA, EngInd, EnvAb, EnvInd, ExcerpMed, FPA, FS&TA, ForAb, HortAb, S&F, SCI, WAE&RSA. *Aud.:* Ac, Sa.

This is "an international journal devoted to basic research into how plants function, ranging from the molecular to the cellular to the whole plant levels, and including the interactions of plants with their biotic and abiotic environments." The journal includes coverage of "development, cell and molecular biology, biochemistry, biophysics, bioenergetics, genetics, and physiology, as well as an understanding of the plant as a whole organism and its interactions with symbionts, pathogens and pests, and the environment." Also covered is content relevant to plant sciences such as "bioinformatics, molecular evolution, functional genomics, genome analysis, proteomics, metabolomics, structural biology, and biotechnology." Access to research articles is free via the journal's web site (www.plantphysiol.org) after 12 months. Free access to tables of contents, abstracts, and "many front-section features" is also available. Stanford University's HighWire Press provides access to *Plant Physiology Online.* This journal should be part of academic or special botany collections.

976. *Systematic Botany.* [ISSN: 0363-6445] 1976. q. USD 155 print & online eds. Ed(s): Alan Whittemore, Leigh Johnson. American Society of Plant Taxonomists, University of Wyoming, Dept. of Botany 3165, Laramie, WY 82071-3165; aspt@uwyo.edu; http://www.aspt.net/. Illus., adv. Refereed. Circ: 1700 Paid. Online: BioOne; CSA; EBSCO Publishing, EBSCO Host; Gale; IngentaConnect; JSTOR (Web-based Journal Archive); OCLC Online Computer Library Center, Inc.; OhioLINK. *Indexed:* Agr, B&AI, BiolAb, CABA, FPA, ForAb, HortAb, S&F, SCI. *Bk. rev.:* Number and length vary. *Aud.:* Ac, Sa.

This journal is published by the American Society of Plant Taxonomists, which "promotes research and teaching in the taxonomy, systematics, and phylogeny of vascular and nonvascular plants." Online access and issue alerts are available through Ingenta Connect. JSTOR coverage, Vols. 1–25 (1976–2000), has a moving wall of five years. Suitable for academic and special botany collections.

■ BUILDING AND CONSTRUCTION

See also Architecture; Home; and Interior Design and Decoration sections.

Nicholas Wharton, Reference and Circulation Librarian, Mortensein Library, University of Hartford, 200 Bloomfield Ave., Hartford, CT 06117

Introduction

This section covers technical and specialized magazines that will be of interest to professional builders, land and building developers, general contractors, engineers, designers, and architects. The journals' information ranges from installation specifications to laws and guidelines, to mathematical ratios for load bearing or estimating, to architectural designs, and to mixture formulas for concrete. Journals cover a wide array of specialized information that concerns building specialties that include welding, plumbing, restoration carpentry, and masonry. Other information includes tips on running a business; discussion of economic trends in the specific field; tips on installations and designs; or showcasing of new products.

Many of the titles have specific audiences and may be useful to special or public libraries that have a building and construction clientele, academic libraries with design or architecture degrees and coursework, or large corporate libraries at design or construction firms. Each of the magazines highlighted in this section has an online presence. Many of these web sites lead to more extensive information in the field or to more general or specialized construction information, product lists, plans, industry news, how to's, and help guides. Many of the publisher sites offer limited or free access to the journals, while others offer a fee-per-article service; all have subscription information.

This section attempts to cull together a wide array of specialized building and construction magazines. Although the list is not comprehensive, the major titles in the field are represented. For related topics, see the Architecture, Home, and Interior Design and Decoration sections.

Basic Periodicals

Sa: *Builder, Building Design & Construction, Constructor, Old House Journal, Professional Builder.*

Basic Abstracts and Indexes

Applied Science and Technology Index, Engineering Index.

977. *A C I Materials Journal.* Supersedes in part (Mar. 1987): *American Concrete Institute. Journal.* [ISSN: 0889-325X] 1929. bi-m. USD 142 domestic; USD 150 foreign. Ed(s): Rebecca A Hartford. American Concrete Institute, PO Box 9094, Farmington Hills, MI 48333; webmaster@aci-int.org; http://www.aci-int.org. Illus., index, adv. Refereed. Circ: 11700. Online: EBSCO Publishing, EBSCO Host. *Indexed:* AS&TI, C&ISA, CerAb, ChemAb, EngInd, H&SSA, HRIS, IAA, SCI. *Aud.:* Ac, Sa.

This journal, published by the American Concrete Institute (ACI), is geared to the professionals, engineers, and architects for structural information regarding building materials. It contains articles and tips on design trends in the field, and a means of technical support. Topics include concrete behaviors with reinforcement additives and environmental effects on grout, reinforcements, and sealants. A monthly feature is a meeting list for various structural interest groups. In addition, all ACI standards and committee reports are published. The web site (www.concrete.org) contains a searchable abstracts database, and full-text articles may be viewed by subscribers or purchased by nonsubscribers. A free student e-membership is now available. Also, the ACI web site has added a career center for prospective job seekers and employers.

978. *A C I Structural Journal.* Supersedes in part (Mar. 1987): *American Concrete Institute. Journal.* [ISSN: 0889-3241] 1929. bi-m. USD 142 domestic; USD 150 foreign. Ed(s): Rebecca A Hartford. American Concrete Institute, PO Box 9094, Farmington Hills, MI 48333; webmaster@aci-int.org; http://www.aci-int.org. Illus., index, adv. Refereed. Circ: 17400. Microform: PQC. Online: OCLC Online Computer Library Center, Inc.; ProQuest LLC (Ann Arbor). *Indexed:* AS&TI, ApMecR, C&ISA, CerAb, ChemAb, EngInd, ExcerpMed, H&SSA, HRIS, IAA, SCI. *Aud.:* Ac, Sa.

Contains articles and tips geared to general contractors and structural engineers for design, field trends, and technical support for concrete and beam construction. Topics include precast concrete, seismic testing and behavior, polymer reinforcement, and tension stiffening effects. A monthly feature is a meeting list for various structural interest groups. ACI standards and committee reports are also published. The web site (www.concrete.org) contains a searchable abstracts database, and full-text articles may be viewed by subscribers or purchased by nonsubscribers. A free student e-membership is now available. Also, the ACI web site has added a career center for prospective job seekers and employers.

Air Conditioning, Heating & Refrigeration News. See Business/Trade and Industry section.

979. *Builder (Washington): NAHB, the voice of America's housing industry.* Former titles: *N A H B Builder; Builder (Washington); N A H B Journal-Scope;* Which was formed by the merger of: *N A H B Journal; N A H B Washington Scope.* [ISSN: 0744-1193] 1942. m. USD 29.95 domestic; USD 35.95 Canada; USD 192 elsewhere. Ed(s): Boyce Thompson. Hanley Wood, LLC, One Thomas Circle, NW, Ste 600, Washington, DC 20005-5701; http://www.hanleywood.com. Illus., adv. Circ: 141457 Paid and controlled. Microform: PQC. Online: Florida Center for Library Automation; Gale; OCLC Online Computer Library Center, Inc.; ProQuest K-12 Learning Solutions; ProQuest LLC (Ann Arbor); H.W. Wilson. *Indexed:* ABIn, API, BPI, LRI. *Aud.:* Ac, Sa.

This publication is marketed toward residential home construction and is published by the National Association of Home Builders (NAHB). Topics range from new construction ideas and plans to growth and slow-down potential to economic costs to trends for special interests such as the elderly and pets. Monthly features include "The Outer Limits," which is on the top growth markets; "Local Leaders"; and "Best Selling Communities." An online subscription is not accessible to the public, but the web site has links to past issues and full-text articles, discussion groups, a products guide, plans, and other building news.

980. *Building Design & Construction: the magazine for the building team.* Formerly (until 1958): *Building Construction.* [ISSN: 0007-3407] 1950. m. USD 119 domestic; USD 164.90 Canada; USD 159.90 Mexico. Ed(s): David Barista. Reed Business Information, 2000 Clearwater Dr, Oak Brook, IL 60523; http://www.reedbusiness.com. Illus., index, adv. Circ: 76006 Controlled. Microform: CIS. Online: EBSCO Publishing, EBSCO Host; Factiva, Inc.; Florida Center for Library Automation; Gale; LexisNexis; Northern Light Technology, Inc.; OCLC Online Computer Library Center, Inc.; ProQuest LLC (Ann Arbor); H.W. Wilson. *Indexed:* ABIn, ArchI, BPI, LRI. *Aud.:* Ac, Sa.

This journal focuses on large construction projects and deals with topics of interest to nonresidential building owners, project building teams, engineers, architects, project managers, and general contractors. It is not geared to the homeowner looking for design ideas. Topics include industry news and trends, emerging design, law, salary structures, cost projections, and industry downturns on a global scale. Monthly features include an editorial and a "News and Trends" section. The web site (www.bdcnetwork.com) contains further product resources, an events page, job and education links, and a searchable database for viewing abstracts or purchasing online articles from past issues.

981. *Buildings: the source for facilities decision-makers.* [ISSN: 0007-3725] 1906. m. USD 70 domestic; USD 85 Canada; USD 125 elsewhere. Ed(s): Jana J Madsen. Stamats Buildings Media, Inc., 615 Fifth St, SE, Cedar Rapids, IA 52401. Illus., index, adv. Circ: 72000 Controlled. Vol. ends: Dec. Microform: PQC. Online: The Dialog Corporation; EBSCO Publishing, EBSCO Host; Florida Center for Library Automation; Gale; Northern Light Technology, Inc.; OCLC Online Computer Library Center, Inc.; ProQuest K-12 Learning Solutions; ProQuest LLC (Ann Arbor); H.W. Wilson. *Indexed:* ABIn, AgeL, BPI, C&ISA, CerAb, IAA. *Aud.:* Ac, Sa.

This journal focuses on all aspects of commercial or industrial construction, including construction materials, scope of building use, liability, increasing productivity, and industry trends. It is targeted to building owners, developers, engineers, architects, project managers, and general contractors. Highlighted building projects are large in scope. Topics include industry news and trends, salary structures, cost projections, and industry downturns. Monthly features include an editorial and "Smarter Buildings," "Industry411," and "Tools of the Trade." The web site (www.buildings.com) contains further product resources, an events and industry news page, "Career Center," a "Buyer's Guide," and topical webinars. There is also a searchable database for viewing abstracts or purchasing online articles from past issues.

982. *Concrete Construction.* Former titles (until Nov.1999): *Aberdeen's Concrete Construction;* (until 1990): *Concrete Construction.* [ISSN: 1533-7316] 1956. m. USD 30 domestic; USD 39 in Canada & Mexico; USD 93 elsewhere. Ed(s): William D Palmer, Jr. Hanley Wood, LLC, 426 S Westgate St, Addison, IL 60101; http://www.hanleywood.com. Illus., index, adv. Circ: 73580 Paid. Microform: PQC. Online: Florida Center for Library Automation; Gale; OCLC Online Computer Library Center, Inc.; ProQuest LLC (Ann Arbor); H.W. Wilson. *Indexed:* AS&TI, EngInd, HRIS. *Aud.:* Ac, Sa.

This journal focuses on industry trends for use of concrete in all construction projects, residential and commercial. The main audience for this publication is concrete contractors, architects, structural engineers, and general contractors. Topics include industry news and trends, highlighted building projects, and technical developments. Features include a "What's New" section and "Problem Clinic Questions." The web site (www.concreteconstruction.net) contains further product resources, a searchable "Problem Clinic," an industry events calendar, "Career Center," and "WCC Bookstore." There is also a searchable database for viewing abstracts and articles from past issues.

983. *Concrete International.* Formerly: *Concrete International - Design and Construction.* [ISSN: 0162-4075] 1979. m. USD 151. Ed(s): Rex C Donahey, Keith A. Tosolt. American Concrete Institute, 38800 Country Club Dr, Farmington Hills, MI 48331; webmaster@aci-int.org; http://www.aci-int.org. Adv. Refereed. Circ: 17000. *Indexed:* AS&TI, C&ISA, CerAb, ChemAb, HRIS, IAA. *Aud.:* Ac, Sa.

This journal, published by the American Concrete Institute (ACI), is geared to the professionals, engineers, and architects for structural information regarding concrete materials. It contains articles and tips on design trends in the field, and a means of technical support. Topics include concrete behaviors with cracking and repairs, use of reinforcements, and general behaviors of different concretes. In addition, all ACI standards and committee reports are published. The web site (www.aci-int.org) contains a searchable abstracts database, and full-text articles may be viewed by subscribers or purchased by nonsubscribers. Also, the ACI web site has added a career center for prospective job seekers and employers.

984. Construction Equipment. Former titles: *Construction Equipment Magazine; Construction Equipment and Materials Magazine.* [ISSN: 0192-3978] 1949. 13x/yr. USD 99.90 domestic (Free to qualified personnel). Ed(s): Rod Sutton. Reed Business Information, 2000 Clearwater Dr, Oak Brook, IL 60523; http://www.reedbusiness.com. Illus., index, adv. Circ: 80000 Controlled. Online: EBSCO Publishing, EBSCO Host; Florida Center for Library Automation; Gale; Northern Light Technology, Inc.; OCLC Online Computer Library Center, Inc.; ProQuest LLC (Ann Arbor). *Indexed:* ABIn. *Aud.:* Sa.

This journal is targeted to those concerned with the acquisition and maintenance of construction equipment such as trucks, heavy machinery, graders, loaders, and mixers. Topics include new products and trends, safety concerns, costs, and new legislation. The magazine and its web site (www.constructionequipment-.com) are filled with advertising, but subscriptions are free. The web site offers a subscription sign-up page for either print or digital publications and contains further product resources, news headlines, guidelines, and other publications for sale.

985. Construction Specifier: solutions for the construction industry. [ISSN: 0010-6925] 1950. m. USD 48 domestic; USD 58 Canada. Ed(s): Erik Missio. Construction Specifications Institute, 289 - 266 Elmwood Ave, Buffalo, NY 14222; csi@csinet.org; http://www.csinet.org. Illus., index, adv. Circ: 26005 Paid. *Indexed:* ArchI, C&ISA, CerAb, EngInd, IAA. *Aud.:* Sa.

The Construction Specifications Institute (CSI) offers authoritative information on construction standards. CSI gears this publication to architects, general contractors, installers, or other construction professionals involved in specification processes. There are a wide range of topics including discussions of specifications rules and guidelines, use of alternative products, working with public bid specs, and conservation ideas. Monthly features include "Industry News," "Coming Events," and "Specifications," mediated by qualified editors. The web site (www.constructionspecifier.com) offers a subscription sign-up page, and an "Exchange" and "Classifieds" page for swapping or selling equipment, and online subscription ordering for non-members and members or students.

986. Constructor: the construction management magazine. [ISSN: 0162-6191] 1919. m. Members, USD 15; Non-members, USD 250. Ed(s): Mark Shaw, Benjamin Harring. A G C, 333 John Carlyle St, Ste 200, Alexandria, VA 22314-5745; info@agc.org; http://www.agc.org. Illus., index, adv. Circ: 43780 Paid and controlled. *Indexed:* HRIS. *Aud.:* Sa.

This is the official trade magazine of the Associated General Contractors of America (AGC). The publication was relaunched in 2005 as a quarterly business journal in partnership with McGraw-Hill Construction. The journal focuses on a broad range of construction topics, and it is the forum for updating members on the association's activities and by-laws. Articles highlight major projects and discuss trends. Features include "Guest and Legal Commentaries" and AGC program and activity reports. The web site (constructoragc.construc-tion.com) offers the current issue and archive of previous issues and information about AGC.

987. Contractor: the newsmagazine of mechanical contracting. [ISSN: 0897-7135] 1954. m. USD 105 foreign (Free to qualified personnel). Penton Media, Inc., 1300 E 9th St, Cleveland, OH 44114-1503; information@penton.com; http://www.penton.com/. Illus., adv. Circ: 50377 Controlled. Online: EBSCO Publishing, EBSCO Host; Florida Center for Library Automation; Gale; Northern Light Technology, Inc.; OCLC Online Computer Library Center, Inc.; ProQuest K-12 Learning Solutions; ProQuest LLC (Ann Arbor). *Indexed:* ABIn. *Aud.:* Sa.

This magazine is designed for the mechanical contractor and the general contractor. The publication focuses on a broad range of construction topics, including trends and regulations, treatment of workers, environmental concerns and laws, and rules and regulations, with information and commentary. The web site (contractormag.com) offers construction news, a product guide, links to related web sites, a classified section, and a list of contributing columnists. Subscriptions to the magazine are free to residents of the United States and Canada.

988. Custom Home. Incorporates (1976-1999): *Custom Builder.* [ISSN: 1055-3479] 1991. 7x/yr. USD 36 in US & Canada (Free to qualified personnel). Ed(s): Jennifer R Goodman, Leslie Ensor. Hanley Wood, LLC, One Thomas Circle, NW, Ste 600, Washington, DC 20005-5701; tjackson@hanleywood.com; http://www.hanleywood.com. Illus., adv. Circ: 40000 Paid and free. Online: Gale. *Aud.:* Sa.

This magazine is designed for the custom home contractor, architect, or potential home owner/builder. Topics range from home design to kitchen and bathroom designs to barbecue grills to landscaping. Sections include letters, editorials, and a calendar of events. "On Your Mind" discusses the business of custom home building, and "The Last Detail" closes each issue with a highlight from inside a specific custom home. The web site (www.customhomeonli-ne.com) offers news, a product guide, a database for subscribers to receive feedback on plans, and links to outside sources. Subscriptions are free to certain contractors and architects, or discounted for the "do-it-yourself consumer."

989. E C & M. Incorporates (in 2002): *Power Quality Assurance;* Formerly (until 199?): *Electrical Construction & Maintenance.* [ISSN: 1082-295X] 1901. m. Free to qualified personnel. Ed(s): Mike Eby, Ellen Parson. Prism Business Media, 9800 Metcalf Ave, Overland Park, KS 66212-2216; inquiries@prismb2b.com; http://www.prismbusinessmedia.com. Illus., adv. Circ: 104000 Controlled. Online: EBSCO Publishing, EBSCO Host; Gale; LexisNexis; OCLC Online Computer Library Center, Inc.; ProQuest LLC (Ann Arbor); H.W. Wilson. *Indexed:* AS&TI, EngInd, RiskAb. *Aud.:* Ac, Sa.

Contains highly technical information regarding designing and installing electrical systems. Geared to engineers and practitioners for all types of system projects, large and small. Topics include commentary on installation guidelines, energy efficiencies, codes, contracts, and system design and installation. Each issue has a "Product Spotlight" section, "Ask the Experts" from the field, and an "Industry Viewpoint." The web site (ecmweb.com) contains further resource guides, tips, and a buyer's guide. Subscription is free in print or online/e-mail.

The Family Handyman. See Do-It-Yourself section.

990. Heating-Piping-Air Conditioning Engineering. Formerly (until 1999): *Heating, Piping and Air Conditioning.* [ISSN: 1527-4055] 1929. m. USD 70 domestic (Free to qualified personnel). Ed(s): Scott Arnold. Penton Media, Inc., 1300 E 9th St, Cleveland, OH 44114-1503; information@penton.com; http://www.penton.com/. Illus., adv. Circ: 56000 Controlled. Microform: PQC. Online: EBSCO Publishing, EBSCO Host; Gale; OCLC Online Computer Library Center, Inc.; ProQuest LLC (Ann Arbor); H.W. Wilson. *Indexed:* ABIn, AS&TI, ApMecR, C&ISA, CerAb, ChemAb, EngInd, ExcerpMed, H&SSA, IAA. *Aud.:* Ac, Sa.

Contains highly technical information regarding designing and installing HVAC, refrigeration, and water pumping systems. This journal is geared to engineers and practitioners on commercial or large system projects. Topics include commentary on installation guidelines, energy efficiencies, contracts, and design and installation of HVAC, plumbing, and piping systems. Each issue has a section for product highlights, "War Stories" from the field, and a calendar for upcoming conferences. The web site (www.hpac.com) contains further resource guides, tips, and information on getting an e-mail newsletter.

991. *Journal of Light Construction (New England Edition).* Supersedes in part (in 1989): *Journal of Light Construction;* Which was formerly (until 1988): *New England Builder.* [ISSN: 1050-2610] 1982. m. USD 39.95 domestic; USD 59.95 foreign. Ed(s): Jill Mason, Dan Jackson. Hanley Wood, LLC, 186 Allen Brook Ln, Williston, VT 05495; tjackson@ hanleywood.com; http://www.hanleywood.com. Illus., index, adv. Sample. Circ: 64148 Paid. *Aud.:* Sa.

Intended for contractors, builders, and remodelers of residential and light construction projects, this journal features articles ranging from how-to pieces to product highlights to discussions of how construction options affect and are affected by the environment. Featured monthly are letters, a Q&A section, and "On the Job," which details real-life experiences of contractors. The web site (www.jlconline.com) offers news, a product guide called "Online Toolbox," an e-newsletter, and has RSS Feed capability. Many of the articles are available for free dating back to 1986.

992. *Masonry Construction.* Former titles: *Aberdeen's Magazine of Masonry Construction;* (until 1990): *Magazine of Masonry Construction.* 1988. 10x/yr. USD 30 domestic; USD 39 in Canada & Mexico; USD 93 elsewhere. Ed(s): Rick Yelton. Aberdeen Group, 426 S Westgate St, Addison, IL 60101; cschierhorn@wocnet.com; http://www.worldofmasonry.com. Illus., index, adv. Circ: 30000 Paid. Online: Florida Center for Library Automation; Gale; OCLC Online Computer Library Center, Inc.; H.W. Wilson. *Indexed:* AS&TI, C&ISA, CerAb, EngInd, IAA. *Aud.:* Sa.

Masons and bricklayers are the intended audience for this publication featuring articles on everything from paving and bricklaying techniques to architectural and patio design. There are new product features and discussions of economic and building trends that affect the industry, as well as discussions of technical processes and standards. Special features in each issue include the "Mason's Toolbag" and "Brickbats." An annual buyer's guide is also published. The web site (www.masonryconstruction.com) contains free access to articles with a searchable interface and links to web "how-to" videos and a project gallery.

Old-House Journal. See Do-It-Yourself section.

993. *P M Engineer.* [ISSN: 1080-353X] 1994. 10x/yr. USD 79 domestic (Free to qualified personnel). Ed(s): Kelly Johnson. B N P Media, 2401 W Big Beaver Rd, Ste 700, Troy, MI 48084; http://www.bnpmedia.com. Adv. Circ: 26500 Controlled. Online: Florida Center for Library Automation; Gale; OCLC Online Computer Library Center, Inc.; ProQuest LLC (Ann Arbor). *Aud.:* Ac, Sa.

This journal contains highly technical information regarding the design of plumbing systems that include drainage systems, filters, and sprinkler systems. It also contains features geared to engineers and practitioners. Topics include commentary on installation guidelines and codes, system efficiencies, and design and installation problems and successes. Each issue has a section for product highlights, industry news, and editorials. The web site (www.pmengineer.com) features online showrooms, webinars, classifieds, and industry links.

994. *Plumbing Engineer.* [ISSN: 0192-1711] 1973. 12x/yr. USD 300 elsewhere (Free to qualified personnel). Ed(s): Mark Bruno. T M B Publishing, 1838 Techny Ct, Northbrook, IL 60062; info@tmbpublishing.com; http://plumbingengineer.com/. Illus., adv. Circ: 23000 Controlled. Microform: PQC. *Aud.:* Ac, Sa.

The journal claims to be "the authoritative source for plumbing, hydronics, fire protection and PVF" and covers the design of plumbing systems, sprinkler systems, and fire prevention systems. Plumbing engineers and practitioners will find useful information on industry trends, news, and product information. Each issue features a section titled "Designers Guide," "Fire Protection," and "Modern Hydronics," as well as a product news section and an events calendar. The web site (www.plumbingengineer.com) features industry links, advertiser information, a newsletter archive, and an issue archive back to 2006.

995. *Professional Builder.* Former titles (until 1993): *Professional Builder and Remodeler;* (until 1990): *Professional Builder;* (until 1985): *Professional Builder and Apartment Business;* (until 1972): *Professional Builder;* (until 1967): *Practical Builder.* [ISSN: 1072-0561] 1936. 17x/yr.

USD 109.90 domestic (Free to qualified personnel). Ed(s): Heather McCune. Reed Business Information, 2000 Clearwater Dr, Oak Brook, IL 60523; http://www.reedbusiness.com. Illus., adv. Circ: 127277 Paid and controlled. Microform: CIS. Online: EBSCO Publishing, EBSCO Host; Florida Center for Library Automation; Gale; Northern Light Technology, Inc.; OCLC Online Computer Library Center, Inc.; ProQuest LLC (Ann Arbor); H.W. Wilson. *Indexed:* ABIn, BPI, C&ISA, CerAb, EnvAb, IAA. *Aud.:* Sa.

Topics included in this journal report on economic and industry trends, highlights of interesting homes, new products, floor plans, and other design ideas for home contractors, builders, and architects. The scope is wide-ranging, and many of the issues are topically dedicated to bathroom remodeling, additions and expansions, and highlighting a specific industry innovation or company. The web site (www.housingzone.com) features relevant news stories, house plans, a special advertising section called "HousingZone MarketPlace," and links to pertinent information for various types of builders. The print subscription is free, and there is access to the archives online back to 1999.

996. *Qualified Remodeler.* Incorporates (1985-1991): *Kitchen and Bath Concepts.* [ISSN: 0098-9207] 1975. a. Free to qualified personnel. Ed(s): Patrick O'Toole. Cygnus Business Media, Inc., 1233 Janesville Ave, Fort Atkinson, WI 53538-0803. Illus., adv. Circ: 85000 Paid and controlled. *Indexed:* ABIn. *Aud.:* Sa.

The journal specializes in remodeling existing buildings and homes and is geared to general contractors and carpenters in the field. Topics include remodeling tips and trends, product guides, promoting the business, building client relationships, and organizational skills, as well as highlights of successful remodeling. Monthly features include "Letters," "Marketing," "Resources," and "Industry News." The web site (www.qualifiedremodeler.com) contains further resource guides and tips, video advertisements from different vendors, a blog list entitled the "market memo," and industry news links.

997. *Remodeling.* Formerly: *Remodeling World;* Incorporates (1948-1987): *Remodeling Contractor (Washington);* Which was formerly (until 1983): *Home Improvement Contractor;* (until 1976): *Home Improvements;* (until 1969): *Building Specialties and Home Improvements.* [ISSN: 0885-8039] 1985. m. USD 24.95 domestic (Free to qualified personnel). Ed(s): Sal Alfano, Christine Hartman. Hanley Wood, LLC, One Thomas Circle, NW, Ste 600, Washington, DC 20005-5701; tjackson@hanleywood.com; http://www.hanleywood.com. Illus., adv. Circ: 82456 Controlled. Microform: PQC. Online: Florida Center for Library Automation; Gale. *Aud.:* Sa.

This journal reports on the trends, ideas, market assessments, and new products for contractors as well as the do-it-yourself remodelers. Information is sometimes technical and sometimes anecdotal. Monthly features include a section for product highlights, industry news, a section called "Ways + Means," "Bottom Line," and "Field Notes," which records best practices by contractors. Subscriptions are free to licensed contractors and available for a fee to others. The web site (www.remodelingmagazine.com) features a product guide, a link to code specifications, and access to current and back issues online.

This Old House. See Do-It-Yourself section.

998. *Welding Journal.* Formerly (until 1937): *American Welding Society Journal.* [ISSN: 0043-2296] 1922. m. Free to members; Non-members, USD 120. Ed(s): Andrew Cullison. American Welding Society, 550 NW LeJeune Rd, Miami, FL 33126; http://www.aws.org. Illus., adv. Circ: 50000 Paid. Microform: PMC; PQC. Online: OCLC Online Computer Library Center, Inc.; H.W. Wilson. *Indexed:* AS&TI, ApMecR, C&ISA, CerAb, ChemAb, EngInd, ErgAb, ExcerpMed, IAA, SCI, SSCI. *Aud.:* Sa.

The American Welding Society publishes this journal encompassing news, technological advances, and trends in welding and metal fabrication. The journal examines techniques such as soldering and brazing; and provides advice on general maintenance, repair, inspection, and testing. It also offers advice on ways to economize time and money. It does all this through in-depth reporting and full-color illustrations. The web site (www.aws.org/wj) offers a buyer's guide, access to the current issue, news, classifieds, subscription information, and an index to past articles.

■ BUSINESS

General/Computer Systems and Forecasting/Ethics/International/Small Business/State and Regional/Trade and Industry

See also Accounting and Taxation; Advertising and Public Relations; Economics; Finance; Management, Administration, and Human Resources; and Real Estate sections.

Brian DeHart, Reference/Instruction Librarian, DePaul University Libraries, 1 E. Jackson Blvd., Chicago, IL 60604; bdehart@depaul.edu

Introduction

The magazines included in this section provide timely news and insight that impact not just large corporations and industries, but also individuals, small businesses, organizations, and governments. The information and analysis they provide are invaluable to institutional as well as personal investors looking to monitor trends and innovations. For their part, scholarly journals report best practices, research findings, and theories that advance the understanding of how business dynamics interact with each other and the world at large.

Publishers now frequently offer additional web-based content that complements their printed issues. Exclusive online features can include access to archives, daily news updates, buyers' guides, rankings, and industry statistics. More and more publishers are offering RSS feeds used to deliver a continuous stream of information tailored to a reader's needs and interests.

Basic Periodicals

GENERAL. Ga: *Barron's, Business 2.0, Business Week, The Economist, Fast Company, Forbes, Fortune, IndustryWeek, Survey of Current Business, Wall Street Journal.* Ac: *Business History Review, Business Horizons, Harvard Business Review, The Journal of Business Research, Journal of Education for Business, Journal of Retailing.*

COMPUTER SYSTEMS AND FORECASTING. Ga: *CIO, eWEEK.* Ac: *International Journal of Forecasting, MIS Quarterly*

ETHICS. Ac: *Business and Society Review, Journal of Business Ethics.*

INTERNATIONAL. Ga: *The Economist, Financial Times, Journal of Commerce.* Ac: *Journal of International Business Studies, Journal of World Business.*

SMALL BUSINESS. Ga: *Franchising World, Entrepreneur, Inc.* Ac: *Entrepreneurship: Theory and Practice, The Journal of Business Venturing, Journal of Small Business Management.*

STATE AND REGIONAL. Will vary.

TRADE AND INDUSTRY. Will vary.

Basic Abstracts and Indexes

ABI/Inform, Business and Company Resource Center, Business Source, Business and Industry, Wilson Business Abstracts.

General

999. *American Journal of Business.* Formerly (until 2007): *Mid-American Journal of Business;* Which was formed by the merger of (1971-1985): *Ball State Business Review;* (1929-1982): *Ball State Journal for Business Educators;* Which was formerly (until 1965): *Ball State Commerce Journal.* [ISSN: 1935-5181] 1985. s-a. Mar. & Sep. USD 40 (Individuals, USD 25; USD 30 foreign). Ed(s): Ashok Gupta, Judy Lane. Ball State University, Bureau of Business Research, 2000 W University Ave, Muncie, IN 47306-0360; jlane@bsu.edu; http://www.bsu.edu. Illus., index, adv. Refereed. Circ: 1800 Paid and free. Microform: PQC. Online: EBSCO Publishing, EBSCO Host; OCLC Online Computer Library Center, Inc.; ProQuest LLC (Ann Arbor); H.W. Wilson. *Indexed:* ABIn, BPI, PAIS, PsycInfo. *Bk. rev.:* 1, length varies. *Aud.:* Ac.

Formerly *Mid-American Journal of Business*, this title continues to be aimed at researchers, practicing managers, and instructors of general business administration in the United States. Articles running 8–10 pages in length are the norm, along with editorials, "Dean's Forum," "Executive Viewpoint," and one book review rounding out each issue. Occasional special issues present specific management themes. Academic libraries and faculty will benefit most from this title.

1000. *Barron's: the Dow Jones business and financial weekly.* Former titles (until vol.74, no.13, 1994): *Barron's National Business and Financial Weekly;* (until 1942): *Barron's.* [ISSN: 1077-8039] 1921. w. USD 179; USD 4 newsstand/cover per issue. Ed(s): Richard Rescigno, Edwin A Finn, Jr. Dow Jones & Company, 200 Liberty St, New York, NY 10281; http://www.dowjones.com. Illus., adv. Circ: 304658 Controlled. Vol. ends: Dec. Microform: BHP; PQC. Online: OCLC Online Computer Library Center, Inc.; ProQuest K-12 Learning Solutions; ProQuest LLC (Ann Arbor). *Indexed:* ABIn, ATI, BPI, BRI, CBRI, EnvAb, LRI, NewsAb. *Bk. rev.:* Various number and length. *Aud.:* Ga, Ac, Sa.

This weekly newspaper format provides general business information that serves the needs of investors. Articles on current business, economic, and political trends are accompanied by reports on industries, individual companies, and people in the news. The "Market Week" center pull-out section covers securities analysis and performance statistics, including stock tables, economic indicators, commodities, money markets, and major indexes. This is a core business and investment title for public and academic libraries.

1001. *Business 2.0.* Formed by the merger of (2000-2001): *eCompany Now;* (1995-2001): *Business 2.0 (Brisbane);* Which was formerly (until 1998): *The Net - Your Cyberspace Companion.* [ISSN: 1538-1730] 2001. m. USD 6.99 domestic; CND 9.65 Canada; USD 3.99 newsstand/cover. Ed(s): James Aley, Ned Desmond. Time Inc., Fortune Group, 1 California St., San Francisco, CA 94111; http://www.business2.com. Illus., adv. Sample. Circ: 550000. Vol. ends: Dec. *Indexed:* ABIn, MicrocompInd. *Aud.:* Ga.

Strives to discover and report on innovative business practices and the people behind them. The cover story and feature articles are accompanied by columns reporting on trends (what's next) in the marketplace, management best practices (what works), and reviews of products and lifestyle (what's cool). More inclusion by the major periodical indexes would improve visibility; selected content is available online at www.business2.com.

1002. *Business Communication Quarterly.* Former titles (until 1994): *Association for Business Communication. Bulletin;* (until 1985): *A B C A Bulletin (American Business Communication Association); A B W A Bulletin (American Business Writing Association).* [ISSN: 1080-5699] 1935. q. USD 314. Ed(s): Dr. Robert J Myers, Kathryn Riley. Sage Publications, Inc., 2455 Teller Rd, Thousand Oaks, CA 91320; info@sagepub.com; http://www.sagepub.com. Illus., index, adv. Sample. Refereed. Circ: 2475. Microform: PQC. Online: EBSCO Publishing, EBSCO Host; Florida Center for Library Automation; Gale; HighWire

Press; Northern Light Technology, Inc.; OCLC Online Computer Library Center, Inc.; SAGE Publications, Inc., SAGE Journals Online; SwetsWise Online Content. Reprint: PSC. *Indexed:* ABIn, BPI, CommAb, HRA, PAIS. *Bk. rev.:* 2-3, 750-1000 words. *Aud.:* Ac, Sa.

This interdisciplinary journal is aimed primarily at an international readership involved directly in the teaching of business communication. As with its sister publication, *Journal of Business Communication*, submissions are invited from educators in a wide variety of fields including management, rhetoric, organizational behavior, composition, speech, mass communication, psychology, linguistics, advertising, sociology, information technology, education, and history. Topics cover teaching methods in a variety of settings: technical institutes, community colleges, four-year colleges, universities, and corporate training programs. Article formats include case studies of specific classroom techniques, reports on program development strategies, research on classroom teaching and assessment, and book reviews of textbooks and other titles of interest to faculty.

Business Economics. See Economics section.

1003. *Business Education Forum.* [ISSN: 0007-6678] 1947. q. Oct., Dec., Feb. & Apr. Free to members. Ed(s): Susan O'Brien. National Business Education Association, 1914 Association Dr, Reston, VA 20191-1596; nbea@nbea.org; http://www.nbea.org. Illus., index, adv. Circ: 15300 Paid. Vol. ends: Apr. Microform: PQC. *Indexed:* ABIn, EduInd. *Aud.:* Ac.

Official publication of the National Business Education Association. Articles range from 1,500 to 2,500 words and cover business education issues in high schools, technical schools, colleges, and universities. The Curriculum Forum section includes articles on accounting, basic business, communication, international business, marketing, methods, and technology. Special sections appear quarterly: research (October), student organizations (December), entrepreneurship (February), and administration and supervision (April). Association news, a professional leadership directory, and award announcements are also included.

1004. *Business Facilities: the location advisor.* Formerly: *A I P R (American Industrial Properties Report).* [ISSN: 0746-0023] 1968. m. USD 30 domestic (Free to qualified personnel). Ed(s): Karim Khan, Mary Ellen McCandless. Group C Communications, 44 Apple St, Ste 3, Tinton Falls, NJ 07724; connie@groupc.com; http://www.groupc.com. Illus., adv. Circ: 43500 Controlled and free. *Aud.:* Ga, Sa.

This magazine is aimed at executives responsible for the expansion or relocation of their companies. Emphasis is placed on covering the general business climates in local communities, states, and regions spotlighted as business-friendly and prime for growth. Short features and longer special reports focus on specific industries, commercial real estate trends, and infrastructure. Each issue reports on news of corporate moves. Follow links to the sister publication, *Today's Facility Manager,* and the *TFM Show* (formerly *Facility Forum*), the premier conference event for this industry. An important magazine for the corporate location scout; a bargain for public library browsing collections; not recommended, however, for academic collections because of the lack of commercial indexing.

1005. *Business Forum (Los Angeles).* Formerly (until 1982): *Los Angeles Business and Economics.* [ISSN: 0733-2408] 1975. q. USD 99. Ed(s): Jane Park. California State University, Los Angeles, School of Business & Economics, 5151 State University Dr, Los Angeles, CA 90032-8120; http://cbe.calstatela.edu/publication/index.htm. Illus., index, adv. Refereed. Circ: 8500 Paid and controlled. Microform: PQC. Online: Florida Center for Library Automation; Gale; OCLC Online Computer Library Center, Inc.; ProQuest LLC (Ann Arbor). *Indexed:* ABIn, PAIS. *Bk. rev.:* Irregular. *Aud.:* Ga, Ac.

Each issue contains five to seven short features providing expert commentary and innovative solutions without being overly technical. Interdisciplinary submissions are encouraged; articles might relate to specific industries, government policy and regulation, or contemporary social and environmental concerns. Issues are occasionally thematic.

1006. *Business History.* [ISSN: 0007-6791] 1959. q. GBP 486 print & online eds. Routledge, 4 Park Sq, Milton Park, Abingdon, OX14 4RN, United Kingdom; info@routledge.co.uk; http://www.routledge.com. Illus., index, adv. Refereed. Microform: PQC. Online: EBSCO Publishing, EBSCO Host; Florida Center for Library Automation; Gale; IngentaConnect; Northern Light Technology, Inc.; OCLC Online Computer Library Center, Inc.; SwetsWise Online Content. Reprint: PSC. *Indexed:* ABIn, AmH&L, AmHI, ArtHuCI, BAS, BPI, BrHumI, HistAb, IBR, IBSS, IBZ, JEL, PAIS, SSA, SSCI, SociolAb. *Bk. rev.:* Approx. 25 per issue, each a single page in length. *Aud.:* Ac.

Each issue contains five feature articles 20–40 pages in length, with an emphasis on U.K. and European history. Subject coverage includes profiles of companies in historical context, analysis of industrial development and practices over time, and the evolution of economic integration. Toward the back of each issue, a single critical book review is followed by 25 shorter summary reviews. Because of the pervasive nature of business in society, this title is of potential interest to all social scientists and historians.

1007. *Business History Review.* Formerly (until 1954): *Business Historical Society. Bulletin.* [ISSN: 0007-6805] 1926. q. USD 130 (Individuals, USD 50; Students, USD 30). Ed(s): Walter A Friedman, Jeffrey Jones. Harvard Business School Publishing, Soldier's Field Rd, Boston, MA 02163; info@hbs.edu. Illus., index, adv. Refereed. Circ: 2000 Paid and controlled. Vol. ends: No. 4. Microform: PQC. Online: Chadwyck-Healey Inc.; The Dialog Corporation; Florida Center for Library Automation; Gale; JSTOR (Web-based Journal Archive); Northern Light Technology, Inc.; OCLC Online Computer Library Center, Inc.; ProQuest LLC (Ann Arbor); H.W. Wilson. *Indexed:* ABIn, ABS&EES, ATI, AmH&L, ArtHuCI, BAS, BPI, BRD, BRI, CBRI, HistAb, IBR, IBSS, IBZ, JEL, LRI, PAIS, SSCI. *Bk. rev.:* 25-30, 750-1,000 words. *Aud.:* Ac.

Each issue is comprised of three feature articles 40–50 pages in length along with numerous book reviews. Subjects cover biographical profiles, corporate culture, and studies of specific industries with emphasis on North American history. Photographs and illustrations appear on the cover and accompany some articles. The online archives at www.hbs.edu/bhr offer article abstracts back to 1954 and pdf images of book reviews back to 2002. Of interest to all social scientists, historians, and fans of Americana.

1008. *Business Horizons.* [ISSN: 0007-6813] 1957. 6x/yr. EUR 339. Ed(s): Catherine M. Dalton. Elsevier Inc., 360 Park Ave S, New York, NY 10010-1710. Illus., index, adv. Circ: 3000 Paid. Vol. ends: No. 6. Microform: PQC. Online: EBSCO Publishing, EBSCO Host; Florida Center for Library Automation; Gale; IngentaConnect; Northern Light Technology, Inc.; OCLC Online Computer Library Center, Inc.; OhioLINK; ScienceDirect; SwetsWise Online Content; H.W. Wilson. *Indexed:* ABIn, ABS&EES, ATI, AgeL, BAS, BLI, BPI, BRD, BRI, CBRI, EAA, ExcerpMed, FutSurv, IBR, LRI, LogistBibl, PAIS, PMA, RI-1, SSCI. *Bk. rev.:* 0-3, 1,500 words. *Aud.:* Ga, Ac.

This bimonthly title is edited by the Kelley School of Business, Indiana University. Approximately ten scholarly articles seven to ten pages in length address a wide range of business disciplines, ethics, and the impact of business on society. Editors strive to strike a balance between the practical and the academic; contributors are encouraged to avoid nontechnical language. Each issue contains a cumulative index for the current volume year. Of interest to all libraries.

1009. *Business Today (Princeton).* [ISSN: 0007-7100] 1968. 3x/yr. USD 9; USD 3.99 newsstand/cover. Ed(s): Meaghan Muntean. Foundation for Student Communication, Inc., 48 University Pl, Princeton, NJ 08544-1011; http://www.princeton.edu/~fscint. Illus., adv. Circ: 200000 Controlled. Microform: MIM; PQC. *Aud.:* Ac.

This student-run magazine serves as a forum for diverse topics and is designed to give undergraduates a broader understanding of business leadership, industry innovation, government policies, international perspectives, and career track advice. The content will appeal to a wider college audience, not just business majors; ideal for browsing collections in academic libraries.

1010. *Business Week.* [ISSN: 0007-7135] 1929. w. USD 64 domestic; CND 94.95 Canada; USD 199 in Asia. McGraw-Hill Companies, Inc., 1221 Ave of the Americas, New York, NY 10020; http://www.mcgraw-hill.com. Illus., index, adv. Circ: 1160000 Paid. Microform: PQC. Online: EBSCO Publishing, EBSCO Host; Florida Center for Library Automation; Gale; LexisNexis; Northern Light Technology, Inc.; OCLC Online Computer Library Center, Inc. *Indexed:* ABIn, ATI, AgeL, Agr, BLI, BPI, BRI, BrTechI, C&ISA, CBRI, CPerI, CWI, CerAb, ChemAb, EnvInd, FLI, FutSurv, IAA, ISTA, LRI, MASUSE, MicrocompInd, PAIS, PRA, RGPR, RI-1, SD. *Bk. rev.:* Various number and length. *Aud.:* Ga.

This title profiles industries, companies, and individuals; tracks political and legal issues; analyzes the impact of information technology; and reports on major developments in international business and foreign markets. Other sections offer commentary on social issues and lifestyle topics, such as travel and consumer product reviews. Editorials generally take a moderate position. The table of contents also highlights unique content available online at www.businessweek.com. In fact, some commercial database vendors now index *Business Week Online* separately from the weekly newsstand title. Articles are written at a level appreciated by a general readership. If a library could purchase only one business magazine, this would be it.

1011. *The Conference Board Review: a magazine of ideas and opinion.* Former titles (until 2006): *Across the Board;* (until 1976): *Conference Board Record;* Supersedes: *Conference Board Business-Management Record.* 1939. bi-m. Members, USD 39; Non-members, USD 59. Ed(s): Albert Vogl. Conference Board, Inc., 845 Third Ave, New York, NY 10022; atb@conference-board.com; http://www.conference-board.org. Illus., index, adv. Circ: 35000. Vol. ends: Dec. Online: EBSCO Publishing, EBSCO Host; Northern Light Technology, Inc.; OCLC Online Computer Library Center, Inc.; ProQuest K-12 Learning Solutions; H.W. Wilson. *Indexed:* ABIn, ABS&EES, ATI, AgeL, BAS, BLI, BPI, FutSurv, PAIS, PMA, SSCI. *Bk. rev.:* 1-2, 1,500 words. *Aud.:* Ga, Ac.

For more than 90 years the Conference Board, whose membership is comprised of thousands of business leaders from around the world, has promoted a better understanding of the changing complexities of the business environment. Whereas this magazine offers best practices and analysis primarily to corporate executives, its content will also appeal to a more general audience. Articles are written in an irreverent and accessible style and address a wide range of subject matter. Only selected features and departments from the current and previous issues are available in full text through www.conference-board.com.

Consumer Reports. See Consumer Education section.

The Economist. See Economics section.

1012. *Fast Company.* [ISSN: 1085-9241] 1995. m. USD 10 domestic; USD 27 Canada. Ed(s): John Byrne. Fast Company, Inc., 375 Lexington Ave, New York, NY 10017; subscriptions@fastcompany.com. Illus., adv. Circ: 750000. Online: EBSCO Publishing, EBSCO Host; Florida Center for Library Automation; Gale; LexisNexis; OCLC Online Computer Library Center, Inc.; ProQuest K-12 Learning Solutions; ProQuest LLC (Ann Arbor); H.W. Wilson. *Indexed:* ABIn, BPI, MicrocompInd. *Aud.:* Ga.

The tag line "How smart people work" really does permeate each issue. Articles of varying lengths profile executives, managers, and business owners who drive innovation. Not surprisingly, emphasis is placed on covering the new, novel, and trendy in the business world. The writing style is decidedly irreverent. Bold graphics and content that are pushed to the very edges of the page speak to a reader who is most likely comfortable multitasking. Conclusions are frequently enumerated or distilled to bullet points; lists of companies or products are ranked, all for the purpose of providing information—fast. Online access to the current issue and archives is available through the web site where articles can be found complemented by video and other exclusives.

1013. *Forbes.* [ISSN: 0015-6914] 1917. bi-w. USD 19.99 domestic; CND 32.09 Canada; USD 4.99 newsstand/cover. Ed(s): Tim W. Ferguson, Paul Maidment. Forbes, Inc., 60 Fifth Ave, New York, NY 10011; http://www.forbes.com/forbes. Illus., index, adv. Circ: 819884. Vol. ends:

Dec. Microform: PQC. Online: The Dialog Corporation; EBSCO Publishing, EBSCO Host; Florida Center for Library Automation; Gale; OCLC Online Computer Library Center, Inc.; ProQuest LLC (Ann Arbor). *Indexed:* ABIn, ATI, AgeL, Agr, BLI, BPI, BRI, ChemAb, EnvAb, FLI, ISTA, LRI, MASUSE, MicrocompInd, PRA, RGPR, RI-1, SSCI. *Aud.:* Ga, Ac.

The focus of this title is on news and analysis impacting executives, managers, and investors. In addition to the cover story, a typical issue contains numerous short articles, each analyzing economic trends or profiling industries, corporations, and key individuals. Recurring sections include Marketing, Entrepreneurs, Technology, Money and Investing, and Health. The table of contents highlights exclusive web features available at www.forbes.com. This is a core title for both public and academic libraries. A subscription is complemented by occasional supplements: *Forbes Asia*, and *Forbes Life*, containing lifestyle features.

1014. *Fortune.* [ISSN: 0015-8259] 1930. bi-w. USD 19.99; USD 4.99 newsstand/cover. Time Inc., Business Information Group, 1271 Ave of the Americas, New York, NY 10020; letters@fortune.com; http://www.fortune.com. Illus., index, adv. Circ: 818791 Paid. Vol. ends: Dec. Microform: PQC. Online: EBSCO Publishing, EBSCO Host; Florida Center for Library Automation; Gale; LexisNexis; OCLC Online Computer Library Center, Inc.; ProQuest LLC (Ann Arbor); H.W. Wilson. *Indexed:* ABIn, ABS&EES, ATI, AgeL, Agr, BLI, BPI, BRI, CBRI, CPerI, EnvAb, ExcerpMed, ISTA, LRI, MASUSE, MicrocompInd, PAIS, RGPR, RI-1, SSCI. *Bk. rev.:* Various number and length. *Aud.:* Ga, Ac, Sa.

Less news-driven than *Business Week*, this title offers lengthier features analyzing major corporate and industry developments. It tends to cover smaller companies and more industry sectors than *Forbes*. Emphasis is on investing and personal finance. Thus, articles inform the reader about general concepts and issues related to the economy, financial markets, and management. Articles are frequently accompanied by explanatory sidebars and additional commentary. The April issue, which contains the *Fortune 500* ranking, is much anticipated; other thematic rankings appear regularly throughout the year. This is a core title for all business collections.

1015. *Harvard Business Review.* [ISSN: 0017-8012] 1922. m. USD 99. Ed(s): Thomas A Stewart. Harvard Business School Publishing, 60 Harvard Way, Boston, MA 02163; corpcustserv@hbsp.harvard.edu; http://www.hbsp.harvard.edu. Illus., index, adv. Circ: 250000 Paid. Vol. ends: Dec. Microform: PQC. Online: DataStar; EBSCO Publishing, EBSCO Host; Florida Center for Library Automation; Gale; ProQuest K-12 Learning Solutions. *Indexed:* ABIn, ABS&EES, ASIP, ATI, AgeL, BAS, BLI, BPI, BRI, CBRI, CommAb, CompR, EnvAb, ExcerpMed, FutSurv, IBR, IBZ, JEL, LogistBibl, PAIS, PMA, RGPR, SSCI. *Bk. rev.:* Various number and length. *Aud.:* Ga, Ac.

Each issue contains about a dozen articles, ten pages in length, along with a short case study. *HBR* provides readers with the current thinking of scholars and industry leaders on the topics of human resources management, manufacturing, strategic planning, globalization of markets, competitiveness, and related general business interests. Articles—although rarely containing footnotes—are highly regarded if not considered scholarly. This is a core business title for academic libraries and larger public libraries.

Inc. See under Small Business, this section.

1016. *Industrial and Corporate Change.* [ISSN: 0960-6491] 1991. bi-m. EUR 522 print or online ed. Ed(s): J. Chytry. Oxford University Press, Great Clarendon St, Oxford, OX2 6DP, United Kingdom; jnl.orders@oup.co.uk; http://www.oxfordjournals.org. Illus., index, adv. Refereed. Circ: 950. Online: EBSCO Publishing, EBSCO Host; Gale; HighWire Press; IngentaConnect; OCLC Online Computer Library Center, Inc.; OhioLINK; Oxford Journals; ProQuest LLC (Ann Arbor); SwetsWise Online Content; H.W. Wilson. Reprint: PSC. *Indexed:* ABIn, BPI, HRA, IBSS, JEL, SSCI. *Bk. rev.:* Various number and length. *Aud.:* Ac, Sa.

The scope of this interdisciplinary journal aimed at industrial historians and business scholars spans sociology, political science, social psychology, economics, and organization theories. The eight to ten articles in each issue are quite lengthy, running 25–40 pages. According to the publisher's web site, topics addressed include "the internal structures of firms; the history of technologies; the evolution of industries; the nature of competition; the decision rules and strategies; the relationship between firms' characteristics and the institutional environment; the sociology of management and of the workforce; the performance of industries over time; the labour process and the organization of production; the relationship between, and boundaries of, organizations and markets; the nature of the learning process underlying technological and organizational change." Recommended for academic libraries offering advanced degrees in the social sciences.

1017. *IndustryWeek: the management resource.* Incorporates (1985-1995): *Electronics;* Which was formerly (1984-1985): *Electronics Week;* (1930-1984): *Electronics.* [ISSN: 0039-0895] 1882. 22x/yr. USD 66 domestic (Free to qualified personnel). Ed(s): Patricia Panchak, Tonya Vinas. Penton Media, Inc., 1300 E 9th St, Cleveland, OH 44114-1503; information@penton.com; http://www.penton.com/. Illus., index, adv. Circ: 236248 Controlled. Vol. ends: Dec. Microform: PQC. Online: The Dialog Corporation; EBSCO Publishing, EBSCO Host; Factiva, Inc.; Florida Center for Library Automation; Gale; LexisNexis; Northern Light Technology, Inc.; OCLC Online Computer Library Center, Inc.; ProQuest K-12 Learning Solutions; ProQuest LLC (Ann Arbor); H.W. Wilson. *Indexed:* ABIn, AS&TI, AgeL, BPI, CWI, EnvAb, LRI, LogistBibl, MASUSE. *Aud.:* Ga, Ac, Sa.

This trade magazine profiles individuals and companies active in manufacturing industries. Approximately five feature articles in each issue cover a wide range of topics of interest to executives and managers, including innovation, competition, infrastructure, globalization, supply chains, distribution, labor relations, regulatory pressures, and best practices in management and marketing. Recurring departments address emerging technologies, leadership, e-business, continuous improvement, and economic policies. Features and departments from the current and previous issues are freely available online at www.industryweek.com. Web-only content is highlighted alongside the magazine's table of contents. Of interest to all business collections.

1018. *Journal of Applied Business Research.* [ISSN: 0892-7626] 1985. q. USD 300. Ed(s): Ronald C Clute. Western Academic Press, PO Box 620760, Littleton, CO 80162; cluter@wapress.com; http://www.wapress.com. Adv. Sample. Refereed. Circ: 600. *Indexed:* ABIn, ATI, AgeL, BAS, BPI, IBSS, JEL. *Aud.:* Ac.

Each issue of this refereed journal contains approximately ten articles, 10–15 pages in length. Both theoretical and applied research manuscripts are considered for publication. Topics cover all areas of business and economics and can include ethical, pedagogical, and technological analysis. Recommended for all academic business collections.

1019. *Journal of Business and Economic Statistics.* [ISSN: 0735-0015] 1983. q. USD 135 print & online eds, Libraries, USD 115 (Members, USD 56 print & online eds). American Statistical Association, 1429 Duke St, Alexandria, VA 22314-3415; asainfo@amstat.org; http://www.amstat.org/publications/index.html. Illus. Refereed. Vol. ends: Oct. *Indexed:* ABIn, BPI, CCMJ, IBSS, JEL, MSN, MathR, SCI, SSCI, WAE&RSA. *Aud.:* Ac.

One of the official journals from the American Statistical Association, this scholarly title focuses on a broad range of topics in applied economics and business statistical problems. Using empirical methods, authors of these highly technical articles presume a reader's knowledge of mathematical theory. Topics covered include demand and cost analysis, forecasting, economic modeling, stochastic theory control, and impact of societal issues on wages and productivity. Recommended for academic libraries.

Journal of Business Communication. See Communication section.

1020. *Journal of Business Research.* Formerly (until 1978): *Southern Journal of Business.* [ISSN: 0148-2963] 1973. 12x/yr. EUR 1788. Ed(s): Arch G Woodside, M Laroche. Elsevier Inc., 360 Park Ave S, New York, NY 10010-1710; usinfo-f@elsevier.com; http://www.elsevier.com. Illus., index, adv. Refereed. Circ: 1750 Paid. Vol. ends: Nov. Microform: PQC. Online: EBSCO Publishing, EBSCO Host; Gale; IngentaConnect; OhioLINK; ScienceDirect; SwetsWise Online Content. *Indexed:* ABIn, AgeL, BPI, CommAb, IBSS, JEL, PAIS, PMA, PsycInfo, SSCI. *Aud.:* Ac, Sa.

Each issue presents a dozen articles 8–20 pages in length covering theoretical and empirical advances in buyer behavior, finance, organizational theory and behavior, marketing, risk and insurance, and international business. Issues are frequently devoted to a theme, e.g., cross-cultural consumer studies, electronic marketing theory, Asian business research, etc. Emphasis is placed on linking theory with practical solutions. Intended for executives, researchers, and scholars alike.

Journal of Business Strategy. See Management, Administration, and Human Resources/Strategic Analysis section.

Journal of Commerce. See under International, this section.

Journal of Consumer Research. See Advertising, Marketing, and Public Relations section.

1021. *Journal of Education for Business.* Formerly (until 1985): *Journal of Business Education.* [ISSN: 0883-2323] 1924. bi-m. USD 122 (Individuals, USD 62 print & online eds.; USD 19 newsstand/cover). Ed(s): Jamie R Kunkle. Heldref Publications, 1319 18th St, NW, Washington, DC 20036-1802; subscribe@heldref.org; http://www.heldref.org. Illus., adv. Refereed. Circ: 660 Paid. CD-ROM: ProQuest LLC (Ann Arbor). Online: EBSCO Publishing, EBSCO Host; Florida Center for Library Automation; Gale; Northern Light Technology, Inc.; OCLC Online Computer Library Center, Inc.; ProQuest K-12 Learning Solutions; ProQuest LLC (Ann Arbor); H.W. Wilson. Reprint: PSC. *Indexed:* ABIn, BRI, CBRI, CWI, ERIC, EduInd, IBR, IBZ, MRD, PAIS, PsycInfo, SWA. *Bk. rev.:* Irregular; 500-750 words. *Aud.:* Ac.

A forum for authors reporting on innovative teaching methods and curricula or proposing new theories and analyses of controversial issues. Each issue contains eight to ten features that aid educators in preparing business graduates who will need new competencies and leadership skills to thrive. Thus, this publication is of most interest to higher education administrators and faculty members.

1022. *Journal of Retailing.* [ISSN: 0022-4359] 1925. 4x/yr. EUR 384. Ed(s): Dhruv Grewal, Michael Levy. Pergamon, The Boulevard, Langford Ln, East Park, Kidlington, OX5 1GB, United Kingdom. Illus., index, adv. Refereed. Circ: 3200. Vol. ends: Winter. Microform: PQC. Online: The Dialog Corporation; EBSCO Publishing, EBSCO Host; Florida Center for Library Automation; Gale; IngentaConnect; Northern Light Technology, Inc.; OCLC Online Computer Library Center, Inc.; OhioLINK; ScienceDirect; SwetsWise Online Content; H.W. Wilson. *Indexed:* ABIn, ATI, AgeL, BPI, CABA, IBR, IBZ, PAIS, PsycInfo, RRTA, RiskAb, SSCI, WAE&RSA. *Aud.:* Ac, Sa.

Each issue offers five or six articles 20–25 pages in length. Retailing is defined as the act of selling products and/or services to consumers for their personal or family use. Thus, the scope of this journal is explicitly limited to consumer behavior, retail strategy, marketing channels, location analysis, the marketing mix, merchandise management, store and operations management, store atmospheric issues, and retail services. Other topics may be addressed so long as retailing is the focus of the submission. Examples include emerging technologies, supply chain management, relationships with third-party service providers, and public policy issues. There is liberal use of mathematical models for the benefit of other academicians; a general readership will appreciate the nontechnical executive summaries.

1023. *Portfolio (New York).* [ISSN: 1936-0916] 2007. 5x/yr. USD 15. Conde Nast Publications, Inc., 4 Times Sq, 14th Fl, New York, NY 10036; http://www.condenast.com. Adv. Circ: 300000. *Aud.:* Ga, Sa.

A brand new title that appeared on the scene in May 2007, this monthly looks to go beyond the likes of *Fortune* and *Forbes* by providing deeper research and analysis. Geared toward executives, it chronicles how business shapes the world, profiles business leaders, and offers a business angle in every story, from politics to art, technology to entertainment. A companion web site at www.portfolio.com presents news updates and online exclusives. A general readership will also find the writing accessible and the format visually attractive.

1024. *The Service Industries Journal.* [ISSN: 0264-2069] 1981. 8x/yr. GBP 745 print & online eds. Ed(s): Gary Akehurst, Nicholas Alexander. Routledge, 4 Park Sq, Milton Park, Abingdon, OX14 4RN, United Kingdom; journals@routledge.com; http://www.routledge.co.uk. Adv. Sample. Refereed. Microform: PQC. Online: EBSCO Publishing, EBSCO Host; Gale; IngentaConnect; Northern Light Technology, Inc.; OCLC Online Computer Library Center, Inc.; ProQuest LLC (Ann Arbor); SwetsWise Online Content. Reprint: PSC. *Indexed:* ABIn, BrHumI, CABA, CommAb, DSA, FS&TA, H&TI, HRA, IBR, IBZ, PRA, RRTA, SSCI, SWA, WAE&RSA. *Bk. rev.:* 5-6, 750-1000 words. *Aud.:* Ac.

The publisher's web site claims that "service industries generate over two-thirds of GNP and employment in developed countries, and their importance is growing in developing countries. Service industries include retailing and distribution; financial services, including banking and insurance; hotels and tourism; leisure, recreation and entertainment; professional and business services, including accountancy, marketing and law." Each issue contains approximately ten articles 20–30 pages in length. Geographic emphasis is split between Europe and the United States. Of interest primarily to academic collections supporting business programs.

1025. *Site Selection.* Former titles (until 1994): *Site Selection and Industrial Development;* (until 1984): *Site Selection Handbook;* (until 1977): *Industrial Development's Site Selection Handbook;* (until 1976): *Site Selection Handbook;* (until 1970): *Industrial Development's Site Selection Handbook;* Incorporated (in 1984): *Industrial Development;* Which was formerly (until 1967): *Industrial Development and Manufacturers Record;* Which was formed by the 1958 merger of: *Manufacturers Record;* (1954-1958): *Industrial Development.* [ISSN: 1080-7799] 1956. bi-m. USD 85 per issue domestic; USD 125 per issue foreign. Ed(s): Adam Bruns, Mark Arend. Conway Data, Inc., 6625 The Corners Pkwy, Ste 200, Norcross, GA 30092; http://www.sitenet.com. Illus., adv. Circ: 45000. Microform: PQC. Online: OCLC Online Computer Library Center, Inc.; H.W. Wilson. *Indexed:* ABIn, BPI, LRI, PAIS. *Aud.:* Ac, Sa.

Offers original research and analysis, interviews, and case studies for expansion-planning decision makers: CEOs, corporate real estate executives, facility planners, human resource managers, and consultants. Industry overviews provide forecasts and address key topics such as new plant construction, utilities and other infrastructure concerns, political and business climates, and labor demographics. Detailed economic development reports on specific cities, states, regions, and foreign countries fill out each issue. Exclusive web content is offered at www.siteselection.com.

1026. *Survey of Current Business.* [ISSN: 0039-6222] 1921. m. USD 63 domestic; USD 25 per issue domestic; USD 35 per issue foreign. U.S. Department of Commerce, Bureau of Economic Analysis, 1441 L St NW, Washington, DC 20230; http://www.bea.doc.gov/bea/. Illus., index. Circ: 7600 Paid. Vol. ends: Dec. Microform: CIS. Online: The Dialog Corporation; EBSCO Publishing, EBSCO Host; Factiva, Inc.; Florida Center for Library Automation; Gale; Northern Light Technology, Inc.; OCLC Online Computer Library Center, Inc.; ProQuest K-12 Learning Solutions; ProQuest LLC (Ann Arbor); H.W. Wilson. *Indexed:* ABIn, AmStI, BPI, IUSGP, JEL, PAIS. *Aud.:* Ga, Ac.

Each monthly issue provides trends in business, industry, and the general economy. It is primarily comprised of charts and tables displaying National Income and Product Accounts (NIPA) data. These statistics include current and historical figures on U.S. international trade in goods and services, gross domestic product, personal income and outlays, foreign direct investment, and similar statistics. Two or three feature articles analyze specific industries or sectors. Available in print through the Federal Depository Libraries program. Most patrons will find the online version at www.bea.gov/scb more timely and appreciate the ability to download tables as spreadsheets.

Wall Street Journal. See Newspapers/General section.

Computer Systems and Forecasting

Information technology is treated in most general business magazines whereas this subsection highlights those titles that specialize in business systems and modeling. See also the Functional Management and Operations Research subsections under Management, Administration, and Human Resources along with Computers and Information Technology in general.

1027. *Business Communications Review.* [ISSN: 0162-3885] 1971. m. USD 45 in US & Canada; USD 70 elsewhere. Ed(s): Eric Krapf, Fred S Knight. C M P Media LLC, 600 Community Dr, Manhasset, NY 11030; http://www.cmp.com. Illus., adv. Circ: 13759 Paid and free. Microform: PQC. Online: EBSCO Publishing, EBSCO Host; Florida Center for Library Automation; Gale; Northern Light Technology, Inc.; OCLC Online Computer Library Center, Inc.; ProQuest K-12 Learning Solutions; ProQuest LLC (Ann Arbor); H.W. Wilson. *Indexed:* ABIn, BPI. *Aud.:* Ac, Sa.

Aimed at professionals working in the enterprise network and telecommunications fields, *BCR* offers analysis of the technologies, trends, management issues, pricing, and regulation that helps managers break down the complex combination of factors for easier decision making. Limited content is available online through the web site at www.bcr.com.

1028. *C I O: the magazine for information executives.* Incorporates (1995-1997): *WebMaster.* [ISSN: 0894-9301] 1987. s-m. 23/yr. USD 95 in US & Canada (Free to qualified personnel). Ed(s): Tom Field, Abbie Lundberg. C X O Media Inc., 492 Old Connecticut Path, PO Box 9208, Framingham, MA 01701-9208; lundberg@cio.com; http://www.cio.com. Illus., adv. Circ: 140000 Paid and controlled. Online: EBSCO Publishing, EBSCO Host; Factiva, Inc.; OCLC Online Computer Library Center, Inc.; ProQuest LLC (Ann Arbor). *Indexed:* ABIn, CompLI, FLI, LogistBibl, MicrocompInd. *Aud.:* Ga, Ac, Sa.

This major trade title provides semi-monthly industry updates, news and events, tips, trends, and opinions by and for managing executives in the information technology and computer systems departments of medium to large organizations. Feature articles cover management skills, outsourcing, recruiting and other human resource management topics, emerging technologies, e-commerce, and IT strategies. Although aimed at the working professional, *CIO* is well suited for public libraries that serve the business community and academic libraries supporting advanced business degrees and computer science programs.

1029. *Computers in Industry.* [ISSN: 0166-3615] 1980. 9x/yr. EUR 1177. Ed(s): J. C. Wortmann. Elsevier BV, Radarweg 29, Amsterdam, 1043 NX, Netherlands; nlinfo-f@elsevier.nl; http://www.elsevier.nl. Illus., index, adv. Refereed. Vol. ends: No. 44 - No. 46. Microform: PQC. Online: EBSCO Publishing, EBSCO Host; Gale; IngentaConnect; OhioLINK; ScienceDirect; SwetsWise Online Content. *Indexed:* ABIn, AS&TI, C&ISA, CEA, CerAb, CompLI, CompR, EngInd, EnvAb, ErgAb, IAA, SCI, SSCI. *Aud.:* Ac, Sa.

The main thrust of this journal is the unique application of information and communication technology (ICT) in business processes such as design, engineering, manufacturing, purchasing, physical distribution, production management, and supply chain management. It includes research in integration of business process support, such as in enterprise modelling, ERP, and EDM. Articles that link industrial use of ICT with knowledge intensive fields such as quality control, logistics, engineering data management, and product documentation are encouraged. The writing is technical and requires a strong background in information systems and computer science, making this strictly a scholar's journal.

Decision Sciences. See Management, Administration, and Human Resources/Operations Research and Management Science section.

1030. *Decision Support Systems.* [ISSN: 0167-9236] 1985. 8x/yr. EUR 1044. Ed(s): A B Whinston. Elsevier BV, North-Holland, Sara Burgerhartstraat 25, Amsterdam, 1055 KV, Netherlands; nlinfo-f@ elsevier.nl; http://www.elsevier.nl. Illus., index, adv. Refereed. *Indexed:* ABIn, AS&TI, C&ISA, CJA, CerAb, CompLI, CompR, EngInd, ErgAb, IAA, PollutAb, PsycInfo, SCI, SSCI. *Aud.:* Ac.

Highly technical and scholarly journal covering the concept of using computers for supporting the managerial decision process. Articles discuss artificial intelligence, cognitive science, computer-supported cooperative work, database management, decision theory, economics, linguistics, management science, mathematical modeling, operations management psychology, and user interface management systems. The relatively high subscription price and theoretical focus limit holdings to academic libraries offering programs in advanced business administration, MIS, or computer science.

eWEEK. See Computers and Information Technology/Popular Titles section.

1031. *Government Technology: solutions for state and local government in the information age.* [ISSN: 1043-9668] 1987. m. USD 269 elsewhere (Free to qualified personnel). Ed(s): Jessica Jones, Steve Towns. e.Republic, Inc., 100 Blue Ravine Rd, Folsom, CA 95630-4703; getinfo@govtech.net; http://www.govtech.net/. Illus., adv. Circ: 72201 Controlled. *Indexed:* CompLI. *Aud.:* Sa.

Aimed at executives and managers, this magazine offers a network of integrated products and services for technology providers in the government IT sector. Features include interviews with key personnel in local and national government departments and agencies who apply technology to improve service to citizens. Areas covered include justice, welfare, transportation, human services and homeland security. News, case studies, conferences and events, product reviews, and sourcing round out each issue. Of primary interest to municipal, state, and federal libraries; public and academic libraries will have no problem affording the free print subscription. Articles and columns, both current and archived, are readily available online at www.govtech.net.

1032. *Information & Management.* Incorporates (1981-1985): *Systems, Objectives, Solutions;* Former titles (until 1977): *Management Datamatics;* (until 1975): *Management Informatics;* (until 1972): *I A G Journal.* [ISSN: 0378-7206] 1968. 8x/yr. EUR 711. Ed(s): E H Sibley. Elsevier BV, North-Holland, Sara Burgerhartstraat 25, Amsterdam, 1055 KV, Netherlands; nlinfo-f@elsevier.nl; http://www.elsevier.nl. Illus., index, adv. Refereed. Circ: 2500. Microform: PQC. Online: EBSCO Publishing, EBSCO Host; Gale; IngentaConnect; OCLC Online Computer Library Center, Inc.; OhioLINK; ScienceDirect; SwetsWise Online Content. *Indexed:* ABIn, AS&TI, CompLI, CompR, EngInd, FR, ISTA, PsycInfo, SCI, SSCI. *Bk. rev.:* Various number and length. *Aud.:* Ac, Sa.

Aimed at managers, database administrators, and senior executives, this scholarly journal covers a wide range of developments in applied information systems such as knowledge management, data mining, and CRM. Articles focus on trends in evaluation methodology and models; managerial policies, strategies, and activities of business, public administration, and international organizations; and guidelines on how to mount successful information technology initiatives through case studies. The technical nature of the writing will appeal primarily to researchers and practitioners active in the MIS field.

1033. *International Journal of Forecasting.* [ISSN: 0169-2070] 1985. 4x/yr. EUR 626. Ed(s): Rob J. Hyndman. Elsevier BV, North-Holland, Sara Burgerhartstraat 25, Amsterdam, 1055 KV, Netherlands. Adv. Refereed. Microform: PQC. Online: EBSCO Publishing, EBSCO Host; Gale; IngentaConnect; OhioLINK; ScienceDirect; SwetsWise Online Content. *Indexed:* ABIn, BAS, FPA, IBSS, JEL, PAIS, PSA, RiskAb, SSCI. *Bk. rev.:* Various number and length. *Aud.:* Ac, Sa.

This official publication of the International Institute of Forecasters is the leading journal of forecasting for all aspects of business. It strives to bridge the gap between theory and practice for those policy and decision makers who utilize forecasting methods. Articles by international scholars are featured each quarter along with notes, book and software reviews, and reviews of current research in forecasting. At half the cost, this is a better buy than the *Journal of Forecasting.* Recommended for academic libraries.

1034. *International Journal of Technology Management.* [ISSN: 0267-5730] 1986. 16x/yr. EUR 1320 (print or online ed.). Ed(s): Dr. Mohammed A Dorgham. Inderscience Publishers, IEL Editorial Office, PO Box 735, Olney, MK46 5WB, United Kingdom; editor@inderscience.com; http://www.inderscience.com. Illus., index, adv. Refereed. Circ: 20000. *Indexed:* ABIn, Agr, BPI, BrTechI, C&ISA, CerAb, CompLI, EngInd, EnvAb, EnvInd, IAA, IBSS, ISTA, SCI, SSCI. *Bk. rev.:* Various number and length. *Aud.:* Ac, Sa.

This refereed journal disseminates advances in the science and practice of technology management, with the goal of fostering communication between government officials, technology executives, and academic experts worldwide. Each issue contains research reports and case studies on technology transfers, supply chain management, sourcing, R&D systems, and information technology. Geared to academics, researchers, professionals, and policy makers, *IJTM* is best suited to academic libraries with advanced degree programs in the management sciences.

1035. *The Journal of Business Forecasting.* Formerly (until 2005): *Journal of Business Forecasting Methods and Systems.* [ISSN: 1930-126X] 1981. q. USD 85 domestic; USD 110 foreign. Ed(s): Chaman L Jain. Graceway Publishing Co., PO Box 670159, Flushing, NY 11367-0159; info@ibf.org; http://www.ibf.org. Illus., index, adv. Circ: 3500. Vol. ends: No. 4. Microform: PQC. Online: EBSCO Publishing, EBSCO Host; OCLC Online Computer Library Center, Inc. *Indexed:* ABIn, ATI, RiskAb. *Bk. rev.:* 1, 750 words. *Aud.:* Ac, Sa.

Executives and managers comprise the primary audience of this highly specialized publication. Clearly written and jargon-free articles provide practical information for decision makers on inventory control, supply chain management, production scheduling, budgeting, marketing strategies, and financial planning. Also featured are international and domestic economic outlooks and corporate earnings analysis by industry. Of most interest to academic business collections and corporate libraries.

1036. *Journal of Forecasting.* [ISSN: 0277-6693] 1981. 8x/yr. USD 1455 print or online ed. Ed(s): Derek Bunn. John Wiley & Sons Ltd., The Atrium, Southern Gate, Chichester, PO19 8SQ, United Kingdom; customer@wiley.co.uk; http://www.wiley.co.uk. Illus., adv. Refereed. Vol. ends: Nov. Reprint: PSC. *Indexed:* ABIn, CCMJ, EngInd, IBSS, IndVet, JEL, MSN, MathR, PAIS, RiskAb, SSCI, VB. *Aud.:* Ac, Sa.

Edited by an international board of scholars, this title offers a forum for practical, theoretical, and computational forecasting methods. As in the many journals dealing with forecasting, this title is concerned with the relationship of decision-making processes to forecasting systems. Feature articles in each issue cover a variety of theoretical and empirical applications in the fields of technology, government, business, and the environment. Presupposes a knowledge of mathematical theory; appropriate for academic and corporate libraries.

1037. *Journal of Intelligent Information Systems: integrating artificial intelligence and database technologies.* [ISSN: 0925-9902] 1992. bi-m. EUR 908 print & online eds. Ed(s): Larry Kerschberg, Maria Zemankova. Springer New York LLC, 233 Spring St, New York, NY 10013-1578; service-ny@springer.com; http://www.springer.com/. Illus., adv. Refereed. Microform: PQC. Online: EBSCO Publishing, EBSCO Host; Gale; IngentaConnect; OCLC Online Computer Library Center, Inc.; OhioLINK; ProQuest LLC (Ann Arbor); Springer LINK; SwetsWise Online Content. Reprint: PSC. *Indexed:* ABIn, CompLI, CompR, EngInd, ErgAb, ISTA, SCI. *Aud.:* Ac, Sa.

The mission of *JIIS* is to present results of research and development on the integration of artificial intelligence and database technologies. Articles address such topics as foundations and principles; methodologies for analysis and design; data representation; expert systems; logic and databases; storage and retrieval; distributed systems; data mining and knowledge management; and user models and visual representation. Submissions describing theoretical aspects, systems architectures, analysis and design tools and techniques, and implementation experiences in intelligent information systems are typical. Shorter articles that discuss emerging issues are welcome. Strictly a scholar's journal.

Long Range Planning. See Management, Administration, and Human Resources/Strategic Analysis section.

1038. *Manufacturing Business Technology.* Former titles (until 2005): *M S I;* (until 2001): *Manufacturing Systems;* (until 198?): *Manufacturing Operations.* [ISSN: 1554-3404] 1983. m. USD 85 domestic (Free to qualified personnel). Ed(s): Kevin Parker. Reed Business Information, 2000 Clearwater Dr, Oak Brook, IL 60523; http://www.reedbusiness.com. Illus., adv. Circ: 97179 Controlled. Online: EBSCO Publishing, EBSCO Host; Gale; LexisNexis; OCLC Online Computer Library Center, Inc.; ProQuest LLC (Ann Arbor); H.W. Wilson. *Indexed:* ABIn, AS&TI, C&ISA, CerAb, CompLI, H&SSA, IAA. *Aud.:* Sa.

This trade monthly spotlights how information technology enhances manufacturing management. Cover stories typically profile company success stories, best practices, or individuals driving innovation. The "Views from the Front" section reports the latest industry news. Features address applications and services; network security; performance and productivity analysis; and integration and infrastructure. Columnists provide commentary and opinion on new technologies. Aimed at industrial managers who develop or oversee systems, this title is recommended for special libraries supporting the manufacturing sector or IT vendors.

MIS Quarterly. See Management, Administration, and Human Resources/Functional Management section.

1039. *Technological Forecasting and Social Change.* Formerly (until 1970): *Technological Forecasting.* [ISSN: 0040-1625] 1969. 9x/yr. EUR 941. Ed(s): J P Martino, Harold A Linstone. Elsevier Inc., 360 Park Ave S, New York, NY 10010-1710; usinfo-f@elsevier.com; http://www.elsevier.com. Illus., adv. Refereed. Vol. ends: No. 66 - No. 68. Microform: PQC. Online: EBSCO Publishing, EBSCO Host; Gale; IngentaConnect; OhioLINK; ScienceDirect; SwetsWise Online Content. *Indexed:* ABS&EES, Agr, ArtHuCI, BAS, BPI, C&ISA, EAA, EngInd, ExcerpMed, FutSurv, HRIS, IPSA, JEL, PSA, SSA, SSCI, SUSA, SociolAb. *Bk. rev.:* 0-2, 1,000-2,500 words. *Aud.:* Ac.

A major international forum for those wishing to deal directly with the methodology and practice of technological forecasting and future studies as planning tools combining social, environmental, and technological factors. Of interest to architects, urban planners, industrial engineers, systems engineers, political scientists, sociologists, military experts, futurologists, corporate planners, and marketers. Included here as a bit of a stretch, but complementary to the other business forecasting titles listed in this section. Articles frequently do have an explicit business angle. Issues are occasionally thematic.

Ethics

The impact of the Sarbanes-Oxley Act of 2002 has created renewed interest in the discussion of business ethics and corporate governance. Titles included here offer both scholarly analysis as well as more popular access to the debate on what constitutes corporate social responsibility.

1040. *Business & Professional Ethics Journal.* Incorporates (1992-2004): *Professional Ethics.* [ISSN: 0277-2027] 1981. q. USD 95 (Individuals, USD 30). Ed(s): Robert J Baum. University of Florida, Center for Applied Philosophy and Ethics in the Professions, PO Box 15017, Gainesville, FL 32604; http://web.phil.ufl.edu. Illus., index, adv. Refereed. Circ: 800 Paid. *Indexed:* BPI, LRI, PAIS, PhilInd, RI-1. *Bk. rev.:* Various number and length. *Aud.:* Ac.

Published by the Center for Applied Philosophy and Ethics in the Professions and broadly interdisciplinary in aim. Lengthy articles explore "the similarities and differences between the ethical situations that arise in two or more professions," including marketing, health care, human resource management, global labor, socially responsible investing, and business ethics. Half of the issues are devoted to reprinting selected papers from professional ethics conferences around the globe. Because of the pervasive awareness of applied ethics in society, this journal will be useful in all academic libraries.

1041. *Business & Society: a journal of interdisciplinary exploration.* [ISSN: 0007-6503] 1960. q. GBP 311. Ed(s): John F Mahon. Sage Publications, Inc., 2455 Teller Rd, Thousand Oaks, CA 91320; info@sagepub.com; http://www.sagepub.com. Illus., index, adv. Refereed. Circ: 700 Paid and free. Microform: PQC. Online: CSA; EBSCO Publishing, EBSCO Host; Florida Center for Library Automation; Gale; HighWire Press; OCLC Online Computer Library Center, Inc.; ProQuest LLC (Ann Arbor); SAGE Publications, Inc., SAGE Journals Online; SwetsWise Online Content. Reprint: PSC. *Indexed:* ABIn, BPI, C&ISA, CerAb, CommAb, CompR, FR, HRA, IAA, IPSA, PAIS, PMA, PRA, PSA, RiskAb, SSA, SociolAb, V&AA. *Bk. rev.:* 1-3, 750-1,000 words. *Aud.:* Ac.

Official journal of the International Association for Business and Society presenting the latest theory, empirical research, and analysis on the ways in which business and society affect each other. Topics covered include business ethics and values, business/government relations, corporate governance, corporate social responsibility, environmental issues, and the international dimensions of business and society relationships. Topical issues generally include several feature articles, one to three lengthy signed book reviews, and related dissertation abstracts.

1042. *Business and Society Review: journal of the Center for Business Ethics at Bentley College.* Formerly (until 1974): *Business and Society Review/Innovation;* Which was formed by the merger of (1962-1972): *Innovation; Business and Society Review.* [ISSN: 0045-3609] 1972. q. GBP 193 print & online eds. Ed(s): Robert E Frederick. Blackwell Publishing, Inc., Commerce Place, 350 Main St, Malden, MA 02148; customerservices@blackwellpublishing.com; http://www.blackwellpublishing.com. Illus., adv. Circ: 3000 Paid. Microform: PQC. Online: Blackwell Synergy; EBSCO Publishing, EBSCO Host; Gale; IngentaConnect; OCLC Online Computer Library Center, Inc.; OhioLINK; SwetsWise Online Content; H.W. Wilson. Reprint: PSC. *Indexed:* ABIn, ATI, AgeL, ApEcolAb, BPI, CLI, CompR, FutSurv, ILP, LRI, PAIS, PMA, PRA, PhilInd, RI-1. *Bk. rev.:* Irregular, 500-2,500 words. *Aud.:* Ga, Ac.

This scholarly publication includes a dozen articles 8–20 pages in length covering a wide range of ethical issues, corporate citizenship, and social responsibility. Some issues are thematic. Articles are of interest to business people, academics, and others involved in the contemporary debate about the proper role of business in society. Expect to find this title in academic collections supporting business programs and in larger public libraries.

1043. *Business Ethics: a European review.* [ISSN: 0962-8770] 1992. q. GBP 684 print & online eds. Ed(s): Christopher Cowton. Blackwell Publishing Ltd., 9600 Garsington Rd, Oxford, OX4 2ZG, United Kingdom; customerservices@blackwellpublishing.com; http://www.blackwellpublishing.com. Illus. Refereed. Online: Blackwell Synergy; EBSCO Publishing, EBSCO Host; IngentaConnect; OCLC Online Computer Library Center, Inc.; OhioLINK; SwetsWise Online Content. Reprint: PSC. *Indexed:* ABIn, ApEcolAb, IBSS, PhilInd, PsycInfo, RiskAb. *Bk. rev.:* Brief. Number varies. *Aud.:* Ac.

This primarily European-focused journal provides a forum for dialogue through original theoretical research and refereed scholarly papers. The range of contributions reflects the variety and scope of ethical issues faced by businesses and organizations worldwide. Articles address ethical challenges and solutions, analyze business policies and practices, and explore the concept of good ethical thinking. Submissions that are responsive to changing concerns and emerging issues are encouraged. Interviews, brief book reviews, comments, and responses to previously published articles round out the content.

1044. *Business Ethics Quarterly.* [ISSN: 1052-150X] 1991. q. USD 160 (Individuals, USD 60; Students, USD 30). Ed(s): George Brenkert. Philosophy Documentation Center, PO Box 7147, Charlottesville, VA 22906-7147. Refereed. Circ: 900. Microform: PQC. Online: EBSCO Publishing, EBSCO Host; OCLC Online Computer Library Center, Inc.; H.W. Wilson. Reprint: PSC. *Indexed:* ABIn, ABS&EES, BPI, IBR, IBSS, IBZ, LRI, PhilInd, RI-1, SSCI. *Bk. rev.:* 2-3, 1,000-2,000 words. *Aud.:* Ac.

This official journal of the Society for Business Ethics looks at how business ethics in particular are influenced by gender, race, ethnicity, and nationality. Article submissions addressing global business and economic concerns are encouraged. There are approximately 6–12 feature articles in each issue, accompanied by one or more review articles. Of most interest to academic business collections.

1045. *C R O: corporate responsibility officer.* Incorporates (1987-2006): *Business Ethics.* [ISSN: 1933-5903] 2006. q. Free to members. C R O Corp. LLC., 37 W. 20th St., Ste. 904, New York, NY 10011; http://www.thecro.com/. Adv. Sample. Circ: 10000 Paid and free. *Indexed:* AltPI. *Bk. rev.:* 2-3; 150-250 words. *Aud.:* Ga, Ac, Sa.

Sporting a new name and now glossier in appearance, this quarterly contains three or four features and several departments including News & Trends, Legal, Corporate Social Responsibility, Ethics & Governance, Diversity, NGO Profile, and On the Move, which notes members' career advancement. Content is of primary interest to corporate executives; however, the discussions and case studies will also interest students in academic libraries with browsing collections. The annual ranking of the "100 Best Corporate Citizens" and analysis of socially responsible investing (SRI) will also appeal to a more general readership. Selected articles and online exclusives are available at the web site.

1046. *Ethikos: examining ethical and compliance issues in business.* Incorporates (1991-1999): *Corporate Conduct Quarterly.* [ISSN: 0895-5026] 1987. s-m. USD 175. Ed(s): Andrew W Singer. Ethikos, Inc., 154 E Boston Post Rd, Mamaroneck, NY 10543. Adv. Online: Northern Light Technology, Inc.; ProQuest K-12 Learning Solutions; ProQuest LLC (Ann Arbor). *Bk. rev.:* 1, 1,000-1,500 words. *Aud.:* Ac, Sa.

Analysis of federal regulatory compliance, reports on corporate policies/practices, and case studies are written primarily by the editors; outside contribution is limited. Each issue also contains an extensive review article. Of interest to academic libraries and special libraries supporting corporate compliance efforts. Selected articles from previous issues are available online at www.ethikosjournal.com.

1047. *International Journal of Value-Based Management.* [ISSN: 0895-8815] 1988. 3x/yr. EUR 211 for print or online ed. Ed(s): Anthony F Libertella, Samuel M Natale. Kluwer Academic Publishers, van Godewijckstraat 30, PO Box 17, Dordrecht, 3300 AA, Netherlands; services@wkap.nl; http://www.wkap.nl. Refereed. Circ: 500. *Indexed:* ABIn, PAIS, RiskAb. *Aud.:* Ac.

A forum for clarifying the role of values in organizational behavior and in the process of decision making. Each issue contains approximately six case studies and empirical research articles 10–20 pages in length. Comparative cultural points of view are encouraged from contributors worldwide. Of interest to academic collections supporting international business programs.

1048. *Journal of Business Ethics.* Incorporates (1997-2004): *Teaching Business Ethics;* (1988-2004): *International Journal of Value-Based Management.* [ISSN: 0167-4544] 1982. 28x/yr. EUR 2060 print & online eds. Ed(s): Alex C Michalos, Deborah C Poff. Springer Netherlands, Van Godewijckstraat 30, Dordrecht, 3311 GX, Netherlands; http://www.springeronline.com. Illus., adv. Refereed. Vol. ends: Dec. Microform: PQC. Online: Chadwyck-Healey Inc.; EBSCO Publishing, EBSCO Host; Gale; IngentaConnect; OCLC Online Computer Library

Center, Inc.; OhioLINK; ProQuest LLC (Ann Arbor); Springer LINK; SwetsWise Online Content. Reprint: PSC. *Indexed:* ABIn, ATI, AgeL, ArtHuCI, BPI, CJA, CommAb, IBR, IBSS, IBZ, PAIS, PRA, PhilInd, PsycInfo, RI-1, RiskAb, SSCI. *Aud.:* Ac.

From its inception, this journal has aimed to improve the human condition by providing a public forum for discussion and debate about ethical issues related to business. The number of submissions and general interest in ethics have greatly expanded in recent years; two sister publications have been absorbed and new section editors have been named to handle business law, codes of ethics, corporate governance, gender issues, philosophic foundations, small business, teaching business ethics, and value-based management. An important title for collections supporting academic programs in business.

1049. *The Journal of Corporate Citizenship.* [ISSN: 1470-5001] 2001. q. GBP 150 (Individuals, GBP 75). Ed(s): Sandra Waddock. Greenleaf Publishing, Aizlewood Business Centre, Aizlewoods Mill, Nursery St, Sheffield, S3 8GG, United Kingdom; http://www.greenleaf-publishing.com. Illus., adv. Sample. Refereed. Circ: 750 Paid. *Indexed:* ABIn, IBSS. *Bk. rev.:* 1, 1,000-1,500 words. *Aud.:* Ac.

This newer peer-reviewed quarterly seeks to integrate theory about corporate citizenship with management practice. Topics can include partnerships; decision making and leadership; accountability standards; economics of sustainable development; human rights; history of corporate social responsibility; market and nonmarket drivers; and image and identity. A key feature is commentaries and essays labeled "Turning Points," which address important contemporary issues that are too new yet to be the subject of empirical and theoretical studies. A good complement to established business ethics collections.

1050. *Multinational Monitor.* Supersedes: *Elements.* [ISSN: 0197-4637] 1980. m. Individuals, USD 25; Corporations, USD 40; Non-profit organizations, USD 30. Ed(s): John Richard, Robert Weissman. Essential Information, PO Box 19405, Washington, DC 20036. Illus., index, adv. Refereed. Circ: 10000. Microform: PQC. Online: EBSCO Publishing, EBSCO Host; Florida Center for Library Automation; Gale; Northern Light Technology, Inc.; OCLC Online Computer Library Center, Inc.; ProQuest LLC (Ann Arbor). *Indexed:* ABIn, AltPI, IBR, IBZ, LeftInd, PAIS. *Bk. rev.:* 0-1, 750-1,500 words. *Aud.:* Ga, Sa.

Provides coverage, often in a highly critical fashion, of the impact multinational corporations have on society and the environment. Articles and interviews address topics involving labor, pollution, corporate crime, government policy, regulatory issues, legislation, developmental finance, and banking. Of interest to general and academic collections with a focus on business ethics. Corporate libraries will find it useful to monitor themselves and competitors in the court of public opinion. Access to current issue contents and archives is available for free at www.multinationalmonitor.org.

International

African Business. See Africa section.

1051. *B R W.* Incorporates (1935-1987): *Rydge's;* (1985-1987): *Rydge's Management and Marketing Update;* (1984-1986): *Today's Computers.* [ISSN: 0727-758X] 1980. w. AUD 199 domestic. Ed(s): Tony Featherstone. Fairfax Business Media, 469 La Trobe St, Melbourne 3000, NSW 3000, Australia; http://www.fxj.com.au/. Illus., index, adv. Circ: 63578. *Indexed:* ABIn, PAIS. *Aud.:* Ga.

Australia's leading business magazine, covering economic, financial, management, marketing, and e-business topics each week. Company and individual profiles spotlight successes—and failures. An index of names on the back inside cover indicates whether the report was negative, positive, or neutral. Online access to magazine content at www.brw.com.au is limited for the most part to print subscribers.

1052. *Business Latin America: weekly report to managers of Latin American operations.* [ISSN: 0007-6880] 1966. w. USD 1420 print or online ed.; USD 955 print or online ed. Ed(s): Anna Szterenfeld, Steven Murphy. Economist Intelligence Unit, 111 W 57th St, New York, NY 10019; newyork@eiu.com; http://www.eiu.com. Illus. Microform: PQC. *Indexed:* ABIn. *Aud.:* Ac, Sa.

This fortnightly report provides news briefs that feature political and economic analysis of Central and South American countries, giving important insights for companies that wish to operate in those regions. Segments include Investment Environment, Industry Monitor, Infrastructure, and Business Outlook, which forecasts the business climate of individual countries. The editorial board consists of executives from large multinational corporations. A vital source of international business intelligence, although it is cost-prohibitive to all but the largest academic and corporate libraries. Similar titles exist from this publisher for other regions/countries, e.g., Africa, Middle East, Asia, India, China, Europe, and Eastern Europe.

Business Strategy Review. See Management, Administration, and Human Resources/Strategic Analysis section.

Business Times. See Asia and the Pacific/Southeast Asia section.

1053. *Business Today.* 1992. fortn. USD 100. Ed(s): Aroon Purie. Living Media India Pvt. Ltd., F-14-15, Connaught Place, New Delhi, India; wecare@intoday.com; http://www.indiatoday.com. Adv. Circ: 127378. *Aud.:* Ga, Ac.

India's leading fortnightly, which covers all aspects of Indian business with emphasis on information systems and technologies. Articles are written clearly, for a general audience, and are accompanied by colorful, detailed graphics. Each issue also includes news and trends, profiles of people, case studies, policy analysis, and discussions on career development. Of interest to larger public libraries and academic collections supporting international business programs or South Asian Studies. Online content at www.business-today.com is privileged access for print subscribers only.

Canadian Business. See Canada section.

Euromoney. See Finance/Investment section.

Far Eastern Economic Review. See Asia and the Pacific/General section.

Financial Times. See Newspapers/General section.

International Small Business Journal. See under Small Business, this section.

1054. *International Trade Forum.* [ISSN: 0020-8957] 1964. q. USD 50. Ed(s): Natalie Domeisen. International Trade Centre, Plais des Nations, Geneva, 1211, Switzerland; itcreg@intracen.org; http://www.intracen.org. Illus., index. Circ: 30000. Microform: PQC. Online: EBSCO Publishing, EBSCO Host; Florida Center for Library Automation; Gale; Northern Light Technology, Inc.; OCLC Online Computer Library Center, Inc.; ProQuest LLC (Ann Arbor); H.W. Wilson. *Indexed:* ABIn, BPI, CABA, FS&TA, HortAb, LRI, PAIS, RRTA, WAE&RSA. *Aud.:* Ga, Ac.

Published by the International Trade Centre (ITC), the cooperative agency of the United Nations Conference on Trade and Development (UNCTAD) and the World Trade Organization (WTO). This quarerly seeks to explore the links between trade development, current events, and societal trends. The magazine continues a 40-year tradition of providing business-like, practical "news you can use." Current content and archives are readily available online at www.tradeforum.org, complemented by enhancements including collections of articles by theme, links to web sites of partner organizations, and a selection of links to major trade topics.

1055. *Japan Journal (English Edition).* Formerly (until 2004): *Look Japan.* 1953. m. JPY 950 newsstand/cover. Ed(s): Chiba Hitoshi. The Japan Journal, Ltd., Kosei Bldg. (4F), 2-2-5 Uchikanda, Tokyo, 101-0047, Japan. Illus., index. Circ: 75000. Vol. ends: Dec. Online: Gale. *Indexed:* BAS, PAIS. *Bk. rev.:* Various number and length. *Aud.:* Hs, Ac, Sa.

Each issue contains a cover story and several features in each of the main sections: Economy and Business, Society and Culture, and Science and Technology. Opinion pieces address such topics as the Japanese economy and politics, Japan–U.S. relations, globalization, small business development, and the impact of technology. There are news reports, interviews, company profiles, and new product announcements. Of interest to high school and public libraries because of the general coverage on the society. Academic collections supporting international studies or business programs will find value in having access to a Japanese perspective written in English. Only print subscribers have access to full content of articles online at www.japanjournal.jp/tjje.

1056. *Japan Spotlight: Economy, Culture & History.* Formerly (until 2003): *Journal of Japanese Trade and Industry.* [ISSN: 1348-9216] 1982. bi-m. JPY 6000; JPY 1200 newsstand/cover. Japan Economic Foundation, 11th Fl, Jiji Press Bldg., 5-15-8 Ginza Chuo-Ku, Tokyo, 104-0061, Japan; info@jef.or.jp; http://www.jef.or.jp/. Illus., adv. Circ: 35000. *Indexed:* BAS, BPI, EnvAb, PAIS. *Aud.:* Ac, Sa.

Covers not only economy, industry, and trade, but also international politics, history, culture, and other topics that fit the primary goal of the Japan Economic Foundation, i.e., to create a deeper understanding of Japan and the world. Writers include business executives, government officials, university professors, specialist researchers, and leading journalists. The cover story sets the theme of the business-oriented features inside. Current issue contents and searchable archives are only available online at www.jef.or.jp/journal to print subscribers. Recommended for academic collections supporting programs in international business or Japanese Studies; a must for corporations doing business with Japan.

1057. *The Journal of Commerce.* Formerly (until 2002, vol.3, issue 42): *J o C Week;* Which was superseded in part (until 2000): *Journal of Commerce;* Which was formerly (until 1996): *Journal of Commerce and Commercial;* (until 1927): *Journal of Commerce.* [ISSN: 1542-3867] 1827. w. USD 195 domestic. Ed(s): Joseph Bonney. Journal of Commerce, Inc., 33 Washington St, 13th Fl, Newark, NJ 07102. Adv. Circ: 22000 Paid. Microform: PQC. Online: The Dialog Corporation; EBSCO Publishing, EBSCO Host; Gale; OCLC Online Computer Library Center, Inc.; H.W. Wilson. *Indexed:* ABIn, BPI, ChemAb, LRI, LogistBibl, PAIS. *Aud.:* Ga, Ac, Sa.

This weekly provides authoritative editorial content for international business executives to help them plan their global supply chain and better manage their day-to-day international logistics and shipping needs. This information is delivered through news, analysis of the political landscape surrounding the latest regulatory issues, case studies, and perspective pieces. Recommended for all international business and transportation collections. Only the table of contents of the current issue can be viewed online at www.joc.com. There is a searchable archive feature, but an instant desktop reprint must be purchased in order to view each article.

1058. *Journal of International Business Studies.* [ISSN: 0047-2506] 1970. 8x/yr. USD 340 print & online eds. Ed(s): Lorraine Y Eden. Palgrave Macmillan Ltd., Houndmills, Basingstoke, RG21 6XS, United Kingdom; journal-info@palgrave.com; http://www.palgrave-journals.com/. Adv. Refereed. Circ: 4100. Microform: PQC. Online: EBSCO Publishing, EBSCO Host; Florida Center for Library Automation; Gale; IngentaConnect; JSTOR (Web-based Journal Archive); Micromedia ProQuest; Northern Light Technology, Inc.; OCLC Online Computer Library Center, Inc.; ProQuest LLC (Ann Arbor); SwetsWise Online Content; H.W. Wilson. Reprint: PSC. *Indexed:* ABIn, ABS&EES, BAS, BPI, CPerI, IBSS, JEL, PAIS, RiskAb, SSCI. *Aud.:* Ac.

This journal publishes empirical and hypothetical research articles that are frequently interdisciplinary in nature. Also included are case studies of corporate activities, strategies, and managerial processes that cross national boundaries; submissions that focus on the interactions of such firms with their economic, political, and cultural environments are encouraged. Recommended for all academic business collections.

1059. Journal of Teaching in International Business. [ISSN: 0897-5930] 1989. q. USD 450 print & online eds. Ed(s): Erdener Kaynak. International Business Press, 10 Alice St, Binghamton, NY 13904; getinfo@ haworthpress.com; http://www.haworthpress.com/. Adv. Sample. Refereed. Circ: 242 Paid. Reprint: HAW. *Indexed:* ABIn, IBR, IBZ. *Aud.:* Ac.

Examines issues, problems, opportunities, and solutions related to teaching and learning in international business. Enables educators to acquire the nuts and bolts of developing successful courses in international business for different cultural milieus, areas, or regions of the world. Some issues are thematic and are simultaneously published as monographs. Of most interest to business curriculum developers in higher education worldwide.

1060. Journal of World Business. Formerly (until 1997): *Columbia Journal of World Business.* [ISSN: 1090-9516] 1965. 4x/yr. EUR 353. Ed(s): J W Slocum, Jr., F. Luthans. Pergamon, The Boulevard, Langford Ln, East Park, Kidlington, OX5 1GB, United Kingdom. Illus., index, adv. Refereed. Circ: 3500. Vol. ends: No. 4. Microform: PQC. Online: EBSCO Publishing, EBSCO Host; Florida Center for Library Automation; Gale; IngentaConnect; OCLC Online Computer Library Center, Inc.; OhioLINK; ScienceDirect; SwetsWise Online Content; H.W. Wilson. *Indexed:* ABIn, ABS&EES, ATI, BLI, BPI, CommAb, IBSS, JEL, PAIS, PMA, PRA, PsycInfo, RRTA, RiskAb, SSCI, WAE&RSA. *Aud.:* Ac.

Each issue includes half a dozen articles written by leading academic researchers, top government officials, and prominent business leaders on issues related to financial markets, free trade, transition economies, emerging markets, privatization, joint ventures, mergers and acquisitions, human resource management, and marketing. Separate editorial boards are designated for contributors in the United States, Europe, Latin America, and the Pacific Rim. Recommended for all academic collections supporting international business studies.

1061. Latin Trade: your business source for Latin America. Formerly (until 1996): *U S - Latin Trade.* [ISSN: 1087-0857] 1993. m. Ed(s): Sabrina R Crow. Freedom Publications, Inc. (Miami), 200 S Biscayne Blvd, Ste 1150, Miami, FL 33131; lattrade@aol.com; http://www.latintrade.com. Illus., adv. Circ: 74000. Online: EBSCO Publishing, EBSCO Host; Factiva, Inc.; Florida Center for Library Automation; Gale; LexisNexis; Northern Light Technology, Inc.; OCLC Online Computer Library Center, Inc.; ProQuest LLC (Ann Arbor). *Indexed:* ABIn, CWI. *Bk. rev.:* Various number and length. *Aud.:* Ac, Sa.

This newsmagazine covers all aspects of corporate business in Central and South America. Feature articles tend to be few and short in length. Four departments fill out the remainder of each issue, providing timely information, statistics, and opinion pieces on people, companies, regulations, technology, import/export, and various trade and industry topics of the region. Special issues include the annual Bravo Awards, which recognize outstanding leadership in Latin America, and the annual ranking of Latin America's 100 largest publicly traded companies. The web site, www.latintrade.com, contains regional trade information and access to articles from the print version.

1062. Multinational Business Review. [ISSN: 1525-383X] 1993. s-a. USD 120 (Individuals, USD 60). Ed(s): Seung H Kim. Saint Louis University, John Cook School of Business, DuBourg Hall, Rm 39, 221 N Grand Blvd, Saint Louis, MO 63103-2097; http://business.slu.edu. CD-ROM: ProQuest LLC (Ann Arbor). Microform: PQC. Online: EBSCO Publishing, EBSCO Host; OCLC Online Computer Library Center, Inc.; ProQuest LLC (Ann Arbor); H.W. Wilson. *Indexed:* ABIn, BPI, PAIS. *Aud.:* Ac.

Publishes feature-length and shorter articles as well as case studies that explore contemporary international issues in finance, accounting, management, marketing, and economics. By focusing on practical applications in operations

management, investing, debt management, and importing and exporting, this journal provides a bridge between business theory and practice. Best suited for academic libraries with international business programs.

1063. The Nikkei Weekly. Former titles (until June 1991): *Japan Economic Journal;* (until 1970): *Nihon Keizai Shimbun (International weekly Edition).* [ISSN: 0918-5348] 1962. w. JPY 21600 domestic; USD 129 United States; CND 195 Canada. Ed(s): Nobuo Oneda. Nihon Keizai Shimbun Inc., 1-9-5 Ote-Machi, Chiyoda-ku, Tokyo, 100-0004, Japan; http://www.nikkei-bookdirect.com/. Illus., index, adv. Circ: 36500. Online: LexisNexis. *Indexed:* ChemAb, EnvAb. *Aud.:* Ga, Ac, Sa.

This newspaper is the leading English-language source of information about business and trade from a Japanese perspective. Similar in format to the *Financial Times*, it provides coverage of the economic, political, science and technology, industrial, management, labor, and financial sectors. Regular reports profile people, corporations, and new products. Summaries of business conditions in other Asian and Pacific Rim markets are provided as well.

Pakistan and Gulf Economist. See Asia and the Pacific/South Asia section.

1064. Project Finance. Formed by the merger of (1992-1997): *Infrastructure Finance;* (1990-1997): *Project and Trade Finance (London, 1989);* Which was formerly (until 1990): *Trade Finance and Banker International;* Which was formed by the 1989 merger of: *Trade Finance; Banker International;* Which was formerly (until 1987): *Euromoney Bank Report.* [ISSN: 1462-0014] 1997. 10x/yr. GBP 1200 combined subscription domestic print & online eds.; EUR 1750 combined subscription in Europe print & online eds.; USD 2250 combined subscription elsewhere print & online eds. Ed(s): Sean Keating, Tom Nelthorpe. Euromoney Institutional Investor Plc., Nestor House, Playhouse Yard, London, EC4V 5EX, United Kingdom; information@euromoneyplc.com; http://www.euromoney.com. Illus., index, adv. Circ: 6000. Microform: PQC. Online: EBSCO Publishing, EBSCO Host; Factiva, Inc.; Gale; OCLC Online Computer Library Center, Inc.; ProQuest LLC (Ann Arbor). *Indexed:* ABIn, BLI. *Aud.:* Ac, Sa.

Self-proclaimed "the global authority for the project finance industry," this trade title offers news and short features covering people, agencies, countries, deals analysis, and developments by large corporations and regional authorities worldwide related to infrastructure, trade, and project finance. Aimed at corporate insiders, this title might appeal to academic libraries with programs in international strategic planning and risk management. Online access to articles at www.projectfinancemagazine.com is limited to print subscribers.

1065. Thunderbird International Business Review. Formerly (until 1998): *International Executive;* Incorporates (1988-2001): *Global Focus;* Which was formerly (until 1999): *Global Outlook;* (until 1998): *Business and the Contemporary World.* [ISSN: 1096-4762] 1959. bi-m. USD 599 domestic; USD 659 in Canada & Mexico; USD 710 elsewhere. Ed(s): Yahia H Zoubir. John Wiley & Sons, Inc., 111 River St, Hoboken, NJ 07030-5774; uscs-wis@wiley.com; http://www.wiley.com. Adv. Refereed. Circ: 1000 Paid. Microform: PQC. Online: EBSCO Publishing, EBSCO Host; OhioLINK; ProQuest LLC (Ann Arbor); SwetsWise Online Content; Wiley InterScience. Reprint: PSC. *Indexed:* ABIn, ABS&EES, BPI, PAIS, RiskAb. *Bk. rev.:* 0-8, 450-2,000 words. *Aud.:* Ac, Sa.

With the goal of exchanging ideas and research between scholars and practitioners worldwide, this refereed journal has a target audience of international managers, academicians, and executives in business and government. Articles and case studies address a wide range of topics: analysis of multinational corporations, small business development, marketing ethics, market entry, doing business in specific countries, and international trade policies. Issues are frequently thematic.

Small Business

Black Enterprise. See African American section.

1066. *Entrepreneur (Irvine).* Formerly (until 1977): *Insider's Report.* [ISSN: 0163-3341] 1973. m. USD 15.97 domestic; USD 31.97 foreign; USD 4.99 newsstand/cover. Ed(s): Karen Axelton, Maria Valdez. Entrepreneur Media, Inc., 2445 McCabe Way, Ste 400, Irvine, CA 92614; http://www.entrepreneur.com. Illus., adv. Sample. Circ: 556831 Paid. Online: EBSCO Publishing, EBSCO Host; Florida Center for Library Automation; Gale. *Indexed:* BPI, PAIS. *Aud.:* Ga, Sa.

A leading magazine covering trends, issues, and problems associated with starting and running a business. Short features written in an engaging style include individual and company profiles; success stories; strategies for improvement; and rankings of top companies and individuals. News coverage includes national, global, women-oriented, industry-specific, and hot topics. Each issue contains tips on technology, money, management, marketing, classified ads, and a products and services directory. The web site, www.entre-preneur.com, contains full-text features and columns from the current issue along with online exclusives. Archival content is available back to 1997. A core title for business collections in most public and academic libraries.

1067. *Entrepreneurship & Regional Development: an international journal.* [ISSN: 0898-5626] 1989. bi-m. GBP 337 print & online eds. Ed(s): Bengt Johannisson. Routledge, 4 Park Square, Milton Park, Abingdon, OX14 4RN, United Kingdom; info@routledge.co.uk; http://www.routledge.co.uk. Adv. Refereed. Online: EBSCO Publishing, EBSCO Host; Gale; IngentaConnect; OCLC Online Computer Library Center, Inc.; SwetsWise Online Content. Reprint: PSC. *Indexed:* ABIn, IBSS, JEL, SSCI. *Bk. rev.:* Infrequent. *Aud.:* Ac.

Focuses on the diverse and complex characteristics of local and regional economies (primarily European) that lead to entrepreneurial vitality. Provides a multidisciplinary forum for researchers, students, and practitioners in the fields of entrepreneurship and small to medium-sized enterprise (SME) development within the larger context of economic growth and development. Each issue contains four or five articles, each 15–25 pages in length. Of interest to academic collections catering to small business studies or economics.

1068. *Entrepreneurship: Theory and Practice.* Formerly (until vol.12): *American Journal of Small Business.* [ISSN: 1042-2587] 1976. bi-m. GBP 311 print & online eds. Ed(s): D Bagby. Blackwell Publishing, Inc., Commerce Place, 350 Main St, Malden, MA 02148; customerservices@ blackwellpublishing.com; http://www.blackwellpublishing.com. Illus., index, adv. Circ: 1600 Paid. Vol. ends: No. 4. Microform: PQC. Online: Blackwell Synergy; EBSCO Publishing, EBSCO Host; Gale; IngentaConnect; OCLC Online Computer Library Center, Inc.; OhioLINK; SwetsWise Online Content; H.W. Wilson. Reprint: PSC. *Indexed:* ABIn, ATI, ApEcolAb, BPI, IBSS, PAIS, RiskAb, SSCI. *Aud.:* Ac.

Blending theoretical and applied methods, this official journal of the U.S. Association for Small Business and Entrepreneurship features refereed articles on a wide range of topics in the field of entrepreneurship studies, including creation of enterprises, management of small firms, and issues in family-owned businesses. Case studies, research notes, announcements, and guest editors' commentary occur sporadically throughout the year. Most appropriate for academic libraries.

1069. *Family Business Review.* [ISSN: 0894-4865] 1988. q. GBP 180 print & online eds. Ed(s): Joseph H Astrachan. Blackwell Publishing, Inc., Commerce Place, 350 Main St, Malden, MA 02148; customerservices@ blackwellpublishing.com; http://www.blackwellpublishing.com. Illus., index. Sample. Refereed. Circ: 1300. Vol. ends: No. 4. *Indexed:* ABIn, CWI, RiskAb, SSCI. *Bk. rev.:* Various number and length. *Aud.:* Ac, Sa.

An international editorial board oversees this scholarly publication from the Family Firm Institute dedicated to furthering knowledge and increasing interdisciplinary skills of educators, consultants, and researchers of family-owned businesses. Four features, comprised of method papers and case studies, are presented in each issue along with invited commentaries, interviews, and book reviews. Occasional special issues are devoted to family-owned business practices in a particular region of the world. Recommended for academic libraries supporting entrepreneurship programs.

1070. *Franchising World.* Former titles: *Franchising Opportunities;* (until 1989): *Franchising World; International Franchise Association. Quarterly Legal Bulletin; International Franchise Association. Legal Bulletin.* [ISSN: 1524-4814] 1960. 8x/yr. USD 50. Ed(s): Terry Hill. International Franchise Association, 1350 New York Ave, NW, Ste 900, Washington, DC 20005; ifa@franchise.org; http://www.franchise.org. Adv. Circ: 12000. Microform: PQC. Online: EBSCO Publishing, EBSCO Host; Florida Center for Library Automation; Gale; Northern Light Technology, Inc.; OCLC Online Computer Library Center, Inc.; ProQuest K-12 Learning Solutions; ProQuest LLC (Ann Arbor); H.W. Wilson. *Indexed:* ABIn, BPI. *Aud.:* Ga.

Official publication of the International Franchise Association. Each issue contains eight articles offering practical advice for both franchisors and franchisees. Anybody interested in franchising as a small business opportunity will want to consult this publication. Regular columns address management and operations, industry trends, case studies, legal and regulatory issues, minority ownership opportunities, international development, and association events and activities.

Hispanic Business Magazine. See Latino Studies section.

1071. *Home Business Magazine: the home-based entrepreneur's magazine.* Formerly: *National Home Business.* [ISSN: 1092-4779] 1993. bi-m. 6 issues per volume. USD 15 domestic; USD 50 Canada; USD 70 foreign. Ed(s): Stacy Ann Henderson. United Marketing & Research Company, Inc., 9582 Hamilton Ave, PMB 368, Huntington Beach, CA 92646. Illus., adv. Circ: 100000. *Aud.:* Ga.

Featuring five or six articles on strategy along with an individual success story, this magazine exudes practical advice. There is a strong online presence at www.homebusinessmag.com, a useful bookmark in libraries that do not subscribe to this bimonthly in print. Information is organized by channels: Start Up, Marketing/Sales, Money Corner, Management, Home Office, Telecommuting, and Community. High resolution digital images of recent issues permit online viewing page by page. Of most interest to public libraries.

1072. *In Business (Emmaus): the magazine for environmental entrepreneuring.* [ISSN: 0190-2458] 1979. bi-m. USD 33 domestic; USD 51 foreign. Ed(s): Nora Clark, Jerome Goldstein. J G Press, Inc., 419 State Ave, Emmaus, PA 18049; advert@jgpress.com; http://www.jgpress.com. Illus., adv. Circ: 3000 Paid and controlled. Vol. ends: No. 6. Online: EBSCO Publishing, EBSCO Host; OCLC Online Computer Library Center, Inc.; ProQuest K-12 Learning Solutions; ProQuest LLC (Ann Arbor). *Indexed:* ABIn. *Bk. rev.:* Various number and length. *Aud.:* Ga, Sa.

Profiling individuals who have created "green" enterprises, this environmentally conscious publication presents practical advice for business growth. A dozen articles cover trends in the green business industry and highlight new products, renewable energy sources, recycling programs, financing options, and environmental and conservation news. An important source of sustainable business practices and alternative products for the owner of small to medium-sized companies. Content from 2004 to the present is freely available at www.jgpress.com/inbusiness.

1073. *Inc: the handbook for the American entrepreneur.* Incorporates (1995-1998): *Self-Employed Professional.* [ISSN: 0162-8968] 1979. m. USD 12 domestic; USD 31 Canada; USD 50 elsewhere. Ed(s): Jane Berentson. Inc., 7 World Trade Centre, New York, NY 10007-2195. Illus., index, adv. Sample. Circ: 650000 Paid. Vol. ends: Dec. Microform: CIS. Online: The Dialog Corporation; EBSCO Publishing, EBSCO Host; Factiva, Inc.; Florida Center for Library Automation; Gale; LexisNexis; OCLC Online Computer Library Center, Inc.; ProQuest K-12 Learning Solutions; ProQuest LLC (Ann Arbor); H.W. Wilson. *Indexed:* ABIn, ATI, Agr, BPI, BRI, CBRI, EnvAb, LRI, LogistBibl, MASUSE. *Bk. rev.:* 0-2, 200-1,000 words. *Aud.:* Ga, Ac, Sa.

The premier magazine aimed at owners and managers of small to mid-sized businesses. Articles feature individuals and companies and their proven strategies for success in marketing, management, finance, and customer relations. Each issue includes a dozen columns and departments that provide timely information on small business trends, new technology, tips from CEOs, recommended web sites, advice on managing people, and editorials. *Inc. Technology* is a supplemental issue appearing three or four times per year. Current issue contents and archives are available for free online at www.inc.com along with web exclusives, services, and tools. This core business title is well suited for all libraries.

1074. *International Small Business Journal.* Formerly (until 1983): *European Small Business Journal.* [ISSN: 0266-2426] 1982. bi-m. GBP 685. Ed(s): Dr. Robert Blackburn. Sage Publications Ltd., 1 Oliver's Yard, 55 City Rd, London, EC1 1SP, United Kingdom; info@sagepub.co.uk; http://www.sagepub.co.uk. Illus., adv. Refereed. Online: CSA; EBSCO Publishing, EBSCO Host; Florida Center for Library Automation; Gale; HighWire Press; Northern Light Technology, Inc.; OCLC Online Computer Library Center, Inc.; ProQuest K-12 Learning Solutions; SAGE Publications, Inc., SAGE Journals Online; SwetsWise Online Content; H.W. Wilson. Reprint: PSC. *Indexed:* ABIn, BPI, CJA, IBSS, PAIS, RiskAb, SSCI. *Bk. rev.:* 0-2, 500-1,500 words. *Aud.:* Ac, Sa.

Provides a forum and focus for the discussion and dissemination of views and research on the small business sector throughout the world. The emphasis is on systematic studies that help to improve the general understanding of small business and so contribute to more effective policies for and management of small business. Articles cover theoretical and methodological developments, empirical studies, practical applications, and reviews of relevant literature. The journal is intended for academics and teachers, policy makers at all levels, trade and business associations, financial institutions, small firms' representative bodies, and planning and industrial development authorities. Recommended for academic and corporate libraries, especially those with an entrepreneurship focus.

1075. *Journal of Business Venturing.* [ISSN: 0883-9026] 1985. 6x/yr. EUR 861. Ed(s): S Subramony, S Venkataraman. Elsevier Inc., 360 Park Ave S, New York, NY 10010-1710; usinfo-f@elsevier.com; http://www.elsevier.com. Illus., index, adv. Refereed. Circ: 675 Paid and free. Microform: PQC. Online: EBSCO Publishing, EBSCO Host; Gale; IngentaConnect; OhioLINK; ScienceDirect; SwetsWise Online Content. *Indexed:* ABIn, RiskAb, SSCI. *Aud.:* Ac, Sa.

Leading scholars and practitioners contribute rigorously developed theoretical and empirical studies to fulfill the editor's stated aims of knowledge advancement in four key areas: entrepreneurship, new business development, industry evolution, and technology management. Approximately five refereed articles 20–30 pages in length make up each issue; occasionally included are invited papers by selected authors with a topic of special concern. The last issue of each volume includes a cumulative index for the volume year. An important journal for academic libraries offering advanced degrees in business.

1076. *Journal of Developmental Entrepreneurship: an international publication devoted to issues of microenterprise development.* [ISSN: 1084-9467] 1996. q. SGD 401 print & online eds. (Individuals, SGD 95). Ed(s): Peter Koveos. World Scientific Publishing Co. Pte. Ltd., 5 Toh Tuck Link, Singapore, 596224, Singapore; http://www.worldscientific.com. Refereed. *Indexed:* ABIn, RiskAb. *Aud.:* Ac, Sa.

Provides a forum for the dissemination of descriptive, empirical, and theoretical research that focuses on issues concerning microenterprise and small business development, especially under conditions of adversity. Scholars are not the only intended audience for *JDE*, but also professionals involved in governmental and NGO efforts to facilitate entrepreneurship in economic and community development programs. Particular attention is given to articles that address challenges and opportunities unique to minority and female entrepreneurs; legislation, regulation, and tax policy; activity in the informal economic sector; education and training; and international and cooperative efforts. Recommended for academic libraries.

1077. *Journal of Small Business Management.* [ISSN: 0047-2778] 1963. q. GBP 200 print & online eds. Ed(s): Chandra S Mishra. Blackwell Publishing, Inc., Commerce Place, 350 Main St, Malden, MA 02148; customerservices@blackwellpublishing.com;

http://www.blackwellpublishing.com. Illus., index, adv. Sample. Refereed. Circ: 3500. Vol. ends: Nov. Online: Blackwell Synergy; EBSCO Publishing, EBSCO Host; Gale; IngentaConnect; Northern Light Technology, Inc.; OCLC Online Computer Library Center, Inc.; OhioLINK; ProQuest K-12 Learning Solutions; ProQuest LLC (Ann Arbor); SwetsWise Online Content; H.W. Wilson. Reprint: PSC. *Indexed:* ABIn, AgeL, BLI, BPI, CJA, CWI, LRI, PAIS, PMA, PsycInfo, RiskAb, SSCI. *Aud.:* Ac, Sa.

This official journal of the International Council for Small Business publishes research in entrepreneurship studies and fosters education in small business management, including financial, strategic, operational, and cultural issues. Divided into two sections, each issue contains five or six rigorously researched articles that include "pragmatic advice for practitioners." Three or four smaller articles follow that focus on small enterprise endeavors outside the United States. Aimed at the international academic community, this title is appropriate for academic collections, especially those offering advanced degrees in business administration.

1078. *Minority Business Entrepreneur.* [ISSN: 1048-0919] 1984. bi-m. USD 18. Ed(s): Christen Liebenberg. Minority Business Entrepreneur, 3528 Torrance Blvd, Ste 101, Torrance, CA 90503-4803; mbewbe@ix.netcom.com; http://www.mbemag.com. Illus., index, adv. Circ: 28000. Vol. ends: No. 6. *Indexed:* ENW. *Bk. rev.:* Various number and length. *Aud.:* Ga, Ac.

This title serves to inform, educate, and inspire business owners who are women or in an ethnic minority. Articles profile individual entrepreneurs, report on success stories, analyze failures, and provide best-practice examples designed to enhance small business management. Typical articles describe corporate and government programs and the positive benefits of supplier diversity. Ideal for public libraries serving small businesses; of interest to academic collections supporting entrepreneurship programs.

1079. *Small Business Economics: an international journal.* [ISSN: 0921-898X] 1989. 10x/yr. EUR 1116 print & online eds. Ed(s): David B Audretsch, Zoltan J Acs. Springer New York LLC, 233 Spring St, New York, NY 10013-1578; service-ny@springer.com; http://www.springer.com/. Illus., index, adv. Sample. Refereed. Microform: PQC. Online: EBSCO Publishing, EBSCO Host; Gale; IngentaConnect; OCLC Online Computer Library Center, Inc.; OhioLINK; ProQuest LLC (Ann Arbor); Springer LINK; SwetsWise Online Content. Reprint: PSC. *Indexed:* ABIn, IBR, IBSS, IBZ, JEL, RiskAb, SSCI. *Bk. rev.:* 0-1, 750-1,000 words. *Aud.:* Ac.

Aimed at scholars, this title provides a forum for studies in the activity of small and mid-sized firms. Each issue features six to eight articles of research and analysis on the links between firm size and performance; the distinct roles of differently sized firms; how and why firm behavior and strategy vary with size; the relationship between firm size and innovation; and the determinants of the formation, growth, and dissolution of firms. The scope is interdisciplinary and cross-national; submissions focusing on institutions and public policy are welcome. Of most interest to academic libraries.

1080. *Technovation.* [ISSN: 0166-4972] 1981. 12x/yr. EUR 1512. Ed(s): G Hayward, R M Mason. Pergamon, The Boulevard, Langford Ln, East Park, Kidlington, OX5 1GB, United Kingdom. Illus., adv. Refereed. Vol. ends: No. 166 - No. 4972. Online: EBSCO Publishing, EBSCO Host; Gale; IngentaConnect; OCLC Online Computer Library Center, Inc.; OhioLINK; ScienceDirect; SwetsWise Online Content. *Indexed:* ABIn, EngInd, RiskAb, SCI, SSCI. *Bk. rev.:* 1-3, 500-1,000 words. *Aud.:* Ac.

All facets of the process of technological innovation from conceptualization through commercial utilization are covered. Topics include technological trends and breakthroughs, availability of capital for new product development and introduction, displacement of existing products, management of entrepreneurial ventures, management of innovation in medium-sized and large organizations, investment strategies related to new science- or technology-based enterprises, the innovator as an individual and as a personality type, and technology transfer to developing nations. Case studies that illustrate how innovation occurs from business and technical standpoints are also included, together with reviews and analyses of governmental and industrial policy that inhibit or stimulate technological innovation. Recommended for academic collections supporting small business studies.

State and Regional

Most states and many cities produce some form of business newsmagazine. The Alliance of Area Business Publications provides a directory of members' titles at their web site, www.bizpubs.org. Only a select few are included here. See also the City and Regional section.

1081. *Alaska Business Monthly.* [ISSN: 8756-4092] 1985. m. USD 21.95. Ed(s): Ron Dalby. Alaska Business Publishing Co., PO Box 241288, Anchorage, AK 99524-1288. Illus., index, adv. Circ: 10000. Online: The Dialog Corporation; Florida Center for Library Automation; Gale; Northern Light Technology, Inc.; OCLC Online Computer Library Center, Inc.; ProQuest LLC (Ann Arbor). *Indexed:* ABIn. *Aud.:* Ga, Ac, Sa.

This title covers issues and trends affecting Alaska's business sector and features stories on the individuals, organizations, and companies that shape the Alaskan economy. Each issue carries current news, interviews, human interest stories, and reports on a major industry sector such as tourism, commercial fishing, construction, technology, manufacturing, mining, oil, gas, and timber. Online content is slow to appear at www.akbizmag.com and is limited for the most part to cover stories.

1082. *Business & Economic Review.* [ISSN: 0007-6465] 1954. q. Free. Ed(s): Jan K Collins. University of South Carolina, Darla Moore School of Business, 1705 College St, Columbia, SC 29208; janc@darla.badm.sc.edu. Illus., index. Circ: 5419. Microform: PQC. Online: EBSCO Publishing, EBSCO Host; Northern Light Technology, Inc.; ProQuest LLC (Ann Arbor); H.W. Wilson. *Indexed:* ABIn, AgeL, BPI, PAIS, PMA. *Aud.:* Ga, Ac.

Published by the Moore School of Business at the University of South Carolina, this magazine addresses general trends and management techniques while at the same time discussing current business and economic topics of particular interest to South Carolina and the Southeast. Along with an economic outlook and statistics, features include personal finance, health care, technology, and environmental reports. Academic libraries that support business programs generally have this type of business school publication in their collections; also of interest to public libraries in the state and region.

1083. *ColoradoBiz.* Former titles (until 1999): *Colorado Business Magazine;* (until 1986): *Colorado Business.* [ISSN: 1523-6366] 1973. m. USD 24 in North America; USD 78 elsewhere. Ed(s): Mike Taylor, Robert Schwab. Wiesner Media, LLC, 7009 S Potomac St, Ste 200, Centennial, CO 80112; http://www.wiesnermedia.com. Illus., adv. Circ: 20019 Paid. Microform: PQC. Online: The Dialog Corporation; EBSCO Publishing, EBSCO Host; Florida Center for Library Automation; Gale; OCLC Online Computer Library Center, Inc. *Indexed:* ABIn, LRI, PAIS. *Aud.:* Sa.

The cover story of this handsome monthly is usually accompanied by five feature articles emphasizing business and industry trends statewide; general topics are usually put into a Colorado context. Departments include Attitude/Altitude, shorter reports on statewide business activities; SmallBiz; Colorado Career, a day-in-the-life type profile of an individual businessperson or government official; and ITech, which reports on information technology trends. Of interest to libraries in the Rocky Mountain region. Online archives at www.cobizmag.com lead to content from the past two years. The web site also provides access to several "top" lists.

1084. *Crain's Chicago Business.* Incorporates (1993-1997?): *Crain's Small Business (Chicago Edition).* [ISSN: 0149-6956] 1978. w. Mon. USD 94.95 combined subscription domestic IL, IN, MI & WI; USD 109 combined subscription domestic other states; USD 148 combined subscription foreign. Ed(s): Joe Cahill, Jeff Bailey. Crain Communications, Inc., 360 N Michigan Ave, Chicago, IL 60601-3806; info@crain.com; http://www.crain.com. Adv. Circ: 50528. Microform:

PQC. Online: The Dialog Corporation; EBSCO Publishing, EBSCO Host; Florida Center for Library Automation; Gale; Northern Light Technology, Inc.; OCLC Online Computer Library Center, Inc.; ProQuest K-12 Learning Solutions; ProQuest LLC (Ann Arbor); H.W. Wilson. *Indexed:* ABIn, BPI, CWI, LRI. *Aud.:* Ga, Ac, Sa.

Premier business newsmagazine for the greater Chicago area. Clearly written articles profile companies and individuals, report on industry trends, and examine the general economic situation in the city and suburbs beyond. Each issue contains a Crain's List—a topical ranking of companies. Of most interest to public, academic, and corporate libraries maintaining business collections within the metropolitan area. Larger libraries outside the area might consider subscribing in acknowledgement of Chicagoland's business acumen.

1085. *Crain's New York Business.* Former titles (until 1985): *Citybusiness;* (until 1984): *New York CityBusiness.* [ISSN: 8756-789X] 1984. w. Mon. USD 59.79 domestic; USD 124.95 foreign; USD 3 newsstand/cover. Ed(s): Rance Crain, Greg David. Crain Communications, Inc., 711 Third Ave, New York, NY 10017-4036; info@crain.com; http://www.crain.com. Adv. Circ: 62000. Online: The Dialog Corporation; EBSCO Publishing, EBSCO Host; Gale; LexisNexis; Northern Light Technology, Inc.; OCLC Online Computer Library Center, Inc.; ProQuest K-12 Learning Solutions; ProQuest LLC (Ann Arbor); H.W. Wilson. *Indexed:* ABIn, BPI, CWI, LRI. *Aud.:* Ga, Sa.

Similar in format to *Crain's Chicago Business.* In addition to news items, editorials, and columnists, recurring departments include IT, real estate, executive moves, small business, restaurant reviews, and the week in review. Of interest to libraries in the Northeast and others that support large business collections.

1086. *Florida Trend: magazine of Florida business.* [ISSN: 0015-4326] 1958. m. Free. Ed(s): Mark R Howard, John Annunziata. Trend Magazine, Inc., 490 First Avenue S., St. Petersburg, FL 33701. Illus., adv. Circ: 50000. Microform: PQC. Online: The Dialog Corporation; Florida Center for Library Automation; Gale; Northern Light Technology, Inc.; OCLC Online Computer Library Center, Inc.; ProQuest K-12 Learning Solutions; ProQuest LLC (Ann Arbor). *Indexed:* ABIn, AgeL, PAIS. *Aud.:* Ga.

Created in the 1950s when agriculture and tourism dominated the Florida economy (and they still do, but are now joined by high tech), this title chronicles business in what has become one of the most populous states in the country. The publisher's aim is to "create a sense of community in Florida, tying together Florida's diverse, competitive and often difficult-to-understand regions in a statewide context." A cover story is accompanied by two to three features; the "Talk of Florida" section spotlights news, companies, and individuals; each issue also contains a topical ranking of businesses. The current issue and archives are available online at www.floridatrend.com.

1087. *Indiana Business Review.* [ISSN: 0019-6541] 1926. q. Free. Ed(s): Morton J Marcus. Indiana University, School of Business, 107 S Indiana Ave, Bloomington, IN 47405. Illus. Circ: 4000. Microform: CIS. Online: EBSCO Publishing, EBSCO Host; Florida Center for Library Automation; Gale; Northern Light Technology, Inc.; OCLC Online Computer Library Center, Inc.; ProQuest K-12 Learning Solutions; ProQuest LLC (Ann Arbor). *Indexed:* ABIn, JEL, PAIS, PMA. *Aud.:* Ga, Ac.

Published by the Indiana Business Research Center, this title provides analysis and insight on economic and demographic issues in the state. However, it is of interest to a wider audience than just Hoosiers; articles spotlight trends and draw conclusions applicable to the country at large. Of interest to all libraries in the Midwest and to larger business collections nationwide.

1088. *Los Angeles Business Journal.* [ISSN: 0194-2603] 1979. w. Mon. USD 99.95 combined subscription print & online eds. Ed(s): Mark Lacter, Mark Lacter. California Business Journals, 5700 Wilshire Blvd., Ste. 170, Los Angeles, CA 90036. Adv. Circ: 40000. Microform: PQC. Online: Florida Center for Library Automation; Gale; Northern Light Technology, Inc.; ProQuest LLC (Ann Arbor). *Aud.:* Ga.

This weekly newspaper covers local business activity in the second largest metropolitan area in the United States. Regular columns feature articles on media and technology, small business, finance, investment, and real estate. Each issue has a special report containing several brief articles on a specific industry or subject. Topical rankings of companies known as "The Lists," along with selected articles from the current newsstand issue, are now available online after free registration through the web site www.labusinessjournal.com. Links are provided to regional editions covering Orange County, San Diego, and the San Fernando Valley.

1089. *New Jersey Business.* [ISSN: 0028-5560] 1954. m. USD 21 domestic; USD 22 foreign; USD 2.50 newsstand/cover. Ed(s): Anthony Birritteri. New Jersey Business Magazine, 310 Passaic Ave, Fairfield, NJ 07004. Illus., adv. Circ: 28000 Paid. Online: Northern Light Technology, Inc.; OCLC Online Computer Library Center, Inc.; ProQuest K-12 Learning Solutions; ProQuest LLC (Ann Arbor). *Indexed:* ABIn, PAIS. *Aud.:* Ga, Sa.

This glossy title covers every angle of the Garden State's economy—from major industries and top executive interviews to environmental issues, government, health care, banking, real estate, advertising, public relations, and corporate promotions. A dozen features and regular departments offer practical business advice and solutions. Only the current issue's cover story is accessible online at www.njbmagazine.com.

1090. *Oregon Business Magazine.* [ISSN: 0279-8190] 1978. m. USD 19.95. Ed(s): Christina Williams, Mitchell Hartman. MediAmerica, Inc., 610 SW Broadway, Ste 200, Portland, OR 97205. Illus., adv. Circ: 19200 Paid and controlled. Microform: PQC. Online: Florida Center for Library Automation; Gale; OCLC Online Computer Library Center, Inc.; ProQuest LLC (Ann Arbor). *Indexed:* ABIn. *Bk. rev.:* Various number and length. *Aud.:* Ga, Sa.

Oregon is home to an increasing number of small and medium-sized businesses, and this title is dedicated to helping them grow. Each issue includes a cover story, features, interviews, company and industry profiles, advice, savvy marketing strategies, and a business ranking called the "Power List." Other "top" lists and selected article content are accessible in full text at www.oregon-business.com.

Trade and Industry

1091. *Air Conditioning, Heating & Refrigeration News: the HVACR contractor's weekly newsmagazine.* Incorporates (1959-1969): *Air Engineering.* [ISSN: 0002-2276] 1926. w. Mon. USD 87 domestic; USD 117 Canada; USD 169 elsewhere. Ed(s): Chris King, Mark Skaer. B N P Media, 2401 W Big Beaver Rd, Ste 700, Troy, MI 48084; http://www.bnpmedia.com. Illus., index, adv. Sample. Circ: 34608 Paid. Microform: CIS; PQC. Online: EBSCO Publishing, EBSCO Host; Gale; OCLC Online Computer Library Center, Inc.; ProQuest LLC (Ann Arbor). *Indexed:* ABIn. *Aud.:* Ac, Sa.

This tabloid-style magazine reports heating, ventilating, and air conditioning (HVAC) industry news with a half dozen articles on training and education, contracting, manufacturing, and management in addition to featuring a particular HVAC system, e.g., rooftop cooling. Regular departments include updates on energy matters, historical practices, views and opinions, industry newsmakers, and classified ads. Appropriate for public libraries serving patrons in regions with active construction and renovation industries, as well as academic libraries supporting programs in engineering, architecture, and related fields.

Airline Business. See Transportation section.

1092. *American Machinist: strategies & innovations for competitive manufacturing.* Former titles (until 1988): *American Machinist and Automated Manufacturing;* (until 1986): *American Machinist;* (until 1968): *American Machinist - Metalworking Manufacturing;* (until 1960): *American Machinist.* [ISSN: 1041-7958] 1877. m. USD 90 domestic (Free to qualified personnel). Ed(s): Patricia L Smith. Penton Media, Inc., 1300 E 9th St, Cleveland, OH 44114-1503; information@ penton.com; http://www.penton.com/. Illus., index, adv. Circ: 82000 Paid and controlled. Microform: PMC; PQC. Online: EBSCO Publishing, EBSCO Host; Florida Center for Library Automation; Gale; Northern Light Technology, Inc.; OCLC Online Computer Library Center, Inc.; ProQuest K-12 Learning Solutions; ProQuest LLC (Ann Arbor); H.W. Wilson. *Indexed:* ABIn, AS&TI, C&ISA, CerAb, ChemAb, IAA, LRI. *Bk. rev.:* Various number and length. *Aud.:* Sa.

Feature articles provide overviews on new tools, manufacturing equipment, materials, production management, and quality control issues. Extensive coverage of products and services, plus numerous departments relating to business and technology trends, software and hardware developments, testing and measurement advancements, practical ideas, casebooks, and liability and regulatory updates, as well as reader service and advertising information, make this a valuable trade magazine to the cutting and tooling machine industry. Current issue content and archives are available on the web site: www.ameri-canmachinist.com.

Beverage Industry. See Food Industry section.

1093. *Beverage World.* Former titles (until 1975): *Soft Drinks;* (until 1966): *National Bottler's Gazette.* [ISSN: 0098-2318] 1882. m. USD 79 domestic (Free to qualified personnel). Ed(s): Andrew Kaplan. Nielsen Business Publications, 770 Broadway, New York, NY 10003-9595; bmcomm@vnuinc.com; http://www.nielsenbusinessmedia.com. Illus., index, adv. Circ: 34000 Paid and controlled. Vol. ends: Dec. Microform: PQC. Online: The Dialog Corporation; EBSCO Publishing, EBSCO Host; Factiva, Inc.; Florida Center for Library Automation; Gale; OCLC Online Computer Library Center, Inc.; ProQuest LLC (Ann Arbor); H.W. Wilson. *Indexed:* ABIn, BPI, ExcerpMed, H&TI, PAIS. *Aud.:* Ac, Sa.

Tracks all aspects of the U.S. beverage industry: manufacturers, bottlers, distributors, and retailers of soft drinks, fruit juices, iced teas, coffees, wines, spirits, and bottled waters. Articles and interviews cover diverse topics including industry statistics, market share, packaging, vending, quality control, consumer preferences, marketing efforts, and fleet management. Sister publications are *Beverage World International* and *Beverage World en Espanol.* In addition to searchable archives with access to full content, exclusive features are offered online at www.beverageworld.com, including "Reports & Analysis," daily industry headlines, a cumulative list of recent new beverage announce-ments, and a buyers' guide, "Databank Directory."

Billboard. See Music section.

Boxoffice. See Films section.

Broadcasting & Cable. See Television, Video, and Radio section.

Builder. See Building and Construction section.

1094. *Chain Store Age: the news magazine for retail executives.* Former titles (until 1995): *Chain Store Age Executive with Shopping Center Age;* (until 1975): *Chain Store Age Executives Edition Including Shopping Center Age.* [ISSN: 1087-0601] 1925. m. USD 105 domestic; USD 125 Canada; USD 165 foreign. Ed(s): M Nannery, Murray Forseter. Lebhar-Friedman, Inc., 425 Park Ave, New York, NY 10022; info@lf.com; http://www.lf.com. Illus., adv. Circ: 35000 Paid and controlled. Vol. ends: Dec. Microform: CIS. Online: EBSCO Publishing, EBSCO Host; Gale; OCLC Online Computer Library Center, Inc.; ProQuest LLC (Ann Arbor); H.W. Wilson. *Indexed:* ABIn, BPI, CWI, LogistBibl. *Aud.:* Ga, Ac, Sa.

This title, from the same publisher as *Retailing Today* (below in this section), serves the decision makers who manage chain stores and shopping centers. Nearly two dozen short articles in each issue discuss current news, events, and issues related to real estate, store planning, operations, electronic retailing, payment systems, related products, and technologies. Appropriate for larger public libraries and for academic libraries that support business programs. Free registration is required to access published article content and detailed industry data at www.chainstoreage.com.

Chemical Market Reporter. See Advertising, Marketing, and Public Relations section.

1095. Chemical Week. Former titles (until 1952): *Chemical Industries Week;* (until 1951): *Chemical Industries;* (until 1933): *Chemical Markets.* [ISSN: 0009-272X] 1914. w. 49/yr. USD 159 domestic; USD 180 Canada; USD 319 in Latin America. Ed(s): Andrew Wood, Peter Sairley. Chemical Week Associates, 110 William St, New York, NY 10038-3910. Illus., index, adv. Circ: 46440 Paid and controlled. Vol. ends: Dec. Microform: PQC. Online: EBSCO Publishing, EBSCO Host; Factiva, Inc.; Florida Center for Library Automation; Gale; LexisNexis; Northern Light Technology, Inc.; OCLC Online Computer Library Center, Inc.; ProQuest K-12 Learning Solutions; ProQuest LLC (Ann Arbor); H.W. Wilson. *Indexed:* A&ATA, ABIn, Agr, BPI, C&ISA, CEA, CWI, CerAb, ChemAb, EngInd, EnvInd, ExcerpMed, IAA. *Aud.:* Sa.

Weekly news source for chemical manufacturers and related industries including pharmaceuticals and plastics. A cover story running two or three pages accompanies brief business and finance news articles organized by region: United States/Americas, Europe/Mideast, Asia/Pacific. Other sections cover construction projects, mergers and acquisitions, information technology, speciality chemical production, environmental issues, laws and regulations, company and market profiles, management trends, and newsmakers in the industry. Most online content at www.chemweek.com is restricted to current subscribers only.

1096. Coal Age. Formerly (until 1996): *Coal;* Which was formed by the merger of (1911-1988): *Coal Age;* (1984-1988): *Coal Mining;* Which was formerly (1964-1984): *Coal Mining and Processing.* [ISSN: 1091-0646] 1988. m. USD 56 domestic (Free to qualified personnel). Ed(s): Steve Fiscor. Mining Media, Inc., 13544 Eads Rd, Prairieville, LA 70769; info@mining-media.com; http://www.mining-media.com. Illus., index, adv. Circ: 19038 Paid and free. *Indexed:* ABIn, AS&TI, BPI, ChemAb, EngInd, EnvAb, EnvInd, ExcerpMed, LRI. *Aud.:* Sa.

Reports on the development of mines, mining technologies, and processing of coal. Two or three brief articles each week feature production operations, maintenance, and transportation issues of U.S. companies. Other departments include people, worldwide company news, a market watch, regulatory matters, new media, classified ads, and association and conference news. Of interest to libraries that are located in mining regions or that collect in areas of energy production and industrial trends.

Constructor. See Building and Construction section.

1097. Customer Interaction Solutions. Incorporates (199?-2002): *Communications Solutions;* Which was formerly (until 2000): *C T I;* Former titles (until 2000): *C@ll Center C R M Solutions;* (until 1999): *Call Center Solutions;* (until 1998): *Telemarketing & Call Center Solutions;* (until 1996): *Telemarketing.* [ISSN: 1533-3078] 1982. m. Free. Technology Marketing Corp., One Technology Plaza, Norwalk, CT 06854; tmc@tmcnet.com; http://www.tmcnet.com. Adv. Circ: 50000 Paid and free. Online: Florida Center for Library Automation; Gale; OCLC Online Computer Library Center, Inc. *Indexed:* ABIn, BPI, C&ISA, CerAb, IAA, MicrocompInd. *Aud.:* Ac, Sa.

This is the primary trade title for call center (also known as contact center) management. With the advent of e-commerce, customer relationship management (CRM) has evolved into a sophisticated industry and is changing the face of direct marketing. Articles cover topics including call center design, products and technologies, best practices, and outsourcing. An annual buyers' guide is published in December. Deep archives and some exclusive web content are available at www.tmcnet.com/call-center.

1098. Dealerscope: product & strategy for consumer technology retailing. Former titles (until Mar. 2000): *Dealerscope Consumer Electronics Marketplace;* (until Oct. 1995): *Dealerscope Merchandising;* Which was formed by the merger of (1958-1986): *Dealerscope;* (1964-1986): *Merchandising;* Which was formerly (until 1976): *Merchandising Week; Electrical Merchandising Week.* [ISSN: 1534-4711] 1986. m. USD 79 domestic (Free to qualified personnel). Ed(s): Jeff O'Heir. North

American Publishing Co., 1500 Spring Garden St., Ste 1200, Philadelphia, PA 19130-4094; http://www.napco.com. Illus., index, adv. Sample. Circ: 20000 Paid. Vol. ends: Nov. Online: The Dialog Corporation; Gale; OCLC Online Computer Library Center, Inc.; H.W. Wilson. *Indexed:* ABIn, BPI. *Aud.:* Ga, Sa.

In the past, this title primarily featured new product announcements in the fields of consumer electronics, major appliances, and computing products; it was light on business solutions and management advice. A renewed mission is to inform readers how to market more profitably selling consumer electronics, as well as assist manufacturers and distributors in communicating best-practice strategies to retail. It should continue to be of interest to general readers who like to keep up with the latest electronic gadgets and innovations. Retail professionals should find the enhanced content more relevant than ever. Web exclusives, current articles, and searchable archives require free registration to view at www.dealerscope.com.

Electronic News. See Electronics section.

ENR. See Engineering and Technology/Civil Engineering section.

Farm Journal. See Agriculture section.

Fleet Owner. See Transportation section.

Folio. See Serials section.

1099. Footwear News. [ISSN: 0162-914X] 1945. w. USD 72 domestic; USD 62 domestic to retailers; USD 145 in Canada & Mexico. Ed(s): Wayne Niemi. Fairchild Publications, Inc., 7 W 34th St, New York, NY 10001-8191; customerservice@fairchildpub.com; http://www.fairchildpub.com. Illus., adv. Circ: 23000 Paid. Online: The Dialog Corporation; EBSCO Publishing, EBSCO Host; Factiva, Inc.; Florida Center for Library Automation; Gale; Northern Light Technology, Inc.; OCLC Online Computer Library Center, Inc.; ProQuest LLC (Ann Arbor). *Indexed:* ABIn, CWI. *Aud.:* Ga, Ac, Sa.

The readership of this weekly includes designers, retailers, manufacturers, importers, wholesalers, suppliers, tanners, finishers, and members of related fields. It offers extensive coverage of trends in women's, men's, and children's footwear across the dress, casual, and athletic categories. A typical issue is more visual than textual in content; articles tend to be brief profiles of designer lines and manufacturers. The web site at www.footwearnews.com offers only a few features and current news items; it lacks the graphic punch of its print counterpart. Of most interest to libraries collecting in fashion design.

1100. Global Cosmetic Industry. Former titles (until 1999): *D C I;* (until May 1997): *Drug and Cosmetic Industry;* Which incorporated (1931-1997): *Drug and Cosmetic Catalog.* [ISSN: 1523-9470] 1914. 13x/yr. USD 43 domestic (Free to qualified personnel). Ed(s): Karen Newman. Allured Publishing Corp., 336 Gundersen Dr, Carol Stream, IL 60188-2403; allured@allured.com; http://www.allured.com. Illus., index, adv. Circ: 16129 Paid. Vol. ends: Dec. Microform: PMC; PQC. Online: The Dialog Corporation; EBSCO Publishing, EBSCO Host; Factiva, Inc.; Florida Center for Library Automation; Gale; Northern Light Technology, Inc.; OCLC Online Computer Library Center, Inc.; ProQuest LLC (Ann Arbor); H.W. Wilson. *Indexed:* ABIn, BPI, CWI, ChemAb, H&SSA. *Aud.:* Ga, Ac, Sa.

GCI, primarily intended for cosmetics and personal-care product professionals, is a showcase of research and development, market trends, and marketing efforts. Features are short and mix the practical (product application) with the technical (formulas and ingredient analysis). Of interest to academic collections supporting marketing programs and to special libraries supporting personal-care product manufacturers, marketers, and retailers. Also somewhat of interest to public libraries because of the practical information imparted to consumers, e.g., new product previews and general fashion forecasts. Current issue contents and archives available at www.gcimagazine.com.

1101. *H F N: the newsweekly of home products retailing.* Former titles (until 1994): *H F D - Home Furnishing Daily; H F D - Retailing Home Furnishings;* (until 1976): *Home Furnishings Daily.* [ISSN: 1082-0310] 1929. w. USD 69 domestic to retailers; USD 109 domestic; USD 245 in Canada & Mexico. Ed(s): Warren Shoulberg. Macfadden Communications Group, LLC, 333 Seventh Ave, 11th Fl, New York, NY 10001; http://www.macfad.com. Illus., index, adv. Sample. Circ: 20027 Paid and controlled. Online: The Dialog Corporation; Factiva, Inc.; Florida Center for Library Automation; Gale; OCLC Online Computer Library Center, Inc.; ProQuest LLC (Ann Arbor). *Indexed:* ABIn, CWI. *Aud.:* Ac, Sa.

This is a key news source for suppliers, manufacturers, wholesalers, and retailers in and associated with the interior design industry. It covers the broad spectrum of what constitutes home furnishings. In addition to the obvious furniture, there are major appliances, housewares, tableware, bedding, floor coverings, lighting and decorative accessories, do-it-yourself decorating products, and giftware. Articles address new materials, products, and processes; news and newsmakers; market conditions; and industry trends. Online content at www.hfnmag.com is limited to article summaries from the current week's issue only. However, today's news briefs, job postings, and a trade show calendar will nicely complement a paid print subscription. Of interest to larger business collections.

Hotel and Motel Management. See Hospitality/Restaurant section.

1102. *Household & Personal Products Industry: the magazine for the detergent, soap, cosmetic and toiletries, wax, polish and aerosol industries.* Formerly: *Detergents and Specialties.* [ISSN: 0090-8878] 1964. m. USD 55 (Free to qualified personnel). Rodman Publishing, Corp., 70 Hilltop Rd, 3rd Fl, Ramsey, NJ 07446. Illus., adv. Circ: 18000 Controlled. *Indexed:* ChemAb, ExcerpMed. *Aud.:* Sa.

Covering soaps, detergents, cosmetics and toiletries, fragrances, waxes and polishes, insecticides, aerosols, and related chemical specialties, *HAPPI* appeals to readers involved in the personal care, household, industrial, and institutional fields. The subject matter of articles can range from hair and skin care and sun protection to the seemingly disparate laundry detergents and household cleaners. Four to six features join regular columns and departments including patent reviews, regulations, marketing, and packaging. Selected content from the current and past issues, complemented by online exclusives, is available at www.happi.com.

IndustryWeek. See under General, this section.

Logistics Management. See Transportation section.

1103. *Meetings and Conventions: perfection in planning.* Incorporates: *Incentive World.* [ISSN: 0025-8652] 1966. m. plus annual directory. USD 82.90. Ed(s): Lori Cioffi, Lori Edelstein. Northstar Travel Media LLC, 500 Plaza Dr, Secaucus, NJ 07094; http://www.ntmllc.com. Illus., adv. Sample. Circ: 70019 Paid and controlled. Vol. ends: Dec. *Indexed:* ABIn, CWI, H&TI. *Bk. rev.:* Various number and length. *Aud.:* Sa.

Meeting and convention planning has become an increasingly more visible and more competitive industry. Four or five feature articles cover a wide range of topics including economic outlook, best practices in both marketing and management, along with career guidance for planners. Several departments report on industry events, newsmakers, travel advice, and legal issues. Each issue includes extensive destination guides. Current issue content and access to archives is available for free online at www.mcmag.com.

1104. *Modern Plastics.* Formerly (until 1935): *Plastic Products.* [ISSN: 0026-8275] 1925. m. Free to qualified personnel. Canon Communications LLC, 11444 W Olympic Blvd, Ste 900, Los Angeles, CA 90064-1549. Illus., index, adv. Circ: 75782 Paid. Vol. ends: Dec. *Indexed:* A&ATA, ABIn, AS&TI, C&ISA, CWI, CerAb, ChemAb, EngInd, SSCI. *Aud.:* Sa.

Covering all aspects of the plastics industry, each issue reports on international news, research and development, product innovations, manufacturing equipment and processes, marketing, distribution, industry trends, and conferences and trade shows. An annual buying guide is filled with company contacts, industry information, and specifications. Most cover stories, selected

features, and other content are available online at www.modplas.com. Of most interest to corporate libraries; also recommended for academic libraries supporting programs in chemistry and engineering.

1105. *Packaging Digest.* Incorporates (1983-1994): *Packaging;* Which was formerly: *Package Engineering Including Modern Packaging;* Which was formed by the merger of (1927-1979): *Modern Packaging;* (1956-1979): *Package Engineering;* Which incorporated (in 1974): *Package Engineering New Products;* Which superseded (1972-1973): *Package Engineering New Products News.* [ISSN: 0030-9117] 1963. m. USD 119.90 domestic (Free to qualified personnel). Ed(s): Mary Ann Falkman. Reed Business Information, 2000 Clearwater Dr, Oak Brook, IL 60523; http://www.reedbusiness.com. Illus., adv. Sample. Circ: 105728. Vol. ends: Dec. Microform: PQC. Online: EBSCO Publishing, EBSCO Host; Factiva, Inc.; Gale; Northern Light Technology, Inc.; OCLC Online Computer Library Center, Inc.; ProQuest LLC (Ann Arbor); H.W. Wilson. *Indexed:* ABIn, AS&TI, BPI, EngInd, LRI. *Aud.:* Ga, Ac, Sa.

Aimed at managers, marketers, and manufacturers in the packaging industry, this monthly tabloid presents the fusion of art, design, and functionality. Ten to 12 short articles feature company and product information; new materials, technologies, and manufacturing methods; environmental concerns; and retail display. Recurring departments report on industry news, pending legislation, regulatory pressures, and new product spotlights. Illustrations abound. Current and past issue articles, daily news updates, industry links, and a few web-based exclusives are available online at www.packagingdigest.com. An important source for marketing and advertising trends; recommended for all libraries.

1106. *Progressive Grocer (New York, 2002).* Formed by the merger of (1922-2002): *Progressive Grocer (New York, 1922);* (1979-2002): *Supermarket Business;* Which was formerly (1969-1979): *Supermarketing;* (1946-1969): *Food Topics.* 2002. 18x/yr. USD 129 domestic (Free to qualified personnel). Ed(s): Stephen Dowdell, Bridget Goldschmidt. Nielsen Business Publications, 770 Broadway, New York, NY 10003-9595; bmcomm@vnuinc.com; http://www.nielsenbusinessmedia.com. Illus., adv. Circ: 40082 Paid and controlled. *Indexed:* ABIn, BPI. *Aud.:* Ga, Ac, Sa.

Intended for the supermarket manager, this title covers such topics as personnel and labor issues, security, customer service, new products, store design, and market conditions in general. Retailers, both foreign and domestic, utilizing unique approaches to management are spotlighted in a "Store of the Month" feature. Articles are categorized as grocery, fresh food, or nonfoods business. Regular departments address consumer preferences, in-store promotions, technology, equipment, distribution, and issues unique to independent stores. Of interest to academic libraries supporting marketing and management programs and to public libraries because of the general appeal of food. Current issue contents and daily news updates are available online at www.progressivegrocer.com.

1107. *Recycling Today.* Formerly: *Recycling Today (Scrap Market Edition);* Which superseded in part (in May 1990): *Recycling Today;* Which was formerly: *Secondary Raw Materials.* [ISSN: 1096-6323] 1963. m. USD 30 domestic (Free to qualified personnel). Ed(s): Brian Taylor, DeAnne Toto. G I E Media Inc., 4020 Kinross Lakes Pkwy Ste 201, Richfield, OH 44286; http://www.giemedia.com. Illus., adv. Circ: 15000 Paid and controlled. Online: Florida Center for Library Automation; Gale; OCLC Online Computer Library Center, Inc. *Indexed:* AS&TI, C&ISA, CerAb, EngInd, EnvAb, EnvInd, ExcerpMed, IAA. *Aud.:* Ga, Ac, Sa.

This title addresses social, political, and environmental issues impacting and impacted by recycling efforts from both a local and global perspective. Articles monitor trends in waste management technologies and processes, environmental regulations, and the volatility of recycled commodity prices. Each issue provides updates on the status of the nonmetallic, ferrous, nonferrous, paper, electronics, scrap, and construction/demolition debris sectors. Current issue contents and archives are available to subscribers at www.recyclingtoday.com/magazine; nonsubscribers may register there for free online access.

Restaurant Business. See Hospitality/Restaurant section.

1108. *Retail Merchandiser.* Formerly (until May 2000): *Discount Merchandiser.* [ISSN: 1530-8154] 1961. m. USD 99 domestic; USD 109 Canada; USD 171 elsewhere. Ed(s): Deborah Garbato, Greg Masters. Nielsen Business Publications, 770 Broadway, New York, NY 10003-9595; bmcomm@vnuinc.com; http://www.nielsenbusinessmedia.com. Illus., adv. Circ: 34188 Controlled. Vol. ends: Dec. Microform: PQC. Online: EBSCO Publishing, EBSCO Host; Florida Center for Library Automation; Gale; Northern Light Technology, Inc.; OCLC Online Computer Library Center, Inc.; ProQuest LLC (Ann Arbor); H.W. Wilson. *Indexed:* ABIn, BPI, PAIS. *Aud.:* Ga, Ac, Sa.

All aspects of merchandising are covered in this publication, including manufacturing, distribution, marketing, advertising, and sales. Articles discuss product lines, famous brands, private labels, store security, technology enhancements, staffing, and related issues. Industry news, newsmakers, and competition are spotlighted. The special convention issue contains 20 pages of editorial commentary on the current and future state of mass retailing. Online content available only to subscribers at www.retail-merchandiser.com.

1109. *Retail Traffic.* Formerly (until May 2003): *Shopping Center World;* Incorporates (1975-1991): *Shopping Center World Product and Service Directory.* [ISSN: 1544-4236] 1972. m. USD 115 domestic (Free to qualified personnel). Ed(s): Beth Karlin, David Bodamer. Prism Business Media, 249 W 17th St, New York, NY 10011; inquiries@prismb2b.com; http://www.prismbusinessmedia.com. Illus. Circ: 36553 Controlled. Microform: PQC. Online: EBSCO Publishing, EBSCO Host; Gale; Northern Light Technology, Inc.; OCLC Online Computer Library Center, Inc.; ProQuest K-12 Learning Solutions; ProQuest LLC (Ann Arbor); H.W. Wilson. *Indexed:* ABIn, BPI. *Aud.:* Sa.

This trade title caters to commercial real estate executives, shopping center developers, owners and managers, retail chain store executives, construction personnel, marketing professionals, leasing agents, brokers, architects, and designers. Articles report on successful shopping center properties, projects proposed and underway, specific design elements and materials, financing, and retail store profiles. Regular departments include Shows and Events, Retail Design Trends, Lease Language, International News, and Sales Figures of Major Retailers. Content is available online at www.retailtrafficmag.com, grouped by topic rather than individual issue.

1110. *Retailing Today.* Former titles: *D S N Retailing Today; Discount Store News.* 1962. fortn. 22/yr. USD 119 domestic (Free to qualified personnel). Ed(s): Tim Craig, Bernadette Casey. Lebhar-Friedman, Inc., 425 Park Ave, New York, NY 10022; info@lf.com; http://www.lf.com. Illus., adv. Circ: 32805. Microform: CIS; PQC. Online: The Dialog Corporation; EBSCO Publishing, EBSCO Host; Factiva, Inc.; Florida Center for Library Automation; Gale; Northern Light Technology, Inc.; OCLC Online Computer Library Center, Inc.; ProQuest LLC (Ann Arbor). *Indexed:* ABIn, CWI, PAIS. *Aud.:* Sa.

Targeted toward managers of all mass retail segments including full-line discount department stores, catalog showrooms, specialty chains, off-price retailers, mid-tier department stores, membership warehouse clubs, and supercenters. Articles report on apparel, home products, soft and hard lines, hot ticket items, new product developments, licensing agreements, merchandising and store plans, operations, market share, and industry trends in general. Regular departments provide classified advertising, columns from the perspective of buyer and seller, and reports on regulatory and market news and newsmakers. Special reports focus on the activities of specific companies and strategic business groups. Free registration is required in order to access deep, full-text archives as well as complementary content at www.retailingtoday.com.

1111. *Rock Products: the aggregate industry's journal of applied technology.* [ISSN: 0747-3605] 1897. m. USD 36 domestic (Free to qualified personnel). Ed(s): Rick Markley. Prism Business Media, 330 N Wabash Ave, Ste 2300, Chicago, IL 60611; inquiries@prismb2b.com; http://www.prismbusinessmedia.com. Illus., adv. Circ: 19000 Controlled. Vol. ends: Dec. Microform: PQC. Online: Gale; Northern Light Technology, Inc.; OCLC Online Computer Library Center, Inc.; ProQuest LLC (Ann Arbor). *Indexed:* ChemAb, EngInd, ExcerpMed. *Aud.:* Sa.

Topics covered are of interest to readers associated with the quarried stone, sand, gypsum, lightweight aggregate, and earthmoving industries. Regular features include a handful of articles on manufacturing technologies, processes, business practices, and labor, regulatory, and safety issues. Additional trade-specific departments include industry news, environmental issues, a Washington letter, new products, and a calendar of events, in additon to an annual buyers' guide and dealer directory. An important title for the aggregate industry. Current and previous issues available online at www.rockproducts.com. Libraries serving communities with these trades should consider subscribing.

1112. *Rubber World.* [ISSN: 0035-9572] 1889. 16x/yr. USD 34 domestic; USD 39 Canada; USD 89 elsewhere. Ed(s): Jill Rohrer, Don R Smith. Lippincott & Peto, Inc., 1867 W Market St, Akron, OH 44313; http://www.rubberworld.com/rwol/rwol.htm. Illus., adv. Circ: 11400 Controlled. Vol. ends: Dec. Microform: PMC; PQC. Online: EBSCO Publishing, EBSCO Host; Factiva, Inc.; Florida Center for Library Automation; Gale; Northern Light Technology, Inc. *Indexed:* C&ISA, ChemAb, EngInd, RRTA, WAE&RSA. *Aud.:* Sa.

Feature articles provide up-to-date technical service information for rubber chemists and formulators, give R&D personnel current technical know-how, and inform plant engineering personnel about the latest equipment and production technology. Regular departments include Business Briefs, Patent News, Market Focus, Tech Service, Process Machinery, Supplies Showcase, Meetings, and Calendar of Events. The subscription includes additional quarterly issues devoted to special topics. Digital edition of the current issue is offered after free registration at www.rubberworld.com; articles from previous issues must be ordered. Libraries that support industrial marketing research, chemistry, and engineering should find this title useful in their collections.

Sea Technology. See Marine Science and Technology section.

Snack Food & Wholesale Bakery. See Food Industry section.

1113. *Special Events Magazine.* Formerly: *Special Events.* [ISSN: 1079-1264] 1982. m. USD 48 domestic (Free to qualified personnel). Ed(s): Lisa Hurley. Prism Business Media, 9800 Metcalf Ave, Overland Park, KS 66212-2216; inquiries@prismb2b.com; http://www.prismbusinessmedia.com. Circ: 5763 Paid and controlled. Online: Florida Center for Library Automation; Gale; OCLC Online Computer Library Center, Inc.; H.W. Wilson. *Indexed:* BPI. *Aud.:* Ga, Sa.

A resource for event professionals who design and produce social, corporate, and public events in hotels, resorts, banquet facilities, and other venues. Coverage of galas is extensive; photos are a feast for the eyes. Departments provide practical advice on event management and tout new products and innovative ideas. The publication has a cooperative alliance with the International Special Events Society. In each issue, five pages are reserved for news and promotion of the society's web site. Contents of the current issue and archived articles arranged by subject are available online at www.specialevents.com.

1114. *Stores.* [ISSN: 0039-1867] 1912. m. USD 120 (Free to qualified personnel). Ed(s): Susan Reda. N R F Enterprises, Inc., 325 7th St, NW, Ste 1000, Washington, DC 20004-2802; http://www.stores.com/. Illus., adv. Circ: 35000 Paid. Vol. ends: Dec. Online: OCLC Online Computer Library Center, Inc. *Indexed:* ABIn, BPI, PAIS. *Aud.:* Ga, Ac, Sa.

This title features corporate and industry news for all kinds of retail chain stores and wholesale clubs, restaurants, drug stores, direct mail, and marketing firms engaged in specialty and general merchandising. The focus is on technology, management, and operations. Special issues include ranked lists of department stores in July and specialty chains in August, both including sales and earnings figures. Current issue contents, archives, and rankings are available at www.stores.org. Appropriate for larger public libraries and for academic libraries that support business programs.

1115. *Street & Smith's SportsBusiness Journal.* [ISSN: 1098-5972] 1998. w. USD 291 domestic; USD 346 Canada; USD 456 elsewhere. Ed(s): Barry Lovette. American City Business Journals, Street & Smith, 120 W Morehead St, Ste 310, Charlotte, NC 28202; info.sportsbiz@amcity.com; http://www.sportsbusinessjournal.com. Illus., adv. *Indexed:* SD. *Aud.:* Ac, Sa.

In addition to numerous news blurbs and short articles on events, individual athletes, and advertising campaigns, each issue contains "Pro Sports Tracker," showing stadium attendance to date. The year-end "By the Numbers" special issue serves as a cumulation of industry statistics. Special libraries supporting advertising agencies, marketing firms, professional teams, and sports associations will want to subscribe. Of possible interest to academic libraries supporting marketing programs and collegiate athletic departments. Online access to content is only available to print subscribers.

1116. *Telephony: intelligence for the broadband economy.* Incorporates (in 2005): *Wireless Review;* (in 2001): *Upstart.* [ISSN: 0040-2656] 1901. bi-w. Free. Ed(s): Vince Vittore, Nikki Golden. Prism Business Media, 330 N Wabash Ave, Ste 2300, Chicago, IL 60611; inquiries@prismb2b.com; http://www.prismbusinessmedia.com. Illus., index, adv. Circ: 62761 Controlled. Microform: PQC. Online: EBSCO Publishing, EBSCO Host; Florida Center for Library Automation; Gale; OCLC Online Computer Library Center, Inc.; ProQuest K-12 Learning Solutions; ProQuest LLC (Ann Arbor); H.W. Wilson. *Indexed:* ABIn, BPI, EngInd, LRI, MicrocompInd. *Bk. rev.:* Various number and length. *Aud.:* Ga, Ac, Sa.

This title covers all aspects of the rapidly evolving broadband industry that includes telecommunications, wireless and PCS technologies, cable, DSL, optics, and VOIP. Each issue contains current news that impacts businesses, alliances, product development, policies, practices, and regulation. Only current issue content is available at www.telephonyonline.com, complemented by extensive industry news items. Given the importance of the digital economy and the technology behind it all, this magazine will be of interest to most libraries.

1117. *Textile World.* Former titles (until 1931): *Textile Advance News;* (until 1924): *Textiles;* (until 1923): *Posselt's Textile Journal;* (until 1921): *Textile World Journal;* Which was formed by the merger of (1903-1915): *Textile World Record;* (1894-1915): *Textile Manufacturers Journal.* [ISSN: 0040-5213] 1915. m. Free. Ed(s): Jim Borneman. Billian Publishing, Inc., 2100 Powers Ferry Rd, Ste 300, Atlanta, GA 30339; info@billian.com; http://www.billian.com. Illus., adv. Circ: 32340 Paid and controlled. Vol. ends: Dec. Microform: PMC; PQC. Online: EBSCO Publishing, EBSCO Host; Florida Center for Library Automation; Gale; OCLC Online Computer Library Center, Inc.; ProQuest K-12 Learning Solutions; ProQuest LLC (Ann Arbor); H.W. Wilson. *Indexed:* ABIn, AS&TI, BPI, ChemAb, EngInd, ExcerpMed. *Aud.:* Sa.

Included in this title are reports on technologies such as yarn manufacturing; fabric forming; chemical treatment and finishing; industrial and specialty textiles; carpet manufacturing and marketing; manufacturing systems; and management issues on an international basis. Articles and advertisements introduce suppliers, new products, innovative techniques, and industry trends. Recurring departments provide industry news, statistics, legal developments, legislation, profiles of companies, interviews with executives, and occasional special reports. The current issue and archives are freely available online at www.textileworld.com.

1118. *Vending Times: vending - feeding - coffee service - music & games.* Incorporates (in 1974): *Vend; V-T Music and Games.* [ISSN: 0042-3327] 1961. m. USD 35. Ed(s): T.R. Sanford, Nick Montano. Vending Times, Inc., 1375 Broadway, 6th Fl, New York, NY 10018-7001; http://www.vendingtimes.com. Illus. Circ: 17500 Paid. Microform: PQC. *Aud.:* Sa.

Vending in some form is evident in most areas of the public landscape: commercial and industrial establishments, hospitals, schools, airports and other transportation hubs, hotels and motels, restaurants and bars, and family entertainment centers. Readership is broadly based and can include independent and national-chain vending and manual foodservice operators, mobile caterers, office refreshment service operators, music and amusement operators, and bulk vending operators, as well as manufacturers, suppliers, distributors, and brokers

of equipment, products, and support services to the industry. Each monthly issue includes sections presenting news, market trends, product innovations, interviews, and coverage of industry events. Extensive web-only content; the current issue and archives are available at www.vendingtimes.com.

1119. *W W D: the retailer's daily newspaper.* Formerly (until 197?): *Women's Wear Daily.* [ISSN: 0149-5380] 1892. d. (Mon.-Fri.). USD 99 domestic to retailers; USD 135 domestic to manufacturers; USD 295 in Canada & Mexico. Fairchild Publications, Inc., 7 W 34th St, New York, NY 10001-8191; customerservice@fairchildpub.com; http://www.fairchildpub.com. Illus., adv. Circ: 161386. Microform: PQC. Online: The Dialog Corporation; EBSCO Publishing, EBSCO Host; Factiva, Inc.; Florida Center for Library Automation; Gale; OCLC Online Computer Library Center, Inc.; ProQuest LLC (Ann Arbor). *Indexed:* ABIn, CWI, LRI. *Aud.:* Ga, Ac, Sa.

This newspaper-format publication provides extensive coverage of the women's apparel and couture fashion industries. Each weekday issue focuses on a rotating theme of accessories, ready-to-wear, sportswear, or beauty, along with commentary on the season's colors, styles, and fabrics. Designers are profiled, and their runway shows are lavishly photographed. There is extensive reporting on the social scene that is intrinsic to the concept of "image." Manufacturing and distribution problems, marketing, distribution channels, and retail issues are discussed in brief. Extensive daily news items are available at www.wwd.com, but access to an archive of 75,000 articles requires a separate subscription. Of interest to libraries with a flair for fashion.

1120. *Wines and Vines: the authoritative voice of the grape and wine industry.* [ISSN: 0043-583X] 1919. m. USD 32.50 domestic; USD 50 foreign. Hiaring Co., 1800 Lincoln Ave, San Rafael, CA 94901-1298. Illus., adv. Circ: 4000 Paid and free. *Indexed:* ChemAb. *Bk. rev.:* Various number and length. *Aud.:* Ga, Ac, Sa.

Published since 1919, this trade title even managed to survive the lean years of Prohibition. Although aimed at wine producers, this monthly publication is enjoyed by all wine aficionados. Each monthly issue includes topical industry news along with editorial columns on political, legal, and regulatory developments. Emphasis is on boutique wine production trends and techniques in North America including profiles of notable winemakers and grape growers. A few news headlines and very limited content from recent issues are offered at www.winesandvines.com.

1121. *Wood & Wood Products: furniture, cabinets, woodworking and allied products management and operations.* [ISSN: 0043-7662] 1896. 13x/yr. USD 55. Ed(s): Richard Christianson. Vance Publishing Corp., 400 Knightsbridge Pkwy, Lincolnshire, IL 60069; http://www.vancepublishing.com. Illus., adv. Circ: 52500 Controlled. Microform: PQC. Online: EBSCO Publishing, EBSCO Host; Florida Center for Library Automation; Gale; Northern Light Technology, Inc.; OCLC Online Computer Library Center, Inc.; H.W. Wilson. *Indexed:* AS&TI, ExcerpMed, FPA, ForAb. *Aud.:* Sa.

This publication is intended for management and operating personnel in the woodworking industry. Articles address machining trends and developments; management and marketing techniques; and automation, hardware, and design for the residential furniture, business and institutional furniture, cabinet, millwork, and panel markets. Current issue contents, archives, industry news, and related links are available online at www.wwpmagazine.com.

■ CANADA

Erica Burnham and Alexander Jerabek, McGill University Libraries, 3459 McTavish St., Montreal, PQ, Canada H3A 1Y1; erica.burnham@ mcgill.ca, alexander.jerabek@mcgill.ca

Introduction

This section is composed of a selection of magazines published in Canada containing articles about Canada and Canadians. The listing is a sample of the best, most representative magazines from all Canadian provinces. Magazines and journals were selected based on their overall quality and appearance, their availability in Canadian libraries, and countrywide circulation figures. Titles with general content describing the cultural, regional, and political diversity of the country were selected. The list also includes a selection of academic titles that contain the best research and scholarly articles about Canada and Canadian life. Canadian publications of a specialized consumer or academic nature are found in the subject listings elsewhere in this volume. The editors have excluded split-run publications for the entries, i.e., foreign magazines containing some Canadian content and advertising, for example, *Time, Reader's Digest,* and *Sports Illustrated.*

The Canadian magazine and journal publishing industry has historically received financial assistance from the Canadian federal government's Department of Canadian Heritage. The Canadian Magazine Fund provides editorial content support and the Publications Assistance Program provides mailing and distribution support. Many of the magazines selected also receive financial support from the Canada Council for the Arts and arts councils in their province of publication. Recently, raises in postal rates and cuts to funding subsidies have been causes of concern to publishers, but the readership continues to grow, and subscribers remain loyal to large national titles and small regional publications alike. Despite the fact that newsstands still include large amounts of U.S. titles, Canadian magazine subscriptions, circulation, readership, and launches continue to increase. And while a venerable title such as *Saturday Night* has suspended publication, other recently launched magazines such as *The Walrus* and *Maisonneuve* have received critical acclaim and captured public interest.

The two national associations representing magazine publishers, the Canadian Magazine Publisher's Association, a membership lobby group for the industry, and Magazine Canada, a nonprofit marketing board, merged under the name Magazines Canada in June 2005. The name change reflects the association's broader approach to changing publication and business environments.

Magazines Canada (www.magazinescanada.ca) operates in both official languages, reflecting increased growth in the association's French-language membership. The association has undertaken advertising campaigns, developed a project office, expanded marketing efforts, and initiated other activities. A new web site was launched with both a consumer-oriented Canadian magazine directory and a news and information site about the organization.

Masthead Online (www.mastheadonline.ca), "The Magazine About Magazines," follows developments in the Canadian magazine publishing industry and reports on a variety of industry-related topics. A regular e-mail bulletin broadcasts headlines from the week's news and job postings.

Most of the magazines and journals selected in this section also have web sites with complementary content summaries, indexes, interactive features, directories, and subscription and online renewal information.

Basic Periodicals

Hs, Ga, Ac: *Canadian Business, Maclean's.*

Basic Abstracts and Indexes

CPI.Q, Canadian Business & Current Affairs - Fulltext Reference.

1122. *Acadiensis: journal of the history of the Atlantic region.* [ISSN: 0044-5851] 1971. s-a. CND 37.45 (Individuals, CND 26.75; CND 9.95 per issue). Ed(s): Bill Parenteau. University of New Brunswick, Department of History, PO Box 4400, Fredericton, NB E3B 5A3, Canada; http://www.unbf.ca/arts/History. Illus., index, adv. Sample. Refereed. Circ: 850. Vol. ends: Spring (No. 2). Microform: MML. *Indexed:* AmH&L, ArtHuCI, CBCARef, CPerI, HistAb, IBR, IBSS, IBZ, SSCI. *Bk. rev.:* 2-4, 12-24 pages. *Aud.:* Ga, Ac.

Acadiensis is a bilingual, semi-annual journal devoted to Eastern Canadian history and regional studies. The journal publishes original research articles by scholars in the fields of history, geography, political science, folklore, literature, sociology, economics, and other areas. Each issue includes reviews and review essays of publications in Canadian Studies. Discussions by scholars are presented in an occasional forum section. An authoritative bibliography compiled by librarians is also included. Articles range in scope from "Music, Song and Dance in Cape Breton" to "The British Military's Building of

Wellington Barracks and Brick Construction in 19th-Century Halifax." The journal's web site provides access to *The Acadiensis Index,* a comprehensive subject and author index to the contents of the journal since the publication of the first issue in 1971. *Acadiensis*'s focus on specialized and neglected areas of study makes it an appropriate choice for special and academic libraries.

1123. *L'Actualite.* Incorporates (in 1976): *Maclean;* Which was formerly (1961-1971): *Magazine Maclean;* Formerly (until 1959): *Ma Paroisse.* [ISSN: 0383-8714] 1945. 20x/yr. CND 35 domestic; CND 56 United States; CND 116 elsewhere. Ed(s): Carole Beaulieu. Rogers Media Publishing Ltd, Rogers Healthcare & Financial Services Group, 1200, ave McGill College, bureau 800, Montreal, PQ H3B 4G7, Canada; http://www.rogers.com. Illus., adv. Circ: 240000. Microform: MML. Online: Gale; LexisNexis; Micromedia ProQuest; ProQuest LLC (Ann Arbor). *Indexed:* CBCARef, CPerI, PdeR. *Bk. rev.:* 1, 1-2 pages, signed. *Aud.:* Hs, Ga, Ac.

L'Actualite is the most popular French-language news magazine in Canada, with a subscription base of over 240,000. The magazine focuses on events and issues in the province of Quebec and also includes stories of significant international interest. Each 100-page issue has regular columns, synopses of world events, opinion essays, health and personal finance items, and a calendar of events for the province. The magazine frequently uses a question and answer format for in-depth feature interviews with politicians, policy makers, business people, scientists, and media personalities. A section titled "L'entretien" interviews an expert on an issue of international political concern. Every two months, the Royal Canadian Geographical Society publishes an insert called "Geographica," a colorful description with maps of a particular Canadian region or city. The January issue spotlights Quebec personalities of the year and winners of an amateur geographical photography contest. The online version of the magazine contains full texts of the feature articles. *L'Actualite* is recommended for libraries wishing to offer information about French-Canadian culture and is suitable for French-language readers in high school and public libraries.

1124. *Alberta History.* Formerly (until 1975): *Alberta Historical Review.* [ISSN: 0316-1552] 1953. q. CND 25. Ed(s): Hugh A Dempsey. Historical Society of Alberta, 95 Holmwood Ave, NW, Calgary, AB T2K 2G7, Canada. Illus., index. Sample. Refereed. Circ: 1200 Paid. Vol. ends: No. 4. Microform: PQC. Online: Gale. *Indexed:* AmH&L, CBCARef, CPerI, HistAb. *Bk. rev.:* 15-20, 1-2 pages. *Aud.:* Ga, Ac.

Alberta History, originally known as the *Alberta Historical Review,* is a quarterly magazine published by the Historical Society of Alberta with assistance from the Alberta Historical Resources Foundation. Primary source material by pioneers and settlers is presented along with scholarly articles about historical figures and events. Although the focus is on Alberta history, the occasional paper will address current concerns and issues. Social aspects of early settlement, reflections on settlers' accounts and writings, and original research make this journal a valuable addition to large public libraries and to academic libraries with strong collections specializing in North American history. The society's web site provides access to sample articles and tables of contents.

1125. *Arctic.* [ISSN: 0004-0843] 1947. q. USD 20 per issue. Ed(s): Karen M McCullough. Arctic Institute of North America, University of Calgary, MLT 11th Fl, 2500 University Dr NW, Calgary, AB T2N 1N4, Canada; kmccullo@acs.ucalgary.ca; http://www.ucalgary.ca/aina. Illus., index. Sample. Refereed. Circ: 2000. Vol. ends: Dec (No. 4). Microform: PQC. Online: Florida Center for Library Automation; Gale; Micromedia ProQuest; ProQuest LLC (Ann Arbor). *Indexed:* ABS&EES, AbAn, AmH&L, AnthLit, ApEcolAb, BiolAb, CABA, CBCARef, CPerI, ChemAb, DSA, EnvAb, EnvInd, ExcerpMed, FPA, ForAb, HistAb, HortAb, IBR, IndVet, M&GPA, OceAb, PetrolAb, PollutAb, RRTA, S&F, SCI, SSCI, SWRA, VB, WAE&RSA, ZooRec. *Bk. rev.:* 7-10, 1-3 pages. *Aud.:* Ac.

Arctic is a cross-disciplinary journal of original scholarship dealing with issues affecting the circumpolar world. Each issue includes "peer-reviewed articles, reviews of new books on the North, profiles of significant people, places and Northern events, and topical commentaries." The subject scope covers anthropology, astronomy, biology, ecology, education, engineering, fine arts, humanities, medicine, and paleoethnology, resulting in the journal being widely indexed. While the scope of articles is broad and covers all aspects of arctic research, the articles themselves can be highly specialized and technical. Although most articles are clearly intended for specialists, for example, "Levels of cadmium, lead, mercury and 137caesium in caribou (Rangifer tarandus) tissues from Northern Quebec," some articles may be of more popular interest, such as an account of the creation of an exhibition about Rockwell Kent, "painter, printmaker, illustrator, and architect; a designer of books, ceramics, and textiles, and a prolific writer." Also included in each issue is a general-interest section titled "Info North" containing an essay of Northern interest, Northern news, and institute news. The journal's web site contains sample articles from recent issues and a full contents listing with bilingual abstracts. *Arctic* is supported in part by a grant from the Social Sciences and Humanities Research Council of Canada. It is suitable for large academic libraries and specialized collections.

1126. *B C Studies: the British Columbian quarterly.* [ISSN: 0005-2949] 1969. q. CND 55 (Individuals, CND 40; Students, CND 25). Ed(s): Carlyn Craig, Robert R J McDonald. University of British Columbia, Buchanan E162, 1866 Main Mall, Vancouver, BC V6T 1Z1, Canada; write_us@bcstudies.com; http://www.interchange.ubc.ca/bcstudie. Illus., index, adv. Sample. Refereed. Circ: 600. Vol. ends: Summer. Microform: MML; PQC. Online: EBSCO Publishing, EBSCO Host; Micromedia ProQuest; ProQuest LLC (Ann Arbor); H.W. Wilson. Reprint: PSC. *Indexed:* AbAn, AmH&L, CBCARef, CPerI, HistAb, IBSS. *Bk. rev.:* 4-20, 2-6 pages, signed. *Aud.:* Ga, Ac.

Since 1969, *BC Studies* has published interdisciplinary research dealing with British Columbia's cultural, economic, and political life, past and present. Each issue includes articles, review essays, book reviews, interviews, poetry, and a bibliography of recent publications. Articles cover a broad range and are of interest to a wide audience. Issues are occasionally thematic, covering such topics as "Perspectives on Aboriginal Culture" or "Scientific Expedition into BC Interior." A section titled "Digital Domain" provides links to selected Internet resources on subjects covered. The web site also provides a cumulative subject index and book review index. The journal's authoritative and informative content makes it a suitable resource for academic and large public libraries.

1127. *The Beaver: Canada's history magazine.* [ISSN: 0005-7517] 1920. bi-m. CND 29.95 domestic; CND 37.95 United States; CND 44.95 elsewhere. Ed(s): Annalee Greenberg. Canada's National History Society, 167 Lombard Ave, # 478, Winnipeg, MB R3B 0T6, Canada; editors@ historysociety.ca. Illus., index, adv. Sample. Circ: 49300. Vol. ends: Dec/Jan (No. 6). Microform: MML. Online: EBSCO Publishing, EBSCO Host; Gale; Micromedia ProQuest. *Indexed:* AICP, AbAn, AmH&L, AnthLit, BRI, CBCARef, CBRI, CPerI, HistAb, MASUSE. *Bk. rev.:* 3-6, 1-3 pages. *Aud.:* Hs, Ga, Ac.

The Beaver is one of Canada's oldest history magazines. It contains articles on Canadian history, famous Canadians, and literary, art, and political history, as well as interviews with prominent Canadians. Features include "Currents" and "Explorations," columns devoted to current events related to history and Canada. Splendid illustrations and photographs accompany articulate and well-written pieces. Reviews of books, films, exhibits, and events are included. The journal's web site contains the feature article of each issue and history lesson plans suitable for junior and secondary teaching. This highly readable and handsome journal is well suited for a broad audience and is appropriate for most libraries and collections.

Books in Canada. See Books and Book Reviews section.

1128. *Border Crossings: a magazine of the arts.* Formerly: *Arts Manitoba.* [ISSN: 0831-2559] 1982. q. CND 27 domestic; USD 32 foreign. Ed(s): Meeka Walsh. Arts Manitoba Publications Inc., 500 70 Arthur St, Winnipeg, MB R3B 1G7, Canada; bordercr@escape.ca; http://www.cmpa.ca/va1.html. Illus., index, adv. Sample. Circ: 3300 Paid. Vol. ends: No. 4. Microform: MML. Online: EBSCO Publishing, EBSCO Host; Micromedia ProQuest; OCLC Online Computer Library Center, Inc.; H.W. Wilson. *Indexed:* ABM, AmHI, ArtInd, CBCARef, CPerI. *Bk. rev.:* 1-3, 2 pages, signed. *Aud.:* Ga, Ac.

This award-winning contemporary arts magazine has been profiling Canadian artists and their work for nearly 25 years. Art is defined broadly to include all visual, performing, and literary arts, painting, photography, architecture, film, drama, dance, music, poetry, and fiction. Each issue is centered on a particular national or international theme. Examples of themes from past issues include love, censorship, technology, First Nations art, and landscapes. There are regular columns describing current artists, exhibits, projects, and publications. Photographic portfolios with color reproductions of art works and extensive interviews with established artists are regular sections in each 100-page issue. The journal's web site contains article abstracts and photographs from the most recent issue. *Border Crossings* continues to be one of the top grant recipients for funding from the Canada Council for the Arts and has now received 50 National and Western Canadian Magazine Awards. This magazine will be of interest to large public and academic libraries.

1129. *British Columbia Magazine.* Formerly (until 2002): *Beautiful British Columbia.* [ISSN: 1709-4623] 1959. q. CND 19.95 domestic; CND 26.95 foreign. Ed(s): Anita Willis. Tourism British Columbia, 802-865 Hornby St, Vancouver, BC V6Z 2G3, Canada; Yvette.Chamberlain@ tourism.bc.ca; http://www.tourism.bc.ca. Illus., adv. Circ: 244000 Paid. Online: EBSCO Publishing, EBSCO Host; Gale; Northern Light Technology, Inc. *Indexed:* CBCARef, CPerI. *Aud.:* Hs, Ga.

This magazine is famous for its high-quality color photography and well-researched articles on beautiful places, remarkable people, and intriguing wildlife in Canada's most western province. Each issue contains photo essays, educational articles, and useful travel information on the magnificent scenery, parks, wilderness, wildlife, geography, ecology, and heritage of the province. The editors pride themselves on seeking out "the exotic, unknown, rare and surprising." A supplement titled "Beautiful BC Traveller" is included with selected issues. The magazine's web site contains highlights of the most recent issue and a subject index of more than 20,000 records for all articles and photographs published. The magazine has a worldwide subscriber base and is suitable for high school and public libraries.

1130. *C A R P Fifty Plus.* Former titles (until 2001): *C A R P News Fifty Plus;* (until 1999): *C A R P News;* (until 1994): *C A R P;* (until 1992): *C A R P News;* (until 1986): *C A R P News Letter.* [ISSN: 1701-3674] 1985. m. CND 7.95; CND 2.50 newsstand/cover per issue. Ed(s): Bonnie Baker Cowan. Canadian Association of Retired Persons, 27 Queen St E, Ste 1304, Toronto, ON M5C 2M6, Canada; info@50plus.com; http://www.50plus.com/. Circ: 43000. *Indexed:* CBCARef, CPerI. *Aud.:* Ga, Ac, Sa.

The Canadian Association for Retired People (CARP) is a nonprofit organization that acts as a national voice for over 400,000 Canadians. The association and its magazine are autonomous and do not accept operating funds from any level of government. The magazine is a compendium of information on health, nutrition, money matters, travel, and community affairs. In each 100-page issue, CARP also provides members an update on their advocacy work and governmental legislation and financial changes effecting people over 50. The magazine includes special reports on seniors' concerns such as safety of food, aging well, and fighting cancer. Three focused issues on retirement, finance, and travel are published throughout the year. CARP negotiates member discounts for accommodations, insurance, and other products, and the magazine highlights these services. Additional services, directories, community chat rooms, discussion forums, and a subject search index are available on the association's web site. This magazine will be of interest to public libraries.

1131. *C M Magazine: Canadian review of materials.* Former titles (until Dec. 1994): *C M: Canadian Materials for Schools and Libraries;* (until 1979): *Canadian Materials.* [ISSN: 1201-9364] 1995. bi-w. Free. Ed(s): Dave Jenkinson. Manitoba Library Association, 606 100 Arthur St, Winnipeg, MB R3B 1H3, Canada; cm@mts.net; http://www.umanitoba.ca/cm. Illus., adv. Online: EBSCO Publishing, EBSCO Host; Micromedia ProQuest. *Indexed:* BRD, BRI, CBCARef, CBRI, CEI, CPerI, MRD. *Bk. rev.:* 30, 1 page, signed. *Aud.:* Ems, Ga, Ac.

Published by the Manitoba Library Association, this web periodical will be of special interest to children, parents, teachers, and librarians. It contains reviews of Canadiana material (books, videos, audio and CD-ROM recordings) suitable for children and young adults. Non-Canadian material is included for review if the subject, author, or illustrator is Canadian. The entire archive of *C M Magazine*'s print predecessor is also available on the web site. It is possible to browse author, title, media, date, age/grade, and features indexes. Keyword searching is available for both the current and past issues. Both public libraries and academic libraries with children's literature collections will find this publication a useful addition.

1132. *Canada. Statistics Canada. Canadian Social Trends.* [ISSN: 0831-5698] 1982. q. CND 39. Ed(s): Susan Crompton. Statistics Canada, Operations and Integration Division, Circulation Management, 120 Parkdale Ave, Ottawa, ON K1A 0T6, Canada; infostats@statcan.ca; http://www.statcan.ca/english/IPS/data/11-008-XPE.htm. Illus., index, adv. Vol. ends: No. 4. Microform: MML. Online: EBSCO Publishing, EBSCO Host; Micromedia ProQuest. *Indexed:* AmH&L, CBCARef, CPerI, HistAb, PAIS, PdeR. *Aud.:* Hs, Ga, Ac, Sa.

This bilingual journal is published and compiled by Statistics Canada's Housing, Family, and Social Statistics Division, and features articles on social, economic, and demographic conditions in Canada. The focus is on statistics and statistical analyses of major social, demographic, and economic indicators. Far from being dry statistical descriptions, the articles discuss relevant topics including culture, education, family, health, income, justice, labor, population, and trends. Charts, graphs, and other representations of data illustrate the articles. Examples of recent subjects include "Studying and working," "Motherhood and paycheques," and "Family violence against seniors." A section called "Educator's Notebook" provides resources and lesson plans for teachers. New publications by Statistics Canada are listed in the bulletin "Keeping Track." There is an online edition. A worthwhile addition to all libraries.

Canadian Art. See Art/General section.

1133. *Canadian Business.* Former titles (until 1977): *Canadian Business Magazine;* (until 1972): *Canadian Business;* (until 1932): *Commerce of the Nation;* Incorporates (1981-1982): *Energy.* [ISSN: 0008-3100] 1928. bi-w. CND 34.95 domestic; CND 64.95 United States; CND 129.95 overseas. Rogers Media Publishing Ltd, One Mount Pleasant Rd, 11th Fl, Toronto, ON M4Y 2Y5, Canada; http://www.rogers.com. Illus., index, adv. Sample. Circ: 83000 Paid. Vol. ends: Dec (No. 12). Microform: MML. Online: EBSCO Publishing, EBSCO Host; Florida Center for Library Automation; LexisNexis; Micromedia ProQuest; Northern Light Technology, Inc.; OCLC Online Computer Library Center, Inc.; ProQuest K-12 Learning Solutions; ProQuest LLC (Ann Arbor); H.W. Wilson. *Indexed:* ABIn, BPI, CBCARef, CPerI, LRI, MASUSE, PAIS, SD. *Bk. rev.:* 2-3, 1-3 pages. *Aud.:* Ga, Ac.

Canadian Business covers all aspects of investing, industry analyses, and technology as they relate to Canadian business and the Canadian economy. It also provides timely topical management information on ideas and opportunities for senior executives. Each issue has a lengthy cover article. There are several feature articles, personal profiles, commentaries, and industry reports. The magazine is supported by full-page color advertising and includes smaller business ads and job postings. There are a number of special issues throughout the year: "The Investor 500," annual best investments; "The Tech 100," annual top technology firms; and "MBA Guide," an annual review of Canadian MBA schools. The magazine's web site provides access to the online addition. Libraries that require a general magazine documenting and predicting the future of Canadian business will find this magazine useful.

1134. *Canadian Dimension: for people who want to change the world.* [ISSN: 0008-3402] 1963. bi-m. CND 37 (Individuals, CND 26.50; Students, CND 19.50). Dimension Publishing Inc., 91 Albert St, Rm 2 B, Winnipeg, MB R3B 1G5, Canada. Illus., index, adv. Sample. Circ: 3200. Vol. ends: Nov/Dec (No. 6). Microform: MML; PQC. Online: EBSCO Publishing, EBSCO Host; Florida Center for Library Automation; Gale; Micromedia ProQuest; Northern Light Technology, Inc.; ProQuest LLC (Ann Arbor). *Indexed:* AltPI, AmH&L, BAS, CBCARef, CPerI, HistAb. *Bk. rev.:* 2-4, 1 page, signed. *Aud.:* Hs, Ga, Ac.

Canadian Dimension has been an "avowedly radical, anti-capitalist magazine" since 1963. As the oldest alternative and independently published magazine in Canada, it consistently challenges mainstream public opinion. The magazine has an editorial collective dedicated to bringing about social change by encouraging open debate in Canadian society. The magazine's readership is broadly based. A recent survey reveals subscribers from four political generations who describe themselves as activists with concerns for globalization, environment, health care, labor, and human rights. Each issue contains 48 pages of ad-free articles written by Canadians about Canadian and international issues. Color advertisements are confined to the magazine's cover pages. Each black-and-white issue has political cartoons, illustrations, and photographs. The journal's web site offers a portion of the current issue online. This magazine is a valuable addition to high school, public, and academic library collections, providing a well-written alternative political viewpoint.

1135. *Canadian Ethnic Studies.* [ISSN: 0008-3496] 1969. 3x/yr. CND 100 (Individuals, CND 70; Students, USD 35). Ed(s): A W Rasporich, James Frideres. Canadian Ethnic Studies Association, c/o Dept. of History, University of Calgary, 2500 University Dr, NW, Calgary, AB T2N 1N4, Canada; ces@ucalgary.ca; http://www.ss.ucalgary.ca/ces. Illus., index, adv. Sample. Refereed. Circ: 800 Paid. Vol. ends: No. 3. Microform: MML; PQC. Online: EBSCO Publishing, EBSCO Host; Florida Center for Library Automation; Gale; Micromedia ProQuest; ProQuest K-12 Learning Solutions; ProQuest LLC (Ann Arbor); H.W. Wilson. Reprint: PSC. *Indexed:* ABS&EES, AICP, AgeL, AmH&L, AmHI, CBCARef, CPerI, ENW, HistAb, IBSS, L&LBA, MASUSE, MLA-IB, PAIS, PSA, RILM, SSA, SociolAb. *Bk. rev.:* 15-20, 1-4 pages, signed. *Aud.:* Ga, Ac.

Canadian Ethnic Studies is a bilingual, refereed journal "devoted to the study of ethnicity, immigration, inter-group relations and the history and cultural life of ethnic groups in Canada." It publishes original research articles. Conference reports, evaluations, case studies, critical essays, practitioner reflections, and reviews are listed in separate sections such as "Ethnic Voice" or "Perspective/ Opinions." Book and occasional film reviews are included, and there is an annual bibliography. Each issue contains lists of contributors, books received, and an index. Issues may have a thematic focus such as diversity and identity, education for a pluralistic society, or Canadian immigration. The journal's web site provides access to the current table of contents and abstracts of upcoming articles. This journal's interdisciplinary nature makes it a valuable addition to academic and public libraries.

1136. *Canadian Gardening.* [ISSN: 0847-3463] 7x/yr. CND 24.56 domestic; CND 37.95 United States; CND 57.95 overseas. Ed(s): Beckie Fox. Avid Media Inc., 340 Ferrier St, Ste 210, Markham, ON L3R 2Z5, Canada; howe@avidmediainc.com; http://www.canadiangardening.com. Adv. Circ: 135000 Paid. *Indexed:* CBCARef, GardL. *Bk. rev.:* 1-2, 1 page, signed. *Aud.:* Hs, Ga.

This home gardening magazine will interest beginners and veterans alike. It has plant profiles, practical advice on gardening techniques, beautiful photographic tours of unique Canadian gardens, and descriptions of new trends in flower and vegetable gardening. Both the urban and country gardener will find articles of interest that provide information specific for growing in Canadian climatic conditions. A small recipe section is included in each issue. Gardening events, fairs, and society meetings from across Canada are included by region in the calendar of events. Sources for all products and plants featured in each issue are listed. The journal's web site is a useful complement to the magazine, providing seed catalogues, lists of Canadian garden clubs and societies, a chat forum, and selected stories from issues since 2000. This colorful magazine is recommended for public libraries.

1137. *Canadian Geographic.* Formerly (until 1978): *Canadian Geographical Journal.* [ISSN: 0706-2168] 1930. 6x/yr. CND 32.66 domestic; CND 42.95 United States; CND 54.95 overseas. Ed(s): Rick Boychuk. Canadian Geographical Enterprises, 39 McArthur Ave, Ottawa, ON K1L 8L7, Canada; editorial@canadiangeographic.ca. Illus., index, adv. Sample. Circ: 240000 Paid. Vol. ends: Nov/Dec (No. 6). Online: EBSCO Publishing, EBSCO Host; Florida Center for Library Automation; Gale; Micromedia ProQuest; Northern Light Technology, Inc.; OCLC Online

Computer Library Center, Inc.; ProQuest K-12 Learning Solutions; ProQuest LLC (Ann Arbor); H.W. Wilson. *Indexed:* ABS&EES, AmH&L, BAS, BRI, CBCARef, CBRI, CPerI, HistAb, MASUSE, PAIS, RGPR. *Bk. rev.:* 1-5, 1 page, signed. *Aud.:* Hs, Ga, Ac.

The Royal Canadian Geographical Society, a nonprofit educational organization founded in 1929, publishes *Canadian Geographic*. Its editorial goal is "to make Canada better known to Canadians," and it does this superbly. The subject of this magazine is Canada, its people, resources, environment, heritage, and any major issue of concern, with a significant geographical dimension. Each 100-page issue has five features, often related to a similar theme, and it is well illustrated with color photographs and maps. Biographies of the Canadian contributors and web sites for background reading for the feature stories are also included. *Canadian Geographic* sponsors an annual amateur photographic contest and publishes the winning photos. There is a small amount of advertising and adventure classified ads in each issue. The magazine's web site provides access to article summaries, photographs, and related Internet resources. This magazine is a valuable geographic resource for high school, public, and academic collections.

1138. *Canadian Historical Review.* Formerly (until 1920): *Review of Historical Publications Relating to Canada.* [ISSN: 0008-3755] 1896. q. CND 115 domestic; USD 115 United States; USD 135 elsewhere. Ed(s): Sylvie Depatie, Arthur Ray. University of Toronto Press, Journals Division, 5201 Dufferin St, Toronto, ON M3H 5T8, Canada; journals@ utpress.utoronto.ca; http://www.utpjournals.com. Illus., index, adv. Sample. Refereed. Circ: 2580. Vol. ends: Dec (No. 4). Microform: MML; PMC; PQC. Online: EBSCO Publishing, EBSCO Host; Gale; Micromedia ProQuest; OCLC Online Computer Library Center, Inc.; OhioLINK; Project MUSE; SwetsWise Online Content. Reprint: PSC. *Indexed:* ABS&EES, AbAn, AmH&L, AmHI, ArtHuCI, BRD, BRI, CBCARef, CBRI, CPerI, FR, HistAb, HumInd, IBR, IBSS, IBZ, PSA, RILM, SSA, SSCI, SociolAb. *Bk. rev.:* 20-30, 1-3 pages, signed. *Aud.:* Ga, Ac.

Canadian Historical Review covers a broad range of subjects. Issues include five to eight scholarly articles, a listing of new publications on Canadian history, occasional film reviews, and forum debates. Bilingual abstracts are provided for the main articles. Topics discussed vary, covering multiculturalism, politics, the environment, religion, gender studies, and people and events of note. A comprehensive bibliography lists new materials (including CD and video media) and dissertations from a range of authoritative sources. The bibliography includes a subject index. Book reviews are provided by experts in the field. The journal's web site contains a table of contents and a link to UTPJOURNALS Online, the searchable bibliographic database of University of Toronto publications. This journal is suitable for both academic and public libraries.

1139. *Canadian House & Home.* Formerly: *House and Home.* [ISSN: 0826-7642] 1982. 8x/yr. CND 26.95 domestic; CND 28.96 in Nova Scotia, Newfoundland & New Brunswick; CND 46.95 United States. Ed(s): Cobi Ladner. Canadian Home Publishers, 511 King St W, Ste 120, Toronto, ON M5V 2Z4, Canada; mail@canhomepub.com; http://www.canadianhouseandhome.com. Adv. Circ: 110700. *Indexed:* CBCARef, CPerI. *Bk. rev.:* 5-10, 100 words. *Aud.:* Hs ,Ga.

This magazine contains the latest trends in decorating and renovating with a Canadian focus. A popular consumer magazine for those who desire stylish living, each issue contains ideas and practical information for transforming living spaces and decorating homes. There are color photographs of interior rooms and exterior landscaping of model Canadian homes, as well as interviews with interior design experts describing their favorite trends and showcasing samples of their work. A small recipe section, decorating advice for entertaining, and a cross-Canada listing of sources for new products and material featured in the articles is also included. The journal's web site provides a table of contents for the current issue. This general-interest magazine is suitable for public library collections.

1140. *Canadian Issues.* Incorporates (until 1999): *A C S Bulletin;* Which was formerly (until 1994): *A C S Newsletter;* (1979-1981): *Association for Canadian Studies. Association Newsletter.* [ISSN: 0318-8442] 1975. q. Free to members. Ed(s): Gregory Slogar. Association for Canadian

Studies, PO Box 8888, Montreal, PQ H3C 3P8, Canada; c1015@er.ugam.ca. Adv. Refereed. Circ: 1500. Online: LexisNexis; Micromedia ProQuest; ProQuest K-12 Learning Solutions. *Indexed:* AmH&L, CBCARef, CEI, CPerI, HistAb, IPSA, PdeR. *Bk. rev.:* 1-2, 1 page, signed. *Aud.:* Hs, Ga, Ac.

This journal is a bilingual publication of the Association for Canadian Studies, a nonprofit scholarly society dedicated to disseminating knowledge about Canada through research and publications. As a general magazine of public opinion, it is readable and informative. Each issue has a dozen opinion essays written by distinguished academics, politicians, or lawyers surrounding a theme. Examples of past themes include cities, sports and Canadian identity, Canada and the world after 9/11, and Canadian rights and freedoms. Not all essays are translated; however, there is an English abstract for all French-language material. Color photographs add to the readability of each 50-page issue. Advertising is limited to forthcoming books from university presses, meeting announcements, and university recruitment. The association's web site provides access to the table of contents of issues published since 1999. This journal will be of interest to high school, public, and academic libraries.

1141. *Canadian Living.* [ISSN: 0382-4624] 1975. m. CND 27.80 domestic; CND 38 United States. Transcontinental Media, Inc., 25 Sheppard Ave West, Ste 100, Toronto, ON M2N 6S7, Canada; info@transcontinental.ca; http://www.transcontinental-gtc.com/en/ home.html. Adv. Circ: 555118 Paid. *Indexed:* CBCARef, CPerI, GardL. *Aud.:* Hs, Ga.

This is the most popular Canadian family magazine, with a circulation of over half a million. Its colorful articles and advertising are primarily focused on three areas, food and nutrition, health and wellness, and family and community. By far the largest component is the recipe section prepared by the *Canadian Living* Test Kitchens, 50 to 75 recipes per issue, collected from across the country, including a nutritional analysis of each dish. Readers are invited to contribute stories about individuals in their community who deserve recognition for their accomplishments, and a regular "O Canada" column provides an opportunity for readers to share experiences about being Canadian. Each issue includes a read-out-loud family story. Practical parenting and relationship advice organized by children's ages is included in every 100-page issue. The magazine's web site allows readers to preview content. This magazine is suitable for public library collections.

1142. *Canadian Public Policy.* [ISSN: 0317-0861] 1975. q. CND 160 domestic; USD 160 United States; USD 180 foreign. Ed(s): James Davies. University of Toronto Press, Journals Division, 5201 Dufferin St, Toronto, ON M3H 5T8, Canada; journals@utpress.utoronto.ca; http://www.utpjournals.com. Illus., index, adv. Sample. Refereed. Circ: 1800 Paid. Vol. ends: Dec (No. 4). Microform: MML. *Indexed:* ABIn, ASG, AgeL, AmH&L, ArtHuCI, CBCARef, CPerI, DSA, EAA, FPA, ForAb, FutSurv, HRA, HistAb, IBR, IBZ, IPSA, JEL, PAIS, PSA, RRTA, SSA, SSCI, SUSA, SWA, SociolAb, WAE&RSA. *Bk. rev.:* 15-25, 1-2 pages, signed. *Aud.:* Ga, Ac.

This refereed journal publishes works in economics, political science, law, sociology, anthropology, geography, social work, administrative and public sciences, and business. The scholarly but accessible articles strive to "stimulate research and discussion of public policy problems in Canada." Featured articles discuss a broad range of topics from employment and income issues to gambling to technological change. Each issue includes reviews and editorials, notices of new and forthcoming publications in the field, and indexes. The journal's web site contains online abstracts, published simultaneously with the print version. Online versions of the articles appear on the web site with a one-year delay. The web site also provides a keyword search index to all volumes. Recommended for academic and public libraries.

1143. *Canadian Wildlife.* Formerly: *International Wildlife (Canadian Edition);* Incorporates: *Wildlife Update;* Formerly: *Canadian Chronicle;* Supersedes: *Wildlife News.* [ISSN: 1201-673X] 1965. 5x/yr. CND 29 domestic; CND 45 United States; CND 55 elsewhere. Ed(s): Martin Silverstone. Canadian Wildlife Federation, 350 Michael Cowpland Dr, Kanata, ON K2M 2W1, Canada; info@cwf-fcf.org; http://www.cwf-fcf.org. Circ: 77000. *Indexed:* CBCARef, CPerI, MASUSE. *Aud.:* Hs, Ga, Ac.

This magazine is a colorful introduction to Canadian wildlife, published by the Canadian Wildlife Federation, an association dedicated to "fostering awareness and enjoyment of our natural world." The wide range of subjects covered include wildlife, wild areas, nature-related research, endangered species, wildlife management, land-use issues, character profiles, and the politics of conservation. Of particular interest are the profiles and behind-the-scenes interviews with prominent scientists. Each 50-page issue has five feature articles and regular editorial columns. For children, the field guide trivia contest and backyard habitat sections encourage reading and interest in nature close to home. The color photographs and text layout are excellent. Advertising is very minimal. Recommended for all high school, public, and academic libraries.

Canadian Woman Studies. See Gender Studies section.

1144. *Journal of Canadian Studies.* [ISSN: 0021-9495] 1966. 3x/yr. CND 105 domestic; USD 105 United States; USD 125 elsewhere. Ed(s): Donald Wright, Renee Hulan. Trent University, 751 George St. N., Ste. 104, Peterborough, ON K9H 7P5, Canada; http://www.trentu.ca. Illus., index, adv. Refereed. Circ: 1400. Vol. ends: No. 4. Microform: MML. Online: EBSCO Publishing, EBSCO Host; Micromedia ProQuest; Northern Light Technology, Inc.; OCLC Online Computer Library Center, Inc.; ProQuest K-12 Learning Solutions; ProQuest LLC (Ann Arbor); H.W. Wilson. *Indexed:* AbAn, AgeL, AmH&L, AmHI, ArtHuCI, BEL&L, CBCARef, CPerI, FR, HistAb, HumInd, IBR, IBSS, IBZ, MLA-IB, RILM, SSCI. *Bk. rev.:* 1-2, 8-15 pages, signed. *Aud.:* Ga, Ac.

This journal is now published by the University of Toronto Press. Articles are of moderate length, bilingual, of both scholarly and general interest, and deal with "some aspect of Canada or Canadian life." Issues include several main articles, bilingual abstracts, and book reviews. There is a useful listing of new books organized by subject. There is also a "Canadian Studies News and Notes" section that lists events of note. The Council of Editors of Learned Journals recently awarded this publication the runner-up prize for the Phoenix Award for Significant Editorial Achievement, and determined that the journal's special Millennium Series, a four-issue set commemorating the journal's 35th anniversary, was an outstanding example of scholarly work. The journal's web site provides table of contents information for issues since 2001. The *Journal of Canadian Studies* is highly recommended for both public and academic libraries.

1145. *Labour: journal of Canadian labour studies - revue d'etudes ouvrieres Canadiennes.* [ISSN: 0700-3862] 1976. s-a. CND 35 (Individuals, CND 25; Students, CND 15). Ed(s): Bryan D Palmer. Canadian Committee on Labour History, Faculty of Arts Publications, FM 2005, Memorial University of Newfoundland, St. John's, NF A1C 5S7, Canada; cclh@mun.ca. Illus., index, adv. Sample. Refereed. Circ: 1200. Vol. ends: No. 2. *Indexed:* AltPI, AmH&L, ArtHuCI, CBCARef, CPerI, HRA, HistAb, IBSS, LeftInd, PAIS, PRA, SFSA, SSCI, SociolAb, V&AA. *Aud.:* Ga, Ac.

This bilingual, interdisciplinary journal has a goal of fostering "imaginative approaches to both teaching and research in labour studies." Articles cover a broad range of labor-related subjects. Issues also include obituaries, research reports, critiques, book and film reviews, announcements, minutes, abstracts, and a history section. A short feature called "Notebook/Carnet" provides room for op-ed pieces and brief essays and commentaries. The bibliography section is organized by publication format. The journal's web site contains tables of contents and abstracts for all issues since 1976. Recommended for general and academic collections.

1146. *Literary Review of Canada: a review of Canadian books on culture, politics and society.* [ISSN: 1188-7494] 10x/yr. CND 70 domestic; USD 75 foreign. Ed(s): Bronwyn Drainie. Literary Review of Canada Inc., 581 Markham St, Ste 3A, Toronto, ON M6G 2L7, Canada. Circ: 5000. *Indexed:* CBCARef. *Bk. rev.:* 12, 1-2 pages, signed. *Aud.:* Ac.

Literary Review of Canada is a pre-eminent journal for the discussion of Canadian politics, culture, and society. Each issue is devoted to review essays of books about Canadian subjects, books by Canadian authors, or international books reviewed by Canadian reviewers. The journal also publishes essays, poetry, and original art. The *Literary Review of Canada* web site provides access

to the table of contents of all issues since 2002. This scholarly journal is aimed at readership demanding serious thought and intellectual debate. It is suitable for large public and academic library collections.

1147. *Maclean's: Canada's weekly newsmagazine.* Former titles (until 1911): *Busy Man's Magazine; Business Magazine.* [ISSN: 0024-9262] 1905. w. CND 34.95 domestic. Rogers Media Publishing Ltd, One Mount Pleasant Rd, 11th Fl, Toronto, ON M4Y 2Y5, Canada; http://www.rogers.com. Illus., index, adv. Sample. Circ: 503497. CD-ROM: ProQuest LLC (Ann Arbor). Microform: MML; NBI; PQC. Online: CanWest Interactive Inc., FPInfomart; EBSCO Publishing, EBSCO Host; Factiva, Inc.; Florida Center for Library Automation; Gale; LexisNexis; Micromedia ProQuest; Northern Light Technology, Inc.; OCLC Online Computer Library Center, Inc.; ProQuest K-12 Learning Solutions; ProQuest LLC (Ann Arbor); H.W. Wilson. *Indexed:* ABIn, BRI, CBCARef, CBRI, CPerI, LRI, MASUSE, MRD, PAIS, RGPR. *Bk. rev.:* 1-2, 2-4 pages. *Aud.:* Hs, Ga, Ac.

This is the most widely read news magazine in Canada and in 2005 celebrated 100 years of publishing. Each issue summarizes world events and highlights Canadian events in politics, health, sport, and science. It is designed in an easy-to-read, three-column format and includes many color photographs and some advertising. Each issue has commentaries, essays, and opinion pieces written by politically informed Canadians. There are regular columns reviewing the best picks in Canadian books, movies, music, and art. Awards, medals, deaths, and nominations are included in the "Passages" column. The "Maclean's Guide to Universities" is an award-winning special issue published each year, ranking and evaluating Canadian universities based on resources and reputation. This guide is an essential selection tool for students and parents evaluating post-secondary educational choices. *Maclean's* is recommended for all high school, public, and academic libraries for its general coverage of Canadian current affairs and world events from a Canadian perspective. The magazine's web site provides access to an online edition.

1148. *Manitoba History.* Formerly (until 1980): *Manitoba Pageant.* [ISSN: 0226-5044] 1956. s-a. CND 19.80 domestic; CND 20.50 United States; CND 22.50 elsewhere. Ed(s): Bob Coutts, Morris Mott. Manitoba Historical Society, 470 167 Lombard Ave, Winnipeg, MB R3B 0T6, Canada. Illus. Sample. Refereed. Circ: 1000. Vol. ends: Fall (No. 2). *Indexed:* AmH&L, CBCARef, CPerI, HistAb. *Bk. rev.:* 4-8, 1-3 pages. *Aud.:* Hs, Ga, Ac.

This journal is devoted primarily to Manitoba history. Longer main articles are accompanied by photographs and illustrations, shorter articles, and both substantial and brief reviews. The articles are scholarly and well documented, and the subject scope is varied. Certain issues may have a focus or theme, such as "The North in Manitoba History" or the historical role of women in the province. The publication is attractively presented, with care given to art reproductions and graphics. It combines articles of scholarly interest with articles and reviews of popular appeal in a well-designed format. An annual bibliography serves researchers in this area well. The Manitoba Historical Society's web site provides table of contents information for all issues. This journal is recommended for academic and larger public libraries and special collections.

1149. *Newfoundland Studies.* [ISSN: 0823-1737] 1985. s-a. CND 20 (Individuals, CND 15). Ed(s): Richard Buehler. Memorial University of Newfoundland, Department of English, Arts and Administration 3026, Elizabeth Ave, St. John's, NF A1C 5S7, Canada; irenew@plato.ucs.mun.can; http://www.ucs.mun.ca/~nflds/. Illus., index, adv. Sample. Refereed. Circ: 250. Vol. ends: Fall (No. 2). *Indexed:* AmH&L, CBCARef, CPerI, HistAb. *Bk. rev.:* 6-7, 2-5 pages, signed. *Aud.:* Ac.

This is an "interdisciplinary journal devoted to publishing essays about the society and culture of Newfoundland, past and present." Published semi-annually, issues present refereed scholarly articles, original documents with introductions and annotations, and book reviews and review articles. A yearly comprehensive bibliography of Newfoundlandia is published. Occasionally, special theme issues are published, most recently "a 308-page volume containing eight specially commissioned articles written to commemorate and analyze the first fifty years of Newfoundland's presence in the Canadian confederation." The journal's web site provides a searchable author and title index for all issues. Suitable for academic and large public libraries.

1150. Ontario History. Formerly (until 1946): *Ontario Historical Society. Papers and Records.* [ISSN: 0030-2953] 1899. s-a. Members, CND 21.40; Non-members, CND 32.10. Ed(s): Gabriele Scardellato. Ontario Historical Society, 34 Parkview Ave, Willowdale, ON M2N 3Y2, Canada; oh5@ontariohistoricalsociety.ca; http://www.ontariohistoricalsociety.ca. Illus., index, adv. Refereed. Circ: 1200. Vol. ends: Dec (No. 4). Reprint: PSC. *Indexed:* AmH&L, CBCARef, CPerI, HistAb. *Bk. rev.:* 5-12, 500-1,000 words. *Aud.:* Ga, Ac.

Ontario History is a publication of the Ontario Historical Society assisted by funding from the Ontario Ministry of Culture and the Social Sciences and Humanities Research Council of Canada. Articles cover political, military, and constitutional history as well as First Nations history, women's history, immigration and ethnic history, labor history, and "other recently developed areas of the discipline." Several research articles about an aspect of Ontario history are presented in each issue, often with accompanying photographs and illustrations. There is a book review section and list of books received. The Ontario Historical Society's web site provides access to the journal's index since 1899. Suitable for academic and public libraries.

1151. Outdoor Canada: the total outdoor experience. [ISSN: 0315-0542] 1972. 8x/yr. CND 25.98 domestic; CND 39 United States; CND 69 overseas. Ed(s): James Little. Avid Media Inc., 340 Ferrier St, Ste 210, Markham, ON L3R 2Z5, Canada; oceditorial@outdoorcanadamagazine.com; http://www.outdoorcanada.ca. Illus., adv. Sample. Circ: 93000 Paid. Vol. ends: Nov/Dec. Microform: MML. Online: Micromedia ProQuest; ProQuest K-12 Learning Solutions. *Indexed:* CBCARef, CPerI. *Aud.:* Hs, Ga.

Outdoor Canada is the country's most widely read publication for the traditional outdoor sportsman. The magazine describes hunting, fishing, canoeing, exploring, and winter sports in the top sporting destinations across Canada. Each issue is well illustrated with color photographs and has four feature articles on an outdoor sport, wildlife, or conservation topic. Regular columns highlight the latest in gear and transportation for outdoor recreation, and authoritative experts provide techniques and answer readers' questions concerning all aspects of hunting and fishing. The publication has a lively opinion column that is reproduced on the magazine's web site. Suitable for high school and public libraries.

1152. Parachute: contemporary art magazine. [ISSN: 0318-7020] 1975. q. CND 125 (Individuals, CND 57). Ed(s): Chantal Pontbriand. Editions Parachute, 4060 bd St Laurent, Ste 501, Montreal, PQ H2W 1Y9, Canada; parachut@citenet.net; http://www.parachute.ca. Adv. Circ: 5000. *Indexed:* ABM, ArtInd, CBCARef, CPerI, PdeR. *Bk. rev.:* 10 -12, 200 - 500 words, signed. *Aud.:* Ga, Ac.

Parachute is among the finest avant-garde visual-arts journals in the world. It is noted for its graphic design and color reproductions. Each issue is bilingual and presents contemporary Canadian and international art and critical essays of substance. Its contributors are both Canadian and international. Interviews with artists, exhibits, book reviews, and an opinionated debate section are regular components of the magazine. Once a year, a special issue is devoted to a city where artistic practices of particular interest are in the process of developing. The authors examine the art of the city by profiling leading artists and individuals. The back pages of each issue are devoted to gallery exhibition announcements. The journal's web site contains abstracts and photographs from all issues published. This journal of art "ideas" will be of interest to large public library and academic collections.

1153. Policy Options. [ISSN: 0226-5893] 1979. 10x/yr. CND 39.95 domestic; CND 54.95 United States; CND 59.95 elsewhere. Ed(s): William Watson. Institute for Research on Public Policy, 1470 Peel St, Ste 200, Montreal, PQ H3A 1T1, Canada; policy@irpp.org; http://www.irpp.org. Illus. Sample. Circ: 2500. Vol. ends: Dec (No. 10). *Indexed:* CBCARef, CPerI, PAIS. *Bk. rev.:* 0-1, 500 words. *Aud.:* Ga, Ac.

This bilingual journal publishes independent research on a broad range of public policy issues ranging from bank mergers to social determinants of health. It is sponsored by the Institute for Research on Public Policy, an independent, national, nonprofit organization that funds original research. Each issue has short articles on current topics that dominate Canadian media headlines as well as in-depth analyses of longer-term issues. Short book reviews of relevant titles are also included in each issue. This useful and informative publication is appropriate for academic and larger public libraries. The journal's web site contains abstracts and full-text articles in pdf format since 1997.

1154. Prairie Forum. [ISSN: 0317-6282] 1976. s-a. CND 29.96 (Individuals, CND 24.61; CND 14.50 newsstand/cover per issue). Ed(s): Patrick Douaud. Canadian Plains Research Center, University of Regina, Regina, SK S4S 0A2, Canada; canadian.plains@uregina.ca; http://www.cprc.ca. Illus., index, adv. Sample. Refereed. Circ: 350. Vol. ends: Fall (No. 2). Microform: MML. *Indexed:* ABS&EES, AmH&L, CBCARef, CPerI, HistAb. *Bk. rev.:* 2-10, 2-4 pages. *Aud.:* Ga, Ac, Sa.

Prairie Forum publishes research devoted to the Northern Plains region. This interdisciplinary journal spans provincial boundaries and covers a range of subjects and disciplines dealing with the prairies. "The journal of the Canadian Plains Research Center is seen as an important step towards bridging both the geographic and disciplinary boundaries." Topics covered include art and culture, farming, history, economic development, and sociology. Occasionally, special issues have dealt with "Changing Prairie Landscapes" and "Prairie Theatre and Drama." Issues include research articles with abstracts, essays, review articles, book reviews, forums, and editorial notes and introductions. The journal's web site provides access to the table of contents of all issues since 1996. Appropriate for academic libraries, special collections, and public libraries.

1155. Queen's Quarterly: a Canadian review. [ISSN: 0033-6041] 1893. q. CND 40 (Individuals, CND 20; CND 6.50 newsstand/cover per issue). Ed(s): Boris Castel. Queen's Quarterly, Queen's University, Kingston, ON K7L 3N6, Canada; http://info.queensu.ca/quarterly. Illus., adv. Sample. Refereed. Circ: 3000. Vol. ends: No. 4. Microform: MML; PQC. Online: Florida Center for Library Automation; Gale; Micromedia ProQuest; ProQuest K-12 Learning Solutions. *Indexed:* ABS&EES, AmH&L, ArtHuCI, BAS, BEL&L, BRI, CBCARef, CBRI, CPerI, HistAb, IBR, IBZ, IPSA, MLA-IB, PAIS, RILM, SSCI. *Bk. rev.:* Number and length vary. *Aud.:* Ga, Ac.

Since *Queen's Quarterly* was founded in 1893, "the journal's commitment has always been to offer both the academic and the general reader a lively collection of analysis and reflection, in fields as diverse as international relations, science policy, literary criticism, travel writing, economics, religion, short fiction, and poetry." Over the years, it has published works by such eminent Canadians as Ed Broadbent, Gwynne Dyer, Michael Ignatieff, Margaret Laurence, and Joyce Carol Oates. Issues include an editorial, several main articles, and sections on photography, reviews, science, and short fiction. It is "always trying to satisfy the curiosity of the congenial reader, the general reader who wants to be both educated and entertained, a reader who appreciates an intellectual overview of the world." Suitable for academic and large public libraries. The journal's web site provides an excerpt from the current issue and biographical notes about the authors.

1156. Quill and Quire: Canada's magazine of book news and reviews. Incorporates (in 1989): *Books for Young People.* [ISSN: 0033-6491] 1935. m. CND 59.95 domestic; CND 95 foreign; CND 4.95 newsstand/cover per issue. Ed(s): Scott Anderson. Key Publishers Co. Ltd., 70 The Esplanade, 4th Fl, Toronto, ON M5E 1R2, Canada; quill@idirect.com; http://www.quillandquire.com. Illus., adv. Circ: 6244. Microform: MMP; MML. Online: Gale; LexisNexis; Micromedia ProQuest. *Indexed:* BRD, BRI, CBCARef, CBRI, CPerI. *Bk. rev.:* Number and length vary. *Aud.:* Hs, Ga, Ac.

Established in 1935, *Quill and Quire* is a periodical whose aim is to be the "leading source of information about the Canadian book industry." Each issue includes news and feature articles, opinion columns, book reviews, and bestseller lists. *Q&Q* also provides a twice-weekly newsletter with breaking news stories about Canadian publishing sent to subscribers via e-mail. This journal is of interest to "booksellers, librarians, publishers, writers, educators and anyone interested in books and the book industry." Feature articles cover such topics as marketing to the United States, the fate of nonfiction, and the state of book reviewing. Interviews with notable figures are often included. The magazine's web site provides access to story summaries only, and a subscription is required for the online edition. Highly readable and informative, *Q&Q* is well suited for academic and public libraries.

1157. *Report on Business Magazine.* Former titles (until 1985): *Report on Business; Report on Business 1000.* [ISSN: 0827-7680] 1984. m. Free with subscr. to the Globe and Mail. Ed(s): Patricia Best. Globe and Mail Publishing, 444 Front St W, Toronto, ON M5V 2S9, Canada; bbalfour@ globeandmail.ca; http://www.robmagazine.com. Illus., adv. Circ: 318000. *Indexed:* CBCARef, CPerI. *Bk. rev.:* 1-3, 500 words, signed. *Aud.:* Hs, Ga, Ac.

This business magazine is published monthly in Canada's national newspaper, *The Globe and Mail.* Each 100-page issue focuses on Canadian business personalities, the individuals and the corporations they lead, with in-depth reporting on the successes, scandals, and failures in the Canadian economy. Some international stories are also included. The regular columnists also provide critical commentary of business practices and government policies. The magazine is printed on recycled paper, with many color photographs of the profiled individuals. There is advertising throughout each issue. Regular columns track trends, review hotels and golf courses, and provide city profiles for business travelers. There is also an online edition. Public and academic libraries will find this readable magazine a reliable source of background information about Canadians in business.

1158. *Saltscapes.* [ISSN: 1492-3351] 2000. bi-m. CND 24.95 domestic; CND 34.95 United States; CND 34.95 elsewhere. Ed(s): Diane leBlanc. Saltscapes Publishing Limited, 40 Alderney Dr, Ste 303, Dartmouth, NS B2Y 2N5, Canada; subscriptions@saltscapes.com; http://www.saltscapes.com. *Aud.:* Hs, Ga.

This family-owned magazine profiles the people, places, and culture of Atlantic Canada's four eastern provinces: Nova Scotia, New Brunswick, Prince Edward Island, and Newfoundland. Subjects included in each 100-page issue are people, recreation, crafts, gardens, and traditions of the region. Writers and photographers are from across Atlantic Canada. Professional chefs' and favorite home-cooking recipes are included, as well as projects and profiles of craftspeople. The magazine has adjusted to readers' opinions and appears to have the right formula as a solid general-interest magazine for those who live in the region as well as for those who don't. The letters-to-the-editor column and the back page, authored by well-known columnist Harry Bruce, are popular with readers. The magazine's web site provides table of contents information only. Suitable for high school and public libraries.

1159. *Saskatchewan History.* [ISSN: 0036-4908] 1948. s-a. CND 16.05 domestic; CND 17.50 foreign. Ed(s): Bruce Dawson. Saskatchewan Archives Board, Murray Building, University of Saskatchewan, Saskatoon, SK S7N 5A4, Canada; info.saskatoon@archives.gov.sk.ca. Illus., index, adv. Sample. Refereed. Circ: 700. Vol. ends: No. 2. *Indexed:* AmH&L, CBCARef, CPerI, HistAb. *Bk. rev.:* 7-8, 1-2 pages. *Aud.:* Ga, Ac.

This journal is published by Saskatchewan Archives and dedicated to the province's history. "The magazine has established itself as a pre-eminent source of information and narration about Saskatchewan's unique heritage." Each issue contains scholarly research and general-interest articles, book reviews, heritage and archives news, and illustrations and photographs. Articles have dealt with such topics as "the fur trade era, ethnic groups and immigration, pioneer life, the history of medical care, business and trade unionism, religion on the prairies, women's history, First Nations and Metis history." The journal's web site contains table of contents listings for all issues since its inception in 1948. Suitable for academic and public libraries.

1160. *This Magazine: because everything is political.* Former titles (until 1998): *This Magazine - Education, Culture, Politics;* (until 1973): *This Magazine Is About Schools.* [ISSN: 1491-2678] 1966. 6x/yr. CND 37 (Individuals, CND 23.99; CND 4.95 newsstand/cover per issue). Ed(s):

Julie Crysler. Red Maple Foundation, 401 Richmond St W. Ste 396, Toronto, ON M5V 3A8, Canada. Illus., index, adv. Sample. Microform: MML; PQC. Online: Gale; Micromedia ProQuest. *Indexed:* AltPI, CBCARef, CEI, CPerI. *Bk. rev.:* 1-2 pages. *Aud.:* Hs, Ga, Ac.

The Red Maple Foundation, a registered charity with support from the Canadian Race Relations Foundation, publishes *This Magazine.* The magazine's independent roots allow the distinguished editorial board to publish critical and intelligent writing about culture, politics, and art in Canada. Its contributors come from all Canadian provinces and include well-known authors Margaret Atwood, Linda McQuaig, and Rick Salutin. The magazine's feature articles provide an alternative interpretation to mainstream political analysis of cultural and political issues. Recent issues feature arctic poverty, recreation, gambling, shopping, the politics of science, and fund raising. Each year in the fall issue, the magazine hosts the "Great Canadian Literary Hunt," judging submissions from across Canada and publishing the winning new poetry. Each 50-page issue is printed on recycled paper. *This Magazine* will provide readers in high school, public, and academic libraries a fresh perspective on Canadian culture. Its web site provides access to the current issue.

1161. *Toronto Life.* Incorporates (1969-1982): *Toronto Calendar Magazine;* (1962-1966): *Ontario Homes and Living.* [ISSN: 0049-4194] 1966. m. CND 25.68 domestic; CND 44 foreign; CND 3.95 newsstand/cover per issue. Ed(s): John Macfarlane. Toronto Life Publishing Co. Ltd., 111 Queen St East, Toronto, ON M5C 1S2, Canada; http://www.torontolife.com. Illus., index, adv. Sample. Circ: 93872. Microform: MML. Online: Gale; LexisNexis; Micromedia ProQuest; ProQuest K-12 Learning Solutions. *Indexed:* ASIP, CBCARef, CPerI. *Aud.:* Hs, Ga.

This magazine highlights culture, politics, and personalities in Canada's largest city. There are five feature articles in each issue written by well-known Canadian journalists on such urban topics as municipal politics, transportation, health care, real estate, sports, and entertainment. The focus of each feature is on the individual personalities in the stories. The calendar of arts events lists theater openings, music, dance, and nightlife in Toronto. Advertisements are sprinkled throughout the magazine. There are classified ads on the back pages, and the best shopping and restaurants are highlighted in regular columns. *Toronto Life* provides a trendy, urban perspective for high school and public library collections. The magazine's web site provides a selection of feature articles from recent issues.

University of Toronto Quarterly. See Literature section.

Windspeaker. See Native Americans section.

YES Mag. See Children section.

■ CARTOGRAPHY, GIS, AND IMAGERY

See also Environment and Conservation; and Geography sections.

Cheryl LaGuardia, Research Librarian, Widener Library, Harvard University, Cambridge, MA 02138

Christine Oka, Coordinator of Bibliographic Instruction, Snell Library, Northeastern University, Boston, MA

Introduction

We are introducing this new section in the 16th edition of *Magazines for Libraries* to acknowledge the rising interest in, and importance of, geographic information systems (GIS) and global positioning systems (GPS), as well as the dynamic nature of the cartographic environment worldwide. This environment is involved in so many aspects of twenty-first century life: economic, environmental, political, and social. We have seen a number of cartographic publications come and go, while other titles have morphed into new entities, because this subject area itself has changed so much, and so rapidly, over the past several decades. Be sure to consult the Geography section of this volume for related titles, and the editors would be interested in hearing from readers about new titles of great importance to your researchers.

Basic Periodicals

Cartography and Geographic Information Science, GISScience and Remote Sensing, Imago Mundi.

Basic Abstracts and Indexes

Geo Abstracts, GEOBASE, GeoRef, SCOPUS.

1162. *A C S M Bulletin: promoting advancement in the collection, analysis and graphic representation of geospatial data.* Formerly (until 1980): *American Congress on Surveying and Mapping. Bulletin.* [ISSN: 0747-9417] 1950. bi-m. Free to members; Non-members, USD 80. Ed(s): Ilse Alipui. American Congress on Surveying and Mapping, 6 Montgomery Village Ave, Ste 403, Gaithersburg, MD 20879; infoacsm@acsm.net; http://www.acsm.net. Illus., adv. Circ: 10000. *Aud.:* Ac, Sa.

This title covers a range of technical and managerial topics in the areas of cartography, geodesy, GIS, GPS, and related fields. It reflects the interest of four ACSM professional organizations: the American Association for Geodetic Surveying (AAGS), the Cartography and Geographic Information Society (CaGIS), the Geographic and Land Information Society (GLIS), and the National Society of Professional Surveyors (NSPS). For academics and practitioners.

1163. *A R C News.* [ISSN: 1064-6108] 1987. q. Free. Ed(s): Thomas K Miller. Environmental Systems Research Institute, Inc., 380 New York St, Redlands, CA 92373. Adv. Circ: 100000. *Aud.:* Ac, Sa.

Meant for those interested in geographic information systems (GIS) and mapping, this title covers new computer mapping applications, conferences, and other trends in GIS teaching and learning. Its target audience is the ESRI user community, but others will find material of interest here. The electronic version (www.esri.com/news/arcnews/arcnews.html) now offers articles exclusively online. Recent articles have included "ArcGIS Goes Mobile: Build and Deploy Server-Based Mobile Applications," "Bring Back Geography!," "Designing a Global GIS Strategy: ESRI Enterprise Advantage Program Lends a Helping Hand at The Nature Conservancy," and "ArcGIS Online Is Ready to Use!"

1164. *The Cartographic Journal.* [ISSN: 0008-7041] 1964. q. USD 415. Ed(s): Ken Field. Maney Publishing, Ste. 1C, Joseph's Well, Hanover Walk, Leeds, LS3 1AB, United Kingdom; maney@maney.co.uk; http://www.maney.co.uk. Illus., index, adv. Sample. Refereed. Circ: 2000. Vol. ends: Dec. Reprint: PSC. *Indexed:* ArtHuCI, IBR, SSCI. *Bk. rev.:* Number and length vary. *Aud.:* Ga, Ac, Sa.

This longstanding title includes authoritative articles and professional papers on cartography, mapping and spatial data display, digital mapping, geographical information systems, related remote-sensing technologies, and global-positioning systems. Each issue also covers international cartographic news, contains book and software reviews, and has a list of recent maps and atlases. Geared toward scholarly readers.

1165. *Cartographic Perspectives.* Former titles (until 1989): *Cartographic Information; Map Gap.* [ISSN: 1048-9053] 1981. 3x/yr. USD 72 (Individuals, USD 42; Students, USD 20). Ed(s): Scott Freundschuh. North American Cartographic Information Society, PO Box 399, Milwaukee, WI 53201; sfreunds@d.umn.edu. Refereed. Circ: 400 Paid. *Aud.:* Ga, Ac, Sa.

Cartographic Perspectives addresses a wide audience, including map publishers and designers, map curators, academics, and amateurs. It contains authoritative articles and papers that deal with all aspects of cartography and related topics. The journal also covers cartographic news and reviews of recent books and software. Important for academic libraries that support a map collection or geography department, and for special libraries that support cartographic work.

1166. *Cartographica: international journal for geographic information and geovisualization.* Incorporates (1964-1980): *Canadian Cartographer;* Which was formerly (until 1968): *Cartographer.* [ISSN: 0317-7173] 1971. q. CND 185 domestic; USD 185 United States; USD 205 elsewhere. Ed(s): Peter Keller, Roger Wheate. University of Toronto Press, Journals Division, 5201 Dufferin St, Toronto, ON M3H 5T8, Canada; journals@utpress.utoronto.ca; http://www.utpjournals.com. Illus., index, adv. Sample. Refereed. Circ: 600. Vol. ends: No. 4. Microform: MML. Online: EBSCO Publishing, EBSCO Host; Micromedia ProQuest. Reprint: PSC. *Indexed:* CBCARef, CPerI, IBR, IBZ. *Bk. rev.:* Number and length vary. *Aud.:* Ac, Sa.

This quarterly, from the University of Toronto Press, publishes articles on cartographic thought, the history of cartography, and cartography and society, as well as material on geovisualization research. Each volume includes two or three regular issues and one or two single-topic monographs (these focus on a particular area of cartography). Regular issues include book reviews and listings of new cartographic publications globally. Abstracts are in both English and French. For a scholarly audience.

1167. *Cartography and Geographic Information Science.* Former titles (until Jan. 1999): *Cartography and Geographic Information Systems;* (until 1990): *American Cartographer.* [ISSN: 1523-0406] 1974. q. Non-members, USD 110. Ed(s): Ilse Genovese. American Congress on Surveying and Mapping, 6 Montgomery Village Ave, Ste 403, Gaithersburg, MD 20879; infoacsm@acsm.net; http://www.acsm.net. Illus., adv. Sample. Refereed. Circ: 2950 Paid. Vol. ends: Oct. *Indexed:* ABS&EES, EngInd, SSCI. *Aud.:* Ac, Sa.

This is the official publication of the Cartography and Geographic Information Society (CaGIS), which is a member organization of the American Congress on Surveying and Mapping (ACSM). It "supports research, education, and practices that improve the understanding, creation, analysis, and use of maps and geographic information." *CaGIS* became one of the three official journals of the International Cartographic Association (ICA) in 2004, and has since expanded coverage globally, inviting international submissions to the journal as well as international participation in the editorial and review processes. This journal "houses" the U.S. National Report to the ICA (you will find more about the U.S.-ICA National Committee at http://www.usnc-ica.org).

1168. *Coordinates. Series A: online journal of the map and geography round table.* [ISSN: 1553-3247] 2005. irreg. Free. American Library Association, 50 E Huron St, Chicago, IL 60611-2795; http://www.ala.org. Refereed. *Aud.:* Ac, Sa.

This electronic-only ALA publication from the Map and Geography Round Table publishes pieces on the history of cartography, map bibliography, cataloging, map and GIS librarianship, map reading and interpretation, and new developments in online mapping. It is aimed at a broad range of cartographic readers, from the amateur to the professional. Articles in this Series A section are original and peer-reviewed. A core title for any mapping library collection, this may be found online at: http://www.sunysb.edu/libmap/coordinates.htm.

1169. *Coordinates. Series B: online journal of the map and geography round table.* [ISSN: 1553-3255] 2005. irreg. Free. American Library Association, 50 E Huron St, Chicago, IL 60611-2795; http://www.ala.org. Refereed. *Aud.:* Ac, Sa.

Another electronic-only ALA publication from the Map and Geography Round Table, Coordinates: Series B also publishes pieces on the history of cartography, map bibliography, cataloging, map and GIS librarianship, map reading and interpretation, and new developments in online mapping (see Series A, earlier). This, too, is aimed at a broad range of cartographic readers, from the amateur to the professional. Articles in this Series B include shorter pieces, technical notes, previously published articles, and other material of interest to a cartographic audience. This, along with Series A, is a core title for any mapping library collection, and may also be found online at: http://www.sunysb.edu/libmap/coordinates.htm.

1170. *Geo World.* Formerly (until 1998): *GIS World;* Which incorporated (1997-1997): *GeoDirectory. Vol. 1 Products and Services;* Which superseded in part (1989-1997): *GIS World Sourcebook;* Which was formerly (until 1995): *International GIS Sourcebook;* (until 1992): *GIS Sourcebook.* [ISSN: 1528-6274] 1988. m. USD 72 domestic; USD 90 in Canada & Mexico; USD 138 elsewhere. m2media360, 760 Market St, Ste 432, San Francisco, CA 94105. Illus., adv. Circ: 25050 Controlled. Online: Gale. *Indexed:* AS&TI, EnvAb, SWRA. *Aud.:* Ac, Sa.

Geo World offers articles on recent technological and application developments in geographic information systems. Articles also describe new and ongoing projects involving GIS, its management, and policy implications. Several columns and departments present unusual uses of GIS, business trends, news of the profession, software and web site reviews, schedules of events, and government geospatial data activities. This journal is important for any library—academic, public, or special—that supports work in any of the numerous applications of GIS.

1171. GIScience and Remote Sensing. Former titles (until 2004): *Mapping Sciences & Remote Sensing;* (until 1980): *Geodesy, Mapping and Photogrammetry;* (until 1972): *Geodesy and Aerophotography.* [ISSN: 1548-1603] 1962. 4x/yr. USD 489 (Individuals, USD 92). Ed(s): John R. Jensen. Bellwether Publishing, Ltd., 8640 Guilford Rd, Ste 200, Columbia, MD 21046; bellpub@bellpub.com; http://www.bellpub.com. Illus. Circ: 300. *Indexed:* ChemAb, ForAb, M&GPA, OceAb, PollutAb, SCI, SWRA. *Aud.:* Ac, Sa.

This quarterly journal publishes original, peer-reviewed articles related to cartography, geographic information systems (GIS), remote sensing of the environment, geocomputation, spatial data mining and statistics, and geographic environmental modeling. The specialized content includes articles on "Markov Chain Modeling of Multinomial Land-Cover Classes" and "Trend Analysis of Time-Series Phenology of North America Derived from Satellite Data." Articles are written for scholarly audiences.

1172. Imago Mundi: the international journal for the history of cartography. [ISSN: 0308-5694] 1935. s-a. GBP 147 print & online eds. Ed(s): Dr. Catherine Delano-Smith. Routledge, 4 Park Square, Milton Park, Abingdon, OX14 4RN, United Kingdom; info@routledge.co.uk; http://www.routledge.co.uk. Illus., index, adv. Refereed. Circ: 700. Reprint: PSC. *Indexed:* AmH&L, AmHI, BrHumI, FR, HistAb, IndIslam. *Bk. rev.:* Number and length vary. *Aud.:* Ac, Sa.

Imago Mundi is a scholarly journal on the history of maps worldwide in all periods. It publishes research and occasional review articles as well as obituaries. Each issue includes book reviews, an indexed bibliography of current literature, and an extensive news and notices section on conferences, exhibits, map acquisitions, etc. The editorship is largely American and British, with an international editorial board. Important for academic libraries that support a geography department or map collection.

1173. Surveying and Land Information Science: an official journal of ACSM devoted to the science of surveying and mapping, land information, and related fields. Former titles (until 2002): *Surveying and Land Information Systems;* (until 1990): *Surveying and Mapping.* [ISSN: 1538-1242] 1941. q. Non-members, USD 110. Ed(s): Joseph C. Loon. American Congress on Surveying and Mapping, 6 Montgomery Village Ave, Ste 403, Gaithersburg, MD 20879; infoacsm@acsm.net; http://www.acsm.net. Illus., index, adv. Sample. Refereed. Circ: 9000. Vol. ends: Dec. Microform: PQC. Online: OCLC Online Computer Library Center, Inc.; ProQuest LLC (Ann Arbor); H.W. Wilson. *Indexed:* AS&TI, HRIS. *Bk. rev.:* Number and length vary. *Aud.:* Ac, Sa.

This journal is published by the National Society of Professional Surveyors, with the American Association for Geodetic Surveying and the Geographic and Land Information Society. It keeps its readers up to date on theoretical, technical, and policy developments in surveying, mapping, and land information systems (including geodesy and hydrography) through research articles, book reviews, current literature lists, and comments and discussion. Topics of current interest, such as global positioning systems (GPS) and total stations, are emphasized. There is a regular section on surveying and mapping education. Issues on special topics are occasionally published. Important for any library, academic, public, or special, that supports research or teaching in any of the numerous applications of GIS and related technologies.

■ CHEMISTRY

General/Analytical/Inorganic/Organic/Physical

Susan M. Braxton, Illinois Natural History Survey Library, 1816 S. Oak St., Champaign, IL 61820, braxton@inhs.uiuc.edu

Introduction

In October 2004, the Chemical Sciences Roundtable, of the Board on Chemical Sciences and Technology of the National Academy of Sciences, sponsored a workshop, "Are Chemistry Journals Too Expensive and Inaccessible?" The published summary (Heindel et al., 2005, National Academies Press) describes the many challenges peculiar to the chemistry literature as well as those facing scholarly publishing in general. In chemistry, there is much emphasis on rapid publication and access, but older literature is widely read and cited. Chemists were said to rely on their abstracting and indexing sources more than researchers in other disciplines, but also to be avid browsers. Because chemistry research is central to many other disciplines, chemistry research not only must be sufficiently detailed for evaluation by chemists, but also must be accessible to non-chemists. Complex graphical information and the unique "language" of chemistry requires both special authoring and special search and retrieval tools.

Providing sufficient data to allow others to make use of published research is challenging in traditional print formats. Journal proliferation was identified as an important aspect that influences the cost of collection development and access to research in chemistry and throughout the sciences. The summary reads like a debate transcript with the often contradictory viewpoints of participating publishers, researchers, administrators, and librarians. As a primer on past, current, and proposed models of scholarly communication, it is highly recommended reading, and not just for chemistry bibliographers.

It is true that the number of chemistry journals is growing. *Ulrich's Periodicals Directory* lists 65 refereed, non-monographic, English-language serials with "chemistry" in the subject that began publication in 1997–2006, and cessation of 27 such titles during the same period. The prior decade, 1987–1996, saw the start of 99 titles and the loss of only eight. Whether this can be taken as evidence of a slowing growth rate is unclear. Nearly 30 percent of the 559 active, refereed, English-language titles in *Ulrich's* with "chemistry" in the subject heading began publication between 1987 and 2006, and nearly 12 percent began publication between 1997 and 2006.

The chemistry journal literature has also grown in complexity, as chemistry research thrives at interfaces with other disciplines. Identification of "chemistry" titles is a challenge. Active, refereed, English-language journals in *Ulrich's* with chemistry subject headings may also have subject headings with engineering (11 percent of titles), physics (9 percent), biology (7 percent), or medical sciences/pharmacy (6 percent), among many others.

While the cost of chemistry titles is often lamented, some notoriously costly titles have been forced to compete with alternatives, and there are free titles worthy of note. The American Chemical Society partnered with the Scholarly Publishing and Academic Resource Coalition (SPARC) to develop *Organic Letters* (1999) and *Crystal Growth and Design* (2001) as alternatives to Elsevier's *Tetrahedron Letters* and *Journal of Crystal Growth*, respectively. *Organic Letters* ranks fifth among organic chemistry titles by 2005 impact factor, well above *Tetrahedron Letters. Crystal Growth and Design* ranks second among crystallography titles by 2005 impact factor, also well above its Elsevier counterpart. Although the free *Internet Journal of Chemistry* is no longer published, the archive remains freely available, with contents indexed in both Chem Abstracts and ISI products. The archive of *Aldrichimica Acta* is also freely available online. This review title publishes only a few articles per year, and was originally offered as a marketing tool by the publisher, Aldrich Chemical, but nevertheless had the highest 2005 impact factor of any organic chemistry title. The recently launched *Beilstein Journal of Organic Chemistry* (2005) from Beilstein Institut and PubMed Central is entirely open-access.

Online access has become ubiquitous, to the point that mentioning it in annotations is superfluous, although at least one title, *Chemistry & Industry,* appeared not to offer site-wide access at the time of review. Widespread assignment of Digital Object Identifiers (DOIs), participation by many major publishers in digital archiving initiatives such as Portico, consortial print archiving agreements, and the prohibitive cost of maintaining subscriptions in two formats have, to some degree, quieted concerns over digital content stability. Anecdotal evidence from a search for print review copies suggests that print in larger libraries is less common than it was as recently as two years ago.

Numerous publishing developments bear mentioning, all related to online publication. The open-access movement has had an influence on key chemistry publishers. The Royal Society of Chemistry has implemented OpenScience, an author-pays model for offering open access. The American Chemical Society (ACS), through "Articles on Request," grants authors the right to post a unique e-print URL that allows 50 free downloads of published pdfs in the first 12 months and unlimited downloads thereafter. This was billed as open access "for all practical purposes" in a recent editorial in *Macromolecules*. The result is access for researchers at least to a subset of chemistry content, whether or not their institutions can afford to license journals, though in the case of ACS, locating the content may not be straightforward.

Two years ago, *Internet Journal of Chemistry*, a SPARC leading-edge partner, ended its run. *IJC*'s editor noted that the journal had intended to demonstrate the benefits of electronic over print publication, for example, with respect to graphical content not easily rendered on the printed page, yet lamented that the potential of electronic publication had not been fully realized.

Most of the titles reviewed here offer supplementary information online, and although much of it is offered in pdf format (flat and printable), chemical image files, video content, and data sets can be found. The assignment of Document Object Identifiers (DOIs) to research articles is increasingly widespread, as is the use of DOIs to provide links to cited and citing references through services such as CrossRef and ChemPort. It is worth noting, however, that forward linking may make use of proprietary platforms; for example, citing references for articles from Elsevier titles are from Scopus records. Also, most journals now offer e-mail and RSS alerts of new content; some even offer alerts when an article has been cited.

Deep backfiles are filling in—for example, the ACS Legacy Backfiles, a development that improves access for those whose libraries can offer them and generates revenue for publishers who sell them separately. As well, the ACS has signed with Portico for safeguarding perpetual archiving of digital content, weakening one rationale for continuing ACS print subscriptions. Note, however, that ACS did not name Portico as a mechanism to fill post-cancellation access.

OpenURL link resolution standards have been widely adopted, and the key publishers can support article-level linking from citations to full text. Lastly, most publishers in this section are also compliant with COUNTER for usage statistics reporting (www.projectcounter.org), at least to some degree.

In the following annotations, if no mention of DOIs is made, it is because the reviewer was unable to find any evidence of DOIs assigned to articles. For more information on DOIs, see www.doi.org. *Journal Citation Reports* for 2005 (Thomson-ISI) was used to gather supporting evidence for inclusion and recommendation of journals; where impact factors and total citations are mentioned outside of publisher quotes, they are from this source.

OpenURL linking levels are reported from the targets list compiled and posted by Ex Libris on their web site as found in April–May 2007; reporting these data does not constitute endorsement. COUNTER compliance was reported from the list of compliant vendors on the Project COUNTER web site as found in April–May 2007.

Basic Periodicals

Ac: *Accounts of Chemical Research, Analytical Chemistry, Chemical Reviews, Inorganic Chemistry, Journal of Chemical Education, The Journal of Organic Chemistry, The Journal of Physical Chemistry Part A, American Chemical Society. Journal.*

Basic Abstracts and Indexes

Chemical Abstracts; Current Contents/Physical; Chemical and Earth Sciences; Science Citation Index.

General

1174. Accounts of Chemical Research. [ISSN: 0001-4842] 1968. m. USD 641 print & online eds. Ed(s): Joan Selverstone Valentine. American Chemical Society, 1155 16th St, NW, Washington, DC 20036; service@ acs.org; http://pubs.acs.org. Illus., index. Sample. Refereed. Circ: 4997

Paid. Vol. ends: Dec. Online: Pub.; EBSCO Publishing, EBSCO Host; OhioLINK; SwetsWise Online Content. *Indexed:* CABA, ChemAb, DSA, EnvAb, ExcerpMed, GSI, SCI. *Aud.:* Ac, Sa.

Accounts of Chemical Research offers short, readable accounts of "basic research and applications in all areas of chemistry and biochemistry" that "describe current developments, clarify controversies, and link the latest advances with past and future research." About 100 articles are published annually, each about nine pages long. Annual volumes may include one or more thematic special issues; recent examples include "Amyloid Assembly and Structure" and "Computational & Theoretical Chemistry." The title ranked third among multidisciplinary chemistry journals in 2005 impact factor, a drop from second in this category since 2003. Recommended for academic libraries that support chemistry programs and special libraries. Further, site-wide online access is available with or without print and includes post-review preprints (ASAP Articles). Electronic Supporting Information (ESI) provides "details that are too voluminous to be printed" but apparently not for complex graphic content. E-mail alerts and RSS feeds are available. DOIs assigned, with cited references linked via ChemPort, CrossRef, and others. Article-level openURL linking via CrossRef DOI. Publisher is COUNTER compliant.

1175. American Chemical Society. Journal. Supersedes in part (in 1914): *American Chemical Journal); (in 1893): Journal of Analytical and Applied Chemistry.* [ISSN: 0002-7863] 1879. w. USD 3858 print & online eds. Ed(s): Peter J Stang, Charlotte Sauer Steigers. American Chemical Society, 1155 16th St, NW, Washington, DC 20036; service@ acs.org; http://pubs.acs.org. Illus., index, adv. Refereed. Circ: 13000 Paid. Vol. ends: Dec. Microform: PMC. Online: Pub.; EBSCO Publishing, EBSCO Host; OhioLINK; SwetsWise Online Content. *Indexed:* AS&TI, ApMecR, BiolAb, CABA, ChemAb, DSA, EngInd, ExcerpMed, FS&TA, GSI, HortAb, PetrolAb, S&F, SCI. *Bk. rev.:* Number and length vary. *Aud.:* Ac, Sa.

The flagship journal of the American Chemical Society is "devoted to the publication of research papers in all fields of chemistry and publishes approximately 17,000 pages of new chemistry a year." The number of pages has increased since the prior review. As of 2005, it was cited more than any other chemistry journal in the Journal Citation Reports (by an order of magnitude), and ranked sixth among multidisciplinary chemistry journals in impact factor. Issues (51 per year) include articles, communications, and book and computer software reviews (the latter at the invitation of the editor). Recommended for academic libraries that support chemistry. Site-wide online access is available with or without print and includes post-review preprints (ASAP Articles). There is a vast amount of supporting information online, which includes text, image, and video files. DOIs assigned, with cited items linked via CrossRef, ChemPort, and others. Article-level openURL linking via CrossRef DOI. Publisher is COUNTER compliant. E-mail alerts and RSS feeds available.

1176. Angewandte Chemie (International Edition). Formerly (until 1998): *Angewandte Chemie: International Edition in English.* [ISSN: 1433-7851] 1961. 52x/yr. EUR 4630. Ed(s): Peter Goelitz. Wiley - VCH Verlag GmbH & Co. KGaA, Boschstr 12, Weinheim, 69469, Germany; subservice@wiley-vch.de; http://www3.interscience.wiley.com/cgi-bin/ home. Illus., index, adv. Sample. Refereed. Circ: 3453 Paid and controlled. Vol. ends: Dec. Online: EBSCO Publishing, EBSCO Host; OhioLINK; SwetsWise Online Content; Wiley InterScience. *Indexed:* ChemAb, EngInd, FS&TA, HortAb, IndVet, SCI, VB. *Bk. rev.:* 1 or 2 per issue, 1-2 pages in length. *Aud.:* Ac, Sa.

The International Edition is the English translation of the German-language publication of the Gesellschaft Deutscher Chemiker. *Angewandte Chemie International Edition* offers a "mixture of review articles, highlights and communications" and Nobel lectures in chemistry and related fields. Communications, which are "critically selected and report on the latest research results," comprise most of the content. Approximately 8,000 pages are published per year, with nearly 1,500 articles in 2005. Ranked fifth in 2005 impact factor among multidisciplinary chemistry journals. Online access includes Early View, preprints of "articles judged by the referees or the editor as being either very important or very urgent" and prior issues to 1998, and institutional subscriptions include free access to *Chemistry—An Asian Journal.* Backfile, 1962-1997, sold separately. DOIs assigned, and links to cited references are provided through ChemPort and CrossRef among others.

OpenURL linking at the journal level. E-mail alerts available, and RSS feeds announced in the first 2007 issue. Recommended for academic and special libraries supporting research in chemistry.

1177. Canadian Journal of Chemistry. Formerly (until 1951): *Canadian Journal of Research. Section B: Chemical Sciences;* Which superseded in part (in 1935): *Canadian Journal of Research.* [ISSN: 0008-4042] 1929. m. CND 1099 (Individuals, CND 315). Ed(s): Robert H Lipson, Dr. Dick Puddephatt. N R C Research Press, National Research Council of Canada, Ottawa, ON K1A 0R6, Canada; pubs@nrc-cnrc.gc.ca; http://pubs.nrc-cnrc.gc.ca. Illus., index, adv. Refereed. Circ: 1488. Vol. ends: Dec. Microform: MML; PMC; PQC. Online: EBSCO Publishing, EBSCO Host; Gale; IngentaConnect; Micromedia ProQuest; OCLC Online Computer Library Center, Inc.; Ovid Technologies, Inc.; ProQuest K-12 Learning Solutions; ProQuest LLC (Ann Arbor); SwetsWise Online Content; H.W. Wilson. *Indexed:* CBCARef, CPerI, ChemAb, DSA, EngInd, ExcerpMed, FPA, ForAb, GSI, HortAb, IndVet, PetrolAb, S&F, SCI. *Aud.:* Ac, Sa.

The principal medium of publication of research papers for the Canadian Society for Chemistry, *Canadian Journal of Chemistry (Revue Canadienne de Chimie)* publishes "outstanding research articles and comprehensive reviews by international contributors in analytical, inorganic, organic, and physical-theoretical chemistry." Features award lectures and one or more special tribute issues per year. More than 200 articles published in 2005. Site-wide online access is available, with or without the print; a substantial backfile to 1951 (vol. 29) was added in April 2006. Supplementary data (text and graphics) from many articles available online. Forthcoming articles published online, and RSS feeds are available for new content. OpenURL linking at the article level.

ChemComm. See *Chemical Communications.*

1178. Chemical & Engineering News: the newsmagazine of the chemical world. Former titles (until 1942): *American Chemical Society. News Edition;* (until 1940): *Industrial and Engineering Chemistry. News Edition.* [ISSN: 0009-2347] 1923. w. USD 273 print & online eds. Ed(s): Rudy M Baum, Pamela S Zurer. American Chemical Society, 1155 16th St, NW, Washington, DC 20036; service@acs.org; http://pubs.acs.org. Illus., index, adv. Refereed. Circ: 136000 Paid. Vol. ends: Dec. Online: EBSCO Publishing, EBSCO Host. *Indexed:* A&ATA, ABIn, AS&TI, Agr, BPI, BiolDig, C&ISA, CEA, CerAb, ChemAb, EngInd, EnvAb, EnvInd, ExcerpMed, FS&TA, IAA, ISTA, M&GPA, PetrolAb, PollutAb, RILM, S&F, SCI, SSCI, WRCInf. *Bk. rev.:* 1–2 per month. *Aud.:* Ga, Ac, Sa.

A weekly providing concise, accessible articles for current awareness in chemistry. Articles summarize research reports from chemistry journals, related findings from other disciplines, and current events. The "News of the Week" section highlights news headlines from a chemistry angle, with references to published research, where applicable. Regular sections address business, education, and government policy; within these sections, numerous, paragraph-long "concentrates" cover relevant news, along with a few longer, by-lined features. Also included are award announcements and ACS news. Redesign launched with vol. 84:42 (October 16, 2006) features new typography and layout for improved readability, new size, plus "adoption of C&EN as the official logo of the magazine"—now more prominent on the cover than the title. Site-wide online access is available with or without print. Online version includes links to companies, agencies, individuals discussed, but not to cited research. OpenURL linking is at the issue level from the publisher. COUNTER compliant, with limitations. Recommended for academic libraries supporting science curricula.

1179. Chemical Communications. Former titles (until 1996): *Journal of the Chemical Society - Chemical Communications;* (until 1972): *Chemical Communications.* [ISSN: 1359-7345] 1965. w. bi-w. until 2005. GBP 1951 combined subscription print & online eds.; USD 3882 combined subscription print & online eds. Ed(s): Dr. Sarah Thomas. Royal Society of Chemistry, Thomas Graham House, Science Park, Milton Rd, Cambridge, CB4 0WF, United Kingdom; sales@rsc.org;

http://www.rsc.org. Illus., index, adv. Sample. Refereed. Vol. ends: Dec. Microform: PQC. Online: EBSCO Publishing, EBSCO Host; OCLC Online Computer Library Center, Inc.; OhioLINK; SwetsWise Online Content. *Indexed:* ChemAb, ExcerpMed, PollutAb, SCI. *Aud.:* Ac, Sa.

In January 2005, marking its 40th year of publication, *ChemComm* changed from two-page to three-page communications, and increased from 24 to 48 issues per year. The latter change improved upon the notable rapid publication record of this "fastest publisher of articles providing information on new avenues of research." Typical issues of *ChemComm* now include a feature article and 30–40 communications. The title boasts international authorship and readership. Recommended for academic and research libraries. Site-wide online access is available with or without print and includes post-review preprints (Advance Articles) and content back to 1996. Subscriptions (print and online) include the new RSC title *Molecular Biosystems.* E-mail alerts and RSS feeds available. DOIs assigned, with cited and citing reference linking via ChemPort, CrossRef, and others. Article-level openURL linking via CrossRef DOI. RSC is COUNTER compliant.

1180. Chemical Reviews. [ISSN: 0009-2665] 1924. m. USD 1183 print & online eds. Ed(s): Josef Michl. American Chemical Society, 1155 16th St, NW, Washington, DC 20036; service@acs.org; http://pubs.acs.org. Illus., index, adv. Sample. Refereed. Circ: 5297 Paid. Vol. ends: Dec. Online: Pub.; EBSCO Publishing, EBSCO Host; OhioLINK; SwetsWise Online Content. *Indexed:* AS&TI, ApMecR, ChemAb, DSA, EngInd, ExcerpMed, GSI, S&F, SCI. *Aud.:* Ac, Sa.

A core title, which as of 2005 had the highest impact factor of any chemistry journal. *Chemical Reviews* provides "comprehensive, authoritative, critical, and readable reviews of important recent research in organic, inorganic, physical, analytical, theoretical, and biological chemistry." Thematic issues are published each year (seven in 2006) and are available for purchase separately; recent examples include "DNA Damage and Repair" and "Chemical Oceanography." Recommended for academic libraries serving chemistry departments and special libraries. Site-wide online access is available with or without print and includes post-review preprints (ASAP Articles) and issues back to 1996. Pre-1996 content is part of the ACS Legacy Archives, sold separately. E-mail alerts and RSS feeds available. Supporting information (primarily text) for some papers available online at no charge. DOIs assigned; cited references linked via ChemPort, CrossRef, and others. Article-level openURL linking via CrossRef DOI. Publisher is COUNTER compliant.

1181. The Chemical Society of Japan. Bulletin. [ISSN: 0009-2673] 1926. m. Institutional members, JPY 69000; Individual members, JPY 10200. Ed(s): Kohei Tamao. Chemical Society of Japan, 1-5, Kanda-Surugadai 1-Chome, Chiyoda-ku, Tokyo, 101-0062, Japan; info@chemistry.or.jp; http://www.chemistry.or.jp/. Illus., index. Refereed. Circ: 3500. Vol. ends: Dec. Microform: PMC; PQC. Online: EBSCO Publishing, EBSCO Host; J-Stage. *Indexed:* ApMecR, CABA, ChemAb, DSA, EngInd, ExcerpMed, ForAb, HortAb, M&GPA, PetrolAb, S&F, SCI, SWRA. *Aud.:* Ac, Sa.

An English-language title which celebrated its 77th anniversary in 2004. Each issue includes invited reviews of awardees' work ("Award accounts"), invited reviews of a specific research topic ("Accounts"), and completed original research ("Articles" and "Short articles"). As of 2005, the latter two were no longer categorized by subdiscipline. New in 2005, one "BCSJ Award Article" per issue was selected by the editorial board as the best of the month, and featured on the cover; some nominated articles are given an honorable mention with a "Selected article" designation. Pages per volume has dropped from a peak of 2,698 in 2002 to under 2,000 in 2006. In the United States it is no longer distributed via the American Chemical Society, but through Maruzen International Co., Ltd. Online access is via the JSTAGE (Japan Science and Technology Information Aggregator, Electronic) platform, which offers openURL linking at the journal level and is partially COUNTER compliant. DOIs assigned; cited references linked via JSTAGE link center. Articles may be published as open access via an author-pays model, beginning in 2006; ten such articles have been published as of this review. Additional "free access" articles are included in each issue of the 2006 and 2007 volumes.

1182. Chemical Society Reviews. Superseded: *Chemical Society, London. Quarterly Reviews; Royal Institute of Chemistry Reviews.* [ISSN: 0306-0012] 1972. m. GBP 514 combined subscription print & online eds.; USD 995 combined subscription print & online eds. Ed(s): Dr. Robert D Eagling. Royal Society of Chemistry, Thomas Graham House, Science Park, Milton Rd, Cambridge, CB4 0WF, United Kingdom; sales@rsc.org; http://www.rsc.org. Illus., index. Refereed. Vol. ends: Dec. *Indexed:* ApMecR, ChemAb, DSA, FS&TA, SCI. *Aud.:* Ac, Sa.

Chemical Society Reviews "publishes accessible, succinct and reader-friendly articles on topics of current interest in the chemical sciences." Includes both critical and tutorial reviews, the latter appropriate for advanced undergraduates or researchers new to the field, as well as well as experts. Publishes articles of "social interest" (e.g., "Automotive fuels" and "Advances in chemistry applied to forensic science") broadening the potential user base beyond research chemists. Began including RSC Awards reviews in 2006. Guest-edited themed issues are published; recent examples include "Nanostructured assemblies," "Liquid crystals," and a celebration of the "Supramolecular chemistry" 20th anniversary. Ranks second in 2005 impact factor among multidisciplinary chemistry journals, with a rising trend in both impact factor and relative rank in recent years, rising above its ACS competitor, *Accounts of Chemical Research,* in 2006. Expanded publication to nine issues in 2004, then to 12 in 2005. Additional title, *Chemical Science,* included with print or online subscription. Recommended for academic and research libraries with chemistry collections. Site-wide online access is available with print or alone at a slightly reduced rate, and includes post-review preprints (Advance Articles). Some Open Access content available as a result of RSC's author-pays "OpenScience" option. Backfiles of preceding titles to 1947 may be purchased. E-mail alerts and RSS feeds available. DOIs assigned; cited and citing reference linking via ChemPort and CrossRef. Article-level openURL linking via CrossRef DOI, except for the backfile, which supports issue-level linking. Publisher is COUNTER compliant.

1183. Chemistry: A European Journal. [ISSN: 0947-6539] 1995. 36x/yr. EUR 4145. Ed(s): Neville Compton. Wiley - VCH Verlag GmbH & Co. KGaA, Boschstr 12, Weinheim, 69469, Germany; subservice@wiley-vch.de; http://www3.interscience.wiley.com/cgi-bin/home. Illus., index, adv. Sample. Refereed. Vol. ends: Dec. Online: EBSCO Publishing, EBSCO Host; OhioLINK; SwetsWise Online Content; Wiley InterScience. *Indexed:* BAS, ChemAb, EngInd, SCI. *Bk. rev.:* Usually 1 to 5 per issue. *Aud.:* Ac, Sa.

Aimed at "chemists of all disciplines," *Chemistry* celebrated its tenth anniversary in 2005. The "international forum for the publication of outstanding Full Papers from all areas of chemistry and related fields" is one of the more highly cited chemistry journals, ranking eighth in 2005 impact factor among multidisciplinary chemistry journals. The "Concepts" section, aimed at nonspecialists, offers a "conceptual guide to unfamiliar areas and experts with new angles on familiar problems." Increased from 24 to 36 issues in 2006. Recommended for academic and research libraries. Online access is available in various package options, and includes "Early View" of articles online ahead of print. Earliest volumes (1–3) offered in a separate backfile. DOIs assigned, and cited references are linked via CrossRef and ChemPort, among others. OpenURL linking is at the journal level. E-mail alerts and RSS feeds available.

1184. Chemistry & Industry. [ISSN: 0009-3068] 1881. s-m. USD 750. Ed(s): Neil Eisberg. Society of Chemical Industry, 14 Belgrave Sq, London, SW1X 8PS, United Kingdom; enquiries@chemind.org; http://www.soci.org. Illus., adv. Sample. Circ: 9161 Paid. Vol. ends: No. 24. Online: EBSCO Publishing, EBSCO Host; Factiva, Inc.; Florida Center for Library Automation; Gale; OCLC Online Computer Library Center, Inc.; H.W. Wilson. *Indexed:* AS&TI, BrTechI, C&ISA, CABA, CEA, CerAb, ChemAb, DSA, EnvInd, ExcerpMed, FPA, FS&TA, HortAb, IAA, IndIslam, IndVet, PetrolAb, S&F, SCI, SSCI, VB, WAE&RSA. *Bk. rev.:* 1-5 per issue. *Aud.:* Ac, Sa.

A useful current awareness source for industrial chemists, clearly tailored to industry needs and interests. Two issues per month cover news, patents, people (e.g., high-level corporate hires), and include reviews and commentary (a recent issue includes commentary on Al Gore's *An Inconvenient Truth*). The "Highlights" section summarizes recent publications from the scholarly literature. Online access is available to institutional print subscribers for a small extra fee, but is limited to five password-protected user accounts, rendering the publisher's access impractical for academic library settings. Some full text is available from several aggregators, though coverage is not complete in at least some of these.

Chemistry in Britain. See *Chemistry World.*

1185. Chemistry World. Formerly (until 2004): *Chemistry in Britain;* Which was formed by the merger of (1950-1964): *Royal Institute of Chemistry. Journal;* Which was formerly: *Royal Institute of Chemistry of Great Britain and Ireland. Journal and Proceedings;* (1957-1964): *Chemical Society. Proceedings;* Which superseded in part (in 1877): *Chemical Society. Journal.* [ISSN: 1473-7604] 1965. m. GBP 643 print & online eds. Ed(s): Mark Peplow. Royal Society of Chemistry, Thomas Graham House, Science Park, Milton Rd, Cambridge, CB4 0WF, United Kingdom; sales@rsc.org; http://www.rsc.org. Illus., index, adv. Refereed. Circ: 45000. Vol. ends: Dec. *Indexed:* A&ATA, BrTechI, ChemAb, DSA, EnvAb, EnvInd, ExcerpMed, FS&TA, RILM, S&F, SCI, SSCI, SWRA. *Bk. rev.:* 6 or more per issue. *Aud.:* Ga, Ac, Sa.

Formerly *Chemistry in Britain,* this title underwent a transformation in 2004 with its name change. In October 2004, the Association of Learned and Professional Society Publishers (ALPSP) awarded *Chemistry World* the ALPSP/Charlesworth Award for Best New Journal. Named best monthly business and professional magazine of the year at the PPA 2006 Magazine Awards. Offers "articles on all aspects of the chemical sciences, regular company and individual profiles, job vacancies, commercial technology reports." Publishes several feature articles per issue on timely or timeless topics related to chemistry, plus news items from current research and an editorial/opinion section (a recent topic is global climate change). An excellent source for current awareness in chemistry and the myriad related disciplines, this title is especially well suited for a broad academic audience including undergraduates and seasoned researchers. Site-wide online access is available free with institutional print subscriptions. Web site offers RSS feeds, and podcasts and the *Chemistry World* Blog were added in 2006. OpenURL linking is at the issue level. Publisher is COUNTER compliant.

1186. Green Chemistry. [ISSN: 1463-9262] 1999. m. GBP 947 print & online eds. Ed(s): Sarah Ruthven. Royal Society of Chemistry, Thomas Graham House, Science Park, Milton Rd, Cambridge, CB4 0WF, United Kingdom; sales@rsc.org; http://www.rsc.org. Refereed. *Indexed:* CABA, ChemAb, DSA, EnvAb, EnvInd, FPA, ForAb, HortAb, S&F, SCI. *Aud.:* Ac, Sa.

Green Chemistry publishes "cutting-edge research that reduces the environmental impact of the chemical enterprise by developing alternative sustainable technologies." Peer-reviewed content includes original research papers, communications, perspectives, and review articles. Title expanded to 12 issues in 2004. Beginning in 2005, a separate publication of the RSC, *Chemical Technology,* was included as a separately paginated insert in issues of this and some other RSC titles. Planned themed issues for 2007 feature papers from the Green Chemistry for Fuel Synthesis and Processing Symposium (held at the 2006 ACS meeting) and from an international Green Solvents for Processes symposium held in October 2006 in Friedrichshafen, Germany. Audience is intended to be broad, from chemists to technologists to upper-level undergraduate students. Recommended for academic libraries supporting chemistry or environmental science curricula. Site-wide online access is available with print, or alone at a slightly reduced rate. Backfile 1999–2004 sold separately. Online includes galley-proofed preprints of accepted papers ("Advance Articles"). Articles may be open access through RSC's OpenScience initiative, via an author-pays option. Newly enhanced html in the online version allows readers to obtain information about compounds mentioned in articles, for example, downloadable structures. Electronic supplementary information for articles is available free of charge and includes text and graphics. DOIs assigned; reference linking via ChemPort and CrossRef to both cited and citing articles. Cited references available only with licensed content, but links to citing articles are free to all. OpenURL linking is at the issue level. Publisher is COUNTER compliant. E-mail alerts and RSS feeds available.

1187. Journal of Chemical Education. [ISSN: 0021-9584] 1924. m. USD 348 Educational granting Ph.D. in chemistry or related sciences; commercial or industrial; government laboratory (Individuals, USD 45). Ed(s): J W Moore. American Chemical Society, 1155 16th St, NW, Washington, DC 20036; service@acs.org; https://portal.chemistry.org/. Illus., index, adv. Sample. Refereed. Circ: 15000 Paid. Vol. ends: Dec. Microform: PMC; PQC. Online: Pub.; EBSCO Publishing, EBSCO Host;

Northern Light Technology, Inc.; OCLC Online Computer Library Center, Inc.; ProQuest LLC (Ann Arbor). *Indexed:* A&ATA, ABIn, BRI, CBRI, ChemAb, DSA, ERIC, EduInd, EngInd, ExcerpMed, GSI, IndIslam, SCI, SSCI. *Bk. rev.:* One or more critical book/media reviews (700+ words each) per issue; 40 per year. *Aud.:* Hs, Ac, Sa.

"The world's premier chemistry education academic journal." Monthly issues of 150–200 pages are populated with "a wide range of interesting articles and activities useful in both the classroom and laboratory." Topical coverage runs the gamut from classroom techniques to scholarship of teaching and learning chemistry to new chemical science appropriate for the classroom. Monthly theme offers a cluster of articles on a given subdiscipline (e.g., analytical chemistry, electrochemistry), in addition to non-themed content. "Chemistry for Everyone" features novel ways of making chemical concepts accessible; a recent article describes teaching the periodic table as a literary text. True to its mission of supporting education, *JCE* has liberal use policies for print and online content. Highly recommended for academic libraries supporting chemistry, chemistry education, or general science education curricula, as well as for high school chemistry educators. Institutional print subscription includes online access via IP recognition or a lower cost name/password option (the latter available only to institutions not offering graduate degrees). Extensive online backfile and supplementary content included. Searchable article index extending back to 1924 available. Web site also offers *JCE* subscribers downloadable software and other tools useful for teachers. Web site also offers reader discussion forums and targeted content for high school teachers. Annual volumes also available on CD-ROM.

Journal of Chemical Research. Synopses (Print Edition). See *Journal of Chemical Research.*

1188. *Journal of Chemical Theory and Computation.* [ISSN: 1549-9618] 2005. m. USD 1189 print & online eds. Ed(s): William Jorgensen. American Chemical Society, 1155 16th St, NW, Washington, DC 20036; service@acs.org; http://pubs.acs.org. Circ: 3147. *Indexed:* SCI. *Aud.:* Ac, Sa.

JCTC was initiated to provide a single forum for "articles, letters, and reviews reporting new theories based on physical laws, advances in computational methods, and important applications to problems in chemistry (editor William Jorgensen in inaugural issue)." Aimed at an audience of theoretical and computational chemists, articles are categorized by topic within issues. Regularly represented topics include dyamics, molecular mechanics, statistical mechanics, quantum chemistry, reaction mechanisms, spectroscopy and excited states, thermodynamics, polymers, biomolecular systems, structure prediction and nanochemistry. Supporting information, primarily textual, is available for some papers online at no charge. Too new to have an impact factor, *JCTC* was cited 99 times and published 134 articles in its first year, according to the 2005 Journal Citation Reports. The number of pages published increased by almost 400 between volumes 1 and 2. Site-wide online access is available with or without print and includes post-review preprints (ASAP Articles). E-mail alerts and RSS feeds available. DOIs assigned, and cited references are linked via ChemPort and CrossRef, among others. Article-level openURL linking via CrossRef DOI; publisher is COUNTER compliant.

1189. *Journal of Physical and Chemical Reference Data.* [ISSN: 0047-2689] 1972. 4x/yr. USD 940 combined subscription domestic print & online eds.; USD 975 combined subscription foreign print & online eds. Ed(s): Robert L Watters, Malcolm Chase, Jr. U.S. Department of Commerce, National Institute of Standards and Technology, 100 Bureau Dr, Gaithersburg, MD 20899-2500; inquiries@nist.gov; http://www.nist.gov. Illus., index. Refereed. Circ: 220. Vol. ends: Dec. Online: American Institute of Physics, Scitation; EBSCO Publishing, EBSCO Host; OhioLINK; SwetsWise Online Content. *Indexed:* AS&TI, ApMecR, CPI, ChemAb, S&F, SCI. *Aud.:* Ac, Sa.

Published by the American Institute of Physics (AIP) for the National Institute of Standards and Technology (NIST), the purpose of this publication is "to provide critically evaluated physical and chemical property data, fully documented as to the original sources and the criteria used for evaluation." *JPCRD* includes critical reviews of measurement techniques, reports of new estimation or prediction techniques, and contributions originating from the National Standard Reference Data System (NSRDS) administered by the National Institute of Standards and Technology under the Standard Reference Data Act (Public Law 90-396). Articles tend to be 20 pages or longer, most with extensive tabular data. Publication reduced from bimonthly to quarterly in 2002, but new content is added online daily. Although the 2005 impact factor was relatively low, it was well above the median for the multidisciplinary chemistry journals, and the importance of this title in particular may be difficult to assess by citations. Site-wide online access (from vol. 28, 1999) is available with the print or alone at a slightly reduced rate; tiered pricing is offered. DOIs assigned, and both cited and citing (via Scitation and CrossRef) works are linked from online articles. Fully openURL compliant for article level linking. AIP is a COUNTER compliant vendor. Recommended for academic and special libraries serving research programs in chemistry and related disciplines.

1190. *Lab On a Chip: miniaturisation for chemistry and biology.* [ISSN: 1473-0197] 2001. 6x/yr. GBP 1014 print & online eds. Ed(s): Harpal Minhas. Royal Society of Chemistry, Thomas Graham House, Science Park, Milton Rd, Cambridge, CB4 0WF, United Kingdom; sales@rsc.rg; http://www.rsc.org. Adv. Refereed. *Indexed:* BiolAb, ChemAb, ExcerpMed, FS&TA, SCI. *Aud.:* Ac, Sa.

This multidisciplinary title began in 2001 to publish "work related to miniaturisation (on or off chips) at the micro- and nano-scale across a variety of disciplines including: chemistry, biology, bioengineering, physics, electronics, clinical/medical science, chemical engineering and materials science." The audience includes industrial and academic sectors engaged in research in pharmaceuticals, medicine, analytical science, synthetic chemistry, biotechnology, physics, materials science, (bio)engineering, and electronics. Accepts communications, full papers, technical notes, critical/tutorial reviews, and mini-reviews. The title has quickly established itself, and ranked seventh by 2005 impact factor among 125 multidisciplinary chemistry journals. Publication frequency doubled to monthly in 2005, and submissions for 2006 continued to increase. *Chemical Technology* is included as a free supplement incorporated into print issues, and subscriptions also include online access to *Molecular Biosystems*. Site-wide online access available with or without print, and includes pre-prints. E-mail and RSS alerts of new content are available. Supplementary data freely available online. On the web site, the moderated Chips and Tips resource offers "practical tips and tricks to solve everyday laboratory issues that never see the light of day in full research publications." DOIs assigned. Cited references linked, and users may also search for citing articles, including both RSC and non-RSC items. Article-level openURL linking is possible. Publisher is COUNTER compliant.

1191. *Pure and Applied Chemistry.* Formerly: *International Congress of Pure and Applied Chemistry. Lectures.* [ISSN: 0033-4545] 1960. m. USD 1500 (Individuals, USD 99). Ed(s): James R Bull, Bernardo J Harold. International Union of Pure and Applied Chemistry, IUPAC Secretariat, PO Box 13757, Research Triangle Park, NC 27709-3757. Illus., index, adv. Sample. Refereed. Circ: 845. Vol. ends: Dec. Microform: PQC. Online: Blackwell Synergy; EBSCO Publishing, EBSCO Host; OCLC Online Computer Library Center, Inc.; SwetsWise Online Content. *Indexed:* A&ATA, CABA, ChemAb, DSA, ExcerpMed, FPA, FS&TA, ForAb, HortAb, IndVet, S&F, SCI, VB. *Aud.:* Ac, Sa.

The official monthly journal of the International Union of Pure and Applied Chemistry (IUPAC) has "responsibility for publishing works arising from those international scientific events and projects that are sponsored and undertaken by the Union." *Pure and Applied Chemistry* publishes IUPAC nomenclatural recommendations, IUPAC Technical Reports on standardization and related matters, and IUPAC sponsored symposium or other event proceedings. Covers "all aspects of pure and applied chemistry." Occasional special topic features are published, approximately one per year, comprising "research papers and short, critical reviews organized around a central compelling theme" with papers submitted by invitation; a recent example: "Natural Products and Biodiversity." Online access is included with print, or alone for a reduced price. Institutional subscription includes *Chemistry International*. DOIs assigned, and new web design available for 2005 and later links to cited references using DOIs. New design includes author and keyword indexing, and chronological browsing of IUPAC Technical Reports and Recommendations, the pdfs of which are free.

Revue canadienne de chimie. See *Canadian Journal of Chemistry.*

CHEMISTRY

Analytical

1192. Acta Crystallographica. Section A: Foundations of Crystallography. Formerly (until 1982): *Acta Crystallographica. Section A: Crystal Physics, Diffraction, Theoretical and General Crystallography;* Which superseded in part (until 1967): *Acta Crystallographica.* [ISSN: 0108-7673] 1948. bi-m. USD 693 print & online eds. Ed(s): John R Helliwell, Dieter Schwarzenbach. Blackwell Munksgaard, Rosenoerns Alle 1, PO Box 227, Copenhagen V, 1502, Denmark; customerservice@munksgaard.dk; http://www.munksgaard.dk/. Illus., index. Refereed. Circ: 1500. Microform: PMC. Online: Blackwell Synergy; EBSCO Publishing, EBSCO Host; Gale; IngentaConnect; OCLC Online Computer Library Center, Inc.; SwetsWise Online Content. Reprint: PSC. *Indexed:* C&ISA, CCMJ, CerAb, ChemAb, IAA, MSN, MathR, MinerAb, S&F, SCI. *Bk. rev.:* Number and length vary. *Aud.:* Ac, Sa.

Acta Crystallographica Section A. Foundations of Crystallography is published by the International Union of Crystallographers, and features "experimental and theoretical studies of the properties and arrangements of atoms, ions and molecules in condensed matter, ideal or real, and of their symmetry." Other sections under the collective title are *Section B: Structural Science, Section C: Crystal Structure Communications, Section D: Biological Crystallography, Section E: Structure Reports,* and *Section F: Structural Biology and Crystallization Communications.* In 2004, all *Crystallography* journals online implemented an open-access policy, intended to maintain lower subscription costs, and to allow authors to make their papers freely available online for a fee. Institutions may purchase open-access memberships that allow the institution's authors to publish open-access articles. There is, as a result, a mix of open-access and subscriber-only content available online for these titles from 2004 forward. Book reviews appear to be open access. Site-wide online access is available with print or alone at a slightly reduced price. DOIs assigned. Cited references are linked via ChemPort and CrossRef. Citing references in other IUCr journals are also linked. Supplementary content accompanies articles, including three-dimensional images. E-mail alerts and RSS feeds available from the publisher web site. OpenURL linking at the article level via the Blackwell Science Synergy platform, and Blackwell is COUNTER compliant.

1193. The Analyst. Incorporates (1996-2000): *Analytical Communications;* Which was formerly (1981-1996): *Analytical Proceedings;* (1975-1981): *Chemical Society. Analytical Division. Proceedings;* (1964-1975): *Society for Analytical Chemistry. Proceedings.* [ISSN: 0003-2654] 1876. m. GBP 1200 combined subscription print & online eds.; USD 2388 combined subscription print & online eds. Ed(s): Niamh O'Connor. Royal Society of Chemistry, Thomas Graham House, Science Park, Milton Rd, Cambridge, CB4 0WF, United Kingdom; sales@rsc.org; http://www.rsc.org. Illus., index, adv. Refereed. Vol. ends: Dec. Microform: PQC. Online: EBSCO Publishing, EBSCO Host; OCLC Online Computer Library Center, Inc.; OhioLINK; SwetsWise Online Content. *Indexed:* A&ATA, C&ISA, CABA, CerAb, ChemAb, DSA, ExcerpMed, FPA, FS&TA, ForAb, HortAb, IAA, IndIslam, IndVet, S&F, SCI, VB, WAE&RSA, WRCInf. *Bk. rev.:* Variable number (1 in 2004, 9 in first 4 months of 2005), 350-750 words. *Aud.:* Ac, Sa.

The Analyst offers "the latest developments in theory and application of analytical and bioanalytical techniques." Publishing urgent communications, full papers, and review articles, it is billed by the publisher as a "core teaching tool." The "i-section" was launched in 2003 and is offered in every issue, with reviews, profiles, overviews, and trends articles intended to be accessible to nonspecialists. A few concise and fast-tracked communications for dissemination of preliminary research findings and numerous longer papers are included in each issue. Communications may be subsequently featured in *Chemical Science* or *Chemical Technology.* Site-wide online access is available with the print edition or alone at a slightly reduced price, and includes post-review, pre-publication "Advance Articles." RSS feeds and e-mail alerts available. The RSC backfile for this title extends to volume 1, 1876. DOIs are assigned, with links to both cited and citing references via ChemPort and CrossRef, among others. Article-level openURL linking via CrossRef DOI, except for the backfile, which supports issue-level linking. Publisher is COUNTER compliant.

1194. Analytica Chimica Acta. Incorporates: *Analytica Chimica Acta - Computer Technique and Optimization.* [ISSN: 0003-2670] 1947. 52x/yr. EUR 8864. Ed(s): L Buydens, P R Haddad. Elsevier BV, Radarweg 29, Amsterdam, 1043 NX, Netherlands; nlinfo-f@elsevier.nl; http://www.elsevier.nl. Illus., index, adv. Sample. Refereed. Microform: PQC. Online: EBSCO Publishing, EBSCO Host; Gale; IngentaConnect; OhioLINK; ScienceDirect; SwetsWise Online Content. *Indexed:* BioEngAb, BiolAb, C&ISA, CABA, CerAb, ChemAb, DSA, EngInd, ExcerpMed, FPA, FS&TA, ForAb, HortAb, IAA, IndVet, M&GPA, PollutAb, S&F, SCI, SWRA, VB, WRCInf. *Aud.:* Ac, Sa.

"*Analytica Chimica Acta* provides a forum for the rapid publication of original research, and critical reviews dealing with all aspects of fundamental and applied modern analytical science." Emphasis is on innovative methodologies, rather than application of existing methods to new systems. Issues contain varying numbers of full articles eight pages in length, with occasional reviews by prior agreement with the editors. Topics covered are myriad and include various types of chromatography, spectrometry, and spectroscopy, chemical and biosensors, microfluidics, and chemometrics. Special issues feature proceedings from conferences or workshops; recent examples include papers from the Fourth International Workshop of Molecularly Imprinted Polymers and the 2005 Instrumental Methods of Analysis conference. Recommended for libraries supporting analytical chemistry research programs. Online site-wide access available with or without print, and includes proofed articles in press. A separate backfile to 1947 is available. E-mail alerts available. DOIs assigned, and cited references are linked via CrossRef. Both cited and citing references are linked via Scopus records. OpenURL linking is at the article level. Publisher is COUNTER compliant with some limitations.

1195. Analytical Chemistry. Incorporates: *Analytical Chemistry News & Features;* Formerly (until 1946): *Industrial and Engineering Chemistry. Analytical Edition;* Which superseded in part (in 1929): *Industrial & Engineering Chemistry.* [ISSN: 0003-2700] 1929. s-m. plus Review Issue and Labguide. USD 1675 print & online eds. Ed(s): Royce W Murray. American Chemical Society, 1155 16th St, NW, Washington, DC 20036; service@acs.org; http://pubs.acs.org. Illus., index, adv. Refereed. Circ: 7734. Vol. ends: Dec. Online: Pub.; EBSCO Publishing, EBSCO Host; OhioLINK; SwetsWise Online Content. *Indexed:* AS&TI, BioEngAb, CABA, CJPI, ChemAb, DSA, EngInd, EnvAb, EnvInd, ExcerpMed, FPA, FS&TA, ForAb, GSI, HortAb, IndVet, MinerAb, OceAb, PetrolAb, PollutAb, RRTA, S&F, SCI, SSCI, SWRA, VB, WAE&RSA, WRCInf. *Bk. rev.:* Varying number and length, 24 total in 2006 in 4 issues. *Aud.:* Ac, Sa.

Analytical Chemistry "explores the latest concepts in analytical measurements and the best new ways to increase accuracy, selectivity, sensitivity, and reproducibility." Covering analytical measurements research in "bioanalysis, electrochemistry, mass spectrometry, microscale systems, environmental analysis, separations, and spectroscopy," this title was the most highly cited and had the highest 2005 impact factor among journals in the analytical chemistry or crystallography categories. The first issue each month offers "features and news articles about new analytical concepts, novel apparatus, research published in other international journals, developments in computers and on the web, and evolving approaches to analytical chemistry education." Book, software, and product reviews are included in a few issues each year. Fast-tracked research (accelerated articles) and research articles are published in every issue. Recommended for academic libraries supporting chemistry and related curricula. Site-wide online access is available with or without print and includes post-review preprints (ASAP Articles). Backfile to 1947 also available. Supporting information for some papers is available online at no charge. E-mail alerts, RSS feeds, and audio content available on the web site. DOIs assigned; cited references linked via ChemPort and CrossRef among others. Article-level openURL linking via CrossRef DOI. Publisher is COUNTER compliant.

1196. Journal of Applied Crystallography. [ISSN: 0021-8898] 1968. bi-m. USD 755 print & online eds. Ed(s): Peter Strickland. Blackwell Munksgaard, Rosenoerns Alle 1, PO Box 227, Copenhagen V, 1502, Denmark; fsub@mail.munksgaard.dk; http://www.munksgaard.dk/. Illus., adv. Refereed. Circ: 1250. Reprint: PSC. *Indexed:* A&ATA, C&ISA, CerAb, ChemAb, CompLI, IAA, SCI. *Aud.:* Ac, Sa.

Covers crystallography technique and theory. Billed by the publisher bills as "main vehicle for the publication of small-angle scattering papers and powder diffraction techniques" and the "primary place where crystallographic computer program information is published." Research papers cover "all areas of science where crystallographic methods are used." Occasional conference proceedings offered as supplements, a recent example is entirely open access on the IUCr web site. Celebrating its 40th anniversary in 2007, the title had the highest 2005 impact factor of among crystallography journals with a trend of increasing impact. Site-wide online access is available with print or alone at a slightly reduced price. DOIs assigned. Cited references are linked via ChemPort and CrossRef. Citing references in other IUCr journals are also linked. Supplementary content accompanies articles, including three-dimensional images. E-mail alerts and RSS feeds available from the publisher web site. OpenURL linking at the article level via the Blackwell Science Synergy platform, and Blackwell is COUNTER compliant.

1197. *Journal of Chromatography A.* Incorporates: *Chromatographic Reviews;* Supersedes (in 1958): *Chromatographic Methods.* [ISSN: 0021-9673] 1956. 78x/yr. EUR 13510. Ed(s): R W Giese, J G Dorsey. Elsevier BV, Radarweg 29, Amsterdam, 1043 NX, Netherlands; nlinfo-f@elsevier.nl; http://www.elsevier.nl. Illus., index, adv. Refereed. Circ: 1700. Microform: PQC. Online: EBSCO Publishing, EBSCO Host; Gale; IngentaConnect; OhioLINK; ScienceDirect; SwetsWise Online Content. *Indexed:* Agr, BiolAb, CABA, ChemAb, DSA, EngInd, ExcerpMed, FPA, FS&TA, ForAb, HortAb, IndVet, PollutAb, RRTA, S&F, SCI, SSCI, VB, WAE&RSA, WRCInf. *Aud.:* Ac, Sa.

Journal of Chromatography A publishes "original research and critical reviews on all aspects of fundamental and applied separation science." Covers "chromatography and related techniques, electromigration techniques (e.g. electrophoresis, electrochromatography), hyphenated and other multi-dimensional techniques, sample preparation, and detection methods such as mass spectrometry." Most articles are regular, full-length research papers, but issues may also offer short communications, discussions, technical notes, invited review articles, and a regular news/calendar section. Articles are arranged by techniques covered, including sample preparation, column liquid chromotography, gas chromatography, and electrophoresis and electrochromatography. Symposium volumes are published. The second and final issue of each volume contains a subject index for the volume. The audience for this title comprises analytical chemists, biochemists, clinical chemists, and others "concerned with the separation and identification of mixtures or compounds in mixtures." Online site-wide access is available with or without the print, and includes articles in press. Backfile to 1958 is available separately. E-mail alerts available. DOIs assigned; cited and citing references are linked. OpenURL linking is at the article level. Publisher is COUNTER compliant with some limitations.

Inorganic

1198. *Coordination Chemistry Reviews.* [ISSN: 0010-8545] 1966. 24x/yr. EUR 5392. Ed(s): Dr. A. B.P. Lever. Elsevier BV, Radarweg 29, Amsterdam, 1043 NX, Netherlands; nlinfo-f@elsevier.nl; http://www.elsevier.nl. Illus., adv. Refereed. Vol. ends: No. 206 - No. 223. Microform: PQC. Online: EBSCO Publishing, EBSCO Host; Gale; IngentaConnect; OhioLINK; ScienceDirect; SwetsWise Online Content. *Indexed:* CerAb, ChemAb, SCI. *Aud.:* Ac, Sa.

Publishes review articles of current research topics and techniques in coordination chemistry, including organometallic, theoretical, and bioinorganic chemistry. Main group and transitional metal group chemistry are also covered. Themed special issues are published; recent examples include anion complexation, and metallocene complexes as catalysts. Issues may also be dedicated to publication of conference proceedings or invited conference lectures. The audience is comprised of inorganic and organometallic chemists. Ranks second among the 43 inorganic and nuclear chemistry titles by 2005 impact factor. Recommended for academic and research libraries supporting research in coordination chemistry. Site-wide online access available with print or alone and includes articles in press. E-mail and RSS alerts of new web site content are available. DOIs assigned. Cited references are linked via Scopus, ScienceDirect, and CrossRef. Citing references are linked via Scopus. Article-level openURL linking is possible. Publisher is COUNTER compliant.

1199. *Dalton Transactions (Print Edition): an international journal of inorganic chemistry.* Former titles (until 2003): *Journal of the Chemical Society. Dalton Transactions (Print Edition);* (until 2001): *Dalton (Cambridge);* Incorporates in part (in Jan. 2000): *Acta Chemica Scandinavica;* Which was formed by the 1989 merger of: *Acta Chemica Scandinavica. Series A: Physical and Organic Chemistry; Acta Chemica Scandinavica. Series B: Organic Chemistry and Biochemistry;* Which superseded in part (1947-1973): *Acta Chemica Scandinavica; Dalton Transactions;* Supersedes in part: *Chemical Society, London. Journal. Section A: Inorganic, Physical and Theoretical Chemistry.* [ISSN: 1477-9226] 1972. w. GBP 2352 print & online eds. Ed(s): Dr. Jamie Humphrey. Royal Society of Chemistry, Thomas Graham House, Science Park, Milton Rd, Cambridge, CB4 0WF, United Kingdom; sales@rsc.org; http://www.rsc.org. Illus., index, adv. Refereed. Vol. ends: Dec. Microform: PQC. Online: EBSCO Publishing, EBSCO Host; OCLC Online Computer Library Center, Inc.; OhioLINK; SwetsWise Online Content. *Indexed:* AS&TI, ChemAb, EngInd, SCI. *Aud.:* Ac, Sa.

Dalton Transactions covers "all aspects of the chemistry of inorganic and organometallic compounds." Papers at the interfaces of inorganic chemistry with other disciplines, such as biomedicine and materials science, are encouraged. Scope includes organometallics and catalysis, bioinorganic chemistry, solid state and coordination chemistry, inorganic materials, and properties and reactions. Publication frequency increased from semi-monthly to weekly in 2006. Publishes full papers, communications, and letters. Perspective and Frontier articles are invited, and editors have recently increased the frequency of these. *Dalton Transactions* retains its claim to the shortest time from submission to publication for inorganic chemistry, with a typical publication time from receipt to publication of 80 days for full papers, and 45 days for communications. Site-wide online access is available with full institutional subscription or alone, and includes pre-publication "Advance Articles." Web site features "Web Themes," clusters of articles selected by guest editors on a particular topic, intended to complement Dalton Discussion theme issues in print. E-mail alerts and RSS feeds available. Some open access content available through an author pays model. DOIs assigned; cited and citing references linked via ChemPort, CrossRef, and others. OpenURL linking is at the issue level. Publisher is COUNTER compliant.

1200. *European Journal of Inorganic Chemistry.* Formed by the merger of part of (1947-1998): *Chemische Berichte;* Which was formed by the merger of part of (1929-1947): *Berichte der Deutschen Chemischen Gesellschaft Abteilung A: Vereins-Nachrichten;* Part of (1929-1947): *Berichte der Deutschen Chemischen Gesellschaft Abteilung B: Abhandlungen;* Both of which superseded (1868-1928): *Berichte der Deutschen Chemischen Gesellschaft;* Part of (1871-1998): *Gazzetta Chimica Italiana;* Part of (1905-1998): *Revista Portuguesa de Quimica;* Part of (1951-1998): *Acta Chimica Hungarica: Models in Chemistry;* Part of (1907-1998): *Societe Chimique de France. Bulletin;* Which was formerly (until 1946): *Bulletin de la Societe Chimique de France. Memoires;* Part of (1972-1998): *Hemika Hronika. Nea Seira;* Which was formerly (1969-1970): *Hemika Hronika. Epistemonike Ekdosis;* Part of (1882-1998): *Recueil des Travaux Chimiques des Pays-Bas;* Which was formerly (until 1920): *Recueil des Travaux Chimiques des Pays-Bas et de la Belgique;* (until 1897): *Recueil des Travaux Chimiques des Pays-Bas;* Part of (1945-1998): *Societes Chimiques Belges. Bulletin;* Which was formerly (until 1944): *Societe Chimique de Belgique. Bulletin;* (1887-1903): *De l'Association Belge des Chimistes. Bulletin;* Part of (1990-1998): *Anales de Quimica;* Which was formed by the merger of (1989-1990): *Anales de quimica. Serie A, Quimica Fisica e Ingenieria Quimica;* Which was formerly (until 1989): *Anales de Quimica. Serie A, Quimica Fisica y Quimica Tecnica;* (1903-1990): *Anales de Quimica. Serie B, Quimica Inorganica y Quimica Analitica;* (1903-1990): *Anales de Quimica. Serie C, Quimica Organica y Bioquimica;* All of which superseded in part (in 1980): *Anales de Quimica;* Which was formerly (until 1967): *Anales de la Real Sociedad Espanola de Fisica y Quimica. Serie B, Quimica;* Which superseded in part (in 1948): *Anales de Fisica y Quimica;* Which was formerly (1903-1940): *Anales de la Sociedad Espanola de Fisica y Quimica.* [ISSN: 1434-1948] 1998. 36x/yr. EUR 3559.

Ed(s): Karen J Hindson. Wiley - VCH Verlag GmbH & Co. KGaA, Boschstr 12, Weinheim, 69469, Germany; subservice@wiley-vch.de; http://www3.interscience.wiley.com/cgi-bin/home. Illus., index, adv. Sample. Refereed. Vol. ends: Dec. Online: EBSCO Publishing, EBSCO Host; OhioLINK; SwetsWise Online Content; Wiley InterScience. *Indexed:* ChemAb, SCI. *Aud.:* Ac, Sa.

European Journal of Inorganic Chemistry expanded from 12 to 24 issues per year in 2003, and 36 issues have been planned for 2007. Celebrating its tenth anniversary in its current form, *EurJIC* is "the fastest growing journal in inorganic chemistry." The title is published by Wiley on behalf of 13 professional societies throughout Europe. Covering "the entire spectrum of inorganic, organometallic, bioinorganic, and solid-state chemistry" with microreviews, short communications, and full papers, the intended audience is "chemists of all disciplines." Site-wide online access is available with or without print, and it includes "Early View" in press articles, a feature implemented in 2003. RSS feeds and e-mail alerts are available. DOIs assigned, and cited references are linked. Citing references within the Wiley Interscience platform are also linked via Wiley's "citation tracking" feature, available to subscribers only. OpenURL linking is at the article level via CrossRef DOI. OpenURL linking is at the journal level.

1201. *Inorganic Chemistry.* [ISSN: 0020-1669] 1962. 24x/yr. USD 3174 print & online eds. Ed(s): Richard Eisenberg, Arlene Bristol. American Chemical Society, 1155 16th St, NW, Washington, DC 20036; service@acs.org; http://pubs.acs.org. Illus., index, adv. Refereed. Circ: 4000 Paid. Vol. ends: Dec. Online: Pub.; EBSCO Publishing, EBSCO Host; OhioLINK; SwetsWise Online Content. *Indexed:* ChemAb, ExcerpMed, GSI, S&F, SCI. *Aud.:* Ac, Sa.

"*Inorganic Chemistry* publishes fundamental studies in all phases of inorganic chemistry," both experimental and theoretical, with emphasis on "synthesis, structure, thermodynamics, reactivity, spectroscopy, and bonding properties of significant new and known compounds." Bioinorganic chemistry, relevant aspects of organometallic chemistry, solid-state phenomena, chemical bonding, materials, and nanochemistry are all considered within its scope. Accepts brief communications and full articles. Up to three thematic forum issues per year on a "multidisciplinary topic of growing interest." In the category of inorganic and nuclear chemistry, this title published the most articles in 2005, had the most cumulative citations as of 2005, and ranked sixth in 2005 impact factor. A core title for academic and research libraries supporting inorganic chemistry programs. Supplementary information for some papers, including text and images, is available online at no charge. Site-wide online access is available with or without print, and it includes post-review preprints (ASAP Articles). DOIs assigned; cited references are linked. OpenURL linking is at the issue level. Publisher is COUNTER compliant.

1202. *Inorganica Chimica Acta.* Incorporates: *Chimica Acta Reviews.* [ISSN: 0020-1693] 1967. 15x/yr. EUR 8996. Ed(s): U. Belluco, R J Puddephat. Elsevier BV, Radarweg 29, Amsterdam, 1043 NX, Netherlands; nlinfo-f@elsevier.nl; http://www.elsevier.nl. Illus., index, adv. Sample. Refereed. Microform: PQC. Online: EBSCO Publishing, EBSCO Host; Gale; IngentaConnect; OhioLINK; ScienceDirect; SwetsWise Online Content. *Indexed:* ChemAb, ExcerpMed, S&F, SCI. *Aud.:* Ac, Sa.

Inorganica Chimica Acta publishes "research in all aspects of Inorganic Chemistry" in the form of full research articles, short research reports (notes), and regular reviews. Topical scope includes synthesis and reactivity of coordination and metallorganic compounds, various properties of inorganic molecules, catalytic reactions, electron transfer and electrochemical investigations involving inorganic systems. Audience comprises inorganic, organometallic, bioinorganic, and catalytic chemists. A frequent offering is "Protagonists in Chemistry," featuring profiles of researchers in the field. Online site-wide

access is available with or without print, and includes in-press articles. E-mail alerts available. DOIs assigned; cited and citing references are linked. OpenURL linking is at the article level. Publisher is COUNTER compliant with some limitations.

1203. *Polyhedron.* Incorporated: *Journal of Inorganic and Nuclear Chemistry; Inorganic and Nuclear Chemistry Letters.* [ISSN: 0277-5387] 1982. 18x/yr. EUR 7328. Ed(s): C. E. Housecroft, G. Christou. Pergamon, The Boulevard, Langford Ln, East Park, Kidlington, OX5 1GB, United Kingdom; nlinfo-f@elsevier.nl. Illus., index. Sample. Refereed. Microform: MIM; PQC. Online: EBSCO Publishing, EBSCO Host; Gale; IngentaConnect; OhioLINK; ScienceDirect; SwetsWise Online Content. *Indexed:* ChemAb, SCI. *Aud.:* Ac, Sa.

Polyhedron publishes original experimental and theoretical papers in "synthetic chemistry, coordination chemistry, organometallic chemistry, bioinorganic chemistry, and solid-state and materials chemistry." Although placed with inorganic chemistry in this review, the target audience includes both inorganic chemists and biochemists. Includes several commissioned review articles ("Polyhedron Reports") each year, and collections of research papers on timely themes ("Polyhedron Symposia-in-Print"). Occasional thematic issues honor prominent researchers; a recent example is an issue honoring Michael B. Hursthouse. Online site-wide access available with or without print, and includes in-press articles. Separate backfile available. E-mail alerts available. DOIs assigned; cited and citing references are linked. OpenURL linking is at the article level. Publisher is COUNTER compliant.

Organic

1204. *Aldrichimica Acta.* Formerly: *Kardinex Sheets.* [ISSN: 0002-5100] 1967. q. Free. Ed(s): Alfonse Runquist. Aldrich, 1001 W St Paul Ave, Milwaukee, WI 53233; aldrich@sial.com; http://www.sigma-aldrich.com. Illus., adv. Circ: 200000 Controlled. *Indexed:* ChemAb, SCI. *Aud.:* Ac, Sa.

"*Aldrichimica Acta* publishes review articles on innovative chemistry research that are written by leading experts." Currently celebrating its 40th year of publication, this title, which began as a marketing tool for Aldrich, boasts the highest 2005 impact factor of organic chemistry titles listed in the Journal Citation Reports. Advertising is extensive and exclusively for Sigma-Aldrich products, but Aldrich, in an interesting take on the question of who pays for open access to scholarly output, has made its entire archive available online at no charge. That and the fact that articles are all extensive reviews may account for the high impact of the title relative to other titles in its subcategory. A recommended addition to the online collections of academic and special libraries that support work in pure and applied chemistry.

1205. *Beilstein Journal of Organic Chemistry.* [ISSN: 1860-5397] 2005. irreg. Free. Ed(s): Jonathan Clyden. Beilstein - Institut zur Foerderung der Chemischen Wissenschaften, Trakehner Str 7/9, Frankfurt am Main, 60487, Germany; info@beilstein-institut.de; http://www.beilstein-institut.de. Refereed. *Indexed:* SCI. *Bk. rev.:* Number and length vary. *Aud.:* Ac, Sa.

Beilstein Journal of Organic Chemistry is a peer-reviewed online journal covering "organic chemistry in its broadest sense, including: organic synthesis, organic reactions, natural products chemistry, supramolecular chemistry and chemical biology." Publishes full research papers, brief preliminary communications, short evaluative book reviews, focused commentaries on recent research findings or other contemporary issues, debate articles featuring arguments "not essentially based on practical research," and invited reviews. All content is open access. DOIs assigned.

1206. *Biomacromolecules.* [ISSN: 1525-7797] 2000. m. USD 1532. Ed(s): Ann-Christine Albertsson. American Chemical Society, 1155 16th St, NW, Washington, DC 20036; service@acs.org; http://pubs.acs.org. Refereed. *Indexed:* BiolAb, ChemAb, EngInd, ExcerpMed, SCI. *Aud.:* Ac, Sa.

Biomacromolecules is an "interdisciplinary journal publishing original research that explores the interactions of macromolecules with biological systems and their environments as well as biological approaches to the design of polymeric materials." Research in a range of applied areas is published, "including consumer products, biosensors, biocompatible surfaces, multifunctional surfaces, polymeric drugs, and polymers for engineering applications." This title has achieved an impressive citation record in a short time and is ranked eighth by 2005 impact factor among organic chemistry titles. Frequency increased to 12 issues per year in 2006, up from six in 2005. Content comprises primarily research articles, but includes critical reviews, brief communications, and notes. Issues may include symposium or other proceedings. Recommended for libraries supporting polymer research or related programs in biochemistry or molecular biology. Site-wide online access is available with or without print, and includes post-review preprints (ASAP articles). Supporting information for some papers is available online at no charge, and includes some image and video files. DOIs assigned; cited references linked via ChemPort and CrossRef, among others. Article-level openURL linking via CrossRef DOI. Publisher is COUNTER compliant.

1207. *European Journal of Organic Chemistry.* Formed by the merger of part of (1818-1998): *Liebigs Annalen;* Which was formerly (until 1995): *Liebigs Annalen der Chemie;* (until 1978): *Justus Liebigs Annalen der Chemie;* (until 1840): *Annalen der Pharmacie;* (until 1832): *Magazin fuer Pharmacie;* (until 1825): *Magazin fuer die Neuesten Erfahrungen, Entdeckungen und Berichtigungen im Gebiete der Pharmacie;* (until 1823): *Allgemeine Bordische Annalen der Chemie fuer die Freunde der Naturkunde und Arzneiwissenschaft im Russischen Reiche;* Part of (1907-1998): *Societe Chimique de France. Bulletin;* Which was formerly (until 1946): *Bulletin de la Societe Chimique de France. Memoires;* Part of (1945-1998): *Societes Chimiques Belges. Bulletin;* Part of (1871-1998): *Gazzetta Chimica Italiana;* Part of (1990-1998): *Anales de Quimica;* Part of (1905-1998): *Revista Portuguesa de Quimica;* Part of (1970-1998): *Hemika Hronika. Nea Seira;* Which was formerly (1969-1970): *Hemika Hronika. Epistemonike Ekdosis;* Part of (1951-1998): *Acta Chimica Hungarica: Models in Chemistry;* Part of (1882-1998): *Recueil des Travaux Chimiques des Pays-Bas;* Which was formerly (until 1920): *Recueil des Travaux Chimiques des Pays-Bas et la Belguique;* (until 1897): *Recueil des Travaux Chimiques des Pays-Bas.* [ISSN: 1434-193X] 1998. 36x/yr. EUR 4330. Ed(s): Haymo Ross. Wiley - VCH Verlag GmbH & Co. KGaA, Boschstr 12, Weinheim, 69469, Germany; adsales@wiley-vch.de; http://www3.interscience.wiley.com/cgi-bin/home. Illus., index, adv. Sample. Refereed. Online: EBSCO Publishing, EBSCO Host; OhioLINK; SwetsWise Online Content; Wiley InterScience. *Indexed:* CABA, ChemAb, DSA, FPA, ForAb, HortAb, IndVet, PollutAb, S&F, SCI, VB, ZooRec. *Aud.:* Ac, Sa.

"*European Journal of Organic Chemistry* publishes full papers, short communications, and microreviews from the entire spectrum of synthetic organic, bioorganic and physical-organic chemistry." It is aimed at "chemists of all disciplines." In 1998, eight titles were merged to form this and a companion title, *European Journal of Inorganic Chemistry,* both of which are co-owned by 13 of 14 European societies comprising the Editorial Union of Chemical Societies. Publication frequency will increase from 24 issues in 2006 to 36 in 2007. Themed issues are published, and one is planned for the tenth anniversary of the title featuring papers from the 15th European Symposium on Organic Chemistry. Site-wide online access is available with or without print, and includes "Early View" pre-prints. E-mail alerts and RSS feeds available. DOIs assigned, and cited references are linked. Citing references within the Wiley Interscience platform are also linked via Wiley's "citation tracking" feature, available to subscribers only. Article-level openURL linking via CrossRef DOI.

1208. *The Journal of Organic Chemistry.* [ISSN: 0022-3263] 1936. 24x/yr. USD 2608 print & online eds. Ed(s): C Dale Poulter. American Chemical Society, 1155 16th St, NW, Washington, DC 20036; service@acs.org; http://pubs.acs.org. Illus., index, adv. Refereed. Circ: 9000 Paid. Vol. ends: Dec. Online: Pub.; EBSCO Publishing, EBSCO Host; OhioLINK; SwetsWise Online Content. *Indexed:* BiolAb, CABA, ChemAb, DSA, EngInd, ExcerpMed, FPA, FS&TA, ForAb, GSI, HortAb, IndVet, S&F, SCI, VB. *Aud.:* Ac, Sa.

In 26 issues per year, *Journal of Organic Chemistry* publishes "novel, important findings of fundamental research in all branches of the theory and practice of organic and bioorganic chemistry" in the form of full articles and notes, invited topical mini-reviews, and invited contributions from recipients of national ACS

awards in organic chemistry. Bibliographies of recent reviews, listed by source publication, are published approximately quarterly. Boasts the highest cumulative citations in the organic chemistry category and ranked seventh by 2005 impact factor. A core title for the subdiscipline, it is recommended for academic libraries supporting graduate chemistry programs. Site-wide online access is available with or without print and includes post-review preprints (ASAP articles). Supplementary information including text and image files is offered online. DOIs assigned; cited references linked via ChemPort, CrossRef, and others. Article-level openURL linking via CrossRef DOI. Publisher is COUNTER compliant.

1209. *Macromolecules.* [ISSN: 0024-9297] 1968. 24x/yr. USD 3183 print & online eds. Ed(s): Timothy P Lodge. American Chemical Society, 1155 16th St, NW, Washington, DC 20036; service@acs.org; http://pubs.acs.org. Illus., index, adv. Refereed. Circ: 4447 Paid. Vol. ends: Dec. Online: Pub.; EBSCO Publishing, EBSCO Host; OhioLINK; SwetsWise Online Content. *Indexed:* BioEngAb, C&ISA, CerAb, ChemAb, EngInd, FS&TA, IAA, SCI. *Aud.:* Ac, Sa.

Macromolecules publishes on "fundamentals of polymer science, including synthesis, polymerization mechanisms and kinetics, chemical modification, and solution/melt/solid-state characteristics, as well as surface properties of organic, inorganic, and naturally occurring polymers." Comprehensive reports, brief communications, and technical notes are published in 26 issues per year. Celebrating its 40th year in 2007, this title boasts the most cumulative citations of any journal in the polymer science category, and ranked third by 2005 impact factor in that category. Recommended for academic libraries supporting polymer research. Site-wide online access is available with or without print and includes post-review preprints (ASAP Articles). From the January 2007 editorial, supplementary information is available online at no charge, and includes text, data sets, and image files. E-mail alerts and RSS feeds available. DOIs assigned; cited references linked via ChemPort, CrossRef, and others. Article-level openURL linking via CrossRef DOI. Publisher is COUNTER compliant.

1210. *Organic & Biomolecular Chemistry.* Formed by the merger of (2001-2002): *Royal Chemical Society. Journal. Perkin Transactions 1;* Which was formerly (until 2001): *Perkin 1;* (until 1999): *Royal Society of Chemistry. Journal: Perkin Transactions 1;* (until 1971): *Chemical Society, London. Journal. Section C. Organic Chemistry;* (2001-2002): *Royal Chemical Society. Journal. Perkin Transactions 2;* Which was formerly (until 2001): *Perkin 2;* (until 1999): *Royal Society of Chemistry. Journal: Perkin Transactions 2;* (until 1971): *Chemistry Society, London. Journal. Section B. Physical Organic Chemistry;* Both of which superseded in part (1848-1877): *Chemical Society. Journal;* Which was formerly (until 1862): *The Chemical Society of London. Quarterly Journal;* (until 1847): *Chemical Society of London. Memoirs and Proceedings;* Which was formed by the 1843 merger of: *Chemical Society of London. Memoirs; Chemical Society of London. Proceedings;* Perkin Transactions 1 incorporated (1994-1998): *Contemporary Organic Synthesis;* Perkin 1 & Perkin 2 incorporated in part (in Jan. 2000): *Acta Chemica Scandinavica;* Which was formed by the merger of (1986-1988): *Acta Chemica Scandinavica A: Physical and Inorganic Chemistry;* Which was formerly (until 1986): *Acta Chemica Scandivavica. Series A: Physical and Inorganic Chemistry;* (1986-1988): *Acta Chemical Scandinavica B: Organic Chemistry and Biochemistry;* Which was formerly (until 1986): *Acta Chemica Scandinavica. Series B: Organic and Biochemistry;* Both of which superseded in part (1947-1973): *Acta Chemica Scandinavica.* [ISSN: 1477-0520] 2003. 24x/yr. GBP 2725 print & online eds. Ed(s): Dr. Vikki Allen. Royal Society of Chemistry, Thomas Graham House, Science Park, Milton Rd, Cambridge, CB4 0WF, United Kingdom; rsc1@rsc.org; http://www.rsc.org. Adv. Refereed. *Indexed:* CABA, ChemAb, EngInd, ForAb, SCI. *Aud.:* Ac, Sa.

Organic & Biomolecular Chemistry publishes "fundamental work on synthetic, physical and biomolecular organic chemistry as well as all organic aspects of: chemical biology, medicinal chemistry, natural product chemistry, supramolecular chemistry, macromolecular chemistry, theoretical chemistry, and catalysis." Rapid, brief communications and full papers are accepted. Boasts the "shortest time to publication in the field." Critical reviews of two types, "Emerging Areas" and "Perspectives," are published by invitation from the editor. *Chemical Science*, launched in 2004, is included as a free supplement with the print of this and several other RSC titles. Recommended for academic libraries supporting chemistry or biochemistry curricula and for research libraries. Site-wide online access is available with or without print and includes and post-review preprints (Advance Articles). E-mail alerts and RSS feeds available. DOIs assigned; cited references linked via ChemPort, CrossRef, and others. Article-level openURL linking via CrossRef DOI. Publisher is COUNTER compliant.

1211. *Organic Letters.* [ISSN: 1523-7060] 1999. 24x/yr. USD 4098 print & online eds. Ed(s): Carol Carr, Amos B Smith. American Chemical Society, 1155 16th St, NW, Washington, DC 20036; service@acs.org; http://pubs.acs.org. Adv. Refereed. Circ: 5500 Paid. Online: Pub.; EBSCO Publishing, EBSCO Host; OhioLINK; SwetsWise Online Content. *Indexed:* BiolAb, ChemAb, SCI, ZooRec. *Aud.:* Ac, Sa.

Organic Letters publishes "brief reports of significant research concerning organic chemistry, including organic synthesis, organometallic, natural product, physical organic, bioorganic, and medicinal chemistry." Emphasis is on rapid communication of research. It covers theory and practice of organic chemistry (including organometallic and materials chemistry), physical and theoretical organic chemistry, natural products isolation and synthesis, new synthetic methodology, and bioorganic and medicinal chemistry. Established as a Scholarly Publishing and Academic Resource Coalition (SPARC) alternative to Elsevier's *Tetrahedron Letters*, to bring the "highest-quality research in organic chemistry to those who need it the most, as quickly as possible, and at a significantly lower price than other journals in that category." The title has gained wide acceptance since its 1999 launch, ranking fifth among organic chemistry journals by 2005 impact factor and by total citations. It is, according to ACS, the "highest-impact communications journal in Organic Chemistry and has been for the past six years." Recommended for academic and other libraries supporting organic chemistry research. Site-wide online access is available with or without print and includes post-review preprints (ASAP articles). Supporting information is available online at no charge, and includes text and image files. DOIs assigned; cited references linked via ChemPort, CrossRef, and others. Article-level openURL linking via CrossRef DOI. Publisher is COUNTER compliant.

1212. *Organometallics.* [ISSN: 0276-7333] 1982. 24x/yr. USD 2992 print & online eds. Ed(s): Dr. Dietmar Seyferth. American Chemical Society, 1155 16th St, NW, Washington, DC 20036; service@acs.org; http://pubs.acs.org. Illus., adv. Refereed. Circ: 3945 Paid. Online: Pub.; EBSCO Publishing, EBSCO Host; OhioLINK; SwetsWise Online Content. *Indexed:* ChemAb, EngInd, SCI. *Aud.:* Ac, Sa.

Organometallics records advances in organometallic, inorganic, organic, and materials chemistry, covering "synthesis, structure, bonding, chemical reactivity and reaction mechanisms, and applications of organometallic and organometalloidal compounds," as well as applications such as "organic and polymer synthesis, catalytic processes, and synthetic aspects of materials science and solid-state chemistry." Brief communications, articles, plus occasional notes and reviews are published for an intended audience of organometallic, inorganic, organic, and materials chemists. Correspondence is also published. The title ranks high in total citations and 2005 impact factor among both organic chemistry and inorganic and nuclear chemistry titles. Recommended for libraries supporting research chemists. Site-wide online access is available with or without print and includes post-review preprints (ASAP articles). Separate backfile available. E-mail alerts and RSS fields available. Supporting information for some papers is available online at no charge, and includes text and images. DOIs assigned; cited references linked via ChemPort, CrossRef, and others. Article-level openURL linking via CrossRef DOI. Publisher is COUNTER compliant.

1213. *Synlett: accounts and rapid communications in synthetic organic chemistry.* [ISSN: 0936-5214] 1989. 20x/yr. EUR 1104.90 (Individuals, EUR 284.90; Students, EUR 69). Ed(s): Dr. K P C Vollhardt. Georg Thieme Verlag, Ruedigerstr 14, Stuttgart, 70469, Germany; kunden.service@thieme.de; http://www.thieme.de/chemistry. Illus., index, adv. Sample. Refereed. Circ: 1950 Paid and controlled. Vol. ends: Dec. Online: EBSCO Publishing, EBSCO Host; OCLC Online Computer Library Center, Inc.; OhioLINK; SwetsWise Online Content. *Indexed:* ChemAb, ExcerpMed, SCI. *Aud.:* Ac, Sa.

Synlett reports "research results and trends in synthetic organic chemistry in short personalized reviews and preliminary communications" in areas that involve organic synthesis. As with *Organic Letters* and *Tetrahedron Letters,* the emphasis is on rapid publication. Content comprises reviews of important recent work written by the researchers, clusters of letters on rapidly evolving topics in designated areas of research, "new tools in synthesis" highlighting techniques and methods in synthetic chemistry, and spotlights on reagents important in current research, chosen by postgraduates. Spotlights are freely available online. In 2006, special issues were published dedicated to Richard Heck and research in China, both featuring invited submissions. International authorship is diverse, but primarily Asian, according to an editiorial in the first 2007 issue. Single-site online access available with print; includes acepted preprints (eFirst). RSS feeds available. DOIs assigned; cited references linked via ChemPort and CrossRef. Article-level openURL linking via CrossRef DOI. Thieme-connect platform usage statistics are COUNTER compliant.

1214. *Synthesis: journal of synthetic organic chemistry.* [ISSN: 0039-7881] 1969. 24x/yr. EUR 1623.90 (Individuals, EUR 458.90; Students, EUR 79). Ed(s): D Enders. Georg Thieme Verlag, Ruedigerstr 14, Stuttgart, 70469, Germany; kunden.service@thieme.de; http://www.thieme.de. Illus., index, adv. Sample. Refereed. Circ: 2500 Paid and controlled. Vol. ends: Dec. Microform: PQC. Online: EBSCO Publishing, EBSCO Host; OCLC Online Computer Library Center, Inc.; OhioLINK; SwetsWise Online Content. *Indexed:* CABA, ChemAb, EngInd, ExcerpMed, HortAb, IndVet, S&F, SCI, VB. *Bk. rev.:* 1 per issue; 500+ words. *Aud.:* Ac, Sa.

Synthesis is "devoted to the advancement of the science of synthetic chemistry, covering all fields of organic chemistry, such as organometallic, organoheteroatom, medicinal, biological, and photochemistry, but also related disciplines." Rising submissions led to increase in publication frequency in 2005 from 18 to 20 issues. Content comprises reviews of recent developments, short papers, feature articles, "Practical Synthetic Procedures (PSP)" with concise descriptions of procedures, and synthesis alert abstracts covering new substances or novel reactions taken from recent literature. There are occasional thematic issues. Print may be purchased alone or with single-site online access. Accepted articles are available online ahead of print publication (eFirst). "Practical Synthetic Procedures (PSP)," synthesis alerts, and book reviews appear to be freely available online. DOIs assigned; cited references linked via ChemPort and CrossRef. Thieme-connect platform usage statistics are COUNTER compliant.

1215. *Tetrahedron.* [ISSN: 0040-4020] 1957. 52x/yr. EUR 15154. Ed(s): L Ghosez. Pergamon, The Boulevard, Langford Ln, East Park, Kidlington, OX5 1GB, United Kingdom. Illus., adv. Refereed. Circ: 3000. Microform: MIM; PQC. Online: EBSCO Publishing, EBSCO Host; Gale; IngentaConnect; OhioLINK; ScienceDirect; SwetsWise Online Content. *Indexed:* BiolAb, CABA, ChemAb, DSA, ExcerpMed, FPA, ForAb, HortAb, IAA, S&F, SCI, ZooRec. *Aud.:* Ac, Sa.

Tetrahedron publishes "experimental and theoretical research results of outstanding significance and timeliness in the field of organic chemistry and its application to related disciplines especially bio-organic chemistry." Topical coverage includes organic synthesis, organic reactions, natural products chemistry, studies of reaction mechanism and various aspects of spectroscopy. Publishes full research papers and critical reviews (Tetrahedron Reports), which are commissioned and may be quite lengthy. As parent of the "Tetrahedron Family" bundle, which includes *Tetrahedron Letters*, *Tetrahedron Asymmetry*, and two bioorganic/medicinal titles, it is notorious for cost, but widely accepted as a core title. Ranks third in total citations among organic chemistry journals, but its 2005 impact factor was near the category aggregate for organic chemistry. Recommended for libraries supporting substantial research programs in organic or bio-organic chemistry. Online site-wide access available with or without print, and includes preprints. RSS alerts available. DOIs assigned; cited and citing references linked via Scopus. Article-level openURL linking. Publisher is partially COUNTER compliant.

1216. *Tetrahedron Letters.* [ISSN: 0040-4039] 1959. 52x/yr. EUR 12058. Ed(s): B Ganem, Lin Guo Qiang. Pergamon, The Boulevard, Langford Ln, East Park, Kidlington, OX5 1GB, United Kingdom. Illus., index, adv. Refereed. Circ: 3380. Vol. ends: Dec (No. 42). Microform: MIM; PQC. Online: EBSCO Publishing, EBSCO Host; Gale; IngentaConnect; OhioLINK; ScienceDirect; SwetsWise Online Content. *Indexed:* Agr, BiolAb, CABA, ChemAb, DSA, ExcerpMed, FPA, ForAb, HortAb, IndVet, S&F, SCI, VB, ZooRec. *Aud.:* Ac, Sa.

Tetrahedron Letters offers coverage of "developments in techniques, structures, methods and conclusions in experimental and theoretical organic chemistry." Emphasis is on rapid publication of short communications. Published 1,956 articles in 2005, more than in any other organic chemistry title. In 2005, ranked second in total cites among organic chemistry journals, topped only by *Journal of Organic Chemistry.* Like *Tetrahedron,* known both for its high price and its standing among research chemists. Recommended for libraries supporting substantial organic or bio-organic chemistry research programs, but note the SPARC alternative *Organic Letters.* Site-wide online access available with or without print, and includes preprints. RSS feeds available. DOIs assigned; cited and citing references are linked via Scopus records. Article-level openURL linking. Publisher is partially COUNTER compliant.

Physical

1217. *Chemical Physics Letters.* [ISSN: 0009-2614] 1967. 102x/yr. EUR 12859. Ed(s): D C Clary, A Zewail. Elsevier BV, North-Holland, Sara Burgerhartstraat 25, Amsterdam, 1055 KV, Netherlands; nlinfo-f@elsevier.nl; http://www.elsevier.nl/homepage/about/us/regional_sites.htt. Illus., index, adv. Refereed. Microform: PQC. Online: EBSCO Publishing, EBSCO Host; Gale; IngentaConnect; OhioLINK; ScienceDirect; SwetsWise Online Content. *Indexed:* ChemAb, EngInd, IAA, MathR, SCI. *Aud.:* Ac, Sa.

"*Chemical Physics Letters* publishes brief reports of significant, original and timely research in the field of chemical physics," emphasizing "the structures, properties and dynamics of molecules, solid surfaces, interfaces, condensed phases, polymers, nanostructures and biomolecular systems." Articles in five categories are published: gaseous molecules, condensed phases, nanostructures and materials, biomolecules, and new experimental or theoretical methods. The intended audience is chemical and molecular physicists and physical chemists. Within each volume, two pieces comprising six "issues" are published, so that in total about 33 pieces are received each year. The title ranks fourth in the JCR physical chemistry category in number of articles published in 2005. As of 2003, this title had been cited more than any journal in the JCR physical chemistry category (although it was not included in that category). By 2005, when it had been added to the physical chemistry category, it ranked third in total cites. Recommended for academic and research libraries supporting physical chemistry or related research programs. Site-wide online access is available with or without print. Accepted articles are available online in advance of print. E-mail alerts of new content are available. DOIs assigned. Cited and cited references are linked via records in Scopus. Article level openURL linking possible. Publisher is COUNTER compliant.

1218. *Chemistry of Materials.* [ISSN: 0897-4756] 1989. 24x/yr. USD 1700 print & online eds. Ed(s): Leonard V Interrante. American Chemical Society, 1155 16th St, NW, Washington, DC 20036; service@acs.org; https://portal.chemistry.org/. Illus., index, adv. Sample. Refereed. Circ: 3847 Paid. Vol. ends: Dec. Online: Pub.; EBSCO Publishing, EBSCO Host; OhioLINK; SwetsWise Online Content. *Indexed:* C&ISA, ChemAb, EngInd, SCI. *Aud.:* Ac, Sa.

Offering "molecular-level perspective at the interface of chemistry, chemical engineering, and materials science," *Chemistry of Materials* publishes 26 issues annually, increasing from monthly publication in 2003. "Research areas of interest are solid-state chemistry, both inorganic and organic, and polymer chemistry, especially as directed to the development of materials with novel and/or useful optical, electrical, magnetic, catalytic, and mechanical properties." Publishing both theoretical and experimental work, typical issues offer several short communications and 30–40 or more full articles. There are occasional thematic issues; "Templated Materials" is a planned topic for 2008. An increasingly important title supporting materials-related research across a range of disciplines; in 2005 was most cited journal in the multidisciplinary materials science category. Editors reported increased submissions in 2006, with a notable increase in international submissions. Site-wide online access is available with or without print and includes post-review preprints (ASAP articles). Supporting information for some papers is available online at no charge. OpenURL linking at the journal level; COUNTER compliant usage reports. DOIs assigned, with links to cited references via ChemPort and CrossRef, among others.

Journal of Chemical Physics. See Physics section.

1219. *The Journal of Physical Chemistry Part A: Molecules, Spectroscopy, Kinetics, Environment and General Theory.* Supersedes in part (in 1997): *Journal of Physical Chemistry;* Which was formerly (until 1952): *Journal of Physical and Colloid Chemistry;* (until 1946): *Journal of Physical Chemistry.* [ISSN: 1089-5639] 1896. 51x/yr. USD 6289 print & online eds. Ed(s): George C Schatz. American Chemical Society, 1155 16th St, NW, Washington, DC 20036; service@acs.org; http://pubs.acs.org. Index, adv. Refereed. Circ: 4862. Online: Pub.; EBSCO Publishing, EBSCO Host; OhioLINK; SwetsWise Online Content. *Indexed:* AS&TI, CEA, ChemAb, DSA, EngInd, FS&TA, GSI, IAA, M&GPA, OceAb, PetrolAb, S&F, SCI, SWRA, WRCInf. *Aud.:* Ac, Sa.

The parent title *Journal of Physical Chemistry* was divided into two parts in 1997. *JPC:A* emphasizes research on molecular "dynamics, spectroscopy, gaseous clusters, molecular beams, kinetics, atmospheric and environmental physical chemistry, molecular structure, bonding, quantum chemistry, and general theory," plus two new categories for 2007, excited states and green chemistry. *JPC:B* covers "nanostructures, micelles, macro-molecules, statistical mechanics and thermodynamics of condensed matter, biophysical chemistry, and general physical chemistry" and has become a venue for "soft matter, surfactants, membranes, thermodynamics, medium effects and biophysical chemistry." A third section, *JPC:C (Nanomaterials and Interfaces)* began publication in 2007, covering "nanomaterials, interfaces, catalysis, and special topics such as electron transport, electronic and optical devices and energy conversion and storage." All three titles are published weekly and include brief letters, full articles, and feature articles. Frequent festschrifts are published; 11 total were published in 2006 in *JPC:A* and JPC:B. As of 2005, *JPC:B* ranked first by total cites in the physical chemistry category, while *JPC:A* ranked fifth. Site-wide online access is available with or without print and includes post-review preprints (ASAP articles). Electronic Supporting Information (ESI) for some papers is available online at no charge. E-mail and RSS alerts of new content are available. DOIs assigned. Cited references are linked using a variety of services (e.g., CrossRef, Medline).

1220. *Langmuir: the A C S journal of surfaces and colloids.* [ISSN: 0743-7463] 1985. 24x/yr. USD 3550 print & online eds. Ed(s): David G Whitten. American Chemical Society, 1155 16th St, NW, Washington, DC 20036; service@acs.org; http://pubs.acs.org. Illus., index, adv. Refereed. Circ: 3936. Vol. ends: Dec. Online: Pub.; EBSCO Publishing, EBSCO Host; OhioLINK; SwetsWise Online Content. *Indexed:* C&ISA, ChemAb, EngInd, SCI. *Aud.:* Ac, Sa.

Langmuir offers "new and original experimental and theoretical research in the fields of colloids, surfaces, and interfaces." Topical coverage includes "structure, properties, and reactivity of colloidal systems (micelles, vesicles, emulsions, gels, polymers, nanoparticles and surfactants), electrochemistry, imaging, forces and spectroscopy, films, biological colloids and interfaces, biopolymers, nanostructures, multicomponent systems, polymers, and materials (including crystal growth, nucleation, and liquid crystals)." Twenty-six issues per year offer brief letters and full articles. As of 2005, ranked second in cumulative citations in the JCR physical chemistry category. Recommended for academic and research libraries supporting research in physical chemistry. Site-wide online access is available with or without print and includes post-review preprints (ASAP articles). Supporting information for some papers is available online at no charge. E-mail and RSS alerts of new content are available. DOIs assigned. Cited references are linked via a variety of services. Article-level openURL linking is possible via CrossRef DOI. COUNTER compliant.

1221. Physical Chemistry Chemical Physics. Formed by the merger of (1990-1998): *Journal of the Chemical Society. Faraday Transactions;* Which was formed by the merger of (1972-1989): *Journal of the Chemical Society. Faraday Transactions I;* (1972-1989): *Journal of the Chemical Society. Faraday Transactions II;* Incorporates (1968-1984): *Faraday Society. Symposia;* Which superseded (1905-1971): *Faraday Society Transactions;* and (1897-1998): *Berichte der Bunsen-Gesellschaft;* Which was formerly (until 1980): *Berichte der Bunsengesellschaft fur Physikalische Chemie;* (until 1962): *Zeitschrift fuer Elektrochemie;* (until 1951): *Zeitschrift fuer Elektrochemie und Angewandte Physikalische Chemie.* [ISSN: 1463-9076] 1999. w. 48/yr. GBP 2273 print & online eds. Ed(s): Mr. Philip Earis. Royal Society of Chemistry, Thomas Graham House, Science Park, Milton Rd, Cambridge, CB4 0WF, United Kingdom; sales@rsc.org; http://www.rsc.org. Illus., index. Sample. Refereed. Online: EBSCO Publishing, EBSCO Host; OCLC Online Computer Library Center, Inc.; OhioLINK; SwetsWise Online Content. *Indexed:* C&ISA, CEA, ChemAb, S&F, SCI. *Aud.:* Ac, Sa.

PCCP publishes rapid communications, invited articles, and research papers on a broad array of topics at the interface of physics and chemistry, including biophysical chemistry. Frequent themed issues are published; a series of themed issues was offered in 2006 on nanoscience and nanotechnology. Publication frequency increased from biweekly to weekly in 2006, with a concurrent increase in the number of themed issues and invited articles. This title boasts a very rapid time from submission to publication that outpaces other physical chemistry letters and communications journals. Run by an ownership board with equal representation from 14 owner societies, mostly European and none North American. Biophysical papers in *PCCP* are simultaneously published in *Chemical Biology* (www.rsc.org/chembiolvj), and as a result of high biophysical content, *PCCP* was recently selected for indexing in MEDLINE. Print issues of *PCCP* incorporate *Chemical Science* and *Chemical Technology* as free supplements. Recommended for academic libraries supporting graduate curricula in chemistry or physics. Site-wide online access is available with or without print and includes and post-review preprints (Advance Articles). E-mail and RSS alerts of new content are available. DOIs assigned; reference linking via ChemPort and CrossRef. Article-level openURL linking possible via CrossRef DOI. Publisher is COUNTER compliant.

■ CHILDREN

See also Parenting; and Teenagers sections.

Lucy Duhon, Serials Librarian, Carlson Library, University of Toledo, Toledo, OH 43606; lucy.duhon@utoledo.edu

Introduction

Magazines for children today cover a variety of topics and serve wide audiences. But most have one thing in common: enticing children to read and learn about their environment by engaging them with articles, illustrations, interactive features, and opportunities for creativity and feedback. While scores of children's magazines have ceased publication over the last decade, perhaps because of market saturation or intense competition with the Internet, or even because of demographic shifts, the ones that thrive are high-quality and have successfully made the transition to engaging the Internet generation, with most running complementary web sites alongside their print publications. A dozen or so continue to be flagships even after more than a quarter century of publication.

Serial publications for children are written either for dedicated audiences or for general readers; some reach wide audiences via commercial channels while others are aimed at much smaller, more specialized audiences. Most of the highest-quality publications listed below contain no advertising. Preschool magazines are generally aimed at either the child alone or at the caretaker and child. The ones listed below are aimed primarily at the child; those meant for adult readers (with child participation) are more appropriately listed in the Classroom Magazines section.

Most magazines to some degree offer features that encourage reader participation, such as games, puzzles, opportunities for submitting artwork or poetry, riddles, essays and letters, and opportunities for feedback in advice columns and in letters to the editor. Many titles differ very little in this regard. A handful of publications are actually produced in large part by children themselves, as is noted below. As with magazine publication for the general population, children's magazine publication has become increasingly specialized, aimed at ever-narrowing audiences and specific markets. Meanwhile, the more general publications have become increasingly competitive and similar in style and quality. Overall, this is good for children, whose main difficulty will now be selecting what to read!

Titles reviewed in this section were selected based on their overall quality, their presence in existing libraries (or appropriateness for library collections), and on their performance in parent and teacher circles (such as those winning various awards), as well as on their unique contributions to the discriminating youth market. The majority of the magazines included below are of high quality and specialize in promoting academic pursuits such as literature and creative writing, science, nature and social studies, healthy living, culture, and the arts; a smaller number exist to provide pure entertainment—but these continue to have a place in libraries as well.

The list below represents reading material for children from preschool through the junior high school level (roughly ages 2–14). Some magazines aimed at teenagers are also popular with pre-teens but have been excluded from this section. Also excluded are magazines whose primary purpose is to support teaching or curriculum, as are magazines aimed at parents, teachers, caretakers, and homeschoolers. These are best used in the classroom, or read by an adult guiding a child. The titles listed below are clearly meant to be read or viewed by the children themselves.

Some titles better suited for individual subscriptions have also been excluded from this section; others are equally appropriate for libraries or homes. Most magazines listed below have supplementary content and online indexing available via publisher web sites.

Basic Periodicals

American Girl, AppleSeeds, Ask, BabyBug, Biography for Beginners, Boys' Life, Calliope, Chickadee, ChildArt, Chirp, Click, Cobblestone, Creative Kids, Cricket, Crinkles, Cyberkids, Dig, Faces, Girl Tech, Highlights for Children, Know, Ladybug, Muse, National Geographic Kids, New Moon, Odyssey, Owl, Ranger Rick, Skipping Stones, Spider, Sports Illustrated for Kids, Stone Soup, Wild, Wild Animal Baby, Yes Mag, Your Big Backyard, Zoobooks.

Basic Abstracts and Indexes

Children's Magazine Guide, Magazine Article Summaries, Primary Search and Middle Search, Reader's Guide for Young People, Readers' Guide to Periodical Literature, Vertical File Index.

1222. American Girl. [ISSN: 1062-7812] 1992. bi-m. USD 22.95 domestic; USD 29 foreign. Ed(s): Kristi Thom. American Girl Publishing, 8400 Fairway Pl, Middleton, WI 53562; readermail@ab.pleasantco.com; http://www.americangirl.com. Illus. Circ: 665523 Paid. Vol. ends: Nov/Dec. *Indexed:* ICM, MASUSE. *Aud.:* 6-12 yrs.

As the largest magazine dedicated exclusively to pre-teen girls, this is a highly engaging bimonthly filled with activities. This colorful publication prides itself on being an "age-appropriate alternative to teen magazines," and strives to bolster self-esteem and encourage creativity. Its message is, "You're great—just the way you are!" Activities include contests, puzzles, and crafts, and reader participation is invited through letters, artwork, and jokes. The publication is highly interactive, thus many readers submit photos along with their personal anecdotes. Departments include "Friendship Matters," "Heart to Heart,"

"Craft," and "Quiz." "Brainwaves" features activities and puzzles pages. "Help!" is an advice column. A recent issue focuses entirely on animals; special features included a quiz on cats and how to make animals out of pipe cleaners. One feature-length fiction article is also included in a recent issue. The magazine also features girl-centered polls and reviews. Highly recommended for personal subscriptions and also for public libraries.

1223. *AppleSeeds.* [ISSN: 1099-7725] 1998. 9x/yr. USD 29.95 domestic; USD 41.95 foreign; USD 4.95 per issue domestic. Ed(s): Susan Buckley. Carus Publishing Company, 315 Fifth St, Peru, IL 61354; custsvc@ cobblestone.mv.com; http://www.cricketmag.com. Illus., index. Sample. Circ: 5000 Paid. Vol. ends: May. *Indexed:* ICM. *Bk. rev.:* 3-5, 20-40 words. *Aud.:* 7-9 yrs.

This richly illustrated elementary social studies magazine contains numerous articles of varying length. Articles include factual, personal anecdotes from real diaries, accounts of life and experiences from other times and lands, and historical fiction and folklore tales. Articles are written so as to bring young readers into the experience, and included are interesting sidebars, some focusing on special vocabulary words. Regular features include "Reading Corner," "Where in the World," and "Fun Stuff." Illustrators contribute in a variety of styles, including cartoons. An annual subject index lists previous issues by theme. This magazine contains no advertisements. An advisory board made up of educational and subject specialists ensures the quality of this publication. Each issue also has an academic consulting editor. Highly recommended for both school and public libraries.

1224. *Ask: arts and sciences for kids.* [ISSN: 1535-4105] 2002. 9x/yr. USD 32.97 domestic; USD 44.97 foreign. Ed(s): Lonnie Plecha. Carus Publishing Company, 315 Fifth St, Peru, IL 61354; custsvc@ cobblestone.mv.com; http://www.cricketmag.com. *Indexed:* ICM. *Aud.:* 7-10 yrs.

This joint venture between Cricket Magazine Group and the Smithsonian Institution aims to answer children's questions about the natural and man-made world around them, focusing primarily on science, technology, and inventions. Departments include "Scoops" (a science and culture news column), "Nestor's Dock" (an environmentally focused comic strip), "Ask Jimmy and the Bug," contests, and letters and artwork. There are also numerous feature articles on topics such as how things work. Also includes hands-on activities related to featured articles. This magazine contains no advertisements. Highly recommended for both school and public libraries.

1225. *Babybug.* [ISSN: 1077-1131] 1994. 10x/yr. USD 35.97 domestic; USD 47.97 foreign. Ed(s): Marianne Carus, Paula Morrow. Carus Publishing Company, 315 Fifth St, Peru, IL 61354; custsvc@ cobblestone.mv.com; http://www.cricketmag.com. Illus. Circ: 47000 Paid. *Aud.:* 6 mos.-2 yrs.

This small, sturdy, 20-page monthly with rounded page edges contains nursery rhymes and simple stories just right for infants and toddlers and their caretakers. Some stories continue from issue to issue. Gently but brightly designed—frequently by award-winning illustrators—this magazine strives to "begin a lifelong love of books" and is an excellent introduction to reading. Each back cover carries summarizing pictures for the child to locate within the issue. This beginner magazine from the Cricket Group teaches children simple concepts about the world around them and fosters an appreciaton for being read to, which is the foundation for reading and learning. Appropriate for public libraries.

1226. *Biography for Beginners: sketches for early readers.* [ISSN: 1081-4973] 1995. s-a. USD 40. Ed(s): Laurie Harris. Favorable Impressions, PO Box 69018, Pleasant Ridge, MI 48069; danh@favimp.com; http://www.favimp.com. Illus., index. Sample. Circ: 4000. Vol. ends: May/Oct. *Aud.:* 6-9 yrs.

This award-winning, 100-page reference publication is written specifically for early elementary readers. Each issue contains nine or ten biographical sketches covering a variety of well-known people, including children's authors, actors, musicians, sports stars, political figures, and scientists. Written in an easy-to-read format and style, with age-appropriate vocabulary, this sturdy magazine engages curious minds with interesting information about people they would

like to know more about. Unfamilar terms are defined for young readers, and pronunciation is provided. Sketches are substantial and generously illustrated, with numerous quotations included. Information about the subject's early life and schooling is included within each sketch. Cumulative name, subject, and birthday indexes are included in each issue, while upcoming biographies are announced. Addresses and web sites are included for classroom writing projects. Appropriate for school and public libraries.

1227. *Boys' Life: the magazine for all boys.* [ISSN: 0006-8608] 1911. m. USD 21.60 domestic; USD 3.60 newsstand/cover per issue. Ed(s): J D Owen, William E Butterworth, IV. Boy Scouts of America, PO Box 152079, Irving, TX 75015-2079. Illus., adv. Circ: 1300000 Paid. Microform: NBI; PQC. Online: EBSCO Publishing, EBSCO Host; Gale; OCLC Online Computer Library Center, Inc.; ProQuest K-12 Learning Solutions; ProQuest LLC (Ann Arbor). *Indexed:* ASIP, CPerI, ICM, IHTDI, MASUSE. *Aud.:* 8-18 yrs.

Published by the Boy Scouts of America, this magazine is filled with captivating informational articles of varying length on space and aviation, nature, technology, and health. It also includes historical and faith-based stories, true stories of scouts in action to promote public service values, and puzzles, mazes, games, comics, and other activities for the various ranks of scouts. Regular features include "Nature," "News and Notes," and "Collecting." Boys actively contribute to jokes and reader mail. Limited advertising at the end of each issue is aimed at scouts and their leaders. Most suitable for personal subscriptions and scouts, but true to its name, this magazine is of value to all boys.

1228. *Boys' Quest.* [ISSN: 1078-9006] 1995. bi-m. USD 27.95 domestic; USD 36.95 foreign; USD 5.95 newsstand/cover domestic. Ed(s): Marilyn Edwards. Bluffton News Printing & Publishing Co., PO Box 164, Bluffton, OH 45817-0164. Illus. Circ: 12000 Paid. Vol. ends: Apr/May. *Indexed:* ICM. *Aud.:* 5-13 yrs.

This small-format, glossy, 50-page magazine prides itself on no violence and no advertising. Among its goals is to "instill traditional family values in elementary-age boys." It does this by helping children identify and develop their interests and abilities and by building confidence through literacy and reading comprehension. Each issue aims to promote fun, brainy activities revolving around a single theme. Regular features include "Fred's World" (an inspriational column), "Science" (featuring hands-on experiments), "Computer Quest" (a puzzler), "Chef's Corner," "T.A.I.L.S. Comics," "Workshop" (real projects), "Collecting" (tips on hobbies), and "Ticklers and Teasers." *Boys' Quest* also includes numerous fiction articles and poems associated with the topic for that issue. Both *Boys' Quest* and *Hopscotch for Girls* are published in months alternating with those of their sister magazine, *Fun for Kidz.* Highly recommended for personal subscriptions but also appropriate for public libraries.

1229. *Calliope (Peru): exploring world history.* Formerly (until 1990): *Classical Calliope.* [ISSN: 1050-7086] 1981. 9x/yr. USD 29.95 domestic; USD 41.95 foreign; USD 4.95 per issue domestic. Ed(s): Lou Waryncia, Rosalie Baker. Carus Publishing Company, 315 Fifth St, Peru, IL 61354; custsvc@cobblestone.mv.com; http://www.cricketmag.com. Illus., index. Circ: 11000 Paid. Vol. ends: May. *Indexed:* AmHI, ICM, MASUSE. *Bk. rev.:* 5, 50-75 words. *Aud.:* 9-15 yrs.

This magazine "explores world history." Regular features include "Musings," "Map," "Fun with Words" (word origins and uses), and "Off the Shelf" (book reviews for further reading). There is also an informational "Ask Calliope" page. A recent themed issue on Rembrandt included not only lengthy articles on the painter, but information on Dutch life during his time, as well as interesting tidbits related to Dutch culture, such as interesting sidebars and notes on word origins. Also included are puzzles and hands-on activities related to the theme. An annual subject index guides readers to themed issues of the previous year. This magazine contains no advertisements. An advisory board made up of educational and subject specialists ensures the quality of this publication. Each issue also has an academic consulting editor. Highly recommended for both school and public libraries.

1230. *Chickadee.* [ISSN: 0707-4611] 1979. 10x/yr. CND 29.95 domestic; CND 32.19 in Maritimes & Quebec; USD 22 United States. Ed(s): Hilary Bain. Bayard Canada, The Owl Group, 49 Front St E, 2nd Fl,

Toronto, ON M5E 1B3, Canada; bayard@owl.on.ca; http://www.owlkids.com/. Illus., index, adv. Circ: 100000. Vol. ends: Dec. *Indexed:* CBCARef, CPerI, ICM. *Bk. rev.:* Number and length vary. *Aud.:* 6-9 yrs.

Winner of several distinguished achievement awards, this bright and colorful magazine helps early elementary school children learn about the world around them. It does this by bringing the world of nature, science, art, and culture to the beginning reader through puzzles, fiction, and factual articles. Richly illustrated with cartoons, photographs, and large typeface, each issue presents a theme with humor and interesting facts. Departments include "Did You Know," "Discovery," "Animal of the Month," "Puzzles and Fun," and "Dr. Zed Science," as well as a variety of puzzles, comics, and fiction articles. A recent issue features a page of book reviews as well. Reader-submitted riddles and artwork are also included. Recommended for school and public libraries, as well as personal subscriptions.

1231. *Child Life: the children's own magazine.* Incorporates: *Young World;* Which was formerly: *Golden Magazine.* [ISSN: 0009-3971] 1921. bi-m. USD 15.95 domestic; USD 19.95 foreign. Ed(s): Jack Gramling. Children's Better Health Institute, 1100 Waterway Blvd, PO Box 567, Indianapolis, IN 46206; g.joray@cbhi.org; http://www.cbhi.org. Illus., index, adv. Sample. Circ: 25622 Paid. Vol. ends: Dec. Microform: PQC. Online: EBSCO Publishing, EBSCO Host; Florida Center for Library Automation; Gale; Northern Light Technology, Inc.; ProQuest K-12 Learning Solutions; ProQuest LLC (Ann Arbor). *Indexed:* ICM, MASUSE. *Bk. rev.:* 2-4, 40-50 words. *Aud.:* 9-11 yrs.

This classic magazine for middle-grade elementary school readers focuses on "educating and entertaining readers" while "promoting good health and fitness." It includes book reviews, web site reviews, word puzzles, and reader-submitted artwork. Also featured are poems and factual and fictional articles on a variety of topics, such as history and sports—but many of these are reprints from past issues. True to its mission, this magazine hosts an annual spelling bee and fitness event; details are covered within the publication. This magazine closes with a two-page column, "Ask Dr. Cory." Magazine content is a bit old-fashioned in style; the stories and illustrations may not reflect the racial and ethnic diversity of its readers. Best suited for personal subscriptions but of value to public and school libraries as well.

1232. *ChildArt: the magazine of the International Child Art Foundation.* [ISSN: 1096-9020] 1998. q. USD 30 domestic; USD 40 foreign. Ed(s): Ashfaq Ishaq. International Child Art Foundation, 1350 Connecticut Ave, NW, Washington, DC 20036-1702; childart@icaf.org; http://www.icaf.org/. *Aud.:* 8-12 yrs.

The International Child Art Foundation's mission is "to prepare children for a creative and cooperative future," recognizing that art is the key to universal communication and understanding among cultures. Understanding that we are living in the age of creativity, this magazine "endeavors to create peace, utilizing the power of the arts to develop the innate creativity and intrinsic empathy of children." Issue themes are determined and planned by children. Most content relates to specific peace and art activities around the globe, with articles about real-life accomplishments and groundbreaking events. The magazine regularly features crafts and activities related to a particular theme. The publishing foundation sponsors an annual "Arts Olympiad," a global initiative providing free art lesson plans to educators, and involving art competitions, exhibitions, and international events. Most appropriate for schools and school libraries, but of value to public libraries as well.

1233. *Children's Digest.* Former titles (Mar.-Nov. 1980): *Children's Digest and Children's Playcraft;* (Until 1980): *Children's Digest (1950).* [ISSN: 0272-7145] 1950. bi-m. USD 17.95 domestic; USD 1.25 per issue. Ed(s): Daniel Lee. Children's Better Health Institute, 1100 Waterway Blvd, PO Box 567, Indianapolis, IN 46206; g.joray@cbhi.org; http://www.cbhi.org. Illus., index, adv. Circ: 80000 Paid. Vol. ends: Dec. Microform: PQC. Online: EBSCO Publishing, EBSCO Host; Gale; Northern Light Technology, Inc.; ProQuest K-12 Learning Solutions; ProQuest LLC (Ann Arbor). *Indexed:* ICM, MASUSE. *Bk. rev.:* 3-5, 80-100 words. *Aud.:* 10-12 yrs.

This colorful newsprint magazine promotes good health and fitness for pre-teen readers. Regular features include stories, puzzles, and interesting articles on health, sports, science, nature, and culture. Readers may submit original poetry, jokes, and riddles. Each issue contains several pages of book reviews, some of them submitted by young readers. The two-page "Ask Dr. Cory" column offers an opportunity for reader-initiated health questions, some of them on sensitive topics. This is one of the few children's magazines containing commercial product reviews. A bit old-fashioned in style, the stories and illustrations may not reflect the racial and ethnic diversity of its readers. Because of the abundance of in-issue workbook style activities and puzzles, this publication is best suited for personal subscriptions, but could be of value to public libraries as well.

1234. *Children's Playmate.* Formerly (until 1935): *Play Mate.* [ISSN: 0009-4161] 1929. bi-m. USD 15.95 domestic; USD 19.95 foreign. Ed(s): Terry Harshman. Children's Better Health Institute, 1100 Waterway Blvd, PO Box 567, Indianapolis, IN 46206; g.joray@cbhi.org; http://www.cbhi.org. Illus., index, adv. Circ: 115000 Paid. Vol. ends: Dec. Microform: PQC. Online: EBSCO Publishing, EBSCO Host; Gale; Northern Light Technology, Inc.; ProQuest LLC (Ann Arbor). *Indexed:* ICM. *Aud.:* 6-8 yrs.

This colorful newsprint magazine aims to promote health, fitness, and wholesomeness through stories, games, recipes, and activities. It invites the creative work of early elementary school-age children and publishes their pictures, poems, jokes, and riddles. A bit old-fashioned in style, the stories and illustrations may not not reflect the racial and ethnic diversity present among its readers. Because of the abundance of in-issue workbook style activities and puzzles, this publication is best suited for personal subscriptions, but could be of value to public libraries as well.

1235. *Chirp.* Formerly: *Tree House.* [ISSN: 1206-4580] 1992. 10x/yr. CND 29.95 domestic; CND 32.19 in Maritimes & Quebec; USD 22 United States. Ed(s): Hilary Bain. Bayard Canada, The Owl Group, 49 Front St E, 2nd Fl, Toronto, ON M5E 1B3, Canada; bayard@owl.on.ca; http://www.owlkids.com/. Circ: 50000. *Aud.:* 3-6 yrs.

This introductory children's magazine from Bayard Canada carries a variety of challenges and exciting activities for the various levels of ability in this very early age group. Each issue includes "ABC fun," based on the issue's theme. The gentle but colorfully illustrated two-page comic "Adventures of Chirp and Friends" draws the very young into reading, while the "Robbie and Emily" comic for older children teaches values and addresses small children's concerns. Crafts, puzzles, riddles, and longer stories challenge older children and advanced readers, while "Look and Learn" is a regular feature for the youngest learners. This "see and do, laugh and learn magazine" is appropriate for public libraries as well as personal suscriptions.

1236. *Click: opening windows for young minds.* [ISSN: 1094-4273] 1998. 9x/yr. USD 32.97 domestic; USD 44.97 foreign; USD 4.95 per issue domestic. Carus Publishing Company, 315 Fifth St, Peru, IL 61354; custsvc@cobblestone.mv.com; http://www.cricketmag.com. Illus. Vol. ends: Dec. Online: EBSCO Publishing, EBSCO Host; ProQuest K-12 Learning Solutions; ProQuest LLC (Ann Arbor). *Indexed:* ICM. *Bk. rev.:* 12-16, length varies. *Aud.:* 3-7 yrs.

This glossy, 40-page magazine opens up the world of science, nature, history, and culture for the most elementary of learners. A joint publication of the Cricket Group and *Smithsonian Magazine,* themed issues are guided by comic-strip character "Click" the mouse and his friends, as he leads children on different discovery adventures. Informational, fact-rich articles cover science, technology, and the surrounding world, aiming to satisfy a child's natural curiosity. Substantial theme-related stories satisfy the eager reader as well. Generously illustrated with photographs and paintings alike. End-of-issue take-out pages double as games for the reader. Special issues cover biographies. A helpful parent's companion section includes follow-up activities, plus additional related book titles. Appropriate for public libraries or individual subscriptions.

1237. *Cobblestone: discover American history.* [ISSN: 0199-5197] 1980. 9x/yr. USD 29.95 domestic; USD 41.95 foreign; USD 4.95 per issue domestic. Ed(s): Meg Chorlian. Carus Publishing Company, 315 Fifth St,

Peru, IL 61354; custsvc@cobblestone.mv.com; http://www.cricketmag.com. Illus., index. Circ: 31000. Vol. ends: Dec. *Indexed:* ICM, MASUSE. *Bk. rev.:* 10, length varies. *Aud.:* 9-14 yrs.

This richly illustrated, award-winning magazine for upper elementary and junior high school students focuses on history. Issues are themed, focusing in depth on a single topic. Departments include "Did You Know?," "Geographically Speaking," and "Going Global," which compares cultures. "Digging Deeper" provides further reading, both in books and online. Unfamiliar words are highlighted in the text and defined in sidebars throughout the magazine. An annual subject index points readers to the appropriate themed issues for the previous year. This magazine contains no advertisements. An advisory board made up of educational and subject specialists ensures the quality of this publication. Each issue also has an academic consulting editor. Highly recommended for both school and public libraries.

1238. *Creative Kids: the national voice for kids.* Formerly: *Chart Your Course.* [ISSN: 0892-9599] 1980. q. USD 19.95 domestic; USD 29.95 foreign. Ed(s): Jenny Robins. Prufrock Press Inc., PO Box 8813, Waco, TX 76714-8813; http://www.prufrock.com. Circ: 35000 Paid. Online: EBSCO Publishing, EBSCO Host; Gale. *Indexed:* MASUSE. *Bk. rev.:* Number and length vary. *Aud.:* 8-14 yrs.

This small-format magazine is created by children; even its advisory board is composed entirely of children. Columns include "Dare to Dream Big" (real-life stories of children who have helped change their communities in some way), "Pen-Pals," and "Speak Out" (children write in response to provocative questions). "Write-On" is an opinion column. This highly interactive magazine includes book reviews, poetry, creative writing, short stories, artwork, and puzzles by and for children. It also provides opportunities for input for contest ideas. Like a "little magazine" for children, this publication is highly recommended for public libraries.

1239. *Cricket: the magazine for children.* [ISSN: 0090-6034] 1973. m. USD 35.97 domestic; USD 47.97 foreign. Ed(s): Marianne Carus, Julia Messina. Carus Publishing Company, 315 Fifth St, Peru, IL 61354; custsvc@cobblestone.mv.com; http://www.cricketmag.com. Illus. Circ: 80000 Paid. Vol. ends: Aug. Online: EBSCO Publishing, EBSCO Host. *Indexed:* CPerI, ICM. *Aud.:* 9-14 yrs.

This beautifully illustrated, award-winning magazine for older elementary through junior high school readers specializes in literature, poetry, science fiction, folktales, and fantasy, as well as historical and contemporary fiction. Substantial factual and scientific articles are presented as well. Regular activities include crossword puzzles, crafts, and recipes. Opportunities for reader participation include a letters-to-the-editor section and reader contests. The cartoon cricket character resides in the margins and explains unfamiliar terms to the reader. *Cricket* is also available on audiocassette. Highly recommended for both school and public libraries as well as personal subscriptions.

1240. *Crinkles: because learning makes crinkles in your brain.* [ISSN: 1522-5631] 1998. bi-m. USD 30 domestic; USD 45 foreign; USD 5 newsstand/cover. Ed(s): Deborah D. Levitov. Libraries Unlimited, Inc., 88 Post Road W, Westport, CT 06881; lu-books@lu.com; http://www.lu.com/. Illus., adv. Sample. Refereed. Circ: 6500 Paid. *Indexed:* ICM. *Bk. rev.:* Number and length vary. *Aud.:* 7-11 yrs.

"Learning makes crinkles in your brain," states the editor of this magazine. The magazine covers a variety of topics in science, nature, culture, history, and technology, and its themed issues include the regular departments "People," "Places," "Events," and "Things." Each bimonthly topic is supplemented by related book reviews, crafts, and other activities, while lengthy articles are followed by references and web links and recommendations to visit the library. This densely printed magazine contains mostly black-and-white but also some color illustrations. Each issue is chock-full of information and challenging activity and provides ample opportunity for reader interaction through jokes, puzzles, and contests. Highly recommended for public libraries as well as personal subscriptions.

1241. *Cyberkids.* 1995. q. Mountain Lake Software, 298 Fourth Ave., San Francisco, CA 94118; http://www.cyberkids.com. *Bk. rev.:* Number and length vary. *Aud.:* 7-12 yrs.

This web site includes clear guidelines for children. Registration is not necessary. The "Creative Works" section publishes original art, poetry, and other works from children around the world. A link to a young composers web site even includes original music. "Fun and Games" includes brain teasers, puzzles, and jokes. There is currently no active shopping section. "Kids Connect," an online community center and message board, has also been discontinued. "Launchpad" remains a useful jumping-off point for children who seek quality additional online information on a variety of topics. There is even a link to museums and libraries, including the Library of Congress and the Internet Public Library. In "CyberViews," children can submit their own book, media, software, and product reviews. "Learning Center" is a place children can search for help with schoolwork. This web site is most appropriate for personal use, but may be useful on public workstations in children's libraries as well.

1242. *Dig.* Formerly (until 2001): *Archaeology's Dig.* [ISSN: 1539-7130] 1999. m. 9/yr. USD 32.97 domestic; USD 44.97 foreign; USD 4.95 per issue domestic. Ed(s): Rosalie Baker. Carus Publishing Company, 315 Fifth St, Peru, IL 61354; custsvc@cobblestone.mv.com; http://www.cricketmag.com. Illus. Sample. Circ: 20000. *Indexed:* ICM. *Aud.:* 9-14 yrs.

Published in partnership with *Archaeology Magazine*, this glossy and richly illustrated publication introduces children to the world of history, culture, and anthropology. Lengthy and colorful feature articles are supported by stunning photographs and supplemented by related crafts and activities. Regular departments include "Dr. Dig," which answers children's questions about archaeology, and "Stones and Bones," short pieces covering discoveries, facts, and myths. Each month, the one-page "Art-i-facts" column highlights a "fantastic factoid about ancient sites, historical objects, and amazing discoveries." Also included are games, puzzles, and opportunities to submit artwork. This magazine contains no advertisements. An advisory board made up of educational and subject specialists ensures the quality of this publication. Each issue also has an academic consulting editor. Highly recommended for public libraries and personal subscriptions.

1243. *Discovery Girls: a magazine created by girls, for girls.* [ISSN: 1535-3230] 2000. bi-m. USD 19.95 domestic; USD 24 Canada; USD 32 elsewhere. Ed(s): Sarah Virney. Discovery Girls, 4300 Stevens Creek Blvd Ste 190, San Jose, CA 95129. Illus., adv. *Indexed:* ICM. *Bk. rev.:* Number and length vary. *Aud.:* 8-13 yrs.

This popular, award-winning bimonthly for pre-teens provides entertainment, advice, and social support for growing girls. Most issues contain at least one article focusing on friendship, and quizzes let girls test their social savvy. Regular departments that encourage reader participation include "The Great Debate," "Embarrassing Moments," "The Worst Day," and "Young Writer's Corner," which solicits stories, poems, and essays. The magazine also includes games, puzzles, and book and product reviews, as well as an advice column and profiles of readers from other cultures in "Over There." Although somewhat more fashion- and pop-culture-oriented than similar girls' magazines, this is nonetheless a quality publication for the delicate pre-teen age. Includes advertising. Recommended for public libraries.

1244. *Disney Adventures.* [ISSN: 1050-2491] 1990. 10x/yr. USD 15 domestic; USD 23 Canada; USD 25 elsewhere. Ed(s): Amy Weingartner. Disney Publishing Worldwide, 114 Fifth Ave, 16th Fl, New York, NY 10011-5690; http://www.disney.com/. Illus., adv. Circ: 1200000 Paid. *Indexed:* ICM. *Bk. rev.:* Number and length vary. *Aud.:* 8-13 yrs.

This small-format, popular companion to the Disney Channel is purely an entertainment magazine for elementary and middle school age children, although it does contain some puzzles and brain-teaser activities. Very densely and colorfully printed, it's also heavily interrupted by advertising. Much of the magazine consists of celebrity profiles and behind-the-scenes looks at television programs. Also includes reader mail, book and movie reviews, a viewing calendar, jokes and comics, and sports and video game departments. Recommended for public libraries.

1245. *Faces: people, places, & cultures.* Formerly: *Faces Rocks.* [ISSN: 0749-1387] 1984. m. USD 29.95 domestic; USD 41.95 foreign. Cobblestone Publishing, 30 Grove St, Ste C, Peterborough, NH 03458; custsvc@cobblestone.mv.com; http://www.cobblestonepub.com. Illus., index. Circ: 12000. *Indexed:* ICM, MASUSE. *Bk. rev.:* 5, 35-50 words. *Aud.:* 9-14 yrs.

This award-winning publication aims to expose middle-grade readers to the beliefs, lifestyles, and cultures of people around the world. Glossy, colorful thematic issues focus on a variety of cultures and countries. Each issue explores a theme in-depth through articles, folk tales, photographs, maps, timelines, recipes, and crafts. Sidebars cover "critical thinking," "did you know," and "fast facts." Regular departments include "High Five" (fascinating facts about the theme topic), "At a Glance," and a one-box comic called "Face Facts," which dispels myths or points out interesting or unusual trivia regarding the themed topic. "Through Time" provides a timeline of historical happenings related to the topic. "Ask Faces" allows readers to ask general questions about culture. "Further Exploring" contains book reviews and suggestions for additional topical reading. An annual subject index points readers to themed issues for the previous year. This magazine contains no advertisements. An advisory board made up of educational and subject specialists ensures the quality of this publication. Each issue also has an academic consulting editor. Highly recommended for both school and public libraries.

1246. *Fun for Kidz.* [ISSN: 1536-898X] 2000. bi-m. USD 27.95 domestic; USD 36.95 foreign; USD 5.95 newsstand/cover domestic. Ed(s): Marilyn Edwards. Bluffton News Printing & Publishing Co., PO Box 227, Bluffton, OH 45817. Adv. *Indexed:* ICM. *Aud.:* 5-13 yrs.

This small-format, glossy, 50-page magazine prides itself on no violence and no advertising. Its philosophy is to "promote purposeful fun." As a companion (and published in alternate months) to its sister publications, *Boys' Quest* and *Hopscotch for Girls,* this magazine encourages children to follow directions and solve problems by providing challenging problems, puzzles, and activities with real-life applications and meaning. Also included are informational articles, fiction, and poems relating to the theme of the issue. Regular departments include "Science" (featuring hands-on experiments), "Computer Quest" (a puzzler), "Collecting" (tips on hobbies), and "Workshop" (a real project). Highly recommended for personal subscriptions but also appropriate for public libraries.

1247. *Fun to Learn - Playroom.* Formerly (until 2001): *Preschool Playroom.* [ISSN: 1477-805X] 2001. bi-m. Redan Publishing Ltd., Canon Court E, Abbey Lawn, Shrewsbury, SY2 5DE, United Kingdom; sam@redan.co.uk. *Aud.:* 2-6 yrs.

This bright magazine brings characters such as Arthur, Barney, Spot, Caillou, and others to life within its activity-filled pages. It features "read-together" stories, and stories with pictures. Each issue also includes a center workbook containing counting, coloring, ABCs, mazes, and matching games as well as parent and child activities. Readers may send in artwork. A key in the table of contents guides parents and teachers as to the learning value of each feature within the magazine. This magazine is perhaps best for personal subscriptions and preschools because of the high level of workbook activity within each issue, but it should also be popular with public libraries.

1248. *Girl Tech.* 1996. m. Radica Games, Ltd., http://www.girltech.com. *Bk. rev.:* Number and length vary. *Aud.:* Ems, Hs.

This highly interactive web site is devoted to encouraging technology use by girls and to raising awareness and confidence in using technology. It publishes material on topical issues, health matters, and women in sports and other professions, and provides fun science, math, word, and other games. Profiles of women in various professions offer readers a glimpse of possibilities for themselves. Girls can submit their own reviews of books, music, software, video games, and movies in "Girl's View." The "Sports" page allows girls to learn about a variety of sports, be inspired by female role models, and even submit their own thoughts and stories. Meanwhile, "Chick Chat" fills the need for young girls to compare notes and seek advice from one another. A good personal subscription e-journal, but also useful in creative writing, music, and art classes.

Girls' Life. See Teenagers section.

1249. *A Girl's World.* 1996. m. A Girl's World Productions, Inc., 825 College Blvd. PMB 102-442, Oceanside, CA 92057; http://www.agirlsworld.com. *Bk. rev.:* Number and length vary. *Aud.:* Ems, Hs.

Written and edited by girls, this bright and flashy web site, "where girls and teens rule the web!," encourages and empowers girls from ages 7 to 17 to become active contributors through a variety of opportunities. These include writing contests, articles, quizzes, opinion polls, and essays. Meanwhile, regular columns such as "Advice Alley," "Pen Pals," "Diaries," and "Celebrities" provide girls with much-appreciated entertainment and social support. Girls are encouraged to submit their own movie and book reviews. This web site also has an e-mail option to connect girls who have similar experiences, problems, or challenges without making their contact information public. Best for personal subscription use.

1250. *Highlights for Children: fun with a purpose.* Incorporates: *Children's Activities.* [ISSN: 0018-165X] 1946. m. USD 29.64 domestic; USD 3.95 newsstand/cover per issue. Ed(s): Christine French Clark, Judy Burke. Highlights for Children, Inc., 1800 Watermark Dr, PO Box 269, Columbus, OH 43216-0269. Illus., index. Circ: 2500000 Paid. Vol. ends: Dec. Microform: PQC. Online: EBSCO Publishing, EBSCO Host; Gale; Northern Light Technology, Inc.; ProQuest K-12 Learning Solutions; ProQuest LLC (Ann Arbor). *Indexed:* ICM. *Aud.:* 4-11 yrs.

A winner of numerous awards, this 44-page, simple classic for children continues to maintain high standards with excellent stories, articles, activities, and crafts. Original pictures, poetry, and stories are solicited from readers in "Your Own Pages." "Dear Highlights" gives readers an opportunity to express their concerns. Although a longstanding publication, and considered by some to be outdated, *Highlights* has updated its feel, including the classic "Goofus and Gallant" feature, which has recently re-emerged with a contemporary look. "Hidden Pictures" and "The Timbertoes" continue to charm, especially young readers. A special key in the table of contents indicates to parents and teachers the particular scope of the articles, features, and departments that follow, as to age-level appropriateness, creative thinking, or moral values. A subscription to *Highlights for Children* grants access to HighlightsKids.com. Highly recommended for personal subscriptions, but also appropriate for school and public libraries.

1251. *Hopscotch (Bluffton): for girls.* [ISSN: 1044-0488] 1989. bi-m. USD 27.95 domestic; USD 36.95 foreign; USD 5.95 newsstand/cover per issue domestic. Ed(s): Marilyn Edwards. Bluffton News Printing & Publishing Co., PO Box 164, Bluffton, OH 45817-0164. Illus., adv. Sample. Circ: 14000 Paid. Vol. ends: Apr/May. Online: EBSCO Publishing, EBSCO Host; Gale. *Indexed:* ICM. *Aud.:* 6-10 yrs.

This small-format, glossy, 50-page magazine prides itself on no violence and no advertising. Among its goals is to "emphasize and develop the childhood interests and values" of pre-teen girls. The publisher states that "well-rounded children with down-to-earth, wholesome principles and interests can more easily handle the pressures brought on by the changes of adolescence." This magazine allows girls to explore their own interests and abilities without the influence of the fast-paced world or peer-pressure. Just like its counterpart, *Boys' Quest,* each issue of *Hopscotch* is meant "to be read, not scanned." Regular features include "Science" (featuring hands-on experiments), "Girl Power" (a comic), "Cooking," "Potsy's Pen Pal Club," and "Potsy's Post Office" (reader mail). Each issue also includes numerous fiction and nonfiction articles, poems, crafts, puzzles, brain-teasers, and other activities associated with the topic for that issue. Both *Hopscotch for Girls* and *Boys' Quest* are published in months that alternate with those of their sister magazine, *Fun for Kidz.* Highly recommended for personal subscriptions but also appropriate for public libraries.

1252. *Humpty Dumpty's Magazine.* Formerly (until 1979): *Humpty Dumpty's Magazine for Little Children.* [ISSN: 0273-7590] 1952. bi-m. USD 15.95 domestic; USD 19.95 foreign. Ed(s): Phyllis Lybarger. Children's Better Health Institute, 1100 Waterway Blvd, PO Box 567,

Indianapolis, IN 46206; g.joray@cbhi.org; http://www.cbhi.org. Illus., index, adv. Circ: 200000. Vol. ends: Dec. Microform: PQC. Online: EBSCO Publishing, EBSCO Host; Gale; Northern Light Technology, Inc.; ProQuest K-12 Learning Solutions; ProQuest LLC (Ann Arbor). *Indexed:* ICM. *Aud.:* 4-6 yrs.

This engaging newsprint magazine aims to promote good health among very young children. It includes fiction, poetry, informational health articles, and science activities based on a monthly theme, as well as coloring pages, spelling words, and matching games and puzzles. Regular features include the "Ask Dr. Cory" column, which answers questions on very young readers' health concerns. Includes reader-submitted artwork. Because of the workbook nature of many of the activites in this magazine, it may be best suited for personal subscriptions, but is of value to public libraries as well.

1253. *Jack and Jill (Inkprint Edition).* [ISSN: 0021-3829] 1938. bi-m. USD 15.95 domestic; USD 19.95 foreign. Ed(s): Daniel Lee. Children's Better Health Institute, 1100 Waterway Blvd, PO Box 567, Indianapolis, IN 46206; g.joray@cbhi.org; http://www.cbhi.org. Illus., adv. Circ: 215000. Microform: PQC. Online: EBSCO Publishing, EBSCO Host; Gale; ProQuest LLC (Ann Arbor). *Indexed:* ICM. *Bk. rev.:* Number and length vary. *Aud.:* 7-10 yrs.

This colorful newsprint magazine promotes health and safety for elementary-grade readers. Each issue includes fictional, informational, biographical, and how-to articles, book reviews, poems, crafts, recipes, puzzles, and activities relating mostly to safety and health issues. Includes a jokes and riddles department with reader contributions, as well as a reader poetry page. Regular features include the "Ask Dr. Cory" column, which answers questions on children's health concerns. Because of the workbook nature of many of the activities in this magazine, it may be best suited for personal subscriptions, but is of value to public libraries as well.

1254. *Junior Baseball: America's youth baseball magazine.* Formerly (until Jan. 1999): *Junior League Baseball.* [ISSN: 1522-8460] 1996. 6x/yr. USD 17.70 domestic; USD 27.70 in Canada & Mexico; USD 47.70 elsewhere. Ed(s): Dave Destler. 2 D Publishing, 22026 Gault St, Canoga Park, CA 91303; editor@juniorbaseball.com. Illus., adv. Circ: 20000 Paid. *Bk. rev.:* 8-10, 20 words. *Aud.:* 5-17 yrs.

This glossy, trade-type publication is directed at young players and their parents and coaches. Articles cover a range of topics from technique and safety to ethics, as well as real-life accounts of personalities and teams. A number of articles are reserved for specific age groups. "Rookie Club" addresses 5- to 8-year-old readers, "All Stars" the 9- to 13-year-olds, and "Hot Prospects" the 14- to 17-year-old crowd. Also includes interviews with and biographies of famous players. A baseball equipment buyers guide is published annually as part of one issue. "Coaches Clinics" and "In the Stands" are written for parents and coaches. Product and book reviews are also included, as are a crossword puzzle and comic. "Players Story" allows children to submit essays about their experience with the sport. Recommended for public libraries.

1255. *Kids Discover.* [ISSN: 1054-2868] 1991. m. USD 26.95 domestic; USD 35.95 foreign. Ed(s): Stella Sands. Kids Discover, 149 5th Ave, 12th Fl, New York, NY 10010. Illus. Circ: 500000 Paid and controlled. *Indexed:* ICM, MASUSE. *Aud.:* 6-12 yrs.

Winner of several awards, this 20-page magazine is written for elementary and junior-high school age readers, and covers a wide variety of subject areas, including science, nature, technology, culture, and history. Each issue focuses tightly on a single topic and includes numerous short articles, diagrams, and activities concerning this theme. Color photographs and illustrations are abundant and highly engaging. Also includes puzzles, do-it-yourself activities, and a list of further reading. Each issue relies on educational and subject consultants. Although the publication is not very lengthy, its layout could be improved with a table of contents. Most suitable for readers in the classroom, but also recommended for public libraries.

1256. *KidZone.* [ISSN: 1547-2019] 2000. bi-m. USD 19.95 domestic; USD 27.95 foreign. Scott Publications, 30595 Eight Mile, Livonia, MI 48152-1798; contactus@scottpublications.com; http://www.scottpublications.com. Illus., adv. *Aud.:* 4-12 yrs.

This inviting, colorful magazine is meant to be shared by families by sharing "quality time together—creating, playing, cooking, learning, and exploring." Regular departments include "Culture Zone," "Fun Zone," and "Chomp Zone." Other features consist of a variety of crafts, games, puzzles, and science projects, as well as contributed artwork and riddles. The cover sports thumbnails with page numbers of features within the issue. This magazine includes limited advertising for educators and caretakers. Especially recommended for school and public libraries.

1257. *Know.* [ISSN: 1715-751X] 2006. bi-m. CND 22 domestic; CND 28 United States; CND 34 elsewhere. Ed(s): Adrienne Mason, Shannon Hunt. Peter Piper Publishing Inc., 501-3960 Quadra St., Victoria, BC V8X 4A3, Canada. *Indexed:* ICM. *Bk. rev.:* 2-4, 50-100 words. *Aud.:* 6-9 yrs.

This colorful, 32-page, glossy magazine takes curious children on a journey from inside their bodies to outer space. The photographs in particular are stunning, and the magazine's attractive layout and large typeface make the very brief articles eye-catching and easy to read. Departments include "Know News," "Know It," "Know You," and "Know Them." "Know How" is a regular experiment column, while "Know and Tell" includes submitted artwork. Also includes book reviews by children. Highly recommended for public libraries.

1258. *Ladybug: the magazine for young children.* [ISSN: 1051-4961] 1990. m. USD 35.97 domestic; USD 47.97 foreign; USD 4.95 newsstand/cover domestic. Ed(s): Marianne Carus, Paula Morrow. Carus Publishing Company, 315 Fifth St, Peru, IL 61354; custsvc@cobblestone.mv.com; http://www.cricketmag.com. Illus. Circ: 127000 Paid. Vol. ends: Aug. Online: EBSCO Publishing, EBSCO Host. *Indexed:* ICM. *Aud.:* 2-6 yrs.

Taking up where *BabyBug* leaves off, this magazine for very young children provides an introduction to the literary world. It consists mostly of stories, songs, and poetry, with accompanying illustrations that are bright and engaging. To accommodate different introductory reading levels, articles range from very short stories with pictures filling in for words, to those several pages in length with challenging words. Some are fiction and some are factual. The "Mop and Family" comic series takes children on reading adventures. Special activity takeout pages at the end involve learning based on concepts within the issue. Recommended for both public libraries and personal subscriptions.

1259. *Muse (Chicago).* [ISSN: 1090-0381] 1996. 10x/yr. USD 32.97 domestic; USD 44.97 foreign; USD 4.95 newsstand/cover per issue domestic. Carus Publishing Company, 315 Fifth St, Peru, IL 61354; http://www.cricketmag.com. Illus., adv. Vol. ends: Dec. *Indexed:* ICM. *Aud.:* 10-14 yrs.

Another joint publication by the Cricket Group and the Smithsonian Institution, this glossy, 50-page, science-oriented magazine engages elementary and middle-school-age readers with provocative topics and humor. Lengthy but highly interesting articles are supported by photographs, pictures, and diagrams plus suggested further reading via web sites and book titles. Article subjects are varied but based on a loose theme in each issue. Regular departments include "Bo's Page" (science in the news), "Kokopelli & Company" (a comic strip), and "Muse Mail." Highly recommended for school and public libraries as well as for personal subscriptions.

1260. *National Geographic Kids.* Formerly (until Oct. 2002): *National Geographic World.* [ISSN: 1542-3042] 1975. 10x/yr. USD 15 domestic; USD 22 Canada; USD 25 elsewhere. Ed(s): Melina Gerosa Bellows, Julie VonBurgh-Agnoe. National Geographic Society, 1145 17th St, NW, Washington, DC 20036; ngsforum@nationalgeographic.com; http://www.nationalgeographic.com. Illus., index, adv. Circ: 1000000. Microform: PQC. Online: EBSCO Publishing, EBSCO Host; Gale; OCLC Online Computer Library Center, Inc.; ProQuest K-12 Learning Solutions; ProQuest LLC (Ann Arbor); H.W. Wilson. *Indexed:* CPerI, ICM, MASUSE, RGPR. *Aud.:* 6-14 yrs.

This high-interest children's geography magazine from the National Geographic Society covers topics in science, travel, wildlife, exploration, history, anthropology, careers, and biography, and includes just-for-fun articles. Departments include "Guinness World Records," "Weird But True," "Silly Pet

Tricks," "Pet Vet," "Cool Inventions," and "What in the World?" One regular feature, "Kids Did It," relates accomplishments of children, accompanied by their photographs. Each issue also includes tear-out collectors' cards. "Art Department" displays reader-submitted art in response to the magazine's request for a particular theme. There is some advertising. Recommended for public and school libraries, though perhaps slightly better suited for personal subscriptions.

1261. Nature Friend. [ISSN: 0888-4862] 1983. m. USD 25 domestic. Dogwood Ridge Outdoors, 4253 Woodcock Ln, Dayton, VA 22821; mailbox@naturefriendmagazine.com; http://www.dogwoodridgeoutdoors.com. Circ: 9000. *Aud.:* 6-12 yrs.

This understated but attractive and educational magazine aims to balance the investigation and study of nature and science with a belief in God. It does this without being narrowminded or preachy. Regular features include "Invisibles" (a sort of hidden-pictures puzzle), "Pictures and Poems" with reader contributions, and "The Mailbox." "You Can Draw" is a particularly delightful department that features a different step-by-step study of nature every month. Feature-length articles delve into the mysteries of various animal and plant life. Also includes projects and puzzles. Perhaps more appropriate for personal subscriptions, but may be of value to libraries as well, due to its high quality.

1262. New Moon: the magazine for girls and their dreams. [ISSN: 1069-238X] 1993. bi-m. USD 24.95 domestic; USD 5.50 newsstand/ cover. Ed(s): Katy Freeborn. New Moon Publishing, 2 W First St, Ste 101, Duluth, MN 55802. Illus., index. Circ: 22000 Paid. Vol. ends: Jul/Aug. *Indexed:* AltPI, CWI, GendWatch, ICM, MASUSE. *Bk. rev.:* Number and length vary. *Aud.:* 8-14 yrs.

This publication offers a strong positive image for pre-teen and early adolescent girls. Advised by an all-girl editorial board, this magazine is international in flavor and content, with features and articles on customs, ceremonies, biographies, and women's work around the world. Also includes biographies and interviews with inspirational female role models. Opportunities for reader participation include the submission of opinions, ideas, advice, book reviews, poetry, and fiction as well as artwork and letters. "Body Language" answers girls' most sensitive health questions. In "Voice Box," girls sound off on hot topics. Includes a couple of comic strips. Highly recommended for school and public libraries as well as for personal subscriptions.

1263. Nickelodeon Magazine. [ISSN: 1073-7510] 1993. 10x/yr. USD 19.99 domestic; USD 32.90 Canada; USD 33.90 elsewhere. Ed(s): Laura Galen. Nickelodeon Magazine, Inc., 1515 Broadway, New York, NY 10036; NickEditor@aol.com; http://www.nick.com/. Illus., adv. Vol. ends: Dec. *Aud.:* 8-14 yrs.

This monthly print companion to the cable television network is highly entertaining but also educational. It opens with a "Celeb Page," which asks stars a different question every month. This magazine includes numerous games, puzzles, and activities, and each issue is laced with novelty or spoof pages and occasionally with collector cards. It includes several regular comic strips but also offers loads of educational articles and tidbits as well as profiles of authors and other well-known personalities. Caption contests and other opportunities for reader contributions abound, including opportunities to submit artwork. There are a few advertisements, but they are generally labeled as such. Best suited for personal subscriptions, but should also be a popular choice with public libraries.

1264. Odyssey (Peru): adventures in science. [ISSN: 0163-0946] 1979. 9x/yr. USD 29.95 domestic; USD 41.95 foreign; USD 4.95 newsstand/ cover per issue domestic. Ed(s): Elizabeth Lindstrom. Carus Publishing Company, 315 Fifth St, Peru, IL 61354; http://www.cricketmag.com. Illus., adv. Sample. Circ: 24000 Paid. *Indexed:* ICM. *Aud.:* 9-14 yrs.

This glossy, 50-page publication for upper elementary and middle school students focuses on science, especially earth science and space. The magazine incorporates scientific principles into everday life, such as sports. While each issue focuses on a particular theme, regular features include "Brain Strain" (a science puzzler), "Science Scoops" (a news piece), and fiction articles concerning the theme topic. Each issue includes "What's Up," a regular astronomy feature announcing upcoming events in the heavens. "Stargazing" is

a regular comic with Jack Horkheimer, while "Kids Picks" offers substantial book reviews written by readers. The color illustrations and photography throughout each issue add interest, while sidebars expand on unfamiliar terms. Reader participation is encouraged. This magazine contains no advertisements. An advisory board made up of educational and subject specialists ensures the quality of this publication. Each issue also has an academic consulting editor. Recommended for school and public libraries and personal subscriptions.

1265. Owl: the discovery magazine for kids. [ISSN: 0382-6627] 1976. 10x/yr. CND 29.95 domestic; CND 32.19 in Maritimes & Quebec; USD 22 United States. Ed(s): Hilary Bain. Bayard Canada, The Owl Group, 49 Front St E, 2nd Fl, Toronto, ON M5E 1B3, Canada; bayard@owl.on.ca; http://www.owlkids.com/. Illus., index. Circ: 100000. *Indexed:* CBCARef, CPerl, ICM. *Aud.:* 8-14 yrs.

This is a brightly illustrated popular discovery magazine for pre-teens who have graduated from the companion magazine, *Chickadee*. It contains entertaining and informative articles, projects, and lots of activities to interest readers. There are pen-pal opportunities, photography and art contests, an opinion page, and usually a removable poster. Every issue includes a "Wow Shot" photograph featuring science or nature, drawing readers in. "Weird Zone" highlights antics of nature or humans, while "Hot Topic" presents a controversial issue for discussion and debate. "Talk About it" allows readers to participate in giving advice to one another. Includes comics and jokes pages. Recommended for school and public libraries and personal subscriptions.

Plays. See Theater section.

1266. Ranger Rick. Formerly (until 1983): *Ranger Rick's Nature Magazine.* [ISSN: 0738-6656] 1967. m. USD 19.95 domestic; USD 31.95 foreign. Ed(s): Gerry Bishop. National Wildlife Federation, 11100 Wildlife Center Dr, Reston, VA 20190-5362; pubs@nwf.org; http://www.nwf.org. Illus., index, adv. Circ: 600000 Paid. Vol. ends: Dec. Microform: NBI; PQC. Online: EBSCO Publishing, EBSCO Host; Gale; Micromedia ProQuest; Northern Light Technology, Inc.; ProQuest K-12 Learning Solutions; ProQuest LLC (Ann Arbor). *Indexed:* CBCARef, CPerl, ICM, MASUSE. *Aud.:* 7-12 yrs.

This high-interest, 48-page nature magazine for elementary school readers is published by the National Wildlife Federation. It is filled with short stories and articles of varying length, accompanied by colorful, often full-page pictures and illustrations. Articles are frequently supplemented by "fast fact" sidebars. Other regular features include reader mail, recipes, informational articles, nature-related puzzles, games and riddles, and a comic series. The corresponding web site includes a number of departments and sample activities from the current month's print publication. Highly recommended for school and public libraries and for individual subscriptions.

1267. Sesame Street. [ISSN: 0049-0253] 1971. 10x/yr. USD 14.97. Ed(s): Rebecca Herman. Sesame Workshop, 1 Lincoln Plaza, New York, NY 10023; http://www.sesameworkshop.org/. Illus., adv. Circ: 800000. Vol. ends: Dec. *Aud.:* 2-6 yrs.

From the publishers of *Parenting,* this engaging magazine employs familiar characters from the television show to draw preschool children in to reading and learning. It includes several parent-child activity pages that promote such skills as cutting, tracing, and coloring. The "Play with Me" feature uses physical activity to teach children to use their bodies and senses to explore their world. Every issue focuses on a particular letter and numeral. "Big Bird's Gallery" displays children's artwork and invites questions and drawings from readers. "Sesame Street Parents" is included with each subscription. This magazine is most suitable for individual subscriptions, but it is useful in preschools and will be popular in some public libraries as well.

1268. Skipping Stones: a multicultural magazine. [ISSN: 0899-529X] 1988. 5x/yr. USD 35 (Individuals, USD 25). Ed(s): Arun N Toke. Skipping Stones, PO Box 3939, Eugene, OR 97403-0939; editor@skippingstones.org. Illus., adv. Circ: 2500. *Bk. rev.:* 16, 30-50 words. *Aud.:* 8-14 yrs.

This award-winning, nonprofit, no-frills magazine "encourages cooperation, creativity and celebration of cultural and linguistic diversity." Much of the writing is contributed by children ages 8–15. Regular departments include "Health Rocks!," "What's on your Mind," and "Skipping Stones Stew," which features reader poetry. Also included are regular book reviews, essays, and exchanges of cultural tradition, such as recipes, games, and projects. The magazine also features pen-pal opportunities, and letters to "Dear Hanna," seeking advice and guidance. Highly recommended for school and public libraries.

1269. *Spider: the magazine for children.* [ISSN: 1070-2911] 1993. m. USD 35.97 domestic; USD 47.97 foreign. Ed(s): Heather Delabre. Carus Publishing Company, 315 Fifth St, Peru, IL 61354; custsvc@cobblestone.mv.com; http://www.cricketmag.com. Illus. Circ: 77000 Paid. Vol. ends: Dec. Online: EBSCO Publishing, EBSCO Host. *Indexed:* ICM. *Bk. rev.:* Number and length vary. *Aud.:* 6-10 yrs.

Another quality magazine from the Cricket Group, this is a general-interest publication featuring realistic and fantasy fiction, folktales, poetry, crafts, and puzzles specially designed to interest newly independent readers. It also includes interesting informational articles. The large, lovely illustrations enhance the text, while insect characters inhabiting the sidebars add their own comments. Included also are a book review page and a reader artwork page. Special activity takeout pages at the end involve learning based on concepts within the issue. Recommended for both public libraries and personal subscriptions.

1270. *Sports Illustrated for Kids.* [ISSN: 1042-394X] 1989. m. USD 29.99 domestic; USD 39.95 Canada; USD 49 elsewhere. Ed(s): Neil Cohen. Sports Illustrated For Kids, 135 W 50th St, New York, NY 10020-1393. Illus., adv. Circ: 934000 Paid. *Indexed:* CPerI, ICM, MASUSE, PEI. *Aud.:* 8-14 yrs.

This commercial publication is aimed at boys and girls who are interested in all kinds of sports. Chock-full of articles of varying lengths, it is colorful, with plenty of stunning action photographs. Articles include human-interest stories about professional athletes and other sports figures, and there are short summaries and photos of children who participate in sports. Regular features include "Freeze Frame," large full-color photographs that catch sports figures in action, and "Comic Cards," which prints captions submitted by readers along with the photos. "End Zone" includes trivia quizzes, hypothetical game rule questions, and reader-submitted artwork. Collector cards are included. This magazine contains a large amount of advertising, but it is labeled as such. The accompanying online site contains content that changes at least daily and contains news, games, and interactive features. Recommended for school and public libraries as well as personal subscriptions.

1271. *Stone Soup: the magazine by young writers and artists.* [ISSN: 0094-579X] 1973. bi-m. USD 34 domestic; USD 38 in Canada & Mexico; USD 42 elsewhere. Ed(s): William Rubel, Gerry Mandel. Children's Art Foundation, PO Box 83, Santa Cruz, CA 95063. Illus., adv. Circ: 20000 Paid. Vol. ends: Summer. Online: EBSCO Publishing, EBSCO Host; Gale. *Indexed:* CPerI, ICM. *Bk. rev.:* Number and length vary. *Aud.:* 8-13 yrs.

Called "the *New Yorker* of the 8–13 set," this small-format, 50-page magazine provides young writers and artists a wonderful opportunity to submit their own creative work for publication. All of the stories, poetry, book reviews, and artwork found in this magazine are the original work of the young contributors. Readers are encouraged to submit writing and artwork based on their own experiences and observations. Photographs of the writers and artists are included with their creations. This magazine publishes approximately eight original fiction articles per issue, interspersed with several pages of original poetry and book reviews. "Mailbox" allows readers to provide feedback on pieces they have read. *Stone Soup* is also available in a Braille edition. Highly recommended for school libraries, especially.

Time for Kids. See Classroom Magazines section.

1272. *Turtle Magazine for Preschool Kids.* [ISSN: 0191-3654] 1979. bi-m. USD 15.95 domestic; USD 19.95 foreign. Ed(s): Terry Harshman. Children's Better Health Institute, 1100 Waterway Blvd, PO Box 567, Indianapolis, IN 46206; g.joray@cbhi.org; http://www.cbhi.org. Illus., adv. Circ: 370000. Vol. ends: Dec. *Aud.:* 2-6 yrs.

Written with a focus on health, safety, and physical fitness, this colorful newsprint magazine is perfect for preschool children. Content includes "Fun to Read," which includes articles of varying length and reading ability, and "Fun to Do" activities, such as dot-to-dot, hidden pictures, mazes, matching games, spelling words, simple science experiments, recipes, and coloring pages. Two regular features display children's artwork. "Ask Doctor Cory" answers health-related questions for parents and teachers. Due to the cut-out and workbook style activities in this magazine, it may be best suited for personal subscriptions, although it is of value to public libraries as well.

1273. *U S Kids.* [ISSN: 0895-9471] 1987. 8x/yr. USD 22.95 domestic; USD 32.95 Canada. Ed(s): Daniel Lee. Children's Better Health Institute, 1100 Waterway Blvd, PO Box 567, Indianapolis, IN 46206; g.joray@cbhi.org; http://www.cbhi.org. Adv. Circ: 225000. *Indexed:* ICM. *Aud.:* 5-10 yrs.

This colorful newsprint magazine promotes health and fitness to early elementary school children. It includes fictional articles, matching games, puzzles, brain-teasers, and poetry, as well as fun, educational articles mostly concerning health, nutrition, and fitness. Unfamiliar words are explained with a guide to pronunciation. "U.S. Kids Mailbox" includes children's letters and creative contributions, while "Dr. Cory" answers questions on children's health concerns. Perhaps most suitable for individual subscriptions but of value to public libraries as well.

1274. *Wild: canada's wildlife magazine for kids.* Formerly (until 1995): *Ranger Rick.* [ISSN: 1492-014X] 1984. 8x/yr. CND 25 domestic; CND 45 United States; CND 58 elsewhere. Ed(s): Nancy Payne. Canadian Wildlife Federation, 350 Michael Cowpland Dr, Kanata, ON K2M 2W1, Canada; info@cwf-fcf.org; http://www.cwf-fcf.org. Circ: 30000 Paid. Online: EBSCO Publishing, EBSCO Host. *Indexed:* CBCARef, CPerI, MASUSE. *Aud.:* 7-12 yrs.

This colorful, 36-page magazine is generously illustrated with stunning photographs and other pictures to captivate children's interest in the natural world around them. A two-page, sparely designed table of contents points children directly to articles of interest with thumbnail pictures. The magazine also includes children's letters and artwork as well as questions submitted by readers. Articles are lengthy and fully illustrated. The center page consists of a full-color wildlife poster. Includes games, puzzles, quizzes, and jokes appropriate for the various reading levels; answers are provided at the end of the issue. Highly recommended for public libraries.

1275. *Wild Animal Baby.* [ISSN: 1526-047X] 1999. 10x/yr. USD 19.95 domestic; USD 31.95 foreign. Ed(s): Lori Collins. National Wildlife Federation, 11100 Wildlife Center Dr, Reston, VA 20190-5362; pubs@nwf.org; http://www.nwf.org. Illus., adv. *Aud.:* 1-4 yrs.

Just right for infants through preschoolers, this small-format, chunky magazine brings the world of wildlife to the earliest learners. Published by the National Wildlife Federation, it includes brief informational articles on wild animals; short fictional articles; matching, color, and counting games; "I Spy"; and parent-child interactive games. Each issue features a letter of the alphabet on the back cover, represented by a wild animal. The end of each issue also challenges children to find pictures within the pages of the issue. Highly recommended for public libraries.

1276. *YES Mag: Canada's science magazine for kids.* [ISSN: 1203-8016] 1996. bi-m. CND 22 domestic; CND 28 United States; CND 34 elsewhere. Ed(s): Shannon Hunt. Peter Piper Publishing Inc., 501-3960 Quadra St., Victoria, BC V8X 4A3, Canada. Adv. Circ: 17000 Paid. *Indexed:* CBCARef, CPerI. *Bk. rev.:* Number and length vary. *Aud.:* 8-14 yrs.

This glossy, 32-page magazine is for readers who have graduated from its sister publication, *Know.* It takes adventurous minds on fascinating and educational science journeys that feature highly interesting articles of varying length accompanied by stunning photographs. Regular departments include "Sci and Tech Watch," "Eye on the Sky," and "Science Photo of the Month." The magazine's attractive and eye-catching layout makes for inviting reading. It also includes reader mail, at-home experiments, and reader book reviews. Highly recommended for public libraries.

Young Rider. See Horses section.

1277. *Your Big Backyard.* [ISSN: 0886-5299] 1979. m. USD 19.95 domestic; USD 27 foreign. Ed(s): Lori Collins. National Wildlife Federation, 11100 Wildlife Center Dr, Reston, VA 20190-5362; pubs@nwf.org; http://www.nwf.org. Illus. Circ: 500000. *Indexed:* ICM. *Bk. rev.:* 1-2. *Aud.:* 3-7 yrs.

This quality magazine from the National Wildlife Federation contains informational articles written at levels appropriate for the very young reader. Accompanying photographs are very large and captivating. Also included are whimsical games and quizzes, cut-out activities, and poetry. "Backyard Buddies" features reader-submitted artwork as well as photographs of readers' personal experiences with wildlife. The "Family Fun Guide" section includes recipes, songs, crafts, and other activities, and also reviews a "Book of the Month." This magazine is an excellent introduction to wildlife and environmental topics. Recommended for public libraries and personal subscriptions.

1278. *Zoobooks.* [ISSN: 0737-9005] 1980. m. USD 20.95. Ed(s): Ed Shadek. Wildlife Education Ltd., 12233 Thatcher Ct, Poway, CA 92064; animals@zoobooks.com; http://www.zoobooks.com. Illus. Circ: 275000 Paid. *Indexed:* ICM. *Aud.:* 4-12 yrs.

Guided by scientific consultants, this colorful, award-winning, 16-page monthly filled with interesting text and pictures focuses in-depth on a different animal every issue. Habitat and species variations are also discussed. Captivatingly illustrated, this magazine is appropriate for both very young readers and older ones ready to absorb many new and exciting facts. Illustrations include musculoskeletal diagrams of the animals presented as well as many large and stunning photographs, including a centerfold in every issue. Each issue also contains a four-page paper insert filled with learning games, activities, crafts, and "Kids Correspondence" (children's artistic and creative contributions). The publication also includes several subscriber-only online features, such as quizzes ("20 Questions"), games, and many additional contributor poems and stories. Each issue announces the next month's animal. Perfect for use in the classroom, in the home, and as a library resource for school projects.

■ CIVIL LIBERTIES

General/Bioethics: Reproductive Rights, Right-to-Life, and Right-to-Die/ Freedom of Expression and Information/Freedom of Thought and Belief/Groups and Minorities/Political-Economic Rights

See also Alternatives; News and Opinion; and Political Science sections.

Catherine Kaye, Government Documents Section, California State University, Fullerton, CA 92834; ckaye@fullerton.edu.

Marie F. Jones, Extended Campus Services Librarian, East Tennessee State University, Johnson City, TN 37614; jonesmf@mail.etsu.edu

Introduction

The journals reviewed in this section document the crucial role of civil liberties in democracy. Civil liberties—the rights to freedom of thought, expression, and action without interference from government—have been at the forefront of debate in the United States since the Founding Fathers wrote the Bill of Rights with the specific intent to safeguard individual liberties against the power of a strong central government.

Civil liberties have traditionally been concerned with freedom of expression and due process, but the specific focus has changed as public attitudes have shifted from one generation to the next. Civil liberties have expanded and, during times of national crisis such as war, have contracted. Judicial activism has had significant impact on civil liberties. The Warren Court (1953–1969)

carved out the constitutional right of privacy that later became the basis of *Roe v. Wade.* The Burger Court shifted rightward and weakened civil liberties, notably in the area of criminal procedure protections. Toward the end of the twentieth century, technology became the First Amendment battleground. Free speech on the Internet and the right to privacy relating to individuals' genetic profiles entered the debate. The terrorist attacks of September 11, 2001, and the USA PATRIOT Act, giving government unprecedented investigative powers, heightened civil liberties concerns. Government actions to prevent future terrorist attacks have made the defense of civil liberties more complex than at any time in our history.

In 1822, James Madison wrote, "A people who mean to be their own governors must arm themselves with the power which knowledge gives." Articles in journals in this section give historical review of civil liberties issues and also chronicle contemporary discussion by intellectuals and policymakers. Intelligent design, RFID technology, secret government surveillance, racial profiling, holiday displays in public places, x-raying of luggage at airports, tracking the contacts of people with HIV, mandatory drug testing of workers whose impairment endangers others, and the civil liberties scorecard of the current administration are issues that citizens, students, and scholars need to examine in depth so that they may effectively participate in American democracy. Journals in this section inform Americans about issues that touch on their daily lives and on the future of their country.

Librarians should review titles in other sections of *Magazines for Libraries*, most notably the ones dedicated to individual groups (African Americans, Asian Americans, Disabilities, Latino Studies, Native Americans, and Women) to augment titles in this section.

Basic Periodicals

Hs: *Amnesty International, Human Rights (Chicago), Liberty (Hagerstown), Newsletter on Intellectual Freedom, Reason;* Ga: *Amnesty International, Cultural Survival Quarterly, Free Inquiry, Human Rights (Chicago), Index on Censorship, Liberty (Hagerstown), Newsletter on Intellectual Freedom, Northwestern Journal of International Human Rights, Reason;* Ac: *Amnesty International, Bioethics, Constitutional Commentary, Cultural Survival Quarterly, Harvard Civil Rights—Civil Liberties Law Review, Human Rights (Chicago), Human Rights & Human Welfare, Human Rights Quarterly, Index on Censorship, Journal of Law and Religion, Law & Inequality, Newsletter on Intellectual Freedom, Northwestern Journal of International Human Rights, Reason;* Sa: *Bioethics, Constitutional Commentary, Free Inquiry, Harvard Civil Rights—Civil Liberties Law Review, Human Rights Quarterly, Issues in Law and Medicine, Journal of Law and Religion, Law & Inequality, Northwestern Journal of International Human Rights.*

Basic Abstracts and Indexes

Alternative Press Index.

General

1279. *Constitutional Commentary.* [ISSN: 0742-7115] 1984. 3x/yr. USD 22; USD 9 newsstand/cover per issue. Ed(s): Daniel Farber. Constitutional Commentary Inc., 229 19th Ave S, Minneapolis, MN 55455; webmaster@law.umn.edu; http://www.law.umn.edu/. Illus., adv. Circ: 600. Vol. ends: Winter. Microform: WSH. Online: EBSCO Publishing, EBSCO Host; Florida Center for Library Automation; Gale; William S. Hein & Co., Inc.; LexisNexis; Northern Light Technology, Inc.; Thomson West. Reprint: WSH. *Indexed:* CLI, ILP, LRI. *Bk. rev.:* 1-4, 2,000-10,000 words. *Aud.:* Ac, Sa.

One of the few faculty-edited law school journals in the country, *Constitutional Commentary* enjoys a wide following among legal scholars, historians, political scientists, and others interested in constitutional law and history. Articles are short and "less ponderous" than ones in traditional law reviews and tend to be topical rather than focus on individual cases. Review essays, book reviews, and a popular column titled "Buf cf...," offering amusing tidbits from historical writings, are featured. Recent issues examine the constitutionality of the filibuster, direct-tax clauses, and separation of powers in the Rehnquist and Burger Courts. Available in print and electronic formats.

Criminal Justice Ethics. See Criminology and Law Enforcement section.

1280. *Harvard Civil Rights - Civil Liberties Law Review.* [ISSN: 0017-8039] 1966. 2x/yr. USD 30 domestic; USD 38 Canada; USD 36 elsewhere. Ed(s): Laura Weinrib, Elena Goldstein. Harvard University, Law School, Publications Center, 1541 Massachusetts Ave, Cambridge, MA 02138; hlscrc@law.harvard.edu; http://www.law.harvard.edu/. Illus., adv. Circ: 1100. Vol. ends: Summer. Microform: WSH; PMC; PQC. Online: EBSCO Publishing, EBSCO Host; LexisNexis; OCLC Online Computer Library Center, Inc.; Thomson West; H.W. Wilson. Reprint: WSH. *Indexed:* ArtHuCI, CJA, CLI, HRA, IBR, IBZ, ILP, LRI, PAIS, PSA, RI-1, SSCI, SUSA, SociolAb. *Bk. rev.:* 1, 2,800-4,500 words. *Aud.:* Ac, Sa.

This law journal was founded in the mid-sixties during the wave of constitutional reform produced by the Warren Court and has tracked the erosion of those civil rights and liberties through the years. As editors change every two years, so do editorial viewpoints, but the common themes of social justice and civil liberties continue throughout, making the journal an "instrument to enhance personal freedoms and human dignities." Articles are written by professors, practitioners, and students. Book reviews appear in every other issue; student book notes appear in each issue. Recent issues examine wrongful birth and wrongful life, RFID's threat to consumer privacy, the right to protest in the aftermath of September 11, the rights of detainees to due process, and First Amendment challenges to cross burning. Available in print and electronic formats.

1281. *Human Rights & Human Welfare: an international review of books and other publications.* [ISSN: 1533-0834] 2001. q. Free. Ed(s): Daniel Whelan, Laura Hebert. Center on Rights Development, University of Denver, Graduate School of International Studies, Denver, CO 80208; cord-mail@du.edu. *Aud.:* Ga, Ac, Sa.

HRHW publishes thematic review essays, book notes, and a review digest on current literature dealing with major issues in overlapping areas of human rights, encompassing international relations, economic and social development, comparative politics, comparative political economy, and political theory. The journal reviews monograph and non-monograph materials, including World Bank reports, research studies, and policy documents. It also covers information currently available on the Internet, with a focus on content, complexity, and ease of use. The Review Digest, an annotated bibliography, lists recent publications and serves as a critical guide to help readers identify areas where new approaches are needed. Articles are peer reviewed. The journal is hosted by the Graduate School of International Studies at the University of Denver in cooperation with an International Consortium of Human Rights Centers. URL: www.du.edu/gsis/hrhw

1282. *Human Rights (Chicago).* [ISSN: 0046-8185] 1970. q. USD 25 (Individuals, USD 18). Ed(s): Vicki Quade. American Bar Association, 321 N Clark St, Chicago, IL 60610; quadev@attmail.com; http://www.abanet.org. Illus., index, adv. Circ: 7000. Microform: WSH. Online: EBSCO Publishing, EBSCO Host; OCLC Online Computer Library Center, Inc.; ProQuest LLC (Ann Arbor); Thomson West. Reprint: WSH. *Indexed:* AgeL, ArtHuCI, CLI, IBR, IBZ, ILP, LRI, PAIS, SSCI. *Aud.:* Hs, Ga, Ac.

Each issue of this journal features articles and special reports surrounding a theme, providing background and analysis on an area of individual rights of current interest. Recent themes include current challenges in public education, the human right to adequate housing, renewal of the Voting Rights Act, and the need for a constitutional amendment to address child poverty. Although published by the American Bar Association Section of Individual Rights and Responsibilities for their section members, the format of this publication, more glossy trade magazine than heavy legal journal, makes it suitable for all types of libraries.

1283. *Human Rights Quarterly: a comparative and international journal of the social sciences, humanities and law.* Formerly (until 1981): *Universal Human Rights.* [ISSN: 0275-0392] 1979. q. USD 170. Ed(s): Bert B Lockwood, Jr. The Johns Hopkins University Press, 2715 N Charles St, Baltimore, MD 21218-4363; http://muse.jhu.edu. Illus., index, adv. Sample. Refereed. Circ: 1436. Vol. ends: Nov. Microform: WSH;

IDC; PQC. Online: Chadwyck-Healey Inc.; EBSCO Publishing, EBSCO Host; Florida Center for Library Automation; Gale; William S. Hein & Co., Inc.; JSTOR (Web-based Journal Archive); OCLC Online Computer Library Center, Inc.; OhioLINK; Project MUSE; ProQuest LLC (Ann Arbor); SwetsWise Online Content. Reprint: PSC; WSH. *Indexed:* ABCPolSci, ABS&EES, AmH&L, ArtHuCI, BAS, CJA, CLI, HistAb, IBR, IBSS, IBZ, ILP, IPSA, IndIslam, LRI, PAIS, PRA, PSA, PhilInd, RI-1, RiskAb, SSA, SSCI, SociolAb. *Bk. rev.:* 1-4, 1,100-3,000 words. *Aud.:* Ac, Sa.

This international journal addresses the complex issues of human rights from an interdisciplinary perspective. Basing its vision on the Universal Declaration of Human Rights, the journal provides a forum for noted international experts in the fields of law, philosophy, and the sciences to present comparative and international research on public policy. Articles are edited to be understood by the intelligent reader. The quarterly provides up-to-date information on the United Nations and regional human rights organizations, both governmental and nongovernmental, and includes human rights research and policy analysis, book reviews, and philosophical essays on the nature of human rights. Recent articles explore the connection between domestic violence and housing rights, the human rights of stateless persons, the crisis of humanitarian intervention in Sudan, and the human right to a safe environment. Highly recommended for academic libraries. Available in print and electronic formats.

Journal of Criminal Law & Criminology. See Law section.

1284. *Law & Inequality: a journal of theory and practice.* [ISSN: 0737-089X] 1981. 2x/yr. USD 18; USD 10 newsstand/cover per issue. Ed(s): Shilesh Muralidhara, Helen Hu. University of Minnesota, Law School, 229 19th Ave S, Minneapolis, MN 55455; http://www.law.umn.edu. Illus., adv. Refereed. Circ: 5600. Vol. ends: Jun. Microform: WSH. Online: LexisNexis. Reprint: WSH. *Indexed:* CLI, ILP, LRI, RI-1. *Bk. rev.:* 1, 2,000 words. *Aud.:* Ac, Sa.

Published by the law students of University of Minnesota, this journal examines the social impact of law on disadvantaged people. Articles are written by legal scholars and practitioners, law students, and non-lawyers. Topics include gender, sexuality, age, ability, race, and socioeconomic status, always with a legal emphasis. Articles appear in standard law journal formats or in personal essays. Recent issues examine Florida's gay adoption ban, the use and abuse of laws in the war on terrorism, and gender equality in reproductive healthcare. Recommended for academic libraries. Available in print and electronic formats.

New Perspectives Quarterly. See News and Opinion section.

1285. *Northwestern Journal of International Human Rights.* [ISSN: 1549-828X] 2003. s-a. Free. Ed(s): Emily Stewart. Northwestern University, School of Law, 357 E Chicago Ave, Chicago, IL 60611; law-web@law.northwestern.edu; http://www.law.northwestern.edu. Reprint: WSH. *Aud.:* Ga, Ac, Sa.

Northwestern University School of Law publishes this interdisciplinary journal dedicated to providing a forum for discussion of human rights issues and international human rights law. Authors are professionals, scholars, and experienced field workers writing on law, business, political science, public policy, economics, sociology, and religion. Recent articles explore the international politics of sexuality and religion, the application of international human rights law to energy access, bringing justice to Cambodia's Khmer Rouge, and sexual trafficking near U.S. military bases. URL: www.law.northwestern.edu/journals/jihr

Social Philosophy and Policy. See Philosophy section.

Social Theory and Practice. See Cultural Studies section.

Bioethics: Reproductive Rights, Right-to-Life, and Right-to-Die

1286. *Bioethics.* [ISSN: 0269-9702] bi-m. GBP 613 print & online eds. Ed(s): Dr. Udo Schueklenk, Ruth Chadwick. Blackwell Publishing Ltd., 9600 Garsington Rd, Oxford, OX4 2ZG, United Kingdom; customerservices@blackwellpublishing.com; http://www.blackwellpublishing.com. Illus. Refereed. Online: Blackwell Synergy; EBSCO Publishing, EBSCO Host; Gale; IngentaConnect; OCLC Online Computer Library Center, Inc.; OhioLINK; SwetsWise Online Content. Reprint: PSC. *Indexed:* ASSIA, ApEcolAb, ArtHuCI, CINAHL, ExcerpMed, GSI, IBR, IBSS, IBZ, IndIslam, PSA, PhilInd, PsycInfo, RI-1, RiskAb, SCI, SSA, SSCI, SWA, SociolAb. *Bk. rev.:* 6-10, 400-1,300 words. *Aud.:* Ac, Sa.

This official journal of the International Association of Bioethics discusses ethical issues raised in the biological and medical sciences. Each issue of the scholarly, refereed journal contains articles, discussion, and book reviews, from an international perspective. Articles are either theoretical or practical in nature, and often offer opposing viewpoints within a single issue. Topics range from AIDS to euthanasia, genomics, informed consent, organ transplants, and stem cell research. Recent articles examine wrongful disability, artificial life support, polio eradication, preparing for an influenza epidemic, and biodefense. Issues sometimes focus on a theme, such as a recent one on infectious diseases. The journal is available in print and electronic formats. The publisher makes available online the table of contents of issues from 1997 to the present and also a sample issue in its entirety (www.blackwellpublishing.com/journals/BIOETHICS).

Hastings Center Report. See Public Health section.

1287. *Issues in Law and Medicine.* [ISSN: 8756-8160] 1985. 3x/yr. USD 99. Ed(s): James Bopp, Jr., Barry A. Bostrom. National Legal Center for the Medically Dependent and Disabled, Inc., Bopp, Coleson & Bostrom, 1 South Sixth St, Terre Haute, IN 47807-3510; bcb@bopplaw.com. Illus., adv. Refereed. Circ: 1000. Vol. ends: Spring. Microform: WSH. Online: EBSCO Publishing, EBSCO Host; Florida Center for Library Automation; Gale; William S. Hein & Co., Inc.; LexisNexis; OCLC Online Computer Library Center, Inc.; ProQuest LLC (Ann Arbor); Thomson West; H.W. Wilson. Reprint: WSH. *Indexed:* AgeL, ArtHuCI, BiolAb, CINAHL, CJA, CLI, ECER, HRA, ILP, LRI, PRA, RI-1, SSCI, SUSA, SWR&A, V&AA. *Bk. rev.:* 5, 200-1,000 words. *Aud.:* Ac, Sa.

This peer-reviewed professional journal has recently shifted its focus away from exclusively discussing medical treatment rights of persons with disabilities and in need of life sustaining treatment toward more general bioethics topics. Articles are sometimes technical in nature because the target audience of the publication is attorneys, healthcare professionals, educators, and administrators. The editorial policy opposes euthanasia and assisted suicide. A wider audience will appreciate the juxtaposition of opposing views on controversial topics and the abstracts of relevant articles from other journals. Available in print and electronic formats.

Freedom of Expression and Information

1288. *Index on Censorship: for free expression.* [ISSN: 0306-4220] 1972. q. GBP 149 print & online eds. Ed(s): Ursula Owen, Judith Vidal-Hall. Routledge, 4 Park Sq, Milton Park, Abingdon, OX14 4RN, United Kingdom; info@routledge.co.uk; http://www.routledge.co.uk. Illus., index, adv. Circ: 10000. Vol. ends: Nov/Dec. Online: EBSCO Publishing, EBSCO Host; SwetsWise Online Content. Reprint: PSC. *Indexed:* AltPI, AmHI, ArtHuCI, BAS, BrHumI, FLI, IBR, IBZ, IndIslam, L&LBA, LISA, MASUSE, MLA-IB, PAIS, RILM, SSA, SSCI. *Aud.:* Ga, Ac.

Index on Censorship reports on freedom of speech, censorship, and censored topics worldwide and acts as a political forum on a broad range of topics. "International in outlook, outspoken in comment," articles and essays take an approach to controversial issues not found in mainstream news and political commentary resources. Regular features include examples of banned literature, factual reports, and comment. Most notably, every issue includes the 30-page "Index Index," which chronicles censorship and free-expression abuses around the world country-by-country. Photo essays documenting the lives of the people and groups reported on are frequently published, and dramatic cover art has become a trademark of the publication. Available in print and electronic formats.

Journal of Information Ethics. See Library and Information Science section.

1289. *Newsletter on Intellectual Freedom.* [ISSN: 0028-9485] 1952. 6x/yr. USD 70 domestic; USD 80 foreign; USD 85 combined subscription domestic print & online eds. Ed(s): Judith F Krug. American Library Association, 50 E Huron St, Chicago, IL 60611-2795; http://www.ala.org. Illus., index. Circ: 3200. Vol. ends: Jan. Microform: PQC. Online: EBSCO Publishing, EBSCO Host; OCLC Online Computer Library Center, Inc.; ProQuest K-12 Learning Solutions; ProQuest LLC (Ann Arbor); H.W. Wilson. *Indexed:* LibLit. *Bk. rev.:* 1-4, 500-700 words. *Aud.:* Hs, Ac, Ga.

American Library Association's Office of Intellectual Freedom publishes this newsletter covering intellectual freedom infringements in the United States and worldwide. The only journal that reports attempts to remove materials from school and library shelves across the United States, it also features "Censorship Dateline," a state-by-state survey of challenges and bannings, arranged by location; "Is It Legal?" and "From the Bench," listing important developments in federal and state laws affecting librarians, teachers, students, authors, and journalists; and "The Intellectual Freedom Bibliography," a guide to current articles and books on freedom of expression in the United States. Recent issues report on public support of the USA PATRIOT Act, intellectual freedom as a casualty of war, Internet filters in libraries, targeting of gay-themed books, intelligent design in the classroom, RFID technology, and privacy issues. This bi-monthly newsletter is available online (www.members.ala.org/nif).

Freedom of Thought and Belief

1290. *Free Inquiry.* [ISSN: 0272-0701] 1980. 11x/yr. USD 19.98 domestic; USD 29.97 foreign. Ed(s): Timothy Madigan, Lewis Vaughn. Council for Secular Humanism, PO Box 664, Amherst, NY 14226-0664; freeinquiry@secularhumanism.org; http://www.secularhumanism.org. Illus., index, adv. Circ: 23000 Paid. Vol. ends: Fall. Microform: PQC. Online: Florida Center for Library Automation; Gale; Northern Light Technology, Inc.; OCLC Online Computer Library Center, Inc.; ProQuest LLC (Ann Arbor). *Indexed:* IBR, IBZ, PAIS, PhilInd. *Bk. rev.:* 3-5, 500-1,500 words. *Aud.:* Hs, Ga, Sa.

Published by the Council for Secular Humanism, *Free Inquiry* focuses on the positive and affirmative aspects of the naturalistic, secular, and humanistic outlook. Editor Paul Kurtz, in support of the position that "secular humanism and scientific naturalism can contribute immensely to the growth of democracy and the improvement of the human condition," presents articles that argue the need to defend free inquiry in all areas of human endeavor. Controversial issues such as church-state separation and the rights of religious minorities are dealt with as ethical matters rather than as political concerns. Readers include scholars, researchers, and others with an interest in secular issues. Recent articles include "The Republican War on Science," "Twisting Scripture: When Translators Distort the Bible," and "The Best Antidote for Religious Fanaticism." Available in print and electronic formats.

The Humanist. See Religion section.

Journal of Church and State. See Religion section.

1291. *Journal of Law and Religion.* [ISSN: 0748-0814] 1983. s-a. USD 35 (Individuals, USD 25; Students, USD 12). Ed(s): Marie A Failinger. Hamline University, School of Law, 1536 Hewitt Ave, St Paul, MN 55104-1284; http://web.hamline.edu/law/. Illus., index, adv. Refereed. Microform: WSH; PMC. Online: EBSCO Publishing, EBSCO Host; William S. Hein & Co., Inc.; JSTOR (Web-based Journal Archive). Reprint: WSH. *Indexed:* CLI, ILP, LRI, NTA, PRA, PSA, R&TA, RI-1, SociolAb. *Bk. rev.:* 1-2, 2,000 words. *Aud.:* Ac, Sa.

Journal of Law and Religion offers an international, interdisciplinary forum on law in its social context, including moral and religious views of law and life for policymakers, scholars, and educators. Examining the "intersection and interaction" of law and religion, this peer-reviewed journal includes a broad range of types of topics, including historical studies, theoretical questions of jurisprudence and theology, essays on the meaning of justice and rights, power and authority, and studies of law and religion in the social arena. In seeking out voices from all religious and legal traditions throughout the world and bringing them into conversations with one another, the journal offers a constructive response to the major issues of the times. Recent articles include "Natural Law and Natural Rights in Islamic Law" and "The Death of Children by Faith-Based Medical Neglect." Available in print and electronic formats.

1292. *Liberty (Hagerstown): a magazine of religious freedom.* [ISSN: 0024-2055] 1906. bi-m. USD 7.95. Ed(s): Lincoln Steed. Review and Herald Publishing Association, 55 W Oak Ridge Dr, Hagerstown, MD 21740-3790; info@rhpa.org; http://www.rhpa.org. Illus., adv. Circ: 200000. Vol. ends: Nov/Dec. Microform: PQC. *Aud.:* Hs, Ga.

Published by the Seventh Day Adventist Church, this magazine is dedicated to the principle that "The God-given right of religious liberty is best exercised when church and state are separate." This readable magazine speaks strongly on issues of separation of church and state, sometimes presenting opposing viewpoints. Articles have touched on topics such as intelligent design, conscientious objection, prayer in school, and whether "under God" should be in the Pledge of Allegiance. The magazine is not proselytizing, and treats issues with "quiet diplomacy." Its online edition (www.libertymagazine.org) includes full text of current articles and archives, with printer-friendly versions and e-mail options.

Mental and Physical Disability Law Reporter. See Law section.

Groups and Minorities

The Advocate. See Gay, Lesbian, Bisexual, and Transgender section.

American Indian Law Review. See Native Americans section.

Children's Legal Rights Journal. See Sociology and Social Work/General section.

Columbia Journal of Gender and the Law. See Law section.

1293. *Cultural Survival Quarterly: world report on the rights of indigenous peoples and ethnic minorities.* Formerly (until 1982): *Cultural Survival Newsletter.* [ISSN: 0740-3291] 1976. q. USD 40; USD 60. Ed(s): Amy Stoll. Cultural Survival, Inc., 215 Prospect St, Cambridge, MA 02139; culturalsurvival@cs.org; http://www.culturalsurvival.org/. Illus., index, adv. Circ: 10000. Vol. ends: Winter. Reprint: PSC. *Indexed:* ABS&EES, AICP, AltPI, AnthLit, CABA, ENW, ForAb, RILM, WAE&RSA. *Bk. rev.:* 1-3, 300-700 words. *Aud.:* Ga, Ac.

CSQ began in 1981 as a newsletter for Cultural Survival, an organization that "has helped indigenous people and ethnic minorities deal as equals in their encounters with industrial society." Since then, the quarterly has expanded to report on the interconnected issues that affect indigenous and ethnic minority communities around the world, including environmental destruction, land rights, sustainable development, and cultural integrity. News, resources, book and media reviews, and notes from the field are included in each issue. All authors are indigenous or are professionals who work with indigenous peoples. Recent articles cover genetic research on human migration, the Alaska Arctic Wildlife Refuge, and indigenous communities and technology. Available in print and electronic formats.

Disability & Society. See Disabilities section.

Lesbian-Gay Law Notes. See Gay, Lesbian, Bisexual, and Transgender section.

Mainstream. See Disabilities section.

Migration World. See Ethnic Studies section.

Mouth. See Disabilities section.

National Black Law Journal. See Law section.

Off Our Backs. See Gender Studies section.

Ragged Edge. See Disabilities section.

Southern California Review of Law and Women's Studies. See Law section.

Political-Economic Rights

Clearinghouse Review. See Law section.

Employee Relations Law Journal. See Labor and Industrial Relations section.

Progressive. See News and Opinion section.

1294. *Reason: free minds and free markets.* [ISSN: 0048-6906] 1968. m. USD 19.97 domestic; USD 29.97 foreign; USD 3.50 newsstand/cover per issue. Ed(s): Nicholas Gillespie. Reason Foundation, 3415 S Sepulveda Blvd, Ste 400, Los Angeles, CA 90034-6060; michaelo@reason.com; http://www.reason.org/pwatch.html. Illus., index, adv. Circ: 50000. Vol. ends: Apr. Microform: PQC. Online: EBSCO Publishing, EBSCO Host; Factiva, Inc.; Florida Center for Library Automation; Gale; Northern Light Technology, Inc.; OCLC Online Computer Library Center, Inc.; ProQuest K-12 Learning Solutions; ProQuest LLC (Ann Arbor); H.W. Wilson. *Indexed:* ABS&EES, AmH&L, BRI, CBRI, HistAb, LRI, MRD, PAIS, PhilInd, RGPR. *Bk. rev.:* 3-4, 1,500-2,500 words. *Aud.:* Hs, Ga, Ac.

Published by Reason Foundation, a nonprofit research and educational organization promoting libertarian principles, *Reason* is an editorially independent and nonpartisan magazine whose writers represent a range of political affiliations. This magazine reports on public policy and popular culture through a mix of news, analysis, commentary, and reviews, attempting to provide an alternative to right-wing and left-wing opinion magazines while "making a principled case for liberty and individual choice in all areas of human activity." Discussions have included homeland security spending, why poor countries are poor, immigration policy, corporate environmentalism, and trade barriers. The journal is available online (www.reason.com), providing full text of past issues in a searchable archive.

The Review of Black Political Economy. See Labor and Industrial Relations section.

■ CLASSICAL STUDIES

See also Archaeology; Art; History; Linguistics; and Literature sections.

Fred W. Jenkins, Head of Collection Management, Roesch Library, University of Dayton, Dayton, OH 45469; fred.jenkins@udayton.edu

Introduction

Although displaced from the central role in education that it once enjoyed, classical scholarship has continued to flourish. University faculty and graduate students produce and consume a large volume of scholarly papers in a variety of journals. Latin and the study of classical civilization have also maintained a modest presence in schools and colleges, although relatively few periodicals are directed toward this audience.

The journal-publishing environment in classical studies remains a stable one. Most journals are well-established titles that have existed for decades, although there are the inevitable shifts in quality and character among them. The few new classical journals introduced in recent years have been devoted largely to highly specialized subdisciplines. Associations and university presses issue the bulk of the titles; there are few commercial publishers in the field. As a result, nearly all the journals aim at an academic audience. Many are highly technical in content, contain extensive passages of untranslated Latin and Greek, and will interest only professional scholars. *Amphora, Arethusa, Arion, Classics Ireland,* and *Greece and Rome* are among the few exceptions that might appeal to a broader audience.

Two particular groups of journals deserve comment. First, there are several good periodicals aimed at teachers of the classics at the high school and college levels. *Classical Journal, Classical Outlook,* and *Classical World* all offer articles and columns of pedagogical interest. Classical studies are also well served by journals devoted solely to book reviews and bibliographical essays. These include *Bryn Mawr Classical Review, Classical Review, Gnomon,* and *Lustrum.* Librarians and scholars alike will find these to be valuable resources.

Classics was also one of the first disciplines to experiment with electronic publishing. *Bryn Mawr Classical Review,* a notable success in this arena, claims to be the second-oldest online scholarly journal in the humanities. While a majority of the print journals found below now have online avatars, new freestanding electronic journals have been slow to appear. Among those that seem to be establishing a lasting presence, three deserve note. *Amphora* is a new publication that seeks to promote the classics to students and the general public. *Ancient Narrative* is an experiment in ongoing peer review; articles are posted online for a year of comment and revision before a final version is archived. *Liverpool International Classical Studies* is an offshoot of an annual seminar; it offers expanding thematic clusters of articles and working papers. With the exception of *Ancient Narrative,* all of the electronic titles discussed here are available without charge on the Internet.

Journals listed below include the most important English-language titles for students and scholars. Only a handful of European journals are noted—those that publish a substantial number of studies in English or provide exceptional bibliographical resources. Because classics has always been an international discipline, libraries supporting research programs in classics will need many additional foreign-language journals.

Basic Periodicals

Hs: *Amphora, Classical Journal, Classical Outlook, Classical World, Greece and Rome.* Ac: *American Journal of Philology, Amphora, Bryn Mawr Classical Review Online, Classical Journal, Classical Outlook, Classical Philology, Classical World, Greece and Rome, Transactions of the American Philological Association.*

Basic Abstracts and Indexes

L'Annee Philologique, Arts and Humanities Citation Index, Humanities Index, TOCS-IN.

1295. *American Journal of Philology.* [ISSN: 0002-9475] 1880. q. USD 160. Ed(s): Barbara K Gold. The Johns Hopkins University Press, 2715 N Charles St, Baltimore, MD 21218-4363; myq@press.jhu.edu; http://muse.jhu.edu. Illus., index, adv. Sample. Refereed. Circ: 961 Paid. Vol. ends: Winter. Microform: IDC; PMC. Online: EBSCO Publishing, EBSCO Host; Florida Center for Library Automation; Gale; JSTOR (Web-based Journal Archive); OCLC Online Computer Library Center, Inc.; OhioLINK; Project MUSE; ProQuest LLC (Ann Arbor); SwetsWise Online Content. Reprint: PSC. *Indexed:* AmHI, ArtHuCI, BRI, CBRI, FR, HumInd, IBR, IBZ, IPB, IndIslam, L&LBA, LingAb, NTA, NumL, PhilInd, RILM, SSCI. *Bk. rev.:* 8-10, 2-5 pages. *Aud.:* Ac.

One of the oldest and most prestigious American journals in the field, the *American Journal of Philology* publishes scholarly contributions in all areas of classical studies, with special emphasis on languages and literature. Contents include both substantial articles and book reviews. These are aimed at professional scholars and generally require a good working knowledge of Latin and Greek. Tables of contents for recent issues and sample issues are available on the publisher's web site. Indispensable for any academic collection that supports a classics program.

1296. *American Philological Association. Transactions.* Supersedes in part (until 1972): *American Philological Association. Transactions and Proceedings;* Which was formerly (until 1986): *American Philological Association. Transactions.* [ISSN: 0360-5949] 1870. s-a. USD 100. Ed(s): Paul Allen Miller. The Johns Hopkins University Press, 2715 N Charles St, Baltimore, MD 21218-4363; http://muse.jhu.edu. Illus., adv. Refereed. Circ: 2576 Paid. Microform: PMC. Online: EBSCO Publishing, EBSCO Host; JSTOR (Web-based Journal Archive); OCLC Online Computer Library Center, Inc.; OhioLINK; Project MUSE; ProQuest LLC (Ann Arbor); SwetsWise Online Content. *Indexed:* AmHI, ArtHuCI, IBR, IBZ, L&LBA, NTA. *Aud.:* Ac.

As the official journal of the American Philological Association (APA), the major professional association for American classicists, this is one of the most widely read titles in the field. It covers all aspects of classical studies and usually offers a good mix of articles on classical literature and history, although literature has predominated in recent years. After more than 130 years as an annual publication, the *Transactions* has now become a semi-annual publication. A typical issue has a six to nine articles. With the change in frequency, other changes have also ensued. The Spring 2005 issue was a first-ever theme issue for this title, consisting largely of papers from a conference on new directions in the study of Roman literature. The publications section of the association's web site (www.apaclassics.org) includes useful materials on the *Transactions,* including tables of contents and abstracts from the recent volumes. A basic title for any academic library.

1297. *Amphora.* [ISSN: 1542-2364] 2002. s-a. American Philological Association, University of Pennsylvania, 292 Logan Hall, Philadelphia, PA 19104-6304; apaclassics@sas.upenn.edu; http://www.apaclassics.org. Illus. *Bk. rev.:* 1-2. *Aud.:* Hs, Ga, Ac.

Amphora represents a relatively new publishing venture by the American Philological Association. It is a lively, illustrated periodical aimed at the general public, students, and scholars. Its contents include articles on classical topics of general interest such as mythology, Pompeii, and films on classical themes. *Amphora* also offers reviews of popular works of classical interest ranging from the classical Greek translations of Harry Potter to a recent biography of Livia. It is available without charge on the APA web site. Back issues are available in pdf format.

1298. *Ancient Narrative.* [ISSN: 1568-3532] 2001. 3x/yr. EUR 96 (Individuals, EUR 48). Ed(s): Dr. Maaike Zimmerman. Barkhuis Publishing, Zuurstukken 37, Eelde, 9761 KP, Netherlands; info@barkhuis.nl; http://www.barkhuis.nl. Refereed. *Aud.:* Ac.

Ancient Narrative is a relatively new journal devoted to the novel in antiquity and its subsequent reception and influence. It covers Jewish, early Christian, and Byzantine narrative texts as well as classical Latin and Greek writings. Contributors take a wide range of approaches, ranging from traditional philological and historical studies to those applying critical theory and methods drawn from the social sciences. This primarily electronic journal represents something of a hybrid. Articles are posted continuously on the web, taken down periodically to allow the authors to revise them in light of comments received, and then appear in final form in the annual volume (both in print and in the electronic archive of *Ancient Narrative*). The journal also publishes numerous supplements that include both *Festschriften* and thematic collections of essays.

1299. *Arethusa.* [ISSN: 0004-0975] 1968. 3x/yr. USD 100. Ed(s): Madeleine S Kaufman, Martha Malamud. The Johns Hopkins University Press, 2715 N Charles St, Baltimore, MD 21218-4363; http://muse.jhu.edu. Illus., adv. Sample. Refereed. Circ: 526 Paid. Vol. ends: Fall. Microform: PQC. Online: Chadwyck-Healey Inc.; EBSCO Publishing, EBSCO Host; OCLC Online Computer Library Center, Inc.; OhioLINK; Project MUSE; ProQuest LLC (Ann Arbor); SwetsWise Online Content. Reprint: PSC. *Indexed:* AmHI, ArtHuCI, HumInd, IBR, IBZ, L&LBA, MLA-IB. *Aud.:* Ac.

Focusing on literary criticism, this journal includes both traditional and new approaches to classical literature. Although scholarly, the articles are often accessible to general readers and students. Thematic issues are not uncommon; recent examples have focused on deixis in Greek lyric poetry and the personal voice in classical scholarship. A typical issue includes four to eight articles. Tables of contents and sample issues are available electronically through the publisher's web site. Recommended for all academic collections.

1300. *Arion: a journal of humanities and the classics.* [ISSN: 0095-5809] 1962. 3x/yr. USD 35 (Individuals, USD 19; Students, USD 12). Ed(s): Herbert Golder. Boston University, 10 Lenox St, Brookline, MA 02146; arion@acs.bu.edu; http://web.bu.edu/arion/. Illus., adv. Circ: 800 Controlled. Vol. ends: Fall. Microform: PQC. Reprint: PSC. *Indexed:* AmHI, ArtHuCI, IAPV, MLA-IB, PhilInd, RILM. *Bk. rev.:* 2-5, 5-20 pages. *Aud.:* Ac.

One of the more lively and controversial journals in the field, *Arion* covers classical literature and its influence. It tends to avoid the technical baggage found in most classical journals and often features nontraditional and comparative approaches. Recent issues have included many articles on the reception of the classics in various eras. Original poetry and translations from Greek and Latin literature also appear in most issues. Tables of contents for current and past issues are available on the journal's web site. *Arion* would be a good addition to any academic library supporting literature programs, as well as a worthwhile selection for larger public libraries.

1301. *Bryn Mawr Classical Review.* [ISSN: 1063-2948] 1990. irreg. Free. Bryn Mawr College, 101 N Merion Ave, Bryn Mawr, PA 19010; http://www.ccat.sas.upenn.edu/bmcr. Illus. Refereed. *Bk. rev.:* 1,500-2,000 words. *Aud.:* Ac.

Claiming to be the "second oldest online scholarly journal in the humanities," this journal provides book reviews that are both timely and scholarly. It is the best single source for evaluations of recent books in classical studies; *BMCR* reviewed over 500 books in 2005. Reviewers, who are normally specialists in the relevant area, offer substantial, detailed, and critical treatments. Important or controversial books sometimes receive multiple reviews; authors' responses are also published. In addition to reviews, the journal includes occasional announcements concerning items of professional interest. Access to the *Review* is free. Subscribers receive new reviews irregularly by e-mail, as they become available. The backfiles are maintained on the publisher's web site and are searchable. An electronic subscription form is available at the *Review* web site. The journal's print version ceased publication in 1998.

1302. *Classical and Modern Literature.* [ISSN: 0197-2227] 1980. s-a. USD 29 (Individuals, USD 26). Ed(s): Daniel M. Hooley. C M L, c/o Daniel Hooley, Editor, Dept of Classical Studies, University of Missouri-Columbia, Columbia, MO 65211-4150. Illus., adv. Refereed. Circ: 500. Vol. ends: Fall. *Indexed:* AmHI, BEL&L, BRI, CBRI, HumInd, IBR, IBZ, MLA-IB, RILM. *Bk. rev.:* 1-2. *Aud.:* Ac.

This journal focuses on the relation of classical and modern literatures. The modern literatures involved are, for the most part, English and Western European. Articles take a variety of approaches, from theoretical to the more traditional study of allusion and influence. Subjects include both high and pop culture; contributions discuss the influence of the classics in film as well as literature. Students and general readers will find most of the contents accessible; quotations from classical and European literature are usually accompanied by translations. The journal also offers occasional translations from the classics. A useful addition to any collection that supports literary studies.

1303. *Classical Antiquity.* Formerly (until 1982): *California Studies in Classical Antiquity.* [ISSN: 0278-6656] 1968. s-a. USD 158 print & online eds. USD 87 newsstand/cover. Ed(s): Mark Griffith. University of California Press, Journals Division, 2000 Center St, Ste 303, Berkeley, CA 94704-1223; journals@ucpress.edu; http://www.ucpress.edu/journals. Illus., index, adv. Sample. Refereed. Circ: 592 Paid. Vol. ends: Oct. Microform: PQC. Online: Chadwyck-Healey Inc.; EBSCO Publishing, EBSCO Host; Florida Center for Library Automation; OCLC Online Computer Library Center, Inc.; ProQuest LLC (Ann Arbor); SwetsWise Online Content; H.W. Wilson. *Indexed:* AmHI, ArtHuCI, HumInd, IBR, IBZ, NTA, SSCI. *Aud.:* Ac.

This journal covers all aspects of ancient Greek and Roman civilization, although literature receives the most attention. Editorial preference is for articles with a broad view of the subject over strictly technical pieces, which enhances the journal's appeal. A typical issue includes five or six articles; there are no book reviews. A good general title, appropriate for most academic libraries.

1304. *Classical Bulletin.* [ISSN: 0009-8337] 1925. s-a. USD 50 (Individuals, USD 25; USD 20 newsstand/cover per issue). Ed(s): Ladislaus J Bolchazy. Bolchazy - Carducci Publishers, Inc, 1000 Brown St, Unit 101, Wauconda, IL 60084; info@bolchazy.com; http://www.bolchazy.com. Illus., index, adv. Refereed. Circ: 700. Microform: PQC. Online: Chadwyck-Healey Inc.; EBSCO Publishing, EBSCO Host; Northern Light Technology, Inc.; ProQuest K-12 Learning Solutions; ProQuest LLC (Ann Arbor). *Indexed:* ABS&EES, AmHI, ArtHuCI, BEL&L, NTA, SSCI. *Bk. rev.:* 8-10, 1,000-2,000 words. *Aud.:* Ac.

For many years a general classics title of average quality suitable for high school and college students, *Classical Bulletin* has undergone extensive transformations in recent years since passing into the hands of commercial publishers (Ares in 1987, and then the present owner in 1992). Various changes in format, subtitles, and content have followed. The journal currently publishes articles on all aspects of classical studies, with the most recent issues focusing on Greek and Latin literature. A useful, but not essential, title.

1305. *Classical Journal.* [ISSN: 0009-8353] 1905. bi-m. USD 45 in US & Canada; USD 50 elsewhere; USD 20 per issue. Ed(s): S Douglas Olson. Classical Association of the Middle West and South, Inc., c/o Anne H. Groton, St. Olaf College, Dept. of Classics, Northfield, MN 55057-1574. Illus., index, adv. Refereed. Circ: 2300 Paid. Vol. ends: May. Microform: PMC; PQC. Online: JSTOR (Web-based Journal Archive); OCLC Online Computer Library Center, Inc.; H.W. Wilson. *Indexed:* ABIn, AmHI, ArtHuCI, BRI, CBRI, EduInd, HumInd, IIMP, MLA-IB, NTA, NumL, PhilInd. *Bk. rev.:* 3-5, 1-5 pages. *Aud.:* Hs, Ac.

As the official journal of the largest regional classical association in the United States, *Classical Journal* aims at a broad audience of scholars, teachers, and students. Its contents normally include three or four articles, "The Forum" (a regular column dealing with pedagogical matters), various association announcements, and a number of book reviews. The articles and reviews, which focus primarily on classical literature and history, are scholarly but usually well within the grasp of college students. This title belongs in any library that supports a classics program.

1306. *Classical Outlook.* [ISSN: 0009-8361] 1923. q. Membership, USD 45; USD 10 newsstand/cover per issue. Ed(s): Richard La Fleur. American Classical League, Miami University, Oxford, OH 45056; info@aclclassics.org; http://www.aclclassics.org. Illus., adv. Circ: 4250. Vol. ends: Summer. *Indexed:* BRI, CBRI. *Bk. rev.:* 6-8, 300-1,000 words. *Aud.:* Hs, Ac.

Intended for teachers of classical studies at all levels from elementary school through college, this journal mainly addresses pedagogical concerns. A typical issue contains three or four articles focusing on practical aspects of teaching Latin or classical civilization. Several regular columns discuss teaching materials and electronic resources for the study of the classics. A poetry section includes original verse on classical themes, translations from Greek and Latin, and original Latin verse. Also, *Classica Americana*, which appears on an occasional basis, offers biographical sketches of prominent American classicists. A necessary publication for high schools where Latin is taught and for colleges that train Latin teachers.

1307. *Classical Philology.* [ISSN: 0009-837X] 1906. q. USD 197 domestic; USD 212.82 Canada; USD 203 elsewhere. Ed(s): Elizabeth M. Adkins, Elizabeth Asmis. University of Chicago Press, Journals Division, PO Box 37005, Chicago, IL 60637; subscriptions@press.uchicago.edu; http://www.journals.uchicago.edu. Illus., index, adv. Sample. Refereed. Circ: 1100 Paid. Vol. ends: Oct. Microform: IDC. Online: EBSCO

Publishing, EBSCO Host; Florida Center for Library Automation; Gale; JSTOR (Web-based Journal Archive); OCLC Online Computer Library Center, Inc.; ProQuest LLC (Ann Arbor). Reprint: PSC. *Indexed:* AmHI, ArtHuCI, HumInd, IBR, IBZ, IPB, L&LBA, LRI, NTA, NumL, SSCI. *Bk. rev.:* 4-6, 3-5 pages. *Aud.:* Ac.

Long regarded as one of the premier journals in the field, *Classical Philology* is an important resource for advanced students and scholars. Each issue includes three to five full-length articles and as many brief notes. Several substantial book reviews and the occasional review essay round out the contents. Articles tend to focus on language and literature, although history and philosophy are not neglected. The sometimes technical nature of the contents and the large amount of untranslated Greek and Latin make the journal somewhat difficult for general readers and beginning students. The journal's web site offers a variety of information, including tables of contents for recent issues. Required for all academic libraries that support classics programs.

1308. *The Classical Quarterly.* [ISSN: 0009-8388] 1906. s-a. GBP 99 print & online eds. Ed(s): Judith Mossman, Miriam Griffin. Cambridge University Press, The Edinburgh Bldg, Shaftesbury Rd, Cambridge, CB2 2RU, United Kingdom; journals@cambridge.org; http://www.journals.cambridge.org. Illus., index, adv. Refereed. Circ: 1600. Microform: PQC. Online: Pub.; EBSCO Publishing, EBSCO Host; Florida Center for Library Automation; Gale; HighWire Press; IngentaConnect; JSTOR (Web-based Journal Archive); Northern Light Technology, Inc.; OCLC Online Computer Library Center, Inc.; ProQuest LLC (Ann Arbor); SwetsWise Online Content. Reprint: PSC. *Indexed:* AmHI, ArtHuCI, BrArAb, BrHumI, FR, HumInd, IBR, IBZ, IPB, LRI, MLA-IB, MSN, NTA, NumL, PhilInd, RI-1, RILM, SSCI. *Aud.:* Ac.

Sponsored by the Classical Association of Great Britain, this austere journal is one of the most highly regarded in the field. Although historical and philosophical topics make an occasional appearance, the primary focus of the journal is Greek and Latin philology. The level of scholarship is high and the content sometimes technical; those with "small Latin and less Greek" will find relatively little of benefit. A typical number includes about 20 articles and another dozen brief notes. There are no book reviews; these appear in a sister publication, *Classical Review.* Essential for libraries that support strong programs in classics.

1309. *The Classical Review.* [ISSN: 0009-840X] 1886. s-a. GBP 106 print & online eds. Ed(s): Neil Hopkinson, Roy Gibson. Cambridge University Press, The Edinburgh Bldg, Shaftesbury Rd, Cambridge, CB2 2RU, United Kingdom. Illus., index, adv. Refereed. Circ: 1600. Vol. ends: Winter. Microform: PMC; PQC. Online: Pub.; EBSCO Publishing, EBSCO Host; Gale; HighWire Press; IngentaConnect; JSTOR (Web-based Journal Archive); OCLC Online Computer Library Center, Inc.; SwetsWise Online Content. Reprint: PSC. *Indexed:* AmHI, ArtHuCI, BRD, BRI, BrHumI, CBRI, HumInd, IBR, IBZ, IPB, MLA-IB, NumL, PhilInd, RI-1, SSCI. *Bk. rev.:* 150, 100-2,000 words. *Aud.:* Ac.

Devoted solely to book reviews, this journal covers works in all areas of classical studies and in a variety of languages. Reviews are normally in English, with occasional exceptions. They tend to be quite scholarly and are frequently critical. A typical issue includes approximately 90 full reviews and 60 brief notices. Tables of contents are available at the journal's web site. Although highly respected and extensive in its coverage, *Classical Review* is rarely timely: Reviews often appear several years after the initial appearance of a book. In spite of this, it remains an important collection development tool for libraries and belongs in any collection that supports a classics program.

1310. *Classical World.* Formerly (until 1957): *Classical Weekly.* [ISSN: 0009-8418] 1907. q. USD 50 (Individuals, USD 35). Ed(s): Matthew S Santirocco. Classical Association of the Atlantic States, University of the Sciences, 600 S 43rd St, Philadelphia, PA 19104-4495; classics@usip.edu; http://www.caas-cw.org/. Illus., index, adv. Refereed. Circ: 3000. Vol. ends: Jun/Aug. Microform: MIM; PQC. Online: Chadwyck-Healey Inc.; OCLC Online Computer Library Center, Inc.; Project

MUSE; SwetsWise Online Content; H.W. Wilson. Reprint: PSC. *Indexed:* AmHI, ArtHuCI, BRD, BRI, CBRI, EduInd, IBR, IBZ, IPB, NTA, NumL, PhilInd, RILM, SSCI. *Bk. rev.:* 15-20, 300-500 words. *Aud.:* Hs, Ac.

Aimed at high school and college teachers of classics, this journal covers all aspects of classical civilization, with primary emphasis on literature and history. In addition to scholarly articles in these areas, *Classical World* includes several regular features that deal with pedagogical topics and an extensive "Notes and News" column that provides information about study programs, conferences, fellowships, and scholarships. The journal is also well known for the many valuable bibliographical surveys that it publishes. These include annual surveys of audiovisual materials and classical textbooks, as well as review essays on particular authors and topics. Accessible to a wide audience, including students and general readers, *Classical World* is suitable for high school, college, and larger public libraries.

1311. *Classics Ireland.* [ISSN: 0791-9417] 1994. a. GBP 5. Ed(s): David Woods. Classical Association of Ireland, Department of Classics, Rm. K210, University College, Dublin, 4, Ireland; andrewsmith@ucd.ie. Illus. Refereed. Circ: 400. *Indexed:* AmHI, NTA. *Bk. rev.:* 6-10, 500-800 words. *Aud.:* Ga, Ac.

The lively and well-written articles in *Classics Ireland* cover a variety of topics: classical literature and its influence, ancient history, classical archaeology, the study of classical antiquity in Ireland, and, occasionally, Byzantine Studies. While the contributors are mostly professional scholars, they tend to aim at a broad audience. *Classics Ireland* is one of the few titles in the field that can be warmly recommended to beginning students and general readers. The full text of the first seven volumes (1994–2000) is available at www.ucd.ie/~classics/ClassicsIreland.html.

1312. *Didaskalia: ancient theater today.* [ISSN: 1321-4853] 1994. irreg. Free. Ed(s): Hugh Denard, C W Marshall. Didaskalia, c/o Hugh Denard, Ed, School of Theatre Studies, Coventry, CV4 AL, United Kingdom; didaskalia@csv.warwick.ac.uk; http://www.warwick.ac.uk/didaskalia/. Illus. *Bk. rev.:* 2-3, 1,000-2,000 words. *Aud.:* Ga, Ac.

Didaskalia publishes articles about staging and performance aspects of Greek and Roman drama, dance, and music, both in antiquity and today. It also includes announcements and reviews of current productions and reviews of books about ancient drama. The character of contributions varies widely; some are scholarly, others are more popular in nature. Most recent issues have been thematic; in the last few years, issues have focused on Tantalus, Electra, trends in research, and electronic research initiatives. *Didaskalia* is a very useful source of information, particularly for those interested in seeing or reading about contemporary productions of the ancient plays.

1313. *Electronic Antiquity: communicating the classics.* [ISSN: 1320-3606] 1993. irreg. Free. Ed(s): Terry Papillon. Digital Library and Archives at Virginia Polytechnic Institute and State University, Department of Classics, 331 Major Williams Hall, Blacksburg, VA 24061-0225; electronic.antiquity@vt.edu; http://scholar.lib.vt.edu/ejournals/ElAnt/. Illus., adv. Refereed. *Bk. rev.:* 2-4; 1,500-4,000 words. *Aud.:* Ac.

One of the first electronic classical journals to appear, *Electronic Antiquity* was intended to facilitate rapid communication in the field. It once offered a selection of brief articles, book reviews, and news items in each issue, but this is no longer the case. New issues have appeared sporadically in recent years and now average about one per year. A typical issue includes one or two articles followed by half a dozen book reviews. The book reviews tend to be substantial and are the most attractive feature of *EA*'s current manifestation. All back issues are available on the journal's web site.

1314. *Glotta: Zeitschrift fuer griechische und lateinische Sprache.* [ISSN: 0017-1298] 1909. 2x/yr. EUR 56; EUR 32.90 newsstand/cover. Vandenhoeck und Ruprecht, Robert-Bosch-Breite 6, Goettingen, 37079, Germany; info@v-r.de; http://www.vandenhoeck-ruprecht.de. Illus., index, adv. Refereed. Circ: 500 Paid and controlled. Reprint: SCH. *Indexed:* ArtHuCI, FR, IBR, IBZ, IndIslam, MLA-IB, RILM. *Aud.:* Ac.

The only journal to focus solely on Greek and Latin linguistics, *Glotta* will interest students of Indo-European and Romance linguistics as well as classicists. Articles are generally written in German or English, and the contents tend to be rather technical. There are no book reviews. A keyword index, arranged by language, appears in the final issue of each volume. For academic libraries that support strong programs in classics or linguistics.

1315. Gnomon: kritische Zeitschrift fuer die gesamte klassische Altertumswissenschaft. [ISSN: 0017-1417] 1924. 8x/yr. EUR 154. Ed(s): H W Noerenberg, Ernst Vogt. Verlag C.H. Beck oHG, Wilhelmstr 9, Munich, 80801, Germany; abo.service@beck.de; http://www.beck.de. Illus., index, adv. Circ: 1400 Paid and controlled. *Indexed:* ArtHuCI, IBR, IBZ, IPB, MLA-IB, NTA, NumL, RI-1, RILM. *Bk. rev.:* 20-25. *Aud.:* Ac.

This review journal is an invaluable bibliographical resource. It covers books in all areas of classical studies. A typical issue includes a dozen substantial scholarly book reviews and as many more brief reviews. Most are in German. Odd-numbered issues include the *Bibliographische Beilage,* a detailed subject bibliography of recent publications that includes both books and articles. Its entries often provide table-of-contents information for conference proceedings, *Festschriften,* and collected papers. These listings are perhaps the most timely printed source of bibliography in the field. The publisher now produces an electronic bibliographical database based on the backfiles (without the reviews) on CD-ROM. Also, a smaller version of the database (about 15 percent of the total content), covering 1997 forward, is available online at www.gnomon.ku-eichstaett.de/Gnomon/en/Gnomon.html. An indispensable journal for any library that supports serious research in the classics.

1316. Greece and Rome. [ISSN: 0017-3835] 1931. s-a. GBP 83 print & online eds. Ed(s): John Taylor. Cambridge University Press, The Edinburgh Bldg, Shaftesbury Rd, Cambridge, CB2 2RU, United Kingdom; journals@cambridge.org; http://www.journals.cambridge.org. Illus., adv. Sample. Refereed. Circ: 1600. Vol. ends: Oct. Microform: PQC. Online: Pub.; EBSCO Publishing, EBSCO Host; Florida Center for Library Automation; Gale; HighWire Press; IngentaConnect; JSTOR (Web-based Journal Archive); OCLC Online Computer Library Center, Inc.; ProQuest K-12 Learning Solutions; ProQuest LLC (Ann Arbor); SwetsWise Online Content. Reprint: PSC. *Indexed:* AmHI, ArtHuCI, BrArAb, BrHumI, HumInd, IBR, IBZ, IPB, NTA, RILM. *Bk. rev.:* 2-3, 500-1,000 words. *Aud.:* Hs, Ga, Ac.

One of the most readable classical journals, *Greece and Rome* aims "to publish scholarly but not technical articles that will be of use to all those who are interested in Classical Civilization, whether or not they are professionally engaged in its study, whether or not they can read Greek or Latin." It succeeds. A typical issue includes about six articles, evenly divided between literature and history, along with an occasional piece on archaeology and several book reviews. In addition to individual book reviews, each issue also includes a varying number of "subject reviews," covering such areas as Greek and Roman history and literature, archaeology and art, philosophy, and general works. These brief review essays cover important recent works in summary fashion. Subscribers to *Greece and Rome* also receive *New Surveys in the Classics,* a series of extended bibliographical essays on individual ancient authors and topics. An excellent journal that belongs in all libraries.

1317. Greek, Roman and Byzantine Studies. Formerly (until 1959): *Greek and Byzantine Studies.* [ISSN: 0017-3916] 1958. q. USD 30 domestic; USD 36 foreign. Ed(s): E. L. Wheeler, Kent J Rigsby. Duke University, Department of Classical Studies, PO Box 90199, Durham, NC 27708-0199. Illus., adv. Refereed. Circ: 850. Vol. ends: Winter. Microform: PQC. Online: Chadwyck-Healey Inc.; OCLC Online Computer Library Center, Inc.; ProQuest LLC (Ann Arbor). Reprint: PSC. *Indexed:* AmHI, ArtHuCI, HumInd, IBR, IBZ, NTA, NumL, RI-1, RILM. *Aud.:* Ac.

The use of "Roman" in this journal's title is somewhat misleading because "articles concerned primarily with Latin are excluded." Its focus is on the Greek world from the prehistoric period through Byzantine times. In practice, the majority of contributions deal with classical Greek literature and history, although a significant number of articles fall into the realm of later Greek

Studies. Many of the articles require a working knowledge of Greek. A typical issue includes four to six articles. The journal does not publish book reviews. Recommended for academic libraries that support a strong classics program.

1318. Harvard Studies in Classical Philology. [ISSN: 0073-0688] 1890. irreg. Ed(s): Albert Henrichs. Harvard University, Department of the Classics, Boylston 320, Cambridge, MA 02138; http://www.fas.harvard.edu/~classics/hscp.html. Illus. Refereed. *Indexed:* ArtHuCI, IBR, NTA, PhilInd, RI-1. *Aud.:* Ac.

This somewhat irregularly issued annual has traditionally published articles by Harvard faculty and graduate students. In recent years, the cast of contributors has expanded, although the majority still have Harvard connections. Most articles concern Greek and Latin language and literature, although there are occasional excursions into ancient history and archaeology. *Harvard Studies* often includes lengthy articles; papers of 50 pages or more are not uncommon. Summaries of recent Harvard dissertations in classical philology appear at the end of most volumes.

1319. Helios: a journal devoted to critical and methodological studies of classical culture, literature, and society. [ISSN: 0160-0923] 1974. s-a. USD 48 (Individuals, USD 27). Ed(s): Steve M Oberhelman. Texas Tech University Press, 2903 4th St, PO Box 41037, Lubbock, TX 79409-1037; ttup@ttu.edu; http://www.ttup.ttu.edu. Illus., adv. Refereed. Circ: 536. Reprint: PSC. *Indexed:* AmHI, ArtHuCI, BEL&L, IBR, IBZ, NTA. *Aud.:* Ac.

Once a nondescript classical periodical of middling quality, *Helios* has found a niche for itself as a venue for "innovative approaches to the study of classical culture." These approaches include "anthropological, deconstructive, feminist, reader response, social history, and text theory." Although contributors tend to overuse trendy jargon and occasionally have blatant political agendas, they do sometimes offer fresh and interesting perspectives on the classics. Greek and Latin are usually translated. *Helios* should be of interest to a wide range of cultural and literary scholars. Suitable for most academic libraries.

1320. International Journal of the Classical Tradition. [ISSN: 1073-0508] 1994. q. EUR 238 print & online eds. Springer Netherlands, Van Godewijckstraat 30, Dordrecht, 3311 GX, Netherlands; http://www.springeronline.com. Illus., adv. Refereed. Circ: 800. Vol. ends: Spring. Online: EBSCO Publishing, EBSCO Host; OCLC Online Computer Library Center, Inc.; OhioLINK; SwetsWise Online Content. Reprint: PSC. *Indexed:* AmHI, IBR, IBZ, RILM. *Bk. rev.:* 5, 2-5 pages. *Aud.:* Ac.

As the official journal of the International Society for the Classical Tradition, this title focuses on the influence of classical antiquity on other cultures and on the reception of the classical heritage from ancient times to the present. Articles cover a wide range of topics, including art, literature, history, music, and philosophy. In addition, the journal offers review articles, book reviews, and news of professional interest (conference announcements, calls for papers, etc.). Students and scholars from all areas of the humanities are likely to find something of interest in its pages.

1321. Journal of Hellenic Studies. [ISSN: 0075-4269] 1880. a. GBP 55 & libraries. Ed(s): Robert Fowler. Society for the Promotion of Hellenic Studies, Senate House, Malet St, London, WC1E 7HU, United Kingdom; office@hellenicsociety.org.uk; http://www.hellenicsociety.org.uk/. Illus., adv. Refereed. Circ: 3000. Microform: PQC. Online: JSTOR (Web-based Journal Archive). Reprint: PSC. *Indexed:* AICP, AmHI, ArtHuCI, ArtInd, BrHumI, HumInd, IBR, IBZ, IPB, IndIslam, LRI, MLA-IB, NTA, NumL, PhilInd, RI-1, SSCI. *Bk. rev.:* 60-70, 1,000-2,000 words. *Aud.:* Ac.

This venerable and highly regarded journal publishes studies in Greek literature, history, archaeology, and philosophy. Contributors traditionally have been predominantly British, although more American and European scholars now appear among them. A typical issue includes about ten articles, many of substantial length. The extensive book review section is a particularly valuable feature; it covers most important books on classical Greek Studies in English and western European languages. Frequently, there are one or two review articles that discuss several books on related themes. Subscriptions also include the annual publication *Archaeological Reports,* which consists largely of reports on current British excavations of classical sites.

1322. *Journal of Roman Studies.* [ISSN: 0075-4358] 1911. a. GBP 45 (Individuals, GBP 36). Ed(s): M D Goodman. Society for the Promotion of Roman Studies, The Roman Society, Senate House, Malet St, London, WC1E 7HU, United Kingdom; http://www.romansociety.org/. Illus., adv. Refereed. Circ: 3200. Reprint: PSC. *Indexed:* AmHI, ArtHuCI, BrArAb, BrHumI, FR, HumInd, IBR, IBZ, NTA, NumL, SSCI. *Bk. rev.:* 60, 1,000-2,000 words. *Aud.:* Ac.

This companion publication to the *Journal of Hellenic Studies* covers all aspects of Roman civilization. The primary emphasis is on history, although important work on archaeology and Latin literature also appears. Its content is scholarly and sometimes technical. An issue usually offers about eight articles (often quite lengthy), one or more substantial surveys or review articles on a specific topic, and a large number of book reviews. The reviews continue to cover most important works in English on Roman Studies, but with fewer European-language titles than in the past. This is an important title for any library that supports a program in ancient history or the classics.

1323. *Leeds International Classical Studies.* [ISSN: 1477-3643] 2002. irreg. Free. Ed(s): Malcolm Heath, Roger Brock. University of Leeds, School of Classics, Leeds, LS2 9JT, United Kingdom; classics@leeds.ac.uk. *Aud.:* Ac.

This online journal is an outgrowth of the Leeds International Classical Seminar. Although it publishes papers from the seminar, the journal publishes neither all nor only Leeds Seminar papers. It includes "articles and interim discussion papers on all aspects of Greek and Roman antiquity, and of the history of the classical tradition." These typically fall into thematic groupings, most based on topics from the seminar. Additional themes are added from time to time. Current themes include comedy, epigram, Lucretius, marriage, pastoral, rhetoric, tragedy, and Vergil. While all articles of a scholarly cast, they range from the accessible to the highly technical.

1324. *Lustrum: Internationale Forschungsberichte aus dem Bereich des Klassischen Altertums.* [ISSN: 0024-7421] 1956. irreg. Ed(s): Hubert Petersmann, Hans Gaertner. Vandenhoeck und Ruprecht, Robert-Bosch-Breite 6, Goettingen, 37079, Germany; info@v-r.de; http://www.vandenhoeck-ruprecht.de. Illus., index, adv. Refereed. Circ: 750 Paid and controlled. *Indexed:* IBR, IBZ. *Aud.:* Ac.

An important source of bibliographical information for researchers, *Lustrum* publishes extensive annotated bibliographies and review essays that focus on particular classical authors or topics. They are generally written by well-known specialists. Often the bibliographies attempt exhaustive coverage for a period of years. Most issues include two or three works, although a few contain only a single book-length bibliography. Unfortunately, this journal's publication schedule has been erratic in recent years. Recommended for libraries that support a strong classics program.

1325. *Mnemosyne: a journal of classical studies.* [ISSN: 0026-7074] 1852. q. EUR 378 print & online eds. (Individuals, EUR 112). Ed(s): G J Boter, A Chaniotis. Brill, PO Box 9000, Leiden, 2300 PA, Netherlands; cs@brill.nl; http://www.brill.nl. Illus., index. Refereed. Vol. ends: Nov. Microform: SWZ. Online: Chadwyck-Healey Inc.; EBSCO Publishing, EBSCO Host; Gale; IngentaConnect; OCLC Online Computer Library Center, Inc.; OhioLINK; Springer LINK; SwetsWise Online Content. Reprint: PSC. *Indexed:* AmHI, ArtHuCI, FR, HumInd, IBR, IBZ, IPB, MLA-IB, NTA. *Bk. rev.:* 10-12, 500-1,500 words. *Aud.:* Ac.

As befits one of the oldest journals in the field, *Mnemosyne* continues to offer traditional studies of Greek and Latin literature. The articles tend to be philological and technical, although most are now written in English rather than the Dutch or Latin of years gone by. Most issues offer three to five articles, as many more short notes (Miscellanea), and a dozen substantial book reviews. A valuable journal, but primarily for collections that cater to graduate students and scholars.

1326. *Mouseion: journal of the Classical Association of Canada.* Formerly (until 2000): *Classical Views/Echos du Monde Classique.* [ISSN: 1496-9343] 1956. 3x/yr. CND 40 (Individuals, CND 25). Ed(s): James Butrica, Mark Joyal. University of Calgary Press, University of Calgary, 2500 University Dr NW, Calgary, AB T2N 1N4, Canada; whildebr@ucalgary.ca; http://www.uofcpress.com. Adv. Refereed. Circ: 750 Paid and free. *Indexed:* CBCARef, IBR, IBSS, IBZ, NTA. *Bk. rev.:* 8-10, 2-5 pages. *Aud.:* Ac.

Mouseion, one of the two journals sponsored by the Classical Association of Canada, began life under the title *Echos du Monde Classique/Classical News and Views* as a source of news items and pedagogical articles for teachers of classics in Canada. In recent years it has evolved into a scholarly journal of good quality. A typical issue includes three to five articles and several substantial book reviews. These cover a wide range of topics, including Greek and Latin literature, ancient history, and classical archaeology. Most articles are in English with the remainder in French. This title is appropriate for academic libraries that support strong classics programs.

1327. *Phoenix (Toronto, 1946).* [ISSN: 0031-8299] 1946. q. CND 100 (Individuals, CND 70). Ed(s): A M Keith. Classical Association of Canada, Trinity College, University of Toronto, Toronto, ON M5S 1H8, Canada; phoenix@chass.utoronto.ca; http://www.chass.utoronto.ca. Illus., index, adv. Refereed. Circ: 1250 Paid and controlled. *Indexed:* ArtHuCI, CBCARef, FR, IBR, IBZ, IPB, IndIslam, L&LBA, MLA-IB, NumL, PhilInd. *Bk. rev.:* 15-20, 500-1,000 words. *Aud.:* Ac.

This journal covers primarily Greek and Latin literature, with sporadic ventures into history and philosophy. Articles are scholarly but generally accessible to a wider audience; Greek and Latin are usually translated. As one would expect of a journal published by the Classical Association of Canada, contributors are predominantly Canadian and write mostly in English, occasionally in French. A typical issue includes half a dozen articles and a selection of book reviews. Suitable for most academic libraries.

1328. *Ramus: critical studies in Greek and Roman literature.* [ISSN: 0048-671X] 1972. s-a. AUD 46.50 (Individuals, AUD 32.50). Ed(s): Anthony James Boyle. Aureal Publications, PO Box 49, Bendigo North, VIC 3550, Australia; http://www.latrobe.edu.au/arts/ramus/aureal.html. Illus., adv. Refereed. Circ: 300 Paid. Online: RMIT Publishing. *Indexed:* AmHI, ArtHuCI, IBR, IBZ. *Aud.:* Ac.

Ramus covers Greek and Latin literature, with an emphasis on literary criticism rather than philology. The articles are both scholarly and readable. A typical issue includes four to six articles; there are no book reviews or other features. The journal occasionally publishes theme-oriented issues, most recently on "Rethinking Terence." Recommended for any academic library that supports programs in literature.

1329. *University of London. Institute of Classical Studies. Bulletin.* [ISSN: 0076-0730] 1954. a. GBP 50 per issue. University of London, Institute of Classical Studies, School of Advanced Study, Senate House, Malet St, London, WC1E 7HU, United Kingdom; icls.publications@sas.ac.uk; http://www.sas.ac.uk/icls/institute/. Illus. *Indexed:* ArtHuCI, NumL. *Aud.:* Ac.

Although the substantial volumes of this annual cover all aspects of classical studies, emphasis tends to be on Greek literature and history, ancient philosophy, and Bronze Age archaeology. Roman Studies receive limited attention. Most contributors are connected to the University of London in some capacity. Each issue includes eight to ten substantial articles; there are no book reviews. This is an important title for collections that support large programs in classical studies.

1330. *Vergilius.* Former titles (until 1959): *Vergilian Digest;* (until 1940): *Vergilius.* [ISSN: 0506-7294] 1938. a. USD 100 (Individuals, USD 20). Ed(s): Patricia A Johnston. Vergilian Society, 22 Bluetop Rd., Setauket, NY 11733; VergSoc@aol.com; http://www.vergil.clarku.edu. Illus., adv. Refereed. Circ: 1400. Reprint: PSC. *Bk. rev.:* 6-8, 2-4 pages. *Aud.:* Ac.

Everything in this journal relates to the poet Vergil in one way or another. In addition to contributions directly concerned with his life and writings, there are studies of his later influence. Over time, the contents have ranged from general interest to scholarly; but in recent years, scholarly articles have predominated, most assuming some knowledge of Latin. An important feature is the annual bibliography of Vergilian studies. There are also notices about the society's programs and activities.

■ CLASSROOM MAGAZINES

Art/Foreign Language/Language Arts/Life Skills/Mathematics/Science/ Social Studies and Current Events/Teacher and Professional

See also Children; Education; and Teenagers sections.

Terry Taylor, Instruction Coordinator, DePaul University, 2350 N. Kenmore Ave., Chicago, IL 60614-3274; ttaylor@depaul.edu

Introduction

Creating or selecting appropriate lesson plans and curricular activities is a significant and time-consuming part of K–12 teachers' class preparation. This section highlights magazines that provide practical classroom information and material to assist in that process. Most classroom magazines are written for students at appropriate reading levels and are available as classroom sets at a discounted per-issue or subscription price. Often these titles are accompanied by supplementary teacher resources, such as audio CDs for foreign-language titles and teacher's guides containing activities, learning goals, and assessment methods. Several publishers offer web sites with material to complement the content of the printed magazines. Student titles are listed by subject in this section. Other classroom magazines are written for teachers and provide resources and ideas for classroom use. Examples of classroom activities that lend themselves to interactivity, collaborative learning, and interdisciplinary instruction in the classroom make these magazines ready-to-use practical tools for developing and enriching curriculum. These titles are listed in this section under the category "Teacher and Professional." Some classroom magazines appear primarily or solely online.

Classroom magazines are geared to the practical application of current theory and standards to classroom activity. Periodicals that cover primarily educational issues or theory are described in the Education section of this volume or in the appropriate subject discipline, e.g., Mathematics. Magazines that may be used in the classroom but that are more likely to be personal subscriptions are described in the Children and Teenagers sections.

Basic Periodicals

Select by subject and audience level.

Basic Abstracts and Indexes

ProQuest, Children's Magazine Guide, Current Index to Journals in Education/ ERIC, MAS Ultra-School Edition, Primary Search, Education Index/Wilson Education Full Text, InfoTrac, Readers' Guide to Periodical Literature.

Art

Dramatics. See Theater section.

1331. *Scholastic Art.* Formerly (until 1992): *Art and Man;* Incorporates: *Artist Junior.* [ISSN: 1060-832X] 1970. 6x/yr. USD 8.95. Ed(s): Susanne McCabe. Scholastic Inc., 557 Broadway, New York, NY 10012; http://www.scholastic.com. Illus., index. Sample. Circ: 245000. Vol. ends: Apr/May. Microform: PQC. Online: Northern Light Technology, Inc.; ProQuest K-12 Learning Solutions; ProQuest LLC (Ann Arbor). *Indexed:* ICM. *Aud.:* Ems, Hs.

Published in cooperation with the National Gallery of Art, this beautifully illustrated magazine introduces junior high and high school students to classical and contemporary art and artists from around the world. The "Artist of the Month" column features an interview with a student artist from among the winners of the Scholastic Art and Writing Award. Each issue features a "Masterpiece of the Month" with a poster of the featured artist's work in the teacher's edition and mini-posters in each student issue. "Art Spotlight" and "Critics Corner" are regular skills features. The teacher's edition (free with orders of ten or more student subscriptions) includes discussion questions, an answer key for the skills sections, a lesson plan for the "Art Workshop," a reproducible question sheet for the featured theme, and a list of the National Content Standards for the Visual Arts to which each article correlates. An additional teacher's edition for working with students in grades 4–6 is also included. The web site (teacher.scholastic.com) includes an editorial calendar with topics and artists for the year's upcoming issues that teachers can use to plan future lessons.

Stone Soup. See Children section.

Foreign Language

1332. *Authentik en Francais.* Formerly (until 1990): *Authentik (Authentique en Francais);* Which was formed by the 1987 merger of: *Authentik (Authentique en Francais Irish Edition); Authentik (Authentique en Francais British Edition);* Both of which superseded in part (in 1984): *Authentik.* [ISSN: 0791-3729] 1978. 5x/yr. USD 35.95 Print & audio CD. Ed(s): Ian Rodmell. Delta Publishing Company, 1400 Miller Pkwy, McHenry, IL 60050-7030; http://www.delta-systems.com. *Aud.:* Hs.

Authentik Language Learning Resources Ltd., a campus company of Trinity College Dublin, publishes this series of foreign-language magazines in French, German, and Spanish. The magazines titled *Authentik* are the advanced level in each of the languages. Issues are 40 pages of up-to-date material and authentic articles. Each issue is accompanied by a 60-minute audio CD. The magazines promote cultural awareness and learner independence. The audio CD contains extracts from radio news, discussions, advertisements, and specially commissioned interviews with native speakers. A transcript of the audio CD and answers are provided along with teachers notes. Intermediate level magazines are available for all three languages (three 32-page issues with 30-minute audio CDs / $16.95 for magazine only, $25.95 with CD): *Katapult* (German), *Etincelle* (French), and *La Cometa* (Spanish). Web-based resource banks for both intermediate and advanced levels are available for site licensing for those who prefer an online language learning experience. Prices range from $250/$350 for one level to $475 for both levels. Discounted pricing is available for purchase of multiple issues for classroom use as well as for web ordering of the online resource banks.

1333. *Ciao Italia: il mensile per il tuo italiano.* [ISSN: 0997-0290] 6x/yr. European Language Institute (E L I), Casella Postale 6, Recanati, 62019, Italy; editorial@elionline.com; http://www.elimagazines.com. Illus. *Aud.:* Ems, Hs.

One of many foreign-language magazines from this publisher, *Ciao Italia* is intended for students in their second year of Italian ("lower intermediate" level). Other magazines target various levels of language proficiency from elementary school through college. All include comic strips, puzzles, and games to teach vocabulary. Topical articles provide reading practice and enhance comprehension.

Elementary-level magazines include pullout pages with stickers for use in classroom activities, and many include a collectible poster with each issue. Intermediate levels place greater emphasis on civilization and culture and contain articles about music, sports, movies, and the Internet. More advanced levels provide excerpts from contemporary literature, enhanced glossaries, and a wider variety of articles. Teachers' guides and audio CDs accompany classroom orders.

Other magazines from this publisher include:

Italian: *Azzurro* for students of various ages beginning to learn Italian, *Ragazzi* (intermediate), *Tutti Insieme* (upper intermediate), *Oggitalia* for advanced students.

German: *Fertig...los* for students beginning to study German, *Kinder* (lower intermediate), *Freunde* (intermediate), *Zusammen* (upper intermediate).

Spanish: *Vamos!* for students beginning to study Spanish, *Chicos* (lower intermediate), *Muchachos* (intermediate), *Todos Amigos* (upper intermediate).

French: *Voila* for beginning French in elementary school, *C'est Facile* for the next level of beginning study, *Mome* (lower intermediate), *Jeunes* (intermediate), *Ensemble* (upper intermediate), *Presse-Papiers* for advanced students.

Latin: *Adulescens*—for students with a beginning knowledge of Latin, *Iuvenis* (lower intermediate).

Russian: *Davai* for students studying Russian at an intermediate level.

For students of English as a Second Language, ELI publishes *Ready for English* for primary school, *Let's Start* for secondary beginners, *A Tot for English* (lower intermediate), *Kid* (intermediate), *Teen* (upper intermediate), *Sure!* — for advanced students.

The web site, www.elimagazines.com, also includes teacher resources, such as reading texts, song lyrics, activities, and professional development materials. The "Play & Learn" section has games, comics, picture dictionaries, tests in the various languages and e-mail postcards.

1334. *Que Tal.* Formerly: *Oye.* [ISSN: 0033-5940] 1963. 6x/yr. USD 7.95 Includes workbook. Mary Glasgow Magazines, Commonwealth House, 1-19 New Oxford St, London, WC1A 1NU, United Kingdom; http://www.link2english.com. Illus. Vol. ends: May/Jun. Microform: PQC. *Aud.:* Hs.

Distributed through Scholastic, this colorful Mary Glasgow (London) magazine is aimed at first-year students of Spanish. Teen-interest content—such as interviews, activities, puzzles, and games—helps build language proficiency and cultural awareness. Some foreign-language magazines from this publisher include activity workbooks with orders of ten or more student copies. Teacher's Notes (in English), free with class subscriptions, provides additional assignments and a table that correlates content to teaching topics, activities, and national standards, where applicable. For the first two levels, a free CD is also provided to help with pronunciation and accent.

Other Mary Glasgow magazines include:

Spanish: *Ahora*—for advanced beginners, *El Sol*—for intermediate and advanced learners

French: *Allons-y!*—beginners and near beginners, *Bonjour*—advanced beginners, *Ca Va?*—intermediate, *Chez Nous*—advanced

German: *Das Rad*—beginners and near beginners, *Schuss*—intermediate, *Actuell*—advanced

Language Arts

Cricket. See Children section.

1335. *Literary Cavalcade.* [ISSN: 0024-4511] 1948. 8x/yr. USD 8.95 per academic year. Ed(s): Judy Goldberg. Scholastic Inc., 557 Broadway, New York, NY 10012. Illus., index, adv. Sample. Circ: 200000 Paid. Vol. ends: May. *Indexed:* AmHI, MASUSE. *Aud.:* Hs.

An excellent introduction to literary forms for high school students. *Literary Cavalcade* offers a variety of readings in prose (fiction and nonfiction), poetry, and drama, including selections from literary works and authors' insights into the writing process. As students read, they also build their vocabulary, develop language arts skills, and prepare for the SAT and ACT tests. Articles and activities correspond to standards for vocabulary development, literary response and analysis, writing strategies, writing applications, and written English conventions. The web site (http://teacher.scholastic.com/writeit/teachercenter.htm) includes an archive of lessons from *Literary Cavalcade* arranged for access by publication date, genre, author, and skills focus.

1336. *Read Magazine (Stamford).* [ISSN: 0034-0359] 1951. 18x/yr. USD 13.80 per semester; USD 3.98 per semester for 10 or more subscriptions. Weekly Reader Corp., 200 First Stamford Pl, PO Box 120023, Stamford, CT 06912-0023; science@weeklyreader.com; http://www.weeklyreader.com. Illus. Sample. Circ: 380750 Paid. Vol. ends: May. Online: EBSCO Publishing, EBSCO Host; ProQuest K-12 Learning Solutions; ProQuest LLC (Ann Arbor). *Aud.:* Ems, Hs.

This language arts magazine for junior high and high school includes plays, short stories, poetry, and nonfiction, both classical and contemporary. It introduces students to literature while developing vocabulary, comprehension, and critical-thinking skills. The "Reader's Theater" feature in each issue reinforces both reading comprehension and verbal skills. Questions and quizzes help students to understand what they have read, and a teacher's guide contains more discussion questions and extension activities as well as recommendations for accommodating the needs of ESOL students. *Word*, the official blog for Weekly Reader's *Read* and *Writing* magazines can be found at www.readandwriting.com. *Read*'s web site contains supplementary material for some of the readings as well as sample articles and stories from the magazine. An online planning calendar (also in the teacher's guide) correlates specific topics, standards, and skills in upcoming issues.

1337. *Scholastic Action.* [ISSN: 0163-3570] 1977. 14x/yr. USD 8.15. Ed(s): Janice Behrans. Scholastic Inc., 557 Broadway, New York, NY 10012; http://www.scholastic.com. Illus. Sample. Circ: 230000. Microform: PQC. Online: EBSCO Publishing, EBSCO Host; Northern Light Technology, Inc.; ProQuest K-12 Learning Solutions; ProQuest LLC (Ann Arbor). *Indexed:* MASUSE. *Aud.:* Hs.

A reading and language arts magazine covering teen topics for remedial and below-level readers in grades 6–12 with an accessible 3–5 reading level. Celebrity profiles, debate topics, and real-life skill activities such as job hunting and Internet safety tips provide engaging reading material for teens. A series of read-aloud plays based upon current movies, TV shows, and classic books is designed to be integrated into the curriculum and help students with decoding, fluency, and class participation. The "True Teen" nonfiction articles highlight teens who have overcome personal and social challenges. A new feature is the "My True Teen Story" writing program in which students can submit their personal story to be included in a future issue of *Action*. Graphic organizers and other tools accompanying the articles help students to improve their reading comprehension and suggest strategies for reading, writing, and vocabulary building. The teacher's edition includes "Issue at a Glance," which ties articles to skills, activities, and related standards. It contains lesson plans and reproducible worksheets as well as a planning calendar.

1338. *Scholastic Let's Find Out.* Formerly (until 1995): *My First Magazine.* [ISSN: 0024-1261] 32x/yr. USD 4.95 per issue. Scholastic Inc., 557 Broadway, New York, NY 10012; http://www.scholastic.com. Illus. Sample. Circ: 615000. Vol. ends: May/Jun. *Aud.:* Ems.

Each month, *LFO* provides teaching ideas for the five critical areas of early reading: phonemic awareness, phonics, fluency, vocabulary, and comprehension in four themed issues. Pictures, stories, and activities help pre-K and kindergarten children discover the world around them. Each activity in the children's magazine has a teacher's note outlining points to emphasize in teaching. Regular sections include "Kids Can Do It," "Science," "People and Places," and "Early Reader." There is also a "Look What I'm Learning at School" section with activities to be done with parents or family and instructions in both English and Spanish. The teacher's guide, included with each subscription, contains cross-curricular activities, NAEYC guidelines, and connections to state and national standards. Additional materials provided each month include special "See-Through" issues that teach children about places not usually visible to the naked eye, "Try-Along Time," to get children up and moving with an activity, song, chant, or finger play, and free classroom posters in full color. There is also a Spanish edition of *LFO* [ISSN: 1076-6766].

1339. *Scholastic Scope.* [ISSN: 0036-6412] 1964. 18x/yr. USD 8.50 per issue with 10 or more student subscr. Ed(s): Diane Weber, Mary Harvey. Scholastic Inc., 557 Broadway, New York, NY 10012; http://www.scholastic.com. Illus., adv. Circ: 424843. Microform: PQC. Online: EBSCO Publishing, EBSCO Host; Northern Light Technology, Inc.; ProQuest LLC (Ann Arbor). *Indexed:* ICM. *Aud.:* Ems.

Scholastic Scope provides literature and writing activities for sixth- to tenth-grade students who read on a sixth- to eighth-grade level, including read-aloud plays, writing workshops, vocabulary builders, and reading strategies. The "Debate" feature in each issue encourages students to think critically by presenting two sides of a controversial issue and asking students to write in with their opinion on the subject. Each issue provides writing prompts, puzzles, a "Readers Theater" play, and regular features such as inspiring real-life accounts in "True Teens," "Writers Toolbox" writing activities to build writing skills, and the "Scope 100," challenging words taken from SAT/ACT lists. The "Have Your Say" writing program invites readers to submit their writing for publication in the magazine. Skill-building features and test-preparation lessons are tied to state and national standards. *Scholastic Scope* works on skills such as sequencing, listening, graph reading, and comprehension. The teacher's edition includes lesson plans with pre-reading activities and post-reading discussion questions as well as reproducible pages.

1340. *Storyworks.* [ISSN: 1068-0292] 1993. 6x/yr. USD 6.95. Scholastic Inc., 557 Broadway, New York, NY 10012; http://www.scholastic.com. Illus. Sample. Vol. ends: Apr/May. *Indexed:* BRI, MASUSE. *Bk. rev.:* 4-5, 125 words. *Aud.:* Ems.

A literature magazine for grades 3–6, *Storyworks* features fiction, nonfiction, poetry, plays, and illustrations by award-winning children's authors and artists. Activities that develop grammar, writing, vocabulary, and test-taking skills complement the readings. "Reviews by You" publishes students' reviews of books they've read. "Sentence Chef" supplies writing skills exercises. "Vocab-U-Larry" introduces new words and tricks for memorizing text, "Grammar Cop" provides practice with grammatical concepts (e.g., homophones), and "Micro Mysteries" build reading comprehension and higher-order critical-thinking skills. Writing activities in the new "Yesterday and Today" feature side-by-side articles for students to compare and contrast. Contests and author interviews offer students the opportunity to experience literature in more active and personal ways. The teacher's guide's "At a Glance" feature lists articles with corresponding themes and standards. The web site has additional lessons, quizzes, activities, and contests.

1341. *Writing (Stamford): the magazine of effective communication.* Formerly (until 1981): *Current Media.* [ISSN: 0279-7208] 1974. 6x/yr. USD 13.80 per academic year. Weekly Reader Corp., 200 First Stamford Pl, PO Box 120023, Stamford, CT 06912-0023; http://www.weeklyreader.com. Illus. Sample. Circ: 127343 Paid. Vol. ends: May. Online: Chadwyck-Healey Inc.; EBSCO Publishing, EBSCO Host; Gale; ProQuest LLC (Ann Arbor). *Aud.:* Ems, Hs.

A magazine aimed at helping students in grades 6–10 build effective communication skills through learning the craft of writing. Each issue links reading and writing with high-interest articles focusing on aspects of one subject per issue, such as music, movies and screenplays, or advertising. Most of the articles are categorized with one of three important aspects of writing: aims, language, and process. Suggestions for writing exercises accompany the articles to spark students' creativity and get them started on their own writing. Student writing is highlighted, as is analysis of the work of well-known authors to illustrate such literary elements as plot, setting, perspective, and style. The "Teacher's Guide" provides suggested discussion questions, pre-reading/ pre-writing and extension activities, and link content to NCTE/IRA standards. *Word*, the official blog for Weekly Reader's *Writing* and *Read* magazines, can be found at www.readandwriting.com. The *Writing* web site (www.weeklyreader.com/teachers/writing) contains archives of the issues as well as a link to the Student Writing Showcase, which includes a Writing Center with creative writing by students and a Publishing Center to provide tips for young writers who want to see their work published.

Life Skills

Career World. See Occupations and Careers section.

1342. *Current Health 1: the beginning guide to health education.* [ISSN: 0199-820X] 1974. 8x/yr. USD 34.50 per academic year; USD 10.15 per academic year 15 or more subscriptions. Weekly Reader Corp., 200 First Stamford Pl, PO Box 120023, Stamford, CT 06912-0023; http://www.weeklyreader.com. Illus. Sample. Circ: 300000 Paid. Vol. ends: May. Online: EBSCO Publishing, EBSCO Host; Northern Light Technology, Inc.; ProQuest K-12 Learning Solutions; ProQuest LLC (Ann Arbor). *Indexed:* ICM, MASUSE. *Aud.:* Ems, Hs.

This magazine is a wonderful resource for teachers looking for engaging material for health education. *Current Health 1* covers topics in personal health, fitness and exercise, diet and nutrition, diseases and disorders, and first aid and safety. Filled with full-color photographs, it focuses on health issues relevant to students and follows most state health curricula for grades 4–7. Each month the feature article provides an in-depth treatment of a current topic such as the effects of climate change on health, pets and health, or how to maintain a healthy

body image. Regular columns such as "Pulse" and "Safety Zone" help students explore health-related issues and questions. The teacher's guide provides key objectives, links to National Health Education standards and relevant subject areas, and a planning calendar.

Current Health 2 [ISSN: 0163-156X] provides health information in a similar format for issues and health topics of interest to grades 7–12. There is an optional Human Sexuality supplement to complement *Current Health 2* that explores sensitive issues such as relationships, peer pressure, and reproductive health from a teenager's perspective.

1343. *Imagine (Baltimore): opportunities and resources for academically talented youth.* [ISSN: 1071-605X] 1993. 5x/yr. USD 35 (Individuals, USD 30). Ed(s): Melissa Hartman. Johns Hopkins University, Center for Talented Youth, 3400 N Charles St, Baltimore, MD 21218. Adv. Sample. *Bk. rev.:* Number and length vary. *Aud.:* Hs.

This exciting periodical for middle and high school students won the Parents Choice Award in the spring of 2003. Each issue focuses on a general subject area, such as robotics, storytelling, mathematics, medicine, or the performing arts. Emphasis is given to activities that students can do *now* to pursue that interest as well as career opportunities in that field. Each issue includes articles about summer programs and extracurricular activities across the country (written by student participants), student reviews of selective colleges, advice on planning for college, career profiles of accomplished professionals, puzzles, web resources, and book reviews written by students.

1344. *Scholastic Choices: personal development & living skills.* Incorporates (in 1999): *Health Choices;* Supersedes (in 1985): *Co-Ed;* Incorporates (in 1991): *Forecast for the Home Economist;* Which superseded (in 1986): *Forecast for Home Economics;* (1963-1966): *Practical Forecast for Home Economics.* [ISSN: 0883-475X] 1956. 6x/yr. USD 8.75 for 10 copies or more. Ed(s): Maura Christopher. Scholastic Inc., 557 Broadway, New York, NY 10012; http://www.scholastic.com. Illus., index, adv. Sample. Circ: 180000 Paid. Vol. ends: May. Microform: PQC. Online: The Dialog Corporation; EBSCO Publishing, EBSCO Host; Gale; OCLC Online Computer Library Center, Inc.; ProQuest K-12 Learning Solutions; ProQuest LLC (Ann Arbor); H.W. Wilson. *Indexed:* ABIn, EduInd, ICM, MASUSE, MRD, RGPR, RILM. *Aud.:* Ems, Hs.

This magazine for grades 7–12 features articles about health and nutrition, family life, decision making, careers, and personal development, using examples of interest to this age group. Eating disorders, single parenthood, safe surfing, and cell phone etiquette are some of the topics covered. Each article includes an activity that encourages students to apply what they've learned. Features include "Sticky Situation," in which students help students as positive peer role models with issues such as substance abuse and personal relationships, and "Recipe 101," featuring recipes from an 18-year-old chef. The teacher's edition summarizes the articles, ties them to applicable standards, and provides discussion questions and additional activities for the featured stories. The tone is upbeat and not condescending; difficult issues are presented honestly. Because of the high interest of the subject matter, this magazine could be used as discussion material in a variety of subjects or settings, for example, language arts, health, or social studies.

Mathematics

Micromath. See *Mathematics Teaching* in the Mathematics section.

1345. *Scholastic Dynamath.* Formerly (until 1982): *Scholastic Math Power.* [ISSN: 0732-7773] 8x/yr. USD 6.95 with 10 or more student subscr. Ed(s): Jack Silbert. Scholastic Inc., 557 Broadway, New York, NY 10012; http://www.scholastic.com. Illus. Circ: 200000 Paid and free. Vol. ends: May. *Aud.:* Ems.

A workbook/magazine for grades 3–6, *Dynamath* reinforces basic math skills with colorful pictures, problems, and puzzles. Telling time, measurements, map reading, and problem solving are among the skills taught. Features include "Math on the Job," "Numbers in the News," and a "Read-Aloud Play" to help students with problem solving. The web site (www.scholastic.com/dynamath) provides skill review quizzes, web links related to the current issue, and bonus pages with timely online articles and resources. The teacher's edition includes an answer key, lesson plans, a "Problem of the Day" planning calendar to introduce math lessons with a warm-up exercise, and a table that correlates math features with national math standards (National Council for Teachers of Mathematics; NCTM).

1346. *Scholastic Math.* [ISSN: 0198-8379] 1980. 12x/yr. USD 8.15. Ed(s): Jack Silbert. Scholastic Inc., 557 Broadway, New York, NY 10012; http://www.scholastic.com. Illus. Circ: 200000 Paid. Microform: PQC. Online: EBSCO Publishing, EBSCO Host; ProQuest K-12 Learning Solutions; ProQuest LLC (Ann Arbor). *Indexed:* ICM, MASUSE. *Aud.:* Ems, Hs.

Scholastic Math for grades 6–9 is designed to prepare junior high students for pre-algebra. Math problems are illustrated in articles on age-appropriate topics. Every issue includes "Fast Math" brainteasers and "Sports by the Numbers." Other features include "Math at Work," "Math Mystery Comix," "Math Around the World," and "Past Math," highlighting unique number systems from other cultures and math history. Skills exercises, quizzes, and practice tests help prepare students for standardized tests. Movies, celebrities, sports, consumer math, and math-related news make complex concepts accessible and entertaining. The teacher's edition contains teaching tips, extension activities, and a skills guide that correlates the articles to National Council for Teachers of Mathematics (NCTM) standards covered in each issue.

Science

1347. *Current Science.* [ISSN: 0011-3905] 1927. 8x/yr. USD 22.95. Weekly Reader Corp., 200 First Stamford Pl, PO Box 120023, Stamford, CT 06912-0023; science@weeklyreader.com; http://www.weeklyreader.com. Illus., index. Sample. Circ: 400000 Paid. Online: EBSCO Publishing, EBSCO Host; Gale; Northern Light Technology, Inc.; OCLC Online Computer Library Center, Inc.; ProQuest K-12 Learning Solutions; ProQuest LLC (Ann Arbor); H.W. Wilson. *Indexed:* ChemAb, FS&TA, ICM, IndVet, MASUSE, RGPR, SCI, SSCI, VB. *Aud.:* Ems, Hs.

Published biweekly, this heavily illustrated magazine uses current news to make science more accessible to students in grades 6–10. Each issue contains sections dealing with physical science, life science, and earth science as well as health and technology. Hands-on activities, reinforcing the National Science Education standards, help students to apply what they have learned in the featured articles. Science trivia, puzzles, and mystery photos are regular features. Each issue comes with a free Planning Guide and Teacher's Guide that contains additional background information and answers to quizzes. Two full-color classroom posters are also included.

1348. *National Geographic Explorer.* Formerly (until 2003): *National Geographic for Kids.* [ISSN: 1541-3357] 10x/yr. National Geographic Society, 1145 17th St, NW, Washington, DC 20036; ngsforum@ nationalgeographic.com; http://www.nationalgeographic.com. Illus. *Aud.:* Ems.

National Geographic offers two editions of this colorful magazine that helps students to develop nonfiction reading skills using science, social studies, and geography content. The *Pioneer Edition* is written at a second- to third-grade reading level and the *Pathfinder Edition* is written for fourth- to sixth-graders. Both editions look alike and feature the same topics, maps, graphs, and illustrations but vary the text and concepts in terms of length and complexity. The editions can be used separately for a specific grade level or combined for differentiated instruction. The standards-based articles help teachers to meet NCLB goals. The Teacher's Guide, included with each issue, contains suggested teaching strategies, "fast facts" about the featured subject matter, reproducible worksheets for checking comprehension, and extension activities for writing practice and making connections between disciplines. Supplementary content, such as games, e-cards, puzzles, and additional links can be found on the web site (www.nationalgeographic.com/ngexplorer). There is also a *National Geographic Young Explorer* (ISSN 1930-8116) geared to a kindergarten–grade 1 reading level. This magazine develops literacy skills and introduces

word patterns and rhymes through poetry while teaching standards-based science and social studies content. Also, new in 2007–2008 is *National Geographic Extreme Explorer*, an edition of the magazine for reluctant readers in grades 6–8.

1349. *Science News: the weekly newsmagazine of science.* Former titles (until 1966): *Science News Letter; Science News Bulletin.* [ISSN: 0036-8423] 1922. w. USD 54.50 domestic; USD 72.50 foreign; USD 3 per issue. Ed(s): Julie Ann Miller. Science Service, 1719 N St, NW, Washington, DC 20036; subnews@sciserv.org. Illus., index, adv. Circ: 133000 Paid. Vol. ends: Dec. Microform: PQC. Online: EBSCO Publishing, EBSCO Host; Florida Center for Library Automation; Gale; LexisNexis; Micromedia ProQuest; Northern Light Technology, Inc.; OCLC Online Computer Library Center, Inc.; ProQuest K-12 Learning Solutions; ProQuest LLC (Ann Arbor); H.W. Wilson. *Indexed:* ABIn, AgeL, Agr, BiolDig, CBCARef, CPerI, ChemAb, EnvInd, GSI, GardL, IAA, MASUSE, RGPR. *Bk. rev.:* 6-8, 125 words. *Aud.:* Hs, Ga.

A slim magazine (16 pages), *Science News* contains approximately 20 news articles and is packed with information about what's happening in the science community. It has three main sections. "News of the Week" contains brief articles on current science news topics, and each issue features two longer articles. "Notes" addresses current research in specific disciplines. *Science News Online* (www.sciencenews.org) provides an archive of past issues with free access to cover stories and additional access for subscribers. Also available on the web site are special features, such as blogs, book listings, and links to "Most Viewed Articles." Podcasts (weekly digital audio) covering biology, astronomy, physical sciences, behavioral sciences, math and computers, chemistry, and earth science are downloadable to an MP3 player, Pocket PC, iPod, or your computer, or on CDs you burn yourself. Although the magazine is not specifically aimed at K–12 students, it is very popular in middle and high schools and is highly recommended.

1350. *Science World.* Former titles (until 1987): *Scholastic Science World;* (until 1974): *Science World;* (until 1965): *Senior Science and Science World.* [ISSN: 1041-1410] 1959. 13x/yr. USD 9.25. Scholastic Inc., 557 Broadway, New York, NY 10012; http://www.scholastic.com. Illus., index, adv. Sample. Circ: 390298. Vol. ends: May. Microform: PQC. Online: EBSCO Publishing, EBSCO Host; Gale; Northern Light Technology, Inc.; OCLC Online Computer Library Center, Inc.; ProQuest K-12 Learning Solutions; ProQuest LLC (Ann Arbor). *Indexed:* ICM, MASUSE. *Aud.:* Ems.

A science magazine with articles and hands-on experiments for grades 6–10. Each issue features interesting articles on topics in the physical, earth/space, life/health, and environmental sciences as well as technology. Hands-on experiments with photos, diagrams, maps, graphs, and charts are regular features, as are puzzles, quizzes, and brainteasers that help students understand scientific processes. The teacher's edition provides lesson plans and a table connecting content to appropriate National Science Education Standards. It also contains an answer key, reproducible skills pages, and additional quizzes to test vocabulary, reading comprehension, and understanding of graphs and maps.

1351. *SuperScience.* Formed by the merger of (1989-1997): *SuperScience Blue;* (1989-1997): *SuperScience Red.* 1997. 8x/yr. USD 6.95 per student for 10 or more copies. Ed(s): Britt Norlander. Scholastic Inc., 557 Broadway, New York, NY 10012; http://www.scholastic.com. Illus., index. Sample. Vol. ends: Apr/May. *Indexed:* ICM, MASUSE. *Aud.:* Ems.

A cross-curricular science news magazine for grades 3–6, *SuperScience* is theme based and includes many color photos that teach earth, life, and physical science concepts. Hands-on activities, experiments, and quizzes on the news stories actively engage students in the content. The teacher's guide provides background information, teaching strategies, discussion prompts, additional activities, reproducible worksheets, and answer keys. Regular features include "Science Mystery," where students read a fictional text, then use scientific method and data to solve the case, and the "You Asked" column that answers a student-generated question in each issue. Feature articles are tied to curriculum areas through process skills addressed in each activity (e.g., observe, compare, use numbers, hypothesize, etc.). *SuperScience* features help teachers meet local, state, and National Science Education Standards. The web site provides extension activities and live web interviews.

1352. W R Science. 2007. 8x/yr. USD 6.95. Weekly Reader Corp., 200 First Stamford Pl, PO Box 120023, Stamford, CT 06912-0023; science@weeklyreader.com; http://www.weeklyreader.com. *Aud.:* Ems.

WR Science is the new classroom magazine from Weekly Reader for grades 3–5 that encourages students to develop critical-thinking skills through science. Its colorful issues include high-interest science news and teacher-tested experiments. The "Sci-Triv Game" makes learning fun by awarding points for identifying correct answers. "Kids in Science" highlights student work from science fairs and issues contain mini-posters. Each issues is accompanied by a teacher's guide.

Social Studies and Current Events

1353. Biography Today (General Series): profiles of people of interest to young readers. [ISSN: 1058-2347] 1992. 3x/yr. USD 60. Ed(s): Cherie D. Abbey. Omnigraphics, Inc., 615 Griswold St, Detroit, MI 48226; info@omnigraphics.com; http://www.omnigraphics.com. Illus., index. Circ: 12000. Vol. ends: Sep (No. 3). *Indexed:* ICM. *Aud.:* Ems.

Written for the young reader, age nine and above, each issue includes profiles of 10–12 current, high-profile individuals, many from the arts, sports, or politics. Each entry provides at least one picture of the person. Biographical information traces the person's life from childhood, including education, first jobs, marriage and/or family, memorable experiences, hobbies, and accomplishments (e.g., honors and awards). Each profile includes a short bibliography for further reading and a current address as well as a web site address, where available. Librarians and teachers submit suggestions for subjects to be included. An advisory board comprised of librarians, children's literature specialists, and reading instructors reviews each issue. A cumulative index in every issue contains the names of all individuals who have appeared in either the general series or the subject series as well as listings of occupations, nationalities, and ethnic origins. The edition of *Biography Today* reviewed here is the general series, which is available as a three-issue subscription, hardcover annual cumulation, or subscription plus cumulation. Special subject series have been published in the following categories: artists, authors, business leaders, performing artists, scientists and inventors, sports figures, and world leaders. These series expand and complement the general series but do not duplicate any of the entries. The subject series are available as individual hardbound volumes, usually published annually. Highly recommended for elementary and middle school libraries as well as children's collections in public libraries. Beginning in 2003, a selection of current profiles was published in Spanish as *Biografías Hoy!* Vol. 1, ISBN 0-7808-0664-6, $39.00.

Cobblestone. See Children section.

1354. Current Events. [ISSN: 0011-3492] 1902. 25x/yr. USD 22.95. Weekly Reader Corp., 200 First Stamford Pl, PO Box 120023, Stamford, CT 06912-0023; science@weeklyreader.com; http://www.weeklyreader.com. Illus., index. Sample. Circ: 205153 Paid. Vol. ends: May. Online: EBSCO Publishing, EBSCO Host; Gale; Northern Light Technology, Inc.; OCLC Online Computer Library Center, Inc.; ProQuest K-12 Learning Solutions; ProQuest LLC (Ann Arbor). *Indexed:* ICM, MASUSE. *Aud.:* Ems, Hs.

This weekly publication (25 issues) highlights current issues in national and international news for students in grades 6–10. Photographs and maps aid in recognition of important places and people and illustrate the ideas presented. Articles present various perspectives and encourage debate about controversial issues. Special reports provide comprehensive coverage of key news stories. The accompanying teacher's guide contains more background information, a quiz, a crossword puzzle, and a planning guide that targets specific social studies, geography, and language arts skills. Supplementary online features include Classroom Newsbreak E-mails (reports and lesson plans sent directly to the teacher's mailbox) and a *Current Events* news blog.

1355. Junior Scholastic. [ISSN: 0022-6688] 1937. 18x/yr. USD 8.25 for orders of 10 or more copies; USD 12.75 for orders of 1-9 copies; USD 21.75 for teacher's edition. Ed(s): Lee Baier, Susanne McCabe. Scholastic Inc., 557 Broadway, New York, NY 10012; http://www.scholastic.com. Illus., index, adv. Sample. Circ: 570000 Paid. Vol. ends: May. Microform: PQC. Online: EBSCO Publishing, EBSCO Host; Gale; ProQuest K-12 Learning Solutions; ProQuest LLC (Ann Arbor). *Indexed:* ICM. *Aud.:* Ems.

A colorful current-events magazine for grades 6–8, *Junior Scholastic* features U.S. and world news, biographical profiles, first-person reports, and excellent maps. Articles focus on people in the news, and the many photos and illustrations help students understand complex issues. History and geography features are included in each issue. The "News Debate" feature presents a controversial question with pro and con viewpoints to initiate classroom discussion. Additional features include activities at the end of each article to enhance comprehension and a puzzle on a related topic. The teacher's edition contains a planning calendar and lesson plans based on the stories in the issue with references to additional resources (print, video, web), skills masters, activities, quizzes, and answer keys. The *Junior Scholastic* page on the *Scholastic News* web site (www.juniorscholastic.com) contains news updates, special reports, games and quizzes, links to other web sites, and teacher tips.

1356. Know Your World Extra. Formerly (until 1977): *Know Your World.* [ISSN: 0163-4844] 1967. bi-m. USD 22.95. Weekly Reader Corp., 200 First Stamford Pl, PO Box 120023, Stamford, CT 06912-0023; http://www.weeklyreader.com. Illus. Sample. Circ: 129353 Paid. Online: EBSCO Publishing, EBSCO Host; Gale; Northern Light Technology, Inc.; ProQuest K-12 Learning Solutions; ProQuest LLC (Ann Arbor). *Indexed:* ICM. *Aud.:* Ems, Hs.

A high–low magazine for preteens and teenagers who read at a second- or fourth-grade level (2.0–4.0). *Extra* covers a wide range of high-interest topics and challenging activities that encourage students to read. Action photography, age-appropriate stories, and controlled vocabulary help students with special needs stay engaged and enjoy reading success. Features include news stories, science articles, true-life adventures, games, and a "Readers' Theater" play in every issue to help students develop language and critical thinking skills while reading aloud. A teacher's guide links content to state and NCTE/IRA standards and includes recommendations for accommodating ESOL students. A planning calendar and reproducible activities to build reading skills are also included.

1357. The New York Times Upfront (Student Edition): the news magazine for teens. Formerly (until 1999): *Scholastic Update;* Which was formed by the merger of (1972-1983): *Scholastic Search;* (1920-1983): *Senior Scholastic;* Which incorporated: *American Observer; World Week.* [ISSN: 1525-1292] 1983. 14x/yr. Individuals, USD 8.95; USD 2.25 newsstand/cover. Ed(s): Peter S Young. Scholastic Inc., 557 Broadway, New York, NY 10012; http://www.scholastic.com. Illus., index, adv. Sample. Circ: 297029 Paid and free. Vol. ends: May. Microform: PQC. Online: The Dialog Corporation; EBSCO Publishing, EBSCO Host; Gale; OCLC Online Computer Library Center, Inc.; ProQuest K-12 Learning Solutions; ProQuest LLC (Ann Arbor). *Indexed:* LRI, MASUSE, RGPR. *Aud.:* Hs.

Upfront is a newsmagazine for teens featuring in-depth coverage of current events, entertainment, and trends. Informative articles about national and international events, special reports, and interviews encourage high school students to consider various points of view. Recent articles examine the immigration debate, universal health insurance, Native American casinos, and nuclear proliferation. The teacher's edition includes lesson plans for the national, international, and history sections with teaching objectives, classroom strategies, writing prompts, and quizzes. The "Voices" column gives students a forum in which to share personal stories. Each issue includes political cartoons from around the country and a debate question with pro and con viewpoints. A subscription also includes two special series: "Coming of Age," which focuses on the challenges teens face in the world today, and "We the People," which looks at the role of the Constitution in American life. The web site supplements the print newsletter and links to additional teacher resources (http://teacher.scholastic.com/upfront).

1358. *Scholastic News. Grade 5/6 Edition.* Formed by the merger of (1952-1998): *Scholastic News (Edition 6);* Which was formerly (until 1993): *Scholastic Newstime;* (until 1989): *Scholastic News (Newstime Edition);* (until 1982): *Scholastic Newstime;* (1941-1998): *Scholastic News (Citizen Edition);* Which was formerly (until 1982): *Scholastic News Citizen;* (until 1973): *Young Citizen.* [ISSN: 1554-2440] 1998. 24x/yr. USD 3.95 per issue. Ed(s): Lucille Renwick. Scholastic Inc., 557 Broadway, New York, NY 10012; http://www.scholastic.com. Illus., index. Microform: PQC. Online: EBSCO Publishing, EBSCO Host. *Indexed:* ICM. *Aud.:* Ems.

A colorful current-events weekly published in several editions to target various reading levels and interests. *Scholastic News*, first-grade and second-grade editions (32 issues per year), help students learn phonics, vocabulary, fluency, and comprehension skills by introducing them to real-world events, seasons, and holidays. Grade 1 and 2 editions also include posters, take-home activity pages, graphic organizers for teachers, and big issues for guided reading. Editions 3 and 4 (26 issues each per year) build on those skills and introduce science, history, and geography topics. Both include a "Test Prep Program" with reproducibles and diagnostic tests to help focus on improving standardized testing skills. Grade 3 includes monthly Magic Schoolbus science stories, and Grade 4 focuses on current events and geography. Also, the senior edition, aimed at fifth- and sixth-grade students, adds read-aloud plays on U.S. history themes plus graphs, puzzles, contests, and political cartoons. Editions sometimes include two-sided posters, and all have teacher's guides with lesson plans, reproducible pages, and additional resources. All content can be extended with material from the *Scholastic News Online* web site (www.scholasticnews-.com).

Scholastic News en espanol for grades 1–3 provides parallel English and Spanish text. Every issue has "Exploring Your World" sidebars that connect topics to Latino cultures and "For the Family" pages that feature reading tips that parents can use with their children. The teacher's edition contains "It's Great to Be Bilingual" reproducible pages to reinforce spelling and vocabulary.

1359. *Time for Kids World Report.* Supersedes in part (in 1997): *Time for Kids.* 1995. w. USD 24.95. Time, Inc., 1271 6th Ave., 22nd Fl., New York, NY 10020. Illus. Sample. Vol. ends: May. *Indexed:* ICM. *Aud.:* Ems.

Time for Kids is a weekly news magazine that is published in three editions: Grades K–1 for ages 4–7, grades 2–3 for ages 7–10, and grades 4–5 for ages 10–12. Each colorful issue is theme based and contains articles, puzzles, and contests relating to the featured topic. Recent themes include "Making the World a Greener Place," "Doctors Who Deliver" (focusing on bringing health care to those who can't afford it), and "Sailing Into History," about the founding of Jamestown on the occasion of its 400th anniversary. Issues also include spotlights on people with notable accomplishments, short book reports, and opinion columns. The web site (www.timeforkids.com) contains highlights from the issues, quizzes, a teacher's guide, and worksheets.

1360. *Weekly Reader. Grade 1 Edition.* Former titles (until 1999): *Weekly Reader, Edition 1; Buddy's Weekly Reader; My Weekly Reader 1.* [ISSN: 1525-4984] 1928. 32x/yr. USD 24.95; USD 3.55 per student for 10 or more subscr. Weekly Reader Corp., 200 First Stamford Pl, PO Box 120023, Stamford, CT 06912-0023; science@weeklyreader.com; http://www.weeklyreader.com. Circ: 1359345 Paid. Online: Gale. *Aud.:* Ems.

Weekly Reader publishes six editions of its newsmagazine covering pre-K through sixth grade. *Weekly Reader* Pre-K and Kindergarten editions (28 issues) develop pre-reading, critical thinking, and citizenship skills and are written to NAEYC guidelines. *Weekly Reader* Editions 1 and 2 (32 issues) offer high-interest, theme-based content that support the curriculum and continue to build reading and vocabulary skills. Edition 3 and the Senior Edition (grades 4–6), now called "WR News" (28 issues), provide more sophisticated and engaging nonfiction and help students build skills while gaining a greater understanding of the world. Content in Editions 1 through Senior covers NCTE/IRA, NCSS, and NSES standards. All editions include a free teacher's guide with curriculum correlations, and a planning calendar to facilitate incorporating the magazine into lesson plans. Editions 1, 2, 3, and Senior include periodic Reading Assessment Tests. Free access to the Weekly Reader web site provides story updates, extension activities, blogs, games, and more.

Teacher and Professional

Arts and Activities. See Education/Specific Subjects and Teaching Methods, The Arts section.

1361. *Connected Newsletter.* Former titles (until 2003): *Classroom Connect Newsletter;* (until 1999): *Classroom Connect.* [ISSN: 1554-4583] 1994. 9x/yr. USD 59. Ed(s): Christine Hofer Borror. Classroom Connect, Inc., 8000 Marina Blvd., Ste. 400, Brisbane, CA 94005-1885. Illus., index. Sample. Vol. ends: Jun. *Aud.:* Sa.

Published nine times a year. Each issue of this newsletter is filled with prescreened web sites, lesson plans, and activities that are designed to help K–12 educators integrate technology and the Internet into their teaching. Regular columns such as "Lesson Plan Goldmines" and "A+ Web Gallery" review web sites. The "Internet Activities" section provides detailed instructions that include learning goals, activities, and suggestions for assessment. "Destinations" provides thematic units. Feature articles focus on topics such as technology and differentiated instruction, learning through gaming, and Web 2.0 in the classroom. Technical articles offer helpful instruction in using web-based software and other Internet tools. Other columns present news about upcoming Internet projects in which classes may participate. First published in 1994, *Connected Newsletter* continues to be a valuable and practical resource for helping teachers incorporate technology into their classrooms.

1362. *Early Childhood Today.* Formerly (until 1993): *Scholastic Pre-K Today.* [ISSN: 1070-1214] 1986. 8x/yr. USD 19.95; USD 4 per issue. Scholastic Inc., 557 Broadway, New York, NY 10012; http://www.scholastic.com. Illus., adv. Circ: 55000 Paid. *Indexed:* ABIn, ERIC, EduInd. *Aud.:* Ac, Sa.

A leading magazine for childcare center owners and directors and early childhood educators, *Early Childhood Today* features research, teaching tips, activities, and management strategies. Articles focus on leadership issues as well as behavior and development. The "Hands-On Activities" section includes ideas for group time as well as age-appropriate activity plans. Columns are flagged with a mouse symbol to indicate when additional web content is available. The web site (http://teacher.scholastic.com/products/ect) contains online activities for ages 3–4, 4–5, 5–6, and mixed ages, as well as professional resources that include articles by experts in behavior and development in children from birth to age six, reports from the field, and product reviews.

Instructor. See Education/General, K-12 section.

1363. *Learning and Leading with Technology.* Formerly (until 1995): *Computing Teacher.* [ISSN: 1082-5754] 1979. 8x/yr. Free to members. Ed(s): Kate Conley. International Society for Technology in Education, 480 Charnelton St, Eugene, OR 97401-2626; iste@iste.org; http://www.iste.org. Illus., index, adv. Sample. Refereed. Circ: 12000. Vol. ends: May. Microform: PQC. Online: Florida Center for Library Automation; Gale; OCLC Online Computer Library Center, Inc.; H.W. Wilson. *Indexed:* ABIn, ERIC, EduInd, ISTA, MicrocompInd. *Aud.:* Sa.

This membership publication of the International Society for Technology in Education (ISTE) is for K–12 teachers and teacher educators with a broad range of experience integrating technology into the classroom. Articles emphasize practical applications of technology. "Learning Connections" focuses on uses of technology for specific subjects (language arts, social studies, math, science, physical education) and service learning. "Leading Connections" offers teacher-to-teacher advice on technology issues, professional development topics, and projects for the connected classroom. Each issue reviews new hardware and software releases. The web site (www.iste.org) provides members with access to the full text of articles.

1364. *The Mailbox: the idea magazine for teachers.* [ISSN: 0199-6045] 1972. bi-m. USD 29.95 domestic; USD 40.95 foreign. Ed(s): Angie Kutzer. Education Center, Inc., 3515 W Market St, Ste 200, PO Box 9753, Greensboro, NC 27403; http://www.themailboxcompanion.com. Illus., index, adv. Sample. Vol. ends: Dec/Jan. *Aud.:* Sa.

A colorful and engaging resource for teachers, *The Mailbox* is published in four editions: Preschool, Kindergarten–Grade 1, Grades 2–3, and Intermediate. The Preschool edition includes arts and crafts, storytime, circle time, songs, and science, among other activities that promote counting and pre-reading skills. A fold-out centerfold activity is included in each issue. The Kindergarten–Grade 1 edition contains many reproducibles as well as a centerfold pullout and focuses on basic math and reading skills. The Grade 2–3 edition takes the math, reading, science, and cross-curricular activities to the next level with puzzles, short writing exercises, and teacher resources. The Intermediate edition features activities in language arts and math as well as a section on science and social studies. It also has regular features on "Management Tips and Timesavers." *Mailbox Companion Online* is a free online service for subscribers that complements the print issue and contains a homepage personalized specifically for the subscriber's edition of the magazine, skill-based reproducibles, forms for classroom management, clip art, and other magazine extenders to complement the units in every issue. A new e-mail service, "The Mailbox Select," provides weekly, grade-specific activities directly to the teacher's inbox (www.themailboxselect.com).

Teacher's Helper: classroom skill builders [ISSN 1078-6570] 6/yr. USD 24.95. The Education Center, P.O. Box 9753, Greensboro, NC 27429-0753; www.themailbox.com. Illus. Vol. ends: Dec./Jan. *Aud:* Sa. Provides skill-based reproducible activity worksheets in four editions: kindergarten, grade 1, grades 2–3, and grades 4–5.

1365. *Mailbox Bookbag: literacy ideas for teachers.* [ISSN: 1088-6397] 1996. bi-m. USD 39.95. Ed(s): Christine Thuman. Education Center, Inc., 3515 W Market St, Ste 200, PO Box 9753, Greensboro, NC 27403. Illus. Sample. Vol. ends: Jun/Jul. *Aud.:* Sa.

An excellent resource for elementary and middle school teachers and librarians, *Mailbox Bookbag* provides brief descriptions of books and suggests activities for each title. Reproducible worksheets reinforce reading vocabulary and comprehension skills and make connections to writing and math skills where applicable. The "Bulletin Boards" section illustrates classroom displays designed to attract students' attention while encouraging them to read. A subscription includes free access to *The Bookbag Companion,* an online resource that contains a searchable (and printable) archive of *Bookbag* issues, editors' monthly picks of author reviews, literature units, and bulletin board ideas as well as publishers' special literature sections created just for *Bookbag* subscribers.

Mathematics Teacher. See Mathematics section.

Mathematics Teaching in the Middle School. See Mathematics section.

Media & Methods. See Media and AV section.

1366. *MultiMedia & Internet at Schools: the media and technology specialists' guide to electronic tools and resources.* Formerly (until 2003): *MultiMedia Schools.* [ISSN: 1546-4636] 1994. 6x/yr. USD 42.95 domestic; USD 57 in Canada & Mexico; USD 66 elsewhere. Ed(s): Kathie Felix, David Hoffman. Information Today, Inc., 143 Old Marlton Pike, Medford, NJ 08055-8750; custserv@infotoday.com; http://www.infotoday.com. Illus., adv. *Indexed:* ABIn, CPerI, EduInd, ISTA, MicrocompInd. *Bk. rev.:* 4. *Aud.:* Ac, Sa.

A practical how-to magazine for librarians, teachers, and media specialists, *MultiMedia & Internet@Schools* reports on, reviews, and discusses a wide array of electronic media, including Internet resources and online services, library systems, curriculum software, and administrative systems and tools to improve learning. Articles and columns address issues associated with using electronic information resources in K–12 schools. Features include "Cyberbee," informing on web resources for classroom use, "The Pipeline," focusing on new technologies and new uses of current technologies, and various "Watch" columns highlighting product and industry news. All are contributed by practicing educators who use new technologies in the classroom or media center. *Multimedia & Internet@Schools* is addressed primarily to K–12 librarians and media specialists, but it also will be of interest to technology coordinators, principals, and other administrators. Register for a free account on

the web site (www.mmischools.com) for links to current and archived content from the magazine with free full text for some articles (the rest available on a pay-per-view basis) and all product reviews. You can also sign up to receive the *MMIS Xtra* Newsletter via e-mail.

1367. *The Onestop Magazine: the magazine for English language teachers.* d. Ed(s): Tim Bowen. Macmillan Education, Macmillan Oxford, Between Towns Rd, Oxford, OX4 3PP, United Kingdom; elt@mhelt.com; http://www.macmillaneducation.com. *Aud.:* Sa.

The Onestop Magazine, organized and run by Macmillan Education, publishes materials developed by teachers in the classroom in order to provide a platform for sharing classroom experience. Material comes from competitions, such as "Lesson Share," and the rest is commissioned. The site offers a range of free resources, including lesson plans, podcasts, study skills extensions, and teaching strategies in the "Methodology" archive. There is a "Teacher Support" section for teachers to share anecdotes, find links to other relevant web sites, and even to ask grammar questions. There is a "Quick Search" feature that allows searching the materials on the site by Age Group, British or American English, Ability Level (beginner, intermediate, advanced), Language Focus (grammar, vocabulary, tests, skills), and Theme. Beginning in 2007, the "Archive" stores all of the monthly newsletters. Also, there are three ways to access *Onestop* resources: You can browse the categories for free—all material is available for downloading for use in the classroom. You can sign up as a registered user (also free) for access to expanded content, an interactive forum in which to share ideas with teachers around the world, and a monthly newsletter with up-to-date information about what's new on the site. Currently there are approximately 420,000 registered users. Finally, you can subscribe as a "Staff Room member" for new content created by expert authors, including weekly news lessons published in conjunction with the *Guardian Weekly* (a digest of four newspapers—*The Guardian, The Observer, The Washington Post,* and *Le Monde*). Other features available for Staff Room members include downloadable flashcards, games and activities, and monthly lesson plans in key content areas. Staff Room membership costs GBP 24 for a year's subscription. A full-featured site for ESL instruction, this is a very useful resource for teachers and students. URL: www.onestopenglish.com.

1368. *Scholastic.com.* Formerly: *Scholastic Network.* w. Scholastic Inc., 557 Broadway, New York, NY 10012. *Aud.:* Ems, Sa.

An excellent source of information and classroom resources with separate areas for each of its target audiences (kids, parents, teachers, administrators, and librarians), the *Scholastic.com* web site emphasizes participation and interaction. The teacher's section (teacher.scholastic.com) includes lesson plans, reproducibles, thematic units, and activities for pre-K through 12th grade. Information about assessment, multiculturalism and diversity, working with young writers, and communicating with parents are some of topics covered under the "Teaching Strategies" section. The "Tools" section provides teaching templates for creating rubrics, flash cards, and graphic organizers. The site also includes a "Classroom Homepage Builder" and "Global Classport," a secure meeting place for connecting and collaborating with classrooms and teachers around the world.

School Arts. See Education/Specific Subjects and Teaching Methods, The Arts section.

1369. *Science and Children: the journal for elementary school science teachers.* Formerly (until 1963): *Elementary School Science Bulletin.* [ISSN: 0036-8148] 1963. 8x/yr. USD 77 (Members, USD 72). Ed(s): Monica Zerry, Joan McShane. National Science Teachers Association, 1840 Wilson Blvd, Arlington, VA 22201; membership@nsta.org; http://www.nsta.org/. Illus., index, adv. Circ: 23500 Paid. Vol. ends: May. *Indexed:* ABIn, ECER, ERIC, EduInd, MRD, WSA. *Bk. rev.:* 7, 300 words. *Aud.:* Sa.

A peer-reviewed journal from the National Science Teachers Association (NSTA) for elementary science teachers, science teacher administrators, and teacher educators, *Science and Children* features articles that discuss pedagogy and educational issues relevant to science teaching. "In the News" highlights discoveries and current research of interest to the science community. Regular features include "Finds & Sites," a list of free or inexpensive materials, publications, and events; "Teaching Through Trade Books," activities inspired by children's literature; and "Every Day Science Calendar," a monthly calendar with "facts and challenges for the science explorer." "Science 101" experts answer teachers' questions about everyday science. "NSTA Recommends" reviews both student texts and professional literature for science teachers. These reviews and others are also available online at www.nsta.org/recommends.

1370. *Science Scope: a journal for middle-junior high science teachers.*
Formerly: *Middle Jr. High Science Bulletin.* [ISSN: 0887-2376] 1978. 8x/yr. Members, USD 72. Ed(s): Kenneth L Roberts. National Science Teachers Association, 1840 Wilson Blvd, Arlington, VA 22201; membership@nsta.org; http://www.nsta.org/. Illus., index, adv. Sample. Refereed. Circ: 15000 Paid. Vol. ends: May. Online: EBSCO Publishing, EBSCO Host; Gale; OCLC Online Computer Library Center, Inc.; ProQuest LLC (Ann Arbor); H.W. Wilson. *Indexed:* ABIn, ERIC, EduInd, MRD. *Bk. rev.:* 2-3, 300 words. *Aud.:* Sa.

A professional journal for middle level and junior high school science teachers. Peer-reviewed articles provide ready-to-use activities and teaching strategies for life science, physical science, and earth science. Regular features include "Science Sampler," descriptions and templates for classroom activities and field trips; "After the Bell," extracurricular science activities; "Tech Trek," incorporating technology in the classroom; "Scope on Safety," safety information for the classroom, and "Scope's Scoops," summaries of recent scientific research. "NSTA Recommends" highlights trade books. These reviews and others are available online at www.nsta.org/recommends.

Teacher Magazine. See Education/General, K-12 section.

Teaching Children Mathematics. See Mathematics section.

Teaching Exceptional Children. See Disabilities section.

Teaching Pre K-8. See Education/General, K-12 section.

The Science Teacher. See Astronomy section.

Today's Catholic Teacher. See Education/General, K-12 section.

1371. *Web Feet (Online Edition): the Internet traveler's desk reference.*
Formerly (until 2006): *Web Feet (Print Edition).* 1998. m. Gale, 27500 Drake Rd, Farmington Hills, MI 48331-3535; http://gale.cengage.com. *Aud.:* Ems, Hs, Ac, Sa.

Acquired by Thomson Gale in 2004, *Web Feet* is a multidisciplinary guide to web sites that have been reviewed and annotated by librarians, educators, subject specialists, and editors. It is an excellent source of up-to-date curriculum resources. This valuable collection is available in several editions: K–8 (appropriate for elementary and middle schools and public libraries), K–12 (for K–12 schools and districts and public libraries), the Core Collection (for K–12 schools and districts, public and academic libraries), an Academic Library Collection, a Public Library Collection, and a specialized Health Collection (for K–12 schools and districts, and public, academic, and medical libraries). All editions are available online and as downloadable MARC records that can be integrated into a library catalog. A ready-reference section has been added to each collection. Subscribers to any *Web Feet* product have access to "Spotlight," which highlights timely and frequently studied topics in *Web Feet.* Featured topics change every other week and previous Spotlights are archived. "Educator Resources" includes Internet resources for teachers, librarians, and parents. The monthly newsletters "Web Feet WIRE" and "Duck Soup" are no longer separately published. Instead there is a *Web Feet* component in each of the Gale newsletters (*Galementary* for elementary schools, *Curriculinks* for secondary schools, and *In the Loop* for APA libraries). Also, *Web Feet Online* provides browsing capability by LC subject, author/sponsor, site title, and LC or Dewey call number. The expanded search feature supports more complex keyword searching options. Search tips provide help with searches by grade level or curriculum area. An online guided tour helps users to orient themselves to searching *Web Feet Online.* Highly recommended for school, public, and academic libraries.

■ COMIC BOOKS

Publications about Comics

Allen Ellis, Professor of Library Services, W. Frank Steely Library, Northern Kentucky University, Highland Heights, KY 41099-6101; ellisa@nku.edu

Doug Highsmith, Reference/Instruction Librarian, University Library, California State University–East Bay, Hayward, CA 94542; doug.highsmith@csueastbay.edu

Roger C. Adams, Associate Professor, Special Collections, Hale Library, Kansas State University, Manhattan, KS 66506, rcadams@ksu.edu

Introduction

Libraries and comic books have long had a rocky relationship. Early references to comic books in the professional library literature made it seem as if comics were no more than promotional pamphlets for Hell. That stance has evolved over the years to the point that comic art is now largely (but, mind you, not completely) accepted as library fare (for an examination of the comics/libraries relationship, see contributors Ellis and Highsmith's "About Face: Comic Books in Library Literature" in *Serials Review,* 2000, vol. 26, Issue 2, pp. 21–43).

Part of this evolution is based upon the tremendous popularity of comic book properties in other media. Just since 2000, comics characters or series that have appeared in live-action or animated big screen movies and/or television adaptations include X-Men, Witchblade, Static, Monkeybone, *Smallville, Ghost World From Hell,* The Tick, Justice League, Blade, Spider-Man, Men in Black, *Road to Perdition,* Corto Maltese, Birds of Prey, Daredevil, Bulletproof Monk, The Hulk, League of Extraordinary Gentlemen, Teen Titans, *American Splendor,* Hellboy, The Punisher, Elektra, Constantine, The Mask, *Sin City,* Krypto the Superdog, Man-Thing, Batman, Fantastic Four, The Crow, *A History of Violence, MirrorMask,* Painkiller Jane, *V for Vendetta,* Superman, Legion of Super-Heroes, *Art School Confidential,* Ghost Rider, *300,* Teenage Mutant Ninja Turtles, Pathfinder, *30 Days of Night,* and *The Haunted World of El Superbeasto.* In addition, films, television, and other media often feature works that are clearly comics-inspired even if they are not direct adaptations—witness television shows like NBC's popular *Heroes;* novels such as Michael Chabon's Pulitzer Prize–winning *The Amazing Adventures of Kavalier and Clay;* and M. Night Shyamalan's *Unbreakable,* as well as a wide variety of other movies. And the end is nowhere in sight.

The cross-pollination works in both directions, of course. Comics have offered adaptations or continuations of both blockbusters and cult favorites. *Predator, Alien, Star Trek, Xena, Warrior Princess, Star Wars, Highlander, Army of Darkness, Nightmare on Elm Street, Buckaroo Banzai, Kolchak: The Night Stalker,* and *Powerpuff Girls* are only some examples. Writer Joss Whedon has even continued the official saga of TV's *Buffy the Vampire Slayer* in the comic book medium with the *Buffy, Season Eight* limited series from Dark Horse Comics.

All of this has caught the attention of the mainstream media, and, before that, scholars such as those in the Comic Art and Comics area of the Popular Culture Association (who produced *Comic Art in Scholarly Writing: A Citation Guide,* seen at http://home.earthlink.net/~comicsresearch/CAC/cite.html), and those who participate on the *Comix-Scholars' Discussion List* at http://web.english.ufl.edu/comics/scholars.

So, whether it is in the format of the traditional periodical pamphlets, graphic novels (which may be reprinted collections of comic book stories or original material—although certainly not always fictional, as "novels" suggests), or quality hardbound or CD reprint collections of classic comic book stories, comic books are frequently recognized as tools to encourage the reluctant reader, or as works of art in their own right, to say nothing of their role in the world of collectibles. As a result, they have earned a position in the world of libraries. Still, comic books are rarely a part of library schools' curriculum, and many librarians would benefit from a crash course in the medium, such as can be found, along with reviews of comics written *by* librarians *for* librarians, at the *Comic Books for Libraries* blog (http://comicbooksforlibraries.blogspot.com).

Whether libraries provide comic books or not, they may wish to provide periodicals that supplement the medium. The first magazine about comic books was 1947's *The Comic Collectors' News.* Prior to that time, such material could sometimes be found in science fiction fanzines. Into the 1960s, as comics readership matured and more adults took interest in comics, fanzines came and went, evolving in the 1970s into professional magazines about comics. Since then, despite the terrific influx of Internet fan sites, print publications continue to thrive, and like the media they examine or celebrate, they have a place in most libraries.

Publications about Comics

1372. *Alter Ego.* [ISSN: 1932-6890] 1999. m. USD 78. Ed(s): Roy Thomas. TwoMorrows, 10407 Bedfordtown Dr, Raleigh, NC 27614; roydann@ntinet.com; http://twomorrows.com. *Aud.:* Hs, Ga.

Since 1994, TwoMorrows Publishing has been "Celebrating the Art & History of Comics," establishing itself as a leader in publishing books and periodicals celebrating the comics medium." *Alter Ego,* named after one of the earliest comics fanzines of the 1960s, is tailored to anyone interested in premodern comic books. The emphasis is on history, be it of a character, title, publisher, creator, genre, or theme. Interviews with creators and prodigious reproduction of art (often rare or unpublished, but, alas, not in color) are among the hallmarks of this title, along with a regular Fawcett Collectors of America feature, focusing on Fawcett Publications, the Golden Age publisher best known for the original Captain Marvel (of "SHAZAM!" fame). Editor Roy Thomas has extensive credentials as a comics professional and fan, and his love for the medium permeates each issue. An excellent choice for those interested in Silver Age or Golden Age comics, or in comics history in general. (AE)

1373. *Back Issue.* [ISSN: 1932-6904] 2003. bi-m. USD 36. Ed(s): Michael Eury. TwoMorrows, 10407 Bedfordtown Dr, Raleigh, NC 27614; roydann@ntinet.com; http://twomorrows.com. *Aud.:* Hs, Ga, Ac.

One of TwoMorrows Publishing's most successful offerings, *Back Issue!* focuses on comic books of the 1970s to the present, with each heavily illustrated issue having a specific theme or focus. (Recent issues look at "Comics Go Hollywood"; "Dynamic Duos"; "The Devil You Say" [demonic-themed or -named comics characters]; and "Secret Identities.") As is true of most of the publisher's other offerings, *Back Issue!* does not limit itself solely to writing about comic books, but will also feature articles or interviews dealing with related popular culture topics such as Star Wars, Star Trek, and comics-related movies and television shows. *Back Issue!* should be of interest to most comics fans, especially those who wish to know more about the history behind some of today's comics and characters. While the publisher has not as yet gathered together materials from the magazine into any "best of" compilations, older individual issues are available for purchase at the publisher's web site. (DH)

Comic Art. See Anime, Graphic Novels, and Manga section.

1374. *Comic Shop News.* 1987. w. Free via comics retail stores. Ed(s): Ward Batty, Cliff Biggers. Comic Shop News, Inc., 2770 Carillon Crossing, Marietta, GA 30066; http://www.csnsider.com. *Aud.:* Hs, Ga.

Every week for 20 years, Comic Shop News has delivered reviews of comics, articles by leading writers, artists, and publishers, interviews, comics publisher news, and product reviews. This full-color, tabloid newsprint publication is as familiar to every denizen of reputable comic shops as the scents of patchouli and body odor are to members of a hippie drum circle. The publication manages to cram an incredible amount of valuable information into its 8–12 pages every week. *Comic Shop News'* unbiased presentation is especially valuable to librarians looking to make decisions about which comics to order for their libraries. Whether a comic title is a one-shot, graphic novel, limited series, or continuing series, CSN will highlight nearly all mainstream press titles. For librarians uninterested in the non-mainstream titles and comics paraphernalia covered by *Previews,* CSN is the go-to, ordering shortcut resource. CSN is not available for subscription, as it is sold in bundles of 100 or 50 copies for about 10 cents each to comic shop owners, over 600 of whom distribute the title free of charge in North America. (RA)

1375. *Comics Buyer's Guide.* Incorporates: *Comics Buyer's Guide Price Guide.* [ISSN: 0745-4570] 1971. m. USD 29.95 domestic; USD 50.95 Canada; USD 65.95 elsewhere. Ed(s): Maggie Thompson. Krause Publications, Inc., 700 E State St, Iola, WI 54990-0001; info@krause.com; http://www.krause.com. Illus., adv. Sample. Circ: 8794 Paid and free. Microform: PQC. *Bk. rev.:* Various number and length. *Aud.:* Ems, Hs, Ga, Ac.

"The World's Longest-Running Magazine about Comics," the *Comics Buyer's Guide* (CBG) was for many years the weekly trade paper for the comics industry, until it began publishing as a monthly magazine in 2004. What uniqueness it lost was only in frequency and format, as it is still *the* source for news and information on the ever-changing comics scene, including mainstream and independent comics, graphic novels and Manga, anime, films, television and video, trading cards, action figures, and animation. Along with advertisements from publishers, retailers, and collectors, each issue is packed with news, reviews, columns, industry information, Internet guides, convention schedules, comics price guides, and a consistently fascinating letters column (a neutral forum wherein various viewpoints are shared on such wide-ranging topics as literacy, censorship, the moral responsibilities of publishers and retailers, perceptions of comics readers by non–comics readers, as well as discussions of comics in general). The annual *CBG* Fan Awards are a popular barometer of what fans are enjoying. Editor Maggie Thompson, with her late husband Don, was among the founders of comics fandom and is an articulate supporter of both comics and literacy in general. The voice and marketplace of comics fandom (and pros as well), *CBG* is often more interesting than the comics they celebrate. There is plenty for young and old followers of comics to enjoy. Adapting a cliche, if you must have *one* magazine about comics, *CBG* is the one to have. (AE)

1376. *Comics Journal: the magazine of comics news & criticism.* [ISSN: 0194-7869] 1976. m. USD 72 domestic; USD 100 foreign. Ed(s): Gary Groth. Fantagraphics Books, Inc., 7563 Lake City Way, Seattle, WA 98115; tcjnews@tcj.com; http://www.tcj.com. Illus., adv. Circ: 12000. *Aud.:* Hs, Ga, Ac.

The Comics Journal is considered an essential read by many in the comics industry, on both the creative and the publishing sides. In nearly 200 pages of each issue of this large-format journal are critical and historical articles, interviews, and reviews of comics, graphic novels, indie comics, and underground comix. An article about the earliest newspaper comic strips might be sandwiched between an interview with an up-and-coming artist/writer and a historiographical essay about lesbian-themed comic books. And although *TCJ* boasts an impressive list of over 50 columnists and contributing writers, bylines about the writers do not accompany the articles, leaving the reader to determine if the writer has serious credentials or is just another fanboy with an ax to grind. And frequently, reviews and other critical essays have a decidedly negative tone that may be more about the writer's dislike of the subject than pure objectivity. Despite the appearance of mean-spiritedness, *TCJ* is a valuable resource. Finally, the magazine's production values are generally high, although the quality of image reproduction—even black-and-white illustrations—are frequently not what one would expect from a journal of this caliber. (RA)

1377. *Draw!* [ISSN: 1932-6882] 2001. q. USD 24. Ed(s): Mike Manley. TwoMorrows, 10407 Bedfordtown Dr, Raleigh, NC 27614; http://twomorrows.com. *Aud.:* Hs, Ga, Ac.

Edited by veteran comics writer/artist Mike Manley, *Draw!* has as its primary audience aspiring comics artists, cartoonists, and animators. Its focus is on "how-to" articles and tutorials, as well as lengthy interviews with comics professionals (which are, as might be expected, usually accompanied by numerous illustrations demonstrating the interviewee's work). Artists in the spotlight have included such well-established pros as Kyle Baker, Doug Mahnke, and Steve Rude. Both editor Manley and fellow comics pro Bret Blevins contribute regular features on drawing styles and techniques. As is true with other titles from this publisher, individual issues are substantial, averaging 80–100 pages in length. Given its "how-to-draw" focus, this publication has a fairly specialized appeal, but would certainly be of interest to academic libraries supporting art/illustration programs, and public libraries with a significant clientele of aspiring artists. Two volumes of *The Best of Draw!* are available from the publisher (volume 1 takes materials from issues 1 and 2 of the magazine; volume 2 has material taken from issues 3 and 4). Also available are individual back issues. (DH)

1378. *Hogan's Alley: the magazine of the cartoon arts.* [ISSN: 1074-7354] 1994. s-a. USD 22.95 domestic for 4 nos.; USD 30.95 foreign for 4 nos.; USD 6.95 newsstand/cover per issue. Ed(s): Tom Heintjes. Bull Moose Publishing Corp., PO Box 47684, Atlanta, GA 30362; http://www.cagle.com/. Illus., adv. Circ: 5000 Paid. *Aud.:* Hs, Ga, Ac.

Subtitled "The magazine for cartooning arts," the somewhat-annual *Hogan's Alley* is literate in approach and solid in its research, while being eclectic in its coverage. Although it focuses primarily on comic strips, it also provides coverage of comic books, animation, and political cartooning. For instance, issue #14 offers a feature article about *Dennis the Menace* along with the last interview of Thurl Ravenscroft, voice of Tony the Tiger; an article on martial arts ads in comics books; and a wide variety of other items. Earlier issues include contents that run the gamut from an article on the car crash that took the life of cartoonist Alex Raymond to a celebration of the 40th "birthday" of Fred Flintstone to a feature on "Comics in the Comics" (i.e., the comic book careers of Bob Hope, Jerry Lewis, and others) to an interview with *Bizarro* artist Dan Piraro. Given the variety of topics it covers and the overall quality of its writing and research, *Hogan's Alley* is of potential interest to all fans and students of the cartoon arts. The online version of the magazine is available on the MSNBC web site, where it is titled *Hogan's Alley: The Online Magazine of the Cartoon Arts.* While the printed magazine does offer content unavailable on the free web site, the site offers "web extras"—materials that either did not make it into the print version, or appeared there in black-and-white, rather than the color version available on the web site. Also available on the web site are most of the contents of the first two sold-out issues of the magazine. (DH)

1379. *ImageTexT.* [ISSN: 1549-6732] 2004. irreg. Free. University of Florida, Department of English, 4008 Turlington Hall, Gainesville, FL 32611. Refereed. *Indexed:* MLA-IB. *Bk. rev.:* Number and length vary. *Aud.:* Hs, Ga, Ac.

ImageTexT is one of the most sublime web publications available about comics. This peer-reviewed, open-access journal brings together a panoply of scholars working in the fields of textual studies, cultural studies, popular culture, literary criticism, history, and art. Published almost quarterly since Spring 2004, *ImageTexT* is a rich resource for some of the finest writing ever produced about comics, comic strips, and animation. Anyone who would dare state that comics studies are as serious as a Lindsay Lohan rehab stint need only peruse one issue to realize that's simply not true. Each article is easily accessed, reproduced in a large, readable font, and supplied with one-click, printer-friendly links, as well as an MLA Style citation link. A complete, free archive is available and searchable using keywords or keyphrases, unlike the resource you're using to read this review. Authors have the freedom to use many full-color images to accompany their articles and hypertext links within articles to further enhance the experience of this publication. Finally, *ImageTexT* is also an excellent resource for unavailable English-language translations of important essays on comics theory. (RA)

1380. *International Journal of Comic Art.* [ISSN: 1531-6793] 1999. s-a. USD 45 (Individuals, USD 30). John A. Lent, Ed & Pub, 669 Ferne Blvd, Drexel Hill, PA 19026. Illus., adv. *Indexed:* MLA-IB. *Bk. rev.:* Various number and length. *Aud.:* Ac.

Considering the multidisciplinary nature of the growing academic interest in comic art, *International Journal of Comic Art* is an especially worthwhile selection for college and university libraries. Scholarly articles on comics appear in such publications as the *Journal of Popular Culture,* but *IJOCA* serves as the primary scholarly journal serving the growing field of comic art scholarship. Editor John A. Lent is professor of communications at Temple University and an authority on the international aspects of comic art, and "scholarly, but not stuffy" is his aim. Recent article titles include "Death and the Superhero: The Silver Age and Beyond"; "9-11-01: Truth, Justice and Comic Books"; "Manga in Italy: History of a Powerful Hybridization"; "Theorizing Comics Journalism"; and "Speaking the 'Truth' of Sex: Moore & Gebbie's *Lost Girls.*" As the last example suggests, some material is for a decidedly mature audience. (AE)

1381. *The Jack Kirby Collector.* [ISSN: 1932-6912] 1994. q. USD 44. Ed(s): John Morrow. TwoMorrows, 10407 Bedfordtown Dr, Raleigh, NC 27614; roydann@ntinet.com; http://twomorrows.com. *Aud.:* Hs, Ga, Ac.

Some comics artists were more accomplished stylists, and many other writers were superior wordsmiths, but no one surpassed the impact on the comics industry provided by the man who, over the course of a 50-plus-year career, created or co-created such characters as Captain America, the Fantastic Four, the X-Men, The Hulk, Thor, the Avengers, the New Gods, Kamandi, the Silver Surfer, the Black Panther, the Challengers of the Unknown, and the immortal Devil Dinosaur. That man, of course, is Jack "King" Kirby, a veritable one-man "Idea Factory." Each issue of the tabloid-formatted *The Jack Kirby Collector* reprints a generous sampling of the King's work, along with a variety of articles about his life, career, and comic book contemporaries, as well as interviews with current comics creators, who discuss Kirby's influence on their work. Kirby biographer and former collaborator Mark Evanier contributes a regular column. Even though Kirby died over a dozen years ago, his influence is still very much felt in the comic book industry. This ongoing legacy makes the *The Jack Kirby Collector* of potential interest to both casual fans and serious students and researchers. Materials from individual issues are gathered together in *The Collected Jack Kirby Collector.* The five volumes of the *Collected Collector* published to date reprint materials appearing in the first 22 issues. These are available for purchase on the web site, as are individual back issues of the magazine. (DH)

1382. *Official Overstreet Comic Book Price Guide.* Former titles (until 2002): *The Overstreet Comic Book Price Guide;* (until 1992): *Official Overstreet Comic Book Price Guide;* (until 1987): *Comic Book Price Guide.* [ISSN: 1551-403X] 1970. a. USD 35 newsstand/cover per issue. Ed(s): J C Vaughn. Gemstone Publishing, Inc., 1966 Greenspring Dr., Ste. 405, Timonium, MD 21093-4117. Illus. Circ: 150000. *Aud.:* Ems, Hs, Ga, Ac.

For nearly 40 years, this annual, commonly referred to simply as *Overstreet,* has been regarded as the bible of the comic book hobbyist, investor, collector, student, and fan. Most mainstream comic books from 1900 to the present (recent editions have increasingly examined pre–twentieth century comic art) are represented, with their current valuation based upon condition. There are other comics price guides available, but *Overstreet* is still the standard. Each issue, besides featuring articles on significant series, publishers, or characters, provides an omnibus of information ranging from invaluable historical and bibliographic data to guidelines for obtaining, grading, storing, and selling comic books. Highly recommended as a reference tool, whether a library offers comics or not. (AE)

1383. *Previews (Timonium).* 1991. m. USD 4.50 newsstand/cover per issue. Ed(s): Marty Grosser. Diamond Comic Distributors, 1966 Greenspring Dr, Ste 300, Timonium, MD 21093; http://www.diamondcomics.com. *Aud.:* Ems, Hs, Ga.

Previews describes itself as the "your ultimate source for all the merchandise available from your local comic book specialty retailer." It is a preview of comics scheduled for shipment to comics shops two months hence; not only comics, but also trading cards (including sports cards), games, toys, apparel, videos, posters, magazines, books, collectibles, collectors supplies, and other products at least loosely related to the world of comics, graphic novels, Manga, and anime. Provided in the 500-plus pages are short descriptions of content and format, price, and expected delivery date, supplemented with articles and interviews promoting coming products. Available primarily through comics specialty shops and subscription services, it includes ordering forms for retailers. This system is a good way for libraries to customize a comics-ordering program. Even if not used as an ordering tool, *Previews* is still fun to browse through, but if you are making it available to your public, be aware that there are many images of human beings in various stages of what is commonly considered undress. The publisher, Diamond Comic Distributors, is particularly accommodating to librarians. Their web site provides such information as "How to Start a Comic Collection," "Starting a Graphic Novel Collection," and "Cataloging Graphic Novels" (see http://bookshelf.diamondcomics.com/public/default.asp?t=1&m=1&c=20&s=181&ai=37802). (AE)

1384. *Rough Stuff.* [ISSN: 1931-9231] 2006. q. USD 26. Ed(s): Bob McLeod. TwoMorrows, 10407 Bedfordtown Dr, Raleigh, NC 27614; roydann@ntinet.com; http://twomorrows.com. *Aud.:* Hs, Ga, Ac.

With long-time comics penciller/inker Bob McLeod at the helm, *Rough Stuff* is (along with *Draw!*) one of two publications of TwoMorrows Publishing that focuses on comic book art. Less focused than its sister publication on the nuts-and-bolts of succeeding as a comic book artist, *Rough Stuff* takes a more historical approach, and attempts to provide its readers with some never-before published comics pages from various eras of the industry (often pages in unfinished or "rough" form). Along with a featured interview with a well-known comic book artist, issues of *Rough Stuff* offer columns, art critiques, and short news items/reports. Less a "how to" publication than is *Draw!*, *Rough Stuff* should have somewhat greater appeal to casual comics fans, as opposed to aspiring artists. All issues of *Rough Stuff* published to date are available for purchase at the web site—either individually or in multi-issue "bundles." (DH)

1385. *Wizard: the comics magazine.* [ISSN: 1065-6499] 1991. m. USD 28 domestic; CND 55 Canada; USD 80 elsewhere. Ed(s): Patricia McCallum. Wizard Entertainment, 151 Wells Ave, Congers, NY 10920; customerservice@WizardUniverse.com. Illus., adv. Sample. Circ: 208000. *Bk. rev.:* Number and length vary. *Aud.:* Hs, Ga.

As the recent change in subtitle suggests, *Wizard* is no longer simply "the Comics Magazine," but now encompasses "Comics, Entertainment and Pop Culture." Modern superhero comics are still the focus, but their relationship to such allied areas as video games, toys and other collectibles, DVDs, anime, and other merchandise is emphasized (especially interpretations of comics characters in film and television—a major concern of many fans). Although it lacks the depth, breadth, and sophistication of the *Comics Buyers Guide*, *Wizard* is a slick, well-produced news/opinion fanzine suitable for teen fans and collectors, loaded with information. Features may provide in-depth examinations of particular creators, publishers, characters, and series, while regular departments spotlight news and reviews, as well as readers' letters. Humor is often attempted, sometimes achieved. Similar fanzines come and go, but with its price and content, *Wizard* maintains its edge. (AE)

1386. *Write Now!* [ISSN: 1555-502X] 2002. q. USD 24. Ed(s): Danny Fingeroth. TwoMorrows, 10407 Bedfordtown Dr, Raleigh, NC 27614; roydann@ntinet.com; http://twomorrows.com. *Aud.:* Ems, Hs, Ga, Ac.

What TwoMorrows Publishing's *Draw!* is for aspiring comics artists and animators, the same publisher's *Write Now!* is for those wanting to pursue or advance a career in comic book writing. Its aim is to provide its readers with a look at both the creative and business sides of writing for comics (or related media), and to give them insight into producing the types of stories that both readers and editors will want. Obviously, simply reading *Write Now!* is no guarantee that aspiring writers will find success, but editor Danny Fingeroth's own experience as a writer in the industry can only enhance the credibility of what he includes in each issue, and presumably stands him in good stead in attracting other pros to contribute to or be interviewed for his publication. The magazine's regular "Nuts & Bolts" section offers examples of past and current comics script and art from a variety of creators. All issues of *Write Now!* published to date are available for purchase at the web site, either individually or in multi-issue "bundles." (DH)

■ COMMUNICATION

See also Education; Journalism and Writing; Media and AV; and Television, Video, and Radio sections.

Laura A. Sullivan, Grants Coordinator, Northern Kentucky University, Steely Library, Highland Heights, KY 41099; sullivanl@nku.edu; FAX: 859-572-6181

Nancy F. Campbell, Assistant to the Associate Provost for Library Services, Northern Kentucky University, Steely Library, Highland Heights, KY 41099; campbelln@nku.edu; FAX: 859-572-6181

Michael J. Providenti, Web Development Librarian, Steely Library, Highland Heights, KY 41099; providenti@nku.edu; FAX: 859-572-6181

Introduction

This section features critical, representative publications in the discipline of communication. Titles chosen reflect scholarship and analysis in all fields of communication: mass, speech, interpersonal, organizational, rhetorical, and applied, among others. All titles of the National Communication Association are featured (it is the oldest and largest national organization to advance communication scholarship and education), including their online publications, two of which are additions to this update. In general, the listing offers many well-known core periodicals within the discipline. While it is recognized that there are numerous communication periodicals that focus on a specific type of communication, such as political, business, visual, health, etc., for purposes of consistency the current list concentrates on the key, general publications, though these titles certainly publish articles on individual communication areas. Future updates will consider adding specialized titles. As with other disciplines, communication has a number of electronic titles in the field, and many of the print titles have an online counterpart. Emphasis is obviously on academic titles, but that is where the concentration of communication titles lies. However, the necessary titles for public libraries are included here as well.

Basic Periodicals

Ac: *Argumentation and Advocacy, Communication Education, Communication Monographs, Communication Quarterly, Communication Reports, Communication Research, Communication Research Reports, Critical Studies in Media Communication, Human Communication Research, Journal of Applied Communication Research, Journal of Communication, Quarterly Journal of Speech, Southern Communication Journal, Western Journal of Communication.*

Basic Abstracts and Indexes

Communication Abstracts, Communication & Mass Media Complete, ERIC, Humanities Index, Psychological Abstracts, Social Sciences Index, Sociological Abstracts.

1387. *American Communication Journal.* [ISSN: 1532-5865] 1996. 3x/yr. Free. Ed(s): Robert L Schrag. American Communication Association, c/o Stephanie Coopman, San Jose State University, San Jose, CA 95192-0112; acjournal@email.com; http://www.americancomm.org/. Refereed. *Indexed:* CommAb. *Bk. rev.:* Irreg. *Aud.:* Ac, Sa.

As described by the editor, this journal is "dedicated to the conscientious analysis and criticism of significant communication artifacts." In appreciation of the multiplicity of methodologies and research interests within the field of communication, essays on any relevant topic may be included. *American Communication Journal* is a blind-reviewed academic journal that organizes each issue around a central theme. A search engine provides easy access to keywords across the journal's entire publication period.

1388. *Argumentation & Advocacy: journal of the American Forensic Association.* Formerly (until vol.25, 1989): *American Forensic Association. Journal.* [ISSN: 1051-1431] 1964. q. USD 20 students members (Institutional members, USD 70; Individual members, USD 75). Ed(s): Randall A Lake. American Forensic Association, PO Box 256, River Falls, WI 54022-0256; amforensicassoc@aol.com;

http://www.americanforensics.org. Illus., adv. Sample. Refereed. Circ: 1000. Vol. ends: Spring. Microform: PQC. Online: EBSCO Publishing, EBSCO Host; Florida Center for Library Automation; Gale; Northern Light Technology, Inc.; OCLC Online Computer Library Center, Inc.; ProQuest K-12 Learning Solutions; ProQuest LLC (Ann Arbor). *Indexed:* AmHI, CommAb, LRI. *Bk. rev.:* 2-5, lengthy. *Aud.:* Ac.

This "flagship" journal of the American Forensic Association advances the study of argumentation. Any research methodology is encouraged in the areas of argumentation theory, public and political argument, legal argument, critical and cultural perspectives, and forensics and pedagogy. Special issues occur occasionally (e.g., televised political debates), and book reviews are included. A title for academic collections.

Broadcasting & Cable. See Television, Video, and Radio section.

Columbia Journalism Review. See Journalism and Writing section.

1389. *Communication and Critical/Cultural Studies.* [ISSN: 1479-1420] 2004. q. GBP 174 print & online eds. Ed(s): Robert L Ivie. Routledge, 325 Chestnut St, Ste 800, Philadelphia, PA 19106; journals@ routledge.com; http://www.tandf.co.uk/journals. Reprint: PSC. *Indexed:* CommAb. *Bk. rev.:* 1+, lengthy. *Aud.:* Ac.

A journal of the National Communication Association, *CCCS* offers scholarship that focuses on communication and our democratic culture. Within that framework, topics may include class, race, ethnicity, gender, the public sphere, nation, globalization, and environment. The journal features "critical inquiry that cuts across academic boundaries to focus on social, political, and cultural practices from the standpoint of communication." Recent article titles include "Rethinking the Globalization Movement: Toward a Cultural Theory of Contemporary Democracy and Communication," "Cultural Studies, Public Pedagogy," and "The Strategic Rhetoric of an 'At-Risk' Educational Identity: Interviewing Jane." *CCCS* publishes occasional reviews of major new books as well as research essays. A relevant publication for today's world, this journal belongs in comprehensive communication collections.

1390. *Communication Education.* Formerly (until 1976): *Speech Teacher.* [ISSN: 0363-4523] 1952. q. GBP 193 print & online eds. Ed(s): Patricia Kearney. Routledge, 325 Chestnut St, Ste 800, Philadelphia, PA 19106; journals@routledge.com; http://www.tandf.co.uk/journals. Illus., index, adv. Sample. Refereed. Circ: 3700. Vol. ends: Oct. Microform: PQC. Online: EBSCO Publishing, EBSCO Host; Gale; IngentaConnect; Northern Light Technology, Inc.; OCLC Online Computer Library Center, Inc.; SwetsWise Online Content. Reprint: PSC. *Indexed:* ABIn, BRI, CBRI, CommAb, EAA, ERIC, EduInd, FLI, IBR, IBZ, L&LBA, LISA, MLA-IB, MRD, PsycInfo, SSA, SSCI. *Aud.:* Ac, Sa.

This journal covers scholarship in communication and instruction. Areas of focus include technology in mediated instruction, classroom discourse, life-span development of communication competence, and diverse backgrounds of learners and teachers in instructional settings. The current editor intends to advance the areas of general instruction and specifically communication education by "encouraging systematic and programmatic research, theoretically grounded projects, rigorous literature reviews and meta-analyses, and interesting methodological and pedagogical papers." Scholarship beyond the classroom, such as community service learning and distance learning is also examined. An important note in the April 2006 issue is that book reviews will no longer be provided in *CE*. This is a critical publication for communication faculty and researchers. Valuable for its focus, and a necessary resource for academic libraries.

1391. *Communication Monographs.* Formerly (until vol.42): *Speech Monographs.* [ISSN: 0363-7751] 1934. q. GBP 167 print & online eds. Ed(s): Alan Sillars. Routledge, 270 Madison Ave, New York, NY 10016; info@routledge-ny.com; http://www.routledge-ny.com. Illus., index. Refereed. Circ: 3400. Vol. ends: Dec. Microform: PQC. Online: EBSCO Publishing, EBSCO Host; Gale; IngentaConnect; Northern Light

Technology, Inc.; OCLC Online Computer Library Center, Inc.; SwetsWise Online Content. Reprint: PSC. *Indexed:* ABIn, AmH&L, ArtHuCI, BAS, CommAb, ECER, EduInd, FLI, HistAb, L&LBA, LT&LA, MLA-IB, PsycInfo, SFSA, SSA, SSCI, SociolAb, V&AA. *Aud.:* Ac.

Communication Monographs publishes original research (qualitiative or quantitative), theoretical papers, original reviews, or methodological articles on human communication processes. An "ideal" article, according to the current editor, would address concepts and issues on core communication problems, address issues that are socially and theoretically signicant, offer extensive data sets and/or intense analysis, and be concisely written. Recommended for academic libraries.

1392. *Communication Quarterly.* Formerly: *Today's Speech.* [ISSN: 0146-3373] 1953. q. USD 217 print & online eds. Ed(s): Jerry L Allen. Routledge, 325 Chestnut St, Ste 800, Philadelphia, PA 19106; journals@ routledge.com; http://www.tandf.co.uk/journals. Illus., index, adv. Refereed. Circ: 3000. Vol. ends: Fall. Microform: PQC. Online: EBSCO Publishing, EBSCO Host; Florida Center for Library Automation; Gale; Northern Light Technology, Inc.; OCLC Online Computer Library Center, Inc.; ProQuest K-12 Learning Solutions; ProQuest LLC (Ann Arbor); SwetsWise Online Content; H.W. Wilson. Reprint: PSC. *Indexed:* AmH&L, AmHI, CommAb, FLI, HumInd, L&LBA, LRI, PRA, RI-1, RILM, SSA, SWA, SociolAb. *Aud.:* Ac.

This journal publishes all types of manuscripts (topical interest papers, research reports, state-of-the-art reviews, supported opinion, critical studies) that advance the understanding of human communication. A good mix of topics are covered; recent articles include "Classroom Communication: The Influence of Instructor Self-Disclosure on Student Evaluations" and "Men, Women, and Televised Violence: Predicting Viewer Aggression in Male and Female Television Viewers." Six to eight articles are published in each issue. *Communication Quarterly* is a regional communication association publication and a core title for academic libraries.

1393. *Communication Reports.* [ISSN: 0893-4215] 1988. s-a. GBP 114 (Individuals, GBP 27). Ed(s): Walter Zakahi. Routledge, 4 Park Sq, Milton Park, Abingdon, OX14 4RN, United Kingdom; journals@ routledge.com; http://www.routledge.com. Illus., adv. Vol. ends: Summer. Online: EBSCO Publishing, EBSCO Host; Florida Center for Library Automation; Gale; Northern Light Technology, Inc.; ProQuest LLC (Ann Arbor); SwetsWise Online Content. Reprint: PSC. *Indexed:* CommAb, L&LBA, PsycInfo, SSA, SociolAb. *Aud.:* Ac.

This journal seeks short, original, data-based articles on broadly defined human communication topics. Theoretical or speculative reports are not accepted; rather, emphasis should be on research data analysis, and a submission should reflect this. Recommended for academic collections.

1394. *Communication Research.* [ISSN: 0093-6502] 1974. bi-m. GBP 502. Ed(s): Michael E Roloff, Pamela Shoemaker. Sage Publications, Inc., 2455 Teller Rd, Thousand Oaks, CA 91320; info@sagepub.com; http://www.sagepub.com. Illus., index, adv. Refereed. Circ: 800 Paid. Vol. ends: Dec. Reprint: PSC. *Indexed:* ABIn, AbAn, AgeL, AmHI, ArtHuCI, CJA, CommAb, EAA, FLI, HRA, HumInd, IBSS, L&LBA, PRA, PSA, PsycInfo, RILM, SFSA, SSA, SSCI, SUSA, SWA, SociolAb, V&AA. *Aud.:* Ac.

The editorial goal of *Communication Research* is "to offer a special opportunity for reflection and change in the new millennium." While requiring submissions of theoretically driven communication research, the journal is not limited to a specific methodology and is receptive to original research efforts, as long as that research is "directly linked to the most important problems and issues facing humankind." Although the title is expensive, it should be required for academic collections.

1395. *Communication Research Reports.* [ISSN: 0882-4096] 1984. a. USD 198 (Individuals, USD 32). Ed(s): Dr. Lisa Sparks. Routledge, 325 Chestnut St, Ste 800, Philadelphia, PA 19106; journals@routledge.com;

http://www.tandf.co.uk/journals. Illus., index, adv. Refereed. Circ: 1500. Microform: PQC. Online: EBSCO Publishing, EBSCO Host; SwetsWise Online Content. Reprint: PSC. *Indexed:* CommAb, L&LBA, PSA, PsycInfo, SSA, SociolAb. *Aud.:* Ac.

A publication of the Eastern Communication Association, *Communication Research Reports* publishes ten or more brief, empirical articles in each issue. Studies on human communication in a wide variety of areas are accepted, including intercultural, interpersonal, aging / life span, health, organizational, persuasive, political, nonverbal, instructional, relational, or mediated. Articles emphasize the reporting and interpretation of the results rather than theory. A title for academic collections.

1396. Communication Studies. Formerly (until 1989): *Central States Speech Journal.* [ISSN: 1051-0974] 1949. q. GBP 144 print & online eds. Ed(s): Jim L Query, Jr. Routledge, 4 Park Sq, Milton Park, Abingdon, OX14 4RN, United Kingdom; journals@routledge.com; http://www.routledge.com. Illus., index, adv. Refereed. Circ: 2700. Vol. ends: Winter. Online: EBSCO Publishing, EBSCO Host; Florida Center for Library Automation; Gale; IngentaConnect; Northern Light Technology, Inc.; OCLC Online Computer Library Center, Inc.; ProQuest K-12 Learning Solutions; ProQuest LLC (Ann Arbor); SwetsWise Online Content. Reprint: PSC. *Indexed:* CommAb, MLA-IB, PRA, RILM, SSA, SSCI, SociolAb. *Aud.:* Ac.

A publication of the Central States Communication Association, *Communication Studies* publishes high quality original research on communication theory and research processes, with the expectation that the essays and studies advance human communication scholarship. Article topics vary (e.g., "Sensemaking and Emotions in Organizations: Accounting for Emotions in a Rational(ized) Context," "Regenerating Masculinity in the Construction of Hindu Nationalist Identity: A Case Study of Shiv Sena") and reflect communication studies in broad contexts. An important title for academic libraries.

1397. Communication Teacher (Online). [ISSN: 1740-4630] q. GBP 22. Ed(s): Deanna Sellnow. Routledge, 4 Park Square, Milton Park, Abingdon, OX14 4RN, United Kingdom. Sample. Refereed. *Aud.:* Ac.

Published by the National Communication Association, *Communication Teacher* is "a quarterly publication dedicated to the identification, assessment and promotion of quality teaching practices in the K-12, community college, and university communication classrooms. Teaching practices are explored in depth: the rationale, objectives and identification of courses for which the practice is intended, a full explanation of the practice, appraisal, references, and suggested readings. Courses covered include communication research methods, communication technologies, communication theory, family, gender, health, interpersonal, intercultural, mass, organizational, public relations, rhetoric and small group, in addition to the basic/hybrid communication courses." Each issue is available electronically to current subscribers in January, April, July, and October. Subscribers then receive a printed volume at the end of the year.

1398. Communication Theory. [ISSN: 1050-3293] 1991. q. GBP 154 print & online eds. Ed(s): Francois Cooren. Blackwell Publishing, Inc., Commerce Place, 350 Main St, Malden, MA 02148; customerservices@blackwellpublishing.com; http://www.blackwellpublishing.com. Illus., adv. Refereed. Circ: 4100. Vol. ends: Nov. Reprint: PSC. *Indexed:* ArtHuCI, CJA, CommAb, IBR, IBSS, IBZ, L&LBA, PSA, PsycInfo, SSA, SSCI, SociolAb. *Aud.:* Ac, Sa.

This journal publishes "high quality, original research into the theoretical development of communication." Many disciplines are represented, including communication studies, psychology, cultural/gender studies, sociology, political science, philosophy, linguistics, and literature. Articles are in-depth and lengthy, with some yearly special issues (e.g., "Succeeding Failure: Openings in Communication and Media Studies"). Recommended for larger research libraries.

1399. Communication World. Former titles (until 1982): *Journal of Communication Management;* (until 1981): *Journal of Organizational Communication;* (until 1974): *I A B C Journal.* [ISSN: 0744-7612] 1973. 7x/yr. USD 150 Free to members; USD 270. Ed(s): Natasha Spring. International Association of Business Communicators, One Hallidie

Plaza, Ste 600, San Francisco, CA 94102; ggordon@iabc.com; http://www.abc.com. Illus., adv. Circ: 45000 Paid and free. Vol. ends: Dec. Online: The Dialog Corporation; EBSCO Publishing, EBSCO Host; Florida Center for Library Automation; Gale; Northern Light Technology, Inc.; OCLC Online Computer Library Center, Inc.; ProQuest K-12 Learning Solutions; ProQuest LLC (Ann Arbor). *Indexed:* ABIn. *Aud.:* Ga, Ac, Sa.

These official publications of the International Association of Business Communicators combine practical articles with global communication issues in the area of communication management. *CW Online* is the electronic interactive magazine, updated regularly; *Communication World* is published bimonthly. Articles in both serve an international audience and include interviews with communication innovators and case studies on current topics. A wide variety of topics are covered including marketing communication, strategic planning, crisis communication, and speechwriting/presentations. Both publications' goals are to "stay on the forefront of developments in the communication profession and report them in an informative, timely and entertaining way to assist and inspire readers." For large public libraries and academic business and communication collections.

1400. Critical Studies in Media Communication. Formerly (unti 1999): *Critical Studies in Mass Communication.* [ISSN: 1529-5036] 1984. 5x/yr. GBP 188 print & online eds. Ed(s): Linda Steiner. Routledge, 325 Chestnut St, Ste 800, Philadelphia, PA 19106; journals@routledge.com; http://www.tandf.co.uk/journals. Illus., index, adv. Sample. Refereed. Circ: 3000 Paid. Vol. ends: Dec. Online: EBSCO Publishing, EBSCO Host; Gale; IngentaConnect; OCLC Online Computer Library Center, Inc.; SwetsWise Online Content. Reprint: PSC. *Indexed:* ABS&EES, AmH&L, AmHI, ArtHuCI, CJA, CommAb, FLI, HistAb, HumInd, IBR, IBSS, IBZ, PRA, PSA, RI-1, RILM, SSA, SSCI, SociolAb. *Aud.:* Ac.

Critical Studies publishes original research, analytical, and theoretical articles that reflect a concentration on mediated communication research. Recent titles include "Hurricane Katrina and Bush's Vacation: Contexts for Decoding" and "The Bachelor: Whiteness in the Harem." A publication of the National Communication Association, this is a valuable source for academic libraries due to its expansive approach to mass communication theory and research.

1401. Discourse & Society: an international journal for the study of discourse and communication in their social, political and cultural contexts. [ISSN: 0957-9265] 1990. bi-m. GBP 549. Ed(s): Teun A van Dijk. Sage Publications Ltd., 1 Oliver's Yard, 55 City Rd, London, EC1 1SP, United Kingdom; info@sagepub.co.uk; http://www.sagepub.co.uk. Adv. Refereed. Reprint: PSC. *Indexed:* ASSIA, ArtHuCI, CommAb, EAA, FLI, HRA, IBR, IBSS, IBZ, IPSA, IndIslam, L&LBA, LingAb, MLA-IB, PRA, PSA, PsycInfo, SFSA, SSA, SSCI, SUSA, SWA, SociolAb, V&AA. *Bk. rev.:* Number and length vary. *Aud.:* Ac.

Discourse & Society is an international, multidisciplinary journal of discourse analysis. The journal studies "society through discourse and discourse through an analysis of its sociopolitical and cultural functions or implications." Social, political, or cultural problems of the day that require a multidisciplinary approach are featured. The journal requires accessibilty as one criterion; that is, articles should be accessible to readers of various levels of expertise and specialization, and to readers from varied disciplines and countries. Articles from a recent issue include "Critical discourse analysis of political press conferences" and "Historical representations of aboriginal people in the Canadian news media." Book reviews are included, and issues are occasionally devoted to special topics. Recommended for large academic collections.

1402. Electronic Journal of Communication Online. Communication Institute for Online Scholarship, PO Box 57, Rotterdam Junction, NY 12150; http://www.cios.org/www/ejcmain.htm. *Bk. rev.:* Occasional. *Aud.:* Ac, Sa.

Presented in English with French abstracts, this academic journal addresses all areas of communication studies including theory, research, practice, and policy. Each issue is devoted to a theme and has its own editor. Nonsubscribers may access the editor's introduction to the issue and view abstracts for each article. A subscription is required to access the articles and the search engine that indexes every word in the issue. Occasionally, an issue will include special features with book reviews.

Howard Journal of Communications. See African American section.

1403. Human Communication Research. [ISSN: 0360-3989] 1974. q. GBP 237 print & online eds. Ed(s): James P Dillard. Blackwell Publishing, Inc., Commerce Place, 350 Main St, Malden, MA 02148; http://www.blackwellpublishing.com. Illus., adv. Sample. Refereed. Circ: 4400. Vol. ends: Jun. Microform: PQC. Online: Blackwell Synergy; Chadwyck-Healey Inc.; EBSCO Publishing, EBSCO Host; Florida Center for Library Automation; Gale; HighWire Press; IngentaConnect; OCLC Online Computer Library Center, Inc.; OhioLINK; ProQuest LLC (Ann Arbor); SwetsWise Online Content. Reprint: PSC. *Indexed:* ASG, AbAn, AgeL, ArtHuCI, CommAb, ERIC, FLI, FR, IMFL, L&LBA, LRI, PRA, PsycInfo, SFSA, SSA, SSCI, SociolAb, V&AA. *Aud.:* Ac, Sa.

This official journal of the International Communication Association has a broad social science focus to the study of human communication. It is touted as one of the top two journals in human communication, and articles emphasize human symbolic processes in the areas of interpersonal, nonverbal, organizational, intercultural, and mass communication; language and social interaction; new technologies; and health communication. Emphasis is on theory-driven research and the development of new theoretical communication models and methods of observing/measuring communication behavior. The journal will appeal not only to communication studies scholars but also to those in psychology, sociology, linguistics, and anthropology. For large public and academic libraries.

1404. Journal of Applied Communication Research. [ISSN: 0090-9882] 1973. q. GBP 193 print & online eds. Ed(s): Tim Sellnow. Routledge, 325 Chestnut St, Ste 800, Philadelphia, PA 19106; journals@routledge.com; http://www.tandf.co.uk/journals. Illus., adv. Sample. Refereed. Circ: 2000. Vol. ends: Nov. Microform: PQC. Online: EBSCO Publishing, EBSCO Host; Gale; IngentaConnect; Northern Light Technology, Inc.; OCLC Online Computer Library Center, Inc.; SwetsWise Online Content. Reprint: PSC. *Indexed:* ASG, AgeL, CommAb, EAA, ERIC, HRA, L&LBA, PRA, PsycInfo, SFSA, SSA, SSCI, SociolAb, V&AA. *Aud.:* Ac, Sa.

This journal publishes articles that study actual communication situations or show results that can be applied to the solution of communication problems. Articles can be any of the following: original research applied to practical situations/problems; application articles that offer ways of improving or expanding upon a particular communication setting through specific research or theory; or commentaries on applied communication issues. Any methodological or theoretical approach is considered, though rigorous application is expected. Examples of articles include "Mobile Phone Use in AA Networks: An Exploratory Study" and "Effects of Mass and Interpersonal Communication on Breast Cancer Screening: Advancing Agenda-Setting Theory in Health Contexts." Valuable for its pertinent topics, and recommended for academic libraries.

1405. Journal of Communication. [ISSN: 0021-9916] 1951. q. USD 1072 print & online eds. Ed(s): Michael Pfau. Blackwell Publishing, Inc., Commerce Place, 350 Main St, Malden, MA 02148; customerservices@blackwellpublishing.com; http://www.blackwellpublishing.com. Illus., index, adv. Refereed. Circ: 6150 Paid. Microform: PQC. Online: Blackwell Synergy; Chadwyck-Healey Inc.; EBSCO Publishing, EBSCO Host; Gale; HighWire Press; IngentaConnect; Northern Light Technology, Inc.; OCLC Online Computer Library Center, Inc.; OhioLINK; ProQuest K-12 Learning Solutions; ProQuest LLC (Ann Arbor); SwetsWise Online Content. Reprint: PSC. *Indexed:* ABIn, ABS&EES, AgeL, AmH&L, AmHI, ArtHuCI, BAS, BRI, CBRI, CJA, CommAb, ExcerpMed, FLI, FR, FutSurv, HRA, HistAb, HumInd, IBR, IBSS, IBZ, IIFP, IPSA, ISTA, L&LBA, LISA, MLA-IB, PRA, PSA, PsycInfo, RILM, SFSA, SSA, SSCI, SWA, SociolAb. *Bk. rev.:* 4+, length varies. *Aud.:* Ac.

Considered a flagship journal in the communication studies field, this publication is interdisciplinary and concentrates broadly on communication theory, research, practice, and policy. The journal is "especially interested in research whose significance crosses disciplinary and sub-field boundaries." Articles are written by scholars, professors from a variety of disciplines, and

graduate and doctoral students. Recent issues include articles on parental mediation of children's television viewing in low-income families and a social skill account of problematic Internet use. The valuable "Review and Criticism" section is extensive, with review essays and shorter book reviews. A necessary publication for large public libraries and academic libraries.

1406. Journal of Communication Inquiry. [ISSN: 0196-8599] 1974. q. GBP 194. Ed(s): Yu Shi. Sage Publications, Inc., 2455 Teller Rd, Thousand Oaks, CA 91320; info@sagepub.com; http://www.sagepub.com. Illus., adv. Sample. Refereed. Circ: 1000 Paid. Vol. ends: Oct. Reprint: PSC. *Indexed:* AmH&L, AmHI, CommAb, FLI, HistAb, HumInd, IBR, IBZ, MLA-IB, PRA, PSA, RILM, SSA, SWA, SociolAb, V&AA. *Bk. rev.:* 1-3, lengthy. *Aud.:* Ac.

This journal approaches the study of communication and mass communication from cultural and historical perspectives. The interdisciplinary aspects of communication are emphasized as articles reflect a variety of approaches, from philosophical to empirical to legal. International contributors regularly represent such diverse areas as mass communication, cultural studies, journalism, sociology, philosophy, and political science. The journal also publishes thematic special issues on any of the following critical topics: deconstructing popular culture; technology and culture; feminist cultural studies; and race, media, and culture. Valuable for its commitment to providing a place for alternative viewpoints on communication and media studies. Includes critical essays and book reviews. For large research collections.

1407. Journal of Computer-Mediated Communication. [ISSN: 1083-6101] q. Free. Ed(s): Dr. Susan C Herring, Rafaeli Sheizaf. Hebrew University of Jerusalem, School of Business Administration, Jerusalem, 91905, Israel; http://jcmc.huji.ac.il. Illus., index. Refereed. Online: EBSCO Publishing, EBSCO Host. *Indexed:* CommAb, L&LBA, PsycInfo, SSCI. *Aud.:* Ac, Sa.

This journal provides a broad interdisciplinary forum for research and essays based on any of the social sciences on the topic of computerized communication. Each issue is devoted to a specific aspect of computer-mediated communication such as online journalism, electronic commerce, and Internet research. An integrated search engine is useful for the researcher searching for keywords or concepts across the full run of issues.

1408. Journal of Nonverbal Behavior. Formerly (until 1979): *Environmental Psychology and Nonverbal Behavior.* [ISSN: 0191-5886] 1976. q. EUR 817 print & online eds. Ed(s): Howard Friedman. Springer New York LLC, 233 Spring St, New York, NY 10013-1578; service-ny@springer.com; http://www.springer.com/. Illus., adv. Sample. Refereed. Vol. ends: Winter. Microform: PQC. Online: EBSCO Publishing, EBSCO Host; Gale; IngentaConnect; OCLC Online Computer Library Center, Inc.; OhioLINK; ProQuest K-12 Learning Solutions; ProQuest LLC (Ann Arbor); Springer LINK; SwetsWise Online Content. Reprint: PSC. *Indexed:* AgeL, CJA, CommAb, EAA, HRA, IBR, IMFL, L&LBA, MLA-IB, PRA, PsycInfo, SFSA, SSA, SSCI, SWA, SWR&A, SociolAb, V&AA. *Aud.:* Ac, Sa.

This specialized journal publishes research on the varying components of nonverbal communication—interpersonal, distance, gaze, facial expressiveness, kinesics, paralanguage, posture, gestures, and related behaviors. Research submitted can be empirical, theoretical, or methodological. The journal recognizes the interdisciplinary nature of nonverbal communication, and manuscripts are welcomed from a variety of research fields. This publication also includes a "Brief Report" section that publishes short informal reports, reviews, and notes. Special issues are also published. An expensive but worthwhile title for comprehensive research collections.

Journalism and Mass Communication Educator. See Journalism and Writing/Journalism section.

1409. Mass Communication and Society. Formerly (until 1998): *Mass Communications Review.* [ISSN: 1520-5436] 1973. q. GBP 286 print & online eds. Ed(s): James Shanahan. Lawrence Erlbaum Associates, Inc., 325 Chestnut St, Ste. 800, Philadelphia, PA 19106; journals@

erlbaum.com; http://www.leaonline.com. Illus., adv. Sample. Refereed. Vol. ends: Summer/Fall. Reprint: PSC. *Indexed:* AmHI, CJA, CommAb, PSA, PsycInfo, SSA, SociolAb. *Bk. rev.:* 1+, lengthy. *Aud.:* Ac.

This is the official journal of the Mass Communication and Society Division of the Association for Education in Journalism and Mass Communication. Research and scholarship is published on mass communication theory from various perspectives, although the macrosocial perspective (i.e., societal, institutional, cross-cultural, global) is encouraged. This is a cross-disciplinary publication drawing from sociology, law, philosophy, history, psychology, and anthropology. Examples of article titles are "News Coverage of Social Protests and the Effects of Photographs and Prior Attitudes" and "Letters to the Editor in the 'War on Terror': A Cross-National Study." A worthwhile title for academic collections.

Philosophy and Rhetoric. See Philosophy section.

1410. *Popular Communication.* [ISSN: 1540-5702] 2003. q. GBP 227 print & online eds. Ed(s): Sharon R Mazzarella, Norma Pecora. Lawrence Erlbaum Associates, Inc., 325 Chestnut St, Ste. 800, Philadelphia, PA 19106; journals@erlbaum.com; http://www.leaonline.com. Adv. Reprint: PSC. *Indexed:* CommAb, SociolAb. *Bk. rev.:* 1-4, lengthy. *Aud.:* Ac, Sa.

Emphasis is, naturally, on popular communication and its texts, artifacts, audiences, events, and practices, including "the Internet, youth culture, representation, fandom, film, sports, spectacles, the digital revolution, sexuality, advertising/consumer culture, television, radio, music, magazines, and dance." The publication is relevant to many fields—mass communication, media studies, sociology, gender studies, etc. Diverse scholarly perspectives are welcome. Book reviews are included, as is an occasional "Review Essay." A title to round out academic communication collections due to the influence of popular culture in society today.

1411. *Qualitative Research Reports in Communication.* [ISSN: 1745-9435] 2000. a. GBP 120 (Individuals, GBP 17). Ed(s): Susan J Drucker. Routledge, 4 Park Sq, Milton Park, Abingdon, OX14 4RN, United Kingdom; info@routledge.co.uk; http://www.routledge.co.uk. Refereed. Reprint: PSC. *Indexed:* CommAb. *Aud.:* Ac.

An Eastern Communication Association journal, *QRRC* publishes numerous qualitative and critical research essays covering the spectrum of human communication topics (legal, interpersonal, rhetorical, intercultural, media, political, and organizational). The brief essays are 2,500 words or less. Recent articles are "Diabetes Management: An Exploration into the Verbal Support Attempts of Relational Others" and "Dialogue in the Lecture Hall: Teacher?Student Communication and Students' Perceptions of Their Learning." A solid title for academic collections.

1412. *Quarterly Journal of Speech.* Former titles (until 1927): *Quarterly Journal of Speech Education;* (until 1917): *Quarterly Journal of Public Speaking.* [ISSN: 0033-5630] 1915. q. GBP 153 print & online eds. Ed(s): David Henry. Routledge, 325 Chestnut St, Ste 800, Philadelphia, PA 19106; journals@routledge.com; http://www.tandf.co.uk/journals. Illus., index, adv. Refereed. Circ: 5400. Vol. ends: Nov. Microform: PMC; PQC. Online: EBSCO Publishing, EBSCO Host; IngentaConnect; Northern Light Technology, Inc.; OCLC Online Computer Library Center, Inc.; SwetsWise Online Content. Reprint: PSC. *Indexed:* ABS&EES, AmH&L, AmHI, ArtHuCI, BEL&L, BRI, CBRI, CommAb, ECER, ERIC, FLI, FR, HRA, HistAb, HumInd, IBR, IBZ, L&LBA, LT&LA, MLA-IB, PRA, PSA, PhilInd, PsycInfo, RI-1, RILM, SSA, SSCI, SUSA, SociolAb, V&AA. *Bk. rev.:* 5+, lengthy. *Aud.:* Ac.

A respected and established journal in the field, *QJS* publishes articles on "rhetoric in all its forms from diverse theoretical perspectives and methods of analysis." Humanistic in approach, the journal seeks essays that aid understanding of discourse practices and that investigate alternative approaches to discourse study, whether that be oral or written, public or private, direct or mediated, historical or contemporary. Each issue may include a book review essay and additional critical book reviews. A necessary title for academic libraries.

1413. *The Review of Communication.* [ISSN: 1535-8593] 2001. q. GBP 148. Ed(s): Raymie McKerrow. Routledge, 325 Chestnut St, Ste 800, Philadelphia, PA 19106; journals@routledge.com; http://www.routledge.com. Refereed. *Aud.:* Ac, Sa.

This refereed publication from the National Communication Association provides "reviews of essays covering multiple publications bearing a common theme or issue, which will be the basis for exploration and comment on a wide range of contemporary research and writing within the field." *The Review of Communication* also provides analyses of books and a list of recently published books in the field of communication.

1414. *Rhetoric Society Quarterly.* Formerly: *Rhetoric Society Newsletter.* [ISSN: 0277-3945] 1968. q. GBP 120 print & online eds. Ed(s): Gregory Clark. Taylor & Francis Inc., 325 Chestnut St, Ste 800, Philadelphia, PA 19016; orders@taylorandfrancis.com; http://www.taylorandfrancis.com. Illus., index, adv. Refereed. Circ: 700 Paid. Vol. ends: Oct. Reprint: PSC. *Indexed:* MLA-IB. *Bk. rev.:* 3-6, length varies. *Aud.:* Ac.

A publication of the Rhetoric Society of America, *RSQ* presents cross-disciplinary scholarship on all aspects of rhetorical studies. Approaches to rhetoric include historical, theoretical, pedagogical, and practical criticism. Editorial expectations are that the scholarship submitted will advance and/or contribute to a multidisciplinary field. To serve its mission as a publication for the society, *RSQ* also publishes book reviews, announcements, and general information. A solid journal in its field, and recommended for academic collections.

1415. *Southern Communication Journal.* Former titles (until 1988): *Southern Speech Communication Journal;* (until 1971): *Southern Speech Journal.* [ISSN: 1041-794X] 1935. q. GBP 107 print & online eds. Ed(s): Craig Smith. Taylor & Francis Inc., 325 Chestnut St, Ste 800, Philadelphia, PA 19016; orders@taylorandfrancis.com; http://www.taylorandfrancis.com. Illus., index, adv. Refereed. Circ: 2500. Vol. ends: Summer. Microform: PQC. Online: EBSCO Publishing, EBSCO Host; Northern Light Technology, Inc.; OCLC Online Computer Library Center, Inc.; ProQuest LLC (Ann Arbor). Reprint: PSC. *Indexed:* AmH&L, CommAb, HistAb, L&LBA, MLA-IB, PRA, RILM, SSA, SociolAb, V&AA. *Bk. rev.:* 3-10, medium length. *Aud.:* Ac.

A well-established publication of a regional communication association, *SCJ* publishes original scholarly research on human communication. The journal is not limited to any topic, simply those topics of interest to scholars, researchers, teachers, and practitioners in the communication field. Any methodological and theoretical orientation is welcomed, as long as the topic is established as important, the methodology is sound, and the theoretical viewpoint is appropriate. An affordable, recommended title for academic libraries.

1416. *Text and Performance Quarterly.* Formerly (until 1989): *Literature and Performance.* [ISSN: 1046-2937] 1980. q. GBP 161 print & online eds. Ed(s): Michael S Bowman. Routledge, 4 Park Sq, Milton Park, Abingdon, OX14 4RN, United Kingdom; journals@routledge.com; http://www.routledge.co.uk. Illus. Sample. Refereed. Vol. ends: Oct. Reprint: PSC. *Indexed:* AmHI, CommAb, HumInd, L&LBA, MLA-IB, RILM, SSA, SociolAb. *Aud.:* Ac, Sa.

This journal publishes readable scholarship that examines and advances the study of performance as a "social, communicative practice; as a technology of representation and expression; and as a hermeneutic." Material is often presented in diverse styles, such as narratives, interviews, performance texts/scripts, and photographic essays. A variety of perspectives to performance are considered—historical, ethnographic, feminist, rhetorical, political, aesthetic. A featured section is "Performance in Review," which analyzes performances from all types of venues. This title is recommended for rounding out communication collections in academic libraries.

1417. *The Toastmaster: for better listening, thinking, speaking.* Formerly: *The Toastmasters International.* [ISSN: 0040-8263] 1933. m. USD 20 (Free to members). Ed(s): Donna H Groh, Suzanne Frey. Toastmasters International, 23182 Arroyo Vista, Rancho Santa Margarita, CA 92688; pubs@toastmasters.org; http://www.toastmasters.org/. Illus., index, adv. Sample. Circ: 200041 Controlled. Vol. ends: Dec. *Aud.:* Ga, Sa.

This is a monthly magazine for members of Toastmasters International, a nonprofit educational organization, although libraries may purchase a subscription. The publication provides helpful information and practical tips to those interested in learning and improving their communication and leadership skills. Newsy article topics include humor, speaking techniques, leadership, famous speakers, self-development, and language usage. Since the majority of readers are experienced and knowledgeable public speakers, only well-researched and well-written articles are accepted for publication. Notices and articles about the activities of the organization are also included. Of benefit to business professionals and other people with these special interests, this is a title for public libraries.

1418. *Vital Speeches of the Day.* [ISSN: 0042-742X] 1934. m. USD 75 domestic; USD 95 foreign. Ed(s): Thomas Dealy. McMurry, Inc., 1010 E Missouri Ave, Phoenix, AZ 85014-2601; info@mcmurry.com; http://www.mcmurry.com. Circ: 9000 Paid and free. Microform: PMC. Online: EBSCO Publishing, EBSCO Host; Florida Center for Library Automation; Gale; Northern Light Technology, Inc.; OCLC Online Computer Library Center, Inc.; ProQuest K-12 Learning Solutions; ProQuest LLC (Ann Arbor); H.W. Wilson. *Indexed:* ABIn, AgeL, BAS, ConsI, FutSurv, LRI, MASUSE, RGPR, RI-1. *Aud.:* Hs, Ga, Ac.

Vital Speeches prints the "best thought of the best minds on current national questions" twice a month. Speeches are printed in full, and editorial policy is committed to covering both sides of public questions in the areas of politics, education, sociology, government, criminology, finance, business, taxation, health, law, labor, economics, etc. Important addresses from a wide variety of national leaders are published; a recent issue includes speeches by George W. Bush ("Gulf Coast Reconstruction") and Jeffrey P. Von Arx, president of Fairfield University ("The Intersection of Faith and Public Life"). Not only is this title important for the general public, it is also an excellent resource for the student of public speaking. Recommended for public and academic libraries.

1419. *Web Journal of Mass Communication Research.* 1997. q. Free. Ed(s): Guido Stempel, Robert Stewart. Ohio University, E. W. Scripps School of Journalism, Athens, OH 45701-2979. Refereed. *Aud.:* Ac, Sa.

Publishes scholarly investigations in mass communication research. Topics from past issues have ranged from a study of integrated marketing communication to the effects of television viewing on college students' use of alcohol. Each issue consists of a single article.

1420. *Western Journal of Communication.* Former titles (until 1991): *Western Journal of Speech Communication;* (until 1976): *Western Speech Communication; Western Speech.* [ISSN: 1057-0314] 1937. bi-m. GBP 125. Ed(s): Daniel Canary. Routledge, 4 Park Sq, Milton Park, Abingdon, OX14 4RN, United Kingdom; journals@routledge.com; http://www.routledge.com. Illus., index, adv. Sample. Refereed. Circ: 2400. Vol. ends: Fall. Microform: PQC. Online: EBSCO Publishing, EBSCO Host; Florida Center for Library Automation; Gale; Northern Light Technology, Inc.; OCLC Online Computer Library Center, Inc.; ProQuest LLC (Ann Arbor); SwetsWise Online Content. Reprint: PSC. *Indexed:* AmH&L, BAS, CommAb, ERIC, HistAb, L&LBA, PhilInd, PsycInfo, SSA, SSCI, SociolAb. *Aud.:* Ac.

One of two scholarly journals of the Western States Communication Association, *WJC* publishes original scholarly articles in all areas of human communication—rhetorical and communication theory, interpersonal communication, gender studies, small-group communication, language behavior, cultural and critical theory, oral interpretation, freedom of speech, and applied communication. All methodological and theoretical perspectives are encouraged. Editorial policy encourages research that is accessible both to a scholarly audience and a learned public. A good title for academic libraries.

1421. *Women's Studies in Communication.* [ISSN: 0749-1409] 1977. s-a. USD 60 (Individuals, USD 35; Students, USD 15). Ed(s): Celeste Condit, Bonnie Dow. Organization for Research on Women and Communication, c/o Bonnie Dow, Celeste Condit, Eds, Department of

Speech Comm, CSU, Long Beach, CA 90840-2407; sdowney@sculb.edu. Illus., adv. Refereed. Circ: 700. Vol. ends: Fall. *Indexed:* AmHI, CWI, CommAb, FLI, FemPer, HumInd, MLA-IB, RILM, WSA. *Bk. rev.:* Various number and length. *Aud.:* Ac, Sa.

The editorial policy of *WSC* states that it provides a "feminist forum for research, reviews, and commentary that advances our understanding of the relationships between communication and women, gender, and feminisms." This journal seeks research from all communication scholars on the above topic in any area of communication (interpersonal, media, organizational, small group, rhetorical theory, etc.). The publication is open to any methodology, perspective, scope, and context, as long as there is a connection between communication and gender/women/the feminine. The editors also encourage submissions from novice scholars. Also included is a "Conversation and Commentary" section. As the journal of the Organization for Research on Women and Communication of the Western Speech Communication Association, this is a worthwhile title for all-inclusive academic collections.

■ COMPUTERS AND INFORMATION TECHNOLOGY

Professional Journals/Popular Titles

See also Business; Electronics; Engineering and Technology; and Library and Information Science sections.

Andy Firpo, Infrastructure and Facilities Integrations, Technology Integration Group, Washington Mutual Inc.; andy.firpo@wamu.net.

Ellen Finnie Duranceau, Digital Resources Acquisitions Librarian, MIT Libraries, Room 14E-210A, 77 Massachusetts Ave., Cambridge, MA 02139-4307; efinnie@mit.edu.

Helene Williams, freelance editor, Seattle, WA, hwilliam@fas.harvard.edu.

Hilary Kline, Manager of Reformatting Support Services, Preservation & Imaging Department, Widener Library, Harvard University; kline@fas.harvard.edu.

Christine Oka, Library Instruction Coordinator, 270 Snell Library, Northeastern University, Boston, MA 02115; c.oka@neu.edu

Introduction

This section contains entries that represent the core computing publications for professional, academic, and public libraries, although some titles may cross audience boundaries. We have categorized the professional and academic publications as those titles that lean toward the technical or conceptual, intended largely for computer scientists and researchers who are pushing the envelope of computing and programming capabilities and examining the theoretical, or philosophical, aspects of computer use. Magazines in the Popular Titles subsection provide more practical information for the "average" computer user, whether at home or at work.

While the use of various types of computing and information technology for the "average" computer user has become increasingly diverse and sophisticated with mobile technology, social networking software, digital photography, home networks, and GPS, we have avoided the explosion of multiple periodicals that cover niche technologies. The review process involved looking at basic titles that are included in smaller academic libraries that support computer engineering programs and public libraries, as well as including a selective list of magazines that cover the most popular operating systems and associated software.

Basic Periodicals

Ems: *Smart Computing English;* Hs: *Byte.com, PC World;* Ga: *Byte.com, MacWorld, PC Magazine, PC World, Smart Computing;* Ac: *Association for Computing Machinery. Journal; Byte.com, The Computer Journal, Computerworld.*

Basic Abstracts and Indexes

Computer and Control Abstracts (INSPEC), Computer Literature Index, Computing Reviews, Internet & Personal Computing Abstracts.

Professional Journals

1422. *A C M Computing Surveys: the survey and tutorial journal of the ACM.* Formerly: *Computing Surveys.* [ISSN: 0360-0300] 1969. q. Non-members, USD 185. Ed(s): Peter Wegner. Association for Computing Machinery, Inc., 2 Penn Plaza, Ste 701, New York, NY 10121-0701; sigs@acm.org; http://www.acm.org. Illus., index. Refereed. Circ: 4323. Vol. ends: No. 4. Microform: PQC. Online: Association For Computing Machinery, Inc., A C M Digital Library; EBSCO Publishing, EBSCO Host; Florida Center for Library Automation; Gale; OCLC Online Computer Library Center, Inc.; OhioLINK; ProQuest LLC (Ann Arbor). *Indexed:* ABIn, AS&TI, CerAb, CompLI, CompR, EngInd, ErgAb, IAA, MathR, SCI. *Aud.:* Ac, Sa.

This publication "publishes surveys, tutorials, and special reports on all areas of computing research." Articles focus primarily on the existing literature in the field, although they do cover a variety of interests in the study of computer science. While surveys tend to be conceptual and aimed at the more knowledgeable reader, tutorials are written for those with less experience, and have specific examples on a particular subject. Recent examples include "Lineage retrieval for scientific data processing: a survey," "Access control in collaborative systems," and "Optimistic replication." Short articles of about 1,000 words are sometimes included, on any topic deemed of interest to the ACM membership. Issues usually include up to six scholarly articles and an introductory "About This Issue" piece. Sometimes an entire issue is devoted to a particular symposium topic and may contain more articles. The web site includes the complete table of contents for present and past issues. Full-text content of the actual articles is available to members in pdf format.

1423. *A C M Queue: tomorrow's computing today.* [ISSN: 1542-7730] 2003. 10x/yr. Individuals, USD 75. Ed(s): Alda Trabucci. Association for Computing Machinery, Inc., 2 Penn Plaza, Ste 701, New York, NY 10121-0701; sigs@acm.org; http://www.acm.org. Adv. Refereed. Circ: 30000 Paid and controlled. *Indexed:* ABIn, C&ISA, CerAb, IAA. *Bk. rev.:* 2; 250 words. *Aud.:* Ac, Sa.

Similar in look and feel to the other ACM publications, this title is aimed at the purely practical: it aims to define and frame technical challenges, spurring innovative solutions to problems. Issues are theme-based and have recently covered topics such as databases, system errors, and RFID. Generally there are four or five articles on the theme topic, along with standard columns, interviews, and reviews. ACM is offering free print subscriptions to non-ACM members who are residents of the United States or Canada, and much of the journal's content is also available free at www.acmqueue.org. (EFD)

1424. *A C M Transactions on Computer Systems.* [ISSN: 0734-2071] 1983. q. Non-members, USD 195. Ed(s): Carla Ellis, Roma Simon. Association for Computing Machinery, Inc., 2 Penn Plaza, Ste 701, New York, NY 10121-0701; sigs@acm.org; http://www.acm.org. Illus. Refereed. Circ: 1851 Paid. Vol. ends: No. 4. Online: Association For Computing Machinery, Inc., A C M Digital Library; EBSCO Publishing, EBSCO Host; Florida Center for Library Automation; Gale; OhioLINK; ProQuest LLC (Ann Arbor). *Indexed:* ABIn, AS&TI, C&ISA, CerAb, CompLI, CompR, EngInd, IAA, SCI. *Aud.:* Ac, Sa.

The charter of this publication of the Association for Computing Machinery is to publish "the newest findings of the computing research field. Papers published in Transactions on Computer Systems are theoretical and conceptual explorations of operating systems, distributed systems and networks. Readers will find design principles, case studies and experimental results in specification, processor management, memory and communication management, implementation techniques and protocols." Security and reliability issues are also discussed. The presentations cover the individual experiences of the researchers as well as recent developments for designers and users of computer systems. Issues usually contain three scholarly papers on various subjects. Recent topics include "Comprehensive multiprocessor cache miss rate generation using multivariate models," "Nonblocking memory management support for dynamic-sized data structures," and "Improved latency and accuracy for neural branch prediction." Occasional special issues focus on a single topic, such as operating system design or system architecture. The web site includes tables of contents for recent issues, with full text of articles available to subscribers.

1425. *A C M Transactions on Database Systems.* [ISSN: 0362-5915] 1976. q. Non-members, USD 194. Ed(s): Richard T Snodgrass, Roma Simon. Association for Computing Machinery, Inc., 2 Penn Plaza, Ste 701, New York, NY 10121-0701; usacm@acm.org; http://www.acm.org. Illus., index. Refereed. Circ: 3300. Vol. ends: No. 4. Microform: PQC. Online: Association For Computing Machinery, Inc., A C M Digital Library; EBSCO Publishing, EBSCO Host; Florida Center for Library Automation; Gale; OhioLINK. *Indexed:* ABIn, AS&TI, C&ISA, CerAb, CompLI, CompR, EngInd, ErgAb, IAA, ISTA, MathR, SCI, SSCI. *Aud.:* Ac, Sa.

This journal "is a key publication for computer scientists working in data abstraction, data modeling and designing data management systems," presenting research on computerized data storage and processing. Articles may focus on database management theory, or design and implementation of database systems, or real-world experience with database systems administration. Most articles "address the logical and technical foundation of data management." Recent topics have included "Exchanging intensional XML data," "Advanced SQL modeling in RDBMS," and "TinyDB: an acquisitional query processing system for sensor networks." Issues usually contain up to five scholarly articles that span a variety of approaches to database system research. The web site includes tables of contents for current and past issues as well as full-text content in pdf format available to members.

1426. *A C M Transactions on Graphics.* [ISSN: 0730-0301] 1982. q. Non-members, USD 195. Ed(s): John Hart, Roma Simon. Association for Computing Machinery, Inc., 2 Penn Plaza, Ste 701, New York, NY 10121-0701; usacm@acm.org; http://www.acm.org. Illus., index. Refereed. Circ: 2025 Paid. Vol. ends: No. 4. Online: Association For Computing Machinery, Inc., A C M Digital Library; EBSCO Publishing, EBSCO Host; OhioLINK. *Indexed:* ABIn, AS&TI, C&ISA, CerAb, CompLI, CompR, EngInd, IAA, SCI. *Aud.:* Ac, Sa.

This journal "is the foremost peer-reviewed journal in the graphics field." Unlike other ACM publications, it is published in color, with articles on "breakthroughs in computer-aided design, synthetic image generation, rendering, solid modeling and other areas." Each issue contains up to six articles in three sections: original refereed papers in "Research"; articles on use and implementation in "Practice and Experience"; and shorter articles on how humans interact with graphics applications. Recent topics include "Error-resilient transmission of 3D models," "Quadric-based simplification in any dimension," "Image-based spatio-temporal modeling and view interpolation of dynamic events," and "Mood swings: expressive speech animation." Some issues focus on a single topic of specific interest. Tables of contents can be found on the web site, and members can find full text in pdf format.

1427. *A C M Transactions on Information Systems.* Formerly (until 1988): *Transactions on Office Information Systems.* [ISSN: 1046-8188] 1983. q. Non-members, USD 195. Ed(s): Roma Simon. Association for Computing Machinery, Inc., 2 Penn Plaza, Ste 701, New York, NY 10121-0701; sigs@acm.org; http://www.acm.org. Illus., adv. Refereed. Circ: 4573 Paid. Vol. ends: No. 4. Online: Association For Computing Machinery, Inc., A C M Digital Library; EBSCO Publishing, EBSCO Host; Florida Center for Library Automation; Gale; OhioLINK. *Indexed:* ABIn, AS&TI, ArtHuCI, C&ISA, CerAb, CompLI, CompR, EngInd, ErgAb, IAA, ISTA, LISA, SCI, SSCI. *Aud.:* Ac, Sa.

The scope of this journal "encompasses all aspects of computerized information systems," with articles that cover "issues in information retrieval and filtering, information interfaces and information systems design." Each issue contains up to four articles; recent examples include "Evaluating implicit measures to improve web search," "Ad Hoc, self-supervising peer-to-peer search networks," and "CrimeNet explorer: a framework for criminal network knowledge discovery." Some issues focus on a single topic of specific interest. Tables of contents can be found on the web site, and members can find full text in pdf format.

1428. *A C M Transactions on Modeling and Computer Simulation.*
[ISSN: 1049-3301] 1991. q. Non-members, USD 185. Ed(s): Roma Simon. Association for Computing Machinery, Inc., 2 Penn Plaza, Ste 701, New York, NY 10121-0701; usacm@acm.org; http://www.acm.org. Illus. Refereed. Circ: 1193 Paid. Vol. ends: No. 4. Online: Association For Computing Machinery, Inc., A C M Digital Library; EBSCO Publishing, EBSCO Host; OhioLINK. *Indexed:* ABIn, AS&TI, C&ISA, CerAb, CompLI, CompR, EngInd, IAA, SCI. *Aud.:* Ac, Sa.

This journal focuses on systems modeling and computer simulation concepts, two of the important tools for development and troubleshooting in computer science. "Emphasizing discrete event simulation, this journal publishes applications, reviews, and tutorials on such topics as combined, distributed, and hybrid simulation, simulation and computer graphics, process generators, and random number generation." Issues usually contain up to four articles, and recent topics include "An alternative time management mechanism for distributed simulations," "Simulating Markov-reward processes with rare events," and "Comparison with a standard via fully sequential procedures." Occasionally, issues are published that focus on a single topic, such as "Computer automated multi-paradigm modeling." Correspondence is often included and provides a forum for criticism and defense of published concepts. Full text of articles is available to members in pdf format on the web page, which also includes tables of contents and abstracts for articles in current and recent issues.

1429. *A C M Transactions on Programming Languages and Systems.*
Incorporates (1992-1993): *Letters on Programming Languages and Systems.* [ISSN: 0164-0925] 1979. bi-m. Non-members, USD 250. Ed(s): Ron Cytron, Roma Simon. Association for Computing Machinery, Inc., 2 Penn Plaza, Ste 701, New York, NY 10121-0701; usacm@acm.org; http://www.acm.org. Illus., index. Refereed. Circ: 7077 Paid. Vol. ends: No. 6. Online: Association For Computing Machinery, Inc., A C M Digital Library; EBSCO Publishing, EBSCO Host; Florida Center for Library Automation; Gale; OhioLINK. *Indexed:* ABIn, AS&TI, C&ISA, CerAb, CompLI, CompR, EngInd, ErgAb, IAA, SCI. *Aud.:* Ac, Sa.

The focus of this journal is "to present research results on all aspects of the design, definition, implementation, and use of programming languages and programming systems." The scope of the articles presented includes "programming languages and their semantics; programming systems (systems to assist the programming task, such as compilers, runtime systems and language environments); storage allocation and garbage collection." Recent topics include "Symbolic bounds analysis of pointers, array indices, and accessed memory regions," "Polymorphic predicate abstraction," and "A systematic approach to static access control." The web site contains tables of contents and abstracts for current and recent issues, and full text of articles is available for members in pdf format.

1430. *A C M Transactions on Software Engineering and Methodology.*
[ISSN: 1049-331X] 1992. q. Non-members, USD 175. Association for Computing Machinery, Inc., 2 Penn Plaza, Ste 701, New York, NY 10121-0701; usacm@acm.org; http://www.acm.org. Illus. Refereed. Circ: 2234 Paid. Vol. ends: No. 4. Online: Association For Computing Machinery, Inc., A C M Digital Library; EBSCO Publishing, EBSCO Host; OhioLINK. *Indexed:* ABIn, AS&TI, C&ISA, CerAb, CompLI, CompR, EngInd, IAA, SCI. *Aud.:* Ac, Sa.

This journal publishes papers on all aspects of designing and building large, complex software systems, including specification, design, development, and maintenance. "It covers tools and methodologies, languages, data structures, and algorithms...reports on successful efforts, noting practical lessons that can be scaled and transferred to other projects, and often looks at applications of innovative technologies." Issues usually contain up to four articles, with recent topics including "A scalable formal method for design and automatic checking of user interfaces," "Software reuse for scientific computing through program generation," and "A comprehensive approach for the development of modular

software architecture description languages." The web site contains tables of contents and abstracts for current and recent issues, and full text of articles is available for members in pdf format.

1431. *Association for Computing Machinery. Journal.* [ISSN: 0004-5411] 1954. bi-m. Non-members, USD 245. Ed(s): Prabhakar Raghavan. Association for Computing Machinery, Inc., 2 Penn Plaza, Ste 701, New York, NY 10121-0701; sigs@acm.org; http://www.acm.org. Illus., index. Refereed. Circ: 2674 Paid. Microform: PQC. Online: Association For Computing Machinery, Inc., A C M Digital Library; EBSCO Publishing, EBSCO Host; Florida Center for Library Automation; Gale; OCLC Online Computer Library Center, Inc.; OhioLINK; ProQuest LLC (Ann Arbor). *Indexed:* ABIn, AS&TI, C&ISA, CCMJ, CerAb, CompR, EngInd, ErgAb, IAA, ISTA, MSN, MathR, SCI, SSCI. *Aud.:* Ac, Sa.

As an overt effort to combat the growing parochialism and fragmentation in computer science, the goal of this journal is to "provide coverage of the most significant work going on in computer science, broadly construed." The focus is on the "careful presentation of theoretical research in the core areas of computing: complexity of algorithms, computer architecture, system modeling, AI, data structures, database theory and graph theory." It also includes articles by authors who are "world class scientists, writing to other scientists about advances, methods and findings behind the fundamentals." In this way, the Association for Computing Machinery strives to make this journal the computer science analogue of *Science* or *Nature*. Issues usually present four to ten scholarly papers, and recent topics include "Lower bounds for linear degeneracy testing," "Simple extractors for all min-entropies and a new pseudorandom generator," and "An information-theoretic approach to normal forms for relational and XML data." The web site provides article abstracts and full text in pdf format (for subscribers) from recent issues, as well as tables of contents going back to 1954!

1432. *Computer Graphics World.* Formerly (until 1980): *Computer Graphics (Eugene).* [ISSN: 0271-4159] 1978. m. USD 55 domestic (Free to qualified personnel). C O P Communications, 620 West Elk Ave, Glendale, CA 91204; info@copprints.com; http://www.copprints.com. Illus., adv. Circ: 40000 Controlled. Vol. ends: Dec. Microform: PQC. Online: The Dialog Corporation; EBSCO Publishing, EBSCO Host; Florida Center for Library Automation; Gale; Northern Light Technology, Inc.; OCLC Online Computer Library Center, Inc.; ProQuest LLC (Ann Arbor). *Indexed:* AS&TI, BrTechI, EngInd, MASUSE, MicrocompInd, SCI. *Aud.:* Ga, Ac, Sa.

This publication is billed as "The Magazine for Digital Content Professionals," *Computer Graphics World* provides content on computer graphics, 3-D modeling, CAD, animation, and visual computing. Topics covered range across a broad spectrum, including the use of computer-generated imagery as an art medium, commercial application of image-processing hardware and software, process descriptions, product reviews, and editorial content on various facets of industries that use these media, processes, and products. Many detailed images are provided along with text content in both the print and web page versions. On computers with slower connections to the Internet, this can cause somewhat long page-loading times, but the high quality and relevance to the topic being covered make the wait well worth it even on these systems, and a pure delight on computers with broadband or networked access. Most issues provide four feature articles; recent examples are "Thriving on Chaos," a discussion of how Ubisoft has added new realism to computer gaming in its Splinter Cell series, and "Mechbelieve," a description of the process by which the movie studio Fox/Blue Sky created a watchmaker's world with mechanical CG people for its latest feature film, *Robots*. The same issue contains another article about the film industry, "Talk With the Animals," which details the digital effects involved in creating talking animals for the live-action film "Racing Stripes."

1433. *The Computer Journal.* [ISSN: 0010-4620] 1958. bi-m. EUR 939 print or online ed. (Individuals, EUR 939). Ed(s): F Murtagh. Oxford University Press, Great Clarendon St, Oxford, OX2 6DP, United Kingdom; enquiry@oup.co.uk; http://www.oxfordjournals.org. Illus., index, adv. Refereed. Circ: 3000. Vol. ends: No. 8. Microform: PQC. Online: EBSCO Publishing, EBSCO Host; Gale; HighWire Press; IngentaConnect; OCLC Online Computer Library Center, Inc.;

OhioLINK; Oxford Journals; ProQuest LLC (Ann Arbor); SwetsWise Online Content; H.W. Wilson. Reprint: PSC. *Indexed:* ABIn, AS&TI, BRI, BrTechI, C&ISA, CerAb, ChemAb, CompLI, CompR, EngInd, ErgAb, ExcerpMed, IAA, MLA-IB, MathR, SCI, SSCI. *Aud.:* Ac, Sa.

This is one of the oldest and most respected scholarly journals in the field. *The Computer Journal* is published by Oxford University Press for the British Computer Society, and it "publishes research papers in a full range of subject areas, as well as regular feature articles and occasional themed issues...[that provide] a complete overview of developments in the field of Computer Science." Issues generally include up to eight articles, and examples from the current issue are "The Teaching and Learning of Programming: A Survey of Supporting Software Tools," "Cyberworld Security—the Good, the Bad and the Ugly," "On the Minimality of Finite Automata and Stream X-machines for Finite Languages," "Perfect Hashing Schemes for Mining Association Rules," "Analytical Honeycomb Geometry for Raster and Volume Graphics," "Self-Adjusting of Ternary Search Tries Using Conditional Rotations and Randomized Heuristics," "On Approximate Algorithms for Distance-Based Queries using R-trees," and "Group Mutual Exclusion in Token Rings." The themed issues have all papers focused on a specific topic. The web site offers the usual abstracts and tables of contents, with full text for subscribers, as well as the very unusual resource of abstracts and tables of contents for issues going back to 1958! Older issues provide abstracts as well as full text presented via scans in tiff format, and there is a large group of issues from 1973 to 1992 not available.

1434. *Computer (New York).* Formerly (until 1970): *IEEE Computer Group News.* [ISSN: 0018-9162] 1966. m. USD 1350. IEEE, Computer Society, 445 Hoes Ln., Piscataway, NJ 08855-1331; customer.service@ieee.org; http://www.computer.org. Illus., adv. Refereed. Circ: 96859 Paid. Vol. ends: Dec. Online: EBSCO Publishing, EBSCO Host; IEEE. *Indexed:* AS&TI, C&ISA, CerAb, CompLI, CompR, EngInd, ErgAb, IAA, SCI, SSCI. *Bk. rev.:* 5, 500 words. *Aud.:* Ac, Sa.

This is the flagship publication of the IEEE Computer Society. *Computer* "publishes highly acclaimed peer-reviewed articles written for and by professionals representing the full spectrum of computing technology from hardware to software and from current research to new applications." Each issue has 15–20 brief (two to five pages each) articles on topics that range from the popular to the technical, with writing and illustrations that are accessible to readers from all backgrounds. Topics have included the architecture of virtual machines, misleading architecting tradeoffs, monitoring virtual machines, and an essay entitled "Me and My Theremin." Of all the IEEE publications, this has the most appeal to a general audience. Subscribers can access the full text of issues from 1988 to the present from the web site.

1435. *Computers & Society (Online Edition).* Former titles (until 2004): *Computers & Society (Print Edition); S I G C A S Newsletter.* q. USD 56. Ed(s): Richard S Rosenberg. Association for Computing Machinery, Inc., 2 Penn Plaza, Ste 701, New York, NY 10121-0701; sigs@acm.org; http://www.acm.org. Illus. Circ: 1500. Vol. ends: Dec. *Indexed:* CompR, ErgAb. *Bk. rev.:* 1-2, 500-750 words. *Aud.:* Ac, Sa.

This is a quarterly newsletter for members of the Special Interest Group on Computers and Society (SIGCAS) of the Association for Computing Machinery. It also serves "the public at large . . . to address concerns and raise awareness about the ethical and societal impact of computers . . . [and] to gather and report information, thus stimulating the exchange and dissemination of ideas. . . ." Issues may contain articles on a variety of topics or a single specific topic, as well as book excerpts or reviews, student papers, and case studies. The journal may also include proceedings from the various conferences sponsored by the Special Interest Group. Recent articles include "A Justification for Software Rights," "Object Oriented Goodness: A Response to Mathieson's 'What Is Information Ethics,'" and "Economics of Disclosure." The web site provides an index to articles and tables of contents with full text available for members; and through the "Related Links" section, it also acts as a portal to a wealth of information on social and ethical concerns.

1436. *Dr. Dobb's Journal: software tools for the professional programmer.* Incorporates (1993-2006): *Software Development;* Former titles (until 1989): *Dr. Dobb's Journal of Software Tools for the Professional*

Programmer; (until 1985): *Dr. Dobb's Journal;* (until 1984): *Dr. Dobb's Journal for the Experienced in Microcomputing;* (until 1984): *Dr. Dobb's Journal for Users of Small Computer Systems;* (until 1981): *Dr. Dobb's Journal of Computer Calisthenics and Orthodontia.* [ISSN: 1044-789X] 1977. m. USD 25 domestic (Free to qualified personnel). Ed(s): John Jainschigg, Deirdre Blake. C M P Media LLC, 600 Harrison St, 6th Fl., San Francisco, CA 94107; http://www.cmp.com. Illus., adv. Circ: 117039 Paid. Microform: PQC. Online: EBSCO Publishing, EBSCO Host; OCLC Online Computer Library Center, Inc.; ProQuest LLC (Ann Arbor). *Indexed:* AS&TI, C&ISA, CerAb, CompR, EngInd, IAA, ISTA, MicrocompInd, SCI. *Bk. rev.:* 2-6, 100-200 words. *Aud.:* Ac, Sa.

This journal is focused on "Software Tools for the Professional Programmer," covering all languages, platforms, and tools, it has been in print since 1976. The authors and the intended audience are "professional software developers who want to revise proposed standards, explore new technologies, argue over programming style, and share tricks of the trade." The web site provides some of the content of the print version, as well as tables of contents and a full-text search of articles from present issues back through 1988. It also contains additional content not in the print version, such as a developer network and additional source code that could not be published in print.

1437. *IEEE - A C M Transactions on Networking.* [ISSN: 1063-6692] 1993. bi-m. USD 595. Ed(s): Ellen Zegurba. IEEE, 445 Hoes Ln, Piscataway, NJ 08854-1331; subscription-service@ieee.org; http://www.ieee.org. Illus., adv. Refereed. Vol. ends: No. 6. Online: Pub.; Association For Computing Machinery, Inc., A C M Digital Library; EBSCO Publishing, EBSCO Host; OhioLINK; SwetsWise Online Content. *Indexed:* ABIn, AS&TI, C&ISA, CerAb, CompLI, CompR, EngInd, IAA, SCI. *Aud.:* Ac, Sa.

A collaborative publication between IEEE and ACM, *Transactions on Networking* succeeds in combining the speed of online publishing with the scholarship of a peer-reviewed publication. Issues focus on "broad coverage of research and experience in network architecture and design, communication protocols, network software and technologies, services and applications, and network operations and management." There are at least ten articles per issue, and all are aimed at the practitioner or researcher. The writing is highly technical, and though some articles espouse new theories, nearly all of them have practical application to today's networking technologies. Recent topics include systems stability, security issues, network protocols, and flow management. Abstracts and past tables of contents are available free at the web site, www.ton.cc.gatech.edu, and subscribers can access the full text of articles from the journal's inception in 1993 to the present.

1438. *IEEE Computer Graphics and Applications.* [ISSN: 0272-1716] 1981. bi-m. USD 875. Ed(s): John Dill, Robin Baldwin. IEEE, 445 Hoes Ln, Piscataway, NJ 08854-1331; subscription-service@ieee.org; http://www.computer.org. Illus., adv. Refereed. Circ: 8000 Paid. Vol. ends: Nov/Dec. Online: Pub.; EBSCO Publishing, EBSCO Host. *Indexed:* AS&TI, C&ISA, CerAb, CompLI, EngInd, ErgAb, IAA, MicrocompInd, SCI, SSCI. *Aud.:* Ac, Sa.

This title is aimed at specialized readers with some experience in computer graphics. *Computer Graphics and Applications* presents information on the applications for computer graphics. Each issue provides about a dozen articles that range from three to ten pages, covering thematic topics such as digital art, web-based shape modeling, and CAD challenges. Some articles are quite technical, but the extensive illustrations help make them accessible. New application and product reviews, as well as conference announcements, keep readers updated, although this information is not all available in the web version. The online subscription version does include the full text of articles from 1988 to the present.

1439. *IEEE Design & Test of Computers.* [ISSN: 0740-7475] 1984. bi-m. USD 625. Ed(s): Yervent Zorian. IEEE, 445 Hoes Ln, Piscataway, NJ 08854-1331; subscription-service@ieee.org; http://www.ieee.org. Illus., adv. Refereed. Circ: 6000 Paid. Vol. ends: No. 4. Online: Pub.; EBSCO Publishing, EBSCO Host. *Indexed:* C&ISA, CerAb, CompLI, EngInd, IAA, SCI. *Bk. rev.:* 1, 100 words. *Aud.:* Ac, Sa.

COMPUTERS AND INFORMATION TECHNOLOGY

Co-published by the IEEE Computer Society and IEEE Circuits and Systems Society, this journal "offers original works describing the body of methods used to design and test electronic product hardware and supportive software." The intended audience is users, developers, and researchers who design and test chips, assemblies, and integrated systems. Issues contain about a dozen articles of seven to ten pages each; guest editors introduce the issue and the three or four feature articles, which are linked by subject. Recent thematic contributions include reconfigurable computing systems and design verification issues. Not all announcements appear in the online subscription version, but the full text of articles and reviews from 1988 to the present is available online.

1440. IEEE Intelligent Systems: putting A I into practice. Former titles (until 2000): *IEEE Intelligent Systems and Their Applications;* (until 1997): *IEEE Expert.* [ISSN: 1541-1672] 1986. bi-m. USD 850. IEEE, Computer Society, 10662 Los Vaqueros Circle, PO Box 3014, Los Alamitos, CA 90720-1314; customer.service@ieee.org; http://www.ieee.org. Illus., adv. Refereed. Circ: 6864. Vol. ends: Dec. Online: EBSCO Publishing, EBSCO Host; IEEE. *Indexed:* AS&TI, BRI, C&ISA, CerAb, CompLI, EngInd, ErgAb, IAA, LISA, PollutAb, RiskAb, SCI, SSCI. *Bk. rev.:* 5-7, 750 words, signed. *Aud.:* Ac, Sa.

This journal emphasizes current techniques and tools as well as research and development from across the spectrum of intelligent systems, from knowledge-based systems to data mining to robotics. Articles are aimed at professionals who deal with any aspect of intelligent systems, from designing and testing, to maintaining, teaching, and managing. Several articles in each issue are oriented to a theme, such as creating and planning with templates, and agent-based technologies. There are regular features that cover industry and research news; and issue-based editorials help connect the technological discussions with the larger world. Full text of articles from 1998 to the present is available with an online subscription.

1441. IEEE Micro. [ISSN: 0272-1732] 1981. bi-m. USD 760. Ed(s): Ken Sakamura, Stephen L Diamond. IEEE, 445 Hoes Ln, Piscataway, NJ 08854-1331; subscription-service@ieee.org; http://www.ieee.org. Illus., index, adv. Refereed. Circ: 6246 Paid. Vol. ends: No. 6. Online: Pub.; EBSCO Publishing, EBSCO Host. *Indexed:* AS&TI, C&ISA, CerAb, CompLI, EngInd, ErgAb, IAA, RILM, SCI, SSCI. *Aud.:* Ac, Sa.

IEEE Micro focuses on the design, performance, and application of microcomputer and microprocessor systems. Each issue generally has a collection of articles on one theme, introduced by a guest editor, such as papers from a microarchitecture conference, or research on network processors. Other features include news, reviews, legal aspects of microprocessing research and use, and standards. The articles are technical, and are aimed at practitioners and researchers rather than the general reader. Subscribers can access online the full text of articles back to 1988.

1442. IEEE MultiMedia Magazine. [ISSN: 1070-986X] 1994. q. USD 685. Ed(s): Robin Baldwin, William Grosky. IEEE, 445 Hoes Ln, Piscataway, NJ 08854-1331; subscription-service@ieee.org; http://www.ieee.org. Illus., adv. Refereed. Circ: 10000 Paid. Vol. ends: Dec. Online: Pub.; EBSCO Publishing, EBSCO Host. *Indexed:* C&ISA, CerAb, CompLI, EngInd, ErgAb, IAA, SCI. *Aud.:* Ac, Sa.

This journal provides technical information on a wide range of multimedia systems and applications issues, including hardware and software for media compression, storage, and transport, workstation support, and data modeling. One of the goals of this journal is to make even technical material easily understood by the non-specialist reader. Each issue covers a variety of conceptual and practical topics; some recent articles include "Superimposing Pictorial Artwork with Projected Imagery," "Interoperable Adaptive Multimedia Communication," and "On-demand Learning for a Wireless Campus." Issues also contain new product descriptions and reviews, and conference and workshop announcements. Subscribers to the online version can access the full text of articles from 1994 to the present.

1443. IEEE Software. [ISSN: 0740-7459] 1984. bi-m. USD 895. Ed(s): Warren Harrison, Dale Strok. IEEE, 445 Hoes Ln, Piscataway, NJ 08854-1331; subscription-service@ieee.org; http://www.ieee.org. Illus.,

adv. Sample. Refereed. Circ: 23000 Controlled and free. Vol. ends: No. 6. Online: Pub.; EBSCO Publishing, EBSCO Host. *Indexed:* ABIn, AS&TI, C&ISA, CerAb, CompLI, EngInd, ErgAb, IAA, SCI, SSCI. *Bk. rev.:* 4-5, 500 words. *Aud.:* Ac, Sa.

The mission of this publication is to be the "authority on translating software theory into practice, [positioning] itself between pure research and pure practice, transferring ideas, methods, and experiences among researchers and engineers." IEEE views this as a magazine more than a scholarly journal, with an emphasis on shorter, readable articles. All aspects of the software industry are covered, including project management, process improvement, software maintenance, web applications, testing, and usability. Each issue presents eight to ten brief articles on specific themes, such as requirements of engineering or software dependability. Other regular features include interviews and book reviews, which, along with the full text of articles from 1988 to the present, are available online.

International Journal of Robotics and Automation. See Robotics section.

1444. Operating Systems Review. [ISSN: 0163-5980] 1970. 5x/yr. USD 30. Ed(s): William Waite. Association for Computing Machinery, Inc., 2 Penn Plaza, Ste 701, New York, NY 10121-0701; sigs@acm.org; http://www.acm.org. Illus., index, adv. Circ: 8000. *Indexed:* C&ISA, CompR, EngInd. *Aud.:* Ac, Sa.

This publication is "an informal publication of the ACM Special Interest Group on Operating Systems (SIGOPS), whose scope of interest includes: computer operating systems and architecture for multiprogramming, multiprocessing, and time sharing; resource management; evaluation and simulation; reliability, integrity, and security of data; communications among computing processors; and computer system modeling and analysis." Issues include articles on a broad range of topics within the scope, and vary from scholarly to practical. Recent examples include "A new pattern for flexible worker threads with in-place consumption message queues," "A study of initialization in Linux and OpenBSD," and "Two attacks on a user friendly remote authentication scheme with smart cards." The web page provides tables of contents and abstracts, with full text in pdf format available for subscribers. (AF)

1445. S I A M Journal on Computing. [ISSN: 0097-5397] 1972. bi-m. USD 480 (Individual members, USD 92). Ed(s): M Yannakakis. Society for Industrial and Applied Mathematics, 3600 University City Science Center, Philadelphia, PA 19104-2688; siam@siam.org; http://www.siam.org. Illus., adv. Refereed. Circ: 1711. Vol. ends: Dec. *Indexed:* AS&TI, ApMecR, C&ISA, CCMJ, CompLI, CompR, EngInd, MSN, MathR, SCI, SSCI. *Aud.:* Ac, Sa.

This scholarly journal "contains research articles on the mathematical and formal aspects of computer science and nonnumerical computing," Typical topics covered include analysis and design of algorithms, data structures, computational complexity, computational algebra, computational aspects of combinatorics and graph theory, computational geometry, computational robotics, the mathematical aspects of programming languages, artificial intelligence, computational learning, databases, information retrieval, cryptography, networks, distributed computing, parallel algorithms, and computer architecture. Issues usually contain at least ten articles. The web site provides abstracts and tables of contents, with full content in several formats available for subscribers. A composite sample issue is available free online, made up of a collection of two papers from a recent issue of each SIAM journal. (EFD)

1446. Software: Practice & Experience. [ISSN: 0038-0644] 1971. 15x/yr. USD 3903 print or online ed. Ed(s): Douglas E Comer, A Wellings. John Wiley & Sons Ltd., The Atrium, Southern Gate, Chichester, PO19 8SQ, United Kingdom; customer@wiley.co.uk; http://www.wiley.co.uk. Illus., index, adv. Refereed. Circ: 1800. Vol. ends: No. 15. Microform: PQC. Online: EBSCO Publishing, EBSCO Host; OhioLINK; SwetsWise Online Content; Wiley InterScience. Reprint: PSC. *Indexed:* AS&TI, BrTechI, C&ISA, CerAb, CompLI, CompR, EngInd, IAA, ISTA, SCI. *Aud.:* Ac, Sa.

The focus of this scholarly journal is "the dissemination and discussion of practical experience with new and established software for both systems and applications." This publication emphasizes practical experience and is intended for sophisticated programmers. Topics cover software design and implementation, case studies describing the evolution of systems and the thinking behind them, and critical appraisals of software systems. Issues usually contain about four articles, and can also include short communications in addition to longer research articles. The web site provides tables of contents and abstracts, with full text in pdf format available for subscribers. A sample issue can be downloaded. (EFD)

Popular Titles

1447. Byte.com. Supersedes (1975-1999): *Byte (Print Edition);* (1995-1999): *Byte on CD-ROM.* 1975. w. 0 membership. C M P Media LLC, 600 Community Dr, Manhasset, NY 11030. Illus., index, adv. Circ: 500000. Microform: PQC. Online: EBSCO Publishing, EBSCO Host; Gale. *Indexed:* ABIn, ABS&EES, AS&TI, BPI, BRI, C&ISA, CBCARef, CBRI, CPerI, ConsI, ErgAb, IHTDI, LRI, MASUSE, MRD, MicrocompInd, RGPR, RILM, SCI. *Aud.:* Hs, Ga, Ac, Sa.

Not available in print since 1998, *Byte* (or rather *BYTE.com*) is a fee-based web site that is usually updated weekly. Although the homepage is a bit busy, it offers subscribers links to very current information on a variety of topics in categories of "In The News," features, and regular columns, as well as the entire content of past weekly editions since 1999. Columns include or have included "Mr. Computer Language Person," "Advanced Software and Technologies," "New Products," "Conference Report," "Portable Computing," and "Media Lab," among others. An interesting aspect of this resource is that, unlike most of the other titles in the Popular Titles subsection, *Byte* provides information on personal computer platforms other than Apple Macintosh and the various Windows releases, including AmigaOS, BeOS, DOS, FreeBSD, Linux, Solaris, and Unix.

1448. Computerworld: newsweekly for information technology leaders. [ISSN: 0010-4841] 1967. w. Mon. USD 99 domestic; USD 130 Canada; USD 250 in Central America. Ed(s): Don Tennant. Computerworld, Inc., 500 Old Connecticut Path, Box 9171, Framingham, MA 01701-9171; http://www.computerworld.com. Illus., adv. Circ: 250707. Vol. ends: Dec. Microform: PQC. Online: EBSCO Publishing, EBSCO Host; Florida Center for Library Automation; Gale; LexisNexis; Northern Light Technology, Inc.; OCLC Online Computer Library Center, Inc.; ProQuest K-12 Learning Solutions; ProQuest LLC (Ann Arbor); H.W. Wilson. *Indexed:* ABIn, BPI, ISTA, LRI, MASUSE, MicrocompInd. *Aud.:* Ga, Ac, Sa.

This weekly tabloid/magazine describes itself as "America's #1 publication for IT leaders" and is available by paid subscription, free subscription (to professionals with almost any conceivable connection to computing), and web site. Vast amounts of timely information are provided on a wide range of topics of interest to "IT executives and professionals who are at the forefront of the move to e-business and adoption of new technologies." Focus areas include news and features, analysis, and "Knowledge Centers": integrated print and online information packages that consist of in-depth coverage of a specific topic in the weekly print issue as well as ongoing coverage of the same topic in a section of the web site. These include Business Intelligence, Careers, Customer Relationship Management, Development, E-Business, Government, Hardware, IT Management, Mobile & Wireless, Outsourcing, Security, Return On Investment, Web Site Management, and others. Other content includes commentary, editorials, and letters to the editor. While almost all of the content of the print version is available on the web site, the electronic version has considerable content not in the print version, and also allows for updates more frequently than weekly. This is a good source for anyone trying to stay current on hardware, software, and industry news and trends.

1449. eWEEK: the enterprise newsweekly. Incorporates (1994-2001): *Inter@ctive Week;* Formerly (until 2000): *P C Week.* [ISSN: 1530-6283] 1984. w. USD 195 domestic (Free to qualified personnel). Ed(s): Matthew Rothenberg. Ziff Davis Media Inc., 28 E 28th St, New York, NY 10016-7930; info@ziffdavis.com; http://www.ziffdavis.com. Illus.,

adv. Circ: 445000 Paid and controlled. Microform: PQC. Online: EBSCO Publishing, EBSCO Host; Florida Center for Library Automation; Gale; OCLC Online Computer Library Center, Inc.; ProQuest K-12 Learning Solutions; H.W. Wilson. *Indexed:* BPI, C&ISA, CerAb, ConsI, IAA, ISTA, LRI, MicrocompInd, PAIS. *Aud.:* Ac, Sa.

eWEEK (published as *PC Week* until 2000) is "the leading weekly resource for IT professionals." The intended audience is largely already within the computing industries. The main focus is on news, analysis, editorials, and discussion; there is almost nothing in the way of retail product reviews. The print version and web page are both organized into "Top Stories," "Breaking News," "Latest Special Reports," "Topic Centers," and "Industry Centers," among others. Recent articles include "Industry Looks into Cloudy Future for Authentication," "ID Theft Bill Widens Encryption Rules," and "Attacks Distract People from More-Likely Threats." The web page provides content from current and archived print issues.

1450. Information Today: the newspaper for users and producers of electronic information services. [ISSN: 8755-6286] 1983. 11x/yr. USD 79.95 domestic; USD 106 in Canada & Mexico; USD 116 elsewhere. Ed(s): Barbara Brynko. Information Today, Inc., 143 Old Marlton Pike, Medford, NJ 08055-8750; custserv@infotoday.com; http://www.infotoday.com. Illus., adv. Circ: 10000 Paid. Vol. ends: No. 11. Microform: PQC. Online: EBSCO Publishing, EBSCO Host; Factiva, Inc.; Florida Center for Library Automation; Gale; Northern Light Technology, Inc.; OCLC Online Computer Library Center, Inc.; ProQuest K-12 Learning Solutions; ProQuest LLC (Ann Arbor); H.W. Wilson. *Indexed:* ABIn, CINAHL, CWI, ISTA, LISA, LRI, LibLit, MicrocompInd, SD. *Bk. rev.:* 10, 100 words. *Aud.:* Ac, Sa.

This monthly newspaper is similar in format and layout to *Computerworld,* but the intended audience is different: it bills itself as "[t]he most widely read publication in the information industry," and its primary focus is on topics of interest to librarians and other information professionals. "*Information Today* delivers total coverage of late-breaking news and long-term trends in the information industry." Issues include features, book reviews, product news and reviews, and interviews. There are also regular columns titled "NewsBytes," "NewsBreak Update," "Legal Issues," "Internet Waves," "Focus on Publishing," and "Database Review." Also included are conference reports, previews, and registration announcements. Recent tables of contents are available on the web site, as are the full text of selected articles and additional web-only content.

1451. InfoWorld: defining technology for business. Formerly (until 1981): *Intelligent Machines Journal.* [ISSN: 0199-6649] 1979. w. USD 195 domestic (Free to qualified personnel). Ed(s): Kathy Badertscher. InfoWorld Media Group, 501 Second St, San Francisco, CA 94107; http://www.infoworld.com. Illus., index, adv. Circ: 370000. Vol. ends: Dec. *Indexed:* ABIn, BPI, C&ISA, CBCARef, CerAb, ConsI, IAA, ISTA, MASUSE, MicrocompInd. *Aud.:* Ac, Sa.

The web site for this journal is very similar to those of *Computerworld* and *Datamation* in terms of content and layout, making differentiation difficult; the print version is also very close to that of *Computerworld* (*Datamation* is only available via web site). Recent articles include "Plotting your future in the Global IT Job Market," "Why You Should Get Closer to the Customer," and "Seven Keys to Job Security." This is another good source for anyone trying to stay current on hardware, software, and industry news and trends.

1452. MacWorld: the Macintosh magazine for the network professional. Incorporates (1985-1997): *MacUser;* Which was formerly: *MacLetter.* [ISSN: 0741-8647] 1984. m. USD 19.97 domestic; CND 29.97 Canada; USD 44.97 foreign. Ed(s): Jason Snell, Dan Miller. Mac Publishing, L.L.C., 501 Second St, 5th Fl, San Francisco, CA 94107; customer_service@macworld.com; http://www.macworld.com. Illus., adv. Circ: 356681 Paid. Vol. ends: Dec. Microform: NBI; PQC. Online: EBSCO Publishing, EBSCO Host; Florida Center for Library Automation; Gale; Northern Light Technology, Inc.; OCLC Online Computer Library Center, Inc.; ProQuest K-12 Learning Solutions; ProQuest LLC (Ann Arbor). *Indexed:* ABIn, BPI, ConsI, ISTA, MASUSE, MRD, MicrocompInd, RGPR. *Aud.:* Hs, Ga, Ac, Sa.

This title focuses on a common non-Microsoft operating system platform. *Macworld* ("The Mac Product Experts") provides in-depth coverage of the Apple operating system and the Macintosh line of personal computers. Issues contain feature articles on Mac-specific hardware, software, and other products; product reviews are prevalent and extensive. Departments include "Opinion," with editorial content and letters to the editor; and "Secrets," with how-to information organized into sections including "Create," "Help Desk," "Mobile Mac," "Working Mac," and "Geek Factor." The web site offers much of the content from the current issue, a limited archive of past issues, and search engines for products and articles. Another Mac-focused magazine that is very similar in content, layout, and intent is *MacAddict*, which is equally deserving of consideration. (AF)

1453. P C Magazine: the independent guide to personal computing and the Internet. Formerly (until 1986): *P C: The Independent Guide to I B M Personal Computers.* [ISSN: 0888-8507] 1982. bi-w. 22/yr. USD 19.97; USD 5.99 newsstand/cover per issue. Ed(s): Jim Lauderback, Stephanie Chang. Ziff Davis Media Inc., 28 E 28th St, New York, NY 10016-7930; info@ziffdavis.com; http://www.ziffdavis.com. Illus., adv. Circ: 700000. Online: EBSCO Publishing, EBSCO Host; Florida Center for Library Automation; Gale; OCLC Online Computer Library Center, Inc.; ProQuest K-12 Learning Solutions; ProQuest LLC (Ann Arbor); H.W. Wilson. *Indexed:* ConsI, ISTA, LRI, MASUSE, MRD, MicrocompInd, RGPR. *Aud.:* Hs, Ga, Ac, Sa.

This biweekly magazine provides content for a wide range of users, from beginners to professionals. A strong focus on new product reviews is provided in the "First Looks" section; other sections include "Pipeline," "Opinion," and "Personal Technology." The "User to User Solutions" section offers articles in response to specific reader requests. Many of the articles in a given issue can speak to a cover "theme"; recent examples are "All-Time Best Windows Tips," "How to Make Great Digital Photos," and "Security Made Simple." The web site provides content from current and archived issues, as well as some web-only content. (AF)

1454. P C World. Incorporates (2004-2006): *Digital World;* Which Incorporated (1985-1995): *P C World. Lotus Edition;* Which was formerly (until 1992): *Lotus;* (1987-1990): *P C Resource.* [ISSN: 0737-8939] 1982. m. USD 19.97 domestic; CND 34.97 elsewhere; USD 6.99 newsstand/cover. Ed(s): Harry McCracken, Edward Albro. I D G Communications Inc., 501 Second St, Ste 600, San Francisco, CA 94107-4133; http://www.idg.com/. Illus., adv. Circ: 1103839 Paid. Vol. ends: Dec. Microform: PQC. Online: EBSCO Publishing, EBSCO Host; Factiva, Inc.; Florida Center for Library Automation; Gale; OCLC Online Computer Library Center, Inc.; ProQuest K-12 Learning Solutions; ProQuest LLC (Ann Arbor); H.W. Wilson. *Indexed:* BPI, CPerI, ConsI, EngInd, ISTA, LRI, MASUSE, MicrocompInd, RGPR. *Aud.:* Hs, Ga, Ac, Sa.

Similar to *PC Magazine,* this publication caters to a broad spectrum of computing users, but almost completely within the consumer market. The magazine is largely focused on product reviews; there are also news stories and editorial content that cover the latest technology in the personal computer market. A common feature is the comparison of the latest hardware and software in table format, including performance, vendor service, price, and overall customer satisfaction—most comparisons are offered in top-ten format. Also included, in the "Here's How" section, is a regular offering of helpful hints geared toward solving computer application problems, operating system issues, and resolution of hardware issues. Departments include "Up Front," "Letters to PC World," "Consumer Watch," "Privacy Watch," "Hassle-Free PC," and "Bugs and Fixes." Content from both current and archived issues is available on the web site. (AF)

1455. Smart Computing. Formerly (until May 1997): *P C Novice.* [ISSN: 1093-4170] 1990. m. USD 29 domestic; USD 37 Canada; USD 69 elsewhere. Ed(s): Ronald D Kobler. Sandhills Publishing Co., 120 W Harvest Dr, Lincoln, NE 68521. Illus., adv. Circ: 205837. Vol. ends: Dec. *Indexed:* ISTA, MicrocompInd, RGPR. *Aud.:* Ems, Hs, Ga.

This journal and its "Learning Series" and "Reference Series" titles represent information that is specifically tailored to the very beginning personal computer user, presented in a format that minimizes the jargon and potential intimidation

of the technical aspects of computing. The continued rise in the number of U.S. households with computers will likely make this type of information more important to a growing number of users for some time to come. Topics include basic training on common operating system functions and usage, practical information on purchasing peripherals (printers, scanners, digital cameras, etc.) and software, and in-depth help using popular personal computer applications. Content is organized into "Featured Articles," "Reviews," "General Computing," "Plugged In," "PC Projects," "Tech Support," "Quick Studies," and "PC Operating Instructions," among others. The web site includes a search engine for product reviews, a computing dictionary and encyclopedia, "Daily Tip" and "Web log" archives, and selected content from and tables of contents for current print issues. There is also web-only content. (AF)

Wired. See World Wide Web section.

■ CONSUMER EDUCATION

Hilary Kline, Manager of Reformatting Support Services, Preservation & Imaging Department, Widener Library, Harvard University

Introduction

According to the *Encyclopaedia Britannica Online,* consumerism is the "movement or polities aimed at regulating the products, services, methods, and standards of manufacturers, sellers, and advertisers in the interests of the buyer." The titles in this section aim to focus on just that. In addition to the particular titles listed here, librarians will be well served in knowing about the following web sites:

www.Recalls.gov, "Your Online Resource for Recalls," provides instant information on recalled products.

www.consumeraction.gov, "The Federal Citizen Information Center's Consumer Action Website" offers a vast number of resources to consumers; it includes a Resource Directory and information targeted to specific audiences (military, teachers, persons with disabilities, media).

www.firstgov.gov, the U.S. government's official web portal, has an entire section on "Consumer Guides and Protection" at www.firstgov.gov/Citizen/Topics/Consumer_Safety.shtml. Areas covered range from "Air Travel Problems and Complaints" to "Workplace Safety Policies and Regulations (OSHA)," with such notable links in between as "Consumer RSS Feeds," "Long Term Care Ombudsman, by State," and "Stopping Unsolicited Mail, Telemarketing, and E-mail." The bonanza of consumer information available here makes it a "must-know-about" for every U.S. citizen, let alone every librarian.

Basic Periodicals

Hs: *Consumer Reports*; Ga: *Consumer Reports*; Ac: *Consumer Reports, Journal of Consumer Affairs.*

Basic Abstracts and Indexes

Consumers Index to Product Evaluations and Information Sources.

Adbusters. See Alternatives/General section.

1456. Co-op America Quarterly. Formerly (until 1991): *Building Economic Alternatives.* 1985. q. Members, USD 60; Non-members, USD 20. Ed(s): Dennis Greenia. Co-op America Inc., 1612 K St, NW, Ste 600, Washington, DC 20006; info@coopamerica.org; http://www.coopamerica.org. Illus., adv. Sample. Circ: 60000 Paid. *Indexed:* AltPI. *Aud.:* Ga, Ac.

Co-op America Quarterly is dedicated to creating a just and sustainable society by harnessing economic power for positive change. Its unique approach involves "working with both the consumer (demand) and business (supply) sides of the economy simultaneously." This publication reminds us that consumer education is not just about saving money, but also about using our purchasing power to buy wisely—by knowing which companies run sweat shops or are harmful to the environment and which companies are socially and environmentally responsible. A recent issue dedicates more than half its pages to citing the numerous reasons why consumers should not support Wal-Mart. In addition to articles, there are a number of provocative advertisements (revealing definite positions against large oil companies and gas-guzzling, oversized vehicles). There is also a listing of "green" web sites for companies and nonprofit organizations. Some readers may find the content here to be a bit "preachy," but for those firmly committed to social and environmental change, it is a highly worthwhile publication.

1457. Consumer Reports. [ISSN: 0010-7174] 1936. m. except s-m. Dec. USD 26; USD 4.95 newsstand/cover. Ed(s): Julia Kagan. Consumers Union of the United States, Inc., 101 Truman Ave, Yonkers, NY 10703-1057; http://www.consumerreports.org. Illus., index. Sample. Circ: 4100000 Paid. Vol. ends: Dec. Microform: NBI. Online: The Dialog Corporation; EBSCO Publishing, EBSCO Host; Gale; LexisNexis; Micromedia ProQuest; ProQuest LLC (Ann Arbor). *Indexed:* ABIn, AgeL, Agr, BLI, CBCARef, CINAHL, CPerI, ConsI, EnvAb, FLI, HRIS, LRI, MASUSE, PAIS, RGPR. *Aud.:* Hs, Ga, Ac.

Consumer Reports' mission is "to work for a fair, just, and safe marketplace for all consumers and to empower consumers to protect themselves." To achieve this and maintain impartiality, all products tested and reviewed here are purchased—no free samples are accepted, and no revenue is generated from outside advertising. That makes for a highly objective, dependable review. Major areas of testing include appliances, automobiles, baby and child products, electronics, foods, health and family-oriented materials, and recreation and home improvement products and services. In addition to the product testing, readers are surveyed on the reliability of products they use. Any dangers uncovered during testing are reported to consumers and to appropriate government and consumer agencies, which may lead to recalls and improved standards. *Consumer Reports* is probably the most recognizable and most popular consumer magazine on the market, and deservedly so. Definitely a must for anyone comparing products before making a purchase, this title belongs in every library collection.

1458. F D A Consumer. Formerly (until 1972): *F D A Papers.* [ISSN: 0362-1332] 1967. bi-m. USD 14 domestic; USD 19.60 foreign. Ed(s): Dori Stehlin. U.S. Department of Health and Human Services, Food and Drug Administration, 5600 Fishers Ln., Rockville, MD 20857; http://www.fda.gov. Illus., index. Sample. Circ: 28000 Paid. Vol. ends: Dec. *Indexed:* AgeL, Agr, BiolDig, CINAHL, ConsI, DSA, ExcerpMed, FS&TA, GSI, IUSGP, IndVet, LRI, MASUSE, PAIS, RGPR, VB, WAE&RSA. *Aud.:* Ga.

The official magazine of the Food and Drug Administration, *FDA Consumer* "reports on current FDA activities to ensure that the products the agency regulates—food, human and animal drugs, medical devices, cosmetics, radiation-emitting products, biologics—are fit to use." It also provides "information on how to get healthy and stay healthy." This free online journal aims to inform the public on guidelines and best practices, resulting from science-based information, for the improvement of health. In earlier years, the magazine had a decidedly scientific tone, however the most recent issues are written in a much more accessible, consumer-based style. A recent issue has an article about the recently approved inhaled insulin product and an article on preventing and treating common foot problems. As with any government publication, the reader should be aware that there is the potential for political bias in the writing—governments have their agendas. URL: www.fda.gov/fdac/default.htm

1459. Journal of Consumer Affairs. [ISSN: 0022-0078] 1967. s-a. GBP 354 print & online eds. Ed(s): Jack Rotfeld. Blackwell Publishing, Inc., Commerce Place, 350 Main St, Malden, MA 02148; customerservices@blackwellpublishing.com; http://www.blackwellpublishing.com. Illus. Sample. Refereed. Circ: 1500. Vol. ends: Winter. Microform: MIM; PQC. Online: Blackwell Synergy; EBSCO Publishing, EBSCO Host; Florida Center for Library Automation; Gale; IngentaConnect; Northern Light Technology, Inc.; OCLC Online Computer Library Center, Inc.; ProQuest K-12 Learning Solutions; ProQuest LLC (Ann Arbor);

SwetsWise Online Content; H.W. Wilson. Reprint: PSC. *Indexed:* ABIn, AgeL, Agr, ArtHuCI, BPI, BRI, CABA, CBRI, CommAb, ConsI, DSA, H&SSA, HortAb, IBR, IBSS, IBZ, IndVet, JEL, PAIS, PsycInfo, RRTA, RiskAb, SSCI, WAE&RSA. *Bk. rev.:* 12-13, 1,000-2,000 words. *Aud.:* Ga, Ac.

This scholarly research publication covers "topics that can be addressed from the consumer's point of view, including economics, nutrition, public policy, consumer education, business law and ethics, consumer psychology, communications and marketing." Articles include a description of the methodology, data, conclusions/implications, and references used in the "analysis of individual, business, and/or government decisions and actions that impact upon the interests of consumers." A recent issue contains "Vehicle Acquisitions: Leasing or Finance?" reporting on a study conducted to see which demographics lease and which finance cars, and the major factors affecting the decision. In another recent issue appears "The Emergence of Biometrics and its Effect on Consumers," speculating on positive and negative impacts experienced from the increased use of biometric authentication systems. This is a consumer journal definitely meant for the academic researcher, but some articles will benefit a discerning general public.

1460. Journal of Consumer Policy: consumer issues in law, economics and behavioral sciences. Formerly (until 1983): *Zeitschrift fuer Verbraucherpolitik.* [ISSN: 0168-7034] 1977. q. EUR 493 print & online eds. Ed(s): Alan Mathios, Geoffrey Woodroffe. Springer New York LLC, 233 Spring St, New York, NY 10013-1578; service-ny@springer.com; http://www.springer.com/. Adv. Refereed. Microform: PQC. Online: EBSCO Publishing, EBSCO Host; Gale; IngentaConnect; OCLC Online Computer Library Center, Inc.; OhioLINK; ProQuest LLC (Ann Arbor); Springer LINK; SwetsWise Online Content. Reprint: PSC. *Indexed:* ABIn, Agr, H&SSA, IBR, IBSS, IBZ, JEL, LRI, PAIS, RiskAb, SSCI, WAE&RSA. *Bk. rev.:* 2-4, both extended and brief. *Aud.:* Ac.

This journal covers a broad range of consumer affairs issues with a scholarly focus. It is refereed and international in scope. Articles tend to be theoretical, mainly about empirical research on consumer and producer conduct, and concerned especially with matters of law, economics, and behavioral sciences. The journal will be useful to academic consumer researchers and those in special libraries studying consumer behaviors, the legal and broader economic issues of consumerism, and the ethics of those producing consumer products.

Kiplinger's Personal Finance. See Finance/Investment section.

1461. Refundle Bundle: your bi-monthly guide to refund and coupon offers. [ISSN: 0194-0139] 1973. bi-m. USD 23.87. Ed(s): Stephen M Samtur. Refundle Bundle, PO Box 140, Yonkers, NY 10710. Illus., adv. Sample. Circ: 70000. *Aud.:* Ga.

Refundle Bundle is a well-established bimonthly publication that consolidates many of the offers promoted by companies, including both those that require a form to receive a refund and those that do not. In addition to informing the consumer of what potential savings are available, *Refundle Bundle* also provides a list of qualifiers ("you need to send in 3 UPC seals, your receipt, and your first-born") and the addresses to which requests should be sent. Recent offers listed run the gamut from pharmaceutical products to DVDs to apple sauce. There is even a section for "Computer Technology and Office Supplies," making this a publication of interest not just in the home but also in the office. For those willing to spend the time to save some extra money, *Refundle Bundle* will be a valuable resource for finding refunds and coupons.

■ COOKING AND COOKERY

Amy J. Watson, Information Specialist, PPG Industries Inc., GTC Library, GTC - Guys Run Road, Pittsburgh, PA 15238; amywatson@ppg.com

Introduction

This new section is the result of dividing the Food and Wine section into two new sections—one centered on food and the other on beverages.

According to the March 5, 2007, issue of *Home Channel News,* there is a growing $303 billion global housewares market, and one subset of that market—cookware—has grown by nearly 8 percent year after year. It is no wonder that almost every popular cooking magazine features not only recipes but also reviews of kitchen equipment and tools. Additionally, according to a May 1, 2007, *Business Wire* release, the luxury-sales spending of first quarter 2007—especially on kitchen appliances and cookware—increased 8 percent over the fourth quarter 2006. This trend can also be seen in several of the magazines reviewed in this section that have a definite focus on the good things in life—travel, dining, and kitchen renovations.

The August 21, 2006, issue of *Publishers Weekly* features an article titled "A Little Bit of Country," which details the changes in the American cookbook market—many of which are also reflected in the magazines reviewed here. A trend toward comfort cooking and easy, quick recipes can be seen in more than one of the popular recipe-focused titles. Another trend is the popularity of Food Network celebrities—noted here as well. According to the same article, the cookbook market increased 12 percent from 2005 to 2006—it is not a leap to believe that the popularity of cooking magazines will make a similar increase.

The magazines in this section tend toward a popular and general-interest focus, though they cover a variety of levels of depth and detail. Each title listed has an accompanying web site that often offers additional subscriber features and online resources.

Basic Periodicals

Ga: *Bon Appetit, Cook's Illustrated, Cuisine at Home, Taunton's Fine Cooking.*

Basic Abstracts and Indexes

Readers' Guide to Periodical Literature.

1462. Betty Crocker Magazine. Formerly: *Betty Crocker Creative Recipes.* 198?. m. USD 19.95; USD 3.99 newsstand/cover per issue domestic; USD 5.50 newsstand/cover per issue Canada. Ed(s): Heidi Losleben, Jackie Sheehan. General Mills, Inc., PO Box 200, Minneapolis, MN 55440; http://www.generalmills.com. Illus., index. *Aud.:* Ga.

This title offers what in essence is a small subject-specific cookbook on a monthly basis. Recipes are organized in "chapters," and a coded index is also provided (low-fat, quick). This magazine has beautiful photographs, and each recipe features a full-page picture. Nutritional information and dietary exchanges are provided at the end of each recipe. While the magazine is advertisement-free, keep in mind that the recipes are based on Betty Crocker ingredients. URL: http://www.bettycrocker.com.

1463. Bon Appetit: America's food and entertaining magazine. [ISSN: 0006-6990] 1956. m. USD 15 domestic; USD 30 foreign; USD 3.99 newsstand/cover per issue domestic. Conde Nast Publications, Inc., 750 3rd Ave, New York, NY 10017; http://www.condenast.com. Illus., index, adv. Circ: 1300000 Paid. Vol. ends: Dec. *Indexed:* ASIP, CBCARef, ConsI, FLI, RGPR. *Aud.:* Ga, Ac, Sa.

Bon Appetit embraces not just cooking, but an entire lifestyle. Recipes are presented as part of entire menu and entertaining suggestions, and they are accompanied by beautiful photography. Cookery and gadgets are addressed in multiple columns, covering new-to-the-market items, kitchen design, and home decor. Restaurant suggestions are part of glossy and inspirational travel spreads. A column of special note is "R.S.V.P.," which features readers' favorite restaurant recipes. Shopping information and codes (low-calorie, low-cholesterol, low-fat, high-fiber, low saturated fat, vegetarian) are included. The companion web site features additional recipes, interactive features, and downloadable podcasts. URL: http://www.bonappetit.com.

1464. Chile Pepper: the magazine of spicy foods. Former titles (until Jan. 1990): *Whole Chile Pepper; Whole Chile Pepper Catalog.* [ISSN: 1069-7985] 1986. bi-m. USD 24.95 domestic; USD 34.95 foreign. Ed(s): Gretchen VanEsselstyn. Goodman Media Group, Inc., 250 W 57th St, Ste 710, New York, NY 10107-0799; info@goodmanmediagroup.com; http://www.goodmanmediagroup.com. Illus., index, adv. Circ: 85000. Vol. ends: Nov/Dec. *Bk. rev.:* Number and length vary. *Aud.:* Ga.

At the outset, a reader could assume that *Chile Pepper* is a "one trick pony" of a magazine. Nothing could be further from the truth. It is a lifestyle magazine, and its columns include coverage of growing your own peppers, recipes of a surprisingly wide variety, and travel coverage, to name a few. Wine and spirit suggestions are provided in separate columns, as are reviews of the newest gadgets in grilling. Cookbook reviews are a regular feature, and these provide recipe samples. The recipe index is organized by course (beverages, desserts, seafood, etc.) and each is rated by the "zest factor." URL: http://www.chilepepper.com.

1465. Chocolatier: a taste of the good life. [ISSN: 0887-591X] 1984. 4x/yr. USD 23.95 domestic; USD 30.95 foreign. Ed(s): Tish Boyle. Haymarket Group Ltd., 45 W 34th St, Ste 600, New York, NY 10001; hpg@haymarketgroup.com; http://www.haymarketgroup.com. Illus., index, adv. Circ: 150000. Vol. ends: Dec. *Indexed:* H&TI. *Aud.:* Ga, Ac, Sa.

Turning the pages of *Chocolatier* is the perfect eye candy for anyone with a sweet tooth. Coverage is not specific to chocolate, though the emphasis on it remains strong. Regular features include cookbook reviews and beautifully photographed showcase recipes. The "Latest Scoop" column addresses current trends in chocolates, sweets, and kitchen items of interest. This magazine is appropriate both for public patrons and for culinary professionals. Recipe index is coded (easy, intermediate, advanced) and provides key information on chocolate and other ingredients. URL: http://www.chocolatiermagazine.com or http://www.chocolate.com.

1466. Cooking with Paula Deen. [ISSN: 1558-1853] 2005. bi-m. USD 19.98 domestic; USD 29.98 Canada. Ed(s): Cindy Cooper. Hoffman Media, LLC., 1900 International Park Dr., Ste. 50, Birmingham, AL 35243; http://www.hoffmanmedia.com. Adv. *Aud.:* Ga.

This vanity title from the Food Network celebrity chef Paula Deen is more than just her cooking program come to print. The magazine embraces an entire lifestyle, including cooking and entertaining, but also travel, restaurant reviews, home decor, and shopping. A glossy and beautiful magazine, it is a delight to flip through, and descriptions of the meals are often mouthwatering. A very basic recipe index is provided, as are readers' resources for item procurement. URL: http://www.pauladeenmagazine.com.

1467. Cook's Country. [ISSN: 1552-1990] 2005. bi-m. USD 19.95 domestic; USD 25.95 Canada; USD 31.95 elsewhere. Ed(s): Christopher Kimball. Boston Common Press, 17 Station St, Brookline, MA 02445. *Aud.:* Ga, Ac, Sa.

Cook's Country is brought to the public by the editors of *Cook's Illustrated* and has a slightly different focus than its predecessor. Instead of black-and-white drawings and tireless testing of recipes, *Cook's Country* offers lively color photography and more "down-home" cuisine. Readers take part here just as in *Cook's Illustrated,* with shortcut and recipe request submissions. "Know How" sidebars offer tips and techniques reminiscent of *Cook's Illustrated,* but the recipe cards are a novel addition. Other key features are the in-depth equipment and product reviews and the "Getting to Know" column addressing foodstuffs. A lovely photographic recipe index is provided. Recommended. URL: http://www.cookscountry.com.

1468. Cook's Illustrated. Former titles (until 1990): *Cook's;* (until 1985): *Cook's Magazine.* [ISSN: 1068-2821] 1980. bi-m. USD 24.95 domestic; USD 30.95 Canada; USD 36.95 elsewhere. Ed(s): Christopher Kimball. Boston Common Press, 17 Station St, Brookline, MA 02445. Illus., index. Circ: 600000 Paid. *Indexed:* H&TI. *Aud.:* Ga, Ac, Sa.

Cook's Illustrated is the companion magazine to the public television program *America's Test Kitchen.* A favorable comparison would be to call this title the *Consumer Reports* of cooking magazines. Each recipe is tirelessly researched and modified until the cooks believe that they've reached perfection. This advertisement-free title features basic black-and-white drawings or photography. A column of interest is "Notes from Readers," where feedback from readers, and in turn the editors, is provided. Reviews are provided for kitchen equipment, and quick tips on useful techniques are demonstrated in detail. URL: http://www.cooksillustrated.com.

1469. Cuisine at Home. Former titles (until 2001): *Cuisine;* (until 2000): *August Home's Cuisine.* [ISSN: 1537-8225] 1996. bi-m. USD 24 domestic; USD 34 foreign; USD 4.99 newsstand/cover. Ed(s): John Meyer. August Home Publishing Co., 2200 Grand Ave, Des Moines, IA 50312-5306; cuisine@cuisinemag.com; http://www.Augusthome.com/cuisine.htm. Illus. Sample. Circ: 528 Paid. Vol. ends: Nov. *Aud.:* Ga, Ac, Sa.

Cuisine at Home's biggest strength is in the detailed photography, showing step-by-step processes through each recipe. Nutritional information is provided for each recipe, and each issue features an "all about" section with detailed focus on a specific foodstuff. Reviews of kitchenware and gadgets are included. Tips and techniques are addressed, making this an ideal magazine for home cooks interested in improving their skills. This title is advertisement-free, but it does not include a recipe index. Of special note are the accompanying online videos to demonstrate techniques further. Strongly recommended. URL: http://www.cuisineathome.com.

1470. Diabetic Cooking. [ISSN: 1526-0291] 1999. bi-m. USD 23.94; USD 29.94. Publications International Ltd., 7373 N Cicero Ave, Lincolnwood, IL 60646; mbowen@pubint.com. Illus., index, adv. Circ: 250000. *Aud.:* Ga.

Diabetic Cooking is a must-have title for cooks with diabetes. Its being printed with a larger font than traditional magazines enables easy reading, and symbols denote recipes of special interest (low-fat, low-sodium, low-carbohydrate, high-fiber). The useful "recipe makeover," where a traditional recipe is altered to be a healthier choice, is a special highlight. All recipes include nutritional information and dietary exchanges. Handy reviews of items commonly available in the grocery aisles are found in each issue. Many of the recipes feature attractive photographs. URL: http://www.diabeticcooking.com.

1471. Every Day with Rachael Ray. [ISSN: 1932-0590] 2005. bi-m. USD 18; USD 3.99 newsstand/cover. Ed(s): Rachael Ray. Reader's Digest Association, Inc, Reader's Digest Rd, Pleasantville, NY 10570-7000; http://www.rd.com. Adv. Circ: 650000 Controlled. *Aud.:* Ga.

Rachael Ray is probably best known for being the bubbly girl next-door on Food Network. Her magazine, *Every Day with Rachael Ray,* is a print personification of her television shows and personality. The beginning of each issue features more lifestyle-oriented content—product reviews, favorite items as shopping recommendations, and celebrity appearances. It is when you get to the core four sections of the magazine that the true value becomes apparent. "Ready?Set" focuses on tools and techniques, "Cook" features recipes, and a noteworthy seven-day menu planner, "Get Together," provides entertaining and party suggestions. "Go Away" offers travel ideas with a culinary slant. This title features a recipe index, suggested wine-pairing index, and a shopping resource guide. Recommended for public libraries. URL: http://www.rachaelraymag.com.

1472. Flavor and Fortune: dedicated to the art and science of Chinese cuisine. [ISSN: 1078-5361] 1992. q. USD 21.50 domestic; USD 41.50 Canada; USD 50 elsewhere. Ed(s): Jacqueline M. Newman. Institute for the Advancement of the Science and Art of Chinese Cuisine, PO Box 91, Kings Park, NY 11754-0091. Illus., adv. Circ: 2400 Paid. *Indexed:* H&TI. *Bk. rev.:* Number and length vary. *Aud.:* Ga, Ac, Sa.

Flavor and Fortune is published by the nonprofit Institute for the Advancement of the Science and Art of Chinese Cuisine, and as such is perhaps a more scholarly journal than others reviewed in this section. This title covers Chinese cuisine from every angle—basic ingredients, detailed recipes, and extensive book reviews. One of the more entertaining features is the restaurant review section, which often includes menus from around the world. While many other cooking magazines simply offer recipes, this title goes in depth with detailed explanations and the history behind ingredients and techniques. This title makes for good reading, as well as good cooking. URL: http://www.flavorandfortune.com.

1473. Food & Wine. Former titles (until 1983): *Monthly Magazine of Food and Wine;* (until 1981): *International Review of Food and Wine.* [ISSN: 0741-9015] 1978. m. USD 37 domestic; USD 49 foreign. Ed(s): Pamela Kaufman, Mary Ellen Ward. American Express Publishing Corp., 1120 Ave of the Americas, 9th Fl., New York, NY 10036; ashields@amexpub.com; http://www.foodandwine.com. Illus., index. Circ: 840100. Vol. ends: Dec. *Indexed:* ASIP. *Aud.:* Ga, Ac, Sa.

Major features of this title lean more toward dining while traveling, as opposed to simple lists of recipes. This journal is geared toward a discriminating lifestyle, and its columns are written with a specific reader in mind—though columns vary from issue to issue. Food and wine pairings are a significant focus, though recipes and wines are indexed separately. Both indexes are coded for ease of use. The online edition offers access to more than 8,000 recipes and 1,700 wine pairings. Other topics can include trends, chef recipes made easy, and entertaining. URL: http://www.foodandwine.com.

1474. Home Cooking. Formerly: *Women's Circle Home Cooking.* [ISSN: 1071-4782] 1973. m. USD 21.97 domestic; USD 3.99 newsstand/cover per issue. Ed(s): Carol Tannehill. Dynamic Resource Group (DRG), 306 E Parr Rd, Berne, IN 46711-2159; http://www.drgnetwork.com. Illus., adv. *Aud.:* Ga, Ac, Sa.

The most impressive feature of *Home Cooking* is most certainly the sheer quantity of recipes in each issue—well over 80 in each of the reviewed issues. Regular columns include recipes that are "almost homemade," "mouth-watering make ahead," "bake sale bestsellers," and "slow cooker recipes," to name only a few. Unique features include a reader-submitted recipe-and-request swap, product reviews, and cut-out recipe cards. A particularly nice point is the index, which features thumbnail images of each recipe. Recommended. URL: http://www.homecookingmagazine.com.

1475. Saveur. [ISSN: 1075-7864] 1994. 9x/yr. USD 19.95 domestic; USD 28.95 Canada; USD 37.95 elsewhere. World Publications LLC, 460 N Orlando Ave, Ste 200, Winter Park, FL 32789; info@worldpub.net; http://www.worldpub.net. Illus., index, adv. Circ: 381585 Paid. *Aud.:* Ga, Ac, Sa.

Saveur embraces a complete lifestyle around cuisine—it is so much more than just a monthly list of recipes. Feature articles cover a variety of topics about eating, drinking, and travel—and all are lushly photographed. Among columns of interest are the reader-submitted kitchen designs and an international agenda of culinary events. Recipes are interspersed through the articles, but are indexed. A guide to resources is also featured. Strongly recommended for public libraries. URL: http://www.saveur.com.

1476. Taste of Home: edited by a thousand country cooks. [ISSN: 1071-5878] 1993. bi-m. USD 19.98 domestic; USD 23.98 Canada; USD 25.98 elsewhere. Ed(s): Kathy Pohl, Ann Kaiser. Reiman Media Group, Inc., 5400 S 60th St, Greendale, WI 53129; subscriberservices@reimanpub.com; http://www.reimanpub.com. Illus., index, adv. Sample. Circ: 4500000 Paid. Vol. ends: Nov/Dec. *Aud.:* Ga.

Flipping through the pages of *Taste of Home* is like walking into your grandmother's Sunday dinner, or a warm and welcoming church potluck. More than 1,000 field editors across the country, as well as a section in which readers request lost recipes, contribute to the feeling that this magazine is a community effort. The index is listed by meal course, and denotes if nutritional facts are provided. Recipe-heavy, this attractively photographed magazine includes feature sections such as "Comforting Casseroles" and "The Great Cupcake Challenge," as well as a clip-and-save section. The column "Touring Country Kitchens" features readers' kitchen renovations and can inspire new ideas for your own kitchen. URL: http://www.tasteofhome.com.

1477. Taste of Home's Cooking for 2. [ISSN: 1557-3664] 2005. q. USD 19.98. Reiman Media Group, Inc., 5400 S 60th St, Greendale, WI 53129; subscriberservices@reimanpub.com; http://www.reimanpub.com. Circ: 900000. *Aud.:* Ga.

The focus of this magazine is on meals for two diners, from appetizers and entrees to downsized desserts. Every recipe is attractively photographed, with nutrition facts provided. Among the useful features are handy tips and supermarket shopping for the small family unit. Kitchen remodels and gadget reviews are featured in both issues, the former allowing readers to show off their inspirational spaces. The indexes are a particular strength, one offering a basic course separation with coding (quick, light, diabetic-friendly, easy to lighten), and another listing items by common ingredients. Also provided are tips for using "one-time" ingredients as recommended by the issue's recipes. Strongly

recommended for public libraries. URL: http://www.cookingfor2.com.

1478. *Taste of Home's Light & Tasty.* [ISSN: 1537-0038] 2001. bi-m. USD 14.98 domestic; CND 19.98 Canada; USD 25.98 elsewhere. Ed(s): Kathy Pohl. Reiman Media Group, Inc., 5400 S 60th St, Greendale, WI 53129; subscriberservices@reimanpub.com; http://www.reimanpub.com. Adv. *Aud.*: Ga.

This is a recipe-heavy magazine with a focus on lower-calorie meals that still taste delicious. Food is attractively photographed, and each recipe includes both nutrition facts and diabetic exchanges. A daily nutrition guide is provided as part of the helpful index (with coding to indicate 30-minute-or-less meals). Across the board, the focus here is on health—from snacking, to lowering sodium, healthy hints, and a Q&A with a dietician. Of special note is the "Test Kitchen Makeover," where reader-submitted recipes are modified to cut the fat and calories, yet keep flavor—including a nutritional breakdown of calories/fat that are eliminated. URL: http://www.lightandtasty.com.

1479. *Taunton's Fine Cooking: for people who love to cook.* [ISSN: 1072-5121] 1994. 7x/yr. USD 29.95 in US & Canada; USD 36 elsewhere; USD 6.95 newsstand/cover. Ed(s): Sarah Jay. Taunton Press, Inc., 63 South Main St, Newtown, CT 06470-5506; publicrelations@ taunton.com; http://www.taunton.com. Illus., index, adv. Circ: 240000 Paid. *Indexed:* ASIP, H&TI. *Aud.*: Ga, Ac, Sa.

The subtitle of *Taunton's Fine Cooking* is wholly appropriate—this is a magazine *for people who love to cook*. Coverage of food features in-season and fresh ingredients, as well as detailed coverage of specific ingredient recipes. Complete menus and party planning provide useful information for cooks of many skill levels. Almost equally covered are kitchen implements—each issue features a detailed review of equipment, as well as reviews of new gadgets and tools in brief reviews. The recipe index is a strength for this title—coded for quick, make-ahead, mostly make-ahead, and vegetarian. Also useful are the nutritional analysis, and "where to buy it" sections. Readers will find the reader's tips and Q&A sections both practical and informative. URL: http://www.finecooking.com.

1480. *Vegetarian Journal.* Formerly: *Baltimore Vegetarians.* [ISSN: 0885-7636] 1982. q. bi-m until 2002. USD 20; USD 4.50 newsstand/ cover per issue. Ed(s): Keryl Cryer. Vegetarian Resource Group, PO Box 1463, Baltimore, MD 21203; vrg@vrg.org; http://www.vrg.org. Illus., index. Sample. Circ: 20000. Online: EBSCO Publishing, EBSCO Host; Gale; OCLC Online Computer Library Center, Inc.; H.W. Wilson. *Indexed:* BRI, CINAHL, RGPR. *Bk. rev.:* Number and length vary. *Aud.*: Ga, Ac, Sa.

Vegetarian Journal is a product of the Vegetarian Resource Group, a nonprofit organization that educates about vegetarianism and related issues. This magazine is a wonderful reflection of their educational purpose. Articles that include recipes also include well-written introductions explaining the whys and hows of each cuisine, and other columns such as "The Scientific Update" lead readers to a safe and healthy lifestyle. Product and book reviews are present, but no recipe index. URL: http://www.vrg.org.

■ CRAFT

General/Clay and Glass/Fiber/Jewelry-Metal/Knitting and Crochet/Needlework/Quilting/Wood

Mary Frances Angelini, Electronic Resources Librarian, Godfrey Lowell Cabot Science Library, Harvard University, One Oxford St., Cambridge, MA 02138; angelini@fas.harvard.edu

Cheryl LaGuardia, Research Librarian, Widener Library, Harvard University, Cambridge, MA 02138

Introduction

Fine craft is an art. Its practitioners are artists, and many have works displayed in fine craft magazines as well as in museums. Home crafting is often considered a form of folk art. Some crafts are based on skills formerly necessary to create useful items (quilting, embroidery, gold and silversmithing) and require specialized tools and training. Useful crafts can certainly also be beautiful, as artisans of the guilds have shown.

There is a plethora of craft resources available online. The majority of these, however, are not crafts journals. *American Craft* has an online counterpart (available through Dialog) as does the *Professional Crafter's Market Guide* (available on the web at http://www.auntie.com/craftzine/main.asp). What is available on the web is a range of people and stores selling items, information about crafts in locations around the globe, museums and exhibitions, and various suppliers' catalogs, as well as the various Usenet chat groups and listservs. All of these resources are valuable, and while they do some of the same things as a magazine, they fill quite a different niche from the traditional magazines listed in this resource.

What is on the Internet tends to be more personal, more surface than substance. This should not be construed as disapproval; the Internet does allow individuals to show their own works and talk about why they do what they do; and it may even help them sell their works. It also allows groups and consortia of individuals to do the same—all without having to break through the old barriers of galleries.

What you may not find—and what I did not find—are substantive articles. I found displays, projects, and personal opinions in great profusion, but rarely did I see detailed technical discussions, historical perspectives, or studies of styles and trends. Given these differences—and the fact that there are few traditional magazines on the Internet—I will not give a list of online magazines that I have reviewed and given some kind of seal of approval. What I will do is give you places to explore or bookmark in your library. Remember that these are just guides; there is so much out there and it is changing all the time.

If you want to bookmark places to start, try search engines such as Yahoo (http://www.yahoo.com) in either the recreation: hobbies and crafts section or the arts: design arts section. Both of these sections list individual crafts as well as magazines. Excite (http://www.excite.com) also indexes sites, but the sites listed here are given ratings, and there are far fewer of them. The sections of potential interest are hobbies (http://www.excite.com/Reviews/Hobbies) and arts (http://www.excite.com/Reviews/Arts). Excite also offers the option of just searching the Internet for whatever is out there, which can also be done from many search sites. My advice is to start from the indexed sites and then use the big search engines to find all kinds of other stuff. Remember to bookmark what you like or you may never see it again! Happy searching, and I hope you find both what you want and what you did not know you wanted.

Basic Periodicals

GENERAL. *American Craft, Crafts.*

CLAY. *Ceramic Review, Ceramics Monthly.*

FIBER. *Fiberarts, Threads.*

JEWELRY-METAL. *Beadwork, Lapidary Journal.*

KNITTING AND CROCHET. *Knitter's.*

NEEDLEWORK. *Piecework, Stitcher's World.*

QUILTING. *Quilter's Newsletter Magazine.*

WOOD. *Fine Woodworking, Woodsmith.*

Basic Abstracts and Indexes

Art Index, Artbibliographies Modern, Index to How to Do It Information, Magazine Article Summaries.

General

1481. *American Craft.* Former titles (until 1979): *Craft Horizons with Craft World;* (until 1979, vol.39, no.3): *Craft Horizons;* Incorporates: *Craft World.* [ISSN: 0194-8008] 1941. bi-m. USD 40 domestic; USD 55 foreign; USD 5 newsstand/cover per issue. Ed(s): Andrew Wagner. American Craft Council, 72 Spring St, New York, NY 10012; council@craftcouncil.org; http://www.craftcouncil.org. Illus., adv. Circ: 40000 Paid and free. Vol. ends: Dec/Jan. CD-ROM: ProQuest LLC (Ann Arbor). Microform: PQC. Online: Northern Light Technology, Inc.; OCLC Online Computer Library Center, Inc.; ProQuest K-12 Learning Solutions; ProQuest LLC (Ann Arbor). *Indexed:* ABM, ArtInd, BAS, BRI, CBRI, DAAI, FLI, IBZ, MRD, RGPR. *Bk. rev.:* 3-4, 500 words, critical, signed. *Aud.:* Ga, Ac, Sa.

It would be difficult to overstate the depth and breadth of this journal. It covers crafts from the contemporary to the historical to the prehistoric in any medium and analyzes the current state of craft in America. While it concentrates on American crafts and artisans, *American Craft* also looks at trends and artisans from all over the world. There are about five feature articles that focus on artists, collectors, technique, the history of a genre or technique, or trends and philosophies. The "Portfolio" section looks at the work of practicing artisans. The "Gallery" section shows photographs submitted by galleries, museums, and individuals to announce upcoming exhibits. The "Focus" section reviews two or three exhibits around the nation. American Craft Council news has its own section. Galleries and museums take out full-page ads to list upcoming shows where other magazines would have commercial ads. And there are lots of these; in fact, there are more gallery notices than there are articles. A beautiful, glossy publication full of ideas, inspiration, and information for artists, craftspeople, students, and the interested public.

1482. *Craft.* [ISSN: 1932-9121] 2006. q. USD 34.95 combined subscription domestic print & online eds.; USD 39.95 combined subscription Canada print & online eds.; USD 49.95 combined subscription elsewhere print & online eds. Ed(s): Carla Sinclair. O'Reilly Media, Inc., 1005 Gravenstein Hwy N, Sebastopol, CA 95472; http://www.oreilly.com/. Adv. Circ: 35992 Paid. *Aud.:* Ga.

This is an interesting and fun craft magazine, although it may not fit in all crafts collections. According to the "welcome" from the editor-in-chief, it is supposed to be "a one-off craft-themed issue of *Make* magazine, featuring some cool but 'craftier' DIY projects." In keeping with the DIY feel of *Make*, about half the projects are "typical" craft projects, although they might have an unusual goal. Many people crochet and felt; not so many crochet robots or think about felting a cocoon for their iPod. Some projects challenge the idea of what a craft is—articles on making chain mail and on brewing cider do not often appear in craft magazines. Other projects take a traditional craft and add DIY aspects to take it in a nontraditional direction. Want to make programmable LED clothing? There is a project for just such a blouse, complete with materials list and thorough instructions—including a section on how to test a circuit. Some of the projects are more DIY than craft, such as making an ant-farm room divider. In addition to projects, *Craft* has thought-provoking and well-written opinion, editorial, and interview sections. There are some ads, but they are confined to the back in a "Marketplace" section. If you have a large craft section, or have a need for a quirky, nontraditional craft magazine, this is for you. If you have a small craft collection and a tight budget, it may not be for you, but it is worth a review.

1483. *S A C Newsmonthly: national news and listings of art & craft shows.* Incorporates: *Art and Crafts Catalyst;* Former titles: *National Arts and Crafts Network; National Calendar of Open Competitive Exhibitions; Lisa's Report; Craft Show Bulletin.* 1986. m. USD 24 print edition only; USD 36 print and online editions. Ed(s): Wayne Smith. S A C, Inc, PO Box 159, Bogalusa, LA 70429-0159; http://www.SACNewsmonthly.com. Adv. Circ: 4000. *Aud.:* Ga, Sa.

This publication is only available online. It lists art and craft show events for the current month and for the next 11 months. Listings are by month, then by state, and then in chronological order. Event information is concise, giving dates, times, the name of the event, location, contact phone numbers, and any other pertinent entry or display requirements. While there is not much information about each listing, the number of listings is remarkable; it is national in scope, updated each issue, and very affordable. There are some news articles on various events, but the focus, and the importance, of this publication is its events listings. An excellent resource for craftspeople and artisans looking to sell their works, and for those who enjoy attending these events.

Clay and Glass

1484. *Ceramic Review.* [ISSN: 0144-1825] 1970. bi-m. GBP 32; GBP 37 overseas. Ed(s): Emmanuel Cooper. Ceramic Review Publishing Ltd., 21 Carnaby St, London, W1V 1PH, United Kingdom; http://www.gold.net/users/dj94/creview.html. Illus., index, adv. Circ: 8300. *Indexed:* ABM, ArtInd, C&ISA, CerAb, DAAI, IAA. *Bk. rev.:* 5-6, critical. *Aud.:* Ac, Sa.

Ceramic Review is a beautiful, thought-provoking, and practical British journal. It includes technical and practical information about methods, materials, and equipment for clay, glazes, and kilns. There are critical articles on practicing potters, reviews of exhibitions, and tips and techniques. There are also articles on historical influences and techniques and the craft as it is practiced in other parts of the world. The ads, which are numerous but confined to the front and back of the magazine, the classified section, and the gallery listings are as critical to the magazine's functionality as the articles themselves—although not as useful for readers on the Western shore of the Atlantic. The web site has good general information and makes content available for purchase. *Ceramic Review* belongs in most crafts collections, and any ceramics collection.

1485. *Glass on Metal: the enamelist's magazine.* [ISSN: 1083-6888] 1982. 5x/yr. USD 45 domestic; USD 52 in Canada & Mexico; USD 59.10 in Europe. Ed(s): Tom Ellis. Enamelist Society, PO Box 310, Newport, KY 41072; http://www.craftweb.com/org/enamel/enamel.htm. Illus., adv. Refereed. Circ: 1100 Paid. Vol. ends: Dec. *Indexed:* ABM, ArtInd. *Bk. rev.:* Occasional, descriptive and critical. *Aud.:* Sa.

Glass on Metal is a publication of the Enamelist Society. There are anywhere from four to eight feature articles in each issue. Most articles are short, about two pages, and society news articles can run to three or four pages. The topics are varied, from works to gallery and museum reviews to techniques to news of the craft and artisans. The web site includes an introduction to enameling and some past articles. This is an unusual specialty journal that is well worth reviewing if your readers include jewelers, crafts people, or metalworkers.

Fiber

1486. *Handwoven.* Incorporates (197?-1981): *Interweave.* [ISSN: 0198-8212] 1979. 5x/yr. USD 24 domestic; USD 28 Canada; USD 31 elsewhere. Ed(s): Madelyn van der Hoogt. Interweave Press, LLC., 201 E Fourth St, Loveland, CO 80537; customerservice@interweave.com; http://www.interweave.com. Illus., adv. Circ: 36000. *Indexed:* IHTDI. *Bk. rev.:* 4-5, critical. *Aud.:* Ga, Ac, Sa.

Handwoven is for the serious weaver, for those who want to be, and for those who follow the craft. There are many projects, sometimes centered on a particular type of material or theme. These themes may be about a weaving technique, a nation's or a people's historic method of weaving or creating cloth, or projects for a season. Regular columns such as "Beginner's Corner" give simple, clear explanations of techniques, and a calendar lists exhibits, shows, and sales by state. There is extensive advertising. A "Project Guide" in each issue has many projects to try. The web site is much like other Interweave Press sites, with some content available for free. If fiber arts are a focus, or even just an aspect of your collection, consider adding this title.

1487. *Sew Stylish.* [ISSN: 1935-8482] 2007. q. USD 6.99 domestic; USD 8.99 Canada. Taunton Press, Inc., 63 South Main St, Newtown, CT 06470-5506; http://www.taunton.com. *Aud.:* Ga.

This glossy new magazine from powerhouse craft publisher Taunton Press is very similar to its elder sister, *Threads.* In fact, in the first two issues there were a couple of articles that were similar to ones that appeared in *Threads.* There are about 20 articles in each issue, and each issue covers a particular theme or topic, such as sewing basics or formal occasions. There are four or so projects in each issue. While *Sew Stylish* has the excellent writing and production values one expects from Taunton, the page layout is more crowded than *Thread* and the style is breezier and more informal. This magazine is in its initial year, so changes will probably occur as the editors find their voice. Still, it is well worth a review to see if it is suited to your readership.

1488. *Spin-Off: the magazine for handspinners.* [ISSN: 0198-8239] 1977. 4x/yr. USD 24 domestic; USD 28 Canada; USD 31 elsewhere. Ed(s): Amy C. Clarke. Interweave Press, LLC., 201 E Fourth St, Loveland, CO 80537; customerservice@interweave.com; http://www.interweave.com. Illus., adv. Circ: 18000. Vol. ends: Dec. *Indexed:* IHTDI. *Bk. rev.:* 5, 300-350 words, critical and descriptive. *Aud.:* Ga, Ac, Sa.

This magazine encompasses many aspects of fiber art. There are in-depth feature articles on various animal fibers (e.g., alpaca) and animals; rare breeds, their wool, and their historical/cultural importance; carding and spinning techniques; caring for items made from natural fibers; museums and their collections; and artist interviews. Included are six or more projects that range from knitting to dyeing to felting. There are also regular columns such as a calendar section that lists festivals, exhibits, conferences, instructional opportunities, and travel items. The extensive classified section lists everything from carding supplies to animals. There are ads throughout the magazine, and they are occasionally distracting from the otherwise excellent content. The web site is found on the main Interweave Press site and lists the monthly table of contents, has some free articles and other offers such as travel, and some ads.

1489. *Threads.* [ISSN: 0882-7370] 1985. bi-m. USD 32.95 in US & Canada; USD 38.95 elsewhere; USD 6.99 newsstand/cover. Taunton Press, Inc., 63 South Main St, Newtown, CT 06470-5506; publicrelations@taunton.com; http://www.taunton.com. Illus., index, adv. Circ: 130000 Paid. Vol. ends: Dec. *Indexed:* ASIP, DAAI, IHTDI. *Bk. rev.:* 1,350 words, critical. *Aud.:* Ga, Sa.

Threads covers all aspects of sewing: clothing, non-clothing, measuring, software, tools and equipment, fabrics, decoration, machine embroidery, and so on. It is not a project magazine *per se*; projects seem designed to teach techniques, style, and design concepts rather than being there for their own sake. There are regular columns such as "Notions" and "Tips." Advertising is found in the first and fourth quarter of the magazine, but not in the feature articles section. The magazine leans more toward the tailoring and structural details of sewing. Online content overlaps with the print magazine content in that there are article previews, but there is some web-only content such as videos and a feature library with articles ordered by subject. This reliably excellent and important

resource for sewers is preferred to its younger sister publication, *Sew Stylish,* if only because of its cleaner presentation. Both are worth reviewing, and, if budget constraints mean you can't have both, choose the better fit for your readers.

Jewelry-Metal

1490. *The Anvil's Ring.* [ISSN: 0889-177X] 1973. q. USD 35 (Individuals, USD 45; Senior citizens, USD 40). Ed(s): Rob Edwards. Artists-Blacksmith Association of North America, Inc., PO Box 816, Farmington, GA 30638-0816; abana@abana.org; http://www.abana.org. Illus., adv. Circ: 5000 Paid. *Bk. rev.:* 1-3, 100-300 words, critical. *Aud.:* Ga, Sa.

If you have thought at all about blacksmithing, you have probably thought that all it involved was shoeing horses, historical reenactment, and that it is a dying art. These thoughts are partially correct, but are a long way from the truth. The artistry of blacksmithing is alive and on display in this magazine. There are four to five feature articles in each issue, covering topics such as blacksmith artists, equipment, blacksmiths from other parts of the world, and examples of blacksmithing's art. Regular departments include "New Works" and "International Report." There are black-and-white and color photos throughout. The advertisements are plentiful and should prove useful for those practicing the craft. There is also a classified section and a "Calendar of Events" listing exhibitions, classes, and courses, organized by date.

1491. *Bead & Button: creative ideas and proffects for the art of beads and jewelry.* [ISSN: 1072-4931] 1994. bi-m. USD 28.95 domestic; USD 38 foreign; USD 5.95 newsstand/cover. Ed(s): Alice Korach. Kalmbach Publishing Co., 21027 Crossroads Circle, PO Box 1612, Waukesha, WI 53187-1612; webmaster@kalmbach.com; http://www.kalmbach.com. Illus., adv. Circ: 161973 Paid. *Indexed:* IHTDI. *Aud.:* Ga.

Bead & Button is devoted to beading, and is not limited to jewelry, but covers the full range of objects that can be decorated with or created with beads and beading techniques. All but one or two of the articles are projects; the others are artists' profiles or information about materials. The projects are very appealing, and the instructions are clear and well written. The regular columns are also quite good, covering such topics as computers; ethnic, cultural, or historical beads and techniques; tool and equipment reviews; a calendar; and basic stitches. The only drawback is that the layout is very crowded and overly busy, with ads scattered throughout the magazine. There is also a web site associated with the magazine; it requires registration to access any meaningful content or features. If your library is in need of a beading projects magazine, *Bead & Button* is an excellent choice.

1492. *Beadwork.* Formerly (until 1998): *Interweave Beadwork.* [ISSN: 1528-5634] 1997. bi-m. USD 19.95 domestic; USD 24.95 Canada; USD 29.95 elsewhere. Ed(s): Jean Campbell, Danielle Fox. Interweave Press, LLC., 201 E Fourth St, Loveland, CO 80537; customerservice@interweave.com; http://www.interweave.com. Illus., adv. Vol. ends: Fall. *Aud.:* Ga.

This is a project magazine focused primarily on jewelry. There are 12-15 projects in each issue, three feature articles, and a variety of regular columns. The projects are not rated for difficulty, but most seem to be accessible to beginners. Each project has a materials and notions list and clear directions that include diagrams. The departments include a calendar of events, calls for entries, basic stitches, columns, letters to the magazine, and readers' works. There is an online index available from the magazine's web site. There is some content, mostly projects, available online without registration—some of the projects are exclusive to the web site. A very good general-interest beading magazine geared toward the beginner hobbyist rather than the professional.

1493. *Step by Step Beads.* [ISSN: 1549-0688] 2003. bi-m. USD 19.95. Interweave Press, LLC., 300 Chesterfield Pkwy, Ste. 100, Malvern, PA 19355; customerservice@interweave.com; http://www.interweave.com. Adv. *Aud.:* Ga.

This is a magazine about the art and craft of making and using beads. There are plenty of projects, 12-15 of them, but some involve the creation of beads through lampwork and polymer clay, in addition to creating jewelry and objects out of beads that one can buy. All projects are rated for skill level. The instructions are detailed and clearly explained. There are also some non-project articles on topics such as organizing one's stash and reviews of media. This is quite a nice, well-rounded journal that has a somewhat narrow focus. It is not for all craft sections—it is a touch too narrow for that—but for any collection that needs more coverage in the beading and jewelry making area, this is worth a look.

Knitting and Crochet

1494. *Cast On.* 1984. 5x/yr. Membership, USD 25. Ed(s): Jean Lampe. Knitting Guild of America, 1100H, Brandywine Blvd, Zanesville, OH 43701; tkga@tkga.com; http://www.tkga.com. Illus., adv. Circ: 10000. *Indexed:* IHTDI. *Bk. rev.:* 2-4, descriptive. *Aud.:* Ga.

Cast On is the official publication of the Knitting Guild of America. Its content has become more focused on projects, with around 18–20 patterns in each issue, each rated for difficulty. There are also four or five articles on topics ranging from designers to knitting with kids to new-product reviews and techniques. The "Guild" section covering news, conventions, and individuals has been greatly reduced and moved to the back of the magazine. While this is still more than just a pattern magazine, that has defiantly become *Cast On*'s focus, bringing it into competition with other more mainstream knitting magazines. The quality and variety of the projects along with their very clear instructions make *Cast On* an excellent choice for your collection if there is a lot of interest in this handicraft.

1495. *Crochet!* Formed by the merger of (199?-2002): *Annie's Crochet to Go;* Which was formerly (199?-199?): *Annie's Quick & Easy Crochet to Go;* (199?-199?): *Annie's Quick & Easy Pattern Club;* (1980-199?): *Annie's Pattern Club Newsletter;* (1999-2002): *Crochet Home & Holiday;* Which was formerly (1989-1999): *Crochet Home;* (1987-1989): *Crochet Fun.* [ISSN: 1539-011X] 1987. bi-m. USD 19.97 domestic; USD 24.97 Canada. Ed(s): Donna Robertson. Dynamic Resource Group (DRG) 306 E Parr Rd, Berne, IN 46711-2159; http://www.drgnetwork.com Circ: 68000. *Aud.:* Ga.

This is a very good, general purpose crochet pattern magazine. And make no mistake—this is a pattern magazine even though it is the official publication of the Crochet Guild of America, although there appears to be no guild news. There are a few home decor patterns (doilies and afghans), but the majority of the patterns are for clothing. With the resurgence in popularity of crocheting as a hobby and a clothing style, this would be a good choice for your collection.

1496. *Interweave Crochet.* [ISSN: 1937-0008] 2005. a. USD 7.99 newsstand/cover. Interweave Press, LLC., 201 E Fourth St, Loveland, CO 80537; customerservice@interweave.com; http://www.interweave.com. *Bk. rev.:* about 6, descriptive, 60-150 words. *Aud.:* Ga.

Like many other Interweave Press publications, this one is a mixture of predominantly projects with three or so feature articles. The feature articles could be on designers, techniques, history, or cultures. The projects run the gamut from clothing—including scarves, boleros, and sweaters—to accessories such as purses and hats; most patterns indicate a skill level. Interestingly, there were no afghan patterns in the issue reviewed. The patterns are well designed and generally fashionable. *Interweave Crochet* has a nicely uncluttered layout, like all Interweave Press publications. A good choice if you need more crochet magazines in your collection.

1497. *Interweave Knits.* [ISSN: 1088-3622] 1996. q. USD 21 domestic; USD 25 Canada; USD 28 elsewhere. Ed(s): Pam Allen. Interweave Press, LLC., 201 E Fourth St, Loveland, CO 80537; customerservice@ interweave.com; http://www.interweave.com. Illus., adv. Circ: 51500 Paid and controlled. *Bk. rev.:* 7, 100-150 words, descriptive. *Aud.:* Ga.

This is a project magazine. There are two or three feature articles and more than 20 projects. The articles might be about wool or other materials, or artist profiles, or histories of knitting around the world. There is a "News and Views" section that has several short articles, but the focus is clearly on the projects. The projects include sweaters, socks, toys, scarves, purses, and pillows—however, they are not rated for difficulty. All projects have detailed instructions and

diagrams of new or difficult stitches and techniques. The "Departments" section has a glossary with explanations and diagrams of the stitches, as well as a "Beyond the Basics" column. The ads are numerous—if readers cannot find the product they are seeking, it will not be for lack of listings. The web site has a link to a "Community" section that has a free newsletter called *Knitting Daily*. Like the other Interweave Press publications, the layout and design of the magazine are very good.

1498. *Knit 'n Style.* Formerly (until 1997): *Fashion Knitting.* [ISSN: 1096-5408] 1981. bi-m. USD 24.97 domestic; USD 30.97 Canada; USD 36.97 elsewhere. Ed(s): Penelope Taylor. All American Crafts, Inc., 7 Waterloo Rd, Stanhope, NJ 07874-2621; editors@allamericancrafts.com; http://www.allamericancrafts.com. Illus., adv. Circ: 55000 Paid. *Aud.:* Ga.

This is a pattern magazine. There are five or so feature articles, but there are more than 25 patterns per issue. The feature articles may be about needles, yarn, yarn companies, designers, or knitting techniques. The patterns are tempting and attractive, are rated for difficulty, and the instructions are well written. This magazine is a direct competitor to *Interweave Knits* and should be reviewed with it. There is not much difference between the two—layout and production values are similar. Choose the one that has patterns that your readers will enjoy the most, although this choice may be difficult. If there is room in the budget, choose both.

1499. *Vogue Knitting International.* [ISSN: 0890-9237] 1982. q. USD 19 domestic; USD 25 Canada; USD 30 elsewhere. Soho Publishing Company, 233 Spring St, 8th flr., New York, NY 10013. Illus., adv. *Aud.:* Ga.

This is a knitting magazine that is fairly evenly divided between patterns and feature articles. Non-pattern articles cover such topics as techniques, designer profiles, information about yarn types, handling difficult stitches in garments, and events and conferences. The majority of the patterns are for clothing. The instructions are clear and easy to understand, rated for difficulty, and have pictures of the yarns used in the project. At the beginning of the pattern instruction section is a guide and information section about the yarns used in the issue, techniques, and abbreviations. As one would expect from a publication with the name *Vogue,* the magazine is also an excellent resource for what is fashionable, both for clothing and home decor. The online content is sparse, and the site functions more as an advertisement for subscription. *Vogue Knitting* is a fine choice for knitting patterns that are both trendy and timeless.

Needlework

1500. *Cross-Stitch and Needlework.* Former titles (until 2006): *Stitcher's World;* (until 1999): *Stitchery Magazine.* [ISSN: 1932-2720] 1995. bi-m. USD 19.99 domestic; USD 21.99 Canada; USD 35.99 elsewhere. Baywood Publishing, Plover, WI 54467. *Aud.:* Ga.

This is the new name of *Stitcher's World*. The title change is very reflective of a change in content that sees an increased focus on cross stitch at the expense of other types of needlework. There are still needlepoint, drawn thread, hardanger, and other types of needlework projects, but they are fewer in number and less interesting. The instructions are clear and the charts are in color. There are also designer profiles and some wonderful columns about technique. Web site content is only available by subscription. This is still a solid magazine for a collection with readers interested in needlework, even if the overall focus and difficulty of the projects have changed.

1501. *Just Cross Stitch.* [ISSN: 0883-0797] 1983. bi-m. USD 19.98 domestic; USD 29.98 Canada; USD 39.98 foreign. Ed(s): Phyllis Hoffman, Lorna Reeves. Hoffman Media, LLC., 1900 International Park Dr., Ste. 50, Birmingham, AL 35243; http://www.hoffmanmedia.com. Illus., adv. Circ: 68000 Paid. *Aud.:* Ga.

Just Cross Stitch is a project magazine, and a good one. There are 10 or 11 articles per issue, one of which comes with a needle-artist profile. There is a good variety of difficulty, and the designs are attractive, the instructions are clear, and all materials are listed. The explanation of basic stitches is also clear and well written. Although there are some advertisements, they are limited and do not interrupt the flow of the designs. A good choice for a library looking to add to this area of their collection.

1502. *Lace.* [ISSN: 0308-3039] 1976. q. GBP 21 domestic; GBP 25 in Europe; GBP 29 elsewhere. Ed(s): D Robinson. Lace Guild, The Hollies, 53 Audnam, Stourbridge, DY8 4AE, United Kingdom; http://www.laceguild.org. Illus., adv. Sample. Circ: 6000. *Bk. rev.:* 3, 120-140 words, critical. *Aud.:* Ga.

This magazine from the Lace Guild is principally devoted to bobbin lace. The content is varied; there are articles on lace makers, design issues, and collections, and there are also some projects that include pricking patterns. In addition, there are plentiful guild news and information about guild courses and workshops. Advertising is confined to the back so that it does not distract from the content. There are some shortened articles available online, but not much more than that. If there are lace makers in your community or you are looking for an interesting or unusual addition to your crafts collection, try reviewing this publication.

1503. *Needle Arts.* [ISSN: 0047-925X] 1970. q. Membership, USD 24. Ed(s): Jody Jeroy. Embroiderers Guild of America, 335 W Broadway, Ste 100, Louisville, KY 40202; egahq@aol.com. Illus., adv. Circ: 21000. Vol. ends: Dec (No. 4). *Indexed:* A&ATA. *Bk. rev.:* 3-4, 150-300 words, some descriptive, some critical. *Aud.:* Ga.

This is the official publication of the Embroiderers' Guild of America (EGA) for its members. As such, there is quite a lot of guild news including classes, correspondence courses, gatherings, competitions, a newsletter, and the like. There are some projects, but this is not really a project magazine. There are about eight feature articles in each issue ranging from two to four pages long and covering a variety of topics such as members' activities, artist profiles, shows, a particular work, historical techniques, conservation of works, and the history of needlework. Columns that appear in every issue include "Letters," the "EGA Marketplace," "Chapter News," and the "EGA Master Calendar." The online site has an education section that lists upcoming classes and registration, a members area, and a shop. Overall, a good magazine for needle artists, since the outreach and class sections provide links to communities that may be of interest to readers.

1504. *Piecework: needlework's living legacy.* [ISSN: 1067-2249] 1993. bi-m. USD 24.95 domestic; USD 29.95 Canada; USD 34.95 elsewhere. Ed(s): Jeane Hutchins. Interweave Press, LLC., 201 E Fourth St, Loveland, CO 80537; customerservice@interweave.com; http://www.interweave.com. Illus., adv. Circ: 47000 Paid and controlled. *Indexed:* AICP, ArtInd. *Bk. rev.:* 6-9, critical. *Aud.:* Ga, Sa.

The purpose of this magazine seems to be to promote historical and ethnic handwork by providing articles on history, techniques, and individual items and people, and then offering projects based on the articles using techniques such as needlework, knitting, quilting, crocheting, beading, drawn thread, and other crafts. Occasionally, issues are devoted to a single theme. The projects all have clear instructions and are well designed. This is not a magazine that will teach a technique in simple terms; if the reader is at all shy about picking up new techniques, then some of the projects may be difficult. The web site content is sparse. The magazine, however, is full of useful information and is devoted to the history and the current state of common and ethnic handicraft arts. It would be a wonderful, interesting addition to any craft collection.

Quilting

1505. *American Quilter.* [ISSN: 8756-6591] 1985. q. Membership, USD 19.95. Ed(s): Christine Brown. American Quilter's Society, 5801 Kentucky Dam Rd, PO Box 3290, Paducah, KY 42002-3290; http://www.aqsquilt.com. Adv. Circ: 56000 Paid. *Aud.:* Ga.

There are many, many project magazines available. This one, although there are lots of projects in it, is not really about the projects. Projects are seen as a way of teaching a technique, showing how one might design a quilt, or demonstrating some aspect of the process. The projects serve a educational end. They manage to do this while being attractive and interesting, and having all the usual extras such as ratings for difficulty, a complete materials lists, and lots of helpful hints. There are also occasional non-pattern articles on topics such as the history of quilting or buying a sewing machine or designer profiles. There is very little

guild news, which is somewhat sad since quilting, historically, has been about a community of quilters (generally women) who get together to share what they do. Still, this is a worthy addition to any quilting collection.

1506. *Fons and Porter's Love of Quilting.* Former titles (until 1999): *Fons and Porter's Sew Many Quilts;* (until 1998): *Sew Many Quilts.* [ISSN: 1525-1284] 1996. bi-m. USD 19.97. Love of Quilting, Inc., PO Box 171, Winterset, IA 50273; http://www.fonsandporter.com/. Circ: 100000. *Aud.:* Ga.

This is a well-designed, high-quality publication focused on projects. There are around ten projects in each issue and about five feature articles. The articles are usually short (one to three pages) and are usually about design or techniques. The project instructions are clear and easy to read, with good pictures and assembly instructions. There are several columns appearing in each issue that cover tips, techniques, and products. There are ads, but they are no more obtrusive or plentiful than in other craft project magazines. The quilting duo responsible for this magazine, Marianne Fons and Liz Porter, also record shows for television, some of which are available via streaming video on the magazine's web site. In addition, the web site has quilting tips and tricks, and everything is available without registration or subscription. Well worth adding to your quilting collection, especially if the television show airs in your area.

1507. *The Quilter Magazine.* Formerly (until 2000): *Traditional Quilter.* [ISSN: 1531-5630] 1989. bi-m. USD 24.97 domestic; USD 31.97 Canada; USD 38.47 elsewhere. Ed(s): Laurette Koserowski. All American Crafts, Inc., 7 Waterloo Rd, Stanhope, NJ 07874-2621; http://www.allamericancrafts.com. Illus., adv. Circ: 65000 Paid. *Bk. rev.:* 3, 100-125 words, descriptive. *Aud.:* Ga.

This is a pattern magazine. The majority of the patterns are for full-sized quilts, although there are some mini-quilts toward the back of the magazine. There are well over 15 projects in every issue, with a good mix of traditional and modern styles. Some projects require special-order fabrics. Some projects have alternative suggestions at the end—some were for block quilts using the same patterns, others for mini-quilts. In addition to the plethora of projects, there are a couple of articles on history, another on tips and techniques, and a designer profile. All in all, this is a good choice if you need more quilting magazines in your craft section.

Wood

1508. *Fine Woodworking.* Incorporates (in 1998): *Home Furniture;* Which superseded (in 1997): *Taunton's Home Furniture;* (1994-1996): *Fine Woodworking's Home Furniture.* [ISSN: 0361-3453] 1975. bi-m. USD 34.95 in US & Canada; USD 41.95 elsewhere. Ed(s): Mark Schofield, Asa Christiana. Taunton Press, Inc., 63 South Main St, Newtown, CT 06470-5506; http://www.taunton.com. Illus., index, adv. Circ: 292000 Paid. Vol. ends: Nov/Dec. *Indexed:* ASIP, ArtInd, DAAI, IHTDI. *Bk. rev.:* 2-4, critical. *Aud.:* Ga, Sa.

Fine Woodworking is for the professional carpenter or cabinetmaker, those who would like to be, and those with an interest in this craft. The magazine uses projects as examples of techniques or as the basis of articles rather than as projects for the reader to do—materials lists and measured drawings are not provided, but there are plenty of diagrams and pictures. Other articles review tools and equipment, discuss health and safety issues, look at designs of current or historic importance, and occasionally profile people or groups—past or present—of woodworkers that are important to the craft. There is an extensive Q&A section, and the "Methods of Work" and "Notes and Comment" sections are also substantial. Of special interest to the practicing woodworker are the supplier advertisements. The web site has some content available without registration, including video clips. Taunton Press has excellent production quality; thus, this magazine is not only a joy to read for content but also for presentation. This belongs in every crafts collection.

1509. *ShopNotes.* [ISSN: 1062-9696] 1992. bi-m. USD 27.95 domestic; CND 37.95 foreign. Ed(s): Tim Robertson. August Home Publishing Co., 2200 Grand Ave, Des Moines, IA 50312-5306; orders@augusthome.com; http://www.augusthome.com. Illus. Circ: 175000 Paid. Vol. ends: Nov. *Indexed:* IHTDI. *Aud.:* Ga.

This is not a project magazine; it is a magazine about all the aspects of woodworking, and there are some projects included. There are tool tests, articles about wood, organizing a workshop, and anything else pertaining to the craft of woodworking. The projects are usually geared to some aspect of the running of a woodworking shop. There are tips and techniques for using and maintaining tools and equipment, wood management, and shop management. The magazine's web site has copies of the projects, including plans and cutting diagrams. If there is a woodworking section in your library, consider adding this title to it.

The Woodenboat. See Boats and Boating section.

1510. *Woodshop News.* [ISSN: 0894-5403] 1986. m. USD 21.95 domestic; USD 33.95 foreign. Ed(s): Tod Riggio. Soundings Publications, L L C, 10 Bokum Rd, Essex, CT 06426; http://www.soundingspub.com. Illus., adv. Circ: 90000 Paid. Vol. ends: Jan. *Aud.:* Ga, Sa.

Woodshop News is a newsmagazine for the professional woodworker and the serious hobbyist. This is not a project magazine; the information it contains is as much a tool for the practicing woodworker as is a hammer. It tracks wood markets and job markets, reviews new tools and other products, tracks legislation, and discusses all aspects of wood and the wood industry. Feature articles cover individual rare-wood species suppliers and dealers, and individual woodworkers or communities. There are regular columns that cover health, ergonomic, and design issues. The web site has some of the articles and columns that appear in the magazine, but no additional content. If there are serious woodworkers in your community, this magazine is worth adding to your collection.

1511. *Woodsmith.* [ISSN: 0164-4114] 1979. bi-m. USD 24.95 domestic; CND 34.95 foreign. Ed(s): Terry Strohman. August Home Publishing Co., 2200 Grand Ave, Des Moines, IA 50312-5306; http://www.augusthome.com. Illus., adv. Circ: 263000 Paid. Vol. ends: Dec. *Indexed:* IHTDI. *Aud.:* Ga.

This is a project magazine, and an excellent one at that. There are four or so projects in each issue with detailed instructions, cutting lists, and diagrams. Of these projects, one or two are designed to teach a technique or process. Every issue contains a "Tips and Techniques" section that has short explanations on general topics. The web site has online extras, listed by magazine issue, which include material and supplies lists and cutting diagrams and videos of some projects. In addition to having useful, well-designed projects, there is no advertising—a welcome change. An excellent choice for your woodworking section.

1512. *Woodwork.* [ISSN: 1045-3040] 1989. bi-m. USD 17.95 domestic; USD 24 foreign. Ed(s): John Lavine. Ross Periodicals, 42 Digital Dr, Ste 5, Novato, CA 94949. Illus., adv. Circ: 50000. Vol. ends: Nov. *Indexed:* IHTDI. *Aud.:* Ga, Sa.

Woodwork is more for the serious hobbyist than the professional carpenter, but the latter might find it useful as well. In each issue there are about nine articles, and they cover all aspects of woodworking from furniture, toys, and turned pieces to species of wood, joining techniques, and profiles of current craftspeople. There are also one or two projects in each issue, complete with measured drawings and materials lists. There is also a "Gallery" where readers can submit finished works for display. The "Events" section lists classes, apprenticeship opportunities, shows, and juried shows by state. The online site has only limited content from the magazine. *Woodwork* is a direct competitor to *Fine Woodworking* and is at least worth a review—it is worth purchase if you have many woodworkers in your community.

■ CRIMINOLOGY AND LAW ENFORCEMENT

See also Law; and Sociology and Social Work sections.

Clark N. Hallman, Professor, Head of Public Services, Briggs Library, South Dakota State University, Brookings, SD 57007-1098; clark.hallman@sdstate.edu

Mary Kraljic, Professor, Access Services Librarian, Briggs Library, South Dakota State University, Brookings, SD 57007-1098; mary.kraljic@sdstate.edu

Introduction

Edwin Sutherland et al. define criminology as " . . . the body of knowledge regarding crime and delinquency as a social phenomenon. It includes within its scope the processes of making laws, breaking laws, and reacting to the breaking of laws" (1992, p. 3). This section describes many fine criminology journals that present scholarly material from many perspectives including those of sociology, psychology, social work, and others. It also includes titles that deal with the agencies of social control, for example, police and corrections, which Marvin Zalman (1981, p. 9) would categorize as criminal justice. These include many titles addressing the needs of practitioners, for example, police officers, corrections officers, probation officers, and social workers, and the needs of law enforcement administrators and/or public administrators involved with criminal justice institutions, as well as the needs of offenders and their victims. Also, a few titles cover news, judicial decisions, and other recent developments, which may be useful to practitioners as well as to students and interested laypersons.

The periodicals described here are representative samples of useful publications from subgroups covering most aspects of criminology and its related agencies. They were chosen as the most prestigious, highest-quality, and/or most useful periodicals from each subgroup. As part of this process, three studies that assessed criminology and criminal justice journals were consulted (Sorensen et al., 2006; Tewksbury et al., 2005; Williams et al., 1995). A few publications were chosen because they are unique in their representation of specific practice areas, theoretical perspectives, or type of content. These periodicals cover law enforcement and corrections administration and practice; criminal behavior; characteristics, etiology, and prevention of crime; ethics; and other components of criminology and the criminal justice arena.

Although jurisprudence, which can be broadly defined as the science of law, is certainly relevant to criminology and criminal justice, its periodicals are more appropriately covered in the Law section. Likewise, sociology journals publish much information of interest to criminology, but they are also given their own section. Therefore, titles like *Deviant Behavior, Law and Society Review,* and *Social Problems* are not included here. As stated above, the titles listed here are not limited to those for a scholarly audience. Many are oriented toward practitioners in the field, and many general readers would find these titles to be of interest.

The criminology and law enforcement periodicals included in this section of *Magazines for Libraries* reflect some of the same trends occurring in the periodicals publishing industry as a whole. For example, many titles that were once published by professional organizations have now gone to large commercial publishers. The ninth edition (1997) of *Magazines for Libraries* covered 45 criminology and law enforcement titles from 32 publishers. This edition includes 51 criminology and law enforcement titles from just 24 publishers. A comparison of the subscription costs for the publications listed in the ninth edition with the subscription costs for 2007 reveals a significant increase. For 2007, prices for "electronic access only" were used if available, followed by "electronic access with paper subscription" prices if "electronic only" prices were not available. If neither of the electronic options was available, the "paper only" price was used. The average library subscription for a title in this section cost approximately $92 in 1997, compared to $425 per title in 2007. However, this is still a relatively inexpensive field for purchasing journals. The basic periodicals listed below cost an average of just $307 per title. The basic general adult (Ga) periodicals cost an average of $32 per title and the basic academic (Ac) periodicals cost an average of $482 per title.

REFERENCES

Sorensen, J., Snell, C., & Rodriguez, J.J. (2006). An assessment of criminal justice and criminology journal prestige. *Journal of Criminal Justice Education,* 17(2), 297-322.

Sutherland, E.H., Cressey, D.R., & Luckenbill, D.F. (1992). *Principles of Criminology* (11th ed.). Dix Hills, NY: General Hall, Inc.

Tewksbury, R., DeMichele, M.T., & Miller, J.M. (2005). Methodological orientations of articles appearing in criminal justice's top journals: who publishes what and where? *Journal of Criminal Justice Education,* 16(2), 265-279.

Williams, F.P. III, McShane, M.D., & Wagoner, C.P. (1995). Differences in assessments of relative prestige and utility of criminal justice and criminology journals. *American Journal of Criminal Justice,* 19, 215-238.

Zalman, M. (1981). *A Heuristic Model of Criminology and Criminal Justice.* Chicago: Joint Commission on Criminology Education and Standards, Univ. of Illinois at Chicago Circle.

Basic Periodicals

Ga: *American Jails, Corrections Compendium, Corrections Today, FBI Law Enforcement Bulletin, Law and Order Magazine, Police Chief, Sheriff Magazine;* Ac: *The British Journal of Criminology, Crime & Delinquency, Criminal Justice & Behavior, Criminal Justice Ethics, Criminology, The Howard Journal of Criminal Justice, Journal of Offender Rehabilitation, Journal of Research in Crime and Delinquency, Justice Quarterly, Policing and Society, The Prison Journal.*

Basic Abstracts and Indexes

Criminal Justice Abstracts, Criminal Justice Periodical Index.

1513. *American Jails: the magazine of the American Jail Association.*
[ISSN: 1056-0319] 1987. bi-m. USD 48 domestic; USD 54 Canada; USD 66 elsewhere. Ed(s): Ken Kerle. American Jail Association, 1135 Professional Ct., Hagerstown, MD 21740-5853; jails@worldnet.att.net; http://www.aja.org. Illus., index, adv. Sample. Circ: 5000. Vol. ends: Nov/Dec. *Indexed:* CJA, CJPI. *Bk. rev.:* 3-4, signed. *Aud.:* Ga, Ac, Sa.

Ken Kerle, managing editor of *American Jails* since its founding in 1987, has pointed out that the men and women who operate more than 3,000 jails in the United States face issues that are unique to corrections work. And yet most criminal justice education programs do not offer coursework geared toward jail studies. So this attractively designed magazine, published by the American Jail Association (AJA), fills a need not only to support and promote the work of jail employees, but also to educate those new to this field. It remains "the only magazine geared solely to jail issues." Up to 25 percent of the articles are contributed by academics. Criminal justice professionals write the remaining 75 to 80 percent. Each thematic issue covers topics such as program evaluation, special problems of small jails, and new products, services and training in jails. Many articles focus on the day-to-day operations of local correctional facilities. Others deal with broader issues such as mental health, work stress, crowding, or women in jails. *American Jails* focuses primarily on facilities, personnel, and inmates in the United States; however, at least one article per issue is dedicated to foreign coverage. Although not peer-reviewed, several well-researched articles with complete references appear in each issue. Informative regular departments include "Sanitarian's File," written by an expert in institutional environmental health and epidemiology, "Jail Industries," and "Chaplain's Corner." Practitioners, faculty, and students of criminal justice will find the news items and lengthier articles useful in their work or study. The general public will also find much of interest here, including articles related to the history of jails. Each January/February issue includes an insert for AJA's annual Training Conference and Jail Expo. Individual issues may be purchased at reasonable cost. Further information and inexpensive article reprints are available through AJA's web site. Highly recommended for collections supporting criminal justice studies.

1514. *Australian and New Zealand Journal of Criminology.* [ISSN: 0004-8658] 1968. 3x/yr. Individuals, AUD 200. Ed(s): Dr. John Pratt. Australian Academic Press Pty. Ltd., 32 Jeays St, Bowen Hills, QLD 4006, Australia; info@australianacademicpress.com.au;

http://www.australianacademicpress.com.au. Illus., index, adv. Sample. Refereed. Vol. ends: No. 3. *Indexed:* CBRI, CJA, CJPI, CLI, HRIS, IBSS, ILP, LRI, PSA, PsycInfo, SSA, SSCI, SociolAb, V&AA. *Bk. rev.:* 2-3, 1,000 words, signed. *Aud.:* Ac, Sa.

This is the official journal of the Australian and New Zealand Society of Criminology. It is a peer-reviewed journal, which helps the society fulfill its purpose of fostering training and research in criminology in institutions of learning, and in law enforcement, judicial, and correctional agencies; encouraging communication within the field of criminology; and promoting understanding of criminology by parliaments, governments, and the public. For over 30 years, the journal has promoted quality research and debate on crime and criminal justice by publishing theoretical and methodological articles and current ethical and ideological debates from multidisciplinary perspectives including criminology, psychology, sociology, law, politics, history, and forensic sciences. The focus is on crime, law enforcement, corrections, and courtroom practices in both countries; and most (but certainly not all) authors are Australian or New Zealand academicians. Many topics are area-specific, such as an Australian national evaluation of the effects of pharmacotherapies for opioid dependence on participants' criminal behavior, importance of ex-prisoner housing and associated social factors in their integration and possible recidivism in New South Wales and Victoria, or prisoner rehabilitation policy and practice in Queensland. But the concepts, theories, and methodologies have wider application, and many articles make no mention of geography. The journal also publishes occasional special issues focused on specific issues or related topics, such as a recent one focusing on developmental pathways to criminal behaviour. The journal is aimed at university-affiliated readers and criminal justice professionals and policymakers. It would be useful in any international or comparative criminology collection and anywhere there is interest in Australia or New Zealand. The publisher's web site provides free access to tables of contents and article abstracts back to 2002 and pdf articles via subscription or individual article purchases.

1515. *The British Journal of Criminology: an international review of crime and society.* Formerly (until 1960): *British Journal of Delinquency.* [ISSN: 0007-0955] 1950. bi-m. EUR 449 print or online ed. (Individuals, EUR 99 print & online eds.). Ed(s): Pat Carlen. Oxford University Press, Great Clarendon St, Oxford, OX2 6DP, United Kingdom; jnl.orders@ oup.co.uk; http://www.oxfordjournals.org. Illus., adv. Refereed. Circ: 2000. Vol. ends: Oct. Online: Chadwyck-Healey Inc.; EBSCO Publishing, EBSCO Host; Florida Center for Library Automation; Gale; William S. Hein & Co., Inc.; HighWire Press; IngentaConnect; Northern Light Technology, Inc.; OCLC Online Computer Library Center, Inc.; OhioLINK; Oxford Journals; ProQuest LLC (Ann Arbor); RMIT Publishing; SwetsWise Online Content; H.W. Wilson. Reprint: PSC; WSH. *Indexed:* ASSIA, AgeL, BrEdI, CJA, CJPI, CLI, IBR, IBSS, ILP, IMFL, LRI, PAIS, PSA, PsycInfo, RiskAb, SSA, SSCI, SWA, SociolAb, V&AA. *Bk. rev.:* 8-10, signed. *Aud.:* Ac, Sa.

In January 2007, editor Pat Carlen announced the addition of a subtitle to the *British Journal of Criminology: An International Review of Crime and Society* to reflect the "increasingly international nature of its contents." And in fact, a perusal of recent contents reveals papers submitted by academicians and researchers in a variety of fields from the United Kingdom, West Indies, United States, Australia, and elsewhere around the globe. Each issue of the journal presents 8–12 lengthy, well-documented articles examining all aspects of crime and society, especially those written from sociological, philosophical, geographical, psychological, cultural, political, or policy perspectives. In addition, each issue includes eight to ten in-depth book reviews with emphasis on British publications. The occasional special issue presents articles that revolve around a common theme such as "Risk and Crime" or "Regulating the Moral Economy." Other recent topics include the fear of crime, crime in Iraq, and a prisoner mutiny at Dartmoor in the 1930s. This journal's multidisciplinary approach makes it important for academic social science collections as well as crime and delinquency collections. It is valuable for research in criminology, probation, and social work, criminal justice, and penology. Free indexing back to 1960 is available online from *BJC*'s web site (http://bjc.oxfordjournals.org) along with free abstracts (1985 to present). The "Advance Access" feature on the web site provides abstracts for upcoming articles. A sample issue may be requested and accessed online. This highly ranked, quality journal published by

Oxford University Press for the Centre for Crime and Justice Studies should be a top choice for collections lacking international coverage in this field.

1516. *Campus Law Enforcement Journal: professional publication for campus law enforcement administrators, campus safety, security adm.* [ISSN: 0739-0394] 1970. bi-m. USD 30 in North America; USD 35 foreign. Ed(s): Karen E Breseman, Peter J Berry. International Association of Campus Law Enforcement Administrators, 342 N Main St, West Hartford, CT 06117-2507; kbreseman@iaclea.org; http://www.iaclea.org. Illus., adv. Sample. Circ: 1700. Vol. ends: Nov/Dec. Microform: PQC. *Indexed:* CJPI. *Aud.:* Ac, Sa.

CLEJ is a publication of the International Association of Campus Law Enforcement Administrators (IACLEA). In today's world, college and university officials must take a proactive and professional approach to crime prevention and public safety on their campuses. IACLEA works to advance public safety for higher-education institutions by providing educational resources, advocacy, and professional development opportunities. The organization believes that campus law enforcement officers should have sufficient expertise to investigate allegations of criminal wrongdoing, make arrests, and make referrals to the local criminal justice system as appropriate. It has more than 1,000 institutional members, i.e., colleges and universities in 20 countries, and about 1,600 individual members. The individual members include campus law enforcement staff, criminal justice faculty, municipal chiefs of police, and individuals from private companies or organizations offering products and services relevant to campus law enforcement. *Campus Law Enforcement Journal* serves as the voice of the campus law enforcement and security community and as a forum for the study of new ideas, trends in law enforcement, and relevant legislation. It seeks to promote professional ideals and standards of practice among law-enforcement personnel at institutions of higher education. Its in-depth articles may deal with all aspects of campus security, public safety, and law enforcement with a primary emphasis on the promotion of professional ideals and standards for law enforcement in the higher-education environment. *CLEJ*'s target audience includes IACLEA members and others interested in campus public safety issues. Practitioners write most articles with an emphasis on practical information and program reviews. It is an attractively packaged, professional magazine with many photographs, relevant advertising, and some organizational news. The IACLEA web site provides additional information about *CLEJ* including article submission guidelines, subscription information, and advertising rates.

1517. *Canadian Journal of Criminology and Criminal Justice.* Former titles (until 2003, vol.45): *Canadian Journal of Criminology;* (until vol.19): *Canadian Journal of Criminology and Corrections;* (until vol.13): *Canadian Journal of Corrections.* [ISSN: 1707-7753] 1958. q. CND 125 domestic; USD 125 United States; USD 145 elsewhere. Ed(s): M Peter Carrington. Canadian Criminal Justice Association, 1750, Courtwood Crescent, Ste 308, Ottawa, ON K2C 2B5, Canada; ccja@bellnet.ca; http://www.ccja-acjp.ca. Illus., index, adv. Sample. Refereed. Circ: 1300. Vol. ends: Oct. Microform: PQC. Online: EBSCO Publishing, EBSCO Host; Florida Center for Library Automation; Gale; Northern Light Technology, Inc.; OCLC Online Computer Library Center, Inc.; ProQuest LLC (Ann Arbor). *Indexed:* ASSIA, AmH&L, CBCARef, CJA, CJPI, CLI, CPerI, EAA, HRA, HistAb, IBSS, LRI, PRA, PdeR, PsycInfo, RiskAb, SFSA, SSA, SSCI, SUSA, SWR&A, SociolAb, V&AA. *Bk. rev.:* 5-8, 500-1,000 words, signed. *Aud.:* Ac, Sa.

As stated on the Canadian Criminal Justice Association's web site, this publication will appeal to "justice administrators, researchers and practitioners, academics, and to anyone wishing to keep abreast of recent criminological findings and opinions." The organization exists to promote informed debate and discussion regarding a more humane, equitable, and effective justice system. Until 1970, the *Canadian Journal of Criminology*'s focus was on corrections. Since then, it has broadened its focus to become an interdisciplinary journal containing articles based on research and experimentation and covering all aspects of criminology and criminal justice. Title changes over the years have reflected this shift. Although most articles are relevant to any geographical area, preference is given to papers with Canadian content or that are related to Canadian institutions, projects, or practices. Most articles are in English (with French and English abstracts), a few are in French; all are well documented. Some issues of *CJC* include invited commentaries on articles published in the journal. In addition, commentaries on other matters of interest and lists of coming events may also appear. Book reviews are listed in the print journal, but appear in full only on the journal's two (French and English) web sites. Recent special thematic issues have addressed critical criminology and crime and the media. The web site (www.ccja-acjp.ca/en/cjc.html) provides tables of contents for *CJC* from 1997 to the present.

1518. *Corrections Compendium: the national journal for corrections.* [ISSN: 0738-8144] 1976. bi-m. USD 75. Ed(s): Susan L. Clayton. American Correctional Association, 206 N Washington St, Ste 200, Alexandria, VA 22314; gdaley@aca.org; http://www.aca.org. Illus., adv. Sample. Circ: 500 Paid and controlled. Vol. ends: Dec. *Indexed:* CJA, CJPI. *Aud.:* Ga, Ac, Sa.

The American Correctional Association is a multi-disciplinary organization of more than 20,000 members from all facets of corrections and criminal justice, including federal, state, and military correctional facilities and prisons, county jails and detention centers, probation/parole agencies, and community corrections/halfway houses. The membership believes in the following principles as they relate to corrections: humanity, justice, protection, opportunity, knowledge, competence and accountability. *Corrections Compendium* is the organization's peer-reviewed, researched-based journal. Each bimonthly issue is packed with fascinating and useful information covering potentially any aspect of corrections. Feature articles and brief articles present research findings and trends, examine events in corrections and criminal justice, and often present information derived from statistical data. The author guidelines state that the journal publishes primarily articles that are research-based and scholarly. In addition, all articles should help readers better understand their profession and the critical issues they face. Therefore, each article must have at least one author who is a corrections practitioner employed by a public agency or nonprofit organization, or currently working in an adult/juvenile institutional or academic setting. State and national corrections news, including legal case reports and commentary, are also published, and international profiles examine corrections and criminal justice agencies around the world. A unique aspect of this publication is that each issue publishes statistical data or other information related to specific corrections concerns from a national survey of correctional systems. These surveys are especially useful to policymakers and analysts, corrections administrators, legislators at all levels, faculty and students of criminal justice, and business professionals involved with corrections. The surveys cover U.S. state and federal correctional facilities as well as Canadian correctional systems (52 U.S. and six Canadian correctional systems). The 2007 surveys address prison construction and renovation, re-entry, hiring requirements and wages of correctional officers, background investigations and search procedures for correctional officers, health care, and budgets. The 2006 survey topics were juveniles, foreign inmates, staff recruitment/work force issues, violence in prisons, health care and communicable diseases, and budgets. The data presented in these surveys make this publication desirable in almost any library where social problems are of interest, and its low subscription price is a bargain. More information about *Corrections Compendium* is available on the American Correctional Association web site.

1519. *Corrections Today.* Former titles (until 1979): *American Journal of Correction;* (until 1954): *Prison World;* (until 1941): *Jail Association Journal.* [ISSN: 0190-2563] 1939. 6x/yr. USD 25 Free to members. Ed(s): Susan Clayton. American Correctional Association, 206 N Washington St, Ste 200, Alexandria, VA 22314; gdaley@aca.org; http://www.aca.org. Illus., index, adv. Sample. Circ: 16500 Controlled. Vol. ends: Dec. Microform: MIM; PQC. Online: EBSCO Publishing, EBSCO Host; Factiva, Inc.; Florida Center for Library Automation; Gale; Northern Light Technology, Inc.; OCLC Online Computer Library Center, Inc.; ProQuest LLC (Ann Arbor); H.W. Wilson. Reprint: PSC. *Indexed:* ABS&EES, CJA, CJPI, PAIS. *Bk. rev.:* 1, 300-500 words, signed. *Aud.:* Ga, Ac, Sa.

This official publication of the American Correctional Association (ACA) provides a forum for the discussion of issues related to the advancement of corrections. Its scope is extremely broad and includes topics from administration and management to community programs, minorities, history and philosophy, probation and parole, correctional industries, volunteer organizations, high-profile inmates, and others. Each issue contains several feature articles on a central theme (e.g., female offenders, inmate re-entry, or the future of the work force). The magazine provides a forum for reader opinions and on-the-job experiences in two regular columns: "Speak Out" and "A View from the Line." Other departments cover industry news, job announcements, conferences and events, book reviews, legislative issues, and research notes. Most articles are short, lightly documented, focused on the practical, and written by corrections professionals or practitioners. An annual buyers' guide of correctional products and services is published in the July issue and is searchable online. *Corrections Today* is not intended for in-depth research, but the clearly written articles and the broad spectrum of its contents—along with its glossy magazine format and numerous photographs—make it appealing to a large audience. The ACA web site provides full-text access to sample articles from each issue of *Corrections Today* dating back to 2003. The low-cost subscription includes *On the Line*, a bimonthly newsletter from ACA.

1520. *Crime & Delinquency.* Formerly (until 1960): *National Probation and Parole Association Journal.* [ISSN: 0011-1287] 1955. q. GBP 511. Ed(s): Elizabeth Piper Deschenes. Sage Publications, Inc., 2455 Teller Rd, Thousand Oaks, CA 91320; info@sagepub.com; http://www.sagepub.com. Illus., index, adv. Sample. Refereed. Circ: 1400 Paid. Vol. ends: Oct. Microform: WSH; PMC. Online: CSA; EBSCO Publishing, EBSCO Host; Florida Center for Library Automation; Gale; HighWire Press; OCLC Online Computer Library Center, Inc.; OhioLINK; SAGE Publications, Inc., SAGE Journals Online; SwetsWise Online Content. Reprint: PSC. *Indexed:* ABS&EES, ASSIA, AgeL, CJA, CJPI, CLI, ExcerpMed, IBSS, ILP, IMFL, LRI, PAIS, PRA, PsycInfo, RI-1, RILM, RiskAb, SFSA, SSA, SSCI, SUSA, SociolAb, V&AA. *Aud.:* Ac, Sa.

Sage publishes *Crime & Delinquency* in cooperation with the National Council on Crime and Delinquency (NCCD), the oldest criminal justice research organization in America. NCCD believes, "Crime control policies must be based on data and best practices, not political rhetoric. The crime rate in the U.S. is intolerably high and will remain so under current criminal justice, economic, educational, and social welfare policies. The correctional system can only have a limited impact on crime rates. Our prisons must be used sparingly for those offenders who are a threat to public safety and cannot be safely managed in the community." *Crime & Delinquency* is policy oriented and presents literate, well-documented articles on all aspects of crime and the administration of justice, including etiology, prevention, corrections, and rehabilitation. It is intended for professionals with direct involvement in the criminal justice field, including policymakers, scholars, administrators, and researchers. Its articles address policy or program implications; social, political, or economic implications; the victim and the offender; and the criminal justice response including the use of sanctions. Both quantitative and qualitative articles are published, but all articles must be presented in a manner that is understandable to practitioners. Both adult and juvenile offenses are discussed. A multidisciplinary view of crime is presented, with an emphasis on society's interrelationships with and responses to its crime problems. Most authors are academics, usually from the fields of criminal justice, sociology, public and policy studies, and social services. Recent topics include inmate-on-inmate victimization among older male prisoners, a multidimensional examination of campus safety, the effect of divorce on domestic crime, old criminal records and predictions of future criminal involvement, the link between age and criminal history in sentencing, long-run trends in incarceration of drug offenders in the United States, and preventing parolees from returning to prison through community-based reintegration. *Crime & Delinquency* occasionally publishes guest-edited special issues, which focus on topics of pressing social concern. More information about this journal is available at the NCCD and Sage web sites. Sage provides free tables of contents with abstracts and subscription full-text pdf access to this journal back to 1955. *Crime & Delinquency* was ranked sixth in criminal justice and criminology journals prestige studies by Sorensen et al. in 2006 and Williams et al. in 1995. This scholarly publication should not be limited to criminal justice collections. It is valuable to policymakers, administrators, and scholars in most social sciences disciplines.

1521. *Crime, Law and Social Change: an interdisciplinary journal.* Formerly: *Contemporary Crises;* Incorporates (1986-1992): *Corruption and Reform.* [ISSN: 0925-4994] 1977. 8x/yr. EUR 1152 print & online eds. Ed(s): Nikos Passas, Peter K Manning. Springer Netherlands, Van

Godewijckstraat 30, Dordrecht, 3311 GX, Netherlands; http://www.springeronline.com. Illus., adv. Sample. Refereed. Microform: PQC. Online: Chadwyck-Healey Inc.; EBSCO Publishing, EBSCO Host; Gale; IngentaConnect; OCLC Online Computer Library Center, Inc.; OhioLINK; Ovid Technologies, Inc.; ProQuest LLC (Ann Arbor); Springer LINK; SwetsWise Online Content. Reprint: PSC. *Indexed:* ABCPolSci, ABIn, AmH&L, ArtHuCI, BAS, CJA, CJPI, FR, HistAb, IBR, IBSS, IBZ, IPSA, LeftInd, PAIS, PSA, RiskAb, SSA, SSCI, SociolAb. *Aud.:* Ac, Sa.

Crime, Law and Social Change publishes essays and reviews of the political economy of organized crime from transnational to local levels anywhere in the world. In the critical, leftist tradition, the journal addresses financial crime, political corruption, environmental crime, and the exploitation of developing nations. The journal is a forum for scholars in criminology, sociology, anthropology, history, law, and political science. Its international coverage of human rights and social problems makes it useful to a broad social science audience. Unfortunately, the subscription price is quite high, but libraries considering this title should also examine *Critical Criminology* (below in this section). More information about *Crime, Law and Social Change*, including tables of contents back to volume 1, can be found at the Springer web site.

1522. *Criminal Justice & Behavior.* Supersedes: *Correctional Psychologist.* [ISSN: 0093-8548] 1973. bi-m. GBP 470. Ed(s): Dr. Curt R Bartol. Sage Publications, Inc., 2455 Teller Rd, Thousand Oaks, CA 91320; info@sagepub.com; http://www.sagepub.com. Illus., index, adv. Refereed. Circ: 1247 Paid. Vol. ends: Dec. Microform: WSH; PMC; PQC. Online: CSA; EBSCO Publishing, EBSCO Host; Florida Center for Library Automation; Gale; HighWire Press; OCLC Online Computer Library Center, Inc.; OhioLINK; SAGE Publications, Inc., SAGE Journals Online; SwetsWise Online Content. Reprint: PSC. *Indexed:* ASSIA, AgeL, BRI, CBRI, CJA, CJPI, CLI, CommAb, ExcerpMed, HRA, LRI, PAIS, PRA, PsycInfo, RiskAb, SFSA, SSA, SSCI, SUSA, SociolAb, V&AA. *Aud.:* Ac, Sa.

Criminal Justice and Behavior: An International Journal is the "Official Publication of the American Association for Correctional and Forensic Psychology" (AACFP). The AACFP's behavioral scientists and practitioners encourage the delivery of high-quality mental health services to criminal offenders, and they promote and disseminate research on the etiology, assessment, and treatment of criminal behavior. *Criminal Justice and Behavior* is an excellent scholarly journal that examines the interface between the behavioral sciences and the criminal justice system. It provides research to support the development of successful services and programs in assessment, offender classification, crime prevention, intervention, and treatment. Although the journal emphasizes correctional psychology, topics may include etiology of crime, the processes of law violation, victimology, deterrence, the psychology of policing, and other concerns. Indeed, any behavioral aspect of criminal justice could be included. Although original empirical research is emphasized, theoretical and integrative review articles, analyses of innovative programs and practices, and commentaries may also be included. In 2007 the journal began publishing monthly, and each issue now contains eight well-documented articles written mostly by academicians. Recent article topics include treatment progress and therapeutic outcomes among adolescents with psychopathic features, physical violence inside prisons, religiosity and desistance from drug use, inmate emotion coping and psychological and physical well-being, psychopathy and the perception of affect and vulnerability, taking stock of criminal profiling, and managing occupational stress of correctional officers. More information about this journal is available at the AACFP and Sage web sites. Sage provides free tables of contents with abstracts and subscription full-text pdf access to this journal back to 1982. *Criminal Justice and Behavior* was ranked tenth in the criminal justice and criminology journals prestige study by Sorensen et al. in 2006 and 11th in the study by Williams et al. in 1995. This is a fine addition to any criminal justice or corrections collection and is potentially useful to any behavioral scientist or criminal justice practitioner.

1523. *Criminal Justice Ethics.* [ISSN: 0731-129X] 1982. s-a. USD 12.50 student & senior citizen members (Institutional members, USD 50; Individual members, USD 15). Ed(s): William Heffernan, John Kleinig. Institute for Criminal Justice Ethics, John Jay College / CUNY, 555 West 57th St, Ste 607, New York, NY 10019-1029; cjethics@jjay.cuny.edu;

http://www.lib.jjay.cuny.edu. Illus. Sample. Refereed. Circ: 1200 Paid. Vol. ends: Summer/Fall. Microform: PQC. Online: Chadwyck-Healey Inc.; EBSCO Publishing, EBSCO Host; Factiva, Inc.; Florida Center for Library Automation; Gale; Northern Light Technology, Inc.; OCLC Online Computer Library Center, Inc.; ProQuest K-12 Learning Solutions; ProQuest LLC (Ann Arbor); H.W. Wilson. *Indexed:* CJA, CJPI, CLI, IBZ, LRI, PhilInd, RI-1. *Bk. rev.:* 1-2, review essays. *Aud.:* Ac, Sa.

The Institute for Criminal Justice Ethics at John Jay College of Criminal Justice publishes this scholarly publication to meet a widespread interest in the moral choices faced by those in the criminal justice system. Intended for philosophers and scholars, criminal justice professionals, lawyers, judges, and the general public, each issue contains a regularly featured "Commentary" and two or three thought-provoking, documented feature articles. *Criminal Justice Ethics* serves as a forum for diverse viewpoints. Articles focusing on the same general topic, such as police gratuities or reintegration, are sometimes presented together as an an "Exchange" or "Symposium." "In the Literature" contains review essays covering recent literature of importance. This journal belongs in all academic collections and anywhere there is a serious examination of "our concern for the proper treatment of those accused of wrongdoing." Sample articles and indexing are available from the journal's web site.

1524. Criminal Justice Policy Review. [ISSN: 0887-4034] 1986. q. GBP 463. Ed(s): David L Myers. Sage Publications, Inc., 2455 Teller Rd, Thousand Oaks, CA 91320; info@sagepub.com; http://www.sagepub.com. Adv. Refereed. Online: CSA; EBSCO Publishing, EBSCO Host; HighWire Press; OCLC Online Computer Library Center, Inc.; OhioLINK; SAGE Publications, Inc., SAGE Journals Online; SwetsWise Online Content. Reprint: PSC. *Indexed:* CJA, CJPI, PSA, RiskAb, SSA, SociolAb, V&AA. *Bk. rev.:* Number and length vary. *Aud.:* Ac, Sa.

Criminal Justice Policy Review, now in its 18th volume, is published by Sage in association with the Department of Criminology at Indiana University of Pennsylvania, where the editor, David L. Meyers, is an Associate Professor and Graduate Director of Criminology. The journal is multidisciplinary and publishes scholarly articles using diverse methodologies, both experimental and nonexperimental, to address criminal justice policy issues. In addition, *CJPR* publishes essays, research notes, interviews, and book reviews to provide more eclectic and accessible material of interest to practitioners and students as well as academics. Special features may present commentaries, transcripts of significant panels or meetings, position papers, and legislative information. The editor advised that the journal is aimed at criminal justice researchers, policymakers, and practitioners. In the latest four issues of the journal, university researchers authored, or coauthored with other criminal justice professionals, 92.6 percent of the articles, and 7.4 percent of the articles were written solely by other criminal justice professionals. Recent topics include system reform and wrongful conviction; a criminal justice policy approach to budgets, institutions, and change; parenting programs for incarcerated parents; the efficacy of victim services programs; contextualizing the criminal justice policymaking process; and moral justifications on the Rehnquist court. *CJPR* provides a useful forum for criminal justice policy–oriented information. More information about this journal is available on the Sage web site. The electronic version is available from Sage.

1525. Criminal Justice Review. [ISSN: 0734-0168] 1976. 3x/yr. GBP 147. Ed(s): Richard Terrill. Sage Publications, Inc., 2455 Teller Rd, Thousand Oaks, CA 91320; info@sagepub.com; http://www.sagepub.com. Adv. Refereed. Circ: 1200. Microform: PQC. Online: CSA; EBSCO Publishing, EBSCO Host; William S. Hein & Co., Inc.; HighWire Press; OCLC Online Computer Library Center, Inc.; SAGE Publications, Inc., SAGE Journals Online; SwetsWise Online Content; H.W. Wilson. Reprint: PSC; WSH. *Indexed:* CJA, CJPI, CLI, ILP, PAIS, PSA, PsycInfo, RiskAb, SFSA, SSA, SSCI, SUSA, SociolAb, V&AA. *Bk. rev.:* 1-2 review essays, 15-20, 700-1,000 word, signed reviews. *Aud.:* Ac, Sa.

Since 2005, *Criminal Justice Review* has been published by Sage in association with Georgia State University College of Health and Human Sciences. Previously it had been published by Georgia State University since 1976. Editorial control remains at Georgia State University, where Richard J. Terrill was reinstated as editor in 2006. Dr. Terrill, Professor of Criminal Justice, had previously served as the editor during 1987–1992 and 1997–2000. *Criminal Justice Review* is a peer-reviewed journal that addresses a broad spectrum of criminal justice topics. Potentially any aspect of crime or the justice system may be covered in three to five articles in each issue. Local, state, and national concerns may be addressed using either quantitative or qualitative methods. Articles, research notes, commentaries, and comprehensive essays that focus on crime and broadly defined justice-related topics are encouraged. Each issue of *CJR* publishes 15–20, 700–1,000 word, signed book reviews, and a fair number of issues include book review essays that may reach more than 3,000 words. The journal also includes essays on recent legal decisions focusing on specific criminal justice concerns and more general wrap-up pieces covering such topics as the recent decisions of the U.S. Supreme Court. Recent articles address development of neighborhood-restorative community justice, communication policy changes in state adult correctional facilities, the decision to incarcerate in juvenile and criminal courts, urban police use of force, and an examination of the degree to which sex offenders kill. This journal complements *International Criminal Justice Review* (below in this section), which shares the same editor and publisher. Sage provides free tables of contents with abstracts and subscription pdf access to the contents of this journal back to 1976.

1526. Criminal Justice Studies: a critical journal of crime, law and society. Formerly: *The Justice Professional.* [ISSN: 1478-601X] 1986. q. GBP 214 print & online eds. Ed(s): Roslyn Muraskin. Routledge, 325 Chestnut St, Ste 800, Philadelphia, PA 19106; journals@routledge.com; http://www.tandf.co.uk/journals. Refereed. Reprint: PSC. *Indexed:* CJA, IBSS, PAIS, PSA, PsycInfo, SSA, SociolAb. *Aud.:* Ac, Sa.

Previously published as *The Justice Professional*, this journal changed its title to *Criminal Justice Studies* in 2003 to reflect its broader focus on quantifiable and qualitative research in criminal justice. The editorial board invites papers on all substantive criminal justice concerns, but it also welcomes articles outside the field that are relevant to criminal justice, including those that cover public administration, public policy, and public affairs issues. Preference is given to academic authors and researchers in the field, although articles from professionals are also considered. In addition, *Criminal Justice Studies* publishes literature reviews, research notes and summary reports of innovative research projects. One special issue is planned each year covering topics such as capital punishment, minorities, and Latinos. The Taylor & Francis web site provides tables of contents and article abstracts from 2002 to the present, a free e-mail contents alert service, a free online sample, and electronic access to the journal.

1527. Criminology: an interdisciplinary journal. Formerly: *Criminologica.* [ISSN: 0011-1384] 1963. q. USD 250 print & online eds. Ed(s): Denise Gottfredson. Blackwell Publishing, Inc., Commerce Place, 350 Main St, Malden, MA 02148; http://www.blackwellpublishing.com. Illus., index. Sample. Refereed. Circ: 4000. Vol. ends: Nov. Microform: PQC. Online: Blackwell Synergy; EBSCO Publishing, EBSCO Host; IngentaConnect; Northern Light Technology, Inc.; OCLC Online Computer Library Center, Inc.; ProQuest K-12 Learning Solutions; ProQuest LLC (Ann Arbor); SwetsWise Online Content. Reprint: PSC; WSH. *Indexed:* AgeL, CJA, CJPI, CLI, ExcerpMed, H&SSA, IBR, IBSS, IBZ, ILP, LRI, PAIS, PsycInfo, RiskAb, SSA, SSCI, SWR&A, SociolAb. *Aud.:* Ac, Sa.

Since 2005, *Criminology* has been published by Blackwell Publishing, but it is still "the Official Publication of the American Society of Criminology" (ASC). With this journal and *Criminology and Public Policy* (below in this section), the ASC tries to create a multidisciplinary forum that fosters the study and research of criminology. This scholarly journal provides excellent, thoroughly documented articles examining crime and deviant behavior as described in many disciplines, including criminal justice, sociology, psychology, history, design, systems analysis, decision theory, law, and others. Each issue contains seven to nine articles, which usually reflect the journal's major emphasis of empirical research and scientific methodology. However, articles which review previously published literature, address theoretical issues, or suggest future criminological research needs, strategies, or methods may also be included. In addition, the journal publishes ASC presidential addresses and occasional commentary. Most authors are from criminal justice/criminology or sociology departments at academic institutions, but occasional contributions from professionals or practitioners in the criminal justice field are also included. Recent topics include the relationship between adolescent employment and antisocial behavior, neighborhood social control through direct intervention or calling the authorities, gender differences and the consequences of delinquent behavior for adulthood functioning and well-being, images of God and public support for capital punishment, and how citizens assess just punishment for police misconduct. The Blackwell and ASC web sites provide additional information about this journal, including tables of contents, article abstracts, and subject and author indexes back to 1963. Blackwell Synergy provides electronic full-text subscription access to this journal from 1963 to the present. This journal was ranked number one in criminal justice and criminology journals prestige studies by Sorensen et al. in 2006 and Williams et al. in 1995. It belongs in any higher-education environment where there is an interest in criminology or criminal justice.

1528. *Criminology and Public Policy.* [ISSN: 1538-6473] 2001. q. GBP 138. Ed(s): Todd R Clear. Blackwell Publishing, Inc., Commerce Place, 350 Main St, Malden, MA 02148; http://www.blackwellpublishing.com. Reprint: PSC; WSH. *Indexed:* CJA, CJPI, FR, RiskAb. *Aud.:* Ac, Sa.

Still a relatively young journal, *Criminology and Public Policy* began in 2001 as an official publication of the American Society of Criminology (ASC). This interdisciplinary journal is devoted to the study of criminal justice policy and practice. The editorial policy states that the journal attempts to "strengthen the role of research findings in the formulation of crime and justice policy by publishing empirically based, policy-focused articles." Its unique format introduces each topic with an editorial outlining the significant policy implications of one or more articles that follow. Some articles are followed by brief "Reaction Essays" by invited specialists. Recent topics include race and policing, public preference for rehabilitation, faith-based prison programs, and parental criminal justice involvement. The ASC web site provides subject and author indexes and abstracts for all articles published in the journal. This is a very interesting addition to the literature of criminology and criminal justice from ASC and a valuable complement to the society's other official publication, *Criminology* (above in this section). Even as a newcomer to the field, this journal has been rated among the top 15 most prestigious criminal justice and criminology journals published in the United States (Sorensen et al., 2006).

1529. *Critical Criminology: international journal.* Formerly: *Journal of Human Justice.* [ISSN: 1205-8629] 1989. 3x/yr. EUR 385 print & online eds. Ed(s): Barbara Sims. Springer Netherlands, Van Godewijckstraat 30, Dordrecht, 3311 GX, Netherlands; http://www.springeronline.com. Adv. Refereed. Circ: 300. Online: EBSCO Publishing, EBSCO Host; Gale; IngentaConnect; OCLC Online Computer Library Center, Inc.; OhioLINK; Springer LINK; SwetsWise Online Content. Reprint: PSC. *Indexed:* CBCARef, CJA. *Bk. rev.:* 2, 1,500-2,500 words, signed. *Aud.:* Ac, Sa.

Both the American Society of Criminology (ASC) and the Academy of Criminal Justice Sciences have a section on critical criminology. In fact, both these organizations share a web site (www.critcrim.org) to address this important paradigm in criminology. They strive to foster research and theory development in the field, provide a forum for discussion and exchange of information, and enhance teaching methods and development of curricula on critical criminology. Now in its 18th year of publication, *Critical Criminology* is the official journal of ASC's Division of Critical Criminology. It is aimed at academics and researchers interested in social, political, and economic justice. Anarchistic, cultural, feminist, integrative, Marxist, peace-making, postmodernist, and left-realist criminological issues are addressed. The journal broadens the definition of crime to include such issues as social harm and social justice, including problems related to class, gender, race/ethnicity, and heterosexism. Alternative methodologies and theories such as chaos theory, nonlinear analysis, and complex systems science are applied to the study of crime and criminal justice in the pages of this journal. The journal is international, and the new editor is Shahid Alvi, University of Ontario, Canada. In addition, Mark Israel, Flinders University, Adelaide, Australia, is editor for the Pacific Rim, Joanna S. Goodey, Vienna International Centre, Austria, is the European editor, and many other countries are represented on the editorial board. Recent topics include an exploration of how gender is treated in mainstream criminology journals and the implications this has for feminist criminology, the role of trauma and disrupted attachments in the development of adolescent girls' violent behavior, Latinos/as in the criminal and juvenile justice systems, safety crimes (criminal liability for managerial failure to prevent harm to employees) in post-communist European Union states, under-enforcement and

over-enforcement of the law with respect to Native American communities, and a critical examination of the digital music sharing phenomenon. A recent special issue presents six articles focusing on ethnic profiling, and the editor advises that he is planning to publish one special issue of the journal each year to allow more exhaustive analysis of important topics. Most issues contain four or five articles and two lengthy book reviews or review essays. This journal complements *Crime, Law and Social Change* (above in this section). More information about *Critical Criminology* can be found on the Springer web site. Springer also provides subscription pdf access to the contents of this journal.

1530. *European Journal of Criminology.* [ISSN: 1477-3708] 2004. q. GBP 346. Ed(s): David J Smith. Sage Publications Ltd., 1 Oliver's Yard, 55 City Rd, London, EC1 1SP, United Kingdom; info@sagepub.co.uk; http://www.sagepub.co.uk. Adv. Refereed. Reprint: PSC. *Indexed:* CJA, PRA, RiskAb, SociolAb, V&AA. *Aud.:* Ac, Sa.

There has been an intense growth of criminology in Europe presumably due to the rising profile of crime control, criminal justice, security, and human rights concerns because of terrorist activities. In addition, the transnational nature of crime has created a need to exchange information and to work towards common standards, and cooperation. Therefore, the European Society of Criminology, which was founded in 2000 by criminologists from wider Europe (within the E.U. and beyond), partnered with Sage to begin publication of *European Journal of Criminology* in 2004. This refereed journal provides a forum for research and scholarship on crime and criminal justice institutions with an emphasis on articles that are relevant to wider Europe. It helps the ESC provide an English-language forum for discussions between criminologists from many different linguistic groups. *EJC* publishes discussions of theory, analyses of quantitative data, comparative studies, systematic evaluations of interventions, studies of criminal justice institutions, and analyses of policy. Most issues of this journal present four or five articles including a country survey, which describes the criminal justice system, reviews trends in crime and punishment, and discusses major publications in recent years in a specific country. The current editor is at the University of Oxford, and most European countries and the United States are represented on the editorial and/or international advisory boards. Recent articles address crime dynamics at Lithuanian borders, parenting and family characteristics and delinquency of male young adults, group sex offending by juveniles, a comparison of social equality and perceptions of insecurity in two European countries, and assessing the regulation of private security across Europe. Although this journal emphasizes material related to Europe, most of the concepts and theories covered in its articles are certainly of interest to researchers in other locations. It presents a very informative and interesting look at criminological study and research in Europe, and it would be useful anywhere European society or social problems are of interest or anywhere international or comparative criminology is of interest. More information about this journal is available on the Sage web site, and Sage provides free tables of contents with abstracts and subscription pdf access to the content of this journal back to its inception in 2004.

1531. *F B I Law Enforcement Bulletin.* [ISSN: 0014-5688] 1932. m. USD 36 domestic; USD 45 foreign. Ed(s): John E Ott. U.S. Federal Bureau of Investigation, 935 Pennsylvania Ave NW, Ste 7350, Washington, DC 20535; http://www.fbi.gov. Illus., index. Sample. Circ: 43000. Vol. ends: Dec. Microform: MIM; PQC. Online: EBSCO Publishing, EBSCO Host; Florida Center for Library Automation; Gale; OCLC Online Computer Library Center, Inc.; ProQuest K-12 Learning Solutions; ProQuest LLC (Ann Arbor); H.W. Wilson. *Indexed:* AgeL, CJA, CJPI, ExcerpMed, IUSGP, PAIS. *Bk. rev.:* Occasional, 400-500 words. *Aud.:* Ga, Ac, Sa.

The Federal Bureau of Investigation publishes this informative and attractively packaged 35-page bulletin primarily for law enforcement professionals. Each issue contains three or four feature articles on either operations or management issues, such as current police techniques, crime problems, personnel, and management techniques and problems, equipment, and training. The articles are well written by law enforcement professionals and most are footnoted. The attractive format, use of photographs, and choice of topics make it similar to *Law and Order* (below in this section), but the lack of advertising in the *Bulletin* and its use of footnoting make it a slightly more scholarly publication. The *Bulletin* is very suitable for an academic environment, although laypersons will also be interested in much of the content. Recent articles cover such topics as use of intelligence for airport security, human trafficking operations, working with the media during a crisis, license plate recognition technology, and Fourth Amendment boundaries for law officers. There are numerous recurring departments including "VICAP Alert," which allows the FBI's Violent Criminal Apprehension Program to ask other law enforcement agencies to review their case files for information that may be helpful on specific cases; "Bulletin Reports," which briefly describes selected criminal justice studies, reports, and project findings; "Perspective," which allows law enforcement professionals to address ethical, legal, or management issues or suggest improvement methods; "Crime Data," which presents statistical data; "Police Practices," which describes methods and procedures used by police departments around the country to address specific problems; "Leadership Spotlight," which provides brief essays on professional behavior written by faculty members of the FBI Academy's Leadership Development Institute; and "The Bulletin Notes," which recognizes officers who rescue citizens or make arrests at unusual risk to the officer's safety. This title is appropriate anywhere there is interest in criminal justice or law enforcement. Taxpayers fund its publication, and the FBI web site provides free access to the full text of the *Bulletin* from 1996 to the present. Paper subscriptions are also available for a modest price.

1532. *Federal Probation: a journal of correctional philosophy and practice.* Formerly (until 1937): *U.S. Probation System. News Letter.* [ISSN: 0014-9128] 1937. 3x/yr. USD 16.50 domestic; USD 22.40 foreign. Ed(s): Ellen Wilson Fielding. Administrative Office of the United States Courts, Federal Corrections and Supervision Division, 1 Columbus Circle, NE, Washington, DC 20544. Illus., index. Sample. Circ: 6500. Vol. ends: Dec. Microform: MIM; PQC. Online: EBSCO Publishing, EBSCO Host; William S. Hein & Co., Inc.; Northern Light Technology, Inc.; OCLC Online Computer Library Center, Inc.; ProQuest LLC (Ann Arbor); H.W. Wilson. Reprint: WSH. *Indexed:* AgeL, BRI, CBRI, CJA, CJPI, CLI, ExcerpMed, IBR, ILP, IUSGP, LRI, PAIS, PsycInfo, SSCI, V&AA. *Bk. rev.:* 2-3, 900-1,500 words, signed. *Aud.:* Ga, Ac, Sa.

Published three times a year, in June, September, and December, each issue of *Federal Probation* contains eight to ten shorter, but well-documented, articles most of which are written by academics, although practitioners also publish here. Contributions comprise a mix of theoretical, philosophical, and research-based papers, but the editors encourage submissions "describing experience or significant findings regarding the prevention and control of delinquency and crime." The publication's main audience consists of criminal justice and corrections professionals, students, academicians, and social service professionals. The September special topic issues edited by guest editors focus on aspects of corrections or criminal justice such as risk assessment. Regular departments include "Juvenile Focus," a review of recent health and safety research about infants and children of all ages; "Reviews of Periodicals," which presents signed reviews of selected articles from various professional journals; and an excellent "Your Bookshelf on Review" section. Although not refereed, this is a quality journal that takes a scholarly approach. It is useful to anyone with a serious interest in probation and corrections. As with other U.S. government publications, the price is affordable for any library collection.

1533. *Homicide Studies: an interdisciplinary & international journal.* [ISSN: 1088-7679] 1997. q. GBP 361. Ed(s): Thomas Petee, Jay Corzine. Sage Publications, Inc., 2455 Teller Rd, Thousand Oaks, CA 91320; info@sagepub.com; http://www.sagepub.com. Illus., adv. Refereed. Reprint: PSC. *Indexed:* ASG, CJA, CJPI, H&SSA, IBR, IBZ, PRA, PSA, PsycInfo, RiskAb, SFSA, SSA, SSCI, SUSA, SociolAb, V&AA. *Bk. rev.:* Occasional, signed, 800-1,000 words. *Aud.:* Ac, Sa.

Homicide Studies is published in association with Homicide Research Working Group (HRWG), which was formed at the 1991 American Society of Criminology (ASC) meeting by homicide experts from public health, criminology, geography, medicine, political science, sociology, criminal justice, and a variety of other disciplines. This international group now includes hundreds of scholars and practitioners devoted to the study of homicide. The HRWG attempts to forge links between research, epidemiology, and practical programs to reduce levels of mortality from violence; promote improved data quality and the linking of diverse homicide data sources; foster collaborative, interdisciplinary research on lethal and nonlethal violence; encourage more efficient sharing of techniques for measuring and analyzing homicide; create and maintain a communication network among those collecting, maintaining, and analyzing

homicide datasets; and generate a stronger working relationship among homicide researchers. The journal *Homicide Studies* plays a major role in helping HRWG achieve those goals. It is a specialized, scholarly, multidisciplinary journal focusing on research, public policy, and applied knowledge related to homicide. It presents both qualitative and quantitative studies, along with occasional theoretical papers, research summaries, and public policy reviews. In addition, an occasional book review essay is published. All articles must focus on homicide, but other violent behaviors may be covered if a relationship between those behaviors and homicide is shown. Twenty-eight lengthy, well-documented articles, three short book reviews, and one book review essay of more then 7,500 words were published in the last eight journal issues. The following are examples of recent topics from the journal: the influence of cultural and structural variables on male serial homicide; using ground-penetrating radar to locate clandestine graves of homicide victims; the influence of social and economic disadvantage on racial patterns in youth homicide; patterns of homicide in East St. Louis; economic inequality, legitimacy, and cross-national homicide rates; exploring the difference between male and female intimate-partner homicides; and battered women who kill. More information about this fine specialized journal is available at the Sage and HRWG web sites. Sage provides free tables of contents with abstracts and subscription pdf access to the content of this journal back to its inception in 1997.

1534. *The Howard Journal of Criminal Justice.* Formerly (until Feb. 1984): *Howard Journal of Penology and Crime Prevention.* [ISSN: 0265-5527] 1941. 5x/yr. GBP 377 print & online eds. Ed(s): Tony Fowles, J Robert Lilly. Blackwell Publishing Ltd., 9600 Garsington Rd, Oxford, OX4 2ZG, United Kingdom; customerservices@ blackwellpublishing.com; http://www.blackwellpublishing.com. Illus. Sample. Refereed. Circ: 1700. Vol. ends: Nov. Microform: PQC. Online: Blackwell Synergy; EBSCO Publishing, EBSCO Host; Gale; IngentaConnect; OCLC Online Computer Library Center, Inc.; OhioLINK; SwetsWise Online Content. Reprint: PSC. *Indexed:* ASSIA, AmHI, ApEcolAb, BrHumI, CJA, CJPI, CLI, IBR, IBSS, IBZ, LRI, PAIS, PSA, PsycInfo, RiskAb, SSA, SociolAb. *Bk. rev.:* 5-8, 700-1,200 words. *Aud.:* Ac, Sa.

This journal is sponsored by the Howard League for Penal Reform, founded in 1866, the oldest penal reform organization in the United Kingdom. The league works independently of government funding to establish a more humane and effective penal system through research and publications on criminal justice policy and practice, hosted conferences and debates, and programs in schools and prisons. *The Howard Journal of Criminal Justice,* a long-standing social science journal, combines articles with comments and reviews, providing coverage of both the theory and practice of criminal justice and the study of crime and criminals. With few foreign contributions, the journal emphasizes research and analysis of the criminal justice system in the United Kingdom, although the recent addition of a co-editor from the United States may signal a broadening of its geographic scope. Most authors are from academic institutions, and they reflect the principal audience for the journal. However, policymakers and administrators in government departments and practitioners in the field also read the journal and often contribute material. The articles are of excellent quality, covering complex material, yet the writing style makes them uniquely accessible even to lay readers. The regular "Penal Policy File" column provides summaries of recent developments in penal policy in the United Kingdom. There are also review articles and an excellent book review section that emphasizes books published in the United Kingdom. Recent topics include Muslim converts in prison, penal policy transfer in the Ukraine, prison dining, and institutional racism. Tables of contents and abstracts from 1997 to the present may be found at the publisher's web site.

1535. *International Criminal Justice Review.* [ISSN: 1057-5677] 1991. q. GBP 147. Ed(s): Richard Terrill. Sage Publications, Inc., 2455 Teller Rd, Thousand Oaks, CA 91320; info@sagepub.com; http://www.sagepub.com. Adv. Refereed. Reprint: PSC; WSH. *Indexed:* CJA, CJPI, PAIS, SSA, SUSA, SociolAb. *Bk. rev.:* 15-20, 800-1,300 words, signed. *Aud.:* Ac, Sa.

International Criminal Justice Review has been published by Sage, in association with Georgia State University, since 2005. Previously it was created in 1991 and published by the Department of Criminal Justice at GSU until Sage acquired it. Editorial control remains at GSU, where Richard Terrill serves as editor of both *ICJR* and *Criminal Justice Review* (above in this section). The journal was published twice each year but switched to a quarterly publication schedule in 2007. It presents peer-reviewed, scholarly articles about trends and problems related to crime and justice throughout the world. Its interdisciplinary content emphasizes an international and/or comparative context, innovative and advanced research methodologies, and findings that are potentially useful to policymakers. Articles, research notes, commentaries, and comprehensive essays may focus on a single country or compare issues affecting two or more countries. Both qualitative and quantitative methodology pieces are published, and they may address either contemporary or historical topics. As in *Criminal Justice Review*, book reviews and review essays comprise an important part of this journal's content. Each issue presents two articles and 15–20 lengthy book reviews and an occasional review essay. Recent topics include a comparative view of the law of interrogation in England, Canada, France, Germany, Russia, and China; adult incarcerated drug offenders in Iran; a review essay on the global reach of organized crime; indigenous-run legal services in Australia and Canada; operational policing of domestic violence in Singapore; informal money transfer systems in South Asia and the Middle East; and an analysis of homicide victims, offenders, and events in Russia. This journal complements *Criminal Justice Review*. Sage provides free tables of contents with abstracts and subscription pdf access to the content of this journal back to 1991.

1536. ***International Journal of Offender Therapy and Comparative Criminology.*** Former titles (until 1972): *International Journal of Offender Therapy;* (until 1966): *Journal of Offender Therapy;* (until 1961): *Association for Psychiatric Treatment of Offenders. Journal.* [ISSN: 0306-624X] 1957. bi-m. GBP 423. Ed(s): George Palermo. Sage Publications, Inc., 2455 Teller Rd, Thousand Oaks, CA 91320; info@sagepub.com; http://www.sagepub.com. Illus., index, adv. Sample. Refereed. Circ: 650 Paid and free. Vol. ends: Winter. Microform: PQC. Online: CSA; EBSCO Publishing, EBSCO Host; HighWire Press; OCLC Online Computer Library Center, Inc.; OhioLINK; SAGE Publications, Inc., SAGE Journals Online; SwetsWise Online Content. Reprint: PSC. *Indexed:* ABS&EES, ASSIA, AgeL, CJA, CJPI, CLI, ExcerpMed, H&SSA, IBR, IBSS, IBZ, ILP, IMFL, LRI, PSA, PsycInfo, RiskAb, SFSA, SSA, SSCI, SUSA, SociolAb, V&AA. *Bk. rev.:* Occasional, 300-1,000 words, signed. *Aud.:* Ac, Sa.

For five decades *International Journal of Offender Therapy and Comparative Criminology* has provided an international forum for research and discussion of all variables associated with the treatment of offenders. This scholarly journal publishes both theoretical and clinical practice papers from the fields of corrections, criminal justice, criminology, law, psychiatry, psychology, social work, sociology, and related health sciences professions. The journal addresses psychological treatment aspects because serious psychological disorders are very common among prisoners and offenders. It recognizes the important effects that genetic/biological influences have on prisoners and offenders. It also recognizes that environment (or life history) is critical to understanding prisoners and offenders. *IJOTCC* promotes the use of all three types of variables, i.e., psychological, biological, and environmental, to develop treatment approaches that apply credible research to practice. Each issue usually presents an editorial with six to eight articles and occasional commentary. Recent editorials address personality disorders and criminal responsibility, a possible alternative therapy for childhood aggressivity, and DNA typing as a most useful forensic tool. Recent article topics include identifying subgroups at high risk of dropping out of domestic batterer treatment, definitions of and beliefs about wife abuse among undergraduate students of social work, public defenders in Israel's juvenile courts, family role in the reintegration process of recovering drug addicts, provincial laws on the protection of women in China, capital punishment views in China and the United States, rehabilitation and resettlement case management in Birmingham (United Kingdom), and the meaning of anger for Australian indigenous offenders. This journal is similar to, and complements, both *Criminal Justice and Behavior* (above in this section) and *Journal of Offender Rehabilitation* (below in this section), but it is perhaps more international. If possible, all three titles should be included in any collection where there is a scholarly interest in criminal psychology, rehabilitation, or corrections. More information about this journal is available at the Sage web site. Sage provides free tables of contents with abstracts and subscription pdf access to the content of this journal back to 1968.

1537. ***Jane's Police Review.*** [ISSN: 0309-1414] 1893. w. GBP 84; USD 255. Ed(s): Catriona Marchant. Jane's Information Group, Sentinel House, 163 Brighton Rd, Coulsdon, CR5 2YH, United Kingdom; info@janes.co.uk; http://www.janes.com. Illus., index, adv. Sample. Circ: 25000 Paid. *Indexed:* ASSIA, CLI, HRIS, ILP. *Aud.:* Ga, Ac, Sa.

A high-circulation trade magazine published for over 100 years, *Jane's Police Review* provides useful and interesting insights into law enforcement in the United Kingdom. It focuses on news and current affairs relevant to British police forces. The weekly issues typically include ten pages of news, news briefs, letters, and commentary, followed by three to five feature articles expounding the realities of law enforcement in the United Kingdom. Most are written by magazine staff or police practitioners. Regular departments cover questions of law and procedural matters, ethical dilemmas in police work, brief interviews with personalities in the news, and practice questions for promotion exams. The online version of *Police Review* is available from the publisher.

1538. ***Journal of Contemporary Criminal Justice.*** [ISSN: 1043-9862] 1978. q. GBP 290. Ed(s): Chris Eskridge. Sage Publications, Inc., 2455 Teller Rd, Thousand Oaks, CA 91320; info@sagepub.com; http://www.sagepub.com. Illus., adv. Sample. Refereed. Circ: 400 Paid. Vol. ends: Nov. Online: CSA; EBSCO Publishing, EBSCO Host; HighWire Press; OCLC Online Computer Library Center, Inc.; OhioLINK; SAGE Publications, Inc., SAGE Journals Online; SwetsWise Online Content. Reprint: PSC. *Indexed:* CJA, CJPI, IBR, IBZ, PRA, PSA, PsycInfo, RiskAb, SSA, SUSA, SociolAb, V&AA. *Aud.:* Ac, Sa.

When this journal was published at California State University–Long Beach, a theme-based format was developed that enabled each issue to present an in-depth exploration of a critical topic by devoting all articles to it. Sage has published *Journal of Contemporary Criminal Justice* since 1997, and fortunately they have maintained that unique theme-based format. Authoritative guest editors assemble four to six articles providing interdisciplinary, thorough coverage of the specified theme for each issue of the journal. Recent and upcoming themes include evidence-based practices for responding to victimization, gender-responsive approaches to the classification and treatment of women offenders, theory and practice of racial profiling, theory and practice of responding to terrorism, desistance from crime and deviant behavior, criminological perspectives on Latin America, methodological issues in conducting comparative research in criminology, and stress among correctional and police officers. The journal's interdisciplinary nature (including perspectives from economics, history, political science, psychology, sociology and other disciplines in addition to criminal justice/criminology) and its one-theme-per-issue format make it very useful for a scholarly or research audience. The current editor is at the University of Nebraska–Lincoln, where the journal's web site presents tables of contents with article abstracts and subject and author indexes back to 1987. In addition, the web site lists upcoming themes and guest editors. More information about this journal is available at the Sage web site. Sage provides free tables of contents with abstracts and subscription pdf access to the content of this journal back to 1978.

1539. ***Journal of Correctional Education.*** [ISSN: 0740-2708] 1949. q. USD 55 CEA individual membership; USD 95 CEA institutional membership; USD 35 CEA student membership. Ed(s): John J Dowdell, Russell L Craig. Ashland University, 401 College Ave, Ashland, OH 44805. Illus., index, adv. Sample. Refereed. Circ: 3300. Vol. ends: Dec. Microform: PQC. Online: EBSCO Publishing, EBSCO Host; OCLC Online Computer Library Center, Inc.; ProQuest LLC (Ann Arbor); H.W. Wilson. *Indexed:* CJA, CJPI, ERIC, EduInd. *Aud.:* Ac, Sa.

Since 1942, the Correctional Education Association, the largest affiliate of the American Correctional Association, has striven to enhance the effectiveness and skills of those who provide educational services in correctional settings. Its goals include providing an active and supportive network of leaders in the field of correctional education, providing technical assistance and advocacy to help increase the quality of correctional education programs and services, distributing timely and practical information to fellow staff members, and representing the collective interest of correctional education to the government, the press, and the public. *Journal of Correctional Education* addresses all aspects of correctional education and stresses the necessary interaction between disciplines and services to treat inmates. It emphasizes the publication of relevant research that will increase understanding and help shape policy and practice in correctional education. In addition, the journal's editorial staff recognizes the need to include practical information that will be immediately useful to those who teach in correctional settings. Therefore, both specific programs and broader theoretical treatments are included. Most of the articles include references and come from college and university researchers, but some come from librarians and instructors at correctional facilities. Most issues contain four or five articles and usually include a U.S. Department of Education update regarding recent programs and activities relevant to correctional education. Recent articles address effects of moderate physical activity on offenders in a rehabilitative program, evaluating the effectiveness of correctional education programs, employers of ex-offenders, education in rural county jails, narrative as a teaching strategy, and literacy-level English language learners in correctional education settings. Occasional special issues may focus on specific topics such as the June 2007 issue's coverage of international correctional education issues. This specialized journal addresses an important segment of successful correctional programs. More information is available at the journal's web site at Ashland University, where the editor is a professor, and at the Correctional Education Association's web site. Full-text articles from this journal are available from EBSCOhost and ProQuest databases.

1540. Journal of Criminal Justice. [ISSN: 0047-2352] 1973. 6x/yr. EUR 1015. Ed(s): Kent B Joscelyn. Pergamon, The Boulevard, Langford Ln, East Park, Kidlington, OX5 1GB, United Kingdom. Illus., index, adv. Sample. Refereed. Circ: 3000. Vol. ends: No. 6. Microform: PQC. Online: EBSCO Publishing, EBSCO Host; Gale; IngentaConnect; OhioLINK; ScienceDirect; SwetsWise Online Content. *Indexed:* ASSIA, AgeL, CJA, CJPI, CLI, IBR, IBZ, ILP, LRI, PAIS, PsycInfo, SSCI, SociolAb, V&AA. *Aud.:* Ac, Sa.

Like several other publications reviewed in this section, the *Journal of Criminal Justice* is a fine, multidisciplinary journal covering all aspects of the criminal justice system, but it places special emphasis on the interactions between crime and individual elements within the criminal justice system. The editors encourage articles that "reflect the application of new disciplines or analytical methodologies to the problems of criminal justice." In that vein, recent topics include the genetic connection with delinquent behavior, the connection between low self-control and parole failure, and assessing faith-based efforts to improve prisoner reentry. The journal strives to be international as well. Approximately 10 percent of articles in recent volumes were written by authors from outside of the United States and Canada. Most contributors to this journal are academicians. This is an excellent addition to any criminal justice collection. It has ranked among the top 15 titles in three separate studies of criminal justice and criminology journals since 1981. Unfortunately, the subscription price is prohibitively high for many libraries. The publisher's web site provides a sample issue and free indexing and abstracts for all issues, 1973 to present.

1541. Journal of Criminal Justice Education. [ISSN: 1051-1253] 1990. 3x/yr. GBP 241 print & online eds. Ed(s): Dr. Craig Hemmens. Routledge, 4 Park Sq, Milton Park, Abingdon, OX14 4RN, United Kingdom; journals@routledge.com; http://www.routledge.com. Illus., index. Sample. Refereed. Circ: 3000. Vol. ends: Fall. Reprint: PSC; WSH. *Indexed:* CJA, CJPI. *Aud.:* Ac, Sa.

Routledge Journals (part of the Taylor & Francis Group) began publishing *JCJE* in 2005, but the journal is the official publication of the Academy of Criminal Justice Sciences (ACJS), and editorial control remains with the academy. In addition to fostering excellence in higher education in criminal justice and criminology, the ACJS encourages understanding and cooperation among those engaged in teaching and research and practitioners in criminal justice agencies. *JCJE* is a scholarly journal that seeks to provide a forum for the examination, discussion, and debate of issues concerning postsecondary education in criminal justice, criminology, and related areas. Its overall goal is to enhance the quality of higher education in these fields by encouraging new empirical research and debate. The journal includes articles dealing with best practices in teaching methods, educational innovations, and academic research. In addition to seven or eight theoretical or conceptual articles, several articles focusing on teaching methods and review articles covering materials useful to CJ education are usually included along with occasional commentary. The current editor, J. Mitchell Miller (Ph.D., Department of Criminal Justice, University of Texas, San Antonio) will finish his three-year term in September 2008. *JCJE* expanded to three issues annually, beginning with volume 18 (2007). The first issue of

volume 18 is a thematic issue covering the history of criminal justice education, and Dr. Miller advises that a second thematic issue is planned for volume 19 on scholarly influences in criminal justice. Recent topics have included academic integrity and distance learning, creating a teaching and learning environment in criminal justice courses, criminal justice and moral issues, and criminology/criminal justice representation in the discipline of sociology. An article of particular interest may be "An Assessment of Criminal Justice and Criminology Journal Prestige," which was published in the October 2006 issue. The popularity and proliferation of criminal justice programs in colleges and universities in recent years, along with concerns about the quality of all educational programs, make this an important journal. Check the ACJS web site and the Taylor & Francis web site for more information. Full-text articles from this journal are available from EBSCOhost and ProQuest databases.

Journal of Criminal Law & Criminology. See Law section.

1542. Journal of Interpersonal Violence: concerned with the study and treatment of victims and perpetrators of physical and sexual violence. [ISSN: 0886-2605] 1986. m. GBP 661. Ed(s): Jon R Conte. Sage Publications, Inc., 2455 Teller Rd, Thousand Oaks, CA 91320; info@sagepub.com; http://www.sagepub.com. Illus., index, adv. Sample. Refereed. Circ: 1000 Paid and free. Vol. ends: Dec. Reprint: PSC. *Indexed:* ASG, ASSIA, AgeL, CINAHL, CJA, CJPI, ERIC, IBR, IBZ, IMFL, PsycInfo, RiskAb, SFSA, SSA, SSCI, SWA, SWR&A, SociolAb, V&AA. *Bk. rev.:* 1, 700-1,000 words, signed. *Aud.:* Ac, Sa.

This scholarly, interdisciplinary journal, now over 20 years old, uniquely focuses on both victims and perpetrators, exploring theoretical links between all types of interpersonal violence. Contributors address the concerns and activities of professionals interested in domestic violence, child sexual abuse, rape and sexual assault, physical child abuse, and other violent crimes. The journal examines the causes, effects, treatment, and prevention of all types of violence, using perspectives from a variety of disciplines including psychology, sociology, social work, and medicine. It publishes both qualitative and quantitative research articles, but with an emphasis on the quantitative. While most authors are academicians, many articles are written by or in collaboration with practitioners in hospitals, prisons, and private practice, law enforcement officials, and researchers in the nonprofit sector. Each issue contains 6–12 articles and an occasional lengthy book review. Other irregular features that may appear include "Brief Notes," describing ongoing research projects into such areas as child hostages, child sexual abuse accommodation syndrome, and violence in teen dating; "Notes from Practice," which reports innovations from practical experience; and "Commentary" on current concerns such as videotaping interviews with children or reporting child abuse. A recent special issue deals with partner violence, employment, and the workplace. The *Journal of Interpersonal Violence* appeared among the top-ranked journals in this field in a study by Sorensen et al. published in 2006. The international scope and interdisciplinary nature of this publication make it useful in any social science collection as well as criminology collections.

1543. Journal of Offender Rehabilitation: a multidisciplinary journal of innovation in research, services, and programs in corrections and criminal justice. Former titles (until 1990): *Journal of Offender Counseling, Services and Rehabilitation;* (until 1980): *Offender Rehabilitation.* [ISSN: 1050-9674] 1976. q. USD 530 print & online eds. Ed(s): Creasie Finney Hairston. Haworth Press, Inc., 10 Alice St, Binghamton, NY 13904-1580; getinfo@haworthpress.com; http://www.haworthpress.com. Illus., adv. Sample. Refereed. Circ: 328 Paid. Vol. ends: Spring/Summer. Microform: PQC. Online: EBSCO Publishing, EBSCO Host; OCLC Online Computer Library Center, Inc.; SwetsWise Online Content. Reprint: HAW. *Indexed:* AltPI, CJA, CJPI, H&SSA, HRA, IBR, IBZ, IMFL, PRA, PsycInfo, RiskAb, SFSA, SSA, SUSA, SWA, SWR&A, SociolAb, V&AA. *Aud.:* Ac, Sa.

Journal of Offender Rehabilitation is an interdisciplinary journal that deals with all aspects of the treatment of offenders and the reentry of ex-offenders into society. The journal's primary focus is the use of research to improve practice. Therefore its articles strive to define the theoretical and empirical basis for practice models and establish connections between research findings and needed interventions and services. It provides an international forum for scientific information that focuses on such topics as community reentry and reintegration; alcohol, substance abuse, and mental health treatment interventions; services for correctional populations with special needs; recidivism prevention strategies; educational and vocational programs; families and incarceration; culturally appropriate practice and probation and parole services, and other rehabilitative treatment of offenders and ex-offenders in correctional facilities and inpatient and outpatient settings. It includes empirical research and conceptual analyses of issues relevant to offender rehabilitation. Each issue contains five or six well-documented articles, which are usually 20–30 pages in length. Many issues of the journal are edited by guest editors, and their articles focus on various aspects of the same broad topic such as mental health issues in the criminal justice system, current trends in probation and parole, and the use of arbitration intervention services. Other recent articles cover implementation and effectiveness of a violent-offender reentry initiative, community reentry for youth offenders, job-related stress and satisfaction among juvenile correctional employees, perceptions of administrative support among prison treatment staff, male batterer profiles, family support of reentry of former prisoners, and self-esteem in the treatment of offenders. This publication is highly recommended for any corrections or social services collection, and its interdisciplinary approach makes it desirable for all collections with an interest in social problems. It is similar to, but somewhat narrower in scope than, the *International Journal of Offender Therapy and Comparative Criminology* (above in this section). The journal seems to have ended its long-time editorial connection with Rutgers University, where it was founded. The current editor is Prof. Creasie Finney Hairston, University of Illinois at Chicago. More information, including tables of contents back to 1990, is available at the Haworth Press web site. An electronic version of this journal is also available from Haworth Press.

1544. *Journal of Quantitative Criminology.* [ISSN: 0748-4518] 1984. q. EUR 850 print & online eds. Ed(s): Matthew D Fetzer, David McDowall. Springer New York LLC, 233 Spring St, New York, NY 10013-1578; service-ny@springer.com; http://www.springer.com/. Illus., index, adv. Sample. Refereed. Vol. ends: Dec. Microform: PQC. Online: EBSCO Publishing, EBSCO Host; Gale; IngentaConnect; OCLC Online Computer Library Center, Inc.; OhioLINK; Ovid Technologies, Inc.; ProQuest LLC (Ann Arbor); Springer LINK; SwetsWise Online Content. Reprint: PSC. *Indexed:* CJA, CJPI, PsycInfo, SSA, SSCI, SociolAb. *Aud.:* Ac, Sa.

Among the most prestigious journals in the field of criminology, *JQC* focuses on research advances from such fields as statistics, sociology, geography, political science, economics, and engineering, as well as criminology. Each issue presents four to five papers "that apply quantitative techniques of all levels of complexity to substantive, methodological, or evaluative concerns of interest to the criminological community." This journal would be most useful to an academic readership (especially graduate level and above). Virtually all authors are from academic institutions. In addition to its unique emphasis on quantitative methods, this journal is broader in scope than other scholarly research journals such as the *Journal of Research in Crime and Delinquency* or *Justice Quarterly* (both below in this section). Recent topics that bear this out include the impact of crime on housing prices; a longitudinal analysis of low self-control and risk of victimization; dasymetric mapping for crime data; and effects of gender and race/ethnicity on sentencing. The Springer web site provides tables of contents back to volume 1, 1985, and free e-mail contents alerts.

1545. *Journal of Research in Crime and Delinquency.* [ISSN: 0022-4278] 1964. q. GBP 368. Ed(s): Clayton Hartjen. Sage Publications, Inc., 2455 Teller Rd, Thousand Oaks, CA 91320; info@sagepub.com; http://www.sagepub.com. Illus., index, adv. Sample. Refereed. Circ: 1100 Paid. Vol. ends: Nov. Microform: WSH; PMC. Online: CSA; EBSCO Publishing, EBSCO Host; Florida Center for Library Automation; Gale; HighWire Press; OCLC Online Computer Library Center, Inc.; OhioLINK; SAGE Publications, Inc., SAGE Journals Online; SwetsWise Online Content. Reprint: PSC. *Indexed:* ASSIA, AgeL, CJA, CJPI, CLI, ExcerpMed, IBR, IBSS, IBZ, ILP, IMFL, PRA, PsycInfo, RILM, RiskAb, SFSA, SSA, SSCI, SUSA, SWA, SWR&A, SociolAb, V&AA. *Aud.:* Ac, Sa.

Journal of Research in Crime and Delinquency is another excellent product of the cooperation between Sage and the National Council on Crime and Delinquency (NCCD). The NCCD promotes crime control policies based on data and best practices, not political rhetoric, and believes the crime rate in the United States will remain intolerably high if current policies continue. It also believes prisons should be used sparingly for those offenders who are a threat to public safety and cannot be safely managed in the community. This long-standing scholarly publication focuses on original research in crime and delinquency or critical analyses of either old or new theories or concepts. In addition, methodological studies, experimental results, statistical analyses, evaluation research, and empirical research are included to enhance the knowledge of crime and society's relationship with it. The journal provides an excellent sampling of research using a variety of methods, both qualitative and quantitative, and it illustrates the application of sophisticated analytic techniques. It is interdisciplinary, with perspectives from economics, psychology, public administration, social work, and sociology, as well as criminology and criminal justice. The articles deal with both the etiology and characteristics of crime and criminals, and the criminal justice system itself. Review essays, research notes, and commentaries are occasionally included. Recent articles address determinants of the levels of nonlethal force employed by police, impact of gang formation on local patterns of crime, neighborhood influence on felony sentencing, an analysis of state corrections spending, the continuing significance of race in capital punishment, and predicting community motor vehicle theft rates. This journal is very useful in an academic setting for graduate/advanced student and faculty research and in other research settings. Its presentation of a variety of research methods and theoretical models and concepts makes it appealing to a broader audience than the *Journal of Quantitative Criminology* (above in this section). More information about this journal is available at the NCCD and Sage web sites. Sage provides free tables of contents with abstracts and subscription full-text pdf access to this journal back to 1964. *Journal of Research in Crime and Delinquency* was ranked third in criminal justice and criminology journals prestige studies by Sorensen et al. in 2006 and fifth by Williams et al. in 1995. Sage and the NCCD also produce *Crime and Delinquency* (above in this section), which is more policy-oriented.

1546. *Justice Quarterly.* [ISSN: 0741-8825] 1984. q. GBP 313 print & online eds. Ed(s): Richard Tewksbury. Routledge, 4 Park Sq, Milton Park, Abingdon, OX14 4RN, United Kingdom; journals@routledge.com; http://www.routledge.com. Illus., adv. Sample. Refereed. Circ: 3000. Vol. ends: Dec. Online: EBSCO Publishing, EBSCO Host; Gale; William S. Hein & Co., Inc.; IngentaConnect; ProQuest LLC (Ann Arbor); SwetsWise Online Content. Reprint: PSC; WSH. *Indexed:* CJA, CJPI, PRA, RiskAb, SFSA, SSA, SSCI, SUSA, SociolAb, V&AA. *Bk. rev.:* 2, 1,000-2,000 words, signed. *Aud.:* Ac, Sa.

This official organ of the Academy of Criminal Justice Sciences (ACJS) has improved in quality over the past 10–15 years to become a premier journal and major forum for criminal justice–related scholarship. It has become both prestigious and difficult to publish in *JQ*. The in-depth articles are written overwhelmingly by and for academics. Occasional review essays address an emerging issue in the field, sometimes serving as "think pieces" that help to outline directions for future research. Befitting the mission of the ACJS, this journal focuses more on the justice system than does the *Journal of Research in Crime and Delinquency* (above in this section), which includes much about the etiology of crime and the traits of criminals. However, the research articles in *JQ* compare favorably with the National Council on Crime and Delinquency title. Both journals should be a part of academic library collections that support graduate level or advanced research.

1547. *Justice Resource Update.* 2004. q. Free registration. National Criminal Justice Reference Service, PO Box 6000, Rockville, MD 20849-6000; http://tellncjrs.ncjrs.org. *Aud.:* Ga, Ac, Sa.

The *Justice Resource Update,* while it publishes just one article per issue, is an important resource for criminal justice because it contains abstracts, URLs, and ordering information for online and paper publications, posters, brochures, and other materials available from the National Criminal Justice Reference Service (NCJRS). NCJRS is the national clearinghouse for information sponsored by the National Institute of Justice. In fact, it is one of the most extensive criminal justice information sources in the world. Beginning in fall 2004, the *Justice Resource Update* replaced the now-ceased *NCJRS Catalog.* Although the first issues were available in paper, news releases described the *Update* as "an online quarterly publication that highlights significant initiatives, priorities, products, web sites, and announcements of funding information of interest to the field." The cover story in the first issue for 2007 discusses the use of geographic information systems (GIS) to analyze crime data. Abstracts are included for a gangs toolkit and reports on international parental kidnapping, training programs for corrections professionals, using grants to address school crime, and burglary at construction sites. Albeit in a briefer format, the *Update* maintains its predecessor's purpose as a useful and free current-awareness listing of government resources, most of which are available free in pdf or html format online. It is available at www.ncjrs.org/justiceresupd.html.

1548. Law and Order Magazine: the magazine for police management.
[ISSN: 0023-9194] 1953. m. USD 25 domestic; USD 85 foreign. Hendon Publishing Company, 130 N Waukegan Rd, Ste 202, Deerfield, IL 60015; info@hendonpub.com. Illus., index, adv. Sample. Circ: 35000 Controlled. Vol. ends: Dec. Microform: PQC. Online: ProQuest LLC (Ann Arbor). *Indexed:* CJA, CJPI. *Bk. rev.:* 0-5, 75-150 words. *Aud.:* Ga, Ac, Sa.

For 54 years, *Law and Order* has been a management-oriented publication that emphasizes practical solutions to problems encountered by law enforcement agencies. Its concise, well-written articles provide information that top and middle law enforcement management can use to help them make decisions to improve law enforcement operations. Working law enforcement officers and practitioners from affiliated agencies and services write most of the articles, although magazine staff members write some. According to the *Law and Order* media kit, Editorial Director Ed Sanow is currently the only editor in the industry that is active in law enforcement. He's a team leader for a multi-agency SWAT team and he continues to participate in monthly law enforcement training activities. In each issue, "Focus" and "Special Report" sections bring together three to seven mostly undocumented articles that address the same broad topics. Additional feature articles covering other topics may also be presented, and regular departments provide brief practical information covering national and international news, law enforcement training, computer equipment and applications, other police equipment, commentary, and more. "Focus" or "Special Report" topics during 2007 include weapons/optics/accessories, body armor and swat equipment; investigations, low-light conditions; technology solutions, biometrics, facial recognition, DNA; homeland security, surveillance equip and tech, night vision equipment; officer training, accredited LE programs, community relations; communications, interoperability, data sharing; computers and software, mobile computing; and best practices, industry outlook, hiring and retention. The magazine also presents detailed information about the IACP conference and the February issue presents the annual buyer's guide. The magazine contains much useful advertising relevant to law enforcement products and services and some job ads. This publication's broad scope and its modest price make it appropriate wherever there is an interest in law enforcement, and especially where working law enforcement management and officers are present. The publisher's web site provides additional information about *Law and Order*, including an article archive with a search interface and free access to full-text articles. Full-text pdf articles from *Law and Order* are also available from ProQuest. This magazine is similar to, and complements, *The Police Chief* (below in this section).

1549. Law Officers' Bulletin. [ISSN: 0145-6571] 1976. bi-w. USD 169. Ed(s): Mary B Murphy. Pike & Fischer, Inc., 1010 Wayne Ave, Ste 1400, Silver Spring, MD 20910; pike@pf.com; http://www.pf.com. Illus. Sample. Vol. ends: No. 26. *Indexed:* CJPI. *Aud.:* Ga, Ac, Sa.

Law Officers' Bulletin is now published by Thomson/West, and it remains a legal digest that presents brief interpretations of constitutional and statutory law, focusing on summaries of recent court decisions from local, state, and federal jurisdictions. Coverage could include any court decision that might impact law enforcement procedures including arrest, search and seizure, interrogation, right to counsel, and others. In addition, U.S. Supreme Court decisions, possible trends created by multiple decisions pertaining to the same important issues, and law officers' constitutional and legal problems are often addressed. Reports are grouped by broad topics and cases are also listed alphabetically. "You Be the Judge" presents real-life scenarios to test the reader's knowledge of federal or state court decisions. Special feature issues provide more in-depth coverage of specific topics. The focus on case law makes this digest narrower in scope than most news digests that address criminal justice topics. This legal digest is written in an informative and understandable manner that makes it useful

anywhere there is interest in the legal ramifications of law enforcement practice. More information is available on the publisher's web site.

1550. National Institute of Justice Journal. irreg. Ed(s): Nancy Ritter. U.S. Department of Justice, National Institute of Justice, 810 Seventh St, NW, Washington, DC 20531; http://www.ojp.usdoj.gov/nij/. *Aud.:* Ga, Ac, Sa.

The National Institute of Justice (NIJ) is the primary research and development agency of the U.S. Department of Justice within the Office of Justice Programs. It is dedicated to researching crime control and justice issues, and it sponsors special projects, research, and programs designed to improve and strengthen the criminal justice system. NIJ also conducts evaluations to determine the effectiveness of programs, especially those funded by the Institute, and recommends programs for continuation or implementation at other locations. *NIJ Journal* publishes information about NIJ research, and programs in an attempt to ensure that research findings influence practice. Each issue presents four to six interesting, well-written, feature articles emphasizing policy-relevant research and initiatives. In addition, recurring columns provide much useful information. "Publications of Interest from NIJ" briefly describes recent NIJ publications, which are often available free on the web. "Books in Brief" presents brief information about books, which derive information for NIJ-funded research. "Features NIJ Articles" provides online access to articles that were written by NIJ staff and published in other publications such as *Corrections Today.* "At-A-Glance" presents brief information about NIJ research in progress or recently completed research including some data and findings or conclusions. Recent feature articles address missing persons and unidentified remains, building trust and confidence in the police, sexual assault in abusive relationships, online DNA training for lawyers and judges, criminal justice in 2040, and the affect of parental incarceration on a child's risk for foster care placement. This journal is useful anywhere crime and criminal justice concerns are relevant, and it's free. The NIJ web site provides online full-text access to this journal back to 1995 and a free e-mail subscription will provide links to the publication as each issue becomes available. In addition, the web site provides access to many other NIJ publications.

1551. Police: the law enforcement magazine. Formerly: *Police Product News.* [ISSN: 0893-8989] 1976. m. USD 25 domestic; USD 40 Canada; USD 60 elsewhere. Ed(s): David Griffith. Bobit Business Media, 3520 Challenger St, Torrance, CA 90503; order@bobit.com; http://www.bobit.com. Illus., adv. Sample. Circ: 52484 Paid. Vol. ends: Dec. *Indexed:* CJPI. *Aud.:* Ga, Ac, Sa.

Police: The Law Enforcement Magazine is one of North America's leading periodicals for working police officers of all ranks. Each issue of *Police* contains five to seven thought-provoking feature articles, law enforcement news, tactical instruction, officer survival tips, and reviews of weapons, gear, and technology. Recent articles encourage police organizations to plan and conduct major incident drills, explain the psychological and emotional tolls of undercover work, and describe the body's reactions to deadly threat. The publisher's well-developed web site, policemag.com, includes a searchable archive with selected full-text articles from 1999 to the present, news briefs, discussion forums, and product information. Like *Law and Order*, *Police* is appropriate in any collection supporting an interest in practical matters regarding law enforcement.

1552. Police Chief: professional voice of law enforcement. [ISSN: 0032-2571] 1934. m. USD 25. Ed(s): Dan Rosenblatt, Charles E Higginbotham. International Association of Chiefs of Police, Inc., 515 N Washington St, Alexandria, VA 22314-2340; information@theiacp.org; http://www.theiacp.org/. Illus., index. Circ: 25000. Vol. ends: Dec. Microform: PQC. Online: EBSCO Publishing, EBSCO Host. *Indexed:* CJA, CJPI, HRIS, PAIS, SSCI. *Aud.:* Ga, Ac, Sa.

Police Chief is the official publication of the International Association of Chiefs of Police (IACP). Since 1893, IACP has worked to advance the science and practice of police services through the development of improved administrative, technical, and operational practices in police work; the encouragement of police cooperation and the exchange of information among police administrators; the enhancement of recruitment and training in the police profession; and the encouragement of police adherence to high professional standards of performance and conduct. Since 1934, *Police Chief* has provided a forum for law enforcement practitioners to share their collective expertise. The publication's mission is to enhance the reader's understanding of the latest trends and practices in law enforcement. Each issue includes five to ten feature articles and often groups several articles together to focus on a specific theme, such as cybercrimes, terrorist threats in the United States and worldwide, and innovations in smaller police agencies. In addition, many very interesting regular columns/departments are included. "Legislative Alert" covers legislation relevant to laws enforcement. "Chief's Counsel" examines case law and liability issues. "Technology Talk" and "Product Update" address new technology and products. "Survivors' Club" documents the benefits of protective devices such as seatbelts and body armor. The magazine is attractively packaged, with feature articles from a supervisory/command viewpoint, some membership news and job ads, and much advertising. Articles are contributed by practitioners in law enforcement and related fields, and are concise and not heavily footnoted. The April issue contains the annual "Buyers' Guide," which presents a directory of law enforcement equipment, products, and service providers. This magazine is particularly useful for law enforcement executives or administrators. However, it is also very useful in academic collections where law enforcement administration is taught, and it would be useful to anyone interested in or studying law enforcement. More information about the IACP and *Police Chief*, including full-text access back to September 2003, is available at the IACP web site. This magazine is similar to, and complements, *Law and Order* (above in this section).

1553. The Police Journal: a quarterly review for the police forces of the Commonwealth and English-speaking world. [ISSN: 0032-258X] 1927. q. USD 224. Ed(s): John Jones. Vathek Publishing, Mairwen Lloyd-Williams, Bridge House, Dolby, IM5 3BP, United Kingdom; http://www.vathek.com. Illus., index, adv. Sample. Refereed. Circ: 400. Vol. ends: Oct/Dec. *Indexed:* ASSIA, BAS, CJA, CJPI, ExcerpMed, HRIS. *Bk. rev.:* 2-4 lengthy, signed. *Aud.:* Ga, Ac, Sa.

For 80 years, *The Police Journal* has been providing informed and practical information for police officers and police management in the Commonwealth. The publication is aimed at decision-makers and policymakers, both within the police service and those organizations, agencies, and government officials associated with law enforcement. Therefore, many articles are written from a management viewpoint. However, the content is also of interest to frontline law enforcement officers. Both academics and practitioners write articles for *The Police Journal*, most of them from the United Kingdom. Each issue presents a "Commentary" article, three or four feature articles, "Recent Judicial Decisions" summarizing relevant British court decisions, and two to four substantial book reviews. The range of subjects runs from police procedure and crime statistics to IT and new laws affecting policy. Recent topics include Generation X police officers, humanistic education and diversity training, and violence against conservation officers. This publication is similar to *The Police Chief* and *Policing* (both in this section) regarding its usefulness to law enforcement management, but its main focus is the United Kingdom, and it is less scholarly and more accessible than *Policing*.

1554. Police Quarterly. [ISSN: 1098-6111] 1998. q. GBP 306. Ed(s): Dennis Kenney. Sage Publications, Inc., 2455 Teller Rd, Thousand Oaks, CA 91320; info@sagepub.com; http://www.sagepub.com. Adv. Refereed. Reprint: PSC. *Indexed:* CJA, RiskAb, V&AA. *Bk. rev.:* 1-2, signed, 2-6 pages. *Aud.:* Ac, Sa.

Published by Sage in association with the Police Executive Research Forum (www.policeforum.org) and the police section of the Academy of Criminal Justice Sciences (www.acjs.org/police.htm), *Police Quarterly* emphasizes policy-oriented research of value to both practitioners and academicians. It publishes all types of police scholarship: theoretical, empirical, qualitative, and quantitative research, and historical and comparative analyses. In addition, the journal includes critiques, descriptions of innovative programs, debates, and reviews of books related to policing. Recent articles address anomia among police chiefs, a comparison of police supervisors in America and Taiwan, and gender diversity in police organizations. *Police Quarterly* continues to be the only journal of its kind published in North America.

1555. Police Times. Former titles: *Police Times and Police Command; Police Times.* 1966. q. USD 18. Ed(s): Jim Gordon. American Federation of Police & Concerned Citizens, 6250 Horizon Dr, Titusville, FL 32780. Illus., adv. Circ: 50000. Vol. ends: Nov/Dec. *Bk. rev.:* 2, 350-450 words. *Aud.:* Ga, Sa.

Police Times is a visually appealing, low-cost magazine that presents thought-provoking articles to a large readership. It is the official voice of the American Federation of Police and Concerned Citizens (AFP&CC), an organization of more than 100,000 law enforcement and security personnel and concerned citizens. AFP&CC is dedicated to the prevention of crime and the apprehension of criminals. It also assists family members of officers killed in the line of duty, promotes the training of police reserves, encourages citizen volunteers, and educates the public about the contributions and sacrifices of law enforcement professionals. The publication presents news, essays, and editorials on issues relevant to law enforcement, often focusing on what's being done and where. Police procedures, programs, equipment, and education and training; crime demographics; and political/policy implications are discussed. The editor actively seeks articles with special emphasis on smaller police departments or individuals who have made important contributions to law enforcement, past or present. Regular sections cover legislative and judicial issues, technological innovations, recent facts, and off-the-wall items. Although OCLC shows very few libraries holding this periodical (perhaps because of its large circulation among practitioners), *Police Times* has potential readership among academics and the general public in addition to its many law enforcement readers. A sample issue is available from the publisher for $2.50.

1556. Policing and Society: an international journal of research & policy. [ISSN: 1043-9463] 1991. q. GBP 546 print & online eds. Ed(s): Martin Innes. Routledge, 4 Park Sq, Milton Park, Abingdon, OX14 4RN, United Kingdom; info@routledge.co.uk; http://www.routledge.co.uk. Illus. Refereed. Online: EBSCO Publishing, EBSCO Host; Gale; IngentaConnect; OCLC Online Computer Library Center, Inc.; SwetsWise Online Content. Reprint: PSC. *Indexed:* CJA, IBSS, PSA, PsycInfo, SSA, SociolAb. *Aud.:* Ac, Sa.

Policing and Society is a scholarly journal concerned with all aspects of policing in their social contexts. Any subject relevant to law enforcement may be covered, although a substantial part of the material presents social scientific investigations of police policy, legal analyses of police powers and their constitutional status, and management-oriented research. Recent topics cover internationalization of crime control, policing and cybersociety, police leadership, and historical policing topics. Occasional special issues focus on various aspects of a broad theme, e.g., reassurance and community policing. The editorial/advisory board includes members from many countries where significant research and inquiry into policing take place. The publication is genuinely global, with recent articles spanning research in Australia, Brazil, Serbia, and the United States, as well as the United Kingdom. Each issue presents five or six well-written and documented articles, most written by college or university faculty. This international journal is of potential use to police, other criminal justice practitioners, and academics from most social science disciplines. However, the price may be too high for many libraries. The publisher's web site provides an online sample copy, tables of contents, and article abstracts from 2002 to present.

1557. Policing (Bradford): an international journal of police strategies and management. Formerly (until 1997): *Police Studies;* Incorporates (1981-1997): *American Journal of Police.* [ISSN: 1363-951X] 1978. q. EUR 2659 combined subscription in Europe print & online eds.; USD 2599 combined subscription in North America print & online eds.; AUD 4199 combined subscription in Australasia print & online eds. Ed(s): Lawrence F Travis, III. Emerald Group Publishing Limited, Howard House, Wagon Ln, Bingley, BD16 1WA, United Kingdom; information@ emeraldinsight.com; http://www.emeraldinsight.com. Illus. Sample. Refereed. Microform: PQC. Online: Pub.; Chadwyck-Healey Inc.; EBSCO Publishing, EBSCO Host; Gale; William S. Hein & Co., Inc.; IngentaConnect; OCLC Online Computer Library Center, Inc.; OhioLINK; ProQuest LLC (Ann Arbor); SwetsWise Online Content. Reprint: PSC; WSH. *Indexed:* ABS&EES, CJA, CJPI, IBSS, PAIS, PRA, PSA, SSA, SSCI, SUSA, SociolAb, V&AA. *Bk. rev.:* 1, 900-1,500 words, signed. *Aud.:* Ac, Sa.

Policing is an interdisciplinary scholarly journal covering theory and research related to law enforcement, which aims to provide global and comparative perspectives of police policy, practice, management, operations, education, training, and science and technology. It was formed in 1997 by the merger of *American Journal of Police*, which focused on policing in the United States, and *Police Studies*, which emphasized comparative and international law enforcement. The result of that merger provides a scholarly examination of law enforcement concerns useful to senior law enforcement officers, policymakers, and especially academics. *Policing* is very useful in libraries where there is an academic or research interest in law enforcement or the social sciences. Unfortunately, its high price might dissuade many libraries from subscribing. Each issue usually contains seven to ten refereed articles. A "Perspectives on Policing" section provides summary abstracts of research published in other journals, and "Policing on the Web" describes web sites useful to law enforcement. Other regular sections include an occasional lengthy book review relevant to law enforcement. Recent topics include suicide by cop, police detectives' perceptions of giving evidence in court, traits of a good investigative interviewer of children, the political economy of American police and policing, geographical information systems and policing in South Africa, organizational commitment levels of police officers in Australia, and police responses to persons with a mental illness. More information about the journal is available on the publisher's web site, including tables of contents and article abstracts back to 1997. The web site also provides a free table of contents e-mail alert service and the ability to purchase online access to single articles. Online subscriptions are available from the publisher, and full-text articles are available from ProQuest databases.

1558. The Prison Journal. Supersedes: *Journal of Prison Discipline and Philanthropy.* [ISSN: 0032-8855] 1845. q. GBP 292. Ed(s): Rosemary L Gido. Sage Publications, Inc., 2455 Teller Rd, Thousand Oaks, CA 91320; info@sagepub.com; http://www.sagepub.com. Illus., index, adv. Sample. Refereed. Circ: 1000. Vol. ends: Dec. Microform: PQC. Online: CSA; EBSCO Publishing, EBSCO Host; Florida Center for Library Automation; Gale; HighWire Press; OCLC Online Computer Library Center, Inc.; OhioLINK; SAGE Publications, Inc., SAGE Journals Online; SwetsWise Online Content. Reprint: PSC. *Indexed:* ASG, AltPI, CJA, CJPI, H&SSA, PAIS, PRA, PsycInfo, RiskAb, SSA, SSCI, SUSA, SociolAb, V&AA. *Aud.:* Ac, Sa.

The Prison Journal: An International Forum on Incarceration and Alternative Sanctions was begun by the Pennsylvania Prison Society, founded in 1787 and the oldest prison reform organization in the United States. For more than 150 years the journal served as the official publication of the society, whose members believe that offenders should be held accountable for breaking laws, although punishments should be constructive. Although this long-standing, well-respected interdisciplinary journal has been published by Sage for several years, it had maintained its connection to the Pennsylvania Prison Society. However, the journal is no longer the official publication of the society, and the society's web site no longer makes mention of the journal. The publication retains a major focus on studies, ideas, and discussion of adult and juvenile confinement, treatment interventions, and alternative sanctions. Articles, research notes, and review essays will present theoretical treatments, research, policy analyses, historical analyses, and practice descriptions and evaluations. Articles are well documented and are contributed by both academic authors and practitioners, including correctional employees, attorneys, and others. Recent article topics include prison-based animal programs, an ethnographic study of staff members in a juvenile correctional facility, gender differences and aggression levels among correctional officers, implications of co-occurring mental illness and substance abuse for local jurisdictions in the criminal justice system, and setting aside (expunging) criminal convictions in Canada to enhance offender reintegration. The journal has continued its practice of publishing occasional special issues focusing on specific aspects of corrections. A recent special issue presented six articles on the Criminal Justice Drug Abuse Treatment Studies (CJ-DATS). Sage has maintained the quality of this fine publication, and it should be of interest to the corrections community and anyone interested in current correctional practices, theories, or reforms. It should be part of any collection emphasizing corrections. Sage provides free tables of contents with abstracts and subscription pdf access to the content of this journal back to 1922.

1559. Probation Journal: the journal of community and criminal justice. Formerly: *Probation.* [ISSN: 0264-5505] 1913. q. GBP 268. Ed(s): Hindpal Singh Bhui. Sage Publications Ltd., 1 Oliver's Yard, 55 City Rd, London, EC1 1SP, United Kingdom; info@sagepub.co.uk; http://www.sagepub.co.uk. Adv. Refereed. Circ: 8600. Reprint: PSC. *Indexed:* ASSIA, CJA, IBR, IBZ, RiskAb. *Bk. rev.:* 5-6, signed, 300-600 words. *Aud.:* Ac, Ga, Sa.

This journal was once described as a "newsletter," but it has developed into a solid scholarly journal, written in a style accessible to a wide audience. Although it is now published by Sage, *Probation Journal* continues its association with Napo, the professional organization of probation officers in England, Wales, and Northern Ireland. Now a century old, Napo has inspired respect in other countries and serves as a model to those seeking effective ways to work with offenders. Each issue includes five or six full-length, documented articles and shorter comment articles. In addition, readers are invited to send submissions for "Practice Notes," describing a recent practice-related issue in brief; "Research and Reports," summarizing recent empirical research, conference papers, or working papers; "Resources," reviewing new videos, handbooks, guides, and the like; and "In Court," detailing important decisions and legal developments in the United Kingdom. Unlike the U.S. publication *Federal Probation* (above in this section), which includes many articles of a theoretical or philosophical nature, most articles in *Probation Journal* are grounded in the practice of everyday work with offenders. Topics covered are of interest to students, academics, and researchers everywhere. Recently covered are the rise in anti-social behavior, offender reading programs, working with sex offenders, and the revival of interest in offenders' inner emotional experiences. Although coverage focuses on the United Kingdom, the United Kingdom's long tradition of probation services make this publication an important addition to all collections supporting research and studies in probation services. The publisher offers full-text access to all volumes back to 1929.

1560. Punishment & Society: the international journal of penology. [ISSN: 1462-4745] 1999. q. GBP 412. Ed(s): Jonathan Simon, Malcolm M Feeley. Sage Publications Ltd., 1 Oliver's Yard, 55 City Rd, London, EC1 1SP, United Kingdom; info@sagepub.co.uk; http://www.sagepub.co.uk. Adv. Refereed. Circ: 1200. Reprint: PSC. *Indexed:* ASSIA, CJA, IBR, IBSS, IBZ, PRA, PSA, RiskAb, SSA, SSCI, SUSA, SociolAb, V&AA. *Bk. rev.:* 4-5, signed, lengthy. *Aud.:* Ac, Sa.

Punishment & Society, now in its ninth year, quickly established itself as an important forum for international research and scholarship dealing with punishment, penal institutions, and penal control. By 2005 it was already ranked 13 out of the top 27 journals in Criminology and Penology in *Journal Citation Reports.* This journal seeks to advance the body of work that has emerged in the field of penology over the last 20 years, while also serving as a source of informed commentary and criticism of contemporary penal policies and practices. The journal includes theoretical and empirical papers from a range of perspectives, including criminology, penology, sociology, history, law, and philosophy. In addition to the thoroughly documented research articles, each issue includes a substantial book review section along with occasional review essays, symposia, debates, and shorter reviews to keep readers up-to-date on what is being published in the field. The current editors, both at the University of California, have stated plans to aggressively solicit articles from throughout the world to further the international scope of the journal, which makes this a fine complement to the North American focus of the corrections periodicals in this section. Recent topics include youth crime in Canada, capital punishment in Japan, politics of crime in Spain, and women prisoners' mental health. The Sage web site includes a recent sample issue, an e-mail alert service, and additional information about this journal.

Sexual Abuse. See Psychology section.

1561. Sheriff Magazine. Formerly (until 1991): *National Sheriff.* [ISSN: 1070-8170] 1948. bi-m. USD 30. Ed(s): Mike Terault. National Sheriffs' Association, 1450 Duke St, Alexandria, VA 22314-3490; nsamail@sherrifs.org; http://www.sheriffs.org/. Illus., adv. Sample. Circ: 21300 Paid and free. Vol. ends: Nov/Dec. *Indexed:* CJA, CJPI. *Aud.:* Ga, Ac, Sa.

Sheriff Magazine is the official publication of the National Sheriffs' Association (NSA), a nonprofit organization that has worked for over 60 years to raise the level of professionalism among sheriffs, their deputies, and others in the field of criminal justice and public safety. Articles deal with best practices, procedures, and research in law enforcement, corrections, and court security. Each issue has a special focus featuring two to four articles that address a chosen theme such as illegal immigration or school violence. Two to four more articles address other current concerns of law enforcement. Special issues include the January-February "Buyers' Guide" and the May–June NSA conference issue. Regular departments provide coverage of successful law enforcement programs, laws and legislation, NSA member news, activities, and a calendar of events. Sheriffs and other law enforcement professionals write most of this content from a practitioner's point of view. Although *Sheriff Magazine* focuses on the concerns of sheriffs and their personnel, it has broad appeal to anyone interested in law enforcement, including investigators, court officers, corrections officials, police officers, and even the general public.

1562. Theoretical Criminology: an international journal. [ISSN: 1362-4806] 1997. q. GBP 419. Ed(s): Eugene McLaughlin, Lynn Chancer. Sage Publications Ltd., 1 Oliver's Yard, 55 City Rd, London, EC1 1SP, United Kingdom; info@sagepub.co.uk; http://www.sagepub.co.uk. Illus., adv. Refereed. Vol. ends: Nov. Reprint: PSC. *Indexed:* CJA, CJPI, IBR, IBZ, PsycInfo, RiskAb, SFSA, SSA, SSCI, SUSA, SWA, SociolAb, V&AA. *Bk. rev.:* 5, 1,400 words, signed. *Aud.:* Ac, Sa.

Theoretical Criminology is a scholarly journal, now in its 11th year of publication, dealing with concepts and theories focusing on criminal behavior, social deviance, criminal law, morality, justice, social regulation, and related concerns. The journal aims to foster theoretical debate, explore the relationship between theory and data in empirical research, and advance the link between criminological analysis and general social and political theory. It is interdisciplinary, presenting perspectives from criminology, sociology, law, history, psychology, anthropology, philosophy, economics, and other disciplines. As would be expected, the journal's scope is broad, including information about the nature of crime and justice, penal policy, the history of crime and criminal justice, comparisons of local and international forms of crime and social control, and the relationships between crime and social development. One of the journal's co-editors is at a university in the United States and the other is at a university in the United Kingdom. In addition, the editorial board consists of associate editors and international advisory editors from many countries, including Australia, Canada, Germany, Italy, Japan, New Zealand, Norway, and Spain. Presumably, this international editorial board has contributed to this journal's ability to publish the scholarship of an international group of authors. Sixty percent of the papers that were published in the last six issues of this journal were written by authors from outside the United States. Occasional theme issues focus on specific topics. One recent special issue focuses on public criminologies and their relationship to public policy formation and intellectual practice. Another recent special issue focuses on a feminist perspective on restorative justice. *Theoretical Criminology* was ranked ninth in a criminal justice and criminology journals prestige study by Sorensen et al. in 2006. More information about this journal, including tables of contents with article abstracts, is available at the Sage web site. Subscription pdf access to the content of this journal, back to 1997, is also available from Sage.

Violence Against Women. See Gender Studies section.

1563. Women & Criminal Justice. [ISSN: 0897-4454] 1989. q. USD 430 print & online eds. Ed(s): Donna C Hale. Haworth Press, Inc., 10 Alice St, Binghamton, NY 13904-1580; getinfo@haworthpress.com; http://www.haworthpress.com. Illus., adv. Sample. Refereed. Circ: 397 Paid. Vol. ends: No. 2. Microform: PQC. Online: EBSCO Publishing, EBSCO Host; OCLC Online Computer Library Center, Inc.; ProQuest LLC (Ann Arbor); SwetsWise Online Content. Reprint: HAW. *Indexed:* AltPI, CJA, CJPI, CWI, FemPer, GendWatch, IBR, IBZ, IMFL, PAIS, SFSA, SSA, SUSA, SWA, SociolAb, V&AA, WSA. *Bk. rev.:* 5-10, 500-1,500 words. *Aud.:* Ac, Sa.

This interdisciplinary, international publication is still the only refereed journal that deals with all areas of women and criminal justice. Topics range from women in criminal justice professions (including education), to women as victims or perpetrators, to women in crime and punishment literature, to examination of incarcerated women and female minors: their legal rights, programs, pregnancy, AIDS, children, old age, and women on death row. In addition, the journal contains biographical essays on women who have made contributions to the criminal justice field as practitioners, criminologists, or theorists. *Women & Criminal Justice* publishes high quality, thoroughly documented articles presenting historical, theoretical, cross-cultural, and empirical research. Book review essays appear only occasionally but are substantial and well written. Because of its unique focus within the fields of criminal justice and women's studies, *Women & Criminal Justice* fills an important research niche. The Haworth Press web site provides tables of contents with article abstracts and a recent sample issue online for those wishing to review the title for purchase.

■ CULTURAL STUDIES

See also History; Literature; and Political Science sections.

Vanette M. Schwartz, Social Sciences Librarian, 8900 Milner Library, Illinois State University, Normal, IL 6l790-8900; vmschwa@ilstu.edu

Introduction

The intersection of cultural and social studies has formed the foundation for a wide-ranging and intellectually challenging body of literature. The exploration of cultural diversity and conflict, along with its impact on society, has become a major part of much of the research in academia. Issues of race, ethnicity, class, and gender influence many disciplines as well as everyday life and popular culture. Culture wars and social conflict are an integral part of the political landscape of nations and the global scene. These factors have built and enhanced the writing and publications in cultural studies.

Many cultural studies publications are both interdisciplinary and international. Every publication in this section addresses issues of race, class, and gender. Many cultural studies journals blend philosophy, history, politics, and literature with social issues; others emphasize popular culture and future studies. Many journals cover history, theory, and research in social science disciplines, while other publications focus on postmodernism and post colonialism. Aesthetics, the arts, and criticism also play a vital role in cultural studies. Alternative formats, styles, and modes of expression are increasing. Especially in electronic journals, photography, film, music, and computer graphics are on the rise. The journal literature of cultural studies offers a unique blend of theoretical, philosophical, and critical writing for scholars, students, and general readers.

Basic Periodicals

Hs: *The Futurist;* Ga: *The Futurist, Humanities, Journal of Popular Culture;* Ac: *American Quarterly, Critical Inquiry, Humanities, Journal of Popular Culture, Postmodern Culture.*

Basic Abstracts and Indexes

America: History and Life, Humanities Index, MLA International Bibliography, PAIS, Social Sciences Index, Sociological Abstracts.

1564. American Quarterly. [ISSN: 0003-0678] 1949. q. USD 145. Ed(s): Curtis Marez. The Johns Hopkins University Press, 2715 N Charles St, Baltimore, MD 21218-4363; http://www.press.jhu.edu. Illus., index, adv. Refereed. Circ: 5299 Paid. Vol. ends: Dec (No. 4). Microform: PQC. Online: Chadwyck-Healey Inc.; EBSCO Publishing, EBSCO Host; JSTOR (Web-based Journal Archive); OCLC Online Computer Library Center, Inc.; OhioLINK; Project MUSE; ProQuest LLC (Ann Arbor); SwetsWise Online Content. Reprint: PSC. *Indexed:* AgeL, AmH&L, AmHI, ArtHuCI, BAS, BEL&L, BRD, BRI, CBRI, FLI, HistAb, HumInd, IBR, IBZ, MLA-IB, PSA, RI-1, RILM, SSA, SSCI, SociolAb. *Bk. rev.:* 5-8, essay length. *Aud.:* Ac.

With a publication history spanning over 55 years, this journal has become the premier publication in the field of American Studies. *American Quarterly* publishes lengthy research articles and review essays on American culture. Recent articles cover such topics as transnational American Studies, public memorials, and empire in early U.S. history. In addition to book reviews, exhibition reviews appear in each issue. A series of articles titled "Currents" features commentaries on timely social and political issues related to American Studies. Special issues are published each September focusing on themes such as technology in American Studies and "Legal Borderlands." This journal covers the activities of the American Studies Association and serves as the major avenue of scholarship in the discipline.

1565. American Studies. Former titles (until 1970): *Midcontinent American Studies Journal;* (until 1961): *Central Mississippi Valley American Studies Association. Journal.* [ISSN: 0026-3079] 1960. 3x/yr. USD 35 (Individuals, USD 20; Students, USD 8). Ed(s): Norman Yetman, David Katzman. University of Kansas, American Studies Department, 213 Bailey Hall, Lawrence, KS 66045-2117; http://www.urc.ukansas.edu/. Illus., index, adv. Refereed. Circ: 1300 Paid. Vol. ends: No. 3. Microform: PQC. *Indexed:* AmH&L, AmHI, HistAb, HumInd, IBR, IBZ, LRI, MLA-IB, PAIS, RILM. *Bk. rev.:* 10-45, 400-500 words, in some issues. *Aud.:* Ac, Ga.

The focus of *American Studies* is on broadly based research that provides insights into American society or culture. Research articles on U.S. literature and the arts, politics, social issues, and popular culture are the foundation of this journal. Recent articles explore such topics as movies in American Studies, Pan-Americanism in the 1940s, and the integration of baseball. Some issues are devoted to a single theme, such as "Indigeneity at the Crossroads of American Studies." Review essays and book reviews appear in most issues. The Mid-America American Studies Association and the University of Kansas jointly publish *American Studies.* The aim of this journal is to be cross-disciplinary and to widen the field of American Studies discourse. Both specialists and nonspecialists will find engaging articles here.

1566. Atlantic Studies: literary, cultural and historical perspectives. [ISSN: 1478-8810] 2004. s-a. GBP 268 print & online eds. Ed(s): William Boelhower, Dorothea Fischer-Hornung. Routledge, 4 Park Square, Milton Park, Abingdon, OX14 4RN, United Kingdom; info@routledge.co.uk; http://www.routledge.co.uk. Reprint: PSC. *Indexed:* AmH&L, AmHI, HistAb, IBSS. *Aud.:* Ac.

This international journal brings together scholarship on the cultures and societies of the overall Atlantic world, in particular the countries of Africa, the Americas, and Europe. It deals primarily with the areas of history and literature along with cultural studies and critical theory, and includes both research studies and debate on current issues. *Atlantic Studies* is the official journal of the Society for Multi-Ethnic Studies: Europe and the Americas. Articles in recent issues cover topics such as French Caribbean literature, the Chesapeake in the seventeenth century, the Cape Verde Islands and the African Atlantic, and Cuban slaves in the nineteenth century. The diasporic, historical, and literary studies of ethnic groups in the Atlantic region form the basis for the writing in this journal. Recommended for academic libraries with an emphasis on this region.

Behaviour and Information Technology. See Psychology section.

1567. Body & Society. [ISSN: 1357-034X] 1995. q. GBP 417. Ed(s): Bryan Turner, Mike Featherstone. Sage Publications Ltd., 1 Oliver's Yard, 55 City Rd, London, EC1 1SP, United Kingdom; info@sagepub.co.uk; http://www.sagepub.co.uk. Adv. Refereed. Circ: 800. Reprint: PSC. *Indexed:* ASSIA, AltPI, IBR, IBSS, IBZ, PEI, SSA, SSCI, SWA, SociolAb, V&AA. *Bk. rev.:* Occasional, 1-4 reviews, 500-1,000 words. *Aud.:* Ac.

This heavily theoretical publication covers disciplines from art and cultural history to health studies, sociology, and philosophy. Focusing on the social and cultural analysis of the human body, articles in this journal center on themes of feminism, postmodernism, medicine, ethics, and consumerism. The Theory, Culture and Society Centre at Nottingham Trent University sponsors this journal along with its joint publication, *Theory, Culture and Society.* Recent

articles in *Body and Society* cover such topics as cosmopolitanism and travel, collective memory, tattooing, and disability and religious tradition. For scholars interested in a wide-ranging combination of theory, society, culture, and science.

1568. Cabinet. [ISSN: 1531-1430] 2000. q. Individuals, USD 28. Ed(s): Sina Najafi. Immaterial Incorporated, 181 Wyckoff St, Brooklyn, NY 11217; subscriptions@immaterial.net; http://www.immaterial.net. *Aud.:* Ga, Ac.

The focus of *Cabinet* is the "margins of culture." An incredibly wide-ranging magazine, this publication covers primarily art and culture, but combines many other aspects into the mix. Both international and interdisciplinary, each issue contains regular columns and essays along with interviews, photography, works of art, and postcards. Issues begin with columns on "Colors," "Ingestion," and "Inventory." The main section includes both articles and art projects ranging from color-music to eye drawings and from the common cold to German photographs. A thematic section is featured in each issue on subjects such as insects, fruits, shadows, and insecurity. Contributors range from academics to freelance writers, artists, filmmakers, sound designers, and musicians. The magazine's web site contains a table of contents and information on contributors, along with additional readings, artwork, sound tracks, and musical works. Named best art and culture magazine by New York Press in 2001 and 2003, this publication provides fascinating reading, engaging art and photography, and something to tickle everyone's fancy.

1569. Canadian Review of American Studies. Formerly (until 1970): *C A S Bulletin.* [ISSN: 0007-7720] 1965. 3x/yr. CND 90 domestic; USD 90 United States; USD 110 elsewhere. Ed(s): Priscilla Walton. University of Toronto Press, Journals Division, 5201 Dufferin St, Toronto, ON M3H 5T8, Canada; journals@utpress.utoronto.ca; http://www.utpjournals.com. Illus., index, adv. Refereed. Circ: 400. Vol. ends: No. 3. Reprint: PSC. *Indexed:* AmH&L, AmHI, ArtHuCI, CBCARef, FLI, HistAb, IBR, IBSS, IBZ, MLA-IB, PSA, RILM, SSCI, SociolAb. *Bk. rev.:* 2-3, 1,000-1,500 words. *Aud.:* Ac.

American culture from the perspective of our northern neighbors is the focus of this publication by the Canadian Association for American Studies in conjunction with the University of Calgary and the University of Windsor. This journal emphasizes cross-disciplinary studies of U.S. culture from both historical and contemporary perspectives. It also includes articles on the relationship between U.S. and Canadian cultures. Each issue includes research articles and review essays written primarily by Canadian academics, with some content by U.S. and international scholars. Many articles focus on literary works or films, while others explore social and cultural issues. Recent articles cover such topics as Chinese American writers, the African American jeramiad, woman suffrage, Vietnam War poetry, and the language of taste. Libraries with an emphasis on American Studies scholarship from varying viewpoints will want to include this journal in their collection.

1570. Comparative American Studies. [ISSN: 1477-5700] 2003. q. USD 636. Ed(s): Richard Ellis. Maney Publishing, Ste. 1C, Joseph's Well, Hanover Walk, Leeds, LS3 1AB, United Kingdom; maney@maney.co.uk; http://www.maney.co.uk. Adv. Reprint: PSC. *Indexed:* AmHI, CommAb, IBR, IBZ, IPSA, SociolAb. *Bk. rev.:* 2-6 reviews, essay length. *Aud.:* Ac.

Scholarship on American Studies from outside the United States is the focus of *Comparative American Studies.* The journal aims to place the discourse on American culture into an international framework. With the contemporary focus on globalization and on the relationship between the United States and other nations, *Comparative American Studies* seeks to draw out the conflicts and common themes, especially in the areas of literature, film, popular culture, photography, and visual arts. Each issue contains six to eight articles on topics such as America in the post-9/11 era, American literature in other languages, and the black Atlantic. Some articles cover comparative themes in the works of U.S., Canadian, and Latin American writers and artists. Since its beginning in 2003, this journal has filled a major gap in the literature of American Studies by providing a much-needed international viewpoint.

1571. *Critical Discourse Studies.* [ISSN: 1740-5904] 2004. s-a. GBP 314 print & online eds. Ed(s): Norman Fairclough, Ruth Wodak. Routledge, 4 Park Square, Milton Park, Abingdon, OX14 4RN, United Kingdom; info@routledge.co.uk; http://www.tandf.co.uk/journals. Refereed. Reprint: PSC. *Indexed:* AmHI, IBSS, L&LBA, LingAb, PSA, SociolAb. *Aud.:* Ac.

Reaching far beyond language and linguistic studies, this publication has something for every discipline in the social sciences, as well as literary and media studies and racial, ethnic and gender studies. This journal aims to "publish critical research that advances our understanding of how discourse figures into social processes, social structures and social change." Connecting academic research with discussion of practical and activist approaches is an additional goal of *Critical Discourse Studies*. Recent articles cover such topics as news reports on human rights, weather discourse, computer war games, teaching household Spanish, and race in British political discourse. Each issue is primarily composed of original articles, although some issues include book reviews and debate sections. This journal enhances the range of scholarship on critical discourse, a vital expanding area of interdisciplinary study.

1572. *Critical Inquiry.* [ISSN: 0093-1896] 1974. q. USD 182 domestic; USD 198.92 Canada; USD 194 elsewhere. Ed(s): W J T Mitchell. University of Chicago Press, Journals Division, PO Box 37005, Chicago, IL 60637; subscriptions@press.uchicago.edu; http://www.journals.uchicago.edu. Illus., index, adv. Refereed. Circ: 2700. Vol. ends: Summer. Microform: PMC; PQC. Online: Chadwyck-Healey Inc.; EBSCO Publishing, EBSCO Host; Florida Center for Library Automation; Gale; JSTOR (Web-based Journal Archive); OCLC Online Computer Library Center, Inc.; ProQuest LLC (Ann Arbor). Reprint: PSC. *Indexed:* ABM, ABS&EES, AmH&L, AmHI, ArtHuCI, BEL&L, CJA, FLI, HistAb, HumInd, IBR, IBZ, L&LBA, LRI, MLA-IB, MRD, PSA, PhilInd, RILM, SSA, SSCI, SociolAb. *Aud.:* Ac.

For over 30 years, *Critical Inquiry* has set the standard for publishing interdisciplinary criticism in the arts and humanities. Each issue includes several articles on topics from the arts, philosophy, literature, film, history, politics, and social issues. Recent issues include articles on such subjects as secularism, conceptual art, Islamic law and feminism, occidentalism, and dissent in Israel. Some volumes include a special section on a single topic or a specific author such as Edward Said or Jacques Derrida. This journal provides a forum for both traditional and currently developed ideas. In *Critical Inquiry*, authors engage in theoretical debate and spar in critical responses. A significant journal for most academic libraries.

1573. *Critical Review (Columbus): an interdisciplinary journal of politics and society.* [ISSN: 0891-3811] 1987. q. GBP 214 print & online eds. Ed(s): Jeffrey Friedman. Routledge, 325 Chestnut St, Ste 800, Philadelphia, PA 19106; journals@routledge.com; http://www.tandf.co.uk/journals. Illus., index, adv. Refereed. Circ: 2000 Paid. Vol. ends: Fall. Microform: PQC. Online: Chadwyck-Healey Inc.; Northern Light Technology, Inc.; ProQuest LLC (Ann Arbor). Reprint: PSC. *Indexed:* AmH&L, ArtHuCI, BRI, HistAb, IBR, IBSS, IBZ, IPSA, JEL, L&LBA, LeftInd, PAIS, PRA, PSA, PhilInd, SSA, SSCI, SociolAb. *Bk. rev.:* 1-3, review essays in some issues. *Aud.:* Ac.

This journal will interest academics in all areas of the social sciences, especially political scientists and economists. *Critical Review* focuses on "researching and debating the nature and role of the modern state." Contributors are primarily from U.S. academic circles, with a few authors from other countries. Articles are theoretical or historical but do not advocate or criticize policies. Each issue concentrates on a particular theme, such as democracy, law and political reality, bias, and ignorance in politics and science. Each issue contains several research articles or essays, well written and extensively documented. Articles explore topics such as belief systems, media bias, and critical realism. One or more review essays are included in most issues. This journal presents lively writing and debate on major political, economic, and social ideas.

1574. *Cross-Cultural Research: the journal of comparative social science.* Former titles (until 1993): *Behavior Science Research; Behavior Science Notes.* [ISSN: 1069-3971] 1966. q. GBP 319. Ed(s): Melvin Ember. Sage Publications, Inc., 2455 Teller Rd, Thousand Oaks, CA 91320; info@sagepub.com; http://www.sagepub.com. Illus., index, adv. Refereed.

Circ: 550 Paid and free. Vol. ends: Nov. Microform: PQC. Online: EBSCO Publishing, EBSCO Host; HighWire Press; OCLC Online Computer Library Center, Inc.; SAGE Publications, Inc., SAGE Journals Online; SwetsWise Online Content; H.W. Wilson. Reprint: PSC. *Indexed:* ABIn, ABS&EES, AICP, AbAn, AgeL, AnthLit, BAS, CJA, CommAb, EI, FR, HRA, IBR, IBSS, IBZ, IMFL, IPSA, L&LBA, PRA, PSA, PsycInfo, SSA, SSCI, SociolAb, V&AA. *Aud.:* Ac.

Cross-Cultural Research aims to publish comparative studies in many areas of the social and behavioral sciences from anthropology, education, psychology, and sociology to subdisciplines such as human and political ecology and evolutionary biology. The journal stresses the methodology of the research and requires that articles include statistical measures linking dependent and independent variables. Recent articles cover such topics as war and the socialization of children, hunting and gathering, sexually transmitted disease and gender roles, and mail order brides. Occasional special issues are published on such themes as corporal punishment or comparative research in anthropological sciences. The journal is sponsored by Human Relations Area Files, Inc., and is the official journal of the Society for Cross-Cultural Research. Scholars in many areas of the social sciences will find this publication valuable for its analysis and range of coverage.

1575. *Cultural & Social History.* [ISSN: 1478-0038] 2004. 3x/yr. GBP 155 GBP 30 per issue domestic. Ed(s): Alexandra Shepard, Anthony McElligott. Berg Publishers, Angel Court, 1st Fl, 81 St Clements St, Oxford, OX4 1AW, United Kingdom; enquiry@bergpublishers.com; http://www.bergpublishers.com/. Illus., adv. Sample. Refereed. Reprint: PSC. *Indexed:* BrHumI, IBR, IBZ, PSA, SociolAb. *Bk. rev.:* 10-12, essay length. *Aud.:* Ac.

This journal is sponsored by the Social History Society and based in the United Kingdom. The purpose of this publication is to blend the historical study of culture and society beyond the traditional borders of these two areas of history. Although many articles focus on aspects of British or Irish history, the journal also has international coverage including recent articles on Russia, East Asia, and Africa. Most contributors are from Britain, the United States, or Western Europe. Each issue includes research articles, a debate forum, a review essay, and several individual book reviews. Articles cover such topics as witchcraft, crime, social status, and religion. With contemporary shifts in historical research toward more emphasis on the interweaving of cultural and social aspects, this journal is right in step with changes in the discipline. *Cultural & Social History* will be of interest to scholars and students in history and related areas such as literature, art, and cultural studies.

1576. *Cultural Critique: an international journal of cultural studies.* [ISSN: 0882-4371] 1985. 3x/yr. USD 78 (Individuals, USD 30). Ed(s): Keya Ganguly, Jochen Schulte-Sasse. University of Minnesota Press, 111 Third Ave S, Ste 290, Minneapolis, MN 55401-2520; ump@umn.edu; http://www.upress.umn.edu. Illus., index, adv. Sample. Refereed. Circ: 700. Vol. ends: Oct. Microform: PQC. Online: EBSCO Publishing, EBSCO Host; JSTOR (Web-based Journal Archive); OCLC Online Computer Library Center, Inc.; OhioLINK; Project MUSE; SwetsWise Online Content. *Indexed:* ABS&EES, AltPI, AmH&L, AmHI, ArtHuCI, FLI, HistAb, HumInd, IBR, IBSS, IBZ, IPSA, LeftInd, MLA-IB, PSA, RI-1, RILM, SSA, SSCI, SociolAb. *Aud.:* Ac.

This journal includes culture in the broadest sense and critique encompassing analysis and interpretation, rather than strictly criticism. An international and interdisciplinary publication, *Cultural Critique* deals with "intellectual controversies, trends, and issues in culture, theory and politics." Most contributors are scholars from U.S. institutions, although some international writers and researchers are included. Most issues are devoted to a single topic, or a few main subjects. Some articles involve literary criticism, while others focus on sociological, anthropological, and philosophical issues. Both historical topics and contemporary social and aesthetic studies are included. Recent articles cover such subjects as the feminization of globalization, religious fundamentalism, and the future of the research university. *Cultural Critique* will appeal to scholars in literature, film, politics, media, art, and sociology.

1577. *Cultural Sociology.* [ISSN: 1749-9755] 2007. 3x/yr. GBP 270. Ed(s): David Inglis, Andrew Blaikie. Sage Publications Ltd., 1 Oliver's Yard, 55 City Rd, London, EC1 1SP, United Kingdom; info@sagepub.co.uk; http://www.sagepub.co.uk. *Aud.:* Ac.

This is a groundbreaking journal merging the fields of sociology and cultural studies into a specialized venue for the first time. An official publication of the British Sociological Association, *Cultural Sociology* aims to "consolidate, develop and promote the arena of sociological understandings of culture." The editors and contributors are primarily from universities in the United Kingdom, with some from the United States and Europe; however, the journal deals with sociology and culture internationally. Articles on the construction of inequality, the work of culture, cultural genealogy, taste and sociology, and cultural consumption analysis, comprise the initial issue. Although scholarship in culture and sociology has been published in many other types of journals, this publication promises to provide a gathering place for research and discourse in this expanding area. Scholars in sociology, cultural studies, and related fields will find this new journal of great interest.

1578. *Cultural Studies.* [ISSN: 0950-2386] 1987. bi-m. GBP 435 print & online eds. Ed(s): Della Pollock, Lawrence Grossberg. Routledge, 4 Park Square, Milton Park, Abingdon, OX14 4RN, United Kingdom; info@routledge.co.uk; http://www.routledge.com. Illus., adv. Refereed. Circ: 1650. Vol. ends: Oct. Online: EBSCO Publishing, EBSCO Host; Gale; IngentaConnect; OCLC Online Computer Library Center, Inc.; SwetsWise Online Content. Reprint: PSC. *Indexed:* ASSIA, AltPI, AmHI, ArtHuCI, BrHumI, CommAb, FR, HumInd, IBSS, PRA, PSA, RI-1, RILM, SSA, SSCI, SWA, SociolAb, V&AA. *Bk. rev.:* 2-6; essay length. *Aud.:* Ac.

During its 20-year history, *Cultural Studies* has consistently sought to be on the cutting edge of writing in this interdisciplinary area. Its aim is to "explore the relation between cultural practices, everyday life, material, economic, political, geographical and historical contexts." This journal emphasizes race, class, and gender, while addressing major questions of community, identity, agency, and change. Contributors are mainly from the United States, the United Kingdom, and Australia, with occasional articles by authors from other countries. Each issue contains several original articles, with book reviews included in some. Frequently, special issues concentrate on single themes such as coloniality, secrecy, security, and intellectual property. Articles have explored such topics as contemporary surveillance, safe households, virtual reality, and African diaspora spaces. *Cultural Studies* will be of interest to scholars and students seeking dynamic, international coverage of cultural issues.

1579. *Cultural Studies - Critical Methodologies.* [ISSN: 1532-7086] 2001. q. USD 454. Ed(s): Norman K Denzin. Sage Publications, Inc., 2455 Teller Rd, Thousand Oaks, CA 91320; info@sagepub.com; http://www.sagepub.com. Adv. Reprint: PSC. *Indexed:* IBSS, PSA, SociolAb. *Aud.:* Ac.

While other titles concentrate on the wider range of cultural studies, or the specific area of cultural critique, this journal combines both with an emphasis on methodology. Such issues as "local and global, text and context, voice, writing for the other, and the presence of the author in the text" are the underlying focus of many contributions to this journal. Each issue is composed of several original articles on topics such as Hurricane Katrina and the collapse of civil society, secrecy and the war in Iraq, and critical pedagogy. Analysis of popular culture, media, and new technologies is also integral to the writing in this publication. *Cultural Studies—Critical Methodologies* blends methodology with the full expanse of cultural studies and cultural critique to make a vital and spirited addition to the literature in this interdisciplinary field.

1580. *Futures.* [ISSN: 0016-3287] 1968. 10x/yr. EUR 1037. Ed(s): Zia Sardar. Pergamon, The Boulevard, Langford Ln, East Park, Kidlington, OX5 1GB, United Kingdom. Illus., index, adv. Sample. Refereed. Vol. ends: Dec. Microform: PQC. Online: EBSCO Publishing, EBSCO Host; Gale; IngentaConnect; OhioLINK; ScienceDirect; SwetsWise Online Content. *Indexed:* ABIn, ArtHuCI, FutSurv, HortAb, IBR, IBZ, ISTA, PSA, PhilInd, RRTA, RiskAb, SSA, SSCI, SociolAb, WAE&RSA. *Bk. rev.:* 2-4, 500-1,500 words. *Aud.:* Ac, Sa.

This journal covers future studies from a cultural, social, scientific, economic, political, and environmental perspective. *Futures* has an international advisory board, but authors are mainly from the United States and the United Kingdom, with some from other countries. The papers that begin each issue cover such subjects as the future workplace, environmental policies, and futures literacy. Many volumes include special issues on such themes as transformative initiatives, Australia's futures, and the future of bioregions. Shorter review articles, essays, and reports are included along with book reviews. *Futures* aims "to examine possible and alternative futures of all human endeavors." This journal will appeal to scholars in the sciences and social sciences and to members of the business and government communities.

1581. *Futures Research Quarterly.* Formerly (until 1985): *World Future Society Bulletin.* [ISSN: 8755-3317] 1967. q. Members, USD 77; Non-members, USD 99. Ed(s): Timothy Mack. World Future Society, 7910 Woodmont Ave, Ste 450, Bethesda, MD 20814; info@wfs.org; http://www.wfs.org/. Illus. Refereed. Circ: 1700. Microform: PQC. Online: EBSCO Publishing, EBSCO Host. *Indexed:* FutSurv. *Bk. rev.:* 3-8, 300-1,000 words. *Aud.:* Ga, Ac.

Futures Research Quarterly, a publication of the World Future Society, seeks to stimulate and advance discourse in many disciplines and areas of future studies. The focus of this journal is on applications of futures research, theory, and methodology. The role of futures research in long-range planning and overall decision-making is also a central theme of this publication. Each issue includes scholarly articles on such topics as prediction and forecasting, leisure in the twenty-first century, futures studies, and strategic issue management. Most issues also contain special features including book reviews and reports on worldwide initiatives and strategies. Contributors are primarily from colleges and universities and research institutes. This journal will be of interest to researchers as well as to planners and decision makers in the public sector and private industry.

1582. *Futurics: a quarterly journal of futures research.* [ISSN: 0164-1220] 1976. q. USD 65 in North America; USD 82 elsewhere. Ed(s): Earl C Joseph. Minnesota Futurists, 825 Summit Ave., Minneapolis, MN 55403; josep027@tc.umn.edu; http://www.mnfuturists.org. Illus., adv. Refereed. Circ: 300. Vol. ends: Oct/Dec. Microform: PQC. Online: Northern Light Technology, Inc.; ProQuest LLC (Ann Arbor). *Indexed:* FutSurv. *Bk. rev.:* 2-6, 250-500 words. *Aud.:* Ga, Ac.

Exploration of alternative futures is the focus of *Futurics*. This regional publication includes full-length articles, responses to articles, short notes, reviews of books and films, and information on recent developments in futures research. Articles cover such topics as urban spaces, trends in computer hardware, Internet usage in China, and e-learning. *Futurics* is published by the Minnesota chapter of the World Future Society. Most contributors are academics from selected institutions in the metropolitan Minneapolis area. Many of the articles are reviews of the literature on a specific topic rather than empirical research. A state and regional publication, this journal will be of greatest interest to libraries in Minnesota and Midwestern areas.

1583. *The Futurist: a journal of forecasts, trends, and ideas about the future.* [ISSN: 0016-3317] 1967. bi-m. USD 55 & institutions Free to members. Ed(s): Cynthia G Wagner, Edward S Cornish. World Future Society, 7910 Woodmont Ave, Ste 450, Bethesda, MD 20814; info@wfs.org; http://www.wfs.org/. Illus., index, adv. Refereed. Circ: 25000 Paid and controlled. Vol. ends: Dec. Microform: PQC. Online: The Dialog Corporation; EBSCO Publishing, EBSCO Host; Florida Center for Library Automation; Gale; Northern Light Technology, Inc.; OCLC Online Computer Library Center, Inc.; ProQuest LLC (Ann Arbor); H.W. Wilson. *Indexed:* ABIn, AgeL, ArtHuCI, BRI, CBRI, CPerI, EAA, EIP, EnvAb, EnvInd, FutSurv, IBR, IBZ, MASUSE, RGPR, RI-1, SSCI, SWR&A. *Bk. rev.:* 1-3, 400-1,000 words. *Aud.:* Hs, Ga, Ac.

The World Future Society is perhaps the leading organization in future studies. For 40 years the society's popular publication, *The Futurist,* has been publishing articles and reports on many aspects of this interdisciplinary area. Each issue includes several engaging articles on such topics as global terrorism, digital currency, visual culture, and sports media. Articles are written by noted researchers and writers in the field. The "World Trends and Forecasts" section offers brief reports in the categories of government, economics, and demography, as well as technology, the environment, and society. "Tomorrow in Brief" presents notices, comments, and news items, some of which are gleaned from other publications. The December issue includes an outlook section compiling forecasts for the coming year. This magazine will appeal to a range of readers from the general public to students at many levels.

Gender & Society. See Gender Studies section.

1584. *History of the Human Sciences.* [ISSN: 0952-6951] 1988. q. GBP 548. Ed(s): James Good. Sage Publications Ltd., 1 Oliver's Yard, 55 City Rd, London, EC1 1SP, United Kingdom; info@sagepub.co.uk; http://www.sagepub.co.uk. Illus., index, adv. Refereed. Circ: 750. Vol. ends: Nov. Reprint: PSC. *Indexed:* ASSIA, AmH&L, AmHI, ArtHuCI, BrHumI, HistAb, IBR, IBSS, IBZ, IPB, IPSA, PSA, PhilInd, PsycInfo, SCI, SSA, SSCI, SociolAb, V&AA. *Bk. rev.:* 1-2, essay length. *Aud.:* Ac.

Based on a broad definition of the human sciences, this publication offers a range of scholarly articles linking research from traditional social science disciplines, including sociology, psychology, anthropology, and political science, with the areas of philosophy, literary criticism, art history, linguistics, psychoanalysis, aesthetics, and law. Some issues focus on one theme, such as sociology and related disciplines, reflexivity, or Holocaust studies. Other issues cover a variety of topics, such as secular morality and progressive politics, psychological adaptation and instinct, biopolitics, and serial killing and identity. Reviews of individual books as well as review essays appear regularly. Most contributors are academics from British, European, and U.S. institutions. This journal will appeal to scholars and advanced students interested in the complex relationships between social science and humanities research.

1585. *Humanities: the magazine of the national endowment for the humanities.* [ISSN: 0018-7526] 1980. bi-m. USD 24. Ed(s): Mary Lou Beatty. U.S. National Endowment for the Humanities, 1100 Pennsylvania Ave, NW, Washington, DC 20506; info@neh.gov; http://www.neh.gov. Illus., index. Sample. Circ: 12000. Vol. ends: Nov/Dec. Microform: PQC. Online: EBSCO Publishing, EBSCO Host; Northern Light Technology, Inc.; OCLC Online Computer Library Center, Inc.; ProQuest K-12 Learning Solutions; ProQuest LLC (Ann Arbor); H.W. Wilson. *Indexed:* AmHI, FLI, HumInd, IUSGP, MASUSE, RI-1, RILM, RRTA. *Aud.:* Hs, Ga, Ac.

This publication reports on the activities and projects sponsored by U.S. government's National Endowment for the Humanities (NEH). *Humanities* includes articles on history, literature, music, art, film, theater, and photography. Contributors are academics, freelance writers, and NEH staff and administrators. Many issues feature one or more sections on specific topics, such as the American West, the power of music, intrepid women, and the Jamestown settlement. A section labeled "Around the Nation" describes exhibits, lectures, festivals, and programs sponsored by state humanities councils. The "Calendar" section describes and pictures current endowment-sponsored exhibitions. The "Deadlines" page lists NEH grants, fellowships, seminars, etc., with application dates. This publication includes engaging, well-illustrated articles that will appeal to a general readers as well as scholars interested in obtaining NEH funding.

1586. *International Journal of Politics, Culture, and Society.* Formerly (until 1987): *State, Culture, and Society.* [ISSN: 0891-4486] 1984. q. EUR 785 print & online eds. Ed(s): Jeffrey Goldfarb, Vera Zolberg. Springer New York LLC, 233 Spring St, New York, NY 10013-1578; service-ny@springer.com; http://www.springer.com/. Illus., index, adv. Refereed. Circ: 500. Vol. ends: Summer. Microform: PQC. Online: EBSCO Publishing, EBSCO Host; Gale; IngentaConnect; OCLC Online Computer Library Center, Inc.; OhioLINK; Springer LINK; SwetsWise Online Content. Reprint: PSC. *Indexed:* AmH&L, HistAb, IBSS, IMFL, IPSA, IndIslam, PAIS, PSA, RiskAb, SSA, SWA, SWR&A, SociolAb. *Bk. rev.:* essay length, in some issues. *Aud.:* Ac.

This journal interweaves scholarship on global and regional political issues with social and cultural theory and conflict. Each issue includes essays and research articles on one or more themes such as institutional change, ethnic and religious groups, and social transformation. Recent articles cover issues such as the new sociological imagination, religion and globalization, the Palestinian–Israeli

conflict, the Balkan states, and gender equity. Essay-length book reviews or a review and commentary section are included in some issues. The journal's editorial board is centered at the New School for Social Research, but contributors are drawn from many countries. Articles frequently cover political and social issues in the context of a particular nation or region. This publication will appeal to social scientists and scholars interested in societal change, especially as it relates to international political and cultural issues.

1587. *International Review of Social History.* Formerly (until 1956): *International Institute for Social History. Bulletin.* [ISSN: 0020-8590] 1937. 3x/yr. GBP 132. Ed(s): Marcel van der Linden. Cambridge University Press, The Edinburgh Bldg, Shaftesbury Rd, Cambridge, CB2 2RU, United Kingdom; journals@cambridge.org; http://www.journals.cambridge.org. Adv. Refereed. Microform: PQC. Online: Pub.; EBSCO Publishing, EBSCO Host; OCLC Online Computer Library Center, Inc.; OhioLINK; SwetsWise Online Content. *Indexed:* AmH&L, ArtHuCI, HistAb, IBR, IBSS, IBZ, IPSA, IndIslam, PSA, SSA, SSCI, SWA, SociolAb. *Bk. rev.:* 8-12, 1,000 words, some essay length. *Aud.:* Ac.

For 70 years this journal has published much of the leading scholarship in social history. The International Institute for Social History, based in the Netherlands, sponsors the journal. Contributors are mainly from American and British institutions, with some from European countries. The research articles that begin each issue cover a range of countries, usually Britain, the United States, or European states, but also Africa, Israel, and Australia. Many articles explore issues of workers' groups and labor history, but other topics from worldwide migration and social class to refugees and rebel armies are also included. Articles are in English, with occasional reviews in French or German. The extensive annotated bibliography of books on many aspects of social history is a vital section of this journal. Covering some 30 pages, the bibliography begins with a general section and is then subdivided by continent and country. The annual supplement is another strength of the journal; this special issue draws together articles on a major theme such as labor history in India and South Asia, or marriage and social class. The journal will appeal to historians and social scientists, especially scholars with an interest in labor history.

1588. *International Social Science Journal.* Formerly (until 1959): *International Social Science Bulletin.* [ISSN: 0020-8701] 1949. q. GBP 202 print & online eds. Blackwell Publishing Ltd., 9600 Garsington Rd, Oxford, OX4 2ZG, United Kingdom; customerservices@ blackwellpublishing.com; http://www.blackwellpublishing.com. Illus., index, adv. Sample. Refereed. Circ: 4500. Vol. ends: Dec. Microform: MIM; PQC. Online: Blackwell Synergy; EBSCO Publishing, EBSCO Host; Gale; IngentaConnect; OCLC Online Computer Library Center, Inc.; OhioLINK; SwetsWise Online Content. Reprint: PSC. *Indexed:* ABCPolSci, AICP, ASSIA, AbAn, AgeL, AmH&L, ApEcolAb, ArtHuCI, BAS, CJA, EI, ERIC, ExcerpMed, FutSurv, HistAb, IBR, IBSS, IBZ, IPSA, IndIslam, JEL, MLA-IB, PAIS, PRA, PSA, PsycInfo, RRTA, SFSA, SSA, SSCI, SWA, SociolAb, WAE&RSA. *Aud.:* Ga, Ac.

Policy questions form the basis for most of the writing in this journal. *International Social Science Journal* provides a venue for scholarship that "reviews, reflects and discusses the results of relevant research." Issued for the United Nations Educational, Social and Cultural Organization (UNESCO), this journal is published in six languages (French, Spanish, Chinese, Arabic, English, and Russian), and the contributors are drawn from many countries. Each issue is devoted to one or two major topics such as remembering slavery, cultural diversity and biodiversity, or social science perspectives on HIV/AIDS. Several articles explore regional and worldwide issues related to the overall theme. Occasionally other sections are included. "Continuing Debate" follows up on previous articles or presents contrasting views on major questions. "Social Science Sphere" offers articles on the social sciences as a whole, concentrating on interdisciplinary aspects. "Open Forum" presents shorter articles on topics other than the theme of the issue. This journal will appeal primarily to academics and policy makers interested in global policy issues.

1589. *Journal for Early Modern Cultural Studies.* [ISSN: 1531-0485] 2001. s-a. USD 37.50 (Individuals, USD 25). Ed(s): Bruce Boehrer. Indiana University Press, 601 N Morton St, Bloomington, IN 47404; http://www.indiana.edu/~iupress. *Indexed:* AmHI, HumInd, MLA-IB. *Bk. rev.;* 2, 1000-1500 words. *Aud.:* Ac.

Although other publications in cultural-social studies focus on history, this journal specializes in the late fifteenth century to the late nineteenth century. As the official publication of the Group for Early Modern Cultural Studies, this publication combines scholarship from many areas of the humanities, social sciences, and area studies with research on gender and postmodernism. Editors and contributors are largely from U.S. and Canadian universities. Beginning with the 2005 volume, one issue per year is devoted to the earlier centuries within the journal's chronological period, while the other issue covers the later centuries. Issues of the journal often emphasize an overall theme such as Shakespeare and English Renaissance drama or post-colonialism. Recent articles have focused on topics from clowns in English drama to trade and diplomacy with China and Japan. This journal will be of interest to scholars in many disciplines whose research centers on the early modern time period.

1590. *Journal of Aesthetic Education.* [ISSN: 0021-8510] 1966. q. USD 88 print & online eds. (Individuals, USD 45 print & online eds.). Ed(s): Pradeep A. Dhillon. University of Illinois Press, 1325 S Oak St, Champaign, IL 61820-6903; journals@uillinois.edu; http://www.press.uillinois.edu. Illus., index, adv. Refereed. Circ: 900 Paid. Vol. ends: Winter. Microform: MIM; PQC. Online: EBSCO Publishing, EBSCO Host; Northern Light Technology, Inc.; OCLC Online Computer Library Center, Inc.; OhioLINK; Project MUSE; ProQuest LLC (Ann Arbor); SwetsWise Online Content. *Indexed:* ABIn, ABM, AmHI, ArtHuCI, ArtInd, BAS, BEL&L, BRI, CBRI, ERIC, EduInd, FLI, IBR, IBZ, PhilInd, RILM, SSCI. *Bk. rev.:* 3-5, 500-1,500 words. *Aud.:* Ac.

Journal of Aesthetic Education draws together the threads of philosophy, theory, and pedagogy as applied to the full range of the arts. The journal provides a forum to explore issues in aesthetic education, both in instructional settings and in society at large. Contributors cover issues of aesthetics and public policy, cultural administration, arts and humanities instruction, aesthetics and new communications media, and the art of teaching and learning. Individual issues include articles on theory and philosophy, and analysis of specific works in literature, art, or music. Recent issues feature articles on such topics as imitation in art, social aspects of violence in relation to art, environmental architecture, and justifying the arts. Special issues have covered themes from aesthetics in drama and theatre education to aesthetic education in Japan to the arts and academic achievement. Some issues contain commentary sections with brief essays or responses to earlier articles. This journal will appeal to scholars and artists as well as to teachers and administrators in arts education.

1591. *Journal of Aesthetics and Art Criticism.* [ISSN: 0021-8529] 1941. q. GBP 144 print & online eds. Ed(s): Susan Feagin. Blackwell Publishing, Inc., Commerce Place, 350 Main St, Malden, MA 02148; customerservices@blackwellpublishing.com; http://www.blackwellpublishing.com. Illus., index, adv. Refereed. Circ: 2700 Paid. Vol. ends: Fall. Microform: MIM; PQC. Online: Blackwell Synergy; EBSCO Publishing, EBSCO Host; Gale; IngentaConnect; JSTOR (Web-based Journal Archive); OCLC Online Computer Library Center, Inc.; OhioLINK; SwetsWise Online Content. Reprint: PSC. *Indexed:* ABM, ABS&EES, AmHI, ArtHuCI, ArtInd, BAS, BRD, BRI, CBRI, FLI, FR, HumInd, IBR, IBZ, IIMP, IIPA, IPB, IndIslam, MLA-IB, MusicInd, PhilInd, RILM, SSCI. *Bk. rev.:* 7-15, 1,000-2,000 words. *Aud.:* Ac.

Although the title of this journal may indicate a quite specific publication, the *Journal of Aesthetics and Art Criticism* instead takes a very wide-ranging view. Both fine and decorative arts are included as well as film, photography, performance, and popular culture. Most issues include several research articles, occasional discussion segments, and book reviews. Articles cover theoretical and philosophical research on aesthetics as well as critical analyses of specific works and artists, historical treatment of the arts, and social and political questions related to aesthetics. Some issues include symposia, a collection of several articles on one theme such as Monroe Beardsley's legacy on aesthetics, or how museums do things with artworks, or the historicity of the eye.

Occasional special issues are published on topics including global theories of the arts and aesthetics, and film as philosophy. As the journal of the American Society for Aesthetics, this publication will appeal to scholars in the philosophy of the arts, to critics of art, and more broadly to students of aesthetics.

Journal of American Ethnic History. See Ethnic Studies section.

1592. *Journal of American Studies.* Formerly (until 1967): *British Association for American Studies. Bulletin.* [ISSN: 0021-8758] 1967. 3x/yr. GBP 166. Ed(s): S. Jay Kleinberg, Susan Castillo. Cambridge University Press, The Edinburgh Bldg, Shaftesbury Rd, Cambridge, CB2 2RU, United Kingdom; journals@cambridge.org; http://www.journals.cambridge.org. Illus., index, adv. Refereed. Vol. ends: Dec. Microform: PQC. Online: Pub.; EBSCO Publishing, EBSCO Host; OCLC Online Computer Library Center, Inc.; OhioLINK; SwetsWise Online Content. Reprint: PSC. *Indexed:* AmH&L, AmHI, ArtHuCI, BRI, BrHumI, CBRI, CJA, FLI, HistAb, HumInd, IBR, IBSS, IBZ, IPSA, LRI, MLA-IB, PSA, RI-1, RILM, SSA, SSCI, SociolAb. *Bk. rev.:* 30-40, 250-750 words. *Aud.:* Ac.

American Studies from the perspective of British scholars are the focus of this publication. U.S. literary works, politics, history, and economics are covered, as are art, music, film, and popular culture. Most contributors are from British universities, although some articles are by U.S. and European authors. Many articles explore American literary classics or historical topics, but cross-disciplinary and comparative cultural studies are also included. Recent articles cover such topics as race and the politics of memory, male empowerment in the 1930s, and Chinese diaspora poetry in America. Each issue includes many book reviews; review essays also appear in some issues. The journal is sponsored by the British Association for American Studies. Biennially, the journal publishes a list of theses on American Studies in progress or completed at British universities. This journal will be of interest to scholars of American Studies in the United Kingdom and the United States.

1593. *Journal of British Studies.* Incorporates (1969-2005): *Albion.* [ISSN: 0021-9371] 1961. q. USD 218. Ed(s): Anna Clark. University of Chicago Press, Journals Division, PO Box 37005, Chicago, IL 60637; http://www.journals.uchicago.edu. Illus., index, adv. Refereed. Circ: 1500 Paid. Vol. ends: Oct. Microform: PQC. Online: Chadwyck-Healey Inc.; EBSCO Publishing, EBSCO Host; Florida Center for Library Automation; Gale; JSTOR (Web-based Journal Archive); ProQuest LLC (Ann Arbor). Reprint: PSC. *Indexed:* AmH&L, AmHI, ArtHuCI, BrArAb, HistAb, HumInd, IBSS, LRI, MLA-IB, RI-1, RILM, SSCI. *Bk. rev.:* 3-5, essay length. *Aud.:* Ac.

Often described as "the premier journal devoted to the study of British history and culture," this journal includes a range of research articles, review essays, and book reviews. Although the editorial board is composed mainly of scholars from U.S. universities and colleges, contributors to the journal include authors from Canada, Australia, and Britain as well as other Western countries. Articles most often cover British history in combination with politics, economics, religion, and social issues. More recently the journal has included articles on comparative history, gender and cultural studies, the arts, and health and disease. Geographically, most writing in this journal deals with England; however, some articles focus on Ireland as well as areas of the former British Empire. Recent articles cover such topics as begging in eighteenth-century London, the public and private in early modern Britain, films of the Second World War, and sites of modern gay history. Sponsored by the North American Conference on British Studies, this journal will be of significant interest internationally to students and scholars of the culture, society, and history of the United Kingdom.

1594. *Journal of Popular Culture.* [ISSN: 0022-3840] 1967. bi-m. GBP 167 print & online eds. Ed(s): Gary C Hoppenstand. Blackwell Publishing, Inc., Commerce Place, 350 Main St, Malden, MA 02148; customerservices@blackwellpublishing.com; http://www.blackwellpublishing.com. Illus., index, adv. Refereed. Circ: 3500. Vol. ends: Spring. Microform: PQC. Online: Blackwell Synergy; Chadwyck-Healey Inc.; EBSCO Publishing, EBSCO Host; Florida Center for Library Automation; Gale; IngentaConnect; Northern Light Technology, Inc.; OCLC Online Computer Library Center, Inc.;

OhioLINK; ProQuest K-12 Learning Solutions; ProQuest LLC (Ann Arbor); SwetsWise Online Content; H.W. Wilson. Reprint: PSC. *Indexed:* ABS&EES, AmH&L, AmHI, ApEcolAb, ArtHuCI, BAS, BEL&L, BRI, CABA, CBRI, CJA, CommAb, DAAI, FLI, FR, HistAb, HumInd, IBR, IBSS, IBZ, IIMP, IIPA, MLA-IB, MRD, MusicInd, PRA, RI-1, RILM, RRTA, SFSA, SSCI, SociolAb, V&AA. *Bk. rev.:* 15-20, 100-500 words. *Aud.:* Ga, Ac.

The articles in this journal explore popular culture and its effects on people and society as a whole. The journal brings to the forefront the aspects of "low culture" that fascinate and consume so much of contemporary U.S. and global society. Each issue contains several articles on a wide variety of topics ranging from comic books to pulp fiction, from television shows to popular movies, and from advertisements to rap music. In addition to its interdisciplinary coverage of U.S. culture, the *Journal of Popular Culture* also has an international focus. Recent articles focus on Japanese cinema and post-war German festivals and narratives. This journal is the official publication of the Popular Culture Association. Scholars studying popular literature, film, and television will be interested in this publication, as will students and general readers who are aficionados of pop culture.

1595. *Journal of the History of Ideas: an international quarterly devoted to intellectual history.* [ISSN: 0022-5037] 1940. q. USD 130.20 print & online. Ed(s): Martin Burke, Anthony Grafton. University of Pennsylvania Press, 4200 Pine St, Philadelphia, PA 19104-4011; http://www.pennpress.org. Illus., index, adv. Sample. Refereed. Circ: 1943 Paid. Vol. ends: Oct/Dec. Microform: PMC; PQC. Online: Chadwyck-Healey Inc.; EBSCO Publishing, EBSCO Host; JSTOR (Web-based Journal Archive); OCLC Online Computer Library Center, Inc.; OhioLINK; Project MUSE; ProQuest LLC (Ann Arbor); SwetsWise Online Content. *Indexed:* ABS&EES, AmH&L, AmHI, ArtHuCI, BAS, BRI, CBRI, CCMJ, ChemAb, FR, HistAb, HumInd, IBR, IBSS, IBZ, IPB, IPSA, IndIslam, MLA-IB, MSN, MathR, NTA, PRA, PSA, PhilInd, RI-1, RILM, SSCI. *Aud.:* Ga, Ac, Sa.

Intellectual history, very broadly defined, is the focus of this publication, which aims to explore the "evolution of ideas and their influence on historical developments" in philosophy, literature, the social sciences, religion, and the arts. Each issue contains several scholarly articles covering such topics as luxury in French political thought, German philosophy and British public policy, idolatry and religion, and histories of science. Most articles deal with philosophical writings, historiography, theology, scientific theories, or literary works. Contributors to the journal are academics, mostly historians, with some authors from the fields of philosophy, classics, and literature. This journal, sponsored by the Society for the History of Ideas, contains superior research and writing that will appeal to scholars in several areas of the humanities.

Journal of Thought. See Education/General, K-12 section.

1596. *Knowledge, Technology and Policy: the international journal of knowledge transfer and utilization.* Former titles (until 1998): *Knowledge and Policy;* (until 1991): *Knowledge in Society.* 1988. q. EUR 300 print & online eds. Springer Netherlands, Van Godewijckstraat 30, Dordrecht, 3311 GX, Netherlands; http://www.springeronline.com. Illus., index, adv. Refereed. Circ: 400. Vol. ends: Winter. Reprint: PSC. *Indexed:* IBR, IBSS, IBZ, IPSA, LISA, PSA, SociolAb. *Bk. rev.:* 2-6; 500-1,000 words. *Aud.:* Ac, Sa.

The influence of technology on society and contemporary culture continues to grow exponentially. This journal provides a forum for interweaving concepts and strategy with the spectrum of technological development. *Knowlege, Technology and Policy* covers technological aspects of how people think, how they organize, access, and use information, and the policy implications of these processes. The journal is aimed at people working in the areas of policy analysis, program evaluation, and technology assessment. Each issue includes several scholarly articles, often centered on a specific theme or overarching issue. Theme issues have focused on such topics as mobile phones and mass communications, policy transfer in developing countries, and social mobility, migration, and technology workers. Article topics include government policy and open source software, innovation studies, and information technology and diplomacy. Some authors are from universities, while others are from business,

the government sector, and research institutes. This journal will be of interest to those teaching and working with developing technologies as well as researchers and policy makers in the public and private sectors.

1597. *Midwest Quarterly: a journal of contemporary thought.* [ISSN: 0026-3451] 1961. q. USD 15 domestic; USD 20 foreign; USD 5 newsstand/cover per issue. Ed(s): James B M Schick. Pittsburg State University, Midwest Quarterly, 406b Russ Hall, 1701 S Broadway, Pittsburg, KS 66762. Index. Refereed. Circ: 570 Paid. Vol. ends: Summer. Microform: PQC. Online: EBSCO Publishing, EBSCO Host; Florida Center for Library Automation; Gale; Northern Light Technology, Inc.; OCLC Online Computer Library Center, Inc.; ProQuest LLC (Ann Arbor); H.W. Wilson. *Indexed:* AmH&L, AmHI, ArtHuCI, BAS, FLI, HistAb, HumInd, IAPV, IBR, IBZ, LRI, MLA-IB, PAIS, RI-1, RILM, SSCI. *Bk. rev.:* 2-5, 500-750. *Aud.:* Ac.

For nearly five decades, the *Midwest Quarterly* has published both writings of literary analysis and a substantial amount of original poetry. Although many, but not all, articles in this publication are written by Midwesterners, the content of Midwest Quarterly has no geographical limitations. This journal focuses on "analytical and speculative treatment of its topics, rather than heavily documented research studies." Most articles analyze specific literary themes and works, although some cover philosophical, social, and historical topics. Recent articles explore the writings of playwrights Langford Wilson, David Rabe, Sam Shepard, and David Mamet, as well as Kate Chopin and Henry David Thoreau. Other articles cover such subjects as discontent in Shaker writings of Isaac Youngs, gender issues of automobile drivers, and Neville Chamberlain and the Munich Crisis. Poetry is a major emphasis of this journal, with each issue including several poems by well-known writers. This journal will appeal to poets as well as scholars in literature and the humanities in general.

1598. *Modern Intellectual History.* [ISSN: 1479-2443] 2004. 3x/yr. GBP 127. Ed(s): Charles Capper, Nicholas T Phillipson. Cambridge University Press, The Edinburgh Bldg, Shaftesbury Rd, Cambridge, CB2 2RU, United Kingdom; journals@cambridge.org; http://www.cup.cam.ac.uk/. Reprint: PSC. *Indexed:* AmH&L, HistAb. *Bk. rev.:* 3-5 review essays per issue, c. 5,000 words. *Aud.:* Ac.

The modern period of intellectual history from 1650 to the present is the time frame covered by this journal. European and American history are the major areas of focus, but articles on transnational history of other regions are also included. As the journal has developed since its beginning in 2004, it has begun to include coverage of non-Western history. The journal draws upon writings from a wide range of disciplines including not only the social sciences and literature, but also "political thought, philosophy, religion, literature, the social sciences, the natural sciences and the visual arts." Each issue contains several scholarly articles along with review essays and an occasional forum containing articles and commentary on a specific theme. Recent articles cover the intellectual history of India, John Dewey and the Soviet Union, Rousseau's Second Discourse, and Jerrold Seigel's "The Idea of the Self." This journal will be of interest to scholars in many disciplines, most especially history, philosophy, and political science.

1599. *Modernism/Modernity.* [ISSN: 1071-6068] 1994. q. USD 140. Ed(s): Jeffrey T Schnapp, Cassandra Laity. The Johns Hopkins University Press, 2715 N Charles St, Baltimore, MD 21218-4363; http://muse.jhu.edu. Illus., index, adv. Refereed. Circ: 1062. Vol. ends: Sep. Online: Chadwyck-Healey Inc.; EBSCO Publishing, EBSCO Host; OCLC Online Computer Library Center, Inc.; OhioLINK; Project MUSE; ProQuest LLC (Ann Arbor); SwetsWise Online Content. Reprint: PSC. *Indexed:* ABM, AmH&L, AmHI, ArtHuCI, ArtInd, BEL&L, HistAb, HumInd, IBR, IBZ, MLA-IB, PSA, RILM, SSA, SociolAb. *Bk. rev.:* 10-20, 500-1,500 words. *Aud.:* Ac.

This journal is an interdisciplinary forum for scholars of modernist studies to explore the theories, methods, philosophy, and history of the late nineteenth to the early mid-twentieth century. The coverage of *Modernism/Modernity* is international and cross-disciplinary, encompassing primarily the arts and history along with other areas of the humanities. Many articles are devoted to literary works of modernist writers such as James Joyce, Virginia Woolf, T.S. Eliot, Ezra Pound, Thomas Mann, and Gertrude Stein. Other articles cover art, music, theater, philosophy, and politics. Recent articles focus on modernism and language reform, aesthetics and film criticism, and modernism and postcolonialism. Some issues center around a particular theme such as Jewish modernism, modernism and transnationalisms, and archaeologies of the modern. This publication is the journal of the Modernist Studies Association. *Modernism/Modernity* will mainly appeal to academics and literary scholars studying this time period in general and its prominent writers and trends.

1600. *New Formations: a journal of culture/theory/politics.* [ISSN: 0950-2378] 1987. 3x/yr. GBP 140 print & online eds. (Individuals, GBP 40 print & online eds.). Ed(s): Scott McCracken. Lawrence & Wishart Ltd, 99a Wallis Rd, London, E9 5LN, United Kingdom; office@lwbooks.co.uk; http://www.l-w-bks.co.uk/. Illus., adv. Refereed. Circ: 1500. Vol. ends: Winter. *Indexed:* AltPI, HistAb, IBSS, MLA-IB, RI-1, RILM. *Bk. rev.:* 2-3; 1,000-3,000 words, plus Book Notes, 2-3, c. 500 words. *Aud.:* Ac.

As the subtitle suggests, this journal uses the basis of cultural studies and examines it through the critical lens of theory and politics. The purpose of this publication is to explore and critically investigate contemporary culture, its ideology, its politics, and its impact. Each issue includes several articles and essays, many of which focus on one specific theme, such as eugenics, the Iraq War and postcolonialism, spatial imagery, and critical realism. Themes are explored from many points of view—from political and social to literary and philosophical. Articles range from modern applications of classical philosophy to popular culture essays. *New Formations* provides a fresh perspective on historical and contemporary international culture and politics. This journal will be of interest to cultural studies scholars especially in politics and philosophy.

1601. *Other Voices (Philadelphia): the (e)journal of cultural criticism.* [ISSN: 1094-2254] 1997. irreg. Free. Ed(s): Vance Bell. Other Voices (Philadelphia), Box 31907, Philadelphia, PA 19104; http://www.othervoices.org/. *Indexed:* AmHI, MLA-IB. *Bk. rev.:* 1-3, essay length. *Aud.:* Ac.

An exclusively electronic journal, *Other Voices* effectively utilizes the Internet in publishing a journal that combines traditional text with electronic text, audio lectures, photography, and a virtual roundtable. The focus of *Other Voices* is cultural criticism in the arts and humanities, including literature, art, film, photography, and music, as well as philosophy and theory. The journal is "dedicated to fostering interdisciplinary dialogues while maintaining respect for the strengths of traditional academic disciplines." Scholarly essays, commentaries, lectures, interviews, reviews of books and exhibitions, and electronic text projects make up the contents. Each issue focuses on a central theme such as recycling culture, engagements, and discrete objects. Essays and commentaries begin each issue, covering such subjects as Nazi imagery in Jewish art, subjectivity, and Serbian history and popular culture. The "Theorizing" section contains several lectures on philosophical and historical topics. A review section concludes each issue. Founded by faculty and students at the University of Pennsylvania, this journal encourages submissions from students. As a free, electronic publication, *Other Voices* makes a valuable contribution to the trend toward alternative modes of publishing in academia.

1602. *Postmodern Culture: an electronic journal of interdisciplinary criticism.* [ISSN: 1053-1920] 1990. 3x/yr. USD 90. Ed(s): Lisa Brawley, James F English. The Johns Hopkins University Press, 2715 N Charles St, Baltimore, MD 21218-4363; http://muse.jhu.edu. Illus. Refereed. Online: EBSCO Publishing, EBSCO Host; OCLC Online Computer Library Center, Inc.; OhioLINK; Project MUSE; SwetsWise Online Content. *Indexed:* AmHI, ArtHuCI, BEL&L, HumInd, MLA-IB. *Bk. rev.:* 5-7, essay length. *Aud.:* Ga, Ac.

A pioneer among scholarly electronic-only journals, *Postmodern Culture* has continued to set high standards for writing in cultural studies. The focus of this journal is literature, philosophy, art, film, and social issues of the late twentieth and early twenty-first centuries. Cultural criticism and theory form the basis for most articles, along with essays and commentary on specialized texts and media. Each issue features essays or creative works on such topics as ethnic bodies and identities, addiction and women's desires, and post–Cold War paranoia. Reviews of films, exhibitions, and performances are included along with book reviews. A "Related Readings" section provides links to other popular-culture sites, collections, journals, newsgroups, and readings. An interactive, annotated "Bibliography of Postmodernism and Critical Theory" is available with each issue. Readers who register with the database may add new items to the bibliography. This journal will appeal to scholars and students in literature, gender studies, politics, art, film, and philosophy.

1603. *Public Culture: society for transnational cultural studies.* [ISSN: 0899-2363] 1988. 3x/yr. USD 166 (Individuals, USD 37). Ed(s): Dilip Parameshwar Gaonkar, Claudio Lomnitz. Duke University Press, 905 W Main St, Ste 18 B, Durham, NC 27701; subscriptions@dukeupress.edu; http://www.dukeupress.edu. Illus., index, adv. Refereed. Circ: 1000 Paid. Vol. ends: Spring. Online: EBSCO Publishing, EBSCO Host; Gale; HighWire Press; OCLC Online Computer Library Center, Inc.; OhioLINK; Project MUSE; SwetsWise Online Content. Reprint: PSC. *Indexed:* ABS&EES, AICP, AltPI, AmHI, AnthLit, ArtHuCI, CABA, CommAb, FLI, HumInd, IBR, IBSS, IBZ, IPSA, LeftInd, MLA-IB, PSA, RRTA, S&F, SSA, SSCI, SociolAb. *Aud.:* Ac.

This journal focuses on cultural studies from a global perspective. *Public Culture* includes research articles and essays on cultural, social, and political issues including contemporary media, urban issues, consumerism, and advertising. Articles cover such topics as the privatization of risk or sexual politics in the public sphere. Photos, drawings, and paintings often accompany articles. Each issue begins with editorials in a section called "Doxa at Large." Two or three articles are often grouped into segments on a common theme such as mediating visibility, or urban reproduction, or sexualities, ethics, and politics. Photo-essays are included in each issue. The "Arts in Circulation" section has both shorter reports and lengthier essays on innovative aspects of the arts. The "From the Field" section features photos, drawings, or paintings that conclude some issues of the journal. Sponsored by the Society for Transnational Cultural Studies, this publication will appeal to readers with an interest in globalization and the internationalization of cultural studies.

1604. *Renaissance Quarterly.* Incorporated (1954-1974): *Studies in the Renaissance;* Formerly (until 1967): *Renaissance News.* [ISSN: 0034-4338] 1954. q. Free to members. Renaissance Society of America, 365 5th Ave., # 5400, New York, NY 10016-4309; rsa@is.nyu.edu; http://www.rsa.org. Illus., index, adv. Refereed. Circ: 3500 Paid. Vol. ends: Winter. Microform: PQC. Online: Chadwyck-Healey Inc.; Florida Center for Library Automation; Gale; JSTOR (Web-based Journal Archive); Northern Light Technology, Inc.; OCLC Online Computer Library Center, Inc.; ProQuest K-12 Learning Solutions; ProQuest LLC (Ann Arbor). Reprint: PSC. *Indexed:* AmH&L, AmHI, ArtHuCI, BEL&L, BRI, CBRI, HistAb, HumInd, IBR, IBZ, MLA-IB, RI-1, RILM, SSCI. *Bk. rev.:* 40-50, 400-500 words. *Aud.:* Ac.

As the leading journal in Renaissance studies, this publication offers research studies, review essays, and a large section of book reviews. Literary works and themes are the focus of many articles, in addition to specialized studies in the arts, religion, or social aspects of the Renaissance. Recent articles cover such topics as beheading in Irish literature, funeral monuments in fourteenth-century Florence, the early Italian press, and early modern art history. Review essays and reviews of individual works make up nearly half of each issue. English-language works predominate, but some titles in French and Italian are included. As the official publication of the Renaissance Society of America, reports of society meetings are also included. This journal will interest scholars and students of the Renaissance both for its scholarly articles and extensive reviews of current books.

1605. *Representations.* [ISSN: 0734-6018] 1983. q. USD 205 print & online eds. USD 56 newsstand/cover. Ed(s): Catherine Gallagher, Thomas Laqueur. University of California Press, Journals Division, 2000 Center St, Ste 303, Berkeley, CA 94704-1223; journals@ucpress.edu; http://www.ucpress.edu/journals. Illus., index, adv. Refereed. Circ: 1244. Microform: PQC. Online: Chadwyck-Healey Inc.; EBSCO Publishing, EBSCO Host; JSTOR (Web-based Journal Archive); OCLC Online Computer Library Center, Inc.; ProQuest LLC (Ann Arbor); SwetsWise Online Content. *Indexed:* ABM, AmH&L, AmHI, ArtHuCI, ArtInd, BEL&L, FLI, HistAb, MLA-IB, PSA, RILM, SSA, SSCI, SociolAb. *Aud.:* Ac.

For over 20 years, *Representations* has provided a multidisciplinary forum for scholars of literature, culture, and history. Most issues include several articles on a variety of topics, with occasional issues focusing on one particular theme. Many articles analyze aspects of a particular literary or philosophical writing, while other essays examine historical, political, or social issues. Recent articles explore topics ranging from realist fiction to trauma and visuality, and from justice in aesthetics to culture and moral change in London after World War II. The essays are written in a very engaging style and present original perspectives on literary, historical, or social subjects. Occasional special issues focus on such themes as "Mimesis East and West," "Redress," and "Crimes, Lies and Narrative." Most contributors are scholars in English or other areas of the humanities. This journal will appeal to a wide range of academics, especially in literature and the humanities.

Sexualities. See Sexuality section.

Social Epistemology. See Philosophy section.

1606. *Social Identities: journal for the study of race, nation and culture.* [ISSN: 1350-4630] 1995. bi-m. GBP 569 print & online eds. Ed(s): Pal Ahluwalia, Toby Miller. Routledge, 4 Park Sq, Milton Park, Abingdon, OX14 4RN, United Kingdom; info@routledge.co.uk; http://www.routledge.co.uk. Illus., index, adv. Sample. Refereed. Vol. ends: Dec. Online: EBSCO Publishing, EBSCO Host; Gale; IngentaConnect; OCLC Online Computer Library Center, Inc.; SwetsWise Online Content. Reprint: PSC. *Indexed:* ASSIA, IBSS, IPSA, PSA, PsycInfo, SSA, SWA, SociolAb. *Bk. rev.:* 1-3, essay length. *Aud.:* Ac.

Current international conflicts and hostilities underscore the critical role of race and ethnicity in contemporary societies. *Social Identities* provides a forum to address global racial, ethnic, and national issues in the context of social and cultural studies. Postmodernism and postcolonialism underscore much of the writing in this journal, as do the theories of how racial, national, and cultural identities are developed, changed, and affected by political and economic power. Each issue begins with several research articles on topics ranging from British culture wars to women in Pakistan, and from racism in Australia to the Rwandan genocide. Special issues are published occasionally on such themes as emergent subjects of neoliberal global capitalism and dialogue with Jacques Derrida. Contributors are mainly from U.S. and U.K. universities, with some writers from Latin America, the Middle East, and Africa. This journal will be of interest to scholars and students in many disciplines, especially politics, history, and sociology, but also humanities and the arts.

1607. *Social Justice Research.* [ISSN: 0885-7466] 1986. q. EUR 716 print & online eds. Ed(s): John T Jost. Springer New York LLC, 233 Spring St, New York, NY 10013-1578; service-ny@springer.com; http://www.springer.com/. Illus., index, adv. Refereed. Vol. ends: Dec. Microform: PQC. Online: EBSCO Publishing, EBSCO Host; Gale; IngentaConnect; OCLC Online Computer Library Center, Inc.; OhioLINK; Springer LINK; SwetsWise Online Content. Reprint: PSC. *Indexed:* ASSIA, BAS, CJA, IBR, IBSS, IBZ, PSA, PsycInfo, SSA, SociolAb. *Bk. rev.:* 2-3, essay length. *Aud.:* Ac.

The theory and practice of social justice has become an expanding area of contemporary social science research and scholarship. This journal aims to explore "the origins, structures and consequences of justice in human affairs." This publication takes a cross-disciplinary view of justice, covering social science and policy studies nationally and internationally. Each issue includes articles on the application of justice to such areas as human rights, conflict of interest, immigration policies, and public views of restorative justice. Recent articles cover topics from criminal sanctions to corporal punishment in schools and from systems of fairness to a framework for thinking about oppression. The articles are well written and thoroughly documented. Contributors are mainly from U.S., Canadian, and European universities. This journal will be of interest to scholars in the social sciences, particularly in political science, criminal justice, sociology, and law.

1608. *Social Science History.* [ISSN: 0145-5532] 1976. q. USD 120 (Individuals, USD 60). Ed(s): Katherine A Lynch. Duke University Press, 905 W Main St, Ste 18 B, Durham, NC 27701; subscriptions@dukeupress.edu; http://www.dukeupress.edu. Illus., index, adv. Sample. Refereed. Circ: 1500. Vol. ends: Winter. Online: EBSCO Publishing, EBSCO Host; Gale; HighWire Press; JSTOR (Web-based Journal Archive); Northern Light Technology, Inc.; OCLC Online Computer Library Center, Inc.; OhioLINK; Project MUSE; ProQuest LLC (Ann Arbor); SwetsWise Online Content. Reprint: PSC. *Indexed:* ABS&EES, AgeL, AmH&L, ArtHuCI, BAS, CJA, HistAb, IBR, IBSS, IBZ, IPSA, PSA, SSA, SSCI, SUSA, SWA, SociolAb. *Aud.:* Ac.

Social aspects of history have become a major focus of contemporary scholarship within the discipline. This publication focuses on interdisciplinary studies that combine history with the fields of sociology, economics, political science, anthropology, and geography. Articles include "a blend of empirical research and theoretical work" as well as comparative and methodological studies. Research covers the family, demography, economic issues, social classes, the labor force, crime, and poverty. Each issue includes articles on such subjects as Mexican immigration, the development of height and weight tables, U.S. political party systems and their realignments. Frequently, an issue is devoted to a single theme, such as the continuing problems of health insurance. Some issues also contain a special section of articles on a single theme such as the politics of method in the human sciences. Many articles focus on U.S. historical research, but British and European history are also covered. As the official journal of the Social Science History Association, this journal will have broad appeal not only to historians, but also to scholars in related social science fields.

1609. *Social Science Information: information sur les sciences sociales.* Formerly: *Social Sciences Information - Information sur les Sciences Sociales.* [ISSN: 0539-0184] 1954. q. GBP 410. Ed(s): Anna Rocha Perazzo. Sage Publications Ltd., 1 Oliver's Yard, 55 City Rd, London, EC1 1SP, United Kingdom; info@sagepub.co.uk; http://www.sagepub.co.uk. Illus., index, adv. Refereed. Vol. ends: Dec. Reprint: PSC. *Indexed:* ABCPolSci, AICP, ASSIA, AmH&L, BAS, CABA, FR, HRA, HistAb, IBR, IBSS, IBZ, IPSA, MLA-IB, PAIS, PSA, PhilInd, RRTA, SFSA, SSA, SSCI, SociolAb, WAE&RSA. *Aud.:* Ac.

With an international focus, this journal publishes research on theory and method in the social sciences, often emphasizing comparative and cross-cultural research. Articles on such subjects as sociology's contributions to economics, components of happiness, and cross-cultural differences in emotions and language reforms and gender indicate the range of issues covered by *Social Science Information.* Occasionally, special issues or symposia are published on such topics as people and the sea, ethology and ethnology, and social sciences in Latin America. Special sections on the areas of rationality and society, biology and social life, studies of science, theory and methods, and trends and developments are included in various issues. Text of articles may be in English or French. This journal is affiliated with the Fondation Maison des Sciences de l'Homme in Paris and will appeal to researchers across a broad spectrum of the social sciences.

1610. *The Social Science Journal.* Formerly (until 1976): *Rocky Mountain Social Science Journal.* [ISSN: 0362-3319] 1963. 4x/yr. EUR 400. Ed(s): N. P. Unnithan. Pergamon, The Boulevard, Langford Ln, East Park, Kidlington, OX5 1GB, United Kingdom; nlinfo-f@elsevier.nl; http://www.elsevier.nl. Illus., index, adv. Refereed. Circ: 2000. Vol. ends: Oct. Online: EBSCO Publishing, EBSCO Host; Florida Center for Library Automation; Gale; IngentaConnect; Northern Light Technology, Inc.; OCLC Online Computer Library Center, Inc.; OhioLINK; ScienceDirect; SwetsWise Online Content; H.W. Wilson. *Indexed:* ABCPolSci, ABS&EES, AbAn, AgeL, AmH&L, ArtHuCI, CJA, CommAb, HistAb, IBR, IBZ, IPSA, PAIS, PRA, PSA, PsycInfo, RiskAb, SSA, SSCI, SWA, SWR&A, SociolAb. *Aud.:* Ac.

Although this publication began as a regional journal, over the past 40 years of its history, *The Social Science Journal* has expanded into a national and international forum. This journal publishes research articles, statistical analyses, and case studies. Articles on society, history, economics, politics, and gender are included, along with coverage of social theories, research methods, and curricular issues. Representative articles have covered such subjects as Eastern

European immigrants in the United States, impacts of privatization, civic education in France and America, and third-party success in gubernatorial elections. Research notes on works-in-progress are also included covering topics such as unemployment and suicide, family planning in Kenya, socio-cultural life of Gypsies, and Internet usage by local government employees. As the official publication of the Western Social Science Association, this journal will be of interest to scholars and students in all geographical areas and in many fields of the social sciences and beyond.

1611. *Social Science Quarterly.* Formerly (until 1968): *Southwestern Social Science Quarterly.* [ISSN: 0038-4941] 1920. q. GBP 232 print & online eds. Ed(s): Nita Lineberry, Robert Lineberry. Blackwell Publishing, Inc., Commerce Place, 350 Main St, Malden, MA 02148; customerservices@ blackwellpublishing.com; http://www.blackwellpublishing.com. Illus., index, adv. Refereed. Circ: 3000. Vol. ends: Dec. Microform: PQC. Online: Blackwell Synergy; Chadwyck-Healey Inc.; EBSCO Publishing, EBSCO Host; Florida Center for Library Automation; Gale; IngentaConnect; OCLC Online Computer Library Center, Inc.; OhioLINK; ProQuest LLC (Ann Arbor); SwetsWise Online Content. Reprint: PSC. *Indexed:* ABCPolSci, ABS&EES, ASSIA, AgeL, AmH&L, ApEcolAb, ArtHuCI, BAS, BRI, CBRI, CJA, CommAb, EAA, FR, H&SSA, HRA, HistAb, IBR, IBSS, IBZ, ILP, IMFL, IPSA, JEL, LRI, PAIS, PRA, PSA, PsycInfo, RI-1, RiskAb, SFSA, SSA, SSCI, SUSA, SWA, SociolAb, V&AA, WAE&RSA. *Bk. rev.:* 10-15, 500 words. *Aud.:* Ga, Ac.

For over 85 years, *Social Science Quarterly* has published top-quality research in a wide range of the social sciences. The journal is international in scope and covers social and public policy issues, including both theoretical approaches and quantitative research. General interest articles explore such topics as racial differences in networks, nonprofit advocacy organizations, black mayors in urban America, and spousal care giving. Frequently, articles are combined around a specific theme such as social and policy issues, the environment, race and ethnicity, politics or comparative perspectives. In 2004, the journal began to publish an additional supplementary issue at the end of the year focusing on themes such as ethnicity and social change; income, poverty, and opportunity; and social science examination of education. This journal offers superior coverage of contemporary social questions from a research standpoint. *Social Science Quarterly* is the official publication of the Southwestern Social Science Association. This journal will interest scholars and students as well as policy researchers.

1612. *Social Science Research.* [ISSN: 0049-089X] 1972. 4x/yr. EUR 816. Ed(s): James D Wright. Academic Press, 525 B St, Ste 1900, San Diego, CA 92101-4495; apsubs@acad.com; http://www.elsevier.com/. Illus., index, adv. Refereed. Vol. ends: Dec. Online: EBSCO Publishing, EBSCO Host; Gale; IngentaConnect; OCLC Online Computer Library Center, Inc.; OhioLINK; ScienceDirect; SwetsWise Online Content. *Indexed:* ABCPolSci, AgeL, AmH&L, ArtHuCI, BAS, CJA, HistAb, IBR, IBSS, IBZ, PSA, PsycInfo, RiskAb, SSA, SSCI, SWA, SociolAb. *Aud.:* Ac.

Although qualitative studies have expanded in the social sciences, much of the current research in these fields remains heavily quantitatively based. This journal covers quantitative research studies as well as methodologies in all areas of the social sciences. Empirical research is the focus of this publication, especially research that emphasizes cross-disciplinary issues or methods. Each issue offers lengthy articles on such topics as immigrants' employment in Germany, student mobility and school dropouts, effects of religion and race on marriage, and reproductive health in developing countries. Occasional feature articles appear, as do special issues on topics such as contemporary research on the family. Contributors are drawn from both U.S. colleges and universities as well as from universities abroad and from private research groups. *Social Science Research* will appeal to scholars and upper level students in the disciplines of sociology, economics, politics, criminal justice, and demography.

1613. *Social Text.* [ISSN: 0164-2472] 1979. q. USD 172 (Individuals, USD 33). Ed(s): Randy Martin, Brent Edwards. Duke University Press, 905 W Main St, Ste 18 B, Durham, NC 27701; subscriptions@dukeupress.edu; http://www.dukeupress.edu. Illus., adv. Refereed. Circ: 650. Vol. ends: Winter. Online: EBSCO Publishing, EBSCO Host; Gale; HighWire Press;

JSTOR (Web-based Journal Archive); OCLC Online Computer Library Center, Inc.; OhioLINK; Project MUSE; SwetsWise Online Content. Reprint: PSC. *Indexed:* ABS&EES, AltPI, AmHI, FR, HumInd, LeftInd, MLA-IB, PSA, RI-1, RILM, SSA, SociolAb. *Aud.:* Ac.

Social Text offers a cutting-edge perspective on current political, social, and cultural trends and issues. Addressing cultural theory with an emphasis on "questions of gender, sexuality, race and the environment" is the journal's focus. Contributors are largely U.S. scholars, critics, artists, and writers, although works of international writers are also included. Articles deal with such topics as neoliberalism, kinship and college students, and discrimination against South Asian immigrants. Special issues on one theme are common and have covered such subjects as the perils of academic freedom, Latina/o migration and employment, queer studies, surveillance and global cities of the South. *Social Text* places current social issues in the larger context of national and international cultural transformation. This journal will appeal to scholars and students interested in the latest cultural theory applied to the critical areas of race, sex, and class.

1614. *Social Theory and Practice: an international and interdisciplinary journal of social philosophy.* [ISSN: 0037-802X] 1970. q. USD 52 (Individuals, USD 28; Students, USD 20). Ed(s): Margaret Dancy, Russell Dancy. Florida State University, Department of Philosophy, 151 Dodd Hall, Tallahassee, FL 32306-1500; journals@mailer.fsu.edu; http://www.fsu.edu/~philo/STP. Illus., index, adv. Sample. Refereed. Circ: 700. Microform: PQC. Online: Chadwyck-Healey Inc.; EBSCO Publishing, EBSCO Host; Florida Center for Library Automation; Gale; OCLC Online Computer Library Center, Inc.; ProQuest K-12 Learning Solutions; ProQuest LLC (Ann Arbor); H.W. Wilson. *Indexed:* ABCPolSci, ABS&EES, ASSIA, AmH&L, FR, HistAb, IBR, IBZ, IPB, IPSA, PRA, PSA, PhilInd, RI-1, SSA, SSCI, SociolAb. *Aud.:* Ac.

Social Theory and Practice has been published by the Department of Philosophy at Florida State University for over 35 years. This journal seeks to address "theoretical and applied questions in social, political, legal, economic, educational and moral philosophy." The articles examine theories of historical figures in philosophy including Aristotle, Hobbes, Kant, Hegel, and Locke, as well as more contemporary theorists such as Rawls, Habermas, and Foucault. Other writings address questions on human rights, responsibilities of soldiers in war, defending liberalism, and disabilities. Occasional special issues have appeared on topics such as cosmopolitanism and the state, and religion and ethics. Most contributors are from American and Canadian universities. The writing is scholarly and encompasses a broad range of the humanities and social sciences as well as public policy issues. This journal will be of interest to scholars and students of philosophy, but also to academics in many other disciplines.

1615. *Southern Quarterly: a journal of the arts in the South.* [ISSN: 0038-4496] 1962. q. USD 35 (Individuals, USD 18). Ed(s): Noel Polk. University of Southern Mississippi, 118 College Drive #5078, Hattiesburg, MS 39406-5078; http://www.usm.edu. Illus., index, adv. Refereed. Circ: 950. Vol. ends: Summer. Microform: PQC. Online: Chadwyck-Healey Inc.; OCLC Online Computer Library Center, Inc.; ProQuest LLC (Ann Arbor); H.W. Wilson. *Indexed:* AmH&L, AmHI, ArtHuCI, BEL&L, FLI, HistAb, HumInd, IBR, IBZ, JEL, MLA-IB, PhilInd, RI-1, RILM. *Bk. rev.:* 4-10, 400-1,000 words. *Aud.:* Ga, Ac.

The arts and culture of the Southern United States is the focus of this journal, including the areas of the fine arts, film, photography, and popular culture, as well as folklore, history, anthropology, and material culture. Each issue presents articles on Southern writers and artists, including interviews, critical analyses of particular works, or themes from Southern literature, music, visual arts, or cultural studies. Frequently, special issues or features on one theme or author are published. Recent special issues have focused on Southern food and drink, imagining the Atlantic world, voices of the storm (Hurricane Katrina), and free people of color. *Southern Quarterly* also contains review essays and bibliographies, along with photographic essays, book reviews, and occasional film and exhibition reviews. "A Bibliography of the Visual Arts and Architecture in the South" appears in the fall issue of each volume. *Southern Quarterly* is a fascinating and thoroughly enjoyable publication for readers in the South and across the country.

1616. *Systems Research and Behavioral Science.* Formed by the merger of (1984-1997): *Systems Research;* (1956-1997): *Behavioral Science.* [ISSN: 1092-7026] 1984. bi-m. USD 690 print or online ed. Ed(s): Mike C Jackson. John Wiley & Sons Ltd., The Atrium, Southern Gate, Chichester, PO19 8SQ, United Kingdom; customer@wiley.co.uk; http://www.wiley.co.uk. Illus., adv. Sample. Refereed. Vol. ends: No. 4. Microform: PQC. Online: EBSCO Publishing, EBSCO Host; Florida Center for Library Automation; Gale; OhioLINK; ProQuest LLC (Ann Arbor); SwetsWise Online Content; Wiley InterScience. Reprint: PSC. *Indexed:* ABIn, AgeL, BAS, ExcerpMed, IBSS, IPSA, PsycInfo, SSCI. *Bk. rev.:* 5-6, 700-1,000 words, in some issues. *Aud.:* Ac.

This journal is the official publication of the International Federation for Systems Research. Its purpose is to publish theoretical and empirical articles on "new theories, experimental research, and applications relating to all levels of living and non-living systems." The journal has a very broad, interdisciplinary scope, covering systems in society, organizations, business and management, as well as systems related to social cognition, modeling, values, and the quality of life. Each issue includes research articles on such topics as natural resource management, military retention and recruitment, data mining, and theories of viability. Some issues include shorter news items or "Notes and Insights," along with book reviews. Special issues appear occasionally on such subjects as knowledge management in the ERP (enterprise resource planning) era, James Grier Miller's living systems theory, and systems dynamics modeling for organizations. The well-written and documented articles range from highly technical studies to theoretical approaches. This journal will be of interest to scholars as well as researchers in business, government, and technology.

1617. *Thesis Eleven: critical theory and historical sociology.* [ISSN: 0725-5136] 1980. q. GBP 421. Ed(s): Peter Beilharz, Peter Murphy. Sage Publications Ltd., 1 Oliver's Yard, 55 City Rd, London, EC1 1SP, United Kingdom; info@sagepub.co.uk; http://www.sagepub.co.uk. Illus., index, adv. Sample. Refereed. Vol. ends: Nov. Microform: PQC. Online: CSA; EBSCO Publishing, EBSCO Host; HighWire Press; OCLC Online Computer Library Center, Inc.; OhioLINK; SAGE Publications, Inc., SAGE Journals Online; SwetsWise Online Content. Reprint: PSC. *Indexed:* AltPI, HRA, IBR, IBSS, IBZ, IPB, IPSA, LeftInd, PAIS, PSA, RILM, SSA, SUSA, SociolAb. *Bk. rev.:* 4-6, 1,000-3,000 words. *Aud.:* Ac.

For over 25 years, *Thesis Eleven* has published some of the leading work in the field of social theory. "The journal is international and interdisciplinary, with a central focus on theories of society, culture, politics and the understanding of modernity." Incorporating both social sciences and liberal arts disciplines, from sociology and politics to philosophy, cultural studies, and literature, this publication includes European social theory as well as theory from other areas of the world. The editors are from Australian universities, while contributors to the journal are primarily from Europe, Canada, Australia, and the United States. Several research articles make up each issue, along with review essays and book reviews. Shorter essays or commentaries on earlier articles are also included. Recent articles have focused on topics such as computer game aesthetics, war and violence, technical gadgetry, civilizations, and the public university. This journal will appeal to academics, especially in the fields of sociology, politics, and philosophy.

■ DANCE

Mary Augusta Thomas, Associate Director, Readers Services and Strategic Planning, Smithsonian Institution Libraries, Washington, DC 20560-0154

Introduction

Current dance magazines reflect a strong international dance community. Both the popular titles and academic research journals incorporate articles on dance worldwide, discussing companies, performances, and history, and ranging from South Africa to the Middle East to China. In the United States, competitive dance for school children has grown in popularity, and includes Irish dance and

dance teams. Ballroom dancing is a regular feature on national television. The number of dance schools and dance programs continues to increase, while dance competitions and dance companies entertain many communities.

Journals in dance serve a diverse group of students, researchers, and dance professionals as well as the dance audience. Many journals have embraced the idea of the universality of dance, without boundaries of technique, venue, or nationality. Since scholars in other disciplines study how dance relates to fields as diverse as archaeology, psychology, sociology, and medicine, dance periodicals have increased their own scope.

The sense of community is strong in most dance magazines and is most evident in the online environment. Dance magazine editors encourage reader interaction by providing links to commercial suppliers, to individual dancers' web sites, and to audition information. Most online journals in dance are based on a print title or focused on a single company, geographic area, or dance style. Online versions of print publications are noted in the appropriate print title annotation. There are some excellent regional dance web sites, including www.danceadvance.org for the Philadelphia area and www.nyfa.org for New York state, with national resources included.

www.danceusa.org is the web site for Dance/USA, "an organization founded in 1982 following the release of a report by the Task Force for a National Dance Organization, which called for the establishment of a national service organization for professional dance. Dance/USA's members include over 400 ballet, modern, ethnic, jazz, and tap companies, dance service and presenting organizations, individuals, and other organizations nationwide." Dancer Online, www.danceronline.com, is a monthly publication that includes reviews, interviews, and news about all types of dance. The online archives go back to 2002.

Basic Periodicals

Ems: *Dance Magazine;* Hs: *Dance and the Arts, Dance Magazine, Dance Spirit, Pointe;* Ga: *Dance Now, Dance Magazine, Dance Spirit, Dance Teacher, Dance Today!, Pointe;* Ac: *Ballet Review, Ballettanz, Dance Chronicle, Dance Now, Dance Research Journal, Dance Theatre Journal, Dancing Times, Pointe;* Sa: *American Journal of Dance Therapy, Dance Research Journal, Dance Teacher, DanceView.*

Basic Abstracts and Indexes

American Bibliography of Slavic and Eastern European Studies, Arts and Humanities Citation Index, Current Contents, Humanities Index, Index to Dance Periodicals, International Index to the Performing Arts, Music Index.

1618. *American Journal of Dance Therapy.* Supersedes (in 1977): *American Dance Therapy Association. Monograph.* [ISSN: 0146-3721] 1968. s-a. EUR 388 print & online eds. Ed(s): Deborah Welsh, Cathy Appel. Springer New York LLC, 233 Spring St, New York, NY 10013-1578; service-ny@springer.com; http://www.springer.com/. Illus., index, adv. Sample. Refereed. Online: EBSCO Publishing, EBSCO Host; Gale; IngentaConnect; OCLC Online Computer Library Center, Inc.; OhioLINK; Springer LINK; SwetsWise Online Content. Reprint: PSC. *Indexed:* AgeL, ArtHuCI, ExcerpMed, IIPA, PEI, PsycInfo, RILM, SSCI. *Bk. rev.:* 4-5, 500 words. *Aud.:* Ac, Sa.

Behavior and movement are closely linked. Essays and original research in this journal reflect the important role of dance and movement in therapeutic practice. Articles present original, scholarly research on the psychology of movement and dance, which is becoming more intertwined with other areas of dance research. As the relationship between movement and psychological health becomes better understood, use of dance in therapy has been steadily growing to deal with physical and mental illness, societal problems like homelessness, and individual personal development. Recent issues include research on dance in Japan, and an analysis of the effects of various music styles on body movement. Clinicians and educators in dance therapy serve as journal contributors. This is a good source for administrators, psychiatrists, psychologists, social workers, and creative-arts therapists in the disciplines of music, art, and drama.

1619. *American SquareDance: the international magazine of square dancing.* Former titles (until 1972): *New Square Dance;* (until 1968): *Square Dance.* [ISSN: 0091-3383] 1945. m. USD 27.50 domestic; USD

35 Canada; USD 92 elsewhere. Ed(s): Randy Boyd, William Boyd. American Squaredance, 34 E Main St, Apopka, FL 32703. Illus., adv. Circ: 12000 Paid. Microform: PQC. *Bk. rev.:* Occasional, short. *Aud.:* Hs, Ga.

For more than 60 years, this magazine has covered square dance worldwide. Regular features report on contra dance and round dance as well as mainstream dance. Contributors cover conventions, clubs, and dance news. The "Caller Lab" presents tips on steps and patterns. Each issue also includes notes on travel, events, and a calendar of dances.

1620. *Ballet Review.* [ISSN: 0522-0653] 1965. q. USD 25 domestic; USD 33 foreign. Ed(s): Francis Mason. Dance Research Foundation, Inc., 37 W 12th St 7J, New York, NY 10011; info@balletreview.com; http://www.balletreview.com. Illus., adv. Circ: 2000 Paid. Microform: PQC. *Indexed:* ABS&EES, AmHI, ArtHuCI, HumInd, IIPA, RILM. *Bk. rev.:* Various number and length. *Aud.:* Ac, Sa.

Founded by Arlene Croce, famed dance critic for *The New Yorker*, this periodical remains central to academic and specialized collections. Not limited only to classical ballet, recent issues include modern dance and avant-garde companies in city by city reviews written by both researchers and practitioners. The blend of familiarity and scholarship makes the information accessible and entertaining. The clear, readable, well-researched text, often with unusual historic and contemporary black-and-white photographs and drawings, and the contributions of leading dance historians and critics combine to lend credibility to this journal as a major resource for dance criticsm. Topics for the six or seven longer articles in each issue include dance history, choreography, trends in dance criticism, and biographical features on important dancers, dance music, costumes, and company performances.

1621. *Ballettanz: Europe's leading dance magazine.* Formerly (until 2002): *Ballett International - Tanz Aktuell;* Which was formed by the merger of (1986-1994): *Tanz Aktuell;* (1982-1994): *Ballett International;* Which incorporated (1990-1991): *Tanz International;* (1958-1989): *Tanz.* [ISSN: 1612-6890] 1994. m. 11/yr. EUR 110 domestic; EUR 120 foreign; EUR 8 newsstand/cover. Ed(s): Hartmut Regitz, Arnd Wesemann. Friedrich Berlin Verlagsgesellschaft mbH, Reinhardtstr 29, Berlin, 10117, Germany; verlag@friedrichberlin.de; http://www.friedrichberlin.de. Illus., adv. Sample. Circ: 12000 Paid. Vol. ends: Dec. *Indexed:* ArtHuCI, IBR, IBZ, IIPA, RILM, SSCI. *Bk. rev.:* 2-3 short reviews. *Aud.:* Ac.

Europe's leading dance magazine serves as "a forum for international discussion on the classical ballet and contemporary dance" and appears in German with a few short articles in English. Online readers may choose an English or German web version. The journal's scope emphasizes the work of companies from Europe to the Far East, which makes it especially valuable for the serious student of dance criticism or history. Recently, a full issue was devoted to contemporary dance in African countries and its relationship to the European dance world. The editor presents features that cross both geographic and thematic boundaries to include politics, strategic planning, and finance, and that offer interesting insights into the European arts community. Reviews of all companies performing in a region or country, both contemporary and classical, are supported by excellent photographs. The European calendar of performances, auditions, and schools will help those seeking dance careers abroad. For any sizable collection, this journal is important for its wide range and contemporary dance perspective.

1622. *Contact Quarterly: a vehicle for moving ideas.* [ISSN: 0198-9634] 1975. 2x/yr. USD 25 (Individuals, USD 20). Ed(s): Lisa Nelson, Nancy Stark Smith. Contact Collaborations, Inc., PO Box 603, Northampton, MA 01060. Illus., index, adv. Sample. Circ: 2400. Vol. ends: Fall. *Indexed:* IIPA. *Bk. rev.:* Number and length vary. *Aud.:* Ac, Sa.

Started over 30 years ago as a journal to cover the then relatively unknown field of dance improvisation, *Contact Quarterly* represents all forms of movement improvisation. Substantial and well-designed, it may be the only dance performance magazine to deal with a broad range of social issues, providing studies on the philosophical and psychological dimensions of movement for all people, including those with mental or physical disabilities. Fiction and poetry are included, along with pieces on health and alternative healing, to emphasize the all-encompassing nature of movement. *Contact Quarterly*, one of the few sources of analytical writing about movement as opposed to formal choreogra-

phy, also provides information on small nontraditional companies, especially those in improvisation. The editors cover worldwide events, festivals, and schools, documenting what teachers of movement improvisation are doing internationally.

1623. *Dance and the Arts.* Former titles (until 1995): *Dance Pages Magazine;* (until 1989): *Dance Pages.* 1983. bi-m. USD 18 domestic; USD 30 Canada; USD 36 in Europe. Ed(s): Donna Gianell. Dance Pages, Inc., 1818 20 Amsterdam Ave, New York, NY 10031; http://www.arts-online.com/danceart.htm. Adv. *Bk. rev.:* 3-5, short. *Aud.:* Hs, Ga, Ac.

Aimed at both professionals and the public, this journal contains numerous short articles and photographs covering many types of dance in performance. One of its strengths is the inclusion of Broadway musicals and show dancing, which are often overlooked in other dance periodicals. Teachers and students of tap dance, tango, salsa, and other popular dance styles will find regular features that include an events calendar, short news notes from teachers and dance companies, and book and video reviews.

1624. *Dance Chronicle: studies in dance & the related arts.* [ISSN: 0147-2526] 1978. 3x/yr. GBP 575 print & online eds. Ed(s): George Dorris, Jack Anderson. Taylor & Francis Inc., 325 Chestnut St, Ste 800, Philadelphia, PA 19016; orders@taylorandfrancis.com; http://www.taylorandfrancis.com. Illus., index, adv. Sample. Circ: 450. Vol. ends: Winter. Microform: RPI. Online: Chadwyck-Healey Inc.; EBSCO Publishing, EBSCO Host; JSTOR (Web-based Journal Archive); OCLC Online Computer Library Center, Inc.; SwetsWise Online Content. Reprint: PSC. *Indexed:* ABS&EES, AmHI, ArtHuCI, HumInd, IIPA, MusicInd, PEI, RILM. *Bk. rev.:* 3-5 signed, 500-1,000 words. *Aud.:* Ac, Sa.

With topics ranging in time from classical antiquity to Broadway, this is the oldest journal devoted exclusively to scholarship in dance. The research found here is essential for serious students of dance history, choreography, performance, and criticism. The contents address all periods and styles of dance and the interplay between dance and music. Detailed research on costuming and staging is also presented. The style is highly polished and readable, with extensive references to sources for further study. Dance experts, established dance historians, and scholars review books in lengthy and carefully supported articles. Contents of several other scholarly dance journals are listed, along with books received. Although this is the most expensive dance journal, it must be included in any serious dance collection.

1625. *Dance Europe.* 1995. m. GBP 33.50 domestic; GBP 43 in Europe; GBP 55 elsewhere. Ed(s): Emma Manning. Dance Europe, PO Box 12661, London, E5 9TZ, United Kingdom. Adv. *Aud.:* Hs, Ga, Ac, Sa.

Dance Europe, founded in 1995, is published monthly in London. The editorial policy aims to provide "unbiased platforms for dance throughout Europe and beyond," and many of the contributors are professional dancers or ex-dancers. Handsomely designed and illustrated, it covers ballet and modern dance from many of the smaller companies across Europe. Well-written interviews with dancers and choreographers will open access to European trends to U.S. students. More political in tone, recent articles ranged from a plea for an end to terrorism to the closing of a major Portugese dance company. Each issue includes a Japanese summary page. There are lists of auditions and a performance diary. *Dance Europe* may be the broadest source for European dance that is currently available. The online version at www.danceeurope.net includes numerous links to dancers and companies.

1626. *Dance Magazine.* Former titles (until 1948): *Dance;* (until 1945): *Dance Magazine;* (until 1943): *Dance;* (until 1942): *The American Dancer.* [ISSN: 0011-6009] 1927. m. USD 34.95 domestic; USD 46.95 Canada; USD 66.95 foreign. Ed(s): Wendy Perron, Hanna Rubin. Macfadden Performing Arts Media, LLC., 110 William St, 23rd Fl., New York, NY 10038; http://dancemedia.com/. Illus., index, adv. Sample. Circ: 50828 Paid and controlled. Vol. ends: Dec. Microform: PQC. Online: EBSCO Publishing, EBSCO Host; Florida Center for Library

Automation; Gale; Northern Light Technology, Inc.; OCLC Online Computer Library Center, Inc.; ProQuest K-12 Learning Solutions; H.W. Wilson. *Indexed:* ABS&EES, AmHI, ArtHuCI, BRI, CBRI, FLI, HumInd, IIPA, MASUSE, MRD, PEI, RGPR, RILM. *Bk. rev.:* 250-2,500 words. *Aud.:* Ems, Hs, Ga, Ac.

Dance Magazine remains the one journal that any collection must include to provide information on current dance in performance and dance education in the United States. With in-depth coverage of all regions and companies, its sections on people, events, an annual audition calendar, and even gossip make this a basic tool. As the oldest continuously published dance periodical (almost 80 years) in the country, it attracts leading dance writers from all over the world and is the first magazine consulted by professionals and dance aficionados. Because of its panoramic coverage of ballet, modern, and theatrical styles throughout the country, it is required reading for the professional dancer and teacher. Clive Barnes, the dean of dance critics, serves as senior consulting editor. Each issue provides listings of jobs and schools nationwide. An online version at www.dancemagazine.com contains a vast amount of additional content including up-to-the-minute reviews.

1627. *Dance Now.* [ISSN: 0966-6346] 1992. q. GBP 15 domestic; GBP 17.50 foreign. Ed(s): David Leonard. Dance Books Ltd., The Old Bakery, 4 Lenten St, Alton, GU34 1HG, United Kingdom; dl@dancebooks.co.uk; http://www.dancebooks.co.uk. Illus., adv. Circ: 5000 Paid. Vol. ends: Winter. *Indexed:* IIPA, RILM. *Bk. rev.:* 2-3, short. *Aud.:* Ga, Ac.

Britain's liveliest dance magazine continues to present contributions by well-known writers and critics. The lengthy profiles of dancers and companies, reviews of the season, readable histories of dance in performance, and interviews with dancers, choreographers, and critics meet the needs of students, professional dancers, and the general reader. The Kirov Ballet is the focus of a recent issue, which contains five articles on their season. It may be the best source in the English language for information on current dance in Russia, with regular reviews of many ballet companies.

1628. *Dance Research Journal.* Formerly: *C O R D News.* [ISSN: 0149-7677] 1969. s-a. USD 115 domestic; USD 127 foreign. Ed(s): Ann Dils. University of Illinois Press, 1325 S Oak St, Champaign, IL 61820-6903; journals@uillinois.edu; http://www.press.uillinois.edu. Illus. Sample. Refereed. Circ: 850. *Indexed:* ABS&EES, AICP, AmHI, ArtHuCI, BRI, CBRI, HumInd, IIPA, RILM. *Bk. rev.:* 5-8. *Aud.:* Ac.

Dance Research Journal, published by the Congress on Research in Dance for its members, is an academic journal on all aspects of dance. Written by well-regarded dance historians at major institutions, it presents current research that employs quantitative and qualitative analysis of international dance and related fields. With its focus on scholarship in dance, the journal includes dance studied through deconstruction, ethnography, linguistics, and semiotics. Papers are well documented and usually accompanied by bibliographies. One of the strongest attributes is the book review section, which contains many in-depth reviews that are signed and often accompanied by additional references, making this journal a major source for bibliographic information. A regular feature lists papers of major conferences and descriptions of research collections and archives. Research on Middle Eastern dance in a recent issue meets a largely unfilled need for more understanding of the region and culture.

1629. *Dance Spirit.* [ISSN: 1094-0588] 1997. 10x/yr. USD 16.95 domestic; USD 28 foreign; USD 4.99 newsstand/cover per issue. Ed(s): Sara Jarrett. Macfadden Performing Arts Media, LLC., 110 William St, 23rd Fl., New York, NY 10038; http://dancemedia.com/. Adv. Circ: 93066 Paid and controlled. *Indexed:* MASUSE. *Aud.:* Hs, Ga, Ac, Sa.

Dance Spirit covers the entire field of dance, and its audience includes dancers in training, dance teachers, and professional dancers from the Broadway stage to the ballet to graduate dance programs. Short features illustrated with color photography meet the needs of dance amateurs interested in tap dance, swing dance, ballroom dancing, and hip-hop, as well as students on dance teams. Each issue includes news on dance competitions, business and agents, and dance events. Lifestyle Media, the publisher, also produces *American Cheerleader, Dance Spirit In Motion, Dance Teacher*, and *Pointe*.

1630. *Dance Teacher: the magazine for dance professionals.* Formerly (until 1999): *Dance Teacher Now.* [ISSN: 1524-4474] 1979. 10x/yr. USD 24.95 domestic; USD 38 in Canada & Mexico; USD 48 elsewhere. Macfadden Performing Arts Media, LLC., 110 William St, 23rd Fl., New York, NY 10038; http://dancemedia.com/. Illus., index, adv. Circ: 25000 Paid. *Indexed:* ABS&EES, IIPA. *Bk. rev.:* 5, 250 words. *Aud.:* Ga, Ac.

Dance Teacher is the only national magazine addressed to dance teachers of all disciplines. Articles on tap, ballroom, Irish dance, and aerobics, ballet, and modern performance appear. Since it covers such a wide range, the content is useful for teachers with students from grade school through college. Profiles of dance teaching institutions, a higher-education guide, classified advertising for training courses, and good articles on dance music make this a fine resource for all dance teachers. There is a nice online version at www.dance-teacher.com. Lifestyle Media, the publisher, is responsible for a string of dance-related publications ranging from ballet to cheerleading to drill teams.

1631. *Dance Theatre Journal.* Formerly (until 1983): *Labanews.* [ISSN: 0264-9160] 1982. q. GBP 25 (Individuals, GBP 15). Ed(s): Martin Hargreaves. Laban, Creekside, London, SE8 3DZ, United Kingdom; info@laban.org; http://www.laban.org. Illus., index, adv. Circ: 2000. Vol. ends: Dec. *Indexed:* ArtHuCI, BrHumI, IIPA, RILM. *Bk. rev.:* Number and length vary. *Aud.:* Ga, Ac, Sa.

A sophisticated journal that aims to both cover dance and foster critical debate among a community of dance intellectuals, *Dance Theatre* focuses on contemporary dance and dance theater in Europe, especially England, and incorporates dance, drama, music, and visual art. Interviews and in-depth articles cover the entire setting of dance performances, detailing not only choreography but cutting-edge design for costumes, sets, lighting, and music. The contents are wide ranging, with a recent issue providing coverage of a South African festival. Extensive footnotes provide material for further research. The articles and reviews encompass ballet, modern dance, and contemporary hybrids, described in a lively fashion for performers, dance writers, and a general audience. Well-written text and visually stimulating black-and-white photographs support the lengthy signed reviews and interviews.

1632. *Dance Today!* Formerly (until 2001): *Ballroom Dancing Times.* [ISSN: 1475-2336] 1956. m. GBP 16 domestic; GBP 18 foreign; GBP 1.10 newsstand/cover per issue. Ed(s): Sylvia Boerner. Dancing Times Ltd., Clerkenwell House, 45-47 Clerkenwell Green, London, EC1R 0EB, United Kingdom; http://www.dt-ltd.dircon.co.uk. Illus., adv. Vol. ends: Sep. *Indexed:* IIPA. *Aud.:* Ga, Sa.

Dance Today! editors include flamenco, sequence, musical theater, and salsa as well as ballroom dance in this glossy magazine. It claims to be *the* magazine for people who love to dance and watch dancing. For ballroom/social dancers in England, this remains the main source for news on national competitions. Despite its new, lovelier look, it retains its most useful sections for dancers and judges, which are well-illustrated and -described scripts and sequences performed by competition winners. Tips on how to improve ballroom dancing may benefit any amateur or professional. Recent issues have included reviews of compact discs and videos.

1633. *DanceView: a quarterly review of dance.* Formerly (until 1992): *Washington Danceview.* [ISSN: 1077-0577] 1988. q. USD 50 (Individuals, USD 30). Ed(s): Alexandra Tomalonis. DanceView, PO Box 34435, Washington, DC 20043. Illus. Vol. ends: Winter. Online: Chadwyck-Healey Inc. *Indexed:* ABS&EES, IIPA. *Bk. rev.:* 10, length varies. *Aud.:* Ac, Sa.

DanceView covers companies and dance events worldwide. It includes thoughtful, in-depth interviews with dancers, often conducted by other dancers and dance writers, and reviews of exhibitions and other forms of research on dance and dance history. Its contributors, Mary Cargill, Robert Greskovic,and others, are professional dance critics who provide analysis of the major companies in the United States, England, and occasionally Russia. Features include regular reports from New York, London, and the Bay Area. Each issue provides overviews of the season, video reviews, and complete book reviews that are a satisfying read. This would be a good addition to serious dance collections serving dance devotees. Its online counterpart, www.danceviewtimes.com, reviews dance in New York, the San Francisco Bay area, and Washington, D.C., and is updated every Monday.

1634. Dancing Times. [ISSN: 0011-605X] 1910. m. GBP 30 domestic; GBP 35 foreign. Ed(s): Mary Clarke. Dancing Times Ltd., Clerkenwell House, 45-47 Clerkenwell Green, London, EC1R 0EB, United Kingdom; http://www.dt-ltd.dircon.co.uk. Illus., adv. Circ: 12000. *Indexed:* ArtHuCI, IIPA, RILM. *Bk. rev.:* 4-5. *Aud.:* Hs, Ga, Ac.

For nearly 100 years, readers interested in theatrical/classical dance, especially British companies and the season, have relied on this magazine, the oldest continuing periodical on dance in existence. Britain remains a major center for dance performance with a strong audience for contemporary dance, which is fully reflected in *Dancing Times*. Because dance students from the United States often study abroad, the coverage of British dance schools is especially valuable. Regular sections are devoted to dance on video and television. "Into Dance!" is a regular section for children that makes dance themes more approachable by profiling young dancers and recent ballets. Although the emphasis is on education and training, frequent articles about the great companies, their history, and past critical evaluations broaden its usefulness to research collections. In-depth reviews of principal dancers from the major companies continue, along with notes on all the schools, competitions, and awards. There is much to offer U.S. audiences, particularly regular reporting from Russia. Its online version at www.dancing-times.co.uk includes archives and additional information on dance education.

1635. Folk Music Journal. Formerly (until 1965): *English Folk Dance and Song Society. Journal;* Which was formed by the merger of (1???-1931): *English Folk Dance Society. Journal;* (1899-1931): *Folk-Song Society. Journal.* [ISSN: 0531-9684] 1931. a. Free to members; GBP 7.50 per issue. Ed(s): David Atkinson. English Folk Dance and Song Society, Cecil Sharp House, 2 Regents Park Rd, London, NW1 7AY, United Kingdom; info@efdss.org; http://www.efdss.org/. Illus., index. Refereed. Circ: 5000. Microform: PQC. Online: Chadwyck-Healey Inc.; EBSCO Publishing, EBSCO Host; OCLC Online Computer Library Center, Inc.; ProQuest LLC (Ann Arbor); H.W. Wilson. Reprint: PSC. *Indexed:* AmHI, ArtHuCI, BrHumI, HumInd, IBR, IBZ, IIMP, IIPA, MLA-IB, MusicInd, RILM, SSCI. *Bk. rev.:* Number varies, 500 words, signed, shorter notices section. *Aud.:* Ac, Sa.

In 1911, Cecil Sharp formed the English Dance and Song Society, which serves to "collect, research and preserve our heritage of folk dances, songs, and music." Their handsomely redesigned journal continues the society's tradition of almost 100 years in presenting carefully researched articles on the history of English folk dance and music, with texts and musical scores. The consistent, well-written style makes this of interest to historians, to the audience for folk music and dancing, and to the many people who are active in folk music and dance as a hobby. The emphasis on considering dance and music together reflects the interdisciplinary approach in most current dance scholarship and incorporates social and cultural history. Recent issues include identifying the earliest reference to morris dancing. Its value to serious students lies not only in the articles but also in the accompanying extensive references. Scholarly reviews of new books and sound recordings are, in effect, research essays. Subscribers become members of the society and also receive the quarterly *English Dance and Song*, which contains shorter informational articles, events calendars, and news items.

1636. Pointe: ballet at its best. Formerly: *Points.* [ISSN: 1529-6741] 2000. bi-m. USD 26; USD 7.99 newsstand/cover. Macfadden Performing Arts Media, LLC., 110 William St, 23rd Fl., New York, NY 10038; http://dancemedia.com/. Illus., adv. Circ: 30000 Paid. *Indexed:* ABS&EES, MASUSE. *Aud.:* Hs, Ga, Ac, Sa.

Pointe, published six times a year, is intended as an international ballet periodical exclusively for those with a serious interest in dance. The focus is on individual dancers as opposed to companies, with articles that discuss the business of ballet. Subjects range from contracts to technique, as well as the most recent developments in health care and the prevention of injuries, each handled by a practitioner/expert in the field. Since the focus is on working

dancers and students, its style is crisp and clear, with very good photographs and illustrations. *Pointe* will also inform the ballet fan who wants to understand more about the dancer's craft and preparations for performance.

■ DEATH AND DYING

See also Medicine section.

Patricia Newland, Catalog/Technical Services Librarian, Francis Harvey Green Library, West Chester University of Pennsylvania, West Chester, PA 19383; Hospice volunteer; pnewland@wcupa.edu

Introduction

Dame Cicely Saunders, who founded the hospice movement as we know it today, died July 14, 2005, at St. Christopher's, the hospice she began almost 40 years ago. Since that time, the hospice movement has grown and spread around the world, fostering her ideal of minimizing pain while providing emotional support for both dying patients and their families (Saxon, Wolfgang. "Cicely Saunders Dies at 87: Reshaped End-of-Life Care." *New York Times* 4 Aug. 2005, late ed.: A17). The physical and social aspects of death and dying form the main research thrusts of the journals reviewed here. Key themes are improving the control of pain associated with chronic or terminal illness, and understanding and providing for the emotional needs of terminally ill patients and their families and caregivers.

Relatively few Americans may have been aware of Dame Cicely's death, but another recent death caught the attention of the entire country. The highly publicized dying and death of Terri Schiavo brought to the forefront the kinds of complex legal and ethical issues that are discussed in these journals. Interest in issues related to death and dying continues to increase, in part due to the constant presence of death, explicit or implicit, in media coverage of war, terrorism, natural disasters, starvation, potential and actual epidemics, etc. These publications present a variety of viewpoints, advice, information, and research on issues that may touch us all.

Basic Periodicals

Ac, Sa: *American Journal of Hospice and Palliative Care; Compassion and Choices Magazine; Death Studies; European Journal of Palliative Care; Illness, Crisis, & Loss; Journal of Pain & Palliative Care Pharmacotherapy; Journal of Palliative Care; Journal of Palliative Medicine; Journal of Social Work in End-of-Life & Palliative Care; Omega; Palliative Medicine; Suicide and Life-Threatening Behavior.*

Basic Abstracts and Indexes

AgeLine, Family Index, MEDLINE, PsycINFO, SCOPUS, Social Work Abstracts.

1637. The American Journal of Hospice and Palliative Medicine. Former titles (until 2004): *The American Journal of Hospice and Palliative Care;* (until 1990): *American Journal of Hospice Care;* Incorporates (2002-2003): *Journal of Terminal Oncology.* 1983. bi-m. GBP 318. Ed(s): Robert Enck. Sage Science Press (US), 2455 Teller Rd, Thousand Oaks, CA 91320; sagescience@sagepub.com; http://www.sagepub.com/journals.nav. Illus., index, adv. Sample. Refereed. Circ: 3000. Vol. ends: Nov/Dec. Reprint: PSC. *Indexed:* AgeL, CINAHL, PsycInfo, SWR&A. *Bk. rev.:* Number and length vary. *Aud.:* Ga, Ac, Sa.

This peer-reviewed journal publishes original research, news briefs, discussions of cases with ethical issues, and life stories of patients/hospice workers. Regular features include updates on palliative care for patients with cancer, pharmaceutical developments, and pain and symptom management in general. The journal is interdisciplinary and would be of interest to all those involved in the care of the dying. While the contents are generally aimed at practitioners and students in the health care and counseling professions, hospice volunteers would also find some features interesting. Recent articles suggest the wide scope of this journal: "Hispanic Access to Hospice Services in a Predominantly Hispanic Community," "Role of the Doctor in Relieving Spiritual Distress at the End of

Life," "Systematic Radionuclide Therapy in Pain Palliation," "Tactical Reframing to Reduce Death Anxiety in Undergraduate Nursing Students," and "Control and End-of-life Care: Does Ethnicity Matter?" Abstracts for volume 10 (1993) to the present are available via a link on the journal's web site.

1638. Compassion and Choices Magazine. Former titles (until 2004): *End-of-Life Choices;* (until 2002): *Timelines;* (until 1994): *Hemlock Quarterly.* 1980. q. Ed(s): Judith Fleming. Compassion & Choices, PO Box 101810, Denver, CO 80250-1810; info@compassionandchoices.org; http://www.compassionandchoices.org. Adv. Circ: 40000. *Aud.:* Ga.

The title change in 2005 from *End-of-Life Choices* to *Compassion and Choices Magazine* reflects a change in the organization that publishes this periodical. End-of-Life Choices, formerly the Hemlock Society, has combined with another organization, Compassion in Dying, to form Compassion and Choices. The organization focuses on direct support of the dying and their families, legislative efforts, and education of the general public on issues involved in choices for the dying. This publication fosters the work of the organization and is aimed at a general adult audience, as well as lawmakers and health care workers. Each issue contains news of the organization's work, updates on news media coverage of issues related to choice in dying, updates on state and national legislation affecting choices for the dying, and narratives of personal experiences of members and their families. Recent issues are freely available online in pdf format at www.compassionandchoices.org/educationcenter/publication.php.

1639. Death Studies: counseling - research - education - care - ethics. Formerly (until 1985): *Death Education.* [ISSN: 0748-1187] 1977. 10x/yr. GBP 435 print & online eds. Ed(s): Robert A Neimeyer. Routledge, 325 Chestnut St, Ste 800, Philadelphia, PA 19106; journals@routledge.com; http://www.tandf.co.uk/journals. Illus., index. Sample. Refereed. Circ: 800. Vol. ends: Dec. Microform: PQC. Online: EBSCO Publishing, EBSCO Host; Factiva, Inc.; Gale; IngentaConnect; OCLC Online Computer Library Center, Inc.; ProQuest LLC (Ann Arbor); SwetsWise Online Content. Reprint: PSC. *Indexed:* ASG, AgeL, CINAHL, CJA, ERIC, ExcerpMed, LRI, PsycInfo, RI-1, SFSA, SSA, SSCI, SWA, SWR&A, SociolAb, V&AA. *Bk. rev.:* Number and length vary. *Aud.:* Ac, Sa.

This peer-reviewed journal is interdisciplinary and would be relevant to a broad spectrum of researchers and students in disciplines as far ranging as medicine, philosophy, religion, psychology, sociology, and education. It contains original research, news related to the field, updates on the latest in professional practice, and in-depth book reviews. Original research examines the effects of age, gender, and ethnicity on beliefs about and reactions to death. Cross-cultural similarities and differences are the subject of regular investigation (see, for instance, such recent studies as "Terrorism and Resilience: Adolescents' and Teachers' Responses to September 11, 2001," "Psychological and Religious Coping Strategies of Mothers Bereaved by the Sudden Death of a Child," "Narratives of Grieving African-Americans About Racism in the Lives of Deceased Family Members," and "Religiosity and Death Obsession in Palestinians"). A recent issue was devoted to the Terri Schiavo case. An online sample issue and tables of contents for volumes 21 (1997) to the present are available from links on the journal's web site. An author/title search is available on the table of contents page.

1640. European Journal of Palliative Care. [ISSN: 1352-2779] 1994. bi-m. GBP 210 (Individuals, GBP 70; Members, GBP 60 EAPC). Ed(s): Bethan France, Dr. Andrew Hoy. Hayward Medical Communications Ltd., Rosalind Franklin House, The Oaks Business Park, Fordham Rd, Newmarket, CB8 7XN, United Kingdom; admin@hayward.co.uk; http://www.hayward.co.uk. Illus., adv. Circ: 2000. *Indexed:* CINAHL. *Aud.:* Ac, Sa.

This publication is the official journal of the European Association for Palliative Care, and serves as a vehicle for communication about the work of the organization and related events within the European palliative care community. The journal publishes review articles in English (there is a French version of this publication as well) on current research in palliative care. The multidisciplinary review articles are not limited in geographic scope; there is a notable concern with palliative care in developing countries. An interesting feature of this journal is its case-study master class. Each issue describes a clinical case and

asks the reader to respond to questions posed about the case; in the next issue, specialists in the field provide answers to these questions, based on the actual conduct of the case. These case studies could be useful for both practitioners and students in the field of palliative medicine. Recent review articles include "Managing Phantom Limb Pain," "Aging, Pain and Palliative Care," and "Opioids and the Control of Breathing: What Do We Know?" An index to articles beginning with volume 5 (1998) is available from a link on the journal's web site. The association's empirical research focus is largely the domain of the journal *Palliative Medicine*, which the association also sponsors.

1641. Illness, Crisis, and Loss. [ISSN: 1054-1373] 1991. q. USD 599. Ed(s): Gerald R Cox, Timothy Gongaware. Baywood Publishing Co., Inc., 26 Austin Ave, PO Box 337, Amityville, NY 11701-0337; info@baywood.com; http://www.baywood.com. Illus., adv. Sample. Refereed. *Indexed:* ASG, ASSIA, CINAHL, HRA, IBR, IBZ, PsycInfo, SFSA, SSA, SociolAb, V&AA. *Bk. rev.:* Number and length vary. *Aud.:* Ac, Sa.

Sponsored by the Center for Death Education and Bioethics, an affiliate of the Sociology/Archaeology Department of the University of Wisconsin, La Crosse, this peer-reviewed journal changed publishers in 2005, and is now published by Baywood Publishing Company, the publisher of *Omega: Journal of Death and Dying.* The focus of *Illness, Crisis, & Loss* is on the psychological, social, and ethical issues involved in serious illness, trauma, death and dying, and the grief they bring. The journal would be of interest to practitioners and students in the fields of counseling, social work, medicine, and ethics. Recent articles reflect the concerns of this journal: "Bounded Grief at Work: Working and Caring for Children with Chronic Illness," "Bits Of Falling Sky and Global Pandemics: Moral Panic and Severe Acute Respiratory Syndrome (SARS)," and "Overcome by or Overcoming Loss: A Call for the Development of Therapy for Individuals Mourning Vocational Loss in Schizophrenia." Tables of contents beginning with volume 7 (1999) are available from a link on the journal's web site; also available is the ability to search across citations and abstracts in these volumes. A sample issue can be accessed from the table of contents page after free registration.

1642. Journal of Pain & Palliative Care Pharmacotherapy. Formerly (until 2002): *Journal of Pharmaceutical Care in Pain & Symptom Control;* Incorporates (1985-2002): *The Hospice Journal.* [ISSN: 1536-0288] 1993. q. USD 580 print & online eds. Ed(s): Arthur G Lipman. The Haworth Medical Press, 10 Alice St, Binghamton, NY 13904; getinfo@haworthpress.com; http://www.haworthpress.com. Illus., adv. Sample. Refereed. Circ: 529 Paid. Reprint: HAW. *Indexed:* BiolDig, CINAHL, ExcerpMed, PsycInfo. *Bk. rev.:* Number and length vary. *Aud.:* Ac, Sa.

This peer-reviewed interdisciplinary journal on the management of pain in both chronic and acute illness, as well as in the dying, includes original research, review articles, and news from the field. Question and answer columns and other advice articles are written so that they can be shared directly with patients and their families. Special reports and updates cover legal issues involved in pain management and discuss standards in the field. There are reviews of books, web sites, and other media. An interesting new feature is each issue's full-color cover art depicting pain or its amelioration. Recent article titles include "Opioid Analgesics in the Substance Abuser: Pros and Cons," "Opioid Expenditures and Utilization in the Medicaid System," and "Assessing the Value of Hospice Care: Is Documentation of Cost Savings Necessary?" Tables of contents beginning with volume 16 (2002) are available from a link on the journal's web site, as is the ability to search by author, article title, and assigned keywords. Also available is a sample issue in pdf format.

1643. Journal of Palliative Care. [ISSN: 0825-8597] 1985. q. CND 125 (Individuals, CND 85). Ed(s): Dr. David J Roy. Centre for Bioethics - Clinical Research Institute of Montreal, 110 Pine Ave W, Montreal, PQ H2W 1R7, Canada; Carole.Marcotte@ircm.qc.ca; http://www.ircm.qc.ca/bioethique/english/publications/journal_of_palliative_care.html. Illus. Sample. Refereed. Vol. ends: Winter. Microform: MML. Online: Micromedia ProQuest; Northern Light Technology, Inc.; ProQuest LLC (Ann Arbor). *Indexed:* AgeL, CBCARef, CINAHL, CPerl, PsycInfo, RILM, SCI, SSCI. *Bk. rev.:* Number and length vary. *Aud.:* Ac, Sa.

A publication of the Centre for Bioethics of the Clinical Research Institute of Montreal, this peer-reviewed journal contains original research, reviews of current issues in the field, regular features such as the Global Exchange, and occasional abstracts from relevant conference proceedings. The journal provides an international perspective on hospice care and palliative medicine, and seeks to educate health professionals involved with the dying. It also would be of interest to students in social work, counseling, and medicine, and hospice volunteers would find many articles interesting as well. Occasional thematic issues such as "Palliative Care . . . for Whom?" and "Dignity at the End of Life" explore critical aspects of palliative care. Recent article titles include "Lower Limb Lymphedema: Experiences and Perceptions of Cancer Patients in the Late Palliative Stage," "Children's Perspectives of a Pediatric Hospice Program," and "Physicians' and Pharmacists' Attitudes Toward the Use of Sedation at the End of Life: Influence of Prognosis and Type of Suffering." All articles are in English; abstracts are available in both English and French. Complete tables of contents from volume 1 (1985) to the present are available from a link on the journal's web site, as is a sample issue.

1644. *Journal of Palliative Medicine.* [ISSN: 1096-6218] 1998. bi-m. USD 765. Ed(s): Charles F von Gunten. Mary Ann Liebert, Inc. Publishers, 140 Huguenot St, 3rd Fl, New Rochelle, NY 10801-5215; info@liebertpub.com; http://www.liebertpub.com. Illus., adv. Sample. Refereed. Circ: 3000 Paid. Vol. ends: Winter. Reprint: PSC. *Indexed:* CINAHL, ExcerpMed, PsycInfo, SCI. *Bk. rev.:* Number and length vary. *Aud.:* Ac, Sa.

This peer-reviewed publication is the official journal of the American Academy of Hospice and Palliative Medicine. It covers palliative care for the dying and ethical and legal issues involved in end-of-life care. It would be of interest to professionals in the health care and counseling fields, as well as students and faculty in programs preparing health, counseling, and social work practitioners. Although American hospice programs and end-of-life issues in the United States are covered in depth, there are also cross-cultural examinations of hospice programs and these same issues in other countries. Each issue of over 200 pages includes original research, reviews of current practice and research, a "Fast Facts and Concepts" column, updates from the field, case studies, book and media reviews, and columns recounting personal experiences of practitioners working with the dying. Recent issues include articles such as "The Impact of Gender and Marital Status on End-of-Life Care: Evidence from the National Mortality Follow-Back Survey," "Elder Abuse at End of Life," and "Promoting Advance Directives among African Americans: A Faith-Based Model." A sample issue and tables of contents going back to volume 1 (1998) are available from the journal's web site. It is possible to search the full text of articles from this web page as well.

1645. *Journal of Social Work in End-of-Life & Palliative Care.* Formerly (until 2005): *Loss, Grief & Care.* [ISSN: 1552-4256] 1986. q. USD 365 print & online eds. Ed(s): Ellen Csikai. Haworth Press, Inc., 10 Alice St, Binghamton, NY 13904-1580; getinfo@haworthpress.com; http://www.haworthpress.com. Illus., adv. Sample. Refereed. Circ: 232 Paid. Vol. ends: Winter. Microform: PQC. Online: EBSCO Publishing, EBSCO Host; OCLC Online Computer Library Center, Inc.; SwetsWise Online Content. Reprint: HAW. *Indexed:* ASG, ASSIA, CINAHL, IBR, IBZ, IMFL, IPSA, SFSA, SSA, SWR&A, SociolAb. *Bk. rev.:* Number and length vary. *Aud.:* Ac, Sa.

This peer-reviewed journal publishes original research and reviews of the literature on the role of social workers in assisting the dying and individuals with chronic illness of all ages, genders, and ethnicities. It reviews professional standards, guidelines and education in this field of social work. While social work practitioners and faculty and students in social work programs are the primary audience for this publication, many articles would also be of interest to health professionals in other disciplines, as well as to hospice volunteers. Recent issues include articles such as "Social Work Competencies in Palliative and End-of-Life Care," "What Matters to Older African Americans Facing End-of-Life Decisions: A Focus Group Study," "Pediatric Palliative and End-of-Life Care: The Role of Social Work in Pediatric Oncology," and "Social Workers' Use of Spiritual Practices in Palliative Care." Tables of contents beginning with volume 1 (2005) are available from a link on the journal's web site, as is the ability to search by author, article title, and assigned keywords. Also available is a sample issue in pdf format.

1646. *Omega: Journal of Death and Dying.* [ISSN: 0030-2228] 1969. 8x/yr. USD 443. Ed(s): Jane Geraldine Pierre, Kenneth Doka. Baywood Publishing Co., Inc., 26 Austin Ave, PO Box 337, Amityville, NY 11701-0337; info@baywood.com; http://www.baywood.com. Illus., index, adv. Sample. Refereed. Vol. ends: No. 4. *Indexed:* ASG, ASSIA, AbAn, AgeL, ArtHuCI, CINAHL, CJA, ExcerpMed, IBR, IBZ, PsycInfo, RI-1, RILM, SSA, SSCI, SociolAb, V&AA. *Bk. rev.:* Number and length vary. *Aud.:* Ac, Sa.

An official journal of the Association for Death Education and Counseling, this interdisciplinary, peer-reviewed journal would be of interest to therapists, social work practitioners, educators, and health professionals, as well as students of a wide range of disciplines such as psychology, sociology, anthropology, and medicine. Original research presents cross-cultural perspectives on dying, grief, and customs related to death and mourning. Occasional thematic issues, such as a recent one on complicated grief, cover critical aspects of this field. Recent issues include such articles as "The Effect of Bereavement Due to Suicide on Survivors' Depression: A Study of Chinese Samples," "An Exploratory Study of Post-Traumatic Stress Disorder Symptoms among Bereaved Children," "How Family Members Respond to Residents' Wish to Die," and "Life Regrets and Death Attitudes in College Students." Tables of contents beginning with volume 1 (1970) are available from a link on the journal's web site; also available is the ability to search across citations and abstracts in these volumes. A sample issue can be accessed from the table of contents page after free registration.

1647. *Palliative Medicine: a multiprofessional journal.* [ISSN: 0269-2163] 1987. 8x/yr. GBP 810. Ed(s): Geoffrey Hanks. Sage Science Press (UK), 1 Oliver's Yard, 55 City Rd, London, EC1Y 1SP, United Kingdom; info@sagepub.com; http://www.sagepub.co.uk/. Illus., index, adv. Sample. Refereed. Circ: 1400. Vol. ends: Dec. Online: EBSCO Publishing, EBSCO Host; Gale; HighWire Press; IngentaConnect; OCLC Online Computer Library Center, Inc.; OhioLINK; ProQuest LLC (Ann Arbor); SwetsWise Online Content. Reprint: PSC. *Indexed:* ASSIA, BiolAb, CINAHL, ExcerpMed, IMFL, PsycInfo, SCI. *Bk. rev.:* Number and length vary. *Aud.:* Ac, Sa.

This publication is the peer-reviewed research journal of the European Association for Palliative Care, which also sponsors the *European Journal of Palliative Care. Palliative Medicine* contains original research, case studies, and book reviews of interest to those working in all areas of palliative care. Although the content is in English, the editors have begun to accept abstracts in languages other than English to increase accessibility to its international readership; many authors are from non-European countries, and the journal provides an international research perspective on palliative care. Recent article titles include "Shelter-Based Palliative Care for the Homeless Terminally Ill," "Patient Work in End-Stage Heart Failure: A Prospective Longitudinal Multiple Case Study," "Being a Hospice Volunteer," and "Making Sense Of Dying: A Review Of Narratives Written Since 1950 by People Facing Death from Cancer and Other Diseases." An online sample issue and tables of contents beginning with volume 12 (1998) are available from links on the journal's web site.

1648. *Suicide and Life-Threatening Behavior: the official journal of the American Association of Suicidology.* Former titles: *Suicide; Life Threatening Behavior.* [ISSN: 0363-0234] 1970. bi-m. USD 575 (Individuals, USD 115). Ed(s): Morton Silverman. Guilford Publications, Inc., 72 Spring St, 4th Fl, New York, NY 10012; info@guilford.com; http://www.guilford.com. Illus., index, adv. Refereed. Circ: 2000. Microform: PQC. Online: EBSCO Publishing, EBSCO Host; OCLC Online Computer Library Center, Inc.; ProQuest LLC (Ann Arbor); SwetsWise Online Content. *Indexed:* ASG, AbAn, AgeL, BiolAb, CJA, CommAb, ERIC, ExcerpMed, FR, HRA, PRA, PsycInfo, RILM, SFSA, SSA, SSCI, SUSA, SociolAb, V&AA. *Bk. rev.:* Number and length vary. *Aud.:* Ac, Sa.

This peer-reviewed publication is the official journal of the American Association of Suicidology, an organization whose mission is understanding and preventing suicide. The journal is interdisciplinary in nature, drawing from the fields of sociology, psychology, statistics, biology, and public health. Practitioners and students in the fields of mental health, social work, and pastoral work would find this journal of interest, as would physicians, nurses, and others in the field of medicine. It consists of original research that examines suicide, attempted suicide, and other life-threatening acts, and their ramifications on the social networks in which a suicidal person is involved. Many articles consider suicide in the context of the age, gender, ethnicity, or nationality of those who commit suicide or who are affected by another's suicide. Recent issues have included articles such as "Integratively Assessing Risk and Protective Factors for Adolescent Suicide," "Belief in the Inevitability of Suicide: Results from a National Survey," and "Suicides in the Developing World: Case Study from Pakistan." A sample issue and tables of contents beginning with volume 31 (2001) are available from links on the journal's web site.

■ DISABILITIES

See also Education; and Medicine and Health sections.

Sharon Naylor, Education Librarian, Milner Library, Illinois State University, Campus Box 8900, Normal, IL 61790-8900; sknaylor@ilstu.edu

Introduction

Although several titles have been added, the list of journals included in this section does not differ greatly from the list in the previous edition. However, some observations can be made and some minor shifts in emphasis can be identified. The number of journals available only electronically has not increased at the rate that might have been expected. In fact, there are fewer electronic periodicals that target a general or special audience listed in this edition than were listed in the previous edition. This by no means should be taken as an indication that less information about disabilities is now available on the Internet. In fact, just the opposite is true. There are numerous blogs, web forums, and association web sites that target persons with disabilities, and it is sometimes difficult to draw the line between online magazines and other Internet formats. The one new nonacademic online magazine added in this edition, *Ouch!*, falls into this category. In general, however, few new online magazines are appearing, and several titles that had appeared in previous editions have ceased to exist. Titles that are exceptions to this observation are *LD Online* and *The Special Ed Advocate Newsletter,* two titles that target teachers and parents, which have survived and thrived for several years. Two other exceptions to this general observation are *DeafDigest* and *Ragged Edge,* online magazines that have appeared in several previous editions.

With the exception of *Information Technology and Disabilities*, a title that first moved online in 1994, electronic-only journals targeting more academic or professional audiences have been somewhat slower to appear. *Assistive Technology Outcomes and Benefits* and *International Journal of Disability, Community & Rehabilitation* are two relative newcomers. Major indexing services have been slow to include online-only titles, however, and this limits their visibility and could impede their success. It will be interesting to see whether open-access academic journals become more successful than free online magazines appear to be. It should also be noted that online availability takes numerous forms. Some journal subscriptions include both paper and electronic access, or they allow for a choice of either the paper or online version. Numerous publications are now part of aggregator services (e.g., EBSCO's Academic Search Premier). Thus, while online access is becoming increasingly available, the most common model appears to be offering both paper subscriptions and/or electronic access.

The introduction of programs in disabilities studies that are emerging on college campuses may be responsible for some subtle shifts in direction. Perhaps the most noticeable shift is toward a more international outlook. Although library literature has noted a trend toward globalization for several years, the journals in this section have not reflected this trend. Many of the titles are published by organizations, most notably the Council for Exceptional Children, that are located in North America. Another contributing factor may be that a number of the journals are education-related, and generally education does not have an international focus. However, this attitude seems to be slowly changing. *Disabilities Studies Quarterly* and *International Journal of Disability, Community & Rehabilitation,* two recent additions to the list in this section that are representative of the approach taken by disabilities studies programs, are international in scope. The rise in the diagnosis of autism spectrum disorders has resulted in the addition of several related titles, including *Autism,* a title with an international focus. A considerable amount of research about autism is being conducted in the United Kingdom and Australia, a factor that will also contribute toward a more international point of view in this area of study. Usually, academic journals are more likely to have an international focus than popular periodicals. However, the e-zine *Disability World*, which started in 2000, has a strong international focus.

Previous essays in this section have commented on the interdisciplinary nature of disabilities journals, and this characteristic seems even more pronounced with the involvement of disabilities studies programs. In addition to the fields of education, psychology, medicine, and computer science (fields that have traditionally written about disabilities), disabilities studies extends to even more areas, including women's studies, literature, art, and public policy. Another trend noted in previous editions, a broadening of the definition of the term "disability," also seems even more pronounced. "Disability" means different things to different people, and who does or does not have a disability may depend on who is doing the defining and for what purpose. Governmental bodies that fund projects and provide financial assistance may define the term more narrowly than independent organizations. Certainly, those in disabilities studies programs are likely to use the broadest possible interpretation. In keeping with the interdisciplinary nature of the field, researchers will need to consult a wide variety of indexes, and several indexes have been added to the list with this edition. Sadly, *Exceptional Child Education Resources* no longer appears, since its sponsoring body, the Council for Exceptional Children, stopped updating it in November of 2004. This is truly a loss, and hopefully another group will step forward to take this over.

A conscious attempt has been made to include magazines and journals that represent a wide variety of publications and viewpoints. There are highly technical and scholarly works as well as breezy, consumer-oriented, self-help publications. Some of the popular titles have a positive, "can do" point of view, while others represent the voice of those who are demanding their rights and railing against what they see as abuses. Some of the academic titles are focused on diagnosis, interventions, and technologies, while others (notably those associated with disabilities studies programs) may include articles and other materials representative of those in various disability rights movements. In keeping with the interdisciplinary nature of disabilities, a wide variety of indexes are suggested. Researchers should keep in mind, however, that online publications may not be indexed and that they will need to employ a variety of strategies when searching for information.

Basic Periodicals

Ga: *New Mobility*; Ac: *American Annals of the Deaf, Journal of Deaf Studies and Deaf Education, American Journal on Mental Retardation, Education and Training in Developmental Disabilities, Focus on Exceptional Children, Journal of Speech, Language, and Hearing Research, Journal of Visual Impairment and Blindness, RE:View.*

Basic Abstracts and Indexes

ERIC, Excerpta Medica, Linguistics and Language Behavior Abstracts, Psychological Abstracts, Education Abstracts, Sociological Abstracts, CINAHL, PsycINFO, SPORTDiscus, SSCI.

1649. 360: your online source for the disability community. Formerly: *360 Degrees: The Magazine with Every Angle (Print Edition).* 1993. q. Free. 360 Magazine, PO Box 922, Clifton, NJ 07014; editor@360usainc.com; http://www.360usainc.com. Adv. Circ: 40000. *Aud.:* Sa.

360 calls itself an "interactive ezine that challenges the traditional views of people in wheelchairs." It covers all topics related to the wheelchair community, and the overall tone is informal, informative, and entertaining. It is geared toward "wheelers" between the ages of 18 and 45 and includes short articles on sports, travel, nutrition and health, sex and relationships, and a "Why Me" column in which readers share their stories. Users must register, but registration is free. The web site includes the magazine archives, a resources directory, several reader forums, and a marketplace. E-mail alerts are sent when new issues are made available. URL: www.360mag.com

1650. *Ability.* [ISSN: 1062-5321] 1992. bi-m. USD 29.70. Ed(s): Chet Cooper, Jane Wollman-Rusoff. C.R. Cooper Publishing, 1001 W 17th St, Costa Mesa, CA 92627. Illus., adv. Sample. Circ: 165000 Paid. *Aud.:* Hs, Ga, Sa.

Ability claims to be "the first publication focusing on disabilities to crossover into mainstream America." Each issue includes an interview with a high-profile personality who is either an advocate for a particular disability or health-related issue or who has successfully dealt with a disability or health problem. Paul Sorvino, Loni Anderson, and Jane Pauley are among those recently interviewed. Also included are articles about new technologies, the Americans with Disabilities Act, travel, employment, nutrition, and human-interest stories. The web site includes the full text of the featured interviews and other selected articles, suggested links, and suggested resources. This inexpensive magazine is a good choice for libraries that want to add a popular title that will appeal to people with a variety of disabilities.

AccessWorld. See Blind and Visually Impaired section.

1651. *Adapted Physical Activity Quarterly.* [ISSN: 0736-5829] 1984. q. USD 240 (Individuals, USD 60 print & online eds.). Ed(s): Terry Rizzo. Human Kinetics, PO Box 5076, Champaign, IL 61825-5076; orders@hkusa.com; http://www.humankinetics.com. Illus., index, adv. Sample. Refereed. Circ: 977 Paid and free. Vol. ends: Oct. Reprint: PSC. *Indexed:* CINAHL, ECER, ExcerpMed, IBR, IBZ, PEI, PsycInfo, RILM, SCI, SD, SSCI. *Bk. rev.:* Number and length vary. *Aud.:* Ac, Sa.

This scholarly, multidisciplinary journal is the official journal of the International Federation of Adapted Physical Activity, and it publishes "the latest scholarly inquiry related to physical activity for special populations." Populations that are considered range from the infant to the elderly. The focus of the articles may be on an adaptation of the equipment, activity, facility, methodology, or setting. Most issues include from five to seven research articles and one "Viewpoint" article that contains commentary on current opinions, legislation, and trends in the profession. Issues also include book and media reviews and abstracts. An author index is included in the October issue. Contents information and abstracts are available on the magazine's web site.

1652. *ADDitude: attention deficit.* [ISSN: 1529-1014] 2000. bi-m. USD 19.99; USD 6.95 newsstand/cover per issue. Ed(s): Ellen Kingsley. New Hope Media, LLC, 39 W 37th St, 15th Fl, New York, NY 10018-6217; lertters@additudemag.com. Adv. Circ: 45100. *Aud.:* Sa.

This magazine is a lifestyle and self-help publication written primarily for the parents of children with Attention Deficit Disorder or adults who have AD/HD themselves. Most articles are relatively short and offer practical advice. For example, recent cover stories include "How to Survive Summer Vacation," "Coach your Coach," and "Bedtime Battles." The magazine does not endorse any particular approach, and it notes that they are "leery of claims for treatments and interventions that have not been tested in controlled, clinical trials." They also note that most of the people who work at *ADDitude* are parents of AD/HD children or have AD/HD themselves. Each issue includes regular columns, classified ads, and an ADD Resource Library. The magazine's web site includes the tables of contents of all issues, the full text of selected articles, and instructions for ordering back issues. A good choice for public libraries.

1653. *American Annals of the Deaf.* Formerly: *American Annals of the Deaf and Dumb.* [ISSN: 0002-726X] 1847. 5x/yr. USD 90 (Individuals, USD 50; USD 30 newsstand/cover per issue in US & Canada). Ed(s): Donald F Moores. Gallaudet University Press, 800 Florida Ave, N E, Washington, DC 20002. Illus., index, adv. Refereed. Circ: 4000 Paid and controlled. Vol. ends: Dec. Microform: PQC. Online: EBSCO Publishing, EBSCO Host; Northern Light Technology, Inc.; OCLC Online Computer Library Center, Inc.; OhioLINK; Project MUSE; ProQuest K-12 Learning Solutions; ProQuest LLC (Ann Arbor); SwetsWise Online Content; H.W. Wilson. *Indexed:* ABIn, AgeL, CINAHL, EAA, ECER, ERIC, EduInd, ExcerpMed, L&LBA, PAIS, PsycInfo, SSCI, SWA. *Aud.:* Ac, Sa.

First published in 1847, this is the official publication of the Convention of American Instructors of the Deaf and of the Conference of Educational Administrators of Schools and Programs for the Deaf. It is directed and administered by a committee made up of members of the executive committees of both of these organizations, and the intended audience is primarily professional educators. Topics covered include communication methods and strategies, language development, mainstreaming and residential schools, parent-child relationships, teacher training, and teaching skills. Topics also extend to covering the broad interests of educators in the general welfare of deaf children and adults. Each year, the *Annals* publishes four literary issues (March, July, October, and December) and an annual reference issue that lists schools and programs in the United States and Canada for students who are deaf or hard-of-hearing (April). The reference issue also provides demographic, audiological, and educational data about students who are deaf and hard-of-hearing and the schools they attend. An annual author and subject index is included in the December issue. The web site includes abstracts of articles in the current issue and a subject/author/volume and issue number index to previous issues. This key journal should be included in libraries that support programs for the hearing impaired.

1654. *American Journal of Occupational Therapy.* Former titles (until 1978): *A J O T: The American Journal of Occupational Therapy;* (until 1977): *American Journal of Occupational Therapy.* [ISSN: 0272-9490] 1947. 6x/yr. USD 182.50 (Individuals, USD 114). Ed(s): Mary A Corcoran. American Occupational Therapy Association, Inc., 4720 Montgomery Ln, PO Box 31220, Bethesda, MD 20814-3425; members@aota.org; http://www.aota.org. Illus., index, adv. Refereed. Circ: 40000. Vol. ends: Nov/Dec. Microform: PQC. Online: EBSCO Publishing, EBSCO Host; Ovid Technologies, Inc. *Indexed:* ASG, ASSIA, AgeL, CINAHL, ECER, ExcerpMed, IMFL, PsycInfo, RILM, SSCI. *Bk. rev.:* Various number and length. *Aud.:* Ac, Sa.

The *American Journal of Occupational Therapy* is an official publication of the American Occupational Therapy Association. Intended for practitioners, it focuses on research, practice, and health care issues in the field of occupational therapy. Issues include news and features about hands-on approaches, clinical technique and technology updates, careers and continuing education, legislative issues, and professional trends. Information about the association, edited speeches, and editorials representing differing viewpoints are also included. There are occasional issues centered around a theme. The November/December issue includes an author and subject index for the year and a listing of educational programs. Tables of contents and article abstracts are available on the journal web site. This journal is recommended for academic, medical, and special libraries.

1655. *American Journal of Physical Medicine and Rehabilitation.* Formerly (until 1988): *American Journal of Physical Medicine.* [ISSN: 0894-9115] 1921. m. USD 465 (Individuals, USD 293). Ed(s): Bradley R Johns, Walter R Frontera. Lippincott Williams & Wilkins, 530 Walnut St, Philadelphia, PA 19106-3621; custserv@lww.com; http://www.lww.com. Illus., adv. Refereed. Circ: 4828. Online: EBSCO Publishing, EBSCO Host; Ovid Technologies, Inc.; SwetsWise Online Content. *Indexed:* BioEngAb, CINAHL, ChemAb, ErgAb, ExcerpMed, PEI, SCI, SD, SSCI. *Aud.:* Ac, Sa.

The *American Journal of Physical Medicine and Rehabilitation* is the official journal of the Association of Academic Physiatrists (AAP). Issues usually include seven research articles and one special research article that is selected by the editors to be published as an educational activity. The journal focuses on the physical treatment of neuromuscular impairments and the use of electrodiagnostic studies. Tables of contents and article abstracts are available on the journal web site. It is a good choice for hospital libraries and academic libraries.

1656. *American Journal of Speech - Language Pathology: a journal of clinical practice.* [ISSN: 1058-0360] 1991. q. USD 127 & libraries (Individuals, USD 46). Ed(s): Jeannette Holt. American Speech - Language - Hearing Association, 10801 Rockville Pike, Rockville, MD 20852-3226; subscribe@asha.org; http://www.asha.org. Illus., adv. Circ: 39640 Controlled. Microform: PQC. Online: EBSCO Publishing, EBSCO Host; HighWire Press; ProQuest K-12 Learning Solutions; ProQuest LLC (Ann Arbor). *Indexed:* CINAHL, ECER, L&LBA, PsycInfo, SSCI. *Aud.:* Ac.

This journal is published by the American Speech-Language-Hearing Association and pertains to all aspects of clinical practice in speech-language pathology. Articles address screening, assessment, and treatment techniques; prevention; professional issues; supervision; and administration. They may appear in the form of clinical forums, clinical reviews, letters to the editor, or research reports that emphasize clinical practice. Issues generally include from three to five research articles. Tables of contents, together with abstracts and key words of all articles for all issues published since February 2001 are available at www.asha.org/about/publications/journal-abstracts/ajslp. Recommended for academic libraries.

1657. American Journal on Mental Retardation. Former titles (until 1987): *American Journal of Mental Deficiency;* (until 1939): *American Association on Mental Deficiency. Proceedings and Addresses of the Annual Session.* [ISSN: 0895-8017] 1876. bi-m. USD 260 print & online eds. for schools & public libraries. Ed(s): William Maclean. American Association on Mental Retardation, 444 N Capitol St, Ste 846, Washington, DC 20001-1512; orders@allenpress.com; http://www.allenpress.com. Illus., adv. Refereed. Circ: 8000. Vol. ends: Nov. Microform: PQC. Online: Allen Press Inc.; EBSCO Publishing, EBSCO Host; OCLC Online Computer Library Center, Inc.; H.W. Wilson. *Indexed:* ABIn, AgeL, BRI, CBRI, ChemAb, EAA, ECER, EduInd, ExcerpMed, FR, L&LBA, PsycInfo, SCI, SSA, SSCI, SWA, SWR&A, V&AA. *Bk. rev.:* 2-3, 600-1,000 words. *Aud.:* Ac, Sa.

This journal is published by the American Association on Mental Retardation. Articles include reports of empirical research on characteristics of people with mental retardation, reviews and theoretical interpretations of relevant research literature, and reports of evaluative research on new treatment procedures. In general, the approach is scientific, experimental, and theory oriented. Bibliographies, case studies, and descriptions of treatment procedures or programs are generally not included. Each issue includes abstracts of the articles in French. An author, subject, and book review index for the year appears in the November issue. Since researchers and professional educators are the target audience, this is primarily recommended for academic libraries.

1658. Annals of Dyslexia: an interdisciplinary journal of specific language disability. Formerly (until 1981): *Orton Society. Bulletin.* [ISSN: 0736-9387] 1951. a. EUR 179 print & online eds. Ed(s): Che Kan Leong. Springer New York LLC, 233 Spring St, New York, NY 10013-1578; journals@springer-ny.com; http://www.springer.com. Refereed. Circ: 10000. Microform: PQC. Online: EBSCO Publishing, EBSCO Host; OCLC Online Computer Library Center, Inc.; ProQuest K-12 Learning Solutions; ProQuest LLC (Ann Arbor); H.W. Wilson. Reprint: PSC. *Indexed:* ABIn, EAA, ECER, ERIC, EduInd, L&LBA, PsycInfo, SSCI. *Aud.:* Ac, Sa.

Published annually by the International Dyslexia Association, the *Annals* contains updates on current research and selected proceedings from the association's conferences. The focus of the journal is "the understanding and remediation of written language difficulties (reading, writing, spelling, handwriting) and related areas." Most articles discuss original research and are written for the scholar. A subject and name index is included at the end of each volume. Recommended for academic libraries.

1659. Archives of Physical Medicine and Rehabilitation. Former titles (until 1953): *Archives of Physical Medicine;* (until 1945): *Archives of Physical Therapy;* (until 1938): *Archives of Physical Therapy, X-Ray, Radium;* (until 1926): *Journal of Radiology;* (until 1920): *The Journal of Roentgenology.* [ISSN: 0003-9993] 1918. 12x/yr. USD 464. Ed(s): Dr. Kenneth M Jaffe, Michael A. Vasko. W.B. Saunders Co., Independence Sq W, Ste 300, The Curtis Center, Philadelphia, PA 19106-3399; http://www.elsevier.com. Illus., index, adv. Refereed. Circ: 10700 Paid. Vol. ends: Dec. *Indexed:* AgeL, CABA, CINAHL, ChemAb, DSA, ErgAb, ExcerpMed, FPA, ForAb, HortAb, IndVet, PEI, RILM, RRTA, SCI, SD, SSCI. *Bk. rev.:* Various number and length. *Aud.:* Ac, Sa.

This journal is published jointly by the American Congress of Rehabilitation Medicine and the American Academy of Physical Medicine and Rehabilitation. It disseminates organizational news and presents current research. The majority of the articles are research based and intended for the professional clinician or researcher. Each issue also includes a section titled "Clinical Notes," which

includes shorter articles that report on an observation that is "interesting, new, or sufficient to warrant attention." Journal subscriptions include print and online versions. This is an important title for medical and academic libraries.

1660. Assessment for Effective Intervention. Formerly: *Diagnostique.* [ISSN: 1534-5084] 1976. q. GBP 76. Ed(s): Linda K. Elksnin. Sage Publications, Inc., 2455 Teller Rd, Thousand Oaks, CA 91320; info@sagepub.com; http://www.sagepub.com. Illus., adv. Refereed. Circ: 1800. Vol. ends: Summer. Microform: PQC. *Indexed:* ECER, L&LBA, PsycInfo. *Aud.:* Ac, Sa.

Assessment for Effective Intervention is the official journal of the Council for Educational Diagnostic Services, a division of the Council for Exceptional Children. The primary purpose of the journal is to publish empirical research that has implications for practitioners. Articles describe relationships between assessment and instruction, innovative assessment strategies, diagnostic procedures, relationships between existing instruments, and review articles of assessment techniques. Recommended primarily for academic libraries.

1661. Assistive Technology Outcomes and Benefits. [ISSN: 1938-727X] 2004. s-a. Ed(s): Phil Parette. Assistive Technology Industry Association, 401 N Michigan Ave, Chicago, IL 60611-4267; Info@ATIA.org; http://www.atia.org/. *Aud.:* Ac, Sa.

Assistive Technology Benefits and Outcomes is a peer-reviewed, cross-disability journal that publishes articles related to the benefits and outcomes of assistive technology (AT). It does not focus on the technology itself, but aims to foster communication among vendors, AT professionals, family members, and consumers with disabilities; to facilitate dialogue regarding effective AT practices; and to help practitioners, consumers, and family members advocate for effective AT practices. Articles include original papers that address benefits or outcomes related to assistive technology devices and services. These may include the findings of original scientific research; marketing research conducted relevant to specific devices; technical notes regarding AT product development; qualitative studies, such as focus groups and structured interviews; and project or program descriptions in which AT outcomes and benefits have been documented. URL: www.atia.org/atob/ATOBWeb/index.htm

1662. Augmentative and Alternative Communication. [ISSN: 0743-4618] 1986. q. GBP 255 print & online eds. Ed(s): John Todman. Informa Healthcare, Mortimer House, 37-41 Mortimer St, London, W1T 3JM, United Kingdom; healthcare.enquiries@informa.com; http://www.tandf.co.uk/journals/. Adv. Refereed. Circ: 1600. Reprint: PSC. *Indexed:* AmHI, CBCARef, CINAHL, ECER, EngInd, L&LBA, LingAb, PsycInfo, SSCI. *Aud.:* Ac.

This is the official journal of the International Society for Augmentative and Alternative Communication. The scholarly journal publishes original articles with direct application to people with complex communication needs for whom augmentative and alternative communication techniques may be appropriate. It includes research and synthesis articles; forum notes; case studies; research, technical, and intervention notes; articles related to the organization's governance; and reviews of the literature. Recent articles include "Job-Related Social Networks and Communication Technology" and "Identifying Patterns of Communicative Behaviors in Girls with Rett Syndrome." Recommended primarily for comprehensive collections supporting programs related to communication disorders or assistive technology.

1663. Autism: the international journal of research and practice. [ISSN: 1362-3613] 1997. 6x/yr. GBP 471. Ed(s): Dermot M Bowler, Lonnie Zwaigenbaum. Sage Publications Ltd., 1 Oliver's Yard, 55 City Rd, London, EC1 1SP, United Kingdom; info@sagepub.co.uk; http://www.sagepub.co.uk. Adv. Refereed. Circ: 2300. Reprint: PSC. *Indexed:* BrEdI, CINAHL, ERIC, ExcerpMed, FR, L&LBA, PsycInfo, SFSA, SSCI, SWR&A. *Bk. rev.:* Number and length vary. *Aud.:* Ac.

The number of children being diagnosed with autism has dramatically increased over the past few years, and this journal helps fill the need for scholarly, research-based information. Interdisciplinary and international in approach, it focuses on evaluative research in all areas, including intervention, diagnosis, training, case study analyses of therapy, education, neurological issues, evaluation of particular therapies, quality of life issues, family issues and family services, medical and genetic issues, and epidemiological research. Most issues are organized around a given topic, and many include at least one substantial book review. The web site includes tables of contents with abstracts back to 1999 as well as a searchable database. It also lists the "most cited" and "most read" articles. An online sample copy can be downloaded from the web site. Both paper and online subscriptions are available. Recommended for academic libraries.

1664. *Autism Spectrum Quarterly.* Former titles (until 2004): *Jenison Autism Journal;* (until 2002): *The Morning News.* [ISSN: 1551-448X] 2004. q. USD 34.95 in US & Canada; USD 32 United Kingdom; USD 33 in Europe except the UK. Ed(s): Diane Twachtman-Cullen. Starfish Specialty Press, PO Box 799, Higganum, CT 06441-0799; info@starfishpress.com; http://www.starfishpress.com/. *Bk. rev.:* Number and length varies. *Aud.:* Ga, Ac, Sa.

New in 2004, *Autism Spectrum Quarterly* aims to appeal to a wide audience, including families and caregivers, educators, counselors, and therapists. Although highly readable, articles are substantive and are in many cases written by professionals whose names will be recognized by readers familiar with the field of autism. The advisory board includes recognized authorities like Tony Atwood, Carol Gray, and Brenda Smith Myles, and the editors are Diane Twachtman-Cullen and Liane Holliday Willey. Articles in recent issues include "Drug Free Approach to Asperger's" and "The Autism Response Team: A Concept Whose Time Has Come". With the growing incidence of and interest in Autism Spectrum Disorders, this title should generate considerable readership. Unfortunately, however, it is not currently indexed by any of the major indexing serices and is only available through a paper subscription, which limits its usefulness for academic libraries. Primarily recommended for public libraries.

Behavior Modification. See Psychology section.

1665. *Behavioral Disorders.* [ISSN: 0198-7429] 1976. q. USD 50 (Individuals, USD 20; USD 54 foreign). Ed(s): Jo Hendrickson, Gary Sasso. Council for Exceptional Children, 1110 N Glebe Rd, Ste 300, Arlington, VA 22201-4795; http://www.cec.sped.org/. Adv. Refereed. Circ: 9000. Microform: PQC. Online: ProQuest K-12 Learning Solutions; ProQuest LLC (Ann Arbor). *Indexed:* ABIn, CJA, ECER, EduInd, PsycInfo, SSCI. *Aud.:* Ac, Sa.

Behavioral Disorders is published by the Council for Children with Behavioral Disorders, a Division of the Council for Exceptional Children. It publishes reports of research, program evaluations, and position papers related to children and youth with emotional and behavioral disorders. The emphasis is on applied research, especially studies related to assessment and intervention. The articles are directed primarily to educators, teachers, psychologists, administrators, and researchers. There are occasional special or theme issues. One recent special issue is titled "Cognitive-Behavioral Interventions." Articles in other recent issues include "Promoting Expressive Writing Among Students with Emotional and Behavioral Disturbance Via Dialogue Journals," "Threats of Violence by Students in Special Education," and "Academic and Behavioral Outcomes for Students at Risk for Emotional and Behavioral Disorders." Recommended for libraries that serve special-education programs.

The Braille Forum. See Blind and Visually Impaired section.

1666. *Career Development for Exceptional Individuals.* [ISSN: 0885-7288] 1978. s-a. GBP 74. Ed(s): Bob Algozzine, David Test. Sage Publications, Inc., 2455 Teller Rd, Thousand Oaks, CA 91320; info@sagepub.com; http://www.sagepub.com. Illus. Circ: 2700. Microform: PQC. Online: EBSCO Publishing, EBSCO Host; Gale; IngentaConnect; ProQuest LLC (Ann Arbor). *Indexed:* ECER, PsycInfo. *Bk. rev.:* 10, 200 words. *Aud.:* Ac, Sa.

Career Development for Exceptional Individuals is the official journal of the Division on Career Development and Transition, a division of the Council for Exceptional Children. The journal specializes in the fields of secondary education, transition, and career development for persons with disabilities. Articles emphasize their roles as students, workers, consumers, family members, and citizens. The journal includes original quantitative and qualitative research, scholarly reviews, and program descriptions and evaluations. Transitioning students with disabilities is an important topic for educators and practitioners, and this journal should be a welcome addition to libraries serving professional educators, counselors, and researchers.

1667. *Closing the Gap: assistive technology resources for children and adults with special needs.* [ISSN: 0886-1935] 1982. bi-m. USD 35 domestic; USD 50 in Canada & Mexico. Ed(s): Budd Hagen. Closing the Gap, PO Box 68, Henderson, MN 56044; info@closingthegap.com; http://www.closingthegap.com. Adv. Circ: 10000. Online: Northern Light Technology, Inc. *Indexed:* CWI. *Aud.:* Ac, Sa.

Closing the Gap is a tabloid-style publication that provides information about assistive technology products for children and adults with special needs. The articles are written in a style that is accessible to the general public and cover all aspects of assistive technology as it relates to special education, rehabilitation, and independent living. The primary focus is on hardware, software applications, and procedures that are currently available for immediate use. Readers are provided with practical strategies and solutions to tackle their technology implementation problems. The web site contains the table of contents of the current issue and the full text for members only. The web site also hosts numerous forums where readers can ask questions and share information. The intended audience is professionals as well as persons with disabilities. This important publication is a good choice for libraries that serve populations or programs related to assistive technology.

1668. *DeafDigest.* 1996. w. Free. Ed(s): Barry Strassler. DeafDigest. *Aud.:* Sa.

This free weekly newsletter is available through e-mail subscription. Information on subscribing is available on the web site (www.deafdigest.com), which includes the text of the current issue. Brief articles include news items of interest to the deaf community and information about upcoming events. Job openings appropriate for the deaf and hard-of-hearing are included. *DeafDigest* subscribers can also subscribe to the *DeafSportZine* newsletter.

1669. *Disability & Society.* Formerly (until 1993): *Disability, Handicap and Society.* [ISSN: 0968-7599] 1986. 7x/yr. GBP 881 print & online eds. Ed(s): Len Barton. Routledge, 4 Park Sq, Milton Park, Abingdon, OX14 4RN, United Kingdom; info@routledge.co.uk; http://www.routledge.com. Illus., index, adv. Sample. Refereed. Online: EBSCO Publishing, EBSCO Host; Gale; IngentaConnect; Northern Light Technology, Inc.; OCLC Online Computer Library Center, Inc.; ProQuest LLC (Ann Arbor); SwetsWise Online Content. Reprint: PSC. *Indexed:* ASSIA, AgeL, ArtHuCI, BrEdI, CINAHL, ECER, IBSS, L&LBA, PSA, PsycInfo, RI-1, SSA, SSCI, SWA, SociolAb. *Bk. rev.:* Number and length vary. *Aud.:* Ac, Sa.

Disability & Society is "an international journal providing a focus for debate about such issues as human rights, discrimination, definitions, policy and practices." A custodial approach is viewed as unacceptable, and an emphasis is placed on community care and integration. Recent articles include "The Lives of Disabled Women in Nepal: Vulnerability without Support," "Feminist Disability Theory: Domestic Democracy and Dilemmas of Self Determination," "Applying a Barriers Approach to Monitoring Disabled People's Employment: Implications for the Disability Discrimination Act," and "Democracy and Dilemmas of Self Determination." In addition to the main articles, there is a "Current Issues" section that is intended to give people the opportunity to write about things that concern them in a less formal and academic way. Substantial book reviews are included in each issue. The publisher's web site includes a request form for a sample copy and table of contents information. This expensive title is primarily for comprehensive collections or for academic libraries that support programs in disability studies.

1670. *Disability Studies Quarterly.* [ISSN: 1041-5718] 1982. q. Ed(s): David Pfeiffer. Center on Disability Studies, 1776 University Ave, Honolulu, HI 96822; cg16@uic.edu. Adv. Circ: 500 Paid. Online: EBSCO Publishing, EBSCO Host. *Indexed:* MLA-IB. *Aud.:* Ac, Sa.

DISABILITIES

Disability Studies Quarterly is the journal of the Society for Disability Studies. It is multidisciplinary and international and offers both peer-reviewed and non-peer-reviewed articles. Non-peer-reviewed material might be commentary, essays, research in progress, poetry, or fiction. Most issues are based around a theme. Themes have included "The State of Disability in Israel/ Palestine," "Religion, Spirituality, and Disability Studies," and "Disability and Humor." A table of contents is available free back to Fall 2000 on the journal's web site, and subscribers also have access to full text. Primarily for academic libraries that support programs in disability studies.

1671. *Disability World.* 2000. m. Free. Ed(s): Barbara Duncan. National Institute for Disability and Rehabilitation Research, 400 Maryland Ave SW, Washington, DC 20202. *Aud.:* Sa.

Disability World is an online magazine dedicated to advancing an exchange of information and research about the international independent-living movement of people with disabilities. It is part of a larger project, IDEAS for the New Millennium, funded in 1999 by the National Institute on Disability and Rehabilitation Research. Departments include "Country Perspectives," "Topical Perspectives," "International News & Views," "Interviews of Leaders and Influential Individuals," "Humor," and "Artwork." Articles are short and informative. The international focus sets this apart from other e-zines. URL: www.disabilityworld.org/

1672. *Education and Training in Developmental Disabilities.* Former titles (until 2003): *Education and Training in Mental Retardation and Developmental Disabilities;* (until 1994): *Education and Training in Mental Retardation;* (until Dec. 1986): *Education and Training of the Mentally Retarded.* [ISSN: 1547-0350] 1966. q. USD 100 (Individuals, USD 30; USD 104.50 foreign). Ed(s): Stanley H Zucker. Council for Exceptional Children, Division on Developmental Disabilities, Special Education Program, PO Box 872011, Tempe, AZ 85287-2011. Illus., index, adv. Circ: 6500 Controlled. Vol. ends: Dec. Microform: PQC. Online: OCLC Online Computer Library Center, Inc.; H.W. Wilson. *Indexed:* ABIn, AgeL, EAA, ECER, EduInd, ExcerpMed, L&LBA, PsycInfo, SSA, SSCI, SWR&A. *Aud.:* Ac, Sa.

This is the publication of the Division on Developmental Disabilities, a division of the Council for Exceptional Children. The journal's focus is on the education and welfare of persons who have developmental disabilities. Topics covered include identification and assessment, educational programming, training of instructional personnel, rehabilitation, community understanding and provisions, and legislation. Articles may be either theory based or practice oriented. Recent articles include "Teaching Special Education Teachers How to Conduct Functional Analysis in Natural Settings," "Predicting Poor Achievement in Early Grade School Using Kindergarten Scores on Simple Cognitive Tasks," and "Self-Injurious Behavior and Functional Analysis: Ethics and Evidence." The primary audience is professional educators. Recommended for academic libraries.

Exceptional Parent. See Family and Marriage section.

1673. *Exceptionality: a special education journal.* [ISSN: 0936-2835] 1990. q. GBP 280 print & online eds. Ed(s): Edward J Sabornie. Lawrence Erlbaum Associates, Inc., 325 Chestnut St, Ste. 800, Philadelphia, PA 19106; journals@erlbaum.com; http://www.leaonline.com. Illus., index, adv. Refereed. Reprint: PSC. *Indexed:* ABIn, ECER, ERIC, EduInd, L&LBA, PsycInfo. *Aud.:* Ac, Sa.

Exceptionality publishes scholarly articles related to special education. Subjects include persons of all ages with mental retardation, learning disabilities, behavior disorders, speech and language disorders, hearing and/or visual impairment, physical limitations, and giftedness. Areas of scholarship published in the journal include quantitative, qualitative, and single-subject research designs, reviews of the literature, discussion pieces, invited works, and position papers. Articles in recent issues include "Intelligence and Behavior among Individuals Identified with Attention Deficit Disorders" and "Mathematical Difficulties and ADHD." Occasionally, issues are oriented around a theme. Recommended for academic libraries that support teacher education programs.

1674. *Focus on Autism and Other Developmental Disabilities.* Formerly (until vol.11, 1996): *Focus on Autistic Behavior.* [ISSN: 1088-3576] 1986. q. GBP 91. Ed(s): Paul Alberto, Juane Heflin. Sage Publications, Inc., 2455 Teller Rd, Thousand Oaks, CA 91320; info@sagepub.com. Illus., adv. Sample. Refereed. Circ: 5700 Paid and free. Microform: PQC. Online: EBSCO Publishing, EBSCO Host; Florida Center for Library Automation; Gale; IngentaConnect; OCLC Online Computer Library Center, Inc.; ProQuest K-12 Learning Solutions; ProQuest LLC (Ann Arbor); H.W. Wilson. Reprint: PSC. *Indexed:* ECER, ERIC, EduInd, IBR, IBZ, L&LBA, PAIS, PsycInfo. *Bk. rev.:* Occasional. *Aud.:* Ac, Sa.

Focus on Autism and Other Developmental Disabilities addresses issues concerning individuals with autism and other developmental disabilities and their families. Included are original research reports, position papers, effective intervention procedures, and descriptions of successful programs. Most issues contain seven articles, and some issues include a book review. Articles cover topics throughout the life span in home, school, work, and community settings. Recent issues include articles on respite care, development of communication skills, Supplemental Security Income, managed care, and workplace supports. Two recent issues devoted to a special theme include one on multicultural aspects related to educating autistic children and a special issue on Asperger Syndrome. Recommended primarily for academic libraries.

1675. *Focus on Exceptional Children.* [ISSN: 0015-511X] 1969. 9x/yr. USD 48 (Individuals, USD 36). Ed(s): Edwin S Ellis, Chriss Walther-Thomas. Love Publishing Co., 9101 E Kenyon Ave, Ste 2200, PO Box 22353, Denver, CO 80237; lpc@lovepublishing.com; http://www.lovepublishing.com/. Illus., index, adv. Circ: 3000. Vol. ends: May. Microform: PQC. Online: EBSCO Publishing, EBSCO Host; Florida Center for Library Automation; Gale; Northern Light Technology, Inc.; OCLC Online Computer Library Center, Inc.; ProQuest K-12 Learning Solutions; ProQuest LLC (Ann Arbor); H.W. Wilson. *Indexed:* ABIn, CWI, ECER, ERIC, EduInd, SSCI. *Aud.:* Ac, Sa.

Published monthly except June, July, and August. Each newsletter features one scholarly, but not necessarily research-based, article on a topic of current interest to teachers, special educators, administrators, or others concerned with the education of exceptional children. The focus is on practice rather than theory. Recent articles include "School Principals and Special Education: Creating the Context for Academic Success" and "Personalized Grading Plans: A Systematic Approach to Making the Grades of Included Students More Accurate and Meaningful." One concern is that the publication seems to consistently run behind, with the most recent issue often being dated over a year prior to the current date. However, this inexpensive, practice-oriented title is a good choice for libraries that serve teachers and teacher educators.

1676. *Hearing Health: the voice on hearing issues.* Formerly (until 1992): *Voice.* 1984. q. USD 24 domestic; USD 43 foreign; USD 4.95 newsstand/cover per issue. Ed(s): Paula Bonillas. Voice International Publications, Inc., 2989 Main St, Box V, Ingleside, TX 78362-0500. Illus., adv. Circ: 20000. *Indexed:* L&LBA. *Aud.:* Sa.

Hearing Health's mission is to increase awareness of real-world applications of research, technology, and trends, and to educate people about the effects of hearing loss on health and quality of life. The language is nontechnical, and articles are written for persons with hearing impairments and their families. The full text of selected articles and an advice column are available on the magazine's web site. Recent articles include "Today's Sound Technology, Tomorrow's Hearing Technology" and "Bad Bugs, Bad Bugs, Whatcha Gonna Do?" Recommended for libraries that serve populations with the deaf or hard-of-hearing.

1677. *Hearing Loss: the journal of self help for hard of hearing people.* Former titles: *S H H H Journal; Shhh.* [ISSN: 1090-6215] 1980. bi-m. Individuals, USD 25. Ed(s): Barbara Kelley. Self Help for Hard of Hearing People, Inc., 7910 Woodmont Ave, Ste 1200, Bethesda, MD 20814; http://www.shhh.org. Adv. Circ: 30000. *Indexed:* AgeL, CINAHL, ECER. *Aud.:* Sa.

Hearing Loss is published by the organization SHHH (Self Help for Hard of Hearing People), which has 250 chapters throughout the United States and claims to represent over 26 million consumers. At the local level, SHHH chapters provide self-help programs, technical information, social activities, and referrals. At the national level, the organization sponsors conferences and an annual convention, and publishes *Hearing Loss,* a magazine that seeks "to make mainstream society more accessible to people who are hard-of-hearing" and "to improve the quality of life for hard-of-hearing people through education, advocacy, and self-help." It includes short, informative articles and updates on a variety of subjects related to hearing loss. Recent articles have included "Call Me Ear-Responsible" and "When I Knew I Needed Hearing Help." Much of the information relates to technological and medical advances. Recommended for libraries serving deaf or hard-of-hearing populations.

1678. *Information Technology and Disabilities.* [ISSN: 1073-5127] 1994. q. Free. Ed(s): Tom McNulty. E A S I: Equal Access to Software and Information, PO Box 818, Lake Forest, CA 92609; http://www.rit.edu/~easi/itd.html. Illus. Refereed. *Indexed:* EduInd, ISTA. *Aud.:* Ac, Sa.

EASI (Equal Access to Software and Information) was originally formed in the late 1980s as part of EDUCOM. In 2000, it became an independent, nonprofit organization. It publishes *Information Technology and Disabilities* free on its web site. Notification of new issues is available by e-mail. EASI's mission is to serve as a resource to the education community by providing both practical and theoretical information and guidance in the area of access to information technologies for individuals with disabilities. It attempts to keep readers informed about developments and advancements within the adaptive computer technology field. Recent articles include "Steps Toward Making Distance Learning Accessible to Students and Instructors With Disabilities" and "Universal Design for Learning: A Statewide Improvement Model for Academic Success." Recommended for professionals in the fields of computing and adaptive technology.

1679. *Intellectual Developmental Disabilities: journal of policy, practice, and perspectives.* Formerly (until 2006): *Mental Retardation.* [ISSN: 1934-9491] 1963. bi-m. USD 246 print & online eds. Ed(s): Steven Taylor. American Association on Mental Retardation, 444 N Capitol St, Ste 846, Washington, DC 20001-1512; http://www.aamr.org. Illus., index, adv. Refereed. Circ: 7500. Vol. ends: Dec. Online: Allen Press Inc.; EBSCO Publishing, EBSCO Host; OCLC Online Computer Library Center, Inc.; H.W. Wilson. *Indexed:* ABIn, AgeL, EduInd, ExcerpMed, FR, L&LBA, PsycInfo, SSA, SSCI, SociolAb. *Bk. rev.:* 3-4, 750-1,200 words. *Aud.:* Ac, Sa.

Mental Retardation is a peer-reviewed journal that includes "policy, practices, and perspectives in the field of mental retardation." It is the official publication of the American Association on Mental Retardation, and some association business is published in the journal. Topics covered include new teaching approaches, program developments, administrative tools, program evaluation, service utilization studies, community surveys, public policy issues, training and case studies, and research. Although it is research oriented, the focus is on applied research. The editors state that two main criteria for acceptance include "relevance to policy or practice" and "potential reader interest." The "Perspectives" section offers short, non-research-based articles. "Trends and Milestones" includes current demographic information. A subject index and tables of contents and abstracts for articles back to 1990 are also available on the web site. Researchers and practitioners are the intended audience. Recommended for academic and special libraries.

1680. *International Journal of Disability, Community & Rehabilitation.* Former titles (until 2002): *International Journal of Practical Approaches to Disability;* (until 1995): *Journal of Practical Approaches to Developmental Handicap.* [ISSN: 1703-3381] 1977. 3x/yr. USD 20. Ed(s): Val Lawton, Aldred Neufeldt. University of Calgary, Rehabilitation Studies, c/o Community Rehabilitation & Disability Studies, Education Tower 4th Fl, University of Calgary, Calgary, AB T2N 1N4, Canada; http://www.crds.org. Illus., adv. Refereed. Circ: 450. Microform: MML. *Indexed:* ASSIA, CBCARef, CEI. *Bk. rev.:* Number and length vary. *Aud.:* Ac.

The *International Journal of Disability, Community and Rehabilitation* is an electronic journal that publishes "papers of research and critical analyses of issues at the intersection of disability, community and rehabilitation." It was preceded by the "International Journal of Practical Approaches to Disability," which was published in a print format for 24 years. The electronic version starts with Spring 2002. International and scholarly in its approach, the journal

includes both research articles and shorter articles "From the Field." Abstracts of relevant doctoral dissertations and masters theses primarily completed in Canada and Australia are also included in selected issues. Most issues provide at least one book review. Author and title indexes and a list of book reviews are available on the web site. There are occasional theme issues. A recent issue is devoted to the aging workforce. Primarily of interest to libraries supporting programs in disability studies.

1681. *International Journal of Disability, Development and Education.* Former titles (until 1990): *Exceptional Child; Slow Learning Child.* [ISSN: 1034-912X] 1954. q. GBP 327 print & online eds. Ed(s): Christa van Kraayenoord. Routledge, 4 Park Sq, Milton Park, Abingdon, OX14 4RN, United Kingdom; info@routledge.co.uk; http://www.routledge.co.uk. Illus., index, adv. Sample. Refereed. Circ: 1400. Microform: PQC. Online: EBSCO Publishing, EBSCO Host; Gale; IngentaConnect; OCLC Online Computer Library Center, Inc.; RMIT Publishing; SwetsWise Online Content; H.W. Wilson. Reprint: PSC. *Indexed:* ABIn, ASSIA, ECER, ERIC, EduInd, IBR, IBZ, L&LBA, PsycInfo, SSCI, SWA. *Aud.:* Ac, Sa.

This scholarly journal is multidisciplinary and has an international focus. Research and review articles that concern "all aspects of education, human development, special education, and rehabilitation" are published. Recent articles include "Children with Attention Deficit Hyperactivity Disorder and their Teachers: A Review of the Literature" and "Influencing the Life Trajectories of Children with Asperger's Syndrome." An online sample issue, an order form, and contents information are located on the journal's web site. Recommended for academic libraries.

1682. *International Journal of Rehabilitation Research.* [ISSN: 0342-5282] 1977. q. USD 509 (Individuals, USD 201). Ed(s): Juhani Wikstroem. Lippincott Williams & Wilkins, 530 Walnut St, Philadelphia, PA 19106-3621; http://www.lww.com. Illus., index, adv. Refereed. Circ: 1000. Vol. ends: Dec. Online: EBSCO Publishing, EBSCO Host; OCLC Online Computer Library Center, Inc.; Ovid Technologies, Inc.; SwetsWise Online Content. *Indexed:* AgeL, CINAHL, CJA, ECER, ERIC, EngInd, ErgAb, ExcerpMed, SSCI. *Bk. rev.:* Various number and length. *Aud.:* Ac, Sa.

This is the official journal of the European Federation for Research in Rehabilitation. As such, it is international in scope and includes research information on both industrialized and third world countries. Most issues include at least five original articles and several brief research reports. The journal is interdisciplinary and targets such fields as rehabilitation medicine, nursing, social and vocational rehabilitation, special education, social policy, social work and social welfare, sociology, psychology, psychiatry, and rehabilitation technology. Areas of interest include disability throughout the life cycle; rehabilitation programs for persons with physical, sensory, mental, and developmental disabilities; measurement of disability; special education and vocational rehabilitation; equipment, access, and transportation; independent living; and consumer, legal, economic, and sociopolitical aspects of disability. The December issue includes annual author and keyword indexes. For comprehensive collections.

1683. *Intervention in School and Clinic.* Former titles (until 1990): *Academic Therapy;* (until 1968): *Academic Therapy Quarterly.* [ISSN: 1053-4512] 1965. 5x/yr. GBP 83. Ed(s): Kyle Higgins, Randall Boone. Sage Publications, Inc., 2455 Teller Rd, Thousand Oaks, CA 91320; info@sagepub.com; http://www.sagepub.com. Illus., index, adv. Sample. Refereed. Circ: 2500. Vol. ends: May. Microform: PQC. Online: EBSCO Publishing, EBSCO Host; Florida Center for Library Automation; Gale; IngentaConnect; OCLC Online Computer Library Center, Inc.; ProQuest LLC (Ann Arbor); H.W. Wilson. Reprint: PSC. *Indexed:* ABIn, ASSIA, ArtHuCI, EAA, ECER, ERIC, EduInd, IBR, IBZ, L&LBA, SFSA, SSCI, SWA. *Bk. rev.:* 4, 150 words. *Aud.:* Ac, Sa.

This practitioner-oriented publication is designed to provide practical, research-based ideas to those who work with students having severe learning disabilities or emotional/behavioral problems and for whom typical classroom instruction is not effective. Issues usually include four main articles. Topics frequently deal with assessment, curriculum, instructional techniques, management, social interventions, and vocational issues. Recent articles are "Creating School-Wide Conditions for High-Quality Learning Strategy Classroom Instruction,"

"Improving Educational Prospects for Youth in Foster Care: The Education Liaison Model," and "Aligning Assessments with State Curriculum Standards and Teaching Strategies." Regular columns are "20 Ways to . . . ," a brief listing of 20 techniques related to a specific theme; "What Works for Me," suggestions from practitioners on effective instructional strategies; and "Conference Dateline," a list of various upcoming conferences. Recent issues include "20 Ways to Eliminate Bullying in Your Classroom" and "What Works for Me—Integrated Processing: A Strategy for Working Out Unknown Words." Highly recommended for libraries that serve teachers, administrators, and teacher educators.

1684. *Journal of Autism and Developmental Disorders.* Formerly (until 1979): *Journal of Autism and Childhood Schizophrenia.* [ISSN: 0162-3257] 1971. bi-m. EUR 1273 print & online eds. Ed(s): Gary B Mesibov. Springer New York LLC, 233 Spring St, New York, NY 10013-1578; service-ny@springer.com; http://www.springer.com/. Illus., index, adv. Refereed. Vol. ends: Dec. Microform: PQC. Online: EBSCO Publishing, EBSCO Host; Gale; IngentaConnect; OCLC Online Computer Library Center, Inc.; OhioLINK; Ovid Technologies, Inc.; Springer LINK; SwetsWise Online Content. Reprint: PSC. *Indexed:* ABIn, ASSIA, BiolAb, CINAHL, ChemAb, ECER, ERIC, EduInd, ExcerpMed, FR, IMFL, L&LBA, PsycInfo, SSCI, SWR&A. *Aud.:* Ac, Sa.

This scholarly journal covers all the severe psychopathologies in childhood, including autism and childhood schizophrenia. Original articles discuss experimental studies on the biochemical, neurological, and genetic aspects of a particular disorder; the implications of normal development for deviant processes; and interaction between disordered behavior of individuals and social or group factors. The journal also features research and case studies involving the entire spectrum of interventions (including behavioral, biological, educational, and community aspects) and advances in the diagnosis and classification of disorders. A recent issue includes the articles "Can Spectro-Temporal Complexity Explain the Autistic Pattern of Performance on Auditory Tasks?" and "Sensory Integration and the Perceptual Experience of Persons with Autism." An online sample copy and contents information for recent issues are available on the web site. For medical and academic libraries.

1685. *The Journal of Deaf Studies and Deaf Education.* [ISSN: 1081-4159] 1996. q. USD 312 print or online ed. Ed(s): Marc Marschark. Oxford University Press, 2001 Evans Rd, Cary, NC 27513; jnlorders@oup-usa.org; http://www.us.oup.com. Adv. Refereed. Circ: 450 Paid. Reprint: PSC. *Indexed:* CINAHL, ERIC, EduInd, FR, L&LBA, PsycInfo, SSCI. *Bk. rev.:* Number and length vary. *Aud.:* Ac, Sa.

The *Journal of Deaf Studies and Deaf Education* is international in focus and publishes original, scholarly manuscripts relevant to deaf persons. It includes topics such as development, education, communication, culture, and clinical or legal issues. Although research-oriented, most articles have a basis in practice and have implications for practitioners. Each issue contains three sections: "Theory/Review Articles" are reviews or treatments of research, theory, or application; "Empirical Articles" present basic, applied, and clinical research in relevant areas; and "Endnotes" provides a forum for brief commentary, historical notes, book reviews, and other information of general interest. Recent articles include "Implications of Utilizing a Phonics-Based Reading Curriculum with Children Who Are Deaf or Hard-of-Hearing" and "The Relative Difficulty of Signed Arithmetic Story Problems for Primary Level Deaf and Hard-of-Hearing Students." There are occasional theme issues. An e-mailed table of contents alert is available. This is a key journal that should be owned by libraries that support deaf education programs.

Journal of Developmental Education. See Education/Higher Education section.

1686. *Journal of Disability Policy Studies.* [ISSN: 1044-2073] 1990. 4x/yr. GBP 83. Ed(s): Bille Jo Rylance, Craig Fiedler. Sage Publications, Inc., 2455 Teller Rd, Thousand Oaks, CA 91320; info@sagepub.com; http://www.sagepub.com. Illus., adv. Refereed. Circ: 500 Paid and free. Reprint: PSC. *Indexed:* CINAHL, CWI, ECER, EduInd, PAIS, PSA, PsycInfo, SSA, SociolAb. *Aud.:* Ac, Sa.

This journal discusses disability policy topics and issues and addresses ethics, policy, and law related to individuals with disabilities. Regular features include "From My Perspective," which provides readers with discussions of the issues currently confronting a particular disability discipline or area, and "Disability Policy Newsbreak!," which offers a listing of the activities of specific disability organizations. Occasionally, special series discuss current problems or areas that need more in-depth research. Past topics have included rehabilitation for people with psychiatric impairments, political participation of people with disabilities, and the status of policy affecting women with disabilities. Recommended for comprehensive collections and colleges supporting programs in disability studies.

1687. *Journal of Early Intervention.* Formerly (until 1989): *Council of Exceptional Children. Division for Early Childhood. Journal.* [ISSN: 1053-8151] 1979. q. GBP 116. Ed(s): Patricia Snyder. Sage Publications, Inc., 2455 Teller Rd, Thousand Oaks, CA 91320; info@sagepub.com; http://www.sagepub.com. Illus., index, adv. Refereed. Circ: 7000. Vol. ends: Fall. *Indexed:* CINAHL, ECER, ERIC, PsycInfo, SFSA, SSCI. *Bk. rev.:* 2-3, 600-900 words. *Aud.:* Ac.

This journal publishes articles related to research and practice in early interventions for infants and young children with special needs and their families. The age under consideration might begin at birth, or even before birth for some prevention programs, and extend through the years when children traditionally begin elementary school. Articles are generally research reports, scholarly reviews, or policy analyses. Most articles relate directly to or have a clear relevance for practice. Articles designated "Innovative Practices" are sometimes included. These describe unique or innovative programs, curricula, techniques, or practices related to any aspect of early intervention. Tables of contents for current and past issues are included on the journal's web site. The web site includes tables of contents back through 1993 and abstracts of articles from 2000 to the present. For academic and special libraries.

1688. *Journal of Fluency Disorders.* [ISSN: 0094-730X] 1974. 4x/yr. EUR 617. Ed(s): E G Conture. Elsevier Inc., 360 Park Ave S, New York, NY 10010-1710; usinfo-f@elsevier.com; http://www.elsevier.com. Adv. Refereed. Microform: PQC. Online: EBSCO Publishing, EBSCO Host; Gale; IngentaConnect; OhioLINK; ScienceDirect; SwetsWise Online Content. *Indexed:* AgeL, BiolAb, CINAHL, CommAb, ExcerpMed, FR, L&LBA, LingAb, MLA-IB, PsycInfo, RILM, SSCI. *Bk. rev.:* Number and length vary. *Aud.:* Ac.

This scholarly quarterly serves as the official journal of the International Fluency Association. It provides comprehensive coverage of the clinical, experimental, and theoretical aspects of stuttering, including information about remediation techniques. Most issues contain three to five original research articles and may include film reviews, book reviews, or letters to the editor, as well as some organizational information. The last issue of the year provides an author index and tables of contents for the whole year. Recent articles include "Unassisted Recovery from Stuttering" and "A Comparative Investigation of the Speech-Associated Attitude of Preschool and Kindergarten Children Who Do and Do Not Stutter." Recommended primarily for academic and health libraries that support related programs.

1689. *Journal of Intellectual and Developmental Disability.* Former titles (until 1995): *Australia and New Zealand Journal of Developmental Disabilities;* (until vol.7, 1981): *Australian Journal of Developmental Disabilities;* (until vol.6, Mar. 1980): *Australian Journal of Mental Retardation.* [ISSN: 1366-8250] 1970. q. GBP 329 print & online eds. Ed(s): Roger J Stancliffe. Informa Healthcare, Mortimer House, 37-41 Mortimer St, London, W1T 3JM, United Kingdom; healthcare.enquiries@informa.com; http://www.tandf.co.uk/journals/. Illus., adv. Refereed. Circ: 1400. Microform: PQC. Online: EBSCO Publishing, EBSCO Host; Gale; IngentaConnect; OCLC Online Computer Library Center, Inc.; SwetsWise Online Content. Reprint: PSC. *Indexed:* CINAHL, CJA, ECER, ERIC, ExcerpMed, IMFL, L&LBA, PsycInfo, SSCI. *Bk. rev.:* 2-3. *Aud.:* Ac.

This scholarly quarterly is the official journal of the Australasian Society for the Study of Intellectual Disability. It is international and multidisciplinary in scope, and publishes original research papers, literature reviews, and conceptual articles. Issues generally contain four or five research articles and one or two brief reports. Recent research articles include "The Relationship Between Food Refusal and Social Skills in Persons with Intellectual Disabilities" and "Parents' Perspectives on the Communication Skills of their Children with Severe Disabilities." Also included in some issues are "Data Briefs" that contain summaries of significant current data (usually national data) on trends in demographics, service provision, expenditure, and other issues. There is also an opinions and perspectives section that provides a forum for discussion and debate about current issues. Most issues include two or three book reviews. There are occasional special or theme issues. Recommended for comprehensive academic collections.

Journal of Learning Disabilities. See Education/Educational Psychology and Measurement, Special Education, Counseling section.

1690. *Journal of Positive Behavior Interventions.* [ISSN: 1098-3007] 1999. q. GBP 83. Sage Publications, Inc., 2455 Teller Rd, Thousand Oaks, CA 91320; info@sagepub.com; http://www.sagepub.com. Adv. Circ: 1600 Paid and free. Reprint: PSC. *Indexed:* EduInd, PsycInfo, SSCI. *Aud.:* Ac.

What distinguishes this title from many others is the emphasis on interventions. It is an important title for both professionals and family members who are looking for research-based information about positive behavior support. Generally, each issue includes six research-based articles. Recent articles include "Using Social Stories to Improve the Social Behavior of Children with Asperger Syndrome" and "Effects of Response Cards on Disruptive Behavior and Academic Responding during Math Lessons by Fourth-Grade Urban Students." In addition to the research articles, a forum section encourages communication among readers by providing for an exchange of opinions and ideas. This title will be of interest to a variety of constituencies, including educators, researchers, social workers, and parents. It is highly recommended for both academic and public libraries.

1691. *Journal of Rehabilitation.* [ISSN: 0022-4154] 1935. q. USD 75 domestic; USD 85 Canada; USD 100 elsewhere. Ed(s): Leon Russ, Daniel Curtiz. National Rehabilitation Association, 633 S Washington St, Alexandria, VA 22314-4109; info@nationalrehab.org; http://www.nationalrehab.org. Illus., adv. Refereed. Circ: 10000 Controlled. Vol. ends: Oct/Dec. Microform: PQC. Online: EBSCO Publishing, EBSCO Host; Florida Center for Library Automation; Gale; Northern Light Technology, Inc.; OCLC Online Computer Library Center, Inc.; ProQuest K-12 Learning Solutions; ProQuest LLC (Ann Arbor); H.W. Wilson. *Indexed:* AgeL, BRI, CINAHL, ECER, ExcerpMed, SSCI. *Bk. rev.:* Number and length vary. *Aud.:* Ac, Sa.

This journal serves as the official publication of the National Rehabilitation Association and is included as part of membership. Most issues contain from six to eight articles that cover a broad range of disability-related issues. A recent issue includes articles dealing with such topics as AIDS, schizophrenia, deafness, disability disclosure on job applications, and job placement. Articles are frequently international in scope, and are research based and practice oriented. Organization news; job advertisements; and book, audiovisual, and software reviews are included in some issues. Contents information and article abstracts from 1999 to the present are available on the journal's web site. This inexpensive and well-indexed title is primarily for academic and hospital libraries.

1692. *Journal of Rehabilitation Research and Development.* Former titles (until 198?): *Journal of Rehabilitation R and D;* (until 1982): *Prosthetics Research. Bulletin.* [ISSN: 0748-7711] 1964. q. Free to qualified personnel. Department of Veterans Affairs, Veterans Health Administration, 103 S Gay St, Baltimore, MD 21202-3517; mail@rehab-balt.med.va.gov; http://www.va.gov. Illus., index. Refereed. Circ: 27000. Microform: PQC. Online: EBSCO Publishing, EBSCO Host; OCLC Online Computer Library Center, Inc.; ProQuest K-12 Learning Solutions; ProQuest LLC (Ann Arbor). *Indexed:* AgeL, ApMecR, BRI, BioEngAb, C&ISA, CBRI, CINAHL, ECER, EngInd, ExcerpMed, H&SSA, HRIS, PEI, SCI, SD, SSCI. *Aud.:* Ac, Sa.

The mission of the *Journal of Rehabilitation Research and Development* is "to responsibly evaluate and disseminate scientific research findings impacting the rehabilitative healthcare community." Priority areas are prosthetics, amputations, orthotics, and orthopedics; spinal cord injury and other neurological disorders; communication, sensory, and cognitive aids; geriatric rehabilitation; and functional outcome research. This publication will primarily be of interest to researchers. Many libraries previously received it as a government depository item. It is now available free online through the Directory of Open Access Journals.

1693. *Journal of Speech, Language, and Hearing Research.* Formerly (until 1996): *Journal of Speech and Hearing Research;* Which incorporates (1948-1991): *Journal of Speech and Hearing Disorders;* Which was formerly (1936-1947): *Journal of Speech Disorders.* [ISSN: 1092-4388] 1958. bi-m. USD 382 domestic to libraries & institutions (Individuals, USD 134). Ed(s): Craig Champlin. American Speech - Language - Hearing Association, 10801 Rockville Pike, Rockville, MD 20852-3226; subscribe@asha.org; http://www.asha.org. Illus., index, adv. Refereed. Circ: 17611 Paid and controlled. Microform: PQC. Online: EBSCO Publishing, EBSCO Host; Florida Center for Library Automation; Gale; HighWire Press; OCLC Online Computer Library Center, Inc.; ProQuest K-12 Learning Solutions; ProQuest LLC (Ann Arbor); H.W. Wilson. *Indexed:* ABIn, ASSIA, AgeL, ArtHuCI, BiolAb, CINAHL, ChemAb, ECER, ERIC, EduInd, ExcerpMed, L&LBA, LingAb, MLA-IB, PsycInfo, RILM, SSCI. *Bk. rev.:* Number and length vary. *Aud.:* Ac, Sa.

The American Speech-Language-Hearing Association publishes this journal. Each issue is divided into three major categories: speech, language, and hearing. Each of these categories has a separate editor, and most issues feature from three to nine significant articles in each area. Articles "pertain broadly to studies of the processes and disorders of speech, language, and hearing, and to the diagnosis and treatment of such disorders." Articles may be reports of original research; theoretical, tutorial, or review articles; or research notes. Topics covered include screening, assessment, treatment techniques, prevention, professional issues, supervision, and administration. Author, title, and subject indexes are included in each December issue. Contents information and abstracts back to February 1999 are available on the web site. This is an important and well-indexed journal that should be owned by academic libraries supporting programs in related disciplines.

1694. *Journal of Visual Impairment & Blindness.* Formed by the merger of (1951-1977): *New Outlook for the Blind;* (1962-1977): *A F B Research Bulletin.* [ISSN: 0145-482X] 1977. m. USD 180 (Individuals, USD 130). Ed(s): Alan J Koenig. American Foundation for the Blind, 11 Penn Plaza, Suite 300, New York, NY 10001; afbinfo@afb.net; http://www.afb.org. Illus., adv. Refereed. Circ: 7000. Vol. ends: Nov/Dec. Online: EBSCO Publishing, EBSCO Host; OCLC Online Computer Library Center, Inc.; ProQuest LLC (Ann Arbor); H.W. Wilson. *Indexed:* ABIn, AgeL, ArtHuCI, CINAHL, ECER, ERIC, EduInd, ExcerpMed, L&LBA, PsycInfo, SSCI, SWR&A. *Bk. rev.:* Brief. Number varies. *Aud.:* Ac, Sa.

This journal includes research articles and shorter pieces of interest to practitioners as well as news coverage about the field of visual impairment. Two sections of *JVIB* are available free online to the public: "Speaker's Corner" and "Perspectives." These columns are platforms for members of the blindness field who are invited to express their points of view about timely, important, and controversial issues. December issues include an annual subject and name index. A free sample is available online, and a table of contents and article abstracts are available on the journal's web site. There are occasional theme issues. Also available in braille and on cassette. Essential for libraries that serve the visually impaired or programs that train persons to work with the visually impaired.

1695. *L D Online.* w. L D Online, http://www.ldonline.org. *Aud.:* Ac, Sa.
Updated weekly, this colorful and well-designed web site features articles geared to families, teachers, and students dealing with learning disabilities. The "Finding Help" section lists national organizations, federal agencies, state-by-state resource guides, Canadian resources, and resources by phone. The "LD in Depth" section features articles written by leading experts, research findings reported by top researchers, and the latest news in the field. A special section for kids features art submitted by children with learning disabilities and includes suggested books for kids and fun activities. The "Getting Started" section

answers frequently asked questions and provides basic information about learning disabilities. Guest columnists and "First Person" essays offer opinions and firsthand experiences about dealing with the challenges of learning disabilities. Numerous bulletin boards on such topics as "Parenting a Child With ADHD" and "Teaching Students with LD and ADHD" are also available. Other features include the "Yellow Pages" and an online store. This well-established source was initiated over ten years ago and has become an important and respected source of information. It will appeal to parents, teachers, and children, and is highly recommended.

Learning Disability Quarterly. See Education/Educational Psychology and Measurement, Special Education, Counseling section.

Mental and Physical Disability Law Reporter. See Law section.

1696. Mouth: voice of the disability nation. [ISSN: 1071-5657] 1990. bi-m. USD 48 (Individuals, USD 18). Ed(s): Lucy Gwin. Free Hand Press, Inc., 61 Brighton St, Rochester, NY 14607; mouthoff@ mouthmag.com. Illus. Circ: 7500 Paid. Online: ProQuest LLC (Ann Arbor). *Indexed:* AltPI. *Aud.:* Sa.

Formerly an e-zine, *Mouth* now describes itself as "the only disability rights-oriented magazine put to printed page." It features investigative journalism, news updates, and interviews with disability rights activists. It is highly critical of persons in what it terms the "helping professions." A sample issue is available online, as are numerous interviews with activists. The tone of this publication perhaps may best be described with the following quotation taken from the magazine's web site: "Mouth brings the conversation down to street level, where well-intentioned 'special' programs wreak havoc in the lives of ordinary people. People talk about calling a spade a spade. We call Jack Kevorkian a serial killer. And when maggots outnumber nurses' aides at what others call a 'care facility,' we call it a hellhole. We say it out loud: if special education is so darned special, every kid in every school ought to have the benefit of it." Mouth also publishes original poetry and essays written by people with disabilities. The link to the original poetry section warns the reader not to enter if they prefer a life without obscenity. *Mouth* is not currently owned by many libraries, but it is included in this section as as being representative of an outspoken and irreverent segment of the disability rights movement. *Mouth* and *Ragged Edge* probably best represent the activist stance now taken by some in the disability community.

1697. N I H Senior Health. a. National Institute on Aging and National Library of Medicine, National Institute on Aging Bldg 31, Rm 5C27, Bethesda, MD 20892; custserv@nlm.nih.gov; http://nihseniorhealth.gov. *Aud.:* Ga.

NIH SeniorHealth is an online resource designed specifically for older adults and developed by the National Institute on Aging (NIA) and the National Library of Medicine (NLM), both part of the National Institutes of Health (NIH). The web site makes reliable, easy-to-understand, aging-related health information easily accessible for those seeking it. *NIH SeniorHealth* features authoritative and up-to-date health information from the institutes and centers at NIH. In addition, the American Geriatrics Society provides expert and independent review of some of the material located on the web site. New topics are added on a regular basis. The senior-friendly web site features large type, short, easy-to-read segments of information and clear navigation tools. A "talking" function reads the text aloud, and special buttons to enlarge the text or to turn on high contrast make text more readable. The web site is a valuable addition to any public library that serves the aging population.

1698. New Mobility. Former titles (until 1994): *Spinal Network's New Mobility;* (until 1992): *Spinal Network EXTRA.* [ISSN: 1086-4741] 1989. m. USD 27.95 domestic; USD 35.95 Canada; USD 57.95 elsewhere. Ed(s): Douglas Lathrop, Tim Gilmer. No Limits Communications Inc., PO Box 220, Horsham, PA 19044-0220. Illus., adv. Sample. Circ: 27000 Paid and free. *Aud.:* Ga, Ac, Sa.

This glossy, upbeat magazine helps fill the need for popular, general-interest publications for people with disabilities, especially for those with mobility impairments. *New Mobility* covers medical news and current research; jobs; benefits; civil rights; sports, recreation and travel; and fertility, pregnancy, and

child care. Feature articles from current issues can be read on the magazine's web site. The site also features a search engine for the magazine and several interactive options, including a users' message center, an advertising board, an online chat option, an "Ask an Expert" section, and classified ads. It also includes a well-developed list of links to other sites. Both the magazine and the web site represent an upbeat and positive lifestyle. *New Mobility* is a good choice for public libraries.

1699. O T J R: Occupation, Participation and Health. Formerly (until 2002): *Occupational Therapy Journal of Research.* [ISSN: 1539-4492] 1981. q. USD 215 (Individuals, USD 95; USD 37 per issue). Ed(s): Helene J Polatajko, Eileen Anderer. Slack, Inc., 6900 Grove Rd, Thorofare, NJ 08086-9447; customerservice@slackinc.com; http://www.slackinc.com. Illus., index, adv. Refereed. Circ: 2000 Paid. Vol. ends: Fall. *Indexed:* AgeL, CINAHL, ExcerpMed, H&SSA, PsycInfo, SSCI. *Bk. rev.:* Number and length vary. *Aud.:* Ac, Sa.

Published by the American Occupational Therapy Foundation, *OTJR* offers original research articles of professional interest to the occupational therapist. It includes three or four full-length feature articles; brief reports; letters to the editor; book, monograph, and journal reviews; and technical notes. The fall issue includes annual title and author indexes. The web site has subscription information, requests for a trial subscription, and links to nursing and health professionals' resources. It is a well-indexed title and is recommended for academic and medical libraries.

1700. Odyssey: new directions in deaf education. Former titles (until 2000): *Perspectives in Education and Deafness;* (until 1989): *Perspectives for Teachers of the Hearing Impaired.* [ISSN: 1544-6751] 1982. s-a. Free. Ed(s): Cathryn Carroll. Gallaudet University, Laurent Clerc National Deaf Education Center, 800 Florida Ave, NE, Washington, DC 20002-3695; Oluyinka.Fakunle@gallaudet.edu; http://clerccenter.gallaudet.edu. Illus., index, adv. Refereed. Circ: 4000. Vol. ends: May/Jun. *Indexed:* ECER. *Aud.:* Hs, Ac, Sa.

Odyssey is now published twice a year by the Laurent Clerc National Deaf Education Center at Gallaudet University and is distributed free of charge. The full text of issues back to winter 2000 is available on the magazine's web site. *Odyssey* offers practical assistance, advice, and support to parents and professionals involved in the education of deaf students, preschool through secondary school. Articles are written in a practical, conversational style and cover a wide range of topics. Most articles describe effective teaching techniques and strategies, learning activities, and innovative projects for classrooms, residential, and mainstream programs. Other articles describe research, information, and personal experiences that relate to current issues in education, deafness, and raising deaf children. Recommended for academic libraries that serve teacher education programs and any libraries serving deaf or hard-of-hearing children and their parents.

1701. Ouch!: ...it's a disability thing. 2002. 1 Base Vol(s) irreg. Free. Ed(s): Damon Rose. B B C Worldwide Ltd., 80 Wood Ln, London, W12 0TT, United Kingdom; http://www.bbc.co.uk. *Aud.:* Sa.

Ouch! is part of BBC's Learning & Interactive department. In one of his posts, the editor notes that he has been following *Ragged Edge* from "our friends over there in the U S of A," and *Ouch!* probably more closely resembles *Ragged Edge* than any other publication. Although it describes itself as a "magazine," *Ouch!* has elements of a blog. To quote the editor, "Ninety-nine percent of the stuff on here is clearly from the perspective of disabled people and written by disabled people." He goes on to note that *Ouch!* is not a help or support site and that if he had to give it a label, he would probably call it a lifestyle magazine. The tone is reflected in his statement that "We're about personal stuff, minutiae of everyday life, and that fantastic dark sense of humour and inevitable cynicism that we disabled people tend to have. Oh, and we don't shy away from subjects that other people might be a bit wary of." It has ten sections: News, Features, Columnists, Close Up, Weblog, Life Files, Play, YourSpace, TV & Radio, and Links. *Ouch!* will be of interest to those who follow *Ragged Edge* and who are interested in an outspoken lifestyle magazine for persons with disabilities.

1702. P N. Formerly (until 1992): *Paraplegia News;* Which incorporated: *Journal of Paraplegia.* 1946. m. USD 23 domestic; USD 32 foreign. Ed(s): Cliff Crase. P V A Publications, 2111 E Highland Ave. Ste 180,

Phoenix, AZ 85016-4702; http://www.pvamagazines.com. Illus., index, adv. Circ: 30000. Vol. ends: Dec. Online: EBSCO Publishing, EBSCO Host; Gale; Northern Light Technology, Inc. *Indexed:* CINAHL, SD. *Aud.:* Ga, Ac, Sa.

This appealing magazine is published by the Paralyzed Veterans of America and is used as a vehicle for relaying organization news and for presenting all news concerning paraplegics (civilians and veterans) and wheelchair living. The format includes numerous color photographs, and topics target the latest on spinal-cord-injury research, new products, legislation, people with disabilities, accessible travel, and computers. The publisher's web site features an index of articles from previous issues, an extensive list of resources, and a calendar of upcoming events. This inexpensive title is a good choice for libraries that serve persons with spinal cord injuries.

1703. Palaestra: forum of sport, physical education and recreation for those with disabilities. [ISSN: 8756-5811] 1984. q. USD 26.95 (Individuals, USD 19.95). Ed(s): William Lorton, David P Beaver. Challenge Publications, Ltd., Circulation Department, PO Box 508, Macomb, IL 61455-0508; challpub@macomb.com; http://www.palaestra.com. Illus., index, adv. Circ: 5500. Microform: PQC. Online: EBSCO Publishing, EBSCO Host; Factiva, Inc.; Gale; Northern Light Technology, Inc.; OCLC Online Computer Library Center, Inc.; ProQuest LLC (Ann Arbor). *Indexed:* PEI, SD. *Bk. rev.:* 5-7, 150-200 words. *Aud.:* Ac, Sa.

This colorful magazine has a threefold mission: "To enlighten parents in all aspects of physical activity, making them the best advocates for their children during IEP [Individual Education Plan] discussions with school or community recreation staffs; to increase the knowledge base of professionals working with children or adults with disabilities, making them aware of the 'can do' possibilities of their students/clients; and to show the value physical activity holds for adult readers' increased wellness." The emphasis is on practical research and descriptions of successful programs or suggested techniques for use with a wide variety of disabilities. Sports nutrition, new-product updates, legislative updates, and training tips are regular features. An author and title index is included in the fall issue. Recommended for public and academic libraries that serve programs in special education, physical education, or therapeutic recreation.

1704. Physical Therapy. Former titles (until 1964): *American Physical Therapy Association. Journal;* Which superseded in part (in 1962): *The Physical Therapy Review;* Which was formerly (until 1948): *Physiotherapy Review;* (until 1927): *P.T.Review.* [ISSN: 0031-9023] 1921. m. USD 110 (Individuals, USD 85; Free to members). Ed(s): Jan P Reynolds, Dr. Jules Rothstein. American Physical Therapy Association, 1111 N Fairfax St, Alexandria, VA 22314-1488; ptunderscorejournal@apta.org; http://www.apta.org. Illus., index, adv. Refereed. Circ: 75000 Paid and controlled. Vol. ends: Dec. Microform: PQC. Online: EBSCO Publishing, EBSCO Host; Florida Center for Library Automation; Gale; HighWire Press; Northern Light Technology, Inc.; OCLC Online Computer Library Center, Inc.; ProQuest LLC (Ann Arbor). *Indexed:* AgeL, CINAHL, ECER, ExcerpMed, GSI, PEI, SCI, SD, SSCI. *Bk. rev.:* Number and length vary. *Aud.:* Ac, Sa.

The official journal of the American Physical Therapy Association. Articles include case reports that describe an element of practice not previously documented in the literature; reports on original research; technical reports that describe and document the specifications or mechanical aspects of a device used by physical therapists; literature reviews; papers that present clinical perspectives on a specific clinical approach; and discussions of issues in physical therapy, health care, and related areas. Book, software, and video reviews; letters to the editor; product news; and association business are included. December issues provide a list of education programs that lead to qualification as a physical therapist. The journal's web site also includes a search engine, abstracts of articles published since January 1995, and free full-text access to many articles. Primarily for academic and special libraries.

1705. Preventing School Failure. Formerly (until 1989): *Pointer (Washington).* [ISSN: 1045-988X] 1956. q. USD 141 (Individuals, USD 60 print & online eds.; USD 34 newsstand/cover). Ed(s): Stephanie F Todd. Heldref Publications, 1319 18th St, NW, Washington, DC 20036-1802;

subscribe@heldref.org; http://www.heldref.org. Illus., index, adv. Refereed. Circ: 444 Paid. CD-ROM: ProQuest LLC (Ann Arbor). Online: EBSCO Publishing, EBSCO Host; Florida Center for Library Automation; Gale; OCLC Online Computer Library Center, Inc.; ProQuest K-12 Learning Solutions; ProQuest LLC (Ann Arbor); H.W. Wilson. Reprint: PSC. *Indexed:* ABIn, ECER, ERIC, EduInd, IBR, IBZ. *Aud.:* Ac, Sa.

Preventing School Failure is designed "for educators and other professionals seeking strategies to promote the success of students who have learning and behavior problems." It includes examples of programs and practices that help children and youth in schools, clinics, correctional institutions, and other settings. Each issue presents six to eight articles that detail classroom applications and practical examples of successful teaching strategies. Recent articles include "Bridging the Gap between High School and College: Strategies for the Successful Transition of Students with Learning Disabilities" and "Twelve Practical Strategies to Prevent Behavioral Escalation in Classroom Settings." There are occasional theme issues. Teachers and teacher educators write most of the articles, and the emphasis is on practice as opposed to theory. An annual author and title index is provided in the summer issue. Highly recommended for libraries that serve teachers and teacher educators.

1706. R E: view: rehabilitation and education for blindness and visual impairment. Former titles: *Education of the Visually Handicapped; International Journal for the Education of the Blind.* [ISSN: 0899-1510] 1969. q. USD 130 (Individuals, USD 35 print & online eds.). Ed(s): Helen Strang. Heldref Publications, 1319 18th St, NW, Washington, DC 20036-1802; subscribe@heldref.org; http://www.heldref.org. Illus., index, adv. Refereed. Circ: 3528 Paid. CD-ROM: ProQuest LLC (Ann Arbor). Online: EBSCO Publishing, EBSCO Host; Florida Center for Library Automation; Gale; OCLC Online Computer Library Center, Inc.; ProQuest K-12 Learning Solutions; ProQuest LLC (Ann Arbor); H.W. Wilson. Reprint: PSC. *Indexed:* ABIn, ECER, ERIC, EduInd, IBR, IBZ, PsycInfo, SSCI. *Bk. rev.:* Signed. Number and length vary. *Aud.:* Ac, Sa.

RE:view is a peer-reviewed journal published in conjunction with the Association for Education and Rehabilitation of the Blind and Visually Impaired. The intended audience is "people concerned with services to individuals of all ages with visual disabilities, including those with multiple disabilities and deaf-blindness." Although written for professionals, the articles are accessible to the general public. Articles include reports on useful practices and controversial issues, research findings, experiments, and professional experiences. Topics cover education and rehabilitation, administrative practices, counseling, technology, and other services to people with visual disabilities. The editors encourage contributions from people who have visual impairments. "Springboard" is a regular column designed for practitioners to use to get their ideas out in front of their peers. The winter issue provides a title and author index. Libraries serving institutions that have programs for the visually impaired should own this key title.

1707. Ragged Edge (Online Edition). Former titles (until 2004): *Ragged Edge (Print Edition);* (until 1997): *Disability Rag and Resource; Disability Rag.* 1980. bi-m. Ed(s): Mary Johnson. Advocado Press, PO Box 145, Louisville, KY 40201. Adv. Circ: 3000 Paid. Online: ProQuest LLC (Ann Arbor). *Indexed:* AltPI. *Bk. rev.:* Various number and length. *Aud.:* Sa.

Ragged Edge is the successor to *Disability Rag*, one of the first and most vocal vehicles to take a strong stance supporting disability rights. It examines current and emerging public issues from a disability perspective: civil rights, politics, culture, humor, sexuality, art, and technology. It publishes freelance journalism, essays, poetry, and fiction. The bimonthly print edition of *Ragged Edge* magazine ceased publication with the November/December 2003 issue, and it is now exclusively online. Readers wishing a print edition of the material published on the web site can purchase the *Disability Rag/Ragged Edge Reader.* Readers can also sign up to receive a free electronic newsletter twice each month. Persons who have been mistreated or underserved by current systems write many of the stories, and a wide variety of conditions are included. The web site provides an archive of issues back to September/October 1997, and features a section where readers can post personal statements and poetry. *Ragged Edge* is probably the best-known and longest-running publication representing the disability rights movement. URL: www.ragged-edge-mag.com/

1708. Reading and Writing Quarterly: overcoming learning difficulties.
Former titles (until 1992): *Journal of Reading, Writing, and Learning Disabilities International;* (until 1984): *Chicorel Abstracts to Reading and Learning Disabilities.* [ISSN: 1057-3569] 1975. q. GBP 289 print & online eds. Ed(s): Howard Margolis. Taylor & Francis Inc., 325 Chestnut St, Ste 800, Philadelphia, PA 19016; orders@taylorandfrancis.com; http://www.taylorandfrancis.com. Illus., index. Refereed. Vol. ends: Oct/Dec. Microform: PQC. Online: EBSCO Publishing, EBSCO Host; Gale; IngentaConnect; OCLC Online Computer Library Center, Inc.; SwetsWise Online Content. Reprint: PSC. *Indexed:* ECER, ERIC, L&LBA, PsycInfo. *Aud.:* Ac, Sa.

Reading and Writing Quarterly "disseminates critical information to improve instruction for regular and special education students who have difficulty learning to read and write." Articles address such issues as adjustments for language-learning style, literature-based reading programs, teaching reading and writing in the mainstream, study strategies, language-centered computer curricula, oral language connections to literacy, cooperative learning approaches to reading and writing, direct instruction, curriculum-based assessment, the impact of environmental factors on instructional effectiveness, and improvement of self-esteem. The emphasis is practical rather than theoretical. Most issues have a theme. Recent themes have included peer tutoring and the timing of literacy instruction. A sample issue is available at the publisher's web site. Recommended for libraries that serve professional educators.

Remedial and Special Education. See Education: Educational Psychology and Measurement, Special Education, Counseling section.

1709. Research and Practice for Persons with Severe Disabilities. Former titles (until 2002): *The Association for Persons with Severe Handicaps. Journal;* (until 1983): *Association for the Severely Handicapped. Journal (JASH);* (until vol.5, no.1): *A A E S P H Review (American Association for the Education of the Severely-Profoundly Handicapped).* [ISSN: 1540-7969] 1975. q. USD 280 membership (Individuals, USD 98 membership). Ed(s): Linda Bambara. T A S H, 29 W Susquehanna Ave, Ste 210, Baltimore, MD 21204-5201; http://www.tash.org. Illus., adv. Refereed. Circ: 3800. Vol. ends: Winter. Microform: PQC. Online: EBSCO Publishing, EBSCO Host; OCLC Online Computer Library Center, Inc.; H.W. Wilson. *Indexed:* ABIn, AgeL, ECER, EduInd, L&LBA, PsycInfo, SSCI. *Aud.:* Ac, Sa.

This scholarly journal publishes "original research, comprehensive reviews, conceptual and practical position papers that offer assessment and intervention methodologies, and program descriptions." Although the journal is research based, putting theory into practice is emphasized. It includes articles on such topics as inclusion, alternative and augmentative communication, supported living and employment, self-advocacy, and positive behavioral practices. Some issues are theme oriented. For example, recent themes have been self-determination and supported employment. Tables of contents are available on the journal's web site. An important title for libraries that support programs for persons with severe disabilities.

1710. The Review of Disability Studies: an international journal. [ISSN: 1553-3697] 2004. q. USD 100 (Individuals, USD 50; Students, USD 25). Ed(s): Robert A. Stodden. Center on Disability Studies, 1776 University Ave, Honolulu, HI 96822; http://www.cds.hawaii.edu. Refereed. *Bk. rev.:* Number and length vary. *Aud.:* Ac, Sa.

The Review of Disability Studies supports the emerging field of disability studies and was established to address the need for an internationally focused academic journal. It contains research articles, essays, and bibliographies relating to the culture of disability and people with disabilities. It also publishes forums on disability topics brought together by forum editors. Poetry, short stories, creative essays, photographs, and art work related to disability are also included. Invited book, film, and video reviews are included in each issue. The journal is published quarterly, and each issue runs approximately 100 pages. The full text is available on the web site as well as through paper subscriptions.

1711. Rural Special Education Quarterly. [ISSN: 8756-8705] 1984. q. Institutional members, USD 100; Individual members, USD 75; Students, USD 25 membership. Ed(s): Barbara Ludlow. American Council on Rural Special Education (A C R S E), Montana Center on Disabilities/

MSU Billings, 1500 Univesity Dr, Billings, MT 59101; inquiries@acres-sped.org; http://www.acres-sped.org. Illus., index. Circ: 650. Vol. ends: Fall. Online: EBSCO Publishing, EBSCO Host; OCLC Online Computer Library Center, Inc.; ProQuest LLC (Ann Arbor); H.W. Wilson. *Indexed:* Agr, EduInd. *Aud.:* Ac, Sa.

Rural Special Education Quarterly is a scholarly journal produced by the American Council on Rural Special Education. The aim is to provide rural educators and administrators with information about federal initiatives, service systems, and other events relevant to rural persons with disabilities. It publishers research reports, program descriptions, position papers, reports of promising practices, and viewpoints. Issues are occasionally centered around a theme. Recent issues include two or three research articles and two or three shorter articles that described direct implementations by practitioners under the category "Promising Practices." An archive of article abstracts back to winter 1992 is available on the journal's web site. This modestly priced periodical is recommended for libraries that serve teacher education programs or special educators in rural areas.

1712. Sexuality and Disability: a journal devoted to the psychological and medical aspects of sexuality in rehabilitation and community settings. [ISSN: 0146-1044] 1978. q. EUR 678 print & online eds. Ed(s): Sigmund Hough. Springer New York LLC, 233 Spring St, New York, NY 10013-1578; service-ny@springer.com; http://www.springer.com/. Illus., index, adv. Sample. Refereed. Vol. ends: Winter. Microform: PQC. Online: EBSCO Publishing, EBSCO Host; Gale; IngentaConnect; OCLC Online Computer Library Center, Inc.; OhioLINK; ProQuest LLC (Ann Arbor); Springer LINK; SwetsWise Online Content. Reprint: PSC. *Indexed:* AgeL, CINAHL, ExcerpMed, IMFL, PsycInfo, SFSA, SSA, SSCI, SWA, V&AA. *Bk. rev.:* Number and length vary. *Aud.:* Ac, Sa.

This international scholarly journal publishes articles "that address the psychological and medical aspects of sexuality in the field of rehabilitation." It covers developments in the areas of sexuality related to a wide range of disabilities. Articles include clinical practice reports, case studies, research and survey data, guidelines for clinical practice, developments in special programs in sex education, and counseling for disabled individuals. Although scholarly, most articles are accessible to the general public. Issues will occasionally focus on a theme. Contents information and abstracts from fall 1998 are available on the web site. Primarily for comprehensive academic collections.

Sharing Solutions. See Blind and Visually Impaired section.

1713. Sign Language Studies. [ISSN: 0302-1475] 1972. q. USD 95 (Individuals, USD 55). Ed(s): David Armstrong. Gallaudet University Press, 800 Florida Ave, NE, Washington, DC 20002-3695; gupress@gallaudet.edu; http://gupress.gallaudet.edu/. Illus., adv. Refereed. Circ: 485. Online: EBSCO Publishing, EBSCO Host; OCLC Online Computer Library Center, Inc.; OhioLINK; Project MUSE; ProQuest LLC (Ann Arbor); SwetsWise Online Content; H.W. Wilson. *Indexed:* AICP, AmHI, BAS, ECER, ERIC, HumInd, IBR, L&LBA, LT&LA, LingAb, MLA-IB, PsycInfo. *Bk. rev.:* 1-2. *Aud.:* Ac, Sa.

Published by Gallaudet University Press, this scholarly journal generally includes in each issue three or four research articles and one or two book reviews. Topics include linguistics, anthropology, semiotics, deaf culture, and deaf history and literature. Two recent articles are "The Political Uses of Sign Language: The Case of the French Revolution" and "The Visible and the Vocal: Speech and Gesture on a Continuum of Communicative Actions." This is a popular title for academic libraries and libraries that serve programs in sign language.

1714. The Special Ed Advocate Newsletter. [ISSN: 1538-3202] 1998. irreg. Free. Ed(s): Pamela Wright. Wrightslaw, webmaster@wrightslaw.com; http://www.wrightslaw.com/. *Aud.:* Sa.

The Special Ed Advocate is a free online newsletter. Each issue includes updates on special education law, new court cases, and information about effective advocacy. The newsletter and Wrightslaw web site are operated by a lawyer who represents children with special needs and his wife, a psychotherapist with training in psychology and clinical social work. Although the Wrights use the web site and newsletter as vehicles for advertising their books and seminars, the information they disseminate without cost provides an important service to professionals attempting to keep abreast of legal issues and to parents who want to learn how to become effective advocates for their children with special needs. Back issues of newsletters back to 1998 are available on the web site. This relatively longstanding electronic newsletter has emerged as an important resource.

1715. *SpeciaLiving Magazine.* [ISSN: 1537-0747] 2002. q. USD 12. Ed(s): Betty Garee. SpeciaLiving, PO Box 1000, Bloomington, IL 61702-1000; garee@aol.com; http://www.SpeciaLiving.com. Illus., adv. Circ: 12000. *Indexed:* CINAHL. *Aud.:* Sa.

SpeciaLiving Magazine is a colorful publication written primarily for the mobility impaired. It focuses on products, travel, accessible housing, people, inspiration, and humor. Short articles feature practical advice and consumer information. Columns provide information about the lifestyles, careers, experiences, and situations encountered by physically challenged individuals. One longtime regular column written by Joni Eareckson Tada offers inspirational advice. Cartoons, humor, and new-product information are also included. This inexpensive and useful publication is recommended primarily for public libraries.

1716. *Sports 'n Spokes: the magazine for wheelchair sports and recreation.* [ISSN: 0161-6706] 1975. 6x/yr. USD 21 domestic; USD 27 foreign. Ed(s): Cliff Crase. P V A Publications, 2111 E Highland Ave. Ste 180, Phoenix, AZ 85016-4702; http://www.pvamagazines.com. Illus., index, adv. Sample. Circ: 9000. *Indexed:* PEI, SD. *Aud.:* Hs, Ga, Sa.

This glossy, upbeat magazine will appeal to the wheelchair athlete and to any adult or teen having a disabling condition and an interest in sports. There are numerous color photographs and short, informative articles on a variety of current topics. The focus is on coverage of wheelchair competitive sports, but other sports covered include bowling, fencing, handcycling, hockey, racing, sailing, shooting, skiing, rugby, fishing, and tennis. Other topics covered include nutrition and assistive devices used in sports and recreation. Each issue includes a list of sports associations for the disabled. A calendar of sporting events and a well-developed list of resources are available on the web site. This is a good choice for school, public, and academic libraries.

1717. *Teaching Exceptional Children.* [ISSN: 0040-0599] 1968. bi-m. Non-members, USD 75. Ed(s): Chris Jesse. Council for Exceptional Children, 1110 N Glebe Rd, Ste 300, Arlington, VA 22201-4795; http://www.cec.sped.org/. Illus., index, adv. Refereed. Circ: 55000. Vol. ends: Jul/Aug. Microform: PQC. Online: EBSCO Publishing, EBSCO Host; Northern Light Technology, Inc.; OCLC Online Computer Library Center, Inc.; ProQuest K-12 Learning Solutions; ProQuest LLC (Ann Arbor); H.W. Wilson. *Indexed:* ABIn, ECER, EduInd, IBR, IBZ. *Aud.:* Ac, Sa.

This colorful magazine is published specifically for teachers and administrators. It provides information on technology, assistive technology, and procedures and techniques for teaching students with exceptionalities. The focus of its practical content is on immediate application. Recent articles include "Friendship-Facilitation Strategies: What Do Students in Middle School Tell Us?" and "Guidelines for Using Volunteer Literacy Tutors to Support Reading Instruction for English Language Learners." Contents information, a keyword search, and some full-text articles are available on the journal's web site. Libraries that serve teacher education programs or special educators should own this popular title.

1718. *Therapeutic Recreation Journal.* [ISSN: 0040-5914] 1967. q. USD 60 (Members, USD 28; Non-members, USD 66). Ed(s): Colleen Deyell Hood. National Recreation and Park Association, 22377 Belmont Ridge Rd, Ashburn, VA 20148-4501; info@nrpa.org; http://www.nrpa.org. Illus., index. Refereed. Circ: 4000. Microform: PQC. Online: Northern Light Technology, Inc.; ProQuest K-12 Learning Solutions; ProQuest LLC (Ann Arbor). *Indexed:* ASSIA, AgeL, CABA, CINAHL, PEI, PsycInfo, RRTA, SD. *Bk. rev.:* 1-2, 600-1,000 words. *Aud.:* Ac, Sa.

Therapeutic Recreation Journal is the official publication of the National Therapeutic Recreation Society, a branch of the National Recreation and Park Association. Some society business is included in the journal. Articles are "scholarly and substantive" and relevant to the field of therapeutic recreation.

The journal web site includes the table of contents of the current issue, the full text of the research updates back to January 2003, and a listing of the research updates back to January 1999. Occasionally, there will be a theme-based issue. Articles are designated as either a "Conceptual Paper" or a "Practice Perspective." Most issues include one substantive book review. This journal will be of interest primarily to professionals and educators, but it is a key title in its field and should be owned by libraries that serve therapeutic recreation programs.

1719. *Today's Caregiver.* 1995. m. USD 18 domestic; USD 26 Canada. Ed(s): Gary Barg. Caregiver Media Group, Ste 3006, 6365 Taft St, Hollywood, FL 33024; info@caregiver.com. Adv. *Aud.:* Ga, Sa.

Today's Caregiver provides information, support, and guidance for family and professional caregivers. In addition to publishing the magazine, the publisher also sponsors a caregivers conference and a web site at caregiver.com that includes topic-specific newsletters, online discussion lists, articles from the magazine, chat rooms, and an online store. Many issues include an interview with a celebrity, and the focus is on practical advice and coping. Caregivers have relatively few sources of practical advice, and this title should be a welcome addition for them. Public libraries may want to consider adding this title.

1720. *Topics in Early Childhood Special Education.* [ISSN: 0271-1214] 1981. q. GBP 80. Ed(s): Judith Carta. Sage Publications, Inc., 2455 Teller Rd, Thousand Oaks, CA 91320; info@sagepub.com; http://www.sagepub.com. Illus., index, adv. Refereed. Circ: 1300 Paid and free. Vol. ends: Winter. Microform: PQC. Online: EBSCO Publishing, EBSCO Host; Florida Center for Library Automation; Gale; IngentaConnect; OCLC Online Computer Library Center, Inc.; ProQuest K-12 Learning Solutions; ProQuest LLC (Ann Arbor); H.W. Wilson. Reprint: PSC. *Indexed:* ABIn, ASSIA, EAA, ECER, ERIC, EduInd, IBR, IBZ, IMFL, L&LBA, PsycInfo, SFSA, SSCI, SWA. *Aud.:* Ac, Sa.

This journal "provides program developers, advocates, researchers, higher education faculty, and other leaders with the most current, relevant research on all aspects of early childhood education for children with special needs." Articles discuss such issues as personnel preparation, policy issues, the operation of intervention programs, and strategies for engaging professionals and family members. Articles are scholarly and generally research based. Recent articles include "Early Head Start and Access to Early Intervention Services: A Qualitative Investigation" and "A Descriptive Analysis of Positive Behavioral Intervention Research with Young Children with Challenging Behavior." Practitioners and professional educators are the targeted audience. Recommended primarily for academic libraries.

1721. *Topics in Language Disorders.* [ISSN: 0271-8294] 1981. q. USD 292 (Individuals, USD 92.95). Ed(s): Katherine G Butler. Lippincott Williams & Wilkins, 530 Walnut St, Philadelphia, PA 19106-3621; custserv@lww.com; http://www.lww.com. Illus., adv. Refereed. Circ: 4550 Paid. Vol. ends: Aug. *Indexed:* ABIn, AgeL, CINAHL, ECER, ERIC, EduInd, L&LBA, PsycInfo, SSCI. *Bk. rev.:* Number and length vary. *Aud.:* Ac, Sa.

This journal publishes scholarly but not always research-based articles. The emphasis is on "bridging the gap between theory, research, and everyday practice." Each issue has selected editors who select from three to six articles based on a central theme. Recent themes have been "Reading Comprehension's New Look: Influences of Theory and Technology on Practice" and "Responsiveness to Intervention and the Speech-Language Pathologist." The journal also provides information about continuing education credit sponsored by the American Speech-Language Hearing Association. Professional educators and practitioners are the intended audience.

1722. *The Volta Review.* [ISSN: 0042-8639] 1898. q. USD 62 (Members, USD 50; Non-members, USD 60). Ed(s): Lea Lakins. Alexander Graham Bell Association for the Deaf and Hard of Hearing, Inc., 3417 Volta Place, NW, Washington, DC 20007; http://www.agbell.org. Illus. Sample.

Refereed. Circ: 12500 Paid. Vol. ends: Fall. Microform: PQC. Online: EBSCO Publishing, EBSCO Host; OCLC Online Computer Library Center, Inc.; ProQuest LLC (Ann Arbor). *Indexed:* ABIn, CINAHL, ECER, EduInd, L&LBA, PsycInfo, SSCI. *Bk. rev.:* 4-7, length varies. *Aud.:* Ac, Sa.

The Volta Review is the official journal of the Alexander Graham Bell Association. Two issues each year generally contain four research articles. Recent articles include "Early Literacy in Children with Hearing Loss: A Comparison between Two Educational Systems" and "Reading Recovery for Children with Hearing Loss." A third issue, a longer "monograph," centers on a specific theme and has a special editor. A recent theme was "Mechanisms of Aminoglycoside Ototoxicity and Strategies for Prevention." Monographs include scholarly articles that present original research or describe successful programs. Contents information back to 1994 is located on the web site. This scholarly journal is recommended for libraries serving researchers and professionals who work with hearing-impaired children and adults.

1723. *Volta Voices.* Formed by the merger of (1976-1994): *Newsounds;* (1982-1994): *Our Kids Magazine.* [ISSN: 1074-8016] 1994. 6x/yr. Membership, USD 50. Alexander Graham Bell Association for the Deaf and Hard of Hearing, Inc., 3417 Volta Place, NW, Washington, DC 20007; http://www.agbell.org. Adv. Circ: 5900 Paid. *Indexed:* CINAHL. *Aud.:* Sa.

Published by the Alexander Graham Bell Association, *Volta Voices* is written for families of children with hearing loss, adults who are deaf and hard-of-hearing, and professionals in the field of deafness. It is published in conjuction with the association's more scholarly publication, *The Volta Review,* and includes the latest information about hearing aids and cochlear implants, professional guidance and classroom tips, legislative updates, social concerns and interactive dialogue, medical updates, parent testimonies, and technological advances. Articles are short and nontechnical. Regular columns are "Connections," the latest news from relevant association sections; "The Kids' Zone," where children can submit drawings, paintings, writings, jokes, or photos; and "Tech Talk." Recommended for libraries serving the deaf or hard-of-hearing and for academic libraries supporting related programs.

1724. *World Around You.* [ISSN: 0199-8293] 1978. 3x/yr. Free. Ed(s): Cathryn Carroll. Gallaudet University, National Deaf Educ Network & Clearinghouse, 800 Florida Ave, NE, KDES PAS 6, Washington, DC 20002-3695; cmcarrol@gallux.gallaudet.edu; http://clerccenter.gallaudet.edu/. Adv. Circ: 6500. *Aud.:* Hs.

World Around You has been published at Gallaudet University since 1978, and the intended audience is deaf teens. Each issue has stories by and about deaf teens and adults who are succeeding in today's world. Other features include information about careers, role models, technology, laws, and deaf culture. The full text of the current issue and most back issues dating to November/December 1996 are available on the magazine's web site. Teachers' guides are available. Although the magazine is designed to be used in the classroom, libraries that serve teacher education programs may want to consider adding this title.

■ DO-IT-YOURSELF

See also Building and Construction; Craft; Home; and Interior Design and Decoration sections.

Carrie M. Macfarlane, Reference and Instruction Librarian for the Sciences, Middlebury College, Middlebury, VT 05753; cmacfarl@middlebury.edu

Introduction

More men and women are reaching for their tool belts these days, and your library can take on the important task of keeping them informed. Do-it-yourself projects always take longer than expected, so you can be sure that your patrons will be looking for good instructions. The titles I have selected provide practical and easy-to-follow advice on projects ranging from fixing a leaky faucet to building an oscillating robot to chopping down a tree.

Be sure to consider your environment (urban or rural?) and your target populations (beginners or seasoned homeowners?) when making your selections. Each publication has a different scope, but this section as a whole offers something for everyone.

For professionals and serious hobbyists, librarians will want to consult other sections such as Building and Construction, and Craft. For those interested in homemaking, entertaining in the home, and interior design, useful titles can be found in sections such as Home, and Interior Design and Decoration.

Basic Periodicals

Ga: *BackHome, The Family Handyman, This Old House.*

Basic Abstracts and Indexes

Index to How to Do It Information, Readers' Guide to Periodical Literature.

1725. *BackHome: your hands-on guide to sustainable living.* [ISSN: 1051-323X] 1990. bi-m. USD 21.97 domestic; USD 30.97 foreign; USD 4.95 newsstand/cover per issue domestic. Ed(s): Lorna K Loveless. WordsWorth Communications Inc., PO Box 70, Hendersonville, NC 28793; info@backhomemagazine.com; http://www.backhomemagazine.com. Illus., adv. Circ: 26000 Paid. *Aud.:* Ga.

BackHome will appeal to the environmentally conscious do-it-yourselfer interested in a healthy lifestyle. With its contributors from across the country described as "everyday folks sharing their real-world experiences," the articles attend to the home, the garden, and even the great outdoors. The magazine provides basic step-by-step instructions for small projects such as planting seedlings and sewing a window quilt. But it also tackles bigger jobs such as building a straw-bale house and making your own maple syrup—and for these it offers just enough information to pique your interest. A number of projects and stories in each issue are family oriented. The table of contents and some full-text articles from the most recent issue are available on the magazine's web site. Recommended for public libraries that serve small town and rural communities.

1726. *Extreme How-To.* [ISSN: 1540-5346] m. 10/yr. USD 18.97 domestic; USD 33.97 Canada; USD 38.97 elsewhere. Ed(s): Matt Weber. Latitude3 Media, 33 Inverness Center Pkwy Ste 120, Birmingham, AL 35242. *Aud.:* Ga.

Homeowners without basic carpentry and building skills will think this magazine is indeed "extreme." But those who regularly commune with table saws, drill presses, and drywall will find it full of real advice for home, garden, and auto repair. As the magazine says, "Our readers are serious." Recent issues have included tips for building a patio, winterizing a home and installing crown molding, and all instructions assume prior knowledge. Even though it's only been around for a few years, *Extreme How-To* seems to have found its niche. If your library is frequented by builders, carpenters, and serious do-it-yourselfers, this magazine is worth reviewing. A selection of full-text articles and product reviews is available on the magazine's web site.

1727. *The Family Handyman: tons of projects, tips and tools.* Incorporates (in 1951): *Home Garden's Natural Gardening Magazine;* Which was formerly (until 1972): *Home Garden;* (until 1967): *The Flower Grower.* [ISSN: 0014-7230] 1951. 10x/yr. USD 19.98 domestic; USD 28.97 foreign; USD 2.99 newsstand/cover. Ed(s): Ken Collier, Spike Carlsen. Home Service Publications, Inc., 2915 Commers Dr, Ste 700, Eagan, MN 55121-2398. Illus., index, adv. Circ: 1000000 Paid. Vol. ends: Dec. *Indexed:* ConsI, IHTDI, RGPR. *Aud.:* Ga.

This is a great read for do-it-yourself homeowners. Issues are packed with illustrated step-by-step instructions for projects and repairs for the home and garden, helpful tips, reviews of new products, and even a humorous "Great Goofs" page where readers share their mistakes so that others may learn from them. Instructions are complete with a breakdown of skill level, tools, and time required. Everyone from the novice with a few hand tools to the expert with a full-sized workshop will find a useful tidbit in each issue. Highly recommended for all public libraries. The magazine's web site offers a significant amount of content, including the table of contents and some full-text articles from the most recent issue, a five-year index, and a categorized "How-To Library" of previously published articles.

1728. HANDY. Former titles (until 2000): *Handyman How-To;* (until 2000): *American How-To.* [ISSN: 1531-569X] 1993. bi-m. Free to members. Ed(s): Larry Okrend. North American Media Group, Inc., 12301 Whitewater Dr, Minnetonka, MN 55343; mail@handymanclub.com; http://www.namginc.com/. Adv. Circ: 925000 Paid. *Aud.:* Ga.

This is the magazine of the Handyman Club of America, and it is available only to paying members. The contents are not for the uninitiated, either. Although it provides extensive comparison reviews and feature articles of interest to any homeowner, most projects are not suitable for a novice with a scant collection of power tools. Still, avid do-it-yourselfers will appreciate the current awareness this title provides. For example, a recent issue highlights products unveiled at a recent International Builders' Show. If your library acquires a membership, this magazine will be delivered to your door just like any other subscription title. Libraries that serve serious do-it-yourselfers may want to check this out. A ten-year index is available on the members-only web site.

1729. Make: technology on your time. [ISSN: 1556-2336] 2005. q. USD 34.95 domestic; USD 39.95 Canada; USD 49.95 elsewhere. Ed(s): Mark Frauenfelder, Dale Dougherty. O'Reilly Media, Inc., 1005 Gravenstein Hwy N, Sebastopol, CA 95472. Illus., adv. *Aud.:* Ga.

We all know at least one of them: those independent thinkers who would rather spend hours soldering together a waffle iron-toaster bedside lamp than go out for a leisurely weekend breakfast. If you've seen any in your library lately, then consider subscribing to this niche magazine. *Make* is a new title for do-it-yourself electronics geeks. Solar-powered robots, audio loopers, and LED throwies are just steps away from reality. Each colorful issue contains instructions for projects such as these, plus do-it-yourself news and technology updates. The web site provides tables of contents and web extras such as reader-submitted projects and a discussion forum.

Mother Earth News. See Environment and Conservation section.

1730. Old-House Journal. [ISSN: 0094-0178] 1973. 6x/yr. USD 21.97 domestic; USD 31.97 Canada; USD 51.97 elsewhere. Ed(s): Gordon Bock. Restore Media LLC, 1000 Potomac St, NW, Ste 102, Washington, DC 20007. Illus., adv. Circ: 100000 Paid. *Indexed:* A&ATA, API, GardL, IHTDI, RGPR. *Aud.:* Ga.

The intellectual do-it-yourselfer will find a treasure trove of information in *Old House Journal.* As its title suggests, it is best suited for old-house aficionados. A study of the colors used in the Arts and Crafts Movement (one section is titled "What's So Keen About Olive Green?") is a perfect illustration of the beauty of this magazine: It can be appealing to homeowners and armchair enthusiasts alike. Product reviews keep readers up-to-date on the latest in home improvement tools and accessories. While some projects are do-it-yourself, others simply give tips and advocate hiring a professional. Highly recommended for libraries in communities with old and historic homes. The web site offers a significant amount of content, including the full text of recent feature articles, product reviews, and searchable floor plans.

1731. ReadyMade: instructions for everyday life. [ISSN: 1544-2950] 2001. bi-m. USD 19.95 domestic. Ed(s): Shoshana Berger. ReadyMade, 2824 Eighth St, Berkeley, CA 94710. Adv. *Aud.:* Ga.

ReadyMade is a relatively new do-it-yourself title that makes reuse and reinvention fun. Found on magazine racks in trendy clothing shops, art supply warehouses, and organic food co-ops, it targets hipsters with a social conscience. Create a ski chalet atmosphere in your home with a fake bear skin rug (instructions on assembly provided) and a firewood tote made from worn-out jeans. Then, depending on whom you're inviting, you'll want to add either a compact disc–encrusted party disco ball or a solid oak "head-banging headboard." Although some projects are less than practical, on the whole the retro look and creative content of this colorful magazine will be appealing to

urban twenty- and thirtysomethings; if your library is trying to reach out to this demographic, then you'll want to take a look. The magazine's web site offers tables of contents and the full text of selected articles, plus an active do-it-yourself blog.

1732. This Old House. Incorporates (in 2001): *Today's Homeowner Solutions;* Which was formerly (until 2001): *Today's Homeowner;* (until 1996): *Home Mechanix;* (until 1984): *Mechanix Illustrated;* Which incorporated: *Electronics Illustrated.* [ISSN: 1086-2633] 1995. 10x/yr. USD 15.96 domestic; USD 25.96 Canada; USD 8.94 per issue. Ed(s): Donna Sapolin. Time4 Media, Inc., 1185 Ave of the Americas, 27th Fl, New York, NY 10035. Illus., adv. Circ: 672754 Paid. Online: EBSCO Publishing, EBSCO Host; OCLC Online Computer Library Center, Inc.; ProQuest LLC (Ann Arbor). *Indexed:* MASUSE, RGPR. *Aud.:* Ga.

The name-recognition factor of this title is enormous due to its long-running affiliated television program. The glossy full-color magazine makes reference to the show, but its scope stretches beyond it. It focuses on maintenance of older homes, with interior and exterior design advice, fix-it projects, and product reviews. Most projects are appropriate for weekend do-it-yourselfers, but some take a big-picture approach and assume readers will hire contractors to do the dirty work. This is a good all-around title for libraries with home maintenance and interior design collections. The web site offers tables of contents and the full text of selected articles, plus related do-it-yourself information.

1733. Workbench: woodworking to improve your home. [ISSN: 0043-8057] 1954. bi-m. USD 22 domestic; CND 32 foreign. Ed(s): Tim Robertson. August Home Publishing Co., 2200 Grand Ave, Des Moines, IA 50312-5306; orders@augusthome.com; http://www.augusthome.com. Illus., adv. Circ: 300000 Paid. *Indexed:* ConsI, IHTDI, MASUSE, RGPR. *Aud.:* Ga.

While many woodworking magazines focus on one type of woodworking such as cabinetmaking, carving, or whittling, *Workbench* focuses on one type of product: furniture and accessories for the home. Do-it-yourselfers with woodworking skills will appreciate plans and instructions for projects such as built-in book nooks, kitchen utensil racks and adjustable picture rails. Product reviews, tool tips and a Q&A column also are useful. Most projects require power tools and know-how, but "bench basics" skill-building articles will help a novice get up to speed over time. Recommended for libraries in urban areas with continuing education woodworking programs, and for any library in a non-urban area. The magazine's web site provides the table of contents of the most recent issue as well as supplemental woodworking resources.

■ EARTH SCIENCES AND GEOLOGY

See also Agriculture; Engineering and Technology; Geography; and Paleontology sections.

Edward F. Lener, College Librarian for the Sciences, University Libraries, Virginia Tech, P.O. Box 90001, Blacksburg, VA 24062; lener@vt.edu

Flora G. Shrode, Head, Reference and Instruction Services, Merrill-Cazier Library, Utah State University, Logan, UT 84322; flora.shrode@usu.edu

Introduction

Due to heavy media coverage of natural disasters such as floods, earthquakes, and landslides, geologic hazards such as these are often the first thing that comes to mind when one mentions the earth sciences. In fact, this is only one part of the picture. The earth sciences touch on many aspects of daily life, from the water that we drink to the energy and mineral resources that power our industries and vehicles. Research ranges from simple field reconnaissance, using the traditional rock hammer, compass, and hand lens, to advanced computer modeling techniques and laboratory equipment designed to simulate conditions deep within the earth. The earth sciences are also highly interdisciplinary, drawing on work in biology, chemistry, geography, physics, and mathematics.

As a general rule, publications in the earth sciences tend to have a long lifespan of usefulness. The importance of older literature is reflected by the fact that indexing coverage in the American Geological Institute's GeoRef database extends back over 200 years for North America. Of course, while much of the older research and descriptive material is still valid, new theories and analytical techniques are more refined and often allow for a better understanding of the underlying processes involved. Also, the increasing use of color illustrations and computer-generated graphics in earth science journals can help readers to grasp complex visual information more easily.

The number of publications for general audiences continues to be limited, but there are many excellent academic and specialist journals in the field. When selecting materials in the earth sciences, it is also necessary to consider the issues of geographic coverage and time frame. Work done at sites from around the world and examining different periods of geologic history are essential to developing a well-rounded collection. Obtaining a good mix of both theoretical and applied research is also important. There are still relatively few electronic-only journals in the earth sciences, but most now offer full text of recent articles online. The GeoScience World collection, launched in 2005, features over 30 titles, including those of many professional societies in the field. The full list may be viewed at their web site (www.geoscienceworld.org).

The American Geological Institute maintains a list of "priority journals." These are serial titles recommended by the GeoRef Users Group Steering Committee to receive highest priority for database indexing as new issues come out. These are indicated in the annotations where applicable. While this is a good general indication of the importance of these titles, one should always be cautious about relying too heavily on any single selection criterion. For the full list of priority journals, go to the American Geological Institute's web site (www.agiweb.org/georef/priorjs.html).

Basic Periodicals

Hs, Ga: *Geology Today, Geotimes, Rocks and Minerals;* Ac, Sa: *Geological Society. Journal, Geological Society of America. Bulletin, Geology, Geophysics, Journal of Geology.*

Basic Abstracts and Indexes

GeoRef.

1734. *A A P G Bulletin.* Former titles (until 1973): *The American Association of Petroleum Geologists Bulletin;* (until 1966): *American Association of Petroleum Geologists. Bulletin.* [ISSN: 0149-1423] 1917. m. Members, USD 16; Non-members, USD 290. Ed(s): John Lorenz, Carol Christopher. American Association of Petroleum Geologists, 1444 S Boulder, Tulsa, OK 74119; http://www.aapg.org. Illus., index, adv. Refereed. Circ: 31000 Paid. Vol. ends: Dec (No. 12). Microform: PMC; PQC. Online: EBSCO Publishing, EBSCO Host; HighWire Press. *Indexed:* ABS&EES, AS&TI, C&ISA, ChemAb, EngInd, EnvAb, MinerAb, OceAb, PetrolAb, PollutAb, SCI, SSCI, SWRA. *Bk. rev.:* 0-4, 300-700 words, signed. *Aud.:* Ac, Sa.

This serves as the official journal of the American Association of Petroleum Geologists (AAPG) and is targeted toward the association's members as well as other professionals in the field. The high-quality research and technical articles address such topics as reservoir characterization, well logging, depositional environments, and basin modeling. The AAPG web site requires registration for most features. Citations are available on GeoScience World from 1921 forward, with full text for 2000 to the present. Suitable for academic and specialized collections. A GeoRef priority journal.

1735. *American Journal of Science: an international earth science journal.* Former titles (until 1880): *American Journal of Science and Arts;* (until 1820): *American Journal of Science (1818).* [ISSN: 0002-9599] 1818. 10x/yr. USD 185 print & online ed. (Individuals, USD 75 print & online ed.; Students, USD 35 print & online ed.). Ed(s): Jay J Ague, Danny M Rye. American Journal of Science, 217 Kline Geology Laboratory, Yale University, PO Box 208109, New Haven, CT 06520-8109; ajs@hess.geology.yale.edu; http://love.geology.yale.edu/.

Illus., index. Refereed. Circ: 1727 Paid. Vol. ends: Dec (No. 10). Microform: PMC; PQC. Online: HighWire Press. *Indexed:* AS&TI, AmH&L, CABA, ChemAb, EnvAb, ExcerpMed, ForAb, GSI, IBR, MinerAb, OceAb, PetrolAb, S&F, SCI, SSCI, SWRA. *Aud.:* Ac, Sa.

The oldest continuously published journal in the United States devoted to the geological sciences. It publishes articles from around the world, presenting results of major research from all earth sciences. Readers are primarily earth scientists in academia and government institutions. There are occasional special issues, with some past topics including functional morphology and evolution, Proterozoic evolution and environments, microbial biogeochemistry, and studies in metamorphism and metasomatism. The journal's web site, through Highwire, provides abstracts from 1945 forward and full text for 1963 to the present. Author and subject indexes, tables of contents, and full text of articles in issues published from 1990 to 2004 are also available online through Yale University. Appropriate for academic and research collections. A GeoRef priority journal.

1736. *American Mineralogist: an international journal of earth and planetary materials.* Superseded in part (1894-1909): *The Mineral Collector;* Which was formerly (until 1893): *Minerals;* Which incorporated (1889-1893): *Mineralogists' Monthly;* Which was formerly: *Exchanger's Monthly.* [ISSN: 0003-004X] 1894. 8x/yr. USD 725. Ed(s): Rachel A Russell, Robert Dymek. Mineralogical Society of America, 3635 Concorde Pkwy Ste 500, Chantilly, VA 20151-1125; business@minsocam.org; http://www.minsocam.org. Illus., index, adv. Sample. Refereed. Circ: 3000 Paid and free. Vol. ends: Nov/Dec (No. 11 - No. 12). Reprint: PSC. *Indexed:* AS&TI, ChemAb, IBR, MinerAb, OceAb, PetrolAb, PhotoAb, S&F, SCI, SWRA. *Bk. rev.:* 0-3, 500-1,200 words, signed. *Aud.:* Ac, Sa.

A key title in the field of mineralogy, this journal is an official publication of the Mineralogical Society of America. Research articles cover many topics, including crystal structure, crystal chemistry, and mineral occurrences and deposits. Work in closely related areas such as crystallography, petrology, and geochemistry is also included. In addition, most issues include a section featuring newly named minerals, with a brief description and citation to the literature for each of them. Tables of contents for journal issues published from 1916 to the present are available on the Mineralogical Society web site. Full text of articles published from 1967 to 2004 are freely accessible online; the latest few years are accessible only to subscribers and society members. The GeoScience World web site also provides full text to subscribers from 1998 forward. A GeoRef priority journal.

1737. *Annales Geophysicae: atmospheres, hydrospheres and space sciences.* Formed by the merger of (1983-1988): *Annales de Geophysicae. Serie A: Upper Atmosphere and Space Sciences;* (1983-1988): *Annales Geophysicae. Serie B: Terrestrial and Planetary Physics;* Both of which superseded in part (in 1985): *Annales Geophysicae;* Which was formed by the merger of (1944-1983): *Annales de Geophysique;* (1948-1983): *Annali di Geofisica.* [ISSN: 0992-7689] 1983. m. EUR 1950. Ed(s): Wlodek Kofman. Copernicus GmbH, Max-Planck Str 13, Katlenburg-Lindau, 37191, Germany; info@copernicus.org; http://www.copernicus.org. Illus., index, adv. Sample. Refereed. Circ: 600. Vol. ends: Dec (No. 12). Online: EBSCO Publishing, EBSCO Host; OhioLINK; Springer LINK; SwetsWise Online Content. *Indexed:* ChemAb, M&GPA, SCI, WRCInf. *Aud.:* Ac, Sa.

This official journal of the European Geosciences Union presents research articles and short communications on a broad range of topics in geophysics. Areas of major emphasis include atmospheric physics and dynamics, the magnetosphere and ionosphere of the earth, solar and heliospheric physics, and the oceans and their physical interactions with the land and air. Special issues may feature conference papers or an in-depth report on selected geophysical studies. This monthly also makes extensive use of color illustrations where appropriate. Online access is available to subscribers for articles published from late 1996 forward.

1738. *Applied Geochemistry.* [ISSN: 0883-2927] 1986. 12x/yr. EUR 1206. Ed(s): Ron Fuge. Pergamon, The Boulevard, Langford Ln, East Park, Kidlington, OX5 1GB, United Kingdom. Illus., index. Sample. Refereed. Vol. ends: Nov (No. 6). Microform: PQC. Online: EBSCO Publishing,

EBSCO Host; Gale; IngentaConnect; OhioLINK; ScienceDirect; SwetsWise Online Content. *Indexed:* ChemAb, EngInd, EnvAb, EnvInd, ForAb, HortAb, M&GPA, MinerAb, PetrolAb, PollutAb, S&F, SCI, SWRA, WRCInf. *Bk. rev.:* 0-2, 400-2,000 words. *Aud.:* Ac, Sa.

This international journal emphasizes research in geochemistry and cosmochemistry that has practical applications to areas such as environmental monitoring and preservation, waste disposal, and exploration for resources. Reports of original research, rapid communications, and some reviews are published in the fields of inorganic, organic, and isotope geochemistry. As the official publication of the International Association of GeoChemistry, some issues include reports of association activities. This journal is appropriate for academic or corporate research collections. The web site provides free access to tables of contents and abstracts for issues published from 1986 to the present, with full-text articles available to libraries that purchase access through ScienceDirect. A GeoRef priority journal.

1739. Basin Research. [ISSN: 0950-091X] 1988. q. GBP 684 print & online eds. Ed(s): Hugh D Sinclair, Peter DeCelles. Blackwell Publishing Ltd., 9600 Garsington Rd, Oxford, OX4 2ZG, United Kingdom; customerservices@blackwellpublishing.com; http://www.blackwellpublishing.com. Illus., index, adv. Sample. Refereed. Circ: 700. Vol. ends: No. 4. Microform: PQC. Online: Blackwell Synergy; EBSCO Publishing, EBSCO Host; Gale; IngentaConnect; OCLC Online Computer Library Center, Inc.; OhioLINK; SwetsWise Online Content. Reprint: PSC. *Indexed:* CABA, ForAb, PetrolAb, S&F, SCI, SWRA. *Bk. rev.:* 0-4, 500-1,500 words, signed. *Aud.:* Ac, Sa.

This journal is a joint publication of the European Association of Geoscientists and Engineers and the International Association of Sedimentologists. It features interdisciplinary work on sedimentary basins that addresses such important issues as sediment transport, fluid migration, and stratigraphic modeling. Special thematic issues are also published from time to time. Free tables of contents can be found on the web site beginning with late 1996, with the full text of articles available for print subscribers, on a per-article basis, or through some aggregator services. Recommended for comprehensive collections, but libraries on a tight budget may first want to consider its more general counterpart *Sedimentology,* also published by Blackwell Science Ltd., for the International Association of Sedimentologists.

1740. Biogeosciences. [ISSN: 1726-4170] 2003. bi-m. EUR 430; EUR 79 newsstand/cover. Copernicus GmbH, Max-Planck Str 13, Katlenburg-Lindau, 37191, Germany; info@copernicus.org; http://www.copernicus.org. Refereed. *Indexed:* BiolAb, CABA, ForAb, M&GPA, S&F, SCI, SWRA, ZooRec. *Aud.:* Ac, Sa.

This open-access journal is dedicated to the publication of research articles, short communications, and review papers on all aspects of the interactions of biological, chemical, and physical processes with the geosphere, hydrosphere, and atmosphere. Some topics include biogeochemistry, global elemental cycles, gas exchange, interactions between microorganisms and rocks, biomineralization, and responses to global change. The web site also allows for interactive discussion of recent article postings.

1741. Boreas: an international journal of quaternary research. [ISSN: 0300-9483] 1972. q. GBP 177 print & online eds. Ed(s): Jan A Piotrowski. Taylor & Francis A S, Biskop Gunnerusgate 14A, PO Box 12 Posthuset, Oslo, 0051, Norway; journals@tandf.no; http://www.tandf.co.uk. Illus., index, adv. Sample. Refereed. Circ: 700. Vol. ends: Dec (No. 4). Microform: PQC. Online: EBSCO Publishing, EBSCO Host; Gale; IngentaConnect; OCLC Online Computer Library Center, Inc.; SwetsWise Online Content. Reprint: PSC. *Indexed:* AbAn, ApEcolAb, BiolAb, BrArAb, ChemAb, IBR, M&GPA, NumL, S&F, SCI, SWRA, ZooRec. *Bk. rev.:* 0-3, 500-1,200 words, signed. *Aud.:* Ac, Sa.

Sponsored by a partnership of geologists in several Nordic countries, this journal deals exclusively with research on the Quaternary period. This extends from about two million years ago to the present, and many of the topics covered, such as climatic variations and sea-level changes, are of particular relevance today. Other papers examine the stratigraphy, glacial dynamics and landforms, and the flora and fauna of the period. Full-text web access beginning with 1999 is available to subscribers. A GeoRef priority journal.

1742. Bulletin of Volcanology. Formerly (until 1984): *Bulletin Volcanologique.* [ISSN: 0258-8900] 1924. 8x/yr. EUR 1468 print & online eds. Ed(s): T H Druitt, J Stix. Springer, Tiergartenstr 17, Heidelberg, 69121, Germany. Illus., index, adv. Sample. Refereed. Vol. ends: Jul (No. 8). Online: EBSCO Publishing, EBSCO Host; OhioLINK; Springer LINK; SwetsWise Online Content. Reprint: PSC. *Indexed:* ChemAb, MinerAb, SCI. *Aud.:* Ac, Sa.

The official journal of the International Association of Volcanology and Chemistry of the Earth's Interior. As suggested by its title, the emphasis is on volcanoes, including their characteristics, behavior, and associated hazards. Coverage is international in scope and includes related material on magmatic systems and igneous petrology. Each issue also contains a useful summary of recent volcanic activity based on data from the Smithsonian Institution's Global Volcanism Network. The web site offers free tables of contents and abstracts as well as full-text access from 1938 forward for subscribers or on a per-article basis. A GeoRef priority journal.

1743. Canadian Journal of Earth Sciences. [ISSN: 0008-4077] 1963. m. CND 936 (Individuals, CND 250). Ed(s): Dr. Brian Jones. N R C Research Press, National Research Council of Canada, Ottawa, ON K1A 0R6, Canada; pubs@nrc-cnrc.gc.ca; http://pubs.nrc-cnrc.gc.ca. Illus., index, adv. Refereed. Circ: 1572. Vol. ends: Dec (No. 12). Microform: MML; PMC; PQC. Online: EBSCO Publishing, EBSCO Host; Gale; IngentaConnect; LexisNexis; Micromedia ProQuest; OCLC Online Computer Library Center, Inc.; Ovid Technologies, Inc.; ProQuest K-12 Learning Solutions; ProQuest LLC (Ann Arbor); SwetsWise Online Content; H.W. Wilson. *Indexed:* AS&TI, C&ISA, CBCARef, CerAb, ChemAb, EngInd, EnvInd, FR, GSI, HRIS, IAA, IBR, M&GPA, MinerAb, PetrolAb, PollutAb, S&F, SCI, SWRA, ZooRec. *Aud.:* Ac, Sa.

Published monthly by the National Research Council of Canada, the majority of the articles are in English, and those in French include English abstracts. Articles are more technical than those found in *Geoscience Canada.* As one might expect, for site-specific topics the focus is heavily on Canadian geology, but many of the underlying principles are transferable to other regions. The web site offers free tables of contents and abstracts from 1998 on, with full-text access for subscribers. A GeoRef priority journal.

1744. Canadian Mineralogist: crystallography, geochemistry, mineralogy, petrology, mineral deposits. Formerly (until 1957): *Contributions to Canadian Mineralogy.* [ISSN: 0008-4476] 1921. bi-m. CND 495 print & online eds. Mineralogical Association of Canada, 490 Rue de la Couronne, Ottawa, ON G1K 9A9, Canada; office@mineralogicalassociation.ca; http://www.mineralogicalassociation.ca. Illus. Sample. Refereed. Circ: 2000. Vol. ends: Dec. *Indexed:* C&ISA, CerAb, ChemAb, EngInd, IAA, IBR, MinerAb, PetrolAb, SCI. *Bk. rev.:* 0-2, 300-1,000 words. *Aud.:* Ac, Sa.

Publishes research papers on crystallography, geochemistry, mineralogy, mineral deposits, and petrology. Averages one thematic issue each year, usually reporting on symposia sponsored by the Mineralogical Association of Canada. Similar in content to *American Mineralogist, European Journal of Mineralogy,* and *Mineralogical Magazine,* this journal places a slightly greater emphasis on ore minerals and deposits and has more of a regional focus. Text is primarily in English with French summaries. Abstracts for papers from 2000 to present may be viewed on the association web site, and full-text access is available to subscribers. A GeoRef priority journal.

1745. Canadian Petroleum Geology. Bulletin. Former titles (until 1962): *Alberta Society of Petroleum Geologists. Journal;* (until 1954): *A.S.P.G. News Bulletin.* [ISSN: 0007-4802] 1953. q. CND 120 domestic; CND 140 per issue United States; CND 170 per issue elsewhere. Ed(s): Glen Stockmal. Canadian Society of Petroleum Geologists, No 160, 540 Fifth Ave SW, Calgary, AB T2P 0M2 , Canada; jaime.croftlarsen@cspg.org; http://www.cspg.org. Illus., index, adv. Refereed. Circ: 3500. Vol. ends: Dec (No. 4). *Indexed:* ChemAb, EngInd, PetrolAb, SCI, ZooRec. *Bk. rev.:* 0-4, 500-1,200 words, signed. *Aud.:* Ac, Sa.

As the official publication of the Canadian Society of Petroleum Geologists, many issues devote some space to society business such as awards and a report of activities. More importantly, the journal also features high-quality research articles on various aspects of petroleum geology in a wide range of geologic environments. Articles are well illustrated and feature color where appropriate. Regional coverage emphasizes Canada and Alaska, but the title is still a valuable addition to larger academic or special libraries. Online access is available for a fee via the AAPG/Datapages portal or through GeoScience World.

1746. Chemical Geology. Incorporates (in 1993): *Chemical Geology. Isotope Geoscience Section;* Which was formerly (1983-1985): *Isotope Geoscience.* [ISSN: 0009-2541] 1966. 44x/yr. EUR 4000. Ed(s): Dr. Steven L. Goldstein, Don Dingwell. Elsevier BV, Radarweg 29, Amsterdam, 1043 NX, Netherlands; nlinfo-f@elsevier.nl; http://www.elsevier.nl. Illus., index, adv. Sample. Refereed. Vol. ends: No. 4. Microform: PQC. Online: EBSCO Publishing, EBSCO Host; Gale; IngentaConnect; OhioLINK; ScienceDirect; SwetsWise Online Content. *Indexed:* ChemAb, MinerAb, OceAb, PetrolAb, PollutAb, S&F, SCI, SWRA. *Aud.:* Ac, Sa.

This title serves as the official publication of the European Association for Geochemistry. It has an international scope and aims to provide broad coverage of the growing field of organic and inorganic geochemistry, including reports about Earth and other planets. Papers address topics such as low temperature geochemistry, organic/petroleum geochemistry, analytical techniques, isotope studies, environmental geochemistry, and experimental petrology and geochemistry. The web site provides free access to tables of contents and abstracts for all articles from the journal's inception in 1966. Full-text access from 1995 forward is available through ScienceDirect. A GeoRef priority journal.

1747. Clay Minerals: journal of the European Clay Groups. Formerly (until 1964): *Clay Minerals Bulletin.* [ISSN: 0009-8558] 1947. q. issue numbers 1-4 last issue includes index. GBP 221 combined subscription domestic print & online eds.; GBP 250 combined subscription foreign print & online eds. Ed(s): J M Adams. Mineralogical Society, 41 Queens Gate, London, SW7 5HR, United Kingdom; info@minersoc.org; http://www.minersoc.org. Illus., index. Refereed. Circ: 1500. Vol. ends: Dec (No. 4). *Indexed:* C&ISA, CerAb, ChemAb, EngInd, IAA, MinerAb, S&F, SCI. *Bk. rev.:* 0-2, 600-1,000 words, signed. *Aud.:* Ac, Sa.

Published by the Mineralogical Society of Great Britain, this journal represents the combined efforts of several clay research groups based primarily in Europe. Papers are occasionally written in French, German, or Spanish but are predominantly in English. Many articles focus on research concerning hydrothermal interactions related to clay weathering and diagenesis. Analytical techniques and their use in the determination of structure and physical properties of clay minerals are also emphasized. The society's web site offers full-text articles for subscribers from 1998 to present as well as a cumulative index for 1948–1997. Abstracts from mid-1975 onward and full text from mid-1996 forward are available online to subscribers of GeoScience World.

1748. Clays and Clay Minerals. Formerly: *Clay Minerals Society. Annual Proceedings.* [ISSN: 0009-8604] 1968. bi-m. USD 275 print & online eds. Ed(s): Derek C Bain, Kevin Murphy. The Clay Minerals Society, PO Box 460130, Aurora, CO 80046; cms@clays.org; http://www.clays.org. Illus., index, adv. Refereed. Circ: 1400. Vol. ends: Dec (No. 6). Online: EBSCO Publishing, EBSCO Host; Gale; HighWire Press; IngentaConnect. Reprint: PSC. *Indexed:* C&ISA, CABA, CerAb, ChemAb, EngInd, ExcerpMed, ForAb, IAA, MinerAb, PetrolAb, S&F, SCI, SWRA. *Aud.:* Ac, Sa.

This journal serves as the official publication of the Clay Minerals Society and was originally issued as an annual proceedings volume. Clays are important because of their unusual chemical and physical properties, and this journal focuses on all aspects of clay science. The publisher's web site offers free tables of contents and abstracts from 1956 forward, with full text available to subscribers for the same period. GeoScience World offers free tables of contents and abstracts beginning with 1975, and subscribers may view full text from 2000 forward. Coverage is similar to that of *Clay Minerals* but with a greater emphasis on interdisciplinary applications. Together, the two journals provide very thorough coverage of the field. A GeoRef priority journal.

1749. The Compass (Norman): an honorary scientific society magazine devoted to the earth sciences. Formerly: *Compass of Sigma Gamma Epsilon.* [ISSN: 0894-802X] 1920. q. Ed(s): R Nowell Donovan. Society of Sigma Gamma Epsilon, c/o Charles J Mankin, University of Oklahoma, Norman, OK 73019; bbellis-sge@ou.edu. Illus., index. Sample. Refereed. Circ: 1800. *Indexed:* PetrolAb. *Aud.:* Ac.

Sigma Gamma Epsilon is an honorary scientific society devoted to the earth sciences. Published since 1920, this quarterly presents society- and chapter-related news and historical information. This small journal also features research articles on a wide range of topics, with many of them written by students presenting their findings. Research papers are refereed and indexed in the major sources. Given the modest price, this title is one that most academic libraries should strongly consider, particularly if they have graduate programs in earth sciences.

1750. Computers & Geosciences. Incorporates: *Geocom Programs.* [ISSN: 0098-3004] 1975. 10x/yr. EUR 2262. Ed(s): Graeme Bonham-Carter. Pergamon, The Boulevard, Langford Ln, East Park, Kidlington, OX5 1GB, United Kingdom. Illus., index, adv. Refereed. Circ: 1100. Vol. ends: Dec (No. 27). Microform: PQC. Online: EBSCO Publishing, EBSCO Host; Gale; IngentaConnect; OhioLINK; ScienceDirect; SwetsWise Online Content. *Indexed:* AS&TI, C&ISA, CABA, CerAb, ChemAb, CompLI, CompR, EngInd, ForAb, HortAb, IAA, ISTA, M&GPA, PetrolAb, PollutAb, S&F, SCI, SSCI, SWRA. *Bk. rev.:* 0-4, 500-2,500 words. *Aud.:* Ac, Sa.

This journal publishes papers on all aspects of scientific computing in the geosciences and often makes data sets and source code available to readers via the Internet. Articles address all types of computational activities in the fields of geology, geochemistry, geophysics, oceanography, hydrology, geography, GIS, and remote sensing. Some example topics are computer algorithms, data structures, numerical methods, simulation models, image analysis, and expert systems. Thorough software reviews appear in most issues. The web site provides free access to tables of contents and abstracts beginning with 1975 issues. Full text from 1995 to the present is available to subscribers on ScienceDirect; articles can also be purchased individually. A GeoRef priority journal.

1751. Contributions to Mineralogy and Petrology. Former titles (until 1965): *Beitraege zur Mineralogie und Petrographie;* (until 1957): *Heidelberger Beitraege zur Mineralogie und Petrographie.* [ISSN: 0010-7999] 1947. m. EUR 3868 print & online eds. Ed(s): J Hoefs, T L Grove. Springer, Tiergartenstr 17, Heidelberg, 69121, Germany. Illus., index, adv. Refereed. Vol. ends: No. 6. Microform: PQC. Online: EBSCO Publishing, EBSCO Host; OhioLINK; Springer LINK; SwetsWise Online Content. Reprint: PSC. *Indexed:* ChemAb, IBR, MinerAb, PetrolAb, SCI. *Aud.:* Ac, Sa.

This journal provides in-depth technical coverage on the petrology and genesis of all major rock types. Heavy emphasis is placed on geochemistry and many of the articles consist of theoretical and experimental work such as determining mineral phase relations and chemical equilibria. Related areas such as isotope geology and element partitioning are also featured. The web site offers free tables of contents and abstracts from 1947 on, with full-text access for subscribers or individual article purchase. A GeoRef priority journal.

1752. Cretaceous Research. [ISSN: 0195-6671] 1980. 6x/yr. EUR 1230. Ed(s): D. J. Batten, Douglas J. Nichols. Academic Press, Harcourt Pl, 32 Jamestown Rd, London, NW1 7BY, United Kingdom; apsubs@acad.com; http://www.elsevier.com/. Illus., index, adv. Sample. Refereed. Vol. ends: Dec (No. 6). Online: EBSCO Publishing, EBSCO Host; Gale; IngentaConnect; OCLC Online Computer Library Center, Inc.; OhioLINK; ScienceDirect; SwetsWise Online Content. *Indexed:* BiolAb, ChemAb, PetrolAb, SCI, ZooRec. *Bk. rev.:* 0-2, 700-1,000 words, signed. *Aud.:* Ac, Sa.

Like *Quaternary Research,* this journal is interdisciplinary and focuses on a single major geological time period. The Cretaceous ended about 65 million years ago, a time best known for the extinction of the dinosaurs. Several of the articles focus on this "K/T boundary," but this is by no means the only subject covered. Stratigraphy and paleontology in particular receive considerable attention. Special topical issues on significant sites or geologic events during the

Cretaceous Period are also featured. The web site provides free access to tables of contents and abstracts beginning with 1980 issues. Full-text articles from 1995 to the present are available to libraries that purchase access through ScienceDirect, or articles may be purchased individually.

1753. *E O S.* Formerly (until 1969): *American Geophysical Union. Transactions.* [ISSN: 0096-3941] 1919. w. USD 465 Free to members. Ed(s): A F Spilhaus, Jr. American Geophysical Union, 2000 Florida Ave, NW, Washington, DC 20009-1277; http://www.agu.org. Illus., index, adv. Sample. Circ: 35000 Paid. Vol. ends: No. 52. *Indexed:* A&ATA, C&ISA, CerAb, EnvAb, HRIS, IAA, M&GPA, PetrolAb, SCI. *Bk. rev.:* 0-2, 100-400 words. *Aud.:* Ac, Sa.

This tabloid-format weekly publishes on items of current interest in geophysics research. Along with the feature articles, there are announcements from the American Geophysical Union, news, book reviews, a calendar of events, and information on grants, fellowships, and employment opportunities. A hardcover volume published annually contains the articles, news, and editorials from the weekly issues. An electronic supplement available at www.agu.org/pubs/eos.html provides deeper coverage of selected items. Recommended for academic and corporate libraries. A GeoRef priority journal.

1754. *Earth and Planetary Science Letters.* [ISSN: 0012-821X] 1966. 48x/yr. EUR 3961. Ed(s): H Elderfield. Elsevier BV, Radarweg 29, Amsterdam, 1043 NX, Netherlands; nlinfo-f@elsevier.nl; http://www.elsevier.nl. Illus., index. Sample. Refereed. Vol. ends: No. 4. Microform: PQC. Online: EBSCO Publishing, EBSCO Host; Gale; IngentaConnect; OhioLINK; ScienceDirect; SwetsWise Online Content. *Indexed:* BrArAb, C&ISA, CerAb, ChemAb, EngInd, ExcerpMed, IAA, M&GPA, MinerAb, OceAb, PetrolAb, PollutAb, SCI, SWRA, ZooRec. *Aud.:* Ac, Sa.

Publishes research in physical, chemical, and mechanical properties of the Earth's crust and mantle, atmosphere, and hydrosphere, as well as papers on lunar studies, plate tectonics, ocean floor spreading, and continental drift. The journal focuses on shorter communications with rapid turnaround. The web site offers free access to tables of contents and article abstracts from 1966 to the present. Background data sets are provided online. Full-text articles from 1995 forward are available to libraries that subscribe via ScienceDirect, or they may be purchased individually. A GeoRef priority journal.

1755. *Earth Surface Processes and Landforms.* Formerly (until Jan. 1981): *Earth Surface Processes.* [ISSN: 0197-9337] 1976. 14x/yr. USD 3500 print or online ed. Ed(s): Michael J Kirkby. John Wiley & Sons Ltd., The Atrium, Southern Gate, Chichester, PO19 8SQ, United Kingdom; customer@wiley.co.uk; http://www.wiley.co.uk. Illus., index, adv. Refereed. Circ: 1050. Vol. ends: Winter (No. 13). Microform: PQC. Online: EBSCO Publishing, EBSCO Host; OhioLINK; SwetsWise Online Content; Wiley InterScience. Reprint: PSC. *Indexed:* C&ISA, CABA, CerAb, ChemAb, EngInd, FPA, FR, ForAb, HortAb, IAA, M&GPA, PollutAb, RRTA, S&F, SCI, SWRA, WAE&RSA. *Bk. rev.:* 0-2, 200-600 words, signed. *Aud.:* Ac, Sa.

This wide-ranging journal publishes on all aspects of earth surface science and geomorphology. This encompasses the complex process of landform evolution by the processes of weathering, erosion, transport, and deposition. Landslides and other natural hazards are also considered. Much of the work is highly interdisciplinary in nature and shows how different chemical, mechanical, and hydrologic factors have interacted to shape the landscape both in the past and in the present. Free tables of contents and abstracts from 1976 forward are provided at the web site, with full-text access for subscribers and the option to purchase articles individually. A GeoRef priority journal.

1756. *Economic Geology and the Bulletin of the Society of Economic Geologists.* Formerly (until 1930): *Economic Geology;* Which superseded in part (in 1906): *American Geologist.* [ISSN: 0361-0128] 1905. 8x/yr. Free to members. Ed(s): Mark D Hannington. Society of Economic Geologists, Inc., 7811 Shaffer Pkwy, Littleton, CO 80127-3732; seg@segweb.org; http://www.segweb.org. Illus., index, adv. Sample.

Refereed. Circ: 5000 Paid. Vol. ends: Dec (No. 8). Microform: PMC; PQC. Online: EBSCO Publishing, EBSCO Host; HighWire Press. *Indexed:* AS&TI, ChemAb, EngInd, IBR, IBZ, MinerAb, PetrolAb, SCI, SWRA. *Bk. rev.:* 0-4, 600-1,000 words. *Aud.:* Ac, Sa.

Articles feature research on theoretical and experimental aspects of economic geology; these are balanced with papers on field research. This bulletin also contains selected tables of contents from journals in related fields and a calendar of relevant events. GeoScience World provides free tables of contents from 1919 forward and full-text articles from 2000 to the present for subscribers. A GeoRef priority journal.

1757. *Elements: an international magazine of mineralogy, geochemistry, and petrology.* Formed by the merger of (1985-2005): *The Lattice;* (1961-2005): *M A C Newsletter; C M S News.* [ISSN: 1811-5209] 2005. q. USD 125 Free to individual members. Ed(s): Pierrette Tremblay. Mineralogical Association of Canada, 490 Rue de la Couronne, Ottawa, ON G1K 9A9, Canada; office@mineralogicalassociation.ca; http://www.mineralogicalassociation.ca. Refereed. *Indexed:* C&ISA, CABA, CerAb, IAA, S&F, SCI, SWRA. *Aud.:* Ac, Sa.

Elements replaces earlier society publications: *The Lattice*, the *MAC Newsletter*, and the *CMS News*. The editors aim to publish applied research studies as a means to forge links among researchers in academic settings and those in industry. Truly international in scope, the editorial advisory board and executive committee represent a wide range of specialties and countries. Each issue features a theme, for example: teaching mineralogy, petrology, and geochemistry; arsenic; water on Mars; and energy, a geoscience perspective. Includes news of society events, short courses, awards, conference reports, and society policy. Members of any of the sponsoring societies and institutional subscribers to the societies' journals receive *Elements* free of charge. Full text available online to subscribers. Affordably priced, this title belongs in academic libraries that support earth science programs and in larger public libraries.

1758. *Engineering Geology.* Incorporates (1983-1991): *Mining Science and Technology.* [ISSN: 0013-7952] 1965. 28x/yr. EUR 1911. Ed(s): R Shiemon, G B Crosta. Elsevier BV, Radarweg 29, Amsterdam, 1043 NX, Netherlands; nlinfo-f@elsevier.nl; http://www.elsevier.nl. Illus., index, adv. Sample. Refereed. Vol. ends: No. 4. Microform: PQC. Online: EBSCO Publishing, EBSCO Host; Gale; IngentaConnect; OhioLINK; ScienceDirect; SwetsWise Online Content. *Indexed:* ApMecR, C&ISA, CerAb, ChemAb, EngInd, ExcerpMed, HRIS, IAA, OceAb, PetrolAb, PollutAb, SCI, SWRA. *Bk. rev.:* 0-2, 500-1,000 words. *Aud.:* Ac, Sa.

This international journal publishes studies relevant to engineering geology and related topics such as environmental concerns and geological hazards. These include research papers, case histories, and reviews. The web site provides free access to tables of contents and abstracts beginning with 1965 issues. Full-text articles are available to libraries that purchase access via ScienceDirect. A GeoRef priority journal.

1759. *Environmental and Engineering Geoscience: serving professionals in engineering, environmental, and ground-water geology.* Former titles (until 1995): *Association of Engineering Geologists. Bulletin;* (until 1968): *Engineering Geology.* [ISSN: 1078-7275] 1963. q. Non-members, USD 175. Ed(s): Normetan R Tilford. Geological Society of America, 3300 Penrose Pl, Boulder, CO 80301-1806; http://www.geosociety.org. Illus., index, adv. Sample. Refereed. Circ: 3500. Vol. ends: Dec (No. 4). *Indexed:* C&ISA, CerAb, ChemAb, ExcerpMed, HRIS, IAA, OceAb, SCI, SWRA. *Bk. rev.:* 0-9, 800-3,000 words. *Aud.:* Ac, Sa.

Publishes research articles and technical papers and notes in areas of interest to hydrologists, environmental scientists, and engineering geologists. Topics include site selection, feasibility studies, design or construction of civil engineering projects, waste management, and ground water. Appropriate for corporate and academic collections. Tables of contents are available on the web from 1995 to the present; abstracts are available from 2002. Full text of articles from 2002 is available to libraries that purchase access via GeoScience World. A GeoRef priority journal.

1760. *Environmental Geology: international journal of geosciences.*
Former titles (until 1993): *Environmental Geology and Water Sciences;*
(until 1984): *Environmental Geology.* [ISSN: 0943-0105] 1975. 16x/yr.
EUR 2368 print & online eds. Ed(s): Gunter Doerhoefer. Springer,
Tiergartenstr 17, Heidelberg, 69121, Germany. Illus., index, adv. Sample.
Refereed. Microform: PQC. Online: EBSCO Publishing, EBSCO Host;
OhioLINK; Springer LINK; SwetsWise Online Content. Reprint: PSC.
Indexed: AS&TI, Agr, BiolAb, CABA, ChemAb, EngInd, EnvAb,
EnvInd, ExcerpMed, FPA, ForAb, HRIS, HortAb, M&GPA, MinerAb,
OceAb, PetrolAb, PollutAb, RRTA, S&F, SCI, SSCI, SWRA,
WAE&RSA. *Bk. rev.:* 2-7, 300-1,800 words, signed. *Aud.:* Ac, Sa.

The application of geological principles and data to environmental issues has
become an increasingly important area of emphasis. This international journal
includes both research articles and applied technical reports on specific cases
and solutions. Much of the work is multidisciplinary in nature and covers such
areas as soil and water contamination, radioactive waste disposal, remediation
techniques, and the effects of mining and industrial activities. Special topical
issues often focus in greater detail on one of these specific subject areas. The
web site offers tables of contents and abstracts from 1975 to the present, with
full-text access available for subscribers or individual purchase. A GeoRef
priority journal.

1761. *Episodes: journal of international geoscience.* Supersedes: *Interna-
tional Union of Geological Sciences. Geological Newsletter.* [ISSN:
0705-3797] 1978. q. USD 24. Ed(s): Hongren Zhang. International
Union of Geological Sciences, 26 Baiwanzhuang Road, PO Box 82,
Beijing, 100037, China. Illus., index, adv. Sample. Refereed. Circ: 3000.
Vol. ends: Dec (No. 4). *Indexed:* CABA, ChemAb, ExcerpMed,
M&GPA, PetrolAb, RRTA, S&F, SCI, SWRA, WAE&RSA. *Bk. rev.:* 0-4,
500-1,500 words. *Aud.:* Ga, Ac, Sa.

Articles generally have more international orientation than those in *Geotimes,*
and cover developments of regional and global importance in earth science
research programs and techniques, organizations, and science policy. The
International Union of Geological Sciences is a large nongovernmental
scientific organization that facilitates international and interdisciplinary
cooperation in the earth sciences, promoting and supporting study of geological
problems of world-wide significance. Each issue of *Episodes* includes a
calendar of future international geoscience events and training opportunities,
and many issues include brief reports from international conferences and
meetings. Tables of contents and abstracts are accessible for issues from 1997
to the present at the IUGS web site.

1762. *European Journal of Mineralogy.* Formed by the merger of
(1950-1988): *Fortschritte der Mineralogie;* (1968-1988): *Rendiconti
della Societa Italiana di Mineralogia e Petrologia;* (1878-1988): *Bulletin
de Mineralogia;* Which was formerly (until 1978): *Societe Francaise de
Mineralogie et de Cristallographie. Bulletin;* (until 1949): *Societe
Francaise de Mineralogie. Bulletin;* (until 1886): *Societe Mineralogique
de France. Bulletin.* [ISSN: 0935-1221] 1988. 6x/yr. USD 487. Ed(s):
Christian Chopin. E. Schweizerbart'sche Verlagsbuchhandlung,
Johannesstr 3A, Stuttgart, 70176, Germany; mail@schweizerbart.de;
http://www.schweizerbart.de. Illus., index, adv. Sample. Refereed. Vol.
ends: Nov/Dec (No. 6). *Indexed:* C&ISA, CerAb, ChemAb, ExcerpMed,
IAA, IBR, MinerAb, SCI. *Aud.:* Ac, Sa.

The result of a cooperative publication effort among several European
mineralogical societies, this journal replaced their individual journals when it
began publication in 1989. Contributions are primarily in English but articles in
French, German, and Italian are also accepted. Papers are international in scope,
with an emphasis on European localities. They cover a wide range of topics in
mineralogy, petrology, and crystallography. Occasional thematic issues have
included such topics as gemstones, experimental mineralogy, fluid interactions,
and mineral surface reactivity. Free tables of contents from 1989 forward are
available, along with full text for subscribers on Geoscience World. A GeoRef
priority journal.

1763. *Exploration & Mining Geology: journal of the Geological Society
of C I M.* [ISSN: 0964-1823] 1992. q. CND 325 (Members, CND 35
CIM; Non-members, CND 140). Canadian Institute of Metallurgy, 3400

de Maisonneuve Blvd, W, Ste 1210, Montreal, PQ H3Z 3B8, Canada;
cim@cim.org; http://www.cim.org/. Illus., index. Refereed. Microform:
PQC. Online: HighWire Press; OhioLINK. *Indexed:* ChemAb, MinerAb.
Aud.: Ac, Sa.

Published for the Geological Society of the Canadian Institute of Mining,
Metallurgy, and Petroleum (CIM), this journal presents papers on mineral
deposits, mining geology, and ore reserves from around the world. Although
nearly all papers are published in English, a few are in French. Abstracts of the
annual CIM meeting are also included. Appropriate for specialized academic
and corporate research collections. GeoScience World provides tables of
contents from 1992 forward, with full text for subscribers from 2000 to the
present.

1764. *G3: Geochemistry, Geophysics, Geosystems: an electronic journal
of the earth sciences.* [ISSN: 1525-2027] 1999. m. Members, USD 66.
Ed(s): Williams White, Laurent D. Labeyrie. American Geophysical
Union, 2000 Florida Ave, NW, Washington, DC 20009-1277;
http://www.agu.org. *Indexed:* SCI. *Aud.:* Ac, Sa.

Sponsored by the American Geophysical Union and the Geochemical Society,
this electronic-only journal publishes original research, reviews, and technical
briefs in geophysics and geochemistry. The focus is on interdisciplinary work
pertaining to understanding the earth as a system, and contributions span a wide
range of topics. Many submissions include material such as large data sets,
sound clips, or movies that could not be included in a print journal. Some
articles are organized into "themes" much like special issues of more traditional
journals. Access to abstracts is available free from the web site, but full-text
articles are accessible only to subscribers or for a fee. A GeoRef priority journal.

1765. *Geo-Marine Letters: an international journal of marine geology.*
[ISSN: 0276-0460] 1980. bi-m. EUR 933 print & online eds. Ed(s): Burg
W Flemming. Springer, Tiergartenstr 17, Heidelberg, 69121, Germany.
Illus., index, adv. Sample. Refereed. Vol. ends: No. 4. Microform: PQC.
Online: EBSCO Publishing, EBSCO Host; OhioLINK; ProQuest LLC
(Ann Arbor); Springer LINK; SwetsWise Online Content. Reprint: PSC.
Indexed: ChemAb, EngInd, IBR, OceAb, PetrolAb, PollutAb, SCI,
SWRA. *Bk. rev.:* 0-3, 700-1,200 words, signed. *Aud.:* Ac, Sa.

Newer analytical techniques and equipment have finally opened up the vast
areas of the earth under the oceans to intensive study. *Geo-Marine Letters*
publishes studies and reviews "dealing with processes, products, and techniques
in marine geology, geophysics, and geochemistry." Major topics of coverage
include depositional environments, sedimentary processes, stratigraphy, and
post-depositional movement. Other areas of emphasis include marine
geochemistry and geophysics. Recent topical issues highlight such subjects as
continent-ocean margins, turbidite deposits, and deep-sea sedimentation. The
web site offers free tables of contents and abstracts from 1981 to the present,
with full-text access available for subscribers or individual purchase.

1766. *Geochemical Transactions.* [ISSN: 1467-4866] 2000. q. Free. Ed(s):
Scott Wood. BioMed Central Ltd., Middlesex House, 34-42 Cleveland
St, London, W1T 4LB, United Kingdom; info@biomedcentral.com;
http://www.biomedcentral.com. Refereed. *Indexed:* CPI, M&GPA, SCI,
SWRA, WRCInf. *Aud.:* Ac, Sa.

The official journal of the Geochemistry Division of the American Chemical
Society, this open-access electronic journal is freely available online and ranks
highly among titles in geochemistry and geophysics disciplines. A vehicle for
rapid publication, *Geochemical Transactions* publishes peer-reviewed articles
on topics in chemistry related to terrestrial and extraterrestrial systems such as
organic geochemistry, inorganic geochemistry, marine and aquatic chemistry,
chemical oceanography, biogeochemistry, applied geochemistry, astrobiology,
and environmental geochemistry. Readers may create an account to save
searches on the journal web site and comment on articles in the journal's
discussion area. RSS feeds and e-mail alerts are available. An important
electronic journal for academic libraries that support earth science research and
teaching.

1767. *Geochemistry: Exploration, Environment, Analysis.* [ISSN:
1467-7873] 2001. q. GBP 167 in Europe; USD 321 United States; GBP
190 elsewhere. Ed(s): Gwendy Hall, Diana Swan. Geological Society

Publishing House, Unit 7, Brassmill Enterprise Centre, Brassmill Ln, Bath, BA1 3JN, United Kingdom; rebecca.toop@geolsoc.org.uk; http://www.geolsoc.org.uk. Illus. Sample. Refereed. Circ: 1000 Paid. *Indexed:* SCI, SWRA. *Aud.:* Ac, Sa.

This quarterly is produced by the Geological Society of London and the Association of Applied Geochemists. It covers the application of geochemistry to the exploration and study of mineral resources. Some topics include geochemical exploration, sampling and analytical techniques, and dispersion processes in and around mineralized deposits. Recommended for academic and special libraries. Full text for subscribers is available on GeoScience World along with free abstracts going back to volume one.

1768. Geochemistry International. Formerly (until 1963): *Geochemistry.* [ISSN: 0016-7029] 1956. m. EUR 3535 print & online eds. Ed(s): Igor' D Ryabchikov. M A I K Nauka - Interperiodica, Profsoyuznaya ul 90, Moscow, 117997, Russian Federation; compmg@maik.ru; http://www.maik.ru. Illus., index, adv. Refereed. Circ: 675. Vol. ends: Dec (No. 12). Microform: PQC. Online: Springer LINK; SwetsWise Online Content. *Indexed:* EngInd, ExcerpMed, MinerAb, OceAb, PetrolAb, PollutAb, SCI, SWRA. *Aud.:* Ac, Sa.

The American Geophysical Union and the American Geological Institute together with the Russian Academy of Sciences sponsor publication of this journal. Articles are translated from the Russian journal *Geokhimiya.* Concentrating on the geology of the Eurasian continent, research papers in the journal address theoretical and applied topics such as cosmochemistry; geochemistry of magmatic, metamorphic, hydrothermal, and sedimentary processes; organic geochemistry; and chemistry of the environment. Occasional reports appear from symposia and international meetings. The publisher's web site provides tables of contents and article abstracts beginning with 1996 issues. Full-text is available to subscribers through SpringerLink beginning with 2006. Appropriate for comprehensive collections.

1769. Geochimica et Cosmochimica Acta. [ISSN: 0016-7037] 1950. 24x/yr. EUR 2751. Ed(s): F A Podosek, L Trower. Pergamon, The Boulevard, Langford Ln, East Park, Kidlington, OX5 1GB, United Kingdom. Illus., index, adv. Sample. Refereed. Circ: 3800. Vol. ends: No. 24. Microform: PQC. Online: EBSCO Publishing, EBSCO Host; Gale; IngentaConnect; OhioLINK; ScienceDirect; SwetsWise Online Content. *Indexed:* C&ISA, CerAb, ChemAb, ExcerpMed, ForAb, IAA, IBR, M&GPA, MinerAb, OceAb, PetrolAb, PollutAb, S&F, SCI, SWRA, WRCInf. *Aud.:* Ac, Sa.

Publishes research papers in the areas of terrestrial geochemistry, meteoritics, and planetary geochemistry. Topics include chemical processes in Earth's atmosphere, hydrosphere, biosphere, and lithosphere; organic and isotope geochemistry; and lunar science. The web site provides free access to tables of contents and abstracts beginning with 1950 issues. Full-text articles from 1995 to the present are available to libraries that purchase access via ScienceDirect. Appropriate for academic and corporate research collections. A GeoRef priority journal.

1770. Geofluids. [ISSN: 1468-8115] 2001. q. GBP 378 print & online eds. Ed(s): John Parnell, Grant Garven. Blackwell Publishing Ltd., 9600 Garsington Rd, Oxford, OX4 2ZG, United Kingdom; customerservices@ blackwellpublishing.com; http://www.blackwellpublishing.com. Adv. Reprint: PSC. *Indexed:* CABA, S&F, SCI. *Aud.:* Ac, Sa.

Geofluids emphasizes the chemical, mineralogical, and physical aspects of subsurface fluids in the earth's crust. Some areas of focus include composition and origin of fluids, groundwater flow regimes, rock fracturing and structural controls on fluid migration, and the geochemistry of dissolution, transport, and precipitation. Free tables of contents and abstracts can be found on the web site along with full text for subscribers from the first volume forward.

1771. Geological Journal. Formerly (until 1964): *Liverpool and Manchester Geological Journal.* [ISSN: 0072-1050] 1966. 5x/yr. USD 1464 print or online ed. Ed(s): Ian D. Somerville. John Wiley & Sons Ltd., The Atrium, Southern Gate, Chichester, PO19 8SQ, United

Kingdom; customer@wiley.co.uk; http://www.wiley.co.uk. Illus., index, adv. Refereed. Circ: 700. *Indexed:* ChemAb, EnvAb, EnvInd, IBR, MinerAb, PetrolAb, PollutAb, SCI, SWRA, ZooRec. *Bk. rev.:* 0-7, 500-2,000 words. *Aud.:* Ac, Sa.

This journal provides broad coverage of geology with an emphasis on interdisciplinary work and regional case studies. The United Kingdom and other areas of Europe receive the most attention, although studies from around the world are included. This title is a good complement to others of a general nature such as *Geology* or *Geological Magazine* and is appropriate for comprehensive collections. Free tables of contents and abstracts from 1996 to the present are provided on the web site, along with full-text access for subscribers or those who pay to download individual articles.

1772. Geological Magazine. Formerly (until 1864): *Geologist.* [ISSN: 0016-7568] 1842. bi-m. GBP 430. Ed(s): M B Allen, I. N. McCave. Cambridge University Press, The Edinburgh Bldg, Shaftesbury Rd, Cambridge, CB2 2RU, United Kingdom; journals@cambridge.org; http://www.journals.cambridge.org. Illus., index, adv. Sample. Refereed. Vol. ends: Nov (No. 6). Microform: BHP. Online: Pub.; EBSCO Publishing, EBSCO Host; HighWire Press; OCLC Online Computer Library Center, Inc.; OhioLINK; SwetsWise Online Content. Reprint: PSC. *Indexed:* ChemAb, ForAb, GSI, IBR, MASUSE, MinerAb, PetrolAb, PollutAb, SCI, SWRA, ZooRec. *Bk. rev.:* 5-12, 100-500 words. *Aud.:* Ac, Sa.

A strong general journal in the field, this title publishes research and review articles in all areas of earth sciences and emphasizes interdisciplinary papers of interest to geologists from several specialties. Each issue also features several signed book reviews. The publisher's web site offers free tables of contents and abstracts along with full text for subscribers from 1997 forward. Full text is also available on GeoScience World from 2000 forward. A GeoRef priority journal.

1773. Geological Society. Journal. Former titles (until 1971): *Geological Society of London. Quarterly Journal;* (until 1845): *Geological Society of London. Proceedings.* [ISSN: 0016-7649] 1826. bi-m. GBP 602 domestic; GBP 687 foreign; USD 1322 foreign. Ed(s): Rob Strachan. Geological Society Publishing House, Unit 7, Brassmill Enterprise Centre, Brassmill Ln, Bath, BA1 3JN, United Kingdom; rebecca.toop@ geolsoc.org.uk; http://www.geolsoc.org.uk. Illus., index, adv. Refereed. Circ: 5200. Vol. ends: Nov (No. 6). *Indexed:* BrArAb, ChemAb, MinerAb, PetrolAb, SCI, ZooRec. *Aud.:* Ac, Sa.

This is the flagship journal of the Geological Society of London, one of the oldest geological societies in the world. It is international in scope, with papers covering the full range of the earth sciences. These include both full-length research articles and shorter, rapid-publication "specials." The editors also often publish thematic sets of papers as all or part of an issue. Top-quality throughout and heavily cited, this journal is highly recommended for academic and special library collections. Full-text access is available as part of the GeoScience World collection, with full text from 1971 forward. Archival coverage back to 1845 is available as part of the Lyell collection. A GeoRef priority journal.

1774. Geological Society of America. Bulletin. Formerly (until 1961): *Bulletin of the Geological Society of America.* [ISSN: 0016-7606] 1890. m. USD 560 domestic; USD 575 foreign; USD 710 combined subscription domestic print & online ed. Geological Society of America, 3300 Penrose Pl, Boulder, CO 80301-1806; pubs@geosociety.org; http://www.geosociety.org. Illus., adv. Sample. Refereed. Circ: 7500. Vol. ends: Dec (No. 12). Microform: PMC; PQC. Online: Allen Press Inc.; EBSCO Publishing, EBSCO Host; HighWire Press. *Indexed:* AS&TI, C&ISA, CerAb, ChemAb, EngInd, EnvInd, GSI, HRIS, IAA, M&GPA, MinerAb, OceAb, PetrolAb, S&F, SCI, SWRA, ZooRec. *Aud.:* Ac, Sa.

This journal is the more research-oriented periodical published by the Geological Society of America (GSA) and contains longer articles than *Geology.* Although coverage of international projects is included, work in North America is emphasized. Large-format inserts (usually maps) appear in some issues. The GSA web site provides tables of contents and article abstracts beginning in 1945, with full-text access for subscribers or individual purchase. Also included is a free data repository of supplementary files for selected articles. Full text is available on GeoScience World from 1988 forward. Strongly recommended for academic and corporate collections. A GeoRef priority journal.

1775. Geology (Boulder). [ISSN: 0091-7613] 1973. m. Non-members, USD 560. Geological Society of America, 3300 Penrose Pl, Boulder, CO 80301-1806; pubs@geosociety.org; http://www.geosociety.org. Illus., adv. Sample. Refereed. Circ: 9500. Vol. ends: Dec (No. 12). Microform: PQC. Online: Allen Press Inc.; EBSCO Publishing, EBSCO Host; HighWire Press. *Indexed:* A&ATA, AS&TI, ChemAb, EngInd, ExcerpMed, GSI, IAA, M&GPA, OceAb, PetrolAb, PollutAb, SCI, SWRA, ZooRec. *Aud.:* Ac, Sa.

This title publishes short, thought-provoking articles (about 20 per issue) on a wide range of geological topics of interest to a broad audience. *Geology* is oriented more toward new investigations and recent discoveries in the field than *Geological Society of America Bulletin*. A new "Research Focus" feature highlights additional information on research issues related to selected articles. Abstracts are accessible on the GSA web site from 1973 to the present, with full-text access for subscribers or for purchase. Full text is also available on GeoScience World from 1988 forward. Strongly recommended for academic and corporate collections. A GeoRef priority journal.

1776. Geology Today. [ISSN: 0266-6979] 1985. bi-m. GBP 425 print & online eds. Ed(s): Peter Doyle. Blackwell Publishing Ltd., 9600 Garsington Rd, Oxford, OX4 2ZG, United Kingdom; customerservices@blackwellpublishing.com; http://www.blackwellpublishing.com. Illus., index, adv. Sample. Refereed. Circ: 2550. Microform: PQC. Online: Blackwell Synergy; EBSCO Publishing, EBSCO Host; Gale; IngentaConnect; OCLC Online Computer Library Center, Inc.; OhioLINK; SwetsWise Online Content. Reprint: PSC. *Indexed:* GSI, MASUSE, ZooRec. *Bk. rev.:* 0-10, 200-500 words. *Aud.:* Ga, Ac.

Published on behalf of the Geologists' Association and the Geological Society of London, this journal is similar in many respects to *Geotimes*. News and current awareness briefings are provided and supplemented by short feature articles. The latter often gravitate toward popular topics but are generally well written and illustrated. Free tables of contents with abstracts can be found on the web site beginning with 1996. Full-text access is available for subscribers and articles are also available for individual purchase. A GeoRef priority journal.

1777. Geomorphology. [ISSN: 0169-555X] 1987. 40x/yr. EUR 2124. Ed(s): R. A. Marston. Elsevier BV, Radarweg 29, Amsterdam, 1043 NX, Netherlands; nlinfo-f@elsevier.nl; http://www.elsevier.nl. Illus., adv. Sample. Refereed. Microform: PQC. Online: EBSCO Publishing, EBSCO Host; Gale; IngentaConnect; OhioLINK; ScienceDirect; SwetsWise Online Content. *Indexed:* FR, ForAb, M&GPA, OceAb, S&F, SCI, SWRA. *Bk. rev.:* 0-3, 500-1,000 words. *Aud.:* Ac, Sa.

Publishes research papers, review articles, and book reviews on landform studies of all types and scales, including extraterrestrial settings. Special issues present papers on such topics as landscape processes, ice sheet geomorphology, and sediment budgets. The web site provides free access to tables of contents and abstracts beginning with 1987 issues and including articles in press. Full text access is available to subscribers from 1995 forward through ScienceDirect. Appropriate for academic collections.

1778. Geophysical Journal International. Formerly (until 1989): *Geophysical Journal;* Which was formed by the 1987 merger of part of: *Annales Geophysicae. Series B: Terrestrial and Planetary Physics; Royal Astronomical Society Geophysical Journal;* Which was formerly (until 1958): *Royal Astronomical Society. Monthly Notices. Geophysical Supplement.* [ISSN: 0956-540X] 1958. m. GBP 1183 print & online eds. Ed(s): C J Ebinger. Blackwell Publishing Ltd., 9600 Garsington Rd, Oxford, OX4 2ZG, United Kingdom; customerservices@blackwellpublishing.com; http://www.blackwellpublishing.com. Illus., adv. Refereed. Circ: 1585. Microform: PQC. Online: Blackwell Synergy; EBSCO Publishing, EBSCO Host; Gale; IngentaConnect; OCLC Online Computer Library Center, Inc.; OhioLINK; SwetsWise Online Content. Reprint: PSC. *Indexed:* C&ISA, CerAb, ChemAb, IAA, M&GPA, MSN, PetrolAb, SCI. *Bk. rev.:* 0-2, 700-1,500 words, signed. *Aud.:* Ac, Sa.

Formed by a merger of three journals, this title continues the numbering of the *Geophysical Journal of the Royal Astronomical Society.* It endeavors to "promote the understanding of the earth's internal structure, physical properties, evolution, and processes." Subject areas covered include seismology, crustal structure, geomagnetism, and rock rheology. Tables of contents can be found on the web site beginning with 1922. Full-text access is available for subscribers, and articles are available for individual purchase. A GeoRef priority journal.

1779. Geophysical Prospecting. [ISSN: 0016-8025] 1953. bi-m. GBP 660 print & online eds. Ed(s): R E White. Blackwell Publishing Ltd., 9600 Garsington Rd, Oxford, OX4 2ZG, United Kingdom; customerservices@blackwellpublishing.com; http://www.blackwellpublishing.com. Illus., adv. Refereed. Circ: 4750. Microform: PQC. Online: Blackwell Synergy; EBSCO Publishing, EBSCO Host; Gale; IngentaConnect; OCLC Online Computer Library Center, Inc.; OhioLINK; SwetsWise Online Content. Reprint: PSC. *Indexed:* C&ISA, CABA, ChemAb, EngInd, PetrolAb, S&F, SCI. *Aud.:* Ac, Sa.

Published on behalf of the European Association for Geoscientists and Engineers, *Geophysical Prospecting* covers research on geophysics as applied to exploration. Many articles report on work in the oil and mineral industries and have a practical emphasis. However, the journal is also appropriate for academic researchers in geophysics. Free tables of content from 1953 to the present are available at the web site, along with full-text access for subscribers or for individual article purchase.

1780. Geophysical Research Letters. [ISSN: 0094-8276] 1974. s-m. USD 2100. Ed(s): James S. Famiglietti. American Geophysical Union, 2000 Florida Ave, NW, Washington, DC 20009-1277; http://www.agu.org. Illus., index. Sample. Refereed. Vol. ends: Dec. Online: EBSCO Publishing, EBSCO Host. *Indexed:* C&ISA, CABA, CerAb, ChemAb, EngInd, ExcerpMed, FPA, ForAb, IAA, M&GPA, MinerAb, OceAb, PetrolAb, PollutAb, S&F, SCI, SWRA, WAE&RSA. *Aud.:* Ac, Sa.

Aimed at scientists in diverse disciplines related to geophysics, issues contain topics such as atmospheric science, oceans, and climate; solid earth and planets; and hydrology and climate. Manuscripts are of limited length in order to expedite review and publication. Special sections address hot topics of broad interest to the geophysics research community. Tables of contents and abstracts are available back to 1974 on the American Geophysical Union web site. Full-text articles from 1994 to the present are available for library subscribers, with earlier ones available for individual purchase. A GeoRef priority journal.

1781. Geophysics. [ISSN: 0016-8033] 1936. bi-m. USD 500 print & online eds. Ed(s): Yonghe Sun. Society of Exploration Geophysicists, PO Box 702740, Tulsa, OK 74170-2740; books@seg.org; http://www.seg.org. Illus., index, adv. Refereed. Circ: 3500 Paid. Vol. ends: Nov/Dec (No. 6). Microform: PQC. Online: American Institute of Physics, Scitation; EBSCO Publishing, EBSCO Host. *Indexed:* AS&TI, ApMecR, C&ISA, ChemAb, EngInd, PetrolAb, PollutAb, SCI, SWRA, WRCInf. *Aud.:* Ac, Sa.

Published by the Society of Exploration Geophysicists, this is one of the leading journals in the field. Many of the articles focus on seismic data acquisition, processing, and interpretation. Other areas such as mechanical properties of rock, borehole geophysics, and remote sensing are also covered. Extensive use is made of color figures and illustrations. Access to tables of contents and article abstracts from 1936 to the present are free at the web site. Full-text articles are available to subscribers. Highly recommended. A GeoRef priority journal.

1782. Geoscience Canada. Formerly (until 1974): *Geological Association of Canada. Proceedings.* [ISSN: 0315-0941] 1948. q. USD 110; CND 117.70. Ed(s): G Nowlan. Geological Association of Canada, c/o Dept. of Earth Sciences, Memorial Univ. of Newfoundland, St. John's, NF A1B 3X5, Canada; http://www.gac.ca. Illus., adv. Sample. Refereed. Circ: 3300. Vol. ends: Dec (No. 4). Microform: PQC. Online: Gale. *Indexed:* CABA, CPerI, EngInd, HortAb, PetrolAb, S&F, SCI, SWRA. *Bk. rev.:* 1-7, 400-1,200 words, signed. *Aud.:* Ac, Sa.

This engaging quarterly is the main journal of the Geological Association of Canada and is geared toward the nonspecialist. Many of the papers deal with historical and policy issues related to the geology of Canada. Others address topics of broader interest, such as sedimentation processes, glacial geology, geothermal energy, and plate tectonics. For many years, this journal has published an excellent series on mineral deposit models; other series feature such topics as environmental marine geoscience, igneous rock associations, and even geology and wine.

1783. *Geosphere.* [ISSN: 1553-040X] 2005. bi-m. Free. Ed(s): Matt Hudson. Geological Society of America, 3300 Penrose Pl, Boulder, CO 80301-1806; pubs@geosociety.org; http://www.geosociety.org. *Indexed:* S&F, SCI. *Aud.:* Ac, Sa.

Casting a broad net, *Geosphere* publishes research articles in all fields of earth and geosciences, especially papers that take advantage of the online format to include multimedia files, vivid color illustrations, and links to supplementary data. Themes in recent issues include modeling flow and transport, geoinformatics, and Great Basic tectonics and metallogeny. All article abstracts and most articles from all but the latest volume are freely available online; only a selected feature article from the latest issue is free. Subscribers may view full text of all articles. Readers may purchase individual articles and set up an e-mail alert to receive notification when new issues are published.

1784. *Geothermics.* [ISSN: 0375-6505] 1972. 6x/yr. EUR 1249. Ed(s): M J Lippmann. Pergamon, The Boulevard, Langford Ln, East Park, Kidlington, OX5 1GB, United Kingdom. Illus., index, adv. Sample. Refereed. Circ: 1075. Vol. ends: Dec. Microform: PQC. Online: EBSCO Publishing, EBSCO Host; Gale; IngentaConnect; OhioLINK; ScienceDirect; SwetsWise Online Content. *Indexed:* C&ISA, CABA, CerAb, ChemAb, EngInd, EnvAb, EnvInd, ForAb, HortAb, IAA, PetrolAb, PollutAb, S&F, SCI, SWRA, WAE&RSA. *Bk. rev.:* 0-2, 400 words. *Aud.:* Ac, Sa.

This journal publishes articles on theory, exploration methods, and all aspects of the use of geothermal resources. Occasional special issues concentrate on one region of the world or a particular technique or application. Each issue also includes a calendar of meetings in the discipline. The web site provides free access to tables of contents and abstracts beginning with 1972. Full text of all content is available to libraries that purchase access through ScienceDirect, or articles can be purchased individually. Appropriate for academic and specialized collections.

1785. *Geotimes: earth, energy and environment news.* [ISSN: 0016-8556] 1956. m. USD 85 (Individuals, USD 42.95; Members, USD 24.95). Ed(s): Anne Bolen. American Geological Institute, 4220 King St, Alexandria, VA 22302-1502; agi@agiweb.org; http://www.agiweb.org/pubs. Illus., index, adv. Sample. Circ: 15000. Vol. ends: Dec (No. 12). Microform: PQC. *Indexed:* BiolDig, C&ISA, CerAb, GSI, IAA, OceAb, PetrolAb, SCI, SSCI, SWRA. *Bk. rev.:* 1-3, 500-1,000 words. *Aud.:* Ga, Ac, Sa.

This monthly magazine provides reports on geoscience research and education, recent geological phenomena, political developments, technological advances, and other news. Articles are aimed at both geologists and the general public. Books, maps, audiovisual material, and software are reviewed. Issues include classified ads and a calendar of events, and these along with news items are accessible at the web site. Strongly recommended for academic and corporate collections.

1786. *Ground Water.* [ISSN: 0017-467X] 1963. bi-m. GBP 279 print & online eds. Ed(s): Mary P Anderson. Blackwell Publishing, Inc., Commerce Place, 350 Main St, Malden, MA 02148; customerservices@blackwellpublishing.com; http://www.blackwellpublishing.com. Illus., index, adv. Refereed. Circ: 11000. Vol. ends: Nov/Dec (No. 6). Microform: PQC. Online: Blackwell Synergy; EBSCO Publishing, EBSCO Host; Florida Center for Library Automation; Gale; IngentaConnect; Northern Light Technology, Inc.; OCLC Online Computer Library Center, Inc.; ProQuest K-12 Learning Solutions; ProQuest LLC (Ann Arbor); SwetsWise Online Content. Reprint: PSC. *Indexed:* AS&TI, Agr, C&ISA, CABA, CerAb, ChemAb, EngInd, EnvAb, EnvInd, ExcerpMed, ForAb, HortAb, IAA, PetrolAb, PollutAb, S&F, SCI, SWRA, WAE&RSA, WRCInf. *Bk. rev.:* 0-5, 300-800 words, signed. *Aud.:* Ac, Sa.

This is an official journal of the Association of Ground Water Scientists and Engineers, a division of the National Ground Water Association. Emphasis is on modeling of ground water hydrology in aquifers and other geologic environments. Chemical interactions and solution transport are also given considerable attention. Monitoring and remediation techniques, however, are largely dealt with in its sister publication, *Ground Water Monitoring and Remediation.* Tables of contents are available on the web site from 1963 forward, with full text available through Blackwell's Synergy. A GeoRef priority journal.

1787. *Hydrogeology Journal.* Formerly: *Applied Hydrogeology.* [ISSN: 1431-2174] 1992. bi-m. EUR 826 print & online eds. Ed(s): Clifford Voss. Springer, Tiergartenstr 17, Heidelberg, 69121, Germany. Illus., index, adv. Sample. Refereed. Vol. ends: No. 6. Online: EBSCO Publishing, EBSCO Host; OhioLINK; Springer LINK; SwetsWise Online Content. Reprint: PSC. *Indexed:* C&ISA, CerAb, IAA, PollutAb, SCI, SWRA. *Aud.:* Ac, Sa.

This journal addresses an increasingly important area of interest in the earth sciences. *Hydrogeology Journal* is the official journal of the International Association of Hydrogeologists and publishes theoretical and research-oriented papers as well as applied reports. The first issue of each year is a thematic one. Recent topics include social and economic aspects of groundwater governance, remote sensing and GIS in hydrogeology, and the future of hydrogeology. The web site offers full-text access from the start of publication for subscribers, along with a free table of contents and abstracts.

1788. *Hydrological Processes: an international journal.* [ISSN: 0885-6087] 1987. 26x/yr. USD 4233 print or online ed. Ed(s): M G Anderson. John Wiley & Sons Ltd., The Atrium, Southern Gate, Chichester, PO19 8SQ, United Kingdom; customer@wiley.co.uk; http://www.wiley.co.uk. Illus., adv. Refereed. Circ: 600. Microform: PQC. Online: EBSCO Publishing, EBSCO Host; OhioLINK; SwetsWise Online Content; Wiley InterScience. Reprint: PSC. *Indexed:* C&ISA, CABA, CerAb, DSA, EngInd, EnvAb, EnvInd, FPA, ForAb, HortAb, IAA, M&GPA, PollutAb, RRTA, S&F, SCI, SWRA, WAE&RSA. *Bk. rev.:* 0-1, 500-1,000 words. *Aud.:* Ac, Sa.

This international journal publishes original scientific and technical papers in hydrology. Articles present research on physical, biogeochemical, mathematical, and methodological aspects of hydrological processes as well as reports on instrumentation and techniques. Occasional special issues address such topics as "Hydrology in the urban environment" and "Land use and climate impacts on fluvial systems." The journal includes a rapid-communications section called *HPToday* that provides invited commentaries, letters to the editor, refereed scientific briefings, current awareness, book reviews, lists and reviews of web sites and software, and conference listings. Full-text articles are available online to subscribers or on a pay-per-view basis.

1789. *Hydrological Sciences Journal.* Former titles (until 1981): *Hydrological Sciences Bulletin;* (until 1971): *International Association of Scientific Hydrology. Bulletin.* [ISSN: 0262-6667] 1956. bi-m. GBP 180 domestic; USD 300 foreign. Ed(s): Zbigniew Kundzewicz. I A H S Press, Centre for Ecology and Hydrology, Wallingford, OX10 8BB, United Kingdom; frances@iahs.demon.co.uk; http://iahs.info. Illus., index. Sample. Refereed. Circ: 700. Vol. ends: Dec (No. 6). *Indexed:* C&ISA, CABA, ChemAb, EngInd, EnvAb, ExcerpMed, ForAb, IBR, IBZ, M&GPA, PollutAb, RRTA, S&F, SCI, SWRA, WAE&RSA, WRCInf. *Bk. rev.:* Number and length vary. *Aud.:* Ac, Sa.

Issued by the International Association of Hydrological Sciences, this journal publishes scientific papers that are primarily written in English but also include some in French. The range of topics covered is quite broad and includes modeling of hydrologic systems, use of water resources, runoff and erosion, and groundwater pollution and chemistry. The journal also features announcements, book reviews, and a handy "diary" of forthcoming hydrology-related events. The web site offers free tables of contents and abstracts along with author and keyword indexes. Full text for recent volumes is available to subscribers.

1790. *Hydrology and Earth System Sciences.* [ISSN: 1027-5606] 1997. q. EUR 500; EUR 85 newsstand/cover. Ed(s): Hubert H G Savenijeh, Kurt Roth. Copernicus GmbH, Max-Planck Str 13, Katlenburg-Lindau, 37191, Germany; info@copernicus.org; http://www.copernicus.org. Refereed. *Indexed:* Agr, ForAb, M&GPA, PollutAb, RRTA, SCI, SWRA, WRCInf. *Aud.:* Ac, Sa.

This interdisciplinary journal takes a broad approach and publishes research in all areas of hydrology with an emphasis on human interactions with physical, chemical, and biological processes. Some topics covered include the hydrological cycle, transport of dissolved and particulate matter, water budgets and fluxes, climate and atmospheric interactions, and the effects of human activity. Articles in special issues address themes such as sediment dynamics and channel change in rivers and estuaries, advances in flood forecasting, and a view from the watershed revisited. Full text is freely available online following an open-access model.

1791. *International Geology Review.* [ISSN: 0020-6814] 1958. m. USD 1498. Ed(s): Brian J Skinner, W G Ernst. Bellwether Publishing, Ltd., 8640 Guilford Rd, Ste 200, Columbia, MD 21046; bellpub@bellpub.com; http://www.bellpub.com. Illus., index, adv. Refereed. Circ: 500. Vol. ends: Dec (No. 12). *Indexed:* ChemAb, OceAb, PetrolAb, PollutAb, SCI, SWRA. *Aud.:* Ac, Sa.

This monthly is published in association with the International Division of the Geological Society of America. It features in-depth review articles and original research. Specific areas of emphasis include petrology, tectonics, and mineral and energy resources. Coverage is global in scope, but the editors particularly encourage submission of papers about less-frequently studied areas such as Africa, Asia, and South America, making this an especially useful resource. Full text is available online to subscribers.

1792. *International Journal of Coal Geology.* [ISSN: 0166-5162] 1981. 16x/yr. EUR 2099. Ed(s): S Dai, J C Hower. Elsevier BV, Radarweg 29, Amsterdam, 1043 NX, Netherlands; nlinfo-f@elsevier.nl; http://www.elsevier.nl. Illus., adv. Sample. Refereed. Vol. ends: No. 4. Microform: PQC. Online: EBSCO Publishing, EBSCO Host; Gale; IngentaConnect; OhioLINK; ScienceDirect; SwetsWise Online Content. *Indexed:* C&ISA, ChemAb, EngInd, EnvAb, MinerAb, PetrolAb, SCI. *Bk. rev.:* 0-2, 500-1,000 words. *Aud.:* Ac, Sa.

Publishes both basic and applied research articles on the geology and petrology of coal from around the world. Some areas of special focus are the geology of coal measures, coal genesis and modern coal-forming environments, and coalbed gases and methane and carbon dioxide sequestration. Proceedings of symposia appear in some issues. The web site provides free access to tables of contents and abstracts from volume one forward. Full-text articles are also available online through ScienceDirect. Appropriate for comprehensive research collections. A GeoRef priority journal.

1793. *International Journal of Earth Sciences.* Formerly (until 1998): *Geologische Rundschau.* [ISSN: 1437-3254] 1910. bi-m. EUR 1048 print & online eds. Ed(s): Wolf-Christian Dullo. Springer, Tiergartenstr 17, Heidelberg, 69121, Germany. Illus., index, adv. Sample. Refereed. Vol. ends: Dec (No. 4). Microform: BHP. Online: EBSCO Publishing, EBSCO Host; OhioLINK; Springer LINK; SwetsWise Online Content. Reprint: IRC; PSC. *Indexed:* ChemAb, IBR, MinerAb, PetrolAb, PollutAb, SCI, SWRA, ZooRec. *Aud.:* Ac, Sa.

This bimonthly publishes "process-oriented original and review papers on the history of the earth." Some areas of particular focus include tectonics, volcanology, sedimentology, mineral deposits, and surface processes. Coverage is international in scope but with a European emphasis. Most papers are in English, but articles in German and French are also accepted. Examples of thematic issue topics include carbonate mounds on the northwest European margin, simulation and visualization of geoprocesses, and the dynamics of alpine mountain belts. A special supplementary volume in 2002 featured milestone papers from the early history of the journal with English translations. The web site offers tables of contents and abstracts for all volumes and full-text access for subscribers. Listed as a GeoRef priority journal under its earlier title, *Geologische Rundschau.*

1794. *Journal of Applied Geophysics.* Formerly (until 1992): *Geoexploration.* [ISSN: 0926-9851] 1963. 12x/yr. EUR 1149. Ed(s): M Chouteau, A. Hoerdt. Elsevier BV, Radarweg 29, Amsterdam, 1043 NX, Netherlands; nlinfo-f@elsevier.nl; http://www.elsevier.nl. Illus., adv. Refereed. Microform: PQC. Online: EBSCO Publishing, EBSCO Host; Gale; IngentaConnect; OhioLINK; ScienceDirect; SwetsWise Online Content. *Indexed:* ChemAb, EngInd, ExcerpMed, OceAb, PetrolAb, PollutAb, SCI, SWRA. *Aud.:* Ac, Sa.

Originally published primarily for mining geophysicists, this journal now emphasizes environmental, geotechnical, engineering, and hydrological aspects of geophysics and petrophysics, including soil and rock mechanical properties. Special issues focus on current topics and conference reports. Recent examples are geophysics applied to detection and discrimination of unexploded ordnance, and electrical and electromagnetic studies in geothermally active regions. The web site provides free access to tables of contents and abstracts back to volume one. Full-text articles from 1992 to the present are available to subscribers through ScienceDirect.

1795. *Journal of Geochemical Exploration.* [ISSN: 0375-6742] 1972. 12x/yr. EUR 1442. Ed(s): R Swennen. Elsevier BV, Radarweg 29, Amsterdam, 1043 NX, Netherlands; nlinfo-f@elsevier.nl; http://www.elsevier.nl. Illus., index. Sample. Refereed. Vol. ends: No. 3. Microform: PQC. Online: EBSCO Publishing, EBSCO Host; Gale; IngentaConnect; OhioLINK; ScienceDirect; SwetsWise Online Content. *Indexed:* ChemAb, EngInd, EnvAb, ExcerpMed, MinerAb, PetrolAb, PollutAb, S&F, SCI, WRCInf. *Bk. rev.:* 0-2, 800-2,000 words. *Aud.:* Ac, Sa.

This journal emphasizes the application of geochemistry to the exploration and study of mineral resources and related fields, including geochemistry of the environment. Papers present international research on geochemical exploration, sampling and analytical techniques, and geochemical distributions and dispersion in rocks, soils, and waters. Free access to tables of contents and article abstracts from volume one (1972) is on the web site. Full-text articles are available online through ScienceDirect. Appropriate for comprehensive and research collections. A GeoRef priority journal.

1796. *Journal of Geodynamics.* [ISSN: 0264-3707] 1984. 10x/yr. EUR 1690. Ed(s): R Stephenson. Pergamon, The Boulevard, Langford Ln, East Park, Kidlington, OX5 1GB, United Kingdom. Adv. Refereed. Circ: 900. Microform: PQC. Online: EBSCO Publishing, EBSCO Host; Gale; IngentaConnect; OhioLINK; ScienceDirect; SwetsWise Online Content. *Indexed:* IAA, M&GPA, SCI, SSCI. *Aud.:* Ac, Sa.

This journal provides an international forum for research in the solid earth sciences with an emphasis on large-scale processes. Papers address a wide range of topics, such as physical properties of rocks and changes with pressure and temperature, mantle convection and heat flow, plate tectonics and kinematics, and magma generation, transport, and emplacement. Occasional issues report on symposia or feature a special topic. Recent examples are *Potential Fields in Geostatics and Geodynamics* and "Hotspot Iceland," respectively. Tables of contents and abstracts are available free on the web site from volume one (1984). Full text is available for all volumes through ScienceDirect.

1797. *The Journal of Geology.* [ISSN: 0022-1376] 1893. bi-m. USD 182 domestic; USD 201.92 Canada; USD 197 elsewhere. Ed(s): Alfred T Anderson, Jr. University of Chicago Press, Journals Division, PO Box 37005, Chicago, IL 60637; subscriptions@press.uchicago.edu; http://www.journals.uchicago.edu. Illus., index, adv. Sample. Refereed. Circ: 1600 Paid. Vol. ends: Nov. Microform: PMC; PQC. Online: EBSCO Publishing, EBSCO Host; Gale; ProQuest LLC (Ann Arbor). Reprint: PSC. *Indexed:* AS&TI, ChemAb, GSI, IAA, IBR, M&GPA, MinerAb, OceAb, PetrolAb, PollutAb, S&F, SCI, SSCI, SWRA, ZooRec. *Bk. rev.:* 0-4, 300-750 words. *Aud.:* Ac, Sa.

This prestigious journal, in print since 1893, is a true necessity for academic and special libraries. Contents address all aspects of geology and are chosen in part for their broad applicability. Both the full-length articles and the shorter geological notes reflect high editorial standards, adding to the archival value of this outstanding publication. Tables of contents are available on the web site beginning with 1996, and full text is accessible to subscribers beginning with 1997. A GeoRef priority journal.

1798. *Journal of Geophysical Research.* Former titles (until 1949): *Terrestrial Magnetism and Atmospheric Electricity;* (until 1899): *Terrestrial Magnetism.* [ISSN: 0148-0227] 1896. m. USD 3150. Ed(s): Richard Arculus, Patrick Taylor. American Geophysical Union, 2000 Florida Ave, NW, Washington, DC 20009-1277; service@agu.org; http://www.agu.org. Refereed. *Indexed:* ApEcolAb, C&ISA, CABA, CerAb, ForAb, HortAb, IAA, M&GPA, MinerAb, OceAb, PetrolAb, PollutAb, S&F, SCI, SWRA. *Aud.:* Ac, Sa.

This comprehensive, interdisciplinary journal presents research on the physics and chemistry of the earth, its environment, and the solar system. *JGR* is published in several parts, available either as a package or separately, including atmospheres, biogeosciences, earth surface, oceans, planets, solid earth, and space physics. Individual issues often contain special sections with multiple papers devoted to one topic. Full-text articles from 1994 to the present are available for subscribers on the American Geophysical Union web site. Parts *B: Solid Earth, C: Oceans,* and *E: Planets* are GeoRef priority journals.

1799. *Journal of Geophysics and Engineering.* [ISSN: 1742-2132] 2004. q. USD 1395 print & online eds. Ed(s): Jian Guo, Mike Warner. Institute of Physics Publishing, Dirac House, Temple Back, Bristol, BS1 6BE, United Kingdom; custserv@iop.org; http://www.iop.org. Refereed. *Indexed:* SCI. *Aud.:* Ac, Sa.

Publishes research articles in all areas of geophysics with an emphasis on applied science and engineering. Covers topics like global geophysics, applied and engineering geophysics, geodynamics, seismology, oil, gas and mineral exploration, petrophysics, and reservoir geophysics. Engineering papers focus on earth subsurface in areas of petroleum engineering, rock mechanics, remote sensing, instrumentation, and sensor design. Newly published articles are freely accessible online for 30 days from the date of online publication. Subscribers may view full text of all articles, while abstracts and reference lists are freely available.

1800. *Journal of Geoscience Education.* Formerly (until vol.44, 1996): *Journal of Geological Education.* [ISSN: 1089-9995] 1951. 5x/yr. USD 55 domestic individuals & libraries; USD 67 foreign individuals & libraries. Ed(s): Carl N Drummond. National Association of Geoscience Teachers, c/o Carl Drummond , Editor, Dept of Geosciences, Fort Wayne, IN 46805-1499; jge@ipfw.edu; http://www.nagt.org. Illus., index, adv. Refereed. Circ: 2800 Paid. Vol. ends: Nov (No. 5). Microform: PQC. *Indexed:* ABIn, ChemAb, EduInd, ExcerpMed. *Bk. rev.:* 5-10, 200-800 words. *Aud.:* Ac, Sa.

Earth science teachers from elementary school through college are the target audience for this journal, which reports on techniques, resources, and innovations useful for both formal and informal instruction. Other features include reviews of web resources, new books for geoscientists, and museum and gallery information, as well as a column on errors in geoscience textbooks. Author and subject indexes beginning with 1980 and full text of volumes since 2001 (articles appear online one year after publication) are available on the web site of the National Association of Geoscience Teachers. A GeoRef priority journal.

1801. *Journal of Glaciology.* [ISSN: 0022-1430] 1947. q. GBP 259. Ed(s): T H Jacka. International Glaciological Society, Lensfield Rd, Cambridge, CB2 1ER, United Kingdom; http://www.igsoc.org/. Illus., index. Refereed. Circ: 1300. *Indexed:* ChemAb, IBR, M&GPA, SCI, SSCI, SWRA. *Bk. rev.:* 0-1, 600-1,200 words. *Aud.:* Ac, Sa.

This journal of the International Glaciological Society publishes findings and theories on all aspects of snow and ice, with particular emphasis on studies of glaciers and their formation, movement, and changes over time. Some issues also include a section called "Instruments and Methods," which describes new techniques and equipment for glacial investigation. Free table-of-contents information is available for all volumes (beginning with 1947) on the society web site, with full text beginning in 2000 for subscribers. Appropriate for comprehensive academic and specialized collections.

1802. *Journal of Hydrology.* [ISSN: 0022-1694] 1963. 64x/yr. EUR 5421. Ed(s): C Neal, G Vachaud. Elsevier BV, Radarweg 29, Amsterdam, 1043 NX, Netherlands; nlinfo-f@elsevier.nl; http://www.elsevier.nl. Illus.,

index, adv. Sample. Refereed. Vol. ends: No. 4. Microform: PQC. Online: EBSCO Publishing, EBSCO Host; Gale; IngentaConnect; OhioLINK; ScienceDirect; SwetsWise Online Content. *Indexed:* Agr, ApMecR, BiolAb, C&ISA, CABA, CerAb, ChemAb, DSA, EngInd, EnvAb, EnvInd, ExcerpMed, FPA, ForAb, HortAb, IAA, M&GPA, OceAb, PollutAb, RRTA, S&F, SCI, SWRA, WAE&RSA, WRCInf. *Aud.:* Ac, Sa.

Publishes research papers and reviews on topics related to all areas of the hydrological sciences, such as physical, chemical, biogeochemical, and systems aspects of surface and groundwater hydrology. Special issues focus on such topics as rainfall microstructure; palaeoflood hydrology and historical data in flood risk analysis; and catchment modeling. Tables of contents and abstracts are available on the web site from volume one (1963), and full-text articles are available through ScienceDirect. Appropriate for comprehensive academic and research collections. A GeoRef priority journal.

1803. *Journal of Metamorphic Geology.* [ISSN: 0263-4929] 1982. 9x/yr. GBP 1147 print & online eds. Ed(s): Doug Robinson, Donna Whitney. Blackwell Publishing Ltd., 9600 Garsington Rd, Oxford, OX4 2ZG, United Kingdom; customerservices@blackwellpublishing.com; http://www.blackwellpublishing.com. Illus., adv. Refereed. Circ: 364. Vol. ends: Nov (No. 6). Online: Blackwell Synergy; EBSCO Publishing, EBSCO Host; Gale; IngentaConnect; OCLC Online Computer Library Center, Inc.; OhioLINK; SwetsWise Online Content. Reprint: PSC. *Indexed:* ChemAb, MinerAb, SCI. *Aud.:* Ac, Sa.

This title publishes papers on a full range of metamorphic topics. Research is presented on properties of metamorphic minerals, theoretical and experimental studies of metamorphic reactions, structural deformation and geochemical changes associated with metamorphism, and regional analysis of metamorphic terrains. The web site provides free tables of contents and abstracts from volume one (1983); full-text access to articles is available for subscribers. A GeoRef priority journal.

Journal of Paleontology. See Paleontology section.

1804. *Journal of Petroleum Geology.* [ISSN: 0141-6421] 1978. q. USD 578 print & online eds. Ed(s): Christopher Tiratsoo. Blackwell Publishing Ltd., 9600 Garsington Rd, Oxford, OX4 2ZG, United Kingdom; customerservices@blackwellpublishing.com; http://www.blackwellpublishing.com. Illus., index, adv. Sample. Refereed. Vol. ends: Oct (No. 4). Online: Blackwell Synergy; EBSCO Publishing, EBSCO Host; Gale; IngentaConnect. Reprint: PSC. *Indexed:* ChemAb, EngInd, MinerAb, OceAb, PetrolAb, SCI. *Bk. rev.:* 0-3, 500-1,200 words, signed. *Aud.:* Ac, Sa.

This quarterly compares quite favorably with its competitors from larger publishing houses. Articles present research on the geology of oil and gas, especially in world regions outside of North America. Topics emphasize geochemical and geophysical studies of petroleum exploration operations, basin modeling, and reservoir evaluation. Each issue includes a calendar of international events. Free tables of contents and abstracts are available on the web site for issues beginning with 2002, and full text is available to subscribers. A GeoRef priority journal.

1805. *Journal of Petrology.* [ISSN: 0022-3530] 1960. m. EUR 1194 print or online ed. Ed(s): Marjorie Wilson. Oxford University Press, Great Clarendon St, Oxford, OX2 6DP, United Kingdom; jnl.orders@ oup.co.uk; http://www.oxfordjournals.org. Illus., index, adv. Sample. Refereed. Circ: 930. Vol. ends: Dec (No. 12). Microform: PQC. Online: EBSCO Publishing, EBSCO Host; Gale; HighWire Press; IngentaConnect; OCLC Online Computer Library Center, Inc.; OhioLINK; Oxford Journals; ProQuest LLC (Ann Arbor); SwetsWise Online Content. Reprint: PSC. *Indexed:* BAS, ChemAb, IBR, MinerAb, SCI. *Bk. rev.:* 0-2, 600-1,000 words, signed. *Aud.:* Ac, Sa.

This highly cited journal from Oxford University Press features research in igneous and metamorphic petrology and is recommended for academic and special libraries. Subjects covered include magmatic processes, petrogenesis, trace element and isotope geochemistry, and experimental studies and theoretical modeling. Occasional issues feature special themes or publish selected papers from conferences. Tables of contents with abstracts beginning with volume one (1969) are freely accessible on the web site, and full-text articles are available to subscribers. A GeoRef priority journal.

1806. *Journal of Quaternary Science.* [ISSN: 0267-8179] 1986. 8x/yr. USD 1770 print or online ed. Ed(s): C J Caseldine. John Wiley & Sons Ltd., The Atrium, Southern Gate, Chichester, PO19 8SQ, United Kingdom; customer@wiley.co.uk; http://www.wiley.co.uk. Illus., index, adv. Refereed. Circ: 700. Vol. ends: No. 8. Microform: PQC. Online: EBSCO Publishing, EBSCO Host; Florida Center for Library Automation; OhioLINK; SwetsWise Online Content; Wiley InterScience. Reprint: PSC. *Indexed:* C&ISA, CerAb, EnvAb, EnvInd, IAA, IBR, M&GPA, S&F, SCI, SWRA, ZooRec. *Bk. rev.:* 2-10, 300-1,000 words, signed. *Aud.:* Ac, Sa.

Published for the Quaternary Research Association, this journal focuses on the earth's history during the last two million years. This time period is the same as that covered by the journal *Boreas,* and there are many similarities between the two. Papers span a wide range of topics and many are interdisciplinary in nature. In particular, there is an emphasis on the stratigraphy, glaciation, and paleoclimatology of the period. Occasional special issues focus on a particular region or environment. Full-length research papers, short contributions intended for rapid communication, and invited reviews are all included. Free tables of contents and abstracts from 1994 to the present are provided on the web site along with access to full-text articles for subscribers.

1807. *Journal of Sedimentary Research.* Formed by the merger of (1994-1996): *Journal of Sedimentary Research. Section A: Sedimentary Petrology and Processes;* (1994-1996): *Journal of Sedimentary Research. Section B: Stratigraphy and Global Studies;* Both superseded in part (1931-1994): *Journal of Sedimentary Petrology.* [ISSN: 1527-1404] 1996. bi-m. Members, USD 70; Non-members, USD 210; Students, USD 35. Ed(s): Colin P North, Kitty L Milliken. S E P M - Society for Sedimentary Geology, 6128 E. 38th St., Ste. 308, Tulsa, OK 74135-5814; http://www.sepm.org. Illus., adv. Refereed. Circ: 5000. Microform: PMC; PQC. Online: EBSCO Publishing, EBSCO Host; HighWire Press. *Indexed:* ChemAb, ExcerpMed, M&GPA, MinerAb, OceAb, PetrolAb, PollutAb, S&F, SCI, SWRA. *Bk. rev.:* 0-3, 200-600 words. *Aud.:* Ac, Sa.

This primary journal of the Society for Sedimentary Geology publishes papers on topics from all branches of sedimentary geology, including inherent characteristics of sediments themselves, their impacts on other aspects of the sediment record, and sedimentary processes. These range from detailed papers that concentrate on very specific, often small-scale topics to "big picture" reports about research on larger spatial and temporal scales. Each issue includes research articles, research methods papers, and discussions. Tables of contents, abstracts, and full-text searching are available on the web site from 1931 forward, and subscribers have access to full-text articles. A GeoRef priority journal.

1808. *Journal of Seismology.* [ISSN: 1383-4649] 1997. q. EUR 445 print & online eds. Ed(s): Augustin Udias. Springer Netherlands, Van Godewijckstraat 30, Dordrecht, 3311 GX, Netherlands; http://www.springeronline.com. Adv. Refereed. Microform: PQC. Online: EBSCO Publishing, EBSCO Host; Gale; IngentaConnect; OCLC Online Computer Library Center, Inc.; OhioLINK; Ovid Technologies, Inc.; Springer LINK; SwetsWise Online Content. Reprint: PSC. *Indexed:* C&ISA, CerAb, H&SSA, IAA, RiskAb, SCI, SWRA. *Aud.:* Ac, Sa.

This international journal specializes in the study of earthquakes and their occurrence. Areas of particular focus include seismicity and seismotectonics, earthquake prediction, seismic hazards, and earthquake engineering. Many papers are regional or historical studies. However, broader theoretical work is also included, along with short communications on new analytical techniques and instrumentation. The web site provides free table of contents and abstracts from volume one (1995) to the present, and subscribers may view full text of articles.

1809. *Journal of Structural Geology.* [ISSN: 0191-8141] 1979. 12x/yr. EUR 1613. Ed(s): C W Passchier. Pergamon, The Boulevard, Langford Ln, East Park, Kidlington, OX5 1GB, United Kingdom. Illus., adv. Sample. Refereed. Circ: 2000. Vol. ends: Dec (No. 12). Microform:

PQC. Online: EBSCO Publishing, EBSCO Host; Gale; IngentaConnect; OhioLINK; ScienceDirect; SwetsWise Online Content. *Indexed:* ApMecR, C&ISA, CerAb, ChemAb, EngInd, IAA, MinerAb, PetrolAb, SCI, SWRA. *Bk. rev.:* 0-2, 500-1,000 words. *Aud.:* Ac, Sa.

This international journal publishes research and review articles on structural geology, tectonics, and the associated rock deformation processes. Some specific topics include faults, folds, fractures, strain analysis, rock mechanics, and theoretical and experimental modeling. Regional structural accounts are published when they are of broad interest. Tables of contents and article abstracts are accessible free on the web site from volume one (1979), and full-text articles are available through ScienceDirect. A GeoRef priority journal.

1810. *Journal of Volcanology and Geothermal Research.* [ISSN: 0377-0273] 1976. 40x/yr. EUR 3029. Ed(s): M T Mangan, L Wilson. Elsevier BV, Radarweg 29, Amsterdam, 1043 NX, Netherlands; nlinfo-f@elsevier.nl; http://www.elsevier.nl. Illus., index, adv. Sample. Refereed. Vol. ends: No. 4. Microform: PQC. Online: EBSCO Publishing, EBSCO Host; Gale; IngentaConnect; OhioLINK; ScienceDirect; SwetsWise Online Content. *Indexed:* ChemAb, EngInd, EnvAb, IAA, MinerAb, PetrolAb, PollutAb, SCI, SWRA. *Aud.:* Ac, Sa.

Publishes recent research on geochemical, petrological, geophysical, economic, tectonic, and environmental aspects of volcanic activity. Occasional special issues address particular processes, environments, or locales, e.g., interaction between volcanoes and their basement, and magma genesis and volcanological processes of Arenal volcano in Costa Rica. Tables of contents and abstracts are available free on the web site from volume one (1976), and full-text articles are accessible through ScienceDirect. A GeoRef priority journal.

Lethaia. See Paleontology section.

1811. *Lithos.* [ISSN: 0024-4937] 1968. 28x/yr. EUR 1570. Ed(s): I Buick, A C Kerr. Elsevier BV, Radarweg 29, Amsterdam, 1043 NX, Netherlands; nlinfo-f@elsevier.nl; http://www.elsevier.nl. Illus., index, adv. Sample. Refereed. Circ: 1000. Vol. ends: No. 4. Microform: PQC. Online: EBSCO Publishing, EBSCO Host; Gale; IngentaConnect; OhioLINK; ScienceDirect; SwetsWise Online Content. *Indexed:* ChemAb, MinerAb, PollutAb, SCI, SSCI. *Bk. rev.:* 1-3, 800-1,000 words. *Aud.:* Ac, Sa.

Publishes research papers, reviews, discussions, and book reviews in the fields of mineralogy, petrology, and geochemistry, with an emphasis on applications to petrogenetic problems. Occasional special issues publish proceedings of meetings, such as *The Origin, Evolution and Present State of Subcontinental Lithosphere,* and *The Role of Accessory Minerals in Rocks: Petrogenetic Indicators of Metamorphic and Igneous Processes.* Free access to tables of contents and article abstracts from volume one (1968) to the present is available on the web site. Full-text articles are accessible through ScienceDirect. A GeoRef priority journal.

1812. *Marine and Petroleum Geology.* Former titles (until 1983): *Underwater Information Bulletin;* (until 1973): *Underwater Journal Information Bulletin;* Which was formed by the merger of: *Underwater Science and Technology Journal; Underwater Science and Technology Information Bulletin; Underwater Journal and Information Bulletin.* [ISSN: 0264-8172] 1971. 10x/yr. EUR 2053. Ed(s): O Catouneanu, D. G. Roberts. Elsevier Ltd., The Boulevard, Langford Ln, Oxford, OX5 1GB, United Kingdom. Illus., index, adv. Sample. Refereed. Microform: PQC. Online: EBSCO Publishing, EBSCO Host; Gale; IngentaConnect; OhioLINK; ScienceDirect; SwetsWise Online Content. *Indexed:* ChemAb, EngInd, EnvAb, EnvInd, OceAb, PetrolAb, SCI. *Aud.:* Ac, Sa.

Multidisciplinary forum for those concerned with marine and petroleum geology to exchange interpretations and techniques on research in areas of basin analysis and evaluation, geophysical interpretation, estimation of reserves, sedimentology, seismic stratigraphy, continental margins, and well logging. Full-color illustrations and fold-out seismic sections and maps enhance many issues of the print journal. Thematic issues are occasionally published on selected basins or depositional environments; recent examples are economic applications of sedimentology and the Gulf of Lions (France). Tables of contents and abstracts from volume one (1984) to the present are available free at the web site; full-text articles are also accessible through ScienceDirect.

Marine Geology. See Marine Science and Technology section.

1813. *Mathematical Geoscience (Print Edition).* Former titles (until 2008): *Mathematical Geology (Print Edition); (until 1986): International Association for Mathematical Geology. Journal.* [ISSN: 1874-8961] 1969. 8x/yr. EUR 1217 print & online eds. Springer New York LLC, 233 Spring St, New York, NY 10013-1578; journals@springer-ny.com; http://www.springer.com. Illus., adv. Refereed. Vol. ends: Nov (No. 8). Microform: PQC. Online: EBSCO Publishing, EBSCO Host; Gale; IngentaConnect; OCLC Online Computer Library Center, Inc.; OhioLINK; Ovid Technologies, Inc.; Springer LINK; SwetsWise Online Content. Reprint: PSC. *Indexed:* ApMecR, C&ISA, CCMJ, CerAb, ChemAb, IAA, MSN, MathR, PetrolAb, SCI, SWRA, ZooRec. *Bk. rev.:* 0-5, 400-700 words, signed. *Aud.:* Ac, Sa.

This is one of the main journals of the International Association for Mathematical Geology, which also publishes *Computers and Geosciences* and *Natural Resources Research.* The ability to work efficiently with large quantities of numerical data has become especially important in recent years. As suggested by the title, papers in *Mathematical Geology* are primarily concerned with the application of math, statistics, and computing in the earth sciences. Some specific areas of concentration include modeling and simulation, fluid mechanics, filtering techniques, fractals, and spatial analysis. Tables of contents and article abstracts from volume one (1969) forward are on the web site, with full-text access available for subscribers. A GeoRef priority journal.

Micropaleontology. See Paleontology section.

1814. *Mineralium Deposita: international journal of geology, mineralogy, and geochemistry of mineral deposits.* [ISSN: 0026-4598] 1966. 8x/yr. EUR 1498 print & online eds. Ed(s): Lawrence D Meinert, Bernd Lehmann. Springer, Tiergartenstr 17, Heidelberg, 69121, Germany. Illus., index, adv. Sample. Refereed. Vol. ends: No. 8. Microform: PQC. Online: EBSCO Publishing, EBSCO Host; OhioLINK; Springer LINK; SwetsWise Online Content. Reprint: PSC. *Indexed:* ChemAb, IBR, MinerAb, PollutAb, SCI. *Bk. rev.:* 0-5, 400-700 words, signed. *Aud.:* Ac, Sa.

This is the official journal of the Society for Geology Applied to Mineral Deposits. It focuses on economic geology including field studies, mineralogy, experimental and applied geochemistry, and ore deposit exploration. Issues contain a mixture of full-length papers, rapid-communication letters and notes, news, and meeting reports. Many of the illustrations are in color, especially those of mineral thin sections. Coverage is international in scope and includes such often under-represented areas as Africa, Asia, Australia, and South America. There are also thematic issues on selected ore deposits or other topics of general interest. The web site offers free tables of contents and abstracts from volume one (1966) to the present and full-text access articles for subscribers. A GeoRef priority journal.

1815. *Mineralogical Magazine.* Formerly (until 1969): *Mineralogical Magazine and Journal of the Mineralogical Society.* [ISSN: 0026-461X] 1876. bi-m. GBP 353 combined subscription domestic print & online eds.; GBP 381 combined subscription foreign print & online eds. Ed(s): M D Welch. Mineralogical Society, 41 Queens Gate, London, SW7 5HR, United Kingdom; http://www.minersoc.org. Illus., index, adv. Sample. Refereed. Circ: 2000. Vol. ends: Dec (No. 6). Microform: BHP. Online: EBSCO Publishing, EBSCO Host; Gale; HighWire Press; IngentaConnect; OCLC Online Computer Library Center, Inc.; SwetsWise Online Content. *Indexed:* ChemAb, EngInd, IBR, MinerAb, SCI. *Bk. rev.:* 3-8, 500-900 words. *Aud.:* Ac, Sa.

Published by the Mineralogical Society, this well-respected journal has been in print for more than 130 years. Topics covered span not only the field of mineralogy but also related areas such as geochemistry and petrology. Both full-length original research papers and shorter letters for rapid communication are included. Along with *American Mineralogist,* this title is highly

recommended for larger academic library collections. Tables of contents and abstracts from 1998 to the present are available on the web through Ingenta; subscribers may view full-text articles from any of several vendors. A GeoRef priority journal.

1816. *The Mineralogical Record.* [ISSN: 0026-4628] 1970. bi-m. USD 175 (Individuals, USD 55). Ed(s): Wendell E Wilson, Thomas P Moore. Mineralogical Record, Inc., 4631 Paseo Tubutama, Tucson, AZ 85750; minrec@aol.com; http://www.minrec.org. Illus., index, adv. Sample. Refereed. Circ: 7400. Vol. ends: Nov/Dec (No. 6). Microform: PQC. Online: Florida Center for Library Automation; Gale; Northern Light Technology, Inc.; OCLC Online Computer Library Center, Inc.; ProQuest K-12 Learning Solutions; ProQuest LLC (Ann Arbor); H.W. Wilson. *Indexed:* ChemAb, GSI, MinerAb. *Bk. rev.:* 0-4, 100-800 words. *Aud.:* Ga, Ac, Sa.

Publishes both nontechnical and technical articles for mineral collectors, curators, and researchers. Each issue has numerous high-quality color photographs, and even many of the advertisements are visually stunning. Reports from mineral shows around the world appear in a column called "What's New in Minerals," and special issues focus on single topics such as minerals of a particular region, equipment used by mineralogists, and historically significant mines. The International Mineralogical Association regularly publishes abstracts of new mineral descriptions in *The Mineralogical Record.* The web site provides searchable tables of contents back to the first issue, published in 1970. Recommended for public and academic libraries.

1817. *Natural Hazards and Earth System Sciences.* [ISSN: 1561-8633] bi-m. Free. Ed(s): Fausto Guzzetti. Copernicus GmbH, Max-Planck Str 13, Katlenburg-Lindau, 37191, Germany. Refereed. *Indexed:* M&GPA, RiskAb, SCI, SWRA. *Aud.:* Ac, Sa.

Publishes interdisciplinary research concerning natural hazards and their risks. Papers include such topics as flooding, landslides, tsunamis, earthquakes, avalanches, volcanic eruptions, and the impact of climate change on natural risks. Full text is available to all on the web site for this open-access, peer-reviewed journal.

1818. *Netherlands Journal of Geosciences.* Former titles: *Geologie en Mijnbouw; (until 1931): Mijnwezen; (until 1928): Mijnwezen en Metallurgie; (until 1925): Mijnwezen;* Incorporates (1946-1999): *Nederlands Instituut voor Toegepaste Geowetenschappen T N O. Mededelingen;* Which was formerly (until 1997): *Rijks Geologische Dienst. Mededelingen; (until 1977): Rijks Geologische Dienst. Mededelingen. Nieuwe Serie; (until 1968): Geologische Stichting. Mededelingen. Nieuwe Serie.* 1921. q. EUR 278. Ed(s): Theo Wong. Netherlands Journal of Geosciences Foundation, PO Box 80015, Utrecht, 3508 TA, Netherlands; http://www.nitg.tno.nl. Illus., index, adv. Refereed. Circ: 2250. Vol. ends: No. 4. Microform: SWZ; PQC. Online: EBSCO Publishing, EBSCO Host; Gale; IngentaConnect; OCLC Online Computer Library Center, Inc.; OhioLINK; Springer LINK; SwetsWise Online Content. *Indexed:* BiolAb, ChemAb, IBR, OceAb, PetrolAb, SCI, SWRA, ZooRec. *Aud.:* Ac, Sa.

This is the official journal of the Royal Geological and Mining Society of the Netherlands, and it represents a merger of two titles, *Geologie en Mijnbouw* and *Mededelingen Nederlands Instituut voor Geowetenschappen–TNO* and began publication in March 2000. Articles feature research on geology and mining with emphasis on the Netherlands, the North Sea, and neighboring areas. A special strength is in geological aspects of coastal and deltaic lowlands, both ancient and modern. Tables of contents, abstracts, supplementary material, and selected full-text articles are available on the web site. Listed as a GeoRef priority journal under its earlier title, *Geologie en Mijnbouw.*

1819. *Organic Geochemistry.* [ISSN: 0146-6380] 1978. 12x/yr. EUR 3178. Ed(s): L R Snowden, J R Maxwell. Pergamon, The Boulevard, Langford Ln, East Park, Kidlington, OX5 1GB, United Kingdom. Illus., index, adv. Sample. Refereed. Circ: 1100. Vol. ends: No. 32. Microform: PQC.

Online: EBSCO Publishing, EBSCO Host; Gale; IngentaConnect; OhioLINK; ScienceDirect; SwetsWise Online Content. *Indexed:* C&ISA, CABA, ChemAb, EngInd, ExcerpMed, FPA, ForAb, HortAb, M&GPA, PetrolAb, PollutAb, S&F, SCI, SWRA, WRCInf. *Bk. rev.:* 0-2, 300-1,000 words. *Aud.:* Ac, Sa.

The official journal of the European Association of Organic Geochemists, this monthly publishes papers on all phases of organic geochemistry, including biogeochemistry, environmental geochemistry, and geochemical cycling. Types of articles include original research papers, comprehensive reviews, technical communications, and discussions and replies. The web site provides free tables of contents and article abstracts from volume one (1979), and full-text articles are available through ScienceDirect. A GeoRef priority journal.

Palaeogeography, Palaeoclimatology, Palaeoecology. See Paleontology section.

Palaeontology. See Paleontology section.

1820. *Petroleum Geoscience.* [ISSN: 1354-0793] 1995. q. GBP 245 in Europe; USD 255 United States; GBP 280 elsewhere. Ed(s): A G Dore. Geological Society Publishing House, Unit 7, Brassmill Enterprise Centre, Brassmill Ln, Bath, BA1 3JN, United Kingdom; enquiries@geolsoc.org.uk; http://www.geolsoc.org.uk. Illus., index, adv. Refereed. Circ: 3500. Vol. ends: Nov (No. 4). *Indexed:* C&ISA, CerAb, IAA, MinerAb, PetrolAb, SCI. *Bk. rev.:* 0-6, 250-600 words, signed. *Aud.:* Ac, Sa.

This quarterly is published by the Geological Society of London and the Petroleum Division of the European Association of Geoscientists and Engineers. It covers a full range of geoscience aspects involved in the "exploration, exploitation, appraisal, and development of hydrocarbon resources." Coverage is international in scope and includes both theoretical and applied articles. Color is used to good effect for many illustrations. Tables of contents and abstracts are freely accessible through Ingenta from 1999 to the present; full-text access is available through several vendors.

1821. *Physics and Chemistry of Minerals.* [ISSN: 0342-1791] 1977. 10x/yr. EUR 2180 print & online eds. Ed(s): C McCammon, P C Burnley. Springer, Tiergartenstr 17, Heidelberg, 69121, Germany. Illus., index, adv. Sample. Refereed. Vol. ends: No. 10. Microform: PQC. Online: EBSCO Publishing, EBSCO Host; OhioLINK; Springer LINK; SwetsWise Online Content. Reprint: PSC. *Indexed:* ChemAb, EngInd, MinerAb, S&F, SCI. *Aud.:* Ac, Sa.

This journal is published in cooperation with the International Mineralogical Association. Papers focus on the chemistry and physics of minerals and related solids. Some areas of emphasis include atomic structure, mineral surfaces, spectroscopy, chemical reactions and bonding, and analysis of physical properties. Recommended for larger academic or special libraries. The web site offers free access to tables of contents and article abstracts from volume one (1977) to the present; full-text access to articles is available to subscribers. A GeoRef priority journal.

1822. *Physics of the Earth and Planetary Interiors.* [ISSN: 0031-9201] 1967. 24x/yr. EUR 2778. Ed(s): D Rubie, K Zhang. Elsevier BV, Radarweg 29, Amsterdam, 1043 NX, Netherlands; nlinfo-f@elsevier.nl; http://www.elsevier.nl. Illus., index. Sample. Refereed. Vol. ends: No. 124 - No. 129. Microform: PQC. Online: EBSCO Publishing, EBSCO Host; Gale; IngentaConnect; OhioLINK; ScienceDirect; SwetsWise Online Content. *Indexed:* ChemAb, EngInd, IAA, M&GPA, PetrolAb, SCI. *Bk. rev.:* 0-1, 300-800 words. *Aud.:* Ac, Sa.

This journal is devoted to studies of the planetary physical and chemical processes, and the papers it contains present observational and experimental studies along with theoretical interpretation. Occasional special issues present papers from symposia or thematic reports on special topics. Some recent examples include magnetic field modeling, dynamics of subduction zones, high-pressure mineral physics, and accurate earthquake location. The web site offers free access to tables of contents and abstracts for issues from volume one (1967), and full-text articles are through ScienceDirect. A GeoRef priority journal.

1823. *Precambrian Research.* [ISSN: 0301-9268] 1974. 32x/yr. EUR 2756. Ed(s): P A Cawood, R R Parrish. Elsevier BV, Radarweg 29, Amsterdam, 1043 NX, Netherlands; nlinfo-f@elsevier.nl; http://www.elsevier.nl. Illus., index, adv. Sample. Refereed. Vol. ends: No. 4. Microform: PQC. Online: EBSCO Publishing, EBSCO Host; Gale; IngentaConnect; OhioLINK; ScienceDirect; SwetsWise Online Content. *Indexed:* ChemAb, MinerAb, PetrolAb, SCI, ZooRec. *Bk. rev.:* 0-2, 200-600 words. *Aud.:* Ac, Sa.

The Precambrian era is believed to have lasted for some four billion years, representing a substantial majority of Earth's history on the geological time scale. This journal emphasizes interdisciplinary studies and publishes research on all aspects of the early history and development of Earth and its planetary neighbors. Topics include the origin of life, evolution of the oceans and atmosphere, the early fossil record, paleobiology, geochronology, and Precambrian mineral deposits. Tables of contents and abstracts are available on the web site from volume one (1974). Full-text articles are available through ScienceDirect. A GeoRef priority journal.

1824. *Pure and Applied Geophysics.* Formerly: *Geofisica.* [ISSN: 0033-4553] 1939. m. EUR 2998 print & online eds. Ed(s): Renata Dmowska, Brian J Mitchell. Birkhaeuser Verlag AG, Viaduktstr 42, Postfach 133, Basel, 4051, Switzerland; info@birkhauser.ch; http://www.birkhauser.ch/journals. Illus. Refereed. Vol. ends: No. 4. Online: EBSCO Publishing, EBSCO Host; OhioLINK; Springer LINK; SwetsWise Online Content. Reprint: PSC. *Indexed:* ApMecR, BAS, ChemAb, ExcerpMed, IAA, M&GPA, PetrolAb, SCI, SWRA. *Bk. rev.:* 0-12, 400-1,200 words, signed. *Aud.:* Ac, Sa.

Often referred to as *PAGEOPH*, this journal features full-length papers on all aspects of geophysics. The vast majority of articles are in English, although contributions in French and German are also accepted. Special issues, sometimes representing multiple numbers within a volume, feature themes like earthquake hazards and urban planning, mechanical and other properties of fractured rock, and induced seismicity. The web site offers free tables of contents and abstracts from 1939 forward and access to full-text articles subscribers. Strongly recommended for academic and special libraries. A GeoRef priority journal.

1825. *Quarterly Journal of Engineering Geology and Hydrogeology.* Formerly (until 1999): *Quarterly Journal of Engineering Geology.* [ISSN: 1470-9236] 1967. q. GBP 305 domestic; GBP 348 foreign; USD 670 foreign. Ed(s): M Packman. Geological Society Publishing House, Unit 7, Brassmill Enterprise Centre, Brassmill Ln, Bath, BA1 3JN, United Kingdom; http://www.geolsoc.org.uk. Illus., index, adv. Refereed. Circ: 3300. Vol. ends: Nov (No. 4). *Indexed:* C&ISA, CerAb, ChemAb, EngInd, ExcerpMed, HRIS, IAA, MinerAb, SCI, SWRA. *Bk. rev.:* 0-7, 300-800 words, signed. *Aud.:* Ac, Sa.

Upholding the high standards of publications from the Geological Society of London, this title focuses specifically on geology as applied to civil engineering, mining, and water resources. This makes it of considerable value to both engineers and earth scientists. Coverage is international in scope. In addition to original research, it includes review articles, technical notes, and lectures. Occasional supplements to the regular issues are published. Tables of contents and abstracts are freely available on the web from volume one (1967) to present on GeoScience World, and subscribers may view full text articles from any of several vendors. Listed as a GeoRef priority journal under its earlier title, *Quarterly Journal of Engineering Geology.*

1826. *Quaternary International.* [ISSN: 1040-6182] 1989. 17x/yr. EUR 1061. Ed(s): N R Catto. Pergamon, The Boulevard, Langford Ln, East Park, Kidlington, OX5 1GB, United Kingdom. Illus. Refereed. Vol. ends: Dec (No. 4). Microform: PQC. Online: EBSCO Publishing, EBSCO Host; Gale; IngentaConnect; OhioLINK; ScienceDirect; SwetsWise Online Content. *Indexed:* M&GPA, SCI, ZooRec. *Aud.:* Ac, Sa.

Publishes international, interdisciplinary research on global climate changes and the succession of glacial and interglacial ages during the Quaternary period, approximately the last two million years of the earth's history. Environmental changes and interactions are studied, with appropriate connections to both present processes and future climatological implications. Most issues are thematic, often presenting collected papers from symposia and workshops sponsored by the International Union for Quaternary Research. Free access to tables of contents and abstracts is available on the web site from volume one (1989), and full-text articles are accessible through ScienceDirect.

1827. Quaternary Research. [ISSN: 0033-5894] 1970. 6x/yr. EUR 1034. Ed(s): E Steig, D B Booth. Academic Press, 525 B St, Ste 1900, San Diego, CA 92101-4495; apsubs@acad.com; http://www.elsevier.com/. Illus., index. Sample. Refereed. Vol. ends: Nov (No. 3). Online: EBSCO Publishing, EBSCO Host; Gale; IngentaConnect; OCLC Online Computer Library Center, Inc.; OhioLINK; ScienceDirect; SwetsWise Online Content. *Indexed:* AbAn, Agr, AnthLit, ApEcolAb, ArtHuCI, BiolAb, BrArAb, CABA, ChemAb, FPA, FR, ForAb, HortAb, M&GPA, OceAb, RRTA, S&F, SCI, SWRA, WAE&RSA, ZooRec. *Bk. rev.:* 0-2, 500-1,000 words. *Aud.:* Ac, Sa.

Papers in this journal present interdisciplinary studies in the earth and biological sciences that cover the Quaternary period. Articles explore topics in areas of geoarcheology, geochemistry and geophysics, geochronology, geomorphology, glaciology, paleobotany and paleoecology, paleoclimatology, and paleogeography. Free access to tables of contents and abstracts for articles from volume one (1970) is available on the web site. Full-text articles are accessible through ScienceDirect. Recommended for college and university libraries. A GeoRef priority journal.

1828. Rocks and Minerals: mineralogy, geology, lapidary. [ISSN: 0035-7529] 1926. bi-m. USD 127 (Individuals, USD 51). Ed(s): Marie Huizing. Heldref Publications, 1319 18th St, NW, Washington, DC 20036-1802; subscribe@heldref.org; http://www.heldref.org. Illus., index. Sample. Refereed. Circ: 3755 Paid. Vol. ends: No. 6. CD-ROM: ProQuest LLC (Ann Arbor). Online: EBSCO Publishing, EBSCO Host; Florida Center for Library Automation; Gale; OCLC Online Computer Library Center, Inc.; ProQuest K-12 Learning Solutions; ProQuest LLC (Ann Arbor); H.W. Wilson. Reprint: PSC. *Indexed:* BRI, CBRI, ChemAb, GSI, MASUSE, MinerAb, PetrolAb. *Bk. rev.:* 0-7, 100-800 words, signed. *Aud.:* Hs, Ga, Ac, Sa.

Spectacular full-color photographs and a modest price make this an ideal choice for libraries of all sizes. The emphasis is on minerals more than on rocks, and the specimens featured in the articles are generally of "museum quality." There is also a considerable amount of other material to interest collectors, such as mineral localities, sample preparation, and historical background. Museum notes, announcements, and a calendar of upcoming events are also included. The web site offers free tables of contents and abstracts and a searchable archive. Access to full text of articles can be purchased.

1829. Sedimentary Geology. [ISSN: 0037-0738] 1967. 40x/yr. EUR 3161. Ed(s): K A W Crook, B W Sellwood. Elsevier BV, Radarweg 29, Amsterdam, 1043 NX, Netherlands; nlinfo-f@elsevier.nl; http://www.elsevier.nl. Illus., index, adv. Sample. Refereed. Vol. ends: No. 4. Microform: PQC. Online: EBSCO Publishing, EBSCO Host; Gale; IngentaConnect; OhioLINK; ScienceDirect; SwetsWise Online Content. *Indexed:* ChemAb, IBR, M&GPA, OceAb, PetrolAb, PollutAb, SCI, SWRA, ZooRec. *Bk. rev.:* 0-4, 300-3,000 words. *Aud.:* Ac, Sa.

Publishes research papers on all aspects of sediments and sedimentary rocks. Examples of topics addressed include analytical techniques such as numerical modeling, regional studies of sedimentary systems, and chemical sedimentology. Some recent special issues have focused on sedimentary records of catastrophic events and deformation of soft sediments in nature and the laboratory, and have presented conference papers from *Drylands: Linking Landscape Processes to Sedimentary Environment*. Articles tend to emphasize the Eurasian region more than *Journal of Sedimentary Research*. Tables of contents and abstracts are available at the web site, from volume one (1967). Full-text articles are available through ScienceDirect. A GeoRef priority journal.

1830. Sedimentology. [ISSN: 0037-0746] 1952. bi-m. GBP 820 print & online eds. Ed(s): Peter Swart, Paul A Carling. Blackwell Publishing Ltd., 9600 Garsington Rd, Oxford, OX4 2ZG, United Kingdom; customerservices@blackwellpublishing.com; http://www.blackwellpublishing.com. Illus., index. Sample. Refereed. Circ: 2870. Vol. ends: Dec (No. 6). Microform: PQC. Online: Blackwell

Synergy; EBSCO Publishing, EBSCO Host; Gale; IngentaConnect; OCLC Online Computer Library Center, Inc.; OhioLINK; SwetsWise Online Content. Reprint: PSC. *Indexed:* CABA, ChemAb, ForAb, M&GPA, OceAb, PetrolAb, PollutAb, S&F, SCI, SWRA. *Aud.:* Ac, Sa.

This bimonthly publication is the official journal of the International Association of Sedimentologists. Full-length papers deal with every aspect of sediments and sedimentary rocks. These are well illustrated and of consistently high quality. Virtually all are in English, but contributions in French and German are also accepted. This journal is recommended for academic and special library collections. Free tables of contents and abstracts from volume one (1962) are accessible on the web site. Full-text articles are available for subscribers. A GeoRef priority journal.

1831. Seismological Society of America. Bulletin. [ISSN: 0037-1106] 1911. bi-m. USD 540 (print & online eds.). Ed(s): Andrew Michael. Seismological Society of America, 201 Plaza Professional Bldg, El Cerrito, CA 94530-4003; info@seismosoc.org; http://www.seismosoc.org. Illus., index. Sample. Refereed. Circ: 2500 Paid. Vol. ends: Dec (No. 6). Online: HighWire Press; OCLC Online Computer Library Center, Inc. *Indexed:* AS&TI, ApMecR, CCMJ, EngInd, IAA, MSN, MathR, PetrolAb, S&F, SCI. *Aud.:* Ac, Sa.

Publishes research papers, reviews, short notes, comments, and replies in the areas of seismology, earthquake geology, and earthquake engineering. Specific topics include investigation of earthquakes; theoretical and observational studies of seismic waves; seismometry; earthquake hazard and risk estimation; and seismotectonics. The web site provides free tables of contents and abstracts from 1911 to the present. Society members and subscribers may view the full-text articles. A GeoRef priority journal.

1832. Stratigraphy. [ISSN: 1547-139X] 2004. q. USD 280 (Individuals, USD 140). Ed(s): John A Van Couvering. Micropaleontology Press, 256 Fifth Ave, New York, NY 10001; http://micropress.org/. Refereed. *Aud.:* Ac, Sa.

This is the journal of record for the North American Commission on Stratigraphic Names, the International Association of Stratigraphic Geologists, and the International Commission on Stratigraphy. Publishes research articles on all aspects of stratigraphy, including chronostratigraphy, biostratigraphy, cyclostratigraphy, sequence stratigraphy, tectonostratigraphy, chemostratigraphy, lithostratigraphy, and others. Selected articles are freely accessible online, while subscribers may view full text.

1833. Tectonics. [ISSN: 0278-7407] 1982. m. USD 650. Ed(s): Kip V Hodges, Onno Oncken. American Geophysical Union, 2000 Florida Ave, NW, Washington, DC 20009-1277; service@agu.org; http://www.agu.org. Illus., index. Sample. Refereed. Vol. ends: Dec (No. 6). Online: EBSCO Publishing, EBSCO Host. *Indexed:* IAA, PetrolAb, SCI. *Aud.:* Ac, Sa.

Cosponsored by the American Geophysical Union (AGU) and the European Geophysical Society, this journal publishes reports of original analytical, synthetic, and integrative studies on the structure and evolution of the terrestrial lithosphere. Emphasis is on continental tectonics, including such topics as thrusting and faulting, mountain building, volcanism, and rifting. The AGU web site provides full-text articles from 1994 to the present for subscribers. Recommended for academic research collections. A GeoRef priority journal.

1834. Tectonophysics. [ISSN: 0040-1951] 1964. 68x/yr. EUR 5176. Ed(s): J P Burg, H Thybo. Elsevier BV, Radarweg 29, Amsterdam, 1043 NX, Netherlands; nlinfo-f@elsevier.nl; http://www.elsevier.nl. Illus., adv. Sample. Refereed. Vol. ends: No. 327 - No. 343. Microform: PQC. Online: EBSCO Publishing, EBSCO Host; Gale; IngentaConnect; OhioLINK; ScienceDirect; SwetsWise Online Content. *Indexed:* C&ISA, CerAb, ChemAb, IAA, IBR, M&GPA, MinerAb, OceAb, PetrolAb, PollutAb, SCI, SSCI, SWRA. *Bk. rev.:* 0-3, 400-1,500 words. *Aud.:* Ac, Sa.

Publishes research papers on geology and physics of the earth's crust and interior, addressing topics such as regional and plate tectonics, seismology, crustal movements, rock mechanics, and structural features. Journal issues frequently include large-scale geological maps, seismic sections, and other diagrams. The web site provides free access to tables of contents and abstracts from volume one (1964). Full-text articles are also available through ScienceDirect. A GeoRef priority journal.

1835. *Terra Nova: the European journal of geosciences.* [ISSN: 0954-4879] 1989. bi-m. GBP 567 print & online eds. Ed(s): Max Coleman, Adolphe Nicolas. Blackwell Publishing Ltd., 9600 Garsington Rd, Oxford, OX4 2ZG, United Kingdom; customerservices@blackwellpublishing.com; http://www.blackwellpublishing.com. Illus., index, adv. Sample. Refereed. Circ: 1765. Vol. ends: No. 6. Microform: PQC. Online: Blackwell Synergy; EBSCO Publishing, EBSCO Host; Gale; IngentaConnect; OCLC Online Computer Library Center, Inc.; OhioLINK; SwetsWise Online Content. Reprint: PSC. *Indexed:* ArtHuCI, PetrolAb, SCI, ZooRec. *Aud.:* Ac, Sa.

Terra Nova is the result of a collaboration between the European Union of Geosciences and 18 national geoscience societies throughout Europe. It includes a mix of original papers and review articles that cover the solid earth and planetary sciences, including interfaces with the hydrosphere and atmosphere. Except for the review articles, all contributions are 2,500 words or less. Free tables of contents and abstracts are available on the web site beginning with 1997. Full-text articles are accessible to subscribers or for others on a per-article basis.

1836. *Water Resources Research.* [ISSN: 0043-1397] 1965. m. USD 1300. Ed(s): Marc B. Parlange. American Geophysical Union, 2000 Florida Ave, NW, Washington, DC 20009-1277; http://www.agu.org. Illus., index. Sample. Refereed. Circ: 4000. Vol. ends: No. 12. Online: EBSCO Publishing, EBSCO Host. *Indexed:* AS&TI, Agr, ApMecR, BioEngAb, CABA, ChemAb, EngInd, EnvAb, EnvInd, ExcerpMed, FPA, ForAb, HortAb, IAA, JEL, M&GPA, OceAb, PetrolAb, PollutAb, RRTA, S&F, SCI, SSCI, SWRA, WAE&RSA, WRCInf. *Aud.:* Ac, Sa.

Articles present interdisciplinary research on water-related studies that spans the social and natural sciences. Areas of focus include the physical, chemical, and biological sciences in hydrology as well as economics, policy analysis, and law. Issues include original research articles along with technical notes, commentaries, and replies. Tables of contents and abstracts from 1990 to the present are freely accessible on the web site. Full-text articles are accessible to subscribers and to members of the American Geophysical Union. A GeoRef priority journal.

■ ECOLOGY

See also Biology; Botany; and Zoology sections.

Kristen LaBonte, Digital Resources and GIS Librarian, Broome Library, California State University Channel Islands, Camarillo, CA 93012

Introduction

Ecology journals can be comprehensive or focused on a certain aspect of the discipline. The publications are all technical in nature and are all peer-reviewed with rigorous publication policies. They are appropriate for academic libraries sponsoring ecology programs, special libraries, and personal libraries of professional ecologists and scientists of related disciplines.

Basic Periodicals

Ac: *Ecology, Journal of Animal Ecology, Journal of Ecology.*

Basic Abstracts and Indexes

Biological Abstracts, Biological Abstracts/RRM, Biological and Agricultural Index, Current Contents/Life Sciences, Science Citation Index, Zoological Record.

1837. *American Midland Naturalist.* Formerly (until 1909): *Midland Naturalist.* [ISSN: 0003-0031] 1909. q. USD 85 N. & S. America & the Caribbean (Individuals, USD 45; Students, USD 25). Ed(s): William Evan. University of Notre Dame, Department of Biological Sciences, Rm 285 GLSC Box 369, Notre Dame, IN 46556. Illus., index. Refereed. Circ: 1400. Microform: IDC; PQC. Online: BioOne; CSA; EBSCO Publishing, EBSCO Host; Florida Center for Library Automation; Gale; JSTOR (Web-based Journal Archive); Northern Light Technology, Inc.; OCLC Online Computer Library Center, Inc.; OhioLINK; ProQuest K-12 Learning Solutions; ProQuest LLC (Ann Arbor); H.W. Wilson. *Indexed:* Agr, AnBeAb, ApEcolAb, B&AI, BiolAb, CABA, ChemAb, DSA, FPA, ForAb, GSI, GardL, HortAb, IBR, IndVet, RRTA, S&F, SCI, SSCI, SWRA, VB, WAE&RSA, ZooRec. *Aud.:* Ac, Sa.

American Midland Naturalist publishes original field and experimental biology articles as well as "review articles of a critical nature on topics of current interest in biology." Published since 1909 by the University of Notre Dame, this academic journal no longer is limited in geographic scope to the middle of America. Rather, it covers the North American continent and has occasional articles from other continents. Two volumes containing two issues each are published per year. The issues are composed of many full-length articles and a few short "Notes and Discussions." All subject areas related to plant and animal ecology are covered in this diverse journal.

1838. *The American Naturalist.* [ISSN: 0003-0147] 1867. m. USD 470 domestic; USD 520.20 Canada; USD 510 elsewhere. Ed(s): Michael C Whitlock. University of Chicago Press, Journals Division, PO Box 37005, Chicago, IL 60637; subscriptions@press.uchicago.edu; http://www.journals.uchicago.edu. Illus., index, adv. Refereed. Circ: 2600 Paid. Microform: IDC; PMC; PQC. Online: EBSCO Publishing, EBSCO Host; Florida Center for Library Automation; Gale; JSTOR (Web-based Journal Archive); ProQuest LLC (Ann Arbor). Reprint: PSC. *Indexed:* Agr, AnBeAb, ApEcolAb, B&AI, BiolAb, BiolDig, CABA, ChemAb, DSA, ForAb, GSI, GardL, HortAb, IndVet, MathR, OceAb, S&F, SCI, SSCI, VB, WAE&RSA, ZooRec. *Aud.:* Ac, Sa.

Advancing the knowledge of organic evolution and examining broad biological principles are the focus of publication for *The American Naturalist*. Articles relating to "community and ecosystem dynamics, evolution of sex and mating systems, organismal adaptation, and genetic aspects of evolution" are published. The journal emphasizes articles in "sophisticated methodologies and innovative theoretical syntheses." The journal has recently revived the section called "Natural History Miscellany," which includes notes pertaining to the natural history of a species that also have "relevance to important or conceptual issues or understanding of the dimensions of biological diversity." The enhanced electronic edition offers a citation manager, RSS, pdfs, direct Medline and CrossRef linking, table and figure galleries, and ASCII versions of tables. Published for the American Society of Naturalists, this journal is appropriate for academic libraries and professionals.

1839. *Ecology.* Formerly (until 1919): *Plant World.* [ISSN: 0012-9658] 1897. m. Members, USD 65. Ed(s): Robert K Peet. Ecological Society of America, 1707 H St, NW, Ste 400, Washington, DC 20006; esahq@esa.org. Illus., index, adv. Refereed. Circ: 6400. Vol. ends: Dec. Microform: IDC; PMC; PQC. Online: Allen Press Inc.; EBSCO Publishing, EBSCO Host; Gale; JSTOR (Web-based Journal Archive); OCLC Online Computer Library Center, Inc.; ProQuest K-12 Learning Solutions; ProQuest LLC (Ann Arbor). *Indexed:* AbAn, Agr, AnBeAb, ApEcolAb, B&AI, BRI, BiolAb, CABA, CBRI, ChemAb, ExcerpMed, FPA, FS&TA, ForAb, GSI, GardL, HortAb, IBR, IndVet, M&GPA, OceAb, RI-1, S&F, SCI, SSCI, SWRA, VB, WAE&RSA, ZooRec. *Bk. rev.:* 5-7, 500-1,000 words. *Aud.:* Ac, Sa.

Ecology focuses on the publishing of concise articles that contain "research and synthesis that lead to generalizations potentially applicable to other species, populations, communities, or ecosystems." Research and synthesis papers from all areas of ecology are published "with particular emphasis on papers that develop new concepts in ecology that test ecological theory or lead to an increased appreciation for the diversity of ecological phenomena." The current trend of the publication is to reduce the number and length of articles and to increase the number of reports to enable greater content per page printed. The journal is a core title for academic and special libraries supporting ecologists.

1840. *Freshwater Biology.* [ISSN: 0046-5070] 1971. m. GBP 2510 print & online eds. Ed(s): Dr. Alan G. Hildrew, Dr. Colin R. Townsend. Blackwell Publishing Ltd., 9600 Garsington Rd, Oxford, OX4 2ZG, United Kingdom; customerservices@blackwellpublishing.com; http://www.blackwellpublishing.com. Illus., index. Sample. Refereed. Circ: 840. Microform: PQC. Online: Blackwell Synergy; EBSCO Publishing, EBSCO Host; Gale; IngentaConnect; OCLC Online Computer Library Center, Inc.; OhioLINK; SwetsWise Online Content. Reprint: PSC. *Indexed:* ApEcolAb, B&AI, BiolAb, BiolDig, CABA, ChemAb, EnvAb, EnvInd, ExcerpMed, FPA, ForAb, HortAb, IndVet, PollutAb, RRTA, S&F, SCI, SWRA, VB, WAE&RSA, WRCInf, ZooRec. *Bk. rev.:* 0-3, 500-2,000 words. *Aud.:* Ac, Sa.

Freshwater Biology publishes standard research papers related to all ecological aspects of inland waters. Studies can be focused at any level in the ecological hierarchy relating to "micro-organisms, algae, macrophytes, invertebrates, fish and other vertebrates, as well as those concerning whole ecosystems and related physical and chemical aspects of the environment." Review articles and discussion (editorial) papers are also printed. Special issues dedicated to a topic or theme are also occasionally published. Applied science papers related to the management and conservation of inland waters are also published in this journal. Appropriate for academic and special libraries that support ecologists, limnologists, biologists, and environmental scientists.

1841. *Journal of Animal Ecology.* [ISSN: 0021-8790] 1932. bi-m. GBP 607 print & online eds. Ed(s): Ken Norris, Dave Raffaelli. Blackwell Publishing Ltd., 9600 Garsington Rd, Oxford, OX4 2ZG, United Kingdom; customerservices@blackwellpublishing.com; http://www.blackwellpublishing.com. Illus., index, adv. Refereed. Circ: 2715. Vol. ends: Nov. Microform: PQC. Online: Blackwell Synergy; EBSCO Publishing, EBSCO Host; Gale; IngentaConnect; JSTOR (Web-based Journal Archive); OCLC Online Computer Library Center, Inc.; OhioLINK; SwetsWise Online Content. Reprint: PSC. *Indexed:* AbAn, AnBeAb, ApEcolAb, B&AI, BiolAb, CABA, ChemAb, FPA, FS&TA, ForAb, HortAb, IndVet, MathR, S&F, SCI, SWRA, VB, ZooRec. *Bk. rev.:* 0-8, 300-1,200 words. *Aud.:* Ac, Sa.

The British Ecological Society offers original research related to all aspects of animal ecology in the *Journal of Animal Ecology.* The topics of evolutionary ecology, behavioral ecology, population ecology, molecular ecology, community ecology, and physiological ecology are covered. In addition, "field, laboratory, and theoretical studies based upon terrestrial freshwater or marine systems" are included. Each article has a numbered point-by-point overview instead of a standard abstract, which allows browsing to be more efficient. The journal is appropriate for academic programs focusing on animal ecology and for professionals.

1842. *Journal of Ecology.* [ISSN: 0022-0477] 1913. bi-m. GBP 639 print & online eds. Ed(s): David J Gibson, Michael J Hutchings. Blackwell Publishing Ltd., 9600 Garsington Rd, Oxford, OX4 2ZG, United Kingdom; customerservices@blackwellpublishing.com; http://www.blackwellpublishing.com. Illus., index, adv. Refereed. Circ: 3190. Vol. ends: Dec. Microform: PQC. Online: Blackwell Synergy; EBSCO Publishing, EBSCO Host; Gale; IngentaConnect; JSTOR (Web-based Journal Archive); OCLC Online Computer Library Center, Inc.; OhioLINK; SwetsWise Online Content. Reprint: PSC. *Indexed:* Agr, AnBeAb, ApEcolAb, B&AI, BiolAb, BrArAb, CABA, ChemAb, EnvAb, EnvInd, ExcerpMed, FPA, ForAb, GSI, GardL, HortAb, IBR, OceAb, PollutAb, RRTA, S&F, SCI, SWRA, WRCInf, ZooRec. *Aud.:* Ac, Sa.

The British Ecological Society offers original research related to the ecology of plants in the *Journal of Ecology.* Experimental papers using any kind of ecological approach are welcomed, along with those focusing on theoretical approaches or papers with historical or descriptive accounts. Papers relating to the cultivation of plants are not published in the *Journal of Ecology.* Each article has a numbered point-by-point overview instead of an abstract, which makes browsing more efficient. Papers from all geographical regions are published, along with essay reviews and forum (opinion) articles. The journal is appropriate for academic programs related to plant ecology and for professionals.

1843. *Oecologia.* Formerly: *Zeitschrift fuer Morphologie und Oekologie der Tiere.* [ISSN: 0029-8549] 1924. 16x/yr. EUR 4674 print & online eds. Ed(s): James R Ehleringer, Craig W Osenberg. Springer, Tiergartenstr 17, Heidelberg, 69121, Germany. Illus., adv. Sample. Refereed. Microform: PQC. Online: EBSCO Publishing, EBSCO Host; OhioLINK; Springer LINK; SwetsWise Online Content. Reprint: PSC. *Indexed:* Agr, AnBeAb, ApEcolAb, B&AI, BiolAb, CABA, DSA, ExcerpMed, FPA, ForAb, HortAb, IndVet, OceAb, S&F, SCI, SWRA, VB, WAE&RSA, ZooRec. *Aud.:* Ac, Sa.

Oecologia publishes "reviews, advances in methodology, and original contributions" related to plant and animal ecology. Issues are divided into the sections of ecophysiology, population ecology, plant and animal interactions, ecosystem ecology, community ecology, global change and conservation ecology, and behavioral ecology. Rapid communications of broad interest to the ecological community are also published in this academic journal. Appropriate for scholars and professionals.

1844. *Oikos: a journal of ecology.* [ISSN: 0030-1299] 1948. 12x/school-academic yr. GBP 708 print & online eds. Ed(s): Per Lundberg, Maria Persson. Blackwell Publishing Ltd., 9600 Garsington Rd, Oxford, OX4 2ZG, United Kingdom; customerservices@blackwellpublishing.com; http://www.blackwellpublishing.com. Illus., adv. Refereed. Circ: 1550. Online: Blackwell Synergy; EBSCO Publishing, EBSCO Host; Gale; IngentaConnect; OCLC Online Computer Library Center, Inc.; OhioLINK; Ovid Technologies, Inc.; SwetsWise Online Content. Reprint: PSC. *Indexed:* AnBeAb, ApEcolAb, BiolAb, CABA, ChemAb, FPA, ForAb, GSI, HortAb, IBR, IndVet, M&GPA, OceAb, S&F, SCI, SWRA, VB, WAE&RSA, ZooRec. *Aud.:* Ac, Sa.

The Nordic Ecologic Society issues *Oikos: a journal of ecology.* Theoretical and empirical work related to all aspects of ecology from all regions of the world can be accepted for publication. The journal also has a forum section, an opinion section, and mini-reviews. The forum section is "intended for short notes on new ideas or new ways of interpreting existing information." The opinion section is available to comment, make suggestions, and discuss published papers or to discuss important current issues in ecology. The mini-reviews summarize current topics in ecology where "rapid and significant changes are occurring." Book reviews are not published in this journal. Appropriate for academic institutions with an ecology program or for professionals.

■ ECONOMICS

Gwyneth H. Crowley, Librarian for Economics & Sociology, Coordinator of Collection Development, Social Science Libraries and Information Services, Yale University; gwyneth.crowley@yale.edu

Introduction

After reviewing economics journals this year for *MFL*, I have noticed certain trends: disappearing book reviews; previous multi-language journals are English-only now; there is a new way of ranking economic journals by Kodrzycki and Yu (a delightful obsession with economists); and overall, economists are being more introspective about their professions and abstractions. New journals continue to abound! The American Economic Association has started several online journals to help disseminate information faster and will be "competing" with Berkley Online Press journals. Other new titles? My favorite is the *Journal of Happiness Studies.* Or how about *Basic Income Studies*? There are certainly more interdisciplinary, focused, and international journals being included in ECONLIT. Also, this year for *MFL,* I have cross-referenced quite a few energy- and health-related journals, as these have become ever more important in today's society.

Basic Periodicals

Ga: *The American Prospect, Challenge, Contemporary Economic Policy, The Economist, Journal of Economic History, Journal of Economic Literature, Journal of Economic Perspectives, OECD Observer, Review of Black Political Economy, Review of Political Economy, World Bank Research Observer;* Ac: *American Economic Review, Brookings Papers on Economic Activity,*

ECONOMICS

Cambridge Journal of Economics, Econometrica, Economic History Review, The Economic Journal, Economica, International Economic Review, Journal of Econometrics, Journal of Economic Literature, Journal of Economic Perspectives, Journal of Economic Theory, Journal of Monetary Economics, Journal of Political Economy, Journal of Public Economics, Manchester School, OECD Observer, Public Choice, Quarterly Journal of Economics, RAND Journal of Economics, The Review of Economic Studies, The Review of Economics and Statistics, The Review of Economics and Statistics, The World Bank Economic Review.

Basic Abstracts and Indexes

ABI/Inform, EconLit, International Bibliography of the Social Sciences, Public Affairs Information Service International, RePEc, Social Science Citation Index, Wilson Social Science Index, Wilson Business Abstracts, World Agricultural Economics and Rural Sociology.

The American Economic Review (Print Edition). See Labor and Industrial Relations section.

1845. American Economist. [ISSN: 0569-4345] 1956. s-a. USD 40 (Individuals, USD 20). Ed(s): Michael Szenberg. Omicron Delta Epsilon, PO Box 1486, Hattiesburg, MS 39403-1486; odecf@aol.com. Sample. Refereed. Circ: 6500 Paid. Microform: PQC. Online: EBSCO Publishing, EBSCO Host; Florida Center for Library Automation; Gale; Northern Light Technology, Inc.; OCLC Online Computer Library Center, Inc.; ProQuest LLC (Ann Arbor); H.W. Wilson. *Indexed:* ABIn, ABS&EES, AgeL, BPI, JEL, PAIS, RiskAb, SSCI. *Bk. rev.:* Number and length vary. *Aud.:* Ac, Sa.

In its 50th volume, this is the journal of The International Honor Society in Economics: Omicron Delta Epsilon. Book reviews and a general index are included. The spring issue has a chapter roll. There are gems! Robert C. Merton, 1997 Nobel Prize–winner in Economic Science, contributed an article about Paul Samuelson and financial economics in the fall 2006 issue to celebrate his 90th birthday. The web site has issues from 2002 to 2005. Good for college and university libraries.

1846. American Journal of Agricultural Economics. Formerly (until 1968): *Journal of Farm Economics.* [ISSN: 0002-9092] 1919. 5x/yr. GBP 263 print & online eds. Ed(s): Ian M Sheldon, Stephen K Swallow. Blackwell Publishing, Inc., Commerce Place, 350 Main St, Malden, MA 02148; customerservices@blackwellpublishing.com; http://www.blackwellpublishing.com. Illus., index, adv. Refereed. Circ: 7000. Microform: PMC. Online: Blackwell Synergy; EBSCO Publishing, EBSCO Host; Florida Center for Library Automation; Gale; IngentaConnect; JSTOR (Web-based Journal Archive); Northern Light Technology, Inc.; OCLC Online Computer Library Center, Inc.; OhioLINK; SwetsWise Online Content; H.W. Wilson. Reprint: PSC. *Indexed:* ABIn, AgeL, Agr, B&AI, BAS, BPI, CABA, CJA, DSA, EnvInd, ExcerpMed, FPA, FS&TA, ForAb, HortAb, IBSS, IndVet, JEL, PAIS, PollutAb, RRTA, RiskAb, S&F, SCI, SSCI, VB, WAE&RSA. *Bk. rev.:* 5, 600-700 words, signed. *Aud.:* Ac, Sa.

This well-respected journal contains 15 or so articles in each issue on "the economics of agriculture, natural resources and the environment, and rural and community development." The authors are usually American academics, but the journal include international coverage as well as invited papers, conference proceedings, book reviews, comments and replies, and biographies of recent fellows. Now, the December issue carries the proceedings from the annual meeting of the American Agricultural Association. Substantial signed book reviews are included. A recent issue included the articles: "Brand-Supermarket Demand for Breakfast Cereals and Retail Competition" and "Is There Persistence in the Impact of Emergency Food Aid? Evidence on Consumption, Food Security and Assets in Rural Ethiopia." The Core Historical Literature of Agriculture collection at Cornell University's Albert R. Mann Library offers free electronic access to back issues from 1919 through 1995. Recommended for all colleges and universities with agricultural economics and related programs.

1847. American Journal of Economics and Sociology. [ISSN: 0002-9246] 1941. 5x/yr. GBP 153 print & online eds. Ed(s): Laurence S Moss. Blackwell Publishing, Inc., Commerce Place, 350 Main St, Malden, MA 02148; customerservices@blackwellpublishing.com; http://www.blackwellpublishing.com. Illus., index. Sample. Refereed. Circ: 2200. Vol. ends: Nov. Microform: PQC. Online: Blackwell Synergy; EBSCO Publishing, EBSCO Host; Florida Center for Library Automation; Gale; IngentaConnect; OCLC Online Computer Library Center, Inc.; OhioLINK; SwetsWise Online Content; H.W. Wilson. Reprint: PSC. *Indexed:* ABCPolSci, ABIn, ABS&EES, AgeL, AmH&L, ApEcolAb, ArtHuCI, BAS, BRI, CBRI, CJA, EIP, FR, FS&TA, HRA, HistAb, IBR, IBSS, IBZ, IMFL, IPSA, IndIslam, JEL, PAIS, PRA, PSA, RRTA, RiskAb, S&F, SSA, SSCI, SUSA, SWA, SWR&A, SociolAb, V&AA, WAE&RSA. *Bk. rev.:* 1, 50-100 words. *Aud.:* Ga, Ac.

This esteemed journal is a "forum for continuing discussion of issues emphasized by the American political economist, social philosopher, and activist, Henry George (1839-1897)." In the April 2007 issue, economists are looking at themselves with intriguing research. Two articles to illustrate are: "Economists' Opinions of Economists' Work" and "What Do Economists Talk About?" Each issue contains 8–11 articles by distinguished scholars. Every year, there is a special thematic issue that is turned into a book. Next year, gambling and probability theory! There is an index at the volume's end. Recommended for large public and university libraries.

1848. The American Prospect: literal intelligence. [ISSN: 1049-7285] 1990. 10x/yr. USD 19.95 domestic; USD 29.95 Canada; USD 34.95 elsewhere. The American Prospect, Inc., 2000 L St NW, Ste 717, Washington, DC 20036. Adv. Circ: 55000 Paid and free. Microform: PQC. Online: Florida Center for Library Automation; Gale; LexisNexis; Northern Light Technology, Inc.; OCLC Online Computer Library Center, Inc.; ProQuest LLC (Ann Arbor); H.W. Wilson. *Indexed:* ABS&EES, AgeL, AltPI, JEL, LRI, LeftInd, PAIS, PRA, RI-1, SWR&A. *Aud.:* Hs, Ga, Ac, Sa.

With a moderate left-wing slant, this passionate and informative magazine is for the general reader, and began publishing in 1990. Conventionally, its aim is to present "a practical and convincing vision of liberal philosophy, politics and public life." Self-described: "Through dogged reporting, cool analysis, witty commentary and passionate argument, the *Prospect* strives to beat back the right wing and to build a majority of true patriots who understand what really makes America great." It is now published every month except August, and there are frequent special reports and features. The online version includes the "group blog, TAPPED." A valuable resource and recommended for browsing and reading in high school, public, academic, and special libraries.

1849. American Review of Political Economy. [ISSN: 1551-1383] 2002. s-a. Free. Ed(s): Zagros Madjd-Sadjadi. University of Washington, 1900 Commerce St, Tacoma, WA 98402; http://www.washington.edu. Refereed. *Indexed:* JEL. *Bk. rev.:* Proposed. *Aud.:* Ac, Sa.

Online only, and free, the *American Review of Political Economy* contains "three to six double-blind peer-reviewed articles" and uses *JEL* (*Journal of Economic Literature*) codes to classify articles. Acceptance criteria are broadly defined "with the goal of creating a rich dialogue." Members of the editorial board mainly come from U.S. institutions.

American Statistical Association. Journal. See Statistics section.

1850. Applied Economics. [ISSN: 0003-6846] 1969. 21x/yr. GBP 5643 print & online eds. Ed(s): Lucio Sarno, Mark P Taylor. Routledge, 4 Park Sq, Milton Park, Abingdon, OX14 4RN, United Kingdom; info@routledge.co.uk; http://www.routledge.com. Illus., index, adv. Sample. Refereed. Vol. ends: Dec. Online: EBSCO Publishing, EBSCO Host; Florida Center for Library Automation; Gale; IngentaConnect; Northern Light Technology, Inc.; OCLC Online Computer Library Center, Inc.; SwetsWise Online Content. Reprint: PSC. *Indexed:* ABIn, AgeL, BAS, BPI, CABA, CJA, DSA, FPA, ForAb, HortAb, IBR, IBSS, IBZ, IndVet, JEL, PAIS, PRA, RRTA, RiskAb, S&F, SSCI, VB, WAE&RSA. *Aud.:* Ac, Sa.

Applied Economics, a peer-reviewed monthly, "encourages the application of economic analysis to specific problems in both public and private sectors" and it contains about 13 articles, mainly quantitative, by international academicians. The subscription to *Applied Economics* includes subscriptions to the monthly *Applied Economics Letters* and the bimonthly *Applied Financial Economics*. They may both be purchased separately. The former publishes "short accounts of new original research that may include theory and methodology." *Applied Financial Letters* publishes "research papers, short articles, notes and comments on financial economics, banking and monetary economics." Its scope is international, with developing and transitional economies gaining interest. Multiple issues have been combined, making for a hefty journal. Two recent articles include interesting research, "Do the sick retire early? Chronic illness, asset accumulation and early retirement" and "Risk coping and starvation in rural China." Although there has been discussion about the journal's high cost per page, it is still recommended for academic libraries.

1851. *The B E Journal in Theoretical Economics.* Formerly: *The B E Journals in Theoretical Economics;* Incorporates (in 2006): *Frontiers of Theoretical Economics; Advances in Theoretical Economics; Contributions to Theoretical Economics; Topics in Theoretical Economics.* [ISSN: 1935-1704] 2001. a. USD 300 (Individuals, USD 35). Ed(s): Aaron S Edlin. Berkeley Electronic Press, 2809 Telegraph Ave, Ste 202, Berkeley, CA 94705; info@bepress.com; http://www.bepress.com. *Indexed:* CCMJ, MSN, MathR. *Aud.:* Ac, Sa.

The Berkeley Electronic Press initiated this project to "create a new standard in scholarly publishing." There are three web-based economics journals to peruse, each has four subsections, and all articles are peer reviewed. *The BE Journals in Theoretical Economics* cover "all areas of economic theory, including decision theory, game theory, general equilibrium theory, and the theory of economic mechanisms." *The BE Journals in Macroeconomics* "publishes in both theoretical and applied macroeconomics." A wide range of topics is covered, including business cycles, economic growth, monetary economics, labor economics, finance, development economics, political economics, public economics, and econometric theory. *The BE Journals in Economic Analysis & Policy*'s scope is microeconomics issues in business and public policy. Topics of interest include "the interaction of firms, the functioning of markets, the formulation of domestic and international policy, and the design of organizations and institutions. Articles can be on corporate finance, industrial organization, international trade, public finance, law and economics or other related fields." There is a nominal fee for the author to publish in these journals, and there is a small growing number of articles available. BE Press has also morphed other publications into *The BE Journals in Macroeconomics* and *The BE Journals in Economic Analysis and Policy*. For institutions, there is a new pricing model for all BE Press journals. Check it out.

1852. *Basic Income Studies: an international journal of basic income research.* [ISSN: 1932-0183] 2006. irreg. USD 325 (Individuals, USD 35). Ed(s): Rafael Pinilla-Palleja, Xavier Fontcuberta Estrada. Berkeley Electronic Press, 2809 Telegraph Ave, Ste 202, Berkeley, CA 94705; info@bepress.com; http://www.bepress.com. Refereed. *Bk. rev.:* Number and length vary. *Aud.:* Ac, Sa.

An exciting new journal from Berkeley Electronic Press! Congratulations to them for thinking of this first, a much-needed journal on "basic income and related issues of poverty relief and universal welfare" and social policy. As an economic concept, *basic income* is defined as a "universal income grant available to every citizen without means test or work requirement," and is a concern for NGOs, politicians, and grass roots movements. Articles are written in a clear style for all, economists and noneconomists alike; and topics are at the leading front of discussions and include subjects such as poverty, political theory, welfare reform, ethics, and public policy. This journal will be welcomed by researchers as an outlet for research. Subscribe now to this e-only journal! For universities, college, special, and larger public libraries.

1853. *Brookings Papers on Economic Activity.* [ISSN: 0007-2303] 1970. s-a. USD 65 (Individuals, USD 50; USD 25 per issue). Ed(s): William C Brainard, George L Perry. Brookings Institution Press, 1775 Massachusetts Ave, NW, Washington, DC 20036-2188. Illus., index. Refereed. Microform: PQC. Online: EBSCO Publishing, EBSCO Host; Florida Center for Library Automation; Gale; JSTOR (Web-based Journal

Archive); Northern Light Technology, Inc.; OCLC Online Computer Library Center, Inc.; OhioLINK; Project MUSE; ProQuest LLC (Ann Arbor); SwetsWise Online Content; H.W. Wilson. *Indexed:* ABIn, ABS&EES, AgeL, BPI, HRA, IBR, IBSS, IBZ, JEL, PAIS, SFSA, SSCI, WAE&RSA. *Aud.:* Ga, Ac.

This esteemed publication from the Brookings Institution, an independent organization, is a forum for "nonpartisan research, education, and publication in economics, government, foreign policy, and the social sciences generally" and works to help develop "sound public policies and to promote public understanding of issues of national importance." The journal is composed exclusively of invited contributions and "articles, reports, and highlights of the discussions from conferences of the Brookings Panel on Economic Activity." Publication has been lagging the past year. Highly recommended for universities and colleges.

1854. *Business Economics: designed to serve the needs of people who use economics in their work.* [ISSN: 0007-666X] 1965. q. EUR 147. Ed(s): Robert Thomas Crow. Springer New York LLC, 233 Spring St, New York, NY 10013-1578; journals@springer-ny.com; http://www.springer.com/. Illus., index, adv. Circ: 4700. Vol. ends: Oct. Microform: PQC. Online: EBSCO Publishing, EBSCO Host; Florida Center for Library Automation; Gale; Northern Light Technology, Inc.; OCLC Online Computer Library Center, Inc.; ProQuest K-12 Learning Solutions; ProQuest LLC (Ann Arbor); Springer LINK; SwetsWise Online Content; H.W. Wilson. Reprint: SCH. *Indexed:* ABIn, BLI, BPI, JEL, PAIS. *Bk. rev.:* 1-4, 1,000-1,500 words. *Aud.:* Ga, Ac.

Published by the National Association for Business Economists, this journal "provides resources and practical information to people who use economics in their jobs," and was created to provide a forum. Each issue typically has five articles, and focus papers. Signed book reviews are included. All very accessible to the non-economist. Papers are mostly invited. Academic and large public libraries should consider this journal for their collections.

1855. *Cambridge Journal of Economics.* [ISSN: 0309-166X] 1977. bi-m. EUR 431 print or online ed. Ed(s): Ann Newton. Oxford University Press, Great Clarendon St, Oxford, OX2 6DP, United Kingdom; jnl.orders@oup.co.uk; http://www.oxfordjournals.org. Illus., index, adv. Refereed. Circ: 1750. Vol. ends: Nov. Online: Chadwyck-Healey Inc.; EBSCO Publishing, EBSCO Host; Gale; HighWire Press; IngentaConnect; OCLC Online Computer Library Center, Inc.; OhioLINK; Oxford Journals; ProQuest LLC (Ann Arbor); SwetsWise Online Content; H.W. Wilson. Reprint: PSC. *Indexed:* ABIn, ArtHuCI, BAS, CABA, IBR, IBSS, IBZ, JEL, PAIS, PSA, RRTA, SSA, SSCI, SociolAb, WAE&RSA. *Bk. rev.:* Occasional, 6-8 pages. *Aud.:* Ac, Sa.

The Cambridge Political Economy Society founded this journal in 1977 "in the tradition of Marx, Keynes, Kalecki, Joan Robinson, and Kaldor." It focuses on "theoretical, applied, policy, and methodological research," with a strong emphasis on economic and social issues. Critical thinking is emphasized in the process of analyzing data, the development of theory, and the construction of policy. The journal's scope and editors are international. Five to eight articles per issue is typical. Material is solicited in the areas of "unemployment, inflation, the organisation of production, the distribution of social product, class conflict, economic underdevelopment, globalisation and international economic integration, changing forms and boundaries of markets and planning, and uneven development and instability in the world economy." This journal is an excellent addition for academic libraries.

1856. *Canadian Journal of Economics.* Supersedes in part (1928-1967): *Canadian Journal of Economics and Political Science;* Which was formerly (until 1934): *Contributions to Canada Economics.* [ISSN: 0008-4085] 1968. q. GBP 120 print & online eds. Ed(s): Dwayne Benjamin. Blackwell Publishing, Inc., Commerce Place, 350 Main St, Malden, MA 02148; customerservices@blackwellpublishing.com; http://www.blackwellpublishing.com. Illus., index. Refereed. Circ: 2600. Microform: MML. Online: Blackwell Synergy; EBSCO Publishing, EBSCO Host; Gale; IngentaConnect; JSTOR (Web-based Journal Archive); OCLC Online Computer Library Center, Inc.; OhioLINK;

SwetsWise Online Content. *Indexed:* ABIn, ABS&EES, AgeL, BAS, CBCARef, CLI, CPerI, DSA, IBR, IBSS, IBZ, ILP, JEL, PAIS, RRTA, RiskAb, SSCI, SWA, WAE&RSA. *Bk. rev.:* 2-4, 1,500-2,200 words. *Aud.:* Ac, Sa.

Published for the Canadian Economics Association, this journal is the "primary academic economics journal" in Canada, with material written mostly in English and some French. An average of fourteen articles are presented along with "Viewpoint," a commissioned piece. Because of an issue with Daniel Hamermesh's "Viewpoint" item, "Replication in Economics" (August 2007), there will be a stricter policy on data replication availability in this journal. Some recent topics are snow removal auctions, unionization and plant closures, human capital accumulation, and international trade. The November issue includes minutes from the annual meeting of the Canadian Economics Association. This widely recognized journal—comparable to the *American Economic Review* —would be an excellent addition to large academic libraries. The *CJE* archive contains full articles since 1999 and abstracts since 1987. Browsing is free. Access is to subscribers only. Free print publication to members of the Canadian Economics Association.

The Cato Journal. See Political Science/Comparative and American Politics section.

1857. *Challenge* (Armonk): the magazine of economic affairs. [ISSN: 0577-5132] 1952. bi-m. USD 315 print & online eds. Ed(s): Jeffrey Madrick. M.E. Sharpe, Inc., 80 Business Park Dr, Armonk, NY 10504; custserv@mesharpe.com; http://www.mesharpe.com. Illus., index, adv. Sample. Refereed. Circ: 5000. Vol. ends: Nov/Dec. Microform: PQC. Online: EBSCO Publishing, EBSCO Host; Florida Center for Library Automation; OCLC Online Computer Library Center, Inc.; ProQuest LLC (Ann Arbor); SwetsWise Online Content; H.W. Wilson. Reprint: PSC. *Indexed:* ABIn, ASIP, BAS, BPI, IBR, IBSS, IBZ, JEL, PAIS. *Bk. rev.:* 1, 2-4 pages. *Aud.:* Hs, Ga, Ac.

Challenge presents a "wide range of views on national and international economic affairs in the belief that an informed dialogue can result in more rational and effective public policy." Many agree this is the "insightful and eclectic" journal to keep you informed on the latest economic policy and issues. Written in a clear, nontechnical manner, the articles are by prestigious economists and well-respected scholars, and the editorial board includes four Nobel laureates. In-depth book reviews are also included. Highly recommended for high school, public, academic, and government libraries. Defintely worth the money!

1858. *Contemporary Economic Policy.* Formerly (until 1994): *Contemporary Policy Issues.* [ISSN: 1074-3529] 1982. q. USD 275 print & online eds. Ed(s): Wade Martin. Blackwell Publishing, Inc., Commerce Place, 350 Main St, Malden, MA 02148; customerservices@blackwellpublishing.com; http://www.blackwellpublishing.com. Illus., index, adv. Refereed. Circ: 3000. Vol. ends: Oct. Microform: PQC. Online: EBSCO Publishing, EBSCO Host; Florida Center for Library Automation; Gale; HighWire Press; IngentaConnect; Northern Light Technology, Inc.; OCLC Online Computer Library Center, Inc.; OhioLINK; Oxford Journals; ProQuest K-12 Learning Solutions; ProQuest LLC (Ann Arbor); SwetsWise Online Content; H.W. Wilson. Reprint: PSC. *Indexed:* ABIn, ABS&EES, AgeL, AmH&L, CABA, CJA, ForAb, HRA, HistAb, IBR, IBSS, IBZ, JEL, PAIS, PRA, RI-1, RRTA, S&F, SSCI, SUSA, WAE&RSA. *Aud.:* Ga, Ac.

This solid journal publishes scholarly research and analysis on current policy issues for business, government, and decision makers. Membership in the Western Economic Association International includes subscriptions to this journal and *Economic Inquiry* (see below). Each issue contains about ten articles. Special topics are included. In January 2007, Government Accountability Office economists published articles in *CEP* to illustrate the policy work being done there. Another special section was on "Monetary Policy Issues of New EU-Member and Candidate Countries." A very solid recommendation for public, academic, and government libraries.

1859. *Ecological Economics.* [ISSN: 0921-8009] 1989. 16x/yr. EUR 1693. Ed(s): Cutler J. Cleveland. Elsevier BV, Radarweg 29, Amsterdam, 1043 NX, Netherlands; nlinfo-f@elsevier.nl; http://www.elsevier.nl. Refereed.

Indexed: ApEcolAb, ArtHuCI, BAS, BiolAb, CABA, CJA, DSA, EnvAb, EnvInd, FPA, ForAb, HortAb, IBSS, IndVet, JEL, M&GPA, PRA, PollutAb, RI-1, RRTA, S&F, SCI, SSCI, SUSA, SWA, SWRA, VB, WAE&RSA, ZooRec. *Bk. rev.:* Number and length vary. *Aud.:* Ac, Sa.

After watching and pondering over this journal for so many years, I have decided to add it. Rankings are higher but that reflects the ever-growing importance of the subject matter. The scope is "the study and management of 'nature's household' (ecology) and 'humankind's household' (economics)" and to help policy be more productive. Some areas of interest are valuation of natural resources, sustainable agriculture and development, renewable resource management and conservation, consequences of genetically engineered organisms, alternative principles for valuing natural wealth, and integrating natural resources and environmental services into national income and wealth accounts. Very important, indeed. Please review this for your academic and special libraries.

1860. *Econometric Theory.* [ISSN: 0266-4666] 1985. bi-m. GBP 392. Ed(s): Peter C B Phillips. Cambridge University Press, The Edinburgh Bldg, Shaftesbury Rd, Cambridge, CB2 2RU, United Kingdom; journals@cambridge.org; http://www.journals.cambridge.org. Illus., adv. Refereed. Microform: PQC. Online: Pub.; EBSCO Publishing, EBSCO Host; OCLC Online Computer Library Center, Inc.; OhioLINK; SwetsWise Online Content. Reprint: PSC. *Indexed:* ABIn, CCMJ, IBSS, JEL, MSN, MathR, SSCI. *Bk. rev.:* Number and length vary. *Aud.:* Ac, Sa.

This leading international journal publishes "original theoretical contributions in all major areas of econometrics." Its scope includes, but is not limited to, "statistical theory of estimation, testing, prediction, and decision procedures in traditionally active areas of research, such as linear and nonlinear modeling, simultaneous equations theory, time series, studies of robustness, nonparametric methods, inference under misspecification, finite-sample econometrics," etc. Also included are "historical studies in the evolution of econometric thought," interviews with leading scholars, and periodic book reviews. There is also a distinguished "ET Interviews" series with "pre-eminent scholars in the field." Highly recommended for libraries with mathematical economic programs and scholars.

1861. *Econometrica: journal of the Econometric Society.* [ISSN: 0012-9682] 1933. bi-m. GBP 302 print & online eds. Ed(s): Eddie Dekel. Blackwell Publishing Ltd., 9600 Garsington Rd, Oxford, OX4 2ZG, United Kingdom; customerservices@blackwellpublishing.com; http://www.blackwellpublishing.com. Illus., index. Refereed. Circ: 6000. Vol. ends: Nov. Microform: PMC; PQC. Online: Blackwell Synergy; EBSCO Publishing, EBSCO Host; Gale; JSTOR (Web-based Journal Archive); OCLC Online Computer Library Center, Inc.; OhioLINK; ProQuest LLC (Ann Arbor); SwetsWise Online Content. Reprint: PSC. *Indexed:* ABIn, AgeL, BAS, CABA, CCMJ, IBR, IBSS, IBZ, IPSA, JEL, MSN, MathR, RRTA, RiskAb, SCI, SSCI, WAE&RSA. *Aud.:* Ac, Sa.

Highly ranked by the Journal Citation Reports, this excellent, technical journal "promotes the unification of the theoretical-quantitative and the empirical-quantitative approach to economic problems." It publishes original, refereed articles for the Econometric Society "in all branches of economics." Recent topics include: business cycle accounting, decision theory, and market entry costs. Also included is a directory of fellows, and news/notes on "scholarly societies in economics, econometrics, mathematics, and statistics." Highly recommended for universities and special libraries.

1862. *Economic Development and Cultural Change.* [ISSN: 0013-0079] 1952. q. USD 260 domestic; USD 282.60 Canada; USD 269 elsewhere. Ed(s): John Strauss. University of Chicago Press, Journals Division, PO Box 37005, Chicago, IL 60637; http://www.journals.uchicago.edu. Illus., index, adv. Refereed. Circ: 2000 Paid. Vol. ends: Jul. Microform: PMC; PQC. Online: Chadwyck-Healey Inc.; EBSCO Publishing, EBSCO Host; Florida Center for Library Automation; Gale; JSTOR (Web-based Journal Archive); ProQuest LLC (Ann Arbor). Reprint: PSC. *Indexed:* ABCPolSci, ABIn, ABS&EES, AICP, ASSIA, AbAn, AgeL, Agr,

AmH&L, BPI, CABA, DSA, EI, FPA, ForAb, HAPI, HRA, HRIS, HistAb, HortAb, IBR, IBSS, IBZ, IMFL, IPSA, IndIslam, JEL, PAIS, PRA, PSA, RRTA, S&F, SFSA, SSA, SSCI, SUSA, SWA, SociolAb, WAE&RSA. *Bk. rev.:* 8-9, lengthy. *Aud.:* Ga, Ac, Sa.

From the highly-respected University of Chicago Press, a "multidisciplinary journal of development economics that disperses scientific evidence about policy issues related to economic development." Articles are on developing nations in regard to the social and economic forces that affect culture. Book reviews are included. Scholars and researchers in economics, sociology, political science, and geography consider this journal very important. Scholars can view back titles in JSTOR.

Economic Geography. See Geography section.

1863. *Economic History Review: a journal of economic and social history.* [ISSN: 0013-0117] 1927. q. GBP 184 print & online eds. Ed(s): Richard Smith, Jane Humphries. Blackwell Publishing Ltd., 9600 Garsington Rd, Oxford, OX4 2ZG, United Kingdom; customerservices@ blackwellpublishing.com; http://www.blackwellpublishing.com. Illus., index, adv. Refereed. Circ: 5000. Vol. ends: Nov. Microform: IDC; PQC. Online: Blackwell Synergy; EBSCO Publishing, EBSCO Host; Gale; IngentaConnect; JSTOR (Web-based Journal Archive); OCLC Online Computer Library Center, Inc.; OhioLINK; SwetsWise Online Content. Reprint: PSC. *Indexed:* ABIn, AgeL, AmH&L, AmHI, ApEcolAb, ArtHuCI, BrArAb, BrHumI, HistAb, IBR, IBSS, IBZ, IndIslam, JEL, NumL, PAIS, PSA, SSA, SSCI, SociolAb. *Bk. rev.:* 28-40, 600-1,200 words. *Aud.:* Ga, Ac, Sa.

The top journal in the history of the social sciences. A typical issue of *Economic History Review* contains a long essay in the "Surveys and Speculations" section that "discusses a particular problem in economic and social history in an adventurous way," five to six articles, "Notes and Comments," and a plethora of signed book reviews. Recently, a 50-year review was written. While it has increased in size and scope (with social history), the author of the electronic age will treat it well. This well-written, easy-to-understand journal is recommended to historians, students, and researchers alike.

1864. *Economic Inquiry.* Formerly (until 1974): *Western Economic Journal.* [ISSN: 0095-2583] 1962. q. USD 345 print & online eds. Blackwell Publishing, Inc., Commerce Place, 350 Main St, Malden, MA 02148; customerservices@blackwellpublishing.com; http://www.blackwellpublishing.com. Illus., index, adv. Sample. Refereed. Circ: 3550. Vol. ends: Oct. Microform: PQC. Online: Chadwyck-Healey Inc.; The Dialog Corporation; EBSCO Publishing, EBSCO Host; Florida Center for Library Automation; Gale; HighWire Press; IngentaConnect; Northern Light Technology, Inc.; OCLC Online Computer Library Center, Inc.; OhioLINK; Oxford Journals; ProQuest K-12 Learning Solutions; ProQuest LLC (Ann Arbor); SwetsWise Online Content; H.W. Wilson. Reprint: PSC. *Indexed:* ABIn, AgeL, AmH&L, BAS, CABA, CJA, HRA, HistAb, IBR, IBSS, IBZ, JEL, LRI, PAIS, PRA, RRTA, RiskAb, SSCI, SUSA, V&AA, WAE&RSA. *Aud.:* Ac, Sa.

A journal of the Western Economic Association. The stated goal of this scholarly journal is "to make each article understandable to economists who are not necessarily specialists in the article's topic areas." It covers all areas of economics, and always has intriguing and applicable articles. A few are "When Are Women More Generous than Men?," "Do Newly Retired Workers in the United States Have Sufficient Resources to maintain Wellbeing?," and "The Labor Market Effects of Sex and Race Discrimination Laws." Academic and special libraries would greatly benefit from a subscription, which also includes four issues of *Contemporary Economic Policy* (above in this section).

1865. *The Economic Journal.* [ISSN: 0013-0133] 1891. 8x/yr. GBP 365 print & online eds. Ed(s): Andrew Scott, Steve Machin. Blackwell Publishing Ltd., 9600 Garsington Rd, Oxford, OX4 2ZG, United Kingdom; customerservices@blackwellpublishing.com; http://www.blackwellpublishing.com. Illus., index, adv. Sample. Refereed. Circ: 7000. Vol. ends: Nov. Microform: PMC; PQC. Online: Blackwell Synergy; EBSCO Publishing, EBSCO Host; Gale; IngentaConnect; JSTOR (Web-based Journal Archive); OCLC Online Computer Library

Center, Inc.; OhioLINK; SwetsWise Online Content. Reprint: PSC. *Indexed:* ABIn, AmH&L, BAS, BRI, CABA, CBRI, CJA, ExcerpMed, HRIS, HistAb, IBR, IBSS, IBZ, JEL, PAIS, RRTA, RiskAb, SSCI, WAE&RSA. *Bk. rev.:* 25, lengthy. *Aud.:* Ac, Sa.

In publication since 1891, this classic and frequently cited periodical continues to be a preeminent source on economic issues, both theoretical and empirical. Each issue typically contains 9–11 papers. A discussion forum, datasets, and book notes can be found on its web site. Selected papers from the annual conference of the Royal Economic Society (the journal's sponsor) and the Association of University Teachers of Economics comprise an annual issue. A recent issue had these sexier-sounding articles: "Sustaining Cooperation in Trust Games," "Equilibrium in the Jungle," and "A Theory of Clearance Sales." Highly recommended for academic, government, business, and financial libraries.

1866. *Economic Policy: a European forum.* [ISSN: 0266-4658] 1985. q. GBP 324 print & online eds. Ed(s): Giuseppe Bertola, Paul Seabright. Blackwell Publishing Ltd., 9600 Garsington Rd, Oxford, OX4 2ZG, United Kingdom; customerservices@blackwellpublishing.com; http://www.blackwellpublishing.com. Illus., index, adv. Refereed. Microform: PQC. Online: Blackwell Synergy; EBSCO Publishing, EBSCO Host; Gale; IngentaConnect; JSTOR (Web-based Journal Archive); OCLC Online Computer Library Center, Inc.; OhioLINK; SwetsWise Online Content. Reprint: PSC. *Indexed:* ABIn, ApEcolAb, BAS, CABA, IBSS, IPSA, JEL, PAIS, RRTA, RiskAb, SSCI, WAE&RSA. *Aud.:* Ga, Ac, Sa.

This reputable journal delivers relevant policy analysis combined with economics to help policy-makers. Mainly focusing on larger international issues and an European perspective, pieces are commissioned. The entire issue is discussed by a panel before publication, insuring quality. The web version has lots of value-added features such as a browsable archive, Web Essays, and papers from panel meetings. This journal is published for CEPR (Centre for Economic Policy Research), the Center for Economic Studies of the University of Munich (CES), and Paris-Jourdan Sciences Economiques (PSE) in association with the European Economic Association. Readership consists of economists, policy makers, researchers, government officials, business leaders, and students.

1867. *The Economic Record.* [ISSN: 0013-0249] 1925. q. GBP 154 print & online eds. Ed(s): Harry Bloch, Glenn Otto. Blackwell Publishing Asia, 550 Swanston St, Carlton South, VIC 3053, Australia; subs@blackwellpublishingasia.com; http://www.blackwellpublishing.com. Illus., index, adv. Refereed. Circ: 3800. Vol. ends: Dec. Microform: PQC. Online: Blackwell Synergy; EBSCO Publishing, EBSCO Host; Florida Center for Library Automation; Gale; IngentaConnect; OCLC Online Computer Library Center, Inc.; OhioLINK; ProQuest LLC (Ann Arbor); RMIT Publishing; SwetsWise Online Content. Reprint: PSC. *Indexed:* ABIn, BAS, IBR, IBSS, IBZ, JEL, PAIS, RRTA, RiskAb, SSCI, SWA, WAE&RSA. *Bk. rev.:* 3-7, lengthy, signed. *Aud.:* Ac, Sa.

Published by the Economic Society of Australia (and also covering New Zealand), this is a general economics journal that provides a forum for research on the Australian economy. The articles have a very long half-life citation. This journal publishes theoretical, applied, and policy papers in all fields of economics. Six articles are typical, and book reviews are included. Recommended for economists and university libraries with international interests.

1868. *Economic Theory.* [ISSN: 0938-2259] 1991. 8x/yr. EUR 1530 print & online eds. Ed(s): Charalambos D Aliprantis. Springer, Tiergartenstr 17, Heidelberg, 69121, Germany. Illus., adv. Sample. Refereed. Online: EBSCO Publishing, EBSCO Host; OhioLINK; ProQuest LLC (Ann Arbor); Springer LINK; SwetsWise Online Content. Reprint: PSC. *Indexed:* ABIn, AgeL, CCMJ, IBSS, JEL, MSN, MathR, SSCI. *Aud.:* Ac, Sa.

The official journal of the Society for the Advancement of Economic Theory covers all areas of economics and could include "classical and modern equilibrium theory, cooperative game theory, macroeconomics, social choice and welfare, uncertainty and information, intertemporal economics (including dynamical systems), public economics, international and developmental economics, financial economics, money and banking, and industrial organization." This journal also includes the section "Exposita," which are notes of noteworthy works. A recent special issue honored Edward Prescott. He is "one of the most influential economists in the history of macroeconomics." Advertised as online first, and publication is ahead of schedule! For economists and graduate students.

1869. *Economica.* [ISSN: 0013-0427] 1921. q. GBP 205 print & online eds. Ed(s): Frank Cowell, Alan Manning. Blackwell Publishing Ltd., 9600 Garsington Rd, Oxford, OX4 2ZG, United Kingdom; customerservices@blackwellpublishing.com; http://www.blackwellpublishing.com. Illus., index, adv. Sample. Refereed. Circ: 3800. Vol. ends: Nov. Online: Blackwell Synergy; EBSCO Publishing, EBSCO Host; Gale; IngentaConnect; JSTOR (Web-based Journal Archive); OCLC Online Computer Library Center, Inc.; OhioLINK; SwetsWise Online Content. Reprint: PSC. *Indexed:* ABIn, AmH&L, ApEcolAb, ArtHuCI, BAS, CJA, EIP, ExcerpMed, HistAb, IBR, IBSS, IBZ, IPSA, JEL, PAIS, RRTA, RiskAb, SSCI, WAE&RSA. *Bk. rev.:* 5-11, 275-1,800 words. *Aud.:* Ac, Sa.

Always a top economics journal, this is published on behalf of the London School of Economics and Political Science. This highly cited journal is international in scope and covers "all branches of economics." Some recent topics are risk aversion, educational investments, school quality, and consumption risk-sharing. In addition to the articles, the journal contains numerous book reviews and an annual author/title index. There will be a special conference and issue to honor the 75th anniversary of Lionel Robbins' "Essay on the Nature and Significance of Economic Science." You can also download two famous articles for free on the Philips Curve and Coase's Theory of the Firm. Recommended for academic libraries, professional economists, and researchers.

1870. *Economics and Human Biology.* [ISSN: 1570-677X] 2003. 3x/yr. EUR 385. Ed(s): John Komlos. Elsevier BV, North-Holland, Sara Burgerhartstraat 25, Amsterdam, 1055 KV, Netherlands; nlinfo-f@ elsevier.nl; http://www.elsevier.nl/homepage/about/us/regional_sites.htt. *Indexed:* CABA, DSA, ExcerpMed, JEL, SCI, SSCI, WAE&RSA. *Aud.:* Ac, Sa.

As economists are branching out, new journals are being born. One of the most intriguing is *Economics and Human Biology,* which "explores the effect of socio-economic processes on human beings as biological organisms." Recent articles include "Does Body Weight Affect Wages?" and "The Vanishing Weight Gap: Trends in Obesity among Adult Food Stamp Participants." This journal is very interdisciplinary and covers "health and economic systems, measurement of poverty, malnutrition and psychological deprivation, and effects of government intervention programs." Please review for your library. You'll be intrigued.

1871. *Economics and Philosophy.* [ISSN: 0266-2671] 1985. 3x/yr. GBP 126. Ed(s): Geoffrey Brennan, Luc Bovens. Cambridge University Press, The Edinburgh Bldg, Shaftesbury Rd, Cambridge, CB2 2RU, United Kingdom; journals@cambridge.org; http://www.journals.cambridge.org. Illus., index, adv. Refereed. Vol. ends: Oct. Microform: PQC. Online: Pub.; EBSCO Publishing, EBSCO Host; OCLC Online Computer Library Center, Inc.; OhioLINK; SwetsWise Online Content. Reprint: PSC. *Indexed:* ABIn, IBSS, IPB, JEL, PhilInd, SSCI. *Bk. rev.:* 3-7, 4-8 pages. *Aud.:* Ac, Sa.

Created for the synergistic study of economics and philosophy. The core of this growing journal is substantial essays from esteemed scholars, and articles link the disciplines of economics and philosophy. The current editors continue the tradition of publishing about "the methodology and epistemology of economics, the foundations of decision theory and game theory, the nature of rational choice in general, historical work on economics with a philosophical purpose, ethical issues in economics, the use of economic techniques in ethical theory, and many other subjects." Very scholarly, for large academic libraries.

1872. *Economics & Politics.* [ISSN: 0954-1985] 1988. 3x/yr. GBP 397 print & online eds. Ed(s): B Peter Rosendorff. Blackwell Publishing Ltd., 9600 Garsington Rd, Oxford, OX4 2ZG, United Kingdom; customerservices@blackwellpublishing.com;

http://www.blackwellpublishing.com. Illus., index, adv. Sample. Refereed. Circ: 300. Vol. ends: Oct. Online: Blackwell Synergy; EBSCO Publishing, EBSCO Host; Gale; IngentaConnect; OCLC Online Computer Library Center, Inc.; OhioLINK; SwetsWise Online Content. Reprint: PSC. *Indexed:* ABIn, ApEcolAb, BAS, CABA, IBSS, IPSA, JEL, PRA, PSA, RiskAb, WAE&RSA. *Bk. rev.:* Number varies, 20 pages. *Aud.:* Ac, Sa.

Analytical political economy here is "broadly defined as the study of economic phenomena and policy in models that include political processes." It is covered in each issue of this solid journal, which contains six or seven technical articles and an extensive book review section. Readers are professionals and students in economics, political science, sociology, and psychology.

1873. *Economics Bulletin.* [ISSN: 1545-2921] 2001. irreg. Free. Ed(s): John Conley. Economics Bulletin, c/o John Conley, Dept. of Economics, 414 Calhoun Hall, Nashville, TN 37235; j.p.conley@vanderbilt.edu. *Indexed:* JEL. *Aud.:* Ac, Sa.

This journal is available e-only, and created to encourage free and fast scientific communication to all research economists. *Economics Bulletin* publishes original notes, comments, and preliminary results. Submissions are refereed, and a decision to publish is made within eight weeks. Accepted papers are published immediately. Also included are letters to the editor, announcements of conferences, and research announcements. There is a handy e-mail notification in your subject of interest. Hopefully, this publication will continue to grow and compete more effectively with the expensive *Economics Letters* (below).

1874. *Economics Letters.* [ISSN: 0165-1765] 1978. 12x/yr. EUR 2125. Ed(s): Dr. Eric Maskin. Elsevier BV, North-Holland, Sara Burgerhartstraat 25, Amsterdam, 1055 KV, Netherlands; nlinfo-f@ elsevier.nl; http://www.elsevier.nl. Illus., index, adv. Sample. Refereed. Vol. ends: Dec. Microform: PQC. Online: EBSCO Publishing, EBSCO Host; Gale; IngentaConnect; OhioLINK; ScienceDirect; SwetsWise Online Content. *Indexed:* AgeL, CCMJ, CJA, IBSS, JEL, MSN, MathR, SSCI, WAE&RSA. *Aud.:* Ac, Sa.

This journal is designed to "provide a means of rapid and efficient dissemination of new results, models, and methods in all fields of economic research." Each contribution is limited to four pages, with a four-month turnover time for publication. An author/subject index is published in the last issue of every volume. This mathematics-oriented journal is intended for researchers and those wanting to know the latest trends. Expensive and neccessary. Recommended for university and special libraries.

1875. *Economics Research Network.* irreg. Social Science Electronic Publishing, Michael_Jensen@ssrn.com; http://www.ssrn.com. *Aud.:* Ga, Ac, Sa.

The Social Science Research Network's goal is "rapid worldwide dissemination of social science research." It has 11 subject networks, and the network for economics has an Abstract Database containing more than 155,000 scholarly working papers. Also, the Electronic Paper Collection has over 122,000 full-text papers. Most articles are free as authors load papers for free, and those can be downloaded for free. Others have a modest fee. Your library may already subscribe to them. Also, SSRN provides "free subscriptions to all of their abstracting journals to users in developing countries on request." *Economics Research Network* is a key resource for economists. Professional announcements, calls for papers, and job openings are listed. A must for economic researchers and academic libraries. URL: www.ssrn.com/ern.

1876. *The Economist.* [ISSN: 0013-0613] 1843. w. 51/yr. GBP 83 domestic; USD 98 United States; USD 200 Mexico. Ed(s): Bill Emmott. Economist Newspaper Ltd, 25 St James's St, London, SW1A 1HG, United Kingdom; letters@economist.com; http://www.economist.com. Illus., index, adv. Sample. Circ: 722984 Paid. Vol. ends: Dec. CD-ROM: Chadwyck-Healey Inc. Microform: PQC. Online: EBSCO Publishing, EBSCO Host; Florida Center for Library Automation; Gale; LexisNexis; Micromedia ProQuest; Newsbank, Inc.; OCLC Online Computer Library Center, Inc.; ProQuest LLC (Ann Arbor). *Indexed:* ABIn,

ASSIA, AgeL, AmHI, BAS, BLI, BPI, BRD, BRI, BrHumI, BrTechI, CABA, CBRI, CPerI, DSA, EnvAb, FLI, FPA, ForAb, FutSurv, HortAb, IAA, IndVet, LogistBibl, MASUSE, PAIS, RI-1, RRTA, S&F, WAE&RSA. *Bk. rev.:* 3-4, 450-500 words. *Aud.:* Ems, Hs, Ga, Ac, Sa. Very informative and easy to read, this journal was founded more than 150 years ago to support free trade and is read in more than 180 countries. This journal is well respected and authoritative for information on "world politics, global business, finance and economics, science and technology, and the arts." It includes 16 news categories, including summaries on politics and business, short articles on world leaders, science, technology, finance and economics, surveys of countries and regions, obituaries, etc. Well known in the back of each issue are handy economic, financial, and market indicators. A must-have for all libraries.

1877. *The Economists' Voice.* [ISSN: 1553-3832] 2004. 3x/yr. USD 300 (Individuals, USD 20). Ed(s): Joseph Stiglitz. Berkeley Electronic Press, 2809 Telegraph Ave, Ste 202, Berkeley, CA 94705; info@bepress.com; http://www.bepress.com. *Indexed:* JEL. *Aud.:* Ga, Ac, Sa.

To be of general interest, *The Economists' Voice* was created in 2004 to provide a nonpartisan forum for leading economists on important issues. Articles are 600–2,000 words in length, and are accessible to the general reader. The journal publishes several columnists with varying political viewpoints and a "Features" section written by a professional economist. The journal is peer-reviewed. Dialogue is encouraged, and letters to the editor are welcomed. Economists, policy makers and analysts, and students of economics will be interested in this online journal. It is heartily recommended for academic and public libraries. URL: www.bepress.com/ev.

Economy and Society. See Sociology and Social Work/General section.

Energy Economics. See Energy section.

The Energy Journal. See Energy section.

1878. *European Economic Association. Journal.* [ISSN: 1542-4766] 2003. bi-m. USD 458 print & online eds. Ed(s): Xavier Vives. M I T Press, 238 Main St., Ste. 500, Cambridge, MA 02142; journals-info@mit.edu; http://mitpress.mit.edu. Refereed. *Indexed:* IBSS, JEL, SSCI. *Aud.:* Ac, Sa.

The European Economic Association (EEA) started an entirely new journal in January 2003 titled *Journal of the European Economic Association* to replace the *European Economic Review* as the association's journal. This journal is fully owned by the EEA and operated via MIT Press. It publishes the papers and proceedings of the annual EEA Congress, and it is making a nice transition as distinguished economists are contributing. It is already indexed in ECONLIT, SSCI, and IBSS. A new initiative is in place to have it be a "truly global outlet for the best research in economics, competing for the very best general-interest manuscripts." Thus it aims to be an outlet for theoretical and empirical work with global relevance and for the development and application of economics as a science, as well as a means of communication and exchange among teachers, researchers, and students in economics. Each annual volume will include a double issue that includes the proceedings from the previous year. Online, the Editor's Report is lacking for 2005 and 2006. Highly recommended for academic institutions, and SPARC-endorsed.

1879. *European Economic Review.* [ISSN: 0014-2921] 1969. 8x/yr. EUR 1589. Ed(s): G A Pfann, Z. Eckstein. Elsevier BV, North-Holland, Sara Burgerhartstraat 25, Amsterdam, 1055 KV, Netherlands; nlinfo-f@elsevier.nl; http://www.elsevier.nl. Illus., index, adv. Sample. Refereed. Vol. ends: Dec. Microform: PQC. Online: EBSCO Publishing, EBSCO Host; Gale; IngentaConnect; OCLC Online Computer Library Center, Inc.; OhioLINK; ScienceDirect; SwetsWise Online Content. *Indexed:* ABIn, AgeL, ArtHuCI, BAS, CJA, IBSS, JEL, PAIS, RRTA, RiskAb, SSCI, WAE&RSA. *Aud.:* Ac, Sa.

This journal's goal is to help "the development of economics as a science." Over ten articles by international authors are included in each issue. Since January 2003, this journal is no longer the official journal of the European Economic Association (EEA). See the *Journal of the European Economic Association* for the fully owned and directly governed EEA journal. Very mathematical and still recommended for econometricians, theorists, and economists.

1880. *Experimental Economics.* [ISSN: 1386-4157] 1998. q. EUR 398 print & online eds. Ed(s): Arthur J H C Schram, Timothy Cason. Springer New York LLC, 233 Spring St, New York, NY 10013-1578; service-ny@springer.com; http://www.springer.com/. Adv. Refereed. Online: EBSCO Publishing, EBSCO Host; Gale; IngentaConnect; OCLC Online Computer Library Center, Inc.; OhioLINK; ProQuest LLC (Ann Arbor); Springer LINK; SwetsWise Online Content. Reprint: PSC. *Indexed:* ABIn, IBSS, JEL, SSCI. *Aud.:* Ac, Sa.

Experimental Economics, a journal of the Economic Science Association, is a relatively new venue for the "growing number of economists who use laboratory methods in experimental research in economics and related fields (i.e., accounting, finance, political science, and the psychology of decision making)." A recent special issue centered on behavioral economics. This journal is recommended for universities and colleges with strong mathematics or economics departments.

1881. *Explorations in Economic History.* Formerly: *Explorations in Entrepreneurial History.* [ISSN: 0014-4983] 1963. 4x/yr. EUR 715. Ed(s): R A Margo. Academic Press, 525 B St, Ste 1900, San Diego, CA 92101-4495; apsubs@acad.com; http://www.elsevier.com/. Illus., index, adv. Refereed. Vol. ends: Oct. Online: Chadwyck-Healey Inc.; EBSCO Publishing, EBSCO Host; Gale; IngentaConnect; OCLC Online Computer Library Center, Inc.; OhioLINK; ScienceDirect; SwetsWise Online Content. *Indexed:* ABIn, ABS&EES, Agr, AmH&L, ArtHuCI, BAS, HistAb, IBR, IBSS, IBZ, JEL, PAIS, SSCI, SWA. *Aud.:* Ac, Sa.

This journal has traditionally accepted articles that apply economic analysis to historical events. The scope is wide, including "all areas of economic change, all historical periods, all geographical locations, and all political and social systems." A bonus is the "Essays in Exploration" section, which surveys the recent literature. The authors are economists, economic historians, demographers, geographers, and sociologists. Recommended for libraries with collection interests in history and economics.

1882. *Feminist Economics.* [ISSN: 1354-5701] 1995. q. GBP 267 print & online eds. Ed(s): Diana Strassmann. Routledge, 4 Park Square, Milton Park, Abingdon, OX14 4RN, United Kingdom. Illus., adv. Sample. Refereed. Vol. ends: No. 3. Online: EBSCO Publishing, EBSCO Host; Gale; IngentaConnect; OCLC Online Computer Library Center, Inc.; SwetsWise Online Content. Reprint: PSC. *Indexed:* ABIn, AgeL, AltPI, AmHI, BAS, BrHumI, CWI, FemPer, IBR, IBSS, IBZ, JEL, PSA, SSA, SSCI, SWA, SociolAb. *Bk. rev.:* 0-12, length varies, signed. *Aud.:* Ac.

This journal of the International Association for Feminist Economics applies a feminist perspective to new and diverse areas of economic inquiry in order to enrich and develop economics and to improve living conditions for all. Coverage is interdisciplinary and international. The journal aims to "examine the relationship between gender and power and the construction and legitimization of economic knowledge." Contents include scholarly articles, book reviews, conference announcements, and explorations of special topics such as teaching feminist economics. A free contents alerting service is available on the publisher's web site.

Futures: news, analysis, and strategies for futures, options and derivatives traders. See Finance/Investment section.

1883. *Games and Economic Behavior.* [ISSN: 0899-8256] 1989. 8x/yr. EUR 1034. Ed(s): S. Neff, Ehud Kalai. Academic Press, 525 B St, Ste 1900, San Diego, CA 92101-4495; apsubs@acad.com; http://www.elsevier.com/. Illus., index, adv. Refereed. Vol. ends: Nov.

Online: EBSCO Publishing, EBSCO Host; Gale; IngentaConnect; OCLC Online Computer Library Center, Inc.; OhioLINK; ScienceDirect; SwetsWise Online Content. *Indexed:* ABIn, ArtHuCI, CCMJ, IBSS, JEL, MSN, MathR, PsycInfo, RiskAb, SSCI. *Aud.:* Ac, Sa.

The leading journal in game theory, this technical and highly cited journal has a wide scope, since it covers game modeling in psychology, political science, biology, computer science, and mathematical sciences. The "cross-fertilization between theories and applications" of game theory is this journal's goal, and it has consistently attracted the best papers in interdisciplinary studies.

Gender and Development. See Gender Studies section.

Harvard Business Review. See Business/General section.

1884. *History of Political Economy.* [ISSN: 0018-2702] 1969. q. USD 362 (Individuals, USD 70). Ed(s): Neil De Marchi, Craufurd D W Goodwin. Duke University Press, 905 W Main St, Ste 18 B, Durham, NC 27701; subscriptions@dukeupress.edu; http://www.dukeupress.edu. Illus., index, adv. Refereed. Circ: 1350 Paid. Vol. ends: Winter. Microform: MIM; PQC. Online: EBSCO Publishing, EBSCO Host; Gale; HighWire Press; Northern Light Technology, Inc.; OCLC Online Computer Library Center, Inc.; OhioLINK; Project MUSE; ProQuest K-12 Learning Solutions; ProQuest LLC (Ann Arbor); SwetsWise Online Content. Reprint: PSC. *Indexed:* ABIn, AmH&L, ArtHuCI, BAS, CCMJ, CJA, FR, HistAb, IBR, IBSS, IBZ, JEL, MSN, PAIS, PSA, PhilInd, SSCI. *Bk. rev.:* 3-7, 1-3 pages. *Aud.:* Ga, Ac, Sa.

The leading journal in its field, the scholarly articles focus on topics such as the development of economic thought, the historical background behind major figures, and the interpretation of economic theories. Early political economists such as Marshall, Adam Smith, Keynes, Malthus, Ricardo, and Marx are heavily featured. Each issue usually has six or seven articles and signed book reviews. Recommended for academic libraries.

The Independent Review. See Political Science/Comparative and American Politics section.

1885. *International Economic Review.* [ISSN: 0020-6598] 1960. q. GBP 301 print & online eds. Ed(s): Charles Y Horioka, Randall Wright. Blackwell Publishing, Inc., Commerce Place, 350 Main St, Malden, MA 02148; customerservices@blackwellpublishing.com; http://www.blackwellpublishing.com. Illus., index, adv. Refereed. Circ: 2000. Vol. ends: Nov. Online: Blackwell Synergy; EBSCO Publishing, EBSCO Host; Gale; IngentaConnect; JSTOR (Web-based Journal Archive); OCLC Online Computer Library Center, Inc.; OhioLINK; SwetsWise Online Content. Reprint: PSC. *Indexed:* ABIn, ABS&EES, AgeL, AmStI, ApEcolAb, BAS, BPI, CCMJ, CJA, IBSS, JEL, MSN, MathR, PAIS, RiskAb, SSCI. *Aud.:* Ac, Sa.

This journal was started in 1960 and is published jointly by the University of Pennsylvania Economics Department and the Osaka (Japan) University Institute of Social and Economic Research Association. The *International Economic Review* focuses on quantitative economics. Issues contain about 12 articles by economics scholars worldwide. Cutting-edge articles in economet- rics, economic theory, and macro and applied economics are sought for inclusion. Recommended for universities with strong econometrics programs.

1886. *International Journal of Economic Theory.* [ISSN: 1742-7355] 2005. q. GBP 282 print & online eds. Ed(s): Makoto Yano, Kazua Nishimura. Blackwell Publishing Ltd., 9600 Garsington Rd, Oxford, OX4 2ZG, United Kingdom; customerservices@ blackwellpublishing.com; http://www.blackwellpublishing.com. Reprint: PSC. *Indexed:* RiskAb. *Aud.:* Ac, Sa.

Launched in 2005, this is the official journal of the International Society for Economic Theory, and it aims high to be a leader for international readers in economic theory. It covers microeconomics, macroeconomics, game theory, general equilibrium, welfare economics, public economics, industrial organiza- tion, intertemporal economics, international economics, development economics, behavioral and experimental economics, and mathematical methods for economics. With an international board of editors, it intends to encourage the

work of young researchers who are not yet established in the profession. *IJET* is produced in cooperation with Keio University and Kyoto University as a joint project of the research programs funded by the Ministry of Education.

1887. *International Journal of Game Theory.* [ISSN: 0020-7276] 1971. q. EUR 548 print & online eds. Ed(s): William Thomson. Physica-Verlag GmbH und Co., Postfach 105280, Heidelberg, 69042, Germany; physica@springer.de. Illus., adv. Refereed. Microform: PQC. Online: EBSCO Publishing, EBSCO Host; OhioLINK; ProQuest LLC (Ann Arbor); Springer LINK; SwetsWise Online Content. Reprint: PSC. *Indexed:* ABIn, CCMJ, IBSS, JEL, MSN, MathR, SCI, SSCI. *Aud.:* Ac, Sa.

This highly cited journal (albeit with a low impact factor) covers "game theory and its applications" in mathematical economics, management science, political science, and biology from a methodological, conceptual, or mathematical point of view. A must for academic libraries with advanced programs in economics and other covered fields. Comparatively reasonably priced.

1888. *International Monetary Fund. Staff Papers.* Formerly (until 1998): *International Monetary Fund. Staff Papers.* [ISSN: 1020-7635] 1950. q. USD 128 print & online eds. Ed(s): Robert Flood. Palgrave Macmillan, 175 Fifth Ave, New York, NY 10010; http://www.palgrave-usa.com. Illus., index, adv. Sample. Refereed. Circ: 5000. Microform: CIS; PQC. Online: Chadwyck-Healey Inc.; EBSCO Publishing, EBSCO Host; Florida Center for Library Automation; Gale; OCLC Online Computer Library Center, Inc.; ProQuest LLC (Ann Arbor); H.W. Wilson. *Indexed:* ABIn, AgeL, AmH&L, BAS, BLI, BPI, EIP, HistAb, IBR, IBSS, IBZ, IndIslam, JEL, PAIS, RRTA, SSCI, WAE&RSA. *Aud.:* Ga, Ac, Sa.

The official research journal for the International Monetary Fund, it is written for a "general audience including policymakers and academics." The authors are IMF staff, primarily professional economists, and invited guests. The "Special Data" section has had an increasing presence. An example is "Core Inflation: Measurement and Statistical Issues in Choosing Among Alternative Measures," by Mick Silver. The focus on policy is illustrated by these two recent titles: "Labor Policies to Raise Employment" and "Foreign Aid Policy and Sources of Poverty: A Quantitative Framework." Starting in June 2007, this journal was to be published online with Palgrave-Macmillan. A great bargain for large public, special, and academic libraries.

1889. *International Review of Applied Economics.* [ISSN: 0269-2171] 1987. 5x/yr. GBP 756 print & online eds. Ed(s): Malcolm Sawyer. Routledge, 4 Park Sq, Milton Park, Abingdon, OX14 4RN, United Kingdom; info@routledge.co.uk; http://www.routledge.co.uk. Illus., index, adv. Refereed. Vol. ends: Jun. Online: EBSCO Publishing, EBSCO Host; Factiva, Inc.; Florida Center for Library Automation; Gale; IngentaConnect; Northern Light Technology, Inc.; OCLC Online Computer Library Center, Inc.; ProQuest K-12 Learning Solutions; ProQuest LLC (Ann Arbor); SwetsWise Online Content. Reprint: PSC. *Indexed:* ABIn, BAS, IBR, IBSS, IBZ, JEL, PAIS, SociolAb, WAE&RSA. *Bk. rev.:* 2, several pages. *Aud.:* Ac, Sa.

This journal is "devoted to the practical applications of economic ideas . . . [It] associates itself broadly with the non-neoclassical tradition." It is not formally associated with any specific school of thought. An important feature of the papers is "interaction between empirical work and economic policy." Written in a "rigorous analytic style, yet nontechnical," the journal is suitable for large college and university libraries. Very reasonably priced.

1890. *Issues in Political Economy: undergraduate student research in Economics.* a. Issues in Political Economy, c/o Steven Greenlaw, Professor and Chair of Economics, Fredericksburg, VA 22401; http://www.elon.edu/ipe/. Refereed. *Aud.:* Ac.

This electronic annual is written, edited, and refereed entirely by undergradu- ates, with oversight from faculty at Mary Washington College and Elon University, in the time-honored belief "that the best way to learn economics is to do economics." They are to be commended for keeping this project going. All papers go through a double-blind review and must be related to economics. Definitely worth a look. URL: www.elon.edu/ipe.

1891. *J E I.* [ISSN: 0021-3624] 1967. q. USD 55 (Individuals, USD 45; Students, USD 15). Ed(s): Glen Atkinson. Association for Evolutionary Economics, Department of Economics, University of Nevada, Reno, NV 89507; afee@bucknell.edu; http://www.orgs.bucknell.edu/afee. Illus., index, adv. Sample. Refereed. Circ: 2000 Paid. Vol. ends: Dec. Microform: PQC. Online: EBSCO Publishing, EBSCO Host; Florida Center for Library Automation; Gale; OCLC Online Computer Library Center, Inc.; ProQuest K-12 Learning Solutions; ProQuest LLC (Ann Arbor); H.W. Wilson. Reprint: PSC. *Indexed:* ABIn, ABS&EES, AgeL, BPI, CJA, CWI, ForAb, IBR, IBSS, IBZ, JEL, LRI, MCR, PAIS, PSA, SSA, SSCI, SociolAb, WAE&RSA. *Bk. rev.:* 15-19, 1-4 pages. *Aud.:* Ac, Sa.

Sponsored by the Association for Evolutionary Economics (AEE), this journal focuses on institutional and evolutionary economics, which includes "the organization and control of diverse economic systems, economic development, environmental and econological issues, economic stabilization, labor relations, monetary management and major economic policies." Early economists Veblen and Commons "laid the foundation." This journal is international in scope and also includes "Notes and Communications" and book reviews. The June issue contains the papers presented at the annual meeting of the AEE. This journal will be of interest to university faculty and graduate students.

Journal of Accounting and Economics. See Accounting and Taxation section.

1892. *Journal of Applied Econometrics.* [ISSN: 0883-7252] 1986. 7x/yr. USD 1485 print or online ed. Ed(s): M Hashem Pesaran. John Wiley & Sons Ltd., The Atrium, Southern Gate, Chichester, PO19 8SQ, United Kingdom; customer@wiley.co.uk; http://www.wiley.co.uk. Illus., index, adv. Sample. Refereed. Circ: 1300. Vol. ends: Dec. Reprint: PSC. *Indexed:* ABIn, AgeL, BAS, CCMJ, IBSS, JEL, MSN, MathR, RiskAb, SSCI, WAE&RSA. *Bk. rev.:* 2, 750-3,500 words. *Aud.:* Ac, Sa.

An international journal that publishes papers that apply econometric techniques to a wide variety of problems, covering measurement, estimation, testing, forecasting, and policy analysis. Scholarly work is emphasized, and an unique feature is that authors are requested to share their data sets for replicability. A typical issue contains five to nine articles followed by book and software reviews, announcements, forthcoming papers, and the call for papers. This journal is recommended for libraries that serve econometricians and interested mathematicians.

1893. *Journal of Asian Economics.* [ISSN: 1049-0078] 1990. 6x/yr. EUR 463. Ed(s): M. Dutta. Elsevier BV, North-Holland, Sara Burgerhartstraat 25, Amsterdam, 1055 KV, Netherlands; nlinfo-f@elsevier.nl; http://www.elsevier.nl. Illus., adv. Refereed. Microform: PQC. Online: EBSCO Publishing, EBSCO Host; Gale; IngentaConnect; OhioLINK; ScienceDirect; SwetsWise Online Content. *Indexed:* BAS, IndIslam, JEL, PAIS. *Aud.:* Ac, Sa.

Published for the American Committee on Asian Economic Studies, this journal provides a forum for this growing research area. Concentrating on innovative paradigms and comparative studies for Asia, and other developing areas. "Economic theory, applied econometrics, international trade and finance, economic development, and comparative economic systems" are well covered. Authors are usually academic economists from Asia, Australia, and the United States. Reasonably priced and recommended for large university and business libraries.

Journal of Banking & Finance. See Finance/Scholarly section.

The Journal of Business. See Business/General section.

Journal of Business and Economic Statistics. See Business/General section.

Journal of Business Ethics. See Business/Ethics section.

1894. *Journal of Comparative Economics.* [ISSN: 0147-5967] 1977. 4x/yr. EUR 786. Ed(s): H. B. Bonin, John P Bonin. Academic Press, 525 B St, Ste 1900, San Diego, CA 92101-4495; apsubs@acad.com; http://www.elsevier.com/. Illus., index, adv. Refereed. Vol. ends: Dec. Online: EBSCO Publishing, EBSCO Host; Gale; IngentaConnect; OCLC Online Computer Library Center, Inc.; OhioLINK; ScienceDirect; SwetsWise Online Content. *Indexed:* ABIn, ABS&EES, BAS, CJA, IBSS, JEL, PAIS, RRTA, SSCI, WAE&RSA. *Bk. rev.:* 2-23, 500-2,000 words. *Aud.:* Ac, Sa.

This major journal is published for the Association for Comparative Economic Studies. While it is "devoted to the analysis and study of contemporary, historical and hypothetical economic systems, primarily socialist and transition economies," a new orientation on the "comparison of economic effects of the various institutions of capitalism on law, politics, culture" will broaden its perspective. Each issue has at least eight articles, five or six lengthy signed book reviews, and an author index for each volume. The association owns the copyrights for the individual articles. Recommended for universities and large institutions with international programs.

Journal of Consumer Research. See Advertising, Marketing, and Public Relations section.

1895. *Journal of Development Economics.* [ISSN: 0304-3878] 1974. 6x/yr. EUR 1783. Ed(s): Mark R Rosenzweig. Elsevier BV, North-Holland, Sara Burgerhartstraat 25, Amsterdam, 1055 KV, Netherlands; nlinfo-f@elsevier.nl; http://www.elsevier.nl. Illus., index, adv. Sample. Refereed. Vol. ends: Oct. Microform: PQC. Online: EBSCO Publishing, EBSCO Host; Gale; IngentaConnect; OhioLINK; ScienceDirect; SwetsWise Online Content. *Indexed:* ABIn, BAS, CJA, H&SSA, HortAb, IBR, IBSS, IBZ, JEL, PAIS, PollutAb, RRTA, RiskAb, SSCI, WAE&RSA. *Bk. rev.:* Number and length vary. *Aud.:* Ac, Sa.

With a high impact factor, this journal "publishes papers relating to all aspects of economic development, from immediate policy concerns to structural problems of underdevelopment." The emphasis is on quantitative work. Issues contain well-written, lengthy book reviews and eight or more articles, sometimes followed by "Notes and Comments." There is an annual author index. This journal is recommended for larger academic institutions—but review closely due to price.

1896. *Journal of Econometrics.* [ISSN: 0304-4076] 1973. 12x/yr. EUR 2696. Ed(s): A. R. Gallant, T. Amemiya. Elsevier BV, North-Holland, Sara Burgerhartstraat 25, Amsterdam, 1055 KV, Netherlands; nlinfo-f@elsevier.nl; http://www.elsevier.nl. Illus., index, adv. Refereed. Microform: PQC. Online: EBSCO Publishing, EBSCO Host; Gale; IngentaConnect; OhioLINK; ScienceDirect; SwetsWise Online Content. *Indexed:* ABIn, AgeL, BAS, CCMJ, DSA, EngInd, IBR, IBSS, IBZ, JEL, MSN, MathR, RRTA, RiskAb, SCI, SSCI, WAE&RSA. *Aud.:* Ac, Sa.

With a very high impact factor, this journal covers theoretical and applied econometrics, of course, and its scope includes estimation, other methodological aspects, and the use of "substantive areas of economics." Also, "[n]ewly developing areas of social experimentation" are also encouraged. The *Annals of Econometrics* are a supplement and the topic is selected by the editor of the issue. Extremely expensive, but very useful for econometricians and large universities.

1897. *Journal of Economic Behavior & Organization.* [ISSN: 0167-2681] 1980. 12x/yr. EUR 2228. Ed(s): J. B. Rosser, Jr. Elsevier BV, North-Holland, Sara Burgerhartstraat 25, Amsterdam, 1055 KV, Netherlands; nlinfo-f@elsevier.nl; http://www.elsevier.nl. Illus., index, adv. Sample. Refereed. Vol. ends: Dec. Microform: PQC. Online: EBSCO Publishing, EBSCO Host; Gale; IngentaConnect; OhioLINK; ScienceDirect; SwetsWise Online Content. *Indexed:* ABIn, ArtHuCI, CJA, ForAb, IBSS, JEL, PsycInfo, RiskAb, SSCI. *Bk. rev.:* 2-3, several pages. *Aud.:* Ac, Sa.

Written by academic economists, this interdisciplinary journal covers both "theoretical and empirical research concerning economic decision, organization, and behavior and to economic change in all its aspects." The goal is to understand how humans can influence organizations and economies, how leading features of an economy can lead to macro and micro behaviors, and how changes can occur. Studies using biology, psychology, law, anthropology, sociology, and mathematics are included. Issues have seven to nine articles and include lengthy, in-depth book reviews. Recommended for large universities and researchers.

1898. *Journal of Economic Dynamics and Control.* [ISSN: 0165-1889] 1979. 12x/yr. EUR 1609. Ed(s): W. J. Den Haan, C Chiarella. Elsevier BV, North-Holland, Sara Burgerhartstraat 25, Amsterdam, 1055 KV, Netherlands; nlinfo-f@elsevier.nl; http://www.elsevier.nl. Illus., index, adv. Refereed. Vol. ends: Nov. Microform: PQC. Online: EBSCO Publishing, EBSCO Host; Gale; IngentaConnect; OhioLINK; ScienceDirect; SwetsWise Online Content. *Indexed:* ABIn, CCMJ, IBR, IBSS, IBZ, JEL, MSN, MathR, RRTA, RiskAb, SSCI, WAE&RSA. *Aud.:* Ac, Sa.

This is widely recognized as the most influential journal in this field. Its scope includes the "development and use of computational methods in economics and finance," and this could include "artificial intelligence, databases, decision support systems, genetic algorithms, modelling languages, neural networks, and qualitative reasoning." This journal is no longer divided into sections, and a recent issue had 16 articles. A reader's being well-rounded in economics would be very helpful for reading this journal. Recommended for universities—but review closely due to price.

1899. *Journal of Economic Growth.* [ISSN: 1381-4338] 1996. q. EUR 629 print & online eds. Ed(s): Oded Galor. Springer New York LLC, 233 Spring St, New York, NY 10013-1578; service-ny@springer.com; http://www.springer.com/. Adv. Refereed. Online: EBSCO Publishing, EBSCO Host; Gale; IngentaConnect; OCLC Online Computer Library Center, Inc.; OhioLINK; ProQuest LLC (Ann Arbor); Springer LINK; SwetsWise Online Content. Reprint: PSC. *Indexed:* ABIn, BAS, IBSS, JEL, SSCI. *Aud.:* Ac, Sa.

The scope is simple, economic growth and dynamic macroeconomics. Empirical and theoretical, the range is wide and deals with international economics, growth models, urban economics, migration, and development. It ranks very high in the widely recognized RepEc (Research Papers in Economics) and the Journal Citation Reports. There are prominent researchers on the editorial board, including (among others) Alberto Alesina, Philippe Aghion, Robert Barro, Paul Romer, Jagdish Bhagwati, and Paul Krugman. Highly recommended for academic and special libraries.

1900. *The Journal of Economic History.* [ISSN: 0022-0507] 1941. q. GBP 130. Ed(s): C Knick Harley, Jeremy Atack. Cambridge University Press, The Edinburgh Bldg, Shaftesbury Rd, Cambridge, CB2 2RU, United Kingdom; journals@cambridge.org; http://www.journals.cambridge.org. Illus., index, adv. Refereed. Vol. ends: Dec. Microform: MIM; PQC. Online: Pub.; EBSCO Publishing, EBSCO Host; JSTOR (Web-based Journal Archive); OCLC Online Computer Library Center, Inc.; OhioLINK; SwetsWise Online Content. *Indexed:* ABIn, ABS&EES, AgeL, Agr, AmH&L, ArtHuCI, BAS, BRI, CBRI, HistAb, IBR, IBSS, IBZ, IndIslam, JEL, PAIS, SSCI, WAE&RSA. *Bk. rev.:* 39-63, 600-1,800 words. *Aud.:* Ac, Sa.

This journal is the official publication of the Economic History Association in Great Britain. Of interest to economists and economic, social, and demographic historians, the journal has a broad coverage in terms of methodology and geography, including such topics as "money and banking, trade manufacturing, technology, transportation, industrial organization, labor, agriculture, servitude, demography, education, economic growth, and the role of government and regulation." This excellent journal will appeal to both the student and the general public. Recommended for colleges, universities, and public libraries.

1901. *Journal of Economic Literature.* Formerly (until 1968): *Journal of Economic Abstracts.* [ISSN: 0022-0515] 1963. q. Free to members. Ed(s): Mary Kay Akerman, Roger Gordon. American Economic Association, 2014 Broadway, Ste 305, Nashville, TN 37203; http://www.vanderbilt.edu/AEA/. Illus., index, adv. Circ: 17267 Paid. Vol. ends: Dec. CD-ROM: SilverPlatter Information, Incorporated.

Microform: PQC. Online: EBSCO Publishing, EBSCO Host; Gale; IngentaConnect; JSTOR (Web-based Journal Archive); ProQuest LLC (Ann Arbor). *Indexed:* ABIn, ABS&EES, AgeL, AmH&L, BRD, BRI, CBRI, HistAb, IBSS, JEL, PAIS, SSCI. *Bk. rev.:* 40, lengthy. *Aud.:* Ac, Sa.

The *Journal of Economic Literature* is received by all members of the American Economic Association (AEA) and libraries everywhere. It contains four to six research articles written by outstanding economists, numerous book reviews, and new book listings by JEL classification. *e-JEL*, the electronic edition, has the current issue hyperlinks. The December issue lists dissertations and recipients of doctoral degrees in economics conferred in U.S. and Canadian universities during the previous academic year. Highly recommended for colleges, universities, and larger public and special libraries. A print subscription is required for the online version, purchased separately, at a low cost.

1902. *Journal of Economic Perspectives.* [ISSN: 0895-3309] 1987. q. Free to members. Ed(s): Alan B Krueger. American Economic Association, 2014 Broadway, Ste 305, Nashville, TN 37203; http://www.vanderbilt.edu/AEA/. Illus., index, adv. Refereed. Vol. ends: Nov. Online: EBSCO Publishing, EBSCO Host; Gale; IngentaConnect; JSTOR (Web-based Journal Archive); OCLC Online Computer Library Center, Inc.; ProQuest LLC (Ann Arbor). *Indexed:* ABIn, ABS&EES, AgeL, AmH&L, BAS, BPI, CJA, HistAb, IBR, IBSS, IBZ, JEL, PAIS, SSCI, WAE&RSA. *Aud.:* Ga, Ac, Sa.

This journal "attempts to fill a gap between the general interest press and most other academic economics journals," including the goal to "synthesize and integrate lessons learned from active lines of economic research and economic analysis of public policy issues." A membership in the American Economic Association also includes two other highly regarded journals, the *Journal of Economic Literature* and the *American Economic Review*. A typical issue contains a lecture, articles, recommendations for further reading and retrospectives, and "Notes" of association announcements and the call for papers. *e-JEP*, the electronic edition, combines the current issue with hyperlinks. This journal is heartily recommended for large public and academic libraries. A print subscription is required for online and must be purchased separately, at a low cost. It's a bargain!

1903. *Journal of Economic Psychology.* [ISSN: 0167-4870] 1981. 6x/yr. EUR 576. Ed(s): D Read, G Antonides. Elsevier BV, North-Holland, Sara Burgerhartstraat 25, Amsterdam, 1055 KV, Netherlands; nlinfo-f@elsevier.nl; http://www.elsevier.nl. Adv. Refereed. Microform: PQC. Online: EBSCO Publishing, EBSCO Host; Gale; IngentaConnect; OhioLINK; ScienceDirect; SwetsWise Online Content. *Indexed:* ABIn, CJA, FR, FS&TA, HRIS, HortAb, IBSS, JEL, PsycInfo, SSCI, WAE&RSA. *Aud.:* Ac, Sa.

Published for the International Association for Research in Economic Psychology, this journal publishes papers that use behavioral science methods for the study of economic behavior, especially the socio-psychological aspects of economic events and processes such as consumption, preferences, choices, and decisions. The study of an individual's actions and society's as a whole has made and will continue to make tremendous impact on economic theory, hence the inclusion of this journal. This is a most interesting area of study, and economists, sociologists, and policy makers will appreciate this leading-edge journal. A very good selection for academic and special libraries.

1904. *Journal of Economic Theory.* [ISSN: 0022-0531] 1969. 6x/yr. EUR 3523. Ed(s): A Lizzeri, Karl Shell. Academic Press, 525 B St, Ste 1900, San Diego, CA 92101-4495; apsubs@acad.com; http://www.elsevier.com/. Adv. Refereed. Online: EBSCO Publishing, EBSCO Host; Gale; IngentaConnect; OCLC Online Computer Library Center, Inc.; OhioLINK; ScienceDirect; SwetsWise Online Content. *Indexed:* ABIn, AgeL, CCMJ, IBSS, JEL, MSN, MathR, PhilInd, RiskAb, SSCI. *Aud.:* Ac, Sa.

This well-established, heavily-cited, core scholarly journal publishes "research on economic theory and emphasizes the theoretical analysis of economic models, including the related mathematical techniques." There are usually four to six articles followed by notes, comments, letters to the editor, announcements, a list of papers to appear in forthcoming issues, and an author index. An excellent journal for libraries that support theoretical economics. Still a must! A competitive journal, *Review of Economic Theory,* was launched in spring 2003 by ELSSS and is endorsed by SPARC.

1905. *Journal of Economics.* Formerly (until 1986): *Zeitschrift fuer Nationaloekonomie.* [ISSN: 0931-8658] 1930. 9x/yr. EUR 1398 print & online eds. Ed(s): Dieter Boes. Springer Wien, Sachsenplatz 4-6, Vienna, A-1201, Austria; journals@springer.at; http://www.springer.at. Illus., index, adv. Sample. Refereed. Microform: PQC. Online: Chadwyck-Healey Inc.; EBSCO Publishing, EBSCO Host; OhioLINK; ProQuest LLC (Ann Arbor); Springer LINK; SwetsWise Online Content. Reprint: PSC. *Indexed:* ABIn, CJA, IBR, IBSS, IBZ, JEL, MathR, PAIS, SSCI. *Bk. rev.:* 6-8, lengthy. *Aud.:* Ac.

Focusing on mathematical economic theory, this excellent journal has technical articles that cover mainly microeconomics and some macroeconomics. Level of difficulty is from medium to hard, in their own estimation. A typical issue has five extensive articles and six to eight lengthy book reviews. Additional supplemental issues are devoted to current issues. Authors are academic and international. For well-versed economists and readers in large academic libraries.

1906. *Journal of Environmental Economics and Management.* [ISSN: 0095-0696] 1975. 6x/yr. EUR 1341. Ed(s): J. A. Herriges. Academic Press, 525 B St, Ste 1900, San Diego, CA 92101-4495; apsubs@acad.com; http://www.elsevier.com/. Illus. Refereed. Online: EBSCO Publishing, EBSCO Host; Gale; IngentaConnect; OCLC Online Computer Library Center, Inc.; OhioLINK; ScienceDirect; SwetsWise Online Content. *Indexed:* ABIn, Agr, ApEcolAb, CABA, EngInd, EnvAb, EnvInd, ExcerpMed, FPA, ForAb, IBSS, IndVet, JEL, M&GPA, PAIS, PollutAb, RRTA, S&F, SCI, SSCI, SWRA, VB, WAE&RSA. *Aud.:* Ac, Sa.

Very highly regarded, this is the official journal of the Association of Environmental and Resource Economists. Devoted to the worldwide coverage of theoretical and empirical research, it "concentrates on the management and/or social control of the economy in its relationship with the management and use of natural resources and the natural environment." The majority of authors are academic economists, and it includes interdisciplinary papers from fields of interest. This journal is recommended for university and large public libraries.

The Journal of Finance. See Finance/Scholarly section.

Journal of Financial and Quantitative Analysis. See Finance/Scholarly section.

Journal of Financial Economics. See Finance/Scholarly section.

1907. *Journal of Health Economics.* [ISSN: 0167-6296] 1982. 6x/yr. EUR 1174. Ed(s): R. Frank, A J Culyer. Elsevier BV, North-Holland, Sara Burgerhartstraat 25, Amsterdam, 1055 KV, Netherlands; nlinfo-f@elsevier.nl; http://www.elsevier.nl. Illus., adv. Refereed. Microform: PQC. Online: EBSCO Publishing, EBSCO Host; Gale; IngentaConnect; OhioLINK; ScienceDirect; SwetsWise Online Content. *Indexed:* ABIn, ASG, ASSIA, AgeL, ExcerpMed, H&SSA, HRA, IBSS, JEL, MCR, PAIS, PEI, PRA, RiskAb, SCI, SFSA, SSCI, V&AA. *Aud.:* Ac, Sa.

The focus of this journal is health and medical care, which is taken to encompass the "production of health services; demand and utilization; financing of; services of; measurement of; behavioral models of demanders and suppliers; manpower planning and forecasting; the prevention of sickness; cost-benefit and cost-effectiveness analyses and issues of budgeting; and efficiency and distributional aspects of health policy." Very useful and informative for economists and students in the field, as well as for health care administrators.

1908. *Journal of Human Development: alternative economics in action.* [ISSN: 1464-9888] 2000. 3x/yr. GBP 232 print & online eds. Ed(s): Khadija Haq, Sakiko Fukuda-Parr. Routledge, 4 Park Sq, Milton Park, Abingdon, OX14 4RN, United Kingdom; info@routledge.co.uk;

http://www.routledge.co.uk. Online: EBSCO Publishing, EBSCO Host; Gale; IngentaConnect; OCLC Online Computer Library Center, Inc.; SwetsWise Online Content. Reprint: PSC. *Indexed:* IBR, IBSS, IBZ, JEL, PSA, SociolAb. *Aud.:* Ac, Sa.

This refereed journal was started in 2000, and its contents reflect human development as a new school of thought in economics, and as such is a must-purchase for academic libraries. Its scope covers the challenges of dealing with development and poverty eradication, including human well-being, markets, growth, social justice, and human rights. Amartya Sen is on the editorial advisory board; he won the 1998 Nobel Prize in economics for his "contributions to welfare economics"; and the lead editor is from The New School. Affiliated with the United Nations Development Programme, this journal will be gaining circulation and respect.

Journal of Human Resources. See Management, Administration, and Human Resources/Human Resources section.

1909. *The Journal of Industrial Economics.* [ISSN: 0022-1821] 1952. q. GBP 162 print & online eds. Ed(s): Pierre Regibeau. Blackwell Publishing Ltd., 9600 Garsington Rd, Oxford, OX4 2ZG, United Kingdom; customerservices@blackwellpublishing.com; http://www.blackwellpublishing.com. Illus., index, adv. Sample. Refereed. Circ: 1850. Vol. ends: Dec. Microform: MIM; PQC. Online: Blackwell Synergy; EBSCO Publishing, EBSCO Host; Gale; IngentaConnect; JSTOR (Web-based Journal Archive); OCLC Online Computer Library Center, Inc.; OhioLINK; SwetsWise Online Content. Reprint: PSC. *Indexed:* ABIn, ApEcolAb, BAS, BPI, CABA, HRA, IBR, IBSS, IBZ, JEL, PAIS, PRA, RiskAb, SSCI, V&AA. *Aud.:* Ac, Sa.

Started in 1952 to promote the analysis of modern industry, especially the behavior of firms and market functions, this widely circulated journal is primary in its field. International economics, labor economics, and law are also covered tangentially. Both theoretical and empirical works are published, covering everything from organization of industry and applied oligopoly theory to regulation, monopoly, merger, and technology policy. Large business collections and universities will want to review this important journal.

1910. *Journal of Institutional and Theoretical Economics.* Formerly (until 1986): *Zeitschrift fuer die Gesamte Staatswissenschaft.* [ISSN: 0932-4569] 1844. q. EUR 284 (Individuals, EUR 164). Ed(s): Rudolf Richter. Mohr Siebeck, Wilhelmstr 18, Tuebingen, 72074, Germany; info@mohr.de; http://www.mohr.de/jite.html. Illus., index, adv. Refereed. Circ: 1070 Paid and controlled. Vol. ends: Dec. *Indexed:* ABIn, AgeL, ArtHuCI, BAS, CJA, IBR, IBSS, IBZ, IPSA, JEL, PAIS, PSA, SSCI, WAE&RSA. *Bk. rev.:* 10-14, 600-2,200 words. *Aud.:* Ga, Ac, Sa.

As institutional economics has grown to importance, this leading journal with a diversity of opinions has covered the "economics of property rights and of institutional evolution, transaction cost economics, contract theory, economic history and interdisciplinary studies." Articles and book reviews may be in English or German, but most are in English; papers have a summary in both languages. Notable are the papers from the Symposium on New Institutional Economics, presented in a single issue annually. Recommended for very large public and university libraries.

1911. *Journal of Institutional Economics.* [ISSN: 1744-1374] 2005. s-a. GBP 148. Ed(s): Geoffrey M Hodgson. Cambridge University Press, The Edinburgh Bldg, Shaftesbury Rd, Cambridge, CB2 2RU, United Kingdom; journals@cambridge.org; http://www.journals.cambridge.org. Online: Pub.; EBSCO Publishing, EBSCO Host; SwetsWise Online Content. *Aud.:* Ac, Sa.

Established in 2005, this interdisciplinary journal focuses on the study of the nature, role, and evolution of institutions in the economy, including firms, states, markets, money, households, and other vital institutions and organizations, recognizing the vital importance that institutions have to everyday economics and life. The editorial and advisory boards are international and accept contributions from all schools of thought. The journal will be of interest to academics in economics and business. A good complement to the *Journal of Institutional and Theoretical Economics,* noted above.

1912. *Journal of International Economics.* [ISSN: 0022-1996] 1971. 6x/yr. EUR 1315. Ed(s): C. M. Engel, J. Eaton. Elsevier BV, North-Holland, Sara Burgerhartstraat 25, Amsterdam, 1055 KV, Netherlands; nlinfo-f@ elsevier.nl; http://www.elsevier.nl. Illus., index, adv. Refereed. Vol. ends: May/Nov. Microform: PQC. Online: EBSCO Publishing, EBSCO Host; Gale; IngentaConnect; OhioLINK; ScienceDirect; SwetsWise Online Content. *Indexed:* ABIn, BAS, IBSS, JEL, PAIS, RRTA, RiskAb, SSCI, WAE&RSA. *Aud.:* Ac, Sa.

This journal has a highly significant impact factor, and its articles pertain to "trade patterns, commercial policy, exchange rates, international institutions, open economy macroeconomics, international finance, international factor mobility." Empirical studies are encouraged for submission. Four frequently downloaded articles in early 2007 include: "Do free trade agreements actually increase members' international trade?"; "The effect of trade liberalization on child labor"; "Economic geography and international inequality"; and "The new open economy macroeconomics: a survey." Each issue has 11 or so articles. Academic instituions with economic programs should subscribe despite the price.

Journal of Labor Economics. See Labor and Industrial Relations section.

Journal of Law and Economics. See Law section.

1913. *Journal of Macroeconomics.* [ISSN: 0164-0704] 1979. 4x/yr. EUR 308. Ed(s): Theodore Palivos, Douglas McMillin. Elsevier BV, North-Holland, Sara Burgerhartstraat 25, Amsterdam, 1055 KV, Netherlands; nlinfo-f@elsevier.nl; http://www.elsevier.nl. Illus., index, adv. Sample. Refereed. Circ: 950. Vol. ends: Fall. Microform: PQC. Online: EBSCO Publishing, EBSCO Host; Gale; IngentaConnect; Northern Light Technology, Inc.; OhioLINK; ScienceDirect; SwetsWise Online Content. *Indexed:* ABIn, IBR, IBSS, IBZ, JEL, SSCI. *Bk. rev.:* 12-16, 75-100 words. *Aud.:* Ac, Sa.

Begun in 1979, the *Journal of Macroeconomics,* published for the E. J. Ourso College of Business Administration at Louisiana State University, is devoted to "economic growth, economic fluctuations, the effects of monetary and fiscal policy, the political aspects of macroeconomics, exchange rate determination and other elements of open economy macroeconomics, the macroeconomics of income inequality, and macroeconomic forecasting." Subscribers will be academic, business, and government libraries.

1914. *Journal of Mathematical Economics.* [ISSN: 0304-4068] 1974. 8x/yr. EUR 1634. Ed(s): F. Delbaen, J. Geanakoplos. Elsevier BV, North-Holland, Sara Burgerhartstraat 25, Amsterdam, 1055 KV, Netherlands; nlinfo-f@elsevier.nl; http://www.elsevier.nl. Illus., adv. Refereed. Microform: PQC. Online: EBSCO Publishing, EBSCO Host; Gale; IngentaConnect; OhioLINK; ScienceDirect; SwetsWise Online Content. *Indexed:* ABIn, CCMJ, IBSS, JEL, MSN, MathR, RiskAb, SCI, SSCI. *Aud.:* Ac, Sa.

Published since 1974, the current goal of this journal "is to provide a forum for work in economic theory which expresses economic ideas using formal mathematical reasoning." This involves any field of economics or school of economic thought. The editor defends the journal on its web site by stating, "[T]he formal mathematical expression of economic ideas is of vital importance to economics. Such an expression can determine whether a loose economic intuition has a coherent, logical meaning." This illustrates an ideological division among economists. Subscriptions are for academic libraries with economic programs and special libraries.

1915. *Journal of Monetary Economics.* Incorporates (1978-2002): *Carnegie-Rochester Conference Series on Public Policy.* [ISSN: 0304-3932] 1975. 8x/yr. EUR 1788. Ed(s): Charles Plosser, Robert G. King. Elsevier BV, North-Holland, Sara Burgerhartstraat 25, Amsterdam, 1055 KV, Netherlands; nlinfo-f@elsevier.nl; http://www.elsevier.nl. Illus., index, adv. Sample. Refereed. Vol. ends: Dec. Microform: PQC. Online: EBSCO Publishing, EBSCO Host; Gale; IngentaConnect; OhioLINK; ScienceDirect; SwetsWise Online Content. *Indexed:* ABIn, BLI, IBR, IBSS, IBZ, JEL, LRI, PAIS, RiskAb, SSCI. *Aud.:* Ac, Sa.

With ever-growing interest in the monetary analysis and the "working and structure of financial institutions." This journal aims to publish selected papers in the growing area of monetary analysis, focusing on "the role of various institutional arrangements, the consequences of specific changes in banking structure, and the welfare aspects of structural policies." The operation of credit markets and the behavior of rates of return on assets are explored as well. The journal is published in collaboration with the University of Rochester's Graduate School of Business Administration and the Department of Economics at Boston University. As a reminder, as of 2002, the journal includes the Carnegie Rochester Conference Series on Public Policy. Although it is expensive, libraries that support programs in banking and finance will want it for their collections.

1916. *Journal of Money, Credit & Banking.* [ISSN: 0022-2879] 1969. 8x/yr. USD 474 print & online eds. Blackwell Publishing, Inc., Commerce Place, 350 Main St, Malden, MA 02148; customerservices@ blackwellpublishing.com; http://www.blackwellpublishing.com. Illus., index, adv. Refereed. Circ: 3500 Paid. Vol. ends: Feb/Nov. CD-ROM: ProQuest LLC (Ann Arbor). Microform: PQC. Online: EBSCO Publishing, EBSCO Host; Florida Center for Library Automation; Gale; JSTOR (Web-based Journal Archive); OCLC Online Computer Library Center, Inc.; OhioLINK; Project MUSE; ProQuest LLC (Ann Arbor); SwetsWise Online Content; H.W. Wilson. Reprint: SCH. *Indexed:* ABIn, ATI, BLI, BPI, IBR, IBSS, IBZ, JEL, PAIS, RiskAb, SSCI. *Bk. rev.:* 1-5, 2-4 pages. *Aud.:* Ac, Sa.

A classic, and sponsored by the Ohio State University Department of Economics, this widely read and cited journal presents "major findings in the study of monetary and fiscal policy, credit markets, money and banking, portfolio management, and related subjects." Ben Bernanke, Chairman of the Federal Reserve Board, is on the advisory board. A newer section called "Shorter Papers, Discussions, and Letters" is for quickly publishing concise new results, models, and methods. Online is a data archive for papers' empirical findings. Both JSTOR and Project Muse have archives. Recommended for policy makers, professional and academic economists, and bankers.

1917. *Journal of Political Economy.* [ISSN: 0022-3808] 1892. bi-m. USD 232 domestic; USD 359.92 Canada; USD 244 elsewhere. Ed(s): Canice Prendergast, Steven D Levitt. University of Chicago Press, Journals Division, PO Box 37005, Chicago, IL 60637; subscriptions@ press.uchicago.edu; http://www.journals.uchicago.edu. Illus., index, adv. Refereed. Circ: 6100. Vol. ends: Dec. Microform: MIM; PMC; PQC. Online: EBSCO Publishing, EBSCO Host; Florida Center for Library Automation; Gale; JSTOR (Web-based Journal Archive); ProQuest LLC (Ann Arbor). Reprint: PSC. *Indexed:* ABCPolSci, ABIn, AgeL, AmH&L, ArtHuCI, BAS, BLI, BRD, BRI, CBRI, CJA, ERIC, HistAb, IBR, IBSS, IBZ, IPSA, IndIslam, JEL, PAIS, PSA, RI-1, RRTA, SSCI, SWA, SociolAb, WAE&RSA. *Bk. rev.:* 1-2, 2-4 pages. *Aud.:* Ac, Sa.

One of the most prestigious economic journals and connected with the Department of Economics and the Graduate School of Business at the University of Chicago, the *Journal of Political Economy* publishes "analytical, interpretive, and empirical studies" in such traditional areas as monetary theory, fiscal policy, labor economics, planning and development, micro- and macroeconomics theory, international trade and finance, industrial organization, history of economic thought, and social economics. The journal has an excellent reputation and is one of the three top journals in the field. Authors are from international academic institutions and government agencies such as the Federal Reserve Board. Each issue includes five or six articles, occasionally followed by review articles, comments, and book reviews. It would be wise for academic and larger public libraries to subscribe to this publication.

1918. *Journal of Post Keynesian Economics.* [ISSN: 0160-3477] 1978. q. USD 380 print & online eds. Ed(s): Paul Davidson, Sidney Weintraub. M.E. Sharpe, Inc., 80 Business Park Dr, Armonk, NY 10504; custserv@ mesharpe.com; http://www.mesharpe.com. Illus., index, adv. Refereed. Circ: 1700. Vol. ends: Winter. Reprint: PSC. *Indexed:* ABIn, FutSurv, IBR, IBSS, IBZ, JEL, SSCI. *Aud.:* Ac, Sa.

Founded by Sidney Weintraub and Paul Davidson (at The New School), this journal concentrates on post–World War II economic theory, including the "treatment of post-Keynesian economics in the history of economic thought," and hence it "is committed to theory that is continuously subjected to scrutiny in terms of its ability both to explain the real world and to provide a reliable guide to public policy." Each issue usually has eight technical articles, an editor's corner, and possibly a symposium. Authors are usually economics professors. The audience for this journal will be professional economists. John Kenneth Galbraith was the founding chairman. Well worth the low price.

1919. *Journal of Public Economic Theory.* [ISSN: 1097-3923] 1999. 5x/yr. GBP 548 print & online eds. Ed(s): Myrna Holtz Wooders, John P Conley. Blackwell Publishing, Inc., Commerce Place, 350 Main St, Malden, MA 02148; customerservices@blackwellpublishing.com; http://www.blackwellpublishing.com. Adv. Refereed. Online: Blackwell Synergy; EBSCO Publishing, EBSCO Host; Gale; IngentaConnect; OCLC Online Computer Library Center, Inc.; OhioLINK; SwetsWise Online Content. Reprint: PSC. *Indexed:* ABIn, JEL. *Aud.:* Ac, Sa.

A new edition to *MFL* this year. Blackwell publishes this important, fairly new (since 1999) platform on behalf of the Association for Public Economic Theory. It is interdisciplinary in nature, and political scientists will also be interested. Theoretical and original papers are accepted in all areas of public economics, including "public goods, local public goods, club economies, externalities, taxation, growth, public choice, social and public decision making, voting, market failure, regulation, project evaluation, equity, and political systems." Methodology sought after includes: general equilibrium theory, game theory, evolution, experimentation, control theory and dynamics, simulation, axiomatic characterization, and first-order and comparative static methods. The editorial board is filled with well-known scholars. Definitely a new addition for academic libraries.

1920. *Journal of Public Economics.* [ISSN: 0047-2727] 1972. 12x/yr. EUR 2208. Ed(s): J. Poterba, R. Boadway. Elsevier BV, North-Holland, Sara Burgerhartstraat 25, Amsterdam, 1055 KV, Netherlands; nlinfo-f@elsevier.nl; http://www.elsevier.nl. Illus., index, adv. Refereed. Vol. ends: Oct. Microform: PQC. Online: EBSCO Publishing, EBSCO Host; Gale; IngentaConnect; OhioLINK; ScienceDirect; SwetsWise Online Content. *Indexed:* ABIn, ASG, AgeL, CJA, EAA, ExcerpMed, HRA, IBR, IBSS, IBZ, JEL, LRI, PAIS, PRA, SSCI, SUSA. *Aud.:* Ac, Sa.

The *Journal of Public Economics* aims to foster original scientific thought on questions of public economics in such fields as education, environmental policies, and tax enforcement. The emphasis is on the application of current theory and quantitative analysis. Also, during the past few years, empirical papers have comprised 40 percent of the journal. The audience is generally scholars, theorists, public economists, and policy makers. A subscription is suggested for universities, but review due to price.

1921. *Journal of Regulatory Economics.* [ISSN: 0922-680X] 1989. bi-m. EUR 890 print & online eds. Ed(s): Michael A Crew. Springer New York LLC, 233 Spring St, New York, NY 10013-1578; service-ny@springer.com; http://www.springer.com/. Illus., index, adv. Refereed. Vol. ends: Dec. Microform: PQC. Online: Chadwyck-Healey Inc.; EBSCO Publishing, EBSCO Host; Gale; IngentaConnect; OCLC Online Computer Library Center, Inc.; OhioLINK; ProQuest LLC (Ann Arbor); Springer LINK; SwetsWise Online Content. Reprint: PSC. *Indexed:* ABIn, IBSS, JEL, SSCI. *Aud.:* Ac, Sa.

Since partial deregulation, this journal is more important than ever. The *Journal of Regulatory Economics* is a forum for the analysis of regulatory theories and institutions. Theoretical and applied papers are included. Topics include the "traditional problems of natural monopoly; antitrust and competition policy, incentive regulation, deregulation, auction theory, new policy instruments, health and safety regulation, environmental regulation, insurance and financial regulation, hazardous and solid waste regulation, universal service obligation, and consumer product regulation." This journal will be read by researchers, policy makers, and professional economists, so large universities and special libraries will be the subscribers.

Journal of Risk and Insurance. See Finance/Insurance section.

Journal of Sports Economics. See Sports/Physical Education, Coaching, and Sports Sciences section.

Journal of Transport Economics and Policy. See Transportation section.

1922. *Journal of Urban Economics.* [ISSN: 0094-1190] 1974. 6x/yr. EUR 1484. Ed(s): Jan K Brueckner. Academic Press, 525 B St, Ste 1900, San Diego, CA 92101-4495; apsubs@acad.com; http://www.elsevier.com/. Illus., index. Refereed. Vol. ends: May/Nov. Online: EBSCO Publishing, EBSCO Host; Gale; IngentaConnect; OCLC Online Computer Library Center, Inc.; OhioLINK; ScienceDirect; SwetsWise Online Content. *Indexed:* ABIn, AgeL, BPI, CJA, ExcerpMed, IBR, IBSS, IBZ, JEL, PAIS, PRA, RiskAb, SSCI, SUSA. *Aud.:* Ac, Sa.

A respected journal in its field, the *Journal of Urban Economics* publishes scholarly work on a wide range of topics and approaches. Three recent articles illustrate this scope: "A simple theory of smart growth and sprawl," "Immigration and housing rents in American cities," and "Depreciation of housing capital, maintenance, and house price inflation: Estimates from a repeat sales model." Also featured are brief notes and an index in the last issue of each volume. This journal has some technical articles. Primarily for economists, but those interested in urban economic issues such as local public finance, transportation, and housing will also benefit.

1923. *Kyklos.* [ISSN: 0023-5962] 1943. q. GBP 340 print & online eds. Ed(s): Rene L Frey. Blackwell Publishing Ltd., 9600 Garsington Rd, Oxford, OX4 2ZG, United Kingdom; customerservices@blackwellpublishing.com; http://www.blackwellpublishing.com. Illus., index. Refereed. Circ: 2600. Vol. ends: Nov. Microform: PQC. Online: Blackwell Synergy; EBSCO Publishing, EBSCO Host; Gale; IngentaConnect; OCLC Online Computer Library Center, Inc.; OhioLINK; SwetsWise Online Content; H.W. Wilson. Reprint: PSC. *Indexed:* ABIn, ApEcolAb, ArtHuCI, BAS, ExcerpMed, HistAb, IBR, IBSS, IBZ, IPSA, JEL, PAIS, PRA, PSA, RRTA, SSA, SSCI, SociolAb, WAE&RSA. *Bk. rev.:* 15-20, 550-1,600 words. *Aud.:* Ga, Ac, Sa.

This journal is widely recognized around the world, and published by an international nonprofit organization whose main purpose is "to analyze socio-economic problems of our time and to bridge the gap between scholarship and economic policy makers by means of public conferences and publications." Authors are most international, and a new "Forum of Ideas" calls for short essays that show new and unconventional ideas, even if not fully worked out or formalized in a neat model. Each issue has about seven articles. Researchers, economists, sociologists, policy makers, and students appreciate this journal. Now entirely in English, even the subtitle. Also for larger public libraries.

1924. *Land Economics: a quarterly journal devoted to the study of economic and social institutions.* Formerly (until 1948): *Journal of Land and Public Utility Economics.* [ISSN: 0023-7639] 1925. q. USD 239 print & online eds. (Individuals, USD 85 print & online eds.). Ed(s): Daniel Bromley. University of Wisconsin Press, Journal Division, 1930 Monroe St, 3rd Fl, Madison, WI 53711-2059; journals@uwpress.wisc.edu; http://www.wisc.edu/wisconsinpress/journals. Illus., index, adv. Refereed. Circ: 1800. Vol. ends: Nov. Microform: PQC. Online: EBSCO Publishing, EBSCO Host; Florida Center for Library Automation; Gale; IngentaConnect; JSTOR (Web-based Journal Archive); Northern Light Technology, Inc.; OCLC Online Computer Library Center, Inc.; ProQuest LLC (Ann Arbor); H.W. Wilson. Reprint: PSC. *Indexed:* ABIn, AgeL, Agr, AmH&L, BAS, BPI, CABA, DSA, EI, EnvAb, EnvInd, ExcerpMed, FPA, ForAb, HistAb, HortAb, IBR, IBSS, IBZ, JEL, LRI, PAIS, PRA, PollutAb, RRTA, RiskAb, S&F, SSCI, SUSA, WAE&RSA. *Bk. rev.:* 1-2, 1-6 pages. *Aud.:* Ac, Sa.

Land Economics is "dedicated to the study of land use, natural resources, public utilities, housing, and urban land issues." One of oldest American economic journals and started by Richard Ely, the founder of the American Economic Association. Its topics include "transportation, energy, urban and rural land use, housing, environmental quality, public utilities, and natural resources." Highly recommended for scholars and economists in government, business, finance, and universities.

Managerial and Decision Economics. See Management, Administration, and Human Resources/Operations Research and Management Science section.

1925. The Manchester School. Formerly: *Manchester School of Economic and Social Studies.* [ISSN: 1463-6786] 1930. bi-m. GBP 341 print & online eds. Ed(s): Keith Blackburn, Eyal Winter. Blackwell Publishing Ltd., 9600 Garsington Rd, Oxford, OX4 2ZG, United Kingdom; customerservices@blackwellpublishing.com; http://www.blackwellpublishing.com. Illus., index, adv. Refereed. Circ: 1300. Vol. ends: Dec. Online: Blackwell Synergy; EBSCO Publishing, EBSCO Host; Gale; IngentaConnect; OCLC Online Computer Library Center, Inc.; OhioLINK; SwetsWise Online Content. Reprint: PSC. *Indexed:* ABIn, AmH&L, HistAb, IBR, IBSS, IBZ, JEL, PAIS, RRTA, RiskAb, SSCI, WAE&RSA. *Bk. rev.:* 20-30, 250-1,500 words. *Aud.:* Ac, Sa.

This general, international journal enjoys an excellent reputation, and covers the theoretical and applied in microeconomics, macroeconomics, econometrics, and labor. Included is an annual supplement of papers reflecting the proceedings of the Money, Macroeconomics, and Finance Research Group. Electronic archives will be available through Blackwell for purchase. Graduate students and economists will appreciate this scholarly publication.

Mathematical Finance. See Finance/Scholarly section.

Meridians. See Gender Studies section.

1926. N B E R Reporter OnLine. q. National Bureau of Economic Research, 1050 Massachusetts Ave, 3rd Fl, Cambridge, MA 02138-5398; http://www.nber.org/reporter/. *Aud.:* Ac, Sa.

The National Bureau of Economic Research (NBER), founded in 1920, is a private, nonprofit, nonpartisan research organization. Numerous American Nobel Prize winners in economics have been researchers at the NBER. With this reputation, it is hard to pass up any information produced by them. The *NBER Reporter OnLine* includes research summaries and program reports from the recent issues of the *NBER Reporter*, a print source that covers broad areas of research. Also, there are archives of two other publications, *NBER Digest* and a searchable index to *NBER Working Papers*. These are available at no additional cost to print subscribers (free or low-cost to begin with). These are a print publication and a web site not to be missed for current trends, issues, and information. Also on the NBER web site are great new features: e-mail notifications of new economic releases and working paper notification. URL: www.nber.org/reporter.

1927. National Institute Economic Review. [ISSN: 0027-9501] 1959. q. GBP 296. Ed(s): Martin Weale. Sage Publications Ltd., 1 Oliver's Yard, 55 City Rd, London, EC1 1SP, United Kingdom; info@sagepub.co.uk; http://www.sagepub.co.uk. Illus., index. Circ: 1700. Vol. ends: Nov. Online: EBSCO Publishing, EBSCO Host; Florida Center for Library Automation; Gale; HighWire Press; Northern Light Technology, Inc.; OCLC Online Computer Library Center, Inc.; SAGE Publications, Inc., SAGE Journals Online; SwetsWise Online Content; H.W. Wilson. Reprint: PSC. *Indexed:* ABIn, BPI, IBR, IBSS, IBZ, JEL, PAIS, RRTA, WAE&RSA. *Aud.:* Ga, Ac, Sa.

This periodical was established in 1959 and from one of Britain's oldest established independent economic research institutes. It covers quantitative research that illustrates a "deeper understanding of the interaction of economic and social forces that affect peoples' lives so that they may be improved." The institute receives no funding from private or public sources. There are six basic sections: "Economic Overview," "Commentary," "The UK Economy," "The World Economy," "Research Articles," and "Main Economic Events." The last is a statistical appendix that gives series information on the GDP, output volumes, prices, unemployment, imports and exports, monthly economic indicators, and financial indicators. There is also a new online forum! Strongly recommended for libraries with large economics collections or those that support international studies.

National Tax Journal. See Accounting and Taxation/Taxation section.

1928. Netnomics. [ISSN: 1385-9587] 1999. 3x/yr. EUR 229 print & online eds. Ed(s): Anna Nagurney, Hans M Amman. Springer New York LLC, 233 Spring St, New York, NY 10013-1578; service-ny@springer.com; http://www.springer.com/. Illus., adv. Sample. Refereed. Online: EBSCO Publishing, EBSCO Host; Gale; IngentaConnect; OCLC Online Computer Library Center, Inc.; OhioLINK; Springer LINK; SwetsWise Online Content. Reprint: PSC. *Indexed:* JEL. *Aud.:* Ac.

Still going strong since 1999, this innovative journal has addressed "pricing schemes for electronic services, electronic trading systems, data mining and high frequency data, real-time forecasting, filtering, economic software agents, distributed database applications, digicash-ecash systems, and many more." Available in paper and/or on the web. Strongly recommended to all those dealing with these new problems and issues as a whole new field of research is emerging.

1929. New Political Economy. [ISSN: 1356-3467] 1996. q. GBP 392 print & online eds. Ed(s): Anthony Payne, Anthony Payne. Routledge, 4 Park Sq, Milton Park, Abingdon, OX14 4RN, United Kingdom; info@routledge.co.uk; http://www.routledge.co.uk. Refereed. Reprint: PSC. *Indexed:* ABIn, AltPI, IBR, IBSS, IBZ, IPSA, IndIslam, JEL, LeftInd, PSA, SSCI, SociolAb. *Bk. rev.:* Number and length vary. *Aud.:* Ac, Sa.

Started in early 1996 on the "belief that a new stage in the development of the world economic and political system has commenced," this interdisciplinary international journal has three or four referred articles in each issue, plus a Special Section for focused topics. It aims to combine "the breadth of vision which characterised the classical political economy of the nineteenth century with the analytical advances of twentieth century social science." The journal is indexed in the Social Science Citation Index. The demands of globalization require the type of information that this journal offers. Highly recommended for academic institutions.

1930. OECD Observer. [ISSN: 0029-7054] 1962. bi-m. EUR 64 combined subscription print & online eds.; USD 75 combined subscription print & online eds.; GBP 43 combined subscription print & online eds. Organisation for Economic Cooperation and Development (OECD), 2 Rue Andre Pascal, Paris, 75775 Cedex 16, France; http://www.oecd.org. Illus., index, adv. Circ: 25000. Vol. ends: Dec/Jan. Online: Chadwyck-Healey Inc.; EBSCO Publishing, EBSCO Host; Florida Center for Library Automation; Gale; IngentaConnect; OCLC Online Computer Library Center, Inc.; ProQuest LLC (Ann Arbor); SwetsWise Online Content; H.W. Wilson. *Indexed:* ABIn, BPI, CABA, DSA, EIP, EnvInd, ExcerpMed, FutSurv, HRIS, IBR, IBZ, PAIS, PdeR, PollutAb, RRTA, SWA, WAE&RSA. *Bk. rev.:* 1-2. *Aud.:* Hs, Ga, Ac.

The Organisation for Economic Co-operation and Development (OECD), an international organization comprised of 30 member-countries, "is a unique forum permitting governments of the industrialised democracies to study and formulate the best policies possible in all economic and social spheres." In contributing to this goal, it "collects and analyses a unique body of data that allows comparison of statistics across countries and provides macro-micro economic research and policy advice in fields that mirror policy-making ministries in governments." All of this research is made available through a large publishing mechanism, and this publication is part of that mechanism. Other excellent publications include *OECD Foreign Trade Statistics, OECD Main Economic Indicators, OECD Economic Studies,* and *OECD Economic Outlook.* The *OECD Observer* is written for a popular audience. It has a wealth of information on the member countries, and it also covers transitional economies, dynamic nonmember economies, and the developing world. It has a wide scope, encompassing "economic growth, labour markets, education, social policy, demography, industry, services, energy, finance trade, fiscal policy, public-sector management, environment, science and technology, investment and multinational enterprises, transport, agriculture and fisheries, taxation, competition and consumer policy, research and development, urban affairs, telecommunications, tourism, and rural development." Every issue has an editorial, articles on a theme, and additional titles. A very useful feature is the two to six pages of current statistics on the GDP, the consumer price index, and the leading indicators. Each year, subscribers receive a pocket book called *OECD in Figures,* a handy 60-page guide of statistics. Highly recommended for high school, academic, and public libraries.

1931. *Oxford Bulletin of Economics and Statistics.* Former titles (until 1973): *Oxford University. Institute of Economics and Statistics. Bulletin;* (until 1963): *Oxford University. Institute of Statistics. Bulletin.* [ISSN: 0305-9049] 1939. 5x/yr. GBP 399 print & online eds. Ed(s): Jonathan Temple, Christopher Adam. Blackwell Publishing Ltd., 9600 Garsington Rd, Oxford, OX4 2ZG, United Kingdom; customerservices@blackwellpublishing.com; http://www.blackwellpublishing.com. Illus., index, adv. Refereed. Circ: 1500. Vol. ends: Dec. Online: Blackwell Synergy; EBSCO Publishing, EBSCO Host; Gale; IngentaConnect; OCLC Online Computer Library Center, Inc.; OhioLINK; SwetsWise Online Content. Reprint: PSC. *Indexed:* ABIn, CABA, CJA, FPA, ForAb, IBSS, JEL, PAIS, RRTA, RiskAb, SCI, SSCI, WAE&RSA. *Aud.:* Ac, Sa.

This bulletin's aim is to publish "international research papers on current practical issues in applied economics." An emphasis is placed on quality and the practicality of "practical importance, theoretical interest and policy relevance" of each article. The journal covers applied economics very broadly, including both developed and developing countries. British economists are usually the authors, but Europeans and Americans are included as well. Free online access to developing worlds is offered via United Nations programs. Academics, professionals, and students in the area of international economics will appreciate this journal.

1932. *Oxford Economic Papers.* [ISSN: 0030-7653] 1938. q. EUR 341 print or online ed. Ed(s): J Forder, A. Banerjee. Oxford University Press, Great Clarendon St, Oxford, OX2 6DP, United Kingdom; jnl.orders@oup.co.uk; http://www.oxfordjournals.org. Illus., index, adv. Sample. Refereed. Circ: 1900. Vol. ends: Oct. Microform: PQC. Online: EBSCO Publishing, EBSCO Host; Gale; HighWire Press; IngentaConnect; JSTOR (Web-based Journal Archive); Northern Light Technology, Inc.; OCLC Online Computer Library Center, Inc.; OhioLINK; Oxford Journals; ProQuest K-12 Learning Solutions; ProQuest LLC (Ann Arbor); SwetsWise Online Content; H.W. Wilson. Reprint: PSC. *Indexed:* ABIn, AmH&L, BAS, CABA, CJA, ExcerpMed, HistAb, IBR, IBSS, IBZ, JEL, PAIS, RRTA, S&F, SSCI, WAE&RSA. *Aud.:* Ac, Sa.

A general journal, *Oxford Economic Papers* publishes material in a wide range of areas in theoretical and applied economics. Contributions are accepted "in economic theory, applied economics, econometrics, economic development, economic history, and the history of economic thought." Special issues are regularly published, covering topics such as financial markets, public economics, and quantitative economic history. Although a great deal of this material centers on the United Kingdom, some of it focuses on other countries' problems. An issue typically has 8–11 articles. University and large college libraries should include this esteemed journal in their holdings.

1933. *Oxford Review of Economic Policy.* [ISSN: 0266-903X] 1985. q. EUR 357 print or online ed. Ed(s): Tim Jenkinson, Christopher Allsopp. Oxford University Press, Great Clarendon St, Oxford, OX2 6DP, United Kingdom; jnl.orders@oup.co.uk; http://www.oxfordjournals.org. Illus., adv. Refereed. Circ: 1600. Online: Chadwyck-Healey Inc.; EBSCO Publishing, EBSCO Host; Gale; HighWire Press; IngentaConnect; OCLC Online Computer Library Center, Inc.; OhioLINK; Oxford Journals; ProQuest LLC (Ann Arbor); SwetsWise Online Content. Reprint: PSC. *Indexed:* ABIn, AmHI, BrHumI, IBSS, JEL, PAIS, SSCI. *Aud.:* Ac, Sa.

Resized smaller in 2007, this journal still packs a wallop of information. Each issue has a theme, and a recent topic is the Solow growth model and its 50 years of invention. Refreshing, current worldwide policy discussions (such as productivity, fiscal restraint and the welfare state, regulation and pensions) are the mainstay. Both macro and micro are represented. Readers would include a wide audience from among academics, government, business, and policy-makers.

1934. *Petroleum Economist: the international energy journal.* Formerly: *Petroleum Press Service.* [ISSN: 0306-395X] 1934. m. GBP 625 combined subscription domestic print & online eds.; EUR 675 combined subscription in Europe print & online eds.; USD 1230 combined subscription elsewhere print & online eds. Ed(s): Tom Nicholls. Euromoney Institutional Investor Plc., Nestor House, Playhouse Yard, London, EC4V 5EX, United Kingdom; information@euromoneyplc.com;

http://www.euromoney.com. Illus., adv. Sample. Circ: 4400. Vol. ends: Dec. Microform: PQC. Online: EBSCO Publishing, EBSCO Host; Florida Center for Library Automation; Gale; LexisNexis; Northern Light Technology, Inc.; OCLC Online Computer Library Center, Inc.; ProQuest LLC (Ann Arbor); H.W. Wilson. *Indexed:* ABIn, BPI, PAIS, PetrolAb. *Aud.:* Ga, Ac, Sa.

The scope of this specialized trade journal is the world oil and gas industry, but it has expanded coverage to include financial, accounting, and legal issues. Also, it provides a macro-economic and geopolitical analysis of the industry. Each issue has world oil and gas production and power summaries in "News in Brief" and "Analysis." As the foremost international journal in the energy industry, this title would benefit related special libraries and public, university, and government libraries.

Post-Communist Economies. See Slavic Studies section.

Post-Soviet Affairs. See Slavic Studies section.

1935. *Public Choice.* Formerly (until 1968): *Papers on Mon-Market Decision-Making.* [ISSN: 0048-5829] 1966. 16x/yr. EUR 1595 print & online eds. Ed(s): Charles K Rowley, Robert D Tollison. Springer New York LLC, 233 Spring St, New York, NY 10013-1578; service-ny@springer.com; http://www.springer.com/. Illus., index, adv. Sample. Refereed. Vol. ends: Dec. Microform: PQC. Online: EBSCO Publishing, EBSCO Host; Gale; IngentaConnect; OCLC Online Computer Library Center, Inc.; OhioLINK; ProQuest LLC (Ann Arbor); Springer LINK; SwetsWise Online Content. Reprint: PSC. *Indexed:* ABCPolSci, ABIn, AgeL, ArtHuCI, HRA, IBR, IBSS, IBZ, IPSA, JEL, PAIS, PRA, PSA, RiskAb, SSA, SSCI, SUSA, SociolAb. *Bk. rev.:* 1-7, 500-2,000 words. *Aud.:* Ga, Ac, Sa.

Public Choice is an interdisciplinary journal of economics and political science. It was founded when economists and political scientists started to apply economic methods to problems in the realm of political science. "It has retained strong traces of economic methodology, but new and fruitful techniques have been developed which are not recognizable by economists." Each issue contains numerous articles, signed book reviews, an author index for each volume, and the call for papers. For larger public libraries and academic collections.

1936. *Quarterly Journal of Economics.* [ISSN: 0033-5533] 1886. q. USD 400 print & online eds. (Individuals, USD 50 print & online eds.). Ed(s): Lawrence Katz, Edward Glaeser. M I T Press, 238 Main St., Ste. 500, Cambridge, MA 02142; journals-info@mit.edu; http://mitpress.mit.edu. Illus., index. Refereed. Circ: 5100 Paid. Vol. ends: Nov. Microform: PQC. Online: EBSCO Publishing, EBSCO Host; Florida Center for Library Automation; Gale; IngentaConnect; JSTOR (Web-based Journal Archive); OCLC Online Computer Library Center, Inc.; SwetsWise Online Content; H.W. Wilson. Reprint: PSC. *Indexed:* ABIn, AgeL, AmH&L, BAS, BPI, CJA, ExcerpMed, HRA, HistAb, IBR, IBSS, IBZ, JEL, MathR, RRTA, RiskAb, SSCI, SUSA, SWR&A, WAE&RSA. *Aud.:* Ac, Sa.

Edited at the Department of Economics at Harvard University, this is "the oldest journal of economics in the English language"; it is also the second-highest cited of all economic journals. The traditional focus on microtheory has been "expanded to include both empirical and theoretical macroeconomics." Statistical methods and models are often used. A typical issue has 11 lengthy articles, sometimes controversial and always interesting. The authors are leading American economists, often affiliated with Harvard. This prestigious journal is essential for libraries that serve professionals, academic economists, and students of economics.

1937. *The Quarterly Review of Economics and Finance.* Former titles (until 1992): *Quarterly Review of Economics and Business; Current Economic Comment.* [ISSN: 1062-9769] 1960. 5x/yr. EUR 468. Ed(s): J E Finnerty, R J Arnould. Elsevier BV, North-Holland, Sara Burgerhartstraat 25, Amsterdam, 1055 KV, Netherlands; nlinfo-f@elsevier.nl; http://www.elsevier.nl. Illus., index, adv. Circ: 2000. Vol. ends: Winter. Microform: MIM; PQC. Online: EBSCO Publishing, EBSCO Host; Florida Center for Library Automation; Gale;

IngentaConnect; OCLC Online Computer Library Center, Inc.; OhioLINK; ScienceDirect; SwetsWise Online Content; H.W. Wilson. *Indexed:* ABIn, AgeL, AmH&L, BPI, HistAb, IBSS, JEL, PAIS, PMA, RRTA, SSCI, WAE&RSA. *Aud.:* Ac, Sa.

This is the official journal of the Midwest Economic Association and the Midwest Finance Association, and it is published for the Bureau of Economic and Business Research at the University of Illinois–Urbana-Champaign. Covering theoretical, empirical, or policy-related ideas, this scholarly journal includes American academic economists. A special feature is "Focus," which often contains papers presented at a regional, national, or international meeting. An issue could have seven to nine articles. A special issue each year has guest editor. Calls for papers, association news, and other tidbits are included. Professional and academic economists appreciate this journal.

1938. *RAND Journal of Economics.* Former titles (until 1984): *Bell Journal of Economics;* (until 1974): *Bell Journal of Economics and Management Science.* [ISSN: 0741-6261] 1970. q. USD 180 domestic; USD 195 foreign. Ed(s): James R Hosek. Rand Journal of Economics, 1700 Main St, Box 2138, Santa Monica, CA 90407-2138; rje@rand.org; http://www.rje.org. Illus., index. Refereed. Circ: 3000 Paid. Vol. ends: Winter. Microform: PQC. Online: EBSCO Publishing, EBSCO Host; Florida Center for Library Automation; Gale; JSTOR (Web-based Journal Archive); OCLC Online Computer Library Center, Inc.; ProQuest LLC (Ann Arbor); H.W. Wilson. Reprint: PSC. *Indexed:* ABIn, ATI, BPI, CompR, HRA, HRIS, IBSS, JEL, MathR, PAIS, PRA, RRTA, RiskAb, SSCI, SUSA, V&AA, WAE&RSA. *Aud.:* Ac, Sa.

Puibslished by the RAND Corporation, this journal supports and encourages research "in the behavior of regulated industries, the economic analysis of organizations, and applied microeconomics." Empirical and theoretical papers in law and economics are accepted. Authors are usually connected to American universities. Usually it contains about 13 articles; there could be symposium papers as well. Highly recommended for large academic, government, business, and public libraries.

The Review of Black Political Economy. See Labor and Industrial Relations section.

1939. *The Review of Economic Studies.* [ISSN: 0034-6527] 1933. q. GBP 232 print & online eds. Ed(s): Bernard Salanie, Juuso Valimaki. Blackwell Publishing Ltd., 9600 Garsington Rd, Oxford, OX4 2ZG, United Kingdom; customerservices@blackwellpublishing.com; http://www.blackwellpublishing.com. Illus., index, adv. Sample. Refereed. Vol. ends: Oct. Online: Blackwell Synergy; EBSCO Publishing, EBSCO Host; Gale; IngentaConnect; JSTOR (Web-based Journal Archive); Northern Light Technology, Inc.; OCLC Online Computer Library Center, Inc.; OhioLINK; ProQuest K-12 Learning Solutions; ProQuest LLC (Ann Arbor); SwetsWise Online Content. Reprint: PSC. *Indexed:* ABIn, AgeL, ApEcolAb, CCMJ, CJA, IBR, IBSS, IBZ, JEL, LRI, MSN, MathR, PAIS, RRTA, RiskAb, SSCI, WAE&RSA. *Aud.:* Ac, Sa.

Originated in 1933 by a group of then-young British and American economists, this journal covers the scope of "behavior of regulated industries, the economic analysis of organizations, and more generally, applied microeconomics. Both theoretical and empirical manuscripts in economics and law are encouraged." An issue may have seven or eight articles with extensive bibliographies. There is an author index in the last issue of each volume. This highly technical journal would be a valuable acquisition for professional and academic economists and large academic collections.

1940. *The Review of Economics and Statistics.* Formerly (until 1948): *The Review of Economics Statistics.* [ISSN: 0034-6535] 1966. q. USD 415 print & online eds. (Individuals, USD 60 print & online eds.). M I T Press, 238 Main St., Ste. 500, Cambridge, MA 02142; journals-info@mit.edu; http://mitpress.mit.edu. Illus., index, adv. Sample. Refereed. Circ: 3500. Vol. ends: Nov. Microform: PQC. Online: EBSCO Publishing, EBSCO Host; Florida Center for Library Automation; Gale; IngentaConnect; JSTOR (Web-based Journal Archive); OCLC Online

Computer Library Center, Inc.; OhioLINK; SwetsWise Online Content; H.W. Wilson. *Indexed:* ABIn, AgeL, Agr, AmH&L, BAS, BPI, CJA, ExcerpMed, HRA, HistAb, IBR, IBSS, IBZ, IPSA, JEL, LRI, MCR, PAIS, PRA, RILM, RRTA, RiskAb, SSCI, SUSA, SWA, WAE&RSA. *Aud.:* Ac, Sa.

Trustworthy to say the least, and edited by the Department of Economics at Harvard University, this general journal covers "applied (especially quantitative) economics." The editorial board and the authors are academic or professional economists. Each issue has 14–18 articles, and the "Notes" section contains one to eight papers. An important journal for university libraries, and very reasonably priced.

Review of Financial Studies. See Finance/Scholarly section.

1941. *Review of Income and Wealth.* Supersedes: *Income and Wealth Series.* [ISSN: 0034-6586] 1966. q. GBP 161 print & online eds. Ed(s): Stephan Klasen, Bart van Ark. Blackwell Publishing Ltd., 9600 Garsington Rd, Oxford, OX4 2ZG, United Kingdom; customerservices@blackwellpublishing.com; http://www.blackwellpublishing.com. Refereed. Circ: 2000. Reprint: PSC. *Indexed:* ABIn, ATI, AgeL, BAS, IBR, IBSS, JEL, PAIS, RiskAb, SSCI. *Aud.:* Ac, Sa.

Begun in 1966, this scholarly journal covers an area of economics that is increasingly being studied by economists everywhere. It covers issues such as: "national and social accounting, microdata analyses of income and wealth and its distribution, the integration of micro and macro systems of economic, financial, and social statistics, international and intertemporal comparisons of income, wealth, inequality, poverty, well-being, and productivity related problems of measurement and methodology." Recommended for academic libraries with economic programs and special institutes.

1942. *Review of Industrial Organization.* [ISSN: 0889-938X] 1984. 8x/yr. EUR 759 print & online eds. Ed(s): Lawrence J White. Springer New York LLC, 233 Spring St, New York, NY 10013-1578; service-ny@springer.com; http://www.springer.com/. Illus., index, adv. Sample. Refereed. Vol. ends: Dec. Microform: PQC. Online: EBSCO Publishing, EBSCO Host; Gale; IngentaConnect; OCLC Online Computer Library Center, Inc.; OhioLINK; ProQuest LLC (Ann Arbor); Springer LINK; SwetsWise Online Content. Reprint: PSC. *Indexed:* ABIn, CABA, IBR, IBSS, IBZ, JEL, SSA, SSCI, WAE&RSA. *Bk. rev.:* 5-7, 500-2,000 words. *Aud.:* Ac, Sa.

Published for the Industrial Organization Society, this review aims "to publish papers on all aspects of industrial organization, broadly defined. The main focus is on competition and monopoly and their effects on efficiency, innovation, and social conditions." Topics range from antitrust, regulation, and deregulation to public enterprise and privatization in any physcial location. This journal can benefit readers at larger academic institutions.

1943. *Review of Political Economy.* [ISSN: 0953-8259] 1989. q. GBP 487 print & online eds. Ed(s): Steve Pressman, Gary Mongiovi. Routledge, 4 Park Sq, Milton Park, Abingdon, OX14 4RN, United Kingdom; journals@routledge.com; http://www.routledge.co.uk. Illus., index, adv. Refereed. Vol. ends: Oct. Online: EBSCO Publishing, EBSCO Host; Gale; IngentaConnect; Northern Light Technology, Inc.; OCLC Online Computer Library Center, Inc.; ProQuest LLC (Ann Arbor); SwetsWise Online Content. Reprint: PSC. *Indexed:* ABIn, CJA, IBR, IBSS, IBZ, JEL, PSA, SSA, SociolAb. *Bk. rev.:* 2-5, 500-3,000 words. *Aud.:* Ga, Ac, Sa.

This review includes "all areas of political economy, including the Post Keynesian, Sraffian, Marxian, Austrian, and Institutionalist traditions." Both theoretical and empirical research are utilized, and mathematics is limited due to editorial policy. Book reviews are also still included. Highly recommended for college, university, and public libraries.

1944. *Review of Social Economy.* [ISSN: 0034-6764] 1948. q. GBP 189 print & online eds. Ed(s): Wilfred Dolfsma, Martha Starr. Routledge, 4 Park Sq, Milton Park, Abingdon, OX14 4RN, United Kingdom; journals@routledge.com; http://www.routledge.co.uk. Illus., adv. Refereed. Circ: 2000. Microform: PQC. Online: EBSCO Publishing,

EBSCO Host; Florida Center for Library Automation; Gale; IngentaConnect; Northern Light Technology, Inc.; OCLC Online Computer Library Center, Inc.; SwetsWise Online Content. Reprint: PSC. *Indexed:* ABIn, ABS&EES, ASSIA, AgeL, AmH&L, ArtHuCI, BAS, BrHumI, CABA, CPL, HistAb, IBR, IBSS, IBZ, IPSA, JEL, PAIS, PRA, PSA, PsycInfo, RRTA, SSA, SSCI, SociolAb, WAE&RSA. *Bk. rev.:* 5-6, signed. *Aud.:* Ac, Sa.

Sponsored by the Association for Social Economics, this journal "investigates the relationship between social values and economics and the relation of economics to ethics, and focuses upon the social economy that encompasses the market economy." Themes covered include justice, need, poverty, income distribution, freedom, gender, environment, humanism, and more. Announcements and the call for papers are included. Strongly recommended for academic libraries.

1945. Review of World Economics. Formerly: *Weltwirtschaftliches Archiv.* [ISSN: 1610-2878] 1914. q. EUR 199 print & online eds. Ed(s): Harmen Lehment, Horst Siebert. Springer, Tiergartenstr 17, Heidelberg, 69121, Germany. Illus., index, adv. Refereed. Circ: 1800. Vol. ends: No. 4. *Indexed:* ABIn, BAS, IBR, IBSS, IBZ, JEL, PAIS, SSCI. *Bk. rev.:* 10-16, 700-2,100 words. *Aud.:* Ac, Sa.

Internationally renowned and affiliated with the esteemed Kiel Institute of World Economics, *Review of World Economics* focuses on the empirical. Topics include "trade and trade policies, international factor movements and international business, international finance, currency systems and exchange rates, monetary and fiscal policies in open economies, economic development, technological change and growth." Well-known scholars contribute. Each issue has six or seven articles, shorter papers, comments, reports, book reviews, and announcements of new books. This scholarly journal is an excellent choice for international economists and graduate students.

1946. Scandinavian Journal of Economics. Former titles (until 1976): *Swedish Journal of Economics;* (until 1965): *Ekonomisk Tidskrift.* [ISSN: 0347-0520] 1899. q. GBP 233 print & online eds. Ed(s): Espen R Moen, Jonas Agell. Blackwell Publishing Ltd., 9600 Garsington Rd, Oxford, OX4 2ZG, United Kingdom; customerservices@ blackwellpublishing.com; http://www.blackwellpublishing.com. Adv. Refereed. Circ: 1100. Online: Blackwell Synergy; EBSCO Publishing, EBSCO Host; Gale; IngentaConnect; OCLC Online Computer Library Center, Inc.; OhioLINK; SwetsWise Online Content. Reprint: PSC. *Indexed:* ABIn, AgeL, AmH&L, HistAb, IBSS, JEL, PAIS, RiskAb, SSCI. *Bk. rev.:* Number and length vary. *Aud.:* Ac, Sa.

"One of the oldest and most distinguished economic journals," this publication covers all areas of economics and related fields, and features theory and policy. The authors are international, and a special issue on a current topic is featured every year. Surveys of the work done by Nobel Memorial Prize–winners in economics are a notable feature. Book reviews included. Highly recommended for academic libraries and special libraries.

1947. Scottish Journal of Political Economy. [ISSN: 0036-9292] 1954. 5x/yr. GBP 202 print & online eds. Ed(s): Robert A Hart, Campbell Leith. Blackwell Publishing Ltd., 9600 Garsington Rd, Oxford, OX4 2ZG, United Kingdom; customerservices@blackwellpublishing.com; http://www.blackwellpublishing.com. Illus., index, adv. Sample. Refereed. Circ: 1500. Vol. ends: Nov. Online: Blackwell Synergy; EBSCO Publishing, EBSCO Host; Gale; IngentaConnect; OCLC Online Computer Library Center, Inc.; OhioLINK; SwetsWise Online Content. Reprint: PSC. *Indexed:* ABIn, AmH&L, AmHI, ApEcolAb, BAS, BrHumI, HistAb, IBR, IBSS, IndVet, JEL, PAIS, PSA, RRTA, RiskAb, SSA, SSCI, SociolAb, WAE&RSA. *Bk. rev.:* 6-9, 700-1,000 words. *Aud.:* Ga, Ac, Sa.

Sponsored by the Scottish Economic Society, this is "a generalist journal with an explicitly international reach." The wide scope includes microeconomics, macroeconomics, labor, monetary, industrial, and international trade and finance. Contributions are worldwide. Typically, each issue has four to eight articles, followed occasionally by review articles and/or book reviews. There is also a special conference issue each year. An excellent journal, recommended for professional and academic economists and for large academic economics programs.

1948. Socio-Economic Planning Sciences. [ISSN: 0038-0121] 1967. 4x/yr. EUR 799. Ed(s): Barnett R Parker. Pergamon, The Boulevard, Langford Ln, East Park, Kidlington, OX5 1GB, United Kingdom. Illus., index, adv. Refereed. Circ: 1700. Microform: MIM; PQC. Online: EBSCO Publishing, EBSCO Host; Gale; IngentaConnect; OhioLINK; ScienceDirect; SwetsWise Online Content. *Indexed:* ABCPolSci, AgeL, CABA, CJA, EAA, ExcerpMed, FPA, ForAb, IBSS, IPSA, MCR, PAIS, PSA, RRTA, RiskAb, S&F, SSA, SSCI, SUSA, SociolAb, WAE&RSA. *Bk. rev.:* Number and length vary. *Aud.:* Ac.

Published as a journal for the Society for the Advancement of Socio-Economics, this aims to be a new platform where an interdisciplinary dialogue between sociology, economics, political science, and moral philosophy is very engaging and enriching. Articles "explore how the economy is or should be governed by social relations, institutional rules, political decisions, and cultural value, and how the economy in turn affects the society of which it is part." One example of these phenomena is breaking up old institutional forms and giving rise to new ones. Recommended for academic audiences.

1949. Southern Economic Journal. [ISSN: 0038-4038] 1933. q. Non-members, USD 130. Ed(s): Laura Razzolini. Southern Economic Association, c/o Laura Razzolini, Virginia Commonwealth University, School of Business, Richmond, VA 23284; lrazzoloni@vcu.edu. Illus., index, adv. Sample. Refereed. Circ: 4000 Paid. Vol. ends: Apr. Microform: MIM; PQC. Online: EBSCO Publishing, EBSCO Host; Florida Center for Library Automation; Gale; JSTOR (Web-based Journal Archive); Northern Light Technology, Inc.; OCLC Online Computer Library Center, Inc.; ProQuest K-12 Learning Solutions; ProQuest LLC (Ann Arbor); H.W. Wilson. Reprint: PSC. *Indexed:* ABIn, ABS&EES, AgeL, AmH&L, ArtHuCI, BPI, CJA, HistAb, IBSS, JEL, PAIS, RRTA, SSCI, SUSA, WAE&RSA. *Bk. rev.:* 24-26, 750-2,250 words. *Aud.:* Ac, Sa.

Published by the Southern Economic Association, College of Business Administration, Oklahoma State University–Stillwater, this solid journal typically includes 11–13 authoritative articles in both theoretical and applied economics. Each issue still includes numerous book reviews and syposium papers. Highly recommended for academic collections and professional and academic economists.

1950. Student Economic Review. 1987. irreg. University of Dublin, Regents House, Trinity College, House 6, Trinity College, Dublin, 2, Ireland; http://econserv2.bess.tcd.ie/SER/. *Aud.:* Ac.

An annual online, this unique journal is edited and run by third-year students from the Department of Economics, Trinity College, Dublin, and written by juniors and seniors. Due to its nature, full-text articles are on a wide range of economic topics from the Irish economy to neuroeconomics. Essays are usually chosen by professors from class assignments, but there is some independent research as well. Worthy new features this year are a debate between Oxford and Yale and a guest speaker from the Bank of England. Coverage is from 1994. URL: www.tcd.ie/Economics/SER.

1951. Studies in Nonlinear Dynamics and Econometrics (Online Edition). Formerly (until 1996): *Studies in Nonlinear Dynamics and Econometrics (Print).* [ISSN: 1558-3708] 1996. q. USD 280 (Individuals, USD 35). Ed(s): Bruce Mizrach. Berkeley Electronic Press, 2809 Telegraph Ave, Ste 202, Berkeley, CA 94705; info@bepress.com; http://www.bepress.com. Refereed. *Indexed:* ABIn, IBSS, JEL, SSCI. *Aud.:* Ac, Sa.

It's hard to believe that this e-journal, published by the Berkeley Electronic Press, has been in *MFL* for ten years now since its inception! The scope covers theoretical and applied papers in the fields of "statistics and dynamical systems theory that may increase our understanding of economic and financial markets." "Algorithms and rapid communications are also published." The entire back set of issues is available. Professional economists and researchers will appreciate this technical journal. URL: www.bepress.com/snde.

Theory and Decision. See Philosophy section.

Transitions Online. See Slavic Studies section.

1952. *The World Bank Economic Review.* [ISSN: 0258-6770] 1986. 3x/yr. USD 173 (academic) print or online ed. Corporations, USD 259 print & online eds.). Ed(s): Jaime de Melo. Oxford University Press, 2001 Evans Rd, Cary, NC 27513; http://www.us.oup.com. Illus. Refereed. Circ: 11000. Microform: PQC. Online: EBSCO Publishing, EBSCO Host; Gale; HighWire Press; IngentaConnect; Northern Light Technology, Inc.; OCLC Online Computer Library Center, Inc.; OhioLINK; Oxford Journals; ProQuest LLC (Ann Arbor); SwetsWise Online Content. Reprint: PSC. *Indexed:* ABIn, AbAn, BAS, CABA, FPA, ForAb, HortAb, IBR, IBSS, IBZ, JEL, PAIS, PRA, PSA, S&F, SSCI, WAE&RSA. *Aud.:* Ac, Sa.

A very widely read scholarly publication, *World Bank Economic Review* is a professional journal for the dispersion of World Bank–sponsored research on policy analysis and choice. The international readers are "economists and social scientists in government, business, international universities, and development research institutions." Policy is emphasized over theoretical or methodological issues. Readers need to be familiar with economic theory and analysis but not necessarily proficient in mathematics. Six to nine articles are written by World Bank staff and economists. There are occasionally special issues by non-Bank specialists. Highly recommended for academic libraries and larger public libraries.

1953. *World Bank Research Observer.* [ISSN: 0257-3032] 1986. s-a. EUR 133 (academic) print or online ed. Corporations, EUR 198 print or online ed.). Ed(s): Shantayanan Devarajan. Oxford University Press, Great Clarendon St, Oxford, OX2 6DP, United Kingdom; jnl.orders@oup.co.uk; http://www.oxfordjournals.org. Illus., adv. Refereed. Circ: 10600. Microform: CIS; PQC. Online: The Dialog Corporation; EBSCO Publishing, EBSCO Host; Gale; HighWire Press; IngentaConnect; Northern Light Technology, Inc.; OCLC Online Computer Library Center, Inc.; OhioLINK; Oxford Journals; ProQuest LLC (Ann Arbor); SwetsWise Online Content; H.W. Wilson. Reprint: PSC. *Indexed:* ABIn, ABS&EES, AbAn, BPI, CABA, ForAb, IBSS, IndIslam, JEL, PAIS, S&F, SSCI, WAE&RSA. *Aud.:* Ga, Ac, Sa.

Written for the nonspecialist and published by the World Bank, this journal is intended for anyone who has an interest in development issues. Articles are written by well-established economists, and key issues in development economics research and policy are examined. Surveys of the latest literature and World Bank research are included. The editorial board is drawn from the international community of economists. Each issue has six to eight articles. Highly recommended for public and academic libraries.

1954. *World Development.* Incorporates: *New Commonwealth.* [ISSN: 0305-750X] 1973. 12x/yr. EUR 2100. Ed(s): Oliver T. Coomes. Pergamon, The Boulevard, Langford Ln, East Park, Kidlington, OX5 1GB, United Kingdom; nlinfo-f@elsevier.nl; http://www.elsevier.nl. Illus., adv. Refereed. Circ: 1600. Vol. ends: No. 29. Microform: PQC. Online: EBSCO Publishing, EBSCO Host; Gale; IngentaConnect; OhioLINK; ScienceDirect; SwetsWise Online Content. *Indexed:* ABCPolSci, ABIn, ABS&EES, Agr, AmHI, BAS, BrHumI, CABA, CJA, DSA, EI, EnvAb, FPA, FS&TA, ForAb, FutSurv, HortAb, IBR, IBSS, IBZ, IPSA, JEL, PAIS, PRA, PSA, PollutAb, RRTA, RiskAb, S&F, SSA, SSCI, SWA, SociolAb, WAE&RSA. *Aud.:* Ac.

Widely respected, this multidisciplinary journal covers ways to improve the human condition; so its topics are wide-ranging and include poverty, unemployment, malnutrition, disease, lack of shelter, environmental problems, and conflicts at all levels. Development processes occur in different ways and at all levels: inside the family, the firm, and the farm; and locally, provincially, nationally, and globally. A solid recommendation for planners, social scientists, and academic and special libraries—but review due to price.

1955. *Yale Economic Review.* [ISSN: 1932-037X] 2005. q. USD 39.99 domestic; USD 60 foreign. Ed(s): Jon Rhinesmith. Yale Economic Review, PO Box 206533, New Haven, CT 06520; info@yaleeconomicreview.com. Adv. *Aud.:* Ac.

Started in 2005, this student-run journal, a nonprofit organization, now accepts submissions from academic economists and researchers from around the world. It has a wide scope and is meant for a broad audience. In the sample Fall 2006 issue, one can read an interview with Robert Schiller, author of *Irrational*

Exuberance. Other exciting writers and interviews include Nobel Laureate Paul Samuelson; John Thain, CEO of the New York Stock Exchange; and Pulitzer Prize–winning author Daniel Yergin. Includes abstracts for recent economic research at Yale. Free to Yale students. I have worked with these dedicated students and ask you to take a look!

■ EDUCATION

General, K-12/Comparative Education and International/Educational Psychology and Measurement, Special Education, Counseling/Higher Education/Homeschooling/Specific Subjects and Teaching Methods

See also Classroom Magazines; and Parenting sections.

Gladys I. Dratch, Head of Collection Development, Monroe C. Gutman Library, Graduate School of Education, Harvard University, Cambridge, MA 02138.

Deborah S. Garson, Head of Research and Instruction Services, Monroe C. Gutman Library, Graduate School of Education, Harvard University, Cambridge, MA 02138

Introduction

As a field, education is both interdisciplinary and inclusive of teaching and learning for pre-K to older learners. Within the social sciences, education relates particularly to the fields of psychology and sociology, as the selection of titles below indicates. By virtue of the teaching and learning components of education, however, the connections to other fields are evident, and readers may wish to examine subject-specific sections of this publication. As a discipline, the field of education is grounded in the traditional research frameworks of philosophy, theory, and methodology that form the basis for applications in many types of educational settings.

The education journals represent a broad range of publications, from the academic and scholarly to those intended for practical applications in the classroom and other learning environments. Journal contents reflect current educational trends and issues, as well as historical analyses of educational theory and practice. Current topics focus on educational reform, e-learning principles and practices, teacher and student assessment, global trends in education, international education, educational counseling, and educational technology.

Publishers are responding to current journal research needs and authors' publishing opportunities as well as their own for-profit requirements by developing electronic collections comparable to the print versions, with all the technological enhancements available to them. A wide variety of options is available for any user of journal collections, ranging from subscription-based models to freely available titles or collections. With the development of the open-access journals, there have been some innovative publishers' responses as well as institutional responses. These initiatives are reflective of the current movement to provide to a global audience open-access journals in education as well as all disciplines.

Basic Periodicals

Ems (teachers): *The Elementary School Journal, Middle School Journal, The Reading Teacher, School Arts, Teaching Pre K-8*; (teachers): Hs: *American Biology Teacher, American Secondary Education, English Journal, The High School Journal, History Teacher*; Ga: *Change, The Education Digest, The ERIC Review, Phi Delta Kappan*; Ac: *Academe, American Journal of Education, The Chronicle of Higher Education, College English, Harvard Educational Review, Lingua Franca, Teachers College Record.*

Basic Abstracts and Indexes

Current Index to Journals in Education, Education Index, Resources in Education.

General, K-12

1956. *American Educational Research Journal.* [ISSN: 0002-8312] 1964. q. GBP 177. Sage Publications, Inc., 2455 Teller Rd, Thousand Oaks, CA 91320; info@sagepub.com; http://www.sagepub.com. Illus., adv. Refereed. Circ: 19800. Vol. ends: Winter. Microform: PQC. Online: JSTOR (Web-based Journal Archive); OCLC Online Computer Library Center, Inc.; ProQuest K-12 Learning Solutions; ProQuest LLC (Ann Arbor); H.W. Wilson. Reprint: PSC. *Indexed:* ABIn, ArtHuCI, CJA, CommAb, ECER, ERIC, EduInd, FR, HEA, IBR, IBZ, L&LBA, PsycInfo, RILM, SSA, SSCI, SWA. *Aud.:* Ac.

Within each issue, articles are published in two sections under separate editorships and editorial boards: "Social and Institutional Analysis" and "Teaching, Learning, and Human Development." Addressing an audience of researchers, practitioners, and policymakers from many disciplines, the articles are lengthy and substantive, generally 20–30 or more pages long, representing the publication's stated focus on original empirical and theoretical studies and analyses in education. In the first section, the research centers on major political, cultural, social, economic, and organizational issues in education. This section is followed by articles that examine various aspects of teaching, learning, and human development in different types of educational settings. Eight or nine articles per issue provide in-depth research findings and analyses with extensive notes, tables, figures, and references. This is an essential resource for advanced undergraduates, graduate students, and academicians. URL: www.aera.net/publications/?id=315.

1957. *American Educator.* [ISSN: 0148-432X] 1977. q. USD 10. Ed(s): Ruth Wattenberg. American Federation of Teachers, 555 New Jersey Ave, NW, Washington, DC 20001; online@aft.org; http://www.aft.org/. Illus., adv. Circ: 850000. Vol. ends: Fall. *Indexed:* ABS&EES, FLI, MLA-IB. *Bk. rev.:* 1, 2,500 words. *Aud.:* Ga, Ac.

Aimed at an audience of teachers and other school and higher-education professionals, this American Federation of Teachers publication contains a variety of articles on topics for a wide range of reader interests. There are opinion pieces on parenting and on student attitudes; practical and informational articles for applications in school settings; and discussions on the national or international school scene, covering such topics as achievement gap, state standards, and schools with low test scores. Issues often have biographical essays and tributes to important historical figures, educators, and authors that are helpful for professional development and classroom use. Recommended for public, academic, and school libraries. URL: www.aft.org/pubs-reports/american_educator/index.html.

1958. *American Journal of Education.* Formerly (until vol.88, Nov. 1979): *School Review.* [ISSN: 0195-6744] 1893. q. USD 121 domestic; USD 133.26 Canada; USD 127 elsewhere. Ed(s): Marilyn Begley, William Lowe Boyd. University of Chicago Press, Journals Division, PO Box 37005, Chicago, IL 60637; subscriptions@press.uchicago.edu; http://www.journals.uchicago.edu. Illus., index, adv. Sample. Refereed. Circ: 1800 Paid. Vol. ends: Aug. Microform: PMC; PQC. Online: EBSCO Publishing, EBSCO Host; Florida Center for Library Automation; Gale; JSTOR (Web-based Journal Archive); OCLC Online Computer Library Center, Inc.; ProQuest K-12 Learning Solutions; ProQuest LLC (Ann Arbor). Reprint: PSC. *Indexed:* ABIn, AmH&L, ArtHuCI, BRI, CBRI, EAA, ERIC, EduInd, HistAb, IBR, IBZ, IMFL, L&LBA, PhilInd, PsycInfo, SSA, SSCI, SWA, SociolAb. *Bk. rev.:* 3-5, 500 words. *Aud.:* Ga, Ac.

This journal publishes scholarly articles on educational topics meant to encourage discussion and debate among scholars and practitioners. Articles range from the methodological and theoretical to matters of administration and policy in the schools. Historical and current perspectives for all school settings are represented. Particularly emphasized are research reports, theoretical statements, philosophical arguments, critical syntheses, and integration of educational inquiry, policy, and practice. Articles have focused on collective bargaining, teacher evaluation, language skills and standardized tests, and the relationship between high school graduation and the various state policies of assessment and accountability. The book reviews are lengthy, and most issues also have a review essay. This is a basic title for graduate students, faculty, and practitioners. URL: www.journals.uchicago.edu/AJE/home.html.

1959. *American School Board Journal.* [ISSN: 0003-0953] 1891. m. USD 57. Ed(s): Sally Zakariya, Glenn Cook. National School Boards Association, 1680 Duke St, Alexandria, VA 22314-3493; info@nsba.org; http://www.nsba.org. Illus., index, adv. Sample. Circ: 40000 Paid. Vol. ends: Dec. Microform: PQC. Online: EBSCO Publishing, EBSCO Host. *Indexed:* ABIn, EAA, EduInd, PAIS, RILM. *Bk. rev.:* 1, 300-1,200 words. *Aud.:* Ga, Sa.

This journal of the American School Boards Association publishes articles on current issues in the field and topics in the news. Authored by faculty and practitioners, articles are directed at an audience of school board members and school administrators. Some topics have been NAEP test scores, the rising number of youth suicides, children at risk, and issues of homework. Regular departments include letters from readers, research findings on particular topics, school law rulings on specific cases, a new section of education news and trends, and book reviews. Special supplements for subscribers of *ASBJ* are the Magna Awards, a yearly recognition of programs for major school district initiatives nationwide, and the annual supplement, *Education Vital Signs*, which focuses on school data. Recommended for school, public, and academic libraries with an education program. URL: www.asbj.com.

1960. *American Secondary Education.* [ISSN: 0003-1003] 1970. 3x/yr. USD 30 domestic; USD 40 foreign; USD 10 newsstand/cover per issue. American Secondary Education, Ashland University, Dwight Schar College of Education Rm 231, Ashland, OH 44805-3702; gvanderz@ashland.edu; http://www3.ashland.edu. Adv. Sample. Refereed. Circ: 400 Paid. Microform: PQC. Online: EBSCO Publishing, EBSCO Host; OCLC Online Computer Library Center, Inc.; ProQuest LLC (Ann Arbor); H.W. Wilson. *Indexed:* ABIn, ERIC, EduInd, SWA. *Bk. rev.:* Number and length vary. *Aud.:* Ac.

This journal examines current secondary school issues for teachers, administrators, and all those involved in public and private secondary education. Written by practitioners and researchers in the field, articles focus on theories, research, and practice, with discussions on such topics as in-school suspension, school bullying, middle school models, promoting young adult literature, implementing critical-thinking instruction, a qualitative study of magnet schools, and teaching through assessment and feedback. Most issues have a column for an opinion or commentary, and suggestions on techniques for handling student harassment in a high school setting. Book reviews are included. Recommended for school and academic libraries with an education program. URL: www3.ashland.edu/academics/education/ase/index.html.

1961. *Childhood Education.* Incorporates (1981-1991): *A C E I Exchange.* [ISSN: 0009-4056] 1924. bi-m. USD 65 non-members. Ed(s): Robert Burke, Anne Watson Bauer. Association for Childhood Education International, 17904 Georgia Ave, Ste 215, Olney, MD 20832-2277; headquarters@acei.org; http://www.acei.org. Illus., adv. Circ: 11500 Paid. Microform: PMC; PQC. Online: Florida Center for Library Automation; Gale; OCLC Online Computer Library Center, Inc.; ProQuest K-12 Learning Solutions; ProQuest LLC (Ann Arbor); H.W. Wilson. *Indexed:* ABIn, BRI, CBRI, ECER, ERIC, EduInd, IMFL. *Bk. rev.:* 40-50, 75-400 words, signed. *Aud.:* Ga, Ac, Sa.

The Association for Childhood Education International's refereed journal is focused on the development and education of children from infancy through early adolescence. It is geared toward an audience of teachers, teacher educators, parents, child care workers, administrators, librarians, and others with an interest in the field. The editors encourage articles on practices in the classroom and in other settings, international programs and practices, and reviews of research. Articles have covered a wide range of useful topics, including biracial children's development of identity; phonemic awareness; child sexual abuse; conflict resolution in a Head Start classroom; child care and education in Ghana; teaching early childhood education online; and interactive toys and children's development. Columns address issues in education, the needs of parents, and teaching strategies. Includes reviews of books for children, reviews and lists of professional books, special publications and reports, and discussions on technology in the classroom. Offers two annual theme issues, such as an international issue on schooling in countries throughout the world. Highly recommended for school, public, and academic libraries. URL: www.acei.org/cehp.htm.

1962. *The Clearing House: a journal of educational strategies, issues, and ideas.* [ISSN: 0009-8655] 1925. bi-m. USD 120 (Individuals, USD 54 print & online eds.; USD 19 newsstand/cover). Ed(s): Sarah Erdreich. Heldref Publications, 1319 18th St, NW, Washington, DC 20036-1802; subscribe@heldref.org; http://www.heldref.org. Illus., index, adv. Sample. Refereed. Circ: 1112 Paid. CD-ROM: ProQuest LLC (Ann Arbor). Online: EBSCO Publishing, EBSCO Host; Florida Center for Library Automation; Gale; Northern Light Technology, Inc.; OCLC Online Computer Library Center, Inc.; ProQuest K-12 Learning Solutions; ProQuest LLC (Ann Arbor); H.W. Wilson. Reprint: PSC. *Indexed:* ABIn, ASIP, EAA, ENW, ERIC, EduInd, FLI, LRI, V&AA. *Aud.:* Ac.

This peer-reviewed and well-indexed journal is geared to the interests of middle-level and high school teachers and administrators. The articles are based on research and school practices with a wide range of educational trends and issues, including school effectiveness, learning styles, curriculum, guidance and counseling, special education, instructional leadership, testing and measurement, and international education. Some issues have a special section with articles focusing on a special theme, such as school choice. Occasionally there are articles that present opinions on current issues of concern and debate. Articles are authored by academicians, administrators, and consultants in the field. Recommended for school libraries and academic libraries with education programs. URL: www.heldref.org/tch.php.

1963. *Curriculum Review.* Former titles (until Dec. 1975): *C A S Review; C S Review.* [ISSN: 0147-2453] 1960. m. USD 169. Ed(s): Frank Sennett. PaperClip Communications, 125 Paterson Ave, Little Falls, NJ 07424; info@paper-clip.com; http://www.paper-clip.com. Illus., adv. Circ: 4800. Vol. ends: Sep/May. Microform: PQC. Online: EBSCO Publishing, EBSCO Host; Florida Center for Library Automation; Gale; OCLC Online Computer Library Center, Inc.; ProQuest LLC (Ann Arbor); H.W. Wilson. *Indexed:* ABIn, BRI, CBRI, ERIC, EduInd, MRD. *Bk. rev.:* 15-25, 150-500 words. *Aud.:* Ga, Ac.

This is a practical report issued monthly during the school year. It aims to assist K–12 teachers and administrators with ideas for the classroom, tips on resources, information about successful schools and projects, and news in the area of Federal Education Budget information. There are columns that present readers' ideas and experiences, technology updates, useful techniques that point out what's working in schools and classrooms, some highlights of education news, interviews with educators, and reviews of school web sites. A section on resources for the classroom provides an abstract of useful books for students and a CD-ROM review. This is a useful publication for school libraries and libraries that serve programs in undergraduate or graduate education. URL: www.paper-clip.com/curriculumreview/default.asp.

1964. *Early Childhood Education Journal.* Formerly (until 1995): *Day Care and Early Education.* [ISSN: 1082-3301] 1973. 6x/yr. EUR 623 print & online eds. Springer New York LLC, 233 Spring St, New York, NY 10013-1578; journals@springer-ny.com; http://www.springer.com. Illus., adv. Sample. Refereed. Circ: 10000 Paid. Vol. ends: Summer. Microform: PQC. Online: EBSCO Publishing, EBSCO Host; Gale; IngentaConnect; OCLC Online Computer Library Center, Inc.; OhioLINK; Ovid Technologies, Inc.; Springer LINK; SwetsWise Online Content. Reprint: PSC. *Indexed:* ABIn, BRI, CBRI, EAA, ECER, ERIC, EduInd, ExcerpMed, L&LBA, MRD, PEI, PsycInfo, SWR&A. *Bk. rev.:* 1-5, 50-500 words, signed. *Aud.:* Ac, Sa.

Intended for early childhood practitioners such as classroom teachers and child care providers, this peer-reviewed publication focuses on the education and care of young children from birth through age eight. The journal publishes articles that address the issues, trends, policies, and practices of the field. Contributors have covered topics of curriculum; child care programs; administration; staff development; equity issues; health and nutrition; facilities; and child development. Recent issues consider literacy development; family child care in the United States; social skills; and writing skills in young children. Highly recommended for academic libraries that serve education programs and for libraries that serve early childhood professional institutions or organizations. URL: http://springerlink.metapress.com.

1965. *Education.* [ISSN: 0013-1172] 1880. q. USD 80 (Individuals, USD 70). Ed(s): George Uhlig. Project Innovation, Inc., PO Box 8508, Mobile, AL 36689-0508; guhlig007@yahoo.com; http://www.projectinnovation.biz. Index, adv. Circ: 3500 Paid. Microform: PMC; PQC. Online: EBSCO Publishing, EBSCO Host; Florida Center for Library Automation; Gale; Northern Light Technology, Inc.; OCLC Online Computer Library Center, Inc.; ProQuest LLC (Ann Arbor); H.W. Wilson. *Indexed:* ABIn, EAA, ERIC, EduInd, L&LBA, SSA, SociolAb. *Aud.:* Ac.

This journal presents a wide range of studies and theoretical papers on all areas of teaching and learning in school and university settings. Brief and lengthy articles cover such topics as math anxiety; diversity in teacher education programs; school district policy on child maltreatment; alternative teacher certification programs; higher education leadership; effective teaching; Hispanic Americans in higher education; professional development schools; and e-portfolios for student learning. Issues have focused on school psychology; the prevention of delinquency through high school programs; and historically black colleges and universities. Recommended for school and academic libraries. URL: http://journals825.home.mindspring.com/education.html.

1966. *Education and Urban Society: an independent quarterly journal of social research.* [ISSN: 0013-1245] 1968. bi-m. GBP 446. Corwin Press, Inc., 2455 Teller Rd, Thousand Oaks, CA 91320-2218; info@sagepub.com; http://www.sagepub.com/. Illus., index, adv. Refereed. Circ: 600 Paid. Vol. ends: Aug. Microform: PQC. Online: CSA; EBSCO Publishing, EBSCO Host; Gale; HighWire Press; OCLC Online Computer Library Center, Inc.; OhioLINK; SAGE Publications, Inc.; SAGE Journals Online; SwetsWise Online Content. Reprint: PSC. *Indexed:* ABCPolSci, ABIn, ASSIA, AmH&L, CJA, EAA, ERIC, EduInd, FR, HRA, HistAb, IBR, IBSS, IBZ, IMFL, L&LBA, PAIS, SFSA, SSA, SSCI, SUSA, SWA, SWR&A, SociolAb. *Aud.:* Ac, Sa.

This peer-reviewed journal provides a multidisciplinary forum for research articles focused on the role of education in society. The intended audience includes school board members, sociologists, educational administrators, urban anthropologists, political scientists, and other professionals in fields aligned with education. The emphasis is on current issues in the field and new ideas regarding educational practices. Topics have included such subjects as religion and education; changing demographics and policy implications; school choice; and school emergency preparedness. This is an important resource for academic libraries. URL: http://eus.sagepub.com.

1967. *The Education Digest: essential readings condensed for quick review.* [ISSN: 0013-127X] 1934. 9x/yr. USD 48 domestic; USD 58 foreign. Ed(s): Kenneth Schroeder, Kenneth Schroeder. Prakken Publications, Inc., 832 Phoenix Dr, Ann Arbor, MI 48108-2221. Illus., index, adv. Sample. Circ: 9500 Paid and free. CD-ROM: ProQuest LLC (Ann Arbor). Microform: PQC. Online: EBSCO Publishing, EBSCO Host; Northern Light Technology, Inc.; OCLC Online Computer Library Center, Inc.; ProQuest K-12 Learning Solutions; ProQuest LLC (Ann Arbor); H.W. Wilson. *Indexed:* ABIn, ECER, ERIC, EduInd, IBR, IBZ, LRI, RGPR, RILM. *Bk. rev.:* 4, 100 words. *Aud.:* Ga, Ac.

This publication provides a condensation of current articles on the themes chosen for the individual-issue *ED* issues. It thus allows educators, students, and other interested readers an opportunity to quickly update their knowledge of particular education topics such as Tech-Ed and the No Child Left Behind Act. In addition, there are regular columns such as the free-ranging discussions in "The Teachers' Lounge," capsules of education news in Washington and elsewhere, book reviews, a calender of events, and web resources. This is a handy, pocket-sized resource that is useful for school and public libraries. URL: www.eddigest.com.

1968. *Education Finance and Policy.* [ISSN: 1557-3060] 2006. q. USD 295 print & online eds. (Individuals, USD 123 print & online eds.). Ed(s): David H. Monk, David N. Figlio. M I T Press, 238 Main St., Ste. 500, Cambridge, MA 02142; journals-info@mit.edu; http://mitpress.mit.edu. *Aud.:* Ac.

This publication is the official journal of the American Education Finance Association. It includes scholarly articles that will inform and impact research and policy in the area of education finance. Articles present theoretical, statistical, and qualitative research from many different viewpoints. Authors have addressed the salaries of public school teachers; the field of school finance; inflation's effect on wages and school finance equity; and teacher retirement decisions and pension incentives. Policy briefs have focused on current education issues such as charter schools; national board teachers; education adequacy cost studies; and modifying the No Child Left Behind Act. Recommended for academic and research institutions.

1969. *Education Policy Analysis Archives.* [ISSN: 1068-2341] 1993. irreg. Free. Ed(s): Sherman Dorn, Gene V Glass. Arizona State University, College of Education, Education Policy Studies Laboratory, PO Box 872411, Tempe, AZ 85287-2411; glass@asu.edu. Refereed. *Indexed:* EduInd, HEA. *Aud.:* Ac.

A peer-reviewed journal that publishes articles on educational policy at all educational levels worldwide. Articles are in Spanish, Portuguese, or English. Article abstracts appear at the beginning of each article. The site has a search utility to aid in finding articles of interest. Issues cover topics of educational policy such as policy, practice, and national board certification; policymakers' online use of academic research; high-stakes testing and the history of graduation; emerging ethnocentric charter schools in Hawaii; an analysis of education policy in Portugal; financing of higher education in the Czech Republic; and teacher community in charter public and traditional public schools. Highly recommended for academic libraries. URL: http://epaa.asu.edu/epaa.

1970. *Education Week: American education's newspaper of record.* [ISSN: 0277-4232] 1981. 44x/yr. Individuals, USD 79.94. Ed(s): Gregory Chronister, Ms. Virginia B Edwards. Editorial Projects in Education Inc., 6935 Arlington Rd, Ste 100, Bethesda, MD 20814-5233; http://www.edweek.org. Illus., index, adv. Sample. Circ: 54000. Vol. ends: Aug. Online: EBSCO Publishing, EBSCO Host; Factiva, Inc.; OCLC Online Computer Library Center, Inc.; ProQuest K-12 Learning Solutions; ProQuest LLC (Ann Arbor). *Indexed:* ABIn, ERIC, EduInd. *Aud.:* Ga, Ac.

This weekly provides full coverage of state and national education news in a newspaper format. There are articles on current topics and issues in the field, information about recent education reports, profiles and interviews, and weekly commentaries. It contains letters to the editor; events listings; advertisements, including books and curriculum products and services; and job postings. From time to time, there is an in-depth report that appears as a series. *EW* also provides several special issues, such as the yearly review of education in the 50 states, *Quality Counts.* This is essential weekly reading for graduate education students, educators, and administrators in the field. Highly recommended for school, public, and academic libraries. URL: www.edweek.org.

1971. *Educational Administration Quarterly.* [ISSN: 0013-161X] 1964. 5x/yr. GBP 392. Ed(s): Diana G Pounder. Corwin Press, Inc., 2455 Teller Rd, Thousand Oaks, CA 91320-2218; info@sagepub.com; http://www.sagepub.com/. Illus., index, adv. Refereed. Circ: 1200 Paid. Vol. ends: Nov. Microform: PQC. Online: CSA; EBSCO Publishing, EBSCO Host; HighWire Press; OCLC Online Computer Library Center, Inc.; OhioLINK; SAGE Publications, Inc., SAGE Journals Online; SwetsWise Online Content. Reprint: PSC. *Indexed:* ABIn, EAA, ERIC, EduInd, FR, IBR, IBZ, SSCI, SWA. *Bk. rev.:* 0-3, essay length. *Aud.:* Ac, Sa.

The *EAQ* seeks scholarly articles that include empirical investigations, conceptual and theoretical perspectives, policy and legal analyses, reviews of research and practice, and analyses of methodology related to broad concepts of administration in education. The editors are especially interested in papers on educational leadership; governance and reform in colleges of education; teaching of educational administration; and the professional preparation of educational administrators. Faculty, principals, and teachers, national and international, have contributed research articles on topics such as: accountability under systemic reform; teacher teams and distributed leadership; implementation of innovative programs in schools; and school accountability. The articles are lengthy, generally 20–30 pages, with extensive references, and with tables and figures. Some issues have a book review or review essay. There are special issues that focus on a topic, such as one devoted to social justice and another on

non-traditional research methods. This journal is published in cooperation with the University Council for Educational Administration and the University of Kentucky. Highly recommended for academic and school libraries. URL: http://eaq.sagepub.com.

1972. *Educational Assessment, Evaluation and Accountability (Print Edition).* Formerly (until 2008): *Journal of Personnel Evaluation in Education.* [ISSN: 1874-8597] 1987. q. EUR 425 print & online eds. Ed(s): Douglas Davis. Springer Netherlands, Van Godewijckstraat 30, Dordrecht, 3311 GX, Netherlands; http://www.springeronline.com. Illus., index, adv. Sample. Refereed. Vol. ends: Dec. Microform: PQC. Online: EBSCO Publishing, EBSCO Host; Gale; IngentaConnect; OCLC Online Computer Library Center, Inc.; OhioLINK; ProQuest LLC (Ann Arbor); Springer LINK; SwetsWise Online Content. Reprint: PSC. *Indexed:* ABIn, AgeL, EAA, ERIC, HEA, PsycInfo. *Bk. rev.:* Various number and length. *Aud.:* Ac, Sa.

Offers discussion and analyses of current issues, programs, and research on personnel evaluation in education settings, both national and international. This journal encourages studies that focus on the theory, research, and practice of personnel evaluation pertaining to K–12 teachers, administrators, support personnel, and faculty in colleges and universities. Articles have featured the findings of a qualitative field study of a teacher assessment system in an urban school district; a discussion of teacher evaluation and merit pay; a student survey of K–12 teachers; ethical considerations in evaluating teachers; and an assessment and evaluation of university faculty. Recent special issues have focused on international comparisons pertaining to educational effectiveness, evaluation and improvement variables, and student evaluation of higher education faculty. Includes notes and reports on the annual conference of the Consortium for Research on Educational Accountability and Teacher Evaluation (CREATE). Occasional book reviews. Recommended for academic libraries. URL: www.springeronline.com.

1973. *Educational Evaluation & Policy Analysis: a quarterly publication of the American Educational Research Association.* [ISSN: 0162-3737] 1979. q. GBP 177. Ed(s): Jane Hannaway. Sage Publications, Inc., 2455 Teller Rd, Thousand Oaks, CA 91320; info@sagepub.com; http://www.sagepub.com. Illus., adv. Refereed. Circ: 6000. Vol. ends: Winter. Microform: PQC. Online: JSTOR (Web-based Journal Archive); OCLC Online Computer Library Center, Inc.; ProQuest LLC (Ann Arbor); H.W. Wilson. Reprint: PSC. *Indexed:* ABIn, CJA, ERIC, EduInd, PsycInfo, SSCI. *Bk. rev.:* 1-2, 500-1,200 words. *Aud.:* Ac.

This journal of the American Educational Research Association publishes theoretical and practical articles for the interest and benefit of researchers involved in educational evaluation or policy analysis. In brief, the editorial instructions for submission indicate that contributions should include economic, demographic, financial, and political analyses of education policies; syntheses of policy studies, evaluation theories, and methodologies; results of important evaluation efforts; and overviews of evaluation studies. Authored by faculty, graduate students, and professionals in the field, well-referenced articles have covered such topics as the impact of foreign-born students; instructional practices in mathematics; report on reading reform model; Success for All; politics in the adoption of school reform models; allocation of school district resources; and enrollment practices in charter schools. An important resource for academic libraries. URL: www.aera.net/publications/?id=316.

1974. *The Educational Forum.* [ISSN: 0013-1725] 1936. q. GBP 76 print & online eds. Ed(s): Jan Robertson. Routledge, 4 Park Sq, Milton Park, Abingdon, OX14 4RN, United Kingdom; info@routledge.co.uk; http://www.routledge.co.uk. Illus., index, adv. Refereed. Circ: 7000. Vol. ends: Summer. Microform: MIM; PQC. Online: OCLC Online Computer Library Center, Inc.; ProQuest LLC (Ann Arbor); H.W. Wilson. *Indexed:* ABIn, BRI, CBRI, EAA, ERIC, EduInd, PhilInd. *Bk. rev.:* 1-3, 700-1,600 words. *Aud.:* Ga, Ac.

This journal of the Kappa Delta Pi, International Honor Society in Education, has as its mission to provide scholarly inquiries on issues of importance for educational improvement. It serves as a forum for discussion by providing differing viewpoints. The audience is university faculty and graduate students in education, educational leaders, K–12 practitioners, and the general educational community. There are themed issues, such as "Sustainable Educational

Leadership," with an introductory overview of the theme. Issues are generally organized into sections: a discussion forum, critical perspectives, and research in practice, with an average eight articles per issue. Includes an open forum, featuring an opinion letter to the editor, and book reviews. This is a valuable resource for undergraduate and graduate education libraries and K–12 schools. URL: www.kdp.org/publications/educational.php.

1975. Educational Foundations. [ISSN: 1047-8248] 1986. 4x/yr. USD 80 (Individuals, USD 50). Ed(s): William T Pink. Caddo Gap Press, 3145 Geary Blvd, PMB 275, San Francisco, CA 94118; info@caddogap.com; http://www.caddogap.com. Illus., adv. Sample. Refereed. Circ: 400 Paid. Vol. ends: Fall. *Indexed:* ABIn, ERIC, EduInd, IBR, IBZ, SSA. *Bk. rev.:* Number and length vary. *Aud.:* Ac.

This journal serves as a forum for members of the American Educational Studies Association, which is composed mainly of college and university professors whose research and teaching in education is closely connected to such liberal arts disciplines as philosophy, history, politics, sociology, anthropology, economics, and comparative and international studies. The publication seeks articles and essays exploring the foundation disciplines and various aspects of the combined fields; a focus on particular topics of significance as they apply to the disciplines; methodological issues; and new research in these fields, with particular reference to the interdisciplinary aspects. Articles have discussed the school reform movement; historically black colleges and universities; charter schools; women educators in the nineteenth and early twentieth centuries; foundations courses for teachers; multicultural education; and educational research in the arts. Books reviews are written by scholars and graduate students. Recommended for academic libraries. URL: www.njcu.edu/edfoundations.

1976. Educational Horizons. [ISSN: 0013-175X] 1921. q. USD 18 domestic; USD 25 foreign; USD 5 per issue. Ed(s): Juli Knutson. Pi Lambda Theta, Inc., 4101 E Third St, PO Box 6626, Bloomington, IN 47407-6626; publications@pilambda.org; http://www.pilambda.org/. Illus., index, adv. Sample. Refereed. Circ: 13000. Vol. ends: Summer. Microform: PQC. Online: OCLC Online Computer Library Center, Inc.; H.W. Wilson. *Indexed:* ABIn, ECER, ERIC, EduInd. *Bk. rev.:* 4-7, 300-500 words. *Aud.:* Ga, Ac.

This journal aims to serve as a forum for educational, social, and cultural issues that offer educators new perspectives, research findings, and scholarly essays. It is broadly directed at K–12 teachers/administrators and practitioners, as well as faculty and staff of higher education institutions. Issues generally have themes that unify the articles, such as testing concerns, safety in the schools, parental choice, and educating at-risk students. Book reviews appear in every issue along with several regular columns that present commentaries on topics of current interest. This is a good mix of readable articles and columns for academic, public, and school libraries. URL: www.pilambda.org/horizons/publications%20index.htm.

1977. Educational Leadership. [ISSN: 0013-1784] 1943. 8x/yr. USD 36. Ed(s): Margaret M Scherer. Association for Supervision and Curriculum Development, 1703 N Beauregard St, Alexandria, VA 22311; update@ascd.org; http://www.ascd.org. Illus., adv. Circ: 175000 Paid. Vol. ends: May. Microform: PQC. Online: EBSCO Publishing, EBSCO Host; Florida Center for Library Automation; Gale; OCLC Online Computer Library Center, Inc.; ProQuest LLC (Ann Arbor); H.W. Wilson. *Indexed:* ABIn, AgeL, BRI, CBRI, EAA, ECER, ERIC, EduInd, IBR, IBZ, L&LBA, MASUSE, RILM, SSCI. *Bk. rev.:* 5, 300 words. *Aud.:* Ga, Ac, Sa.

EL's focus is on educators with leadership roles in elementary, middle, and secondary education and all those with an interest in curriculum, instruction, supervision, and leadership in the schools. Authored by teachers, administrators, higher education faculty, and other professionals in the field, articles and essays (generally three to six pages) are organized under such themes as the prepared graduate; teaching to student strengths; improving professional practice; assessment to promote learning; and changing demographics. Departments include a section on perspectives written by the editor, a research feature that provides an article/commentary, book reviews, letters to the editor, and descriptions of useful web sites. Each issue contains a wide selection of illustrated and referenced articles, and advertisements of interest to teachers and administrators. This is an important resource for academic, public, and school libraries. URL: www.ascd.org/portal/site/ascd.

1978. Educational Researcher. [ISSN: 0013-189X] 1972. 9x/yr. GBP 190. Ed(s): Stafford Hood, Michele L Foster. Sage Publications, Inc., 2455 Teller Rd, Thousand Oaks, CA 91320; info@sagepub.com; http://www.sagepub.com. Illus., index, adv. Refereed. Circ: 22500 Controlled. Vol. ends: Dec. Microform: PQC. Online: JSTOR (Web-based Journal Archive); OCLC Online Computer Library Center, Inc.; ProQuest LLC (Ann Arbor); H.W. Wilson. Reprint: PSC. *Indexed:* ABIn, EAA, ECER, ERIC, EduInd, HEA, IBR, IBZ. *Bk. rev.:* 1-3, 1,200-2,000 words. *Aud.:* Ac.

This American Educational Research Association (AERA) journal publishes scholarly articles of significance to educational researchers from many disciplines. The features section contains articles that may report, analyze, or synthesize research inquiries or explore developments of importance to the field of research in education. The section titled "Research News and Comment" is under separate editorship and seeks articles that analyze trends, policies, and controversies regarding educational research. Responses to articles within an issue may appear, offering a dialogue highlighting divergent approaches and interpretations. Book reviews are included in every issue. Provides AERA news, with annual meeting highlights, council minutes, and meeting events. Contains advertisements for job openings. This is an important journal for graduate education students, faculty, and researchers in the field. URL: www.aera.net/publications/?id=317.

1979. Educational Studies: a journal of the American Educational Studies Associations. [ISSN: 0013-1946] 1970. bi-m. GBP 258 print & online eds. Ed(s): Rebecca Martusewicz. Lawrence Erlbaum Associates, Inc., 325 Chestnut St, Ste. 800, Philadelphia, PA 19106; journals@erlbaum.com; http://www.leaonline.com. Illus., index, adv. Refereed. Circ: 1300. Microform: PQC. Online: EBSCO Publishing, EBSCO Host; Gale; OCLC Online Computer Library Center, Inc.; OhioLINK; SwetsWise Online Content; H.W. Wilson. Reprint: PSC. *Indexed:* ABIn, ABS&EES, ArtHuCI, BRD, BRI, CBRI, ERIC, EduInd, PhilInd, PsycInfo, SSCI. *Bk. rev.:* 20, essay length. *Aud.:* Ac.

Educational Studies has expanded its traditional book review format to include academic articles that focus on the interdisciplinary field of educational foundations as well as media reviews, essay reviews, and poetry. Articles may focus on teaching within this field, research methodologies, or report on significant findings. Articles have discussed the politics of community participation in a public school; educational biography; integrating computer technology; professional teaching standards; and social foundations of education. Each issue contains lengthy book reviews. This is a valuable journal for undergraduate and graduate education students and faculty. URL: www3.uakron.edu/aesa/publications/edstudies.html.

1980. Educational Theory: a medium of expression. [ISSN: 0013-2004] 1951. q. GBP 120 print & online eds. Ed(s): Nicholas C Burbules. Blackwell Publishing, Inc., Commerce Place, 350 Main St, Malden, MA 02148; customerservices@blackwellpublishing.com; http://www.blackwellpublishing.com. Illus., index, adv. Refereed. Circ: 2200 Paid. Vol. ends: Fall. Microform: PQC. Online: Blackwell Synergy; EBSCO Publishing, EBSCO Host; Gale; IngentaConnect; OCLC Online Computer Library Center, Inc.; ProQuest LLC (Ann Arbor); SwetsWise Online Content. Reprint: PSC. *Indexed:* ABIn, ApEcolAb, BRI, CBRI, ERIC, EduInd, IBR, IBZ, IPB, PhilInd, SSA, SSCI, SWA. *Bk. rev.:* 1-2, essay length. *Aud.:* Ac.

Founded by the John Dewey Society and the Philosophy of Education Society, this journal fosters ongoing development of educational theory and discussion of theoretical problems in the education profession. *ET* seeks scholarly articles and studies on the educational foundations of education and related disciplines that contribute to the advancement of educational theory. Issues may present articles on a single theme, such as "A Half-Century of *Educational Theory*: Perspectives on the Past, Present, and Future" and "A Symposium on Globalization and Education," or a collection of articles on a variety of topics. Topics covered have been the university as a cultural system; developmental liberalism; emotional intelligence; and knowledge in the postmodern university. Recommended for academic libraries. URL: www.blackwellpublishing.com/journal.asp?ref=0013-2004&site=1.

1981. *The Elementary School Journal.* Former titles (until 1914): *Elementary School Teacher;* (until 1902): *Elementary School Teacher and Course of Study;* (until 1901): *Course of Study.* [ISSN: 0013-5984] 1900. 5x/yr. USD 151 domestic; USD 165.06 Canada; USD 158 elsewhere. Ed(s): Gail M Hinkel, Thomas L Good. University of Chicago Press, Journals Division, PO Box 37005, Chicago, IL 60637; subscriptions@press.uchicago.edu; http://www.journals.uchicago.edu. Illus., index, adv. Refereed. Circ: 2200 Paid. Microform: PMC; PQC. Online: EBSCO Publishing, EBSCO Host; Gale; JSTOR (Web-based Journal Archive); ProQuest LLC (Ann Arbor). Reprint: PSC. *Indexed:* ABIn, EAA, ECER, ERIC, EduInd, L&LBA, PsycInfo, SSCI. *Aud.:* Ac.

The *ESJ* seeks original studies that provide data about school and classroom processes in elementary or middle schools, as well as articles focused on educational theory and research and the implications for teaching. This publication is directed toward an audience of researchers, teacher educators, and practitioners. Articles with references, data, and tables have covered a wide range of topics, such as grade retention, vocabulary development, after-school program engagement, and a proposal to improve classroom teaching. Themed issues are also published, such as one on No Child Left Behind. This is a major title for academic and school libraries. URL: www.journals.uchicago.edu/ESJ/home.html.

Gender and Education. See Gender Studies section.

1982. *Harvard Educational Review.* Formerly (until 1937): *Harvard Teachers Record.* [ISSN: 0017-8055] 1931. q. USD 139 (Individuals, USD 59). Harvard University, Graduate School of Education, 8 Story St, 1st Fl, Cambridge, MA 02138; hepg@harvard.edu; http://gseweb.harvard.edu/~hepg/her.htm/. Illus., index, adv. Refereed. Circ: 6250 Paid and free. Vol. ends: Nov. Microform: PQC. Online: EBSCO Publishing, EBSCO Host; Northern Light Technology, Inc.; OCLC Online Computer Library Center, Inc.; ProQuest LLC (Ann Arbor). *Indexed:* ABIn, AgeL, AmH&L, ArtHuCI, BAS, BRD, BRI, CBRI, CJA, EAA, ECER, ERIC, EduInd, FR, HistAb, IBR, IBZ, IPSA, L&LBA, PAIS, PSA, PhilInd, PsycInfo, SSA, SSCI, SWA, SWR&A, SociolAb. *Bk. rev.:* Number and length vary. *Aud.:* Ac.

HER, a journal of opinion and research, seeks articles on teaching and practice in the United States and international educational settings. Articles and other contributions are authored by teachers, practitioners, policy makers, scholars, and researchers in education and related fields. Authors have focused on such topics as urban schools; No Child Left Behind; educating immigrant children; teacher unions and state testing scores; and methods for ethnographic research. An occasional feature, "Voices Inside Schools," serves as a forum for teachers, students, and others to share their research and perspectives on issues from within school settings. Contains book reviews of recent publications. *HER* is published by an editorial board of doctoral students at the Harvard Graduate School of Education. Highly recommended for academic libraries. URL: www.hepg.org/main/her/Index.html.

1983. *The High School Journal.* [ISSN: 0018-1498] 1917. bi-m. Oct.-May. USD 54 (Individuals, USD 34). Ed(s): Danielle Cook, Howard Machtinger. University of North Carolina Press, 116 S. Boundary St, Chapel Hill, NC 27514-3808; uncpress_journals@unc.edu; http://www.uncpress.unc.edu. Illus., index. Sample. Refereed. Circ: 750 Paid and free. Vol. ends: Apr/May. Microform: PQC. Online: EBSCO Publishing, EBSCO Host; Florida Center for Library Automation; Gale; Northern Light Technology, Inc.; OCLC Online Computer Library Center, Inc.; OhioLINK; Project MUSE; ProQuest LLC (Ann Arbor); SwetsWise Online Content; H.W. Wilson. Reprint: PSC. *Indexed:* ABIn, EAA, ERIC, EduInd, PsycInfo, SWA. *Bk. rev.:* 1, 500 words. *Aud.:* Ac.

This journal seeks reflective articles that examine the field of secondary education and report on research, informed opinions, and, occasionally, successful practices. Special issues have focused on particular topics, such as high schools in the twenty-first century and the use of narratives for teaching.

Other issues contain a collection of topics of interest for teacher educators and other professionals and individuals interested in adolescent growth and development and secondary schools. Authors have researched secondary instruction and literacy; school principals; high school teacher attitudes about inclusion; high school course-taking; student participation in decision making; and constructivism in theory and practice. Recommended for school and academic libraries that serve education programs. URL: http://uncpress.unc.edu/bm-journals.html.

1984. *History of Education Quarterly.* Formerly (until 1961): *History of Education Journal.* [ISSN: 0018-2680] 1949. q. USD 136 print & online eds. Ed(s): James D Anderson. Blackwell Publishing, Inc., Commerce Place, 350 Main St, Malden, MA 02148; customerservices@blackwellpublishing.com; http://www.blackwellpublishing.com. Illus., index, adv. Sample. Refereed. Circ: 1800. Vol. ends: Winter. Online: EBSCO Publishing, EBSCO Host; JSTOR (Web-based Journal Archive); OCLC Online Computer Library Center, Inc.; ProQuest LLC (Ann Arbor). Reprint: PSC. *Indexed:* ABIn, AmH&L, ArtHuCI, BAS, ERIC, EduInd, HistAb, IBR, IBZ, RILM, SSCI. *Bk. rev.:* 10-30, 500 words. *Aud.:* Ac.

This publication of the international and scholarly History of Education Society covers topics spanning the history of education, both formal and nonformal, including the history of childhood, youth, and the family. The articles are universal in scope and greatly vary in content and time period. There are two or three lengthy articles per issue in addition to a historiographical essay. Research topics have included charity education in the eighteenth century; race and gender in higher education, 1940–1955; social history of the school principal; American women's higher education from 1945 to 1965; Asian Americans in the history of education; a study of Amherst College from 1850 to 1880; national identity in mid-Victorian Wales; and religious schooling in America. Offers an average of 15 book reviews per issue. This is a major journal for education historians. Recommended for academic libraries. URL: www.ed.uiuc.edu/hes/index.htm.

1985. *Independent School.* Formerly (until 1976): *Independent School Bulletin.* [ISSN: 0145-9635] 1941. 3x/yr. Members, USD 25; Non-members, USD 35. Ed(s): Michael Brosnan. National Association of Independent Schools, 1620 L St, NW, Washington, DC 20036-5605; info@nais.org; http://www.nais.org. Adv. Circ: 7500 Paid. Microform: PQC. Online: EBSCO Publishing, EBSCO Host; OCLC Online Computer Library Center, Inc.; H.W. Wilson. *Indexed:* ABIn, EduInd, MRD. *Bk. rev.:* 2. *Aud.:* Ac, Sa.

IS is published to provide an open forum for the exchange of general information about elementary and secondary education and to focus particularly on independent schools. Issues feature news and research articles that report on such topics as what we teach; school culture and climate; athletics and education; the public purpose of private schools; and sexuality education. Contains interviews, profiles, opinion pieces, and a narrative section about books. Each issue includes an insert of *The Reporter,* the independent school newsletter of the National Association of Independent Schools. Includes a classified section for job postings. Recommended for academic, public, and school libraries. URL: www.nais.org/index.cfm.

1986. *Instructor (New York).* Formed by the merger of (1996-1999): *Instructor: Primary Edition;* (1996-1999): *Instructor: Intermediate Edition;* Both of which superseded in part (1981-1996): *Instructor (New York, 1990);* Which was formerly (until 1989): *Instructor and Teacher (Cleveland);* (until 1989): *Instructor (Cleveland);* (until 1986): *Instructor and Teacher (Dansville);* Which was formed by the merger of (1931-1981): *Instructor (Dansville);* (1972-1981): *Teacher (Stamford);* Which was formerly: *Grade Teacher.* [ISSN: 1532-0200] 1981. 8x/yr. USD 8 domestic; USD 32 foreign; USD 3 newsstand/cover. Ed(s): Jennifer O Prescott, Terry Cooper. Scholastic Inc., 557 Broadway, New York, NY 10012; http://www.scholastic.com. Illus., index, adv. Sample. Circ: 254361 Paid. Vol. ends: May/Jun. Microform: PQC. Online: EBSCO Publishing, EBSCO Host; Gale; Northern Light Technology, Inc.; OCLC Online Computer Library Center, Inc.; ProQuest LLC (Ann Arbor); H.W. Wilson. *Indexed:* ABIn, BRI, CBRI, CPerI, ECER, ERIC, EduInd, MRD. *Bk. rev.:* 10, 50-100 words. *Aud.:* Ga.

This resource for elementary and middle school teachers includes helpful articles with information for professional development, as well as tips, strategies, lesson plans, and activities for use in the classrooms. A section on ready-to-use material includes a poster, reproducible activities, theme units, and a variety of aids for classroom projects. Issues have featured math software, heroes of history, a teacher's technology guide with information about software, hardware, and multimedia reference tools. They have also featured articles and strategies for teaching science. Issues are packed with advertisements for all types of products for classroom use. Recommended for school libraries and academic libraries that serve education programs. URL: http://teacher.scholastic.com/products/instructor.

1987. *International Electronic Journal for Leadership in Learning.* [ISSN: 1206-9620] 1997. a. w/frequent updates. Free. Ed(s): Charles F Webber, Kent Donlevy. University of Calgary Press, University of Calgary, 2500 University Dr NW, Calgary, AB T2N 1N4, Canada; whildebr@ucalgary.ca; http://www.uofcpress.com. Refereed. *Indexed:* CEI, EduInd. *Aud.:* Ems, Hs.

A refereed academic journal dedicated to promoting the study and discussion of current leadership issues related to educational communities. Articles, reviews, and commentaries focus on topics of concern to schools. Contributors have considered mission statements of two-year and four-year higher education institutions; school system evaluation; collaborative international research; skills for success in college; improving university-provided teacher in-service; and strengthening family-school relationships. A broad readership includes teachers, administrators, parents, community members, academics, and those involved with the governance of schools, such as school trustees. An important journal for all libraries that serve the field of education. URL: www.ucalgary.ca/~iejll.

1988. *Journal of Classroom Interaction.* Formerly: *Classroom Interaction Newsletter.* [ISSN: 0749-4025] 1965. s-a. USD 45 (Individuals, USD 40; USD 67 combined subscription in North America for print & online). Journal of Classroom Interaction, c/o Dr H Jerome Freiberg, Ed, College of Education, University of Houston, Houston, TX 77204-5872; http://www.coe.uh.edu/. Illus., index, adv. Sample. Refereed. Circ: 1000 Paid and controlled. Vol. ends: Winter. Microform: PQC. Online: OCLC Online Computer Library Center, Inc.; ProQuest LLC (Ann Arbor); H.W. Wilson. *Indexed:* ABIn, ERIC, EduInd, PsycInfo. *Aud.:* Ac.

This semi-annual journal publishes articles on empirical research and theory dealing with observation techniques, student and teacher behavior, and other issues connected with classroom interaction. Geared for an audience of faculty, practitioners, and graduate education students, this journal has presented a range of investigations and studies authored by national and international researchers and teacher educators. Topics have included importance of teacher interpersonal behavior; classroom heterogeneity and instructional time in Dutch secondary schools; the development of a learning environment questionnaire; construction of science knowledge; and how classes influence the participation of students in college classrooms. Themed issues have focused on mathematics in elementary and secondary school classrooms and democratic classroom practices. Recommended for academic and school libraries. URL: www.coe.uh.edu/cmcd/coejci/index.htm.

1989. *Journal of Education.* [ISSN: 0022-0574] 1875. 3x/yr. USD 45 (Individuals, USD 35; USD 15 per issue domestic). Ed(s): Dr. Edwin Delattre, Joan Dee. Boston University, School of Education, 605 Commonwealth Ave, Boston, MA 02215; bjued@bu.edu. Illus., adv. Circ: 2000. Vol. ends: Fall. Microform: PQC. Online: EBSCO Publishing, EBSCO Host. *Indexed:* ABIn, BRI, CBRI, CommAb, EAA, ERIC, EduInd, L&LBA, PAIS, SWA. *Bk. rev.:* 1, essay length. *Aud.:* Ac.

The journal was established in 1875, and follows a historic tradition of addressing policies and practices in the field. It has a focus on research, scholarship, reflection, and analysis for an audience of scholars and practitioners. Its editorial board seeks to publish a wide range of topics; and each issue addresses an important theme or topic. Recent issues have highlighted school sports and cyberethics. The journal invites readership suggestions for potential subjects relevant to the field of education.

1990. *The Journal of Educational Research.* [ISSN: 0022-0671] 1920. bi-m. USD 172 (Individuals, USD 75 print & online eds.; USD 27 newsstand/cover). Ed(s): Jeanne Bebo. Heldref Publications, 1319 18th St, NW, Washington, DC 20036-1802; subscribe@heldref.org; http://www.heldref.org. Illus., index, adv. Refereed. Circ: 1877 Paid. CD-ROM: ProQuest LLC (Ann Arbor). Microform: PMC. Online: Chadwyck-Healey Inc.; EBSCO Publishing, EBSCO Host; Florida Center for Library Automation; Gale; OCLC Online Computer Library Center, Inc.; ProQuest LLC (Ann Arbor); H.W. Wilson. Reprint: PSC. *Indexed:* ABIn, BAS, EAA, ECER, ERIC, EduInd, FR, HEA, IBR, IBZ, L&LBA, PsycInfo, SSCI, SWA, V&AA. *Aud.:* Ac.

JER publishes research articles that are expressly relevant to educational practice in elementary and secondary schools. Articles by national and international faculty have provided studies on professional development schools, teachers as readers and writers, gender in schools, an update of the Early Childhood Longitudinal Study, teacher and learner perceptions of geometry programs, facilitating academic achievement in the classroom, and parents' conceptions of kindergarten readiness. Contains five or six well-illustrated and referenced articles per issue. A valuable resource for academic and school libraries. URL: www.heldref.org/jer.php.

1991. *Journal of Thought.* [ISSN: 0022-5231] 1966. 4x/yr. USD 80 (Individuals, USD 50). Ed(s): Douglas Simpson. Caddo Gap Press, 3145 Geary Blvd, PMB 275, San Francisco, CA 94118; info@caddogap.com; http://www.caddogap.com. Illus., index, adv. Sample. Refereed. Circ: 300 Paid. Vol. ends: Winter. Microform: PQC. Online: Gale; OCLC Online Computer Library Center, Inc.; ProQuest LLC (Ann Arbor). *Indexed:* IBR, IBZ, PhilInd, SSA, SSCI. *Aud.:* Ac.

This journal reflectively and philosophically examines worldwide educational issues and problems from the perspective of many different disciplines. It welcomes the work of scholars that represent a variety of methodologies, approaches, cultures, and nationalities. Essays that offer analyses and critiques of arguments or that report on significant research of interest to the field are encouraged. The articles are written by and directed at an audience of faculty in higher education institutions and practitioners. Issues may explore a variety of topics or offer a common thematic thread such as the achievement gap. Examples of themed issues include a consideration of John Dewey and Lawrence Cremin and technology in the schools. Each issue contains an essay introduction by the editor. Recommended for academic libraries. URL: www.educ.ttu.edu/online/dsimpson/journalofthought/index.html.

1992. *Kappa Delta Pi Record.* [ISSN: 0022-8958] 1964. q. Free to members; Non-members, USD 18. Ed(s): Kathie-Jo Arnoff. Kappa Delta Pi, 3707 Woodview Trace, Indianapolis, IN 46268-1158; pubs@kdp.org; http://www.kdp.org. Illus. Refereed. Circ: 55000 Paid and controlled. Online: OCLC Online Computer Library Center, Inc.; ProQuest LLC (Ann Arbor); H.W. Wilson. *Indexed:* ABIn, EAA, ECER, ERIC, EduInd. *Bk. rev.:* Number and length vary. *Aud.:* Ac.

This publication of the Kappa Delta Pi International Honor Society in Education offers articles on current issues, classroom practices, and general educational concerns about teaching and learning. The journal's current areas of interest include the dropout problem and prevention, differentiated learning, action research, and teaching children in poverty. Articles are authored by faculty, teachers, administrators, parents, and others involved in the schools. Themed issues have featured articles on middle and high school topics such as flexible schedules and specific teacher preparation programs. Non-themed issues have offered articles on preservice teaching; education reform efforts; tips for publishing research findings; and the classroom environment. Includes information about Kappa Delta Pi, letters to the editor, opinion pieces, a section on programs in practice, and book reviews. Recommended for school and academic libraries. URL: www.kdp.org/publications/kdp.php.

1993. *Middle School Journal.* Formerly: *Midwest Middle School Journal.* [ISSN: 0094-0771] 1970. 5x/yr. USD 40. Ed(s): Tom Erb. National Middle School Association, 4151 Executive Pkwy, Ste 300, Westerville, OH 43081-3871; info@nmsa.org; http://www.nmsa.org. Illus., index, adv. Sample. Refereed. Circ: 27000 Paid. Vol. ends: May. *Indexed:* ABIn, EduInd. *Bk. rev.:* 1-4, 500-1,800 words. *Aud.:* Ga, Ac.

The articles in this official journal of the National Middle School Association are focused on middle level education and the educational and developmental needs of youngsters aged 10–15. Written by teacher educators and professionals in the field and directed at an audience of practitioners, articles report on successful programs or discuss effective practices and research applications, and there are reflective essays. Issues may be thematic or of general interest to the readership. Coverage of topics has included engaging instruction to captivate students and celebrating teachers and learning. Discussions have centered on advisory sessions for urban young adolescents; interdisciplinary team training for middle grades teachers; aggressive students; national board certification; and equity in mathematics classrooms. Departments include an editorial and a section on "What Research Says." Recommended for school libraries and academic libraries that serve education programs. URL: www.nmsa.org/services/midjournal.htm.

1994. *Mind, Brain, and Education.* [ISSN: 1751-2271] 2007. q. USD 300 print & online eds. Ed(s): Kurt W. Fischer. Blackwell Publishing, Inc., Commerce Place, 350 Main St, Malden, MA 02148; customerservices@ blackwellpublishing.com; http://www.blackwellpublishing.com. Refereed. *Aud.:* Ac.

This new, interdisciplinary, peer-reviewed journal combines education, biology, and cognitive science to introduce the new field of mind, brain, and education. Research and practice in the area of mind, brain, and education will contribute to the synergy between scientific research and educators' practical knowledge. The inaugural issue features scholarly articles on the relevance of affective and social neurosciences to education; genetic links between mind, brain, and education; how genomics can inform education; and searching for universal laws of psychology to inform cognition. In the first issue, there is an introductory section, "Dialogue," which is authored by the editor, followed by articles in two sections, "Concepts" and "Research." The research section focuses on whether there are separate neural systems for spelling. Highly recommended for academic and research institutions.

1995. *Momentum (Washington).* Formerly: *Catholic School Bulletin.* [ISSN: 0026-914X] 1970. 4x/yr. USD 20; USD 5 per issue. Ed(s): Brian E. Gray. National Catholic Educational Association, 1077 30 St, NW, Ste 100, Washington, DC 20007; nceaadmin@ncea.org; http://www.ncea.org. Illus. Circ: 25000. Microform: PQC. Online: OCLC Online Computer Library Center, Inc.; ProQuest LLC (Ann Arbor); H.W. Wilson. *Indexed:* ABIn, CPL, EduInd, PAIS. *Bk. rev.:* 3-6, 400-600 words. *Aud.:* Sa.

Geared to Catholic educators and parents, this journal offers news and articles pertinent to current issues in education, with a particular focus on Catholic schools. Each issue includes a special section that presents articles on such topics as social justice, the learning process, Catholic identity, the vocation of Catholic education, and Catholic education and public policy. Written by teachers, administrators, clergy, and professionals in the field, the articles provide practical news and information about school programs and practices for K–12 schools. Recommended for parochial school libraries and academic libraries that serve education programs. URL: www.nameorg.org/publications.html.

1996. *Multicultural Education: the magazine of the National Association for Multicultural Education Planning.* [ISSN: 1068-3844] 1993. q. Ed(s): Alan H Jones. Caddo Gap Press, 3145 Geary Blvd, PMB 275, San Francisco, CA 94118; info@caddogap.com; http://www.caddogap.com. Illus., adv. Sample. Refereed. Circ: 1000 Paid. Vol. ends: Summer. *Indexed:* ABIn, ERIC, EduInd, IBR, IBZ, L&LBA, MRD, SWA. *Bk. rev.:* 6-8, length varies. *Aud.:* Ac.

This publication provides articles on all aspects of multicultural education, innovative practices, opinion pieces, personal perspectives, reviews of books and other media, and news items and announcements about conferences, events, and programs. Authored by college and university faculty, teachers, doctoral students, and administrators within schools and organizations, articles have discussed high-stakes schooling; minority parents and school culture; Asian American teachers; multicultural literature; technology and multiculturalism; state requirements for the preparation of teachers working with diversity;

multicultural teaching by African American faculty; promoting bilingualism; recruiting students of color to teach; and a report on the role of the arts in multicultural settings. Recommended for school and academic libraries. URL: http://caddogap.com.

1997. *Multicultural Perspectives.* [ISSN: 1521-0960] 1999. q. GBP 207 print & online eds. Ed(s): Penelope L Lisi. Lawrence Erlbaum Associates, Inc., 325 Chestnut St, Ste. 800, Philadelphia, PA 19106; journals@erlbaum.com; http://www.leaonline.com. Illus., adv. Reprint: PSC. *Indexed:* L&LBA. *Bk. rev.:* Number and length vary. *Aud.:* Ac.

This official journal of the National Association for Multicultural Education is geared to an audience of K–12 educators, social scientists, social service personnel, and teacher educators, and all those involved in multicultural education. Articles are written primarily by college and university faculty and have focused on multiracial and multiethnic students; multicultural lesson plans; art and multicultural education; cultural heritage and academic achievement; bilingual and bicultural narratives for teacher research; and culturally responsive pedagogy in citizenship education. Includes reviews of books and other media. Highly recommended for school and academic libraries. URL: www.erlbaum.com/shop/tek9.asp?pg=products&specific=1521-0960.

1998. *N A S S P Bulletin.* Formerly: *National Association of Secondary School Principals. Bulletin.* [ISSN: 0192-6365] 1916. m. Sep.-May. GBP 156. Ed(s): Len Foster. Corwin Press, Inc., 2455 Teller Rd, Thousand Oaks, CA 91320-2218; info@sagepub.com; http://www.corwinpress.com. Illus., adv. Refereed. Circ: 40000 Paid. Vol. ends: Dec. Microform: PQC. Online: HighWire Press; OCLC Online Computer Library Center, Inc.; ProQuest LLC (Ann Arbor); H.W. Wilson. Reprint: PSC. *Indexed:* ABIn, BRI, CBRI, CJA, EAA, ECER, ERIC, EduInd, LRI, RILM, SWA, V&AA. *Bk. rev.:* 2-3 pages. *Aud.:* Ac.

This National Association of Secondary School Principals publication supports the decision making and practices of middle level and high school principals. Its articles address current issues and emphasize effective administration and leadership. Issues contain research and scholarly articles authored by faculty and professionals in the field. Various themes are explored, such as implementing high school grades and advanced placement; mobile students and academic achievement; technology standards for school administrators; supporting student teachers; preventing school violence; developing teacher leaders; and after-school and summer programs. The editors have given priority to particular topics, for example, middle level principalship; reading to learn; altering school start times; funding and equity; literacy in the middle level and high school; and teacher effectiveness, recruitment, and retainment. Includes book reviews. Highly recommended for school and academic libraries that serve education programs. URL: www.principals.org/s_nassp/sec_abstracts.asp?CID= 42&DID=42.

1999. *N A S S P Leadership for Student Activities.* [ISSN: 1040-5399] 1988. m. USD 12 newsstand/cover per issue. National Association of Secondary School Principals, 1904 Association Dr, Reston, VA 20191-1537; http://nasccms.principals.org. *Aud.:* Ac.

This publication of the National Association of Secondary School Principals Department of Student Activities is geared for student activities advisers and student leaders. Articles written by teachers, student council advisers, guidance counselors, and educational consultants offer practical information about successful programs for developing student leadership. Articles have discussed programs for the student council; a specific high school leadership conference; local area organizations that teach leadership; how to identify and develop leaders; and student profiles. Issues include leader resources, middle level activities, projects, national news, scholarships and awards, information about school honor societies, and an exchange of information about activities. Recommended for school libraries.

2000. *N A S S P Newsleader.* Formerly: *N A S S P Newsletter.* [ISSN: 0278-0569] 1971. m. Sep.-May. USD 180 (Individuals, USD 148). Ed(s): James Rourke. National Association of Secondary School Principals, 1904 Association Dr, Reston, VA 20191-1537; http://www.nassp.org. Illus., index, adv. Sample. Circ: 42000 Controlled. Vol. ends: May. *Bk. rev.:* 1-3, 500-1,000 words. *Aud.:* Ac.

In a newspaper format, this publication provides articles on current issues, news, and events for an audience of school leaders in middle level and high school education. It also includes coverage of the National Association of Seconary School Principals (NASSP) conferences, awards, organizational events, speeches, and elections, and available professional opportunities. This is an important resource for secondary school principals, as is the NASSP web site, which provides timely complementary information.

2001. *P J E, Peabody Journal of Education.* Formerly (until 1970?): *Peabody Journal of Education.* [ISSN: 0161-956X] 1923. q. GBP 277 print & online eds. Ed(s): James W Guthrie. Lawrence Erlbaum Associates, Inc., 325 Chestnut St, Ste. 800, Philadelphia, PA 19106; journals@erlbaum.com; http://www.leaonline.com. Illus., adv. Sample. Refereed. Circ: 2000 Paid. Vol. ends: Summer. Reprint: PSC. *Indexed:* ABIn, AgeL, BAS, ECER, ERIC, EduInd, L&LBA, PhilInd, PsycInfo, SSA, SSCI, SociolAb. *Aud.:* Ga, Ac.

PJE publishes symposia in the broad area of education and human development. The journal is one of America's oldest educational publications. Issues focus on themes with contributed articles by practitioners, academicians, policy makers, and researchers and scholars in the social sciences. The intended audience is similarly broad and diverse. Topics explored include newly emerging global issues, the No Child Left Behind Act, the relations between schools and their constituents, and access and equity in postsecondary education. Lengthy and well-referenced articles offer in-depth examination of the selected themes. This is an important journal for academic libraries. URL: http://peabody.vanderbilt.edu/news_and_events/journal.htm.

2002. *Phi Delta Kappan.* Formerly: *Phi Delta Kappan Magazine.* [ISSN: 0031-7217] 1915. 10x/yr. USD 65 (Individuals, USD 58). Ed(s): Rise Koben. Phi Delta Kappa International, 408 N Union St, PO Box 789, Bloomington, IN 47402-0789; publications@pdkintl.org; http://www.pdkintl.org. Illus., index. Circ: 60000 Paid. Vol. ends: Sep/Jun. Microform: CIS; PQC. Online: EBSCO Publishing, EBSCO Host; Florida Center for Library Automation; Gale; Northern Light Technology, Inc.; OCLC Online Computer Library Center, Inc.; ProQuest K-12 Learning Solutions; ProQuest LLC (Ann Arbor); H.W. Wilson. *Indexed:* ABIn, ABS&EES, ArtHuCI, BRD, BRI, CBRI, EAA, ECER, ERIC, EduInd, FutSurv, IBR, IBZ, LRI, RGPR, SSCI. *Aud.:* Ga, Ac.

PDK publishes articles on education research and leadership, with an emphasis on current issues, trends, and policy. Authored by faculty, practitioners, independent researchers, and consultants in the field, articles report on research or provide commentary on topics of concern and interest for educators at all levels. Articles have focused on bridging the gap between research and practice; low-achieving students; the standards movement; tenure in schools of education; professional certification; technological literacy; and teacher education. Departments include a Washington commentary; state news; information on current research; legal perspectives; and technology. A section titled "Backtalk" provides an opportunity for readers to submit comments on *PDK* articles. This is an important resource for educators. URL: www.pdkintl.org/kappan/kappan.htm.

2003. *Principal (Alexandria).* Formerly (until Sep. 1980): *National Elementary Principal.* [ISSN: 0271-6062] 1921. 5x/yr. Free to members; Non-members, USD 8. Ed(s): Rebecca Kesner, Leon E Greene. National Association of Elementary School Principals, 1615 Duke St, Alexandria, VA 22314-3483; lgreene@naesp.org; http://www.naesp.org. Illus., index. Circ: 29000 Paid and controlled. Vol. ends: May. Microform: PQC. Online: OCLC Online Computer Library Center, Inc.; H.W. Wilson. *Indexed:* ABIn, ECER, ERIC, EduInd. *Bk. rev.:* 350 words. *Aud.:* Ac.

This journal is published to serve elementary and middle school educators. Articles are written by teachers, principals, administrators, and other professionals to address current issues and to present ideas and information for practical applications in the schools. Regular columns include feature articles and commentaries for practitioners, a focus on the middle grades, technology trends, the reflective principal, and school law issues. Books of interest to principals are reviewed. Articles have discussed the confidentiality of student records, interviewing for the principalship, and safe schools. Issues may also have a theme, such as arts in the core curriculum and quality physical education

programs. Articles have also focused on the resilient principal, geography education, and foreign language instruction. Recommended for school and academic libraries that serve education programs. URL: www.naesp.org/ContentLoad.do?contentId=288.

2004. *Principal Leadership (High School Edition).* Formed by the merger of (1993-2000): *The High School Magazine;* (1981-2000): *Schools in the Middle.* [ISSN: 1538-9251] 2000. m. Sep.-May. USD 180 (Individuals, USD 148). Ed(s): Patricia George. National Association of Secondary School Principals, 1904 Association Dr, Reston, VA 20191-1537; http://nasccms.principals.org. Adv. *Indexed:* ABIn, BRI, CBRI, EduInd. *Aud.:* Ac.

This title is published in two separate editions, middle level and high school, and replaces two former NASSP publications, *Schools in the Middle* and *The High School Magazine.* The stated focus is supporting and enhancing the leadership capability of high school and middle level principals, assistant principals, and other school leaders with articles and practical information based on research and best practices. Issues have provided articles, authored by practitioners and professionals in the field, addressing developing and sustaining teachers, managing substitute teachers, school climate, and cocurricular activities. Regular departments include a discussion of a legal problem; a focus on technology issues; an update on court decisions related to school matters; and tips for principals on various topics. The two editions of this title are nearly identical, with the exception of two to four articles specific to the editions within the contents of each of the four different issues examined. The covers are exactly the same except for the edition label. With this unusual format, the potential for confusion is unfortunate and inevitable, to say nothing of the dilemma for libraries with regard to retention of largely duplicate editions. This title is only a partial replacement for *Schools in the Middle,* which had a more direct focus on middle schools. Nonetheless, this is a title recommended for school and academic libraries that serve education programs. URL: www.principals.org/s_nassp/sec_abstracts.asp?CID=43&DID=43.

2005. *Radical Teacher: a socialist and feminist journal on the theory and practice of teaching.* [ISSN: 0191-4847] 1975. 3x/yr. USD 20 domestic; USD 28 in Canada & Mexico; USD 39 elsewhere. Ed(s): Pamela Annas. Center for Critical Education, PO Box 382616, Cambridge, MA 02238; info@radicalreacher.org. Illus., adv. Refereed. Circ: 2400 Paid. Vol. ends: Winter. *Indexed:* ABIn, AltPI, CWI, EduInd, LeftInd, MLA-IB, SSA. *Bk. rev.:* 1-2, 1,000-2,000 words. *Aud.:* Ac, Sa.

This journal presents articles written by and for educational workers at all education levels in a variety of institutional settings. Since 1975 the journal has provided a forum for the exploration and discussion of peace, social justice, and equality. Some issues have emphasized particular themes such as repression and resistance in higher education, teaching in a time of war, and race in the classroom. Several regular columns are reviews of books for professional reading, current education news, and teaching notes. Recommended for school and academic libraries that serve education programs. URL: www.radicalteacher.org.

2006. *Review of Educational Research.* [ISSN: 0034-6543] 1931. q. GBP 177. Ed(s): Beverly Gordon, Joyce King. Sage Publications, Inc., 2455 Teller Rd, Thousand Oaks, CA 91320; info@sagepub.com; http://www.sagepub.com. Illus., index, adv. Refereed. Circ: 18400. Vol. ends: Winter. Microform: PMC; PQC. Online: JSTOR (Web-based Journal Archive); Northern Light Technology, Inc.; OCLC Online Computer Library Center, Inc.; ProQuest LLC (Ann Arbor); H.W. Wilson. Reprint: PSC. *Indexed:* ABIn, CommAb, EAA, ECER, ERIC, EduInd, FR, HEA, IBR, IBZ, L&LBA, LT&LA, PsycInfo, SSA, SSCI, SociolAb. *Aud.:* Ac.

RER publishes critical reviews and interpretations of educational research literature on substantive and methodological issues. The reviews of research relevant to education may be from any discipline. Authored by faculty, doctoral students, and professionals in the field, well-referenced articles have reviewed teacher recruitment and retention; classroom diversification; online education; postmodern perspectives on teaching freedom; the principal's role in creating inclusive schools; gender roles in school employment for over a century; and anti-oppressive education. Four to five articles per issue offer thought-provoking reviews and analyses for the American Educational Research Association (AERA) members and readers of this AERA publication. Highly recommended for academic libraries. URL: www.aera.net/publications/?id=319.

2007. Roeper Review: a journal on gifted education. [ISSN: 0278-3193] 1978. q. USD 80 (Individuals, USD 50). Ed(s): Ruthan Brodsky. Roeper School, PO Box 329, Bloomfield Hills, MI 48303. Illus., index, adv. Sample. Refereed. Circ: 3000 Paid. Vol. ends: Jun. *Indexed:* ABIn, EAA, ECER, ERIC, EduInd, IBR, IBZ, PsycInfo, RILM, SWA. *Bk. rev.:* 4-5, 200-800 words. *Aud.:* Ga, Ac, Sa.

As the mission and contents indicate, this journal publishes articles that reflect on research, observation, experience, theory, and practice with regard to the growth, emotions, and education of gifted and talented learners. Faculty authors and professionals in the field have contributed to one issue's theme cultural context and high ability with articles on cultural dimensions of giftedness and talent, leadership and intelligence, and motivational aspects of giftedness. Other issues offered articles that explored the themes of influences of parents, teachers, and the media on the development of gifted students, and the use of online technologies for gifted secondary students. Issues generally include a section that presents one or more in-depth research articles and/or a brief research article. This is an informative and important journal in gifted education. Recommended for academic libraries that serve education programs. URL: www.roeperreview.org.

2008. School Administrator: the monthly magazine for school system leaders. Incorporates: *D C Dateline.* [ISSN: 0036-6439] 1943. m. 11/yr. Members, USD 9; Non-members, USD 10. Ed(s): Jay P Goldman. American Association of School Administrators, 801 N Quincy St, Ste 700, Arlington, VA 22208-1730; magazine@aasa.org; http://www.aasa.org. Adv. Circ: Controlled. Online: EBSCO Publishing, EBSCO Host; Gale; Northern Light Technology, Inc.; OCLC Online Computer Library Center, Inc.; ProQuest LLC (Ann Arbor); H.W. Wilson. *Indexed:* ABIn, ERIC, EduInd. *Bk. rev.:* Number and length vary. *Aud.:* Ac.

This American Association of School Administrators (AASA) monthly magazine for school leaders is focused on topics and news related to school district administration and is directed primarily at an audience of school superintendents. Authored by superintendents, faculty, and other professionals, articles provide practical information and discussions on important topics and often support a particular theme. Issues have offered articles on technology costs and benefits, personal technology, the meaning of the new economy for education and educators, and school health issues, such as nursing needs and indoor air quality. There are guest columns on pertinent subjects, president's corner, tech leadership, organization news, book reviews, and other resources. Issues contain an insert, the AASA *Bulletin: A Supplement to the School Administrator,* which includes organization news, conference news, calls for proposals, and job postings. An important resource for school and academic libraries that serve education programs. URL: www.aasa.org/publications/sa/index.htm.

2009. Teacher Magazine. [ISSN: 1046-6193] 1989. bi-m. USD 17.94. Ed(s): Ms. Virginia B Edwards. Editorial Projects in Education Inc., 6935 Arlington Rd, Ste 100, Bethesda, MD 20814-5233; http://www.edweek.org. Illus., adv. Sample. Circ: 100000. Vol. ends: May/Jun. Online: EBSCO Publishing, EBSCO Host; OCLC Online Computer Library Center, Inc.; ProQuest LLC (Ann Arbor). *Indexed:* ABIn, ERIC, EduInd. *Bk. rev.:* 4, 100-400 words. *Aud.:* Ga.

This magazine for K–12 educators contains articles on current news and education topics of interest. It includes information about programs in particular schools, profiles of educators, interviews for reports on a particular subject, opinions, comments, and letters by the readership, and book reviews. Teachers, other education professionals, and writers contribute to this magazine. *Teacher* includes a calendar for grants, fellowships, award and contest deadlines, and events information. It also includes advertisements and general information on curriculum aids, school supplies, various products, professional development, and job postings. This is a useful K–12 resource. Recommended for school, public, and academic libraries that serve education programs. URL: www.edweek.org/tm/index.html.

2010. Teachers College Record: a professional journal of ideas, research and informed opinion. Former titles (until 1970): *The Record, Teachers College, Columbia University;* (until 1967): *Teachers College Record.* [ISSN: 0161-4681] 1900. m. USD 621 & Carribean, print & online eds. (Individuals, USD 89 & Carribean, print & online eds.; Students, USD 63 & Carribean, print & online eds.). Ed(s): Jeff Frank, Robert Calfee. EBSCO Publishing, 10 Estes St, Ipswich, MA 01938; information@ebscohost.com; http://www.epnet.com/. Illus., index, adv. Sample. Refereed. Circ: 2500. Microform: MIM; PQC. Online: Blackwell Synergy; EBSCO Publishing, EBSCO Host; Gale; IngentaConnect; OCLC Online Computer Library Center, Inc.; OhioLINK; SwetsWise Online Content; H.W. Wilson. *Indexed:* ABIn, AmH&L, ApEcolAb, ArtHuCI, BRD, BRI, CBRI, EAA, ECER, ERIC, EduInd, FutSurv, HEA, HistAb, IBR, IBZ, MLA-IB, PhilInd, PsycInfo, SSA, SSCI, SWA, SociolAb, V&AA. *Bk. rev.:* 6-8, 750 words. *Aud.:* Ac.

TCR is a scholarly journal of research, analysis, and commentary on a broad range of issues and topics in the field of education. Articles have focused on teacher induction policy, peace education, learning portfolios, gender equity in the sciences, teachers' learning communities, standards in early childhood education, learning to lead, reflective journal writing, and knowledge management for school leaders. *TCR* also publishes theme issues, such as two recent ones on distance learning and online education and youth development and social identity in the twenty-first century. A recent issue is entirely devoted to book reviews organized topically under administration, assessment and evaluation, curriculum, diversity, early childhood education, higher education, learning, research methods, social context, teacher education, teaching, and technology. Highly recommended for academic libraries. URL: www.blackwellpublishing.com/journal.asp?ref=0161-4681.

2011. Teaching K-8: the professional magazine for teachers. Former titles: *Teaching Pre K-8; Early Years - K-8;* (until 1987): *Early Years.* 1971. m. 8/yr. USD 23.97 domestic; USD 33.97 foreign. Early Years, Inc., 40 Richards Ave, Norwalk, CT 06854-2309; TeachingK8@aol.com; http://www.teachingk-8.com. Illus., adv. Sample. Circ: 101000. Vol. ends: May. Microform: PQC. Online: EBSCO Publishing, EBSCO Host; Northern Light Technology, Inc.; OCLC Online Computer Library Center, Inc.; ProQuest K-12 Learning Solutions; ProQuest LLC (Ann Arbor); H.W. Wilson. *Indexed:* ABIn, BRI, ECER, ERIC, EduInd. *Bk. rev.:* 8-12, length varies. *Aud.:* Ga.

This resource provides practical articles, tips and teaching strategies, news and classroom activities authored by teachers, education faculty, librarians, parents, and members of the teaching editorial staff. Each issue contains a section of skill-building activities, and regular departments with ideas for teaching in the middle school, teaching math, art in the curriculum, teaching reading and writing, issues in literacy and learning, and a newsletter for parents. There is information about web sites, software, and children's books. The online publication is entitled *Teaching Pre K-8.* Recommended as a useful resource for school and academic libraries that serve graduate and undergraduate education programs.

2012. Theory into Practice. Supersedes: *Educational Research Bulletin.* [ISSN: 0040-5841] 1962. q. GBP 103 print & online eds. Ed(s): Anita Woolfolk Hoy. Lawrence Erlbaum Associates, Inc., 325 Chestnut St, Ste. 800, Philadelphia, PA 19106; journals@erlbaum.com; http://www.leaonline.com. Illus., index, adv. Refereed. Circ: 1500. Microform: PQC. Online: EBSCO Publishing, EBSCO Host; Florida Center for Library Automation; Gale; JSTOR (Web-based Journal Archive); Northern Light Technology, Inc.; OCLC Online Computer Library Center, Inc.; OhioLINK; Project MUSE; ProQuest K-12 Learning Solutions; ProQuest LLC (Ann Arbor); SwetsWise Online Content; H.W. Wilson. Reprint: PSC. *Indexed:* ABIn, CJA, EAA, ERIC, EduInd, SFSA, SSCI. *Aud.:* Ac.

Each issue of *TIP* offers a comprehensive overview of a particular education topic, with articles representing a range of viewpoints on the subject. Articles authored by faculty and other professionals in the field are directed at an audience of teachers, education researchers, students, professors, and administrators. Editors provide an introduction to the topic for each issue. The topic of the Reggio Emilia approach to early childhood education is the focus of a recent issue, which offers ten articles and additional resources. An issue about multiple literacies offers articles on the meaning of multiple literacies, becoming literate in a second langauge, and multiple literacies in connection with teacher education. Recommended for academic libraries that serve education programs. URL: www.coe.ohio-state.edu/TIP.

2013. *Today's Catholic Teacher.* [ISSN: 0040-8441] 1967. bi-m. USD 14.95 domestic; USD 19.95 foreign. Ed(s): Mary Noschang. Peter Li Education Group, 2621 Dryden Rd, Ste 300, Dayton, OH 45439-1661; service@peterli.com; http://www.peterli.com. Illus., adv. Sample. Circ: 50000 Paid. Vol. ends: Apr. *Indexed:* BiolDig, CPL. *Aud.:* Ac.

Addressing K–12 Catholic school teachers, this journal provides articles on special topics such as technology in the Catholic schools and an educator development series on the vocation of teaching, as well as practical articles related to classroom activities. It includes news, ideas for class projects, resources, and other helpful aids for academic and religious lesson plans. It contains extensive advertising information on products and services for classroom use. Recommended for Catholic school libraries. URL: www.peterli.com/tct/index.shtm.

2014. *Urban Education.* [ISSN: 0042-0859] 1966. bi-m. GBP 469. Ed(s): Kofi Lomotey. Corwin Press, Inc., 2455 Teller Rd, Thousand Oaks, CA 91320-2218; info@sagepub.com; http://www.sagepub.com/. Illus., adv. Refereed. Circ: 750 Paid. Vol. ends: Jan. Microform: PQC. Online: CSA; EBSCO Publishing, EBSCO Host; HighWire Press; OCLC Online Computer Library Center, Inc.; OhioLINK; SAGE Publications, Inc., SAGE Journals Online; SwetsWise Online Content. Reprint: PSC. *Indexed:* ABIn, BRI, CJA, EAA, ERIC, EduInd, FR, HRA, IBR, IBZ, L&LBA, PsycInfo, SFSA, SSA, SSCI, SUSA, SWA, SWR&A, SociolAb, V&AA. *Bk. rev.:* 2, 10 pages. *Aud.:* Ac.

This journal provides articles that examine issues of concern for city schools. Subjects include: student motivation and teacher practice; restructuring in large urban schools; school-to-work programs; and mental health needs of urban students. Topics explored have been a study of Chicana and Chicano students in an urban setting; the depiction of Native Americans in trade books; student achievement in the Chicago schools; mentoring for urban youth; African American male students enrolled in alternative school programs; and students with special needs in three profiled high schools. Includes book reviews. A special annual issue provides in-depth coverage of an important issue in urban education, such as the issue on historical perspective on activism, empowerment, and reform in urban public schools. Recommended for academic libraries. URL: http://uex.sagepub.com.

2015. *Vitae Scholasticae: the journal of educational biography.* [ISSN: 0735-1909] 1982. s-a. Ed(s): Lucy F Townsend. Caddo Gap Press, 3145 Geary Blvd, PMB 275, San Francisco, CA 94118; caddogap@aol.com. Illus., index, adv. Sample. Refereed. Circ: 150 Paid. Vol. ends: Fall. *Indexed:* AmH&L, HistAb, IBR, IBZ. *Aud.:* Ac.

As the journal of the International Society for Educational Biography, this publication offers scholarly articles on all aspects of educational biography. Articles have focused on the lives of Emma Ducie and Flora White; considered the case of a nineteenth-century traveler with respect to experiential education; and explored the topic of autobiography and identity. Issues reflect a wide range of research interests for graduate education students and faculty. Recommended for academic libraries that serve education programs. URL: http://caddogap.com/journals.htm.

2016. *Voices from the Middle.* [ISSN: 1074-4762] 1994. q. USD 20. Ed(s): Kylene Beers. National Council of Teachers of English, 1111 W Kenyon Rd, Urbana, IL 61801-1096; cschanche@ncte.org; http://www.ncte.org. Adv. Circ: 10000 Paid. *Indexed:* ABIn, ERIC, EduInd. *Bk. rev.:* Number and length vary. *Aud.:* Ac.

Recognizing that middle school teachers are challenged with "a unique set of circumstances and issues," this journal is dedicated to supporting the middle school educator. Each issue provides a forum for the sharing of ideas, practices, reflections, solutions, and theories from classroom teachers and others involved with middle school students. Thematic issues consider middle school topics such as standards of learning and teaching, teaching for social justice, and social and emotional learning. Each issue has a featured theoretical article with

additional articles focused on classroom practices for grades six to eight. Regular columns of professional book reviews, student book reviews, worldwide resources, and a news-and-notes section contribute to the journal's forum orientation. Specifically for middle schools with a professional library, as well as education libraries. URL: www.ncte.org/pubs/journals/vm.

2017. *Y C - Young Children.* Formerly (until 2002): *Young Children.* [ISSN: 1538-6619] 1944. bi-m. USD 95 (Individuals, USD 60; Free to members). Ed(s): Polly Greenberg. National Association for the Education of Young Children, 1313 L St N.W., Ste 500, Washington, DC 20036-1426; http://www.naeyc.org. Illus., index, adv. Refereed. Circ: 90000. Vol. ends: Sep. Microform: PQC. Online: OCLC Online Computer Library Center, Inc.; ProQuest LLC (Ann Arbor). *Indexed:* ABIn, AgeL, Agr, EAA, ECER, ERIC, EduInd, L&LBA, MRD, SFSA, SSCI. *Bk. rev.:* 1-8, 400-800 words. *Aud.:* Ac.

This journal of the National Association for the Education of Young Children (NAEYC) addresses an audience of teachers and directors of programs involved with children from birth through age eight within child care, preschool, Head Start, and primary grade settings. It is also directed at teacher educators, local and state decision makers, and researchers in child development. Practical articles provide ideas for teaching children and administering programs, and scholarly articles refer to current research and theory as a basis for practical recommendations. Articles also describe program changes that have occurred as an outcome of experts' experience and research about how young children learn. Essays discuss important issues and ideas concerning the education, care, and development of young children. Issues include NAEYC organization information, brief book reviews, letters from readers, and a calendar of conferences. Recommended for school, public, and academic libraries. URL: www.journal.naeyc.org.

Comparative Education and International

2018. *Adults Learning.* [ISSN: 0955-2308] 1989. 10x/yr. GBP 56 (Individuals, GBP 34). Ed(s): Stephenie Hughes. The National Institute of Adult Continuing Education (NAICE), Renaissance House, 20 Princess Rd. W, Leicester, LE1 6TP, United Kingdom; enquiries@niace.org.uk; http://www.niace.org.uk. Illus., index, adv. Sample. Circ: 3000. Vol. ends: Jun. Online: EBSCO Publishing, EBSCO Host. *Indexed:* BrEdI. *Bk. rev.:* 6-7, 500 words. *Aud.:* Ac, Sa.

This official publication of the National Institute of Adult Continuing Education (NIACE) in England and Wales provides national news of conferences and events, notes or reviews of publications, web site reviews, commentaries, and brief articles on current issues in the field. Articles by adult education consultants, university professors, and NIACE personnel have discussed social purpose in adult education; the idea of a language for education; distance and lifelong learning; the findings of a report on attitudes of young adults concerning basic skills; language learning in the United Kingdom; skills training; and global learning. Recommended for academic and public libraries. URL: www.niace.org.uk/publications/Periodicals/AdultsLearning/Default.htm.

2019. *Australian Journal of Education.* [ISSN: 0004-9441] 1957. 3x/yr. AUD 164 (Individuals, AUD 99). Ed(s): Simon Marginson. Australian Council for Educational Research, Private Bag 55, Camberwell, VIC 3124, Australia; sales@acer.edu.au; http://www.acer.edu.au. Illus., index, adv. Sample. Refereed. Circ: 1000. Vol. ends: Nov. *Indexed:* AgeL, EAA, EduInd, FR, HEA, IBR, IBZ, L&LBA, MLA-IB, SSA, SSCI, SWA, SociolAb. *Bk. rev.:* 6, 800-1,500 words. *Aud.:* Ac.

AJE publishes papers on the theory and practice of education utilizing various methodologies and conceptual frameworks. Its main focus is on Australian education. Although primarily from Australia, the authors represent an international corps of scholars from a broad range of disciplines, such as philosophy, psychology, political science, economics, history, anthropology, medicine, and sociology. Articles have discussed systemic racism; perceptual motor programs in Australian schools; motivational goals and school achievement; policy development in Aboriginal education; distance education for students in isolated schools; leadership dilemmas of Hong Kong principals; and programs for gifted students in Australia. Articles have also reviewed publications and citation data to evaluate the contribution of Australian educational research to major international journals. A special issue on inequality and public policy offers articles on restructuring educational opportunity in England, curriculum policy with respect to post-compulsory education and training, and a study of mathematics achievement in the United States and Australia. Most issues contain several book reviews. Recommended for academic libraries. URL: www.acer.edu.au/publications/acerpress/AJE/AJEOverview.html.

2020. *British Educational Research Journal.* Formerly (until vol.4, 1978): *Research Intelligence.* [ISSN: 0141-1926] 1975. bi-m. GBP 928 print & online eds. Ed(s): Pat Sikes. Routledge, 4 Park Sq, Milton Park, Abingdon, OX14 4RN, United Kingdom. Illus., index, adv. Refereed. Online: EBSCO Publishing, EBSCO Host; Gale; IngentaConnect; JSTOR (Web-based Journal Archive); Northern Light Technology, Inc.; OCLC Online Computer Library Center, Inc.; ProQuest LLC (Ann Arbor); SwetsWise Online Content. Reprint: PSC. *Indexed:* BrEdI, EAA, ERIC, FR, IBR, IBSS, IBZ, L&LBA, LT&LA, PsycInfo, SFSA, SSA, SSCI, SWA, SociolAb, V&AA. *Bk. rev.:* Number and length vary. *Aud.:* Ac, Sa.

This major publication of the British Educational Research Association is interdisciplinary in its approach and includes reports of experiments and surveys, discussions of methodological and conceptual issues in educational research for all sectors of education, and descriptions of research in progress. Scholarly articles are primarily focused on British education, although the journal's scope is international. Articles have examined school violence, national test reading scores, ability grouping placement in secondary schools, and differential attainment by gender for students in Wales. Other subjects have been international comparative studies of student achievement, primary mathematics in England and Russia, and the influence of politics in developing the curriculum. An entire issue is devoted to subject knowledge and application. Includes book reviews. Recommended for academic libraries. URL: www.bera.ac.uk/berj.html.

2021. *British Journal of Educational Studies.* [ISSN: 0007-1005] 1952. q. GBP 293 print & online eds. Ed(s): Paul Croll. Blackwell Publishing Ltd., 9600 Garsington Rd, Oxford, OX4 2ZG, United Kingdom; customerservices@blackwellpublishing.com; http://www.blackwellpublishing.com. Illus., index, adv. Refereed. Circ: 1300. Vol. ends: Nov. Microform: PQC. Online: Blackwell Synergy; EBSCO Publishing, EBSCO Host; Gale; IngentaConnect; JSTOR (Web-based Journal Archive); OCLC Online Computer Library Center, Inc.; OhioLINK; SwetsWise Online Content. Reprint: PSC. *Indexed:* ABIn, AmH&L, ApEcolAb, ArtHuCI, BAS, BrEdI, EAA, ERIC, EduInd, HistAb, IBR, IBSS, IBZ, L&LBA, SSA, SSCI, SociolAb. *Bk. rev.:* 12-15, 500-1,000 words. *Aud.:* Ac.

BJES seeks articles on major education topics and principles of general interest, particularly current developments in education policy in the United Kingdom and elsewhere. Empirical research reports are not included unless they are basic to the discussion of an important topic. Articles represent a wide range of perspectives in the areas of educational philosophy, history, psychology, sociology, management, administration, and comparative studies. They are also written for an audience of nonspecialists in the field, in keeping with the journal's interest in clearly expressed and nontechnical contributions to scholarship. Articles have discussed educationally meaningful curricula; education and the middle classes; the chartered teacher; a Scottish perspective of social capital; social inclusion and changing social contexts; the validity of the National Curriculum assessment in England; the writing skills and formal education needed for properly functioning in the workplace; a critical exploration of educational reforms in Western countries; and research and contemporary school leadership in England. Recommended for academic libraries. URL: www.blackwellpublishing.com/journal.asp?ref=0007-1005.

2022. *British Journal of Sociology of Education.* [ISSN: 0142-5692] 1980. 5x/yr. GBP 1162 print & online eds. Ed(s): Len Barton. Routledge, 4 Park Sq, Milton Park, Abingdon, OX14 4RN, United Kingdom; info@routledge.co.uk; http://www.routledge.com. Illus., index, adv. Refereed. Online: EBSCO Publishing, EBSCO Host; Gale; IngentaConnect; JSTOR (Web-based Journal Archive); Northern Light Technology, Inc.; OCLC Online Computer Library Center, Inc.; ProQuest LLC (Ann Arbor); SwetsWise Online Content. Reprint: PSC. *Indexed:* ASSIA, ArtHuCI, BrEdI, EAA, ERIC, FR, IBR, IBSS, IBZ, PSA, PsycInfo, RILM, SSA, SSCI, SWA, SociolAb. *Bk. rev.:* Number and length vary. *Aud.:* Ac, Sa.

This journal publishes scholarly articles that reflect the range of current perspectives on both theory and empirical research in the sociology of education. International academic authors have contributed articles on home environment and second language; a case study of policy-making in Queensland; games of subversion and sabotage; globalization and e-learning in higher education; the improvement of university teaching; nontraditional adult learners; and a longitudinal study of Australian secondary school students. Each issue generally contains a review essay, an extended review, and a review symposium on a major book or a collection of books. Recommended for academic libraries. URL: www.tandf.co.uk/journals/titles/01425692.asp.

2023. *Canadian Journal of Education.* [ISSN: 0380-2361] 1976. q. Free to members; Non-members, CND 100; CND 25 per issue. Ed(s): Samuel Robinson, Francois Larose. Canadian Society for the Study of Education, 260 Dalhousie, Ste 204, Ottawa, ON K1N 7E4, Canada; csse@csse.ca; http://www.scee.ca. Illus., index. Sample. Refereed. Circ: 1460. Vol. ends: Fall. Microform: MML. Online: JSTOR (Web-based Journal Archive); Micromedia ProQuest; OCLC Online Computer Library Center, Inc.; ProQuest LLC (Ann Arbor); H.W. Wilson. *Indexed:* ABIn, CBCARef, CEI, CPerI, EAA, ERIC, EduInd, IBR, IBZ, L&LBA, PAIS, PsycInfo, SSA, SWA, SociolAb. *Bk. rev.:* 3-7, 600-1,500 words. *Aud.:* Ac.

CJE publishes articles broadly but not exclusively related to Canadian education. Included are short research notes, discussions on topics, and book reviews. Articles are published either in English or French, with the abstracts in both languages. Topics covered have been financial accountability and educational attainment; large-scale assessment outcomes in British Columbia; democracy and education; student achievement; gender issues in education; boys and literacy; indigenous education contexts; and evidence of Canadians' declining confidence in public education. This is an important and well-indexed Canadian education journal. Recommended for academic libraries. URL: www.csse.ca/CJE/home.htm.

2024. *Child Education.* [ISSN: 0009-3947] 1924. m. GBP 37.50 domestic; GBP 49.95 foreign. Scholastic Ltd., Villiers House, Clarendon Ave, Leamington Spa, CV32 5PR, United Kingdom; enquiries@scholastic.co.uk; http://www.scholastic.co.uk. Illus., index, adv. Circ: 59926. Vol. ends: Dec. Microform: PQC. *Indexed:* ABIn, EduInd. *Bk. rev.:* 15-20, 50-200 words. *Aud.:* Ac.

This publication provides lesson plans, colorful posters, and reproducible activities geared for classroom use in primary schools in the United Kingdom. Articles offer tips on teaching strategies and ideas to enhance the curriculum. Throughout there is useful current information about U.K. education news, publications, and resources. Each monthly issue is organized with activities under literacy, arts workshop, project, and numeracy. Book reviews include professional reading and children's books. Recommended for school and public libraries. URL: www.scholastic.co.uk/magazines/childed.htm.

2025. *Chinese Education and Society: a journal of translations.* Formerly (until Jan. 1993): *Chinese Education.* [ISSN: 1061-1932] 1968. bi-m. USD 1284 print & online eds. Ed(s): Stanley Rosen. M.E. Sharpe, Inc., 80 Business Park Dr, Armonk, NY 10504; custserv@mesharpe.com; http://www.mesharpe.com. Illus., index, adv. Refereed. Vol. ends: Nov/Dec. Microform: PQC. Online: EBSCO Publishing, EBSCO Host; OCLC Online Computer Library Center, Inc.; SwetsWise Online Content; H.W. Wilson. Reprint: PSC. *Indexed:* ABIn, AgeL, BAS, EAA, ERIC, EduInd, FR, IBR, IBZ, SSCI. *Aud.:* Ac, Sa.

This journal provides unabridged English translations of important articles on education in China from Chinese journals, newspapers, and collections of articles in book form. The translated names of the sources used are *Education Research, People's Education,* and *Chinese Education News,* as well as other national and local newspapers and magazines. Issues have focused on such topics as environmental education in China; women in the teaching profession; gender equality in China; women students' culture and psychology; qualitative research; women's education and employment; and education and the economy. There was also coverage of the brain drain, which discusses the problem of sending students abroad and then attracting them back. Recommended for academic libraries. URL: www.mesharpe.com/mall/results1.asp?acr=ced.

2026. Comparative Education: an international journal of comparative studies. [ISSN: 0305-0068] 1965. q. GBP 836 print & online eds. Ed(s): Michael Crossley. Routledge, 4 Park Sq, Milton Park, Abingdon, OX14 4RN, United Kingdom; info@routledge.co.uk; http://www.routledge.com. Illus., index, adv. Refereed. Circ: 1200. Vol. ends: Oct. Online: EBSCO Publishing, EBSCO Host; Gale; IngentaConnect; JSTOR (Web-based Journal Archive); Northern Light Technology, Inc.; OCLC Online Computer Library Center, Inc.; ProQuest LLC (Ann Arbor); SwetsWise Online Content. Reprint: PSC. *Indexed:* ABIn, BAS, BrEdI, EAA, ERIC, EduInd, FR, IBR, IBSS, IBZ, L&LBA, RRTA, SSA, SSCI, SWA, SociolAb, WAE&RSA. *Bk. rev.:* Number and length vary. *Aud.:* Ac, Sa.

This international journal provides current information and analyses of significant world problems and trends in the field of education, with particular emphasis on comparative studies for policy making and implementation. It also has an interest in the associated disciplines of government, management, sociology, technology, and communications, with a view to the impact of these areas on educational policy decisions. The instructions to contributors have a long list of suggested themes, including educational reform, post-compulsory education, curricular content, education for the disadvantaged, higher education, and teacher preparation. Article topics have included culture, instruction, and assessment; western influences on Chinese educational testing; the impact of the West on post-Soviet Russian education; classroom reform in India; recent initiatives in school science and technology; a comparative study of educational reforms in Hong Kong and mainland China; a comparative view of the National Curriculum standards in primary schools; secondary schooling in France and Australia; and schooling's contribution to social capital in Bolivia. A special issue reflects on comparative and international research for the twenty-first century. Includes book reviews. Recommended for academic libraries. URL: www.tandf.co.uk/journals/carfax/03050068.html.

2027. Comparative Education Review. [ISSN: 0010-4086] 1957. q. USD 208 domestic; USD 225.48 Canada; USD 216 elsewhere. Ed(s): Mark Ginsburg, Heidi Ross. University of Chicago Press, Journals Division, PO Box 37005, Chicago, IL 60637; subscriptions@press.uchicago.edu; http://www.journals.uchicago.edu. Illus., index, adv. Refereed. Circ: 2200 Paid. Vol. ends: Nov. Microform: PQC. Online: EBSCO Publishing, EBSCO Host; Florida Center for Library Automation; Gale; JSTOR (Web-based Journal Archive); ProQuest K-12 Learning Solutions; ProQuest LLC (Ann Arbor). Reprint: PSC. *Indexed:* ABIn, ABS&EES, BAS, CABA, EAA, ERIC, EduInd, FR, IBR, IBZ, L&LBA, PAIS, RRTA, SSA, SSCI, SociolAb, WAE&RSA. *Bk. rev.:* 9-11, 800-2,000 words. *Aud.:* Ac.

The official journal of the Comparative and International Education Society, this publication seeks to advance knowledge of education policies and practices throughout the world and the teaching of comparative education studies. Articles authored by international faculty and researchers have discussed school leadership in Trinidad and Tobago; governing transnational education; education in Azerbaijan and Central Asia; the evaluation of school improvement in Indonesia; a comparative view of barriers to academic women; vocational education in eastern Germany; education and social transformation in Israel and South Africa; and educational change in the Czech Republic. Issues contain one or more essay reviews and a number of book reviews. The August 2006 special issue on Islam and education includes an essay review and book reviews on the topic. Recommended for academic libraries. URL: www.journals.uchicago.edu/CER/home.html.

2028. Current Issues in Comparative Education (CISE). [ISSN: 1523-1615] 1998. s-a. Free. Columbia University, Teachers College, 525 W 120th St, New York, NY 10027. *Indexed:* EduInd. *Aud.:* Ac.

An international open-access journal dedicated to publishing scholarly debate and discussion on educational policies and comparative studies. With academic and practical experience–based contributions, the journal has a wide and diverse audience. Each themed issue has a minimum of five articles with an online commentary. Issue topics have included the education of immigrants,

gender-centered theorizing; education and social exclusion; political violence and education; and HIV/AIDS education. Recommended for academic libraries. URL: www.tc.columbia.edu/cice.

2029. Curriculum Inquiry. Formerly: *Curriculum Theory Network.* [ISSN: 0362-6784] 1971. q. GBP 291 print & online eds. Ed(s): Ming Fang He, F Michael Connelly. Blackwell Publishing, Inc., Commerce Place, 350 Main St, Malden, MA 02148; customerservices@blackwellpublishing.com; http://www.blackwellpublishing.com. Illus., index, adv. Refereed. Circ: 1700. Vol. ends: Winter. Online: Blackwell Synergy; EBSCO Publishing, EBSCO Host; Gale; IngentaConnect; JSTOR (Web-based Journal Archive); OCLC Online Computer Library Center, Inc.; OhioLINK; SwetsWise Online Content. Reprint: PSC. *Indexed:* ABIn, ArtHuCI, CEI, EAA, ERIC, EduInd, IBR, IBZ, SSCI, SWA. *Bk. rev.:* 1-2, essay length. *Aud.:* Ac.

This journal sponsored by the Ontario Institute for Studies in Education focuses on the study of educational research, development, evaluation, and theory. Within each issue, international authors from a variety of disciplines offer articles on a wide range of issues and topics such as Israeli kindergarten teachers coping with terror and war; storytelling as pedagogy; case studies on preservice teachers' service learning; a collaborative relationship with teachers at an elementary school; writing as inquiry through workshops; arts and urban schools; and the selection of curricular contents of school projects in Spain. Equally important in this journal are critical book reviews, for which there are extensive instructions for in-depth essays. Editorial introductions are substantive. Recommended for academic libraries. URL: www.blackwellpublishing.com/journal.asp?ref=0362-6784.

2030. Discourse (Abingdon): studies in the cultural politics of education. [ISSN: 0159-6306] 1980. q. GBP 408 print & online eds. Ed(s): Robert Lingard, Victoria Carrington. Routledge, 4 Park Sq, Milton Park, Abingdon, OX14 4RN, United Kingdom; info@routledge.co.uk; http://www.routledge.com. Illus., adv. Refereed. Circ: 500. Online: EBSCO Publishing, EBSCO Host; Gale; IngentaConnect; OCLC Online Computer Library Center, Inc.; SwetsWise Online Content. Reprint: PSC. *Indexed:* AmHI, CommAb, L&LBA, MLA-IB, PSA, SSA, SWA, SociolAb. *Bk. rev.:* Number and length vary. *Aud.:* Ac, Sa.

With its emphasis on international critical inquiry and dialogue on the cultural politics of education, this journal offers scholarly articles on a range of current topics of interest and concern. Articles have discussed politics, culture, and school curriculum; deparochializing education; student identities and schooling; gender gap; language, literacy, and performance; critical cultural studies; storytelling as a teaching strategy for teacher education; gifted education in South Australia; discourse though the drawings of teachers and students; Asian women's experiences in contemporary British schooling and society; and youth at risk. Includes review essays and book reviews. Recommended for academic libraries. URL: www.tandf.co.uk/journals/titles/01596306.asp.

2031. Economics of Education Review. [ISSN: 0272-7757] 1982. 6x/yr. EUR 796. Ed(s): Dr. Elchanan Cohn. Pergamon, The Boulevard, Langford Ln, East Park, Kidlington, OX5 1GB, United Kingdom. Illus., adv. Refereed. Circ: 525. Microform: PQC. Online: EBSCO Publishing, EBSCO Host; Gale; IngentaConnect; OhioLINK; ScienceDirect; SwetsWise Online Content. *Indexed:* ASG, BAS, EAA, ERIC, HEA, HRA, JEL, SSCI, SWA. *Bk. rev.:* 0-3, 600-1,000 words. *Aud.:* Ac.

EER provides a forum to share ideas and research findings in the economics of education. It also seeks to encourage theoretical, empirical, and policy research that points out the role of economic analysis for an improved understanding of educational problems and issues. The articles are authored by international faculty, documented with references, tables, and other data, and cover a wide range of topics. Articles have focused on race, poverty, and teacher mobility; student data in efficiency analysis; health effects of education; grades as information; an analysis of the *U.S. News & World Report* rankings of colleges and universities; efficiency of Australian universities; costs and other factors in year-round versus traditional school schedules; educational attainment and gender wage gap; and a merit pay model for college faculty. Includes book reviews. Recommended for academic libraries. URL: www.elsevier.com.

2032. Educational Research. [ISSN: 0013-1881] 1958. 3x/yr. GBP 297 print & online eds. Ed(s): Alison Lawson, Dr. Seamus Hegarty. Routledge, 4 Park Square, Milton Park, Abingdon, OX14 4RN, United Kingdom; info@routledge.co.uk; http://www.routledge.co.uk. Illus., index, adv. Refereed. Circ: 2500. Vol. ends: Nov. Microform: SWZ. Online: EBSCO Publishing, EBSCO Host; Gale; IngentaConnect; OCLC Online Computer Library Center, Inc.; SwetsWise Online Content. Reprint: PSC. *Indexed:* ABIn, ArtHuCI, BrEdI, CJA, EAA, ERIC, EduInd, FR, IBR, IBSS, IBZ, LT&LA, PsycInfo, SSCI, SWA. *Bk. rev.:* 7, 600 words. *Aud.:* Ac.

This journal is published by the National Foundation for Education Research in England and Wales (NFER), a major British research institution. It seeks articles on contemporary issues in education that convey research findings in language that is understandable for its non-expert readership. With its objective of comprehensively describing for readers the problems and the research outcomes of a wide range of concerns in all areas of education, this forum for NFER is meant to assist professionals in making practical decisions. Faculty authors and researchers have written articles on student stress in secondary education; restorative justice in New Zealand schools; students' construction of science knowledge; English teachers' understanding of the development of imagination in the classroom; the impact of school departments on secondary science teaching; training expert teachers; the influence of television and videos on children's imagination; and classroom influences on bullying. This publication also includes short research reports and book reviews. Recommended for academic libraries. URL: www.tandf.co.uk/journals/titles/00131881.asp.

2033. European Education: issues and studies. Formerly (until 1991): *Western European Education.* [ISSN: 1056-4934] 1969. q. USD 920 print & online eds. Ed(s): Edward F Bodine, Bernhard Streitwieser. M.E. Sharpe, Inc., 80 Business Park Dr, Armonk, NY 10504; custserv@mesharpe.com; http://www.mesharpe.com. Illus., adv. Refereed. Circ: 220 Paid. Vol. ends: Dec. Reprint: PSC. *Indexed:* ABIn, ERIC, EduInd, IBR, IBZ. *Aud.:* Ac.

This publication contains selected articles from major journals drawn from the member states of the Council of Europe. It also includes research reports and documents (some abridged) from various research centers and school systems. Its education scope is broad, with a particular focus on experiments and innovations including the following subject areas: higher education in transition; reform and restructing in post-communist systems; and European integration and education policy. Themed issues have addressed post–Cold War studies in comparative education; higher education in the Balkans; comparative European perspectives on school–state relationships; and education in postnational Europe. Recommended for academic libraries. URL: www.mesharpe.com/mall/results1.asp.

2034. European Journal of Education: research, development and policies. Formerly: *Paedagogica Europaea.* [ISSN: 0141-8211] 1964. q. GBP 928 print & online eds. Ed(s): Jean Gordon, Jean-Pierre Jallade. Blackwell Publishing Ltd., 9600 Garsington Rd, Oxford, OX4 2ZG, United Kingdom; customerservices@blackwellpublishing.com; http://www.blackwellpublishing.com. Illus., index, adv. Refereed. Online: Blackwell Synergy; EBSCO Publishing, EBSCO Host; Gale; IngentaConnect; JSTOR (Web-based Journal Archive); OCLC Online Computer Library Center, Inc.; OhioLINK; SwetsWise Online Content. Reprint: PSC. *Indexed:* ABIn, ApEcolAb, BrEdI, EAA, ERIC, EduInd, FR, HEA, IBR, IBZ, SSA, SWA. *Aud.:* Ac.

This is the journal of the European Institute for Education and Social Policy, which commissions the contributed papers from a range of specialists in the field. The aim is to offer a European perspective on policy making. The institute edits *EJE* and acts through an international board of editors. Each issue has a theme, such as issues on graduate employment; the futures of learning; reforms in doctoral education; and national qualifications frameworks. Individual articles have focused on the history of EU cooperation in the field of education and training; equal opportunities in educational systems; the changing demand for skills; multiculturalism as a pedagogical problem; university research policy in Norway; Finnish higher education; and German as a second language. Recommended for academic libraries. URL: www.blackwellpublishing.com/journal.asp?ref=0141-8211.

2035. Higher Education: the international journal of higher education and educational planning. [ISSN: 0018-1560] 1971. 8x/yr. EUR 994 print & online eds. Ed(s): Grant Harman. Springer Netherlands, Van Godewijckstraat 30, Dordrecht, 3311 GX, Netherlands; http://www.springeronline.com. Illus., index, adv. Sample. Refereed. Vol. ends: No. 4. Microform: PQC. Online: EBSCO Publishing, EBSCO Host; Gale; IngentaConnect; OCLC Online Computer Library Center, Inc.; OhioLINK; Springer LINK; SwetsWise Online Content. Reprint: PSC. *Indexed:* ABIn, BrEdI, CABA, EAA, ERIC, EduInd, HEA, IBR, IBSS, IBZ, IPSA, LT&LA, SSA, SSCI, SWA, WAE&RSA. *Bk. rev.:* Number and length vary. *Aud.:* Ac.

This publication provides a forum for the exchange of information, experiences, and research results worldwide among professionals in the field. International authors reflect on higher education problems and issues; offer comparative reviews and analyses of country policies and education systems; and consider how these contributions may impact future planning. Articles have discussed the role of government intervention in Australian international education; the prediction of international students' academic success; academic careers of immigrant women professors in the United States; cross-border flows of students for higher education; gender-earning gap among European higher education graduates; the restructuring of the University of Botswana, 1990–2000; and international student perceptions of discrimination. Includes book reviews. Recommended for academic libraries. URL: www.springerlink-.com.

2036. International Education Webzine. Formerly: *Teacher's Internet Pages.* 1996. bi-m. International Educators' Network Association, c/o Bucknell, 25 Tudor City Place, New York, NY 10017; http://members.iteachnet.org/webzine/index.php. *Bk. rev.:* Number and length vary. *Aud.:* Ac.

A daily magazine reporting on international education news and events. With a large number of feature stories relevant to international education, the magazine is a vital resource. Articles have included project-based learning and education reform. Sections cover book reviews, conferences, house swaps, jobs, and job seekers. Daily news is provided with links to media such as the *New York Times International* and *Science Daily.* An events calendar includes recruitment fairs. Recommended for all academic and school libraries. URL: http://members.iteachnet.org/webzine.

2037. International Journal of Leadership in Education: theory & practice. [ISSN: 1360-3124] 1998. q. GBP 323 print & online eds. Ed(s): Dr. Duncan Waite. Taylor & Francis Ltd., 4 Park Sq, Milton Park, Abingdon, OX14 4RN, United Kingdom; info@tandf.co.uk; http://www.tandf.co.uk/journals. Adv. Refereed. Online: EBSCO Publishing, EBSCO Host; Gale; IngentaConnect; OCLC Online Computer Library Center, Inc.; SwetsWise Online Content. Reprint: PSC. *Indexed:* BrEdI. *Bk. rev.:* Number and length vary. *Aud.:* Ac.

This international journal provides a forum for theoretical and practical discussions of educational leadership. It considers conceptual, methodological, and practical issues in a variety of settings. Its stated goal is to publish cutting-edge research on instructional supervision, curriculum and teaching development, and educational administration. It presents alternative theoretical perspectives, methodologies, and leadership experiences. Its broad definition of leadership includes teachers as leaders, shared governance, site-based decision making, and community-school collaborations. Issue sections include peer-reviewed, theoretically-based research papers; practical shorter articles from academicians and practitioner-researchers; commentary; and book reviews. Articles have covered such topics as middle leadership in U.K. schools; principals' perceptions of politics; barriers to science education reform; traditional and personal admissions criteria; and evaluating school-based management. Recommended for academic libraries. URL: www.tandf.co.uk/journals/titles/13603124.asp.

2038. International Review of Education. [ISSN: 0020-8566] 1955. bi-m. EUR 375 print & online eds. Ed(s): Orrin F Summerell. Springer Netherlands, Van Godewijckstraat 30, Dordrecht, 3311 GX, Netherlands; http://www.springeronline.com. Illus., index, adv. Sample. Refereed. Vol. ends: Dec (No. 6). Microform: PQC. Online: EBSCO Publishing, EBSCO Host; Gale; IngentaConnect; OCLC Online Computer Library

Center, Inc.; OhioLINK; Springer LINK; SwetsWise Online Content. Reprint: PSC. *Indexed:* ABIn, AgeL, BAS, BrEdI, CABA, ERIC, EduInd, FR, IBR, IBSS, IBZ, IndIslam, L&LBA, LT&LA, SSA, SSCI, SociolAb, WAE&RSA. *Bk. rev.:* 8, 800 words. *Aud.:* Ac.

This UNESCO publication is directed at institutes of education, teacher training institutions and ministries, nongovernment organizations, and individuals throughout the world. It provides an informational forum for scholarly articles on educational policy issues, trends, and innovations in the field. Several journal issues have focused on work and learning research; literacy in the information age; and education and human rights. Article contributors have discussed teaching and learning of values through television; schooling for all in South Africa; the feminization of primary education; self-reporting and test discrepancy; nonformal education and distance education; multigraded schools; adult literacy; and curricula for rural areas in developing countries. A few articles within an issue may be non-English, but with an English abstract. Includes book reviews. Recommended for academic libraries. URL: www.springerlink.com.

2039. *Irish Journal of Education.* [ISSN: 0021-1257] 1967. a. EUR 7 in Europe; USD 10 elsewhere. Ed(s): Thomas Kellaghan. St. Patrick's College, Educational Research Centre, Drumcondra, Dublin, 9, Ireland; info@erc.ie; http://www.erc.ie. Illus., index, adv. Sample. Refereed. Circ: 1000. Vol. ends: Winter. Microform: PQC. Online: H.W. Wilson. *Indexed:* BrEdI, EduInd, FR, L&LBA, SSA, SSCI. *Aud.:* Ac.

This journal is intended for an audience of teachers at all education levels and other readers interested in the field. It presents research articles with a focus on education in Ireland as well as developments in educational theory and practice in other countries. Subject areas covered include philosophy, history and sociology of education, educational and child psychology, comparative education, and curriculum studies. Articles have explored the college in the community; middle management in primary schools; leisure activities of pupils in relation to their reading achievement; science curriculum and policies in Ireland; Irish music education; primary school evaluation; student participation in Australian secondary school mathematics courses; and an overview of the PISA 2003 findings in Ireland. Recommended for academic libraries. URL: www.erc.ie/IJE%20main%20page%20text.htm.

2040. *J E T: Journal of Educational Thought.* Formerly: *Journal of Educational Thought.* [ISSN: 0022-0701] 1967. 3x/yr. CND 90 (Individuals, CND 80; CND 30 per issue). Ed(s): Linda Lentz, Ian Winchester. University of Calgary, Faculty of Education, 2500 University Dr NW, Calgary, AB T2N 1N4, Canada; http://external.educ.ucalgary.ca/ jet/jetaug.html. Illus., adv. Sample. Refereed. Circ: 575. Vol. ends: Dec. Microform: MML; PQC. Online: Micromedia ProQuest; OCLC Online Computer Library Center, Inc.; ProQuest LLC (Ann Arbor); H.W. Wilson. Reprint: PSC. *Indexed:* ABIn, CEI, EAA, EduInd, L&LBA, PhilInd, SSA, SSCI, SWA, SociolAb. *Bk. rev.:* 6-8, 700-1,500 words. *Aud.:* Ac.

This journal presents research articles on the theory and practice of education. Subject areas explored by mainly Canadian and American faculty vary widely and include administration, comparative education, curriculum, evaluation, instructional methodology, intercultural education, philosophy, psychology, and sociology. Authors have discussed native people and the social work profession; the moral dimensions of citizenship education; the relevancy of poetry in school leadership; constructivist learning; multicultural teacher education curriculum; technology and inequality in U.S. school systems; integrity within the university; vocational education in Canadian public schooling; and the portrayal of private schools in selected feature films. All articles have French and English abstracts, with occasional articles entirely in French. Each issue contains an editorial and book reviews. Recommended for academic libraries. URL: www.educ.ucalgary.ca/research/jet/jet.html.

2041. *Journal of Philosophy of Education.* Formerly: *Philosophy of Education Society of Great Britain. Proceedings.* [ISSN: 0309-8249] 1966. q. GBP 513 print & online eds. Ed(s): Paul Standish. Blackwell Publishing Ltd., 9600 Garsington Rd, Oxford, OX4 2ZG, United Kingdom; customerservices@blackwellpublishing.com; http://www.blackwellpublishing.com. Illus., index, adv. Refereed. Vol. ends: No. 2. Online: Blackwell Synergy; EBSCO Publishing, EBSCO

Host; Gale; IngentaConnect; OCLC Online Computer Library Center, Inc.; OhioLINK; SwetsWise Online Content. Reprint: PSC. *Indexed:* ABIn, ApEcolAb, BrEdI, EAA, ERIC, EduInd, FR, IBR, PhilInd, RI-1, SSCI, SWA. *Bk. rev.:* 1-2, 1,000-2,000 words. *Aud.:* Ac.

This journal is published for the Philosophy of Education Society of Great Britain. Authors discuss basic philosophical issues related to education, or they may provide critical examinations of current educational practices or policies from a philosophical perspective. The authors are international, as is the editorial board. Articles have focused on such topics as knowledge and skills for PISA; thinking about environmental studies; propositional thinking; well-being and education; the meanings of education and pedagogy; schools and moral education; schools as communities; and Nietzsche's educational legacy. Special issues devoted to a particular theme have presented articles on the philosophical problems of online education and the idea of "high culture" within education. Generally includes a book review or review article. Recommended for academic libraries. URL: www.blackwellpublishing.com/journal.asp?ref= 0309-8249.

2042. *Prospects: quarterly review of comparative education.* Formerly: *Prospects in Education.* [ISSN: 0033-1538] 1969. q. EUR 109 print & online eds. Springer Netherlands, Van Godewijckstraat 30, Dordrecht, 3311 GX, Netherlands; http://www.springeronline.com. Illus. Circ: 2125. Reprint: PSC. *Indexed:* ABIn, BrEdI, EduInd, IBR, IBZ, SSCI. *Bk. rev.:* 1-2, essay length. *Aud.:* Ac.

This publication of the UNESCO International Bureau of Education provides articles on education throughout the world by scholars, practitioners, policy makers, and administrators. Themed issues have focused on school autonomy and evaluation, education in Asia, professionalism in teaching, and education for sustainable development. Each issue begins with at least one opening article that offers an opinion on a controversial topic. Some issues have a section that discusses education trends based on particular case studies, for example, modern education in Afghanistan, child rights and education in Japan, and higher education in Nigeria. This journal is currently available in a number of foreign language editions: Arabic, Chinese, French, Russian, and Spanish. Recommended for academic libraries. URL: www.ibe.unesco.org/International/ Publications/Prospects/proshome.htm.

2043. *Times Educational Supplement.* [ISSN: 0040-7887] 1910. w. GBP 56; GBP 1.20 newsstand/cover per issue. Ed(s): Patricia Rowan. T S L Education Ltd., Admiral House, 66-68 E Smithfield, London, E1 1BX, United Kingdom; http://www.tsleducation.co.uk. Illus., index, adv. Circ: 135000. CD-ROM: Chadwyck-Healey Inc. Microform: RPI. *Indexed:* ABIn, BRI, BrEdI, CBRI, EduInd, FLI, LT&LA, RILM. *Bk. rev.:* 8-12, 400-800 words. *Aud.:* Ac, Sa.

TES is the British version of the American publication, *Education Week.* It is the United Kingdom's major weekly publication for news concerning "primary, secondary, and further education." It includes background analyses of a wide range of current issues in education, local and national news, and a section on job openings for predominantly K–12 and also higher-education positions. It provides frequent special supplements to the news edition, such as separate job advertising supplements that include international openings; a curriculum special on mathematics; a special issue on computers in education; feature supplements with a focus on human interest stories; news; and articles of interest. It also contains reviews of adult and children's books, TV and radio, theater, and curriculum resources. Highly recommended for academic libraries. URL: www.tes.co.uk.

2044. *Times Higher Education Supplement.* [ISSN: 0049-3929] 1971. w. Free to members. Ed(s): John O'Leary. T S L Education Ltd., Admiral House, 66-68 E Smithfield, London, E1 1BX, United Kingdom; http://www.tsleducation.co.uk. Illus., index, adv. Circ: 25000. CD-ROM: Chadwyck-Healey Inc. Microform: RPI. Online: EBSCO Publishing, EBSCO Host. *Indexed:* ABIn, AmHI, BRI, BrEdI, BrHumI, EduInd, LISA, LT&LA, MLA-IB, PhilInd. *Bk. rev.:* 35, 300-1,200 words. *Aud.:* Ac.

This title is the British version of the American publication *Chronicle of Higher Education.* *THES* states it is "designed specifically for professional people working in higher education and research." Articles cover a range of higher-education topics including governmental policy, international news and views, scientific theory, and copyright. Its review section has two distinctly British columns, "Whistleblowers" and "Soapbox," as well as more general features such as international news, opinion and letters, and book reviews. The section on teaching with theoretical and practical articles has covered the teaching of grammar, constructing a teaching portfolio, and team problem-solving. Each issue has a book review section focused on a particular area such as "Cultural and Media Studies," "Psychology and Psychiatry," "Women's and Gender Studies," and "Mathematics and Physics." As with the *Chronicle of Higher Education*, *THES* includes job advertisements with some international vacancies. This British weekly is a standard for any academic library, higher education institute, or organization. URL: www.thes.co.uk.

Educational Psychology and Measurement, Special Education, Counseling

2045. *Applied Measurement in Education.* [ISSN: 0895-7347] 1988. q. GBP 352 print & online eds. Ed(s): Barbara S Plake, James C Impara. Lawrence Erlbaum Associates, Inc., 325 Chestnut St, Ste. 800, Philadelphia, PA 19106; journals@erlbaum.com; http://www.leaonline.com. Illus., adv. Refereed. Vol. ends: No. 4. Reprint: PSC. *Indexed:* ABIn, EAA, ERIC, EduInd, PsycInfo, SSCI, SWA. *Aud.:* Ac.

Sponsored by the Oscar and Luella Buros Center for Testing, this research journal focuses on educational and psychological testing articles. The intended audience of researchers and practitioners will find articles on applied research, educational measurement problems and considered solutions, and research reviews of current issues in testing. Research studies with accompanying tables, figures, graphs, and other supporting material address topics such as alignment methodologies; selected methods of scoring classroom assessments; the assessment of graduate-level writing skills; the structure and scoring of mathematics performance assessments; an analysis of faculty evaluation data; and the use of standard calculators in testing situations. Contributors are from academic and testing institutions such as the American Council of Testing and the Education Testing System. Strongly recommended for libraries that serve teachers and related education professionals. URL: https://www.erlbaum.com/shop/tek9.asp?pg=products&specific=0895-7347.

2046. *Counselor Education and Supervision.* [ISSN: 0011-0035] 1961. q. USD 80. Ed(s): William Kline. American Counseling Association, 5999 Stevenson Ave, Alexandria, VA 22304-3300; http://www.counseling.org. Illus., index, adv. Refereed. Circ: 3500. Vol. ends: Jun. Microform: PQC. Online: EBSCO Publishing, EBSCO Host; Florida Center for Library Automation; Gale; OCLC Online Computer Library Center, Inc.; ProQuest LLC (Ann Arbor); H.W. Wilson. Reprint: PSC. *Indexed:* ABIn, AgeL, CWI, ERIC, EduInd, PsycInfo, SSCI, SWA. *Bk. rev.:* Number and length vary. *Aud.:* Ac, Sa.

This official publication of the Association for Counselor Education and Supervision (ACES) is designed for professionals engaged in the teaching and supervising of counselors. The journal's scope encompasses a broad range of workplaces, from schools to agencies to private institutions. Each issue contains about six articles written by authors predominantly from academe. Articles range from pedagogical methods to practical teaching methods such as teaching research integrity in the field of education, using screenwriting techniques for realistic role plays. The journal has two regularly featured sections: one on counselor preparation and the other on counselor supervision. The inclusion of ACES executive council minutes supports the professional orientation of the journal. A focused journal for a specific audience. URL: www.ohiou.edu/che/ces.

2047. *Educational Measurement: Issues and Practice.* Supersedes: *National Council on Measurement in Education. Measurement News;* Formerly: *N C M E Newsletter.* [ISSN: 0731-1745] 1982. q. Ed(s): Steve Ferrara. Blackwell Publishing, Inc., Commerce Place, 350 Main St, Malden, MA 02148; customerservices@blackwellpublishing.com; http://www.blackwellpublishing.com. Illus. Refereed. Circ: 2600. Vol. ends: Winter. Reprint: PSC. *Indexed:* ABIn, ERIC, EduInd, PsycInfo. *Bk. rev.:* 1, 5,000 words. *Aud.:* Ac.

A journal of the National Council on Measurement in Education (NCME) designed to both highlight and inform its professional audience on issues and practices in the field of educational measurement. Each issue contains three articles ranging in length from five to ten pages. Journal articles cover such topics as models of cognition used in educational measurement; security of web-based assessments; practice analysis for credentialing examinations; the meaning of student achievement in relation to the TIMSS international survey data; evaluation criteria for teacher certification tests; large-scale testing in other countries; and issues in large-scale writing assessments. As a membership publication, the journal also reports on NCME member activities, the annual conference, and organizational news. This journal supports practitioners in the field of testing. URL: www.ncme.org/pubs/emip.ace.

2048. *Educational Psychology Review.* [ISSN: 1040-726X] 1989. q. EUR 679 print & online eds. Ed(s): Kenneth A Kierwa. Springer New York LLC, 233 Spring St, New York, NY 10013-1578; service-ny@springer.com; http://www.springer.com/. Illus., adv. Sample. Refereed. Vol. ends: Dec. Microform: PQC. Online: EBSCO Publishing, EBSCO Host; Gale; IngentaConnect; OCLC Online Computer Library Center, Inc.; OhioLINK; Springer LINK; SwetsWise Online Content. Reprint: PSC. *Indexed:* ABIn, CJA, ERIC, EduInd, L&LBA, PsycInfo, SSCI, SWA. *Aud.:* Ac, Sa.

An international peer-reviewed publication that supports the field of general educational psychology. Averaging four to six substantial and well-referenced articles per issue, this journal covers the history, the profession, and the issues of the educational psychology field. Two recent special issues cover collaborative learning and classroom motivation. A regular feature, "Reflections on the Field," provides an arena for interviews and discussion with leading educational psychologists. Article authors are predominantly from institutions of higher education. Academic libraries that serve education and psychology faculty and graduate students will want this title. URL: www.springerlink.com.

2049. *J E M.* Former titles (until 1978): *Journal of Educational Measurement;* (until 1964): *National Council on Measurement in Education. Yearbook.* [ISSN: 0274-838X] 19??. q. GBP 201 print & online eds. Ed(s): Michael J Kolen. Blackwell Publishing, Inc., Commerce Place, 350 Main St, Malden, MA 02148; customerservices@blackwellpublishing.com; http://www.blackwellpublishing.com. Illus., index, adv. Refereed. Circ: 3500. Vol. ends: Winter. Microform: PQC. Online: Blackwell Synergy; EBSCO Publishing, EBSCO Host; Gale; IngentaConnect; JSTOR (Web-based Journal Archive); OCLC Online Computer Library Center, Inc.; ProQuest LLC (Ann Arbor); SwetsWise Online Content. Reprint: PSC. *Indexed:* ABIn, ERIC, EduInd, HEA, IBR, IBZ, PsycInfo, SSCI. *Bk. rev.:* 2, 600-1,200 words. *Aud.:* Ac.

Published by the National Council on Measurement, this journal intends to "promote greater understanding and improved use of measurement techniques." The journal's content format is based on research studies and reports on educational measurement such as a study to investigate standard error measurement with testlets. There is a review section for books, software, and published tests and measurements. In addition, the journal asks for and publishes comments on previously published articles and reviews. The authors come from a broad range of testing and measurement backgrounds, such as the National Board of Medical Examiners, Microsoft Corporation, Research Triangle Institute, and CTB/McGraw-Hill. A scholarly research journal for those in the field of educational testing and measurement. URL: www.ncme.org/pubs/jem.ace.

2050. *Journal of Educational and Behavioral Statistics.* Formerly (until vol.19, no.3, 1994): *Journal of Educational Statistics.* [ISSN: 1076-9986] 1976. q. GBP 142. Ed(s): Ginny Maisch. Sage Publications, Inc., 2455 Teller Rd, Thousand Oaks, CA 91320; info@sagepub.com; http://www.sagepub.com. Illus., index, adv. Refereed. Circ: 3700. Vol. ends: Winter. Microform: PQC. Online: JSTOR (Web-based Journal Archive); OCLC Online Computer Library Center, Inc.; ProQuest LLC (Ann Arbor); H.W. Wilson. Reprint: PSC. *Indexed:* ABIn, ERIC, EduInd, PsycInfo, SSCI. *Aud.:* Ac.

This journal is sponsored by the American Educational Research Association and the American Statistical Association. Intended for the statistician working in the field of educational or behavioral research, the journal publishes papers on methods of analysis as well as reviews of current methods and practices. *JEBS* articles inform readers about the use of statistical methods: the "why, when, and how" of statistical methodology. Four to five articles are included per issue along with the occasional column titled "Teachers Corner," which presents brief essays on the teaching of educational and behavioral statistics. A focused journal important to those in academe, whether researcher or practitioner. URL: www.apa.org/journals/edu.

2051. *Journal of Educational Psychology.* [ISSN: 0022-0663] 1910. q. USD 450 (Non-members, USD 161). Ed(s): Dr. Karen R Harris. American Psychological Association, 750 First St, N E, Washington, DC 20002-4242; journals@apa.org; http://www.apa.org. Illus., adv. Sample. Refereed. Circ: 6000 Paid. Vol. ends: Feb. Microform: PMC; PQC. Online: Pub.; CSA; EBSCO Publishing, EBSCO Host; OCLC Online Computer Library Center, Inc.; OhioLINK; Ovid Technologies, Inc.; ProQuest LLC (Ann Arbor); ScienceDirect. Reprint: PSC. *Indexed:* ABIn, AgeL, ArtHuCI, CommAb, EAA, ECER, ERIC, EduInd, FR, HEA, IBR, IBZ, L&LBA, LT&LA, MLA-IB, PsycInfo, SFSA, SSA, SSCI, SWA. *Aud.:* Ac.

The journal's stated purpose is to publish current research as well as theoretical and review articles in the field of educational psychology. Each issue has 15–20 well-referenced research articles supported by tables, figures, and appendixes. Most articles have multiple authors. Article coverage includes learning, cognition, instruction, motivation, social issues, emotion, and special populations at all education levels. The journal has published such articles as preschool instruction and children's emergent literacy growth; teaching phonics; interactive writing intervention with kindergarten children; adolescents' perception of the classroom environment; a comparison of five urban early childhood programs; and a study that identified and described middle school students' goals. Published by the American Psychological Association, this is an academic research journal for students, researchers, and practitioners in the field of educational psychology.

2052. *The Journal of Experimental Education.* [ISSN: 0022-0973] 1932. q. USD 143 (Individuals, USD 63 print & online eds.; USD 40 newsstand/cover). Ed(s): Page Pratt. Heldref Publications, 1319 18th St, NW, Washington, DC 20036-1802; subscribe@heldref.org; http://www.heldref.org. Illus., index, adv. Sample. Refereed. Circ: 1066 Paid. CD-ROM: ProQuest LLC (Ann Arbor). Microform: PMC. Online: Chadwyck-Healey Inc.; EBSCO Publishing, EBSCO Host; Florida Center for Library Automation; Gale; OCLC Online Computer Library Center, Inc.; ProQuest K-12 Learning Solutions; ProQuest LLC (Ann Arbor); H.W. Wilson. Reprint: PSC. *Indexed:* ABIn, EAA, ERIC, EduInd, FR, HEA, IBR, IBZ, L&LBA, MASUSE, PsycInfo, SSCI, SWA. *Aud.:* Ac.

This journal publishes research studies that use quantitative or qualitative methodologies in the behavioral, cognitive, and social sciences. Intended for researchers and practitioners, the journal is dedicated to promoting educational research in areas such as teaching, learning, and schooling. Contributed articles are divided into three sections: learning and instruction; motivation and social processes; and measurement, statistics, and research design. Articles have covered such topics as motivation and self-regulation as predictors of achievement; cooperative college examinations; the effects of test anxiety on college students; and video case construction with pre-service teacher education programs. A journal intended for and useful to the professional researcher in the field of education and related social sciences. URL: www.heldref.org/jexpe.php.

2053. *Journal of Learning Disabilities.* [ISSN: 0022-2194] 1967. bi-m. GBP 124. Sage Publications, Inc., 2455 Teller Rd, Thousand Oaks, CA 91320; info@sagepub.com; http://www.sagepub.com. Illus., adv. Refereed. Circ: 4100 Paid and free. Vol. ends: Dec. Microform: PQC. Online: EBSCO Publishing, EBSCO Host; Florida Center for Library Automation; Gale; IngentaConnect; OCLC Online Computer Library Center, Inc.; ProQuest K-12 Learning Solutions; ProQuest LLC (Ann Arbor); H.W. Wilson. Reprint: PSC. *Indexed:* ABIn, ASSIA, BRI, CINAHL, EAA, ECER, ERIC, EduInd, ExcerpMed, FR, HEA, IBR, IBZ, IMFL, L&LBA, MLA-IB, PAIS, PsycInfo, SSCI, SWA. *Aud.:* Ac, Sa.

Dedicated to the field of learning disabilities, the journal publishes articles on practice, research, and theory. Articles are organized into categories such as international studies, instructional/intervention, research, definitional issues, assessment, and special issues. Each issue averages about six to eight well-referenced articles. In covering the multidisciplinary field of learning disabilities, articles have presented topics such as learning disability assessment across ethnic groups; impaired visual attention in children with dyslexia; inattentive behavior in young children; identifying interventions to remediate reading difficulties of children with learning disabilities; and examining an apprenticeship relationship in a collaborative writing context. A recent special issue covers IQ discrepancy and the LD diagnosis. Includes a classified advertising section with professional position postings. A professional calendar lists seminars and conferences on learning disabilities. An academic journal that covers the field. URL: www.ingentaconnect.com/content/proedcw/jld.

2054. *Learning Disability Quarterly.* [ISSN: 0731-9487] 1978. q. USD 114 non-member Free to members. Ed(s): David Edgburn. C L D, 11184 Antioch, Suite 405, Overland Park, KS 66210; http://www.cldinternational.org/. Illus., adv. Refereed. Circ: 3500. Vol. ends: Fall. Online: EBSCO Publishing, EBSCO Host; Florida Center for Library Automation; Gale; JSTOR (Web-based Journal Archive); OCLC Online Computer Library Center, Inc.; ProQuest LLC (Ann Arbor); H.W. Wilson. *Indexed:* ABIn, ECER, ERIC, EduInd, PsycInfo, SSCI, SWA. *Aud.:* Ac, Sa.

Published by The Council for Learning Disabilities, an international organization, this journal focuses on educational practices and theories as applied to disabilities. Articles cover a broad range of formats including assessment or remediation reports; literature reviews; theory and issue papers; original or applied research; and professional education program models. With usually six articles an issue, the journal contents cover professional development, current issues in the field, the development of effective teaching methods, teaching in inclusive classrooms, and increasing student achievement. Figures, tables, and appendixes support the research methodology used by authors. An important journal of value to both the academician and practitioner.

2055. *Professional School Counseling.* Formed by the merger of (1965-1997): *Elementary School Guidance and Counseling;* (1954-1997): *School Counselor;* Which superseded (1953-1954): *Elementary Counselor.* [ISSN: 1096-2409] 1997. 5x/yr. Free to members; Non-members, USD 115. American School Counselor Association, 1101 King St, Ste 625, Alexandria, VA 22314-2957; http://www.schoolcounselor.org. Illus., index, adv. Sample. Refereed. Vol. ends: May. Online: EBSCO Publishing, EBSCO Host; Florida Center for Library Automation; Gale; Northern Light Technology, Inc.; OCLC Online Computer Library Center, Inc.; ProQuest LLC (Ann Arbor); H.W. Wilson. *Indexed:* ABIn, AgeL, ERIC, EduInd, PsycInfo, SFSA, SWR&A. *Bk. rev.:* Number and length vary. *Aud.:* Ga, Ac.

The journal is dedicated to presenting the most current theory, research, practice, techniques, materials, and ideas for school counselors. Articles are research-based, but the journal also publishes theoretical and philosophical pieces as well as literature reviews. Each issue has eight or more articles. Article topics have included school counselors and crisis intervention; multicultural group supervision; body image in the middle school; a case study in elementary school counseling; the counseling of at-risk adolescent girls; and the importance of promoting a professional identity. A regular feature, "Perspectives from the Field," gives a brief overview of current issues or practices of concern to school counselors. Books and other resources are reviewed. This is a very relevant title for school counselors or other professionals concerned with the well-being of all elementary and high school students. URL: www.schoolcounselor.org/content.asp?contentid=235.

2056. *Psychology in the Schools.* [ISSN: 0033-3085] 1964. 8x/yr. USD 602. Ed(s): David E. McIntosh. John Wiley & Sons, Inc., 111 River St, Hoboken, NJ 07030-5774; uscs-wis@wiley.com; http://www.wiley.com. Illus., index, adv. Sample. Refereed. Circ: 1700. Vol. ends: Oct. Microform: PQC. Online: EBSCO Publishing, EBSCO Host; OhioLINK; SwetsWise Online Content; Wiley InterScience. *Indexed:* ABIn, ABS&EES, AgeL, ECER, EduInd, FR, IBR, IBZ, IMFL, L&LBA, PsycInfo, SSCI, SWA. *Bk. rev.:* 1-5, 600-2,000 words. *Aud.:* Ac.

This peer-reviewed journal is intended for the school practitioner and others working in educational institutions, including psychologists, counselors, and administrators. Articles are organized into categories of evaluation and assessment, educational practices and problems, strategies for behavioral change, and general issues. Categories are indicative of article content such as evaluation and assessment focusing on testing practices and issues. Recent testing articles cover preparing school psychologists for crisis intervention; assessing giftedness with the WISC-III and SB-IV; teacher behavior toward failing students; a review of diversity research literature in school psychology from 2000 to 2003; predicting reading levels for low-SES English-speaking children; looking at early screening profile validity; and the learning and study strategies of college students with ADHD. Two special issues are published annually that cover current topics such as psychoeducational and psychosocial functioning of Chinese children, and school psychology in the twenty-first century. Occasional test and book reviews. An important journal for school and academic libraries. URL: www3.interscience.wiley.com/cgi-bin/jhome/32084.

2057. *Remedial and Special Education.* Formed by the merger of (1981-1984): *Topics in Learning and Learning Disabilities;* (1980-1984): *Exceptional Education Quarterly;* (1978-1983): *Journal for Special Educators;* Which was formed by the 1978 merger of: *Special Children; Journal for Special Educators of the Mentally Retarded;* Which was formerly: *Digest of the Mentally Retarded;* Incorporates: *Retarded Adult.* [ISSN: 0741-9325] 1984. bi-m. GBP 114. Sage Publications, Inc., 2455 Teller Rd, Thousand Oaks, CA 91320; info@sagepub.com; http://www.sagepub.com. Illus., index, adv. Sample. Refereed. Circ: 1700 Paid and free. Microform: PQC. Online: EBSCO Publishing, EBSCO Host; Florida Center for Library Automation; Gale; IngentaConnect; OCLC Online Computer Library Center, Inc.; ProQuest LLC (Ann Arbor); H.W. Wilson. Reprint: PSC. *Indexed:* ABIn, ASSIA, CJA, EAA, ECER, ERIC, EduInd, IBR, IBZ, L&LBA, PsycInfo, SSCI. *Bk. rev.:* Number and length vary. *Aud.:* Ac, Sa.

A journal dedicated to the issues and practices of remedial and special education. Each issue averages five to six articles, which may be literature reviews, position papers, or research reports. Topics cover a broad range of issues concerning the population of underachieving and exceptional individuals. Recent article topics include inclusionary education in Italy; effects of training in universal design for learning; social skills interventions for young children with disabilities; inclusive schooling and community-referenced learning; mediated activities and science literacy; charter school enrollment of students with disabilities; and the legal and practical issues of high school graduation for students with disabilities. A special series considers peer-mediated instruction and intervention. Contributing authors are predominantly academics, including graduate students. Book reviews and a professional calendar are regular features. A journal of importance for the special education teacher and regular classroom teacher as well as those teaching in the field.

2058. *Studies in Educational Evaluation.* [ISSN: 0191-491X] 1974. 4x/yr. EUR 686. Ed(s): David Nevo. Pergamon, The Boulevard, Langford Ln, East Park, Kidlington, OX5 1GB, United Kingdom. Illus., adv. Sample. Refereed. Vol. ends: No. 3. Microform: PQC. Online: EBSCO Publishing, EBSCO Host; Gale; IngentaConnect; OhioLINK; ScienceDirect; SwetsWise Online Content. *Indexed:* ABIn, BrEdI, ERIC, EduInd, HEA, RILM. *Aud.:* Ac.

An internationally authored journal that publishes reports on evaluation studies for practitioners, students, and researchers. Focused on presenting both empirical and theoretical studies, the journal seeks articles that report on international educational systems, evaluation practices, and current evaluation issues of educational programs, institutions, personnel and student assessment. Additionally, the journal covers topics both general to the field and specific to a country or countries. Topics presented have included anti-bullying programs; evaluation of science and mathematics teacher professional development program; school composition and achievement in primary education; evaluation of an alternative teacher licensing assessment program; program evaluation using video; and Brazil's basic education evaluation system. Two thematic issues cover the findings and assessment methods of the Third International

Mathematics and Science Study (TIMSS). This is a focused journal with international coverage that is recommended for libraries that serve testing and education organizations or institutions.

Higher Education

2059. *A A U W Outlook.* Former titles (until 1988): *Graduate Woman;* (until 1978): *A A U W Journal.* [ISSN: 1044-5706] 1962. q. Non-members, USD 15. Ed(s): Jodi Lipson. American Association of University Women, 1111 16th St, NW, Washington, DC 20036; ads@aauw.org; http://www.aauw.org. Illus., adv. Circ: 150000 Paid and free. Vol. ends: Nov/Dec. Microform: PQC. *Indexed:* AgeL, PAIS. *Bk. rev.:* 1-2, 200-500 words. *Aud.:* Ga, Ac, Sa.

Published by the American Association of University Women for its members, this magazine informs and promotes the organization's mission of "equity for all women and girls, lifelong education, and positive societal changes." Regular features include an equity watch and "Word Has It," which gives the history of word definitions relating to women. Illustrated throughout with photos, the magazine has classified ads that include job opportunities. Featured brief articles have considered AAUW in the postwar era; issues of women and tech-savvy; the struggle for pay equity; 30 years of Title IX; AAUW members' reflections on voting experiences over eight decades; and the Violence Against Women Act. Member surveys, the President's Message, and an issue devoted to the AAUW's annual conference exemplify the outreach focus of the magazine to its members. An important magazine for academic libraries and for libraries that serve women's organizations. URL: www.aauw.org/outlook/index.cfm.

2060. *Academe.* Incorporates (1967-1978): *Academe;* Former titles (until 1978): *A A U P Bulletin;* (until 1955): *American Association of University Professors. Bulletin.* [ISSN: 0190-2946] 1915. bi-m. USD 68 domestic; USD 72 foreign. Ed(s): Gwendolyn Bradley, Wendi A Maloney. American Association of University Professors, 1012 14th St, NW, Ste 500, Washington, DC 20005-3465; aaup@aaup.org; http://www.aaup.org. Illus., index, adv. Refereed. Circ: 45000 Paid. Vol. ends: Nov/Dec. Microform: PMC; PQC. Online: EBSCO Publishing, EBSCO Host; Northern Light Technology, Inc.; OCLC Online Computer Library Center, Inc.; ProQuest LLC (Ann Arbor). *Indexed:* ABIn, AbAn, AgeL, AmH&L, EAA, ERIC, EduInd, HEA, HistAb, MLA-IB, PAIS, RI-1, SSCI. *Bk. rev.:* 3-4, 800-1,500 words. *Aud.:* Ac.

The journal of the American Association of University Professors (AAUP) is dedicated to presenting faculty views on issues concerning higher education. Each issue has a theme such as globalization and the university, ethics and higher education, professors and intellectual property, and assessment and accountability of faculty and institutions. Five or six featured articles cover such important topics as scientific misconduct, intellectual property and the AAUP, copyrighted materials and the web, and diversity and affirmative action, part-time and non–tenure-track faculty, and faculty retirement policy. Regular departments report on government policy and legislation pertaining to higher education, current legal issues facing academe, book reports, and censured higher education administrations. The association provides brief reports on its committees, its council, and annual meetings. The invaluable annual report on the "economic status of the profession" keeps the higher education professional informed as to faculty economic well-being. New and noteworthy items of interest are highlighted in a regular column titled "Nota Bene." A required journal for all academic libraries and special libraries. URL: www.aaup.org/publications/Academe.

2061. *Change: the magazine of higher learning.* Formerly (until 1970): *Change in Higher Education.* [ISSN: 0009-1383] 1969. bi-m. USD 151 (Individuals, USD 58; USD 24 newsstand/cover). Heldref Publications, 1319 18th St, NW, Washington, DC 20036-1802; subscribe@heldref.org; http://www.heldref.org. Illus., index, adv. Refereed. Circ: 12868 Paid. CD-ROM: ProQuest LLC (Ann Arbor). Online: EBSCO Publishing, EBSCO Host; Factiva, Inc.; Florida Center for Library Automation; Gale; Northern Light Technology, Inc.; OCLC Online Computer Library Center, Inc.; ProQuest LLC (Ann Arbor); H.W. Wilson. Reprint: PSC. *Indexed:* ABIn, AgeL, AmH&L, BRI, CBRI, CWI, EAA, ERIC, EduInd, HEA, HistAb, IBR, IBZ, RGPR. *Aud.:* Ac.

With editorial guidance from the American Association of Higher Education, *Change* presents views and opinions on current higher education issues. This journal is intended for all practitioners in higher education institutions, organizations, and government offices, and its focus is on discussion and analysis of educational programs and practices. Articles cover all aspects of higher education, including teaching methods, curriculum, students, educational philosophy, economics and finance, higher education management and administration, public policy, and professional development. Each issue contains about six articles, ranging from a brief point of view to a featured article. Article topics have included de facto privatization of public higher education; work/family policies in academia; the Carnegie Classification System; the demographics of higher education; pay equity for faculty; academic audits; evaluating state higher education performance; and changing admissions policies. Regular departments feature an editorial and a column of items of current interest to those in the field. A title important to all those in the field of higher education from administrators to department heads to faculty. URL: www.aahe.org/change.

2062. The Chronicle of Higher Education. [ISSN: 0009-5982] 1966. w. 49/yr. USD 82.50 domestic; USD 135 Canada; USD 275 elsewhere. Ed(s): Philip Semas. Chronicle of Higher Education, Inc., 1255 23rd St, NW, Ste 700, Washington, DC 20037. Illus., index, adv. Sample. Circ: 92000 Paid. Vol. ends: Aug. Microform: CIS; PQC. Online: EBSCO Publishing, EBSCO Host; Gale; LexisNexis; Northern Light Technology, Inc.; OCLC Online Computer Library Center, Inc.; ProQuest LLC (Ann Arbor); H.W. Wilson. *Indexed:* A&ATA, ABIn, ABS&EES, Agr, BRI, CBRI, CWI, ERIC, EduInd, ISTA, LRI, NTA, PRA, RI-1, RILM. *Aud.:* Ga, Ac.

Published weekly, *The Chronicle of Higher Education* is academe's resource for news and information. Although the journal is intended for higher education faculty and administrators, the contents are relevant for others interested in the field of higher education such as researchers, students, federal and state legislators, government policy makers, and taxpayers. The weekly is organized into sections: current developments and issues in higher education; regular features on faculty, research, money and management, government and politics, international, students, and athletics; the chronicle review, with letters to the editor and opinion articles; and the section on career networking, with hundreds of job listings. Additionally, twice a year *Events in Academe* indexes meetings, events, and deadlines for fellowships, grants, papers, and prizes. An annual almanac issue covers facts and statistics about U.S. higher education at both the national and state level. *CHE* is available online with a searchable archive of more than 12 years. A required standard for all academic libraries as well as higher education institutions and organizations. URL: http://chronicle.com.

2063. College and University. [ISSN: 0010-0889] 1925. q. Non-members, USD 50. Ed(s): Saira Burki, Roman S Gawkoski. American Association of Collegiate Registrars and Admissions Officers, One Dupont Circle, NW, Ste 520, Washington, DC 20036-1135; pubs@aacrao.org; http://www.aacrao.com. Illus., index, adv. Circ: 9500. Vol. ends: Summer. Microform: PQC. Online: ProQuest LLC (Ann Arbor). *Indexed:* ABIn, AgeL, BRI, CBRI, EAA, ERIC, EduInd, HEA, SSCI. *Bk. rev.:* Number and length vary. *Aud.:* Ac.

This journal of the American Association of Collegiate Registrars and Admissions Officers publishes scholarly and educational policy articles. The journal's focus is emerging and current issues, innovative practices and techniques, and administrative information technology in the profession. Each issue contains three or four featured articles. Regular features are letters to the editor, guest commentary, and book reviews. Articles have considered influence of peer groups on academic success; race and diversity in higher education; predicting final GPA of graduate school students; evaluation of enrollment management models; using non-cognitive assessment in college recruiting; and the mission of the registrar. Articles reflect the professional experience of the contributing academic authors. This journal is required for libraries that serve those working or studying in the field of higher education admissions and registration. URL: www.aacrao.org/publications/candu/c&u.htm.

2064. College Board Review. [ISSN: 0010-0951] 1947. q. USD 25. Ed(s): Paul Barry. College Board, 45 Columbus Ave, New York, NY 10023; http://www.collegeboard.com/. Illus., index. Sample. Circ: 15500. Microform: PQC. *Indexed:* ABIn, EduInd, HEA. *Aud.:* Ga, Ac.

This journal published by the College Board offers opinions and ideas on current issues and topics in the field of education. It is intended for teachers, faculty, and administrators, and its scope includes guidance, testing, financial aid, and teaching and learning. Each issue has a focus with one or more supporting articles on themes such as the SAT writing section; college admissions as big business; the affirmative action debate; and *Brown v Board of Education*. Articles are usually short opinion pieces or experience-based essays written by authors from varied higher education backgrounds. Such authors include an education editor of a newspaper, a member of the Board of Regents of the University of California, a college president, a director of college advising, and an economist with the Consortium on Financing Higher Education. An important journal for those involved or interested in the field of higher education. URL: www.collegeboard.com/about/news_info/publications.html.

2065. College Teaching. Formerly (until 1985): *Improving College and University Teaching*. [ISSN: 8756-7555] 1953. q. USD 129 (Individuals, USD 58 print & online eds.; USD 31 newsstand/cover). Ed(s): Sarah Erdreich. Heldref Publications, 1319 18th St, NW, Washington, DC 20036-1802; subscribe@heldref.org; http://www.heldref.org. Illus., adv. Refereed. Circ: 1302 Paid. CD-ROM: ProQuest LLC (Ann Arbor). Online: EBSCO Publishing, EBSCO Host; Florida Center for Library Automation; Gale; Northern Light Technology, Inc.; OCLC Online Computer Library Center, Inc.; ProQuest K-12 Learning Solutions; ProQuest LLC (Ann Arbor); H.W. Wilson. Reprint: PSC. *Indexed:* ABIn, EAA, ERIC, EduInd, HEA, IBR, IBZ. *Bk. rev.:* 2-4, 800-1,200 words. *Aud.:* Ac.

A journal dedicated to exploring the issues of teaching at the undergraduate and graduate level. Articles cover interdisciplinary topics that have a focus on application, such as active learning, teaching techniques, new classroom practices, evaluations of innovative programs and practices, and professional development. Ranging from 750 to 5,000 words, articles address such teaching issues as English literacy problems for Asian graduate students; using features films as a teaching tool; team teaching a graduate course; inclusiveness in the classroom; and Internet assignments in a political science course. Regular departments are an editorial or opinion piece and a brief column presenting a teaching idea or technique for the classroom. With a broad range of topics, this journal covers the higher education classroom. An important and informative tool for higher education instructors. URL: www.heldref.org/ct.php.

2066. Community College Journal. Former titles (until 1991): *Community, Technical, and Junior College Journal; Community and Junior College Journal; Junior College Journal*. [ISSN: 1067-1803] 1930. bi-m. USD 28 domestic. Ed(s): Cheryl Gamble. American Association of Community Colleges, One Dupont Circle, NW, Ste 410, Washington, DC 20036-1176; http://www.aacc.nche.edu. Illus., index, adv. Sample. Circ: 11000 Paid. Vol. ends: Jun/Jul. Microform: PQC. Online: ProQuest LLC (Ann Arbor). *Indexed:* ABIn, AgeL, EAA, EduInd, HEA. *Bk. rev.:* 4-7, 100-300 words. *Aud.:* Ac.

As the advocate for community colleges, the American Association of Community Colleges publishes this journal to support the advancement of community colleges as institutions of higher learning. The journal contents include feature articles, opinion pieces, news items, and issues in the field of higher education. Each issue is dedicated to a theme with five or six brief articles. Recent themes include workforce and economic development; resource development such as funding challenges; the community college student; and legislative advocacy. The intended audience of presidents, board members, administrators, faculty, and staff at two-year institutions is presented with practical content. Articles focus on trends and issues in the field such as training future faculty, community colleges and changing technology needs, and the public image of community colleges. For all community college libraries and graduate education program libraries that support those working in or preparing to work in the field. URL: www.aacc.nche.edu.

2067. *Community College Review.* [ISSN: 0091-5521] 1973. q. GBP 144. Ed(s): George B Vaughan. Sage Publications, Inc., 2455 Teller Rd, Thousand Oaks, CA 91320; info@sagepub.com; http://www.sagepub.com. Illus. Refereed. Circ: 1325 Paid. Vol. ends: Spring. Microform: PQC. Online: EBSCO Publishing, EBSCO Host; Florida Center for Library Automation; Gale; HighWire Press; OCLC Online Computer Library Center, Inc.; ProQuest K-12 Learning Solutions; ProQuest LLC (Ann Arbor); H.W. Wilson. Reprint: PSC. *Indexed:* ABIn, EAA, ERIC, EduInd, HEA, MLA-IB. *Bk. rev.:* Number and length vary. *Aud.:* Ac.

This is a refereed journal publishing articles of 12–24 pages in length on research and practice of interest to community college educators. It is intended for a broad readership including community college presidents, administrators, graduate students, and faculty. The journal articles are primarily qualitative or quantitative research. Both scholars and practitioners contribute to the journal, with topics covering faculty life at community colleges; community college and university transfer partnerships; instructional technology practices of community college faculty; a qualitative analysis of community college faculty careers; the recruitment of community college faculty; and race and ethnic relations among community college students. Regular features are a literature review on a specific topic and book reviews. An important title for libraries that serve the higher education community.

2068. *Innovative Higher Education.* Formerly (until 1983): *Alternative Higher Education.* [ISSN: 0742-5627] 1976. 5x/yr. EUR 750 print & online eds. Springer New York LLC, 233 Spring St, New York, NY 10013-1578; journals@springer-ny.com; http://www.springer.com. Illus., index, adv. Sample. Refereed. Vol. ends: Summer. Microform: PQC. Online: EBSCO Publishing, EBSCO Host; Gale; IngentaConnect; OCLC Online Computer Library Center, Inc.; OhioLINK; Springer LINK; SwetsWise Online Content. Reprint: PSC. *Indexed:* ABIn, ERIC, EduInd, HEA, HRA, IBR, IBZ, SWA. *Aud.:* Ga, Ac.

A refereed academic journal dedicated to emerging and current trends in higher education. Its focus is on providing practitioners and scholars with current strategies, programs, and innovations to enhance the field of higher education. The publication focuses on four designated types of articles: those that consider current innovative trends and practices with application beyond the context of higher education; those that discuss the effect of innovations on teaching and students; those that present scholarship and research methods broadly defined; and those that cover practice and theory appropriate for both faculty and administrators. Recent issues feature topics relevant to the field such as diversity education; allocating university resources to create on-line learning environments; use of PowerPoint technology in higher education; and flexible learning environments. This scholarly journal is highly recommended for libraries at higher education institutions or organizations. URL: www.uga.edu/ihe/ihe.html.

2069. *Journal of College Student Development.* Formerly (until 1987): *Journal of College Student Personnel.* [ISSN: 0897-5264] 1959. bi-m. USD 140. Ed(s): Florence Hamrick. The Johns Hopkins University Press, 2715 N Charles St, Baltimore, MD 21218-4363; myq@press.jhu.edu; http://www.press.jhu.edu. Illus., adv. Refereed. Circ: 695 Paid. Vol. ends: Nov. Microform: PQC. Online: EBSCO Publishing, EBSCO Host; OCLC Online Computer Library Center, Inc.; OhioLINK; Project MUSE; ProQuest K-12 Learning Solutions; ProQuest LLC (Ann Arbor); SwetsWise Online Content. Reprint: PSC. *Indexed:* ABIn, AgeL, EAA, ERIC, EduInd, HEA, PsycInfo, RILM, SSCI, SWR&A. *Bk. rev.:* 0-4, 700-1,500 words. *Aud.:* Ac, Sa.

This publication of the American College Personnel Association is focused on student development, professional development, administrative issues, and innovative programs to enhance student services. Authors contribute quantitative or qualitative research articles, research reviews, and essays on theoretical, organizational, and professional topics. A regular column describes new practices related to theory and research, programs, and techniques. Each issue generally contains about seven articles with a wide range of college student topics of interest such as understanding of binge drinking behavior; a literature review of college alcohol use and sexual behavior; predicting minority academic performance; research to determine the expectations for due process

in a campus disciplinary hearing; and a study that examines student perceptions of faculty teaching as an indicator of student persistence. Includes book reviews. A professional journal recommended for academic libraries. URL: www.jcsdonline.org.

2070. *Journal of Computers in Mathematics and Science Teaching.* [ISSN: 0731-9258] 1981. q. USD 165 (Members, USD 55; USD 40 student members). Ed(s): Ed Dubinsky. Association for the Advancement of Computing in Education, PO Box 1545, Chesapeake, VA 23327-1545; info@aace.org; http://www.aace.org. Illus., adv. Sample. Refereed. Circ: 950 Paid. Online: EBSCO Publishing, EBSCO Host; Florida Center for Library Automation; Gale; OCLC Online Computer Library Center, Inc.; ProQuest LLC (Ann Arbor); H.W. Wilson. *Indexed:* ABIn, CompLI, CompR, EAA, ERIC, EduInd, MicrocompInd, PsycInfo. *Aud.:* Ac, Sa.

An academic journal providing a venue for information on using information technology in teaching mathematics and science. It is published by the Association for the Advancement of Computing in Education, and its aim is to promote the teaching and learning of computing technologies. With an international authorship, the journal is directed to faculty, researchers, classroom teachers, and administrators. Article format includes research papers, case studies, courseware experiences, review papers, evaluations, and opinions. Issues have four to six well-referenced articles on such topics as: interactive learning in mathematics education; personalized computer-assisted problem-solving; technology and teaching, such as gender and computer-mediated communications; technology and manipulatives; the principles for design and use of simulation software in science learning; and technologies with hands-on science activities in the United States, Japan, and the Netherlands. A subject-specific journal of value to both practitioner and researcher at all education levels. URL: www.aace.org/pubs/jcmst/default.htm.

2071. *Journal of Developmental Education.* Formerly (until 1984): *Journal of Developmental and Remedial Education.* [ISSN: 0894-3907] 1978. 3x/yr. USD 37 (Individuals, USD 32). Ed(s): Milton G Spann. Appalachian State University, National Center for Developmental Education, Reich College of Education, Boone, NC 28608; http://www.ncde.appstate.edu/index.htm. Illus., index. Refereed. Circ: 5000. Vol. ends: Jan. Online: EBSCO Publishing, EBSCO Host; Northern Light Technology, Inc.; OCLC Online Computer Library Center, Inc.; ProQuest K-12 Learning Solutions; ProQuest LLC (Ann Arbor); H.W. Wilson. *Indexed:* ABIn, ERIC, EduInd, HEA, MLA-IB. *Aud.:* Ac, Sa.

The National Center for Developmental Education's publication is dedicated to the education of the academically at-risk college community. The intended readers are educators involved with academically at-risk college students including faculty, administrators, and others at postsecondary institutions. The editorial focus is on articles that relate educational theory to the practice of teaching, evaluative studies, and the dissemination of research and news in the field. Articles have examined learning disabled students' access to higher education; critical thinking; developmental mathematics in four-year institutions; program evaluation studies; comprehension monitoring for mathematical problem solving; developmental education activities; and student counseling. In addition to about four articles per issue, there are regularly featured columns listing professional conferences and workshops, and a review of computer use in the developmental classroom. An important title for all academic libraries. URL: www.ncde.appstate.edu/jde.htm.

2072. *Journal of Higher Education.* [ISSN: 0022-1546] 1930. bi-m. USD 164. Ed(s): Jason Gray, Leonard L Baird. Ohio State University Press, 180 Pressey Hall, 1070 Carmack Rd, Columbus, OH 43210-1002; ohiostatepress@osu.edu; http://www.ohiostatepress.org. Illus., adv. Refereed. Circ: 4200 Paid. Vol. ends: Nov/Dec. CD-ROM: ProQuest LLC (Ann Arbor). Microform: PMC; PQC. Online: EBSCO Publishing, EBSCO Host; Florida Center for Library Automation; Gale; JSTOR (Web-based Journal Archive); Northern Light Technology, Inc.; OCLC Online Computer Library Center, Inc.; OhioLINK; Project MUSE; ProQuest K-12 Learning Solutions; ProQuest LLC (Ann Arbor);

SwetsWise Online Content; H.W. Wilson. *Indexed:* ABIn, AgeL, AmH&L, BRI, CBRI, ChemAb, EAA, ERIC, EduInd, HEA, HistAb, MLA-IB, PhilInd, RI-1, SSA, SSCI, SWA, SWR&A. *Bk. rev.:* 4-12, 700-1,500 words. *Aud.:* Ac.

A membership journal for several higher-education associations, this is the standard title in the field of higher education. It publishes research or technical papers, professional practice papers, literature reviews, and policy papers. Article content focuses on topics of interest and importance to the higher education community. A small number of substantial articles cover the current trends and issues in the field such as women of color in academe; critical thinking through effective teaching; assessment of institutional performance; gender bias in student evaluations of teaching; faculty time allocations; dual-career couples; and racial differences in the selection of an academic major. Occasional special issues examine topics in depth, such as research and methodology, the faculty in the new millennium or higher education's social role in the community at large. Each issue contains several lengthy book reviews and a review essay. A highly recommended journal for all libraries that serve higher education institutions and organizations. URL: www.ohiostatepress.org/journals/JHE/jhemain.htm.

2073. *Liberal Education.* Incorporates: *Forum for Liberal Education;* Former titles (until 1958): *Association of American Colleges. Bulletin;* (until 1939): *Bulletin of the Association of American Colleges.* [ISSN: 0024-1822] 1915. q. Members, USD 36; Non-members, USD 50. Ed(s): Bridget Puzon. Association of American Colleges and Universities, 1818 R St, NW, Washington, DC 20009; http://www.aacu.org/. Illus., index. Circ: 5000. Vol. ends: Nov/Dec. Microform: PQC. Online: EBSCO Publishing, EBSCO Host; Florida Center for Library Automation; Gale; Northern Light Technology, Inc.; ProQuest K-12 Learning Solutions; ProQuest LLC (Ann Arbor). *Indexed:* ABIn, AgeL, AmH&L, ERIC, EduInd, HEA, HistAb, MLA-IB, SSCI. *Aud.:* Ac.

A journal of the Association of American Colleges and Universities, dedicated to improving undergraduate education. This journal is a voice of the association and a resource for the higher education community, and its contents highlight liberal education theory and its practical application. Three sections include a featured topic with three or four supporting articles, a perspective section with how-to pieces, and an opinion article. Featured topics have been the Bringing Theory to Practice Project; faculty work; academic freedom; and educating for personal and social responsibility. For all libraries that serve the undergraduate education community and graduate schools of education. URL: www.aacu.org/liberaleducation/index.cfm.

2074. *Research in Higher Education.* [ISSN: 0361-0365] 1973. 8x/yr. EUR 1028 print & online eds. Ed(s): John C Smart. Springer New York LLC, 233 Spring St, New York, NY 10013-1578; journals@springer-ny.com; http://www.springer.com. Illus., adv. Refereed. Vol. ends: No. 4. Microform: PQC. Online: EBSCO Publishing, EBSCO Host; Gale; IngentaConnect; OCLC Online Computer Library Center, Inc.; OhioLINK; Springer LINK; SwetsWise Online Content. Reprint: PSC. *Indexed:* ABIn, AgeL, EAA, ERIC, EduInd, HEA, IBR, IBZ, SSCI, SWA. *Aud.:* Ac.

The journal of the Association for Institutional Research is dedicated to improving the functioning of higher education institutions. Articles are written for an audience of higher education personnel, including institutional planners, administrators, and student personnel specialists. Professional papers focus on quantitative studies of higher education procedures. Areas of focus include administration and faculty, curriculum and instruction, student characteristics, and recruitment and admissions. Each issue contains about five lengthy, well-referenced articles addressing subjects such as scholarship of teaching and learning; dropout behavior for college undergraduates; educational attainment for blacks and whites; research on college students' academic coping style and academic performance; evaluating MBA program admissions criteria; institutional approaches to student assessment; and a study focusing on student preference for private over public institutions. A standard journal for all academic libraries and higher education institutions and organizations. URL: http://airweb.org/page.asp?page=89.

2075. *The Review of Higher Education.* Formerly (until 1978): *Higher Education Review.* [ISSN: 0162-5748] 1977. q. USD 160. Ed(s): Amaury Nora. The Johns Hopkins University Press, 2715 N Charles St, Baltimore, MD 21218-4363; http://muse.jhu.edu. Illus., adv. Refereed. Circ: 2184 Paid. Microform: PQC. Online: Chadwyck-Healey Inc.; EBSCO Publishing, EBSCO Host; OCLC Online Computer Library Center, Inc.; OhioLINK; Project MUSE; ProQuest LLC (Ann Arbor); SwetsWise Online Content. Reprint: PSC. *Indexed:* EAA, ERIC, HEA, IBR, IBZ, PsycInfo, SSCI, SWA. *Bk. rev.:* Occasional, essay length. *Aud.:* Ac.

The Association for the Study of Higher Education publishes this scholarly journal to report on the issues and trends affecting the field of higher education. The *RHE* contains peer-reviewed articles, essays, studies, and research findings. Issues are analyzed, examined, investigated, and described in articles focusing on topics important to the study of higher education. Recent issues have included Hispanic college degree attainment; shaping institutional environments; college freshmen and social adjustment; graduate student unionization; the roles and challenges of deans of higher education; current demographics of higher education; an analysis of gender differences in faculty salaries; and fiscal ability of public universities to compete for faculty. The review essay looks at recently published titles on a topic such as a historical perspective on higher education planning. Available in an online edition. An important journal to inform all those working or interested in the field of higher education. URL: www.press.jhu.edu/journals/review_of_higher_education.

2076. *Student Affairs Journal Online.* 1996. irreg. Ed(s): Steve Eubanks. Student Affairs Journal Online, PO Box 1682, Glendora, CA 91740; connect@digiserve.com; http://www.digiserve.com/connect/sajo/. *Indexed:* HEA. *Bk. rev.:* Number and length vary. *Aud.:* Ac.

A journal focused on technology and Student Affairs. This is intended for practitioners, researchers, and professionals in the field, and it contributes to a better understanding of college students and how to support and serve them. Scholarly articles consider primary research, new and innovative programs, and technology issues. Contributors have written on how students are using technology to be politically and socially active; the YouTube phenomenon; best practices for student affairs professionals who are members of online networking communities; things to consider when using Facebook; what motivates students to enroll in online courses; the use of bulletin boards as community-building tools; an argument for historical research in student affairs; and Japanese students' adjustment to American colleges based on gender differences. Regular reviews cover books, software, and web resources. With a broad coverage of issues and resources, this title is highly recommended for the student affairs practitioner, researcher, and academic community. URL: http://studentaffairs.com/ejournal.

Homeschooling

2077. *Eclectic Homeschool Online.* 1996. irreg. Eclectic Homeschool Association, PO Box 5304, Fallon, NV 89407-5304. *Aud.:* Ga.

Published from a Christian worldview, this magazine promotes creative homeschooling through unique resources, teaching methods, and online tips. The editor states that articles and resources are not limited to purely Christian material. There is a discussion list and newsletter. A recent issue contains tips for motivating children; a feature on the composer Richard Wagner; applying math principles for solving word problems; and an art history unit. Recommended for public libraries and the homeschooling community. URL: www.eho.org.

2078. *Home Education Magazine.* [ISSN: 0888-4633] 1984. bi-m. USD 32. Ed(s): Helen E Hegener. Home Education Magazine, PO Box 1083, Tonasket, WA 98855. Illus., adv. Sample. Circ: 28000. Vol. ends: Dec. *Aud.:* Ga.

This journal is one of the oldest homeschooling magazines. Each issue presents feature articles, columns by various contributors, political commentary, and issues affecting homeschooling. Columns and articles have covered such topics as regulation of homeschooling; classic homeschooling books; advice on a weekly park day; writing group strategies; and the relationship between schools and homeschools. It also contains interviews, resources, and reviews. The web site offers subscription information, current issue content, a blog, and an archive of selected articles and columns. Highly recommended for public libraries and the homeschooling community. URL: www.homeedmag.com.

2079. Home Educator's Family Times. 1993. bi-m. USD 12. Home Educator's Family Times, Inc., PO Box 6442, Brunswick, ME 04039. *Aud.*: Ga.

A homeschool publication focused on new or veteran homeschool families. Content covers research on education and home school issues, homeschool strategies, how-to articles, special education needs, recommended curriculum resources, and highlights from the New England Regional Conference. The article archives currently date back to 1995 with selected issues. Current issue articles cover such topics as college and homeschooling; evaluating learning progress; and homeschooling and family unity. Recommended for public libraries and the homeschooling community. URL: www.homeeducator.com/FamilyTimes.

2080. Homeschooling Horizons Magazine. [ISSN: 1499-187X] 2000. m. 10/yr. CND 23.95 domestic; USD 23.95. A H M B Horizons, 42 Prevost RR 7, Vaudreuil-Dorion, PQ J7V 8P5, Canada. *Aud.*: Ga.

This magazine focuses on offering practical advice and encouragement to homeschooling parents, both new and veteran home educators. Although based in Canada, this magazine has a U.S. readership. It sponsors annual fall conventions. The editors strive for innovative ideas and a global perspective in its content. Regular features include letters from readers; a spotlight on Canadian authors; curriculum reviews; project and activity pages; and a monthly specialty section on a variety of topics. Recommended for public libraries and the homeschooling community. URL: www.homeschoolinghorizons.com.

2081. Homeschooling Today. [ISSN: 1073-2217] 1992. bi-m. USD 21.99 domestic; USD 31.99 foreign. Ed(s): Stacy McDonald, Marilyn Rockett. Family Reformation, LLC, PO Box 436, Barker, TX 77413; service@homeschooltoday.com. Adv. Circ: 30000. *Aud.*: Ga.

Focused on the mechanics, mission, and metrics of homeschooling. A recent issue focuses on literature and includes articles on the lost art of narration, a unit study on authors, and organizing a home library. Other issues have covered homeschooling for single parents; life after homeschool; homeschooling special-needs children; the church as a support group; and the Jamestown legacy as a unit study. Recommended for public libraries and the homeschooling community. URL: www.homeschooltoday.com.

2082. Practical Homeschooling. [ISSN: 1075-4741] 1993. bi-m. USD 29 USD 19.95 domestic. Home Life, Inc., PO Box 1190, Fenton, MO 63026-1190; editor@home-school.com. *Indexed*: CPerI. *Aud.*: Ga.

Offers detailed product reviews, news shorts, and special features. URL: www.home-school.com/.

Specific Subjects and Teaching Methods

ADULT EDUCATION

2083. Adult Basic Education and Literacy Journal. Former titles (until 2007): *Adult Basic Education;* (until vol.14, no.3, 1990): *Adult Literacy and Basic Education.* [ISSN: 1934-2322] 1977. 3x/yr. USD 70 (Individuals, USD 65). Ed(s): Ken Melichar. Commission on Adult Basic Education, 1320 Jamesville Ave, Syracuse, NY 13210; http://www.coabe.org/. Illus., index, adv. Sample. Refereed. Circ: 1500 Paid. Vol. ends: Fall. Microform: PQC. Online: EBSCO Publishing, EBSCO Host; Northern Light Technology, Inc.; ProQuest LLC (Ann Arbor). *Indexed*: ABIn, AgeL, BRI, ERIC, EduInd. *Bk. rev.*: 1, 1,000 words, signed. *Aud.*: Ac, Sa.

A peer-reviewed scholarly journal dedicated to improving educators' efforts with adult literacy. The journal's audience consists of adult educators working in volunteer-based, community-based, and institution-based literacy programs. Written for the practitioner, this journal publishes critical essays, research reviews, and theoretical or philosophical articles. With an emphasis on practical

relevance, contents have considered the welfare-to-work curriculum; refining family literacy practice; teaching reading to adults; adult numeracy education; reading strategies; a research study with resulting guidelines and practical applications for using technology in the classroom; a review process for reviewing the adult literacy provision at the community provider level; and practitioner-based inquiry. A highly recommended title for libraries that serve adult literacy educators. URL: www.coabe.org/index.cfm?fuseaction=journal.html.

2084. Adult Education Quarterly: a journal of research and theory. Formerly (until 1983): *Adult Education;* Which was formed by the 1950 merger of: *Adult Education Journal; Adult Education Bulletin;* Which was superseded in part (in 1941): *Journal of Adult Education.* [ISSN: 0741-7136] 1950. q. GBP 171. Ed(s): Robert J Hill, Bradley C Courtenay. Sage Publications, Inc., 2455 Teller Rd, Thousand Oaks, CA 91320; info@sagepub.com; http://www.sagepub.com. Illus., index, adv. Sample. Refereed. Circ: 5000. Vol. ends: Summer. Microform: PQC. Online: CSA; EBSCO Publishing, EBSCO Host; Gale; HighWire Press; OCLC Online Computer Library Center, Inc.; OhioLINK; SAGE Publications, Inc., SAGE Journals Online; SwetsWise Online Content; H.W. Wilson. Reprint: PSC. *Indexed*: ABIn, AgeL, BRI, BrEdI, CBRI, EAA, EduInd, L&LBA, PsycInfo, RI-1, SSCI, SWA. *Bk. rev.*: 3, 1,000 words. *Aud.*: Ac, Sa.

A refereed journal dedicated to promoting the practice and understanding of adult and continuing education. Geared to scholars and practitioners, the journal aims to be inclusive regarding adult and continuing education topics and issues. Articles cover a wide range of research, including surveys, experimental designs, case studies, ethnographic observations, theory, historical investigations, or analyses. The present editors' goal is to increase the diversity of scholarly research to include newer forms such as feminist or postmodernist research, and to include international and interdisciplinary investigations. Each issue reflects the publication's focus on research and theory with, for example, adult learning in new social movements; the postmodern theory of lifelong learning; international humanitarian workers; Cambodian women's participation in adult ESL programs; a focus on workplace pedagogy; an assessment study of worker education programs and globalization; and a field study of nonparticipation in literacy programs among Mayan adults. The book review policy of the journal is also inclusive, seeking to define the field of adult and continuing education as multidisciplinary and broad-based. Book reviews consider publications indirectly related, such as cultural studies, work and the economy, distance learning, and international development. A standard title for academic libraries as well as adult education organizations. URL: http://aeq.sagepub.com.

Educational Media International. See Media and AV section.

2085. Journal of Adolescent and Adult Literacy. Former titles (until 1995): *Journal of Reading;* (until 1964): *Journal of Developmental Reading.* [ISSN: 1081-3004] 1957. 8x/yr. USD 122 (Individuals, USD 61; Students, USD 37). Ed(s): Todd Goodson. International Reading Association, 800 Barksdale Rd, Newark, DE 19714-8139; journals@reading.org; http://www.reading.org. Illus., index, adv. Refereed. Circ: 15000 Paid. Vol. ends: May. Microform: PQC. Online: EBSCO Publishing, EBSCO Host; Florida Center for Library Automation; Gale; OCLC Online Computer Library Center, Inc.; ProQuest K-12 Learning Solutions; ProQuest LLC (Ann Arbor); H.W. Wilson. *Indexed*: ABIn, ABS&EES, AgeL, ArtHuCI, BEL&L, BRI, CBRI, ECER, ERIC, EduInd, L&LBA, MLA-IB, MRD, RILM, SSCI, SWA. *Bk. rev.*: 3, 800 words. *Aud.*: Ac.

A peer-reviewed journal dedicated to providing a forum for educators working in the field of literacy and language arts for older learners. Published by the International Reading Association, the focus is on innovative methods of teaching and researching literacy, and the issues and concerns of literacy professionals. Original articles present practical, theoretical, or research topics such as extracurricular reading habits of college students in Taiwan; preservice teacher understandings of adolescent literacy development; engaging student teachers to address illiteracy in content area classrooms; teaching English and literature to ESL students; a survey of content area reading strategies; cross-age tutoring; a workshop format and instruction strategy for struggling adolescent readers; and adolescent vocabulary development. Regularly featured columns present opinions and viewpoints, technology issues, and literacy requirements in the current work environment. Each issue contains lengthy reviews of books for adolescents, professional materials, and classroom materials. Recommended for school and academic libraries. URL: www.reading.org/publications/journals/jaal.

Learning and Leading with Technology. See Classroom Magazines/Teacher and Professional section.

THE ARTS

2086. Art Education. Incorporates (1970-1980): *Art Teacher.* [ISSN: 0004-3125] 1948. bi-m. USD 50 domestic; USD 75 foreign. Ed(s): Thomas A Hatfield, Lynn Ezell. National Art Education Association, 1916 Association Dr, Reston, VA 20191-1590; kemery@naea-reston.org; http://www.naea-reston.org. Illus., index, adv. Refereed. Circ: 20000 Controlled. Vol. ends: Nov. Microform: PQC. Online: JSTOR (Web-based Journal Archive); Northern Light Technology, Inc.; OCLC Online Computer Library Center, Inc.; ProQuest LLC (Ann Arbor); H.W. Wilson. *Indexed:* ABIn, ERIC, EduInd, IBR, IBZ. *Aud.:* Hs, Ac.

This journal of the National Art Education Association supports the association's goal of promoting art education. Articles on current issues and exemplary practices in visual arts education serve the professional needs and interests of art educators at all educational levels. Theme-focused issues have addressed topics such as exemplary content, curricula, and criteria for assessment in art education, defining art education as a field, mediating culture, secondary art education, visual culture, museum education, art education in and beyond the classroom, and art education around the world. In addition to the three or four themed articles, each issue has instructional resources, including four full-color art reproductions and a lesson plan. Position advertisements are a regular item. Highly recommended for school and academic libraries. URL: www.naea-reston.org.

2087. Arts and Activities: the nation's leading arts education magazine. Formerly: *Junior Arts and Activities.* [ISSN: 0004-3931] 1932. m. Sep.-June. USD 30 domestic; USD 44.95 foreign. Ed(s): Maryellen Bridge. Publishers Development Corp., 12345 World Trade Dr, San Diego, CA 92128. Illus., index. Sample. Circ: 22000. Microform: PQC. Online: EBSCO Publishing, EBSCO Host; Florida Center for Library Automation; Gale; OCLC Online Computer Library Center, Inc.; ProQuest K-12 Learning Solutions; ProQuest LLC (Ann Arbor); H.W. Wilson. *Indexed:* ABIn, EduInd, MRD. *Bk. rev.:* 2-6, 50-100 words. *Aud.:* Ems, Hs, Ga, Ac.

A magazine dedicated to providing an exchange of professional experiences, opinions, and new ideas for art educators. Contributors share strategies for art instruction, approaches to art history, techniques for engaging students in evaluating art, and programs and lessons to expand students' appreciation of art. Articles have covered a broad range of topics such as art appreciation, ceramics, computer art, drawing and painting, mixed media, papier-mache, collage, and three-dimensional design for grades K–12. A regular feature is a pullout clip-and-save art print. For the practitioner, the magazine publishes an annual buyers' guide and a listing of summer art programs. Recommended for school libraries and academic libraries with art education programs. URL: www.artsandactivities.com.

2088. Arts Education Policy Review. Former titles (until 1992): *Design for Arts in Education;* (until 1977): *Design.* [ISSN: 1063-2913] 1879. bi-m. USD 135 (Individuals, USD 62 print & online eds.). Heldref Publications, 1319 18th St, NW, Washington, DC 20036-1802; subscribe@heldref.org; http://www.heldref.org. Illus., index, adv. Refereed. Circ: 882 Paid. CD-ROM: ProQuest LLC (Ann Arbor). Microform: PQC. Online: Chadwyck-Healey Inc.; EBSCO Publishing, EBSCO Host; Florida Center for Library Automation; Gale; Northern Light Technology, Inc.; OCLC Online Computer Library Center, Inc.; ProQuest K-12 Learning Solutions; ProQuest LLC (Ann Arbor); H.W. Wilson. Reprint: PSC. *Indexed:* ABIn, ArtInd, BRI, ERIC, EduInd, IBR, IBZ, RGPR, RILM. *Bk. rev.:* 1, essay length. *Aud.:* Ac.

This journal provides a forum for the discussion of arts education policy issues in grades preK–12, nationally and internationally. With a focus on presenting current and controversial ideas and issues, articles focus on the application of policy analysis to arts education topics. Contributors present a broad range of perspectives and ideas on arts education. Articles cover music teacher education in the twenty-first century; values and voice in dance education; technology as arts-based education; re-envisioning the Arts Ph.D.; and issues from the improvement of music teacher education to national theater standards. A recent issue of the journal offers a symposium on arts education from past to present. Readership includes teachers, university faculty, education students, graduate students, policymakers, and others interested in arts in education. Recommended for all school and academic libraries. URL: www.heldref.org/aepr.php.

2089. School Arts: the art education magazine for teachers. [ISSN: 0036-6463] 1901. m. Sep.-May. USD 24.95 domestic; USD 34.95 Canada; USD 39.95 elsewhere. Ed(s): Nancy Walkup. Davis Publications, Inc. (Worcester), 50 Portland St, Printers Bldg, Worcester, MA 01608; contactus@davis-art.com; http://www.davis-art.com. Illus., index, adv. Sample. Circ: 20000 Paid and controlled. Vol. ends: May/Jun. Microform: NBI; PQC. Online: Florida Center for Library Automation; Gale. *Indexed:* ABIn, ASIP, BRI, CBRI, ERIC, EduInd, MRD. *Aud.:* Ga, Ac.

A magazine dedicated to inspiring art and classroom teachers at the elementary and secondary level. Each issue has a theme such as art for life and work, which includes articles on literacy learning, art criticism, bookmaking and papermaking, and art and poetry. Short focused articles present curriculum ideas and plans, art technique applications, exemplary art programs, instruction and assessment methods, teaching art to special populations, and professional development. With the practitioner as audience, the magazine contains classroom instructional materials organized by educational level, and extensive advertisements for art materials. Highly recommended for all school libraries. URL: www.davis-art.com/Portal/SchoolArts/SAdefault.aspx.

2090. Studies in Art Education: a journal of issues and research in art education. [ISSN: 0039-3541] 1959. q. USD 25 domestic; USD 45 foreign. Ed(s): Candice Stout. National Art Education Association, 1916 Association Dr, Reston, VA 20191-1590; http://www.naea-reston.org. Illus., index. Refereed. Circ: 3500. Vol. ends: Summer. Microform: PQC. Online: JSTOR (Web-based Journal Archive); Northern Light Technology, Inc.; OCLC Online Computer Library Center, Inc.; ProQuest K-12 Learning Solutions; ProQuest LLC (Ann Arbor); H.W. Wilson. *Indexed:* ABIn, ABM, ERIC, EduInd, SWA. *Bk. rev.:* 1-3, 500-1,000 words. *Aud.:* Ac.

Published by the National Art Education Association, this scholarly journal supports the association's goal to promote art education through professional development and to disseminate knowledge and information about the field. The journal reports on historical, philosophical, or empirical research in the field of art education as well as applicable research in related disciplines. An interdisciplinary approach to art education is a focus of the journal's content. Issues cover a wide variety of topics and reflect the trends and issues of art education research. Articles have examined the place of content in teaching adolescent artists, mentoring in the art classroom, and the retention of good art teachers in the public school classrooms. Highly recommended for all academic libraries.

2091. Visual Arts Research: educational, historical, philosophical and psychological perspectives. Former titles (until 1982): *Review of Research in Visual Arts Education;* (until 1975): *Review of Research in Visual and Environmental Education.* [ISSN: 0736-0770] 1973. s-a. USD 55 (Individuals, USD 45). Ed(s): Elizabeth Delacruz. University of Illinois at Urbana-Champaign, School of Art and Design, 143 Art and Design Bldg, 408 E Peabody Dr, Champaign, IL 61820; http://www.art.uiuc.edu/a+d/index.html. Illus., adv. Refereed. Circ: 400. Vol. ends: Fall. *Indexed:* ABIn, EduInd, PsycInfo. *Aud.:* Ac.

A journal dedicated to research on teaching and learning in the visual arts. Article contents cover critical and cultural studies, curriculum research and development, art education history, research, and theory, aesthetics, and phenomenology. A regular column reports on published dissertations that are relevant to the field of visual arts instruction. Academic contributors, predominantly from the United States, present papers concerned with current issues and ideas such as aesthetic thinking of young children and adolescents; art and incarcerated women; an assessment tool for an inner-city arts program; and art education as multicultural education. A recent special issue contains versions of papers from a visual culture gathering in November 2004. A focused journal for a specific audience.

BIOLOGY

2092. *The American Biology Teacher.* [ISSN: 0002-7685] 1938. 9x/yr. Membership, USD 90. Ed(s): Cheryl Merrill, Ann Haley Mackenzie. National Association of Biology Teachers, Inc., 12030 Sunrise Valley Dr, Ste 110, Reston, VA 20191; office@nabt.org; http://www.nabt.org. Illus., index, adv. Refereed. Circ: 12000 Paid. Vol. ends: Nov/Dec. Microform: PQC. Online: BioOne; CSA; OCLC Online Computer Library Center, Inc.; OhioLINK; ProQuest K-12 Learning Solutions; ProQuest LLC (Ann Arbor). *Indexed:* ABIn, ABS&EES, Agr, BRI, BiolDig, CABA, DSA, ERIC, EduInd, EnvAb, EnvInd, ForAb, GSI, GardL, HortAb, IndVet, MRD, RILM, S&F, SCI, SSCI, VB. *Bk. rev.:* 4-8, 300-800 words. *Aud.:* Ems, Hs, Ac.

This is the official journal of the National Association of Biology Teachers, and it is aimed at teachers of high school and undergraduate biology students. Most authors are biology educators (mainly at the college level, though some are high school teachers) or professional biologists. The journal publishes three to five articles monthly. These may include reviews of biology research or topics of current interest, discussion of social and ethical issues in biology education, results of studies on teaching techniques, or approaches for use in the classroom. The "How-to-Do-It" section includes four to six articles focusing on specific projects for the laboratory or field. Most issues have reviews of audiovisual materials or computer resources in "Classroom Technology Reviews." "Biology Today" presents essays by the section editor on interesting topics of current interest. Announcements and society news are also featured. Given the concern about science education in this country, this title should be of interest to anyone teaching undergraduate introductory biology courses, junior and senior high teachers, and even parents home-schooling older children.

COMMUNICATION ARTS

2093. *College Composition and Communication.* [ISSN: 0010-096X] 1950. q. Members, USD 25; Non-members, USD 75; Students, USD 12.50. Ed(s): Deborah Holdstein. National Council of Teachers of English, 1111 W Kenyon Rd, Urbana, IL 61801-1096; membership@ncte.org; http://www.ncte.org. Illus., index, adv. Refereed. Circ: 10000. Vol. ends: Dec. Microform: PQC. Online: Chadwyck-Healey Inc.; EBSCO Publishing, EBSCO Host; JSTOR (Web-based Journal Archive); ProQuest LLC (Ann Arbor). *Indexed:* ABIn, AbAn, AmHI, ArtHuCI, BRI, CBRI, ERIC, EduInd, IBR, IBZ, L&LBA, MLA-IB, SSCI, SWA. *Bk. rev.:* 1, essay length. *Aud.:* Ac.

This academic journal, published by the Conference on College Composition and Communication, addresses the issues and concerns of college composition instructors. Articles provide a forum for critical work on the study and teaching of college-level composition and reading. Article content covers all aspects of the profession, including teaching practices, the historical or institutional background of an educational practice, and current issues and trends in related disciplines. Although focused on those responsible for the teaching of composition at the college level, this journal will be of interest to administrators of composition programs, community college instructors, researchers, technical writers, graduate assistants, and others involved with college writing instruction. Each issue contains featured articles, review essays, book reviews, and contributor responses to published research theory or practice. Contributors have considered visual communication in the teaching of writing; service learning programs; plagiarism in policy and pedagogy; economics of academic staffing for first-year writing courses; and responding to student writing. A highly recommended title for academic libraries. URL: www.ncte.org/groups/cccc.

2094. *College English.* [ISSN: 0010-0994] 1939. bi-m. Members, USD 25; Non-members, USD 75; Students, USD 12.50. Ed(s): John Schilb. National Council of Teachers of English, 1111 W Kenyon Rd, Urbana, IL 61801-1096; cnimz@ncte.org; http://www.ncte.org. Illus., index, adv. Refereed. Circ: 8000. Vol. ends: Dec. Microform: PMC; PQC. Online: Chadwyck-Healey Inc.; EBSCO Publishing, EBSCO Host; JSTOR (Web-based Journal Archive); OCLC Online Computer Library Center, Inc.; ProQuest LLC (Ann Arbor). *Indexed:* ABIn, AbAn, AmHI, ArtHuCI, BEL&L, BRI, ECER, ERIC, EduInd, HumInd, IAPV, IBR, IBZ, L&LBA, LT&LA, MLA-IB, PhilInd, SSCI. *Bk. rev.:* 1-3, essay length. *Aud.:* Ac.

This refereed journal of the College Section of the National Council of Teachers of English (NCTE) provides a forum for scholars on English Studies. Topics covered include but are not limited to literature, linguistics, literacy, critical theory, reading theory, rhetoric, composition, pedagogy, and professional issues. Each issue has three or four articles as well as occasional opinion pieces, book reviews, reader comments and author responses, and NCTE news and announcements. Authors have published literary articles on topics such as autistic students and appropriate pedagogy, and D. H. Lawrence and the dialogical principal. Other issues have covered creative nonfiction and an empirical study on composition. A standard for all academic libraries. URL: www.ncte.org/pubs/journals/ce.

2095. *English Education: official journal of the Conference on English Education and Communication.* Formerly (until 1968): *Conference on English Education. Selected Addresses Delivered.* [ISSN: 0007-8204] 1963. 4x/yr. USD 75 (Individuals, USD 25). Ed(s): LouAnn Reid. National Council of Teachers of English, 1111 W Kenyon Rd, Urbana, IL 61801-1096; rsmith@ncte.org; http://www.ncte.org. Illus., index, adv. Sample. Refereed. Circ: 3100. Vol. ends: Dec. Microform: PQC. Online: EBSCO Publishing, EBSCO Host; ProQuest LLC (Ann Arbor). *Indexed:* ABIn, ERIC, EduInd, SSCI. *Aud.:* Ac.

Dedicated to the education of teachers of English, reading, and language arts, the Conference on English Education focuses its journal on preservice training and in-service development. Issues relevant to the profession are considered such as preservice and in-service education, professional development, student teacher evaluation, English curriculum, and trends in teacher education programs nationwide. Each issue has three or four articles covering such topics as expressive language and the art of English teaching; self-motivated student literacies; intertextual composition; and preparation of English-teacher educators. Readership is aimed at a broad range of teacher education personnel, including college and university instructors of teachers; in-service educators; teacher consultants; curriculum coordinators; and classroom teachers supervising student teachers. A highly recommended journal for libraries that serve education programs. URL: www.ncte.org/pubs/journals/ee.

2096. *English Journal.* [ISSN: 0013-8274] 1912. bi-m. Members, USD 25; Non-members, USD 75; Students, USD 12.50. Ed(s): Margaret Chambers, Virginia Monseau. National Council of Teachers of English, 1111 W Kenyon Rd, Urbana, IL 61801-1096; rsmith@ncte.org. Illus., index, adv. Sample. Refereed. Circ: 51000 Paid. Vol. ends: Dec. Microform: PMC; PQC. Online: EBSCO Publishing, EBSCO Host; JSTOR (Web-based Journal Archive); OCLC Online Computer Library Center, Inc.; ProQuest LLC (Ann Arbor). *Indexed:* ABIn, BRI, CBRI, ECER, ERIC, EduInd, FLI, IAPV, L&LBA, LRI, LT&LA, MLA-IB, MRD, SSCI. *Bk. rev.:* 6, 500-700 words. *Aud.:* Ac.

A publication of the National Council of Teachers of English (NCTE), this journal serves an audience of middle school, junior high school, and senior high school teachers, as well as supervisors and teacher educators. This refereed publication covers current practices and theory in teaching composition, reading skills, oral language, literature, and varied media use. Featured articles may focus on a particular issue or topic while regular columns review books and classroom material; provide a forum for the exchange of teaching suggestions and ideas; and inform as to NCTE news and activities. With 15 or more articles per issue, the featured topic is well covered by both practical applications and theoretical perspectives. Topics have included extracurricular and co-curricular English; Shakespeare for a new age; cultural issues relevant to the study of language; the issues and challenges of technology as a teaching tool; and the school and the community. A recommended journal for school and academic libraries. URL: www.ncte.org/pubs/journals/ej.

2097. Kairos: a journal for teachers of writing in webbed environment.
[ISSN: 1521-2300] 1996. 3x/yr. Free. Ed(s): Douglas Eyman, James A. Inman. Kairos, jinman@english.cas.usf.edu; http://129.118.38.138/kairos/default.htm. Refereed. *Indexed:* MLA-IB, OTA. *Aud.:* Ac, Sa.

A refereed "product" dedicated to exploring writing, learning, and teaching in hypertextual environments. This journal is intended for teachers, researchers, and writing tutors at the higher education level, and its focus is technical and business writing, professional communication, creative writing, composition, and literature. Contributions to the journal must be written in/for hypertext on the web. The journal's contributions cover empirical research reports, sample syllabi, theoretical essays, commentary, and software reviews. Each issue has a themed focus with regular columns for news and reviews. Features have considered critical issues in computers and writing, technology and the language arts in the K–12 classroom, and hypertext fiction/hypertext poetry. A highly recommended resource for the secondary education and higher education community. URL: http://english.ttu.edu/kairos.

2098. Language Arts. Former titles (until 1975): *Elementary English;* (until 1946): *Elementary English Review.* [ISSN: 0360-9170] 1924. bi-m. Members, USD 25; Non-members, USD 75; Students, USD 12.50. Ed(s): Gloria Kauffman, Jean Schroeder. National Council of Teachers of English, 1111 W Kenyon Rd, Urbana, IL 61801-1096; http://www.ncte.org. Illus., index, adv. Sample. Refereed. Circ: 11500. Vol. ends: Dec. Microform: PQC. Online: EBSCO Publishing, EBSCO Host; OCLC Online Computer Library Center, Inc.; ProQuest LLC (Ann Arbor). *Indexed:* ABIn, BRI, CBRI, ERIC, EduInd, L&LBA, LT&LA, MLA-IB, MRD. *Bk. rev.:* 30-35 children's books. *Aud.:* Ac.

A title published by the National Council of Teachers of English for elementary teachers and teacher educators of language arts. Original articles focus on all aspects of language arts learning and teaching from preschool through middle school age levels. Issues are theme focused with the exception of a single non-themed issue per volume. Recent themes consider NCLB and literacy practices in teacher education; local languages and literacies; the cross-cultural convergence with language arts; new theories and ideas on writing instruction; and literacy, logic, and intuition. Each issue gives classroom strategies, methods, research reports, and opinions. Recommended for school and academic libraries that serve an education program.

2099. Learning, Media & Technology (Online Edition). Formerly (until 2005): *Journal of Educational Media (Online Edition).* [ISSN: 1743-9892] 2000. 3x/yr. GBP 615. Routledge, 4 Park Sq, Milton Park, Abingdon, OX14 4RN, United Kingdom; info@routledge.co.uk; http://www.routledge.co.uk. *Bk. rev.:* Number and length vary. *Aud.:* Ac.

This title, incorporating the former journal, *Education, Communication, & Media,* is an international peer-reviewed publication focused on innovative media and educational technologies. Recent special issues have included media education and digital technologies, and researching the overlap between computer games and education. Articles include a case study on children learning new media skills, remixing multimodal resources in Norway, computer games and media learning, and digital media production in informal learning situations. Another issue covers topics such as teaching technology within an Art & Design higher education curriculum, feminizing technology, development of a video database for language education, and effective pedagogy for using an interactive whiteboard with mathematics and modern languages. The journal includes an editorial, a section entitled "Viewpoints," and book reviews. Highly recommended for academic and research institutions.

2100. Reading Improvement: a journal for the improvement of reading teaching. Formerly: *Reading in High School.* [ISSN: 0034-0510] 1963. q. USD 50 (Individuals, USD 40). Ed(s): George Uhlig. Project Innovation, Inc., PO Box 8508, Mobile, AL 36689-0508; guhlig007@yahoo.com; http://www.projectinnovation.biz. Illus., index, adv. Sample. Refereed. Circ: 1100 Paid. Vol. ends: Winter. Microform: PQC. Online:

EBSCO Publishing, EBSCO Host; Florida Center for Library Automation; Gale; OCLC Online Computer Library Center, Inc.; ProQuest LLC (Ann Arbor); H.W. Wilson. *Indexed:* ABIn, ERIC, EduInd, L&LBA, RILM. *Bk. rev.:* 0-3, 200-300 words. *Aud.:* Ac.

A journal dedicated to improving the pedagogy and practice of the teaching of reading. Covering all levels of instruction, the journal publishes investigative reports and theoretical papers. Each issue contains five to seven articles with a broad range of topics, such as secondary students' recreational reading patterns; English language learners and content reading; successful implementation of the America Reads Program; reading English as a foreign language; recommendations for reading improvement and achievement in multicultural settings; and computer literacy for workplace development. Recommended for school and academic libraries.

2101. Reading Research and Instruction. Former titles (until vol.25): *Reading World; Journal of the Reading Specialist.* [ISSN: 0886-0246] 1961. q. Membership, USD 100. Ed(s): Sherry Kragler, Carolyn Walker. College Reading Association, c/o John A. Smith, Department of Elementary Education, Logan, UT 84322-2805; http://www.collegereadingassociation.org/. Illus., index, adv. Refereed. Circ: 1200. Online: OCLC Online Computer Library Center, Inc.; ProQuest LLC (Ann Arbor); H.W. Wilson. *Indexed:* ABIn, ERIC, EduInd, PsycInfo, SSCI. *Bk. rev.:* Number and length vary. *Aud.:* Ac.

A refereed journal of the College Reading Association, which publishes articles on reading research and related literacy fields. Articles include discussions of current issues, research reports, instructional practices, book reviews, and news from the field. Each issue has four or five lengthy articles on such topics as classroom spelling instruction; learning through multicultural literature; a study done to understand preservice elementary education teachers' beliefs about struggling readers; a research study to give preservice teachers a better understanding of the classroom writing process; and current findings from a study of middle school readers participating in literacy events. Highly recommended for school and academic libraries that serve education programs.

2102. Reading Research Quarterly. [ISSN: 0034-0553] 1965. q. USD 122 (Individuals, USD 61; Students, USD 37). Ed(s): David Reinking, Donna E. Alvermann. International Reading Association, 800 Barksdale Rd, Newark, DE 19714-8139; journals@reading.org; http://www.reading.org. Illus., index, adv. Refereed. Circ: 14388 Paid. Vol. ends: Fall. Microform: PQC. Online: EBSCO Publishing, EBSCO Host; Florida Center for Library Automation; Gale; JSTOR (Web-based Journal Archive); Northern Light Technology, Inc.; H.W. Wilson. *Indexed:* ABIn, AgeL, ArtHuCI, CommAb, EAA, ECER, ERIC, EduInd, FR, L&LBA, LT&LA, LingAb, MLA-IB, PsycInfo, SFSA, SSCI. *Bk. rev.:* 1, 10 pages. *Aud.:* Ac.

Published by the International Reading Association, *RRQ* is a peer-reviewed scholarly journal dedicated to presenting and examining the issues of literacy for all learners. Articles include qualitative and quantitative research, integrative reviews, and conceptual pieces that promote and contribute to the understanding of literacy and literacy research. Each issue reflects a broad range of academic literacy research, with topics and issues such as integrative review of teaching reading in Kenyan primary schools; assessing narrative comprehension in young children; the tutoring of young at-risk readers by minimally trained college students; and a historical definition of social constructionism. Responding to an international readership, the journal provides a brief abstract of each featured article in six languages. Letters to the editor and commentaries contribute to the journal's dialogue on literacy research. Available online. Highly recommended for academic and school libraries. URL: www.reading.org/publications/journals/rrq.

2103. The Reading Teacher: a journal of the International Reading Association. Formerly (until 1951): *International Council for the Improvement of Reading Instruction. Bulletin.* [ISSN: 0034-0561] 1948. 8x/yr. USD 122 (Individuals, USD 61 print & online eds.). Ed(s): Judith Mitchell, D Ray Reutzel. International Reading Association, 800 Barksdale Rd, Newark, DE 19714-8139; journals@reading.org; http://www.reading.org. Illus., index, adv. Refereed. Circ: 55000 Paid. Vol. ends: May. Microform: PQC. Online: EBSCO Publishing, EBSCO Host; Florida Center for Library Automation; Gale; Northern Light

Technology, Inc.; OCLC Online Computer Library Center, Inc.; ProQuest LLC (Ann Arbor); H.W. Wilson. *Indexed:* ABIn, AgeL, AmHI, ArtHuCI, BRI, CBRI, ECER, ERIC, EduInd, L&LBA, MLA-IB, MRD, RILM, SSCI. *Bk. rev.:* Number and length vary. *Aud.:* Ga, Ac.

A peer-reviewed journal by the International Reading Association, *RT* considers practices, research, and trends in literacy education and related disciplines. This journal is published for educators and other professionals involved with literacy education for children to the age of 12. Individual issues have five or six featured articles, teaching ideas, and children's book review columns, as well as the occasional annotated bibliography of books and children's literary work. A recent themed issue covers literacy instruction in the United States and worldwide. The journal's goal to promote and affect literacy education is realized with article topics such as improving students' reading performance through standards-based school reform; measurement of attitudes toward writing; and high-stakes testing in reading. An important journal for school and academic libraries. URL: www.reading.org/publications/journals/rt.

2104. *Research in the Teaching of English.* [ISSN: 0034-527X] 1967. q. USD 20. Ed(s): Michael Smith, Peter Smagorinsky. National Council of Teachers of English, 1111 W Kenyon Rd, Urbana, IL 61801-1096; cschanche@ncte.org; http://www.ncte.org. Illus., adv. Sample. Refereed. Circ: 4100. Vol. ends: Dec. Microform: PQC. Online: EBSCO Publishing, EBSCO Host; ProQuest LLC (Ann Arbor). *Indexed:* ABIn, ArtHuCI, ERIC, EduInd, L&LBA, LT&LA, SSCI. *Aud.:* Ac.

RTE's definition of research in the teaching of English is broad and inclusive. The journal is dedicated to publishing multiple approaches to conducting research such as teacher-based research, historical articles, narratives, and current methodology. Additionally, the journal seeks articles that consider literacy issues regardless of language, within schools or other settings, and in other disciplines. General themes are supported with scholarly, well-referenced articles. A semi-annual selected bibliography of recent research in the teaching of English further supports *RTE*'s mission. Recommended for academic libraries. URL: www.ncte.org/pubs/journals/rte.

2105. *T E S L - E J.* [ISSN: 1072-4303] 1994. q. Free. Ed(s): Maggie Sokolik. T E S L - E J, University of California, Berkeley, College Writing Programs, Berkeley, CA 94720-2500; sokolik@socrates.berkeley.edu; http://www.kyoto-su.ac.jp/information/tesl-ej. Illus., index. Refereed. *Indexed:* BRI, CBRI, EduInd, L&LBA, LingAb, MLA-IB. *Bk. rev.:* Number and length vary. *Aud.:* Ac.

A refereed academic journal focused on the research and practice of English as a second or foreign language. *TESL-EJ* covers a broad range of issues from research to classroom practices for all education levels. Wide-ranging topics covered include the current status and standards of English grammar teaching; adult education and literacy; curriculum development and evaluation; and employment issues for EFL/ESL teachers. Issues present original articles, book or media reviews, and a forum for discussion. Featured articles range from 9 to 16 pages in length. Authors have written on such issues as teaching literature in the Muslim world; an interactive information literacy course for international students; the nature of peer-response variation in EFL and ESL students; and second-language writing and research. A standard journal for the field of ESL. URL: http://tesl-ej.org.

ENVIRONMENTAL EDUCATION

2106. *The Journal of Environmental Education.* Formerly (until 1971): *Environmental Education.* [ISSN: 0095-8964] 1969. q. USD 149 (Individuals, USD 66 print & online eds.; USD 36 newsstand/cover). Ed(s): Stephanie F Todd. Heldref Publications, 1319 18th St, NW, Washington, DC 20036-1802; subscribe@heldref.org; http://www.heldref.org. Illus., index, adv. Sample. Refereed. Circ: 1145 Paid. CD-ROM: ProQuest LLC (Ann Arbor). Online: EBSCO Publishing, EBSCO Host; Florida Center for Library Automation; Gale; Northern Light Technology, Inc.; OCLC Online Computer Library Center, Inc.; ProQuest K-12 Learning Solutions; ProQuest LLC (Ann Arbor); H.W. Wilson. Reprint: PSC. *Indexed:* ABIn, ERIC, EduInd, EnvAb, EnvInd, ExcerpMed, IBR, IBZ, PollutAb, PsycInfo, RI-1, SSCI, SWRA. *Bk. rev.:* 1-2, 500 words. *Aud.:* Ac, Sa.

With a focus on environmental education, this journal publishes original articles that promote and inform on instruction, theory, methods, and practice from primary grades through college. Peer-reviewed research articles include project reports, programs, review articles, critical essays, analyses, and qualitative or quantitative studies. The emphasis is on how to instruct on environmental issues and how to evaluate existing programs. There are four to six articles per issue, and topics have included: environmental literacy in teacher training; teaching through modeling; building environmental literacy; developing effective environmental education; considering culture as a determinant of environmental attitudes; and examining a meta-analysis of classroom interventions and improved environmental behavior. Regular columns include a review of resources and a summary of a current innovative research study. Readership consists of teachers and others involved with environmental education programs for schools, parks, camps, recreation centers, and businesses. Recommended title for schools and programs that serve environmental education. URL: www.heldref.org/jenve.php.

MORAL EDUCATION

2107. *Journal of Moral Education.* [ISSN: 0305-7240] 1971. q. GBP 202 print & online eds. Ed(s): Monica J Taylor. Routledge, 4 Park Sq, Milton Park, Abingdon, OX14 4RN, United Kingdom; info@routledge.co.uk; http://www.routledge.co.uk. Illus., index, adv. Sample. Refereed. Vol. ends: Dec. Online: EBSCO Publishing, EBSCO Host; Gale; IngentaConnect; Northern Light Technology, Inc.; OCLC Online Computer Library Center, Inc.; ProQuest LLC (Ann Arbor); SwetsWise Online Content. Reprint: PSC. *Indexed:* ABIn, ASSIA, ArtHuCI, BrEdI, CJA, EAA, ERIC, EduInd, FR, HEA, IBR, IBSS, IBZ, PhilInd, PsycInfo, R&TA, RI-1, SSA, SSCI, SWA, SociolAb. *Bk. rev.:* 5-10, 600-1,500 words. *Aud.:* Ac.

A journal focused on all aspects of moral education and development. A multidisciplinary approach and inclusive age range contribute to the journal's broad content scope. Authors provide philosophical analyses, empirical research reports, evaluations of educational practice, and overviews of international moral education theories and practices. Five or six articles per issue cover moral education research such as moral education at the movies; character education in a public high school; a critical analysis of the meaning of dominance; an exploration of language-based socialization patterns; and children's development of moral and social knowledge. Curriculum materials and book reviews as well as special thematic issues further the academic value of the journal. A standard journal for all academic libraries.

SOCIAL STUDIES (INCLUDING HISTORY AND ECONOMICS)

2108. *History Teacher.* [ISSN: 0018-2745] 1967. q. USD 63 (Individuals, USD 32; Students, USD 22). Ed(s): Jane A Dabel. Society for History Education, 1250 Bellflower Blvd, PO Box 1578, Long Beach, CA 90840; trj@csulb.edu. Illus., index, adv. Sample. Refereed. Circ: 2000. Vol. ends: Aug. Microform: PQC. Online: EBSCO Publishing, EBSCO Host; JSTOR (Web-based Journal Archive); OCLC Online Computer Library Center, Inc.; H.W. Wilson. *Indexed:* ABIn, ABS&EES, AmH&L, BAS, EduInd, FLI, HistAb, IBR, IBZ, MRD. *Bk. rev.:* 12-15, 600-1,200 words. *Aud.:* Ac.

A membership journal of the Society for History Education, this title is dedicated to the teaching of history in the secondary and higher education classroom. The journal focuses on professional analyses of current and innovative teaching techniques. Issues have included counterfactual thought experiments and articles on history teaching at the community college; digital history in the history/social studies classroom; the craft of teaching; historiography; and the state of the profession. An extensive review section covers textbooks, readers, films, computer programs, and other material. Recommended for academic libraries.

2109. *The Journal of Economic Education.* [ISSN: 0022-0485] 1969. q. USD 154 (Individuals, USD 68 print & online eds.; USD 37 newsstand/cover). Ed(s): Rosalind Springsteen. Heldref Publications, 1319 18th St, NW, Washington, DC 20036-1802; subscribe@heldref.org; http://www.heldref.org. Illus., index, adv. Refereed. Circ: 1391 Paid.

CD-ROM: ProQuest LLC (Ann Arbor). Online: Chadwyck-Healey Inc.; EBSCO Publishing, EBSCO Host; Florida Center for Library Automation; Gale; JSTOR (Web-based Journal Archive); Northern Light Technology, Inc.; OCLC Online Computer Library Center, Inc.; ProQuest K-12 Learning Solutions; ProQuest LLC (Ann Arbor); H.W. Wilson. Reprint: PSC. *Indexed:* ABIn, AgeL, EAA, ERIC, EduInd, IBR, IBZ, JEL, PAIS, SSCI. *Bk. rev.:* 1-2, 300-3,000 words. *Aud.:* Ac.

This journal offers original articles on innovations in and evaluations of teaching techniques, materials, and programs in economics. Designed for instructors of beginning through graduate level economics courses, issues feature sections on research, economic instruction, and economic content. Contributed articles include theoretical and empirical studies, substantive issues, new ideas, innovations in pedagogy, interactive exemplary material, and reports on the status and events that influence academic economists. Recent article topics explore modelling financial innovation and economic growth; self-reports of cheating; teaching inflation targeting; risk aversion and the value of information; graduate program ranking and job market success; high school students' opportunities for economic research; student evaluations; and the use of music to teach economics. Recommended for academic libraries. URL: www.indiana.edu/~econed.

2110. *Social Education: the official journal of the National Council for the Social Studies.* [ISSN: 0037-7724] 1937. 7x/yr. Institutional members, USD 75; Individual members, USD 55. Ed(s): Kristen Page, Michael Simpson. National Council for the Social Studies, 8555 16th St, Ste 500, Silver Spring, MD 20910; ncss@ncss.org; http://www.ncss.org. Illus., index, adv. Sample. Circ: 29000 Paid. Vol. ends: Nov/Dec. Microform: PQC. Online: Florida Center for Library Automation; Gale; Northern Light Technology, Inc.; OCLC Online Computer Library Center, Inc.; ProQuest K-12 Learning Solutions; ProQuest LLC (Ann Arbor). *Indexed:* ABIn, ABS&EES, ASSIA, AgeL, AmH&L, BAS, BRI, CBRI, ERIC, EduInd, FLI, HistAb, IndIslam, LRI, MRD, PhilInd, RILM, SSCI. *Bk. rev.:* 1-6, 200-800 words. *Aud.:* Ac.

A journal published by the National Council for the Social Studies (NCSS) to support the council's mission "to provide leadership, service, and support" for social studies instructors. The journal's content is focused on classroom practices at all levels: elementary, middle, high school, and university. Featured articles have presented teaching economics in U.S. history, digital voices, simulations, and connections for classroom teaching, a consideration of the practice and theory of instructional technology, and a ten-year study of citizenship education in five countries. Significant journal content is given to classroom curriculum such as a study unit on the Great Depression; an oral history project to explore immigration; and a critique of NCSS curriculum standards. Regularly includes book reviews, lesson plans, the Internet as an instruction tool, and a journal supplement, *Middle Level Learning*, all of which contribute to the classroom focus of this publication. Highly recommended for school and academic libraries that serve education programs.

2111. *The Social Studies.* [ISSN: 0037-7996] 1909. bi-m. USD 119 (Individuals, USD 60 print & online eds.; USD 19 newsstand/cover). Ed(s): Helen Kress. Heldref Publications, 1319 18th St, NW, Washington, DC 20036-1802; subscribe@heldref.org; http://www.heldref.org. Illus., index, adv. Refereed. Circ: 1260 Paid. Microform: PQC. Online: Chadwyck-Healey Inc.; EBSCO Publishing, EBSCO Host; Florida Center for Library Automation; Gale; Northern Light Technology, Inc.; OCLC Online Computer Library Center, Inc.; ProQuest K-12 Learning Solutions; ProQuest LLC (Ann Arbor); H.W. Wilson. Reprint: PSC. *Indexed:* ABIn, AmH&L, ArtHuCI, BRD, BRI, CBRI, ENW, ERIC, EduInd, HistAb, IBR, IBZ, PAIS, PSA, RILM, SSCI. *Bk. rev.:* 0-1, 400 words. *Aud.:* Ac.

This peer-reviewed journal publishes articles concerned with the subjects of social studies, social sciences, history, and interdisciplinary studies for grades K-12. The journal seeks articles that give new perspectives, practical applications, and insights on issues concerning social studies curriculum and instruction. With five to seven articles per issue, *TSS* covers a broad range of topics from research-based to classroom practice. Articles have focused on the achievement gap in social studies and science; author studies in children's literature to explore social justice issues; critical thinking for students; strategies for student-centered classroom dialogue; a review of social studies/history

curriculum, 1892–1937; the use of instructional methods and curriculum in the classroom such as studying history on the Internet; a teacher's guide for a unit on Appalachia; and using student-designed oral history. Recommended for school and academic libraries. URL: www.heldref.org/tss.php.

TEACHER EDUCATION

2112. *Action in Teacher Education.* [ISSN: 0162-6620] 1978. q. USD 90 individual membership; USD 130 domestic institutional membership; USD 150 foreign institutional membership. Ed(s): John J Chiodo, Priscilla Griffith. Association of Teacher Educators, P O Box 793, Manassas, VA 20113; ate1@aol.com; http://www.ate1.org. Illus., index, adv. Sample. Circ: 4000. Vol. ends: Winter. Microform: PQC. Online: OCLC Online Computer Library Center, Inc.; H.W. Wilson. *Indexed:* ABIn, ERIC, EduInd. *Aud.:* Ac.

A refereed journal published by the Association of Teacher Educators, an organization dedicated to the improvement of teacher education for both school and higher education instructors. Intended to serve as a forum for issues, ideas, and trends concerning the improvement of teacher education, this journal is for the practitioner. Articles are focused on the theory, practice, and research of teacher education. With practitioners as audience, the content is on the applications and implications of research and practice. Issues are both thematic and nonthematic, with 10–14 articles per issue. Themed issues have featured partnerships; alternative routes to certification; indigenous perspectives on teacher education; reflective practices; preparation and professional development of teachers and the impact on student learning; and three different perspectives on teaching and teacher education. Non-themed issues have covered a broad range of issues from professional identity to writing federal grant proposals to redesigning teacher education programs. For all school and academic libraries. URL: www.ou.edu/action.

2113. *Journal of Education for Teaching: international research and pedagogy.* Formerly (until 1980): *British Journal of Teacher Education.* [ISSN: 0260-7476] 1975. q. GBP 710 print & online eds. Ed(s): Peter Gilroy, Edgar Stones. Routledge, 4 Park Sq, Milton Park, Abingdon, OX14 4RN, United Kingdom; info@routledge.co.uk; http://www.routledge.co.uk. Adv. Refereed. Online: EBSCO Publishing, EBSCO Host; Gale; IngentaConnect; Northern Light Technology, Inc.; OCLC Online Computer Library Center, Inc.; ProQuest LLC (Ann Arbor); SwetsWise Online Content. Reprint: PSC. *Indexed:* ABIn, BrEdI, ERIC, EduInd, HEA, L&LBA, LT&LA, SSCI, SWA. *Aud.:* Ac.

JET publishes original articles on the subject of teacher education. The journal's definition of teacher education is inclusive of initial training, in-service education, and professional staff development. Primarily British but with an international orientation, the journal seeks to promote academic discussion of issues, trends, research, opinion, and practice on teacher education. Contributors have assessed such issues as teacher education for sustainable education; global influences on teacher education in Scotland; teacher authority in Finnish schools; the role of higher education in the training of secondary school teachers in Great Britain; and development and change with science teachers' practice in Egyptian classrooms. Recommended for all academic libraries. URL: www.tandf.co.uk/journals/online/0260-7476.asp.

2114. *Journal of Teacher Education: the journal of policy, practice, and research in teacher education.* [ISSN: 0022-4871] 1950. 5x/yr. GBP 259. Ed(s): Hilda Borko, Jennifer Whitcomb. Corwin Press, Inc., 2455 Teller Rd, Thousand Oaks, CA 91320-2218; info@sagepub.com; http://www.corwinpress.com. Illus., adv. Sample. Refereed. Circ: 7876 Paid. Vol. ends: Nov/Dec. Microform: PQC. Online: CSA; EBSCO Publishing, EBSCO Host; Florida Center for Library Automation; Gale; HighWire Press; OCLC Online Computer Library Center, Inc.; OhioLINK; SAGE Publications, Inc., SAGE Journals Online; SwetsWise Online Content. Reprint: PSC. *Indexed:* ABIn, ArtHuCI, BRI, CBRI, EAA, ECER, ERIC, EduInd, FR, IBR, IBZ, SSCI, SWA. *Bk. rev.:* 1-3, 1,000 words. *Aud.:* Ac.

A professional journal of the American Association of Colleges for Teacher Education, *JTE* considers teacher education as a field of study. As noted in the journal's subtitle, the focus is on policy, practice, and research in teacher education. Articles address such topics as the success of academic searches for the next generation of teacher educators; reflective teaching; field experiences of preservice teachers; quality in preservice teacher portfolios; teacher education faculty; student teaching; and other professional interests. Themed issues have considered multicultural education, and teacher education and society with scholarly papers integrating research, practice, and theory on the topic. Highly recommended for all libraries that serve teacher education programs.

2115. Teacher Education Quarterly. Formerly (until 1983): *California Journal of Teacher Education.* [ISSN: 0737-5328] 1972. 4x/yr. USD 100 (Individuals, USD 60; Institutional members, USD 140). Ed(s): Thomas G Nelson. Caddo Gap Press, 3145 Geary Blvd, PMB 275, San Francisco, CA 94118; info@caddogap.com; http://www.caddogap.com. Illus., adv. Sample. Refereed. Circ: 1000 Paid. Vol. ends: Fall. Microform: PQC. Online: Gale; OCLC Online Computer Library Center, Inc.; ProQuest LLC (Ann Arbor); H.W. Wilson. *Indexed:* ABIn, EduInd, IBR, IBZ. *Aud.:* Ac.

A refereed research journal that focuses on current educational research and practice as well as educational policy and reform issues. Published by the California Council on Teacher Education, an organization dedicated to supporting and promoting teacher educators. *TEQ* supports the council's mission with relevant, interesting, and challenging articles related to the field of teacher education and teacher professional development. Contributors from university researchers to teacher education practitioners cover issues such as preservice teachers' experiences and beliefs about writing instruction; preparing for multicultural schools; an approach to professional development schools; arts-based curriculum; teacher preparation for inclusive environments; interdisciplinary team teaching as professional development; and current policy initiatives and innovative teacher education practices. Recommended for all libraries that serve teacher education programs.

2116. Teaching and Teacher Education. [ISSN: 0742-051X] 1985. 8x/yr. EUR 999. Ed(s): Michael J Dunkin, N L Gage. Pergamon, The Boulevard, Langford Ln, East Park, Kidlington, OX5 1GB, United Kingdom. Illus., index. Sample. Refereed. Vol. ends: Nov (No. 17). Microform: PQC. Online: EBSCO Publishing, EBSCO Host; Gale; IngentaConnect; OhioLINK; ScienceDirect; SwetsWise Online Content. *Indexed:* ABIn, BrEdI, ERIC, EduInd, IBR, IBZ, PsycInfo, SSCI. *Aud.:* Ac.

This international journal covers all aspects and levels of teaching and teacher education. With its broad coverage, the journal is of value to all concerned with teaching, including researchers in teacher education, educational and cognitive psychologists, and policy makers and planners. The journal is committed to promoting teaching and teacher education through the publication of theory, research, and practice. Academic authors support the journal's commitment, with scholarly articles ranging from classroom practice to professional development to preservice teachers. Each issue contains seven or eight articles focused on topics such as: the impact of service learning and literacy tutoring on pre-service teachers; developing whole-school pedagogical values; collaborative action research and project work; the peer review process; a diversity study using narrative methodology; a collaborative research project exploring an innovative professional development program; and a case study of student teaching in an inner-city school. Recommended for all libraries that serve teacher education programs.

2117. Teaching Education. [ISSN: 1047-6210] 1987. q. GBP 280 print & online eds. Ed(s): Allan Luke, Diane Mayer. Routledge, 4 Park Sq, Milton Park, Abingdon, OX14 4RN, United Kingdom; journals@ routledge.com; http://www.routledge.co.uk. Illus., index, adv. Sample. Refereed. Circ: 1200 Controlled. Vol. ends: Spring/Summer. Online: EBSCO Publishing, EBSCO Host; Gale; IngentaConnect; OCLC Online Computer Library Center, Inc.; SwetsWise Online Content; H.W. Wilson. Reprint: PSC. *Indexed:* ABIn, EduInd. *Bk. rev.:* 3-5, 300-500 words. *Aud.:* Ac.

Dedicated to providing a forum for innovative practice and research in teacher education, the journal focuses on challenge and change in teacher education. Contributors address social, cultural, practical, and theoretical issues of teacher education from school to university. The journal's contents include critical and theory-based research; scholarly reflections on current teacher education issues;

innovative approaches to undergraduate and graduate teaching; and new practices in the K–12 classroom. Research and scholarship topics have addressed media literacy for preservice teachers; case writing in teacher education; teaching action research to preservice teachers; the politics of pedagogy; and developing critical writing practices. Innovative approaches to curriculum have included the city as a multicultural classroom and a course on student assistance training for preservice teachers. Recommended for all academic libraries.

TECHNOLOGY

2118. Educational Technology: the magazine for managers of change in education. Formerly: *Teaching Aids News.* [ISSN: 0013-1962] 1961. bi-m. USD 139 domestic; USD 159 foreign. Ed(s): Lawrence Lipsitz. Educational Technology Publications, 700 Palisade Ave, PO Box 1564, Englewood Cliffs, NJ 07632-0564; edtecpubs@aol.com; http://www.bookstoread.com/etp/. Illus., adv. Sample. Circ: 2500 Paid. Vol. ends: Nov/Dec. *Indexed:* ABIn, CompLI, EAA, ECER, EduInd, FLI, MRD, MicrocompInd, SSCI. *Aud.:* Ac.

This magazine publishes articles that report on research and practical applications in the field of educational technology. It is focused on a readership of school administrators, trainers, designers, and others involved with educational technology. With nine or ten articles per issue, varied aspects of educational technology are covered, such as blended learning programs; Web 2.0 for educational applications; online collaboration; dimensions of e-learning; instructional design; interactive multimedia instruction; web-based learning; and knowledge management for teachers. Beginning in 2006, new features include a column on education and innovative technology; biographical studies of major figures in the field; and a question-and-answer feature with educational technology leaders. There are also occasional columns by leaders from interdisciplinary fields related to educational technology, and special issues on developing trends in the field. A recent special issue focuses on highly mobile computing. Recommended for all academic and school libraries.

2119. Educational Technology Research & Development. Formed by the merger of (1977-1989): *Journal of Instructional Development;* (1953-1989): *Educational Communications and Technology Journal;* Which was formerly (unil 1978): *A V Communication Review;* (until 1963): *Audio Visual Communication Review.* [ISSN: 1042-1629] 1989. bi-m. EUR 232 print & online eds. Ed(s): Michael Spector, Steven M Ross. Springer New York LLC, 233 Spring St, New York, NY 10013-1578; service-ny@springer.com; http://www.springer.com/. Illus., index, adv. Refereed. Circ: 5000 Paid. Vol. ends: No. 4. Microform: PQC. Online: EBSCO Publishing, EBSCO Host; OCLC Online Computer Library Center, Inc.; ProQuest LLC (Ann Arbor); Springer LINK; SwetsWise Online Content; H.W. Wilson. Reprint: PSC. *Indexed:* ABIn, ArtHuCI, CommAb, EAA, ERIC, EduInd, FLI, FR, L&LBA, PsycInfo, SSCI. *Bk. rev.:* 4, essay length. *Aud.:* Ac.

A publication of the Association for Educational Communications and Technology, the journal serves to promote educational technology and its application to the learning process. Each issue has five or six articles that cover research and development topics. Recent topics include cultural competence and instructional design; web-based learning environment and student motivation; computer-based tools for instructional design; project-based learning with the web; reflections on the current state of educational technology; a design theory of problem solving; and cultural connections in a distance-learning community. A regular department features issues and trends in the field of educational technology in other countries. Recommended for all academic and school libraries.

2120. From Now On - the Educational Technology Journal. 1990. m. Free. Ed(s): Jamie McKenzie. From Now On - the Educational Technology Journal, 917 12th St, Bellingham, WA 98225. *Aud.:* Ems, Hs, Ga.

A journal committed to the use of technologies for information literacy and for student learning and reasoning. Articles are written for a broad audience of parents, educators, administrators, and others involved with educational technology. Issues have covered the topics of assessment, curriculum, grants, research, staff development, technology planning, virtual museums, and web site development. Short, concise articles have focused on finding the deep web;

online research modules; inspired writing and inquiry; topical research as an instructional method; strategies to encourage student questioning; assessment of staff technology competencies; and the development of district technology plans. Recommended for school and academic libraries. URL: www.fno.org.

2121. *Journal of Educational Computing Research.* [ISSN: 0735-6331] 1984. 8x/yr. USD 467. Ed(s): Robert H Seidman. Baywood Publishing Co., Inc., 26 Austin Ave, PO Box 337, Amityville, NY 11701-0337; info@baywood.com; http://www.baywood.com. Illus., index, adv. Sample. Refereed. *Indexed:* ABIn, ArtHuCI, CompLI, EAA, ERIC, EduInd, IBR, IBZ, L&LBA, PsycInfo, SSCI, SWA. *Bk. rev.:* 0-2, essay length. *Aud.:* Ac.

This refereed journal publishes original articles on various aspects of educational computing: development and design of new hardware and software; interpretation and implications of research; and theory and history. Informative interdisciplinary articles are intended for a readership of practitioners, researchers, scientists, and educators from classroom teachers to faculty. Each issue's well-referenced articles advance knowledge and practice in the field of educational computing with empirical research, analyses, design and development studies, and critical reviews. Authors have presented recent research on sustainable online communities for teacher professional development; a retrospective of the research in instructional technology literature from 2000 through 2004; literature-related electronic networks and systemic school reform; enabling student accomplishment online; a review of published evaluation instruments used in online formal courses; and an evaluative study of a network-based hypertext discussion tool. A special issue has focused on important issues in the K–12 environment such as digital media literacy standards. An important title for libraries that serve the K–12 community and for academic libraries that serve education programs.

2122. *Journal of Interactive Media in Education.* [ISSN: 1365-893X] 1996. irreg. Free. Ed(s): Tamara Sumner, Simon Buckingham Shum. Open University, Knowledge Media Institute, Milton Keynes, MK7 6AA, United Kingdom; jime@open.ac.uk; http://www-jime.open.ac.uk. Illus. Refereed. *Indexed:* EduInd, PsycInfo. *Bk. rev.:* Occasional, 1,600 words, signed. *Aud.:* Ac.

A journal focused on the role and contribution of interactive media to the field of learning. With an interest in the integration of technology and education, the journal publishes articles that develop theory, critique existing work, or analyze various aspects of educational technology. Articles have presented collaborative learning on the web; rhetoric in a digital media; and narrative in an information and communication technology course. Articles can have an interactive component, such as examples of interactive media or access to qualitative data. Special issues focus on advances in learning design and learner and teacher experiences with mobile devices. Book reviews include responses by authors and other readers. Recommended for academic libraries. URL: www-jime.open.ac.uk.

2123. *Meridian (Raleigh): a middle school computer technologies journal.* [ISSN: 1097-9778] 1998. s-a. Free. Ed(s): Beckey Reed. North Carolina State University, College of Education, Poe Hall, Box 7801, Raleigh, NC 27695-7801. *Indexed:* EduInd. *Aud.:* Ems, Sa.

A journal focused on the research and practice of computer technology in the middle school classroom. Articles feature research, practical application, commentary, and book excerpts for the middle school practitioner, administrators, and others involved with middle school students. Two issues a year consider topics and issues such as using GPS and geocaching; games and education; cultural diversity and technology; using graphing calculators; and information and communication technology (ICT) and academic rigor. A recent issue establishes an interactive forum intended to create an evolving article with readers' response on the topic of the issues in educational web design. An important journal for teachers in the middle schools.

2124. *Tech Directions: the magazine linking education to careers.* Former titles (until May 1992): *School Shop - Tech Directions;* (until May 1990): *New School Shop - Tech Directions;* (until May 1989): *School Shop.* [ISSN: 1062-9351] 1941. 10x/yr. USD 30 domestic; USD 40 foreign. Ed(s): Susanne Peckham. Prakken Publications, Inc., 832 Phoenix Dr, Ann Arbor, MI 48108-2221; http://www.techdirections.com. Illus., index,

adv. Sample. Circ: 35000 Paid and controlled. Vol. ends: May. Microform: PQC. Online: EBSCO Publishing, EBSCO Host; Northern Light Technology, Inc.; OCLC Online Computer Library Center, Inc.; ProQuest K-12 Learning Solutions; ProQuest LLC (Ann Arbor); H.W. Wilson. *Indexed:* ABIn, ERIC, EduInd, MRD. *Bk. rev.:* 6, 150 words. *Aud.:* Ga, Ac.

A publication focused on the fields of technology, industrial, and vocational education. Contributors cover teaching techniques, school-to-work transition, industrial arts, and current issues in the field. The magazine is intended for technology and vocational technical educators at all educational levels, and its articles and columns are curriculum oriented. Topics have included robot building with kits; scale model house construction; applied science; solar power; and technology concepts, as well as model school programs and an annual guide to training and certification programs. Recommended for academic and school libraries with vocational education programs. URL: www.techdirections.com.

2125. *Techniques.* Former titles (until 1996): *American Vocational Association.Techniques;* (until 1996): *Vocational Education Journal;* (until 1985): *VocEd;* (until 1978): *American Vocational Journal.* [ISSN: 1527-1803] 1926. 8x/yr. Non-members, USD 48. Ed(s): Peter Magnuson, Susan Reese. Association for Career and Technical Education, 1410 King St, Alexandria, VA 22314. Adv. Circ: 30000 Paid. CD-ROM: ProQuest LLC (Ann Arbor). Microform: PQC. Online: EBSCO Publishing, EBSCO Host; Florida Center for Library Automation; Gale; OCLC Online Computer Library Center, Inc.; ProQuest LLC (Ann Arbor); H.W. Wilson. *Indexed:* ABIn, BRI, ERIC, EduInd, MRD, PEI. *Bk. rev.:* 1, 500 words. *Aud.:* Ga, Ac, Sa.

Published by the Association for Career and Technical Education (ACTE), this magazine covers issues of career and technical education. Content is aimed at ACTE members with current news about legislation, profiles of educators, featured articles about programs and issues, and association news and events. Issues have examined career and technical education with special needs students; the history and future of school-to-career; a series on accountability and assessment; and emergency telecommunicator training for high school students. Recommended for all libraries that serve career and technical education programs. URL: www.techdirections.com.

2126. *The Technology Teacher.* Former titles (until 1983): *Man - Society - Technology; Journal of Industrial Arts Education.* [ISSN: 0746-3537] 1939. 8x/yr. Free to members; Non-members, USD 70. Ed(s): Kathleen de la Paz. International Technology Education Association, 1914 Association Dr, Ste 201, Reston, VA 20191-1539; itea@iteaconnect.org; http://www.iteaconnect.org/index.html. Illus., index, adv. Sample. Refereed. Circ: 5000 Paid. Vol. ends: May/Jun. Microform: PQC. Online: EBSCO Publishing, EBSCO Host; Gale; Northern Light Technology, Inc.; OCLC Online Computer Library Center, Inc.; ProQuest K-12 Learning Solutions; ProQuest LLC (Ann Arbor); H.W. Wilson. *Indexed:* ABIn, ERIC, EduInd, MRD. *Bk. rev.:* 1, 100 words. *Aud.:* Ac.

This is the journal of the International Technology Education Association, and its goal is to be a resource tool for technology education practitioners. The audience ranges from elementary school to high school classroom teachers, as well as teacher educators. Article content is focused on the sharing of classroom ideas and applications. With the practitioner as audience, article content has covered web site creation, telemedicine, computer upgrade tips, designing robots, industrial design activities, and biotechnology curriculum projects. As a membership journal, it also includes association events and news. Recommended for all school and academic libraries.

■ ELDER ISSUES

Janet A. Ohles, Associate Director of Library Services, Western Connecticut State University, Danbury, CT 06810

Introduction

In January of 2000, 78 million baby boomers began to turn 60. In 2000, 10–14.9 percent of the population was age 65 or older. U.S. Census Bureau projections show that by 2025, 20–30 percent of the population will be 60 or older in more than 30 states. There are many issues that are unique to this elder population.

The *Merriam-Webster OnLine Dictionary* defines an issue as a final outcome that usually constitutes a solution to a problem or the resolution of a difficulty. The 2005 White House Conference on Aging identified the "Top 50 Resolutions" that will guide recommendations for national aging policies over the next ten years.

This section identifies popular and general-interest magazines that address the broad topics identified in these Top 50 Resolutions: health care, the workplace (paid and volunteer), retirement, finances, nutrition, civic and social engagement, housing, quality of life, and caregiving.

Basic Periodicals

A A R P: The Magazine, Ageing and Society, Generations (San Francisco).

Basic Abstracts and Indexes

Abstracts in Social Gerontology, AGELINE.

2127. A A R P: The Magazine. Formed by the merger of (2001-2003): *My Generation;* (2002-2003): *A A R P Modern Maturity;* Which was formerly (until Mar. 2002): *Modern Maturity;* (until 1960): *We; Journal of Lifetime Living;* Modern Maturity incorporated (in 1986): *Dynamic Years;* Which was formerly (1965-1977): *Dynamic Maturity.* [ISSN: 1541-9894] 2003. bi-m. Membership, USD 12.50; USD 3.50 per issue. Ed(s): Hugh Delehanty, John Stoltenberg. American Association of Retired Persons (A A R P), 601 E St, NW, Washington, DC 20049; http://www.aarp.org. Circ: 2150000. *Indexed:* AgeL, RGPR. *Aud.:* Ga.

Since 2002, the American Association for Retired Persons (AARP) has published *AARP The Magazine* bimonthly. The magazine is a benefit for the more than 35 million AARP members, ages 50 and older. It covers a broad range of topics important to the age group, including coverage of legislative, consumer, and legal topics. Each issue has several general-interest feature stories geared toward the older adult. There are also several regular columns such as health, nutrition, and finance, along with a travel log. The magazine is published in three editions focusing on different decades: the 50s edition, 60s edition, and 70s edition. The association also publishes *AARP Segunda Juventud,* which is produced and edited for Hispanics, and is written in Spanish with English summaries for cross-cultural families. Appropriate for public libraries.

2128. A O A eNews. 2003. m. U.S. Department of Health and Human Services, Administration on Aging, 200 Independence Ave, SW, Washington, DC 20201; http://www.aoa.dhhs.gov. *Aud.:* Ga.

The Administration on Aging (AoA) began publishing *eNews* in 2003 to provide important information to state and area agencies on aging, members of the Leadership Council on Aging organizations, grantees, tribal organizations, and service providers. The newsletter presents brief descriptions of federal policy and program updates, news of national and regional AoA events, and information about local services and programs that meet the needs of the aging population. An archive of previous issues is maintained on the AoA web site. The newsletter is available in pdf and Word formats and may be read online or through e-mail. Reading *AoA eNews* is an easy way for those interested in governmental programs and services that impact the aging to keep up-to-date on key news affecting this population.

2129. Ageing International: information bulletin of the International Federation on Ageing. [ISSN: 0163-5158] 1973. q. EUR 268 print & online eds. Ed(s): S Levkoff. Springer New York LLC, 233 Spring St, New York, NY 10013-1578; service-ny@springer.com; http://www.springer.com/. Illus., index, adv. Sample. Circ: 900. Vol. ends: Winter. Reprint: PSC. *Indexed:* ASG, AgeL, EAA, ErgAb, SSA, SociolAb. *Aud.:* Ga, Ac.

Ageing International is a quarterly publication that is produced in cooperation with the International Federation on Ageing. The journal accepts articles that 1) are research oriented on broad topics relevant to aging from the perspective of the social and behaviorial sciences; 2) describe innovative service delivery programs and/or professional practice innovations that improve quality of life

or address concerns of aging populations; or 3) are well-documented scholarly briefs that present viewpoints or a critical analysis on a topical issue that has relevance to aging populations worldwide. The journal focuses on social and economic issues, public policies, and the use of resources. Appropriate for large public libraries, special libraries that serve public and health policy professionals, general gerontology collections, and academic collections that support aging and public-health disciplines.

2130. Assisted Living Executive. Formerly (until 2005): *Assisted Living Today.* [ISSN: 1553-8281] 1993. 9x/yr. Free to members; Non-members, USD 60. Ed(s): Angela Hickman Brady. Assisted Living Federation of America, 1650 King St, Ste 602, Alexandria, VA 22314-2747; info@alfa.org; http://www.alfa.org. Adv. Circ: 9000 Paid and controlled. *Indexed:* AgeL. *Aud.:* Sa.

Assisted Living Executive is a monthly trade publication written by and for assisted living professionals. The journal includes articles on current concerns being addressed in assisted living communities, including regulatory, educational, legal, and residential issues. Interviews with experts in the field, surveys and trends relevant to assisted living, and management topics are also covered. Products and services promoting assisted living communities, and medical devices and equipment are promoted in the journal. While directed toward professionals working in the field, *Assisted Living Executive* will interest health policy practitioners, aging and housing advocates, and individuals interested in learning more about assisted living. Appropriate for large public libraries.

2131. Generations (San Francisco). [ISSN: 0738-7806] 1976. q. USD 71.50 (Individuals, USD 38; Free to members). Ed(s): Mary Johnson. American Society on Aging, 833 Market St, Ste 511, San Francisco, CA 94103-1824; pubsinfo@asaging.org; http://www.asaging.org. Illus., adv. Sample. Refereed. Circ: 10000. Microform: PQC. Online: EBSCO Publishing, EBSCO Host; Florida Center for Library Automation; OCLC Online Computer Library Center, Inc.; ProQuest K-12 Learning Solutions; ProQuest LLC (Ann Arbor); H.W. Wilson. Reprint: PSC. *Indexed:* ASG, AbAn, AgeL, BRI, CBRI, CINAHL, HRA, PAIS, RI-1, SFSA, SSA, SSCI, SWR&A, SociolAb. *Aud.:* Ac, Ga.

Published quarterly, *Generations* is the journal of the American Society on Aging. It features thematic issues that cover topics important to both the aging population and public health, such as nutrition, housing, and cultural competence. Each issue covers a topic in-depth and from a variety of perspectives, including overview articles, manuscripts that cover policy and research issues, specific concerns and recent developments relevant to the topical theme, and programs and practice concepts. *Generations* is a core journal for academic collections and large public libraries supporting programs, administrators, policy makers, and planners in all settings dealing with aging and serving older adults.

2132. Kiplinger's Retirement Report. [ISSN: 1075-6671] 1994. m. USD 59.95. Ed(s): Knight A Kiplinger, Priscilla Brandon. Kiplinger Washington Editors, Inc., 1729 H St, NW, Washington, DC 20006; http://www.kiplinger.com/clients. *Indexed:* ATI, RGPR. *Aud.:* Ga.

Published monthly, *Kiplinger's Retirement Report* is a newsletter for the retired consumer with articles on finances, investments, health, household management, and travel, as well as on taxes, Social Security, and pensions. The first Kiplinger newsletter was published in 1923 by W.M. Kiplinger, an AP reporter who went to Washington to cover economic issues. A small family run business, the Kiplinger Washington editors offer financial advice in four newsletters and one magazine. The basic format of its founder remains today, with short articles that feature a staccato style and underlined phrases. Appropriate for public libraries or those serving a large retired community.

2133. Social Security Bulletin. [ISSN: 0037-7910] 1937. q. USD 56. Ed(s): Marilyn R Thomas. U.S. Social Security Administration, Office of Research, Evaluation and Statistics, 500 E St, SW, 8th Fl, Washington, DC 20254-0001; ores.publications@ssa.gov; http://www.ssa.gov. Illus., index. Sample. Vol. ends: Dec. Microform: MIM; CIS; PMC; PQC. Online: Chadwyck-Healey Inc.; EBSCO Publishing, EBSCO Host; Florida Center for Library Automation; Gale; William S. Hein & Co.,

Inc.; Northern Light Technology, Inc.; OCLC Online Computer Library Center, Inc.; ProQuest K-12 Learning Solutions; ProQuest LLC (Ann Arbor); H.W. Wilson. Reprint: WSH. *Indexed:* ABIn, ASG, AgeL, AmStI, BPI, CLI, ExcerpMed, ILP, IUSGP, JEL, LRI, MCR, PAIS, SSA, SSCI, SWR&A. *Aud.:* Ac, Sa.

The *Social Security Bulletin* is published quarterly by the Social Security Administration (SSA), the federal agency responsible for managing the nation's social insurance program. The SSA pays retirement, disability, and survivor benefits to workers and their families and administers the Social Security Income program. Issues of the bulletin are typically thematic and contain three or four research articles written by SSA staff. The articles typically address a topic, projection, trend, or characteristic of widespread concern to the American public and to policy makers. The articles are well researched, factual, and analytical. They contain extensive use of data and supporting statistical analyses, charts, and tables. The "Perspectives" section of the *Bulletin* contains articles written by non-SSA researchers on topics that may have implications for social policy. Articles are accepted that contribute to "an improved understanding of the Old-Age Survivors Insurance (OASI), Disability Insurance (DI), and the Supplemental Security (SSI) programs and issues related to their beneficiaries and contributors." Articles that feature social insurance themes in other countries are also accepted. An "Annual Statistical Supplement" presents a yearly compilation of current and historical data on Social Security beneficiaries and covered workers, along with the economy in general. Highlights, trends, program descriptions, and legislative history are also included. The *Bulletin* may be included in a federal depository library's holdings or purchased by subscription. It will be of interest to individuals who deal with the aging worker and/or retiree worldwide.

2134. *Spotlight on Caregiving: caregiving newsletter online.* Formerly: *Caregiving Online.* 1997. m. Free. Ed(s): Denise Brown. Tad Publishing Co., PO Box 224, Park Ridge, IL 60068; http://www.caregiving.com/. *Aud.:* Ga.

Spotlight on Caregiving is a free monthly online newsletter that is sent to registered users of the caregiving.com web site. The newsletter is edited and written by Denise M. Brown, with input from experts and readers. The focus of the newsletter is to address caregiver needs; it also includes useful information for the aging population and family and friends of the aged. Dedicated to the caregiver, *Spotlight on Caregiving* has regular columns such as "Dear Denise," where readers may ask the editor for her caregiving suggestions. The newsletter is part of an online community that offers caregivers a connection to others in a similar role through online information and the opportunity to join support groups. Although the web site has a lot of information for readers, it is cumbersome to navigate. The newsletter is recommended for those who care for the aging or those who are involved in advocacy efforts for this population group.

Travel 50 & Beyond. See Travel and Tourism section.

■ ELECTRONICS

Paula M. Storm, Assistant Professor; Science Technology Librarian, Bruce T. Halle Library, Eastern Michigan University, Ypsilanti, MI 48197; pstorm@emich.edu; FAX: 734-487-8861

Introduction

The trade magazines and journals in the field of electronics cover its technical, business, scientific, and consumer aspects. Readers from a variety of backgrounds and educational levels primarily use these publications as a way to keep current in this rapidly changing environment. Those in business need to know how to incorporate electronic equipment into their workflow, how to monitor the electronics industry, and how to improve, assemble, or package their electronic products.

Meanwhile, readers with technical and scientific backgrounds will want to keep updated on current trends and research and use journals to communicate their own findings. Consumers will find the trade magazines invaluable in discovering information on new equipment and on construction and repair, as well as reviews and ratings. Public librarians collecting in the area of electronics will want to include the trade magazines, and those in an academic environment will supplement those titles with scholarly journals, particularly those published by IEEE.

Basic Periodicals

Ga: *Electronic News, Electronics World, Popular Home Automation;* Ac, Sa: *IEEE Transactions on Consumer Electronics, IEEE Transactions on Electron Devices, IEEE Transactions on Industrial Electronics, IEEE Transactions on Power Electronics, Institute of Electrical and Electronics Engineers. Proceedings, International Journal of Electronics, Solid-State Electronics.*

Basic Abstracts and Indexes

ABI/Inform, Applied Science and Technology Index, Business and Company ASAP, Business Source Premier, Business Index, EI Compendex, Electronics and Communications Abstracts, IEEE Explore, INSPEC, NTIS, Physics Abstracts, Science Abstracts. Section B: Electrical and Electronics Abstracts, Science Citation Index, SPIE Digital Library.

2135. *AudioXpress.* Formed by the merger of (1988-2000): *Glass Audio;* (1980-2000): *Speaker Builder;* (199?-2000): *Audio Electronics;* Which was formerly (1970-199?): *Audio Amateur.* [ISSN: 1548-6028] 2001. m. USD 32 domestic; USD 63 per issue foreign; USD 7 newsstand/cover per issue. Ed(s): Edward T Dell, Jr. Audio Amateur Corporation, 305 Union Street, Peterborough, NH 03458; custserv@audioxpress.com. Illus., adv. Sample. Circ: 16000 Paid. *Indexed:* IHTDI. *Aud.:* Hs, Ga.

For the do-it-yourself audiophile, *AudioXpress* covers subjects ranging from amplifiers to vacuum tube technology. Articles feature new projects as well as tips to help upgrade current equipment. Includes reviews of equipment and columns with advice from experts in audio technology.

2136. *Digital Signal Processing.* [ISSN: 1051-2004] 1991. 6x/yr. EUR 606. Ed(s): J. Campbell, M. Rangaswamy. Academic Press, 525 B St, Ste 1900, San Diego, CA 92101-4495; apsubs@acad.com; http://www.elsevier.com/. Illus. Sample. Refereed. Online: EBSCO Publishing, EBSCO Host; Gale; IngentaConnect; OCLC Online Computer Library Center, Inc.; OhioLINK; ScienceDirect; SwetsWise Online Content. *Indexed:* EngInd, SCI. *Aud.:* Ac, Sa.

Consisting of peer-reviewed research articles and reviews that cover new technologies, this journal is for electronic engineers, scientists, and business managers engaged in digital signal processing. The diverse subjects covered include digital signal processing applications in biomedicine, astronomy, telecommunications, geology, and biology. This journal is available online via Swets, Gale, Elsevier, and other vendors.

2137. *E D N World: electronic technology for engineers and engineering managers.* Former titles: *E D N Magazine;* Which incorporated (2000-2002): *CommVerge;* (1962-1971): *Electronic Equipment Engineering - E E E;* (until 1961): *Electrical Design News.* 1956. 28x/yr. USD 149.90 domestic (Free to qualified personnel). Ed(s): Maury Wright. Reed Business Information, 275 Washington St, Newton, MA 02458; http://www.reedbusiness.com. Illus., index, adv. Sample. Circ: 136000 Paid and controlled. Vol. ends: No. 26. *Indexed:* ABIn, AS&TI, C&ISA, CerAb, IAA, MicrocompInd, SCI. *Bk. rev.:* Number and length vary. *Aud.:* Ac, Sa.

Written by and for electronic design engineers, *EDN World* contains practical, technical articles on current design topics, illustrated by numerous images of schematics, charts, and photographs. In addition, this journal has shorter feature articles that highlight the latest news and trends in electronic design. Full text is online at www.edn.com.

2138. *E E Times: the industry newspaper for engineers and technical management.* [ISSN: 0192-1541] 1972. w. USD 280 domestic (Free to qualified personnel). Ed(s): Brian Fuller. C M P Media LLC, 600 Community Dr, Manhasset, NY 11030; http://www.eetimes.com. Adv.

Circ: 150000 Controlled. Microform: PQC. Online: Florida Center for Library Automation; Gale; LexisNexis; OCLC Online Computer Library Center, Inc.; ProQuest K-12 Learning Solutions; ProQuest LLC (Ann Arbor). *Indexed:* ABIn, C&ISA, CWI, CerAb, EngInd, IAA, LRI. *Aud.:* Ga, Ac, Sa.

This trade publication is focused on the key trends and news in the electronics industry. Written for engineers and technical managers, it is a weekly tabloid that contains statistics, charts, and tables on the electronics industry sector.

Electronic Business. See Business/Trade and Industry section.

2139. *Electronic Design.* [ISSN: 0013-4872] 1952. bi-w. USD 100 domestic (Free to qualified personnel). Ed(s): Paul Whytock. Penton Media, Inc., 1300 E 9th St, Cleveland, OH 44114-1503; information@penton.com; http://www.penton.com/. Illus., index, adv. Sample. Circ: 145000 Controlled. Vol. ends: No. 28. Microform: PQC. Online: The Dialog Corporation; EBSCO Publishing, EBSCO Host; Factiva, Inc.; Florida Center for Library Automation; Gale; Northern Light Technology, Inc.; OCLC Online Computer Library Center, Inc.; ProQuest K-12 Learning Solutions; ProQuest LLC (Ann Arbor); H.W. Wilson. *Indexed:* ABIn, AS&TI, C&ISA, CerAb, EngInd, IAA, MicrocompInd. *Bk. rev.:* Number and length vary. *Aud.:* Ac, Sa.

Electronic Design features regular short, practical articles on various subjects of interest to design engineers such as EDA, test and measurement, and communications. Two longer features include "Design Solutions," written by contributors who provide more in-depth advice and problem solutions, and "Technology Report," which addresses current topics in the world of electronic design. Full text is available online via Factiva, Gale, ProQuest, and other vendors.

2140. *Electronic Engineering Design.* Formerly (until 2001): *Electronic Engineering.* 1928. m. GBP 95.48 domestic; USD 214 foreign; GBP 10.09 newsstand/cover per issue domestic. Ed(s): Ron Neale. C M P Europe Ltd, Lutgate House, 245 Blackfriars Rd, London, SE1 9UY, United Kingdom. Illus., adv. Sample. Circ: 25444. Vol. ends: Dec. Microform: PMC; PQC. Online: EBSCO Publishing, EBSCO Host; Gale; OCLC Online Computer Library Center, Inc. *Indexed:* ABIn, AS&TI, BrTechI, CEA, ChemAb, CompLI, ExcerpMed, MicrocompInd. *Aud.:* Ac, Sa.

A British trade publication, *Electronic Engineering Design* focuses on new products and industry news from the United Kingdom, but it covers the United States and other regions as well. Controversial and innovative technologies are highlighted, as are profiles of electronics designers who are currently in the news.

Electronic House. See Home section.

2141. *Electronic News (San Jose).* Former titles (until 1991): *Chilton's Electronic News; Electronic News.* [ISSN: 1061-6624] 1957. w. 51/yr. USD 119 domestic; USD 199 Canada; USD 329 elsewhere. Ed(s): Ed Sperling. Reed Business Information, 1101 S Winchester Blvd, Bldg N, San Jose, CA 95128-3901; http://www.reedbusiness.com. Illus., adv. Sample. Circ: 46250 Paid. Microform: MIM; PQC. Online: The Dialog Corporation; EBSCO Publishing, EBSCO Host; Factiva, Inc.; Florida Center for Library Automation; Gale; LexisNexis; OCLC Online Computer Library Center, Inc.; ProQuest LLC (Ann Arbor); H.W. Wilson. *Indexed:* ABIn, BPI, MASUSE. *Bk. rev.:* 1, 700-1,000 words. *Aud.:* Ac, Sa.

This title is aimed at managers who are involved in businesses that are related in any way to electronics. Features include news and trends in industries such as automotive, telecommunications, defense, packaging, supply chain, medical, and semiconductors. This title is useful for market research, financial information, and government contract news for the electronics industry. Full text is available online.

2142. *Electronics Letters.* [ISSN: 0013-5194] 1965. 25x/yr. USD 1900 in the Americas print or online ed.; GBP 1100 elsewhere print or online ed.; USD 2280 combined subscription in the Americas print & online eds. Ed(s): Chris Toumazou, Ian White. The Institution of Engineering and Technology, Michael Faraday House, Six Hills Way, Stevenage, SG1 2AY, United Kingdom; journals@theiet.org; http://www.theiet.org/. Illus., index, adv. Sample. Refereed. Circ: 2200. Vol. ends: No. 25. *Indexed:* C&ISA, CerAb, ChemAb, EngInd, ExcerpMed, IAA, SCI. *Aud.:* Ac, Sa.

Electronics Letters contains short research papers that address the most current international developments in electronics. This journal is now published by the Institution of Engineering and Technology, a new institution formed by the joining together of the IEE (Institution of Electrical Engineers) and the IIE (Institution of Incorporated Engineers). Each issue contains about 30 papers that cover both the science and technology of electronics. Full text is available online from a variety of vendors.

2143. *Electronics Supply & Manufacturing.* [ISSN: 1549-5752] 2004. m. Free to qualified personnel. Ed(s): Bruce Rayner. C M P Media LLC, 600 Community Dr, Manhasset, NY 11030; http://www.cmp.com. Adv. *Aud.:* Sa.

Written for OEM and EMS middle management, *Electronics Supply & Manufacturing* covers the news, trends, and issues in supply chain management, supply base management, design chain management, manufacturing management, and business management. Articles include best practices, case studies, and industry analysis. Full text is available online back to April 2004, at www.my-esm.com.

2144. *Embedded Systems Design: creative solutions for senior systems designers and their teams.* Formerly (until Oct. 2005): *Embedded Systems Programming.* [ISSN: 1558-2493] 1988. m. USD 55 domestic (Free to qualified personnel). Ed(s): Richard Nass. C M P Media LLC, 600 Harrison St, 6th Fl., San Francisco, CA 94107; http://www.cmp.com. Adv. Circ: 45000. Online: Gale; LexisNexis; ProQuest LLC (Ann Arbor). *Indexed:* CompLI, MicrocompInd. *Aud.:* Ac, Sa.

Embedded Systems Design is a magazine for electronic systems designers who are responsible for selecting, integrating, and building hardware and software components and systems for their companies. Each issue contains short articles that highlight featured products and longer feature articles that address specific problems encountered by system designers. Available full-text online via ProQuest.

Home Theater. See Television, Video, and Radio/Home Entertainment section.

2145. *IEEE Circuits & Devices: the magazine of electronic and photonic systems.* Former titles (until 1990): *IEEE Circuits and Devices Magazine;* (until 1984): *IEEE Circuits and Systems Magazine;* Which superseded: *Circuits and Systems.* 1979. bi-m. USD 275. Ed(s): Ronald W Waynant. IEEE, 445 Hoes Ln, Piscataway, NJ 08854-1331; subscription-service@ieee.org; http://www.ieee.org. Illus., index, adv. Sample. Refereed. Circ: 30725. Vol. ends: Nov. *Indexed:* C&ISA, CerAb, EngInd, IAA, SCI, SSCI. *Bk. rev.:* Number and length vary. *Aud.:* Ac, Sa.

Software and book reviews, new product listings, and a conference calendar are some of the features available in this journal, published by the Circuits and Systems Society, Electron Devices Society, and Lasers and Electro-Optics Society of the IEEE. Articles cover the design, implementation, packaging, and manufacture of micro-electronic and photonic devices, circuits, and systems. Available online via IEEE.

2146. *IEEE Electron Device Letters.* Formerly (until Jan. 1980): *Electron Device Letters.* [ISSN: 0741-3106] 1980. m. USD 815. Ed(s): John R Brews. IEEE, 445 Hoes Ln, Piscataway, NJ 08854-1331; subscription-service@ieee.org; http://www.ieee.org. Illus., index. Sample. Refereed. Online: Pub.; EBSCO Publishing, EBSCO Host. *Indexed:* AS&TI, C&ISA, CerAb, ChemAb, EngInd, IAA, SCI. *Aud.:* Ac, Sa.

ELECTRONICS

This journal is published by the IEEE Electron Device Society, and publishes original research and significant contributions relating to the theory, design, and performance of electron and ion devices, solid state devices, integrated electronic devices, and optoelectronic devices and energy sources. *IEEE Electron Device Letters* was the 15th most cited journal in electrical and electronics engineering according to the annual *Journal Citation Report* (2004).

2147. *IEEE Journal of Quantum Electronics.* [ISSN: 0018-9197] 1965. bi-m. USD 1550. Ed(s): Laura Vansavage. IEEE, 445 Hoes Ln, Piscataway, NJ 08854-1331; subscription-service@ieee.org; http://www.ieee.org. Illus., index. Sample. Refereed. Online: Pub.; EBSCO Publishing, EBSCO Host. *Indexed:* AS&TI, C&ISA, CerAb, ChemAb, EngInd, IAA, SCI. *Aud.:* Ac, Sa.

The annual *Journal Citation Report* (2004) named the *IEEE Journal of Quantum Electronics* the fourth most-cited electronics journal. Each issue highlights specific subjects, and the articles are grouped accordingly. Published by the IEEE Lasers and Electro-Optics Society, this journal covers technology in which quantum electronic devices are used. Available online via IEEE.

2148. *IEEE Transactions on Circuits and Systems Part 1: Regular Papers.* Formerly (until 2003): *IEEE Transactions on Circuits and Systems Part 1: Fundamental Theory and Applications;* Which superseded in part (in 1992): *IEEE Transactions on Circuits and Systems;* Which was formerly (until 1973): *IEEE Transactions on Circuit Theory;* (until 1962): *I R E Transactions on Circuit Theory;* (until 1954): *Professional Group on Circuit Theory. Transactions.* [ISSN: 1549-8328] 1952. m. USD 750. Ed(s): Pier Paolo Civalleri. IEEE, 445 Hoes Ln, Piscataway, NJ 08854-1331; subscription-service@ieee.org; http://www.computer.org. Illus., index. Sample. Refereed. Vol. ends: No. 12. Online: Pub.; EBSCO Publishing, EBSCO Host. *Indexed:* AS&TI, C&ISA, CCMJ, CerAb, ChemAb, CompLI, EngInd, IAA, MSN, MathR, SCI, SSCI. *Aud.:* Ac, Sa.

Published by the IEEE Circuits and Systems Society, *IEEE Transactions on Circuits and Systems* contains peer-reviewed papers on the theory and applications of circuits and systems, both analog and digital. Articles contain numerous charts and tables as well as short biographies of the authors. Available online through IEEE.

2149. *IEEE Transactions on Circuits and Systems. Part 2: Express Briefs.* Formerly (until 2004): *IEEE Transactions on Circuits and Systems Part 2: Analog and Digital Signal Processing;* Which superseded in part (in 1992): *IEEE Transactions on Circuits and Systems;* Which was formerly (until 1973): *IEEE Transactions on Circuit Theory;* (until 1962): *I R E Transactions on Circuit Theory;* (until 1954): *Transactions of the I R E Professional Group on Circuit Theory.* [ISSN: 1549-7747] 1952. m. USD 715. Ed(s): Edgar Sanchez Sinencio. IEEE, 445 Hoes Ln, Piscataway, NJ 08854-1331; subscription-service@ieee.org; http://www.computer.org. Illus., index. Sample. Refereed. Vol. ends: No. 12. Online: Pub.; EBSCO Publishing, EBSCO Host. *Indexed:* AS&TI, C&ISA, CerAb, CompLI, EngInd, IAA, SCI. *Aud.:* Ac, Sa.

The intent of *IEEE Transactions on Circuits and Systems—II: Express Briefs* is rapid dissemination of original innovations and ideas on the subject of digital and analog circuits and systems. If an article is accepted, it is scheduled to be published four months from date of receipt. Authors may send more in-depth articles to the sister publication *IEEE Transactions on Circuits and Systems Part 1: Regular Papers,* (above in this section). Available online via IEEE.

2150. *IEEE Transactions on Consumer Electronics.* Former titles (until 1974): *IEEE Transactions on Broadcast and Television Receivers;* (until 1962): *I R E Transactions on Broadcast and Television Receivers;* (until 1954): *I R E Professional Group on Broadcast and Television Receivers. Transactions.* [ISSN: 0098-3063] 1952. q. USD 270. Ed(s): Wayne C Luplow. IEEE, 445 Hoes Ln, Piscataway, NJ 08854-1331; subscription-service@ieee.org; http://www.ieee.org. Illus., index. Sample. Refereed. Vol. ends: Nov. Online: Pub.; EBSCO Publishing, EBSCO Host. *Indexed:* AS&TI, C&ISA, CerAb, ChemAb, CompLI, EngInd, ErgAb, IAA, MathR, SCI, SSCI. *Bk. rev.:* Number and length vary. *Aud.:* Ac, Sa.

This publication from the IEEE emphasizes new technology in consumer electronics. Consumer electronics includes products and components used for leisure, education, or entertainment. Many of the papers in this journal are those that were presented at the International Conference on Consumer Electronics. It is available electronically through the IEEE.

2151. *IEEE Transactions on Electromagnetic Compatibility.* [ISSN: 0018-9375] 1959. q. USD 380. Ed(s): Motohisa Kanda. IEEE, 445 Hoes Ln, Piscataway, NJ 08854-1331; subscription-service@ieee.org; http://www.computer.org. Illus., index. Sample. Refereed. Vol. ends: Nov. Online: Pub.; EBSCO Publishing, EBSCO Host. *Indexed:* C&ISA, CerAb, ChemAb, EngInd, IAA, MathR, SCI. *Aud.:* Ac, Sa.

According to the *2004 Journal Citation Report, IEEE Transactions on Electromagnetic Compatibility* was the 19th most cited journal in telecommunications. Topics covered in this journal include measurement techniques and standards, spectrum conservation and utilization, and equipment and systems related to electromagnetic compatibility. This IEEE publication includes correspondence, brief articles, and longer papers. Available full-text online via the IEEE.

2152. *IEEE Transactions on Electron Devices.* Former titles (until 1962): *I R E Transactions on Electron Devices;* (until 1954): *I R E Professional Group on Electron Devices. Transactions.* [ISSN: 0018-9383] 1952. m. USD 1350. Ed(s): Renuka P Jindal. IEEE, 445 Hoes Ln, Piscataway, NJ 08854-1331; subscription-service@ieee.org; http://www.ieee.org. Illus., index. Sample. Refereed. Vol. ends: No. 12. Online: Pub.; EBSCO Publishing, EBSCO Host. *Indexed:* AS&TI, C&ISA, CerAb, ChemAb, CompLI, EngInd, ExcerpMed, IAA, MathR, SCI. *Bk. rev.:* Number and length vary. *Aud.:* Ac, Sa.

The IEEE Electron Device Society publishes this monthly journal, which covers the theory, design, performance, and reliability of electron devices. Two types of papers are selected for inclusion: peer-reviewed, in-depth regular papers; and briefs covering preliminary results or reporting of recently completed projects. There is also a section for letters to the editor. Full text is available online through the IEEE.

2153. *IEEE Transactions on Industrial Electronics.* Former titles (until 1981): *IEEE Transactions on Industrial Electronics and Control Instrumentation;* (until 1963): *IEEE Transactions on Industrial Electronics;* (until 1962): *I R E Transactions on Industrial Electronics;* (until 1959): *I R E Professional Group on Industrial Electronics. Transactions.* [ISSN: 0278-0046] 1953. bi-m. USD 765. Ed(s): Marian Kazmierkowski. IEEE, 445 Hoes Ln, Piscataway, NJ 08854-1331; subscription-service@ieee.org; http://www.computer.org. Illus., index. Sample. Refereed. Vol. ends: Nov. Online: Pub.; EBSCO Publishing, EBSCO Host. *Indexed:* AS&TI, ApMecR, C&ISA, CerAb, ChemAb, EngInd, IAA, MathR, SCI. *Bk. rev.:* Number and length vary. *Aud.:* Ac, Sa.

Each issue of *IEEE Transactions on Industrial Electronics* features a special section of reviewed papers that cover a specific topic on the application of electronics to industrial and manufacturing systems and processes. Each special section of papers is preceded by a guest editorial that explains the special topic that is to be covered. Following the special section papers are papers on various topics, letters, and comments. As in all *IEEE Transactions* journals, short biographies and photos of authors are included. Online availability is via IEEE.

2154. *IEEE Transactions on Power Electronics.* [ISSN: 0885-8993] 1986. bi-m. USD 665. Ed(s): Dr. J D Van Wyk. IEEE, 445 Hoes Ln, Piscataway, NJ 08854-1331; subscription-service@ieee.org; http://www.ieee.org. Illus., index. Sample. Refereed. Vol. ends: Oct. Online: Pub.; EBSCO Publishing, EBSCO Host. *Indexed:* C&ISA, CerAb, EngInd, IAA, SCI. *Aud.:* Ac, Sa.

Published by the Power Electronics Society of the IEEE, *IEEE Transactions on Power Electronics* has the highest impact factor of any journal in power electronics, according to its editor-in-chief, Frede Blaabjerg. As of 2006, *IEEE Power Electronics Letters* has merged with this publication, producing one journal that contains both long research papers and the shorter letters that introduce new developments and ideas. Online availability is from IEEE.

2155. *Institute of Electrical and Electronics Engineers. Proceedings.* Former titles (until 1962): *Proceedings of the IRE;* (until 1938): *Proceedings of the Institute of Radio Engineers.* [ISSN: 0018-9219] 1913. m. USD 775; USD 915 combined subscription print & online eds. Ed(s): Fawwaz Ulaby, James Calder. IEEE, 445 Hoes Ln, Piscataway, NJ 08854-1331; subscription-service@ieee.org; http://www.ieee.org. Illus., index, adv. Sample. Refereed. Circ: 25000 Paid. Vol. ends: Dec. Online: Pub.; EBSCO Publishing, EBSCO Host. *Indexed:* AS&TI, BioEngAb, C&ISA, CerAb, ChemAb, EngInd, ErgAb, ExcerpMed, IAA, MathR, PetrolAb, RILM, SCI, SSCI. *Aud.:* Ga, Ac, Sa.

Published since 1913 and renowned as the most highly-cited general interest journal in electrical engineering and computer science, the *Proceedings of the IEEE* contains in-depth tutorial and review articles in the areas of electrical engineering and technology. Also included are survey articles that review an existing technology. Each issue focuses on a special topic, preceded by an editorial that reviews the included papers. Articles are written for the IEEE member or the general reader who has some background in electrical engineering. Available online via IEEE.

2156. *International Journal of Electronics.* Supersedes in part (in 1965): *Journal of Electronics and Control;* Which was formerly (1955-1957): *Journal of Electronics.* [ISSN: 0020-7217] 1965. m. GBP 1866 print & online eds. Ed(s): Dr. Stepan Lucyszyn. Taylor & Francis Ltd., 4 Park Sq, Milton Park, Abingdon, OX14 4RN, United Kingdom; info@tandf.co.uk; http://www.tandf.co.uk/journals. Illus., index. Refereed. Online: EBSCO Publishing, EBSCO Host; Gale; IngentaConnect; OCLC Online Computer Library Center, Inc.; SwetsWise Online Content. Reprint: PSC. *Indexed:* ApMecR, C&ISA, CerAb, ChemAb, EngInd, ExcerpMed, IAA, MathR, SCI. *Aud.:* Ac, Sa.

International Journal of Electronics originates in the United Kingdom and publishes articles in these topic areas of electronics: solid state; power; analogue; RF and microwave; and digital. Each issue contains fewer than ten full-length papers that report a theoretical or experimental perspective on one of the above topics. Full text is available online via various vendors.

2157. *Journal of Active and Passive Electronic Devices.* [ISSN: 1555-0281] 2005. q. USD 498 (print & online eds.) Individuals, USD 122). Ed(s): Robert Castellano, John N Avaritsiotis. Old City Publishing, Inc., 628 N 2nd St, Philadelphia, PA 19123; info@oldcitypublishing.com; http://www.oldcitypublishing.com. Refereed. *Bk. rev.:* Number and length vary. *Aud.:* Ac, Sa.

International in scope, this is a new academic journal that fills the subject gap of active and passive electronic devices. This peer-reviewed journal includes review articles, short communications, long articles, and book reviews on the subject of electronic components. Full text is available online for 2005–2006 at www.oldcitypublishing.com/JAPED/JAPED.html.

2158. *Journal of Electronic Materials.* [ISSN: 0361-5235] 1971. m. EUR 552 print & online eds. Ed(s): Suzanne Mahney. Springer New York LLC, 233 Spring St, New York, NY 10013-1578; journals@springer-ny.com; http://www.springer.com. Illus., index, adv. Sample. Refereed. Circ: 1300. Vol. ends: No. 12. Microform: PQC. Online: EBSCO Publishing, EBSCO Host; Gale; IngentaConnect; OCLC Online Computer Library Center, Inc.; ProQuest K-12 Learning Solutions; ProQuest LLC (Ann Arbor). Reprint: PSC. *Indexed:* AS&TI, C&ISA, CerAb, ChemAb, EngInd, IAA, SCI. *Aud.:* Ac, Sa.

This journal is published by the The Minerals, Metals & Materials Society (TMS) and the Institute of Electrical and Electronics Engineers (IEEE). Written for practicing materials engineers and scientists, the *Journal of Electronic Materials* contains peer-reviewed technical papers about new developments in the science and technology of the materials used in electronics, as well as review papers, letters, and selected papers from conferences and meetings from the TMS. Several special issues are published during the year containing articles that focus on the same aspect of electronic materials. Available in full text from IEEE.

2159. *Microelectronics Journal.* Formerly (until 1978): *Microelectronics;* Incorporates (1983-1991): *Journal of Semi-Custom I Cs;* (1983-1991): *Semi-Custom I C Yearbook.* [ISSN: 0959-8324] 1967. 12x/yr. EUR 1736. Ed(s): Mohamed Henini, Bernard Courtois. Elsevier Ltd., The Boulevard, Langford Ln, Oxford, OX5 1GB, United Kingdom. Illus., index, adv. Sample. Refereed. Circ: 700. Online: EBSCO Publishing, EBSCO Host; Gale; IngentaConnect; OhioLINK; ScienceDirect; SwetsWise Online Content. *Indexed:* C&ISA, ChemAb, EngInd, SCI. *Bk. rev.:* Number and length vary. *Aud.:* Ac, Sa.

International in scope, *Microelectronics Journal* covers the research on and applications of microelectronics circuits, systems, physics, and devices. Review articles are included, as are papers that present an unusual or new system design or device. Papers are peer reviewed and contain an abstract and keywords. Full text is available online through various vendors.

2160. *Nuts & Volts: exploring everything for electronics.* Formerly: *Nuts & Volts Magazine.* [ISSN: 1528-9885] 1979. m. USD 24.95 domestic; USD 31.95 Canada; USD 42.95 elsewhere. T & L Publications, 430 Princeland Ct, Corona, CA 92879; subscribe@nutsvolts.com; http://www.nutsvolts.com. Illus., adv. Sample. Circ: 45000. *Indexed:* BiolDig, IHTDI. *Aud.:* Hs, Ga.

Written for the electronics hobbyist, design engineer, and electronics technician, *Nuts & Volts* contains information on equipment and do-it-yourself projects in robotics, lasers, circuit design, computer control, automation, laser, and data acquisition. There are also columns that feature new technology, products, and electronics news.

2161. *Semiconductor International: the semiconductor industry's technical authority.* Incorporates (in 2006): *Semiconductor Manufacturing Magazine;* Which was formerly (until 2003): *Semiconductor Magazine;* (until 2000): *Channel;* Incorporates (1961-2003): *Electronic Packaging & Production.* [ISSN: 0163-3767] 1978. m. USD 131.99 domestic; USD 178.90 Canada; USD 164.50 Mexico. Ed(s): Pete Singer. Reed Business Information, 2000 Clearwater Dr, Oak Brook, IL 60523; http://www.reedbusiness.com. Illus., adv. Sample. Circ: 43500 Controlled. Vol. ends: No. 14. Microform: PQC. Online: EBSCO Publishing, EBSCO Host; Factiva, Inc.; Gale; LexisNexis; OCLC Online Computer Library Center, Inc.; ProQuest LLC (Ann Arbor); H.W. Wilson. *Indexed:* ABIn, AS&TI, ChemAb, EngInd, MicrocompInd. *Aud.:* Ac, Sa.

A trade publication for the semiconductor industry, *Semiconductor International* provides information on technology, markets, news, and newsmakers for the manager or engineer focused on semiconductors. Each issue provides both feature articles and regular columns that contain numerous color images, charts, and graphs. This magazine is available online full-text from a number of vendors.

2162. *Semiconductor Science and Technology.* [ISSN: 0268-1242] 1986. m. USD 2960 print & online eds. Ed(s): L Molenkamp. Institute of Physics Publishing, Dirac House, Temple Back, Bristol, BS1 6BE, United Kingdom; custserv@iop.org; http://www.iop.org. Illus., index, adv. Sample. Refereed. Circ: 689. Vol. ends: No. 12. Online: EBSCO Publishing, EBSCO Host; Gale; IngentaConnect; OhioLINK; SwetsWise Online Content. *Indexed:* AS&TI, C&ISA, ChemAb, EngInd, SCI. *Aud.:* Ac, Sa.

Published by the Institute of Physics, *Semiconductor Science and Technology* is an international journal that covers semiconductor research and its applications. Research papers, review articles, and rapid communications (replacing "Letters" as of 2006) are all peer reviewed and are written for the scientist or engineer. Occasionally, an issue will cover a specific topic. Two such special issues for 2006 and 2007 are "Carbon Nanotubes" and "Optical Orientation." Full text is available online.

2163. *Solid-State Electronics.* [ISSN: 0038-1101] 1960. 12x/yr. EUR 3201. Ed(s): Y Arakawa. Pergamon, The Boulevard, Langford Ln, East Park, Kidlington, OX5 1GB, United Kingdom. Illus., index, adv. Refereed. Circ: 2400. Vol. ends: No. 12. Microform: MIM; PQC. Online: EBSCO

Publishing, EBSCO Host; Gale; IngentaConnect; OhioLINK; ScienceDirect; SwetsWise Online Content. *Indexed:* AS&TI, C&ISA, ChemAb, EngInd, ExcerpMed, IAA, IBR, SCI, SSCI. *Bk. rev.:* Number and length vary. *Aud.:* Ac, Sa.

This international journal consists of collections of original research papers covering the theory, design, physics, modeling, measurement, preparation, evaluation, and applications of solid-state electronics, crystal growth, semiconductors and circuit engineering. The letters, review papers, and research papers emphasize the new and innovative and the connection of theory and practice. Full text is available online.

2164. *Solid State Technology.* Former titles (until 1968): *Semiconductor Products and Solid State Technology;* (until 1962): *Semiconductor Products.* [ISSN: 0038-111X] 1958. m. USD 234 domestic (Free to qualified personnel). Ed(s): Phil Lo Piccolo, Phil LoPiccolo. PennWell Corporation, 1421 S Sheridan Rd, Tulsa, OK 74112; patrickM@pennwell.com; http://www.pennwell.com. Illus., index, adv. Sample. Circ: 41286 Controlled. Vol. ends: No. 12. Microform: PQC. Online: EBSCO Publishing, EBSCO Host; Florida Center for Library Automation; Gale; Northern Light Technology, Inc.; OCLC Online Computer Library Center, Inc.; ProQuest LLC (Ann Arbor). *Indexed:* ABIn, AS&TI, ChemAb, EngInd, IAA, RiskAb, SCI. *Bk. rev.:* Number and length vary. *Aud.:* Ac, Sa.

Solid State Technology is a trade magazine for managers and engineers in the semiconductor manufacturing industry. Each issue covers the news and technology of such topics as nanotechnology, MEMS, flat panel displays, atomic layer deposition, wafers, and waste handling, as well as the materials, software, products, and processes used in the manufacturing of semiconductors. Occasional special issues cover the state of the industry in specific geographic regions or report on important conferences and trade shows. Available online from a variety of vendors.

2165. *Techliving: your hassle-free way to live.* Former titles (until 2004): *Home Automation;* (until 2001): *Popular Home Automation.* [ISSN: 1550-199X] 1996. 7x/yr. USD 29.95 domestic; USD 70 foreign. Ed(s): Rachel Cericole. E H Publishing, Inc., 111 Speen St, Ste 200, PO Box 989, Framingham, MA 01701-2000; info@ehpub.com; http://www.ehpub.com. Illus., adv. Sample. Vol. ends: No. 6. *Indexed:* IHTDI. *Aud.:* Hs, Ga.

This consumer magazine is written for the reader who wants to keep current in home technology and electronics. Included are do-it-yourself projects and repair and installation tips, as well as reviews of new consumer electronic products such as those for entertainment, communications, home automation, and networking.

■ ENERGY

Sharon L. Siegler, Engineering Librarian, Lehigh University Library & Technology Services, Fairchild/Martindale Library, 8A Packer Ave., Bethlehem, PA 18015; FAX: 610-758-6524; sls7@lehigh.edu

Introduction

The trend in energy research and implementation is toward environmentally friendly fuel sources, such that biomass fuel provides a new twist to the term "green fuel." More energy journals are featuring biomass, wind, wave (or tidal), geothermal, and solar energy, even when these are not the main thrust of the title. Combinations (for instance, diesel fuel and biomass) are common. "Renewables" are stressed in technical and policy journals alike, with concomitant attention to energy conservation. There is even an *International Journal of Green Energy.* The number of publications in energy/power research and application is astounding, even when limited to English-language titles. This section samples the technical aspects of all forms of energy sources, with attention to the legal, public policy, and economic issues as well. Prices range from free (such as the *Monthly Energy Review*) through inexpensive (many of the trade and society magazines), and on to the sometimes astonishingly

expensive scholarly publications. It is difficult to dabble in this field; it is better to pick an area of specialization (oil, policy, conservation and the like) and then acquire the titles that suit the local library collection.

Basic Periodicals

Ga: *Power Engineering, U.S. Energy Information Administration. Monthly Energy Review, World Oil;* Ac: *Energy & Fuels, The Energy Journal, Fuel, Solar Energy Materials and Solar Cells, U.S. Energy Information Administration. Monthly Energy Review.*

Basic Abstracts and Indexes

Applied Science and Technology Abstracts, Engineering Index, Science Abstracts.

2166. *Applied Energy.* [ISSN: 0306-2619] 1975. 12x/yr. EUR 2784. Ed(s): P Walsh, S D Probert. Pergamon, The Boulevard, Langford Ln, East Park, Kidlington, OX5 1GB, United Kingdom. Illus., adv. Refereed. Microform: PQC. Online: EBSCO Publishing, EBSCO Host; Gale; IngentaConnect; OhioLINK; ScienceDirect; SwetsWise Online Content. *Indexed:* ApMecR, C&ISA, ChemAb, EngInd, EnvAb, EnvInd, ExcerpMed, PollutAb, SCI, SSCI. *Aud.:* Ac.

Applied Energy discusses energy conversion, conservation, and management from the engineering point of view. Research here is not to develop new energy sources, but to better utilize the ones presently in use. Each issue contains about half a dozen research articles; the exceptions are special thematic issues, which may have many more. Articles in recent issues examine "environmental advantages of superconducting devices in distributed electricity-generation," "economic feasibility of waste heat to power conversion," and "developing a simplified model for evaluating chiller-system configurations." Articles are lengthier than most, averaging more than 15 pages and often exceeding that. Authors are almost exclusively academics or from government-sponsored research institutions. With some exceptions, the lag time between receipt and publication is quite short—sometimes less than two months—so that much of the work is very current. Mounted in *ScienceDirect*, searching, display, linking (e-mail, references), and RSS feeds features are well implemented. Unfortunately, this is a relatively expensive title in the field and it should be considered only for an extensive academic library collection.

2167. *Applied Thermal Engineering.* Former titles (until vol.16, 1996): *Heat Recovery Systems and C H P (Combined Heat and Power);* (until 1983): *Journal of Heat Recovery Systems.* [ISSN: 1359-4311] 1980. 18x/yr. EUR 2164. Ed(s): David A Reay. Pergamon, The Boulevard, Langford Ln, East Park, Kidlington, OX5 1GB, United Kingdom. Refereed. Microform: PQC. Online: EBSCO Publishing, EBSCO Host; Gale; IngentaConnect; OhioLINK; ScienceDirect; SwetsWise Online Content. *Indexed:* ApMecR, C&ISA, CEA, CerAb, ChemAb, EngInd, EnvAb, H&SSA, IAA, SCI. *Aud.:* Ac, Sa.

This journal covers thermal energy applications in depth, from the theoretical ("The greenhouse effect: A new source of energy") to the extremely practical ("Dishwasher and washing machine heated by a hot water circulation loop"). Usually, though, work involves energy production and large-scale use (such as manufacturing or building heating plants). Although the journal is academic in thrust, many of the authors are from industrial concerns; the editor himself maintains a private practice as well as an academic appointment. Articles are lengthy (often more than 20 pages). The lag time between submission and electronic publication is often within six months of receipt, but print readers can expect to wait over a year. Occasionally, an issue is devoted to the proceedings of a conference, but the bulk of the papers are current, independent research. Occasional conference announcements and patent alerts round out the issues. Those libraries with strong interests in energy and mechanical engineering would find this a welcome title, but compare it to *Applied Energy*.

2168. *Biomass & Bioenergy.* [ISSN: 0961-9534] 1991. 12x/yr. EUR 1524. Ed(s): R P Overend, C P Mitchell. Pergamon, The Boulevard, Langford Ln, East Park, Kidlington, OX5 1GB, United Kingdom. Refereed. Microform: PQC. Online: EBSCO Publishing, EBSCO Host; Gale;

IngentaConnect; OhioLINK; ScienceDirect; SwetsWise Online Content. *Indexed:* BioEngAb, BiolAb, CABA, ChemAb, DSA, EngInd, EnvAb, EnvInd, FPA, ForAb, HortAb, PollutAb, RRTA, S&F, SCI, WAE&RSA. *Aud.:* Ac.

As the title indicates, the coverage of this journal is very mixed. Some articles will appeal mostly to agribusiness endeavors, discussing harvesting methods, agricultural waste, pesticide runoff, and the like. Others will appeal to the energy engineer, with BTU figures and combustion problems associated with biofuels. Still others will appeal to economists and managers, with long-range forecasting of biofuel production and usage. One recent article on "environmental systems analysis of biogas systems: the environmental impact of replacing various reference systems" will appeal to those involved in the popular argument "are biofuels less or more expensive to produce than what they are intended to replace?" Authors are from academia and government-sponsored research laboratories, with a wide range of backgrounds: engineering, agriculture, economics, and more. The publication lag is now approaching two years, even with early posting on the web site. Institutions with strong agriculture as well as energy collections will find this a core title. Some geographic areas will have a strong interest in this type of energy source, while others will find this a niche topic.

2169. *Distributed Energy: the journal for onsite power solutions.* [ISSN: 1546-9751] 2003. bi-m. USD 48 (Free to qualified personnel). Ed(s): John Trotti. Forester Communications, Inc., PO Box 3100, Santa Barbara, CA 93130; http://www.forester.net. Adv. Circ: 18000. *Aud.:* Sa.

"Distributed energy" is also known as "distributed generation of energy," which gives a clearer idea of this relatively new approach to energy delivery and conservation. Although it requires careful engineering to put into practice, it is largely a management issue: how to better utilize energy resources to obtain reliable, less-expensive power. Thus, this isn't likely to be a "home energy" project, but it is eminently suited to large complexes, such as hospitals, campuses (both industrial and academic), high-rise buildings, and even, as California found, the county jail (see the March/April 2007 issue). As much concerned with reliability as with lower cost and efficiency, this approach to power supplies reduces the impact of regional power outages and price fluctuation. *Distributed Energy* may be the only publication specifically devoted to the field, although there are others in electrical power distribution and cogeneration that cover the topic. The articles are short, generally without references, and often by industry-related authors or freelance writers. Many of them describe success stories; others look into policy and economic issues. All articles are presently freely available at the web site. There is also a convenient, simple keyword search engine (which includes all of the publisher's magazines). Designed for the engineer and/or manager specifically engaged in managing power operations, this will be a useful title for many industry libraries.

2170. *Energy.* [ISSN: 0360-5442] 1976. 15x/yr. EUR 2334. Ed(s): Dr. N Lior. Pergamon, The Boulevard, Langford Ln, East Park, Kidlington, OX5 1GB, United Kingdom. Illus., index, adv. Sample. Refereed. Circ: 1100. Vol. ends: Dec. Microform: PQC. Online: EBSCO Publishing, EBSCO Host; Gale; IngentaConnect; OhioLINK; ScienceDirect; SwetsWise Online Content. *Indexed:* AS&TI, AgeL, BAS, BrTechI, C&ISA, CABA, CerAb, ChemAb, DSA, EngInd, EnvAb, ExcerpMed, FPA, ForAb, HortAb, IAA, PollutAb, RRTA, S&F, SCI, SWRA, WAE&RSA. *Aud.:* Ac.

One of the first scholarly journals in the energy field, this title covers the full spectrum: all types of energy sources, all aspects of energy production, plus economic/political/social factors. *Energy* emphasizes development, assessment, and management of energy programs. Most papers involving technical matter average fewer than eight pages; those concerned with economic issues tend to be twice as long. Technical issues often have an economic or societal aspect; economic issues often have a technical flavor. Periodically, an issue will be devoted to a theme (such as "Electricity Market Reform and Deregulation") or a symposium (such as "Sustainable Development of Energy, Water and Environment Systems"). Bibliographies, maps, and statistics abound. Publication delay has shortened to about one year, alleviated somewhat by web posting of accepted articles before print publication. However, the gap between online and print versions is still almost one year. RSS

feeds, openURL linking, and downloading to citation managers are added features. A primary journal, but expensive for all except large academic or industry libraries.

2171. *Energy and Buildings.* [ISSN: 0378-7788] 1978. 12x/yr. EUR 1614. Ed(s): B B Todorovic. Elsevier S.A., PO Box 564, Lausanne, 1001, Switzerland. Illus., index, adv. Sample. Refereed. Vol. ends: No. 6. Microform: PQC. Online: EBSCO Publishing, EBSCO Host; Gale; IngentaConnect; OhioLINK; ScienceDirect; SwetsWise Online Content. *Indexed:* API, C&ISA, EngInd, EnvAb, EnvInd, ExcerpMed, PollutAb, SCI, SUSA. *Aud.:* Ac, Sa.

The emphasis here is on the "buildings," with the "energy" portion largely devoted to energy conservation, architectural design for passive energy use/savings, use of solar energy, manipulation of lighting, insulation materials, and cost/benefit analyses for energy consumption. "Sustainability" has been added to the mix, and it is also a likely source for distributed energy material, so often used in multi-occupant facilities. The buildings can be anything from high-rise complexes to grass huts, from classrooms in the tropics to crawlspaces in Finland. Although scholarly in treatment, this journal is practical in outlook; articles have discussed energy consumption in old school buildings, low-cost insulation, pressure air-flow models for ventilation, and heat transfer in insulated concrete walls. Authorship is international. Articles tend to be short (six to ten pages). Not for all collections, this title is best for libraries with interest in civil engineering or architecture as well as energy.

2172. *Energy & Environment.* [ISSN: 0958-305X] 1990. 8x/yr. GBP 386; GBP 418 combined subscription print & online eds. Ed(s): Sonja Boehmer-Christiansen. Multi-Science Publishing Co. Ltd., 5 Wates Way, Brentwood, CM15 9TB, United Kingdom; sciencem@hotmail.com; http://www.multi-science.co.uk. Refereed. Online: EBSCO Publishing, EBSCO Host; Gale; IngentaConnect; OhioLINK; SwetsWise Online Content. *Indexed:* C&ISA, CerAb, EngInd, EnvAb, EnvInd, IAA, M&GPA, PollutAb. *Aud.:* Ac.

This is a difficult journal. It is described by its editor as an interdisciplinary journal aimed at scientists, engineers, and social scientists, discussing energy's impact on the environment. More to the point, the editor sees it as a forum for all parties to discuss the issues, and actively encourages and publishes their debates. To that end, "Viewpoints and technical communications" is a regular issue feature. Most of the articles are sociopolitical or socioeconomic; the technology issues are raised, but, perforce, at a relatively superficial level. The articles themselves are scholarly treatments, extensively documented, but the authors vary in level of expertise. Very few institutions subscribe to this title, but it deserves a wider audience; regardless of the merits of the debates published here, the fact that the debates occur should help drive out bad science, bad politics, bad economics, and bad blood. Recommended with reservations to libraries with strong programs in economics and politics as well as energy.

2173. *Energy & Fuels.* [ISSN: 0887-0624] 1987. bi-m. USD 1337 print & online eds. Ed(s): Michael T Klein. American Chemical Society, 1155 16th St, NW, Washington, DC 20036; service@acs.org; http://pubs.acs.org. Illus., index, adv. Refereed. Circ: 3440. Vol. ends: Nov/Dec. Online: Pub.; EBSCO Publishing, EBSCO Host; OhioLINK; SwetsWise Online Content. *Indexed:* AS&TI, C&ISA, ChemAb, EngInd, ExcerpMed, PetrolAb, PollutAb, SCI. *Bk. rev.:* 1, 1,000 words. *Aud.:* Ac, Sa.

One of the many American Chemical Society (ACS) journals, this is a scholarly publication interested in both the discovery of non-nuclear fuels and their development as power sources. Each issue's content is arranged by category: Catalysis & Kinetics, Combustion, Environmental, Fossil Fuels, Materials, Process Engineering, and Renewable, with the sections on catalysis, combustion, and fossil fuels predominating. Renewables, however, have been getting more press recently. Individual issues often contain selected papers from symposia, reviews, and "communications" (brief notes on techniques). Authorship is from academia and includes chemists and geologists as well as engineers. Publication is often within one year of receipt of manuscript. ACS has taken advantage of the wide availability of the web: Many articles have supporting material, such as extensive tabular data, that can be accessed at its web site. The site has added RSS feeds and the option to download references to the major bibliographic managers. This is a core, quality title.

2174. *Energy & Power Management: serving the commercial, industrial and institutional markets.* Formerly (until 2005): *Energy User News;* Incorporates: *Energy User News Digest.* [ISSN: 1556-5467] 1976. m. USD 105 (Free to qualified personnel). Ed(s): Kevin Heslin. B N P Media, 2401 W Big Beaver Rd, Ste 700, Troy, MI 48084; http://www.bnpmedia.com. Illus., index, adv. Sample. Circ: 50177 Controlled. Vol. ends: Dec. Online: The Dialog Corporation; EBSCO Publishing, EBSCO Host; Factiva, Inc.; Florida Center for Library Automation; Gale; Northern Light Technology, Inc.; OCLC Online Computer Library Center, Inc. *Indexed:* ABIn, C&ISA, CerAb, IAA. *Aud.:* Ga, Sa.

At one time, this was a thin, glossy tabloid that was mostly advertisements. Although the ads are still very much there (the reason why this is "free to qualified"), *Energy & Power Management* is a good example of what the web can do for what was once basically a "buyers' guide." The "users" here are businesses and industrial concerns. Their problems include high energy costs, pollution, and upgrading their power plants. Each issue has a few topical articles. The web version archives the feature articles for about two years, for free online reading. There is a fee, however, for formatted copies and the rights to add articles to a web site. Also included is a wide array of free ancillary services, such as encyclopedia-type articles on "fundamental issues" that might provide quick answers to student questions. The monthly statistics column provides regional figures for gas and electric utility prices for commercial entities. The buyers' guide is still present, with links to a lengthy list of providers. Public libraries may consider linking to the site from their catalogs; industry libraries will want to subscribe as well.

2175. *Energy Conversion and Management.* Former titles (until 1968): *Energy Conversion; Advanced Energy Conversion.* [ISSN: 0196-8904] 1961. 20x/yr. EUR 3820. Ed(s): Jesse C. Denton, Dr. N Lior. Pergamon, The Boulevard, Langford Ln, East Park, Kidlington, OX5 1GB, United Kingdom. Illus., index, adv. Sample. Refereed. Circ: 1300. Vol. ends: No. 18. Microform: PQC. Online: EBSCO Publishing, EBSCO Host; Gale; IngentaConnect; OhioLINK; ScienceDirect; SwetsWise Online Content. *Indexed:* AS&TI, ApMecR, CABA, CEA, ChemAb, DSA, EngInd, EnvAb, EnvInd, ExcerpMed, FPA, ForAb, HortAb, PollutAb, S&F, SCI, SSCI, SWRA, WAE&RSA. *Aud.:* Ac, Sa.

Another of the many energy-related scholarly publications in the Elsevier stable, this journal is concerned with technical development of all types of fuels and energy resources, ranging from hydrocarbons though biomass, solar, wind, and other renewable sources. The topics are defined broadly, such that "Thermal management on spacecraft" and "Preparation of biodiesel from waste cooking oil" are both likely papers. While its sister publication, *Energy (Oxford),* discusses large-scale management issues, *Energy Conversion* presents detailed technical papers on the ultimate production of many of the same resources. Authorship is international. Papers have become relatively lengthy (often nearly 20 pages) and are well referenced. Although one of the most expensive titles in the field, this publication has a relatively high subscription base, probably because of the emphasis on application and its wide coverage of energy sources.

2176. *Energy Economics.* Incorporates (in 2001): *Journal of Energy Finance and Development.* [ISSN: 0140-9883] 1979. 6x/yr. EUR 977. Ed(s): J P Weyant, R S J Tol. Elsevier BV, North-Holland, Sara Burgerhartstraat 25, Amsterdam, 1055 KV, Netherlands; nlinfo-f@ elsevier.nl; http://www.elsevier.nl. Illus., index, adv. Sample. Vol. ends: No. 6. Microform: PQC. Online: EBSCO Publishing, EBSCO Host; Gale; IngentaConnect; OhioLINK; ScienceDirect; SwetsWise Online Content. *Indexed:* ABIn, EngInd, EnvAb, EnvInd, ExcerpMed, HRIS, IBSS, JEL, PAIS, PollutAb, RiskAb, SSCI, WAE&RSA. *Aud.:* Ac.

True to its name, this scholarly journal discusses the economic and tax issues of energy, generally on the macro scale. Recent issues feature "Oil and energy price volatility" (on everyone's mind these days), "Hourly electricity prices in day-ahead markets," and "Spacial peak-load pricing." Definitely international in scope, the lengthy articles have covered Indian coal, oil-price sticker shock in Europe, price rigidity in the New Zealand petroleum industry, and the Colombian electricity market. This is a journal for larger collections with an active local interest in economics; other libraries should consider *The Energy Journal.*

2177. *Energy Engineering.* Former titles (until 1980): *Building Systems Design;* (until 1969): *Air Conditioning, Heating and Ventilating;* (until 1955): *Heating and Ventilating;* (until 1929): *The Heating and Ventilating Magazine.* [ISSN: 0199-8595] 1904. bi-m. USD 200 in US & Canada; USD 250 elsewhere. Ed(s): Wayne C. Turner. The Fairmont Press, Inc., 700 Indian Trail, Lilburn, GA 30047; linda@fairmontpress.com; http://www.fairmontpress.com. Illus., index, adv. Refereed. Circ: 8771 Paid. Vol. ends: No. 6. Microform: PMC; PQC. Online: EBSCO Publishing, EBSCO Host; Northern Light Technology, Inc.; OCLC Online Computer Library Center, Inc.; ProQuest K-12 Learning Solutions; ProQuest LLC (Ann Arbor); SwetsWise Online Content; H.W. Wilson. *Indexed:* AS&TI, ChemAb, EngInd, EnvAb, ExcerpMed. *Aud.:* Ac, Sa.

This is the energy magazine for the plant engineer, high-rise building supervisor, and town engineer. Articles range from tips on energy auditing to surveys of energy waste minimization over several industries. Most articles are written by practitioners or consultants, but some are by academics. Some have lengthy reference lists and others are obviously "expert-advice" columns. Over the years, coverage has broadened from HVAC fine-tuning and lighting system adjustments to include alternative fuels, fuel cells, cogeneration, energy control systems, and "green systems." Two other journals from the same publisher (not reviewed here) are *Strategic Planning for Energy and the Environment* and *Cogeneration and Competitive Power Journal;* the former is addressed to managers and the latter discusses the technical aspects of "cogeneration" (using the byproduct of one power source to produce yet another form of energy). The publisher now has web access to all of its journals with a browsable, searchable interface; "guest users" may access sample articles. Users who register can obtain an alerting service and pay-per-view of individual articles. A good choice for a large public library and/or undergraduates in an engineering curriculum.

2178. *The Energy Journal.* [ISSN: 0195-6574] 1980. q. USD 350 in US & Canada; USD 375 elsewhere. Ed(s): G. Campbell Watkins, Adonis Yatchew. International Association for Energy Economics (I A E E), 28790 Chagrin Blvd, Ste 350, Cleveland, OH 44122; iaee@iaee.org; http://www.IAEE.org. Illus., index, adv. Sample. Refereed. Circ: 3400. Vol. ends: No. 4. Microform: PQC. Online: EBSCO Publishing, EBSCO Host; Florida Center for Library Automation; Gale; Northern Light Technology, Inc.; OCLC Online Computer Library Center, Inc.; ProQuest K-12 Learning Solutions; ProQuest LLC (Ann Arbor); H.W. Wilson. *Indexed:* ABIn, BPI, BRI, CBRI, EngInd, EnvAb, H&SSA, JEL, PAIS, PetrolAb, PollutAb, RiskAb, SCI, SSCI, SWRA. *Bk. rev.:* 4, 1,000 words. *Aud.:* Ac.

The journal of the International Association for Energy Economics, this is a scholarly publication that covers the economic and social/political aspects of energy. Generally this means electric power, but there is some attention to oil, natural gas, and coal. Representative topics include international comparisons of carbon dioxide emissions, regional oil markets, and cointegration analysis as a tool in economic forecasting. Articles are lengthy, often more than 20 pages, with extensive bibliographies, and charts and graphs as illustrations. Authors are from the international academic and government-policy community. Announcements of association conferences and business complete the issues. There are occasional special issues (available for a modest additional fee). The web site includes tables of contents and subject category indexes for the entire run of the journal, plus the option for subscribers to download issues rather than receive them by mail. This title is available in full text from several sources, and the subscription price remains low; a good choice for libraries with strong energy and economics programs.

2179. *Energy Law Journal.* [ISSN: 0270-9163] 1980. s-a. USD 35 domestic; USD 41 Canada; USD 47 elsewhere. Ed(s): Andrew Butcher. University of Tulsa, College of Law, 3120 E Fourth Pl, Tulsa, OK 74104; http://www.utulsa.edu. Adv. Circ: 2300. Microform: WSH. Online: William S. Hein & Co., Inc.; LexisNexis; OCLC Online Computer Library Center, Inc.; ProQuest LLC (Ann Arbor); Thomson West; H.W. Wilson. Reprint: WSH. *Indexed:* ABIn, CLI, EnvAb, ILP, LRI, PAIS. *Bk. rev.:* 2, 1,000 words. *Aud.:* Ac, Sa.

As much about economics and environment as about law, the *Energy Law Journal* is a scholarly work devoted to lengthy analyses of energy issues and how they affect the law or the law affects them. Issues are not only reviewed but debated as well. Papers are written by attorneys, judges, and experts from government agencies. Most of the discussions involve U.S. law, but there are occasional works specific to other countries or international in scope. Emphasis is on electricity supply with some attention to oil, natural gas, the environment, and alternative energy forms, such as hydrogen. Book reviews, committee reports on energy and administrative law, and what passes for short notes in the legal world (such as "Saginaw Bay Pipeline Company v. United States: Saginaw Wins the Pipeline Depreciation Battle, But is the War Over?") round out the issues. Widely owned by law libraries, it deserves consideration by libraries with strong energy collections and public-policy collections. The web site now has the complete set of volumes mounted, some as html, some as linked pdf.

2180. Energy Materials: materials science & engineering for energy systems. [ISSN: 1748-9237] 2006. q. USD 515 print & online eds. Ed(s): Dr. Fujio Abe, Dr. R Viswanathan. Maney Publishing, Ste. 1C, Joseph's Well, Hanover Walk, Leeds, LS3 1AB, United Kingdom; maney@maney.co.uk; http://www.maney.co.uk. Refereed. *Aud.:* Ac.

A new title from the Institute of Materials, Minerals, and Mining, this journal emphasizes the materials problems and solutions for a wide range of energy sources and systems. With the exception of hydrogen, the content is "post-extraction" of energy, meaning no mining, drilling, or, in the case of biomass, growing. The editors have made hydrogen a special case, as its production for energy use is still in its infancy and it has the promise of being a renewable and green energy source. The initial issues have survey articles or commentary on various still-novel energy sources, such as biomass and wind, and economics and policy considerations. However, most of the standard research articles discuss highly specific metallic materials problems associated with turbines and boilers used in electric, gas, and/or nuclear power production. The web version of the journal is mounted at Ingenta, which nicely includes links to the cited references, but neglects to tell the reader that there are more references in the paper than just the ones that have links. Since references often give an indication of the scope of an article, this "short list" can be misleading. The articles themselves are well written and edited, but the coverage is still uneven and unsettled. Libraries with strong collections in energy should consider it for inclusion in another year or so.

2181. Energy Policy. [ISSN: 0301-4215] 1973. 18x/yr. EUR 1764. Ed(s): Nicky France. Pergamon, The Boulevard, Langford Ln, East Park, Kidlington, OX5 1GB, United Kingdom. Illus., index, adv. Sample. Refereed. Vol. ends: No. 15. Microform: PQC. Online: EBSCO Publishing, EBSCO Host; Gale; IngentaConnect; OhioLINK; ScienceDirect; SwetsWise Online Content. *Indexed:* ABIn, ABS&EES, AgeL, BPI, EngInd, EnvAb, EnvInd, ExcerpMed, ForAb, HRIS, IBSS, PAIS, PollutAb, RI-1, SCI, SSCI. *Aud.:* Ac.

This journal should be compared with *Energy Economics,* also from Elsevier. First, the emphasis is on renewable energy forms (such as wind, solar, biomass), as opposed to the primarily oil and electric power interests of its sister title. Second, the theme is policy decisions, by government and by industry as opposed to financial considerations. Environmental concerns, green energy, and alternative energy forms are much discussed in current issues. Both publications have international authorship and interest, but *Energy Policy* often discusses specific countries and regions while *Energy Economics* is often global in focus. Publication lag is very short, often only two to three months. While most of the articles are research reports, each issue also contains a "Viewpoints" section with one or two persuasive analyses. Recommended for libraries with international relations and public policy collections in conjunction with energy research.

2182. Energy Sources. Part A. Recovery, Utilization, and Environmental Effects. Supersedes in part (1973-2005): *Energy Sources;* Which incorporated (1974-1991): *Energy Systems and Policy.* [ISSN: 1556-7036] 2006. q. USD 3204 print & online eds. Ed(s): James G Speight. Taylor & Francis Inc., 325 Chestnut St, Ste 800, Philadelphia, PA 19016; orders@taylorandfrancis.com; http://www.taylorandfrancis.com. Illus., index, adv. Sample. Refereed. Online: EBSCO Publishing, EBSCO Host; Gale; IngentaConnect;

OCLC Online Computer Library Center, Inc.; SwetsWise Online Content. Reprint: PSC. *Indexed:* ABIn, AS&TI, Agr, BAS, BiolAb, C&ISA, CerAb, ChemAb, EngInd, EnvAb, EnvInd, IAA, PAIS, PetrolAb, PollutAb, SCI. *Aud.:* Ac.

Energy Sources split into two sections in January 2006. Part A, still the major section with 16 issues per year, retained the technical papers; Part B (also reviewed here) covers economics, policy, and planning. Librarians are usually not pleased when a title splits because, aside from the cataloging headaches and user confusion, there is also an automatic price increase. In this case, it is still possible to subscribe to each part separately, so that libraries that emphasize the technical aspects of energy are not required to accept the policy addition (and *vice versa*). There is also a combined subscription option. The journal's theme is fuel sources: carbon-based (petroleum, natural gas, oil tars and shales, organic waste), nuclear, wind, solar, and geothermal. The aspects are extraction and conversion to energy, reporting "completed" research, as opposed to theory or in-process updates. Recent articles cover predicting lignite quality, pyrolysis of sugarcane bagasse, and low enthalpy geothermal heating. Issue topics tend to clump, with a string of issues devoted to carbon-based fuels, then a single that is mostly other forms. There is no statement of submission, revision, acceptance, and publication dates, but reviewing the article references indicates a lag between writing and publication of about two years.

2183. Energy Sources. Part B. Economics, Planning, and Policy. Supersedes in part (1973-2005): *Energy Sources;* Which incorporates (in 1994): *Energy Systems and Policy.* [ISSN: 1556-7249] 2006. a. USD 317 print & online eds. Taylor & Francis Inc., 325 Chestnut St, Ste 800, Philadelphia, PA 19016; orders@taylorandfrancis.com; http://www.taylorandfrancis.com. Refereed. Reprint: PSC. *Indexed:* C&ISA, CerAb, EngInd, IAA. *Aud.:* Ac.

Energy Sources split in 2006 into parts A and B. Part A is the "parent" title and is reviewed in this section; Part B is really a new journal, since the volume numbering begins with one. Unlike many title splits, it is possible to subscribe to each title separately or to get both at a reduced price. Part A contains the highly technical papers; Part B contains the analysis papers. This does not mean that they are light reading; recent titles include "Energy and exergy analyses of a diesel engine fueled with various biodiesels" and "The importance of natural gas as a world fuel." Many of the articles published so far are reviews in nature. Libraries with collections in economics and policy may want to watch this journal for a year or two to see how the content develops.

2184. Fuel. [ISSN: 0016-2361] 1922. 18x/yr. EUR 3056. Ed(s): K. D. Bartle, John W. Patrick. Elsevier Ltd., The Boulevard, Langford Ln, Oxford, OX5 1GB, United Kingdom. Illus., index, adv. Sample. Refereed. Vol. ends: No. 15. Microform: PQC. Online: EBSCO Publishing, EBSCO Host; Gale; IngentaConnect; OhioLINK; ScienceDirect; SwetsWise Online Content. *Indexed:* ApMecR, BrTechI, C&ISA, CerAb, ChemAb, EngInd, EnvAb, EnvInd, ExcerpMed, IAA, PetrolAb, PollutAb, SCI. *Aud.:* Ac.

One of the oldest professional journals devoted to energy sources, *Fuel* publishes highly technical articles on coal (and coal tar), petroleum (oil, oil shale, oil sands, and derivatives), natural gas, and more than a trace of biomass. Most of the articles concern the production of electrical energy, but there is some attention to transportation (gasoline, diesel fuel, and the like). Authorship is international and largely academic, with some coauthors from commercial enterprises. The articles are under ten pages, well referenced, and illustrated with charts, tables, and line drawings. Most of each issue is devoted to "full papers," but the occasional review article, brief communication, or book review pops up. The extra issues in this "monthly" are proceedings of conferences. This is a relatively expensive title but is useful in a number of engineering disciplines and has a proven track record.

2185. Fuel Processing Technology. [ISSN: 0378-3820] 1978. 12x/yr. EUR 2318. Ed(s): G. P. Huffman. Elsevier BV, Radarweg 29, Amsterdam, 1043 NX, Netherlands; nlinfo-f@elsevier.nl; http://www.elsevier.nl. Illus., index. Sample. Refereed. Microform: PQC. Online: EBSCO Publishing, EBSCO Host; Gale; IngentaConnect; OhioLINK; ScienceDirect; SwetsWise Online Content. *Indexed:* C&ISA, CerAb, ChemAb, EngInd, EnvAb, ExcerpMed, IAA, PetrolAb, SCI. *Aud.:* Ac.

Fuel Processing Technology should be compared to its sister publication, *Fuel*. The two titles cover the same types of fuels: hydrocarbons (coal, oil, shale) and biomass. The first title emphasizes "processing" (the conversion of the raw materials to higher forms of fuels), but the second title also includes papers similar in scope. However, *Fuel Processing Technology* uses a less theoretical approach. The articles make dense reading, with such titles as "Solid state NMR investigation of silica aerogel supported Fischer-Tropsch catalysts" and "The influence of Cu, Fe, Ni, Pb and Zn on gum formation in the Brazilian automotive gasoline." However, there are occasional review articles and special issues, such as one on biofuels for transportation. Article authorship, length, illustration, and referencing are also similar. The pair are for those libraries with strong programs in petroleum technology as well as energy.

Geothermics. See Earth Sciences section.

2186. Home Energy. Formerly (until 1987): *Energy Auditor and Retrofitter.* [ISSN: 0896-9442] 1984. bi-m. USD 59 domestic; USD 74 elsewhere. Ed(s): Alan Meier, Jim Gunshinan. Energy Auditor and Retrofitter, Inc., 2124 Kittredge St, #95, Berkeley, CA 94704; http://www.homeenergy.org. Illus., adv. Sample. Circ: 3000 Paid. Vol. ends: Nov/Dec. Online: Florida Center for Library Automation; Gale. *Indexed:* EnvAb, EnvInd. *Aud.:* Ga, Sa.

Home Energy is published by a nonprofit organization, which states that its mission is "to provide objective and practical information for residential energy conservation." Originally intended for the professional home remodeler, since 1997 it has addressed the homeowner as well, partly with consumer guide information and partly with self-help tips. Each issue has a few articles that are factual in nature, cite publications or refer to web links, and include many photographs and line illustrations. The rest of the issue is "Trends," covering product information, an events calendar, industry news, and briefs. The web site is not just a reproduction of the printed product, but includes a do-it-yourself tips section, a blog, and a training directory. Only subscribers have access to the content, although the 1993–1999 archive (searchable) is free to all. There is an extensive list of short, colorfully illustrated information articles for both the consumer and the contractor, plus links to sites of interest. With its wide geographic range, even in states where the winter sun can be hard to find, this is good title for any public library.

2187. Home Power: the hands-on journal of home-made power. [ISSN: 1050-2416] 1987. bi-m. USD 22.50 domestic; USD 30 foreign. Ed(s): Richard Perez. Home Power, Inc., PO Box 520, Ashland, OR 97520-0520; hp.info@homepower.prg; http://www.homepower.com. Illus., adv. Circ: 67883. *Indexed:* ConsI. *Aud.:* Ga, Sa.

Home Power is not so much a magazine as it is an industry. Visiting its web site is as much fun as it is educational. The magazine promulgates "homemade" electric power using renewable energy resources (solar, wind, water). Regular issue features (although not in every issue) are "Ask the Experts," "Code Corner," "Power Politics," "Word Power" (a running encyclopedia of solar energy terms and what they mean), and several discussion columns. Many articles are success stories from the readership. The magazine has become quite sophisticated since its days of desktop publishing. The web site includes the full pdf version of the current issue (a free sample), some useful files/data from earlier issues, links to related sites, and ads for the company's book and CD-ROM publications.

2188. IEEE Power & Energy Magazine. Formed by the merger of (1981-2003): *IEEE Power Engineering Review;* (1988-2003): *IEEE Computer Applications in Power.* [ISSN: 1540-7977] 2003. bi-m. USD 330. Ed(s): Melvin I Olken. IEEE, 445 Hoes Ln, Piscataway, NJ 08854-1331; customer.service@ieee.org. *Indexed:* C&ISA, CerAb, EngInd, IAA. *Bk. rev.:* 1, 1000 words. *Aud.:* Ac, Sa.

This title is another of the highly relevant, highly useful *IEEE Magazines* series (as distinct from the often dense *IEEE Transactions*). It is designed for the "electric power professional." Each issue is based on a theme chosen by the editor, then illustrated with three or four articles. This journal is executed in the usual colorful, glossy style of the *IEEE Magazines,* and its articles are eight to ten pages in length, with extensive bibliographies. The remainder of the issues includes letters, columns (the "Leader's Corner," the "Business Scene"), society and industry news, book reviews, new products, and an events calendar. The

IEEEXplore site now identifies the content type of each title on the contents page, an exceedingly welcome addition when the titles themselves are ambiguous. For instance, a recent issue has the title "Electricity Restructuring" but the identifier was the "Business Scene," clearly a short piece. Well worth considering for many libraries, especially for those where the equivalent *IEEE Transactions* are either too expensive or too weighty.

2189. IEEE Transactions on Energy Conversion. Supersedes in part: *IEEE Transactions on Power Apparatus and Systems.* [ISSN: 0885-8969] 1986. q. USD 585. Ed(s): James L Kirtley. IEEE, 445 Hoes Ln, Piscataway, NJ 08854-1331; subscription-service@ieee.org; http://www.ieee.org. Refereed. Online: Pub.; EBSCO Publishing, EBSCO Host. *Indexed:* AS&TI, C&ISA, CerAb, EngInd, EnvAb, IAA, SCI. *Aud.:* Ac.

The thrust of this journal is efficient conversion of energy-producing mechanisms (usually motors in small or large scale) to electrical energy. Therefore, it contains a significant number of articles that cover wind, solar, and renewable energy production problems. As usual with *IEEE Transactions* publications, the papers are written for and by academics, but there are highly practical problems under discussion, such as "space charge accumulation in induction motor magnet wire." Large engineering collections will be pleasantly surprised to discover they have a good, economical source of material on niche energy topics. Commercial entities in solar or wind power will find this an inexpensive source of research material. It is also a good title for those electric-car enthusiasts found in engineering schools.

2190. I E T Renewable Power Generation. [ISSN: 1752-1416] 2007. q. USD 460 print or online ed. Ed(s): David Infield. The Institution of Engineering and Technology, Michael Faraday House, Six Hills Way, Stevenage, SG1 2AY, United Kingdom; journals@theiet.org; http://www.theiet.org/. *Aud.:* Ac.

In 2006, the Institution of Electrical Engineers (IEE) and the Institution of Incorporated Engineers (IIE) merged to form the Institution of Engineering and Technology (IET), much to the consternation of cataloguers everywhere. The fruits of this merger include many title changes and some new additions to the institution's journal collection. *IET Renewable Power Generation* is one of them, and it promises to be a welcome niche title in a crowded field. Specifically, this research journal discusses the practical generation of power from several renewable energy sources, both from the technical and the managerial sides of the system. The first issue addressed wind, photovoltaic, and wave power as resources, plus the distribution problems associated with them. The scope of the journal also includes solar, marine current, geothermal, biomass, and fuel-cell power sources. Unlike many new titles that have overview articles with broad outlines, *IET Renewable Power Generation* got down to business from the start. IET is using Scitation to mount its journals, taking advantage of both the ability to display and link to article references, but to such new Adobe Acrobat features as internal linking of figures and references and one-click capture of illustrations. The price for a quarterly is steep, especially since the first issue was less than 100 pages, but the first year's issues are free to all, allowing libraries to scrutinize the content before making a final subscription decision.

2191. Institution of Mechanical Engineers. Proceedings. Part A: Journal of Power and Energy. Formerly (until 1990): *Institution of Mechanical Engineers. Proceedings. Part A: Journal of Power Engineering;* Which superseded in part (in 1989): *Institution of Mechanical Engineers. Proceedings. Part A: Power and Process Engineering;* Which superseded in part (1847-1982): *Institution of Mechanical Engineers. Proceedings.* [ISSN: 0957-6509] 1983. 8x/yr. USD 2145 in the Americas; GBP 1106 elsewhere. Ed(s): C J Lawn. Professional Engineering Publishing Ltd., 1 Birdcage Walk, London, SW1H 9JJ , United Kingdom; journals@ pepublishing.com; http://www.pepublishing.com. Illus., index. Sample. Refereed. Circ: 1000. Vol. ends: No. 6. Microform: PMC; PQC. Online: EBSCO Publishing, EBSCO Host; Gale; IngentaConnect; OCLC Online Computer Library Center, Inc.; ProQuest K-12 Learning Solutions; ProQuest LLC (Ann Arbor); SwetsWise Online Content. *Indexed:* AS&TI, ApMecR, BrTechI, C&ISA, CerAb, ChemAb, EngInd, IAA, MathR, OceAb, PollutAb, SCI. *Bk. rev.:* 3, 500 words. *Aud.:* Ac, Sa.

Normally, the journal of a professional society outside the United States would not be included in this section, especially when there are relevant titles available from U.S. equivalents (*IEEE Transactions on Energy Conversion* and *Journal of Solar Energy Engineering,* also reviewed in this section). However, this publication is well worth consideration for a broadly based energy collection. First, it covers a lot of territory: electric power, wind power, ocean wave energy, power production from coal, nuclear energy, gas, fuel cells, solar energy. Its focus is the conversion of energy forms into electricity; much of the content concerns the design and upkeep of mechanical systems that do the actual conversion. Second, although the publisher is a British society, the journal has an international authorship made up of a combination of academic and industry researchers. Third, it has a relatively rapid turnaround from submission to publication. Fourth, the articles are readable (it is indexed in *Applied Science and Technology Abstracts*), well referenced, and well illustrated. A rarity in these times, there are even extensive book reviews. Its major shortcoming is that it is relatively expensive for a college library. Most university collections will already have it, as part of the complete IME *Proceedings,* and therefore at a cheaper rate.

2192. *International Journal of Energy Research.* [ISSN: 0363-907X] 1976. 15x/yr. USD 5320 print or online ed. Ed(s): I Dincer. John Wiley & Sons Ltd., The Atrium, Southern Gate, Chichester, PO19 8SQ, United Kingdom; customer@wiley.co.uk; http://www.wiley.co.uk. Adv. Refereed. Circ: 500. Reprint: PSC. *Indexed:* ApMecR, BrTechI, C&ISA, CerAb, ChemAb, EngInd, EnvAb, EnvInd, ExcerpMed, IAA, OceAb, PollutAb, SCI, SSCI. *Aud.:* Ac.

This is an exceedingly eclectic title. The aims and scope of information of this journal are indicated in the journal's web site with "the Editors do not wish to restrict the areas of energy research suitable for publication," and the range of topics covered in each issue verifies this statement. Article subjects range from cost-efficient control strategies for a confectionery plant (management) to phase-change drywall systems (practical) to performance studies of combustion of gas cycle and rankine cycle engines (thermodynamics)—and these were all in one issue. Micro- and nano-scale developments have been added to the mix, and a recent issue has been devoted to advances in micro and nano energy systems. Articles often run 20 or more pages. Not only are authors international, but it is not unusual to find an article co-authored by a team from three or more institutions. As it is, the price makes this a hard title to justify; it has the dubious distinction of being the most expensive journal reviewed in this section, if not in the entire energy field, without the distinction of the high Impact Factor of other titles. For the comprehensive academic collection.

2193. *International Journal of Green Energy.* [ISSN: 1543-5075] 2004. q. GBP 706 print & online eds. Ed(s): Xianguo Li. Taylor & Francis Inc., 325 Chestnut St, Ste 800, Philadelphia, PA 19016; orders@taylorandfrancis.com; http://www.taylorandfrancis.com. Refereed. Reprint: PSC. *Indexed:* C&ISA, CABA, CerAb, EngInd, EnvAb, FPA, ForAb, HortAb, IAA, S&F, SCI. *Aud.:* Ac.

This journal publishes research on "the forms and utilizations of energy that have no, minimal, or reduced impact on environment and society." To that end, a large percentage of the articles deal with wind, solar, biomass, and other alternative/renewable sources. Financial considerations play a part, illustrated by the wonderful merger of economics and technology in the title "Carbon credits required to make manure biogas plants economic." That title is also indicative of the niche subjects that might make or break the journal. These are not mainstream research thrusts, but the journal has, in only four short years of publication, earned an Impact Factor that is higher than the *Oil and Gas Journal,* a long-time staple in the energy field. Issues are slim, averaging six articles and less than 100 pages. Libraries with interests in sustainable development as well as energy should consider this one.

2194. *International Journal of Hydrogen Energy.* [ISSN: 0360-3199] 1976. 15x/yr. EUR 2758. Ed(s): T Nejat Veziroglu. Pergamon, The Boulevard, Langford Ln, East Park, Kidlington, OX5 1GB, United Kingdom. Illus., adv. Refereed. Circ: 2250. Microform: PMC; PQC. Online: EBSCO Publishing, EBSCO Host; Gale; IngentaConnect; OhioLINK; ScienceDirect; SwetsWise Online Content. *Indexed:* C&ISA, ChemAb, EngInd, EnvAb, IAA, SCI. *Aud.:* Ac.

This may be the only journal (there are a few magazines) devoted to hydrogen as an energy source, and, as such, it covers both the technical aspects and the social aspects (economics, environment, and international impact). Most of the articles are short and highly technical, with much of the discussion concerned with fuel cells. There is also a goodly number of articles on hydrogen-powered vehicles. Recent articles include "Separation of hydrogen from a hydrogen/methane mixture using a PEM fuel cell" and "On the road performance simulation of hydrogen and hybrid cars." Several issues each year include conference papers or are organized around a theme; "fuel cells" is a popular repeat. This is a niche area in energy research and should be considered only by those institutions with like programs.

2195. *International Journal of Photoenergy.* [ISSN: 1110-662X] 1999. s-a. USD 195. Ed(s): S A Abdel-Mottaleb. Hindawi Publishing Corp., 410 Park Ave, 15th Fl, PMB 287, New York, NY 10022; hindawi@hindawi.com; http://www.hindawi.com. Refereed. *Indexed:* C&ISA, CerAb, IAA, SCI. *Aud.:* Ac.

This is a journal with an extremely narrow focus, but one that has caught the attention of many in the photovoltaic and/or solar energy field in its short publishing life. Aimed at the chemistry/chemical engineering researcher, articles cover fine details in photoreactivity, degradation, and, conversely, energizing of materials due to "photoenergy." This is precisely why some researchers in solar energy, fuel cells, and the like read and cite this journal. Resolving materials problems in these fields is critical to success, and much of this is uncharted territory. This title's Impact Factor now ranks it in the middle of ISI's energy category, just below *Solar Energy* and ahead of such consistently important titles as *Applied Energy* and *Journal of Solar Energy.* The web site has some nice features, such as RSS feeds, links to references through the publisher and through Google Scholar, and even a "how to cite" format. This is an Open Access publication and inexpensive as scholarly journals go, but the treatment is so specialized that only libraries with strong solar/photovoltaic collections will find it useful.

2196. *Journal of Energy and Development.* [ISSN: 0361-4476] 1975. s-a. USD 45, Libraries, USD 37 (Students, USD 25). International Research Center for Energy and Economic Development, 850 Willowbrook Rd, Boulder, CO 80302-7439; iceed@stripe.colorado.edu; http://www.iceed.org. Adv. Sample. Refereed. Circ: 2000. Microform: WSH. *Indexed:* ABCPolSci, Agr, BAS, C&ISA, CLI, CerAb, EnvInd, IAA, ILP, JEL, PAIS, PSA, PetrolAb, SSCI. *Bk. rev.:* 4, 500 words. *Aud.:* Ac.

This journal is the chief contribution to the scholarly world of a tiny organization, the International Research Center for Energy and Economic Development (located at the University of Colorado at Boulder). It specializes in review articles on the economic impact of energy (chiefly oil and gas) on the large (national or worldwide) scale. For such a small publication, it has a wide readership in academia, one that cannot be attributed solely to its modest subscription price. Definitely a title to be considered for economics as well as energy collections, but it should be noted that it is running a year behind its own publication schedule. The last issue at time of writing was Autumn 2005, completed in March 2006.

2197. *Journal of Energy Engineering.* Former titles (until 1983): *American Society of Civil Engineers. Energy Division. Journal;* (until 1979): *American Society of Civil Engineers. Power Division. Journal;* Which superseded in part (in 1956): *American Society of Civil Engineers. Proceedings.* [ISSN: 0733-9402] 1873. q. USD 273. Ed(s): Hilary I Inyang. American Society of Civil Engineers, 1801 Alexander Bell Dr, Reston, VA 20191-4400; http://www.asce.org. Illus. Refereed. Circ: 1100. Microform: PQC. Online: American Institute of Physics, Scitation; EBSCO Publishing, EBSCO Host; SwetsWise Online Content. *Indexed:* AS&TI, C&ISA, CerAb, ChemAb, EngInd, EnvInd, ExcerpMed, HRIS, IAA, M&GPA, PollutAb, SCI. *Aud.:* Ac, Sa.

This journal is part of the American Society of Civil Engineers stable of engineering journals and has been focused on energy since 1983. However, worthy as the articles may have been, it was a niche journal until recently. An indicator is that its Impact Factor has jumped, and it has, in only two short years, climbed from very low in the Energy category to the mid-level, in the company of such stalwarts as *Solar Energy* and the *Journal of Energy.* During this time there has been a change in editor, which definitely accounts for emphasis on theme issues, such as sustainable energy generation systems. Issues often contain articles on solar, wind, geothermal, and other alternate energy sources. Improving conservation techniques, distribution methods, and concern for the environment are constant themes. Although meant for the researcher, one of the hallmarks of ASCE journals is the "discussions and closures" where readers comment on earlier articles and the authors reply; this infuses some relevancy to the practicing engineer. Solid energy collections should include this title; libraries with strong interest in civil and mechanical engineering will also find it useful.

2198. *Journal of Energy Finance and Development.* [ISSN: 1085-7443] 1996. s-a. NLG 1336 Combined with Energy Economics. Elsevier Ltd., The Boulevard, Langford Ln, Oxford, OX5 1GB, United Kingdom. Illus., index. Refereed. Online: EBSCO Publishing, EBSCO Host; Gale; IngentaConnect; OhioLINK; ScienceDirect. *Indexed:* JEL. *Aud.:* Ac.

True to its name, this scholarly journal discusses the economic and tax issues of energy, generally on the macro scale. Recent issues feature "Oil and energy price volatility" (on everyone's mind these days), "Hourly electricity prices in day-ahead markets," and "Spacial peak-load pricing." Definitely international in scope, the lengthy articles have covered Indian coal, oil-price sticker shock in Europe, price rigidity in the New Zealand petroleum industry, and the Colombian electricity market. This is a journal for larger collections with an active local interest in economics; other libraries should consider *The Energy Journal.*

2199. *Journal of Power Sources.* [ISSN: 0378-7753] 1976. 24x/yr. EUR 3924. Ed(s): Z Ogumi, C K Dyer. Elsevier S.A., PO Box 564, Lausanne, 1001, Switzerland. Refereed. Microform: PQC. Online: EBSCO Publishing, EBSCO Host; Gale; IngentaConnect; OhioLINK; ScienceDirect; SwetsWise Online Content. *Indexed:* C&ISA, CerAb, ChemAb, EngInd, EnvAb, EnvInd, IAA, PollutAb, SCI. *Aud.:* Ac.

Think photovoltaics: the power sources here are fuel cells and batteries for portable power supplies, electric vehicles, satellites. This journal discusses the conversion of solar, wind, and other energy sources into storage devices such as fuel cells. Much of the work involves materials properties, electrochemical reactions, and the application of photovoltaics to practical devices. Issues are lengthy, often running to 200 pages, and the publication lag is quite short, sometimes under four months but generally around six. The contents are arranged in subject sections, then divided by type (review, article, short communication). Several issues per year are devoted to conference proceedings. This is a high-Impact-Factor journal, but quite expensive (although not on a cost-per-page basis); libraries with strong engineering collections as well as renewable-energy interests should consider it. However, it should be compared with *Progress in Photovoltaics* (below in this section).

2200. *Journal of Solar Energy Engineering.* [ISSN: 0199-6231] 1980. q. Members, USD 50 print & online eds.; Non-members, USD 263 print & online eds. Ed(s): Aldo Steinfeld. A S M E International, Three Park Ave, New York, NY 10016-5990; infocentral@asme.org; http://www.asme.org. Illus., index. Refereed. Vol. ends: Nov. Microform: PQC. Online: American Institute of Physics, Scitation; EBSCO Publishing, EBSCO Host; SwetsWise Online Content. *Indexed:* AS&TI, ApMecR, C&ISA, CEA, CerAb, ChemAb, EngInd, EnvInd, IAA, SCI. *Aud.:* Ac, Sa.

This is an engineering research journal, with short articles (around six pages) on applied research into solar energy production, materials used in solar energy, and applications of solar energy to other engineering problems. Most readers are familiar with the use of solar power to dry fruits and heat water, but many will be surprised to learn that it can also be used in aluminum smelting and fullerene synthesis. The journal should really be titled "Solar and Wind Energy"; every few issues, several articles on wind power are included. Recent articles discuss alignment of parabolic trough solar concentrators, a solar hydrogen power plant, and design loads for wind turbines. This is a good value for the research dollar, and it will be useful at industrial as well as academic sites.

2201. *Journal of Wind Engineering & Industrial Aerodynamics.* Formerly (until 1980): *Journal of Industrial Aerodynamics.* [ISSN: 0167-6105] 1975. 12x/yr. EUR 2859. Ed(s): Ted Stathopoulos. Elsevier BV,

Radarweg 29, Amsterdam, 1043 NX, Netherlands; nlinfo-f@elsevier.nl; http://www.elsevier.nl. Refereed. Microform: PQC. Online: EBSCO Publishing, EBSCO Host; Gale; IngentaConnect; OhioLINK; ScienceDirect; SwetsWise Online Content. *Indexed:* ApMecR, C&ISA, CerAb, EngInd, EnvAb, EnvInd, IAA, M&GPA, PollutAb, SCI. *Aud.:* Ac.

Billing itself as the oldest wind energy journal in English, this publication still reflects its heritage of "industrial aerodynamics." Although many of the articles in this globally oriented journal deal with wind energy generation, a sizable portion cover wind effects on structures, wind tunnel design, wind in the meteorological sense, and fluid flow and turbulence of air. Although useful and relevant, this expensive title is more suited to a structural or aeronautical engineering collection than to energy production. Libraries with smaller collections or more focused interests should consider the other wind power journals covered in this section.

Nuclear Engineering International. See Engineering and Technology/ Nuclear Engineering section.

2202. *Nuclear Technology.* Former titles (until 1970): *Nuclear Applications and Technology;* (until 1969): *Nuclear Applications.* [ISSN: 0029-5450] 1965. m. USD 1700 print & online eds. Ed(s): Nicholas Tsoulfanidis. American Nuclear Society, Inc., 555 N Kensington Ave, La Grange Park, IL 60526-5592; orders@ans.org; http://www.ans.org. Illus., index. Refereed. Circ: 1388 Paid. Vol. ends: No. 3. *Indexed:* A&ATA, AS&TI, C&ISA, CerAb, ChemAb, EngInd, EnvAb, H&SSA, IAA, IBR, PollutAb, SCI, SSCI. *Bk. rev.:* Occasional. *Aud.:* Ac, Sa.

One of several publications from the American Nuclear Society (ANS), *Nuclear Technology* publishes papers on applications of research to the nuclear energy field, as opposed to theoretical work. Each issue is subdivided into sections, such as nuclear reactor safety, fission reactors, radioactive waste management, and others as appropriate. The layout is crisp, and such features as keyword descriptors at the head of each paper help the reader target relevant papers. The authorship is international, often from industry, and publication lag averages about one year. Brief author biographies are included after the bibliographies. Papers rarely run more than ten pages. Occasionally, technical notes (one- or two-page items) are included. Book reviews are encouraged but rarely appear. Libraries with active physics researchers will probably have all of the ANS publications; others may prefer the specialized titles.

2203. *Oil & Gas Journal.* [ISSN: 0030-1388] 1902. 49x/yr. Free to qualified personnel; USD 89 combined subscription domestic print & online eds. Ed(s): Bob Tippee. PennWell Corporation, 1700 W Loop S, Ste 1000, Houston, TX 77027; patrickM@pennwell.com; http://www.pennwell.com. Illus., index, adv. Circ: 70000 Paid. Vol. ends: No. 52. Microform: PMC; PQC. Online: EBSCO Publishing, EBSCO Host; Factiva, Inc.; Florida Center for Library Automation; Gale; LexisNexis; Northern Light Technology, Inc.; OCLC Online Computer Library Center, Inc.; ProQuest LLC (Ann Arbor). *Indexed:* ABIn, AS&TI, BPI, C&ISA, CEA, ChemAb, EngInd, EnvInd, ExcerpMed, HRIS, M&GPA, OceAb, PetrolAb, PollutAb, S&F, SCI. *Aud.:* Ga, Ac, Sa.

Decade after decade, this has been a reliable source for topical industry news, special features, and lots of data. Articles comprise a large portion of the contents, either short reviews (one to three pages) by staff writers or somewhat longer referenced papers by industry specialists. Each issue follows the section format of focus articles, general interest news, exploration and development, drilling and production, and processing and transportation, with columns on equipment and statistics. There are a number of annually repeating issues, such as forecast and review or worldwide refining. Because it is a weekly, its events calendars, industry briefs, government watch items, and people columns are fresh, and the web version offers even later news. On the web site, parts of the current issue, the product guide, and the equipment exchange section are freely accessible; the complete issues, statistical data, and backfiles are available only to subscribers. This is also the place to find a job and to sell new or used equipment. The best section for librarians is the multi-page statistics analysis at the end of each paper issue. American Petroleum Institute data and prices (crude and refined, U.S. and world regions) are reported weekly, but other analyses pop up from time to time, such as country-by-country current/previous-year production comparison figures. There is a three-tiered subscription system, ranging from print-only to print-and-electronic. Libraries will prefer the latter; it is worth the expense because of the backfiles and the statistics.

2204. Oxford Energy Forum: quarterly journal for debating energy issues and policies. [ISSN: 0959-7727] 1990. q. GBP 30 domestic; EUR 50 in Europe; USD 50 elsewhere. Ed(s): Ian Skeet. Oxford Institute for Energy Studies, 57 Woodstock Rd, Oxford, OX2 6FA, United Kingdom; publications@oxfordenergy.org; http://www.oxfordenergy.org/. Circ: 600 Paid. *Indexed:* ABIn, PAIS. *Aud.:* Ac.

The *Forum* uses a debate format to discuss the economic and policy issues associated with energy development. Oil and natural gas are the topics of most issues because of the impact on the world economy, but nuclear and renewables appear occasionally, as well as policy and tax issues. Each issue usually has two themes; a panel of experts is assembled for each theme and short discussions ensue. Although supporting data may be present, this is tangential to the actual purpose of airing the issues. The individual number begins with a short essay describing the "debates," proceeds to the meat of the arguments, then concludes with "Personal Commentary" and "Asinus Muses." The commentary is a reader's or author's reaction or thoughts on any topic that concerns the readership. "Asinus" is that wonderful convention of the dyspeptic observer making brief remarks on (mostly) current energy news. Satirical comments aside, this is another title (see *Energy & Environment,* reviewed above) worthy of consideration in large academic libraries because of the cross-disciplinary treatment of issues.

2205. Power Engineering. Former titles (until 1950): *Power Generation;* (until 1947): *Power Plant Engineering;* (until 1917): *Practical Engineer.* [ISSN: 0032-5961] 1896. m. USD 76 domestic (Free to qualified personnel). Ed(s): David Wagman. PennWell Corporation, 1421 S Sheridan Rd, Tulsa, OK 74112; patrickM@pennwell.com; http://www.pennwell.com. Illus., index, adv. Circ: 58000 Controlled. Vol. ends: Dec. Microform: PQC. Online: EBSCO Publishing, EBSCO Host; Florida Center for Library Automation; Gale; Northern Light Technology, Inc.; OCLC Online Computer Library Center, Inc.; ProQuest K-12 Learning Solutions; ProQuest LLC (Ann Arbor). *Indexed:* ABIn, AS&TI, ApMecR, BiolDig, C&ISA, CerAb, ChemAb, EngInd, EnvInd, ExcerpMed, H&SSA, IAA, SCI, SSCI. *Aud.:* Ga, Ac, Sa.

One of those trade magazines that have been around forever, partly because it knows how to change with the times, *Power Engineering* is concerned with the electric power–producing industry with a concentration on solid fuels. Although it does not ignore the "big picture," its focus is on running the power plant. In addition to short articles, it is chock-full of ads, industry briefs, and regular columns on the environment, business, and field notes (which plant is doing what about which). The articles are often by staff writers but can also be tips from experts in the industry. Although they usually do not include references, the articles are well illustrated with color photographs, charts, tables, and line drawings. The annual buyers' guide now appears in December, but is also available on the web. Other features include the "Project of the Year," the big industry conference, Power-Gen, webcasts, podcasts, and white papers. Free registration at the web site provides access to the issue archives through a nice search interface.

2206. Power (Houston). Incorporates (1981-2007): *European Power News;* Which was formerly (1976-1981): *Power Generation Industrial;* (1977-2007): *International Power Generation;* (1976-2007): *Middle East Electricity.* [ISSN: 0032-5929] 1883. bi-m. USD 59 domestic; USD 64 Canada; USD 159 elsewhere. The TradeFair Group, Inc., 11000 Richmond, Ste. 500, Houston, TX 77042; info@tradefairgroup.com; http://www.tradefairgroup.com/. Illus., index, adv. Circ: 72000 Controlled. Vol. ends: No. 9. Microform: PQC. Online: EBSCO Publishing, EBSCO Host; ProQuest LLC (Ann Arbor). *Indexed:* ABIn, AS&TI, ApMecR, C&ISA, CerAb, ChemAb, EngInd, EnvInd, ExcerpMed, IAA, PetrolAb, PollutAb, SCI. *Aud.:* Ga, Ac, Sa.

After more than a century of publication, McGraw-Hill sold *Power* to the TradeFair Group (Houston, Texas) in 2006. In some areas there have been some big changes, but much of the familiar format remains. Every other issue seems to have a "special report" on something, and there are annual features, such as the "Powerplant Award" and the new "Top Plants" survey. The concentration is

on "traditional" power plants, which run on fossil fuels or nuclear power, but renewable energy sources are also included. Although technical, the articles are written with management in mind, which makes them approachable for the undergraduate or lay reader. Few articles have references; the author's credentials and e-mail contact are the "cited sources." There are columns on fuels, labor, the environment, and the latest technologies and management practices. Obviously a rival to *Power Engineering* (in this section), *Power* seems to have the edge on in-depth special issues, but these are not available at the web site except to registered subscribers.

2207. Progress in Energy and Combustion Science. [ISSN: 0360-1285] 1975. 6x/yr. EUR 1760. Ed(s): Norman A Chigier. Pergamon, The Boulevard, Langford Ln, East Park, Kidlington, OX5 1GB, United Kingdom. Illus., index, adv. Refereed. Microform: PQC. Online: EBSCO Publishing, EBSCO Host; Gale; IngentaConnect; OhioLINK; ScienceDirect; SwetsWise Online Content. *Indexed:* ApMecR, C&ISA, CEA, ChemAb, EngInd, EnvAb, EnvInd, ExcerpMed, IAA, SCI. *Aud.:* Ac.

This is a review journal publishing papers on efficient combustion of fuels (fossil and biomass), with the aim of conserving resources and protecting the environment. Although much of the "conversion" is for power plant energy production, a fair percentage is devoted to jets and internal combustion engines. Articles are not for the fainthearted; the editors solicit articles from experts in the field, and they do a thorough job. It is not unusual for an issue to have only two papers, each of 50 pages or more. This journal is heavily illustrated with tables and charts, and many of these include color for emphasis and easy reading, a virtue of electronic publishing. Thus, this title is consumed by the academic market, but some papers are deliberately designed for the practicing engineer or manager. This is an expensive publication, but with a very high Impact Factor (as befits a review journal), and well worth considering for the complete research collection.

2208. Progress in Photovoltaics: research and applications. [ISSN: 1062-7995] 1993. 8x/yr. USD 1667 print or online ed. Ed(s): P A Lynn. John Wiley & Sons Ltd., The Atrium, Southern Gate, Chichester, PO19 8SQ, United Kingdom; customer@wiley.co.uk; http://www.wiley.co.uk. Adv. Refereed. Microform: PQC. Online: EBSCO Publishing, EBSCO Host; OhioLINK; SwetsWise Online Content; Wiley InterScience. Reprint: PSC. *Indexed:* C&ISA, CerAb, ChemAb, EngInd, EnvAb, IAA, SCI. *Aud.:* Ac.

For "photovoltaics" in the title, the reader should substitute the term "solar cells." This journal promotes quick publication of research articles, brief communications, and short surveys, generally within a year of submission, and often less. There is a deliberate mix of academics, practitioners, and policy makers on the review board to provide the same mix in the journal. Issues are divided into research, broad perspectives, and applications. The articles can be quite practical, as in "PV pumping stations," and experimental, as in "Experimental solar spectral irradiance until 2500 nm." About once a year there will be a theme issue on such topics as "PV crystal-gazing: the next ten years for solar cells." The photovoltaics literature survey section, culled from other research journals in the field, is very current and appears in each issue. This is a good title for universities with strong interests in energy and electrical engineering.

2209. Public Utilities Fortnightly. Former titles (until Sep. 1994): *Public Utilities Reports. Fortnightly;* (until Oct. 1993): *Public Utilities Fortnightly.* [ISSN: 1078-5892] 1929. m. USD 169 domestic; USD 199 foreign. Ed(s): Bruce W Radford, Richard Stavros. Public Utilities Reports, Inc., 8229 Boone Blvd, Ste 401, Vienna, VA 22182; pur_info@pur.com; http://www.pur.com. Adv. Circ: 6500 Paid. Microform: PQC. Online: EBSCO Publishing, EBSCO Host; Florida Center for Library Automation; Gale; LexisNexis; Northern Light Technology, Inc.; OCLC Online Computer Library Center, Inc.; ProQuest LLC (Ann Arbor); Thomson West. *Indexed:* ABIn, ATI, BPI, CLI, EnvAb, EnvInd, LRI, PAIS. *Aud.:* Ga, Sa.

This classic title hasn't been "fortnightly" since 2003; it is now a monthly. Gone are the flimsy newsprint pages (pink, if memory serves), replaced by glossy paper, full-color layouts, and eye-catching advertisements. Issues have three or four articles and several columns, including two on people ("plain" people and "people in power"). The articles average four pages, often with nicely formatted data, and, unless opinion pieces, include numerous references. This is a magazine for the investor, addressing new plant technology, regulatory issues, international economics, and supply/distribution problems for electricity, natural gas, nuclear power, and other large-scale energy suppliers. The brevity of the articles, coupled with the overview approach, makes this a useful source for undergraduates as well. The web site has tables of contents for issues back to 1995; the entire set is searchable, but full text is restricted to subscribers.

2210. Renewable & Sustainable Energy Reviews. [ISSN: 1364-0321] 1997. 6x/yr. EUR 1116. Ed(s): Dr. Lawrence L Kazmerski. Pergamon, The Boulevard, Langford Ln, East Park, Kidlington, OX5 1GB, United Kingdom. *Indexed:* EngInd, EnvAb, SCI. *Aud.:* Ac.

This is an economics and policy journal, which, as the title suggests, features extensive review articles. Papers average 30 pages and can reach 50. Authors are either faculty at universities or researchers for government-supported organizations. The energy sources covered are biomass, geothermics, hydrogen, hydroelectric, ocean/tide, solar, and wind. Illustrations are often tables and graphs, an excellent data source. Libraries should compare this title with its sister publication *Renewable Energy* and *Renewable Energy World* (the latter two both below) to determine which title(s) fit their collections best.

2211. Renewable Energy. Incorporates (1984-1990): *Solar and Wind Technology.* [ISSN: 0960-1481] 1985. 15x/yr. EUR 2041. Ed(s): Ali A M Sayigh. Pergamon, The Boulevard, Langford Ln, East Park, Kidlington, OX5 1GB, United Kingdom. Illus., index, adv. Sample. Refereed. Vol. ends: No. 12. Microform: PQC. Online: EBSCO Publishing, EBSCO Host; Gale; IngentaConnect; OhioLINK; ScienceDirect; SwetsWise Online Content. *Indexed:* C&ISA, EngInd, EnvAb, EnvInd, ExcerpMed, PollutAb, SCI, SWRA. *Bk. rev.:* 1, 1,000 words. *Aud.:* Ac.

At the other end of the spectrum from such magazines as *Home Power* and *Windpower Monthly,* in both type of content and price, *Renewable Energy* is a scholarly publication. Originally emphasizing solar and wind energy (and still heavily cited in the major solar energy titles), it now includes ocean wave and geothermal material. A small percentage of the articles is nontechnical, covering social, political, and economic aspects of renewable energy development, but most articles are technical in nature. The authorship is international, with a high rate of Third World contributors, reflecting the sites that emphasize development and use of low-cost (economically and environmentally) power sources. Issues are arranged by type of article: "article," "technical brief," and "data bank" (the latter designating a summary of extensive data collection and evaluation).

2212. Renewable Energy World. Incorporates (1996-1998): *Sustainable Energy Industry Journal.* [ISSN: 1462-6381] 1996. bi-m. USD 115 in Europe (Free to qualified personnel). PennWell Corporation, 1421 S Sheridan Rd, Tulsa, OK 74112; Headquarters@PennWell.com; http://www.pennwell.com. Illus., adv. Circ: 15000 Controlled. *Aud.:* Ac, Sa.

A colorful trade publication with a well-designed web presence, this magazine covers all of the "renewable" energy sources: biomass, cogeneration, hydroelectric, geothermal, green, solar, wind, and tidal/wave. Although published in Britain, coverage is international, both in terms of articles and of suppliers: it's easy to find wind power companies in, say, Colombia. Each issue emphasizes one or more types in turn. Designed for the practitioner rather than the scholar, issues are crammed with current news, include ten or so articles, and have the usual conference/trade show announcements, letters, editorials, and the like. The web site includes links to suppliers, related material, and archives of selected articles from back numbers. The articles themselves often have the kinds of tables, charts, and engineering data hard to acquire elsewhere, plus sometimes lengthy bibliographies. Those on the web site are free to all, making this a good referral site for undergraduate research. Perhaps a sign of things to come, the subscription page urges readers to "subscribe digitally" and offers a half-price subscription to encourage them. Corporate libraries with interests in any renewable energy sources will want a full subscription; public and academic libraries may find the web site sufficient.

2213. Resource and Energy Economics. Formerly (until 1993): *Resources and Energy.* [ISSN: 0928-7655] 1978. 4x/yr. EUR 640. Ed(s): M. Hoel, Charles D Kolstad. Elsevier BV, North-Holland, Sara Burgerhartstraat 25, Amsterdam, 1055 KV, Netherlands; nlinfo-f@elsevier.nl; http://www.elsevier.nl. Illus., index, adv. Sample. Refereed. Microform: PQC. Online: EBSCO Publishing, EBSCO Host; Gale; IngentaConnect; OhioLINK; ScienceDirect; SwetsWise Online Content. *Indexed:* ABIn, EngInd, EnvAb, EnvInd, ForAb, JEL, M&GPA, PollutAb, SSCI, WAE&RSA. *Aud.:* Ac.

Evidently economists proceed at a different pace than engineers. This slim quarterly publishes four to six articles, averages less than 100 pages per issue, and has a lag time of over two years between submission and publication, yet is one of the most-cited titles in economics and in environmental studies. This journal should be compared with its sister publication *Energy Economics* (above in this section). *Resources and Energy Economics* emphasizes use of resources, of which energy is one. The papers are scholarly and lengthy (often more than 20 pages). Recent topics include "Substitution between energy, capital and labour within industrial companies" and "Heterogeneous capital stocks and the optimal timing for CO2 abatement." Libraries whose interest is primarily in energy will prefer *Energy Economics,* while those with strong economics and/or business collections should consider both journals.

2214. Solar Energy. [ISSN: 0038-092X] 1957. 12x/yr. EUR 2564. Ed(s): D Yogi Goswami. Pergamon, The Boulevard, Langford Ln, East Park, Kidlington, OX5 1GB, United Kingdom. Illus., index, adv. Sample. Refereed. Circ: 13000. Vol. ends: No. 6. Microform: MIM; PQC. Online: EBSCO Publishing, EBSCO Host; Gale; IngentaConnect; OhioLINK; ScienceDirect; SwetsWise Online Content. *Indexed:* API, AS&TI, Agr, ApMecR, C&ISA, CerAb, ChemAb, EngInd, EnvAb, EnvInd, ExcerpMed, M&GPA, SCI, SSCI. *Bk. rev.:* 1, 500 words. *Aud.:* Ac.

Solar Energy was once the premier journal in solar research, encompassing biomass and wind energy as well as the engineering and physical aspects of solar energy. It is strictly a scholarly publication, and most of its authors are academics from all of the engineering disciplines, with a few applied physicists included for good measure. Illustrations are limited to charts, tables, and line drawings, although an occasional candid photograph of field work appears; many of these are enhanced with adept use of color. Every few months there is a topical issue (such as "Urban Ventilation") and the occasional "short note," a brief methodology description. Publication lag time can be over a year, but most of the lag seems to be in the review process; once accepted, an article is promptly published. Since this title was last reviewed, the Impact Factor has declined but the price, inevitably, has increased. Institutions with emphasis on materials and electronics might prefer its sister publication *Solar Energy Materials & Solar Cells* (below).

2215. Solar Energy Materials & Solar Cells. Formerly (until 1992): *Solar Energy Materials;* Incorporates (1979-1991): *Solar Cells.* [ISSN: 0927-0248] 1979. 12x/yr. EUR 2311. Ed(s): C. M. Lampert. Elsevier BV, North-Holland, Sara Burgerhartstraat 25, Amsterdam, 1055 KV, Netherlands; nlinfo-f@elsevier.nl; http://www.elsevier.nl. Illus., index. Sample. Refereed. Vol. ends: No. 4. Microform: PQC. Online: EBSCO Publishing, EBSCO Host; Gale; IngentaConnect; OhioLINK; ScienceDirect; SwetsWise Online Content. *Indexed:* C&ISA, CerAb, ChemAb, EngInd, EnvAb, ExcerpMed, IAA, SCI. *Aud.:* Ac.

Aptly named, this journal publishes highly technical papers on the materials used in solar energy production and products. Aside from solar cells, it includes light control (smart windows), optical and photochemical properties of materials, and photothermal devices (used in energy storage). Unlike *Progress in Photovoltaics* (reviewed above), this is an applications-centered publication. Recent articles discuss growth of ZnO thin films, power loss in a parabolic photovoltaic concentrator, and low band gap polymers used in organic solar cells. An events calendar is a regular feature, and "letters" (brief articles) appear occasionally. This is one of the top ten most-cited journals in energy, but it is best for scholarly collections that encompass materials chemistry as well as energy.

2216. Solar Today: today's energy choices for a cleaner environment. Formerly: *A S E S News.* [ISSN: 1042-0630] 1987. bi-m. USD 29 domestic; USD 39 Canada; USD 49 elsewhere. Ed(s): Regina Johnson.

American Solar Energy Society, Inc., 2400 Central Ave., Ste A, Boulder, CO 80301-2843; ases@ases.org; http://www.ases.org. Illus., index, adv. Circ: 6000. Vol. ends: Nov/Dec. *Indexed:* BiolDig, EnvAb, EnvInd. *Aud.:* Ga, Sa.

This is the members' magazine for the American Solar Energy Society, the "local" for the international, which publishes *Solar Energy*. The latter is for researchers; *Solar Today* is for everybody. As is true of many magazines in the solar field, wind power is included as an also-ran. Many of the articles describe success stories on a small scale, such as "Zero-Energy Home Makeover." Others take the larger view, covering potential world markets for wind energy or green power. Although the topics may be technical, the treatment usually is not. The letters section is extensive, there are lots of ads (for both the contractor and the homeowner), and society news and conference programs complete the issue. The web site includes links to conferences and events, educational and informational sites, government agencies, utilities, businesses (by specialty), and society business and information on the annual National Solar Tour (formerly the National Tour of Solar Buildings). This is an inexpensive title suitable for public libraries, but academic institutions will be better served by *Solar Energy* or *Solar Energy Materials & Solar Cells*.

2217. U.S. Department of Energy. Energy Information Administration. Monthly Energy Review (Print Edition). Formed by the merger of: *P I M S Monthly Petroleum Report; Monthly Energy Indicators;* Incorporates (1975-1982): *Quarterly Report, Energy Information Report to Congress, Required by Public Law 93-319, Amended by Public Law 94-163.* [ISSN: 0095-7356] 1974. m. USD 147 domestic; USD 205.80 elsewhere. U.S. Department of Energy, Energy Information Administration, 1000 Independence Ave, SW, Washington, DC 20585; infoctr@eia.doe.gov; http://eia.doe.gov. Illus., index. Vol. ends: Dec. Online: EBSCO Publishing, EBSCO Host; Florida Center for Library Automation; Gale; OCLC Online Computer Library Center, Inc.; ProQuest LLC (Ann Arbor). *Indexed:* AmStI, EnvAb, EnvInd, IUSGP. *Aud.:* Ga, Ac, Sa.

A merger of print and electronic media for the transmittal of statistical data, the *Monthly Energy Review* has become entirely a creature of the web. Most issues are made up of data on specific forms of energy (coal, oil, gas, electricity, nuclear), their production, consumption, and pricing. Renewable energy sources now have their own section, right there with oil, electricity, and coal. Data are presented monthly for the current and previous two years, then annually for earlier years, back to 1973. Often there are accompanying illustrative charts and graphs. Each section begins with a short introduction highlighting current trends, proceeds through copious data, then ends with explanatory notes and data-source information for specific tables. The site includes conversion tables, various appendixes (such as carbon dioxide emission factors for coal), and an extensive glossary. "Energy Plugs" became a feature in 1996; these are abstracts of lengthy reports compiled by the Energy Information Administration (EIA) that can be ordered in print or obtained, free, at the EIA web site. Individual tables may be downloaded in CSV or Excel formats. Beginning with the November 1996 issue, the entire issue is accessible in pdf format. The web site is easy to navigate and includes a broad range of other EIA data and analyses, including separate annual data compilations. The EIA site includes other publications for each of the energy sources that it monitors that provide more data and more in-depth analyses; libraries may also want to add those that suit local needs. Add this to the Bookmark section of the reference desk browser, and as a direct link from the catalog record.

2218. W S E A S Transactions on Power Systems. [ISSN: 1790-5060] 2006. q. EUR 400 (Individuals, EUR 300). Ed(s): Christian Bouquegneau. World Scientific and Engineering Academy and Society (W S E A S), Ag Ioannou Theologou 17-23, Zographou, 15773, Greece; http://www.wseas.org. *Indexed:* C&ISA, CerAb, IAA. *Aud.:* Ac, Sa.

One of about 20 journals from WSEAS (World Scientific and Engineering Academy and Society), *Power Systems* is a rapidly growing journal with an uneven focus. Most of the articles discuss arcane parts, techniques, and systems in the power production industry, almost exclusively dealing with electrical power. Each issue, though, has a few broader articles, usually on such energy sources as wind, solar, hydropower, and photovoltaic. Occasionally there are economic analyses of power distribution and conservation. Contributions are limited to six pages (with some exceptions) and, although the authorship is international, most papers are from Third World countries. The society itself,

formed in 1996, is eclectic in its interests, which perhaps explains the wide range in the article presentations. Because of the highly specialized content of most of the issues, the journal is best suited to academic libraries with strong programs in power production and those businesses and governments interested in electric power generation and distribution.

2219. Wind Energy. [ISSN: 1095-4244] 1998. bi-m. USD 756 print or online ed. Ed(s): Robert Thresher. John Wiley & Sons Ltd., The Atrium, Southern Gate, Chichester, PO19 8SQ, United Kingdom; customer@wiley.co.uk; http://www.wiley.co.uk. Refereed. Reprint: PSC. *Indexed:* EngInd, EnvAb, SCI. *Aud.:* Ac.

For many years there were only two scholarly journals covering wind sources of energy, the *Journal of Wind Engineering & Industrial Aerodynamics* and *Wind Engineering* (both reviewed in this section). *Wind Energy* was launched in 1998, evidently in direct competition with *Wind Engineering*. They both cover the technical aspects of generating power from wind sources; they both have an international scope, include papers authored largely by academic institutions and government-funded agencies, have lengthy articles and references, and include the occasional historical or economic review. Where they differ is in price and bulk; *Wind Energy* costs a third more than *Wind Engineering* and has half as many pages. Libraries with large collections may want both, but the less expensive title seems the best bet.

2220. Wind Engineering. [ISSN: 0309-524X] 1977. bi-m. GBP 317; GBP 337 combined subscription print & online eds. Ed(s): John Twidell. Multi-Science Publishing Co. Ltd., 5 Wates Way, Brentwood, CM15 9TB, United Kingdom; sciencem@hotmail.com; http://www.multi-science.co.uk. Refereed. *Indexed:* ApMecR, C&ISA, CerAb, EngInd, IAA. *Aud.:* Ac.

Wind Engineering claims to be the oldest English-language journal devoted entirely to the technical issues of wind power, which is largely true, although the *Journal of Wind Engineering & Industrial Aerodynamics* (above in this section) has been in existence longer, beginning as the *Journal of Industrial Aerodynamics*. Topics covered are wind turbines, turbine blade design, and economic and historical aspects of wind energy, and there is a good deal of emphasis on wind farms and offshore wind energy production. The electronic version is mounted by Ingenta and includes the option of an RSS feed of the contents. It is very similar in coverage and quality to *Wind Energy* (above), and libraries with restricted budgets or tangential interest in wind power will want to carefully compare the two. However, *Wind Engineering* is the less expensive of the two and has more content.

2221. Windpower Monthly: news magazine. [ISSN: 0109-7318] 1985. m. USD 195; USD 295 inc. on-line ed.; USD 430 inc. subc. to Windstats Newsletter. Ed(s): Lyn Harrison. Windpower Monthly A/S, Vrinners Hoved, PO Box 100, Knebel, 8420, Denmark; mail@windpower-monthly.com; http://www.windpower-monthly.com. Illus., adv. Sample. Circ: 3000. Vol. ends: No. 12. *Indexed:* EnvAb, EnvInd. *Aud.:* Ac, Sa.

Begun in Denmark, distributed from the United States, and with a web site originating in the United Kingdom, *Windpower Monthly* is truly an international publication. The audience is wind energy businesses, investors, and power plant component manufacturers. Although each issue will have a small number of articles (one of which is the "Focus Article"), the bulk of the magazine is devoted to wind energy news reports, arranged by regions/countries of the world. Some of the news is technical ("Blades Built by Robots"), but most of it is economic or policy news. The "Windicator," a quarterly supplement, is a chart of wind power capacity worldwide, identifying industrial, political, technical, and economic trends. Issues from 1994 to the present can be searched on the web site by keyword, date, and geographic area. Tables of contents for the current three issues include lengthy abstracts, but only print subscribers can access the full text via ID/password. Electronic subscribers have access to the complete backfile.

2222. World Oil. Formerly: *Oil Weekly*. [ISSN: 0043-8790] 1916. m. Free. Ed(s): Kurt Abraham, Perry Fischer. Gulf Publishing Co., PO Box 2608, Houston, TX 77252-2608; publications@gulfpub.com; http://www.gulfpub.com. Illus., adv. Circ: 35563 Paid and controlled. Microform: PQC. Online: EBSCO Publishing, EBSCO Host; Factiva,

Inc.; Florida Center for Library Automation; Gale; Northern Light Technology, Inc.; OCLC Online Computer Library Center, Inc.; ProQuest LLC (Ann Arbor); H.W. Wilson. *Indexed:* ABIn, AS&TI, BPI, C&ISA, ChemAb, EngInd, PAIS, PetrolAb, SSCI. *Aud.:* Ac, Sa.

One of the many petroleum-related trade magazines (see the *Oil & Gas Journal* above in this section), this one covers oil around the world. Each issue follows the pattern of focus articles, feature articles, columns (such as "What's New in Production" and "International Politics"), news, and departments. Focus and feature articles are short (two or three pages), but they are well illustrated in color and often have numerous references. The web site includes supplements (such as "Deepwater Technology") and case studies, plus extensive statistics (both production and price), reference tables, forecasts, and analyses. The data alone are worth the price of subscription. An excellent, inexpensive addition to a good energy collection.

■ ENGINEERING AND TECHNOLOGY

General/Biomedical Engineering/Chemical Engineering/Civil Engineering/Computer, Control, and Systems Engineering/Electrical Engineering/Manufacturing Engineering/Materials Engineering/Mechanical Engineering/Nuclear Engineering

See also Aeronautics and Space Science; Atmospheric Sciences; Biology; Chemistry; Computers and Information Technology; Earth Sciences; Mathematics; Physics; Robotics; and Science and Technology sections.

G. Lynn Berard, Principal Librarian, Science Libraries, Carnegie Mellon University, Pittsburgh, PA 15213-3890

Introduction

Originating in the eleventh century from the Latin "ingeniator," the term "engineer" means "the ingenious one." Imhotep, an Egyptian from about 2550 BC, is credited as the first engineer. Engineering is the product of human innovation and endeavor; therefore, it is the profession that deals with the properties of matter and the sources of power in nature by designing and building machines, devices, and structures useful to humans. Technology is a major application of engineering processes and, in a sense, is the product of engineering. The transfer of technology and engineering knowledge happens by the passing of blueprints, models, designs, patents, and education.

Less obvious, but an equal partner in the dissemination of engineering knowledge, is the formation of professional organizations and the issuing of their publications. As early as the thirteenth century, European monasteries created manuscripts showing various machines and processes. With the invention of the printing press in the fifteenth century, illustrated books and manuals were produced that depicted technical processes. The notebooks of Leonardo da Vinci, Francesco di Giorgio Martini, and Georgius Agricola were filled with sketches of futuristic inventions and were reproduced and circulated among their colleagues. In the last few decades, engineering educators and the nation's engineering schools have broadened the curriculum by adding environmental awareness to their programs. Companies are balancing their responsibilities to their shareholders and the public by supporting the incorporation of sustainable approaches to manufacturing. Industry is hiring environmentally aware engineers and academia is preparing students to balance the tough tradeoffs in a worldwide economy of production costs versus environmental protections.

Engineering has become much less departmentalized and very interdisciplinary in its approach to both practice and the design of educational curricula. This cross-pollination of the field creates a challenge for the selector, who needs to think interdisciplinarily and acknowledge that a journal that is of interest to many may stretch a limited budget. Make use of the subject index at the back of this volume and consider other sections, especially the Environment and Conservation section. This section attempts to provide a map for the selector in making purchase decisions in several areas of engineering, but it is not exhaustive by any means. I urge the reader to study carefully the preface of this book before delving into any particular discipline. The criteria for selection are carefully laid out, and they provide a basis for understanding the content of the individual sections.

Engineering association and society publications are the bricks and mortar of an engineering library collection. Whether one chooses to enroll in a standing-order plan or simply purchase main titles published by a pertinent society will depend in large part on the budget of the purchasing institution. Many societies offer reduced rates for institutional memberships and have flexible order plans. Engineering and technology collections are expensive. Very few U.S. libraries can afford to purchase and maintain research-level collections in engineering.

Electronic publishing has changed the way we can provide access to periodicals in all disciplines; journals in electronic form are the norm. Some are free while others require a subscription fee to access. In the main, all the journals included in this section have some form of electronic access. The Open Access movement is attempting to change publishing's economic model and copyright ownership of the author's intellectual property, thereby enabling free access to scholarly work.

The future holds much promise for electronic publishing and the creation of true digital, paperless libraries. Engineering scholars and students have come to expect electronic full-text access to their pertinent materials and this form of information delivery is still evolving.

Basic Periodicals

BIOMEDICAL ENGINEERING. Ac, Sa: *Biotechnology and Bioengineering.*

CHEMICAL ENGINEERING. Ga, Ac, Sa: *AIChE Journal.*

CIVIL ENGINEERING. Ac, Sa: *Civil Engineering, ENR.*

COMPUTER, CONTROL, AND SYSTEMS ENGINEERING. Ac, Sa: *Association for Computing Machinery. Journal.*

ELECTRICAL ENGINEERING. Ac, Sa: *IEEE Journals, Proceedings, and Transactions.*

MANUFACTURING ENGINEERING. Ac, Sa: *Journal of Manufacturing Systems.*

MATERIALS ENGINEERING. Ac, Sa: *Journal of Materials Research, Metallurgical and Materials Transactions A.*

MECHANICAL ENGINEERING. Ac, Sa: *American Society of Mechanical Engineers. Transactions.*

NUCLEAR ENGINEERING. Ga, Ac, Sa: *Nuclear Engineering International.*

Basic Abstracts and Indexes

Applied Science and Technology Index, Computer & Control Abstracts and Electrical and Electronic Abstracts (INSPEC), Engineering Index, Metals Abstracts.

General

2223. *A S E E Prism.* Formed by the merger of (1974-1991): *Engineering Education News;* (1924-1991): *Engineering Education;* Which was formerly (until 1969): *Journal of Engineering Education (Washington).* [ISSN: 1056-8077] 1991. 10x/yr. Free to members; Non-members, USD 150. Ed(s): Joanne Tulley, Robert Black. American Society for Engineering Education, 1818 N St, NW, Ste 600, Washington, DC 20036; http://www.asee.org. Illus., index, adv. Circ: 12000. Microform: CIS; PQC. Online: OCLC Online Computer Library Center, Inc.; ProQuest LLC (Ann Arbor); H.W. Wilson. *Indexed:* ABIn, ApMecR, C&ISA, CerAb, ChemAb, EduInd, IAA, RI-1. *Bk. rev.:* Number and length vary. *Aud.:* Ac.

This journal for the academic professional presents scholarly research and teaching methods in all disciplines of engineering. It is one of the many communication tools available to the membership of the American Society for

Engineering Education. Membership news, classified job ads, campaign news, and informative articles on teaching techniques are offered. Informative teaching articles. Available online for members at www.prism-magazine.org.

2224. A S H R A E Journal. Incorporates (1929-1959): *American Society of Heating and Air-Conditioning Engineers. Journal;* (1914-1959): *Refrigerating Engineering;* Which was formerly (until 1922): *A S R E Journal.* [ISSN: 0001-2491] 1959. m. Non-members, USD 59. Ed(s): Fred Turner. American Society of Heating, Refrigerating and Air-Conditioning Engineers, Inc. (A S H R A E), 1791 Tullie Circle, NE, Atlanta, GA 30329; http://www.ashrae.org. Illus., index, adv. Refereed. Circ: 54000 Paid. Vol. ends: Dec. Microform: PQC. Online: EBSCO Publishing, EBSCO Host; OCLC Online Computer Library Center, Inc.; ProQuest LLC (Ann Arbor); H.W. Wilson. *Indexed:* AS&TI, ApMecR, C&ISA, CerAb, ChemAb, EngInd, EnvAb, EnvInd, ExcerpMed, H&SSA, IAA, PollutAb, SCI. *Aud.:* Ac, Sa.

Offered to members since 1914, the American Society of Heating, Refrigerating and Air-Conditioning Engineers (ASHRAE) journal was created. Their credo then and now is "A Society like ours should be the guardian of the industry it represents; let us protect it through the Journal." In this publication, ASHRAE informs readers of changes in the HVAC&R field by providing technical papers, discussions, and news of interest. Special sections present current legal and design issues and product updates. There are classified advertisements, news regarding standards development, and a meetings and trade shows calendar. Available online at www.ashrae.org.

2225. Current Nanoscience. [ISSN: 1573-4137] 2005. q. USD 400 print or online ed. (Individuals, USD 160; Corporations, USD 820 print or online ed.). Ed(s): Atta-ur Rahman. Bentham Science Publishers Ltd., P O Box 294, Bussum, AG 1400, Netherlands; sales@bentham.org; http://www.bentham.org. Refereed. *Indexed:* EngInd, ExcerpMed, SCI. *Aud.:* Ac, Sa.

Current Nanoscience publishes authoritative reviews and original research reports, written by experts in the field, on all the most recent advances in nanoscience and nanotechnology. All aspects of the field are represented, including nanostructures, synthesis, properties, assembly, and devices. The journal is essential to all involved in nanoscience and its applied areas. Nanotechnology is the creation of systems for transforming matter, energy, and information that are based on nanometer-scale components with precisely defined molecular features. Applications of nanoscience in biotechnology, medicine, pharmaceuticals, physics, material science, and electronics are also covered.

2226. Graduating Engineer & Computer Careers (Print Edition). Formerly (until 1997): *Graduating Engineer.* 1979. q. USD 50.70. Ed(s): Valerie Anderson. Career Recruitment Media, Inc., 211 W Wacker Dr, Ste 900, Chicago, IL 60606; info@careermedia.com; http://www.careermedia.com/. Illus., adv. Circ: 64000 Controlled. *Aud.:* Ac.

This affordable journal is a must-read for engineering students. Directories abound in this publication, providing clues to which employers are hiring, engineering employers by discipline, and salary expectations. Special features include articles on career advice, how to select a graduate school, and recent graduates' experiences in the work world. Contains lots of job ads in industry and academic areas, and a campus calendar.

2227. Human Factors: the journal of the human factors and ergonomics society. [ISSN: 0018-7208] 1958. q. USD 485 print & online eds. (Individuals, USD 348 print & online eds.). Ed(s): Eduardo Salas. Human Factors and Ergonomics Society, PO Box 1369, Santa Monica, CA 90406-1369; lois@hfes.org; http://www.hfes.org. Illus., index. Refereed. Circ: 6200. Microform: PQC. Online: EBSCO Publishing, EBSCO Host; Florida Center for Library Automation; Gale; IngentaConnect; Northern Light Technology, Inc.; OCLC Online Computer Library Center, Inc.; ProQuest K-12 Learning Solutions; ProQuest LLC (Ann Arbor); H.W. Wilson. *Indexed:* AS&TI, AbAn, AgeL, C&ISA, CerAb, CommAb, CompLI, EngInd, ErgAb, ExcerpMed, FR, H&SSA, HRA, HRIS, IAA, IBR, IBZ, ISTA, PsycInfo, SCI, SSCI, SUSA. *Aud.:* Ac, Sa.

This journal is the official publication of the Human Factors and Ergonomics Society, an interdisciplinary organization of professional workers concerned with the role of humans in complex systems, the design of equipment and facilities, and the development of human-compatible environments. Ergonomics is the study of human capability and psychology in relation to the working environment and the equipment operated by the worker. To disseminate knowledge about human/machine/environment relationships and to promote putting this knowledge to work, the society publishes this journal. Evaluative reviews, articles on methods and quality approaches to human-machine theory, and reports of original research are presented. Free online access, with searchable index, is available at the society's web site.

2228. InterJournal. [ISSN: 1081-0625] 1997. irreg. Free. Ed(s): Y Bar Yam. New England Complex Systems Institute, 24 Mount Auburn St, Cambridge, MA 02138; nesci@necsi.org. Illus. Refereed. *Aud.:* Ac, Sa.

InterJournal is a distributed, self-organizing, refereed electronic journal. Selected topics include complex systems, genetics, polymers, and complex fluids. It is published by the New England Complex Systems Institute (NECSI), an independent educational and research institution dedicated to advancing the study of complex systems. Complex systems have multiple interacting components whose collective behavior cannot be simply inferred from the behavior of components. The recognition that understanding the parts cannot explain collective behavior has led to various new concepts and methodologies that are affecting all fields of science and engineering, and they are being applied to technology, business, and even social policy. The institute's web site is www.interjournal.org.

2229. International Journal for Numerical Methods in Engineering. [ISSN: 0029-5981] 1969. 52x/yr. USD 10235 print or online ed. Ed(s): Roland W Lewis. John Wiley & Sons Ltd., The Atrium, Southern Gate, Chichester, PO19 8SQ, United Kingdom; customer@wiley.co.uk; http://www.wiley.co.uk. Illus., index, adv. Refereed. Circ: 1500. Microform: PQC. Online: EBSCO Publishing, EBSCO Host; SwetsWise Online Content; Wiley InterScience. Reprint: PSC. *Indexed:* ApMecR, C&ISA, CCMJ, CerAb, CompLI, EngInd, IAA, MSN, MathR, SCI. *Bk. rev.:* Number and length vary. *Aud.:* Ac, Sa.

This publication provides a common platform for the presentation of papers and exchange of views on numerical methods used to solve a variety of engineering problems in such areas as heat transfer, structural analysis, fluid mechanics, network theory, electronics, and optimal system design. Available online at Wiley Interscience.

2230. Journal of Elasticity. [ISSN: 0374-3535] 1971. m. EUR 2180 print & online eds. Ed(s): Roger L Fosdick. Springer Netherlands, Van Godewijckstraat 30, Dordrecht, 3311 GX, Netherlands; http://www.springeronline.com. Illus., adv. Refereed. Microform: PQC. Online: EBSCO Publishing, EBSCO Host; Gale; IngentaConnect; OCLC Online Computer Library Center, Inc.; OhioLINK; Springer LINK; SwetsWise Online Content. Reprint: PSC. *Indexed:* ApMecR, CCMJ, EngInd, IAA, MSN, MathR, SCI. *Aud.:* Ac, Sa.

Original and significant discoveries in elasticity are reported in this journal. Full articles and research notes, along with occasional historical essays and classroom notes, are contained within. This basic journal will be of interest to a variety of engineering professionals. Electronic access via SpringerLink.

2231. Journal of Engineering Mathematics. [ISSN: 0022-0833] 1966. m. EUR 1485 print & online eds. Ed(s): H K Kuiken. Springer Netherlands, Van Godewijckstraat 30, Dordrecht, 3311 GX, Netherlands; http://www.springeronline.com. Illus., index, adv. Refereed. Microform: PQC. Online: EBSCO Publishing, EBSCO Host; Gale; IngentaConnect; OCLC Online Computer Library Center, Inc.; OhioLINK; Springer LINK; SwetsWise Online Content. Reprint: PSC. *Indexed:* ApMecR, C&ISA, CCMJ, CerAb, EngInd, IAA, MSN, MathR, SCI. *Bk. rev.:* Number and length vary. *Aud.:* Ac, Sa.

The application of mathematics to physical problems, specifically in the general area of engineering science, is the aim of this journal. Topics include numerical analysis, ordinary and partial differential equations, and computational methods. Applied fields of interest include biomedical engineering, solid mechanics, continuum mechanics, fluid mechanics, and fracture mechanics. Available online via Kluwer.

2232. *Leadership and Management in Engineering.* [ISSN: 1532-6748] 2001. q. USD 209. Ed(s): Charles R Glagola. American Society of Civil Engineers, 1801 Alexander Bell Dr, Reston, VA 20191-4400; http://www.asce.org. *Indexed:* C&ISA, CerAb, EngInd, HRIS, IAA. *Aud.:* Ac, Sa.

A helpful, timely magazine with practical advice on leadership and management in the engineering fields. Features advice on budgeting, strategic planning, marketing, and general management principles. Case studies are often published. Available online at www.pubs.asce.org/journals/lenews.html.

Measurement Science and Technology. See Physics section.

Biomedical Engineering

2233. *Annals of Biomedical Engineering.* Incorporates (1976-197?): *Journal of Bioengineering.* [ISSN: 0090-6964] 1979. m. EUR 958 print & online eds. Ed(s): Larry McIntire. Springer New York LLC, 233 Spring St, New York, NY 10013-1578; journals@springer-ny.com; http://www.springer.com/. Illus., index, adv. Refereed. Circ: 2200. Microform: PQC. Online: EBSCO Publishing, EBSCO Host; Gale; IngentaConnect; OCLC Online Computer Library Center, Inc.; OhioLINK; Springer LINK; SwetsWise Online Content. Reprint: PSC. *Indexed:* ApMecR, BioEngAb, BiolAb, C&ISA, CPI, CerAb, ChemAb, EngInd, ExcerpMed, IAA, SCI. *Bk. rev.:* Number and length vary. *Aud.:* Ac, Sa.

This is the official journal of the Biomedical Engineering Society, and its editorial board is composed mainly of U.S. academics. The journal contains scholarly articles on a wide spectrum of topics such as bioelectric phenomena and quantitative electrophysiology, biomaterials and biomechanics, and information-systems theory applications. Includes original articles, special communications, rapid communications, history and teaching articles, book reviews, and letters to the editor. Available online at www.springerlink.com.

2234. *Biomaterials.* Incorporates (1986-1995): *Clinical Materials;* Which incorporated (in 1991): *Critical Reviews in Biocompatibility.* [ISSN: 0142-9612] 1980. 36x/yr. EUR 3910. Ed(s): D. F. Williams. Elsevier BV, Radarweg 29, Amsterdam, 1043 NX, Netherlands; nlinfo-f@elsevier.nl; http://www.elsevier.nl. Illus., adv. Refereed. Microform: PQC. Online: EBSCO Publishing, EBSCO Host; Gale; IngentaConnect; OhioLINK; ScienceDirect; SwetsWise Online Content. *Indexed:* BioEngAb, BrTechI, C&ISA, CABA, CerAb, ChemAb, DSA, EngInd, ExcerpMed, HortAb, IAA, IndVet, S&F, SCI, VB. *Bk. rev.:* Number and length vary. *Aud.:* Ac, Sa.

Biomaterials is an international journal that covers the science and application of biomaterials and associated medical devices. It is the aim of the journal to provide a peer-reviewed forum for the publication of original papers and authoritative review papers dealing with the most important issues that face the use of materials in clinical practice. The scope of the journal covers the basic science and engineering aspects of biomaterials, including their mechanical, physical, chemical, and biological properties; relevant design and production characteristics of devices constructed of these materials; and their clinical performance. In this context, biomaterials are defined as all those materials used in medical devices in which contact with the tissues of the patient is an important and guiding feature of their use and performance. They include a range of metals and alloys, glasses and ceramics, natural synthetics, polymers, biomimetics, composites, and natural or tissue-derived materials, including combinations of synthetic materials and living tissue components. The journal is relevant to all applications of biomaterials, including implantable medical devices, tissue engineering, and drug delivery systems. Available via Science Direct.

2235. *Biotechnology and Bioengineering.* Formerly (until 1962): *Journal of Biochemical and Microbiological Technology and Engineering.* [ISSN: 0006-3592] 1958. 18x/yr. USD 7345. Ed(s): Douglas S Clark. John Wiley & Sons, Inc., 111 River St, Hoboken, NJ 07030-5774; uscs-wis@wiley.com; http://www.wiley.com. Illus., index, adv. Refereed. Circ: 1700. CD-ROM: The Dialog Corporation. Microform: PQC. Online: EBSCO Publishing, EBSCO Host; OhioLINK; SwetsWise Online Content; Wiley InterScience. *Indexed:* Agr, B&AI, BioEngAb, BiolAb, C&ISA, CABA, CEA, ChemAb, DSA, EngInd, ExcerpMed, FPA, FS&TA, ForAb, HortAb, IndVet, PollutAb, S&F, SCI, SWRA, VB, WAE&RSA, WRCInf. *Aud.:* Ac, Sa.

All aspects of biotechnology are explored in this journal. Topics of interest include cellular physiology, metabolism, enzyme systems and their applications, animal-cell biotechnology, bioseparations, and environmental biotechnology. Approximately ten scholarly papers are offered in each issue, as well as communications. A core journal in the biomedical engineering discipline and available electronically from Wiley Interscience.

2236. *Journal of Biomaterials Science. Polymer Edition.* [ISSN: 0920-5063] 1989. m. EUR 1708 print & online eds. Ed(s): S L Cooper, K Kataoka. V S P, Brill Academic Publishers, PO Box 9000, Leiden, 2300 PA, Netherlands; vsppub@brill.nl; http://www.vsppub.com. Sample. Refereed. Online: EBSCO Publishing, EBSCO Host; Gale; IngentaConnect; OCLC Online Computer Library Center, Inc.; Springer LINK; SwetsWise Online Content. Reprint: PSC. *Indexed:* BioEngAb, BiolAb, C&ISA, CerAb, ChemAb, EngInd, ExcerpMed, IAA, IndVet, SCI, SSCI, VB. *Aud.:* Ac, Sa.

Available online and in print, this monthly journal publishes original research papers, short communications, and review articles with the goal of contributing to future progress in the practical applications of polymers, synthetic and natural, as the most versatile biomaterials. These applications contribute to the science of pharmaceuticals, biomedical devices, and biological systems. Provides an international forum for the discussion of fundamental biomaterials research.

2237. *Journal of Biomechanical Engineering.* [ISSN: 0148-0731] 1977. q. Members, USD 60 print & online eds.; Non-members, USD 430 print & online eds. Ed(s): Frank C Yin. A S M E International, Three Park Ave, New York, NY 10016-5990; infocentral@asme.org; http://www.asme.org. Illus., index, adv. Refereed. Microform: PQC. Online: American Institute of Physics, Scitation; EBSCO Publishing, EBSCO Host; SwetsWise Online Content. *Indexed:* AS&TI, ApMecR, BioEngAb, C&ISA, CEA, CerAb, ChemAb, EngInd, ExcerpMed, IAA, SCI. *Bk. rev.:* Number and length vary. *Aud.:* Ac, Sa.

The mechanics of prosthesis is a wide-open field in engineering. This refereed journal, the official publication of the Institute of Physics and Engineering in Medicine, covers all aspects of new developments in health care, including the instrumentation of function replacement, biomedical computing, clinical engineering, and biological systems. Solutions to particular patient problems are discussed and open to critical examination. Available online at http://scitation.aip.org/ASMEJournals/Biomechanical.

2238. *Journal of Biomechanics.* [ISSN: 0021-9290] 1968. 16x/yr. EUR 3402. Ed(s): Dr. Farshid Guilak, Dr. Rik Huiskes. Pergamon, The Boulevard, Langford Ln, East Park, Kidlington, OX5 1GB, United Kingdom. Illus., index, adv. Refereed. Circ: 1600. Microform: PQC. Online: EBSCO Publishing, EBSCO Host; Gale; IngentaConnect; OhioLINK; ScienceDirect; SwetsWise Online Content. *Indexed:* AbAn, ApMecR, BioEngAb, BiolAb, C&ISA, CABA, EngInd, ErgAb, ExcerpMed, H&SSA, IAA, IndVet, PEI, RILM, SCI, SD, SSCI, VB. *Bk. rev.:* Number and length vary. *Aud.:* Ac, Sa.

Biomechanics is the study of the mechanics of living things. From the biological side, this journal features articles that deal with the dynamics of the musculoskeletal system, the mechanics of soft and hard tissues, the mechanics of bone and muscle, and the mechanisms of cells. From the mechanical aspect, the mechanics of prosthetics and orthotics are presented. Each issue offers research articles along with technical notes describing new techniques. Available online via ScienceDirect. Includes sports-related biomechanics.

2239. *Journal of Biomedical Materials Research. Part A.* Supersedes in part (1966-2002): *Journal of Biomedical Materials Research;* Incorporated (1990-1995): *Journal of Applied Biomaterials.* [ISSN: 1549-3296] 2003. 16x/yr. USD 7982. Ed(s): James Anderson. John Wiley & Sons, Inc., 111 River St, Hoboken, NJ 07030-5774; uscs-wis@wiley.com; http://www.wiley.com. Illus., adv. Refereed. *Indexed:* ApMecR, B&AI, BiolAb, C&ISA, CerAb, ChemAb, ExcerpMed, IAA, SCI. *Aud.:* Ac, Sa.

This is the official journal of the Society for Biomaterials (U.S.), the Japanese Society for Biomaterials, the Australian Society for Biomaterials, and the Korean Society for Biomaterials. It covers such topics as ceramics and alloys, along with dentistry, implanted devices, and surgery. Each article contains graphs, tables, and photos and is highly readable yet scholarly. A noteworthy international effort. Available online through Wiley Interscience.

Chemical Engineering

2240. *A I Ch E Journal.* [ISSN: 0001-1541] 1955. m. USD 1789. Ed(s): Swapna Padhye. John Wiley & Sons, Inc., 111 River St, Hoboken, NJ 07030-5774; uscs-wis@wiley.com; http://www.wiley.com. Illus., index, adv. Refereed. Circ: 3000 Paid. Vol. ends: Dec. Online: EBSCO Publishing, EBSCO Host; OhioLINK; ProQuest LLC (Ann Arbor); ScienceDirect; SwetsWise Online Content; Wiley InterScience. *Indexed:* AS&TI, ApMecR, C&ISA, CEA, CerAb, ChemAb, EngInd, EnvAb, EnvInd, ExcerpMed, IAA, MathR, PetrolAb, PollutAb, S&F, SCI, WRCInf. *Bk. rev.:* Number and length vary. *Aud.:* Ac, Sa.

The main publication of the American Institute of Chemical Engineers, this journal is devoted to fundamental research and developments that have immediate or potential value in chemical engineering. Each issue contains reviews, full-length research papers (both experimental and theoretical), R&D notes, and detailed book reviews. Supplemental materials are provided by contributors when they have referenced works that are not essential to the development of their article or that are not easily accessible elsewhere but are of interest to the reader. These supplemental materials are deposited on microfilm, and a footnote with an access pointer is provided. The journal is available online via Science Direct.

Chemical & Engineering News. See Chemistry/General section.

2241. *The Chemical Engineer: the essential magazine for the chemical & process industries.* Formerly: *Chemical Engineer and Transactions of the Institution of Chemical Engineers;* Which superseded in part (in 1983): *Institution of Chemical Engineers. Transactions;* Which incorporated (1922-1990): *Chemical Engineer Diary and Institution News;* Which was formerly (until 1983): *Institution of Chemical Engineers. Diary.* [ISSN: 0302-0797] 1923. m. GBP 165. Ed(s): Delyth Forsdyke, Claudia Hume. Institution of Chemical Engineers, George E Davis Bldg, 165-189 Railway Terr, Rugby, CV21 3HQ, United Kingdom; http://www.icheme.org/. Illus., index, adv. Refereed. Circ: 25695 Paid. *Indexed:* AS&TI, CEA, ChemAb, EngInd, SCI, WRCInf. *Aud.:* Ac, Sa.

Published by the Institution of Chemical Engineers in the United Kingdom, this magazine is the sister publication to *Chemical & Engineering News* (see Chemistry section) in the United States. News from and about the chemical industry, feature articles, technology reports, plant and equipment developments, a literature showcase, and events of interest to the professional are provided. Great for both the general reader and the specialist. Available online at www.portlandpress.com/pcs/journals/journal.cfm?product=TCE.

2242. *Chemical Engineering Education.* [ISSN: 0009-2479] 1965. q. Members, USD 25; Non-members, USD 80. Ed(s): Tim Anderson. American Society for Engineering Education, Chemical Engineering Division, 227 Chemical Engineering Bldg, P O Box 116005, Gainesville, FL 32611-6005; cee@che.ufl.edu; http://cee.che.ufl.edu. Illus., index, adv. Refereed. Circ: 2850 Paid. Microform: PQC. *Indexed:* C&ISA, ChemAb, EngInd, ExcerpMed. *Bk. rev.:* Number and length vary. *Aud.:* Ac.

Written for the educator, *CEE* publishes papers in the broad field of chemical engineering education. Typical content includes course descriptions, curriculum formats, research programs, and special instruction programs. Views on various topics of interest to the profession along with descriptions of chemical engineer-

ing departments, educators, and laboratory setups are also provided. Available only in print format, with abstracts of major papers back to 1998 available at their web site, http://cee.che.ufl.edu/index.html.

2243. *Chemical Engineering Science.* [ISSN: 0009-2509] 1951. 24x/yr. EUR 5445. Ed(s): A. Bell. Pergamon, The Boulevard, Langford Ln, East Park, Kidlington, OX5 1GB, United Kingdom. Illus., index, adv. Refereed. Circ: 2000 Paid. Microform: PQC. Online: EBSCO Publishing, EBSCO Host; Gale; IngentaConnect; OhioLINK; ScienceDirect; SwetsWise Online Content. *Indexed:* ApMecR, BioEngAb, BrTechI, C&ISA, CEA, CerAb, ChemAb, EngInd, EnvAb, EnvInd, ExcerpMed, IAA, PetrolAb, PollutAb, SCI, WRCInf. *Bk. rev.:* Number and length vary. *Aud.:* Ac, Sa.

The chemical, oil, pharmaceutical, and food industries will find this journal pertinent. Papers found within describe original experiments and theoretical insights. Some core topics are chemical-reaction engineering, applied catalysis, biochemical engineering, fluid mechanics, mathematical modeling and simulation, and multiphase flow. New areas of interest are environmental problems and molecular science related to fundamental chemical engineering. Available online via Science Direct.

Chemical Week. See Business/Trade and Industry section.

2244. *Combustion and Flame.* [ISSN: 0010-2180] 1963. 16x/yr. EUR 1837. Ed(s): J Driscoll, K Kohse-Hoinghaus. Elsevier Inc., 360 Park Ave S, New York, NY 10010-1710; usinfo-f@elsevier.com; http://www.elsevier.com. Illus., index, adv. Refereed. Microform: PQC. Online: EBSCO Publishing, EBSCO Host; Gale; IngentaConnect; OhioLINK; ScienceDirect; SwetsWise Online Content. *Indexed:* ApMecR, C&ISA, CEA, CerAb, ChemAb, EngInd, EnvAb, ExcerpMed, IAA, IBR, PollutAb, SCI. *Bk. rev.:* Number and length vary. *Aud.:* Ac, Sa.

An official publication of the Combustion Institute, this general-interest journal exists for the publication of experimental and theoretical investigations of combustion phenomena and closely allied matters. The contents include scholarly articles, brief communications for the membership, a comments section for the membership, a meetings calendar, and book reviews. Available online via Science Direct.

2245. *Computers & Chemical Engineering.* [ISSN: 0098-1354] 1977. 12x/yr. EUR 2770. Ed(s): G V Reklaitis. Pergamon, The Boulevard, Langford Ln, East Park, Kidlington, OX5 1GB, United Kingdom. Illus., adv. Refereed. Circ: 1000. Vol. ends: No. 25. Microform: PQC. Online: EBSCO Publishing, EBSCO Host; Gale; IngentaConnect; OhioLINK; ScienceDirect; SwetsWise Online Content. *Indexed:* AS&TI, C&ISA, CEA, CerAb, ChemAb, CompLI, EngInd, ExcerpMed, H&SSA, IAA, SCI, SSCI, WRCInf. *Bk. rev.:* Number and length vary. *Aud.:* Ac, Sa.

The application of computing technology to chemical engineering problems is the focus of the professional papers published in this journal. Areas of interest include new developments, design methods for chemical engineering equipment, and the dynamic analysis and control of chemical processes and process operations (e.g., safety, scheduling, and reliability). New computer methods and programs are described. Available online via ScienceDirect.

2246. *International Journal of Chemical Reactor Engineering.* [ISSN: 1542-6580] 2003. s-a. USD 280 (Individuals, USD 35). Ed(s): Franco Berruti, Hugo DeLasa. Berkeley Electronic Press, 2809 Telegraph Ave, Ste 202, Berkeley, CA 94705; info@bepress.com; http://www.bepress.com. Refereed. *Indexed:* C&ISA, CerAb, EngInd, IAA, SCI. *Bk. rev.:* Number and length vary. *Aud.:* Ac, Sa.

The *International Journal of Chemical Reactor Engineering* publishes significant research and scholarship in the broad fields of theoretical and applied reactor engineering. The mandate of the journal is to assemble high-quality papers from the broad research spectrum covered by modern reactor engineering. The range of topics includes single-phase and multi-phase reactor design, operation and control, new chemical reactor concepts, fluid mechanics and fluid dynamics, computational fluid dynamics, catalysis, low- and high-pressure and temperature operation, and environmental and economical implications. Also covered are topics drawn from the substantial areas of overlap between reaction and reactor engineering.

2247. *Journal of Catalysis.* [ISSN: 0021-9517] 1962. 16x/yr. EUR 6233. Ed(s): E. Inglesia. Academic Press, 525 B St, Ste 1900, San Diego, CA 92101-4495; apsubs@acad.com; http://www.elsevier.com/. Illus., adv. Refereed. Online: EBSCO Publishing, EBSCO Host; Gale; IngentaConnect; OCLC Online Computer Library Center, Inc.; OhioLINK; ScienceDirect; SwetsWise Online Content. *Indexed:* AS&TI, CEA, ChemAb, EngInd, ExcerpMed, SCI. *Bk. rev.:* Number and length vary. *Aud.:* Ac, Sa.

Journal of Catalysis emphasizes the publication of original studies in heterogeneous and homogeneous catalysis as well as studies relating catalytic properties to chemical processes at surfaces; studies of the chemistry of surfaces; and engineering studies related to catalysis. This journal features authoritative articles, notes, letters to the editors, and book reviews, and it is the indispensable source of information for chemists and chemical engineers in both applied and academic fields. Publishes manuscripts of archival value.

2248. *Journal of Chemical and Engineering Data.* Formerly (until 1959): *Chemical & Engineering Data Series.* [ISSN: 0021-9568] 1956. m. USD 1107 print & online eds. Ed(s): Dr. Kenneth N Marsh. American Chemical Society, 1155 16th St, NW, Washington, DC 20036; service@acs.org; http://pubs.acs.org. Illus., index, adv. Refereed. Circ: 3777 Paid. Online: Pub.; EBSCO Publishing, EBSCO Host; OhioLINK; SwetsWise Online Content. *Indexed:* AS&TI, CEA, ChemAb, EngInd, PetrolAb, S&F, SCI. *Aud.:* Ac, Sa.

The publication of experimental data and the evaluation and prediction of property values are the main focus of this journal. This title is the only American Chemical Society journal to report experimental data on the physical, thermodynamic, and transport properties of well-defined materials, including complex mixtures of known compositions and systems of environmental and biochemical interest. Available online. A core journal for a special collection.

2249. *Journal of Membrane Science.* [ISSN: 0376-7388] 1977. 40x/yr. EUR 7044. Ed(s): W J Koros. Elsevier BV, Radarweg 29, Amsterdam, 1043 NX, Netherlands; nlinfo-f@elsevier.nl; http://www.elsevier.nl. Illus., index. Refereed. Microform: PQC. Online: EBSCO Publishing, EBSCO Host; Gale; IngentaConnect; OhioLINK; ScienceDirect; SwetsWise Online Content. *Indexed:* BioEngAb, C&ISA, ChemAb, DSA, EngInd, ExcerpMed, FS&TA, PollutAb, SCI, WRCInf. *Aud.:* Ac, Sa.

A highly cited journal for "membranologists," the *Journal of Membrane Science* serves to emphasize the structure and function of nonbiological membranes. This is a practical journal that aims to provide the vehicle for rapid communications among researchers. Regular features include a meetings calendar and author and subject indexes. Available online. Scholarly papers are accepted in the experimental and applications phases of research.

2250. *Plasma Chemistry & Plasma Processing.* Incorporates (1996-2004): *Plasmas and Polymers.* [ISSN: 0272-4324] 1981. bi-m. EUR 1033 print & online eds. Ed(s): Stan Veprek, Emil Pfender. Springer New York LLC, 233 Spring St, New York, NY 10013-1578; service-ny@springer.com; http://www.springer.com/. Illus., adv. Refereed. Microform: PQC. Online: EBSCO Publishing, EBSCO Host; Gale; IngentaConnect; OCLC Online Computer Library Center, Inc.; OhioLINK; Springer LINK; SwetsWise Online Content. Reprint: PSC. *Indexed:* C&ISA, CerAb, ChemAb, EngInd, IAA, SCI. *Aud.:* Ac, Sa.

This international journal offers current scholarly reports on plasma chemistry and plasma processing as well as review articles for the plasma chemistry community. Will be of interest to chemists, chemical engineers, and metallurgists. It encompasses all types of industrial processing plasmas. Available online from Springer.

Civil Engineering

2251. *American Water Works Association. Journal.* [ISSN: 0003-150X] 1914. m. Membership, USD 185; USD 12 per issue foreign. Ed(s): Marcia Lacey. American Water Works Association, 6666 W Quincy Ave, Denver, CO 80235; http://www.awwa.org. Illus. Refereed. Circ: 45100 Controlled. Vol. ends: Dec. Microform: PMC; PQC. Online: ProQuest LLC (Ann Arbor). *Indexed:* ABIn, AS&TI, BioEngAb, BiolAb, ChemAb, EngInd, EnvAb, EnvInd, ExcerpMed, FS&TA, PollutAb, SCI, SWRA, WRCInf. *Aud.:* Ga, Ac, Sa.

This is the official organ of the American Water Works Association. As in other society publications, regular departments include letters, legislation/regulations, news, business updates, product literature, meeting notices, and classified advertisements. This is a valuable, readable magazine that reports new testing procedures, research findings, and product information in the water/environmental arena. A must for an academic or public library. Subscription is generally for members only but exceptions are made for libraries. Online info at www.awwa.org/communications/journal.

2252. *Canadian Journal of Civil Engineering.* [ISSN: 0315-1468] 1973. m. CND 708 (Individuals, CND 165). Ed(s): Donald S Mavinic. N R C Research Press, National Research Council of Canada, Ottawa, ON K1A 0R6, Canada; pubs@nrc-cnrc.gc.ca; http://pubs.nrc-cnrc.gc.ca. Illus., adv. Refereed. Circ: 2686. Microform: MML; PQC. Online: EBSCO Publishing, EBSCO Host; Gale; IngentaConnect; Micromedia ProQuest; OCLC Online Computer Library Center, Inc.; Ovid Technologies, Inc.; ProQuest K-12 Learning Solutions; ProQuest LLC (Ann Arbor); SwetsWise Online Content; H.W. Wilson. *Indexed:* AS&TI, C&ISA, CBCARef, CPerI, CerAb, EngInd, ExcerpMed, H&SSA, IAA, IBR, SCI, SSCI, SUSA, SWRA. *Bk. rev.:* Number and length vary. *Aud.:* Ac, Sa.

Official monthly publication of the Canadian Society for Civil Engineering. Article topics include environmental engineering, hydrotechnical engineering, and basic building and mechanics for civil engineers. A good resource for the study of the history of the field of civil engineering. Features new developments in engineering design and construction. Good resource for the global engineering collection.

2253. *Civil Engineering (Reston): engineered design and construction.* Former titles: *Civil Engineering - A S C E; Civil Engineering (New York).* [ISSN: 0885-7024] 1930. m. USD 230 domestic; USD 275 foreign. Ed(s): Ann Powell. American Society of Civil Engineers, 1801 Alexander Bell Dr, Reston, VA 20191-4400; http://www.asce.org. Illus., index, adv. Refereed. Circ: 101210. Vol. ends: Dec. Microform: PQC. Online: EBSCO Publishing, EBSCO Host; OCLC Online Computer Library Center, Inc.; ProQuest K-12 Learning Solutions; ProQuest LLC (Ann Arbor). *Indexed:* ABIn, AS&TI, ApMecR, C&ISA, CerAb, ChemAb, EngInd, EnvInd, HRIS, IAA, SCI. *Bk. rev.:* Number and length vary. *Aud.:* Ac, Sa.

This is the official news publication for the American Society of Civil Engineers (ASCE). Free to all members, it offers an up-to-date focus on what is happening in the field of civil engineering. Noteworthy departments include upcoming ASCE conferences and a calendar of events, new publications, news briefs, member news, and new products and applications. It offers full-length, semitechnical articles on timely topics. A necessary journal for academic and public libraries. Available online to members at www.asce.org/cemagazine/0407.

2254. *Cold Regions Science and Technology.* [ISSN: 0165-232X] 1979. 12x/yr. EUR 1304. Ed(s): G W Timco. Elsevier BV, Radarweg 29, Amsterdam, 1043 NX, Netherlands; nlinfo-f@elsevier.nl; http://www.elsevier.nl. Refereed. Microform: PQC. Online: EBSCO Publishing, EBSCO Host; Gale; IngentaConnect; OhioLINK; ScienceDirect; SwetsWise Online Content. *Indexed:* ApMecR, C&ISA, CerAb, ChemAb, EngInd, FPA, IAA, M&GPA, PetrolAb, PollutAb, S&F, SCI, SWRA. *Aud.:* Ac, Sa.

Cold Regions Science and Technology is an international journal that deals with the scientific and technical problems of cold environments, including both natural and artificial environments. The primary concern is with problems related to the freezing of water, and especially with the many forms of ice, snow, and frozen ground. The journal serves a wide range of specialists, providing a medium for interdisciplinary communication and a convenient source of reference. Highly cited by ISI. Available electronically via Elsevier Science Direct.

2255. Computers & Structures. [ISSN: 0045-7949] 1971. 32x/yr. EUR 6038. Ed(s): B. H.V. Topping, K J Bathe. Pergamon, The Boulevard, Langford Ln, East Park, Kidlington, OX5 1GB, United Kingdom. Illus., index, adv. Refereed. Circ: 1500. Vol. ends: No. 79. Microform: PQC. Online: EBSCO Publishing, EBSCO Host; Gale; IngentaConnect; OhioLINK; ScienceDirect; SwetsWise Online Content. *Indexed:* ApMecR, C&ISA, CCMJ, CerAb, ChemAb, CompLI, CompR, EngInd, HRIS, IAA, MSN, MathR, SCI. *Aud.:* Ac, Sa.

The application of computers to the solution of scientific and engineering problems related to hydrospace, aerospace, and terrestrial structures is dealt with here. This international journal is designed for the researcher working with the practical engineering aspects of structural analysis, design, and optimization. Each issue offers highly technical articles that deal with design of structures that employ the use of analog, digital, and hybrid computers. The interdisciplinary nature of this journal, along with its internationalism, makes it a valuable addition to any technical civil engineering collection. Available online via Elsevier Science Direct.

2256. E N R: the construction weekly. Formerly (until 1987): *Engineering News-Record;* Which was formed by the merger of (1902-1917): *Engineering News;* (1910-1917): *Engineering Record.* [ISSN: 0891-9526] 1874. w. 46/yr. USD 82 domestic; USD 89 in Canada & Mexico; USD 195 elsewhere. McGraw-Hill Construction Dodge, 2 Penn Plaza, 25th Fl, New York, NY 10121; http://www.fwdodge.com. Illus., adv. Circ: 71255 Paid. Microform: PQC. Online: EBSCO Publishing, EBSCO Host; LexisNexis; ProQuest K-12 Learning Solutions; ProQuest LLC (Ann Arbor). *Indexed:* ABIn, AS&TI, AltPI, BPI, C&ISA, CerAb, ChemAb, EngInd, ExcerpMed, HRIS, IAA, PetrolAb. *Bk. rev.:* Number and length vary. *Aud.:* Ga, Ac, Sa.

Now in its 133rd year of publication, this journal is the staple of the construction industry. Very readable, it offers thoughtful articles on the environment, transportation, business, and building fronts. Mainly written for the construction industry, the articles and regular columns are easily digested by the student and professional alike. Material prices, job ads, editorials, and news from the field are all featured. Excellent for public, special, and academic libraries and a great resource for historical study of the field of engineering. Available online at http://enr.construction.com/Default.asp.

2257. Earthquake Engineering and Structural Dynamics. [ISSN: 0098-8847] 1972. 15x/yr. USD 4665 print or online ed. Ed(s): Anil K Chopra. John Wiley & Sons Ltd., The Atrium, Southern Gate, Chichester, PO19 8SQ, United Kingdom; customer@wiley.co.uk; http://www.wiley.co.uk. Illus., index, adv. Refereed. Circ: 1000. Microform: PQC. Online: EBSCO Publishing, EBSCO Host; OhioLINK; SwetsWise Online Content; Wiley InterScience. Reprint: PSC. *Indexed:* AS&TI, ApMecR, C&ISA, CerAb, EngInd, EnvAb, H&SSA, IAA, IBR, SCI, SUSA, SWRA. *Bk. rev.:* Number and length vary. *Aud.:* Ac, Sa.

The official journal of the International Association for Earthquake Engineering, this journal is scholarly and highly technical and aims to provide a forum for the publication of papers on all aspects of engineering related to earthquakes. Articles are selected with the researcher and designer in mind and reflect the journal's international flavor. Earthquake engineering includes seismicity, ground motion characteristics, soil amplification and failure, methods of dynamic analysis, behavior of structures, seismic codes, and tsunamis. Available online at www3.interscience.wiley.com.

2258. Electronic Journal of Geotechnical Engineering. [ISSN: 1089-3032] 1996. q. Free. Ed(s): Mete Oner. Electronic Journal of Geotechnical Engineering, oner@okway.okstate.edu; http://www. geotech.civen.okstate.edu/ejge. Refereed. *Indexed:* C&ISA, CerAb, EngInd, H&SSA, IAA, PollutAb, SWRA. *Aud.:* Ac, Sa.

An electronic journal created to provide an open forum for rapid, interactive, peer-reviewed information exchange in geotechnical engineering worldwide. Includes job ads, discussion forums, a meetings calendar, and research papers. Available at www.ejge.com/index_ejge.htm.

2259. Electronic Journal of Structural Engineering. [ISSN: 1443-9255] 2001. irreg. Free. E J S E International Ltd., Department of Civil and Environmental Engineering, University of Melbourne, Parkville, VIC 3052, Australia. Refereed. *Indexed:* C&ISA, CerAb, EngInd, H&SSA, IAA, RiskAb. *Aud.:* Ac, Sa.

This journal provides an international forum for leading research and practical applications in structural engineering. It contains research papers, discussions and comments, and news about upcoming conferences and workshops. Will be distributed only in electronic form. Available at www.ejse.org.

Engineering Geology. See Earth Sciences section.

2260. Geotechnique: international journal of soil mechanics. [ISSN: 0016-8505] 1948. 10x/yr. GBP 398 combined subscription domestic print & online eds.; USD 963 combined subscription United States print & online eds.; GBP 459 combined subscription elsewhere print & online eds. Ed(s): Richard Sands. Thomas Telford Ltd., Thomas Telford House, 1 Heron Quay, London, E14 4JD, United Kingdom; journals@ thomastelford.com; http://www.t-telford.co.uk/. Illus., index. Refereed. Circ: 2500. *Indexed:* ApMecR, BrTechI, C&ISA, CerAb, ChemAb, EngInd, HRIS, IAA, IBR, PetrolAb, PollutAb, S&F, SCI, SWRA. *Aud.:* Ac, Sa.

This geotechnical journal features scholarly technical articles in the fields of soil mechanics, geotechnical engineering, and engineering geology. Technical notes and discussion papers are featured in each issue. Every article includes an English and a French abstract. Available online and in print. First published in 1837, *Geotechnique* is one of the 11 subdivision publications of the Proceedings of the Institution of Civil Engineers. Available at www.geotechnique-ice.com.

2261. Journal of Hydraulic Engineering (New York). Formerly (until 1982): *American Society of Civil Engineers. Hydraulics Division. Journal.* [ISSN: 0733-9429] 1956. m. USD 944. Ed(s): Dennis A Lyn. American Society of Civil Engineers, 1801 Alexander Bell Dr, Reston, VA 20191-4400; http://www.asce.org. Illus. Refereed. Circ: 2900. Microform: PQC. Online: American Institute of Physics, Scitation; EBSCO Publishing, EBSCO Host; SwetsWise Online Content. *Indexed:* AS&TI, ApMecR, C&ISA, CABA, CerAb, EngInd, EnvAb, ExcerpMed, FPA, ForAb, H&SSA, HRIS, IAA, M&GPA, OceAb, RRTA, S&F, SCI, SWRA, WAE&RSA, WRCInf. *Aud.:* Ac, Sa.

Suitable for general application in the hydraulic engineering community, this journal hosts articles that describe the analysis and solutions of problems in the field. Topics range from flows in closed conduits to free-surface flow, and it includes environmental fluid dynamics. Presentation of contributions demonstrate concepts, methods, techniques and results that advance knowledge in the field. Available online.

Journal of Hydrology. See Earth Sciences section.

2262. Journal of Structural Engineering. Formerly (until 1982): *American Society of Civil Engineers. Structural Division. Journal.* [ISSN: 0733-9445] 1956. m. USD 1097. Ed(s): Sashi Kunnath. American Society of Civil Engineers, 1801 Alexander Bell Dr, Reston, VA 20191-4400; http://www.asce.org. Illus. Refereed. Circ: 4100. Microform: PQC. Online: American Institute of Physics, Scitation; EBSCO Publishing, EBSCO Host; SwetsWise Online Content. *Indexed:* AS&TI, ApMecR, C&ISA, CerAb, EngInd, EnvAb, FPA, ForAb, H&SSA, HRIS, IAA, OceAb, PetrolAb, SCI. *Aud.:* Ac, Sa.

Journal of Structural Engineering, a journal of the American Society of Civil Engineers, reports on fundamental knowledge that contributes to the state-of-the-art and state-of-practice in structural engineering. Articles cover the art and science of structural design, investigate the physical properties of engineering materials as related to structural behavior, develop methods of analysis, and study the merits of various types of structures and methods of construction. A must-have for both the public and academic professional collection. Available in online format from SciCitation.

Computer, Control, and Systems Engineering

2263. *Artificial Intelligence.* [ISSN: 0004-3702] 1970. 18x/yr. EUR 2527. Ed(s): A G Cohn, C. R. Perrault. Elsevier BV, North-Holland, Sara Burgerhartstraat 25, Amsterdam, 1055 KV, Netherlands; nlinfo-f@elsevier.nl; http://www.elsevier.nl. Illus., adv. Refereed. Circ: 1100. Microform: PQC. Online: EBSCO Publishing, EBSCO Host; Gale; IngentaConnect; OhioLINK; ScienceDirect; SwetsWise Online Content. *Indexed:* AS&TI, BioEngAb, C&ISA, CCMJ, CerAb, CompLI, CompR, EngInd, ErgAb, IAA, ISTA, L&LBA, LISA, MSN, MathR, SCI, SSCI. *Aud.:* Ac, Sa.

The main international journal on artificial intelligence that began publication in 1970 at the very beginnings of the field of computer science, it presents papers in the areas of software engineering, robotics, philosophy and logic, natural languages, vision, and cognitive science. It is a very prestigious and highly cited journal in its field. Accepts papers in automated reasoning, computational theories of learning, and other areas. Available online via ScienceDirect.

Association for Computing Machinery. Journal. See Computers and Information Technology/Professional Journals section.

2264. *Control Engineering: covering control, instrumentation, and automation systems worldwide.* [ISSN: 0010-8049] 1954. m. USD 109.90 domestic; USD 145.90 Canada; USD 139.90 Mexico. Ed(s): Mark T Hoske. Reed Business Information, 2000 Clearwater Dr, Oak Brook, IL 60523; http://www.reedbusiness.com. Illus., adv. Sample. Circ: 88085 Controlled and free. Online: EBSCO Publishing, EBSCO Host; Factiva, Inc.; Florida Center for Library Automation; Gale; LexisNexis; Northern Light Technology, Inc.; OCLC Online Computer Library Center, Inc.; ProQuest LLC (Ann Arbor); H.W. Wilson. *Indexed:* ABIn, AS&TI, C&ISA, CEA, CWI, CerAb, ChemAb, EngInd, EnvInd, IAA, SCI, SSCI. *Bk. rev.:* Number and length vary. *Aud.:* Ac, Sa.

Market updates, news items in the control arena, new control products, software reviews, and business directories are all regular departments in this well-illustrated and newsy magazine. A good choice for public libraries. Available online at www.controleng.com.

2265. *IEEE Network: the magazine of global information exchange.* [ISSN: 0890-8044] 1987. bi-m. USD 375. Ed(s): Jorg Leibeherr. IEEE, 445 Hoes Ln, Piscataway, NJ 08854-1331; subscription-service@ieee.org; http://www.ieee.org. Illus., adv. Refereed. Vol. ends: No. 6. Online: Pub.; EBSCO Publishing, EBSCO Host. *Indexed:* C&ISA, CerAb, CompLI, EngInd, IAA, SCI. *Aud.:* Ac, Sa.

IEEE Network provides the networking community a forum for highlighting and discussing major computer communications issues and developments. This journal covers topics that include network protocols and architecture; protocol design and validation; communications software; network control, signaling, and management; network implementation (LAN, MAN, WAN); and micro-to-host communications. The online version is available at www.comsoc.org/livepubs/ni. Also available via the IEEE Communications Society's Digital Library.

2266. *IEEE Transactions on Systems, Man and Cybernetics, Part C: Applications and Reviews.* Supersedes in part (in 1996): *IEEE Transactions on Systems, Man and Cybernetics;* Which was formed by the merger of (1968-1971): *IEEE Transactions on Man-Machine Systems;* Which was formerly (1963-1967): *IEEE Transactions on Human Factors in Electronics;* (1965-1971): *IEEE Transactions on Systems Science and Cybernetics.* [ISSN: 1094-6977] 1971. bi-m. USD 290. Ed(s): Vladimir Marik. IEEE, 445 Hoes Ln, Piscataway, NJ

08854-1331; subscription-service@ieee.org; http://www.ieee.org. Illus., index, adv. Sample. Refereed. Vol. ends: Dec. Online: Pub.; EBSCO Publishing, EBSCO Host. *Indexed:* AS&TI, C&ISA, CerAb, CompLI, EngInd, ErgAb, IAA, ISTA, SCI. *Bk. rev.:* Occasional, 700-1,000 words. *Aud.:* Ac, Sa.

Systems engineering and science, with cybernetic and man-machine systems, comprise the areas of investigation in this journal. Headline topics of national importance bring together such areas as large-scale systems, learning and adaptive systems, and "complex hardware, behavioral, biological, ecological, educational, environment, health care, management, socio-economic, transportation, and urban systems." There are roughly five to a dozen papers of 5–15 pages, and 5–15 "correspondences" of about three to ten pages each. Theoretical inquiries join forces with pragmatic goals—for example, the uses of artificial intelligence. Articles indicate lavish use, as required, of mathematical systems, including hardware and software. The central value of this periodical is evidenced by its numerous tutorial articles. Available online via the IEEE Xplore database.

2267. *I S A Transactions.* [ISSN: 0019-0578] 1961. q. USD 345. Ed(s): R. Russell Rhinehart. Elsevier Inc., 360 Park Ave S, New York, NY 10010-1710; usinfo-f@elsevier.com; http://www.elsevier.com. Illus., index. Refereed. Microform: PQC. Online: EBSCO Publishing, EBSCO Host; Gale; IngentaConnect; OhioLINK; ScienceDirect; SwetsWise Online Content. *Indexed:* AS&TI, ChemAb, EngInd, ExcerpMed, H&SSA, IAA, RiskAb, SCI. *Aud.:* Ac, Sa.

What's new in the field of instrumentation and control technology? This journal focuses on new developments in topics of importance in industrial measurement, control, and automation. This field is a very dynamic one, and staying current is a competitive task. The journal includes future directions and theories and applications for developing manufacturing processes and equipment. Available online through Science Direct.

2268. *International Journal of Control.* Supersedes in part (in 1965): *Journal of Electronics and Control;* Which was formerly (1955-1957): *Journal of Electronics.* [ISSN: 0020-7179] 1965. m. GBP 3698 print & online eds. Ed(s): Eric Rogers. Taylor & Francis Ltd., 4 Park Sq, Milton Park, Abingdon, OX14 4RN, United Kingdom; info@tandf.co.uk; http://www.tandf.co.uk/journals. Illus., adv. Refereed. Online: EBSCO Publishing, EBSCO Host; Gale; IngentaConnect; OCLC Online Computer Library Center, Inc.; SwetsWise Online Content. Reprint: PSC. *Indexed:* ApMecR, CCMJ, ChemAb, EngInd, IBR, MSN, MathR, SCI. *Bk. rev.:* Number and length vary. *Aud.:* Ac, Sa.

Computer-aided design is the leading-edge technology in engineering prototype ideation. This journal promotes and reports original research in the areas of neurocontrol, robotics, automation, and adaptive control. An excellent journal choice for robotics and CAD-CAM engineering collections. Available online via informaworld at www.informaworld.com, the new online portal for all Taylor & Francis Group journals.

International Journal of Parallel Programming. See Computers and Information Technology/Professional Journals section.

2269. *The Journal of Artificial Intelligence Research.* [ISSN: 1076-9757] 1994. s-a. USD 170. Ed(s): Dr. Martha E Pollack. A I Access Foundation, Inc, Information Sciences Institute, Marina del Rey, CA 90290. Illus., adv. Refereed. Online: EBSCO Publishing, EBSCO Host. *Indexed:* CCMJ, EngInd, MSN, MathR, SCI. *Aud.:* Ac, Sa.

This refereed electronic journal is devoted to all areas of artificial intelligence. It is indexed in INSPEC, ISI, and MathSci. It was established in 1994 as one of the first electronic scientific journals. A complete archive is available online at www.jair.org.

2270. *Journal of Experimental Algorithmics.* [ISSN: 1084-6654] 1996. q. Non-members, USD 159. Ed(s): Bernard M E Moret. Association for Computing Machinery, Inc., 2 Penn Plaza, Ste 701, New York, NY 10121-0701; sigs@acm.org; http://www.acm.org. Illus. Refereed. *Indexed:* CCMJ, CompLI, MSN, MathR. *Aud.:* Ac, Sa.

This online journal is devoted to experimental work in the design and analysis of algorithms and data structures, with two principal aims: to stimulate research in algorithms based on implementation and experimentation, and to distribute programs and testbeds throughout the research community. Areas of focus include combinatorial optimization, computational biology, computational geometry, graph manipulation, graphics, heuristics, network design, parallel processing, routing and scheduling, searching and sorting, and VLSI design. Available at www.jea.acm.org.

2271. *Journal of Graph Algorithms and Applications.* [ISSN: 1526-1719] 1997. irreg. Free. Ed(s): Ioannis G Tollis, Roberto Tamassia. Brown University, Department of Computer Science, 115 Waterman St, Providence, RI 02912-1910; rt@cs.brown.edu; http://www.cs.brown.edu/publications/jgaa/. Illus. Refereed. *Indexed:* CCMJ, MSN, MathR. *Aud.:* Ac, Sa.

An electronic journal for the graph algorithms research community. Topics of interest include design and analysis of graph algorithms, experiences with graph algorithms, and applications of graph algorithms. Available in both print and electronic formats.

2272. *Machine Learning: an international journal.* [ISSN: 0885-6125] 1986. m. EUR 1432 print & online eds. Ed(s): Foster Provost. Springer New York LLC, 233 Spring St, New York, NY 10013-1578; service-ny@springer.com; http://www.springer.com/. Illus., adv. Refereed. Microform: PQC. Online: EBSCO Publishing, EBSCO Host; Gale; IngentaConnect; OCLC Online Computer Library Center, Inc.; OhioLINK; Ovid Technologies, Inc.; Springer LINK; SwetsWise Online Content. Reprint: PSC. *Indexed:* AS&TI, BioEngAb, C&ISA, CerAb, CompLI, CompR, EngInd, IAA, L&LBA, PsycInfo, SCI, SSCI. *Aud.:* Ac, Sa.

Can machines learn? This journal provides an international forum for research on computational approaches to learning. Papers that demonstrate both theory and computer implementation are published. Learning methods of interest include inductive learning methods as applied to classification and recognition; genetic algorithms that demonstrate reasoning and inference; and learning from instruction through robotic and motor control. This is a core journal for any computing, control, and systems professional level collection. Available online via SpringerLink.

2273. *Neural Networks.* [ISSN: 0893-6080] 1988. 10x/yr. EUR 1613. Ed(s): Dr. Stephen Grossberg, John Taylor. Pergamon, The Boulevard, Langford Ln, East Park, Kidlington, OX5 1GB, United Kingdom. Illus., adv. Refereed. Circ: 1053 Paid. Microform: PQC. Online: EBSCO Publishing, EBSCO Host; Gale; IngentaConnect; OhioLINK; ScienceDirect; SwetsWise Online Content. *Indexed:* AS&TI, BioEngAb, BiolAb, C&ISA, CompLI, CompR, EngInd, ExcerpMed, PsycInfo, RILM, SCI, SSCI. *Aud.:* Ac, Sa.

The modeling of the brain and behavioral processes and the application of these models to computer and related technologies are the focus of scholarly articles presented in this highly cited journal. Psychologists, neurobiologists, mathematicians, physicists, computer scientists, and engineers will find this interdisciplinary journal of value. A core journal for any computer science and systems collection. Available online via Elsevier's ScienceDirect product.

Robotics and Autonomous Systems. See Robotics section.

2274. *Ubiquity.* [ISSN: 1530-2180] 2000. w. Free. Ed(s): Suzanne Douglas, John Gehl. Association for Computing Machinery, Inc., 2 Penn Plaza, Ste 701, New York, NY 10121-0701; sigs@acm.org; http://www.acm.org. *Bk. rev.:* Number and length vary. *Aud.:* Ac, Sa.

This is a web-based publication that fosters critical analysis and in-depth commentary on issues related to and of interest to the information technology profession. Departments include book reviews, interviews, and reflections. Available at www.acm.org/ubiquity.

Electrical Engineering

The Institute of Electrical and Electronics Engineers (IEEE) publications are vital to any engineering collection and are among the most highly cited journals in engineering. This society produces technical periodicals, conference papers, standards, reports, tutorials, and other specialized publications. The flagship journal is the *Proceedings of the IEEE* [0018-9219], a monthly that presents papers that have broad significance and long-range interest in all areas of electrical, electronics, and computer engineering. Since 1913, the *Proceedings of the IEEE* has been the leading authoritative resource for in-depth research coverage, tutorial information, and reviews of electrical and computer engineering technology. More than 100 titles are available for purchase. The *Index to IEEE Publications* is an annual publication that indexes by author and subject all the publications of the society. The IEEE Computer Society also publishes materials and should be consulted for selections. A full-text electronic product called *IEEE Xplore* is available from the publisher for all of its journals, proceedings, and standards. Check for current products at http://shop.ieee.org/store.

2275. *IEEE - Signal Processing Magazine.* Formerly (until 1991): *IEEE - A S S P Magazine.* [ISSN: 1053-5888] 1984. bi-m. USD 650. Ed(s): K J Ray Liu. IEEE, 445 Hoes Ln, Piscataway, NJ 08854-1331; subscription-service@ieee.org; http://www.ieee.org. Refereed. Online: Pub.; EBSCO Publishing, EBSCO Host. *Indexed:* C&ISA, CerAb, EngInd, IAA, SCI. *Aud.:* Ac, Sa.

This IEEE magazine publishes tutorial-style articles on signal processing research and applications covering fundamental principles of interest to the diverse concerns of its readers. It strives to deliver articles on emerging and active technical developments, issues, and events to the research, educational, and professional communities. It is also the main society communication platform addressing important issues concerning all members. Suitable for public and academic library collections. Available online via IEEE Xplore.

2276. *IEEE Transactions on Circuits and Systems for Video Technology.* [ISSN: 1051-8215] 1991. m. USD 730. Ed(s): Keshab K Parhi. IEEE, 445 Hoes Ln, Piscataway, NJ 08854-1331; subscription-service@ieee.org; http://www.ieee.org. Refereed. Online: Pub.; EBSCO Publishing, EBSCO Host. *Indexed:* AS&TI, C&ISA, CerAb, EngInd, IAA, SCI. *Aud.:* Ac, Sa.

Topics covered are too numerous to list, but include all aspects of video technology, image analysis, video storage and retrieval, video signal processing, and related topics. Available electronically through the IEEE Xplore database.

2277. *IEEE Transactions on Medical Imaging.* [ISSN: 0278-0062] 1982. m. USD 1095. Ed(s): Michael Vannier. IEEE, 445 Hoes Ln, Piscataway, NJ 08854-1331; subscription-service@ieee.org; http://www.ieee.org. Refereed. Online: Pub.; EBSCO Publishing, EBSCO Host. *Indexed:* BioEngAb, C&ISA, CerAb, EngInd, ErgAb, IAA, SCI. *Aud.:* Ac, Sa.

IEEE Transactions on Medical Imaging is the second-most-cited journal in electrical and electronics engineering, the most-cited in imaging science and photographic technology, and the third-most-cited in biomedical engineering and computer science interdisciplinary applications in 2005. This periodical focuses on imaging of body organs, usually *in situ*, rather than microscopic biological entities, and the associated equipment and techniques, such as instrumentation systems, transducers, computing hardware, and software. Available online via the IEEE Xplore database.

2278. *IEEE Transactions on Pattern Analysis and Machine Intelligence.* [ISSN: 0162-8828] 1979. m. USD 1675. Ed(s): Kirk Kroeker, Kevin Bowyer. IEEE, 445 Hoes Ln, Piscataway, NJ 08854-1331; subscription-service@ieee.org; http://www.ieee.org. Refereed. Circ: 7000 Paid and controlled. Online: Pub.; EBSCO Publishing, EBSCO Host. *Indexed:* AS&TI, C&ISA, CerAb, CompLI, CompR, EngInd, ErgAb, IAA, SCI, SSCI. *Aud.:* Ac, Sa.

This volunteer-edited journal strives to present most important research results in all traditional areas of computer vision and image understanding, all traditional areas of pattern analysis and recognition, and selected areas of machine intelligence. Each issue is carefully peer-reviewed and archived for future generations. Available electronically through the IEEE Xplore database.

Institute of Electrical and Electronics Engineers. Proceedings. See Electronics section.

2279. Optical Engineering. Former titles (until 1972): *S P I E Journal;* (until 1962): *S P I E Newsletter.* [ISSN: 0091-3286] m. USD 835 print & online eds. Ed(s): Karolyn Labes, Dr. Donald C O'Shea. S P I E - International Society for Optical Engineering, 1000 20th St, Bellingham, WA 98225; spie@spie.org; http://spie.org. Illus., index, adv. Refereed. Circ: 9000 Controlled. Online: American Institute of Physics, Scitation; EBSCO Publishing, EBSCO Host; SwetsWise Online Content. *Indexed:* AS&TI, C&ISA, CPI, CerAb, ChemAb, EngInd, ExcerpMed, IAA, PhotoAb, SCI, SSCI. *Bk. rev.:* Number and length vary. *Aud.:* Ac, Sa.

This is the journal of the International Society for Optical Engineering, a technical society dedicated to the advancement of applications of optical, electro-optical, and photoelectronic instrumentation systems and technologies. Optics is the science of light and vision. The editors accept articles that report new research and development, especially new, inventive technologies. Each issue contains 40–50 short articles on such areas as lasers, imaging, holography, biomedical optics, and the like. Book reviews, short courses, and a calendar of meetings are found in each issue. A great bargain for an academic or special library. Available electronically from the society at http://spiedl.aip.org.

2280. Progress in Quantum Electronics. [ISSN: 0079-6727] 1969. 6x/yr. EUR 1115. Ed(s): P T Landsberg, R Sheps. Pergamon, The Boulevard, Langford Ln, East Park, Kidlington, OX5 1GB, United Kingdom. Refereed. Microform: PQC. Online: EBSCO Publishing, EBSCO Host; Gale; IngentaConnect; OhioLINK; ScienceDirect; SwetsWise Online Content. *Indexed:* C&ISA, ChemAb, EngInd, SCI. *Aud.:* Ac, Sa.

An international review journal, *Progress in Quantum Electronics* is devoted to the dissemination of new, specialized topics at the forefront of quantum electronics and its applications. Theoretical and experimental articles are welcomed. Available online from ScienceDirect. Impact factor of 5.176 in 2005 in ISI JCR.

Semiconductor Science and Technology. See Electronics section.

Manufacturing Engineering

2281. Advances in Electronics Manufacturing Technology. [ISSN: 1745-3836] 2004. irreg. Free. Vertilog Ltd., Kings House, 14 Orchad St, Bristol, BS1 5EH, United Kingdom; contactus@vertilog.com; http://www.vertilog.com. Refereed. *Aud.:* Ac, Sa.

This is a peer-reviewed journal specializing in demonstrations of technologies in the industrial supply chain. Coverage includes all areas of electronics and semiconductor and microelectronic component manufacturing technology. All manuscripts are based on empirical data gathered from the field or from in-house testing in applications labs or R&D labs. Publication of articles can happen in less than 45 days, making this journal particularly useful for those interested in rapid industry innovations.

2282. Computers & Industrial Engineering. [ISSN: 0360-8352] 1977. 8x/yr. EUR 2821. Ed(s): M I Dessouky. Pergamon, The Boulevard, Langford Ln, East Park, Kidlington, OX5 1GB, United Kingdom. Illus., index, adv. Refereed. Circ: 1000. Vol. ends: No. 40 - No. 41. Microform: PQC. Online: EBSCO Publishing, EBSCO Host; Gale; IngentaConnect; OhioLINK; ScienceDirect; SwetsWise Online Content. *Indexed:* ABIn, C&ISA, CerAb, CompLI, CompR, EngInd, ErgAb, IAA, SCI, SSCI. *Bk. rev.:* Number and length vary. *Aud.:* Ac, Sa.

In all forms of engineering, computers and their applications have become general tools in the profession. Software is being developed and improved that allows for computer solutions to industrial engineering problems, as well as providing new techniques for design and planning. This journal provides a forum for sharing information to all practitioners on the uses of computers and their programs in industrial applications. It features refereed articles, technical discussions, a software section, and short papers. Available online from Elsevier ScienceDirect.

2283. Journal of Manufacturing Systems. [ISSN: 0278-6125] 1982. 4x/yr. EUR 761. Ed(s): J T Black. Elsevier Ltd., The Boulevard, Langford Ln, Oxford, OX5 1GB, United Kingdom; nlinfo-f@elsevier.nl; http://www.elsevier.com. Illus., index, adv. Refereed. Circ: 1000. Online: Northern Light Technology, Inc.; OCLC Online Computer Library Center, Inc.; OhioLINK; ProQuest LLC (Ann Arbor). *Indexed:* ABIn, AS&TI, ApMecR, EngInd, SCI. *Aud.:* Ac, Sa.

The Society of Manufacturing Engineers produces this journal for its membership and for all professionals interested in the manufacturing industries and R&D organizations. Decreasing plant operation costs, increasing productivity, and producing quality products are a few of the endeavors this society hopes to achieve by sharing the scientific methods developed and presented in this journal. Case studies and general surveys are offered. Technical papers in robotics, machine tooling, inspection, and handling-equipment areas are accepted, along with papers that report important research and new process developments.

2284. Journal of Quality Technology: a quarterly journal of methods, applications and related topics. Supersedes in part (in 1968): *Industrial Quality Control.* [ISSN: 0022-4065] 1944. q. USD 100 (Members, USD 30; Non-members, USD 45). American Society for Quality, 600 N Plankinton Ave, P O Box 3005, Milwaukee, WI 53203-2914; help@asq.org; http://www.asq.org. Illus., index. Refereed. Circ: 22000. Microform: PQC. Online: OCLC Online Computer Library Center, Inc.; ProQuest LLC (Ann Arbor); H.W. Wilson. Reprint: PSC. *Indexed:* ABIn, AS&TI, C&ISA, CerAb, EngInd, FS&TA, IAA, IBR, SCI. *Bk. rev.:* Number and length vary. *Aud.:* Ga, Ac, Sa.

Suitable for practicing engineers, the *Journal of Quality Technology* publishes papers on the practical applicability of new techniques, examples of techniques in practice, and results of historical research. Departments include computer programs, technical aids, and book reviews. This journal is produced for the membership of the American Society for Quality, with the goal of "dedication to the advancement of quality." Available online at www.asq.org/pub/jqt.

2285. Machine Design: magazine of applied technology for design engineering. Incorporates (1982-2001): *Computer-Aided Engineering;* Incorporates (1954-1992): *Penton's Control & Systems;* Which was formerly (until 1991): *Automation;* (until 1987): *Production Engineering;* (until 1977): *Automation.* [ISSN: 0024-9114] 1929. 22x/yr. USD 105 domestic; USD 135 Canada; USD 153 elsewhere. Ed(s): Leland E Teschler, Ronald Khol. Penton Media, Inc., 1300 E 9th St, Cleveland, OH 44114-1503; information@penton.com; http://www.penton.com/. Illus., index, adv. Circ: 191000 Paid and controlled. Microform: PQC. Online: The Dialog Corporation; EBSCO Publishing, EBSCO Host; Florida Center for Library Automation; Gale; Northern Light Technology, Inc.; OCLC Online Computer Library Center, Inc.; ProQuest K-12 Learning Solutions; ProQuest LLC (Ann Arbor); H.W. Wilson. *Indexed:* A&ATA, ABIn, AS&TI, C&ISA, CWI, CerAb, ChemAb, EngInd, EnvAb, ErgAb, ExcerpMed, HRIS, IAA, LRI, PetrolAb. *Aud.:* Ga, Ac, Sa.

This magazine easily wins the prize for reporting on cutting-edge techno-trinkets! With color photos, graphs, and drawings, the latest whiz-kid inventions are featured here alongside many colorful ads for industry tools, software, and services. With a finger on the pulse of the field, this magazine is a must for the technologically inclined. If it's in at least the prototype stage, the device will be found here. A magazine for the "techie" in all of us. Available online at www.machinedesign.com.

2286. Manufacturing Engineering. Former titles (until 1975): *Manufacturing Engineering and Management;* (until 1970): *Tool and Manufacturing Engineer;* (until 1960): *Tool Engineer.* [ISSN: 0361-0853] 1932. m. USD 100 domestic; USD 195 foreign. Ed(s): James D Destefani, Brian J Hogan. Society of Manufacturing Engineers, One SME Dr, PO Box 930, Dearborn, MI 48121-0930; http://www.sme.org/. Illus., adv. Circ: 102500 Controlled. Microform: PQC. Online: Northern Light Technology, Inc.; OCLC Online Computer Library Center, Inc.; ProQuest K-12 Learning Solutions; ProQuest LLC (Ann Arbor); H.W. Wilson. *Indexed:* ABIn, AS&TI, ApMecR, C&ISA, CerAb, EngInd, IAA, SCI, SSCI. *Bk. rev.:* Number and length vary. *Aud.:* Ga, Ac, Sa.

The official publication of the Society of Manufacturing Engineers, this monthly provides feature articles on such topics as machine tools of the future, aspects of machinery (e.g., turning, milling, and cutting-tool speed limits), and the computerization of machines. Advice is given on potential tool purchases. Special departments include a tech update, shop solutions, a news desk, product reviews, and job ads. Useful for the job shop owner or any other manufacturing professional. Available online at www.sme.org/cgi-bin/ find-issues.pl?&&ME&SME&. This site also features archive of former issues back to 2000. Great for a public library collection.

2287. Plant Engineering: the problem-solving resource for plant engineers. [ISSN: 0032-082X] 1947. m. USD 131.99 domestic; USD 163.90 Canada; USD 156 Mexico. Ed(s): Bob Vaura. Reed Business Information, 2000 Clearwater Dr, Oak Brook, IL 60523; http://www.reedbusiness.com. Illus., adv. Circ: 100030 Controlled. Online: The Dialog Corporation; EBSCO Publishing, EBSCO Host; Factiva, Inc.; Florida Center for Library Automation; Gale; LexisNexis; Northern Light Technology, Inc.; OCLC Online Computer Library Center, Inc.; ProQuest K-12 Learning Solutions; ProQuest LLC (Ann Arbor); H.W. Wilson. Indexed: ABIn, AS&TI, CEA, ChemAb, ExcerpMed, H&SSA, LRI, PollutAb. Bk. rev.: Number and length vary. Aud.: Ga, Ac, Sa.

Like similar Cahners publications, *Plant Engineering* is news and advertising driven. An informative tool for industrial professionals, this magazine publishes articles on fluid handling/maintenance, facilities, coatings, HVAC, power transmission, and management topics. One will find the expected new-product news, literature updates, reader inquiry cards, and classifieds. Great for a public library collection. URL: www.manufacturing.net/ple.

2288. Quality Progress. Supersedes in part (in 1968): *Industrial Quality Control.* [ISSN: 0033-524X] 1944. m. Members, USD 55; Non-members, USD 80. Ed(s): Debbie Donaldson. American Society for Quality, 600 N Plankinton Ave, P O Box 3005, Milwaukee, WI 53203-2914; cs@asq.org; http://www.asq.org. Illus., index, adv. Circ: 133000 Paid and controlled. Microform: PQC. Online: OCLC Online Computer Library Center, Inc.; ProQuest LLC (Ann Arbor); H.W. Wilson. Reprint: PSC. Indexed: ABIn, AS&TI, C&ISA, ExcerpMed, SSCI. Aud.: Ga, Ac, Sa.

This publication of the American Society for Quality Control provides information on standards, industry changes, and the society's perspective on current issues. Each issue contains eight to ten feature articles. In an effort to gain membership feedback and to improve the editorial quality of the journal, each article ends with a questionnaire requesting an opinion of the reader on the quality of the featured article. Available online at www.asq.org/pub/ qualityprogress.

Materials Engineering

2289. Acta Materialia. Incorporates (1992-1999): *Nanostructured Materials;* Former titles (until vol.44): *Acta Metallurgica et Materialia;* (until 1990): *Acta Metallurgica.* [ISSN: 1359-6454] 1953. 20x/yr. EUR 3111. Ed(s): Subhash Mahajan, Gunter Gottstein. Pergamon, The Boulevard, Langford Ln, East Park, Kidlington, OX5 1GB, United Kingdom. Illus., index, adv. Refereed. Circ: 2300. Vol. ends: Dec. Microform: PQC. Online: EBSCO Publishing, EBSCO Host; Gale; IngentaConnect; OhioLINK; ScienceDirect; SwetsWise Online Content. Indexed: ApMecR, C&ISA, CerAb, ChemAb, EngInd, IAA, IBR, RILM, SCI. Bk. rev.: Number and length vary. Aud.: Ac, Sa.

This scholarly journal's purpose is to publish original papers that advance the understanding of the properties of such materials as metals and alloys, ceramics, high polymers, and glasses. The experimentation, simulation, and modeling that advance the understanding of the properties of materials are its main mission. Available online via Elsevier ScienceDirect.

2290. Advanced Materials & Processes. Incorporates (1930-1989): *Metal Progress.* [ISSN: 0882-7958] 1983. m. Free to members; Non-members, USD 398; USD 33 newsstand/cover. Ed(s): Margaret W Hunt, Donald F Baxter. A S M International, 9639 Kinsman Rd, Materials Park, OH 44073-0002; cust-srv@asminternational.org;

http://www.asminternational.org. Illus., adv. Circ: 34000 Paid. Vol. ends: Jun/Dec. Online: EBSCO Publishing, EBSCO Host; Florida Center for Library Automation; Gale; OCLC Online Computer Library Center, Inc.; H.W. Wilson. Indexed: AS&TI, C&ISA, CerAb, EngInd, IAA, SCI, SSCI. Aud.: Ac, Sa.

The journal for the American Society for Metals (ASM) members, each issue includes several articles about the manufacture, R&D, and social and economic impacts of engineered materials. ASM news, technological developments, and job ads are also included. Tables of contents, an advertisers index, and an issue summary can be found online at the publisher's web site. Available online from the society at www.asminternational.org.

2291. Composites Part A: Applied Science and Manufacturing. Formerly (until vol.27): *Composites;* Incorporates (1990-1995): *Composites Manufacturing.* [ISSN: 1359-835X] 1969. 12x/yr. EUR 2514. Ed(s): M Wisnom. Pergamon, The Boulevard, Langford Ln, East Park, Kidlington, OX5 1GB, United Kingdom. Adv. Refereed. Microform: PQC. Online: EBSCO Publishing, EBSCO Host; Gale; IngentaConnect; OhioLINK; ScienceDirect; SwetsWise Online Content. Indexed: ApMecR, BrTechI, C&ISA, CerAb, ChemAb, EngInd, IAA, SCI. Aud.: Ac, Sa.

Composites Part A: Applied Science and Manufacturing publishes original research papers, review articles, case studies, short communications, and letters from a wide variety of sources dealing with all aspects of the science and technology of composite materials. This area includes fibrous and particulate reinforcements in polymeric, metallic, and ceramic matrices; aligned eutectics; reinforced cements and plasters; and "natural" composites such as wood and biological materials. Available electronically from Elsevier ScienceDirect.

2292. J O M. Former titles (until 1989): *Journal of Metals;* (until 1977): *J O M;* (until 1974): *Journal of Metals;* Which was formed by the merger of (1934-1949): *Metals Technology;* (1919-1949): *Mining and Metallurgy.* [ISSN: 1047-4838] 1949. m. EUR 243 print & online eds. Ed(s): Maureen Byko, James T Robinson. Springer New York LLC, 233 Spring St, New York, NY 10013-1578; journals@springer-ny.com; http://www.springer.com. Illus., index, adv. Refereed. Circ: 10000 Paid. Vol. ends: Dec. Microform: PQC. Online: EBSCO Publishing, EBSCO Host; Factiva, Inc.; Gale; IngentaConnect; ProQuest LLC (Ann Arbor). Reprint: PSC. Indexed: ABIn, AS&TI, C&ISA, CerAb, ChemAb, EngInd, IAA, IBR, SCI. Bk. rev.: Number and length vary. Aud.: Ac, Sa.

As the primary publication of the Minerals, Metals and Materials Society, this journal covers a broad range of materials science and engineering topics and is of interest to both academic and industrial readers. Business, government, industry, and society news and job advertisements are regular features. *JOM-e* is a by-invitation-only electronic supplement to the journal that publishes papers exclusively on the web rather than producing them in the conventional print version of the journal. Also available electronically via SpringerLink.

2293. Journal of Composite Materials. [ISSN: 0021-9983] 1967. 26x/yr. GBP 3184. Ed(s): H Thomas Hahn. Sage Science Press (UK), 1 Oliver's Yard, 55 City Rd, London, EC1Y 1SP, United Kingdom; info@sagepub.com; http://www.sagepub.co.uk/. Illus., index, adv. Refereed. Circ: 790 Paid. Microform: PQC. Online: CSA; EBSCO Publishing, EBSCO Host; HighWire Press; OCLC Online Computer Library Center, Inc.; SAGE Publications, Inc., SAGE Journals Online; SwetsWise Online Content. Reprint: PSC. Indexed: AS&TI, ApMecR, ArtInd, C&ISA, CerAb, ChemAb, EngInd, IAA, SCI. Aud.: Ac, Sa.

This journal strives to provide a permanent record of achievements in the science, technology, and economics of composite materials. The contents of both upcoming and past issues are available online. Full text is available from the publisher at www.sagefulltext.com.

Journal of Electronic Materials. See Electronics section.

2294. Journal of Materials Research. [ISSN: 0884-2914] 1986. m. USD 870 combined subscription domestic print & online; USD 910 combined subscription foreign print & online. Ed(s): Gordon E Pike. Materials Research Society, 506 Keystone Dr, Warrendale, PA 15086-7573;

info@mrs.org; http://www.mrs.org. Illus., index, adv. Refereed. Vol. ends: Dec. Online: EBSCO Publishing, EBSCO Host. *Indexed:* AS&TI, ApMecR, C&ISA, CerAb, ChemAb, EngInd, IAA, SCI. *Aud.:* Ac, Sa.

This journal focuses on original research, with occasional review articles on the theoretical description, processing, preparation, characterization, and properties of materials with new or unusual structures or properties. In addition to articles, *JMR* publishes communications and short submissions. Available online via the publisher at www.mrs.org/publications/jmr.

2295. *Journal of Materials Science.* Incorporates (1993-2004): *Interface Science;* (1982-1998): *Journal of Materials Science Letters.* [ISSN: 0022-2461] 1966. 24x/yr. EUR 9845 print & online eds. Ed(s): Rees D Rawlings, C Barry Carter. Springer New York LLC, 233 Spring St, New York, NY 10013-1578; service-ny@springer.com; http://www.springer.com/. Illus., index, adv. Refereed. Vol. ends: Dec. Online: EBSCO Publishing, EBSCO Host; Gale; IngentaConnect; OCLC Online Computer Library Center, Inc.; OhioLINK; Springer LINK; SwetsWise Online Content. Reprint: PSC. *Indexed:* A&ATA, AS&TI, ApMecR, C&ISA, CerAb, ChemAb, EngInd, ExcerpMed, IAA, RILM, SCI, WRCInf. *Aud.:* Ac, Sa.

Includes reviews, full-length papers, and short communications recording original research. International and interdisciplinary in scope, the journal covers the areas of metals, ceramics, glasses, polymers, electrical materials, composite materials, fibers, nanostructured materials, nanocomposites, and biological and biomedical materials. Available online via SpringerLink.

2296. *Journal of Testing and Evaluation.* Formerly (until 1973): *Journal of Materials. (J M L S A).* [ISSN: 0090-3973] 1966. bi-m. USD 410 (Individuals, USD 265). Ed(s): Donald Petersen. A S T M International, 100 Barr Harbor Dr, PO Box C700, West Conshohocken, PA 19428-2959; service@astm.org; http://www.astm.org. Illus., index, adv. Refereed. Circ: 400. Vol. ends: Nov. Microform: PMC; PQC. Online: EBSCO Publishing, EBSCO Host; SwetsWise Online Content. *Indexed:* AS&TI, ApMecR, C&ISA, CABA, CerAb, ChemAb, EngInd, ExcerpMed, FPA, ForAb, IAA, RILM, S&F, SCI. *Aud.:* Ac, Sa.

Published by the American Society for Testing and Materials (ASTM), this journal provides a multidisciplinary forum for the applied sciences and engineering fields. Articles feature new technical information; evaluation of materials; and new methods for testing products, services, and materials. They also highlight new ASTM standards. Available online from the society at www.astm.org.

2297. *Metallurgical and Materials Transactions A - Physical Metallurgy and Materials Science.* Formerly (until 1994): *Metallurgical Transactions A - Physical Metallurgy and Materials Science;* Which superseded in part (in 1975): *Metallurgical Transactions;* Which was formed by the merger of: *American Society for Metals. Transactions Quarterly; Metallurgical Society of AIME. Transactions.* [ISSN: 1073-5623] 1970. 13x/yr. EUR 2035 print & online eds. Ed(s): D E Laughlin. Springer New York LLC, 233 Spring St, New York, NY 10013-1578; journals@springer-ny.com; http://www.springer.com. Illus., index. Refereed. Circ: 1500 Paid and controlled. Vol. ends: Dec. Microform: PMC; PQC. Online: EBSCO Publishing, EBSCO Host; Gale; IngentaConnect; OCLC Online Computer Library Center, Inc.; ProQuest K-12 Learning Solutions; ProQuest LLC (Ann Arbor). Reprint: PSC. *Indexed:* AS&TI, C&ISA, CerAb, ChemAb, EngInd, IAA, SCI. *Aud.:* Ac, Sa.

Published jointly by ASM International and the Minerals, Metals and Materials Society, this journal was created with the goal of transferring basic research—performed in physical metallurgy and materials science—from the lab to actual shop fabrication and industrial application. Available online at http://journalsip.astm.org.

Mechanical Engineering

2298. *Acta Mechanica.* Formerly (until 1965): *Oesterreichisches Ingenieur-Archiv.* [ISSN: 0001-5970] 1946. 28x/yr. EUR 4298 print & online eds. Ed(s): H Troger, F Ziegler. Springer Wien, Sachsenplatz 4-6, Vienna, A-1201, Austria; journals@springer.at; http://www.springer.at. Illus., adv.

Sample. Refereed. Microform: PQC. Online: EBSCO Publishing, EBSCO Host; OhioLINK; ProQuest LLC (Ann Arbor); Springer LINK; SwetsWise Online Content. Reprint: PSC. *Indexed:* ApMecR, C&ISA, CerAb, ChemAb, EngInd, IAA, MathR, SCI. *Aud.:* Ac, Sa.

The classic fields within theoretical and applied mechanics—such as rigid-body dynamics, elasticity, plasticity, hydrodynamics, and gas dynamics—are addressed by the original research papers presented in this journal. Special attention is given to recently developed and boundary areas of mechanics. More than a dozen papers are contributed to each issue, along with announcements of upcoming international conferences. A classic mechanical engineering journal. Available online via SpringerLink.

2299. *Aerosol Science and Technology.* Incorporates (1985-1988): *Atomisation and Spray Technology.* [ISSN: 0278-6826] 1982. m. GBP 730 print & online eds. Ed(s): Richard C Flagan. Taylor & Francis Inc., 325 Chestnut St, Ste 800, Philadelphia, PA 19016; orders@taylorandfrancis.com; http://www.taylorandfrancis.com. Refereed. Microform: PQC. Online: EBSCO Publishing, EBSCO Host; Gale; IngentaConnect; OCLC Online Computer Library Center, Inc.; OhioLINK; SwetsWise Online Content. Reprint: PSC. *Indexed:* ApMecR, C&ISA, CEA, CerAb, ChemAb, EngInd, ExcerpMed, H&SSA, IAA, M&GPA, PollutAb, SCI. *Aud.:* Ac, Sa.

The official journal of the American Association for Aerosol Research, *Aerosol Science and Technology* covers theoretical and experimental investigations of aerosol and closely related phenomena. It presents high-quality papers on fundamental and applied topics. Ranked fifth in 2005 ISI journal citation reports. Online access to issues is through Informaworld and IngentaConnect.

2300. *Computer Methods in Applied Mechanics and Engineering.* [ISSN: 0045-7825] 1970. 52x/yr. EUR 8516. Ed(s): T. J.R. Hughes, M. Papadrakakis. Elsevier BV, North-Holland, Sara Burgerhartstraat 25, Amsterdam, 1055 KV, Netherlands; nlinfo-f@elsevier.nl; http://www.elsevier.nl. Illus., index, adv. Refereed. Vol. ends: No. 190. Microform: PQC. Online: EBSCO Publishing, EBSCO Host; Gale; IngentaConnect; OhioLINK; ScienceDirect; SwetsWise Online Content. *Indexed:* AS&TI, ApMecR, C&ISA, CCMJ, CerAb, CompLI, CompR, EngInd, IAA, MSN, MathR, SCI. *Aud.:* Ac, Sa.

This specialist journal publishes scholarly papers on computer applications that address finite element and boundary element methods in applied mechanics and engineering. It is a very specialized publication, found mainly in special library and research collections. Founded over three decades ago, this journal provides a forum for the publication of papers that chronicle the development of computer methods for the solution of scientific and engineering problems.

2301. *Engineering Fracture Mechanics.* [ISSN: 0013-7944] 1968. 18x/yr. EUR 4524. Ed(s): K-H Schwalbe, R. H. Dodds. Pergamon, The Boulevard, Langford Ln, East Park, Kidlington, OX5 1GB, United Kingdom. Illus., index, adv. Refereed. Circ: 1600. Microform: PQC. Online: EBSCO Publishing, EBSCO Host; Gale; IngentaConnect; OhioLINK; ScienceDirect; SwetsWise Online Content. *Indexed:* ApMecR, C&ISA, CerAb, ChemAb, EngInd, H&SSA, IAA, SCI, SWRA. *Bk. rev.:* Number and length vary. *Aud.:* Ac, Sa.

Fracture mechanics is a topic of general interest to engineers in the mechanical, material science, and civil engineering fields. This journal offers a variety of sources of fracture mechanics information to the practitioner, with full scholarly articles of a theoretical and practical nature, as well as book reviews, solutions, formulae, curves of data, and tables. Available online via ScienceDirect.

2302. *International Journal of Heat and Mass Transfer.* [ISSN: 0017-9310] 1960. 26x/yr. EUR 5628. Ed(s): W J Minkowycz, J P Harnett. Pergamon, The Boulevard, Langford Ln, East Park, Kidlington, OX5 1GB, United Kingdom. Illus., index, adv. Refereed. Circ: 2500. Microform: MIM; PQC. Online: EBSCO Publishing, EBSCO Host; Gale; IngentaConnect; OhioLINK; ScienceDirect; SwetsWise Online Content. *Indexed:* AS&TI, ApMecR, C&ISA, CEA, CerAb, ChemAb, EngInd, EnvAb, EnvInd, ExcerpMed, IAA, PetrolAb, SCI. *Bk. rev.:* Number and length vary. *Aud.:* Ac, Sa.

This journal is one of the core titles for a collection that covers heat and mass transfer. Contents include previously unpublished scholarly articles of an analytical, numerical, and/or experimental nature; reviews of new books on heat and mass transfer; and technical notes. A companion journal, *International Communications in Heat and Mass Transfer,* is a much faster medium for notes or short papers. This volume serves as the tool for rapid dissemination of new ideas, techniques, and discussions. A joint subscription price is available. Available online via ScienceDirect.

2303. *International Journal of Mechanical Sciences.* [ISSN: 0020-7403] 1960. 12x/yr. EUR 2960. Ed(s): Stephen R Reid. Pergamon, The Boulevard, Langford Ln, East Park, Kidlington, OX5 1GB, United Kingdom. Illus., index, adv. Refereed. Circ: 1400. Microform: PQC. Online: EBSCO Publishing, EBSCO Host; Gale; IngentaConnect; OhioLINK; ScienceDirect; SwetsWise Online Content. *Indexed:* ApMecR, C&ISA, CerAb, ChemAb, EngInd, H&SSA, IAA, MathR, SCI. *Aud.:* Ac, Sa.

The mechanics of solids and fluids, the forming and processing of those materials, structural mechanics, and thermodynamics provide the scope for this international journal. Mechanical and civil engineers will find it valuable. Available online through ScienceDirect and others. Interdisciplinary.

2304. *International Journal of Solids and Structures.* [ISSN: 0020-7683] 1965. 26x/yr. EUR 7214. Ed(s): Charles Steele. Pergamon, The Boulevard, Langford Ln, East Park, Kidlington, OX5 1GB, United Kingdom. Illus., adv. Refereed. Circ: 1400. Microform: PQC. Online: EBSCO Publishing, EBSCO Host; Gale; IngentaConnect; OhioLINK; ScienceDirect; SwetsWise Online Content. *Indexed:* ApMecR, C&ISA, CCMJ, CerAb, ChemAb, EngInd, H&SSA, IAA, MSN, MathR, SCI. *Aud.:* Ac, Sa.

The mechanics of solids and structures is experiencing considerable growth technologically. This field is at the crossroads of materials, life sciences, mathematics, physics, and engineering design. This journal's aim is to foster the exchange of ideas among workers internationally and among workers who emphasize various aspects of the foundations of the field. Articles are analytical, experimental, and numerical in scope. Available online via Elsevier's ScienceDirect.

2305. *Journal of Aerosol Science.* [ISSN: 0021-8502] 1970. 12x/yr. EUR 2502. Ed(s): G Kasper, E. J. Davis. Pergamon, The Boulevard, Langford Ln, East Park, Kidlington, OX5 1GB, United Kingdom. Adv. Refereed. Circ: 890 Paid and controlled. Microform: PQC. Online: EBSCO Publishing, EBSCO Host; Gale; IngentaConnect; OhioLINK; ScienceDirect; SwetsWise Online Content. *Indexed:* ApMecR, C&ISA, CABA, CEA, ChemAb, EngInd, EnvAb, EnvInd, ExcerpMed, FPA, ForAb, HortAb, M&GPA, PollutAb, S&F, SCI, SWRA. *Aud.:* Ac, Sa.

Journal of Aerosol Science is a long-established, international publication that sets out to encourage and foster all aspects of basic and applied aerosol research by publishing high-quality scientific papers in that very multidisciplinary field. The publication welcomes the submission of original papers that describe recent theoretical and experimental research. Occasional research and tutorial reviews are published that deal with specific aspects of aerosol science or establish links between various relevant disciplines. Available online from ScienceDirect and others.

2306. *Journal of Fluid Mechanics.* [ISSN: 0022-1120] 1956. s-m. GBP 1990. Ed(s): T.J. Pedley, Stephen H Davis. Cambridge University Press, The Edinburgh Bldg, Shaftesbury Rd, Cambridge, CB2 2RU, United Kingdom; journals@cambridge.org; http://www.journals.cambridge.org. Illus., index, adv. Refereed. Microform: PMC; PQC. Online: Pub.; EBSCO Publishing, EBSCO Host; OCLC Online Computer Library Center, Inc.; OhioLINK; SwetsWise Online Content. Reprint: PSC. *Indexed:* AS&TI, ApMecR, C&ISA, CCMJ, CEA, CerAb, ChemAb, EngInd, ExcerpMed, IAA, M&GPA, MSN, MathR, PetrolAb, SCI, SWRA. *Bk. rev.:* 3, length varies. *Aud.:* Ga, Ac, Sa.

Offering a dozen or so full-length scholarly research papers, this interdisciplinary journal explores fundamental fluid mechanics and its application to aeronautics, astrophysics, chemical engineering, mechanical engineering,

colloid science, combustion, hydraulics, and meteorology. A schedule of international conferences on fluid mechanics is listed in the June issue. Availability online is free to print subscribers.

2307. *Journal of Mechanical Design.* Formerly (until 1990): *Journal of Mechanisms, Transmissions and Automation in Design;* Supersedes in part (in 1978): *Journal of Mechanical Design.* [ISSN: 1050-0472] 1978. q. Members, USD 80 print & online eds.; Non-members, USD 545 print & online eds. Ed(s): J M McCarthy. A S M E International, Three Park Ave, New York, NY 10016-5990; infocentral@asme.org; http://www.asme.org. Refereed. *Indexed:* AS&TI, ApMecR, C&ISA, CerAb, EngInd, EnvAb, IAA, SCI. *Aud.:* Ac, Sa.

Covering all aspects of the design of mechanical systems, this journal accepts in-depth scholarly articles on the development and design of machines and mechanical systems. Addresses the areas of robotics, manufacturing design, macro- and nano-scaled mechanical systems, and failure and analysis. Available online from the ASME Digital Library at http://scitation.aip.org/ASMEJournals/MechanicalDesign.

2308. *Mechanical Engineering.* [ISSN: 0025-6501] 1906. m. Non-members, USD 118. Ed(s): Harry Hutchinson. A S M E International, Three Park Ave, New York, NY 10016-5990; infocentral@asme.org; http://www.asme.org. Illus., index, adv. Refereed. Circ: 115000 Paid. Microform: PMC; PQC. Online: EBSCO Publishing, EBSCO Host; Florida Center for Library Automation; Gale; OCLC Online Computer Library Center, Inc.; ProQuest K-12 Learning Solutions; ProQuest LLC (Ann Arbor). *Indexed:* ABIn, AS&TI, ApMecR, C&ISA, CCMJ, CerAb, ChemAb, EngInd, EnvAb, EnvInd, ExcerpMed, H&SSA, HRIS, IAA, M&GPA, PetrolAb, RILM, SCI, SWRA. *Bk. rev.:* Number and length vary. *Aud.:* Ga, Ac, Sa.

Published monthly by the American Society of Mechanical Engineers (ASME), this trade publication acts as the official organ of the society. It communicates news, new products, a calendar of upcoming meetings, publications offered for sale by the society, standards and code changes, and job opportunities. *ASME News* is included as a supplement to a subscription to *Mechanical Engineering.* Necessary for all engineering collections. Some feature stories from the print version are posted on the web site along with late-breaking news items only on the web site. Industry news online at www.memagazine.org.

Progress in Energy and Combustion Science. See Energy section.

Nuclear Engineering

2309. *International Journal of Radiation Biology.* Formerly (until 1988): *International Journal of Radiation Biology and Related Studies in Physics, Chemistry and Medicine.* [ISSN: 0955-3002] 1959. m. GBP 1851 print & online eds. Ed(s): A M Rauth, Richard Hill. Informa Healthcare, Mortimer House, 37-41 Mortimer St, London, W1T 3JM, United Kingdom; healthcare.enquiries@informa.com; http://www.tandf.co.uk/journals/. Illus., adv. Refereed. Online: EBSCO Publishing, EBSCO Host; Gale; IngentaConnect; OCLC Online Computer Library Center, Inc.; SwetsWise Online Content. Reprint: PSC. *Indexed:* BiolAb, ChemAb, DSA, ExcerpMed, FS&TA, HortAb, IndVet, SCI, VB. *Aud.:* Ac, Sa.

The *International Journal of Radiation Biology* was rated the highest-ranked journal for the nuclear sciences in 2005 with an impact factor of 1.923. Focusing on the biological effects of radiation exposure and responses, this journal publishes scholarly articles, technical reports and notes, and reviews, and covers topical issues. Medical uses are also covered for the nuclear community, most notably in the area of the use of radiation for cancer treatment. Published by Taylor & Francis, this title is available online through the parent company, informaworld.

2310. *Journal of Nuclear Materials.* [ISSN: 0022-3115] 1959. 36x/yr. EUR 7361. Ed(s): L K Mansur, S Ishino. Elsevier BV, North-Holland, Sara Burgerhartstraat 25, Amsterdam, 1055 KV, Netherlands; nlinfo-f@elsevier.nl. Illus., adv. Refereed. Microform: PQC. Online: EBSCO

Publishing, EBSCO Host; Gale; IngentaConnect; OhioLINK; ScienceDirect; SwetsWise Online Content. *Indexed:* ApMecR, C&ISA, CerAb, ChemAb, EngInd, EnvAb, EnvInd, H&SSA, IAA, SCI. *Aud.:* Ac, Sa.

Journal of Nuclear Materials publishes high-quality papers in materials research relevant to nuclear fission and fusion reactors and high-power accelerator technologies, and in closely related aspects of materials science and engineering. The journal welcomes both original research and critical review papers that cover experimental, theoretical, and computational aspects of either fundamental or applied nature. The breadth of the field is such that a wide range of processes and properties is of interest to the readership, spanning (for example) atomic lattice defects, microstructures, thermodynamics, corrosion, and mechanical and physical properties. This journal also publishes important conference proceedings. Cited by ISI in 2005 as the number-two-ranked nuclear science publication. Available online from ScienceDirect.

2311. Nuclear Engineering International. Formerly (until 1968): *Nuclear Engineering;* Which incorporated (1956-1963): *Nuclear Power.* [ISSN: 0029-5507] 1956. m. GBP 248 domestic; EUR 381 in Europe; USD 457 in North America. Wilmington Media Ltd., Maidstone Rd, Footscray, Sidcup, DA14 5HZ, United Kingdom; wilmington@wdis.co.uk; http://www.wilmington.co.uk/. Illus., index, adv. Refereed. Circ: 2399. Microform: PQC. Online: EBSCO Publishing, EBSCO Host; Florida Center for Library Automation; Gale; LexisNexis; OCLC Online Computer Library Center, Inc.; ProQuest K-12 Learning Solutions; ProQuest LLC (Ann Arbor). *Indexed:* ABIn, AS&TI, ApMecR, BrTechI, C&ISA, CerAb, ChemAb, EngInd, EnvAb, ExcerpMed, H&SSA, IAA, PollutAb, RiskAb, SCI. *Aud.:* Ga, Ac, Sa.

Get the global perspective in nuclear engineering with the addition of this title to your collection. Features include articles, industry briefs, profiles of national nuclear programs, wall charts, and statistics pertinent to the field as well as news and company profiles. This publisher also issues the *World Nuclear Industry Handbook,* a good reference source for technical details on nuclear power plants and fuel cycle facilities. Recent issues are available online at publisher's web site, wwww.neimagazine.com.

2312. Nuclear Instruments & Methods in Physics Research. Section A. Accelerators, Spectrometers, Detectors, and Associated Equipment. Supersedes in part (in 1984): *Nuclear Instruments and Methods in Physics Research;* Which had former titles (until 1981): *Nuclear Instruments and Methods;* (until 1958): *Nuclear Instruments.* [ISSN: 0168-9002] 1957. 28x/yr. EUR 12801. Ed(s): W Barletta, R Klanner. Elsevier BV, North-Holland, Sara Burgerhartstraat 25, Amsterdam, 1055 KV, Netherlands; nlinfo-f@elsevier.nl. Illus., index, adv. Refereed. Vol. ends: No. 456 - No. 474. Microform: PQC. Online: EBSCO Publishing, EBSCO Host; Gale; IngentaConnect; OhioLINK; ScienceDirect; SwetsWise Online Content. *Indexed:* A&ATA, C&ISA, ChemAb, EngInd, EnvAb, EnvInd, ExcerpMed, IAA, SCI. *Aud.:* Ac, Sa.

This highly cited international scholarly journal publishes papers on particle accelerators and other devices that produce and measure nuclear radiations. Each issue includes numerous articles on such topics as fusion, dosimetry, space radiation, and instruments and methods for high-energy physics. A meetings calendar of interest to professionals in the nuclear industry is provided. A very costly purchase for the specialized collection. Available online from ScienceDirect.

2313. Nuclear Instruments & Methods in Physics Research. Section B. Beam Interactions with Materials and Atoms. Supersedes in part (in 1984): *Nuclear Instruments and Methods in Physics Research;* Which had former titles (until 1981): *Nuclear Instruments and Methods;* (until 1958): *Nuclear Instruments.* [ISSN: 0168-583X] 1957. 24x/yr. EUR 9811. Ed(s): Lynn E Rehn, I C Vickridge. Elsevier BV, North-Holland, Sara Burgerhartstraat 25, Amsterdam, 1055 KV, Netherlands; nlinfo-f@ elsevier.nl. Illus., index, adv. Refereed. Vol. ends: No. 173 - No. 185. Microform: PQC. Online: EBSCO Publishing, EBSCO Host; Gale; IngentaConnect; OhioLINK; ScienceDirect; SwetsWise Online Content. *Indexed:* ArtHuCI, C&ISA, CerAb, ChemAb, EngInd, EnvInd, IAA, RILM, SCI, SSCI. *Bk. rev.:* Number and length vary. *Aud.:* Ac, Sa.

This highly cited technical journal publishes experimental and theoretical papers of original research that span all aspects of the interaction of energetic beams with atoms, molecules, and aggregate forms of matter, including ion beam analysis and modification of materials. Available in electronic form from ScienceDirect.

2314. Progress in Nuclear Magnetic Resonance Spectroscopy. [ISSN: 0079-6565] 1966. 8x/yr. EUR 1267. Ed(s): J Feeney, J W Emsley. Elsevier BV, Radarweg 29, Amsterdam, 1043 NX, Netherlands; nlinfo-f@elsevier.nl; http://www.elsevier.nl. Index. Refereed. Microform: PQC. Online: EBSCO Publishing, EBSCO Host; Gale; IngentaConnect; OhioLINK; ScienceDirect; SwetsWise Online Content. *Indexed:* ChemAb, EngInd, SCI. *Aud.:* Ac, Sa.

Progress in Nuclear Magnetic Resonance Spectroscopy publishes review papers that describe research related to theory and application of NMR spectroscopy. Of importance to the chemistry, physics, biochemistry, and materials science communities, as well as many areas of biology and medicine. Review articles cover applications in all related subjects, as well as in-depth treatments of the fundamental theory and instrumental developments of NMR spectroscopy. Continues to be a highly cited journal in the nuclear industry.

■ ENVIRONMENT AND CONSERVATION

See also Biology; Fishing; Hiking, Climbing, and Outdoor Recreation; Hunting and Guns; and Sports sections.

George E. Clark, Ph.D., Environmental Research Librarian, Research Services, Lamont Library Level B–Harvard Yard, Harvard University, Cambridge, MA 02138; FAX: 617-496-5570; george_clark@harvard.edu

Introduction

Environmental concerns on a planetary scale continue to grow as an important topic, both in public policy circles (with new publications from the Intergovernmental Panel on Climate Change) and in the public consciousness (with the success of the documentary film *An Inconvenient Truth*). At the national, regional, and local levels, the field of environmental studies is also compelling. It is an extremely broad area that focuses on the relationship between people and their surroundings, including the natural world and the built environment, cultural and institutional differences in those relationships, and related public policies. Many environmental researchers study the negatives as well as the positives, so the field also includes topics such as pollution, disease, floods, and famines.

Public libraries and school libraries may want to focus on issues of *metropolitan and regional planning* impacts on the environment (for example, urban blight and suburban sprawl, development, zoning, transportation, parks, recycling, and waste management), *local livelihood* impacts on and relationships to the environment (agriculture, fishing, logging, mining, manufacturing, commerce, business, and tourism), *household impacts and sustainable living,* local and regional *ecosystems and species,* the local geographic and demographic distribution of environmental threats and benefits (a field commonly called *environmental justice*), and the *capacity to deal with emergent environmental threats* (local natural and man-made hazards, public health, toxicity information, risk communication, community organizing, and environmental news).

Many public libraries already receive publications that will help users plan vacations in parks and other appealing natural areas outside the local area. Of course, academic and special libraries will want to adapt their collections according to users' home disciplines and their local, regional, national, international, and global research questions, adding in more technical publications.

Because of the breadth of the environmental field, it is impossible to list serials that would be appropriate for each of the above topics in this section of *Magazines for Libraries.* The publications listed here include many that focus on the environment *per se,* along with a smattering that will begin to convey the true breadth of the field. Many of the other sections in this volume will have references to highly environmentally relevant journals and magazines, and they should be explored as well.

Basic Periodicals

Conservation, Ecology and Society, Environment, Environmental Hazards, Green Teacher, Grist, High Country News, Linkages Update, Natural Hazards Observer.

Basic Abstracts and Indexes

Academic Search Premier, Agricola, BIOSIS, Environment Index, Environmental Sciences and Pollution Management (EnvironmentS), Forestry Abstracts, GeoBase, Medline, Meteorological and Geoastrophysical Abstracts, LexisNexis Environmental, Pollution Abstracts, ProQuest Research Library, Risk Abstracts, TOXNET, and Web of Science.

2315. *Ambio: a journal of the human environment.* [ISSN: 0044-7447] 1972. m. USD 200 Print edition (Individuals, USD 72 Print edition). Ed(s): Elisabeth Kessler. Kungliga Vetenskapsakademien, PO Box 50005, Stockholm, 10405, Sweden; http://www.kva.se. Illus., index, adv. Refereed. Circ: 4000. Vol. ends: Dec. *Indexed:* ApEcolAb, B&AI, BRI, BiolAb, BiolDig, CABA, CBRI, ChemAb, DSA, EnvAb, EnvInd, ExcerpMed, FPA, FS&TA, ForAb, FutSurv, GSI, H&SSA, HortAb, IndVet, M&GPA, OceAb, PollutAb, RRTA, RiskAb, S&F, SCI, SFSA, SSCI, SUSA, SWRA, VB, WAE&RSA, WRCInf, ZooRec. *Aud.:* Ac, Sa.

Ambio is a general, peer-reviewed environmental journal that dates from 1972 and the early consciousness of environment as a global issue. It is sponsored by the Royal Swedish Academy of Sciences and aims to address "scientific, social, economic, and cultural factors that influence the condition of the human environment." Each issue contains about a dozen articles.

American Forests. See Forestry section.

2316. *American Water Resources Association. Journal.* Formerly (until 1997): *Water Resources Bulletin.* [ISSN: 1093-474X] 1965. bi-m. USD 443 print & online eds. Ed(s): Kenneth Lanfear. Blackwell Publishing, Inc., Commerce Place, 350 Main St, Malden, MA 02148; customerservices@blackwellpublishing.com; http://www.blackwellpublishing.com. Illus., adv. Circ: 4000. Microform: PQC. Online: ProQuest LLC (Ann Arbor). Reprint: PSC. *Indexed:* AS&TI, Agr, BAS, CABA, ChemAb, DSA, EngInd, EnvAb, EnvInd, ExcerpMed, FPA, ForAb, HortAb, IndVet, M&GPA, OceAb, PollutAb, RI-1, RRTA, S&F, SCI, SSCI, SWRA, VB, WAE&RSA, WRCInf. *Bk. rev.:* Number and length vary. *Aud.:* Ac, Sa.

Journal of the American Water Resources Association is the premier U.S. academic journal devoted to water. It covers hydrology, watershed management, economics, engineering, groundwater, ecology, water policy, and pollution, among other topics. However, the article count runs heavily toward the physical and technical side. Includes book reviews.

BackHome. See Do-It-Yourself section.

2317. *Biodiversity and Conservation.* [ISSN: 0960-3115] 1991. 14x/yr. EUR 2504 print & online eds. Ed(s): Alan T Bull. Springer Netherlands, Van Godewijckstraat 30, Dordrecht, 3311 GX, Netherlands; http://www.springeronline.com. Illus., adv. Refereed. Online: EBSCO Publishing, EBSCO Host; Gale; IngentaConnect; OCLC Online Computer Library Center, Inc.; OhioLINK; Ovid Technologies, Inc.; Springer LINK; SwetsWise Online Content. Reprint: PSC. *Indexed:* Agr, ApEcolAb, BiolAb, CABA, DSA, EnvAb, EnvInd, FPA, ForAb, GardL, HortAb, IndVet, PollutAb, RRTA, S&F, SCI, SSCI, SWRA, VB, WAE&RSA, ZooRec. *Aud.:* Ac, Sa.

Biodiversity and Conservation is a peer-reviewed academic journal dealing with the biological side of threats to ecosystems and species. It is international in scope and contains technical articles on species diversity, ecological communities, invasive organisms, and other relevant topics. Heavy on statistical analyses.

Climatic Change. See Atmospheric Sciences section.

2318. *Conservation: best minds, best writing.* Former titles (until 2007): *Conservation In Practice;* (until 2002): *Conservation Biology in Practice.* [ISSN: 1936-2145] 2000. q. GBP 45 print & online eds. Ed(s): Kathy Kohm. Blackwell Publishing, Inc., Commerce Place, 350 Main St, Malden, MA 02148; customerservices@blackwellpublishing.com; http://www.blackwellpublishing.com. Index, adv. *Indexed:* AltPI, ApEcolAb, BiolDig, CABA, FPA, ForAb, GardL, HortAb, IndVet, RRTA, S&F, SWRA, WAE&RSA, WRCInf. *Bk. rev.:* Number and length vary. *Aud.:* Hs, Ga, Ac, Sa.

Conservation, formerly *Conservation in Practice,* is a general readership publication of the Society for Conservation Biology that reports on complex and compelling issues such as carbon credits, Amazon forest history, and species extinction. The magazine is international in scope, pleasing to read, and well illustrated. It provides essays, general-interest summaries of academic work, a surprisingly approachable statistical feature, plugs for articles in other journals, and book reviews.

2319. *Daily Environment Report (Print Edition).* [ISSN: 1060-2976] 1992. d. USD 3537. Ed(s): Larry E. Evans, Bernard S Chabel. The Bureau of National Affairs, Inc., 1231 25th St, NW, Washington, DC 20037; customercare@bna.com; http://www.bna.com/. Illus., index. *Aud.:* Ga, Ac, Sa.

Daily Environment Report is for those with a serious interest in the processes of environmental governance in the United States. Along with concise articles on all aspects of environmental policy, this BNA publication prints the Presidential and Congressional calendars, Federal Register headlines, public comment deadlines, and an index to court cases mentioned in the day's issue. Available online in pdf.

2320. *E: the environmental magazine.* [ISSN: 1046-8021] 1990. bi-m. USD 19.95 domestic; USD 29.95 in Canada & Mexico; USD 4.95 newsstand/cover per issue. Ed(s): Brian Howard, Jim Motavalli. Earth Action Network, 28 Knight St, Norwalk, CT 06851. Illus., adv. Sample. Circ: 50000 Paid. Vol. ends: Nov/Dec. Online: EBSCO Publishing, EBSCO Host; Florida Center for Library Automation; Gale; OCLC Online Computer Library Center, Inc.; ProQuest K-12 Learning Solutions; ProQuest LLC (Ann Arbor); H.W. Wilson. *Indexed:* ABS&EES, ASIP, AltPI, BRI, BiolDig, CBRI, CINAHL, EnvAb, EnvInd, GSI, MASUSE, RGPR, SWRA. *Aud.:* Hs, Ga.

E: The Environmental Magazine aims to be "a clearinghouse of information, news, and resources for people concerned about the environment who want to know 'What can I do?'" Issues contain foreign and domestic environmental news, feature pieces, and a guide to "Green Living" with segments on health, food, and other consumer topics.

2321. *EcoHealth.* Formed by the merger of (2000-2004): *Global Change and Human Health;* (1995-2004): *Ecosystem Health.* [ISSN: 1612-9202] 2004. q. EUR 418 print & online eds. Ed(s): Bruce A Wilcox. Springer New York LLC, 233 Spring St, New York, NY 10013-1578; journals@springer-ny.com; http://www.springer.com/. Refereed. Reprint: PSC. *Indexed:* BiolAb, ExcerpMed, H&SSA, PollutAb, RiskAb, SCI, ZooRec. *Bk. rev.:* Number and length vary. *Aud.:* Ac, Sa.

EcoHealth is a peer-reviewed journal focusing on the links between ecosystems and human health. Topics covered include "human health, wildlife health, and ecosystem sustainability." A recent issue includes articles on West Nile virus, bushmeat and disease, and mosquito-borne illness. This journal fills an important niche as society begins to cope with climate change.

2322. *The Ecologist.* Incorporates (1977-1985): *Mazingira;* Formed by the merger of (1978-1979): *New Ecologist;* (1978-1979): *Ecologist Quarterly;* Both of which superseded (in 1978): *Ecologist.* [ISSN: 0261-3131] 1970. 10x/yr. GBP 28 domestic; USD 52 in US & Canada; GBP 38 elsewhere. Ed(s): Zac Goldsmith. Ecosystems Ltd., 18 Chelsea Wharf, 15 Lots Rd, London, SW10 0JZ, United Kingdom. Illus. Sample. Circ: 20000. Microform: PQC. Online: EBSCO Publishing, EBSCO Host; Florida Center for Library Automation; Gale; OCLC Online

Computer Library Center, Inc.; ProQuest K-12 Learning Solutions; ProQuest LLC (Ann Arbor); H.W. Wilson. *Indexed:* AltPI, AmHI, BiolDig, BrHumI, EnvAb, EnvInd, ExcerpMed, ForAb, GSI, IBR, LeftInd, PAIS, PollutAb, S&F, SWRA, VB, WAE&RSA. *Aud.:* Hs, Ga.

The Ecologist is an activist publication on topics such as "food, war, politics, pharmaceuticals, farming, toxic chemicals, corporate fraud, mass media [and] supermarkets." Topics include product labeling, green shopping, health, food, pesticides, and nuclear power. Often entertaining and always provocative.

2323. *Ecology and Society.* Formerly: *Conservation Ecology.* [ISSN: 1708-3087] 1997. 2x/yr. Free. Ed(s): Michelle Lee. Resilience Alliance Publications, PO Box 40037, Waterloo, ON N2J 4V1, Canada; questions@consecol.org; http://www.consecol.org. Illus. Refereed. *Indexed:* ApEcolAb, BiolAb, CABA, CBCARef, FPA, ForAb, GSI, HortAb, PAIS, S&F, SCI, SWRA, WAE&RSA, ZooRec. *Bk. rev.:* Number and length vary. *Aud.:* Ac, Sa.

The editors' goal is to "discuss issues related to the linked and dynamic systems of humans and nature and generate an improved understanding of essential interactions that will enhance our capacity to actively adapt to change." This peer-reviewed academic and professional journal, devoted to the interplay between human and natural systems, takes substantial advantage of its online format. Readers can track issues in progress, and graphics are pleasing, so it is more than just a paper journal that has been put online. Authors include both biologists and social scientists, and articles are a mix of the technical and more readable. Special issues on important topics are common. One fault is the lack of page numbers, even in the pdf versions, which makes precise citation difficult. URL: www.ecologyandsociety.org.

2324. *Ecosystems.* [ISSN: 1432-9840] 1998. 8x/yr. EUR 637 print & online eds. Ed(s): Monica G Turner, Stephen R Carpenter. Springer New York LLC, 233 Spring St, New York, NY 10013-1578; journals@springer-ny.com; http://www.springer.com/. Illus., adv. Sample. Refereed. Reprint: PSC. *Indexed:* Agr, ApEcolAb, BiolAb, CABA, FPA, ForAb, HortAb, IndVet, M&GPA, PollutAb, RRTA, S&F, SCI, SWRA, WAE&RSA, ZooRec. *Aud.:* Ac, Sa.

Ecosystems favors a wide range of ecological articles, particularly those that "integrate natural and social processes at appropriately broad scales." It is a technical, peer-reviewed journal that is appropriate for academic and special libraries with users interested in ecosystem science. Rich in modelling, mapping, and remote sensing.

2325. *Electronic Green Journal: professional journal on international environmental information.* Formerly (until 1994): *Green Library Journal.* [ISSN: 1076-7975] 1992. 2x/yr. Free. Ed(s): Maria Anna Jankowska. University of Idaho Library, University of Idaho Library, Rayburn St, Moscow, ID 83844-2350; majordomo@uidaho.edu; http://egj.lib.uidaho.edu. Illus. Refereed. Circ: 20000 Controlled. *Indexed:* BRI, CBRI, EnvAb, GSI, PAIS, PollutAb, ZooRec. *Bk. rev.:* Number and length vary. *Aud.:* Ga, Ac, Sa.

Electronic Green Journal is a peer-reviewed publication that covers international and regional environmental topics for researchers, professionals, and the interested public. It contains articles, opinion pieces, and many short book reviews. Useful for those interested in building collections of environmental publications. Content comes from practitioners around the globe.

2326. *Emergency Preparedness News: contingency planning - crisis management - disaster relief.* Incorporates (in 2003): *Port & Rail Security International.* [ISSN: 0275-3782] 1977. bi-w. USD 309 in US & Mexico; USD 405 elsewhere; USD 437 combined subscription print & email eds. Ed(s): Deborah Elby. Business Publishers, Inc., 2272 Airport Rd S, Naples, FL 34112; http://www.eliresearch.com. *Aud.:* Ga, Ac, Sa.

"Contingency planning, crisis management, disaster relief." Recent articles include the state of FEMA, lessons learned from Katrina, planning for flu epidemics, and communications interoperability.

2327. *Environment: science and policy for sustainable development.* Formerly (until 1969): *Scientist and Citizen.* [ISSN: 0013-9157] 1958. m. except Jan.-Feb., July-Aug. combined. USD 137 (Individuals, USD 51;

USD 13 newsstand/cover). Ed(s): Barbara Richman. Heldref Publications, 1319 18th St, NW, Washington, DC 20036-1802; subscribe@heldref.org; http://www.heldref.org. Illus., adv. Refereed. Circ: 3752 Paid and controlled. CD-ROM: ProQuest LLC (Ann Arbor). Online: EBSCO Publishing, EBSCO Host; Florida Center for Library Automation; Gale; Northern Light Technology, Inc.; OCLC Online Computer Library Center, Inc.; ProQuest K-12 Learning Solutions; ProQuest LLC (Ann Arbor); H.W. Wilson. Reprint: PSC. *Indexed:* AS&TI, Agr, B&AI, BRI, BiolDig, CABA, CBRI, CPerI, ChemAb, DSA, EnvAb, EnvInd, ExcerpMed, FPA, ForAb, GSI, H&SSA, IBR, IBSS, IBZ, IndVet, LRI, M&GPA, MASUSE, PRA, PollutAb, RGPR, RI-1, RRTA, S&F, SCI, SSCI, VB, WAE&RSA, WRCInf. *Bk. rev.:* Number and length vary. *Aud.:* Hs, Ga, Ac, Sa.

Environment, according to its web site, "analyzes the problems, places, and people where environment and development come together, illuminating concerns from the local to the global. *Environment* offers peer-reviewed articles and commentaries from researchers and practitioners who provide a broad range of international perspectives. The magazine also features in-depth reviews of major policy reports, sustainable development indicators, and guides to the best web sites and books." While *Environment* is peer-reviewed, it is written with a general audience in mind. Advertisements include a guide to graduate programs in environmental studies. Articles run toward transnational sustainable development, but region- and country-based studies may also be found.

2328. *Environment and Development Economics.* [ISSN: 1355-770X] 1996. bi-m. GBP 200. Ed(s): Anastasios Xepapadeas. Cambridge University Press, The Edinburgh Bldg, Shaftesbury Rd, Cambridge, CB2 2RU, United Kingdom; journals@cambridge.org; http://www.cup.cam.ac.uk/. Illus., adv. Refereed. Online: Pub.; EBSCO Publishing, EBSCO Host; OCLC Online Computer Library Center, Inc.; OhioLINK; SwetsWise Online Content. Reprint: PSC. *Indexed:* ABIn, BAS, FPA, ForAb, HortAb, JEL, M&GPA, PAIS, PollutAb, S&F, SSCI, WAE&RSA. *Aud.:* Ac.

Environment and Development Economics is a peer-reviewed, academic economics journal. It contains two types of articles, "Theory and Applications" and "Policy Options." Articles include portions that are quite technical. International in scope, with a developing-country focus.

2329. *Environment and Energy Daily (Online): the best way to track congress.* [ISSN: 1540-790X] 1999. d. USD 1990. Ed(s): Kevin Braun. Environmental and Energy Publishing, LLC, 122 C St, NW, Ste 722, Washington, DC 20001; pubs@eenews.net; http://www.eenews.net. *Aud.:* Hs, Ga, Ac, Sa.

Appropriations and reauthorizations and hearings, oh my! *Environment and Energy Daily* provides these and more—a comprehensive online news source for Congress and the environment. From global warming to fish farms, *E&E Daily* provides (yes) daily coverage of Congress's environmental maneuverings. This service complements house.gov and senate.gov because it provides the analysis and background that the Congressional web sites do not. "Congressional Committee Assignments," "Hill Hearings & Markups This Week," a searchable archive, budget information, and selected key documents are included. URL: www.eenews.net/eed.

2330. *Environmental Conservation: an international journal of environmental science.* [ISSN: 0376-8929] 1974. q. GBP 315. Ed(s): Nicholas Polunin. Cambridge University Press, The Edinburgh Bldg, Shaftesbury Rd, Cambridge, CB2 2RU, United Kingdom; journals@cambridge.org; http://www.journals.cambridge.org. Illus., adv. Sample. Refereed. Vol. ends: Winter. Microform: PQC. Online: Pub.; EBSCO Publishing, EBSCO Host; OCLC Online Computer Library Center, Inc.; OhioLINK; SwetsWise Online Content. *Indexed:* ApEcolAb, B&AI, BAS, BiolAb, BiolDig, C&ISA, CABA, ChemAb, EngInd, EnvAb, EnvInd, ExcerpMed, FPA, ForAb, HortAb, IBR, IBZ, IndVet, M&GPA, OceAb, PollutAb, RRTA, S&F, SCI, SSCI, SWRA, WAE&RSA, ZooRec. *Bk. rev.:* Number and length vary. *Aud.:* Ac, Sa.

Environmental Conservation is a peer-reviewed academic publication. While the journal prominently features the sciences, it also includes management and social science approaches and encourages submissions from all perspectives on the topic. Issues include "Comment" (brief articles and opinion pieces), "Papers" (longer articles), and book reviews.

2331. *Environmental Ethics: an interdisciplinary journal dedicated to the philosophical aspects of environmental problems.* [ISSN: 0163-4275] 1979. q. USD 50 (Individuals, USD 25). Ed(s): Eugene C Hargrove. Environmental Philosophy, Inc., Center for Environmental Philosophy, University of North Texas, Box 310980, Denton, TX 76203-0980; http://www.cep.unt.edu. Illus., index, adv. Refereed. Circ: 1900. Vol. ends: Winter. Microform: PQC. *Indexed:* Agr, AmHI, ArtHuCI, BiolAb, EnvAb, EnvInd, ExcerpMed, GSI, HumInd, IBR, IBZ, IPB, PSA, PhilInd, R&TA, RI-1, SSA, SSCI, SWRA, ZooRec. *Bk. rev.:* Number and length vary. *Aud.:* Ac.

Environmental Ethics is a peer-reviewed academic journal dealing with all aspects of environmental philosophy, including but not limited to ethics. Authors are asked to explain philosophical issues fully enough to be understood by environmental scholars who are not rigorously schooled in philosophy. A recent issue provides articles on wolf reintroduction, cars, and sustainability.

2332. *Environmental Hazards.* Formerly: *Global Environmental Change Part B: Environmental Hazards;* Which superseded in part (in 1999): *Global Environmental Change.* [ISSN: 1747-7891] 1990. 4x/yr. EUR 270. Ed(s): S. L. Cutter, Dr. J. K. Mitchell. Pergamon, The Boulevard, Langford Ln, East Park, Kidlington, OX5 1GB, United Kingdom. *Indexed:* CABA, EnvAb, EnvInd, ForAb, H&SSA, M&GPA, OceAb, PollutAb, RRTA, S&F, SWA, SWRA, WAE&RSA. *Aud.:* Ac, Sa.

An interdisciplinary and international peer-reviewed journal dedicated to "addressing the human and policy dimensions of hazards." Hazards covered include extreme "natural" events from earthquakes to epidemics and "technological failures and malfunctions," including toxic releases. The emphasis on human and policy dimensions means that the journal focuses on rigorous studies of the social science of hazards and not exclusively on the physical and engineering parameters. The journal has a distinguished international board that includes geographers and other social scientists as well as experts from both governmental and nongovernmental organizations. *Environmental Hazards* is for "specialists from a wide range of fields who are interested in the effects of hazard events on people, property, and societies." Appropriate for academic libraries and government and other special libraries with an interest in environmental or disaster policy. Formerly Part B of *Global Environmental Change.*

Environmental Health Perspectives. See Government Periodicals—Federal section.

Environmental History. See Forestry section.

2333. *Environmental Protection: management and problem-solving for environmental professionals.* [ISSN: 1057-4298] 1990. m. USD 99 domestic (Free to qualified personnel). Ed(s): Angela Neville. Stevens Publishing Corporation, 5151 Beltline Rd, 10th Fl, Dallas, TX 75240; custserv@stevenspublishing.com; http://www.stevenspublishing.com/. Illus., index, adv. Circ: 73000 Controlled. Vol. ends: Dec. *Indexed:* BPI, EnvAb, EnvInd, H&SSA, M&GPA, PollutAb, SWRA. *Aud.:* Sa.

An industry-focused magazine that deals with environmental regulation, compliance, and remediation. This publication contains articles that will help environmental officers and consultants deal with environmental problems while maintaining the bottom line.

2334. *Environmental Science & Policy.* [ISSN: 1462-9011] 1998. 8x/yr. EUR 748. Ed(s): Dr. J. C. Briden. Elsevier Inc., 360 Park Ave S, New York, NY 10010-1710; usinfo-f@elsevier.com; http://www.elsevier.com. Illus. Sample. Refereed. Online: EBSCO Publishing, EBSCO Host; Gale; IngentaConnect; OhioLINK; ScienceDirect; SwetsWise Online Content. *Indexed:* ExcerpMed, M&GPA, PollutAb, SCI, WRCInf. *Bk. rev.:* Number and length vary. *Aud.:* Ac, Sa.

A broadly interdisciplinary journal focusing on "environmental issues such as climate change, biodiversity, environmental pollution and wastes, renewable and non-renewable natural resources, and the interactions between these issues." Includes social science approaches. Recent article topics include the carbon cycle, science policy, and invasive species.

Ethics, Place and Environment. See Geography section.

2335. *Global Change Biology.* [ISSN: 1354-1013] 1995. m. GBP 1818 print & online eds. Ed(s): Steve Long. Blackwell Publishing Ltd., 9600 Garsington Rd, Oxford, OX4 2ZG, United Kingdom; customerservices@blackwellpublishing.com; http://www.blackwellpublishing.com. Adv. Refereed. Circ: 425. Online: Blackwell Synergy; EBSCO Publishing, EBSCO Host; Gale; IngentaConnect; OCLC Online Computer Library Center, Inc.; OhioLINK; SwetsWise Online Content. Reprint: PSC. *Indexed:* Agr, ApEcolAb, CABA, DSA, EnvAb, EnvInd, FPA, FS&TA, ForAb, HortAb, IndVet, M&GPA, PollutAb, RRTA, S&F, SCI, SWRA, VB, WAE&RSA, ZooRec. *Aud.:* Ac, Sa.

Global Change Biology aims to address "the interface between all aspects of current environmental change and biological systems," including responses at scales ranging from "molecular to biome." Environmental change is seen as including change in gas concentrations (such as carbon dioxide), change in climate, and the interactions of these with the biosphere. Objects of study featured recently include hurricanes, volcanoes, frogs, and bogs.

2336. *Global Change NewsLetter.* [ISSN: 0284-5865] 1989. q. Free. Ed(s): Clare Bradshaw. Royal Swedish Academy of Science, International Geosphere-Biosphere Programme, IGBP Secretariat, Box 50005, Stockholm, 10405, Sweden; sec@igbp.kva.se; http://www.igbp.kva.se/. Illus. Circ: 10000 Controlled. *Aud.:* Ac, Sa.

Global Change NewsLetter is a free color publication of the International Geosphere-Biosphere Programme (IGBP), an international research program on global environmental change. This is a technical publication that aims to appeal to the broad range of global-change research disciplines. The focus is on IGBP research projects, people, and meetings. A calendar lists a wide range of global change meetings and links readers to the web sites of global change research organizations.

2337. *Global Ecology and Biogeography: a journal of macroecology.* Formerly (until 1998): *Global Ecology and Biogeography Letters.* [ISSN: 1466-822X] 1991. bi-m. GBP 2906 print & online. Ed(s): David J Currie, Tim M Blackburn. Blackwell Publishing Ltd., 9600 Garsington Rd, Oxford, OX4 2ZG, United Kingdom; customerservices@blackwellpublishing.com; http://www.blackwellpublishing.com. Adv. Reprint: PSC. *Indexed:* AnBeAb, ApEcolAb, BiolAb, CABA, EnvAb, FPA, ForAb, HortAb, IBR, IBZ, IndVet, M&GPA, PollutAb, S&F, SCI, SWRA, VB, WAE&RSA, ZooRec. *Bk. rev.:* Number and length vary. *Aud.:* Ac, Sa.

This academic journal covers large-scale ecology. Topics include "broad-scale patterns of biodiversity, ecosystem responses to global climate change, historical and evolutionary biogeography, remote sensing of ecosystem properties, species abundance and species range patterns, and statistical methodologies."

2338. *Global Environmental Change.* [ISSN: 0959-3780] 1990. 4x/yr. EUR 677. Ed(s): Neil Adger. Pergamon, The Boulevard, Langford Ln, East Park, Kidlington, OX5 1GB, United Kingdom. Illus. Sample. Refereed. Vol. ends: Dec. Microform: PQC. Online: DataStar; The Dialog Corporation; EBSCO Publishing, EBSCO Host; Gale; IngentaConnect; OhioLINK; ScienceDirect; SwetsWise Online Content. *Indexed:* ApEcolAb, CABA, EnvAb, EnvInd, FPA, ForAb, HortAb, IBSS, M&GPA, OceAb, PollutAb, RRTA, S&F, SCI, SSCI, SWA, SWRA, WAE&RSA. *Aud.:* Ac, Sa.

Global Environmental Change is an interdisciplinary academic journal that concentrates on the links between the local, regional, and global scales in environmental transformation, including global climate change. Perspectives and topics include "public policy, economics, equity, risk, and resilience, science policy, international development, and health and well-being." This publication fills the gaps in social science and policy approaches that exist in many of the other global change journals, and so it is particularly valuable to policymakers seeking a richer understanding of problems documented by the scientific data.

2339. Green Teacher: education for planet earth. [ISSN: 1192-1285] 1991. q. CND 28.30 domestic; USD 28 foreign; CND 33.30 combined subscription domestic print & online eds. Ed(s): Gail Littlejohn, Tim Grant. Green Teacher, 95 Robert St, Toronto, ON M5S 2K5, Canada; info@greenteacher.com. Illus., adv. Sample. Circ: 6800. *Indexed:* CEI, CPerI, EnvAb, EnvInd. *Bk. rev.:* Number and length vary. *Aud.:* Hs, Ga, Ac.

Green Teacher is a great resource for educators, covering student populations of all school ages. Not only will traditional environmental and science educators appreciate this illustrated publication, but also teachers of language (with a recent stories on social justice and language arts) and teachers of other subjects such as art (art and gardens), health (farm produce programs), and early childhood (pretend games). Each issue is full of pedagogical tips, projects, activities, and readings. Also look for book reviews, picture book reviews, and workshop and conference announcements. Highly recommended for elementary through high school educators.

2340. Greenwire. Former titles: *Environment and Energy Newsline; Environment and Energy Update.* [ISSN: 1540-787X] 1997. d. USD 1795 includes special reports. Ed(s): Kevin Braun. Environmental and Energy Publishing, LLC, 122 C St, NW, Ste 722, Washington, DC 20001; pubs@eenews.net. *Aud.:* Hs, Ga, Ac, Sa.

Greenwire is a thorough online daily that covers environment and energy policy, focusing on the national but covering many international, state, and local issues as well. The publication includes access to a story archive, text of environmental laws, selected documents, and detailed special reports. URL: www.eenews.net/gw.

2341. High Country News: a paper for people who care about the West. [ISSN: 0191-5657] 1970. bi-w. USD 42 (Individuals, USD 32). Ed(s): Greg Hanscom. High Country Foundation, PO Box 1090, Paonia, CO 81428; editor@hcn.org; http://www.hcn.org. Illus., index, adv. Circ: 18000 Paid. Vol. ends: Dec. Online: EBSCO Publishing, EBSCO Host; ProQuest LLC (Ann Arbor). *Indexed:* AltPI, EnvAb, EnvInd. *Bk. rev.:* Number and length vary. *Aud.:* Hs, Ga, Ac, Sa.

A newspaper on environmental issues in the West. Focuses on the 11 westernmost states in the continental United States. Topics include "water, logging, wildlife, grazing, wilderness, growth and other issues changing the face of the West." Classified ads are included. Recommended for public, academic, and special libraries in the Western states and elsewhere in libraries that are national in scope.

2342. Human Ecology (New York): an interdisciplinary journal. [ISSN: 0300-7839] 1972. 6x/yr. EUR 1150 print & online eds. Ed(s): Daniel G Bates. Springer New York LLC, 233 Spring St, New York, NY 10013-1578; service-ny@springer.com; http://www.springer.com/. Illus., index, adv. Refereed. Online: EBSCO Publishing, EBSCO Host; Florida Center for Library Automation; Gale; IngentaConnect; OCLC Online Computer Library Center, Inc.; OhioLINK; Ovid Technologies, Inc.; ProQuest K-12 Learning Solutions; ProQuest LLC (Ann Arbor); Springer LINK; SwetsWise Online Content. Reprint: PSC. *Indexed:* AICP, AbAn, Agr, AnthLit, ApEcolAb, BAS, BiolAb, CABA, DSA, EI, ExcerpMed, FPA, ForAb, HortAb, IMFL, IndVet, PRA, PSA, RRTA, S&F, SFSA, SSA, SSCI, SUSA, SWA, SociolAb, VB, WAE&RSA. *Bk. rev.:* Number and length vary. *Aud.:* Ac, Sa.

Human Ecology is an important academic anthropology journal that is also favored by geographers and other social scientists interested in cultural and political ecology, which is the study of the interplay between ecosystems, cultures, and power over time and space. Articles tend to examine the developing world, although more-developed areas are also included. Producer (often subsistence) occupations such as farming, herding, and forest use feature prominently, as do a variety of coping strategies within and around land-use systems that are institutionally and biophysically constrained.

2343. International Journal of Mass Emergencies and Disasters. [ISSN: 0280-7270] 1983. 3x/yr. USD 55 (Individuals, USD 45). Ed(s): Ronald Perry. International Research Committee on Disasters, c/o Dr. Brenda D. Phillips, 519 Math Science Bldg, Stillwater, OK 74074; http://www.udel.edu/DRC/IRCD.html. Adv. Refereed. *Indexed:* H&SSA, PSA, RiskAb, SSA, SociolAb. *Bk. rev.:* Number and length vary. *Aud.:* Ga, Ac, Sa.

International Journal of Mass Emergencies and Disasters is the peer-reviewed academic and professional journal of the International Sociological Association's Research Committee on Disasters. Although sponsored by this association, the journal seeks research from all disciplines on the social and behavioral aspects of preparing for and coping with "natural," technological, and conflict-induced disasters. This journal should be a core publication for emergency management and security professionals as well as academics in the field.

2344. Journal of Contingencies and Crisis Management. [ISSN: 0966-0879] 1993. q. GBP 363 print & online eds. Ed(s): Alexander Kouzmin, Uriel Rosenthal. Blackwell Publishing Ltd., 9600 Garsington Rd, Oxford, OX4 2ZG, United Kingdom; customerservices@blackwellpublishing.com; http://www.blackwellpublishing.com. Refereed. Online: Blackwell Synergy; EBSCO Publishing, EBSCO Host; Gale; IngentaConnect; OCLC Online Computer Library Center, Inc.; OhioLINK; SwetsWise Online Content. Reprint: PSC. *Indexed:* ABIn, ApEcolAb, H&SSA, IBSS, IPSA, PSA, PsycInfo, RiskAb, SSA, SociolAb. *Bk. rev.:* Number and length vary. *Aud.:* Ac, Sa.

"Contingency planning, scenario analysis, and crisis management." This journal approaches natural, public health, technological, and conflict-based disasters from the perspective of the corporate or government manager. It attempts to address all time phases, from prevention to recovery.

Journal of Environmental Economics and Management. See Economics section.

The Journal of Environmental Education. See Education/Specific Subjects and Teaching Methods: Environmental Education section.

2345. Journal of Environmental Health. [ISSN: 0022-0892] 1938. 10x/yr. USD 135 domestic; USD 160 foreign. Ed(s): Nelson Fabian. National Environmental Health Association, 720 S Colorado Blvd, S Tower, Ste 970, Denver, CO 80246; staff@neha.org; http://www.neha.org. Illus., adv. Refereed. Circ: 7000 Paid and free. Microform: PQC. Online: EBSCO Publishing, EBSCO Host; Florida Center for Library Automation; Gale; Northern Light Technology, Inc.; OCLC Online Computer Library Center, Inc.; ProQuest K-12 Learning Solutions; ProQuest LLC (Ann Arbor); H.W. Wilson. *Indexed:* AS&TI, C&ISA, CABA, CINAHL, CerAb, ChemAb, DSA, EnvInd, ExcerpMed, FS&TA, GSI, H&SSA, IAA, IndVet, PollutAb, RRTA, S&F, SCI, SSCI, SWRA, VB, WAE&RSA. *Aud.:* Ac, Sa.

A magazine for professionals in the public health field. Topics run from contaminants to communities to compliance. Published by the National Environmental Health Association, the journal is split between peer-reviewed technical articles, columns, and news departments such as "library corner," job listings, and "practical stuff."

2346. Journal of Environmental Systems. [ISSN: 0047-2433] 1971. q. USD 324. Ed(s): Sheldon Reaven. Baywood Publishing Co., Inc., 26 Austin Ave, PO Box 337, Amityville, NY 11701-0337; info@baywood.com; http://www.baywood.com. Illus., adv. Sample. Refereed. *Indexed:* BiolAb, C&ISA, CABA, CerAb, EngInd, EnvAb, EnvInd, ExcerpMed, ForAb, HRIS, HortAb, IAA, IBR, IBZ, IndVet, M&GPA, PRA, PollutAb, RRTA, S&F, SSCI, SUSA, SWRA, VB, WAE&RSA. *Aud.:* Ac, Sa.

Journal of Environmental Systems is a peer-reviewed technical journal covering "environmental, energy, and waste problems." Most authors published here take a heavily statistical approach. Despite the range of topics, the highly technical approach makes this publication inappropriate for a general audience.

The Journal of Wildlife Management. See Zoology section.

2347. *Land Letter: the newsletter for natural resource professionals.* [ISSN: 0890-7625] 1982. fortn. USD 795. Ed(s): Kevin Braun. Environmental and Energy Publishing, LLC, 122 C St, NW, Ste 722, Washington, DC 20001; pubs@eenews.net; http://www.eenews.net. Adv. Circ: 600 Paid. Online: LexisNexis. *Aud.:* Hs, Ga, Ac, Sa.

Land Letter is a weekly news service covering natural resources, federal lands, and land management policy, including endangered species, water rights, and mining. From the Bureau of Land Management to the Forest Service, *Land Letter* does for natural resources what its sister publications *Greenwire* and *E&E Daily* do for environmental policy and Congress.

2348. *Linkages Update.* Former titles: *Linkages; Earth Negotiations Bulletin; Earth Summit Bulletin.* 1992. irreg. Free. Ed(s): Langston James "Kimo" Goree, IV. International Institute for Sustainable Development (I I S D), 161 Portage Ave E, 6th Fl, Winnipeg, MB R3B 0Y4, Canada; info@iisd.ca; http://www.iisd.org. *Aud.:* Hs, Ga, Ac, Sa.

Linkages Update is the authoritative semimonthly web and e-mail news record for information on global environmental negotiations and treaties, including global warming, sustainability, biological diversity, endangered species, hydroelectric power, forests, fisheries, energy, and more. Published by the well-respected International Institute for Sustainable Development, the publication is staffed by PhD.s, PhD. candidates, and lawyers. Excellent e-mail lists (including one on Africa) and detailed schedules, history, and archival reporting on past negotiations, as well as links to key publications make this *the* place to go for detailed information on what's really going on at international environmental meetings.

2349. *Local Environment: the international journal of justice and sustainability.* [ISSN: 1354-9839] 1996. bi-m. GBP 559 print & online eds. Ed(s): Bob Evans, Julian Agyeman. Routledge, 4 Park Sq, Milton Park, Abingdon, OX14 4RN, United Kingdom; info@routledge.co.uk; http://www.routledge.co.uk. Refereed. Online: EBSCO Publishing, EBSCO Host; Gale; IngentaConnect; OCLC Online Computer Library Center, Inc.; SwetsWise Online Content. Reprint: PSC. *Indexed:* CABA, EnvAb, EnvInd, ForAb, IBR, IBSS, IBZ, IndVet, PollutAb, RRTA, S&F, VB, WAE&RSA. *Aud.:* Ac, Sa.

Local Environment "is a refereed journal which focuses on local environmental, justice and sustainability policy, politics and action." Recent issues include articles on integrated pest management in an urban setting, ecological footprints, and urban sprawl.

2350. *Mother Earth News: the original guide to living wisely.* [ISSN: 0027-1535] 1970. bi-m. USD 14.95 domestic; USD 15.50 Canada; USD 18 elsewhere. Ed(s): Cheryl Long. Ogden Publications, 1503 SW 42nd St, Topeka, KS 66609-1265; http://www.ogdenpubs.com. Illus., index, adv. Sample. Circ: 400000 Paid. Microform: NBI; PQC. Online: EBSCO Publishing, EBSCO Host; Florida Center for Library Automation; Gale; Northern Light Technology, Inc.; OCLC Online Computer Library Center, Inc.; ProQuest K-12 Learning Solutions; ProQuest LLC (Ann Arbor); H.W. Wilson. *Indexed:* ASIP, CPerI, CWI, ConsI, GardL, IHTDI, MASUSE, RGPR. *Aud.:* Hs, Ga.

Mother Earth News provides users with tips on how to live in an environmentally sustainable and self-reliant way. Solar, wind, and wood power feature prominently, as do building projects, gardening, and food preparation. Consider tow hooks for your truck, chickens for your coop, and solar heaters for your hot water to become thrifty and self-sufficient.

2351. *Natural Hazards Observer.* [ISSN: 0193-8355] 1976. bi-m. Free. Ed(s): Greg Guibert. University of Colorado, Institute of Behavioral Science, Program on Environment and Behavior, Natural Hazards Center, 482 UCB, Boulder, CO 80309-0482. Illus. Circ: 400 Paid. *Indexed:* EnvInd. *Aud.:* Ga, Ac, Sa.

Natural Hazards Observer is an indispensable source of information on natural and technological hazards, especially for those interested in human effects, preparation, and response. Published by the largely federally funded Hazards Center at the University of Colorado, the *Observer* provides invited columns on

current issues from floods to terror from insiders in the emergency planning profession. Each issue also includes a "Washington Update," lists of recently awarded grants and contracts, educational opportunities, and annotated bibliographies of web sites and recent publications sorted by subject. Simply designed and well-illustrated with cartoons by Rob Pudim, *Natural Hazards Observer* is a pleasure to read and an outstanding value. It should receive even more well-deserved recognition in the aftermath of Hurricane Katrina. Academic, government, and public libraries, particularly those in hazard-prone or high-threat areas, should rush to get this publication, which is free within the United States.

2352. *Natural Hazards Review.* [ISSN: 1527-6988] 2000. q. USD 274. Ed(s): James E Beavers. American Society of Civil Engineers, 1801 Alexander Bell Dr, Reston, VA 20191-4400; http://www.asce.org. Refereed. *Indexed:* C&ISA, CABA, CerAb, EngInd, ForAb, H&SSA, HRIS, HortAb, IAA, RiskAb, S&F. *Bk. rev.:* Number and length vary. *Aud.:* Ac, Sa.

Natural Hazards Review attempts to integrate physical science, social science, engineering, and policy perspectives on disasters, including floods, earthquakes, wildfires, and others. Published by the American Society of Civil Engineers in association with the Hazards Center at the University of Colorado at Boulder, this journal is peer reviewed and includes book reviews.

2353. *The Natural Resources Journal.* [ISSN: 0028-0739] 1961. q. USD 40 domestic; USD 45 foreign; USD 15 newsstand/cover per issue. Ed(s): G Emlen Hall. University of New Mexico, School of Law, MSC11 6070, 1 University of New Mexico, Albuquerque, NM 87131-0001; lawrev@law.unm.edu; htttp://lawschool.unm.edu. Illus., adv. Refereed. Circ: 2000. Vol. ends: Fall. Microform: WSH; PMC. Online: William S. Hein & Co., Inc.; LexisNexis; OCLC Online Computer Library Center, Inc.; H.W. Wilson. Reprint: WSH. *Indexed:* ABCPolSci, ABS&EES, Agr, BAS, BRI, CABA, CBRI, CLI, EnvAb, EnvInd, ExcerpMed, FPA, ForAb, IBR, IBSS, IBZ, ILP, JEL, LRI, PAIS, PSA, PetrolAb, PollutAb, RRTA, S&F, SSCI, SUSA, SWRA, WAE&RSA. *Bk. rev.:* Number and length vary. *Aud.:* Ac, Sa.

The Natural Resources Journal is a key environmental law and policy publication targeted to specialists in the field. Articles include complete citations of relevant laws and legal cases. Wide-ranging topics include water resources, endangered species, farm policy, and cross-border disputes.

OnEarth. See Alternatives/General section.

Ranger Rick. See Children section.

2354. *Remote Sensing of Environment.* [ISSN: 0034-4257] 1969. 24x/yr. EUR 2778. Ed(s): Marvin E. Bauer. Elsevier Inc., 360 Park Ave S, New York, NY 10010-1710; usinfo-f@elsevier.com; http://www.elsevier.com. Illus., index, adv. Sample. Refereed. Vol. ends: Mar/Dec. *Indexed:* Agr, ApEcolAb, BioEngAb, BiolAb, C&ISA, CABA, CerAb, CompR, EngInd, EnvAb, EnvInd, ExcerpMed, FPA, ForAb, HortAb, IAA, M&GPA, OceAb, PetrolAb, PhotoAb, PollutAb, RRTA, S&F, SCI, SSCI, SWRA, WAE&RSA. *Aud.:* Ac, Sa.

This journal focuses on analyses of environmental phenomena based on satellite imagery, air photos, and other means of gathering data from afar. Remote sensing is now used in a surprising number of scientific fields, and among those cited by the editors are agriculture, ecology, forestry, geography, geology, hydrology, land use, meteorology, and oceanography. Other areas of interest include image processing techniques, modeling, analysis, and imaging and measuring systems. A selection of articles in a recent issue examines tropical forests, mosquito breeding areas, and digital elevation models.

2355. *Restoration Ecology.* [ISSN: 1061-2971] 1993. q. GBP 363 print & online eds. Ed(s): Richard Hobbs. Blackwell Publishing, Inc., Commerce Place, 350 Main St, Malden, MA 02148; customerservices@ blackwellpublishing.com; http://www.blackwellpublishing.com. Adv. Refereed. Microform: PQC. Online: Blackwell Synergy; EBSCO Publishing, EBSCO Host; Gale; IngentaConnect; OCLC Online

Computer Library Center, Inc.; OhioLINK; SwetsWise Online Content. *Indexed:* ApEcolAb, BiolAb, CABA, EnvAb, EnvInd, FPA, ForAb, GardL, HortAb, IndVet, RRTA, S&F, SCI, SWRA, VB, WAE&RSA, ZooRec. *Bk. rev.:* Number and length vary. *Aud.:* Ac, Sa.

Restoration Ecology is a peer-reviewed publication of the Society for Ecological Restoration International. It includes papers about "assisting the recovery of an ecosystem that has been degraded, damaged, or destroyed." The journal publishes research and applied articles from various disciplinary perspectives on land, freshwater, and seawater settings of many scales.

2356. Wildlife Society Bulletin: perspectives on wildlife conservation and sustainable use. [ISSN: 0091-7648] 1973. 5x/yr. USD 295. Ed(s): Warren Ballard. The Wildlife Society, 5410 Grosvenor Ln, Ste 200, Bethesda, MD 20814; tws@wildlife.org; http://www.wildlife.org. Illus., index, adv. Circ: 6400. Vol. ends: Winter. *Indexed:* Agr, ApEcolAb, BiolAb, CABA, DSA, ExcerpMed, FPA, ForAb, GSI, HortAb, IndVet, PollutAb, RRTA, S&F, SCI, SSCI, SWRA, VB, WAE&RSA, ZooRec. *Bk. rev.:* Number and length vary. *Aud.:* Ac, Sa.

Wildlife Society Bulletin is a peer-reviewed research publication for wildlife managers and scholars. The instructions for authors suggest quite a broad range of appropriate topics for articles. These include wildlife and plant management policies and management and research techniques, contemporary issues and special topics, wildlife law enforcement, education (of wildlife management students, hunters, and other stakeholders), and the economics, sociology, psychology, administration, and philosophy of wildlife management. Both game and nongame species are addressed. In addition to reviews of the literature and book and software reviews, this scholarly journal also includes opinion pieces and news.

2357. World Watch: working for a sustainable future. [ISSN: 0896-0615] 1988. bi-m. USD 27 in North America. Worldwatch Institute, 1776 Massachusetts Ave, NW, Washington, DC 20036; wwpub@worldwatch.org; http://www.worldwatch.org. Illus., index. Circ: 24000. Vol. ends: Nov/Dec. Microform: PQC. Online: EBSCO Publishing, EBSCO Host; Florida Center for Library Automation; Gale; Northern Light Technology, Inc.; OCLC Online Computer Library Center, Inc.; ProQuest K-12 Learning Solutions; ProQuest LLC (Ann Arbor); H.W. Wilson. *Indexed:* ABS&EES, BiolDig, EnvAb, EnvInd, GSI, M&GPA, PAIS, RiskAb, SSCI, SWA. *Bk. rev.:* Occasional. *Aud.:* Hs, Ga, Ac.

World Watch is a magazine published by the Worldwatch Institute, an organization dedicated to finding practical solutions to achieve an "environmentally sustainable and socially just society." Each issue includes feature articles (e.g., carbon offsets, renewable energy certificates, and palm oil cultivation) and departments including letters and life cycle studies.

■ ETHNIC STUDIES

Andrea Imre, Electronic Resources Librarian, Morris Library 6632, Southern Illinois University Carbondale, Carbondale, IL 62901-6632; aimre@lib.siu.edu; FAX: 618-453-3452

Introduction

Ethnicity is a double-edged sword. Ethnicity is responsible for global conflicts throughout the world, and there are barriers to overcome in the acceptance of the various cultural, racial, religious, or linguistic characteristics of ethnic peoples. On the other hand, the identification of certain ideals, beliefs, and traditions among the peoples of ethnic groups results in a diverse and rich cultural environment around the globe. It is this combination of elements, both negative and positive, that requires us to deal with an ever-changing palette, and libraries need to focus on happenings in society that affect us all.

Ethnic-interest journals investigate ethnicity, migration, immigration, multiculturalism, cultural heritage, race relations, and the history of ethnic peoples. They promote diversity and the understanding of different cultures, raise awareness about the cultural heritage of various ethnic groups, investigate the histories of ethnic peoples, and examine the social, economic, and political backgrounds of ethnic conflicts. The journals in this section range from student

interest and weekly trade magazines to highly prestigious scholarly journals. While some journals are geared toward specific ethnic groups, others appeal to a wider audience and are recommended for all types of libraries. Ethnic scholarly journals are often interdisciplinary, and may focus on history, literature, languages, sociology, economy, political science, geology, anthropology, or geography.

Taking the nature of one's clientele into consideration plays a major role when selecting ethnic interest journals. It is easily one of the most vital factors we deal with today, and one that should rightly command our attention.

Basic Periodicals

Ems, Hs: *MultiCultural Review;* Ga: *African- American Yearbook, Annual Editions: Race & Ethnic Relations;* Ac: *Ethnic and Racial Studies, Journal of Intercultural Studies.*

Basic Abstracts and Indexes

America History and Life, Historical Abstracts, Social Sciences Index, Sociological Abstracts, SocINDEX.

Abafazi. See Gender Studies section.

2358. Afghan Communicator: voice of the young generation. irreg. USD 24 in US & Canada; USD 28 elsewhere. Afghan Communicator, PO Box 1159, New York, NY 10011-1159; YoungAfghans@hotmail.com; http://www.angelfire.com/in/AfghanCommunicator/. *Bk. rev.:* Number and length vary. *Aud.:* Ga.

This independent magazine published by and for the young generation of Afghans focuses on education, advocacy, youth leadership, art, and culture. It aims to provide unbiased coverage of political and social issues, reports on important cultural events for the Afghan community, and includes announcements of upcoming events. Recommended for general audiences interested in the contemporary Afghan scene.

2359. African-American Career World. 2001. s-a. USD 18 (Free to qualified personnel). Ed(s): James Schneider. Equal Opportunity Publications, Inc., 445 Broad Hollow Rd, Ste 425, Melville, NY 11747; info@eop.com; http://www.eop.com. Adv. *Aud.:* Ga, Ac.

Published by Equal Opportunities Publications, Inc., this semi-annual "career guidance and recruitment" magazine is intended for African American students and paraprofessionals. Each issue includes columns, departments, and feature articles describing internships, employment opportunities, and career strategies for African Americans. Job advertisements by companies that are actively recruiting graduates in engineering and information technology are also included. Highly recommended for audiences interested in diversity recruitment and employment in technical fields.

African American Review. See African American section.

2360. African American Yearbook: a resource and referral guide for and about African Americans. [ISSN: 1540-1324] 2001. a. USD 29.95 per vol. Ed(s): John Zavala, Angela E. Zavala. T I Y M Publishing Co., Inc., 6718 Whittier Ave, Ste 130, McLean, VA 22101; tiym@tiym.com; http://www.tiym.com/. Adv. Circ: 50000 Controlled. *Aud.:* Ga, Ac.

Now in its sixth year, this yearbook is an important resource guide for and about African Americans. It includes educational and career opportunities for African Americans along with the description, requirements, and listings of minority scholarships, fellowships, and grants offered by various organizations and universities. There are listings of minority business opportunities, African American publications, organizations, radio and TV stations, churches, historically black colleges and universities, and African American conventions and events. Interviews with and listings of prominent African Americans, plus lots of data, including census data, about the African American community are also provided. Highly recommended for all types of libraries.

African Studies Review. See Africa section.

2361. *African Vibes.* [ISSN: 1932-1198] 2006. bi-m. USD 24.95. African Vibes, general@africanvibes.com; http://www.africanvibes.com/. Adv. *Aud.:* Ga.

From fashion to sports, from physiological problems to arts and artistry, this magazine is a potpourri of everything, and aims to "enlighten the world about the African." Many articles focus on Africans in the United States and provide advice on such matters as medical, life, and disability insurance; homeownership; personal relationships; and health matters. Interviews with famous African personalities are also included. Recommended for public libraries.

2362. *Afro-Americans in New York Life and History.* [ISSN: 0364-2437] 1977. s-a. USD 8. Ed(s): Monroe Fordham. Afro-American Historical Association of the Niagara Frontier, PO Box 63, Buffalo, NY 14207; fordham@adelphia.net. Illus. Refereed. Circ: 700 Paid. Vol. ends: Jul. Online: Gale; ProQuest LLC (Ann Arbor). *Indexed:* AmH&L, ENW, HistAb, IIBP, RILM. *Bk. rev.:* Number and length vary. *Aud.:* Ga, Ac.

This interdisciplinary journal publishes analytical, historical, and descriptive articles pertaining to African Americans in New York State. The journal also identifies and publicizes archival sources and research materials to aid researchers of African American history. Extensive book reviews dealing with the life and history of people of African descent are also included. Recommended for academic and public libraries.

2363. *Afro-Hispanic Review.* [ISSN: 0278-8969] 1982. s-a. USD 60 (Individuals, USD 30). Ed(s): William Luis. Vanderbilt University, Department of Spanish and Portuguese, VU Station B 351617, Nashville, TN 37235-1617; spanish-portuguese@vanderbilt.edu. Illus., adv. Sample. Refereed. Circ: 500. Online: Chadwyck-Healey Inc.; EBSCO Publishing, EBSCO Host; Northern Light Technology, Inc.; ProQuest LLC (Ann Arbor). *Indexed:* AmHI, HAPI, IIBP, MLA-IB, RILM. *Bk. rev.:* Number and length vary. *Aud.:* Ga, Ac.

Now published by the Department of Spanish and Portuguese at Vanderbilt University, this bilingual journal includes articles, interviews, testimonies, artwork, poems, and book reviews. The peer-reviewed articles reflect the richness of Afro-Hispanic literature and culture and their influence in the Hispanic world. Recommended for academic and research libraries.

2364. *Alo Hayati.* 2004. q. USD 28; USD 8.95 newsstand/cover per issue. Ed(s): Michael D Lloyd. Unique Image, Inc, 19365 Business Center Dr, Unit #1, Northridge, CA 91324; http://www.uniqueimageinc.com/. Adv. Circ: 62595. *Aud.:* Ga.

This magazine provides a cultural look at happenings in the Middle East and among its community in the United States. More at home in public than academic libraries, it opens up a world of Middle Eastern fashion, culture, art, and entertainment. Published quarterly, it looks at life through community living and intercultural exchanges, while also showcasing certain tourist spots in and around the Middle East. Recommended for public libraries.

Amerasia Journal. See Asian American section.

2365. *Anagram: art and literature of Asian Americans.* s-a. Anagram, 3505 N. Charles St, Baltimore, MD 21218; anagram@jhunix.hcf.jhu.edu; http://www.jhu.edu/~anagram/index.html. *Aud.:* Ac, Sa.

Published by students at the Johns Hopkins University, this literary magazine includes poetry, short fiction, nonfiction, art, and photography by Asian Americans. The journal presents a diverse view of the Asian American cultural landscape. Recommended for academic and research libraries.

2366. *Annual Editions: Race & Ethnic Relations.* [ISSN: 1075-5195] 1991. a. USD 20.31 per vol. Ed(s): John A Kromkowski. McGraw-Hill - Contemporary Learning Series, 2460 Kerper Blvd, Dubuque, IA 52001; customer.service@mcgraw-hill.com; http://www.dushkin.com. Illus. Refereed. *Aud.:* Ga, Ac.

This collection of public press articles promotes the understanding of racial and ethnic issues in the United States. Each issue includes around 50 public press articles grouped into units focusing on race, ethnicity, indigenous ethnic groups, immigration, American legal traditions, and cultural pluralism, among others.

An annotated list of online resources supporting the articles in each issue is also included. Highly recommended for academic and research libraries, as well as for general audiences interested in the subject matter.

2367. *Arab - American Affairs.* Formerly (until 2003): *The News Circle;* Which incorporated (197?-1984): *Mideast Business Exchange.* [ISSN: 1940-1086] 1972. bi-m. USD 100 (Individuals, USD 35; USD 3.95 newsstand/cover). Ed(s): Joseph R. Haiek. News Circle Publishing House, 1250 W Glenoaks Blvd, Unit E, Box 3684, Glendale, CA 91201-0684; newscirc@pacbell.net; http://www.arab-american-affairs.net. Illus., adv. Circ: 5000 Paid and controlled. *Bk. rev.:* Number and length vary. *Aud.:* Ga.

This independent magazine looks at issues from politics to business and culture that affect the Arab American community. Current news, views, profiles, and opinions are also part of the journal, which tries to forge closer ties between the two worlds. Also featured is an Arab American calendar that details social and other events within the community. Recommended for public and academic libraries.

2368. *Arab American Almanac.* [ISSN: 0742-9576] 1974. irreg. Ed(s): Joseph R Haiek. News Circle Publishing House, 1250 W Glenoaks Blvd, Unit E, Box 3684, Glendale, CA 91201-0684; newscirc@pacbell.net; http://www.arab-american-affairs.net. Illus., adv. Circ: 10000. *Bk. rev.:* Number and length vary. *Aud.:* Ga, Ac.

The *Almanac* describes the dealings and state of the Arab American community, and it is a comprehensive reference tool featuring this ethnic group. In addition to material on literature, history, and religion, it provides information on organizations, the media, religious institutions and other selected topics. It is a source for all cultural, political, economic, religious, and social issues within the Arab American community. Recommended for all types of libraries.

2369. *Arab - American Business: the magazine for a culture of success.* 2001. m. USD 29.95 domestic; USD 39.95 foreign. Ed(s): Nidal Ibrahim. A A Business LLC, PO Box 753, Huntington Beach, CA 92648. Adv. *Aud.:* Ga, Ac.

This is a monthly business and trade journal designed to highlight success stories in the Arab American world. It keeps readers abreast of economic and political happenings while also profiling individual careers and certain noteworthy news items that connect the two cultures. Recommended for academic and public libraries.

Asian American Movement Ezine. See Asian American section.

Asian American Policy Review. See Asian American section.

2370. *Asian Ethnicity.* [ISSN: 1463-1369] 2000. 3x/yr. GBP 234 print & online eds. Ed(s): Colin Mackerras. Routledge, 4 Park Sq, Milton Park, Abingdon, OX14 4RN, United Kingdom; info@routledge.co.uk; http://www.routledge.com. Refereed. Online: EBSCO Publishing, EBSCO Host; Gale; IngentaConnect; OCLC Online Computer Library Center, Inc.; SwetsWise Online Content. Reprint: PSC. *Indexed:* IBR, IBSS, IBZ, IPSA, IndIslam, PSA, SSA, SociolAb. *Bk. rev.:* Number and length vary. *Aud.:* Ga, Ac.

This cross-disciplinary journal addresses topics concerned with Asian ethnicity and identity. The peer-reviewed articles deal with ethnic minority groups and ethnic relations in Asia "where questions of ethnicity now loom largest." China, India, and Indonesia, being the most populous countries in the region, are more prominently discussed. Each issue includes several book reviews. Highly recommended for academic and research libraries.

2371. *Asian Fortune.* [ISSN: 1074-8822] 1993. m. USD 30. Asian Fortune, PO Box 578, Haymarket, VA 20168. Adv. Circ: 20000. *Aud.:* Ga.

Serving the Asian communities in the District of Columbia, Maryland, and Virginia, this monthly newspaper devotes its pages to news, weather, events, and classifieds. Education; arts and entertainment; business; and local, national, and international news are some of the areas covered. Recommended for public libraries.

2372. The Asian Reporter. [ISSN: 1094-9453] 1991. w. USD 200 (Individuals, USD 40). Asian Reporter Publications, Inc., 922 N. Killingsworth St., Ste 1-A, Portland, OR 97217-2220; : asianreporter@juno.com; http://www.asianreporter.com. Adv. *Indexed:* ENW. *Aud.:* Ga.

A weekly newspaper featuring articles pertinent to the Asian communities of the Pacific Northwest. The articles chart a varied path, dealing with news items from Asia and opinion pieces about and from the community. A sampling of the job market in the area is also provided. In addition, there is a community calendar with listings of workshops, seminars, auctions, and fundraisers. An ongoing events section keeps the community informed about arts, culture, and entertainment in the area. Recommended for public libraries.

2373. AsianWeek: the voice of Asian America. [ISSN: 0195-2056] 1979. w. USD 29. Ed(s): Ted Fang. Pan Asia Venture Capital Corporation, 809 Sacramento St, San Francisco, CA 94108; advertising@asianweek.com; http://www.pavc.com. Adv. Circ: 45716. Online: Northern Light Technology, Inc.; ProQuest LLC (Ann Arbor). *Indexed:* ENW. *Bk. rev.:* Number and length vary. *Aud.:* Ga.

This weekly consumer newspaper's target audience is the Asian American community in the San Francisco Bay area. The paper includes local, national, and international news coverage, opinion pieces, profiles of and interviews with successful Asian Americans, arts and entertainment listings, classifieds, and more. Recommended for public and academic libraries.

Canadian Ethnic Studies. See Canada section.

2374. Ethnic and Racial Studies. [ISSN: 0141-9870] 1978. bi-m. GBP 375 print & online eds. Ed(s): Martin Bulmer. Routledge, 4 Park Square, Milton Park, Abingdon, OX14 4RN, United Kingdom; info@routledge.co.uk; http://www.routledge.co.uk. Illus., index, adv. Sample. Refereed. Circ: 1550. Vol. ends: Oct. Online: EBSCO Publishing, EBSCO Host; Gale; IngentaConnect; OCLC Online Computer Library Center, Inc.; SwetsWise Online Content. Reprint: PSC. *Indexed:* ABCPolSci, AICP, ASSIA, AbAn, AmH&L, BAS, BRI, CBRI, CJA, CWI, EI, FR, HistAb, IBR, IBSS, IBZ, IIBP, IPSA, L&LBA, PAIS, PRA, PSA, PsycInfo, RI-1, SSA, SSCI, SWA, SWR&A, SociolAb, V&AA. *Bk. rev.:* 11-30, 500-1,000 words. *Aud.:* Ac.

This prominent bimonthly journal highlights a variety of interdisciplinary viewpoints on topics related to race, ethnicity, and nationalism. Peer-reviewed research articles written by a diverse group of international scholars focus on theory and empirical evidence and discuss sociological, economic, and political issues. The journal also includes review articles and book reviews. Highly recommended for academic and research libraries.

Ethnic Groups. See *Identities: global studies in culture and power.*

2375. Ethnic Studies Review. Formed by the merger of (1978-1996): *Explorations in Ethnic Studies;* (1981-1996): *Explorations in Sights and Sounds.* [ISSN: 1555-1881] 1996. 2x/yr. Free to members. Ed(s): Otis L Scott. National Association for Ethnic Studies (NAES), College of Arts and Sciences, Arizona State University, Glendale, AZ 85306-4908; naesi@asu.edu; http://www.ethnicstudies.org. Refereed. *Indexed:* ABS&EES, BAS, Chicano, ENW. *Bk. rev.:* Number and length vary. *Aud.:* Hs, Ac.

Published by the National Association for Ethnic Studies, this journal explores race, ethnicity, and interrelations from a variety of cultures around the world, seeking to promote activities and scholarship that contribute to the development and understanding of ethnic studies. Articles in each issue center around such themes as "Challenges of Identity Formation" and "Fair Access." The journal also includes research notes, essays, and book reviews. Recommended for academic libraries and scholarly research centers.

2376. Ethnohistory. [ISSN: 0014-1801] 1954. q. USD 119 (Individuals, USD 45). Ed(s): Neil L Whitehead. Duke University Press, 905 W Main St, Ste 18 B, Durham, NC 27701; subscriptions@dukepress.edu; http://www.dukeupress.edu. Illus., adv. Refereed. Circ: 1350 Paid. Vol. ends: Winter. Microform: PQC. Online: Chadwyck-Healey Inc.; EBSCO Publishing, EBSCO Host; Gale; HighWire Press; JSTOR (Web-based

Journal Archive); Northern Light Technology, Inc.; OCLC Online Computer Library Center, Inc.; OhioLINK; Project MUSE; ProQuest K-12 Learning Solutions; ProQuest LLC (Ann Arbor); SwetsWise Online Content. Reprint: PSC. *Indexed:* ABS&EES, AICP, AbAn, AmH&L, AmHI, AnthLit, ArtHuCI, BAS, BrArAb, FR, HistAb, HumInd, IBSS, IIBP, IndIslam, PRA, PSA, RI-1, SSA, SSCI, SociolAb. *Bk. rev.:* 10-15, 800-1,200 words. *Aud.:* Ac.

This scholarly journal looks at "indigenous, diasporic, and minority peoples" through the many centuries, charting the flow of cultures and the history associated therein. While most articles take anthropological and historical approaches, geology, geography, archaeology, literature, and sociology are also well represented. Special issues focus around such themes as "Lake Rudolf (Turkana) as Colonial Icon in East Africa," "Outside Gods: History Making in the Pacific," and "Native Peoples and Tourism." Each issue includes review essays and book reviews. Highly recommended for academic and research libraries.

Ethnology. See Anthropology section.

2377. Identities: global studies in culture and power. Formerly (until 1994): *Ethnic Groups;* Incorporates: *Afro-American Studies.* [ISSN: 1070-289X] 1976. q. GBP 261 print & online eds. Ed(s): Thomas M Wilson, Jonathan D Hill. Routledge, 4 Park Square, Milton Park, Abingdon, OX14 4RN, United Kingdom; journals@routledge.com; http://www.routledge.co.uk. Illus., adv. Sample. Refereed. Online: EBSCO Publishing, EBSCO Host; Gale; IngentaConnect; OCLC Online Computer Library Center, Inc.; SwetsWise Online Content. Reprint: PSC. *Indexed:* ABS&EES, ASSIA, AbAn, AmH&L, AnthLit, HistAb, IBR, IBSS, IBZ, IIBP, MLA-IB, PAIS, PSA, RILM, SSA, SSCI, SWA, SociolAb. *Bk. rev.:* 4-5, length varies. *Aud.:* Ac.

This journal looks at issues of racial, national, ethnic, and gender identities from an international perspective. Political, social, cultural, and economic boundaries are also explored. The journal deals with global population movements and their effects on our cultural diversity and interactions. Book and media reviews are included. Recommended for academic libraries.

2378. International Journal of Anglo-Indian Studies. [ISSN: 1327-1652] 1996. irreg. Centre of Anglo-Indian Studies, 1 Kurt Place, Noble Park, VIC 3174, Australia; agilbert@alphalink.com.au. *Bk. rev.:* Number and length vary. *Aud.:* Ga.

This journal probes questions of identity and culture from among those segments of the population who consider themselves to be of mixed European-Indian descent, which is the make-up of the Anglo-Indian. It explores the Anglo-Indians' dissemination into the larger global entity, along with questions of race, ethnicity, and identity. Articles focus on sociological, psychological, and historical perspectives. Recommended for academic and research-oriented libraries.

International Migration Review. See Population Studies section.

International Review of African American Art. See Art/Museum Publications section.

Journal of African American History. See African American section.

2379. Journal of American Ethnic History. [ISSN: 0278-5927] 1981. q. USD 190 print or online ed. (Individuals, USD 45). Ed(s): John J. Bukowczyk. University of Illinois Press, 1325 S Oak St, Champaign, IL 61820-6903; journals@uillinois.edu; http://www.press.uillinois.edu. Illus., index, adv. Refereed. Circ: 1100. Vol. ends: Summer (No. 4). Microform: PQC. Online: Chadwyck-Healey Inc.; EBSCO Publishing, EBSCO Host; Florida Center for Library Automation; Gale; Northern Light Technology, Inc.; OCLC Online Computer Library Center, Inc.; OhioLINK; ProQuest K-12 Learning Solutions; ProQuest LLC (Ann Arbor); SwetsWise Online Content. Reprint: PSC. *Indexed:* ABS&EES, AbAn, AmH&L, AmHI, ArtHuCI, BAS, Chicano, HistAb, HumInd, IBR, IBZ, IIBP, IMFL, PSA, RI-1, RILM, SSA, SSCI, SociolAb. *Bk. rev.:* Number and length vary. *Aud.:* Ac, Sa.

The official publication of the Immigration History Society, this journal deals with various aspects of immigration and ethnic history in the United States. A large number of articles focus on the history, acculturation, and social interaction of ethnic groups at specific locations in the United States, while others examine national immigration policies. In addition, each issue contains review essays and book reviews. Highly recommended for academic and research libraries.

Journal of Asian American Studies. See Asian American section.

2380. *Journal of Black Psychology.* [ISSN: 0095-7984] 1974. q. GBP 329. Ed(s): Shawn O Utsey. Sage Publications, Inc., 2455 Teller Rd, Thousand Oaks, CA 91320; info@sagepub.com; http://www.sagepub.com. Illus., adv. Refereed. Circ: 2600. Microform: PQC. Online: CSA; Chadwyck-Healey Inc.; EBSCO Publishing, EBSCO Host; HighWire Press; OCLC Online Computer Library Center, Inc.; OhioLINK; SAGE Publications, Inc., SAGE Journals Online; SwetsWise Online Content. Reprint: PSC. *Indexed:* ASSIA, AbAn, CINAHL, CJA, ERIC, HEA, HRA, IBSS, IIBP, IMFL, L&LBA, PRA, PsycInfo, RiskAb, SSA, SSCI, SociolAb, V&AA. *Bk. rev.:* Number and length vary. *Aud.:* Ac, Sa.

This journal presents scholarly research and theory on the experiences and behavior of black populations along with the recent advances and developments in the field. Articles, research briefs, essays, commentaries, and book reviews written by distinguished scholars are included. African-centered psychology, personality, education, health and social behavior, diversity, and family issues are some of the areas explored in detail, providing greater understanding of black populations. Highly recommended for academic and research libraries.

2381. *Journal of Black Studies.* [ISSN: 0021-9347] 1970. bi-m. GBP 487. Ed(s): Molefi Kete Asante. Sage Publications, Inc., 2455 Teller Rd, Thousand Oaks, CA 91320; info@sagepub.com; http://www.sagepub.com. Illus., index, adv. Refereed. Circ: 900 Paid. Vol. ends: Jul. Microform: PQC. Online: Chadwyck-Healey Inc.; EBSCO Publishing, EBSCO Host; Florida Center for Library Automation; Gale; HighWire Press; JSTOR (Web-based Journal Archive); OCLC Online Computer Library Center, Inc.; SAGE Publications, Inc., SAGE Journals Online; SwetsWise Online Content. Reprint: PSC. *Indexed:* ASSIA, AgeL, AmH&L, ArtHuCI, BRI, BrArAb, CBRI, CJA, HEA, HRA, HistAb, IBR, IBSS, IIBP, IMFL, IPSA, L&LBA, PAIS, PRA, PSA, PsycInfo, RILM, RiskAb, SFSA, SSA, SSCI, SWR&A, SociolAb, V&AA. *Bk. rev.:* Number and length vary. *Aud.:* Ac, Sa.

Published six times a year, this journal identifies key issues central to the black experience through research articles on Afrocentricity, economics, social issues, literature, politics, and culture, among others. The status and importance of Black Studies in higher education are chronicled through an exhaustive selection of articles. The sociological and economic impact of race and ethnicity and its intercultural exchanges are all extensively discussed, and book reviews present a cross-section of the available literature. Recommended for academic and research libraries.

2382. *Journal of Ethnic and Migration Studies.* Former titles (until 1998): *New Community;* (until 1971): *Community.* [ISSN: 1369-183X] 8x/yr. GBP 763 print & online eds. Ed(s): Russell King. Routledge, 4 Park Sq, Milton Park, Abingdon, OX14 4RN, United Kingdom; info@routledge.co.uk; http://www.routledge.co.uk. Online: EBSCO Publishing, EBSCO Host; Gale; IngentaConnect; OCLC Online Computer Library Center, Inc.; SwetsWise Online Content. Reprint: PSC. *Indexed:* ASSIA, AmHI, BrEdI, BrHumI, CJA, IBSS, IPSA, PSA, RILM, SSA, SSCI, SWA, SociolAb. *Bk. rev.:* 750-1000 words, signed. *Aud.:* Ac.

This peer-reviewed journal looks at all forms of migration and includes articles on "ethnic conflicts, discrimination, racism, nationalism, citizenship, and policies of integration" from an international perspective. A large number of articles present research about ethnic peoples in Europe. Special issues focus on such topics as "Migration and Health in Southern Africa," "Music and Migration," and "Media and Minorities in Multicultural Europe." Each issue includes signed book reviews. Highly recommended for research and academic libraries.

2383. *Journal of Immigrant and Minority Health.* Formerly (until Jan. 2006): *Journal of Immigrant Health.* [ISSN: 1557-1912] 1999. q. EUR 349 print & online eds. Ed(s): Sana Loue. Springer New York LLC, 233 Spring St, New York, NY 10013-1578; service-ny@springer.com; http://www.springer.com/. Adv. Refereed. Online: EBSCO Publishing, EBSCO Host; Gale; IngentaConnect; OCLC Online Computer Library Center, Inc.; OhioLINK; Ovid Technologies, Inc.; ProQuest LLC (Ann Arbor); Springer LINK; SwetsWise Online Content. Reprint: PSC. *Indexed:* ABIn, AgeL, CINAHL, ExcerpMed, H&SSA, PsycInfo, RiskAb. *Bk. rev.:* Number and length vary. *Aud.:* Ac, Sa.

This peer-reviewed journal explores immigrant health from an international perspective through articles that have their basis in the behavioral sciences. Health and medicine in their practical applications and emotional connotations for immigrants are extensively discussed. Law and ethics as well as sociological and historical viewpoints are also presented. Recommended for academic, research, and medical libraries.

2384. *Journal of Intercultural Studies.* Supersedes (in 1980): *Ethnic Studies.* [ISSN: 0725-6868] 1977. q. GBP 380 print & online eds. Ed(s): Michael V. Ure, Jan van Bommel. Routledge, 4 Park Square, Milton Park, Abingdon, OX14 4RN, United Kingdom; info@routledge.co.uk; http://www.routledge.co.uk. Illus., adv. Sample. Refereed. Online: EBSCO Publishing, EBSCO Host; Florida Center for Library Automation; Gale; IngentaConnect; OCLC Online Computer Library Center, Inc.; RMIT Publishing; SwetsWise Online Content. Reprint: PSC. *Indexed:* AICP, BrEdI, IBSS, IndIslam, L&LBA, SSA, SWA, SociolAb. *Bk. rev.:* 15, 400 words. *Aud.:* Ga, Ac.

This international interdisciplinary journal takes a global look at multiculturalism, ethnicity, emerging cultural formations, cultural identity, and intercultural negotiations. Peer-reviewed, theoretically informed articles from the fields of cultural studies, sociology, gender studies, political science, cultural geography, urban studies, and race and ethnic studies are provided. In addition, there are review essays and books reviews. Highly recommended for academic libraries.

Latin Beat Magazine. See Latino Studies section.

Latin Style: the Latin arts and entertainment magazine. See Latino Studies section.

Latina Style. See Latino Studies section.

Latino Leaders. See Latino Studies section.

Lilith. See Cultural Studies section.

MELUS. See Literature/General section.

Meridians. See Gender Studies section.

2385. *Migration News.* [ISSN: 1081-9908] 1994. m. USD 30 domestic; USD 50 foreign. Ed(s): Philip Martin. University of California at Davis, Department of Agricultural Economics, One Shields Ave, Davis, CA 95616; migrant@primal.ucdavis.edu; http://migration.ucdavis.edu. Illus. Circ: 2500. *Aud.:* Hs, Ga.

Focusing on immigration news of the preceding quarter, this newsletter features articles on international immigration and integration developments. Current policies of various governments and their respective repercussions for migrant families and workers are presented, along with reports on immigration. Topics are grouped into four international geographic regions—North America, Europe, Asia, and Other. Recommended for academic and public libraries.

2386. *MultiCultural Review: dedicated to a better understanding of ethnic, racial and religious diversity.* Incorporates (1986-1992): *Journal of Multicultural Librarianship.* [ISSN: 1058-9236] 1992. q. USD 65 (Individuals, USD 29.95; USD 85 foreign). Ed(s): Lyn Miller-Lachmann.

Goldman Group, Inc., 4125 Gunn Hwy, Ste B1, Tampa, FL 33618; todd@ggpubs.com; http://www.ggpubs.com. Illus., index, adv. Sample. Circ: 5000 Paid. *Indexed:* ABIn, ABS&EES, BRD, BRI, CBRI, Chicano, EduInd, IBR, IBZ, IndIslam, MRD, PAIS. *Bk. rev.:* 100, 200-500 words, signed. *Aud.:* Hs, Ac.

Intended for educators and librarians, this quarterly journal is an excellent reviewing tool covering a wide range of materials on multicultural topics. Signed reviews of books, audio materials, videocassettes, and computer software are grouped by subject and include recommendations of intended audience by grade level. Each issue contains five or six peer-reviewed feature articles on multiculturalism, ethnography, multicultural pedagogy, or librarianship. The "Editor's Shelf" looks at new editions, reissues, translations, new volumes in a series, and online reference sources important to the field. A "Chalkboard" section provides curriculum materials and suggestions for the classroom. Highly recommended for public and academic libraries as well as for teachers at the elementary and secondary levels.

The North Star (Poughkeepsie). See African American section.

Race, Gender & Class. See Interdisciplinary Studies section.

■ EUROPE

General/Newspapers

See also Latin America and Spain; and Slavic Studies sections.

Sebastian Hierl, Librarian for Western Europe, Germanic Emphasis, Harvard College Library, Collection Development, Widener Room 140, Cambridge, MA 02138; 617-495-2426, Fax: 617-496-8704; eshierl@fas.harvard.edu

Introduction

This section provides a list of core titles from Western Europe that cover current events, economic and business trends, history, politics, and culture, with a focus on literature and the arts. Following the general division of labor within North American academic institutions, titles from Central and Eastern Europe are described separately in the Slavic Studies section. For linguistic reasons, titles from Spain and Portugal are covered in the Latin America and Spain section.

The publications in this section have been selected for their relevance to the broad field of European Studies and to provide insight into European current events. The titles are aimed toward educated readers who want to keep abreast of developments in Europe, as covered by the major publications in each country. This includes popular magazines that reveal the tastes and concerns of the general public, as well as more demanding and specialized titles that are clearly designed for an academic readership. The scholarly journals in this section do not, however, provide a core list of peer-reviewed, scholarly journals across all fields of study for all Western European Studies. Lists of key scholarly journals by subject are provided in the specific subject sections elsewhere in this volume, such as Literature, History, and Political Science.

The broad and interdisciplinary scope of this section requires selectivity. The magazines, journals, and newspapers listed here have been included based upon previous editions of *Magazines for Libraries* and upon recommendations by colleagues. In many cases, there are references to publications listed in other sections containing similar European titles, such as Newspapers and International Magazines.

Basic Periodicals

Akzente, Central European History, L'Espresso, L'Express, Journal of European Studies, Kursbuch, London Magazine, Merkur, La Nouvelle Revue Francaise, Scandinavian Review, Der Spiegel, Les Temps Modernes, Text und Kritik, Yale French Studies.

Basic Abstracts and Indexes

Annual Bibliography of English Language Literature, Arts and Humanities Citation Index, Bibliography of the History of Art, British Humanities Index, Current Contents, Francis, Humanities Index, IBZ, MLA International Bibliography, PAIS, RILM Abstracts of Music Literature, Zeitungs-Index.

General

2387. *A E I O U.* irreg. Bundesministerium fuer Bildung, Wissenschaft und Kultur, Minoritenplatz 5, Vienna, 1014, Austria; ministerium@bmbwk.gv.at; http://www.bmbwk.gv.at. *Aud.:* Ga.

In German and English. *AEIOU* is more a web portal than an electronic journal, with much information on Austrian cultural events. Supported by the Austrian Ministry of Education, Science and Culture, *AEIOU* is an online "cultural window" to Austria. The site provides access to so-called "albums" that are created by the ministry or various other national cultural institutes. For example, the *Institut fur Musikwissenschaft* in Graz produces the music album, which contains information on instruments, composers, genres, styles, and periods. Other albums cover Sigmund Freud and video clips of historic and cultural events. There is also an encyclopedia of Austria with about 14,000 entries on Austrian history, geography, politics, economics, people, and the arts. The links to all major cultural institutions in Austria are helpful for staying abreast of the latest cultural events, but there is no online summary or newsletter. URL: www.aeiou.at.

2388. *De Academische Boekengids.* Supersedes (in 2000): *Amsterdamse Boekengids.* [ISSN: 1567-7842] 1995. q. EUR 29.50. Ed(s): Bart Funnekotter, Inge Klinkers. Amsterdam University Press, Prinsengracht 747-751, Amsterdam, 1017 JX, Netherlands; info@aup.nl; http://www.aup.nl. Illus., adv. Refereed. *Bk. rev.:* Number and length vary. *Aud.:* Ac.

In Dutch. *De Academische Boekengids* is a scholarly journal that contains essays and reviews of contemporary publications in all subject areas by leading academics and critics. Published by Amsterdam University Press six times a year, the *Academische Boekengids* is produced by and freely distributed to researchers at the universities of Amsterdam, Groningen, Leiden, and Utrecht. Non-affiliates may subscribe to the print for a limited fee or refer to the web site at www.academischeboekengids.nl, which provides free access to the full text from 2000 on, with a delay of four weeks for the latest issues. Fully searchable, the site permits easy browsing and quick access to articles. Covering the whole spectrum of academic publishing, *De Academische Boekengids* is recommended for those wanting to stay abreast of noteworthy publications and to follow the scholarly debate in the Netherlands.

2389. *Airone.* [ISSN: 1124-8343] 1981. m. Ed(s): Nicoletta Salvatori. Editoriale Giorgio Mondadori SpA, Via Tucidide 56, Torre 3, Milan, 20134, Italy; info@cairocommunication.it; http://www.cairocommunication.it. Illus., adv. Circ: 100000. *Aud.:* Hs, Ga, Ac.

In Italian. *Airone* (Italian for "heron") is similar to *National Geographic* and *GEO.* Covering natural history, the environment, and civilization at large, *Airone* usually is comprised of six lengthy, in-depth articles and various shorter pieces. Like *National Geographic, Airone* derives its appeal from the combination of breathtaking photography with stories of adventure and travel. The tendency of the photographs to overshadow the text make *Airone* a wonderful tool for beginners who wish to improve their knowledge of Italian while remaining in awe of the wonders of our world. Recommended for large public libraries.

2390. *Akzente: Zeitschrift fuer Literatur.* [ISSN: 0002-3957] 1954. bi-m. EUR 46.20 domestic; EUR 50 foreign; EUR 7.90 newsstand/cover. Ed(s): Michael Krueger. Carl Hanser Verlag GmbH & Co. KG, Kolbergerstr 22, Munich, 81679, Germany; info@hanser.de; http://www.hanser.de. Illus., index, adv. Sample. Circ: 3300 Paid and controlled. *Indexed:* AmHI, ArtHuCI, IBR, IBZ, MLA-IB, SSCI. *Aud.:* Ac.

In German. *Akzente* is a literary magazine steeped in tradition. Originally published as a poetry magazine, it now focuses on contemporary literary theory and criticism, literature, poetry, and culture in general. The magazine contains no illustrations and presupposes an intensive interest in literature or literary training. Topics range from essays on specific works or authors to larger subjects, such as the notion of beauty or the treatment of a literary movement or country. Contributors are generally authors and academics who focus on literature. *Akzente* used to be distributed more widely, but it has received strong competition from newspapers such as the *Frankfurter Allgemeine Zeitung* and *Die Zeit,* whose "Feuilleton" sections have taken over the role played by literary magazines. Nevertheless, *Akzente* is highly recommended for academic libraries that support German Studies and comparative literature programs, as well as for large public libraries.

2391. Annales (Paris): histoire, sciences sociales. Former titles (until 1946): *Annales d'Histoire Sociale;* (until 1945): *Melanges d'Histoire Sociale;* (until 1942): *Annales d'Histoire Sociale;* (until 1939): *Annales d'Histoire Economique et Sociale.* [ISSN: 0395-2649] 1929. bi-m. EUR 81 domestic; EUR 104 foreign; EUR 100 domestic. Armand Colin, 21 Rue du Montparnasse, Paris, 75283 Cedex 06, France; infos@armand-colin.com; http://www.armand-colin.com. Illus., adv. Sample. Refereed. Circ: 5000. Reprint: PSC; SCH. *Indexed:* AmH&L, ArtHuCI, BrArAb, FR, HistAb, IBR, IBSS, IBZ, IPSA, NumL, PAIS, PSA, RILM, SSA, SSCI, SociolAb. *Bk. rev.:* 15, length varies. *Aud.:* Ac.

In French. *Annales* was created by Lucien Febvre and Marc Bloch in Strasbourg in 1929. It was revolutionary for its time and was one of the most influential historical journals of the twentieth century. Targeted at an international audience and written in a colloquial style previously unheard of, *Annales* rejected the traditional approach of analyzing the history of politics, government, and military campaigns as official history and, instead, broadened its scope of investigation to a deeper analysis of social and economic forces. Articles are mostly in French but include English contributions. Information on the editorial board and a summary of individual issues are available at www.editions.ehess.fr/revues/annales-histoire-sciences-sociales. *Annales* is also included in www.persee.fr, a French research portal similar to JSTOR that permits full-text access to back issues of scholarly journals. *Annales* revolutionized the way history was written, and it remains indispensable to any research library.

2392. Belfagor: rassegna di varia umanita. [ISSN: 0005-8351] 1946. bi-m. EUR 49 domestic; EUR 86 foreign. Ed(s): Carlo F Russo. Casa Editrice Leo S. Olschki, Viuzzo del Pozzetto 8, Florence, 50126, Italy; celso@olschki.it; http://www.olschki.it. Adv. Circ: 3500. *Indexed:* AmH&L, ArtHuCI, HistAb, IBR, IBZ, MLA-IB, RILM, SSCI. *Bk. rev.:* Number and length vary. *Aud.:* Ac.

In Italian. Founded in 1946 by Luigi Russo, literary critic and director of the Scuola Normale Superiore of Pisa, *Belfagor'*s motto is to pursue "seriousness of endeavour and unbiased critical orientation." *Belfagor* publishes contemporary essays and reviews, as well as important historical materials from past critics, on all issues pertaining to history, culture, politics, and the arts. Following the motto, the scope of inquiry is interdisciplinary and international, as are the contributors. The web site at www.olschki.it/riviste/belfagor.htm is mostly informational, but it does provide tables of contents for issues from 1997 on. Recommended for research libraries that support Italian Studies.

2393. Le Canard Enchaine: journal satirique paraissant le mercredi. [ISSN: 0008-5405] 1915. w. EUR 54.90 domestic; EUR 76.20 foreign; EUR 1.20 newsstand/cover per issue. Ed(s): Erik Emptaz, Claude Angeli. Editions Marechal, 173 rue Saint-Honore, Paris, Cedex 1 75051, France. Illus. Circ: 600000. Microform: PQC. *Bk. rev.:* Number and length vary. *Aud.:* Ga, Ac.

In French. Published since 1915, *Le Canard Enchaine* is France's premier satirical magazine and its oldest. Covering national and international politics, news, and society in general, it established a reputation of satirically uncovering corruption by politicians and other public figures in business, sports, and the media. In order to maintain its independence, *Le Canard* (literally "duck," but also the colloquial term for "newspaper" in French) does not contain any advertisements. The web site is informational only, but provides the cover pages of recent issues, as well as of special "dossiers." According to the description,

the site was created only to provide an official web presence to discourage the number of pirate sites and hoaxes claiming to be the real *Le Canard* online. An important part of French culture, *Le Canard* is recommended for large research and public libraries.

2394. Central European History. [ISSN: 0008-9389] 1968. q. GBP 106 print & online eds. Ed(s): Catherine Epstein, Kenneth Ledford. Cambridge University Press, The Edinburgh Bldg, Shaftesbury Rd, Cambridge, CB2 2RU, United Kingdom; information@cambridge.org. Illus., index, adv. Refereed. *Indexed:* ABS&EES, AmH&L, AmHI, ArtHuCI, BRI, CBRI, HistAb, HumInd, IBR, IBSS, IBZ, MASUSE, RILM, SSCI. *Bk. rev.:* 15, length varies. *Aud.:* Ac.

In English. This highly regarded journal is published for the Conference Group for Central European History of the American Historical Association since 1968. International, scholarly, and refereed, it examines the social, cultural, and military history of German-speaking Europe from the medieval era to the present. Includes book and film reviews. Recommended for research libraries.

2395. Cicero: Magazin fuer politische Kultur. 2004. m. EUR 75; EUR 7 newsstand/cover. Ed(s): Wolfram Weimer. Ringier Publishing GmbH, Berliner Str 89, Potsdam, 14467, Germany; http://www.ringier.de. Adv. Circ: 84053 Paid and controlled. *Aud.:* Ga, Ac.

In German. *Cicero,* named after the Roman statesman, lawyer, political theorist, and philosopher, Marcus Tullius Cicero, is a German political and cultural magazine modeled after *The New Yorker* and *The Atlantic Monthly.* Since its launch in 2004, *Cicero* has established itself next to magazines such as *Der Spiegel, Focus,* and *Stern* by focusing on contributions by well-known national and international political figures, academics, and authors. With sections that cover international politics, national politics, the world economy, and mostly German culture, this journal emphasizes political news, presented on glossy paper and with ample illustrations. Though more commercial than *The New Yorker* and *The Atlantic Monthly, Cicero* is recommended to research and large public libraries in conjunction with *Der Spiegel* to cover German political and cultural news.

2396. Contemporary French Civilization. [ISSN: 0147-9156] 1976. s-a. USD 60 (Individuals, USD 30). Ed(s): Lawrence R Schehr. University of Illinois at Urbana-Champaign, Department of French, c/o Professor Lawrence R. Schehr, 2090 FLB, Urbana, IL 61801. Illus., adv. Refereed. Circ: 1100. *Indexed:* AmH&L, AmHI, ArtHuCI, FLI, FR, HistAb, IPSA, PSA, RILM, SSA, SociolAb. *Bk. rev.:* Number and length vary. *Aud.:* Ac.

Primarily in French, but includes some English. *Contemporary French Civilization: a journal devoted to all aspects of civilization and cultural studies in France and the Francophone world* is edited by Lawrence Schehr at the University of Illinois. As the subtitle indicates, this refereed journal is particularly inclusive and covers all French-speaking cultures throughout the world. It publishes research articles, interviews of famous personalities, book reviews, and scholarly, annotated bibliographies. Recommended for all libraries that support research in French Studies.

The Contemporary Review. See News and Opinion section.

2397. Critique: revue generale des publications francaises et etrangeres. [ISSN: 0011-1600] 1946. m. Ed(s): Philippe Roger. Critique, 7 rue Bernard Palissy, Paris, 75006, France. Illus., index, adv. *Indexed:* AmHI, ArtHuCI, DAAI, FR, HistAb, IBR, IBSS, IBZ, IPB, L&LBA, MLA-IB, PSA, RILM, SSA, SSCI, SociolAb. *Bk. rev.:* 5-8, length varies. *Aud.:* Ac.

In French. Published by Editions de Minuit since 1946, *Critique* is an eminent French journal that covers new publications on the arts, history, religion, literature, philosophy, and society. A French equivalent to the *Times Literary Supplement, Critique* was founded by Georges Bataille; the journal is now under the editorial leadership of Philippe Roger, and the editorial board includes leading French intellectuals. An essential publication for research libraries and recommended for large public libraries.

2398. *Le Debat: histoire, politique, societe.* [ISSN: 0246-2346] 1980. 5x/yr. EUR 62.50 domestic; EUR 66.50 foreign. Ed(s): Marcel Gauchet. Editions Gallimard, 15 Rue Sebastien-Bottin, Paris, 75328 Cedex 07, France; catalogue@gallimard.fr; http://www.gallimard.fr. Illus. Sample. Circ: 10000. *Indexed:* AmH&L, FR, HistAb, IBSS, IPSA, PAIS, RILM. *Aud.:* Ac.

In French. This bimonthly journal, published by the eminent publishing house Gallimard, was created by historian Pierre Nora in 1980 with the intention to provide for intellectual debate what the *Nouvelle Revue Francaise* did for literature; that is, to rally brilliant minds around one publication and generate a renewal of French critical thinking on major issues facing the contemporary world. With this rather lofty goal, it covers topics ranging from discussions of political challenges to Western civilization and democracies, to religious and social challenges created by immigration and globalization, to environmental challenges and entropy, to the role and influence of the media in contemporary society, and more. Not wanting to compete with the *Nouvelle Revue Francaise*, another Gallimard publication, this journal has largely ignored literary topics. Providing insight into contemporary French intellectual debate, *Le Debat* is recommended for research libraries supporting French Studies.

Deutschland. See International Magazines section.

2399. *Dutch Crossing: a journal of low countries studies.* [ISSN: 0309-6564] 1977. s-a. GBP 25 (Individuals, GBP 16). Association of the Low Countries Studies in Great Britain and Ireland, Department of Dutch Studies, University of Hull, Hull, HU6 7RX, United Kingdom; s.drop@dutch.hull.ac.uk. Illus., index. Sample. *Indexed:* L&LBA, LT&LA, MLA-IB, PSA, SociolAb. *Bk. rev.:* 12, length varies. *Aud.:* Ac.

In English. This scholarly, multidisciplinary, peer-reviewed journal is the official publication of the Association for Low Countries Studies in Great Britain and Ireland. *Dutch Crossing* covers the Dutch language, literature, history, politics, and art, as well as the media, culture, and society of the Netherlands and Flanders. Particular emphasis is given to the "relations between the Low Countries and the English-speaking world in all periods from the Middle Ages to the present day." Issues include scholarly articles, research reports, translations of literary works, and book reviews. All contributions are in English. The web site describes the editorial board and the scope of the journal, gives tables of contents for recent issues, and provides contact and subscription information. *Dutch Crossing* is recommended for libraries that support research in European Studies and the Low Countries.

The Economist. See Economics section.

2400. *Edinburgh Review.* Formerly (until 1985): *New Edinburgh Review.* [ISSN: 0267-6672] 1969. s-a. GBP 37 (Individuals, GBP 18). Ed(s): Alex Thomson. Edinburgh Review, 22A Buccleuch Pl, Edinburgh, United Kingdom; edinburgh.review@ed.ac.uk. Illus., adv. Refereed. Circ: 1500. Microform: PMC; PQC. *Indexed:* AmHI, BEL&L. *Bk. rev.:* Number and length vary. *Aud.:* Ga, Ac.

In English. *Edinburgh Review* was founded in 1802 by Francis Jeffrey as a review of literary criticism. After a break in publication in the mid–twentieth century, it resurfaced as *New Edinburgh Review* and returned to its earlier title, *Edinburgh Review,* in 1985. Over the course of its history, the review has published the works of such influential figures as Macaulay, Scott, Carlyle, Gladstone, and, more recently, James Baldwin, R. D. Laing, Alasdair Gray, and Tom Nairn. Balancing its Scottish focus with international coverage of intellectual debate, previous issues of the review have looked at such topics as "New Poetry by Angela McSeveney and Paul Grattan," "Theatre in Scotland," and "Voices of Africa." Publishing essays, short fiction, poetry, and reviews, *Edinburgh Review* is considered the leading journal of ideas from Scotland.

Elsevier. See International Magazines section.

2401. *Esperienze Letterarie: rivista trimestrale de critica e di cultura.* [ISSN: 0392-3495] 1976. q. EUR 130 (Individuals, EUR 80). Istituti Editoriali e Poligrafici Internazionali, Via Giosue' Carducci, 60, Ghezzano - La Fontina, 56010, Italy; iepi@iepi.it; http://www.iepi.it. *Indexed:* MLA-IB, RILM. *Bk. rev.:* Number and length vary. *Aud.:* Ac.

In Italian. *Esperienze Letterarie* publishes critical essays on Italian culture and literature, including comparative studies, and reviews of recent publications. Its scope is international, as exemplified by the members of the editorial board, and essays are written by scholars of Italian literature from all continents. Each issue typically includes about six essays, reviews of recently published monographs, and a large section of literary surveys, providing summaries of articles published in approximately 40 periodicals, many of them from abroad. Recommended for research libraries that support Italian Studies.

L'Espresso. See International Magazines section.

2402. *Esprit.* [ISSN: 0014-0759] 1932. m. EUR 23 per issue domestic; EUR 25 per issue foreign. Ed(s): Olivier Mongin. Esprit, 212 rue Saint Martin, Paris, 75003, France. Illus., index, adv. Circ: 10000. *Indexed:* AmH&L, ArtHuCI, BAS, FLI, HistAb, IBR, IBSS, IBZ, IPB, IPSA, IndIslam, MLA-IB, NTA, PAIS, PdeR, RI-1, RILM. *Bk. rev.:* 10-12, length varies. *Aud.:* Ac.

In French. *Esprit* was created in 1932 by a group of intellectuals around the philosopher Emmanuel Mounier as an international magazine to promote the exchange of ideas and the dissemination of the Personalist principles. Beyond that, *Esprit* publishes widely on all contemporary philosophical issues and contains articles and commentary by international philosophers, historians, sociologists, economists, writers, literary critics, and journalists. Contributors have included Paul Ricoeur, Andre Bazin, John Rawls, and Charles Taylor. *Esprit* also contains interviews and reviews of the arts and books. The web site at www.esprit.presse.fr provides access to select articles and audio interviews, tables of contents, a blog, and RSS feeds. *Esprit* is recommended for all research libraries.

2403. *L'Esprit Createur: a critical quarterly of French literature.* [ISSN: 0014-0767] 1961. q. USD 80. Ed(s): Maria Minich Brewer, Daniel Brewer. The Johns Hopkins University Press, 2715 N Charles St, Baltimore, MD 21218-4363; myq@press.jhu.edu; http://www.press.jhu.edu. Illus., index, adv. Sample. Refereed. Circ: 950. Microform: PQC. Reprint: PSC. *Indexed:* AmHI, ArtHuCI, BRI, CBRI, FR, IBR, IBZ, IndIslam, MLA-IB, SSCI. *Bk. rev.:* Number and length vary. *Aud.:* Ac.

In English and French. *L'Esprit Createur* is an American publication with a decidedly French flavor. This peer-reviewed scholarly journal contains critical essays that focus on Francophone literature, criticism, and culture, as well book reviews. With a host of eminent past and present contributors, *L'Esprit Createur* ranks among the premier literary and critical publications and is highly recommended for all academic and public research libraries.

2404. *Europe: revue litteraire mensuelle.* [ISSN: 0014-2751] 1923. m. EUR 75 domestic; EUR 105 foreign. Ed(s): Pierre Gamarra. Europe, 4 Rue Marie Rose, Paris, 75014, France; europe.revue@wanadoo.fr. Illus., index, adv. Sample. Circ: 16000. *Indexed:* ArtHuCI, BEL&L, FR, IBR, IBSS, IBZ, MLA-IB, RILM. *Bk. rev.:* 20, length varies. *Aud.:* Ac.

In French. Founded in 1923 under the leadership of Romain Rolland and having counted Louis Aragon, Paul Eluard, and Elsa Triolet as past editors, *Europe* is a literary review with clout. Covering not only European literature but world literature, it is nevertheless a French publication; most authors are Francophone, and French themes are emphasized. Issues are dedicated to particular themes or authors and include articles on a broad range of topics, such as reviews of national literatures (Turkey, Portugal, etc.) and comparative literature. Short stories, poems, and reviews of contemporary theater, poetry, literature, and film are included. The web site provides tables of contents of current and previous issues back to 1999 and a searchable index of issues from 1923 to 2000. *Europe* is highly recommended for all libraries that support French Studies and comparative literature.

2405. *European Commission. European Union. Bulletin.* 10x/yr. European Commission, Office for Official Publications of the European Union, 2 Rue Mercier, Luxembourg, L-2985, Luxembourg. *Aud.:* Ga, Ac.

This bulletin provides regular summaries of the activities of the European Commission and other institutions. It is updated online several times a month, in English and French. The print version appears ten months a year, and it is published in English, French, and German. The *General Report on the Activities of the European Union* supplements the *Bulletin* by providing an annual overview of E.U. activities. The *Bulletin* permits readers to stay up-to-date on such developments as Turkey's accession to the European Union or the Commission's action on climate change. Access to the web site is free, and archives back to 1996 are available. Recommended to specialists who want to stay abreast of E.U. developments.

2406. European History Quarterly. Formerly (until 1984): *European Studies Review.* [ISSN: 0265-6914] 1971. q. GBP 345. Ed(s): Lucy Riall. Sage Publications Ltd., 1 Oliver's Yard, 55 City Rd, London, EC1 1SP, United Kingdom; info@sagepub.co.uk; http://www.sagepub.co.uk. Illus., index, adv. Sample. Refereed. Circ: 1150. Reprint: PSC. *Indexed:* ABS&EES, AmH&L, AmHI, ArtHuCI, BrHumI, CJA, HistAb, HumInd, IBR, IBSS, IBZ, IPSA, NumL, PSA, RI-1, SSA, SSCI, SociolAb. *Bk. rev.:* 8-10, length varies. *Aud.:* Ac.

In English. The *European History Quarterly* covers European history and social and political thought from the late Middle Ages to the present. Contributions are peer-reviewed by an international editorial board and written by prominent scholars from Europe and North America. Issues generally contain about six scholarly contributions and an extensive book review section and periodically feature review articles, as well as historiographical essays. Recommended for all academic libraries.

2407. European Studies: a journal of European culture, history and politics. Formerly (until 2000): *Yearbook of European Studies.* [ISSN: 1568-1858] 1988. irreg. Ed(s): Menno Spiering. Editions Rodopi B.V., Tijnmuiden 7, Amsterdam, 1046 AK, Netherlands; orders-queries@rodopi.nl; http://www.rodopi.nl. Illus. *Aud.:* Ac.

As its subtitle indicates, *European Studies* is an interdisciplinary journal that covers all aspects of academic inquiry regarding European culture, history, and politics. Published at the University of Amsterdam, it replaces the *Yearbook of European Studies* (also known as *Annuaire d'Etudes Europeennes*). Each issue of *European Studies* is organized around a central theme, ranging from comparative studies of the cultural, political, and economic interactions between New Zealand and Europe to studies of historical figures such as Robespierre and Machiavelli. Examples of issues illustrating *European Studies'* interdisciplinary field of inquiry are "Nation Building and Writing Literary History" and "Food, Drink and Identity in Europe." Recommended for research libraries.

2408. Eurozine: the netmagazine. [ISSN: 1684-4637] 1998. irreg. Ed(s): Carl Henrik Fredriksson. eurozine, Rembrandtstr 31/10, Vienna, 1020, Austria. *Aud.:* Ga, Ac.

Published with the support of the European Union, *eurozine* is both a web portal for European cultural journals and a multilingual magazine of its own. Created through the collaboration of European cultural journals, *eurozine* provides access to about 100 periodicals such as *Kritika & Kontext, Mittelweg36, Ord & Bild, Revista Critica, Samtiden, Transit,* and *Wespennest,* to cite just a few. With the aim to open "a new space for transnational debate," *eurozine* is a nonprofit organization with an editorial office in Vienna and an editorial board composed of the editors of participating journals. The site is well organized, and all articles, including some from archival issues, may be searched by keyword and read in html or pdf format. The site includes biographies of contributors and an impressive list of European cultural journals, with links to their web sites. Recommended for staying abreast of the current cultural debate in Europe. URL: www.eurozine.com.

L'Express. See International Magazines section.

2409. Forum Italicum: a journal of Italian studies. [ISSN: 0014-5858] 1967. s-a. plus irreg. Special Issues, 1-2/yr. USD 33 (Individuals, USD 23). Ed(s): Mario B Mignone. State University of New York at Stony Brook, Center for Italian Studies, Stony Brook, NY 11794-3358; mmignone@notes.cc.sunysb.edu; http://www.italianstudies.org. Illus., adv. Sample. Refereed. Circ: 850. *Indexed:* ArtHuCI, IBR, IBZ, MLA-IB. *Bk. rev.:* 15-20, length varies. *Aud.:* Ac.

In Italian or English. *Forum Italicum* is published in the United States and consequently most contributors are North American, although some Italian and European authors are included. It is peer-reviewed, and issues usually contain five or six scholarly articles, notes, and reviews, as well as poetry, prose, and translations. The web site provides information about the distinguished editorial board and subscriptions, and contains a searchable and comprehensive bibliography of all issues, as well as pdf files of book reviews. Highly recommended for libraries that support Italian and European Studies.

2410. Le Francais dans le Monde. Incorporates (1981-1998): *Diagonales;* Which was formerly (until 1987): *Reponses.* [ISSN: 0015-9395] 1961. 6x/yr. EUR 80. Ed(s): Francoise Ploquin. C L E International, 27 Rue de la Glaciere, Paris, 75013, France; cle@vuef.fr; http://www.cle-inter.com/. Illus., adv. Sample. Circ: 12000. *Indexed:* L&LBA, LT&LA, MLA-IB. *Aud.:* Hs, Ga, Ac.

In French. Published by the French Federation of Teachers of French (Federation internationale des professeurs de francais, or FIPF) and under the sponsorship of the French Foreign Ministry, *Le Francais dans le Monde* is designed for teachers of French throughout the world. The bimonthly issues cover current events and French culture and provide texts specifically designed to be read in class, with accompanying exercises. Articles usually focus on new methods of language instruction and ways to overcome teaching challenges. Also included are reviews of web sites and other multimedia tools devoted to teaching French. Readers will also find a number of advertisements for study and travel abroad, teaching aids, and correspondents. The web site is well organized and contains searchable archives with summaries of articles starting in 1994. *Le Francais dans le Monde* is recommended for academic libraries that support French-language instruction, and for school and public libraries.

2411. France: the quarterly magazine for Francophiles. [ISSN: 0958-8213] 1989. m. GBP 39.95; GBP 3.99 newsstand/cover. Ed(s): Nick Wall. Archant Life, Prospect House, Rouen Rd, Norwich, NR1 1RE, United Kingdom; johnny.hustler@archant.co.uk; http://www.archantlife.co.uk. Illus., adv. Sample. Circ: 53896. *Aud.:* Ga.

In English. *France* has the look and feel of a government-sponsored magazine designed to increase tourism, yet it is actually published by a private British publisher. Similar to *France Today* and *France Magazine* (which is published by the *Maison Francaise* in Washington, D.C., and available free of charge), *France* contains articles on French culture, culinary traditions, and places of interest. The magazine's layout favors large color photographs to showcase the best of France, and short articles provide "insider tips" for travelers. The web site provides summaries of articles and tables of contents back to 1990 and includes a number of useful links. In particular, the "FiloFrance" might come in handy for travelers. It includes, for example, a link to market days for every French city. Published for British Francophiles, the web site and magazine are nevertheless helpful for Americans who want to steep themselves in French (tourist) culture.

2412. French Cultural Studies. [ISSN: 0957-1558] 1990. 3x/yr. GBP 304. Ed(s): Brian Rigby. Sage Publications Ltd., 1 Oliver's Yard, 55 City Rd, London, EC1 1SP, United Kingdom; info@sagepub.co.uk; http://www.sagepub.co.uk. Illus., adv. Sample. Reprint: PSC. *Indexed:* AmHI, BrHumI, HumInd, IBSS, MLA-IB, SSA, SociolAb. *Aud.:* Ac.

In English and French. *French Cultural Studies* intends to cover all aspects of modern French culture, language, and society. The emphasis is on cinema, television, the press, visual arts, and popular culture over the more traditional areas of inquiry such as literature, but latter are not excluded. The journal is edited by an international board of prestigious scholars and focuses on the twentieth century, but the scope of the journal extends to the study of the roots of modern culture. *French Cultural Studies* is part of the Sage Publications database; subscribers receive access to the full text from 1990 to the most recent issue. Recommended for research libraries.

2413. French Forum. [ISSN: 0098-9355] 1976. 3x/yr. USD 100 (Individuals, USD 37). Ed(s): Lydie Moudileno, Gerald Prince. University of Nebraska Press, 1111 Lincoln Mall, Lincoln, NE 68588-0630; journals@unlnotes.unl.edu; http://www.nebraskapress.unl.edu. Illus., adv. Sample. Refereed. Circ: 250. *Indexed:* AmHI, ArtHuCI, IBR, IBZ, MLA-IB, RI-1, RILM. *Bk. rev.:* 6, length varies. *Aud.:* Ac.

In English and French. *French Forum* is a peer-reviewed journal of French and Francophone literature, published by the University of Nebraska and produced by the Romance Languages Department at the University of Pennsylvania. Members of the editorial board are for the most part renowned American professors of French Studies and literature, and articles tend to be mostly in English, although French essays and reviews are always included. Along with articles on French literature and literary criticism, *French Forum* provides book reviews of new titles in the field, as well as a list of books received that may be used both as an overview of new publications and for potential reviewers to chose from. Recommended to research libraries.

2414. *French Historical Studies.* [ISSN: 0016-1071] 1958. q. USD 143 (Individuals, USD 40). Ed(s): Ted Margadant, Jo Burr Margadant. Duke University Press, 905 W Main St, Ste 18 B, Durham, NC 27701; subscriptions@dukeupress.edu; http://www.dukeupress.edu. Illus., index, adv. Sample. Refereed. Circ: 1650 Paid and controlled. Online: Chadwyck-Healey Inc.; EBSCO Publishing, EBSCO Host; Gale; HighWire Press; JSTOR (Web-based Journal Archive); Northern Light Technology, Inc.; OCLC Online Computer Library Center, Inc.; OhioLINK; Project MUSE; ProQuest K-12 Learning Solutions; SwetsWise Online Content. Reprint: PSC. *Indexed:* AmH&L, AmHI, ArtHuCI, HistAb, HumInd, IBR, IBZ, MLA-IB, RILM, SSCI. *Aud.:* Ac.

In English and French. Published by Duke University Press for the Society for French Historical Studies, this is a refereed journal that publishes monographic articles, commentaries, research notes, and book review essays, but not book reviews. Issues also include society news, as well as bibliographies of recent publications in French history and abstracts of the articles contained in the issue, in both English and French. Occasional special issues are supervised by guest editors. The web site provides further society news and contains the table of contents for the current issue. Recommended for academic libraries.

2415. *French History.* [ISSN: 0269-1191] 1987. q. EUR 228 print or online ed. Ed(s): Malcolm Crook. Oxford University Press, Great Clarendon St, Oxford, OX2 6DP, United Kingdom; jnl.orders@oup.co.uk; http://www.oxfordjournals.org. Illus., adv. Sample. Refereed. Circ: 750. Reprint: PSC. *Indexed:* AmH&L, HistAb, PSA, SSA, SociolAb. *Bk. rev.:* 20, length varies. *Aud.:* Ac.

In English. Published by the British Society of the Study of French History, this journal provides a "broad perspective on contemporary debates from an international range of scholars, and covers the entire range of French history from the early Middle Ages to the twentieth century." True to this statement, the editorial board is comprised of international, although mostly British, scholars. Issues include research articles and book reviews only. News of the society is treated in a separate publication, the *French Historian*. The web site at Oxford University Press provides tables of contents and full text (for subscribers only) from the first volume (1987) to the present, as well as RSS and table of contents notification via e-mail. Recommended for research libraries.

2416. *French Review.* [ISSN: 0016-111X] 1927. 6x/yr. USD 38 domestic; USD 43 foreign. Ed(s): Clyde Thogmartin, Christopher P Pinet. American Association of Teachers of French, Mailcode 4510, Southern Illinois University, Carbondale, IL 62901-4510; abrate@siu.edu; http://www.frenchteachers.org. Adv. Circ: 12000 Paid. Microform: PMC; PQC. Online: JSTOR (Web-based Journal Archive). *Indexed:* ABIn, AmHI, ArtHuCI, BRI, CBRI, EduInd, FLI, FR, HumInd, IBR, IBZ, L&LBA, LT&LA, MLA-IB, RILM. *Aud.:* Ac.

The *French Review* is the official journal of the American Association of Teachers of French. According to the web site of the association, the journal has the largest circulation of any scholarly publication on French Studies in the world. Each issue contains articles and reviews on French and Francophone literature, cinema, society and culture, linguistics, technology, and pedagogy. The web site is mostly informational but contains tables of contents of issues going back to 1999. Recommended for academic libraries.

2417. *German Life and Letters.* [ISSN: 0016-8777] 1936. q. GBP 311 print & online eds. Ed(s): Dr. Margaret Littler, Gail Finney. Blackwell Publishing Ltd., 9600 Garsington Rd, Oxford, OX4 2ZG, United Kingdom; customerservices@blackwellpublishing.com; http://www.blackwellpublishing.com. Illus., index, adv. Sample. Refereed.

Circ: 800. Online: Blackwell Synergy; EBSCO Publishing, EBSCO Host; Gale; IngentaConnect; OCLC Online Computer Library Center, Inc.; OhioLINK; SwetsWise Online Content. Reprint: PSC. *Indexed:* AmH&L, AmHI, ApEcolAb, ArtHuCI, BrHumI, HistAb, IBR, IBZ, L&LBA, MLA-IB, RI-1, RILM. *Aud.:* Ac.

In English and German. *German Life and Letters* was founded in England in 1936. After shutting down for the war, it emerged again in 1947 as a scholarly, refereed journal intended to cover "all aspects of German Studies since the Middle Ages, including: literature, language, arts and culture, social history and politics." Thematic issues are published irregularly and cover a wide variety of topics, ranging from German cinema to "Exilliteratur." The web site at Blackwell's provides a free online cumulative index from 1936 to 2006; abstracts and full text are available from 1997 on and reserved for institutions with current subscriptions. Recommended for academic libraries that support research in German Studies.

2418. *The German Quarterly.* [ISSN: 0016-8831] 1928. q. USD 75 domestic; USD 85 foreign; USD 25 newsstand/cover per issue. Ed(s): Dagmar Lorenz. American Association of Teachers of German, Inc., 112 Haddontowne Ct, Ste 104, Cherry Hill, NJ 08034; headquarters@aatg.org; http://www.aatg.org. Index, adv. Sample. Refereed. Circ: 3500 Paid. Microform: PMC; PQC. Online: Chadwyck-Healey Inc.; EBSCO Publishing, EBSCO Host; JSTOR (Web-based Journal Archive); OCLC Online Computer Library Center, Inc.; ProQuest K-12 Learning Solutions; ProQuest LLC (Ann Arbor); H.W. Wilson. *Indexed:* ABIn, ABS&EES, AmHI, ArtHuCI, BRI, CBRI, EduInd, HumInd, IBR, IBZ, L&LBA, LT&LA, MLA-IB, RILM, SSCI. *Bk. rev.:* 35, length varies. *Aud.:* Ac.

In German and English. Published by the American Association of Teachers of German, *The German Quarterly* is a refereed journal designed to address issues of teachers of German at all educational levels. It is essentially multidisciplinary and covers German cultural studies in general. Along with scholarly articles on German language, literature, history, and culture, it provides special reports and extensive book reviews of academic publications. The web site at www.aatg.org is designed to address the needs of all teachers of German and contains numerous helpful links, including a link to teaching resources. *The German Quarterly* should be included in any library that supports German Studies.

2419. *German Studies Review.* [ISSN: 0149-7952] 1978. 3x/yr. Individuals, USD 55; USD 17 newsstand/cover. Ed(s): Diethelm Prowe. German Studies Association, c/o Diethelm Prowe, History Department, Northfield, MN 55057-4025; dprowe@carleton.edu; http://www.g-s-a.org. Illus., adv. Sample. Refereed. Circ: 2400. *Indexed:* ABS&EES, AmH&L, AmHI, ArtHuCI, BRI, HistAb, HumInd, IBR, IBSS, IBZ, L&LBA, MLA-IB, PhilInd, RI-1, RILM, SSA, SSCI, SociolAb. *Bk. rev.:* 60. *Aud.:* Ac.

In English or German. Published by the North American German Studies Association, *German Studies Review* is a refereed journal that covers interdisciplinary scholarship in German, Austrian, and Swiss history, literature, cultural studies, political science, and economics. Issues generally contain about six articles and a large section of book reviews of academic publications. Articles and book reviews are in either English or German, but because most members of the association are from the United States, publications are chiefly in English. The web site is mostly informational, but includes tables of contents and abstracts for current issues and tables of contents back to the first issue (1978). Recommended for academic libraries that support research in German Studies.

2420. *The Germanic Review: literature, culture, theory.* [ISSN: 0016-8890] 1925. q. USD 149 (Individuals, USD 63 print & online eds.; USD 36 newsstand/cover). Heldref Publications, 1319 18th St, NW, Washington, DC 20036-1802; subscribe@heldref.org; http://www.heldref.org. Illus., index, adv. Sample. Refereed. Circ: 666 Paid. Vol. ends: Winter. CD-ROM: ProQuest LLC (Ann Arbor). Microform: PQC. Online: Chadwyck-Healey Inc.; EBSCO Publishing, EBSCO Host; Factiva, Inc.; Florida Center for Library Automation; Gale; Northern Light Technology, Inc.; OCLC Online Computer

Library Center, Inc.; ProQuest K-12 Learning Solutions; ProQuest LLC (Ann Arbor); H.W. Wilson. Reprint: PSC. *Indexed:* ABS&EES, AmHI, ArtHuCI, HumInd, IBR, IBZ, L&LBA, MLA-IB, RILM, SSA. *Bk. rev.:* 3-9, length varies. *Aud.:* Ac.

In English and German. *The Germanic Review* is a refereed journal of international scholarship in German Studies. Edited at Columbia University, it contains articles on German literature, literary theory, and culture, as well as reviews of the latest publications in the field. The web page, at Heldref Publications, is informational only, but includes tables of contents for recent issues. Published since 1925, *The Germanic Review* is an important title for libraries that support German Studies.

2421. Germany Info. d. Ed(s): Jose Schulz. Germany Info, 4645 Reservoir Rd NW, Washington, DC 20007. *Aud.:* Ga.

Germany Info is published cooperatively by the German Embassy, the German Information Center, and the Consulates General in the United States. It is an official government publication that aims to introduce U.S. citizens to German culture and history and promote understanding and business between the two countries. It does not contain critical articles or reviews, but provides a host of information about Germany, from the latest news to cultural information, foreign trade regulations, labor law, and other business-related information, as well as the latest scientific news from German research institutions and a number of links to official German government sites. It is a useful site for those wanting to learn more about Germany in general or preparing to spend a year abroad at a German university, as well as those seeking specific business or travel information. URL: www.germany.info/relaunch/index.html.

2422. De Gids. [ISSN: 0016-9730] 1837. m. EUR 7.75 per issue. Uitgeverij Balans, Postbus 2877, Amsterdam, 1000 CW, Netherlands; balans@uitgeverijbalans.nl; http://www.uitgeverijbalans.nl. Index, adv. Circ: 2500. *Indexed:* AmH&L, BEL&L, HistAb, IBR, MLA-IB, RILM. *Bk. rev.:* Number and length vary. *Aud.:* Ac.

In Dutch. *De Gids,* published since 1837, is one of the most renowned Dutch literary and cultural magazines. Issues contain contemporary poetry and fiction, reviews of new publications, and critical essays on all aspects of intellectual debate, but with a focus on literature. Contributions are international in scope, but authors are mostly Dutch-speaking. Tables of contents are available online from 2001 on through the *Bibliografie van de Literaire Tijdschriften in Vlaanderen en Nederland* at the web site of the National Library of the Netherlands. Highly recommended for research libraries that support Dutch Studies.

2423. Giornale della Libreria. Former titles (until 1993): *G D L. Giornale della Libreria;* (until 1987): *Giornale della Libreria;* (until 1920): *Giornale della Libreria, della Tipografia e delle Arti ed Industrie Affini.* [ISSN: 1124-9137] 1888. m. EUR 63 domestic; EUR 110 foreign. Ediser Srl, Via delle Erbe 2, Milan, 20121, Italy; ediser@ediser.it; http://www.ediser.it. Illus., adv. Sample. Circ: 5000. *Aud.:* Ac.

In Italian. The *Giornale della Libreria* is the official publication of the Italian publishers association. As such—and like *Livres Hebdo* and *Buchreport,* which are the respective organs of the French and German publishers associations—the *Giornale della Libreria* provides the latest editorial and commercial news on the national and international publishing worlds. This includes information on new products and trends in the market, statistical and market research information, and articles on particular publishing houses or personalities. In addition, the *Giornale* lists new books, arranged by author, subject, and publisher, and it functions as an Italian *Books in Print.* Recommended for libraries as a collection development and reference tool, and to stay abreast of new developments in Italian publishing.

2424. Giornale Storico della Letteratura Italiana. [ISSN: 0017-0496] 1883. q. Loescher Editore, Via Vittorio Amedeo II, 18, Turin, 10121, Italy; mail@loescher.it; http://www.loescher.it. Illus., index. Reprint: SCH. *Indexed:* ArtHuCI, IBR, IBZ, MLA-IB, RILM. *Bk. rev.:* 20-25, length varies. *Aud.:* Ac.

In Italian. Published since 1883, the *Giornale Storico della Letteratura Italiana* is a highly reputable literary journal that focuses, as the title indicates, on literary history. Issues contain scholarly articles, notes and discussions,

bibliographies, and announcements, as well as a large section of books reviews. The latter, covering the latest publication in the field, constitutes a useful collection development tool. The web site at www.loescher.it provides tables of contents under "Riviste" from 1999 on. This long-standing, important publication should be made available at research libraries that support Italian Studies.

2425. Granta. [ISSN: 0017-3231] 1979. q. GBP 24.95 in British Isles; GBP 32.95 in Europe; USD 39.95 United States. Ed(s): Ian Jack. Granta Publications Ltd., 2-3, Hanover Yard, Noel Rd, London, N1 8BE, United Kingdom; http://www.granta.com. Illus., adv. Circ: 96000. Microform: PQC. *Indexed:* AmHI, HumInd. *Bk. rev.:* Number and length vary. *Aud.:* Ga, Ac.

In English. *Granta* is an eminent literary journal in the English-speaking world. Published at Cambridge University since 1889, it has published such world-famous authors as E. M. Forster, A. A. Milne, Ted Hughes, Sylvia Plath, Richard Ford, Salman Rushdie, Susan Sontag, John Hawkes, Paul Auster, and Milan Kundera. During the 1970s, *Granta* encountered financial difficulties and was relaunched in its current format in 1979 as a magazine of "new writing" aimed at both writers and a wider audience than the original Cambridge publication. Each issue of this second series of *Granta* is organized around a central theme and contains original fiction, poetry, criticism, opinion, essays, and observations. The web site at www.granta.com provides excerpts from the magazine as well as selected full text and tables of contents for all back issues since 1979. Highly recommended for all academic and public libraries.

L'Hebdo. See International Magazines section.

2426. L'Histoire. [ISSN: 0182-2411] 1978. 11x/yr. Societe d'Editions Scientifiques, 74 Av. du Maine, Paris, 75014, France. Illus., adv. Sample. Circ: 76300. *Indexed:* AmH&L, ArtHuCI, HistAb, IBSS, PdeR, SSCI. *Bk. rev.:* 15, length varies. *Aud.:* Hs, Ac.

In French. *L'Histoire* is a glossy, full-color magazine designed to bring history to a mass audience. With a layout similar to that of a regular newsmagazine, it is nevertheless a serious publication. While articles are mandatorily accompanied by large color photographs, maps, and illustrations to attract the reader and facilitate easy reading, they are generally accompanied by footnotes and end with a bibliography. In addition to special reports and research articles, *L'Histoire* contains a section on current events and book reviews. The web site, at www.histoire.presse.fr, is well organized and without advertisements. It includes access to tables of contents of archival issues back to 1978, as well as a subject and author search feature. More than just a commercial publication, although inappropriate for true scholarly research, *L'Histoire* primarily addresses high school and beginning undergraduate students.

2427. Historische Zeitschrift. [ISSN: 0018-2613] 1859. bi-m. EUR 415 domestic (Students, EUR 148). Ed(s): Lothar Gall. Oldenbourg Wissenschaftsverlag GmbH, Rosenheimer Str 145, Munich, 81671, Germany; vertrieb-zs@verlag.oldenbourg.de; http://www.oldenbourg.de. Illus., index, adv. Circ: 2800. Microform: PQC. *Indexed:* AmH&L, ArtHuCI, HistAb, IBR, IBZ, IndIslam, MLA-IB, SSCI. *Bk. rev.:* 80-100, 1-3 pages. *Aud.:* Ac.

In German. Published since 1859, *Historische Zeitschrift* is one of the premier independent, scholarly journals in the field. Published bimonthly, it usually contains three to five articles and provides a large number of book reviews that cover most of the output in the discipline, organized by period and ranging from ancient history to the present. A wonderful tool for scholars who want to stay abreast of new developments in the field, it is also extremely useful for collection development. The web site at Oldenbourg Verlag provides brief information and access to tables of contents of since 1999, as well as an overview of the special publications, the "Beihefte" and "Sonderhefte," that accompany *Historische Zeitschrift.* Among various indexing services that cover this publication, "Magazine Stacks" at the University of Erlangen provides free indexing of all issues. Highly recommended for academic libraries that support research in German and European history.

Iceland Review. See International Magazines section.

2428. *In Britain.* [ISSN: 0019-3143] 1967. bi-m. GBP 23.70 domestic; GBP 26.70 in Europe; USD 33 United States. Ed(s): Andrea Spain. Romsey Publishing Company Ltd. (London), Jubilee House, 2 Jubilee Pl, London, SW3 3TQ, United Kingdom. Adv. Circ: 45000 Controlled. Online: EBSCO Publishing, EBSCO Host. *Indexed:* H&TI. *Aud.:* Ga.

In English. Published by the British Travel Authority, *In Britain* is a glossy, colorful magazine, filled with images designed to induce you to spend your next vacation in the United Kingdom. *In Britain* is not without tradition, having been published since 1930. Its layout, however, has been updated to include large images and short texts, advertising tourism in Britain. The web site at www.inbritain.co.uk was unavailable at the time of this review, but it previously provided summary abstracts for the current issue and links to an online index going back to 1997, as well as several links to further tourist information.

2429. *L'Infini: litterature, philosophie, art, science, politique.* [ISSN: 0754-023X] 1983. q. EUR 53 domestic; EUR 62.50 foreign. Ed(s): Marcelin Pleynet. Editions Gallimard, 15 Rue Sebastien-Bottin, Paris, 75328 Cedex 07, France; catalogue@gallimard.fr; http://www.gallimard.fr. Illus. *Indexed:* ArtHuCI, FLI, FR, IBR, IBZ, MLA-IB, RILM. *Aud.:* Ac.

In French. *L'Infini,* previously *Tel Quel,* joined Gallimard in 1983, under the leadership of Philippe Sollers. What differentiates *L'Infini* from Gallimard's premier literary journal, *La Nouvelle Revue Francaise,* is that *L'Infini* focuses on new, contemporary authors, whereas the more established and venerable *Nouvelle Revue* publishes the great, contemporary masters. Because *L'Infini* also publishes famous authors, the main difference is that it is co-edited by Sollers, one of France's most celebrated living authors. The journal covers all literature, including criticism, modern poetry, interviews, and essays on philosophy, art, science, and politics. *L'Infini* has published or commented on Julia Kristeva, Philippe Roth, Milan Kundera, Vladimir Nabokov, Alain Finkielkraut, Michel Rio, Chantal Thomas, Philippe Djian, and more. An important title for academic libraries that support French literary programs.

2430. *Irish University Review: a journal of Irish studies.* Formerly (until 1970): *University Review.* [ISSN: 0021-1427] 1954. s-a. Ed(s): Anne Fogarty. Irish University Review, Rm. J210, Department of English, University College, Dublin, 4, Ireland. Illus., adv. Refereed. Circ: 1200. Online: Gale. *Indexed:* ArtHuCI, MLA-IB, RILM, SSCI. *Bk. rev.:* 10, length varies. *Aud.:* Ac.

In English. The *Irish University Review: a journal of Irish studies,* established in 1970, is a refereed, scholarly, literary journal. With an emphasis on contemporary Irish literature, it includes literary essays; short fiction; poetry; interviews with authors, poets, and playwrights; and a large section of book reviews. The semi-annual issues are regularly devoted to Irish authors or themes and include a bibliography on the topic treated, while the book reviews permit readers to stay abreast of current Irish literature. Recommended for academic and large public libraries.

2431. *Italica.* [ISSN: 0021-3020] 1924. q. USD 60 (Individuals, USD 45; Students, USD 25). Ed(s): Andrea Ciccarelli. American Association of Teachers of Italian (A A T I), c/o Maria Rosaria Vitti-Alexander, Nazareth College of Rochester, Rochester, NY 14618; mrvittia@naz.edu; http://www.aati-online.org. Adv. Circ: 1500. Microform: PQC. Online: Chadwyck-Healey Inc.; Gale; JSTOR (Web-based Journal Archive). *Indexed:* ArtHuCI, FLI, IBR, IBZ, L&LBA, LT&LA, MLA-IB, RILM. *Bk. rev.:* Number and length vary. *Aud.:* Ac.

In English and Italian. *Italica* is the official journal of the American Association of Teachers of Italian (AATI). *Italica* contains critical studies on all aspects of Italian language, linguistics, literature, and pedagogy, as well as a section of book reviews. Authors are generally from North America, as preference is given to AATI members. The web site of the AATI provides a host of information, but the section on *Italica* is mostly informational, though it includes tables of contents of select issues. Archival issues may be accessed through JSTOR.

2432. *Journal of European Studies (Chalfont Saint Giles).* [ISSN: 0047-2441] 1971. q. GBP 374. Ed(s): John Flower. Sage Publications Ltd., 1 Oliver's Yard, 55 City Rd, London, EC1 1SP, United Kingdom; info@sagepub.co.uk; http://www.sagepub.co.uk. Illus., index, adv.

Sample. Circ: 550. Microform: PQC. Online: Chadwyck-Healey Inc.; EBSCO Publishing, EBSCO Host; Florida Center for Library Automation; Gale; HighWire Press; OCLC Online Computer Library Center, Inc.; ProQuest K-12 Learning Solutions; SAGE Publications, Inc., SAGE Journals Online; SwetsWise Online Content. Reprint: PSC. *Indexed:* ABIn, AmH&L, AmHI, ArtHuCI, BrHumI, FR, HistAb, HumInd, IBR, IBZ, L&LBA, MLA-IB, RI-1, SSA, SSCI, SociolAb. *Bk. rev.:* 30, length varies. *Aud.:* Ac.

In English. The *Journal of European Studies* is a peer-reviewed journal that covers the literature and cultural history of Europe since the Renaissance. Published quarterly since 1971, *JES* is led by an international editorial board, guaranteeing the quality of articles and review essays. Covering a wide interdisciplinary spectrum, *JES* sometimes dedicates issues to specific topics, such as "The Invasion and Occupation of France 1940–44: Intellectual and Cultural Responses." *JES* publishes mostly in English, but occasional contributions in French or German are found. The web site at Sage Publications provides access to the full text of the journal from 1971 on. Recommended for all research libraries.

Knack. See International Magazines section.

2433. *Kursbuch.* [ISSN: 0023-5652] 1965. 4x/yr. EUR 32; EUR 10 newsstand/cover. Zeitverlag Gerd Bucerius GmbH & Co. KG, Buceriusstr, Eingang Speersort 1, Hamburg, 20095, Germany; zeitmagazin@zeit.de; http://www.zeit.de. Illus., adv. Sample. Circ: 12000 Paid and controlled. *Indexed:* IBR, IBZ, PAIS, PhilInd. *Aud.:* Ac.

In German. *Kursbuch* was founded by writer and leading literary critic Hans Magnus Enzensberger at Germany's renowned Suhrkamp Verlag in 1965. One of Germany's premier critical reviews, *Kursbuch* addresses contemporary issues that range from current social problems to literary criticism, the arts, technology, and other subjects that appeal to critical minds, through high-quality literary/philosophical essays, organized around a central theme. Contributions are usually by German writers, although *Kursbuch* regularly includes translations. The web site at the publisher, Rowohlt, provides tables of contents for the latest issues only. Highly recommended for all academic libraries that support German Studies and literature.

2434. *Lettere Italiane.* [ISSN: 0024-1334] 1949. q. EUR 72 domestic; EUR 98 foreign. Ed(s): C Delcorno, Carlo Ossola. Casa Editrice Leo S. Olschki, Viuzzo del Pozzetto 8, Florence, 50126, Italy; celso@olschki.it; http://www.olschki.it. Illus., adv. Sample. Circ: 1200. *Indexed:* ArtHuCI, IBR, IBZ, MLA-IB, RILM. *Bk. rev.:* 4-6, length varies. *Aud.:* Ac.

In Italian. Founded by the Departments of Italian Studies at the Universities of Padua and Torino and published quarterly since 1949, with Vittore Branca as former editor and an internationally recognized editorial board, *Lettere Italiane* is one of Italy's premier scholarly, refereed literary journals. Covering Italian literature from the Middle Ages to the present, issues contain several lengthy articles written by scholars, a news section that covers literary events in the academic world, book reviews, and a list of titles received. *Lettere Italiane* is of such stature that the journal has developed two highly regarded monographic series: the *Biblioteca di Lettere Italiane* and the *Saggi di Lettere Italiane.* The web site is informational only. Indispensable to research libraries that cover Italian literature, *Lettere Italiane* is recommended for all academic libraries that support Italian Studies.

2435. *Lettre International.* [ISSN: 0945-5167] 1988. q. EUR 37 domestic; EUR 41.12 foreign. Ed(s): Dirk Hoefer, Frank Berberich. Lettre International, Elisabethhof, Portal 3b, Erkelenzdamm 59-61, Berlin, 10999, Germany; lettre@lettre.de; http://www.lettre.de. Adv. Circ: 30000. *Aud.:* Ga, Ac.

In German. *Lettre International* may rightfully claim to be a "European Quarterly." In addition to the German edition, *Lettre International* is published in French, Italian, Spanish, Danish, Romanian, and Hungarian, though the editorial offices in each country work independently and each edition of *Lettre International* stands on its own. The tabloid-size German edition, published since 1988, has established itself as a leading cultural magazine that comments on international subjects and events. Containing mostly translations from artists, writers, journalists, poets, and academics from all over the world, *Lettre*

International provides a truly international and interdisciplinary platform for intellectual debate on all subjects of human inquiry, from history to literature and philosophy, to the world economy, popular culture, and the arts. The web site at www.lettre.de provides tables of contents with excerpts for all issues. Recommended for research libraries and large public libraries.

2436. *Lire: le magazine des livres.* [ISSN: 0338-5019] 1975. m. 10/yr. EUR 27.30 domestic; EUR 41.30 in Europe. Ed(s): Pierre Assouline. Groupe Express-Expansion, 29 Rue de Chateaudun, Paris, 75308, France; http://www.groupe-expansion.com. Illus., adv. Sample. Circ: 140000. *Bk. rev.:* Number and length vary. *Aud.:* Ga.

In French. Published by *L'Express, Lire* is a glossy magazine with the look and feel of a general-interest publication, but is devoted entirely to writing and reading. It is an exceptional resource for those wanting to stay abreast of current French literary affairs. Covering new novels, poetry, theater, and also nonfiction, *Lire* includes interviews with authors and extensive excerpts from their new works. The web site complements the magazine with full text of numerous articles and reviews back to 1995. Also functioning as a portal to web sites relevant to contemporary French literature, www.lire.fr provides a free overview of current events and French literary publications. A very useful collection development tool and an important publication for the understanding of contemporary French literature. Recommended for research and academic libraries.

The Literary Review. See Literary Reviews section.

2437. *Litterature.* [ISSN: 0047-4800] 1971. q. EUR 83 (Individuals, EUR 59). Armand Colin, 21 Rue du Montparnasse, Paris, 75283 Cedex 06, France; infos@armand-colin.com; http://www.armand-colin.com. Illus., index. Sample. *Indexed:* ArtHuCI, FR, IBR, IBZ, MLA-IB, RILM. *Bk. rev.:* 4, length varies. *Aud.:* Ac.

In French. *Litterature* is one of France's premier literary reviews. Published quarterly since 1971 by the French literature department at the University of Paris VIII, issues are organized around a central theme and include research articles, complete with thorough bibliographies of the author or topic discussed. Summaries of all articles are also provided in English at the end of each issue. Recommended for all academic libraries that support French Studies.

2438. *London Magazine (London, 1954).* [ISSN: 0024-6085] 1954. bi-m. GBP 28.50; USD 67; GBP 33.50 foreign. Ed(s): Alan Ross. London Magazine Ltd., 30 Thurloe Pl, London, SW7, United Kingdom. Illus., adv. Sample. Circ: 4000. *Indexed:* FLI. *Bk. rev.:* 20, length varies. *Aud.:* Ga, Ac.

In English. First published in 1732, *London Magazine* is probably one of the oldest literary magazines in existence. Revived in a new series in 1954 and now in its third incarnation, the "new" *London Magazine* is sponsored by Arts Council England and edited by Sebastian Barker and Christopher Arkell. It contains essays, critiques, photographs, drawings, poetry, correspondence, short stories, and reviews. The web site at www.thelondonmagazine.net gives information about back issues with tables of contents and a list of helpful links, as well as subscription information and a summary of the eventful history of the magazine. An essential publication for all research and public libraries that support contemporary English literature and poetry.

2439. *Magazine Litteraire.* [ISSN: 0024-9807] 1966. m. Ed(s): Jean Jacques Brochier. Magazine-Expansion, 40 rue des Saints-Peres, Paris, 75007, France; magazine@magazine-litteraire.com; http://www.magazine-litteraire.com. Illus., adv. Circ: 55000. *Indexed:* IBZ, MLA-IB, PdeR, RILM. *Bk. rev.:* 40 or more. *Aud.:* Ga, Ac.

In French. The direct competitor to *Lire* is *Magazine Litteraire*. It focuses on literature, whereas *Lire* covers the French publishing scene as well. It was on the market before *Lire*, but both magazines cover world literature with an emphasis on contemporary French authors. *Magazine Litteraire* is famous for its in-depth coverage of particular authors, national literatures, genres, or themes every month in its "Dossier" section. In addition, it contains news articles on the latest publications and trends, numerous brief reviews of books, and frequent interviews with contemporary authors such as Henri Troyat and Andrei Makine. The web site is well organized and contains full text of numerous articles and reviews, including a selective archive of previous "Dossiers" that cover the whole span of the magazine's history (some go back as far as the 1960s). More specialized than *Lire, Magazine Litteraire* is highly recommended for research libraries and large public libraries as a collection development tool and to provide insight into the contemporary French literary scene.

2440. *Merkur: Deutsche Zeitschrift fuer europaeisches Denken.* [ISSN: 0026-0096] 1947. m. EUR 106 (Students, EUR 72). Ed(s): Kurt Scheel, Karl Heinz Bohrer. Verlag Klett-Cotta, Rotebuehlstr 77, Stuttgart, 70178, Germany; info@klett-cotta.de; http://www.klett-cotta.de. Illus., adv. Sample. Circ: 4200 Paid and controlled. *Indexed:* AmH&L, ArtHuCI, BAS, FR, HistAb, IBR, IBZ, IPSA, MLA-IB, PAIS, PhilInd, RILM, SSCI. *Aud.:* Ac.

In German. Founded in 1947, *Merkur* is one of Germany's premier cultural reviews, offering critical essays on politics, philosophy, history, and literature, as well as any issues that affect modern society, from cloning to the Internet. With contributors such as Ralf Dahrendorf, Nathalie Sarraute, Jan Philipp Reemtsma, Richard Rorty, and Klaus von Dohnanyi—to name just a few—*Merkur* truly deserves its subtitle: "A German Magazine for European Thought." The web site is mostly informational, but it provides indexes for current and previous issues dating back to 1988. *Merkur* started a collaboration with the Goethe-Institut to publish *Goethe Merkur,* which provides translations of important *Merkur* articles and that are distributed at various branches of the Goethe-Institut throughout the world, as well as online. *Merkur* is essential for any library that supports German Studies.

2441. *Monatshefte: fuer deutschsprachige literatur und kultur.* Formerly (until 1946): *Paedagogische Monatshefte - Zeitschrift fuer das Deutschamerikanische Schulwesen.* [ISSN: 0026-9271] 1899. q. USD 170 print & online eds. (Individuals, USD 65 print & online eds.). Ed(s): Hans Adler. University of Wisconsin Press, Journal Division, 1930 Monroe St, 3rd Fl, Madison, WI 53711-2059; journals@uwpress.wisc.edu; http://www.wisc.edu/wisconsinpress/journals. Illus., index, adv. Sample. Circ: 900. Microform: PMC; PQC. Online: EBSCO Publishing, EBSCO Host. Reprint: PSC. *Indexed:* FLI, IBR, IBZ, L&LBA, MLA-IB. *Bk. rev.:* 15, length varies. *Aud.:* Ac.

In English and German. *Monatshefte* has been published continuously since 1899 at the University of Wisconsin, Madison. A peer-reviewed journal devoted to German literature and culture, it covers topics from all periods of German literature and includes book reviews of current scholarship in German Studies. Once a year, it also publishes news on new hires, retirements, and visiting professors, as well as a comprehensive list of German Studies faculty and departments in North America. The web site at http://german.lss.wisc.edu/~monat/index.shtml is mostly informational, but it contains tables of contents, including abstracts of articles, from 1996 on. Recommended for all academic libraries that support German Studies.

2442. *Le Monde Diplomatique.* [ISSN: 0026-9395] 1954. m. Ed(s): Micheline Paunet. Le Monde S.A., 21 bis, rue Claude Bernard, Paris, 75242 Cedex 5, France. Illus., index, adv. Sample. Circ: 165000. Microform: RPI. Online: EBSCO Publishing, EBSCO Host. *Indexed:* AltPI, PAIS, PdeR. *Aud.:* Ga, Ac.

In French. Starting out as a supplement to the French daily newspaper *Le Monde, Le Monde Diplomatique* has successfully established itself as an independent publication, highly regarded in diplomatic and academic circles. As its name indicates, *Le Monde Diplomatique* covers the world's political, diplomatic, and economic news. Although it is in French, its contributors are international, and an English version is also available as a supplement to *The Guardian.* Providing lengthy, in-depth analysis of worldwide diplomatic events, the particular strength of *Le Monde Diplomatique* lies in its extensive coverage of Africa, Asia, and Latin America. Following its "parent" publication, the general editorial standpoint of *Le Monde Diplomatique* may be characterized as center-left. The web site is well organized and provides free access to the full text of select articles. A core title for libraries that support international and political studies.

2443. *Il Mondo: il settimanale economico Italiano.* [ISSN: 0391-6855] 1949. w. 50 issues. EUR 100. Ed(s): Gianni Gambarotta. R C S Periodici, Via San Marco 21, Milan, 20121, Italy; info@periodici.rcs.it; http://www.rcsmediagroup.it/siti/periodici.php. Illus., index, adv. Sample. Circ: 70000 Paid. *Indexed:* PAIS. *Aud.:* Ga, Ac.

In Italian. *Il Mondo* is a business and finance magazine. Covering primarily business, financial markets, and the economy, *Il Mondo* also features articles on politics, society, and science and technology. The web site provides tables of contents of current issues, with full text of selected articles. Access to the archives dating back to 1986 is free but requires registration. Recommended for academic libraries that support research in international business, and for large public libraries.

2444. *Neue Rundschau.* [ISSN: 0028-3347] 1890. q. EUR 34 domestic; EUR 38 in Europe; EUR 45 elsewhere. Ed(s): Martin Bauer. S. Fischer Verlag GmbH, Hedderichstr. 114, Frankfurt am Main, 60596, Germany; verkauf@s-fischer.de; http://www.s-fischer.de. Illus., index, adv. Sample. Circ: 7000. Microform: BHP. *Indexed:* ArtHuCI, IBR, IBZ, MLA-IB, SSCI. *Aud.:* Ac.

In German. Published since 1890 by S. Fischer Verlag, the quarterly *Neue Rundschau* is one of Germany's premier literary and cultural magazines. Each issue is organized around a theme and contains articles about or primary work from prominent German and international intellectuals such as Gunter de Bruyn, Paul Michael Lutzeler, George Steiner, Pierre Bourdieu, John Barth, and J. M. Coetzee, to name just a few. The web site is mostly informational, but it provides tables of contents back to 1998 and brief descriptions of issues back to 1993. Highly recommended for all libraries that support German Studies and comparative literature.

2445. *New German Critique: an interdisciplinary journal of German studies.* [ISSN: 0094-033X] 1973. 3x/yr. USD 123 (Individuals, USD 33). Ed(s): David Bathrick. Duke University Press, 905 W Main St, Ste 18 B, Durham, NC 27701; orders@dukeupress.edu; http://www.dukeupress.edu. Illus., index, adv. Sample. Circ: 2000. Microform: PQC. Online: EBSCO Publishing, EBSCO Host; HighWire Press; JSTOR (Web-based Journal Archive); ProQuest LLC (Ann Arbor). Reprint: PSC. *Indexed:* ABS&EES, AltPI, AmH&L, AmHI, ArtHuCI, FLI, HistAb, IBR, IBZ, LeftInd, MLA-IB, PSA, PhilInd, SSA, SSCI, SociolAb. *Aud.:* Ac.

In English. The *New German Critique,* published by the Department of German Studies at Cornell University, is interdisciplinary in scope and covers all major contemporary topics pertaining to political and social theory, philosophy, literature, film, media, and the arts. Issues are organized around a theme and include up to eight lengthy scholarly articles. The web site is mostly informational, but it provides tables of contents for all back issues as well as special issues. Highly recommended for all research libraries, in particular those that support collections in contemporary criticism, philosophy, German Studies, and comparative literature.

New Statesman. See News and Opinion section.

2446. *Nineteenth Century French Studies.* [ISSN: 0146-7891] 1972. s-a. 2 double issues. USD 90 (Individuals, USD 50). Ed(s): Marshall C Olds. University of Nebraska Press, 1111 Lincoln Mall, Lincoln, NE 68588-0630; journals@unlnotes.unl.edu; http://www.nebraskapress.unl.edu. Illus., index, adv. Refereed. Circ: 350. Microform: PQC. Online: EBSCO Publishing, EBSCO Host; Florida Center for Library Automation; Gale; OCLC Online Computer Library Center, Inc.; OhioLINK; Project MUSE; SwetsWise Online Content; H.W. Wilson. *Indexed:* AmH&L, AmHI, ArtHuCI, FR, HistAb, HumInd, IBR, IBZ, MLA-IB, RILM. *Bk. rev.:* 10, length varies. *Aud.:* Ac.

In English and French. *Nineteenth Century French Studies* is a peer-reviewed scholarly journal that covers all aspects of nineteenth-century French literature and criticism. It examines new trends and includes reviews (in both French and English) of promising research in a variety of disciplines. The web site, at www.unl.edu/ncfs, provides information on submissions, guidelines, and subscriptions, as well as free access to the full archive of abstracts of articles published since the journal's inception. The journal is available in full text online through Project Muse and other large serials aggregators. A premier resource for nineteenth-century French literary scholarship, it is highly recommended for libraries that support research in French literature.

Norseman. See International Magazines section.

2447. *La Nouvelle Revue Francaise.* [ISSN: 0029-4802] 1908. q. EUR 52. Ed(s): Bertrand Visage. Editions Gallimard, 15 Rue Sebastien-Bottin, Paris, 75328 Cedex 07, France; catalogue@gallimard.fr; http://www.gallimard.fr. Illus. Reprint: PSC. *Indexed:* ArtHuCI, BAS, FR, MLA-IB, RILM, SSCI. *Bk. rev.:* 6, length varies. *Aud.:* Ac.

In French. *La Nouvelle Revue Francaise,* or *NRF,* is one of France's most prestigious literary reviews. It was founded in 1908 by a group of writers, among them Eugene Montfort and Andre Gide. The review counts Romain Rolland, Andre Suares, Paul Claudel, Guillaume Apollinaire, Jean Giraudoux, Marcel Proust, and Paul Valery among its early contributors. Currently published by novelist and critic Michel Braudeau, *NRF* has expanded its scope to include international figures and literatures, with the inclusion of authors such as Claudio Magris, Joyce Carol Oates, and Paul Auster. Issues are regularly dedicated to the literatures of other countries, such as Mexico, Cuba, and the United States. Next to internationally renowned authors, it publishes works by lesser-known contemporary writers. Issues include critical essays, poetry, short stories, and reviews of books, art, theatre, and music. The web site at Gallimard provides tables of contents back to 1953. Because of its importance, particularly for early twentieth-century French literary studies, *NRF* is highly recommended for research libraries and large public libraries.

2448. *Nuova Antologia.* Former titles (until 1926): *Nuova Antologia di Lettere, Scienze e Arti;* (until 1899): *Nuova Antologia di Scienze, Lettere e Arti;* (until 1866): *Antologia.* [ISSN: 0029-6147] 1866. q. EUR 52 domestic; EUR 62 foreign. Casa Editrice Edumond Le Monnier, Via Antonio Meucci 2, Grassina, 50015, Italy; lemonnier@lemonnier.it; http://www.lemonnier.it. Adv. Circ: 8000. *Indexed:* AmH&L, FR, HistAb, IBSS, IndIslam, MLA-IB. *Bk. rev.:* Number and length vary. *Aud.:* Ac.

In Italian. *Nuova Antologia* is one of Italy's oldest and most renowned cultural reviews. Founded in 1866, it is interdisciplinary in scope, with essays on politics, philosophy, religion, anthropology, sociology, literature, the arts, and all topics of contemporary intellectual debate. Coverage is international and includes some of Italy's most well-known scholars, writers, and critics, as well as international figures such as Jacques Delors and Jean Starobinski. A prestigious review, *Nuova Antologia* is highly recommended for libraries that support Italian Studies.

2449. *Poetique: revue de theorie et d'analyse litteraires.* [ISSN: 0032-2024] 1970. q. EUR 15 per issue. Editions du Seuil, 27 Rue Jacob, Paris, 75006, France; contact@seuil.com; http://www.seuil.com. Illus., adv. Sample. *Indexed:* ArtHuCI, IBR, IBZ, MLA-IB, RILM. *Aud.:* Ac.

In French. *Poetique* has been published by L'Ecole Normale Superieure since 1970, with the support of the Centre National du Livre. With Helene Cixous, Gerard Genette, Michael Rifaterre, and other famous literary personalities on the editorial board, *Poetique* is one of France's most renowned literary periodicals. Analyzing and commenting on Western literature, drama, and film, each issue of *Poetique* contains six to nine scholarly articles. Essential for libraries that support French Studies and comparative literature.

Le Point. See International Magazines section.

2450. *Il Politico: rivista italiana di scienze politiche.* [ISSN: 0032-325X] 1950. 3x/yr. EUR 51.65 in the European Union; EUR 77.47 elsewhere. Ed(s): Pasquale Scaramozzino. Casa Editrice Dott. A. Giuffre, Via Busto Arsizio, 40, Milan, 20151, Italy; giuffre@giuffre.it; http://www.giuffre.it. Illus., index, adv. Sample. Circ: 1100. *Indexed:* ABCPolSci, AmH&L, BAS, HistAb, IBSS, IPSA, JEL, PAIS, PSA. *Aud.:* Ac.

In Italian and English. Published as a continuation of *Annali di Scienze Politiche* (*Annals of Political Sciences*), *Il Politico* is generally recognized as one of the more important periodicals in the field, with an emphasis on theory. *Il Politico* is renowned for the quality of its articles, written by internationally renowned authors, and for the wealth of notes and reviews. The essays include brief summaries in English. The web site, at www.giuffre.it, is purely informational. Highly recommended for academic and research libraries that support Italian Studies.

Profil. See International Magazines section.

2451. *Quinzaine Litteraire.* [ISSN: 0048-6493] 1966. fortn. Ed(s): Maurice Nadeau. S E L I S la Quinzaine Litteraire, 135 rue Sain-Martin, Paris, Cedex 4 75194, France. Illus., adv. Sample. Circ: 20000. Microform: PQC. *Indexed:* ArtHuCI, IBR, IBZ, MLA-IB, RILM, SSCI. *Bk. rev.:* 20, length varies. *Aud.:* Ga, Ac.

In French. *Quinzaine Litteraire* was first published in 1966 by Maurice Nadeau and quickly established itself as a serious literary journal with a reputation for tackling the most controversial contemporary authors, through reviews, essays, and original prose and poetry. Beyond literature, issues include reviews of contemporary theater and cinema. Contributors to *Quinzaine Litteraire* are among France's most well-known critics and writers. The web site provides access to the latest issue in full text and to a selection of articles from the archive, as well as to a blog. The complete archives are available online through a separate subscription. An essential title for all libraries that support research in French Studies and literature.

2452. *Revue des Deux Mondes: litterature, histoire, arts et sciences.* Former titles (until 1982): *Nouvelle Revue des Deux Mondes;* (until 1972): *Revue des Deux Mondes.* [ISSN: 0750-9278] 1829. m. Ed(s): Bruno de Cessole. Societe de la Revue des Deux Mondes, 9 rue de Lille, Paris, 75007, France. Illus., index, adv. Circ: 15000. Reprint: PSC. *Indexed:* AmH&L, BAS, HAPI, HistAb, IBR, IBSS, IBZ, MLA-IB, RILM. *Bk. rev.:* 2, length varies. *Aud.:* Ga, Ac.

In French. The *Revue des Deux Mondes* was first published in 1829, with the objective to establish a cultural, economic, and political bridge between France and the United States. Truly multidisciplinary, it covers all major subjects that affect our two societies and is one of the primary agents of intercultural dialogue and debate. Providing commentary and analysis on world events from a mostly French perspective, the journal has over the years accumulated an impressive list of contributors, including such figures as Balzac, Baudelaire, Hugo, Fenimore Cooper, Heine, and Tocqueville, to name just a few. The web site is informational only, but provides tables of contents back to 2004. Older archival issues of the *Revue* are available in digital format from the Bibliotheque Nationale's digital library portal, Gallica. The *Revue des Deux Mondes* is one of the few publications that may rightly claim to be a cultural institution. An essential title for large public libraries and research libraries.

2453. *Revue d'Histoire Moderne et Contemporaine.* Former titles (until 1953): *Etudes d'Histoire Moderne et Contemporaine;* (until 1940): *Revue d'Histoire Moderne;* (until 1914): *Revue d'Histoire Moderne et Contemporaine (1899).* [ISSN: 0048-8003] 1899. 4x/yr. EUR 25 per issue. Ed(s): Pierre Milza, Daniel Roche. Editions Belin et Herscher, 8 Rue Ferou, Paris, 75278 , France; http://www.editions-belin.com. Illus., index. Sample. Refereed. Circ: 1800 Paid. Microform: PQC. Online: Chadwyck-Healey Inc. *Indexed:* AmH&L, ArtHuCI, BAS, FR, HistAb, IBR, IBSS, IBZ, IPSA, IndIslam, PdeR, RILM, SSCI. *Bk. rev.:* 17, length varies. *Aud.:* Ac.

In French. The *Revue d'Histoire Moderne et Contemporaine* is the official journal of the Societe d'Histoire Moderne et Contemporaine. First published by Pierre Caron in 1899, it is supported by the Centre National de la Recherche Scientifique and the Centre National du Livre. Each quarterly issue of this eminent, peer-reviewed journal is comprised of six to ten lengthy research articles and detailed book reviews that deal with topics in European history from the sixteenth century to the present. Examples of research topics include a discussion of the work of Eric J. Hobsbawm and the history of homosexualities in Europe. In addition, the *Revue* contains a list of books received, with summaries in both French and English. The web site at www.editions-belin.com is mostly informational, but it provides tables of contents of current issues back to 2001. Recommended for all libraries that support research in European history.

2454. *Revue Historique.* [ISSN: 0035-3264] 1876. q. EUR 86 (Individuals, EUR 74). Ed(s): J F Sirinelli, Claude Gauvard. Presses Universitaires de France, 6 Avenue Reille, Paris, 75685 Cedex 14, France; revues@puf.com; http://www.puf.com. Illus., index. Microform: PQC. Reprint: PSC. *Indexed:* AmH&L, ArtHuCI, BAS, FR, HistAb, IBR, IBSS, IBZ, IPSA, IndIslam, NumL, PdeR, RILM, SSCI. *Bk. rev.:* 60, length varies. *Aud.:* Ac.

In French. Founded in 1876 by Gabriel Monod, the *Revue Historique* is published by the Presses Universitaires de France. It is France's main publication covering general history and it has had defining impact on the development of the discipline itself. Each issue contains several lengthy, scholarly articles; numerous reviews; and a title list of books received. The December issue contains an annual index. The web site at www.puf.com is mostly informational. Highly recommended for research libraries.

2455. *Rivista di Letterature Moderne e Comparate.* [ISSN: 0391-2108] 1946. q. EUR 60. Ed(s): A Pizzorusso, A R Parra. Pacini Editore SpA, Via A. Gherardesca 1, Ospedaletto, 56121, Italy; pacini.editore@pacinieditore.it; http://www.pacinimedicina.it. Illus., adv. Sample. Circ: 520. *Indexed:* ArtHuCI, FR, IBR, IBZ, MLA-IB. *Bk. rev.:* 13, length varies. *Aud.:* Ac.

In Italian, French, and English. Established by Carlo Pellegrini and Vittorio Santoli, the *Rivista di Letterature Moderne e Comparate* covers the whole spectrum of Western literature since the Renaissance. With about six scholarly articles and numerous book reviews in Italian, French, and English, the *Rivista* addresses comparatists in both Europe and North America. The December issue contains an index for the year. The web site at www.pacinieditore.it is purely informational. Recommended for research libraries that support programs in comparative literature.

2456. *Rivista Storica Italiana.* [ISSN: 0035-7073] 1884. 3x/yr. EUR 117.50 (Individuals, EUR 90.50; EUR 198 foreign). Ed(s): Emilio Gabba. Edizioni Scientifiche Italiane SpA, Via Chiatamone 7, Naples, 80121, Italy; info@edizioniesi.it; http://www.edizioniesi.it/. Illus., index, adv. Sample. Circ: 1600. Reprint: SCH. *Indexed:* AmH&L, ArtHuCI, BAS, HistAb, IBR, IBSS, IBZ, IndIslam, MLA-IB, NumL, RILM, SSCI. *Bk. rev.:* 8-15, length varies. *Aud.:* Ac.

In Italian. Founded in 1884 and published by Edizioni Scientifiche Italiane, *Rivista Storica Italiana* may be considered Italy's premier historical journal. The comprehensive *Rivista* covers all periods of world history, albeit with a focus on Italian history. Each issue contains 6–12 lengthy scholarly articles, usually organized around a theme; a section with historiographical essays; numerous reviews of new publications; and a list of books received. This quarterly is essential to any library that supports historical research.

2457. *Samtiden: tidsskrift for politikk, litteratur og samfunnsspoersmaal.* [ISSN: 0036-3928] 1890. bi-m. NOK 410 (Individuals, NOK 378; Students, NOK 328). Ed(s): Cathrine Sandnes. Aschehoug & Co. (W. Nygaard) AS, P O Box 363, Oslo, 0102, Norway; kundeservice@aschehoug.no; http://www.aschehoug.no. Adv. *Indexed:* AmH&L, BEL&L, HistAb, MLA-IB. *Aud.:* Ac.

In Norwegian. *Samtiden* is Norway's oldest and most renowned cultural review. Covering religion, the media, psychology, philosophy, literature, politics, and the arts, *Samtiden* is truly interdisciplinary and publishes articles with an international scope, although most are written by Norwegian scholars, critics, and artists. The web site at www.samtiden.no is well organized and provides easy access to the tables of contents of current issues, as well as issues back to 1996, with selected articles in full text. Select issues are also available through idunn.no. Highly recommended for libraries that support Scandinavian Studies.

2458. *Scandinavian Journal of History.* Incorporates: *Excerpta Historica Nordica.* [ISSN: 0346-8755] 1976. q. GBP 165 print & online eds. Ed(s): Jari Ojala. Routledge, 4 Park Sq, Milton Park, Abingdon, OX14 4RN, United Kingdom; journals@routledge.com; http://www.routledge.co.uk. Illus., adv. Sample. Online: EBSCO Publishing, EBSCO Host; Gale; IngentaConnect; OCLC Online Computer Library Center, Inc.; SwetsWise Online Content. Reprint: PSC. *Indexed:* AmH&L, AmHI, ArtHuCI, CJA, FR, HistAb, IBSS, SSCI. *Aud.:* Ac.

In English. *Scandinavian Journal of History* is a joint publication of the historical associations of Denmark, Finland, Iceland, Norway, and Sweden. The journal contains scholarly articles and review essays that survey themes in recent Scandinavian historical research. Although most authors are Scandinavian, all articles and reviews are published in English. This journal also contains a books-received section at the back of each issue. Informaworld.com provides tables of contents and full text back to 1998 to subscribers. Recommended for research libraries that support Scandinavian Studies.

2459. *Scandinavian Review.* Formerly (until 1975): *American Scandinavian Review.* [ISSN: 0098-857X] 1913. 4x/yr. USD 15 domestic; USD 22 foreign; USD 5 newsstand/cover. Ed(s): Richard Litell. American-Scandinavian Foundation, 58 Park Ave., New York, NY 10016-3007; http://www.amscan.org. Illus., index, adv. Sample. Circ: 8000 Paid and free. Microform: PQC. Online: Chadwyck-Healey Inc.; Northern Light Technology, Inc.; OCLC Online Computer Library Center, Inc.; ProQuest K-12 Learning Solutions; ProQuest LLC (Ann Arbor). *Indexed:* AmH&L, HistAb, MLA-IB, PAIS, RILM. *Bk. rev.:* 2-5, 450 words. *Aud.:* Hs, Ga, Ac.

In English. *Scandinavian Review* is published by the American-Scandinavian Foundation (ASF), whose mission is to "promote an international understanding by means of educational and cultural exchange between the U.S. and Denmark, Finland, Iceland, Norway, and Sweden." The magazine covers all aspects of contemporary life in Scandinavia, with particular emphasis on art and design; industrial development; and commercial, political, economic, and social innovation. Regular features include articles on a particular theme or person, reviews of Nordic books, and a list of contributors. Subscription information and samples of articles can be found at the ASF web site at www.amscan.org. Contributors to the *Scandinavian Review* comprise leading journalists and writers on both sides of the Atlantic. Because this magazine offers information rarely found in American media about the Nordic countries, it is an excellent addition to any collection that supports European Studies.

2460. *Scandinavian Studies (Provo).* [ISSN: 0036-5637] 1911. q. USD 60 (Individuals, USD 50; Students, USD 25). Society for the Advancement of Scandinavian Study, c/o Steven P Sondrup, Ed, Department of Comparative Literature, Provo, UT 84602-6118; http://www.byu.edu/sasslink. Illus., index, adv. Sample. Refereed. Circ: 1100. Microform: PQC. Online: Chadwyck-Healey Inc.; EBSCO Publishing, EBSCO Host; Gale; OCLC Online Computer Library Center, Inc.; ProQuest K-12 Learning Solutions; ProQuest LLC (Ann Arbor); H.W. Wilson. *Indexed:* AmH&L, AmHI, ArtHuCI, BRI, HistAb, HumInd, IBR, IBZ, LRI, MLA-IB, RILM. *Bk. rev.:* 15, lengthy. *Aud.:* Ac.

Text in English. Published by Brigham Young University, *Scandinavian Studies* is a refereed scholarly journal that covers philological and linguistic problems of Scandinavian languages, medieval and modern; Scandinavian literature; and studies in Scandinavian history, society, and culture. Although the journal accepts submissions in Scandinavian languages, all are translated into English, including the reviews. Contributors are mostly North American. Recommended for research libraries that support Scandinavian Studies.

2461. *Schweizer Monatshefte: Zeitschrift fuer Politik, Wirtschaft, Kultur.* [ISSN: 0036-7400] 1921. m. CHF 110 domestic; CHF 131 foreign. Ed(s): Michael Wirth, Robert Nef. Schweizer Monatshefte, Vogelsangstr 52, Zuerich, 8006, Switzerland. Illus., adv. Circ: 3000. Microform: PQC. *Indexed:* AmH&L, BAS, HistAb, IBR, IBZ, IPSA, MLA-IB, PAIS, RILM. *Bk. rev.:* Number and length vary. *Aud.:* Ac.

In German and sometimes French. *Schweizer Monatshefte* is Switzerland's and one of Europe's premier magazines of critical thinking. Covering politics, the economy, and culture, it has been published since 1931 and has successfully resisted the commercial pressures of today. It is well known for its in-depth treatment and analytical approach to contemporary issues that face Western societies. It has published articles by such famous authors as Friedrich Duerrenmatt and Max Frisch, and includes dossiers on topics ranging from unemployment, to the ethics of modern science, to the future of higher education. Given this, *Schweizer Monatshefte* is a comprehensive, ambitious, and demanding magazine. The web site is well organized and provides tables of contents and sample articles in full text going back to 2003. Highly recommended for research institutions.

2462. *Sinn und Form: Beitraege zur Literatur.* [ISSN: 0037-5756] 1949. bi-m. EUR 39.90 domestic; EUR 50 foreign; EUR 9 newsstand/cover. Ed(s): Sebastian Kleinschmidt. Aufbau-Verlag GmbH, Neue Promenade 6, Berlin, 10178, Germany; info@aufbau-verlag.de; http://www.aufbau-verlag.de. Adv. Refereed. Circ: 2845 Paid and controlled. *Indexed:* ArtHuCI, FR, IBR, IBZ, MLA-IB, RILM, SSCI. *Aud.:* Ac.

In German. *Sinn und Form* is primarily a literary magazine, focusing on literary criticism and theory, but including essays on philosophy and theology, as well as society at large. Hailed by the *Frankfurter Allgemeine Zeitung* as one of the best literary magazines in the German-speaking world, *Sinn und Form* boasts an exceptional list of contributors, including George Steiner, Julien Green, Hans-Georg Gadamer, E. M. Cioran, Jurgen Habermas, Heiner Muller, Ernst Junger, Czeslaw Milosz, Kenzaburo Oe, Emmanuel Levinas, Jorge Semprun, Seamus Heaney, Michel Tournier, Peter Sloterdijk, and Claudio Magris, among others. The web site provides tables of contents back to 1992. Highly recommended for any library that supports research in German Studies and Comparative Literature.

The Spectator. See News and Opinion section.

Der Spiegel. See International Magazines section.

Suomen Kuvalehti. See International Magazines section.

2463. *Les Temps Modernes.* [ISSN: 0040-3075] 1945. bi-m. EUR 71 domestic; EUR 72.50 foreign. Editions Gallimard, 15 Rue Sebastien-Bottin, Paris, 75328 Cedex 07, France; catalogue@gallimard.fr; http://www.gallimard.fr. Illus., adv. *Indexed:* AltPI, AmH&L, ArtHuCI, BAS, HistAb, IBR, IBSS, IBZ, IPSA, IndIslam, MLA-IB, PAIS, PdeR, RILM, SSCI. *Aud.:* Ac.

In French. *Les Temps Modernes* was founded by Jean-Paul Sartre in 1945, in the aftermath of World War II. The original members of the editorial board included Raymond Aron, Simone de Beauvoir, Michel Leiris, Maurice Merleau-Ponty, Albert Olivier, and Jean Paulhan. Currently published by Gallimard and edited by Claude Lanzmann, *Les Temps Modernes* is a cultural review, primarily covering politics, philosophy, and literature, but expanding its analysis to all issues that face the modern world. Over the years, it has published contributions by members of its editorial board, as well as Richard Wright, Francis Ponge, Samuel Beckett, Alberto Moravia, Carlo Levi, James Agee, Boris Vian, and Jean Genet, among others. The web site includes tables of contents from 1995 onward. Of international stature and one of the most important publications of its type, *Les Temps Modernes* is highly recommended for all research libraries.

2464. *Text und Kritik: Zeitschrift fuer Literatur.* [ISSN: 0040-5329] 1962. q. EUR 42. Ed(s): Heinz Ludwig Arnold. Edition Text und Kritik in Richard Boorberg Verlag GmbH & Co. KG, Levelingstr 6A, Munich, 81673, Germany; info@etk-muenchen.de; http://www.etk-muenchen.de. Adv. Circ: 3000 Paid and controlled. *Indexed:* ArtHuCI, IBR, IBZ, MLA-IB, RILM. *Bk. rev.:* Number and length vary. *Aud.:* Ac.

In German. Published since 1963, *Text und Kritik,* founded by Heinz Ludwig Arnold, is a literary review that publishes contemporary authors, as well as critical essays on German literature. The monthly issues focus on a particular author or theme. Topics covered include, for example, the formation of the German literary canon and "pop" literature. Contributors are German literary scholars, critics, and authors, including famous literary figures such as W. G. Sebald, Robert Schindel, or Elfriede Jelinek. The web site, at www.etk-muenchen.de/literatur, is mostly informational, but it contains the tables of contents for selected back issues, starting in the early 1980s. Highly recommended for all research libraries that support German Studies, and for large public libraries with an interest in German literature.

2465. *Wespennest: Zeitschrift fuer brauchbare Texte und Bilder.* [ISSN: 1012-7313] 1969. q. EUR 36 domestic; EUR 40 foreign; EUR 12 newsstand/cover. Ed(s): Walter Famler. Wespennest, Rembrandtstr 31/4, Vienna, 1020, Austria; office@wespennest.at. Adv. Circ: 5000 Controlled. *Aud.:* Ga.

In German. *Wespennest* has published articles by noted authors as well as newcomers on a quarterly basis since 1969. Each issue presents a literary, essayistic, art-theoretical, or political topic. A section titled "Wiener Portraits," despite the name, covers noted figures on the international cultural scene. *Wespennest* also contains interviews and reviews. The web site, at www.wespennest.at, provides full text of select articles and reviews, including tables of contents of all back issues. Recommended for those wanting to stay abreast of Austrian cultural events.

2466. Yale French Studies. [ISSN: 0044-0078] 1948. s-a. Ed(s): Alyson Waters. Yale University Press, PO Box 209040, New Haven, CT 06520; ysm@yale.edu; http://yalepress.yale.edu/yupbooks. Illus., adv. Sample. Circ: 2500. Microform: PQC. Online: JSTOR (Web-based Journal Archive). Reprint: PSC. *Indexed:* ABS&EES, AmHI, ArtHuCI, FLI, FR, HumInd, IBR, IBZ, MLA-IB, RILM, SSCI. *Aud.:* Ac.

Yale French Studies is one of the premier journals on French literature, thought, and civilization in the English language. Each issue has a distinct title and focuses on a single topic. Although essays are mostly contributed by North American scholars, articles by the most well-known contemporary French authors and critics have also been included since its inception. The journal provides a multidisciplinary approach to literature that includes French-speaking cultures outside of France. The full text is accessible through JSTOR with a two-year wall. Indispensable for any library that supports the study of French culture.

Newspapers

Newspapers are popular among Europeans. It has been reported that an average of 31 million newspapers are sold in Germany each day and 80 percent of the German population over the age of 14 reads at least one newspaper daily. Like Germany, the rest of Western Europe has an appetite for reading newspapers. To stay competitive, newspaper publishers have created user-friendly and continuously updated web versions of their products while adding more color and innovative designs to their print editions. Although brief, this section presents newspapers that either have high international readership or are cited as the nation's newspaper of record.

See also the Newspapers section and check the index for specific titles not included here.

2467. Aftenposten. Formerly: *Christiania Adresseblad.* [ISSN: 0804-3116] 1860. d. 2/day. NOK 2546 domestic; NOK 4632 in Scandinavia; NOK 9240 in Europe. Ed(s): Hans Erik Matre, Arild Kvellstad. Aftenposten Forlag AS, Biskop Gunnerus Gate 14 A, Oslo, 0185, Norway; aftenposten@aftenposten.no; http://www.aftenposten.no. Illus., adv. Circ: 251014. *Aud.:* Ga, Ac.

In Norwegian. *Aftenposten* is Norway's main newspaper. Published in Oslo, it covers local, national, and international news, politics, business, the economy, cultural events, sports, and the media. As the country's premier daily and paper of record, *Aftenposten* reports on and shapes the national debate, yet it is full of colorful illustrations and generous white spaces that make it very accessible. The web site provides a number of selected articles for free, including some from past issues, but only subscribers have access to the complete edition. This well-organized site has a link to the news in English, but the ads are a bit overbearing. The site provides RSS feeds. Recommended to all libraries that want to cover Norwegian and international news.

2468. Berlingske Tidende. [ISSN: 0106-4223] 1749. d. DKK 3793. Ed(s): Niels Lunde, Elisabeth Ruehne. Berlingske Dagblade AS, Pilestraede 34, Copenhagen K, 1147, Denmark. Illus., index, adv. Circ: 124000 Controlled. *Aud.:* Ac, Ga.

In Danish. *Berlingske Tidende* is one of Denmark's main three daily newspapers. Founded in 1749, it is one of the oldest newspapers in the world. It reports on national and international news, politics, business and economics, health and medicine, the arts, media, and sports, as well as society at large, including a lifestyle section with articles on travel, fine dining, cars, and more. The web site provides the full text of a number of articles as well as other features one would expect from a leading newspaper, including RSS newsfeeds. Unfortunately, the site is cluttered with ads that make it difficult to read. The

archive goes back to 1990 but is reserved for subscribers only. Considered one of Denmark's premier newspapers, *Berlingske Tidende* is recommended for research collections and large public libraries.

2469. Dagens Nyheter. [ISSN: 1101-2447] 1864. d. SEK 3348 (Students, SEK 1250). Ed(s): Pia Pasternak, Jan Wifstrand. AB Dagens Nyheter, Gjoerwellsgatan 30, Stockholm, 10515, Sweden; info@dn.se; http:/www.dn.se. Illus., adv. Circ: 360000. *Aud.:* Ga, Ac.

In Swedish. Published since 1864, *Dagens Nyheter* is Sweden's premier daily newspaper, covering national and international news, politics, business and economics, culture, the media, and sports. Full of photos and illustrations, including cartoons, it is a family-oriented newspaper that does not sacrifice quality. The web site provides free access to major current articles, as well as features such as RSS feeds and podcasts. Access to articles back to 1992 is reserved for subscribers only. A Sunday-only subscription is available. Recommended for libraries that support research in Swedish Studies or large Swedish-speaking populations.

2470. Le Figaro. [ISSN: 0182-5852] 1828. d. EUR 365 domestic; EUR 504 foreign. Ed(s): Baudouin Bollaert. Societe du Figaro S.A., 14 bd Haussmann, Paris, 75009, France; http://lefigaro.fr. Illus. Circ: 492725 Paid. Microform: PQC. *Aud.:* Ga, Ac.

In French. *Le Figaro* is France's most important daily newspaper after *Le Monde.* It covers national and international news, politics, and cultural events. *Le Monde* is generally perceived as the main independent French national newspaper, with a left-centrist slant, and *Le Figaro* is its main contender, with a more right-of-center orientation. Published in Paris since 1828, *Le Figaro* is probably France's most ancient daily, with a long and turbulent history. Over the years, the paper has spawned several supplements, among them the *Figaro Litteraire,* which dates back to 1946 and counted Paul Claudel, Julien Green, and Colette, among others, as contributors. Since then, *Figaro Magazine,* *Figaro Madame,* and *Le Figaro Etudiants* have complemented the daily paper. *Le Figaro* regularly shares articles with like-minded papers such as *Die Welt* and the *Daily Telegraph,* as well as *ABC* of Spain. The freely accessible web site covers the major news stories and provides access to the archives up to 1997 on a fee-per-article basis. *Le Figaro* is recommended for large research and public libraries that want a diversified collection and a varied take on the news of France.

2471. France - Amerique: edition internationale du Figaro. Incorporates (1996-2007): *Journal Francais;* Which was formerly (1978-1996): *Journal Francais d'Amerique;* Formerly (until 1941): *Courrier des Etats-Unis.* [ISSN: 0747-2757] 1828. w. USD 50 domestic; USD 96 Canada; USD 142 elsewhere. Ed(s): Pascale Richard. FrancePress, Inc., 333 W 39th St, Ste 702, New York, NY 10018. Illus., adv. Circ: 20000 Paid and controlled. *Aud.:* Ga.

In French. Owned by *Le Figaro, France—Amerique* is geared toward French expatriates in the United States. Covering French news, politics, business, sports, the media, culture, and society at large, *France—Amerique* focuses mostly on articles about the French–American relationship. Also covered are French cultural events in the United States and the remnants of French culture in North America. The web site is well organized and contains full text of selected articles. It also includes links to information about visas and other practical issues for French expatriates living in the United States. For public libraries.

2472. Frankfurter Allgemeine: Zeitung fuer Deutschland. [ISSN: 0174-4909] 1949. d. EUR 40 per month. Frankfurter Allgemeine Zeitung GmbH, Hellerhofstr 2-4, Frankfurt Am Main, 60327, Germany; http://www.faz.de. Illus., adv. Circ: 379714. Microform: PQC. Online: Factiva, Inc. *Indexed:* RILM. *Aud.:* Ga, Ac, Sa.

In German. The *Frankfurter Allgemeine Zeitung,* or *FAZ* as it is commonly known, is generally considered Germany's leading daily newspaper. Established in 1949 in then–West Germany's financial and publishing center, Frankfurt am Main, *FAZ* is a paper of exceptional quality, with carefully researched articles on national and international news, politics, business, the economy, sports, and travel. Well known for its cultural section titled "Feuilleton," *FAZ* dominates the intellectual debate, and its literary critics are widely influential. The web site provides non–German speakers with an English version and includes a wide selection of articles summarized from the print version, as well as special "Dossiers" and features such as RSS feeds. The archive goes back to 1993, on a pay-per-article basis. *FAZ* is indispensable for research libraries and recommended for all collections that support German Studies.

The Guardian. See Newspapers/General section.

2473. Helsingin Sanomat. Formerly (until 1904): *Paivalehti.* [ISSN: 0355-2047] 1889. d. EUR 215. Ed(s): Janne Virkkunen. Helsingin Sanomat Oy, Toolonlahdenkatu 2, PO Box 77, Sanoma, 00089, Finland. Illus., adv. Circ: 492385. *Indexed:* MLA-IB. *Aud.:* Ga, Ac.

In Finnish. *Helsingin Sanomat* is generally considered Finland's premier newspaper. It covers national and international affairs, business, the arts and media, sports, and local events. Its evenhanded approach and balancing of viewpoints are exemplary. The paper's layout and design are attractive, and it includes color photographs. The web site has a link to the *Helsingin Sanomat International Edition,* which provides a summary of the major stories in English. The archives for the *Helsingin Sanomat* are limited to subscribers and date back to 1990, while the archives of the English edition are free and go back to 2000. Recommended for libraries that support Scandinavian Studies.

2474. International Herald Tribune: the world's daily newspaper. [ISSN: 0294-8052] 1887. 6x/w. Ed(s): Michael Getler. International Herald Tribune, 6 bis, rue des Graviers, Neuilly-sur-Seine, Cedex 92521, France; iht@iht.com; http://www.iht.com. Illus. Circ: 234722 Paid. Microform: PQC. Online: Florida Center for Library Automation; Gale; Northern Light Technology, Inc.; ProQuest K-12 Learning Solutions; ProQuest LLC (Ann Arbor). *Indexed:* RILM. *Aud.:* Ga, Ac.

In English. Published for American expatriates since 1887, the *International Herald Tribune* is the product of a unique collaboration between *The New York Times* and a number of premier international newspapers, among them *El Pais,* the *Frankfurter Allgemeine Zeitung, Haaretz,* and others. While the newspaper started out as available only in selected locations (e.g., Paris in the 1920s), it is now printed in 21 locations and distributed around the world. The well-organized web site presents the news with a different emphasis depending on the region of interest, and it provides free access to selected full-text articles, including a free archive dating back to 1991. The site further provides access to blogs and RSS feeds. The world's most international paper, it presents a unique summary of world news.

2475. The Irish Times. [ISSN: 0791-5144] 1859. d. Ed(s): Valentine Lamb. Irish Times Ltd., 10-16 D'Olier St., Dublin, 2, Ireland. Illus. Circ: 102460 Paid. Microform: PQC. Online: LexisNexis; Northern Light Technology, Inc. *Indexed:* PAIS. *Aud.:* Ga, Ac.

In English. Published since 1859, *The Irish Times* established itself as Ireland's premier independent newspaper in 1974, when it established a trust to remain free "from any form of personal or party political, commercial, religious or other sectional control." With correspondents all over the world, the paper covers international and national news, politics, the economy, technology, media, sports, the arts, and any other issue of general interest. The fully developed web site provides access to select articles in full text and to a host of services, including a searchable, but restricted archive going back to 1996. Recommended for research and large public libraries or those that cater to a large Irish community.

2476. Liberation. [ISSN: 0335-1793] 1973. d. EUR 265. Liberation, 11 rue Beranger, Paris, Cedex 3 75154, France; espaceslibe@liberation.fr; http://www.liberation.fr. Illus. Circ: 210000 Paid. Microform: PQC. *Indexed:* RILM. *Bk. rev.:* Number and length vary. *Aud.:* Ga.

In French. *Liberation* is one of France's major daily newspapers. Established in 1973 by Jean-Paul Sartre and Serge July in the aftermath of the student protests of May 1968, *Liberation* started as an outspoken, provocative, leftist newspaper that has gradually turned into a more mainstream, national publication. Geared toward younger readers, students, and the intellectual left, it covers daily national and international news as well as cultural events. "*Libe,*" as it is known in France, is recommended for research libraries and for those wanting an alternative to the more established papers *Le Monde* and *Le Figaro.*

2477. Le Monde. [ISSN: 0395-2037] 1944. d. EUR 59. Ed(s): Jean Marie Colombani. Le Monde S.A., 21 bis, rue Claude Bernard, Paris, 75242 Cedex 5, France; redac@lemonde.fr; http://www.lemonde.fr. Illus., index. Circ: 500000. Microform: RPI. *Indexed:* RILM. *Aud.:* Ga, Ac.

In French. *Le Monde* is France's leading newspaper. Established in 1944, after France's liberation, *Le Monde* rose from the ashes of *Le Temps,* following de Gaulle's wish for a new paper of reference. First edited by Hubert Beuve-Mery, *Le Monde* established itself as an independent newspaper through its in-depth, quality reporting on national and international news and politics, business and the economy, the arts, and the media. Its political commentary and section on the arts, including a weekly literary supplement, are widely influential. Over the years, *Le Monde* has developed several supplements and sections to increase readership, such as *Le Monde de l'education.* Other initiatives, such as *Le Monde Diplomatique* and the *Cahiers du Cinema,* have established themselves as successful, independent publications. The free web site is one of the most complete and well-organized online newspaper sites and includes full text of a wide variety of articles. The archive, which can be searched from 1987 to the present, provides full text for a fee. Essential to all research collections and recommended to all libraries as the leading French news source in print.

2478. Morgunbladid. [ISSN: 1021-7266] 1913. d. ISK 8500. Ed(s): Styrmir Gunnarsson. Arvakur h.f., Kringlan 1, Reykjavik, 103, Iceland; mbl@centrum.is; http://www.mbl.is/frettir. Illus., adv. Circ: 55000 Controlled. *Bk. rev.:* Number and length vary. *Aud.:* Ac.

In Icelandic. *Morgunbladid* is Iceland's premier daily newspaper. Covering national and international news, politics, the economy, arts, media, and sports, it also includes reviews of films, plays, music, and books. The web site is well organized and easy to navigate. Recommended for research libraries that cover Icelandic and Scandinavian Studies.

2479. N R C - Handelsblad. [ISSN: 0002-5259] 1970. d. Mon.-Sat. EUR 281.50. Ed(s): F E Jensma. P C M Uitgevers NV, N R C - Handelsblad, Postbus 8987, Rotterdam, 3009 TH, Netherlands. Illus., adv. Circ: 267140. *Bk. rev.:* Number and length vary. *Aud.:* Ga, Ac.

In Dutch. The *NRC - Handelsblad* is the premier daily newspaper in the Netherlands. Created in the 1970s through merger of the *Nieuwe Rotterdamse Courant* and the *Algemeen Handelsblad,* two of the country's major papers, the *NRC* is known for its independent stance and serious approach to national and international news, politics, and the economy. It also covers cultural events in great detail and is a leading source for book reviews. The web site is well organized and provides free access to selected full text, but requires online registration. Access to the full content of the paper, including the archives, is reserved for paying subscribers. A weekend edition is also available. Highly recommended for research libraries and large public libraries that cover international news and Dutch Studies.

2480. Ta Nea. 1946. d. Ed(s): Leon Karapanayiotis. Lambrakis Press SA, Panepistimiou 18, Athens, 106 72, Greece. Illus., adv. *Aud.:* Ac.

In Greek. *Ta Nea* is one of Greece's main daily newspapers. Published in Athens, it covers all major national and international news stories, including the arts, media, and sports. The web site provides access to selected current articles and to archival issues. Recommended for research libraries that support international and contemporary Greek Studies and for public libraries that serve a large Greek community.

2481. Neue Zuercher Zeitung. Formerly (until 1821): *Zuercher Zeitung.* [ISSN: 0376-6829] 1780. d. except Sun. CHF 434. Ed(s): Markus Spillmann. Neue Zuercher Zeitung, Falkenstr 11, Zuerich, 8021, Switzerland; verlag@nzz.ch; http://verlag.nzz.ch. Illus., adv. Circ: 159000 Paid and controlled. Microform: RPI; PQC. Online: LexisNexis. *Indexed:* RILM. *Aud.:* Ac.

In German. Published since 1780, the *Neue Zuercher Zeitung* is one of Europe's oldest and most renowned newspapers. As Switzerland's premier daily, and highly regarded abroad, it provides well-written and well-researched articles on national and international news, the economy, politics, the media, the arts, and sports. Particularly outstanding is its coverage of business and the economy, as well as its cultural pages. The web site is well organized and provides access to selected full text, as well as to the archives from 1993 to date, but access is restricted. The site includes an "English Window," which includes selected full text of articles translated into English. The *Neue Zuercher Zeitung* is an important title for large research and public libraries.

2482. Die Presse: unabhaengige Tageszeitungs fuer Oesterreich.
Formerly: *Neue Freie Press.* 1848. d. Mon.-Sat. EUR 266.90. Ed(s): Michael Fleischhacker. Die Presse Verlagsgesellschaft mbH & Co. KG, Parkring 12a, Vienna, 1015, Austria; geschaeftsfuehrung@diepresse.com. Illus., adv. Circ: 104560 Paid and controlled. Microform: ALP; PQC. *Aud.:* Ac.

In German. *Die Presse* is generally viewed as Austria's most reputable newspaper, although its circulation is less than that of its more popular competitors. Covering national and international news, politics, the economy, the media, culture, arts, sports, technology, and local events in Vienna, it is available in both German and English at www.diepresse.at. Including full text of selected articles, the web site provides a free newsletter service and RSS feeds, and contains numerous subsections. The archive is accessible from 2001 onward. Recommended for large research and public libraries with an interest in Austrian Studies.

2483. La Repubblica. [ISSN: 0390-1076] 1976. d. EUR 250. Gruppo Editoriale l' Espresso SpA, Via Cristoforo Colombo 90, Rome, 00147, Italy; espresso@espressoedit.it; http://www.espressoedit.it. Adv. *Bk. rev.:* Number and length vary. *Aud.:* Ga.

In Italian. *La Repubblica* is Italy's main independent newspaper, covering national and international news, politics, business and economics, the arts, literature, and the media. The paper has several supplements, such as the highly influential literary section, published every Thursday, and the magazine *Venerdi di Repubblica,* which accompanies the paper every Friday and is similar to such American publications as *Time. La Repubblica's* editorial stance is generally perceived as being center-left. Its main national competitor is the *Corriere della Sera.* The web site, www.repubblica.it, provides full text of a fairly large and varied selection of articles, but it is teeming with ads that can render browsing frustrating. The site offers RSS news feeds and podcasts, as well as free access to selected articles in the archives. As the primary independent Italian news source in print, *La Repubblica* is recommended for large public libraries and all research libraries that support Italian Studies.

2484. Die Tageszeitung. Formerly: *Die Tageszeitung (Ausgabe Berlin).* [ISSN: 0941-1526] 1978. 6x/w. EUR 348. Ed(s): Bascha Mika. T A Z Verlagsgenossenschaft e.G., Kochstr 18, Berlin, 10969, Germany; briefe@taz.de; http://www.taz.de. Adv. Circ: 80857 Paid. Online: LexisNexis. *Aud.:* Ga, Ac.

In German. *Die Tageszeitung* is an independent, left-wing national daily published in Berlin by a cooperative that emanates from student, ecological, feminist, and Third World movements of 1968 and the following years. The "Taz," as it is commonly known, is proud of its loud, unabashedly leftist, critical voice. It is published with regional supplements, and includes a monthly supplement of *Le Monde Diplomatique.* The web site is well organized and provides a full-text electronic edition of the current print publication, including all supplements and special reports ("Dossiers"), as well as a blog. Access to the archives is restriced. Because of its unique voice and history, *Die Tageszeitung* is recommended for large research libraries.

The Times. See Newspapers/General section.

TLS: the Times literary supplement. See Newspapers/General section.

2485. Die Zeit: Wochenzeitung fuer Politik, Wirtschaft, Handel und Kultur. [ISSN: 0044-2070] 1946. w. EUR 149.76; EUR 3.20 newsstand/cover. Ed(s): Giovanni di Lorenzo. Zeitverlag Gerd Bucerius GmbH & Co. KG, Buceriusstr, Eingang Speersort 1, Hamburg, 20095, Germany. Illus., adv. Circ: 471707 Paid. Microform: PQC. *Bk. rev.:* Number and length vary. *Aud.:* Ga, Ac.

In German. Published by former chancellor Helmut Schmidt, among others, *Die Zeit* is Germany's most prestigious weekly newspaper. Established in Hamburg in 1946, it is highly regarded in political and cultural circles and is the leading source for academic recruitment advertisements. Published every Thursday, *Die Zeit* reports on the week's national and international news, with a focus on political events, economic issues, culture, the media, and academia. Because it does not cover events on a daily basis, it is known for its careful analysis of the week in review. Having undergone a complete revamping at the end of the 1990s in an effort to appeal to a younger generation and to counter a dwindling subscription list, the paper has lost its formerly austere character by adding color, large images, and new coverage, with sections on travel, food, etc. It remains one of the premier sources for cultural information, and its literary section rivals that of the *Frankfurter Allgemeine.* The freely accessible web site provides full text of a number of articles, and it has established itself as a portal to information on cultural and educational events, as well as classifieds and similar services that are common to major newspapers. Highly recommended for all libraries that support scholarship in German Studies.

■ FAMILY

See also Lesbian, Gay, Bisexual, and Transgender; Marriage and Divorce; Parenting; Psychology; and Sociology and Social Work sections.

Erin K. McCaffrey, Distance Learning Librarian, Regis University, 3333 Regis Blvd., D-20, Denver, CO 80221; emccaffr@regis.edu

Introduction

According to the U.S. Census Bureau report *America's Families and Living Arrangements: 2003* (issued November 2004), growth in American household size has decreased with changes in marriage, divorce, and fertility. Marriage rates have declined as the average age of first marriage has increased. Single-parent childbearing and child rearing are more common, as are unmarried partner households. Definitions of gender roles within the family have changed. The traditional representation of the family is very different from the variety of intimate and partner relationship structures that represent the family today.

The literature in family and marriage also reflects these changes, presenting a broader representation of what constitutes "family." Marital and couples therapy, same-sex couples, gender issues, substance abuse, diversity and cross-cultural examinations of the family, family violence, and therapy and treatment are frequent themes in the current marriage and family literature. Training and supervision is also receiving greater attention.

Family periodicals tend to fall into either the popular or the scholarly category. The popular magazines in this area concentrate on practical self-help for couples and families. Of the scholarly journals represented here, content ranges from theory and research to practice and application. Periodicals in this category are devoting greater coverage to outside influences on marriage, the family, and intimate relationships.

In this section, we focus on periodicals that treat the family as a whole, addressing family studies, family therapy, marital and couples therapy, as well as the broader definition of the contemporary family. Many of the periodicals in this category offer table of contents information and selected full text on their web sites.

Basic Periodicals

Ga: *FamilyFun, Parenting, Parents;* Ac: *Family Process, Family Relations, Journal of Comparative Family Studies, Journal of Family Issues, Journal of Family Psychology, Journal of Marriage and Family;* Sa: *Families in Society, Journal of Marital and Family Therapy, Journal of Sex & Marital Therapy.*

Basic Abstracts and Indexes

Family & Society Studies Worldwide, Psychological Abstracts, Sage Family Studies Abstracts, Social Sciences Citation Index, Social Sciences Index, Social Work Abstracts, Sociological Abstracts.

2486. *American Journal of Family Therapy.* Former titles (until 1979): *International Journal of Family Counseling;* (until 1976): *Journal of Family Counseling.* [ISSN: 0192-6187] 1973. 5x/yr. GBP 169 print & online eds. Ed(s): S Richard Sauber. Routledge, 325 Chestnut St, Ste 800, Philadelphia, PA 19106; journals@routledge.com; http://www.tandf.co.uk/journals. Illus., index, adv. Sample. Refereed. Circ: 2000. Vol. ends: Winter. Microform: PQC. Online: EBSCO Publishing, EBSCO Host; Gale; IngentaConnect; Northern Light Technology, Inc.; OCLC Online Computer Library Center, Inc.; ProQuest LLC (Ann Arbor); SwetsWise Online Content. Reprint: PSC. *Indexed:* AgeL, CINAHL, CJA, ExcerpMed, IMFL, LRI, PsycInfo, SFSA, SSA, SSCI, SWR&A, SociolAb. *Bk. rev.:* 0-4, 600-1,200 words. *Aud.:* Ac, Sa.

The *American Journal of Family Therapy* proposes to be "the incisive, authoritative, independent voice" in family therapy. It is interdisciplinary in scope, and its readership includes marriage and family therapists, psychiatrists, psychologists, allied health and mental health practitioners, counselors, clinical social workers, physicians, nurses, and clergy practitioners. Regular sections include "Family Measurement Techniques," "Family Behavioral Medicine and Health," "Family Law Issues in Family Therapy Practice," "Continuing Education and Training," and "International Department." The journal also includes book and media reviews. Recent topics include parental alcoholism and family unpredictability, men and men's issues in marriage and family therapy programs, mental health practice with Arab families, family interventions with law enforcement officers, and understanding the transition from career to full-time motherhood. This journal is highly recommended for academic libraries seeking more than one scholarly family therapy journal.

2487. *Child & Family Behavior Therapy.* Formerly (until 1982): *Child Behavior Therapy.* [ISSN: 0731-7107] 1978. q. USD 750 print & online eds. Ed(s): Charles Diament, Cyril M Franks. Haworth Press, Inc., 10 Alice St, Binghamton, NY 13904-1580; getinfo@haworthpress.com; http://www.haworthpress.com. Illus., adv. Sample. Refereed. Circ: 387 Paid. Vol. ends: No. 4. Microform: PQC. Online: EBSCO Publishing, EBSCO Host; OCLC Online Computer Library Center, Inc.; SwetsWise Online Content. Reprint: HAW. *Indexed:* CINAHL, CJA, ECER, ERIC, FR, IMFL, PEI, PRA, PsycInfo, RiskAb, SFSA, SSA, SSCI, SWA, SWR&A, SociolAb, V&AA. *Bk. rev.:* 1-4, 600-2,200 words. *Aud.:* Ac, Sa.

Published quarterly, *Child & Family Behavior Therapy* is aimed at counselors, family therapists, teachers, child psychologists, researchers, and others interested in utilizing behavior therapy techniques when working with difficult children and adolescents. Each issue of this peer-reviewed journal contains three to four articles. Researchers will find the considerable book reviews helpful. Articles are lengthy and scientific, yet practical in approach, and include clinical applications, case studies, and original research. Recent articles include "Enhancing the Impact of Parent Training Through Narrative Restructuring," "Evaluation of a Weight Loss Treatment Program for Individuals with Mild Mental Retardation," "Effects of Cognitive-Behavioral Group Therapy for Depressive Mothers of Children with Behavior Problems," and "Externalizing Disorders and the Treatment of Child Anxiety: A Preliminary Study." Recommended for academic libraries.

2488. *Contemporary Family Therapy: an international journal.* Formerly (until 1986): *International Journal of Family Therapy.* [ISSN: 0892-2764] 1979. q. EUR 798 print & online eds. Ed(s): William Nichols. Springer New York LLC, 233 Spring St, New York, NY 10013-1578; service-ny@springer.com; http://www.springer.com/. Adv. Refereed. Online: EBSCO Publishing, EBSCO Host; IngentaConnect; OCLC Online Computer Library Center, Inc.; OhioLINK; Ovid Technologies, Inc.; Springer LINK; SwetsWise Online Content. Reprint: PSC. *Indexed:* ABS&EES, ASG, ASSIA, AgeL, FR, IBR, IBZ, IMFL, PsycInfo, RI-1, SFSA, SSA, SSCI, SWA, SWR&A, V&AA. *Aud.:* Ac.

Contemporary Family Therapy provides current developments in family therapy research, practice, and theory with "an emphasis on examining families within the broader socio-economic and ethnic matrices of which families and their members are a part." The interactions among family systems, society, and individuals are examined. Recent topics include authoritarian parenting style in Asian societies, case studies in sibling incest, marital expectations, work and family conflict, rural marriage and family therapists, and premarital education. A recent issue presents research on family psychotherapy for East Indian families. International in scope, the editorial board also includes broad geographic representation. This journal is recommended for academic libraries supporting family therapy and sociology programs.

2489. *Exceptional Parent: the magazine for families and professionals caring for people with special needs.* [ISSN: 0046-9157] 1971. m. USD 29.95 domestic; USD 54.95 Canada; USD 57.95 elsewhere. Ed(s): Rick Rader. Exceptional Parent, 700 Broadway Ste 76, Westwood, NJ 07675-1674. Illus., index. Sample. Circ: 33000 Controlled. Vol. ends: Dec. Microform: PQC. Online: Gale; Northern Light Technology, Inc.; OCLC Online Computer Library Center, Inc.; ProQuest LLC (Ann Arbor); H.W. Wilson. *Indexed:* ABIn, CINAHL, ECER, EduInd, IMFL. *Aud.:* Ga, Sa.

Exceptional Parent serves individuals with disabilities, as well as their families and caregivers, in addition to physicians, educators, and therapists. Originally focused on children with disabilities, the magazine has expanded its scope to include adults with disabilities and focuses on making life easier for those with disabilities. Each issue includes a special section devoted to in-depth coverage of a particular topic. Recent issues include "Autism Awareness," "Schools, Camps and Residences," "Reducing Stress," "Financial Estate and Tax Planning," and "Family and Community." In addition, *Exceptional Parent* publishes an annual resource guide. Informative articles cover such topics as assistive technology, accessibility, mobility, education, health care and recreation, diet and nutrition, and learning disabilities. Regular columns include "Organizational Spotlight," "Ask the Therapist," "Further Reading," "Idea," and "Living with a Disability." Recommended for large public libraries.

Families in Society. See Sociology and Social Work/Social Work and Social Welfare section.

Family Circle. See Fashion and Lifestyle section.

The Family Handyman. See Do-It-Yourself section.

2490. *The Family Journal: counseling and therapy for couples and families.* [ISSN: 1066-4807] 1993. q. GBP 385. Ed(s): Kaye W Nelson. Sage Publications, Inc., 2455 Teller Rd, Thousand Oaks, CA 91320; info@sagepub.com; http://www.sagepub.com. Refereed. Circ: 7000. Reprint: PSC. *Indexed:* CJA, ERIC, HRA, PsycInfo, RiskAb, SFSA, SSA, SWR&A, SociolAb. *Bk. rev.:* Number and length vary. *Aud.:* Ac, Sa.

The official journal of the International Association of Marriage and Family Counselors, *The Family Journal* presents an assortment of practice, research, and theory in each issue. This blend of coverage, from a family systems perspective, serves educators, practitioners, and researchers involved with couple and family counseling and therapy. "Using Popular Films to Teach Systems Thinking," "Expanding the Use of the Ethical Genogram," "Preparing Counselors-in-Training to Work with Couples," and "Assessing Perturbation and Suicide in Families" are some recent features. In addition to articles, regular sections include counselor training, case consultation, ethics, literature reviews, book reviews, and techniques to share. Interviews with leaders in family therapy are also published here. Recommended for academic libraries.

2491. *Family Process.* [ISSN: 0014-7370] 1962. q. USD 315 print & online eds. Ed(s): Evan Imber-Black. Blackwell Publishing, Inc., Commerce Place, 350 Main St, Malden, MA 02148; customerservices@blackwellpublishing.com; http://www.blackwellpublishing.com. Illus., index, adv. Sample. Refereed. Circ: 3800 Paid. Vol. ends: Dec. CD-ROM: ProQuest LLC (Ann Arbor). Online: Blackwell Synergy; EBSCO Publishing, EBSCO Host; Gale; IngentaConnect; OCLC Online Computer Library Center, Inc.; ProQuest K-12 Learning Solutions; ProQuest LLC (Ann Arbor); SwetsWise Online Content. Reprint: PSC. *Indexed:* ASSIA, AgeL, ApEcolAb, CINAHL, CJA, CommAb, ExcerpMed, FR, IBR, IBZ, IMFL, PsycInfo, SFSA, SSA, SSCI, SWA, SWR&A, SociolAb, V&AA. *Aud.:* Ac, Sa.

One of the foremost journals in the field, *Family Process* began publication when the field of family therapy was in its infancy. A major resource for over 40 years, this multidisciplinary peer-reviewed journal "publishes clinical research, training, and theoretical contributions in the broad area of family therapy." Mental health and social service professionals will find research and clinical ideas on a wide range of psychological and behavioral problems. Recent topics include bullying, ecology of attachment in the family, the practice of community in family therapy, father responsivity, the vulnerability cycle, and family consequences of refugee trauma. Subscribers can access additional material on the *Family Process* web site, including a searchable archive. This journal is recommended for academic libraries that support family therapy, psychiatry, psychology, and social work programs.

2492. Family Relations: interdisciplinary journal of applied family studies. Former titles (until 1979): *Family Coordinator;* (until 1967): *Family Life Coordinator;* (until 1959): *The Coordinator.* [ISSN: 0197-6664] 1952. 5x/yr. Individuals, USD 126 print & online eds. Ed(s): Joyce A Arditti. Blackwell Publishing, Inc., Commerce Place, 350 Main St, Malden, MA 02148; customerservices@blackwellpublishing.com; http://www.blackwellpublishing.com. Illus., index, adv. Refereed. Circ: 4200 Paid. CD-ROM: NISC International, Inc. Microform: PQC. Online: Blackwell Synergy; The Dialog Corporation; EBSCO Publishing, EBSCO Host; IngentaConnect; JSTOR (Web-based Journal Archive); Northern Light Technology, Inc.; OCLC Online Computer Library Center, Inc.; ProQuest K-12 Learning Solutions; ProQuest LLC (Ann Arbor); SwetsWise Online Content. Reprint: PSC. *Indexed:* ASG, AgeL, Agr, ApEcolAb, BRI, CBRI, CJA, ERIC, HRA, IBSS, MRD, PsycInfo, RI-1, RiskAb, SFSA, SSA, SSCI, SWA, SWR&A, SociolAb, V&AA. *Bk. rev.:* 7-18, 500-800 words. *Aud.:* Ac, Sa.

Family Relations is one of two journals published by the National Council on Family Relations (NCFR). It emphasizes "family research with implications for intervention, education, and public policy." It publishes empirical studies, conceptual analysis, and literature reviews written with the needs of practitioners in mind. Articles are interdisciplinary in scope and focus on a diverse range of family issues, including gender and family relationships, cross-cultural issues, aging, and intergenerational family relations. Recent topics include challenges for the wives of firefighters, victims of chronic dating violence, preparing future family professionals, women and work in a rural community, treating difficult couples, and families and communities. Readers are scholars and practitioners, including marriage and family therapists, educators, researchers, and family practitioners. NCFR members can access full-text articles through the NCFR web site. *Family Relations* is routinely cited and is an excellent resource. Highly recommended for academic libraries with programs addressing family research and family studies, psychology, or social work.

2493. Family Safety & Health. Formerly (until 1984): *Family Safety.* [ISSN: 0749-310X] 1961. q. Members, USD 16.75; Non-members, USD 21.80. Ed(s): Melissa Ruminski. National Safety Council, 1121 Spring Lake Dr, Itasca, IL 60143-3201; http://www.nsc.org. Illus., adv. Circ: 550000. Vol. ends: Winter. Microform: PQC. *Aud.:* Hs, Ga.

Published by the National Safety Council, *Family Safety & Health* emphasizes information for living a safe and healthy life. It provides information on home, recreational, and driving safety. It also presents current nutrition, family health, safety tips, and fitness information. Articles address topics that highlight living a safe and healthy life, such as caring for an aging parent, symptoms of mold, neighborhood watch programs in community crime prevention, fireproofing your home, safe skiing, and indoor air quality. Recommended for public and high school libraries.

Family Therapy Networker. See *Psychotherapy Networker.*

FamilyFun. See *Parenting* section.

2494. Journal of Child and Family Studies. [ISSN: 1062-1024] 1992. q. EUR 592 print & online eds. Ed(s): Nirbhay Singh. Springer New York LLC, 233 Spring St, New York, NY 10013-1578; service-ny@springer.com; http://www.springer.com/. Adv. Refereed. Online: EBSCO Publishing, EBSCO Host; Gale; IngentaConnect; OCLC Online

Computer Library Center, Inc.; OhioLINK; Ovid Technologies, Inc.; Springer LINK; SwetsWise Online Content. Reprint: PSC. *Indexed:* ASSIA, CJA, IBSS, PsycInfo, RiskAb, SFSA, SSA, SWR&A, SociolAb, V&AA. *Bk. rev.:* Number and length vary. *Aud.:* Ac, Sa.

The *Journal of Child and Family Studies* addresses all aspects of emotional disorders pertaining to children and adolescents and their effects on families. Clinicians and practitioners will find the basic and applied research, program evaluation, policy issues, and book reviews useful. Recent articles include "Expectancies for Sexually Abused Children: Evidence of Perceiver Bias," "Adherence to Wraparound Principles and Association with Outcomes," and "Quality of Relationships Between Youth and Community Service Providers: Reliability and Validity of the Trusting Relationship Questionnaire." This journal is recommended for academic libraries, particularly those that support programs related to child and adolescent mental health.

2495. Journal of Comparative Family Studies. [ISSN: 0047-2328] 1970. 4x/yr. USD 270 (Individuals, USD 115). Ed(s): George Kurian. University of Calgary, Department of Sociology, 2500 University Dr NW, Calgary, AB T2N 1N4, Canada; cairns@ucalgary.ca. Illus., index, adv. Refereed. Circ: 800. Vol. ends: No. 4. Microform: MIM; MML; PQC. Online: EBSCO Publishing, EBSCO Host; Florida Center for Library Automation; Gale; Micromedia ProQuest; Northern Light Technology, Inc.; OCLC Online Computer Library Center, Inc.; ProQuest K-12 Learning Solutions; ProQuest LLC (Ann Arbor); H.W. Wilson. *Indexed:* ASG, ASSIA, AgeL, AnthLit, ArtHuCI, BAS, CBCARef, CEI, CJA, CPerI, EI, ExcerpMed, IBR, IBSS, IBZ, IMFL, PsycInfo, RILM, RRTA, SFSA, SSA, SSCI, SWA, SociolAb, V&AA, WAE&RSA. *Bk. rev.:* 0-10, 400-1,300. *Aud.:* Ac.

Aimed at scholars of national and international comparative family studies, this peer-reviewed journal "provides a unique cross-cultural perspective on the study of the family." Abstracts are provided in English, French, and Spanish, and the editorial board and authors are international in representation. The journal publishes articles, book reviews, and research notes. Recent articles include "Changing Views on Family Diversity in Urban Korea," "Rampage: The Social Roots of School Shootings," and "Post-Familial Families and the Domestic Division of Labour." The journal also publishes special issues on selected themes, such as "Farm Family Responses to Changing Agricultural Conditions" and "Youth and Family: Intergenerational Tensions and Transfers." The last issue of each year contains a section on books received and an index. Highly recommended for academic libraries that serve anthropology, social psychology, sociology, or multicultural studies programs.

2496. Journal of Family History: studies in family, kinship and demography. Supersedes: *Family in Historical Perspective.* [ISSN: 0363-1990] 1976. q. GBP 378. Ed(s): Roderick Phillips. Sage Publications, Inc., 2455 Teller Rd, Thousand Oaks, CA 91320; info@sagepub.com; http://www.sagepub.com. Illus., index, adv. Sample. Refereed. Circ: 1400. Vol. ends: Oct. Online: Chadwyck-Healey Inc.; EBSCO Publishing, EBSCO Host; Florida Center for Library Automation; Gale; HighWire Press; OCLC Online Computer Library Center, Inc.; SAGE Publications, Inc., SAGE Journals Online; SwetsWise Online Content; H.W. Wilson. Reprint: PSC. *Indexed:* ABS&EES, ASG, AgeL, AmH&L, AmHI, ArtHuCI, EI, HistAb, HumInd, IBR, IBSS, IBZ, IMFL, SFSA, SSA, SSCI, SUSA, SWA, SWR&A, SociolAb, V&AA. *Bk. rev.:* 4-8, 800-1,200 words. *Aud.:* Ac.

International and interdisciplinary in scope, this quarterly journal publishes scholarly research articles "concerning the family as a historical social form with contributions from the disciplines of history, gender studies, economics, law, political science, policy studies, demography, anthropology, sociology, liberal arts and the humanities." Published in association with the National Council on Family Relations, contributions represent the international perspective of historically based research. Book reviews, research notes, and debates are regular features. Recent articles include "Farm Families and the American Revolution," "Was Ancient Rome a Dead Wives Society? What Did the Roman Paterfamilias Get Away With?" and "Does the Sex of Firstborn Children Influence Subsequent Fertility Behavior?: Evidence from Family Reconstitution." Recommended for academic libraries.

2497. *Journal of Family Issues.* [ISSN: 0192-513X] 1980. 8x/yr. GBP 691. Ed(s): Constance Shehan. Sage Publications, Inc., 2455 Teller Rd, Thousand Oaks, CA 91320; info@sagepub.com; http://www.sagepub.com. Illus., index, adv. Sample. Refereed. Circ: 1500 Paid. Vol. ends: Nov. Microform: WSH; PMC. Online: CSA; Chadwyck-Healey Inc.; EBSCO Publishing, EBSCO Host; Florida Center for Library Automation; Gale; HighWire Press; OCLC Online Computer Library Center, Inc.; OhioLINK; SAGE Publications, Inc., SAGE Journals Online; SwetsWise Online Content. Reprint: PSC. *Indexed:* ASG, ASSIA, AgeL, Agr, AmH&L, CINAHL, CJA, ERIC, HEA, HistAb, IMFL, PsycInfo, RiskAb, SFSA, SSA, SSCI, SWR&A, SociolAb, V&AA. *Aud.:* Ac, Sa.

The *Journal of Family Issues* is "devoted to contemporary social issues and social problems related to marriage and family life and to theoretical and professional issues of current interest to those who work with and study families." It publishes current research, analyses, and theory. Articles, advocacy pieces, research developments, and commentaries represent any topic related to family issues and are presented from an interdisciplinary perspective. Recent topics include mothers in Christian academia and their experiences of spousal support, assisted reproduction and the courts, examination of the mental health advantage of the married, and wives' employment and spouses' marital happiness. This scholarly journal is highly recommended for academic libraries.

2498. *Journal of Family Psychology.* [ISSN: 0893-3200] 1987. q. USD 400 (Individuals, USD 126). Ed(s): Dr. Anne E Kazak. American Psychological Association, 750 First St, N E, Washington, DC 20002-4242; journals@apa.org; http://www.apa.org. Illus., index, adv. Refereed. Vol. ends: Feb. Reprint: PSC. *Indexed:* ABIn, ASSIA, CJA, EduInd, FR, IMFL, PsycInfo, SFSA, SSA, SSCI, SWA, SWR&A, SociolAb. *Aud.:* Ac, Sa.

Published by the American Psychological Association, the *Journal of Family Psychology* is regarded as a key journal in family research. It provides original scholarly articles "devoted to the study of the family system from multiple perspectives and to the application of psychological methods of inquiry to that end." Occasionally, the journal publishes literature reviews, case studies, or theoretical articles, but the focus of the journal is empirical research addressing behavioral, biological, cognitive, emotional, and social variables. The journal addresses such topics as family violence and abuse, marital and family assessment, families in transition, family policy, the family and employment, cross-cultural perspectives on the family, and marital and family processes, transitions, and life stages. Recent special issues include "Methodology in Family Science" and "Sibling Relationships Contribute to Individual and Family Well-Being." This widely indexed journal is highly recommended for academic libraries.

2499. *Journal of Family Psychotherapy: the official journal of the International Family Therapy Association.* Formerly (until 1988): *Journal of Psychotherapy and the Family.* [ISSN: 0897-5353] 1985. q. USD 565 print & online eds. Ed(s): Terry S Trepper. Haworth Press, Inc., 10 Alice St, Binghamton, NY 13904-1580; getinfo@ haworthpress.com; http://www.haworthpress.com. Adv. Sample. Refereed. Circ: 272 Paid. Microform: PQC. Online: EBSCO Publishing, EBSCO Host; OCLC Online Computer Library Center, Inc.; SwetsWise Online Content. Reprint: HAW. *Indexed:* BiolDig, ExcerpMed, FR, IMFL, PsycInfo, RiskAb, SFSA, SSA, SWA, SWR&A, SociolAb, V&AA. *Bk. rev.:* Number and length vary. *Aud.:* Ac, Sa.

The *Journal of Family Psychotherapy* fills a niche in the marriage and family therapy literature, focusing on a case study orientation. Case studies, program reports, and descriptions of strategies currently in clinical practice are written by clinicians for practicing clinicians. The journal is divided into sections that include "Minorities and Family Therapy," "Sexuality and the Family," "Applications of Current Research in Family Psychotherapy," and "Transgenerational Family Therapy." It presents articles that are "of immediate practical use to therapists." Thematic issues are published periodically; previous topics include "Education and Training in Solution-Focused Brief Therapy," "Family Therapy Around the World," and "Spirituality and Family Therapy." Book and media reviews are a regular feature. This journal is recommended for academic libraries supporting marriage and family therapy programs.

2500. *Journal of Family Therapy.* [ISSN: 0163-4445] 1979. q. GBP 243 print & online eds. Ed(s): Ivan Eisler. Blackwell Publishing Ltd., 9600 Garsington Rd, Oxford, OX4 2ZG, United Kingdom; customerservices@ blackwellpublishing.com; http://www.blackwellpublishing.com. Illus., index, adv. Refereed. Circ: 2500. Vol. ends: Nov. Online: Blackwell Synergy; EBSCO Publishing, EBSCO Host; Gale; IngentaConnect; OCLC Online Computer Library Center, Inc.; OhioLINK; Ovid Technologies, Inc.; SwetsWise Online Content. Reprint: PSC. *Indexed:* ASSIA, AgeL, ApEcolAb, FR, IBSS, IMFL, PsycInfo, RiskAb, SFSA, SSA, SSCI, SWA, SociolAb, V&AA. *Bk. rev.:* 1-4, 500-1,200 words. *Aud.:* Ac, Sa.

This peer-reviewed journal is the official publication of the Association for Family Therapy and Systemic Practice in the United Kingdom. It seeks to advance "the understanding and treatment of human relationships constituted in systems such as couples, families, professional networks, and wider groups." International contributions to each issue include research papers, training articles, and book reviews and represent all schools of thought within family therapy. Recent papers include "Multiple family therapy for anorexia nervosa: concepts, experiences and results," "A model to coordinate understanding of active autonomous learning," and "Placement of responsibility and moral reasoning in couple therapy." Recent special issues address such topics as eating disorders and the family, and postmodernism and family therapy. The editors welcome new contributors within Europe. Recommended for academic libraries that call for original research in family therapy.

2501. *Journal of Family Violence.* [ISSN: 0885-7482] 1986. bi-m. EUR 868 print & online eds. Ed(s): Vincent B Van Hasselt, Michel Hersen. Springer New York LLC, 233 Spring St, New York, NY 10013-1578; service-ny@springer.com; http://www.springer.com/. Illus., index, adv. Refereed. Vol. ends: Dec. Microform: PQC. Online: EBSCO Publishing, EBSCO Host; Gale; IngentaConnect; OCLC Online Computer Library Center, Inc.; OhioLINK; Ovid Technologies, Inc.; ProQuest LLC (Ann Arbor); Springer LINK; SwetsWise Online Content. Reprint: PSC. *Indexed:* ASG, ASSIA, AgeL, CINAHL, CJA, CJPI, FR, H&SSA, IBR, IBSS, IBZ, IMFL, PRA, PsycInfo, RI-1, RiskAb, SFSA, SSA, SSCI, SUSA, SociolAb, V&AA. *Bk. rev.:* 0-4, 300-1,000 words. *Aud.:* Ac, Sa.

This journal is interdisciplinary in scope, and its clinical and research reports draw from clinical and counseling psychology, criminology, law, marital counseling, psychiatry, public health, social work, and sociology. Papers, case studies, and review articles are also included. The journal addresses "clinical and investigative efforts concerning all forms of family violence and its precursors, including spouse-battering, child abuse, sexual abuse of children, incest, abuse of the elderly, marital rape, domestic homicide, the alcoholic marriage, and general family conflict." Intimate partner violence, gender-role stereotypes in domestic violence, reasons for returning to abusive relationships, the relationship between adolescent physical abuse and criminal offending, and rural versus urban victims of violence are just a few topics recently addressed. Recommended for academic libraries, especially those that support psychology or social work programs.

Journal of Feminist Family Therapy. See Psychology section.

2502. *Journal of Marital and Family Therapy.* Formerly (until 1979): *Journal of Marriage and Family Counseling.* [ISSN: 0194-472X] 1975. q. USD 266 print & online eds. Ed(s): Karen Wampler. Blackwell Publishing, Inc., Commerce Place, 350 Main St, Malden, MA 02148; customerservices@blackwellpublishing.com; http://www.blackwellpublishing.com. Illus., index, adv. Refereed. Circ: 20000. Vol. ends: Oct. Microform: PQC. Online: EBSCO Publishing, EBSCO Host; OCLC Online Computer Library Center, Inc.; ProQuest LLC (Ann Arbor); H.W. Wilson. *Indexed:* ASG, AgeL, ExcerpMed, IMFL, PsycInfo, SFSA, SSA, SSCI, SWA, SWR&A, SociolAb, V&AA. *Bk. rev.:* 3-10, 300-1,000 words, signed. *Aud.:* Ac, Sa.

Published by the American Association for Marriage and Family Therapy, this peer-reviewed journal "publishes articles on research, theory, clinical practice, and training in marital and family therapy." The practical articles, focused on clinical topics, are directed to marriage and family therapists. Recent articles include "Integrating Emotion-Focused Therapy with the Satir Model," "Changing Emotion: The Use of Therapeutic Storytelling," and "Integrating the

Older/Special Needs Adoptive Child into the Family." A recent issue includes a special section on the role of cognitive-behavioral interventions in couple and family therapy. Topics related to clinical practice, theory, and training are often included. As the leading family therapy journal, this is an essential title for academic libraries that serve programs in marriage and family therapy.

2503. Journal of Marriage and Family. Former titles (until 1964): *Marriage and Family Living;* (until 1940): *Living.* [ISSN: 0022-2445] 1939. 5x/yr. GBP 519 print & online eds. Ed(s): Alexis Walker. Blackwell Publishing, Inc., Commerce Place, 350 Main St, Malden, MA 02148; customerservices@blackwellpublishing.com; http://www.blackwellpublishing.com. Illus., index, adv. Refereed. Circ: 6200 Paid. CD-ROM: NISC International, Inc. Microform: PQC. Online: Blackwell Synergy; The Dialog Corporation; EBSCO Publishing, EBSCO Host; Gale; IngentaConnect; JSTOR (Web-based Journal Archive); OCLC Online Computer Library Center, Inc.; ProQuest LLC (Ann Arbor); SwetsWise Online Content. Reprint: PSC. *Indexed:* ABS&EES, ASG, AgeL, Agr, ApEcolAb, BRD, BRI, CBRI, CJA, CommAb, ECER, ERIC, ExcerpMed, FR, HRA, IBSS, IMFL, PsycInfo, RI-1, SFSA, SSA, SSCI, SUSA, SWA, SWR&A, SociolAb, V&AA. *Bk. rev.:* 7-21, 600-1,000 words. *Aud.:* Ac, Sa.

The *Journal of Marriage and Family* is one of two publications of the National Council on Family Relations and a leading resource in family research. According to the *ISI Journal Citation Reports,* it is the most highly cited journal in family studies. It presents original research and theory, research interpretation, and critical discussion related to marriage and the family. Here, marriage and family encompass other forms of close relationships. Contributors come from a diverse array of social science fields, including psychology, anthropology, sociology, history, and economics. All family-related topics are represented, including family structure, partner violence, child support, families formed outside of marriage, work and family demands, the changing family demography, cohabitation, marital satisfaction, and families and social policy. A special issue was published in 2005 on "Theoretical and Methodological Issues in Studying Families." Frequently cited and widely indexed, this journal is highly recommended for all academic libraries.

2504. Marriage & Family Review. [ISSN: 0149-4929] 1978. q. USD 690 print & online eds. Ed(s): Gary W Peterson, Suzanne Steinmetz. Haworth Press, Inc., 10 Alice St, Binghamton, NY 13904-1580; getinfo@haworthpress.com; http://www.haworthpress.com. Adv. Sample. Refereed. Circ: 413 Paid. Microform: PQC. Online: EBSCO Publishing, EBSCO Host; OCLC Online Computer Library Center, Inc.; ProQuest LLC (Ann Arbor); SwetsWise Online Content. Reprint: HAW. *Indexed:* ASG, ASSIA, AgeL, Agr, AmHI, CJA, CWI, FR, GendWatch, IBR, IBZ, IMFL, PsycInfo, SFSA, SSA, SSCI, SWA, SWR&A, SociolAb, V&AA. *Bk. rev.:* Number and length vary. *Aud.:* Ac, Sa.

Marriage & Family Review is an important source for practitioners and researchers, providing current, multidisciplinary coverage of social issues related to marriage and family life. A refereed journal, it is devoted to practice, new research and theory in marriage and family studies, and a wide range of disciplines that include psychology, sociology, social work, child development, education, nursing, and urban and policy studies. It is published primarily in thematic issues, and it has recently included such themes as "Macro-Level Influences on Parent-Youth Relations," "Challenges of Aging on U.S. Families: Policy and Practice Implications," and "Complementary Approaches in Cross-Cultural Parent-Youth Research," as well as course design and teaching strategies and techniques in family studies. Widely indexed, *Marriage & Family Review* is highly recommended for academic libraries.

Modern Bride. See Weddings section.

Mothering. See Parenting section.

Parenting. See Parenting section.

Parents. See Parenting section.

2505. Psychotherapy Networker: the magazine for today's helping professional. Formerly (until Mar. 2001): *Family Therapy Networker.* [ISSN: 1535-573X] 1982. bi-m. USD 24 domestic; USD 30 foreign. Ed(s): Richard Simon. Family Therapy Network, Inc., 5135 MacArthur Blvd NW, Washington, DC 20016. Illus., adv. Circ: 65000. Vol. ends: Nov. *Indexed:* AltPI, SWR&A. *Bk. rev.:* Number and length vary. *Aud.:* Ac, Sa.

Psychotherapy Networker is a trade publication aimed at therapists. Its mission is to inspire therapists and to connect them with their colleagues. Although written for therapists, the articles also are likely to appeal to general readers interested in psychology. Family therapy is a significant subject included in this publication. Feature articles, case studies, clinical methods, and career information, as well as regular columns addressing family matters, consultation, and networking provide practical information for therapists. Reviews of self-help and therapy books are included, as well as current popular film reviews written from a therapist's perspective. Because of its broad appeal, *Psychotherapy Networker* is recommended for academic and special libraries, as well as large public libraries.

Sexual and Relationship Therapy. See Sexuality section.

Studies in Family Planning. See Family Planning section.

Working Mother. See Fashion and Lifestyle section.

■ FAMILY PLANNING

See also Family and Marriage; Health and Fitness; Population Studies; and Pregnancy sections.

Kevin Deemer, Library Director, Kent State University Ashtabula Campus, Ashtabula, OH 44004; kdeemer@kent.edu

Introduction

Family Planning covers a range of topics from personal decisions about birth control and reproductive health to broader issues on global population growth. The journals and magazines selected publish articles relating to women's health, contraception, pregnancy, newborn care, sterilization, infertility, reproductive health, and population growth in both developed and developing countries. All titles selected will be of interest to health science libraries and academic libraries with nursing or related health care programs.

Basic Periodicals

Birth; Journal of Obstetric, Gynecologic, and Neonatal Nursing; Perspectives on Sexual Reproductive Health; Population Reports. English Edition; Studies in Family Planning.

Basic Abstracts and Indexes

Cumulative Index to Nursing and Allied Health Literature, MEDLINE, Population Index.

2506. Birth: issues in perinatal care. Formerly (until 1981): *Birth and the Family Journal.* [ISSN: 0730-7659] 1973. q. GBP 306 print & online eds. Ed(s): Diony Young. Blackwell Publishing, Inc., Commerce Place, 350 Main St, Malden, MA 02148; customerservices@ blackwellpublishing.com; http://www.blackwellpublishing.com. Illus., index, adv. Sample. Refereed. Circ: 3500. Vol. ends: Dec. Microform: PQC. Online: Blackwell Synergy; EBSCO Publishing, EBSCO Host; Gale; IngentaConnect; OCLC Online Computer Library Center, Inc.; OhioLINK; Ovid Technologies, Inc.; SwetsWise Online Content. Reprint: PSC. *Indexed:* ASSIA, ApEcolAb, CABA, CINAHL, DSA, ExcerpMed, PsycInfo, SCI, SSCI. *Bk. rev.:* 2-3. *Aud.:* Ac, Sa.

Birth is a multidisciplinary, refereed journal devoted to issues and practices in the care of childbearing women, infants, and families. The journal is written by and for maternal and neonatal nurses, midwives, physicians, public health workers, doulas, psychologists, social scientists, childbirth educators, lactation counselors, epidemiologists, and other health caregivers and policymakers in perinatal care. In addition to feature articles and columns, *Birth* publishes editorials, media reviews, news, and a calendar of events. Individual and institutional subscribers have access to full-text articles via the publisher's web site. Additional online services such as RSS feeds and the journal's table of contents delivered via e-mail are available to subscribers. This journal is recommended for medical libraries and academic libraries with health care programs.

2507. *Conceive Magazine (Florida).* [ISSN: 1550-8900] 2004. q. USD 19.20 domestic; USD 27.20 Canada; USD 39.20 elsewhere. Ed(s): Beth Weinhouse. Conceive Magazine, 622 E Washington St Ste 440, Orlando, FL 32801. Adv. Circ: 140000. *Aud.:* Sa.

Started in 2004, this glossy lifestyle magazine is "the first magazine for making babies." The audience is primarily women considering or planning to start a family. It provides information about women's health, fertility, infertility, conception, and adoption. Every issue has articles in various departments such as "Conceptual News," "A Fit Conception," "Adam & Eve," "Emotionally Speaking," "Fertabulary," "Boxers & Briefs," and "Legal Briefcase." The magazine's web site (www.conceivemagazine.com) provides additional information and resources like support groups, conception success stories, and expert advice. The articles are short and easy to read. This magazine is unique in its scope and aim. *Conceive Magazine* would be a useful, accessible resource for public libraries looking to provide information on infertility, adoption, and family planning.

2508. *Journal of Obstetric, Gynecologic, and Neonatal Nursing.* Incorporates (1990-1993): *A W H O N N's Clinical Issues in Perinatal and Women's Health Nursing;* Which was formerly (until 1992): *N A A C O G's Clinical Issues Perinatal and Women's Health Nursing;* Former titles (until 1985): *J O G N Nursing; Nurses Association of the American College of Obstetricians and Gynecologists. Bulletin News; Nurses Association of A.C.O.G. Bulletin.* [ISSN: 0884-2175] 1972. bi-m. USD 823 print & online eds. Ed(s): Margaret H Kearney, Nancy K Lowe. Blackwell Publishing, Inc., Commerce Place, 350 Main St, Malden, MA 02148; customerservices@blackwellpublishing.com; http://www.blackwellpublishing.com. Illus., adv. Refereed. Circ: 22862 Paid. Vol. ends: Nov/Dec. CD-ROM: Ovid Technologies, Inc. Microform: PQC. Online: Blackwell Synergy; EBSCO Publishing, EBSCO Host; HighWire Press; OCLC Online Computer Library Center, Inc.; Ovid Technologies, Inc.; SAGE Publications, Inc., SAGE Journals Online; SwetsWise Online Content. Reprint: PSC. *Indexed:* CABA, CINAHL, DSA, PsycInfo, SCI, SFSA, SSCI. *Aud.:* Ac, Sa.

This journal in its 35th year is the official publication of the Association of Women's Health, Obstetric and Neonatal Nurses (AWHONN). It is a scholarly, peer-reviewed publication addressing the latest research practice issues, policies, opinions, and trends affecting women, childbearing families, and newborns. Articles are authored by nurses and emphasize evidence-based and clinical nursing practices. As of 2006, the journal is now published by Blackwell. Individual and institutional subscribers have access to full-text articles via the publisher's web site. Additional online services such as RSS feeds and the journal's table of contents delivered via e-mail are available to subscribers. Institutional subscribers also receive a subscription to another AWHONN publication titled *AWHONN Lifelines. JOGNN* is recommended for academic and health science libraries serving nursing faculty and nursing students.

2509. *M C N: American Journal of Maternal Child Nursing.* [ISSN: 0361-929X] 1976. bi-m. USD 194 (Individuals, USD 50.95). Ed(s): Margaret Comerford Freda. Lippincott Williams & Wilkins, 530 Walnut St, Philadelphia, PA 19106-3621; http://www.lww.com. Illus., index, adv. Sample. Circ: 22000. Vol. ends: Nov/Dec. CD-ROM: Ovid Technologies, Inc. Microform: PQC. Online: EBSCO Publishing, EBSCO Host; Ovid Technologies, Inc.; SwetsWise Online Content. *Indexed:* AgeL, CINAHL, IMFL, PsycInfo, SCI, SSCI. *Aud.:* Ac, Sa.

MCN is a peer-reviewed journal focusing on today's major issues and high priority problems in maternal/child nursing, women's health, and family nursing, with extensive coverage of advanced practice health care issues

relating to infants and young children. The journal is intended for nurses practicing in perinatal, neonatal, midwifery, and pediatric specialties. *MCN* publishes clinically relevant practice and research articles aimed at assisting nurses with evidence-based practice. Individual print subscribers also receive full-text online access to the journal. Recommended for medical libraries and academic libraries serving nurses or nursing students.

2510. *Nursing for Women's Health.* Formerly (until 2007): *A W H O N N Lifelines.* [ISSN: 1751-4851] 1997. bi-m. GBP 106 print & online eds. Ed(s): Ann Katz. Blackwell Publishing, Inc., Commerce Place, 350 Main St, Malden, MA 02148; customerservices@blackwellpublishing.com; http://www.blackwellpublishing.com. Illus., index, adv. Sample. Refereed. Circ: 22431 Paid. Vol. ends: Dec. CD-ROM: Ovid Technologies, Inc. Online: Blackwell Synergy; EBSCO Publishing, EBSCO Host; HighWire Press; Ovid Technologies, Inc.; SAGE Publications, Inc., SAGE Journals Online; SwetsWise Online Content. Reprint: PSC. *Indexed:* CINAHL, SFSA. *Aud.:* Ac, Sa.

A publication of the Association of Women's Health, Obstetric and Neonatal Nurses, *AWHONN Lifelines* publishes articles primarily on women's health, newborn care, and professional nursing issues. It is a refereed publication featuring articles with practical application to the clinical setting rather than original research. Articles are typically authored by nurses and written in concise, practical, and easy-to-read format. As of 2006, *Lifelines* is now published by Blackwell. Individual and institutional subscribers have access to full-text articles via the publisher's web site. Additional online services such as RSS feeds and the journal's table of contents delivered via e-mail are available to subscribers. Institutional subscribers to *Lifelines* also receive a subscription to another AWHONN publication titled *Journal of Obstetric, Gynecologic, & Neonatal Nursing. AWHONN Lifelines* is recommended for libraries serving nurses or nursing students.

2511. *Perspectives on Sexual and Reproductive Health.* Formerly (until 2002): *Family Planning Perspectives.* [ISSN: 1538-6341] 1969. q. Ed(s): Patricia Donovan. Blackwell Publishing, Inc., Commerce Place, 350 Main St, Malden, MA 02148; customerservices@blackwellpublishing.com; http://www.blackwellpublishing.com. Illus., index, adv. Refereed. Circ: 5649 Paid and free. Vol. ends: Nov/Dec. Microform: CIS; PQC. Online: EBSCO Publishing, EBSCO Host; Gale; JSTOR (Web-based Journal Archive); Northern Light Technology, Inc.; OCLC Online Computer Library Center, Inc.; ProQuest K-12 Learning Solutions; ProQuest LLC (Ann Arbor). *Indexed:* AbAn, Agr, BiolDig, CINAHL, CWI, EnvAb, EnvInd, ExcerpMed, HRA, IMFL, PAIS, SFSA, SSCI, SWA, SWR&A. *Bk. rev.:* Number and length vary. *Aud.:* Sa.

Perspectives on Sexual and Reproductive Health publishes peer-reviewed, policy-relevant research articles on sexual and reproductive health and rights in the United States and other industrialized countries. The journal is published by the Guttmacher Institute, a nonprofit organization focused on sexual and reproductive health research, policy analysis, and public education. The institute's mission is to protect the reproductive choices of all women and men throughout the world. Additionally, the institute supports a person's ability to safeguard their health and exercise individual responsibilities in regard to sexual behavior, relationships, reproduction, and family formation. Each issue of *Perspectives on Sexual and Reproductive Health* publishes research articles, an introductory section by the editors called "In This Issue," a "Digest" section, and a section titled "FYI." The Guttmacher Institute's web site provides access to the current issue and a searchable archive. *Perspectives on Sexual and Reproductive Health* is highly recommended for any library wanting to provide information on family planning and reproductive health.

2512. *Population Reports (English Edition).* Formerly: *George Washington University. Population Information Program. Population Reports.* [ISSN: 0887-0241] 1973. 4x/yr. Free to qualified personnel. Johns Hopkins University, Population Information Program, Bloomberg School of Public Health, 111 Market Pl, Ste 310, Baltimore, MD 21202; Poprepts@jhuccp.org; http://www.jhuccp.org. Illus. Sample. Circ: 81000. Vol. ends: Dec. Online: EBSCO Publishing, EBSCO Host; Gale. *Indexed:* MASUSE. *Aud.:* Hs, Ga, Ac, Sa.

The aim of *Population Reports* is to provide an accurate and authoritative overview of important developments in family planning and related health issues. Each issue focuses on a single topic that is assigned to one of ten series: Oral Contraceptives, Intrauterine Devices, Female Sterilization, Male Sterilization, Barrier Methods, Family Planning Programs, Injectables and Implants, Issues in World Health, Special Topics, and Maximizing Access and Quality. *Population Reports* is published in several languages including English, French, Spanish, and Portuguese; some reports are also condensed and translated into Arabic, Indonesian, Russian, and Turkish. Ninety percent of *Population Reports* is distributed to developing countries. The full text of *Population Reports* is available online at www.infoforhealth.org/pr. Each report is well written, accessible, and easy to read. This publication would benefit any public or academic library collection.

2513. Studies in Family Planning. Incorporates: *Current Publications in Family Planning.* [ISSN: 0039-3665] 1963. q. USD 141 print & online eds. Ed(s): Gary Bologh. Blackwell Publishing, Inc., Commerce Place, 350 Main St, Malden, MA 02148; customerservices@ blackwellpublishing.com; http://www.blackwellpublishing.com. Illus., index. Refereed. Circ: 6000 Paid and free. Vol. ends: Dec. Microform: PQC. Online: Blackwell Synergy; EBSCO Publishing, EBSCO Host; Florida Center for Library Automation; Gale; IngentaConnect; JSTOR (Web-based Journal Archive); Northern Light Technology, Inc.; OCLC Online Computer Library Center, Inc.; SwetsWise Online Content. Reprint: PSC. *Indexed:* ABS&EES, ASSIA, ApEcolAb, ArtHuCI, BAS, CABA, CINAHL, CWI, DSA, EIP, EnvAb, EnvInd, ExcerpMed, H&SSA, IBR, IBSS, IBZ, IMFL, IndIslam, JEL, PAIS, PRA, PsycInfo, RRTA, RiskAb, SFSA, SSA, SSCI, SWA, SociolAb, V&AA, WAE&RSA. *Bk. rev.:* 3-4. *Aud.:* Ac, Sa.

Studies in Family Planning is a peer-reviewed, international journal interested in all aspects of reproductive health, fertility regulation, and family planning programs in both developing and developed countries. Each issue contains research articles, reports, individual country data from demographic and health surveys, book reviews, and an occasional commentary. Individual and institutional subscribers have access to full-text articles via the publisher's web site. Additional online services such as RSS feeds and e-mail delivery of the journal's table of contents are also available to subscribers. *Studies in Family Planning* is recommended for academic libraries serving institutions with health-related programs.

■ FASHION AND LIFESTYLE

Monica Fusich, Henry Madden Library, 5200 N. Barton Ave., M/S 34, California State University–Fresno, Fresno, CA 93740-8014.

Charles A. Skewis, Head, Collection & Resource Services, Georgia Southern University, Statesboro, GA 30460-8074; cskewis@georgiasouthern.edu.

Vang Vang, Henry Madden Library, 5200 N. Barton Ave., M/S 34, California State University–Fresno, Fresno, CA 93740-8014; vangv@csufresno.edu.

Thomas L. Kilpatrick, Professor Emeritus, Southern Illinois University Libraries, Carbondale, IL 62901-6632; tkilpatrick@hcis.net.

Cheryl LaGuardia, Research Librarian, Widener Library, Harvard University, Cambridge, MA 02138

Introduction

This section was created by combining titles derived from several former sections (Men, Women: Fashion, etc.) with new publications focused on cultural issues of style.

Why this change? Because it has been an interesting time for the genre of fashion magazines. They have remained competitive by updating their content and keeping current by using celebrities rather than supermodels on their covers. They are also delving into the teen market with the release of *Teen Vogue*

and *Teen Elle*. With youth increasingly interested in clothing and appearance, this is a trend that is sure to continue, as is the appearance of men's style entries such as *Razor*.

The fashion and lifestyle magazine field is very competitive and hard to break into, which was seen with the failed launch of *Suede*, a title that seemed as if it would be popular with urban women. However, it began with a circulation of 250,000, aimed at twenty-something women of color, and folded after a mere four issues.

Fashion and the Internet are a perfect match. The Internet offers instantaneous access to fashion reporting by using web-streaming to highlight fashion shows and designers' collections. The fashion industry quickly saw the value of the Internet as an advertising and information medium and began to develop commercial sites. Most of these offer the table of contents of current issues, with some special features to lure readers to these sites. The growth of fashion reporting from print to the Internet emphasizes the universal interest in fashion.

Basic Periodicals

Cosmopolitan, Elle, Family Circle, Glamour, GQ, Good Housekeeping, InStyle, Marie Claire, Maxim: for men, New Man, Redbook, SharpMan, Vogue.

Basic Abstracts and Indexes

Consumer's Index, Design and Applied Arts Index, Magazine Index Plus, Readers' Guide to Periodical Literature.

2514. Adventure Time Magazine. 1996. m. Ed(s): Gary Winterhalter. Adventure Time Magazine, http://www.adventuretime.com. *Aud.:* Ga.

This title's focus is on activities that challenge strength, endurance, and intelligence. Even if the reader doesn't want to drive a dog team across the frozen tundra or kayak down a dangerous river, men will enjoy the opportunity to read about someone else's adventures in doing those things. Well written, although biased toward difficult sports.

2515. Allure. [ISSN: 1054-7711] 1991. m. USD 15 domestic; USD 34 Canada; USD 39 elsewhere. Ed(s): Linda Wells, Susan Kittenlan. Conde Nast Publications, Inc., 750 3rd Ave, New York, NY 10017; http://www.condenast.com. Illus., adv. Circ: 1014384 Paid. Vol. ends: Feb. Microform: PQC. Online: Gale; LexisNexis; ProQuest LLC (Ann Arbor). *Aud.:* Ga.

Allure has become a mainstream women's fashion, health, and beauty magazine. The magazine lacks the nontraditional approach to the definition of "beauty" that it highlighted at its inception, and it now displays the traditional beauty magazine features: fashion, hair, cosmetics, health, and celebrities. Each issue offers clothes, cosmetics, and accessory tips, products, and trends through features such as "Beauty Insider," "Beauty 101," and "Fashion Report." *Allure* does successfully cover many of the same topics as competitors such as *Elle*. Also, much of the magazine is photographic, although fashion layouts lack the rough edge of the magazine's earlier days. The magazine's web site highlights the contents of the current issue and provides beauty and fashion tips and product reviews, reader forums and polls, and "Talk to Allure."

2516. American Cowboy. Former titles: *American Cowboy Magazine;* (until 1979): *Hoof and Horn.* [ISSN: 1079-3690] 1931. bi-m. USD 14.95 domestic; USD 24.95 Canada; USD 29.95 elsewhere. Ed(s): Jesse Mullins. American Cowboy, L.L.C., 1949 Sugarland Dr, Ste 220, Sheridan, WY 82801-7102; editor@cowboy.com. Illus., adv. Sample. Circ: 85000 Paid. Vol. ends: No. 6. *Bk. rev.:* 5, 200 words, signed. *Aud.:* Ga.

American Cowboy is more about a lifestyle than the horses involved in it, but it is hard to separate the cowboy from his horse. This journal covers Western travel, art, food, entertainment, sports, and more, all through the lens of the cowboy. It finds the cowboy culture alive and well, and provides an opportunity for readers to experience it for themselves through travel recommendations to ranches, events, and more generally, to the American West. Rodeos, trail rides, and cattle drives are regular features. Brightly photographed covers include country music stars and cowboy movie favorites but also the real American cowboy at work and play.

2517. Arena (London): the grown-up magazine for men. [ISSN: 0955-0046] 1986. m. GBP 30.60; GBP 3.40 newsstand/cover. Ed(s): Greg Williams. Emap Metro Ltd, Mappin Ho, 4 Winsley St, London, W1W 8HF, United Kingdom. Illus., adv. *Bk. rev.:* 6, 200 words, signed. *Aud.:* Ga.

Arena is a sophisticated general-interest magazine with a strong male orientation similar to *Esquire,* its American counterpart. Work, leisure, politics, travel, fashion, biography, sports, and other topics of interest to the culture-conscious male are treated in grand style. *Arena* is highly recommended for the library that seeks reading material with an international flair for the sophisticated male. *Arena Homme Plus,* a biannual by the same publisher, will also be enjoyed by men interested in cutting-edge trends in fashion.

Audrey. See Asian American section.

2518. Backwoodsman. 1980. 6x/yr. USD 18. Backwoodsman Press, c/o Charlie Richie, Ed, Box 627, Westcliffe, CO 81252. Adv. Circ: 30000. *Bk. rev.:* 3, 200 words, signed. *Aud.:* Ga.

Backwoodsman is a fascinating magazine, whether or not you're into the outdoor scene. The brief, well-illustrated articles cover all aspects of backwoods life, including fishing and hunting, nature, survival in the wilds, handicrafts (soap making, knife making, fly tying, etc.), building cabins and other types of shelters, hobbies, woods lore, and much more. Although a niche publication, *Backwoodsman* would fit comfortably into the magazine selection of many libraries.

2519. Bust: for women with something to get off their chests. [ISSN: 1089-4713] 1993. bi-m. USD 19.95 domestic; USD 29.95 Canada; USD 39.95 elsewhere. Ed(s): Debbie Stoller. Bust, Inc., PO Box 1016, New York, NY 10276; debbie@bust.com; http://www.bust.com. *Indexed:* FemPer. *Bk. rev.:* 22, 150-300 words. *Aud.:* Hs, Ga.

Bust provides a newsstand antidote to mainstream women's magazines. While many of the topics are the same, the perspective is decidedly alternative, unconventional, and liberal. For example, the subject matter of the "Broadcast" and "Real Life" sections ranges from political activism, honor killings in Pakistan, and abortion, to the history of hair color, instructions for making a charm bracelet, and stereo-buying advice. Each issue has a general theme (e.g., "The Age Issue," "Fight Like a Girl Issue") and includes various takes on that theme through first-person articles, personality profiles, and in-depth, frank celebrity interviews. "The *Bust* Guide" covers a wide range of film, book, and music reviews. A healthy and empowering attitude toward sex is endorsed through sex product advertising, a regular advice column from "sexpert Susie Bright," and "One-Handed Read," a soft-core erotic short story at the end of the issue. The web site is as interesting and varied as the magazine: it offers an online store, information on subscription prices and back issue information (including sample stories from previous issues), a calendar of events, "News from the Net," a chat room, message boards, greeting cards, and personals. Also, a directory of web sites of interest to *Bust* readers called "Girl Wide Web" offers links to sites arranged in subject categories such as "Culture Vulture" and "She-Commerce & Services."

2520. Chatelaine (English Edition). [ISSN: 0009-1995] 1928. m. CND 19.98 domestic; CND 49 United States; CND 54 elsewhere. Ed(s): Rona Maynard. Rogers Media Publishing Ltd, One Mount Pleasant Rd, 11th Fl, Toronto, ON M4Y 2Y5, Canada; http://www.rogers.com. Illus., adv. Circ: 750000. Microform: MIM; MML; PQC. Online: EBSCO Publishing, EBSCO Host; Micromedia ProQuest; ProQuest LLC (Ann Arbor). *Indexed:* CBCARef, CPerI, MASUSE, PdeR. *Aud.:* Ga.

This premier Canadian women's service magazine calls itself "Canada's biggest kitchen table." While it offers many of the same features as the well-known U.S. titles, it takes a distinctly national perspective and has been recognized as a Magazine of the Year by the Canadian National Magazine Awards. The magazine features regular columns that cover business, health, technology, personal financial management, and parenting. Home life is covered through food columns that feature quick recipes, inexpensive crafts, decorating tips, and make-your-own fashions with mail-order patterns. Articles on health and family, relationships, Canadian celebrities, and personal-interest stories round out *Chatelaine.* There is also a French edition [ISSN: 0317-2635]. The

magazine offers an electronic version, *Chatelaine Connects,* that has also achieved recognition as the most-used web site by Canadian women. The site offers a number of features and services organized to reflect the magazine's content. There are links to back issues, discussion groups on health, family, work, and money, and to other web sites. A reader poll, promotions, contests, a buyer's guide, a book club, and an e-mail alerting service round out the site. It is well designed and could serve as a model to emulate for other women's service magazines.

2521. Cigar Aficionado: the good life magazine for men. [ISSN: 1063-7885] 1991. bi-m. USD 19.95 domestic; USD 25.95 Canada; USD 48 elsewhere. Ed(s): Gordon Mott, Marvin R Shanken. Marvin R. Shanken Communications, Inc., 387 Park Ave S, New York, NY 10016; http://www.cigaraficionado.com. Illus., adv. Circ: 290000 Paid. *Aud.:* Ga.

The first thing that strikes the new reader when opening an issue of *Cigar Aficionado* is the fact that there is far more to the magazine than the title implies. Certainly, cigars are much in evidence; information about fine cigars is provided, news affecting cigars and smoking laws is reported, and restaurants in cities around the country that permit cigar smoking are reviewed. However, the target audience for *Cigar Aficionado* is the affluent male who can enjoy a good cigar, along with other life's pleasures, which include travel, dining, the arts, sports, literature, hobbies, collecting, golf, fishing, and more. Each issue contains a personality profile, ranging from President Kennedy to Demi Moore. The pleasures of cigar smoking are seamlessly integrated into this eye-catching magazine, so that a non-smoker can easily enjoy an issue as well as his cigar-smoking friend. Librarians should take a look.

2522. Complex Magazine. [ISSN: 1538-6848] 2002. bi-m. 5/yr. until 2003. USD 14.99 domestic; USD 25 Canada; USD 40 elsewhere. Complex Media LLC, 1350 Broadway, Ste 511, New York, NY 10018; contactus@ complexmagazine.com. Illus., adv. Circ: 300000 Controlled. *Aud.:* Ga.

A shopping guide for the hip-hop culture, *Complex Magazine* covers the current retail market for the up-to-thirties male. Columns and feature articles provide outfitting guidance for the well-appointed young man, from sneakers to baseball caps, with information on the appropriate automobile and the latest in electronic accessories rounding out the perfect image. Young men on the go will devour the information provided here.

2523. Cosmopolitan. Formerly (until 1952): *Hearst's International Combined with Cosmopolitan;* Which was formed by the 1925 merger of (1921-1925): *Hearst's International;* (1886-1925): *The Cosmopolitan.* [ISSN: 0010-9541] 1886. m. USD 18 domestic; USD 42 foreign; USD 3.99 newsstand/cover per issue. Ed(s): Kate White. Hearst Magazines, 300 W 57th St, New York, NY 10019; HearstMagazines@hearst.com; http://www.hearstcorp.com/magazines/. Illus., adv. Circ: 2900000 Paid. Vol. ends: Dec. Microform: PQC. Online: EBSCO Publishing, EBSCO Host; Gale; Northern Light Technology, Inc.; OCLC Online Computer Library Center, Inc.; ProQuest LLC (Ann Arbor). *Indexed:* ASIP, DAAI, LRI, MASUSE, MRD. *Bk. rev.:* 4-6; brief, 500 words. *Aud.:* Ga.

Cosmo continues to adapt to the changing landscape of women's magazine publishing while maintaining its "bad girl" image. The focus is on the "*Cosmo* Girl" and her needs: sex, looks, relationships, success, and more sex as reflected in the advertising as well as the content. Work is less prominently featured, although each issue includes an item or two devoted to careers and personal financial management. Entertainment is featured in "Cosmo Informer," which focuses on trends, films, and celebrity gossip. Much of the magazine is question-and-answer advice columns and regular features like the "Dating Diary" and "Man Manual," which provide male beefcake rivaling *Playgirl* magazine. Feature stories highlight celebrities and sex and relationship articles with a "pop-psych" bent on such topics as extramarital affairs and keeping a man interested. Each issue also includes several reader-contributed features. "Book Club" provides a book adaptation that leans toward soft-core pornography. *Cosmo*'s web site offers various reader advice and survey links, including "Cosmo Quiz," a sex-article archive, "Bedside Astrologer," and a celebrity interview.

2524. Country Woman. Former titles (until 1987): *Farm Woman;* (until 1986): *Farm Woman News;* (until 1985): *Farm Wife News.* [ISSN: 0892-8525] 1971. bi-m. USD 14.98 domestic; USD 19.98 Canada; USD

25.98 elsewhere. Ed(s): Ann Kaiser. Reiman Media Group, Inc., 5400 S 60th St, Greendale, WI 53129; subscriberservices@reimanpub.com; http://www.reimanpub.com. Illus., adv. Sample. Circ: 2300000 Paid. Vol. ends: Dec. *Aud.:* Hs, Ga.

Country Woman describes itself as a magazine "for farm and country women and those who have moved from the country in body but not in heart." Readers are the writers and contributors that create each issue. Through letters, household hints, farm and garden advice, do-it-yourself information, home photos, craft patterns, personality features about women and their hobbies and interests, travel features, and recipes, this magazine provides a means for rural women as well as those interested in country life to network with one another and share experiences and information. Although geared toward women, it appeals to a broad readership. Frequent contests and surveys are offered and promoted. Pleasure reading is provided through short fiction and readers' poetry. A companion web site provides links to a "Country Store," cooking schools, recipes, and tours plus the table of contents and a feature story from the latest issue.

2525. *Details.* [ISSN: 0740-4921] 1982. 10x/yr. USD 9.97 domestic; USD 30 Canada; USD 37.95 elsewhere. Ed(s): Daniel Peres. Fairchild Publications, Inc., 750 3rd Ave, 3rd Fl, New York, NY 10017; customerservice@fairchildpub.com; http://www.fairchildpub.com. Illus., adv. Sample. Circ: 408844 Paid. Vol. ends: No. 12. *Indexed:* ASIP. *Aud.:* Ga, Ac.

This trendy magazine is directed at style-conscious young men in their twenties and thirties. *Details* is outspoken, outrageous, and very readable. Fashion, grooming, style, sex, politics, adventure, and popular culture are highlighted in a slick, attractive, and browsable format that is designed to compete with *GQ* for readership. Public and college libraries will find it very popular.

2526. *Easyriders.* [ISSN: 0046-0990] 1971. m. USD 39.95; USD 6.99 newsstand/cover. Ed(s): Sandie Nilsen, Dave Nichols. Paisano Publications, Inc., 28210 Dorothy Dr, Box 3075, Agoura Hills, CA 91301. Illus., adv. Circ: 31000 Paid. *Bk. rev.:* 4, 100 words. *Aud.:* Ga.

"The world's largest-selling motorcycle magazine for men," *Easyriders* is a popular monthly that will appeal to a different readership than *GQ* or *FHM.* Each issue, written for the motorcycle enthusiast, features the hottest bikes and the prettiest models imaginable. Well-known bikers, bike shows, biker-friendly cities and towns, special road trips, and customized cycles are featured on a regular basis. A 30-page feature called "General Store" contains ads and purchase information for biker clothing and accessories. This is definitely a niche publication, and public librarians might consider it for purchase if its clientele includes a large biker population.

2527. *Elle.* [ISSN: 0888-0808] 1985. m. USD 10 domestic; USD 30 foreign; USD 3.50 newsstand/cover. Ed(s): Roberta Myers. Hachette Filipacchi Media U.S., Inc., 1633 Broadway, New York, NY 10019; http://www.hfmus.com. Illus., adv. Circ: 1014418 Paid. Vol. ends: Aug. *Indexed:* ASIP, MRD. *Bk. rev.:* 8-12, brief. *Aud.:* Hs, Ga.

Elle is a well-rounded fashion magazine that includes lifestyle, relationship, health, fitness, and beauty features. A considerable portion of each issue is also devoted to information on culture, politics, and social issues. Articles cover music, literature, and film as well as a celebrity cover story and fiction. Regular columns such as "Ask E. Jean" provide relationship advice. "Elle First" covers fashion news and trends, and "Fashion Reporter" follows runway news and trends in the industry. Lush, artistic fashion layouts also remain a prominent feature, emphasizing designer wear. Each issue includes a calendar of fashion-related events and museum openings, a retail guide, and numerology and horoscope features. *Elle*'s web site complements the print title by offering online fashion stories, photos from designer collections, an issue preview, events calendar, and a discussion forum and e-mail newsletter.

2528. *Essence (New York): the magazine for today's black woman.* [ISSN: 0014-0880] 1970. m. USD 47.88 domestic; USD 34.96 Canada; USD 13.99 newsstand/cover. Ed(s): Susan L Taylor, Diane Weathers. Essence Communications Inc., 1500 Broadway, 6th Fl, New York, NY 10036-4015; info@essence.com; http://www.essence.com. Illus., adv.

Circ: 950000 Paid. Vol. ends: Dec. Microform: PQC. Online: EBSCO Publishing, EBSCO Host; Gale; LexisNexis; OCLC Online Computer Library Center, Inc.; ProQuest LLC (Ann Arbor). *Indexed:* BRI, CBRI, MASUSE, MRD, RGPR. *Bk. rev.:* 4-5, 75 words; 6, 15 words; unsigned. *Aud.:* Hs, Ac, Sa.

Essence is a well-written, interesting magazine that is marketed to African American women but includes many features of broad interest. Articles are typical of those found in other general-interest women's magazines—male/female relationships, health and fitness, beauty, diet, parenting, financial management, careers, recipes, decorating, fashion, and travel—but they are approached from an African American perspective and in the voices of this population. Several point-of-view and advice columns provide personal perspectives on issues. Each issue contains two or three inspirational articles on prominent African American personalities in the arts, politics, education, and other fields. The magazine also sponsors the annual Essence Awards, highlighting accomplishments of African Americans. There is at least one article in each issue on a social issue relevant to the African American community, such as sexual harassment, AIDS, and gang violence. Each issue also includes "In the Spirit," a long-standing inspirational message from Susan L. Taylor, Editorial Director, and a "Where to Buy" page. *Essence* ranks among the top magazines for readership among African American adults. Its circulation continues to grow, and it appeals to both men and women. The web site provides highlights of the current issue; book, film, and music reviews; celebrity profiles; a calendar of events, polls, and beauty tips. The magazine also features "Essence Cares," a National Mentoring Movement initiative.

2529. *F H M (United States).* [ISSN: 1532-0588] 2000. m. USD 14.97 domestic; USD 20.97 foreign. Ed(s): Scott Gramling, Jonathan Tesser. Emap USA, 110 Fifth Ave, New York, NY 10011. Illus., adv. Circ: 5025000 Paid. *Aud.:* Ga.

This publication for men, which originated in Great Britain in 1985, has now gone international, with an American version sold alongside, or instead of, the British version in the United States. Both the British and the American versions focus on cutting-edge topics and the latest in fashion, entertainment, lifestyles, jobs, celebrities, sports, fast cars, fads, and adventure. The format integrates a wealth of information, opinion, and pointed satire in neat capsules, lavishly illustrated. The Americanization of this title has caused changes in style intended to appeal to an American audience. Collection development librarians may wish to compare the British and the American versions before subscribing.

2530. *Family Circle.* [ISSN: 0014-7206] 1932. 15x/yr. USD 19.98; USD 2.50 newsstand/cover. Ed(s): Linda Fears. Meredith Corp., 1716 Locust St, Des Moines, IA 50309-3023; mimcontact@meredith.com; http://www.meredith.com. Illus., adv. Circ: 3800000 Paid. Vol. ends: Dec. *Indexed:* ASIP, AgeL, ConsI, IHTDI. *Aud.:* Ga.

Family Circle continues to wage war at the checkout counter with *Woman's Day.* Each issue's bright, colorful cover promises tips to make women's lives easier or to help them achieve a goal. In addition, departments provide advice from experts on issues of interest to the contemporary working wife, mother, and homemaker on cooking, decorating and crafts, beauty and fashion, medical news, gardening, health and fitness, travel, and even pet care. *Family Circle* recognizes the dual role of a woman as mother and worker, so recipes and decorating tips are quick, practical, and economical. Regular features include "Circle This," which provides consumer news; "Family Answer Book," which features advice on money, marriage, law, family matters, and other topics; and "Buyer's Guide." One or two lengthy features highlight the life of a celebrity or, in the feature "Women Who Make a Difference," offer an inspiring, real-life story that frequently shows a woman's triumph over adversity. The magazine's web site highlights the contents of current and past issues and links to recipes and gardening, decorating, and other advice.

2531. *Fashion Net.* 1995. w. Triple International Ltd., http://www.fashionnet.com. Illus. *Aud.:* Ga, Sa.

Fashion Net: the Guide to All Things Chic offers weekly fashion news, links to designers, and useful information on the fashion industry for aspiring fashion designers, models, stylists or photographers. *Fashion Net* also includes message boards and job listings, and it e-mails weekly fashion updates.

2532. First for Women. [ISSN: 1040-9467] 1989. 17x/yr. USD 19.97; USD 1.99 newsstand/cover. Bauer Publishing Company, L.P., 270 Sylvan Ave, Englewood Cliffs, NJ 07632; http://www.ffmarket.com. Illus., adv. Circ: 1350000 Paid. *Aud.:* Ga.

First for Women is a quick-read magazine with multiple short articles on a wide variety of topics geared toward "women on the go," the stay-at-home mom, and women who must juggle the responsibilities of work and home. Articles are grouped into three main parts: "You," "Family," and "Fun." *First for Women* has improved on the quality of its advertisers since its inception, and it looks a little less cluttered in recent years, but it still retains the overcrowded, busy look and feel of supermarket tabloids. Each issue is heavy on photographs and light on content, which is delivered primarily in the format of tips, lists, and advice columns. There are no editor's letters or readers' letters concerning the content of past issues. Editorial content is well written, attractively illustrated, and nicely laid out, but this magazine has yet to achieve the circulation of its venerable grocery store competitors, *Family Circle* and *Woman's Day*.

2533. Flare (Toronto): Canada's fashion magazine. Formerly: *Miss Chatelaine*. [ISSN: 0708-4927] 1964. m. CND 19.98 domestic; CND 51.52 United States; CND 54.52 elsewhere. Ed(s): Lisa Tant. Rogers Media Publishing Ltd, One Mount Pleasant Rd, 8th Fl, Toronto, ON M4Y 2Y5, Canada; http://www.rogers.com. Illus., adv. Circ: 201000 Paid. Vol. ends: Dec. Microform: MML. Online: EBSCO Publishing, EBSCO Host; Micromedia ProQuest; ProQuest LLC (Ann Arbor). *Indexed:* CBCARef, CPerI. *Aud.:* Hs, Ga.

Flare is the fashion, beauty, and health magazine for the contemporary Canadian woman. Regular columns and features consist primarily of brief news items and tips on cosmetics, skin and hair care, fitness, health, decorating, and fashion. Fashion layouts have become less practical, more youthful—and more expensive—in recent years, suggesting a marketing move toward a younger readership and away from career women who are seeking more practical and affordable fashion. A buying guide is provided. Also included in each issue are relationship advice; information on decorating, health, and fitness; and personality features. *Flare Online* provides links to fashion, beauty, health information and advice, and fashion resources; there are also links to Canadian fashion theater, gallery, and music events. The site also highlights the current issue of the magazine along with fashion and beauty tips, a horoscope, contests, a store, and reader forums.

2534. G Q: gentlemen's quarterly for men. [ISSN: 0016-6979] 1957. m. USD 12 domestic; USD 37 Canada; USD 38 elsewhere. Ed(s): Mary Gail Pezzimenti. Conde Nast Publications, Inc., 750 3rd Ave, New York, NY 10017; gqmag@aol.com; http://www.gq.com. Illus., adv. Circ: 666450 Paid. Vol. ends: Winter. Microform: PQC. Online: Factiva, Inc.; H.W. Wilson. *Indexed:* ASIP, IIFF, RGPR, RILM. *Aud.:* Hs, Ga, Ac.

The leading fashion magazine for the American male, *GQ* is the first stop for the man-on-the-go with an interest in looking good and being seen in the right places. Quality writing, amply illustrated with eye-catching photography, appeals to the "in crowd." Feature articles emphasize clothing, travel, and dining, with frequent glimpses into the private lives of the current trendsetters. The young, style-conscious male will find useful the regular columns on grooming, finance, fashion, and music, and will enjoy the occasional fiction that finds its way into *GQ*. Librarians will find it a favorite among young men for browsing and in-depth reading.

2535. Giant (New York). [ISSN: 1550-6614] 2004. 10x/yr. USD 7.97 domestic; USD 30 Canada; USD 50 elsewhere. Ed(s): Smokey Fontaine. Giant Magazine, LLC., 440 9th Ave, 11th Fl, New York, NY 10001; info@giantmag.com. Adv. Circ: 200000. *Bk. rev.:* 5, 300 words, signed. *Aud.:* Ga.

A bimonthly media event for men, *Giant* is the most fun a guy can have with a magazine. *Giant* focuses on movies, DVDs, TV, games, print media, and the month's best web sites, with feature articles on entertainment personalities, special events, classic media, and trends, with a secondary emphasis on fashion, all done up in a neat and exciting package for men. The writing is fresh, with a twist of irony, layouts are eye-catching, and the photography is breathtaking. With not a hint of being a gossip mag from the check-out lane of the grocery store, *Giant* is pure class.

2536. Glamour. Incorporates: *Charm*. [ISSN: 0017-0747] 1939. m. USD 15 domestic; USD 36 Canada; USD 41 foreign. Ed(s): Cynthia Leive, Jill Herzig. Conde Nast Publications, Inc., 750 3rd Ave, New York, NY 10017; magpr@condenast.com; http://www.glamour.com. Illus., adv. Circ: 2300000 Paid. Vol. ends: Dec. Microform: PQC. *Indexed:* ASIP, ConsI, LRI, MRD, RGPR. *Bk. rev.:* 5, 75 words, unsigned. *Aud.:* Hs, Ga, Ac.

While not the magazine it once was, with a focus on social issues along with health and beauty coverage, *Glamour* has balanced celebrity and sex features with more intelligent articles. This is not to say, however, that it is still not a strong competitor with *Cosmo* on the sex front. This magazine, it seems, has found its identity as the twenty-something woman's "Miss Manners" and charm-school bible. Therefore, it contains your usual "beautify yourself in ten minutes," "dress for your body type," and "how to go vintage for $200 or less" articles. Personality profiles and celebrity fashion are staples. These articles are generally well written, engaging, and informative. This magazine has also responded to the market by featuring women who are not always pencil-thin, particularly as part of its annual "body confidence" issue, which features women in all shapes and sizes. However, there are still too many advertisements, but for the price it is acceptable. A web site features reader services, polls, and contests, and promotes the recent issue.

2537. Good Housekeeping. Former titles (until 1919): *Good Housekeeping Magazine;* (until 1909): *Good Housekeeping*. [ISSN: 0017-209X] 1885. m. USD 10 domestic; USD 32 foreign; USD 2.50 newsstand/cover per issue. Ed(s): Rosemary Ellis. Hearst Magazines, 300 W 57th St, New York, NY 10019; HearstMagazines@hearst.com; http://www.hearstcorp.com/magazines/. Illus., adv. Circ: 4600000 Paid. Vol. ends: Jun/Dec. Microform: NBI; PQC. Online: EBSCO Publishing, EBSCO Host; Gale; Northern Light Technology, Inc.; OCLC Online Computer Library Center, Inc.; ProQuest K-12 Learning Solutions; ProQuest LLC (Ann Arbor); H.W. Wilson. *Indexed:* AgeL, CINAHL, ConsI, IHTDI, LRI, MASUSE, RGPR. *Aud.:* Ga, Ac.

The *Good Housekeeping* Seal of Approval has stood as the symbol of "unique consumer education and consumer protection" since 1885, and the magazine maintains those ties to consumer information and advice. *Good Housekeeping* is targeted to family-oriented readers who are interested in practical information and a bit of inspiration. Regular departments are written by respected authorities—for example, "Do the Right Thing" by Peggy Post, the "Household Helpline" by Heloise, and "Money Watch" by Jane Bryant Quinn. Consumer information in the way of product recalls, money management, and the environment is provided in each issue. Articles focus on relationships, health, beauty, fitness, and interior decoration as well as celebrity profiles and inspirational personal stories in "Getting Personal." Short stories and novel adaptations are occasional features. And, of course, the extensive recipe section—providing menus, step-by-step guides, and a heavy emphasis on the microwave—has always been a strong selling point. Information from the Good Housekeeping Institute is also provided, featuring consumer information, recalls, and product evaluations. *Good Housekeeping* maintains high editorial standards and strictly reviews all advertising copy before it is accepted for publication. This policy, as well as the magazine's efforts to keep up with a changing society, keeps it one of the premier women's service magazines. The web site complements the magazine with consumer information, a buyer's guide, expert advice, recipes, and the opportunity for reader interaction and advice-sharing.

2538. Harper's Bazaar. [ISSN: 0017-7873] 1867. m. USD 10 domestic; USD 20 Canada; USD 3.50 newsstand/cover per issue. Ed(s): Glenda Bailey. Hearst Magazines, 300 W 57th St, New York, NY 10019; HearstMagazines@hearst.com; http://www.hearstcorp.com/magazines/. Illus., adv. Circ: 700000 Paid. Vol. ends: Dec. Microform: NBI; PMC; PQC. Online: EBSCO Publishing, EBSCO Host; Gale; OCLC Online Computer Library Center, Inc.; ProQuest K-12 Learning Solutions; ProQuest LLC (Ann Arbor); H.W. Wilson. *Indexed:* DAAI, MASUSE, RGPR. *Bk. rev.:* Number and length vary. *Aud.:* Ga, Ac.

Harper's Bazaar, one of America's oldest fashion magazines, balances lavishly illustrated fashion spreads with feature articles. Its iconic place in this history of fashion is shown in every issue, with an archival spread featuring a famous designer or photographer from past issues. The magazine is currently divided into three sections. "Beauty" and "Hottest, Newest, Latest" cover current fashion trends; "Runway Report" covers makeup, hair, and accessories, as well as fashion trends; and "Fashionable Life" focuses on the arts, including film and book reviews, food, and interior design. In addition, well-written interviews with designers or celebrities known for their interest in fashion are included in every issue. *Harper's Bazaar*, a perennial favorite, appeals to women interested in a contemporary interpretation of fashion. The web site provides information on current fashion events, links to advertisers, and excerpts from articles in the current print issue.

2539. *Heartland U S A.* 1991. bi-m. USD 12. Ed(s): Brad Pearson. U S T Publishing, 1 Sound Shore Dr, Ste 3, Greenwich, CT 06830-7251; husaedit@ustnet.com. Adv. Circ: 901511 Controlled. *Bk. rev.:* 3, 200 words. *Aud.:* Ga.

Not just another fashion magazine, *Heartland USA* is a general-interest magazine for the average man who works with his hands, loves to hunt and fish, watches sports on TV, listens to country music, and longs to spend more time with his family. Those areas are the focus of this publication, with emphasis on outdoor activities, wildlife, how-to articles, spectator sports, human interest, and family life. This title will definitely appeal to the jeans-and-flannel-shirt crowd.

2540. *Hint.* w. Ed(s): Lee Carter. Hint Magazine, 121 W 3d St, Apt ER, New York, NY 10012-1287; leecarter@hintmag.com; http://www.hintmag.com. Adv. *Aud.:* Ga, Ac.

Each issue includes interviews and articles on current and cutting-edge fashion trends and designers. Some of the regular columns include "Shoptart," "Jetsetera, the Art of Parties," and "Model Mania." *Hint* uses a variety of visuals such as web streaming, photographs, animated gifs, and graphics to add an edgy and au courant feeling to the site. A message board, chat room, and a weekly newsletter are also included.

2541. *InStyle.* [ISSN: 1076-0830] 1994. m. USD 23.88 domestic; USD 34 Canada; USD 3.99 newsstand/cover. Ed(s): Norman Pearlstine, Maria Baugh. Time, Inc., Time & Life Bldg, Rockefeller Center, 29th Fl, New York, NY 10020-1393; letters@instylemag.com. Illus., adv. Circ: 1660193 Paid. *Indexed:* MASUSE, RGPR. *Aud.:* Ga.

InStyle combines the celebrity profiles and gossip of magazines like *People* with the fashion, beauty, and home entertaining elements of other women's magazines. The packaging is stylish and clean, appealing to an upscale readership. Fashion features like "The Look" use celebrities to highlight fashion trends, accessories, tips, and Q & A. This approach continues through the beauty coverage, with celebrities providing cosmetics and hair advice, including product recommendations. "Instant Style" and "Runway to Reality" provide advice on how to get that celebrity look for yourself, while "Transformations" follows a particular celebrity and her yearly physical and fashion updates. The magazine also focuses on home entertaining and decorating and includes a few recipes. Celebrity interviews are lengthy and accompanied by photographs taken in the celebrity's home. Information on furniture, interior design, and accessories accompany the article. The web site is very rich and includes a daily calendar with links to "Look of the Day," "Parties," and other content areas. It also offers two blogs as well as an RSS feed.

2542. *Jade Magazine: a fresh perspective for Asian women.* 1999. bi-m. Ed(s): Ellen Hwang. JADE Magazine Inc., Village Station, Box 915, New York, NY 10014; info@jademagazine.com. Circ: 10000. *Aud.:* Sa.

Started by two ambitious Asian American women, *Jade* is an e-zine designed to create a place to address young English-speaking Asian women's issues and interests, highlight their contributions, and confront the stereotypes surrounding them. Through its clean, uncluttered presentation and well-written content, *Jade* has grown in readership. Many features are common to women's fashion and beauty magazines—clothes, cosmetics, accessories, health, careers, travel, and entertainment—but all are addressed from a unique Asian perspective. In addition to the more typical women's magazine features, *Jade* also provides daily updates of world news relevant to its readership, events of interest in Asia, Canada, and the United States, and "Open Mike," where readers can share their views. The current online issue is available at no charge; articles from past issues are for sale. *Jade* has recently begun publishing a print edition.

2543. *Jane.* [ISSN: 1093-8737] 1997. 10x/yr. USD 10 domestic; USD 33.95 Canada; USD 37.95 elsewhere. Ed(s): Bill van Parys, Debbie McHugh. Fairchild Publications, Inc., 7 W 34th St, New York, NY 10001-8191; customerservice@fairchildpub.com; http://www.fairchildpub.com. Illus., adv. Circ: 500000. Vol. ends: Dec. *Bk. rev.:* 3-5, brief, unsigned. *Aud.:* Ga.

Launched in 1997 by former *Sassy* editor Jane Pratt, *Jane* has joined the competitive market of women's lifestyle magazines. Its content is similar to that of its competitors: fashion, beauty, personalities, and health, with a heavy dose of gossip, entertainment, and culture through book, film, and music reviews. What made *Jane* unique early on—coverage of "gadgets," automobiles, and other topics usually found in men's magazines, as well as articles of political or social interest—has faded into the background, but the tongue-in-cheek style remains. Celebrities have become a prominent focus, but *Jane*'s quirky interviews and profiles are not what you find in other women's magazines. For example, Pamela Anderson of *Baywatch* fame is a regular columnist. Fashion layouts are artsy and edgy, and the high-quality paper stock brings out the best in the photography. The web site is rather disappointing with difficult-to-read color schemes, distracting graphics, and meager content. The current issue's table of contents is offered; however, other links on the site usually lead to merchandise information. Readers can "Rant" by means of a reader-poll link, or explore "Jane's Dates," a personals service.

2544. *Just for Black Men: for strong, positive caring brothers.* [ISSN: 1090-0365] 1996. bi-m. USD 18 domestic; USD 24 Canada; USD 27 elsewhere. Ed(s): Kate Feguson. Black Men Publications, 46 Violet Ave, Poughkeepsie, NY 12601. Illus., adv. *Bk. rev.:* 3, 200 words. *Aud.:* Ga.

Just for Black Men is one of only a handful of magazines for the young and style-conscious black male. Designed to appeal to the 20-to-40 age group, it is heavily into lifestyle, health and fitness, and sports, with secondary emphasis on the latest in men's fashion, business and financial advice, travel, and black celebrities. *Just for Black Men* oozes sensuality, but does it with class. Photos of African American supermodels stand side-by-side with articles on fatherhood, self-esteem, and health. This is an excellent title for libraries that need materials to appeal to the style-conscious African American male.

2545. *Ladies' Home Journal.* Formerly (until 1889): *Ladies Home Journal and Practical Housekeeper.* [ISSN: 0023-7124] 1883. m. USD 16.97. Ed(s): Diane Salvatore, Pamela Guthrie O'Brien. Meredith Corp., 1716 Locust St, Des Moines, IA 50309-3023; mimcontact@meredith.com; http://www.meredith.com. Illus., adv. Circ: 5000000 Paid. Vol. ends: Dec. Microform: PQC. Online: The Dialog Corporation; ProQuest K-12 Learning Solutions. *Indexed:* CINAHL, ConsI, LRI, MASUSE, RGPR. *Aud.:* Ga, Ac.

LHJ is a consistently popular women's magazine that works to keep itself in step with the changing role of American women while maintaining a sense of its own history. The magazine was recently redesigned and has gone to a larger, more readable format. However, tradition is still maintained between the covers through the long-standing feature "Can This Marriage Be Saved?," which is described as "the most popular, most enduring women's magazine feature in the world" and is prominently placed at the beginning of each issue. A more recent addition is "Was This Marriage Saved?," a follow-up on a couple profiled in an earlier issue that tracks their progress. The remainder of the magazine is heavily focused on woman as wife, mother, sister, friend, and worker, with lengthy, often inspirational stories about marriage and family. *LHJ* is one of the few women's magazines in which content dominates over image. The balance of each issue is devoted to woman as individual through a number of regular departments on beauty, fashion, health, food, and home decorating. A celebrity is featured on the cover with an accompanying profile. As with other service magazines, *LHJ* offers a large food section with recipes, menu planning, and nutritional information. Although *LHJ* is geared to a predominantly white, middle-class audience, efforts have been made to reflect minorities in photographs and advertising. The magazine's web site reprints or supplements articles from recent issues through links on health, beauty, parenting, and food. There is also a shopping guide as well as an opportunity for reader feedback and discussion.

2546. *Latina (New York).* [ISSN: 1099-890X] 1996. m. USD 11.97 domestic; USD 27 foreign; USD 2.95 newsstand/cover. Ed(s): Sylvia A Martinez. Latina Publications LLC, 1500 Broadway, Ste 600, New York, NY 10036; editor@latina.com; http://www.latina.com. Illus., adv. *Aud.:* Sa.

Latina, a bilingual fashion and lifestyle magazine, is the brainchild of Stanford graduate Christy Haubegger, who recognized the need for a publication that addresses the interests of the fastest-growing minority in the United States. The magazine's mission has been to entertain and inspire Hispanic women with award-winning content that covers Latin culture, style, beauty, food, music and celebrities. *Latina* has been very successful in meeting its mission; today, this magazine is a newsstand staple. Fashion, beauty, health, fitness, work, travel, parenting, personal finance, food, and relationships are all included; and celebrity interviews and feature stories can be found in every issue of *Latina.* The arts and entertainment features highlight not only successful Hispanic musicians, artists, dancers, authors, and actors but also lesser-known Latinas too. Social issues such as education, domestic violence, legal rights, health care, and interracial relationships are also covered, although less so in recent issues. In 2005, *Latina* magazine was ranked No.1 in advertising pages among 38 Hispanic publications. A web site covers the areas of "Amor and Sex"; "Our Culture," which links to brief biographies of Latino women primarily in the entertainment field; "Succeed," which offers articles and tips on succeeding in all areas of life; and "Mujeres on the Move," comprising articles on women who make a difference in their and others' lives. There is also the option to receive a weekly newsletter via e-mail from the magazine.

2547. *The Look Online.* irreg. USD 108. Look Online, Inc., 529 E 85th St, New York, NY 10028; look@lookonline.com; http://www.lookonline.com/. *Bk. rev.:* 2-4, 150-200 words, signed. *Aud.:* Sa.

The Look Online is an e-zine for both fashion industry professionals and consumers who want "real insider information about New York fashion and how it works." The site is divided into two parts, one free and the other subscription-based. The "Daily Fashion Report" is free and uses a blog format to provides a fashion reports,new, reviews, photos and videos. The "Look Online," available via six-month subscriptions, offers expanded industry fashion and market reports written by senior fashion editors, a New York fashion events schedule, and a guide to New York public relations firms.

2548. *Lucky: a new magazine about shopping.* [ISSN: 1531-4294] 2000. m. USD 12 domestic; USD 30 Canada; USD 31 elsewhere. Ed(s): Kim France. Conde Nast Publications, Inc., 750 3rd Ave, New York, NY 10017; talktous@luckymag.com; http://www.luckymag.com. Circ: 917598 Paid. *Aud.:* Ga.

Looking for every possible swimsuit style, its cost, and how to buy it? Or are you comparison shopping for strappy high-heeled sandals? Then *Lucky* is for you. More of a catalog than a magazine, *Lucky* targets shopaholics looking for great buys around the country in women's apparel, cosmetics, and home decorating. There is no pretense of providing content comparable to other women's magazines—no relationship stories or sex advice here. Except for an occasional expert tip on topics such as buying jewelry or applying makeup, there is little text in the magazine other than brief descriptions of an item, its cost, and how to order it. It is page after page of products organized into fashion, beauty, and lifestyle sections. "Style Spy" highlights a variety of trendy clothes, shoes, and accessories, and "Beauty Spy" focuses on cosmetics and hair care. Lifestyle coverage is found in sections like "Home Spy," which focuses on decorating, organizing, and do-it-yourself projects. While it hardly matters to the magazine's target readership, it does become difficult to tell where the magazine ends and the advertising begins. Included in each issue is a page of stickers labeled "Yes!" or "Maybe?" for the reader to use to mark items that catch her eye. The magazine's redesigned web site features a catch of the day, bargain browser, shopping directory, a locator service for bargains in different areas of the country, reader forums, issue highlights, events, and promotions.

2549. *Marie Claire.* [ISSN: 1081-8626] 1994. m. USD 12 domestic; USD 32 foreign; USD 3.50 newsstand/cover. Ed(s): Joanna Coles, Lesley Symour. Hearst Magazines, 300 W 57th St, New York, NY 10019;

HearstMagazines@hearst.com; http://www.hearstcorp.com/magazines/. Illus., adv. Circ: 950000 Paid. Online: EBSCO Publishing, EBSCO Host; Gale; ProQuest LLC (Ann Arbor). *Bk. rev.:* 2-3, 25 words. *Aud.:* Ga.

Marie Claire no longer needs to rely on name recognition from its European counterpart, which started in France in the 1930s and is published in 22 countries. It stands on its own in the marketplace with other fashion, beauty, and lifestyle magazines. Fashion and beauty are major emphases, taking up about half of each issue, with health, fitness, relationships, food, decorating, personal finance, and entertainment rounding out the issue. Layouts are bold, contemporary, and daring, and feature young designers. Cosmetics, accessories, and beauty tips also receive significant coverage. Celebrity news and gossip focus on the young and the hip in fashion and the arts. There is an occasional brief nod to work and career advice. *Marie Claire* leans toward the sensational in its articles, with such topics as shaken-baby syndrome and child abduction in its "First Person" and "Special Report" features. The magazine's web site promotes and supplements the current issue and offers reader services including message boards, a chat room, and product promotions and freebies.

2550. *Maxim: for men.* [ISSN: 1092-9789] 1997. m. USD 12 domestic; USD 29.97 Canada; USD 3.95 newsstand/cover. Ed(s): Jimmy Jellinek. Dennis Maxim, Inc., 1040 Ave of the Americas, 23rd Fl, New York, NY 10018. Illus., adv. Sample. Circ: 2500000 Paid. Vol. ends: Dec. *Bk. rev.:* 5, 200 words, signed. *Aud.:* Ga.

Maxim appears regularly on newsstands throughout the United States, and has gradually found its way onto some library periodical racks. It is a slick, good-looking magazine that will attract male readers. Its provocative cover does the trick, but there's as much meat as cheesecake within. Health, holidays, sports, technology, investing, fashion, and sex are all grist for the *Maxim* mill. All types of media are reviewed. A fascination with the slightly offbeat is also apparent. Inquisitive librarians and readers may check out the title through its online full-text web site.

2551. *Men of Integrity.* [ISSN: 1524-1122] 1998. bi-m. USD 19.95. Ed(s): Harry Genet. Christianity Today International, 465 Gundersen Dr, Carol Stream, IL 60188; http://www.christianitytoday.com. *Aud.:* Ga.

A Christian magazine for men by the same company that publishes *Christianity Today, Men of Integrity* is slanted toward the family man of Christian background and faith. Typical articles concern parenting, family life, money management, personal happiness, and setting examples for others.

2552. *Men's Journal.* [ISSN: 1063-4657] 1992. m. USD 9.97 domestic; USD 25.97 foreign; USD 3.95 newsstand/cover. Wenner Media, Inc., 1290 Ave of Americas, New York, NY 10104. Illus., adv. Circ: 566943 Paid. *Indexed:* ASIP, BRI. *Bk. rev.:* 4, 200 words, signed. *Aud.:* Hs, Ga.

A publication for the active male, *Men's Journal* consists of about equal parts sports, action, and travel reading, with a hint of the good life for savor. Known for its exquisite photography and exceptional writing, it is aimed at the active man who wants to get the most out of life. An article about American heroes may stand side-by-side with one about climbing Mt. Everest and a word portrait of author William Vollmann's best friend, along with columns on the latest innovations in digital and other equipment, sports, fashion trends, health, grooming, sex, cars, books, and music. Librarians who browse this title will be won over.

2553. *Menz Magazine.* [ISSN: 1202-7472] 1994. q. CND 15; CND 19.50 foreign. Ed(s): Clayton Anderson. Better One Media, 300 Leo Parizeau, Ste 1901, Montreal, PQ H2W 2N1, Canada; editor@menz.com; http://www.menz.com. Adv. Circ: 50000. *Indexed:* CBCARef. *Bk. rev.:* 2, 200-500 words, signed. *Aud.:* Ga.

Canada's premier magazine for men, *Menz Magazine* is a good-looking, general publication for the average male, focusing on finance, health, fitness, adventure, food, and the Canadian lifestyle. Reviews of new technology, entertainment, cars, and fashion trends round out the journal. Beautiful women are in evidence, but not to the same degree as in American counterparts. Librarians should definitely give this title consideration for its slightly different take on modern males.

2554. *More (New York)*. [ISSN: 1094-7868] 1997. 10x/yr. USD 20 domestic; USD 30 foreign; USD 2.95 newsstand/cover. Ed(s): Susan Crandell. Meredith Corp., 125 Park Ave, 19th Fl, New York, NY 10017; http://www.meredith.com. Illus., adv. Circ: 850000. *Bk. rev.*: Number and length vary. *Aud.*: Ga, Sa.

A spinoff of *Ladies Home Journal, More* is geared to a target audience of women at 40+. Articles focus on the positive aspects of that time of a woman's life, focusing on health, fashion for all sizes and shapes, travel, relationships, and beauty tips. "Notebook" highlights trends, films, books, travel, and the arts, suggesting that the content is geared to women with more leisure time and a fair amount of disposable income on their hands. Interior decorating is also a focus, with work and career de-emphasized. As with *Ladies Home Journal,* a celebrity graces the cover, and other well-known personalities are featured heavily in the magazine. Health-related news and information is a particular strength, through both the "Vital & Vibrant" section and lengthy articles that focus on such topics as breast cancer and osteoporosis. Relationship stories focus on love and sex at middle age and parenting adult children. The web site highlights events and promotions, the current issue, and a reader panel.

2555. *New Man: the magazine about becoming men of integrity*. [ISSN: 1077-3959] 1994. bi-m. USD 19.95; USD 3.95 newsstand/cover. Ed(s): Robert Andrescik. Strang Communications Co., 600 Rinehart Rd, Lake Mary, FL 32746; ministries@strang.com. Illus., adv. Circ: 215000 Paid. *Indexed*: ChrPI. *Bk. rev.*: 4, 200 words, signed. *Aud.*: Ga.

New Man is not just your typical men's magazine; it is a magazine for the Christian male. Topics are far-ranging, from parenting, personal growth, and mental health to finances, software, and automobiles—approached from a religious perspective. *New Man* is a good-looking alternative for the man who is more interested in personal development, family life, and spiritual growth than in just looking good.

2556. *O: The Oprah Magazine*. [ISSN: 1531-3247] 2000. m. USD 19.97 domestic; USD 46 foreign; USD 3.95 newsstand/cover per issue. Ed(s): Amy Gross. Harpo Entertainment Group, 110 N Carpenter St, Chicago, IL 60607. Illus., adv. Circ: 2600000 Paid. Online: EBSCO Publishing, EBSCO Host; Gale; ProQuest LLC (Ann Arbor). *Indexed*: RGPR. *Bk. rev.*: 1 lengthy; 4-5 brief; signed. *Aud.*: Ga.

O is television personality Oprah Winfrey's highly successful foray into publishing. The magazine complements the themes of her popular talk show, emphasizing spirituality, personal development, and celebration. A motivating column from Oprah begins and ends each issue, and the pages in between draw upon many of the same people that have been featured on the television program—for example, Phil McGraw on relationship advice and Suze Orman on personal finance. The magazine combines elements of other popular women's newsstand magazines such as fashion, beauty, health, decorating, family, and celebrities, but adds Oprah's own brand of self-help, inspiration, and faith in the human spirit. As with the audience on television, the magazine's readers play a strong role in the content through reader advice stories and surveys. Another strong feature is inspirational profiles of people overcoming hardships or helping others. "The O List" highlights products for pampering—food, clothes, music, home decor, and the like. Each issue includes an in-depth and intimate interview between Oprah and a well-known personality. The high-quality production and clean, spare cover (with Oprah, of course, featured) set the magazine apart from its competitors and communicate Oprah's sense of style and purpose. A web site highlights the current issue, previews forthcoming issues, and archives back issues. There are links to Oprah's television show web site, chat and message boards, an online photo gallery to which readers can contribute, advice, and recipes.

2557. *Playgirl: entertainment for women*. [ISSN: 0273-6918] 1973. m. USD 21.95; USD 4.99 newsstand/cover. Ed(s): Michele Zipp, Tasha Church. Playgirl, Inc., 801 Second Ave, New York, NY 10017-4706. Illus., adv. Sample. Circ: 350000 Paid. Vol. ends: May. *Bk. rev.*: 2-3, brief, unsigned. *Aud.*: Ga.

Playgirl is an adult magazine that was the 1970s answer to *Playboy* and has probably surprised many with its longevity. As with its male counterpart, *Playgirl* isn't purchased for the articles. Its numerous photo layouts, including a centerfold, feature men (sometimes with women) in provocative nude poses. Readers vote annually for "Man of the Year" and can even send in photos of their favorite guy to the "Real Men" department. The text is dominated by advice columns, reader exchanges, celebrity interviews, and articles with a sexual theme. "Sex Ed" is a cross between "Dear Abby" and "Playboy Advisor," and "Readers' Fantasy Forum" allows readers to share their rich imaginations. Each issue also includes book, music, film, and product reviews and a horoscope. Advertising supports the sexual content of the magazine, promoting 900 telephone numbers, sexual aids and devices, and videos. A web site provides additional nude pictorials. Free access still requires a credit card for identification purposes; a members-only site is accessed with a password.

2558. *Prima*. [ISSN: 0951-8622] 1986. m. GBP 16.99; GBP 2.50 newsstand/cover per issue. Ed(s): Maire Fahey. National Magazine Company Ltd., National Magazine House, 72 Broadwick St, London, W1F 9EP, United Kingdom; http://www.natmags.co.uk. Illus., adv. Circ: 317308 Paid and controlled. *Bk. rev.*: 6-8, brief. *Aud.*: Ga.

Prima, Britain's largest-selling women's monthly, is akin to *Family Circle* and *Woman's Day* in the United States. The magazine takes an affordable, do-it-yourself approach to home and family management in many of its regular features and articles. Topics include health, beauty, family relationships, travel, decorating, gardening, cooking, crafts, and fashion for women on a budget. There are fashion layouts of ready-made, moderately priced clothing as well as patterns for making your own. Consumer and health information is also highlighted. The recipe section is extensive and practical, keeping cost and ease of preparation in mind. The web site promotes the current issue and provides subscription information.

2559. *Red (London): best things in life*. [ISSN: 1461-1317] 1998. m. GBP 33.60 domestic; GBP 60.45 in Europe; GBP 102.30 newsstand/cover per issue elsewhere. Ed(s): Trish Halpin, Sarah Stone. Hachette Filipacchi (UK) Ltd., 64 North Row, London, W1K 7LL, United Kingdom; http://www.hachettefilipacchiuk.co.uk. Illus., adv. *Bk. rev.*: 6, 50-75 words. *Aud.*: Ga.

Red is a popular British women's magazine similar in coverage to lifestyle counterparts such as *Marie Claire* and *Glamour*. Articles focus on celebrities, relationships, style, health and beauty, work, and home and garden. A celebrity interview is included, and entertainment is also covered in the "Talk" section, with brief items on U.S. and U.K. celebrity gossip, music, television, films, and books. "Red Living" focuses on decorating, fashion, food, travel, fitness, and health. *Red* is published in a larger format than U.S. magazines, and there is generally more depth to its content, particularly in the first half of each issue. The web site supplements features in the current issue; offers chat, message boards, and contests; and highlights the "Man of the Month."

2560. *Redbook*. [ISSN: 0034-2106] 1903. m. USD 8 domestic; USD 24 foreign; USD 3.50 newsstand/cover per issue. Ed(s): Stacy Morrison, Janet Siroto. Hearst Magazines, 300 W 57th St, New York, NY 10019; HearstMagazines@hearst.com; http://www.hearstcorp.com/magazines/. Illus., adv. Circ: 2407985 Paid. Microform: NBI; PQC. Online: EBSCO Publishing, EBSCO Host; Gale; Northern Light Technology, Inc.; OCLC Online Computer Library Center, Inc.; ProQuest LLC (Ann Arbor); H.W. Wilson. *Indexed*: ConsI, FLI, MASUSE, RGPR, RI-1. *Aud.*: Ac, Ga.

Redbook targets a younger audience than its sister Hearst publication, *Good Housekeeping,* and it has spicier, sexier content. It attempts to reach young readers who have married and outgrown *Cosmo* but do not yet place themselves in the readership of more traditional titles such as *Ladies' Home Journal* and *Good Housekeeping*. The magazine begins with a focus on that woman and her health, diet, fitness, beauty, and fashion followed by a heavy dose of information and advice on marriage, parenting, and family life, including recipes. Articles focus on sex, relationships, personalities, and personal stories that sometimes border on the sensational, the inspirational, or even the tragic. The web site is similar in content but perhaps a little steamier than the printed magazine, focusing on sex and marriage, reader polls and chats, advice columns, and "Redbook Diaries," which comprises serialized stories with accompanying message boards.

2561. *SharpMan.com: the ultimate guide to men's living*. 1998. w. Ed(s): Y M Reiss. SharpMan Media LLC, 11718 Barrington Ct., No. 702, Los Angeles, CA 90049; http://www.sharpman.com. Circ: 60000. *Aud.*: Ga.

An online lifestyle journal for young men, *SharpMan* emphasizes dating, toys, work, grooming, travel, and health for young men of high school age through age 30. Articles are short, interesting, matter-of-fact, and to the point, and they cover a wide range of topics that young men will find useful in their daily lives. High school librarians especially may want to bookmark this site for future reference.

2562. *Skirt! Magazine.* 1994. m. USD 26. Ed(s): Nikki Hardin. Skirt! Magazine, 455 1/2 King St, Charleston, SC 29403; nikki@skirtmag.com; http://www.skirtmag.com. *Bk. rev.:* Number and length vary. *Aud.:* Ga.

Skirt! began as a print publication in the Charleston area in 1994 but has expanded its focus and readership through its web edition. The magazine is described as "an attitude...spirited, independent, outspoken, serious, playful and irreverent, sometimes controversial, always passionate." The e-zine lives up to its purpose with lively, first-person essays on a wide range of topics—moving back home, living with cancer, even going into the pickle business. Regular departments are entertaining as well. "Short Skirts" offers women's news, "Skirt Salon" highlights entertainment, "Muse Room" provides inspiration, and "Bitch of the Month" invites readers to let off some steam. Recipes, books, and films round out the site. Archives are available, as are reader feedback opportunities through polls and e-mail to the editor.

2563. *Stuff: for men.* [ISSN: 1524-2838] 1998. m. USD 9.97 domestic; USD 19.97 Canada; USD 29.97 elsewhere. Ed(s): Sky Shineman. Dennis Publishing, Inc., 1040 Ave of the Americas, 23rd Fl, New York, NY 10018. Illus., adv. *Bk. rev.:* 2, 200 words. *Aud.:* Ga.

Men's toys, and tools too, are the focus of this upscale consumer shopper's guide produced by the publishers of *Maxim*. The latest in audio, video, online, office, and home technologies are reviewed in detail, along with hiking boots, motorcycles, radar detectors, sporting dogs, and anything else that might appeal to the active male ego. There are articles, too, such as "The 25 Greatest Cars of All Time." The newest films, books, videos, and CDs are reviewed. *Stuff* will intrigue the male population with its cutting-edge information, slick presentations, and beautiful models. There's a British version, too.

2564. *Subject Magazine.* [ISSN: 1472-2879] 2001. 3x/yr. GBP 5.95. Ed(s): Ross Cottingham. Stable Publications Ltd., PO Box 31959, London, W2 5YA, United Kingdom; info@subject-magazine.com; http://www.subject-magazine.com. *Bk. rev.:* 8, 200 words, signed. *Aud.:* Ga.

A men's magazine without skin? It's been done before, but not very often, and that's just one of the reasons that this title focusing on the male reader is such a pleasant surprise. *Subject Magazine* is a publication of considerable substance, with interesting news bites; meaty articles on current topics; biographical sketches of rising stars in the entertainment, business, and science fields; and critical reviews of the newest book, film, television, and music offerings. Articles such as an unofficial tour of London pubs and a search for a good pint add a bit of levity and local color, while a healthy serving of information on entertainment trend-setters ensures a wide readership. The articles are beautifully packaged with superb photography, colorful backgrounds, and eye-catching layouts. Somewhat reminiscent of *Men's Journal*, *Subject Magazine* offers a broader scope with a British flavor.

2565. *Today's Black Woman: your guide to love and relationships.* [ISSN: 1099-582X] 1995. 9x/yr. USD 27 domestic. Ed(s): Kate Ferguson. Enoble Media Group, 210 Rte 4 E, Ste 401, Paramus, NJ 07652. Illus., adv. Circ: 87401. Vol. ends: Dec. *Bk. rev.:* 3-5, 50 words. *Aud.:* Sa.

Today's Black Woman has much in common with other African American women lifestyle magazines. Format and content are also familiar: health, fitness, beauty, money, relationships, sex, work and career, celebrities, travel, and fashion. Articles either focus on getting/keeping a man or promote positive and motivational images of successful women through celebrity features and personal profiles. The magazine places a strong focus on sexuality and intimacy through several articles, Q & A columns, and regular columns such as "Man Talk" and "Men's Room." A book excerpt or short story is included, usually with a romantic theme. A self-test appears in each issue, along with a horoscope. *Today's Black Woman* does not compare in quality to *Essence* and *Ebony* but may appeal to a younger readership looking for a magazine that addresses its needs and interests as African American women.

2566. *Today's Christian Woman.* [ISSN: 0163-1799] 1978. bi-m. USD 17.95 domestic; USD 29.95 foreign. Ed(s): Harold B. Smith, Jane Struck. Christianity Today International, 465 Gundersen Dr, Carol Stream, IL 60188; http://www.christianitytoday.com. Illus., adv. Sample. Circ: 260000 Paid. Vol. ends: Nov/Dec. Online: EBSCO Publishing, EBSCO Host; Gale. *Indexed:* ChrPI. *Bk. rev.:* 6-8, 60 words. *Aud.:* Ga, Sa.

Today's Christian Woman describes itself as "a practical magazine geared for women in their 20s, 30s, and 40s." Its purpose is to address personal and social issues from a biblical perspective to help women cope with issues that arise in family and marital relationships, work life, and personal development. Letters to the editor and regular columns such as "MomSense," "Your Relationships," and "My Story" offer spiritual and practical guidance for the reader on health, marriage, work, finances, and family. Role models and popular Christian authors and celebrities also provide inspiration through profiles and a cover story. Women of color have become more prominently featured in the magazine in recent years. Articles cover such topics as spiritual development, prayer, relationships, careers, family life, and issues such as addiction and birth control. Advertisements are geared to this special audience and include Christian book, music, and video publishers. Each issue also features book, film, and music reviews. A web site offers information from and about the magazine, chat and interactive Bible study links, a prayer network, advice, and reader polls.

2567. *Unleashed.* [ISSN: 1536-8904] 2001. bi-m. USD 12.99 domestic; CND 19.99 Canada; USD 4.99 domestic. Ed(s): Ron Samuel. UNleashed Magazine, 10359 Santa Monica Blvd, 415, Los Angeles, CA 90025. *Aud.:* Ga.

Stunning photography, eye-catching layouts, and exceptional writing are the signature components of this magazine designed for the urban man. Biographical sketches and interviews with people making news in the arts and entertainment industries are interspersed with the latest fashion statements for men, exotic travel destinations described, hot wheels examined, newest gadgets unveiled, and health/personal care prescribed. Once discovered by the fashion-conscious male, this cutting-edge, upscale magazine will become a reading staple.

2568. *Vogue.* [ISSN: 0042-8000] 1892. m. USD 15 domestic; USD 50 Canada; USD 60 elsewhere. Ed(s): Anna Wintour. Conde Nast Publications, Inc., 750 3rd Ave, New York, NY 10017; http://www.condenast.com. Illus., index, adv. Circ: 1260026 Paid. Vol. ends: Dec. Microform: PQC. Online: Gale; LexisNexis; ProQuest LLC (Ann Arbor). *Indexed:* DAAI, FLI, MRD, RGPR, RI-1. *Bk. rev.:* 3-4, 100-200 words. *Aud.:* Ga, Ac.

Vogue, which has been in print over 100 years, is one of the premier international fashion magazines, offering up-to-date information on current fashion and runway trends. Each issue is divided into four main sections: "Fashion," "Beauty, Health and Fitness," "Features," and "People Are Talking About." The "Fashion" section typically includes articles on haute couture and designers as well as an overview of the fashion season by Andre Leon Talley. "Beauty, Health and Fitness" offers information related to fashion such as makeup and hair trends, while the "Features" section includes well-written articles on a variety of topics. "People Are Talking About" covers current events such as museum openings and book and film reviews. The fashion layouts, shot by famous photographers, are always interesting and sometimes controversial. *Vogue* also has Australian, Brazilian, British, French, German, Italian, and Spanish editions. *Vogue* has partnered with *W* to provide a web site called *Style.com*. This site provides slides of fashion shows as well as articles on current trends, people, and parties. *Style.com* also provides a forum for readers to post comments and offers the option to subscribe to a weekly newsletter. This is an essential title for those interested in fashion.

2569. *W.* Incorporates (in Jan. 2007): *Jewelry W*; (1987-1988): *Scene (New York)*. [ISSN: 0162-9115] 1971. m. USD 16.95 domestic; USD 65 Canada; USD 97 elsewhere. Ed(s): Bridgette Foley. Fairchild Publications, Inc., 7 W 34th St, New York, NY 10001-8191; customerservice@fairchildpub.com; http://www.fairchildpub.com. Illus., adv. Circ: 402376 Paid. Vol. ends: Dec. Online: Gale. *Indexed:* ASIP, DAAI, IndIslam. *Aud.:* Ga, Ac.

W is a lavishly illustrated magazine that covers all areas of fashion from designers to current collections. It is divided into sections that highlight trends in cosmetics, accessories, beauty, and interior design. The magazine's large size allows for interesting layouts that complement these articles. In addition to fashion coverage, a large part of the magazine is devoted to the doings of various individuals involved in high society. The "Eye" department describes the openings, dinners, and weddings these celebrities are attending as well as providing information on various actors, directors, and artists. This is the magazine to read to keep up with the lives of newsworthy people while enjoying interesting fashion layouts. *W* has partnered with *Vogue* to create *Style.com,* which highlights features from both magazines while also providing extras such as fashion shows, beauty trends, and people and parties.

2570. *Woman's Day.* [ISSN: 0043-7336] 1937. 17x/yr. USD 10 domestic; USD 30 foreign. Ed(s): Jane Chesnutt, Sue Kakstys. Hachette Filipacchi Media U.S., Inc., 1633 Broadway, New York, NY 10019; http://www.hfmus.com. Illus., adv. Circ: 4279375 Paid. Vol. ends: Dec. Microform: PQC. Online: OCLC Online Computer Library Center, Inc. *Indexed:* ASIP, ConsI, IHTDI, MASUSE. *Aud.:* Ga.

Woman's Day is a perennial checkout-counter competitor with *Family Circle* and, in more recent years, *First for Women* and other titles. While it has updated its content and gone to a cleaner cover look, *Woman's Day*'s approach has remained essentially the same: to provide practical information to middle-class wives and mothers who may or may not be working outside the home. Regular features include the editor's column, "All in a Woman's Day," and numerous tips on housekeeping, parenting, and family relationships. Many of the regular departments offer advice on a number of topics of concern to the thrifty woman: health, nutrition and meal planning, home care, money management, crafts, travel, gardening, and decorating. The magazine's strengths are product and consumer information, inexpensive and practical fashions, and recipes. Editorially, the magazine is conservative and patriotic and projects a subtle religious bent through the biblical quote that tops the table of contents and through inspirational articles and personal profiles. A web site reflects the contents of current and past issues and offers reader polls, chat, contests, product information and promotions, and recipes.

2571. *Women Today Magazine.* m. Free. Ed(s): Claire Colvin. Women Today Magazine, 20385 64th Ave, Langley, BC V2Y 1N5, Canada; editor@womentodaymagazine.com; http://www.womentodaymagazine.com. *Aud.:* Ga.

Women Today is a Canadian e-zine that covers much of the same ground as newsstand service magazines but with an underlying Christian message that is not readily apparent until the site is explored. Information about fashion, beauty, family, career, relationships, health and wellness, recipes, and parenting is helpful and in-depth. New items are labeled as such, and older items stay on the site for a while, sometimes making the lists under each main topic quite long. Live chat, discussion boards, and polls are available to get readers involved in the site. A feature not found in most service magazines but provided by *Women Today* is first-person news about women from around the world. Here is where a strong evangelical Christian message is delivered, directing readers to information on how they can accept Christ into their lives. There is a companion site, *Christian Women Today,* that has a more overt religious message similar to the print magazine *Today's Christian Woman* and its companion web site.

2572. *WomenOf.com.* 1997. w. Ed(s): S Klann. Prosolutions Inc, 7585 W 66th Ave, Arvada, CO 80003. *Aud.:* Ga.

This e-journal provides comprehensive coverage of a wide-ranging number of issues and topics: business, health, family, travel, law, automobiles, sports, money, cooking, and more. Issued weekly, *WomenOf.com* serves as a national edition or digest of sorts for several community-focused e-journals for women. A pull-down menu to these sites is on the home page, and some of the articles are drawn from these local sites. Articles are, for the most part, well written and authoritative, providing a brief author profile and e-mail address, and there is also a "Woman of the Month" feature. A section called "The Directory" provides a promising listing of services such as health care providers, financial services, lawyers, banks, spas, and more (it is currently light on entries in several categories).

2573. *Working Mother: the smart guide for a whole life.* Incorporates (1986-1988): *Baby; McCall's Working Mother.* [ISSN: 0278-193X] 1978. 9x/yr. USD 9.97 domestic; USD 19 Canada; USD 29.97 elsewhere. Ed(s): Susan Lapinski. Working Mother Media, 60 E 42nd St., 27th Fl, New York, NY 10165; http://www.workingmother.com. Illus., adv. Circ: 75000 Paid. Vol. ends: Dec. Microform: PQC. Online: ProQuest LLC (Ann Arbor). *Indexed:* RGPR. *Aud.:* Ga.

Working Mother is a valuable and popular resource for working women who are new mothers or who already have older children. The "Work in Progress" department provides helpful and practical information and advice on health, fitness, beauty, food and nutrition, money, and career and workplace concerns, such as child care, maternity leave, technology, and pay equity. "Go Home" focuses on parenting, including games, projects, and other things to do with children. Recipes pay particular attention to nutritional needs and ease of preparation. Each issue closes with "Back Talk," a personal comment piece. Annually, the magazine reports on the best U.S. companies for working mothers and the status of child care in the 50 states, and a report on the "Best Companies for Women of Color" debuted in 2003. The reports are also available on the magazine's web site, along with current issue highlights and articles, a book club, recipes, and events.

2574. *Zink: the essential element of style.* [ISSN: 1546-4717] 11x/yr. USD 28; USD 3.95 newsstand/cover domestic; USD 4.95 newsstand/cover Canada. Jormic Media Group, Inc., 535 34th St., Ste. 602, New York, NY 10001. Adv. *Bk. rev.:* Number and length vary. *Aud.:* Ga.

Zink, celebrating its fifth anniversary, focuses on contemporary style and how it applies to fashion, beauty, and entertainment. The magazine is divided into five main areas. "Ignition" highlights cutting-edge design; "Style Fusion" offers information on fashion trends and designers; "Combustion" contains book, film, and music reviews; "Well Features" is themed fashion layouts; and "Vaporization" contains columns on relationships, sex, food, and travel. The demographics of *Zink* is 18- to 34-year-olds and this focus is seen in the youthful models and layout. The text is subservient to visuals in this publication, and the photography is truly stunning and innovative.

■ FICTION: GENERAL/MYSTERY AND DETECTIVE

General/Mystery and Detective

Marta A. Davis, Librarian, Morris Library, Mail Code 6632, Southern Illinois University Carbondale, Carbondale, IL 6290; mdavis@lib.siu.edu., FAX: 618- 453-5706

Introduction

Magazines in this section publish prose fiction, usually short stories. Some publications also feature reviews and interviews. Generally, publishers of this genre are either small, independent firms or are connected to an academic institution. The web sites are often substantial, with helpful links for readers, writers, and researchers.

In addition to the web versions of print publications, fiction can be found on personal sites and e-zines. A good web site requires constant maintenance to remain viable. Few receive the attention needed to sustain a recommended quality and quantity of material. One exception is *ClueLass,* an excellent web site that covers the entire mystery world.

Basic Periodicals

GENERAL. Ga, Ac: *Fiction, Fiction International, Zoetrope.*

MYSTERY AND DETECTIVE. Ga, Ac: *ClueLass HomePage, Ellery Queen's Mystery Magazine.*

Basic Abstracts and Indexes

American Humanities Index, MLA International Bibliography, Mystery Short Fiction.

General

This category is composed primarily of journals that publish original works of fiction, usually short stories, by both emerging and established writers. Some only publish fiction, while others include book reviews or interviews. In most cases, the audience is the scholarly or general reader, and the publication has limited circulation.

2575. *Fiction.* [ISSN: 0046-3736] 1972. 2x/yr. USD 18 (Individuals, USD 20; USD 40 foreign). Ed(s): Mark J Mirsky. Fiction, c/o City College of NY, Department of English, New York, NY 10031; http://www.ccny.cuny.edu/fiction/fiction.htm. Illus., index. Circ: 3000. Microform: PQC. *Indexed:* AmHI. *Aud.:* Ga, Ac.

This periodical presents a selection of skillfully crafted short fiction by major American authors as well as first-timers. Published twice a year, issues may include translated works of writers from other countries, previously published pieces, and book excerpts. This is recommended for public libraries and academic libraries supporting creative writing programs. The web site includes excerpts from past issues and subscription information.

2576. *Fiction International.* [ISSN: 0092-1912] 1973. a. USD 24 (Individuals, USD 12). Ed(s): Harold Jaffe. Hignell Book Printing, 488 Burnell St, Winnipeg, MB R3G 2B4, Canada; books@hignell.mb.ca; http://www.hignell.mb.ca. Illus., adv. Circ: 500 Paid. Microform: PQC. Online: EBSCO Publishing, EBSCO Host. *Indexed:* AmHI, BRI, CBRI. *Aud.:* Ga, Ac.

Fiction International combines literary innovation, thought provoking visuals, and progressive politics. This annual publication contains about 30 works on a specific theme. Recent topics include "Sacred/Shamanic," "Women Writers from the Third World," and "American Indian Writers." This magazine is recommended for large public libraries and academic libraries. The web site contains subscriber and contributor information and table of contents of the current issue and selections from past issues.

2577. *Glimmer Train.* [ISSN: 1055-7520] 1991. q. USD 36 domestic; USD 46 Canada; USD 59 elsewhere. Ed(s): Linda Swanson-Davies. Glimmer Train Press, Inc., 1211 NW Glisan St, Ste 207, Portland, OR 97209-3054; eds@glimmertrain.com; http://www.glimmertrain.com. Sample. Circ: 16000 Paid. *Indexed:* AmHI. *Aud.:* Ga, Ac.

Each issue of this attractive quarterly includes eight to ten excellent stories by new and published authors. There are special competitions for very short fiction and traditional-length short fiction. The publication's web site has useful information about submission guidelines, reading fees, and submissions. A good choice for most public and all academic libraries supporting creative writing programs.

Jacket. See Literary Reviews section.

2578. *The Long Story.* [ISSN: 0741-4242] 1982. a. USD 13 for 2 yrs. domestic; USD 15 for 2 yrs. foreign; USD 7 newsstand/cover per issue domestic. Ed(s): R Peter Burnham. Long Story, 18 Eaton St, Lawrence, MA 01843-1110; rpbtls@aol.com; http://www.longstorymagazine.com/. Circ: 1100. *Indexed:* AmHI. *Aud.:* Ga, Ac.

This is the only literary magazine devoted exclusively to longer stories of 8,000 to 20,000 words. Published annually, it presents an eclectic mix of eight to ten stories offering various perspectives on man and society. The web site has subscription and submission information, the table of contents and editorial from the current issue, and an index to past issues. Recommended for large public libraries and academic libraries supporting creative writing programs.

2579. *Other Voices (Chicago): fiction.* [ISSN: 8756-4696] 1985. s-a. USD 30 (Individuals, USD 26; USD 9 newsstand/cover per issue domestic). Ed(s): Gina Frangello. Other Voices, Inc., University of Illinois at Chicago, Department of English, Chicago, IL 60607-7120; othervoices@listserv.uic.edu; http://www.othervoicesmagazine.org. Illus., adv. Circ: 1500. *Indexed:* AmHI. *Aud.:* Ga, Ac.

This magazine "is dedicated to fresh, original and diverse stories, novel-excerpts, and one-act plays." It publishes the work of new and established writers and sponsors an annual short story writing contest. The web site includes selected stories plus information for subscribers and contributors. Recommended for large public libraries and academic libraries supporting creative writing programs.

2580. *Quick Fiction: stories under 500 words.* [ISSN: 1543-8376] 2002. s-a. USD 11; USD 19.50 for 2 yrs.; USD 6.50 newsstand/cover per issue. Ed(s): Brenda Pike. Quick Fiction, PO Box 4445, Salem, MA 01970. Circ: 500 Paid and controlled. *Aud.:* Ga.

This is a well-edited and well-designed little literary magazine. It publishes short "stories and narrative prose poems that, in the space of a single page, set a scene for characters to confront conflict." Each issue includes 15–20 stories and includes biographical information of each author. Many of the contributors are established authors. The web site offers submission and subscription information as well as the table of contents for the current issue. Suitable for general readers, this title would also be appreciated in academic libraries supporting creative writing programs.

2581. *Romantic Times Book Reviews: the magazine for fiction lovers.* Former titles (until 2006): *Romantic Times Book Club;* (until May 2002): *Romantic Times Magazine; Romantic Times;* Which incorporated (1986-1991): *Rave Reviews.* [ISSN: 1933-0634] 1981. m. USD 29.95 domestic; USD 65 foreign. Ed(s): Libby Snitzer, Lorraine Freeney. Romantic Times Publishing Group, 55 Bergen St, Brooklyn, NY 11201. Illus., adv. Circ: 135000. *Bk. rev.:* 120-170, 50-250 words. *Aud.:* Ga.

This glossy magazine covers romance fiction for readers, writers, and booksellers, including publishing industry news and features, profiles of authors, tips for aspiring writers, bookstore news, and reviews of forthcoming books. The web site is very comprehensive and has links to award-winning books, authors, and resources for readers and writers, including a popular message board for readers.

StoryQuarterly. See Little Magazines section.

2582. *Zoetrope: all-story.* [ISSN: 1091-2495] 1997. 4x/yr. USD 19.95 domestic; USD 25.95 in Canada & Mexico; USD 39.95 elsewhere. Ed(s): Adrienne Brodeur. A Z X Publications, 1350 Ave of the Americas 24th Fl, New York, NY 10019; info@all-story.com; http://www.all-story.com. Illus., adv. Sample. Circ: 40000 Controlled. *Aud.:* Ga, Ac.

This is an exceptionally well-crafted, quarterly literary publication founded by film director Francis Ford Coppola with the goal "to explore the intersection of story and art, fiction and film." The magazine purchases not only the print rights of the new stories and one-act plays it publishes, but also options film rights for possible use by Coppola's American Zoetrope production company. Each issue also contains a story that was adapted into a film. The work of well-known artists such as Kiki Smith and David Byrne appear in each issue. This journal would be an excellent teaching tool in academic libraries supporting programs in creative writing and journalism. The entire contents of the current issue and back issues are available on the web site, which allows for online submissions via the Zoetrope Virtual Studio.

Mystery and Detective

Magazines in this section include periodicals that publish original short mystery stories or hard-boiled crime fiction. They may also include book reviews, criticism, interviews and other information of interest to readers and writers of this genre. Magazine web sites include information on subscribing and submissions and a table of contents for the current issue.

2583. *Alfred Hitchcock's Mystery Magazine (Print Edition).* [ISSN: 0002-5224] 1956. 10x/yr. USD 43.90 domestic; USD 53.90 foreign. Ed(s): Linda Landrigin. Penny Publications LLP, 6 Prowitt St., Norwalk, CT 06855. Illus., adv. Circ: 92000 Paid and free. Vol. ends: Dec. *Indexed:* AmHI, MSF. *Bk. rev.:* 2-7, 40-100 words. *Aud.:* Ga.

Founded in 1956, this classic illustrated mystery magazine is a must subscription for all public libraries. Digest-sized and 144 pages long, *AHMM* is published 11 times a year, with a double issue in July/August. Each issue contains seven original, new short stories varying in length from short-shorts to novellas. Each issue also includes a reprinting of a classic mystery tale. Other features include a story contest, puzzles, book reviews, author interviews, and comments from the editor. The magazine accepts cartoons and artwork as well as story submissions on almost any kind of mystery. Manuscripts must be under 14,000 words. The web site has submission guidelines, the table of contents of the current issue, and a featured story of the month.

2584. *Baker Street Journal: an irregular quarterly of Sherlockiana.* [ISSN: 0005-4070] 1946. q. USD 24.95 domestic; USD 27.50 foreign. Ed(s): Steven Rothman. Sheridan Press, PO Box 465, Hanover, PA 17331-0465. Illus., index, adv. Circ: 1600 Paid. Microform: PQC. *Indexed:* AmHI, BEL&L, MLA-IB. *Bk. rev.:* 1-10, 30-90 words. *Aud.:* Ga.

This is the official publication of the major association of Sherlock Holmes fans in the United States. The subtitle describes this periodical as an "irregular quarterly of Sherlockiana." As such, each issue contains ten or so well-researched articles dealing with the life and times of the fictional character Sherlock Holmes. Articles such as "Mrs. Hudson: A Legend" provide thoughtful insights of interest to the avid reader. Because it is geared toward fans of the Holmes novels, this magazine also has a section for assorted announcements and a handy calendar of events.

2585. *ClueLass HomePage.* 1995. m. Ed(s): Kate Derie. Deadly Serious Press, 405 E Wetmore Rd #117-499, Tucson, AZ 85705-1700; http://www.cluelass.com. *Aud.:* Ga, Sa.

This web site (www.cluelass.com) does not publish mystery stories but is an extremely well-organized and easy-to-navigate database for fans and writers of all mystery genres. The site features current nominees and past winners of numerous awards in the mystery field, notices of upcoming conferences and events, links to sites providing factual source information for writers, and other web sites related to mystery, crime, and suspense.

2586. *Clues: a journal of detection.* [ISSN: 0742-4248] 1980. q. USD 134 (Individuals, USD 63 print & online eds.; USD 32 newsstand/cover). Ed(s): Elizabeth Foxwell. Heldref Publications, 1319 18th St, NW, Washington, DC 20036-1802; subscribe@heldref.org; http://www.heldref.org. Illus., adv. Refereed. Circ: 394 Paid. Online: Chadwyck-Healey Inc.; Florida Center for Library Automation; Gale; ProQuest LLC (Ann Arbor). *Indexed:* ABS&EES, AmHI, MLA-IB. *Bk. rev.:* 0-60, 40-300 words. *Aud.:* Ga, Ac.

This peer-reviewed quarterly publishes scholarly articles on all aspects of mystery and detective material in print, television, and film. As such, it features articles of analysis, criticism, and opinion. Some issues feature a particular author's work and include an author interview. This journal is for the well-read mystery reader and students of popular culture. The web site provides submission, publication, and subscription information.

2587. *Crimewave: 100% pure crime fiction.* [ISSN: 1463-1350] 1998. s-a. GBP 11 domestic; GBP 22 foreign; GBP 3 newsstand/cover per issue domestic. Ed(s): Andy Cox, Mat Coward. T T A Press, 5 Martins Ln, Witcham, Ely, CB6 2LB, United Kingdom; ttapress@aol.com; http://www.tta-press.com. Illus., adv. *Aud.:* Ga.

Crimewave is a well-designed British magazine with a sharp, uncluttered layout. It publishes short stories from established crime writers as well as talented new authors. Its byline states, "No reviews, no interviews, no padding, just 100 percent pure crime fiction!" Its web site (www.ttapress.com/publCW.html) includes details on submissions, subscription information, and an index of past issues.

2588. *Ellery Queen's Mystery Magazine (Print Edition): the world's leading mystery magazine.* Former titles (until 1988): *Ellery Queen;* (until 1981): *Ellery Queen's Mystery Magazine.* [ISSN: 1054-8122] 1941. 10x/yr. USD 43.90 domestic; USD 53.90 foreign; USD 3.99 newsstand/cover. Ed(s): Janet Hutchings. Penny Publications LLP, 6 Prowitt St., Norwalk, CT 06855. Illus. Circ: 77270. *Indexed:* AmHI, MSF. *Bk. rev.:* 8-12, 30-70 words. *Aud.:* Ga, Ac.

Published since 1941, *Ellery Queen's Mystery Magazine* publishes stories written by leading crime and mystery writers but also encourages first-story submissions. Each well-edited issue includes 10 to 12 short stories, book reviews, and a puzzle or two. This magazine is recommended for all public libraries and academic libraries supporting creative writing programs.

2589. *Mystery Readers Journal.* Formerly: *Mystery Readers of America Journal.* [ISSN: 1043-3473] 1985. q. USD 28 domestic; USD 40 foreign. Ed(s): Janet A. Rudolph. Mystery Readers International, PO Box 8116, Berkeley, CA 94707-8116. Circ: 1500 Paid. *Indexed:* BRI. *Bk. rev.:* 25-45, 200-900 words. *Aud.:* Ga, Ac.

This interesting quarterly is the official publication of Mystery Readers International. It is unique in that each issue focuses on a single theme. Past examples include "Mysteries Set in Italy," "Art Mysteries," "Culinary Crime," and "Senior Sleuths." Issues include in-depth analysis of the subgenre by established authors, book reviews, author interviews, columns, and a calendar of mystery related events. The web site provides information on subscriptions, an index of past issues, and links to related sites. This magazine would be appreciated in public libraries supporting book clubs.

2590. *Mystery Scene.* [ISSN: 1087-674X] 1985. 6x/yr. USD 32. Ed(s): Ed Gorman. Mystery Scene Magazine, 331 W. 57th St, Ste 148, New York, NY 10019-3101; KateStineNotThisPart@mysteryscenemag.com. Illus., adv. Circ: 8000. *Bk. rev.:* 10-15, 45-80 words. *Aud.:* Ga, Sa.

This entertaining magazine is designed for both readers and authors of mysteries, booksellers, and publishers. Each issue includes author interviews, book reviews, and articles on writing. The reader will also find in-depth feature articles, publishing news, and reviews of current books, movies, and television productions. The web site has details on subscribing, contributing, and advertising, as well as the table of contents of the latest issue.

2591. *Sherlock Holmes Journal.* [ISSN: 0037-3621] 1952. s-a. Membership, GBP 18. Ed(s): Heather Owen, Nicholas Utechin. Sherlock Holmes Society of London, c/o Nicholas Utechin, Highfield Farm House, Headington, OX3 7LR, United Kingdom; Nick@nutechin.freeserve.co.uk; http://sherlock-holmes.org.uk. Illus. Circ: 1600. *Bk. rev.:* 5-10, 80-700 words. *Aud.:* Ga.

This is the official publication of the British Sherlock Holmes Society, a literary and social society devoted to Sherlock Holmes, Dr. John H. Watson, and their world. The society sponsors group tours to the locales of Holmes stories enabling devotees to do their own first-hand research, some of which is published in the society's journal. Thus the publication is an entertaining mix of serious scholarship lightened with reports of social activities. The society's web site is comprehensive, including subscription information, the current issue's table of contents, and a calendar of events.

■ FICTION: SCIENCE FICTION, FANTASY, AND HORROR

Carrie Donovan, Instructional Services Librarian, Herman B Wells Library, Indiana University-Bloomington, cdonovan@indiana.edu

Introduction

Although themes of science fiction, fantasy, and horror pervade the entertainment and publishing industries, magazines and journals related to science fiction and its many sub-genres have not dramatically increased in number in recent years. Those publications that are proven to be steadfast and significant contributors to the creation and critique of science fiction, fantasy, and horror are included here. The titles in this section transcend traditional boundaries to lend an enlightened and informed voice to the conversations surrounding all things speculative, supernatural, fantastic, and frightening.

Authors, fans, and scholars in the field of science fiction, fantasy, and horror create a myriad of content, resulting in publications ranging from the literary to the fantastic. Research-oriented journals make up a small percentage of this subject's periodicals, while resources intended for a more general readership are common. Some publications are available online or have corresponding web sites that offer access to articles, reviews, and archives.

Basic Periodicals

Analog Science Fiction & Fact (print edition), Asimov's Science Fiction (print edition), Fantasy & Science Fiction, Science Fiction Studies.

Basic Abstracts and Indexes

Abstracts of English Studies, American Humanities Index, Arts & Humanities Citation Index, Book Review Index, MLA International Bibliography.

2592. Analog Science Fiction & Fact (Print edition). Former titles (until 1991): *Analog Science Fiction Science Fact;* (until 1965): *Analog Science Fact - Science Fiction;* (until 1961): *Astounding Science Fiction.* [ISSN: 1059-2113] 1930. 12x/yr. USD 32.97 domestic; USD 42.97 foreign. Ed(s): Stanley Schmidt. Dell Magazines, 475 Park Ave S, 11 Fl, New York, NY 10016-6901; juliamcevoy@dellmagazines.com. Illus., index, adv. Sample. Circ: 50000 Paid. Vol. ends: Dec. Online: OCLC Online Computer Library Center, Inc.; ProQuest K-12 Learning Solutions; ProQuest LLC (Ann Arbor). *Indexed:* ASIP, BRI, CBRI, LRI. *Bk. rev.:* 8-12, 300-1,500 words. *Aud.:* Hs, Ga, Ac.

Analog Science Fiction and Fact is one of the leading science fiction magazines today. The publication offers a "more realistic" approach to the genre by combining scientific articles with original fiction. The balance of fiction with fact will appeal to the realistic sensibilities of science fiction fans. In addition to novellas and short stories, each issue includes book reviews, classified advertisements, lists of upcoming events, and letters to and from the editor. Subscriptions and single issues of this publication are now available in a variety of electronic formats (visit www.analogsf.com for more information).

2593. Andromeda Spaceways Inflight Magazine. [ISSN: 1446-781X] 2002. bi-m. AUD 45 domestic; AUD 66 foreign; USD 49 foreign. Andromeda Spaceways Publishing Co-Op, PO Box 127, Belmont, W.A. 6984, Australia; editor@andromedaspaceways.com; http://www.andromedaspaceways.com. *Bk. rev.:* 5-10, 100-500 words. *Aud.:* Ems, Hs, Ga.

With an emphasis on science fiction of a milder sort, *Andromeda Spaceways Inflight Magazine* is a relatively new publication that aims to appeal to a variety of readers, including children and young adults. In addition to many book reviews, interviews, and letters to and from the editor, stories written by young or novice authors are occasionally published. Sample segments from the magazine are available on its companion web site.

2594. Aphelion. 1997. m. Free. Ed(s): Dan Hollifield. Aphelion, vila@america.net; http://www.aphelion-webzine.com. *Aud.:* Ga.

This e-zine emphasizes new works of science fiction that will introduce the public to beginning writers and introduce these first-time writers, in turn, to the criticism of editors and readers. Serialized stories and novelettes, in addition to poetry and fiction, are included. There is also an archive of past issues available and searchable on the web site. This resource is primarily for the author trying to find his or her way, and is recommended as such.

2595. Asimov's Science Fiction (Print Edition). Former titles (until Nov. 1992): *Isaac Asimov's Science Fiction Magazine;* (until 1990): *Isaac Asimov's Science Fiction;* (until 1986): *Isaac Asimov's Science Fiction Magazine.* [ISSN: 1065-2698] 1977. 12x/yr. USD 32.97 domestic; USD 42.97 foreign. Ed(s): Gardner Dozois, Sheila Williams. Dell Magazines, 475 Park Ave S, 11 Fl, New York, NY 10016-6901; juliamcevoy@dellmagazines.com. Illus., index, adv. Sample. Circ: 50000 Paid. Vol. ends: Dec. Microform: PQC. *Indexed:* AmHI. *Bk. rev.:* 6-15, 50-100 words. *Aud.:* Hs, Ga, Ac.

Asimov's Science Fiction remains one of the leading magazines of the genre. It presents original works of science fiction and fantasy by well-known authors, and also newcomers, in the form of novellas, short stories, and poetry. Informational articles and extensive book reviews by regular and guest contributors complete the wide scope of this publication. Also included are a calendar of events and a list of classified advertisements. Subscriptions and single issues of this publication are now available in a variety of electronic formats as well (visit www.asimovs.com for more information).

2596. Black Static. Formerly (until 2006): *The Third Alternative.* 1994. bi-m. USD 40.01. Ed(s): Andy Cox. T T A Press, 5 Martins Ln, Witcham, Ely, CB6 2LB, United Kingdom; ttapress@aol.com; http://www.tta-press.com. Illus., adv. Circ: 6000 Controlled. *Indexed:* PRA. *Bk. rev.:* 15-25, 500-1,000 words. *Aud.:* Ga, Ac.

Published in Great Britain, *Black Static* features interviews, reviews, artwork, cinema features, comment columns, and fiction from new and known authors and artists. This publication will satisfy science fiction fans and scholars alike. Because it often transcends the divide between literary genres, readers of mainstream fiction will also be attracted to *Black Static* for its provocative editorials and groundbreaking fiction.

2597. Cemetery Dance. [ISSN: 1047-7675] 1988. bi-m. USD 27. Cemetery Dance Publications, 132 B Industry Ln, Unit 7, Forest Hill, MD 21050. Illus., adv. Vol. ends: Winter. *Bk. rev.:* 20-40, 200-5,000 words. *Aud.:* Ga.

This award-winning publication includes essays and artwork as well as news and reviews. Contributions by regular columnists, aspiring writers, and well-known authors come in the form of fiction and nonfiction. Readers of horror will appreciate the six to eight original stories that are published in each issue, while fans of the broader genre of science fiction will take interest in this journal's news articles, interviews, and reviews of movies, software, and books.

2598. Chronicle (Radford): S F, fantasy & horror's monthly trade journal. Formerly (until 2004): *Science Fiction Chronicle;* Incorporating (in 1984): *Starship;* Which was formerly: *Algol.* [ISSN: 1552-9983] 1979. m. USD 45 domestic; USD 56 Canada; USD 75 elsewhere. Ed(s): Charles C. Ryan. DNA Publications, Inc., PO Box 2988, Radford, VA 24143-2988; publisher@dnapublications.com; http://www.dnapublicvations.com. Illus., adv. Circ: 12000. Microform: PQC. Online: ProQuest K-12 Learning Solutions; ProQuest LLC (Ann Arbor). *Indexed:* AmHI, BRI, CBRI, MLA-IB. *Bk. rev.:* 20-50, 50-300 words. *Aud.:* Hs, Ga.

Chronicle reports extensively on the labors of those dedicated to the literature of the genre. Feature articles and reviews of books and films, as well as regular market reports and buyers' guides, make this publication an essential resource for anyone wanting to keep current in the field. Announcements and news important to publishers, booksellers, and writers of the genre are also included.

2599. Cinefantastique: the magazine with a sense of wonder. [ISSN: 0145-6032] 1970. 9x/yr. USD 34.95 domestic; USD 44.95 Canada; USD 59.95 elsewhere. Ed(s): Mark A Altman. C F Q Media, LLC, 3740

Overland Ave, Ste E, Los Angeles, CA 90034; mail@cfq.com; http://www.cfq.com. Illus., adv. Circ: 40000. Vol. ends: Dec. *Indexed:* FLI, MRD. *Bk. rev.:* 5, 150-300 words. *Aud.:* Ga.

Cinefantastique (CFQ) reviews science fiction, fantasy, and horror films; television; comics; games; and much more. Insightful interviews and in-depth articles provide honest and thought-provoking perspectives that take readers beyond the mainstream. *CFQ* offers information about upcoming SF conventions and major events such as film and DVD release dates, in order to keep readers current. *Cinefantastique* has a long history of covering the genre's entertainment in general, but it will appeal primarily to those interested in film reviews and previews, as that topic constitutes the bulk of the publication's contents.

2600. *DargonZine: electronic magazine of the Dargon Project.* Formerly (until 1988): *FSFnet.* [ISSN: 1080-9910] 1985. irreg. 8-12/yr. Free. Ed(s): Ornoth Liscomb. Dargon Project, dargon@shore.net; http://www.dargonzine.org. Illus. *Aud.:* Hs, Ga.

DargonZine is the product of the "Dargon Project," a "shared world" of amateur writers who author the fiction featured in this electronic resource. Many authors write with regard to a common milieu, sharing settings, and characters. Stories included in this e-zine are related to Dargon, a fantasy world that is predominantly human, at a late-medieval technology level, where magic is relatively rare. The concept is novel, and the stories are usually compelling and entertaining.

2601. *The Dark Side: the magazine of the macabre and fantastic.* [ISSN: 0960-6653] 199?. m. GBP 38.40 domestic; GBP 44 in Europe; GBP 63 elsewhere. The DarkSide Publishing Ltd., PO Box 35, Liskeard, PL 14 4YT, United Kingdom. Illus., adv. *Aud.:* Ga, Sa.

Advertised as "Britain's best-selling horror magazine," *Dark Side* represents the genre well, with vivid photographs and uncompromising articles that focus on horror films and the people who make them. Interviews and reviews abound in this always informative, but sometimes disturbing, magazine of the macabre and the paranormal. A list of horror film festivals is available, as are classified advertisements. Some adult content is included.

2602. *DreamWatch.* Formerly (until 1994): *DreamWatch Bulletin.* [ISSN: 1356-482X] 1983. m. USD 6.99 newsstand/cover per issue United States; USD 9.99 newsstand/cover per issue Canada. Titan Magazines, Titan House, 144 Southwark St, London, SE1 0UP, United Kingdom; http://www.titanmagazines.co.uk/. Adv. *Bk. rev.:* 8-10, 300-500 words. *Aud.:* Hs, Ga.

Dreamwatch aspires to provide the latest news and information about mainstream science fiction and fantasy entertainment, with a focus on fantasy film and television. Although this publication originates in the United Kingdom, it concentrates on the products of Hollywood, with reviews and highlights of current and upcoming films and television shows. Also included are reviews of comic books, books, and merchandise, as well as news columns and letters to the editor. Public libraries wishing to provide a variety of fan magazines will want to consider adding this publication to the collection.

2603. *Extrapolation.* [ISSN: 0014-5483] 1959. q. USD 28 (Individuals, USD 18). Ed(s): Javier A Martinez. University of Texas at Brownsville and Texas Southmost College, Department of English, 80 Ft Brown, Brownsville, TX 78520; jmartinez@utb.edu. Index, adv. Sample. Refereed. Circ: 1000. Vol. ends: Dec. Microform: PQC. Online: Chadwyck-Healey Inc.; EBSCO Publishing, EBSCO Host; Florida Center for Library Automation; Gale; Northern Light Technology, Inc.; OCLC Online Computer Library Center, Inc.; ProQuest K-12 Learning Solutions; ProQuest LLC (Ann Arbor). *Indexed:* ABS&EES, AmHI, ArtHuCI, BEL&L, BRI, CBRI, FLI, HumInd, IBR, IBZ, MLA-IB. *Bk. rev.:* 3-5, 300-1,500 words. *Aud.:* Ac.

Extrapolation is one of the foremost scholarly journals of science fiction and fantasy, featuring critical articles on innovators in the field, genre studies, and other thought-provoking themes. The quarterly journal includes book reviews, letters, and short editorials. This publication deserves a place in any library that supports science fiction scholars.

2604. *Fangoria.* [ISSN: 0164-2111] 1978. 10x/yr. USD 54.47 domestic; USD 63.97 foreign. Ed(s): Anthony Timpone. Starlog Group, Inc., 1372 Broadway, 2nd Fl, New York, NY 10018; postalzone@starloggroup.com; http://www.starlog.com. Illus., adv. Circ: 214500 Paid. *Bk. rev.:* Number and length vary. *Aud.:* Hs, Ga.

Fans of horror in books, film, and television will appreciate this publication's reviews, photographs, and interviews. *Fangoria* appeals to the reader's interest in gore by including color photographs of terrifying scenes with nearly every article. The reviews of new movies and books are more likely to represent mainstream media than the more alternative experiments of the genre. Some adult content is included.

2605. *Fantasy & Science Fiction.* Formerly (until 1987): *The Magazine of Fantasy and Science Fiction;* Incorporates: *Venture Science Fiction.* [ISSN: 1095-8258] 1949. m. combined Oct.-Nov. USD 44.89 domestic; USD 64.89 foreign; USD 3.99 newsstand/cover per issue. Ed(s): Gordon Van Gelder. Spilogale, Inc., P. O. Box 3447, Hoboken, NJ 07030; FandSF@aol.com; http://www.fsfmag.com. Illus., adv. Sample. Circ: 35000 Paid. Vol. ends: Jun/Dec. Microform: PQC. Online: EBSCO Publishing, EBSCO Host; Gale; OCLC Online Computer Library Center, Inc.; ProQuest LLC (Ann Arbor). *Indexed:* AmHI, BRI, CBRI, MASUSE. *Bk. rev.:* 5-15, 200-1,000 words. *Aud.:* Hs, Ga, Ac.

Each issue of *Fantasy & Science Fiction* features eight to twelve short stories and novellas from famous and not-so-famous authors. The magazine also includes reviews of new and forthcoming books as well as columns by regular contributors. This well-established publication deserves a place in libraries that support and serve readers of the genre. Subscriptions are also available in a variety of electronic formats (visit www.sfsite.com/fsf for more information).

2606. *Femspec.* [ISSN: 1523-4002] s-a. USD 85 (Members, USD 30). Femspec, 1610 Rydalmount Rd, Cleveland Heights, OH 44118. Circ: 300. *Indexed:* AmHI, FemPer, GendWatch, HumInd, IBR, IBZ, MLA-IB. *Bk. rev.:* 2, essay length, signed. *Aud.:* Ga, Ac.

Femspec is an interdisciplinary journal that brings a unique perspective to SF criticism through critiques and creations that are grounded in feminist scholarship. The publication is "dedicated to critical and creative works in the realms of science fiction, fantasy, magical realism, surrealism, myth, folklore, and other supernatural agents." Each issue features fiction, poetry, criticism, interviews, and book reviews.

2607. *Foundation: the review of science fiction.* [ISSN: 0306-4964] 1972. 3x/yr. USD 35.50. Ed(s): Farah Menleshon. Science Fiction Foundation, University of Reading, Department of History, Faculty of Letters and Social Science, Reading, RG1 5PT, United Kingdom; asawyer@ liverpool.ac.uk; http://www.liv.ac.uk/~asawyer/fnd.html. Illus., index, adv. Sample. Refereed. Circ: 1000. Vol. ends: Dec. *Indexed:* IBR, IBZ, MLA-IB. *Bk. rev.:* 10-15, 500-2,500 words. *Aud.:* Ac.

This international journal is published by the Science Fiction Foundation. It combines critical analysis with lively book reviews and editorials. Many well-known science fiction writers are included among the contributors. As one of the few peer-reviewed publications of the genre, *Foundation* is an excellent scholarly resource for academic and research collections.

2608. *Interzone: science fiction and fantasy.* Incorporates (in 1994): *Nexus;* (1991-1993): *Million.* [ISSN: 0264-3596] 1982. m. GBP 42 domestic; EUR 24 in Europe; GBP 36 in Europe. Ed(s): Andy Cox. T T A Press, 5 Martins Ln, Witcham, Ely, CB6 2LB, United Kingdom; ttapress@aol.com; http://www.tta-press.com. Illus., adv. Sample. Circ: 10000. *Bk. rev.:* 7-10, 100-500 words. *Aud.:* Ga, Ac.

The British publication *Interzone* features new science fiction and fantasy stories. One of the first successful British publications of the genre, *Interzone* maintains its credibility among the premier science fiction magazines of today. It has published short stories by many established science fiction writers, but its particular strength has been in the nurturing of newer writers. Interviews, illustrations, and reviews are also included.

2609. *Journal of the Fantastic in the Arts.* Former titles (until 1988): *Fantasy Review;* (until 1984): *Fantasy.* [ISSN: 0897-0521] 1988. q. USD 25 (Individuals, USD 20). Ed(s): William A Senior. Florida Atlantic University, c/o Robert A. Collins, Dorothy F.Schmidt College of Arts & Letters, Boca Raton, FL 33431-0991; collins@fau.edu, http://www.iafa.org/. Illus., index, adv. Sample. Refereed. Circ: 500. *Indexed:* IBR, IBZ, MLA-IB. *Aud.:* Ac.

The focus of this scholarly journal is the study of the fantastic in literature and the arts (drama, film, dance, architecture, and popular media). It includes original artwork and essays on all aspects of the fantastic. Offering an interdisciplinary approach to the study of fantasy, *JFA* publishes quality papers on engaging themes, such as textual comparisons, character studies, and author analyses.

2610. *Locus (Oakland): the magazine of the science fiction and fantasy field.* [ISSN: 0047-4959] 1968. m. USD 59 (Individuals, USD 56; USD 6.50 newsstand/cover). Ed(s): Charles N Brown. Locus Publications, 34 Ridgewood Ln, Oakland, CA 94611. Illus., index, adv. Sample. Circ: 9000 Paid. Vol. ends: Dec. *Indexed:* BRI, CBRI. *Bk. rev.:* 15-30, 200-1,000 words. *Aud.:* Hs, Ga, Ac.

Containing articles, news, and reviews, *Locus* is a vital resource for authors, publishers, and enthusiasts of science fiction and fantasy. This magazine features comprehensive lists of forthcoming books and a section devoted to science fiction magazines. Also included are interviews with authors, reports of conventions and awards, and listings of events. *Locus* does not publish fiction. The scope of this magazine includes the United States and Europe. The web version of this publication allows free access to samples from the current issue of *Locus,* in addition to its own news and reviews.

2611. *Mythlore: a journal of J.R.R. Tolkien, C.S. Lewis, Charles Williams, and mythopoeic literature.* Supersedes (1964-1972): *Tolkien Journal.* [ISSN: 0146-9339] 1969. s-a. USD 38 domestic; USD 42 in the Americas; USD 50 elsewhere. Ed(s): Janet Brennan Croft. Mythopoeic Society, 920 N Atlantic Blvd # E, Alhambra, CA 91801; http://www.mythsoc.org. Index, adv. Sample. Refereed. Circ: 660. Online: Gale. *Indexed:* AmHI, ArtHuCI, BEL&L, MLA-IB, RI-1. *Bk. rev.:* 3-15, 100-300 words. *Aud.:* Hs, Ga, Ac.

In alignment with the goals of its publishing body, *Mythlore* promotes the discussion and enjoyment of fantasy and mythic literature. This journal includes critical articles and features on poetry, art, and bibliographies. The publication's title reflects the specific nature of its content. Libraries that support scholars of this narrow genre will find *Mythlore* invaluable.

2612. *New York Review of Science Fiction.* [ISSN: 1052-9438] 1988. m. USD 36 domestic; USD 38 Canada; USD 47 in Europe. Ed(s): David G Hartwell. Dragon Press, PO Box 78, Pleasantville, NY 10570; dgh@tor.com; http://www.nyrsf.com. Illus., adv. Circ: 1000 Paid. *Indexed:* MLA-IB. *Bk. rev.:* 8-15, 1,000-3,500 words. *Aud.:* Ac.

Along with extensive and thoughtful book reviews, *NYRSF* also includes essays on topics related to literature of the science fiction, fantasy, and horror genre. This publication provides a learned analysis of the genre's authors and their writing. It will be most appropriate for academic libraries with a core science fiction collection.

2613. *Planet Magazine (San Francisco).* q. USD 20 domestic; USD 28 in Canada & Mexico; USD 40 elsewhere. Planet Magazine, 876 Valencia St., Ste B, San Francisco, CA 94110; info@planet-mag.com. *Aud.:* Hs, Ga.

One of the first science fiction e-zines, *Planet Magazine* is a free, award-winning publication of science fiction and fantasy literature written by emerging writers. Content is presented in a reader-friendly, blog-style format. The quality of content varies, ranging from first-rate to amateurish. The publication offers a worthy arena for new writers and digital artists to display their work.

2614. *Realms of Fantasy.* [ISSN: 1078-1951] 1994. bi-m. USD 16.95 domestic; USD 21.95 foreign; USD 3.99 newsstand/cover per issue. Ed(s): Shawna McCarthy. Sovereign Media, 453B Carlisle Dr, Herndon, VA 20170; sovmedia@erols.com; http://www.scifi.com. Illus., adv. Sample. Circ: 53000 Paid. *Bk. rev.:* Number and length vary. *Aud.:* Hs, Ga, Ac.

As the title implies, *Realms of Fantasy* covers the spectrum of fantasy fiction, with six to eight short stories in each issue. Original artwork, book reviews, film reviews, and coverage of computer, board, card, and role-playing games are also included. The contemporary perspective of this publication make it well suited to libraries serving a science fiction and fantasy readership of varying ages and interests.

2615. *S F X: the earth's greatest S F and fantasy magazine.* [ISSN: 0262-2971] 1981. 13x/yr. GBP 35.79 domestic; GBP 48 in Europe; GBP 65 elsewhere. Ed(s): David Bradley. Future Publishing Ltd., Beauford Court, 30 Monmouth St, Bath, BA1 2BW, United Kingdom; customerservice@subscription.co.uk; http://www.futurenet.co.uk. Adv. Circ: 36710. *Bk. rev.:* 5-10, 100-500 words. *Aud.:* Hs, Ga.

As Europe's best-selling science fiction, fantasy, and horror magazine, *SFX* reviews all the latest films, DVDs, videos, and books of the genre. Biting wit and unbiased writing can be found on each page of this publication. Fans of popular, mainstream science fiction films and television shows will appreciate the bright and bold format showcasing the photographs, interviews, and behind-the-scenes coverage found in every issue.

2616. *Sci-Fi.* Formerly (until 1999): *Sci-Fi Entertainment.* [ISSN: 1527-5779] 1994. w. USD 16.95 domestic; USD 21.95 elsewhere. Sovereign Media, 453B Carlisle Dr, Herndon, VA 20170; sovmedia@erols.com. Illus., adv. Sample. Circ: 75000. *Bk. rev.:* 5-10, 800-1,000 words. *Aud.:* Hs, Ga.

Science fiction fans and also readers with broader interests will appreciate *Sci Fi*'s focus on the latest trends and current successes of the genre in film and television. News and interviews of popular shows and stars will engage readers, while the reviews and ratings will inform them. The publication's scope extends beyond the programming of the SciFi Channel to encompass other networks and venues. The wide coverage of this publication makes it a useful addition to any collection needing an infusion of popular culture.

2617. *Sci Fi Weekly.* w. Ed(s): Scott Edelman. Sci Fi Weekly, 128 Bayer Road, Hedgesville, WV 25427. *Bk. rev.:* 3-5. *Aud.:* Ga.

Science Fiction Weekly is an online source for news, reviews, and interviews about the world of science fiction entertainment. Pulling together both newsy and critical content regarding science fiction television, film, games, books, and more, this resource is entertaining and informative. Visitors to the web site who register will receive newsletters, information about upcoming events, and access to an online bulletin board.

2618. *Science Fiction and Fantasy Writers of America. Bulletin.* Former titles (until 1992): *Bulletin of the Science Fiction Writers of America;* (until 1982): *S F W A Bulletin.* [ISSN: 1538-2362] 1965. q. USD 21 domestic; USD 31 in Canada & Mexico; USD 38 elsewhere. Ed(s): Mark Kreighbaum. Science Fiction and Fantasy Writers of America, Inc.(S F W A), PO Box 877, Chestertown, MD 21620; execdir@sfwa.org; http://www.sfwa.org. Illus., adv. Sample. Circ: 2200 Paid and controlled. Microform: PQC. *Bk. rev.:* 2-5, 300-1,500 words. *Aud.:* Ga, Ac.

This publication is geared to writers of science fiction. Published by the Science Fiction and Fantasy Writers of America, the *Bulletin* offers reports and information useful to writers and publishers of science fiction and fantasy. Fiction and essays from professional writers and book reviews are also included.

2619. *Science Fiction Studies.* [ISSN: 0091-7729] 1973. 3x/yr. USD 35 (Individuals, USD 25). Ed(s): Arthur B Evans. S F - T H, Inc., EC L 06, DePauw University, Greencastle, IN 46135-0037; aevans@depauw.edu.

Illus., index, adv. Sample. Refereed. Circ: 1100. Vol. ends: Dec. *Indexed:* ABS&EES, AmHI, ArtHuCI, BRI, CBCARef, CBRI, HumInd, IBR, IBZ, MLA-IB. *Bk. rev.:* 10-20, 500-3,000 words. *Aud.:* Ac.

Science Fiction Studies is a necessity for any academic collection. In addition to the extensive book reviews, essays, and interviews published in this journal, refereed articles provide readers with a scholar's approach to science fiction. The journal includes articles on topics ranging from current technologies to theories of past eras. Offering an international perspective without bias, *Science Fiction Studies* will complement any library's science fiction collection. Tables of contents and article abstracts for current and past issues are available on the publication's companion web site.

2620. *Slayage.* [ISSN: 1546-9212] 2001. q. Ed(s): Rhonda V Wilcox, David Lavery. Middle Tennessee State University, 1301 East Main St, Murfreesboro, TN 37132; http://www.mtsu.edu. *Aud.:* Ga, Ac.

Slayage is an ongoing effort to articulate the meaning and significance behind the themes and context of the television series "Buffy the Vampire Slayer." This e-journal includes essays and articles relating to a variety of aspects of the series and its spinoff "Angel." Much more than a fan site, *Slayage* provides content that is scholarly in tone and reviewed by qualified editors and researchers in the field.

2621. *Starlog.* [ISSN: 0191-4626] 1976. m. 10/yr. USD 56.97 domestic; USD 66.97 foreign; USD 7.99 newsstand/cover per issue. Ed(s): David McDonnell. Starlog Group, Inc., 1372 Broadway, 2nd Fl, New York, NY 10018. Illus., adv. Sample. Circ: 226855. *Bk. rev.:* 10-15, 50-100 words. *Aud.:* Ems, Hs, Ga.

One of the more popular mass-market magazines, *Starlog* covers science fiction, fantasy, and horror in the popular media. This publication includes news and interviews related to both current and classic movies, television series, web sites, and books in the genre. Articles and columns are accompanied by photographs, cartoons, and humor. With the growing popularity of science fiction, fantasy, and horror in television and film, *Starlog* is an asset to libraries that serve large populations. This publication's online presence at www.starlog-.com is expanding to encompass promotion and review material as well.

2622. *Strange Horizons.* 2000. w. Ed(s): Susan Marie Groppi. Strange Horizons, editor@strangehorizons.com. *Bk. rev.:* 15-20. *Aud.:* Ga, Ac.

Strange Horizons is a weekly online magazine of science fiction, fantasy, and science fact. With content spanning a variety of topics concerning science fiction and all its subgenres, this resource includes short fiction, poetry, artwork, reviews, and articles. In addition to an archive of past issues, the site also maintains a forum designed to facilitate discussion among *Strange Horizons* readers and contributors.

2623. *Tangent Online: short fiction review.* Formerly (until 1997): *Tangent (Print).* 1993. bi-m. USD 5. Ed(s): Eugie Foster. Tangent, 824 Stone Arch Dr., Independence, MO 64052-1735; editor@tangentonline.com; http://www.tangentonline.com. Adv. *Bk. rev.:* 60-75, 500-2,000 words. *Aud.:* Hs, Ga, Ac.

Tangent reviews almost all the short fiction published in science fiction and fantasy magazines. Author profiles, regular columns, and articles are also included. This e-zine is currently freely available to the general public without subscription.

2624. *Vector: the critical journal of the British Science Fiction Association.* Incorporates: *Paperback Inferno;* Which was formerly (until 1980): *Paperback Parlour.* [ISSN: 0505-0448] 1958. bi-m. GBP 2.50 per issue. Ed(s): Tony Cullen, Paul Billinger. British Science Fiction Association Ltd., c/o Estelle Roberts, Membership Secretary, 97 Sharp St, Hull, HU5 2AE, United Kingdom; bsfa@enterprise.net; http://www.bsfa.co.uk. Illus., adv. Sample. Circ: 1000. Vol. ends: Dec. *Bk. rev.:* 15-25, 200-1000 words. *Aud.:* Hs, Ga, Ac.

"One of the longest running critical journals of science fiction in the world," *Vector* features incisive articles and in-depth book reviews. Each issue also includes interviews, editorials, and discussions of British science fiction of the past and present. The critical tone and broad coverage of this publication make it a necessity for anyone hoping to stay aware of the genre's latest literary endeavors.

2625. *Weird Tales.* Former titles (until 1998): *Worlds of Fantasy and Horror;* (until 1994): *Weird Tales.* 1923. bi-m. USD 24 domestic; USD 48 foreign. Ed(s): Darrell Schweitzer, George Scithers. Wildside Press, 9710 Traville Gateway Dr. #234, Rockville, MD 18928-0301; weirdtales@comcast.net; http://www.wildsidepress.com/. Illus., adv. Circ: 8000 Paid. *Aud.:* Hs, Ga.

Including original fiction, verse, and illustrations, *Weird Tales* will appeal to readers of classic science fiction and fantasy. This unique magazine has a long tradition of publishing stories by some of the genre's most influential and illustrious authors, including Ray Bradbury and Robert E. Howard. *Weird Tales* is recommended for libraries that serve a solid science fiction readership.

■ FILMS

Caroline M. Kent, Widener Library, Harvard University, Cambridge, MA 02138; cmkent@fas.harvard edu

Susan Oka, Margaret Herrick Library, Center for Motion Picture Studies–Academy of Motion Picture Arts and Sciences, 333 S. La Cienega Blvd., Beverly Hills, CA 90211; soka@oscars.org

Introduction

It is fascinating that a wholly visual medium such as film can generate such a huge body of print publications (digital or not)! Of course, since it is a visual medium, the publications themselves are indeed beautiful, and this may help keep them alive longer than in a discipline that is predominantly text-based. But approaching this body of publications is daunting, to say the least. Film magazines can be approached logically by dividing them into those publications that address a more academic market or formal film studies programs, and those that address the needs of the film buff. True fan magazines have not been included here, although there are some magazines that address the fans of a particular film genre, such as American film classics. There are clear, strong relationships to other disciplines, such as screenwriting (creative writing), animation (art), film music, etc., and many of those journals have been included here. There are also a multitude of business-related publications and technical journals; a few of these have also been included. Any library developing its film journal collection should look carefully at the research and curricula of the programs it serves when determining which few of the many titles should be purchased.

If the number of print journals is daunting, the number of digital publications is almost overwhelming. A visual medium like film logically gives birth to materials in other visual media, such as the web. Not surprisingly, however, this turns out to be very valuable—because of the huge popularity of film, even libraries that serve serious film studies programs could in the past barely dip into the ocean of international publications on film. The rapid increase in film-interest portals and e-journals around the world can help fill this gap. In many ways, the liberal use of the Internet greatly increases our access to important sources in film, sources that were previously unavailable. There are electronic publications on Cuban film, and portals in Urdu and Tamil and Russian—the vast majority of countries have a movie industry, and this is reflected on the web. Some of these publications are true electronic journals, many are gateways.

Gateways or research portals are obviously not the purview of this publication; but we cannot ignore the growing importance of portals such as the Internet Movie Database (www.imdb.com). Making them harder and harder to deal with, portals are also becoming hybrid, including a wide variety of web-publishing formats. There are film sites on the web containing materials that are truly serial in nature, that are portals to other sources, and that are blogs. Cartoon Brew (www.cartoonbrew.com) is a site in blog format, in which the editors keep the content focused on issues, books, and news of interest to the art end of animation. Print publication ain't what it used to be, and neither is electronic publishing. It is shifting as you read this. This is not news to libraries, but we have yet to comfortably accommodate all these new formats—and we must.

Basic Periodicals

Hs: *Animation Magazine, Film Comment, Film Quarterly, Movieline's Hollywood Life, Premiere;* Ga: *Cineaste, Classic Images, Film Comment, Film Quarterly, Movieline's Hollywood Life, Premiere, Sight and Sound;* Ac: *Cineaste, Cinema Journal, Film Comment, Film Quarterly, Journal of Film and Video, Sight and Sound.*

Basic Abstracts and Indexes

Film Literature Index, International Index to Film Periodicals.

2626. American Cinematographer: the international journal of motion picture production techniques. [ISSN: 0002-7928] 1920. m. USD 29.95 domestic; USD 49.95 in Canada & Mexico; USD 69.95 elsewhere. Ed(s): Stephen Pizzello. A S C Holding Corporation, PO Box 2230, Los Angeles, CA 90078; ascmag@aol.com; http://www.cinematographer.com. Illus., index, adv. Circ: 45000 Paid. Vol. ends: Dec. Microform: PQC. Online: Chadwyck-Healey Inc.; OCLC Online Computer Library Center, Inc.; H.W. Wilson. *Indexed:* ABS&EES, ArtInd, ChemAb, FLI, IBR, IBZ, IIFP, IIPA, MRD, RILM. *Bk. rev.:* 8-10, 150 words. *Aud.:* Sa.

This monthly publication of the American Society of Cinematographers not only provides current industry information but also provides interviews with cinematographers of current releases and a behind-the-scenes look at the technical details used to achieve a particular shot. Working cameramen can get reviews of new equipment on the market, and film buffs and burgeoning cinematographers can get detailed information about their new favorite films. Book and DVD reviews, classified ads, and an ad index are in each issue. Titles of recent articles include "Giving Shakespeare an Indian Spin" and "Grace Tells of Emotional Salvation." This journal is for collections addressing the needs of film studies programs and filmmakers.

2627. Animation Magazine. [ISSN: 1041-617X] 1987. m. USD 50 domestic; USD 65 in Canada & Mexico; USD 80 elsewhere. Ed(s): Christine Ferriter. Terry Thoren Publications, D B A Animation Magazine, 30941 W. Agoura Rd., Ste. 102, Westlake Village, CA 91361. Illus., adv. Circ: 40000. *Indexed:* ArtInd. *Bk. rev.:* 1-2, 300-500 words. *Aud.:* Ga, Sa.

Although it claims to be a fan magazine, the level of technical detail and technical ads indicate that it as much an industry magazine. Not too surprisingly for a magazine about a visual art form, it is a gorgeous publication, with wonderful glossy illustrations that have wide appeal. It contains articles on animation's use in feature films, games, and television. There are copious ads, film reviews, and regular articles on industry business and conferences. There is also an annual section on animation academic programs. Some titles of recent feature articles include "Bart Does Nude Scene," "*Ratatouille* Offers Hidden Ingredients," and "Third Time's a Charm for Shrek." Any academic library with a strong art program should consider purchasing this title, as well as any special or academic library that services a film production population.

2628. Asian Cult Cinema. 4x/yr. USD 30 domestic for 6 nos.; USD 50 foreign for 6 nos.; USD 6 newsstand/cover per issue. Asian Cult Cinema, PO Box 16-1919, Miami, FL 33116; ascucinema@aol.com. *Bk. rev.:* Occasional, 300-500 words. *Aud.:* Ga, Sa.

This is not a journal for the faint-hearted, just as many of these films are not for the squeamish. But thanks to Quentin Tarantino, there is greater interest than ever before in Asian cult films, particularly martial arts films. Sometimes an issue is wholly devoted to a particular country or part of the genre, such as one on Thai cinema. Recent articles include "C Tadanobu Asano: I'm Not as Whacked Out as Dragon Eye Morrison," "Flower and Snake 2: A Dialogue," and "Foreign Crimes: Thoughts on the Mr. Moto Films." A word of warning: It is recommended that libraries get sample copies before making decisions to purchase this journal; some of its content, while not pornographic in itself,

certainly reports on pornographic materials. But the journal is recommended for serious academic collections on film, and for more local collections that address the needs of young (not youth!) populations with serious interests in Asian film.

2629. Audience (Online Edition). 1998. irreg. Wilson Associates, PO Box 215, Simi Valley, CA 93062; http://www.audiencemag.com/. Adv. *Bk. rev.:* Number and length vary. *Aud.:* Ga, Ac.

This was a monthly print periodical from July 1968 to September 1998 and became entirely an online publication in December 1998. There is an archive of articles from 1971 to 1995, book and film reviews, festival coverage, short interviews with filmmakers, and a section of films rated by staff critics. Although many of the article entries appear blog-like, this online journal remains much more like a journal than a blog. Recent titles of articles include "Three Is a Magic Number: The 2007 Summer Movie Season" and "Square Pegs & Round Holes; Famously Bad Casting." Any academic or public library with a filmgoing clientele should consider linking to this site.

2630. Boxoffice: the business magazine of the global motion picture industry. [ISSN: 0006-8527] 1920. m. USD 49.95 domestic; USD 64.95 in Canada & Mexico; USD 125 elsewhere. Ed(s): Kim Williamson. Media Enterprises, 351 W Nubbard St., #405, Chicago, IL 60610. Illus., adv. Circ: 7000 Paid and controlled. Vol. ends: Dec. *Indexed:* ABIn, FLI, IIPA. *Aud.:* Sa.

For 87 years, *Boxoffice* has been required reading for every serious player in the industry, from theater owners to studio executives. There is coverage of industry news (national and international), box office grosses, production data on new Hollywood releases, and financial information on the major studios. Also included are numerous reviews of new Hollywood feature films; interviews with filmmakers, screenwriters, executives, actors, producers, and directors; and up-to-date festival information. Although it covers all areas of the film industry, it is definitely skewed toward exhibitors. It lists current and upcoming studio release charts by month. There are short reviews with "exploitips," a guide to new products, and news on concessions. Highly recommended for libraries that need complete coverage of the Hollywood film industry.

2631. Bright Lights (Online Edition): film journal. Formerly (until 1995): *Bright Lights (Print Edition).* 1974. q. Free. Ed(s): Gregory Battle. Bright Lights, PO Box 420987, San Francisco, CA 94142-0987; http://www.brightlightsfilm.com. Illus., adv. Circ: 17500. *Indexed:* FLI, IIFP, MLA-IB, MRD. *Bk. rev.:* Number and length vary. *Aud.:* Ga, Ac.

"A popular-academic hybrid of movie analysis, history and commentary, looking at classical and commercial, independent, exploitation, and international film from a wide range of vantage points from the aesthetic to the political. A prime area of focus is on the connection between capitalist society and the images that reflect, support, or subvert it—movies as propaganda." Included on this site are some highly unusual genres, such as "tranny cinema." It has feature articles, film reviews, book reviews, filmmaker interviews, and film festival coverage. Titles of recent articles include "Mothering of Evil: In Several Hitchcock Films," "Extinguishing Features: The Last Years of Richard Pryor," and "Across the Great Divide: Canadian Popular Cinema in the 21st Century." Any library with serious filmgoing patrons should consider linking to this edgy, interesting journal.

2632. Camera Obscura: a journal of feminism and film theory. [ISSN: 0270-5346] 1976. 3x/yr. USD 114 (Individuals, USD 30). Ed(s): Lynne Joyrich, Amelie Hastie. Duke University Press, 905 W Main St, Ste 18 B, Durham, NC 27701; subscriptions@dukeupress.edu; http://www.dukeupress.edu. Illus., adv. Sample. Refereed. Circ: 630. Vol. ends: Sep. Online: EBSCO Publishing, EBSCO Host; Florida Center for Library Automation; Gale; HighWire Press; OCLC Online Computer Library Center, Inc.; OhioLINK; Project MUSE; ProQuest LLC (Ann Arbor); SwetsWise Online Content. Reprint: PSC. *Indexed:* ABM, AltPI, AmHI, ArtHuCI, ArtInd, BAS, CWI, FLI, FemPer, GendWatch, IBR, IBZ, IIFP, IIPA, MLA-IB, MRD, RILM, SSCI, SWA. *Bk. rev.:* Number and length vary. *Aud.:* Ac.

This title "seeks to provide a forum for dialogue and debate on media, culture, and politics. Specifically, the journal encourages contributions in the following areas: analyses of the conjunctions among gender, race, class, sexuality, and nation, as these are articulated in film, television, popular culture, and media criticism and theory; new histories of film, television, popular culture, and media criticism and theory, as well as contemporary interventions in these fields; politically engaged approaches to visual culture, media production, and contemporary constructions of feminism—inside the academy and in popular culture." Articles are well documented and accompanied by detailed notes. Titles of some recent articles include "Picture This: Lillian Gilbreth's Industrial Cinema for the Home," "Joan Crawford's Padded Shoulders: Female Masculinity in Mildred Pierce," and "Allegory and the Aesthetics of Becoming Woman in Marziyeh Meshkini's *The Day I Became a Woman*." This is a recommended addition to academic film collections.

2633. Canadian Journal of Film Studies. [ISSN: 0847-5911] 1990. s-a. CND 45 (Individuals, CND 35). Ed(s): William C Wees. Film Studies Association of Canada, Department of Art History and Communication Studies, McGill University, Arts Building W225, Montreal, PQ H3A 2T6, Canada; william.wees@mcgill.ca; http://www.film.queensu.ca/ FSAC/CJFS.html. Illus., adv. Refereed. Circ: 300 Paid. *Indexed:* CBCARef, FLI, IIFP, IIPA, MRD. *Bk. rev.:* Number and length vary. *Aud.:* Ac.

The stated aim of this publication is "to promote scholarship on Canadian film and television while . . . publishing articles, book reviews and archival materials relevant to all aspects of film and television." There are good book reviews and lengthy essays in English (or occasionally in French) covering Canadian as well as global cinema. Sometimes issues have central themes, such as a recent one on documentary historiographies. Other recent articles have included "Peter Urquhart and Ira Wagman, Considering Canadian Television: Intersections, Missed Directions, Prospects for Textual Expansion" and "Sounds like Horror: Alejandro Amenabar's Thesis on Audio-Visual Violence."

2634. Cineaction!: radical film criticism & theory. [ISSN: 0826-9866] 1985. 3x/yr. CND 40 (Individuals, CND 21; USD 8 per issue). Cineaction!, 40 Alexander St, Apt 705, Toronto, ON M4Y 1B5, Canada. Illus., index, adv. Sample. Circ: 2500. Online: Florida Center for Library Automation; Gale. *Indexed:* CBCARef, CPerI, FLI, IIFP, IIPA, MLA-IB, MRD. *Bk. rev.:* Number and length vary. *Aud.:* Ac.

This title examines film from various differing viewpoints. Each issue focuses on a central theme, and forthcoming themes are announced, encouraging the submission of articles. In addition to scholarly articles on film theory, there are interviews with filmmakers, film reviews, book reviews, and reports from international film festivals. Some recent article titles include "Erotic Thrillers," "Fellini's Forgotten Masterpiece: *Toby Dammit*," and "In Dreams and the Gothic: The Moment of Collapse."

2635. Cineaste: America's leading magazine on the art and politics of the cinema. [ISSN: 0009-7004] 1967. q. USD 35 (Individuals, USD 20; USD 6 newsstand/cover per issue). Ed(s): Gary Crowdus. Cineaste Publishers, Inc., 304 Hudson St., 6th Fl, New York, NY 10013-1015. Illus., index, adv. Circ: 12000 Paid. Vol. ends: Fall. Microform: PQC. Online: Chadwyck-Healey Inc.; EBSCO Publishing, EBSCO Host; Factiva, Inc.; Florida Center for Library Automation; Gale; OCLC Online Computer Library Center, Inc.; ProQuest K-12 Learning Solutions; ProQuest LLC (Ann Arbor); H.W. Wilson. *Indexed:* ABS&EES, AltPI, ArtHuCI, ArtInd, FLI, IBR, IBZ, IIFP, IIPA, LeftInd, MASUSE, MLA-IB, MRD, SSCI. *Bk. rev.:* Number and length vary. *Aud.:* Ga, Ac.

This publication bills itself as "America's leading magazine on the art and politics of the cinema." It provides interviews with actors and filmmakers as well as film, home video, and book reviews. Recent article titles include "Touchy Subjects: Amir Muhammad's Films on Race and Power in Malaysia," "Contemporary Balkan Cinema," and "Iraq War Documentaries." For serious film studies collections.

Cinefantastique. See Fiction: Science Fiction, Fantasy, and Horror section.

2636. Cinefex: the journal of cinematic illusions. [ISSN: 0198-1056] 1980. q. USD 32 domestic; USD 42 in Canada & Mexico; USD 46 elsewhere. Ed(s): Jody Duncan. Cinefex, PO Box 20027, Riverside, CA 92516; editor@cinefex.com. Illus., adv. Circ: 28000 Paid. Vol. ends: Dec. *Indexed:* FLI, IIFP, IIPA, MRD. *Aud.:* Sa.

"*Cinefex* is a quarterly magazine devoted to motion picture special effects. Since 1980 it has been the bible to professionals and enthusiasts, covering the field like no other publication. Profusely illustrated in color, with as many as 180 pages per issue, *Cinefex* offers a captivating look at the technologies and techniques behind many of our most popular and enduring movies." For the professional, there is a profusion of ads for services and products related to special visual effects. And not too surprisingly, they have an astounding web site! Titles of recent articles include "*Spiderman 3*: The Enemy Within," "Ted Rae on *Apocalypto*," and "*300*: A Beautiful Death." For any library serving the needs of a film studies program.

2637. Cinema Journal. Formerly (until 1967): *Society of Cinematologists. Journal.* [ISSN: 0009-7101] 1961. q. USD 110 (Individuals, USD 44). Ed(s): Jon Lewis. University of Texas Press, Journals Division, 2100 Comal, Austin, TX 78722; journals@uts.cc.utexas.edu; http://www.utexas.edu/utpress/journals/journals.html. Illus., index, adv. Sample. Refereed. Circ: 2750 Paid and controlled. Vol. ends: Aug. Online: Chadwyck-Healey Inc.; EBSCO Publishing, EBSCO Host; JSTOR (Web-based Journal Archive); OCLC Online Computer Library Center, Inc.; OhioLINK; Project MUSE; ProQuest K-12 Learning Solutions; ProQuest LLC (Ann Arbor); SwetsWise Online Content; H.W. Wilson. Reprint: PSC. *Indexed:* ABS&EES, ArtHuCI, ArtInd, FLI, IBR, IBZ, IIFP, IIPA, MLA-IB, MRD, RILM. *Bk. rev.:* Number and length vary. *Aud.:* Ac.

This title "presents recent scholarship by Society for Cinema Studies members. The journal publishes essays on a wide variety of subjects from diverse methodological perspectives. A Professional Notes section informs . . . readers about upcoming events, research applications, and the latest published research." Titles of recent articles include "The Revered Gaze: The Medieval Imaginary of Mel Gibson's *The Passion of The Christ*," "In Focus: Fair Use and Film," and "The Clothes Make the Fan: Fashion and Online Fandom when Buffy the Vampire Slayer Goes to eBay." For all film collections addressing the needs of film studies programs.

2638. Cinema Scope. [ISSN: 1488-7002] 1999. q. USD 40 (Individuals, USD 20). Ed(s): Mark Peranson. Cinema Scope Publishing, 465 Lytton Blvd, Toronto, ON M5N 1S5, Canada; http://www.insound.com. Illus., adv. *Indexed:* FLI. *Bk. rev.:* Number and length vary. *Aud.:* Ac, Sa.

"An independently published quarterly jam-packed with interviews, features, and essays on film and video, *CS* is geared to cinephiles looking for an intelligent forum on world cinema. With unparalleled depth and breadth, *CS* is a real alternative in today's Canadian film scene." Includes DVD reviews, book reviews, and film festival reviews. Titles of recent articles include "Ghost Stories: Wang Bing's Startling New Cinema," "Human, All Too Human: *Battlestar Galactica* Re-imagined," and "Straightening the Picture of Africa: Chad's Mahamat-Saleh Haroun." For any film journal collection addressing the needs of serious film aficionados and students.

2639. Classic Images. Former titles (until 1979): *Classic Film - Video Images;* (until 1978): *Classic Film Collector; Eight MM Collector.* [ISSN: 0275-8423] 1962. m. USD 32 domestic; USD 42 foreign. Ed(s): Bob King. Muscatine Journal, 301 E Third St, Muscatine, IA 52761; classicimages@classicimages.com; http://www.classicimages.com. Illus., index, adv. Circ: 5000. Vol. ends: Dec. Microform: PQC. *Indexed:* FLI, IIFP, IIPA, MRD. *Bk. rev.:* Number and length vary. *Aud.:* Ga.

"The film fan's bible," this is the publication for people who love older, classic films. Each tabloid-format issue is approximately 80 pages in length. It has biographical articles on film stars illustrated with black-and-white production and publicity stills. There are regular monthly features: video and DVD reviews, book reviews, music in film, obituaries, and "this month in movie history." For film buffs and collectors, it has an advertisers' index for film festivals, conventions, video companies, publishers, and memorabilia merchants. Recent titles include "An Evening with Farley Granger" and "Frances Dee: A Kind of Grace." Its tabloid format makes it dubious choice for an archiving library, but if a public library serves a large population of film buffs, this would be a good choice.

2640. Creative Screenwriting. [ISSN: 1084-8665] 1994. bi-m. USD 23.95 domestic; USD 31.95 Canada; USD 42.95 elsewhere. Ed(s): Den Shewman. Inside Information Group, 6404 Hollywood Blvd, Ste 415, Los Angeles, CA 90028; info@creativescreenwriting.com. Illus., adv. Circ: 26000 Paid. *Indexed:* FLI, IIFP, IIPA, MLA-IB. *Bk. rev.:* Number and length vary. *Aud.:* Ac.

This title "publishes critical, theoretical, historical, and practical essays on all aspects of writing for feature films and television. It also publishes critical reviews of books, products, and seminars of interest to the screenwriters. In seeking to bridge the professional and screenwriting literatures, *Creative Screenwriting* welcomes contributions from diverse perspectives." Titles of recent articles include "Seeing the World in Shades of Gray: Micheal Goldenberg on *Harry Potter and the Order of the Phoenix*," "How Brad Bird and Mark Andrews Reshaped a Rat's Tale in *Ratatouille*," and "Away From Her: Actress Sarah Polley Adapts Alice Munro for Her First Screenplay." This is a good addition for library collections that support scriptwriting programs. Many larger public libraries will also want to consider its purchase.

2641. D G A Magazine. Formerly: *D G A News.* 1975. bi-m. USD 30 domestic; USD 45 in Canada & Mexico; USD 60 elsewhere. Ed(s): Ted Elrick. Directors Guild of America, 7920 Sunset Blvd., Hollywood, CA 90046; http://www.dga.org. Illus., adv. Circ: 15000. *Indexed:* FLI, IIFP. *Bk. rev.:* Number and length vary. *Aud.:* Sa.

This is the official magazine of the Directors Guild of America. It reports guild and industry news that affects its membership. There is a section of updates on guild members—deaths, additions, changes. Festivals are covered, and interviews with directors of upcoming major feature films and TV movies are included in each issue. Book and DVD reviews are also included. For academic and special library film studies collections.

2642. Editors Guild Magazine. bi-m. USD 45. Ed(s): Stephanie Argy. Steven Jay Cohen, IATSE Local 700 MPEG, 7715 Sunset Blvd, Ste 200, Hollywood, CA 90046; http://www.editorsguild.com. *Aud.:* Sa.

This is the official magazine of the Editors Guild. It covers industry events impacting guild members. There are interviews with editors, assessments of new equipment and technologies, and a section on technical tips. Regular features in each issue include an index of advertisers, announcements and obituaries, and new signatories. For serious industry and academic film studies collections.

2643. Film & History: an interdisciplinary journal of film and television studies. Supersedes: *Historians Film Committee Newsletter.* [ISSN: 0360-3695] 1970. s-a. USD 80 (Individuals, USD 50). Ed(s): Peter C Rollins. Historians Film Committee, Popular Culture Centre, R R 3, Box 80, Cleveland, OK 74020; RollinsPC@aol.com. Illus., adv. Refereed. Circ: 1000 Paid. Online: Chadwyck-Healey Inc.; EBSCO Publishing, EBSCO Host; OCLC Online Computer Library Center, Inc.; OhioLINK; Project MUSE; ProQuest LLC (Ann Arbor); SwetsWise Online Content. *Indexed:* ABS&EES, AmH&L, ArtInd, FLI, HistAb, IIFP, IIPA, MRD. *Bk. rev.:* Number and length vary. *Aud.:* Ac.

Each issue of this semi-annual publication has a special focus or theme. Two recent issues focus on the Holocaust on film, one covering documentaries, the other covering feature films. Other topics covered have been American sports on film, war on film, and reality TV. There are television, film, and book reviews. A number of the sponsors for this title are publishers, some are university presses. This title is for academic collections.

2644. Film & Video. Former titles (until 1988): *Opticmusic's Film & Video Production;* (until 1987): *Optic Music.* [ISSN: 1041-1933] 1984. m. USD 59 domestic (Free to qualified personnel). Ed(s): Bryant Frazer. Access Intelligence, LLC, 4 Choke Cherry Rd, 2nd Fl, Rockville, MD 20850; clientservices@accessintel.com; http://www.accessintel.com. Illus., adv. Circ: 30000 Controlled. *Aud.:* Ac, Sa.

This title brings the reader up to date on current technology in the film industry. A recent issue has an article spotlighting three relatively new directors who are using new technologies to complete their respective film projects, a National Association of Broadcasters' convention preview of new technologies and products, and the annual directory of stock footage sources. Advertisements for film services and equipment are included in each issue. Some recent titles of articles include "Virtual Sets for Virtually No Budget," "Cool Camerawork in the Arctic North," and "Metadata on my Mind." This will be a welcome addition to any collection that supports a filmmaking program.

2645. Film Comment. Formerly: *Vision.* [ISSN: 0015-119X] 1962. bi-m. USD 24.95 domestic; USD 32 in Canada & Mexico; USD 60 elsewhere. Ed(s): Laurence Abbasi. Film Society of Lincoln Center, 70 Lincoln Center Plaza, New York, NY 10023-6595; rtvfc@aol.com; http://www.filmlinc.com/fcm/fcm.htm. Illus., index, adv. Circ: 40000. Vol. ends: Nov/Dec. CD-ROM: ProQuest LLC (Ann Arbor). Microform: NBI; PQC. Online: Chadwyck-Healey Inc.; EBSCO Publishing, EBSCO Host; Florida Center for Library Automation; Northern Light Technology, Inc.; OCLC Online Computer Library Center, Inc.; ProQuest K-12 Learning Solutions; ProQuest LLC (Ann Arbor). *Indexed:* ABIn, ABS&EES, AmHI, ArtHuCI, ArtInd, BRI, CBRI, FLI, HumInd, IBR, IBZ, IIFP, IIPA, MASUSE, MRD, RGPR, RILM. *Bk. rev.:* Number and length vary. *Aud.:* Hs, Ga, Ac.

This publication by the Film Society of Lincoln Center gives excellent coverage of filmmaking in the United States as well as worldwide. Recent articles include "Lee Marvin: The Hollywood Icon Who Took No Prisoners," "Jean-Daniel Pollet," and "Manuel Yanez on Carlos Saura." For academic collections and public libraries addressing the needs of serious film buffs.

2646. Film Criticism. [ISSN: 0163-5069] 1976. 3x/yr. USD 18 (Individuals, USD 15). Ed(s): I Lloyd Michaels. Allegheny College, 520 N Main St, Meadville, PA 16335; campus@alleg.edu. Illus., adv. Sample. Refereed. Circ: 500. Vol. ends: Spring. *Indexed:* ABS&EES, AmHI, ArtHuCI, ArtInd, BRI, CBRI, FLI, HumInd, IIFP, IIPA, MLA-IB, MRD, RILM, SSCI. *Bk. rev.:* Number and length vary. *Aud.:* Ac.

This refereed journal publishes articles that examine and re-examine films from a variety of critical, political, and aesthetic viewpoints. Unusual aspects of films and symbolism are discussed in great detail. Occasionally, the body of work by a specific filmmaker is analyzed. Recent titles include "The Formal Design of *Brokeback Mountain*," "Shark Porn: Film Genre, Reception Studies, and Chris Kentis' *Open Water*," and "Serbian Cinema." There are book reviews in most issues. For academic libraries serving film studies programs.

2647. Film History: an international journal. [ISSN: 0892-2160] 1987. q. USD 175. Ed(s): Richard Koszarski. Indiana University Press, 601 N Morton St, Bloomington, IN 47404. Illus., index. Sample. Refereed. Vol. ends: Dec. *Indexed:* AmH&L, ArtInd, FLI, HistAb, IIFP, IIMP, IIPA, MRD. *Bk. rev.:* Number and length vary. *Aud.:* Ac.

"The subject of *Film History* is the historical development of the motion picture, and the social, technological and economic context in which this has occurred. Its areas of interest range from the technical and entrepreneurial innovations of early and pre-cinema experiments, through all aspects of the production, distribution, exhibition and reception of commercial and non-commercial motion pictures. In addition to original research in these areas, the journal will survey the paper and film holdings of archives and libraries worldwide, publish selected examples of primary documentation (such as early film scenarios) and report on current publications, exhibitions, conferences, and research in progress. Most future issues will be devoted to comprehensive studies of single themes." Titles of recent articles include "Soviet Cinematic Offensive in the Spanish Civil War," "Dueling for Judy: The Concept of the Double in the Films of Kim Novak," and "Safari Adventure: Forgotten Cinematic Journeys in Africa." For academic libraries with film studies collections.

2648. Film Journal International. Former titles (until 1996): *Film Journal; Independent Film Journal.* [ISSN: 1526-9884] 1934. m. USD 65 domestic; USD 120 foreign. Ed(s): Robert Sunshine. Nielsen Business Publications, 770 Broadway, New York, NY 10003-9595;

http://www.nielsenbusinessmedia.com. Illus., index, adv. Circ: 9200. Vol. ends: Dec. Online: EBSCO Publishing, EBSCO Host; Florida Center for Library Automation; Gale. *Indexed:* FLI, IIPA. *Aud.:* Sa.

The intended audience for this publication is exhibitors: news, articles, and advertisements all relate to aspects of exhibition and concessions. The articles on specific film titles are written for a broader audience, but the main intent is to report on box-office potential. Each issue includes film reviews, film company news, new posts, new products, a buying and booking guide, trade talk, and an index of advertisers. Recent feature titles include "A Redefined Rodent in Paris," "Harry the Fifth," and "Dinner at the Movies." For special libraries and film studies programs that address the business and promotional aspects of film making.

2649. Film Quarterly. Former titles (until 1958): *Quarterly of Film, Radio and Television;* (until 1951): *Hollywood Quarterly.* [ISSN: 0015-1386] 1945. q. USD 162 print & online eds. USD 45 newsstand/cover. Ed(s): Rob White. University of California Press, Journals Division, 2000 Center St, Ste 303, Berkeley, CA 94704-1223; journals@ucpress.edu; http://www.ucpress.edu/journals. Illus., index, adv. Sample. Refereed. Circ: 4550. Vol. ends: Oct. Microform: PQC. Online: Chadwyck-Healey Inc.; EBSCO Publishing, EBSCO Host; Florida Center for Library Automation; Gale; JSTOR (Web-based Journal Archive); Northern Light Technology, Inc.; OCLC Online Computer Library Center, Inc.; ProQuest LLC (Ann Arbor); SwetsWise Online Content; H.W. Wilson. *Indexed:* ABS&EES, ASIP, AmH&L, AmHI, ArtHuCI, ArtInd, BRD, BRI, CBRI, FLI, HumInd, IBR, IBZ, IIFP, IIPA, MLA-IB, MRD, RGPR, RILM. *Bk. rev.:* Number and length vary. *Aud.:* Ga, Ac.

"International in coverage and reputation, *Film Quarterly* offers lively and penetrating articles covering the entire field of film studies. Articles include interviews with innovative film- and videomakers, writers, editors and cinematographers; readable discussion of issues in contemporary film theory; definitive, thoughtful reviews of international, avant garde, national cinemas, and documentaries; and important approaches to film history." Now available online as well. Recent titles include "Deviation Red vs. Blue: The Blood Gulch Chronicles," "Brokering *Brokeback*: Jokes, Backlashes, and Other Anxieties," and "Racial Camp in *The Producers* and *Bamboozled*." For academic libraries serving films studies programs.

2650. Film Score Monthly: music soundtracks for motion pictures and television. [ISSN: 1077-4289] 1990. bi-m. USD 36.95 domestic; USD 42.95 in Canada & Mexico; USD 50 elsewhere. Ed(s): Tim Curran, Jonathan Kopkim. Film Score Monthly, 8503 Washington Blvd, Culver City, CA 90232-7443; lukas@filmscoremonthly.com; http://www.filmscoremonthly.com. Illus., adv. Sample. Circ: 11000. *Indexed:* FLI, IIMP, IIPA, MusicInd. *Aud.:* Sa.

Film Score Monthly provides information for those interested in what is happening in the film music industry: current news, record-label updates on releases, upcoming assignments (who's scoring what for whom), and CD reviews. There are feature articles on composers and behind-the-scenes looks at film music production.

2651. Filmmaker: the magazine of independent film. Formed by the 1992 merger of: *Off-Hollywood Report; Montage.* [ISSN: 1063-8954] 1992. q. USD 40 (Individuals, USD 18). Ed(s): Scott Macaulay. Filmmaker, 104 W 29th St, 12th Fl, New York, NY 10001. Illus., adv. Sample. Circ: 42000. Online: Chadwyck-Healey Inc. *Indexed:* FLI, IIPA, MRD. *Bk. rev.:* Number and length vary. *Aud.:* Sa.

This title is directed toward those interested in independent, smaller-budgeted films and filmmaking. Lesser-known films currently being released are profiled in each issue, along with independent filmmaker interviews and current film festival news. There are advertisements for film products, pre- and postproduction services, and film festivals, plus a handy advertisers' index. This is a nice addition to any collection that supports a film program.

2652. Films of the Golden Age. [ISSN: 1083-5369] 1995. q. USD 18.80. Ed(s): Bob King. Muscatine Journal, 301 E Third St, Muscatine, IA 52761; http://www.classicimages.com/foga. Illus., adv. Vol. ends: Winter. *Indexed:* FLI, IIFP, MRD. *Aud.:* Ga.

How many of us start our interest in film with an addiction to old films? No matter how academic our original interest becomes, publications such as *Films of the Golden Age* have continuing appeal. This publication covers what it defines as the "golden age," that is, films produced in the studio era, from the 1930s through the 1950s. There are biographical articles on both stars and directors. Each issue is chock-full of illustrations, many of them unusual. Public libraries and academic libraries with general film collections should consider purchasing this. One caveat: its large, newspaper format will make processing and storage painful.

2653. Griffithiana. [ISSN: 0393-3857] 1978. s-a. USD 80 (Individuals, USD 40). Ed(s): Peter Lehman, Davide Turconi. Cineteca del Friuli, Via G. Bini, Palazzo Gurisatti, Gemona, 33013, Italy; griffithiana@cinetecadelfriuli.org; http://cinetecadelfriuli.org. Illus., adv. Refereed. Circ: 2500. *Indexed:* AmHI, FLI, IIFP, IIPA, MLA-IB, MRD. *Bk. rev.:* Number and length vary. *Aud.:* Ac.

"An international journal of film history, *Griffithiana* is devoted to the study of animation and silent cinema. It features articles by prominent international film scholars, historians, archivists, and journalists, as well as comprehensive filmographies and reviews of international cinema books. Many issues showcase newly rediscovered and restored films presented at the Pordenone Film Festival." The articles are published in both Italian and English.

2654. Images (Kansas City): a journal of film and popular culture. q. Ed(s): Grant Tracey. Images Journal, 111 E 66th Terrace, Kansas City, MO 64113; info@imagesjournal.com; http://www.imagesjournal.com. *Bk. rev.:* Number and length vary. *Aud.:* Ga.

Images "publishes articles about movies, television, video and the other popular visual arts." It is a quarterly journal, but new articles and reviews are added each week. There are also video, DVD, and book reviews.

2655. The Independent (New York). Former titles (until 2005): *The Independent Film & Video Monthly;* (until 1994): *Independent (New York).* [ISSN: 1557-5799] 1978. q. 10/yr. until 2007. Free to members. Ed(s): Mike Hofman, Erin Trahan. Independent Media Publications, 304 Hudson St, 6th Fl, New York, NY 10013. Illus., adv. Circ: 42000. Vol. ends: Dec. Online: Chadwyck-Healey Inc.; OCLC Online Computer Library Center, Inc.; ProQuest LLC (Ann Arbor). *Indexed:* AltPI, FLI, IIPA, MLA-IB, MRD. *Bk. rev.:* Number and length vary. *Aud.:* Ac, Sa.

This monthly publication of the Foundation for Independent Video and Film is "dedicated to the advancement of media arts and artists." Each issue contains entertainment industry news, technology reports, and book reviews. "Distributor FAQ" and "Funder FAQ" give background information on a spotlighted company. Up-to-date information on foundation events and film festivals is provided. There are advertisements throughout for equipment and postproduction services.

2656. indieWIRE. 1995. d. Ed(s): Eugene Hernandez. indieWIRE LLC, 253 5th Ave, New York, NY 10016; contact@indiewire.com; http://www.indiewire.com. Adv. *Aud.:* Ga, Ac, Sa.

This is an excellent example of the hybrid nature of electronic publishing. Is it a magazine? a newspaper? a mere newsletter? a portal? It contains blogging, but is not a blog per se. *indieWIRE* offers special coverage of the major independent film festivals in such places as Los Angeles and Tribeca. It has routine coverage of special areas, such as world cinema and queer cinema. It includes film business news and information on releases and people. Its articles may be brief, but they are substantive, and all materials are archived. It is, in fact, probably the most up-to-date place for industry information on independent films. This is an invaluable link for any library that supports a film studies or production program.

2657. Intensities: the journal of cult media. [ISSN: 1471-5031] 2001. s-a. Ed(s): Sara Gwenllian Jones. Cardiff University, School of Journalism, Media and Cultural Studies, Cardiff, United Kingdom. *Bk. rev.:* 10-15, 1,000-3,000 words. *Aud.:* Ac, Sa.

This fascinating, peer-reviewed e-journal is not just about movies; as its subtitle suggests, it does cover other forms of media. But film has always figured largely in cult media, and many of its reviews and feature articles are about film. Libraries supporting film studies programs should seriously consider linking to this publication.

2658. International Documentary. [ISSN: 1077-9361] 1986. m. Combined issue for Jan./Feb & Jul./Aug. USD 85 individual membership; USD 150 institutional membership. Ed(s): Thomas White. International Documentary Association, 1201 W 5th St, Ste M320, Los Angeles, CA 90017-1461; membership@documentary.org; http://www.documentary.org/. Illus., adv. Sample. Circ: 7500 Paid and free. Vol. ends: Nov. *Indexed:* FLI, IIFP. *Aud.:* Ac, Sa.

This publication of the International Documentary Association intends to "promote nonfiction film and video and to support the efforts of documentary makers around the world." It provides membership news and reports on festivals. Feature articles on aspects of the documentary filmmaking process are published with the doc filmmaker in mind. Ads for pre- and postproduction services, festivals, and classes in documentary filmmaking are included. Columns formerly included in each issue but now available on the web site are North American Broadcast and Cable Premieres, Events and Screenings, Calls for Entries, Funding, and Jobs and Opportunities.

2659. Journal of Film and Video. Former titles (until 1983): *University Film and Video Association. Journal;* (until 1981): *University Film Association. Journal; University Film Producers Association. Journal.* [ISSN: 0742-4671] 1947. q. USD 40 domestic; USD 50 foreign. Ed(s): Stephen Tropiano. University of Illinois Press, 1325 S Oak St, Champaign, IL 61820-6903; journals@uillinois.edu; http://www.press.uillinois.edu. Illus., index, adv. Refereed. Circ: 1300. Microform: PQC. Online: Chadwyck-Healey Inc.; EBSCO Publishing, EBSCO Host; OCLC Online Computer Library Center, Inc.; ProQuest LLC (Ann Arbor). *Indexed:* ABS&EES, ArtHuCI, ArtInd, CommAb, FLI, IBR, IBZ, IIFP, IIPA, MRD. *Aud.:* Ac.

This refereed journal "focuses on scholarship in the fields of film and video production, history, theory, criticism, and aesthetics." In its call for papers, it requests "articles about film and related media, problems of education in these fields and the function of film and video in society." For academic audiences.

2660. Journal of Popular Film and Television. Formerly (until 1978): *Journal of Popular Film.* [ISSN: 0195-6051] 1971. q. USD 129 (Individuals, USD 59 print & online eds.; USD 31 newsstand/cover). Ed(s): Julia Goodwin. Heldref Publications, 1319 18th St, NW, Washington, DC 20036-1802; subscribe@heldref.org; http://www.heldref.org. Illus., index, adv. Refereed. Circ: 1100 Paid. CD-ROM: ProQuest LLC (Ann Arbor). Online: Chadwyck-Healey Inc.; EBSCO Publishing, EBSCO Host; Florida Center for Library Automation; Gale; OCLC Online Computer Library Center, Inc.; ProQuest K-12 Learning Solutions; ProQuest LLC (Ann Arbor); H.W. Wilson. Reprint: PSC. *Indexed:* ABS&EES, AmH&L, AmHI, ArtHuCI, ArtInd, BRI, CBRI, CWI, CommAb, FLI, HistAb, HumInd, IBR, IBZ, IIFP, IIPA, MLA-IB, MRD, RI-1, RILM, SSCI, V&AA. *Bk. rev.:* Number and length vary. *Aud.:* Ga, Ac.

This title "is dedicated to popular film and television in the broadest sense. Concentration is upon commercial cinema and television: stars, directors, producers, studios, networks, genres, series, the audience, etc." Articles are accompanied by acknowledgements, with notes and works cited. Each year, the journal publishes one theme issue on such subjects as "Media Literacy and Education: The Teacher-Scholar in Film and Television" and "Fantastic Voyages: Horror, Fantasy, and Science Fiction/Speculative Cinema." Book reviews are also included.

2661. Journal of Religion and Film. [ISSN: 1092-1311] 1997. s-a. Free. Ed(s): William L Blizek. University of Nebraska at Omaha, Department of Philosophy and Religion, ASH Building, Omaha, NE 68182-0265; http://www.unomaha.edu. Adv. Refereed. *Indexed:* MLA-IB, RI-1. *Aud.:* Ga, Ac.

The *Journal of Religion and Film* "examines the description, critique, and embodiment of religion in film." The editors "invite articles and discussion on a variety of film types, commercial and academic, foreign and documentary, classic and contemporary." Peer-reviewed articles and analyses of films stressing spiritual aspects are presented. URL: www.unomaha.edu/~wwwjrf.

2662. Movieline's Hollywood Life. Formerly (until Apr. 2003): *Movieline.* [ISSN: 1544-0583] 1989. 10x/yr. USD 13.75 domestic; USD 33 foreign; USD 3.99 newsstand/cover per issue. Line Publications LLC, 10537 Santa Monica Blvd., Ste. 250, Los Angeles, CA 90025-4952. Illus., adv. Circ: 312000. *Indexed:* ASIP, FLI, MRD. *Aud.:* Ga.

This slick magazine presents news of current major studio releases and their stars, covering premieres, festivals, and the celebrity lifestyle. Recent video and DVD releases are showcased, along with upcoming cable TV titles. *Movieline's Hollywood Life* is aimed at general audiences.

2663. Moviemaker: the art and business of making movies. 1993. q. USD 16 domestic; USD 26 Canada; USD 42 elsewhere. Ed(s): Timothy E Rhys. Moviemaker Pub., 2265 Westwood Blvd, Ste 479, Los Angeles, CA 90064; staff@moviemaker.com. Illus., adv. Circ: 50000 Paid and controlled. *Indexed:* FLI, IIPA, MRD. *Aud.:* Ac, Sa.

This title features articles on producers, actors, and directors. It also covers independent film industry issues, such as copyright, technical instruction, festivals, shorts, and documentaries. There are ads for film equipment and services, with an advertisers index. This is a good title for collections that support a film studies program.

2664. Osian's Cinemaya: the Asian film quarterly. Formerly: *Cinemaya.* [ISSN: 0973-2144] 1988. q. USD 55. Osian's - Connoisseurs of Art Pvt. Ltd., 42 A Golf Links, New Delhi, 110 003, India; hq@osians.com; http://www.osians.com. Illus., adv. Circ: 5000 Paid and controlled. Vol. ends: Winter. *Indexed:* FLI, IIFP, MRD. *Aud.:* Ga, Ac.

The official journal of the Network for the Promotion of Asian Cinema, this title provides coverage of Asian film and filmmakers and interviews with filmmakers not commonly found in popular movie magazines. It also provides film festival news and film reviews. Published quarterly.

2665. Post Script (Commerce): essays in film and the humanities. [ISSN: 0277-9897] 1981. 3x/yr. USD 25 (Individuals, USD 15). Ed(s): Gerald Duchovnay. Post Script, Inc., Department of Literature and Languages, Texas A & M University, Commerce, TX 75429-3011; gerald_duchovnay@tamu-commerce.edu; http://www.tamu-commerce.edu/coas/litlang. Illus., index, adv. Refereed. Circ: 400. Online: Chadwyck-Healey Inc.; Gale. *Indexed:* BRI, CBRI, FLI, IIFP, IIPA, MLA-IB, MRD. *Bk. rev.:* Number and length vary. *Aud.:* Ac.

This title publishes "manuscripts on film as language and literature; acting; film music; film as visual art (painting and cinematic style, set design, costuming); film and photography; film history; aesthetics; the response of film and the humanities to technology; interdisciplinary studies in theme and genre; film and American Studies; reappraisals of seminal essays; book reviews and interviews; and responses to articles appearing in *Post Script.*" Occasionally, an issue is devoted to a specific topic.

2666. Quarterly Review of Film and Video. Formerly (until 1989): *Quarterly Review of Film Studies.* [ISSN: 1050-9208] 1976. 5x/yr. GBP 545 print & online eds. Ed(s): Wheeler Winston Dixon, Gwendolyn Audrey Foster. Routledge, 325 Chestnut St, Ste 800, Philadelphia, PA 19106; journals@routledge.com; http://www.tandf.co.uk/journals. Illus., index. Refereed. Online: EBSCO Publishing, EBSCO Host; Gale; IngentaConnect; OCLC Online Computer Library Center, Inc.; SwetsWise Online Content. Reprint: PSC. *Indexed:* ABS&EES, AmHI, ArtHuCI, ArtInd, BRI, CBRI, CommAb, FLI, HumInd, IIFP, MLA-IB, MRD, SSCI. *Bk. rev.:* Number and length vary. *Aud.:* Ac.

This refereed journal is international and interdisciplinary in scope. It publishes "critical, historical, and theoretical essays, book reviews and interviews in the area of moving image studies including film, video, and digital image studies." For academic institutions.

2667. Script (Calabasas): where film begins. [ISSN: 1092-2016] 1995. bi-m. USD 24.95 domestic; USD 32.95 in Canada & Mexico; USD 44.95 elsewhere. Ed(s): Shelly Mellott. Final Draft, Inc., 26707 W. Agoura Rd., Ste. 205, Calabasas, CA 91302; http://www.finaldraft.com/. Illus., adv. Circ: 50000 Controlled. *Indexed:* FLI. *Aud.:* Sa.

The explanation given for the title is, "the (i) in *Scr(i)pt* is used to honor the screenwriter . . . our message to you is that we recognize you as the genesis of film—the inspiration." This publication is for those who are beyond asking for examples of the standard script format. Interviews and articles are included of/by writers of currently released films as well, which makes it a source of practical information for both established and burgeoning screenwriters.

2668. Senses of Cinema. [ISSN: 1443-4059] 1999. bi-m. Free. Ed(s): Scott Murray, Rolando Caputo. Senses of Cinema Inc., Cinema Studies Program, School of Fine Arts, Melbourne, VIC 3010, Australia. Refereed. *Indexed:* MLA-IB. *Bk. rev.:* Number and length vary. *Aud.:* Ac, Sa.

Senses of Cinema is "an online film journal devoted to the serious and eclectic discussion of cinema." It receives financial assistance from the Australian Film Commission, and it has a slight down-under, Aussie bias (the Festivals section is divided into "international festivals" and "Australian festivals"). The journal is building up a "Great Directors" database, with a critical essay on each director along with a filmography, bibliography, and web resources. It includes book and DVD reviews. URL: www.sensesofcinema.com.

2669. Sight and Sound: the international film monthly. Incorporates (1934-1991): *Monthly Film Bulletin.* [ISSN: 0037-4806] 1932. m. GBP 45.75 domestic; GBP 54.75 foreign. British Film Institute, 21 Stephen St, London, W1T 1LN, United Kingdom; http://www.bfi.org.uk. Illus., index, adv. Circ: 26299. Vol. ends: Dec. Microform: MIM; PQC; WMP. Online: Chadwyck-Healey Inc.; EBSCO Publishing, EBSCO Host; OCLC Online Computer Library Center, Inc.; H.W. Wilson. *Indexed:* AmHI, ArtHuCI, ArtInd, BRD, BRI, BrHumI, CBRI, FLI, HumInd, IBR, IBZ, IIFP, IIPA, LISA, MLA-IB, MRD, SSCI. *Bk. rev.:* Number and length vary. *Aud.:* Ga, Ac.

This publication is particularly good in the area of film reviews and credits; it consistently gives the most complete credit listings of any film periodical. Coverage includes major film festivals and filmmakers, American and foreign. It also publishes detailed articles and interviews with directors not usually found in popular movie magazines.

Variety. See Theater section.

2670. The Velvet Light Trap. [ISSN: 0149-1830] 1971. s-a. USD 72 (Individuals, USD 30). University of Texas Press, Journals Division, 2100 Comal, Austin, TX 78722; journals@uts.cc.utexas.edu; http://www.utexas.edu/utpress/journals/journals.html. Illus., index, adv. Sample. Circ: 531. Vol. ends: Sep. Microform: PQC. Online: Chadwyck-Healey Inc.; EBSCO Publishing, EBSCO Host; Florida Center for Library Automation; Gale; OCLC Online Computer Library Center, Inc.; OhioLINK; Project MUSE; SwetsWise Online Content. Reprint: PSC. *Indexed:* AmH&L, AmHI, CommAb, FLI, HistAb, IIFP, IIPA, MLA-IB, MRD, PRA, V&AA. *Bk. rev.:* Number and length vary. *Aud.:* Ac.

This publication is "devoted to investigating historical questions that illuminate the understanding of film and other media." Issues tend to have a single theme, e.g., religion and the media. Articles and interviews are of a scholarly nature and include notes. Book reviews are given in each issue. Recommended for academic collections.

2671. Written By. Former titles (until 1996): *Writers Guild of America, West. Journal;* Formerly (until 1997): *Journal.* [ISSN: 1092-468X] 1997. 10x/yr. USD 40 domestic; USD 45 Canada; USD 50 elsewhere. Ed(s): Tawn E McCarthy. Writers Guild of America, West, 7000 W Third St, W Hollywood, Los Angeles, CA 90048; writtenby@wga.org; http://www.wga.org/. Illus., adv. Circ: 3000 Paid. *Indexed:* FLI, IIPA. *Aud.:* Sa.

The official publication of the Writers Guild of America West, this "actively seeks material from Guild members and other writers." It covers current events and creative issues that affect screen and television writers and offers biographical articles on writers and analyses of current films. A good title for libraries that support a screenwriting program.

■ FINANCE

Banking/Insurance/Investment/Scholarly/Trade Journals

See also Accounting and Taxation; Business; Consumer Education; and Economics sections. For Business Valuation, see also Real Estate section.

Carol J. Elsen, Collection Manager, Andersen Library, University of Wisconsin–Whitewater, Whitewater, WI 53190.

Barbara Esty, Curriculum Services Librarian, Baker Library, Harvard Business School, Boston, MA 02163

Introduction

Finance as a field of study encompasses the management, manipulation, and movement of money or its equivalent in and out of organizations and markets for the benefit of investors, organizations, and governments. Because of the international nature of financial markets, this field is taking on an increasingly global scope. Finance journals range from consumer-oriented personal finance magazines to highly theoretical and quantitative titles of interest to scholars.

Because finance intersects with so many other areas of business, finance journals may be found in other sections of this volume, such as Accounting and Taxation; Business; Real Estate; and Management, Administration, and Human Resources.

Due to the broad scope of finance, titles are presented in five major sections: (1) "Banking" includes titles that focus on banks and other financial institutions that are also geared to practitioners; (2) "Insurance" titles are trade publications for insurance professionals; (3) "Investment" includes titles that are particularly intended for individual and institutional investors and money managers; (4) "Scholarly" titles cover all aspects of finance, including securities markets, financial instruments, financial economics, and strategic financial management; and (5) "Trade" titles are generally targeted toward professionals in various areas of finance.

Most of the scholarly titles are highly technical in nature and require a working knowledge of mathematics, statistics, and finance to truly appreciate the content; these are appropriate for collections that support researchers or graduate programs in finance. The trade, banking, and insurance titles are less technical and are highly practical, since they are written for professionals in the field; many of these titles are appropriate for academic and public libraries. Most titles that target individual investors are reasonably priced and appropriate for all types of libraries to consider. The institutional-investing and money-management titles have a scope suitable for academic and public libraries as well as any library that supports investment professionals. Investors will find that web sites are increasingly useful as the Securities and Exchange Commission (SEC) and an increasing number of content providers provide timely and free (or low-cost) basic financial information via the Internet.

When selecting titles for a particular patron group, keep in mind the skill level required by each title and the cost, because finance titles can be expensive.

This section embeds comments on selected web sites in the annotations.

Basic Periodicals

Ga: *Kiplinger's Personal Finance;* Ac, Sa: *American Banker, Euromoney, Financial Analysts Journal, Institutional Investor, Investor's Chronicle, The Journal of Finance.*

Basic Abstracts and Indexes

ABI/Inform, Business Index, Business Periodicals Index, Journal of Economic Literature/EconLIT, PAIS.

Banking

2672. *A B A Bank Marketing.* Former titles (until 2001): *Bank Marketing;* (until 1972): *Bank Marketing Management.* [ISSN: 1539-7890] 1915. m. combined Jan.-Feb & July-Aug issues. USD 160 foreign (Members, USD 80; Non-members, USD 120). Ed(s): Walt Albro. American Bankers Association, 1120 Connecticut Ave NW, Washington, DC 20036-3971; custserv@aba.com; http://www.aba.com. Illus. Circ: 4015 Paid. Microform: PQC. Online: EBSCO Publishing, EBSCO Host; Gale; Northern Light Technology, Inc.; OCLC Online Computer Library Center, Inc.; ProQuest LLC (Ann Arbor); H.W. Wilson. *Indexed:* ABIn, BLI, BPI. *Bk. rev.:* Number and length vary. *Aud.:* Ga, Ac, Sa.

This delightful, glossy trade publication is filled with coverage of all aspects of retail and corporate bank marketing. Each issue includes industry news and announcements, association news, an events calendar, problems/solutions, new products/services, a half-dozen provider profiles, and special sections that focus on community heroes, brands, customer service surveys, and a wide variety of technical and related service issues, in addition to frequent practitioner-written case studies. Articles often have clever titles, such as "A Cinderella Story." Regular departments include "New Products/Services," "Idea Bank," and "Continuing Education Quiz" to keep professionals up-to-speed. With its numerous, interesting sidebars, this is a great title for browsing collections.

2673. *A B A Banking Journal.* Incorporates: *Banking Buying Guide;* Former titles (until 1979): *Banking; American Bankers Association. Journal.* [ISSN: 0194-5947] 1908. m. USD 50 Free to qualified personnel; USD 35 domestic financial institutions. Ed(s): William W Streeter. Simmons-Boardman Publishing Corp., 345 Hudson St, 12th Fl, New York, NY 10014-4502. Illus., index, adv. Sample. Circ: 31500 Paid. Microform: PQC. Online: EBSCO Publishing, EBSCO Host; Factiva, Inc.; Florida Center for Library Automation; Gale; LexisNexis; OCLC Online Computer Library Center, Inc.; ProQuest LLC (Ann Arbor); H.W. Wilson. *Indexed:* ABIn, ATI, BLI, BPI, LRI, PAIS, RI-1, RiskAb. *Bk. rev.:* Number and length vary. *Aud.:* Ac, Sa.

This industry magazine covers news, trends, and products in commercial and community banking. Columns report on community banking, compliance, mortgage lending, trusts, technology, new-product development, news and newsmakers, regulatory issues, and the general economy. A calendar of events is also included. Recent feature articles examine micropayments, operational risk management in the U.S. banking industry, and data management.

2674. *American Banker.* Incorporates (1999-2002): *Financial Services Marketing.* [ISSN: 0002-7561] 1836. d. 5/wk. USD 895 combined subscription domestic for print & online eds.; USD 950 combined subscription Canada for print & online eds.; USD 1195 combined subscription elsewhere for print & online eds. Ed(s): David Longobardi. SourceMedia, Inc., One State St Plaza, 27th Fl, New York, NY 10004; custserv@sourcemedia.com; http://www.sourcemedia.com. Illus., index, adv. Circ: 40000. Vol. ends: Dec. CD-ROM: The Dialog Corporation. Microform: PQC. Online: DataStar; EBSCO Publishing, EBSCO Host; Florida Center for Library Automation; Gale; Northern Light Technology, Inc.; OCLC Online Computer Library Center, Inc.; ProQuest LLC (Ann Arbor). *Indexed:* ATI, AgeL, BLI, CWI, LRI, NewsAb. *Bk. rev.:* Number and length vary. *Aud.:* Ac, Sa.

This highly regarded daily financial paper reports on trade and industry news and newsmakers. It covers trends in community banking, mortgages, investment products, debt and credit, technology, ATMs, and finance. Bank ratings, marketing, court cases, regulations, and news about movers and shakers in the banking industry are also included. Because of the in-depth coverage of banking and the concise reports of related general business and industry news, this is a must for bankers and for academic as well as larger public libraries.

2675. *Bank Accounting & Finance.* [ISSN: 0894-3958] 1987. bi-m. USD 345. Ed(s): Claire Greene. C C H Tax and Accounting, 2700 Lake Cook Rd, Riverwoods, IL 60015; http://tax.cchgroup.com. Illus., index, adv. Circ: 800 Paid. Vol. ends: No. 6. *Indexed:* ATI, BLI. *Aud.:* Ac, Sa.

This no-nonsense practitioner's magazine addresses core issues related to financial, legislative, and corporate aspects of bank management, so it is primarily of interest to bank accountants and executives. Statements of Financial Accounting Standards are analyzed and case studies are presented. Regular columns provide news on the regulatory climate, merger and acquisition strategies, taxation, SEC regulations, bank management practices, and the Financial Accounting Standards Board and the Emerging Issues Task Force. Several peer-researched feature articles focus on a specific topic, including recent ones on IT automation and integrated compliance, best practices for reducing model risk exposure, and compliance costs in the second year of Sarbanes-Oxley. This title provides timely, insightful information and is suitable for academic libraries that support programs in accounting and finance.

2676. *The Banker.* [ISSN: 0005-5395] 1926. m. GBP 245; EUR 361; USD 441. Ed(s): Stephen Timewell, Brian Caplen. Financial Times Business Information, Magazines, Tabernacle Court, 16-28 Tabernacle St, London, EC2A 4DD, United Kingdom. Illus., index, adv. Circ: 12500. Vol. ends: Dec. Microform: PQC. Online: Florida Center for Library Automation; Gale; LexisNexis; OCLC Online Computer Library Center, Inc.; ProQuest LLC (Ann Arbor). Reprint: SCH. *Indexed:* ABIn, BLI, BPI, PAIS, RRTA, WAE&RSA. *Bk. rev.:* Number and length vary. *Aud.:* Ac, Sa.

This international banking newsmagazine provides insights into the international retail and investment banking climates. Each issue includes summary reports of economic and industry conditions in a dozen or more countries, along with brief reports that cover banking, capital markets, foreign exchange, derivatives, trade finance, risk analysis, technology, and interviews. Recent contents include discussions of covered bonds, the credit derivatives market, the strengthening of firms' compliance departments, and a host of other issues for each geographic region. Ranked lists of top banks and directories of foreign banks are often provided. This is a great choice for any academic or large public library whose patrons are interested in international finance, development, and banking news.

2677. *Banking Strategies.* Former titles (until 1996): *Bank Management;* (until 1990): *Bank Administration;* (until 1986): *Magazine of Bank Administration; Auditgram;* Incorporated (in 1993): *Bankers Monthly.* [ISSN: 1091-6385] 1925. bi-m. USD 66.50 domestic (Free to qualified personnel). Bank Administration Institute, One N Franklin, Ste. 1000, Chicago, IL 60606-3421; info@bai.org; http://www.bai.org. Illus., index, adv. Circ: 32000 Paid and controlled. Vol. ends: Dec. Microform: PQC. Online: Gale; OCLC Online Computer Library Center, Inc.; H.W. Wilson. *Indexed:* ABIn, ATI, BLI, BPI, PAIS. *Aud.:* Ac, Sa.

Published by the Bank Administration Institute, whose directors represent the upper ranks of the banking industry, this magazine targets senior-level bank and financial services managers. It reports on banking and bank management issues such as community banking, retail banking, lending, corporate services, operations, technology, finance/accounting, audit/control, human resources, treasury management, regulatory issues, and strategy development. The magazine presents several 5- to 15-page articles on current topics. Departments cover trends and statistics, human resources, economic perspectives, Washington news, and community banking. The online version of the journal is free. Large public libraries and academic libraries that support programs in finance and banking should consider this title.

2678. *Community Banker.* Former titles (until 2000): *America's Community Bankers;* (until 1995): *Savings and Community Banker;* Which was formed by the merger of (1952-1993): *Savings Institution Magazine;* Which was formerly (until 1983): *Savings and Loan News;* (1983-1993): *Bottomline (Washington);* Which was formed by the merger of (1921-1983): *Savings Bank Journal;* (1974-1983): *National Savings and Community League Journal;* Incorporates: *National League Journal of Insured Savings Associations.* [ISSN: 1529-1332] 1880. m. Members, USD 75; Non-members, USD 95. Ed(s): Debra Cope. America's Community Bankers, 900 19th St, NW, Ste 400, Washington, DC 20006; http://www.americascommunitybankers.org. Illus., adv. Circ:

10000 Controlled. Microform: PQC. Online: EBSCO Publishing, EBSCO Host; Gale; OCLC Online Computer Library Center, Inc.; ProQuest LLC (Ann Arbor); H.W. Wilson. *Indexed:* ABIn, BLI, BPI, H&TI, PAIS. *Aud.:* Ac, Sa.

This trade periodical provides in-depth analysis of current legislative and regulatory developments, economic trends, national news, investment management, marketing, human resources, compliance, tax management, data processing, and personnel. A calendar and general association news and personal profiles are included. Short feature articles recently examined minority-owned businesses as an untapped lending market, and merchant capture services (online deposits for corporate clients). Each issue has a "crash course" article that functions as a continuing education program. Technology and surveys/trends columns keep readers abreast of the competitive landscape. Because it is primarily a practitioner's magazine, only large public libraries or academic libraries that support programs in banking and finance should consider this title.

2679. *Credit Union Magazine: for credit union elected officials, managers and employees.* Formerly: *Credit Union Bridge.* [ISSN: 0011-1066] 1924. m. USD 56. Ed(s): Kathryn Kuehn. Credit Union National Association, Inc., PO Box 431, Madison, WI 53701; http://www.cuna.org/. Illus., index, adv. Circ: 30983. Microform: PQC. Online: EBSCO Publishing, EBSCO Host; Northern Light Technology, Inc.; OCLC Online Computer Library Center, Inc.; ProQuest LLC (Ann Arbor). *Indexed:* ABIn, BLI, PAIS. *Aud.:* Ac, Sa.

This important trade magazine, produced by the Credit Union National Association, reports on news and newsmakers, new products and technologies, target markets, new services, and information related to credit unions in general. Recent topics include discussions of security as a marketing differentiator, targeting the Hispanic market, and indirect lending. This title is worthwhile for large public libraries and academic libraries that support finance programs or a campus credit union. The web site provides free articles from the current issue and archives.

2680. *Independent Banker.* [ISSN: 0019-3674] 1950. m. Members, USD 35; Non-members, USD 50. Ed(s): Nicole Swann, Tim Cook. Independent Community Bankers of America, One Thomas Circle, NW, Ste 400, Washington, DC 20005-5802; info@icba.org; http://www.icba.org. Illus., adv. Circ: 12000 Paid. Microform: PQC. Online: Northern Light Technology, Inc.; ProQuest LLC (Ann Arbor). *Indexed:* ABIn, BLI, PAIS. *Aud.:* Ac, Sa.

The "nation's voice for community banks" is dedicated to the preservation of community banking. Each issue features a cover story on an executive or a timely issue. A recent cover story outlines the House Financial Services Committee Chairman's community bank agenda. A dozen feature articles and columns provide information on investments, technology, cash management, operations, the regulatory environment, and the regional independent banking climate across the United States. Industry insiders can keep current with an industry calendar, news of association activities, and announcements of new products and services. This is a core title for academic libraries that support undergraduate or graduate business programs.

2681. *Mortgage Banking: the magazine of real estate finance managers and employees.* Former titles (until 1981): *Mortgage Banker; M B A News Review.* [ISSN: 0730-0212] 1939. m. USD 74.95 foreign (Members, USD 60; Non-members, USD 69.95). Ed(s): Janet Hewitt, Janet Hewitt. Mortgage Bankers Association, 1919 Pennsylvania Ave NW, Washington, DC 20006-3438; janet_hewitt@mbaa.org; http://www.mbaa.org. Illus., index, adv. Sample. Circ: 10023. Vol. ends: Sep. Microform: CIS; PQC. Online: EBSCO Publishing, EBSCO Host; Factiva, Inc.; Florida Center for Library Automation; Gale; Northern Light Technology, Inc.; OCLC Online Computer Library Center, Inc.; ProQuest LLC (Ann Arbor); H.W. Wilson. *Indexed:* ABIn, ATI, BLI, BPI, PAIS. *Aud.:* Ac, Sa.

This journal provides practical and timely articles about all types of real estate and real estate financing. Departments cover technology, software, key people, the secondary mortgage market, statistics, sources of demographics and research, mortgage revenue bonds, and servicing. There is also a news alert

page. Recent topics include sub-prime lending, early payment defaults, and the nuts and bolts of reverse-mortgage lending. Libraries that support business programs that focus on real estate should consider this title.

2682. *The R M A Journal.* Former titles (until Sep. 2000): *The Journal of Lending & Credit Risk Management;* (until 1996): *Journal of Commercial Lending;* (until 1992): *Journal of Commercial Bank Lending;* (until 1967): *Robert Morris Associates Bulletin.* [ISSN: 1531-0558] 1918. 10x/yr. Members, USD 60; Non-members, USD 85. Ed(s): Beverly Foster. Risk Management Association, One Liberty Place, Ste 2300, 1650 Market St, Philadelphia, PA 19103-7398; bfoster@rmahq.org. Illus., index, adv. Circ: 20000 Paid. Vol. ends: Aug. *Indexed:* ABIn, ATI, BLI, BPI, PAIS, RiskAb. *Bk. rev.:* Number and length vary. *Aud.:* Ac, Sa.

The official journal of the Risk Management Association (RMA), this is a key source of information for commercial loan officers. It covers risk management issues in addition to commercial lending. Each issue contains 10–12 feature articles as well as regular departments on management strategies, commercial lending and risk management issues, accounting actions, and a cautionary case study. Recent article topics include credit risk exposure from a regional bank perspective, problem loans, global banking, and hurricane disasters and recovery. An essential title for libraries that support finance programs and professionals.

2683. *U S Banker.* Incorporates (1997-2002): *FutureBanker;* Incorporates (1886-1997): *Bankers Magazine;* Former titles (until 1977): *United States Investor - Eastern Banker;* (until 1971): *United States Investor.* [ISSN: 0148-8848] 1891. m. USD 89 domestic; USD 95 foreign. Ed(s): Holly Sraeel. SourceMedia, Inc., One State St Plaza, 27th Fl, New York, NY 10004. Illus., index, adv. Sample. Circ: 39000 Controlled. Vol. ends: Dec. Microform: PQC. Online: EBSCO Publishing, EBSCO Host; Factiva, Inc.; Gale; LexisNexis; OCLC Online Computer Library Center, Inc.; ProQuest LLC (Ann Arbor); H.W. Wilson. *Indexed:* ABIn, ATI, BLI, BPI, CWI, LRI, PAIS. *Aud.:* Ac, Sa.

This magazine provides a solid overview and update for students and practitioners who are interested in current banking issues. Profiles of companies and/or interviews with several key people are part of each issue. One or two cover stories are followed by a number of shorter articles on the industry, Washington, relevant new technology, and banking news. Recent topics include the significance of pricing towards rewards given by credit card companies; technology advances for automated teller machines (ATM) for the You Generation; and growth in the banking services to the unbanked. Special features include annual ranked lists, such as the 100 largest U.S. banks, the ten most profitable U.S. banks, and profitability rankings of mid-size U.S. banks. There is a directory of suppliers and professional services in each issue.

Insurance

2684. *Advisor Today.* Formerly (until January 2000): *Life Association News;* Which incorporated (1956-1986): *Probe (Rockville Centre).* [ISSN: 1529-823X] 1906. m. Free to members; Non-members, USD 7. Ed(s): Ayo Mseka, Kevin Sheridan. National Association of Insurance and Financial Advisors, 2901 Telestar Ct, Falls Church, VA 22042-1205; jedwards@naifa.org; http://www.naifa.org. Illus., index, adv. Sample. Circ: 100000 Paid. Vol. ends: Dec. Microform: PQC. Online: EBSCO Publishing, EBSCO Host; OCLC Online Computer Library Center, Inc.; ProQuest LLC (Ann Arbor). *Indexed:* ABIn. *Bk. rev.:* 500-1,000 words. *Aud.:* Ac, Sa.

This trade magazine has the largest circulation among insurance and financial advising magazines and is the official publication of the National Association of Insurance and Financial Advisors. News and updates on sales, law and legislation, selling strategies, managing people and technology in your office, and book reviews are accompanied by reports designed for advisors. Recent articles focus on health insurance for the uninsured, maximizing clients' pensions, hiring tips, and personal interaction with clients. Recommended for academic libraries due to the excellent value for the price.

2685. *Best's Review. Insurance Issues and Analysis.* Formed by the 2000 merger of: *Best's Review. Life - Health Insurance Edition;* Which was formerly (1920-1969): *Best's Insurance News. Life - Health Edition;* (1977-2000): *Best's Review. Property - Casualty Insurance Edition;* Which was formerly: *Best's Review. Property - Liability Edition;* (1938-1969): *Best's Insurance News. Fire and Casualty.* [ISSN: 1527-5914] 2000. m. USD 50. Ed(s): Lynna Goch, Sally Whitney. A.M. Best Co., Ambest Rd, Oldwick, NJ 08858; http://www.ambest.com. Illus., index, adv. Vol. ends: Apr. Online: EBSCO Publishing, EBSCO Host; Factiva, Inc.; Gale; OCLC Online Computer Library Center, Inc.; ProQuest K-12 Learning Solutions; ProQuest LLC (Ann Arbor); H.W. Wilson. *Indexed:* ABIn, BPI, CWI. *Aud.:* Ac, Sa.

This trade magazine, formerly published as separate life/health and property/casualty editions, provides wide coverage of the insurance industry under a single title. This integrated edition includes company and industry news, political and regulatory information, new-product announcements, newsmakers in the industry, and reports of court cases in each issue. This publication "best" represents the insurance industry as a whole and therefore is a core title for large public and academic libraries.

2686. *Business Insurance: news magazine for corporate risk, employee benefit and financial executives.* [ISSN: 0007-6864] 1967. w. USD 97 domestic; USD 130 in Canada & Mexico; USD 230 elsewhere. Ed(s): Regis J. Coccia, Paul D. Winston. Crain Communications, Inc., 711 Third Ave, New York, NY 10017-4036; info@crain.com; http://www.crain.com. Illus., adv. Circ: 45722. Microform: MIM; PQC. Online: EBSCO Publishing, EBSCO Host; Florida Center for Library Automation; Gale; LexisNexis; Northern Light Technology, Inc.; OCLC Online Computer Library Center, Inc.; ProQuest LLC (Ann Arbor); H.W. Wilson. *Indexed:* ABIn, BLI, BPI, CINAHL, CWI, LRI. *Aud.:* Ac, Sa.

Business Insurance serves business executives who are responsible for the purchase and administration of corporate insurance/self-insurance programs, encompassing both property and liability insurance and employee benefit programs, including life, health, and pensions. Each week, this tabloid-style publication includes current news, editorials, and insightful feature articles that would appeal to insurance professionals and students.

2687. *C P C U eJournal.* Former titles (until 2004): *Chartered Property & Casualty Underwriters Society. Journal (Print Edition); Society of Chartered Property and Casualty Underwriters. Annals.* 1949. m. Ed(s): David C Marlett. Chartered Property & Casualty Underwriters Society, 720 Providence Rd, Malvern, PA 19355; membercenter@cpcusociety.org; http://www.cpcusociety.org/. Illus., index. Sample. Vol. ends: Dec. *Indexed:* ABIn, BPI. *Aud.:* Ac, Sa.

The Society of Chartered Property and Casualty Underwriters is the leading professional organization in property and casualty insurance in the United States, and it has strict examination, experience, and ethical requirements for membership. This journal keeps association members informed on current issues, legal requirements, and financial aspects of property and casualty insurance. Feature articles are seven to ten pages in length; opinion pieces are slightly shorter. Articles examine insurance concepts such as professional and practitioner liability and cost containment, including alternative reinsurance, as well as specific forms of insurance, such as automobile, flood, and medical. Regular departments offer information on extended coverages, opinion pieces, and letters. Anyone interested in this area of insurance, but particularly those in academic programs or active in the insurance industry, would enjoy this publication.

2688. *G A M A International Journal.* [ISSN: 1095-7367] 6x/yr. Free to members; Non-members, USD 150. G A M A International, 2901 Telestar Court, Ste 140, Falls Church, VA 22042; http://www.gamaweb.com. *Bk. rev.:* 1-5, 50-100 words. *Aud.:* Sa.

This journal is devoted to the professional development of leaders in the insurance and financial services industry. Articles focus on the leadership and management skills needed to build and maintain successful agencies. Recent article topics include embracing diversity for business growth, positioning

insurance advisors as counselors rather than as salespeople, and dealing with executive recruiters. Recommended for special libraries that support insurance professionals.

2689. *Independent Agent.* Formerly (until 1969): *American Agency Bulletin.* [ISSN: 0002-7197] 1903. m. USD 24. Ed(s): Katie Butler. Independent Insurance Agents of America - M S I, 127 S Peyton St, Alexandria, VA 22314; magazine@iiaa.org; http://www.iiaa.com/. Illus., adv. Sample. Circ: 47000. Vol. ends: Dec. *Aud.:* Ac, Sa.

This title serves the industry-information needs of the Independent Insurance Agents of America. Explored in each issue are reinsurance, basic coverages, liability, licensing and certification, regulatory information, finance, customer service, the competition between independent agencies and direct writers, marketing, and related topics. This magazine provides practical information for agents as well as policyholders, covering the wide scope of the independent agency system. Academic libraries that support insurance education and large public libraries should considered this title for their collections.

2690. *Insurance Law & Litigation Week.* [ISSN: 1550-8927] 2004. w. USD 1917 combined subscription print & online eds. Strafford Publications, Inc., 590 Dutch Valley Rd, N E, Postal Drawer 13729, Atlanta, GA 30324-0729. *Aud.:* Sa.

This newsletter is a comprehensive weekly briefing on key developments in insurance law nationwide—the latest court decisions, new filings and complaints, jury verdicts, out-of-court settlements, pending and enacted legislation, and current agency actions. Areas covered include commercial and general, life and health, property and casualty, auto, homeowner's, title, disability, workers' compensation, and reinsurance. A good selection for law school and academic business libraries.

2691. *Insurance: Mathematics and Economics.* [ISSN: 0167-6687] 1982. 6x/yr. EUR 1189. Ed(s): M J Goovaerts, H. U. Gerber. Elsevier BV, North-Holland, Sara Burgerhartstraat 25, Amsterdam, 1055 KV, Netherlands; nlinfo-f@elsevier.nl; http://www.elsevier.nl. Illus., index, adv. Sample. Refereed. Circ: 1000. Vol. ends: No. 4. Microform: PQC. Online: EBSCO Publishing, EBSCO Host; Gale; IngentaConnect; OhioLINK; ScienceDirect; SwetsWise Online Content. *Indexed:* ABIn, AgeL, CCMJ, IBSS, JEL, MSN, MathR, RiskAb, SCI, SSCI. *Aud.:* Ac, Sa.

Each issue contains five to eight papers of international interest, 10–15 pages in length, concerned with the theory of insurance mathematics or the inventive application of it, including empirical or experimental results. Articles evaluate mathematical and economic applications related to actuarial science and a variety of insurance-related concerns. Libraries that support programs in actuarial science, mathematics, and economics will need to evaluate this journal despite its hefty price.

2692. *Journal of Risk and Insurance.* Formerly (until 1964): *Journal of Insurance;* Which was formed by the merger of (1954-1956): *Review of Insurance Studies;* (1933-1956): *American Association of University Teachers of Insurance. Journal;* Which was formerly (until 1937): *American Association of University Teachers of Insurance. Proceedings of the Annual Meeting.* [ISSN: 0022-4367] 1957. q. GBP 263 print & online eds. Ed(s): Richard MacMinn, Georges Dionne. Blackwell Publishing, Inc., Commerce Place, 350 Main St, Malden, MA 02148; customerservices@blackwellpublishing.com; http://www.blackwellpublishing.com. Illus., index, adv. Refereed. Circ: 2853 Paid and controlled. Vol. ends: Dec. Microform: PQC. Online: Blackwell Synergy; The Dialog Corporation; EBSCO Publishing, EBSCO Host; Florida Center for Library Automation; Gale; IngentaConnect; JSTOR (Web-based Journal Archive); OCLC Online Computer Library Center, Inc.; OhioLINK; ProQuest LLC (Ann Arbor); SwetsWise Online Content; H.W. Wilson. Reprint: PSC. *Indexed:* ABIn, AgeL, BPI, CJA, JEL, LRI, MCR, PAIS, RiskAb, SSCI. *Bk. rev.:* 1-3, 1,000+ words. *Aud.:* Ac.

This is the flagship journal of the American Risk and Insurance Association. Each issue contains roughly ten articles that present original theoretical and empirical research in insurance economics and risk management. The focus is on the organization of markets, managing pure risk, insurance finance, the economics of employee benefits, utility theory, insurance regulation, actuarial and statistical methodology, and economics of insurance institutions. Large public libraries and academic libraries that support business programs should consider this title.

2693. *Life Insurance Selling: the magazine for top life health and financial services producers.* [ISSN: 0024-3140] 1926. m. USD 50 in Canada & Mexico (Free to qualified personnel). Ed(s): Gordon Bess. Summit Business Media LLC, 1801 Park 270 Dr, Ste 550, Maryland Heights, MO 63146; info@SBMediaLLC.com; http://www.sbmediallc.com. Illus., adv. Circ: 50000 Controlled. Vol. ends: Dec. Microform: PQC. *Bk. rev.:* 0-2, 50 words. *Aud.:* Sa.

This magazine for life and health insurance and financial-services producers provides practical and transferable sales ideas and information through both editorial content and advertising. Regular departments describe policies, books, sales aids, computer products, and educational programs designed for producers. This is one of the best introductions to life insurance sales as a career, and it provides important product information for producers.

2694. *National Underwriter. Life & Health.* Former titles (until 2005): *National Underwriter. Life and Health Financial Services;* (until 1986): *National Underwriter. Life and Health Insurance Edition.* [ISSN: 1940-1345] 197?. w. USD 198. Ed(s): Thomas Slattery, Steve Piontek. The National Underwriter Company, 5081 Olympic Blvd, Erlanger, KY 41018; customerservice@nuco.com; http://www.nationalunderwriter.com. Illus., adv. Circ: 49419. Vol. ends: Dec. Microform: PQC. Online: EBSCO Publishing, EBSCO Host; Gale; LexisNexis; OCLC Online Computer Library Center, Inc.; ProQuest LLC (Ann Arbor); H.W. Wilson. *Indexed:* ABIn, BPI, CWI, LRI. *Aud.:* Ac, Sa.

This is a core newspaper for the life, health, and financial-services segments of the insurance industry. A variety of topics are covered—new product information; changes in the tax law; new federal and state legislation; company, agent, and brokerage activities; and trade association meetings. Special in-depth issues are offered throughout the year that focus on particularly hot topics or issues of importance. Public libraries with a balanced business collection and all academic libraries that support insurance programs should have this title.

2695. *National Underwriter. P & C.* Former titles (until 2005): *National Underwriter. Property & Casualty - Risk & Benefits Management Edition;* (until 1989): *National Underwriter. Property and Casualty - Employee Benefits Edition;* (until 1986): *National Underwriter. Property and Casualty Insurance Edition.* [ISSN: 1940-1353] 1896. w. USD 198. Ed(s): Sam Friedman, Susanne Sclafane. The National Underwriter Company, 5081 Olympic Blvd, Erlanger, KY 41018; customerservice@nuco.com; http://www.nationalunderwriter.com. Illus., adv. Circ: 47537. Vol. ends: Dec. Microform: PQC. Online: EBSCO Publishing, EBSCO Host; Florida Center for Library Automation; Gale; LexisNexis; OCLC Online Computer Library Center, Inc.; ProQuest LLC (Ann Arbor); H.W. Wilson. *Indexed:* ABIn, BPI, CWI, LRI. *Aud.:* Ac, Sa.

This is a core newspaper for the international property, casualty, and risk management insurance industry. Regularly featured sections include industry trends, agent and broker activities, corporate risk management, employee benefits, product and marketing information, stock activity, international events, and reinsurance. In addition, special, in-depth issues throughout the year focus on hot topics or issues of importance. Public libraries with a balanced business collection and all academic libraries that support insurance programs should have this title.

Investment

2696. *A A I I Journal.* [ISSN: 0192-3315] 1979. 10x/yr. Free to membership. Ed(s): Maria Crawford Scott. American Association of Individual Investors, 625 N Michigan Ave, Ste 1900, Chicago, IL 60611; members@aaii.com; http://www.aaii.com. Illus., index, adv. Sample. Circ: 150000 Paid. Vol. ends: No. 10. *Indexed:* BPI. *Bk. rev.:* Number and length vary. *Aud.:* Ga, Ac, Sa.

This journal is designed to help individuals become more effective managers of their personal investment portfolios. Each issue presents regular columns on news and events related to technology, capital markets, investment technology, e-commerce, new products, and special operations. A recent issue offers articles on the advantage of preferred stock, "enhanced" index funds, immediate insurance annuities, and brokered certificates of deposit. There is an annual survey of discount brokerage firms that helps investors compare commissions for a range of trades. An educated general audience, as well as scholars and practitioners, will benefit from this journal.

2697. *Better Investing.* [ISSN: 0006-016X] 1951. m. USD 31 domestic; USD 60 Canada; USD 66 elsewhere. Ed(s): Adam Ritt. Betterinvesting, 711 W Thirteen Mile Rd, Madison Heights, MI 48071. Illus., index, adv. Sample. Circ: 220074 Paid. Microform: PQC. Online: ProQuest K-12 Learning Solutions; ProQuest LLC (Ann Arbor). *Indexed:* ABIn. *Bk. rev.:* Number and length vary. *Aud.:* Ga, Ac, Sa.

A popular choice for personal investing collections in public libraries, this title presents news and information related to money management, investment clubs, and National Association of Investors Corporation events. A recent feature article explores the use of company-specific blogs as another angle on researching a company. Each issue includes an editorial, letters to the editor, "Ask Mr. NAIC," a growth fund report, a technology report, and regional notices. The stocks and funds section includes an undervalued stock, a stock to study, a contrary opinion, a "five years ago stock to study," an undervalued feature, and an 18-month undervalued review. Public and academic libraries that serve individual investors or support investment courses should certainly consider this title.

2698. *C F A Digest.* [ISSN: 0046-9777] 1971. q. Members, USD 50; Non-members, USD 75. Ed(s): Daniel J Larocco, Rodney N Sullivan. C F A Institute, 560 Ray C Hunt Drive, Charlottesville, VA 22903; http://www.cfainstitute.org. Illus. Circ: 30000 Controlled. *Aud.:* Ac, Sa.

The Association for Investment Management and Research, composed of the Institute of Chartered Financial Consultants and the Financial Analysts Federation, produces this digest. Each issue provides 600-word abstracts of 30 articles, drawn from a pool of 70 investment-related journals. Scholarly articles on alternative investments, corporate finance, corporate governance, debt investments, derivatives, equity investments, financial markets, investment theory, portfolio management, quantitative tools, and risk measurement and management are included. Publishers' names and addresses and article order forms are included. The editor summarizes the general content and the uses of the research articles in each issue. This is a core title for academic libraries that support programs in investment and finance.

Commercial Investment Real Estate. See Real Estate section.

2699. *Equities.* Former titles (until Sep. 1990): *O T C Review;* (until Feb. 1977): *Over-the-Counter Securities Review.* [ISSN: 1053-2544] 1951. q. USD 19.95. Ed(s): Gregory Bergman. Equities Magazine LLC, 2118 Wilshire Blvd, Ste 722, Santa Monica, CA 90403. Illus., adv. Circ: 5000 Paid. Vol. ends: Dec. Online: EBSCO Publishing, EBSCO Host; Florida Center for Library Automation; Gale. *Indexed:* PAIS. *Bk. rev.:* Number and length vary. *Aud.:* Ac, Sa.

This trade magazine profiles small- to mid-cap public companies that offer a wide variety of unusual and unfamiliar investment opportunities, such as a biotech company that uses adult stem cells to help reverse tissue damage in stroke patients and a company that specializes in eye sculpting. The "Favorites of the Famous" section lists stocks picked by well-known equity analysts. CEO interviews, stock picks in various industry groups, and articles featuring up-and-coming companies highlight each issue. Recent article topics include advice on analyzing biotechnology stocks, diversifying with foreign investments, and the emerging mining industry in Peru. The annual interview with investor Sir John Templeton is popular with readers. Although the magazine production is somewhat amateurish, the investment analysis will appeal to readers in large public and academic libraries.

FINANCE

2700. Euromoney: the monthly journal of international money and capital markets. Incorporates (1994-2006): *Corporate Finance.* [ISSN: 0014-2433] 1969. m. GBP 365 combined subscription domestic print & online eds.; EUR 545 combined subscription in Europe print & online eds.; USD 695 combined subscription elsewhere print & online eds. Ed(s): Clive Horwood. Euromoney Institutional Investor Plc., Nestor House, Playhouse Yard, London, EC4V 5EX, United Kingdom; information@euromoneyplc.com; http://www.euromoney.com. Illus., index. Sample. Circ: 20674. Vol. ends: Dec. Microform: PQC. Online: The Dialog Corporation; EBSCO Publishing, EBSCO Host; Florida Center for Library Automation; Gale; OCLC Online Computer Library Center, Inc.; ProQuest K-12 Learning Solutions; ProQuest LLC (Ann Arbor); H.W. Wilson. *Indexed:* ABIn, BLI, BPI, IBSS, PAIS. *Bk. rev.:* Number and length vary. *Aud.:* Ac, Sa.

This title monitors the global financial marketplace, including financial institutions, securities, and commodities in established and emerging economies. It provides profiles of companies, industries, and the family trees and business interests of the people who control the wealth. Related aspects of international finance are covered. Each issue provides information from a dozen or more countries and regions. Several yearly supplements profile individual countries or key topics—a recent example is a guide to financial supply-chain management. As the title suggests, this journal gives a uniquely European perspective on global financial issues. This is a core industry publication for anyone interested in international finance and is appropriate for academic, special, and larger public libraries that support finance programs or professionals.

2701. Financial Planning. Formerly (until 1983): *The Financial Planner.* [ISSN: 0746-7915] 1972. m. USD 79 domestic; USD 89 foreign. Ed(s): Eric Garland, Jennifer Liptow. SourceMedia, Inc., One State St Plaza, 27th Fl, New York, NY 10004; custserv@sourcemedia.com; http://www.sourcemedia.com. Adv. Circ: 100000 Paid and controlled. Online: EBSCO Publishing, EBSCO Host; Gale; LexisNexis; OCLC Online Computer Library Center, Inc.; ProQuest K-12 Learning Solutions; ProQuest LLC (Ann Arbor). *Indexed:* ABIn, ATI, BLI, PAIS. *Bk. rev.:* Number and length vary. *Aud.:* Ga, Ac, Sa.

As you might imagine, the target audience for this journal is professional financial planners. Regular columns provide insights and advice on industry analysis, investment analysis, client strategies, effective use of human and technology resources, and behavioral finance. CFP licensees can get credits by taking the monthly continuing-education quizzes. Recent articles discuss how financial planners are using the principles of psychology to help them communicate with clients, emerging market bond funds, and Chinese stocks. The web site has news, interactive tools, and full-text articles from current and past issues.

2702. Futures (Chicago): news, analysis and strategies for futures, options and derivatives traders. Formerly (until 1984): *Commodities;* Incorporates (in 199?): *Trends in Futures;* Which was formerly: *Commodity Closeup.* [ISSN: 0746-2468] 1972. m. USD 68 combined subscription in US & Canada print & online eds.; USD 121 combined subscription elsewhere print & online eds. Ed(s): Daniel Collins. Highline Media, Futures Magazine Group Office, 111 W Jackson Blvd Ste 2210, Chicago, IL 60604; http://www.summitbusinessmedia.com. Illus., index, adv. Circ: 62000 Controlled. Vol. ends: Dec. Microform: PQC. Online: EBSCO Publishing, EBSCO Host; Florida Center for Library Automation; Gale; OCLC Online Computer Library Center, Inc.; ProQuest LLC (Ann Arbor); H.W. Wilson. *Indexed:* ABIn, BPI, EAA, PAIS. *Bk. rev.:* 0-3. *Aud.:* Ac, Sa.

This glossy trade title covers the global markets with articles and news reports about the futures/options industry. Contracts, exchanges, brokerage firms, technology, strategy, hot commodities, and trading techniques may be covered by each issue. Recent stories discuss the Trin indicator in short-term moves, embracing the option hedge, understanding demand in cash-based metals, and knowing when to use the Fibonacci and Lucas models in trading stocks. This is a crucial title for libraries that support graduate business programs.

2703. Institutional Investor (America's Edition): the premier magazine of professional finance. Incorporates (1970-1973): *Corporate Financing.* [ISSN: 0020-3580] 1967. m. USD 495 combined subscription print & online eds. Ed(s): Deirdre Brennan, Michael Carroll. Institutional Investor, Inc., 225 Park Ave, S, 7th Fl., New York, NY 10003-1605. Illus., index, adv. Sample. Circ: 101615 Paid and controlled. Vol. ends: Dec. Microform: PQC. Online: EBSCO Publishing, EBSCO Host; Florida Center for Library Automation; Gale; Northern Light Technology, Inc.; OCLC Online Computer Library Center, Inc.; ProQuest LLC (Ann Arbor); H.W. Wilson. *Indexed:* ABIn, ATI, AgeL, BLI, BPI, CWI, EnvAb, PAIS, SSCI. *Bk. rev.:* 1-2, 1,000-1,500 words. *Aud.:* Ac, Sa.

This practitioner's magazine is known for its benchmark rankings and ratings of analysts, asset managers, banks, and country credit globally. These rankings are designed to assist financial professionals in making sound investment decisions. The journal provides detailed coverage of commercial and investment banking and many other areas of finance and investing. It also addresses policies, strategies, and the political activities in the social arenas that influence investment decisions. A cover story and several longer feature articles look at issues such as the decline of the American Stock Exchange, European hedge fund IPOs, and expansion of Chicago futures exchanges overseas. These are accompanied by many smaller pieces on international finance, travel, corporate governance, real state, mutual funds, money management, pensions, global funds, and the impact of financial accounting standards. The magazine's web site is a nice enhancement and well worth a visit. This publication is a must for academic and research libraries that support programs in business and finance.

2704. Investment Dealers' Digest: news magazine of the financial community. Formerly (until 1997): *I D D.* [ISSN: 0021-0080] 1935. w. USD 1095 domestic; USD 1145 Canada; USD 1195 elsewhere. Ed(s): Ken MacFayden, Tom Granahan. SourceMedia, Inc., One State St Plaza, 27th Fl, New York, NY 10004; custserv@sourcemedia.com; http://www.sourcemedia.com. Illus., index, adv. Circ: 50000 Paid. Vol. ends: No. 51. Online: EBSCO Publishing, EBSCO Host; Florida Center for Library Automation; Gale; LexisNexis; OCLC Online Computer Library Center, Inc.; ProQuest K-12 Learning Solutions; ProQuest LLC (Ann Arbor). *Indexed:* ABIn, CWI, PAIS. *Aud.:* Ac, Sa.

This publication is an important tool for keeping abreast of the investment banking and investment communities. Feature articles, usually one or two pages long, examine individuals and their trading practices, trading losses, horror stories, and successes. Each issue features "league tables" of investment banking and M&A deals by industry and also tracks new debt/equity registrations. Additional coverage is provided for news on firms and exchanges, personnel, capital markets, and aftermarket performance that serves the investment community. This newsmagazine is a must for metropolitan libraries and academic libraries with business and finance programs.

2705. Investor's Business Daily. Formerly (until 1991): *Investor's Daily.* [ISSN: 1061-2890] 1984. d. (Mon.-Fri.). USD 295. Ed(s): Wesley Mann. Investor's Business Daily, Inc., 12655 Beatrice St, Los Angeles, CA 90066. Illus., adv. Circ: 264699. *Aud.:* Ga, Ac, Sa.

This daily newspaper provides timely information for individual and institutional investors. It reports on the economic, social, and political trends that drive markets and the individuals, companies, industries, and funds that make up the competitive landscape. Regular features include a weekly list of the 100 top-rated stocks, a list of stocks traded heavily by institutional investors, unbiased market analysis, profiles of innovative companies, and "Investor's Corner," lessons for successful investing. This newspaper is an excellent source for evaluating the global investment climate and is a necessity for academic libraries that support business programs and for large public libraries.

2706. Investors Chronicle (London, 1860). Formerly: *Investors Chronicle and Stock Exchange Gazette;* Incorporates: *Stock Exchange Gazette; Financial World.* [ISSN: 0261-3115] 1860. w. GBP 125 domestic; GBP 4.95 newsstand/cover per issue domestic; GBP 164 in Europe. Ed(s): Matthew Vincent. Financial Times Business Ltd., Maple House, 149 Tottenham Court Rd, London, W1P 9LL, United Kingdom; ceri.jones@ft.com; http://www.ft.com. Illus., adv. Circ: 44770. Vol. ends: Dec.

Microform: RPI; PQC. Online: Gale; LexisNexis; OCLC Online Computer Library Center, Inc.; ProQuest LLC (Ann Arbor). *Indexed:* ABIn, BLI, PAIS. *Bk. rev.:* Number and length vary. *Aud.:* Ac, Sa.

This weekly financial news magazine reports to private and professional investors from a British perspective on international companies, exchanges, strategies for investors, and more. Articles are grouped by category under general business news, features, tips, markets, sectors, and companies. Stock tips, statistics, and a survey article appear in each issue. Special supplements are issued with the subscription that report on insurance, investing for children, and other topics of interest to investors. *Datastream* and *Financial Times* and *Bloomberg* provide many of the charts and data for the magazine.

2707. The Journal of Investing. [ISSN: 1068-0896] 1992. q. USD 380 combined subscription domestic print & online eds.; USD 455 combined subscription foreign print & online eds. Ed(s): Brian Bruce. Institutional Investor, Journals, 225 Park Ave S, 7th Fl., New York, NY 10003-1605; info@iijournals.com; http://www.iijournals.com. Illus., adv. Circ: 2500 Paid. *Indexed:* ABIn, BPI. *Aud.:* Ac, Sa.

This journal presents articles written by expert practitioners for an audience of investment professionals, on the latest developments that affect financial and investment decisions. Articles present research on portfolio strategy, mutual funds, ETFs, socially responsible investing, asset allocation, and performance measurement. Recent articles have discussed baby boomers and financial markets; and unexpected capital gains and the stock market performance at the turn of the century. There was also a survey of demographics and performance in the hedge fund industry. For a trade journal with a decidedly scholarly bent, these articles are highly readable, but the audience will still need a good undergraduate background in finance to appreciate them.

2708. The Journal of Portfolio Management: the journal for investment professionals. [ISSN: 0095-4918] 1975. q. USD 489 combined subscription domestic print & online eds.; USD 564 combined subscription foreign print & online eds. Ed(s): Frank Fabozzi. Institutional Investor, Journals, 225 Park Ave S, 7th Fl., New York, NY 10003-1605; info@iijournals.com; http://www.iijournals.com. Illus., index, adv. Sample. Microform: PQC. Online: EBSCO Publishing, EBSCO Host; Florida Center for Library Automation; Gale; OCLC Online Computer Library Center, Inc.; ProQuest LLC (Ann Arbor); H.W. Wilson. *Indexed:* ABIn, ATI, BLI, BPI, JEL, PAIS, SSCI. *Bk. rev.:* Number and length vary. *Aud.:* Ac, Sa.

This journal for investment professionals is particularly helpful to finance and accounting faculty, CFOs, and portfolio managers. Tightly focused articles discuss particular aspects of portfolio management in clearly written layman's terms. Not longer than 20 pages each, recent articles cover topics including corporate bonds, diversification, and asset allocation. Recommended for academic and large public libraries.

Journal of Real Estate Finance and Economics. See Real Estate section.

2709. Kiplinger's Personal Finance. Former titles (until 2000): *Kiplinger's Personal Finance Magazine;* (until 1991): *Changing Times.* [ISSN: 1528-9729] 1947. m. USD 12 domestic; USD 21.50 Canada; USD 27 elsewhere. Ed(s): Knight A Kiplinger, Janet Bodnar. Kiplinger Washington Editors, Inc., 1729 H St, NW, Washington, DC 20006; magazine@kiplinger.com; http://www.kiplinger.com. Illus., index, adv. Circ: 850000 Paid. CD-ROM: ProQuest LLC (Ann Arbor). Microform: NBI; PQC. Online: The Dialog Corporation; EBSCO Publishing, EBSCO Host; Factiva, Inc.; Florida Center for Library Automation; Gale; LexisNexis; Northern Light Technology, Inc.; OCLC Online Computer Library Center, Inc.; ProQuest K-12 Learning Solutions; ProQuest LLC (Ann Arbor); H.W. Wilson. *Indexed:* ABIn, ATI, AgeL, BPI, BRI, CBRI, CINAHL, ConsI, MASUSE, PAIS, RGPR. *Bk. rev.:* Number and length vary. *Aud.:* Ga, Ac, Sa.

Aimed at Everyman, this title presents practical strategies for managing your money and achieving financial security. Articles cover topics ranging from cars, home mortgage options, and money management to spending and consumer advocacy. Regular departments monitor and report on mutual funds, money

market funds, blue chips, and taxes. Personal-interest columns discuss travel, health, personal finances, and family finances. A handful of articles in each issue discuss general concerns related to investing. Special issues evaluate and chart mutual fund performance. The web site provides online access to selected content.

Money. See General Interest section.

2710. Morningstar FundInvestor. Formerly: *Five Star Investor.* [ISSN: 1099-0402] 1998. m. USD 99 domestic; USD 139 in Canada & Mexico; USD 159 elsewhere. Ed(s): Russel Kinnel. Morningstar, Inc., 225 W Wacker Dr, Ste 400, Chicago, IL 60606; http://www.morningstar.com. Circ: 40000 Paid. *Aud.:* Ga, Ac, Sa.

Morningstar produces both (on the one hand) stock and mutual-fund investment newsletters and (on the other) a user-friendly web site with helpful free content that includes fund data, calculators, and market news. The mutual fund title evaluated here comprises monthly issues that contain detailed coverage of the mutual fund industry, including 500 select funds. This publication offers ratings, statistics, and interviews with top financial planners and fund industry leaders, as well as news, updates, and emerging trends in the industry. All public and academic libraries that provide investment information should have this title.

2711. Pensions & Investments: the newspaper of corporate and institutional investing. Former titles: *Pensions and Investment Age; Pensions and Investments.* [ISSN: 1050-4974] 1973. bi-w. USD 239 domestic; USD 255 Canada; USD 325 elsewhere. Ed(s): Elizabeth Karier, Nancy Webman. Crain Communications, Inc., 711 Third Ave, New York, NY 10017-4036; info@crain.com; http://www.crain.com. Illus., index, adv. Sample. Circ: 50000 Paid and controlled. Microform: CIS; PQC. Online: EBSCO Publishing, EBSCO Host; Florida Center for Library Automation; Gale; LexisNexis; Northern Light Technology, Inc.; OCLC Online Computer Library Center, Inc.; ProQuest LLC (Ann Arbor); H.W. Wilson. *Indexed:* ABIn, ATI, BLI, BPI, CWI, LRI, PAIS. *Aud.:* Ga, Ac, Sa.

This weekly newsmagazine for money managers provides information, explanation, analysis, and updates on all aspects of pensions and institutional investments. Regular departments cover news, interviews, opinions, a "Pensions and Investments" index, and updates on newsmakers. The Annual Databook issue includes ranking of top managers and funds, statistics on pensions plans, mutual funds, savings plans, life insurance, and more. Recent feature articles address real estate investment risk in the coming years, the thriving fixed-income market, and concerns around the OTC derivative market.

2712. Risk. [ISSN: 0952-8776] 1987. m. GBP 670; EUR 1005; USD 1341. Ed(s): Nicholas Sawyer. Incisive Media Plc., Haymarket House, 28-29 Haymarket, London, SW1Y 4RX, United Kingdom; customerservices@incisivemedia.com; http://www.incisivemedia.com/. Illus., adv. Sample. Vol. ends: Dec. *Indexed:* ABIn, RiskAb. *Bk. rev.:* Number and length vary. *Aud.:* Ac, Sa.

This journal provides mathematical detail in its discussions of all forms of risk, including currencies, interest rates, equities, commodities, and credit. Issues include a cover story, an organizational profile, an interview, news, and six to eight articles on fund management, options, and brokers. Topics include the credit market, equity derivatives, interest rate swaps, structured credit, and inflation. Reader polls indicate this journal has higher readership among pension fund managers than does either the *Economist* or *Institutional Investor.* Public libraries with supporting demographics and academic libraries with programs in international business, economics, or finance should consider this title for its practitioner-oriented information.

2713. SmartMoney: the Wall Street Journal magazine of personal business. [ISSN: 1069-2851] 1992. m. USD 3.50 newsstand/cover per issue. Ed(s): Edwin A Finn, Fleming Meeks. Dow Jones & Company, 200 Liberty St, New York, NY 10281. Illus., index, adv. Sample. Circ: 800000 Paid. *Indexed:* ASIP, AgeL, BPI. *Aud.:* Ga, Sa.

Along with *Kiplinger's,* this is another very popular name in personal finance. Published by the *Wall Street Journal,* this magazine is full of useful advice on all topics ranging from business travel to planning a wedding. Stock picks, industry analysis, and recommended investment vehicles are included. Feature articles, each several pages in length, provide human-interest stories on issues like debt management, going green, how to retire early, and successful home renovations. There is a good bit of advertising related to investments and high-end consumer products. A good choice for browsing collections in public and academic libraries. The Internet equivalent is also outstanding.

2714. *The Street.com.* 1996. w. USD 229.95. Ed(s): Dave Kansas. TheStreet.com, 14 Wall St, New York, NY 10005; http://www.weissratings.com/. *Aud.:* Ga.

Backed by *The New York Times,* this is one of the more reliable of scores of online financial-advice sites. Since 1996, it has given solid advice based on financial know-how rather than wild guesses about investments. The site provides insights and advice from well-known market watchers, and the first-rate analysis and in-depth articles will be of interest to anyone serious about Wall Street.

2715. *Worth.* Former titles (until May 2006): *Robb Report Worth;* (until 2003): *Worth;* (until 1992): *Investment Vision;* Which incorporated (1985-1991): *Personal Investor.* [ISSN: 1931-9908] 1986. m. USD 40 domestic; USD 50 Canada; USD 80 elsewhere. Ed(s): Matt Purdue, Elizabeth Ritter. CurtCo Robb Media LLC., 29160 Heathercliff Rd, Ste 200, Malibu, CA 90265; http://www.curtco.com. Illus., adv. Circ: 500000. *Indexed:* ASIP, AgeL, FLI. *Bk. rev.:* Number and length vary. *Aud.:* Ga, Ac, Sa.

This personal investing magazine offers a mix of personal and global investment information in a glossy, popular format. But special features on topics like the 250 wealthiest towns in America, handmade fly rods, and the world's best golf course are what lend this title its irresistible "lifestyles of the rich and famous" appeal. The "Personal Pursuits" section covers alternative investments like second homes, automobiles, airplanes, and art. This section also includes lifestyle articles on luxury travel and fine dining. Recommended for browsing collections in public libraries and larger academic libraries.

Scholarly

2716. *Applied Financial Economics.* [ISSN: 0960-3107] 1991. 18x/yr. GBP 1957 print & online eds. Ed(s): Giorgio Valente, Mark P Taylor. Routledge, 4 Park Sq, Milton Park, Abingdon, OX14 4RN, United Kingdom; info@routledge.co.uk; http://www.routledge.com. Illus., index. Refereed. Online: EBSCO Publishing, EBSCO Host; Gale; IngentaConnect; OCLC Online Computer Library Center, Inc.; SwetsWise Online Content. Reprint: PSC. *Indexed:* ABIn, BAS, BPI, IBR, IBSS, IBZ, JEL, RiskAb. *Aud.:* Ac, Sa.

This peer-reviewed journal serves as an international forum for applied research on financial markets (debt, equity, derivatives, foreign exchange) as well as corporate finance, market structure, and related areas. Each issue includes roughly a half-dozen articles, generally about ten pages in length, that focus on both developed markets and developing economies in Central and Eastern Europe. Topics also include econometric techniques as they relate to financial research, forecasting, and the intersection of real and financial economy. Recent articles look at volatility transmission across markets, trade intensity in the Russian stock market, and banks' riskiness over the business cycle. This highly technical journal will be appreciated in academic and research libraries that support graduate programs or finance professionals.

2717. *Applied Mathematical Finance.* [ISSN: 1350-486X] 1994. q. GBP 975 print & online eds. Ed(s): Dr. William Shaw, Dr. Ben Hambly. Routledge, 4 Park Square, Milton Park, Abingdon, OX14 4RN, United Kingdom; info@routledge.co.uk; http://www.routledge.com. Adv. Refereed. Online: EBSCO Publishing, EBSCO Host; Gale; IngentaConnect; OCLC Online Computer Library Center, Inc.; SwetsWise Online Content. Reprint: PSC. *Indexed:* ABIn, IBR, IBZ, JEL. *Aud.:* Ac, Sa.

Aimed at financial practitioners, academics, and applied mathematicians, this title includes 15- to 20-page articles by worldwide academics that are designed to encourage the "confident use" of applied mathematics and mathematical models for finance. Papers cover such topics as economic primitives (interest rates, asset prices, etc.), market behavior, market strategy (such as hedging), financial instruments, reviews of new developments in financial engineering, general mathematical finance, models and algorithms, new products, and reviews of practical tools. Recent articles explore the Levy swap market model, and American options under the variance gamma process.

2718. *F M.* Formerly (until 1988): *Financial Management.* [ISSN: 1087-7827] 1972. q. USD 300 print & online eds. Ed(s): Bill Christie. Blackwell Publishing, Inc., Commerce Place, 350 Main St, Malden, MA 02148; customerservices@blackwellpublishing.com; http://www.blackwellpublishing.com. Illus., index. Refereed. Circ: 12000. Vol. ends: Winter. Microform: PQC. Online: EBSCO Publishing, EBSCO Host; Gale; OCLC Online Computer Library Center, Inc.; ProQuest LLC (Ann Arbor); H.W. Wilson. Reprint: PSC. *Indexed:* ABIn, ATI, BPI, IBSS, JEL, PAIS, RiskAb, SSCI. *Aud.:* Ac, Sa.

This is a core publication for financial management because of its high-quality, often groundbreaking research. Editors include the most widely published scholars in the field, and each volume addresses a variety of topics related to the practical applications and economic aspects of operating large public companies. Articles report the results of empirical and survey research that examines markets, securities, financial leverage, pricing, trading, lease-purchase options, and cash flow. Sources of data are provided, and some articles are presented as tutorials intended for classroom use. Strictly for academic and research libraries.

2719. *Financial Accountability & Management.* [ISSN: 0267-4424] 1985. q. GBP 364 print & online eds. Ed(s): Irvine Lapsley. Blackwell Publishing Ltd., 9600 Garsington Rd, Oxford, OX4 2ZG, United Kingdom; customerservices@blackwellpublishing.com; http://www.blackwellpublishing.com. Adv. Online: Blackwell Synergy; EBSCO Publishing, EBSCO Host; Gale; IngentaConnect; OCLC Online Computer Library Center, Inc.; OhioLINK; SwetsWise Online Content. Reprint: PSC. *Indexed:* ABIn, ATI, BLI, BPI, PAIS, RiskAb. *Aud.:* Ac, Sa.

This interdisciplinary journal draws from the fields of economics, social and public administration, political science, management sciences, accounting, and finance. The focus is on financial accountability, accounting, and financial and resource management for governmental and nonprofit organizations. A recent article discusses organizational culture and the adoption of management accounting practices in the public sector in Singapore. Recommended for libraries that support upper-level public finance programs or professionals.

2720. *Financial History Review.* [ISSN: 0968-5650] 1994. s-a. GBP 96. Ed(s): Duncan M Ross, Stefano Battilossi. Cambridge University Press, The Edinburgh Bldg, Shaftesbury Rd, Cambridge, CB2 2RU, United Kingdom; journals@cambridge.org; http://www.journals.cambridge.org. Illus., adv. Refereed. *Indexed:* AmH&L, BAS, HistAb, IBSS, JEL. *Bk. rev.:* 3-8, signed, 1,000-2,500 words. *Aud.:* Ac.

Founded by the European Association for Banking History, this title serves as a forum for scholars interested in the development of banking and finance. Each issue begins with article abstracts in English, French, German, and Spanish that are followed by several lengthy articles. Recent topics include the Maria Theresa dollar in the early twentieth-century Red Sea region; social and human capital formation in the German banking elite from 1870 to 1990; and the 1927 Bank Law in Japan. Announcements and occasional bibliographies on financial history are included. Libraries with collections in business history will want this title.

2721. *Financial Market Trends.* [ISSN: 0378-651X] 1977. s-a. EUR 105 combined subscription print & online eds.; USD 132 combined subscription print & online eds.; GBP 72 combined subscription print & online eds. Organisation for Economic Cooperation and Development (OECD), 2 Rue Andre Pascal, Paris, 75775 Cedex 16, France; http://www.oecd.org. Illus., index. Vol. ends: Oct. *Indexed:* ABIn, BLI, PAIS. *Aud.:* Ac, Sa.

This journal analyzes trends and developments in financial markets around the world, with special emphasis on Organization for Economic Cooperation and Development (OECD) countries. Each issue has a section in both French and

English that highlights recent trends in financial markets. The remainder of each issue is in English and focuses on structural and regulatory developments in OECD countries. Financial statistics, charts, and graphs are included in each issue. Recent issues include articles on global saving-investment behavior, assessing the impact of pension funds on financial markets, and factors behind low long-term interest rates.

2722. Financial Markets, Institutions and Instruments. Former titles (until 1992): *Monograph Series in Finance and Economics;* (until 1990): *Salomon Brothers Center for the Study of Financial Institutions. Monograph Series; New York University Institute of Finance. Bulletin.* [ISSN: 0963-8008] 1928. 5x/yr. GBP 347 print & online eds. Ed(s): Mary Jaffier, Anthony Saunders. Blackwell Publishing, Inc., Commerce Place, 350 Main St, Malden, MA 02148; customerservices@ blackwellpublishing.com; http://www.blackwellpublishing.com. Illus., adv. Refereed. Online: Blackwell Synergy; EBSCO Publishing, EBSCO Host; Gale; IngentaConnect; OCLC Online Computer Library Center, Inc.; OhioLINK; SwetsWise Online Content. Reprint: PSC. *Indexed:* BLI, IBSS, JEL, RiskAb. *Aud.:* Ac, Sa.

This journal attempts to bridge the gap between the academic and professional finance communities by covering topics that are relevant to both groups. Contributors include both financial practitioners and academics. Each issue has in-depth articles on a single topic, while the year-end issue features the year's most significant developments in corporate finance, money and banking, derivative securities, and fixed-income securities. Recent articles examine the basic analytics of access to financial services, the asset management industry in Asia, and financial intermediaries and interest rate risk. Recommended for academic and corporate libraries.

2723. The Financial Review (Statesboro). Incorporates: *Eastern Finance Association. Proceedings of the Annual Meeting.* [ISSN: 0732-8516] 1966. q. GBP 217 print & online eds. Ed(s): Arnold R Cowan, Cynthia J Campbell. Blackwell Publishing, Inc., Commerce Place, 350 Main St, Malden, MA 02148; customerservices@blackwellpublishing.com; http://www.blackwellpublishing.com. Illus., index, adv. Refereed. Circ: 2000. Vol. ends: Nov (No. 4). Microform: PQC. Online: Blackwell Synergy; EBSCO Publishing, EBSCO Host; Gale; IngentaConnect; OCLC Online Computer Library Center, Inc.; OhioLINK; ProQuest LLC (Ann Arbor); SwetsWise Online Content. Reprint: PSC. *Indexed:* ABIn, ATI, BLI, BPI, JEL, PAIS, RiskAb. *Bk. rev.:* Number and length vary. *Aud.:* Ac, Sa.

This refereed journal of the Eastern Finance Association publishes "empirical, theoretical and methodological articles on topics of micro- and macro-finance." Each issue contains seven to ten articles of 15–50 pages each. Recent issues examine such topics as asymmetric information in the IPO aftermarket, price movement effects on the state of the electronic limit-order book, and reflections on the efficient market hypothesis. Recommended for libraries that support finance programs and researchers.

2724. Foundations and Trends in Finance. [ISSN: 1930-8248] 2005. 4x/yr. USD 345 in the Americas; EUR 345 elsewhere; USD 385 combined subscription in the Americas print & online eds. Ed(s): George Constantinides. Now Publishers Inc., PO Box 1024, Hanover, MA 02339; sales@nowpublishers.com; http://www.nowpublishers.com. Refereed. *Aud.:* Ac, Sa.

Each issue of this scholarly work is essentially a 50- to 100-page monograph, written by a top-tier finance professor or finance professional. The goal is to provide a tutorial and overview of research on a given finance topic. For instance, Terence Lim (Goldman Sachs), Andrew W. Lo (MIT), Robert C. Merton (Harvard University), and Myron S. Scholes (Stanford University) teamed up to create "The Derivatives Sourcebook." This journal is new, but promises to be a great addition to the field as a teaching tool for complex financial concepts.

2725. Global Finance Journal. [ISSN: 1044-0283] 1989. 3x/yr. EUR 399. Ed(s): M. Shahrokhi. Elsevier BV, North-Holland, Sara Burgerhartstraat 25, Amsterdam, 1055 KV, Netherlands; nlinfo-f@elsevier.nl; http://www.elsevier.nl. Illus., index. Refereed. Microform: PQC. Online:

EBSCO Publishing, EBSCO Host; Gale; IngentaConnect; OhioLINK; ScienceDirect; SwetsWise Online Content. *Indexed:* ABIn, BAS, JEL, RiskAb. *Bk. rev.:* 1, 250-500 words. *Aud.:* Ac, Sa.

The School of Business and Administrative Sciences of California State University–Fresno provides the editorial direction of this journal, which focuses on theories and techniques of global finance. With a target audience of academicians and practitioners, the eight to ten articles in each issue are selected for their clarity and practicality. Recent articles cover such topics as limit orders and the intraday behavior of market liquidity, the cross-section of expected stock returns in the Chinese A-share market, and valuing coins as the sum of the underlying asset and a perpetual American put option.

2726. Government Finance Review. Formed by the merger of (197?-1985): *Government Financial Management Resources in Review;* (1926-1985): *Governmental Finance;* Which was formerly (until 1971): *Municipal Finance.* [ISSN: 0883-7856] 1985. bi-m. USD 35. Ed(s): Anne Spray Kinney, Karen Utterback. Government Finance Officers Association, 203 N LaSalle St, Ste 2700, Chicago, IL 60601-1210; Subscriptions@ gfoa.org; http://www.gfoa.org. Illus., index, adv. Circ: 16000 Paid. Microform: PQC. Online: Florida Center for Library Automation; Gale; Northern Light Technology, Inc.; OCLC Online Computer Library Center, Inc.; ProQuest LLC (Ann Arbor); H.W. Wilson. *Indexed:* ABCPolSci, ABIn, ATI, BLI, BPI, LRI, PAIS. *Bk. rev.:* Number and length vary. *Aud.:* Ac, Sa.

The membership magazine of the Government Finance Officers Association of the United States and Canada reflects a broad spectrum of theory and practice in finance and financial management for state and local governments. Recent article topics include public audit committees, the 2007 revision of the Government Auditing Standards, securities litigation, and the risks and rewards of municipal wireless networks. A core title for public finance collections.

2727. International Financial Statistics. [ISSN: 0020-6725] 1948. m. USD 495; USD 65 newsstand/cover. Ed(s): Carol Carson. International Monetary Fund, Publication Services, 700 19th St, NW, Ste 12-607, Washington, DC 20431; publications@imf.org; http://www.imf.org. Circ: 12500. Microform: BHP; CIS; PMC; PQC. *Indexed:* PAIS. *Aud.:* Ac, Sa.

Published by the Statistics Department of the International Monetary Fund, this is considered the "standard source of statistics on all aspects of international and domestic finance." Statistics are presented monthly, quarterly, and annually in tabular form for specific countries, geographic regions, and world aggregates. Current information on exchange rates, money and banking, prices, government finance, and national accounts are just some of the contents of this important source. The annual yearbook features 12 years of annual data (an unfortunate change, since previous yearbooks offered 30 years of data). Academic and large public libraries should consider this title as it is an invaluable source of country financial data.

2728. International Journal of Finance. [ISSN: 1041-2743] 1988. 4x/yr. USD 150 (Individuals, USD 70). Ed(s): Dilip K Ghosh. International Journal of Finance, 206 Rabbit Run Dr, Cherry Hill, NJ 08003. Illus., index, adv. Vol. ends: No. 4. *Aud.:* Ac, Sa.

This journal concentrates on publishing a handful of lengthy articles in each issue that are related to empirical research in the areas of corporate finance, portfolio analysis, institutions, and global finance. Recent examples of the wide variety of topics include the impact of the Iraq war on emerging markets' bond prices, and intangible investments and the cost of equity capital. Authors are scholars and researchers from many countries. Academic libraries that support programs in international business or finance should consider this title.

2729. International Journal of Finance and Economics. [ISSN: 1076-9307] 1996. q. USD 735 print or online ed. Ed(s): Mark P Taylor, Michael P Dooley. John Wiley & Sons Ltd., The Atrium, Southern Gate, Chichester, PO19 8SQ, United Kingdom; customer@wiley.co.uk; http://www.wiley.co.uk. Illus., adv. Refereed. Vol. ends: Dec. Reprint: PSC. *Indexed:* ABIn, BLI, JEL, SSCI. *Bk. rev.:* 1, signed, 5,000 words. *Aud.:* Ac, Sa.

Each issue includes a small number of lengthy articles on topics related to some aspect of international finance. Each article has a 500-word non-technical abstract. Occasionally, an article will be published that is academically rigorous but less technical. The content of this journal appears to be more empirical than theoretical; it is positioned as a step between practitioner and theoretical titles that focus on similar content. Recent article topics include historical origins of U.S. exchange market intervention policy, central bank intervention and exchange rate volatility, and an empirical model for daily highs and lows of U.S. stock indexes. Although pricey, this title is appropriate for international finance collections in larger libraries.

2730. *International Review of Economics & Finance.* [ISSN: 1059-0560] 1991. 4x/yr. EUR 375. Ed(s): C. R. Chen, H. Beladi. Elsevier BV, North-Holland, Sara Burgerhartstraat 25, Amsterdam, 1055 KV, Netherlands; nlinfo-f@elsevier.nl; http://www.elsevier.nl. Illus., index. Refereed. Microform: PQC. Online: EBSCO Publishing, EBSCO Host; Gale; IngentaConnect; OhioLINK; ScienceDirect; SwetsWise Online Content. *Indexed:* ABIn, BAS, BLI, JEL. *Bk. rev.:* Number and length vary. *Aud.:* Ac, Sa.

This journal presents a truly global perspective in empirical and theoretical papers on financial and market economics. Articles in recent issues explore trade theory and the role of time zones, synthetic money, and sovereign bond markets with political risk and moral hazard. The half-dozen lengthy articles in each issue require a working knowledge of statistics to be fully appreciated. Libraries that support finance students and professionals will want to consider this title.

2731. *International Review of Financial Analysis.* [ISSN: 1057-5219] 1991. 5x/yr. EUR 399. Ed(s): L Nail, J A Batten. Elsevier BV, North-Holland, Sara Burgerhartstraat 25, Amsterdam, 1055 KV, Netherlands; nlinfo-f@elsevier.nl; http://www.elsevier.nl. Illus., index. Refereed. Microform: PQC. Online: EBSCO Publishing, EBSCO Host; Gale; IngentaConnect; OhioLINK; ScienceDirect; SwetsWise Online Content. *Indexed:* ABIn, BAS, BLI, JEL. *Aud.:* Ac, Sa.

This journal is focused primarily on exploring international financial markets from a "broad spectrum of cultural, spatial, institutional, historical, regulatory, and methodological" perspectives to advance the understanding of finance. Recent topics include the co-movement of U.S. and German bond markets, evidence of an asymmetry in the relationship between volatility and autocorrelation, and whether ownership structure affects value. This heavyweight title will support graduate and research programs in finance.

2732. *Journal of Applied Corporate Finance.* Formerly: *Continental Bank Journal of Applied Corporate Finance.* [ISSN: 1078-1196] 1988. q. GBP 218 print & online eds. Ed(s): Donald H Chew, Jr. Blackwell Publishing, Inc., Commerce Place, 350 Main St, Malden, MA 02148; customerservices@blackwellpublishing.com; http://www.blackwellpublishing.com. Illus., index. Refereed. Vol. ends: No. 4. Reprint: PSC. *Indexed:* ATI, BLI, RiskAb. *Aud.:* Ac, Sa.

This journal covers topics related to restructurings, global competition, capital management, financial innovation, and corporate governance. Each issue centers on a theme and contains 8–12 substantive articles. Recent topics include international corporate governance, private equity, value-based management, and corporate risk.

2733. *Journal of Applied Finance: theory, practice, education.* Formerly (until 2001): *Financial Practice and Education.* [ISSN: 1534-6668] 1991. s-a. USD 40 (Individual members, USD 95). Ed(s): Raj Aggrawal. Financial Management Association International, University of South Florida, College of Business Administration, Ste 3331, Tampa, FL 33620-5500; fma@coba.usf.edu; http://www.fma.org. Adv. Refereed. Circ: 4500. Online: EBSCO Publishing, EBSCO Host; OCLC Online Computer Library Center, Inc.; ProQuest LLC (Ann Arbor). *Indexed:* ABIn, BAS, BLI, JEL. *Aud.:* Ac, Sa.

This journal focuses on the theory, practice, and education of finance. Lengthy scholarly articles are geared to practitioners. Recent article topics include

corporate governance, shareholder rights, and manager characteristics and hedge fund performance. Recommended for academic libraries that support finance programs.

2734. *Journal of Banking & Finance.* Incorporates (1985-1989): *Studies in Banking and Finance.* [ISSN: 0378-4266] 1977. 12x/yr. EUR 2550. Ed(s): G. P. Szegoe. Elsevier BV, North-Holland, Sara Burgerhartstraat 25, Amsterdam, 1055 KV, Netherlands; nlinfo-f@elsevier.nl; http://www.elsevier.nl. Illus., index, adv. Sample. Refereed. Vol. ends: Dec. Microform: PQC. Online: EBSCO Publishing, EBSCO Host; Gale; IngentaConnect; OhioLINK; ScienceDirect; SwetsWise Online Content. *Indexed:* ABIn, ATI, BAS, BLI, BPI, IBSS, JEL, PAIS, RiskAb, SSCI. *Bk. rev.:* Number and length vary. *Aud.:* Ac, Sa.

This journal aims to provide a platform for scholarly research that concerns financial institutions and the capital markets in which they function. Many of this journal's issues contain a special section of five or six themed articles and an additional seven to ten regular papers on topics related to financial institutions, money, and capital markets. The editorial board includes top U.S. and international finance faculty as well as some practitioners, mainly from the U.S. Federal Reserve system. Recent articles discuss globalization in emerging economies, market returns, and momentum strategies in commodity futures markets. Although expensive, this is an important title for academic and research collections to consider.

2735. *The Journal of Derivatives.* [ISSN: 1074-1240] 1993. q. USD 395 combined subscription domestic print & online eds.; USD 470 combined subscription foreign print & online eds. Ed(s): Stephen Figlewski. Institutional Investor, Journals, 225 Park Ave S, 7th Fl., New York, NY 10003-1605; info@iijournals.com; http://www.iijournals.com. Illus., index, adv. *Indexed:* ABIn, BLI, BPI, JEL. *Aud.:* Ac, Sa.

Aimed at bridging the gap between academic theory and practice, this title is marketed as the only journal that focuses exclusively on derivatives. Readers need to be well versed in mathematics. Articles range from 10 to 20 pages in length, include charts and graphs, and offer analysis and evaluative commentary on all aspects of the use of derivatives: hedging, management of foreign exchange risk, maximization of transaction costs, measuring swap exposures on a balance sheet, comparison of price models, evaluation of new products, embedded options, arbitrage between cash and futures markets, and similar themes. Recent issues discuss an algorithm for simulating Bermudan option prices on simulated asset prices; calibration risk for exotic options; and a closed-form approach to the valuation and hedging of basket and spread options. This journal is suitable for libraries that support graduate finance programs or for finance professionals.

2736. *Journal of Emerging Market Finance.* [ISSN: 0972-6527] 2002. 3x/yr. GBP 150. Ed(s): Shubhashis Gangopadhyay. Sage Publications India Pvt. Ltd., M-32 Market, Greater Kailash-I, PO Box 4215, New Delhi, 110 048, India; editors@indiasage.com; http://www.indiasage.com/. Refereed. Reprint: PSC. *Indexed:* RiskAb. *Aud.:* Ac.

This journal aims to highlight the theory and practice of finance in emerging markets. Emphasis is on articles that are of practical significance, but the journal covers theoretical and conceptual topics as well. Recent articles examine market efficiency as seen in evidence from the Athens Stock Exchange, the inefficiency of banks in India, and regional integration of stock markets in MENA countries. Academic libraries that support global finance programs should consider this title.

2737. *The Journal of Finance.* [ISSN: 0022-1082] 1946. bi-m. GBP 320 print & online eds. Ed(s): Robert F Stambaugh. Blackwell Publishing, Inc., Commerce Place, 350 Main St, Malden, MA 02148; customerservices@blackwellpublishing.com; http://www.blackwellpublishing.com. Illus., index, adv. Sample. Refereed. Circ: 8000. Vol. ends: Dec. Microform: MIM; PQC. Online: Blackwell Synergy; EBSCO Publishing, EBSCO Host; Gale; IngentaConnect;

JSTOR (Web-based Journal Archive); OCLC Online Computer Library Center, Inc.; OhioLINK; SwetsWise Online Content. Reprint: PSC. *Indexed:* ABIn, ATI, BLI, BPI, BRI, CBRI, IBR, IBSS, IBZ, JEL, MathR, PAIS, RiskAb, SSCI. *Bk. rev.:* 3-4, 1,500-2,000 words. *Aud.:* Ac, Sa.

This is the official publication of the American Finance Association and is a core publication for business collections. It is one of the most highly regarded and widely cited academic journals in finance and economics. A single issue generally includes six to ten feature articles of 20–50 pages in length plus six to ten shorter papers that report on original scholarly research, in addition to announcements, commentaries, and lectures. This journal highlights research from all major fields of financial research. Recent articles examine corporate ownership, global growth opportunities and market integration, and reputation effects in trading on the NYSE.

2738. *Journal of Financial and Quantitative Analysis.* [ISSN: 0022-1090] 1966. q. USD 150 (Individuals, USD 70; Students, USD 25). Ed(s): Paul Malatesta, Hank Bessembinder. University of Washington, School of Business Administration, 115 Lewis Hall, Box 353200, Seattle, WA 981953200. Illus., index, adv. Refereed. Circ: 3200 Paid. Vol. ends: Dec. Microform: PQC. Online: EBSCO Publishing, EBSCO Host; JSTOR (Web-based Journal Archive); ProQuest LLC (Ann Arbor). Reprint: SCH. *Indexed:* ABIn, ATI, BLI, BPI, IBR, IBSS, IBZ, JEL, LibLit, PAIS, SSCI. *Aud.:* Ac, Sa.

Theoretical and empirical research on corporate finance, investments, financial markets, and related concepts are approached from a quantitative perspective in this academic journal. Recent articles discuss why some firms de-list from major exchanges, the impact of overnight periods on option pricing, and IPOs of state-owned enterprises. As articles tend to be data-heavy, knowledge of finance and statistics is needed to fully appreciate this journal. Academic libraries with extensive programs in finance should consider this title.

2739. *Journal of Financial Economics.* [ISSN: 0304-405X] 1974. 12x/yr. EUR 2058. Ed(s): G. William Schwert. Elsevier BV, North-Holland, Sara Burgerhartstraat 25, Amsterdam, 1055 KV, Netherlands; nlinfo-f@elsevier.nl; http://www.elsevier.nl. Illus., index, adv. Sample. Refereed. Vol. ends: No. 2. Microform: PQC. Online: EBSCO Publishing, EBSCO Host; Gale; IngentaConnect; OhioLINK; ScienceDirect; SwetsWise Online Content. *Indexed:* ABIn, ATI, BPI, IBSS, JEL, RiskAb, SSCI. *Bk. rev.:* Number and length vary. *Aud.:* Ac, Sa.

The focus of this journal is on reports of analytical, empirical, or clinical research in capital markets, corporate finance, corporate governance, and economics of organizations and financial institutions. Feature articles are usually 15–50 pages long. Recent articles cover executive stock options and IPO underpricing, geographical segmentation of U.S. capital markets, and portfolio manager ownership and fund performance. Large academic libraries with graduate programs in finance and economics may be the only ones that will want to invest in this costly journal.

2740. *Journal of Financial Education.* Formerly (until 1973): *Financial Education.* [ISSN: 0093-3961] 1972. q. Free to members. Finance Education Association, c/o Dept of Finance, Haub School of Business, Philadelphia, PA 19131; http://www.fea.sju.edu. Adv. Refereed. Circ: 800. *Aud.:* Ac.

The *Journal of Financial Education* is devoted to promoting financial education through publication of articles that focus on educational research, creative pedagogy, and curriculum development. Each peer-reviewed issue contains a case study, lengthy articles that focus on finance pedagogy, and educational research. Recent topics include the undergraduate finance curriculum in the new millennium; distance education and M.B.A. student performance; and teaching Excel VBA to finance students. Libraries that support graduate and undergraduate business programs should consider adding this title to their collection.

2741. *Journal of Financial Intermediation.* [ISSN: 1042-9573] 1990. 4x/yr. EUR 521. Ed(s): Anjan V Thakor. Academic Press, 525 B St, Ste 1900, San Diego, CA 92101-4495; apsubs@acad.com; http://www.elsevier.com/. Illus. Refereed. Online: EBSCO Publishing,

EBSCO Host; Gale; IngentaConnect; OCLC Online Computer Library Center, Inc.; OhioLINK; ScienceDirect; SwetsWise Online Content. *Indexed:* ABIn, BLI, IBSS, JEL, SSCI. *Aud.:* Ac, Sa.

The focus of this title is on the design of financial contracts and institutions. Research topics have included the theory of financial intermediation; informational bases for the design of financial contracts; the role of insurance firms in influencing allocations and the efficiency of market equilibrium; the economics of financial engineering; and interactions between real and financial decisions. Articles are 20–30 pages in length, and recent issues include articles on financial contracting, venture capital investments, loan pricing, and repurchase agreements. This journal would be appropriate for large public libraries that serve educated investors and for many academic libraries.

2742. *Journal of Financial Research.* [ISSN: 0270-2592] 1978. q. GBP 285 print & online eds. Ed(s): William T Moore. Blackwell Publishing, Inc., Commerce Place, 350 Main St, Malden, MA 02148; customerservices@blackwellpublishing.com; http://www.blackwellpublishing.com. Illus., index, adv. Sample. Refereed. Circ: 1900 Paid. Microform: PQC. Online: Blackwell Synergy; EBSCO Publishing, EBSCO Host; Florida Center for Library Automation; Gale; IngentaConnect; Northern Light Technology, Inc.; OCLC Online Computer Library Center, Inc.; OhioLINK; SwetsWise Online Content; H.W. Wilson. Reprint: PSC. *Indexed:* ABIn, ATI, BPI, JEL, RiskAb, SSCI. *Bk. rev.:* Number and length vary. *Aud.:* Ac, Sa.

This journal presents original research in investment and portfolio management, capital markets and institutions, and corporate finance, corporate governance, and capital investment. Each issue contains eight to ten articles that are 15–20 pages long. Recent topics include evidence on the compensation of portfolio managers; price and volume effects of a pure ticker symbol change; and the importance of liquidity as a factor in asset pricing. Large academic libraries that support finance programs and public libraries that serve educated investors should consider this title.

2743. *Journal of Financial Services Research.* [ISSN: 0920-8550] 1987. bi-m. EUR 743 print & online eds. Ed(s): Haluk Unal. Springer New York LLC, 233 Spring St, New York, NY 10013-1578; service-ny@springer.com; http://www.springer.com/. Illus., index, adv. Sample. Refereed. Vol. ends: Oct. Microform: PQC. Online: EBSCO Publishing, EBSCO Host; Gale; IngentaConnect; OCLC Online Computer Library Center, Inc.; OhioLINK; ProQuest LLC (Ann Arbor); Springer LINK; SwetsWise Online Content. Reprint: PSC. *Indexed:* ABIn, BLI, IBSS, JEL, RiskAb, SSCI. *Aud.:* Ac, Sa.

The focus of this title is on theoretical and applied microeconomic analysis specifically related to financial markets and institutions. Papers cover original research on private and public policy questions that arise from the evolution of the financial-services sector. Topics in recent issues include the evaluation of subjectivity in incentive pay, determinants of equity style, and the role and impact of financial advisors on the market for municipal bonds. Libraries that support economics and finance professionals or graduate programs should consider this specialized title.

2744. *The Journal of Fixed Income.* [ISSN: 1059-8596] 1991. q. USD 510 combined subscription domestic print & online eds.; USD 585 combined subscription foreign print & online eds. Ed(s): Stanley J Kon. Institutional Investor, Journals, 225 Park Ave S, 7th Fl., New York, NY 10003-1605; info@iijournals.com; http://www.iijournals.com. Illus., index, adv. *Indexed:* ABIn, ATI, BPI. *Aud.:* Ac, Sa.

The associate editors are mostly academics from prestigious universities but also professionals from investment firms and other financial journals. Each issue contains six to ten articles, each about 20 pages long, that report original applied research on all aspects of fixed-income investing. Articles discuss market conditions and methods of analysis of a variety of fixed-income investments. Recent articles discuss the recent bond market; a case study on default and recovery rates of sovereign bonds; and valuing fixed-rate mortgage loans with default and prepayment options. Libraries that support graduate finance programs or investment professionals should consider this title.

2745. The Journal of Futures Markets. [ISSN: 0270-7314] 1981. m. USD 1933. Ed(s): Robert I Webb. John Wiley & Sons, Inc., 111 River St, Hoboken, NJ 07030-5774; uscs-wis@wiley.com; http://www.wiley.com. Illus., index, adv. Sample. Refereed. Circ: 1100. Vol. ends: Dec. Reprint: PSC. *Indexed:* ABIn, ATI, BLI, BPI, IBSS, JEL, PAIS, RiskAb, SSCI. *Aud.:* Ac, Sa.

Each issue of this journal focuses on futures, options, and other derivatives. Recent topics include the information content of option-implied volatility surrounding the 1997 Hong Kong stock market crash; a simplified approach to modeling the co-movement of asset returns; and long memory models for daily and high-frequency commodity futures returns. Articles include charts and tables. Recommended for academic and research libraries that support finance programs.

2746. Journal of International Financial Management and Accounting. [ISSN: 0954-1314] 1988. 3x/yr. GBP 371 print & online eds. Ed(s): Richard Levich, Frederick Choi. Blackwell Publishing Ltd., 9600 Garsington Rd, Oxford, OX4 2ZG, United Kingdom; customerservices@blackwellpublishing.com; http://www.blackwellpublishing.com. Illus. Refereed. Circ: 600. Online: Blackwell Synergy; EBSCO Publishing, EBSCO Host; Gale; IngentaConnect; OCLC Online Computer Library Center, Inc.; OhioLINK; SwetsWise Online Content. Reprint: PSC. *Indexed:* ABIn, ATI, BPI, IBSS, RiskAb. *Bk. rev.:* 1, 1,500 words. *Aud.:* Ac, Sa.

Each issue contains three to five original research articles, each 20–30 pages long, on topics related to international aspects of financial management and reporting, banking and financial services, auditing, and taxation. Issues sometimes include an "Executive Perspective" (written by a practitioner), a case, comments concerning earlier papers, or a book review. Recent articles discuss the introduction of the Euro and use of derivatives in French firms; analysts' forecasts in Asian-Pacific markets; and "after the 'Bubble'": valuation of telecommunications companies by financial analysts. Libraries that support finance programs and professionals may want to consider this specialized title.

2747. Journal of International Money and Finance. [ISSN: 0261-5606] 1982. 8x/yr. EUR 1090. Ed(s): Michael T Melvin, James R Lothian. Pergamon, The Boulevard, Langford Ln, East Park, Kidlington, OX5 1GB, United Kingdom. Illus., index. Refereed. Vol. ends: Dec. Microform: PQC. Online: EBSCO Publishing, EBSCO Host; Gale; IngentaConnect; OhioLINK; ScienceDirect; SwetsWise Online Content. *Indexed:* ABIn, BLI, IBSS, JEL, PAIS, RiskAb, SSCI. *Bk. rev.:* Number and length vary. *Aud.:* Ac, Sa.

This publication presents research in all areas of international finance, monetary economics, and the increasing overlap between the two. Topics include foreign exchange; balance of payments; international markets; fiscal policy; foreign aid; and international economic institutions. Articles in recent issues discuss global price dispersion; trade liberalization; capital controls, capital flow contractions, and macroeconomic vulnerability; and financial globalization and integration. Each article is roughly 15–30 pages long. The scope of this journal makes it an appropriate choice for academic and research libraries.

2748. Journal of Investment Management. [ISSN: 1545-9144] 2003. q. USD 250 combined subscription domestic print & online; USD 275 combined subscription foreign print & online. Ed(s): H. Gifford Fong. Stallion Press, 3658 Mt. Diablo Blvd. Ste. 200, Lafayette, CA 94549. Refereed. Circ: 13000. *Indexed:* ABIn. *Bk. rev.:* 1-2, 500 words. *Aud.:* Ac, Sa.

This journal features a Nobel-laureate–studded advisory board and editors from the top tier of industry and academia. The journal aims to have multiple categories of presentation, including "Insights," written by leading authorities; "Working papers," where high-quality manuscripts are reviewed; and "Book reviews," which provide a discussion of new and noteworthy books. The journal's mission is to maximize the understanding and use of the material for the practitioner and student through rigorous editorial and presentation standards. An excellent choice for academic and special libraries that support investment management programs and professionals.

2749. Managerial Finance. [ISSN: 0307-4358] 1975. m. EUR 7159 combined subscription in Europe print & online eds.; USD 7999 combined subscription in North America print & online eds.; AUD 6779 combined subscription in Australasia print & online eds. Ed(s): Don T Johnson. Emerald Group Publishing Limited, Howard House, Wagon Ln, Bingley, BD16 1WA, United Kingdom; information@emeraldinsight.com; http://www.emeraldinsight.com. Sample. Refereed. Circ: 400. Reprint: PSC. *Indexed:* ABIn, ATI, PAIS. *Aud.:* Ac, Sa.

If price is not an issue, this is a solid financial management title. Each issue deals with a particular topic such as capital structure, MENA markets, real estate investing, and managing risk. Recommended for libraries that support finance programs that are international in scope.

2750. Mathematical Finance: an international journal of mathematics, statistics and financial economics. [ISSN: 0960-1627] 1991. q. GBP 763 print & online eds. Ed(s): Robert A Jarrow. Blackwell Publishing, Inc., Commerce Place, 350 Main St, Malden, MA 02148; customerservices@blackwellpublishing.com; http://www.blackwellpublishing.com. Illus., index, adv. Sample. Refereed. Circ: 800. Vol. ends: Oct. Online: Blackwell Synergy; EBSCO Publishing, EBSCO Host; Gale; IngentaConnect; OCLC Online Computer Library Center, Inc.; OhioLINK; SwetsWise Online Content. Reprint: PSC. *Indexed:* ABIn, ATI, CCMJ, IBSS, JEL, MSN, MathR, SCI, SSCI. *Bk. rev.:* 0-2, 250-500 words. *Aud.:* Ac, Sa.

This publication aims to provide a bridge between mathematical scientists and economists. Each issue brings together work on the mathematical aspects of finance theory from such diverse fields as finance, economics, mathematics, and statistics. Recent topics include stock loans, the theory and calibration of swap market models, and the duality in optimal investment and consumption problems with market frictions. Libraries that support research in finance and economics should consider this title.

2751. Public Finance Review. Formerly (until 1997): *Public Finance Quarterly.* [ISSN: 1091-1421] 1973. bi-m. GBP 498. Ed(s): James Alm. Sage Publications, Inc., 2455 Teller Rd, Thousand Oaks, CA 91320; info@sagepub.com; http://www.sagepub.com. Illus., adv. Refereed. Circ: 800 Paid. Microform: PQC. Online: EBSCO Publishing, EBSCO Host; Florida Center for Library Automation; Gale; HighWire Press; OCLC Online Computer Library Center, Inc.; SAGE Publications, Inc., SAGE Journals Online; SwetsWise Online Content. Reprint: PSC. *Indexed:* ABIn, ASG, ATI, AgeL, IBSS, JEL, PAIS, PSA, RiskAb, SSCI, SUSA. *Bk. rev.:* Number and length vary. *Aud.:* Ac, Sa.

This scholarly journal explores the theory, policy, and institutions related to the allocation, distribution, and stabilization functions within the public sector of the economy. Each issue includes five lengthy articles in which authors present theoretical and empirical studies of the positive or normative aspects of (primarily) U.S. federal, state, and local government policies. Recent article topics include accounting for spatial error correlation in the 2004 presidential popular vote; criminal investigation enforcement activities and taxpayer noncompliance; and Medicaid's nursing home coverage and asset transfers. Academic libraries that support programs in public administration and finance should consider this title.

2752. Quantitative Finance. [ISSN: 1469-7688] 2001. bi-m. GBP 856 print & online eds. Ed(s): Michael Dempster, Jean-Philippe Bouchaud. Routledge, 4 Park Sq, Milton Park, Abingdon, OX14 4RN, United Kingdom; journals@routledge.com; http://www.routledge.com. Adv. Sample. Refereed. Reprint: PSC. *Indexed:* ABIn, CCMJ, JEL, MSN, MathR, SCI, SSCI. *Bk. rev.:* Number and length vary. *Aud.:* Ac, Sa.

This interdisciplinary journal presents original research that reflects the increasing use of quantitative methods in the field of finance. Just a few of the applications covered in this journal are experimental finance, price formation, trading systems, corporate valuation, risk management, and econometrics. Recent topics include volatility-induced financial growth; scenario-generation methods for an optimal public debt strategy; and dynamic consumption and asset allocation with derivative securities. This journal has a well-respected editorial board from universities and research institutions around the world, and this fact makes this journal a good pick to add depth to quantitative areas in finance collections of research libraries.

2753. The Review of Financial Studies. [ISSN: 0893-9454] 1988. bi-m. EUR 318 (academic) print or online ed. Corporations, EUR 855 print or online ed.). Ed(s): Matthew Spiegel. Oxford University Press, Great Clarendon St, Oxford, OX2 6DP, United Kingdom; jnl.orders@ oup.co.uk; http://www.oxfordjournals.org. Illus., adv. Refereed. Circ: 2750. Online: EBSCO Publishing, EBSCO Host; Gale; HighWire Press; IngentaConnect; JSTOR (Web-based Journal Archive); OCLC Online Computer Library Center, Inc.; OhioLINK; Oxford Journals; ProQuest LLC (Ann Arbor); SwetsWise Online Content. Reprint: PSC. *Indexed:* ABIn, AgeL, BLI, IBSS, JEL, RiskAb, SSCI. *Bk. rev.:* 1, signed, 1,000-2,500 words. *Aud.:* Ac, Sa.

This scholarly journal presents a balance of new theoretical and empirical research in the form of 10–12 lengthy articles. Recent papers examine concepts such as stock return predictability, open market activity, portfolio selection, options and bubbles, and the transmission of information across international equity markets. Academic libraries should consider this a core finance title.

2754. Review of Quantitative Finance and Accounting. [ISSN: 0924-865X] 1991. 8x/yr. EUR 996 print & online eds. Ed(s): Cheng-few Lee. Springer New York LLC, 233 Spring St, New York, NY 10013-1578; service-ny@springer.com; http://www.springer.com/. Illus., adv. Sample. Refereed. Vol. ends: No. 4. Microform: PQC. Online: EBSCO Publishing, EBSCO Host; Gale; IngentaConnect; OCLC Online Computer Library Center, Inc.; OhioLINK; ProQuest LLC (Ann Arbor); Springer LINK; SwetsWise Online Content. Reprint: PSC. *Indexed:* ABIn, ATI, BLI, IBR, IBSS, IBZ, JEL, RiskAb. *Aud.:* Ac, Sa.

The focus of this title is on quantitative theoretical and methodological research and empirical applications. Major themes trace the interaction of finance, accounting, economics, and quantitative methods. Recent articles discuss analysts' forecast revisions and firms' research and development expenses, interday and intraday volatility, and pricing futures on geometric indexes. Since a strong background in mathematics and economic statistics is required to understand these articles, only specialists and research libraries should consider this journal for purchase.

Trade Journals

2755. A F P Exchange. Former titles (until 1999): *T M A Journal (Treasury Management Association); (until Jan. 1994): Journal of Cash Management.* [ISSN: 1528-4077] 1981. bi-m. Individuals, USD 90; Individual members, USD 120. Ed(s): Christy Kincade, John T Hiatt. Association for Financial Professionals, 7315 Wisconsin Ave, Ste 600 W, Bethesda, MD 20814; AFP@AFPonline.org; http://www.AFPonline.org. Illus., index, adv. Sample. Circ: 15000. Vol. ends: No. 6. *Indexed:* ABIn, ATI, BLI, BPI, RiskAb. *Bk. rev.:* Number and length vary. *Aud.:* Ac, Sa.

Certified cash managers and certified public accountants are among the contributors to this association publication, which provides timely, practical information and advice to cash managers in corporations and governments. Regular departments and columns provide a legislative watch, a career section, a buyer's guide, and current news. Recent features include discussions of limiting liquidity risk, cash flow forecasting, and a report on a U.S. Treasury conference that featured top U.S. economists such as Greenspan, Volker, and Paulson. This practitioner's magazine serves as a good introduction and updating service for those interested in government, corporate, and global cash management.

2756. Business Credit. Formerly: *Credit and Financial Management.* [ISSN: 0897-0181] 1898. 10x/yr. USD 54. Ed(s): Caroline Zimmerman. National Association of Credit Management, 8840 Columbia 100 Pkwy, Columbia, MD 21045; http://www.nacm.org. Illus., index, adv. Sample. Circ: 24000 Controlled. Vol. ends: Dec. Microform: PQC. Online: EBSCO Publishing, EBSCO Host; Factiva, Inc.; Florida Center for Library Automation; Gale; Northern Light Technology, Inc.; OCLC Online Computer Library Center, Inc.; ProQuest LLC (Ann Arbor); H.W. Wilson. *Indexed:* ABIn, ATI, BLI, BPI, LRI. *Aud.:* Ac, Sa.

The target audience of this title is the corporate credit and financial professional, with additional emphasis on company finance in general. Each issue includes news on relevant issues, such as legislation, loss prevention, collections, and

technology. Several feature articles present insights on such topics as how to get paid by delinquent customers on the verge of bankruptcy, taking chances on restructuring firms, and fostering an ethical culture in the wake of scandal. Columns on international issues and on professionals at work as well as member profiles present a global yet personalized approach to industry issues. Articles in the international-affairs section give insight into the global-industry environment.

2757. Buyouts. [ISSN: 1040-0990] 1987. bi-w. 25/yr. USD 1845 in US & Canada. Ed(s): David Toll. Thomson Financial, 195 Broadway, New York, NY 10007; http://www.thomsonfinancial.com. *Indexed:* ABIn, CWI. *Aud.:* Ac, Sa.

This trade journal covers news, commentary, data and analysis of leveraged buyouts, managed buyouts, and special situations. In addition to broad coverage of industry news, each issue analyzes a recent deal and features an interview with a key industry player. A recent cover story features LBO and venture capital firms coming together in high-tech deals. Although it is most appropriate for collections that support buyout professionals and graduate business programs, larger business libraries may want to consider this title.

2758. Financial Analysts Journal. [ISSN: 0015-198X] 1945. bi-m. USD 250 domestic print & online eds. Ed(s): Richard M Ennis. C F A Institute, 560 Ray C Hunt Drive, Charlottesville, VA 22903; http://www.cfainstitute.org. Illus., index, adv. Sample. Circ: 40000. Vol. ends: Nov/Dec. Microform: PQC. Online: EBSCO Publishing, EBSCO Host; Northern Light Technology, Inc.; OCLC Online Computer Library Center, Inc.; ProQuest LLC (Ann Arbor). *Indexed:* ABIn, ATI, BPI, IBSS, PAIS, SSCI. *Bk. rev.:* 1-2, 500 words. *Aud.:* Ac, Sa.

Each issue of this title, which is aimed at academicians and practitioners, contains nearly a dozen articles of varying length on financial and investment analysis. Primary emphasis is on valuation, portfolio management, market structure, market behavior, and professional conduct and ethics. Articles also involve accounting, economics, and securities law and regulations. Recent issues include articles on FASB's quick fix for pension accounting, interest rate swaps, and understanding changes in corporate credit spreads. Association content, such as speeches, commentary, and association policy statements, is also included. The editorial board has representatives from highly respected universities and capital management firms. This is a well-regarded title for academic or public libraries that support finance programs or financial analysts.

2759. Financial Executive: for today's global business leader. Former titles (until 1987): *F E: The Magazine for Financial Executives;* (until Jan. 1985): *Financial Executive; Controller.* [ISSN: 0895-4186] 1932. 10x/yr. USD 59 domestic; USD 79 foreign. Ed(s): Jeffrey Marshall, Ellen M. Heffes. Financial Executives International, P.O. Box 674, Florham Park, NJ 07932; http://www.fei.org. Illus., index, adv. Sample. Circ: 17000 Paid. Microform: PQC. Online: The Dialog Corporation; EBSCO Publishing, EBSCO Host; Florida Center for Library Automation; Gale; Northern Light Technology, Inc.; OCLC Online Computer Library Center, Inc.; ProQuest LLC (Ann Arbor); H.W. Wilson. *Indexed:* ABIn, ATI, AgeL, BPI, PAIS. *Bk. rev.:* Number and length vary. *Aud.:* Ac, Sa.

This title targets senior management, particularly chief financial officers. Topics address evolving financial, economic, strategic, and technological trends. Recent articles focus on common mistakes to avoid when selling a private company, turning diversity into a competitive advantage, and companies that eschew top-down finance controls in favor of a new system of budgeting and decision-making. Although aimed at the CFOs of large corporations, many medium-size businesses doing business overseas and businesses without a CFO will benefit from the practical information contained in these pages. Public libraries that serve medium-size to large businesses and academic libraries with programs in finance should consider this title.

2760. FinancialWeek. [ISSN: 1934-2888] 2006. w. USD 79 domestic; USD 149 Canada; USD 199 elsewhere. Crain Communications, Inc., 711 Third Ave, New York, NY 10017-4036; info@crain.com; http://www.crain.com. Adv. Circ: 55000 Controlled. *Aud.:* Ga, Ac, Sa.

This glossy trade publication is a nice addition to the finance field as it has news for finance professionals across the spectrum of industries and functional specialties. Published by Crain Communications, of regional business journal fame, this new title provides the same newsy tone for a national audience. The web version is nicely done and worth using. This journal will get public as well as academic and research library users up-to-speed on national and local happenings in the corporate finance arena that will affect businesses.

2761. *Global Finance.* [ISSN: 0896-4181] 1987. m. USD 375. Ed(s): Paolo Panerai, Dan Keeler. Global Finance Media, Inc., 411 Fifth Ave., 7th Fl, New York, NY 10016. Illus., adv. Circ: 50000 Controlled. Vol. ends: Dec. *Indexed:* ABIn, BLI, PAIS. *Aud.:* Ga, Ac, Sa.

Targeting corporate executives and institutional investors, this magazine features news and analysis of corporate finance, mergers and acquisitions, capital markets, banking, risk management, money management, investor relations, and other topics relevant to the global marketplace. The corporate finance news section covers foreign exchange, mergers and acquisitions, global ADRs, and corporate bonds. Recent feature article topics include a special report on new Arab economies in the Middle East, the annual ranking of the top developed market banks (April issue), and the rise of corporate social responsibility. This is a good title for libraries that support international finance programs and professionals.

2762. *Journal of Business Finance & Accounting.* [ISSN: 0306-686X] 1974. 10x/yr. GBP 821 print & online eds. Ed(s): P F Pope, M Walker. Blackwell Publishing Ltd., 9600 Garsington Rd, Oxford, OX4 2ZG, United Kingdom; customerservices@blackwellpublishing.com; http://www.blackwellpublishing.com. Illus., index, adv. Refereed. Circ: 1350. Vol. ends: Dec. Online: Blackwell Synergy; EBSCO Publishing, EBSCO Host; Gale; IngentaConnect; OCLC Online Computer Library Center, Inc.; OhioLINK; SwetsWise Online Content. Reprint: PSC. *Indexed:* ABIn, ATI, IBSS, JEL, RiskAb, SSCI. *Aud.:* Ac, Sa.

The scope of the *JBFA* covers both theoretical and empirical analysis relating to financial reporting, asset pricing, financial markets and institutions, market microstructure, corporate finance, corporate governance, and the economics of internal organization and management control. Each issue delivers eight to ten feature articles that are 15–20 pages in length. Despite the price and the British focus, the large number of articles and the variety of topics make this an impressive title.

2763. *Journal of Financial Planning.* Formerly (until 1988): *Institute of Certified Financial Planners. Journal.* [ISSN: 1040-3981] 1979. 12x/yr. Non-members, USD 109. Ed(s): Maureen Peck, Ian W. MacKenzie. Financial Planning Association, 4100 E Mississippi Ave Ste 400, Denver, CO 80246; journal@fpanet.org; http://www.fpanet.org. Illus., index, adv. Sample. Circ: 27000 Paid. Vol. ends: No. 4. *Indexed:* ABIn, ATI, AgeL, BPI, PAIS, RiskAb. *Aud.:* Ac, Sa.

This practitioner-focused title serves as a forum for the exchange of ideas and information related to the financial planning profession. Roughly a dozen short articles focus on professional issues, retirement, portfolio management, investment research, technology, noteworthy people, and strategies. Departments report on legal and legislative news, institutional resources, continuing education, letters to the editor, and contacts. The web site includes full-text articles from current and past issues and features additional content that does not appear in the print edition. Academic and large public libraries that support programs and professionals in insurance and finance should consider this title.

2764. *Mergers & Acquisitions (New York, 1965): the dealmakers' journal.* Incorporated (in 1967): *Mergers and Acquisitions Monthly.* [ISSN: 0026-0010] 1965. m. USD 695 domestic; USD 870 foreign. Ed(s): Martin Sikora. SourceMedia, Inc., One State St Plaza, 27th Fl, New York, NY 10004; custserv@sourcemedia.com; http://www.sourcemedia.com. Illus., index, adv. Circ: 3000 Paid. Microform: CIS; PQC. Online: EBSCO Publishing, EBSCO Host; Florida Center for Library Automation; Gale; LexisNexis; Northern Light Technology, Inc.; OCLC Online Computer Library Center, Inc.; ProQuest LLC (Ann Arbor); H.W. Wilson. *Indexed:* ABIn, ATI, BPI, CLI, CWI, LRI, PAIS. *Aud.:* Ac, Sa.

Corporate mergers and acquisitions (M&A) are the specialized focus of this core trade magazine. Joint ventures are reported on but are not regularly charted. Data are gathered from a number of sources, including Thomson's Merger and Corporate Transaction Database, and are used to develop league tables that rank the leading financial advisers in the M&A industries, as well as sales volumes of target companies, industries most attractive to foreign investment, countries with the largest role in M&A in the United States, and the top transactions. Quarterly rosters give data on U.S. acquisitions by SIC code, foreign acquisitions in the United States, and U.S. acquisitions overseas. In addition, this title includes a feature cover story, perspectives "From the Field," current news, LBO watch, and the "industry's most comprehensive calendar of events."

2765. *Private Equity International.* [ISSN: 1474-8800] 2001. 10x/yr. GBP 645 domestic; EUR 970 in Europe; USD 1225 elsewhere. Ed(s): Philip Borel. P E I Media, 2nd Fl, Sycamore House, Sycamore St, London, EC1Y 0SG, United Kingdom; http://www.investoraccess.com/. Circ: 5000. *Aud.:* Ac, Sa.

Private Equity International is written by a team of experienced, international journalists who are dedicated solely to covering the global asset class. Each issue looks at current happenings in each corner of the globe and reports on newsmakers, recent deals, and current issues of interest. Most of the magazine's content is in the form of short articles and charts, with longer profile articles on executives in the field that would appeal to practitioners. Large academic or special libraries that support private equity, venture capital, or entrepreneurship programs or professionals should consider this title.

2766. *Risk Management.* Formerly: *National Insurance Buyer.* [ISSN: 0035-5593] 1954. m. USD 64 domestic; USD 74 Canada. Ed(s): Morgan O'Rance, Jared Wade. Risk Management Society Publishing, Inc., 1065 Ave of the Americas, 13th Fl, New York, NY 10018; http://www.rims.org/rmmag.html. Illus., index, adv. Circ: 15000 Paid and controlled. Vol. ends: Dec (No. 12). Microform: PQC. Online: EBSCO Publishing, EBSCO Host; Florida Center for Library Automation; Gale; Northern Light Technology, Inc.; OCLC Online Computer Library Center, Inc.; ProQuest LLC (Ann Arbor); H.W. Wilson. *Indexed:* ABIn, ATI, BPI, LRI, RiskAb. *Bk. rev.:* 6-9, 20 words. *Aud.:* Ac, Sa.

Articles in this trade journal might typically explore global growth, risk management, and specific examples of companies, operations, and innovators. Regular features include a calendar, quick industry facts and figures, rules and regulations, and an executive forum. Recent article topics include a report on the insurance industry and the Patriot Act, cleaning up an environmental disaster, and the value of web-based claims systems. Academic libraries that support business education, specifically insurance and finance, and public libraries with supporting demographics should consider this title.

2767. *Treasury & Risk.* Formerly (until 2006): *Treasury & Risk Management;* Which incorporated (in 1996): *Corporate Cashflow;* Which was formerly (1980-1988): *Cashflow;* (in 1992): *Corporate Risk Management;* Treasury & Risk Management was formerly (until no.2, 1992): *Treasury.* [ISSN: 1935-7214] 1991. 10x/yr. USD 64 domestic (Free to qualified personnel). Ed(s): Susan Kelly, Kevin Reardon. Wicks Business Information LLC, 1375 Kings Highway E, Ste 450, Fairfield, CT 06824-5398; info@wicksbusinessinfo.com; http://www.wicksbusinessinfo.com. Illus., index, adv. Sample. Circ: 47000 Controlled. Vol. ends: No. 10. Online: EBSCO Publishing, EBSCO Host; Gale; OCLC Online Computer Library Center, Inc. *Indexed:* ABIn, ATI, BLI. *Aud.:* Sa.

This publication targets CEOs, CFOs, presidents, vice-presidents of treasury and finance, controllers, financial managers, cash and credit managers, and risk managers. Each issue has three or four feature articles as well as news and departments that address careers, opinions, and an executive profile. Features discuss specific solutions to practical problems of risk managers. Recent articles include discussions of insurance, the next generation of corporate lenders, and cash management.

2768. *Venture Capital Journal: the only financial analyst of small business investment companies and venture capital companies.* Former titles: *Venture Capital; S B I C - Venture Capital; S B I C-Venture Capital Service.* [ISSN: 0883-2773] 1961. m. USD 1625 in US &

Canada; USD 1680 elsewhere. Ed(s): Lawrence Aragon. Thomson Financial Media, 195 Broadway, New York, NY 10007. Adv. Online: EBSCO Publishing, EBSCO Host; Florida Center for Library Automation; Gale; LexisNexis; OCLC Online Computer Library Center, Inc.; ProQuest K-12 Learning Solutions; ProQuest LLC (Ann Arbor). *Indexed:* ABIn, CWI, LRI. *Aud.:* Ac, Sa.

This is a core journal for libraries that cater to venture capitalists, entrepreneurs, or entrepreneurship programs. It offers news, analysis, and insight into the venture capital and private equity markets, with stories on recent deals, new sources of capital, and fund formations. There are profiles of leading venture capital firms and their portfolios, interviews with institutional investors, and up-to-date reports on the latest venture-backed IPOs.

2769. *Wall Street & Technology: for senior-level executives in technology and information management in securities and investment firms.* Formerly (until 1992): *Wall Street Computer Review;* Which Incorporated (in 1991): *Wall Street Computer Review. Buyer's Guide.* [ISSN: 1060-989X] 1983. m. USD 85 domestic (Free to qualified personnel). Ed(s): Kerry Massaro. C M P Media LLC, 3 Park Ave, New York, NY 10016-5902; http://www.cmp.com. Illus., index, adv. Sample. Circ: 25000 Controlled. Vol. ends: Dec. Online: Factiva, Inc.; Florida Center for Library Automation; Gale; LexisNexis; OCLC Online Computer Library Center, Inc.; ProQuest K-12 Learning Solutions; ProQuest LLC (Ann Arbor); H.W. Wilson. *Indexed:* ABIn, BPI, LRI, MicrocompInd, PAIS. *Bk. rev.:* Number and length vary. *Aud.:* Ac, Sa.

This trade newspaper is one of an important group of niche titles that provide information on the technology of financial services (others include *Insurance & Technology* and *Bank Systems & Technology*). The technology and communications aspects of the financial-services industry are discussed in articles and departments that report on trading, regulation, and money management. The "Buyer's Guide" issue includes generic software and operating systems and a list of products, hardware, materials, and services provided to the financial-services industry, divided into the type of service supported, including general quote services, securities trading by security type, portfolio accounting/management, equity research, and others. The format includes the vendor names and addresses, the products/services with which they are compatible, and product descriptions. Other regular coverage includes risk management, trading and exchange, investment technology, inside operations, and a calendar. Recent articles discuss timely topics such as changing technology infrastructures, digitally protecting research, and energy solutions. The web site has current and past articles arranged by topic and type of article.

■ FIRE PROTECTION

Lian Ruan, Director/Head Librarian, Illinois Fire Service Institute Library, University of Illinois at Urbana–Champaign, 11 Gerty Drive, Champaign, IL 61820; lruan@fsi.uiuc.edu

Diane Richardson, Reference and Training Librarian, Illinois Fire Service Institute Library, University of Illinois at Urbana–Champaign, 11 Gerty Drive, Champaign, IL 61820; dlrichar@fsi.uiuc.edu

Adam Groves, Archivist and Metadata Librarian, Illinois Fire Service Institute Library, University of Illinois at Urbana–Champaign, 11 Gerty Drive, Champaign, IL 61820; agroves@fsi.uiuc.edu

Introduction

We live in an era of heightened concern for public safety, and today's fire service personnel are responsible for a wide range of public safety activities. While fire protection is still the primary concern of the fire service, the profession has evolved to include a variety of additional first-responder duties, such as hazardous materials response, rescue work, emergency medical services, and safety education. In recent years, emergency incident management, terrorism response, and other homeland security activities have emerged as additional key components of the fire service profession. These increased professional activities have, in turn, led to an increase in the information needs of fire service personnel.

This section describes fire protection periodicals of both national and international scope that are mainly geared toward fire service personnel. These publications generally focus on training, administrative, and safety issues related to the fire service, but also provide detailed information about emergency incidents, fire statistics, and professional research. Feature article topics in these publications frequently involve firefighting, rescue operations, fire investigation and prevention, hazardous materials response, homeland security, and emergency incident management, while the publications also contain sections dealing with news, politics, and commercial products. This section also describes a peer-reviewed and internationally recognized scholarly journal focusing on fire protection research and other aspects of fire science.

Basic Periodicals

Ac: *Fire Chief, Fire Engineering, Fire Protection Engineering, Fire Technology, NFPA Journal;* Sa: *Advanced Rescue Technology, Fire Chief, Fire Engineering, Fire Protection Engineering, Fire Rescue Magazine, Fire Technology, Firehouse, Industrial Fire World, NFPA Journal.*

Basic Abstracts and Indexes

Chemical Abstracts, Engineering Index.

2770. *Advanced Rescue Technology.* Formerly: *E M S Rescue Technology.* [ISSN: 1524-0134] 1995. bi-m. USD 12.50. Cygnus Business Media, Inc., 830 Post Rd East, Westport, CT 06880; http://www.cygnusb2b.com. Illus., adv. Circ: 40000 Controlled. *Indexed:* CINAHL. *Bk. rev.:* 400-500 words. *Aud.:* Sa.

Advanced Rescue Technology supports the informational needs of rescue personnel, specifically those involved in rural, urban, water, air, wildland, vehicle, or other search-and-rescue operation activities. Feature articles are typically produced by fire rescue professionals, and frequently describe hands-on training and rescue techniques and procedures. The periodical also regularly contains articles explaining and assessing new developments in rescue technology. Other features include sections on rescue technology news, as well as classified ads and product showcases. *Advanced Rescue Technology* is recommended for fire departments, fire service and rescue personnel, emergency medical services personnel, and special and academic libraries that support rescue personnel.

2771. *Fire Chief: every department, every leader.* Incorporates: *Volunteer Firefighter; Volunteer Fire Chief.* [ISSN: 0015-2552] 1956. m. USD 60 in US & Canada (Free to qualified personnel). Ed(s): Kevin Daniels, Janet Wilmoth. Prism Business Media, 330 N Wabash Ave, Ste 2300, Chicago, IL 60611; inquiries@prismb2b.com; http://www.prismbusinessmedia.com. Illus., adv. Circ: 53000 Controlled. Vol. ends: Dec. Microform: PQC. Online: EBSCO Publishing, EBSCO Host; Factiva, Inc.; Gale; OCLC Online Computer Library Center, Inc.; ProQuest LLC (Ann Arbor); H.W. Wilson. *Indexed:* BPI. *Bk. rev.:* 0-4, 50-300 words. *Aud.:* Ac, Sa.

Fire Chief magazine is designed for fire service officers and administrators, but it is a valuable resource for all fire protection personnel, too. This periodical predominantly features articles that are contributed by fire officers and administrators from throughout the United States, covering topics of interest to all fire service leaders, be they career or volunteer firefighters, or general public safety officials. Frequent article topics include fire prevention, suppression, and investigation; emergency medical response; hazardous materials and terrorism response; public education; and administrative matters such as training and budgeting. The magazine also closely monitors and advocates important professional advances, including the development of new technologies or improvements in firefighter health and safety initiatives. Regular columns in each issue are devoted to a variety of essential topics, including fire protection, technology, training, volunteer firefighting, and legal issues. Other regular features include classified ads and new product descriptions. *Fire Chief* is highly recommended for fire officers, fire service leaders, and public administrators, as well as large public libraries and special and academic libraries that serve fire protection and prevention training programs.

2772. *Fire Engineering: the journal of fire suppression and protection.*
Formerly (until 1926): *Fire Protection;* Incorporates (1903-1926): *Fire and Water Engineering.* [ISSN: 0015-2587] 1877. m. USD 29.95 domestic; USD 42.75 Canada; USD 64.95 elsewhere. Ed(s): Bobby Holton, Diane Feldman. PennWell Corporation, 1421 S Sheridan Rd, Tulsa, OK 74112; patrickM@pennwell.com; http://www.pennwell.com. Illus., index, adv. Sample. Circ: 46647 Paid. Vol. ends: Dec. Microform: PQC. Online: EBSCO Publishing, EBSCO Host; Gale; OCLC Online Computer Library Center, Inc.; ProQuest LLC (Ann Arbor). *Indexed:* ABIn, AS&TI, C&ISA, CerAb, ChemAb, EngInd, ExcerpMed, H&SSA, IAA, SCI. *Aud.:* Ac, Sa.

For more than 100 years, *Fire Engineering* has been a leading learning resource for fire service personnel throughout the world. With an overall concentration on practical, hands-on advice, this periodical focuses on training and management issues facing fire protection and emergency response personnel. Feature articles typically highlight advances in the profession, such as new technologies or innovative training methods and tools. Articles also frequently reference actual fire and emergency incidents, providing case studies that identify valuable lessons learned from the various incidents. In addition to regular columns directed to fire officers, training officers, and volunteers, each issue also includes a roundtable column in which 12 or 15 fire officers from around the United States weigh in with opinions about a single popular issue within the fire service at the time. Moreover, the online version of the magazine is frequently updated, providing up-to-date fire service news and current events. *Fire Engineering* is highly recommended for fire departments and fire service personnel, as well as large public libraries and special and academic libraries that support fire prevention and protection training programs.

2773. *Fire Protection Engineering.* [ISSN: 1524-900X] 1998. q. Free to qualified personnel. Society of Fire Protection Engineers, 7315 Wisconsin Ave., Ste. 620E, Bethesda, MD 20814-3234; sfpehqtrs@sfpe.org; http://www.sfpe.org. Illus., adv. Circ: 11000. Vol. ends: Fall. Online: ProQuest LLC (Ann Arbor); H.W. Wilson. *Indexed:* AS&TI. *Bk. rev.:* 200-300 words. *Aud.:* Ac, Sa.

Fire Protection Engineering, a quarterly publication, is the "Official Magazine of the Society of Fire Protection Engineers." The magazine typically contains scholarly articles and studies on issues concerning the construction and design of fire protection systems and equipment, but the writing is still accessible and understandable to those without advanced degrees or training in engineering. Frequent article topics include building codes and standards, fire detection and suppression systems, and the design of fire safety systems. Additionally, every issue includes industry news briefs and guides to new products and resources. Recommended for special and academic libraries that support fire prevention and protection training programs.

2774. *Fire Technology: an international journal of fire protection research and engineering.* [ISSN: 0015-2684] 1965. q. EUR 372 print & online eds. Ed(s): John M Watts, Jr. Springer New York LLC, 233 Spring St, New York, NY 10013-1578; service-ny@springer.com; http://www.springer.com/. Illus., index, adv. Sample. Circ: 3000. Vol. ends: Oct (No. 4). Microform: PQC. Online: EBSCO Publishing, EBSCO Host; Gale; IngentaConnect; Northern Light Technology, Inc.; OCLC Online Computer Library Center, Inc.; OhioLINK; ProQuest LLC (Ann Arbor); Springer LINK; SwetsWise Online Content. Reprint: PSC. *Indexed:* AS&TI, ChemAb, EngInd, H&SSA, IAA, RiskAb, SCI. *Bk. rev.:* 1, 250-500 words. *Aud.:* Ac, Sa.

The foremost scientific and technical refereed journal in the fire science field, *Fire Technology* publishes original papers that address problems in fire safety and related fields. Its mission is to provide the fire protection community with information on the latest fire-related technical developments and scientific research. Articles address fire detection, suppression and modeling, human behavior, materials testing, and performance standards. Subjects also include technical aspects of fire risk analysis, fire investigation, loss statistics, wildland fires, and municipal fire protection. It is a cross-disciplinary publication that treats fire-related issues from fields such as engineering, ergonomics, chemistry, physics, psychology, sociology, and management science. Technical news, software and book reviews, accounts of current research, editorials, and meeting announcements are also included. Highly recommended for special library and

academic library collections that serve fire protection and prevention programs, or that serve allied fields with a scholarly interest in fire science, such as chemistry, physics, engineering, or ergonomics.

2775. *Firehouse.* [ISSN: 0145-4064] 1976. m. USD 28; USD 5 newsstand/cover. Ed(s): Harvey Eisner. Cygnus Business Media, Inc., 3 Huntington Quadrangle, Ste 301N, Melville, NY 11747-3601. Illus., adv. Circ: 86300 Controlled. Vol. ends: Dec. *Indexed:* ABIn. *Aud.:* Sa.

Firehouse provides timely, in-depth coverage of major emergency incidents and covers other topics of interest to fire service personnel, including training, operations, apparatus, administration, and equipment. It also covers research and offers a calendar of events. The "On the Job" feature describes the progress of fires in detail, including lessons learned. Human interest stories and firefighting history items are also featured. Monthly columns include "Fire Politics," "Close Calls," "EMS," "University of Extrication," and "Thermal Imaging Training." The magazine also publishes career and volunteer run surveys and annual Heroism and Community Service Awards. Highly recommended for fire departments, as well as special and public libraries.

2776. *FireRescue Magazine.* Formed by the merger of (1983-1997): *Firefighter's News;* (1988-1997): *Rescue;* Which was formerly (until 1989): *Rescue Magazine.* [ISSN: 1094-0529] 1997. m. USD 40. Ed(s): Shannon Pieper, Michelle Garrido. Elsevier Public Safety, 525 B St, Ste 1900, San Diego, CA 92101. Adv. Circ: 50733 Paid and controlled. *Indexed:* CINAHL. *Aud.:* Sa.

With a mission of "Read It Today, Use It Tomorrow," *FireRescue* focuses on problem solving with the latest information and techniques for firefighters, technical rescue personnel, fire company officers, and training officers. Each issue includes color photos of firefighters and rescue personnel in action plus tactical tips, editorials, essays, and observations in columns such as "Apparatus Ideas," "Truck Company Operations" and "Company Officer Development." Other monthly features include sections on the latest tools and their use, fire prevention, and fitness. Feature articles include topics such as incident command, extrication, rural operations, volunteer issues, and major incident readiness. Letters to the editor, new products, classifieds, and an advertising index are also included. Recommended for special libraries and large public libraries, fire departments, and fire and emergency medical services professionals.

2777. *Industrial Fire World.* [ISSN: 0749-890X] 1985. bi-m. USD 29.95 domestic; USD 49.95 foreign. Ed(s): Anton Riecher. Industrial Fire World, P O Box 9161, College Station, TX 77842-9161; ind@fireworld.com; http://www.fireworld.com. Adv. Sample. Circ: 31500. *Aud.:* Sa.

The vision of *Industrial Fire World* is to increase responder safety in the field of industrial fire and emergency response by providing research and testing updates, along with lessons learned from actual incidents. Regular columns include "Focus on Hazmat," "EMS Corner," and "Risk Assessment." There is also a service directory and bimonthly editorial by the publisher. The "Incident Log" column provides information on national and international industrial incidents. Recommended for special library and public library collections.

2778. *N F P A Journal.* Formed by the merger of (1907-1991): *Fire Journal;* (1970-1991): *Fire Command;* Which was formerly (until 1984): *Fire Service Today;* (until 1981): *Fire Command.* [ISSN: 1054-8793] 1991. bi-m. Membership, USD 138. Ed(s): John Nicholson. National Fire Protection Association, 1 Batterymarch Park, Quincy, MA 02269; dgfergason@nfpa.org; http://www.nfpa.org. Illus., index, adv. Sample. Circ: 81000 Paid. Vol. ends: Nov/Dec. Microform: PQC. Online: EBSCO Publishing, EBSCO Host; OCLC Online Computer Library Center, Inc.; ProQuest LLC (Ann Arbor). *Indexed:* AS&TI, AgeL, ChemAb, SCI. *Aud.:* Ac, Sa.

The *NFPA Journal* is the official members' magazine of the National Fire Protection Agency, a nonprofit organization that produces codes and standards related to fire, building, and electrical safety. It features in-depth articles on fire protection and life-safety topics, including research and investigation reports. Regular columns also cover sprinkler systems, structural firefighting, fire alarms, and public education. Annual NFPA statistical studies on firefighter injuries and fatalities, multiple-death fires, large-loss fires, and fire loss in the United States are a unique feature. Highly recommended for academic or special libraries and large public libraries.

■ FISH, FISHERIES, AND AQUACULTURE

Michael R. Blake, Associate Director and Head of Instructional Services, Oliver Wendell Holmes Library, Phillips Academy Andover, 180 Main St., Andover, MA 01810; mblake@andover.edu

Lenora Oftedahl, StreamNet Librarian, Columbia River Inter-Tribal Fish Commission, 729 N.E. Oregon St., Suite 190, Portland, OR 97232; OFTL@critfc.org

Introduction

Leave your fly rod at home! Here we are examining the materials that cover the noncontemplative aspects of fishing and fisheries science; management of fisheries, aquaculture, taxonomy, harvesting, genetics, nutrition, physiology, behavior, ecology, conservation, preservation, and overfishing.

Magazines and journals that cover fish, fisheries, and aquaculture tend to be written for the trained researcher or scientist. Very few are considered for the general public, the exception being those magazines devoted to the aquarium trade.

Publishers are increasingly specialized or are governmental agencies working toward the conservation and preservation of the fisheries. Be prepared for higher prices in these much more specialized journals. The electronic forms are also being bundled with the print subscriptions.

Many of the titles listed have electronic counterparts. Most of these add to the cost of the journal. Electronic-only options tend to cost the same or more, depending on the publisher.

Basic Periodicals

Hs, Ga: *Aquaculture Magazine, Fisheries, Freshwater and Marine Aquarium, Tropical Fish Hobbyist, AquaWorld Magazine;* Ac, Sa: *Aquaculture, Aquaculture Research, Canadian Journal of Fisheries and Aquatic Sciences, Fish Physiology & Biochemistry, Fisheries Management and Ecology, Fisheries Research, Fishery Bulletin, Journal of Fish Biology, Reviews in Fisheries Science, American Fisheries Society. Transactions.*

Basic Abstracts and Indexes

Aquaculture and Fisheries Resources, Aquatic Sciences and Fisheries Abstracts, Biological Abstracts, NISC-Aquatic Biology.

2779. *Alaska Fishery Research Bulletin.* Former titles (until 1994): *Alaska. Department of Fish and Game. Fishery Research Bulletin;* (until 1988): *Alaska. Department of Fish and Game. Informational Leaflet.* [ISSN: 1091-7306] 1961. s-a. Free. Ed(s): Doug Eggers. Alaska Department of Fish and Game, Division of Commercial Fisheries, P.O. Box 25526, Juneau, AK 99802-5526. Illus. Sample. Circ: 700. *Indexed:* OceAb, SWRA, ZooRec. *Aud.:* Ac, Sa.

The *Alaska Fishery Research Bulletin* contains 5–15 articles and may contain issues and perspectives, notes, and letters. Like many other states' departments of fish and wildlife (or equivalents), this publication primarily focuses on the Alaska environs. Biological sampling articles are included.

2780. *American Fisheries Society. Transactions.* [ISSN: 0002-8487] 1870. bi-m. Individuals, USD 43. American Fisheries Society, 5410 Grosvenor Ln, Ste 110, Bethesda, MD 20814-2199; journals@fisheries.org; http://www.fisheries.org. Illus., index, adv. Refereed. Circ: 3700. Vol. ends: No. 6. Online: Allen Press Inc.; EBSCO Publishing, EBSCO Host. *Indexed:* AnBeAb, ApEcolAb, B&AI, BiolAb, CABA, ChemAb, EnvAb, EnvInd, ExcerpMed, FPA, ForAb, IndVet, OceAb, PollutAb, RRTA, S&F, SCI, SWRA, VB, WAE&RSA, WRCInf, ZooRec. *Bk. rev.:* Various number and length. *Aud.:* Ac, Sa.

One of the six publications by the American Fisheries Society, this title contains refereed technical papers on all aspects of fisheries science. Coverage is as varied as the membership of the organization. Here we find articles on biology, ecology, genetics, economics, culture, diseases, and other topics about any marine or freshwater finfish, exploitable shellfish, or their respective fisheries. A must for any fisheries scientist.

2781. *Aquacultural Engineering.* [ISSN: 0144-8609] 1982. 8x/yr. EUR 954. Ed(s): Dr. J. van Rijn, J Colt. Elsevier BV, Radarweg 29, Amsterdam, 1043 NX, Netherlands; nlinfo-f@elsevier.nl; http://www.elsevier.nl. Illus., index, adv. Refereed. Vol. ends: No. 6. Microform: PQC. Online: EBSCO Publishing, EBSCO Host; Gale; IngentaConnect; OhioLINK; ScienceDirect; SwetsWise Online Content. *Indexed:* Agr, BioEngAb, BiolAb, CABA, EngInd, EnvAb, EnvInd, ExcerpMed, ForAb, HortAb, IndVet, OceAb, PollutAb, RRTA, S&F, SCI, SWRA, VB, WAE&RSA. *Aud.:* Ac, Sa.

An international engineering journal written for fisheries scientists and marine biologists involved with aquaculture. It covers all aspects of engineering from design and choosing materials and utilization to assessment and evaluation of finished projects. Conservation and recycling efforts are often topics included.

2782. *Aquaculture.* Incorporates (1990-1996): *Annual Review of Fish Diseases.* [ISSN: 0044-8486] 1972. 48x/yr. EUR 3933. Ed(s): R P Wilson. Elsevier BV, Radarweg 29, Amsterdam, 1043 NX, Netherlands; nlinfo-f@elsevier.nl; http://www.elsevier.nl. Illus., index, adv. Refereed. Circ: 650. Microform: PQC. Online: EBSCO Publishing, EBSCO Host; Factiva, Inc.; Gale; IngentaConnect; OhioLINK; ScienceDirect; SwetsWise Online Content. *Indexed:* Agr, B&AI, BiolAb, CABA, ChemAb, DSA, EnvAb, EnvInd, ExcerpMed, FS&TA, FoVS&M, ForAb, HortAb, IndVet, OceAb, PollutAb, RRTA, S&F, SCI, SWRA, VB, WAE&RSA, ZooRec. *Bk. rev.:* Various number and length. *Aud.:* Ac, Sa.

This international journal is written for fisheries scientists and marine biologists. It includes research studies on aquatic life in freshwater and saltwater environments. Occasional special issues focus on a single topic. About four to seven articles appear in each issue.

2783. *Aquaculture Economics & Management.* [ISSN: 1365-7305] 1997. 3x/yr. GBP 264 print & online eds. Ed(s): Clem Tisdell, PingSun Leung. Taylor & Francis Ltd., 4 Park Sq, Milton Park, Abingdon, OX14 4RN, United Kingdom; info@tandf.co.uk; http://www.tandf.co.uk/journals. Adv. Sample. Refereed. Circ: 400. Reprint: PSC. *Indexed:* Agr, BiolAb, CABA, ForAb, HortAb, IndVet, JEL, OceAb, PollutAb, RRTA, S&F, SWRA, VB, WAE&RSA. *Aud.:* Ac, Sa.

A relatively new journal whose primary purpose is to publish papers on aquaculture economic analysis for managers in both the public and private sectors.

2784. *Aquaculture Magazine.* Former titles: *Commercial Fish Farmer and Aquaculture News; Commercial Fish Farmer; Catfish Farmer and World Aquaculture News;* Formed by the merger of: *American Fish Farmer; American Fishes and U.S. Trout News; Catfish Farmer; Catfish Farming Industries.* [ISSN: 0199-1388] 1969. bi-m. USD 24 domestic; USD 30 in Canada & Mexico; USD 60 elsewhere. Ed(s): Greg Gallagher. Richard V. Gallagher, PO Box 1409, Arden, NC 28704. Illus., adv. Circ: 8000 Paid. Vol. ends: No. 6. *Indexed:* Agr, EnvAb, EnvInd, FS&TA, IndVet, MASUSE, OceAb, VB. *Bk. rev.:* Various number and length. *Aud.:* Hs, Ga.

An international publication written for the fish farmer. Each issue contains four or five feature articles and regular features including a calendar of events, catfish production figures, a classified section, and regular columns. There is an annual buyer's guide as well. Useful for high school students researching aquaculture or for anyone else interested in the field.

2785. *Aquaculture Nutrition.* [ISSN: 1353-5773] 1995. bi-m. GBP 516 print & online eds. Ed(s): Dr. Rune Waagbo, Dr. Gro-Ingunn Hemre. Blackwell Publishing Ltd., 9600 Garsington Rd, Oxford, OX4 2ZG, United Kingdom; customerservices@blackwellpublishing.com;

http://www.blackwellpublishing.com. Illus., index, adv. Refereed. Circ: 225. Vol. ends: No. 4. Reprint: PSC. *Indexed:* Agr, BiolAb, CABA, ChemAb, DSA, HortAb, IndVet, OceAb, SCI, VB, WAE&RSA, ZooRec. *Aud.:* Ac, Sa.

An international research publication covering the nutrition of all farmed aquatic animals. The journal accepts review and original research articles. This publication has a rather narrow focus and would be most valuable to those studying the feeding of fish.

2786. *Aquaculture Research.* Former titles (until 1995): *Aquaculture and Fisheries Management;* (until 1985): *Fisheries Management.* [ISSN: 1355-557X] 1970. 16x/yr. GBP 1699 print & online eds. Ed(s): Dr. Ronald W Hardy, Dr. S J de Groot. Blackwell Publishing Ltd., 9600 Garsington Rd, Oxford, OX4 2ZG, United Kingdom; customerservices@ blackwellpublishing.com; http://www.blackwellpublishing.com. Illus., index, adv. Sample. Refereed. Circ: 315. Vol. ends: No. 12. Microform: PQC. Online: Blackwell Synergy; EBSCO Publishing, EBSCO Host; Gale; IngentaConnect; OCLC Online Computer Library Center, Inc.; OhioLINK; SwetsWise Online Content. Reprint: PSC. *Indexed:* Agr, BiolAb, CABA, DSA, EnvAb, EnvInd, ExcerpMed, FPA, ForAb, HortAb, IndVet, OceAb, PollutAb, RRTA, S&F, SCI, VB, WAE&RSA, ZooRec. *Bk. rev.:* Various number and length. *Aud.:* Ac, Sa.

An international journal covering all aspects of aquaculture in marine, freshwater, or brackish water environments. Fish species are in a broad range. Papers can be original research articles, review articles, short communications, or book reviews. Valuable for scientists working in aquaculture.

Aquatic Conservation. See Marine Science and Technology section.

2787. *Canadian Journal of Fisheries and Aquatic Sciences.* Former titles (until 1980): *Fisheries Research Board of Canada. Journal;* (until 1937): *Biological Board of Canada. Journal;* (until 1934): *Contributions to Canadian Biology and Fisheries; Contributions to Canadian Biology.* [ISSN: 0706-652X] 1901. m. CND 954 (Individuals, CND 250). Ed(s): M M Ferguson, J C Roff. N R C Research Press, National Research Council of Canada, Ottawa, ON K1A 0R6, Canada; pubs@nrc-cnrc.gc.ca; http://pubs.nrc-cnrc.gc.ca. Illus., index, adv. Refereed. Circ: 3000. Vol. ends: No. 12. Microform: PQC. Online: EBSCO Publishing, EBSCO Host; Gale; IngentaConnect; Micromedia ProQuest; OCLC Online Computer Library Center, Inc.; Ovid Technologies, Inc.; ProQuest K-12 Learning Solutions; ProQuest LLC (Ann Arbor); SwetsWise Online Content; H.W. Wilson. *Indexed:* AnBeAb, ApEcolAb, B&AI, BiolAb, CABA, CBCARef, CPerI, ChemAb, DSA, EnvAb, EnvInd, ExcerpMed, FPA, FS&TA, ForAb, GSI, HortAb, IBR, IBZ, IndVet, M&GPA, OceAb, PollutAb, RRTA, S&F, SCI, SWRA, VB, WAE&RSA, WRCInf, ZooRec. *Aud.:* Ac, Sa.

A primary research journal that includes "Rapid Communication" and in-depth research articles covering all aspects of fishery biology and aquatic ecosystems. Most articles are in English. Some articles are in French, but all have English and French abstracts. Contains 15–25 research articles per issue. Required reading for those working in fisheries. Ranked among the top three journals in the field for the past decade by ISI.

Copeia. See Zoology section.

2788. *Diseases of Aquatic Organisms.* [ISSN: 0177-5103] 1985. 12x/yr. EUR 800 combined subscription domestic for print & online eds.; EUR 826 combined subscription foreign for print & online eds. Ed(s): Otto Kinne. Inter-Research, Nordbuente 23, Oldendorf, 21385, Germany; ir@int-res.com; http://www.int-res.com. Refereed. *Indexed:* BiolAb, CABA, ChemAb, DSA, FoVS&M, HortAb, IndVet, OceAb, RRTA, S&F, SCI, SWRA, VB, ZooRec. *Aud.:* Ac, Sa.

The articles in this journal will interest all biologists working with pathogens. It covers toxicology, parasites, immunology, and more. Some of the illustrations are in color. All aquatic species (vertebrate and invertebrate) and environments (freshwater, brackish, and marine) are covered.

2789. *Ecology of Freshwater Fish.* [ISSN: 0906-6691] 1992. q. GBP 397 print & online eds. Ed(s): Javier Lobon-Cervia, David C Heins. Blackwell Munksgaard, Rosenoerns Alle 1, PO Box 227, Copenhagen V, 1502, Denmark; info@mks.blackwellpublishing.com; http://www.munksgaard.dk/. Illus., adv. Refereed. Reprint: PSC. *Indexed:* AnBeAb, ApEcolAb, BiolAb, CABA, ForAb, IndVet, S&F, SCI, SWRA, VB, ZooRec. *Bk. rev.:* Number and length vary. *Aud.:* Ac, Sa.

Publishes relevant articles on all aspects of freshwater fish and fisheries, especially ecology. Letters, theoretical papers, and population studies can be found occasionally. Every article has an abstract in Spanish.

2790. *Environmental Biology of Fishes.* [ISSN: 0378-1909] 1976. m. EUR 2258 print & online eds. Ed(s): David L G Noakes. Springer Netherlands, Van Godewijckstraat 30, Dordrecht, 3311 GX, Netherlands; http://www.springeronline.com. Adv. Refereed. Microform: PQC. Online: EBSCO Publishing, EBSCO Host; Gale; IngentaConnect; OCLC Online Computer Library Center, Inc.; OhioLINK; Springer LINK; SwetsWise Online Content. Reprint: PSC. *Indexed:* AnBeAb, ApEcolAb, ArtHuCI, BiolAb, CABA, CJA, ChemAb, EnvInd, ExcerpMed, ForAb, HortAb, IndVet, OceAb, PollutAb, RRTA, S&F, SCI, SWRA, VB, WRCInf, ZooRec. *Aud.:* Ac, Sa.

An international journal that deals with the relationship between fishes and their external and internal environments, whether natural or unnatural. Prefers multidisciplinary papers that advance the scholarly understanding of life.

2791. *Fish and Fisheries.* [ISSN: 1467-2960] 2000. q. GBP 437 print & online eds. Ed(s): Paul J B Hart, Tony J Pitcher. Blackwell Publishing Ltd., 9600 Garsington Rd, Oxford, OX4 2ZG, United Kingdom; customerservices@blackwellpublishing.com; http://www.blackwellpublishing.com. Refereed. Online: Blackwell Synergy; EBSCO Publishing, EBSCO Host; Gale; IngentaConnect; OCLC Online Computer Library Center, Inc.; OhioLINK; SwetsWise Online Content. Reprint: PSC. *Indexed:* ApEcolAb, CABA, IndVet, OceAb, PollutAb, RRTA, S&F, SCI, SWRA, VB, WAE&RSA, WRCInf, ZooRec. *Aud.:* Ac, Sa.

"The purpose of the journal is to provide critical overviews of major physiological, molecular, ecological, and evolutionary issues in the study of fish, and to establish a forum for debate of issues of global concern in world fisheries." Controversies are inevitable, and the editors would like both sides of various issues to publish in the journal for more balanced coverage.

2792. *Fish and Shellfish Immunology.* [ISSN: 1050-4648] 1991. 10x/yr. EUR 936. Ed(s): C Secombes, A E Ellis. Academic Press, Harcourt Pl, 32 Jamestown Rd, London, NW1 7BY, United Kingdom; apsubs@acad.com; http://www.elsevier.com/. Illus., index, adv. Refereed. Online: EBSCO Publishing, EBSCO Host; Gale; IngentaConnect; OCLC Online Computer Library Center, Inc.; OhioLINK; ScienceDirect; SwetsWise Online Content. *Indexed:* BiolAb, CABA, DSA, FoVS&M, HortAb, IndVet, OceAb, SCI, VB, ZooRec. *Aud.:* Ac, Sa.

An international refereed journal focusing on fish and shellfish immunology. Issues contain about six papers. Review articles and short communications are regular features. Full text of this journal is available electronically as well as in print.

2793. *Fish Physiology & Biochemistry.* [ISSN: 0920-1742] 1986. 4x/yr. EUR 511 print & online eds. Ed(s): H J Th Goos. Springer Netherlands, Van Godewijckstraat 30, Dordrecht, 3311 GX, Netherlands; http://www.springeronline.com. Illus., index. Refereed. Vol. ends: No. 4. Online: EBSCO Publishing, EBSCO Host; Gale; IngentaConnect; OCLC Online Computer Library Center, Inc.; OhioLINK; Ovid Technologies, Inc.; Springer LINK; SwetsWise Online Content. Reprint: PSC. *Indexed:* BiolAb, CABA, ChemAb, ExcerpMed, HortAb, IndVet, OceAb, PollutAb, S&F, SCI, SWRA, VB, ZooRec. *Aud.:* Ac, Sa.

An international journal focusing on original, experimental research articles, brief communications, review articles, editorial comments, and announcements on the physiology and biochemistry of fishes. This journal is valuable to anyone studying fish physiology.

2794. Fisheries. Supersedes (in 1976): *American Fisheries Society. Newsletter.* [ISSN: 0363-2415] 1948. m. USD 76 in North America (Free to members). American Fisheries Society, 5410 Grosvenor Ln, Ste 110, Bethesda, MD 20814-2199; journals@fisheries.org; http://www.fisheries.org. Illus., index, adv. Refereed. Circ: 9700 Paid. Vol. ends: No. 12. Online: Allen Press Inc. *Indexed:* B&AI, BiolAb, CABA, ChemAb, EnvAb, EnvInd, ExcerpMed, FPA, ForAb, GSI, HortAb, IndVet, OceAb, PollutAb, RRTA, S&F, SCI, SSCI, SWRA, VB, WAE&RSA, WRCInf. *Bk. rev.:* Number varies, 500 words. *Aud.:* Ac, Sa.

Printed on ten percent post-consumer recycled paper, this monthly publication from the American Fisheries Society contains news about the society, legislative updates, meeting information, current events, editorials, book reviews, and feature articles. Like other newsletters of scientific societies, there is also a job placement center in each issue. This is the "house organ" for the society.

2795. Fisheries Management and Ecology. [ISSN: 0969-997X] 1994. bi-m. GBP 584 print & online eds. Ed(s): Hal Schramm, I Cowx. Blackwell Publishing Ltd., 9600 Garsington Rd, Oxford, OX4 2ZG, United Kingdom; customerservices@blackwellpublishing.com; http://www.blackwellpublishing.com. Illus., index, adv. Refereed. Circ: 245. Vol. ends: No. 4. Reprint: PSC. *Indexed:* ApEcolAb, BiolAb, CABA, EnvAb, FPA, ForAb, IndVet, OceAb, PollutAb, RRTA, S&F, SCI, SWRA, VB, WAE&RSA, ZooRec. *Bk. rev.:* Various number and length. *Aud.:* Ac, Sa.

An international journal covering the management, ecology, and conservation of fisheries: "The aim of this journal is to foster an understanding of how to maintain, develop and manage the conditions under which fish populations can thrive, and how they and their habitat can be conserved and enhanced."

2796. Fisheries Research. [ISSN: 0165-7836] 1982. 18x/yr. EUR 2122. Ed(s): A D McIntyre. Elsevier BV, Radarweg 29, Amsterdam, 1043 NX, Netherlands; nlinfo-f@elsevier.nl; http://www.elsevier.nl. Illus., index, adv. Refereed. Online: EBSCO Publishing, EBSCO Host; Gale; IngentaConnect; OhioLINK; ScienceDirect; SwetsWise Online Content. *Indexed:* BiolAb, CABA, EnvAb, EnvInd, ForAb, IndVet, OceAb, PollutAb, RRTA, S&F, SCI, SWRA, VB, WAE&RSA, ZooRec. *Bk. rev.:* Various number and length. *Aud.:* Ac, Sa.

An international, multidisciplinary journal covering the science, technology, management, and economics of fisheries. The theoretical or practical papers are written for economists, administrators, policy makers, legislators, and fisheries scientists.

2797. Fisheries Science. [ISSN: 0919-9268] 1935. bi-m. GBP 453 print & online eds. Ed(s): Shugo Watabe. Blackwell Publishing Asia, 550 Swanston St, Carlton South, VIC 3053, Australia; subs@blackwellpublishingasia.com; http://www.blackwellpublishing.com. Refereed. Circ: 5400. *Indexed:* BiolAb, CABA, ChemAb, DSA, FPA, FS&TA, ForAb, HortAb, IndVet, S&F, SCI, VB, WAE&RSA, ZooRec. *Aud.:* Ac, Sa.

An international journal sponsored by the Japanese Society of Fisheries Science, this title has a long history of quality articles in all areas of the aquatic sciences. The bulk of the journal contains original research articles but there are also "Short Papers" and the occasional "Review Article."

2798. Fishery Bulletin. [ISSN: 0090-0656] 1881. q. USD 55 domestic; USD 68.75 foreign. Ed(s): Norm Barboo, Sharyn Matriotti. U.S. National Marine Fisheries Service, Scientific Publications Office, 7600 Sand Point Way, N E, Bin C15700, Seattle, WA 98115; http://spo.nwr.noaa.gov. Illus. Refereed. Circ: 2000. Vol. ends: No. 4. Microform: PQC; NTI. Online: Florida Center for Library Automation; Gale; OCLC Online Computer Library Center, Inc.; H.W. Wilson. *Indexed:* B&AI, BiolAb, CABA, ChemAb, EnvAb, EnvInd, FS&TA, IUSGP, IndVet, OceAb, PollutAb, SCI, SWRA, VB, ZooRec. *Aud.:* Ac, Sa.

This quarterly publishes original research articles or technical notes on fisheries science, engineering, and economics. Most of the contributing authors work for the National Marine Fisheries Service, but some articles from other countries

appear. The publication is available free in limited numbers to libraries, research institutions, and state and federal agencies, and in exchange for other scientific publications.

Freshwater and Marine Aquarium. See Pets section.

2799. Journal of Applied Aquaculture. [ISSN: 1045-4438] 1992. q. USD 455 print & online eds. Ed(s): Carl D Webster. Haworth Press, Inc., 10 Alice St, Binghamton, NY 13904-1580; getinfo@haworthpress.com; http://www.haworthpress.com. Illus., adv. Sample. Refereed. Circ: 181 Paid. Vol. ends: No. 4. Reprint: HAW. *Indexed:* Agr, BiolDig, CABA, EnvAb, EnvInd, FS&TA, ForAb, HortAb, IndVet, OceAb, RRTA, S&F, VB, WAE&RSA, ZooRec. *Aud.:* Ac, Sa.

This is a worthwhile journal and valuable to scientists in the field. Contains 5–10 in-depth research articles that cover all aspects of raising fish, lobster, and other aquatic food products from "Production Characteristics of Channel Catfish" to "Aquatic Animal Health Inspection in West Virginia."

2800. Journal of Applied Ichthyology. Incorporates: *Archive of Fishery and Marine Research.* [ISSN: 0175-8659] 1984. bi-m. GBP 534 print & online eds. Ed(s): Dr. H Rosenthal. Blackwell Verlag GmbH, Kurfuerstendamm 57, Berlin, 10707, Germany; verlag@blackwell.de; http://www.blackwell.de. Index. Refereed. Circ: 340. Reprint: PSC. *Indexed:* BiolAb, CABA, ChemAb, DSA, EnvAb, FS&TA, ForAb, HortAb, IndVet, OceAb, RRTA, S&F, SCI, SWRA, VB, WAE&RSA, ZooRec. *Bk. rev.:* Various number and length. *Aud.:* Ac, Sa.

Although this journal is the official journal of the World Sturgeon Conservation Society, coverage is not limited to the fish most often known for caviar, the sturgeon. Articles cover all aspects of aquaculture and fisheries management, the biology and genetics of fish species, and the historical and population studies of fishes of the world. Special emphasis is given to problems occurring in developing countries. A recent special issue covers "Introduced Non-Native Fishes."

2801. Journal of Aquariculture and Aquatic Sciences. Formerly (until 1982): *Journal of Aquariculture.* [ISSN: 0733-2076] 1980. irreg. Ed(s): John Farrell Kuhns. The Written Word, 7601 E. Forest Lake Dr., N.W., Parkville, MO 64152. Illus., index, adv. Refereed. Circ: 800 Paid. *Indexed:* BiolAb, PollutAb, SWRA, ZooRec. *Bk. rev.:* Various number and length. *Aud.:* Ac, Sa.

This journal publishes original research articles, correspondence, short communications, book reviews, and product reviews for the aquarium science and technology field and for the aquatic sciences. "The *Journal of Aquariculture & Aquatic Sciences* is the only peer-reviewed, international, English-language journal covering aquarium science and technology and the affiliated sciences." Published on an irregular basis.

2802. Journal of Aquatic Animal Health. [ISSN: 0899-7659] 1989. q. Individuals, USD 38. Ed(s): Vicki Blazer. American Fisheries Society, 5410 Grosvenor Ln, Ste 110, Bethesda, MD 20814-2199; journals@ fisheries.org; http://www.fisheries.org. Illus., adv. Refereed. Circ: 1500. Online: Allen Press Inc.; EBSCO Publishing, EBSCO Host. *Indexed:* BiolAb, CABA, EnvAb, FoVS&M, HortAb, IndVet, OceAb, S&F, SCI, SWRA, VB, ZooRec. *Aud.:* Ac, Sa.

This is a core title of the American Fisheries Society. Subject coverage includes etiology, epidemiology, prevention and control, toxicology, and treatments of diseases of marine and freshwater organisms. Focused primarily on fish and shellfish, the coverage also includes human interactions with fish in articles such as "Effects of Practices Related to Catch-and-Release Angling." Each issue contains 5–10 research articles and a similar number of "Communications." A basic need for any ichthyologist.

2803. Journal of Fish Biology. [ISSN: 0022-1112] 1969. m. plus supp. GBP 1846 print & online eds. Ed(s): J F Craig. Blackwell Publishing Ltd., 9600 Garsington Rd, Oxford, OX4 2ZG, United Kingdom; customerservices@blackwellpublishing.com; http://www.blackwellpublishing.com. Illus., index, adv. Refereed. Online: Blackwell Synergy; EBSCO Publishing, EBSCO Host; Gale;

IngentaConnect; OCLC Online Computer Library Center, Inc.; OhioLINK; SwetsWise Online Content. Reprint: PSC. *Indexed:* AnBeAb, ApEcolAb, BiolAb, CABA, ChemAb, DSA, EnvInd, ExcerpMed, FS&TA, ForAb, HortAb, IndVet, OceAb, RRTA, S&F, SCI, SWRA, VB, WAE&RSA, WRCInf, ZooRec. *Bk. rev.:* Various number and length. *Aud.:* Ac, Sa.

Published for the Fisheries Society of the British Isles by Blackwell, this international journal is intended to foster the goal of the society to develop liaisons between those active in fisheries biology. It will not publish papers that harm or kill threatened or endangered fish to gather the data.

2804. *Journal of Fish Diseases.* [ISSN: 0140-7775] 1978. m. GBP 1084 print & online eds. Ed(s): R Wootten, R J Roberts. Blackwell Publishing Ltd., 9600 Garsington Rd, Oxford, OX4 2ZG, United Kingdom; customerservices@blackwellpublishing.com; http://www.blackwellpublishing.com. Illus., index, adv. Refereed. Circ: 555. Vol. ends: No. 9. Microform: PQC. Online: Blackwell Synergy; EBSCO Publishing, EBSCO Host; Gale; IngentaConnect; OCLC Online Computer Library Center, Inc.; OhioLINK; SwetsWise Online Content. Reprint: PSC. *Indexed:* BiolAb, CABA, ChemAb, DSA, ExcerpMed, FoVS&M, HortAb, IndVet, OceAb, SCI, VB, ZooRec. *Bk. rev.:* Various number and length. *Aud.:* Ac, Sa.

This international journal publishes research papers, short communications, review articles, and book reviews focusing on the diseases of fish. It would be valuable in a collection serving fish pathologists or environmental researchers.

2805. *Journal of Shellfish Research.* Formerly: *National Shellfisheries Association. Proceedings.* [ISSN: 0730-8000] 1981. s-a. USD 175 (Individual members, USD 75). Ed(s): Sandra E Shumway. National Shellfisheries Association, Inc., c/o University of Connecticut, Marine Science Dept, Groton, CT 06340. Illus., index. Refereed. Circ: 950. *Indexed:* BiolAb, CABA, ChemAb, FPA, ForAb, HortAb, IndVet, OceAb, RRTA, S&F, SCI, VB, WAE&RSA, ZooRec. *Aud.:* Ac, Sa.

This society publication covers all aspects of shellfish research. Technical meeting/symposium abstracts are included in some issues.

2806. *Marine Fisheries Review.* Formerly: *Commercial Fisheries Review.* [ISSN: 0090-1830] 1939. q. USD 19 domestic; USD 26.60 foreign. Ed(s): W L Hobart. U.S. National Marine Fisheries Service, Scientific Publications Office, 7600 Sand Point Way, N E, Bin C15700, Seattle, WA 98115; http://spo.nwr.noaa.gov. Illus., index. Refereed. Circ: 2000. Vol. ends: No. 4. Microform: CIS; NTI. Online: EBSCO Publishing, EBSCO Host; Florida Center for Library Automation; Gale; OCLC Online Computer Library Center, Inc.; H.W. Wilson. *Indexed:* AmStI, B&AI, ChemAb, EnvAb, FS&TA, IUSGP, OceAb, PAIS, SWRA, VB, ZooRec. *Aud.:* Ac, Sa.

This journal concentrates on "in-depth review articles and practical or applied aspects of marine fisheries rather than pure research." Issues usually include about six articles. Valuable for researchers working with marine fisheries. Beginning with Vol. 60, no. 1, the full contents of this title are available online. The print version is running very late.

2807. *North American Journal of Aquaculture.* Formerly (until 1999): *Progressive Fish-Culturist.* [ISSN: 1522-2055] 1934. q. Individuals, USD 38. Ed(s): Bruce A Barton, William L Shelton. American Fisheries Society, 5410 Grosvenor Ln, Ste 110, Bethesda, MD 20814-2199; journals@fisheries.org; http://www.fisheries.org. Illus., index, adv. Refereed. Circ: 2600. Vol. ends: No. 4. Microform: PQC. Online: Allen Press Inc.; EBSCO Publishing, EBSCO Host. *Indexed:* B&AI, BiolAb, CABA, ChemAb, DSA, EnvAb, ExcerpMed, HortAb, IUSGP, IndVet, OceAb, RRTA, S&F, SCI, SWRA, VB, WAE&RSA, WRCInf, ZooRec. *Bk. rev.:* Various number and length. *Aud.:* Ac, Sa.

Produced by the American Fisheries Society, this publication reports on all aspects of commercial aquaculture operations through refereed articles, short communications, and technical notes. Articles about the aquarium trade are not found here. Although most aquaculturists are members of the publishing organization, this is highly recommended for all fisheries scientists.

2808. *North American Journal of Fisheries Management.* [ISSN: 0275-5947] 1981. q. Individuals, USD 43. Ed(s): Carolyn Griswold. American Fisheries Society, 5410 Grosvenor Ln, Ste 110, Bethesda, MD 20814-2199; journals@fisheries.org; http://www.fisheries.org. Illus., index, adv. Refereed. Circ: 3300. Vol. ends: No. 4. Online: Allen Press Inc.; EBSCO Publishing, EBSCO Host. *Indexed:* B&AI, BiolAb, CABA, ChemAb, EnvInd, FPA, ForAb, HortAb, IndVet, OceAb, RRTA, S&F, SCI, SWRA, VB, WAE&RSA, WRCInf, ZooRec. *Aud.:* Ac, Sa.

A quarterly publication to promote information exchanges between fisheries managers. Covers all aspects of finfish and exploitable shellfish fisheries and the many challenges those fisheries face. Contains 20–30 research articles and multiple "Management Briefs." As the journal of one of the world's oldest and largest professional fisheries societies, this title is a must for all fisheries scientists.

2809. *Reviews in Fish Biology and Fisheries.* [ISSN: 0960-3166] q. EUR 783 print & online eds. Ed(s): Jennifer L Nielsen. Springer Netherlands, Van Godewijckstraat 30, Dordrecht, 3311 GX, Netherlands; http://www.springeronline.com. Adv. Refereed. Online: EBSCO Publishing, EBSCO Host; Gale; IngentaConnect; OCLC Online Computer Library Center, Inc.; OhioLINK; Ovid Technologies, Inc.; Springer LINK; SwetsWise Online Content. Reprint: PSC. *Indexed:* AnBeAb, ApEcolAb, CABA, ForAb, HortAb, IndVet, M&GPA, OceAb, RRTA, S&F, SCI, VB, WAE&RSA, ZooRec. *Bk. rev.:* Various number and length. *Aud.:* Ac, Sa.

Publishes four to six papers per issue and book reviews, conference reports, and "Points of View." The journal caters to all those interested in fish as an organism and tries to reach all levels, from the general public to the academic researcher.

2810. *Reviews in Fisheries Science.* [ISSN: 1064-1262] 1992. q. GBP 597 print & online eds. Ed(s): Dr. Robert R Stickney. Taylor & Francis Inc., 325 Chestnut St, Ste 800, Philadelphia, PA 19016; orders@taylorandfrancis.com; http://www.taylorandfrancis.com. Illus., index. Refereed. Vol. ends: No. 4. Reprint: PSC. *Indexed:* C&ISA, CerAb, IAA, OceAb, SCI, ZooRec. *Bk. rev.:* Various number and length. *Aud.:* Ac, Sa.

This journal covers all aspects of fisheries science and provides up-to-date coverage of the latest hot topics. A recent issue focuses on the ecology and impacts of highway construction on stream habitat. Each issue contains 3–5 review articles.

Tropical Fish Hobbyist. See Pets section.

2811. *World Aquaculture Society. Journal.* Former titles: *World Mariculture Society. Journal; World Mariculture Society. Proceedings.* [ISSN: 0893-8849] 1986. q. GBP 201 print & online eds. Ed(s): Carl Webster. Blackwell Publishing, Inc., Commerce Place, 350 Main St, Malden, MA 02148; customerservices@blackwellpublishing.com; http://www.blackwellpublishing.com. Illus. Refereed. Vol. ends: No. 4. Reprint: PSC. *Indexed:* Agr, BiolAb, CABA, DSA, ForAb, HortAb, IndVet, OceAb, RRTA, S&F, SCI, VB, WAE&RSA, ZooRec. *Aud.:* Ac, Sa.

This journal publishes research articles on international aquaculture geared toward fisheries scientists. Articles cover the culture of aquatic plant and animal life, and topics include diseases, economics, genetics, physiology, and reproduction.

■ FISHING

Rachel Crane, Assistant Professor and Librarian, Wichita State University Libraries, Wichita State University, Wichita, KS 67260-0068

Introduction

The titles listed in this section focus on the sport of fishing and are appropriate for public libraries or for personal subscription. These publications represent all methods of fishing—spin, bait, and fly fishing, with titles focusing on diverse fishing-related activities, a variety of species, and/or diverse fishing habitats. Titles examine fishing in general or focus on a single aspect of the sport such as fly tying (*Fly Tyer*), a species (*Bassin'*), or a habitat (*Salt Water Sportsman*). Almost all titles contain information on technique, gear, safety, education, history, conservation, fish biology, literature, news, and legislation. Occasionally, titles incorporate other outdoor activities, notably hunting or boating. Regional information is of prime importance to sport fishermen, and librarians will want to be aware of geographic and species preferences. It should also be noted that those who fly fish often travel to do so, since their prime quarry is often, but not limited to, cold water trout and salmon. No matter the method of fishing, these publications provide wide geographic coverage of fishing in all bodies of water. Most publications found here are not indexed, however this should not deter one from subscribing. Popular by nature, these titles are often enjoyed by browsing, especially since so many have inspiring photographs.

Basic Periodicals

Ems: Field and Stream, Outdoor Life; Hs, Ga, Ac: American Angler, Field and Stream, Fly Fisherman, In-Fisherman, Outdoor Life.

Basic Abstracts and Indexes

Sports Periodicals Index, Readers' Guide to Periodical Literature.

2812. *American Angler: the magazine of fly fishing & fly tying.* Former titles: *American Angler and Fly Tyer; American Fly Tyer; Fly Tyer.* [ISSN: 1055-6737] 1977. bi-m. USD 21.95 domestic; USD 31.95 Canada; USD 41.95 elsewhere. Ed(s): Russ Lumpkin, Phil Monahan. Morris Communications Co., LLC., 725 Broad St, Augusta, GA 30901; http://www.morris.com/. Adv. Circ: 60000 Paid. *Indexed:* PEI. *Aud.:* Hs, Sa.

American Angler is a wonderful publication for fly fishers and tyers of all levels. Although it focuses on cold water species, articles also appear about fishing with a fly for warm water and saltwater species. Regular contributors are the tops in their field. Regular columns and departments cover entomology, casting, warm water fly fishing, fly fishing techniques, fly tying, and new equipment; reflective essays are included as well. Features focus on detailed descriptions of fishing locations and fly fishing tactics. Articles are well written, enjoyable, and accompanied by fine photo illustrations. Highly recommended for all libraries serving a fly fishing population.

2813. *Bassin': official magazine of the weekend angler.* Formerly (until 1985): *Pro Bass.* [ISSN: 0884-4739] 1974. 7x/yr. USD 15.95. Ed(s): Jason Sowards. NatCom, Inc., 7580 E 151st St, Bixby, OK 74008; cs@natcom-publications.com; http://www.natcom-publications.com. Illus., adv. Sample. Circ: 200000 Paid. Vol. ends: Dec. *Aud.:* Ems, Hs, Sa.

This magazine is devoted to bass fishing all over the world. Each issue has seasonal themes plus regular and feature articles. Some of these include letters, association news, tournaments and events, tips and techniques for the young and beginning angler, tackle and boat maintenance, and lure and bait reports. The information is accurate and appropriate for readers of any age. The species most frequently discussed are largemouth, smallmouth, and spotted bass. Periodically, information about white, stripers, Suwanee, pavon, or peacock bass is given. *Bassin'* would be well read in any library, as bass fishing occurs throughout North America. The magazine has a web site, and some features are available there to whet your appetite.

2814. *Crappie World.* Formerly (until 199?): *Crappie.* [ISSN: 1072-9011] 1989. q. USD 15.95. Ed(s): Jason Sowards. NatCom, Inc., 7580 E 151st St, Bixby, OK 74008; cs@natcom-publications.com; http://www.natcom-publications.com. Illus., adv. Sample. Circ: 100000 Paid. Vol. ends: Dec. *Aud.:* Ems, Hs, Sa.

Crappie World is a specialized magazine covering all aspects of crappie fishing. It presents information for all ages of fishermen and all locations where panfish are found. The crappie enthusiast will be updated on coming tournaments and events, recipes, techniques, equipment, and fishing stories. *Crappie World* provides good information for libraries near crappie waters, which are essentially all across North America.

Disabled Outdoors Magazine. See Hiking, Climbing, and Outdoor Recreation/General section.

Field & Stream. See Hunting and Guns section.

2815. *Fish & Fly: for the adventure angler.* [ISSN: 1535-6353] 5x/yr. USD 15.95 domestic; USD 23.95 Canada; USD 35.95 elsewhere. Ed(s): Thomas R Pero. Turnstile Publishing Company, 1500 Park Center Dr, Orlando, FL 32835. Adv. *Aud.:* Sa.

This is a relatively new publication, and it fills a niche for the traveling angler looking to explore new directions. Meant for the fly fisher, in-depth articles focus primarily on fishing destinations from exotic locations to neighborhood streams; as the subtitle says, this magazine is "for the adventure angler." The publication is excellently produced, with enticing feature articles accompanied by wonderful photographs, fly recipes, and local information. Departments include readers' fishing logs, letters, and reports from home waters. Although it has the look of an expensive title, its reasonable subscription price makes it easy for libraries to purchase.

2816. *Fishing and Hunting News: the nation's largest outdoor newspaper.* [ISSN: 0015-301X] 1944. 24x/yr. USD 39.95; USD 3.50 newsstand/ cover per issue. Ed(s): John Marsh. Outdoor Empire Publishing, Inc., 21415 87th St, Woodinville, WA 98072; mliang@outdoorempire.com; http://www.outdoorempire.com. Illus., adv. Sample. Circ: 85000 Paid. Vol. ends: Dec. *Aud.:* Hs, Ga.

Fishing and Hunting News publishes seven region-specific editions: Washington/Alaska, Oregon, California, Colorado, the Great Lakes states (Illinois, Indiana, Ohio, Michigan, Wisconsin), the Mid-Atlantic states (New Jersey, New York, Pennsylvania), and the Rocky Mountain states (Idaho, Montana, Utah, Wyoming, Nevada). The local and timely articles give this magazine characteristics not found in any other periodical in this section. The photographs are well done, and many articles have charts, maps, and statistics. A publication of this quality, full of local expert advice from cover to cover, should not be ignored by libraries. The magazine's web site contains a small selection of features for each of the seven editions.

2817. *Fly Angler's Online: the fly fishing enthusiast's weekly magazine.* w. Free. Fly Angler's Online, P.O. Box 1959, Poulsbo, WA 98370; publisher@flyanglersonline.com. *Aud.:* Hs, Ga.

This online publication for fly fisherpersons is wonderfully thorough and up-to-date. The site contains articles on fly fishing instruction, fly tying, regional fishing information, humor, poetry, and a multitude of diverse features, along with a bulletin board and chat room. Notable are the photographs accompanying fly tying recipes, which are excellent. Overall, the site is easily navigable. It is revised weekly, and past articles are archived in each section. This is the publication to bookmark for both beginning and longtime anglers.

2818. *Fly Fisherman: the leading magazine of fly fishing.* [ISSN: 0015-4741] 1969. 6x/yr. USD 19.95 domestic; USD 32.95 Canada; USD 34.95 elsewhere. Source Interlink Companies, 27500 Riverview Center Blvd, Bonita Springs, FL 34134; edisupport@sourceinterlink.com; http://www.sourceinterlink.com. Illus., adv. Sample. Circ: 151774 Paid. Vol. ends: Nov. *Bk. rev.:* 2-3; 500 words. *Aud.:* Hs, Sa.

Fly Fisherman is devoted solely to the sport of fly fishing. The articles cover fresh or saltwater fly fishing, various species of fish, and information useful to the expert or novice fly fisherperson. A unique feature of this publication is international geographic coverage specific to fly fishing. The magazine has full-color photographs, well-written articles, and a little something for everyone. For some feature articles in full text, other reports, articles on equipment, and a large database of fly patterns, go to the web site at www.flyfisherman.com.

2819. *Fly Tyer.* [ISSN: 1082-1309] q. USD 21.95 domestic; USD 31.95 in Canada & Mexico; USD 41.95 elsewhere. Ed(s): Russ Lumpkin, David Klausmeyer. Morris Communications Co., LLC., 725 Broad St, Augusta, GA 30901; http://www.morris.com/. Adv. *Aud.:* Hs, Sa.

Fly Tyer is unique in its exclusive focus on fly tying. Flies for all species and all tying techniques are presented here. Columns cover tying history, new innovations, tips for new tyers, and materials selection. Features provide in-depth information on fly patterns and tying methods. Patterns are presented in a clear and concise fashion, with outstanding photographic images. This publication is worth its subscription price for the fine photography alone. Recommended for libraries that support fly fishers.

2820. *Flyfishing & Tying Journal.* Former titles (until 1999): *Flyfishing;* (until 1997): *Western Flyfishing;* (until 1996): *Flyfishing.* [ISSN: 1521-7361] 1978. q. USD 18.95 domestic; USD 23.95 foreign; USD 4.99 newsstand/cover per issue. Ed(s): Ms. Kim Koch, Mr. David Hughes. Frank Amato Publications, Inc, 4040 S E Wister St, Portland, OR 97222; info@amatobooks.com; http://www.amatobooks.com. Adv. Circ: 36056 Paid. *Bk. rev.:* 3-5, 200-500 words. *Aud.:* Hs, Sa.

Formerly known as *Western Flyfishing,* this title does emphasize Western waters in the United States, but overall its coverage is international. North America is covered in each issue, and occasionally fishing locations in other countries are featured. As a publication that emphasizes both fishing and tying, the journal covers casting, fly tying, knots, places to fish, conservation, new products, books, videos, and fishing news. Each issue is filled with contributions from outstanding authors in the field, accompanied by excellent, useful illustrations. Fly fishing readers living in the West or traveling to fish in the West will get their money's worth from this publication, and so will libraries. Highly recommended.

Fur-Fish-Game. See Hunting and Guns section.

2821. *Game & Fish.* m. USD 19.97; USD 3.50 newsstand/cover per issue. Source Interlink Companies, 27500 Riverview Center Blvd, Bonita Springs, FL 34134; edisupport@sourceinterlink.com; http://www.sourceinterlink.com. Adv. *Aud.:* Hs, Ga.

Game & Fish produces regional editions for 30 states and/or regions of the continental United States. This publication excels at providing timely, detailed information close to home for both fishers and hunters. There are feature articles covering recommended places to fish, current water conditions, suggested techniques, conservation, and new products pertaining to all species and fishing methods in the appropriate locality. Recommended for libraries that serve those wanting to explore their local fishing resources. Additional information is available at www.gameandfishmag.com.

Gray's Sporting Journal. See Hunting and Guns section.

2822. *In-Fisherman: the journal of freshwater fishing.* [ISSN: 0276-9905] 1975. 8x/yr. USD 16 domestic; USD 29 Canada; USD 31 elsewhere. Source Interlink Companies, 27500 Riverview Center Blvd, Bonita Springs, FL 34134; edisupport@sourceinterlink.com; http://www.sourceinterlink.com. Illus., adv. Sample. Circ: 270994 Paid. Vol. ends: Nov. *Indexed:* ASIP. *Aud.:* Hs, Ga, Ac.

In-Fisherman's coverage is complete, with articles about freshwater fish, lures, tactics, strategies, biology, the science of fisheries, and all kinds of waterways. Each issue of over 100 pages focuses on common fish species such as bass, walleye, pike, muskie, crappie, bluegill, perch, and catfish, with minor species covered in at least one article. Articles are well written by professional, experienced staff and have excellent illustrations. No library could go wrong with a subscription to *In-Fisherman*. It is the Cadillac of fishing magazines for older readers. Four annual guides are produced in addition to the magazine and are worth considering for purchase: *Walleye Guide, Ice-fishing Guide, Bass Guide,* and *Catfish In-sider Guide.* Publication information can be found at the journal's web site: www.in-fisherman.com.

2823. *Musky Hunter Magazine.* [ISSN: 1079-3402] 1989. bi-m. USD 20.95 domestic; USD 23.95 foreign. Ed(s): Jim Saric. Esox Promotions, Inc, 7978 Hwy 70 East, St Germain, WI 54558; info@muskyhunter.com; http://www.muskyhunter.com. Adv. Circ: 32000 Paid. *Aud.:* Hs, Sa.

This is a specialized publication that focuses on muskellunge and musky fishing in all areas of their range in North America. Because muskies are a fish of northern regions, this title would be a particular asset to collections serving this area of the United States or Canada. Articles focus on fishing methods, fishing history, lake profiles, angler interviews, biology, and research. Regular departments highlight reports of big fish catches, tournaments, questions answered by professional fishermen, and new gear. Informative articles are accompanied by excellent photographs that may be enough to influence one to take up the pursuit of muskies. Recommended for public libraries in areas with a substantial population of muskellunge.

Outdoor Life. See Hiking, Climbing, and Outdoor Recreation/General section.

2824. *Salt Water Sportsman.* [ISSN: 0036-3618] 1939. m. USD 24.97 domestic; USD 27.97 Canada; USD 4.99 per issue. Time4 Media, Inc., 2 Park Ave, New York, NY 10016. Illus., adv. Sample. Circ: 168000 Paid. Vol. ends: Jan. Online: EBSCO Publishing, EBSCO Host. *Indexed:* ConsI. *Aud.:* Sa.

Salt Water Sportsman is the only magazine in this section that provides international coverage for all methods of saltwater fishing, including fly fishing, bottom fishing, and trolling. The full-color publication is written by professionals who practice what they preach. Excellent articles and photos present information on fish facts, tales, rigging, techniques, boats, products, destinations, offshore news, and sportfishing news. Feature articles cover more specialized topics on specific fish, equipment, management, and conservation matters. This magazine is a source of saltwater and offshore fishing information that is not found in similar periodicals.

2825. *Saltwater Fly Fishing.* [ISSN: 1082-1295] 1995. bi-m. USD 17.95 domestic; USD 27.95 Canada; USD 37.95 elsewhere. Ed(s): Russ Lumpkin. Morris Communications Co., LLC., 725 Broad St, Augusta, GA 30901; http://www.morris.com/. Adv. *Aud.:* Hs, Sa.

As a specialized publication, *Saltwater Fly Fishing* caters to those who approach the seas with a fly rod and reel. Although it focuses on fly fishing on the coasts of North America, this publication is international in scope. All aspects of the sport are covered. Regular columns discuss casting, gear, fish behavior, fly tying, boating, and tactics. Features consist of regional reports, different fish species, new gear, and angling techniques. All articles are well written and contributed by prominent authors in the sport. Highly recommended for libraries near saltwater locations.

Tropical Fish Hobbyist. See Pets section.

2826. *Walleye In-Sider.* [ISSN: 1068-2112] 1989. 6x/yr. USD 11.98 domestic; USD 24 Canada; USD 26.98 elsewhere. Ed(s): Doug Stange. Source Interlink Companies, 27500 Riverview Center Blvd, Bonita Springs, FL 34134; edisupport@sourceinterlink.com; http://www.sourceinterlink.com. Illus., adv. Circ: 66434 Paid. *Aud.:* Hs, Sa.

This is a specialized publication that covers all aspects of walleye fishing in the United States and Canada. Articles emphasize methods and techniques used in the pursuit of walleye. Regular departments discuss fishing locations, travel, tackle, recipes, fish biology, electronic accessories, boat maintenance, recommended times to fish, and methods of fishing. In addition, lots of tournament information is provided. Articles are well written and provide practical information for anglers of all levels.

■ FOLKLORE

Jean Piper Burton, Technical Services Librarian, FH Green Library, West Chester University of Pennsylvania, West Chester, PA 19383

Introduction

Folklore can be defined as cultural materials that are part of a group of people and are passed by oral communication, customary example, and imitation. Folk traditions can be a part of many generations or of recent developments found in pop culture. Because everyone is a part of some folk-culture group, there is interest in the subject by both laypersons and scholars.

To accommodate both the general reader and the researcher, this section covers a wide variety of publications with differing scopes. Some titles offer examples of a specific geographic area, some take a historical perspective, and others are research oriented. Over the past few years, there have appeared more and more folklore resources on the web. Most societies and many individual folklorists have their own web sites. These sites may include selected publications from the society's journal, tables of contents for both current and past issues, and/or opportunities to subscribe for a fee to the journal in either electronic format or print. A few sites offer their journals for free. Electronic indexing services may offer full-text articles from a variety of titles. In this review section, the journals indicated as electronic resources are samples of e-journals in the area of folklore. Sample selections tend to be published only in electronic form and have shown a stable history. Most provide free access.

Basic Periodicals

Hs: *The Foxfire Magazine*; Ga: *Journal of American Culture, Storytelling Magazine*; Ac: *Ethnologies, Folklore, Journal of American Folklore, Journal of Folklore Research.*

Basic Abstracts and Indexes

America: History and Life, Historical Abstracts, Humanities Index, MFL International Bibliography.

2827. *Asian Folklore Studies.* Formerly (until vol.22, 1963): *Folklore Studies.* [ISSN: 0385-2342] 1942. s-a. JPY 6000 (Individuals, JPY 3000). Nanzan University, Anthropological Institute, 18 Yamazato-cho, Showa-ku, Nagoya, 466-8673, Japan; nuai@ic.nanzan-u.ac.jp; http://www.nanzan-u.ac.jp/JINRUIKEN/index.html. Illus., adv. Refereed. Circ: 350. Vol. ends: No. 2. Microform: IDC. Online: American Theological Library Association; EBSCO Publishing, EBSCO Host; Florida Center for Library Automation; Gale; JSTOR (Web-based Journal Archive); Northern Light Technology, Inc.; OCLC Online Computer Library Center, Inc.; Ovid Technologies, Inc.; ProQuest K-12 Learning Solutions; ProQuest LLC (Ann Arbor); H.W. Wilson. *Indexed:* AICP, AmHI, ArtHuCI, BAS, EI, FR, HumInd, IBR, IBSS, IBZ, MLA-IB, RI-1, RILM, SSCI. *Bk. rev.:* 30, 1,000 words. *Aud.:* Ac.

This journal publishes scholarly research on the folklore of Asian nations, including literary works and the oral tradition; it also discusses folkloric aspects of belief, cultural customs, and art. The journal includes scholarly articles, research materials, communications, and book reviews. Some of the articles are purely descriptive accounts or retellings of folk tales; others are more analytic, based on research, including surveys and textual analysis or comparative study. Examples of recent topics are the rite of second burial in Taiwan, Korean shamanism, the scorpion in Muslim folklore, and folk culture and urban adaption in Bangladesh. Abstracts are included. Most but not all of the articles are in English; some are in French or German. The book reviews are fairly lengthy. Recommended for academic libraries with an interest in Asian literature or arts, folklore, or children's literature. (ChD)

2828. *Australian Folklore: a yearly journal of folklore studies.* [ISSN: 0819-0852] 1987. a. AUD 30 (Individuals, AUD 25). Ed(s): Robert Smith, John S. Ryan. Australian Folklore Association, c/o Prof. J.S. Ryan, Ed., School of English, Communication and Theatre, University Of New England, NSW 2351, Australia; jryan@pobox.une.edu.au; http://www.une.edu.au/arts/FolkloreJournal/AF.htm. Illus., adv. Refereed. Circ: 300 Paid. *Indexed:* IBR, IBZ, MLA-IB, RILM. *Bk. rev.:* 500-700 words. *Aud.:* Ac.

A scholarly journal devoted to mostly Australian folklore with a few articles on British and American folk subjects. Article topics cover a wide range of lore from sport to music and pop culture to traditional customs. Most articles have reference lists and/or bibliographies. Occasional issues are devoted to a single theme or to a noted folklorist and his or her work. Past issues have included the subjects of foodways past and present, tourism, storytelling, quilts, and gathering songs in Australian. Most issues include book reviews. Although not always an easy title to acquire, it does provide an excellent source for students of Australian folklore. Recommended for universities that support a strong folklore program.

2829. *Children's Folklore Review.* [ISSN: 0739-5558] 1979. s-a. Free to members. Ed(s): C W Sullivan, III. East Carolina University, E Fifth St, Greenville, NC 27858-4353; http://www.acls.org/afolks.htm. Circ: 150. *Indexed:* MLA-IB. *Aud.:* Ga, Ac.

Published by the Children's Folklore Section of the American Folklore Society, the scope of this title covers "all aspects of children's traditions—oral, customary, and material." Articles may also deal with the use of folklore in children's literature, education, and pop culture. Issues contain a few lengthy articles plus letters to the editor and section announcements. Although the format consisting of only a small number of feature articles may be limiting, it is a good title for those doing research in children and folklore, especially since titles that deal strictly with children's lore are not plentiful. It is also a good source for those working in critical review of children's literature as a genre.

2830. *Cultural Analysis: an interdisciplinary forum of folklore and popular culture.* [ISSN: 1537-7873] 2000. irreg. Free. Ed(s): JoAnn Conrad. Cultural Analysis, University of California at Berkeley, 232 Kroeber Hall, Berkeley, CA 94720; caforum@socrates.berkeley.edu; http://socrates.berkeley.edu/~caforum/index.html. Refereed. *Indexed:* RILM. *Aud.:* Ac.

This e-journal is an "interdisciplinary, peer-reviewed journal dedicated to investigating expressive and everyday culture." The journal includes research articles, notes, reviews, and responses. It is designed to be cross-disciplinary and international in scope. Available free on the web, the journal is produced in both html and pdf formats. Some feature articles are followed by critics' responses. Articles cover topics such as traditional world music and postcards as souvenirs and collectibles. Each article is abstracted. Reviews average 1,500 to 2,000 words. Some issues are thematic. One of the strengths of this publication is its diversity of authorship, with contributors from around the world. This journal seems to have developed a solid foundation for web access. Recommended for academics with cultural studies programs. URL: http://ist-socrates.berkeley.edu/~caforum/

2831. *Culture & Tradition.* [ISSN: 0701-0184] 1976. a. CND 8. Memorial University of Newfoundland, Arts and Admin. Bldg., P O Box 115, St. John's, NF A1C 5S7, Canada; CULTURE@Kean.ucs.mun.ca. Illus. Circ: 300. *Indexed:* AICP, CBCARef, CPerI, MLA-IB, RILM. *Bk. rev.:* Number and length vary. *Aud.:* Ac.

Published by the graduate students of folklore at Memorial University of Newfoundland, *Culture & Tradition* is Canada's longest-running bilingual folklore journal. Published in English and French, it covers all aspects of folklore from traditional art and music to cultural psychology and sociological structure. Published annually, each volume contains an average of six articles, a section of book reviews, and several media reviews. In the issues with fewer book reviews, the reviews are quite lengthy. Some of the volumes are edited loosely around broad themes such as music or the supernatural. A recent issue covers student life and campus customs. Because it covers more than just regional topics, this is a good title for academic folklore programs.

2832. *Ethnologies.* Formerly: *Canadian Folklore.* [ISSN: 1481-5974] 1979. a. CND 65 membership (Individuals, CND 45 membership; Students, CND 25 membership). Ed(s): Nancy Schmitz. Folklore Studies Association of Canada, CELAT- Faculte des Lettres, c/o Universite Laval, Quebec, PQ G1K 7P4, Canada; cfe@celat.ulaval.ca; http://www.fl.ulaval.ca/celat/acef. Illus., adv. Refereed. Circ: 500. Vol. ends: No. 2. *Indexed:* AmH&L, AmHI, CBCARef, CPerI, HistAb, HumInd, IBSS, MLA-IB, RILM. *Aud.:* Ac.

Published by the Folklore Studies Association of Canada, *Ethnologies* is a continuation of *Canadian Folklore/Folklore Canadien*. There seems to be little change in scope or content. Each issue of this journal is devoted to a specific topic. Themes are wide ranging, from the historic and traditional to current trends in the field. A recent issue on the theme of the geography of space includes articles on Cape Breton Celtic and women alone in an urban landscape. In the several copies reviewed, the number of articles in French and in English varied, but abstracts for each article were in both languages. The review section includes both book and media titles. For academic libraries that support folk studies programs, this free journal is a necessary addition. Recommended for large public libraries with strong folk and culture collections.

2833. *Folklore.* Formed by the merger of (until 1888-1890): *Archaeological Review;* (1883-1889): *The Folk-Lore Journal;* Which was formerly (1878-1882): *The Folk-Lore Record.* [ISSN: 0015-587X] 1890. 3x/yr. GBP 270 print & online eds. Ed(s): Patricia Lysaght. Routledge, 4 Park Square, Milton Park, Abingdon, OX14 4RN, United Kingdom; journals@routledge.com; http://www.tandf.co.uk. Illus., adv. Sample. Refereed. Circ: 1300 Paid. Microform: PMC. Online: Chadwyck-Healey Inc.; EBSCO Publishing, EBSCO Host; Florida Center for Library Automation; Gale; IngentaConnect; JSTOR (Web-based Journal Archive); Northern Light Technology, Inc.; OCLC Online Computer Library Center, Inc.; ProQuest K-12 Learning Solutions; ProQuest LLC (Ann Arbor); SwetsWise Online Content; H.W. Wilson. Reprint: PSC. *Indexed:* AICP, AmHI, ArtHuCI, BEL&L, BRI, BrArAb, BrHumI, FR, HumInd, IBR, IBSS, IBZ, IndIslam, L&LBA, MLA-IB, NumL, RI-1, RILM. *Bk. rev.:* 20, 500-700 words. *Aud.:* Ac.

A British publication, this scholarly journal considers itself a forum for European folk studies and culture, but most articles are on the United Kingdom. In addition to articles, some issues include papers from meetings of the Folklore Society. Bibliographies, articles on recipients of awards in the field, and book reviews are located in the "Review of Folklore Scholarship" section. This journal is for libraries that provide research materials in the area of folk studies.

2834. *Folklore.* [ISSN: 1406-0949] 1996. q. Free. Ed(s): Andres Kuperjanov, Mare Koiva. Eesti Kirjandusmuuseum, Vanemuise St 42-235, Tartu, 51003, Estonia; kirmus@kirmus.ee; http://www.kirmus.ee/. Illus. Refereed. *Indexed:* IBSS, MLA-IB. *Bk. rev.:* Number and length vary. *Aud.:* Ga, Ac.

This journal is the publication of the Folklore Department of the Institute of the Estonian Language and is not to be confused with the British Folklore Society's journal of the same name. Articles cover a wide variety of topics, including religion in Russia, burial tradition, group identity, and the Ingrian Finns. Some issues include book reviews and news. There is a special emphasis on Estonia and neighboring regions. The real appeal is the free electronic version of this publication. Articles are done as pdf files to provide illustrations as well as text. There is online access to both current and back issues. An editorial note welcomes contributors from all countries and contributions on all aspects of folklore. Submission guidelines include a listing of software requirements. Although it has strong Eastern European emphasis, this is a worthy journal and one of the better ones with full online access. Recommended for academic and general adult readers. URL: www.folklore.ee/folklore

2835. *Folklore Forum (Online Edition).* Formerly (until 2004): *Folklore Forum (Print Edition).* 1968. s-a. Ed(s): Danille Christensen Lindquist. Folklore & Ethnomusicology Publications, Inc., 504 N Fess, Bloomington, IN 47408; folkpub@ucs.indiana.edu. Illus., adv. Refereed. Circ: 300 Paid. Vol. ends: No. 2. *Indexed:* ABS&EES, AmH&L, AmHI, BAS, HistAb, HumInd, MLA-IB, RILM. *Bk. rev.:* 5-7, 500-600 words. *Aud.:* Ac.

Edited by graduate students at the Folklore Institute of Indiana University, this journal has changed its format to electronic only. The introductory statement describes it as not a scholarly publication, but rather as a forum for students to explore their ideas and interests in the area of folklore. For the electronic version, several of the articles were reprints from early issues. There are five articles on average, and about as many book reviews. Hopefully, this cross-disciplinary journal will now be able to publish on a regular basis. URL: www.indiana.edu/~folkpub/forum/

The Foxfire Magazine. See Teenagers section.

2836. *Indian Folklife.* [ISSN: 0972-6470] 2000. q. Ed(s): M D Muthukumaraswamy. National Folklore Support Centre, 508, Kaveri Complex, 5th Fl, 96 Mahatma Gandhi Rd, Chennai, 600 034, India; info@indianfolklore.org; http://www.indianfolklore.org. *Bk. rev.:* 500-2000 words. *Aud.:* Ac.

This newsletter is available on the web via open access. According to the web site, "it publishes original and unpublished research papers, book reviews, resource reviews and announcemtns in the discipline of folklore." The scope of the newsletter is India, primarily south and southeastern India. Book reviews average about a page and a half. Issues are usually thematic; a recent issue covers Indian performing arts and education. The National Folklore Support Centre also publishes an annual scholarly journal, *Indian Folklore Research Journal,* with a limited number of articles. Best purchased by academic libraries supporting folklore or world culture programs.

2837. *Journal of American Culture.* Former titles (until 2003): *Journal of American and Comparative Culture;* (until Jun. 2001): *Journal of American Culture.* [ISSN: 1542-7331] 1978. q. GBP 137 print & online eds. Ed(s): William M Jones, Kathy Merlock Jackson. Blackwell Publishing, Inc., Commerce Place, 350 Main St, Malden, MA 02148; customerservices@blackwellpublishing.com; http://www.blackwellpublishing.com. Illus. Refereed. Circ: 1200. Vol. ends: No. 4. Microform: PQC. Online: Blackwell Synergy; Chadwyck-Healey Inc.; EBSCO Publishing, EBSCO Host; Gale; IngentaConnect; Northern Light Technology, Inc.; OCLC Online Computer Library Center, Inc.; OhioLINK; ProQuest K-12 Learning Solutions; ProQuest LLC (Ann Arbor); SwetsWise Online Content; H.W. Wilson. Reprint: PSC. *Indexed:* ABS&EES, AmH&L, AmHI, ApEcolAb, ArtHuCI, BRI, CABA, CBRI, CJA, CommAb, FLI, HistAb, HumInd, IIMP, IIPA, LRI, MLA-IB, PRA, PSA, RILM, RRTA, SSA, SociolAb. *Bk. rev.:* 20-30, 300-500 words. *Aud.:* Ga, Ac.

As the official journal of the American Cultural Association, this publication intends to "promote and facilitate American culture in its broadest sense." Contributors must be members of the association. There is a mix of historic and present-day material. Articles cover traditional folklore themes and pop culture. Some issues are thematic; for example, a recent issue loosely follows the theme of film's and television's influence and heroes. Most issues include short book reviews. With its wide variety of topics and accessible writing style, this title will be of interest to the general reader and the student of folklore.

2838. *Journal of American Folklore.* [ISSN: 0021-8715] 1888. q. USD 105. Ed(s): Harry Berger, Giovanna Del Negro. University of Illinois Press, 1325 S Oak St, Champaign, IL 61820-6903; journals@uillinois.edu; http://www.press.uillinois.edu. Illus., index, adv. Refereed. Circ: 3000 Paid. Vol. ends: No. 4. Microform: MIM; PMC; PQC. Online: Chadwyck-Healey Inc.; EBSCO Publishing, EBSCO Host; JSTOR (Web-based Journal Archive); OCLC Online Computer Library Center, Inc.; OhioLINK; Project MUSE; ProQuest K-12 Learning Solutions; ProQuest LLC (Ann Arbor); SwetsWise Online Content; H.W. Wilson. *Indexed:* ABS&EES, AICP, AmH&L, AmHI, AnthLit, ArtHuCI, BEL&L, BRI, CBRI, FR, HistAb, HumInd, IBR, IBZ, IIMP, IIPA, IndIslam, L&LBA, MLA-IB, MusicInd, RI-1, RILM, SSA, SSCI, SociolAb. *Bk. rev.:* 10, 500-700 words. *Aud.:* Ga, Ac.

Although there is an emphasis on the United States, the scope of this journal is worldwide and varied. Articles past and present include such topics as emerging legends in contemporary society, challenges for the folklore discipline, and folklore in education. Occasional issues are devoted to a single theme. Reviews are lengthy and cover both books and media. One of journal's goals is to "push the boundaries, explore the borders, and expand the parameters of folklore." Academic libraries should select this title for their basic collection, and large public libraries will also want to consider it.

2839. *Journal of Cultural Geography.* [ISSN: 0887-3631] 1980. s-a. Individuals, USD 40. Ed(s): Alyson Greiner. Popular Press, Bowling Green State University, Jerome Library Room 100, Bowling Green, OH 43403; http://www.bgsu.edu/offices/press. Illus., adv. Refereed. Circ: 600. Vol. ends: No. 2. Online: EBSCO Publishing, EBSCO Host; Florida Center for Library Automation; Gale. *Indexed:* AmH&L, BAS, FR, HistAb, MLA-IB, RI-1, RILM, WAE&RSA. *Bk. rev.:* 12, 400-500 words. *Aud.:* Ac.

This journal's articles discuss the influences of culture on the physical world. Topics vary widely, from the historic to current pop culture. Articles cover a wide range of folklore, from changes in American religion to McDonald's hamburgers in the United Kingdom. Some issues are thematic; a recent theme was physical and geographical place in film. Most contributors are professors or graduate students. In addition to articles, there are book reviews and occasional annotated bibliographies. This title should appeal to a wide variety of readers. A good pick for academic libraries and larger public libraries.

2840. *Journal of Folklore Research: an international journal of folklore and ethnomusicology.* Former titles (until 1983): *Folklore Institute. Journal;* (until 1964): *Midwest Folklore.* [ISSN: 0737-7037] 1951. 3x/yr. USD 55 (Individuals, USD 29.50). Ed(s): Moira Smith, John McDowell. Indiana University Press, 601 N Morton St, Bloomington, IN 47404; journals@indiana.edu; http://www.indiana.edu/~iupress. Illus., index, adv. Refereed. Circ: 700. Vol. ends: No. 3. Microform: PQC. Online: Chadwyck-Healey Inc.; EBSCO Publishing, EBSCO Host; Florida Center for Library Automation; Gale; OCLC Online Computer Library Center, Inc.; OhioLINK; Project MUSE; ProQuest LLC (Ann Arbor); SwetsWise Online Content; H.W. Wilson. *Indexed:* AICP, AmH&L, AmHI, ArtHuCI, BEL&L, EI, FR, HistAb, HumInd, IBR, IBSS, IBZ, IIMP, IIPA, MLA-IB, MusicInd, RILM, SSCI. *Bk. rev.:* Number and length varies. *Aud.:* Ac.

This scholarly journal is published by the Indiana University Folklore Institute. Its purpose is to provide a forum for research and theory in the field of folklore. It is international in scope. Issues cover a wide range of topics. Articles are usually related under a central theme or may highlight a noted folklorist. Most of the reviews have been moved to "Booknotes" on the institute's web site. However, more substantial ones still appear in the journal. Abstracts for articles can be located on their web site, but access to the actual article is through Project Muse. This title is a must for libraries serving academic folklore research and folklore programs.

2841. *Journal of Latin American Lore.* [ISSN: 0360-1927] 1975. s-a. USD 50 (Individuals, USD 40). Ed(s): Colleen H Trujillo, Johannes Wilbert. University of California at Los Angeles, Latin American Center, 10343 Bunche Hall, Box 951447, Los Angeles, CA 90095-1447. Illus., index, adv. Refereed. Circ: 325. Vol. ends: No. 2. *Indexed:* AICP, AmH&L, AmHI, AnthLit, ArtHuCI, HAPI, HistAb, HumInd, IBR, MLA-IB, MusicInd, RI-1. *Aud.:* Ac.

This journal is devoted to folk culture in Latin America, and its scope is from prehistoric times to the present day. Article research uses "records of ancient civilizations, indigenous groups, peasant communities, and the elite and popular sectors of modern urban society." Most pieces are scholarly in nature and most are in English. Although its publication schedule is erratic, the table of contents of issues can be found on their web site. This is a good title for academic libraries that support Latin American Studies programs. Large public libraries that serve Latino communities may also want to consider it.

2842. *Louisiana Folklore Miscellany.* [ISSN: 0090-9769] 1958. a. USD 10 (Individuals, USD 7). Ed(s): Marcia Gaudet. Louisiana Folklore Society, c/o Dept of English, Loyola University, New Orleans, LA 70118. *Aud.:* Ga, Ac.

Published under the auspices of the Louisiana Folklore Society, this is described on the society's web site as a publication of "articles, notes, and commentaries on all aspects of Louisiana folklore and folklife." What makes this journal a standout among Southern folklore journals is its wide variety of Southern cultural topics. It is an excellent source for articles on Cajun and Creole social life and customs. Issues have included such topics as quilting, oral narratives, ethnicity in Louisiana product names, Christmas levee bonfires, food, Mardi Gras chase, blues/gospel music, and midwifery. The society's web site offers full text of some articles. This is a great publication for general readers and folklore researchers interested in the traditions of the South. Highly recommended as a Southern folklore title.

2843. *Marvels & Tales: journal of fairy-tale studies.* Formerly (until 1996): *Merveilles et Contes.* [ISSN: 1521-4281] 1987. s-a. USD 52 (Individuals, USD 26). Ed(s): Donald P Haase. Wayne State University Press, The Leonard N Simons Bldg, 4809 Woodward Ave, Detroit, MI 48201-1309; http://wsupress.wayne.edu/. Illus. Refereed. Circ: 100. *Indexed:* AmHI, IBSS, MLA-IB. *Bk. rev.:* Number and length vary. *Aud.:* Ac.

According to its editorial statement, this journal is "committed to promoting advances in fairy-tale studies." Covering a wide variety of cultural groups and disciplines, there are up to five lengthy articles, plus translations of tales and reviews covering both print and media. Some issues are organized by themes,

including "Beauty and the Beast," romantic tales, marriage tests or quests in African oral literature, and the Arabian Nights. A scholarly journal for academic folklore programs or strong children's literature programs.

2844. *Mississippi Folklife.* Formerly: *Mississippi Folklore Register.* 1967. s-a. USD 10. Ed(s): Ted Dunbyn. University of Mississippi, Center for the Study of Southern Culture, Barnard Observatory, PO Box 1848, University, MS 38677-1848; http://imp.cssc.olemiss.edu/publications/missfolf/backissues/. Illus., adv. Circ: 350. Vol. ends: No. 2. *Indexed:* MLA-IB, RILM. *Bk. rev.:* 2-3, 300-500 words. *Aud.:* Ga, Ac.

Stating that it takes "a wide view of what is folk," this title covers subjects from the historical to present-day pop culture. Some issues are thematic, usually broad in scope. Content may include articles, photographic essays, reviews, and field notes. The reviews, both book and media, are well written. Although the scope of the journal is Mississippi and adjoining regions, it is a good title for Southern folklife in general. A must for libraries of its region, and a good bet for libraries interested in Southern folk culture.

2845. *New York Folklore.* Formerly (until 1974): *New York Folklore Quarterly.* [ISSN: 0361-204X] 1945. q. USD 50 (Individuals, USD 35; Students, USD 20). Ed(s): Karen Taussig Lux. New York Folklore Society, 632 W Buffalo St, 2nd Fl, Ithaca, NY 14850; nyfs@nyfolklore.org; http://www.nyfolklore.org. Illus. Refereed. Circ: 650. Vol. ends: No. 2. Microform: PQC. *Indexed:* AmH&L, ArtHuCI, ChemAb, HistAb, IIMP, IIPA, MLA-IB, MusicInd, RILM. *Aud.:* Ga, Ac.

Published by the New York Folklore Society, *Voices* covers New York State and surrounding regions. Most issues include feature articles, columns, society news, announcements, and reviews. The scope of the publication covers a wide variety of topics, from traditional accordian music to urban legends. The editors view the journal as publishing "peer-reviewed, research-based articles, written in an accessible style, on topics related to traditional art and life, including ethnic culture. Informative columns on subjects such as legal issues, photography, sound and video recording, archiving, ethics, and the nature of traditional art and life." For libraries that are interested in Northeastern folklore, this is a good title.

2846. *North Carolina Folklore Journal.* Formerly (until 1972): *North Carolina Folklore.* [ISSN: 0090-5844] 1948. 2x/yr. USD 25 (Individuals, USD 20; Students, USD 15). Ed(s): Dr. Carmine Prioli. North Carolina Folklore Society, P O Box 62271, Durham, NC 27715; http://www.ecu.edu/ncfolk/. Illus. Refereed. Circ: 500. Vol. ends: No. 2. *Indexed:* AmH&L, FR, HistAb, IIMP, IIPA, MLA-IB, MusicInd, RILM. *Bk. rev.:* 1-2, 300 words. *Aud.:* Ga, Ac.

Published by the North Carolina Folklore Society, this title's scope is "folk culture traditions in and related to North Carolina." Topics include the historical, the traditional, and the contemporary. Issues can be thematic, delving into all aspects of a subject from geographic and occupational influences to community and domestic life. There are reviews for books and media and also for exhibits. Although not lengthy, they are well written. This journal is a good choice not only for those interested in North Carolina folk culture but also the folklore of southern Appalachia and the Southeastern coast. Its easy reading style makes it a title for both general and academic library audiences.

2847. *Now & Then: the Appalachian magazine.* [ISSN: 0896-2693] 1984. 3x/yr. USD 25 (Individuals, USD 20 Membership contribution). Ed(s): Nancy Fischman, Jane Harris Woodside. East Tennessee State University, Center for Appalachian Studies and Services, PO Box 70556, Johnson City, TN 37614-0556; woodsidj@etsu.edu; http://cass.etsu.edu/n&t/. Circ: 1500. *Indexed:* AmH&L, FLI, HistAb, MLA-IB, RILM. *Bk. rev.:* 5, 500 words. *Aud.:* Ga.

Sponsored by the Center for Appalachian Studies and Services, this journal is probably the best source of folk culture relating to Appalachia. It is a nice mix of articles, essays, poetry, interviews, and photographs covering views of past and present folk life. Some issues are thematic—youth of Appalachia, media portrayal of the region. Reviews are limited, but additional titles are listed under "Books Worth Mentioning." Current events of the region are listed in an accompanying newsletter. An excellent title, recommended for libraries of the region and for others supporting interest in its folk culture.

2848. *Oral Tradition (Print Edition).* [ISSN: 0883-5365] 1986. s-a. USD
40 (Individuals, USD 30; Students, USD 20). Ed(s): John M Foley.
Slavica Publishers, Inc., 2611 E 10th St, Bloomington, IN 47408-2603;
slavica@indiana.edu; http://www.slavica.com. Illus. Refereed. *Indexed:*
AmHI, HumInd, IBR, IBZ, MLA-IB, RILM. *Bk. rev.:* 100-300 words.
Aud.: Ac.

This journal describes its purpose as a "comparative and interdisciplinary focus
for studies of oral literature and related fields by publishing research and
scholarship on the creation, transmission, and interpretation of all forms of oral
tradition expression." Articles are worldwide in scope, with subjects ranging
from ancient epics and religious texts to modern drama and e-texts. Some issues
are thematic. Begining with the March 2006 issue, free electronic access to the
complete journal was provided. With Vol. 19, the "eCompanions" feature for
articles will be added. This will include "audio, video, photographic, and textual
support to selected contents." This scholarly title is for academic libraries that
support folk literature programs.

2849. *Overland Review: the journal of the Mid-America Folklore Society.*
Former titles (until 2003): *Mid-America Folklore;* (until 1979):
Mid-South Folklore. 1973. 2x/yr. USD 10. Ed(s): Robert Cochran.
Mid-America Folklore Society, Center for Ozark Studies, University of
Arkansas, Fayetteville, AR 72701; http://www.theology.org/APUC/
hjou.html. Illus. Refereed. Circ: 200. Vol. ends: No. 2. *Indexed:*
MLA-IB, RI-1, RILM. *Bk. rev.:* 16, 100-300 words. *Aud.:* Ga, Ac.

This journal is an example of a regional title. While it covers a variety of
subjects, most topics involve interests in the Midwest. Articles cover traditional
folklore topics and pop culture. It is a good source for information on the lore
of the Ozarks area. Signed book reviews are well written and cover a variety of
materials. This is a good title for libraries within the geographic region or those
interested in Midwestern folk culture.

Parabola. See General Editorial section.

2850. *Storytelling Magazine.* Incorporates: *Inside Story;* Which was
formerly: *Yarnspinner;* Formerly (until 1989): *National Storytelling
Journal.* [ISSN: 1048-1354] 1984. bi-m. Membership, USD 50. Ed(s):
Nella Tsacrios. National Storytelling Network, 132 Boone St, Ste 5,
Jonesborough, TN 37659; nsn@storynet.org; http://www.storynet.org/.
Illus., index, adv. Circ: 12000. *Aud.:* Hs, Ga.

Issues are a mix of articles, stories, news, and advertisements. Usually the
stories section has a central theme. Bibliographies of suggested readings that
accompany the articles are from print, media, and Internet sources. The news
section deals with all aspects of the National Storytelling Network, listing
conferences, awards, and calls for stories. There are a fair number of advertisements in the magazine, but all are pertinent to storytellers. A good source for
storytellers and teachers as well as librarians.

2851. *Tennessee Folklore Society. Bulletin.* [ISSN: 0040-3253] 1935. q.
USD 14 (Individuals, USD 10). Ed(s): Charles K Wolfe. Tennessee
Folklore Society, Box 201, Middle Tennessee State University,
Murfreesboro, TN 37132; cwolfe@frank.mtsu.edu. Illus., index.
Refereed. Circ: 425 Paid. Vol. ends: No. 4. *Indexed:* AmH&L, HistAb,
IBR, IBZ, IIMP, IIPA, MLA-IB, MusicInd, RILM. *Bk. rev.:* 2-3, 600
words. *Aud.:* Ga, Ac.

Most of the articles in this journal pertain to folk culture in Tennessee and
neighboring states. However, there are occasional pieces on folklore outside the
United States, and some issues are thematic. In addition to articles, there are
reviews of books and media and a section listing coming events. Issues also
usually contain a section listing publications available from the Tennessee
Folklore Society. This journal is a must for Tennessee libraries and others in the
surrounding geographic region.

2852. *Western Folklore.* Formerly (until 1947): *California Folklore
Quarterly.* [ISSN: 0043-373X] 1942. q. Institutional members, USD 50;
Individual members, USD 40; Students, USD 30. Ed(s): Elliot Oring.
California Folklore Society, 9420 Carrillo Ave, Montclair, CA
91763-2412; http://www.westernfolklore.org/. Adv. Circ: 1200. Online:
Chadwyck-Healey Inc.; JSTOR (Web-based Journal Archive); Northern

Light Technology, Inc.; OCLC Online Computer Library Center, Inc.;
ProQuest K-12 Learning Solutions; ProQuest LLC (Ann Arbor); H.W.
Wilson. *Indexed:* ABS&EES, AmH&L, AmHI, ArtHuCI, BEL&L, BRI,
CBRI, FLI, FR, HistAb, HumInd, IIMP, IIPA, MLA-IB, MusicInd, RI-1,
RILM. *Bk. rev.:* Number and length vary. *Aud.:* Ga, Ac.

This title's geographic scope includes California and neighboring regions. Most
issues are composed of articles and reviews. Some may have a thematic
approach. Topics cover all aspects of folklore, taking a wide interpretation of the
subject, from the pop culture of carnivals to the unmaking of a modern folk hero.
Reviews vary in length from several paragrahs to several pages. Although
publication lags, this journal is a good addition for both academics and the
sophisticated general reader.

■ FOOD AND NUTRITION

*Robert Threlkeld, Resource Management Librarian, Countway Medical
Library, Harvard University, Boston, MA, 02115;
robert_threlkeld@hms.harvard.edu*

Introduction

Titles in this section are generally more appropriate for academic libraries,
especially those with collections supporting research in the health sciences.
Many of these titles are intended for an audience of nutrition researchers or
health professionals, although a few are appropriate for a more general audience
with some interest or background in the area. Content ranges from very
technical discussions of cutting-edge research in nutrition to lighter articles
describing more general issues affecting the fields of nutrition and health. Topics
discussed may include specific effects of new treatments or medications, or
broader issues of how nutrition fits into the greater context of health
maintenence and wellness. Other important issues include health policy,
ensuring the safety of the nation's food supply, healthy eating behaviors, food
allergies, and obesity.

Basic Periodicals

Ga: *Nutrition Action Healthletter, Nutrition News Focus, Nutrition Today,
Vegetarian Journal;* Ac: *American Journal of Clinical Nutrition, Annals of
Nutrition and Metabolism, The British Journal of Nutrition, Journal of
Nutrition, Journal of the American Dietetic Association, Nutrition Reviews.*

Basic Abstracts and Indexes

*Bibliography of Agriculture, Biological Abstracts, CAB Abstracts (primarily
Human Nutrition subset), Current Contents (primarily Life Sciences section),
Index Medicus, Medline, Medline Plus (Nutrition Health Topic), Nutrition
Abstracts and Reviews.*

2853. *American College of Nutrition. Journal.* [ISSN: 0731-5724] 1982.
6x/yr. USD 220 (Individuals, USD 90). Ed(s): Dr. David Klurfeld, Dr.
Richard Caldwell. American College of Nutrition, 300 S Duncan Ave,
Ste 225, Clearwater, FL 33755-6415; http://www.am-coll-nutr.org/jacn/
jacn.htm. Illus., adv. Refereed. Circ: 1600 Paid. Online: EBSCO
Publishing, EBSCO Host; HighWire Press. *Indexed:* Agr, BiolAb,
CABA, ChemAb, DSA, ExcerpMed, FS&TA, ForAb, HortAb, PEI,
RRTA, S&F, SCI, SSCI, WAE&RSA. *Bk. rev.:* Number and length vary.
Aud.: Ac, Sa.

This is the official journal for the American College of Nutrition, so it is
primarily targeted toward professionals and researchers working on current
research in nutrition. The emphasis is on original research that supports the
college's objectives in enhancing knowledge of nutrition and metabolism, and
in applying that knowledge toward health maintenance and the prevention of
disease. Content includes scholarly articles describing original research in the
field, as well as review articles, clinical and laboratory reports, and conference

abstracts. The journal is available online at www.jacn.org, and includes tables of contents, abstracts, and full-text articles available for subscribers. Tables of contents and abstracts are available without subscription at no charge.

2854. American Dietetic Association. Journal. Formerly: *American Dietetic Association. Bulletin.* [ISSN: 0002-8223] 1925. 12x/yr. USD 387. Ed(s): Linda Van Horn. Elsevier Inc., 360 Park Ave S, New York, NY 10010-1710; usinfo-f@elsevier.com; http://www.elsevier.com. Illus., index, adv. Refereed. Circ: 70000 Paid. Microform: PMC; PQC. Online: EBSCO Publishing, EBSCO Host; Florida Center for Library Automation; Gale; IngentaConnect; OCLC Online Computer Library Center, Inc.; OhioLINK; ProQuest K-12 Learning Solutions; ProQuest LLC (Ann Arbor); ScienceDirect; SwetsWise Online Content. *Indexed:* AgeL, Agr, B&AI, CABA, CINAHL, ChemAb, DSA, ExcerpMed, FPA, FS&TA, ForAb, GSI, H&SSA, H&TI, HortAb, IndVet, RRTA, S&F, SCI, SSCI, SWR&A, WAE&RSA. *Bk. rev.:* Number and length vary. *Aud.:* Ac, Sa.

As the official publication of the American Dietetic Association, this journal's primary audience is professional nutritionists and dieticians. The scope of the articles is sufficiently broad, however, that it could appeal to a more general audience that has some familiarity with the content. The journal emphasizes refereed reports of original research on topics related to nutrition and dietetics, such as diet therapy, community nutrition, and education and training. There are also articles of professional interest to practitioners such as reports of association activities and conferences, as well as columns focusing on professional advice.

2855. American Journal of Clinical Nutrition: a journal reporting the practical application of our world-wide knowledge of nutrition. Formerly (until 1954): *The Journal of Clinical Nutrition.* [ISSN: 0002-9165] 1952. m. USD 460 print & online eds. (Individuals, USD 200 print & online eds.). American Society for Nutrition, 9650 Rockville Pike., Rm. L-3503, Bethesda, MD 20814; http://www.nutrition.org. Illus., index, adv. Refereed. Circ: 7250 Paid and controlled. Microform: PMC; PQC. Online: EBSCO Publishing, EBSCO Host; HighWire Press; OCLC Online Computer Library Center, Inc.; ProQuest K-12 Learning Solutions; ProQuest LLC (Ann Arbor). *Indexed:* ABS&EES, AgeL, Agr, B&AI, BiolAb, CABA, CINAHL, ChemAb, DSA, ExcerpMed, FS&TA, ForAb, H&SSA, HortAb, IndVet, PEI, RRTA, SCI, SSCI, VB, WAE&RSA. *Bk. rev.:* 1-4, 500-1,000 words. *Aud.:* Ac, Sa.

This journal, published by the American Society for Clinical Nutrition, is intended to report on and provide a forum for original research in clinical and experimental nutrition, and makes a good addition to core collections in the health sciences. Articles are grouped by research areas such as Energy and Protein Metabolism, Growth, Development, and Pediatrics, Aging, and Nutritional Epidemiology and Public Health. In addition to scholarly articles in these areas, the journal includes editorials, review articles, and book reviews. Tables of contents, abstracts, and full text are available online to subscribers.

2856. Annals of Nutrition and Metabolism: European journal of nutrition, metabolic diseases and dietetics. Formed by the merger of (1947-1981): *Annales de la Nutrition et de l'Alimentation;* (1970-1981): *Nutrition and Metabolism;* Which was formerly (1959-1969): *Nutritio et Dieta.* [ISSN: 0250-6807] 1981. 8x/yr. CHF 2606. Ed(s): Ibrahim Elmadfa. S. Karger AG, Allschwilerstr 10, Basel, 4055, Switzerland; karger@karger.ch; http://www.karger.ch. Illus., index, adv. Sample. Refereed. Circ: 1250. Online: EBSCO Publishing, EBSCO Host; OCLC Online Computer Library Center, Inc.; ProQuest K-12 Learning Solutions; ProQuest LLC (Ann Arbor); SwetsWise Online Content. *Indexed:* Agr, BiolAb, CABA, ChemAb, DSA, ExcerpMed, FPA, FS&TA, ForAb, HortAb, IndVet, RRTA, SCI, VB, WAE&RSA. *Aud.:* Ac, Sa.

This peer-reviewed, scholarly title emphasizes the role of nutrition in health disorders such as hypertension and coronary heart disease. Articles selected for publication often outline basic research or clinical reports that focus on human nutrition from the perspective of molecular genetics. Other articles may explore topics such as the associations between dietary habits and disease, or the effectiveness of diets and dietary supplements. This journal is appropriate for health science collections that support professional or research populations.

2857. The British Journal of Nutrition: an international journal of nutritional science. [ISSN: 0007-1145] 1947. m. GBP 672. Ed(s): P C Calder. Cambridge University Press, The Edinburgh Bldg, Shaftesbury Rd, Cambridge, CB2 2RU, United Kingdom; journals@cambridge.org; http://www.journals.cambridge.org. Illus., index, adv. Refereed. Microform: SWZ; PMC; PQC. Online: EBSCO Publishing, EBSCO Host; Gale; IngentaConnect; OCLC Online Computer Library Center, Inc.; OhioLINK; Ovid Technologies, Inc.; SwetsWise Online Content; H.W. Wilson. *Indexed:* Agr, B&AI, BiolAb, CABA, CINAHL, ChemAb, DSA, ExcerpMed, FPA, FS&TA, ForAb, HortAb, IndVet, RRTA, SCI, VB, WAE&RSA. *Bk. rev.:* 1-2, 500 words, signed. *Aud.:* Ac, Sa.

This peer-reviewed, scholarly journal is international in scope and is appropriate for academic and health science collections. The goal of the Nutrition Society, which publishes the journal, is "the advancement of scientific study of nutrition and its applications to the maintenance of human and animal health." With this goal in mind, the articles published are primarily original research papers and review articles on clinical nutrition, animal nutrition, and basic research as it applies to nutrition. The journal considers nutrition research a multidisciplinary undertaking and accepts papers from a variety of perspectives, including clinical, statistical, agricultural, and experimental research.

2858. Dairy Council Digest: an interpretive review of recent nutrition research. [ISSN: 0011-5568] 1929. bi-m. Free. National Dairy Council, O'Hare International Center, 10255 W Higgins Rd, Ste 900, Rosemont, IL 60018-5616; ndc@dairyinformation.com; http://www.nationaldairycouncil.org. Illus. Sample. Circ: 25000. Vol. ends: Dec. Microform: PQC. Online: Northern Light Technology, Inc.; ProQuest LLC (Ann Arbor). *Indexed:* Agr, DSA. *Aud.:* Ga, Ac, Sa.

In January 1999, this publication became available only online. Each issue covers a single topic, with extensive references. Examples from recent issues are "The Role of Dairy Foods and Activity for Grooming Children," "A New Look at Dietary Patterns and Hypertension," "Health-Enhancing Properties of Dairy Ingredients," and "Health Benefits of Dairy Foods for Minorities." Although targeted at nutrition professionals, this excellent journal contains content of interest to consumers. (MMC)

2859. European Journal of Clinical Nutrition. Formerly (until 1987): *Human Nutrition. Clinical Nutrition;* Which superseded in part (in 1981): *Journal of Human Nutrition;* Which was formerly (until 1976): *Nutrition.* [ISSN: 0954-3007] 1976. m. EUR 812. Ed(s): Jaap C Seidell. Nature Publishing Group, The MacMillan Building, 4 Crinan St, London, N1 9XW, United Kingdom; http://www.nature.com. Illus. Sample. Refereed. *Indexed:* Agr, BiolAb, CABA, DSA, ExcerpMed, FS&TA, GSI, HortAb, IndVet, RRTA, SCI, SSCI, VB, WAE&RSA. *Bk. rev.:* 1-3, length varies, signed. *Aud.:* Ac, Sa.

A scholarly publication suitable for academic and health science collections, this journal covers theoretical aspects of nutrition. The journal focuses on human nutrition exclusively and does not accept papers on animal studies unless they include parallel research conducted on humans. Coverage includes epidemiological research that considers nutritional causes and effects of disease, as well as community nutrition, nutrition education, and determinants of eating behavior. Typical issues include review articles, research reports, and short communications.

International Journal of Food Sciences and Nutrition. See Food Industry section.

2860. Journal of Nutrition. [ISSN: 0022-3166] 1928. m. USD 470 print & online eds. Ed(s): Dr. A Catherine Ross. American Society for Nutrition, 9650 Rockville Pike., Rm. L-3503, Bethesda, MD 20814; staff@dues.faseb.org; http://www.nutrition.org. Illus., index, adv. Sample. Refereed. Circ: 4800 Paid. Vol. ends: Dec. Microform: PMC; PQC. Online: EBSCO Publishing, EBSCO Host; HighWire Press; Northern Light Technology, Inc.; OCLC Online Computer Library Center, Inc.; ProQuest K-12 Learning Solutions; ProQuest LLC (Ann Arbor). *Indexed:* AbAn, Agr, B&AI, BiolAb, BiolDig, CABA, ChemAb, DSA, ExcerpMed, FPA, FS&TA, ForAb, GSI, H&SSA, HortAb, IndVet, RRTA, RiskAb, S&F, SCI, SSCI, VB, WAE&RSA. *Bk. rev.:* Various number and length. *Aud.:* Ac, Sa.

This scholarly journal focuses on original research in nutrition, emphasizing "timely, accurate information on all aspects of nutrition research." Articles are geared toward professionals and researchers, typically discussing advanced concepts such as nutrient-gene interactions and the biochemical and molecular effects of nutrients. Subsections of the journal focus on nutrition from the perspective of specialized research areas such as aging, cancer, neuroscience, and epidemiology. As the official publication of the American Society for Nutrition, subscriptions include supplements providing coverage of conferences or symposia as well as topics of professional interest.

2861. *Journal of Nutrition Education and Behavior.* Formerly: *Journal of Nutrition Education.* [ISSN: 1499-4046] 1969. bi-m. USD 339. Ed(s): Sandra K. Shepherd. Elsevier Inc., 360 Park Ave S, New York, NY 10010-1710; usinfo-f@elsevier.com; http://www.elsevier.com. Illus., index, adv. Refereed. Circ: 2856. *Indexed:* ABIn, AgeL, Agr, CABA, CBCARef, CINAHL, DSA, EduInd, FS&TA, GSI, H&TI, PsycInfo, SCI, SD, SSCI, SWA, WAE&RSA. *Aud.:* Ac, Sa.

This scholarly journal approaches nutrition research from a social science perspective, emphasizing research on factors that influence food behaviors and how these behaviors can be positively modified. Subject coverage includes articles that stress nutritional education and public policy aspects of food science research. It is the official journal of the Society for Nutrition Education, and thus its intended audience is society members, professionals, and educators with an interest in nutrition education.

2862. *The Journal of Nutritional Biochemistry.* Supersedes (in 1990): *Nutrition Reports International.* [ISSN: 0955-2863] 1970. 12x/yr. USD 1607. Ed(s): Dr. B. Hennig. Elsevier Inc., 360 Park Ave S, New York, NY 10010-1710; usinfo-f@elsevier.com; http://www.elsevier.com. Illus., index. Sample. Refereed. Circ: 1000 Paid. Vol. ends: Dec. Microform: PQC. Online: EBSCO Publishing, EBSCO Host; Gale; IngentaConnect; OhioLINK; ScienceDirect; SwetsWise Online Content. *Indexed:* AgeL, Agr, BiolAb, CABA, ChemAb, DSA, ExcerpMed, FS&TA, HortAb, IndVet, RRTA, SCI, VB. *Aud.:* Ac, Sa.

This peer-reviewed, scholarly journal presents original experimental research on nutrition and its relationship to such fields as biochemistry, molecular biology, physiology, pharmacology, and toxicology. A good selection for health science collections, this title is aimed at professionals and researchers and includes articles of professional interest such as conference summaries, symposium reports, and critical reviews.

2863. *Nutrition: an international journal of applied and basic nutritional science.* Formerly (until 1987): *Nutrition International.* [ISSN: 0899-9007] 1985. 12x/yr. USD 637. Ed(s): Dr. Michael M. Meguid. Elsevier Inc., 360 Park Ave S, New York, NY 10010-1710; usinfo-f@elsevier.com; http://www.elsevier.com. Adv. Refereed. Circ: 650 Paid. Vol. ends: No. 17. Online: EBSCO Publishing, EBSCO Host; Gale; IngentaConnect; OhioLINK; ScienceDirect; SwetsWise Online Content. *Indexed:* Agr, CABA, CINAHL, ChemAb, DSA, ExcerpMed, FPA, FS&TA, ForAb, HortAb, IndVet, PEI, RRTA, SCI, VB, WAE&RSA. *Aud.:* Ac, Sa.

This scholarly journal emphasizes basic and applied research in nutrition, and has a broad scope crossing several fields of interest to nutrition researchers. It features articles and columns from clinical as well as experimental and epidemiological perspectives. Typical issues feature review articles and shorter pieces on such topics as public policy, epidemiology, and nutritional statistics. Tables of contents, abstracts, and full text are available online to subscribers.

2864. *Nutrition Research.* Incorporates (1975-1993): *Progress in Food and Nutrition Science;* Which was formerly: *International Encyclopedia of Food and Nutrition.* [ISSN: 0271-5317] 1981. 12x/yr. USD 1878. Ed(s): Bruce A Watkins. Elsevier Inc., 360 Park Ave S, New York, NY 10010-1710; usinfo-f@elsevier.com; http://www.elsevier.com. Illus., adv. Sample. Refereed. Circ: 580 Paid. Vol. ends: Dec (No. 21). Online: EBSCO Publishing, EBSCO Host; Gale; IngentaConnect; OhioLINK; ScienceDirect; SwetsWise Online Content. *Indexed:* Agr, B&AI, BiolAb, CABA, ChemAb, DSA, ExcerpMed, FPA, FS&TA, ForAb, HortAb, IndVet, RRTA, SCI, SSCI, VB, WAE&RSA. *Aud.:* Ac, Sa.

This scholarly journal, intended for a research or professional audience, emphasizes rapid publication of original papers and review articles on research in the nutritional sciences. Subject areas include nutritional biochemistry and metabolism, food intolerance and allergy, nutrition requirements in health and disease, the influence of socioeconomic, political, and cultural factors on individual and community nutrition, and how nutrition affects growth and development. This journal is appropriate for academic or health science libraries supporting nutrition research.

2865. *Nutrition Reviews.* [ISSN: 0029-6643] 1942. m. USD 220 (Individuals, USD 140). Ed(s): Michelle Paolucci, Dr. Robert H Russell. International Life Sciences Institute, One Thomas Circle, 9th Fl., Washington, DC 20005; ilsi@ilsi.org; http://www.ilsi.org. Illus., index, adv. Refereed. Circ: 4000 Paid. Microform: PQC. Online: EBSCO Publishing, EBSCO Host; Gale; IngentaConnect; Northern Light Technology, Inc.; OCLC Online Computer Library Center, Inc.; ProQuest K-12 Learning Solutions; ProQuest LLC (Ann Arbor). *Indexed:* Agr, B&AI, CABA, CINAHL, ChemAb, DSA, ExcerpMed, FS&TA, GSI, H&TI, HortAb, IndVet, RRTA, SCI, SSCI, VB, WAE&RSA. *Aud.:* Ac, Sa.

This journal presents authoritative and critical reviews of current research and other developments in the areas of nutrition science and policy. Coverage includes experimental and clinical research in dietetics, food science, and nutrition in medicine. In addition, a typical issue contains editorials, critical reviews, and nutrition grand rounds. This title will be of interest to an educated general audience and rounds out a health science collection nicely.

2866. *Nutrition Today.* [ISSN: 0029-666X] 1985. bi-m. USD 241 (Individuals, USD 79.95). Ed(s): Johanna T Dwyer. Lippincott Williams & Wilkins, 530 Walnut St, Philadelphia, PA 19106-3621; custserv@lww.com; http://www.lww.com. Illus., index, adv. Refereed. Circ: 4780. Online: EBSCO Publishing, EBSCO Host; Florida Center for Library Automation; Gale; Northern Light Technology, Inc.; OCLC Online Computer Library Center, Inc.; Ovid Technologies, Inc.; SwetsWise Online Content; H.W. Wilson. *Indexed:* AS&TI, Agr, CINAHL, DSA, FS&TA, GSI, PEI, RRTA. *Aud.:* Ga, Ac, Sa.

This journal emphasizes wellness and educational aspects of nutrition research. One of its stated goals is to provide guidance for professional nutritionists in evaluating new diets and nutrition claims. Articles include coverage of research findings and policy issues, and feature conference reports as well as critical discussions. This title is appropriate for an educated general audience.

Vegetarian Journal. See Cooking and Cookery section.

2867. *World Review of Nutrition and Dietetics.* [ISSN: 0084-2230] 1964. irreg. Ed(s): A P Simopoulos. S. Karger AG, Allschwilerstr 10, Basel, 4055, Switzerland; karger@karger.ch; http://www.karger.ch. Refereed. *Indexed:* Agr, ChemAb, DSA, FS&TA. *Aud.:* Ac, Sa.

This series publishes focused, comprehensive reviews of topics related to nutrition. Each volume thoroughly explores an especially fundamental, relevant, or controversial topic considered to be central to nutrition research. Recent topics include nutrition and fitness, nutrigenetics and nutrigenomics, and evolutionary aspects of nutrition and health. Many volumes are available online, and tables of contents and indexes are available without subscription. This series makes a good addition to academic or health science collections.

■ FOOD INDUSTRY

Pamela Palmer, Associate Professor of Libraries, University of Memphis, Memphis, TN 38152; prpalmer@memphis.edu

Introduction

From trade journals to scholarly publications, food industry periodicals cover a wide range of emphases, and their target audiences are similarly varied. Trade journals focus on trends, news, industry analysis, companies, and personalities in the industry. Directed to a broad readership interested in corporate administration, plant operations, manufacturing equipment, and government regulation, they serve to keep insiders current. Use of graphics, photographs, and design features make them as colorful as the products they cover. At the other end of the spectrum, the scholarly journals are highly technical scientific reports of original research and reviews of research on food-related areas of chemistry and microbiology. Most food industry titles have web sites with details about the publication. Some offer access to full-text articles from the current issue, while others provide only tables of contents and abstracts. Other web features offered by some titles include current news items, alerts to topics of personal interest, fee-based article access, and subscriptions to the online version.

Trends over the past two years reflect many of the issues covered by popular news sources. Whether the concern is allergens, packaging, labeling, technology, dietary habits of children, or safety, both trade publications and scholarly journals are focused on making the food industry more safe and productive. In the area of access, scholarly journals continue to offer relatively little full text online, while trade journals are more likely to provide articles in full text to nonsubscribers.

Basic Periodicals

Ac: *Food Technology;* Sa: *Food Technology, Journal of Food Science, Prepared Foods.*

Basic Abstracts and Indexes

Food Science and Technology Abstracts.

2868. Appetite. [ISSN: 0195-6663] 1980. 6x/yr. EUR 1076. Ed(s): S. Thornton, A. Stunkard. Elsevier BV, Life Sciences Department, Molenwerf 1, Amsterdam, 1014 AG, Netherlands; nlinfo-f@elsevier.nl; http://www.elsevier.nl. Illus., index, adv. Refereed. Vol. ends: No. 3. Online: EBSCO Publishing, EBSCO Host; Gale; IngentaConnect; OCLC Online Computer Library Center, Inc.; OhioLINK; ScienceDirect; SwetsWise Online Content. *Indexed:* Agr, AnBeAb, BiolAb, CABA, ChemAb, DSA, ExcerpMed, FS&TA, HortAb, PEI, PsycInfo, RRTA, SCI, SSCI, VB, WAE&RSA. *Bk. rev.:* 1, 300-400 words. *Aud.:* Ac, Sa.

This bimonthly journal is focused on behavioral nutrition and the cultural, sensory, and physiological influences on choices and intakes of food and drinks. It covers normal and disordered eating and drinking, dietary attitudes and practices, and all aspects of the bases of human and animal behavior toward food. The journal provides short communications, book reviews, and abstracts of presentations at major meetings in the social science, psychology, or neuroscience of food consumption, including the Association for the Study of Food in Society, the Society for the Study of Ingestive Behavior, and conferences on Food Choice. Sample articles are "The Stice model of overeating: Tests in clinical and non-clinical samples," "Dietary restraint and cognitive performance in children," and "Experience of dietary advice among Pakistani-born persons with type 2 diabetes in Oslo." Target audiences include academics and other researchers in the areas of psychology, social research, neuroscience, physiology, nutrition, and sensory food science. Access to full text is available through ScienceDirect at www.sciencedirect.com. The *Appetite* web site is at www.elsevier.com/wps/find/journaldescription.cws_home/622785/description#description.

2869. Beverage Industry. Former titles (until 1973): *Soft Drink Industry;* (until 1966): *Bottling Industry.* [ISSN: 0148-6187] 1946. m. USD 85.05 domestic (Free to qualified personnel). Ed(s): Elizabeth Fuhrman, Sarah Theodore. Stagnito Communications, Inc., 155 Pfingsten Rd, Ste 205, Deerfield, IL 60015; info@stagnito.com; http://www.stagnito.com. Illus., index, adv. Circ: 34000 Controlled. Microform: PQC. Online: EBSCO Publishing, EBSCO Host; Florida Center for Library Automation; Gale; Northern Light Technology, Inc.; OCLC Online Computer Library Center, Inc.; ProQuest LLC (Ann Arbor). *Indexed:* ABIn, BPI, H&TI. *Aud.:* Sa.

Beverage Industry is billed as the only feature tabloid serving the entire beverage marketplace. This trade publication's focus is production, marketing, technology, and distribution, including coverage of obstacles facing executives in the corporate suite, on the plant floor, and in the R&D lab. Coverage is broad, including bottled water, juice/juice-type drinks, wine, liquor, alternative

beverages, coffee and tea, dairy, soft drinks, and beer. Issues are chock full of industry information—individual companies' successful sales and marketing approaches, trends and news in product safety, and industry issues, as well as new packaging, logistics, coverage of meetings and shows, marketing trends, and a Supplier's Marketplace. One recent issue has The 2006 Soft Drinks Report as a category focus, and contains a cover story on the super-premium juice brand Odwalla, industry issues on topics ranging from Powerade battles to Coca-Cola's New International Group, Miller's marketing, distribution trends, and other industry topics. Online at www.bevindustry.com.

2870. Candy Industry: the global magazine of chocolate and confectionery. Former titles (until 1982): *Candy and Snack Industry; Baked Snack Industry; Candy.* [ISSN: 0745-1032] 1874. m. USD 70.10 domestic; USD 125 in Canada & Mexico; USD 200 elsewhere. Ed(s): Bernard Pacyniak, Susan Tiffany. Stagnito Communications, Inc., 155 Pfingsten Rd, Ste 205, Deerfield, IL 60015; info@stagnito.com; http://www.stagnito.com. Illus., index, adv. Circ: 6400 Paid and controlled. Vol. ends: Dec. Microform: PQC. Online: The Dialog Corporation; EBSCO Publishing, EBSCO Host; Factiva, Inc.; Florida Center for Library Automation; Gale; Northern Light Technology, Inc.; OCLC Online Computer Library Center, Inc.; ProQuest LLC (Ann Arbor). *Indexed:* ABIn, BPI, DSA, FS&TA, LRI. *Aud.:* Sa.

A trade publication targeted to the global confectionary market, *Candy Industry* offers international coverage of news, key events, and conferences; special reports on segments of the industry; company profiles; plant and processing technology; packaging; new products; and more. As the leading information source for the global confectionary marketplace, the magazine covers large and medium-sized confectionary manufacturers, family and privately owned businesses, and smaller retail confectioners with on-premises manufacturing. A recent issue includes a cover story on Daffin's Candies of Sharon, Pennsylvania, an international profile of Maestrani of Switzerland, a news item on 1-800-Flowers's purchase of Fanny May Confections, and an R&D report on "The Trend Against Trans[fats]." The 2006 Buyers' Guide lists over 640 companies in 480 product areas. Heavily illustrated with many charts and graphs, the magazine is easy to read and informative. It is available online at www.candyindustry.com.

2871. Cereal Chemistry. [ISSN: 0009-0352] 1924. bi-m. USD 450. Ed(s): R Carl Hoseney. American Association of Cereal Chemists, Inc., 3340 Pilot Knob Rd., St. Paul, MN 55121-2097; aacc@scisoc.org; http://www.aaccnet.org. Illus., index, adv. Refereed. Circ: 1438 Paid. Vol. ends: Dec. Microform: PMC; PQC. Online: ProQuest LLC (Ann Arbor). *Indexed:* Agr, B&AI, BiolAb, CABA, ChemAb, DSA, ExcerpMed, FS&TA, HortAb, S&F, SCI, VB. *Aud.:* Sa.

An international research journal published since 1924, *Cereal Chemistry* covers cereal science. Research areas include biochemistry, biotechnology, products, processes, and analytical procedures associated with cereals and other grain crops. The research reported explores raw materials, processes, products utilizing cereal (corn, wheat, oats, rice, rye, etc.), oilseeds, and pulses, as well as analytical procedures, technological tests, and fundamental research in the cereals area. Articles range from comprehensive reviews to reports of original investigations. Published by the American Association of Cereal Chemists (ASCC), the journal is written for a scholarly audience. Recent articles include "Ethanol Production from Pearl Millet Using *Saccharomyces cerevisiae*" and "Using Multivariate Techniques to Predict Wheat Flour Dough and Noodle Characteristics from Size-Exclusion HPLC and RVA Data." On the AACC web site at www.aaccnet.org/cerealchemistry, readers have access to a featured article from the current issue, can view tables of contents of past issues, and can search the journal's abstracts from 1960 to the present, although full text is available online only to subscribers.

2872. Cereal Foods World. Formerly: *Cereal Science Today.* [ISSN: 0146-6283] 1956. bi-m. Nov.-Dec. combined. USD 236. Ed(s): Jody Grider, Jody Grider. American Association of Cereal Chemists, Inc., 3340 Pilot Knob Rd., St. Paul, MN 55121-2097; aacc@scisoc.org; http://www.aaccnet.org. Illus., index, adv. Refereed. Circ: 4660 Paid and controlled. Vol. ends: Dec. Microform: PQC. Online: ProQuest LLC (Ann Arbor). *Indexed:* Agr, BiolAb, CABA, ChemAb, DSA, EnvAb, FS&TA, HortAb, IBSS, RRTA, S&F, SCI, WAE&RSA. *Aud.:* Sa.

Written for food industry professionals, *Cereal Foods World* focuses on industry and product information in the areas of grain-based food science, technology, and new product development. It includes high-quality feature articles and scientific research papers that focus on advances in grain-based food science and the application of these advances to product development and food production practices. Published by the American Association of Cereal Chemists (AACC), *Cereal Foods World* gives tables of contents for previous years at www.aaccnet.org/cerealfoodsworld. Regular features include articles, research reports, and columns on quality assurance, engineering, nutrition, and grain quality; AACC news; and industry profiles and news. Feature articles in recent issues include "Incorporating Distillers Grains in Food Products," "Effects of Barley Consumption on CVD Risk Factors," and "Reformulating Tortillas with Zero Trans Fat." Each bimonthly issue has a different cereal food focus, such as baking or barley.

2873. Chemical Senses. Formerly (until 1980): *Chemical Senses and Flavour.* [ISSN: 0379-864X] 1974. 9x/yr. EUR 1061 print or online ed. (Individuals, EUR 357). Ed(s): Dr. Robyn Hudson, Dr. B. W. Ache. Oxford University Press, Great Clarendon St, Oxford, OX2 6DP, United Kingdom; jnl.orders@oup.co.uk; http://www.oxfordjournals.org. Illus., index, adv. Refereed. Circ: 560. Vol. ends: No. 6. Online: EBSCO Publishing, EBSCO Host; Gale; HighWire Press; IngentaConnect; OCLC Online Computer Library Center, Inc.; OhioLINK; Ovid Technologies, Inc.; Oxford Journals; ProQuest LLC (Ann Arbor); SwetsWise Online Content. Reprint: PSC. *Indexed:* AnBeAb, CABA, ChemAb, DSA, ExcerpMed, FPA, FR, FS&TA, ForAb, HortAb, IndVet, PsycInfo, SCI, SSCI, VB, ZooRec. *Aud.:* Sa.

Chemical Senses publishes original research and review papers on all aspects of human and animal chemoreception. This includes the gross morphology and fine structure of receptors and central chemosensory pathways; the properties of the stimuli and the nature of the chemical-receptor interaction; and the electrical, biochemical, and behavioral correlates (both animal and human) of neural response to chemosensory stimuli. An important part of the journal's coverage is devoted to techniques and the development and application of new methods for investigating chemoreception and chemosensory structures. The journal is associated with the European Chemoreception Research Organization, the Association for Chemoreception Sciences, and the Japanese Association for the Study of Taste and Smell. Geared to a scholarly/professional audience, *Chemical Senses* is international in scope and authorship. A recent article is titled "Cross-Modal Interactions Between Olfaction and Touch." On the journal web site at http://chemse.oupjournals.org, users can search for articles and view abstracts from 1994 forward. Only subscribers have free access to full text (February 1998 to the present); nonsubscribers can order individual articles for a fee. An e-mail alerting service is also available.

2874. Critical Reviews in Food Science and Nutrition. Former titles: *C R C Critical Reviews in Food Science and Nutrition; C R C Critical Reviews in Food Technology.* [ISSN: 1040-8398] 1970. 8x/yr. GBP 1186 print & online eds. Ed(s): Fergus M Clydesdale. Taylor & Francis Inc., 325 Chestnut St, Ste 800, Philadelphia, PA 19016; orders@taylorandfrancis.com; http://www.taylorandfrancis.com. Illus., index. Refereed. Circ: 500. Vol. ends: Dec. Reprint: PSC. *Indexed:* Agr, BioEngAb, C&ISA, CABA, CerAb, ChemAb, DSA, FS&TA, HortAb, IAA, IndVet, SCI, SSCI. *Aud.:* Ac, Sa.

Presenting critical viewpoints of current technology, food science, and human nutrition is the focus of *Critical Reviews in Food Science.* Major areas include food safety, food processing, government regulation and policy, nutrition, fortification, new food products, food and behavior, effects of processing on nutrition, and food labeling. The application of scientific discoveries and the acquisition of knowledge as they relate to nutrition are thoroughly addressed in this comprehensive and authoritative information source. Reviews include issues of national concern, especially to the food science nutritionist and health professional. Published bimonthly with an occasional supplement, issues contain three or four authoritative critical reviews written for a scholarly or expert audience. The journal is international in both scope and authorship. Recent article titles include "Scraped Surface Heat Exchangers" and "Food Allergy in Dogs and Cats: A Review." Tables of contents are available online, and both abstracts and full text are available only to subscribers.

2875. Dairy Foods: innovative ideas and technologies for dairy processors. Formerly (until 1986): *Dairy Record;* Which incorporated (in 1981): *American Dairy Review;* Which was formerly (until 1965): *American Milk Review;* (until 1959): *American Milk Review and Milk Plant Monthly;* Which was formed by the merger of (1930-1958): *Milk Plant Monthly;* (1939-1958): *American Milk Review (Year).* [ISSN: 0888-0050] 1958. m. USD 116 domestic (Free to qualified personnel). Ed(s): Cindy Dubin, David Phillips. B N P Media, 2401 W Big Beaver Rd, Ste 700, Troy, MI 48084; http://www.bnpmedia.com. Illus., index, adv. Circ: 19000 Controlled. Vol. ends: Dec. Microform: PQC. Online: The Dialog Corporation; EBSCO Publishing, EBSCO Host; Florida Center for Library Automation; Gale; Northern Light Technology, Inc.; OCLC Online Computer Library Center, Inc.; ProQuest LLC (Ann Arbor). *Indexed:* ABIn, CABA, DSA, ExcerpMed, FS&TA, RRTA, WAE&RSA. *Aud.:* Ac, Sa.

For more than a century, *Dairy Foods* has served the dairy industry by analyzing and reporting on technologies, trends, and issues and how they affect North America's processors of milk, cheese, frozen desserts, and cultured products. As the leading periodical targeting dairy processors and the companies selling to them, the monthly magazine covers news and trends, new products and marketing, ingredient technology, plant operations, and special features. Recent issues highlight such features as "The Future for Dairy Proteins" and "Lowering pH." Departments include an industry editorial, information on industry movers and shakers, and new products. The web site at dairyfoods.com includes daily news articles from the current issue and an archive of articles from previous issues.

2876. Food Additives and Contaminants: analysis, surveillance, evaluation, control. [ISSN: 0265-203X] 1984. m. GBP 2263 print & online eds. Ed(s): Elke Anklam, T Phillips. Taylor & Francis Ltd., 4 Park Sq, Milton Park, Abingdon, OX14 4RN, United Kingdom; info@tandf.co.uk; http://www.tandf.co.uk/journals. Illus., index, adv. Refereed. Online: EBSCO Publishing, EBSCO Host; Gale; IngentaConnect; OCLC Online Computer Library Center, Inc.; SwetsWise Online Content. Reprint: PSC. *Indexed:* Agr, BiolAb, CABA, CerAb, ChemAb, DSA, EnvAb, ExcerpMed, FPA, FS&TA, ForAb, H&SSA, HortAb, IndVet, S&F, SCI, VB, WAE&RSA. *Bk. rev.:* 2-5, 300-600 words. *Aud.:* Ac, Sa.

Publishing original research papers and reviews, *Food Additives and Contaminants* covers analytical methodology, occurrence, persistence, safety evaluation, detoxication, regulatory control, and surveillance of natural and man-made additives and contaminants in the food chain. Contributions cover the chemistry, biochemistry, and bioavailability of these substances; factors affecting levels of potentially toxic compounds that may arise during production, processing, packaging, storage, and in the development of novel foods and processes; and surveillance data and exposure estimates. It is published in affiliation with the International Society for Mycotoxicology. Readership includes scientists involved in all aspects of food safety and quality including research, analysis, safety evaluation, quality assurance, regulatory aspects, and surveillance. Recent articles include "Neoformation of boldenone and related steroids in faeces of veal calves" and "Typical diffusion behaviour in packaging polymers—application to functional barriers." An e-mail alert service for contents and keywords is available at www.tandf.co.uk/journals/titles/0265203X.asp.

2877. Food and Chemical Toxicology. Formerly (until 1982): *Food and Cosmetics Toxicology.* [ISSN: 0278-6915] 1963. 12x/yr. EUR 2752. Ed(s): Hans Verhagen, Joseph F. Borzelleca. Pergamon, The Boulevard, Langford Ln, East Park, Kidlington, OX5 1GB, United Kingdom. Illus., index, adv. Refereed. Circ: 1900. Microform: PQC. Online: EBSCO Publishing, EBSCO Host; Gale; IngentaConnect; OhioLINK; ScienceDirect; SwetsWise Online Content. *Indexed:* Agr, BiolAb, C&ISA, CABA, CerAb, ChemAb, DSA, ExcerpMed, FPA, FS&TA, ForAb, H&SSA, HortAb, IndVet, PollutAb, S&F, SCI, SSCI, VB, WAE&RSA, WRCInf. *Aud.:* Sa.

An international journal, *Food and Chemical Toxicology* publishes original research and occasional interpretative reviews on the toxic effects, in animals or humans, of natural or synthetic chemicals occurring in the human environment. Other areas covered include studies related to food, water, and other consumer products; papers on industrial and agricultural chemicals and pharmaceuticals, along with new areas such as safety evaluation of novel foods and biotechnologically derived products and inter-relationships between nutrition and toxicology. Given the journal's recognition of the need for high-quality science in support of health and safety decisions, it considers publishing papers of a more regulatory nature, provided they are part of a more general scientific analysis in their "Regulatory Toxicology" section. Target audiences are food scientists, toxicologists, chemists, and researchers working in the pharmaceutical industry. Published since 1963, the journal is scholarly. Issues typically contain a review article and several research articles. Recent titles include "Tooth whitening products and the risk of oral cancer" and "Effects of aminopentol on in utero development in rats." The journal is online at www.elsevier.com/wps/find/journaldescription.cws_home/237/description#description.

2878. Food and Drug Law Journal. Formerly (until 1991): *Food Drug Cosmetic Law Journal.* [ISSN: 1064-590X] 1946. 3x/yr. Members, USD 299; Non-members, USD 379. Ed(s): Stephanie Scott, M Cathryn Butler. Food and Drug Law Institute, 1000 Vermont Ave, NW, Ste 200, Washington, DC 20005; comments@fdli.org; http://www.fdli.org. Illus., index, adv. Refereed. Reprint: WSH. *Indexed:* CABA, CLI, ChemAb, DSA, ExcerpMed, FS&TA, H&SSA, ILP, IndVet, LRI, SCI, SSCI, VB, WAE&RSA. *Aud.:* Ac, Sa.

For over 50 years, this award-winning journal has offered readers scholarly, in-depth, analytical articles, providing insight into the actions of the FDA, FTC, and USDA, how the courts interpret these actions, and the reaction of industry. Articles published in the *Food and Drug Law Journal* are heavily cited and reviewed. Praised for its balance of the scholarly and the practical, the journal focuses on five objectives (1) to clarify the complex regulation and legislation affecting the food, drug, cosmetic, medical device, and healthcare technology industries; (2) to explore the possible future implications of proposed regulations and policy trends; (3) to analyze critical court decisions in food and drug law, including intellectual property, antitrust, constitutional, and criminal law issues related to the health law field; (4) to look beyond our borders to assess how food- and drug-related issues are regulated in other countries; and (5) to provide a neutral forum for intelligent discussion and debate among authors from private industry, government agencies, and academic institutions. Recent articles include "When Food Is Poison: The History, Consequences, and Limitations of the Food Allergen Labeling and Consumer Protection Act of 2004" and "Challenges in Regulating Breakthrough Medical Devices." The journal's web site at www.fdli.org/pubs/Journal%20Online provides tables of contents and article abstracts; articles may be purchased for a fee.

2879. Food Chemistry. Incorporates (1985-1991): *Journal of Micronutrient Analysis.* [ISSN: 0308-8146] 1976. 24x/yr. EUR 4309. Ed(s): G. G. Birch. Elsevier BV, Radarweg 29, Amsterdam, 1043 NX, Netherlands; nlinfo-f@elsevier.nl; http://www.elsevier.nl. Illus., index, adv. Refereed. Microform: PQC. Online: EBSCO Publishing, EBSCO Host; Gale; IngentaConnect; OhioLINK; ScienceDirect; SwetsWise Online Content. *Indexed:* A&ATA, Agr, BiolAb, CABA, ChemAb, DSA, ExcerpMed, FPA, FS&TA, ForAb, HortAb, IndVet, RRTA, S&F, SCI, VB, WAE&RSA. *Aud.:* Ac, Sa.

Aimed at food technologists, scientists, and chemists, *Food Chemistry* publishes original, peer-reviewed research papers. The focus is on six areas: the chemical analysis of food; chemical additives and toxins; chemistry relating to the microbiological, sensory, nutritional, and physiological aspects of food; structural changes in molecules during the processing and storage of foods; direct effects on foods of the use of agrochemicals; and chemical quality in food engineering and technology. In its "Analytical, Nutritional and Clinical Methods" section, the journal covers the measurement of micronutrients, macronutrients, additives, and contaminants in foodstuffs and biological samples. Recent articles include "Yeast derivatives (extracts and autolysates) in winemaking: Release of volatile compounds and effects on wine aroma volatility" and "Nutritional and antinutritional significance of four unconventional legumes of the genus Canavalia—A comparative study." The journal's web site is at www.elsevier.com/locate/foodchem.

2880. Food Engineering: the magazine for manufacturing management. Former titles (until 1998): *Chilton's Food Engineering;* (until 1977): *Food Engineering;* (until 1951): *Food Industries.* [ISSN: 1522-2292] 1928. 11x/yr. USD 79 domestic; USD 105 Canada; USD 119 elsewhere. Ed(s): Joyce Fassl. B N P Media, 2401 W Big Beaver Rd, Ste 700, Troy, MI 48084; http://www.bnpmedia.com. Illus., index, adv. Circ: 53000 Controlled. Vol. ends: Dec. Microform: CIS; PQC. Online: The Dialog Corporation; EBSCO Publishing, EBSCO Host; Gale; OCLC Online Computer Library Center, Inc.; ProQuest K-12 Learning Solutions; ProQuest LLC (Ann Arbor); H.W. Wilson. *Indexed:* ABIn, AS&TI, ChemAb, DSA, FS&TA, H&TI. *Aud.:* Ac, Sa.

Written for the manufacturing team in the food and beverage processing industry, *Food Engineering* is subtitled "The Magazine for Manufacturing Management." It covers flexible manufacturing, advanced information exchange, and the changing role of the food engineer. Now in its 78th year, the trade journal covers the full array of food industry topics, ranging from features and tech updates to issues of packaging, safety, software, R&D, and a variety of special reports. Regular special reports include "Top 100 Food and Beverage Companies," "Annual Packaging Trends Survey," and "State of Food Manufacturing." Cover articles in recent issues include "RFID: Making the Right Moves" and "Allergens & Labeling: Got It Under Control?" Special reports and current issue articles are available on the journal's web site at www.foodengineeringmag.com.

2881. Food in Canada. Former titles (until 1991): *Food (Toronto);* (until 1985): *Food in Canada;* Incorporates: *Canadian Baker; Canadian Food Industries.* [ISSN: 1188-9187] 1941. 9x/yr. CND 77 domestic (Free to qualified personnel). Ed(s): Carolyn Cooper. Rogers Media Publishing Ltd, One Mount Pleasant Rd, 11th Fl, Toronto, ON M4Y 2Y5, Canada; http://www.rogers.com. Illus., adv. Microform: MML. Online: EBSCO Publishing, EBSCO Host; Micromedia ProQuest; Northern Light Technology, Inc.; ProQuest LLC (Ann Arbor). *Indexed:* ABIn, CPerI, ChemAb, DSA, FS&TA, H&TI. *Aud.:* Sa.

Food in Canada is a trade magazine covering all aspects of food and the food industry in that country. Recent articles include "Working With The Grain," "The Family Farm," and "A Cut Above." Departments cover areas such as news, regulations, food law, packaging, and new products. Articles focus on Canada but often discuss Canadian trade with other countries or various countries' policies and laws. Available at www.bizlink.com/food.htm, the publication offers online access to full-text articles in the current and back issues starting with 2004.

2882. Food Protection Trends. Former titles (until 2003): *Dairy, Food and Environmental Sanitation;* (until 1989): *Dairy and Food Sanitation; Food and Fieldmen.* [ISSN: 1541-9576] 1980. m. USD 220 domestic; USD 235 in Canada & Mexico; USD 250 elsewhere. Ed(s): Lisa K. Hovey. International Association for Food Protection, 6200 Aurora Ave, Ste 200W, Des Moines, IA 50322-2864; info@foodprotection.org; http://www.foodprotection.org. Illus., adv. Circ: 3500 Paid and free. Microform: PQC. *Indexed:* Agr, CABA, DSA, FS&TA, H&SSA, HortAb, IndVet, RRTA, RiskAb, S&F, VB, WAE&RSA. *Bk. rev.:* Number and length vary. *Aud.:* Ac.

Published by the International Association for Food Protection, *Food Protection Trends* contains refereed articles on applied research, applications of current technology, and general-interest subjects for food safety professionals. Features include industry and association news, an industry-related products section, and a calendar of meetings, seminars, and workshops. Updates of government regulations and sanitary design are also featured. It is distributed to all 9,000 members of the association. Recent articles include "New England Home Gardeners' Food Safety Knowledge of Fresh Fruits and Vegetables" and "Top Ten Food Safety Problems in the United States Food Processing Industry." Tables of contents for issues back through 1999 are available at the organization's web site at www.foodprotection.org, and abstracts of most articles are available from the tables of contents.

2883. Food Reviews International. [ISSN: 8755-9129] 1985. 4x/yr. GBP 913 print & online eds. Ed(s): Dr. Richard W Hartel. Taylor & Francis Inc., 325 Chestnut St, Ste 800, Philadelphia, PA 19016; orders@taylorandfrancis.com; http://www.taylorandfrancis.com. Illus., index, adv. Refereed. Circ: 350. Vol. ends: No. 4. Microform: RPI. Online: EBSCO Publishing, EBSCO Host; Gale; IngentaConnect; OCLC Online Computer Library Center, Inc.; SwetsWise Online Content. Reprint: PSC. *Indexed:* Agr, BioEngAb, CABA, ChemAb, DSA, FS&TA, H&SSA, H&TI, HortAb, IndVet, S&F, SCI, WAE&RSA. *Bk. rev.:* 1-2, 300-400 words. *Aud.:* Ac, Sa.

Food Reviews International presents state-of-the-art reviews concerned with food production, processing, acceptability, and nutritional values—examining the relationship of food and nutrition to health, as well as the differing problems affecting both affluent and developing nations. Readers are food scientists and technologists, food and cereal chemists, chemical engineers, agriculturalists, and nutritionists. Recent articles include "Structure and Texture Properties of Fried Potato Products" and "Traditional Cassava Foods in Burundi—A Review." Tables of contents are available on the journal's web site at http://taylorandfrancis.metapress.com. There readers can view the abstract, register to use the two-minute preview, and order copies of the articles for a fee.

2884. *Food Technology: a publication of the Institute of Food Technologists.* [ISSN: 0015-6639] 1947. m. USD 145 domestic; USD 155 foreign. Ed(s): Bob Swientek, Neil Mermelstein. Institute of Food Technologists, 525 W. Van Buren St., Ste. 1000, Chicago, IL 60607-3814; http://www.ift.org. Illus., index, adv. Circ: 28400 Paid. Vol. ends: Dec. Microform: PQC. Online: EBSCO Publishing, EBSCO Host. *Indexed:* AS&TI, AgeL, Agr, B&AI, CABA, ChemAb, DSA, EngInd, ExcerpMed, FS&TA, GSI, H&SSA, H&TI, HortAb, IBR, IndVet, SCI, SSCI, VB, WAE&RSA. *Aud.:* Ac, Sa.

Food Technology, published by the Institute of Food Technologists (IFT), is designed to present information on the development of new and improved food sources, products, and processes; their proper utilization by industry and the consumer; and their effective regulation by government agencies. The monthly publication provides news and analysis for food scientists and other interested individuals in the food and supplier industries, government, and academia. It combines serious multidisciplinary content with top-notch photographs and graphics. Contents range from features to departments, columns, and resources. For example, a recent issue includes features on "Reducing Sodium—A European Perspective" and "Nanotechnology in Nutraceuticals and Functional Foods." Departments and columns cover the interests of their audience—news, consumer trends, ingredients, packaging, laboratories, and federal government updates. Visit their web site at www.ift.org to access to the current issue. Access to older issues is limited to IFT members and nonmember subscribers.

2885. *International Journal of Food Sciences and Nutrition.* Former titles: *Food Sciences and Nutrition; Human Nutrition. Food Sciences and Nutrition; Journal of Plant Foods; Plant Foods for Man.* [ISSN: 0963-7486] 1973. 8x/yr. GBP 816 print & online eds. Ed(s): C J K Henry. Informa Healthcare, Mortimer House, 37-41 Mortimer St, London, W1T 3JM, United Kingdom; healthcare.enquiries@informa.com; http://www.tandf.co.uk/journals/. Refereed. Circ: 1000 Controlled. Online: EBSCO Publishing, EBSCO Host; Florida Center for Library Automation; Gale; IngentaConnect; OCLC Online Computer Library Center, Inc.; ProQuest LLC (Ann Arbor); SwetsWise Online Content. Reprint: PSC. *Indexed:* Agr, BiolAb, CABA, ChemAb, DSA, ExcerpMed, FPA, FS&TA, ForAb, GSI, HortAb, PEI, RRTA, S&F, SCI, WAE&RSA. *Aud.:* Ac, Sa.

Designed to integrate food science with nutrition, *International Journal of Food Sciences and Nutrition* publishes research articles and critical reviews in the fields of food science and nutrition, with special emphasis on the emerging interface between the sciences. The journal focuses on ten major areas: (1) impact of nutritional science on food product development, (2) nutritional implications of food processing, (3) bioavailability of nutrients, (4) nutritional quality of novel foods, (5) food-nutrient interactions, (6) use of biotechnology in food science/nutrition, (7) tropical food processing and nutrition, (8) good acceptability and dietary selection, (9) nutritional and physiological aspects of food, and (10) dietary requirements and nutritive value of food. Recent articles include "Comparison of antioxidant activity of roasted tea with green, oolong, and black teas" and "Relation of smoking, physical activity, and residence to body fat and fat distribution in elderly men in Greece." The journal's web site is at www.tandf.co.uk/journals/titles/09637486.asp, where abstracts can be read and articles ordered.

2886. *Journal of Food Protection.* Former titles (until 1977): *Journal of Milk and Food Technology;* (until 1947): *Journal of Milk Technology.* [ISSN: 0362-028X] 1937. m. USD 335 domestic; USD 355 in Canada & Mexico; USD 385 elsewhere. Ed(s): John Sofos, Joseph Frank. International Association for Food Protection, 6200 Aurora Ave, Ste 200W, Des Moines, IA 50322-2864; info@foodprotection.org; http://www.foodprotection.org. Illus., index, adv. Refereed. Circ: 500 Controlled. Microform: PMC; PQC. Online: EBSCO Publishing, EBSCO Host; Gale; IngentaConnect. *Indexed:* Agr, B&AI, BiolAb, CABA, ChemAb, DSA, ExcerpMed, FPA, FS&TA, H&SSA, H&TI, HortAb, IndVet, PollutAb, RRTA, RiskAb, S&F, SCI, VB, WAE&RSA. *Aud.:* Sa.

Meeting its goal of publishing the most up-to-date, original research reports and review articles in food science and technology, the *Journal of Food Protection* publishes papers from scientists worldwide. A leader in the field of food microbiology, the journal is scholarly and research based. Readership exceeds 11,000 scientists from 69 countries. First published in 1937, the journal is a publication of the International Association for Food Protection. Recent articles include "Growth of *Salmonella Enteritidis* Phage Type 30 in Almond Hull and Shell Slurries and Survival in Drying Almond Hulls." and "Inhibition of *Salmonella enterica* by Plant-Associated Pseudomonads In Vitro and on Sprouting Alfalfa Seed." See current and recent contents with abstracts online or search past issues at http://apt.allenpress.com/aptonline/?request=index-html. An online subscription can be purchased separately or in conjunction with the print version.

2887. *Journal of Food Science.* Formerly (until 1961): *Food Research.* [ISSN: 0022-1147] 1936. 9x/yr. Ed(s): Daryl B Lund. Blackwell Publishing, Inc., Commerce Place, 350 Main St, Malden, MA 02148; customerservices@blackwellpublishing.com; http://www.blackwellpublishing.com. Illus., index. Refereed. Circ: 10000 Paid. Microform: PQC. Online: EBSCO Publishing, EBSCO Host. *Indexed:* AS&TI, AbAn, Agr, B&AI, BioEngAb, BiolAb, BiolDig, CABA, ChemAb, DSA, ExcerpMed, FPA, FS&TA, ForAb, GSI, H&SSA, HortAb, IndVet, RRTA, S&F, SCI, SSCI, SWRA, VB, WAE&RSA. *Aud.:* Ac, Sa.

The premier journal of the Institute of Food Technologists, *Journal of Food Science* contains peer-reviewed reports of original research and critical reviews of all basic and applied aspects of food sciences for food professionals. In addition to the research and review articles, a regular segment, "Industrial Aspects of Selected JFS Articles," provides short items. Each issue includes articles in these areas: concise reviews/hypotheses in food science, food chemistry and toxicology, food engineering and physical properties, food microbiology and safety, and sensory and nutritive qualities of food. Recent articles include "Sulfite Formation in Isolated Soy Proteins" and "The Effect of High Dietary Vitamin E on Lipid Stability of Oven-Cooked and Hot-Smoked Trout Fillets." Print subscribers have online access to abstracts and full-text articles at the journal's web site, www.ift.org/cms/?pid=1000341, where nonsubscribers can browse abstracts and download articles for a fee.

2888. *Prepared Foods.* Incorporates in 1986: *Food Plant Equipment;* Former titles (until 1984): *Processed Prepared Foods;* (1895-1977): *Canner Packer;* Incorporates in 1981: *Food Development;* Which was formerly: *Food Product Development.* [ISSN: 0747-2536] 1895. m. USD 116 domestic (Free to qualified personnel). Ed(s): Claudia Dziuk O'Donnell, Julia Gallo-Torres. B N P Media, 2401 W Big Beaver Rd, Ste 700, Troy, MI 48084; http://www.bnpmedia.com. Illus., index, adv. Circ: 50000 Controlled. Vol. ends: Dec. Microform: PQC. Online: EBSCO Publishing, EBSCO Host; Florida Center for Library Automation; Gale; Northern Light Technology, Inc.; OCLC Online Computer Library Center, Inc.; H.W. Wilson. *Indexed:* AS&TI, ChemAb, DSA, FS&TA, H&TI. *Aud.:* Sa.

A trade publication, *Prepared Foods* focuses on development trends and technologies for formulators and marketers. Each monthly issue includes features in the broad areas of food business and marketing, product development, and research/development, as well as special reports and news. Recent issues include articles on "Eating Ethnic," "Fixing the Fiber Gap," and "Fat Magic." Special sections include "Supplier Chef Profiles" and "Nutra Solutions—A Supplement on Solutions for the Development and Marketing of

Nutritional Products." The web site at www.preparedfoods.com provides breaking news and full-text articles, and can be browsed by ingredient, subject, and issue.

2889. Snack Food & Wholesale Bakery. Former titles (until 1997): *Snack & Bakery Foods;* (until 1996): *Snack Food;* (until 1967): *Biscuit and Cracker Baker.* [ISSN: 1096-4835] 1912. m. USD 85.06 domestic (Free to qualified personnel). Ed(s): Deborah Cassell, Dan Malovany. Stagnito Communications, Inc., 155 Pfingsten Rd, Ste 205, Deerfield, IL 60015; info@stagnito.com; http://www.stagnito.com. Illus., index, adv. Circ: 18300 Paid and controlled. Vol. ends: Dec. Online: EBSCO Publishing, EBSCO Host; Florida Center for Library Automation; Gale; OCLC Online Computer Library Center, Inc. *Aud.:* Sa.

Covering the industry leaders in the baked goods and snack food markets, this tabloid trade publication focuses on the people, news, and trends in these growing fields. Issues include two to three features; business and marketing editor's comments, news, market trends, and new products; the SFA section, focused on the Snack Food Association; and technology and development. Recent issues include cover stories on "Swift in Swiss Rolls [Romensky Pastry Plant in Russia]" and "Focus on Your Customers— Wheat Wave." The publication's web site at www.snackandbakery.com offers table of contents access to current and earlier issues, with online content back to 2001. There is a search feature as well.

■ FORENSICS

Jim Hodgson, Tracing Supervisor, Access Services Department, Widener Library, Harvard University, Cambridge, MA 02138; hodgson@fas.harvard.edu

Introduction

Selecting forensics journals appropriate for a general reference collection can be a difficult task. Forensics, or forensic science, is the study and application of scientific method to any subject of public discourse or legal proceeding. Subjects can range from evidence used in audits to studies of engineering failures. Criminology uses "forensics" to investigate and prosecute offenses, in a variety of applications with scientific merit ranging from debatable in the case of fiber analysis and fingerprints, to nearly incontrovertible in the case of DNA/mtDNA comparisons.

Medical forensics includes methods for determining the causes of death and disease in individuals and populations; autopsies and toxicology are very important topics in this field. Forensic psychology concerns human behavior as understood in a legal sense—i.e., intent, responsibility, and knowing right from wrong. Digital forensics is the study of data discovery and recovery. In a larger sense, most science is forensics, because scientific research is usually presented for public debate. The purpose of this section is to provide information on only the most general journals, with an orientation toward criminology.

Basic Periodicals

Forensic Magazine; Forensic Science Communications; Forensic Science International; Journal of Forensic Sciences; International Journal of Legal Medicine (Legal Medicine); Medicine, Science and the Law; Science and Justice.

Basic Abstracts and Indexes

Criminal Justice Abstracts; Criminal Justice Periodical Index (January 1997-); MEDLINE; Science Citation Index; Biology Digest; BIOSIS Previews.

2890. Forensic Magazine. [ISSN: 1553-6262] 2004. bi-m. USD 120 in US & Canada (Free to qualified personnel). Ed(s): Chris Janson. Vicon Publishing, Inc., 4 Limbo Ln, Amherst, NH 03031; http://www.viconpublishing.com. Adv. *Aud.:* Hs, Ga, Sa.

This trade journal publishes stories written in a dramatic narrative style that is suitable for those new to studying this field, or just interested in *CSI* stories. A print version is available but not selected for review, since most if not all content seems to be available free online with non–pop-up advertisements. OCLC shows there is a sparse number of print copies; only six libraries are shown holding this title worldwide. But the articles are well-written case reports by professionals in the field.

2891. Forensic Science Communications. Formerly (until 1999): *Crime Laboratory Digest.* [ISSN: 1528-8005] 1984. s-a. Free. Ed(s): Joseph A DiZinno. U.S. Federal Bureau of Investigation, 935 Pennsylvania Ave NW, Ste 7350, Washington, DC 20535; http://www.fbi.gov. Refereed. Circ: 3000. *Indexed:* SSCI. *Aud.:* Sa.

This open-access journal began in 1999 and is published by FBI Laboratory personnel, and articles are keyword-indexed on a general government search engine. The articles cover subjects that revolve around the criminological aspects of forensic science, with a difficulty level suited to high school audiences and up; but they are a bit dry and technical.

2892. Forensic Science International: an international journal dedicated to the applications of genetics in the administration of justice. Former titles (until vol.13, no.1, 1979): *Forensic Science; Journal of Forensic Medicine.* [ISSN: 0379-0738] 1972. 30x/yr. EUR 2870. Ed(s): P. Saukko. Elsevier Ireland Ltd, Elsevier House, Brookvale Plaza, E. Park, Shannon, Ireland. Illus. Refereed. Microform: PQC. Online: EBSCO Publishing, EBSCO Host; Gale; IngentaConnect; OhioLINK; ScienceDirect; SwetsWise Online Content. *Indexed:* AbAn, BiolAb, CABA, CJA, CLI, ChemAb, DSA, ExcerpMed, ForAb, H&SSA, HRIS, HortAb, ILP, IndVet, LRI, RRTA, RiskAb, S&F, SCI, SSCI, VB, ZooRec. *Bk. rev.:* 0-3, signed. *Aud.:* Ac, Sa.

One of the earliest journals devoted to forensic science, this was also one of the first available online. It publishes original research papers, literature review articles, book reviews, and case reports that cover all legal aspects of general forensics disciplines. The journal also covers (per the journal's mission statement) "investigations of value to public health in its broadest sense, and the important marginal area where science and medicine interact with the law." A sample article title is "A general approach to Bayesian networks for the interpretation of evidence" (volume 139, issue 1, January 2004). Most articles require a strong medical or science background on the part of the reader, but some will be lay-accessible. One nice feature is the diary, a listing of upcoming professional events.

2893. International Journal of Legal Medicine (Online). [ISSN: 1437-1596] 1998. bi-m. Springer, Haber Str 7, Heidelberg, 69126, Germany; orders@springer.de; http://www.springer.de. *Aud.:* Ac, Sa.

In the late nineteenth century, Germany was the predominant nation doing medical and scientific research, and legal medicine evolved from those origins. Most of the articles in this journal (the online version is reviewed here) relate to medicine or lab techniques, but some are specific to criminology, and all are relevant to criminal forensics to a high degree. A strong medical or science background is recommended for the reader, but the wide variety of (albeit mostly medical) topics recommends this journal for inclusion in a core list of forensics publications. A print version is available but was not selected for review here, since all 17 holding libraries with catalog access through OCLC own only online subscriptions.

2894. Journal of Forensic Sciences. Supersedes: *What's New in Forensic Sciences.* [ISSN: 0022-1198] 1956. bi-m. USD 468 print & online eds. Ed(s): Michael A Peat. Blackwell Publishing, Inc., Commerce Place, 350 Main St, Malden, MA 02148; customerservices@blackwellpublishing.com; http://www.blackwellpublishing.com. Illus., index, adv. Refereed. Circ: 6208. Microform: PQC. Online: Blackwell Synergy; EBSCO Publishing, EBSCO Host; SwetsWise Online Content. Reprint: PSC. *Indexed:* A&ATA, AbAn, BiolAb, BiolDig, C&ISA, CABA, CJA, CJPI, CLI, CerAb, ChemAb, DSA, ExcerpMed, ForAb, HRIS, HortAb, IAA, ILP, IndVet, LRI, PsycInfo, RILM, RRTA, S&F, SCI, SSCI, VB, ZooRec. *Bk. rev.:* 0-5, signed. *Aud.:* Ac, Sa.

This is another of the journals that began in the 1950s devoted to forensic science. Its contents are subdivided into "Anthropology," "Criminalistics," "Odontology," "Pathology and Biology," "Psychiatry," "Questioned Documents," "Correspondence," "Book Reviews," and "For the Records" (specific medical studies). All articles require a strong medical or professional criminology background. Sample article title: "Diary of an Astronaut: Examination of the Remains of the Late Israeli Astronaut Colonel Ilan Ramon's Crew Notebook Recovered After the Loss of NASA's Space Shuttle Columbia" (volume 52, issue 3, May 2007).

2895. *Medicine, Science and the Law.* [ISSN: 0025-8024] 1960. q. GBP 60 domestic; GBP 70 foreign. Ed(s): A W Goode. Barnsbury Publishing, PO Box 6314, London, N1 0DL, United Kingdom. Adv. Refereed. Circ: 1600. *Indexed:* AgeL, CABA, CJA, CLI, ChemAb, ExcerpMed, ForAb, HRIS, ILP, LRI, SCI, SSCI. *Bk. rev.:* 0-2. *Aud.:* Ac, Sa.

This small-format journal is chock-full of a wide variety of readable articles intended to "advance the knowledge of forensic science and medicine," per its home page. Articles explore the interactions between society and medicine, while case studies focus on specific deaths or types of death, and medical techniques or devices. Example articles: "Gender identity disorder and its medico-legal considerations" (volume 47, issue 1, January 2007) and "Medical liabilities of the French physician passenger during a commercial air flight" (volume 47, issue 1, January 2007). A regular feature, "Law and Science," presents short abstracts of specific cases, plus there is an occasional diary that lists upcoming U.K. events. Surprisingly, there is scant online presence for this journal, although some (not all) articles are available full-text via MEDLINE.

2896. *Science and Justice.* Formerly: *Forensic Science Society. Journal.* [ISSN: 1355-0306] 1960. q. EUR 208. Ed(s): Robert Forrest. Forensic Science Society, Clark House, 18A Mount Parade, Harrogate, HG1 1BX, United Kingdom; journal@forensic-science-society.org.uk; http://www.forensic-science-society.org.uk/. Illus., index, adv. Refereed. Circ: 2600. *Indexed:* CJA, CLI, ChemAb, ExcerpMed, IndVet, LRI, SCI, SSCI, VB. *Bk. rev.:* 0-4, signed. *Aud.:* Sa.

This journal (with the earlier title *Forensic Science Society*) began publishing in 1960, and was another early entry in the roster of journals devoted to forensic science. In 1995, it switched to a larger, glossy format and changed its name to *Science and Justice.* I found this journal to be superlative. It is international in scope, and provides abstracts at the beginning of each article in multiple languages, but English is predominant throughout. It covers topics related to what the public would think of as "forensics" (i.e., criminalistics), but with a large dose of theory and analysis. Compared to other journals in this field, it is a bit thin, in that it has only four to six articles per publication; but the overall high quality of the writing, and the unabashed emphasis on scientific criminology, more than makes up for this. Articles are written in accessible English, but written by scientists, so having a science background is not necessary but may be helpful for the reader. Table of contents and selected articles are available free online.

■ FORESTRY

Bonnie E. Avery, Forestry and Natural Resources Librarian, Room 121, The Valley Library, Oregon State University, Corvallis, OR 97331-4501; bonnie.avery@oregonstate.edu

Introduction

A broad definition of forestry would include the study of trees and forests and their use by people. Modern, "science-based" forestry began in the nineteenth century when Europeans looked for specialists who could address questions on wood supply and extraction both at home and in their colonies. The threat of forest loss and wood scarcity created concern for increased forest growth as well as management techniques that would improve yield. By 1891, the United States had established publicly owned forest reserves. In 1900, the Society of American Foresters was established, as was the first School of Forestry in North America at Yale University. The U.S. Forest Service was formed three years later. This combination of professional, scholarly, and governmental resources continues to provide the core of U.S. forestry research today.

Since the mid-1940s, the scope of forestry has grown in response to economics, demography, politics, and social change as well as developments in related fields of study. While at one time German was the primary language of forestry, since World War II most research is reported in English. Knowledge of international research and practices has grown in importance since the 1980s, particularly as broader trade in forest products influenced the health of forests. In addressing global forest concerns, international and local researchers have begun to "discover" reservoirs of indigenous knowledge concerning native forests and their use.

Modern forestry education has a tradition of integrating concepts from a variety of disciplines and creating new specialties. These include forest genetics, forest ecology, forest recreation, forest economics, forest engineering, urban forestry, plantation forestry, forest pathology, and wood science. The questions addressed by forestry are often interdisciplinary or require a deep understanding of a complementary discipline. As a result, a forest science collection is most useful when it is in close proximity to a sound collection in the natural, environmental, and agricultural sciences. Likewise, users of a wood science or forest engineering collection will rely on access to collections in the physical sciences and civil, mechanical, and chemical engineering.

Finally, to address the interaction of humans and the forest as a multipurpose resource, whether looking at income generation, recreational use, traditional knowledge and practices, conservation strategies or sustainable practices, a forest researcher will need access to collections in the social sciences.

Given these assumptions about access to other collections, we can define a distinct serial literature for forestry. First, it is anchored in the history of forestry and is composed largely of government document series and international and nongovernmental organization report series. By comparison to these, trade, professional and specialized scholarly journals constitute a highly regarded yet smaller portion of the serial information resources in forestry.

The list of periodicals included here does not include government publications, although these are an important source of technical as well as scientific information. Governmental agencies such as the regional research and experiment stations of the U.S. Forest Service are vital sources of information on all aspects of forestry. Series titles such as the regional *General Technical Reports* are numerous and now are published electronically and made available from the Forest Service's *TreeSearch* web site. Electronic versions of many Canadian government forestry report series are also available free via the web. In addition, Canadian libraries focusing on forestry will benefit from their access to the National Research Council of Canada's many serial publications.

Although they are important sources of information, statistical series and serials available from nongovernmental, nonprofit international organizations and research institutions have not been included in this listing. Several statistical series and *The State of the World's Forests* are available as searchable datasets and in full text from the Food and Agriculture Organization (FAO) Forestry Sector web site.

There are numerous serial report publications now available via the Internet from other nongovernmental, nonprofit agencies. These are particularly important for coverage of "international forestry." The FAO Forestry Sector web site will help identify and serve as a portal to many of these resources, as will the "AgNIC Forestry" web site.

This selection of scholarly, academic, and trade journals for forestry is primarily representative and by no means exhaustive. In 2001, faculty members in the College of Forestry at Oregon State University were asked to list their most used or "top ten" journals. This served to provide confirmation of the multidisciplinary underpinnings of forestry but also to provide a core set of scholarly titles for this list. In general when selecting scholarly titles, I look for those with high impact factor rankings or journals with a long citation half-life as provided by the *Journal Citation Reports* from Thomson ISI. When deciding between comparable titles, I considered the journal subscription price, and gave preference to professional society publications over journals from commercial publishers.

I look for titles that reflect changing concerns in forestry. Recent additions to the list of forestry titles include *International Journal of Wildland Fire,* the *Journal of Forest Products Business Research,* and *Small-Scale Forestry.* Monitoring additions to the Directory of Open Access Journals (DOAJ) serves as an inexpensive entree to international society publications and research journals. For this edition, I have included of these titles *Forest@* and *Revista Arvore* as strong, representative open-access publications.

For anyone new to managing a forestry collection, I recommend *Literature of Forestry and Agroforestry,* published by Cornell University Press in 1996. It provides a useful history of the field and identifies both monographs and serials that have defined "science-based forestry" during the last century. This serves as a good foundation for considering new areas of research and how best to provide a wide array of "evidence-based" forestry information in the future.

Basic Periodicals

Hs: *American Forests, Unasylva*; Ga: *American Forests, Environmental History, Journal of Forestry, Unasylva*; Ac, Sa: *Arboriculture and Urban Forestry, Canadian Journal of Forest Research, Environmental History, Forest Ecology and Management, Forest@, Forest Products Journal, Journal of Forest Products Business Research, Forest Science, International Journal of Wildland Fire, Journal of Forestry, Revista Arvore, Wood and Fiber Science.*

Basic Abstracts and Indexes

Agricola, Bibliography of Agriculture, Biological and Agricultural Index, TreeSearch, Forest Products Abstracts, Forestry Abstracts, Forest Science Database (CABI).

2897. *Agricultural and Forest Meteorology.* Formerly (until 1984): *Agricultural Meteorology.* [ISSN: 0168-1923] 1964. 24x/yr. EUR 2778. Ed(s): K T Paw U. Elsevier BV, Radarweg 29, Amsterdam, 1043 NX, Netherlands; nlinfo-f@elsevier.nl; http://www.elsevier.nl. Illus., index, adv. Sample. Refereed. Microform: PQC. Online: EBSCO Publishing, EBSCO Host; Gale; IngentaConnect; OhioLINK; ScienceDirect; SwetsWise Online Content. *Indexed:* Agr, BiolAb, CABA, DSA, EnvAb, EnvInd, ExcerpMed, FPA, FR, ForAb, HortAb, IndVet, M&GPA, PollutAb, S&F, SCI, SWRA, VB, WAE&RSA. *Bk. rev.:* 1-3, 500-800 words. *Aud.:* Ac, Sa.

This international journal covers meteorology as it is used in the agricultural, forest, and soil sciences. Articles emphasize research relevant to the practical problems of forestry, agriculture, and natural ecosystems. Topics include the effect of weather on forests, soils, crops, water use, and forest fires; the effect of vegetation on climate and weather; and canopy micrometeorology. This journal is heavily used by specialists working in these areas, and as a result it has been assigned a high impact factor by the Institute of Scientific Information. Twenty-four issues appear annually in six volumes, though it is not uncommon for issues to be combined. While this is an expensive journal, a number of thematic, special issues are available for purchase as monographs. With a print subscription, online access to the current year is available through Science Direct Web Editions. Options for more complete online access are available through Science Direct.

2898. *Agroforestry Systems.* Incorporates (1972-1999): *Agroforestry Forum;* Which was formerly (until 1992): *Agroforestry in the U K.* [ISSN: 0167-4366] 1982. 9x/yr. EUR 1177 print & online eds. Ed(s): P K Ramachandran Nair. Springer Netherlands, Van Godewijckstraat 30, Dordrecht, 3311 GX, Netherlands; http://www.springeronline.com. Adv. Refereed. Microform: PQC. Online: EBSCO Publishing, EBSCO Host; Gale; IngentaConnect; OCLC Online Computer Library Center, Inc.; OhioLINK; Springer LINK; SwetsWise Online Content. Reprint: PSC. *Indexed:* Agr, B&AI, BiolAb, CABA, DSA, EnvInd, FPA, ForAb, GardL, HortAb, S&F, SCI, SSCI, SWA, WAE&RSA. *Bk. rev.:* Occasional, 500-1,500 words. *Aud.:* Ac, Sa.

Sponsored in part by the World Agroforestry Center (formerly the International Center for Research in Agroforestry), this is an international, refereed journal. It has grown in reputation during its 20 years of publication and is currently highly cited in the research literature. Three volumes are published annually, each consisting of three issues. Included in each issue are seven to ten reports of original research, critical reviews, and short communications, with periodic book reviews and announcements. Topics include basic and applied research on indigenous species and multipurpose trees, and techniques for integrating systems of trees, crops, and livestock. For inclusion, research results and information presented must have application beyond the specific location studied. This journal would complement collections that support agriculture and environmental studies as well as forestry, particularly those with an international development focus. Online access for an additional fee is available via Kluwer Online. Subscription information and the table of contents of recent issues are available on the journal web site.

2899. *American Christmas Tree Journal.* Formerly: *American Christmas Tree Growers' Journal.* [ISSN: 0569-3845] 1956. 4x/yr. Non-members, USD 50. Ed(s): Becky Rasmussen, Dennis Tompkins. National Christmas Tree Association, 16020 Swingley Ridge Rd, Ste 300, Chesterfield, MO 63017; info@realchristmastrees.org; http://www.realchristmastrees.org. Illus., index, adv. Circ: 1800. Vol. ends: Oct. *Aud.:* Ga.

This trade journal is issued four times annually. It serves as the membership journal for the National Christmas Tree Association. Feature articles are of interest to the woodlot owners who grow and market Christmas trees or related products. State chapters of the National Christmas Tree Association report and announce conferences under "Association News." Grower profiles, marketing, business and regulatory information, and silvicultural advice are covered regularly. The White House Christmas tree is featured annually, and articles with a historical perspective on Christmas trees appear regularly. This journal would be useful in general collections where this industry is part of the local economy.

2900. *American Forests.* Formerly (until 1931): *American Forests and Forest life;* (until 1924): *American Forestry;* (until 1910): *Conservation;* (until 1908): *Forestry & Irrigation;* Which was formed by the 1902 merger of: *National Irrigation;* (1895-1901): *The Forester.* [ISSN: 0002-8541] 1895. q. Membership, USD 25; USD 3 newsstand/cover per issue. Ed(s): Michelle Robbins. American Forests, 734 15th St, NW, Ste 800, Washington, DC 20005-2000. Illus., index, adv. Circ: 25000 Paid. Vol. ends: Winter. Microform: PQC. Online: EBSCO Publishing, EBSCO Host; Florida Center for Library Automation; Gale; Northern Light Technology, Inc.; OCLC Online Computer Library Center, Inc.; ProQuest K-12 Learning Solutions; ProQuest LLC (Ann Arbor); H.W. Wilson. *Indexed:* ABIn, Agr, B&AI, BRI, BiolDig, CBRI, ChemAb, EngInd, EnvInd, FPA, ForAb, GSI, GardL, LRI, MASUSE, RGPR. *Aud.:* Hs, Ga, Ac.

This magazine is the membership organ for one of the oldest conservation organizations in the United States, American Forests. Feature articles are intended for a general audience and address tree planting, tree species profiles, and current policy controversies, as well as the practical aspects of current research and how-to articles. Typical of this magazine's well-illustrated and easily read features are recent articles on the role of urban forests in urban planning and on wildfire recovery efforts in the Southwest. The organization sponsors the work of the "Global ReLeaf Center," "Forest Policy Center," and "Urban Forest Center," and maintains the "National Register of Big Trees." Editorial emphasis is placed on coverage of forests and trees located "on land where people live, work, and relax." Further explanation of sponsored programs and memberships are available on the organization's web site, as is an archive of many of the magazine's articles. This magazine is issued quarterly and would be suitable for public, school, and college libraries.

2901. *Arboriculture and Urban Forestry.* Formerly (until 2005): *Journal of Arboriculture;* Which was formed by the merger of (1935-1975): *Arborist's News; International Shade Tree Conference. Proceedings of the Annual Meeting.* [ISSN: 1935-5297] 1975. bi-m. USD 105. Ed(s): Robert W Miller. International Society of Arboriculture, PO Box 3129, Champaign, IL 61826-3129; isa@isa-arbor.com; http://www.isa-arbor.com. Illus., index, adv. Sample. Refereed. Circ: 8500. Vol. ends: Nov. *Indexed:* Agr, B&AI, BiolAb, CABA, FPA, ForAb, GardL, HortAb, RRTA, S&F, WAE&RSA. *Aud.:* Ac, Sa.

This bimonthly journal (formerly, *Journal of Arboriculture*) is published by the International Society of Arboriculture (ISA). Each issue includes four to six research papers intended for the practitioner, and although scientific in nature, are accessible to the interested layperson. Articles regularly cover such topics as green space, sustainable urban forestry, control of invasive species, landscaping, etc., and would be of interest to urban policymakers as well as urban foresters and park administrators. Of interest to homeowners and gardeners are topics such as street tree inventories, the effect of vegetation on energy use, and topping of trees. Included in each issue is "Arboriculture Abstracts," which summarizes relevant articles in related journals. At this writing, a free backfile for the years 1998 through 2004 is available online at "Arboriculture On-Line" at www.treelink.org/joa. The table of contents for issues from 2002 to date are linked from the ISA web site, although access requires a subscriber password.

2902. *Arborist News.* [ISSN: 1542-2399] 1992. bi-m. Membership, USD 105. International Society of Arboriculture, PO Box 3129, Champaign, IL 61826-3129; isa@isa-arbor.com; http://www.isa-arbor.com. Adv. *Indexed:* GardL. *Aud.:* Hs, Ga, Ac, Sa.

This bimonthly publication covers news of interest to the tree-care professional and is the membership publication of the International Society of Arboriculture. Regular features include the "Tree Industry Calendar," professional profiles, summaries of articles published in the *Journal of Arboriculture,* the "Climbers Corner," and "European News." Continuing-education articles feature general tree-care, current tree-health problems, and business aspects of arboriculture. Selected articles are available in full text on the society's web site, as is membership information needed for subscribing. Articles are timely and readable and would be useful for the general homeowner as well as for the professional arborist. This publication is suitable for a general collection or public library.

2903. *Canadian Forest Industries: Canada's only national publication serving saw and pulpwood logging, sawmilling and allied activities.* Formed by the merger of: *Canada Lumberman; Timber of Canada.* [ISSN: 0318-4277] 1888. 8x/yr. CND 51 domestic; USD 55 United States; CND 75 elsewhere. Ed(s): Scott Jamieson. J C F T Forest Communications, 90 Morgan Rd, Unit 14, Baie d'Urte, PQ H9Y 3A8, Canada; info@forestcommunications.com; http://www.forestcommunications.com. Illus., index, adv. Sample. Circ: 12500. Vol. ends: Dec. Microform: MML; PQC. Online: CanWest Interactive Inc., FPInfomart; Micromedia ProQuest. *Indexed:* CPerI, FPA, ForAb. *Aud.:* Ac, Sa.

This Canadian trade journal serves as the journal of record for the Canadian Woodlands Forum of the Forest Products Association of Canada (formerly the Canadian Pulp and Paper Association). It focuses on the full range of activities associated with logging technology and harvesting systems. Articles are of current interest, and editorial features are common and may give this publication broad appeal among those interested in industry practices suitable for North America. Topics such as environmentally sound road building, wood certification, current forest harvesting practices, and tests of new logging equipment are featured regularly and would be of interest to students in forestry or environmental policy. Regular features also include reviews of new products and literature. Subscription information for this bimonthly publication is available on the journal's web site.

2904. *Canadian Journal of Forest Research.* [ISSN: 0045-5067] 1970. m. CND 922 (Individuals, CND 250). Ed(s): Cindy E Prescott, Doug Maynard. N R C Research Press, National Research Council of Canada, Ottawa, ON K1A 0R6, Canada; pubs@nrc-cnrc.gc.ca; http://pubs.nrc-cnrc.gc.ca. Illus., index, adv. Sample. Refereed. Circ: 862. Vol. ends: Dec. Microform: MML; PQC. Online: EBSCO Publishing, EBSCO Host; Gale; IngentaConnect; Micromedia ProQuest; OCLC Online Computer Library Center, Inc.; Ovid Technologies, Inc.; ProQuest K-12 Learning Solutions; ProQuest LLC (Ann Arbor); SwetsWise Online Content; H.W. Wilson. *Indexed:* Agr, ApEcolAb, B&AI, BiolAb, CABA, CBCARef, CPerI, ChemAb, DSA, EngInd, EnvAb, EnvInd, ExcerpMed, FPA, ForAb, HortAb, IBR, IBZ, M&GPA, PollutAb, RRTA, S&F, SCI, SSCI, SWRA, WAE&RSA, ZooRec. *Aud.:* Ac, Sa.

Consistently in the top ten forestry journal rankings as issued by Institute for Scientific Information, this refereed journal should be a core title for any research collection in this area. International in scope, this journal's articles are in English with French summaries, report on primary research addressing an array of questions, and are accompanied by extensive bibliographies. Each issue is comprised of 15 to 20 articles, often authored by researchers at universities, government forestry agencies, or other research institutions. Subscription information and tables of contents are available on the web site of the National Research Council of Canada. After a 12-month period, the full text of articles in the journal are included in Ebsco's Academic Search packages. Apart from designated Canadian Depository Libraries, complete full-text availability requires an additional fee.

2905. *Environmental History.* Formed by the merger of (1976-1996): *Environmental History Review;* Which was formerly (until 1989): *Environmental Review;* (1957-1996): *Forest and Conservation History;*

Which was formerly (until 1989): *Journal of Forest History;* (until 1974): *Forest History.* [ISSN: 1084-5453] 1996. q. USD 130 (Individuals, USD 55 includes membership). Forest History Society, 701 Williams Vickers Ave, Durham, NC 27701-3162; recluce2@duke.edu; http://www.foresthistory.org. Illus., index, adv. Sample. Refereed. Circ: 2000. Vol. ends: Oct. Microform: PQC. Online: EBSCO Publishing, EBSCO Host; Northern Light Technology, Inc.; OCLC Online Computer Library Center, Inc.; ProQuest K-12 Learning Solutions; ProQuest LLC (Ann Arbor). Reprint: PSC. *Indexed:* Agr, AmH&L, ArtHuCI, CABA, EnvAb, EnvInd, FPA, ForAb, GardL, HistAb, HortAb, IndVet, PollutAb, RRTA, S&F, SSCI, SWRA, WAE&RSA. *Bk. rev.:* 15-20, 500-1,000 words. *Aud.:* Ga, Ac, Sa.

This refereed journal provides a rich resource for those interested in the history of forestry and environmental studies. Each issue includes four or five well-documented historical articles as well as numerous book reviews. Recent issues include articles on the Forest Service and ecosystem management, urban weed control in the early twentieth century, and a history of oaks in eighteenth- and nineteenth-century Sweden. Books, articles, theses and dissertations, and archival material added to the Forest History Society's database of "sources related to environmental history" are reported with brief annotations in the regular feature, "Biblioscope." This is a significant resource for current awareness for the researcher. Moderately priced and accessible to the general reader with an interest in history, it would be a good addition to larger public libraries as well as a standard for collections that support both undergraduate study and graduate research in forestry and environmental studies. Tables of contents, a searchable bibliography, and subscription information are available on the journal's web site.

2906. *Forest Ecology and Management.* [ISSN: 0378-1127] 1977. 24x/yr. EUR 3752. Ed(s): G M J Mohren, R F Fisher. Elsevier BV, Radarweg 29, Amsterdam, 1043 NX, Netherlands; nlinfo-f@elsevier.nl; http://www.elsevier.nl. Illus., index, adv. Sample. Refereed. Microform: PQC. Online: EBSCO Publishing, EBSCO Host; Gale; IngentaConnect; OhioLINK; ScienceDirect; SwetsWise Online Content. *Indexed:* Agr, ApEcolAb, B&AI, BiolAb, CABA, ChemAb, DSA, EngInd, EnvAb, EnvInd, ExcerpMed, FPA, ForAb, HortAb, IndVet, M&GPA, PollutAb, RRTA, S&F, SCI, SSCI, SWRA, WAE&RSA, ZooRec. *Aud.:* Ac, Sa.

This refereed journal is perhaps most representative of the multidisciplinary nature of forestry. Each volume consists of 25 to 45 articles appearing in three issues, although these issues are often combined for publication. There are 15–17 volumes published annually. The journal reports on the "application of biological, ecological and social knowledge to the management of man-made and natural forests." Volumes are often thematic, and typical articles report on research related to tree growth, nutrient cycling, landscape ecology, the forest as habitat, the effect of logging practices, and numerous other subjects. The publisher's web site provides a table of contents to recent years, and a print subscription includes licensed access to the most recent 9 to 12 months of the journal through ScienceDirect. Options for full online access through ScienceDirect Digital Collections are available for subscribers, but require separate license agreements. The heavy use of this journal by scholars and researchers makes it a core title for research-based forestry collections despite its high cost.

2907. *Forest Landowner.* Formerly (until 1996): *Forest Farmer.* [ISSN: 1087-9110] 1941. bi-m. USD 55. Ed(s): Paige Cash. Forest Landowners Association, PO Box 450209, Atlanta, GA 31145-0209; info@forestlandowners.com; http://www.forestlandowners.com. Illus., adv. Circ: 12733 Paid. Vol. ends: Nov/Dec. *Indexed:* EngInd, EnvAb. *Aud.:* Ga.

This bimonthly publication serves as the membership organ for the Forest Landowners Association and presents issues of concern to large and small timberland owners in the southern and eastern United States. A well-illustrated trade journal, it provides feature articles of political as well as technical interest. Recent issues include articles on seedling mortality, riparian zones, consulting foresters, planning, and research on pest detection for forest health. Feature articles from many issues are available on the association's web site. The association is active in lobbying at the local, regional, and national level, and regular columns include information on timber pricing, timber tax issues, government affairs, and hunting and wildlife, as well as new products and organization news. An annual "Seedling Nursery Directory" appears in the September/October issue, and in alternate years the journal issues "Forest Landowner Manual," a directory of dealers, mills, schools, state and federal agencies, and associations related to forestry in southern and eastern United States. In the geographic regions noted, and where the local economy includes small landowners who privately manage timberlands, this publication would be appropriate for a general library collection.

2908. Forest Policy and Economics. [ISSN: 1389-9341] 2000. 8x/yr. EUR 416. Ed(s): M Krott. Elsevier BV, Radarweg 29, Amsterdam, 1043 NX, Netherlands; nlinfo-f@elsevier.nl; http://www.elsevier.nl. Refereed. Online: EBSCO Publishing, EBSCO Host; Gale; IngentaConnect; OhioLINK; ScienceDirect; SwetsWise Online Content. *Indexed:* Agr, BiolAb, CABA, EngInd, FPA, ForAb, HortAb, IBR, IBZ, PollutAb, RRTA, S&F, SCI, WAE&RSA. *Aud.:* Ac, Sa.

This refereed journal is issued quarterly in collaboration with the European Forest Institute (EFI) and fills a niche in the forestry literature by addressing policy issues in an international context. It covers economics and planning as they apply to the forests and forest industries sector, and it seeks to "enhance communications amongst researchers, legislators, decision-makers, and other professionals concerned with formulating and implementing policies for the sector." Each issue consists of 7 to 12 articles as well as occasional conference announcements and EFI news. Special thematic issues have covered such topics as national forestry programs, multipurpose management of mountain forests, and forest-related rural development. As a moderately priced, scholarly forestry title, it will be an important addition to research collections, but may also be a useful for large public library collections where forestry is an important part of the economy. Subscription information and table of contents for recent issues are available on the journal's web site. In addition to print, licensing options for access to articles online are available.

2909. Forest Products Journal. Former titles (until 1955): *Forest Products Research Society. Journal;* (until 1951): *Forest Products Research Society. Proceedings of the National Annual Meeting.* [ISSN: 0015-7473] 1947. 10x/yr. USD 155 domestic; USD 165 in Canada & Mexico; USD 195 elsewhere. Ed(s): Erin Bosch. Forest Products Society, 2801 Marshall Ct, Madison, WI 53705-2295; erin@forestprod.org. Illus., index, adv. Sample. Refereed. Circ: 2000 Paid. Vol. ends: Nov/Dec. Microform: PMC; PQC. Online: EBSCO Publishing, EBSCO Host; Florida Center for Library Automation; Gale; Northern Light Technology, Inc.; OCLC Online Computer Library Center, Inc.; ProQuest LLC (Ann Arbor). *Indexed:* A&ATA, ABIn, Agr, B&AI, CABA, ChemAb, DSA, EngInd, EnvAb, EnvInd, ExcerpMed, FPA, ForAb, HortAb, PollutAb, RRTA, S&F, SCI, SSCI, WAE&RSA. *Bk. rev.:* 0-1, 1,000-2,000 words. *Aud.:* Ac, Sa.

Sponsored by the Forest Products Society, this refereed journal is well respected for its technical coverage of research in wood science and technology. The journal is issued ten times a year. Each includes 10 to 12 technical articles on an array of topics that include management, processes, solid wood products, composites and manufactured wood products, and fundamental disciplines. To put these articles in perspective, a short statement on the relevance of each article is given under the heading "Practicalities and Possibilities." In addition to association news and classified ads, regular feature columns report on international research literature, new publications and computer applications, patents, codes, standards, and regulatory changes. The featured article from each of the most recent three issues is available in full text on the society's web site. Earlier articles are available to society members only through a user ID and password. This lack of IP recognition access may be a problem for libraries wishing to provide online access to their users. Although this journal is a technical publication, many of its articles would be useful to engineers, economists, and those wishing to keep abreast of the forest products industry.

2910. Forest Science: a journal of research and technical progress. [ISSN: 0015-749X] 1955. bi-m. USD 375 (Individuals, USD 130). Ed(s): Matthew Walls, Edwin Green. Society of American Foresters, 5400 Grosvenor Ln, Bethesda, MD 20814; johnsonc@safnet.org; http://www.safnet.org. Illus., index, adv. Sample. Refereed. Circ: 1200 Paid. Vol. ends: Dec. Microform: PQC. Online: EBSCO Publishing, EBSCO Host; Gale; IngentaConnect; OCLC Online Computer Library

Center, Inc.; ProQuest K-12 Learning Solutions; ProQuest LLC (Ann Arbor). *Indexed:* Agr, B&AI, BiolAb, CABA, ChemAb, EngInd, EnvAb, EnvInd, ExcerpMed, FPA, ForAb, HortAb, PollutAb, RRTA, S&F, SCI, SSCI, SWRA, WAE&RSA, ZooRec. *Bk. rev.:* 2-3, 1,000 words. *Aud.:* Ac, Sa.

This bimonthly refereed journal is one of five journals sponsored by the Society of American Foresters. Each issue includes 15 to 25 articles reporting on scientific results from both theoretical and applied research related to silviculture, soils, biometry, disease, recreation, photosynthesis, tree physiology, and all aspects of management and harvesting. International in scope, articles in this journal are both highly cited and consistently cited over a long period of time. It enjoys wide respect within the forestry scientific community and is heavily used by researchers, practitioners, and students alike, who consider this a core title for their work. The general format is open to a wider audience, and articles are readable, making the journal accessible to the general reader as well. Since late 2000, full-text access to articles from this journal is available to subscribers at no additional cost through *ingenta*. There are occasional problems with the timeliness of this online access. Subscription information is available from the society's web site, as is a good deal of other information about the society.

2911. Forest@. [ISSN: 1824-0119] 2004. q. Free. Societa Italiana di Selvicoltura ed Ecologia Forestale, Dipartimento di Produzione Vegetale, Via dell'Ateneo Lucano 10, Potenza, 85100, Italy; http://www.sisef.it. *Bk. rev.:* 1-2; 250-750 words. *Aud.:* Ac, Sa.

Each issue of *Forest@* has three sections: scientific articles, "News and Views," and "News Announcements." Ten to twenty scientific articles are included in each issue. These include reports on original research, literature reviews, and research/technical notes. Coverage includes the fields of silviculture, forest ecology, ecophysiology, conservation genetics, forest biodiversity, and forest management. The "News and Views" section includes editorials, comments, letters, and book reviews. "News Announcements" includes new symposia, meetings, advanced courses, position announcements, etc. As an online journal, *Forest@* is able to offer a communication medium for continuing the scientific discussions raised in articles as well. Although most papers are in Italian with English summaries, articles in English also appear. A recent submission in English discusses the USDA Forest Service Forest Inventory and Analysis Program and provides an interesting history of the U.S. Forest Survey. URL: www.sisef.it/forest@

2912. Forestry Chronicle. [ISSN: 0015-7546] 1925. bi-m. USD 180, Libraries, CND 180 (Individuals, CND 100). Ed(s): Ron Ayling. Canadian Institute of Forestry, 151 Slater St, Ste 606, Ottawa, ON K1P 5H3, Canada; cif@cif-ifc.org; http://www.cif-ifc.org. Illus., index, adv. Sample. Refereed. Circ: 2800. Vol. ends: Nov/Dec. *Indexed:* Agr, CABA, ChemAb, EngInd, EnvAb, EnvInd, FPA, ForAb, HortAb, IndVet, RRTA, S&F, SCI, WAE&RSA, ZooRec. *Bk. rev.:* 1-10, 500-1,500 words. *Aud.:* Ac, Sa.

Published by the Canadian Institute of Forestry, this refereed journal includes both peer-reviewed articles and membership news. Bimonthly issues include 10 to 15 articles in English and, less frequently, in French with English summaries. In recent issues, the ratio of "Professional Papers" to "Scientific and Technical Papers" is two to one. Papers focus on applied and scientific research and occasionally include conference presentations. Announcements of recent publications, forestry education programs, and professional and institute news are regularly included. Online access to this publication is available with a subscription and includes an archive back to 2002. The intended audience for this journal is the professional forester; however, given its modest price, it is an accessible publication for collections that serve undergraduates and the general public.

2913. I A W A Journal. Former titles (until 1993): *I A W A Bulletin; I A W A Publications.* [ISSN: 0928-1541] 1931. q. Free to members. Ed(s): E A Wheeler, P Baas. International Association of Wood Anatomists, PO Box 80102, Utrecht, 3508 TC, Netherlands. Refereed. Circ: 800. *Indexed:* A&ATA, BiolAb, CABA, FPA, ForAb, HortAb, RRTA, S&F, SCI. *Bk. rev.:* 2-3, 500-1,000 words. *Aud.:* Ac, Sa.

Published by the International Association of Wood Anatomists, this refereed journal covers topics in wood anatomy such as the micro-structure of wood, bark, and related plant products including bamboo, rattan, and palms basic to the study of forest products. Published quarterly, each issue is comprised of eight to ten well-documented, illustrated articles on the anatomy and properties of a variety of species, as well as association news, announcements of conferences and workshops, and two or three book reviews. Table of contents and article abstracts for issues published since 2000 are available on the publisher's web site. For specialized and research collections, this highly cited journal is an important and inexpensive addition.

2914. *International Forestry Review.* Formerly (until 1999): *Commonwealth Forestry Review.* [ISSN: 1465-5489] 1921. q. GBP 180. Ed(s): Alan J Pottinger. Commonwealth Forestry Association, PO Box 142, Oxford, OX26 6ZJ, United Kingdom; http://cfa-international.org/publications.html. Illus., adv. Refereed. Circ: 900. *Indexed:* CABA, ChemAb, FPA, ForAb, HortAb, RRTA, S&F, SCI, WAE&RSA. *Bk. rev.:* 5-7, 300-500 words. *Aud.:* Ga, Ac, Sa.

Formerly the *Commonwealth Forestry Review,* this refereed journal is published quarterly by the Commonwealth Forestry Association (CFA). Each issue features 6 to 12 papers reporting on a wide range of research conducted, for the most part, in Asia and Africa. Also regularly featured are short opinion pieces under the heading "Comment," five to seven book reviews, and translations of article summaries in French and Spanish. Occasional issues focus on themes such as "forestry and small island developing states." One of the goals of CFA is to foster public interest in forestry. For that reason, this modestly priced and well-indexed journal is a good introduction to forestry concerns from an international as well as a scientific point of view. While online access is available for subscribers, it requires authentication by password rather than IP recognition. This title would be useful for undergraduate collections that support international programs, and for research collections.

2915. *International Journal of Forest Engineering.* Formerly (until 1999): *Journal of Forest Engineering.* [ISSN: 1494-2119] 1989. s-a. USD 155 domestic; USD 165 in Canada & Mexico; USD 195 elsewhere. Ed(s): Jeremy Rickards. University of New Brunswick, Faculty of Forestry and Environmental Management, PO Box 44555, Fredericton, NB E3B 6C2, Canada; jforeng@unb.ca. Illus. Refereed. Circ: 350 Paid. Vol. ends: Jul. *Indexed:* Agr, CABA, FPA, ForAb, HortAb, S&F, WAE&RSA. *Aud.:* Ac, Sa.

Although articles on forest engineering appear in other forestry journals, this semi-annual refereed publication sponsored by the faculty of Forestry and Environmental Management at the University of New Brunswick is unique in being devoted to the research aspects of this field. The composition of its editorial board is representative of its international scope. Each issue contains, on average, eight technical papers along with occasional technical notes and reviews. Among topics covered are forest operations including harvesting, stand management, machine design, road design and construction, and wood engineering and processing. The column "Tell us about your organization" may prove useful for librarians wishing to better acquaint themselves with this field. Free full-text access is available for the first ten volumes from the journal's web site. Online access to subsequent volumes requires a subscriber user name and password. Modestly priced, this is an important addition to library collections that support practitioners and researchers in forest operations.

2916. *International Journal of Wildland Fire.* [ISSN: 1049-8001] 1991. q. AUD 940 print & online eds. (Individuals, AUD 200 print & online eds.). Ed(s): Mike Flannigan. C S I R O Publishing, 150 Oxford St, PO Box 1139, Collingwood, VIC 3066, Australia; publishing@csiro.au; http://www.publish.csiro.au/. Index. Sample. Refereed. Circ: 800 Paid. *Indexed:* Agr, BiolAb, CABA, EnvAb, FPA, ForAb, H&SSA, HortAb, M&GPA, PollutAb, RRTA, RiskAb, S&F, SCI, WAE&RSA. *Aud.:* Ac, Sa.

This peer-reviewed journal is published commercially by the Commonwealth Scientific and International Research Organisation Australia (CSIRO). It is presented under the auspices of the International Association of Wildland Fire and has an editorial board representative of the North America, Australia, and Europe. Among the areas covered on a regular basis are fire ecology, fire behavior, and fire management systems, as well as modeling of fire in relation to history, climate, landscape, and ecosystems. The journal is well indexed. The increased and sustained interest in fire management in relation to forested lands makes this publication a desirable addition to both specialized forestry

collections and academic collections. Relative to other journals in this field, it is modestly priced. A subscription to the print version includes online access via IP recognition. Online-only access is available at a reduced annual fee, and multi-site licenses are available.

2917. *Journal of Forest Products Business Research (Online Edition).* Formerly (until 2005): *Journal of Forest Products Business Research (Print Edition).* 2004. irreg. USD 100 (Individuals, USD 50). Ed(s): Eric Hansen. Forest Products Society, 2801 Marshall Ct, Madison, WI 53705-2295; http://www.forestprod.org. Refereed. *Aud.:* Ac, Sa.

This electronic journal is currently issued annually with three to ten articles appearing as they are accepted throughout the year. Very modestly priced, it is intended to provide a forum for the publication of scientific research related to forest industry. This is an international journal dedicated to recognition and growth of the academic field of forest products business, particularly management and marketing. Articles may be scientific papers, synthesis papers, and editorials. Access is via a subscriber log in, which may work better for smaller libraries than those that rely on IP authentication for electronic resources. URL: www.forestprod.org/jfpbr.html

2918. *Journal of Forestry.* [ISSN: 0022-1201] 1902. 8x/yr. USD 185 (print & online eds.) Individuals, USD 85; Free to members). Ed(s): Matthew Walls, Keith Moser. Society of American Foresters, 5400 Grosvenor Ln, Bethesda, MD 20814; ziadia@safnet.org; http://www.safnet.org/pubs. Illus., index. Sample. Refereed. Circ: 16500 Controlled. Vol. ends: Dec. Microform: PMC; PQC. Online: EBSCO Publishing, EBSCO Host; Gale; IngentaConnect; Northern Light Technology, Inc.; OCLC Online Computer Library Center, Inc.; ProQuest K-12 Learning Solutions; ProQuest LLC (Ann Arbor). *Indexed:* Agr, B&AI, BiolDig, CABA, ChemAb, EngInd, EnvAb, EnvInd, ExcerpMed, FPA, ForAb, GardL, HRIS, HortAb, PAIS, PollutAb, RRTA, S&F, SCI, SSCI, SWRA, WAE&RSA, ZooRec. *Bk. rev.:* 5-10, 100 words; 0-1, lengthy. *Aud.:* Hs, Ga, Ac.

This is the membership journal of the Society of American Foresters. Themes for each of eight issues are available on the society's web site. Current themes include forest health and ecology, international forestry and sustainable development, education and employment, and forest certification and third-party auditing, as well as two open forums and an issue devoted to technology and practice, with an annual "Professional Resource Guide." Past themes include ethics, GIS, and fire. Feature articles undergo peer review but are written for a broad audience. Regular features include member "Perspectives" and "Focus on," which features more practical information of interest to members in specific sectors of forestry. Of use to librarians for collection development is the regular column on "New Releases," which includes books, reports, and media. Both the writing and range of topics covered make this an important addition to public and college libraries as well as collections that serve the professional forester and researcher. Since late 2000, full-text access to articles from this journal is available to subscribers at no additional cost through *ingenta.* An extensive electronic backfile back to 1905 also being developed. Subscription information is available from the society's web site, as is a good deal of other information about this professional society.

2919. *Journal of Sustainable Forestry.* [ISSN: 1054-9811] 1993. q. USD 375 print & online eds. Ed(s): Graeme P Berlyn. Haworth Food & Agricultural Products Press, 10 Alice St, Binghamton, NY 13904-1580; getinfo@haworthpress.com; http://www.haworthpress.com/. Illus., index, adv. Sample. Refereed. Circ: 152 Paid. Vol. ends: No. 4. Microform: PQC. Online: EBSCO Publishing, EBSCO Host; OCLC Online Computer Library Center, Inc.; SwetsWise Online Content. Reprint: HAW. *Indexed:* AbAn, Agr, BiolDig, CABA, EngInd, EnvAb, EnvInd, FPA, ForAb, GardL, HortAb, IBR, IBZ, PollutAb, RRTA, S&F, SWRA, WAE&RSA. *Bk. rev.:* Occasional, brief. *Aud.:* Ac, Sa.

This international journal is refereed and focuses on research that promotes the sustainability of forests for their products (both wood and non-wood) as well as research that contributes to sustainable agroforestry. It fills a niche in the commercial journal market. Two or more of the four issues that make up each volume may be combined to serve as the record of a conference covering an unusual topic, such as recent issues on "War and Tropical Forests: Conservation in Areas of Armed Conflict," "Illegal Logging in the Tropics: Strategies for

Cutting Crime," and "Plantations and Protected Areas in Sustainable Forestry." These multi-issue titles are often made available as monographs as well. It can be argued that more of this material is now available on the web; however, the fact that this journal is well indexed in the bibliographic databases used by students makes it particularly important for academic collections.

2920. *National Woodlands Magazine.* [ISSN: 0279-9812] 1979. q. USD 25 domestic includes 8 issues of Woodland Report newsletter; USD 35 foreign includes 8 issues of Woodland Report newsletter. Ed(s): Eric Johnson. National Woodland Owners Association, 374 Maple Ave E Ste 310, Vienna, VA 22180; http://www.nationalwoodlands.org. Illus., adv. Circ: 26000 Paid. Vol. ends: Oct. *Aud.:* Ga.

This quarterly magazine serves the membership of the National Woodland Owners Association. This association monitors government activities related to its membership and works with nonprofit groups and professional societies to communicate the concerns and interests of nonindustrial, private woodlot owners. Each issue includes three to five feature articles on such topics as fire management and environmental education, as well as regular political news columns and reports from the "Forest Fire Lookout Association." Regular departments include "Timber and Taxes," "National Historic Lookout Register," and updates to the "National Directory of Consulting Foresters." Though plain in presentation, the magazine has a broad geographic focus within the United States. An inexpensive addition to a general collection, it serves to represent the point of view of the nonindustrial landowner. Membership and subscription information are available from the association's web site, as is the full text of issues from July 2002 forward.

2921. *New Forests: journal of biology, biotechnology, and management of afforestation and reforestation.* [ISSN: 0169-4286] 1986. bi-m. EUR 758 print & online eds. Ed(s): Stephen W Hallgren. Springer Netherlands, Van Godewijckstraat 30, Dordrecht, 3311 GX, Netherlands; http://www.springeronline.com. Illus., index, adv. Sample. Refereed. Microform: PQC. Online: EBSCO Publishing, EBSCO Host; Gale; IngentaConnect; OCLC Online Computer Library Center, Inc.; OhioLINK; Ovid Technologies, Inc.; Springer LINK; SwetsWise Online Content. Reprint: PSC. *Indexed:* Agr, BiolAb, CABA, EngInd, EnvInd, FPA, ForAb, HortAb, PollutAb, RRTA, S&F, SCI, WAE&RSA. *Aud.:* Ac, Sa.

This refereed journal is international in scope and is intended for an audience of scientists and practitioners. Two volumes each of three issues appear annually and contain six to eight papers of reporting on the findings of original research. "New forests" refers to the reproduction of trees and forests by reforestation or afforestation, whether for the purposes of resource protection, timber production, or agroforestry. Topics included are silviculture, plant physiology, genetics, biotechnology, propagation methods and nursery practices, ecology, economics, and forest protection. Although relatively new, it enjoys a good reputation among researchers and should be considered a core title for a research collection. Archival full-text access to issues is available as an alternative to print or in addition to a print subscription for an additional fee through the publisher's web site.

2922. *Northern Journal of Applied Forestry.* [ISSN: 0742-6348] 1984. q. USD 170 (Individuals, USD 75). Ed(s): Matthew Walls, James W Hornbeck. Society of American Foresters, 5400 Grosvenor Ln, Bethesda, MD 20814; safweb@safnet.org; http://www.safnet.org. Illus., index, adv. Sample. Circ: 2000 Paid. Vol. ends: Dec. Microform: PQC. Online: EBSCO Publishing, EBSCO Host; Gale; IngentaConnect; ProQuest LLC (Ann Arbor). *Indexed:* Agr, BiolAb, CABA, ChemAb, EngInd, EnvAb, EnvInd, FPA, ForAb, HortAb, IndVet, RRTA, S&F, SCI, WAE&RSA, ZooRec. *Aud.:* Ac, Sa.

This is one of three regional applied research journals from the Society of American Foresters. It is targeted toward the professional forester and forest landowner in the northeastern and midwestern United States and Canada and the boreal forests of these areas. Emphasis is on management practices and techniques. Quarterly issues contain six to ten peer-reviewed articles on such topics as pest and disease control, wildlife management, and harvesting practices, all focusing on practical research to help the practitioner better manage forests of the region. All three regional journals are modest in price and are important for a research and teaching collection. In areas where forests are

an important part of the local economy, a general collection would be strengthened with the addition of the geographically appropriate title. Since late 2000, full-text access to articles from this journal has been available to subscribers at no additional cost through *ingenta*. Subscription information is available from the society's web site, as is a good deal of other information about the society.

2923. *Revista Arvore.* [ISSN: 0100-6762] 1977. bi-m. Universidade Federal de Vicosa, Av PH Rolfs s/n, Campus Universitario, Vicosa, 36571-000, Brazil; reitoria@mail.ufv.br; http://www.ufv.br. *Indexed:* CABA, FPA, ForAb, HortAb, RRTA, S&F, WAE&RSA, ZooRec. *Aud.:* Ac, Sa.

This well-indexed, technical and scientific journal is published bimonthly by the Sociedade de Investigacoes Florestais (SIF) in Brazil. It contains original papers in the field of forestry and related research. Among other things, this journal offers a local perspective on issues related to the fate of tropical forests particularly in the Brazilian Amazon. The text of most articles is in Portuguese, however informative abstracts are available in English. All aspects of forestry are included in the content of this journal. It is typical of the growing number of institutionally based and discipline-specific publications from other countries that are being made available via the Directory of Open Access Journals.

2924. *Small-Scale Forestry.* Formerly (until 2007): *Small-Scale Forest Economics, Management and Policy.* [ISSN: 1873-7617] 2002. q. EUR 320 print & online eds. Ed(s): J. Bliss, H. Karppinen. Springer Netherlands, Van Godewijckstraat 30, Dordrecht, 3311 GX, Netherlands; http://www.springeronline.com. Refereed. Circ: 1500. *Bk. rev.:* 2-3, substantive. *Aud.:* Ga, Ac, Sa.

This peer-reviewed journal began in 2002 as an effort to address the need to disseminate research findings on management of small-scale private forest woodlots within the International Union of Forest Research Organizations (IUFRO). Issues include six to eight articles on topics related to social and economic aspects of private woodlot management and two to three substantive book reviews. With international coverage and a very modest subscription cost, this journal has the potential to be a welcome addition to academic collections. It should also be of use to general collections where management of private woodlots plays a role in the local economy. A sample issue is available for preview on the publisher's web site, and later issues are available in electronic format with a subscription.

2925. *Southern Journal of Applied Forestry.* [ISSN: 0148-4419] 1977. q. USD 170 (Individuals, USD 75). Ed(s): Matthew Walls, Ian A Munn. Society of American Foresters, 5400 Grosvenor Ln, Bethesda, MD 20814; safweb@safnet.org; http://www.safnet.org. Illus., index, adv. Sample. Refereed. Circ: 1000 Paid. Vol. ends: Nov. Microform: PQC. Online: EBSCO Publishing, EBSCO Host; Gale; IngentaConnect; ProQuest K-12 Learning Solutions; ProQuest LLC (Ann Arbor). *Indexed:* Agr, BiolAb, CABA, ChemAb, EngInd, EnvAb, FPA, ForAb, HortAb, RRTA, S&F, SCI, SWRA, WAE&RSA, ZooRec. *Aud.:* Ac, Sa.

This is one of three regional, applied-research journals from the Society of American Foresters. It is targeted toward the professional forester and forest landowner in a geographic region ranging from Oklahoma and East Texas east to Virginia and Kentucky. Emphasis is on management practices and techniques in this region where plantation forests are more common. Quarterly issues contain six to ten peer-reviewed articles on such topics as pest and disease control, wildlife management, and harvesting practices, all focusing on practical research to help the practitioner better manage forests of the region. All three regional journals are modest in price and are important for a research and teaching collection. In areas in which forests are an important part of the local economy, a general collection would be strengthened with the addition of the geographically appropriate title. Since late 2000, full-text access to articles from this journal has been available to subscribers at no additional cost through *ingenta*. Subscription information is available from the society's web site, as is a good deal of other information about the society.

2926. *Tree Physiology: an international botanical journal.* [ISSN: 0829-318X] 1986. m. CND 1974 print & online eds. Ed(s): Rozanne Poulson. Heron Publishing, 202-3994 Shelbourne St, Victoria, BC V8N 3E2, Canada; publisher@heronpublishing.com; http://heronpublishing.com. Illus., index, adv. Sample. Refereed. Vol.

ends: Dec. Online: The Dialog Corporation; EBSCO Publishing, EBSCO Host. *Indexed:* Agr, ApEcolAb, BiolAb, CABA, ChemAb, EnvAb, EnvInd, FPA, ForAb, GardL, HortAb, PollutAb, S&F, SCI, SWRA. *Bk. rev.:* 0-3, 300-500 words. *Aud.:* Ac, Sa.

This refereed journal is international in scope and distribution. It is issued 18 times a year and is a medium for disseminating theoretical and experimental research results as well as occasional review articles. Each issue consists of eight to ten papers dealing with an array of topics related to tree physiology, including genetics, reproduction, nutrition, and environmental adaptation, as well as those relevant to environmental management, biotechnology, and the economic use of trees. This is an important journal for forest science and botany collections. Online access to the full text of this journal is available at no additional cost to the subscriber. The publisher's web site also provides a cumulative index for downloading.

2927. Trees: structure and function. [ISSN: 0931-1890] 1987. bi-m. EUR 1352 print & online eds. Ed(s): Ulrich E Luettge, Robert D Guy. Springer, Tiergartenstr 17, Heidelberg, 69121, Germany. Illus., index, adv. Sample. Refereed. Vol. ends: Sep. Online: EBSCO Publishing, EBSCO Host; OhioLINK; Springer LINK; SwetsWise Online Content. Reprint: PSC. *Indexed:* Agr, BiolAb, CABA, EngInd, FPA, ForAb, HortAb, RRTA, S&F, SCI, WAE&RSA. *Aud.:* Ac, Sa.

This international, refereed journal is narrowly focused but highly regarded among physiologists in the scholarly community of forestry, horticulture, and botany. Each of its six annual issues includes eight to ten articles on original research in the physiology, biochemistry, functional anatomy, structure, and ecology of trees and woody plants. Review articles are included selectively, as are papers on pathology and technological problems that add to a basic understanding of the structure and function of trees. An online edition of the journal, along with a table-of-contents alerting service, is available from publisher's web site.

2928. Unasylva: international journal of forestry and forest products. [ISSN: 0041-6436] 1947. q. USD 50. Food and Agriculture Organization of the United Nations (F A O), Via delle Terme di Caracalla, Rome, 00100, Italy; FAO-HQ@fao.org; http://www.fao.org. Illus., index. Sample. Circ: 6500. Vol. ends: Dec. Microform: CIS. *Indexed:* B&AI, BAS, BiolDig, CABA, FPA, ForAb, HortAb, RRTA, S&F, SWA, WAE&RSA. *Bk. rev.:* 2-5, 300 words. *Aud.:* Hs, Ga, Ac.

Available in French, Spanish, and English, this international journal is published by the Food and Agriculture Organization (FAO) of the United Nations to promote better understanding of issues in international forestry. Articles are well illustrated and readable and will have broad appeal to an audience that includes students, policymakers, and professional foresters. Each quarterly issue consists of 8 to 12 articles that usually address a theme such as perceptions of forests, sustainable forest management, illegal logging, forest-dependent peoples, etc. Regular departments include new books, reports on FAO forestry activities, and news in the "world of forestry." This would be a good addition to general, high school, and college libraries as well as research collections. The full text of articles in each issue of the journal since 1974 is available on the FAO web site.

2929. Western Journal of Applied Forestry. [ISSN: 0885-6095] 1986. q. USD 170 (Individuals, USD 75). Ed(s): Matthew Walls, Robert Deal. Society of American Foresters, 5400 Grosvenor Ln, Bethesda, MD 20814; safweb@safnet.org; http://www.safnet.org. Illus., adv. Sample. Refereed. Circ: 2500 Paid. Vol. ends: Oct. Microform: PQC. Online: EBSCO Publishing, EBSCO Host; Gale; IngentaConnect; ProQuest LLC (Ann Arbor). *Indexed:* Agr, BiolAb, CABA, DSA, EngInd, EnvAb, FPA, ForAb, HortAb, RRTA, S&F, SCI, WAE&RSA. *Aud.:* Ac, Sa.

This is one of three regional applied research journals from the Society of American Foresters. It is targeted toward the professional forester and landowner in western North America. Emphasis is on management practices and techniques. Quarterly issues contain six to ten peer-reviewed articles on such topics as pest and disease control, wildlife management, and harvesting practices, all focusing on practical research to help the practitioner better manage forests of the region. All three regional journals are modest in price and are important for a research and teaching collection. In areas where forests are an important part of the local economy, a general collection would be strength-

ened with the addition of the geographically appropriate title. Since late 2000, full-text access to articles from this journal has been available to subscribers at no additional cost through *ingenta*. Subscription information is available on the society's web site, as is a good deal of other information about the society.

2930. Wood and Fiber Science. Formerly: *Wood and Fiber.* [ISSN: 0735-6161] 1968. q. USD 250. Ed(s): Geza Ifju. Society of Wood Science and Technology, One Gifford Pinchot Dr, Madison, WI 53726-2398; http://www.swst.org. Illus., index, adv. Sample. Refereed. Circ: 1000. Vol. ends: Oct. Microform: PQC. *Indexed:* Agr, CABA, ChemAb, EngInd, FPA, ForAb, S&F, SCI, SSCI, WAE&RSA. *Bk. rev.:* 1-3, 400-600 words. *Aud.:* Ac, Sa.

This refereed journal is the product of the Society of Wood Science and Technology (SWST). Typical of the range of subjects covered by the 12 to 15 articles in each issue are processing testing, modeling applied to oriented strandboard, wood adhesives, moisture movement, use of engineered wood products in Japan, and properties of wood–plastic composites, plus one or two book reviews. This journal is modestly priced and highly regarded by wood scientists and wood technologists. Particularly with the increase in international research coverage, it is also useful for those interested in following new developments in these areas for product marketing. This journal is recommended for comprehensive research collections as well as those collections needing an economical representative title in this area. A pdf index to the journal is linked from the SWST web site, as are the tables of contents for issues since 2005.

■ GAMES

See also Computers and Information Technology; and Sports sections.

Patrick Jose Dawson, Associate University Librarian, Information and Research Services, UCSB Libraries, University of California, Santa Barbara, CA 93106; dawson@library.ucsb.edu

Introduction

Game magazines cover a very broad spectrum, attempting to capture all that is classified as a "game." As games and the means to play them have changed from board and card games to computer games and on to adventure simulations, so too have magazines that cover the games. The study of games is also a new area of interest in cultural theory and cultural anthropology and sociology, so more academic publications are just beginning to emerge. There are still the traditionally published magazines dealing with time-tested games such as chess and bridge, while the publication explosion of electronic-games magazines reflects the huge increase in the number and types of electronic games.

More-traditional game magazines tend to use print, while electronic and computer games opt for online publishing. However, be aware that online publishing does not mean there will be constant access to some of these publications. Anyone with a computer and an Internet provider has the ability to become a publisher of an online blog, newsletter, podcast, or magazine.

Games and game magazines fall into five basic types: (1) games of chance, (2) adventure games, (3) computer or electronic games, (4) traditional games, and (5) military games. Military games take gaming to a level that includes strategy and logic and are aimed at both the military professional and civilians who enjoy playing war games (board and electronic) as a hobby. Included in military gaming are miniatures (models) and adventure simulations, such as reenacting. The majority of game magazines in print today are devoted to traditional games like chess, checkers, and bridge, due mostly to the large number of worldwide associations that are devoted to these traditional games and the familiarity with devotees of these games to print journals. Military gamers, miniature builders, and reenactors usually do not enjoy the umbrella of an association to gather them together, so they lack a community to share publication information, and therefore these publications can be hard to locate.

As role-playing games—a type of adventure game—have become more prevalent, there has also been an increase in the number of these publications. Many of them deal with the games themselves (e.g., "Dungeons and Dragons," or reenacting battles), while some are concerned with the collections of cards and figures associated with these games. This has become quite lucrative and popular, and a search on eBay will uncover the plethora of items that can be had.

Another type of adventure game is "Paintball," which gives participants the opportunity to hunt, "kill," and "be killed" in a rather safe environment. The same goes for reenacting, where you can kill and die often and even live the life of the soldier or civilian from 1776, 1812, or 1865. There has been an increase, both in print and online, in the number of lottery and game-of-chance magazines as more states conduct lotteries and the number of casinos and Native American tribe–owned casinos has increased, with legalized gambling no longer confined to Las Vegas and Atlantic City. Computer and electronic games are extremely popular, and the number of electronic publications for these games has grown.

Electronic publication of game magazines is becoming the means of choice for many publishers, especially those that deal with computer and electronic games. Use your preferred search engine with the terms "games" or "gaming" and you will find a multitude of titles, including many self-published works. However, many of the hits you do get will not be established publications, most lacking ISSN numbers or any affiliation with a recognized publisher. Many of the print publishers also offer an online equivalent; however, this equivalent is not always included in the cost of the print edition or is an abridged version of the print. Many producers of games have set up web sites with links to game magazines, but the focus of the web site is to sell the games that are discussed in the publication.

The advantages to publishing on the web are that it allows for real-time updates, changing calendars of game events, buying and selling of games, and interactive tutorials and problem solving, not to mention copious "cheats" for winning, and it is a more economical means of publishing, especially for individuals. As the World Wide Web has settled and more people have become familiar with working online, anyone has the potential to publish, but these individual or group publications are inconsistent and tend to come and go. While many of these titles are free, they do require that a "profile" be established so that the sponsors of the magazine or web site are able to send copious e-mail advertising.

Basic Periodicals

Ga: *ACF Bulletin*, *Bridge World*, *Chess Life*, *Games*.

2931. *A C F Bulletin.* [ISSN: 1045-8034] 1952. bi-m. USD 25. Ed(s): Charles C Walker. American Checker Federation, PO Box 365, Petal, MS 39465. Illus. Circ: 1000. *Aud.:* Ems, Hs, Ga, Ac.

The *ACF Bulletin* is the official periodical of the American Checker Federation (ACF). It covers checkers-related news at state, district, national, and international levels. It reports the results of ACF and affiliated tournaments, including annotated accounts of national tournament games. The "Mail Play News" caters to the correspondence checkers player, including news of mail games between Great Britain and the United States as well as local matches. There is a problem-and-solution article each month, and the "Swap Shop" page features books for sale on checkers and checkerboards. The ACF web site is worth looking at for its archived problems, games, and interviews. Available online at www.acfcheckers.com.

2932. *A P C T News Bulletin.* 1967. 6x/yr. USD 18; USD 36 foreign. Ed(s): Helen Warren. American Postal Chess Tournaments, PO Box 305, Western Springs, IL 60558-0305; apct@aol.com. Adv. Circ: 1000. *Bk. rev.:* 3, 50 words. *Aud.:* Hs, Ga, Ac.

American Postal Chess Tournaments (APCT) is geared toward correspondence chess players, offering information on postal and e-mail events. Currently, the APCT has over 1,000 "Postalities" in 50 states and eight foreign countries. The APCT offers 11 distinctive tournaments, ranging from the Pawn Tournaments for more sociable play to the more competitive Queen Tournaments. However, some of the tournaments are for the serious tournament player, as they include entry fees and prize money. The bulletin includes game results, ratings, annotated and nonannotated games, "how to improve" articles, and a listing of new and out-of-print chess books. There is also a section of writing on theory as well as computer chess. The book reviews are particularly good and of interest to all chess players. The APCT is an affiliate of the U.S. Chess Federation.

2933. *Action Pursuit Games.* [ISSN: 0893-9489] 1987. m. USD 33. Ed(s): Dan Reeves. C F W Enterprises, Inc., 4201 Van Owen Pl, Burbank, CA 91505; http://www.cfwenterprises.com. Illus., adv. Circ: 81642 Paid and controlled. *Aud.:* Hs, Ga.

The leading magazine for the game and sport of paintball. This activity rapidly gained popularity in the early-to-mid 1990s. The popularity has somewhat leveled off in recent years, but a large group of core people keeps the hobby active and vital. The game doesn't just attract paintball enthusiasts; some companies have even used the sport as a team-building exercise. This magazine contains feature articles that focus on game strategies, safety, and equipment. Extensive advertisements also point people to places where paintball-related products can be purchased. Users consulting the advertising should probably be aware that most of the products are somewhat on the "high end" and may not be suited to people getting started in the hobby. This publication would be good for public libraries that serve communities with paintball enthusiasts. The related web site is www.actionpursuitgames.com.

2934. *Alnavco Log.* Formerly: *Alnavco Distributors: the Report.* 1966. 3x/yr. Free. Ed(s): Pete Paschall. Alnavco, 10, Belle Haven, VA 23306-0010. Illus. Circ: 2000. *Aud.:* Hs, Ga.

This publication is a newsletter for one of the largest distributors of military miniatures. *Alnavco* specializes in naval models, but it also has a large armored-vehicle product line. The newsletter contains articles on general modelling, painting, and the use of miniatures in wargaming. This newsletter would be a good addition to public libraries that have collections of modelling literature. It is online at www.alnavco.com.

2935. *The Art of War.* irreg. Clash of Arms Games, Byrne Bldg., No. 205, Lincoln & Morgan Sts., Phoenixville, PA 19460. Illus. *Aud.:* Hs, Ga.

The Art of War is a magazine published to support the users of Clash of Arms (COA) gaming systems. Clash of Arms makes a number of elaborate wargames that mainly deal with World War II historical scenarios. The magazine contains articles about military history, tactical gaming situations, and rules updates for COA games. This publication would work best in a public library that serves a visible local military gaming community. What is available from Clash of Arms can be viewed at www.clashofarms.com.

2936. *Battlefleet.* 1966. q. GBP 13.50. Ed(s): Stuart Barnes. Naval Wargames Society, c/o Stuart Barnes, 5 Clifton Pl, Ilfrancombe, EX 349jj, United Kingdom. *Aud.:* Hs, Ga.

Battlefleet is the quarterly journal of the Naval Wargames Society, based in Great Britain. The journal covers a wide range of articles on any aspect of naval wargaming. This publication also contains reviews of gaming systems and updates on naval modelling. *Battlefleet* would be a good addition to a public library that serves an active community of military gamers and naval model builders.

2937. *Blitz Chess.* [ISSN: 1053-3087] 1988. q. USD 4 newsstand/cover per issue domestic; USD 4.50 newsstand/cover per issue in Canada & Mexico; USD 5 newsstand/cover per issue elsewhere. Ed(s): Walter S Browne. World Blitz Chess Association, 8 Parnassus Rd, Berkeley, CA 94708; wbcablitz@aol.com. Illus., adv. Circ: 1200 Paid. *Aud.:* Ga, Ac.

This magazine is devoted to blitz chess, the fastest form of the game, with a five-minute time limit per player. There is coverage of chess and tournament events, including where to play, annotated games, articles about players, articles on blitz tactics, and announcements of tournaments with end-game articles by Pal Benko. The contents are not limited to blitz chess, however. Top international chess events are covered, and there are interesting historical chess problems to solve as well as information on the grand masters. Each issue includes a complete list of members and a quarterly rating list of players.

2938. *The Boardgamer.* 1995. q. USD 13. Ed(s): Bruce Monnin. The Boardgamer, 177 S Lincoln St, Minster, OH 45865-1240. *Aud.:* Hs, Ga.

This magazine is designed to support players of Avalon Hill board games. It also provides a review and commentary of games played at the World Boardgaming Championships. *The Boardgamer* would best be acquired by public libraries that serve an active gaming community.

2939. The Bridge Bulletin. Former titles: *American Contract Bridge League. Bulletin;* (until 1993): *Contract Bridge Bulletin.* [ISSN: 1089-6376] 1935. m. Non-members, USD 20. Ed(s): Paul Linxwiler, Brent Manley. American Contract Bridge League, 2990 Airways Blvd, Memphis, TN 38116-3847; acbl@acbl.org. Illus., adv. Sample. Circ. 147000 Controlled. *Bk. rev.:* 3, 50 words. *Aud.:* Ga.

The Bridge Bulletin is the major source for news and information about contract bridge, including duplicate bridge. *The Bridge Bulletin* publishes articles on strategy, contains interviews with players, and includes a calendar of national and world events. Included are a listing of tournament schedules and results, miscellaneous bridge news, and special instructional sections devoted to novice and intermediate players. This is the publication of the American Contract Bridge League.

2940. Bridge Magazine. Incorporates (1980-200?): *International Popular Bridge Monthly;* Which was formerly (until 1980): *Popular Bridge Monthly;* Former titles (until 1993): *Bridge (London); Bridge International;* (until 1984): *Bridge Magazine;* Which Incorporated: *British Bridge World.* [ISSN: 1351-4261] 1926. m. GBP 39.95 domestic; GBP 49.95 in Europe; USD 80 in US & Canada. Ed(s): Mark Horton. Chess & Bridge Ltd., 369 Euston Rd, London, NW1 3AR, United Kingdom; info@chess.co.uk; http://www.chesscenter.com. Illus., adv. Circ: 10000. *Bk. rev.:* Number and length vary. *Aud.:* Ga, Ac, Sa.

This magazine has a long publishing history, having survived for over 70 years. It has a substantial circulation worldwide for a magazine that only deals with the game of bridge. It contains all that a good magazine on bridge should: articles on bidding and play, as well as instruction articles for playing or learning bridge. It also contains information on competitions, reports on tournaments, and humor related to bridge, as well as hints on how to win and a section that profiles international players. The journal web site, www.bridgemagazine.co.uk, links to the publication and also is a shopping cornucopia for anyone looking for anything associated with playing bridge.

2941. Bridge Today: the magazine for people who love to play bridge. [ISSN: 1043-6383] 1988. 6x/yr. USD 24 domestic; USD 29 Canada; USD 34 elsewhere. Ed(s): Matthew Granovetter. Granovetter Books, 3329 Spindletop Dr NW, Kennesaw, GA 30144-7336. Illus., adv. Sample. Circ: 6000. *Aud.:* Ga.

Bridge Today offers game analyses, problems, and articles on specific aspects of bridge. The distinguishing feature of *Bridge Today* is the clear and entertaining annotations. Each article is a bridge lesson in itself. A list of books available from the *Bridge Today* bookshop is also included. This journal is an excellent complement to *The Bridge Bulletin* and *The Bridge World.* The journal web site, www.bridgetoday.com, has links to the magazine, a bridge question to solve, and an online store.

2942. The Bridge World (Online Edition): the magazine no bridge player should be without. Formerly: *Bridge World (Print Edition).* 1929. irreg. Ed(s): Jeff Rubens. Bridge World Magazine Inc., 717 White Plains Rd., White Plains, NY 10583-5009; mail@bridgeworld.com; http://www.bridgeworld.com. Illus., adv. Circ: 7800. *Bk. rev.:* Number and length vary. *Aud.:* Ga.

This title is aimed at the dedicated player. The publication states that it wants to "teach you, entertain you, challenge you, prepare you and 'smarten' your game." That said, it offers a wide variety of articles, problems, bridge news, and instructional features. The articles, written by a number of well-known bridge analysts, are rather technical but generally informal in style. There is also a section of book reviews, which is of use to the serious player. *The Bridge World* will be appreciated where there is a significant population of serious bridge players.

2943. British Chess Magazine. [ISSN: 0007-0440] 1881. m. GBP 33 domestic; GBP 35 in Europe; GBP 40.25 elsewhere. Ed(s): Murray Chandler. British Chess Magazine Ltd., The Chess Shop, 69 Masbro Rd, London, W14 0LS, United Kingdom; 100561.3121@compuserve.com; http://www.bcmchess.co.uk. Illus., adv. Circ: 4000. Vol. ends: Dec. *Bk. rev.:* 8, 50 words. *Aud.:* Ga, Ac.

This is the leading chess magazine in Great Britain, with a substantial circulation worldwide. It has something for every chess player: reports of current tournaments, historical features, problems and studies, correspondence chess, and opening theory. The *British Chess Magazine* is particularly famous for its deeply annotated games, chosen for instruction and enjoyment. The magazine is written for players at every strength level. It also has an extensive web site that is full of information and allows you to purchase books and chess paraphernalia: www.bcmchess.co.uk.

2944. C3i. 1992. q. USD 22. G M T Games, Box 1308, Hanford, CA 93232. *Aud.:* Hs, Ga.

This magazine is designed for players of GMT board games. GMT makes a number of historical wargames that span a number of different periods. The articles consist of gaming tips, game pieces, and general military history. This publication would well suit a public library that serves an active military gaming group.

2945. Camp Chase Gazette: where the Civil War comes alive. [ISSN: 1055-2790] 1972. 10x/yr. USD 28. Ed(s): Nicky Hughes. Camp Chase Publishing Co., Inc., 1609 W. 1st North St., Morristown, TN 37814. Adv. Sample. Circ: 4200 Paid. *Bk. rev.:* 350 words. *Aud.:* Hs, Ga.

Camp Chase Gazette is the only nationally distributed magazine that deals with the popular hobby of Civil War reenacting. The articles report on topics of interest for reenactors, and they give a national calendar of events for activities happening around the country. A subscription to this publication would most benefit public libraries that cater to a known group of Civil War reenactors or those interested in reading about the kit of Civil War soldiers and civilians.

2946. Card Player. [ISSN: 1089-2044] 1988. fortn. USD 39.95; USD 4.95 per issue. Card Player Media, LLC, 3140 S Polaris Ave, Las Vegas, NV 89102; http:/www.cardplayer.com. Illus., adv. Circ: 5000 Paid. *Aud.:* Ga.

This magazine, published in Las Vegas and host to major poker tournaments, is devoted to poker throughout the world. It includes articles on strategy, interviews, poker stories, poker-themed travel, and tournament schedules and results. Also covered are casino and sports gambling and gambling industry news. An extensive, information-filled web site is at www.cardplayer.com.

2947. Casino Chronicle: a weekly newsletter focusing on the gaming industry. [ISSN: 0889-9797] 1983. w. 48/yr. USD 195 domestic; USD 210 in Canada & Mexico; USD 245 elsewhere. Ed(s): Ben A Borowsky. Casino Chronicle, PO Box 740465, Boynton Beach, FL 33474-0465. Illus., adv. Sample. Circ: 1500 Paid and controlled. *Aud.:* Sa.

This newsletter is aimed at executives in the casino industry and companies and individuals engaged in business with casino hotels. It gives concise, thorough coverage of everything from legislation, company news, and construction to financial information. The major emphasis is on Atlantic City, but this journal also covers Las Vegas and other gambling operations nationwide, including tribal casinos.

2948. Chess Correspondent. [ISSN: 0009-3327] 1926. 6x/yr. USD 16. Ed(s): Joe Ganem. C C L A, PO Box 59625, Schaumburg, IL 60159-0625. Illus., adv. Sample. Circ: 1000. *Bk. rev.:* Number and length vary. *Aud.:* Ac, Sa.

This is the official publication of the Correspondence Chess League of America, a nonprofit organization founded in 1909. It features annotated games, articles on chess fundamentals, book reviews, and ratings, all with an emphasis on correspondence chess. The league sponsors postal and e-mail tournaments. This publication won the 1993 award from the Chess Journalists Association for the Best Magazine on Postal Chess. It also has a web site at www.chessbymail.com.

2949. Chess Life. Formerly (until 1980): *Chess Life and Review;* Incorporates: *Chess Review.* [ISSN: 0197-260X] 1969. m. Free to members. Ed(s): Daniel Lucas. United States Chess Federation, PO Box 3967, Crossville, TN 38557-3967; http://www.uschess.org. Illus., index, adv. Sample. Circ: 70000. Vol. ends: Dec. Microform: PQC. *Bk. rev.:* 2-3, 250 words. *Aud.:* Hs, Ga, Ac.

This official publication of the U.S. Chess Federation provides exhaustive coverage of chess-related news for federation members: workshops, tournaments, and a calendar of national and state events. It covers all aspects of chess: carefully annotated games, interviews, puzzles, and advice. Also included are columns on historical topics, personality profiles (the emphasis is on American players), and short stories. This is a basic chess title, recommended for most libraries. The U.S. Chess Federation also publishes *School Mates,* aimed at young chess players. The U.S. Chess Federation has a web site at www.uschess.org, and there is a link on this site to the magazine.

2950. *The Citizens' Companion: the voice of civilian reenacting.* [ISSN: 1075-9344] 1993. bi-m. USD 24 domestic; USD 30 foreign. Ed(s): Susan Lyons Hughes. Camp Chase Publishing Co., Inc., 1609 W. 1st North St., Morristown, TN 37814. Adv. Sample. Circ: 1200 Paid. *Aud.:* Hs, Ga.

Besides military reenactors, there are also civilian reenactors, and this interesting magazine for civilian reenactors supports the *Camp Chase Gazette,* which is aimed at the military reenactor. This magazine has articles about the role of civilians in the Civil War and pieces about period attire and dress. This would be a good selection for a public library that caters to an active group of Civil War reenactors. Both mentioned publications are linked from the web site www.campchase.com.

2951. *Command Magazine: military history, strategy & analysis.* [ISSN: 1059-5651] 1989. bi-m. USD 19.95; USD 42.95 foreign. Ed(s): Ty Bomba. X T R Corp., PO Box 4017, San Luis Obispo, CA 93403; perello@aol.com. Illus., index, adv. *Aud.:* Hs, Ga.

Still one of the better magazines for this hobby, *Command* combines military history with discussions on general wargaming. Excellent, lavishly illustrated, and well-researched military history articles grace this publication's pages. Many of the military history articles are substantial contributions to their fields. This magazine would be a strong addition for public libraries with an interest in wargaming or general military history. The military history articles may also be of interest to academic readers.

2952. *Competitive Edge.* irreg. USD 14 for 2 issues plus games. Ed(s): Jon Compton. One Small Step, 613 N Morada Ave, West Covina, CA 91790. *Aud.:* Hs, Ga.

A small periodical with general information about wargaming and military miniatures. The content is highly specialized and designed for the experienced gamer. Note that it is published irregularly and may be difficult to obtain.

2953. *Critical Hit.* q. Ed(s): Trevor Holman. Critical Hit, P.O. Drawer 79, Croton Falls, NY 10519. Illus. *Aud.:* Hs, Ga.

This magazine supports the players of "Critical Hit" wargames. This vendor is best known for its popular game called "Squad Leader" and other games based on World War II historical scenarios. This publication has articles on new games, as well as tips for playing games from the current product line. Most of the articles are for hardcore gamers, not collectors of miniatures or occasional gamers. There is an extensive web site at www.criticalhit.com.

2954. *Dragon Magazine.* Formerly: *Dragon (Lake Geneva).* [ISSN: 1062-2101] 1976. m. USD 38.95. Ed(s): Eric Mona. Paizo Publishing LLC, 2700 Richards Rd., Ste. 201, Bellevue, WA 98005-4200; customer.service@paizo.com; http://paizo.com. Illus., adv. Sample. Circ: 50000. *Aud.:* Ems, Hs, Ga.

Dragon Magazine is dedicated to role-playing games in general, not exclusively to Dungeons and Dragons. It is a profusely illustrated publication, full of practical advice on designing scenarios, characters, and environments. It has an exhaustive calendar of events, and it lists sources for role-playing equipment. Paizo Publishing has a web site at www.paizopublishing.com that links to *Dragon Magazine* and *Dungeon Magazine,* as well as products for purchase and downloads.

2955. *The Duelist: the official trading card magazine from Wizards of the Coast.* [ISSN: 1082-8621] 1994. m. USD 24.95; GBP 24.95 in Europe; GBP 34.95 elsewhere. Ed(s): Will McDermott. Wizards of the Coast, Inc., 1801 Lind Ave, PO Box 707, Renton, WA 98057; duelist@wizards.com; http://www.wizards.com/Duelist_Online. Illus., adv. Circ: 100000 Paid. *Aud.:* Ems, Hs, Ga.

Duelist is devoted to "Magic: The Gathering" (the popular trading-card game) and other trading-card games. It contains reviews of new games, articles on the use of individual cards, articles on deck building, and strategy advice. Many of the articles utilize the expertise of top players as well as of game designers and developers. The magazine has promised to cover other, related electronic games. Wizards of the Coast also has an extensive web site that supports its products at www.wizards.com.

2956. *Electronic Gaming Monthly.* Incorporates (in 2007): *Expert Codebook.* [ISSN: 1058-918X] 1986. m. USD 12 domestic; USD 28 foreign; USD 5.99 newsstand/cover. Ed(s): Dan Shoe Hsu, Shane Bettenhausen. Ziff Davis Media Inc., 28 E 28th St, New York, NY 10016-7930; info@ziffdavis.com; http://www.ziffdavis.com. Illus., adv. Circ: 398219 Paid. Online: EBSCO Publishing, EBSCO Host; Gale; ProQuest K-12 Learning Solutions; ProQuest LLC (Ann Arbor); H.W. Wilson. *Indexed:* MASUSE, MicrocompInd, RGPR. *Aud.:* Ems, Hs, Ga.

Electronic Gaming Monthly covers electronic games on all the major game systems, including PlayStation, Xbox, Nintendo, and others. Networked online games are covered by *Computer Gaming World,* another Ziff-Davis publication. Most of the magazine is devoted to game previews and reviews. The evaluations are detailed and objective and provide a good source of consumer information. Libraries should be aware of occasional risque covers and ads. The web site offers an abbreviated free version of the magazine and other gaming information at www.egmmag.com.

2957. *En Passant: Canada's chess magazine.* Former titles: *Chess Canada Echecs; Chess Federation of Canada. Bulletin.* [ISSN: 0822-5672] 1973. 6x/yr. CND 15; CND 18 foreign. Ed(s): Hal Bond. En Passant Publishers Ltd., 2212 Gladwin Cres E 1, Ottawa, ON K1B 5N1, Canada. Illus., adv. Circ: 3000. *Bk. rev.:* 10, 25 words. *Aud.:* Ga, Ac.

This is the official journal of the Chess Federation of Canada (CFC). The mandate of the CFC is to promote and encourage the knowledge, study, and play of chess in Canada. The magazine is aimed at players of all strengths. Regular features include a calendar of events, analysis of major games, interviews, book reviews, listings of other Canadian chess associations and local clubs, reports from the clubs, and ratings of players.

2958. *The Europa Magazine (Colorado Springs).* irreg. G R D Games, 3302 Adobe Court, Colorado Springs, CO 80907-5442. *Aud.:* Hs, Ga.

This publication supports the players of GRD board games. These games are very intense, map-driven historical scenarios that are centered on World War II themes and tactics. The games are almost like "general staff" modules, with very high and complicated standards of play. The publication is aimed at a small, select core group and may not be of interest to other gamers.

2959. *Fire & Movement: the forum of conflict simulation.* [ISSN: 0147-0051] 1976. q. USD 22 domestic; USD 26 Canada; USD 28 elsewhere. Ed(s): David McElhanon. Decision Games, PO Box 21598, Bakersfield, CA 93390; decsion@iwvisp.com; http://www.decisiongames.com. Illus., index, adv. Circ: 2000. *Aud.:* Hs, Ga.

Published by Decision Games, this magazine reviews a wide variety of historical board and online games. This publication has detailed reviews of new wargames, and includes advice on playing and purchasing gaming systems. It is published for the general gaming audience. Decision Games has a link to this publication and to its other publication, *Strategy & Tactics,* on its web site at www.decisiongames.com.

2960. *Game Informer Magazine.* [ISSN: 1067-6392] 1991. m. USD 19.98 domestic; USD 4.99 newsstand/cover per issue domestic; USD 6.99 newsstand/cover per issue Canada. Ed(s): Andrew McNamara, Andrew

Reiner. Game Informer Magazine, 724 N First St, 4th Fl, Minneapolis, MN 55401-2885; customerservice@gameinformer.com; http://www.gameinformer.com. Adv. Circ: 200000 Paid. *Bk. rev.:* Number and length vary. *Aud.:* Ga.

Gamer Informer Magazine advertises itself as the "leading computer game magazine in the world." The monthly publication covers PC, Sony PlayStation 2, Nintendo Game Cube, Microsoft Xbox, and hand-held game news. There are also upcoming game release news and the usual secrets and cheats. Content includes screen shots and drawings of characters from various games, and the text is very appealing to adolescents and young adults.

2961. *Game Report Online.* 1994. q. USD 15 in US & Canada; USD 20 elsewhere. Ed(s): Peter Sarrett. Game Report Online, 1920 N 49th St., Seattle, WA 98103; editor@gamereport.com; http://www.gamereport.com. *Bk. rev.:* Number and length vary. *Aud.:* Hs, Ga.

The editor of this first-class review of games has definite opinions about what is good and what is bad, and he says so without any "ifs" or "buts." The result is a reliable place to turn for information about all types of games, from board games to dice, family games, and strategy games. There are a few features and articles, but most of the focus is on reviews, covering material for all age groups. The web site, www.gamereport.com, has links for acquiring games, books, and other game-related items.

2962. *GamePro: world's largest multiplatform gaming magazine.* [ISSN: 1042-8658] 1989. m. USD 39.95 for 6 mos. Ed(s): Mike Weigand. I D G Communications Inc., 555 12TH St, Oakland, CA 94607-4002; comments.gamepro@gamepro.com. Adv. Circ: 428126. *Aud.:* Ga.

Gamepro is reflective of many of the computer gaming magazines that are on the market. It has news on the operating systems, including PC, Sony PlayStation, Nintendo Game Cube, Microsoft Xbox, and hand-helds. It contains sections on news and reviews of games, previews of forthcoming games, screen shots from games, and game movie trailers. Also on the web site at www.gamepro.com are the journal's top-rated games, links to blogs, and message boards for gamers.

2963. *Games.* [ISSN: 0199-9788] 1977. 10x/yr. USD 29.90 domestic; USD 37.90 Canada; USD 45.90 elsewhere. Ed(s): Jennifer Orehowsky. Games Publications, Inc., PO Box 184, Fort Washington, PA 19034. Illus., adv. Circ: 80000 Paid. *Indexed:* BRI, CBRI. *Bk. rev.:* Number varies, 100 words. *Aud.:* Hs, Ga.

Games includes something for everyone, including its own games, which are some of the most challenging and original puzzles around, and games for one or several players. Puzzle types range from photo identification to intellectual problem-solving. Games are rated for level of difficulty. Features include contests, short articles, and book and game reviews.

2964. *Games Domain Review.* 1994. w. Ed(s): Rich Greenhill. Games Domain Review, 435 Lichfield Rd., Aston, Birmingham, B67 SS, United Kingdom; http://www.gamesdomain.co.uk/help/newsletter.html. *Aud.:* Ga.

Published in England, this magazine has a broader interest for Americans than one might suspect. True, a few news items and reviews of electronic games are of interest only in the United Kingdom, but many will be valued by those in North America. In a typical issue, there are short pieces on such items of universal interest as Star Wars, Starship Titanic, and Alluds: Sealed Mystery, as well as reviews of the latest games. There is an archive of over 1,400 reviews that are as evaluative as they are descriptive. For this reason alone, anyone involved with electronic games should turn to this site for advice and help.

2965. *Games for Windows.* Formerly (until 2006): *Computer Gaming World.* [ISSN: 1933-6160] 1981. 12x/yr. USD 19.97 domestic; USD 35 foreign. Ed(s): Jeff Green, Sean Molloy. Ziff Davis Media Inc., 28 E 28th St, New York, NY 10016-7930; info@ziffdavis.com; http://www.ziffdavis.com. Adv. Circ: 300000 Paid. Online: EBSCO Publishing, EBSCO Host; Florida Center for Library Automation; Gale; ProQuest K-12 Learning Solutions; ProQuest LLC (Ann Arbor). *Indexed:* MASUSE, MicrocompInd. *Aud.:* Ga.

Games for Windows focuses more on networked online gaming than single-use PlayStation or Xbox players, or single-use Internet games. Besides giving gaming advice and information on individual games, this publication contains articles on the latest developments in various types of computer entertainment. It also contains very good reviews of computer hardware, but from a game player's perspective, not from the average user's.

2966. *Games, Games, Games.* [ISSN: 1357-1508] 1986. 10x/yr. GBP 26 domestic; GBP 29 in Europe; GBP 35 United States. Ed(s): Paul Evans. S F C Press (Small Furry Creatures), 17 Crendon St, High Wycombe, HP 136LJ, United Kingdom; http://www.sfcp.co.uk. Illus., adv. *Aud.:* Hs, Ga.

This British publication claims to cover the whole gaming industry, but it mostly covers wargames. The magazine includes reviews and playing tips for all kinds of board and online wargames. This publication has excellent coverage of the wargaming community in Europe. Public libraries with users who have a general interest in gaming would most benefit from this magazine.

2967. *GameWEEK: the newspaper of the interactive entertainment industry.* Formerly (until 1998): *Videogame Advisor.* [ISSN: 1097-394X] 1985. 44x/yr. USD 99 domestic; USD 149 in Europe; USD 200 elsewhere. Ed(s): Mike Davila. CyberActive Publishing, 64 Danbury Rd, Ste 500, Wilton, CT 06897; jim@gameweek.com; http://www.gameweek.com/. Illus., adv. *Aud.:* Ga, Sa.

This large-format trade magazine covers industry news, trade shows, financial news, and projections, using a clear, visually oriented format. There are some game previews and reviews, but far more space is devoted to evaluations of new software and hardware, sales rankings, company profiles, and long interviews. The web site, www.gameweek.com, complements the print publication with daily industry-related press releases and "GameJobs," a listing of job openings in the gaming industry. This journal should be of interest in areas where the gaming industry is a significant factor in the local economy.

2968. *Go World.* [ISSN: 0286-0376] 1977. q. USD 32; USD 50 in Europe. Ed(s): Richard Bozulich. Kiseido Publishing Company, C.P.O. Box 1140, Tokyo, Japan; kiseido@yk.rim.or.jp; http://www.kiseido.com. Illus., adv. Circ: 10500. *Bk. rev.:* Number and length vary. *Aud.:* Hs, Ga.

This quarterly offers instructional articles for beginners and more-advanced players, commentary, news, and articles of general interest about the game Go. Go is an ancient board game that uses simple materials and concepts to generate complex strategies and tactics. The major Go tournaments in Japan, Korea, and China are also covered. The Go web site, kiseido.com, has information on the game and other items available for purchase.

2969. *I M P Bridge Magazine.* 1995. m. EUR 39 domestic; EUR 54 in Europe; EUR 73 elsewhere. Ed(s): Jan Van Cleeff. I M P Bridge Magazine, 2512 GA, The Hague, Netherlands. *Aud.:* Ga, Ac.

This has flourished as a print magazine since 1989. While it is published in the Netherlands, its text is in English and meant for an international group of bridge players. The primary focus is on tournaments, but it also has numerous features on methods of play and defense. The primary audience is the near-expert, not the beginner. However, there are numerous links to other bridge web sites and related bridge magazines that can be used by the person first being introduced to the game. There is an informative web site at www.imp-bridge.nl; however, you need to be able to read Dutch to utilize it.

2970. *Line of Departure.* q. USD 15. Line of Departure, 3835 Richmond Ave, Ste 192, Staten Island, NY 10312. *Aud.:* Hs, Ga.

Line of Departure contains reviews and playing advice for a wide selection of wargames. This publication is geared to the experienced gamer, so be aware that the audience is limited.

2971. *Lottery & Casino News.* Formerly (until 1996): *Lottery Player's Magazine.* [ISSN: 1088-727X] 1981. bi-m. USD 17.75; USD 35.50 foreign. Ed(s): Samuel W Valenza, Jr. Regal Publishing Corporation, PO Box 487, Marlton, NJ 08053-0487; regalpub@lottery-casino-news.com; http://www.lottery-casino-news.com. Illus., adv. Circ: 150000 Paid. *Aud.:* Ga.

Coverage in this publication is not limited to lotteries. It also contains features about other gambling games, ranging from bingo to racing and casino action. The main emphasis is on lotteries, with numerous articles, features, and short pieces giving background information on the subject. Upcoming lotteries and winning numbers in the states that sponsor the games are also provided. Of interest is information provided on legislation concerning lotteries and gaming. Back issues are available by request.

2972. *LottoWorld: America's lottery magazine.* [ISSN: 1077-1840] 1993. m. USD 29.95. Ed(s): Dennis Schroeder. Lottoworld Inc., 201 8th St S Ste 107, Naples, FL 33940-4811; rholman@coconet.com; http://www.lottoworldmagazine.com. Illus., adv. Circ: 250000 Paid. *Aud.:* Ga.

This national lottery magazine has eight regional or state editions as well as a national edition. It includes features on winning strategies, lottery statistics, and interviews. The web site has an abbreviated version of the print magazine.

2973. *Miniature Wargames.* [ISSN: 0266-3228] 1983. m. GBP 37 domestic; GBP 42 foreign; GBP 3.20 newsstand/cover per issue domestic. Ed(s): Iain Dickie. Pireme Publishing Ltd., Wessex House, St Leonards Rd, Bournemouth, BH8 8QS, United Kingdom. Illus., index, adv. Circ: 10000 Paid. *Bk. rev.:* Number and length vary. *Aud.:* Hs, Ga.

A very respected publication that covers miniature wargaming in the United Kingdom. *Miniature Wargames* is packed with colorful illustrations and modelling advice for collectors of military miniatures. The articles cover all historical periods, and naval modelling is also covered in detail. This magazine has something for everyone who might be interested in miniatures. The journal's web site, www.wargames.co.uk, has links to editorials, reviews, information, and, of course, vendors of miniatures.

2974. *New in Chess Magazine.* Supersedes in part (in 1984): *Schaakbulletin (Amsterdam).* [ISSN: 0168-8782] 1968. 8x/yr. EUR 54 domestic; EUR 66 rest of Europe (euro zone); GBP 45 United Kingdom). Ed(s): Jan Timman, Dirk Jan Ten Geuzendam. Interchess B.V., PO Box 1093, Alkmaar, 1810, Netherlands; nic@newinchess.com; http://www.newinchess.com/. Illus., adv. Sample. Vol. ends: Jan. *Bk. rev.:* 3, 100 words. *Aud.:* Hs, Ga, Ac.

This chess title has more of a European focus than *Chess Life* or other U.S. chess magazines. It contains articles on world chess tournament play with detailed game analyses, as well as interviews and articles on the history of chess that may be of interest to the lay reader. There is a supplement (issued four times per year) available for an additional $129. Subscribers may also obtain data disks on the more than 16,000 games that are discussed or cited in the yearbook. Special Nicbase software is required to read the data and replay the games. There is also an extensive web site, www.newinchess.com, linking to the publication and other chess-related materials and items.

2975. *NOSTalgia (Victorville, E-mail Edition).* Formerly: *Nost-Algia (Print Edition).* 1960. q. Membership, USD 20; Members, USD 10. Ed(s): Don Cotten. Knights of the Square Table, c/o Donald Cotten, 13393 Mariposa Rd 248, Victorville, CA 92392-5324; http://www.nostgames.com/. Adv. Circ: 350. *Bk. rev.:* Number and length vary. *Aud.:* Ga, Ac.

NOSTalgia stands for Knights of the Square Table and is a postal games club, primarily chess, but also checkers, shogi, and Go. Regular features include an editorial, chess problems, chess results, checkers problems, a calendar of conventions, and news about members. Secret word ladders, a word game, is also featured in the bulletin. The NOST has been accepted as a member of the U.S. Postal Chess Federation. Includes book reviews.

2976. *P C Gamer.* Former titles (until May 1994): *Game Player's P C Entertainment;* (until 1991): *Game Player's P C Strategy Guide; Game Player's M S - D O S Strategy Guide.* [ISSN: 1080-4471] 1988. m. USD 19.95 domestic includes m. CD-ROM; USD 34.95 Canada includes m. CD-ROM; USD 49.95 elsewhere includes m. CD-ROM. Ed(s): Chuck Osborn. Future U S, Inc., 4000 Shoreline Court, Ste. 400, South San Francisco, CA 94080; http://www.futureus-inc.com. Adv. Circ: 250000 Paid. *Aud.:* Hs, Ga, Ac.

This publication, which originally evaluated educational products for IBM PC and compatible computers, has come to focus more on PC-compatible games. Sections include hints to improve scores, announcements of new games, interviews with game creators, and downloadable previews to new games. The journal's web site at www.pcgamer.com links to the publication, and it lists blogs, forums, and podcasts related to PC gaming.

2977. *Panzerschreck.* irreg. Minden Games, 9573 W Vogel Ave, Peoria, AZ 85345; minden2@hotmail.com; http://www.homestead.com/minden_games/. *Aud.:* Hs, Ga, Ac.

Panzerschreck is an unusual publication; you cannot obtain it with a formal subscription. Each issue must be requested separately. This is a publication for the solitaire gamer, and each issue includes a complete game. The game inserts come with rules, maps, counters, and other assorted game parts. The parts and inserts would create problems for libraries, as they are unique to each game and "magazine." Information on the publication and how to acquire it can be found at www.homestead.com/minden_games.

2978. *Paper Wars.* Formerly (until 1993): *Wargame Collector's Journal.* 1991. bi-m. USD 29.95 domestic; USD 48 in Europe; USD 54 elsewhere. Ed(s): John Burtt. Omega Games, PO Box 2191, Valrico, FL 33595; omegagames@aol.com; http://paperwarsmag.tripod.com/. Illus., adv. *Bk. rev.:* Number and length vary. *Aud.:* Hs, Ga.

Paper Wars is a good reviewing source for wargames from a variety of different companies, and it includes reviews of books on military history. This journal might enhance a public library collection that serves users who have an interest in wargaming or general military history.

2979. *Perfidious Albion.* 1976. triennial. Ed(s): Charles Vasey. Perfidious Albion, 75 Richmond Park Rd, London, SW14 8JY, United Kingdom. *Aud.:* Ga.

This publication provides some clever reviews of a wide variety of board and online wargaming systems. The articles have a strong bent toward the gaming community in the United Kingdom, but a lot of North American gaming products are also examined. This could be a good source of wargame reviews for libraries that have a patron base interested in war games.

2980. *Rolling Good Times Online.* 1995. d. Free. Ed(s): Sue Schneider. RGT Online Inc., 205 S. Main St., St. Charles, MO 63301-2804; rgt@rgtonline.com; http://www.rgtonline.com. Adv. *Aud.:* Ga.

This gamblers' magazine covers a wide spectrum, from where professional gambling is taking place to interviews and comments by the same professionals. The tips on how to win, strategies to follow, and games to watch may or may not be valid, depending on the viewpoint of the reader and the person giving the help. Be that as it may, the magazine does pretty well covering the field. The web site at www.rgtonline.com extensively covers gambling news and strategies and what's on at the major gambling destinations.

2981. *Scrye.* [ISSN: 1540-0565] 1994. m. USD 29.98 domestic; USD 54.98 Canada; USD 5.99 newsstand/cover per issue. Ed(s): Joyce Greenholdt. Krause Publications, Inc., 700 E State St, Iola, WI 54990-0001; info@krause.com; http://www.krause.com. Adv. Circ: 41220 Paid and free. *Aud.:* Hs, Ga.

This is a price and buying guide for collectors of miniatures and card games, with a section for trading, listing your collectibles, and searching for dealers. It also includes news on nationwide conventions, a tournament calendar for deck games, and listings of tournament winners. There is a link to the magazine from the publisher's web site at www.krause.com.

2982. *Simulacrum: a quarterly journal of board wargame collecting & accumulating.* 1999. q. CND 25 domestic; USD 25 United States print & online eds.; USD 30 elsewhere print & online eds. Ed(s): John Kula. Simulacrum, 794 Fort St, RPO Box 38023, Victoria, BC V8W 3N2, Canada. *Aud.:* Hs, Ga.

One of the leading peridicals for collectors of board wargames. The articles are loaded with information on past wargames and tips about finding and collecting the games. This publication would be of interest to public libraries that serve users interested in collecting games and toys. There is an entertaining web site for the magazine at www3.telus.net/Simulacrum/main.html.

2983. Strategist. m. USD 15. Ed(s): Vickie Watson, Tim Watson. Strategy Gaming Society, 87-6 Park Ave, Worcester, MA 01605; http://pages.about.com/strategygames. *Bk. rev.:* Number and length vary. *Aud.:* Hs, Ga.

This publication is the monthly newsletter of the Strategy Gaming Society (SGS). It contains articles about new games, gaming reviews, scenarios, and information about new Internet resources. The articles are of interest to wargamers of all levels.

2984. Strategy and Tactics: the magazine of conflict simulation. Former titles (until 1988): *Strategy and Tactics Magazine;* (until 1982): *Strategy and Tactics.* [ISSN: 1040-886X] 1967. bi-m. USD 29.97 domestic; USD 36 Canada; USD 42 elsewhere. Ed(s): Joseph Miranda. Decision Games, PO Box 21598, Bakersfield, CA 93390; http://www.decisiongames.com. Illus., index, adv. Circ: 10000. *Indexed:* AmH&L, HistAb. *Aud.:* Hs, Ga.

This is one of the most respected publications for wargaming and general military history. *Strategy & Tactics* contains articles from all periods of military history. This magazine also includes articles about possible future conflicts and alternative history scenarios. Reviews of gaming products and advice about wargaming are included; the subjects of feature articles are extensively covered. The content is well researched, and articles are often excellent contributions to the overall field of military history. There is a link to the publication at www.decisiongames.com and a link to the companion publication, *Fire & Movement.*

2985. Tac News. 1987. bi-m. Free. G H Q, 28100 Woodside Rd, Shorewood, MN 55331; customerservice@ghqmodels.com; http://www.ghqmodels.com/. *Aud.:* Hs, Ga.

This interesting newsletter covers military modelling and wargaming with miniatures. The newsletter also contains general military history articles that mostly deal with World War II topics. The web site at www.ghqmodels.com lists all the products you will need to get into military or railroad miniature modelling.

2986. Tournaments Illuminated. [ISSN: 0732-6645] 1967. q. Members, USD 35. Ed(s): Nancy Beattie. Society for Creative Anachronism, PO Box 360789, Milpitas, CA 95036-0789. Illus., adv. Circ: 22000. *Aud.:* Hs, Ga, Ac.

This is the official publication of the Society for Creative Anachronisms. This is one of the largest groups dedicated to medieval reenacting. One of the largest areas of interest is the medieval soldier, and the pages are loaded with articles about the armor and weapons of the medieval period. A good selection for public libraries that serve those interested in historical reenacting. The Society of Creative Anachronisms is active on many college campuses, and academic libraries might also benefit from having this publication. The official web site for the society is at www.sca.org.

2987. Vae Victis. [ISSN: 0242-312X] 1974. bi-m. EUR 35 domestic; EUR 42 elsewhere. Ed(s): Frederic Bey. Histoire et Collection, 5 Av. de la Republique, Paris, 75011, France; fredbey@club-internet.fr; http://livres.histoireetcollections.com. Circ: 15000. *Aud.:* Hs, Ga, Ac.

This French-language publication is one of the better sources for the wargaming and military history scene in Europe. Excellent articles and reviews appear on a broad range of wargaming topics, and well-researched articles are also offered on general military history. This publication would be useful to public and academic libraries that have strong French-language and military history collections. Its web site is at www.vaevictis.com.

2988. Valkyrie. [ISSN: 1355-2767] 1994. m. GBP 3 newsstand/cover per issue. Ed(s): Dave Renton. Partizan Press, 816-818 London Rd, Leigh-on-sea, Southend, SS9 3NH, United Kingdom; partizan@compuserve.com. Illus. Circ: 12000. *Aud.:* Hs, Ga.

Perhaps the leading publication for players of role-playing and fantasy games. Many of these games have strong elements of strategy built in, even if the games may not be centered on historical or current reality. Public libraries that cater to a group of role-playing and fantasy gamers might consider purchasing this publication.

2989. Wargamers Information. 1975. s-a. USD 3 for 12 issues. Ed(s): Rick Loomis. Flying Buffalo Inc., PO Box 1467, Scottsdale, AZ 85252; http://www.flyingbuffalo.com. Circ: 500. *Aud.:* Hs, Ga.

A publication for players of Flying Buffalo games. This magazine reviews new games and suggests playing tips for the current line of products. The vendor of the games makes many card-based and board wargaming products as well as fantasy gaming products. Designed for a hardcore gaming audience, this publication may be best suited to a limited audience. Flying Buffalo games can be found at www.flyingbuffalo.com.

2990. Wargames Illustrated. [ISSN: 0957-6444] 1987. m. GBP 32 domestic; GBP 34 foreign; GBP 2.75 newsstand/cover per issue. Ed(s): Duncan Macfarlane. Stratagem Publications Ltd., 18 Lovers Ln, Newark, NG24 1HZ, United Kingdom; illustrated@wargames.co.uk; http://www.wargames.co.uk. Illus., adv. *Aud.:* Hs, Ga.

This is an interesting British publication that has excellent articles about board and miniature wargaming products. Some of the miniatures features are very well done, with eye-catching illustrations. A possible purchase for public libraries that serve a wargaming community.

2991. White Dwarf. [ISSN: 0265-8712] 1977. m. GBP 40. Ed(s): Paul Sawyer. Games Workshop Ltd., Willow Rd, Lenton, NG7 2WS, United Kingdom; http://www.games-workshop.com. Circ: 60968. *Aud.:* Hs, Ga.

This monthly hobby magazine of Games Workshop is intended to keep the reader informed of new game releases, upcoming games, and what is going on with the workshop. Included are photos of new miniatures and information on trading and prices of miniatures. Games Workshop is online at www.games-workshop.co.uk.

■ GARDENING

See also Agriculture; and Home sections.

Rex J. Krajewski, Reference Services Librarian, Simmons College, 300 The Fenway, Boston, MA 02115; krajewsk@simmons.edu

Introduction

There are myriad reasons people choose to garden. Some garden because their family always has, and it allows them to stay connected to their heritage; some garden because they love the design element plants add to a landscape; some garden because they want to sustain themselves with the fruits of their own labor. The reasons people garden are as diverse as the kinds of gardening they do. Flower gardening remains popular. Flower gardeners may focus on particular kinds of flowers such as perennials, annuals, tropicals, rare specimens, or particular plants like roses or hydrangeas. Vegetable gardening is the other mainstay of gardening; this category often includes fruits and herbs. Other popular categories of gardening include landscape and design, organic and heirloom, and, increasingly, water gardening. Perhaps because gardeners and gardening are so diverse, information about gardening comes from many different disciplines. Literature about gardening tends to encompass the the subject's interdisciplinary nature. Gardeners seek to know more about the science of gardening from fields such as agriculture, horticulture, and biochemistry. Ideas about design and aesthetics come from the worlds of art, architecture, history, and landscaping. Issues such as environmental sustainability; seed and plant copyright; and GMO (genetically modified organisms), organic, and heirloom growing even have a political aspect, and that is covered in the literature. Magazines about gardening may focus on a single aspect or may integrate multiple aspects. Specific topics of magazines might be defined by species, like *The Rose*; by region, like *Northern Gardener*; by environment, like *Rock Gardener*; or by purpose, like *Garden Design*. Even multidisciplinary, or generalist, titles tend to espouse a perspective. So, for example, *Organic*

Gardening deals with many different kinds of gardening, including ornamentals, vegetables, and water gardening, but it does so with the assumption that all will be done using organic techniques and principles. When choosing magazines on gardening, readers are likely to be attracted to the angle and focus. Libraries should be aware of the interests of gardeners in their user population and choose accordingly. In addition to titles that cater to local interests, libraries should have generalist gardening titles from a number of different perspectives to satisfy diverse needs and interests. Provided here is just such list of core generalist titles.

Please note that region-specific titles, those that deal with the growing needs and conditions of a particular area, have been left off this list. Please consider such titles based on the region where your library patrons live. It should be noted, though, that increasingly, general gardening magazines are treating relevant topics from a number of different regional perpectives, rendering regionally specific titles less unique.

There are very few strictly electronic journals in the realm of gardening magazines, though it should be noted that most print garden magazines have some kind of online presence. These might take the form of selected articles and content available to everyone for free, or all articles and content available to subscribers for free. Another variation would be extra content available online to subscribers, such as guides, reader communities or blogs, free offers, and reference material. It is worthwhile for libraries to investigate what garden magazines of interest offer information online, and consider linking to these online resources via library catalogs, subject guides, or other resource-finding vehicles for patrons.

Basic Periodicals

Ga: *The American Gardener, BBC Gardeners' World Magazine, Fine Gardening, The Garden, Garden Gate, Gardening How-To, Horticulture, HortIdeas, National Gardening, Organic Gardening.*

Basic Abstracts and Indexes

Garden Literature Index.

2992. The American Gardener. Former titles: *American Horticulturist; American Horticultural Magazine;* Incorporates: *American Horticultural Society News and Views; Gardeners Forum.* [ISSN: 1087-9978] 1922. bi-m. USD 35 domestic. Ed(s): David J Ellis. American Horticultural Society, 7931 E Boulevard Dr, Alexandria, VA 22308-1300; info@ahs.org; http://www.ahs.org. Illus., index, adv. Circ: 26000. Vol. ends: Nov/Dec. Microform: PQC. *Indexed:* B&AI, BiolDig, GSI, GardL, HortAb, MASUSE. *Bk. rev.:* 3, 500 words. *Aud.:* Ga, Ac.

The American Gardener is the official publication of the American Horticultural Society. It includes regular features on such topics as design, regional issues, conservation, and habitat gardening. Reviews, regional calendars, and vibrant photography round out this mainstay among gardening magazines. A unique perspective offered by *The American Gardener* is the attention paid to gardening for children and families. The magazine is designed for serious gardeners, so topics are treated with great detail and provide sound information.

2993. The Avant Gardener. [ISSN: 0005-1926] 1968. m. USD 24 domestic; USD 30 foreign. Ed(s): Thomas Powell. Horticultural Data Processors, PO Box 489, New York, NY 10028. Index. Sample. Vol. ends: Oct. *Indexed:* GardL. *Bk. rev.:* 3, 50 words. *Aud.:* Sa.

The Avant Gardener is the cute name of a very serious, no-nonsense gardening newsletter. Editor and publisher Thomas Powell compiles research and information from a number of sources all over the country into this monthly newsletter. There are no ads or images in this publication, but it is packed with information on plants, products, techniques, and resources. The information is sound, even if sometimes the spelling and grammar are not. If what you are looking for is just good, solid gardening advice, this is the newsletter for you.

2994. B B C Gardeners' World Magazine. [ISSN: 0961-7477] 1991. m. GBP 28.50; GBP 2.80 newsstand/cover. Ed(s): Adam Pasco. B B C Worldwide Ltd., 80 Wood Ln, London, W12 0TT, United Kingdom; bbcworldwide@bbc.co.uk; http://www.bbcmagazines.com. Illus., index, adv. Sample. Circ: 382816 Paid. Vol. ends: Feb. *Indexed:* GardL. *Aud.:* Ga.

BBC Gardeners' World Magazine is part of a multimedia gardening experience from the British media outlet BBC. Because the magazine is so closely aligned with television, the Internet, and radio, it features celebrity contributors like "Ground Force" alum Alan Titchmarsh. Aimed at a broad market, articles cover a wide range of gardening topics. Regular features include the "Fresh Ideas" section with "creative projects, garden design tips, new plants and great shopping ideas for a brighter and better garden," "What to Do Now," offering a planting and project schedule for Britain's gardening season, and "Problem Solving," a forum for readers to submit questions and receive expert advice.

Canadian Gardening. See Canada section.

2995. Country Gardens. [ISSN: 1068-431X] 1992. bi-m. USD 19.97 for 2 yrs. Ed(s): Carol S Sheehan, Luann Brandsen. Meredith Corp., 1716 Locust St, Des Moines, IA 50309-3023; http://www.meredith.com. Illus., adv. Circ: 325000 Paid. Vol. ends: Fall. *Indexed:* GardL. *Bk. rev.:* 500 words. *Aud.:* Hs, Ga, Ac.

Country Gardens is a product of the well-known mainstream publisher Better Homes and Gardens. With an emphasis on successful personal experiences, this magazine would inspire and motivate even novice gardeners. Tips and projects are basic enough to be tackled by anyone. A more advanced gardener might go to another source for more cutting-edge or sophisticated information, but everyone would enjoy the lush photography and illustrations. Another universally appealing feature is that advertisements are limited to a separate section in the back of the magazine.

2996. Country Living Gardener. [ISSN: 1086-3753] 1993. s-a. Hearst Magazines, 300 W 57th St, New York, NY 10019; HearstMagazines@hearst.com; http://www.hearstcorp.com/magazines/. Illus., adv. Circ: 475000 Paid. Online: EBSCO Publishing, EBSCO Host; Gale; ProQuest LLC (Ann Arbor). *Indexed:* GardL. *Bk. rev.:* 8-10, 100-200 words. *Aud.:* Ga.

Country Living Gardener debuted independently of its parent publication, *Country Living,* in 1993, and it has grown in popularity ever since. Topics covered include gardening of all kinds, landscaping, design, food and entertainment, health and beauty, crafts, travel, and the environment. Designed to appeal to broad audience, it hits the nail on the head. While projects and advice may be more for beginners and novices, the "sumptuous visuals" are irresistible to anyone who loves plants and gardens.

2997. The English Garden: for everyone who loves beautiful gardens. [ISSN: 1361-2840] 1997. m. GBP 37.50 United Kingdom; USD 47.50 elsewhere; USD 4.99 newsstand/cover per issue. Ed(s): Vanessa Berridge. Romsey Publishing Company Ltd. (London), Jubilee House, 2 Jubilee Pl, London, SW3 3TQ, United Kingdom. Adv. Circ: 55656 Paid. *Indexed:* GardL. *Aud.:* Hs, Ga, Ac.

As its subtitle says, *The English Garden* is "for everyone who loves beautiful gardens." Filled with the requisite tips and ideas, this magazine excels in information on enjoying gardens, such as ideas on gardens to visit and descriptions of storied estates. Indeed, regardless of whether or not the style of garden you enjoy is "English" or not, this publication will inspire you with its beautiful, breathtaking images.

2998. Fine Gardening. [ISSN: 0896-6281] 1988. bi-m. USD 29.95 in US & Canada; USD 36 elsewhere; USD 6.99 newsstand/cover. Ed(s): Todd Meier. Taunton Press, Inc., 63 South Main St, Newtown, CT 06470-5506; publicrelations@taunton.com; http://www.taunton.com. Illus., index, adv. Circ: 202163 Paid. *Indexed:* ASIP, BRI, CBRI, GardL, IHTDI. *Bk. rev.:* 4, 250 words. *Aud.:* Ga.

Don't be fooled by the adverbial description in the title of *Fine Gardening.* As far as this publication is concerned, *all* gardening is "fine." Most articles are practical, for example, providing information about plants, step-by-step directions on projects, and techniques for effective gardening. While there are a lot of ads in this magazine, they are appropriate to the content. The publication is sleek in appearance—the color photographs and illustrations are stunning, design ideas are hip, and product features are trendy. However, the content is well written and the information sound, so this general gardening magazine lives up to its own hype.

2999. Garden Design: the fine art of residential landscape architecture. [ISSN: 0733-4923] 1982. bi-m. USD 11.97 domestic; USD 17.97 Canada; USD 23.97 elsewhere. World Publications LLC, 460 N Orlando Ave, Ste 200, Winter Park, FL 32789; info@worldpub.net; http://www.worldpub.net. Illus., adv. Circ: 339725 Paid. Vol. ends: Nov/Dec. *Indexed:* ArtInd, FLI, GardL. *Bk. rev.:* 3-5, 300 words. *Aud.:* Ga.

From its title, it should be clear that the focus of *Garden Design* is design and landscaping in gardens. In fact, if one were to choose a single magazine to represent this perspective on gardening, this would be it. Inspiration is provided by photographs and reports of upscale gardens, but practical advice, ideas, and strategies are given for gardeners of all levels and tastes. The product reviews are for cutting-edge and trendy garden design tools and accessories, and advertisements follow suit. This well-written publication is a must-read for anyone interested in garden design or in just looking at pictures and descriptions of beautiful gardens.

3000. Garden Gate. [ISSN: 1083-8295] 1995. bi-m. USD 24 domestic; KHR 34 foreign. Ed(s): Steven Nordmeyer. August Home Publishing Co., 2200 Grand Ave, Des Moines, IA 50312-5306; orders@augusthome.com; http://www.augusthome.com. Illus. Circ: 495000 Paid. *Indexed:* GardL, IHTDI. *Aud.:* Hs, Ga, Ac.

The unique feature of this general gardening magazine is that it does not include advertisements. Therefore, it appears smaller than other comparable magazines, but, in fact, contains just as much information in each issue. Articles tend to be practical in nature, including a lot of how-to narratives supported by color photographs and sketches. Although *Garden Gate* may not provide as sophisticated or cutting-edge content as some other magazines of its type, it is a good, basic gardening periodical.

3001. Garden History. [ISSN: 0307-1243] 1973. s-a. Membership, GBP 35. Ed(s): Dr. Barbara Simms, Dr. Andrew Eburne. Garden History Society, 70 Cowcross St, London, ECIM 6EJ, United Kingdom; enquiries@gardenhistorysociety.org; http://www.gardenhistorysociety.org. Illus., index. Refereed. Circ: 2750. Vol. ends: Winter. *Indexed:* API, BrArAb, GardL, NumL. *Bk. rev.:* 6, 500-1,000 words. *Aud.:* Ac.

Another British title, *Garden History* is unique among most other gardening titles in two ways. First, it is a journal; content is refereed and produced primarily for a scholarly audience. Second, its focus is not on gardening techniques but on the history of gardening. Despite these distinctions, or perhaps because of the them, this publication is sure to interest most garden enthusiasts. It is the official journal of the Garden History Society, and its purpose is to provide "support to the society's promotion of the study of garden history, landscape gardening and horticulture." Articles cover such important and broadly appealing topics as historical gardens, conservation, regional garden issues, and the intersection of other scholarship with gardens and garden history.

3002. Gardening How-To. [ISSN: 1087-0083] 1996. bi-m. Free to members. Ed(s): Amy Sitze. North American Media Group, Inc., 12301 Whitewater Dr, Minnetonka, MN 55343; http://www.namginc.com/. Adv. Circ: 675000 Paid. *Indexed:* GardL. *Bk. rev.:* Number and length vary. *Aud.:* Ga.

Gardening How-To is the official magazine of the National Gardening Club, which is a paid membership association of home gardening enthusiasts. In many ways, it is not unlike other general consumer magazines, but with more reader-contributed content, including book and product reviews. The how-to and science of horticulture information are more basic than in some other

magazines, but where this publication really shines is in its inclusion of "good ideas," helpful tips and strategies for more effective and efficient gardening. Much of this advice comes from other club members, so content is being generated by the audience.

3003. Gardens Illustrated. [ISSN: 0968-8927] 1993. 10x/yr. GBP 31.20 domestic; GBP 52 in Europe; AUD 79.64 Australia. B B C Worldwide Ltd., 80 Wood Ln, London, W12 0TT, United Kingdom; bbcworldwide@bbc.co.uk; http://www.bbcmagazines.com. *Indexed:* DAAI, GardL. *Aud.:* Hs, Ga, Ac, Sa.

As its name implies, *Gardens Illustrated*'s specialty is its visual depiction of gardens and gardening. While the photography in the magazine is exceptional, the narrative is every bit as worthwhile as the pictures. Gardens from all over the world provide a backdrop for inspiration and information. Regular features include plant profiles, news, product reviews, and recipes.

3004. Green Prints: the weeder's digest. [ISSN: 1064-0118] 1990. q. USD 17.97 domestic; USD 21 in Canada & Mexico; USD 27 United Kingdom. Ed(s): Pat Stone. Green Prints, PO Box 1355, Fairview, NC 28730; http://www.greenprints.com. Illus., adv. Sample. Circ: 10000 Paid. Vol. ends: Winter. *Indexed:* GardL. *Aud.:* Ems, Hs, Ga, Ac.

Green Prints: the Weeder's Digest is another title that fulfills a unique role. Rather than being a how-to publication or one that inspires primarily with stunning imagery, this magazine offers a collection of personal narratives on the topic of gardening. Essays, stories, quotations, relevant ads, and black-and-white illustrations all serve to provide the perfect companion to readers who can't get enough of all things having to do with gardening.

3005. Grow Your Own: fresh food from the garden. [ISSN: 1745-1876] 2005. m. GBP 32 domestic; GBP 59.95 in Europe; GBP 39.95 elsewhere. Ed(s): Georgina Wroe. Aceville Publications Ltd., Castle House, 97 High St, Colchester, CO1 2QN, United Kingdom; http://www.aceville.com. Adv. *Aud.:* Ga.

Grow Your Own is a British gardening magazine that specializes in gardening for food. Regular features include "News" about fruit and vegetable gardening, "Six of the Best," highlighting the best in various gardening categories, and an "Ask the Experts" advice forum. Features cover a variety of topics, including design ideas, cooking advice, plant variety investigations, and how-to instructions. A unique strategy is dividing articles into two sections, one called "Practical Advice" and the other called "The Organic Section." The added value of this layout is that readers can expect content in these focused areas in each issue, as well as more general, diverse content.

3006. Growing Edge Magazine: indoor & outdoor gardening for today's grower. [ISSN: 1043-2906] 1989. bi-m. USD 26.95 domestic; USD 55 Canada; USD 79.50 foreign. Ed(s): Doug Peckenpaugh. New Moon Publishing, Inc., PO Box 1027, Corvallis, OR 97339-1027; http://www.growingedge.com. Adv. Circ: 25000. *Indexed:* GardL. *Bk. rev.:* Number and length vary. *Aud.:* Ga, Sa.

This is the gardening magazine that covers the place where technology and nature collide. Specializing in hydroponics, it also covers other cutting-edge growing strategies like aeroponics, aquaponics, greenhouses, controlled environments, drip irrigation, water conservation, and organic gardening. Content is aimed at all levels of growers, from backyard gardeners to commercial producers. In addition to how-to features, the articles discuss many perspectives in hydroponics and other innovative growing techniques, including personal experiences, political issues, and product and book reviews. This title is a great choice for those interested in high-tech or advanced gardening methodologies.

3007. The Heirloom Gardener Magazine. [ISSN: 1548-1085] 2003. q. USD 12. Ed(s): Jeremiath Gettle. Hill Folk's Publishing, 2278 Baker Creek Rd, Mansfield, MO 65704; heirloomgardener@getgoin.net. *Aud.:* Hs, Ga, Ac.

Since 2003, *The Heirloom Gardener* has been a magazine dedicated to home heirloom gardeners. Interest in heirloom gardening is steadily growing as people become more aware of issues like native heritage and garden history. Also, as concern grows about genetically modified plants, heirloom species have garnered more attention. This magazine's appeal continues to grow. Covering topics listed above, as well as related concerns like organic gardening and preservation, *The Heirloom Gardener* would be a nice addition to a generalist gardening magazine collection because it views the topic through a somewhat alternative lens. The magazine includes charming illustrations reminiscent of old-time seed catalogs. An interesting note: The magazine does not accept advertising from the tobacco, chemical, or automobile industries, or those it sees as counter to its view on responsible citizenship and sustainability.

3008. *Horticulture: gardening at its best.* [ISSN: 0018-5329] 1904. bi-m. USD 19.95 domestic; USD 26.95 foreign; USD 6.99 newsstand/cover. F + W Publications, Inc., 98 N Washington St, Boston, MA 02114; wds@fwpubs.com; http://www.fwpublications.com. Illus., index, adv. Sample. Circ: 300856 Paid and controlled. Vol. ends: Nov/Dec. Microform: MIM; PQC. Online: EBSCO Publishing, EBSCO Host; Florida Center for Library Automation; Gale; OCLC Online Computer Library Center, Inc.; H.W. Wilson. *Indexed:* ASIP, B&AI, BRI, BiolDig, CBRI, ConsI, ExcerpMed, GSI, GardL, IHTDI, MASUSE. *Bk. rev.:* 3, 500 words. *Aud.:* Ga, Ac.

Horticulture is one of the oldest titles in this list, and it could serve as a representative archetype of gardening magazines. While it is beautifully illustrated with inspiring color photographs, the strength of this title is as an information source. Reading this magazine makes one feel like a smarter, better informed gardener with a scientific understanding, artistic knowledge, and technical savvy. Regular features include "Pest Watch," "Plant Index and Pronunciation Guide," and product reviews. *Horticulture* has often defined expectations of gardening magazines, and is leading the way in addressing regional needs with content specific to major growing regions in the United States.

3009. *HortIdeas.* [ISSN: 0742-8219] 1984. m. USD 25 domestic; USD 32 in Canada & Mexico; USD 42 elsewhere. Ed(s): Patricia Williams, Gregory Williams. HortIdeas Publishing, 750 Black Lick Rd, Gravel Switch, KY 40328; gwill@mis.net; http://www.users.mis.net/~gwill. Index. Sample. Circ: 1200 Paid and free. Vol. ends: Dec. *Indexed:* ExcerpMed, GardL. *Bk. rev.:* 3, 500 words. *Aud.:* Ga.

A unique title, *HortIdeas* could almost be understood as an abstracting service for the average grower. Editors "gather the information from hundreds of popular and technical sources, worldwide, and rewrite it so that you can understand it and use it." The idea behind this publication is that there is a lot of good information out there about gardening and horticulture that the average gardener or small-scale grower would never have time to read. So, the staff at *HortIdeas* scan popular and technical publications about gardening, horticulture, agriculture, forestry, ecology, and more to find the very best and most useful information. And that is what this magazine provides, distilled, easy-to-read, up-to-date on the latest research and ideas, and the most important information. There are no color photographs, basic how-to articles, experiential narratives, or advertisements.

3010. *Hortus: a gardening journal.* [ISSN: 0950-1657] 1987. q. GBP 32 United Kingdom; GBP 37 in Europe; USD 68 United States. Ed(s): David Wheeler. The Bryansground Press, Bryan's Ground, Stapleton, Presteigne, LD8 2LP, United Kingdom; all@hortus.co.uk; http://www.hortus.co.uk. Illus., index, adv. Sample. Circ: 3000 Paid. Vol. ends: Winter. *Indexed:* GardL. *Bk. rev.:* Various number, 1,000 words. *Aud.:* Ga.

Hortus is a publication that is inspired by and indulges in the artistic side of gardening. Itself a beautiful specimen, the journal is in black and white on ochre-colored paper. While topics such as historical and notable gardens, plant introductions, gardeners of note, and ideas worth sharing are included, much of the content comes from the place where gardens intersect with art. For example, books about how to garden are reviewed, but so is fiction that features gardens. *Hortus* is for those who believe gardening is a high art, but also for those who only occasionally enjoy losing themselves in the beauty of gardens.

3011. *National Gardening.* Former titles (until 1986): *National Gardening Association; Gardens for All.* [ISSN: 1052-4096] 1979. bi-m. USD 18 domestic; USD 24 foreign. Ed(s): Shila Patel, Michael MacCaskey.

National Gardening Association, 1100 Dorset St, S Burlington, VT 05403-8000; roseg@garden.org; http://www.garden.org. Illus., index, adv. Sample. Circ: 275000. Vol. ends: Nov/Dec. *Indexed:* GardL. *Aud.:* Ga.

National Gardening is a publication of the National Gardening Association (NGA), which "is a nonprofit leader in plant-based education." The magazine includes an exceptional collection of articles that provide useful strategies for growing flowers, fruits, vegetables, and herbs. It also offers advice on landscaping, basic garden care like pest control, and home and health issues like cooking and crafts. Articles are straightforward and practical, and photographs are inspirational because they come from real gardens of home growers. Many of the articles, plus additional useful features can be found on the NGA web site, www.garden.org. Overall, the magazine successfully fulfills the parent organization's mission "to connect people to gardening in five core fields: plant-based education, health and wellness, environmental stewardship, community development, and responsible home gardening."

3012. *Organic Gardening.* Former titles (until 2003): *O G;* (until 2001): *Organic Gardening;* (until 1988): *Rodale's Organic Gardening;* (until 1985): *Organic Gardening;* (until 1978): *Organic Gardening and Farming.* 1942. bi-m. USD 23.96 domestic; CND 32.96 Canada; USD 42 elsewhere. Ed(s): Scott Meyer. Rodale, Inc., 33 E Minor St, Emmaus, PA 18098; info@rodale.com; http://www.rodale.com. Illus., index, adv. Circ: 300000 Paid. Vol. ends: Dec. Microform: NBI; PQC. Online: EBSCO Publishing, EBSCO Host; Florida Center for Library Automation; Gale; OCLC Online Computer Library Center, Inc.; ProQuest LLC (Ann Arbor); H.W. Wilson. *Indexed:* Agr, B&AI, BiolDig, GardL, IHTDI, MASUSE, RGPR. *Aud.:* Ga.

While its focus is organic gardening techniques, all gardeners will find something to like in this magazine. In general, images are less dazzling than in other gardening magazines, but the color sketches and photographs serve the very practical purpose of illustrating the narrative. Regular features include "Letters," with questions answered and advice given, "Cutting Edge," offering new ideas and gardening innovations, "Dig Deeper," which treats a topic in great depth, and "Beyond the Garden," which discusses topics such as natural health and cooking that are related to organic gardening. If you are an organic gardener, *Organic Gardening* is a must; it treats gardening naturally and organically from every angle. If you are a gardener of any sort, it is a great read that offers new ideas and inspiration.

3013. *Studies in the History of Gardens & Designed Landscapes.* Formerly (until 1997): *The Journal of Garden History.* [ISSN: 1460-1176] 1981. q. GBP 527. Ed(s): John Dixon Hunt. Taylor & Francis Ltd., 4 Park Sq, Milton Park, Abingdon, OX14 4RN, United Kingdom; info@tandf.co.uk; http://www.tandf.co.uk/journals. Illus., index, adv. Sample. Refereed. Vol. ends: Winter. Reprint: PSC. *Indexed:* A&ATA, API, AmH&L, ArtHuCI, ArtInd, BrArAb, BrHumI, GardL, HistAb, IBR, IBZ, NumL. *Bk. rev.:* Number and length vary. *Aud.:* Ac.

Studies in the History of Gardens & Designed Landscapes is a scholarly journal on garden history. Readers of this publication are almost exclusively scholars in garden history or related topics such as art, architecture, design, or other histories. The journal's "main emphasis is on documentation of individual gardens in all parts of the world," although it includes other topics such as design, horticulture, technique, and conservation. Also, it is well known for its book reviews. Photography and other illustration are included.

3014. *Water Gardening.* [ISSN: 1090-6827] 1996. bi-m. USD 20; USD 25; USD 30. Ed(s): Sue Speichert. Water Gardeners, PO Box 607, St John, IN 46373. *Indexed:* GardL. *Aud.:* Hs, Ga, Ac, Sa.

A growing area of interest in landscaping and home gardening is water gardening. A good, basic magazine covering the topic is this one. Articles will appeal to water gardeners of all skill levels and interests, and they cover such topics as design, technology, and selection and care of fish and plants. Special attention is given to ecological issues and concerns in water gardening. Letters, product reviews, illustrations, and experiential narratives are also included.

■ GAY, LESBIAN, BISEXUAL, AND TRANSGENDER

Judith Ohles Kooistra, Collection Development Librarian/Associate Professor, Libraries and Media Services, Kent State University Stark Campus, 6000 Frank Ave. N.W., North Canton, OH 44720; jkooistra@stark.kent.edu

Lori L. Allen McGee, Lecturer of Spanish, Department of Modern & Classical Language Studies, Kent State University Stark Campus, 6000 Frank Ave. N.W., North Canton, OH 44720; lmcgee@stark.kent.edu

Introduction

The political climate of the last few years has led to a polarization of the American people. There are very few who are ambivalent about gay, lesbian, bisexual, and transgender issues; most feel very strongly about what they believe, whether those beliefs are positive toward or negative against gays. However, people's beliefs are generally formed from their background, opinions, stereotypes, media perceptions, and the like; very often, facts are not at the forefront of the formation of their convictions. Unfortunately, facts about these issues can often be inadequate at best; too often, facts are simply nonexistent. Most of what people know, or think they know, comes from personal opinion, experience, and one's familial belief system. What is needed is a wide array of materials that present information about GLBT issues so that the vast spectrum of the GLBT experience can be understood.

There are many questions that society has yet to answer about GLBT people, not the least of which involves the marriage issue. With the onslaught of media coverage during the same-sex marriages in San Francisco in 2004 and the subsequent deluge of articles, essays, and debates, one can recognize the importance of having access to current and accurate information. Related to the marriage debate is the issue of gay adoption. With or without society's approval, gays are adopting; one could then argue that society would benefit if those couples could marry and have the same rights and benefits as their heterosexual counterparts. These are just two examples of the topics that are currently making headlines in magazines and being examined at length in scholarly journals.

With the Religious Right on its rampage against GLBT people, another topic people are contemplating is nature vs. nurture. For example, is "gayness" something genetic, like eye color or height, or is it something we learn and can therefore un-learn? This last example is, of course, what the Right would want us to believe; however, there is no gay person in our experience who has said that they somehow learned to be gay. Therefore, it is of the utmost importance that the general public have access to materials that will help them weed out opinions based on religious fervor and find information based as much as possible on fact and data.

Libraries have long been for both of us the largest and most venerable symbol of education that we have as Americans. Education is the key to fighting the ignorance, bigotry, and hatred that abounds in some parts of our society today. We discuss the concept of education as not solely referring to book knowledge but also to that elusive body of knowledge that E.D. Hirsch, Jr. refers to as "cultural literacy." According to Hirsch, "to be culturally literate is to possess the basic information needed to thrive in a modern world."* This information is available to us not only from traditional modes of learning, but also from more mainstream avenues like magazines, newspapers, and journals. Our libraries, especially those libraries that serve schools and universities, should take on the responsibility of maintaining in their collections those magazines and journals that best reflect the needs of the GLBT members of their community.

The magazines and journals in this GLBT section of *Magazines for Libraries* represent some of the best of what is available to provide information for both the general public and gay, lesbian, bisexual, and transgender persons. These titles describe the issues facing GLBT people and their culture and lives. There are several types of magazines represented in this section. Here we have some of the following: publications that provide new research possibilities and oftentimes hope for those suffering with HIV; scholarly journals that seek out the most heavily researched and documented papers about theoretical aspects of various GLBT subject areas; fun and entertaining magazines; and newsmagazines that keep us informed of what is happening in GLBT life and culture. These titles are clearly important for GLBT people so that they can feel connected with one another and know and understand what is happening in their

world. The titles may be just as important to those who are not in the gay, lesbian, bisexual, or transgender community, for it is in these titles where the rest of Americans can find accurate, current information and scholarship about GLBT lives. It is only with this type of information that people can become educated about issues facing GLBT people.

*Hirsch,, E.D., Jr. Cultural Literacy: What Every American Needs to Know Houghton Mifflin Company, Boston, 1987, p. xiii.

Basic Periodicals

Hs: *The Advocate, Oasis (electronic), Out, XY Magazine;* Ga: *The Advocate, Curve, The Gay & Lesbian Review Worldwide, Out;* Ac: *The Advocate, Curve, The Gay & Lesbian Review Worldwide, GLQ, Harrington Gay Men's Fiction Quarterly, Harrington Lesbian Fiction Quarterly, Journal of Bisexuality, Journal of Homosexuality, Journal of Lesbian Studies, Lambda Update.*

Basic Abstracts and Indexes

Alternative Press Index, Academic Search Premier, Expanded Academic ASAP, Gay and Lesbian Abstracts, GenderWatch, GLBT Life With Full Text, MasterFILE Premier, Sexual Diversity Studies.

3015. A & U: America's AIDS magazine. Formerly (until 1996): *Art & Understanding.* [ISSN: 1545-0554] 1991. m. USD 9.95 (Free to qualified personnel). Ed(s): David Waggoner, Chael Needle. Art & Understanding, Inc., 25 Monroe St, Ste 205, Albany, NY 12210-2743. Illus., adv. Circ: 205000. *Indexed:* IAPV. *Bk. rev.:* 2, 600-1,000 words. *Aud.:* Ga.

Subtitled "America's AIDS Magazine," *A&U* has recently featured a celebrity AIDS advocate—in one way or another—in each issue's cover story. In addition, typically three feature articles are included. This glossy magazine includes a number of photographs and advertisements. Regular departments include the health and wellness features "Wellness Watch" (alternative medicines and therapies), "Treatment Horizons," and "The Culture Of AIDS" (reviews). The magazine is a quick read and is geared toward those who are HIV+ and their family and friends. These days, it seems that would mean almost everyone. *A&U* has a companion web site at www.aumag.org that states, "Articles not found in the print version of *A&U* will appear regularly." Recommended for public libraries.

3016. The Advocate (Los Angeles, 1967): the national gay & lesbian newsmagazine. [ISSN: 0001-8996] 1967. bi-w. m. in Jan, Aug. USD 39.97 domestic; USD 69.94 foreign. Ed(s): Judy Wieder, John Jameson. L P I Media, Inc, PO Box 4371, Los Angeles, CA 90078. Illus., adv. Circ: 109947. Online: EBSCO Publishing, EBSCO Host; Florida Center for Library Automation; Gale; OCLC Online Computer Library Center, Inc.; ProQuest LLC (Ann Arbor); H.W. Wilson. *Indexed:* AltPI, BRI, CBRI, CWI, GendWatch, LRI, MASUSE, PAIS, RGPR. *Bk. rev.:* 1-5, 50-100 words. *Aud.:* Hs, Ga, Ac.

A biweekly newsmagazine, *The Advocate*, in existence since 1967, functions as a gay and lesbian version of *Time* or *Newsweek*. Cover stories generally focus on current topics of interest to American gays and lesbians. For example, recent issues have covered such topics as the military's "don't ask, don't tell" policy, the film "Brokeback Mountain," Chicago's Gay Games and Montreal's Outgames, and Rosie O'Donnell's and Kelli Carpenter's R Family Cruises. Regular sections include the following: television, book, and film reviews; "GenQ," which focuses on the younger generation of gays; and "The Advocate Report," which provides up-to-date news items. *The Advocate* is a glossy, easy-to-read publication that actually holds interest for a gay-friendly straight audience as well as a gay and lesbian audience. It is a key magazine for keeping abreast of important gay and lesbian issues in the United States. It also has a well-organized and useful web site at www.advocate.com. In addition to providing archives of past issues, the web site is updated daily and includes a daily news digest, an "Advocate Poll," and a list of current lesbian and gay events throughout the nation. "Gay & Lesbian Resources" provides links to various web sites, divided by general subject area. *The Advocate* is a key resource for libraries. It is a must-have for keeping patrons up-to-date on issues of importance to gays and lesbians, issues that actually resonate beyond the gay and lesbian world. Very highly recommended for all libraries.

3017. Bay Area Reporter. 1971. w. Thu. Free. Ed(s): Cynthia Laird. Benro Enterprise, Inc., 395 Ninth St., San Francisco, CA 94103-3831. Circ: 36500 Paid. *Bk. rev.:* 2, 200-500 words. *Aud.:* Ga.

The *Bay Area Reporter* is the weekly newspaper for the gay, lesbian, bisexual, and transgender population in the San Francisco Bay area and has been a presence there since 1971. Accessible to all GLBT Americans at www.ebar.com, the *Bay Area Reporter* can now keep all Americans abreast of relevant news from the San Francisco area. The *Bay Area Reporter* describes itself in the following way: "San Francisco's oldest and largest local newspaper of record serving the lesbian, gay, bisexual and transgender communities. Founded in 1971, B.A.R. is regarded for its original writing covering news and entertainment relevant to our lives." Regular sections include Community News, Commentary, Obituaries, Classifieds, Arts & Entertainment, and Personals. An important addition for public libraries, particularly those on the West Coast.

3018. Curve: the best-selling lesbian magazine. Formerly (until vol.6, 1996): *Deneuve.* [ISSN: 1087-867X] 1991. 10x/yr. USD 21.95 domestic; USD 33.95 Canada; USD 43.95 elsewhere. Ed(s): Dane Anderson-Minshall. Outspoken Enterprises, Inc., 1550 Bryant St. Ste 510, San Francisco, CA 94103. Illus., adv. Circ: 68200 Paid and free. Online: Florida Center for Library Automation; Gale; OCLC Online Computer Library Center, Inc. *Indexed:* AltPI, CWI. *Bk. rev.:* 4-6, 100-400 words. *Aud.:* Hs, Ga, Ac.

Published ten times a year, *Curve* is a glitzy, entertaining read for lesbians. Brief articles and blurbs make for fun reading, and all of this is peppered with color photographs and interspersed with advertisements. Topics covered include entertainment, lesbian diversity, celebrities, boos, travel, and sex, among others. *Curve* "has been named Best Gay and Lesbian Publication by the Gay and Lesbian Alliance Against Defamation (GLAAD), and we also took top honors in the category of Best Rock Reporting for our behind-the-scenes profile of Melissa Etheridge." Recommended for public libraries that cater to a lesbian clientele.

3019. Electronic Gay Community Magazine. 1988. d. Free. Electronic Gay Community Magazine, http://www.awes.com/egcm. *Aud.:* Hs, Ga, Ac.

In continuous publication since 1988, the *Electronic Gay Community Magazine* is a great free online resource for GLBT people. Simply designed, it is very user-friendly and packed with information. Departments include "Lifestyle," where one can find articles on topics such as pride, ageism, and gay parents; "Politics" and "Judicial," which are currently filled with articles on gay marriage; "Editorials"; "AIDS"; "Youth," which has articles about gay education in schools and gay/straight alliances; "Health"; "Reviews," with commentary about "Brokeback Mountain" and the comedian Margaret Cho; and "Gay TV." There is also a page of links to popular gay and lesbian advocate web sites. *EGCM* is a great resource. URL: www.awes.com/egcm

3020. G L Q: a journal of lesbian and gay studies. [ISSN: 1064-2684] 1993. q. USD 172 (Individuals, USD 38). Ed(s): Annamarie Jagose, Ann Cvetkovich. Duke University Press, 905 W Main St, Ste 18 B, Durham, NC 27701; subscriptions@dukeupress.edu; http://www.dukeupress.edu. Illus., adv. Refereed. Circ: 675 Paid and controlled. Online: EBSCO Publishing, EBSCO Host; Gale; HighWire Press; OCLC Online Computer Library Center, Inc.; OhioLINK; Project MUSE; SwetsWise Online Content. Reprint: PSC. *Indexed:* AltPI, AmHI, ArtHuCI, HumInd, IBSS, IBZ, MLA-IB, SSCI, SWA, SociolAb. *Bk. rev.:* 1-2, 1,200 words. *Aud.:* Ac.

GLQ: A Journal of Lesbian and Gay Studies is considered the preeminent scholarly and theoretical journal in the field of GLBT studies and queer theory. Including in its authors and editorial and advisory boards some of the most important scholars in this growing field, *GLQ* issues contain the latest theoretical research, book and film reviews, and the "GLQ Archives," primary materials that typically have not previously been published. *GLQ* is heavily indexed so that its articles can be easily accessed by serious scholars. In its self-description, the journal characterizes the quarterly in this way: "Providing a much-needed forum for interdisciplinary discussion, *GLQ* publishes scholarship, criticism, and commentary in areas as diverse as law, science studies, religion, political

science, and literary studies. Its aim is to offer queer perspectives on all issues touching on sex and sexuality." This journal should be found in all academic libraries.

3021. The Gay & Lesbian Review Worldwide. Formerly (until 2000): *Harvard Gay & Lesbian Review.* [ISSN: 1532-1118] 1994. bi-m. USD 60 (Individuals, USD 19.75; USD 10 newsstand/cover). Ed(s): Richard Schneider, Jr. Harvard Gay & Lesbian Review Inc., PO Box 180300, Boston, MA 02118; info@glreview.com. Illus., adv. Circ: 9000 Paid. *Indexed:* AltPI, AmHI, BRI, CWI, GendWatch, HumInd, RILM. *Bk. rev.:* 10-15, 500-1000 words. *Aud.:* Ac, Ga.

From six to nine feature articles generally grace this well-written, interesting magazine that rivals titles such as *The New Yorker* in tone and substance. In addition to the features, the magazine includes book reviews, poems, guest opinions, an artist's profile, a lists of conferences/events, and calls for submissions, among other appealing items. Self-identified as addressing gay and lesbian "literary culture," *The Gay & Lesbian Review Worldwide* tackled such interesting topics during the spring and summer of 2006 as "Brokeback Mountain," Barney Frank, Lesbian separatism, artist David Hockney, and singer/songwriter Janis Ian. *The Review* describes its mission in the following way: "to provide a forum for enlightened discussion of issues and ideas of importance to lesbians and gay men; to advance gay and lesbian culture by providing a quality vehicle for its best writers and thinkers; and to educate a broader public on gay and lesbian topics." Considered essential for all public and academic libraries.

3022. Gay Law Net. Formerly: *Gay Law News.* m. Free. Ed(s): David B Allan. Gay Law Net, gaylawnet@labyrinth.net.au; http://www.gaylawnet.com/. *Bk. rev.:* Number and length vary. *Aud.:* Hs, Ga, Ac.

Gay Law Net is by far one of the most comprehensive law sites for GLBT people. It is very user-friendly, especially the index, which has all the information on the site in one place. Some of the departments include "News Archive," "Attorney Listing," and "Laws Worldwide." One of the most interesting departments is the "E-zine" where one can find book reviews, articles on domestic partnering, education, family law, human rights, health, marriage, parenting, religion, and wills and estates, to name just a few. *Gay Law Net* is truly "dedicated to providing general information, news, and resources concerning the law as it affects the global gay, lesbian, bisexual, transsexual, and intersex community." URL: www.gaylawnet.com

3023. Genre Magazine. [ISSN: 1074-5246] 1991. 12x/yr. USD 19.95. Ed(s): Chris Ciompi, Mark Liebermann. Genre Media Llc., 333 Seventh Ave., 4th Fl, New York, NY 10001. Illus., adv. Circ: 50000 Paid. *Bk. rev.:* 3-8, 50-150 words. *Aud.:* Ga.

With fashion shoots, interviews, reviews about all types of media, a large travel section, and plenty of (clean) eye candy for gay men, *Genre* is a hip, glossy magazine geared toward the younger crowd. Interviews with gay-friendly celebrities as well as features such as "It's On! Gay Games Vs. Outgames" and "Coming Out Younger: Is It Any Easier Today?" are also included in the magazine. The *Genre* web site, www.genremagazine.com, includes the "BladeWire" with daily news updates. The web site describes the magazine in the following fashion: "*Genre* is the complete lifestyle sourcebook for gay men. Every month, the magazine throws a spotlight on the hottest, the freshest and the best—in entertainment, the arts, fashion, home design, automotive, technology, health and fitness, grooming and travel." Recommended for public libraries.

3024. Girlfriends: lesbian culture, politics, and entertainment. [ISSN: 1078-8875] 1994. m. Ed(s): Heather Findlay. H A F Publishing, 3415 Cesar Chavez, Ste 101, San Francisco, CA 94110; staff@girlfriendsmag.com; http://www.girlfriendsmag.com. Illus. Sample. Circ: 30000. *Bk. rev.:* 6-9, 80-500 words. *Aud.:* Ga, Ac.

Sometimes described as a *People* for lesbians, *Girlfriends* is a young, hip, fun magazine. "Features" generally includes two to three entertaining articles and "Queer as Life" includes sections on Relationships, Style, Health, and the appropriately and cleverly titled "Dykestinations." In addition, the "Girl Guide" includes reviews of television, film and DVDs, books, and music. *Girlfriends* has a companion web site at www.girlfriendsmag.com that includes parts of the print issue as well as additional online features such as Girlfriends Personals and Classifieds. *Girlfriends'* own mission statement reads: "*Girlfriends* is a national monthly magazine for lesbians. Our mission is to provide entertaining, visually pleasing coverage of culture, politics, and entertainment from an informed and critical lesbian perspective." This title is recommended for public and academic libraries with a lesbian clientele or a popular culture focus.

3025. *Harrington Gay Men's Literary Quarterly.* Formerly (until 2006): *Harrington Gay Men's Fiction Quarterly.* [ISSN: 1556-9241] 1998. q. USD 125 print & online eds. Ed(s): Thomas L Long. Harrington Park Press, 10 Alice St, Binghamton, NY 13904; getinfo@haworthpress.com; http://www.haworthpress.com/. Adv. Sample. Circ: 201 Paid. *Indexed:* AmHI, IBR, IBZ. *Aud.:* Ga, Ac.

With many college and university programs including GLBT studies majors (or at least a few courses that include GLBT authors), there is a demand for journals with diverse literary voices. This is where a title such as the re-named *Harrington Gay Men's Literary Quarterly* comes in. Previously the *Harrington Gay Men's Fiction Quarterly*, this journal provides a venue for established and upcoming GLBT writers. Affiliated with both the Council of Editors of Learned Journals and the GL/Q Caucus of the Modern Language Association, *HGMLQ* provides an aesthetically pleasing blend of prose, poetry, critical essays, and original art. Thematic issues have revolved around such topics as coming out, parenting and family, politics, and relationships. As described on its corresponding web site, *HGMLQ* is "an international journal [that] highlights global queer diversity; rediscovers lost voices, and explores edgy postmodern writing, erotica, poetry, fiction, drama, film, literary and cultural criticism, and memoir. This journal will help anyone—whether a scholar, educator, student, gay fiction/literature fan or writer—gain a better understanding of these genres." Highly recommended for any library that supports a composition program.

3026. *Harrington Lesbian Literary Quarterly.* Formerly (until 2006): *Harrington Lesbian Fiction Quarterly.* [ISSN: 1556-9225] 2000. q. USD 125 print & online eds. Ed(s): Judith Stelboum. Alice Street Editions, 10 Alice St, Binghamton, NY 13904; getinfo@haworthpress.com; http://www.haworthpress.com/. Sample. *Indexed:* AmHI, FemPer, IBR, IBZ, MLA-IB. *Aud.:* Ac, Ga.

International in scope, the *Harrington Lesbian Literary Quarterly* highlights the best of lesbian authors and artists. Any institution of higher education with courses covering lesbian writers will want to include *HLLQ* in its collection, for it covers a wide range of styles of writing, such as short stories, critical essays, drama, poetry, and excerpts from novels. Authors and artists included in the journal are of diverse ages and ethnicities. The publication is both appealing to the eye and interesting to read. In describing the journal, the Haworth web site indicates the following: "Affiliated with the Gay/Lesbian Caucus of the Modern Language Association and the Council of Editors of Learned Journals—and critical for any college or university library where LGBT studies are in the curricula—the *Harrington Lesbian Literary Quarterly* is designed to serve as an essential professional publication for faculty and students engaged in literary and culture studies. It features artwork, graphics, and photography reflecting the themes of lesbian life experiences." Re-titled from the *Harrington Lesbian Fiction Quarterly*, the *HLLQ* is a fine addition to any library in which students need to find quality lesbian writing. Highly recommended.

3027. *Instinct.* [ISSN: 1096-0058] 1997. 10x/yr. USD 14.95 domestic; USD 38.95 foreign. Ed(s): Mike Wood, Robbie Daw. Instinct Publishing, 11440 Ventura Blvd, Ste 200, Studio City, CA 91604-3154. Adv. Circ: 85000. *Aud.:* Ga.

Instinct is a glitzy, colorful, popular magazine for gay males. The covers boast articles that rival those of magazines such as *Cosmopolitan*. For example, covers of recent issues include such attention-grabbers as "Pimp My Pride: We Hook You Up!;" "Hey, Nice Package: 'I Have a Crush On My UPS Guy';" "Golden Guy: Frisky & Fearless After 70!;" and "Addicted to Love? Might as Well Face It . . . You're a Love Sponge." An interesting regular feature includes a write-up on a gay-friendly woman titled "Chick We'd Switch For." Articles in *Instinct* are brief and entertaining. The web site, www.instinctmag.com, includes such features as "Bachelor of the Month" and "Mom of the Month," as well as other interesting tidbits not found in the print magazine. Archives of past issues can also be found on the web site. This monthly magazine is recommended for public libraries with a young gay male clientele.

3028. *Journal of Bisexuality.* [ISSN: 1529-9716] 2000. q. USD 340 print & online eds. Ed(s): Dr. Fritz Klein. Haworth Press, Inc., 10 Alice St, Binghamton, NY 13904-1580; getinfo@haworthpress.com; http://www.haworthpress.com. Adv. Sample. Refereed. Circ: 122 Paid. Reprint: HAW. *Indexed:* AmHI, IBR, IBZ, PAIS, PsycInfo, SFSA, SSA, SWA, SWR&A, SociolAb. *Bk. rev.:* Various number and length. *Aud.:* Ac.

An important title in the GLBT field, the *Journal of Bisexuality* is one of the only titles to cater specifically to the topic of bisexuals and bisexuality. Started in 2000, this quarterly publication is a refereed journal that often focuses on one topic of interest, such as "Plural Loves: Designs for Bi and Poly Living," "Bi Men: Coming Out Every Which Way," and "Current Research on Bisexuality." The thematic issues typically have a guest editor and are usually also offered for purchase as monographic separates. Most issues include several well-researched and extensively documented articles as well as bibliographies and film and book reviews. The *Journal of Bisexuality*, published by the venerable Haworth Press, is heavily indexed and covers various subject areas. It "is the first professional quarterly to publish both professional articles and serious essays on bisexuality and its meaning for the individual, the community, and society." This journal is recommended for academic libraries and for larger public libraries.

3029. *Journal of Gay & Lesbian Mental Health.* Formerly (until 2008): *Journal of Gay & Lesbian Psychotherapy.* [ISSN: 1935-9705] 1988. q. USD 270. Ed(s): Dr. Jack Drescher. Haworth Press, Inc., 10 Alice St, Binghamton, NY 13904-1580; getinfo@haworthpress.com; http://www.haworthpress.com. Illus., adv. Sample. Refereed. Circ: 314 Paid. Microform: PQC. Online: EBSCO Publishing, EBSCO Host; OCLC Online Computer Library Center, Inc.; ProQuest LLC (Ann Arbor); SwetsWise Online Content. Reprint: HAW. *Indexed:* AbAn, CWI, GendWatch, IMFL, PsycInfo, SSA, SWR&A, SociolAb. *Aud.:* Ac.

The official journal of the Association of Gay & Lesbian Psychiatrists, the *Journal of Gay & Lesbian Psychotherapy* is another title from the prolific publishing house, Haworth Press. Published since 1988 and geared toward scholars and practitioners, this quarterly often has themed issues, e.g., "A Gay Man's Guide to Prostate Cancer," "Handbook of LGBT Issues in Community Mental Health," " Gay and Lesbian Parenting," and "Addictions in the Gay and Lesbian Community." These thematic issues are also available as monographic separates through Haworth Press. International in scope and including an impressive roster of scholars and practitioners in the psychiatric, psychological, and mental health fields, the *Journal of Gay & Lesbian Psychotherapy* also appeals to the most well-versed of professionals. "The primary editorial goal of the journal is to present the data of clinical psychotherapy with lesbian and gay patients/clients. While maintaining a strong psychodynamic focus, the journal is also committed to covering the full range of therapeutic assessment and interventions with gay and lesbian patients/clients, including cognitive, behavioral, and eclectic approaches, individual and couples therapy, psychopharmacological intervention, and alcohol and substance abuse treatment." The journal is indexed in a number of impressive academic indexes, and therefore students in various disciplines will be able to access its important contributions. A very important addition to academic libraries supporting medical and psychological collections.

3030. *Journal of Gay & Lesbian Social Services: issues in practice, policy & research.* [ISSN: 1053-8720] 1994. q. USD 330 print & online eds. Ed(s): Jeane W Anastas. Haworth Press, Inc., 10 Alice St, Binghamton, NY 13904-1580; getinfo@haworthpress.com; http://www.haworthpress.com. Illus., adv. Sample. Refereed. Circ: 280 Paid. Microform: PQC. Online: EBSCO Publishing, EBSCO Host; Northern Light Technology, Inc.; OCLC Online Computer Library Center, Inc.; ProQuest LLC (Ann Arbor); SwetsWise Online Content. Reprint: HAW. *Indexed:* AgeL, CABA, CJA, CWI, GendWatch, IBR, IBZ, IMFL, PAIS, PsycInfo, RiskAb, SFSA, SSA, SWA, SWR&A, SociolAb, V&AA. *Bk. rev.:* 0-3, 1,000-2,500 words. *Aud.:* Ac, Sa.

In existence since 1994, this quarterly publication includes on its editorial board an impressive list of scholars in the social services field. It is not surprising, then, that the articles provide well-documented, original scholarship and research for practitioners and academics. Many issues are centered around special themes, such as "Gay Men Living with Chronic Illnesses and Disabilities: From Crisis to Crossroads" and "Gay and Lesbian Rights Organizing: Community-Based Strategies." A list of previous themes is included at the beginning of each issue. These special issues, which are overseen by one or more guest editors, are also offered for purchase as monographic separates. The journal self-identifies as focusing on articles "based on research, qualitative or quantitative," although other forms of scholarly papers are found in the journal as well. Indeed, this is a very important publication in the social services field. Libraries that support significant social services collections should have this title.

3031. *Journal of Homosexuality.* [ISSN: 0091-8369] 1974. q. USD 630 print & online eds. Ed(s): John De Cecco. Harrington Park Press, 10 Alice St, Binghamton, NY 13904; getinfo@haworthpress.com; http://www.haworthpress.com/. Illus., adv. Sample. Refereed. Circ: 811 Paid. Microform: PQC. Online: EBSCO Publishing, EBSCO Host; OCLC Online Computer Library Center, Inc.; ProQuest LLC (Ann Arbor); SwetsWise Online Content. Reprint: HAW. *Indexed:* ASSIA, AbAn, AgeL, AltPI, AmHI, ArtHuCI, BRI, CBRI, CJA, CWI, ExcerpMed, GendWatch, H&SSA, HEA, HRA, IBR, IBSS, IBZ, IMFL, LRI, PAIS, PsycInfo, RI-1, RILM, RiskAb, SFSA, SSA, SSCI, SWA, SWR&A, SociolAb, V&AA, WSA. *Bk. rev.:* 4, 2,000-5,000 words. *Aud.:* Ac.

No academic collection with gay and lesbian periodical titles would be complete without the *Journal of Homosexuality*. This scholarly publication, which has passed its 50th volume, is a preeminent title in the gay and lesbian field. It is self-described as "devoted to scholarly research on homosexuality, including sexual practices and gender roles and their cultural, historical, interpersonal, and modern social contexts." This peer-reviewed journal is generally divided into three major sections: the largest section contains scholarly articles, sometimes encompassing a theme; the second section consists of book reviews; and the third section "is an annotated bibliography of references selected for their importance to research on human sexuality, sexual preference, and social sex roles." The journal is indexed in virtually every index of note, including those covering medical sciences, social sciences, anthropology, and women's studies, to name a few. Grounded mainly in the social sciences, the *Journal of Homosexuality* is a title that has been around for a long time and is here to stay. Its scholarship and research is on a very high level. Highly recommended for academic collections.

Journal of Interdisciplinary Gender Studies. See Gender Studies section.

3032. *Journal of L G B T Youth.* Formerly (until 2007): *Journal of Gay & Lesbian Issues in Education.* [ISSN: 1936-1653] 2003. q. USD 330 print & online eds. Ed(s): James T Sears. Haworth Press, Inc., 10 Alice St, Binghamton, NY 13904-1580; getinfo@haworthpress.com; http://www.haworthpress.com. Adv. Refereed. Reprint: HAW. *Indexed:* EAA, IBR, IBZ, PAIS, SWA. *Aud.:* Ac, Sa.

A quarterly journal published by the esteemed Haworth Press, the *Journal of Gay & Lesbian Issues in Education* includes articles devoted to various issues in education from scholars, administrators, and other practitioners. The editorial board is also made up of the best educational scholars and practitioners. Articles are well researched, providing recent scholarship "directly related to educational policy, professional practice curriculum development, and pedagogy." Many issues revolve around a theme, such as "Trans Youth," "Gay-Straight Alliances," and "Researching Queer Youth." Issues also often include articles about practical applications of theoretical concepts. This combination of scholarly and down-to-earth articles makes the journal an appealing one for both educational scholars and practitioners. In addition to these qualities, the journal has an international youth advisory board made up of GLBT teenagers from ages 16 to 24 who are included to provide a unique and necessary voice. "Every educational practitioner, policymaker, and scholar interested in queer-related issues in elementary, middle, and secondary schools as well as undergraduate level colleges should consider a subscription to this vital journal!" The web site for the journal can be found at www.jtsears.com/jglie.htm. Highly recommended for academic and public library collections with patrons who work in the educational field.

3033. *Journal of Lesbian Studies.* [ISSN: 1089-4160] 1997. q. USD 320 print & online eds. Ed(s): Esther D Rothblum. Harrington Park Press, 10 Alice St, Binghamton, NY 13904; getinfo@haworthpress.com; http://www.haworthpress.com/. Illus., adv. Sample. Refereed. Circ: 220 Paid. Microform: PQC. Online: EBSCO Publishing, EBSCO Host; OCLC Online Computer Library Center, Inc.; ProQuest LLC (Ann Arbor); SwetsWise Online Content. Reprint: HAW. *Indexed:* AmHI, CJA, CWI, FemPer, GendWatch, IBR, IBZ, PAIS, PsycInfo, SSA, SWA, SWR&A, SociolAb. *Bk. rev.:* Various number and length. *Aud.:* Ac.

The *Journal of Lesbian Studies* is a quarterly publication that explores, in scholarly and intellectually significant ways, various aspects of lesbian life and culture. Each issue has a major theme and is compiled by a guest editor or editors. Themed issues have included such topics as "Lesbian Ex-Lovers: The Really Long-Term Relationships" and "Lesbians, Feminisms, and Psychoanalysis: The Second Wave." Articles are written by a variety of scholars and are well researched and referenced. Each issue of the *Journal of Lesbian Studies* is also available as a monographic separate, a useful feature for libraries or individuals who are interested in a few topics or issues covered by the journal but do not want to purchase a subscription. *Journal of Lesbian Studies* offers intriguing, quality articles in a field that otherwise does not receive enough attention. Recommended for academic libraries that support GLBT courses.

3034. *Lambda Update.* [ISSN: 1058-949X] 1976. 3x/yr. USD 40. Ed(s): Joneil Adriano. Lambda Legal Defense & Education Fund, Inc., 120 Wall St, Ste 1500, New York, NY 10005-3904; lambdalegal@lambdalegal.org; http://www.lambdalegal.org. Illus., adv. Circ: 20000. *Aud.:* Ga, Ac.

Lambda Update is an official publication of Lambda Legal, which "is a national organization committed to achieving full recognition of the civil rights of lesbians, gay men, bisexuals, transgender people and those with HIV through impact litigation, education and public policy work." While the organization works towards civil rights for GLBT and HIV-positive people, the *Update* provides a forum for reading about the work that Lambda Legal has undertaken, laws that affect GLBT Americans, and developing public policy. *Lambda Update* is a very important title for libraries to keep patrons abreast of the progress, or lack thereof, of the public policy and legal developments in the GLBT and HIV arenas.

3035. *Lesbian Connection.* [ISSN: 1081-3217] 1974. bi-m. Free to Lesbians worldwide. Elsie Publishing Institute, PO Box 811, E Lansing, MI 48826; elsiepub@aol.com. Illus., adv. Sample. Circ: 23000. *Bk. rev.:* 2-4, 200-300 words. *Aud.:* Hs, Ga.

Small but packed with information, *Lesbian Connection* is truly "for, by and about lesbians." Funded by donations, this publication features such sections as "News Items," which gives general information about lesbians in the news; "Bits & Pieces," containing happenings in cities across the United States; "Passings," presenting heartfelt eulogies of women who have died; "Letters" and "Responses" from readers and members; "Contact Dykes," a mailing list of women "who volunteer to provide information about their area to traveling lesbians or women new to town"; "Festival Forum"; and a large section of "Ads & Announcements" offering information about many topics including stores, art, music, books, lesbian groups, campgrounds, and retreats. Each edition also contains several strips of "Dykes to Watch Out For," a poignant and hilarious look at lesbian life. *Lesbian Connection* is a publication that truly cares about it readers, evidenced by the personal nature of the writing and information. *Lesbian Connection* is also available on tape for readers "who have difficulty with the printed version." The fact that *Lesbian Connection* covers happenings across America makes it a welcome publication for lesbians from coast to coast.

3036. *Lesbian - Gay Law Notes.* [ISSN: 8755-9021] 1980. m. except Aug. USD 55 domestic; USD 60 in Canada & Mexico; USD 70 elsewhere. Ed(s): Arthur S Leonard. Lesbian & Gay Law Association Foundation of Greater New York, 799 Broadway, Ste 340, New York, NY 10003-6811; le-gal@interport.net; http://www.le-gal.org. *Aud.:* Ga, Ac.

Useful to both professionals and laypersons, *Lesbian/Gay Law Notes* provides briefs of recent legal decisions affecting the GLBT community. Published by LeGaL, the Foundation of the Lesbian & Gay Law Association of Greater New York, *Lesbian/Gay Law Notes* reads like a legal newspaper, yet the articles are not difficult to read for those not in the field. Each issue begins with a headline story; for example, a recent headline was "Another N.Y. Appeals Panel Rejects Marriage Bids." There are regular columns, the largest of which is "Lesbian/Gay Legal News." Other regular columns are "AIDS & Related Legal Notes," and "Publications & Announcements." *Lesbian/Gay Law Notes* is a necessary addition to larger public libraries and any university library needing legal publications.

3037. *Lesbian News.* [ISSN: 0739-1803] 1975. m. USD 45 domestic; USD 55 Canada; USD 65 elsewhere. Ed(s): Claudia Piras. L N Publishing Inc., PO Box 55, Torrance, CA 90507. Illus., adv. Circ: 40000 Paid and free. Online: EBSCO Publishing, EBSCO Host. *Indexed:* AltPI, MASUSE. *Bk. rev.:* 8-10, 300-500 words. *Aud.:* Hs, Ga.

Lesbian News is an oversized news magazine with a newsprint interior and glossy cover. The covers generally feature a woman currently making news in the lesbian community. Recent covers have featured rock star Melissa Etheridge and WNBA great Sheryl Swoopes. Inside, readers will find many news articles, including international news and transgender updates. Lifestyle sections include poetry, interviews, culture, humor, and self-help. One regular department is "Lesbians on Location," a photo spread of pages on the "who's who" of the California lesbian scene. Other regular departments are "Ask Dr. Jane," "At the Movies," "Listen to the Music," "Travel," "A Look at Books," "Community Access," "Classifieds," and "Calendar of Events," among others. For those who like to check on lesbian happenings via the Internet, there is also a great companion web site, www.lesbiannews.com, with just as much news as the print magazine, plus links and subscription information. *Lesbian News* boasts that it is the "longest-running national-lesbian publication," currently celebrating 31 years in print. Although most of the advertisements and classifieds pertain to the Southern California area, the breadth of the news and culture covered makes this a useful publication for any lesbian audience.

3038. *Metro Source: a celebration and exploration of urban gay life.* [ISSN: 1529-935X] 1990. 6x/yr. USD 19.95. Ed(s): Richard Walsh. Metrosource Publishing, Inc., 180 Varick St, 5th Fl, New York, NY 10014-4606. Illus., adv. Circ: 15018 Paid. *Bk. rev.:* 6, 240-360 words. *Aud.:* Ga.

Metro Source is an upscale lifestyle magazine geared mostly toward gay men, but it may also be of interest to gay-friendly people as well. Published bimonthly, *Metro Source* comes out in three separate issues each time: one (somewhat thin) national issue and two full issues, one for the New York area and one for Los Angeles. Each issue has an attractive man on the cover, usually a model or celebrity, and the articles revolve around a theme. Recent themes have been "The Art & Design Issue," "The Travel Issue," and "The Pride Issue." Each issue also has regular departments that are fairly self-explanatory: "Metroscope," "Metrodiary," "Metrobooks," "Metromusic," and "MetroDVD," to name a few. The New York and Los Angeles issues include information about area restaurants, hot spots, and business and community resouces. *Metro Source* also has a great web site, www.metrosource.com, where one can find just as much, if not more, information as in the magazine. Libraries on the East and West Coasts will want the New York and Los Angeles issues, respectively, while others with an active gay population will want the national issue.

Michigan Journal of Gender & Law. See Law section.

3039. *New York Blade News.* 1997. w. USD 35 for 6 mos. Ed(s): Lisa Keen, Inga Sorenson. Window Media LLC, 242 W 30th St, 4th Fl, New York, NY 10001; http://www.nyblade.com. Adv. Circ: 50000. *Aud.:* Ga.

The *New York Blade* is, of course, a local newspaper, but its contents are of interest to GLBT people around the nation. With columns about health, religion, legal news, art, theater, DVD and music reviews, plus national and international news, it is a great source of information that gives its readers an idea of the current climate for gays and lesbians in America. Published weekly, the calendar section is useful for anyone in the New York area or anyone planning a trip to the Big Apple. There is also a useful companion web site, www.nyblade.com, where readers can stay up-to-date on all New York and national news. This is not only an important newspaper for the New England area, it is also a great addition for any national library with a metropolitan clientele.

3040. *Out.* [ISSN: 1062-7928] 1992. 12x/yr. USD 17.95 domestic; USD 34.95 foreign; USD 4.99 newsstand/cover. Ed(s): Brendan Lemon. L P I Media, Inc, 245 W. 17th St., Ste. 1200, New York, NY 10011. Illus., adv. Circ: 115429 Paid. Microform: PQC. Online: EBSCO Publishing, EBSCO Host. *Indexed:* PAIS. *Bk. rev.:* 6-9, 50-400 words. *Aud.:* Hs, Ga, Ac.

Owned by the same company that publishes *The Advocate*, *Out* is LPI Media's lifestyle magazine for gay men, and one of the best of its type. Published monthly, with a hot guy on each cover, *Out* provides up-to-date information on style, music, movies, what's hot and what's not, plus advice, horoscopes, and health. Recent cover headlines have been "Swimsuit Special: 18 Pages of Guy Candy," and "White Hot Fashion Sizzles Under the Miami Sky." In its pages one can also find articles about Hollywood actors, film reviews, and art and design. It also has a user-friendly web site, www.out.com, with daily gossip, advice, horoscopes, and reader polls, plus an archive of past issues. *Out* is a must for all libraries.

3041. *Passport.* 2000. bi-m. USD 19.95 United States; USD 25.95 in Canada & Mexico; USD 35.95 elsewhere. Ed(s): Reed Ide. Q Communications, Inc., 584 Castro St, Ste 521, San Francisco, CA 94114. Adv. *Aud.:* Ga.

Colorful and glossy pages and hot models mark *Passport* as one of the top gay travel magazines. Recent cover features have included "What's New in Mexico City," "Ski Parties," "2006 Swimwear, Brazilian Heat!" "Sensational Spring Breaks," and "Romance & Adventure South Africa." Each issue has articles on the hot spots of the (gay) world, and personal accounts from travelers on what was good and bad about their trip. Regular departments include "Curious Traveler," where readers can share tips, comments, and recommendations; "Globetrotting," highlighting one destination in each issue; "Travel Bound," recommendations of books and travel guides; "Special Effects," a look at exciting new products for the traveler; "World Beat," a list of hot spots, events, and celebrations; and "Dreamscape," a featured spa getaway. Perhaps the most practical column is "Business Class," a guide, with the gay business traveler in mind, to hotels, restaurants, entertainment, and the like in various world cities. There is also a companion web site at www.passportmagazine.com with articles, links, and subscription information. *Passport* would be welcomed in larger libraries in metropolitan areas or in libraries with large travel sections.

3042. *Q V Magazine: gay Latino men's journal.* [ISSN: 1522-7588] 1997. bi-m. USD 29.95; USD 4 newsstand/cover per issue. Ed(s): Demetrio Roldan. Q V Magazine, Box 9700, Long Beach, CA 90810. Adv. *Aud.:* Ga.

In Hispanic culture, it is sometimes difficult if not impossible to be gay and Latino at the same time. *Q V Magazine* offers a refuge of sorts for gay Latinos to meet and explore ideas about others like themselves. Published bimonthly, *Q V Magazine*, where the Q V stands for the Latin phrase *Quo Vadis* ("Where are you going?"), claims to be the "nation's largest and most respected gay Latino magazine." Full of articles on social issues, politics, business, travel, and entertainment, *Q V Magazine* presents gay Latinos in a positive light. In its pages are interviews, surveys, advice (from "Dear Papi"), astrology (from "La Chicharona"), and lots of ads with sexy Latino men. For libraries with a Hispanic clientele, this magazine is a must.

3043. *R F D: a country journal for gay men everywhere.* [ISSN: 0149-709X] 1974. q. USD 25 domestic; USD 40 foreign; USD 7.75 newsstand/cover per issue. RFD Press, PO Box 68, Liberty, TN 37095; mail@rfdmag.org. Illus., adv. Circ: 1500 Paid. *Indexed:* AltPI. *Bk. rev.:* 1-2, 400-1,000 words. *Aud.:* Ga.

R F D Magazine is like a *Farmer's Almanac* for the radical-fairie scene. Full of poetry, art, photography (mostly nude), and essays, *R F D* offers a way for those gays on the edge of modern society to express themselves in ways that may not be easily done elsewhere. In many issues, there are also articles that are metaphysical in nature or essays that explore the "hidden" side of life. A recent issue is about the tenth anniversary of the Zuni Mountain Fairies, with most of its content about this way of life. One can also find in *R F D* a number of reader letters, announcements, and remembrances. *R F D* is recommended for any library with a collection of metaphysical or natural health–related titles.

Sexualities. See Sexuality section.

3044. *Trans-Health: the online magazine of health and fitness for transsexual and transgendered people.* 2001. q. Trans-Health, info@trans-health.com; http://www.trans-health.com. *Aud.:* Hs, Ga, Ac, Sa.

Trans-Health is a global transgender and transsexual resource compiled by three people, one from the United States and two from Canada. Under the heading "What's New?" can be found current information about transgender and transsexual happenings around the world. There are also many topics to choose from for more information about transgender and transsexual issues. These topics are "Aging," "Body modification," "Disability," "Fitness and training," "Health and wellbeing," "Health care services," "Hormones," "Mental and emotional health," "Nutrition," "Origins," "Sexuality," "Sports and competition," "Surgery," and "Transitioning." *Trans-Health* is a great resource for transgender and transsexual people, and also for those wishing to learn more about transgender issues. URL: www.trans-health.com

3045. *Transgender Tapestry: the journal for persons interested in crossdressing & transsexualism.* Formerly (until 1995): *Tapestry.* [ISSN: 1083-0006] 1978. q. USD 36. Ed(s): Jean Marie Stine. International Foundation for Gender Education, Inc., PO Box 540229, Waltham, MA 02454; info@ifge.org; http://www.ifge.org. Illus., adv. Circ: 10000 Paid. *Bk. rev.:* 300-1,200 words, signed. *Aud.:* Ga.

Transgender Tapestry is one of the most comprehensive resources around for trangendered people. Published by the International Foundation for Gender Education (IFGE), this magazine provides informative articles and feature stories in each issue. A recent issue covers the IFGE Community Awards, plus articles on transgender issues in the workplace, legal issues, dealing with death, and media coverage of transgender and transsexual people. Regular columns include "And That's the Way It Is," "Ask Ari," "IFGE Synchronicity Bookstore," in addition to reader mail, editorials, professional listings, and community resources. In each issue one can find poetry, humor, fiction, and a personality parade. There is also a wonderful companion web site, www.ifge.org, that has many articles, archives, and links to other resources for transgendered and transsexual people. *Transgender Tapestry* is a great resource for all libraries.

3046. *Trikone Magazine: bisexual, gay and lesbian South Asians.* Formerly (until 1987): *Trikon.* [ISSN: 1042-735X] 1986. q. USD 15 domestic; USD 30 foreign; USD 3.95 newsstand/cover. Ed(s): Sandip Roy. Trikone Magazine, PO Box 14161, San Francisco, CA 94114; trikone-web@trikone.org; http://www.trikone.org. Illus., adv. Circ: 1200 Paid. Online: ProQuest LLC (Ann Arbor). *Indexed:* GendWatch. *Aud.:* Hs, Ga, Ac, Sa.

Thematic in content, *Trikone* "offers a supportive, empowering, and non-judgmental environment where queer South Asians can meet, make connections, and proudly promote awareness and acceptance of their sexuality in society." (South Asia, here, refers to the countries of Afghanistan, Bangladesh, Bhutan, Myanmar, India, Maldives, Nepal, Pakistan, Sri Lanka, Tibet, and the diaspora.) *Trikone,* Sanskrit for "triangle," is a black-and-white quarterly that chooses a theme for each issue, with most of the articles dealing with that one theme. A recent theme was "Movie Buzz," with movie reviews for recent South Asians titles, interviews with directors, and coverage of film conferences. Issues may also contain original poetry and short fiction. Regular departments include "Letters," "Newsnotes," "Classifieds," "Contacts," and "Resources." *Trikone* is an excellent resource for any library with a culturally diverse population.

3047. *Velvet Park: dyke culture in bloom.* [ISSN: 1540-3777] 2002. q. USD 7.75 newsstand/cover per issue. Ed(s): Grace Moon, Diana Cage. Velvet Park Magazine, PO Box. 60248, Brooklyn, NY 11206-0248. *Bk. rev.:* 1, 1,000 words. *Aud.:* Ga.

Velvet Park is truly a "thought-provoking, sexy, trail-blazing magazine of arts, culture and social activism for lesbians." When most people think of lesbians, the image of short-haired, Birkenstock-wearing women comes to mind, but *Velvet Park* shows a different side of lesbian life. Reminiscent of many popular art and culture magazines, *Velvet Park* is slick, artistic, and very "now" for

avant-garde lesbians. It is full of articles about music, art, sex, and literature. It also offers very comprehensive coverage of Showtime's "The L Word," giving bios of the actors, reviews of the show, and a place for readers to comment about the storyline. *Velvet Park* is an excellent magazine for libraries with a cosmopolitan clientele.

3048. *The Washington Blade: the gay weekly newspaper of the nation's capital.* Formerly (until 1980): *Blade.* [ISSN: 0278-9892] 1969. w. Fri. USD 85. Ed(s): Chris Crain, Kevin Naff. Window Media LLC, 1408 U St, NW, 2nd Fl, Washington, DC 20009-3916; webmaster@ washblade.com; http://www.washblade.com. Illus., adv. Sample. Circ: 44000. Microform: PQC. Online: EBSCO Publishing, EBSCO Host; Newsbank, Inc. *Indexed:* SWR&A. *Bk. rev.:* 6-8, 400-600 words. *Aud.:* Hs, Ga, Ac.

The Washington Blade is part serious newspaper and part style magazine. The front half has local and national news, forum pages, local life, book reviews, and the like, while the back half has professional directories, real estate classifieds, job classifieds, and personal ads (some with rather racy photos). The news coverage, while fully covering the D.C. area, also provides excellent stories on national and international news as well. *The Blade* would be an excellent resource for any GLBT people wishing to relocate to the D.C. area. Recommended for any library with an array of national newspapers.

3049. *White Crane: a journal of gay wisdom & culture.* Formerly: *White Crane Newsletter.* [ISSN: 1070-5430] 1989. q. USD 22 in North America; USD 36 elsewhere; USD 6 newsstand/cover per issue in North America. Ed(s): Dan Vera, Bo Young. White Crane Institute, 172 Fifth Ave, #69, Brooklyn, NY 11217; editor@whitecranejournal.com; http://www.whitecranejournal.com. Illus., adv. Sample. Circ: 800 Controlled. *Bk. rev.:* 2, 150-650 words. *Aud.:* Ga.

Highly spiritual in content, *White Crane* is "committed to the certainty that Gay consciousness plays a unique and important role in the evolution of life on Earth." Each issue is thematic in content, beginning with an "Editor's Note" discussing the theme and the ideas for choosing it. A recent theme was "Skepticism & Doubt: Reason, Religion & Reality." The issue, like most others, included interviews, essays, poetry, discussion of culture, book reviews, and some regular columns. These include "Updrafts," letters from readers; "re:Sources," information about further reading and study of the current theme; and "PRAXIS," a final thought about the theme from a regular columnist. *White Crane* also has a companion web site, www.gaywisdom.org, where readers can find out more information about the current topic, contact the editors, and order issues.

3050. *Whosoever: an online magazine for gay, lesbian, bisexual and transgendered christians.* 1996. bi-m. Free. Ed(s): Candace L Chellew. Whosoever, editor@whosoever.org; http://www.whosoever.org. *Aud.:* Hs, Ga, Ac.

Whosoever "exists to provide a safe and sacred space for gay, lesbian, bisexual and transgender Christians to reclaim, rekindle and grow their relationship with God." One look at this site proves that this is true. Sprinkled liberally with quotes from the Bible, *Whosoever* has many resources for GLBT Christians. On the site, readers will find departments such as "Issues," "Christian Agnostic Blog," "Whosoever Store," "Author Index," "Prayer Requests," and "News," to name a few. Two departments are particularly striking: "What We Believe," which is very much like a FAQ page, but with the questions having to do with religion and gays; and "The Ex-Gay Myth," which exposes the Ex-Gay Ministries for what they truly are and cautions readers against them. There is also a link to find a local fellowship and a monthly podcast. An excellent resource for gay Christians everywhere. URL: www.whosoever.org

3051. *Windy City Times.* [ISSN: 1049-698X] 1985. w. Wed. USD 89. Ed(s): Tracy Baim. Lambda Publications, Inc., 1940 W. Irving Park Rd., # 1, Chicago, IL 60613-2468; outlines@suba.com; http://outlineschicago.com. Adv. Circ: 24000 Controlled. Microform: MMP. *Aud.:* Hs, Ga, Ac.

A great local newspaper, *Windy City Times* has been "the voice of Chicago's gay, lesbian, bi and trans community since 1985." Each issue has three general sections: "News," which in recent issues included stories about Stonewall, the

Gay Games, galas, and V-Day; "Entertainment," with articles about music, theater, the Oscars, and Hollywood; and "Outlines," with regular real estate, classified, calendar, connections, and sports sections. *Windy City Times* does offer some national news, but mostly it is just an excellent source of local news and events for Chicago and the surrounding area. Recommended for Midwestern libraries, or for any library with a GLBT newspaper collection.

3052. *XY Magazine.* [ISSN: 1522-8614] 1996. 10x/yr. USD 40 domestic; CND 75 Canada; USD 65 Mexico. Ed(s): Peter Ian Cummings. XY Media, Ltd., 4104 24th St, Ste 900, San Francisco, CA 94114-3615; xypost@xy.com; http://www.xy.com. Illus., adv. *Bk. rev.:* 7-12, 50-500 words. *Aud.:* Hs, Ga, Ac.

In publication since 1996, *XY* is one of the few magazines directed toward young gay men. This glossy, full-color, bimonthly magazine has much to offer, including original photography; essays on politics and culture; film, music, and literature reviews; letters from readers; and advice for surviving as a young gay man in America today. Closely tied in to the magazine is the web site, www.xy.com, which has articles, chat rooms, a place where readers can write in or send photos, and even a page dedicated to suicide prevention. For libraries with a large youth clientele, *XY* is a much-needed publication.

■ GENDER STUDIES

See also Gay, Lesbian, Bisexual, and Transgender; and Sexuality sections.

Lilith R. Kunkel, Library Director, Salem Campus Library, Kent State University Salem Regional Campus, 2491 State Route 45 South, Salem, OH 44460; FAX: 330-332-5086; kunkel@salem.kent.edu

Charles A. Skewis, Head, Collection & Resource Services, Georgia Southern University, Statesboro, GA 30460-8074; cskewis@georgiasouthern.edu

Thomas L. Kilpatrick, Professor Emeritus, Southern Illinois University Libraries, Carbondale, IL 62901-6632; tkilpatrick@hcis.net

Cheryl LaGuardia, Head of Instructional Services for the Harvard College Library, Widener Library, Research Services, Harvard University, Cambridge, MA 02138; claguard@fas.harvard.edu

Introduction

Gender studies is a field of study focusing on issues of sex and gender and on the roles, status, and condition of men and women in socio-cultural and political contexts. From its inception, it has been interdisciplinary and activist in outlook, and is often related to feminist, ethnic, and queer studies. It can be literary, humanistic, or scientific in its approach. Programs vary greatly in their blending of theoretical, empirical, and applied studies. They also vary in their sexual politics and in their attention to diversity in race, ethnicity, and class as well as in sexuality and gender. Critics have sometimes challenged the academic credibility of these programs and provided limited financial support compared to more traditional disciplines.

In choosing gender studies periodicals to meet the needs of library users, selectors need to consider not only the complicated origins of the discipline but also current trends in publishing. The most notable trends are the growth of web-based publishing and the increased availability of online, full-text databases. The number of resources has proliferated as the web makes cheap, fast publishing possible, free of the constraints of mainstream publishing. Many web-based publications prove to be ephemeral, however, and access to their content through major search engines is limited. The growth of databases and full-text services has increased the availability of gender studies periodicals to some degree. The online versions of specialized abstracts and indexes such as *Contemporary Women's Issues, Studies on Women,* and *Gender Abstracts* provide good coverage of these, but their price may be beyond the reach of smaller libraries struggling to meet the costs of the big databases.

The titles listed here have been selected to represent the variety and scope of gender studies. The online publications included are free scholarly journals available only online. This section includes few publications dealing with sexuality; these are covered in the Gay, Lesbian, Bisexual, and Transgender

section and the Sexuality section. Well-established women's health publications are now included in the Health and Fitness section or the Medicine section, while some men's health journals remain in this section.

Basic Periodicals

Ga: *Harvard Men's Health Watch, Today's Father;* Sa: *The Aging Male, International Journal of Men's Health, Journal of Men's Health and Gender, Journal of Men's Studies, Men and Masculinities, Psychology of Men and Masculinities.*

FEMINIST AND WOMEN'S STUDIES. Ems: *New Moon, New Moon Network;* Hs: *Ms., NWSA Journal, Women in Literature and Life Assembly, Women in Sport & Physical Activity;* Ga: *Frontiers, Herizons, Iris, Ms., National NOW Times, Sexing the Political;* Ac: *Critical Matrix, Feminist Economics, Feminist Studies, Frontiers, Gender and Education, Gender and History, Gender Issues, Genders, Health Care for Women International, Hypatia, Journal of Women's History, Legacy, Ms., NWSA Journal, Sexing the Political, Signs, Tulsa Studies in Women's Literature, Violence Against Women, WIN News, Woman's Art Journal, Women & Health, Women & Politics, Women in Sport & Physical Activity Journal, Women's Health Issues, Women's Studies Quarterly, Women's Writing.*

LITERARY AND ARTISTIC. Ga: *Bridges, Calyx, Room of One's Own;* Ac: *Calyx, femspec, Kalliope, n.paradoxa.*

SPECIAL INTEREST. Hs: *Melpomene Journal;* Ga: *Conscience, Lilith, Melpomene Journal;* Ac: *Media Report to Women.*

Basic Abstracts and Indexes

Ac: *Contemporary Women's Issues, Feminist Periodicals, GenderWatch, Studies on Women and Gender Abstracts, Violence & Abuse Abstracts, Women Studies Abstracts, Women's Studies Index, Women's Studies International, Women's Studies on Disc.*

3053. *Affilia: journal of women and social work.* [ISSN: 0886-1099] 1986. q. GBP 326. Ed(s): Miriam Dinerman. Sage Publications, Inc., 2455 Teller Rd, Thousand Oaks, CA 91320; info@sagepub.com; http://www.sagepub.com. Illus., adv. Refereed. Circ: 650 Paid. Vol. ends: Nov. Reprint: PSC. *Indexed:* ASSIA, AgeL, ArtHuCI, CINAHL, CJA, FemPer, HRA, IMFL, SFSA, SSA, SSCI, SWA, SWR&A, SociolAb, V&AA, WSA. *Bk. rev.:* 7-14, 350-900 words, signed. *Aud.:* Ac, Sa.

This scholarly journal addresses the concerns of social work and its clients from a feminist perspective. It aims to provide the knowledge and tools needed to improve the delivery of social services through research reports, empirical articles, opinion pieces, and book reviews. Issues also include news updates and literary works. Full text is available through *Sage Journals Online* to institutions with print subscriptions.

3054. *Asian Journal of Women's Studies.* [ISSN: 1225-9276] 1995. q. KRW 75000 (Individuals, KRW 30000). Ed(s): Philwha Chang. Asian Center for Women's Studies, Ewha Woamns University, #11-1, Daehyun-dong, Seodaemun-gu, Seoul, 120-750, Korea, Republic of; acwsewha@esha.ac.kr; http://ewhawoman.or.kr/acws. Adv. Sample. Refereed. Circ: 700 Paid and controlled. *Indexed:* AltPI, CJA, FemPer, GendWatch, SSCI. *Bk. rev.:* 2, 800-1,000 words, signed. *Aud.:* Ac.

This interdisciplinary journal from the Asian Center for Women's Studies provides a feminist perspective on women's issues in Asia and throughout the world. It aims to communicate scholarly ideas and "to develop women's studies in Asia and expand the horizon of Western-centered women's studies." It includes scholarly articles, country reports, notes on teaching and research, and book reviews.

3055. *Atlantis: a women's studies journal - revue d'etudes sur les femmes.* [ISSN: 0702-7818] 1975. s-a. CND 45 (Individuals, CND 25; CND 12 newsstand/cover per issue). Ed(s): Marilyn Porter, June Corman. Mount Saint Vincent University, Institute for the Study of Women, Halifax, NS B3M 2J6, Canada; atlantis@msvu.ca. Illus., index, adv. Refereed. Circ: 900. Vol. ends: Spring/Summer. Microform: MML. *Indexed:* AltPI, AmH&L, AmHI, CBCARef, CPerI, FemPer, HistAb, LeftInd, MLA-IB, SWA, WSA. *Bk. rev.:* 8, length varies, signed. *Aud.:* Ac.

Atlantis is an established Canadian journal providing critical and creative writing in English and French about women and women's studies. Publication alternates between general, open, and special issues. One recent issue features creative works and essays on the theme "Women, Art, Politics and Power." Its perspective is international and interdisciplinary. Contributors are academics, artists, and feminists.

3056. *Australian Feminist Studies.* [ISSN: 0816-4649] 1986. 3x/yr. GBP 450 print & online eds. Ed(s): Susan Magarey. Routledge, 4 Park Sq, Milton Park, Abingdon, OX14 4RN, United Kingdom; info@routledge.co.uk; http://www.routledge.com. Adv. Refereed. Circ: 600. Online: EBSCO Publishing, EBSCO Host; Gale; IngentaConnect; OCLC Online Computer Library Center, Inc.; RMIT Publishing; SwetsWise Online Content. Reprint: PSC. *Indexed:* AltPI, AmH&L, AmHI, ArtHuCI, FemPer, HistAb, IBSS, PSA, SSA, SSCI, SWA, SociolAb. *Bk. rev.:* 6-8, 500 words, essay length, signed. *Aud.:* Ac.

This international, peer-reviewed journal focuses on feminist scholarship, teaching, and practice. Its contents include research articles, reviews, critiques, and correspondence as well as news of policies affecting women, conference reports, and discussions of teaching. Some articles fall within familiar disciplinary boundaries while others are interdisciplinary. Editorial practice recognizes "difference and diversity among feminisms." A free contents alerting service is available from the publisher.

The Beltane Papers: a journal of women's mysteries. See Sprituality and Well-Being section.

3057. *Bridges: a Jewish feminists journal.* [ISSN: 1046-8358] 1990. s-a. USD 52 (Individuals, USD 32). Ed(s): Clare Kinberg. Indiana University Press, 601 N Morton St, Bloomington, IN 47404; journals@indiana.edu; http://iupjournals.org. Illus. Sample. Circ: 3000. Online: EBSCO Publishing, EBSCO Host; Project MUSE. *Indexed:* AmHI, FemPer, IJP, R&TA. *Bk. rev.:* 2, essay length, signed. *Aud.:* Hs, Ac, Sa.

Now published by Indiana University Press, *Bridges* continues under the direction of the editorial collective that established it in 1990. It is an independent review of Jewish feminist culture and politics. Contents illustrate Jewish feminism in all its diversity and include articles, commentary, essays, fiction, poetry, visual art, and reviews as well as oral histories, interviews, diaries, and letters. Special issues have focused on "Health Matters," "Writings by Israeli Jewish Women on Peace Seeking," and "Writing and Art by Jewish Women of Color."

3058. *Canadian Woman Studies.* Formerly (until vol.3, no.2, 1981): *Canadian Women's Studies.* [ISSN: 0713-3235] 1978. q. CND 53.50 (Individuals, CND 38.52). Ed(s): Luciana Ricciutelli. Inanna Publications and Education Inc., 212 Founders College, York University, 4700 Keele St, Downsview, ON M3J 1P3, Canada; cwscf@yorku.ca; http://www.yorku.ca/org/cwscf/home.html. Illus., adv. Refereed. Circ: 5000. Vol. ends: Winter (No. 4). Microform: MML. Online: Florida Center for Library Automation; Gale; Micromedia ProQuest; OCLC Online Computer Library Center, Inc.; H.W. Wilson. *Indexed:* ABS&EES, AltPI, AmHI, BRI, CBCARef, CPI, CPerI, CWI, FemPer, HumInd, SWA, WSA. *Bk. rev.:* 7, 600-1,100, signed. *Aud.:* Ac, Sa.

This bilingual, feminist quarterly "was founded with the goal of making current writing and research on a wide variety of feminist topics accessible to the largest possible community of women." It seeks to provide a middle ground between theory and activism. Issues are theme based and include scholarly and experiential articles, art, creative writing, and book reviews. Coverage is international.

The editors encourage submissions dealing with the diverse lives of "women of color, Aboriginal women, immigrant women, working class women, women with disabilities, lesbians, and other marginalized women."

Columbia Journal of Gender and the Law. See Law section.

3059. *Critical Matrix: the Princeton journal of women, gender, and culture.* [ISSN: 1066-288X] 1985. s-a. USD 30 (Individuals, USD 25; Students, USD 20). Ed(s): Paul Kelleher, Lisa Fluet. Princeton University, Program in the Study of Women and Gender, 113 Dickinson Hall, Princeton University, Princeton, NJ 08544-1017; matrix@princeton.edu. Illus., index, adv. Refereed. Circ: 500. Vol. ends: No. 2. Online: Gale; OCLC Online Computer Library Center, Inc. *Indexed:* CWI, FemPer, GendWatch, MLA-IB, RI-1, WSA. *Aud.:* Ac.

Critical Matrix is "a forum for research, criticism, theory, and creative work in feminism and gender studies." A forthcoming special issue on "Fates and Futures of Feminism" considers what feminism means today and how present debates depart from and advance feminist studies. This award-winning journal from Princeton's Program in Women's Studies and Gender includes work "by authors at any stage in their careers, with or without academic affiliation."

3060. *Differences: a journal of feminist cultural studies.* [ISSN: 1040-7391] 1989. 3x/yr. USD 114 (Individuals, USD 35). Ed(s): Denise Davis, Elizabeth Weed. Duke University Press, 905 W Main St, Ste 18 B, Durham, NC 27701; dukepress@duke.edu; http://www.dukeupress.edu. Illus., adv. Sample. Refereed. Circ: 610. Vol. ends: Fall. Online: EBSCO Publishing, EBSCO Host; Florida Center for Library Automation; Gale; HighWire Press; OCLC Online Computer Library Center, Inc.; OhioLINK; Project MUSE; ProQuest LLC (Ann Arbor); SwetsWise Online Content; H.W. Wilson. Reprint: PSC. *Indexed:* AltPI, AmHI, CWI, FLI, FemPer, GendWatch, HumInd, IBSS, LeftInd, MLA-IB, PSA, SSA, SSCI, SWA, SociolAb, WSA. *Aud.:* Ac.

This scholarly journal looks at how concepts and categories of "difference" are produced and operate within culture and over time. The main, but not exclusive, focus is women and gender. Articles are interdisciplinary and often theoretical. Special issues include "Difference: Reading with Barbara Johnson," "Derrida's Gift," and "The Question of Embodiment." Now published by Duke University Press with full text available online to institutions with print subscriptions.

3061. *European Journal of Women's Studies.* [ISSN: 1350-5068] 1994. q. GBP 397. Ed(s): Kathy Davis, Mary Evans. Sage Publications Ltd., 1 Oliver's Yard, 55 City Rd, London, EC1 1SP, United Kingdom; info@sagepub.co.uk; http://www.sagepub.co.uk. Illus., adv. Refereed. Vol. ends: Nov. Reprint: PSC. *Indexed:* ABS&EES, ASSIA, AgeL, AmHI, ArtHuCI, BrHumI, CJA, CommAb, FemPer, HRA, IBR, IBSS, IBZ, IPSA, PSA, PsycInfo, SFSA, SSA, SSCI, SWA, SociolAb, V&AA, WSA. *Bk. rev.:* 2-10, length varies, signed. *Aud.:* Ac.

This multidisciplinary, academic journal publishes theoretical and thematic articles dealing with women and feminism in a varied European context. Issues include open letters, book reviews, and conference reports and provide multiple feminist perspectives. Published with the support of WISE (The European Women's Studies Association). Full text is available through *Sage Journals Online.*

3062. *Everyman.* Formerly (until 1992): *Men's Magazine.* [ISSN: 1199-1461] 1992. bi-m. USD 20. Ed(s): David Shackleton. Everyman, PO Box 4617, Ottawa, ON K1S 5H8, Canada. Online: ProQuest LLC (Ann Arbor). *Indexed:* GendWatch. *Bk. rev.:* 3, 400 words, signed. *Aud.:* Ga, Sa.

Everyman is the official magazine of the Canadian men's movement. Its focus is "men's growth toward wholeness and balancing the gender debate," according to editor and publisher David Shackleton. Themes for each issue—love and relationships, aging and death, custody and access, violence, equality, boys, fatherhood, and rights and responsibilities—are indicative of the range of topics addressed by the publication, which features articles, poetry, letters, news, a calendar of events, and reviews. A useful feature is a four-page spread called "Resources for Men," which lists social-service organizations throughout Canada. *Everyman* is an attractive, thought-provoking journal for the man who takes manhood seriously.

Feminism & Psychology. See Psychology section.

3063. *Feminist Collections: a quarterly of women's studies resources.* [ISSN: 0742-7441] 1980. q. USD 55 (Individuals, USD 30). Ed(s): JoAnne Lehman, Phyllis Holman Weisbard. University of Wisconsin System, Women's Studies Librarian, 430 Memorial Library, 728 State St, Madison, WI 53706; wiswsl@library.wisc.edu; http://www.library.wisc.edu/libraries/womensstudies. Illus., adv. Circ: 1000. Vol. ends: Summer. Online: Gale; OCLC Online Computer Library Center, Inc.; ProQuest LLC (Ann Arbor). *Indexed:* AltPI, CWI, FemPer, GendWatch, HEA, LISA, SWA, WSA. *Bk. rev.:* Number varies, essay length, signed. *Aud.:* Ac, Sa.

Feminist Collections provides information on resources for teaching and research in women's studies. It includes reviews of books, periodicals, and audiovisual and Internet resources as well as news about feminist publishing. Recent articles cover topics such as information literacy in the women's studies classroom, gender studies in Russia, and e-sources on women and gender. Regular features include "New Reference Works in Women's Studies" and "Periodical Notes," which provides information about new and ceased publications. A print subscription includes *Feminist Periodicals,* a current-contents listing service (see Abstracts and Indexes in the front matter), and *New Books on Women & Feminism.* An important resource for teaching, research, and collection development.

3064. *Feminist Majority Foundation Online.* 1995. d. Membership, USD 15. Feminist Majority Foundation, 1600 Wilson Blvd, Ste 801, Arlington, VA 22209; femmaj@feminist.org; http://www.feminist.org. *Aud.:* Ga, Ac.

The Feminist Majority Foundation, a nonprofit organization headed by Eleanor Smeal, uses "research and action to empower women economically, socially, and politically." This web site provides an online daily news service that covers U.S. and global feminist news, as well as useful links to organizations involved in a wide range of feminist causes. Its "Feminist Research Center" and "Feminist Internet Gateway" offer access to resources for feminist scholarship. A search engine allows readers to search U.S. news from 1995 to the present and global news from June 2000 to the present.

3065. *Feminist Review.* [ISSN: 0141-7789] 1979. 3x/yr. USD 498 print & online eds. Palgrave Macmillan Ltd., Houndmills, Basingstoke, RG21 6XS, United Kingdom; journal-info@palgrave.com; http://www.palgrave-journals.com/. Illus., adv. Sample. Refereed. Circ: 3500. Online: Chadwyck-Healey Inc.; EBSCO Publishing, EBSCO Host; Gale; IngentaConnect; JSTOR (Web-based Journal Archive); OCLC Online Computer Library Center, Inc.; ProQuest LLC (Ann Arbor); SwetsWise Online Content. Reprint: PSC. *Indexed:* ASSIA, AltPI, AmHI, ArtHuCI, BrHumI, CWI, FR, FemPer, IBR, IBSS, IBZ, IPSA, LeftInd, PSA, RI-1, RILM, SSA, SSCI, SWA, SociolAb. *Bk. rev.:* 4-17, length varies, signed. *Aud.:* Ga, Ac.

This journal publishes scholarly articles, dialogues, review essays, book reviews, and occasional creative writing that covers a range of feminist academic and political concerns. Its perspective is international and interdisciplinary. Recent special issues include one on the nature of the "hystories" created by women authors and activists and another on the debates within contemporary Italian feminism. Contents pages and a contents alerting service are available from the publisher's web site.

3066. *Feminist Studies.* [ISSN: 0046-3663] 1972. 3x/yr. USD 230 (Individuals, USD 35). Ed(s): Claire G. Moses. Feminist Studies, Inc., 0103 Taliaferro Hall, University of Maryland, College Park, MD 20742-7726. Illus., index, adv. Refereed. Circ: 5000 Paid. Vol. ends: Fall (No. 3). Microform: PQC. Online: Chadwyck-Healey Inc.; EBSCO Publishing, EBSCO Host; Florida Center for Library Automation; Gale; JSTOR (Web-based Journal Archive); Northern Light Technology, Inc.; OCLC Online Computer Library Center, Inc.; ProQuest K-12 Learning

Solutions; ProQuest LLC (Ann Arbor); H.W. Wilson. Reprint: PSC. *Indexed:* ABS&EES, ASSIA, AgeL, AltPI, AmH&L, AmHI, AnthLit, ArtHuCI, BAS, BrHumI, CWI, FemPer, GendWatch, HistAb, IBR, IBSS, IBZ, IMFL, MASUSE, MLA-IB, PAIS, PRA, PSA, PhilInd, RI-1, RILM, SFSA, SSA, SSCI, SWA, SociolAb, WSA. *Bk. rev.:* 0-1, essay length, signed. *Aud.:* Ac.

Feminist Studies seeks to promote discussion among feminist scholars, activists, and writers, to develop an interdisciplinary body of knowledge and theory, and to change women's condition. Contents include scholarly research, essays, book reviews, and creative works. A recent issue on "globalization" includes three articles exploring the meaning of the hijab in the Islamic Middle East and in France. Published by an editorial collective in association with the University of Maryland's Women's Studies Program. Contents pages are available from the publisher's web site.

3067. *Feminist Teacher: a journal of the practices, theories, and scholarship of feminist teaching.* [ISSN: 0882-4843] 1984. 3x/yr. USD 85 print & online eds. (Individuals, USD 38 print & online eds.). University of Illinois Press, 1325 S Oak St, Champaign, IL 61820-6903; journals@ uillinois.edu; http://www.press.uillinois.edu. Adv. Refereed. Circ: 600. *Indexed:* ABIn, AltPI, CWI, ERIC, EduInd, FemPer, GendWatch, SWA, WSA. *Bk. rev.:* Number and length vary. *Aud.:* Hs, Ga, Ac.

This journal addresses the theory and practice of feminist teaching and considers issues such as multiculturalism and interdisciplinarity in a feminist context. It is directed toward teachers and administrators at all levels and includes articles, book reviews, review essays, course descriptions, bibliographies, and other resources for teaching.

3068. *Feminist Theology.* [ISSN: 0966-7350] 1992. 3x/yr. GBP 219. Ed(s): Lisa Isherwood, Lillalou Hughes. Sage Publications Ltd., 1 Oliver's Yard, 55 City Rd, London, EC1 1SP, United Kingdom; info@sagepub.co.uk; http://www.sagepub.co.uk. Adv. Online: EBSCO Publishing, EBSCO Host; HighWire Press; SAGE Publications, Inc., SAGE Journals Online; SwetsWise Online Content. Reprint: PSC. *Indexed:* IBR, IBZ, NTA, R&TA, RI-1, SWA. *Bk. rev.:* 6-8, length varies, signed. *Aud.:* Ac, Sa.

Feminist Theology provides an interdisciplinary and feminist perspective on theology, biblical studies, and the sociology of religion. It aims to be accessible to a wide range of readers and "to give a voice to the women of Britain and Ireland in matters of theology and religion." There is a free contents alerting service. Full text is available through *Sage Journals Online.*

3069. *Feminist Theory: an international interdisciplinary journal.* [ISSN: 1464-7001] 2000. 3x/yr. GBP 275. Ed(s): Gabriele Griffin, Sasha Roseneil. Sage Publications Ltd., 1 Oliver's Yard, 55 City Rd, London, EC1 1SP, United Kingdom; info@sagepub.co.uk; http://www.sagepub.co.uk. Illus., index, adv. Refereed. Vol. ends: Dec. Online: EBSCO Publishing, EBSCO Host; HighWire Press; OCLC Online Computer Library Center, Inc.; SAGE Publications, Inc., SAGE Journals Online; SwetsWise Online Content. Reprint: PSC. *Indexed:* FemPer, IBR, IBSS, IBZ, IPSA, PSA, PsycInfo, SSA, SociolAb. *Bk. rev.:* Number and length vary; signed. *Aud.:* Ac.

This international journal focuses on the critical examination and discussion of diverse feminist theoretical and political positions across the humanities and social sciences. Written by feminists from around the world, its contents include articles, shorter "think pieces" on topical issues, interchanges between theorists, and book reviews. Free contents alerting service. Full text is available through *Sage Journals Online.*

3070. *Frontiers (Lincoln): a journal of women studies.* [ISSN: 0160-9009] 1975. 3x/yr. USD 100 (Individuals, USD 37). Ed(s): Gayle Gullett, Susan E Gray. University of Nebraska Press, 1111 Lincoln Mall, Lincoln, NE 68588-0630; journals@unlnotes.unl.edu; http://www.nebraskapress.unl.edu. Illus., index, adv. Refereed. Circ: 350 Paid. Microform: PQC. Online: EBSCO Publishing, EBSCO Host; Florida Center for Library Automation; Gale; OCLC Online Computer

Library Center, Inc.; OhioLINK; Project MUSE; ProQuest LLC (Ann Arbor); SwetsWise Online Content. *Indexed:* ABS&EES, AgeL, AmH&L, AmHI, ArtHuCI, BAS, FLI, FR, FemPer, GendWatch, HRA, HistAb, HumInd, IBR, IBZ, MLA-IB, PAIS, RILM, SSCI, SWA, SociolAb, WSA. *Aud.:* Ac.

This multicultural, cross-disciplinary journal features work in women's studies, history, anthropology, sociology, ethnic studies, and American Studies. It is a mix of scholarly work, personal essays, and creative works. Contributions from authors belonging to racial and ethnic minorities are encouraged. Some issues include sets of articles on themes such as "gender, place, and migration."

3071. Gender and Development. Formerly: *Focus on Gender.* [ISSN: 1355-2074] 1993. 3x/yr. GBP 171 print & online eds. Ed(s): Caroline Sweetman. Routledge, 4 Park Sq, Milton Park, Abingdon, OX14 4RN, United Kingdom; info@routledge.co.uk; http://www.routledge.co.uk. Circ: 100. Online: EBSCO Publishing, EBSCO Host; Gale; IngentaConnect; OCLC Online Computer Library Center, Inc.; SwetsWise Online Content. Reprint: PSC. *Indexed:* CABA, FemPer, HortAb, IBR, IBSS, IBZ, IndIslam, PSA, RRTA, S&F, SSA, SWA, SociolAb, WAE&RSA. *Bk. rev.:* brief, 750 words. *Aud.:* Ac, Sa.

This journal is concerned with the relationship between gender and economic development. Issues are thematic and include articles, case studies, conference reports, interviews, resources, and book reviews. Articles are directed toward development practitioners, policy makers, and academics. A recent issue, for example, focuses on gender-based violence against women and children. Articles describe the problem in Africa, Central America, South Asia, and Soviet Georgia. Contents pages are available free of charge on the publisher's web site. Full text is available through *Ingenta Select.*

3072. Gender and Education. [ISSN: 0954-0253] 1989. 6x/yr. GBP 1010 print & online eds. Ed(s): Becky Francis, Christine Skelton. Routledge, 4 Park Sq, Milton Park, Abingdon, OX14 4RN, United Kingdom; info@routledge.co.uk; http://www.routledge.co.uk. Illus., adv. Sample. Refereed. Vol. ends: Dec (No. 4). Online: EBSCO Publishing, EBSCO Host; Gale; IngentaConnect; OCLC Online Computer Library Center, Inc.; ProQuest LLC (Ann Arbor); SwetsWise Online Content. Reprint: PSC. *Indexed:* ASSIA, BrEdI, CWI, EAA, ERIC, FemPer, IBR, IBSS, IBZ, IndIslam, LT&LA, SSA, SSCI, SWA, SociolAb, V&AA. *Bk. rev.:* 9-15, 500-1,000 words, signed. *Aud.:* Ac.

Gender and Education publishes multidisciplinary research with gender as a main category of analysis. Education is broadly defined as encompassing formal and informal education at all levels and within all contexts. Coverage is international. Tables of contents and an e-mail contents alerting service are available on the publisher's web site. Full text is available online, to institutions with print subscriptions, through the publisher's web site.

3073. Gender and History. [ISSN: 0953-5233] 1989. 3x/yr. GBP 347 print & online eds. Ed(s): Michele Mitchell, Helmut Puff. Blackwell Publishing Ltd., 9600 Garsington Rd, Oxford, OX4 2ZG, United Kingdom; customerservices@blackwellpublishing.com; http://www.blackwellpublishing.com. Illus., adv. Sample. Refereed. Vol. ends: Nov. Online: Blackwell Synergy; EBSCO Publishing, EBSCO Host; Gale; IngentaConnect; OCLC Online Computer Library Center, Inc.; OhioLINK; SwetsWise Online Content. Reprint: PSC. *Indexed:* AmH&L, AmHI, ApEcolAb, CJA, FemPer, HistAb, HumInd, IBSS, IndIslam, NTA, PSA, SSA, SWA, SociolAb, WSA. *Bk. rev.:* Number varies, essay length, signed. *Aud.:* Ac.

This journal offers a historical perspective on gender relations, men and masculinity, and women and femininity. It has a broad chronological and geographical scope. It covers both specific episodes in gender history and broader methodological questions in history. It also includes discussions of teaching gender history and extensive book reviews. Special issues focus on themes such as "Translating Feminisms in China" or "Domestic Service Since 1750." Tables of contents of past issues and a sample issue are available on the publisher's web site.

3074. Gender & Society. [ISSN: 0891-2432] 1987. bi-m. GBP 397. Ed(s): Christine L Williams. Sage Publications, Inc., 2455 Teller Rd, Thousand Oaks, CA 91320; info@sagepub.com; http://www.sagepub.com. Illus., adv. Sample. Refereed. Circ: 1800 Paid. Vol. ends: Dec. Reprint: PSC. *Indexed:* ABS&EES, ASSIA, AgeL, AmH&L, ArtHuCI, CJA, CommAb, FemPer, HRA, HistAb, IBR, IBSS, IBZ, IMFL, IndIslam, PSA, PsycInfo, RI-1, RiskAb, SFSA, SSA, SSCI, SWA, SociolAb, V&AA, WSA. *Bk. rev.:* Number varies, essay length, signed. *Aud.:* Ac.

This official publication of Sociologists for Women in Society presents the latest research and theory on gender and its social and structural implications. Its contents include scholarly articles focused on a particular theoretical or policy issue as well as research reports and book reviews. Topics covered in recent issues include "Gender, Race, and Depression," "Gender and Organizational Culture," and "The Changing Gender Composition of College Majors." Articles are available electronically via *Sage Journals Online* to members of institutions with print subscriptions. *ISI Journal Citation Reports* ranks this journal among the top women's studies journals.

3075. Gender Issues. Formerly (until 1998): *Feminist Issues.* [ISSN: 1098-092X] 1980. q. EUR 290 print & online eds. Springer New York LLC, 233 Spring St, New York, NY 10013-1578; journals@springer-ny.com; http://www.springer.com. Illus., adv. Refereed. Circ: 500. Vol. ends: Fall. Microform: PQC. Online: EBSCO Publishing, EBSCO Host; Florida Center for Library Automation; Gale; Northern Light Technology, Inc.; OCLC Online Computer Library Center, Inc.; OhioLINK; ProQuest LLC (Ann Arbor); SwetsWise Online Content. Reprint: PSC. *Indexed:* ABS&EES, AltPI, AnthLit, CJA, FemPer, HRA, IBR, IBZ, LRI, LeftInd, MASUSE, NTA, PRA, RI-1, SFSA, SSA, SWA, SociolAb, V&AA, WSA. *Bk. rev.:* 2, essay length, signed. *Aud.:* Ac.

Gender Issues publishes basic and applied research relating to gender, gender roles, and the changing roles and statuses of women throughout the industrial and developing nations of the world. It covers a broad range of topics in gender studies and feminism. Recent issues, for example, include articles on women and welfare reform, the effects of cohabitation on children, and college sports and Title IX. It also includes book reviews. Full text is available to individuals and members of subscribing institutions through the publisher's web site.

Gender, Place and Culture. See Geography section.

3076. Gender, Technology & Development. [ISSN: 0971-8524] 1997. 3x/yr. GBP 152. Ed(s): Cecilia Ng, Thanh-Dam Truong. Sage Publications India Pvt. Ltd., M-32 Market, Greater Kailash-I, PO Box 4215, New Delhi, 110 048, India; http://www.indiasage.com/. Illus., index, adv. Sample. Refereed. Circ: 400. Vol. ends: Nov. Reprint: PSC. *Indexed:* IBSS, PSA, SSA, SWA, SociolAb. *Bk. rev.:* 4, length varies, signed. *Aud.:* Ac.

This international, refereed journal focuses on gender relations and technological development in non-Western societies and cultures, particularly Asia. Its intended audience is academics and people working in development and natural resource management. In addition to scholarly articles, it includes book reviews, conference reports, and a listing of recent books on development and technology. A "People's Initiative" section profiles efforts to apply gender theory to real-world development problems. One special issue each year focuses on a theme, such as gender and natural resource governance. Tables of contents of recent issues are available on the publisher's web site.

3077. Gender, Work and Organization. [ISSN: 0968-6673] 1994. bi-m. GBP 547 print & online eds. Ed(s): Deborah Kerfoot, David Knights. Blackwell Publishing Ltd., 9600 Garsington Rd, Oxford, OX4 2ZG, United Kingdom; customerservices@blackwellpublishing.com; http://www.blackwellpublishing.com. Illus., adv. Sample. Refereed. Vol. ends: No. 4. Online: Blackwell Synergy; EBSCO Publishing, EBSCO Host; Gale; IngentaConnect; OCLC Online Computer Library Center, Inc.; OhioLINK; SwetsWise Online Content. Reprint: PSC. *Indexed:* ABIn, ApEcolAb, CJA, ErgAb, FemPer, HRA, IBSS, PsycInfo, RiskAb, SSA, SSCI, SWA, SociolAb. *Bk. rev.:* Number and length vary, signed. *Aud.:* Ac.

This interdisciplinary journal publishes theoretical and research articles relating to gender and work. It is concerned with "gender relations at work, the organization of gender and the gendering of organizations." One recent special issue addressed "Gender as Social Practice: Doing, Saying, and Performing Gender Relations." The journal also includes review articles and book reviews of international publications. Content pages and free e-mail table-of-contents alerts are available on the publisher's web site.

3078. *Genders (Online Edition).* [ISSN: 1936-3249] s-a. Free. Ed(s): Ann Kibbey, Carol Siegel. University of Colorado, Campus Box 226, Boulder, CO 80309. Refereed. *Indexed:* AmHI. *Bk. rev.:* Number varies, essay length, signed. *Aud.:* Ga, Ac.

This e-journal from the University of Colorado and Washington State University publishes "essays about gender and sexualities in relation to artistic, semiotic, political, literary, social, ethnic, racial, economic, rhetorical or legal concerns." Contents include essays on how sexuality is used to support or protect various cultural institutions, historical and cross-cultural analyses of contemporary gender issues, and discussions of particular works of art, literature, or film. One recent issue, for example, includes articles on male flight attendants, gay self-destruction, and cultural definitions of women's physical fitness as well as an essay on the film *My Beautiful Laundrette* and another on Egyptian novelist Ahdaf Soueif's *The Map of Love.* URL: www.genders.org.

Hastings Women's Law Journal. See Law section.

3079. *Hawwa: journal of women of the Middle East and the Islamic world.* [ISSN: 1569-2078] 2003. 3x/yr. EUR 231 print & online eds. (Individuals, EUR 75). Ed(s): Amira Sonbol. Brill, PO Box 9000, Leiden, 2300 PA, Netherlands; cs@brill.nl; http://www.brill.nl. Reprint: PSC. *Indexed:* FemPer. *Aud.:* Ac.

This peer-reviewed journal publishes articles on women and gender issues in the Middle East and the Islamic world. It includes theoretical and methodological as well as topical articles and book reviews. Its main focus is on the contemporary era. Some historical articles are included. A recent issue challenges the contemporary understanding of sexuality in the Islamic World and explores how Victorian attitudes have shaped understandings of sexuality in both Islamic and Western scholarship. Full text available online through *Ingenta Select.*

3080. *Hecate: an interdisciplinary journal of women's liberation.* [ISSN: 0311-4198] 1975. s-a. AUD 154 (Individuals, AUD 35). Ed(s): Carole Ferrier. Hecate Press, PO Box 6099, St Lucia, QLD 4067, Australia. Adv. Refereed. Circ: 2000. Online: EBSCO Publishing, EBSCO Host; Florida Center for Library Automation; Gale; Northern Light Technology, Inc.; OCLC Online Computer Library Center, Inc.; ProQuest K-12 Learning Solutions; ProQuest LLC (Ann Arbor); RMIT Publishing. *Indexed:* AltPI, AmHI, BEL&L, FemPer, GendWatch, IBR, IBZ, LeftInd, SWA, WSA. *Aud.:* Ga, Ac.

This international journal offers a feminist, Marxist, and generally radical perspective on women's experiences in Australia and throughout the world. It focuses on history, culture, sexuality, and politics. A recent special issue commemorates the 50th anniversary of the publication of Simone de Beauvoir's *The Second Sex.* Contents include essays, interviews, and creative works. The journal also publishes the annual *Hecate's Australian Women's Book Review.*

3081. *Herizons: women's news & feminist views.* Formerly (until 1981): *Manitoba women's newspaper.* [ISSN: 0711-7485] 1979. 4x/yr. CND 30 (Individuals, CND 24.99; CND 5.75 newsstand/cover per issue). Ed(s): Penni Mitchell. Herizons, P O Box 128, Winnipeg, MB R3C 2G1, Canada; herizons@escape.ca; http://www.cmpa.ca/f6.html. Illus., adv. Circ: 4500. Online: EBSCO Publishing, EBSCO Host; Florida Center for Library Automation; Gale; Northern Light Technology, Inc.; OCLC Online Computer Library Center, Inc. *Indexed:* AltPI, CBCARef, CPerI, CWI, FemPer, GendWatch, MASUSE, SWA. *Bk. rev.:* 4, 550 words, signed. *Aud.:* Ga, Ac.

This popular Canadian feminist magazine covers topics of interest to feminists worldwide. A recent issue, for example, includes a feature article on globalization and human rights and a related story on work to end violence against women in Nepal. Other sections cover news, opinion, art, music, literature, health, and sexuality. Selected articles from the current and previous issues are posted on the magazine's web site.

3082. *Hypatia: a journal of feminist philosophy.* Supersedes in part (in 1986): *Women's Studies International Forum;* Which was formerly (1978-1981): *Women's Studies International Quarterly.* [ISSN: 0887-5367] 1986. q. USD 110 (Individuals, USD 40). Ed(s): Hilde Lindemann. Indiana University Press, 601 N Morton St, Bloomington, IN 47404. Illus., adv. Sample. Refereed. Circ: 1700. Vol. ends: Fall. Online: Chadwyck-Healey Inc.; EBSCO Publishing, EBSCO Host; Florida Center for Library Automation; Gale; OCLC Online Computer Library Center, Inc.; OhioLINK; Project MUSE; ProQuest K-12 Learning Solutions; ProQuest LLC (Ann Arbor); ScienceDirect; SwetsWise Online Content; H.W. Wilson. Reprint: PSC. *Indexed:* ABS&EES, AltPI, AmHI, CWI, FemPer, GendWatch, HumInd, IBR, IBZ, LeftInd, MLA-IB, PSA, PhilInd, RI-1, SSA, SWA, SociolAb, WSA. *Bk. rev.:* 3-5, 1,000-1,500 words, signed. *Aud.:* Ac.

This journal positions itself at "the intersection of philosophy and women's studies" and strives to promote and develop feminist discourse in philosophy. It is also concerned with reclaiming the work of women philosophers. It is theoretically sophisticated, and interdisciplinary submissions are also welcomed. A recent special issue focuses on "The Reproduction of Whiteness: Race and the Regulation of the Gendered Body." The journal includes book reviews and "Musings" on controversial issues.

3083. *Intersections: gender, history & culture in the Asian context.* [ISSN: 1440-9151] 1998. s-a. Free. Ed(s): Carolyn Brewer, Anne Marie Medcalf. Murdoch University, School of Asian Studies, South St, Perth, W.A. 6163, Australia; intrsect@central.murdoch.edu.au; http://wwwsshe.murdoch.edu.au/hum/as/intersections/. Illus., index, adv. Refereed. *Indexed:* AmHI, HumInd, IBSS, MLA-IB, SociolAb. *Bk. rev.:* 2-7, essay length, signed. *Aud.:* Ac.

This refereed electronic journal provides a forum for research and teaching about the multiple historical and cultural gender patterns of Asia. Papers include photos, maps, or artistic reproductions as well as video or sound where these enhance understanding and allow "for new connections to be made." Contents include research articles, commentary, discussion papers, interviews, poetry, and book and film reviews. One recent theme-based issue focuses on "Of Queer Import(s): Sexualities, Genders, and Rights in Asia" while another looks at "Queer Japan." Author and geographic indexes are available on the journal web site.

3084. *Iris: A Journal about Women.* [ISSN: 0896-1301] 1980. s-a. USD 40 (Individuals, USD 9). University of Virginia, Women's Center, PO Box 800588, Charlottesville, VA 22908; http://www.womenscenter.virginia.edu. Illus., adv. Refereed. Circ: 2500 Paid. Vol. ends: Summer/Fall. *Indexed:* CWI, FemPer, GendWatch, WSA. *Bk. rev.:* 2-12, length varies, signed. *Aud.:* Ga, Ac.

This magazine from the University of Virginia's Women's Center features a new look as "a magazine for and about thinking young women." The new format includes sections on "Your World," "Your Self," and "Your Work" as well as a feature article.

Journal of Couple & Relationship Therapy. See Family and Marriage section.

Journal of Feminist Studies in Religion. See Religion section.

3085. *Journal of Gender Studies.* [ISSN: 0958-9236] 1992. 3x/yr. GBP 412 print & online eds. Ed(s): Diane Dubois, Jenny Wolmark. Routledge, 4 Park Sq, Milton Park, Abingdon, OX14 4RN, United Kingdom; info@routledge.co.uk; http://www.routledge.co.uk. Illus., index, adv. Sample. Refereed. Vol. ends: Nov. Online: EBSCO Publishing, EBSCO Host; Gale; IngentaConnect; Northern Light Technology, Inc.; OCLC

Online Computer Library Center, Inc.; ProQuest K-12 Learning Solutions; ProQuest LLC (Ann Arbor); SwetsWise Online Content. Reprint: PSC. *Indexed:* ASSIA, AmHI, BRI, CJA, CWI, FemPer, IBSS, PSA, PsycInfo, RI-1, SSA, SSCI, SWA, SWR&A, SociolAb. *Bk. rev.:* 8-33, 300-1,500 words, signed. *Aud.:* Ac.

This interdisciplinary, feminist journal uses gender as a framework for analysis in the natural and social sciences, the arts, and popular culture. Articles come from international sources and diverse backgrounds. They provide a variety of perspectives on social and cultural definitions of gender and gender relations. Book reviews and a "Forum" featuring interviews, debates, or responses to articles are also included. An article alert service and contents pages are available online from the publisher.

3086. *Journal of Interdisciplinary Gender Studies.* [ISSN: 1325-1848] 1995. s-a. AUD 80 (Individuals, AUD 40). Ed(s): Wendy Michaels. University of Newcastle, Faculty of Education and Arts, Faculty of Arts and Social Sciences, Newcastle, NSW 2308, Australia; mgams@cc.newcastle.edu.au; http://www.newcastle.edu.au/journal/jigs/ index.html. Refereed. Online: RMIT Publishing. *Bk. rev.:* 800-1,200 words, signed. *Aud.:* Ac.

This refereed journal publishes papers that focus on gender issues in historical and contemporary contexts within and across disciplines. It features contributions from new and established scholars. Articles are concerned with gay and lesbian issues, race, ethnicity, sexuality, and masculinity, as well as with women. A recent special issue examines "Screening the Past: Gender Readings in History and Film." Contents also include poetry and book reviews. Although indexing of this publication is limited, contents information and abstracts are available on the journal's web site.

3087. *Journal of International Women's Studies (Online).* [ISSN: 1539-8706] 1999. s-a. Free. Ed(s): Diana Fox. Bridgewater State College, c/o Diana Fox, Bridgewater, MA 02325; http://www.bridgew.edu. *Indexed:* FemPer, IBSS, MLA-IB, PAIS, SociolAb. *Bk. rev.:* 0-2, essay length, signed. *Aud.:* Ac.

This journal provides an opportunity for scholars, activists, and students to bridge "the conventional divides of scholarship and activism: 'western' and 'third world' feminisms" by exploring "the relationship between feminist theory and various forms of organizing." Contents grow out of conferences and activist meetings and include research articles, essays, and film and book reviews. One recent special issue is titled "Women's Bodies, Gender Analysis, Feminist Politics at the *Forum Social Mundial*." URL: www.bridgew.edu/SoAS/jiws.

3088. *The Journal of Men's Health & Gender.* [ISSN: 1571-8913] 2004. 4x/yr. EUR 550. Ed(s): S Meryn. Elsevier BV, Radarweg 29, Amsterdam, 1043 NX, Netherlands; nlinfo-f@elsevier.nl; http://www.elsevier.nl. Refereed. *Indexed:* ExcerpMed, PsycInfo. *Bk. rev.:* 3, 500 words, signed. *Aud.:* Ac, Sa.

The Journal of Mens's Health & Gender is the newest title in the area of men's studies. Intended for the scholar, it is a research-oriented journal, including peer-reviewed articles on topics as varied as men's physical and mental health, sexuality, attitudes, gender differences, and aging. Each issue contains review and research articles, news items, editorials, commentary, discussion, book reviews, and a calendar of events for the International Society of Men's Health and Gender. Typical of Elsevier publications, the quality is superior; the cost is high. Research and medical libraries will want to subscribe.

3089. *Journal of Men's Studies: a scholarly journal about men and masculinities.* [ISSN: 1060-8265] 1992. 3x/yr. USD 150 (Individuals, USD 50). Ed(s): Dr. James A Doyle. Men's Studies Press, PO Box 32, Harriman, TN 37748-0032; publisher@mensstudies.com; http://www.mensstudies.com. Illus., adv. Sample. Refereed. Circ: 390 Paid. Vol. ends: May. *Indexed:* AmHI, CJA, CWI, GendWatch, HumInd, PsycInfo, SFSA. *Bk. rev.:* 4, 800 words. *Aud.:* Ac, Sa.

This journal concerning men and masculinity helps fill a void in the areas of psychosocial and sexual scholarship. The academic and professional communities constitute the target audience for this essential journal, which offers high-quality, peer-reviewed research that touches on a variety of disciplines, including anthropology, history, literature, psychology, and sociology. The *Journal of Men's Studies* is a first-rate tool to aid in defining modern man in a volatile, ever-changing culture. Every academic and research library should subscribe to this title.

3090. *Journal of Women, Politics & Policy: a quarterly journal of research & policy studies.* Formerly (until 2005): *Women & Politics.* [ISSN: 1554-477X] 1980. q. USD 530 print & online eds. Ed(s): Karen O'Connor. Haworth Press, Inc., 10 Alice St, Binghamton, NY 13904-1580; getinfo@haworthpress.com; http://www.haworthpress.com. Illus., adv. Sample. Refereed. Circ: 566 Paid. Vol. ends: No. 4. Microform: PQC. Online: EBSCO Publishing, EBSCO Host; OCLC Online Computer Library Center, Inc.; ProQuest LLC (Ann Arbor); SwetsWise Online Content; H.W. Wilson. Reprint: HAW. *Indexed:* ABCPolSci, ABS&EES, AgeL, AltPI, AmH&L, ArtHuCI, CWI, CommAb, ExcerpMed, FemPer, GendWatch, HistAb, IBR, IBSS, IBZ, IPSA, LRI, PAIS, PSA, SSA, SSCI, SWA, SWR&A, SociolAb, WSA. *Bk. rev.:* 5-14, 600 words; essay length; signed. *Aud.:* Ac, Sa.

Formerly *Women & Politics,* this journal was retitled to reflect its expanded international and multidisciplinary focus. It is "devoted to the advancement of knowledge about women's political participation and about the development of public policies that affect women and their families." Contents include research and theoretical articles by social scientists and public policy experts as well as book reviews. Widely covered by indexing/abstracting services. Tables of contents and a contents alert service are available on the publisher's web site.

3091. *Journal of Women's History.* [ISSN: 1042-7961] 1989. q. USD 115. Ed(s): Antoinette Burton, Jean Allman. The Johns Hopkins University Press, 2715 N Charles St, Baltimore, MD 21218-4363; http://muse.jhu.edu. Illus., adv. Sample. Refereed. Circ: 761. Vol. ends: Winter. Microform: PQC. Online: Chadwyck-Healey Inc.; EBSCO Publishing, EBSCO Host; Florida Center for Library Automation; Gale; Northern Light Technology, Inc.; OCLC Online Computer Library Center, Inc.; OhioLINK; Project MUSE; ProQuest K-12 Learning Solutions; ProQuest LLC (Ann Arbor); SwetsWise Online Content; H.W. Wilson. Reprint: PSC. *Indexed:* ABS&EES, AltPI, AmH&L, AmHI, ArtHuCI, BRI, CJA, CWI, FLI, FemPer, GendWatch, HistAb, HumInd, IBR, IBSS, IBZ, PSA, RILM, SSA, SWA, SociolAb, WSA. *Bk. rev.:* 2-4, essay length; 23-120 brief abstracts. *Aud.:* Ac.

This scholarly journal features theoretical and research articles about women and gender throughout world history. It publishes research articles and essays on methodological and theoretical topics in women's history. Contents also include "Roundtable" discussions, commentary, review essays, book reviews, and a listing of dissertations in women's history. One recent double-issue focuses on "Women Consumers." Full text is available online from 1999 on. An important journal for historical collections.

3092. *Journeymen.* [ISSN: 1061-8538] 1991. q. USD 18; USD 24 Canada. Ed(s): Paul S Boynton. Journeymen, 513 Chester Turnpike, Candia, NH 03034. Illus., adv. *Bk. rev.:* 1, 2,000 words signed. *Aud.:* Ga.

A small but intriguing magazine, *Journeymen* is described as a "participatory networking publication intended to help men make connections with each other." Within its covers the reader will find addressed such issues as father–son relationships, men's health, marriage, divorce, friendship, language and gender, and intimacy. Literary forms include, but are not limited to, poetry, essays, interviews, and book reviews. *Journeymen* is a sensitive and sensible alternative to the mainstream sex- and fashion-laden publications that permeate the men's magazine market.

3093. *The Liberator (Forest Lake): male call.* Formerly: *Legal Beagle.* [ISSN: 1040-3760] 1968. m. USD 24 in North America; USD 48 elsewhere. Ed(s): Richard F Doyle. Men's Defense Association, 17854 Lyons St, Forest Lake, MN 55025; rdoyle@mensdefense.org; http://www.mensdefense.org/. Illus., adv. Sample. Circ: 2000 Controlled. Vol. ends: Dec. *Bk. rev.:* 28 pages, signed. *Aud.:* Sa.

Pro-male in every respect, *The Liberator* represents a small but growing group of activist men who are dedicated to preserving the rights of males, particularly in such areas as divorce court, child custody, and visitation rights. The editors espouse a traditional view of the family and family values, and of men and masculinity, and they present their views in a straightforward manner with little regard for current trends or political correctness. Topics include domestic relations, feminist trends and legislation, child-abuse cases, the masculine ethic, and parental rights. Some readers will find this journal to be exactly what they want, and others will take offense at its bluntness and conservative views—but rest assured that *The Liberator* will be read.

3094. Lilith: the independent Jewish women's magazine. [ISSN: 0146-2334] 1976. q. USD 21 domestic; USD 27 Canada; USD 29 elsewhere. Lilith Publications, Inc., 250 W 57th St, Ste 2432, New York, NY 10107-0172. Adv. Circ: 10000. Microform: PQC. Online: ProQuest LLC (Ann Arbor). *Indexed:* ABS&EES, AltPI, ENW, FemPer, GendWatch, IJP, SWA, WSA. *Bk. rev.:* 5-14, 300 words, signed. *Aud.:* Ga, Sa.

Lilith is still going strong as one of the earliest magazines of the Second Wave feminist movement of the 1970s. Its nonfiction includes autobiography, biography, interviews, and analyses of wide-ranging topics affecting Jewish women around the world. Reports may focus on local grassroots activism or national and international events. *Lilith* also publishes fiction illuminating the lives of Jewish women and offers an annual fiction prize. Contributors include established authors such as Cynthia Ozick and Grace Paley and new writers. Selected articles, including some in Spanish, are available on the magazine's web site.

3095. Men and Masculinities. [ISSN: 1097-184X] 1998. 5x/yr. GBP 319. Ed(s): Michael S Kimmel. Sage Publications, Inc., 2455 Teller Rd, Thousand Oaks, CA 91320; info@sagepub.com; http://www.sagepub.com. Illus., adv. Sample. Refereed. Vol. ends: Apr (No. 4). Reprint: PSC. *Indexed:* CABA, CJA, CommAb, FPA, ForAb, HRA, IBSS, IndIslam, PSA, PsycInfo, RRTA, SFSA, SSA, SSCI, SWA, SociolAb. *Bk. rev.:* 6, 1,500 words, signed. *Aud.:* Ac, Sa.

Men and Masculinities is an important title in the area of research in men's studies. All topics are considered, including psychology, psychiatry, education, social and family relations, work, and sexuality. With a focus on research and an emphasis on quality, its editors insist that all articles pass the test of blind peer-review before publication. An editorial board made up of scholars from throughout the world ensures a broad base of scholarship and provides a forum for U.S. and international researchers. Research and academic libraries throughout the world should subscribe.

3096. Men's Voices. Former titles (until Sep. 1997): *M.E.N. Magazine; Seattle M.E.N. Newsletter.* [ISSN: 1520-247X] 1981. q. USD 20. Ed(s): Bert H Hoff. White Rock Alternative, 7552 31st Ave, N E, Seattle, WA 98115; berthoff@wln.com; http://www.vix.com/menmag/. Illus., adv. Sample. Circ: 1000. *Bk. rev.:* 6, 200 words, signed. *Aud.:* Ga, Sa.

A local publication that has gone national, *Men's Voices* has become a publishing leader in men's rights and the male experience since its introduction in 1981. Unlike some of its counterparts, *Men's Voices* acknowledges pro-feminist opinions and issues and attempts to treat male/female points-of-view in an unbiased, truthful, and politically correct manner. Articles, poetry, book reviews, and interviews with such leaders of the men's movement as Michael Meade and Robert Bly make this an important title for the library that seeks to provide access to diverse opinions. Check out the web version.

3097. Menstuff: the national men's resource. Former titles: *Menstuff (Print); (until 1993): National Men's Resource Calendar.* 1985. q. Free. Ed(s): Gordon Clay. National Men's Resource Center, PO Box 800, San Anselmo, CA 94979-0800; menstuff@menstuff.org; http://www.menstuff.org. Illus. *Bk. rev.:* Up to 20, 100 words. *Aud.:* Ga, Sa.

Menstuff is the official organ of the National Men's Resource Center, an association founded to support awareness of men's issues and help to end men's isolation. Current news and articles concerning issues such as divorce and child custody, families, abuse, sexuality, violence, and health appear regularly, as do book reviews on as many as 20 books per issue. A calendar of events, lists of

men's service organizations, and other sources of information and assistance for men are regular features. This site is essential for the research directory alone. Every library should have this web site bookmarked or hot-linked for quick and easy access.

3098. Meridians (Middletown): feminism, race, transnationalism. [ISSN: 1536-6936] 2000. s-a. USD 85 (Individuals, USD 30). Ed(s): Paula Giddings. Indiana University Press, 601 N Morton St, Bloomington, IN 47404. Refereed. *Indexed:* AltPI, AmHI, FemPer, GendWatch, HumInd, IIBP, PSA, SociolAb. *Aud.:* Ga, Ac.

Meridians publishes interdisciplinary "scholarship and creative work by and about women of color in the U.S. and international contexts." It focuses on the interplay of feminism, race, and transnationalism. Its contents include articles, essays, a counterpoint section featuring discussions of topical issues, interviews, reports, creative works, and media reviews. Edited at Smith College.

3099. Michigan Feminist Studies. Former titles (until 1987): *New Occasional Papers in Women's Studies;* (until 1983): *Michigan Occasional Paper;* Supersedes (in 1978): *University of Michigan Papers in Women's Studies.* [ISSN: 1055-856X] 1974. a. USD 40. Ed(s): Karen Miller, Cari Carpenter. University of Michigan, Women's Studies Department, 1122 Lane Hall, 204 S State St, Ann Arbor, MI 48109-1290; mfseditors@umich.edu. Illus., adv. Refereed. Circ: 500. *Indexed:* AmHI, FemPer, GendWatch, HumInd, WSA. *Bk. rev.:* 0-4, essay length, signed. *Aud.:* Ac.

This interdisciplinary journal from University of Michigan graduate students publishes original research on women and gender to "advance feminist theory and analysis." Each issue is organized around a theme. Recent issues include "Bodies: Physical and Abstract" and "Gender and Globalisms." Limited indexing.

Michigan Journal of Gender and Law. See Law section.

Ms. See News and Opinion section.

3100. N W S A Journal. [ISSN: 1040-0656] 1988. 3x/yr. USD 140. The Johns Hopkins University Press, 2715 N Charles St, Baltimore, MD 21218-4363; myq@press.jhu.edu; http://www.press.jhu.edu. Illus., adv. Refereed. Circ: 1200. Online: Chadwyck-Healey Inc.; EBSCO Publishing, EBSCO Host; Florida Center for Library Automation; Gale; OCLC Online Computer Library Center, Inc.; OhioLINK; Project MUSE; ProQuest LLC (Ann Arbor); SwetsWise Online Content; H.W. Wilson. Reprint: PSC. *Indexed:* ASSIA, AbAn, AmH&L, AmHI, BRI, CBRI, CJA, CWI, FemPer, GendWatch, HistAb, LeftInd, MLA-IB, PAIS, PSA, RILM, SSA, SWA, SociolAb, WSA. *Bk. rev.:* 9-12, brief and essay length, signed. *Aud.:* Ac.

The journal of the National Women's Studies Association publishes interdisciplinary, multicultural scholarship in women's studies. It seeks to connect feminist scholarship and theory with activism and teaching. In addition to research articles, its contents includes articles about the theory and teaching of women's studies and reviews of books, teaching materials, and films. One recent special issue focuses on "Feminist Activist Art" and its ability to effect change, while another examines "Feminism, Peace, and War."

3101. National N O W Times. Formerly: *Do It N O W.* [ISSN: 0149-4740] 1968. q. Non-members, USD 35. Ed(s): Patricia Ireland. National Organization for Women, 1100 H St NW, 3rd Fl, Washington, DC 20005; publications@now.org; http://www.now.org. Illus., adv. Circ: 250000. Vol. ends: Oct (No. 4). *Indexed:* AltPI. *Bk. rev.:* Number varies, 500 words, signed. *Aud.:* Ga, Ac.

The official newsletter of the National Organization for Women (NOW) provides news about feminist issues and achievements. It offers political commentary, conference reports, and notes on NOW chapter activities. It also includes book reviews, illustrations, and advertising. Full text of current and past issues is available on NOW's web site.

3102. *Nora: Nordic journal of women's studies.* [ISSN: 0803-8740] 1993. 3x/yr. GBP 101 print & online eds. Ed(s): Elisabet Rogg, Susanne V Knudsen. Taylor & Francis A B, Hollaendergatan 20, PO Box 3255, Stockholm, 10365, Sweden; journals@se.tandf.no. Illus., adv. Sample. Refereed. Online: EBSCO Publishing, EBSCO Host; Gale; IngentaConnect; OCLC Online Computer Library Center, Inc.; SwetsWise Online Content. Reprint: PSC. *Indexed:* ASSIA, FemPer, IBR, IBSS, IBZ, SWA. *Bk. rev.:* 6, 700 words-essay length, signed. *Aud.:* Ac.

While focusing on women's experiences in Nordic countries both historically and in the present, this journal is also international and offers discussions of interest to feminist scholars everywhere. One recent issue contains articles on the question of letters in historical research. Another examines how sports reflect and construct gender identities and relations. In addition to research articles, the content includes review essays and short communications. An article-alert service and tables of contents are available on the publisher's web site.

3103. *Off Our Backs: a women's news journal.* [ISSN: 0030-0071] 1970. 6x/yr. USD 40 (Individuals, USD 25; Students, USD 21). Ed(s): Jennie Ruby. Off Our Backs, Inc., 2337B 18th St, NW, Washington, DC 20009-2003. Illus., index, adv. Circ: 15000. Vol. ends: Dec. Microform: PQC. Online: EBSCO Publishing, EBSCO Host; Florida Center for Library Automation; Gale; Northern Light Technology, Inc.; OCLC Online Computer Library Center, Inc.; ProQuest LLC (Ann Arbor). *Indexed:* AltPI, BRI, CBRI, CWI, FemPer, GendWatch, SWA, WSA. *Bk. rev.:* 1-5, 1,000-2,000 words. *Aud.:* Ga, Ac.

This long-running feminist newspaper covers news about women and feminist activism around the world. It serves as a resource for information on feminist and lesbian culture and as a forum for discussion. It also aims to educate the public and to promote social justice and equality. One recent issue includes reports on religious fundamentalism and women's oppression throughout the world. Special features include reviews of books, theater, film, television, and music, and a comic strip called "Dykes to Watch Out For."

3104. *Outskirts (Online Edition): feminisms along the edge.* Formerly (until 1996): *Outskirts (Print Edition).* [ISSN: 1445-0445] 1981. s-a. Free. Ed(s): Delys Bird. University of Western Australia, Centre for Women's Studies, http://www.chloe.uwa.edu.au/outskirts/. Refereed. *Bk. rev.:* Number and length vary. *Aud.:* Ac.

This is a refereed, feminist, cultural-studies e-journal issued from the English Department of the University of Western Australia and the Women's Studies program of the University of Adelaide. Its focus is on a broad range of issues in "feminisms along the edge." Contents include articles, commentaries, conference reports, and reviews of performances and books. Full text is available online from 1996 forward. URL: www.chloe.uwa.edu.au/outskirts.

3105. *Psychology of Men & Masculinity.* [ISSN: 1524-9220] 2000. q. USD 295 (Individuals, USD 80; Members, USD 55). Ed(s): Sam V Cochran. American Psychological Association, 750 First St, N E, Washington, DC 20002-4242; journals@apa.org; http://www.apa.org. Vol. ends: Dec. Online: Pub.; CSA; EBSCO Publishing, EBSCO Host; OCLC Online Computer Library Center, Inc.; OhioLINK; Ovid Technologies, Inc.; ProQuest LLC (Ann Arbor); ScienceDirect. Reprint: PSC. *Indexed:* PsycInfo. *Aud.:* Ac, Sa.

Research, theory, and clinical scholarship concerning men and masculinity constitute this blind-reviewed journal published by the American Psychological Association. Among the topics addressed are men's health, behavior, emotional development, relationships, gender roles, parenting, and sexuality. A rigorous peer-reviewing system ensures the quality of the articles chosen for each issue, making this one of the most prestigious titles in its field.

3106. *Resources for Feminist Research.* Formerly: *Canadian Newsletter of Research on Women.* [ISSN: 0707-8412] 1972. s-a. CND 80 (Individuals, CND 38; Students, CND 27). Ed(s): Philinda Masters. University of Toronto, Ontario Institute for Studies in Education, 252 Bloor St W, Toronto, ON M5S 1V6, Canada. Illus., index, adv. Refereed. Circ: 2000. Vol. ends: Winter. Microform: MML. Online: Florida Center for Library

Automation; Gale; Micromedia ProQuest; OCLC Online Computer Library Center, Inc. *Indexed:* AgeL, AmH&L, AmHI, CBCARef, CEI, CPerI, CWI, FemPer, HistAb, SSA, SWA, SociolAb, WSA. *Bk. rev.:* 5-20, length varies, signed. *Aud.:* Ac.

This bilingual (English/French) journal from the University of Toronto publishes research on issues relating to gender, sexuality, ethnicity, nationality, and class. Its theme-based issues focus on such topics as "Women's Studies and the Internet" and "The Impact of Gender Studies Across the Disciplines." Contents includes research articles, discussion papers or reports, and essays as well as book reviews and poems.

3107. *Sex & Health.* Former titles (until 1997): *Men's Confidential Newsletter;* (until 1993): *Men's Health Newsletter.* [ISSN: 1097-4717] 1985. m. USD 48. Ed(s): Michael Lafavore. Rodale, Inc., 33 E Minor St, Emmaus, PA 18098; http://www.rodale.com. Illus., adv. Circ: 110000 Paid. *Aud.:* Ga.

A newsletter that focuses on medical advice for men, *Sex & Health* addresses health, aging, stress, nutrition, and hygiene, but it places particular emphasis on sexual issues. Most of the articles are brief, very readable, and based on research. Two columns, "Better Sex" and "Ask Sex & Health," address sexual problems with candor and insight. Back issues are available online.

3108. *Signs: journal of women in culture and society.* [ISSN: 0097-9740] 1975. q. USD 245 domestic; USD 275.24 Canada; USD 266 elsewhere. Ed(s): Mary Hawkesworth. University of Chicago Press, Journals Division, PO Box 37005, Chicago, IL 60637; subscriptions@ press.uchicago.edu; http://www.journals.uchicago.edu. Illus., index, adv. Refereed. Circ: 2600 Paid. Vol. ends: Summer. Microform: PMC; PQC. Online: Chadwyck-Healey Inc.; EBSCO Publishing, EBSCO Host; Factiva, Inc.; Florida Center for Library Automation; Gale; JSTOR (Web-based Journal Archive); OCLC Online Computer Library Center, Inc.; ProQuest K-12 Learning Solutions; ProQuest LLC (Ann Arbor). Reprint: PSC. *Indexed:* ABCPolSci, ABS&EES, ASSIA, AgeL, AmH&L, AmHI, AnthLit, ArtHuCI, BAS, BRI, CBRI, CommAb, FR, FemPer, HistAb, IBR, IBSS, IBZ, IMFL, IPSA, LeftInd, MLA-IB, NTA, PSA, PsycInfo, RI-1, RILM, SFSA, SSA, SSCI, SWA, SociolAb, V&AA, WSA. *Bk. rev.:* 2-12, 1,200-2,000 words, signed. *Aud.:* Ac.

This established journal publishes interdisciplinary articles on familiar and new areas of feminist scholarship including gender, sexuality, race, ethnicity, and nationality. Content includes research articles, essays, review essays, book reviews, and notes. Some issues include "Comparative Perspectives Symposia," i.e., sets of articles on themes such as "Gender and Spirituality" or "Women in Refugee Camps." Other articles trace the growth and development of feminist scholarship. Contents pages and full text are available on the publisher's web site from 2002 to date.

3109. *Social Politics: international studies in gender, state, and society.* [ISSN: 1072-4745] 1994. q. EUR 144 print or online ed. Ed(s): Barbara Hobson, Ann Orloff. Oxford University Press, Great Clarendon St, Oxford, OX2 6DP, United Kingdom; jnl.orders@oup.co.uk; http://www.oxfordjournals.org. Illus., index, adv. Refereed. Circ: 850. Vol. ends: No. 3. Microform: PQC. Online: EBSCO Publishing, EBSCO Host; Gale; HighWire Press; IngentaConnect; OCLC Online Computer Library Center, Inc.; OhioLINK; Oxford Journals; Project MUSE; SwetsWise Online Content. Reprint: PSC. *Indexed:* AmH&L, CJA, FemPer, HistAb, IBR, IBSS, IBZ, PAIS, PSA, SSA, SSCI, SWA, SociolAb. *Bk. rev.:* essay length, signed. *Aud.:* Ac, Sa.

This scholarly journal applies a feminist and gender perspective to the analysis of social policy, the state, and society. It is interdisciplinary and multicultural in scope. Articles in one recent issue on "Child Care, East and West" provide new insights into child care policies by examining differences among nations and over time. The publisher's web site provides tables of contents, article abstracts, and an e-mail contents alerting service.

Southern California Review of Law and Women's Studies. See Law section.

3110. *Studies in Gender and Sexuality.* [ISSN: 1524-0657] 2000. q. GBP 156 print & online eds. Ed(s): Ken Corbett. The Analytic Press, Inc., 10 Industrial Ave, Mahwah, NJ 07430; TAP@analyticpress.com; http://www.analyticpress.com. Adv. Refereed. Reprint: PSC. *Indexed:* FemPer, IBR, IBZ, PsycInfo, SWA, SociolAb. *Aud.:* Ac.

This journal looks at gender and sexuality from the perspectives of feminism, psychoanalytic theory, developmental research, and cultural studies. Contents represent a variety of theoretical, clinical, and methodological approaches. Some issues offer roundtable discussions and sets of papers on topics such as the psychological transformation brought by motherhood. Contents pages are available on the publisher's web site. Full text is available from 2000 on.

3111. *Transitions (Minneapolis).* [ISSN: 0886-862X] 1981. bi-m. Membership, USD 30. Ed(s): Jim Lovestar. National Coalition of Free Men, PO Box 582023, Minneapolis, MN 55458; ncfm@ncfm.org; http://www.ncfm.org. Illus., adv. Sample. Online: ProQuest LLC (Ann Arbor). *Indexed:* GendWatch. *Bk. rev.:* 1, 500 words, signed. *Aud.:* Ga, Sa.

"*Transitions* is intended as an educational forum for new ideas and articulation of men's issues," according to its mission statement. The official newsletter of the National Coalition of Free Men, *Transitions* mirrors the goal of the organization, which is to achieve true equity between the sexes. However, because of activist positions among many feminist groups, this journal appears to be at odds with the women's movement. Domestic violence against men, divorce, child custody, and male bashing are frequently dealt with in *Transitions*, as are the changing roles of women and their impact on men. Obviously a publication with an agenda, this journal nevertheless presents well-documented arguments against gender biases by authorities in the area of men's studies and asks thought-provoking questions of leaders and legislators who have pushed the feminist agenda at all costs. Every library that promotes activist women's issues should subscribe to *Transitions* in order to provide perspective.

3112. *Violence Against Women: an international and interdisciplinary journal.* [ISSN: 1077-8012] 1995. m. GBP 575. Ed(s): Claire M Renzetti. Sage Publications, Inc., 2455 Teller Rd, Thousand Oaks, CA 91320; info@sagepub.com; http://www.sagepub.com. Illus., adv. Sample. Refereed. Circ: 700 Paid and free. Vol. ends: Dec. Reprint: PSC. *Indexed:* ASG, ASSIA, CINAHL, CJA, CJPI, FemPer, H&SSA, HRA, IBSS, PsycInfo, RiskAb, SFSA, SSA, SSCI, SUSA, SWA, SociolAb, V&AA. *Bk. rev.:* 2, essay length, signed. *Aud.:* Ga, Ac, Sa.

This journal publishes empirical research and cross-cultural and historical analyses of violence against women and girls. It is concerned with both well-known and lesser-known forms of violence and seeks to promote dialogue among people of diverse backgrounds working in various fields and disciplines. Contents include research articles, review essays, survivor articles and poetry, and clinical, legal, and research notes. The journal also includes book reviews. Two recent special issues explore the themes of "gender-based violence against immigrant women" and "intimate partner violence among Latinos." Articles are available on the publisher's web site to members of institutions with print subscriptions. The publisher also offers a contents alerting service.

3113. *Wagadu: a journal of transnational women's and gender studies.* [ISSN: 1545-6196] 2004. q. Free. Ed(s): Mechthild Nagel. State University of New York at Cortland, P. O. Box 2000, Cortland, NY 13045. Refereed. *Bk. rev.:* Number and length vary. *Aud.:* Ac.

This free, online, peer-reviewed journal provides a postcolonial and transnational perspective on race and gender issues. It is intended as "a medium of exchange and information . . . for scholars and activists." Contents include articles written around a single theme such as "Feminists Confront Empire," "Women in a Global Environment," and "Water and Women in Past, Present and Future," plus book reviews. Articles are predominantly in English but submissions in other languages are also welcomed.

3114. *Women: a cultural review.* [ISSN: 0957-4042] 1990. 3x/yr. GBP 231 print & online eds. Ed(s): Helen Carr, Isobel Armstrong. Routledge, 4 Park Sq, Milton Park, Abingdon, OX14 4RN, United Kingdom; info@routledge.co.uk; http://www.routledge.co.uk. Adv. Circ: 450.

Online: EBSCO Publishing, EBSCO Host; Gale; IngentaConnect; OCLC Online Computer Library Center, Inc.; SwetsWise Online Content. Reprint: PSC. *Indexed:* AltPI, AmHI, BrHumI, CWI, FLI, FemPer, HumInd, IBSS, RI-1. *Bk. rev.:* Number and length vary. *Aud.:* Ac.

The focus of this British journal is on "the role and representation of gender and sexuality in the arts and culture, with a particular focus on the contemporary world." It publishes research articles, essays, review essays, interviews, and book reviews about women and gender in literature, the media, history, education, law, philosophy, psychoanalysis, and the fine and performing arts. Two special issues a year are thematic. The publisher's web site provides tables of contents and an article-alert service.

3115. *Women & Environments International Magazine.* Former titles (until 2001): *W E International Magazine;* (until 1998): *Women and Environments;* (until 1980): *Women and Environments International Newsletter.* [ISSN: 1499-1993] 1976. s-a. CND 35 (Individuals, CND 22; CND 5.95 newsstand/cover). Ed(s): Reggie Modlich, Prabha Khosla. Institute for Women's Studies and Gender Studies, New College, University of Toronto, Toronto, ON M5S 1C6, Canada; we.mag@utoronto.ca; http://www.weimag.com. Illus., adv. Circ: 1850 Paid and controlled. Microform: CML. Online: EBSCO Publishing, EBSCO Host; LexisNexis; Micromedia ProQuest; OCLC Online Computer Library Center, Inc.; ProQuest LLC (Ann Arbor); H.W. Wilson. *Indexed:* AltPI, CBCARef, CPerl, EnvAb, FemPer, GendWatch, MASUSE, SFSA, SWA, WSA. *Bk. rev.:* 1-4, 175-400 words. *Aud.:* Ga, Ac.

This Canadian magazine "examines women's multiple relationships with their environments—natural, built, and social—from feminist perspectives." It provides a forum for discussions among academics, professionals, and activists. Contents include research articles, essays, interviews, news updates, book reviews, art, and poetry. A recent issue features articles on "Women and Global Climate Change." Excerpts from articles in the current issue and contents pages for back issues are available on the journal's web site.

Women and Music. See Music section.

Women & Therapy. See Psychology section.

3116. *Women's History Review.* [ISSN: 0961-2025] 1992. 5x/yr. GBP 364 print & online eds. Ed(s): June Purvis. Routledge, 4 Park Sq, Milton Park, Abingdon, OX14 4RN, United Kingdom; info@routledge.co.uk; http://www.routledge.co.uk. Illus., index, adv. Sample. Refereed. Vol. ends: Dec. Reprint: PSC. *Indexed:* AmH&L, AmHI, ArtHuCI, BRI, BrHumI, FemPer, HistAb, HumInd, IBR, IBZ, PSA, SSA, SWA, SociolAb. *Bk. rev.:* 5-8, length varies, signed. *Aud.:* Ac.

This journal provides an interdisciplinary, feminist perspective on women and gender relations in history. Coverage, while heavily British, also includes U.S., European, and world history. The journal also includes review essays and book reviews. Tables of contents and abstracts are available on the publisher's web site.

3117. *Women's Studies: an interdisciplinary journal.* [ISSN: 0049-7878] 1972. 8x/yr. GBP 613 print & online eds. Ed(s): Wendy Martin. Taylor & Francis Inc., 325 Chestnut St, Ste 800, Philadelphia, PA 19016; orders@taylorandfrancis.com; http://www.taylorandfrancis.com. Illus., adv. Refereed. Microform: MIM. Online: EBSCO Publishing, EBSCO Host; Florida Center for Library Automation; Gale; IngentaConnect; Northern Light Technology, Inc.; OCLC Online Computer Library Center, Inc.; SwetsWise Online Content. Reprint: PSC. *Indexed:* ABS&EES, AbAn, AmH&L, AmHI, BrHumI, CommAb, FLI, FemPer, HistAb, HumInd, IBR, IBSS, IBZ, MLA-IB, RILM, SSA, SWA, SociolAb, WSA. *Bk. rev.:* Number and length vary. *Aud.:* Ac.

This journal publishes articles, essays, and book reviews that focus largely on women in literature and the arts, but it is also interdisciplinary in outlook. Its contents include poetry and film and book reviews. Occasional issues focus on special topics such as "Globalization, Activism, and the Academy: Resisting Complicity, Challenging Backlash." Tables of contents and a contents alerting service are available on the publisher's web site.

3118. Women's Studies International Forum. Former titles (until 1982): *Women's Studies International Quarterly;* (until 1979): *Women's Studies (Oxford).* [ISSN: 0277-5395] 1978. 6x/yr. EUR 655. Ed(s): Christine Zmroczek. Pergamon, The Boulevard, Langford Ln, East Park, Kidlington, OX5 1GB, United Kingdom; nlinfo-f@elsevier.nl; http://www.elsevier.nl. Illus., index, adv. Sample. Refereed. Circ: 1000. Vol. ends: Nov/Dec (No. 24). Microform: PQC. Online: EBSCO Publishing, EBSCO Host; Gale; IngentaConnect; OhioLINK; ScienceDirect; SwetsWise Online Content. *Indexed:* ABS&EES, AbAn, AgeL, AltPI, AmH&L, AmHI, AnthLit, BAS, BrHumI, CJA, CommAb, FemPer, HistAb, IBR, IBSS, IBZ, IndIslam, PSA, PsycInfo, SSA, SSCI, SWA, SociolAb, WSA. *Bk. rev.:* 6-10, length varies, signed. *Aud.:* Ac.

This expensive journal offers truly global coverage of women's studies and feminist research. It publishes research and theoretical articles, review essays, and book reviews. One or more theme-based issues a year address special topics such as "Gender in Commonwealth Higher Education" and "Gendered Violence." The publisher's web site offers tables of contents, abstracts, and a contents alerting service.

3119. Women's Studies Quarterly. Formerly: *Women's Studies Newsletter.* [ISSN: 0732-1562] 1972. 4x/yr. USD 50 (Individuals, USD 40; USD 22 per issue). Ed(s): Cindy Katz. Feminist Press, CUNY Graduate Center, 365 5th Ave, New York, NY 10016; mvaux@gc.cuny.edu; http://www.feministpress.org. Illus., adv. Refereed. Circ: 3000 Controlled. Vol. ends: Fall/Winter (No. 3 - No. 4). Reprint: PSC. *Indexed:* ABIn, ABS&EES, AgeL, AltPI, AmH&L, CJA, EduInd, FemPer, HistAb, PAIS, PSA, RILM, SSA, SWA, SociolAb, WSA. *Bk. rev.:* 0-5, 1,000-1,800 words, signed. *Aud.:* Ga, Ac.

This journal from Feminist Press provides an international and cross-cultural perspective on research and teaching in women's studies. Its contents include research articles and articles about teaching. Theme-based issues provide diverse viewpoints and in-depth coverage of subjects such as "The Global and the Intimate" and "Gender and Culture in the 1950s."

3120. X Y: Men, Masculinities and Gender Politcs. 1999. irreg. Ed(s): Michael Flood. X Y: Men, Masculinities and Gender Politcs, PO Box 473, Blackwood, SA 5051, Australia. *Bk. rev.:* 1, 200 words, signed. *Aud.:* Ac, Sa.

A print journal gone electronic, this title was orginally *XY: Men, Sex, Politics,* published in Canberra, Australia, from 1990 to 1998. During its eight-year history, 397 feature articles were printed in the journal. This web site contains 60 of the best articles from the print journal, and new articles are added to the web site periodically. Issues the journal has explored include the men's movement, masculinity, class, race, sexuality, and domestic violence. Feature articles are peer reviewed. Personal stories, bibliographies, poems, and other literary forms are included. Although originating from Australia, *XY* is popular with contributors and readers from around the world.

■ GENEALOGY

Computers and Genealogy/International and Ethnic-Interest Journals/ National and Regional Journals/State—Alphabetical by State

See also Canada; Europe; and History sections.

Scott Andrew "Drew" Bartley, former archivist and reference librarian at the New England Historic Genealogical Society, now researcher, consultant, editor of the Mayflower Descendant *and* Vermont Genealogy, *Boston, MA; www.yourgenealogist.com*

Introduction

Genealogy is one of the most popular hobbies today. Though claiming interest from all ages, the main group is over 60. This 60-plus group is more computer-literate than other similarly aged groups, and they also focus more time on their passion than other hobbyist groups. For that reason, libraries need to be ready to serve this group of users. Every library needs an adequate genealogical collection. Now, that means library patron access to one of the major genealogical databases (Ancestry.com, Heritage Quest, New England Historic Genealogical Society, etc.). Part of any good collection also includes access to the latest articles written on the subject.

Coverage by genealogical periodicals runs the gamut of topics across geographical locations, ethnicities, and time periods. There are scholarly journals, commercial publications, how-to manuals, society newsletters, and a mixture of all of these. There are so many genealogical periodicals in print today that not all could be presented here. No surname-based journals are included (e.g., the *Smith Family Journal*). Only a few county or local journals are presented when no statewide journal exists. (For a list of those journals, see *Printed Sources: A Guide to Published Genealogical Records* by Kory L. Meyerink [*Ancestry,* 1998], pp. 742–750.) One representative journal from each U.S. state was solicited, and 46 out of 50 states are represented either by their own journal or by a regional journal. Some states have more than one journal, but limited space requires that each state have but one entry, with two exceptions. Journals based on ethnicity were selected from those published in English. There are no comprehensive journals for Irish, Hispanic, or Italian genealogy. Some of these are international publications, but no other international journals were solicited.

Journals on computers and genealogy, as well as e-journals, have continue their evolution. No scholarly journal has yet switched to e-journal only, but some have offered parts that way. The best meta-site for all things genealogical continues to be found at www.CyndisList.com.

As used herein, the term *scholarly* does not apply to an arcane, intellectual journal meant only for the elite. I use the term to designate journals that properly footnote each genealogically significant event to a primary source so a reader may go directly to that source. *Solid* journals are those that footnote a majority of their work, although not completely. In many instances secondary print sources are cited, which forces the researcher to do a double look-up. *Basic* journals do not cite sources; and although they publish worthy material, it is left to the reader to follow up on the journal's research. The term *FASG*, which stands for Fellow of the American Society of Genealogists, follows several of the editors' names in this section. The ASG is the leader in genealogical scholarship, and the journals edited by fellows of that society should be looked upon as models in this field. *Primary-source transcriptions* refers to printed lists of original records for genealogy, such as tax lists, marriage records, Bible records, freeman lists, and the like.

Computers and Genealogy

3121. Genealogical Computing. [ISSN: 0277-5913] 1981. q. USD 25 domestic; USD 30 in Canada & Mexico; USD 35 elsewhere. Ed(s): Elizabeth Kelley Kerstens. MyFamily.com Inc., 360 West 4800 N, Provo, UT 84604; gceditor@ancestry-inc.com; http://www.ancestry.com. Illus., index, adv. Circ: 11000. Vol. ends: Apr. *Aud.:* Ga.

From the publishers of *Ancestry,* this journal focuses on the use of computers to enhance genealogical research. Software, CD-ROMs, scanners, and the Internet are all well-covered topics. Software and CD-ROM reviews are regular features. An annual directory of genealogy software is comprehensive and supplies all the information needed for this field. Recommended for all libraries.

International and Ethnic-Interest Journals

3122. Acadian Genealogical Exchange Newsletter. [ISSN: 0199-9591] 1972. s-a. USD 17 domestic; USD 20 foreign. Ed(s): Janet B Jehn. Acadian Genealogical Exchange, 3265 Wayman Branch Rd, Covington, KY 41015; janjehn@aol.com; http://www.acadiangenexch.com. Illus., adv. Circ: 600. Vol. ends: Oct. *Bk. rev.:* 20/yr. *Aud.:* Ga.

A journal dedicated to Acadian, French Canadian, and Cajun ancestry. Its articles run the gamut from genealogical help on the Internet to family genealogies. Ancestor tables and queries are published. The April and July issues are combined into one magazine.

3123. *Afro-American Historical and Genealogical Society. Journal.*
[ISSN: 0272-1937] 1980. s-a. USD 45 (Individuals, USD 35). Ed(s):
Sylvia Polk-Burriss. Afro-American Historical and Genealogical Society,
PO Box 73086, Washington, DC 20056-3086. Illus., index, adv. Circ:
900. Vol. ends: Summer/Fall. *Indexed:* AmH&L, HistAb, IIBP. *Bk. rev.:*
10/yr. *Aud.:* Ga, Ac.

This scholarly journal provides in-depth methodology for the research of
African American ancestry. Primary source transcriptions are included, as well
as analyses of such data for research. Family genealogies are published, as are
reports of archives with depository materials for African American genealogy.
A cumulative index for 1980–1990 is available.

3124. *American-Canadian Genealogist.* q. Institutional members, USD 50;
Individual members, USD 30. American-Canadian Genealogical Society,
PO Box 6478, Manchester, NH 03108-6478; editor@acgs.org. *Aud.:* Ga.

A basic journal presenting society news, a surname search list, and queries.

3125. *Augustan.* Former titles: *Augustan Society Omnibus; Augustan
Society Information Bulletin; Forbears; Augustan;* Incorporates: *Royalty
and Monarchy; Genealogical Library Journal; Colonial Genealogist;
English Genealogist;* Which was formerly: *English Genealogist Helper;*
Incorporates: *Germanic Genealogist;* Which was formerly: *Germanic
Genealogist Helper;* Incorporates: *Heraldry; Chivalry.* 1957. q. USD 24.
Ed(s): Rodney Hartwell. Augustan Society, Inc., PO Box 75, Daggett,
CA 92327-0075; http://www.augustansociety.org. Illus., index, adv. Vol.
ends: No. 4. *Bk. rev.:* 10/yr. *Aud.:* Sa.

A scholarly journal that focuses on ancient, medieval, and royal European
ancestry. A cumulative index for 1959–1975 is available.

3126. *Avotaynu: the international review of Jewish genealogy.* [ISSN:
0882-6501] 1985. q. USD 35 in North America; USD 43 elsewhere.
Ed(s): Sallyann Admur Sack. Avotaynu Inc., 155 N Washington Ave,
Bergenfield, NJ 07621. Illus., adv. Circ: 3000 Paid. Vol. ends: Winter.
Indexed: IJP. *Bk. rev.:* 15/yr. *Aud.:* Ga, Ac.

A scholarly journal that focuses on Jewish genealogy. Articles concentrate on
resources, both in the United States and abroad, to aid the researcher, as well as
methodology suggestions. Queries, "Ask the Experts," and Internet help are
regular features.

3127. *Family History.* [ISSN: 0014-7265] 1962. q. GBP 15. Ed(s): Cecil R
Humphery Smith. Institute of Heraldic and Genealogical Studies, 79-82,
Northgate, Canterbury, CT1 1BA, United Kingdom; ihgs@ihgs.ac.uk;
http://www.ihgs.ac.uk. Illus., adv. Circ: 1300. Vol. ends: Oct. Microform:
PQC. *Indexed:* ABS&EES, BrArAb, HistAb, NumL. *Bk. rev.:* 35/yr.
Aud.: Ga, Ac.

This scholarly journal reflects the mission of the institute, which is to study the
history and structure of the family. The articles focus on British genealogy,
much of which is medieval and contains heraldic information. The institute's
news and upcoming events are also published.

3128. *The Genealogist: your family history magazine.* [ISSN: 0311-1776]
1974. q. AUD 44. Ed(s): Margaret Rowe-Keys. Australian Institute of
Genealogical Studies, Inc., PO Box 339, Blackburn, VIC 3130, Australia;
info@aigs.org.au; http://www.aigs.org.au/. Circ: 4000. *Aud.:* Ga.

This basic journal from Australia features how-to articles, society news, library
acquisitions, surname interest lists, and a column on web sites.

3129. *Genealogists' Magazine.* [ISSN: 0016-6391] 1925. q. GBP 16
domestic (Free to members). Ed(s): Michael Gandy. Society of Genealogists, 14 Charterhouse Bldgs, Goswell Rd, London, EC1M 7BA, United
Kingdom; http://www.sog.org.uk. Illus., index, adv. Sample. Circ: 16000.
Vol. ends: Dec. *Bk. rev.:* 50/yr. *Aud.:* Ac, Sa.

The national scholarly journal for genealogy in the United Kingdom. Articles
are well cited and focus on methodology and primary sources rather than actual
family genealogies. Queries, library updates, obituaries, and society news
appear in each issue.

3130. *German Genealogical Digest.* [ISSN: 1085-2565] 1985. q. USD 22.
Ed(s): Larry Jensen. Jensen Publications, PO Box 780, Pleasant Grove,
UT 84062. Adv. Circ: 1300. *Bk. rev.:* 10/yr. *Aud.:* Ga.

A well-written scholarly journal for German genealogy written in English. The
articles are well cited and focus on methodology. An "Ask the Experts" section
and queries are regular features. Because more Americans are ethnically
German than anything else, this is an important journal for all libraries.

3131. *Mennonite Family History.* [ISSN: 0730-5214] 1982. q. USD 18.
Ed(s): J Lemar Mast. Masthof Press, 220 Mill Rd, Morgantown, PA
19543; mast@masthof.com. Illus., adv. Circ: 1850. *Aud.:* Ga, Ac.

A scholarly journal featuring primary source and genealogy for Mennonite,
Amish, and Brethren family history. The annual index is published separately.

3132. *Nase Rodina.* [ISSN: 1045-8190] 1989. q. Membership, USD 20
individuals. Czechoslovak Genealogical Society, Intl., PO Box 16225, St.
Paul, MN 55116-0225; http://www.cgsi.org. *Aud.:* Ga.

Nase Rodina, a scholarly journal, promotes genealogy of the ethnic groups that
comprise Czechoslovakia as it was formed in 1918. Those groups include
Czech, Bohemian, Moravian, Slovak, German, Hungarian, Jewish, Rusyn, and
Silesian genealogy. Each issue has a single theme or topic for all articles. Each
includes queries and a calendar of events.

3133. *New Netherland Connections.* [ISSN: 1087-4542] 1996. q. USD 15.
Ed(s): Dorothy A Koenig. New Netherland Connections, 1232 Carlotta
Ave, Berkeley, CA 94707-2707; dkoenig@library.berkeley.edu. Illus.,
index. Sample. Circ: 500. Vol. ends: Nov. *Bk. rev.:* 4/yr. *Aud.:* Ga.

This journal focuses on the families of the New Netherland Colony (New York
and New Jersey) in the colonial period, 1624–1664. Articles include family
genealogies and methodology. Ancestor tables are not published, but queries
and answers are. Corrections to errors in printed genealogies are also a focus of
this journal.

3134. *Palatine Immigrant: Researching German-speaking ancestry.*
[ISSN: 0884-5735] 1975. q. Individuals, USD 28. Ed(s): John T Golden.
The Palatines to America Society, Capital University, Columbus, OH
43209-2394; pal-am@juno.com; http://www.palam.org. Illus., index. Circ:
3000 Paid. Vol. ends: Dec. *Bk. rev.:* 80/yr. *Aud.:* Ga, Ac.

A scholarly journal for German-speaking ancestry, not just Palatine research.
Articles on methodology and primary source transcriptions appear in English.
An immigrant ancestor register is a regular feature, along with upcoming events
for the society.

3135. *Rodziny.* Formerly (until 1992): *Polish Genealogical Society
Newsletter.* [ISSN: 1544-726X] 1979. s-a. Individuals, USD 15. Ed(s):
William Hoffman. Polish Genealogical Society of America, Inc., 984 N
Milwaukee Ave, Chicago, IL 60622; pgsamerica@aol.com;
http://www.pgsa.org. Illus., adv. Circ: 1500. *Indexed:* ABS&EES. *Aud.:*
Ga.

The focus of *Rodziny* is on Polish American ancestry. It is published
semi-annually (May and August) and is more scholarly than its companion
volume, *The Bulletin of the Polish Genealogical Society of America.* The
Bulletin provides society news, queries, and upcoming events and is published
quarterly. All aspects of Polish genealogy are covered.

3136. *The Scottish Genealogist.* [ISSN: 0300-337X] 1954. q. GBP 16
(Individuals, GBP 16). Ed(s): Stuart E Fleming. Scottish Genealogy
Society, 15 Victoria Terrace, Edinburgh, EH1 2JL, United Kingdom;
info@scotsgenealogy.com; http://www.scotsgenealogy.com. Illus., index.
Circ: 2000. Vol. ends: Dec. *Bk. rev.:* 20/yr. *Aud.:* Ga, Ac.

The national scholarly journal for genealogy in Scotland. Articles focus on
methodology and primary source suggestions rather than family genealogies.
Queries, library news, Scottish genealogies in progress, and society news are
also included.

3137. *Swedish American Genealogist: a quarterly journal devoted to Swedish American biography, genealogy and personal history.* [ISSN: 0275-9314] 1981. q. USD 25 in North America; SEK 250 in Scandinavia. Ed(s): Mrs. Elisabeth Thorsell. Swenson Swedish Immigration Research Center, Augustana College, 639 38th St, Rock Island, IL 61201-2296; http://www.augustana.edu/administration/swenson/. Illus., index, adv. Circ: 900. Vol. ends: Dec. *Indexed:* AmH&L, HistAb. *Bk. rev.:* 10/yr. *Aud.:* Ga, Ac.

The scholarly journal is subtitled "devoted to Swedish American biography, genealogy and personal history," and all these areas are covered. It provides methodology articles and primary source materials on Swedes in both the United States and Sweden. Family genealogies, ancestor tables, and queries are included.

National and Regional Journals

3138. *American Genealogist.* Formerly (until 1932): *New Haven Genealogical Magazine.* [ISSN: 0002-8592] 1922. q. USD 30. Ed(s): David L Greene, Robert Charles Anderson. American Genealogist, PO Box 398, Demorest, GA 30535-0398. Illus., index. Refereed. Circ: 1920 Paid and free. Vol. ends: Oct. Microform: PQC. Online: Northern Light Technology, Inc. *Indexed:* BRI, CBRI. *Bk. rev.:* 40/yr. *Aud.:* Ga, Ac.

This scholarly journal focuses on genealogical methodology and problem solving in the context of colonial American families. European origins and some medieval and royal-ancestry articles are also included. There is a query section, but ancestor tables are no longer published. There is a yearly index and a published index of the first 60 volumes (currently out of print). *Periodical Contents Index* includes this journal through the year 1960 (volume 36). Recommended for both academic and public libraries.

3139. *American Genealogy Magazine.* [ISSN: 1049-6696] 1986. bi-m. USD 22.50. Ed(s): Jamese Pylant. Datatrace Systems, 378 S Baxter, Box 1587, Stephenville, TX 76401. Illus., adv. Circ: 1200 Paid. *Aud.:* Ga.

A scholarly journal featuring how-to articles and abstracts of primary sources. Each issue includes a surname-only index.

3140. *Ancestry Magazine.* Formerly: *Ancestry Newsletter.* [ISSN: 1075-475X] 1983. bi-m. USD 24.95 domestic; USD 29.95 in Canada & Mexico; USD 34.95 elsewhere. Ed(s): Jennifer Utley. MyFamily.com Inc., 360 West 4800 N, Provo, UT 84604; http://www.ancestry.com. Illus., adv. Circ: 40000 Paid. Vol. ends: Nov/Dec. *Aud.:* Ga.

This is a sleek, visually beautiful magazine and one of the few genealogy publications found on newsstands. Articles by experts in the field focus on methodology, top research areas, etc., and the scope is national. The publisher also hosts a popular web site on genealogy.

3141. *Association of Professional Genealogists Quarterly.* Former titles (until 1991): *A P G Quarterly; A P G Newsletter;* Supersedes (1975-1979, vol.5, no.3): *Professional Genealogists' News Bulletin.* [ISSN: 1056-6732] 1979. q. USD 50 domestic; USD 55 Canada; USD 70 elsewhere. Ed(s): Pamela Boyer Porter. Association of Professional Genealogists, PO Box 350998, Westminster, CO 80035-0998. Illus., adv. Circ: 1400. Vol. ends: Dec. *Bk. rev.:* 25/yr. *Aud.:* Sa.

This journal provides articles aimed at the professional genealogist, including software reviews, research tips, and writing and editing suggestions. Society news and upcoming events are features. A 20-year (1979–1999) cumulative article index is available online at www.apgen.org/qindex.html.

3142. *Eastman's Online Genealogy Newsletter.* [ISSN: 1544-4090] 1996. w. Ed(s): Richard Eastman. MyFamily.com Inc., 360 West 4800 N, Provo, UT 84604; http://www.myfamilyinc.com/. *Aud.:* Ga.

Now on its own server, this newsletter is still thriving under Eastman's editorship. Everything is discussed, from new books and electronic products to genealogically interesting news items and upcoming events. An archive of columns from May 1998 to September 1999 is available on the web site. Newsletters from April 1999 to the present are found at www.ancestry.com/library/view/columns/eastman/eastman.asp under the archives section. Access to this part of Ancestry.com is still free, although membership gives the viewer access to many databases from this company. The current URL is www.eogn.com/home.

3143. *Everton's Genealogical Helper.* Former titles (until 2004): *Everton's Family History Magazine;* (until 2002): *Everton's Genealogical Helper;* (until 1992): *Genealogical Helper.* [ISSN: 1554-2645] 1947. bi-m. USD 27 domestic; USD 36 foreign. Ed(s): Holly Hanson. Everton Publishers, PO Box 368, Logan, UT 84323-0368; customer_service@everton.com; http://www.everton.com. Illus., index, adv. Circ: 48000. Vol. ends: Nov/Dec. Microform: PQC. *Indexed:* BRI. *Aud.:* Ga.

Often called *Genealogical Helper* or *Genie Helper,* this magazine is "dedicated to helping genealogists." Although there are still large sections devoted to queries and book advertisements, more-substantive articles also appear in each issue. A column for upcoming genealogical events is included, as are over 40 pages in the "Everton's Computer Helper" section. Software reviews, web site URL listings, and computer tips are given. Each issue is separately indexed for subject, locality, and surname. A very useful all-around magazine for genealogy and appropriate for all public libraries. The online version provides the table of contents of the current print issue and a snippet of each article. For the entire article, one must subscribe.

3144. *Family Chronicle: the magazine for families researching their roots.* [ISSN: 1209-4617] bi-m. USD 27 domestic; USD 35 Canada. Moorshead Magazines Ltd., PO Box 194, Niagara Falls, NY 14304; publisher@familychronicle.com. Adv. *Indexed:* CBCARef, CPerI. *Aud.:* Ga.

A slick news journal–like magazine with how-to and computer-topic articles and many business advertisements. This is the perfect magazine for a general public library collection.

3145. *Family Tree Magazine: discover, preserve and celebrate your family history.* [ISSN: 1529-0298] 1999. bi-m. USD 27; USD 5.99 newsstand/cover per issue domestic; USD 8.99 newsstand/cover per issue Canada. Ed(s): Allison Stacy. F + W Publications, Inc., 4700 E Galbraith Rd, Cincinnati, OH 45236; wds@fwpubs.com; http://www.fwpublications.com. Adv. Circ: 80000 Paid. *Bk. rev.:* 20/yr. *Aud.:* Ga.

This is the latest slick newsmagazine-like journal for a general audience. It is ideal for a general public library collection. It is also available at newsstands.

3146. *Federation of Genealogical Societies Forum.* Formerly (until 1989): *Federation of Genealogical Societies Newsletter.* [ISSN: 1531-720X] 1976. q. Members, USD 11; Non-members, USD 17. Ed(s): Sandra H Luebking. Federation of Genealogical Societies, PO Box 200940, Austin, TX 78720-0940; fgs-office@fgs.org; http://www.fgs.org. Illus., adv. Circ: 25000. Vol. ends: Winter. *Bk. rev.:* 60/yr. *Aud.:* Ga.

This journal provides society news, upcoming events, software reviews, book reviews, etc., to its constituent audience: genealogical societies and libraries. Some methodology articles appear, and regular features include records access, state by state, and a family associations update. The *Forum* was a newsletter from 1976 to 1988.

3147. *The Genealogist.* [ISSN: 0197-1468] 1980. 2x/yr. USD 25 domestic; USD 33 foreign. Ed(s): Gale Ion Harris, Charles M Hansen. Picton Press, PO Box 250, Rockport, ME 04856-0250; sales@pictonpress.com; http://www.pictonpress.com. Index, adv. Refereed. Circ: 500. Vol. ends: Fall. *Indexed:* AmH&L, HistAb. *Aud.:* Ac, Sa.

The Genealogist is a highly respected scholarly journal that deals with European origins, royal and medieval ancestry, knotty genealogical problems, complete descendant genealogies, and related studies that are deemed too lengthy by other scholarly journals in the field. Founded in 1980 as a private enterprise with an irregular publishing schedule, it became the official journal of the American Society of Genealogists (ASG) in 1997 (volume 11). Under the aegis of ASG, it has consistently maintained its semi-annual publication as well as its long-standing quality. This is a journal for all academic libraries and public libraries with a major genealogical focus.

3148. *Great Migration Newsletter.* [ISSN: 1049-8087] 1990. q. USD 15. Ed(s): Robert Charles Anderson. New England Historic Genealogical Society, 101 Newbury St, Boston, MA 02116-3007. Illus., adv. Circ: 4000. *Bk. rev.:* 40/yr. *Aud.:* Ac, Sa.

This newsletter provides ongoing information from the Great Migration Study Project. This project has already produced a valuable study of all the immigrants for the years 1620–1633 (available from the New England Historic Genealogical Sociey), and surnames starting with A to F for 1634–1635, and it plans to continue through to 1640, encompassing more than 15,000 people. Articles provide research methodology and analysis of primary source records of each early New England town. Recent literature, including articles, is reviewed by the editor. The first five volumes of this newsletter can be purchased as a monograph for $19.50 from the society.

3149. *Heritage Quest Magazine.* Formerly: *Heritage Quest;* Incorporates: *Pastime & Heritage Quest News.* [ISSN: 1074-5238] 1985. bi-m. USD 28. Ed(s): Patty Meitzler, Leland K Meitzler. Heritage Quest, 549, Centerville, UT 84014-0549; Leland@heritagequest.com; http://www.heritagequest.com. Adv. Circ: 14000 Paid. *Aud.:* Ga.

This journal is designed for a general audience and brings together how-to articles. It is available on CD-ROM for volumes 1–15 (1985–1999).

3150. *Journal of Online Genealogy.* 1996. m. Free. Ed(s): Matthew Helm. Journal of Online Genealogy, mhelm@tbox.com; http://www.onlinegenealogy.com. *Aud.:* Ga.

This is the best of the genealogical e-journals. It features methodology articles for pursuing research online and other news, successful research stories, and press releases of new products. Articles discuss usenet newsgroups, discussion lists, and new web sites. The last year's issues are archived on the site.

3151. *Mayflower Descendant: a magazine of Pilgrim genealogy and history.* [ISSN: 8756-3959] 1985. s-a. USD 25. Ed(s): Scott Andrew Bartley. Massachusetts Society of Mayflower Descendants, Drew Bartley, 100 Boylston St Ste 750, Boston, MA 02116-4610; msmd@tiac.net; http://www.massmayflowersociety.com. Illus., index. Circ: 600. Vol. ends: Jul. *Bk. rev.:* 30/yr. *Aud.:* Ga, Ac.

This scholarly journal was resurrected after a nearly 50-year hiatus (volumes 1–34; 1899–1937). Membership in the Mayflower Society is not necessary to subscribe. Articles focus on Pilgrim families (not just *Mayflower* families), transcriptions of primary source material, methodology, published genealogies, and corrections to the five generations project. Volume 35 to 48 was in an 8 1/2" x 11" format. With volume 49 (2000), the 6" x 9" format and scholarly footnoting started.

3152. *National Genealogical Society Quarterly.* [ISSN: 0027-934X] 1912. q. USD 50 USD 55. Ed(s): Claire Bettag, Thomas W. Jones. National Genealogical Society, 3108 Columbia Pike, Ste 300, Arlington, VA 22204-4304; ngs@ngsgenealogy.org; http://www.ngsgenealogy.org. Illus., index, adv. Refereed. Circ: 18000 Paid. Vol. ends: Dec. Microform: PMC. *Indexed:* AmH&L, BRI, CBRI, HistAb. *Bk. rev.:* 50/yr. *Aud.:* Ga, Ac.

This scholarly journal includes articles that truly run the gamut of American genealogy—all ethnicities, all locales, and all time periods, including the twentieth century. The focus of most are particularly well-written methodology articles that point to hidden and very helpful resources. Updates and corrections to articles appear, as does some primary source material (mostly Bible records). Review essays and regular book reviews are in each issue. The journal's editorial base since 1987 has been the Department of History, University of Alabama. The journal is available on a CD-ROM that includes volumes 1–85 (1912–1997).

3153. *New England Ancestors.* Formerly (until Jan. 2000): *N E H G S Nexus.* [ISSN: 1527-9405] 1984. 5x/yr. USD 40 domestic; USD 50 foreign. Ed(s): Carolyn Oakley. New England Historic Genealogical Society, 101 Newbury St, Boston, MA 02116-3007. Illus., index. Circ: 19000. Vol. ends: Dec. *Bk. rev.:* 5/yr. *Aud.:* Ga.

This companion journal to the society's *Register* provides society news and updates to the society's premier New England library. The well-cited articles focus on topics of interest to all genealogists. Regular columns appear on what's new, computer interests, a pocket librarian (surveying collections across the country), and pilgrim life (a special project focusing on the Mayflower passenger). Recent feature article topics have included genetics and genealogy, ancient lineages, pioneers in computer genealogy, and research in Boston. Family associations, genealogies in progress, and notable kin are highlighted in each issue. There is a query section, with answers, and a section for corrections to genealogies in print.

3154. *New England Historical and Genealogical Register.* [ISSN: 0028-4785] 1847. q. USD 60. Ed(s): Henry Hoff. New England Historic Genealogical Society, 101 Newbury St, Boston, MA 02116-3007; http://www.nehgs.org. Illus., index, adv. Circ: 19000. Vol. ends: Oct. Microform: PQC. *Indexed:* AmH&L, HistAb. *Bk. rev.:* 50/yr. *Aud.:* Ga, Ac.

The doyenne of scholarly genealogical journals, this remains the model against which other journals are judged. The *Register*'s primary focus is colonial New England families, the European origins of those families, and some medieval and royal ancestry for New Englanders. New England primary source material is also abstracted and published. Book reviews are detailed and scholarly. There is a yearly index and cumulative indexes for volumes 1–50 and 51–148. The CD-ROM of the first 148 volumes is full-text and searchable. Microfilms have been created in blocks of five years per reel. Recommended for both academic and public libraries.

3155. *Southern Genealogist's Exchange Society Quarterly.* Formerly (until 2004): *Southern Genealogist's Exchange Quarterly.* [ISSN: 1933-1010] 1957. q. USD 20 domestic; USD 27 in Canada & Mexico; USD 35 elsewhere. Ed(s): Mary Louise Howard. Southern Genealogist's Exchange Society, Inc., PO Box 2801, Jacksonville, FL 32203-2801; sges@juno.com; http://sgesjax.tripod.com. Illus., index, adv. Circ: 300. Vol. ends: Dec. *Bk. rev.:* 150/yr. *Aud.:* Ga.

A regional journal that covers the 12 southern states of Virginia, West Virginia, North Carolina, South Carolina, Georgia, Florida, Kentucky, Tennessee, Alabama, Mississippi, Arkansas, and Louisiana and may extend into any of the other states. Articles cover primary source transcriptions and, to a lesser extent, methodology and family genealogies. Queries are published.

State—Alphabetical by State

ALABAMA

3156. *Alabama Genealogical Society Magazine.* [ISSN: 0568-806X] 1967. s-a. Institutional members, USD 15; Individual members, USD 20. Ed(s): Marcia K Smith Collier. Alabama Genealogical Society, Samford University, Box 2296, Birmingham, AL 35229; jylhardy@bellsouth.net; http://www.archives.state.al.us/ags. Illus., index. Circ: 400 Paid. Vol. ends: Winter. *Bk. rev.:* 20/yr. *Aud.:* Ga.

A solid genealogical journal. The lengthy and substantive articles are well footnoted and scholarly. Primary source transcriptions such as Bible records and census listings are included, and society news and queries are regular features.

ALASKA

3157. *Anchorage Genealogical Society. Quarterly Report.* q. Membership, USD 18 individual. Anchorage Genealogical Society, P O Box 242294, Anchorage, AK 99524-2294; ags@ak.net; http://www.rootsweb.com/~akags/. *Bk. rev.:* 10/yr. *Aud.:* Ga.

A basic journal that publishes abstracts of primary sources from the Anchorage area and society news.

ARIZONA

3158. Copper State Journal. Formerly (until 1997): *Copper State Bulletin.* [ISSN: 1097-7236] 1965. q. USD 14. Ed(s): Rondie R Yancey. Arizona State Genealogical Society, PO Box 42075, Tucson, AZ 85733-2075. Illus., index, adv. Circ: 500. Vol. ends: Winter. *Bk. rev.:* 20/yr. *Aud.:* Ga.

A basic journal that focuses on the publication of primary source material and methodology tips for genealogy in southern Arizona and Pima County. Society news, additions to the society's library, and queries are regular features. Each issue is separately indexed. Selected articles back to 1996 are found on the society's web site.

ARKANSAS

3159. Arkansas Family Historian. [ISSN: 0571-0472] 1962. q. USD 20. Ed(s): Margaret Harrison Hubbard. Arkansas Genealogical Society, Inc., 17653, Little Rock, AR 72222-7653. Illus., index. Circ: 1000. Vol. ends: Dec. *Bk. rev.:* 60/yr. *Aud.:* Ga.

A basic journal that focuses on the publication of primary source material and methodology tips for genealogy in Arkansas. Society news and queries are regular features. Each issue is separately indexed.

COLORADO

3160. Colorado Genealogist. [ISSN: 0010-1613] 1939. q. USD 20 (Individuals, USD 15). Ed(s): Juanita Moston. Colorado Genealogical Society, PO Box 9218, Denver, CO 80209. Illus., index, adv. Circ: 650. Vol. ends: Nov. *Bk. rev.:* 15/yr. *Aud.:* Ga.

A solid genealogical journal. An extensive index to the most recently received periodical issues at the society's library is a wonderful feature.

CONNECTICUT

3161. Connecticut Nutmegger. Formerly (until 1970): *Nutmegger (West Hartford).* [ISSN: 0045-8120] 1968. q. Free to members. Connecticut Society of Genealogists Inc., 175 Maple St, East Hampton, CT 06118. Illus., adv. Circ: 5000 Paid. Vol. ends: Mar. *Bk. rev.:* 100/yr. *Aud.:* Ga.

A solid genealogical journal for research in Connecticut. Methodology and family genealogies are included. Ongoing transcriptions of primary source material are a mainstay of this journal. They are publishing the Barbour Collection of vital records for the state (now being published by GPC). Queries (and a wonderful index to the names in the queries), family Bible records, and an ongoing list of families for which information has been sent in by members (ancestry service) are all published.

DELAWARE

3162. Delaware Genealogical Society. Journal. [ISSN: 0731-3896] 1980. 2x/yr. Institutional members, USD 18; Individual members, USD 14.50. Ed(s): Mary Fallon Richards. Delaware Genealogical Society, 505 N Market St, Wilmington, DE 19801-3091; mfallonr@ix.netcom.com; http://www.delgensoc.org. Illus., index, adv. Circ: 700. Vol. ends: Oct. *Aud.:* Ga.

This semi-annual journal mainly provides primary sources in Delaware genealogy: marriage bonds, cemetery listings, Bible records, church, court, and newspaper death abstracts. Each issue is separately indexed.

FLORIDA

3163. Florida Genealogist. [ISSN: 0161-4932] 1977. q. USD 25. Ed(s): Jackie Hufschmid. Florida State Genealogical Society, Inc., PO Box 10249, Tallahassee, FL 32302-2249. Illus., index. Circ: 800. Vol. ends: Winter. *Bk. rev.:* 5/yr. *Aud.:* Ga.

A basic journal that focuses on the publication of primary source material and methodology tips for genealogy in Florida. Additions to the society's library and queries are regular features. Each issue is indexed separately. The first ten volumes (1978–1988) have a cumulative index available in print or microfiche.

GEORGIA

3164. Georgia Genealogical Society Quarterly. [ISSN: 0435-5393] 1964. q. USD 25. Georgia Genealogical Society, Inc., PO Box 54575, Atlanta, GA 30308-0575. Illus., index, adv. Circ: 1100 Paid. Vol. ends: Winter. *Bk. rev.:* 60/yr. *Aud.:* Ga, Ac.

A solid genealogical journal devoted to the state of Georgia. Most articles present primary source transcriptions, with some methodology articles also included. Queries and additions to the society's library are published. Each issue is separately indexed, and a cumulative index for 1964–1980 ($25) is available from the society.

IDAHO

3165. Idaho Genealogical Society Quarterly. [ISSN: 0445-2127] 1958. q. Membership, USD 20. Ed(s): Steve Barrett. Idaho Genealogical Society, PO Box 1854, Boise, ID 83701-1854; http://www.lili.org/idahogenealogy. Illus., adv. Circ: 400. *Bk. rev.:* 10/yr. *Aud.:* Ga.

A basic journal that focuses on the publication of primary source material and methodology tips for genealogy in Idaho. Society news, additions to the society's library, and queries are regular features.

ILLINOIS

3166. Illinois State Genealogical Society Quarterly. [ISSN: 0046-8622] 1969. q. Individual members, USD 25. Illinois State Genealogical Society, PO Box 10195, Springfield, IL 62791-0195; http://www.tbox.com/ISGS. Illus., index, adv. Circ: 2300. Vol. ends: Winter. *Bk. rev.:* 75/yr. *Aud.:* Ga, Ac.

This solid journal focuses on the publication of primary source material and methodology for genealogy in Illinois. Family genealogies are also included. Additions to the society's library and queries are regular features. Each issue is separately indexed. A 25-year cumulative index is available for 1969–1993 as a county-subject, author-title, and table of contents index. A five-year cumulative index is available for 1969–1973 as a subject–title and name index.

INDIANA

3167. The Hoosier Genealogist. [ISSN: 1054-2175] 1961. q. Members, USD 35. Ed(s): Teresa Baer. Indiana Historical Society, 450 W. Ohio St., Indianapolis, IN 46202-3269; pr@indianahistory.org; http://www.indianahistory.org. Illus., index. Circ: 6000 Paid and controlled. Vol. ends: Dec. *Aud.:* Ga, Ac.

This solid journal focuses on the publication of primary source material for genealogy in Indiana broken down by regions (northern, central, southern), genealogies, family records, and three feature articles. Queries are included.

IOWA

3168. Hawkeye Heritage. [ISSN: 0440-5234] 1966. q. Members, USD 25. Ed(s): Tami Foster. Iowa Genealogical Society, 628 East Grand Ave, Des Moines, IA 50309-1924; igs@iowagenealogy.org; http://www.iowagenealogy.org/. Illus., index, adv. Circ: 3000. Vol. ends: Winter. *Aud.:* Ga.

A basic journal that focuses on the publication of primary source material and methodology tips for genealogy in Iowa. Some family genealogies are also published. Society news, additions to the society's library, and queries are regular features.

GENEALOGY

KANSAS

3169. *The Treesearcher.* 1959. q. USD 12 (Individuals, USD 15; USD 20 families). Kansas Genealogical Society, Inc., 2601 Central, Village Square Mall, P O Box 103, Dodge City, KS 67801-0103; http://www.dodge.city.net/kgs. Circ: 525. *Bk. rev.:* 25/yr. *Aud.:* Ga.

A basic journal that contains some primary material as well as information about genealogical lectures in the area, including the speakers' handouts. Queries are published.

KENTUCKY

3170. *Kentucky Ancestors.* [ISSN: 0023-0103] 1965. q. USD 25. Ed(s): Thomas Stephens. Kentucky Historical Society, 100 W. Broadway St., Frankfort, KY 40601-1931. Illus., index. Circ: 4800. Vol. ends: Spring. *Indexed:* HistAb. *Bk. rev.:* 50/yr. *Aud.:* Ga, Ac.

Some states are lucky to have one genealogical journal, while Kentucky can boast of four. This is the most comprehensive of the four, covering the entire state, while the others concentrate on the western, central, and eastern portions of the state. A solid journal, *Kentucky Ancestors* includes articles on methodology and local history as well as primary source transcriptions. Society news, queries, and additions to the society's library are regularly published.

LOUISIANA

3171. *Louisiana Genealogical Register.* [ISSN: 0148-7655] 1954. q. USD 25 domestic; USD 35 Canada; USD 45 elsewhere. Ed(s): David Howell. Louisiana Genealogical and Historical Society, PO Box 82060, Baton Rouge, LA 70884-2060; bcomeaux@aol.com. Illus., index. Circ: 650. Vol. ends: Dec. *Bk. rev.:* 40/yr. *Aud.:* Ga.

This solid journal provides primary source records and family genealogies for Louisiana. Some but not all articles are footnoted. Ancestor tables, additions to the society's library, and queries are published.

MAINE

3172. *Maine Genealogist.* Formerly: *Maine Seine.* [ISSN: 1064-6086] 1978. q. USD 20. Ed(s): Lois Ware Thurston, Joseph Anderson. Maine Genealogical Society, PO Box 221, Farmington, ME 04938-0221. Illus., index. Circ: 1000 Paid. Vol. ends: Nov. *Bk. rev.:* 15/yr. *Aud.:* Ga, Ac.

This journal is a scholarly publication that deserves its place among the best in the country. Articles focus on Maine families and primary source materials. Includes articles on methodology and queries.

MARYLAND

3173. *Maryland Genealogical Society Bulletin.* [ISSN: 0542-8351] 1960. q. USD 20. Ed(s): Martha Reamy. Maryland Genealogical Society, 201 W Monument St, Baltimore, MD 21201. Illus., index, adv. Circ: 1200. Vol. ends: Fall. *Bk. rev.:* 30/yr. *Aud.:* Ga, Ac.

A scholarly journal that focuses on Maryland families and source materials. Articles are well cited by end notes, and those dealing with family genealogies are given for many generations. Queries and letters to the editor are featured. Each issue is indexed separately.

MICHIGAN

3174. *Detroit Society for Genealogical Research. Magazine: containing records of Michigan and Michigan source states.* [ISSN: 0011-9687] 1937. q. USD 20 domestic; USD 25 Canada; USD 30 elsewhere. Ed(s): Patricia Ibbotson. Detroit Society for Genealogical Research, Inc., c/o Detroit Public Library, Burton Historical Collection, Detroit, MI 48202; http://www.dsgr.org. Illus., index. Circ: 1000. Vol. ends: Summer. Microform: PQC. *Bk. rev.:* 50/yr. *Aud.:* Ga.

This solid journal devotes each issue to records of Michigan and Michigan source states. Short family genealogies and queries are published, although ancestor tables are not. Newspaper abstracts, cemetery records, Bible records, court records, and other specialized resources comprise the bulk of this journal. A cumulative index is available for volumes 1–10, 11–15, 16–20, 21–25, 26–30, and annually after that.

MINNESOTA

3175. *Minnesota Genealogical Journal.* [ISSN: 0741-3599] 1984. 2x/yr. USD 20 domestic; USD 22 Canada; USD 25 elsewhere. Ed(s): Mary Hawker Bakeman. Park Genealogical Books, PO Box 130968, Roseville, MN 55113-0968; mbakeman@parkbooks.com; http://www.parkbooks.com/mgjbroch.html. Adv. Circ: 600 Paid. *Aud.:* Ga.

This solid journal focuses on the transcription of primary material or indexes to the same. The material is arranged by county.

3176. *Minnesota Genealogist.* [ISSN: 0581-0086] 1969. q. Members, USD 25. Ed(s): Erv Chorn. Minnesota Genealogical Society, 5768 Olson Memorial Highway, Golden Valley, MN 55422; mgsdec@mtn.org; http://www.mtn.org/mgs. Illus., adv. Circ: 1800 Paid. *Bk. rev.:* 10/yr. *Aud.:* Ga.

A solid genealogical journal for the state of Minnesota. Articles cover methodology, including Internet research, primary source transcriptions, and some family genealogies. A column for Minnesota connections in printed works, queries, and society news are all featured. A cumulative 30-year index is available.

MISSOURI

3177. *Missouri State Genealogical Association Journal.* [ISSN: 0747-5667] 1981. q. USD 15; USD 25 foreign. Ed(s): Jerry R Ennis. Missouri State Genealogical Association, P O Box 833, Columbia, MO 65205-0833; bdoerr@rollanet.org; http://www.rollanet.org/~bdoerr/ state.htm. Illus., index. Circ: 1000. Vol. ends: No. 4. *Bk. rev.:* 40/yr. *Aud.:* Ga.

A basic journal that focuses on the publication of primary source material and methodology tips for genealogy in Missouri. Editorials and queries are regular features.

MONTANA

3178. *Treasure State Lines.* [ISSN: 1060-0337] 1976. q. USD 20. Ed(s): Alice L Heisel. Great Falls Genealogy Society, 422 2nd St S., Great Falls, MT 59405-1816; gfgs@mcn.net. Illus., index, adv. Circ: 200. Vol. ends: Nov. *Aud.:* Ga.

This basic journal includes primary source transcriptions and methodological articles. Queries are included. A subject index for volumes 1–22 (1976–1998) and a surname index for volumes 1–20 (1976–1996) are available from the society.

NEBRASKA

3179. *Nebraska Ancestree.* 1978. q. USD 15. Ed(s): Mary Bergsten. Nebraska State Genealogical Society, Box 5608, Lincoln, NE 68505-0608. *Aud.:* Ga.

A solid genealogical journal that focuses on Nebraska families. Society news and queries are regularly featured, with a few methodological articles and primary-source transcriptions.

NEVADA

3180. *The Nevada Desert.* 1981. 9x/yr. USD 10. Ed(s): Dee Clem. Nevada State Genealogical Society, 8044 Moss Creek Dr, Reno, NV 89506-3121. *Aud.:* Ga.

This basic society newsletter includes articles on guest speakers, new additions to local family history centers, methodology, and sources.

3181. *The Prospector.* [ISSN: 1085-3707] 1980. q. Membership, USD 16 individual. Clark County Nevada Genealogical Society (CCNGS), P O Box 1929, Las Vegas, NV 89125-1929; ccngs@juno.com; http://www.lvrj.com/communitylink/ccngs/. *Bk. rev.:* 10/yr. *Aud.:* Ga.

A basic journal from Nevada that publishes abstracts statewide, queries, and society news.

NEW HAMPSHIRE

3182. *New Hampshire Genealogical Record.* [ISSN: 1055-0763] 1903. q. Non-members, USD 20. Ed(s): Ann Theopold Chaplin. New Hampshire Society of Genealogists, PO Box 2316, Concord, NH 03302-2316; acnack@aol.com. Illus., index, adv. Circ: 925. Vol. ends: Oct. *Bk. rev.:* 20/yr. *Aud.:* Ga, Ac.

Resurrected in 1990, this scholarly journal focuses on New Hampshire families and source materials. Articles are well cited, and those dealing with family genealogies are given for many generations. The first seven volumes (1903–1910) are available for purchase as a set.

NEW JERSEY

3183. *Genealogical Magazine of New Jersey.* [ISSN: 0016-6367] 1925. 3x/yr. USD 15. Ed(s): Janet T Riemer, Roxanne K Carkhuff. Genealogical Society of New Jersey, PO Box 1291, New Brunswick, NJ 08903. Illus., index. Circ: 875 Paid. Vol. ends: Sep. *Aud.:* Ga, Ac.

This scholarly journal focuses on the publication of primary source material for genealogy in New Jersey. Selected Bible and family records are also published when received by the society.

NEW MEXICO

3184. *New Mexico Genealogist.* [ISSN: 0545-3186] 1962. q. USD 20. Ed(s): Karen S. Daniel. New Mexico Genealogical Society, PO Box 8283, Albuquerque, NM 87198-8283; info@nmgs.org; http://www.nmgs.org. Index. *Aud.:* Ga.

A solid genealogical journal for New Mexico, whose history predates New England's by 22 years. Methodological articles and genealogies are well footnoted and well written. Primary source transcriptions and queries also are included. There is a cumulative subject and surname index for volumes 1–33 (1962–1994). Tables of contents for 1996 to the present appear on the web site of the society.

NEW YORK

3185. *New York Genealogical and Biographical Record.* [ISSN: 0028-7237] 1869. q. USD 30 includes The New York Researcher. Ed(s): Patricia Law Hatcher. New York Genealogical and Biographical Society, 122 E 58th St, New York, NY 10022-1939; publications@nygbs.org; http://www.newyorkfamilyhistory.org/. Illus., adv. Refereed. Circ: 3000 Paid. Vol. ends: Oct. Microform: PQC. *Bk. rev.:* 60/yr. *Aud.:* Ga, Ac.

The second oldest genealogical journal in the United States, *NYGBR* upholds high scholarly standards in dealing with the subject matter of New York State and the Dutch and English colonies that preceded it. Articles run the gamut from transcriptions of source materials, both U.S. and Dutch, to family genealogies. It is a state journal with regional and national importance. Regular features include additions to the society's library and society notes. A subject index was complied by Jean D. Worden for 1870 to 1982 and published independently. This is out of print. The journal is indexed annually with a separate index mailed with the January issue of the following year. There are plans to create a CD-ROM version of the journal.

NORTH CAROLINA

3186. *North Carolina Genealogical Society Journal.* [ISSN: 0360-1056] 1975. q. USD 30. Ed(s): Raymond A Winslow, Jr. North Carolina Genealogical Society, PO Box 1492, Raleigh, NC 27602; ncgs@earthlink.net; http://www.ncgenealogy.org. Illus., index, adv. Circ: 1900. Vol. ends: Nov. *Bk. rev.:* 90/yr. *Aud.:* Ga, Ac.

This scholarly journal focuses on the publication of primary source material for genealogy in North Carolina. Queries and a lengthy "document review" (i.e., book) section are included in each issue, which is separately indexed. A 20-year cumulative index to articles (1975–1995) is available from the society.

NORTH DAKOTA

3187. *North Central North Dakota Genealogical Record.* [ISSN: 0736-5667] 1978. q. USD 15. Mouse River Loop Genealogy Society, P O Box 1391, Minot, ND 58702-1391. *Bk. rev.:* 10/yr. *Aud.:* Ga.

A basic journal publishing abstracts of primary sources, queries, and society news.

OHIO

3188. *Ohio Records & Pioneer Families: the cross road of our nation.* [ISSN: 1063-4649] 1960. q. Members, USD 15; Non-members, USD 20. Ed(s): Susan Dunlap Lee. Ohio Genealogical Society, 713 S Main St, Mansfield, OH 44907-1644; ogs@ogs.org; http://www.ogs.org. Illus., index. Circ: 1600. Vol. ends: No. 4. *Aud.:* Ga.

Ohio is a critical state for anyone pursuing pioneer genealogy. This basic journal focuses on the publication of primary source material and pioneer family genealogies in Ohio. Queries appear in each issue. A ten-year (1985–1994) surname index is available from the society. The society also publishes *Ohio Civil War Genealogy Journal, The Report,* and a society newsletter.

OKLAHOMA

3189. *Oklahoma Genealogical Society Quarterly.* [ISSN: 0474-0742] 1955. q. Members, USD 15. Ed(s): Tracy Jackson. Oklahoma Genealogical Society, PO Box 12986, Oklahoma City, OK 73157. Illus., index. Circ: 1150. Vol. ends: Dec. *Bk. rev.:* 20/yr. *Aud.:* Ga.

A basic journal that focuses on the publication of primary source material and methodology tips for genealogy in Oklahoma. Society news, additions to the society's library, and queries are regular features. Each issue is separately indexed, and a subject index from 1955 to 1990 is available from the society. The journal is also on microfilm from 1955 to 1990.

OREGON

3190. *Oregon Genealogical Society Quarterly.* [ISSN: 0738-1891] 1962. q. USD 25 domestic; USD 30 foreign. Linda Forrest, Ed. & Pub., PO Box 10306, Eugene, OR 97440-2306. Illus., index, adv. Circ: 475. Vol. ends: Winter. *Bk. rev.:* 30/yr. *Aud.:* Ga.

A basic journal that focuses on the publication of primary source material and methodology tips for genealogy in Oregon. Ancestor tables and queries are regular features.

PENNSYLVANIA

3191. *Pennsylvania Genealogical Magazine.* Formerly (until 1948): *Genealogical Society of Pennsylvania. Publications.* [ISSN: 0882-3685] 1895. s-a. Membership, USD 25. Ed(s): Marion F Egge. Genealogical Society of Pennsylvania, 215 S. Broad St., 7 th floor, Philadelphia, PA 19107; gappa@aol.com; http://www.libertynet.org/gspa/. Illus., adv. Refereed. Circ: 1600. Vol. ends: Fall/Winter. *Bk. rev.:* 25/yr. *Aud.:* Ga, Ac.

GENEALOGY

This scholarly journal focuses on the publication of primary source material for genealogy in Pennsylvania. Methodology articles, library updates, and queries are also included. Pennsylvania was a major entry port for immigration, making this journal an important one nationally as well as locally. There is a query section.

RHODE ISLAND

3192. Rhode Island Roots. Formerly (until 1981): *R.I. Roots.* [ISSN: 0730-1235] 1976. q. USD 10. Ed(s): Jane Fletcher Fiske. Rhode Island Genealogical Society, 13 Countryside Dr, Cumberland, RI 02864. Illus., index, adv. Circ: 800 Controlled. Vol. ends: Dec. *Bk. rev.:* Number varies. *Aud.:* Ga, Ac.

This scholarly journal publishes articles on the families of and research in Rhode Island. Primary source transcriptions as well as methodology articles are published. News of the society and queries are regular features. A cumulative index of the first five volumes is available.

SOUTH CAROLINA

3193. South Carolina Magazine of Ancestral Research. [ISSN: 0190-826X] 1973. q. USD 27.50; USD 30. Brent H. Holcomb, Ed. & Pub., PO Box 21766, Columbia, SC 29221. Illus., adv. Circ: 750. Vol. ends: Fall. *Bk. rev.:* 25/yr. *Aud.:* Ga.

A solid genealogical journal that focuses on primary source material and methodology for research in South Carolina. Queries are published.

TENNESSEE

3194. Tennessee Ancestors. [ISSN: 0882-0635] 1985. 3x/yr. USD 15. Ed(s): Rene Jordan. East Tennessee Historical Society, 600 Market Street, PO Box 1629, Knoxville, TN 37902. Illus., index. Circ: 2200. Vol. ends: Dec. *Bk. rev.:* 60/yr. *Aud.:* Ga, Ac.

This scholarly journal focuses on methodology articles on research in Tennessee. Primary source transcriptions and updates to the membership of the First Families of Tennessee Society are included. Queries are published in each issue.

3195. Tennessee Genealogical Magazine: Ansearchin News. Formerly: *Ansearchin' News.* 1954. q. Members, USD 20. Ed(s): Dorothy Roberson. Tennessee Genealogical Society, Davies Plantation, 9114 Davies Plantation Rd, Brunswick, TN 38014-0247. Circ: 1200 Paid. *Aud.:* Ga.

A solid journal that features abstracts of primary sources, queries, book reviews, and society news. The annual index is published separately.

TEXAS

3196. Stirpes. [ISSN: 0039-1522] 1961. q. USD 22. Ed(s): Frances Pryor. Texas State Genealogical Society, 3219 Meadow Oaks Dr, Temple, TX 76502-1752; wdonaldsn@aol.com; http://www.rootsweb.com/~txsgs/. Illus., index, adv. Circ: 850 Controlled. Vol. ends: Dec. *Indexed:* AmH&L, HistAb. *Bk. rev.:* 15/yr. *Aud.:* Ga.

A solid genealogical journal for Texas with primary source transcription, well-footnoted articles, and queries. The index is published separately. A cumulative index (1961–1985) is available from the society. The journal is available on microfilm for 1961 to 1994.

UTAH

3197. Crossroads (Salt Lake City). Formerly (until 2006): *Utah Genealogical Association. Genealogical Journal.* [ISSN: 1935-2328] 1972. q. USD 45 (Individuals, USD 35). Ed(s): Rhonda McClure. Utah Genealogical Association, PO Box 1144, Salt Lake City, UT 84110; info@infouga.org; http://www.infouga.org. Illus., index, adv. Refereed. Circ: 1000. Microform: PQC. *Bk. rev.:* 20/yr. *Aud.:* Ga.

Aimed at a Utah audience, this solid journal covers all geographic areas of the United States and provides methodological help and support for the collections at the Family History Library in Salt Lake City, the largest genealogical library in the world. Other articles focus on Utah's families, research sources, primary source abstracts, and Mormon genealogy. A ten-year (1985–1995) cumulative article index is available at the society's web site.

VERMONT

3198. Vermont Genealogy. Formerly (until 1996): *Branches and Twigs.* [ISSN: 1086-2439] 1972. q. Membership, USD 20. Ed(s): Scott Bartley. Genealogical Society of Vermont, PO Box 14, Randolph, VT 05060; http://www.genealogyvermont.org. Illus., index, adv. Circ: 11300 Paid. Vol. ends: Oct. *Bk. rev.:* 25/yr. *Aud.:* Ga, Ac.

A scholarly journal that focuses on well-cited articles on Vermont families, primary source materials, and methodologies. Queries are still part of this journal, but all society news can now be found in the society's newsletter.

VIRGINIA

3199. Virginia Genealogist. [ISSN: 0300-645X] 1957. q. Individuals, USD 25. Ed(s): John Frederick Dorman. Virginia Genealogist, PO Box 5860, Falmouth, VA 22403-5860. Illus., index. Circ: 715 Paid. Vol. ends: Oct/Dec. *Bk. rev.:* 30/yr. *Aud.:* Ga, Ac.

A scholarly journal that focuses on Virginia families and source materials. The well-cited articles deal with European origins and medieval and royal lineages for Virginia immigrants. There is a query section in each issue. Virginia is to Southern genealogy what Massachusetts is to New England genealogy, so this is an important journal with national appeal. Two consolidated indexes are available from the editor for volumes 1–20 and volumes 21–35. Genealogies are numbered using the Henry system.

WASHINGTON

3200. Seattle Genealogical Society Bulletin. 1952. q. USD 20. Seattle Genealogical Society, 15329, Seattle, WA 98115-0329. Adv. Circ: 1700 Paid. *Bk. rev.:* 30/yr. *Aud.:* Ga.

A basic journal for genealogy. Articles are not limited to the state of Washington (one recent article focused on New York, another on California). A listing of recent acquisitions in the Seattle Public Library is a regular feature. Queries are included.

WEST VIRGINIA

3201. Kanawha Valley Genealogical Society. Journal. [ISSN: 0270-4064] 1977. q. USD 15. Kanawha Valley Genealogical Society, PO Box 8555, South Charleston, WV 25303. *Aud.:* Ga.

A basic journal featuring abstracts of primary sources, queries, and society news.

WISCONSIN

3202. Wisconsin State Genealogical Society Newsletter. [ISSN: 1094-9445] 1954. q. USD 20 (Individuals, USD 18). Ed(s): Virginia V Irvin. Wisconsin State Genealogical Society, Inc., 2109 20 Ave, Monroe, WI 53566; md2609@tds.net; http://www.rootsweb.com/~wsgs/. Circ: 1600 Paid. *Aud.:* Ga.

A basic journal that focuses on the publication of primary source material and methodology for genealogy in Wisconsin. Society news, additions to Wisconsin genealogical libraries, upcoming events, and queries are all regular features. Materials are arranged county by county and designed to be taken apart. There is a second pagination unique to each county.

▪ GENERAL INTEREST

See also Alternatives; Canada; Europe; and News and Opinion sections.

Joe Toth, Collection Development Librarian, Middlebury College, Middlebury, VT 05753; jtoth@middlebury.edu

Introduction

This section lists magazines that represent a variety of subjects, interests, and editorial purposes. Some are well known and need little explanation as to worth. Others may have evaded the discerning eyes of librarians and the reading public, and thus need reviewing perhaps to promote use and enjoyment.

There is seriousness and frivolity, practicality and mirth within these entries. For these reasons, it is hard to typify them and to sum up this section neatly, except to say that, if you had to start a current periodicals collection somewhere, you might begin with many of the listings offered here.

Basic Periodicals

Ems: *National Geographic;* Hs: *National Geographic, Smithsonian, World Press Review;* Ga: *National Geographic, The New Yorker, Smithsonian, World Press Review;* Ac: *American Scholar, Smithsonian, The Wilson Quarterly.*

Basic Abstracts and Indexes

American Humanities Index, Magazine Article Summaries, Magazine Index, Readers' Guide to Periodical Literature.

3203. *A I M.* Former titles (until 1992): *A I M for Racial Harmony & Peace;* (until 1976): *A I M for Racial Harmony.* [ISSN: 1085-5211] 1974. q. USD 12. Ed(s): Myron Apilado. A I M Publishing Association, 7308 Eberhart, Chicago, IL 60619. Illus. Circ: 10000. *Indexed:* AmHI. *Aud.:* Ga, Ac.

The laudable purpose of this magazine is to "purge racism from the human bloodstream by way of the written word." It is simple in format and to-the-point in content, with all of its material offered in support of racial harmony. Its feature articles are short, sometimes sharp (e.g., Michael Parenti's piece on the free market harming New Orleans post-Katrina), and sometimes reflective (e.g., Jimmy W. Hall's rumination on interracial dating and marriage). This magazine presents poetry and fiction on similar themes, and news and viewpoints as well. *AIM* asks readers to participate in its experiment, who often contribute to the recurring sections. Libraries should join the conversation as well.

3204. *American Scholar.* [ISSN: 0003-0937] 1932. q. USD 25 domestic; USD 35 Canada; USD 40 per issue elsewhere. Ed(s): Anne Fadiman. Phi Beta Kappa Society, 1606 New Hampshire Ave, NW, Washington, DC 20009; http://www.pbk.org. Illus., adv. Sample. Refereed. Circ: 23000 Paid. Vol. ends: Fall. Microform: PMC; PQC. Online: Chadwyck-Healey Inc.; EBSCO Publishing, EBSCO Host; Florida Center for Library Automation; Gale; OCLC Online Computer Library Center, Inc.; ProQuest LLC (Ann Arbor); H.W. Wilson. *Indexed:* ABS&EES, AmH&L, AmHI, ArtHuCI, BRD, BRI, CBRI, FLI, HistAb, HumInd, IAPV, IBR, IBZ, IPSA, LRI, MASUSE, MLA-IB, NTA, PAIS, PSA, RGPR, RI-1, RILM, SSCI, SWR&A. *Bk. rev.:* 5-9, essay-length. *Aud.:* Hs, Ga, Ac.

The Phi Beta Kappa Society's *American Scholar* publishes articles by academics and professional writers about issues that are based in academe but extend outward to the general public. (Most scholarship should do as much, but often doesn't.) In its editor's words, *American Scholar* is "a place where the best minds take on the biggest subjects." Race, anti-Semitism, and twenty-first century Christianity were recently featured themes. But even in issues that handled these subjects, there are scores of shorter pieces on class, memoir writing, brain research, refugee camps, and other engaging topics. In addition to feature articles, there are sections on books, arts, and poetry, all with reviews of contemporary works on themes many of which you won't find in the mainstream press. Add editorials and various types of reader responses, and you have a journal that appeals to readers who read to be challenged by confronting topics that often are difficult and open-ended.

3205. *The Atlantic Monthly.* Former titles (until 1993): *Atlantic;* (until 1981): *Atlantic Monthly;* (until 1971): *Atlantic;* (until 1932): *Atlantic Monthly;* Which incorporated (in 1910): *Putnam's Magazine;* (1909): *Putnam's & the Reader;* (until 1908): *Putnam's Monthly;* (until 1907): *Putnam's Monthly & the Critic;* (until 1906): *The Critic;* Which incorpoated (in 1905): *Literary World;* The Critic was formerly (1884): *Critic & Good Literature;* Which was formed by the merger of (1881-1884): *Critic; Good Literature.* [ISSN: 1072-7825] 1857. 10x/yr. USD 24.50 domestic; USD 32.50 Canada; USD 39.50 elsewhere. Ed(s): Cullen Murphy. Atlantic Monthly Co., 600 New Hampshire Ave, NW, Washington, DC 20037. Illus., index, adv. Circ: 459600 Paid. Vol. ends: Jun/Dec. CD-ROM: ProQuest LLC (Ann Arbor). Microform: PMC; PQC. Online: EBSCO Publishing, EBSCO Host; Florida Center for Library Automation; Gale; Micromedia ProQuest; OCLC Online Computer Library Center, Inc.; ProQuest K-12 Learning Solutions; ProQuest LLC (Ann Arbor); H.W. Wilson. *Indexed:* ABS&EES, AgeL, AmH&L, BAS, BRD, BRI, CBCARef, CBRI, CJA, CPerI, FLI, FutSurv, HistAb, IAPV, MASUSE, MRD, NTA, PAIS, PRA, RGPR, RI-1, RILM. *Bk. rev.:* 2-3, 500 words. *Aud.:* Hs, Ga, Ac.

Great magazines call for little explanation, so all that needs be stated here is that the *Atlantic* enlists strong editors and writers to tackle subjects in and beyond the current interests of the public. One set of articles it calls its "agenda," in which foreign affairs and the Washington scene always are covered. The rest of the pieces deal with whatever the writers find interesting and in need of exposure: Internet dating, soldiering in Gaza, pharmaceutical reps, and spies and the NSA, to name a few. The "Critics" section offers more than reviews, with longer articles on authors and books, and the "Pursuits and Retreats" section includes comment on travel, food, and technology. Of course, photographs appear throughout the publication. Simply, the *Atlantic Monthly* should be in the hands of discerning, engaged readers, and thus is essential to all current periodical collections.

3206. *AudioFile: the magazine for people who love audiobooks.* [ISSN: 1063-0244] 1992. 6x/yr. USD 29.95 (Individuals, USD 19.95). Ed(s): Robin F Whitten. AudioFile, 37 Silver St, Box 109, Portland, ME 04112-0109. Illus., adv. Circ: 10000 Controlled. *Indexed:* MRD. *Bk. rev.:* 100 per issue. *Aud.:* Hs, Ga, Ac.

AudioFile offers signed reviews of abridged and unabridged audiobooks and other spoken-word products by educators, performers, and technicians. Reviewers focus on presentation, not content, and often comment on vocal style and characterization. Reviews appear under headings such as fiction, biography and memoir, and history so that readers may skip to favorite material. Issues also include sections on "new releases," but it's the reviews that drive this magazine. While *AudioFile* may be a favorite way for audiobook readers to discover new titles, perhaps its greatest use will be as a reference resource for librarians. Because audiobooks are now more popular and easy to use (with many books now available in mp3 format), librarians have an even greater need to stay abreast of technical developments, audio-booksellers, and reader tastes. *AudioFile* addresses these needs by including a "resources" section that indexes the reviews, identifies contact information for all of the items referred to in the magazine, and provides a directory of advertisers, making *AudioFile* a guide to what audiobooks are available for your library.

3207. *Australian Women's Weekly.* [ISSN: 0005-0458] 1933. m. AUD 69.95; AUD 6.40 newsstand/cover. Ed(s): Deborah Thomas. A C P Magazines Ltd., 54-58 Park St, Sydney, NSW 2000, Australia; research@acpaction.com.au; http://www.acp.com.au. Illus., adv. Circ: 605000 Paid and controlled. *Bk. rev.:* Number and length vary. *Aud.:* Ga.

In the parlance of the magazine trade, the *AWW* is aimed at women's interests, with sections on fashion, food, well-being, and parenthood. It also includes advertising, illustrations, and book and television reviews. But Australia is on the other side of the world, which means that the *AWW*, at the level of example, offers readers fashions, styles, recipes, and rituals from the Anglo-Asian bent that makes up the Australian worldview. For example, tips on gardening include growing passion fruit and selecting Christmas bushes; beauty advice covers beach hair; and the food column contains recipes for kingfish and lamb kofta. Australian celebrities are profiled, as are Aussie TV shows and fiction writers. Perhaps the keenest example that we're not in Kansas anymore is the "Marry a Farmer" contest (or is it a service?), in which reader/contestants write letters to single men on the farms, who then respond with offers to meet. Kudos to *AWW* for doing its part to foster national contentment! Subscribe to *AWW* to offer American women similar yet different perspectives on women's popular culture.

3208. *Bomb: interviews with artists, writers, musicians, directors and actors.* [ISSN: 0743-3204] 1981. q. USD 22 domestic; USD 30 Canada; USD 42 elsewhere. Ed(s): Betsy Sussler, Lucy Raven. New Art Publications, Inc., 80 Hanson Pl, Ste 703, Brooklyn, NY 11217. Illus., adv. Sample. Circ: 25000. *Indexed:* ABM, AmHI, FLI, HumInd, IAPV, MRD. *Aud.:* Hs, Ga, Ac.

Bomb is an arts magazine that presents interviews with and dialogues between artists, fiction writers, musicians, playwrights, directors, actors, photographers, and musicians. It also offers original fiction and poetry, as well as pieces by artists and writers about other artists and writers: Willem Dafoe on Michael Ondaatje, Ron Rifkin on Arthur Miller, and Mary-Louise Parker on Paula Vogel. Generally, *Bomb*'s slant is on the contemporary scene, with most of its subjects among the living, making its interviews occasions for readers to discover not only works but careers in progress. A recent issue includes essays on the philosopher Bernard-Henri Levy, playwright Adam Rapp, filmmaker Judd Ne'eman, and painter Dana Schultz. *Bomb* reminds readers that the world of the arts is far broader, more diverse, and more challenging than the way it is construed in the mainstream press. For this reason, *Bomb* is an important addition to periodical collections in academic and large public libraries.

3209. *The City Journal.* Formerly (until 1992): *N.Y.* [ISSN: 1060-8540] 1990. q. USD 23 domestic; USD 28 foreign. Ed(s): Myron Magnet. Manhattan Institute, Inc., 52 Vanderbilt Ave, New York, NY 10017-3808; http://www.city-journal.org. Adv. Circ: 10000 Paid. *Indexed:* CJA, PAIS. *Aud.:* Hs, Ga, Ac.

The *City Journal* is often described as an urban policy magazine that, while focusing primarily on New York, considers topics and subjects of concern to all urban areas. Each issue contains one or more articles on New York happenings, such as "What Bloomberg Could Still Accomplish," and "How to Save the Subways—Before It's Too Late." But the remainder of the publication extends beyond urban policy to general reportage, with pieces on African Americans and victimology, Mexican consulates and illegal immigration, and the ADA and frivolous lawsuits. While its web site includes a topic archive with a subject list that would make *Britannica* editors proud, the bulk of *CJ* seems to be aimed at politics and social issues, with a smattering of arts and events coverage. *CJ* is a general-purpose publication aimed at exploring issues that define and impinge upon city life. Of course, these issues become more important as urban life enlarges in size and cultural influence.

3210. *Contexts: understanding people in their social worlds.* [ISSN: 1536-5042] 2002. q. USD 176 print & online eds. USD 48 newsstand/cover. Ed(s): David Linker, Jeff Goodwin. University of California Press, Journals Division, 2000 Center St, Ste 303, Berkeley, CA 94704-1223; journals@ucpress.edu; http://www.ucpress.edu/journals. Adv. Circ: 2858. *Indexed:* ABS&EES, ASIP, ENW, SociolAb. *Aud.:* Hs, Ga, Ac.

Contexts is a quarterly magazine published by the American Sociological Association, which right off the bat might scare away those who fear the sometimes abstruse language of academe. Fear not, for *Contexts* presumes that the general public is intelligent and interested, and seeks to engage them by disseminating current research on provocative and important topics. Recent issues have pieces on refinancing political campaigns; a perceived epidemic of mental illness; consumers' unknowing relationships with sweatshops; and speculation on how international conflicts end. Also, there are reviews of all sorts, photo essays, short pieces on trends and themes, and my favorite, a column on "keywords," in which a concept is explored through application and discussion within various disciplines. Raymond Williams would be proud of the aims of this "inquiry into a lexicon." *Contexts* is a fine publication that deserves consideration.

3211. *Daedalus.* Formerly (until 1955): *American Academy of Arts and Sciences. Proceedings.* [ISSN: 0011-5266] 1950. q. USD 110 print & online eds. (Individuals, USD 44 print & online eds.). Ed(s): Stephen R Graubard. M I T Press, 238 Main St., Ste. 500, Cambridge, MA 02142; journals-info@mit.edu; http://mitpress.mit.edu. Illus., index. Sample.

Refereed. Circ: 20000. Vol. ends: Fall. Microform: PQC. Online: Chadwyck-Healey Inc.; EBSCO Publishing, EBSCO Host; Florida Center for Library Automation; Gale; IngentaConnect; Northern Light Technology, Inc.; OCLC Online Computer Library Center, Inc.; ProQuest LLC (Ann Arbor); SwetsWise Online Content. *Indexed:* ABCPolSci, ABS&EES, AmH&L, AmHI, ArtHuCI, BAS, BRI, BrArAb, CBRI, ChemAb, FR, FutSurv, HistAb, HumInd, IBR, IBSS, IBZ, IPSA, LRI, MLA-IB, NTA, PAIS, PSA, PhilInd, RGPR, RI-1, SCI, SSA, SSCI, SWR&A, SociolAb. *Aud.:* Ga, Ac.

Daedalus is located squarely in academe. While its contents include some fiction and poetry, a point/counterpoint dialogue, and notes and letters, the bulk of each issue of the publication deals with a central subject that invited authors, experts in their fields, write about. Recent issues on aging and the state of the humanities reveal the scholarly bent that the editors maintain consistently. The latter topic especially marks *Daedalus* as removed from mainstream concerns at times, but such distance is precisely what expert analysts must assume if they are to provide commentary that pierces commonplace understandings. This magazine is for the serious-minded reader willing to spend time reading multiple articles on a subject offered from different, sometimes contradictory perspectives. Recommended for academic and large public libraries.

3212. *Esquire.* Former titles (until 1979): *Esquire Fortnightly;* (until 1978): *Esquire.* [ISSN: 0194-9535] 1933. m. USD 8 newsstand/cover per issue domestic; USD 20 newsstand/cover per issue foreign. Ed(s): David Granger, John Kennedy. Hearst Magazines, 300 W 57th St, New York, NY 10019; HearstMagazines@hearst.com; http://www.hearstcorp.com/magazines/. Illus., adv. Circ: 700000 Paid. Vol. ends: Dec. Microform: PQC. Online: EBSCO Publishing, EBSCO Host; Florida Center for Library Automation; Gale; OCLC Online Computer Library Center, Inc.; ProQuest LLC (Ann Arbor); H.W. Wilson. *Indexed:* BEL&L, BRI, CBRI, FLI, MASUSE, MLA-IB, MRD, RGPR, RILM. *Aud.:* Ga, Ac.

Does *Esquire* have articles? Does it matter? This magazine is all about men, from paragraph to picture, from essay to advertisement. And it doesn't apologize for the version of manliness it promotes in its pages. *Esquire*'s men are good-looking, fun-loving, adventure-seeking, heterosexual, and successful enough to buy some diversionary toys. They play and work so hard they don't have time to read too deeply on anything—after all, it's external stimuli they crave. And *Esquire* delivers, with cavalcades of images of sexy men and women, fast cars, cool guitars, and gear, gear, gear. In between are interviews with celebrities—good-looking ones—lists of dos and don'ts about women, bodies, and style, and factoids on golf, sneakers, and whatever else. The magazine is a gesture that shouts that "being a man is fun, and if you don't know that, we'll show you." For the sake of men who share this vision, and there are a lot of them, subscribe to *Esquire*.

3213. *German Life.* [ISSN: 1075-2382] 1994. bi-m. USD 22.95 domestic; USD 32 foreign. Ed(s): Mark Slider. Zeitgeist Publishing, 1068 National Hwy, Lavale, MD 21502-7501. Illus., adv. Sample. Circ: 40000 Paid and controlled. Online: Northern Light Technology, Inc.; ProQuest LLC (Ann Arbor). *Indexed:* ENW. *Aud.:* Hs, Ga.

The web site of *German Life* tells us the magazine is "written for all interested in the diversity of German culture, past and present, and in the various ways that North America has been shaped by its German element." In other words, its audience primarily is German-Americans who turn *GL*'s pages with a nostalgic or curious eye about their past. There's even a section on researching your German family history to fuel this interest. But *GL* does present deeper looks into everyday German culture, even if these perspectives are written for potential travelers. Articles on open-air museums, fountains, cities, and regions speak enthusiastically to visitors, but they do so without glossing over bumps, bruises, and other imperfections. *GL* includes reviews of all sorts, and a language section written in German. *German Life*'s web site is "Created and maintained by the German Corner." Perhaps that attribution best describes the editorial slant of *German Life*.

3214. *Grit: American life & traditions.* [ISSN: 0017-4289] 1882. m. USD 12.95 domestic; USD 15.45 foreign. Ed(s): Andrea Skalland. Ogden Publications, 1503 SW 42nd St, Topeka, KS 66609-1265; http://www.ogdenpubs.com. Illus., adv. Sample. Circ: 100000 Paid. Online: Gale. *Aud.:* Ems, Hs, Ga.

Grit is a family magazine "dedicated to bring readers good news." The news in *Grit* comes by way of positive accounts of rural life, on farms, in woods, or with animals. It features "cooks of the month" who speak of crock pots and Dutch-oven baking; short memoirs by folks recounting warm memories; poetry and fiction (the latter sometimes serialized); short pieces on children and pets; and the exploits of gardeners and their triumphs. Humor, wonder, fulfillment through helping others, interesting places—*Grit* champions all of these themes through exploring the coastal roads in Oregon or the patterns of Amish quilts—without apologies. There also are tips on staying healthy and active. And *Grit* is peppered with lots of excellent photographs that supplement its feature articles, to take the reader along for a ride filled with smiles and remembrances. Recommended for public libraries as a counterweight to the cynicism of the times.

3215. Harper's. Former titles (until 1976): *Harper's Magazine;* (until 1913): *Harper's Monthly Magazine;* (until 1900): *Harper's New Monthly Magazine;* Which incorporated (1850-1852): *International Magazine of Literature, Art, and Science.* [ISSN: 0017-789X] 1850. m. USD 14.97 domestic; CND 24 Canada; USD 41 elsewhere. Ed(s): Lewis H Lapham. Harpers Magazine, 666 Broadway, 11th Fl, New York, NY 10012-2317; http://harpers.org/SubscriberCare.html. Illus., adv. Circ: 228000 Paid. Vol. ends: Jun/Dec. CD-ROM: ProQuest LLC (Ann Arbor). Microform: NBI; PMC; PQC. Online: Chadwyck-Healey Inc.; EBSCO Publishing, EBSCO Host; Factiva, Inc.; Florida Center for Library Automation; Gale; Micromedia ProQuest; Northern Light Technology, Inc.; OCLC Online Computer Library Center, Inc.; ProQuest LLC (Ann Arbor); H.W. Wilson. *Indexed:* ABS&EES, AmH&L, BEL&L, BRD, BRI, CBCARef, CBRI, CPerI, FLI, FutSurv, IAPV, LRI, MASUSE, MLA-IB, MRD, PRA, RGPR, RI-1, RILM. *Aud.:* Hs, Ga, Ac.

Harper's consistently publishes some of the best writing on cultural and political subjects found in America, often by some of America's best writers. One memorable piece jumps to mind after ten years: Barry Lopez's "On the Wings of Commerce" was a fascinating account of air freighters, 747s and the like that fly after-hours transporting goods around the world. Such topics show up in *Harper's* among the commentaries, fiction, excerpts from other publications, and the famed Harper's Index, a statistical melange of illuminating facts. Advertisements are few and seriousness is presumed. *Harper's* is a high-quality magazine that is essential to almost all library collections.

3216. Harvard Magazine. Formerly (until 1973): *Harvard Bulletin.* [ISSN: 0095-2427] 1898. bi-m. USD 30 domestic (Free to qualified personnel). Ed(s): John S Rosenberg, Christopher Reed. Harvard Magazine, Inc., 7 Ware St, Cambridge, MA 02138. Illus., adv. Sample. Circ: 218491. Vol. ends: Jul/Aug. *Indexed:* ASIP, EnvAb, NTA, RI-1, RiskAb. *Bk. rev.:* 5-7, 200-650 words. *Aud.:* Ac.

So why include a magazine dedicated to all things Harvard? Because Harvard is the preeminent institution among preeminent institutions, so much so that its shifts in educational outlooks affect the vision of the rest of higher education; its financial dealings—particularly its endowment management—impress not-for-profit foundations and Wall Street alike; and its internal politics and social life generate interest in newspapers coast to coast. The magazine includes feature articles on the Harvard Corporation and how it runs the university, global warming and the coming dependence on coal, and the arrival of women at the Divinity School. There are departments called "The Browser," "The Alumni," and "The College Pump," as well as a commencement and reunion guide and a section called "Treasure" that highlights some of the many art works Harvard owns. Surely a specialty publication, *Harvard Magazine* might add depth to academic and large public library collections.

3217. Hello! [ISSN: 0214-3887] 1988. w. GBP 94 for 6 mos. domestic; GBP 120 for 6 mos. in Europe; GBP 99 in US & Canada. Hello! Ltd., Wellington House, 69-71 Upper Ground, London, SE1 9PQ, United Kingdom. Illus., adv. Circ: 546952 Paid. *Aud.:* Ga.

This fun magazine is kind of a union of *People Weekly* and *Town and Country.* Wonderful celebrity-related pictures of all of the places and things "outsiders" would love to see grace each issue. The focus is international, with an emphasis on Britain and the United States. An impressive insert titled "Seven Days" includes anything and everything about London (worth the price alone). It is very timely, but there is little "real news." There are also sections on fashion,

beauty, and cookery; and a travel section surprisingly includes prices. There is, however, a slant on charity that differentiates it from its American cousins. A "frivolous" and fun inclusion for large public libraries and any that focus on the United Kingdom.

3218. Intelligence Report. Supersedes (in 1996): *Klanwatch Intelligence Report.* 1981. q. USD 99.95. Ed(s): Richard C. Young, Mark Potok. Southern Poverty Law Center, Intelligence Project, PO Box 548, Montgomery, AL 36104-0548; http://www.splcenter.org. Illus. Circ: 380000 Controlled. *Aud.:* Ga.

The *Intelligence Report* publishes information gathered by the Intelligence Project (of the Southern Poverty Law Center) on the activities of "hate groups and extremist activities throughout the United States." Included in its audience are law enforcement agencies, for which the SPLC offers an online course in examining hate crimes. The *Report* profiles specific activities of militia, patriot, white-supremacist, skinhead, and neo-Nazi groups, sending reporters on site—and sometimes undercover—to document transgressions. Direct mail, music labels, political campaigns, legal proceedings: these are all arenas in which hate-crime news occurs, and they are covered. A recent *IR* issue on "The Year in Hate" presents data over a five-year period to show the expansion of hate groups in the United States. A "Hate Groups Map" permits readers to see which groups are where. Recommended for public libraries mostly because they sometimes should house publications that disseminate information for the good of the commonwealth.

3219. Long Term View: a journal of informed opinion. [ISSN: 1066-1182] 1992. q. USD 10; USD 4.95 per issue. Ed(s): Lawrence R Velvel. Massachusetts School of Law at Andover, 500 Federal St, Woodland Park, Andover, MA 01810; vietzke@mslaw.edu; http://www.mslaw.edu. Illus. Sample. Circ: 5000. Vol. ends: Oct/Nov. *Aud.:* Hs, Ga, Ac.

Long Term View devotes each issue to discussion of a single topic in the field of public policy, sometimes in various formats. Future topics or questions are listed in current issues, with an invitation to submit an article on point. Generally, scholars, authors, and government or industry professionals respond. Past topics have included consideration of term limits, the need for a third political party, community and isolation, and "Why we seek war." In addition to articles, interviews with experts on the subject at hand are included. Because *LTV* issues consider single topics, the publication may be a fine resource for academic libraries.

3220. Mental Floss: feel smart again. [ISSN: 1543-4702] 2001. bi-m. USD 21.97 domestic; USD 31.97 Canada; USD 41.97 elsewhere. Ed(s): Neely Harris, Mangesh Hattikudur. Mental Floss L L C, PO Box 528, Novelty, OH 44072. Illus., adv. Circ: 35656. *Aud.:* Hs, Ga, Ac, Sa.

This brain-zine should appeal to nerds, geeks, and "Jeopardy" fans, those folks who have favorite writers and actually look things up in a dictionary. It takes pride in its steady organization, with sections entitled Scatter-Brained, Left Brain, Right Brain, Feature, Spinning the Globe, and Critical Knowledge. You can guess what these cover—if you can't, *Mental Floss* is not for you! In tones irreverent and whimsical, a recent issue of *MF* includes biographies, reviews, and articles on the history of hacking, the Know-Nothing party, and the Green movement in Morocco—and a how-to guide on ways to enjoy the magazine. Try its web site for the Quiz of the Day. There's even an archive for quiz junkies.

3221. Moment: the magazine of Jewish culture, politics, and religion. [ISSN: 0099-0280] 1975. bi-m. USD 14.97 domestic; USD 29.97 foreign. Ed(s): Nadine Epstein. Moment Magazine, 4115 Wisconsin Ave NW, Ste. 102, Washington, DC 20016-2848. Illus., adv. Sample. Circ: 65000. Vol. ends: Jan/Feb. Microform: PQC. Online: Northern Light Technology, Inc.; ProQuest LLC (Ann Arbor). *Indexed:* ABS&EES, ENW, IJP, RILM. *Bk. rev.:* 2-3, 750-1,500 words. *Aud.:* Ga.

Moment announces that it serves as an independent forum for viewpoints that include "Orthodox, Conservative, Reform, Reconstructionist, secular humanist and the non-affiliated movements," as well as "left," "right," and "center." The mere recitation of these titles and tags suggests that its audience has more than a passing familiarity with Jewish religion and history. That *Moment,* as a forum for exchange, seeks to facilitate discussion among its various religious and ethnic stakeholders suggests further that readers should expect to be challenged, perhaps affronted, as well as affirmed and informed. With pieces asserting that whites should pay reparations and that the world has benefited from the Jews' being the chosen people, such is the case. But *Moment* has depth and soul that urge it beyond the religio-political. There are interviews and exposes on interesting people, famous and not-so, ruminations on food and language, poetry, book reviews, and more. *Moment* is a welcome addition to any library, but especially to those located in areas with large Jewish populations.

3222. *Money (New York).* [ISSN: 0149-4953] 1972. 13x/yr. USD 39.89 domestic; USD 39.95 Canada; USD 99.99 elsewhere. Ed(s): Norman Pearlstine, Craig Hilliard. Time, Inc., Time & Life Bldg, Rockefeller Center, 29th Fl, New York, NY 10020-1393; http://www.money.cnn.com. Illus., index, adv. Circ: 1900000 Paid. Vol. ends: Dec. CD-ROM: ProQuest LLC (Ann Arbor). Microform: CIS; PQC. Online: The Dialog Corporation; EBSCO Publishing, EBSCO Host; Factiva, Inc.; Florida Center for Library Automation; Gale; LexisNexis; OCLC Online Computer Library Center, Inc.; ProQuest LLC (Ann Arbor); H.W. Wilson. *Indexed:* ABIn, ATI, BLI, BPI, BRI, CBRI, ConsI, EnvAb, LRI, MASUSE, PAIS, RGPR. *Bk. rev.:* 500-700 words, number varies. *Aud.:* Ga, Ac.

This magazine usually has pictures of couples or families on its covers because the slant of the publication is to personalize money management, to make it less complicated and scary. It has feature articles, not only on strategies for improving your credit and tripling your savings, but on poker players, daredevils, and writers. *Money* gets most of its work done in its recurring sections: Start, Plan, Home, Invest, and Save. Within these, you learn about portfolios, taxes, credit cards, insurance, investment funds, refinancing, and much, much more. *Money* situates some issues in the personal contexts of everyday people, as when they profile a newly married couple that has chosen to combine previously separate assets and investment instruments. *Money* now is a part of the CNNMoney.com family of resources, a web site with sections and material that often amplifies articles presented by *Money*.

3223. *Mother Jones.* [ISSN: 0362-8841] 1976. bi-m. USD 24 domestic; USD 34 Canada. Ed(s): Russ Rymer, Alastair Paulin. Foundation for National Progress, 222 Sutter St, 6th Fl, San Francisco, CA 94108; http://www.motherjones.com. Illus., adv. Circ: 225000 Paid. Vol. ends: Dec. CD-ROM: ProQuest LLC (Ann Arbor). Microform: NBI; PQC. Online: The Dialog Corporation; EBSCO Publishing, EBSCO Host; Florida Center for Library Automation; Gale; Northern Light Technology, Inc.; OCLC Online Computer Library Center, Inc.; ProQuest K-12 Learning Solutions; ProQuest LLC (Ann Arbor); H.W. Wilson. *Indexed:* ASIP, AltPI, BRI, CBRI, CWI, EnvAb, FutSurv, LeftInd, MASUSE, MRD, PAIS, RGPR, RILM, WSA. *Bk. rev.:* 3, 100-400 words. *Aud.:* Ga, Ac.

It's easy to call *Mother Jones* a progressive magazine; after all, it derives most of its support from the Foundation for National Progress. Would that labels were so easily acquired. Instead, *Mother Jones* has earned its progressive stripes through years of providing probing investigations of politicos, corporations, and regimes, and has long championed environmentalism through sustained analysis of farming, foodstuffs, and responsible recreation. Underscoring the latter, recent issues on the fate of oceans and the food chain present several articles on each theme. *Mother Jones* is not overly serious or somber, though, because it handles many of its subjects with quirkiness and irreverence. Well-known writers appear in *MJ*, the style of which still suggests that it's a haven for outcasts of the mainstream who fervently seek better ways for collectives to behave in the world. A unique magazine that is essential to most library collections.

3224. *National Geographic.* Formerly (until 1959): *The National Geographic Magazine.* [ISSN: 0027-9358] 1888. m. USD 19 domestic; CND 33 Canada; USD 37 elsewhere. Ed(s): William L Allen, Chris Johns. National Geographic Society, 1145 17th St, NW, Washington, DC 20036; http://www.nationalgeographic.com. Illus., index, adv. Circ: 9500000 Paid. Vol. ends: Jun/Dec. Microform: PMC; PQC. Online: EBSCO Publishing, EBSCO Host; Florida Center for Library Automation; Gale; OCLC Online Computer Library Center, Inc.;

ProQuest K-12 Learning Solutions; ProQuest LLC (Ann Arbor); H.W. Wilson. *Indexed:* A&ATA, ABS&EES, AICP, AbAn, AnthLit, BEL&L, BiolDig, CBCARef, CPerI, EI, EnvAb, EnvInd, GardL, IBR, ICM, LRI, MASUSE, RGPR, RI-1. *Aud.:* Ems, Hs, Ga, Ac.

MFL has extolled the excellence of *National Geographic* for many years, and this entry will be no different. For a long time, *NG* has conceived of geography in broad terms, wedding the physical and cultural strands within the discipline in feature articles that examine ritual, population shift, climate change, animal behavior, and small-town or village life. It continues to advance the National Geographic Society's mission, which is "to increase and diffuse geographic knowledge while promoting the conservation of the world's cultural, historical, and natural resources," with first-rate research, clear and colorful maps and other graphic displays, and photographs often so riveting and moving that we've marked the times in our own lives by when we first saw this or that picture. But you know all of this because *National Geographic* is now an American institution. What you may not know is that its web site is almost as rich as its magazine, combining some video features we've grown used to from *NG's* televison specials with supplementary texts from its publications. There are other online extras as well. All libraries should subscribe to this magazine.

3225. *New Internationalist.* Formerly: *Internationalist.* [ISSN: 0305-9529] 1970. 11x/yr. Individuals, GBP 28.85. Ed(s): Chris Richards, Richard Swift. New Internationalist Publications Ltd., 55 Rectory Rd, Oxford, OX4 1BW, United Kingdom; mazine@indas.on.ca; http://www.newint.org. Illus., index, adv. Sample. Circ: 75000. *Indexed:* AICP, AltPI, AmHI, BrHumI, CBCARef, CPerI, CWI, IBR, IBZ, MASUSE, PRA, RRTA, V&AA, WAE&RSA. *Bk. rev.:* 2-3, 250-300 words. *Aud.:* Hs, Ga, Ac.

This magazine's power lies in its dogged pursuit of facts and stories that expose the exploitation of people and/or the environment worldwide. *NI* does its work thematically, by assigning single topics to issues, such as Justice After Genocide, Nuclear's Second Wind, and The Challenge to Violence. Seven to ten articles follow, exploring the theme from different viewpoints and locales. Most longer pieces include footnotes to support assertions and to encourage further reading. Also in the magazine, in the "News, Views and Voices" section, are profiles of people and countries, reviews of books, music, and films, a short essay, and letters to the editor. One reader responded with praise for *NI's* continuing coverage of important issues, but admitted that constant exposure inspired melancholy. Perhaps, but such coverage is an important addition to a library's periodical collection.

3226. *The New Yorker.* [ISSN: 0028-792X] 1925. w. USD 47 domestic; USD 90 Canada; USD 112 elsewhere. Ed(s): David Remnick, David Remnick. Conde Nast Publications, Inc., 750 3rd Ave, New York, NY 10017; http://www.condenast.com. Illus., adv. Circ: 813434 Paid. Vol. ends: Dec. Microform: PQC. Online: Chadwyck-Healey Inc.; EBSCO Publishing, EBSCO Host; Florida Center for Library Automation; Gale; LexisNexis; ProQuest K-12 Learning Solutions; ProQuest LLC (Ann Arbor). *Indexed:* ABS&EES, AgeL, BEL&L, BRD, BRI, CBRI, FLI, GardL, IAPV, IIMP, IIPA, LRI, MASUSE, MLA-IB, MRD, MusicInd, NTA, PRA, RGPR, RI-1, RILM. *Bk. rev.:* 0-9, 200-3,000 words. *Aud.:* Hs, Ga, Ac.

Famous for its fiction, facts, reviews and criticism, cartoons, and talk and goings on about the town its title harbors, *The New Yorker* is one of the esteemed publications in America. Its history is rich with great writers, editors, and illustrators, as careers were made and sustained within its pages. And today, the beat goes on in rhythms of intelligent assertion. Its critics regularly attend to all of the arts, with recent issues reviewing the Martha Graham company's latest, vocal renditions of Britten, and of course as many appraisals of films and plays as will fit in designated space. Poets and fiction writers round out the regular fare, as do essays of politics and society. *The New Yorker* still is an excellent publication that deserves to be read by the widest audience possible. Essential to all libraries with a current periodicals section.

3227. *Ode.* [ISSN: 1382-3841] 1995. m. USD 35 in developing nations; USD 59 elsewhere; USD 5.95 newsstand/cover per issue. Ed(s): Jurrian Kamp. Ode International Publishers B.V., PO Box 2402, Rotterdam, 3000 CK, Netherlands. Illus., adv. *Aud.:* Ga.

This magazine takes seriously its charge to write "about people and ideas that are changing the world." For proof, it's published in three languages and posts a history on its web site that includes sections on "the beginning," "the early years," "permission marketing," "service record," "more than just a magazine," and "international adventure." Heady stuff. But *Ode* delivers with curiously enticing articles on monkeys and intelligence, blogging, the new sixties, the healing power of placebos, and much more. I smiled at "The Manifesto of the Cloud Appreciation Society." Additionally, *Ode* has pieces on people and places, and scores of reviews on books, web creations, and music. Its web site is comprehensive, and offers readers abstracts on all past feature articles.

3228. Popular Mechanics. Former titles (until 1952): *Popular Mechanics Magazine;* (until 1913): *Popular Mechanics.* [ISSN: 0032-4558] 1902. m. USD 12 domestic; USD 28 foreign; USD 3.99 newsstand/cover per issue. Ed(s): James B. Meigs, David Dunbar. Hearst Magazines, 300 W 57th St, New York, NY 10019. Illus., index, adv. Circ: 1200000 Paid. Vol. ends: Dec. CD-ROM: ProQuest LLC (Ann Arbor). Microform: NBI; PQC. Online: EBSCO Publishing, EBSCO Host; Florida Center for Library Automation; Gale; Micromedia ProQuest; Northern Light Technology, Inc.; OCLC Online Computer Library Center, Inc.; ProQuest K-12 Learning Solutions; ProQuest LLC (Ann Arbor); H.W. Wilson. *Indexed:* A&ATA, CBCARef, CPerI, ConsI, HRIS, IHTDI, MASUSE, NTA, RGPR. *Aud.:* Hs, Ga.

Long before the DIY movement ushered in by "This Old House" and fostered by Home Depot and Lowe's, *Popular Mechanics* was urging readers (mostly men) to investigate projects, collect tools, and make calculated attempts to build or repair things themselves. *PM* still does as much today, with renewed energy and broader scope. Technology, automobiles, home improvement, applied science, and the outdoors are the general areas covered by the magazine, and with advances in technology and engineering translating into new construction products and techniques, the subdivisions within these areas have multiplied twofold over the years. And yet *PM* still has room for sections on art and photography! Look for "how to" articles on furniture restoration and tuning a car, advice columns offering tips on home and auto improvement, and responses to readers' questions on a range of practical problems encountered while in the DIY trenches. *PM* has longer articles within the aforementioned sections that deal with topics like biofuels, cell phone efficiency, solar heating, gardening, and neutron beams. Anything dealing with applied science and technology goes in *PM,* which presumes that lay readers are intelligent and curious, and rewards them accordingly with practical and incisive reading.

3229. Reader's Digest. [ISSN: 0034-0375] 1922. m. USD 27.98 domestic; USD 38.95 foreign; USD 2.99 newsstand/cover per issue. Ed(s): Jacqueline Leo, Jacob Young. Reader's Digest Association, Inc, Reader's Digest Rd, Pleasantville, NY 10570-7000; http://www.rd.com. Illus., index, adv. Sample. Circ: 15000000. Vol. ends: Dec. Microform: PQC. *Indexed:* CINAHL, CPerI, HRIS, LRI, MASUSE, RGPR, RI-1. *Aud.:* Ems, Ga, Hs.

Two words jump at you when you examine *Reader's Digest* as a publication. The first is that it's a digest in that its subjects are presented in a "just the facts, ma'am" style, short and to the point. Some of pieces are excerpted from longer works in other publications; others are written for *RD.* The second term you recall is inspiration. *RD's* news mostly is positive, with "inspiring" stories of exploits of people very much like your neighbors, recalling famous deeds of past heroes. You'll read about belief in angels, brilliant ideas, hot spots, and cool gear; about survivors, activists, selfless doctors, and caring celebrities. Of course, *RD* is replete with humorous tidbits and stories, recipes, and home-repair advice. There's something for everyone in *Reader's Digest,* whose subtitle states that it's "America in Your Pocket." One minor complaint is that *RD* is hard to leaf through because of the rigid, cardboard-like advertisements that divide its pages, but there probably was a past article that explained how to extract these notices and use the paper to make doilies or spinning wheels!

3230. Red Pepper: raising the political temperature. [ISSN: 1353-7024] 1994. m. USD 60. Ed(s): Hillary Wainwright. Socialist Newspaper (Publications) Ltd., 1b Waterlow Rd, London, N19 5NJ, United Kingdom; redpepper@onlne.rednet.co.uk; http://www.redpepper.org.uk/. Illus., adv. *Indexed:* AltPI. *Aud.:* Hs, Ga, Ac.

"*Red Pepper* is a magazine of information, campaigning and culture. It provides a forum for the left to debate ideas and action." So states the opening of *Red Pepper's* extensive editorial charter of about 3,500 words, a declaration of ideals that permits readers no doubt about where its editors and contributors stand. But proof of a distorted bias is in the reading, and *Red Pepper's* articles, while they depart from the left, arrive to the reader as well written and engaging investigative reports or salient commentaries on issues that deserve examination. *RP* regularly covers the environment, civil liberties, and labor topics within the U.K. scene and beyond. It also attends to international news, with features on the success of the worker's party (Partido dos Trabalhadores) in Brazil and Chinese workers' rights. Europe, the G-8, and the United States also are part of *RP's* standard coverage. Entries on political and cultural events in the United Kingdom and beyond, film reviews, and notes on campaigns of all kinds make their way into *RP's* pages as well. While *RP* has a point of view, it's not strident in its views, but controlled and no-nonsense in its approach to informing the public.

3231. Reunions Magazine. [ISSN: 1046-5235] 1990. bi-m. USD 9.99; USD 3 newsstand/cover. Ed(s): Edith Wagner. Reunions, PO Box 11727, Milwaukee, WI 53211-0727; reunions@execpc.com; http://www.reunionsmag.com. Illus., adv. Sample. Circ: 621 Paid. *Aud.:* Ga.

Reunions is a niche magazine that accomplishes what it sets out to do: to create a cultural space for like-minded people to come together to receive and trade information. Sounds sort of like a reunion, doesn't it? The magazine provides detailed advice and instruction on how to plan for and hold reunions of all sorts: family, class, military, and ethnic. A planner may register his/her reunion with the magazine so that it appears on the web site listing; *Reunions* also provides a directory of companies that serve reunion planners. But the most interesting feature of the magazine is that it's partially a collective endeavor, with *Reunions* offering an open invitation to readers to contribute articles on how they fared in holding their gatherings, as well as to pose questions or to offer advice on the labor-intensive process. *Reunions* is a one-of-a-kind magazine that would fare well in the collections of libraries in high-population areas.

3232. Saturday Evening Post. [ISSN: 0048-9239] 1971. bi-m. USD 14.97 domestic; USD 19.97 foreign; USD 2.95 newsstand/cover. Ed(s): Dr. Cory Servaas, Ted Kreiter. Benjamin Franklin Literary and Medical Society, Inc., 1100 Waterway Blvd, Indianapolis, IN 46202. Illus., adv. Sample. Circ: 339500 Paid. Vol. ends: Dec. Microform: NBI. Online: The Dialog Corporation; EBSCO Publishing, EBSCO Host; Florida Center for Library Automation; Gale; Northern Light Technology, Inc.; OCLC Online Computer Library Center, Inc.; ProQuest K-12 Learning Solutions; ProQuest LLC (Ann Arbor); H.W. Wilson. *Indexed:* BRI, CBRI, CINAHL, MASUSE, RGPR. *Aud.:* Ems, Hs, Ga.

The middle and end of the heyday of the *SEP* had Norman Rockwell illustrating its covers and famous fiction writers contributing to its pages. *SEP* then closed its doors for several years, and reopened in a different time and market. Since the 1970s, it has directed its attention more to the older population, maintaining illustrations and advertisements that give it almost a nostalgic touch, comforting to some readers, I'm sure. Much of the *Post* deals with matters of health. In one issue, I counted 12 articles, both feature and columns, that were health-related. The rest of it contains pieces on just about anything, from the U.S. health care system to *The Chronicles of Narnia.* Perhaps the greatest feature of the *SEP* is that it feels welcoming, inviting readers to comment on contents, responding to their needs with advice on prescription drugs and quality of life, and entertaining them with humor and games.

3233. Smithsonian. [ISSN: 0037-7333] 1970. m. USD 19 domestic; USD 45 New Zealand; USD 55 elsewhere. Ed(s): Carey Winfrey. Smithsonian Magazine, 900 Jefferson Dr, SW, Washington, DC 20560-0406. Illus., index, adv. Circ: 2300000 Paid. Microform: PQC. Online: EBSCO Publishing, EBSCO Host; Florida Center for Library Automation; Gale; Micromedia ProQuest; OCLC Online Computer Library Center, Inc.; ProQuest K-12 Learning Solutions; ProQuest LLC (Ann Arbor); H.W. Wilson. *Indexed:* ABM, ABS&EES, AbAn, AmH&L, AmHI, AnthLit, ArtHuCI, BEL&L, BRD, BRI, BiolDig, CBCARef, CBRI, CPerI, EnvAb, EnvInd, FLI, GardL, HistAb, IBR, IBZ, LRI, MASUSE, PRA, RGPR, RI-1, RILM, SSCI. *Bk. rev.:* 4, 500 words. *Aud.:* Hs, Ga, Ac.

Perhaps the best thing to say about this intelligent and always interesting magazine is that you wish you had a lifetime subscription. Its feature articles span geography, history, archeology, and the arts, with topics such as baby boomers in Saudi Arabia, profiles of Wenzhou and Shenyang, China, the terminus of Homer's *Odyssey,* and the trajectory of the Dada movement. Beyond the topics are descriptions and analysis of subjects at the comfort zone between scientific reporting and good storytelling. In its "departments," *Smithsonian* regularly investigates archeological digs, museum artifacts, photographers and photograph collections, and points of interest for the intrepid traveler. The "Presence of Mind" section usually presents historical topics provocatively and in some detail. The magazine, like its namesake museum, is a pleasure to look at as well, with fine photographs of landscapes, exhibit pieces, and people included throughout each issue. Simply pick up an issue of *Smithsonian* and you'll select it for your library's periodical collection—it's that good.

3234. ***T V Guide.*** [ISSN: 0039-8543] 1953. w. USD 39.52; USD 1.99 newsstand/cover. Ed(s): Ian Birch, Jill Rachlin-Marbaix. Gemstar - TV Guide International, 1211 Ave of the Americas, New York, NY 10036; http://www.tvguide.com. Illus., index, adv. Circ: 9000000. *Indexed:* ASIP, LRI, RGPR. *Aud.:* Ga.

In case you've been out of touch (I have!), *TV Guide* is now the size of a standard magazine—with extra content to fill it! There are plenty of features on TV celebrities that appear in your favorite shows (David Caruso, Hugh Laurie, Teri Hatcher), news from in front of the camera and behind the scenes, a guide for movies on the tube, a list of family-friendly programs, questions and answers, cheers and jeers, highlights, and the customary hourly programming grid. Whew, *TV Guide* has grown—and its web site has even more information! This magazine is a great addition to the popular culture section of a periodicals collection.

3235. ***Tokion.*** bi-m. JPY 48000 domestic; USD 25 United States; USD 40 Canada. Ed(s): Kaori Sakurai. Knee High Media, 1-23-3 Higashi Shibuya-ku, Tokyo, 150-0011, Japan; http://www.tokion.com/. *Aud.:* Hs, Ga, Ac, Sa.

Perhaps *Tokion* magazine represents our time in that it's a publication that's both independent and part of a web assemblage that includes a radio station, a store, a gateway to articles and web sites beyond its virtual walls, and a news list. The magazine announces that it's about creativity, which means it centers on the arts, and more specifically, on people in the arts. Past issues have interviews and short essays on actors (Samantha Morton), directors (John Waters), musicians (Bjork, Brian Eno, Lou Reed), artists (Mike Mills, Kami, Matthew Barney), writers (Douglas Coupland), and other luminaries like Robert Evans and Evel Knievel. Issues are loosely organized around themes, such as Go North, Heroes, and Infamous. There are fashion pieces regularly, and excellent photographs throughout the publication. See *Tokion*'s web site to experience its vibe.

3236. ***Town & Country (New York).*** Incorporates (1901-1992): *Connoisseur.* [ISSN: 0040-9952] 1846. m. USD 12 domestic; USD 36 foreign; USD 4 newsstand/cover per issue. Ed(s): Pamela Fiori, Linda Nardi. Hearst Magazines, 300 W 57th St, New York, NY 10019; HearstMagazines@hearst.com; http://www.hearstcorp.com/magazines/. Illus., adv. Circ: 464415 Paid. Vol. ends: Dec. *Indexed:* ASIP, ArtInd, BAS, BRI, DAAI, IndIslam, MASUSE, RILM. *Aud.:* Ga.

Town & Country is a print travelogue for those journeying to the clean, well-groomed territory of unbounded leisure time. And how to enjoy those environs? A look at *T&C*'s sections will help plan your itinerary: Parties; On the Town; In the Country; Fashion & Style; Jewelry; Watches; Beauty & Health; Arts & Culture; Travel Notebook; Design Trends; Social Graces; Weddings; Fashion and Shopping Information—and Horoscopes. Add to all of these chapters feature articles that describe architecturally stunning coastal escape homes, villas, townhouses, retreats, manses, and other coveted abodes, and you have a magazine that manifests in its pages the life you've always wanted. See it to believe it. Subscribe to keep the dream alive.

3237. ***Vanity Fair.*** [ISSN: 0733-8899] 1983. m. USD 18 domestic; USD 38 Canada; USD 43 elsewhere. Ed(s): Chris Garrett, Krista Margo Smith. Conde Nast Publications, Inc., 750 3rd Ave, New York, NY 10017;

http://www.condenast.com. Illus., adv. Circ: 1182831 Paid. Vol. ends: Dec. *Indexed:* ASIP, DAAI, FLI, MRD, MusicInd, RGPR, RILM. *Bk. rev.:* Number and length vary. *Aud.:* Ga.

Vanity Fair is a magazine that now provides general commentary on the social and political life of the nation and beyond, along the lines of *Atlantic Monthly* and *Harper's.* Unlike its competitors-in-arms, its history permits it to include slick coverage of popular culture, glossy and provocative advertisements, equally provocative and sometimes troubling photographs, and a section called Fanfair that calendars "a month in the life of a culture" with event listings; film, music, and book reviews; and other things expected to be "hot" in the coming 30 days. Recent articles include profiles of Anderson Cooper and Dick Cheney and an excerpt from a new book about Hurricane Katrina. James Wolcott, Christopher Hitchens, Annie Leibovitz, and Herb Ritts are among the many names of exceptional professionals associated with *VF*, a magazine that has the right blend of the serious and the frivolous, of work and fun.

3238. ***The Village Voice.*** [ISSN: 0042-6180] 1955. w. Free in New York City. Ed(s): Donald Forst, Laura Conway. Village Voice Media, Inc., 36 Cooper Sq, New York, NY 10003. Illus., adv. Circ: 253000. Vol. ends: Dec. Microform: PQC. Online: Chadwyck-Healey Inc.; LexisNexis; Northern Light Technology, Inc.; OCLC Online Computer Library Center, Inc.; ProQuest LLC (Ann Arbor). *Indexed:* ASIP, BRI, CBRI, FLI, IIMP, IIPA, MRD, MusicInd, RILM. *Bk. rev.:* 1-7, 500-4,000 words. *Aud.:* Ga, Ac.

It may be that *The Village Voice* invented the counterculture, or at least a version of it. Since the 1950s, *The Voice* has challenged power through editorial and investigative reporting, journalistic style by eschewing undue reverence and formality, and convention by celebrating all of New York's constituents in print and picture. And its format mirrors New York in miniature, so full of information and image that you come away saying that if *The Voice* reflects a week in New York, visitors better prepare for a helluva ride. There's local, regional, and national news coverage, feature articles on subjects such as abortion and online music, heads-up pointers on food and bars, and scores of review pieces, short and long, on film, theatre, music, art, dance, and books. Staff writers, including Nat Hentoff and Tom Robbins, have strong followings in the area and beyond. *The Village Voice* may be the best example of a weekly paper that feeds a city as much as it feeds off it. Couple it with a subscription to the *The New Yorker* to give your library's users sharp insight into the Big Apple, which is still one of the powerful cultural and political engines in America.

3239. ***The Week: all you need to know about everything that matters.*** [ISSN: 1533-8304] 2001. 50x/yr. USD 49.50 domestic; USD 79.50 Canada; USD 127.50 elsewhere. Ed(s): William Flak. The Week Publications, Inc., 1040 6th Ave, 23rd Fl, New York, NY 10012. Adv. Circ: 429401 Paid and controlled. *Aud.:* Hs, Ga, Ac.

The Week is a British digest of the "key" stories appearing in the British and world press in the past seven days. It summarizes articles from other publications and supplements this reporting with analysis of its own. As with all good digests, *The Week* strives to be succinct, to boil down stories to smaller yet still substantial proportions. *The Week* has a "pop culture underbelly" that will please many, with celebrity/royal gossip, tabloid stories, serious and frivolous poll coverage, and revisits with controversies. There are sections on the arts, in which reviews are reviewed; health and science coverage; and city and leisure sections that preview London happenings to come. Subscribe to *The Week* and you'll feel that you're seeing the world in greater detail through British lenses, with a vicarious side jaunt through London Town.

3240. ***The Wilson Quarterly: surveying the world of ideas.*** [ISSN: 0363-3276] 1976. q. USD 20 domestic; USD 35 foreign. Ed(s): James Carman, Steven Lagerfeld. Woodrow Wilson International Center for Scholars, 1 Woodrow Wilson Plaza, 1300 Pennsylvania Ave, NW, Washington, DC 20004-3027. Illus., index, adv. Sample. Circ: 60000. Vol. ends: Nov. Microform: PQC. Online: EBSCO Publishing, EBSCO Host; Florida Center for Library Automation; Gale; Northern Light Technology, Inc.; OCLC Online Computer Library Center, Inc.;

ProQuest K-12 Learning Solutions; ProQuest LLC (Ann Arbor); H.W. Wilson. *Indexed:* ABS&EES, AmH&L, AmHI, BRI, CBRI, HistAb, HumInd, LRI, PAIS, PRA, RGPR, RI-1, RILM. *Bk. rev.:* 11-16, 1,500 words. *Aud.:* Ga, Ac.

The aim of the *Wilson Quarterly* is to address subject areas and issues that affect public life by "presenting the best writing and thinking of academics, specialists, and others to a broad audience." Articles and essays on politics, culture, religion, and science carry titles such as "The Sovereign State of Retirement," "The Resurrection of Pearl Buck," "The Future Is a Foreign Country," and "The Other Sixties." Some issues center on themes, while others present a roster of interesting but unconnected pieces. There also are sections called "Findings," for brief articles on topics; "Current Books," for reviews and discussions about authors; and "In Essence," a survey of articles from other leading journals and periodicals. Major pieces in *WQ* are long and intended for readers willing to invest time reading on complex subjects. The editors seem to stand in the middle of the road, perhaps to coax from both sides the kind of informed but collegial debates they feel will best serve the country. Recommended for large public and all academic libraries.

■ GENERAL INTEREST: NON–ENGLISH LANGUAGE

Enrique Diaz, Designer/Multimedia Specialist, Harvard College Library Communications, Widener Library, Harvard University, Cambridge, MA 02138

Cheryl LaGuardia, Head of Instructional Services for the Harvard College Library, Widener Library, Research Services, Harvard University, Cambridge, MA 02138; claguard@fas.harvard.edu

Introduction

Readers have expressed interest in a section that can help them serve the needs of ESL/non-English-language-speaking populations in transition within their communities, and this section attempts to begin to do that. The editors are very interested in hearing suggestions from *MFL* readers for more languages and titles to be represented here; please do e-mail Cheryl with your suggestions at claguard@fas.harvard.edu.

Basic Periodicals

Buenhogar: Good Housekeeping en Espanol; National Geographic en Espanol; Siempre Mujer; Vanidades.

3241. *Buenhogar.* [ISSN: 0186-422X] 1966. m. USD 53.70; USD 2.95 newsstand/cover per issue. Ed(s): Paolo Merigo. Editorial Televisa, 6355 NW 36th St, Miami, FL 33166; subscriptions@editorialtelevisa.com. Illus., adv. Circ: 150000. *Aud.:* Ga, Sa.

Articles here are on home decorating, cooking, fashion, image, and entertainment. Sections on lifestyle, health, family, celebrities, housekeeping, beauty, and decorating are presented in much the same manner as in the English-language *Good Housekeeping.* Prominent Latinos are often featured in this edition.

3242. *Cosmopolitan en Espanol.* [ISSN: 0188-0616] 1973. m. USD 18 domestic; USD 45.35 foreign. Editorial Televisa, 6355 NW 36th St, Miami, FL 33166; info@editorialtelevisa.com; http://www.editorialtelevisa.us/. Illus., adv. Circ: 52630 Paid. Microform: PQC. *Aud.:* Ga.

A compendium of articles mostly by women, for women, covering the areas of fashion, beauty, work, home, relationships, trendy social issues, and periodic calculations of one's sexual IQ. A staple for any general interest Spanish-speakers' collection.

3243. *E S P N Deportes: la revista.* [ISSN: 1933-947X] 2005. m. USD 18 domestic; USD 43.35 foreign. Editorial Televisa, 6355 NW 36th St, Miami, FL 33166; subscriptions@editorialtelevisa.com; http://www.editorialtelevisa.us/. Adv. Circ: 55000 Paid. *Aud.:* Ems, Hs, Ga, Sa.

This glossy magazine shows a global perspective on every sport—even golf. Features include sports news, interviews with star athletes, award events, sports curiosities ("estranged teams" in Cuba, for example) and regional coverage of individual sports. Sure to serve Spanish-speaking sports enthusiasts well.

3244. *Furia Musical.* 1993. fortn. USD 12 domestic; USD 37.35 foreign. Editorial Televisa, 6355 NW 36th St, Miami, FL 33166; subscriptions@editorialtelevisa.com; http://www.editorialtelevisa.us/. Adv. Circ: 9006 Paid. *Aud.:* Hs, Ga, Sa.

Furia is the Mexican equivalent of *People* magazine. The focus is on music celebrities, featuring bands on tour, and with a heavy slant on Nortena musicians. Regular sections include photo galleries, horoscopes, centerfolds (suitable for general audiences), and music reviews. A mainstay publication that will be of great interest to a Hispanic audience.

3245. *Harper's Bazaar en Espanol.* [ISSN: 0890-9598] 1949. m. USD 18.90; USD 2.95 newsstand/cover per issue. Ed(s): Carols Mendez. Editorial Televisa, 6355 NW 36th St, Miami, FL 33166; info@editorialtelevisa.com; http://www.editorialtelevisa.us/. Illus., adv. Circ: 52000. *Aud.:* Hs, Ga, Sa.

This sophisticated glossy is the ultimate serial salute to high fashion, sandwiching features by famous writers among the pretty pages of couture and cosmetics. Regular features include fashion news, horoscopes, lifestyle notes, interviews with designers, and a page of "what's in and what's out." Sure to please many fashion-conscious Spanish-speaking readers.

3246. *Men's Health en Espanol.* [ISSN: 1547-5638] 1994. m. Editorial Televisa, 6355 NW 36th St, Miami, FL 33166; subscriptions@editorialtelevisa.com. Adv. *Aud.:* Hs, Ga, Sa.

Covers the gamut of male interests: food, sex, sports, fashion, entertainment, health, bodybuilding, exercise, practical lifestyle tips, and unmasking female orgasm-faking. A standard title for libraries serving Spanish-speaking men.

3247. *National Geographic en Espanol.* [ISSN: 1546-8852] 1998. m. USD 34 domestic; USD 45 foreign. Ed(s): Luis Albores. Editorial Televisa, 6355 NW 36th St, Miami, FL 33166; info@editorialtelevisa.com; http://www.editorialtelevisa.us/. Illus., adv. Circ: 36276. *Aud.:* Hs, Ga, Ac, Sa.

Heavily illustrated, with superb essays, this journal is just as important for a Spanish-speaking audience as it is for English speakers. It covers global cultures, wildlife, the environment, advances in technology and science, and world history. An essential subscription for serving Spanish-speaking audiences.

3248. *Prevention en Espanol.* [ISSN: 1529-370X] 1999. m. USD 12 domestic; USD 35.40 foreign. Editorial Televisa, 6355 NW 36th St, Miami, FL 33166; subscriptions@editorialtelevisa.com; http://www.editorialtelevisa.us/. Adv. Circ: 60000 Paid. *Aud.:* Hs, Ga, Sa.

The Spanish-language version of this standard title covers nutrition, women's health, and related interests (fashion, body image, love and sex, etc.) in sections on trends, beauty, food and nutrition, alternative therapies, exercise, family, relationships, and feature articles. An essential source for libraries that serve Spanish-speaking populations.

3249. *Siempre Mujer: !Siempre Mujer!* [ISSN: 1556-2638] 2005. bi-m. USD 2.99 per issue; USD 12. Meredith Corp., 1716 Locust St, Des Moines, IA 50309-3023; http://www.meredith.com. Circ: 350000. *Aud.:* Hs, Ga, Sa.

The publishers of *Siempre Mujer* have come up with a very timely title here. This publication is designed to "reflect the lifestyles, aspirations and dreams of Hispanic women who keep their traditions alive and embrace new American values." (from the publisher's web site) The targeted readership is eight million

Hispanic women in the United States, with a median age of 35, and an annual household income of $35,000. It is a powerful demographic, and this title can provide an excellent bridge for Hispanic households in the United States, 82 percent of which speak Spanish at home (according to the U.S. Census Bureau, 2004). Content focuses on articles and columns on clothing, family and parenting, culture and entertainment, self-development, health and fitness, finances, home decorating, make-up, and food, along with frequent interviews with Hispanic celebrities. Secciones Regulares include: Hablemos (Let's Talk, an editorial), Colaboradores (brief bios of notable Hispanics in the news), De Mujer a Mujer (Woman to Woman), Cultura, Horoscopo, and Toque Final (the Final Touch, a brief philosophical note at the end of the issue). Issues are thematic; recent issues have been the "Travel Special" and the "Bargain Style Special," for example. An excellent addition to public and high school library collections serving significantly sized Hispanic populations.

3250. *T V y Novelas.* [ISSN: 0188-0683] 1982. bi-w. USD 29 domestic; USD 79.70 foreign. Ed(s): Gloria Calzada. Editorial Televisa, 6355 NW 36th St, Miami, FL 33166; info@editorialtelevisa.com; http://www.editorialtelevisa.us/. Adv. Circ: 144994 Paid. *Aud.:* Hs, Ga, Sa.

If you want to attract a teenage Spanish-speaking audience, this is a must-have title. It covers popular Hispanic TV stars, industry gossip, soap opera plotlines, and fashion, fashion, fashion—who's wearing what while being seen with whom.

3251. *Tu Dinero.* 2005. 10x/yr. USD 17.95 domestic; USD 47.28 foreign. Editorial Televisa, 6355 NW 36th St, Miami, FL 33166; subscriptions@ editorialtelevisa.com; http://www.editorialtelevisa.us/. Adv. Circ: 50000 Paid. *Aud.:* Ga, Sa.

Follow the money and you'll find this Spanish-language publication, which covers how to make, invest, and save money. Recent articles discuss e-banks, online investing, interviews with celebrities on how they manage their money, starting your own business, car buying tips, franchising how-tos, and playing games with your kids to demonstrate that compound interest is their very best friend. A solid addition to a Spanish-language collection that will appeal to most adult readers.

3252. *Vanidades.* fortn. Editorial Televisa Argentina, Av Paseo Colon 275, Piso 10, Buenos Aires, 1063, Argentina; http://www.televisa.com.ar. Adv. *Aud.:* Hs, Ga, Sa.

Habla Spanglish? This predominantly Spanish-language publication offers crossover coverage of cultural icons, entertainers, models, musicians, and royal families around the world. Fixed features include Notas (notes), Turismo (travel), Cine (film), Han triunfado (success stories), Camara indiscreta (candid camera), and Horoscopo (you know this). There's a heavily cross-cultural merchandising focus on women's beauty products and fashion: some advertisements are entirely in English, but article text is in Spanish.

■ GEOGRAPHY

See also Population Studies section.

Fred Burchsted, Research Librarian, Research Services Dept., Widener Library, Harvard University, Cambridge, MA 02138; burchst@fas.harvard.edu

Introduction

Geographers study the surface of the earth, the processes that form it (physical geography), and how people modify and are influenced by it (human geography). Concerned with spatial patterns on the earth's surface and how they change, geography straddles the sciences, social sciences, and humanities. It has links with many other disciplines—any subject that has a spatial perspective. Physical geography is closely allied to geology and draws on physical sciences methodology. Human geographers are often more affiliated with related social science fields (economics, sociology, political science) than with any core area of geography. Geography is increasingly infiltrating the humanities with studies of social construction of landscapes and regions, how places are imagined in

literary works, and individual experiences of place. Regional geography explores the features that characterize particular areas. Analytical geographers use quantitative methods to elucidate patterns of settlement and other spatial phenomena. Partly in reaction to the positivistic analytical approach, humanistic, and later cultural, geography arose to take into consideration human feelings and perceptions. Radical geography elucidates spatial aspects of social and economic inequality. There is a strong emphasis on studies of change, especially in the growing area of environmental studies and in work on globalization.

All the areas of geography have in common the use of maps, and more recently, other forms of geospatial technology. This is now a very active field, as many areas outside of academic geography, including marketing, environmental monitoring, and urban and regional planning, use geographical information systems and other technologies. Partly because of these applications, geographical education is burgeoning as geographically trained graduates take jobs in diverse areas.

Comprehensive lists of journals, print and electronic, may be found at Geosource: Web Resources for Human Geography, Physical Geography, Planning, Geoscience and Environmental Science (www.library.uu.nl/ geosource); Resources for Geographers (www.colorado.edu/geography/ virtdept/resources/contents.htm); Oddens' Bookmarks (http://oddens.geog.uu.nl/index.php). The American Geographical Society Library at the University of Wisconsin–Milwaukee lists publications received, including books, periodical articles, pamphlets, maps and atlases, and government documents in *Current Geographical Publications*, with issues since April 2004 available free on their web site (http://geobib.lib.uwm.edu). It is cumulated since 1985 in the Online Geographical Bibliography (GEOBIB). The print version ceased with the December 2003 issue.

All the subdisciplines, approaches, and methodologies are reflected in geography's periodical literature. The following is a selection of the most important general interest, scholarly/research, and trade periodicals in geography.

Basic Periodicals

Hs: *Geographical, National Geographic;* Ga: *Explorers Journal, Geographical, National Geographic;* Ac: *Association of American Geographers. Annals, Geographical Review, Institute of British Geographers. Transactions, The Professional Geographer.*

Basic Abstracts and Indexes

Geographical Abstracts. Online Geographical Bibliography (GEOBIB).

3253. *Acme: an international e-journal for critical geographies.* [ISSN: 1492-9732] 2002. s-a. Free. Ed(s): Lawrence Berg. University of British Columbia - Okanagan, 3333 University Way, Kelowna, BC V1V 1V7, Canada. Refereed. *Indexed:* IBSS. *Aud.:* Ac.

A journal of radical approaches to spatial relationships involved in inequality and social justice. Aimed at fostering social and political change. Articles approach geography from anarchist, anti-racist, environmentalist, feminist, Marxist, postcolonial, queer, and other perspectives. Articles are largely in English, but may be in French, Italian, German, or Spanish. The editorial board is international with a Canadian emphasis. Of interest to any library supporting a geography department with a political or social orientation.

3254. *Antipode: a radical journal of geography.* [ISSN: 0066-4812] 1969. 5x/yr. GBP 501 print & online eds. Ed(s): Melissa Wright, Noel Castree. Blackwell Publishing Ltd., 9600 Garsington Rd, Oxford, OX4 2ZG, United Kingdom; customerservices@blackwellpublishing.com; http://www.blackwellpublishing.com. Illus., index, adv. Sample. Refereed. Circ: 1050. Vol. ends: Oct. Online: Blackwell Synergy; EBSCO Publishing, EBSCO Host; Gale; IngentaConnect; OCLC Online Computer Library Center, Inc.; OhioLINK; SwetsWise Online Content. Reprint: PSC. *Indexed:* AltPI, AmH&L, ApEcolAb, ArtHuCI, CJA, EI, FR, HistAb, IBR, IBSS, IBZ, LeftInd, M&GPA, PRA, PSA, RI-1, SSA, SSCI, SWRA, SociolAb, WAE&RSA. *Bk. rev.:* 3-6, 1,200-2,400 words, signed. *Aud.:* Ac.

Antipode publishes articles from a variety of radical ideological positions, offering dissenting perspectives on environmentalism, feminism, postcolonialism, postmodernism, race, urbanism, war, and other topics. Most issues include focused groups of papers. This journal is devoted to fostering social and political change through activist scholarship and free discussion. Editors and authors are American and British, with an international editorial board. Antipode Online, the journal's new web site, offers several features, including some free content, obituaries of left-wing geographers, and links to left-wing journals and organizations. This journal is important for academic libraries that support geography and political science departments.

3255. Applied Geography. [ISSN: 0143-6228] 1981. 4x/yr. EUR 653. Ed(s): Robert Rogerson. Pergamon, The Boulevard, Langford Ln, East Park, Kidlington, OX5 1GB, United Kingdom. Illus., index. Sample. Refereed. Vol. ends: Oct. Microform: PQC. Online: EBSCO Publishing, EBSCO Host; Gale; IngentaConnect; OhioLINK; ScienceDirect; SwetsWise Online Content. *Indexed:* CABA, CJA, EnvAb, EnvInd, FPA, ForAb, HortAb, PollutAb, RRTA, S&F, SSCI, SUSA, SWRA, VB, WAE&RSA. *Aud.:* Ac, Sa.

Applied Geography focuses geographical thought and methods on human problems that have a spatial component by fostering an understanding of the underlying systems, human or physical. Coverage includes resource management, environmental problems, agriculture, and urban and regional planning. The target audience is planners and policymakers as well as academics. The editorship is British with a British/American/international editorial board. Authorship is international with a British emphasis. Important for libraries that support academic geography departments or agencies concerned with policy and planning.

3256. Arab World Geographer. [ISSN: 1480-6800] 1998. q. USD 145 (Individuals, USD 48; USD 15 newsstand/cover). Ed(s): Ghazi Falah. Centre for Urban and Community Studies, University of Toronto, 455 Spadina Ave, Toronto, ON M5S 2G8, Canada; http://www.library.utoronto.ca/www/cucs. Refereed. *Indexed:* IBSS, IndIslam, M&GPA. *Bk. rev.:* 1-2, 400-800 words, signed. *Aud.:* Ac, Sa.

Arab World Geographer publishes articles on geographical research, both theoretical and applied, on all aspects, cultural and physical, of the human environment in the Arab countries. There is an emphasis on application of research to policy and on the publication of work by Arab geographers. The editorship is American with an international editorial board. Authorship is international. Important for academic libraries that support geography departments or Middle Eastern area studies programs.

3257. Area. [ISSN: 0004-0894] 1969. q. GBP 168 print & online eds. Ed(s): Heather Viles, Alastair Bonnett. Blackwell Publishing Ltd., 9600 Garsington Rd, Oxford, OX4 2ZG, United Kingdom; customerservices@ blackwellpublishing.com; http://www.blackwellpublishing.com. Illus. Refereed. Circ: 2500. Vol. ends: Dec. Reprint: PSC. *Indexed:* ArtHuCI, BAS, BrArAb, CABA, CJA, EI, FR, ForAb, HortAb, IBR, IBSS, IBZ, NumL, RRTA, S&F, SSCI, SWA, WAE&RSA. *Bk. rev.:* 6-20, 1,000-2,000 words, signed. *Aud.:* Ac.

Area is a scholarly journal that features short research and discussion articles on topics of current professional interest and expressions of opinion by geographers on public questions—largely human geography, but some physical. Groups of several articles focusing on special subjects are often published. The "Observation" section features short reviews and opinion pieces on subjects of current debate. This journal aims at a free discussion of geographical ideas, results, and methodology. Authorship and editorship are British. Important for libraries that support a geography department.

3258. Association of American Geographers. Annals. [ISSN: 0004-5608] 1911. q. GBP 643 print & online eds. Ed(s): Anne M. Jones, Robin Friedman. Routledge, 325 Chestnut St, Ste 800, Philadelphia, PA 19106; journals@routledge.com; http://www.tandf.co.uk/journals. Illus., index, adv. Sample. Refereed. Circ: 9000 Paid. Vol. ends: Dec. Microform: PQC. Online: Blackwell Synergy; EBSCO Publishing, EBSCO Host; Gale; IngentaConnect; JSTOR (Web-based Journal Archive); OCLC Online Computer Library Center, Inc.; OhioLINK; SwetsWise Online Content. Reprint: PSC. *Indexed:* ABS&EES, AbAn, Agr, AmH&L, BAS,

BRI, BiolDig, CABA, CBRI, CJA, EI, FPA, FR, ForAb, HistAb, HortAb, IBR, IBSS, IBZ, IPSA, IndIslam, LRI, M&GPA, PRA, PollutAb, RI-1, RRTA, S&F, SSCI, SUSA, SWRA, WAE&RSA. *Bk. rev.:* 10-20, 750-2,000 words, signed. *Aud.:* Ac.

The *Annals* is often considered the leading American research journal in geography. Covering all areas of geography worldwide, it offers research articles, commentaries on published articles, book review forums, and occasional review articles and map supplements. Emphasis is on integrative and cross-disciplinary papers. Editorship/authorship is largely American with some international editors and contributors. Important for all academic and for large public libraries.

3259. Australian Geographer. [ISSN: 0004-9182] 1928. 3x/yr. GBP 312 print & online eds. Ed(s): James Forrest. Routledge, 4 Park Sq, Milton Park, Abingdon, OX14 4RN, United Kingdom; info@routledge.co.uk; http://www.routledge.com. Illus., index, adv. Sample. Refereed. Circ: 1200. Vol. ends: Nov. Online: EBSCO Publishing, EBSCO Host; Gale; IngentaConnect; OCLC Online Computer Library Center, Inc.; ProQuest K-12 Learning Solutions; ProQuest LLC (Ann Arbor); RMIT Publishing; SwetsWise Online Content. Reprint: PSC. *Indexed:* BAS, CABA, CJA, DSA, FPA, FR, ForAb, HortAb, IBR, IBSS, IBZ, M&GPA, PAIS, PollutAb, RRTA, S&F, SSCI, SWRA, WAE&RSA. *Aud.:* Ac.

Published under the auspices of the Geographical Society of New South Wales, *Australian Geographer* offers research articles on human and physical geography, focusing on environmental studies. There is a strong Australian concentration but with articles on the broader Asia-Pacific and Antarctic region. Occasional special issues on focused topics are published. Editorship/ authorship is largely Australian. Important for academic libraries that support geography departments, and environmental or area studies programs with Australasian interests.

Cartographic Perspectives. See Cartography, GIS, and Imagery section.

Cartography and Geographic Information Science. See Cartography, GIS, and Imagery section.

Coordinates: Series B. See Cartography, GIS, and Imagery section.

3260. Cultural Geographies: a journal of cultural geographies. Formerly (until 2001): *Ecumene.* [ISSN: 1474-4740] 1994. q. GBP 360. Ed(s): Philip Crang, Catherine Nash. Sage Publications Ltd., 1 Oliver's Yard, 55 City Rd, London, EC1 1SP, United Kingdom; info@sagepub.co.uk; http://www.sagepub.co.uk. Illus., index, adv. Sample. Refereed. Circ: 900. Vol. ends: Oct. Online: EBSCO Publishing, EBSCO Host; Gale; HighWire Press; IngentaConnect; OCLC Online Computer Library Center, Inc.; OhioLINK; ProQuest LLC (Ann Arbor); SwetsWise Online Content. Reprint: PSC. *Indexed:* AmHI, BrHumI, CABA, HortAb, IBR, IBSS, IBZ, PSA, RRTA, S&F, SSA, SSCI, SociolAb. *Bk. rev.:* 4-8, 700-1,300 words, signed. *Aud.:* Ac.

Drawing on contributors from a wide range of disciplines, *Cultural Geographies* explores thought on the perception, representation, and interpretation of the earth and on "the cultural appropriation of nature, landscape, and environment." Interest in these themes comes from a variety of artistic, humanistic, environmental, and geographical communities. The "Cultural Geographies in Practice" section offers critical reflections from practitioners and academics on how civic, policy, and artistic practices relate to cultural geography. The editorship is American and British with international editorial/ advisory boards. Authorship is international, with the United States, Canada, and the United Kingdom most heavily represented. Important for libraries supporting geography departments and environmental and cultural studies programs.

3261. CyberGEO: revue euroeenne de geographie/European journal of geography. [ISSN: 1278-3366] 1996. irreg. Free. Ed(s): Christine Kosmopoulos. CyberGeo, 13 rue du Four, Paris, 75006, France; vanky@parisgeo.cnrs.fr; http://www.cybergeo.presse.fr/. *Indexed:* FR, IBSS. *Bk. rev.:* 10-20/year, 200-800 words, signed. *Aud.:* Ac.

This is a free online journal publishing articles on the whole range of geography. It offers authors quick publication and immediate reader feedback. Results of reader feedback may be incorporated into or added to articles. There is an associated discussion mailing list. The web site has an English version. Articles have English summaries and are in French, English, and other languages. The editorial board is European, largely French. Of interest to any library supporting a geography department, especially with theoretical or European interests.

Earth Interactions. See Atmospheric Sciences section.

Earth Surface Processes and Landforms. See Earth Sciences section.

3262. *Economic Geography.* [ISSN: 0013-0095] 1925. q. USD 85. Ed(s): Joanne Miller, Bjorn Asheim. Clark University, 950 Main St, Worcester, MA 01610; econgeography@clarku.edu; http://www.clarku.edu/. Illus., index, adv. Refereed. Circ: 1700. Vol. ends: Oct. Microform: PMC; PQC. Online: EBSCO Publishing, EBSCO Host; Florida Center for Library Automation; Gale; JSTOR (Web-based Journal Archive); Northern Light Technology, Inc.; OCLC Online Computer Library Center, Inc.; ProQuest K-12 Learning Solutions; ProQuest LLC (Ann Arbor). *Indexed:* ABIn, ABS&EES, AgeL, AmH&L, BAS, BRI, CBRI, DSA, EI, FR, HRIS, HistAb, IBR, IBSS, IBZ, IPSA, IndIslam, JEL, PAIS, PSA, RRTA, SSCI, SWA, WAE&RSA. *Bk. rev.:* 5-10, 800-1,800 words, signed. *Aud.:* Ac.

Economic Geography publishes theoretical articles and empirical papers that make a contribution to theory. Topics include land use, agriculture, and urban and regional development, with an emphasis on recent approaches that involve gender, environmental issues, and industrial change. The editors wish to make *EG* a focus for debate on the current diversity of theories in economic geography. The editorship and authorship are largely American/British/Commonwealth. Important for libraries that support academic geography and economics departments or urban and regional planning programs.

3263. *Ethics, Place and Environment: a journal of philosophy and geography.* Incorporates (1997-2004): *Philosophy amd Geography.* [ISSN: 1366-879X] 1998. 3x/yr. GBP 261 print & online eds. Ed(s): Tim Unwin, Andrew Light. Routledge, 4 Park Sq, Milton Park, Abingdon, OX14 4RN, United Kingdom; info@routledge.co.uk; http://www.routledge.com. Illus., index, adv. Sample. Refereed. Vol. ends: Oct. Online: EBSCO Publishing, EBSCO Host; Gale; IngentaConnect; OCLC Online Computer Library Center, Inc.; SwetsWise Online Content. Reprint: PSC. *Indexed:* EnvAb, GardL, IBR, IBSS, IBZ, PhilInd, SSA, SUSA, SociolAb. *Bk. rev.:* 4-8, 600-2,000 words, signed. *Aud.:* Ac.

This scholarly journal of geographical and environmental ethics is concerned with human behavior in social/cultural and physical/biological environments. Emphases are on ethical problems of geographical and environmental research, ethical implications of environmental legislation, and business ethics from a geographical/environmental perspective. Both research and review articles are published, together with sets of short communications on special topics, including debates, conference reports, commentaries on published papers, opinions, and book reviews. Absorbed the journal *Philosophy & Geography* in 2005. The editorial board and authors are largely American/British/Commonwealth, with some broader international representation. Important for academic libraries that support geography or philosophy departments and for any library that supports an environmental studies program.

Eurasian Geography and Economics. See Slavic Studies section.

3264. *Explorers Journal.* [ISSN: 0014-5025] 1921. q. USD 24.95. Ed(s): Angela Schuster. Explorers Club, 46 E 70th St, New York, NY 10021; http://www.explorers.org/. Illus., index, adv. Refereed. Circ: 3500. Vol. ends: Dec. Microform: PQC. *Bk. rev.:* 5-7, 100-400 words, signed. *Aud.:* Hs, Ga, Ac.

The Explorers Club, a learned society devoted to the advancement of exploration, promotes all areas of field research by publishing in its journal scholarly articles of high literary and aesthetic quality that communicate the excitement of exploration and field research. Articles are accessible to nonspecialist readers and feature high-quality color illustrations. Also included are brief notes on new discoveries and news of exploration and explorers. Useful for academic and public libraries and for libraries of institutions that undertake overseas field research.

3265. *Gender, Place and Culture: a journal of feminist geography.* [ISSN: 0966-369X] 1994. bi-m. GBP 629 print & online eds. Ed(s): Brenda Yeoh, Linda Peake. Routledge, 4 Park Sq, Milton Park, Abingdon, OX14 4RN, United Kingdom; info@routledge.co.uk; http://www.routledge.co.uk. Illus., index, adv. Sample. Refereed. Vol. ends: Dec. Online: EBSCO Publishing, EBSCO Host; Gale; IngentaConnect; OCLC Online Computer Library Center, Inc.; ProQuest LLC (Ann Arbor); SwetsWise Online Content. Reprint: PSC. *Indexed:* AltPI, AmHI, BrHumI, CJA, CWI, FemPer, IBR, IBSS, IBZ, IndIslam, MASUSE, RILM, SSA, SSCI, SWA, SociolAb. *Bk. rev.:* 5-12, 900-1,500 words, signed. *Aud.:* Ac.

Gender, Place and Culture provides a forum for research and debate concerning the connections of geography and gender issues. Topics include spatial aspects of gender relations; oppression structures; gender construction and politics; and relations between gender and ethnicity, age, class, and other social categories. Articles are theoretical or empirical but with implications for theory. The journal emphasizes the relevance of its subject area for feminism and women's studies. The "Viewpoint" feature offers commentaries on published papers, debates, and other short items. Editorship and authorship are largely American/British/Commonwealth. Important for academic libraries that support geography departments or programs in women's or cultural studies.

Geo World. See Cartography, GIS, and Imagery section.

3266. *Geoforum.* [ISSN: 0016-7185] 1970. 6x/yr. EUR 1122. Ed(s): Andrew Leyshon, J. L. Emel. Pergamon, The Boulevard, Langford Ln, East Park, Kidlington, OX5 1GB, United Kingdom. Illus., adv. Sample. Refereed. Circ: 600. Vol. ends: Nov. Microform: PQC. Online: EBSCO Publishing, EBSCO Host; Gale; IngentaConnect; OhioLINK; ScienceDirect; SwetsWise Online Content. *Indexed:* AgeL, BAS, CABA, CJA, DSA, EI, EnvAb, EnvInd, ExcerpMed, FPA, FR, ForAb, HortAb, IBSS, IndVet, PSA, PollutAb, RILM, RRTA, S&F, SSA, SSCI, SWA, SociolAb, VB, WAE&RSA. *Aud.:* Ac, Sa.

Geoforum addresses the management of the physical and social human environment by focusing on the spatial organization of economic, environmental, political, and social systems at scales from the global to the local. It emphasizes international, interdisciplinary, and integrative approaches and applications to policy. Issues generally focus on special subjects. Appropriate for libraries that support programs in urban/regional planning and environmental programs as well as academic geography.

3267. *Geographical.* [ISSN: 0016-741X] 1935. m. GBP 33 domestic; GBP 39 in Europe; USD 69 in US & Canada. Ed(s): Carolyn Fry. Royal Geographical Society, PO Box 285, Sittingbourne, ME9 8PF, United Kingdom; http://www.rgs.org. Illus., adv. Circ: 30000. Vol. ends: Dec. Microform: WMP. Online: EBSCO Publishing, EBSCO Host; Gale; OCLC Online Computer Library Center, Inc.; H.W. Wilson. *Indexed:* AmHI, BAS, BrHumI, GSI, H&TI, MASUSE, PAIS. *Bk. rev.:* 3-5, 150-300 words, signed. *Aud.:* Ga.

Official magazine of the Royal Geographical Society, *Geographical* publishes colorfully illustrated, popular but scholarly articles on field research in geography, anthropology, environmental studies, and natural history, and on subjects of geographical interest worldwide. Regular features include "In Conversation," interviewing travel writers, environmentalists, etc., and "Geotravel," offering brief news stories and reports on interesting places. The magazine carries news of the activities of the society. Editorship/authorship is largely from the United Kingdom. Important for academic and public libraries and for libraries supporting overseas field research.

3268. *Geographical Analysis: an international journal of theoretical geography.* [ISSN: 0016-7363] 1969. q. GBP 150 print & online eds. Ed(s): Alan T Murray. Blackwell Publishing, Inc., Commerce Place, 350 Main St, Malden, MA 02148; customerservices@

blackwellpublishing.com; http://www.blackwellpublishing.com. Illus., index, adv. Refereed. Circ: 900 Paid. Vol. ends: Jan/Oct. Microform: PQC. Online: Blackwell Synergy; EBSCO Publishing, EBSCO Host; Florida Center for Library Automation; Gale; IngentaConnect; OCLC Online Computer Library Center, Inc.; OhioLINK; Project MUSE; SwetsWise Online Content. Reprint: PSC. *Indexed:* BAS, CJA, FR, IBR, IBSS, IBZ, RRTA, RiskAb, SSCI, SUSA, SWA, WAE&RSA. *Bk. rev.:* Occasional, 700-1,200 words, signed. *Aud.:* Ac.

Geographical Analysis publishes methodological articles and new applications of mathematical and statistical methods in geography, including spatial data analysis and spatial econometrics. Editorship is largely American and British; authorship is international. Appropriate for college and university libraries with programs in quantitative social science research and in geography.

3269. *The Geographical Journal.* Former titles (until 1892): *Royal Geographical Society and Monthly Record of Geography. Proceedings; Which* incorporated (1830-1880): *Royal Geographical Society of London. Journal;* (until 1878): *Royal Geographical Society of London. Proceedings.* [ISSN: 0016-7398] 1857. q. GBP 151 print & online eds. Ed(s): John Briggs. Blackwell Publishing Ltd., 9600 Garsington Rd, Oxford, OX4 2ZG, United Kingdom; customerservices@ blackwellpublishing.com; http://www.blackwellpublishing.com. Illus., index, adv. Refereed. Circ: 8250. Vol. ends: Nov. CD-ROM: ProQuest LLC (Ann Arbor). Microform: PQC. Online: Blackwell Synergy; EBSCO Publishing, EBSCO Host; Florida Center for Library Automation; Gale; IngentaConnect; JSTOR (Web-based Journal Archive); Northern Light Technology, Inc.; OCLC Online Computer Library Center, Inc.; OhioLINK; ProQuest K-12 Learning Solutions; ProQuest LLC (Ann Arbor); SwetsWise Online Content. Reprint: PSC. *Indexed:* AICP, AmH&L, AmHI, ApEcolAb, ArtHuCI, BAS, BRI, BrArAb, BrHumI, CABA, CBRI, DSA, EI, ExcerpMed, FR, ForAb, HistAb, HortAb, IBR, IBSS, IBZ, IPSA, IndIslam, M&GPA, NumL, PAIS, PSA, PollutAb, RRTA, S&F, SCI, SSCI, SUSA, SWRA, WAE&RSA. *Bk. rev.:* 1-8, 400-600 words, signed. *Aud.:* Ga, Ac.

This journal of the Royal Geographical Society publishes articles on all aspects of geography with an emphasis on environment and development. Book reviews, society news, meeting reports, and a substantial section on news of the profession are included. There are frequent topic-focused special issues. Editorship is British; authors are increasingly international. Important for any library that supports geography or area studies departments.

3270. *Geographical Review.* Former titles (until 1916): *American Geographical Society. Bulletin;* (until 1901): *American Geographical Society of New York. Journal;* (until 1872): *American Geographical and Statistical Society. Journal.* [ISSN: 0016-7428] 1859. q. USD 152 (Individuals, USD 88). Ed(s): Craig E Colten. American Geographical Society, 120 Wall St., Ste. 100, New York, NY 10005-3904; ags@amergeog.org; http://www.amergeog.org. Illus., index, adv. Refereed. Circ: 3000. Vol. ends: Oct. Microform: PMC; PQC. *Indexed:* ABS&EES, AbAn, AgeL, AmH&L, ArtHuCI, BAS, BRI, BrArAb, CBRI, ChemAb, EI, FR, HAPI, HistAb, IBR, IBSS, IBZ, IPSA, IndIslam, MASUSE, PAIS, PRA, PollutAb, RRTA, S&F, SSCI, SWA, WAE&RSA. *Bk. rev.:* 14-16, 600-2,000 words, signed. *Aud.:* Ga, Ac.

A publication of the American Geographical Society, *Geographical Review* publishes research articles and numerous book reviews. Regular features include "Geographical Record," short, sharply focused review articles, and "Geographical Field Note," short, local case studies. This journal is designed to present the results of geographical research to the interested nonprofessional as well as to academics. Authorship is largely American and Canadian. Important for most academic and large public libraries.

3271. *Geography: an international journal.* [ISSN: 0016-7487] 1901. 3x/yr. GBP 76.25. Ed(s): Dr. Kenneth Lynch. Geographical Association, 160 Solly St, Sheffield, S1 4BF, United Kingdom; info@geography.org.uk; http://www.geography.org.uk. Illus., index. Refereed. Circ: 5000. Vol. ends: Oct. *Indexed:* AmH&L, AmHI, BAS, BrArAb, BrEdI, BrHumI, CJA, EIP, FR, ForAb, HistAb, HortAb, IBR, IBSS, IBZ, IndIslam, NumL, PollutAb, RRTA, S&F, SSCI, SWA, SWRA, WAE&RSA. *Bk. rev.:* 10-15, 250-500 words, signed. *Aud.:* Ac.

This is the major journal of the Geographical Association, the society devoted to the teaching of geography in Britain at the college and secondary levels. Articles present research results with classroom applications, report on ongoing changes in the earth's human and physical geography, and discuss environmental, policy, and quality issues in geographical education. "This Changing World" features short articles on contemporary issues. New emphasis beginning 2008 on fostering communication among geographical subdisciplines. New features include "Challenging Assumptions," devoted to debunking popular myths, and "Spotlight," which will offer in-depth reviews of educational resources. Editorship and authorship are British. Useful in any library that supports a geography department or teacher education program.

3272. *GeoJournal: an international journal on human geography and environmental sciences.* [ISSN: 0343-2521] 1977. m. EUR 2033 print & online eds. Ed(s): I Max Barlow. Springer Netherlands, Van Godewijckstraat 30, Dordrecht, 3311 GX, Netherlands; http://www.springeronline.com. Illus., index, adv. Refereed. Vol. ends: No. 4. Microform: PQC. Online: EBSCO Publishing, EBSCO Host; Gale; IngentaConnect; OCLC Online Computer Library Center, Inc.; OhioLINK; Ovid Technologies, Inc.; ProQuest LLC (Ann Arbor); Springer LINK; SwetsWise Online Content. Reprint: PSC. *Indexed:* BAS, CABA, CJA, EngInd, FPA, FR, ForAb, H&TI, HortAb, IBR, IBSS, IBZ, M&GPA, OceAb, PollutAb, RRTA, S&F, SWRA, WAE&RSA. *Bk. rev.:* 0-8, 800-1,000 words, signed. *Aud.:* Ac, Sa.

GeoJournal applies the methods and results of human geography and allied fields to problems of social/environmental change and technological development. Applications to forecasting and planning are emphasized. There are frequent special issues with guest editors and occasional review articles. Editors and authors are international. Important for libraries that support geographical/environmental research or management/planning with a spatial emphasis.

Geomundo. See Latin America and Spain section.

Imago Mundi. See Cartography, GIS, and Imagery section.

3273. *Institute of British Geographers. Transactions.* Former titles (until 1964): *Institute of British Geographers. Transactions and Papers;* (until 1938): *Institute of British Geographers. Transactions.* [ISSN: 0020-2754] 1933. q. GBP 316 print & online eds. Ed(s): Adam Tickell. Blackwell Publishing Ltd., 9600 Garsington Rd, Oxford, OX4 2ZG, United Kingdom; customerservices@blackwellpublishing.com; http://www.blackwellpublishing.com. Illus., index. Refereed. Circ: 2600. Vol. ends: No. 4. Online: Blackwell Synergy; EBSCO Publishing, EBSCO Host; Gale; IngentaConnect; JSTOR (Web-based Journal Archive); OCLC Online Computer Library Center, Inc.; OhioLINK; SwetsWise Online Content. Reprint: PSC. *Indexed:* AgeL, BAS, BrArAb, CJA, FR, IBR, IBSS, IBZ, NumL, PAIS, PollutAb, RRTA, S&F, SSCI, SWA, WAE&RSA. *Bk. rev.:* 4-6, 900-1,200 words, signed. *Aud.:* Ac.

The major journal of the leading British research-oriented geographical society, now joined with the Royal Geographical Society, and one of the leading geographical journals. Editorials discuss current trends in geographical research. Although general in scope, it publishes more human than physical geography. Important for any library that supports a geography department.

3274. *Journal of Geography.* [ISSN: 0022-1341] 1917. 6x/yr. USD 203 print & online eds. Ed(s): Catherine M Lockwood. Taylor & Francis Inc., 325 Chestnut St, Ste 800, Philadelphia, PA 19016; http://www.taylorandfrancis.com. Illus., index, adv. Refereed. Circ: 3900 Paid. Vol. ends: Dec. Microform: PQC. Online: Chadwyck-Healey Inc.; OCLC Online Computer Library Center, Inc.; ProQuest K-12 Learning Solutions; ProQuest LLC (Ann Arbor); H.W. Wilson. Reprint: PSC. *Indexed:* ABIn, AgeL, BAS, EduInd, EnvAb, EnvInd, IBR, IBZ, MRD, PRA, RILM, SSCI, SUSA. *Bk. rev.:* 2-5, 500-600 words, signed. *Aud.:* Ac.

Official journal of the National Council for Geographic Education, *Journal of Geography* is concerned with geographical teaching at all levels. It offers articles on teaching methods and strategies as well as educational policy, and contains teaching resources and news of the profession. The "Teacher's Notebook" section offers K–12 teaching strategies. Occasional special theme sections are published. Editorship and authorship are largely American. Useful in any library that supports a geography department or teacher education program.

3275. Journal of Historical Geography. [ISSN: 0305-7488] 1975. 4x/yr. EUR 496. Elsevier Ltd., The Boulevard, Langford Ln, Oxford, OX5 1GB, United Kingdom; http://www.elsevier.com. Illus., index, adv. Sample. Refereed. Vol. ends: Oct. Online: Chadwyck-Healey Inc.; EBSCO Publishing, EBSCO Host; Gale; IngentaConnect; OCLC Online Computer Library Center, Inc.; OhioLINK; ScienceDirect; SwetsWise Online Content. *Indexed:* AbAn, AmH&L, ArtHuCI, BAS, BRI, BrArAb, CBRI, EI, FR, HistAb, IBR, NumL, RI-1, SSCI. *Bk. rev.:* 15-30, 500-750 words, signed. *Aud.:* Ac.

Journal of Historical Geography publishes research papers, methodological contributions, commentaries on published papers, news of the specialty, and occasional review articles. Subjects treated include reconstruction of past human environments, instances of environmental change, geographical aspects of imagination and culture in the past, and historical methodology. Applications to historic preservation are discussed. Editorship and authorship are American/British/Commonwealth. Important for academic libraries that support geography or history departments.

3276. Journal of Latin American Geography. Formerly (until 2003): *Conference of Latin Americanist Geographers Yearbook.* [ISSN: 1545-2476] 1971. s-a. USD 100 (Individuals, USD 60). Ed(s): David J Robinson. University of Texas Press, Journals Division, 2100 Comal, Austin, TX 78722; journals@uts.cc.utexas.edu; http://www.utexas.edu/utpress/journals/journals.html. Illus. Circ: 215. Online: EBSCO Publishing, EBSCO Host; OCLC Online Computer Library Center, Inc.; OhioLINK; Project MUSE; SwetsWise Online Content. *Indexed:* HAPI. *Bk. rev.:* 5-6, 1,000 words, signed. *Aud.:* Ac.

Publishes articles on all aspects of Latin American, but largely human, geography with emphasis on interdisciplinary approaches. The "Forum" section offers a variety of short articles, including preliminary reports of field or archival work, descriptions of field courses, and seminar or conference reports. The awards section profiles recipients of several Conference of Latin Americanist Geographers awards.

Journal of Transport Geography. See Transportation section.

National Geographic. See General Interest section.

3277. Physical Geography. [ISSN: 0272-3646] 1980. 6x/yr. USD 399 (Individuals, USD 90). Ed(s): Antony R Orme. Bellwether Publishing, Ltd., 8640 Guilford Rd, Ste 200, Columbia, MD 21046; bellpub@bellpub.com; http://www.bellpub.com. Illus., index. Sample. Refereed. Circ: 400. Vol. ends: Dec. *Indexed:* FR, M&GPA, SCI, SWRA. *Aud.:* Ac.

Physical Geography offers research papers on geomorphology, climatology, soil science, biogeography, and related subjects. Coverage is worldwide. Review articles and methodological and discussion papers are also published. The editors and editorial board are American/Canadian. Important for academic libraries that support geography, geology, or environmental studies departments.

3278. Polar Geography. Former titles: *Polar Geography and Geology;* (until vol.3, 1979): *Polar Geography.* [ISSN: 1088-937X] 1977. q. GBP 200 print & online eds. Ed(s): David R Yesner. Taylor & Francis Inc., customerservice@taylorandfrancis.com; http://www.taylorandfrancis.com. Illus. Circ: 300. *Indexed:* FR, M&GPA, OceAb, PollutAb. *Bk. rev.:* Occasional, 400-600 words, signed. *Aud.:* Ac, Sa.

Polar Geography publishes scholarly research on physical and human geography of the polar regions, with some emphasis on the Russian Arctic. Particular attention is paid to contextualizing results of international research projects and to interactions of the polar regions with the global climate system. Long papers and substantial review articles are welcomed. Some translations of Russian articles and sources are published. Editorship is American, with an international editorial board; authorship is international.

3279. Political Geography. Formerly (until 1992): *Political Geography Quarterly.* [ISSN: 0962-6298] 1982. 8x/yr. EUR 1104. Ed(s): John O'Loughlin. Pergamon, The Boulevard, Langford Ln, East Park, Kidlington, OX5 1GB, United Kingdom. Illus., index, adv. Sample. Refereed. Vol. ends: No. 8. Microform: PQC. Online: EBSCO Publishing, EBSCO Host; Gale; IngentaConnect; OhioLINK; ScienceDirect; SwetsWise Online Content. *Indexed:* ABCPolSci, AmH&L, ArtHuCI, BRI, CJA, EI, FR, HistAb, IBR, IBSS, IBZ, IPSA, PAIS, PSA, SSCI, SWA, SociolAb. *Bk. rev.:* 3-6, 800-1,400 words, signed. *Aud.:* Ac.

Includes traditional, quantitative, political, economic, poststructuralist, and other approaches. Contributions from nongeographers on spatial aspects of politics are encouraged. Debates on topics of wide interest are published, as are special issues. "Book Forum" offers multiple reviews of a major new book. Editorship and authorship are largely British and American. Important for academic libraries that support geography, political science, or international relations departments.

3280. Population Space and Place. Formerly (until 2003): *International Journal of Population Geography.* [ISSN: 1544-8444] 1995. bi-m. USD 1006 print or online ed. Ed(s): Dr. Allan Findlay, Dr. Paul Boyle. John Wiley & Sons Ltd., The Atrium, Southern Gate, Chichester, PO19 8SQ, United Kingdom; customer@wiley.co.uk; http://www.wiley.co.uk. Illus., index, adv. Sample. Refereed. Vol. ends: Dec. Microform: PQC. Online: EBSCO Publishing, EBSCO Host; OhioLINK; SwetsWise Online Content; Wiley InterScience. Reprint: PSC. *Indexed:* C&ISA, CABA, CJA, CerAb, DSA, EnvAb, IAA, IBSS, RRTA, S&F, SSCI, SWA, WAE&RSA. *Bk. rev.:* 3-4, 800-1,500 words, signed. *Aud.:* Ac.

Population Space and Place publishes research and review articles, book reviews, and articles on current debates. Topics covered include migration, the geography of fertility/mortality, population modeling and forecasting, environmental issues, spatial aspects of labor, housing, minority groups, and historical demography. Planning and policy implications of population research are emphasized. Articles originating in allied disciplines are published. The editorship is largely British, with an international advisory board; the authorship is international. Important for any library that supports research in geography or population studies, or in social science generally.

3281. The Professional Geographer. [ISSN: 0033-0124] 1949. q. Individuals, USD 155 print & online eds. Ed(s): Robin Friedman, Sharmistha Bagchi-Sen. Routledge, 325 Chestnut St, Ste 800, Philadelphia, PA 19106; journals@routledge.com; http://www.routledge.com. Illus., index. Refereed. Circ: 9000 Paid. Vol. ends: Nov. Microform: PQC. Online: Blackwell Synergy; EBSCO Publishing, EBSCO Host; Gale; IngentaConnect; OCLC Online Computer Library Center, Inc.; OhioLINK; SwetsWise Online Content. *Indexed:* ABS&EES, AbAn, AgeL, ArtHuCI, BAS, CJA, FR, ForAb, IBR, IBSS, IBZ, M&GPA, PRA, PollutAb, RRTA, S&F, SSCI, SUSA, SWA, WAE&RSA. *Bk. rev.:* 4-7, 700-1,200 words, signed. *Aud.:* Ac.

A publication of the Association of American Geographers, *The Professional Geographer* publishes short research papers and essays on all aspects of geography. New approaches and alternative perspectives are emphasized. "Focus" is a section for collections of short articles on special topics. The "Commentary" section discusses issues of current interest. Important for all academic and for large public libraries.

3282. Progress in Human Geography: an international review of geographical work in the social sciences and humanities. [ISSN: 0309-1325] 1977. bi-m. GBP 467. Ed(s): Ron J Johnston, Sarah Radcliffe. Sage Publications Ltd., 1 Oliver's Yard, 55 City Rd, London, EC1 1SP, United Kingdom; info@sagepub.co.uk; http://www.sagepub.co.uk. Illus., index, adv. Sample. Refereed. Circ:

1200. Vol. ends: No. 4. Online: EBSCO Publishing, EBSCO Host; Gale; HighWire Press; IngentaConnect; OCLC Online Computer Library Center, Inc.; OhioLINK; ProQuest LLC (Ann Arbor); SwetsWise Online Content. Reprint: PSC. *Indexed:* ASSIA, AgeL, ArtHuCI, BAS, BrArAb, CABA, CJA, EI, FPA, FR, ForAb, H&SSA, IBR, IBSS, IBZ, PSA, PollutAb, RRTA, S&F, SSA, SSCI, SUSA, SWRA, SociolAb. *Bk. rev.:* 9-21, 700-1,600 words, signed. *Aud.:* Ac.

Publishes review articles on trends and developments in human geography and related work in other disciplines. Articles cover the full international literature and discuss possible applications. "Progress Reports" are short reviews of recent work on focused topics. The "Textbooks that Moved Generations" section revisits classic works and assesses their influence. Editorship and authorship are largely British/Commonwealth/American, with an international advisory board. This journal is important for academic libraries that support social science research and geography departments, as well as for large public libraries. Sage also issues a similar title, *Progress in Physical Geography* (ISSN: 0309-1333), which is important for libraries serving geography and geology departments and environmental studies programs.

3283. *Singapore Journal of Tropical Geography.* Supersedes in part: *Journal of Tropical Geography.* [ISSN: 0129-7619] 1980. 3x/yr. GBP 159 print & online eds. Ed(s): Peggy Teo, James D Sidaway. Blackwell Publishing Asia, 550 Swanston St, Carlton South, VIC 3053, Australia; subs@blackwellpublishingasia.com; http://www.blackwellpublishing.com. Illus. Sample. Refereed. Circ: 660. Online: Blackwell Synergy; EBSCO Publishing, EBSCO Host; Gale; IngentaConnect; OCLC Online Computer Library Center, Inc.; OhioLINK; SwetsWise Online Content. Reprint: PSC. *Indexed:* ApEcolAb, BAS, EI, EIP, FR, IBR, IBSS, PSA, PollutAb, RRTA, S&F, SSCI, SociolAb, WAE&RSA. *Bk. rev.:* 4-6, 400-600 words, signed. *Aud.:* Ac.

Edited at the Department of Geography of the University of Singapore, this journal treats human and physical geography and spatial aspects of development from an interdisciplinary perspective. Papers from scholars outside of geography are welcome. It contains more on the Asian tropics than on Africa or South America, and more on human than on physical geography. Authorship is international. Important for academic libraries that support geography departments or area studies programs with interests in the Old World tropics.

Surveying and Land Information Science. See Cartography, GIS, and Imagery section.

3284. *Terrae Incognitae: the journal for the history of discoveries.* [ISSN: 0082-2884] 1969. a. USD 30. Ed(s): Marguerite Ragnow. Society for the History of Discoveries, c/o Dr. Sanford H. Bederman, Sec.-Treas., 5502 Laurel Ridge Drive, Alpharetta, GA 30005; http://www.sochistdisc.org/. Illus., index. Refereed. Circ: 600. *Indexed:* AmH&L, HistAb. *Bk. rev.:* 15-20, 300-1,000 words, signed. *Aud.:* Ac.

This scholarly journal covers the worldwide history of discovery and exploration. It publishes research articles, book reviews, and a bibliography of current literature. Editorship is American, Canadian, and British; authorship is international. Important for academic libraries that support geography and history departments.

3285. *Tijdschrift voor Economische en Sociale Geografie.* [ISSN: 0040-747X] 1910. 5x/yr. GBP 225 print & online eds. Ed(s): Jan van Weesep. Blackwell Publishing Ltd., 9600 Garsington Rd, Oxford, OX4 2ZG, United Kingdom; customerservices@blackwellpublishing.com; http://www.blackwellpublishing.com. Illus., index, adv. Sample. Refereed. Vol. ends: No. 5. Online: Blackwell Synergy; EBSCO Publishing, EBSCO Host; Gale; IngentaConnect; OCLC Online Computer Library Center, Inc.; OhioLINK; SwetsWise Online Content. Reprint: PSC. *Indexed:* ApEcolAb, CABA, DSA, EI, ExcerpMed, FPA, FR, FS&TA, ForAb, HRIS, HortAb, IBR, IBSS, IBZ, PAIS, PSA, RILM, RRTA, RiskAb, S&F, SSCI, SWA, SociolAb, WAE&RSA. *Bk. rev.:* 2-5, 1,000-1,500 words, signed. *Aud.:* Ac.

Published under the auspices of the Royal Dutch Geographical Society, *TESG* offers scholarly articles and subject-focused issues on human geography, emphasizing new approaches emanating from both Continental and Anglo-American traditions. Special sections discuss Dutch and European geographical trends. Each issue carries maps illustrating Netherlands human geography. Editorship is largely Dutch; authorship is international. Important for academic libraries that support geography departments or area studies programs with interests in Western Europe.

Urban Geography. See Urban Studies section.

■ GERIATRICS AND GERONTOLOGICAL STUDIES

Tracey Mayfield, Librarian for Gerontology, Family & Consumer Sciences, Social Work, Recreation & Leisure, Kinesiology, & Human Development at California State University Long Beach, Long Beach, CA 90840-1901; tmayfiel@csulb.edu

Introduction

According to the recent literature, the fastest growing population in the United States is that of persons 65 and older. The study of older persons and the aging process, called gerontology, and the study of health promotion and prevention and treatment of disease of the elderly, called geriatrics, are becoming paramount to understanding this fascinating demographic group. The journals (both electronic and print) and magazines in this section are but a sample of the wealth of information that is available on gerontology and geriatrics. The scope of the journals in this section run the gamut from general interest to spirituality to medical, and the audience for these titles range from students and researchers to practitioners and clinicians to caregivers and the elderly themselves. The core indexing and abstract services are AgeLine (published by the American Association of Retired Persons, or AARP) and Abstracts in Social Gerontology (published in cooperation with the National Council on Aging, or NCoA); however, as gerontology is such an interdisciplinary subject, other indexes and electronic databases can be used depending on the specific subject. Other such subjects include social work, psychology, ethnic studies, education, women's studies, sociology, and public policy.

Basic Periodicals

Geriatrics: Medicine for midlife and beyond, Journal of Aging and Health, Journal of Aging & Social Policy, Journal of Applied Gerontology, Journals of Gerontology: Series A and B.

Basic Abstracts and Indexes

Abstracts in Social Gerontology, AgeLine.

3286. *Activities, Adaptation & Aging: the journal of activities management.* [ISSN: 0192-4788] 1980. q. USD 650 print & online eds. Ed(s): Linnea Couture. Haworth Press, Inc., 10 Alice St, Binghamton, NY 13904-1580; getinfo@haworthpress.com; http://www.haworthpress.com. Illus., adv. Sample. Refereed. Circ: 340 Paid. Vol. ends: Summer. Microform: PQC. Online: EBSCO Publishing, EBSCO Host; OCLC Online Computer Library Center, Inc.; SwetsWise Online Content. Reprint: HAW. *Indexed:* ASG, AbAn, AgeL, CABA, CINAHL, ExcerpMed, HortAb, IBR, IBZ, IMFL, MCR, PEI, PsycInfo, RILM, RRTA, SD, SSA, SWA, SWR&A, SociolAb, WAE&RSA. *Bk. rev.:* 2-3, 600-800 words, signed. *Aud.:* Ac, Sa.

Established as "the primary journal for activity professionals," this journal advances the study and practice of activity for the elderly. While geared toward "activity directors and all health care professionals concerned with the enhancement of the lives of the aged," the journal offers both formal and informal research related to activity for the elderly, which makes it appropriate for both activity directors and health care professionals while also apposite in academic libraries. Interdisciplinary in nature, recent articles include "Determining the Effects of Tai Chi on Dynamic Balance and Fear of Falling in an Elderly Population," and "The Evaluation of an Animal Assisted Therapy

Intervention for Elders with Dementia in Long-Term Care." The journal includes regular features such as book reviews, as well as sections on "Aging, Activities and the Internet," and "Announcements / What's New." Special thematic issues are also published.

3287. Age and Ageing. [ISSN: 0002-0729] 1972. bi-m. Corporations, EUR 464 print or online ed. Ed(s): Roger Francis. Oxford University Press, Great Clarendon St, Oxford, OX2 6DP, United Kingdom; jnl.orders@oup.co.uk; http://www.oxfordjournals.org. Illus., index, adv. Sample. Refereed. Circ: 3275. Vol. ends: Nov. Online: EBSCO Publishing, EBSCO Host; Florida Center for Library Automation; Gale; HighWire Press; IngentaConnect; OCLC Online Computer Library Center, Inc.; OhioLINK; Ovid Technologies, Inc.; Oxford Journals; ProQuest K-12 Learning Solutions; ProQuest LLC (Ann Arbor); SwetsWise Online Content. Reprint: PSC. *Indexed:* ASG, ASSIA, AbAn, AgeL, BiolAb, CABA, CINAHL, ChemAb, DSA, ErgAb, ExcerpMed, H&SSA, RRTA, RiskAb, SCI, SSCI, WAE&RSA. *Aud.:* Ac, Sa.

This is the official journal of the British Geriatrics Society, the sole association in the United Kingdom that focuses on geriatric medicine professionals. The journal is international in scope and publishes original research and commissioned reviews covering topics in geriatric medicine and gerontology. *Age and Ageing* focuses on "research on ageing and clinical, epidemiological and psychological aspects of later life." In addition to the research papers, the journal also includes research letters, case reports, clinical reminders, systematic reviews, and letters. The journal is appropriate for academic libraries with a geriatric medicine collection and is especially fitting for medical libraries.

3288. Ageing and Society: the journal of the centre for policy on ageing and the British society of gerontology. [ISSN: 0144-686X] 1981. 8x/yr. GBP 220. Ed(s): Tony Warnes. Cambridge University Press, The Edinburgh Bldg, Shaftesbury Rd, Cambridge, CB2 2RU, United Kingdom; information@cambridge.org; http://www.journals.cambridge.org. Illus., index, adv. Sample. Refereed. Circ: 1050. Microform: PQC. Online: Pub.; EBSCO Publishing, EBSCO Host; Factiva, Inc.; OCLC Online Computer Library Center, Inc.; OhioLINK; SwetsWise Online Content. Reprint: PSC. *Indexed:* ASG, ASSIA, AgeL, AmH&L, ArtHuCI, EAA, HistAb, IBR, IBSS, IBZ, IPSA, PAIS, PSA, PsycInfo, RI-1, RRTA, SSA, SSCI, SWA, SociolAb, V&AA. *Bk. rev.:* Number and length vary. *Aud.:* Ac.

Ageing and Society is an "interdisciplinary and international journal devoted to publishing papers on the understanding of human ageing and the circumstances of older people in their social and cultural contexts." The journal regularly publishes research articles and an "extensive book review section" and occasionally includes guest editorials, review symposia, and special issues. A recent issue focuses on the vulnerability of older adults, and other recent articles discuss activity and well-being in later life, filial norms and family support, and positive aging and views of middle-aged and older adults in Hong Kong.

3289. The Aging Male. [ISSN: 1368-5538] 1998. q. GBP 219 print & online eds. Ed(s): Bruno Lunenfeld. Informa Healthcare, Mortimer House, 37-41 Mortimer St, London, W1T 3JM, United Kingdom; healthcare.enquiries@informa.com; http://www.tandf.co.uk/journals/. Illus., adv. Sample. Refereed. Circ: 1200 Paid. Vol. ends: No. 4. Online: EBSCO Publishing, EBSCO Host; Gale; IngentaConnect; OCLC Online Computer Library Center, Inc.; ProQuest LLC (Ann Arbor); SwetsWise Online Content. Reprint: PSC. *Indexed:* ExcerpMed, SCI. *Aud.:* Ac, Sa.

The Aging Male is the official journal of the International Society for the Study of the Aging Male. It publishes original, peer-reviewed research with multidisciplinary coverage on a wide range of topics on this emerging specialty in gerontology and geriatrics. Along with the original research articles, editorials and reviews of literature may also be included. Special issues, such as a recent one on the Fifth World Congress of the Aging Male, are also published. Recent articles include "Relationship of testosterone serum levels and lifestyle in aging men," "Aging in Asia: a cultural, socioeconomical and historical perspective," and "Investigation, treatment and monitoring of late-onset hypogonadism in males." Suitable for research and medical libraries.

3290. American Geriatrics Society. Journal. Supersedes (in 1952): *American Therapeutic Society. Transactions.* [ISSN: 0002-8614] 1953. m. GBP 538 print & online eds. Ed(s): Dr. Thomas T Yoshikawa. Blackwell Publishing, Inc., Commerce Place, 350 Main St, Malden, MA 02148; customerservices@blackwellpublishing.com; http://www.blackwellpublishing.com. Illus., index, adv. Sample. Refereed. Circ: 9462. Vol. ends: Dec. Microform: PQC. Online: Blackwell Synergy; EBSCO Publishing, EBSCO Host; Gale; IngentaConnect; M D Consult; OCLC Online Computer Library Center, Inc.; OhioLINK; Ovid Technologies, Inc.; SwetsWise Online Content; H.W. Wilson. Reprint: PSC. *Indexed:* ASG, ASSIA, AgeL, ApEcolAb, BiolAb, CABA, CINAHL, ChemAb, DSA, ExcerpMed, FPA, ForAb, H&SSA, HortAb, PsycInfo, RRTA, RiskAb, S&F, SCI, SFSA, SSA, SSCI, SWR&A, V&AA. *Aud.:* Ac, Sa.

As the title indicates, this monthly journal is published on behalf of the American Geriatrics Society. All articles published in the journal are well organized into sections: Clinical Investigations, Brief Reports, Brief Methodological Reports, Progress in Geriatrics, Nursing, Education and Training, Ethnogeriatrics and Special Populations, Ethics Public Policy and Medical Economics, Clinical Trials and Tribulations, "Old Lives Tale," Special Articles, and a section containing letters to the editor. The journal is heavily indexed and is considered a core journal in geriatrics and gerontology.

3291. American Journal of Geriatric Psychiatry. [ISSN: 1064-7481] 1993. bi-m. USD 965 (Individuals, USD 351). Ed(s): Dr. Dilip V Jeste. Lippincott Williams & Wilkins, 530 Walnut St, Philadelphia, PA 19106-3621; custserv@lww.com; http://www.lww.com. Illus., index, adv. Sample. Refereed. Microform: PQC. Online: EBSCO Publishing, EBSCO Host; HighWire Press; Northern Light Technology, Inc.; Ovid Technologies, Inc.; ProQuest LLC (Ann Arbor); SwetsWise Online Content. *Indexed:* ASG, AgeL, ExcerpMed, PsycInfo, SCI, SSCI. *Aud.:* Ac, Sa.

The official publication of the American Association of Geriatric Psychiatry, this monthly journal "contains peer-reviewed articles on the diagnosis and classification of psychiatric disorders of later life, epidemiological and biological correlates of mental health of older adults, and psychopharmacology and other somatic treatments." In addition to research articles, issues can contain editorials, clinical reviews, brief reports, and letters to the editor. Recent article topics include "Best dementia screening instrument for general practitioners," "Discrepancies in information provided to primary care physicians by patients with and without dementia," and "Outcomes of depressed patients undergoing inpatient pulmonary rehabilitation." The journal is appropriate for academic and medical libraries.

3292. Canadian Journal on Aging. [ISSN: 0714-9808] 1982. q. CND 120 domestic; USD 140 foreign; CND 140 combined subscription domestic print & online eds. Ed(s): Mark Rosenberg. The Canadian Association on Gerontology, 100-824 Meath St, Ottawa, ON K1Z 6E8, Canada; info@cagacg.ca; http://www.cagacg.ca/index.htm. Illus., adv. Sample. Refereed. Circ: 1600 Paid. Vol. ends: Winter. Reprint: PSC. *Indexed:* ASG, AgeL, CBCARef, CINAHL, CPerI, CommAb, ERIC, ExcerpMed, HRA, IBR, IBSS, IBZ, PAIS, PsycInfo, SFSA, SSA, SSCI, SWR&A, SociolAb. *Bk. rev.:* . *Aud.:* Ac.

This refereed quarterly is the official journal of the Canadian Association on Gerontology. It publishes information on "aging concerned with biology, educational gerontology, health sciences, psychology, social sciences, and social policy and practice." The journal itself is published in English, but offers abstracts and keywords in both English and French. Recent articles include "Personality, Cognitive Adaptation, and Marital Satisfaction as Predictors of Well-Being among Older Married Adults" and "Risk Factors for Falling among Community-Dwelling Veterans and Their Caregivers." This journal is appropriate for academic libraries desiring a Canadian perspective.

3293. Clinical Gerontologist: the journal of aging and mental health. Former titles: *Journal of Aged Care;* (until 1981): *Aged Care and Services Review.* [ISSN: 0731-7115] 1977. q. USD 690 print & online eds. Ed(s): Terry L Brink. Haworth Press, Inc., 10 Alice St, Binghamton, NY 13904-1580; getinfo@haworthpress.com; http://www.haworthpress.com. Illus., index, adv. Sample. Refereed. Circ:

350 Paid. Vol. ends: Summer. Microform: PQC. Online: EBSCO Publishing, EBSCO Host; OCLC Online Computer Library Center, Inc.; SwetsWise Online Content. Reprint: HAW. *Indexed:* ASG, ASSIA, AbAn, AgeL, CINAHL, ExcerpMed, FR, H&SSA, IMFL, MCR, PsycInfo, RiskAb, SFSA, SSA, SWR&A, SociolAb, V&AA. *Bk. rev.:* Number varies, under 500 words. *Aud.:* Ac, Sa.

Geared specifically toward professionals and practitioners (psychologists, physicians, nurses, social workers, and counselors) who work with older adults, this journal has a practical emphasis. There is no "poetry or politics" in this publication, whose goal is to provide relevant, timely, and practical information "applicable to the assessment and management of mental disorders in later life." Issues regularly addressed include adjustments to changing roles, issues related to diversity and aging, Alzheimer's disease and dementia, family caregiving, spirituality, cognitive tests and cognitive functioning, comorbidities, depression, hypochondriasis, paranoia, and rehabilitation and education for the elderly. In the articles, authors typically report research, present illustrative case material, and review the field's literature. One unique section in the journal is "Clinical Comments," which "features brief observations and specific suggestions from practitioners" allowing for peer communication and learning. Issues can also feature book, media, and software reviews.

3294. *Geriatrics: medicine for midlife and beyond.* [ISSN: 0016-867X] 1946. m. USD 70 domestic; USD 99 in Canada & Mexico; USD 140 elsewhere. Ed(s): Deborah Kaplan, Peter D'Epiro. Advanstar Communications, Inc., 123 Tice Blvd, Woodcliff Lake, NJ 07677; info@advanstar.com; http://www.advanstar.com. Illus., index, adv. Sample. Refereed. Circ: 77968 Controlled and free. Vol. ends: Dec. Online: EBSCO Publishing, EBSCO Host; Florida Center for Library Automation; Gale; Northern Light Technology, Inc.; OCLC Online Computer Library Center, Inc.; ProQuest K-12 Learning Solutions; ProQuest LLC (Ann Arbor); H.W. Wilson. *Indexed:* ASG, AbAn, AgeL, CABA, CINAHL, ChemAb, ExcerpMed, GSI, H&SSA, RiskAb, SCI, SSCI. *Aud.:* Ga, Ac, Sa.

At first glance, this title appears to be a magazine. However, if you look closely toward the top of the front cover, it explains that it is a monthly, peer-reviewed, evidence-based journal aimed at primary care physicians and geriatricians for use in their practices in providing care for older adults. The articles are organized into sections: Psychiatric Consultant, Cardiology, Clinical Challenge, and Endocrinology. Other journal "departments" include News & Views, "Derm DDx," Medicare Matters, and Editorials. Occasionally, other special sections will appear, such as highlights of meetings integral to the journal's topics. Although the journal claims to be geared toward physicians, anyone studying or working with older adults will benefit.

3295. *The Gerontologist.* [ISSN: 0016-9013] 1961. bi-m. USD 198. Ed(s): Linda S Noelker. Gerontological Society of America, 1030 15th, NW, Ste 250, Washington, DC 20005-1503; geron@geron.org; http://www.geron.org. Illus., index, adv. Sample. Refereed. Circ: 6500 Paid. Microform: PQC. Online: EBSCO Publishing, EBSCO Host; HighWire Press; Northern Light Technology, Inc.; OCLC Online Computer Library Center, Inc.; ProQuest K-12 Learning Solutions; ProQuest LLC (Ann Arbor). *Indexed:* ASG, AgeL, ArtHuCI, CINAHL, CJA, ChemAb, ERIC, ErgAb, ExcerpMed, GSI, IBSS, PsycInfo, SFSA, SSA, SSCI, SUSA, SWR&A, SociolAb. *Bk. rev.:* Number and length vary. *Aud.:* Ac, Sa.

Published by the Gerontological Society of America, this multidisciplinary journal focuses on the social policy, program development, and service delivery aspects of human aging. Further, it seeks to reflect and inform the "broad community of disciplines and professions involved in understanding the aging process and provide service to older people." Disciplines covered include social and psychological sciences, biomedical and health sciences, political science, public policy, economics, education, law, and humanities. Articles are grouped together by topic, which varies from issue to issue. Regular sections in the journal are "Practical Concepts," which focuses on innovative practices and programs, and book reviews. Recent topics covered include elder abuse, improving the workforce, assisted living, falls, marital effects, depression, and nursing homes. This is considered a core title for libraries that service gerontology programs.

3296. *Gerontology & Geriatrics Education.* [ISSN: 0270-1960] 1980. q. USD 620 print & online eds. Ed(s): Pearl M Mosher-Ashley. Haworth Press, Inc., 10 Alice St, Binghamton, NY 13904-1580; getinfo@haworthpress.com; http://www.haworthpress.com. Illus., index, adv. Sample. Refereed. Circ: 300 Paid. Reprint: HAW. *Indexed:* ASG, AbAn, AgeL, CINAHL, EAA, ExcerpMed, IBR, IBZ, IMFL, PsycInfo, SFSA, SSA, SWA, SociolAb, V&AA. *Aud.:* Ac, Sa.

This is the official journal of the Association for Gerontology in Higher Education (which is the educational unit of The Gerontological Society of America). Its focus is on research topics, curriculum development, evaluation (course and program), innovation in the classroom, and other geriatric and gerontological topics that have educational implications. The intended audience is students, teachers, practitioners, administrators, and policy makers, and it is geared toward showcasing best practices and resources for gerontologists and gerontology/geriatrics educators. Articles tend to cover "research results, observations, evaluations, theoretical discussions, and recommendations related to gerontology and geriatric course work, practice placements, and curriculum design and implementation." Topics covered include innovations in the teaching of gerontology and geriatrics; training and supervision of gerontology and geriatrics educators, researchers, and practitioners; new roles for gerontology and geriatrics educators in public and private programs; research and discussion on aging-related issues in gerontological education; and new educational materials and teaching methods in the field of aging. Occasional special thematic issues will be published focusing on in-depth coverage of one topic. Like many journals published by Haworth Press, the table of contents also supplies the article abstracts, which makes for easy review.

3297. *International Journal of Aging & Human Development: a journal of psychosocial gerontology.* Formerly (until 1973): *Aging and Human Development.* [ISSN: 0091-4150] 1970. 8x/yr. USD 443. Ed(s): Bert Hayslip, Jr. Baywood Publishing Co., Inc., 26 Austin Ave, PO Box 337, Amityville, NY 11701-0337; info@baywood.com; http://www.baywood.com. Illus., index, adv. Sample. Refereed. *Indexed:* ASG, ASSIA, AbAn, AgeL, BAS, BRI, CommAb, ERIC, ExcerpMed, FR, HRA, IBR, IBZ, IMFL, PsycInfo, RILM, SFSA, SSA, SSCI, SWR&A, SociolAb. *Bk. rev.:* Number and length vary. *Aud.:* Ac, Sa.

This peer-reviewed journal focuses on answering many broad questions about aging and the development of the human organism. The journal strives to focus on gerontology from both sides of the coin, emphasizing the "psychological and social studies of aging and the aged," and also "research that introduces observations from other fields that illuminate the 'human' side of gerontology" or that "utilizes gerontological observations to illuminate in other fields." As the title indicates, the journal is international in scope, and it includes research articles and book reviews. Recent articles include "College Students' Perceptions of Job Demands, Recommended Retirement Ages, and Age of Optimal Performance in Selected Occupations," "Bringing the Law to the Gerontological Stage: A Different Look at Movies and Old Age," and "Neighborhood Deterioration, Social Skills, and Social Relationships in Late Life."

3298. *Journal of Aging and Health: an interdisciplinary research forum.* [ISSN: 0898-2643] 1989. 8x/yr. GBP 382. Ed(s): Kyriakos S Markides. Sage Publications, Inc., 2455 Teller Rd, Thousand Oaks, CA 91320; info@sagepub.com; http://www.sagepub.com. Illus., index, adv. Refereed. Circ: 750 Paid and free. Reprint: PSC. *Indexed:* ASG, AgeL, CINAHL, ExcerpMed, H&SSA, IMFL, PsycInfo, SSA, SSCI, SociolAb. *Aud.:* Ac.

This interdisciplinary journal examines the "complex and dynamic relationship between gerontology and health." It presents research findings and scholarly exchange in social and behavioral factors related to health and aging and covers both domestic and international topics. The journal has a wide focus that includes the following areas: active life expectancy, diet/nutrition, disease prevention, ethics in health care, health behaviors and beliefs, health service utilization, longevity and mortality, long-term care, mental health, social support and health, the recovery process, alcoholism, and suicide. Although preference is given to manuscripts presenting the findings of original research, review and methodological pieces are also considered.

3299. *Journal of Aging and Physical Activity.* [ISSN: 1063-8652] 1993. q. USD 240 (Individuals, USD 60 print & online eds.). Ed(s): Anthony A Vandervoort, Jessie C. Jones. Human Kinetics, PO Box 5076, Champaign, IL 61825-5076; orders@hkusa.com; http://www.humankinetics.com. Illus., adv. Sample. Refereed. Circ: 745 Paid. Vol. ends: Oct. Reprint: PSC. *Indexed:* ASG, AbAn, AgeL, CABA, CINAHL, ErgAb, ExcerpMed, IBR, IBZ, PEI, PsycInfo, SCI, SD, SSA, SSCI. *Aud.:* Ac, Sa.

This is the official journal of the International Society for Aging and Physical Activity, which investigates the relationship between physical activity and the aging process. This peer-reviewed, multidisciplinary journal is organized into three distinct sections. The Original Research section focuses on scientific studies, investigations, systematic clinical observations, and controlled case studies. The Scholarly Reviews section focuses on reviews that bridge research and practice in the study of physical activity and aging. The Professional Applications section focuses on articles based on experience in working with older populations and the available research on and evidence of program development, program activities, and application of exercise principles. Other sections that may appear in the journal are editorials, a digest of articles from other sources, media reviews, and news announcements.

3300. *Journal of Aging & Social Policy: a journal devoted to aging & social policy.* [ISSN: 0895-9420] 1989. q. USD 565 print & online eds. Ed(s): Francis G Caro. Haworth Press, Inc., 10 Alice St, Binghamton, NY 13904-1580; getinfo@haworthpress.com; http://www.haworthpress.com. Illus., adv. Sample. Refereed. Circ: 402 Paid. Microform: PQC. Online: EBSCO Publishing, EBSCO Host; OCLC Online Computer Library Center, Inc.; SwetsWise Online Content. Reprint: HAW. *Indexed:* ASG, AbAn, AgeL, BiolDig, CINAHL, H&SSA, IBR, IBZ, IMFL, PAIS, PSA, RiskAb, SFSA, SSA, SWR&A, SociolAb. *Aud.:* Ac, Sa.

This journal examines the international policy issues that affect the elderly. The articles "examine and analyze policymaking and the political processes that affect the development and implementation of programs for the elderly from a global perspective." Topics regularly covered in the journal include long-term care and financing, assisted living, financial security, pension coverage, housing, transportation, health care access and financing, and retirement. Special theme issues are usually published annually on a specific topic. Geared toward educators, practitioners, researchers, and administrators who work with the aged, the journal seeks to review the processes for "adopting policies at the state and federal levels." The journal also investigates the "interplay of political and economic forces, legal and regulatory constraints, the pressure of special interests, and the influence of constituencies." The journal is well organized into three distinct sections: Commentary, General Articles, and International View, with abstracts for all articles printed in the table of contents for easy review.

3301. *Journal of Aging Studies.* [ISSN: 0890-4065] 1987. 4x/yr. EUR 391. Ed(s): Dr. J. F. Gubrium. Pergamon, The Boulevard, Langford Ln, East Park, Kidlington, OX5 1GB, United Kingdom. Refereed. Microform: PQC. Online: EBSCO Publishing, EBSCO Host; Florida Center for Library Automation; Gale; IngentaConnect; OCLC Online Computer Library Center, Inc.; OhioLINK; ScienceDirect; SwetsWise Online Content; H.W. Wilson. *Indexed:* ASG, AgeL, IMFL, PAIS, PsycInfo, SFSA, SSA, SSCI, SociolAb. *Aud.:* Ga, Ac, Sa.

This peer-reviewed journal is unique in that articles "need not deal with the field of aging as a whole, but with any defensibly relevant topic pertinent to the aging experience and related to the broad concerns and subject matter of the social and behavioral sciences and the humanities." Therefore, the topics covered in each issue vary in content and scope. In most issues, there is a section called "Of General Interest" that contains varied articles, and the other topical sections vary from issue to issue. Special issues have been published that have a central theme. Two recent special issues focus on "New Directions in Feminist Gerontology" and "Fashioning Age: Cultural Narratives of Later Life," both of which had guest editors. The journal "emphasizes innovation and critique" as well as "new directions in general—regardless of theoretical or methodological orientation, or academic discipline." The editors welcome critical, empirical, or theoretical contributions. Recent articles cover "Sex after 40: Gender, ageism, and sexual partnering in midlife" and "Young athletic bodies and narrative maps of aging."

3302. *Journal of Applied Gerontology.* [ISSN: 0733-4648] 1982. 5x/yr. GBP 466. Ed(s): Dr. Jim Mitchell. Sage Publications, Inc., 2455 Teller Rd, Thousand Oaks, CA 91320; info@sagepub.com; http://www.sagepub.com. Illus., index, adv. Refereed. Circ: 850 Paid. Vol. ends: Dec. Reprint: PSC. *Indexed:* ASG, AgeL, CINAHL, ExcerpMed, H&SSA, HRA, IMFL, PsycInfo, RiskAb, SFSA, SSA, SSCI, SociolAb, V&AA. *Aud.:* Ac.

The official publication of the Southern Gerontological Society, this journal "provides an international forum for information that has clear and immediate applicability to the health, care and quality of life of older persons." The journal "fills a void in the existing literature of gerontology" and covers a wide range of topics including caregiving, exercise, death and dying, health, leisure activities, housing, long-term care, mental health, retirement planning, and sexuality. The journal seeks to bridge research and practice, and its goal is to "publish findings, recommendations, and promising ideas that have general applicability to and significance for enhancing the lives and life circumstances of older persons everywhere."

3303. *Journal of Cross-Cultural Gerontology.* [ISSN: 0169-3816] 1986. q. EUR 499 print & online eds. Ed(s): Margaret Perkinson. Springer New York LLC, 233 Spring St, New York, NY 10013-1578; service-ny@springer.com; http://www.springer.com/. Illus., index, adv. Sample. Refereed. Vol. ends: No. 4. Microform: PQC. Online: EBSCO Publishing, EBSCO Host; Gale; IngentaConnect; OCLC Online Computer Library Center, Inc.; OhioLINK; Ovid Technologies, Inc.; Springer LINK; SwetsWise Online Content. Reprint: PSC. *Indexed:* ASG, AgeL, AnthLit, IBR, IBSS, IBZ, PsycInfo, RiskAb, SFSA, SSA, SociolAb. *Bk. rev.:* Number and length vary. *Aud.:* Ac, Sa.

This "is an international and interdisciplinary journal providing a forum for scholarly discussion of the aging process and the problems of the aged throughout the world." Emphasis is placed on "discussions of research findings, theoretical issues and applied approaches that deal with non-Western populations, as well as articles that provide a comparative orientation to the study of the aging process in its social, economic, historical and biological perspectives." In addition to research articles, issues can contain book reviews, research notes, and editor's notes. Recent articles include "Time is not up: Temporal complexity of older Americans' lives," "Japan's silver human resource centers and participant well-being," and "Growing old in St. Lucia: Expectations and experiences in a Caribbean village."

3304. *Journal of Elder Abuse & Neglect.* [ISSN: 0894-6566] 1988. q. USD 630 print & online eds. Ed(s): Pamela B Teaster, Terry Fulmer. The Haworth Maltreatment & Trauma Press, 10 Alice St, Binghamton, NY 13904; getinfo@haworthpress.com; http://www.haworthpress.com. Illus., adv. Sample. Refereed. Circ: 800 Paid. Microform: PQC. Online: EBSCO Publishing, EBSCO Host; OCLC Online Computer Library Center, Inc.; ProQuest LLC (Ann Arbor); SwetsWise Online Content. Reprint: HAW. *Indexed:* ASG, AgeL, CINAHL, CJA, CJPI, H&SSA, IBR, IBZ, IMFL, PsycInfo, RiskAb, SFSA, SSA, SSCI, SUSA, SWR&A, SociolAb, V&AA. *Bk. rev.:* Number and length vary. *Aud.:* Ga, Ac, Sa.

The official publication of National Committee for the Prevention of Elder Abuse, this journal's focus is the causes, effects, treatment, and prevention of the mistreatment of older people, with an emphasis on the causes of elder abuse and highlighting new and effective treatment methods and preventive strategies. This peer-reviewed quarterly seeks to educate professionals and the public on the issue of elder abuse. Topics covered include preventive strategies for elders; incidence and prevalence studies; mandatory reporting of abuse, neglect, and violence; standards for gerontological nursing practice; family caregiving of older adults; dependent adult children as perpetrators of neglect and abuse; the intergenerational cycle of violence in child and elder abuse; victim assistance programs and evaluations; therapeutic recreation; spousal abuse; and elder self-neglect. In addition to research articles, other recurring features include clinical practice, policy studies, education and training, book reviews, reviews of literature, international issues, and specific disciplines.

3305. *Journal of Geriatric Psychiatry and Neurology.* [ISSN: 0891-9887] 1988. q. GBP 282. Ed(s): Dr. Alan M Mellow. Sage Science Press (US), 2455 Teller Rd, Thousand Oaks, CA 91320; info@sagepub.com;

http://www.sagepub.com/. Illus., adv. Sample. Refereed. Circ: 1295. Online: EBSCO Publishing, EBSCO Host; Gale; HighWire Press; OCLC Online Computer Library Center, Inc.; SAGE Publications, Inc., SAGE Journals Online; SwetsWise Online Content. Reprint: PSC. *Indexed:* ASG, CBCARef, ExcerpMed, HortAb, PsycInfo, SCI, SSCI. *Aud.:* Ac, Sa.

This journal is the official publication of the Alzheimer's Foundation, and its focus is on original research, clinical reviews, and case reports on all aspects of neuropsychiatric care of older adults. Emphasis is placed on age-related biologic, neurologic, and psychiatric illnesses, psychosocial problems, forensic issues, and family care. The intended audience for the journal is clinicians and researchers in geriatric psychiatry, neurology, psychology, nursing, and social work. Topics discussed include Alzheimer's disease and other dementias; behavioral and mood complications of neurological disorders, such as stroke, Parkinson's disease, and primary dementias; delirium, depression, and other mood disorders; late-life addictions; anxiety disorders, sleep disorders, schizophrenia, and other psychotic disorders; adjustment disorders; and complications of bereavement. Occasional special issues are published focusing on a single topic. Suitable for academic and medical libraries.

3306. *Journal of Gerontological Social Work.* [ISSN: 0163-4372] 1978. q. in 2 vols. USD 590 print & online eds. Ed(s): M Joanna Mellor, Rose Dobrof. Haworth Social Work Practice Press, 10 Alice St, Binghamton, NY 13904; getinfo@haworthpress.com; http://www.haworthpress.com/. Illus., adv. Sample. Refereed. Circ: 639 Paid. Microform: PQC. Online: EBSCO Publishing, EBSCO Host; OCLC Online Computer Library Center, Inc.; SwetsWise Online Content. Reprint: HAW. *Indexed:* ASG, ASSIA, AgeL, CINAHL, CJA, CommAb, EAA, ExcerpMed, HRA, IBR, IBZ, IMFL, PSA, PsycInfo, SSA, SSCI, SWR&A, SociolAb, V&AA. *Aud.:* Ac, Sa.

This peer-reviewed journal focuses on social work theory, practice, consultation, and administration in the field of aging. The intended audience is social work administrators, practitioners, consultants, and supervisors in long-term care facilities, acute treatment centers, psychiatric hospitals, mental health centers, family services agencies, senior citizen and community centers, and public health and welfare agencies. Topics covered in the journal include case work and group work with the elderly, hospital geriatric social work, elderly and public welfare, mental health services for the elderly, law and gerontological social work, policy and planning studies, problems of geriatric substance abuse, and factors of class and ethnicity and their affect on service delivery and use. Occasionally, themed issues are published on a single topic. The journal considerably publishes the abstracts of all the articles (including those by the editor) in the table of contents for easy review.

3307. *Journal of Housing for the Elderly.* [ISSN: 0276-3893] 1983. q. USD 560 print & online eds. Ed(s): Benyamin Schwarz. Haworth Press, Inc., 10 Alice St, Binghamton, NY 13904-1580; getinfo@haworthpress.com; http://www.haworthpress.com. Illus., adv. Sample. Refereed. Circ: 179 Paid. Microform: PQC. Online: EBSCO Publishing, EBSCO Host; OCLC Online Computer Library Center, Inc.; SwetsWise Online Content. Reprint: HAW. *Indexed:* API, ASG, ASSIA, AgeL, Agr, CINAHL, IBR, IBZ, IMFL, PAIS, PRA, SFSA, SSA, SUSA, SociolAb. *Aud.:* Ga, Ac, Sa.

This journal covers more than just "houses." It focuses on the research related to housing and aging as well as on residences for the elderly. Topics of research include energy conservation, privacy needs, policy implications of home equity conversion, management issues, housing-related service delivery innovations, case histories of successful housing alternatives, financing strategies, salient housing issues regarding the elderly, case studies on the development of better housing facilities for the elderly, and issues and problems in housing policies for the elderly. The intended audience is scholars, policymakers, legislators, architects and urban planners, lending institutions, religious groups, developers, and the general public.

3308. *Journal of Nutrition for the Elderly.* [ISSN: 0163-9366] 1980. q. USD 690 print & online eds. Ed(s): Annette B Natow. Haworth Press, Inc., 10 Alice St, Binghamton, NY 13904-1580; getinfo@haworthpress.com; http://www.haworthpress.com. Illus., adv. Sample. Refereed. Circ: 354 Paid. Vol. ends: Summer. Microform: PQC. Online:

EBSCO Publishing, EBSCO Host; OCLC Online Computer Library Center, Inc.; SwetsWise Online Content. Reprint: HAW. *Indexed:* ASG, AbAn, AgeL, Agr, BiolAb, CABA, CINAHL, ChemAb, DSA, ExcerpMed, FS&TA, H&SSA, IMFL, MCR, PEI, PsycInfo, RRTA, RiskAb, SWR&A, WAE&RSA. *Aud.:* Ga, Ac, Sa.

This peer-reviewed journal equally serves two distinct audiences: those studying gerontology and those studying nutrition. The focus of the journal is examining the role of nutrition in disease prevention and management, functional performance, and overall quality of life for the elderly, as well as providing information in developing and assessing nutritional educational programs for the older adult. In addition to articles that illustrate best practices and application of the research presented, the journal provides evidence-based interventions and client education suggestions. Recent articles include "Inadequate Intakes of Indispensable Amino Acids among Homebound Older Adults," "Food Workshops, Nutrition Education, and Older Adults: A Process Evaluation," and "Barriers to the Consumption of Fruits and Vegetables among Older Adults."

3309. *Journal of Religion, Spirituality & Aging: the interdisiplinary journal of practice, theory & applied research.* Former titles (until 2004): *Journal of Religious Gerontology;* (until vol.7, 1990): *Journal of Religion and Aging.* [ISSN: 1552-8030] 1985. q. USD 420 print & online eds. Ed(s): James W Ellor. The Haworth Pastoral Press, 10 Alice St, Binghamton, NY 13904; getinfo@haworthpress.com; http://www.haworthpress.com/. Illus., adv. Sample. Refereed. Circ: 380 Paid. Vol. ends: Fall. Reprint: HAW. *Indexed:* ASG, ASSIA, AgeL, AmH&L, ChrPI, HistAb, IBR, IBZ, IMFL, PsycInfo, R&TA, RI-1. *Bk. rev.:* 500-600 words. *Aud.:* Ga, Ac, Sa.

This interdisciplinary, interfaith, international, and professional journal focuses on spirituality, religion, and aging issues with an emphasis on practices, theories, data on religion and spirituality, as well as ethical issues, grief, death, long-term care for the elderly, support systems for families, retirement, and counseling. The intended audience is pastors, religious educators, chaplains, lay spiritual care leaders, pastoral counselors, as well as secular professionals such as administrators, social workers, counselors, psychologists, nurses, physicians, and recreation and rehabilitative therapists who work with the elderly and their families. Topics covered include rituals that enhance older adults' lives, residents' attitudes about on-site religious activities in retirement communities, preaching to senior citizens, creative living in later years, practical theological models for worship with Alzheimer's patients, the meaning of our aging for God, suffering as a practical theological perspective, biblical foundations for a practical theology of aging, and Christian education for the spiritual growth of senior adults. The journal is suitable for public libraries (especially those serving elderly communities), and academic libraries with gerontology programs or religious studies programs.

3310. *Journal of Women and Aging: the multidiciplinary quarterly of psychosocial practice, theory & research.* [ISSN: 0895-2841] 1989. q. USD 475 print & online eds. Ed(s): J Dianne Garner. Haworth Press, Inc., 10 Alice St, Binghamton, NY 13904-1580; getinfo@haworthpress.com; http://www.haworthpress.com. Illus., adv. Sample. Refereed. Circ: 366 Paid. Microform: PQC. Online: EBSCO Publishing, EBSCO Host; OCLC Online Computer Library Center, Inc.; ProQuest LLC (Ann Arbor); SwetsWise Online Content. Reprint: HAW. *Indexed:* ASG, AbAn, AgeL, CINAHL, CWI, EAA, FemPer, GendWatch, H&SSA, IBR, IBZ, IMFL, PsycInfo, SSA, SSCI, SWA, SWR&A, SociolAb, WSA. *Aud.:* Ga, Ac.

This international and interdisciplinary professional journal focuses on the challenges that women face as they age. Contributing authors come from many disciplines, such as gerontology, nursing, medicine, mental health, sociology, and social work, and they present articles that cover all aspects of the aging process for women. Topics covered include osteoporosis, domestic violence, myocardial infarction, hysterectomy and menopause, breast cancer, loss, and terminal illness. Recent articles include "The Experience of Loneliness of Battered Old Women," "Remarriage in Later Life: Older Women's Negotiation of Power, Resources and Domestic Labor," and "Gender Differences in Retirement Decision in Hong Kong." The journal is appropriate for academic libraries with gerontology, women's studies, sociology, and social work programs.

3311. Journals of Gerontology. Series A: Biological Sciences & Medical Sciences. Supersedes in part (in 1995): *Journal of Gerontology.* [ISSN: 1079-5006] 1946. m. USD 578 (Individual members, USD 135). Ed(s): James R Smith. Gerontological Society of America, 1030 15th, NW, Ste 250, Washington, DC 20005-1503; http://www.geron.org. Illus., index, adv. Sample. Refereed. Circ: 3818 Paid and controlled. Vol. ends: Dec. Microform: PQC. Online: EBSCO Publishing, EBSCO Host; HighWire Press; OCLC Online Computer Library Center, Inc.; ProQuest K-12 Learning Solutions; ProQuest LLC (Ann Arbor). *Indexed:* ASG, AbAn, AgeL, ArtHuCI, BRI, CABA, CBRI, CINAHL, ChemAb, DSA, ErgAb, ExcerpMed, FPA, HortAb, IndVet, PAIS, PsycInfo, RRTA, S&F, SCI, SFSA, SSCI, SUSA, SWR&A, VB. *Aud.:* Ac, Sa.

Published by the Gerontological Society of America, the *Journals of Gerontology* were the first journals on aging that were published in the United States. Series A is divided into two distinct, peer-reviewed, scientific journals, each with their own editor and table of contents. The Biological Sciences section of Series A is focused on the biological aspects of aging, and a sample of the topics included are biochemistry, biodemography, exercise sciences, genetics, immunology, morphology, nutrition, pathology, pharmacology, and vertebrate and invertebrate genetics. The Medical Sciences section of Series A focuses on the full range of medical sciences pertaining to aging. A sample of the topics included are basic medical science, clinical research, and health services research for professions such as dentistry, allied health sciences, nursing, and medicine. Four types of articles are published: original research articles, rapid communications, review articles, and guest editorials. These journals are well indexed and are considered core journals for any library with a gerontology or geriatric collection.

3312. Journals of Gerontology. Series B: Psychological Sciences & Social Sciences. Supersedes in part (in 1995): *Journal of Gerontology.* [ISSN: 1079-5014] 1946. bi-m. USD 255 (Individuals, USD 122). Ed(s): Thomas Hess. Gerontological Society of America, 1030 15th, NW, Ste 250, Washington, DC 20005-1503; http://www.geron.org. Illus., index, adv. Sample. Refereed. Circ: 5862 Paid. Vol. ends: Nov. Microform: PQC. Online: EBSCO Publishing, EBSCO Host; HighWire Press; OCLC Online Computer Library Center, Inc.; ProQuest K-12 Learning Solutions; ProQuest LLC (Ann Arbor). *Indexed:* ASG, AbAn, AgeL, ArtHuCI, BRI, CABA, CBRI, CINAHL, CJA, ChemAb, DSA, ErgAb, ExcerpMed, FR, HRA, PAIS, PsycInfo, RRTA, SCI, SFSA, SSA, SSCI, SUSA, SWR&A, SociolAb, V&AA. *Aud.:* Ac, Sa.

Like its sister publication listed above, Series B of the *Journals of Gerontology* consists of two distinct, peer-reviewed, scientific journals under one cover. The Psychological Sciences section of Series B is focused on articles that cover the applied, clinical, counseling, developmental, experimental, and social psychology of aging. Samples of topics include attitudes, cognition, emotion, interpersonal relations, perception, personality, psychometric tests, and sensation. Four types of articles are published: original research articles, brief reports, invited reviews and position papers, and theoretical or methodological contributions. The Social Sciences section of Series B covers the areas of aging in the fields of anthropology, demography, economics, epidemiology, geography, political science, public health, social history, social work, and sociology. There are five types of articles published: original research articles, brief reports, letters to the editor, reviews, and theoretical and methodological contributions. These journals are well indexed and are considered core journals for any library with a gerontology or geriatric collection.

3313. Physical & Occupational Therapy in Geriatrics: current trends in geriatric rehabilitation. [ISSN: 0270-3181] 1980. q. USD 660 print & online eds. Ed(s): Ellen Dunleavey Taira. Haworth Press, Inc., 10 Alice St, Binghamton, NY 13904-1580; getinfo@haworthpress.com; http://www.haworthpress.com. Illus., adv. Sample. Refereed. Circ: 511 Paid. Microform: PQC. Online: EBSCO Publishing, EBSCO Host; OCLC Online Computer Library Center, Inc.; SwetsWise Online Content. Reprint: HAW. *Indexed:* ASG, AgeL, CINAHL, ExcerpMed, IMFL, MCR, PAIS, PEI, PsycInfo, RILM, RiskAb, SD, SWR&A. *Aud.:* Ac, Sa.

Utilizing a balance of research and practical information, this journal focuses on both the physical and mental rehabilitation of older adults. It investigates long-term care in institutional and community settings, crisis intervention, and innovative programming for the range of problems experienced by the elderly,

as well as the current skills needed for working with an aged clientele. Recent articles include "Decisional Balance and Readiness to Change Driving Behavior in Older Adults: A Pilot Study," "The Effect of Tai Chi Inspired Exercise Compared to Strength Training: A Pilot Study of Elderly Retired Community Dwellers," and "Movement Patterns Used by the Elderly When Getting Out of Bed." Occasional thematic issues will focus on a specific challenge in the profession. Past thematic issues have included the following topics: community mobility, driving and the elderly, innovative programs for the impaired elderly, and aging in place. The journal would be an asset to medical libraries and academic libraries with gerontology, social work, and physical therapy programs.

3314. Psychology and Aging. [ISSN: 0882-7974] 1986. q. USD 425 (Individuals, USD 144). Ed(s): Dr. Fredda Blanchard-Fields. American Psychological Association, 750 First St, N E, Washington, DC 20002-4242; journals@apa.org; http://www.apa.org. Illus., index, adv. Sample. Refereed. Vol. ends: Feb. Microform: PQC. Online: Pub.; CSA; EBSCO Publishing, EBSCO Host; OCLC Online Computer Library Center, Inc.; OhioLINK; Ovid Technologies, Inc.; ProQuest LLC (Ann Arbor); ScienceDirect. Reprint: PSC. *Indexed:* ASG, ASSIA, AgeL, CINAHL, ErgAb, ExcerpMed, FR, IMFL, PsycInfo, SSCI, SWR&A. *Aud.:* Ac, Sa.

This journal publishes original articles on adult development and aging, including "reports of research that may be applied, biobehavioral, clinical, educational, experimental (laboratory, field, or naturalistic studies), methodological, or psychosocial." Emphasis is placed on original research investigations, although occasional theoretical analyses of research issues, practical clinical problems, or policy may appear. Critical reviews of content areas in adult development and aging may also be included, and clinical case studies that have theoretical significance are also appropriate. Occasionally, brief reports will be accepted. Recent articles have been published on the following topics: "Treatment of Depression in Low-Income Older Adults," "The Role of Visual Attention in Predicting Driving Impairment in Older Adults," and "Symptoms of Depression in Older Home-Care Patients : Patient and Informant Reports."

3315. Research on Aging: a quarterly of social gerontology and adult development. [ISSN: 0164-0275] 1979. bi-m. GBP 456. Ed(s): Angela O'Rand. Sage Publications, Inc., 2455 Teller Rd, Thousand Oaks, CA 91320; info@sagepub.com; http://www.sagepub.com. Illus., index, adv. Sample. Refereed. Circ: 700 Paid. Vol. ends: Dec. Reprint: PSC. *Indexed:* ASG, AbAn, AgeL, CINAHL, CJA, ExcerpMed, HRA, IMFL, PsycInfo, SFSA, SSA, SSCI, SWR&A, SociolAb. *Aud.:* Ac.

Research on Aging serves as an international forum on the aged and the aging process and provides information on improving practices and policies concerning the elderly. The peer-reviewed articles are both broad in scope and detailed in coverage that encourages development of new knowledge and analysis, while the current state of the field is examined through a range of critical and review articles. In addition to the articles, the journal also features debates on current issues, special issues, practical research findings, and future directions in the field. Topics frequently covered include Alzheimer's disease and caregiver support; age discrimination; migration patterns of the elderly; the aging labor force; aging and social stress; age and inequality; demography of aging; retirement satisfaction; and gender, race, ethnicity, and social support. This journal is well indexed and is considered a core title for academic libraries with a gerontology collection.

3316. Topics in Geriatric Rehabilitation. [ISSN: 0882-7524] 1985. q. USD 314 (Individuals, USD 95.95). Ed(s): Carol B Lewis. Lippincott Williams & Wilkins, 530 Walnut St, Philadelphia, PA 19106-3621; http://www.lww.com. Illus. Sample. Refereed. Circ: 2580 Paid. Online: EBSCO Publishing, EBSCO Host; Florida Center for Library Automation; Gale; Ovid Technologies, Inc.; ProQuest LLC (Ann Arbor). *Indexed:* ASG, AgeL, CINAHL, ExcerpMed, IMFL, SSCI, V&AA. *Aud.:* Ac, Sa.

This peer-reviewed journal "provides hands-on, treatment-related guidance written by and for specialists in all aspects of geriatric care." Each issue is focused on a specific topic, and therefore topics are discussed in great detail. Recent articles include "Strategies and Tools to Enable Safe Mobility for Older

Adults," "Determinants of Older Driver Safety From a Socioecological Perspective," and "Pedestrian Mobility and Safety: A Key to Independence for Older People." Contributing authors are both academics and practitioners, so there is emphasis on both sides of the issues. This journal is suitable for academic libraries with geriatric, gerontology, social work, and physical therapy programs.

■ GLOBALIZATION

Kathryn Johns-Masten, Serials Librarian, Standish Library, Siena College, Albany, NY 12211; kjohns-masten@siena.edu

Introduction

Technological advances have increased many nations' abilities to trade with countries around the world. Globalization, a term first used in the 1980s, describes the idea of economies depending on each other on a global scale. Competition, labor issues, communication, and economics now link countries that in the past were isolated or unaffected by each other. Now, with the ease of completing international transactions, once-disconnected financial markets have distinct, and sometimes disturbing, effects on each other.

This is a new section, and while it contains a small number of titles, they are excellent resources. As more titles are available in this area of study, future editions of this section will expand in length.

Basic Periodicals

Yale Global Online, Globalizations, Global Dialogue.

Basic Abstracts and Indexes

IngentaConnect, Sociological Abstracts.

3317. *Competition and Change: the journal of global political economy.* [ISSN: 1024-5294] 1996. q. USD 366. Ed(s): Sukhdev Johal, Julie Froud. Maney Publishing, Ste. 1C, Joseph's Well, Hanover Walk, Leeds, LS3 1AB, United Kingdom; maney@maney.co.uk; http://www.maney.co.uk. Reprint: PSC. *Indexed:* IBSS, JEL. *Aud.:* Ac, Sa.

This specialized journal combines "research and ideas in global business and political economy in ways that will interest social scientists inside and outside the schools of business and management." The goal is for articles to emanate from a social science perspective and develop from there to illustrate broad business issues that surround globalization and financialization, which impact social conditions. The journal contains full-length peer-reviewed articles; review articles and position pieces; and short items of relevant news and information. Students, faculty, and researchers in business, political science, and the social sciences will find this journal valuable.

3318. *Global Dialogue.* [ISSN: 1450-0590] q. USD 192 (Individuals, USD 60). Centre for World Dialogue, 39 Riga Fereou St, Ag Omologitae, P.O. Box 23992, Nicosia, CY-1687, Cyprus. *Indexed:* IBR, IBSS, IBZ, IPSA, PAIS, PSA, SociolAb. *Bk. rev.:* Number and length vary. *Aud.:* Hs, Ga, Ac.

Global Dialogue is a quarterly publication "dedicated to promoting the exchange of ideas on a broad range of international issues, social, political, economic and cultural." A main tenet of this journal is that debate should be used as a means to solve problems, as opposed to threats or use of force. This journal examines conflicts and issues from all areas of the world and highlights the forces at work internationally that are shaping today's world. It contains articles, a comment section, and book reviews. Good resource for the intelligent general reader.

3319. *Global Media and Communication.* [ISSN: 1742-7665] 2005. 3x/yr. GBP 286. Ed(s): Daya K Thussu, Zhao Zhao. Sage Publications Ltd., 1 Oliver's Yard, 55 City Rd, London, EC1 1SP, United Kingdom; info@sagepub.co.uk; http://www.sagepub.co.uk. Adv. Refereed. *Indexed:* CommAb. *Aud.:* Ac, Sa.

This is an international refereed journal that provides an arena for critical debates and developments in an ever-changing global environment. "Interviews, reviews of recent media developments and digests of policy documents and data reports from a variety of countries" are included. The international area of communications studies, media studies, cultural studies, telecommunications, and public policy are just a few of the subjects covered by this journal. The use of ten regional editors from a variety of countries ensures that multiple perspectives and views are included in the journal. Essential reading for academics, researchers, and students in communications and globalization studies.

3320. *Global Networks (Oxford): a journal of transnational affairs.* [ISSN: 1470-2266] 2001. q. GBP 286 print & online eds. Ed(s): Dr. Alisdair Rogers. Blackwell Publishing Ltd., 9600 Garsington Rd, Oxford, OX4 2ZG, United Kingdom; customerservices@ blackwellpublishing.com; http://www.blackwellpublishing.com. Reprint: PSC. *Indexed:* ApEcolAb, EngInd, IBSS, IPSA, IndIslam, JEL, PSA, RiskAb, SSA, SSCI, SociolAb. *Bk. rev.:* Number and length vary. *Aud.:* Ac, Sa.

This journal provides peer-reviewed "research on global networks, transnational affairs and practices, and their relation to wider theories of globalization." Its regional editors ensure that issues of worldwide interest and relevance are addressed. Subjects vary from the scope and powers of the states in a period of globalization to issues of sociocultural interest, to the political economy of global networks. The intended audience includes academics, international NGOs, business networks, and international foundations.

Global Social Policy. See Sociology and Social Work section.

3321. *Globalization and Health.* [ISSN: 1744-8603] 2005. irreg. Free. Ed(s): Greg Martin. BioMed Central Ltd., Middlesex House, 34-42 Cleveland St, London, W1T 4LB, United Kingdom; info@biomedcentral.com; http://www.biomedcentral.com. Refereed. *Indexed:* ExcerpMed, H&SSA. *Bk. rev.:* Number and length vary. *Aud.:* Ac, Sa.

This open-access journal contains research that considers both the positive and negative influences of globalization on health. Seeking to provide a balanced arena for debate that is challenging and rational, this journal contains research articles, book reviews, commentaries, debate articles, invited reviews, and short reports. As technological advances continue at a rapid pace and economies are more closely linked, issues of health care and welfare on a local scale affect communities worldwide. While other publications discuss similar topics, this journal provides a dedicated outlet for this subject. Recommended for researchers and academic libraries.

3322. *Globalizations.* [ISSN: 1474-7731] 2004. 4x/yr. GBP 288 print & online eds. Ed(s): Barry Gills. Routledge, 4 Park Square, Milton Park, Abingdon, OX14 4RN, United Kingdom; journals@routledge.com; http://www.routledge.co.uk. Refereed. Reprint: PSC. *Aud.:* Ac, Sa.

This peer-reviewed journal is published quarterly and seeks to publish "the best work exploring new meanings of globalizations, bringing fresh ideas to the concept, broadening its scope, and contributing to shaping debates of the future." A wide variety of disciplines is covered, including natural, environmental, medical, public health science, social science, and the humanities. Seeking a variety of interpretations and exploring globalization from many perspectives, this journal is necessary for academic libraries and researchers in the field of globalization.

3323. *Yale Global Online.* 200?. irreg. Free. Yale University, Center for the Study of Globalization, The Betts House, 393 Prospect St, New haven, CT 06521. *Bk. rev.:* Number and length vary. *Aud.:* Ga, Ac, Sa.

This free publication of the Yale Center for the Study of Globalization is available on the web for all to access. Its aim is to "analyze and promote debate on all aspects of globalization through publishing original articles and multi-media presentations." *Yale Global* republishes articles on the topic of globalization and other related disciplines. Selections of slide show presentations, video clips, and Flash presentations of speakers from Yale and elsewhere are available. Selected translations are available. Book reviews and excerpts, academic papers, and links to resources by topic make this a very robust source of information on globalization. Recommended for academics and people interested in globalization.

■ GOVERNMENT PERIODICALS—FEDERAL

Rosemary L. Meszaros, Coordinator, Government Information and Law, Western Kentucky University, Bowling Green, KY 42101; rosemary.meszaros@wku.edu; 270-745-6441

Introduction

The official federal printer, the U.S. Government Printing Office, is known familiarly by its initials, GPO. The Federal Depository Library Program that is within GPO distributes documents to more than 1,000 libraries across the country. While predictions of the demise of GPO and the Federal Depository Library Program have been made for some time, especially with the advent of the Internet, the federal agencies are still abiding by Title 44 of the United States Code and cooperating with GPO in providing online access to federal documents, including online access.

GPO is archiving the online resources under a Persistent Uniform Resource Locator (PURL). See http://purl.access.gpo.gov for an explanation. This move counterbalances the apprehension experienced by some in the depository community concerning the stability of online access. To paraphrase Mark Twain, the Depository Program and GPO's demise have been prematurely exaggerated.

GPO continues its publishing pace by publishing and disseminating the reports, studies, testimony, hearings, analyses, and surveys—in short, the very words uttered and written by our federal public servants. The many federal agencies in the executive branch, the Congress and its agencies, and the Supreme Court all offer something for every interest. Law, military, politics, education, environment, business, economics, agriculture, weather, science, demographics, large print, audio and Braille bibliographies, consumer information, statistics—all are represented in the array of magazines and journals published, distributed, and sold by GPO.

While GPO is not slowing down its pace, it is transforming its mode of dissemination from primarily print to the digital format. GPO maintains a gateway web site, *GPO Access*, at www.gpoaccess.gov.

GPO has recognized that some titles should remain available in print. Thus they have assembled the Essential Titles for Public Use in Paper Format, www.access.gpo.gov/su_docs/fdlp/pubs/estitles.html. Several depository libraries have assisted with the electronic transition. A very useful alphabetical list of federal government periodicals with clickable links is maintained by the University of Louisville Libraries at http://library.louisville.edu/government/periodicals/periodall.html. This list includes publications that have ceased.

Two other gateways seek to facilitate access to web-based information: *USA.gov* from the General Services Administration, www.usa.gov, and the Library of Congress's web site, http://loc.gov. Finally, the Federal Citizen Information Center in Pueblo, Colorado, www.pueblo.gsa.gov, continues to provide quick and easy access to their consumer publications.

GPO marches on with digital dissemination.

Basic Periodicals

Ga: *U.S. Congress. Congressional Record, U.S. Office of the Federal Register. Weekly Compilation of Presidential Documents;* Ac: *U.S. Congress. Congressional Record, Morbidity and Mortality Weekly Report, U.S. Office of the Federal Register. Weekly Compilation of Presidential Documents;* Sa: *Morbidity and Mortality Weekly Report.*

Basic Abstracts and Indexes

LexisNexis Government Periodicals, LexisNexis Statistical, Public Affairs Information Service International.

3324. *AgExporter (Print Edition).* (until 1989): *Foreign Agriculture.* [ISSN: 1047-4781] 1937. q. USD 44. U.S. Department of Agriculture, Foreign Agricultural Service, Information Division, Rm 4638 S, Washington, DC 20250-1000; http://ffas.usda.gov/info/agexporter/agexport.html. Illus., index. Sample. Circ: 1800. Vol. ends: No. 12. Online: Florida Center for Library Automation; Gale; Northern Light Technology, Inc.; OCLC Online Computer Library Center, Inc.; ProQuest K-12 Learning Solutions; ProQuest LLC (Ann Arbor); H.W. Wilson. *Indexed:* ABIn, ABS&EES, Agr, AmStI, B&AI, DSA, HortAb, IUSGP, PAIS, RRTA, WAE&RSA. *Aud.:* Sa.
This journal is written by U.S. Department of Agriculture staff for businesses selling farm products overseas. It provides tips on exporting, descriptions of markets with the greatest sales potential, and information on export assistance available from the USDA. The audience is U.S. agricultural producers, exporters, trade organizations, state departments of agriculture, and any other export-oriented organization. It has had electronic access since 1996 when it was called *AgExporter*. URL: www.fas.usda.gov/info/fasworldwide/maghome.htm.

Agricultural Research. See Agriculture section.

3325. *Alcohol Research & Health.* Formerly (until 1999): *Alcohol Health & Research World.* [ISSN: 1535-7414] 1975. q. USD 25 domestic. Ed(s): Dianne M Welsh. U.S. National Institute on Alcohol Abuse and Alcoholism, 6000 Executive Blvd, Bethesda, MD 20892-7003; http://www.niaaa.nih.gov. Illus., index. Refereed. Circ: 3700 Paid. Vol. ends: No. 4. Online: EBSCO Publishing, EBSCO Host; Florida Center for Library Automation; Gale; OCLC Online Computer Library Center, Inc.; ProQuest LLC (Ann Arbor); H.W. Wilson. *Indexed:* AgeL, Agr, AmStI, CINAHL, CJA, CWI, ChemAb, HRIS, IUSGP, MASUSE, PAIS, PsycInfo, SSCI, SWR&A. *Aud.:* Ac, Sa.
Each issue is devoted to a particular topic in alcohol research, e.g., children of alcoholics, chronobiology, circadian rhythms and alcohol use, and alcohol and comorbid mental health disorders. This quarterly, peer-reviewed scientific journal is available in full text from 1997 to date on the web site of the National Institute on Alcohol Abuse and Alcoholism. Online since 1994. URL: www.niaaa.nih.gov/Publications/AlcoholResearch.

Amber Waves. See Agriculture section.

The Astronomical Almanac. See Astronomy section.

3326. *C R M (Washington).* Formerly (until 1991): *C R M Bulletin.* [ISSN: 1068-4999] 1978. bi-m. Free. U.S. Department of the Interior, National Parks Service, Culture Resources, 1849 C Street NW Ste. 350NC, Washington, DC 20240. *Indexed:* A&ATA, AmH&L, ArtInd, HistAb, RILM. *Bk. rev.:* Number and length vary. *Aud.:* Ga, Ac, Sa.
CRM Journal is produced under a cooperative agreement with the National Conference of State Historic Preservation Officers and the National Park Service. A sister publication to *Common Ground: Preserving Our Nation's Heritage, CRM Journal* is peer reviewed and addresses the history of, development of, trends in, and emerging issues in cultural resource management in the United States and abroad. Its purpose is to broaden the intellectual foundation of the management of cultural resources. It is written for practitioners in the cultural resources fields, including history, architecture, curation, ethnography, archeology, cultural landscapes, folklore, and related areas. It is also for scholars in colleges and universities who teach, study, and interpret cultural resources, and other members of the heritage community. Full text online since 2001. URL: http://crmjournal.cr.nps.gov/Journal_Index.cfm.

3327. *Cityscape (Washington, D.C.): a journal of policy development and research.* [ISSN: 1936-007X] 1994. 3x/yr. USD 5 per issue. U.S. Department of Housing and Urban Development, Office of Policy Development and Research, 451 Seventh St, SW, Washington, DC 20410-6000. *Indexed:* JEL. *Aud.:* Ga, Ac, Sa.

Cityscape: A Journal of Policy Development and Research strives to share HUD-funded and other research on housing and urban policy issues with scholars, government officials, and others involved in setting policy and determining the direction of future research. This journal focuses on innovative ideas, policies, and programs that show promise in revitalizing cities and regions, renewing their infrastructure, and creating economic opportunities. A typical issue consists of articles that examine various aspects of a theme of particular interest to its audience, such as home equity conversion mortgage or reverse mortgage, housing discrimination, assisted housing, etc. It has been online since its first issue in August 1994. URL: www.huduser.org/periodicals/cityscape.html.

3328. *Common Ground (Washington, DC): preserving our nation's heritage.* Former titles (until 1996): *Federal Archeology;* (until 1994): *Federal Archeology Report.* [ISSN: 1087-9889] 1988. q. Free. U.S. Department of the Interior, National Park Service, National Center for Cultural Resources, 1849 C Street NW, Washington, DC 20240; NPS_HeritageNews@nps.gov; http://www.cr.nps.gov. Circ: 12000. *Indexed:* RGPR. *Aud.:* Ga, Ac, Sa.

This award-winning magazine from the National Parks Service archaeology program has had two name changes: from *Common Ground: Archeology and Ethnography in the Public Interest* and, prior to that, *Federal Archaeology.* Expanding its scope beyond archaeology and ethnography, *Common Ground* now offers an in-depth look at the nationwide effort to preserve our heritage in all its forms. Stories focus not only on preservation, but on the people making it happen—on public and tribal lands and in cities, towns, and neighborhoods across the nation. Readers will find a wealth of useful information—from the nuts and bolts of approaches that work, to where to get grants, to the latest research findings. It is written in a jargon-free, to-the-point style. Quality artwork and photography provide an intimate portrait of America's heritage. Full text online; archived online since 2003. URL: http://commonground.cr.nps.gov/Index.cfm.

3329. *Congressional Record: proceedings and debates of the Congress.* [ISSN: 0363-7239] 1873. d. when Congress is in session. USD 503 domestic; USD 704.20 foreign. U.S. Government Printing Office, 732 N Capitol St NW, Washington, DC 20401; http://www.gpo.gov. Illus., index. Microform: WSH. *Aud.:* Ac, Sa.

The *Congressional Record* is the most widely recognized published account of the debates, proceedings, and activities of the United States Congress. Currently averaging more than 200 pages a day, it is a substantially verbatim account of the proceedings of Congress. It is published daily when either or both houses of Congress are in session. It may be thought of as the world's largest daily newspaper because it contains an account of everything that is said and done on the floors of the House and Senate, extensive additional reprinting of inserted materials, and, since 1947, a resume of congressional activity (the *Daily Digest*). Available and searchable online through *GPO Access* from 1994 to current at www.gpoaccess.gov/crecord/index.html; and through the Library of Congress's THOMAS database from 1989 to present at http://thomas.loc.gov.

3330. *Consumer Product Safety Review.* Former titles (until 1996): *N E I S S Data Highlights; N E I S S News.* [ISSN: 1555-1172] 1976. q. USD 18 domestic; USD 25.20 foreign. Ed(s): Ed Kang. U.S. Consumer Product Safety Commission, Washington, DC 20207. Circ: 1300 Paid. *Indexed:* AmStI. *Aud.:* Ga, Sa.

This quarterly journal offers an in-depth look at the latest hazards associated with 15,000 types of consumer products under the agency's jurisdiction, both home and recreational products, as well as the most significant current product recalls. Available from its first issue in Summer 1996 to its current issue. URL: www.cpsc.gov/cpscpub/pubs/cpsr.html.

3331. *Emerging Infectious Diseases (Print Edition).* [ISSN: 1080-6040] 1995. m. Free. Ed(s): D Peter Drotman, Kenneth S Korach. U.S. Department of Health and Human Services, Centers for Disease Control and Prevention, 1600 Clifton Rd, Atlanta, GA 30333; http://www.cdc.gov. Illus. Refereed. Circ: 23500. Vol. ends: No. 4. Online: EBSCO Publishing, EBSCO Host; Gale; OCLC Online Computer Library Center, Inc.; H.W. Wilson. *Indexed:* ABS&EES, BiolAb, BiolDig, CABA, DSA, ExcerpMed, FS&TA, ForAb, GSI, H&SSA, IndVet, PollutAb, RRTA, RiskAb, S&F, SCI, SWRA, VB, WAE&RSA, ZooRec. *Bk. rev.:* Number and length vary. *Aud.:* Ga, Sa.

This is a monthly peer-reviewed journal tracking and analyzing disease trends. It has a very high citation rate and ranking in its field. In addition to dispatches on the latest epidemiology of infectious diseases, the issues contain research articles, columns, letters, commentary, and book reviews. Available in full text beginning with its inaugural issue in 1995 from the Centers for Disease Control and Prevention web site. URL: www.cdc.gov/ncidod/EID/index.htm.

3332. *Endangered Species Bulletin (Print Edition).* Formerly (until 1994): *Endangered Species Technical Bulletin.* [ISSN: 1091-7314] 1976. 4x/yr. Ed(s): Michael Bender. U.S. Fish and Wildlife Service, Division of Endangered Species, 452 Arlington Sq, Washington, DC 20240; http://www.fws.gov. Illus. *Indexed:* Agr, EnvAb, EnvInd, GardL. *Aud.:* Ga, Ac.

The *Endangered Species Bulletin* was created in 1976 to meet the growing demand for news of developments in the endangered-species program. It is the primary means by which the U.S. Fish and Wildlife Service disseminates information on rule makings (listings, reclassifications, and delistings), recovery plans and activities, regulatory changes, interagency consultations, changes in species' status, research developments, new ecological threats, and a variety of other issues. The Fish and Wildlife Service distributes the *Bulletin* free to federal, state, and local agencies and official contacts of the endangered-species program. Online in varying degrees of completeness since 1994. URL: www.fws.gov/endangered/bulletin.html. It is also reprinted by the University of Michigan as part of its own publication, *The Endangered Species Update.* URL: www.fws.gov/Endangered/bulletin.html.

3333. *Engineer (Fort Leonard Wood): the professional bulletin of Army engineers.* [ISSN: 0046-1989] 1971. q. USD 19 domestic; USD 26.60 foreign. U.S. Army Maneuver Support Center, Development Support Department, 320 Manscen Loop, Ste 210, Fort Leonard Wood, MO 65473-8929. *Indexed:* ABIn, AUNI, C&ISA, CerAb, IAA, IUSGP. *Bk. rev.:* Number and length vary. *Aud.:* Sa.

Engineer is a professional-development bulletin designed to provide a forum for exchanging information and ideas within the Army engineer community. Articles are by and about officers, enlisted soldiers, warrant officers, Department of the Army civilian employees, and others. Writers discuss training, current operations and exercises, doctrine, equipment, history, personal viewpoints, or other areas of general interest to engineers. Articles may share good ideas and lessons learned or explore better ways of doing things. In addition to regular columns from the Commandant of the U.S. Army Engineer School and from the Command Sergeant Major, and a book review column, there is also a column entitled "Dedication," which lists those in the Army Corps of Engineers who have been lost in the global war on terrorism. Full-text electronic coverage as of February 2001. URL: http://www.wood.army.mil/ENGRMAG/Default.html.

3334. *Environmental Health Perspectives.* Incorporates (in 2003): *E H P Toxicogenomics.* [ISSN: 0091-6765] 1972. m. inc. quarterly suppl. and annual review. Individuals, USD 263; Students, USD 89. Ed(s): Thomas J Goehl. U.S. Department of Health and Human Services, National Institute of Environmental Health Sciences, PO Box 12233, Research Triangle Park, NC 27709; http://niehs.nih.gov/. Illus., adv. Refereed. Circ: 6500. Vol. ends: Dec (No. 12). Online: EBSCO Publishing, EBSCO Host; Gale; National Library of Medicine; OCLC Online Computer Library Center, Inc.; ProQuest LLC (Ann Arbor); H.W. Wilson. *Indexed:* ABS&EES, Agr, BiolAb, CABA, CINAHL, ChemAb, DSA, EnvAb, EnvInd, ExcerpMed, FPA, FS&TA, ForAb, GSI, H&SSA, HortAb, IndVet, M&GPA, PollutAb, RRTA, RiskAb, S&F, SCI, SSCI, SWRA, VB, WAE&RSA, WRCInf, ZooRec. *Bk. rev.:* Number and length vary. *Aud.:* Ac.

This peer-reviewed journal is dedicated to the discussion of the effects of the environment on human health. It contains articles, commentary, news, editorials, and a research forum. It publishes 12 issues annually. It includes monthly sections devoted to children's health and environmental medicine; a toxicogenomics research section, published in coordination with toxicogenomics news in separate quarterly issues; and an annual review issue. A quarterly Chinese-language edition is also published, as well as occasional special issues. *EHP* is an open-access journal, meaning all articles are freely available online. URL: www.ehponline.org.

F B I Law Enforcement Bulletin. See Criminology and Law Enforcement section.

FDA Consumer. See Health and Fitness section.

Federal Probation. See Criminology and Law Enforcement section.

3335. *Federal Reserve Bulletin.* [ISSN: 0014-9209] 1915. q. U.S. Federal Reserve System, Board of Governors, Publications Services, Rm MS 138, Washington, DC 20551; http://www.federalreserve.gov. Circ: 26000. Microform: MIM; CIS; PMC; PQC. Online: The Dialog Corporation; EBSCO Publishing, EBSCO Host; Florida Center for Library Automation; Gale; William S. Hein & Co., Inc.; Northern Light Technology, Inc.; OCLC Online Computer Library Center, Inc.; ProQuest K-12 Learning Solutions; ProQuest LLC (Ann Arbor); H.W. Wilson. Reprint: WSH. *Indexed:* ABIn, AgeL, AmStI, BLI, BPI, CLI, IBSS, ILP, IUSGP, JEL, PAIS, WAE&RSA. *Aud.:* Ac, Sa.

Staff members of the Board of Governors of the Federal Reserve prepare the articles for this publication. In general, they report and analyze economic developments, discuss bank regulatory issues, and present new data. Available in full text online since 1997 on the Federal Reserve Board web site. The quarterly paper version of the *Bulletin* is no longer published in print. However, the board produces an annual compilation in print for sale. URL: www.federalreserve.gov/pubs/bulletin.

Fishery Bulletin. See Fish, Fisheries, and Aquaculture section.

3336. *Forum: English teaching.* Former titles (until 2000): *U.S. Department of State. Bureau of International Information Programs. Forum;* (until 1982): *United States. International Communication Agency. Forum;* (until 197?): *United States Information Agency. Forum;* (until 1978): *English Teaching Forum.* [ISSN: 1559-663X] 1963. q. USD 19 domestic; USD 26.60 foreign. U.S. Department of State, Bureau of Education and Cultural Affairs, 2201 C St NW, Washington, DC 20520. Illus. Circ: 100000. *Indexed:* IUSGP, LT&LA. *Bk. rev.:* 4. *Aud.:* Ga, Ac, Sa.

A quarterly journal published by the U.S. Department of State for teachers of English as a foreign or second language. Over 60,000 copies of the magazine are distributed in 100 countries. In 2002, the *Forum* celebrated its 40th anniversary. Most of the authors published in the journal are classroom teachers and regular readers of the journal. Submissions from English-language teachers around the world are welcomed. Book reviews are a half-page in length. Articles from issues of the *Forum* dating back to 1993 are available online through *GPO Access* or directly at the U.S. Department of State web site. URL: http://exchanges.state.gov/education/engteaching/eal-foru.htm.

3337. *Health Care Financing Review.* [ISSN: 0195-8631] 1979. q. USD 48 domestic; USD 62.20 foreign; USD 23 per issue domestic. Ed(s): Linda F Wolf. U.S. Health Care Financing Administration, 7500 Security Blvd. C3-24-07, Baltimore, MD 21244-1850; lwolf@cms.hhs.gov; http://www.hcfa.gov/. Illus. Vol. ends: Summer (No. 4). Microform: CIS; PQC. Online: EBSCO Publishing, EBSCO Host; Florida Center for Library Automation; Gale; Northern Light Technology, Inc.; OCLC Online Computer Library Center, Inc.; ProQuest LLC (Ann Arbor); H.W. Wilson. *Indexed:* ABIn, ASG, AgeL, AmStI, BPI, ExcerpMed, IUSGP, MCR, PAIS, SCI, SSCI, SWR&A. *Aud.:* Ac, Sa.

The Health Care Financing Administration was renamed the Centers for Medicare and Medicaid Services in 2001, but the journal retains the familiar name. It highlights the results of policy-relevant research and provides a forum for a broad range of viewpoints to stimulate discussion among a diverse audience that includes policy makers, planners, administrators, insurers, researchers, and health care providers. Topics include managed and community-based care, Medicaid reform, and prescription drugs. Many articles include statistics. Available in full text online since the Fall 1998 issue from the Centers for Medicare and Medicaid Services web site. URL: www.cms.hhs.gov/HealthCareFinancingReview.

3338. *Heritage News (Washington, D.C.).* [ISSN: 1555-2748] 2003. m. U.S. Department of the Interior, National Park Service, National Center for Cultural Resources, 1849 C Street NW, Washington, DC 20240; NPS_HeritageNews@nps.gov; http://www.cr.nps.gov. *Aud.:* Ga, Ac, Sa.

Heritage News is a monthly e-newsletter published by the National Park Service to deliver timely information on topics including grant opportunities, new laws or policies, events, and activities of interest to the national heritage community. It updates its sister publications *Common Ground: Preserving Our Nation's Heritage* and *CRM: The Journal of Heritage Stewardship.* Also includes information on significant legislation. Online since August 2003. URL: http://heritagenews.cr.nps.gov/index/Index.cfm.

Humanities: the magazine of the national endowment for the humanities. See Cultural Studies section.

Journal of Rehabilitation. See Disabilities section.

3339. *M M W R.* Formerly (until 1976): *U.S. National Communicable Disease Center. Morbidity and Mortality.* [ISSN: 0149-2195] 1951. w. USD 373 domestic; USD 522 foreign. Ed(s): Frederic E Shaw. U.S. Department of Health and Human Services, Centers for Disease Control and Prevention, Epidemiology Program Office, 1600 Clifton Rd NE, Atlanta, GA 30333; http://www.cdc.gov. Illus., index. Circ: 30000 Paid. Microform: CIS; PQC. Online: EBSCO Publishing, EBSCO Host; Factiva, Inc.; Florida Center for Library Automation; Gale; ProQuest LLC (Ann Arbor). *Indexed:* AmStI, BiolAb, BiolDig, CABA, CINAHL, CJA, CWI, DSA, EnvAb, FS&TA, ForAb, H&SSA, HortAb, IndVet, PEI, RRTA, RiskAb, S&F, VB, WAE&RSA. *Aud.:* Ac, Sa.

Contains data on specific diseases as reported by state and territorial health departments, and reports on infectious and chronic diseases, environmental hazards, natural or human-generated disasters, occupational diseases and injuries, and intentional and unintentional injuries. Also included are reports on topics of international interest and notices of events of interest to the public health community. No longer distributed in paper to federal depository libraries. Available online from 1982 on the Centers for Disease Control's own web site at www.cdc.gov/mmwr/mmwr_wk.html.

Marine Fisheries Review. See Fish, Fisheries, and Aquaculture section.

Mariners Weather Log. See Marine Science and Technology section.

Military History. See Military section.

Military Review. See Military section.

3340. *National Institute of Standards and Technology. Journal of Research.* Former titles (until 1988): *U.S. National Bureau of Standards. Journal of Research;* Formed by the 1977 merger of: *U.S. National Bureau of Standards. Journal of Research. Section A. Physics and Chemistry; U.S. National Bureau of Standards. Journal of Research. Section B. Mathematical Sciences;* Which was formerly (until 1967): *U.S. National Bureau of Standards. Journal of Research. Section B. Mathematics and Mathematical Physics;* Which superseded in part (in 1959): *U.S. National Bureau of Standards. Journal of Research.* [ISSN: 1044-677X] 1927. bi-m. USD 47 domestic; USD 65.80 foreign. Ed(s): Theodore V Vorburger. U.S. Department of Commerce, National Institute of Standards and Technology, 100 Bureau Dr, Gaithersburg, MD 20899-2500; inquiries@nist.gov; http://www.nist.gov. Illus., index. Circ: 2000 Paid and controlled. Vol. ends: Nov/Dec. Microform: PQC. Online: Florida Center for Library Automation; Gale; OCLC Online Computer Library Center, Inc.; ProQuest K-12 Learning Solutions; ProQuest LLC (Ann Arbor); H.W. Wilson. *Indexed:* AS&TI, ApMecR, C&ISA, CABA, CerAb, ChemAb, EngInd, FS&TA, ForAb, HortAb, IAA, IUSGP, MathR, S&F, SCI. *Aud.:* Ac, Sa.

This journal reports on National Institute of Standards and Technology (NIST) research and development in metrology and related fields of physical science, engineering, applied mathematics, statistics, biotechnology, and information technology. Papers cover a broad range of subjects, with the major emphasis on measurement methodology and the basic technology that underlies standardization. Also included, on occasion, are articles on topics closely related to the institute's technical and scientific program. NIST was formerly the National Bureau of Standards. Full text of all articles since 1948 is available on the NIST web site. URL: http://nvl.nist.gov/nvl3.cfm?doc_id=89&s_id=117.

Occupational Outlook Quarterly. See Occupations and Careers section.

Parameters. See Military section.

3341. *Peace Watch.* Formerly (until 1994): *United States Institute of Peace. Journal.* [ISSN: 1080-9864] 1988. bi-m. Ed(s): David Aronson. U.S. Institute of Peace, 1200 17th St NW, Ste 200, Washington, DC 20036-3011; http://www.usip.org. Illus. Circ: 15000. Vol. ends: Oct (No. 6). *Indexed:* ABS&EES. *Aud.:* Ga, Ac, Sa.

The Institute of Peace is an independent, nonpartisan federal institution created by Congress to promote the prevention, management, and peaceful resolution of international conflicts. Articles are written by the institute's staff and focus on news of conflicts worldwide, as well as report on symposia held under the sponsorship of the institute. Full text since 1996 is available online at its web site. URL: www.usip.org/peacewatch/index.html.

Prologue. See Archives and Manuscripts section.

Public Health Reports. See Public Health section.

Public Roads. See Transportation section.

Science & Technology Review. See Science and Technology section.

Social Security Bulletin. See Elder Issues section.

3342. *State Magazine.* Former titles (until 1996): *State;* (until 1980): *U.S. Department of State. Newsletter.* [ISSN: 1099-4165] 1961. m. except Aug.-Sep. combined issue. USD 40 domestic; USD 56 foreign. Ed(s): Carl Goodman. U.S. Department of State, HR/ER/SMG, SA-1, Rm H-236, Washington, DC 20522-0602. Illus. Microform: MIM; PQC. *Indexed:* ABS&EES, IUSGP, PAIS. *Aud.:* Ga, Sa.

State Magazine is published to facilitate communication between management and employees of the State Department at home and abroad and to acquaint employees with developments that may affect operations or personnel. The magazine is also available to persons interested in working for the Department of State and to the general public. While the magazine serves the members of the State Department, it contains interesting articles about people and places all over the world. Online since 1996. URL: http://purl.access.gpo.gov/GPO/LPS356.

Survey of Current Business. See Business/General section.

3343. *Treasury Bulletin.* Incorporates (in 1945): *Annual Report on the Financial Condition and results of the Operations of the Highway Trust Fund.* [ISSN: 0041-2155] 1939. q. USD 46. U.S. Department of the Treasury, Financial Management Service, 3700 East West Highway, Rm 515C, Hyattsville, MD 20782; http://www.fms.treas.gov. Circ: 1900. Microform: CIS; PMC. Online: Factiva, Inc.; OCLC Online Computer Library Center, Inc.; ProQuest LLC (Ann Arbor). *Indexed:* ABIn, AmStI, BLI. *Aud.:* Ga, Sa.

This is a quarterly synopsis of U.S. Department of the Treasury activities, covering financing operations, budget receipts and expenditures, debt operations, cash income and outgo, IRS collections, capital movements, yields of long-term bonds, ownership of federal securities, and other Treasury activities. There are lots of charts and graphs. Regular features include "Profile of the Economy," "Market Yields," "International Statistics," "Capital Movements," "Foreign Currency Positions," and "Federal Debt." Online since March 1996. URL: www.fms.treas.gov/bulletin/index.html.

U.S. Bureau of Labor Statistics. Monthly Labor Review. See Labor and Industrial Relations section.

U.S. Energy Information Administration. Monthly Energy Review. See Energy section.

3344. *Weekly Compilation of Presidential Documents.* [ISSN: 0511-4187] 1965. w. USD 133 domestic; USD 186.20 foreign. U.S. Office of the Federal Register, National Archives and Records Administration, Eighth St and Pennsylvania Ave, NW, Washington, DC 20408; http://www.access.gpo.gov/nara/nara003.html. Illus., index. Circ: 7000. Vol. ends: No. 52. *Indexed:* MASUSE, PAIS. *Aud.:* Ga, Ac, Sa.

Issued every Monday from the White House, this journal contains statements, messages, proclamations, executive orders, radio addresses, speeches, press conferences, communications to Congress and federal agencies, statements regarding bill signings and vetoes, appointments, nominations, reorganization plans, resignations, retirements, acts approved by the president, nominations submitted to the Senate, and White House announcements and press releases. Available in full text online since 1993 and searchable through *GPO Access.* URL: www.gpo.gov/nara/nara003.html.

■ GOVERNMENT PERIODICALS—STATE AND LOCAL

General/State and Municipal Associations

See also City and Regional; Political Science; and Urban Studies sections.

Rosemary L. Meszaros, Coordinator, Government Information and Law, Western Kentucky University, Bowling Green, KY 42101; FAX: 270-745-6175; rosemary.meszaros@wku.edu

Introduction

Most states do not maintain a depository system such as the federal depository program. California, Florida, Virginia, Michigan, South Carolina, and Texas are among the few having a regular arrangement for distributing state documents to designated libraries within their respective states. Documents librarians who specialize in state and local governments are detectives at heart. The trail of many documents, however, leads straight to the web. The Internet has given rise to many states using the web as their publishing medium of choice. The ease of access, the cost savings, and the universality of the Internet makes it an attractive alternative to print. State and local periodicals are focused and give a home-grown coverage that national periodicals do not. Online access is the key to wider distribution, but it is also a worrisome medium to librarians, historians, and others with archival leanings. One daily online service of note is Stateline-e.org: where policy and politics news click (www.stateline.org/live), which is funded by the Pew Charitable Trust. The staff of professional journalists delivers news on state policy innovations and trends, and nourish public debate on state-level issues such as health care, tax and budget policy, environment, and other important issues.

The periodicals in this section cover a variety of local and state issues. Budgeting, the environment, infrastructure, technology, telecommunications, and health care are topics of commonality. Besides these communal concerns, some of the periodicals feature articles on how the policies of the federal government may impact them on a local basis, such as immigration issues. Many also profile state and local government officials. While some of the periodicals in this section may be of interest primarily to state and local officials, most are of interest to residents of the areas. Companion sections in this volume include City and Regional and Urban Studies.

Basic Periodicals

Ga: *Nation's Cities Weekly, State Government News;* Ac: *Governing, Spectrum, State and Local Government Review, State Legislatures.*

Basic Abstracts and Indexes

Lexis-Nexis, Political Science Abstracts, Public Affairs Information Service. Bulletin, Sage Urban Studies Abstracts, Urban Affairs Abstracts.

General

American City & County. See Urban Studies section.

3345. *C P A News (Washington, D.C., Online Edition).* Formerly (until 2002): *Alternatives (Online Edition).* m. Free. Center for Policy Alternatives, 1875 Connecticut Ave, NW, Ste 710, Washington, DC 20009-5728; http://www.stateaction.org. *Aud.:* Ga, Ac, Sa.

The publisher, the Center for Policy Alternatives, describes itself as the nation's only nonpartisan, nonprofit organization working to strengthen the capacity of state legislators to lead and achieve progressive change. Their web site covers links to 130 state policy issues from absentee voting to worker freedom from mandatory meetings. The web site also provides online access to all issues of *CPA News* and its print predecessor, *Alternatives,* after registration. URL: www.stateaction.org/publications.

3346. *CommonWealth: politics, ideas and civic life in Massachusetts.* 1996. q. USD 50. Ed(s): Robert David Sullivan, Michael Jonas. The Massachusetts Institute for a New Common Wealth, 18 Tremont St, Ste 1120, Boston, MA 02108; info@massinc.org; http://www.massinc.org. *Bk. rev.:* Number and length vary. *Aud.:* Ga, Ac, Sa.

The mission of MassINC, publisher of *CommonWealth,* is to develop a public agenda for Massachusetts that promotes the growth and vitality of the middle class. MassINC has four primary initiatives: economic prosperity, lifelong learning, safe neighborhoods, and civic renewal. The publication includes articles, interviews, news, and book reviews. *CommonWealth* calls itself the Bay State's leading political magazine. A *Boston Globe* journalist has called it "snazzy and fair-minded." Web access has been available since summer 1996. Subscribers to the print version are asked for a $50 donation to become a friend of MassINC. Online access is free, but registration is required. URL: www.massinc.org.

3347. *County News.* Formerly: *N A C O News and Views.* [ISSN: 0744-9798] 1970. bi-m. Mon. USD 90. Ed(s): Beverly Schlotterbeck. National Association of Counties, 25 Massachusetts Ave, NW, Washington, DC 20001. Illus. Circ: 27000 Controlled. Vol. ends: Dec. *Aud.:* Sa.

Published by the National Association of Counties (NACo), this journal evaluates issues and policies of interest to county officials nationwide. Sections include "Financial Services News," "HR (Human Resources) Doctor," "Job Market," "News from the Nation's Counties," "Notices," "NACo on the Move," "Profiles in Service" (profiles of county officials), "Research News," and "Web Watch." Full text available online since February 1994 at NACo's web site. URL: www.naco.org/CountyNewsTemplate.cfm?Section=County_News.

3348. *Empire State Report: the magazine of politics and public policy in New York State.* Former titles (until 1989): *Changing Faces;* (until 1985): *Empire State Report Weekly;* (until 1983): *Empire State Report;* (until 1979): *Empire;* (until 1978): *Empire State Report.* [ISSN:

0747-0711] 1974. 10x/yr. USD 19.95 domestic; USD 75 foreign; USD 4.50 newsstand/cover per issue. Ed(s): Stephen H Acunto, Sr. Empire State Report Inc, 25-35 Beechwood Ave, Mt Vernon, NY 10553; epire@cinn.com. Circ: 15600 Paid and controlled. *Indexed:* PAIS. *Bk. rev.:* Number and length vary. *Aud.:* Ga, Ac, Sa.

This magazine of politics, policy, and the business of government in New York State reaches the state's senior municipal and town executives and financial decision makers (mayors, town supervisors, village managers, comptrollers, etc.). Readers also include statewide elected officials, state agency and authority heads, state government managers and senior staff, local and town government officials, public school and college/university administrators, private association executives, and business leaders across the state. *Empire State Report* dissects legislative issues from all angles and presents ideas in an objective fashion to incite balanced and beneficial change. Not available online.

3349. *Governing: the states and localities.* [ISSN: 0894-3842] 1987. m. USD 39.95 domestic (Free to qualified personnel). Ed(s): Peter Harkness. C Q Press, Inc., 1100 Connecticut Ave, Ste 1100, Washington, DC 20036; customerservice@cqpress.com; http://www.cqpress.com. Illus., adv. Circ: 86000 Paid and controlled. Vol. ends: Sep. Online: LexisNexis; OCLC Online Computer Library Center, Inc.; H.W. Wilson. *Indexed:* AgeL, HRIS, LRI, PAIS, RGPR. *Aud.:* Ac, Sa.

The men and women who set policy for and manage the day-to-day operations of cities, counties, and states, as well as such governmental bodies as school boards and special districts, are the primary audience for *Governing,* published by Congressional Quarterly. A past recipient of a *Folio* magazine Editorial Excellence Award, *Governing* also has been nominated several times for National Magazine Awards in the public-interest category and for general excellence in the under-100,000 circulation category. *Governing* posts stories from leading newspapers nationwide on management, policy, technology, and current news, along with links to web sites of interest, such as on city planning, deregulation, tourism, and more. Highlights online at http://governing.com.

3350. *Illinois Issues: a magazine of government and politics.* [ISSN: 0738-9663] 1975. m. USD 35.95 domestic; USD 94.95 foreign. Ed(s): Peggy Boyer Long. University of Illinois at Springfield, PO Box 19243, Springfield, IL 62794-9243; http://www.uis.edu. Illus., adv. Circ: 6500. Vol. ends: Dec. *Indexed:* PAIS. *Bk. rev.:* 1, 1,000 words. *Aud.:* Ga, Ac.

This magazine's mission is to provide fresh, provocative analysis of public policy in Illinois. With a special focus on Illinois government and politics, it pays close attention to current trends and legislative issues and examines the state's quality of life. It also engages its readers in dialogue, enhancing the quality of public discourse in Illinois. A not-for-profit monthly magazine published by the University of Illinois at Springfield, *Illinois Issues* also sponsors and promotes other appropriate public affairs educational activities. Available in full text online since March 2002. The web site also features a blog. URL: http://illinoisissues.uis.edu/index.html.

3351. *Maine Policy Review.* [ISSN: 1064-2587] 1991. 3x/yr. Donation. Ed(s): Jonathan Rubin, Greg Gallant. Margaret Chase Smith Center for Public Policy, 5715 Coburn Hall, University of Maine, Orono, ME 04469-5715; mcsc@umit.maine.edu; http://www.umaine.edu/mcsc/mpr.htm. *Aud.:* Ga, Ac, Sa.

A joint publication of the Margaret Chase Smith Center for Public Policy at the University of Maine. The majority of articles in *Maine Policy Review* are written by Maine citizens, many of whom are readers of the journal. It publishes independent analyses of public policy issues relevant to Maine by providing accurate information and thoughtful commentary. Issues range from snowmobiling to housing. Most issues since 1994 are on the web site. URL: www.umaine.edu/mcsc/MPR/archives/Archive.htm.

3352. *Nation's Cities Weekly.* Formed by the merger of (1978-1978): *City Weekly;* (1963-1978): *Nation's Cities.* [ISSN: 0164-5935] 1978. w. Free to members; Non-members, USD 96. Ed(s): Cyndy Liedtke, Amy Elsbree. National League of Cities, 1301 Pennsylvania Ave, NW, Ste

550, Washington, DC 20004; http://www.nlc.org. Illus., adv. Circ: 30000 Paid and free. Vol. ends: Dec. Microform: PQC. Online: Florida Center for Library Automation; Gale; Northern Light Technology, Inc. *Indexed:* LRI, PAIS. *Aud.:* Ga, Sa.

This tabloid provides up-to-the-minute news on how national developments will affect cities, in-depth reports and case studies on how local governments are finding innovative solutions to today's municipal problems, and special editorial features by urban affairs experts. It includes regular reporting on developments in Congress and the Bush administration, the courts, and state government. To supplement this extensive coverage, *Nation's Cities Weekly* provides special reports throughout the year on key topics of interest to local government leaders on finance, the environment, housing, technology, economic development, and telecommunications, as well as extensive coverage of the National League of Cities' two annual conventions. Regular monthly columns feature news about technologies, products, and services of interest to local governments and a roundup of news about how cities are solving today's problems and improving services to citizens. Online since 2003 on the National League of Cities web site. URL: www.nlc.org/articles/current_issue.aspx.

3353. *North Carolina Insight.* 1978. s-a. Free to members. Ed(s): Mebane Rash Whitman. North Carolina Center for Public Policy Research, Inc., PO Box 430, Raleigh, NC 27602; http://www.nando.net/insider/nccppr. Adv. Circ: 1000 Paid. *Indexed:* AgeL, PSA. *Aud.:* Ga, Ac, Sa.

The mission of the North Carolina Center for Public Policy Research is to create a more well-informed public and more effective, accountable, and responsive government by examining public policy issues that face North Carolina and enrich the dialogue among three constituencies: the public, the media, and policy makers. Based on their research and published studies, the center sometimes makes recommendations on public policy issues. *North Carolina Insight* features pro and con debates on issues such as education, the lottery, infrastructure, funding for the arts, voter turnout, and elections. Not available online.

3354. *Pennsylvania Township News.* [ISSN: 0162-5160] 1948. m. USD 34. Ed(s): Ginni Linn. Pennsylvania State Association of Township Supervisors, 4855 Woodland Dr, Enola, PA 17025; psatsweb@psats.org; http://www.psats.org. Illus., adv. Circ: 10000 Paid and free. Vol. ends: Dec. *Aud.:* Sa.

Regular features of *Pennsylvania Township News* include "Legislative Update," "Environmental Digest," "Newsworthy Items," "One Source Municipal Training?" (a listing and description of courses offered to township officials), and a "Questions & Answers" column. Articles deal with common interests to the over 1,450 Pennsylvania member townships: stormwater drainage, animal control, recycling, etc. There are also interviews with top-ranking township officials. Table of contents is online. Articles online available to subscribers only.

3355. *Popular Government.* [ISSN: 0032-4515] 1931. 3x/yr. USD 20. Ed(s): John B Stephens. University of North Carolina at Chapel Hill, School of Government, Knapp-Sanders Bldg, CB #3330, Chapel Hill, NC 27599-3330; khunt@sog.unc.edu; http://www.sogpubs.unc.edu. Illus., index. Circ: 7700 Paid and free. Microform: PQC. Online: EBSCO Publishing, EBSCO Host. *Indexed:* CJA, HRIS, PAIS. *Bk. rev.:* 1, 2,000 words. *Aud.:* Ga, Ac.

Directed to approximately 7,500 North Carolina state and local public officials, *Popular Government* contains articles on tax and finance, budgeting and purchasing, management and personnel, social services, education, justice and corrections, environmental protection, land use, and other topics of importance to governmental administration and public policy. Many of the articles are written by members of the faculty of the Institute of Government of the University of North Carolina at Chapel Hill. Others are written by specialists and practitioners in appropriate fields. Selected articles online since 1999. URL: www.iog.unc.edu/popgov.

3356. *Privatization Watch.* Formerly (until 1988): *Fiscal Watchdog.* 1976. m. USD 135 (Individuals, USD 135; Non-profit organizations, USD 75). Ed(s): Jacobs Fellow. Reason Foundation, 3415 S Sepulveda Blvd, Ste 400, Los Angeles, CA 90034-6060; chrism@reason.com; http://www.reason.org/pwatch.html. Adv. Circ: 25000. *Aud.:* Ga, Ac.

Each issue concerns a specific topic: education, environment, corrections, public safety, and other subjects of interest. Published by the Public Policy Institute of the Reason Foundation, a public policy think tank promoting choice, competition, and a dynamic market economy as the foundation for human dignity and progress. Coverage of public-private partnerships is worldwide. Articles are full-text online since 2004 at www.reason.org/pw.shtml. From December 2002, issues are online at www.rppi.org/privwatch.shtml.

3357. *Public Management: devoted to the conduct of local government.* [ISSN: 0033-3611] 1918. m. 11/yr. USD 36 domestic; USD 52 foreign. Ed(s): Beth Payne. International City/County Management Association, 777 N Capitol St, N E Ste 500, Washington, DC 20002-4201; http://www.icma.org. Illus., adv. Circ: 13000 Paid. Vol. ends: Dec. Microform: MIM; PQC. Online: EBSCO Publishing, EBSCO Host; Florida Center for Library Automation; Gale; Northern Light Technology, Inc.; OCLC Online Computer Library Center, Inc.; ProQuest LLC (Ann Arbor); H.W. Wilson. *Indexed:* ABIn, BPI, PAIS, PRA. *Aud.:* Ga, Sa.

The International City/County Management Association (ICMA) is the publisher of *Public Management.* ICMA is the professional and educational organization for chief appointed managers, administrators, and assistants in cities, towns, counties, and regional entities throughout the world. Feature articles are written from the local government manager's point of view. The intent of the articles is to allow other local government managers to adapt solutions to fit their own situations. Regular sections include letters to the editor, profiles of individual officials and corporate entities, book reviews, an ethics column, and FYI news briefs. Articles online are passworded but available to ICMA members and subscribers to *Public Management.* Online since 2003. URL: www.icma.org/pm/info/about.cfm.

3358. *State and Local Government Review: a journal of research and viewpoints on state and local government issues.* Supersedes: *Georgia Government Review.* [ISSN: 0160-323X] 1968. 3x/yr. USD 35 (Individuals, USD 22). Ed(s): Michael Scicchitano. University of Georgia, Carl Vinson Institute of Government, 201 N Milledge Ave, Athens, GA 30602-5482; http://www.cviog.uga.edu/. Illus., index. Refereed. Circ: 1000. Vol. ends: Fall. *Indexed:* ABCPolSci, HRA, IBR, IBZ, IPSA, PAIS, PRA, PSA, SUSA. *Bk. rev.:* 1, 1,000 words. *Aud.:* Ac, Sa.

State and Local Government Review is jointly sponsored by the Carl Vinson Institute of Government of the University of Georgia and the Section on Intergovernmental Administration and Management (SIAM) of the American Society for Public Administration (ASPA). SIAM is the section of ASPA dedicated to state and local as well as intergovernmental teaching and research. Membership in SIAM includes a subscription to *State and Local Government Review.* Issues include feature stories and the "Practitioner's Corner," offering practical advice for government officials on issues such as local government, federalism, telecommunications, utility deregulation, etc. This is one of the few scholarly journals in this field. Contents and abstracts of articles are available for the most recent issue. Full text is available for previous issues from 1993 forward through the Carl Vinson Institute of Government. Online since 1993. Abstracts only, 1993-1996; abstracts and full text, 1997 to the present. URL: www.cviog.uga.edu/publications/slgr/issues.php.

3359. *State Legislatures.* [ISSN: 0147-6041] 1975. m. 10/yr. USD 49 domestic; USD 55 Canada. Ed(s): Sharon Randall, Karen Hansen. National Conference of State Legislatures, 7700 E First Pl, Denver, CO 80230; http://www.ncsl.org. Illus., adv. Circ: 18208. Vol. ends: Dec. Online: Florida Center for Library Automation; Gale; LexisNexis; Northern Light Technology, Inc.; OCLC Online Computer Library Center, Inc.; ProQuest K-12 Learning Solutions; ProQuest LLC (Ann Arbor). *Indexed:* MASUSE, PAIS, SUSA. *Aud.:* Ga, Ac.

The trends, issues, solutions, personalities, innovations, and challenges of managing a state—they will all be found in *State Legislatures* magazine, published by the National Conference of State Legislatures. This national magazine of state government and policy provides lively, insightful articles encompassing vital information on public policies. From agriculture to cloning to transportation, a wide variety of topics are covered. Only excerpts are available online for nonsubscribers; full access for subscribers. URL: www.ncsl.org/magazine.

3360. *State Net Capitol Journal.* [ISSN: 1521-8457] 1998. w. USD 1800 Online ed. (Free to qualified personnel Online ed.). Ed(s): Rich Ehisen. State Net, 2101 K St, Sacramento, CA 95816; statenet@statenet.com; http://www.statenet.com. *Aud.:* Ga, Ac, Sa.

State Net produces *State Net Capitol Journal*, which provides a comprehensive look at the issues and politics driving state governments all over the country. The 50-state edition covers major trends in the spotlight, from Augusta to Honolulu, featuring original reporting from its team of editors, from governors' agendas to legislative hot topics. It also provides an entertaining and informative array of notes and quotes, selecting information from numerous publications around the country. Subscriptions are free to qualified readers, that is, government affairs professionals. URL: www.statenet.com/resources.

3361. *State News (Lexington).* Formerly: *State Government News;* Which incorporated (in 1978): *Legislative Session Sheet.* [ISSN: 1549-3628] 1958. m. USD 55. Ed(s): Elaine Stuart. Council of State Governments, 2760 Research Park Dr, Box 11910, Lexington, KY 40578-1910; info@csg.org; http://www.csg.org/. Illus., adv. Circ: 17000. Vol. ends: Nov/Dec. Microform: WSH. Online: EBSCO Publishing, EBSCO Host; Gale. *Indexed:* AgeL, PAIS, SUSA. *Aud.:* Ga, Sa.

For more than 40 years, *State News* magazine, formerly called *State Government News*, has been a source of nonpartisan information. It offers updates and in-depth analyses of state programs, policies, and trends in the executive, legislative, and judicial branches in areas such as health and human services, environment and natural resources, agriculture and rural policy, public safety and justice, education, energy, transportation, telecommunications, digital government, fiscal policy, economic development, state leadership, state management and administration, federalism and intergovernmental relations, interstate relations, election coverage, emergency management, and more. Online since 2000. URL: www.csg.org/pubs/statenews.aspx.

3362. *State Politics & Policy Quarterly.* [ISSN: 1532-4400] 2000. q. USD 120 print & online eds. (Individuals, USD 42 print & online eds.). Ed(s): Richard Winters, Ronald Weber. University of Illinois Press, 1325 S Oak St, Champaign, IL 61820-6903; journals@uillinois.edu; http://www.press.uillinois.edu. Refereed. *Indexed:* AmH&L, HistAb, IBSS, PAIS, PSA, SSCI, SociolAb. *Bk. rev.:* Number and length vary. *Aud.:* Ac, Sa.

The mission of *State Politics & Policy Quarterly* is to stimulate research on state politics and policy and to provide an institutional structure to develop a progressive and coherent research agenda in the field. Online access to subscribers. All may view tables of contents and abstracts online. URL: http://cspl.uis.edu/InstituteForLegislativeStudies/SPPQ.

3363. *Virginia Review.* Formerly (until 1981): *Virginia Municipal Review.* [ISSN: 0732-9156] 1924. bi-m. USD 18. Ed(s): Alyson L Taylor White. Review Publications, Inc., 4218 Old Hundred Rd, Chester, VA 23831; rhabeck@mindspring.com; http://www.reviewnet.com. Illus., adv. Circ: 5000 Paid and controlled. Vol. ends: Nov/Dec. *Aud.:* Sa.

A professional journal for officials at all levels of government in the Commonwealth of Virginia, *Virginia Review* prints articles describing specific problems faced by localities and how the problems were solved, as well as employee relations, planning for growth, and economic development, among other topics. Each issue focuses on a specific theme. The journal does not include political articles or those that have the sole purpose of selling a product or concept. Online since March/April 2004. URL: www.vareview.com/index2.asp.

State and Municipal Associations

The primary objectives for periodicals from State and Municipal Associations are to offer a medium for the exchange of ideas and information and a discussion

forum on issues of interest to local officials. Common problems and issues such as legislation, growth, lotteries, traffic, crime, disaster preparedness, economy, energy, immigration, telecommunications and leadership usually form the substance of feature articles. In addition, many include a calendar, a solutions column, and a legal advice column. Many of them have an upbeat, enthusiastic, optimistic tone winding through them but most contain matter-of-fact articles on confronting and solving problems. Practitioners and observers of municipal government are the principal audience for these periodicals.

3364. *Actionlines Magazine.* 4x/yr. USD 50. Indiana Association of Cities and Towns, 200 S Meridian, Ste 340, Indianapolis, IN 46225; http://www.citiesandtowns.org. Circ: 4500. *Aud.:* Ga, Ac, Sa.

Actionlines is the official magazine of the Indiana Association of Cities and Towns. It includes relevant, timely articles about issues affecting Indiana cities and towns and municipal government. Not available online.

3365. *Alabama Municipal Journal.* [ISSN: 0002-4309] 1935. m. USD 24. Ed(s): Carrie Banks. Alabama League of Municipalities, 535 Adams Ave, Box 1270, Montgomery, AL 36102. Illus., adv. Circ: 4500 Paid and controlled. Vol. ends: Jun. *Aud.:* Sa.

From the Alabama League of Municipalities, the articles in this periodical highlight the practical issues faced by local governments in Alabama and spotlight common problems, solutions, trends, and legal information. It offers reprints of speeches and articles from other publications from time to time. Unrestricted Internet access since the June 2006 issue. URL: www.alalm.org/Journal/Journal%20Archive.htm.

3366. *Cities and Villages.* [ISSN: 0009-7535] 1953. 6x/yr. USD 10. Ed(s): Cynthia L Grant. Ohio Municipal League, 175 S Third St, Ste 510, Columbus, OH 43215-5134; http://www.omlohio.org/. Illus., index. Circ: 10000. *Aud.:* Ga, Ac, Sa.

The official publication of the Ohio Municipal League, *Cities and Villages* is read by officials who are directly involved in every aspect of municipal management and service. The magazine keeps the leadership of Ohio's cities and villages informed about current developments and the latest techniques for solving municipal problems. Not available online.

3367. *City & Town.* Formerly: *Arkansas Municipalities.* [ISSN: 0193-8371] 1947. m. USD 15; USD 1.50 newsstand/cover per issue. Arkansas Municipal League, PO Box 38, North Little Rock, AR 72115-0038; jkw@arml.org; http://www.arml.org. Illus., index, adv. Circ: 6800 Paid and free. Vol. ends: Dec. *Aud.:* Sa.

Designed to provide a forum for municipal officials to exchange ideas and compare notes on accomplishments and problems in Arkansas, *City & Town* is sent to elected officials, city administrators and managers, police chiefs, fire chiefs and other department heads, and state officials, local newspapers, chambers of commerce, and other offices and persons who are interested in municipal affairs. Employment opportunities and classified ads are spotlighted in the "Municipal Mart" section. Selected articles for 2005 and pdf full text from 2006 appear online at www.arml.org/publications_city_town.html.

3368. *City Magazine.* Former titles: *Kentucky City;* (until 1968): *Kentucky City Bulletin.* 1929. q. Ed(s): Sylvia L Lovely, Robert S Bryant. Kentucky League of Cities, 101 E Vine St, Ste 600, Lexington, KY 40507-3700; city@klc.org; http://www.klc.org. Illus., adv. Circ: 27130 Controlled. *Aud.:* Sa.

This award-winning magazine is the official magazine of the Kentucky League of Cities (KLC) and is Kentucky's only magazine dedicated specifically to city and municipal issues. It covers critical topics, profiles people, events and innovative initiatives and practices in Kentucky's cities. Each issue has one primary theme, such as the impact of immigration, disaster planning, the brain drain, aging population, and environment. Lavishly illustrated. Online since 2004. URL: www.klc.org/sectionArticles.asp?section=100&article=280&bct=Home/KLC%20Publications/Magazines%20%26%20Newsletters/City%20Magazine.

3369. City Scan (Bismarck). Formerly (until 1996): *North Dakota League of Cities Bulletin.* [ISSN: 1094-5784] 1969. 10x/yr. Free to qualified personnel. Ed(s): Connie Sprynczynatyk. North Dakota League of Cities, 410 E. Front Ave., Bismarck, ND 58504; http://www.ndlc.org/. Illus., adv. Circ: 2850. *Aud.:* Sa.

Written specifically for city and park district officials and designed to promote best municipal practices, the magazine regularly features information about technology, cost-saving ideas, innovative programs, leadership issues, and products and services that help city leaders increase the efficiency and effectiveness of municipal operations. Selected articles online only. URL: www.ndlc.org/index.asp.

3370. Cityscape (Des Moines). Formerly (until 1995): *Iowa Municipalities.* [ISSN: 1088-5951] 1960. m. Free to members. Ed(s): Betsy Knoblock. Iowa League of Cities, 317 Sixth Ave, Ste 800, Des Moines, IA 50309-4111. Illus., adv. Circ: 5500 Paid. Vol. ends: Jun. *Indexed:* AmStI, CJA, JEL. *Aud.:* Sa.

Cityscape is part of the membership benefits of the Iowa League of Cities. The publication contains articles about city government issues in Iowa and serves as a communication tool for local government officials. Some of the articles featured in *Cityscape* are available online in a Q&A section on the league's web site. Full text not available online.

3371. Colorado Municipalities. [ISSN: 0010-1664] 1925. bi-m. USD 20. Ed(s): Traci Stoffel. Colorado Municipal League, 1144 Sherman St, Denver, CO 80203-2207; http://www.cml.org. Illus., adv. Circ: 4900. *Indexed:* PAIS. *Bk. rev.:* Number and length vary. *Aud.:* Ga, Ac, Sa.

This is the flagship magazine of the Colorado Municipal League. Its target audience is Colorado municipal government officials. Each issue runs to about 30 pages and is packed with in-depth coverage of the topics and issues important to those officials. Not available online.

3372. Connecticut Town & City. 19??. bi-m. Free to members; Non-members, USD 18. Connecticut Conference of Municipalities, 900 Chapel St, New Haven, CT 06510; ccm@ccm-ct.org; http://www.ccm-ct.org. Circ: 7000. *Aud.:* Sa.

Reports on major intergovernmental issues, new ideas in municipal management, and cost-saving measures by towns. Regular features include Regional and Intermunicipal Cooperation, Innovative Ideas For Managing Local Governments, Civic Amenities (which includes beautification projects, noise and litter abatement, and other ideas to make communities better places), Volunteers, Municipal Ethics Quiz, What's New, and Public-Private Cooperation. Not available online.

3373. Creating Quality Cities. Formerly (until 199?): *City Report.* bi-m. Ed(s): Ken Harward. Association of Idaho Cities, 3100 S. Vista Ave., Ste. 310, Boise, ID 83705-7335; tclark@idahocities.org; http://www.idahocities.org. Adv. *Aud.:* Ga, Ac, Sa.

News, job openings in city government from around Idaho, a calendar of events listing conferences, workshops and institutes, profiles of city officials, grant opportunities, and a Q&A section on legislative issues makes this newsletter of interest to government officials and citizens alike. Online issues begin with March 2004. URL: www.idahocities.org/index.asp?Type=B_BASIC&SEC=%7B2A5B670F-2B72-4DCC-9521-A0A6AEF6402A%7D.

3374. Georgia's Cities. Former titles: *Urban Georgia; Georgia Municipal Journal.* 1951. m. USD 36. Georgia Municipal Association, 201 Pryor St, SW, Atlanta, GA 30303-3606; info@gmanet.com; http://www.gmanet.com. Adv. Circ: 7300 Free. *Aud.:* Ga, Ac, Sa.

Georgia's Cities is sometimes referred to as *Georgia's Cities Newspaper* and resembles a newspaper in layout. The articles follow the newspaper format; there are several columns including a question-and-answer column, district roundup, and city desk. Online since April 2006. URL: www.gmanet.com/georgia_cities_newspaper.

3375. Illinois Municipal Review: the magazine of the municipalities. [ISSN: 0019-2139] 1922. m. USD 10 (Free to members). Ed(s): Ken Alderson, Gary Koch. Illinois Municipal League, PO Box 5180, Springfield, IL 62705-5180; gkoch@iml.org; http://www.iml.org. Illus., adv. Circ: 13500 Controlled. Vol. ends: Dec. *Aud.:* Sa.

A legal Q&A, municipal calendar, exchange column, editorials, and a variety of articles of interest to local Illinois government officials make up this long-running magazine. Available online back to 1956. URL: www.lib.niu.edu/ipo/imlistyrs.html.

3376. Kansas Government Journal. [ISSN: 0022-8613] 1914. m. USD 30. Ed(s): Kim Gulley. League of Kansas Municipalities, 300 SW Eighth St, Topeka, KS 66603-3912; kgulley@lkm.org; http://www.lkm.org. Illus., index, adv. Circ: 6200 Paid. Vol. ends: Dec. *Aud.:* Sa.

This periodical keeps Kansas officials up-to-date on federal and statewide legislation as well as economic developments and budgetary procedures impacting municipalities. It also focuses on new ways of solving problems and assisting citizens. A subject index appears in the December issue. Not available online.

3377. Local Focus. m. USD 44. Ed(s): Kevin Toon. League of Oregon Cities, PO Box 928, Salem, OR 97308; loc@orcities.org; http://www.orcities.org. *Aud.:* Ga, Ac, Sa.

Includes regular updates on state and federal matters, League of Oregon Cities news, city happenings and best practices, feature articles, a calendar of events, helpful publications, summaries of legal cases, and a list of job openings. Issues since January 2005 are available online. URL: www.orcities.org/Publications/Newsletters/tabid/873/Default.aspx

3378. Louisiana Municipal Review. [ISSN: 0164-3622] 1938. m. Ed(s): Tom Ed McHugh. Louisiana Municipal Association, PO Box 4327, Baton Rouge, LA 70821; lamunicipalassociation@compuserve.com; http://www.lamunis.org. Adv. Circ: 3300 Paid and controlled. *Aud.:* Ga, Ac, Sa.

The official publication of the Louisiana Municipal Association, a statewide league of villages, towns, and cities in Louisiana, *Louisiana Municipal Review* serves as a medium of exchange of ideas and information on municipal affairs for the public officials of Louisiana. It includes news articles, features, obituaries, and a column written by the state's governor. Online for one calendar year. URL: http://lma.org/LMR/lmr.htm.

3379. Michigan Municipal Review. [ISSN: 0026-2331] 1928. 10x/yr. Free to members. Ed(s): Judi C Lintott. Michigan Municipal League, 1675 Green Rd, Ann Arbor, MI 48106; http://www.mml.org/. Illus., index, adv. Circ: 11300 Controlled. Vol. ends: Dec. Microform: PQC. *Indexed:* PAIS. *Aud.:* Sa.

This periodical aims to provide a forum to Michigan officials for the exchange of ideas and information. Municipal officials, consultants, legislators, and staff members of the Michigan Municipal League contribute to the publication. Want ads, a marketplace column, a municipal calendar, and legal spotlights round out the issues. Online to members only. There is an RSS feed on the web. URL: www.mml.org/rss/subscribe.htm.

3380. Minnesota Cities. Formerly (until 1976): *Minnesota Municipalities.* [ISSN: 0148-8546] 1916. 10x/yr. USD 40. Ed(s): Erica Norris Perlman. League of Minnesota Cities, 145 University Ave W, St Paul, MN 55103-2044; webmaster@lmnc.org; http://www.lmnc.org. Illus., adv. Circ: 7300 Controlled. *Indexed:* PAIS. *Aud.:* Ga, Ac, Sa.

The League of Minnesota Cities' monthly magazine includes articles on a wide range of city-related topics. Each issue is based on a theme—for example, human resources, technology, and winter. Highlights of the current issue are on their web site. URL: www.lmnc.org/library/magazine.cfm.

3381. Mississippi Municipalities. [ISSN: 0026-6337] 1955. bi-m. USD 16. Ed(s): Hollidae M Robinson. Mississippi Municipal League, 600 E Amite St, Ste 104, Jackson, MS 39201-1906. Illus., adv. Circ: 3300. *Aud.:* Ga, Ac, Sa.

Mississippi Municipalities contains feature articles as well as an auditor's column and a column about tax collections. The second issue is the annual conference issue. Online since Fall 2006. URL: www.mmlonline.com.

3382. Missouri Municipal Review. [ISSN: 0026-6647] 1936. 10x/yr. USD 25. Ed(s): Katie Bradley. Missouri Municipal League, 1727 Southridge Dr, Jefferson City, MO 65109; http://www.mocities.com. Illus., index, adv. Circ: 6250 Paid and free. *Aud.:* Ga, Ac, Sa.

Designed to meet the needs and interests of municipal officials in Missouri, it features articles on all phases of municipal government and serves as a medium through which member officials can exchange ideas on current issues. Selected articles available online. Three special issues are published each year: Parks and Recreation (May), Public Works (June), and Pre-Conference (August). Feature articles only are online at www.mocities.com/default.asp?SectionID=53.

3383. Municipal Advocate. Formerly (until 1988): *Municipal Forum.* [ISSN: 1046-2422] 1980. q. Members, USD 49; Non-members, USD 99. Ed(s): John Ouellette. Massachusetts Municipal Association, 60 Temple Place, Boston, MA 02111. Adv. Circ: 4525. *Aud.:* Ga, Ac, Sa.

Presents in-depth articles about important and timely municipal issues, such as budgeting, technology, management, infrastructure maintenance, education, and legal issues. An emphasis is placed on innovative solutions and problem-solving strategies. Not available online.

3384. Municipal Bulletin. 1941. bi-m. Ed(s): Jennifer Purcell. New York Conference of Mayors and Municipal Officials. Circ: 7000. *Aud.:* Ga, Ac, Sa.

Municipal Bulletin, a resource for expanded coverage of NYCOM activities and events, reports on legislative and other developments at the state and federal levels, presents in-depth analysis of special issues, affiliate news, and the latest information on the municipal legal front. Available online only to members.

3385. Municipal Maryland. Formerly: *Maryland Municipal News.* [ISSN: 0196-9986] 1948. 9x/yr. USD 35. Ed(s): Karen Bohlen. Maryland Municipal League, Inc., 1212 West St, Annapolis, MD 21401. Adv. Circ: 2000. *Aud.:* Ga, Ac, Sa.

Municipal Maryland features articles on a variety of city/town topics such as downtown revitalization, public works, financial management, conducting effective council meetings, consensus building, legal and personnel issues, recreation, and public safety. Regular columns include Small Town News, Innovations, and City Beat (news about large municipalities). The November issue features articles summarizing the general sessions and most of the workshops from the Maryland Municipal League's annual summer convention. Registration information for the annual convention is published in the March issue; registration information for the league's legislative conference is published in the July/August issue. Selected articles are available online. URL: www.mdmunicipal.org/publications/magazine.cfm.

3386. The Municipality. [ISSN: 0027-3597] 1900. m. USD 18; USD 1.75 per issue. Ed(s): Jean Staral. League of Wisconsin Municipalities, 122 W Washington Ave, Ste 300, Madison, WI 53703; http://www.lwm-info.org. Illus., index, adv. Circ: 9600 Paid and controlled. Vol. ends: Dec. *Indexed:* PAIS. *Aud.:* Sa.

From mosquito control to complex legal matters, this periodical showcases issues of interest to local government officials in Wisconsin. News about local officials, web links of interest, and a calendar are also included. Full text of the current edition can be found on the web under Resources at www.wileague.govoffice2.com.

3387. Nebraska Municipal Review. [ISSN: 0028-1905] 1930. m. USD 50; USD 5 per issue. Ed(s): Lynn Marienau. League of Nebraska Municipalities, 1335 L St, Lincoln, NE 68508; info@lonm.org; http://www.lonm.org. Illus., adv. Circ: 3300. *Indexed:* PAIS. *Bk. rev.:* Number and length vary. *Aud.:* Ga, Ac, Sa.

This official publication of the League of Nebraska Municipalities features articles on laws and issues affecting local government, government officials, leadership, and training. Not available online.

3388. New Hampshire Town & City. [ISSN: 0545-171X] m. 10/yr. Members, USD 22; Non-members, USD 30. Ed(s): Eleanor M Baron. New Hampshire Municipal Association, 25 Triangle Park Dr, PO Box 617, Concord, NH 03302-0617; nhma@nhmunicipal.org; http://www.nhmuicipal.org. Adv. Circ: 2800. *Aud.:* Ga, Ac, Sa.

Provides local officials and others with 40–60 pages of timely information on legal issues, legislative issues, upcoming programs, and services of the local government center. Selected articles from past issues are available online through topical links, such as Finance and Taxation, Land Use, Liability, and Governance. URL: www.nhlgc.org/LGCWebSite/InfoForOfficials/townandcityarticles.htm.

3389. New Jersey Municipalities. [ISSN: 0028-5846] 1917. m. Oct.-Jun. Members, USD 16; Non-members, USD 18. Ed(s): William G Dressel, Jr. New Jersey State League of Municipalities, 222 W State St, Trenton, NJ 08608. Illus., index, adv. Circ: 8200. Vol. ends: Dec. *Indexed:* PAIS, SFSA, SUSA. *Aud.:* Sa.

Typical lead articles are on such topics as public-private partnerships, energy, and urban sprawl. Columns include "Legal Q&A," "Legislative Update," "Labor Relations," "Washington Watch," job notices, and a calendar. Selected articles are available online at www.njslom.org/maghome.html.

3390. New Mexico Municipal League. Municipal Reporter. [ISSN: 0028-6257] 1959. m. USD 20. Ed(s): William F Fulginiti. New Mexico Municipal League, 1229 Paseo de Peralta, Box 846, Santa Fe, NM 87504-0846. Adv. Circ: 1700. *Aud.:* Ga, Ac, Sa.

The New Mexico Municipal League has produced this monthly newsletter for many years. There is a link to municipal job openings, and a regular column titled *HR Insights* tackles personnel policy and problems in a Q&A format. Online publication begins with the October 2006 edition. URL: www.nmml.org/2006%20Municipal%20Reporter.htm.

3391. Quality Cities. Formerly: *Florida Municipal Record.* [ISSN: 0892-4171] 1928. 6x/yr. Members, USD 10; Non-members, USD 20. Ed(s): Beth Mulrennan. Florida League of Cities, Inc., 301 S Bronough St, Ste 300, Tallahassee, FL 32301. Illus., adv. Circ: 4700 Paid. Vol. ends: May. *Aud.:* Ga, Sa.

Quality Cities serves as a medium for exchange of ideas and information for Florida's municipal officials. Reporting addresses legislation affecting cities, current municipal issues, and innovative local-government ideas. The two summer issues cover the post-legislative session report and the Florida League of Cities conference. Not available online.

3392. South Dakota Municipalities. [ISSN: 0300-6182] 1934. m. USD 30. Ed(s): Carrie Harer. South Dakota Municipal League, 214 E Capitol, Pierre, SD 57501. Adv. Circ: 2800 Paid and free. *Aud.:* Ga, Ac, Sa.

The magazine contains articles on legislation, court decisions, attorney general opinions, and issues that affect municipal operations on a daily basis. Not available online.

3393. Tennessee Town and City. [ISSN: 0040-3415] 1950. s-m. USD 15; USD 1 per issue. Ed(s): Gael B Stahl. Tennessee Municipal League, 226 Capitol Blvd, Ste 710, Nashville, TN 37219-1894; gstahl@tml1.org; http://www.tml1.org. Illus., index, adv. Circ: 6250 Controlled. *Indexed:* PAIS. *Aud.:* Ga, Ac, Sa.

Tennessee Town and City looks like a newspaper. It has numerous photographs of the subjects of its news items. There is a classified ad section. In addition to distribution by subscription, free copies of *Tennessee Town and City* can be picked up in various newspaper stands in Nashville in the Legislative Plaza and the State Capitol. Online since July 2006. URL: www.tml1.org/tn_town_city/index.htm.

3394. Texas Town & City. Former titles (until 1994): *T M L Texas Town & City;* (until 1984): *Texas Town & City.* [ISSN: 1084-5356] 1914. 11x/yr. USD 30. Ed(s): Karla Vining. Texas Municipal League, 1821 Rutherford Ln, Ste 400, Austin, TX 78754-5128. Illus., adv. Circ: 11800 Controlled. *Indexed:* SUSA. *Aud.:* Ga, Ac, Sa.

The official publication of the Texas Municipal League, it sets its sights on alerting member cities to important governmental or private sector actions or proposed actions that may affect city operations. Not available online.

3395. The Touchstone. q. Ed(s): Jeremy Woodrow. Alaska Municipal League, 217 Second St, Ste 200, Juneau, AK 99801-1267; http://www.akml.org. *Aud.:* Ga, Ac, Sa.

Legislative matters, job openings, a business card section, and news of the Alaska Municipal League's conference dominate this official newsletter. When the Alaska State Legislature is in session, *The Touchstone* is supplemented by the electronic weekly *AML Legislative Bulletin*. These publications are sent free to member municipalities, associates, and affiliates. Available online since January 2006. URL: www.akml.org/touchstone.html.

3396. U S Mayor. Former titles: *Mayor; United States Municipal News.* [ISSN: 1049-2119] 1934. s-m. USD 35. Ed(s): J Thomas Cochran. United States Conference of Mayors, 1620 Eye St, NW, Washington, DC 20006. Illus., adv. Circ: 5000. *Aud.:* Sa.

Although its present title includes the word newspaper, this publication takes the form of a newsletter or news magazine. Sections include Front Page, Executive Director's Column, About the Mayor (featuring a particular mayor), Washington Outlook, U.S. Mayor Articles (usually about a dozen articles on mayors around the nation), and a Calendar of Events. Online since August 1996. URL: www.usmayors.org/uscm/us_mayor_newspaper.

3397. Virginia Town & City. [ISSN: 0042-6784] 1966. m. Members, USD 8; Non-members, USD 16. Ed(s): David Parsons. Virginia Municipal League, PO Box 12164, Richmond, VA 23241-0164. Illus., adv. Circ: 5000 Paid and controlled. *Bk. rev.:* Number and length vary. *Aud.:* Ga, Ac, Sa.

Each issue is devoted to a single theme. Typical themes include the digital divide, terrorism, budgets, urban planning, and records management. Available on the web since September 2006. URL: www.vml.org/VTC/VTCindex.html.

3398. W A M News. Former titles (until 1979): *W A M News Bulletin;* (until 1961): *News Bulletin.* 19??. m. Free to members. Ed(s): Ginger Newman. Wyoming Association of Municipalities, 315 W 27th St, Cheyenne, WY 82001. Circ: 2000. *Aud.:* Ga, Ac, Sa.

WAM News is the official newsletter of the Wyoming Association of Municipalities and serves as an exchange of ideas and information for officials of municipalities. It has a broad audience of local and state elected officials, along with state agencies, businesses, and associations involved in local government. In addition to news, there is a calendar of events, a professional directory, and municipal ads, including job vacancies. Online since April 2007. URL: www.wyomuni.org.

3399. Western City. Formerly (until 1976): *Western City Magazine.* [ISSN: 0279-5337] 1924. m. USD 39 domestic (Students, USD 26.50). Ed(s): Jude Hudson. League of California Cities, 1400 K St, 4th Floor, Sacramento, CA 95814-3916; http://www.cacities.org. Illus., index, adv. Circ: 10500 Paid and controlled. Vol. ends: Dec. *Indexed:* HistAb, PAIS. *Aud.:* Sa.

Both practical ideas and bigger-picture policy issues and trends are the twin goals of *Western City*. The magazine's stated mission is to support and serve elected and appointed city officials (and those interested in local government), and to examine the policy, process, and fiscal issues that affect local government, and to do so from a number of angles, including individual city success stories, legal analyses, and statewide perspectives. Online since September 2004. URL: www.westerncity.com/index.jsp?displaytype=?ion=art&zone=wcm&sub_sec=art_past.

■ HEALTH AND FITNESS

Jennifer Pollock, Assistant Librarian, Yale Center for British Art, Yale University, New Haven, CT 06511, jennifer.pollock@yale.edu

Introduction

With obesity being on the verge of surpassing smoking as the number one cause of preventable death in the United States, human health and fitness are becoming a subject that we the people are finally paying attention to. Furthermore, we are increasingly seeking information regarding the health and fitness of the planet as the consequences of our careless and aggressive consumption of the earth's resources are seemingly just now becoming realized. Therefore, a lot of information in the form of health and fitness publications is out there, helping people learn how to eat well, exercise, and reduce global warming by way of making minor, and sometimes major, lifestyle adjustments.

Many publications highlighted in this section are "popular," some are focused on women's issues, and some are focused on men. Many are directed toward a wide-ranging, general readership. Some are stylish, light, and fun, while others are serious and academic, but each offers something for someone. Also, almost every publication included in this section has a web site that offers some free info and tips, general information about the publication itself, and sometimes, full-text articles. My hope is that you find this section useful in selecting the health and fitness publications that best suit your particular interests and needs.

Basic Periodicals

ConsumerReports on Health; F D A Consumer; Fitness; Harvard Health Letter; Health; Prevention, Self, Shape.

Basic Abstracts and Indexes

AgeLine, AltHealth Index, Cumulative Index to Nursing and Allied Health Literature, Index Medicus.

3400. Alternative Medicine Magazine. Formerly: *Alternative Medicine Digest.* 1994. 10x/yr. USD 69 (Individuals, USD 24.95). Alternative Medicine, 951 Front St., Novato, CA 94945-3236; http://www.alternativemedicine.com. Illus., adv. Circ: 170000. *Indexed:* CINAHL. *Aud.:* Ga.

Alternative Medicine Magazine is geared toward career- and family-minded women who want to live, eat, and maintain optimal physical and spiritual health in the most "unsynthetic" way possible. This 100-page magazine runs articles and stories that focus on important health topics such as bone health and how to help save the planet from global warming, and it also includes lighter topics such as raw foods diets, lifting brain fog, and mineral makeup. Advertisements for organic and "natural" dietary supplements and health aids abound, as do tips for cultivating naturally healthier pets and children. Despite the heavy drug advertisements, articles that cover important issues such as global warming, cancer prevention, healthy pregnancy, and Wal-Mart's selling of organic products make *Alternative Medicine Magazine* a good one for the shelves.

3401. Body & Soul: balanced living in a busy world. Former titles: *New Age;* (until 1998): *New Age Journal;* (until 1983): *New Age Magazine; New Age Journal.* [ISSN: 1539-0004] 1974. bi-m. plus a. special issue. USD 4.95 domestic; USD 5.99 Canada; USD 14.95 domestic. Martha Stewart Living Omnimedia LLC, 11 W. 42nd St., 25th Fl, New York, NY 10036. Illus., adv. Sample. Circ: 200000 Paid. Vol. ends: Nov/Dec. Microform: PQC. *Indexed:* AgeL, AltPI, BRI, CBRI. *Aud.:* Ga.

Body & Soul is exactly the type of magazine that we've all come to expect from the publishers of *Martha Stewart Living*, It is very well designed with elegant color tones that are easy on the eyes, chock-full of simply perfect images of food and plants and tea, and beautiful women in yoga positions. The articles are focused on simple, uplifting stories that speak to young mothers on the go who want to create a healthy, non-toxic home environment; working women who love to entertain and give thoughtful gifts to friends for no special reason; and wives who want to stay young, healthy, stress free, and sexy—forever. Even the advertisements are well designed. As a matter of fact, they are so alluring and they blend into the magazine so well that you barely know you're looking at ads for organic foods, yoga retreat centers, and sunlight saunas. Probably almost all women between the ages of 30 and 50 will love *Body & Soul*. Appropriate for public libraries.

3402. *Child Health Alert.* [ISSN: 1064-4849] 1983. 10x/yr. USD 29 domestic; USD 34 in Canada & Mexico. Ed(s): Allen A Mitchell. Child Health Alert, PO Box 610228, Newton, MA 02461. Illus., index. Sample. Vol. ends: Jun. Online: EBSCO Publishing, EBSCO Host; Gale; Northern Light Technology, Inc.; OCLC Online Computer Library Center, Inc.; ProQuest K-12 Learning Solutions; ProQuest LLC (Ann Arbor). *Aud.*: Ga.

The mission statement of *Child Health Alert* says that it is an independent newsletter evaluating the latest developments that affect the health and safety of children, that the goal is to present and interpret current health information, and that its contents are not intended to provide medical advice regarding individual diagnosis or treatment, which should be obtained from a physician. That said, articles are co-written by teams of health care professionals, doctors, and RNs. Health educators translate technical, health-related research and advances into accessible and user-friendly language for a general readership. The newsletter's focus is on children's diet and child obesity, new vaccines and booster shot information, child safety and product recalls, and resource information on neighborhood safety networks. The web site, www.childhealthalert.com, is a good source of articles and links to related resources that complement the printed newsletter. Issues dating back to January 1996 are freely available in full text on the web site. *Child Health Alert* is appropriate for public libraries, medical libraries (with a child and/or consumer health focus), and school libraries.

3403. *Consumer Reports on Health.* Formerly (until 1991): *Consumer Reports Health Letter.* [ISSN: 1058-0832] 1989. m. USD 19. Ed(s): Ronni Sandroff. Consumers Union of the United States, Inc., 101 Truman Ave, Yonkers, NY 10703-1057; http://www.consumerreports.org. Illus., index. Sample. Circ: 360000. Vol. ends: Dec. Online: EBSCO Publishing, EBSCO Host; Factiva, Inc.; LexisNexis; ProQuest LLC (Ann Arbor). *Indexed*: BiolDig, CINAHL, CPerI, MASUSE. *Aud.*: Ga.

Consumer Reports on Health is nonprofit and does not accept advertising, and what this means for the reader is that the information is "truthful" or at least is not sponsored by doctors or drug companies. That said, this newsletter, which is touted as being known for unbiased advice on health, fitness, and goods and services related to health, does not have very good customer service, and the contents have received mixed reviews by readers. *Consumer Reports on Health* offers up-to-date, although not breakthrough, information on diet and nutrition, diseases and symptoms, doctors and health-care providers, exercise and fitness, and wellness and alternative medicine. The companion web site, www.consumerreports.org/main/crh/home.jsp, is a nice complement to the newsletter, and it is free with a yearly subscription to the print edition. The online version includes a searchable archive that goes back four years. Column authors and consultants include health authorities, medical researchers, and medical experts. Some typical article titles are "Healthy sex: his and hers," "How to keep your brain sharp and youthful," and "Staying well—at your age." This newsletter is recommended for public libraries.

3404. *Environmental Nutrition: the newsletter of food, nutrition and health.* Formerly: *Environmental Nutrition Newsletter.* [ISSN: 0893-4452] 1977. m. USD 39 domestic; USD 49 Canada; USD 59 elsewhere. Ed(s): Susan Male Smith. Belvoir Media Group, LLC, 800 Connecticut Ave, Norwalk, CT 06854-1631; customer_service@belvoir.com; http://www.belvoir.com. Illus., index. Sample. Circ: 85000. Online: EBSCO Publishing, EBSCO Host; Florida Center for Library Automation; Gale; Northern Light Technology, Inc. *Indexed*: Agr, BiolDig, CINAHL. *Aud.*: Ga.

Environmental Nutrition has been supplying the general public with dependable commentary about the environment and its connection to food and our health and nutrition since 1977. This eight-page newsletter, printed on recycled paper with soy ink, offers an abundance of interesting facts about topics such as how prostate health can be enhanced by consuming veggies, how one's waistline is the best measure of one's health, and how to get four "prediseases" under control ("prediabetes," "prehypertension," osteopenia, and obesity). Also, *EN*

offers practical guidance related to cookies, margarine, raw milk, and chick peas. The editorial team consists of doctors, nurses, health-focused academics, dieticians, and medical experts. These experts and professionals review and analyze information from research reports to provide readers informed guidance that is easy to comprehend. Every issue includes "Nutrition Comparison" charts that give tips for shopping shortcuts by check-marking the most nutritious, longest lasting, and best buys among brand-name foods. The web site, www.environmentalnutrition.com, offers subscribers access to current issues, a searchable index, and an online archive back to August 1996. *EN* is highly recommended for public and medical libraries.

3405. *Exercise for Men Only.* [ISSN: 0882-4657] 1985. bi-m. USD 31.15 domestic; USD 40.95 foreign; USD 5.99 newsstand/cover. Ed(s): Cheh N Low. Chelo Publishing, Inc., 350 Fifth Ave, Ste 3323, New York, NY 10118; editorial@exercisegroup.com; http://www.exercisegroup.com. Illus., adv. Circ: 110258 Paid. Vol. ends: No. 6. *Aud.*: Ga.

You can judge this magazine by its cover, but not its title. Why? Because this mag is less about exercise than it is about pumping your every manly muscle up, "Schwarzenegger style." Like many of the dozens of macho male muscle and bodybuilding magazines, this one is dominated by images of hairless, chiseled chests and absolutely fabulous abs—and how you, too, men, can get the look. But wait. . .there's more to this mag than young and tan men in bikinis. *Exercise for Men Only* is a very focused look at how to safely, effectively, and efficiently build up your bod so that in no time at all you can look like Adonis. Articles concerning bodybuilding, nutrition, sports medicine, men's health, psychology, and grooming are enhanced with glossy, color images of very strapping men. I'd say that *Exercise for Men Only* is the only hardcore muscle mag for men that any public library needs.

3406. *Fitness: mind - body - spirit for women.* Formerly (until 1992): *Family Circle's Fitness Now.* [ISSN: 1060-9237] 1983. m. USD 16.97; USD 29.97 Canada; USD 3.50 newsstand/cover. Meredith Corp., 1716 Locust St, Des Moines, IA 50309-3023; http://www.meredith.com. Illus., adv. Sample. Circ: 1500000 Paid. Vol. ends: Dec. *Aud.*: Ga.

Fitness, one of America's top women's health and fitness magazines, is designed for health-minded women in their child-bearing years. Regular features include sections on weight loss, beauty and style, body sculpting, nutrition, health, and articles that offer upbeat stories of how women are fighting to lose weight or otherwise make a difference in the world. *Fitness* and its many advertisements focus on exercise, fashion, diet and nutrition, sports, health, medicine, psychology, children, and beauty. And while there are many interesting factoids and bits of health-related information, none of it is necessarily cutting-edge, and the magazine lacks depth. That said, it is a fun and light read designed to help a woman feel and look her best by way of commonsense advice and feel-good stories delivered via news/product information columns, quick tips, and lists. Training features offer step-by-step workout instructions and advice. Inspiration is provided by success stories from celebrities and readers. In addition to equipment and gear evaluations in each issue, there is an annual buyer's guide. The web site for *Fitness* complements the magazine with exercise tips, health and diet news, a recipe finder, reader polls and quizzes, a calculator for target heart rate and other health factors, and message boards, along with subscription information.

3407. *A Friend Indeed: for women in the prime of life.* [ISSN: 0824-1961] 1984. bi-m. CND 35 domestic; USD 30 United States; USD 40 elsewhere. Ed(s): June O'Leary Rogers. A Friend Indeed Publications Inc., 419 Graham Ave, Main Fl, Winnipeg R3C 0M3, MB R3C 0M3, Canada. Illus., index. Sample. Circ: 6000 Paid. Vol. ends: Feb. *Indexed*: CBCARef, CINAHL, CPerI, CWI, GendWatch. *Bk. rev.*: Number and length vary. *Aud.*: Ga.

A Friend Indeed: for women in the prime of life is a free web site now fully dedicated to issues related to menopause. This knowledge database provides a vast amount of practical and readable information and support for anyone (not only women) interested in boning up on the issues that surround the menopausal transition and midlife. In addition to menopause videos, there are six sections under which all of the information falls: Menopause Information, Menopause Effects, Signs and Symptoms, Treatments, Causes, and Remedies.

3408. *The Harvard Health Letter: a publication for the general readership, designed to provide accurate and timely health information.* Formerly (until 1990): *Harvard Medical School Health Letter.* [ISSN: 1052-1577] 1975. m. USD 28 domestic; USD 40 Canada; USD 47 elsewhere. Ed(s): Thomas H Lee, Peter Wehrein. Harvard Health Publications Group, 164 Longwood Ave, Boston, MA 02115; hhp@hms.harvard.edu; http://www.health.harvard.edu. Illus., index. Sample. Circ: 250000 Paid. Vol. ends: Oct. Online: EBSCO Publishing, EBSCO Host; Factiva, Inc.; Florida Center for Library Automation; Gale; Northern Light Technology, Inc. *Indexed:* Agr, BiolDig, CINAHL, ConsI, MASUSE, RGPR. *Bk. rev.:* Number and length vary. *Aud.:* Hs, Ga, Ac.

The Harvard Health Letter is an eight-page newsletter from Harvard Medical School that deals with a wide range of health issues. The information is breakthrough, well researched, and well written. Article topics range from your health and the planet's health to back surgery, obesity, pain relievers, and the good, bad, and the ugly about fish. The editorial board is comprised of medical doctors, the articles are written in easy-to-understand language, and the subject matter is wide-ranging. Articles provide carefully researched clarifications of medical terminology and procedures, and the web site, www.health.harvard.edu, provides an abundance of information in the form of articles, book reviews, and special reports. A searchable index is also available to subscribers, as well as back issues of the print edition (for a fee). *The Harvard Health Letter* is highly recommended for public libraries, health libraries, and medical libraries with a consumer health focus.

3409. *Harvard Heart Letter.* [ISSN: 1051-5313] 1990. m. USD 28 domestic; USD 40 Canada; USD 47 elsewhere. Ed(s): Thomas H Lee, P J Skerrett. Harvard Health Publications Group, 10 Shattuck St, 6th Fl, Boston, MA 02115-6011. Illus. Sample. Circ: 113000. Vol. ends: Aug. Online: EBSCO Publishing, EBSCO Host; Factiva, Inc.; Florida Center for Library Automation; Gale; Northern Light Technology, Inc. *Indexed:* BiolDig, MASUSE. *Aud.:* Ga.

Harvard Heart Letter is a distinctive newsletter from Harvard Medical School that concentrates on cardiac health. It offers first-rate information and respected and trustworthy advice to people who may already suffer from heart disease or are concerned about their risk and wish to take positive steps toward change. Regular sections include "Heart Beat," short, sound bites of information dedicated to interesting health breakthroughs and products as they pertain to cardiac health. Also, a section titled "Ask the Doctor" answers questions posed by readers. Typical titles from recent issues include "Nine ways to protect your heart when diabetes threatens it" and "Different shades of gray for post-heart attack depression." This newsletter, although limited in scope, is highly recommended for public, health, and medical libraries.

3410. *Harvard Men's Health Watch.* [ISSN: 1089-1102] 1996. m. USD 24 domestic; USD 40 Canada; USD 47 elsewhere. Ed(s): Anthony L Komaroff, Dr. Harvey B Simon. Harvard Health Publications Group, 10 Shattuck St, 6th Fl, Boston, MA 02115-6011; http://www.health.harvard.edu. Circ: 100000 Paid. Online: EBSCO Publishing, EBSCO Host; Florida Center for Library Automation; Gale. *Indexed:* CINAHL, PEI. *Aud.:* Ga, Sa.

Harvard Men's Health Watch, yet another excellent source of information from Harvard Medical School, is a fusion of current medical research specific to men's health issues and popular topics of interest to men, such as DHEA and the health benefits of pomegranates and red wine. The articles are brief, but not because they lack depth. Rather, the writing is succinct, and therefore the information can be quickly read and easily understood by the layman. Typical topics covered in this newsletter are diet and exercise, DHEA, sexual dysfunction, prostate issues and cancer, and diabetes and aging. The information and advice is clear and no-nonsense, and the newsletter is highly recommended for public and medical libraries, doctor's and dentist's offices, and other waiting rooms.

3411. *The Harvard Mental Health Letter.* Formerly (until 1990): *Harvard Medical School Mental Health Letter.* [ISSN: 1057-5022] 1984. m. USD 59 domestic; USD 80 Canada; USD 87 elsewhere. Ed(s): Michael Craig Miller. Harvard Health Publications Group, 10 Shattuck St, 6th Fl, Boston, MA 02115-6011; http://www.health.harvard.edu. Illus. Sample. Circ: 53000 Paid. Vol. ends: Jun. Online: EBSCO Publishing, EBSCO Host; Florida Center for Library Automation; Gale; Northern Light Technology, Inc. *Indexed:* BiolDig, CINAHL, MASUSE. *Aud.:* Hs, Ga, Ac.

The Harvard Mental Health Letter is a newsletter that presents current topics and research on a vast range of mental health issues. However, don't be fooled into thinking that it is only for audiences who treat, work with, or care for people suffering from impaired mental health. This newsletter also covers topics that one may not think to categorize as "mental health issues," such as violence among children, depression at menopause, and the effects of name-calling. Mental health care is a constantly evolving field, and this newsletter serves as a reliable information source for the general public and for psychiatrists, psychologists, social workers, and mental health specialists of all kinds. Highly recommended for health and medical libraries as well as public libraries.

3412. *Health.* Formed by the merger of (1990-1992): *In Health;* (1969-1991): *Health (New York);* Which was formerly (1969-1981): *Family Health;* Which incorporated (1950-1976): *Today's Health;* Which was formerly: *Hygeia.* [ISSN: 1059-938X] 1992. 10x/yr. USD 15.97 domestic; USD 25.95 foreign; USD 5.50 newsstand/cover per issue. Ed(s): Lisa Delaney, Jerry Guillery. Southern Progress Corp., 2100 Lakeshore Dr, Birmingham, AL 35209; http://corp.southernprogress.com/spc/. Illus., adv. Sample. Circ: 1350000 Paid. Vol. ends: Nov/Dec. Microform: PQC. Online: EBSCO Publishing, EBSCO Host; Gale; OCLC Online Computer Library Center, Inc. *Indexed:* AgeL, BiolDig, CBCARef, CINAHL, CPerI, ConsI, GSI, H&SSA, MASUSE, PEI, RGPR, SD. *Aud.:* Hs, Ga.

Health is a popular, glossy magazine for women that presents health-related information in a fun and interesting way. News, tips, and articles are divided into categories such as "Healthy Looks," "Healthy Moves," "Healthy Body," "Healthy Weight," "Healthy Balance," "Healthy Eating," and "In Every Issue." Recent article titles include "Eat more, feel full, weigh less," "More time for you," "Keep your heart healthy," and "Time to play! Scrapbooking, hiking, yoga, cooking classes—hobbies help busy women find happiness." The web site, www.health.com, is a nice companion to the print edition. Full-text articles are made available online (with a subscription), and a place is provided to submit questions electronically to the editorial staff and to browse offers for cookbooks, DVDs, and fitness-related events happening around the country. The publication's target audience is women in their thirties and forties. Recommended for public libraries.

3413. *HealthFacts.* [ISSN: 0738-811X] 1976. m. USD 25 domestic; USD 29 in Canada & Mexico; USD 36 in Europe. Ed(s): Maryann Napoli. Center for Medical Consumers, 239 Thompson St, New York, NY 10012-1090; http://www.medicalconsumers.org. Illus., index. Sample. Circ: 12000. Vol. ends: Dec. Online: EBSCO Publishing, EBSCO Host; Florida Center for Library Automation; Gale; Northern Light Technology, Inc.; OCLC Online Computer Library Center, Inc.; ProQuest K-12 Learning Solutions; ProQuest LLC (Ann Arbor). *Indexed:* CINAHL, MASUSE. *Aud.:* Ga.

HealthFacts is a six-page newsletter published by the Center for Medical Consumers, a nonprofit advocacy group founded in 1976 and active on the local and national level to improve the American health-care system and individual health care. This newsletter is less about fitness than it is about health, health care, drugs, and surgery. The organization that publishes it is funded by private donations, by newsletter subscriptions, and by the Judson Memorial Church. It accepts no funding from the drug or medical device industries. Recent article topics include using statin-treatment guidelines, the link between long-term use of Prilosec and hip fractures, and how a bone-loss drug ad combines fear and half truth. *HealthFacts* is written by Maryann Napoli and Arthur A. Levin, and although it is accessible and the language is seemingly unbiased, the information does not reflect medical research findings. The Center for Medical Consumers web site, www.medicalconsumers.org, is chock-full of health-related information, and it serves as a fine companion to this newsletter.

3414. *International Journal of Men's Health.* [ISSN: 1532-6306] 2002. 3x/yr. USD 55 domestic; USD 70 foreign; USD 70 combined subscription domestic (print & online eds.). Ed(s): Miles Groth. Men's Studies

Press, PO Box 32, Harriman, TN 37748-0032; http://www.mensstudies.com. Index, adv. Sample. Refereed. *Indexed:* CABA, CINAHL, ExcerpMed, GendWatch, PsycInfo, RRTA. *Aud.:* Ga, Sa.

International Journal of Men's Health is a peer-reviewed, scholarly journal that consists of research findings in the form of articles. These articles cover every aspect of men's health and fitness, be it mental health, physical health, sexual health, or social health. The primary audience for this publication includes educators, students, researchers, and professionals in the fields of medicine, health sciences, behavioral and social sciences, and public health. Every academic and research library with any sort of health collection should subscribe to this important research journal.

3415. *Johns Hopkins Medical Letter Health after 50.* [ISSN: 1042-1882] 1989. m. USD 24. Ed(s): Patrice Benneward. Rebus Inc., 632 Broadway, 11th Fl, New York, NY 10012; health_after_50@enews.com. Illus. Sample. Circ: 475000 Paid. Vol. ends: Feb. *Indexed:* BiolDig, CINAHL. *Aud.:* Ga.

Johns Hopkins Medical Letter Health after 50 is expressly designed for the health-conscious individual over the age of 50. Recent article titles include "Two Parkinson's drugs that cause heart valve damage?," "Is it time to see a geriatrician?," and "Does depression feel different for men?" The newsletter regularly features four major articles and three sections, titled "Remedies," "Longevity Facts," and "Drugstore Aisle," that offer useful tips and info sound bites. The eight-page publication, edited by medical and health experts, is comprised of up-to-date, reliable medical information based on trustworthy medical research. This newsletter, put out by Johns Hopkins Medical School, is nicely complemented by www.johnshopkinshealthalerts.com, a mostly unrestricted web site that showcases a variety of recent health and fitness news and other valuable information. Highly recommended for public libraries, health libraries, and medical libraries.

3416. *Mayo Clinic Health Letter: reliable information for a healthier life.* [ISSN: 0741-6245] 1983. 12x/yr. USD 27 domestic; USD 34 in Canada & Mexico; USD 42 elsewhere. Ed(s): Aleta Capelle. Mayo Medical Ventures, 200 First St, SW, Centerplace 5, Rochester, MN 55905; http://www.mayoclinic.com/. Illus., index. Circ: 700000 Paid and controlled. Vol. ends: Dec. *Indexed:* BiolDig, CINAHL, ConsI, RGPR. *Aud.:* Hs, Ga.

The *Mayo Clinic Health Letter* is an elegant looking, full-color, eight-page newsletter edited by the highly acclaimed medical experts at the Mayo Clinic. The newsletter consists of well-researched and well-written information on health, fitness, and medical advice. Recent articles cover such topics as pancreatitis, adult attention deficit disorder, hypnosis, and tips for making healthy dietary choices. Each issue features sections titled "Health Tips," in which a common health topic is explored; "News and Views," highlighting medical research results and news from the Mayo Clinic's researchers and doctors; and "Second Opinion," a column dedicated to answering questions submitted by subscribers. A subscription to the *Mayo Clinic Health Letter* provides 12 monthly issues, three medical essays in which the editors focus on timely health topics, and a year-end index that alphabetically organizes all topics covered throughout the year. Highly recommended for public libraries, health libraries, and medical libraries.

3417. *Men's Health (United States Edition): tons of useful stuff.* Formerly (until 1987): *Prevention Magazine's Guide to Men's Health.* [ISSN: 1054-4836] 1986. 10x/yr. USD 24.94 domestic; CND 39.50 Canada; USD 49.07 elsewhere. Ed(s): David Zinczenko, Peter Moore. Rodale, Inc., 33 E Minor St, Emmaus, PA 18098; info@rodale.com; http://www.rodale.com. Illus., adv. Circ: 1665038 Paid. Vol. ends: Dec (No. 10). Online: EBSCO Publishing, EBSCO Host; Gale; OCLC Online Computer Library Center, Inc.; ProQuest LLC (Ann Arbor); H.W. Wilson. *Indexed:* CINAHL, MASUSE, RGPR. *Aud.:* Hs, Ga, Ac.

David Wright, third baseman for the New York Mets, is on the cover of a recent edition of *Men's Health*, with a quote that reads, "I want to do everything above average." This quote, and Wright's easy-going, fit, smart, good looks pretty much sums up what the magazine is all about. In other words, it is meant for the man who wants to be healthy and fit, sexy and sophisticated, a good lover and a caring partner, stylish, confident, and rich. Articles such as "Need to grow a

pair?," "Are you failing enough?: If you can't be great, be a total screw-up. But never, ever be good enough," "Defend your manhood," and "Build a better breakfast" wittily cover important topics related to mental health, work stress, diet, and physical health. A quality fitness magazine, and recommended for public libraries.

3418. *Prevention: smart ways to live well.* [ISSN: 0032-8006] 1950. m. USD 15.97 domestic; USD 26.94 Canada; USD 2.99 newsstand/cover per issue. Rodale, Inc., 33 E Minor St, Emmaus, PA 18098; info@rodale.com; http://www.rodale.com. Illus., index, adv. Sample. Circ: 3200000. Vol. ends: Dec. Microform: PQC. Online: EBSCO Publishing, EBSCO Host; Florida Center for Library Automation; Gale; OCLC Online Computer Library Center, Inc.; ProQuest K-12 Learning Solutions; ProQuest LLC (Ann Arbor); H.W. Wilson. *Indexed:* CPerI, GSI, MASUSE, RGPR. *Aud.:* Hs, Ga.

Prevention, a magazine that has been published for more than 57 years, is an extraordinarily popular health and fitness magazine that people of any age can enjoy, but it is mostly geared toward middle-aged women. The approximately 200-page, purse-sized magazine offers up-to-date information on health, diet and nutrition, beauty, fitness, and mental health. There are extensive "special sections" that provide tips and information on hot topics such as walking for exercise, hormone issues, organic cooking, and deadly beauty treatments. The web site, www.prevention.com, complements the magazine and features full-text samples of articles, but some of the information is password protected and only available to subscribers of the print magazine. *Prevention* is a popular American standard and a tried and true source for women's health and fitness news. Recommended for public libraries.

3419. *Self.* [ISSN: 0149-0699] 1979. m. USD 12 domestic; USD 27 Canada; USD 30 elsewhere. Ed(s): Lucy Danziger, Kate Westerreck. Conde Nast Publications, Inc., 750 3rd Ave, New York, NY 10017; magpr@condenast.com; http://www.condenast.com. Illus., adv. Sample. Circ: 1314270 Paid. Vol. ends: Dec. Microform: PQC. *Aud.:* Hs, Ga.

Self is aimed at contemporary women who are looking for an upbeat lifestyle magazine that emphasizes fitness and health along with fashion and beauty coverage. It has evolved over the years from a magazine that included fiction and coverage of political and social issues to one with a strong fitness and health focus. *Self* has now settled into the more broadly focused lifestyle magazine market while returning, at least in some degree, to its roots by covering issues of importance to women such as abortion, body image, and bioengineering in foods. Coverage balances health, beauty, style, and diet while remaining strong in its treatment of fitness with workout routines and other exercise advice. The web site highlights current and past issues along with a tip of the day, health calculator, workout slide show, and links to reader surveys and forums.

3420. *Shape.* [ISSN: 0744-5121] 1981. m. USD 14.97 domestic; USD 29.97 Canada; USD 41.97 foreign. Ed(s): Katherine M Tomlinson, Elizabeth Tuner. A M I - Weider Publications, 1 Park Ave, 3d Fl, New York, NY 10016; http://www.amilink.com. Illus., adv. Sample. Circ: 1692690 Paid. Vol. ends: Aug. *Indexed:* PEI, SD. *Aud.:* Hs, Ga, Ac.

Shape is a popular women's health and exercise magazine. Its target audience is women in their twenties, thirties, and forties. The focus of articles and stories is on weight loss; toning up through exercise, yoga, and sports; beauty and fashion for the young, active woman; the right athletic gear and sportswear; maintaining proper health by way of an organic diet; and travel with an emphasis on health spas and yoga and meditation retreats. *Shape* has a variety of sections in which tips, news, and features appear: "Shape your Life," "Look Great," "Live Healthy," "Get Fit," and "Eat Right." Much attention is given to training, exercise, and proper technique; regular features such as "Do It Right" and "Target Training" teach proper form for various exercises using a "reader model" to illustrate the activity. Product evaluations are useful, and the "Buyer's Guide" advertises a variety of products and services. A companion publication, *Fit Pregnancy*, is published quarterly.

3421. *Today's Diet & Nutrition.* [ISSN: 1559-5110] 2005. q. USD 9.99 domestic; USD 14.99 Canada; USD 24.99 elsewhere. Ed(s): Kate Jackson. Great Valley Publishing Company, Inc., 3801 Schuylkill Rd, Spring City, PA 19475-2224; http://www.gvpub.com. Adv. Circ: 83000. *Aud.:* Ga.

Today's Diet & Nutrition is a 100-page publication dedicated to providing the earthy woman with information about natural and organic nutrition, food, cooking, health, fitness, and beauty aids. The magazine is divided into six departments: "health," "nutrition," "fitness," "lifestyle," "beauty," and "cuisine." Articles, stories, and advertisements are focused on how natural, organic, and other healthy foods, cooking products, and dietary supplements can help a woman feel, look, and be her best, inside and out. Recommended.

3422. Today's Health and Wellness. [ISSN: 1531-8044] 2000. bi-m. Free to members. Ed(s): Claire Lewis. North American Media Group, Inc., 12301 Whitewater Dr, Minnetonka, MN 55343; namghq@namginc.com; http://www.namginc.com/. Adv. Sample. Circ: 225000 Paid. *Aud.:* Ga.

Today's Health and Wellness is another magazine that targets women in their thirties, forties, and fifties; however, the emphasis is on wellness rather than fitness per se. Therefore, you won't find how-to guides to getting better abs. Instead, there are articles on such topics as maintaining a healthy weight, EGCG in green tea, and tennis elbow. The magazine encourages women to stay fit and healthy by actively pursuing the activities that they've always enjoyed, such as tennis, skiing, and dancing. One article titled "The energy of optimism" explores 11 ways to snap out of a negative frame of mind. While this magazine offers no new or breakthrough medical information, it is a source for quality reminders about how to live a full and healthy life. Recommended.

3423. Total Health: for longevity. Formerly (until 1980): *Trio.* [ISSN: 0274-6743] 1979. bi-m. USD 16.95 domestic; USD 23.95 foreign. Ed(s): Lyle Hurd, Jr. Total Health Holdings LLC, 165 N 100 St E, Ste 2, Saint George, UT 84770-2505. Adv. Circ: 95000. Microform: PQC. Online: EBSCO Publishing, EBSCO Host; Gale; Northern Light Technology, Inc.; OCLC Online Computer Library Center, Inc.; ProQuest K-12 Learning Solutions; ProQuest LLC (Ann Arbor). *Indexed:* CINAHL, MASUSE. *Aud.:* Ga.

Total Health, published and edited by Lyle Hurd, is dedicated to "helping its readers achieve and maintain optimum health and longevity by adopting a self-managed natural health program which includes diet, nutritional supplementation, exercise, spirituality, and commitment to community." The magazine encourages middle-aged folks to follow non-invasive, drug-free, nutrition-based medical approaches, and all advertisements, articles, and stories are dedicated to furthering this cause. For example, upon opening the cover, one is faced with two advertisements: one for a fish oil supplement and one for a vitamin-enriched, avocado-based pet food. This magazine offers a fresh, naturopathic look at health, fitness, and nutrition for everyone in the family—including Fido. Recommended.

3424. Tufts University Health & Nutrition Letter. Formerly (until 1997): *Tufts University Diet and Nutrition Letter.* [ISSN: 1526-0143] 1983. m. USD 18 domestic; USD 35 Canada; USD 40 elsewhere. Tufts University, School of Nutrition, Medford, MA 02155. Illus. Sample. Circ: 150000 Paid. Microform: PQC. Online: EBSCO Publishing, EBSCO Host; Florida Center for Library Automation; Gale; OCLC Online Computer Library Center, Inc.; ProQuest LLC (Ann Arbor). *Indexed:* Agr, BiolDig, CINAHL, ConsI, MASUSE, SD. *Aud.:* Hs, Ga.

Tufts University Health & Nutrition Letter is a trustworthy, eight-page newsletter that offers reliable, scientifically tested information on general health and fitness. The editorial advisory board is comprised of medical doctors and other respected health experts affiliated with Tufts University Medical School. Well-researched, easy-to-read articles cover topics like how brisk walking can rebuild the brain, how 22 percent of U.S. calories come from beverages, nine keys to living to a healthy 85-plus, and how coffee is linked to lowered diabetes risk. The web site, www.healthletter.tufts.edu, offers a few sample articles to nonsubscribers, and subscribers have access to an online archive of full-text articles back to January 2003 and a master index organized by topic. This newsletter is highly recommended for public libraries, health libraries, and medical libraries.

3425. University of California, Berkeley. Wellness Letter: the newsletter of nutrition, fitness, and stress management. [ISSN: 0748-9234] 1984. m. USD 24. Ed(s): Dale A Ogar. Health Letter Associates, PO Box 412,

New York, NY 10012-0007. Illus. Sample. Circ: 500000 Paid. Vol. ends: Sep. Online: EBSCO Publishing, EBSCO Host; Florida Center for Library Automation; Gale. *Indexed:* BiolDig, CINAHL, ConsI. *Aud.:* Hs, Ga.

University of California, Berkeley. Wellness Letter is an authoritative yet easy-to-read newsletter. Much like the *Tufts University Health & Nutrition Letter*, the *Mayo Clinic Health Letter*, and the *Harvard Health Letter*, it offers up-to-date, well-researched information that draws upon the expertise of the top medical researchers at Berkeley and worldwide. Sample articles from recent issues include "What should you believe about salt?," "Heading off migraines," and "A rough guide to fiber." The web site, www.wellnessletter.com, offers a few full-text articles, but otherwise the information is password protected. Subscribers can immediately access any article in the three-year index, which is organized by topic. This newsletter is highly recommended for public libraries as well as health and medical libraries.

3426. Women & Health: the multidisciplinary journal of women's health issues. [ISSN: 0363-0242] 1976. q. 2 vols./yr. USD 665 print & online eds. Ed(s): Jeanne Mager Stellman. The Haworth Medical Press, 10 Alice St, Binghamton, NY 13904; getinfo@haworthpress.com; http://www.haworthpress.com. Illus., adv. Sample. Refereed. Circ: 596 Paid. Vol. ends: No. 4. Microform: PQC. Online: EBSCO Publishing, EBSCO Host; OCLC Online Computer Library Center, Inc.; ProQuest LLC (Ann Arbor); SwetsWise Online Content. Reprint: HAW. *Indexed:* AbAn, AgeL, AltPI, BAS, BiolDig, CABA, CINAHL, CJA, CWI, DSA, ExcerpMed, FemPer, GSI, GendWatch, H&SSA, HEA, IBR, IBZ, IMFL, MCR, PAIS, PEI, PsycInfo, RRTA, RiskAb, SFSA, SSA, SSCI, SWA, SWR&A, SociolAb, V&AA, WAE&RSA, WSA. *Bk. rev.:* 8-12, length varies, signed. *Aud.:* Ac, Sa.

This international scholarly journal is an important resource for current research on issues relating to women's health and well-being. Written for researchers, policy planners, and health care practitioners, it examines women's physical and psychological well-being, the socio-cultural factors contributing to health problems, and issues of prevention, early diagnosis and treatment, limitation of disability, and rehabilitation. Some issues are theme based. Contents pages and abstracts are available on the journal's web site. Article titles include "The association between disordered eating and substance use and abuse in women: A community-based investigation," "Barriers to physical activity among women in the rural Midwest," and "Healthy eating, exercise, and weight: Impressions of sexual minority women." This scholarly journal is highly recommended for academic collections and medical libraries.

3427. Women's Adventure. Formerly: *Dandelion.* 2003. bi-m. USD 18. Women's Adventure, 709 Baseline Rd, Boulder, CO 80305. Adv. Circ: 1000 Paid and controlled. *Aud.:* Ga.

On page four of *Women's Adventure,* Michelle Theall, the founding editor and publisher of the magazine, tells an exhilarating story of how she went from watching grizzlies fight for salmon from a viewing platform to watching a grizzly run directly at her on a trail only moments later. In another issue, she discusses the adventure that is motherhood. These experiences she describes are an indication of what the rest of the magazine is like. Filled with stories, advertisements, articles, and news related to skiing, snowboarding, rock climbing, travel to exotic lands, kayaking, and how you can do it all with a baby if need be, this magazine is for the true adventuress and for women who are not afraid to experience a little pain for a lot of heady pleasure. The magazine is only 50–60 pages long, but it's filled to the brim with positively stimulating and inspirational ideas and ways that women can live fit, healthy, exciting lives. Recommended.

3428. Women's Health Issues. [ISSN: 1049-3867] 1991. 6x/yr. USD 355. Ed(s): Dr. Anne Rossier Markus. Elsevier Inc., 360 Park Ave S, New York, NY 10010-1710; usinfo-f@elsevier.com; http://www.elsevier.com. Illus., adv. Refereed. Circ: 700 Paid. Vol. ends: Nov (No. 11). Microform: PQC. Online: EBSCO Publishing, EBSCO Host; Gale; IngentaConnect; OhioLINK; ScienceDirect; SwetsWise Online Content. *Indexed:* AgeL, CINAHL, ExcerpMed, H&SSA, PEI, PsycInfo, RiskAb, SSA, SSCI, SWA, SociolAb. *Aud.:* Ac, Sa.

Women's Health Issues is a scholarly journal from the Jacobs Institute of Women's Health at The George Washington University Medical Center. The primary focus is on women's health care and policy. Typically highlighted in research articles are gender differences in specific diseases or conditions and the socioeconomic, ethnic, and cultural factors affecting the health and well-being of women. Published are well-researched, peer-reviewed articles, conference reports, and editorials and opinion pieces on issues relating to women's health and wellness. The audience for this journal consists of health professionals, policy makers, social scientists, and students and researchers. Tables of contents and abstracts are available on the journal's web site. Highly recommended for academic, research, and medical libraries.

■ HEALTH CARE ADMINISTRATION

Health Professions; Nursing.

Vivienne B. Piroli, School for Health Studies Librarian, Beatley Library, Simmons College, Boston, MA 02115

Introduction

The journals in this field are directed at those individuals involved in the health-care industry. That covers a broad range of professionals from clinical practitioners—the dentists, physicians, nurses, and laboratory staff—to executive and financial officers of health-care systems. In addition to these audiences, several of the journals look to serve the needs of students on track to become managers in the industry, or physicians who will eventually run their own practices.

There are an array of journals that deal with health care from a variety of perspectives. The following selections focus strongly on the health business aspect of the industry and largely ignore those publications with a public policy or a social or legal approach. The emphasis here is on accounting, business, finance, theoretical models of management, quality and safety issues, technical excellence, implementation of legal and/or ethical obligations, and awareness of federal laws.

Most of the journals here have a specialized audience. Publications with a weekly presence and that offer an update into current trends and information would serve interested patrons in a public library setting. The majority of titles are well suited to academic libraries that support medical, dental, health science, health-care administration, or public health programs. Those journals with a scholarly output are necessary for researchers in higher education. Many of the included titles are supplied to practitioners as part of their subscription to professional associations and are at the forefront of providing insights into upcoming trends and practices and would be ideal in hospital library settings.

Some of the journals offer online counterparts with a dizzying array of access options. Most require a subscription-based access. Others offer free access to the current issue for 30 days, and charge for articles from their archive. All of the journals have web sites that detail the level and cost of access via the publisher or the related association.

This list is a strong representation of journals currently in publication that support and lead the field of health-care administration and are capable of enhancing many types of libraries, particularly academic and hospital ones.

Basic Periodicals

Ga: *Modern Healthcare;* Ac: *Health Care Mangement Review, Healthcare Financial Management, Inquiry;* Sa: *The Joint Commission Journal on Quality Improvement, Journal of Healthcare Management, Journal of Nursing Administration.*

Basic Abstracts and Indexes

Cumulative Index to Nursing and Allied Health Literature, Index Medicus.

3429. Dental Economics. Formerly (until 196?): *Oral Hygiene.* [ISSN: 0011-8583] 1911. m. USD 115 domestic (Free to qualified personnel). Ed(s): Kevin Henry, Joseph A Blaes. PennWell Corporation, 1421 S Sheridan Rd, Tulsa, OK 74112; Headquarters@PennWell.com;

http://www.pennwell.com. Illus., index, adv. Sample. Circ: 109000 Controlled. Vol. ends: Dec. Online: Northern Light Technology, Inc.; ProQuest LLC (Ann Arbor). *Indexed:* ATI. *Aud.:* Ac, Sa.

This journal prides itself on being the "Nation's Leading Business Journal" for dentists. It is published monthly and contains regular columns as well as features. The monthly columns deal with topics facing most dentists in practice, such as incorporating emerging technologies; finding ways to improve a practice; and advising on how to maintain fiscal health in a practice. The journal does not shy away from product endorsements, and it reviews a variety in each issue. Features cover topics relating to current trends such as staff management, increasing business, or adopting new treatment techniques. The tone of this publication is colloquial and personalized toward the reader. It is written with the understanding that dentists are clinicians and not businesspeople. Therefore, business concepts and management techniques are explained in the context of dental practice issues. The value of this journal is in its currency of topics. Its relevancy to practitioners is highlighted by the use of case studies and examples. The journal is circulated on a complimentary basis to dentists in practice. Its web site is http://de.pennnet.com.

3430. Frontiers of Health Services Management. [ISSN: 0748-8157] 1984. q. USD 95 domestic; USD 105 foreign; USD 27 newsstand/cover per issue. Ed(s): Audrey Kaufman. Health Administration Press, 1 North Franklin St, Ste 1700, Chicago, IL 60606-4425; ache@ache.org; http://www.ache.org/hap.cfm. Illus. Sample. Circ: 2500 Paid. Vol. ends: Summer. Microform: PQC. Online: EBSCO Publishing, EBSCO Host; Northern Light Technology, Inc.; OCLC Online Computer Library Center, Inc.; ProQuest LLC (Ann Arbor). *Indexed:* ABIn, AgeL, ExcerpMed. *Aud.:* Ac, Sa.

This journal provides current information and in-depth discussion of topics written by both experts and scholars in the field of health services management. Each issue contains a feature article followed by substantive commentaries from three other authors. Within the same issue, the author(s) of the original article has the opportunity to provide a response to the commentators. The journal is a quarterly and published by the Foundation of the American College of Healthcare Executives. It is scholarly in tone and references are included at the end of articles. Each issue is thematic and deals with overarching topics in health-care management, such as electronic records or the use of an evidence-based management approach. This journal is well suited to an academic environment and those involved in strategic planning within health-care management. Its web site is www.ache.org/pubs/frontiers.cfm.

3431. H F M Magazine. Former titles: *Healthcare Financial Management;* (until 1982): *Hospital Financial Management;* (until 1968): *Hospital Accounting.* 1946. m. USD 135 (Individuals, USD 114; USD 198 foreign). Ed(s): Eric Reese. Healthcare Financial Management Association, 2 Westbrook Corporate Center, Ste 700, Westchester, IL 60154-5700; http://www.hfma.org. Illus., index, adv. Sample. Circ: 32000 Paid and controlled. Vol. ends: Dec. Microform: PQC. Online: The Dialog Corporation; EBSCO Publishing, EBSCO Host; Florida Center for Library Automation; Gale; Northern Light Technology, Inc.; OCLC Online Computer Library Center, Inc.; ProQuest LLC (Ann Arbor); H.W. Wilson. *Indexed:* ABIn, ATI, AgeL, BPI, CINAHL, ExcerpMed, LRI. *Bk. rev.:* 4, 1,000 words. *Aud.:* Ac, Sa.

HFM is the official journal of the Healthcare Financial Management Association. It is published monthly and, within the year, a 13th issue is produced in December. This journal is focused specifically on the financial aspects of health care—with topics ranging from patient billing to absorbing the cost of uncompensated care, to maximizing margins in hospitals and health-care systems. Like many other publications in this genre, *HFM* also contains a section that refers to action and advocacy on health-care issues in government, "Eye on Washington." Articles are written by professionals in the field and offer solutions to common problems and challenges faced by health-care administrators. The tone of the publication is businesslike, and it uses charts, graphs, and some abstract art to provide visual interest. In addition to advertisements, the journal provides up-to-date listings of career openings for professionals in this field. This is an informative and current source of information for financial officers and administrators. Its web site is www.hfma.org/hfm.

3432. *Health Care Management Review.* [ISSN: 0361-6274] 1976. q. USD 286 (Individuals, USD 95.95). Ed(s): L. Michele Issel. Lippincott Williams & Wilkins, 323 Norristown Rd, Ste 200, Ambler, PA 19002; custserv@lww.com; http://www.lww.com. Illus., adv. Sample. Refereed. Circ: 2400 Paid. Vol. ends: Fall. Microform: PQC. Online: EBSCO Publishing, EBSCO Host; Florida Center for Library Automation; Gale; OCLC Online Computer Library Center, Inc.; Ovid Technologies, Inc.; ProQuest LLC (Ann Arbor). *Indexed:* ABIn, AgeL, BPI, CINAHL, ExcerpMed, H&SSA, MCR, SSCI. *Bk. rev.:* Number and length vary. *Aud.:* Ac, Sa.

This is a peer-reviewed, quarterly publication that aims to be a leader in the field. Its goal is to present articles that will inform and direct its readership. Within the editorial section of each issue it is clear that the content is not centered on anecdotal reporting but emphasizes reflection and analysis of current topics and issues. This journal is aimed at both practitioners and researchers. Interestingly, the subjects of many articles in recent issues are nursing-home facilities and not just large hospital and health-care systems. All articles include bibliographies and brief abstracts. Manuscript guidelines are strict and authors must limit their articles to 18 pages, 25 references, and no more than four figures or tables. This leads to tight and well-focused issues with even balance from one article to the next. Health services managers would benefit from this publication, as it shows how theoretical models can be applied in real-world settings.

3433. *The Health Care Manager.* Former titles: *Health Care Supervisor; Health Care Supervisors Journal.* [ISSN: 1525-5794] 1982. q. USD 286 (Individuals, USD 95.95). Ed(s): Charles R McConnell. Lippincott Williams & Wilkins, 530 Walnut St, Philadelphia, PA 19106-3621; http://www.lww.com. Illus., adv. Refereed. Circ: 3500 Paid. Vol. ends: Jun. Online: EBSCO Publishing, EBSCO Host; Florida Center for Library Automation; Gale; OCLC Online Computer Library Center, Inc.; Ovid Technologies, Inc.; ProQuest LLC (Ann Arbor). *Indexed:* ABIn, CINAHL, PsycInfo. *Aud.:* Ac, Sa.

Produced for managers of health-care systems, this is a quarterly, peer-reviewed publication. This journal has an editorial board comprising individuals from higher education in the fields of health, medicine, information management, and business. This journal's purpose is to offer practical management guidance for health-care managers. Each article is preceded by a short but detailed abstract. To assist the flow of content and the reader, articles contain major and minor subheadings. Some articles contain references and others do not. Those that do not have references tend to be less scholarly and focus more on explaining or evaluating a trend or an issue. In recent issues, some of the topic areas covered were college on the Internet, and succession planning. In general the articles are not lengthy and the subject matter tends to be practical. Busy managers would quickly understand current management theories and see how they could be applied. Due to its pragmatic nature, this is a very relevant journal to managers in health care, but it is also useful to the individual seeking to learn about applied management theory in a practical context.

3434. *Health Progress.* Formerly (until 1984): *Hospital Progress.* [ISSN: 0882-1577] 1920. bi-m. USD 50 domestic; USD 60 foreign. Ed(s): Carrie Stetz. Catholic Health Association of the United States, 4455 Woodson Rd., St. Louis, MO 63134-3797; http://www.chausa.org. Illus., index, adv. Sample. Circ: 12000. Vol. ends: Dec. Microform: PQC. Online: EBSCO Publishing, EBSCO Host; Northern Light Technology, Inc.; ProQuest LLC (Ann Arbor). *Indexed:* ASG, AgeL, CINAHL, CPL, ExcerpMed, MCR, SWR&A. *Bk. rev.:* 2, 500-1,000 words. *Aud.:* Ga, Ac, Sa.

This bimonthly journal is the official journal of the Catholic Health Association of the United States. The journal features many case studies and first-person narratives as well as regularly featured columns. The publication is infused with a Catholic perspective and treats issues of patient safety and quality health care through the perspective of ethics and social justice. One of the regular columns on communications strategies was changed in 2006 to focus on communications in the context of Catholic health care rather than generalized information on health-care marketing strategy. While many of the articles are written by laypeople, a considerable number are by health-care professionals who are also priests and nuns. Advertisers are those who are connected or affiliated with the Catholic Health Association. The emphasis is on presenting successful

approaches to issues in health care and providing models of excellence. Articles are footnoted and also include useful summaries for readers. The web site is www.chausa.org/Pub/MainNav/News/HP.

3435. *Hospital & Health Networks.* Incorporates (1999-2003): *Health Forum Journal;* Which was formerly (1987-1999): *Healthcare Forum Journal;* (1985-1987): *Healthcare Forum;* (1958-1985): *Hospital Forum;* Formerly (until 1993): *Hospitals.* [ISSN: 1068-8838] 1936. m. Individuals, USD 89; Free to qualified personnel. Ed(s): Alden Solovy, Bill Santamour. Health Forum, Inc., One N Franklin, 29th Fl, Chicago, IL 60606; hfcustsvc@healthforum.com; http://www.healthforum.com/. Illus., index, adv. Sample. Circ: 70499 Paid and controlled. Vol. ends: Dec. Microform: PQC. Online: The Dialog Corporation; EBSCO Publishing, EBSCO Host; Factiva, Inc.; Gale; OCLC Online Computer Library Center, Inc.; ProQuest LLC (Ann Arbor); H.W. Wilson. *Indexed:* ABIn, ATI, AgeL, BPI, CINAHL, CWI, ChemAb, ExcerpMed, LRI, MCR, SCI, SSCI. *Aud.:* Ga, Ac, Sa.

This journal, published monthly, has a very businesslike tone and structure. Its target audience includes hospital managers and administrators. Content is heavily focused on the role of information technology in matters relating to strategic planning, organizational structure, and marketing. Many of the columns deal with organizational problems and offer survey data to highlight issues with colorful charts and graphs. Part of the intention of this approach is to offer hospital administrators some documented facts to assist them in implementing change at local levels. Other, regular columns examine ethical dilemmas with commentary, with potential solutions offered from physicians and administrators. This publication features advertisements heavily, and each issue contains a glossy fold-out advertisement. Its content is timely and relevant to managers and administrators in a hospital setting. Its web site is www.hhnmag.com/hhnmag/index.jsp.

3436. *Inquiry (Rochester): the journal of health care organization, provision and financing.* [ISSN: 0046-9580] 1963. q. USD 125 (Individuals, USD 75). Ed(s): Katherine Swartz, Ronny Frishman. Excellus Health Plan, Inc., 165 Court St, Rochester, NY 14647; http://www.inquiryjournal.org. Illus., index, adv. Refereed. Circ: 1200. Vol. ends: Winter. Microform: PQC. Online: Allen Press Inc.; EBSCO Publishing, EBSCO Host; OCLC Online Computer Library Center, Inc.; ProQuest LLC (Ann Arbor). *Indexed:* ABIn, AgeL, BPI, CINAHL, ExcerpMed, HRA, IBR, IBZ, JEL, MCR, PAIS, SCI, SSCI. *Bk. rev.:* 3-6, length varies. *Aud.:* Ac, Sa.

A quarterly publication, *Inquiry* broadly focuses on the health-care industry. This journal attempts to provide substantive and scholarly articles on topics concerned with the organization and structure of the industry, health-care delivery, and business management. Each year, the Winter issue calls for research papers on specific issues that have been topical in the prior year. Some such requests are for papers on the effects of Hurricane Katrina and on public policy topics. The articles in each issue are well researched and provide detailed bibliographies as well as graphs and charts supporting data. Due to the broad scope of this journal, it is suitable for a wide audience from the hospital executive to clinical managers, to scholars and students alike. Its web site is www.inquiryjournal.org.

3437. *The Joint Commission Journal on Quality and Patient Safety.* Former titles (until Jan 2005): *The Joint Commission Journal on Quality and Safety;* (until 2003): *The Joint Commission Journal on Quality Improvement;* (until 1993): *Q R B - Quality Review Bulletin.* [ISSN: 1553-7250] 1974. m. USD 250 combined subscription domestic print & online eds.; USD 270 combined subscription in Canada & Mexico print & online eds.; USD 325 combined subscription elsewhere print & online eds. Ed(s): Steve Berman. Joint Commission Resources, Inc., 1 Renaissance Blvd., Oakbrook Terrace, IL 60181; http://www.jcrinc.com. Illus., index, adv. Sample. Refereed. Circ: 7955. Vol. ends: Dec. Online: EBSCO Publishing, EBSCO Host; Gale; IngentaConnect. *Indexed:* AgeL, CINAHL, ExcerpMed, MCR, SSCI, SWR&A. *Aud.:* Ac, Sa.

This monthly journal is a publication of the Joint Commission on Accreditation of Healthcare Organizations. This independent body offers accreditation to hospitals, health-care facilities, laboratories, and providers of medical care, as well as providers of medical equipment and device suppliers. This journal is concerned with maintaining the highest standards for quality and safety in all areas of health care. The journal publishes content that illustrates this goal through case studies, descriptions of innovative methodologies, or research into new or improved practices. This publication seeks to be on the leading edge of literature and research into quality methods and patient safety. All articles are peer-reviewed and the journal has a scholarly feel to it. Advertisement space is limited to the inside of the back cover. The web site is www.jcrinc.com/subscribers/journal.asp?durki=32.

3438. *Journal of Health Care Finance.* Formerly (until 1994): *Topics in Health Care Financing.* [ISSN: 1078-6767] 1974. q. USD 279. Ed(s): Judith J. Baker, James J Unland. Aspen Publishers, Inc., 111 Eighth Ave., 7th Fl, New York, NY 10011; customer.service@aspenpubl.com; http://www.aspenpublishers.com. Illus., adv. Sample. Circ: 3700 Paid. Vol. ends: Summer. Microform: PQC. Online: EBSCO Publishing, EBSCO Host; Florida Center for Library Automation; Gale; OCLC Online Computer Library Center, Inc.; Ovid Technologies, Inc.; ProQuest LLC (Ann Arbor). *Indexed:* ABIn, AgeL, BPI, CINAHL, ExcerpMed, LRI, MCR, RiskAb. *Aud.:* Ac, Sa.

The goal of this journal is to provide its readership with carefully researched and quality information. Despite this aim, the publishers do not accept legal responsibility for the content of the articles. The editorial board consists of persons from the business and accounting world and from medicine. The journal is very much concerned with presenting articles that support the business of running a hospital or health system. The articles are scholarly in nature and offer content summaries and author-supplied keywords for indexing. Brief biographical details and affiliations are offered for each of the authors as well as acknowledgements for sponsored research. All articles are thoroughly referenced and contain graphs and charts where appropriate. The content centers on themes and questions relating to cost containment and reduction and budgets, and offers representations of theoretical models in areas such as econometrics and diversification. This would be an essential journal for any library with a health business collection.

3439. *Journal of Healthcare Management.* Former titles (until 1997): *Hospital and Health Services Administration;* (until 1975): *Hospital Administration.* [ISSN: 1096-9012] 1956. bi-m. USD 95 domestic; USD 105 foreign; USD 27 newsstand/cover. Ed(s): Kyle Grazier. Health Administration Press, 1 North Franklin St, Ste 1700, Chicago, IL 60606-4425; ache@ache.org; http://www.ache.org/hap.cfm. Illus. Sample. Refereed. Circ: 28000 Paid. Microform: PQC. Online: EBSCO Publishing, EBSCO Host; Florida Center for Library Automation; Gale; OCLC Online Computer Library Center, Inc.; ProQuest LLC (Ann Arbor). *Indexed:* ABIn, ATI, AgeL, CINAHL, ExcerpMed, LRI, MCR, SSCI. *Bk. rev.:* 8, 250-400 words. *Aud.:* Ac, Sa.

This scholarly journal is published by the American College of Healthcare Executives, which despite its moniker is an international body. Each issue follows a similar format with an editorial; an interview with a health-care executive; columns on pay for performance, competencies, and perspective; articles; and a fellow project. Articles include thorough references in addition to charts, tables, and graphs. The tone is scholarly and the content presents much empirical data. This publication is most suited to professionals with management responsibilities in health-care systems and hospitals, but it is not restricted to this group. Physicians and advanced practice nurses with managerial charges would also benefit from the content. This source would provide students of health management with careful insights on theoretical concepts in practice. Its web site is www.ache.org/pubs/jhmsub.cfm.

3440. *The Journal of Nursing Administration.* [ISSN: 0002-0443] 1971. 11x/yr. USD 399 (Individuals, USD 107). Ed(s): Suzanne P Smith. Lippincott Williams & Wilkins, 530 Walnut St, Philadelphia, PA 19106-3621; custserv@lww.com; http://www.lww.com. Illus., index, adv. Sample. Refereed. Circ: 11397. Vol. ends: Dec. CD-ROM: Ovid Technologies, Inc. Microform: PQC. Online: EBSCO Publishing, EBSCO Host; Ovid Technologies, Inc.; SwetsWise Online Content. *Indexed:* AgeL, CINAHL, ExcerpMed, SCI, SSCI. *Bk. rev.:* Number and length vary. *Aud.:* Ac, Sa.

Though essentially a monthly, *JONA* publishes 11 issues per year; the July/August issue is a combined one. Content is provided by highly qualified authors, who are experienced as nurse administrators and educators. Articles are scholarly and research-based and include detailed reference lists. The journal's subtitle is "Innovations in Healthcare Executive Leadership and Management." Therefore, it is not surprising that the articles attempt to provide case studies and research to help deal with common challenges. In recent issues the journal has focused on topics such as quality improvement, nurse retention, and organizational strategies. This journal is useful to nursing administrators, nurse educators, and graduate students in the fields of both nursing and health-care management.

3441. *Laboratory Medicine.* Formed by the 1970 merger of: *Bulletin of Pathology; Registry of Medical Technologists. Technical Bulletin;* Incorporates: *Technical Improvement Service Bulletin.* [ISSN: 0007-5027] 1965. m. USD 125 print & online eds. (Individuals, USD 105 print & online eds.). American Society for Clinical Pathology, 2100 W Harrison St, Chicago, IL 60612; info@ascp.org; http://www.ascp.org. Illus., adv. Refereed. Circ: 72000 Paid. Vol. ends: Dec. Microform: PQC. Online: EBSCO Publishing, EBSCO Host. *Indexed:* CABA, CINAHL, ChemAb, ExcerpMed, IndVet, SCI, SSCI. *Aud.:* Ac, Sa.

Published monthly, this journal serves medical technologists and laboratory professionals. It bills itself as a newsmagazine, which is shown in its coverage of current topics, product endorsements, and a manufacturers' index. The scope of the journal is beyond just management topics, as it aims to highlight the scientific, technical, and educational aspects of clinical laboratories. Each issue contains a column called "The Washington Report" that details the various legislative initiatives and votes that occur each month in Congress. The journal also publishes reviewed research articles on topics of interest to clinical pathologists. Many of the other regular columns are practically written and include scenarios from professional situations. The web site is www.labmedicine.com.

3442. *M G M A Connexion.* Former titles (until 2001): *Medical Group Management Journal;* (until 1987): *Medical Group Management.* [ISSN: 1537-0240] 1953. 10x/yr. Individuals, USD 95; Free to members. Ed(s): Brenda Hull. Medical Group Management Association, 104 Inverness Terr. E, Englewood, CO 80112; beh@mgma.com; http://www.mgma.com. Illus., index, adv. Sample. Circ: 32000 Paid and free. Vol. ends: Nov/Dec. Microform: PQC. Online: EBSCO Publishing, EBSCO Host; ProQuest LLC (Ann Arbor). *Indexed:* AgeL, ExcerpMed, MCR. *Bk. rev.:* 1-3, length varies. *Aud.:* Ac, Sa.

This publication is aimed directly at practitioners in the medical field. By including contributions from this group, this journal attempts to faithfully represent the practice manager's perspective. The journal is divided into three areas of content–features, columns, and departments. Members of the Medical Group Management Association can also receive a digest of each issue on the member web site, www.mgma.com. While heavy on advertisements, this publication has great relevance to its audience, as it promotes the most current trends and thinking for managers and physicians in group practice. One of the regular columns deals with legislative issues at the federal level and acts as a means to galvanize support for particular causes, as well as providing information on changes and interpretations of the law. In addition to addressing legal matters, the journal provides subscribers with relevant resources on information technology and continuing education opportunities as well as marketing and risk management models. This is a monthly publication and of great relevance to group practitioners. Its specific web site is www.mgma.com/about/connexion.cfm.

3443. *Medical Economics.* [ISSN: 0025-7206] 1923. s-m. USD 109 domestic (Free to qualified personnel). Ed(s): David Azevedo, Marianne D Mattera. Advanstar Communications, Inc., 131 W First St, Duluth, MN 55802-2065; info@advanstar.com; http://www.advanstar.com. Illus., adv. Circ: 160806 Free. Vol. ends: Dec. Microform: RPI; PQC. Online: The Dialog Corporation; Factiva, Inc.; Florida Center for Library Automation; Gale; Northern Light Technology, Inc.; OCLC Online Computer Library Center, Inc.; H.W. Wilson. *Indexed:* ABIn, ATI, AgeL, BPI, CINAHL, LRI, MCR, PAIS. *Aud.:* Ac, Sa.

The central tenet of this publication is proving the link between the business of medical practice and higher standards of patient care. Published every two weeks, this breezy journal seeks to provide physicians with knowledge and support for their practices in what is acknowledged as a competitive market. The journal covers topics in the areas of practice management, finance, and patient relations, and has a segment on advice from an expert panel. In 2006, it also includes a new section on the latest research in a variety of clinical practice areas, offering citations and annotations for the recommended readings. Advertisements are prominent, and indexed classifieds are also included. The web site is www.memag.com/memag.

3444. *Modern Healthcare: the newsmagazine for administrators and managers in hospitals, and other healthcare institutions.* Formed by the merger of (1967-1976): *Modern Healthcare (Long-Term Care);* Which was formerly (until 1974): *Modern Nursing Home;* (1913-1976): *Modern Healthcare (Short-Term Care);* Which was formerly (until 1974): *Modern Hospital.* [ISSN: 0160-7480] 1976. w. USD 154 domestic. Ed(s): Neil McLaughlin, David Burda. Crain Communications, Inc., 360 N Michigan Ave, Chicago, IL 60601-3806; info@crain.com; http://www.crain.com. Illus., index, adv. Sample. Circ: 71580 Paid and controlled. Vol. ends: Dec. Online: EBSCO Publishing, EBSCO Host; Florida Center for Library Automation; Gale; LexisNexis; OCLC Online Computer Library Center, Inc.; ProQuest LLC (Ann Arbor); H.W. Wilson. *Indexed:* ABIn, API, ATI, AgeL, BPI, CINAHL, CWI, ExcerpMed, LRI. *Aud.:* Ga, Ac, Sa.

This journal bills itself as the only weekly business source for the health-care industry. As such, it is brief in content with short, newsy articles and complemented by copious advertisements. The articles focus on both the executives in the industry and issues that are making headlines that week. Recurring headings are Medicare, technology, finance, and insurers. The features area of the journal is also quite brief and acts more as a forum for presenting summaries of review articles and details of surveys on items such as leading executives in the industry. This journal is useful for busy executives, as it allows the reader to be informed on the latest industry happenings without expending a large time commitment. It is useful for finding fast information on the health-care industry and becoming familiar with the major players and the current issues and trends affecting the industry. Its web site is www.modern-healthcare.com.

3445. *Nursing Administration Quarterly.* [ISSN: 0363-9568] 1976. q. USD 316 (Individuals, USD 102). Ed(s): Barbara J Brown. Lippincott Williams & Wilkins, 530 Walnut St, Philadelphia, PA 19106-3621; custserv@lww.com; http://www.lww.com. Illus., adv. Refereed. Circ: 2500 Paid. Vol. ends: Summer. Microform: PQC. Online: EBSCO Publishing, EBSCO Host; Florida Center for Library Automation; Gale; Ovid Technologies, Inc.; ProQuest LLC (Ann Arbor). *Indexed:* AgeL, CINAHL. *Bk. rev.:* 2-3, 500-1,000 words, signed. *Aud.:* Ac, Sa.

As its title indicates, this publication comes out four times annually. It is highly scholarly in nature and provides a forum in which nursing educators, clinical instructors, and health-care executives can publish their research. Each issue contains articles that are central to a particular theme. These themes have ranged from ethics to magnet systems to technology in recent issues. The articles presented are moderated by guest editors who maintain knowledge and expertise in these themed areas. Tables, charts, and graphs support the data within these research articles as well as comprehensive reference lists. The inclusion of a section with book reviews adds practical value to each issue for the nurse administrator. Advertisements are minimal and non-intrusive. This title would be a welcome addition to most library collections that have a focus on nursing or health-care administration.

3446. *Nursing Economics: the journal for health care leaders.* [ISSN: 0746-1739] 1983. bi-m. USD 70 (Individuals, USD 54). Ed(s): Kenneth J Thomas, Connie R Curran. Jannetti Publications, Inc., E Holly Ave, PO Box 56, Pitman, NJ 08071-0056; NEJRNL@ajj.com; http://www.ajj.com/. Illus., index. Sample. Refereed. Vol. ends: Nov. Online: EBSCO Publishing, EBSCO Host; Florida Center for Library Automation; Gale; Northern Light Technology, Inc.; Ovid Technologies, Inc.; ProQuest LLC (Ann Arbor). *Indexed:* AgeL, CINAHL, SCI, SSCI. *Aud.:* Ac, Sa.

This bimonthly journal is directed at nursing managers and those with key decision-making roles for nurses. Its goal is to provide examples and information for those currently in positions of responsibility as well as offer mentoring support to leaders of the future. This journal highlights topics in the areas of policy, economic analysis, emerging technologies, and examples of best practices. Each issue includes articles and corresponding exercises for advanced practice nurses that enable them to earn continuing education credits and certificates for specific numbers of contact hours. Articles include executive summaries, tables and charts, and extensive bibliographies. This journal is of most use to the practitioner, and it actively supports the advancement of nurses into administrative roles. It also offers a clear and well-researched insight into the issues faced by advanced practice nurses and nurse administrators. This is an essential publication for those in either role. Its web site is www.nursingeconomics.net/cgi-bin/WebObjects/NECJournal.woa.

■ HEALTH PROFESSIONS

Health Care Administration, Medicine; Nursing; and Public Health sections.

Eleanor P. Randall, Science Reference Librarian, Baron-Forness Library, Edinboro University of Pennsylvania, Edinboro, PA 16444; eprandall@edinboro.edu

Introduction

Periodicals selected for inclusion in this section consistently include aspects of the economic, educational, political, and social conditions impacting the health professions. Some have been selected on the basis of providing guidance to those considering entering a health career. Currently, the main source of career guidance is provided by specialized web sites designed by organizations of health professionals such as the American Medical Association and the American Nurses Association. Frequent newsletters and electronic transmissions have become the norm for rapid dissemination of information on issues of immediate concern. Mindful that most professional societies also include similar information impacting on the health professions, see also the Medicine section in this volume.

Basic Abstracts and Indexes

Cumulative Index to Nursing and Allied Health Literature, Medline.

3447. *American Dental Association. Journal.* Formery (until 1939): *The Journal of the American Dental Association and the Dental Cosmos;* Which was formed by the merger of (1859-1936): *The Dental Cosmos;* (1922-1936): *American Dental Association. Journal;* Which was formerly (until 1922): *National Dental Association. Journal.* [ISSN: 0002-8177] 1913. m. USD 153 (Individuals, USD 122). Ed(s): Dr. Michael Glick, Michael Glick. American Dental Association, 211 E Chicago Ave, Chicago, IL 60611; adapub@ada.org; http://www.ada.org. Illus., index, adv. Refereed. Circ: 138000 Paid. Vol. ends: Dec. Microform: PQC. Online: EBSCO Publishing, EBSCO Host; Gale; HighWire Press. *Indexed:* AbAn, BiolAb, CABA, CINAHL, ChemAb, GSI, MCR, SCI, SSCI. *Aud.:* Ac, Sa.

The monthly *JADA* is considered the nation's foremost dental journal. Sponsored by the American Dental Association (www.ada.org), each issue contains peer-reviewed articles that cover all the latest aspects of dentistry. Dentists and others will find the reviews, clinical reports, dental research, and editorials extremely useful. A continuing education program with related articles is also offered in each issue. Items covered include the following broad categories: "Cosmetic and Restorative Care," "Research," "Clinical Practice," "Continuing Education," and "Informatics and Technology." Additionally, there are the sections "Views," "Letters to the Editor," and "News." Illustrations are in color, and a dental calendar of events is provided. Especially for dentists and any researchers or consumers seeking dental information.

American Journal of Nursing. See Nursing section.

3448. Diversity: Allied Health Careers. 2002. q. Free to qualified personnel. Ed(s): Vicki Chung. Career Recruitment Media, Inc., 211 W Wacker Dr, Ste 900, Chicago, IL 60606; info@careermedia.com; http://www.careermedia.com/. Adv. *Bk. rev.:* Number and length vary. *Aud.:* Hs, Sa.

Diversity: Allied Health Careers addresses issues of recruitment and academic advising. Free subscriptions are provided to job applicants and career services counselors. A salary review of allied health professions is published annually. Regular features include "A Day in the Life," book reviews, web sites, and scholarship and meeting announcements. Freely accessible on the web at www.diversityalliedhealth.com.

International Nursing Review. See Nursing section.

3449. The Internet Journal of Allied Health Sciences and Practice: a journal dedicated to allied health professional practice and education. [ISSN: 1540-580X] 2003. q. Free. Ed(s): Dr. Richard E Davis. Nova Southeastern University, 3200 S University Dr, Fort Lauderdale, FL 33328; ron@nsu.nova.edu. Refereed. *Indexed:* CINAHL. *Aud.:* Ac, Sa.

This is a scholarly online forum for the advancement of allied health professions. It presents an interdisciplinary approach to initiatives involving the science, practice, and education of allied health professionals. Discussion of clinical procedures is included, and online archives are searchable. All articles are registered and submitted on CD-ROM to the Library of Congress Catalog of Publications. URL: http://ijahsp.nova.edu

Journal of Practical Nursing. See Nursing section.

3450. L P N (Year): the journal for excellence in practical nursing. [ISSN: 1553-0582] 2005. bi-m. USD 118 (Individuals, USD 25.90). Ed(s): Richard R Gibbs. Lippincott Williams & Wilkins, 16522 Hunters Green Pkwy, Hagerstown, MD 21740; custserv@lww.com; http://www.lww.com. Illus. Refereed. *Aud.:* Ac, Sa.

The publisher describes *LPN 2006* as "the new, peer-reviewed resource that focuses on the skills needed by practical nurses to safely deliver bedside care to their patients in any practice setting. *LPN 2006* helps the practical nurse strengthen his or her clinical skills and build confidence while also offering advice on documentation, practice issues, and career development."

3451. Men in Nursing. [ISSN: 1558-6243] 2006. bi-m. USD 116 (Individuals, USD 29.95). Ed(s): Bob Kepshire. Lippincott Williams & Wilkins, 530 Walnut St, Philadelphia, PA 19106-3621; custserv@lww.com; http://www.lww.com. Adv. *Aud.:* Ac, Sa.

Launched in February of 2006, *Men in Nursing* was created to focus on the support of male nurses and their colleagues. As a peer-reviewed journal, it is described as "the first journal of its kind" written by men for their male colleagues. Feature articles and editorials in the first issue include a broad range of topics from issues of personal finance to men's health to the recruitment of men into the profession. Opportunities for earning continuing education credit and contact hours will be available in each issue. This title should occupy a niche in all academic institutions with a nursing and/or gender studies program.

3452. Minority Nurse. [ISSN: 1076-7223] 1993. q. USD 19.95. Ed(s): Pam Chwedyk. Career Recruitment Media, Inc., 211 W Wacker Dr, Ste 900, Chicago, IL 60606; info@careermedia.com; http://www.careermedia.com/print/mn.html. Adv. Circ: 30000. *Indexed:* CINAHL. *Aud.:* Ga, Ac, Sa.

Representing the health care and professional issues of minority nurses, *Minority Nurse* publishes columns discussing diversity concerns in nursing schools, second opinions on a wide range of controversial topics, special reports, and feature articles on nursing careers. Scholarship and employment opportunities are included. The nation's largest hospitals and 1,800 nursing programs receive complimentary copies. Academic counselors, administrators, nursing students, and health professionals, regardless of minority status, will benefit from this publication.

3453. Nursing Forum: an independent voice for nursing. [ISSN: 0029-6473] 1961. q. GBP 121 print & online eds. Blackwell Publishing, Inc., Commerce Place, 350 Main St, Malden, MA 02148; customerservices@blackwellpublishing.com; http://www.blackwellpublishing.com. Illus., adv. Refereed. Circ: 2050. Microform: PQC. Online: Blackwell Synergy; EBSCO Publishing, EBSCO Host; Florida Center for Library Automation; Gale; Northern Light Technology, Inc.; OCLC Online Computer Library Center, Inc.; Ovid Technologies, Inc.; ProQuest LLC (Ann Arbor); SwetsWise Online Content. Reprint: PSC. *Indexed:* AgeL, CINAHL, ExcerpMed. *Aud.:* Ac, Sa.

An international board of notable health professionals provides the venue for the presentation of current professional practice issues. A regular feature, "Said Another Way," presents viewpoints on controversial subjects related to all areas of the career of nursing. Feature articles include clinical and research-based information. Suitable for all nurses, particularly advanced practice nurses (APNs). *Nursing Forum* presents a global approach to current issues and the future status of nursing.

3454. Nursing Outlook. [ISSN: 0029-6554] 1953. 6x/yr. USD 160. Ed(s): Marion E Broome. Mosby, Inc., 11830 Westline Industrial Dr, St Louis, MO 63146-3318; elspcs@elsevier.com; http://www.us.elsevierhealth.com. Illus., index, adv. Sample. Refereed. Circ: 6000 Paid and controlled. Vol. ends: Nov/Dec. Microform: PQC. Online: EBSCO Publishing, EBSCO Host; OCLC Online Computer Library Center, Inc.; ScienceDirect; SwetsWise Online Content. *Indexed:* AgeL, CINAHL, ECER, MCR, SCI, SSCI, SWR&A. *Aud.:* Ac.

As the official journal of the American Academy of Nursing (AAN), this publication is of primary interest to practicing nurses and nurse educators. A regular feature on key issues is "AAN News and Opinion." Topics range from the inclusion of more nursing journals in the ISI Web of Knowledge to the nursing faculty shortage. Tables of contents and abstracts are free of charge at www.nursingoutlook.org. A well-respected title with a broad range of up-to-date information on policy and practice in nursing.

3455. Policy, Politics & Nursing Practice. [ISSN: 1527-1544] q. GBP 259. Ed(s): David M Keepnews. Sage Publications, Inc., 2455 Teller Rd, Thousand Oaks, CA 91320; info@sagepub.com; http://www.sagepub.com. Adv. Refereed. Online: CSA; EBSCO Publishing, EBSCO Host; HighWire Press; OCLC Online Computer Library Center, Inc.; SAGE Publications, Inc., SAGE Journals Online; SwetsWise Online Content. Reprint: PSC. *Indexed:* CINAHL. *Aud.:* Ac, Sa.

The scope of *Policy, Politics & Nursing Practice* is defined by the title. It is described as a forum that includes topics that "affect nursing practice in all venues of care delivery." International health policy issues, interviews, commentaries, and case studies broaden the audience benefiting from this scholarly approach. The recent article titled "Mid-Career Opportunity for Nurses: Learning and Growing Through a Health Policy Internship" is of direct value to many professional health care providers reevaluating career options. All academic nursing faculty, heath care administrators, health care workers in positions of leadership, and students would find this journal professionally satifying to read on a regular basis.

■ HIKING, CLIMBING, AND OUTDOOR RECREATION

General/Association Magazines/Association Newsletters

Pauline Baughman, Reference Librarian, Multnomah County Library, 801 S.W. Tenth Ave., Portland, OR 97205-2597; paulineb@multcolib.org; FAX: 503-988-5226

Introduction

Whether ice climbing in the Canadian Rockies, backpacking through the Canyons of the Escalante, or hiking local trails, outdoor recreation in all forms is enjoyed by both the casual and extreme participants alike. Although most outdoor-related publications focus on specific activities, a few focus on outdoor recreation in general. A number of the titles below will be enjoyed by a general audience, but most are specialized and aimed at a specific audience. Outdoor magazines included in this section focus on a broad range of issues and activities, including conservation and environmental issues. Aimed at the general consumer, they are attractive and contain many color photographs.

The commercial climbing magazines listed here focus primarily on the United States, with some international coverage. Most titles include equipment reviews, climbing tips, maps, and route information, along with stunning color photos. Association magazines, on the other hand, contain accounts of trips and expeditions, together with general interest and regional articles.

Like commercial climbing magazines, commercial hiking publications cover large geographic regions and include a wide range of articles of interest to many hikers, including product reviews, technique tips, and destination guides. Association magazines fill the local and regional information gap left by commercial publishers by focusing on specific regions and trails.

In addition to the annotated list of commercial publications and association magazines below, there is an unannotated selection of hiking, climbing, and outdoor recreation association newsletters. Most association magazines and newsletters focus on club events and activities in the particular geographic region where the organization is based. Librarians are advised to seek out and collect publications from those local organizations that will be of most interest to their patrons.

Basic Periodicals

Hs: *Backpacker;* Ga: *American Hiker, Backpacker, Climbing, Outside (Santa Fe), Rock & Ice;* Ac: *Alpine Journal, American Alpine Journal, Backpacker, Canadian Alpine Journal, Climbing, Outside (Santa Fe), Rock & Ice.*

Basic Abstracts and Indexes

Ingenta.

General

3456. *Backpacker: the magazine of wilderness adventure.* Former titles (until 1980): *Backpacker Including Wilderness Camping;* (until 1979): *Backpacker (1973);* Incorporates (1971-19??): *Wilderness Camping.* [ISSN: 0277-867X] 1973. 9x/yr. USD 19.97 domestic; USD 34 Canada; USD 3.99 per issue domestic. Ed(s): Jonathan Dorn. Active Interest Media, 33 E Minor St, Emmaus, PA 18098; http://www.aimmedia.com/. Illus., adv. Sample. Circ: 280000 Paid. Vol. ends: Nov/Dec. Microform: PQC. Online: EBSCO Publishing, EBSCO Host; Florida Center for Library Automation; Gale; Northern Light Technology, Inc.; OCLC Online Computer Library Center, Inc.; ProQuest K-12 Learning Solutions; ProQuest LLC (Ann Arbor); H.W. Wilson. *Indexed:* ASIP, ConsI, MASUSE, PEI, RGPR, SD. *Bk. rev.:* 2-3, 100-200 words. *Aud.:* Hs, Ga, Ac.

Backpacker focuses primarily on hiking and backpacking, but it is a magazine that will appeal to many outdoor enthusiasts. Along with detailed information on planning trips, this magazine contains articles on nature, health and nutrition, and first aid and safety, as well as recipes and product reviews. The annual "Gear Guide" contains equipment and clothing reviews. *Backpacker's* web site does not contain articles from the print edition of the magazine, but it features daily news items, a weekend wilderness guide, and an online version of the annual gear guide.

3457. *Backpacking Light: the magazine of lightweight hiking and backcountry travel.* [ISSN: 1550-4417] 2004. q. Ed(s): Matt Colon. Beartooth Mountain Press, 1627 W Main St, Bozeman, MT 59715. *Aud.:* Ga.

Dedicated to lightweight backpacking enthusiasts who are interested in lightening their load, this magazine and web site feature editorials, gear guides and checklists, product reviews, and news articles. Lightweight backpacking is defined by a pack weight of less than 20 pounds without food and water. The content of the print magazine and the online site is entirely different.

3458. *Climber.* Former titles (until 1995): *Climber and Hillwalker; Climber; Climber and Rambler; Climber.* [ISSN: 1358-5207] 1961. m. GBP 32 domestic; GBP 45 in Europe; GBP 58 elsewhere. Ed(s): Bernard Newman. Warners Group Publications Plc, The Maltings, West St, Bourne, PE10 9PH, United Kingdom; subscriptions@warnersgroup.co.uk; http://www.warnersgroup.co.uk. Illus., adv. Sample. Circ: 15549. Vol. ends: Dec. *Indexed:* SD. *Bk. rev.:* 2-4, 300-800 words. *Aud.:* Ac, Sa.

This magazine has very limited coverage of North America, but it will be of interest to those who climb internationally. Each issue contains news items, route descriptions, profiles of climbers, advice from experts, information on competitions, and gear reviews.

3459. *Climbing.* [ISSN: 0045-7159] 1970. 9x/yr. USD 29.95 domestic; USD 39.95 Canada; USD 44.95 elsewhere. Source Interlink Companies, 27500 Riverview Center Blvd, Bonita Springs, FL 34134; edisupport@sourceinterlink.com; http://www.sourceinterlink.com. Illus., adv. Sample. Circ: 38263 Paid. Vol. ends: Dec/Jan. *Bk. rev.:* 4-5, 100-300 words. *Aud.:* Ac, Sa.

Climbing contains a variety of articles related to sport, traditional, alpine, and ice climbing in the United States, with some international coverage. Each issue contains interviews, a detailed expedition plan to a climbing destination, equipment reviews, competition results, and spectacular photos. One issue a year is dedicated to gear and product reviews. The web site contains much of the full text of the print magazine and includes news, an events calendar, and an index to past issues of the magazine.

3460. *Disabled Outdoors Magazine.* [ISSN: 1067-098X] 1987. q. USD 14; USD 20 Canada. Ed(s): Carolyn Dohme. John Kopchik, Jr., HC 80, Box 395, Grand Marais, MN 55604. Illus., adv. Circ: 7800. Vol. ends: Dec. *Bk. rev.:* 1-4, 500-1,500 words. *Aud.:* Ems, Hs, Ac, Sa.

Disabled Outdoors is the only magazine in the United States dedicated specifically to the outdoors and the disabled person. Articles are written by people with disabilities for people of all ages and with all types of disabilities. Topics cover the United States and Canada and include camping, mountaineering, hunting, fishing, boating, and snow and water skiing.

3461. *Explore (Calgary): Canada's outdoor adventure magazine.* Formerly: *Explore Alberta.* [ISSN: 0714-816X] 1981. 7x/yr. CND 26.95 domestic; USD 32.95 United States; USD 36.95 elsewhere. Ed(s): James Little. Quarto Communications, 54 St Patrick St, Toronto, ON M5T 1V1, Canada. Adv. Circ: 25550 Paid. Microform: MML. Online: Gale; LexisNexis. *Indexed:* CBCARef, CPerI, SD. *Bk. rev.:* Number and length vary. *Aud.:* Ga.

Focusing on travel, adventure, and gear, this magazine primarily features articles on outdoor recreation opportunities in Canada. Articles focus on backpacking, skiing, bicycling, canoeing, and kayaking; the magazine also includes information on environmental issues and reviews of outdoor equipment and clothing.

Field & Stream. See Hunting and Guns section.

3462. *Gripped.* [ISSN: 1488-0814] m. Ed(s): David Chaundy-Smart. Gripped Inc., 344 Bloor St. West, 510, Toronto, ON M5S 3A7, Canada; gripped@gripped.com. Adv. *Bk. rev.:* 2-3, 100-200 words. *Aud.:* Ga.

Canada's first climbing magazine covers all aspects of technical climbing including gym climbing, cragging, ice climbing, big walls, and mountaineering, with a focus on climbing in Canada and abroad. Includes articles for beginners, profiles of Canadian climbers, mini-guides and routes, travel, product reviews, and exciting color photos.

3463. *High Mountain.* Former titles: *High Mountain Sports; High Magazine.* 1982. m. GBP 28 domestic; GBP 45 foreign; GBP 2.99 newsstand/cover per issue. Ed(s): Geoff Birtles. Greenshires Publishing Limited, Telford Way, Kettering, NN16 8UN, United Kingdom; http://www.greenshirespublishing.com. Illus., adv. Sample. Circ: 14000. Vol. ends: Dec. *Bk. rev.:* 2-4, 400-1,200 words. *Aud.:* Ac, Sa.

Focusing primarily on Britain, *High Mountain* is a commercial journal that publishes the British Mountaineering Council's news and notes. Each issue contains articles related to rock climbing and mountaineering, as well as interviews and equipment reviews.

3464. *Outdoor Life.* [ISSN: 0030-7076] 1898. m. USD 10 domestic; CND 16 Canada; USD 3.99 newsstand/cover. Time4 Media, Inc., 2 Park Ave, New York, NY 10016. Illus., adv. Sample. Circ: 1350000 Paid. Vol. ends: Dec. CD-ROM: ProQuest LLC (Ann Arbor). Microform: NBI; PQC. Online: The Dialog Corporation; EBSCO Publishing, EBSCO Host; Gale; Northern Light Technology, Inc.; OCLC Online Computer Library Center, Inc.; ProQuest K-12 Learning Solutions; ProQuest LLC (Ann Arbor); H.W. Wilson. *Indexed:* ConsI, MASUSE, RGPR. *Aud.:* Ems, Hs, Ga, Ac.

Outdoor Life has been providing readers with articles on hunting and fishing for over 100 years. There are four regional editions: East, Midwest, South, and West; the edition subscribers receive is determined by address. Content includes information on techniques, gear and product reviews, and the occasional article on conservation and the environment. Coverage is primarily of North America and Canada. The web site, which is also the web site for *Field & Stream*, will be of interest to fans of either magazine.

3465. *Outside (Santa Fe).* Formerly (until 1980): *Mariah - Outside;* Which was formed by the merger of (1976-1979): *Mariah;* (1977-1979): *Outside (San Francisco).* [ISSN: 0278-1433] 1976. m. USD 18 domestic; USD 35 Canada; USD 45.97 elsewhere. Ed(s): Lawrence J Burke, Katie Arnold. Mariah Media Inc., Outside Plaza, 400 Market St, Santa Fe, NM 87501; http://www.outsidemag.com/. Illus., adv. Circ: 575000. Microform: PQC. *Indexed:* ASIP, RI-1, SD. *Aud.:* Hs, Ga.

Outside magazine covers all aspects of outdoor activities, including camping, climbing, hiking, cycling, and fishing. Included are articles that cover the United States and the globe, as well as photographs, gear reviews, and fitness tips. The advertising section "Active Traveler Directory" lists recreational opportunities across the world. *Outside* won the National Magazine Award for General Excellence 1996–1998. The online version of the magazine includes many of the same features as the print edition.

3466. *Rock & Ice: the climber's magazine.* [ISSN: 0885-5722] 1984. 9x/yr. USD 25.95; USD 5.99 newsstand/cover per issue. Ed(s): Matt Samet. Big Stone Publishing, 1101 Village Rd, Ste UL-4D, Carbondale, CO 81623. Illus., adv. Sample. Circ: 32000 Paid and controlled. Vol. ends: Nov/Dec. *Bk. rev.:* 5-8, 300-500 words. *Aud.:* Ac, Sa.

Aimed at the serious climber, *Rock & Ice* provides general articles on climbing and climbers as well as detailed information on climbing areas, primarily in the United States, including locations, routes, and interviews. There are also articles on techniques, product reviews, and an impressive photo gallery. Special issues include an annual guide to road trips and a "SuperGuide" that covers international climbing. The *Rock & Ice* web site features news, notice of climbing events, technical tips, and reader responses to controversial climbing topics.

3467. *Sierra: exploring, enjoying and protecting the planet.* Formerly: *Sierra Club Bulletin.* [ISSN: 0161-7362] 1893. bi-m. USD 12 (Individuals, USD 15). Ed(s): Joan Hamilton, Robert Schildgen. Sierra Club, 85 Second St, 2nd Fl, San Francisco, CA 94105-3441; information@ sierraclub.org; http://www.sierraclub.org. Illus., index, adv. Circ: 730000 Controlled. Vol. ends: Nov/Dec. Microform: PQC. Online: EBSCO Publishing, EBSCO Host; Florida Center for Library Automation; Gale; Northern Light Technology, Inc.; OCLC Online Computer Library Center, Inc.; ProQuest LLC (Ann Arbor); H.W. Wilson. *Indexed:* AltPI, BAS, BRI, BiolDig, CBRI, EnvInd, GSI, LRI, M&GPA, MASUSE, RGPR. *Aud.:* Hs, Ga, Ac.

The Sierra Club, founded in 1892, is well known for its commitment to protecting the earth's ecosystems. *Sierra,* the official publication of the club, contains well-researched articles that are usually written by freelance journalists

or Sierra Club members, combined with numerous color photographs. The "Mixed Media" feature reviews selected environmental books, web sites, and videos. Many of the articles found in *Sierra* are available on the Sierra Club web site.

Association Magazines

3468. *A M C Outdoors.* Formerly (until 1993): *Appalachia Bulletin;* Which superseded: *A M C Times.* [ISSN: 1067-5604] 1907. 10x/yr. Members, USD 50. Ed(s): Ed Winchester. Appalachian Mountain Club, 5 Joy St, Boston, MA 02108; http://www.outdoors.org. Illus., adv. Sample. Circ: 84000 Controlled. *Bk. rev.:* 2-4, 400-1,200 words. *Aud.:* Ac, Sa.

Published by the Appalachian Mountain Club (see *Appalachia Journal* below, the club journal), this magazine features articles on hiking areas and conservation issues in the Northeast. Each issue contains club news and information on club activities, profiles of members, technique tips, and equipment recommendations.

3469. *A T Journeys: the magazine of the Appalachian Trail Conservancy.* Formerly (until Aug.2005): *Appalachian Trailway News.* [ISSN: 1556-2751] 1939. bi-m. USD 15. Ed(s): Martin Bartels. Appalachian Trail Conservancy, PO Box 807, Harpers Ferry, WV 25425-0807; http://www.atconf.org. Illus. Circ: 29000 Paid. Vol. ends: Nov/Dec. *Bk. rev.:* 1-2, 200-400 words. *Aud.:* Ga.

Focusing primarily on preserving and maintaining the Appalachian Trailway, this magazine covers conservation and environmental issues, trail-building efforts, hiking experiences, and club news.

3470. *Adirondac.* [ISSN: 0001-8236] 1945. 6x/yr. Non-members, USD 20. Ed(s): Neal Burdick. Adirondack Mountain Club, Inc., 814 Goggins Rd, Lake George, NY 12845-4117; pubs@adk.org; http://www.adk.org. Illus., index, adv. Sample. Circ: 18500 Controlled. Vol. ends: Nov/Dec. *Indexed:* EnvAb. *Bk. rev.:* 2-3, 200-400 words. *Aud.:* Ga.

This magazine is dedicated to "promoting the protection and enlightened use of state park and forest preserve lands." Focusing on the Adirondack and Catskill mountain regions, this title contains articles on current environmental topics; personal accounts of hiking, climbing, and canoeing trips; and club news and programs.

3471. *Alpine Journal: a record of mountain adventure and scientific observation.* Incorporates (in 1982): *Alpine Climbing;* (in 1977): *Ladies Alpine Club. Journal.* [ISSN: 0065-6569] 1863. a. GBP 18.50. Ed(s): Johanna Merz. Cordee Books & Maps, 3a De Montfort St, Leicester, LE1 7HD, United Kingdom. Illus., index, adv. Sample. Circ: 1500. *Bk. rev.:* 30-45, 50-1,500 words. *Aud.:* Ac, Sa.

International in scope, this annual publication presents detailed accounts of expeditions and climbs throughout the world, encompassing all aspects of mountains and mountaineering, including those related to art, literature, geography, history, geology, medicine, and ethics in the mountain environment. *Alpine Journal* contains numerous illustrations and maps accompanying its general-interest articles and club notes.

3472. *American Alpine Journal.* [ISSN: 0065-6925] 1929. a. USD 30. Ed(s): Christian Beckwith. American Alpine Club, 710 10th St, Ste 100, Golden, CO 80401-1022; aaj@americanalpineclub.org; http://www.americanalpineclub.org. Illus., index. Circ: 8000. Microform: PQC. *Bk. rev.:* 20-30, 200-1,200 words. *Aud.:* Ac, Sa.

As the premier annual record of significant mountaineering and rock climbing ascents worldwide, this journal features 15–20 personal narratives of mountaineering expeditions around the world. Most articles include photos and maps of routes and a summary of area and new-route statistics. Each issue contains a lengthy "Climbs and Expeditions" section, which gives details of major climbs and attempts throughout the world, and concludes with summaries of club activities and member obituaries.

3473. *American Alpine News.* Formerly: *A A C News.* [ISSN: 0147-9288] 1950. q. USD 5 domestic; USD 10 foreign. Ed(s): Hilary Maitland, Gene Ellis. American Alpine Club, 710 10th St, Ste 100, Golden, CO 80401-1022; getinfo@americanalpineclub.org; http://www.americanalpineclub.org. Illus., adv. Sample. Circ: 6000. Vol. ends: Dec. *Indexed:* CINAHL. *Bk. rev.:* 1-2, 200-250 words. *Aud.:* Ac, Sa.

Like most of the other association magazines in this section, *American Alpine News* contains club and expedition news, a calendar of events, and features on club members. It includes articles on topics of interest to climbers, reports of climbs, and classified ads.

3474. *American Hiker: the magazine of American Hiking Society.* Formerly (until 1993): *American Hiker News.* [ISSN: 0279-9472] 1977. bi-m. USD 25. Ed(s): David Lillard. American Hiking Society, PO Box 20160, Washington, DC 20041-2160; info@americanhiking.org; http://www.americanhiking.org. Illus., adv. Sample. Circ: 10000. Vol. ends: Dec. *Aud.:* Ga, Ac, Sa.

The American Hiking Society, a nonprofit organization, is dedicated to preserving America's hiking trails. Its magazine covers a wide geographic area and contains national and regional news on trail issues, features on conservation, society news, and equipment information.

3475. *Appalachia Journal.* [ISSN: 0003-6587] 1876. 10x/yr. USD 10. Ed(s): Lucille Daniels. Appalachian Mountain Club, 5 Joy St, Boston, MA 02108. Illus., index, adv. Sample. Circ: 13000 Paid. Vol. ends: Winter. *Indexed:* HistAb. *Bk. rev.:* 5-10, 200-400 words. *Aud.:* Ga, Ac, Sa.

Because of its broad geographic scope, *Appalachia Journal* will appeal to many hikers and climbers. Described as "America's oldest journal of mountaineering and conservation," it contains articles on hiking and climbing experiences, conservation, and natural history. Also included are club notes, poetry, book reviews, and analyses of hiking and climbing accidents.

3476. *British Columbia Mountaineer.* [ISSN: 0045-2998] 1917. biennial. CND 12. Ed(s): M C Feller. British Columbia Mountaineering Club, PO Box 2674, Vancouver, BC V6B 3W8, Canada. Illus., adv. Circ: 500. *Aud.:* Ac, Sa.

British Columbia Mountaineer, a club journal, reports on recent climbs in British Columbia, camps, and expeditions. It is illustrated with black-and-white photos and maps. A different publication, the newsletter, is published ten times a year and contains club news, trip schedules, and access information.

3477. *Bruce Trail News.* [ISSN: 0383-9249] 1963. q. CND 12; USD 12. Ed(s): Norman Day. Trail News Inc., 17 Marlborough Ave, Toronto, ON M5R 1X5, Canada. Illus., adv. Sample. Circ: 10000 Controlled. *Bk. rev.:* 2-4, 100-500 words. *Aud.:* Ga.

The Bruce Trail consists of more than 800 kilometers of hiking trails on the Niagara Escarpment between Niagara Falls and Tobermory, Canada. This publication offers club news, trail updates, personal narratives related to the trail, and general-interest articles related to the environment and nature. The association's web site provides general information about the trail as well as events and accommodations along the trail and membership information.

3478. *Canadian Alpine Journal.* [ISSN: 0068-8207] 1907. a. CND 28.95. Ed(s): Geoff Powter. Alpine Club of Canada, P O Box 8040, Canmore, AB T1W 2T8, Canada; alpclub@teluspianet.net; http://www.AlpineClubfCanada.ca. Illus., index, adv. Sample. Circ: 3500. *Bk. rev.:* 3-4, 500-800 words. *Aud.:* Ac, Sa.

The *Canadian Alpine Journal* features accounts of mountaineering expeditions in Canada and of Canadian mountaineers. Also included are adventures in other countries, essays, stories, club news, and obituaries.

3479. *Mountaineer (Seattle): to explore, study, preserve and enjoy the natural beauty of the Northwest and beyond.* [ISSN: 0027-2620] 1907. m. plus special issues. USD 20. Ed(s): Brad Stracener. Mountaineers, Inc., 300 Third Ave W, Seattle, WA 98119-4117. Illus., adv. Sample. Circ: 15000. Vol. ends: Dec. *Bk. rev.:* 1-3, 200-400 words. *Aud.:* Ac, Sa.

Mountaineer is the monthly publication of the Seattle Mountaineers club. Issues consist primarily of information about club activities, trips, and classes. Each issue contains four or five articles related to local issues of interest and reports of legislative news related to the environment.

3480. *Signpost for Northwest Trails.* Formerly: *Signpost for Northwest Hikers.* [ISSN: 8750-1600] 1966. m. USD 25. Ed(s): Dan Nelson. Washington Trails Association, 2019 3rd Ave., Ste. 100, Seattle, WA 98121-2430; http://pasko.physiol.washington.edu/wta/. Illus., index, adv. Sample. Circ: 3500 Paid. Vol. ends: Dec. *Aud.:* Ga.

Focusing on the Pacific Northwest, this magazine includes descriptions of hikes, hiking techniques, news on environmental legislation, and activity reports of the Washington Trails Association. It is most useful for its reader-contributed reports on trail conditions.

3481. *Trail and Timberline.* [ISSN: 0041-0756] 1918. m. Non-members, USD 15. Ed(s): Scott Stebbinson. Colorado Mountain Club, 710 10th St, Ste 200, Golden, CO 80401-1022. Illus., index, adv. Circ: 7500. Vol. ends: Dec. *Bk. rev.:* 1-2, 100-400 words. *Aud.:* Ga.

This association magazine reports the activities and news of the Colorado Mountain Club. It includes personal narratives of club members and occasional articles on environmental issues and natural history.

Association Newsletters

Adirondack Forty-Sixer Peeks. 1948. s-a. Free to members. P.O. Box 180, Cadyville, NY 12918-0180.

Adirondack Trail Improvement Society Newsletter. 1897. s-a. Free to members. Adirondack Trail Improvement Soc., P.O. Box 565, Keene Valley, NY 12943.

American Alpine News. [ISSN: 0147-9288] 1950. 4/yr. $10. Amer. Alpine Club, 710 Tenth St., Ste. 100, Golden, CO 80401; http://www.americanalpineclub.org.

American Hiker. [ISSN: 0164-5722] 1979. bi-m. Free to members (Nonmembers, $25). Amer. Hiking Soc., 1422 Fenwick Ln., Silver Spring, MD 20910-3328.

Apex to Zenith. q. Free to members. Highpointers Club, P.O. Box 6364, Sevierville, TN 37864.

B.C. Mountaineer Newsletter. [ISSN: 0045-2998] 1917. 10/yr. Free to members. Michael Feller, British Columbia Mountaineering Club, P.O. Box 2674, Vancouver, BC, Canada V6B 3W8.

Buckeye Trailways Newsletter. bi-m. James W. Sprague, Buckeye Trail Association, P.O. Box 254, Worthington, OH 43085.

California Explorer. [ISSN: 0164-8748] 1978. bi-m. $28.50. Kay Graves, Harold Chevrier, 1135 Terminal Way, Suite 209, Reno, NV 89502.

Chicago Mountaineer. 1945. m. Free to members (Nonmembers, $10). Robert White, Chicago Mountaineering Club, 1845 N. Orleans, Apt. 2R, Chicago, IL 60614.

Desert Trails. 1975. q. Free to members. Anne Garrison, Desert Trail Assn., P.O. Box 34, Madras, OR 97741.

DIVIDEnds. [ISSN: 1069-6660] 1980. s-a. $7.50. Gary Grey, Continental Divide Trail Soc., 3704 N. Charles St. #601, Baltimore, MD 21218; www.gorp.com/dcts.

FLT News. q. Free to members. Gene Bavis, Finger Lake Trail Conference, 6111 Visitor Center Road, Mt. Morris, NY 14510.

Footprint. [ISSN: 1064-0681] 1966. bi-m. Free to members. Peter Durnell, Florida Trail Assn., 5415 SW 13th St., Gainesville, FL 32608.

Gazette of the Alpine Club of Canada. [ISSN: 0833-0778] 1986. q. Free to members. Zac Bolan, Alpine Club of Canada, Indian Flats Rd., P.O. Box 8040, Canmore, AB, Canada T1W 2T8.

Iowa Climber. 1940. s-a. Free to members. John Ebert, Iowa Mountaineers, P.O. Box 163, Iowa City, IA 52244.

Long Trail News. 1922. q. Free to members (Nonmembers, $24). Sylvia Plumb, Green Mountain Club, Inc., 4711 Waterbury-Stowe Rd., Waterbury Center, VT 05677.

Mazama. [ISSN: 0275-6226] 1896. m. $15. The Mazamas, 909 N.W. 19th Ave., Portland, OR 97209.

Mountaineer: to explore, study, preserve and enjoy the natural beauty of the Northwest and beyond. 1907. m. $15. Brad Stracener. Mountaineers, Inc., 300 Third Ave. W., Seattle, WA 98119-4117.

North Star: the newsletter of the North Country Trail Association. 1981. q. Free to members. North Country Trail Assn., 229 E. Main St., Lowell, MI 49331.

Outdoor Report. [0826-3019] 1977. q. $10. Norma Wilson, Outdoor Recreation Council of B.C., 334-1367 W. Broadway, Vancouver, BC, Canada V6H 4A9; www.orcbc.bc.ca.

Ozark Highlands Trail Association Newsletter. m. Tim Ernst, HC 33, Box 50-A, Pettigrew, AR 72752; www.hikearkansas.com/ohta.html.

Pathways Across America. 1988. q. Free. Gary Werner, Amer. Hiking Soc., 1422 Fenwick Lane, Silver Spring, MD 20910; www.americanhiking.org/news.

Potomac Appalachian. [ISSN: 0092-2226] 1932. m. $6. Linda Shannon-Beaver, Potomac Appalachian Trail Club, 118 Park St. S.E., Vienna, VA 22180; www.patc.net.

Prairie Club Bulletin. [ISSN: 0032-6607] 1908. 6/yr. Free to members (Nonmembers, $15). Susan Messer, The Prairie Club, 533 W. North Ave., No. 10, Elmhurst, IL 60126.

Ridgeline. 1987. bi-m. Free to members (Nonmembers, $1). Superior Hiking Trail Assoc., P.O. Box 4, Two Harbors, MN 55616; www.shta.org.

Skyliner. 1933. m. Free to members. Skyline Hikers of the Canadian Rockies, P.O. Box 3814, Spruce Grove, AB, Canada T7X 3B1.

Trail Tracks. [ISSN: 1082-8308] 1971. q. Free to members (Nonmembers, $35). Stuart H. Macdonald, American Trails, P.O. Box 11046, Prescott, AZ 86304; www.americantrails.org/trailtracks/index.html.

Trail Walker: news of hiking and conservation. [ISSN: 0749-1352] 1963. bi-m. Free to members. New York-New Jersey Trail Conference, 156 Ramapo Valley Rd., Rte. 202, Mahwah, NJ 07430.

Trailblazer. 1985. q. Free to members. Rails-to-Trails Conservancy, 1100 17th St. N.W., 10th Floor, Washington, DC 20036.

Trailhead. 1974. bi-m. Free to members (Nonmembers, $10). Bernice E. Paige, Idaho Trails Council, P.O. Box 1629, Sun Valley, ID 83353.

Trails Advocate. q. $15. Tom Neenan, Iowa Trails Council, Inc., P.O. Box 131, Center Point, IA 52213.

Up Rope. 1944. m. $15. Mountaineering Section of the Potomac Appalachian Trail Club, 118 Park St. S.E., Vienna, VA 22180.

Voyageur Trail News. [ISSN: 1040-8541] 3/yr. Free to members. Cheryl Landmark, 150 Churchill Blvd., P.O. Box 20040, Sault Sainte Marie, ON, Canada P6A 6W3; www3.sympatico.ca/voyageur.trail/newsletter.html.

■ HISTORY

Loraine Wies, Periodicals/Acquisitions Library, Schaffer Library, Union College, Schenectady, NY 12308

Introduction

We often hear the aged chestnut of wisdom—that in order to understand where we are today, we need to understand where we have been. Such is the study of history. The chronicling of mankind's history has been offered in many ways—in written documentation and oral storytelling as well as through artistic interpretation and expression.

The journals chosen for this section offer high-quality presentations of historical research for both academics and laypersons. For many journals, it is apparent from their titles that a relationship between disciplines is a focus of the publication, e.g., *Journal of the History of Sexuality* or *Comparative Studies in Society and History, Literature and History.* For other not-so-descriptive titles, I have attempted to provide an overview of the interdisciplinary relationships highlighted within.

With a primary focus on American history, the list includes some British and international titles as well. Many of the titles are accessible in a full-text version through a variety of subscription-based aggregators such as JSTOR and Proquest. Generally, I have not provided information on how to submit an article or a review but have included a URL where this information can often be obtained. [Editor's note: *American Heritage Magazine* suspended publication

of the print version with the April/May 2007 issue. The web site, at American-Heritage.com, continues to publish, and we refer you and your researchers to it, since this has been a standard historical journal for many years.]

Basic Periodicals

Ems: *American History(Leesburg);* Hs: *American History, History Today;* Ga: *American History (Leesburg), History News, History Today;* Ac: *American Historical Review, English Historical Review, Hispanic American Historical Review, The Historian (East Lansing), History, History Today, Journal of American History, Journal of Contemporary History, Journal of Modern History, Journal of Urban History, William and Mary Quarterly.*

Basic Abstracts and Indexes

America: History and Life, Arts and Humanities Citation Index, Historical Abstracts.

3482. *Alaska History: a publication of the Alaska Historical Society.* [ISSN: 0890-6149] 1984. s-a. Non-members, USD 12. Ed(s): James H Ducker. Alaska Historical Society, PO Box 100299, Anchorage, AK 99510-0299; ahs@alaska.net; http://www.alaskahistoricalsociety.org/. Illus. Sample. Refereed. Circ: 700. *Indexed:* AmH&L, HistAb. *Bk. rev.:* 6-20, 350-600 words. *Aud.:* Ga, Ac.

Various aspects of the history of the state of Alaska are covered in this semi-annual journal, published by the Alaska Historical Society. Authors are both laypersons and academics. Illustrations, especially photographs, are plentiful and useful, and maps are also included when relevant. The book reviews cover titles about the northwestern United States as well as Alaska. In addition, the section titled "Alaskana" provides basic bibliographic information about new works on Alaskan history and culture. Recent articles in the journal include "Symbolic Acts and the Claiming of Alaska," "The Gold of Russian America: The Gold Rush that Didn't Happen," and "George Holt: First White Man Across the Chilkoot Pass."

3483. *American Heritage.* [ISSN: 0002-8738] 1954. 8x/yr. USD 12 domestic. Ed(s): Frederick Allen, Richard F Snow. American Heritage, 90 Fifth Ave, New York, NY 10011; http://www.americanheritage.com. Illus., index, adv. Circ: 280000 Paid. *Indexed:* ABS&EES, AmH&L, AmHI, ArtHuCI, BEL&L, BRI, CBRI, FLI, HistAb, LRI, MASUSE, MLA-IB, RGPR, RILM, SSCI. *Aud.:* Ems, Hs, Ga, Ac.

This popular magazine of American history is a standard, and should be readily accessible in most public and academic libraries. It covers a broad range of topics in American Studies. Well-known authors of historical pieces such as Stephen Sears and Harold Holzer have occasionally been contributors. Articles on topics as wide-ranging as Alfred Hitchcock; Wildwood, New Jersey; and Benedict Arnold have appeared in recent issues. The writing style is informative and appealing without pandering to the audience. Departments such as "Time Machine" and "History Now" further enhance the publication's appeal, and most articles and columns are amply illustrated. This well-loved magazine has made a successful transition to the twenty-first century, and, in fact, is no longer available in print, but is an e-journal only. To subscribe, go to www.americanheritage.com/contact.

3484. *American Historical Review.* [ISSN: 0002-8762] 1895. 5x/yr. USD 280 domestic; USD 310.80 Canada; USD 305 elsewhere. Ed(s): Robert A. Schneider. University of Chicago Press, Journals Division, PO Box 37005, Chicago, IL 60637; subscriptions@press.uchicago.edu; http://www.journals.uchicago.edu. Illus., index, adv. Refereed. Circ: 18000. Vol. ends: Dec. Microform: PQC. Online: EBSCO Publishing, EBSCO Host; JSTOR (Web-based Journal Archive); OCLC Online Computer Library Center, Inc.; ProQuest LLC (Ann Arbor). Reprint: PSC. *Indexed:* ABS&EES, AbAn, AmH&L, AmHI, ArtHuCI, BAS, BRD, BRI, BrArAb, CBRI, CJA, FLI, HistAb, HumInd, IBR, IBSS, IBZ, IPSA, IndIslam, JEL, MASUSE, NumL, PRA, RI-1, RILM, SSCI, SUSA, SWA. *Bk. rev.:* 250-275, 450 words. *Aud.:* Ac, Sa.

Study of the full range of history would not be possible without this journal, which is the official publication of the American Historical Association. The articles in *American Historical Review* represent the leading edge in scholarly writing on American and world history. Each issue contains from two to six major articles; numerous book reviews occupy at least 50 percent of each issue, and there is also a section of film reviews. Occasional special features such as "AHR Forum" and "Forum Essay" focus on particular issues. Recent articles have covered topics as diverse as African-American rights in the nineteenth century, elocution, and Western masculinity. Each issue has a topical table of contents, a convenient feature for those seeking to browse the subject contents. "In This Issue" presents a useful, brief description of each of the major articles and an overview of the entire issue. Additionally, there is a supplement listing the tables of contents for all volumes published for the year.

3485. *American History (Leesburg).* Formerly (until 1995): *American History Illustrated.* [ISSN: 1076-8866] 1966. bi-m. USD 19.95 domestic; USD 27.95 foreign; USD 4.99 per issue. Ed(s): Roger Vance. Weider History Group, 741 Miller Dr, S E, Ste D-2, Leesburg, VA 20175. Illus., index, adv. Circ: 100000 Paid. Microform: NBI; PQC. Online: EBSCO Publishing, EBSCO Host; Florida Center for Library Automation; Gale; OCLC Online Computer Library Center, Inc.; ProQuest K-12 Learning Solutions; ProQuest LLC (Ann Arbor). *Indexed:* AmH&L, AmHI, ArtHuCI, HistAb, IIFP, MASUSE, RGPR, RILM, SSCI. *Bk. rev.:* 2-29, 200-300 words. *Aud.:* Ems, Hs, Ga.

American History is aimed at a general audience and makes extensive use of accompanying illustrations to supplement the articles on various historical topics. Recent articles include "'The Birth of a Nation,' When Hollywood Glorified the KKK" and "Abraham Lincoln: The Lawyer." A few books and other historical media are reviewed in each issue. This journal is a good place to begin for students researching topics in American history, and a good source of information for adults with an interest in the subject.

3486. *American Jewish History.* Former titles: *American Jewish Historical Society. Publications; American Jewish Historical Quarterly.* [ISSN: 0164-0178] 1893. q. USD 125. Ed(s): Eli Faber. The Johns Hopkins University Press, 2715 N Charles St, Baltimore, MD 21218-4363; http://muse.jhu.edu. Illus., index, adv. Refereed. Circ: 1743 Paid and controlled. Vol. ends: Dec. Microform: PQC. Online: Chadwyck-Healey Inc.; EBSCO Publishing, EBSCO Host; Gale; Northern Light Technology, Inc.; OCLC Online Computer Library Center, Inc.; OhioLINK; Project MUSE; ProQuest K-12 Learning Solutions; ProQuest LLC (Ann Arbor); SwetsWise Online Content; H.W. Wilson. Reprint: PSC. *Indexed:* ABS&EES, AmH&L, AmHI, ArtHuCI, FLI, FR, HistAb, HumInd, IBR, IBZ, IJP, MLA-IB, NTA, PSA, RI-1, SSA, SSCI, SociolAb. *Bk. rev.:* 5-10, 1 page each. *Aud.:* Ga, Ac.

The American Jewish Historical Society is the sponsor of this scholarly journal, published quarterly, and examination of the full range of American Jewish Studies is the goal of the organization and the publication. Entire issues are often devoted to the discussion of a single topic. Recent articles have included "Reading Rothko's Christological Imagery" and "Jewish Diversity During the 'German' Period." Regular features in each issue include several book reviews and an occasional review essay. Contributor profiles, located at the beginning of each issue, are a helpful addition. The wide range of topics in this journal makes it appealing to both scholars and laypersons.

3487. *The Annals of Iowa: a quarterly journal of history.* [ISSN: 0003-4827] 1863. q. USD 19.95. Ed(s): Marvin Bergman. State Historical Society of Iowa, 402 Iowa Ave, Iowa City, IA 52240; http://www.culturalaffairs.org. Illus., index. Refereed. Circ: 1200. Microform: PQC. *Indexed:* AmH&L, HistAb, IBR, IBZ. *Bk. rev.:* 17-19, 500-2,750 words. *Aud.:* Ac, Sa.

Although the history of Iowa is the primary focus of the articles in this publication, the book reviews included in each issue cover a much wider geographic area and a broader range of topics. Contributors include both academics and informed laypersons. A recent issue includes an article on the impact of the YMCA and YWCA associations on life at Penn College. Articles are informative, scholarly, and well written, and lack the density seen in some similar publications.

3488. *Arkansas Historical Quarterly.* [ISSN: 0004-1823] 1942. q. Free to members; USD 5.50 per issue. Ed(s): Jeannie M Whayne. Arkansas Historical Association, University of Arkansas, Department of History,

Fayetteville, AR 72701; dludlow@uark.edu; http://www.uark.edu/depts/arkhist/home. Illus., index, adv. Refereed. Circ: 1600. Microform: PQC. Online: EBSCO Publishing, EBSCO Host; ProQuest K-12 Learning Solutions; ProQuest LLC (Ann Arbor). Reprint: PSC. *Indexed:* AmH&L, AmHI, ArtHuCI, BEL&L, HistAb, IBR, IBZ, RILM, SSCI. *Bk. rev.:* 1-26, 450 words. *Aud.:* Ac, Sa.

As with many other state historical journals, the focus of this publication is on a single state—Arkansas, in this case. The book reviews, however, cover a wider range of subjects and geography. Recent articles include "Women Locked the Doors, Children Screamed, and Men Trembled in their Boots: Black Bears and People in Arkansas" and "Thunder Across the Arkansas Prairie: Shelby's Opening Salvo in the 1864 Invasion of Missouri." Other regular features of the journal are "Arkansas Listings in the National Register of Historic Places" and "Resources in Arkansas History," which contains information on primary source materials about Arkansas in various repositories. This is an important bibliographical resource for those interested in the history of one of the more colorful Southern states.

3489. *Biography (Honolulu): an interdiscliplinary quarterly.* [ISSN: 0162-4962] 1978. q. USD 50 (Individuals, USD 30). Ed(s): Craig Howes. University of Hawaii Press, Journals Department, 2840 Kolowalu St, Honolulu, HI 96822-1888; uhpjourn@hawaii.edu; http://www.uhpress.hawaii.edu/. Illus., index. Sample. Refereed. Circ: 450. Vol. ends: Fall (No. 4). Online: Chadwyck-Healey Inc.; EBSCO Publishing, EBSCO Host; Florida Center for Library Automation; Gale; OCLC Online Computer Library Center, Inc.; OhioLINK; Project MUSE; ProQuest K-12 Learning Solutions; ProQuest LLC (Ann Arbor); SwetsWise Online Content. Reprint: PSC. *Indexed:* ABS&EES, AmH&L, ArtHuCI, BRI, CBRI, HistAb, IBR, IBSS, IBZ, MLA-IB, SSCI. *Bk. rev.:* Number varies, 2-4 pages, signed. *Aud.:* Ac.

This scholarly journal publishes articles of significant length on theoretical, generic, historical, and cultural dimensions of life-writing, encompassing biography, autobiography, journal writing, and other forms. Recent issues feature essays on such topics as "From Epitaph to Obituary: The Death Politics of T.S. Elliot and Ezra Pound." Each issue provides approximately 100 excerpted reviews of life-writing works published elsewhere, and a "Lifelines" section that announces publishing, conference, and grant opportunities. An annual bibliography of recent biographical writing appears in the fall issue, and the winter issue is devoted to special topics. Recommended for all academic collections, especially those that specialize in literature, history, or life-writing. Tables of contents and abstracts back to the Winter 1995 issue are available on the University of Hawaii Press web site.

3490. *British Heritage.* Incorporates (1979): *British History Illustrated.* [ISSN: 0195-2633] 1974. bi-m. USD 19.95 domestic; USD 21.95 foreign; USD 4.99 newsstand/cover. Ed(s): Dana Huntley. Weider History Group, 741 Miller Dr, S E, Ste D-2, Leesburg, VA 20175. Illus., index, adv. Circ: 70000 Paid. Microform: PQC. Online: EBSCO Publishing, EBSCO Host; Factiva, Inc.; Florida Center for Library Automation; Gale; ProQuest K-12 Learning Solutions; ProQuest LLC (Ann Arbor). *Indexed:* AmH&L, HistAb, MASUSE. *Bk. rev.:* 3-4, 300-400 words. *Aud.:* Hs, Ga.

Any library that serves the general public and any academic library that serves an undergraduate population will find *British Heritage* a valuable addition to their collection. This colorful magazine includes articles on all periods and eras of British history. The history of Boy Scouting, the Welsh National Eisteddford Festival, and planting an English garden are just some of the topics in recent issues. Articles are heavily illustrated, but not to the detriment of the text. Regular departments such as "Brit Tips" and "Notable Britons" provide further information. "Brit Tips" is particularly useful for those contemplating a trip to the United Kingdom. This is a thoroughly enjoyable magazine for laypersons, and scholars will also find useful material here. Also helpful for students beginning research on a topic in British history or culture.

3491. *California History (San Francisco).* Former titles (until 1978): *California Historical Quarterly; California Historical Society Quarterly.* [ISSN: 0162-2897] 1922. q. Members, USD 11.68; Non-members, USD 13.30. Ed(s): Janet R Fireman. California Historical Society, 678 Mission

St, San Francisco, CA 94105; info@calhist.org; http://www.calhist.org. Illus., index, adv. Refereed. Circ: 6000. Microform: LIB. Online: Florida Center for Library Automation; Gale. *Indexed:* AmH&L, ArtHuCI, BAS, CJA, HistAb, MLA-IB, RILM, SSCI. *Bk. rev.:* 8-12, length varies. *Aud.:* Ga, Ac.

Although its primary geographic focus is the state of California, this journal has a much broader cultural view. "California Checklist" is a useful bibliographic feature, listing recent publications on all aspects of the history of California. The activities of the California Historical Society are fully reported. Article authors may be academics, laypersons, or staff members of the society. The separation of endnotes from their articles in a section toward the back of the journal is workable, but not helpful. A well-written and recommended addition to general and academic libraries.

3492. Canadian Journal of History. [ISSN: 0008-4107] 1966. 3x/yr. CND 40 (Individuals, CND 32; Students, CND 15). Ed(s): Linda Dietz, Christopher Kent. University of Saskatchewan, Dept of History, 9 Campus Dr, 707 Arts Bldg, Saskatoon, SK S7N 5A5, Canada; cjh@duke.usask.ca; http://www.usask.ca/history/cjh. Illus., adv. Refereed. Circ: 700. Vol. ends: Dec. CD-ROM: H.W. Wilson. Microform: MML. Online: Chadwyck-Healey Inc.; EBSCO Publishing, EBSCO Host; Florida Center for Library Automation; Gale; Micromedia ProQuest; Northern Light Technology, Inc.; OCLC Online Computer Library Center, Inc.; ProQuest K-12 Learning Solutions; ProQuest LLC (Ann Arbor); H.W. Wilson. Reprint: PSC. *Indexed:* ABS&EES, AmH&L, AmHI, ArtHuCI, BAS, CBCARef, CPerI, HistAb, HumInd, IBR, LRI, MASUSE, MLA-IB, PSA, RILM, SociolAb. *Bk. rev.:* 50, 1,000 words. *Aud.:* Ac, Sa.

Articles in this scholarly journal are generally about some aspect of British or Western European history. In spite of its title, Canada itself seems rarely to be the subject of the journal. Recent articles include "Parliament Intends to Take Away the King's Life: Print and the Decision to Execute Charles I" and "'Leather' and the Fighting Spirit: Sport in the British Army in World War I." Book reviews and review essays are regular features of each issue. Article texts are in English, with abstracts in both French and English. Given the chronological and geographic scope of this publication, it is recommended for most academic libraries.

3493. Catholic Historical Review. [ISSN: 0008-8080] 1915. q. USD 60 (Individuals, USD 50). Ed(s): Nelson H Minnich. Catholic University of America Press, 620 Michigan Ave, NE, 240 Leahy Hall, Washington, DC 20064; cua-press@cua.edu; http://cuapress.cua.edu. Index, adv. Refereed. Circ: 1892. Microform: PMC; PQC. Online: EBSCO Publishing, EBSCO Host; Gale; Northern Light Technology, Inc.; OCLC Online Computer Library Center, Inc.; OhioLINK; Project MUSE; ProQuest K-12 Learning Solutions; ProQuest LLC (Ann Arbor); SwetsWise Online Content; H.W. Wilson. *Indexed:* ABS&EES, AmH&L, AmHI, ArtHuCI, BEL&L, BRI, CBRI, CPL, FR, HistAb, HumInd, IBR, IBZ, MASUSE, MLA-IB, OTA, R&TA, RI-1, SSCI. *Bk. rev.:* 30-50, 1-2 pages. *Aud.:* Ac, Sa.

The Roman Catholic church and its missionaries have had a significant impact on the historical development of numerous countries and population groups. This scholarly journal published by the American Catholic Historical Association covers not only the history of the Roman Catholic church, but also its social, political, cultural, and historical impact. Recent articles include "St. Paul's Shipwreck and Early Christianity in Malta" and "The American College of Louvain." Book reviews and a periodical listing of relevant journal articles are included in each issue. Given the scope of topics covered here, this journal is recommended for academic libraries.

3494. Civil War History: a journal of the middle period. [ISSN: 0009-8078] 1955. q. USD 35 (Individuals, USD 25). Ed(s): William Blair. Kent State University Press, 307 Lowry Hall, PO Box 5190, Kent, OH 44242-0001; sclarki@kent.edu; http://www.kent.edu:80/history/. Illus., index, adv. Refereed. Circ: 1800. Microform: MIM; PQC. Online: EBSCO Publishing, EBSCO Host; Florida Center for Library Automation; Gale; Northern Light Technology, Inc.; OCLC Online

Computer Library Center, Inc.; OhioLINK; Project MUSE; ProQuest K-12 Learning Solutions; ProQuest LLC (Ann Arbor); SwetsWise Online Content; H.W. Wilson. *Indexed:* AmH&L, AmHI, ArtHuCI, BEL&L, HistAb, HumInd, IBR, RI-1, SSCI. *Bk. rev.:* 7-13, 1-2 pages. *Aud.:* Ga, Ac.

The Civil War continues to be a topic of strong interest for scholars and laypersons. This journal has three or four major articles and 10–15 book reviews in each issue. Although this is the scholarly companion to *Civil War Times*, the information contained herein will be useful to anyone who desires more in-depth knowledge of Civil War topics. Articles cover many aspects of the war, such as "The Dilemma of Quaker Pacificism in a Slaveholding Republic" and "An Experimental Station for Lawmaking." Although more suitable for the advanced reader, this journal should be included in academic and general library collections.

3495. Civil War Times: a magazine for persons interested in the American Civil War, its people, and its era. Formerly (until 2002): *Civil War Times Illustrated.* [ISSN: 1546-9980] 1959. 10x/yr. USD 24.95 domestic; USD 36.95 foreign; USD 4.99 newsstand/cover. Ed(s): Chris Lewis. Weider History Group, 741 Miller Dr, S E, Ste D-2, Leesburg, VA 20175. Illus., index, adv. Circ: 145000. Online: EBSCO Publishing, EBSCO Host; Factiva, Inc.; Florida Center for Library Automation; Gale; ProQuest K-12 Learning Solutions; ProQuest LLC (Ann Arbor). *Indexed:* AmH&L, HistAb, MASUSE. *Bk. rev.:* 2-3, length varies. *Aud.:* Hs, Ga.

Civil War publications have a large and loyal readership, and *Civil War Times* is one of the most popular. This is another of the publications produced by the Weider History Group. The extensive use of illustrations supplement such topics as the mapmaking, Lincoln's legacy, and issues of national security. Numerous advertisements make it sometimes difficult to follow a story from one part of the magazine to another. Regular features such as "Gallery," "Travel," and "My War," as well as book reviews, enhance the magazine's appeal. Intended primarily for the general reader and Civil War enthusiast, this publication would also be helpful to high school and junior college students beginning research on a Civil War topic.

3496. Clio (Ft. Wayne): a journal of literature, history, and the philosophy of history. [ISSN: 0884-2043] 1971. q. USD 60 (Individuals, USD 27). Ed(s): Lynette Felber. Indiana University, Department of English and Linguistics, 2101 E. Coliseum Blvd., Fort Wayne, IN 46805-1499; http://www.ipfw.edu. Illus., index, adv. Refereed. Circ: 800. Microform: PQC. Online: Chadwyck-Healey Inc.; Factiva, Inc.; Florida Center for Library Automation; Gale; OCLC Online Computer Library Center, Inc.; ProQuest K-12 Learning Solutions; ProQuest LLC (Ann Arbor); H.W. Wilson. *Indexed:* AmH&L, AmHI, ArtHuCI, BRI, CBRI, HistAb, HumInd, IBR, IBZ, MLA-IB, PhilInd, SSA. *Bk. rev.:* 10-12, 2-3 pages. *Aud.:* Ac, Sa.

This quarterly, published by Indiana and Purdue Universities, takes an unusual approach to the study of history. The focus is on history as it impacts, and is influenced by, both literature and the philosophy of history. This view is reflected in such recent articles as "History out of Joint: Essays on the Use and Abuse of History" and "The Relation of Culture to History: A Review of Marshall Sahlins's Apologies to Thucydides and William Sewell's Logic of History." Book reviews and review essays cover a broad range of eras and literary genres. This publication is most suited for academic and special libraries and for upper-level undergraduates, advanced readers, and scholars.

3497. Comparative Studies in Society and History: an international quarterly. [ISSN: 0010-4175] 1959. q. GBP 112. Ed(s): Andrew Shryock. Cambridge University Press, The Edinburgh Bldg, Shaftesbury Rd, Cambridge, CB2 2RU, United Kingdom; journals@cambridge.org; http://www.journals.cambridge.org. Illus., index, adv. Refereed. Vol. ends: Nov. Microform: PQC. Online: Pub.; EBSCO Publishing, EBSCO Host; JSTOR (Web-based Journal Archive); OCLC Online Computer Library Center, Inc.; OhioLINK; SwetsWise Online Content. *Indexed:* ABCPolSci, ABS&EES, AICP, AmH&L, AmHI, AnthLit, ArtHuCI, BAS, CABA, DSA, EI, FR, ForAb, HistAb, HortAb, HumInd, IBR, IBSS, IBZ, IMFL, IPSA, IndIslam, PRA, PSA, RI-1, RILM, RRTA, S&F, SSA, SSCI, SWA, SociolAb, WAE&RSA. *Aud.:* Ac, Sa.

This quarterly journal is "a forum for new research and interpretation concerning problems of recurrent patterning and change in human societies through time and in the contemporary world." Article topics cover either historical or other social science aspects, and issues are based on themes, such as "Voicing," "Political Moralities/Moral Politics," and "Sovereignities and Subordinations." Authors are usually academics from North American and European institutions. Articles are well documented, and abstracts are located at the front of each issue. The interdisciplinary nature of this journal makes it particularly useful for those concerned with the study of history as it interconnects with other disciplines. Strongly recommended for academic libraries.

Continuity and Change. See Population Studies section.

3498. *Delaware History.* [ISSN: 0011-7765] 1946. s-a. Non-members, USD 15. Ed(s): Carol Hoffecker. Historical Society of Delaware, 505 Market St, Wilmington, DE 19801; http://www.hsd.org. Illus., index. Refereed. Circ: 1600 Paid. Reprint: PSC. *Indexed:* AmH&L, HistAb, IBR, IBZ, RILM. *Aud.:* Ga, Ac.

This twice-yearly publication by the Historical Society of Delaware is typical of many state historical journals. Each issue usually has three lengthy articles on some aspect of Delaware history, and the fourth issue in each volume contains a bibliography of Delaware history. The activities of the society are reported here as well. However, the publication is not geared specifically to the needs of genealogists. Articles are accompanied by illustrations and often make extensive use of primary source materials. This journal is primarily for libraries with patrons interested in Delaware history.

3499. *Delaware Review of Latin American Studies.* [ISSN: 1536-1837] 1999. irreg. Free. University of Delaware, Department of Foreign Languages and Literatures, 325 Smith Hall, Newark, DE 19716. *Indexed:* MLA-IB, PAIS. *Bk. rev.:* 3-10 per issue. *Aud.:* Ac, Sa.

The *Delaware Review of Latin American Studies* is a "refereed scholarly journal on the Internet about all aspects of Latin American society, culture and history." Each issue has several articles and book reviews that generally revolve around a central theme. Recent themes have included the examination of "Latin America within a vast continental context and within the most specific context of a single city" and "the issue of identity and the effect of national and racial parameters upon its formation." All articles and book reviews are indexed by volume and are searchable from the highly navigable web site. As well, occasional volumes also have a "Profile" section with an interview of a scholar of Latin American Studies. Submissions are written in English, Spanish, or Portuguese, and this adds to the global appeal of this journal.

3500. *Diplomatic History: the journal of the Society for Historians of American Foreign Relations.* [ISSN: 0145-2096] 1977. 5x/yr. GBP 257 print & online eds. Ed(s): Robert D Schulzinger, Thomas W Zeiler. Blackwell Publishing, Inc., Commerce Place, 350 Main St, Malden, MA 02148; customerservices@blackwellpublishing.com; http://www.blackwellpublishing.com. Illus., adv. Refereed. Circ: 1750. Vol. ends: Oct. Online: Blackwell Synergy; EBSCO Publishing, EBSCO Host; Gale; IngentaConnect; OCLC Online Computer Library Center, Inc.; OhioLINK; SwetsWise Online Content. Reprint: PSC. *Indexed:* ABS&EES, AmH&L, AmHI, ApEcolAb, ArtHuCI, BAS, HistAb, HumInd, IBR, IBSS, IBZ, IPSA, PRA, PSA, SSCI. *Bk. rev.:* 4-5, 3-8 pages. *Aud.:* Ac, Sa.

This scholarly journal contains articles on U.S. diplomatic history from the country's founding to the present day. Issues may focus on themes, such as "Diplomatic History Forum: The United States and Japan in the Twentieth Century," and subscribers to an affiliated online forum are invited to participate in further discussions of the topics. In addition, there is a review essay and four or five signed book reviews in each issue. Recent issues include articles on "Anglo-American Rivalry and the Origins of U.S. China Policy," "The Perils and Possibilities of Wartime Neutrality on the Edges of Empire: Iroquois and Acadians between the French and British in North America," and "Wither Japan's Military Potential? The Nixon Administration's Stance on Japanese Defense Power." This journal is of interest to those involved with the history of U.S. diplomacy, and it will be most useful in academic and special libraries.

3501. *Eighteenth-Century Life.* [ISSN: 0098-2601] 1974. 3x/yr. USD 108 (Individuals, USD 27). Ed(s): Cedric D Reverand, Mark Booth. Duke University Press, 905 W Main St, Ste 18 B, Durham, NC 27701; subscriptions@dukeupress.edu; http://www.dukeupress.edu. Illus., adv. Refereed. Circ: 575. Online: EBSCO Publishing, EBSCO Host; Gale; HighWire Press; OCLC Online Computer Library Center, Inc.; OhioLINK; Project MUSE; SwetsWise Online Content. Reprint: PSC. *Indexed:* AmH&L, AmHI, ArtHuCI, BEL&L, CJA, HistAb, HumInd, IBR, LRI, MLA-IB, RI-1, RILM, SSA. *Bk. rev.:* Number and length vary. *Aud.:* Ga, Ac.

Dedicated to the interdisciplinary study of "all areas of eighteenth-century life outside of North America—art, history, literature, politics, science and so on," the articles presented reflect a wide range of scholarly and cultural interests. Recent articles include "Mutinous Behavior on Voyages to the South Seas and Its Impact on Eighteenth-Century Civil Society" and "*Letters of Mr. Alexander Pope* and the Curious Case of Modern Scholarship and the Vanishing Text." Each issue contains four or five articles, with an additional review essay including one or more book reviews. Many volumes also present an extensive bibliography of books received.

3502. *English Historical Review.* [ISSN: 0013-8266] 1886. 6x/yr. EUR 300 print or online ed. Ed(s): Dr. G W Bernard, Martin Conway. Oxford University Press, Great Clarendon St, Oxford, OX2 6DP, United Kingdom; jnl.orders@oup.co.uk; http://www.oxfordjournals.org. Illus., index, adv. Refereed. Circ: 2550. Vol. ends: Nov. Microform: IDC; PMC; PQC. Online: Chadwyck-Healey Inc.; EBSCO Publishing, EBSCO Host; Florida Center for Library Automation; Gale; HighWire Press; IngentaConnect; JSTOR (Web-based Journal Archive); Northern Light Technology, Inc.; OCLC Online Computer Library Center, Inc.; OhioLINK; Oxford Journals; ProQuest K-12 Learning Solutions; ProQuest LLC (Ann Arbor); SwetsWise Online Content; H.W. Wilson. Reprint: PSC. *Indexed:* AmH&L, AmHI, ArtHuCI, BAS, BRD, BRI, BrArAb, BrHumI, CBRI, HistAb, HumInd, IBR, IBZ, IndIslam, MLA-IB, NumL, PSA, RI-1, SSCI, SociolAb. *Bk. rev.:* Number and length vary. *Aud.:* Ac, Sa.

English Historical Review covers a range of topics in English medieval and modern history. Articles are generally quite dense, with the usual scholarly apparatus. Each issue has a "Notes and Documents" section, with one or two articles analyzing one or multiple archival documents. Numerous book reviews are also included. Recent issues include such articles as "English Lords in Late Thirteenth and Early Fourteenth Century Ireland: Roger Bigod and the de Clare Lords of Thomond" and "Prince Charles and the Second Session of the 1621 Parliament." This is certainly one of the best journals on the subject of British history and is recommended for all academic libraries.

3503. *Florida Historical Quarterly.* [ISSN: 0015-4113] 1908. q. USD 55 (Corporations, USD 500; Members, USD 40). Ed(s): Dr. Craig Thompson Friend. Florida Historical Society, 435 Brevard Ave, Cocoa, FL 32922; wynne@flahistory.net; http://www.florida-historical-soc.org. Illus., index. Circ: 2500. *Indexed:* AbAn, AmH&L, HistAb, IBR. *Bk. rev.:* 14-18, 1-2 pages. *Aud.:* Ac, Sa.

Florida played an important role in the early history of the United States; hence, this journal is particularly recommended for libraries with in-depth collections in American history. Each issue has three or four major articles plus book reviews, book notes, and a section on recent primary source acquisitions by Florida institutions. The major articles generally involve some aspect of Florida history, while the book reviews cover a broader geographic area. This is a very useful research and bibliographic tool for those interested in Florida history or the impact of broader topics in Southern history on the state of Florida.

Gender and History. See Gender Studies section.

3504. *Georgia Historical Quarterly.* [ISSN: 0016-8297] 1917. q. USD 40 (Individuals, USD 45; Students, USD 25). Ed(s): Anne J Bailey. Georgia Historical Society, 501 Whitaker St, Savannah, GA 31499; ghs@georgiahistory.com; http://www.georgiahistory.com. Illus., index, adv. Refereed. Circ: 3200. Vol. ends: Winter. Microform: MIM; PMC; PQC. Online: EBSCO Publishing, EBSCO Host. *Indexed:* AmH&L, AmHI, BEL&L, HistAb. *Bk. rev.:* 8-24, 1-2 pages. *Aud.:* Ac, Sa.

This quarterly publication of the Georgia Historical Society generally covers historical matters pertaining to the state of Georgia. Recent issues have included such articles as "The Georgia Navy's Dramatic Victory of April 19, 1778" and "Post-Civil War Violence in Atlanta." The book reviews in each issue cover a broader geographic area. Articles analyzing primary source materials are also included in some issues. Although this journal is intended for those interested in Georgia historical subjects, there are occasionally articles and topics with relevance to students pursuing other research, particulary Southern history.

3505. *Hispanic American Historical Review.* [ISSN: 0018-2168] 1921. q. USD 297 (Individuals, USD 44). Ed(s): Barbara Weinstein, Mary Vaughan. Duke University Press, 905 W Main St, Ste 18 B, Durham, NC 27701; subscriptions@dukepress.edu; http://www.dukepress.edu. Illus., index, adv. Refereed. Circ: 2200 Paid. Microform: MIM; PMC; PQC. Online: EBSCO Publishing, EBSCO Host; Gale; HighWire Press; JSTOR (Web-based Journal Archive); Northern Light Technology, Inc.; OCLC Online Computer Library Center, Inc.; OhioLINK; Project MUSE; ProQuest LLC (Ann Arbor); SwetsWise Online Content. Reprint: PSC. *Indexed:* AmH&L, AmHI, ArtHuCI, BRI, CBRI, HAPI, HistAb, HumInd, IBR, IBSS, IBZ, MLA-IB, NumL, RILM, SSCI. *Bk. rev.:* Numerous, 1 page. *Aud.:* Ac, Sa.

This scholarly journal covers the field of Latin American history from the colonial era to the present. Articles in recent issues include "Reconstructing the City, Constructing the State: Government in Valparaiso after the Earthquake of 1906" and "The Melodramatic Nation: Integration and Polarization in the Argentine Cinema of the 1930's." Each issue usually has three lengthy articles and numerous book reviews. The book reviews are arranged chronologically by historical period and are very helpful for the compilation of bibliographies. Occasionally, a research report such as "Making History Count: The Guadalajara Census Project (1791-1930)" appears. This is one of the major journals in English on the topic of Latin American history, and, as such, it is highly recommended for all academic libraries and for public libraries whose clientele may find this source useful.

3506. *The Historian (East Lansing): a journal of history.* [ISSN: 0018-2370] 1938. q. GBP 120 print & online eds. Ed(s): David Carr. Blackwell Publishing, Inc., Commerce Place, 350 Main St, Malden, MA 02148; customerservices@blackwellpublishing.com; http://www.blackwellpublishing.com. Illus., adv. Refereed. Circ: 18000. Vol. ends: Aug. Microform: PQC. Online: Blackwell Synergy; Chadwyck-Healey Inc.; EBSCO Publishing, EBSCO Host; Gale; IngentaConnect; OCLC Online Computer Library Center, Inc.; OhioLINK; SwetsWise Online Content; H.W. Wilson. Reprint: PSC. *Indexed:* ABS&EES, AmH&L, AmHI, ApEcolAb, ArtHuCI, BAS, BRI, BrArAb, CBRI, HistAb, HumInd, LRI, MASUSE, NumL, PRA, PSA, RI-1, RILM. *Bk. rev.:* 40-60, 400-500 words. *Aud.:* Ga, Ac.

This publication is from Phi Alpha Theta, the International Honor Society in History. It is issued quarterly and contains five to ten lengthy articles, an interview with a well-known historian, many book reviews arranged by geographic area, and, occasionally, a review essay in each issue. Recent issues include such articles as "The Other White Gold: Salt, Slaves, the Turks and Caicos Islands, and British Colonialism" and "Genocide and Ethnic Cleansing? The Fate of Russian 'Aliens and Enemies' in the Finnish Civil War in 1918." Clearly, the range of historical topics covered is very broad. Given the nature of its contents and their relevance to readers and scholars of all levels, *The Historian* is recommended for all libraries.

3507. *Historical Journal.* Formerly (until 1957): *Cambridge Historical Journal.* [ISSN: 0018-246X] 1923. q. GBP 234. Ed(s): Robert Tombs, Peter Mandler. Cambridge University Press, The Edinburgh Bldg, Shaftesbury Rd, Cambridge, CB2 2RU, United Kingdom; journals@cambridge.org; http://www.journals.cambridge.org. Illus., index, adv. Circ: 1500. Vol. ends: Dec. Microform: PQC. Online: Pub.; EBSCO Publishing, EBSCO Host; JSTOR (Web-based Journal Archive); OCLC Online Computer Library Center, Inc.; OhioLINK; SwetsWise Online Content. Reprint: PSC. *Indexed:* AmH&L, AmHI, ArtHuCI, BAS, BEL&L, BrArAb, BrHumI, CJA, HistAb, HumInd, IBR, IBSS, IBZ, IndIslam, LRI, NumL, PRA, PSA, RI-1, SSCI, SociolAb. *Bk. rev.:* 5-28, lengthy. *Aud.:* Ac, Sa.

Officially, this publication "covers all aspects of European and world history since the 15th century." In practice, the principal focus is Great Britain. The contents consist of lengthy book review essays, including a historiographical review article, and six or seven scholarly and generally esoteric articles. Recent issues have included such articles as "The First Evangelical Tract Society" and "Love and Courtship in mid-Twentieth Century England." Recommended for academic and special libraries.

3508. *Historical Methods: a journal of quantitative and interdisciplinary history.* Formerly (until 1977): *Historical Methods Newsletter.* [ISSN: 0161-5440] 1967. q. USD 182 (Individuals, USD 71 print & online eds.; USD 43 newsstand/cover). Ed(s): Barbara Kahn. Heldref Publications, 1319 18th St, NW, Washington, DC 20036-1802; subscribe@heldref.org; http://www.heldref.org. Illus., index, adv. Refereed. Circ: 467 Paid. Vol. ends: Winter. CD-ROM: ProQuest LLC (Ann Arbor). Online: Chadwyck-Healey Inc.; EBSCO Publishing, EBSCO Host; Florida Center for Library Automation; Gale; Northern Light Technology, Inc.; OCLC Online Computer Library Center, Inc.; ProQuest K-12 Learning Solutions; ProQuest LLC (Ann Arbor); H.W. Wilson. Reprint: PSC. *Indexed:* ABS&EES, AmH&L, AmHI, ArtHuCI, BAS, ExcerpMed, HistAb, HumInd, IBR, IBZ, MASUSE, PSA, SSCI, SociolAb. *Bk. rev.:* Number and length vary. *Aud.:* Ac, Sa.

The title is descriptive of the scope and purpose of this journal. There are usually two or three lengthy articles that stress the positive and negative aspects of historical methodology. Articles such as "Counting Nineteenth-Century Maternal Deaths: The Case of Tasmania" indicate the international aspects of the journal. Articles are typically filled with graphs, tables, and/or mathematical formulas, and are generally divided into categories such as "Perfecting Data" and "Database Developments." The journal's contents principally focus on economic and social issues. Book reviews are not generally included, but the Fall issue is solely devoted to presenting book reviews. There are occasional lengthy criticisms of methodologically important works.

3509. *Historical Research.* Formerly (until 1987): *University of London. Institute of Historical Research. Bulletin.* [ISSN: 0950-3471] 1923. q. GBP 165 print & online eds. Ed(s): David Bates. Blackwell Publishing Ltd., 9600 Garsington Rd, Oxford, OX4 2ZG, United Kingdom; customerservices@blackwellpublishing.com; http://www.blackwellpublishing.com. Illus., adv. Refereed. Circ: 1400. Vol. ends: Nov. Microform: IDC. Online: Blackwell Synergy; EBSCO Publishing, EBSCO Host; Gale; IngentaConnect; OCLC Online Computer Library Center, Inc.; OhioLINK; SwetsWise Online Content. Reprint: PSC. *Indexed:* AmH&L, AmHI, ApEcolAb, ArtHuCI, BrArAb, BrHumI, HistAb, HumInd, IBR, IBZ, NumL, PSA, RI-1, SSA, SSCI, SociolAb. *Aud.:* Ac, Sa.

Sponsored by the Institute of Historical Research at the University of London, this journal concentrates on medieval and modern history in most parts of the world, but particularly in Britain, the Commonwealth, and the United States. Four or five articles of 15–20 pages each present such topics as "'The pooreste and simpleste sorte of people'? The selection of parish offices during the personal rule of Charles I" and "Imagining Muslim futures: Debates over state and society at the end of the Raj." Recommended for academic and special libraries; this journal serves both students and scholars as a basic source of research ideas.

3510. *History: the journal of the Historical Association.* [ISSN: 0018-2648] 1912. q. USD 486 print & online eds. Ed(s): Joseph Smith. Blackwell Publishing Ltd., 9600 Garsington Rd, Oxford, OX4 2ZG, United Kingdom; customerservices@blackwellpublishing.com; http://www.blackwellpublishing.com. Illus., adv. Sample. Refereed. Circ: 5300. Vol. ends: Oct. Microform: MIM; IDC; PQC. Online: Blackwell Synergy; EBSCO Publishing, EBSCO Host; Gale; IngentaConnect; OCLC Online Computer Library Center, Inc.; OhioLINK; SwetsWise Online Content. Reprint: PSC. *Indexed:* AmH&L, AmHI, ApEcolAb, ArtHuCI, BAS, BRD, BrArAb, BrEdI, BrHumI, HistAb, HumInd, IBR, IBSS, IBZ, IPSA, IndIslam, NumL, PSA, SSA, SSCI, SociolAb. *Bk. rev.:* 36-95, lengthy. *Aud.:* Ac, Sa.

This is the official journal of England's prestigious Historical Association. Three or four research and review articles normally comprise about half of each issue, and the other half is devoted to book reviews. The focus of the articles is largely on modern European (particularly British) events, while the reviews cover a wider geographic range. For example, a typical issue may include such articles as "Reluctant Kings and Christian Conversion in Seventh-Century England" and "An Overlooked *Entente*: Lord Malmesbury, Anglo-French Relations and the Conservatives' Recognition of the Second Empire, 1852." Considering the large number of evaluative book reviews, *History* is a valuable tool for the bibliographer.

3511. *History and Theory: studies in the philosophy of history.* [ISSN: 0018-2656] 1960. q. GBP 173 print & online eds. Ed(s): Brian C Fay. Blackwell Publishing, Inc., Commerce Place, 350 Main St, Malden, MA 02148; customerservices@blackwellpublishing.com; http://www.blackwellpublishing.com. Index, adv. Refereed. Vol. ends: Dec. Microform: PQC. Online: Blackwell Synergy; EBSCO Publishing, EBSCO Host; Gale; IngentaConnect; JSTOR (Web-based Journal Archive); OCLC Online Computer Library Center, Inc.; OhioLINK; SwetsWise Online Content; H.W. Wilson. Reprint: PSC. *Indexed:* ABS&EES, AmH&L, AmHI, ApEcolAb, ArtHuCI, BAS, BRI, CBRI, FR, HistAb, HumInd, IBR, IBSS, IBZ, IPB, IPSA, MASUSE, NTA, PSA, PhilInd, RI-1, RILM, SSA, SSCI, SociolAb. *Bk. rev.:* Number varies, essay length. *Aud.:* Ac, Sa.

Articles, review essays, and summaries of books mainly in the areas of "critical philosophy of history, speculative philosophy of history, history of historiography, historical methodology, critical theory, time and culture," and "related disciplines" are the stated focus of this quarterly. Four articles, four lengthy book review essays, and shorter book reviews appear in a typical issue. The fourth issue of each volume is a "theme issue" or, every few years, a bibliography of books and articles on the philosophy of history. Recent articles have included "Nietzsche's Relation to Historical Methods and Nineteenth-Century German Historiography" and "Is There a Chinese Mode of Historical Thinking? A Cross-Cultural Analysis." The scholarly quality and reputation of this journal are outstanding. It has an interdisciplinary appeal for historians and philosophers, as well as for social scientists interested in questions of methodology.

3512. *History News: the magazine of the American Association for State and Local History.* [ISSN: 0363-7492] 1940. q. Institutional members, USD 75; Individual members, USD 50. Ed(s): Bob Beatty. American Association for State and Local History, 1717 Church St, Nashville, TN 37203-2991; membership@aaslh.org; http://www.aaslh.org. Illus., index, adv. Circ: 7000. *Indexed:* A&ATA, AmH&L, HistAb. *Bk. rev.:* Occasional. *Aud.:* Ga, Ac.

Described as "the magazine for historical agency and museum professionals and volunteers." The aim of the association responsible for this important information journal is "advancing knowledge, understanding and appreciation of local history in the U.S. and Canada." *History News* participates in this goal by providing news on local or, to use the broader term, "nearby history" activities. Each issue contains "Faces and Places," focusing on happenings of interest to the preservationist, curator, educator, archivist, local historian, or administrator. An occasional feature is "The Bookshelf," consisting of reviews of a few books relevant to local history and historical associations. Recent feature articles have included "Revolutionary City Comes to Colonial Williamsburg" and "The Future of History Organizations." There are numerous photographs that supplement the text and contribute to the reader's enjoyment. This magazine is suitable for all types of libraries.

3513. *History Today.* [ISSN: 0018-2753] 1951. m. GBP 42; GBP 71.38 combined subscription print & online eds. Ed(s): Peter Furtado. History Today Ltd., 20 Old Compton St, London, W1D 4TW, United Kingdom; admin@historytoday.com. Illus., index, adv. Refereed. Circ: 35000 Paid. Vol. ends: Dec. CD-ROM: ProQuest LLC (Ann Arbor). Microform: NBI. Online: Chadwyck-Healey Inc.; EBSCO Publishing, EBSCO Host; Florida Center for Library Automation; Gale; Northern Light Technology, Inc.; OCLC Online Computer Library Center, Inc.; ProQuest K-12

Learning Solutions; ProQuest LLC (Ann Arbor); H.W. Wilson. *Indexed:* AmH&L, AmHI, ArtHuCI, BAS, BEL&L, BRD, BRI, BrArAb, BrHumI, CBRI, HistAb, HumInd, IBR, IBZ, IndVet, LRI, MASUSE, NTA, NumL, PRA, RGPR, RI-1, RILM, SSCI. *Bk. rev.:* 3-7. *Aud.:* Ga, Ac.

This is the English equivalent of *American Heritage,* although it is more scholarly. *History Today* is suitable for both the layperson and the professional historian who wishes to learn more about British history. The half-dozen articles are written in a journalistic, popular fashion, although they are always accurate and sometimes supported with bibliographic data. Most of the emphasis is on the British Isles, although occasionally the authors cover other parts of the world such as Turkey and Spain. Features, which run from a paragraph to a page in length, include regular columns and news notes. Handsomely illustrated.

3514. *History (Washington): reviews of new books.* [ISSN: 0361-2759] 1972. q. USD 181 (Individuals, USD 79 print & online eds.; USD 43 newsstand/cover). Ed(s): Chelsea Jennings. Heldref Publications, 1319 18th St, NW, Washington, DC 20036-1802; subscribe@heldref.org; http://www.heldref.org. Illus., index, adv. Refereed. Circ: 373 Paid. CD-ROM: ProQuest LLC (Ann Arbor). Online: EBSCO Publishing, EBSCO Host; Florida Center for Library Automation; Gale; Northern Light Technology, Inc.; ProQuest LLC (Ann Arbor). *Indexed:* ABS&EES, AmH&L, ArtHuCI, BRI, CBRI, HistAb, IBR, IBZ, MASUSE. *Bk. rev.:* Number varies, 450 words. *Aud.:* Hs, Ga, Ac.

This book review source provides an authoritative and helpful selection tool for any library acquiring historical works. It provides reasonably current "informative evaluations" of books 1–12 months after publication. Books about all time periods and all geographic areas are reviewed. The reviews, written and signed by specialists, discuss content, strengths and weaknesses, authors' credentials, and the audience addressed; as well, complete bibliographic information is provided. The 100 reviews published each quarter average approximately 450 words each. There is an author index plus a lengthy "feature review" in each issue.

3515. *History Workshop Journal.* Formerly (until 1995): *History Workshop.* [ISSN: 1363-3554] 1976. s-a. EUR 140 print or online ed. Ed(s): Bertie Mandelblatt. Oxford University Press, Great Clarendon St, Oxford, OX2 6DP, United Kingdom; jnl.orders@oup.co.uk; http://www.oxfordjournals.org. Illus., adv. Refereed. Circ: 1200. Online: Chadwyck-Healey Inc.; EBSCO Publishing, EBSCO Host; Gale; HighWire Press; IngentaConnect; OCLC Online Computer Library Center, Inc.; OhioLINK; Oxford Journals; Project MUSE; SwetsWise Online Content. Reprint: PSC. *Indexed:* AltPI, AmH&L, ArtHuCI, EI, HistAb, LeftInd, PSA, RILM, SSA, SSCI, SWA, SociolAb. *Bk. rev.:* 10-20, length varies. *Aud.:* Ga, Ac, Sa.

This journal concerns itself with "the fundamental elements of social lifework and material culture, close relations and politics, sex divisions, family, school and home." True to the "workshop" aim of demystifying historical production, the editors encourage critical dialogue and debate through a variety of features. The editors also insist that contributors write in a clear, accessible style, avoid jargon, and not assume prior knowledge or specialized interest among the readership. There are generally four or five articles and essays with such titles as "Rogues, Conycatching and the Scribbling Crew" or "Jews and the British Empire c. 1900." Articles are arranged in subcategories such as "Feature Periodization: Then and Now," "Historians in the Street," and "Historic Passion"; these subcategories vary from issue to issue. This is an outstanding journal for both experts and laypersons.

3516. *Indiana Magazine of History.* Formerly (until 1913): *The Indiana Quarterly Magazine of History.* [ISSN: 0019-6673] 1905. q. USD 18 domestic; USD 24 foreign. Ed(s): Eric Sandweiss. Indiana University, Department of History, 742 Ballantine Hall, 1020 E Kirkwood Ave, Bloomington, IN 47405-7103; imaghist@indiana.edu. Illus., adv. Refereed. Circ: 11000. Online: EBSCO Publishing, EBSCO Host. *Indexed:* AmH&L, BEL&L, BRI, HistAb, IBR, IBZ. *Bk. rev.:* 12-18, 500-750 words. *Aud.:* Ac, Sa.

Published by the Indiana University Department of History in cooperation with the Indiana Historical Society, this journal is a mixture of scholarly and popular articles. Some issues focus on a special topic, e.g., "The Civil War," with a series of articles revolving around a single document, in this instance the war diary of a Hoosier soldier. Typical articles of interest are "Not Southern Scorn but Local Pride: The Origin of the Word *Hoosier* and Indiana's River Culture" and "Mr. Halleck's New Deal: Congressman Charles Halleck and the Limits to Reform." Lively, well edited, and usually much broader in scope than Indiana topics, this is a good general title for large and medium-sized libraries in the region.

3517. *The International History Review.* [ISSN: 0707-5332] 1979. q. USD 230 (Individuals, USD 55). Ed(s): Terence Ollerhead, Edward Ingram. International History Review, EAA 2010, Simon Fraser Univ, Burnaby, BC V5A 1S6, Canada. Illus., adv. Refereed. Circ: 1000 Paid and controlled. *Indexed:* ABS&EES, AmH&L, AmHI, ArtHuCI, BAS, CBCARef, CPerI, HistAb, HumInd, IBR, IBSS, IBZ, IPSA, IndIslam, PRA, SSCI. *Bk. rev.:* 70-80, length varies. *Aud.:* Ac.

An impressive overview of world history is found here, matched only by the extensive book reviews, which may run from a page to several pages in length. Coverage, ranging from Roman and Byzantine eras to modern times, is international and includes all periods. This journal is a bibliographer's dream and an ideal source of reliable, and often imaginative, new ideas about world history. Each issue is 200-plus pages long and contains: four scholarly articles and at least one review article; "Notes with Documents"; often an "Essay and Reflection"; and about 80 book reviews. Recent articles have included "On the American Empire from a British Imperial Perspective" and "The Surrogate War between the Savoys and the Medici: Sovereignty and Precedence in Early Modern Italy." Required for any large history collection.

3518. *Irish Historical Studies.* [ISSN: 0021-1214] 1938. s-a. Ed(s): Mary Ann Lyons, David Hayton. Irish Historical Society, Department of Modern History, Trinity College, Dublin, 2, Ireland. Refereed. Circ: 900. *Indexed:* AmH&L, AmHI, ArtHuCI, BrArAb, BrHumI, HistAb, IBR, IBZ, MLA-IB, NumL, RILM, SSCI. *Bk. rev.:* 15-23, length varies. *Aud.:* Ac, Sa.

Although published in Dublin, this semi-annual journal is co-sponsored by the Ulster Society for Irish Historical Studies. Five or more learned articles in each issue cover most periods of Ireland's turbulent past from medieval times through the early twentieth century. Contemporary history is not often covered. Recent articles have included "Historical revision: Was O'Connell a United Irishman?" and "Football and Sectarianism in Glasgo during the 1920's and 1930's." One number of each volume provides a classified list of theses written in Irish universities. As "the only scholarly journal exclusively devoted to the study of Irish History," this journal belongs in any collection that seeks serious treatment of the subject.

3519. *Journal of American History.* Formerly (until 1964): *Mississippi Valley Historical Review.* [ISSN: 0021-8723] 1914. q. USD 170 (Individuals, USD 45). Organization of American Historians, 112 N Bryan Ave, PO Box 5457, Bloomington, IN 47407-5457; http://www.oah.org. Illus., index, adv. Refereed. Circ: 12000. Vol. ends: Dec. Microform: PMC; PQC. Online: EBSCO Publishing, EBSCO Host; JSTOR (Web-based Journal Archive); Northern Light Technology, Inc.; OCLC Online Computer Library Center, Inc.; ProQuest LLC (Ann Arbor). Reprint: PSC. *Indexed:* ABS&EES, AmH&L, AmHI, ArtHuCI, BAS, BRD, BRI, CBRI, HistAb, HumInd, IBR, IBZ, LRI, MLA-IB, RI-1, RILM, SSA, SSCI, SociolAb. *Bk. rev.:* 100, 1-5 pages. *Aud.:* Ac, Sa.

The publisher of this important title is the primary scholarly organization for American history specialists. Unlike *The American Historical Review* (above in this section), the *Journal* is exclusively devoted to America's past. The scholarly articles presuppose some knowledge of American history. In addition to numerous book and film reviews, each issue provides a list of recent dissertations and published bibliographies and a classified listing of recent articles. Recent articles include such topics as the "The Passion of Sacco and Vanzetti: A Global History" and "Military History, Democracy and the Role of the Academy." This is a substantive bibliographic source and a basic journal for any library collecting in the field. Institutional subscribers also receive *OAH Newsletter* and the *Magazine of History* (below in this section), which is aimed at history teachers. In addition, OAH members are provided access to a fully searchable database that contains citations from the "Recent Scholarship" section of the journal dating back to June 1999.

3520. *Journal of Contemporary History.* [ISSN: 0022-0094] 1966. q. GBP 391. Ed(s): Richard J Evans, Niall Ferguson. Sage Publications Ltd., 1 Oliver's Yard, 55 City Rd, London, EC1 1SP, United Kingdom; info@sagepub.co.uk; http://www.sagepub.co.uk. Illus., adv. Refereed. Circ: 2000. Microform: PQC. Online: Chadwyck-Healey Inc.; EBSCO Publishing, EBSCO Host; HighWire Press; JSTOR (Web-based Journal Archive); Northern Light Technology, Inc.; OCLC Online Computer Library Center, Inc.; ProQuest K-12 Learning Solutions; SAGE Publications, Inc., SAGE Journals Online; SwetsWise Online Content. Reprint: PSC. *Indexed:* ABCPolSci, ABS&EES, AmH&L, AmHI, ArtHuCI, BAS, BrHumI, HistAb, HumInd, IBR, IBSS, IBZ, IPSA, IndIslam, PRA, PSA, SSA, SSCI, SUSA, SociolAb. *Bk. rev.:* 6-12. *Aud.:* Ga, Ac.

Europe is the primary (although not exclusive) focus of this "international forum for the analysis of twentieth-century European history." Occasionally, there are special theme issues, e.g., "Domestic Dreamworlds: Notions of Home in Post-1945 Europe" and "War." This scholarly quarterly consciously attempts to bridge the gap between the professional historian and the general student of history. Although the subject matter of the journal is relatively narrow, it includes topics of wide appeal, since accessibility to a broad audience is one of its hallmarks.

Journal of Ecclesiastical History. See Religion section.

3521. *The Journal of Imperial and Commonwealth History.* [ISSN: 0308-6534] 1972. 4x/yr. GBP 373 print & online eds. Ed(s): A J Stockwell, Peter Burroughs. Routledge, 4 Park Sq, Milton Park, Abingdon, OX14 4RN, United Kingdom; info@routledge.co.uk; http://www.routledge.co.uk. Illus., index, adv. Refereed. Vol. ends: Sep. Microform: PQC. Online: EBSCO Publishing, EBSCO Host; Gale; IngentaConnect; OCLC Online Computer Library Center, Inc.; SwetsWise Online Content. Reprint: PSC. *Indexed:* AmH&L, AmHI, ArtHuCI, BAS, BrHumI, HistAb, IBR, IBSS, IBZ, IndIslam, PSA, SSA, SSCI, SociolAb. *Bk. rev.:* Number varies, 350-600 words. *Aud.:* Ac.

This title is an important, although pricey, source for the scholar or layperson interested in the history of British colonialism. Four or five studies in each issue, written by academics, deal with such topics as imperial policy and diplomacy, the growth of nationalism, decolonization, and the evolution of the Commonwealth. Considering the length and geographical extent of British rule, this journal touches on the history of the entire world, including, of course, today's developing nations. The bibliographic and historical information provided in each volume offers complete coverage of this field. Recent articles have included such topics as "Integration and Disintegration: The Attempted Incorporation of Malta into the United Kingdom in the 1950's" and "Capitalism, Nationalism and the New American Empire."

Journal of Interdisciplinary History. See Interdisciplinary Studies section.

3522. *Journal of Medieval and Early Modern Studies.* Formerly (until 1996): *Journal of Medieval and Renaissance Studies.* [ISSN: 1082-9636] 1971. 3x/yr. USD 210 (Individuals, USD 38). Ed(s): David Aers, Valeria Finucci. Duke University Press, 905 W Main St, Ste 18 B, Durham, NC 27701; subscriptions@dukepress.edu; http://www.dukepress.edu. Illus., adv. Refereed. Circ: 1000. Vol. ends: Fall. Microform: PQC. Online: EBSCO Publishing, EBSCO Host; Gale; HighWire Press; OCLC Online Computer Library Center, Inc.; OhioLINK; Project MUSE; ProQuest K-12 Learning Solutions; ProQuest LLC (Ann Arbor); SwetsWise Online Content. Reprint: PSC. *Indexed:* AmH&L, AmHI, ArtHuCI, BEL&L, HistAb, HumInd, IBR, IBZ, MLA-IB, NTA, RI-1, RILM, SSCI. *Aud.:* Sa.

The purpose of this title is to publish "work across the disciplines on topics ranging from late antiquity to the seventeenth century, work that is both historically grounded and informed by the broad intellectual shifts that have occurred in the academy." Recent articles titles have reflected a shift from primarily European history to an inclusion of Western Asian topics, as well. There are no book reviews.

3523. *Journal of Medieval History.* [ISSN: 0304-4181] 1975. 4x/yr. EUR 584. Ed(s): A E Curry. Elsevier BV, Radarweg 29, Amsterdam, 1043 NX, Netherlands; nlinfo-f@elsevier.nl; http://www.elsevier.nl. Illus., index. Refereed. Microform: PQC. Online: EBSCO Publishing, EBSCO Host; Gale; IngentaConnect; OhioLINK; ScienceDirect; SwetsWise Online Content. *Indexed:* AmHI, ArtHuCI, BrArAb, CJA, FR, IBR, IBZ, NumL, SSCI. *Aud.:* Ac, Sa.

The *Journal of Medieval History* "aims at meeting the need for a major publication devoted exclusively to the history of Europe in the Middle Ages." Medieval Europe, including Britain and Ireland, from the fall of the Roman Empire to the Renaissance, comprises the subject matter of this publication. The editorial goal is to make "continental work in medieval history better known and more accessible, especially in Britain and North America." Most of the three to five articles in each issue are in English, with English summaries provided for articles in French or German. Each issue also contains a review article or essay on the historiography of the Middle Ages.

3524. *Journal of Mississippi History.* [ISSN: 0022-2771] 1939. q. USD 25 domestic; USD 35 foreign. Ed(s): Elbert R Hilliard, Kenneth McCarty. Mississippi Historical Society, Department of Archives and History, PO Box 571, Jackson, MS 39205-0571; http://www.mdah.state.ms.us/admin/jmh.html. Illus., index, adv. Refereed. Circ: 1500. Microform: PQC. *Indexed:* AmH&L, HistAb, IBR, IBZ, RILM. *Bk. rev.:* 6-10. *Aud.:* Ac, Sa.

This title is published jointly by the Mississippi Department of Archives & History and the Mississippi Historical Society. It follows the typical pattern of regional historical journals; first, it has three or four articles such as "Movie Theaters in Twentieth-Century Jackson, Mississippi" and "Recent Manuscript Accessions at Mississippi Colleges and University Libraries." The articles are followed by a section on "Historical News and Notices" and a section of book reviews (1–2 1/2 pages long) that are well written, although not all that current. An annual bibliography of dissertations relating to Mississippi history is included in the first issue of each volume.

3525. *Journal of Modern History.* [ISSN: 0022-2801] 1929. q. USD 222 domestic; USD 242.32 Canada; USD 234 elsewhere. Ed(s): John W Boyer. University of Chicago Press, Journals Division, PO Box 37005, Chicago, IL 60637; subscriptions@press.uchicago.edu; http://www.journals.uchicago.edu. Illus., index, adv. Refereed. Circ: 3000 Paid. Vol. ends: Dec. Microform: PMC; PQC. Online: EBSCO Publishing, EBSCO Host; Florida Center for Library Automation; Gale; JSTOR (Web-based Journal Archive); ProQuest K-12 Learning Solutions; ProQuest LLC (Ann Arbor). Reprint: PSC. *Indexed:* ABS&EES, AmH&L, AmHI, ArtHuCI, BAS, BEL&L, BRI, CBRI, HistAb, HumInd, IBR, IBSS, IBZ, IPSA, IndIslam, PRA, PSA, RI-1, RILM, SSCI, SociolAb. *Bk. rev.:* 40-50, 1-2 pages. *Aud.:* Ac, Sa.

The need perceived by the American Historical Association for a journal exclusively devoted to modern history brought about this publication in 1929. It is published in cooperation with the association's Modern European History Section, and its scope was originally confined generally to modern Europe since the Renaissance, with a distinct emphasis on Western Europe. Today, it is devoted to "historical analysis from a global point of view," and it "features comparative and cross-cultural scholarship." An average issue contains four or five articles that can run as much as 50 pages each, plus review articles and lengthy book reviews. Typical topics include "Democracy and War: Political Regime, Industrial Relations, and Economic Preparations for War in France and Britain up to 1940" and "State Socialist Bodies: East German Nudism from Ban to Boom."

3526. *Journal of Social History.* [ISSN: 0022-4529] 1967. q. USD 99 (Individuals, USD 40; Students, USD 25). Ed(s): Peter N. Stearns. George Mason University, 4400 University Dr, Fairfax, VA 22030; ataylor@gmu.edu; http://www.gmu.edu/. Illus., adv. Refereed. Circ: 1500. Vol. ends: Summer. Microform: MIM; PQC. Online: Chadwyck-Healey Inc.; EBSCO Publishing, EBSCO Host; Florida Center for Library Automation; Gale; Northern Light Technology, Inc.; OCLC Online Computer Library Center, Inc.; OhioLINK; Project MUSE; ProQuest

K-12 Learning Solutions; ProQuest LLC (Ann Arbor); SwetsWise Online Content; H.W. Wilson. *Indexed:* ABS&EES, AgeL, AmH&L, AmHI, ArtHuCI, BAS, BRI, CBRI, CJA, HistAb, HumInd, IBR, IBSS, IBZ, PSA, RI-1, RILM, SFSA, SSA, SSCI, SWA, SociolAb. *Bk. rev.:* 25-30, lengthy. *Aud.:* Ac, Sa.

The content is a reflection of the impact that the social sciences have had on contemporary historical research. Articles are often replete with statistical tables and graphs. The nineteenth and twentieth centuries are the typical (although not exclusive) focus of most of the research published in this journal. A typical issue includes six or more articles divided by topical sections, review essays, and relevant book reviews. Recent articles include "The Smoke and Mirrors: Willy Clarkson and the Role of Disguises in Inter-war England" and "Paid Mothering in the Public Domain: Dutch Dinner Ladies and Their Difficulties." A journal of interdisciplinary scholarly value, particularly for the academic library collection.

3527. *Journal of Southern History.* [ISSN: 0022-4642] 1935. q. USD 35 (Individuals, USD 25). Ed(s): John B Boles. Southern Historical Association, Rice University, Box 1892, Houston, TX 77251; jinscoe@arches.uga.edu; http://www.uga.edu/~sha. Illus., index, adv. Refereed. Circ: 5000 Paid. Vol. ends: Nov. Online: EBSCO Publishing, EBSCO Host; Florida Center for Library Automation; Gale; JSTOR (Web-based Journal Archive); ProQuest LLC (Ann Arbor). *Indexed:* AbAn, AmH&L, AmHI, ArtHuCI, BRI, CBRI, HistAb, HumInd, IBR, IBZ, IIBP, RI-1, RILM, SSCI. *Bk. rev.:* 30-40, 500-600 words. *Aud.:* Ac, Sa.

This is the distinguished scholarly journal for students of the South's rich history. Each issue features four research articles written by history professors from all over the United States. No topic or time period is ignored, from the culture of slavery to the modern civil rights movement. An annual feature is a bibliography of articles about Southern history. Such special features, together with the numerous book reviews, make the journal a convenient bibliographic source for the study of the South. One of the finest regional journals, it is highly recommended, particularly for the academic library.

3528. *Journal of the Early Republic.* [ISSN: 0275-1275] 1981. q. USD 110. Ed(s): Roderick A McDonald. University of Pennsylvania Press, 4200 Pine St, Philadelphia, PA 19104-4011; http://www.upenn.edu/pennpress/. Illus., index, adv. Refereed. Circ: 1500 Paid. Online: EBSCO Publishing, EBSCO Host; JSTOR (Web-based Journal Archive); Northern Light Technology, Inc.; OCLC Online Computer Library Center, Inc.; Project MUSE; ProQuest K-12 Learning Solutions; ProQuest LLC (Ann Arbor); SwetsWise Online Content; H.W. Wilson. *Indexed:* AmH&L, AmHI, ArtHuCI, CJA, HistAb, HumInd, IBR, IBZ, LRI, RI-1. *Bk. rev.:* 15-20, 1-3 pages. *Aud.:* Ac, Sa.

This journal is "committed to the history and culture of the United States from 1776 to 1861." According to editorial policy, "the terms history and culture are interpreted broadly, and contributions in political, economic, social, cultural and other fields are welcome." Four articles typically appear in each issue with a substantial number of book reviews included as well. Recent topics have included "American Sinner/Canadian Saint? The Further Adventures of the Notorious Stephen Burroughs, 1790-1840" and "Cholera, Christ and Jackson: The Epidemic of 1832 and the Origins of Christian Politics in Antebellum America." Listings of recently completed dissertations and articles published in other journals about the early American republic are an annual feature. The journal is scholarly, and it is aimed at the professional historian who has a particular interest in this period. Such individuals will also be interested in *William and Mary Quarterly* (see below in this section).

3529. *Journal of the History of Sexuality.* [ISSN: 1043-4070] 1990. 3x/yr. USD 180 (Individuals, USD 45). Ed(s): Mathew Kuefler. University of Texas Press, Journals Division, 2100 Comal, Austin, TX 78722; journals@uts.cc.utexas.edu; http://www.utexas.edu/utpress/journals/journals.html. Illus., adv. Sample. Refereed. Circ: 746. Vol. ends: Nov. Reprint: PSC. *Indexed:* ABS&EES, AgeL, AmH&L, AmHI, ArtHuCI, CJA, FR, HistAb, HumInd, IBR, IBSS, IBZ, IPSA, MLA-IB, NTA, RI-1, SSA, SSCI, SWA, SociolAb. *Bk. rev.:* 11-16, 2-3 pages. *Aud.:* Ac, Sa.

This journal seeks to illuminate sexuality "in all its expressions, recognizing differences of class, culture, gender, race, and sexual preference" within a scope transcending "temporal and geographic boundaries." Articles include studies on

"Chaussons in the Streets: Sodomy in Seventeenth-Century Paris" and "Heterosexuality as a Threat to Medieval Studies." The entire content is a reflection of first-rate scholarship. Occasionally, there is a critical commentary or debate relevant to a previous article. The book reviews, book lists, and review essays provide a comprehensive bibliographic source.

3530. *Journal of the Southwest.* Formerly (until 1987): *Arizona and the West.* [ISSN: 0894-8410] 1959. q. USD 24 (Individuals, USD 18). Ed(s): Joseph C Wilder. University of Arizona, Southwest Center, 1052 N Highland, Tucson, AZ 85721-0185; swct@email.arizona.edu; http://www.uapress.arizona.edu/. Illus., index, adv. Refereed. Circ: 900. Microform: PQC. Online: Florida Center for Library Automation; Gale; OCLC Online Computer Library Center, Inc.; ProQuest LLC (Ann Arbor); H.W. Wilson. *Indexed:* AmH&L, AmHI, ArtHuCI, HistAb, HumInd, MLA-IB, RILM, SSCI. *Bk. rev.:* 9-15, 500 words. *Aud.:* Ga, Ac, Sa.

Scholarly articles related to all areas of the greater Southwest, including northern Mexico, make up the content of this journal. Its stated mission is to publish "broadly across disciplines, including: intellectual and social history, anthropology, literary studies, folklore, historiography, politics, borderlands studies, and regional natural history." Photographs and other illustrations add to the overall appeal of this well-edited journal. The book reviews comprise a useful bibliographical source for the study of the region.

3531. *Journal of the West: an illustrated quarterly of Western American history and culture.* [ISSN: 0022-5169] 1962. q. USD 60 (Individuals, USD 45). A B C-Clio, 130 Cremona Dr, Ste C, Santa Barbara, CA 93117-5505; sales@abc-clio.com; http://www.abc-clio.com. Illus., index, adv. Refereed. Circ: 4500. Vol. ends: Oct. *Indexed:* AmH&L, AmHI, ArtHuCI, FLI, HistAb, HumInd, IBR, IBZ, RILM, SSCI. *Bk. rev.:* 30-50, 250-500 words. *Aud.:* Ga, Ac.

This quarterly is aimed at both the layperson and the historian. Its contents are well documented and, somewhat unusually, written in a popular style. Each issue consists of 100–125 pages, with numerous black-and-white illustrations to support the dozen or so articles. A wide range of subject matter is considered, and each issue is given over to a single topic such as "Teaching about the West." The "Western Forum" column in each issue provides a space for historians and others to discuss particular, provocative topics. This is a general-interest publication that should be considered by many different types of libraries, particularly in the western United States.

3532. *Journal of Urban History.* [ISSN: 0096-1442] 1974. bi-m. GBP 505. Ed(s): David R Goldfield. Sage Publications, Inc., 2455 Teller Rd, Thousand Oaks, CA 91320; info@sagepub.com; http://www.sagepub.com. Illus., index, adv. Refereed. Circ: 800 Paid. Vol. ends: Sep. Online: CSA; Chadwyck-Healey Inc.; EBSCO Publishing, EBSCO Host; Florida Center for Library Automation; Gale; HighWire Press; OCLC Online Computer Library Center, Inc.; SAGE Publications, Inc., SAGE Journals Online; SwetsWise Online Content. Reprint: PSC. *Indexed:* ABCPolSci, ABS&EES, AmH&L, AmHI, ArtHuCI, BAS, BRI, CBRI, CJA, CommAb, HistAb, HumInd, IBR, IBSS, IBZ, IIBP, PSA, RILM, SSA, SSCI, SUSA, SWR&A, SociolAb. *Bk. rev.:* 3-4, essay length. *Aud.:* Ac.

Devoted to "the history of cities and urban societies throughout the world in all periods of human society," this journal pays special attention to studies "offering important new insights or interpretations; utilizing new research techniques or methodologies; comparing urban societies over space and/or time." The contents of each volume generally meet these demanding editorial criteria, although there is an overall emphasis on modern history. There are three or four articles per issue, treating such topics as city planning history, migration, and urban growth. Additionally, some issues have Special Sections (with guest editors) devoted to such topics as "Public Housing in the Americas" and "On Black Milwaukee." Books are critically reviewed in three or four lengthy review essays. This is a fine scholarly journal of interdisciplinary value that does justice to a crucial subject of international importance.

Journal of Women's History. See Gender Studies section.

3533. *Journal of World History: official journal of the World History Association.* [ISSN: 1045-6007] 1990. q. USD 75 (Individuals, USD 60; Students, USD 25). Ed(s): Jerry H Bentley. University of Hawaii Press, Journals Department, 2840 Kolowalu St, Honolulu, HI 96822-1888; uhpjourn@hawaii.edu; http://www.uhpress.hawaii.edu/. Illus., adv. Sample. Refereed. Circ: 1800. Online: EBSCO Publishing, EBSCO Host; Florida Center for Library Automation; Gale; Northern Light Technology, Inc.; OCLC Online Computer Library Center, Inc.; OhioLINK; Project MUSE; ProQuest K-12 Learning Solutions; ProQuest LLC (Ann Arbor); SwetsWise Online Content. *Indexed:* AmH&L, AmHI, ArtHuCI, HistAb, IBR, IBSS, IBZ, PSA, SSA, SociolAb. *Bk. rev.:* 10, 1-4 pages. *Aud.:* Ac, Sa.

This title is "devoted to historical analysis from a global point of view." The journal recognizes the limitations of the predominant national focus of historical scholarship on such topics as movements in population, climate change, imperial expansion, the spread of religion and ideas, etc. Occasional volumes of this title offer a topical forum such as "Social History, Women's History and World History." This journal is an important addition to scholarly publishing and should be considered for inclusion in all college and university libraries.

3534. *Kansas History.* Supersedes (1931-1977): *Kansas Historical Quarterly.* [ISSN: 0149-9114] 1978. q. Members, USD 30. Ed(s): Virgil W Dean. Kansas State Historical Society, Center for Historial Research, 6425 SW 6th Ave, Topeka, KS 66615-1099; vdean@kshs.org; http://www.kshs.org. Illus., index. Refereed. Circ: 3800 Paid. Microform: PQC. Online: EBSCO Publishing, EBSCO Host. *Indexed:* ABS&EES, AmH&L, HistAb, IBR, IBZ, RILM. *Bk. rev.:* 5-26, 300-2,600 words. *Aud.:* Ga, Ac, Sa.

The editors of this well-illustrated journal publish "political, social, intellectual, cultural, economic and institutional histories," and "biographical and historio-graphical interpretations and studies of archeology, the built environment and material culture." The subtitle notwithstanding, the contents are primarily concerned with the "Sunflower State" and focus on all eras from the prehistoric period to the present time. This is a local-history title with some imagination. Although the feature articles are chiefly on Kansan historical topics, the book reviews cover a broader geographical area. Noteworthy are the personal journals and memoirs that are occasionally published here. Numerous photographs add to the appeal.

3535. *Literature & History.* [ISSN: 0306-1973] 1975. s-a. GBP 67 (Individuals, GBP 27). Ed(s): John King, Roger Richardson. Manchester University Press, Oxford Rd, Manchester, M13 9NR, United Kingdom; http://www.manchesteruniversitypress.co.uk/. Illus. Refereed. Circ: 600. Online: Chadwyck-Healey Inc.; EBSCO Publishing, EBSCO Host; SwetsWise Online Content. *Indexed:* AmH&L, AmHI, ArtHuCI, BRI, CBRI, HistAb, HumInd, MLA-IB. *Bk. rev.:* 3-4, essays and short notices. *Aud.:* Ac.

The aim of this scholarly semi-annual journal is to explore "the relations among writing, history and ideology." Issues contain such articles as "Joining the 'Crusade Against the Giants': Keir Hardie's Fairy Tales and the Socialist Child Reader" and "Richard Carlile's Working Women: Selling Books, Politics, Sex and *The Republican*." Analyzing the political and ideological content of literary texts is a current trend in many academic institutions, and this journal undoubtedly has a niche in such places.

3536. *Louisiana History.* [ISSN: 0024-6816] 1960. q. Free to members. Ed(s): Carl A Brasseux. Louisiana Historical Association, PO Box 42808, Lafayette, LA 70504; http://cls.louisiana.edu/lahist.html. Illus., adv. Circ: 1400. *Indexed:* ABS&EES, AmH&L, HistAb, RILM. *Bk. rev.:* 5-15, 1-3 pages. *Aud.:* Ga, Ac, Sa.

Amateur and professional historians are contributors to this solid local publication. The four or five documented studies in a typical issue deal with all conceivable aspects of Louisiana's rich history, including the periods of Spanish and French colonization. Much of the content emphasizes the antebellum and Civil War periods. This is a scholarly and readable journal that should be considered by public and academic libraries in the South as well as libraries with geographically broader historical collections.

3537. *Magazine of History: for teachers of history.* [ISSN: 0882-228X] 1985. q. USD 40 (Members, USD 20; Non-members, USD 30). Organization of American Historians, 112 N Bryan Ave, PO Box 5457, Bloomington, IN 47407-5457; magazine@oah.org; http://www.oah.org. Illus., adv. Refereed. Circ: 6500. Microform: PQC. Online: EBSCO Publishing, EBSCO Host; ProQuest K-12 Learning Solutions; ProQuest LLC (Ann Arbor). *Indexed:* ABIn, AmH&L, BRI, EduInd, HistAb, IBR, IBZ. *Bk. rev.:* 2-4, 1/2-1 page. *Aud.:* Hs, Ga, Ac.

This publication is directed to high school, middle school, and college history and social studies teachers. Its editorial guidelines call for articles on recent scholarship, curriculum, and education methodology "written in a style that is readable and accessible" to this audience. Issues are devoted to special themes. Specifics of these subjects are further illustrated with model lesson plans. The editors particularly welcome material of multicultural interest. This title is highly recommended, particularly for curriculum collections or other library collections that support teacher training. The Organization of American Historians (OAH) also publishes the highly regarded, scholarly *Journal of American History* (see above in this section). Institutional subscribers to that publication also receive this one, as well as the *OAH Newsletter.*

3538. *Maryland Historical Magazine.* [ISSN: 0025-4258] 1906. q. Individual members, USD 45; Students, USD 35. Ed(s): Robert I Cottom. Maryland Historical Society, 201 W Monument St, Baltimore, MD 21201; press@mdhs.org; http://www.mdhs.org. Illus., index, adv. Circ: 5300. Vol. ends: Dec. *Indexed:* AmH&L, HistAb, IBR, IBZ, PSA, SociolAb. *Bk. rev.:* 4-10, 500-1,000 words. *Aud.:* Ga, Ac.

Although the focus is primarily on Maryland history, some article topics involve broader, national issues. There are book reviews of a page or more, and sometimes excerpts from one of the titles reviewed. The journal is currently only available in print format; meanwhile, the publishers are seeking back copies of the publication in order to expand availability to the Internet. Useful for both the scholar and the layperson.

3539. *Mediaeval Studies.* [ISSN: 0076-5872] 1939. a. EUR 78.50 in the European Union; EUR 83.50 elsewhere. Ed(s): Dr. Jonathan Black. Pontifical Institute of Mediaeval Studies, 59 Queens Park Crescent E, Toronto, ON M5S 2C4, Canada. Refereed. Circ: 1100. *Indexed:* ABS&EES, AmHI, ArtHuCI, CPL, FR, IBR, IBZ, IPB, IndIslam, MLA-IB, PhilInd, RI-1, RILM. *Aud.:* Ac, Sa.

Through the "publication of extensive studies in a wide spectrum of disciplines," the editors of *Mediaeval Studies* strive to present articles of "original research which make contributions of lasting significance for scholarship in the Middle Ages." Each issue is divided into three sections—"Texts," "Articles," and "Mediaevalia"—each devoted to the publication of, and scholarly comment on, both unedited and edited manuscript and archival materials. The journal does not include book reviews.

3540. *Minnesota History.* Formerly (until 1925): *Minnesota History Bulletin.* [ISSN: 0026-5497] 1915. q. USD 20. Ed(s): Anne R Kaplan, Marilyn Ziebarth. Minnesota Historical Society, 345 Kellogg Blvd W, St Paul, MN 55102; http://www.mnhs.org/market/mhspress/mnhistory.html. Illus., index. Refereed. Circ: 15000. Microform: MIM; PQC. *Indexed:* ABS&EES, AmH&L, HistAb. *Bk. rev.:* 5-25, 450 words. *Aud.:* Ga, Ac.

This journal emphasizes the history of the state of Minnesota and the history of the Upper Midwest. It is published by the Minnesota Historical Society, and the authors of the refereed articles range from academics to well-informed amateurs. The large number of illustrations included in each issue richly supplement the prose but do not overwhelm it. Recent topics include an account of The Beatles' tour in Minnesota in 1965 and the effects of the Cold War on a university professor. Special sections in each issue discuss artifacts from the Minnesota Historical Society's collections. A well-written regional journal with broad appeal.

3541. *Montana: the magazine of western history.* [ISSN: 0026-9891] 1951. q. USD 37 foreign (Non-members, USD 29). Ed(s): Molly Holz. Montana Historical Society, 225 N Roberts St, PO Box 201201, Helena,

MT 59620-1201; http://www.montanahistoricalsociety.org. Illus., index, adv. Refereed. Circ: 10000 Paid and free. *Indexed:* AmH&L, ArtHuCI, HistAb, SSCI. *Bk. rev.:* 10-20, 500-1,000 words. *Aud.:* Ga, Ac.

This handsome and entertaining magazine contains information not geographically confined to the borders of "The Treasure State." Each issue consists largely of four interpretive, documented articles presented in an attractive format, supplemented by numerous photographs and other illustrations. This title has both academic and popular appeal, and it would enhance almost any general library collection in the Western states, or collections elsewhere with a collecting strength in that area.

3542. *New England Quarterly: a historical review of New England life and letters.* [ISSN: 0028-4866] 1928. q. USD 94 (Individuals, USD 40). Ed(s): Linda Smith Rhoads. M I T Press, 238 Main St., Ste. 500, Cambridge, MA 02142; journals-info@mit.edu; http://mitpress.mit.edu. Illus., index, adv. Refereed. Circ: 2500 Paid. Vol. ends: Dec. Microform: PMC; PQC. Online: Chadwyck-Healey Inc.; JSTOR (Web-based Journal Archive); Northern Light Technology, Inc.; OCLC Online Computer Library Center, Inc.; ProQuest LLC (Ann Arbor). *Indexed:* AmH&L, AmHI, ArtHuCI, BEL&L, BRD, BRI, CBRI, HistAb, HumInd, IBR, IBZ, L&LBA, MLA-IB, R&TA, RI-1, RILM. *Bk. rev.:* 6-20, 2-4 pages. *Aud.:* Ac, Sa.

The focus of this highly regarded journal is the history and culture of a single region. Many of the articles are about famous New Englanders, and some actually fall into the category of literary criticism. The contents are not limited to any time period, but the colonial period and the nineteenth century receive the most emphasis. Among the six or seven features per issue are an occasional review essay and "Memoranda and Documents," which features short articles or a historical document with commentary. Considering the importance of New England's history and culture through all periods of American history, this is a journal whose appeal extends beyond the region. A key title for both American history and literature collections.

3543. *New Jersey History: a magazine of New Jersey history.* Formerly (until 1967): *New Jersey Historical Society. Proceedings.* [ISSN: 0028-5757] 1845. s-a. USD 30 (Members, USD 15). Ed(s): Kathryn Grover. New Jersey Historical Society, 52 Park Pl, Newark, NJ 07102-4302; http://www.jerseyhistory.org. Illus., adv. Refereed. Circ: 1200 Paid. Microform: BHP; PQC. *Indexed:* AmH&L, BEL&L, HistAb, MLA-IB. *Bk. rev.:* 3-30, length varies. *Aud.:* Ga, Sa.

Amateur and professional historians are among the writers for this publication, which publishes original contributions about New Jersey's rich history. Two to four articles appear in each issue. The "Notes and Documents" section often contains an edited document illuminating some aspect of New Jersey's past.

3544. *The New Mexico Historical Review.* [ISSN: 0028-6206] 1926. q. USD 50 (Individuals, USD 30; Students, USD 20). Ed(s): Durwood Ball. University of New Mexico, 1013 Mesa Vista Hall, Albuquerque, NM 87131-1186; http://www.unm.edu/. Illus., index, adv. Refereed. Circ: 1500 Paid. Microform: BHP; PQC. *Indexed:* AICP, AmH&L, AmHI, ArtHuCI, CJA, Chicano, HistAb, IBR, RILM. *Bk. rev.:* 9-25, 1 page. *Aud.:* Ga, Sa.

This quarterly journal publishes "original articles dealing with Southwestern history and culture from the earliest pre-history to the present." Much of the content deals with what is today the state of New Mexico and the area of northern Mexico. The style is scholarly, but the contents also have a high degree of popular appeal. Book reviews, review essays, and book notes supplement the information in this distinguished journal.

3545. *New York History: quarterly journal of the New York State Historical Association.* Former titles (until 1931): *New York State Historical Association. Quarterly Journal;* (until 1917): *New York State Historical Association. Proceedings.* [ISSN: 0146-437X] 1902. q. Members, USD 30; Non-members, USD 37.50. Ed(s): Daniel Goodwin. New York State Historical Association, PO Box 800, Cooperstown, NY

13326; http://www.nysha.org. Illus., index. Circ: 4000. Vol. ends: Oct. Microform: PQC. Online: Chadwyck-Healey Inc. *Indexed:* AmH&L, AmHI, ArtHuCI, CJA, HistAb, MLA-IB, RI-1, RILM, SSCI. *Bk. rev.:* 8-10, 1-2 pages. *Aud.:* Ac.

Throughout its long history, this journal has consistently demonstrated quality in both scholarship and writing. Members of the New York State Historical Association receive this journal as part of their membership benefits. A typical issue will feature three scholarly articles. In addition to the lengthy book reviews, the "Books-in-Brief" section provides shorter critiques of relevant publications. Highly recommended for academic and public library collections, even those outside the Empire State.

3546. North Dakota History: journal of the Northern Plains. Formerly (until 1945): *North Dakota Historical Quarterly.* [ISSN: 0029-2710] 1926. q. USD 35 domestic; USD 42 Canada; USD 50 elsewhere. Ed(s): Susan Dingle. State Historical Society of North Dakota, North Dakota Heritage Center, Bismarck, ND 58505. Illus., index. Refereed. Circ: 2000. Microform: PQC. *Indexed:* AmH&L, HistAb, RILM. *Bk. rev.:* 4-16, 1-2 pages. *Aud.:* Ga, Ac.

A regional history journal whose scope extends beyond the state of North Dakota to include the northern plains. Recent articles include "Family, Politics, and Show Business: The Photographs of Sitting Bull" and "The Corps of Discovery and the Final Challenges in Reaching the Pacific Ocean." This title is amply illustrated and includes book reviews. Well written and suitable for laypersons and professionals alike.

3547. Oregon Historical Quarterly. [ISSN: 0030-4727] 1900. q. USD 50 (Individuals, USD 38). Ed(s): Marianne Keddington-Lang. Oregon Historical Society, 1200 SW Park Ave, Portland, OR 97205. Illus., index. Refereed. Circ: 7500. Microform: PMC. Online: Florida Center for Library Automation; Gale. *Indexed:* ABS&EES, AmH&L, AmHI, ArtHuCI, FLI, HistAb, HumInd, IBR, SSCI. *Bk. rev.:* 2-28, 250-800 words. *Aud.:* Ga, Ac.

This is a "popular historical publication containing research and essays on the history and culture of the Pacific Northwest, particularly the state of Oregon." Amateur and professional historians alike are the authors and book reviewers, and the writing is exceptionally good. Three or four articles with illustrations appear in each issue. Typical articles include "Cast Aside the Automobile Enthusiast: Class Conflict, Tax Policy and the Preservation of Nature in Progressive-Era Portland" and "Pioneering Water Pollution Control in Oregon." Perhaps the most interesting aspect is the number of personal reminiscences published here. Issues also include short biographical sketches of contributors as well as letters to the editor. Recommended particularly for public and academic libraries in the Pacific Northwest.

3548. Pacific Historical Review. [ISSN: 0030-8684] 1932. q. USD 151 print & online ed. USD 41 newsstand/cover. Ed(s): Carl Abbott, David A Johnson. University of California Press, Journals Division, 2000 Center St, Ste 303, Berkeley, CA 94704-1223; journals@ucpress.edu; http://www.ucpress.edu/journals. Illus., index, adv. Refereed. Circ: 1448 Paid. Vol. ends: Nov. Microform: PQC. Online: Chadwyck-Healey Inc.; EBSCO Publishing, EBSCO Host; Florida Center for Library Automation; Gale; OCLC Online Computer Library Center, Inc.; ProQuest LLC (Ann Arbor); SwetsWise Online Content; H.W. Wilson. *Indexed:* ABS&EES, AmH&L, AmHI, ArtHuCI, BAS, BRI, CBRI, CJA, ENW, HistAb, HumInd, IBR, IBSS, IBZ, RILM, SSCI. *Bk. rev.:* 25-30, 1-5 pages. *Aud.:* Ac, Sa.

The scope of this review is "the history of American expansionism to the Pacific and beyond, and the post-frontier developments of the twentieth-century American West." Articles are also published on "historians' methodologies and philosophies." There are usually three or four major features in each issue, e.g., "Sir William Drummond Stewart: Aristocratic Masculinity in the American West" and "Cities of Color: The New Racial Frontier in California's Minority-Majority Cities." Articles are followed by research notes and detailed book reviews. This is the official publication of the Pacific Coast Branch of the American Historical Association. As such, it is one of the more important scholarly publications devoted to U.S. history and is a valuable tool for the serious student of the American West and the Far East. Recommended for all academic libraries.

3549. Past and Present: A Journal of Historical Studies. [ISSN: 0031-2746] 1952. q. EUR 195 print or online ed. Ed(s): Chris Wickham, Lyndal Roper. Oxford University Press, Great Clarendon St, Oxford, OX2 6DP, United Kingdom; jnl.orders@oup.co.uk; http://www.oxfordjournals.org. Illus., index, adv. Sample. Refereed. Circ: 3500. Reprint: PSC. *Indexed:* AmH&L, AmHI, ArtHuCI, BAS, BEL&L, BrArAb, BrHumI, CJA, FR, HistAb, HumInd, IBR, IBSS, IBZ, IndIslam, L&LBA, NTA, NumL, PSA, SSA, SSCI, SociolAb. *Bk. rev.:* Number and length vary. *Aud.:* Ac, Sa.

Published on behalf of the Past and Present Society, this journal is associated with the British academic left wing. In terms of readability and intellectual level, it is a scholarly publication of high quality oriented toward the historian and the educated layperson. One of the journal's aims is to present material that can be the subject of debate and controversy. The content of each volume, regarding time and place, is eclectic, with a certain emphasis on social history. Recent articles include "Freedom and Unfreedom in Early Medieval Francia: The Evidence of Legal Formulae," "Resurrecting by Numbers in Eighteenth-Century England," and "Mass Culture and Divided Audiences: Cinema and Social Change in Inter-War Germany." Book reviews do not appear regularly, but there are occasional lengthy review articles.

3550. Pennsylvania History: a journal of Mid-Atlantic studies. [ISSN: 0031-4528] 1933. q. USD 30 (Individuals, USD 20). Ed(s): Paul Douglas Newman. Pennsylvania Historical Association, 108 Weaver Bldg, Penn State University, State College, PA 16802; jbf2@psu.edu; http://www3.la.psu.edu/histrlst/journals/ph.htm. Illus., index, adv. Refereed. Circ: 850 Paid. Vol. ends: Fall. Microform: PQC. *Indexed:* AmH&L, AmHI, HistAb, HumInd, IBR, IBZ, RI-1, RILM. *Bk. rev.:* 5-12, 1-2 pages. *Aud.:* Ga, Ac.

The official publication of the Pennsylvania Historical Association, *Pennsylvania History* contains two to four studies in each issue "dealing with the social, intellectual, economic, political and cultural history of Pennsylvania and the Middle Atlantic region." A regular feature of this publication is the inclusion of edited documentary material. The contributors are mostly academics, but the well-documented articles are selected for their appeal to both the specialist and the general reader. Readers should also be aware of *The Pennsylvania Magazine of History and Biography,* another scholarly quarterly, published since 1877 by the Historical Society of Pennsylvania (1300 Locust St., Philadelphia, PA 19107).

3551. Radical History Review. [ISSN: 0163-6545] 1973. 3x/yr. USD 120 (Individuals, USD 35). Duke University Press, 905 W Main St, Ste 18 B, Durham, NC 27701; subscriptions@dukeupress.edu; http://www.dukeupress.edu. Illus., adv. Refereed. Circ: 1200 Paid. Online: EBSCO Publishing, EBSCO Host; Gale; HighWire Press; OCLC Online Computer Library Center, Inc.; OhioLINK; Project MUSE; SwetsWise Online Content. Reprint: PSC. *Indexed:* ABS&EES, AltPI, AmH&L, AmHI, ArtHuCI, BAS, BRI, FLI, HistAb, HumInd, IBSS, LeftInd, PSA, RILM, SSA, SSCI, SociolAb. *Bk. rev.:* Number and length vary. *Aud.:* Ac.

Editorially presented as a publication that stands "at the point where rigorous historical scholarship and active political engagement converge," the *Radical History Review* explores topics of "gender, race, sexuality, imperialism, and class, stretching the boundaries of historical analysis to explore Western and non-Western histories." Each issue is devoted to a particular thematic topic such as "Performance, Politics and History" or "Truth Commissions: State Terror, History, and Memory." A recurring feature of interest to college faculty is "Teaching Radical History," which offers suggestions for course contents and model syllabi. This journal is highly recommended for academic libraries.

3552. Review (Binghamton). [ISSN: 0147-9032] 1977. q. USD 125. Ed(s): Richard E Lee. Fernand Braudel Center for the Study of Economies, Historical Systems, and Civilizations, Binghamton University, P.O. Box 6000, Binghamton, NY 13902-6000; http://fbc.binghamton.edu. Illus., adv. Refereed. Circ: 1100. *Indexed:* ABS&EES, AltPI, AmH&L, HistAb, IBR, IBSS, IBZ, IPSA, LeftInd, PSA, SSA, SociolAb. *Aud.:* Ac.

"We hope to make our journal a forum that will reflect the true diversity of contemporary world scholarship." Committed to "the primacy of analysis of economies over long historical process, and the transitory (heuristic) nature of theories," the journal features five or six articles in each issue with such titles as "New Imperialism or New Capitalism?" and "Secular Trends, Long Waves, and the Cost of the State: Evidence from the Long-Term Movement of the Profit Rate in the U.S. Economy." All articles are scholarly, original, and well written.

3553. *Reviews in American History.* [ISSN: 0048-7511] 1973. q. USD 138. Ed(s): Louis P Masur. The Johns Hopkins University Press, 2715 N Charles St, Baltimore, MD 21218-4363; http://muse.jhu.edu. Illus., index, adv. Circ: 2550 Paid. Vol. ends: Dec. Microform: PQC. Online: EBSCO Publishing, EBSCO Host; Florida Center for Library Automation; Gale; JSTOR (Web-based Journal Archive); OCLC Online Computer Library Center, Inc.; OhioLINK; Project MUSE; ProQuest LLC (Ann Arbor); SwetsWise Online Content. Reprint: PSC. *Indexed:* ABS&EES, AmH&L, AmHI, ArtHuCI, BRD, BRI, CBRI, HistAb, HumInd, IBR, IBZ, RILM, SSCI. *Bk. rev.:* 30-40, lengthy. *Aud.:* Ac, Sa.

Each quarterly issue "presents more than 20 comparative and interpretive essays analyzing recent research published on all specialties of American history, including economics, military history, women in American history, law, political philosophy, and religion." References are made to earlier works, and complete bibliographic information is provided. Retrospective essays that examine landmark works by major historians are also regularly featured. This is a convenient, authoritative source for keeping abreast of important scholarship in the field of American history, and a useful tool for any library ordering selectively in this subject area. Also useful for colleges where students are required to produce research-length papers on topics in American history.

3554. *The Scottish Historical Review.* [ISSN: 0036-9241] 1903. s-a. GBP 76. Ed(s): Dr. E Cameron, Dr. D Broun. Edinburgh University Press, 22 George Sq, Edinburgh, EH8 9LF, United Kingdom; http://www.eup.ed.ac.uk. Illus., index, adv. Refereed. Circ: 900. Vol. ends: Oct. Microform: IDC; PQC. Online: Chadwyck-Healey Inc.; EBSCO Publishing, EBSCO Host; ProQuest K-12 Learning Solutions. Reprint: PSC. *Indexed:* AmH&L, AmHI, ArtHuCI, BrArAb, BrHumI, HistAb, IBR, NumL, RI-1. *Bk. rev.:* 10-20, length varies. *Aud.:* Ac, Sa.

Intended as an equivalent to the *English Historical Review* (above in this section), this review covers all aspects of Scotland's long and often tumultuous history. Few of the scholarly studies in each issue, however, go beyond the nineteenth century. Each issue contains several lengthy articles, such as the recent "The Bannatyne Club and the Publication of Scottish Ecclesiastical Cartularies," and multiple book reviews. Special features include a classified bibliography of articles on the history of Scotland published each year, and occasional "Notes and Comments" regarding relevant documentary sources. This is the only learned journal exclusively devoted to this subject. It is also a useful tool for the bibliographer collecting in this area. Most appropriate for academic libraries with collections and curricula in this area.

3555. *Social History.* [ISSN: 0307-1022] 1976. q. GBP 326 print & online eds. Ed(s): Keith Nield, Janet Blackman. Routledge, 4 Park Sq, Milton Park, Abingdon, OX14 4RN, United Kingdom; journals@routledge.com; http://www.routledge.co.uk. Illus., index, adv. Circ: 1000. Online: EBSCO Publishing, EBSCO Host; Gale; IngentaConnect; OCLC Online Computer Library Center, Inc.; SwetsWise Online Content. Reprint: PSC. *Indexed:* ABS&EES, AmH&L, AmHI, ArtHuCI, BrHumI, CBCARef, HistAb, HumInd, IBR, IBSS, IBZ, PSA, SSA, SSCI, SociolAb. *Bk. rev.:* 10-13, lengthy. *Aud.:* Ac, Sa.

"Articles, reviews and debates of high quality historical analysis without restriction on place, period or viewpoint" is the editorial description of this journal. Years ago, the editors also proclaimed that "*Social History* has established a firm and stable place among the handful of English-language journals publishing historical material of the highest quality." Indeed, the editors have successfully published studies that "encourage an interdisciplinary approach to historical questions, and are concerned to provide an opportunity for critical analysis of the concepts and methods of the social sciences as they bear on the work of the social historian." British social history receives the most attention. In addition to the original research articles, there are several regular features and review essays. The latter, together with the excellent book reviews and a list of books received, provide an inclusive bibliographical source.

3556. *The South Carolina Historical Magazine.* Formerly (until 1951): *The South Carolina Historical and Genealogical Magazine.* [ISSN: 0038-3082] 1900. q. USD 55 domestic; USD 75 foreign. Ed(s): W. Eric Emerson. South Carolina Historical Society, 100 Meeting St, Charleston, SC 29401; info@schistory.org; http://www.schistory.org. Illus., index. Circ: 5500. Vol. ends: Oct. Microform: PQC. Online: ProQuest K-12 Learning Solutions. *Indexed:* AmH&L, HistAb, IBR, IBZ. *Bk. rev.:* 5-10, 1-2 pages. *Aud.:* Ac, Sa.

The South Carolina Historical Society was founded in 1855 for the purpose of collecting "information respecting every portion of the state, to preserve it and when deemed advisable, to publish it." The society's scholarly journal successfully meets this worthy mandate in service of a state that was in many respects a crucible of the South's and the nation's development. In addition to one- to two-page book reviews, the journal features "recently processed manuscripts" as well as articles of biographies and memoirs.

3557. *Southwestern Historical Quarterly.* [ISSN: 0038-478X] 1897. q. USD 108 (Individuals, USD 52). Ed(s): Randolph B. Campbell. University of Texas Press, Journals Division, 2100 Comal, Austin, TX 78722; journals@uts.cc.utexas.edu; http://www.utexas.edu/utpress/ journals/journals.html. Illus., index, adv. Circ: 3430 Paid and free. Vol. ends: Apr. Microform: PQC. Online: EBSCO Publishing, EBSCO Host. *Indexed:* AbAn, AmH&L, AmHI, ArtHuCI, BRI, HistAb, HumInd, RILM, SSCI. *Bk. rev.:* 1-12, 1-5 pages. *Aud.:* Ac, Sa.

"Scholarly research on the history of Texas and the Southwest is the focus of *SHQ*, the oldest scholarly journal in Texas." This journal of the highest caliber typically features three articles, an edited contemporary document, and a book review essay. It is somewhat misnamed because the contents deal largely with Texas history and the contributors are mostly Texas historians. Recent articles have been entitled "Perhaps the Most Incorrect of Any Land Line in the United States: Establishing the Texas-New Mexico Boundary Along the 103rd Meridian" and "Under the Influence: The Texas Business Men's Association and the Campaign Against Reform, 1906-1915." Because of the attractive layout, typography, and accompanying photographs, this is a handsome publication compared with similar scholarly titles.

3558. *True West.* Incorporates (1923-1981): *Frontier Times.* [ISSN: 0041-3615] 1953. 10x/yr. USD 29.95; USD 5.99 newsstand/cover per issue. Ed(s): Bob Boze Bell. True West Publications, 6702 E Cave Creek Rd Ste 5, Cave Creek, AZ 85331; truepublications@aol.com; http://www.truewestmagazine.com. Illus., index, adv. Sample. Circ: 50000 Paid and controlled. Vol. ends: Dec. *Bk. rev.:* 4-25, 300-600 words. *Aud.:* Hs, Ga.

This magazine attempts to provide a feeling of the Wild West by covering Western history and culture from pre–Civil War days to the present. It is easy reading, with good, authentic photographs and illustrations. Aimed at a general audience, it is suitable for high schools and public libraries. The style is popular, the illustrations are excellent, and the material is nicely presented. The scope is obvious from the title. *True West* includes factual accounts, reviews of nonfiction books, columns on Western films and travel, sections on family history and cooking, and a section of queries asking readers to share information. In addition to the eight issues per year, the magazine publishes two special issues, a travel issue and a "Best of the West" issue, which are included with an annual subscription. Further supplemental materials can also be accessed at the journal's web site.

3559. *Virginia Magazine of History and Biography.* [ISSN: 0042-6636] 1893. q. Membership, USD 38. Ed(s): Paul A Levengood, Nelson D Lankford. Virginia Historical Society, PO Box 7311, Richmond, VA 23221; http://www.vahistorical.org. Illus., index, adv. Circ: 8100. Vol. ends: Oct. Microform: PMC; PQC. Online: EBSCO Publishing, EBSCO Host; OCLC Online Computer Library Center, Inc.; ProQuest LLC (Ann Arbor). Reprint: PSC. *Indexed:* AmH&L, AmHI, ArtHuCI, HistAb, HumInd, IBR, MASUSE, MLA-IB, SSCI. *Bk. rev.:* 4-40, 200-500 words. *Aud.:* Ac, Sa.

Because of Virginia's importance in the colonial and Civil War periods in American history, a significant portion of the studies in this quarterly fall in the period from the seventeenth through the nineteenth centuries. Many of the heavily footnoted articles and other features in each issue are biographical or contain biographical aspects. Occasionally, an issue is devoted to a single topic. Recent articles include "Mr. Jefferson's University: Women in the Village" and "Rediscovered: Robert E. Lee's Earliest-Known Letter." The contents are nicely illustrated with numerous black-and-white photographs. A valuable addition to academic libraries that support courses in early American history.

3560. *Western Historical Quarterly.* [ISSN: 0043-3810] 1969. q. USD 70. Ed(s): David Rich Lewis. Western History Association, Utah State University, 0710 Old Main Hill, Logan, UT 84322-0740; whq@hass.usu.edu; http://www.usu.edu/~history/text/whq.htm. Illus., index, adv. Circ: 2500. Vol. ends: Winter. Online: EBSCO Publishing, EBSCO Host; JSTOR (Web-based Journal Archive). *Indexed:* ABS&EES, AUNI, AmH&L, AmHI, ArtHuCI, BRI, CBRI, HistAb, HumInd, RI-1, RILM, SSCI. *Bk. rev.:* 30-40, 375 words. *Aud.:* Ga, Ac, Sa.

This title's purpose is "to promote the study of the North American West in its varied aspects and broadest sense." The geographic focus encompasses not only the United States but Canadian Provinces, as well. Recent articles include "The Pachua Panic: Sexual and Cultural Battlegrounds in World War II Los Angeles" and "'When We First Came Here It All Looked Like Prairie Land Almost': Prairie Fire and Plains Settlements." Book reviews (often extensive), book notices, and similar features are found. This journal offers a wide variety of information about the West for both scholars and laypersons from a variety of social science disciplines.

3561. *William and Mary Quarterly: a magazine of early American history and culture.* Formerly: *William and Mary College Quarterly Historical Magazine.* [ISSN: 0043-5597] 1892. q. USD 75 (Individuals, USD 40; Students, USD 17.50). Ed(s): Christopher Grasso. Omohundro Institute of Early American History & Culture, PO Box 8781, Williamsburg, VA 23187-8781; ieahc1@wm.edu; http://www.wm.edu/oieahc. Illus., index, adv. Refereed. Circ: 3700. Vol. ends: Oct. Microform: PQC. Online: EBSCO Publishing, EBSCO Host; JSTOR (Web-based Journal Archive). Reprint: PSC. *Indexed:* AmH&L, AmHI, ArtHuCI, BRI, CBRI, HistAb, HumInd, IBR, IBZ, MLA-IB, PhilInd, R&TA, RI-1, RILM, SSCI. *Bk. rev.:* 13-20, 1,000 words. *Aud.:* Ac, Sa.

Although American history before 1815 is the chief focus of this well-established and respected quarterly, the editors also encourage contributions in the areas of literature, ethnohistory, and the arts. Its articles, notes and documents, and reviews range from British North America and the United States to Europe, West Africa, the Caribbean, and the Spanish American borderlands. Forums and topical issues, including a recent one on "Colonial History and National History: Reflections on a Continuing Problem," address topics of active interest in the field. An important journal for all levels of academic libraries and for public libraries with an emphasis on American history.

3562. *Wisconsin Magazine of History.* [ISSN: 0043-6534] 1917. q. USD 55 membership (Individuals, USD 37.50 membership). Ed(s): Kent J Calder. Wisconsin Historical Society, 816 State St, Madison, WI 53706; http://www.shsw.wisc.edu. Illus., index. Circ: 7000. Microform: MIM; PQC. Reprint: PSC. *Indexed:* ABS&EES, AmH&L, HistAb, IBR, IBZ, MLA-IB. *Bk. rev.:* 12-15, 500-1,000 words. *Aud.:* Ac, Sa.

"Collecting, advancing and disseminating knowledge of Wisconsin and of the trans-Allegheny West" is the mission of the historical society that publishes this fine scholarly journal. *Wisconsin Magazine of History* does much to carry out this responsibility. The articles are written by both amateur and professional historians, and the contents frequently go beyond regional interests. A recent issue with four lead articles includes "When the Braves of Bushville Ruled Baseball: Celebrating Andy Pafko and the 1957 Milwaukee Braves" and "Made-to-Order Farms: Benjamin Faast's Vision for Northern Wisconsin." Each issue also contains a "Wisconsin History Checklist," materials added to the society's library, and a detailed listing of new manuscript accessions. Selected articles are available online at the journal's web site. A valuable addition to all research collections in the area of American history.

Women's History Review. See Gender Studies section.

■ HOME

See also Do-It-Yourself; and Interior Design and Decoration sections.

Pamela Matz, Reference Librarian, Widener Library, Harvard University, Cambridge, MA 02138

Introduction

Although the boom in the housing market may be slowing, interest in making—and making over—our homes remains strong, with most shelter magazines maintaining or growing in circulation. The field's three broad categories also remain, and libraries will want to collect in all three, if possible. First are the traditional shelter magazines, such as *Better Homes and Gardens*, *House Beautiful*, and *Traditional Home*, and the traditional magazines with a country slant, *Country Living*, *Country Home*, and *Country Almanac*. These cover a broad range of topics (decorating, entertaining, remodeling, collecting, travel) and show readers the beautiful and interesting homes of both celebrities and the less famous. Next are the more contemporary magazines that mix home and lifestyle topics, such as *Real Simple*, *Martha Stewart Living*, and *Mary Engelbreit's Home Companion*. These magazines combine decorating, cooking, and fashion information with advice about how to live with simplicity, with creative flair, and with cheer and balance. Finally, there are magazines that address very specific communities. Libraries can please their readers by choosing the right fit from *Dwell* to *Metropolitan Home*, both aimed, in different ways, at a more hip, younger audience, or *Natural Home* and *Backwoods Home*, both for the outdoor-minded and self-reliant, or the many others described in the section that follows. Libraries should also consider replacements for two popular titles that ceased publication in 2006. Readers mourning the demise of *Budget Living* and *Organic Style* might welcome *Domino*, a magazine that focuses on stylish but cost-conscious shopping for the home, and *Readymade*, a do-it-yourself magazine with a funky style and a surprising scope (see Do-It-Yourself section).

Many print home magazines both showcase features from current issues on their web sites and offer other resources that are only available electronically. These web sites are worth noting. *Better Homes and Gardens*, for example, offers a "Home Care Tracker" and a "Stain Solver," while the *Martha Stewart Living* web site provides a weekly calendar of household activities with directions, and the *This Old House* web site includes a resource directory of products, supplies, and services used in the show.

Basic Periodicals

Hs: *Better Homes and Gardens;* Ga: *Better Homes and Gardens, The Family Handyman, House Beautiful, Martha Stewart Living;* Ac: *Electronic House, Traditional Home, Victorian Homes.*

Basic Abstracts and Indexes

Magazine Index, Periodical Abstracts, Readers' Guide to Periodical Literature.

3563. *Backwoods Home Magazine: practical ideas for self reliant living.* [ISSN: 1050-9712] 1989. bi-m. USD 17.90. Ed(s): Dave Duffy. David J. Duffy, Ed. & Pub., PO Box 712, Gold Beach, OR 97444. Illus., adv. Circ: 60000. Vol. ends: Dec. *Bk. rev.:* 1, 200 words. *Aud.:* Ga.

Backwoods Home offers features on owner-built housing, independent energy, gardening, health, self-employment, and country living, all advocating a self-reliant lifestyle. For example, recent articles discuss how to keep bees, how to combine a nursing career and a backwoods way of life, and how to use solar power for a weekend cabin. The editor's political views (conservative and libertarian, according to his own description) are often evident; whether readers agree or disagree, those interested in an independent, rural lifestyle will find *Backwoods Home* valuable.

3564. *Better Homes and Gardens.* [ISSN: 0006-0151] 1922. m. USD 22 domestic; USD 35 foreign; USD 3.99 newsstand/cover. Ed(s): Gayle Goodson Butler, Kitty Morgan. Meredith Corp., 1716 Locust St, Des Moines, IA 50309-3023; http://www.meredith.com. Illus., adv. Circ:

7600000 Paid. Vol. ends: No. 12. Microform: PQC. Online: Gale; OCLC Online Computer Library Center, Inc.; ProQuest LLC (Ann Arbor). *Indexed:* CINAHL, ConsI, GardL, IHTDI, RGPR. *Aud.:* Hs, Ga, Ac.

There is a strong chance that whatever home project readers are planning, it will be covered by *Better Homes and Gardens*. The magazine's strength is its combination of extensive scope and fine detail. Each issue includes features on gardening, interior design, building, family matters, food, and health; and across the range of topics, articles include precise technical information. This magazine would be a good choice for most public libraries. *Better Homes and Gardens* also publishes titles focusing on particular aspects of the home and home ownership.

3565. *Cottage Living.* [ISSN: 1550-2562] 2001. 9x/yr. USD 16; USD 3.99 newsstand/cover per issue. Ed(s): Eleanor Griffin. Southern Progress Corp., 2100 Lakeshore Dr, Birmingham, AL 35209; http://corp.southernprogress.com/spc/. Adv. Circ: 500000. *Aud.:* Ga.

A new entry into the field in 2004, *Cottage Living* aims at those in their 30s and 40s who are interested in seeking "a little more relaxed way of living," according to editor Eleanor Griffin. The words "comfortable," "simple," "cozy," and "fresh" tend to appear frequently in this magazine, which looks at traditional topics from its own particular perspective. A recent "Welcome Home" column by editor Griffin is a good illustration of the magazine's style. Quoting one of the issue's contributors, Griffin begins, "I love a sofa that still looks good after my kids have jumped on it." Apparently many readers feel the same way, because circulation has been jumping.

3566. *Country Almanac.* [ISSN: 1058-3734] 1981. bi-m. USD 24.97; USD 6.95 newsstand/cover. Ed(s): Jodi Zucker. Harris Publications, Inc., 1115 Broadway, 8th Fl, New York, NY 10010; comments@harris-pub.com; http://www.harris-pub.com/. Illus., adv. Circ: 400000. Vol. ends: No. 4. *Bk. rev.:* Various number and length. *Aud.:* Ga.

Each issue of *Country Almanac* includes articles on collecting and decorating with country details (both original and reproduction), tours of charming houses with a country look, and do-it-yourself projects. *Country Almanac* emphasizes the affordability and ease of projects, and it praises country style for providing both "down-home" qualities and forms of creative self-expression. Readers enjoy the combination of decor ideas with instructions for achieving a cozy, country feeling in their own homes.

3567. *Country Home.* [ISSN: 0737-3740] 1979. 10x/yr. USD 21.97 domestic; USD 29.97 foreign; USD 4.95 newsstand/cover domestic. Ed(s): Carol S Sheehan. Meredith Corp., 1716 Locust St, Des Moines, IA 50309-3023; http://www.meredith.com. Illus., index, adv. Circ: 1250000 Paid. Vol. ends: No. 6. Microform: NBI. *Indexed:* ASIP, GardL. *Aud.:* Ga.

Redefining itself as a broader, modern lifestyle magazine, *Country Home* introduced new design and editorial elements in 2003. Now subtitled "Be Creative. Be Yourself.," the magazine continues to encourage readers to draw on traditional artifacts and styles to enrich contemporary homes, but it also includes fashion, make-up, and shopping tips. Still reporting on life's pleasures, still targeted at an upper-middle-class audience, *Country Home* now has a more contemporary flair and a more browsable quality. Of the three "country" home publications, this is the one likely to appeal to younger, urban readers.

3568. *Country Living (New York).* Formerly: *Good Housekeeping's Country Living.* [ISSN: 0732-2569] 1978. m. USD 12 domestic; USD 28 foreign; USD 3.50 newsstand/cover per issue. Ed(s): Nancy Mernit Soriano. Hearst Magazines, 300 W 57th St, New York, NY 10019; HearstMagazines@hearst.com; http://www.hearstcorp.com/magazines/. Illus., adv. Circ: 1600000 Paid. Vol. ends: Dec. *Indexed:* GardL, MASUSE. *Aud.:* Ga.

According to *Media Week* in 2003, *Country Living* had the largest circulation and longest history of the country-focused shelter periodicals. *Country Living* defines its scope broadly, including not only decorating, home building, gardening, and antiques, but also collecting, shopping, cooking, travel, and crafts. Distinctive features include an emphasis on items just becoming collectible—such as nineteenth- and twentieth-century lawn games and giveaway juice glasses—and do-it-yourself projects in a range of budget categories. *Country Living* has a broad appeal.

3569. *Dwell.* [ISSN: 1530-5309] 2000. 10x/yr. USD 19.95 domestic; USD 29.95 Canada; USD 35.95 elsewhere. Ed(s): Allison Arieff. Dwell LLC, 99 Osgood Pl., San Francisco, CA 94133. Illus., adv. Circ: 300000 Paid. *Indexed:* ASIP. *Aud.:* Ga.

A 2005 National Magazine Award winner and one of *Library Journal*'s best new magazines of 2000, *Dwell* continues to be refreshing, showcasing home architecture and furnishings of surprising kinds in surprising locations. Recent issues report on a furniture fair in Stockholm, a Texas country house designed to recycle every possible drop of water, and a Japanese vacation home with vast windows offering a view of Mount Fuji. *Dwell* readers are likely to be younger than followers of *Better Homes and Gardens* or the various country journals. The magazine has an environmentally conscious slant; a hip, contemporary look; and an imaginative way of marrying design consciousness to practical information. Libraries with readers who seek out these qualities will want to include *Dwell* in their collections.

3570. *Electronic House: fast track to the connected lifestyle.* [ISSN: 0886-6643] 1986. 10x/yr. USD 19.95. Ed(s): Cindy Davis. E H Publishing, Inc., 111 Speen St, Ste 200, PO Box 989, Framingham, MA 01701-2000; info@ehpub.com; http://www.ehpub.com. Illus., adv. Circ: 75000. Vol. ends: No. 6. *Indexed:* IHTDI. *Aud.:* Ga, Sa.

Written for consumers who enjoy technology but aren't necessarily engineers, *Electronic House* includes articles on both extravagant and affordable smart homes. Some electronic controls cover a whole house, while others manage subsystems such as lighting, security, home theater, energy use, and telecommunications. *Electronic House* evaluates products and provides price information, tips, and guidelines. It is a valuable resource for readers interested in electronic home innovations.

Elle Decor. See Interior Design and Decoration section.

The Family Handyman. See Do-It-Yourself section.

3571. *Home: the remodeling and decorating resource.* Former titles (until 1981): *Hudson Home Magazine;* (until 1980): *Hudson Home Guides;* Incorporates: *Home Building and Remodeling; Home Planning and Design; Home Improvement and Repair; Home Plans and Ideas; Kitchens, Baths and Family Rooms.* [ISSN: 0278-2839] 1955. 8x/yr. USD 8 domestic; USD 20 foreign; USD 3.50 newsstand/cover per issue. Ed(s): Donna Sapolin. Hachette Filipacchi Media U.S., Inc., 1633 Broadway, New York, NY 10019; http://www.hfmus.com. Illus., adv. Circ: 1000000 Paid. Vol. ends: No. 10. *Aud.:* Ga.

Home emphasizes home design and renovation and is aimed primarily at middle-income homeowners. It provides descriptions of whole-house renovations and of smaller room-by-room redos, with detailed product evaluations. This magazine focuses less than others in this category on lifestyle but emphasizes practical aspects of home ownership, such as financing and insuring. Recommended for libraries in communities where many homeowners are remodeling.

3572. *House Beautiful.* [ISSN: 0018-6422] 1896. m. USD 12 domestic; USD 28 foreign; USD 3.95 newsstand/cover per issue. Ed(s): Stephen Dricker, Deborah Martin. Hearst Magazines, 300 W 57th St, New York, NY 10019; HearstMagazines@hearst.com; http://www.hearstcorp.com/magazines/. Illus., adv. Circ: 850000 Paid. Vol. ends: No. 12. Microform: NBI; PQC. Online: EBSCO Publishing, EBSCO Host; Gale; Northern Light Technology, Inc.; OCLC Online Computer Library Center, Inc.; ProQuest K-12 Learning Solutions; ProQuest LLC (Ann Arbor); H.W. Wilson. *Indexed:* ASIP, ConsI, FLI, GardL, MASUSE, RGPR. *Aud.:* Ga.

House Beautiful had another makeover in 2005, intended to make the magazine warmer and more service-oriented and adding how-to tips and product options, while maintaining its traditional mainstream focus. As in the past, *House Beautiful* continues to feature articles on home decorating and remodeling, architecture, entertaining, and gardening that guide readers in creating comfortable homes expressing their personal styles. Projects primarily draw on high-end materials, with some more cost-conscious features. Many public libraries will want to include this publication.

3573. *Living Home.* 1995. irreg. Ed(s): Kim Garretson. Novo Media Group, http://www.livinghome.com. *Aud.:* Ga.

Living Home is an interesting—and free—compendium of home and garden information, now going through an update to reflect a new emphasis on technology. Links to commercial products sometimes seem to blur editorial boundaries, but the site offers lively writing and a fresh approach to home-related topics. It is fun to browse.

3574. *Martha Stewart Living.* [ISSN: 1057-5251] 1990. m. USD 28 domestic; CND 38 Canada; USD 54 elsewhere. Ed(s): Margaret Roach, Amy Conway. Martha Stewart Living Omnimedia LLC, 11 W. 42nd St., 25th Fl, New York, NY 10036; mstewart@marthastewart.com; http://www.marthastewart.com. Illus., adv. Circ: 1894134 Paid. Vol. ends: No. 12. *Indexed:* GardL, RGPR. *Aud.:* Ga.

With Martha Stewart's release from prison in 2005, the magazine she founded began to rebuild from the advertising and circulation woes that had plagued it during the years of Ms. Stewart's legal troubles. Martha Stewart's insistence that the magazine could continue to deliver what it had become known for has been proven true. Middle-class readers are still finding in *Martha Stewart Living* a beautifully illustrated set of directions for creating a home that is gracious, comfortable, and orderly, as well as guides for recognizing and making "good things" that have persuasive appeal. A strong choice for many public libraries.

3575. *Mary Engelbreit's Home Companion: leading the artful life.* [ISSN: 1096-5289] 1996. bi-m. USD 19.95 domestic; USD 36.95 Canada; USD 28.95 elsewhere. Home Companion Publishing Group LLC, 6358 Delmar Blvd, Ste 450, St Louis, MO 63130; contactus@maryengelbreit.com; http://www.maryengelbreit.com. Illus., adv. Circ: 525000 Paid. *Aud.:* Ga.

Founded and edited by Mary Engelbreit, whose whimsical drawings are a familiar sight on greeting cards and other products, *Home Companion* is aimed at middle-class baby-boomers with a creative streak. Issues include do-it-yourself crafts, recipes, and visits to artists' and collectors' homes. However, this standard fare is presented with surprising twists, and the featured homes reflect their owners' flair and individuality. The look is bright, the attitude is cheerful and easygoing, and Engelbreit's drawings are sprinkled throughout. Libraries that can add this title to a mix of more traditional shelter magazines will probably have pleased readers.

3576. *Metropolitan Home: style for our generation.* Former titles (until 1981): *Apartment Life;* (until 1970): *Apartment Ideas.* [ISSN: 0273-2858] 1969. 10x/yr. USD 10 domestic; USD 22 foreign; USD 4.50 newsstand/ cover per issue. Ed(s): Donna Warner. Hachette Filipacchi Media U.S., Inc., 1633 Broadway, New York, NY 10019; http://www.hfmus.com. Illus., adv. Circ: 600000 Paid. Vol. ends: Dec. Microform: PQC. Online: OCLC Online Computer Library Center, Inc. *Indexed:* ASIP, ArtInd, GardL, IHTDI. *Aud.:* Ga.

Metropolitan Home includes articles on the familiar mix of decorating, remodeling, collecting, cooking, designing, and entertaining, but its look and focus are decidedly urban, upscale, contemporary, and clean. Articles focus on design-conscious elegance in a variety of metropolitan settings, including one or two international locations per issue. *Metropolitan Home* would be welcome in libraries where readers have an interest in more sophisticated home styles.

3577. *Natural Home.* Former titles (until 2006): *Natural Home and Garden;* (until 2005): *Natural Home.* [ISSN: 1933-1134] 1996. bi-m. USD 19.95 domestic; USD 22.50 foreign; USD 4.99 newsstand/cover. Ogden Publications, 1503 SW 42nd St, Topeka, KS 66609-1265; http://www.ogdenpubs.com. Illus., adv. Circ: 150000 Paid. *Aud.:* Ga.

Natural Home and Garden addresses home and lifestyle issues for a middle-class, environmentally conscious readership. It aims to inspire and inform a mainstream audience with the message that what is good for the planet can also be delightful, convenient, and comfortable. Topics covered in each issue include innovative homebuilding, cooking, gardening, uses of salvaged materials, and responsible product choices. Readers will find articles here that

they would be unlikely to see anyplace else, such as plans for keeping chickens in an urban backyard. *Natural Home and Garden* will appeal to a niche readership, but for those interested in these topics, it will be invaluable.

3578. *Real Simple: the magazine for a simpler life - home - body - soul.* [ISSN: 1528-1701] 2000. 10x/yr. USD 28.68 domestic; USD 41.95 Canada; USD 4.50 newsstand/cover. Ed(s): Kristin van Ogtrop, Nancy Hawley. Time, Inc., Time & Life Bldg, Rockefeller Center, 29th Fl, New York, NY 10020-1393; letters@realsimple.com. Illus., adv. Sample. Circ: 1550000 Paid. *Aud.:* Ga.

Since its 2000 debut, *Real Simple* has become an icon of contemporary middle-class life, offering realistic solutions for simplifying complex lives. The design is distinctive: muted colors, large pictures, a lucid layout. Short features with a friendly, authoritative tone offer solutions to a range of problems, from finding the time and space to sort and store children's artwork, to buying jeans that fit, to researching investment decisions without giving up all your spare time to do it. Active, middle-class women are the target audience, and the focus is on fashion and beauty articles, but men striving to manage personal, professional, and community commitments may be interested as well. Public libraries should consider subscribing.

3579. *Remodeling Online.* Hanley Wood, LLC, One Thomas Circle, NW, Ste 600, Washington, DC 20005-5701. *Aud.:* Ga.

Remodeling Online (http://remodeling.hw.net) serves and promotes the community of remodelers. It offers content from the print magazine *Remodeling*, from other publications of the parent company Hanley-Wood, and articles from other remodeling sources. Do-it-yourself remodelers will find useful information, such as the annual report on returns related to the cost of remodeling projects. As in other vendor-sponsored electronic journals, editorial and advertising content are not strictly separated.

3580. *Romantic Homes.* Formerly: *Victorian Sampler.* [ISSN: 1086-4083] 1983. m. USD 29.95 domestic; USD 3.99 newsstand/cover per issue. Ed(s): Catherine Yarnovich, Eileen Paulin. A P G Media, 265 S Anita Dr, Ste 120, Orange, CA 92868. Illus., adv. Circ: 130000 Paid. Vol. ends: No. 12. *Aud.:* Ga.

Romantic Homes is aimed at readers who want to create a warm, casually elegant, home haven. It emphasizes using items from other cultures or periods (original or reproduction) to bring a special flair to home decorating. Most issues focus on a particular "romantic" style, such as British Colonial, Caribbean Island, or Country Life. Not a substitute for, but a useful supplement to, the shelter magazines with broader scopes.

Southern Accents. See Interior Design and Decoration section.

Sunset. See General Editorial/General section.

This Old House. See Do-It-Yourself section.

3581. *Traditional Home.* Formerly (until 1985): *Traditional Home Ideas.* [ISSN: 0883-4660] 1978. 8x/yr. USD 24; USD 4.95 newsstand/cover. Ed(s): Mark Mayfield, Michael Diver. Meredith Corp., 125 Park Ave, 19th Fl, New York, NY 10017; http://www.meredith.com. Illus., adv. Circ: 950000 Paid. Vol. ends: No. 6. Microform: NBI. *Aud.:* Ga.

Like *Country Home* and *Romantic Homes* (above in this section), *Traditional Home* addresses the technique of combining elements of classic decor with realities of contemporary life in renovating, decorating, and entertaining. However, this magazine is more substantial and upscale than *Romantic Homes*, combining rich pictorials with detailed text; and *Traditional Home*'s featured designs include both country styles and more classic and formal examples. Aimed toward an affluent, older audience, *Traditional Home* offers expert advice on antiques; art; and, uniquely, etiquette. Worth consideration by libraries with strong home collections.

3582. *Veranda: a gallery of fine design.* [ISSN: 1040-8150] 1987. bi-m. USD 15. Ed(s): Lisa Newsom. Hearst Magazines, 300 W 57th St, New York, NY 10019; HearstMagazines@hearst.com; http://www.hearstcorp.com/magazines/. Illus., adv. Circ: 447000 Paid. Vol. ends: No. 4. *Indexed:* GardL. *Aud.:* Ga.

Acquired by the Hearst Corporation in May 2002, *Veranda* has dropped the word "Southern" from its subtitle, indicating an even more national focus. *Veranda* features beautiful (and undoubtedly expensive) homes throughout the United States in a variety of lush styles. The magazine is gorgeous, featuring artful photography of interiors, gardens, table settings, and floral arrangements. Articles focus on decorative arts, books, collectibles, luxury goods, unusual travel destinations, art exhibitions, architects, and the latest in furnishings. There is no discussion of remodeling or renovating. A good candidate for public libraries with strong home magazine collections.

3583. *Victorian Homes.* [ISSN: 0744-415X] 1982. bi-m. USD 19.95 domestic; USD 34.95 Canada; USD 44.95 elsewhere. Ed(s): Erika Kotite. A P G Media, 265 S Anita Dr, Ste 120, Orange, CA 92868. Illus., adv. Circ: 100000 Paid. Vol. ends: No. 6. *Indexed:* GardL. *Aud.:* Ga, Sa.

Victorian Homes combines well-illustrated articles with instructive text, cultivating understanding and appreciation of Victorian architecture and artifacts and the culture that gave them life. Included are discussions of Victorian building materials, ways to shop for and care for particular kinds of antiques, and guides for choosing period fixtures and replicas. An annual sourcebook of companies offering products and services for the Victorian revival market may be especially useful to owners of nineteenth- and early-twentieth-century homes.

■ HORSES

Linda Collins, Head of Access Services, Lamont Library, Harvard University, Cambridge, MA 02138

Introduction

The horse plays an important role in the American economy. Diverse equine interests represent a 25 billion dollar industry. From the Western ranges to Virginia's Hunt Country and in suburban communities across the nation, we continue our love affair with this noble beast. The recreational uses of the horse cannot be clearly defined by region. The country is a melting pot of equine activity, from horse racing and show jumping to Western reining and dressage. Across the country, 4-H and Pony Clubs continue to introduce children to riding, showing, and the basics of horse care and management.

From general-interest to breed-specific titles, there are many journals that support all types of equine involvement. The nonprofit American Horse Publications Association (www.americanhorsepubs.org) is a great source of information about equine publications. Another excellent resource is the American Horse Council (www.horsecouncil.org), the national trade association representing the horse industry in Washington, D.C.

The highest-quality electronic journals are related to the major publishers of standard equine publications. Primedia, Inc., publisher of *Equus, Practical Horseman, Arabian Horse World,* and *Horse Illustrated,* also publishes two electronic journals: *EquiSearch* (www.equisearch.com) and *Arabian Horse World* (www.ahwmagazine.com), both worth a visit. The Blood-Horse, Inc., publisher of *The Blood-Horse, Equine Images,* and *The Horse—Your Guide to Equine Health,* also has a wonderful e-journal, *The Horse Interactive* (www.thehorse.com). There are other, more specialized web journals such as *DRF.com* (www.drf.com), published by the *Daily Racing Form. The Equestrian Times* (www.equestriantimes.com) specializes in international competition. To find other sites, visit *The Horse Source* (http://source.bloodhorse.com/thehorse), published by The Blood-Horse, Inc. This is an excellent resource.

Basic Periodicals

Ga: *Equus, Horse & Rider, Horse Illustrated, Practical Horseman, Western Horseman.*

American Cowboy. See Fashion and Lifestyle section.

3584. *American Farriers Journal.* [ISSN: 0274-6565] 1974. 8x/yr. USD 47.95 domestic; USD 57.95 Canada; USD 79.95 elsewhere. Ed(s): Pat Tearney, Frank Lessiter. Lessiter Publications, 225 Regency Court, Ste 200, Brookfield, WI 53045; info@lesspub.com; http://www.lesspub.com/. Adv. Circ: 7000 Paid. *Aud.:* Sa.

This trade publication features articles of interest not only to farriers but to equine practitioners and all those who manage horses. Article topics include current therapies, the latest in shoeing techniques, the anatomy and physiology of the horse, and information about national trade shows and conferences. Where there are horses, there are farriers. This publication is a valuable resource for all those involved in the care of horses.

3585. *The American Quarter Horse Journal.* Formerly (until Jun. 2001): *Quarter Horse Journal.* [ISSN: 1538-3490] 1948. m. USD 25 domestic; USD 50 Canada; USD 80 foreign. Ed(s): Jim Bret Campbell. American Quarter Horse Association, PO Box 200, Amarillo, TX 79168; http://www.aqha.com. Illus., index, adv. Sample. Circ: 66000 Paid. Vol. ends: Sep. Microform: PQC. *Bk. rev.:* 3, 250 words. *Aud.:* Sa.

This comprehensive journal is the official publication of the American Quarter Horse Association. Covering all disciplines, it speaks to the versatility of this popular horse. With more registered quarter horses than any other breed, this journal has a strong following. Because the quarter horse plays an important and influential role in many cross-breeding programs, the stallion issue is of interest to horsemen across the country.

3586. *The American Saddlebred.* [ISSN: 0746-6153] 1983. bi-m. Non-members, USD 25. Ed(s): Mary Kirkman. American Saddlebred Horse Association, 4093 Iron Works Pike, Lexington, KY 40511. Illus., adv. Sample. Circ: 7200. Vol. ends: Dec. *Bk. rev.:* 2, 150 words. *Aud.:* Sa.

The official journal of the American Saddlebred Horse Association, this publication does not stray far from its primary focus—the breeding, training, showing, and promotion of these flashy, charismatic horses. The journal is the primary communication tool of the association and serves as a platform for interesting and continued discussions. The articles are well written and educational, including everything from legal responsibilities to understanding the direction of the breed past and present. Exceptional color photographs enhance the cover. Included are a calendar of events, classified ads, and association notes and updates. A must for all American saddlebred enthusiasts and libraries where this style of horsemanship is prevalent.

3587. *Appaloosa Journal.* Formerly: *Appaloosa News.* [ISSN: 0892-385X] 1946. m. USD 29.95 domestic (Free to membership). Ed(s): Diane Rice. Appaloosa Horse Club, 2720 W Pullman Rd, Moscow, ID 83843-0903; journal@appaloosa.com; http://www.appaloosa.com. Adv. Sample. Circ: 21341 Paid and free. Vol. ends: Dec. Microform: PQC. *Aud.:* Sa.

Appaloosa Journal is the official publication of the national breed association and registry for Appaloosa horses. Its stated mission is to advance and improve the breeding and performance of the Appaloosa horse. To this end, the journal includes information on Appaloosa breeding, listing leading sires and incentive programs. An extensive show calendar includes class lists for each event and current national standings. Feature articles on training help to improve the performance of the horse. Each issue has information on all disciplines of this versatile breed, including Appaloosa stakes racing and news from the regional associations.

3588. *Arabian Horse World: the magazine for owners, breeders and admirers of fine horses.* [ISSN: 0003-7494] 1960. m. USD 40 domestic; USD 72 Canada; USD 88 elsewhere. Source Interlink Companies, 1316 Tamson Dr, Ste 101, Cambria, CA 93428; edisupport@sourceinterlink.com; http://www.sourceinterlink.com. Illus., index, adv. Sample. Circ: 10000 Paid. Vol. ends: Dec. *Aud.:* Sa.

Arabians are one of the oldest, purest breeds and have been admired for centuries for their classic beauty, strength, and stamina. *Arabian Horse World* is a publication as exquisite as the breed it represents. Artistic color photographs enhance every issue. Profiles of top breeders, leading sires, and prominent

Arabian farms are featured. The versatility of the Arab is apparent, with articles on racing and endurance riding. This comprehensive journal often has over 300 pages and is of particular interest to those involved in the breeding of these lovely horses.

3589. The Blood-Horse. [ISSN: 0006-4998] 1916. w. USD 89 domestic except Kentucky; USD 94.34 in Kentucky; USD 164.78 Canada. Ed(s): Raymond S Paulick, Dan Liebman. The Blood-Horse, Inc., PO Box 4030, Lexington, KY 40544. Illus., index, adv. Sample. Circ: 24000 Paid. Vol. ends: Dec. Microform: PQC. *Aud.:* Sa.

The Blood-Horse is the primary publication of the international thoroughbred industry. Published for 85 years, this weekly journal dedicates itself to the improvement of thoroughbred breeding and racing. This is the bible of the sport of horseracing. It is of interest to racing professionals, those involved in breeding programs, handicappers, and fans. Race results, statistics, information on top lineage, sales, and biographies fill each issue. A must for all communities with ties to the thoroughbred industry. The electronic version (www.blood-horse.com) includes news, racing results, sales and breeding information, and links to stud farms. There is a 12-month archive for subscribers.

3590. Carriage Journal. [ISSN: 0008-6916] 1963. 5x/yr. Membership, USD 45. Ed(s): Jill Ryder. Carriage Association of America, Inc., 177 Pointers Auburn Rd, Salem, NJ 08079. Illus., index, adv. Sample. Circ: 3200. Vol. ends: Spring. *Bk. rev.:* 3-4, 500 words. *Aud.:* Sa.

Published by the Carriage Association of America five times a year, this journal has a very international feel, with reports from England, South Africa, Germany, Argentina, and many other countries. It is apparent that carriage horse enthusiasts will travel great distances in pursuit of their sport. Articles are extremely well researched and authoritative, and cover a vast array of topics in great detail. Black-and-white photographs accompany most articles. An updated calendar lists events, trips, shows, and sales. Classified ads include everything from harnesses to horses to carriages. Because of its commitment to carriages from Roman times to the present, this publication may be of interest to historians as well as to driving enthusiasts.

3591. The Chronicle of the Horse. [ISSN: 0009-5990] 1937. w. USD 59 domestic; USD 79 foreign; USD 2.95 newsstand/cover per issue. Ed(s): Tricia Booker, John Strassburger. Chronicle of the Horse, Inc., PO Box 46, Middleburg, VA 20118. Illus., index, adv. Sample. Circ: 20000 Paid. Vol. ends: Dec. Microform: PQC. *Bk. rev.:* Occasionally, 3-4, 300 words. *Aud.:* Ga, Sa.

This weekly publication is to the show-horse crowd what *The Blood-Horse* is to thoroughbred racing enthusiasts, a primary source for events, results, and the participants. Focusing on show jumping, dressage, eventing, driving, and hunter jumpers, this is a first-rate professional publication. The extensive classified ads offer horses, ponies, real estate, jobs, vans, and trailers. Each issue is packed with interesting feature articles on the personalities involved in the sport. The online version (www.chronofhorse.com) provides access to the same reliable source of current news and results for the entire sport-horse community.

3592. Cutting Horse Chatter. Former titles (until Apr. 1993): *Cutting Horse;* (until 1991): *Cuttin' Hoss Chatter.* [ISSN: 1081-0951] 1948. m. USD 5 newsstand/cover per issue. Ed(s): Peggy Riggle. National Cutting Horse Association, 260 Bailey Ave., Fort Worth, TX 76107-1862. Illus., adv. Sample. Circ: 12000. Vol. ends: Dec. *Aud.:* Sa.

Cutting Horse Chatter is the official publication of the governing body of the sport of cutting, a competition that comes from the Western tradition of cattle handling. Much of the business of the National Cutting Horse Association is carried in the journal. Half of the almost 400 pages are devoted to show results, standings, upcoming events, and issues related to association management. Feature article topics include training, personality profiles, and cattle management. Interest in the sport of cutting is definitely on the increase, with events and clinics being held regularly in such unlikely locations as New England.

3593. The Draft Horse Journal. [ISSN: 0012-5865] 1964. q. USD 30 domestic; USD 35 Canada; USD 40 elsewhere. Ed(s): Lynn Telleen. Draft Horse Journal, PO Box 670, Waverly, IA 50677; http://www.horseshoes.com. Illus., index, adv. Sample. Circ: 21100 Paid and controlled. Vol. ends: Winter. *Bk. rev.:* 1, 200 words. *Aud.:* Sa.

This quarterly publication represents the heavyweight division: Belgians, Percherons, Clydesdales, and Shires. Focusing on breeding and sales, it also covers the draft horse shows and the county fair circuit of horse pulls. Feature articles discuss the nuances of the eight-horse hitch, harness and tack, and the history and use of these big horses in logging, agriculture, and transportation. *The Draft Horse Journal* is a unique and important resource that boasts subscribers from all over the world.

3594. Dressage Today. [ISSN: 1079-1167] 1994. m. USD 19.95 domestic; USD 31.95 foreign. Ed(s): Patricia Lasko. Source Interlink Companies, 656 Quince Orchard Rd, Ste 600, Gaithersburg, MD 20878; edisupport@sourceinterlink.com; http://www.sourceinterlink.com. Illus., adv. Sample. Circ: 42700 Paid. Vol. ends: Aug. *Indexed:* SD. *Bk. rev.:* 1-2, 300 words. *Aud.:* Ga, Sa.

Dressage brings the training of the horse to an art form. At the most advanced levels, it is the pinnacle of harmony between horse and rider, but more basic levels of dressage training can serve as the foundation for all other styles of riding. *Dressage Today* features articles related to the sport of dressage but also includes a wealth of training information that easily relates to other disciplines. Interviews with leaders in the sport, information on national and international competitions, and articles on the selection and care of the dressage horse are just some of the contents. As the nationwide interest in dressage grows, this journal enjoys increased popularity.

3595. The Equestrian Times. 1995. d. USD 40. Ed(s): Nicole Graf. International Equestrian News Network, P O Box 227, Marshfield Hills, MA 02051; info@ienn.com; http://www.ienn.com/ienn/contact.html. *Aud.:* Ga, Sa.

The Equestrian Times (www.equestriantimes.com) is an online publication of the International Equestrian News Network, covering international equestrian events, show results, reports, feature articles, interviews, and photos. Available by subscription only, it provides a wealth of information, with archives going back to January 1997. *The Equestrian Times* provides electronic access to the most comprehensive coverage of the international world of equine sport.

Equine Veterinary Journal. See Veterinary Science.

3596. Equus. [ISSN: 0149-0672] 1977. m. USD 19.95 domestic; USD 31.95 foreign. Ed(s): Laurie Prinz. Source Interlink Companies, 656 Quince Orchard Rd, Ste 600, Gaithersburg, MD 20878; edisupport@sourceinterlink.com; http://www.sourceinterlink.com. Illus., index, adv. Sample. Circ: 150404 Paid. Microform: PQC. *Indexed:* SD. *Aud.:* Ga.

If you were to select only one general horse publication, this is the classic. A repeat winner of the American Horse Publications Awards, *Equus* provides horsemen with sound advice on horse health. Feature articles by leaders in the industry are consistently well written and researched. "The Medical Front" is a monthly column describing the latest therapies, drugs, and procedures in laymen's terms. "Case Reports" are particularly good horse/human-interest stories. *Equus* has a licensed veterinarian on its editorial board to ensure the accuracy of its medical reports. This publication has wide appeal to a broad range of horse enthusiasts.

3597. Hoof Beats. [ISSN: 0018-4683] 1933. m. Members, USD 16.50; Non-members, USD 32.50. Ed(s): Nicole Kraft. United States Trotting Association, 750 Michigan Ave, Columbus, OH 43215; dhoffman@ustrotting.com; http://www.ustrotting.com. Illus., index, adv. Sample. Circ: 13588 Paid and free. Vol. ends: Feb. *Bk. rev.:* 1, 300 words. *Aud.:* Sa.

Hoof Beats is as important to the standardbred racing industry as *The Blood-Horse* is to thoroughbred racing. The official publication of the United States Trotting Association, this monthly publication carries features about leading drivers and winning trotters and pacers. Also included are regular articles on the business of the sport, including legislative changes that affect parimutuel wagering and taxes. Information on top stallions, successful breeding lines, and statistics round out the offerings. This is an important publication for anyone with ties to the harness racing community.

3598. Hoofcare & Lameness: the journal of equine foot science. Former titles (until 1992): *Hoofcare and Lameness Quarterly Report;* (until 1991): *F Y I.* [ISSN: 1076-4704] 1985. q. USD 59 domestic; USD 65 Canada; USD 75 elsewhere. Ed(s): Fran Jurga. Hoofcare Publishing, 19 Harbor Loop, PO Box 660, Gloucester, MA 01930. Illus., adv. Circ: 1500 Paid. *Bk. rev.:* 3-4, 250 words. *Aud.:* Ac, Sa.

This journal of equine foot science is a focused quarterly publication for the professional farrier, veterinarian, or anyone involved with the care of the performance horse. "No hoof, no horse" is the popular saying that this publication addresses, with an international board of consulting editors who are not shy about challenging conventional practice and hoof care theory. This scholarly journal's 15-year index is a virtual who's who and what's what in the history of horseshoeing and lameness. If you are interested in examining the horse from the ground up, this is an excellent place to begin. *Hoofcare & Lameness* also has a web presence (www.hoofcare.com), with access to news and events, book and video reviews, and past articles.

3599. The Horse: your guide to equine health care. Formerly (until 1995): *Modern Horse Breeding.* [ISSN: 1081-9711] 1984. m. 10/yr. plus a. edition. USD 24 domestic; USD 40.45 Canada; USD 45 elsewhere. Ed(s): Kimberly S Graetz, Christie West. The Blood-Horse, Inc., 3101 Beaumont Centre Circle, Lexington, KY 40513; http://www.bloodhorse.com. Adv. Circ: 41334. *Indexed:* IndVet. *Aud.:* Ga, Ac, Sa.

Published by *The Blood-Horse*, this independent journal relies on the expertise of the American Association of Equine Practitioners. Focusing on health, it has regular features on sports medicine, nutrition, and equine behavior. It includes reports from recent symposiums, association meetings, and current research. This is an important publication of interest to equine practitioners and horse owners who are concerned about the health and welfare of their animals.

3600. Horse & Rider. Incorporates (1981-1991): *Performance Horseman.* [ISSN: 0018-5159] 1968. m. USD 15.95 domestic; USD 27.95 Canada; USD 30.95 elsewhere. Ed(s): Darrell Dodds. Source Interlink Companies, 9036 Brittany Way, Tampa, FL 33619; edisupport@sourceinterlink.com; http://www.sourceinterlink.com. Illus., index, adv. Circ: 175000 Paid. Vol. ends: Dec. *Indexed:* MASUSE, SD. *Bk. rev.:* 1, 50 words. *Aud.:* Ga.

Horse & Rider is a self-proclaimed magazine for the Western rider, but its broad scope makes it so much more. Articles include training tips from professionals across the disciplines, the latest information on horse care, and regular features on horse people from chiropractors to authors. This is a high-quality publication with wonderful photographs enhancing the feature articles. It is well written and researched. A comprehensive index published annually in the January issue is an extremely useful tool, making this a publication well worth collecting.

3601. Horse Illustrated. [ISSN: 0145-9791] 1976. m. USD 12 domestic; USD 30 foreign. Ed(s): Liz Moyer, Moira Harris. BowTie, Inc., 2401 Beverly Blvd, PO Box 57900, Los Angeles, CA 90057; http://www.animalnetwork.com/. Illus., index, adv. Circ: 197772 Paid and controlled. Vol. ends: Dec. *Bk. rev.:* 2, 150 words. *Aud.:* Ga.

This general-interest horse magazine does an exceptional job of providing articles of interest to all disciplines. Whether the focus is Western pole bending or top-level dressage, the articles always find the common ground. They are accompanied by rich color photographs. The quality of writing aside, this publication beats the other general-interest magazines in its sheer size. A recent issue was a full 140 pages with nine feature articles of six to eight pages each. Regular columns include the latest industry news and guest editorials on controversial topics. This is a great all-around publication that will be of interest to all horse owners and enthusiasts.

3602. Horse Journal. Formerly (until 199?): *Michael Plumb's Horse Journal.* [ISSN: 1097-6949] 1994. m. USD 49 in US & Canada; USD 67 elsewhere. Belvoir Media Group, LLC, 800 Connecticut Ave, Norwalk, CT 06854-1631; customer_service@belvoir.com; http://www.belvoir.com. Illus., index, adv. Sample. Vol. ends: Dec. *Aud.:* Ga.

This publication describes itself as the product, care, and service guide for people who love horses. It is the *Consumer Reports* of the equine crowd, accepting no commercial advertising. The product recommendations are unbiased and firmly based on field trials and experience. In the same authoritative, no-nonsense style, articles inform readers on nutrition, health care, training, and the latest technological advances. Every issue is packed with valuable practical advice. Subscribers also have access to *Horse Journal* online.

3603. The Morgan Horse. [ISSN: 0027-1098] 1941. m. USD 31.50 domestic; USD 53.50 in Canada & Mexico; USD 61.50 elsewhere. Ed(s): Christina Kollander. American Morgan Horse Association, 122 Bostwick Rd, PO Box 960, Shelburne, VT 05482-0960; info@morganhorse.com; http://www.morganhorse.com. Illus., index, adv. Sample. Circ: 15000. Vol. ends: Jan. *Bk. rev.:* 2, 100 words. *Aud.:* Sa.

The official journal of the Morgan Horse Breed Association, this publication has all the information one needs for breeding, showing, or just enjoying this versatile horse. Articles include information about the Morgan in harness, as a park horse, and in the hunter/jumper division; English and Western pleasure; and dressage. There are extensive show results and regional reports. Leading personalities, past and present, are profiled, as well as prominent Morgan horse farms. The popularity of this breed has spread from its origins in Vermont and enjoys a strong following across the country.

3604. N A R H A Strides. [ISSN: 1541-0188] 1995. 4x/yr. Membership, USD 40. North American Riding for the Handicapped Association, Inc., PO Box 33150, Denver, CO 80233; http://www.narha.org. Illus., adv. Circ: 4500. *Aud.:* Sa.

The official publication of the North American Riding for the Handicapped Association, this nonprofit journal concerns itself with industry standards, program accreditation, and certification of instructors. Articles include a wide range of topics, such as the correct training of horses for use in these types of programs, insurance policy limitations and general liability, crisis management, and a definition of terms used in therapeutic applications. It also features very heartwarming success stories of young riders who gain increased confidence and physical ability as a direct result of their participation in the riding program. This publication would be of interest to administrators of handicapped riding facilities, mental health professionals, instructors, barn managers, volunteers, fundraisers, sponsors, and the participants and their parents.

3605. N R H A Reiner. [ISSN: 0199-6762] 1980. bi-m. Members, USD 40. Ed(s): Sharon Barr. National Reining Horse Association, 3000 N.W. Tenth St., Oklahoma, OK 73107-5302. Illus., adv. Sample. Circ: 6000. Vol. ends: Mar. *Aud.:* Sa.

The National Reining Horse Association (NRHA) is the governing body of the sport of reining. Its mission is to enforce the standards of competition and educate the public on the proper performance of a reining horse. *NRHA Reiner*, the association's official publication, presents association news and regional reports and highlights the major reining events across the country. Proper training is emphasized, as well as communication between horse and rider. The sport of reining is growing, with enthusiasts nationwide and over 350 sanctioned events.

3606. Paint Horse Journal. [ISSN: 0164-5706] 1962. m. Non-members, USD 30. Ed(s): Jennifer Nice. American Paint Horse Association, PO Box 961023, Ft. Worth, TX 76161-0023; ddodds@apha.com; http://www.apha.com. Illus., index, adv. Sample. Circ: 32000 Paid. Vol. ends: Dec. *Bk. rev.:* 1-3, 200 words. *Aud.:* Sa.

The official publication of the American Paint Horse Association, this is the magazine for owners and breeders who appreciate a little splash of color in their barn. The popularity of the paint horse has skyrocketed in recent years, making it the second-largest registered breed in the country, just behind the American

Quarter Horse. The breeding of paints is a study in genetics, and this journal is an important resource, including all recent research in this area. Covering all aspects of breeding, training, showing, and racing, this journal is a must for paint horse enthusiasts.

3607. *Polo Players' Edition*. m. Ed(s): Gwen Rizzo. Rizzo Management Corp., 3500 Fairlane Farms Rd, Ste 9, Wellington, FL 33414. Circ: 6500 Paid. *Aud.:* Ga.

This is a magazine by polo players for polo players. Articles include advice on training for players and their horses, reports on events, and features on celebrity players. More important are tournament results, the calendar of upcoming matches, and news from the polo scene. The polo community's commitment to philanthropy is evidenced by the number of articles reporting on fundraising and other charitable events. Published within *Polo—Players' Edition* is the *USPA Bulletin*, the official publication of the U.S. Polo Association.

3608. *Practical Horseman*. [ISSN: 0090-8762] 1973. m. USD 19.95 domestic; USD 31.95 foreign. Ed(s): Sandy Oliynyk. Source Interlink Companies, 656 Quince Orchard Rd, Ste 600, Gaithersburg, MD 20878; edisupport@sourceinterlink.com; http://www.sourceinterlink.com. Illus., adv. Sample. Circ: 78021 Paid. Vol. ends: Dec. *Indexed:* SD. *Aud.:* Ga.

Practical Horseman bills itself as the "number one resource for English riders," and there is no better in its class. The articles on training of both horse and rider are comprehensive and accompanied by exceptional color photographs. The monthly jumping clinic is a great exercise in developing a keen eye for evaluating the athleticism of both horse and rider. The journal is packed full of sage advice for beginners and seasoned professionals. It also serves as a platform for discussion on topics that affect the industry. This publication is valuable for those involved in all aspects of English riding, from the trail to the show ring.

3609. *Saddle & Bridle: the oldest name in show horse magazine*. [ISSN: 0036-2271] 1927. m. USD 64; USD 7.50 newsstand/cover. Ed(s): Mary Bernhardt. Saddle and Bridle, Inc., 375 Jackson Ave., St. Louis, MO 63130-4243. Illus., adv. Circ: 5200 Paid. *Bk. rev.:* Number and length vary.

Saddle and Bridle is the oldest publication devoted to showing gaited horses. For almost 80 years, owners of saddlebreds, hackneys, roadsters, and other gaited breeds have used it as a major resource for show results, sales, and breeding information. This publication features the champions of the sport and the people behind these elegant animals. Articles explain and examine show rules, provide information on breeding, training, and horse care, and feature those involved in the sport. Regional editors from all parts of the country closely follow the show circuit. This is a tried-and-true journal for those involved in the sport.

3610. *The Trail Rider*. Former titles (until 198?): *Trail Rider;* (until 1986): *The New England Trail Rider.* [ISSN: 0892-3922] 1970. bi-m. USD 19.97 domestic; USD 46 Canada; USD 60 elsewhere. Ed(s): Rene Riley. Horse Media Group, 730 Front St., Louisville, CO 80027; http://www.horsemediagroup.com/. Adv. Circ: 3000 Paid. *Aud.:* Sa.

This publication is as rough and ready as the horsemen it's written for. Billed as America's premier trail riders' information source, it concerns itself with recreational and competitive trail riding and the horses bred and sold for this purpose. The protection of the land and trails they ride on is a major focus, as well as popular destinations for trail-riding adventures.

3611. *Western Horseman*. [ISSN: 0043-3837] 1936. m. USD 22 domestic; USD 32 Canada; USD 42 elsewhere. Ed(s): Fran D Smith, A J Mangum. Western Horseman, Inc., 3850 N Nevada Ave, Colorado Springs, CO 80907-5339. Illus., index, adv. Sample. Circ: 215000 Paid. Vol. ends: Dec. Microform: PQC. *Indexed:* ASIP, B&AI. *Bk. rev.:* 3-4, 300 words. *Aud.:* Ga.

This granddaddy of the industry bills itself as "the world's leading horse magazine since 1936" and has the readership to prove it. A tremendously popular general-interest horse magazine with a decidedly Western slant, this publication features a wide array of articles that cover training, health care, equipment, events, ranching, and personality profiles. There is something here

for everyone, including a column for young horsemen; a "Political Watch" that informs readers of legislative changes affecting them; and even a column on Western art. Every issue includes product reviews, a cartoon of the month, a calendar of events, show results, and classified ads. *Western Horseman* online (www.westernhorseman.com) includes a search engine for equestrian events across the country, current point standings, and a link to numerous breed registries.

3612. *Young Rider: the magazine for horse and pony lovers*. [ISSN: 1098-2442] 1995. bi-m. USD 12.99 domestic; USD 28.97 foreign. Ed(s): Lesley Ward. BowTie, Inc., 2401 Beverly Blvd, PO Box 57900, Los Angeles, CA 90057; http://www.animalnetwork.com/. Illus., adv. Circ: 82699 Paid. *Bk. rev.:* 1, 100 words. *Aud.:* Ems.

Young Rider is arguably the best equine publication for young people. Directed toward 8- to 14-year-old readers, the articles are informative, interesting, and intelligent. The magazine is valuable to children who ride at public stables, English riders, Western riders, those who show, those who compete in gymkhanas, and those who just plain like horses. The articles are colorfully presented and accompanied by many photographs. There is an ever-present emphasis on safety and responsible behavior. Each edition includes large, removable color posters. It is not heavy with advertisements, and those found are age-appropriate. Overall, this is a wonderful publication for young people who are interested in horses.

■ HOSPITALITY/RESTAURANT

Amy J. Watson, Information Specialist, PPG Industries Inc., GTC Library, GTC - Guys Run Road, Pittsburgh, PA, 15238, amywatson@ppg.com

Introduction

According to "DataMonitor Industry Market Research" (December 2004), the leading revenue source for the United States hotel and restaurant industry in 2003 was the restaurant market, which accounted for 47.5 percent of the sector's value. Looking to the future, this subsector is forecast to have reached a value of $473.1 billion by 2008. Among the difficulties facing the restaurant industry is the backlash for perceived marketing of unhealthful foods and the fragmentation of industry statistics due to regional offerings.

The hotel industry in the United States is expected to expand by nearly 49 percent over the 2001–2010 time period. Despite negative growth in 2002 related to decreased travel following the events of September 11, 2001, the United States market has bounced back well. Many major chains have slashed prices in order to attract more leisure travelers, and others are diversifying their product offerings to attract business clientele. In addition, gyms, health spas, and the like are bringing in a revenue stream from nonmembers who live locally. Tourism is key to this industry's growth, however the current instability in the global arena has led to changes in the way Americans perceive leisure travel. An increase in domestic demand and travel by road has led to a decrease of revenue due to the threat of terrorism or epidemic disease. ("DataMonitor Industry Market Research," December 2005)

In the United States in the past 25 years, the number of post-secondary institutions offering hospitality, travel, and tourism programs has more than quadrupled. This has resulted in a wide variety of philosophies and approaches being taught at the university level. According to "College Source Online," as of May 2006, over 250 schools in the United States offer some sort of course of study in the hospitality and restaurant field. The broad emphasis in this field is one that covers both the basic principles and processes of the industry, as well as keeping individuals abreast of current, cutting-edge trends.

The magazines and journals in this section cover both the hotel and restaurant industries with a variety of focuses and depths. There are several refereed journals that offer research and analysis from a high quality, in-depth perspective. Additionally, the diverse assortment of trade publications keeps those in the industry abreast of cutting-edge information and breaking news. The gamut of information needs are well covered with titles that address such topics as management, human resources, hospitality trends, design and decor, and security issues. The majority of titles listed have accompanying web sites that offer useful additional information and interactive tools.

Basic Periodicals

Ac: *The Cornell Hotel & Restaurant Administration Quarterly, Journal of Hospitality & Tourism Research;* Sa: *Nation's Restaurant News, Hotel & Motel Management, Lodging, Restaurants and Institutions.*

Basic Abstracts and Indexes

Lodging, Restaurant and Tourism Index.

3613. Chef Magazine. Former titles (until 1994): *Chef Institutional;* (until 1971): *Chef Magazine.* [ISSN: 1087-061X] 1956. m. USD 32; USD 47 for 2 yrs. Talcott Communications Corporation, 20 W Kinzie, 12th Fl, Chicago, IL 60610; talcottpub@talcott.com; http://www.talcott.com. Adv. Circ: 47000 Controlled and free. *Indexed:* H&TI. *Aud.:* Sa.

Celebrating its 50th year, this tabloid-sized magazine serves the information needs of the chef and restaurant hospitality community. A recent merger with *Equipment Solutions* magazine now allows the logical exploration of an even broader range of foodservice concepts. With regular departments that include such topics as beverage/spirits, catering, nutrition, and a technology update, this title is a must for those in the industry. The feature articles address interesting topics in-depth, and many articles include sample recipes. The new-equipment section reviews and highlights cutting-edge culinary technology. The accompanying web site offers useful interactive tools. This title is highly recommended to libraries that aid those in the culinary and hospitality fields.

3614. Cornell Hospitality Quarterly. Formerly (until 2008): *The Cornell Hotel & Restaurant Administration Quarterly.* [ISSN: 1938-9655] 1960. q. GBP 251. Ed(s): Michael Sturman. Sage Publications, Inc., 2455 Teller Rd, Thousand Oaks, CA 91320; info@sagepub.com; http://www.sagepub.com. Illus., index, adv. Sample. Refereed. Circ: 2717 Paid. Vol. ends: Nov/Dec (No. 42). Online: CSA; EBSCO Publishing, EBSCO Host; Factiva, Inc.; Florida Center for Library Automation; Gale; HighWire Press; OCLC Online Computer Library Center, Inc.; OhioLINK; ProQuest LLC (Ann Arbor); SAGE Publications, Inc., SAGE Journals Online; ScienceDirect; SwetsWise Online Content. Reprint: PSC. *Indexed:* ABIn, ABS&EES, ATI, BAS, BPI, CABA, FS&TA, H&TI, LRI, PAIS, RRTA, S&F, WAE&RSA. *Aud.:* Ac, Sa.

A high quality, scholarly, and important title, *CQ* is published quarterly by the School of Hotel Administration, Cornell University. It is highly recommended for information centers that serve researchers and professionals in the hospitality and tourism field. The primary audience for *CQ* is "hospitality managers at the corporate or property level." This respected and refereed title includes research findings, applied theories, and editorial content covering a wide range of topics such as marketing, international development and human resources. Each issue includes executive summaries of feature articles for ease of use. A standout title in the field.

3615. Hotel and Motel Management: the leading newsmagazine of the hospitality industry. Incorporates: *Motor Inn Journal.* [ISSN: 0018-6082] 1875. 21x/yr. USD 53.50 domestic; USD 74 in Canada & Mexico; USD 130 elsewhere. Ed(s): Jeff Higley. Questex Media Group Inc., 600 Superior Ave E, Ste 1100, Cleveland, OH 44114; questex@sunbeltfs.com; http://www.questex.com. Illus., index, adv. Circ: 60000 Controlled. Vol. ends: Dec. Microform: PQC. Online: The Dialog Corporation; EBSCO Publishing, EBSCO Host; Factiva, Inc.; Florida Center for Library Automation; Gale; OCLC Online Computer Library Center, Inc.; ProQuest LLC (Ann Arbor); H.W. Wilson. *Indexed:* ABIn, ATI, BPI, CWI, H&TI. *Aud.:* Sa.

With regular columns focusing on a wide variety of topics such as technology, design and decor, trends and statistics, and travel trends, this biweekly tabloid will be of interest to hotel professionals. Additional areas of interest include "Supplier News," "People on the Move," and "Transactions," which can easily be used to track the changes and trends of the competition. A guest column features input from a variety of industry professionals. The web edition complements the print version, and features a searchable directory and other interactive tools. As a whole, this title is a good way for professionals to stay up-to-date on the latest industry news.

3616. Hotel Business. [ISSN: 1065-8432] 1992. 26x/yr. USD 200 domestic (Free to qualified personnel). Ed(s): Dennis Nessler. I C D Publications, 45 Research Way, Ste 106, East Setauket, NY 11733. Illus., adv. Circ: 42500 Controlled. *Indexed:* H&TI. *Aud.:* Sa.

A tabloid-sized publication, *Hotel Business* is geared toward decision makers in all aspects of hotel ownership and operations. A variety of topics are covered in each issue, such as amenities, furnishings, security, and bedding and linens, as well as a focus on market size, such as mid-market or economy. There is a strong focus on industry news, balanced equally with advertising and classifieds. An annual "Greenbook" containing exclusive research is included with a print subscription. The corresponding web site brings breaking news, a searchable index, a calendar, and other interactive tools. This is an up-and-coming title in the field.

3617. International Journal of Hospitality and Tourism Administration. Supersedes (in 2000): *Journal of International Hospitality, Leisure and Tourism Management.* [ISSN: 1525-6480] 1997. q. USD 300 print & online eds. Ed(s): Dr. Kaye S Chon, Dr. Clayton W Barrows. Haworth Hospitality Press, 10 Alice St, Binghamton, NY 13904-1580; getinfo@haworthpress.com; http://www.haworthpress.com/. Adv. Refereed. Circ: 173 Paid. Microform: PQC. Online: EBSCO Publishing, EBSCO Host; OCLC Online Computer Library Center, Inc.; SwetsWise Online Content. Reprint: HAW. *Indexed:* CABA, FR, ForAb, H&TI, IBR, IBZ, PAIS, PEI, RRTA, S&F, WAE&RSA. *Aud.:* Ac, Sa.

A respected refereed journal with an international focus, this quarterly seeks to address "critical competency areas that will help practitioners be successful." Published by the University of Guelph School of Hotel and Food Administration, the journal can be counted on to cover best practices in the hospitality and tourism management field. Articles are scholarly and well researched, and cover topics ranging from consumer behavior to security and safety. Highly recommended for libraries that support research and studies in this field.

3618. Journal of Foodservice Business Research. Formerly (until 2002): *Journal of Restaurant & Foodservice Marketing.* [ISSN: 1537-8020] 1994. q. USD 295 print & online eds. Ed(s): Amarjit Basra, H Parsa. Haworth Food & Agricultural Products Press, 10 Alice St, Binghamton, NY 13904-1580; getinfo@haworthpress.com; http://www.haworthpress.com/. Adv. Refereed. Circ: 146 Paid. Reprint: HAW. *Indexed:* Agr, CABA, FS&TA, H&TI, IBR, IBZ, RRTA, WAE&RSA. *Bk. rev.:* Number and length vary. *Aud.:* Ac, Sa.

This refereed journal blends cutting-edge information with research from respected individuals in the field. Somewhat international in scope, this quarterly covers a wide range of topics: finance, law, human resources, and information systems. Uniquely, it includes reviews of foodservice-related Internet resources, books, and software. Special themed issues address specific topics in great depth. A well-respected journal, recommended for libraries that support researchers in the hospitality and foodservice industry.

3619. Journal of Hospitality & Tourism Research. Formed by the merger of (1989-1997): *Hospitality and Tourism Educator;* (1990-1997): *Hospitality Research Journal;* Which was formerly: *Hospitality Education and Research Journal;* (1976-1983): *Journal of Hospitality Education.* [ISSN: 1096-3480] 1997. q. GBP 240. Ed(s): Kaye Chon. Sage Publications, Inc., 2455 Teller Rd, Thousand Oaks, CA 91320; info@sagepub.com; http://www.sagepub.com. Illus., adv. Refereed. Circ: 1300 Paid and free. Reprint: PSC. *Indexed:* H&TI, RRTA, SUSA. *Bk. rev.:* Number and length vary. *Aud.:* Ac, Sa.

This is the professional journal of the International Council on Hotel, Restaurant and Institutional Education (www.chrie.org), an educational association in the field of hospitality and tourism. The quarterly contains in-depth, refereed articles on a broad variety of topics, from strategic management issues to legal issues to cross-cultural and multicultural management issues. There are also book and software reviews, research notes, industry viewpoints, and conference reviews. Geared toward researchers and scholars in this field, it is recommended for libraries that support such users.

3620. *Lodging.* Former titles (until 1993): *Lodging Magazine;* (until 1990): *Lodging.* [ISSN: 1078-5795] 1975. 12x/yr. Free to members. Ed(s): Philip Hayward. McNeill Group. Inc., 385 Oxford Valley Rd, Ste 420, Yardley, PA 19067; http://www.mcneill-group.com. Illus., adv. Circ: 35000 Paid. *Indexed:* H&TI. *Aud.:* Sa.

This slick, high quality publication is a benefit of membership in the American Hotel and Lodging Association. Regular departments include a spotlight on facility openings, financial topics, and governmental affairs, as well as rotating columns on such topics as marketing, technology, and design and construction. Feature articles on current issues in the industry are well written and include attractive photography. Recommended for all corporate and property managers in the field, as well as libraries serving them. The online edition features a useful article archive.

3621. *Lodging Hospitality.* Former titles: *Hospitality Lodging; Hospitality-Food and Lodging; Hospitality-Restaurant and Lodging; American Motel Magazine.* [ISSN: 0148-0766] 1949. m. USD 80 domestic; USD 100 Canada; USD 150 elsewhere. Ed(s): Ed Watkins. Penton Media, Inc., 1300 E 9th St, Cleveland, OH 44114-1503; information@penton.com; http://www.penton.com/. Illus., index, adv. Sample. Circ: 50976 Controlled. Vol. ends: Dec. Microform: CIS; PQC. Online: The Dialog Corporation; EBSCO Publishing, EBSCO Host; Florida Center for Library Automation; Gale; Northern Light Technology, Inc.; OCLC Online Computer Library Center, Inc.; ProQuest LLC (Ann Arbor); H.W. Wilson. *Indexed:* ABIn, ATI, BPI, CWI, H&TI. *Aud.:* Sa.

Serving the domestic lodging industry, this title offers coverage geared toward managers and executives of properties with more than 50 rooms. Stunning photography accompanies articles focused on future and cutting-edge developments in design. Several regular departments rotate focus on such areas as branding, marketing, and technology. The online version has several additional features, such as a buyer's guide and a career center. A good title for those who want to keep their finger on the pulse of the industry.

3622. *Nation's Restaurant News: the newsweekly of the food service industry.* [ISSN: 0028-0518] 1967. w. Mon., 50/yr. USD 164 domestic (Qualified personnel, USD 89.95). Ed(s): Ellen Koteff. Lebhar-Friedman, Inc., 425 Park Ave, New York, NY 10022; info@lf.com; http://www.lf.com. Illus., index, adv. Circ: 90000. Vol. ends: Dec. Microform: CIS; PQC. Online: EBSCO Publishing, EBSCO Host; Factiva, Inc.; Florida Center for Library Automation; Gale; Northern Light Technology, Inc.; OCLC Online Computer Library Center, Inc.; ProQuest LLC (Ann Arbor); H.W. Wilson. *Indexed:* ABIn, BPI, CWI, H&TI, LRI. *Aud.:* Sa.

This newsweekly contains an incredible amount of information in each issue. Densely packed with news, illustrations, and advertising, it is designed to keep restaurant professionals in the know. Regular departments include coverage on supplier news, current culinary trends, marketing, and consumer trends. An online edition features breaking news, a recipe index, and other useful interactive features. Recommended for libraries serving those with an interest in the restaurant field.

3623. *Restaurant Business: street smarts for the entrepreneur.* Formerly (until 1974): *Fast Food.* [ISSN: 0097-8043] 1902. m. USD 119 domestic (Free to qualified personnel). Ed(s): Ralph Raffio. Ideal Media LLC, 303 E Wacker Dr, 21st Fl, Chicago, IL 60601. Illus., adv. Circ: 77000 Controlled. Microform: CIS; PQC. Online: EBSCO Publishing, EBSCO Host; Factiva, Inc.; Florida Center for Library Automation; Gale; Northern Light Technology, Inc.; OCLC Online Computer Library Center, Inc.; ProQuest K-12 Learning Solutions; ProQuest LLC (Ann Arbor); H.W. Wilson. *Indexed:* ABIn, Agr, BPI, FS&TA, H&TI, LRI. *Aud.:* Sa.

This lively and informative monthly caters to the information needs of those in the commercial foodservice industry. In conjunction with the online version, it provides quality coverage and analysis of the emerging trends in the field. The print edition features both colorful and in-depth cover stories as well as regular departments. Notable among these are the "20 Minute University" by the Culinary Institute of America, and "The Foodservice Buyer," which includes

product reviews and profiles. The online edition offers breaking news, interactive resources, and downloadable reports. This is a quality trade publication, recommended for libraries that serve patrons in the hospitality field.

3624. *Restaurants & Institutions.* Incorporates (in 1986): *Bar Business;* Former titles: *Institutions; Institutions - Volume Feeding; Institutions - Volume Feeding Management.* [ISSN: 0273-5520] 1937. s-m. USD 165 domestic; USD 214 Canada; USD 203 Mexico. Ed(s): Patricia B Dailey. Reed Business Information, 2000 Clearwater Dr, Oak Brook, IL 60523; http://www.reedbusiness.com. Illus., index, adv. Circ: 167508 Controlled. Vol. ends: Dec. Microform: CIS. Online: EBSCO Publishing, EBSCO Host; Factiva, Inc.; Florida Center for Library Automation; Gale; LexisNexis; OCLC Online Computer Library Center, Inc.; ProQuest LLC (Ann Arbor); H.W. Wilson. *Indexed:* ABIn, AgeL, BPI, H&TI, LRI. *Aud.:* Sa.

This glossy title provides equal parts content and advertising. Named the magazine of the year by the American Society of Business Publication Editors in 2005, it features consistent writing and greater user-friendliness following a recent redesign. This is a good source of information on food and business trends as well as research and editorial coverage. The online version provides an RSS feed on headline news and is part of a larger site including "Foodservice 411," "Chain Leader," and "Foodservice Equipment & Supplies." A daily e-newsletter is also available. A highly recommended title for those in the field and libraries that serve them.

■ HUMOR

Donna Burton, Associate Professor, Schaffer Library, Union College, Schenectady, NY 12308; burtond@union.edu

Introduction

Laughter is universal; it crosses age, gender, and social lines and is a physical response to humor. What individuals find humorous, however, is a very subjective emotion based on personal psychological perception and interpretation. E-mail and the Internet have facilitated the propagation of humor spam and the genesis of humor/satire/parody/jokes/cartoon web sites created by existing publishers, entrepreneurs, entities with specific social or political agendas, and even ordinary folks with a sense of fun or unusual interests.

Between online access and newsstand issues, there really is something for everyone in the humor genre. Choices range from printed materials (and their online issues and archives) or the Internet-only presences, all of which convey humor in its various forms (parody, satire, anecdotes, poetry, etc.), to those technical or scholarly resources that take humor seriously and study, analyze, and interpret it rather than generate it. There are relative newcomers, *MadKids* or *The Believer,* and grizzled veterans, *MAD* or *JIR,* both in their fifties, and a variety in between.

In this age of political correctness, the lines between funny and edgy and offensive have become more difficult to navigate than ever, and the balancing act for libraries may be a slightly tricky one in this genre. Nevertheless we are in a position, when life gets difficult, to do as Joel Goodman, founder and director of the HUMOR Project, Inc., Saratoga Springs, New York (wwww.humorproject.com), has suggested, and remember that "Humor can be a powerful antidote to stress—in the midst of challenging times, it can help us to move from a 'grim and bear it' mentality to a 'grin and share it' orientation."

Basic Periodicals

Hs: *Mad;* Ga: *Mad, The Onion;* Ac: *The Annals of Improbable Research.*

3625. *The Annals of Improbable Research: the journal of record for inflated research and personalities.* [ISSN: 1079-5146] 1995. bi-m. USD 33 domestic; USD 39 in Canada & Mexico; USD 49 elsewhere. Ed(s): Marc Abrahams. Annals of Improbable Research, PO Box 380853, Cambridge, MA 02238; info@improbable.com; http://www.improbable.com. Illus. Refereed. *Aud.:* Hs, Ac, Sa.

Sporting the Holmesian pronouncement, "When all other contingencies fail, whatever remains, however improbable, must be the truth," this journal requires detailed perusal—the wit and humor abound. For example, this journal's editorial masthead and letters to the editor are entitled, respectively, AIRheads and AIR Vents, not to mention the absurdist "Unclassified Ads." Colorful front and back covers may display the Mona Lisa with colored contact lenses or show the spray pattern of projectile penguin poop. The rest of the publication, running 32 pages, is solely in black-and-white text, likewise the illustrations, diagrams or photographs; and there is no outside advertising. Serious research is lampooned and "many of the other articles are genuine, too, but [the editors] don't know which ones." The bimonthly issues are thematic, ranging from painting to fish and chips to smells, beauty, astronomy, or cats. Recent articles have included "Is the Grand Canyon Fake?," "Why Engineers Paint," "Pringles in Your Ear," and the annual "Ig Noble Prize Winners," which honors "achievements that first make people laugh, and then make them think." Also don't miss the web site, which has a daily updated blog and issue archives from volume one, 1995, with sample articles viewable in each issue. Excellent for college and large public libraries and even high school libraries (since the editors encourage copying, sharing, and discussing favorite articles with classes in the *AIR* Teachers' Guide).

3626. *The Believer.* [ISSN: 1543-6101] 2003. 10x/yr. USD 45 domestic; USD 75 foreign; USD 8 newsstand/cover. Ed(s): Andrew Leland, Heidi Julavits. McSweeney's, 826 Valencia St., San Francisco, CA 94110; custservice@mcsweeneys.net; http://www.mcsweeneys.net. Illus., adv. Indexed: MLA-IB. *Bk. rev.:* Number and length vary. *Aud.:* Ac, Sa.

"*The Believer* is a monthly magazine where length is no object. There are book reviews that are not necessarily timely, and that are very often very long. There are interviews that are also very long. *The Believer* contains no ads and is printed in four colors on heavy stock paper." This is stated succinctly on the web site. There are also articles, poems, and columns, with drawn illustrations sprinkled throughout, and the format is elegantly simple and the text clean. On the web, tables of contents from the inaugural June 2003 issue to the present are available at www.believermag.com/issues, with excerpts for almost everything and full text for some things. Contributors cover a broad spectrum of novelists, poets, musicians, actors, and freelancers, and can be searched by issue or name through the web site or the MLA index. Recent articles include "Stuff I've Been Reading," "Reality Hunger: A Manifesto," "A Brief Take on Genetic Screening," and "Fat Fiction," about overweight people as a championless oppressed minority. This is not an in-your-face type of humor publication—it's more chuckles than guffaws. The editors state that they will focus on writers and books they like and will give people and books the benefit of the doubt. Its appeal will most likely be for those with a literary bent in large public or academic libraries.

3627. *Humor: international journal of humor research.* Former titles: *World Humor and Irony Movement Serials Yearbook; World Humor and Irony Membership Serial Yearbook; Western Humor and Irony Membership Serial Yearbook.* [ISSN: 0933-1719] 1988. q. EUR 182; EUR 209 combined subscription print & online eds.; EUR 46 newsstand/ cover. Ed(s): Salvatore Attardo. Mouton de Gruyter, Genthiner Str 13, Berlin, 10785, Germany; mouton@degruyter.de; http://www.degruyter.de. Illus., index, adv. Refereed. Reprint: PSC. Indexed: AgeL, AmHI, ArtHuCI, BRI, CBRI, IBR, IBSS, IBZ, L&LBA, MLA-IB, PsycInfo, SSCI. *Bk. rev.:* 2-4, 350-400 words. *Aud.:* Ac.

This journal "...was established as an international interdisciplinary forum for the publication of high quality research papers on humor as an important and universal human faculty," and "contributions will be in the form of empirical observational studies, theoretical discussions, presentations of research, short notes, reactions/replies to recent articles, book reviews, and letters to the editor," according to the cover blurb. This is a truly scholarly journal that is not only refereed but indexed in at least 11 commercial indexes. Although published in Germany, it is available in English. Relevant graphics, charts, and tables may be included with text, and the advertising is minimal and unobtrusive. Article titles range from "The masking effects of humor on audience perception of message organization" to "Medical merriment in the works of Enrique Jardiel Poncela," to "'One of the last vestiges of gender bias': The characterization of women through the telling of dirty jokes in Ally McBeal." Book reviews cover

interesting titles from folktales to cinema to farce to the psychopathology of humor. Academic and research collections should consider this title, especially in view of the extensive indexing.

3628. *Humor Times.* [ISSN: 1076-8610] m. USD 17.95. Ed(s): James Israel. Comic Press News, PO Box 162429, Sacramento, CA 95816; info@humortimes.com; http://www.humortimes.com. *Aud.:* Ga, Ac.

Enjoy political cartoons? Don't miss this monthly compilation published by Sacramento's Comic Press. In 16 pages of tabloid-sized newsprint, you can find a plethora of them by a variety of cartoonists from a number of places. According to the SCP web page, "Some of the country's finest editorial cartoonists take a look at what's happening on the world stage, while adding their own commentary via the irreverent art of cartooning. Also featured are humor columnists such as nationally known comedian Will Durst and others. In addition, there are lots of great panel cartoons from the likes of Dave Coverly (*Speed Bump*) and Dan Reynolds (*Reynolds Unwrapped*). And we finish off with a whole page of the absurdly funny world view of Dan Piraro and his cartoon panels known as *Bizarro*." In black and white, except for the cover and centerfold pages, this journal contains no advertising, and the cartoons speak for themselves. Additional cartoons can be accessed from the web site for free. This should be considered for high schools, public libraries, and academic insitutions; it is for anywhere and for anyone interested in political and social satire on current events.

3629. *Journal of Irreproducible Results: the science humor magazine.* [ISSN: 0022-2038] 1955. bi-m. USD 39 (Individuals, USD 26.95). Journal of Irreproducible Results, 413 Poinsettia Ave, San Mateo, CA 94403-2803. Illus., index, adv. Circ: 2000. Vol. ends: No. 6. *Aud.:* Ac, Sa.

While you don't really have to be an Einstein to enjoy this magazine, it is subtitled "The Science Humor Magazine," and the articles are made to look and sound complex, so an interest or background in the field certainly wouldn't hurt. The colorful covers and wild variations in font types inside make for interesting viewing, uncomplicated by little, if any, advertising. Articles range from "How to survive a robot uprising" to "Acoustic oscillations in Jell-O, with and without fruit, subjected to varying levels of stress." There are also "Risk factor correlations with respect to cat defenestration" (i.e., the risk of throwing a cat out of the window); "Parents' and researchers' views of children's invisible imaginary companions" (the entire article is "This space left intentionally blank"); and "A saucepan under observation never reaches a phase transition." *JIR*'s editor, Norman Sperling, states that readers will "get more new ideas, perspectives, and viewpoints per issue from *JIR* than from any other scientific publication. *JIR* can spur new insights into real science." Occasional poems and song parodies are included, as are crossword puzzles, cartoons ("Deep space hand salutes"), and illustrations and/or photos accompanying the articles. *JIR* is both interesting and fun and should be in the collections of college, university, hospital, and research libraries. High school libraries and public libraries should consider it, too.

3630. *Light.* [ISSN: 1064-8186] 1992. q. USD 22 domestic; USD 38 foreign; USD 6 newsstand/cover. Ed(s): John Mella. Light Quarterly, PO Box 7500, Chicago, IL 60680-7500. Illus., adv. Circ: 1100 Paid. *Indexed:* AmHI, IAPV. *Bk. rev.:* Number and length vary. *Aud.:* Ga.

According to *Light*'s web site, their contributors include not only well-known poets such as John Updike, W. D. Snodgrass, and Wendy Cope, among many others, but also exciting new talent. The publication's goal is to restore "lightness, understandability, and pleasure to the reading of poems." At this it does succeed. Even non–poetry lovers can enjoy these light and amusing poems; there is everything from parodies to puns to limericks to haiku and sonnets. Each quarterly issue, about the dimensions of a trade paperback, runs around 60 pages, the first eight to ten of which contain poems all of which are by the "Featured Poet." The subsequent pages contain groups of poems playfully categorized under titles such as "Beasties," "Fractured Language," "Short and Sour," and "Just Kidding." The journal concludes with "Reviews and Reflections," a section of book reviews and ruminations, followed by very abbreviated letter and news sections. This would be a good selection for an academic library or large public library. Some poems may not be appropriate for all ages.

3631. *Mad.* [ISSN: 0024-9319] 1952. m. USD 16 domestic; USD 30 foreign; USD 3.99 newsstand/cover per issue. Ed(s): John Ficarra. E.C. Publications, Inc., 1700 Broadway, New York, NY 10019. Illus. Circ: 500000 Paid. *Aud.*: Hs, Ga.

This over-50-year-old iconoclastic publication directed to adolescents and young adults, and written by "the usual gang of idiots," is no longer your black-and-white newsprint magazine from the old days. Graphics range from funny to gross—delivered in glossy color throughout the magazine. Perennial favorites continue, with features such as the clever fold-in back cover, Spy vs. Spy, and the amusing "marginals" cartoon sketches that literally have you perusing every inch of this magazine. With fun poked at virtually anything from current movies to dating to politics and parent/child relationships, very little is sacred in the world of *MAD,* while it's stayed fresh and funny and contemporary. Although this may not be your Dad's (or Granddad's) *MAD,* some things never change; letters to the editor still complain about parents confiscating *MAD.* Now parents have a new incarnation to worry about, *MadKids,* not to mention the previously semi-annual *Mad Classics,* which is now published eight times a year, with selections from previous issues. Surely popular in school and public libraries; the main problem may be keeping it until the next month's issue.

3632. *Mad Kids.* 2005. q. USD 12.99; USD 4.99 newsstand/cover. Ed(s): John Ficarra. E.C. Publications, Inc., 1700 Broadway, New York, NY 10019. Adv. *Aud.*: Ems, Ga.

Following in the footsteps of its venerable predecessor, this new version is targeted to the 6- to 11-year-old set. It's full of jokes, celebrity interviews, games, posters, and contests. Its appearance is bright, colorful, and busy, but it is fairly heavy on the advertising (of course). Boogers (history's most famous) and flatulence and zits add up to a very high grossness quotient—just the way kids like it, but parents may not agree. Some material seems too juvenile for 11-year-olds, and some seems too advanced for 6-year-olds. There's no back page fold-in, but there are special centerfold goodies such as posters or door knob hangers or bookmarks to cut out. There are also a number of other interactive pages where one puts words in the mouth of "Dumb Steve," fills in the punchline of a cartoon, tries to solve "spot what's wrong" picture puzzles, or takes an "Are you a slob?" quiz. Other features include a celebrity chat room (i.e., questions and answers by kiddie fave celebs), "Spy vs. Spy Junior," "The Continuing Adventures of Willy Nilly," and segments like "15 reasons to hate school" or "Games that make really bad video games" (like hide-and-seek or virtual yo-yo). Libraries may want to sample first before deciding whether to subscribe, since to fully enjoy this magazine, kids will want to cut some pages up and fill others in. Some parents may find some material objectionable.

3633. *McSweeney's.* q. USD 55 domestic; USD 85 foreign. Ed(s): Timothy McSweeney. McSweeney's, 826 Valencia St., San Francisco, CA 94110; custservice@mcsweeneys.net; http://www.mcsweeneys.net. *Aud.*: Ga, Ac.

Also known, according to the web site, as *McSweeney's Quarterly Concern,* this journal "publishes on a roughly quarterly schedule, and we try to make each issue very different from the last. One issue came in a box, one was Icelandic, and one looks like a pile of mail." In all, we give you groundbreaking fiction and much more." This journal definitely isn't pedestrian; the bundle-of-mail issue (#17) contained the following: "a recent issue of Yeti Researcher; a large envelope, called Envelope, containing fine oversized reproductions of new art; a sausage-basket catalog; a flyer for slashed prices on garments that are worn by more than one person at a time; a new magazine of experimental fiction called Unfamiliar; [and] a couple of letters." More "regular" issues contain fiction by authors such as Roddy Doyle and Joyce Carol Oates, yet the publisher is also "committed to finding new voices...and promoting the work of gifted but underappreciated writers." In the review copy there was no advertising or illustrations, although the latter were present in the bundle-of-mail issue (#17) and another issue (#13) that is all comics. *McSweeney's* won't be for everyone, but for those liking short fiction pieces and occasional quarterly surprises, this is an obvious one for large public and academic libraries to consider. Odd formats may make for problematic retention or storage.

3634. *The Onion.* [ISSN: 1534-6978] w. USD 39.95 domestic; USD 110 Canada; USD 200 elsewhere. Ed(s): Scott Dikkers. Onion, Inc., 33 University Sq, Ste 270, Madison, WI 53715; infomat@theonion.com; http://www.theonion.com. *Aud.*: Ga.

Self-described in the media kit on its web site, "*The Onion* is a national publication and website that offers award-winning news and views that readers can't get anywhere else. Every week, our attention-grabbing headlines and renowned photojournalism paint a picture of the world that informs the educated and the stupid alike." Whether you're one of the residents of Madison or six other cities with access to a free weekly copy, a paid subscriber, or a dedicated peruser of the web site, you come to find that *The Onion,* subtitled "America's finest news source," is a fun outlet for social humor and political satire. However, this publication does sport a disclaimer that it is "not intended for readers under 18 years of age." *The Onion* reflects a mastery of looking like legitimate news, enough that you often have to do a double-take at sensationalistic headlines such as "Rotation of earth plunges entire North American continent into darkness," or "48-hour Internet outage plunges nation into productivity." In newsprint, these tabloid-sized issues run 30 to 40 pages, and the covers and ads sport color images while the rest is in black-and-white (except on the web site). It is fairly heavy on the advertising, and much of it is local for Madisonites. Also local is "AV Club," an entertainment calendar section that comprises a good half to two-thirds of each hard-copy issue. This journal also includes cinema, DVD, and CD reviews that would be of general reader interest. The archive web site allows search by issue, topic, section, or simply keyword, encompassing August 1996 to the present (over 350 issues). RSS feeds for new content are available. Since much of the content is replicated and/or expanded on online, and a fair portion is of local interest, a print subscription probably shouldn't be considered vital unless there is patron demand in public and academic libraries.

3635. *Studies in American Humor.* Incorporates (1974-1984): *American Humor.* [ISSN: 0095-280X] 1974. a. Membership, USD 20. Ed(s): M Thomas Inge. American Humor Studies Association, c/o Joseph Alvarez, Sec-Treas, 900 Havel Ct, Charlotte, NC 28211-4253; joe_alvarez@ cpcc.cc.nc.us. Illus., index, adv. Refereed. Circ: 500. *Indexed*: AmH&L, AmHI, HistAb, HumInd, MLA-IB. *Bk. rev.*: 2-4, 400-600 words. *Aud.*: Ac.

Founded over 30 years ago and issued only once a year by the American Humor Studies Association, this journal "publishes essays, review essays, and book reviews on all aspects of American humor" (per the web site). Most years, in addition to the main content, a nice feature section, "The year's work in American humor studies," gives a summary of the types of articles on humor published during the preceeding year that aren't in specifically humor-oriented sources, as well as new books on various aspects of humor. This journal is peer-reviewed and is indexed in several literature indexes such as *MLA* and *Humanities Index,* with no advertising and generally little in the way of illustrations. Representative articles include "Playing like a man: Noncompetitive manhood and frontier humor," "A muse of their own: The satirical poetry of nineteenth-century feminists," and "Defying limits: Subversive humor in the texts of American minorities and women." In terms of web presence, former editor Jack Rosenbalm has undertaken scanning the full text of previous issues and has so far made available tables of contents from the old and new series of this title (between 1974 and 1989) and even some of the articles at www.compedit.com/toc.htm. The subscription rate is very reasonable and includes membership in the association. Recommended for research and academic libraries.

3636. *The Toque: Canada's source for humour and satire.* w. Free. The Toque Entertainment. *Aud.*: Hs, Ga, Ac, Sa.

Subtitled "[t]he world leader in Canadian humor, parody & satire," *The Toque* (meaning "hat," and which is featured on its logo—along with a maple leaf, hockey stick, and bottle of beer) seems somewhat like a north-of-the-border version of *The Onion* (see above). The journal states, "We are willing to satirize any subject matter, and our material should not be construed as defamatory, derogatory, or racist in nature. Everything and everyone is equal, and thus a fair target. However, you'll find that most of our writing is friendly and fun anyhow, and not as caustic as other sites can be." The main menu includes Canadian jokes, fake images, funny pictures, and news bits. The site claims daily updating, and there is an RSS feed option. High school and public libraries at least may want to carefully consider access issues. *The Toque* itself provides the disclaimer that "The material in *The Toque* is intended for adults, or those of adult age with maturity issues. It is not meant for those under 18 years of age."

So please don't sue us because you let your kid read our website," and there is adult content advertising readily visible. It certainly could find a niche among general or academic library clientele.

3637. *The White House.* d. Ed(s): John A Wooden. The White House, http://whitehouse.org. *Aud.:* Ga, Ac.

Be careful—www.whitehouse.org is the URL, but www.whitehouse.gov is The White House in Washington, D.C. "Chickenhead is Earth's preeminent purveyor of loathesome and hopelessly puerile parody, produced by a detestable clique of New York City failures, who toil ineffectually in abject poverty and much-deserved obscurity," and they're not totally kidding. Be it "Dead-Eye Dick (Cheney's) Hunt Club" hunting safety rules, government (i.e., "crony") jobs such as FEMA's Michael Brown or Harriet Miers for the Supreme Court, or an outrageous draft registration form, all is fodder for satirizing today's news and politics. Although there is a "disclaimer on age appropriateness: [that the web site] should not be accessed by persons under 18 years of age or White House attorneys with nothing better to do than squander taxpayer dollars by composing empty intimidation letters to political satirists," at the same time there is no required age declaration or hindrance to ready access, which some libraries may particularly want to consider.

■ HUNTING AND GUNS

Joseph A. Molendyke, Librarian, Kent State University Trumbull Campus Library; 4314 Mahoning Ave NW, Warren, OH 44483; 330-675-8879; molenj@trumbull.kent.edu

John E Popadak II, Library Associate, Kent State University Trumbull Campus Library; 4314 Mahoning Ave NW, Warren, OH 44483; 330-675-8816; jpopadak@kent.edu

Introduction

Hunting and Guns is somewhat of a misnomer, since the subject includes a multitude of outdoor sporting interests rather than simply a deer hunter in the field. Many of the magazines and journals do focus on firearms, but there is also something for the bow-hunter and trapper, as well as the knife enthusiast and dog lover. As for firearms, the subject stretches from primitive black-powder rifles to new offerings in the handgun, shotgun, and rifle arsenal. Most of the magazines offer detailed articles on these firearms, along with technical data and field testing. Ammunition is scrutinized as well, with in-depth articles from *Rifle's Handloader*, for example. Feature articles are often written by experienced staff writers. Submissions from experts in the field and the reader/ enthusiast round out article offerings. Virtually all magazines have regular "departments" for new products, equipment reviews, and regional reports. Gun legislation, land management, and hunter safety are often the subject of articles and op-ed pieces. Color photography is impressive, featuring both the firearm, the prey, and the vast outdoors. Drawings, maps, and charts are used when applicable, particularly in a publication like *Muzzleloader* where historic articles abound. Focus is also directed to the game being hunted, be it white-tail, elk, or wild turkey. Articles on animal behavior and habitat are frequently found.

This popular genre has been expanding to include the youthful hunter, the outdoor sports–minded woman, and the disabled enthusiast. Offerings such as *Wheelin' Sportsman* and *Women in the Outdoors* should bear strong consideration for inclusion in a library's hunting and outdoor enthusiast collection. As one would expect, almost all of these titles have associated web sites, and offer selected online access to feature articles.

Basic Periodicals

Ems: *American Hunter, Field & Stream, Outdoor Life;* Hs, Ga, Ac: *American Hunter, American Rifleman, Blade, Bow and Arrow Hunting, Bowhunting World, Field & Stream, Fur-Fish-Game, Guns & Ammo, Muzzle Blasts, Outdoor Life, Petersen's Hunting, Shotgun Sports.*

Basic Abstracts and Indexes

Magazine Index, Readers' Guide to Periodical Literature.

3638. *American Hunter.* [ISSN: 0092-1068] 1973. m. Membership, USD 35; USD 2 newsstand/cover domestic. Ed(s): J Scott Olmstead. National Rifle Association of America, 11250 Waples Mill Rd, Fairfax, VA 22030; http://www.nra.org. Illus., adv. Sample. Circ: 1300000 Paid. Vol. ends: Dec. *Indexed:* ConsI. *Bk. rev.:* 1-4, 500 words. *Aud.:* Hs, Ga, Ac.

According to the National Rifle Association (NRA), *American Hunter* is about "tactics, adventure, great places to hunt, the latest hunting gear, and a special emphasis on the guns hunters love—all delivered by experts in the field." This magazine is one of the two official journals of the NRA. As with the other official journal, *American Hunter* has launched a TV show. Once a week readers and viewers are treated to expert hunters giving tips and instruction. This magazine is loaded with information for hunters of all types of prey, especially pheasant, turkey, deer, and elk as well as other big game. This magazine is recommended for any hunter and any library that services hunters. Access to some feature articles is available online.

3639. *American Rifleman.* [ISSN: 0003-083X] 1885. m. Membership, USD 35. Ed(s): Mark A Keefe, IV. N R A Publications, 11250 Waples Mill Rd, Fairfax, VA 22030-9400; membership@nrahq.org; http://www.nrahq.org/. Illus., adv. Sample. Circ: 1600000. Vol. ends: Dec. Microform: PQC. Online: Northern Light Technology, Inc.; OCLC Online Computer Library Center, Inc.; ProQuest K-12 Learning Solutions. *Indexed:* ConsI, FLI. *Bk. rev.:* 3-7, 150-250 words. *Aud.:* Hs, Ga, Ac.

American Rifleman is one of two magazines published by the National Rifle Association. Safety is one of the key issues in the magazine. Articles may include such topics as gunsmithing, handguns, shotguns, rifles, police training, gun collecting, handloading, and competitive shooting. This magazine has been published since 1923 and has been a big part of America's enthusiasm for guns. There are more than 12 regular departments and columns. As with *Field and Stream*, *American Rifleman* has become so popular that the editors have taken the magazine to television. Recommended for any gun enthusiast. Access to some feature articles is available online.

3640. *American Shooting Magazine.* 1996. m. Ed(s): David A Pierce. Silver Bullet Industries, Inc., 45303 Margate, Macomb, MI 45304; dapierce@rust.net; http://www.americanshooting.com. *Aud.:* Ems, Hs, Ga.

This web site is quite primitive compared to others, but that is not necessarily a bad thing. It is very easy to navigate, and the links scroll right down the page so there is no looking for the right link in a different area of the site. It is divided into four parts: Departments, Features, Advertisers, and Classifieds. If an article is new to the site, it is marked with a "New" designation. Since this is a free publication, it is recommended for any library that has hunters and/or shooters as clientele.

3641. *American Trapper.* [ISSN: 1050-4036] 1955. bi-m. USD 25. Ed(s): Tom Krause. National Trappers Association, 3200 Lewis Rd, P O Box 513, Riverton, WY 82501-0513; TKrause@wyoming.com. Illus., adv. Sample. Circ: 20000 Paid. Vol. ends: Dec. *Aud.:* Sa.

American Trapper is published four times a year by the National Trappers Association (NTA) and is the official publication of the association. Feature articles are written by trappers from across the country who earn their living as trappers. Articles cover ways of trapping, types of animals to trap, and evaluations of equipment used in trapping. "Exclusive Stories" are articles written by members detailing their experiences while trapping. Other regular features include letters to the editor, classified ads, "In Passing," and "NTA Family Album." Each issue also contains at least two articles written by staff and two articles written by NTA officers.

3642. *Blade.* Formerly: *Blade Magazine;* Which incorporated: *Edges;* Which was formerly (until 1982): *American Blade.* [ISSN: 1064-5853] 1973. m. USD 19.98 domestic; USD 36.98 Canada; USD 47.98 elsewhere. Ed(s): Steve Shackleford. Krause Publications, Inc., 700 E State St, Iola, WI 54990-0001; info@krause.com; http://www.krause.com. Illus., adv. Circ: 38068 Paid and free. *Indexed:* CBCARef. *Bk. rev.:* Number and length vary. *Aud.:* Hs, Ga, Ac.

Feature articles in this monthly magazine include information on blade and knife shows, throwing, cover making, history, metals, and materials for handles. Some articles may be reviews of blades and knives, or of books about blades and knives. Each issue may have articles on knives (military, hunting, etc.), stars, swords, axes, and any other type of blade one can think of. With over 15 regular departments including "Unsheathed," "Guild Directions," "Blade Shoppe and Blade List," and "The Knife I Carry," this magazine contains a wealth of knowledge for the blade community. It is a must for any blade enthusiast. Access to some feature articles is available online.

3643. *Bow and Arrow Hunting: the world's leading archery magazine.* Formerly (until 1985): *Bow and Arrow.* [ISSN: 0894-7856] 1963. 9x/yr. USD 21.95 domestic; USD 32.95 Canada; USD 46.95 elsewhere. Ed(s): Jeff Howe, Joe Bell. A P G Media, 265 S Anita Dr, Ste 120, Orange, CA 92868. Illus., adv. Circ: 9700 Paid. *Bk. rev.:* 1-3, 200-500 words. *Aud.:* Hs, Sa.

Bow and Arrow Hunting is published nine times a year by Action Pursuit Group. Feature articles include all aspects of hunting with bow and arrow. They may be reviews of arrows or bows, tips from experts who hunt with bow and arrow, information on bowhunting safety, or tips on competition shooting. Articles are written by both professional and amateur bowhunters. Regular departments and columns include "Mail Pouch," "Questions & Answers," "Reflections," and "Hi-Spirit." Access to some feature articles is available online.

3644. *Bowhunting World: the archery equipment authority.* Formerly (until 1989): *Archery World.* [ISSN: 1043-5492] 1952. 9x/yr. USD 15.97 domestic; USD 24.97 foreign; USD 3.99 newsstand/cover per issue domestic. Ed(s): Mark Melotik, Mike Strandlund. Grand View Media Group, Inc., 200 Croft St, Ste 1, Birmingham, AL 35242-1824; webmaster@grandviewmedia.com; http://www.grandviewmedia.com. Illus., index, adv. Sample. Circ: 130000 Paid and controlled. Vol. ends: Dec. *Indexed:* ConsI, PEI. *Aud.:* Sa.

Bowhunting World is published nine times a year by Grand View Media Group. Feature articles may deal with arrow making, shaft making, equipment reviews, or tips from experts, and deal with bowhunting any type of animal, from bears to deer to elk, even fish. Every issue contains the very informative "Exclusive Bow Report," which tests and analyzes a specific bow each month. Regular departments include "Home Bow Mechanic," "Backcountry," "New Gear," and the "IBO Newsletter." A nice feature of *Bowhunting World* is the monthly "Field Test" section. The staff take new bowhunting gear and/or accessories out in the field, test them, and then review each item. There are also two special issues each year—a buyer's guide and a bowhunter's guide. A must for any library that maintains a collection for bowhunters.

3645. *Bugle (Missoula): journal of elk and the hunt.* [ISSN: 0889-6445] 1984. bi-m. USD 35. Ed(s): Dan Crockett. Joy Publications, LLC, 2291 W Broadway, PO Box 8249, Missoula, MT 59807-8249. Illus., adv. Sample. Circ: 195000 Paid. Vol. ends: Dec. *Aud.:* Ga, Ac.

Bugle, a publication of the Rocky Mountain Elk Foundation, is about "all things Elk." The foundation stresses conservation and education to secure the health of the wildlife habitat for future generations. Feature articles are therefore tailored to these subjects, and are written by experienced authors with backgrounds in conservation, land management, and environmental concerns. Other feature articles focus on elk and elk hunting. Interesting articles can also be found in monthly departments such as "Women in Elk Country," "Bows and Arrows," "Habits and Habitat," and "Gear," to name a few. Articles are accompanied by many spectacular color photographs of awe-inspiring environments and wildlife, predominately elk. Selected feature articles are available online. The Elk Foundation also sponsors "Elk Country Journal," a television series on the Outdoor Life Network. This publication will serve library patrons with an interest in hunting as well as land conservation and wildlife habitat.

3646. *The Chase: a full cry of hunting.* [ISSN: 0009-1952] 1920. 11x/yr. USD 30 domestic; USD 32 Canada; USD 34 elsewhere. Ed(s): JoAnn Stone. Chase Publishing Co., Inc., 1150 Industry Rd, PO Box 55090, Lexington, KY 40555; chasepubl@aol.com. Illus., adv. Sample. Circ: 3300 Paid. Vol. ends: Jun. *Aud.:* Sa.

The Chase is an oversized monthly publication (combined issue for December/January) that promotes itself as the "authoritative magazine of foxhunting." Issues focus on field trial and bench show results nationwide as reported by contributing authors/participants, and are accompanied by black-and-white photos. Interspersed are advertisements for hounds at stud and notices for upcoming hunts and shows. Each issue concludes with copious lists of kennel registrations and monthly transfers. *The Chase* clearly lives up to its billing as authoritative, and it is invaluable to the foxhunting enthusiast. Should appeal to any library serving this clientele.

3647. *Deer & Deer Hunting: practical & comprehensive information for white-tailed deer hunters.* [ISSN: 0164-7318] 1977. 9x/yr. USD 19.99 domestic; USD 29.99 Canada; USD 34.99 elsewhere. Ed(s): Joe Shead, Daniel E Schmidt. Krause Publications, Inc., 700 E State St, Iola, WI 54990-0001; info@krause.com; http://www.krause.com. Illus., adv. Sample. Circ: 116292 Paid. Vol. ends: Aug. *Bk. rev.:* Occasional, up to 2,000 words. *Aud.:* Hs, Sa.

For the bow and arrow and gun hunting enthusiast, the magazine of choice should be *Deer & Deer Hunting*. This periodical has a wealth of informative articles written by field editors and experienced freelance contributors. Article subjects range from diverse hunting destinations to deer environs to wildlife education, with regular pieces on personal deer encounters. There is an abundance of color photography, with many full-page spreads. Shorter departmental articles address issues of white-tail management, deer behavior, and bow hunting tips and tactics. For all libraries serving the deer hunting community.

Disabled Outdoors Magazine. See Hiking, Climbing, and Outdoor Recreation/General section.

3648. *Field & Stream. Northeast Edition.* Supersedes in part (in 1984): *Field and Stream;* Incorporates: *Living Outdoors.* [ISSN: 8755-8580] 1895. m. USD 12 domestic; USD 27.97 Canada; USD 34.97 foreign. Time4 Media, Inc., 2 Park Ave, New York, NY 10016. Illus., adv. Circ: 1500000 Paid. Microform: NBI; PQC. *Indexed:* ConsI, MASUSE, RGPR. *Bk. rev.:* 4-6, 200-300 words. *Aud.:* Ems, Hs, Ga.

Field & Stream is published 11 times a year by Time4 Media, Inc. "It celebrates the outdoor experience with great stories, compelling photography, and sound advice, and it honors the traditions hunters and fisherman have passed down for generations." This magazine has been around for more than 100 years, so it must be doing something right. With so many informative and accessible articles, it is a must for any public library. Feature articles deal with anything having to do with the outdoors, from fishing to hunting to boating to equipment reviews to conservation. The magazine has become so popular that there is a televion show with the same name. Each issue contains regular departments such as "Bullet Points," "Rifles," "Fishing," "Shotguns," and "Conservation." Each issue also has a "Field Test," which compares and analyzes new equipment after using it. A must for any outdoorsman. Access to some feature articles is available online.

Fishing and Hunting News. See Fishing section.

3649. *Full Cry: published exclusively for the American coon hound and trail hound enthusiast.* [ISSN: 0016-2620] 1939. m. USD 23; USD 3 newsstand/cover. Ed(s): Terry Walker. C & H Publishing, PO Box 777, Sesser, IL 62884. Illus., adv. Sample. Circ: 20200 Paid. Vol. ends: Jan. *Aud.:* Sa.

Full Cry is a monthly publication dedicated to the coon hound and tree dog sport. The bulk of each issue contains reports from the many associations that exist nationwide. Reports are written by association members, and include updates on activities along with black-and-white photos. General-interest articles appear throughout, submitted by members, and include personal stories of travels and hunts. Regular columns appear for classified advertising, a "Quick Locator" for finding breeders and related services, and "Photo Happenings" for reader photo submissions. Breeder advertising and association events are sprinkled throughout each issue. *Full Cry* is truly an "enthusiast-friendly" magazine. Libraries serving patrons with sporting dog interests should have this magazine.

3650. *Fur - Fish - Game. Harding's Magazine.* [ISSN: 0016-2922] 1925. m. USD 16.95. Ed(s): Mitch Cox. A.R. Harding Publishing Co., 2878 E Main St, Columbus, OH 43209; ffgservice@ameritech.net. Illus., adv. Sample. Circ: 113000 Paid. Vol. ends: Dec. *Aud.:* Hs, Ga, Ac.

Fur-Fish-Game is published 12 times a year by Harding Publishing. This magazine deals with all aspects of the outdoors. From fishing to trapping to hunting (of all types) to camping to hiking to boating, this magazine covers it all. Regular departments include "Letters from the Reader," "News and Notes," "Fish and Tackle," "Fur Market Report," "The Trapline," and "The Gun Rack." *Fur-Fish-Game* is a venerable publication with a long history and a loyal readership. It covers more aspects of the outdoors than any other magazine on the market. A must for any library.

3651. *Gray's Sporting Journal.* [ISSN: 0273-6691] 1975. 7x/yr. USD 36.95 domestic; USD 46.95 Canada; USD 56.95 elsewhere. Ed(s): James R Babb. Morris Communications Co., LLC., 725 Broad St, Augusta, GA 30901; http://www.morris.com/. Illus., adv. Sample. Circ: 35000. Vol. ends: Jan. *Bk. rev.:* 1-3; 500+ words. *Aud.:* Ac, Sa.

Gray's Sporting Journal purports to be more a literary publication for the "discerning reader" than a firearms-driven magazine for the die-hard hunter. In this capacity it succeeds admirably. Well-written first-hand articles about fishing and hunting treks are interspersed with "photographic journals," paintings and drawings of the sporting outdoors, and poetry. Each issue has "The Listing," an alphabetical presentation of state and territorial outfitters and lodges for the travel-minded sportsperson. Thoughtful book reviews are a staple as well. Selected feature articles are available online. "Gray's Sporting Journal Television" can be seen on the Outdoor Life Network.

3652. *Gun Dog: upland bird and waterfowl dogs.* [ISSN: 0279-5086] 1981. bi-m. USD 24.97 domestic; USD 34.97 Canada; USD 36.97 elsewhere. Source Interlink Companies, 27500 Riverview Center Blvd, Bonita Springs, FL 34134; edisupport@sourceinterlink.com; http://www.sourceinterlink.com. Illus., adv. Sample. Circ: 52971. Vol. ends: Dec/Jan. *Aud.:* Hs, Sa.

For the waterfowl hunting enthusiast and bird dog lover, *Gun Dog* is the magazine that clearly addresses their needs. Articles cover dog breeds, their handling and training, health aspects, and some historical discussion. Animal behavior, education thereof, and competitions are also subject material. There are regular departments for veterinary information, training tips, and conservation issues. This magazine would be useful to any library serving the gun dog and upland bird hunting fan. Selected feature articles are available online.

3653. *Gun Dogs Online.com.* m. Free. Gundogs Online.Com, P.O. Box 444, Southbury, CT 06488-0444; support@gundogsonline.com. *Bk. rev.:* Number and length vary. *Aud.:* Hs, Ga.

Gun Dogs Online (www.gundogsonline.com) is "committed to being the Internet's best source of hunting dog supplies and information relating to hunting dogs." With links to dog training collars, dog supplies, dog doors and fences, training books, and shooting supplies, among others, this site covers everything the hunting dog owner might need. The many articles are written by both experts and laypersons. The site is easy to navigate, and there is access to a complete archive. A wonderful site for owners of hunting dogs.

3654. *Gun-Knife Show Calendar.* Formerly: *Gun Show Calendar.* [ISSN: 1522-9572] 1979. q. USD 14.95 domestic; USD 23.95 foreign. Krause Publications, Inc., 700 E State St, Iola, WI 54990-0001; info@krause.com; http://www.krause.com. Illus., adv. Sample. Circ: 5758 Paid and free. Vol. ends: Dec. *Aud.:* Sa.

The quarterly *Gun-Knife Show Calendar* is a list of gun and knife shows throughout the United States. Each issue has "The Battle Plan," which provides dates for military gun and knife shows. Each issue also has a special section for blade shows (sponsored by *Blade Magazine*) as well as a blank three- or six-month calendar so enthusiasts can plan their show schedules. Each listing provides the dates and addresses of the shows, and usually the show hours and admission prices. For dealers, the promoter's number is generally listed as well. The magazine may also list shows up to a year in advance, which gives both dealers and enthusiasts time to plan. For anyone who has interest in attending gun and/or knife shows.

3655. *Gun List: the indexed firearms paper.* [ISSN: 0894-8119] 1984. bi-w. USD 37.98 domestic; USD 113.98 Canada; USD 171.98 elsewhere. Krause Publications, Inc., 700 E State St, Iola, WI 54990-0001; info@krause.com; http://www.krause.com. Illus., index, adv. Sample. Circ: 81120 Paid and free. Vol. ends: Dec. *Aud.:* Sa.

The biweekly *Gun List* is the ultimate gun buying guide. It has thousands upon thousands of guns for sale from all over the world. There is an index on the front cover, allowing quick access to the type of gun you are looking for. The index also lists knives, books on guns, gun accessories, and scopes and binoculars. Each issue also contains articles addressing all aspects of the gun world, plus many columns including "Reader's Range," "Gun Value Tracker," and "NRA Update." This newspaper-style publication also contains many gun-related advertisements. This title is geared for people looking to buy and sell guns, and for those looking to stay up-to-date on gun news and prices.

3656. *Gun World: for the firearms & hunting enthusiast.* [ISSN: 0017-5641] 1960. m. USD 23.95 domestic; USD 38.95 Canada; USD 48.95 elsewhere. Ed(s): Jeff Howe, Jan Libourel. A P G Media, 265 S Anita Dr, Ste 120, Orange, CA 92868. Illus., adv. Circ: 130000. Vol. ends: Dec. *Bk. rev.:* 1, 200-300 words. *Aud.:* Ga.

Firearms enthusiasts are sure to find something to their liking in *Gun World*. This publication runs the gamut of firearms and regularly reviews handguns, shotguns, and rifles. Featured reviews may be of exotic contemporary pieces or guns of yesteryear. Tactical firearms are reviewed, and there are reports from the field. Reviews are thorough and detailed, with photos and target results. Regular departments include new gun products and tactical gear, along with technical how-to advice. The photography is excellent, with some full-page spreads. Recommended for any library with patrons interested in firearms.

3657. *Guns & Ammo.* Incorporates (1995-1996): *Performance Shooter.* [ISSN: 0017-5684] 1958. m. USD 17.94; USD 30.94 Canada; USD 32.94 elsewhere. Ed(s): Scott Rupp. Source Interlink Companies, 27500 Riverview Center Blvd, Bonita Springs, FL 34134; edisupport@ sourceinterlink.com; http://www.sourceinterlink.com. Illus., index, adv. Circ: 590238 Paid. Vol. ends: Dec. Microform: PQC. Online: The Dialog Corporation; Gale. *Aud.:* Hs, Ga, Ac.

For general, all-around coverage of firearms and related issues, libraries would do well to include *Guns & Ammo* in their collections. The scope reaches all levels of shooter experience. Articles routinely address issues involving firearms and shooting, ammunition and reloading, collectible guns, and relevant technical data. Firearms safety and legislative issues are also reported. Selected feature articles are available online.

3658. *Hunter & Shooting Sports Education Journal.* Former titles (until 2004): *Hunter Education Journal;* (until 1998): *Hunter Education Instructor;* (until 1989): *Hunter Safety Instructor;* (until 1983): *Hunter Safety News.* 1973. 3x/yr. Corporations, USD 100 member; Members, USD 25 volunteer. International Hunter Education Assocation (I H E A), 3725 Cleveland Ave, PO Box 490, Wellington, CO 80549; info@ihea.com; http://www.ihea.com. Illus., adv. Circ: 65000 Controlled. *Aud.:* Ems, Hs, Ga.

Hunter & Shooting Sports Education Journal is published three times a year by the International Hunter Education Association (IHEA). The primary focus is on hunter safety and education, with a particular emphasis on the youthful hunter. Feature articles are often written by experienced and respected administrators in the hunter safety field. Topics may include hunting laws, historical pieces on established safety programs, wildlife management, and safe hunting techniques. Regular departments such as the "Bulletin Board" list happenings and events from around the country with accompanying color photos, and "Teaching 101" and "Wild Game Recipes" also appear regularly. Each issue also includes opinion pieces and commentary by IHEA leadership. This journal should be in any library serving hunting interests, particularly the young. Archived issues dating from 2002 are available online.

3659. *Muzzle Blasts.* [ISSN: 0027-5360] 1939. m. Membership, USD 40. Ed(s): Eric Bye, Terri Trowbridge. National Muzzle Loading Rifle Association, PO Box 67, Friendship, IN 47021; nmlra@nmlra.org. Illus., index, adv. Sample. Circ: 21000 Controlled. Vol. ends: Aug. *Bk. rev.:* 1, 1,000 words. *Aud.:* Hs, Sa.

Muzzle Blasts is the official publication of the National Muzzle Loading Rifle Association. Feature articles cover all aspects of the sport of muzzle loading, including data on various antique weapons and features on fur trading, buffalo hunting, and Indian encounters, all from a historical perspective. Also included are features on current association activities such as youth programs and calendars of events. Regular departments juxtapose brief historical articles on black-powder weapons, knives, and powder horns with current legislative affairs and web sites of particular interest to the sport. Most articles and how-to pieces are accompanied by black-and-white photos and drawings. Will serve library patrons with an interest in historical hunting methods and techniques. Selected feature articles are available online.

3660. *Muzzleloader: publication for black powder shooters.* [ISSN: 0274-5720] 1974. bi-m. USD 23 domestic; USD 29 foreign. Ed(s): Bill Scurlock. Scurlock Publishing Co., Inc., 1293 Myrtle Springs Rd, Texarkana, TX 75503-9403; jason@scurlockpublishing.com; http://www.muzzleloadermag.com. Illus., index, adv. Sample. Circ: 15000 Paid. Vol. ends: Feb. *Bk. rev.:* 2-4, 500-1,500 words. *Aud.:* Hs, Sa.

Muzzleloader is a bimonthly publication for the black-powder enthusiast. The emphasis is more on the firearm as a part of eighteenth-century history than the nuts and bolts of the rifle itself. In fact, most articles revolve around frontier history—the fur trade industry, the French and Indian war, Indians versus settlers on the frontier, and the daily life of the colonial woodsman. Feature articles are written by experienced staff writers and are often appended with reference notes. Most articles include black-and-white photos, and maps and drawings when applicable. Regular features include book reviews, technical how-to advice, and period-piece product offerings. This publication would serve any library with collections in early American history and firearms.

3661. *North American Whitetail: the magazine devoted to the serious trophy deer hunter.* [ISSN: 0746-6250] 1982. 8x/yr. USD 14.97; USD 2.99 newsstand/cover per issue domestic; USD 3.99 newsstand/cover per issue Canada. Ed(s): Gordon Whittington. Primedia Enthusiast Group, 2250 Newmarket Pkwy, Ste 110, Marietta, GA 30067; information@primedia.com; http://www.primedia.com. Illus., adv. Sample. Circ: 130000 Paid. Vol. ends: Feb. *Aud.:* Hs, Sa.

North American Whitetail is published eight times a year by Primedia Enthusiast. Informative, interesting feature articles deal with "getting the big one." Articles may also be product reviews, dog training tips, and anything else related to whitetail deer hunting. Regular departments include "Headlines," "NAW Television," "Trails and Tails," and "Hall of Fame." Each issue also has advertisements geared specifically to the whitetail hunter. Recommended for any library where whitetail hunting is a popular recreational activity.

Outdoor Life. See Hiking, Climbing, and Outdoor Recreation/General section.

3662. *Petersen's Hunting.* [ISSN: 0146-4671] 1973. 10x/yr. USD 14.97 domestic; USD 27.97 Canada; USD 29.97 elsewhere. Ed(s): Scott Rupp, Bob Sarber. Source Interlink Companies, 6420 Wilshire Blvd, Los Angeles, CA 90048; edisupport@sourceinterlink.com; http://www.sourceinterlink.com. Illus., adv. Circ: 380798 Paid. Microform: PQC. Online: Gale. *Bk. rev.:* Occasional. *Aud.:* Hs, Ga, Ac.

Petersen's Hunting attempts to be all things to all hunters, and it does a remarkable job. This comprehensive hunting magazine is filled with well-written articles on a variety of subjects, including firearms profiles and reviews, hunting techniques, guides, outfitters, and game recipes. Featured game include both large and small prey, turkey, and waterfowl, with worldwide expedition reports. An obvious choice for any library's general hunting and outdoor sports collection. Selected feature articles are available online.

3663. *Pheasants Forever: journal of upland game conservation.* [ISSN: 1079-7041] 1982. 5x/yr. USD 25. Ed(s): Mark Herwig. Pheasants Forever Inc., 1783 Buerkle Circle, St. Paul, MN 55110-5254. Illus., adv. Circ: 100000. *Aud.:* Ac, Sa.

For the upland game-bird hunter and wildlife habitat enthusiast, *Pheasants Forever* is a fine choice. Article topics range from shotgun and bird dog handling to pheasant biology and behavior. Issues also focus on conservation, habitat management, and environmental and legislative concerns. Public education is always an interwoven theme. Articles are written by experienced authors, and handsome photography abounds. A good addition to any library serving bird hunters. Selected feature articles are available online.

3664. *Precision Shooting: dealing exclusively with extreme rifle accuracy.* [ISSN: 0048-5144] 1956. m. USD 37; USD 3.95 newsstand/cover per issue. Ed(s): David D Brennan. Precision Shooting, Inc., 222 McKee St, Manchester, CT 06040. Illus., adv. Sample. Circ: 18000 Paid. *Aud.:* Ac, Sa.

Precision Shooting indeed focuses on "extreme rifle accuracy." Articles are written mainly from a pool of respected authors and cover a variety of shooting-related topics, including rifle and cartridge reviews, optics, and shooting improvement skills. Many articles are technically oriented, accompanied by photos, charts, and graphs. There are occasional articles from a historical perspective and contributions written from the field. The magazine reports regularly on shooting competitions, scores, records, and results. It will serve library patrons with an interest in hunting sports. Selected feature articles are available online.

3665. *Rifle: the sporting firearms journal.* Formerly: *Rifle Magazine.* [ISSN: 0162-3583] 1968. bi-m. USD 19.97 domestic; USD 26 foreign; USD 4.99 newsstand/cover per issue. Ed(s): Dave Scovill. Wolfe Publishing Co., 2625 Stearman Rd., Ste. A, Prescott, AZ 86301-6155. Illus., adv. Sample. Circ: 113000. Vol. ends: Dec. *Bk. rev.:* 3-5, 250-500 words. *Aud.:* Hs, Sa.

Rifle is a bimonthly publication that covers everything of interest to the hunting and firearms fan. Reviews of rifles (many of them vintage), cartridges, and shooting accessories are written by veteran contributors and knowledgeable staff. Articles are lengthy and enhanced by color photos highlighting minute details. Featured regularly are shorter articles on new products, optics, basic gunsmithing, and how-to advice. *Rifle* would be a fine addition to libraries with collections in hunting and firearms sports. Selected feature articles are available online.

3666. *Rifle's Handloader: ammunition reloading journal.* Formerly: *Handloader.* 1966. bi-m. USD 22.97 domestic; USD 29 foreign; USD 4.99 newsstand/cover per issue. Ed(s): Dave Scovill. Wolfe Publishing Co., 2625 Stearman Rd., Ste. A, Prescott, AZ 86301-6155. Illus., index, adv. Sample. Circ: 110000 Paid. Vol. ends: Jan. *Aud.:* Ac, Sa.

Rifle's Handloader is a bimonthly publication that focuses on cartridges and shells for rifles, handguns, and shotguns. Articles are written by a highly knowledgeable and experienced staff. Firearms of historic significance are often received, along with performance statistics. A majority of articles detail hand-loading techniques and thoroughly evaluate factory cartridges and cartridge loads. In fact, the number of cartridge types and loads is mind-boggling to the neophyte. All articles are accompanied by color photos, graphs, and charts. Regular departments include new-product reviews and a very informative Q&A section. This publication would be a welcome addition to any library that serves the hunting and firearms fan. Select feature articles are available online. *Rifle's Handloader* is also available from the publisher on DVD from inception (1966-).

3667. *S H O T Business: shooting, hunting & outdoor trade.* [ISSN: 1081-8618] 1993. m. USD 25 domestic (Free to qualified personnel). World Publications LLC, PO Box 8500, Winter Park, FL 32790; info@worldpub.net; http://www.worldpub.net. Illus., adv. Circ: 20500 Controlled. Vol. ends: Dec. *Bk. rev.:* 6-8, 500-1,000 words. *Aud.:* Ac, Sa.

The official publication of the National Shooting Sports Foundation, *S H O T Business* is the magazine of choice for those in the shooting sports and retailing business. Feature articles highlight the latest in manufacturer's wares, such as optics and ammo. Additional features address issues of successful retailing. There are regular departments for human resources concerns, regional sales trends, and new-product reviews. The foundation is actively involved in firearms safety education and the promotion of programs that introduce young people and their parents to shooting sports and the outdoors.

3668. *Shotgun Sports: America's leading shotgun magazine.* [ISSN: 0744-3773] 1976. m. USD 32.95 domestic; USD 39.95 foreign; USD 4.95 newsstand/cover. Ed(s): Frank Kodl. Shotgun Sports, PO Box 6810, Auburn, CA 95604. Illus., adv. Sample. Circ: 108000. Vol. ends: Dec. *Aud.:* Hs, Sa.

For the shotgun enthusiast, *Shotgun Sports* is clearly one of the magazines of choice. Trap shooting, sporting clays, skeet shooting, and hunting are covered, offering something of interest to the recreational user as well as the diehard shotgun hunter. In-depth reviews of shotguns, both new and classic, are by experienced and knowledgeable authors. Ammo and reloading techniques are also a staple. Occasional articles appear for the youthful hunter and the sportswoman, too. The large number of feature articles are supplemented by a like number of regular columns and departments. Selected feature articles are available online.

3669. *Trap & Field: the official publication of the Amateur Trapshooting Association.* [ISSN: 0041-1760] 1890. m. USD 25 domestic; USD 37 foreign. Ed(s): Terry Heeg. Curtis Magazine Group, Inc., 1000 Waterway Blvd, Indianapolis, IN 46202-2157. Illus., adv. Sample. Circ: 14000 Paid. Vol. ends: Dec. *Indexed:* SD. *Aud.:* Ems, Hs, Sa.

Trap & Field is the official publication of the Amateur Trapshooting Association. Feature articles have to do with anything related to trapshooting including legislation, advice from experts, and competition winners. The magazine contains more than 14 regular departments including "Gun Exchange," "Honor Roll," "Shoot Directory," and "Shooter's Marketplace." It also features columns written by trapshooters. Recommended for anyone interested in the sport, from beginners to experts. Access to some feature articles is available online.

3670. *Trapper & Predator Caller: practical information for experienced dedicated trappers & predator callers.* Formerly (until 1984): *Trapper.* [ISSN: 8750-233X] 1975. 10x/yr. USD 18.95 domestic; USD 29.95 Canada; USD 35.95 foreign. Ed(s): Paul Wait. Krause Publications, Inc., 700 E State St, Iola, WI 54990-0001; info@krause.com; http://www.krause.com. Illus., adv. Sample. Circ: 38260 Paid and free. Vol. ends: Dec. *Aud.:* Ems, Hs, Sa.

Trapper & Predator Caller's feature articles are informative, written by actual trappers, and can have anything to do with trapping and predator calling. This newspaper publication contains recent trapping news and the latest information on predator calling. Articles may contain tips from experts on how to trap, what equipment to use, and what clothing to wear while trapping. Each issue also contains several regular departments such as "The Market Report," "The Answer Men," "New Products," "Calendar of Events," and "Furbearer Behavior." There is also association news from each state and classified ads. Access to some feature articles is available online.

3671. *Turkey & Turkey Hunting: practical & comprehensive information for wild turkey hunters.* Incorporates (in 1992): *Turkey Hunter;* Which was formerly (1984-198?): *Turkey.* [ISSN: 1067-4942] 1983. 6x/yr. USD 15.95 domestic; USD 22.95 Canada; USD 27.95 foreign. Ed(s): James Schlender. Krause Publications, Inc., 700 E State St, Iola, WI 54990-0001; info@krause.com; http://www.krause.com. Illus., adv. Sample. Circ: 68962 Paid and free. *Bk. rev.:* 1, 5,000 words. *Aud.:* Hs, Sa.

Turkey hunting lore is replete with quirks and strategies, and there is no better resource than *Turkey & Turkey Hunting* magazine to bring these to print. Each issue has feature articles highlighting hunting tips and tactics and hunting in various geographic regions and terrains. Articles are well written and include many full-page color photos. Feature articles are augmented by regular departments including "Turkey Biology," "Favorite Calls," and new gear. Recommended for libraries with hunting and outdoor sports collections. Selected feature articles are available online.

3672. *Wheelin' Sportsmen.* [ISSN: 1538-1218] 2002. q. Members, USD 25. Ed(s): Karen Lee. National Wild Turkey Federation, Inc., 770 Augusta Rd, Edgefield, SC 29824-0530; kroop@nwtf.net; http://www.nwtf.net. Adv. Circ: 29000. *Bk. rev.:* 2-4, 200-400 words. *Aud.:* Hs, Ga, Sa.

Wheelin' Sportsmen is a welcome publication for and about disabled hunters and outdoor sports enthusiasts, and it fills a void. Published by the National Wild Turkey Federation (NWTF), *Wheelin' Sportsmen* contains many feature articles about sportsmen and sportswomen, many youthful, living with various disabilities while enjoying their favorite outdoor sports. Articles are accompanied by color photographs of the participants and their able-bodied companions. There are regular departments on available gear, nutrition and health, outdoor crafts, and NWTF events, both national and regional. A fine addition to any library's outdoor sports collection. Selected feature articles are available online.

3673. *Wildfowl: the magazine for duck & goose hunters.* [ISSN: 0886-0637] 1985. 7x/yr. USD 24.97 domestic; USD 37.97 Canada; USD 39.97 elsewhere. Source Interlink Companies, 27500 Riverview Center Blvd, Bonita Springs, FL 34134; edisupport@sourceinterlink.com; http://www.sourceinterlink.com. Illus., adv. Sample. Circ: 40553 Paid. Vol. ends: Jul. *Bk. rev.:* Various number and length. *Aud.:* Hs, Sa.

For duck and goose hunters and waterfowlers of all kinds, *Wild Fowl* is the magazine of choice. Articles are written by an array of experienced authors, and cover such topics as hunting methodology, how-to information, and locations for successful hunts. Articles on conservation education and habitat can also be found. Product reviews and game recipes help round out the offerings. Photography is liberally included. This would make a fine addition to any library with an outdoor sport hunting collection. Selected feature articles are available online.

3674. *Wildlife Harvest: the magazine for gamebird production & improved hunting.* [ISSN: 0886-3458] 1970. m. USD 35. Ed(s): Peggy Mullin Boehmer. Wildlife Harvest Publications, PO Box 96, Goose Lake, IA 52750. Illus., adv. Sample. Circ: 2500 Paid. Vol. ends: Dec. *Bk. rev.:* 1-3, 100-200 words. *Aud.:* Hs, Ga.

Wildlife Harvest is published monthly and is geared toward anyone with an interest in wild birds. Each issue contains information on how to raise and market game birds, how to hunt game birds, equipment and gear, hunting dogs, and other topics, plus advertisements. Membership in the North American Gamebird Association includes a free subscription to the magazine. Access to some feature articles is available online.

3675. *Women & Guns Magazine.* [ISSN: 1045-7704] 1989. bi-m. USD 18; USD 3.95 newsstand/cover. Ed(s): Peggy Tartaro. Second Amendment Foundation, 267 Linwood Ave, Buffalo, NY 14209; http://www.saf.org. Illus., adv. Sample. Circ: 18000 Paid. Vol. ends: No. 6. *Bk. rev.:* 1, 300 words. *Aud.:* Sa.

Women gun owners, and women with an interest in firearms for personal protection to those who are competitive shooters, will be avid readers of *Women & Guns Magazine*. Articles are often written by experienced contributing editors, and cover such topics as types of firearms and their uses, recreational and competitive shooting, handgun safety and skills, and women and guns from a historical perspective. "Legally Speaking" appears in each issue and is a comprehensive look at firearm issues with Second Amendment implications. Selected feature articles are available online, as well as selected articles from archived issues.

3676. *Women in the Outdoors.* [ISSN: 1526-8217] q. Members, USD 25. Ed(s): Karen Lee. National Wild Turkey Federation, Inc., 770 Augusta Rd, Edgefield, SC 29824-0530; kroop@nwtf.net; http://www.nwtf.net. Circ: 50000. *Aud.:* Hs, Ga, Sa.

Women in the Outdoors is published four times a year by the National Wild Turkey Federation (NWTF) and is the official publication of the NWTF Women in the Outdoors Program. Feature articles are always well written and very informative. Articles may focus on camping, boating, fishing, hunting, hiking, skiing, and dog sledding. Some of the magazine's regular features are a section on the "Outdoor Woman," a gear guide, health hints, mail from the members, and a scrapbook. This magazine should be in any library in areas where there are outdoor activities for women.

■ INFORMATICS

Robert C. Threlkeld, Resource Management Librarian, Countway Library of Medicine, Harvard University, Boston, MA 02115

Meghan Dolan, Head of Numeric Data Services, Social Sciences Program, Harvard College Library, Harvard University, Cambridge, MA 02138

Introduction

Informatics can be described broadly as the application of information processing perspectives and techniques to a particular discipline. It might also be described in terms of the organization and transformation of information. Medical informatics, as defined by the American Medical Informatics Association, has to do with "all aspects of understanding and promoting the effective organization, analysis, management, and use of information in health care."

In the course of our research, we found that the term *informatics* had wide and accepted use within the medical sciences, and that medical informatics as a discipline has been rapidly growing and changing. Medical informatics is a very broad field encompassing topics such as the organization and use of medical records, medical education, data collection and statistical analysis, and imaging technology. It also forms an intersection between fields such as computational biology and biomedical engineering, as well as the clinical sciences and public health. Journals in the field of medical informatics can therefore touch on many different disciplines and perspectives; some focus on developments in information technology, software, and data analysis, while others focus on effective decision-making strategies or methods to improve medical education. Many of these titles will be most appropriate for academic or research libraries that support clinical or scientific research.

Basic Periodicals

BMC Medical Informatics and Decision Making, Health Information and Libraries Journal, International Journal of Medical Informatics, Journal of the American Medical Informatics Association (JAMIA), Journal of Biomedical Informatics, Journal of Medical Internet Research, Journal of Medical Systems, Medical Informatics and the Internet in Medicine, Methods of Information in Medicine Teaching and Learning in Medicine.

Basic Abstracts and Indexes

Index Medicus/Medline/PubMed, Current Contents/Clinical Medicine, Current Contents/Engineering Computing & Technology, BIOSIS, Cinahl, Computer Contents, EMBASE, BIOBASE, INSPEC, Pascal et Francis (INST-CNRS), Information Science Abstracts, INSPEC, Scopus, Science Citation Index Expanded, PsycINFO, LISTA.

3677. American Medical Informatics Association. Journal. [ISSN: 1067-5027] 1994. 6x/yr. USD 429. Ed(s): Dr. Randolph A Miller. Hanley & Belfus, Inc., 210 S 13th St, Philadelphia, PA 19107; http://www.elsevierhealth.com. Illus., adv. Refereed. Circ: 5000 Paid. Online: EBSCO Publishing, EBSCO Host; HighWire Press; National Library of Medicine; ProQuest K-12 Learning Solutions; ProQuest LLC (Ann Arbor). *Indexed:* AgeL, BioEngAb, CINAHL, CompLI, ErgAb, ExcerpMed, H&SSA, ISTA, RiskAb, SCI, SSCI. *Bk. rev.:* Number and length vary. *Aud.:* Ac.

Published bimonthly, the *Journal of the American Medical Informatics Association: JAMIA* is the official journal of the just-named AMIA. Members of the AMIA have access to the online edition of the journal at no cost, but must pay a reduced fee for the print edition. *JAMIA* is also available to subscribers without AMIA membership. *JAMIA* is a peer-reviewed, interdisciplinary journal that will be of interest to medical staff, researchers, public health analysts, health-care computing specialists, and medical educators. The content is divided into three sections: "The Practice of Informatics," which includes review papers, position papers, and viewpoint papers; "Original Investigations," which comprises research papers, methods papers, and case studies; and "Special Sections," which are devoted to specific topics or subjects (typically five to seven papers per topic). The journal also includes book reviews and software reviews. Recent papers published in this journal have included "Implementing Pediatric Growth Charts into an Electronic Health Record System," "Clinical Computing in General Dentistry," and "Who Are the Informaticians? What We Know and Should Know."

3678. B M C Medical Informatics and Decision Making. [ISSN: 1472-6947] 2001. irreg. Free. Ed(s): Dr. Melissa Norton. BioMed Central Ltd., Middlesex House, 34-42 Cleveland St, London, W1T 4LB, United Kingdom; info@biomedcentral.com; http://www.biomedcentral.com. Illus., index. Refereed. *Indexed:* BioEngAb, ExcerpMed, SCI. *Aud.:* Ac, Sa.

BMC Medical Informatics and Decision Making is an online, peer-reviewed journal that publishes articles on information management, systems, and technology in health care, as well as medical decision making. Submission of articles, as well as peer review and publication, are all carried out online, so articles are published rather quickly relative to print journals. This journal takes advantage of the online submission process, allowing researchers to submit datasets or other supplementary information such as tables and figures along with the text of the article. Datasets are made available to other researchers seeking to confirm or replicate article findings independently. Recent articles have covered topics such as electronic distribution of summary health-care data, evaluation of software tools used in decision making and data analysis, and a discussion of data-mining strategies.

3679. Health Information and Libraries Journal (Print Edition). Formerly (until 2001): *Health Libraries Review (Print Edition).* [ISSN: 1471-1834] 1984. q. GBP 355 print & online eds. Ed(s): Graham Walton. Blackwell Publishing Ltd., 9600 Garsington Rd, Oxford, OX4 2ZG, United Kingdom; customerservices@blackwellpublishing.com; http://www.blackwellpublishing.com. Illus., adv. Refereed. Circ: 580. Microform: PQC. Online: Blackwell Synergy; EBSCO Publishing, EBSCO Host; Gale; IngentaConnect; OCLC Online Computer Library Center, Inc.; OhioLINK; Ovid Technologies, Inc.; SwetsWise Online Content. Reprint: PSC. *Indexed:* CINAHL, ISTA, LISA, SSCI. *Bk. rev.:* 1 per issue. *Aud.:* Ac.

Health Information and Libraries Journal is directed more toward library and information professionals working in the health field than clinicians or researchers. Its purpose is to provide a forum for discussing evidence-based approaches to health-care and information management practices. This journal's scope includes topics such as managing programs and services in a changing health environment, information technology in health, and education and outreach. Recent articles include discussions of publishing trends in Chinese medicine, the development of efficient search strategies, and the use of PDAs in clinical settings.

3680. International Journal of Medical Informatics. Formerly (until 1997): *International Journal of Bio-Medical Computing.* [ISSN: 1386-5056] 1971. 12x/yr. EUR 2407. Ed(s): J Talmon, C Safran. Elsevier Ireland Ltd, Elsevier House, Brookvale Plaza, E. Park, Shannon, Ireland. Illus., adv. Refereed. Online: EBSCO Publishing, EBSCO Host; Gale; IngentaConnect; OhioLINK; ScienceDirect; SwetsWise Online Content. *Indexed:* BioEngAb, BiolAb, CABA, ChemAb, CompLI, CompR, DSA, EngInd, ExcerpMed, MathR, SCI, SSCI. *Aud.:* Ac.

The *International Journal of Medical Informatics* is the official journal of the International Medical Informatics Association (IMIA) and the European Federation of Medical Informatics (EFMI). Researchers from the fields of medicine, health policy, and computer science as well as medical educators will be interested in the content of the journal as it addresses "information (including national/international registration) systems; hospital information systems; departmental and/or physician's office systems; document handling systems; electronic medical record systems; standardization; systems integration; organizational, economic, social, ethical and cost-benefit aspects of IT applications in health care; computer-aided medical decision support systems using heuristic, algorithmic and/or statistical methods as exemplified in decision theory, protocol development, artificial intelligence, etc.; [and] evaluations of educational computer based programs pertaining to medical informatics or medicine in general." Recent articles have included: assessing medical residents' usage and perceived needs for personal digital assistants;

empowering patients with essential information and communication support in the context of diabetes; an investigation into health informatics and related standards in China; and a Bayesian model for triage decision support.

3681. *Journal of Biomedical Informatics.* Formerly (until 2001): *Computers and Biomedical Research.* [ISSN: 1532-0464] 1969. 6x/yr. EUR 817. Ed(s): Dr. E. H. Shortliffe. Academic Press, 525 B St, Ste 1900, San Diego, CA 92101-4495; apsubs@acad.com; http://www.elsevier.com/. Illus., index, adv. Sample. Refereed. Online: EBSCO Publishing, EBSCO Host; Gale; IngentaConnect; OCLC Online Computer Library Center, Inc.; OhioLINK; ScienceDirect; SwetsWise Online Content. *Indexed:* ApMecR, BioEngAb, BiolAb, ChemAb, CompR, EngInd, ExcerpMed, IndVet, SCI, SSCI, VB. *Aud.:* Ac.

The *Journal of Biomedical Informatics* emphasizes descriptions of new techniques and methodologies that have an overall impact across the various informatics subfields, rather than focusing on a specific discipline. Articles lean more toward the general theoretical underpinnings of research techniques than toward their specific clinical applications. Typical articles have discussed new information resources, strategies for managing electronic health records, and processes for interpreting radiological images.

3682. *Journal of Medical Internet Research.* [ISSN: 1438-8871] 1999. q. Free. Ed(s): Gunther Eysenbach. Journal of Medical Internet Research, Centre for Global eHealth Innovation, Toronto General Hospital, Toronto, ON M5G 2C4, Canada. Illus., adv. Refereed. *Indexed:* BioEngAb, CommAb, ExcerpMed, ISTA, LISA, PsycInfo, SCI. *Aud.:* Ga, Ac.

The *Journal of Medical Internet Research* was established in 1999 as the first open-access, peer-reviewed medical informatics journal. Although it is primarily an open-access journal, there is also a membership option that allows individuals or institutions to subscribe to it. See the journal web site for more information about membership benefits. This multidisciplinary journal is international in scope and focuses on "all aspects of research, information and communication" in the field of health-care and consumer health informatics. The papers published within the journal will be of interest to medical and health-care practitioners, researchers, consumers, hospital administrators, medical educators, librarians, and health-care policy makers. The journal may also be of interest to the general public, as there are often papers published that focus on consumer e-health web sites, Internet use for health-related queries, and information on e-health communities. Recent articles published have included "A Case Analysis of INFOMED: The Cuban National Health Care Telecommunications Network and Portal," "eHealth Literacy: Essential Skills for Consumer Health in a Networked World," and "The Internet as a Vehicle to Communicate Health Information During a Public Health Emergency: A Survey Analysis Involving the Anthrax Scare of 2001." Due to the web-based delivery and access of this journal, the publishers are able to provide statistics relating to the number of viewers who accessed a specific article as well as the top five to 20 articles viewed per month. The publishers also provide statistics concerning the number of unique readers per month, the number of article/paper submissions per month, and the percentage of articles/papers that are published. The journal also provides (for a fee) peer review of research protocols and grant proposals. See the journal web site for more information regarding submission guidelines and costs.

3683. *Journal of Medical Systems.* [ISSN: 0148-5598] 1977. bi-m. EUR 1030 print & online eds. Ed(s): Ralph R Grams. Springer New York LLC, 233 Spring St, New York, NY 10013-1578; service-ny@springer.com; http://www.springer.com/. Illus., index, adv. Refereed. Vol. ends: Nov/Dec. Microform: PQC. Online: EBSCO Publishing, EBSCO Host; Gale; IngentaConnect; OCLC Online Computer Library Center, Inc.; Ovid Technologies, Inc.; Springer LINK; SwetsWise Online Content. Reprint: PSC. *Indexed:* C&ISA, CINAHL, CerAb, CompLI, CompR, ExcerpMed, H&SSA, IAA, ISTA, LISA, MCR, MicrocompInd, SCI, SSCI. *Aud.:* Ac.

The *Journal of Medical Systems* is the one journal in this section that focuses most strongly on the tools and systems that organize and disseminate medical data. The electronic delivery of health care and the information systems that store, retrieve, and deliver medical data figure most prominently in the articles and papers published in this journal. The journal also publishes a separate

section that provides status reports on these systems. Education is also a recurring theme. This journal would be of most interest to health-care computing specialists, medical staff, students and researchers, and hospital administrators. Recent articles published have included "A Review on Diffusion of Personal Digital Assistants in Healthcare," "A Tool for Improving the Web Accessibility of Visually Handicapped Persons," and "Comparing GIS-Based Methods of Measuring Spatial Accessibility to Health Services."

3684. *Medical Informatics and the Internet in Medicine: an international journal of computing in health care.* Former titles (until 1999): *Medical Informatics;* (until 1985): *Medecine et Informatique.* [ISSN: 1463-9238] 1976. q. GBP 635 print & online eds. Ed(s): John Bryant. Informa Healthcare, Mortimer House, 37-41 Mortimer St, London, W1T 3JM, United Kingdom; healthcare.enquiries@informa.com; http://www.tandf.co.uk/journals/. Illus., adv. Refereed. Online: EBSCO Publishing, EBSCO Host; Gale; IngentaConnect; OCLC Online Computer Library Center, Inc.; SwetsWise Online Content. Reprint: PSC. *Indexed:* BioEngAb, BiolAb, CINAHL, CompLI, ErgAb, ExcerpMed, IndVet, LISA, SCI, SSCI. *Bk. rev.:* Number and length vary. *Aud.:* Ac.

Medical Informatics and the Internet in Medicine "promotes the application of analysis, inference and reasoning of medical information." The journal also focuses on how data and knowledge are organized and how this organization can be applied to medical education. The journal is multidisciplinary in scope, as its content will appeal to researchers in medicine, public health, computer science, education, and librarianship. The journal publishes review articles, original research papers, and technical notes. Articles contain illustrations, charts, diagrams, and tables of data. Current issues have included research on e-learning in medicine, home monitoring of chronically ill patients using the Internet, and developing cooperative web-based work environments. Titles of recently published research papers are "Mobile healthcare informatics," "Quality of websites in Spanish public hospitals," and "Health literacy and the World Wide Web: Comparing the readability of leading incident cancers on the Internet."

3685. *Teaching and Learning in Medicine: an international journal.* [ISSN: 1040-1334] 1989. q. GBP 396 print & online eds. Ed(s): Jerry Colliver. Lawrence Erlbaum Associates, Inc., 325 Chestnut St, Ste. 800, Philadelphia, PA 19106; journals@erlbaum.com; http://www.leaonline.com. Illus., adv. Refereed. Reprint: PSC. *Indexed:* CINAHL, PsycInfo, SCI, SWA. *Bk. rev.:* Number and length vary. *Aud.:* Ac.

Teaching and Learning in Medicine publishes scholarly articles on the purposes and processes involved in medical education. This journal focuses on the acquisition and maintenance of usable knowledge and skills under the complex and rapidly changing demands of the clinical sciences, targeting an audience of medical school faculty, administrators, and residency program directors. Emphasis is placed on articles that empirically test the quality of medical education programs, and allow administrators to make informed, practical decisions about how best to provide quality medical education. Recent articles include discussions of print versus electronic journals and whether format makes a difference in knowledge acquisition; effective teaching strategies; and educational reform.

■ INTERDISCIPLINARY STUDIES

Courtney L. Young, Reference Librarian, Beaver Campus Library, The Pennsylvania State University, Monaca, PA 15061; cly11@psu.edu

Introduction

The creation and inclusion of a section titled Interdisciplinary Studies reflects both the increase in scholarship that employs the use of multiple approaches and the scholastic conversations taking place across disciplines. In many ways, this section is a complement to sections that focus on and incorporate diverse fields of study. While racial and gender diversity are often equated with interdisciplinary studies, broader disciplines within the sciences, social sciences, and humanities are also bridging the gaps. This area focuses on cross-disciplinary education and the facilitation of conversations among educators in a variety of fields.

The emphasis of the journals included here is on science, approaches to education, and the understanding that one approach is really a strategy among many approaches. A large number of journals include "interdisciplinary" as a subtitle but are better suited for other sections.

Another challenge in editing this section was the large number of journals with a sporadic publishing history or journals that had simply ceased. While you are encouraged to explore the many sections that more directly focus on specific disciplines and types of diversity, consider these periodicals as a starting point when building collections to integrate these important types of resources. Suggestions for expanding this list are encouraged.

Basic Periodicals

Ac: *Issues in Integrative Studies.*

Basic Abstracts and Indexes

EBSCO Academic Premiere; ProQuest Research Library; Project MUSE.

American Quarterly. See Cultural Studies section.

American Scholar. See General Interest section.

American Studies. See Cultural Studies section.

Critical Inquiry. See Cultural Studies section.

Discourse. See Education/Comparative Education and International section.

Film & History. See Films section.

3686. *Interdisciplinary Environmental Review.* [ISSN: 1521-0227] 1999. a. USD 100 (Individuals, USD 50; Students, USD 35). Ed(s): Demetri Kantarelis, Kevin Hickey. Interdisciplinary Environmental Association, Department of Economics and Foreign Affairs, Assumption College, Worcester, MA 01615-0005; http://www.desu.edu/mreiter/iea.htm. *Bk. rev.:* Number and length vary; signed. *Aud.:* Ac.

Published by the Interdisciplinary Environmental Association, *IER* publishes "research and survey papers" in all disciplines concerning the "natural environment." Each annual issue features seven or eight articles. Scholarship on ethics, religion, gender, and globalization as they relate to the environment are but a handful of diverse topics included in each publication. Submission information encourages authors to write their manuscripts in a manner that will "facilitate communication between disciplines." A journal sure to serve a variety of researchers.

3687. *Interdisciplinary Literary Studies: a journal of criticism and theory.* [ISSN: 1524-8429] s-a. USD 35 (Individuals, USD 25). Ed(s): Kenneth Womack. Interdisciplinary Literary Studies, c/o Kenneth Womack, Penn State Altoona, Altoona, PA 16601-3760. *Indexed:* MLA-IB. *Bk. rev.:* Number and length vary; signed. *Aud.:* Ac.

This journal publishes research exploring "the interconnections between literary studies and other disciplines, ideologies, and cultural methods of critique." Its scholarship focuses on discussing the "pedagogical possibilities of interdisciplinary literary studies." Also included are book reviews and interviews with important scholars in the field.

3688. *Interdisciplinary Science Reviews.* [ISSN: 0308-0188] 1976. q. USD 746. Ed(s): Howard Cattermole. Maney Publishing, Ste. 1C, Joseph's Well, Hanover Walk, Leeds, LS3 1AB, United Kingdom; maney@maney.co.uk; http://www.maney.co.uk. Refereed. Circ: 400 Paid. Reprint: PSC. *Indexed:* C&ISA, CerAb, ChemAb, IAA, RILM, SCI, SSCI. *Bk. rev.:* Number and length vary; signed. *Aud.:* Ac.

Founded in 1976, *ISR* aims to "foster inclusive pluralistic appreciation and understanding of scientific activity." This is accomplished through submissions by scholars with diverse research interests, which include the physical and biological sciences, social sciences, and humanities. Faculty and research from around the world contribute frequently. Special issues are often published, with themes including "Science and Theatre" and "Radioactive Waste." Most issues are heavily illustrated. Book reviews and letters to the editor round out each issue. A fascinating and essential journal for interdisciplinary collections.

3689. *Interdisciplinary Studies in Literature and Environment.* [ISSN: 1076-0962] 1993. s-a. USD 25 (Individual members, USD 25). Ed(s): Patrick Barron, Scott Slovic. Association for the Study of Literature and Environment, Department of English/098, University of Nevada, Reno, Reno, NV 89557; http://www.asle.umn.edu. Adv. *Indexed:* AmHI, MLA-IB. *Bk. rev.:* Number and length vary; signed. *Aud.:* Ac.

Another journal with a focus on the increasing research and scholarship on the environment, *ISLE* "seeks to bridge the gap between scholars, artists, students, and the public." Produced by the Association for the Study of Literature and Environment since 1993, *ISLE* bridges the gap with scholarship on advertising, poetry, religion, the environment, and representations of nature in literature. Book reviews and an annotated list of recent books are included.

3690. *Issues in Integrative Studies: an interdisciplinary journal.* [ISSN: 1081-4760] 1982. a. Free to members. Ed(s): Dr. Joan Fiscella. Association for Integrative Studies, Miami University, Oxford, OH 45056; aisorg@muohio.edu; http://www.units.muohio.edu/aisorg. Adv. Refereed. Circ: 550 Paid. *Indexed:* HEA. *Bk. rev.:* Number and length vary; signed. *Aud.:* Ac.

While other journals take an interdisciplinary approach to the study of disciplines, research in *Issues in Integrative Studies* explores what, exactly, the field of interdisciplinary studies is all about. Each publication examines the challenges of exploring this area of study, including "interdisciplinary theory and methodology; the nature, means, and problems of integrative research, especially on the human experience; and special pedagogical approaches for enhancing interdisciplinary/integrative comprehension, perspectives, knowledge, and utilization." This is an impressive, key journal for institutions with interdisciplinary studies programs, which has applications for education programs.

Journal of Interdisciplinary Gender Studies. See Gender Studies section.

3691. *Journal of Interdisciplinary History.* [ISSN: 0022-1953] 1969. q. USD 276 print & online eds. (Individuals, USD 54 print & online eds.). Ed(s): Theodore K Rabb, Robert I Rotberg. M I T Press, 238 Main St., Ste. 500, Cambridge, MA 02142; journals-info@mit.edu; http://mitpress.mit.edu. Illus., index, adv. Refereed. Circ: 1700. Microform: PQC. Online: EBSCO Publishing, EBSCO Host; Gale; IngentaConnect; JSTOR (Web-based Journal Archive); OCLC Online Computer Library Center, Inc.; OhioLINK; Project MUSE; SwetsWise Online Content; H.W. Wilson. Reprint: SCH. *Indexed:* ABCPolSci, ABS&EES, AmH&L, AmHI, ArtHuCI, BAS, BRI, BrArAb, CBRI, FR, HistAb, HumInd, IBR, IBSS, IBZ, IPSA, NumL, PRA, PSA, RILM, SSA, SSCI, SUSA, SWA, SociolAb. *Bk. rev.:* 30-45, 2-3 pages, signed. *Aud.:* Ac, Sa.

Incorporating "contemporary insights on the past," articles in this journal employ a diverse approach to analysis and methodology in historical scholarship. Sample titles of articles, clearly influenced by an interdisciplinary approach to research, include "The Mulatto Advantage: The Biological Consequences of Complexion in Rural Antebellum Virginia"; "Nutritional Success on the Great Plains: Nineteenth-Century Equestrian Nomads"; and "Urban Identity in Medieval English Towns." Book reviews, research notes, and review essays continue to be a strength of the journal. While remaining an important journal in the discipline of history, the *Journal of Interdisciplinary History* is a solid contributor to interdisciplinary studies.

Journal of the History of Ideas. See Cultural Studies section.

Literature and History. See History section.

Philosophy and Literature. See Philosophy section.

Postmodern Culture. See Cultural Studies section.

3692. *Race, Gender & Class: an interdisciplinary journal.* Formerly (until 1994): *Race, Sex and Class.* [ISSN: 1082-8354] 1993. q. USD 40 (Individuals, USD 24). Ed(s): Jean Ait Belkhir. Southern University at New Orleans, Department of Social Sciences, 6400 Press Dr, New Orleans, LA 70126; jbelkhir@suno.edu; http://www.suno.edu/sunorgc. Circ: 1200. *Indexed:* AltPI, ENW, FemPer, GendWatch, HEA, PSA, SSA, SWR&A, SociolAb. *Bk. rev.:* Number and length vary; signed. *Aud.:* Ac.

This interdisciplinary, multicultural journal from Southern University of New Orleans publishes articles and review essays that focus on issues of race, gender, and class in society. It also publishes proceedings of the annual Race, Gender, and Class Conference. The journal aims to publish materials that "have practical implications, direct or indirect, for education" and "that are accessible to undergraduates in introductory and general education classes." Unusual for its focus on race and class. Limited coverage in indexes.

Social Theory and Practice. See Cultural Studies section.

Studies in the Decorative Arts. See Art/General section.

■ INTERIOR DESIGN AND DECORATION

See also Home section.

Holly Stec Dankert, Readers' Services Librarian, John M. Flaxman Library, School of the Art Institute of Chicago, 37 S. Wabash, Chicago, IL 60603; hdankert@artic.edu; FAX: 312-899-1465

Introduction

Trade magazines aimed at professional designers provide the backbone of interior design publications; however, consumer-oriented titles play an important role in providing product information and consumer trends to practitioners while bringing design principles to the masses. Both types of magazines are central to interior design.

Trade publications serve to inform decorators, designers, and architects of current practices, trends, and new products and services in both commercial and residential interiors. Most of these trade titles include reader-service information, professional development opportunities, new technology advancements in furnishings and materials, calendars of professional events, and reviews of new publications in interior design. In addition, these publications provide many full-color illustrations of interiors and the materials used for their creation. The field's professional literature is best suited to academic libraries that offer degrees in interior design or decorating and public and special libraries that support their local design community.

Consumer-oriented titles target the affluent buyer as well as the professional decorator or designer, and generally devote a great deal more copy space to photography of the featured interiors and to advertisements that highlight furnishings, appliances, wall coverings, textiles, flooring, and interior architecture. Many from this second group focus on the homes of celebrities and renowned designers or collections of art, antiques, and custom furnishings, and they are almost exclusively devoted to residential interiors.

The hallmark of all titles in this section is the extensive use of lush, full-color illustrations. The web sites of the trade titles continue to provide more relevant content to their constituents than do the consumer titles, which provide

subscriber services and little more; however, more content is being added year by year. Magazines in this section will appeal to all library users but are aimed at working designers and a clientele in search of professional design services.

Basic Periodicals

Ga: *Architectural Digest, House & Garden;* Ac: *Architectural Digest, Contract, ID Magazine, Interior Design, Interiors & Sources, Journal of Interior Design.*

Basic Abstracts and Indexes

Art Abstracts/Index, Avery Index to Architectural Periodicals.

3693. *American Style: the art of living creatively.* [ISSN: 1078-8425] 1995. q. USD 24.99 domestic; USD 33 Canada; USD 36 elsewhere. Ed(s): Hope Daniels. Rosen Group, 3000 Chestnut Ave, Baltimore, MD 21211-2743; http://www.americanstyle.com. Illus., adv. Sample. Circ: 60000. Vol. ends: Summer. *Aud.:* Ga, Sa.

American Style provides designers, decorators, and collectors with beautifully photographed residential interiors by highlighting American craft art—pottery, ceramic sculpture, art glass, jewelry, wearable art, and fine gifts. Showcasing artists, each issue features the homes of collectors, artists, and gallery owners, giving prominence to the objects they collect or create. There is information on gallery shows, museum exhibitions, craft fairs, arts festivals throughout the United States, and segments that highlight an artist or location. The web site, www.americanstyle.com, provides resources including links to art events by state, a collector's corner, preferred dealers, and portions of the print magazine's articles. Blending art and interior design, *American Style* is recommended for all public and academic libraries that serve collectors or the design community.

3694. *Architectural Digest: the international magazine of interior design.* [ISSN: 0003-8520] 1920. m. USD 24 domestic; USD 59.95 Canada; USD 64.95 elsewhere. Ed(s): Paige Rense. Conde Nast Publications, Inc., 750 3rd Ave, New York, NY 10017; http://www.condenast.com. Illus., adv. Circ: 812892 Paid. Vol. ends: Dec. Microform: PQC. Online: OCLC Online Computer Library Center, Inc.; H.W. Wilson. *Indexed:* A&ATA, ABS&EES, ASIP, AmHI, ArtHuCI, ArtInd, FLI, GardL, MASUSE, RGPR, RILM. *Aud.:* Ga, Ac.

Lavish homes decorated by renowned interior designers are captured in this classic interior design magazine. International in scope, each issue features residences exquisitely furnished with expensive, often one-of-a-kind antiques, objets d'art, and premium designer furniture. Occasional issues are devoted to a particular style or period and feature luxurious hideaways around the world; not to be missed is the summer issue devoted to American country houses. With its glossy advertising of luxury products; showcase for antiques, designer, and collector items; and sophisticated international locations, *Architectural Digest* is aimed at the rich and cosmopolitan. Many readers, regardless of income, will find it appealing. A standard design magazine recommended for all libraries.

3695. *Contract.* Former titles (until 2000): *Contract Design;* (until 1990): *Contract.* [ISSN: 1530-6224] 1960. m. USD 79 domestic (Free to qualified personnel). Ed(s): Diana Mosher. Nielsen Business Publications, 770 Broadway, New York, NY 10003-9595; bmcomm@vnuinc.com; http://www.nielsenbusinessmedia.com. Illus. Sample. Circ: 30000. Vol. ends: Dec. Microform: PQC. Online: EBSCO Publishing, EBSCO Host; Gale; OCLC Online Computer Library Center, Inc.; H.W. Wilson. *Indexed:* ArtInd. *Bk. rev.:* Number and length vary. *Aud.:* Ac, Sa.

Contract is an important venue for industry information aimed at the design professional that focuses on commercial interiors. Sweeping, carefully lit, full-color interior photos illustrate trends in corporate, retail, hospitality, health care, entertainment, government, educational, and institutional design. The journal also covers new-product information on floor and wall coverings, textiles, lighting, and furniture. Professional interior designers will value the wide variety of briefs on current practices, resources, materials, trends, and industry news, along with articles on such topics as specifying systems furniture and tips for starting your firm. An annual source guide comes out in December of each year. Most useful is the web site, www.contractmagazine.com, which offers current design projects, industry updates, a searchable vendor database, conferences, trade shows, and professional associations. The web site offers everything needed to stay current in nonresidential design, plus the table of contents and some articles from the current issue at no charge. Aimed at the architecture and design community, this core title is a must-have for all libraries that serve architects, design professionals, and students.

Dwell. See Home section.

3696. Elle Decor. [ISSN: 1046-1957] 1989. 8x/yr. USD 10 domestic; USD 22 foreign; USD 4.99 newsstand/cover per issue. Ed(s): Margaret Russell. Hachette Filipacchi Media U.S., Inc., 1633 Broadway, New York, NY 10019; http://www.hfmus.com. Illus., adv. Sample. Circ: 500000 Paid. Vol. ends: Nov. *Indexed:* ASIP. *Aud.:* Ga.

Elle Decor exudes a younger, more chic spirit than other magazines in this section. Posh interiors, modern renovations, urban town homes, and country retreats highlighted by sleek, colorful photography are the focus of the dozen or so articles that feature artists and designers and their affluent clients of a younger generation. *Elle Decor* includes a panoply of artful objects, kitchen gadgets, bed-and-bath linens, furniture, and fixtures for the style-conscious individual. Each issue includes trend-setting designs that are inspirational and attainable. Resource contacts and reader services make this title valuable for both professionals and do-it-yourself decorators. Elledecor.com is a wonderful web site that highlights some print content plus fun sections on "What's Hot," "Trend Alert," "Truth in Decorating," "Elle Decor Style," and "Promo/Events." Suitable for public libraries and all libraries that serve design professionals.

3697. Frame. [ISSN: 1388-4239] 1997. bi-m. EUR 79 in Europe; EUR 85 in US & Canada; EUR 109 elsewhere. BIS Publishers, Postbus 323, Amsterdam, 1000 AH, Netherlands; info@bispublishers.nl; http://www.bispublishers.nl. Illus., adv. Circ: 34150. *Indexed:* DAAI. *Bk. rev.:* 5-7, 300 words. *Aud.:* Sa.

A glossy European magazine bursting with full-color photos, *Frame: The Great Indoors* focuses on radical and ultra-contemporary designed objects and interiors from around the world. *Frame* succeeds in looking very different, intentionally, from other professional interiors magazines and is enhanced with artful advertising from a wide range of European furniture, lighting and designed objects manufactures. Regular features include an in-depth portrait of new interior designers and/or architects, a handful of articles on new commercial interiors, and a multitude of briefs on new industrial designs from retail displays to automobiles. The web site, www.framemag.com, gives much of the print content at no cost but very few illustrations. Recommended for design collections.

3698. House & Garden. Former titles (until 1998): *Conde Nast House & Garden;* (until 1993): *House and Garden;* Which incorporates (in 1915): *American House and Garden;* Which was formerly (until 1905): *Scientific American Building Monthly;* (until 1901): *Scientific American.* [ISSN: 1522-0273] 1885. m. USD 12 domestic; USD 33.97 Canada; USD 38.97 elsewhere. Ed(s): Elizabeth Pochoda, Dominique Browning. Conde Nast Publications, Inc., 750 3rd Ave, New York, NY 10017; http://www.condenast.com. Illus., index, adv. Sample. Circ: 770325 Paid. Vol. ends: Dec. Microform: PQC. *Indexed:* API, DAAI, FLI, GardL, RGPR. *Aud.:* Ga.

Monothematic treatments predominate each month in the quintessential *House & Garden,* which provides in its regular departments an astonishing array of gadgets for the home, culinary foodstuffs, fabrics, flora, and outdoor furnishings to tempt consumers and decorators alike. Offering a range of mid-priced objects, this Conde Nast publication is a foil for the publisher's more upscale *Architectural Digest.* Feature articles highlight apartments, houses, estates, gardens, and collections owned or designed by famous people. Although aimed at the consumer, this magazine is also of value to professional residential designers. Recommended for public libraries.

3699. I.D: the international design magazine. Former titles (until 1984): *Industrial Design;* (until 1983): *Industrial Design Magazine;* (until vol. 26, 1979): *Industrial Design.* [ISSN: 0894-5373] 1954. 8x/yr. USD 30 domestic; USD 45 Canada; USD 60 elsewhere. Ed(s): Julie Lasky, David Sokol. F + W Publications, Inc., 38 E 29th St, 3rd Fl, New York, NY

10016; wds@fwpubs.com; http://www.fwpublications.com. Illus., adv. Sample. Circ: 19500 Paid. Vol. ends: Dec. Microform: PQC. Online: ProQuest LLC (Ann Arbor). *Indexed:* ABM, AS&TI, ArtInd, DAAI, FLI, IBR, IBZ. *Bk. rev.:* 2-3, 300 words. *Aud.:* Ac, Sa.

I.D. has provided over 50 years of critical coverage of "the art, business and culture of design." An international magazine of industrial design, it brings new products to interior and contract designers, as well as to the target industrial designer audience. Thematic issues celebrate such diverse design challenges as water (building a snow house, swim goggles, and razors) and health (children's products, spa design, and body imaging). Annual issues include December's directory/buyer's guide for design professionals, the "Design Sourcebook"; the July/August juried recognition of hundreds of products with design merit, the "Annual Design Review"; the "Student Design Review" (October); and the "Interactive Media Design Review" (November). Regular features include six to ten brief articles about consumer products, furniture, equipment, living/working spaces, packaging, and graphic design. There are also editorials, briefs on research and development, new and noteworthy designs, items on expositions, and more. The well-designed web site, www.id-mag.com, continues to provide a mix of free articles and content for subscribers only. Having won numerous design awards itself, this magazine provides a rich source of ideas and is a welcome addition to libraries with art and design collections and those that serve design professionals and students.

3700. Interior Design. [ISSN: 0020-5508] 1932. m. USD 64.95 domestic; USD 79.95 Canada; USD 172.95 elsewhere. Ed(s): Cindy Allen. Reed Business Information, 360 Park Ave South, New York, NY 10010; http://www.reedbusiness.com. Illus., adv. Circ: 55420 Paid. Vol. ends: Dec. Microform: CIS; PQC. Online: EBSCO Publishing, EBSCO Host; Factiva, Inc.; Florida Center for Library Automation; Gale; LexisNexis; Northern Light Technology, Inc.; OCLC Online Computer Library Center, Inc.; ProQuest K-12 Learning Solutions; ProQuest LLC (Ann Arbor); H.W. Wilson. *Indexed:* ABIn, ArchI, ArtInd, DAAI. *Bk. rev.:* 4-5, 150 words. *Aud.:* Ac, Sa.

Interior Design leads professional interior design literature in terms of having the largest circulation among designers and specifiers. It is renowned for its extensive coverage of commercial and residential interior design projects, and its advertising space abounds with products from premier interior-furnishings manufacturers, both U.S. and international. The print edition offers lengthy (10–15 pages) feature articles that focus on notable projects or design firms with beautifully shot interiors, primarily in the United States. Regular departments include industry awards, news, brief bios, new projects, technology, and the latest innovations in furnishings from international manufacturers. A subscription includes fall and spring "Market Tabloids" and the annual "Interior Design Buyers Guide." The web site, www.interiordesign.net, serves the professional interior design community with industry news, new product updates, a buyer's guide (searchable by company name and keyword), topical features, reader services, and archives of the print edition. Recommended for all libraries and a must for those that support the interior design community.

3701. Interiors & Sources. Former titles (until 2004): *I S Magazine;* (until 2002): *Interiors & Sources.* 1990. bi-m. Free. Ed(s): Robert Nieminen. Stamats Business Media, 615 5th St, S E, Cedar Rapids, IA 52401; http://www.stamatscorp.com. Illus., index, adv. Sample. Circ: 27800 Controlled. Vol. ends: Nov/Dec. *Indexed:* ArtInd. *Aud.:* Ac, Sa.

Catering to the professional designer and architect, *Interiors & Sources* concentrates on commercial interiors. The magazine employs the novel approach of featuring an individual designer or design team and their current projects on the cover, plus additional articles on noteworthy commercial and residential interiors, coverage of professional events, conferences, industry news, troubleshooting tips, and fairly extensive product sources. Practitioners will appreciate "ASID Update," "IIDA Notes," "IDEC Report," and "NCIDQ News," plus sections on health and green design. The web site provides professional trade news and information including an archive dating back to 1995. Recommended for academic libraries with a design focus and public libraries that serve the local interior design/architecture community.

3702. Journal of Interior Design. Formerly: *Journal of Interior Design Education and Research.* [ISSN: 1071-7641] 1976. s-a. Ed(s): Jo Ann Asher Thompson. Interior Design Educators Council, Inc., 7150 Winton

Drive, Suite 300,, Indianapolis, IN 46268; info@idec.org; http://www.idec.org/. Illus., index, adv. Sample. Refereed. Circ: 700. *Indexed:* ABM, ArtInd, ErgAb. *Bk. rev.:* 4-5, 500 words. *Aud.:* Ac.

This journal has the distinction of being the only scholarly title for the interior design profession. Published by the Interior Design Educators Council, it focuses on education, practice, research, and theory, providing scholars and teachers with a forum for "scientific applications of design principles," historical research, and design processes in theory and practice. Regular reports give readers current practices and techniques for classroom and studio education plus reviews of new books, technology, and other media. The council's web site, www.idec.org, provides annual conference, membership, and graduate program and other information pertinent to design educators. Recommended for all academic collections that serve design programs.

3703. Southern Accents: the magazine of fine Southern interiors and gardens. [ISSN: 0149-516X] 1977. bi-m. USD 28 domestic; USD 34 foreign; USD 5.99 newsstand/cover per issue. Ed(s): Frances MacDougall, Dawn Cannon. Southern Progress Corp., 2100 Lakeshore Dr, Birmingham, AL 35209; http://corp.southernprogress.com/spc/. Illus., adv. Circ: 400000 Paid. Vol. ends: Nov/Dec. *Indexed:* GardL. *Aud.:* Ga.

Featuring elegant gardens and homes located in the southern United States, this publication caters to decorators and clients of a traditional sensibility. Six or seven articles illustrate classic and traditional interiors decorated by professionals. Tips on entertaining, antiques, flowers, travel, gardening, and collecting are regular departments, with a calendar, a sourcebook, and trade show listings rounding out each issue. More entertaining and decorating ideas are available at www.southernaccents.com, which is for subscribers only. Recommended for public libraries and academic design collections.

3704. V M & S D. Former titles: *Visual Merchandising & Store Design;* (until 1982): *Visual Merchandising;* (until 1973): *Display World.* [ISSN: 1072-9666] 1922. m. USD 42 domestic; USD 62 Canada; USD 65 elsewhere. Ed(s): Carole Winters, Steve Kaufmann. S T Publications Inc., 407 Gilbert Ave, Cincinnati, OH 45202; cwinters@stpubs.com; http://www.stmediagroup.com. Illus., adv. Sample. Circ: 27000 Paid and controlled. Vol. ends: Dec. *Indexed:* BPI. *Aud.:* Ac, Sa.

VM & SD is the trade magazine for interior designers, owners, managers, and marketers of retail establishments. Typical of most trade magazines, it provides a wealth of industry-related news and feature articles, frequently with a single-topic theme. Other industry content—a calendar of events, an annual survey of top fixture manufacturers of signage, graphics, and props, plus the annual buyer's guide (January issue)—round out this important resource to merchandisers. Not to be missed is the accompanying web site, www.visual-store.com, that serves the retail profession. Recommended for academic libraries that serve interior design programs or public libraries that cater to local retailers.

Veranda: a gallery of fine design. See Home section.

3705. The World of Interiors. [ISSN: 0264-083X] 1981. m. GBP 29.90 domestic; GBP 65 in Europe; GBP 44 United States. Ed(s): Harriet Paterson. Conde Nast Publications Ltd., Vogue House, Hanover Sq, London, W1S 1JU, United Kingdom; http://www.worldofinteriors.co.uk. Illus., adv. Circ: 71691. Vol. ends: Dec. *Indexed:* ArtInd, DAAI, RILM. *Bk. rev.:* 5-6, 500 words. *Aud.:* Ga, Sa.

This lush British monthly offers international coverage of residential interior design. Regular departments with catchy titles provide design trends, auction and fair dates, merchandise, and suppliers for the U.K. market. Articles often feature renowned personalities and showcase royal abodes, historic homes, modern penthouses, and whimsical to formal gardens throughout the world, but predominantly in Britain. Fine art and antiques collections are also featured. Aimed at designers in the United Kingdom and their clients, this journal is best suited to large libraries that serve the design community.

■ INTERNATIONAL MAGAZINES

Elizabeth McKeigue, Research Librarian, Widener Library, Harvard University, Cambridge, MA 02138

Introduction

This section recommends titles of popular general-interest magazines from outside the United States or magazines produced in the United States but directed toward non-U.S. nationals. It endeavors to include publications that have a broad appeal in a variety of languages. A number of the magazines chosen are indexed in major American-produced indexes like LexisNexis and Academic Search Premier. A major criterion for selection of titles for this section is whether the magazine would be useful for students learning a new language. In the United States, the most popular languages taught in both high schools and colleges are the major European ones (Spanish, French, German, and Italian) but that may be changing. Existing sections in *Magazines for Libraries* that focus on a particular geographic area or a specific country (e.g., Canada, Asia, Europe) often include references to general-interest periodicals. For example, most general-interest magazines in Spanish can be found in the Latin America section, magazines from China and Japan in the Asia section, and so forth. In future editions, the hope is to provide a less Eurocentric focus and to include more Asian and African titles. Recommendations from experts and natives of foreign countries are welcome, so please contact me.

Basic Periodicals

Ga: *The Bulletin* (Australia), *Bunte* (Germany), *Elsevier* (Netherlands), *L'Espresso* (Italy), *L'Express* (France), *Hello!* (United Kingdom), *Impacto* (Mexico), *International Express* (United Kingdom), *Ogonek* (Russia), *Paris Match* (France), *Proceso* (Mexico), *The Spectator* (United Kingdom), *Der Spiegel* (Germany), *Stern* (Germany).

Australian Women's Weekly. See General Interest section.

3706. The Bulletin with Newsweek. Formerly: *Bulletin;* Which incorporates: *Newsweek (International, Pacific Edition);* And (1961-1962): *Australian Financial Times.* [ISSN: 1440-7485] 1880. w. AUD 129.90; AUD 5.95 newsstand/cover. Ed(s): John Lehmann. A C P Magazines Ltd., 54-58 Park St, Sydney, NSW 2000, Australia; research@ acpaction.com.au; http://www.acp.com.au. Illus., adv. Circ: 58615 Paid. Microform: PQC. Online: EBSCO Publishing, EBSCO Host. *Aud.:* Ga.

In English, from Australia. One of the most widely read magazines in Australia, it is indeed, as its title implies, the Australian version of *Newsweek*. Like its American counterpart, it contains reporting and commentary in the areas of politics, public affairs, economics and business, information technology, health and science, the arts, and sport. Some of its regular features include Home, Upfront (news commentary), News, Features, Columns, The Investor, Sport, and Time Off. Found online at http://bulletin.ninemsn.com.au, only a portion of each article can be viewed, and for full access online, one must subscribe. Recommended for large public libraries and academic libraries with programs that study Australia, New Zealand, and the Pacific Rim of Asia.

3707. Bunte. Incorporates: *Bunte Oesterreich;* Formerly: *Bunte Illustrierte.* [ISSN: 0172-2050] 1948. w. EUR 130; EUR 2.50 newsstand/cover. Ed(s): Patricia Riekel. Hubert Burda Media Holding GmbH & Co. KG, Arabellastr 23, Munich, 81925, Germany; http://www.burda.de. Illus., adv. Sample. Circ: 742592 Paid. Microform: ALP. Online: LexisNexis. *Aud.:* Ga.

In German, from Germany. As one of the most popular general-interest magazines in Germany, *Bunte* is Germany's answer to *People* magazine. It's great for students of German who are looking for some "fun" reading. Articles run the gamut of pop culture subjects, from Paris's and Lindsay's latest catfight to detailed updates of Brad's and Angelina's baby. But aside from the ubiquitous celebrity chatter, there are also sections on Sports, Business, Technology, Travel, and Health. At www.bunte.de, you'll find some of the same features of the print magazine. The travel advice section online is particularly good. Recommended for libraries that support elementary German-language programs or that cater to a German-speaking population.

3708. *Caras.* [ISSN: 0104-396X] 1993. w. BRL 306.80 domestic; USD 279 foreign. Editora Abril, S.A., Avenida das Nacoes Unidas 7221, Pinheiros, Sao Paulo, 05425-902, Brazil; abrilsac@abril.com.br; http://www.abril.com.br. Illus., adv. Circ: 326400. *Bk. rev.:* Number and length vary. *Aud.:* Ga.

In Portuguese, from Brazil. If *Bunte* is Germany's *People* agazine, then *Caras* is the Brazilian *Bunte*! This magazine provides news and general-interest stories. Contents include feature articles and interviews with and photographs of celebrities. There are even some stories about ordinary people as newsmakers. Rich with advertising, photos, book reviews, film and some theater reviews, and music reviews, *Caras* is pretty to look at and great for popular culture news from Brazil. The web site at www.caras.com.br requires a subscription in order to see anything beyond an RSS news feed and some splashy photos. Recommended for public libraries serving Brazilian Portuguese-speaking communities and for academic libraries supporting Portuguese-language programs.

Contenido. See Latin America and Spain section.

3709. *Dani.* [ISSN: 1512-5130] 1992. w. BAM 115 domestic; USD 195 foreign. Ed(s): Vildana Selimbegovic. Civitas d.o.o., Skenderija 31A, Sarajevo, 71000, Bosnia & Herzegovina. Illus., adv. *Bk. rev.:* Number and length vary. *Aud.:* Ga.

In Serbo-Croatian, from Bosnia and Herzegovina. *Nezavisni* is a weekly magazine that has been in print since 1992. It is also known by the English translation of its title, *Independent Magazine Dani.* Articles cover topics such as news (in BiH and beyond), social issues, interviews, and book, film, music, video, DVD, and television reviews. Recommended for public libraries serving an immigrant Balkan population and for academic libraries supporting Slavic Studies programs.

3710. *Deutschland (English Edition): magazine on politics, culture, business and science.* Former titles (until 1993): *Scala;* (until 1973): *Scala International.* [ISSN: 0945-6791] 1961. bi-m. Free. Ed(s): Peter Hintereder. Frankfurter Societaets-Druckerei GmbH, Frankenallee 71-81, Frankfurt Am Main, 60327, Germany; verlag@fsd.de; http://www.fsd.de. Illus., adv. Circ: 500000. *Indexed:* WAE&RSA. *Bk. rev.:* Number and length vary. *Aud.:* Ga.

In English, from Germany. This primarily English-language magazine is great way for non-German-speaking Germany lovers to learn about today's Germany. Article topics focus on political, economic, scientific, and cultural events in Germany, and are written by German journalists. Recent topics include interviews with prominent Germans, opinion pieces (especially about German and American politics), and history, such as an article on preparations for the World Cup finals and a featured look at Germany's role as the third largest economy in the world. This magazine also includes advertising, photos, interesting photographic essays, and book and film reviews. Another great feature is that the online version at www.magazine-deutschland.de is available in a variety of languages, including French, Arabic, Spanish, and Portuguese. Because this magazine is in English, it is highly recommended for large public and all academic libraries.

The Economist. See Economics section.

3711. *Elsevier.* Incorporates (in 1998): *Elseviers Weekblad;* Formerly (until 1987): *Elseviers Magazine.* [ISSN: 0922-3444] 1944. w. Ed(s): Peter Moennink. Reed Business Information bv, Van de Sande, Bakhuyzenstraat 4, Amsterdam, 1061 AG, Netherlands; info@reedbusiness.nl; http://www.reedbusiness.nl. Illus., adv. Circ: 192409 Paid. *Aud.:* Ga.

In Dutch, from the Netherlands. A primary news magazine in the Netherlands, *Elsevier* is the publication that lent its name to the well-known publishing company. Articles present research and commentary on a variety of social, political, and cultural topics. This glossy magazine is easily browsable and is probably most reminiscent of *Time* or *Newsweek.* Many issues focus on business and the European economy. Another popular topic is American politics, particularly the relationship between the United States and the European Union. *Elsevier* is an excellent resource for Dutch-reading students of Europe and politics. Recommended for research and large academic libraries.

3712. *L'Espresso: settimanale di politica, cultura, economia.* [ISSN: 0423-4243] 1955. w. EUR 60 domestic. Ed(s): Claudio Rinaldi. Gruppo Editoriale l' Espresso SpA, Via Cristoforo Colombo 90, Rome, 00147, Italy; espresso@espressoedit.it; http://www.espressoedit.it. Illus., adv. Sample. Circ: 500000. Microform: PQC. *Indexed:* PAIS. *Aud.:* Ga.

In Italian, from Italy. This newsmagazine provides articles on a variety of general-interest topics, such as art, culture, business, health, society, sports, and world news (from an Italian point of view). There is a regular feature on the activities of the Vatican. Recent issues in *L'Espresso* include coverage of the Italian parliamentary elections and of Pope Benedict XVI's trip to Poland. Although heavy on advertising, this magazine nonetheless provides nice photographic essays, detailed articles, and book/DVD/movie/music recommendations. The well-designed web site at www.espressonline.it has full text of current issues freely available (in both Italian and English) and now includes a section of blogs on various topics (in Italian only). The web site also has video and audio files freely available for viewing with media players. Strongly recommended for libraries with Italian-speaking patrons or students of Italian.

3713. *L'Express.* [ISSN: 0014-5270] 1953. w. EUR 72.80 domestic; EUR 103.30 in the European Union; EUR 129.30 in US & Canada. Ed(s): Denis Jeambar. Groupe Express-Expansion, 29 Rue de Chateaudun, Paris, 75308, France; http://www.groupe-expansion.com. Illus., adv. Sample. Circ: 530000. Microform: PQC. Online: LexisNexis. *Indexed:* PAIS, PdeR. *Aud.:* Ga.

In French, from France. In print since 1953, this news and current affairs magazine offers investigative articles and point-of-view pieces on a variety of political and social debates, both in France and the wider world. It is available online at www.lexpress.fr. Specific sections include world news, French issues, society, science and health, media (television and film), and photographic essays. Like its Italian counterpart *L'Espresso*, *L'Express* has a very good web site, and complete articles from the current edition are available for free. Both the print and the online versions include advertising, and articles are frequently punctuated with photos, graphs, charts, and illustrations. Highly recommended for large public and most academic libraries.

3714. *Focus (Munich): das moderne Nachrichtenmagazin.* [ISSN: 0943-7576] 1993. w. EUR 140.40; EUR 2.90 newsstand/cover. Ed(s): Uli Baur, Helmut Markwort. Focus Magazin Verlag GmbH, Arabellastr 23, Munich, 81925, Germany; medialine@focus.de; http://www.focus.de. Illus., adv. Sample. Circ: 752118 Paid. *Aud.:* Ga, Ac.

In German, from Germany. This news magazine is similar in style and scope to *U.S. News & World Report.* Articles include in-depth reporting on world news (from a German perspective), business, technology, health, culture, and sports. *Focus* also has an annual ranking of the top German universities. Each issue includes many photographs, statistics, charts, and graphs. Recent issues present articles on how red wine has been proven by Italian researchers to help regulate sleep patterns and a feature on mobile phones of the future. The letters to the editor give a good idea of current topics of political debate in Germany. Found online at http://focus.msn.de, it includes full text of the current issue for free. The online version also now features a blog and video downloads of recent news stories from "Focus Online TV." Recommended primarily for academic and research libraries. Public libraries may want to consider this magazine if they support a user population of German speakers.

3715. *H P - De Tijd.* Formed by the merger of (1974-1990): *De Tijd;* (19??-1990): *H P - Haagse Post;* Which was formerly (until 1969): *Haagse Post.* [ISSN: 0924-9648] 1990. w. Audax Publishing B.V., Joan Muyskenweg 6-6a, Amsterdam, 1096 CJ, Netherlands; info@publishing.audax.nl; http://www.audax.nl. *Bk. rev.:* Number and length vary. *Aud.:* Ga.

In Dutch, from the Netherlands. This popular general-interest magazine has a large annual circulation and includes news features, interviews, and opinion columns. In the *Cultuur* section there are literature and film reviews, as well as lists of the top-selling books and DVDs in the Netherlands. In addition to culture, another major topic covered is health. A recent article discusses some reasons why people are living longer in some parts of the Netherlands than others. Unlike its primary Dutch-language competitor *Elsevier*, *HP* focuses more on societal issues than on politics or world news. For example, there is a section dedicated to recommendations for children's books, and articles on parenting issues. On the web at www.hpdetijd.nl, this magazine is recommended for large public and academic libraries.

Harper's Bazaar en Espanol. See Latin America and Spain section.

3716. *L'Hebdo: magazine suisse d'information.* [ISSN: 1013-0691] 1981. w. CHF 205. Ed(s): Alain Jeannet. Ringier Romandie, Pont Bessieres 3, Case postale 3733, Lausanne, 1002, Switzerland; ringier.romandie@ringier.ch; http://www.ringier.ch. Illus., adv. Sample. Circ: 47911 Paid and controlled. *Aud.:* Ga.

In French, from Switzerland. *L'Hebdo* covers news, culture, technology, and business from a Swiss perspective. There is a German-language version of this publication called *Die Woche* that has essentially the same content. *L'Hebdo* includes lots of advertising, photos, and illustrations, both in print and on the web at www.hebdo.ch. Only the current issue is available in full online. Recent articles include an interview with Swiss politician Doris Leuthard and Jean Studer. Articles focus primarily on societal issues and political issues. Features include science and technology, the world, society, culture, business, media (film and TV), and travel. The web site now features a blog written by the journalists at *L'Hebdo*. Recommended for large public and academic libraries.

Hello! See General Interest section.

3717. *Iceland Review (1985): the magazine of Iceland.* Former titles (until 1985): *Atlantica and Iceland Review;* (until 1967): *Iceland Review (1963).* [ISSN: 1670-004X] 1963. q. ISK 3400 domestic; EUR 36 in Europe; USD 34.50 elsewhere. Ed(s): Anna Margret Bjoernsson. Iceland Review, Borgartuni 23, Reykjavik, 105, Iceland; icelandreview@icelandreview.com; http://www.icelandreview.com. Illus., adv. Sample. *Indexed:* RGPR. *Bk. rev.:* Number and length vary. *Aud.:* Ga.

In English and some Icelandic, from Iceland. *Iceland Review* is everything you wanted to know about Iceland, and it's in English! Articles focus on Icelandic nature, culture, art, literature, and daily life. The print version states that the online version is available at www.icelandreview.is. Each issue includes advertising, interviews, classifieds, book reviews, and at least one mention of Bjork. The primary focus of the magazine is promoting tourism in Iceland. The listing of hotels and restaurants is quite extensive. Articles are very interesting, although authors try very hard to say only positive things—for example, a cheery article about foreign workers in the highlands of Iceland where there are blizzard conditions every day in winter. An article in another issue talks about how the "Government Cracks Down on Immigration" and implies that it is a positive reason to visit Iceland. Recommended for libraries supporting Scandinavian Studies or libraries serving a significant population of Scandinavian Americans.

Impacto. See Latin America and Spain section.

India Today. See Asia and the Pacific/South Asia section.

3718. *Knack.* [ISSN: 0772-3210] 1971. w. EUR 134. Roularta Media Group, Research Park, Zellik, 1731, Belgium; communication@roularta.be; http://www.roularta.be. Illus., adv. Circ: 150000 Paid. *Aud.:* Ga, Ac.

In Dutch, from Belgium. This glossy popular magazine covers news, politics, business, literature, films, celebrity news, and sports in Belgium. Each issue of *Knack* includes lists of the top-selling books, films, music CDs, and DVDs in Belgium. Those lists and the full text of most articles from the current issue are also found on the web at www.knack.be. Sections include news this week, film, music, TV and radio, books, letters, lifestyle, business and finance, and sport. Recommended for large public libraries and for large academic libraries supporting European Studies programs.

Maclean's. See Canada section.

3719. *Norseman: a review of current events.* Incorporates (1907-1984): *Nordmanns-forbundet.* [ISSN: 0029-1846] 1907. 5x/yr. NOK 250 (Students, NOK 200; Senior citizens, NOK 200). Ed(s): Harry Cleven, Gunnar Gran. Nordmanns-Forbundet, Radhusgata 23 B, Oslo, 0158, Norway; norseman@online.no. Illus., adv. Circ: 10000. *Bk. rev.:* Number and length vary. *Aud.:* Ga.

In English and some Norwegian, from Norway. Written more for Norwegian Americans than for Norwegians, *Norseman* includes feature articles, interviews, photos, advertising, illustrations, and book reviews. The focus is primarily on cultural and historical issues. It is published by Nordmanns Forbundet under the patronage of His Majesty the King of Norway. The masthead of this magazine declares that *Norseman* "promotes solidarity between Norway and Norwegians abroad and furthers the cause of Norwegian culture and interests." Included are letters to the editor, articles on business (particularly shipping), Norway's relationship to the United States and Norwegian Americans, the history of Norway and Scandinavia, travel, and sports. Recommended for libraries that support a population of Scandinavian Americans or academic libraries supporting Scandinavian Studies programs.

3720. *Novoe Vremya: ezhenedel'nyi zhurnal.* [ISSN: 0137-0723] 1943. w. RUR 440.99 for 6 mos. domestic; USD 242 foreign. Ed(s): Aleksandr Pumpyanskii, Sergei Goliakov. Izdatel'stvo Novoe Vremya, ul Tverskaya dom 7, Moscow, 127994, Russian Federation. Illus., adv. Circ: 25000. Microform: BHP; EVP; MIM; PQC. *Indexed:* PAIS, RILM. *Bk. rev.:* Number and length vary. *Aud.:* Ga.

In Russian, from Russia. This magazine includes feature articles on a variety of topics of interest to Russian emigres and to students of the Russian language. It is packed with glossy photos and advertising (especially in the post-Soviet issues since 1991), as well as charts, illustrations, and book, film, and music reviews. Recommended for public libraries serving a Russian-speaking population and for academic libraries supporting Slavic Studies programs.

3721. *Oggi.* [ISSN: 0030-0705] 1945. w. EUR 88.40. Ed(s): Paolo Occhipinti. R C S Periodici, Via San Marco 21, Milan, 20121, Italy; info@periodici.rcs.it; http://www.rcsmediagroup.it/siti/periodici.php. Illus. Circ: 4138000. *Aud.:* Ga.

In Italian, from Italy. This current-affairs journal features articles by some of Italy's top journalists. According to the publisher's web site, *Oggi* is the "traditional weekly magazine of the Italian family for over 50 years." As such, it features investigative reports and interviews of interest to the average, working Italian.

3722. *Ogonek.* [ISSN: 0131-0097] 1899. w. USD 273 foreign. Ed(s): Vladimir Pekin. Izdatel'stvo Ogonek, Bumazhnyi pr 14, Moscow, 101456, Russian Federation. Illus., adv. Circ: 50000. Vol. ends: Dec. Microform: EVP. Online: East View Information Services. *Indexed:* CDSP. *Aud.:* Ga, Ac.

In Russian, from Russia. Published since 1899, this weekly magazine features articles on current news events and interviews with people in the news. Articles are also available at the magazine's web site at www.ropnet.ru/ogonyok/win/welcome.html. Highly recommended for libraries serving a Russian-speaking population and for most academic libraries.

3723. *Paris Match.* Former titles (until 1976): *Nouveau Paris Match;* (until 1972): *Paris Match.* [ISSN: 0397-1635] 1949. w. EUR 99. Ed(s): Didier Rapaud. Hachette Filipacchi Medias S.A., 149/151 Rue Anatole France, Levallois-Perret, 925340, France; lgardere@interdeco.fr; http://www.lagardere.com. Illus., adv. Circ: 772000 Paid. *Indexed:* PdeR. *Aud.:* Ga.

In French, from France. *Paris Match* is one of the most widely read magazines in France. With its combination of news, current affairs, celebrity interviews, and great photography, this magazine is also a favorite of Francophones (and Francophiles) all over the world. There is a stylish web site at www.parismatch-.com where one can find a number of articles from the current and past issues in full text without a subscription. It is also one of the few commercial web sites with a bare minimum of annoying pop-up advertisements. However, *Paris Match* is best enjoyed in print. Highly recommended for public and academic libraries everywhere.

People en Espanol. See Latin America and Spain section.

3724. *Le Point.* [ISSN: 0242-6005] 1972. w. EUR 117 domestic; EUR 117 in Belgium & Luxembourg; EUR 139 in Europe. Ed(s): Jean Schmitt. Sebdo Le Point, 74 av. du Maine, Paris, 75014, France; cyber@lepoint.tm.fr; http://www.lepoint.fr. Illus. Circ: 355000 Paid. Microform: PQC. *Indexed:* PAIS, PdeR. *Aud.:* Ga, Ac.

In French, from France. The primary competitor of *L'Express* for the distinction of being France's top newsmagazine, *Le Point* has been covering news and current-interest stories since 1972. Main features include editorials, letters, world news, news from France, society, business, economics, and media/technology. Most issues also include essays on travel, food, wine, cinema, literature, and art. The table of contents for the current issue can be found at www.lepoint.fr. One must subscribe to the magazine to receive access to the full text of the current issue online. *Le Point* is an important resource for the study of current events and issues in France. Highly recommended for large public libraries and most academic libraries.

Proceso. See Latin America and Spain section.

3725. *Profil: das unabhaengige Nachrichtenmagazin Oesterreichs.* [ISSN: 1022-2111] 1970. w. EUR 79.90 (Students, EUR 45). Ed(s): Reinhard Tramontana, Liselotte Palme. Verlagsgruppe News Gesellschaft mbH, Taborstr 1-3, Vienna, 1020, Austria; redaktion@news.at; http://www.news.at. Illus., adv. Sample. Circ: 77255 Paid. *Aud.:* Ga.

In German, from Austria. This popular newsmagazine features Austrian current-affairs issues, world news, sport, people, money, weather, technology, women's issues, food and wine, travel, home and garden, and classifieds. It is also available online at www.profil.at—however, make sure you have a good browser that can eliminate pop-ups, because in *Profil* they are prolific. The print version is also rife with advertising, photos (especially of celebrities), and illustrations. There is also a separate section devoted to TV and film reviews. Recommended as a good light news and entertainment magazine, especially in public or school libraries supporting the study of the German language.

The Spectator. See News and Opinion section.

3726. *Der Spiegel.* [ISSN: 0038-7452] 1947. w. EUR 171.60 domestic; EUR 226.20 per issue in Europe; EUR 304.20 per issue elsewhere. Ed(s): Stefan Aust. Spiegel-Verlag Rudolf Augstein GmbH und Co. KG, Brandstwiete 19, Hamburg, 20457, Germany. Illus., adv. Sample. Circ: 1062462 Paid. *Indexed:* BAS, PAIS, RILM. *Aud.:* Ga, Ac.

In German, from Germany. Packed with over 200 pages of text, this magazine is one of the most popular in Germany. With text entirely in German, each issue includes many articles (both short pieces and longer features) on politics (both German and worldwide), business, current affairs, culture, technology, and sport. Think of this journal as *Time* magazine in German. *Der Spiegel* is known for its superior investigative reporting, especially in the area of German and European politics. The online version at www.spiegel.de is updated daily and includes the full text of the current weekly print issue. If you can purchase just one magazine in German, this should be it. Strongly recommended for academic, research, and public libraries.

3727. *Stern.* [ISSN: 0039-1239] 1948. w. EUR 135.20; EUR 2.80 newsstand/cover. Ed(s): Thomas Osterkorn, Andreas Petzold. Gruner und Jahr AG & Co., Am Baumwall 11, Hamburg, 20459, Germany. Illus., adv. Sample. Circ: 1018146 Paid. Microform: ALP; PQC. *Aud.:* Ga, Ac.

In German, from Germany. *Stern* is a current-affairs magazine that provides articles on news and culture but seems to focus primarily on lifestyle issues, particularly stories about ordinary Germans faced with extraordinary circumstances. Articles report from both both scientific and humanistic points of view. A unique feature of *Stern* is its bestseller list that ranks the week's 20 most popular books, films, DVDs, and music CDs in Germany. The electronic version at www.stern.de includes the full text of the current issue and an archive of articles appearing in the past six months. As one of the most intellectually accessible magazines in Germany, *Stern* is highly recommended for academic and public libraries.

3728. *Suomen Kuvalehti.* [ISSN: 0039-5552] 1916. w. EUR 145. Ed(s): Tapani Ruokanen. Yhtyneet Kuvalehdet Oy, Maistraatinportti 1, Helsinki, 00015, Finland; http://www.kuvalehdet.fi/. Illus., adv. Circ: 101380. *Bk. rev.:* Number and length vary. *Aud.:* Ga, Ac.

In Finnish, from Finland. This newsmagazine is the most popular and well respected in Finland. It is reminiscent of other newsmagazines known for their strong current-affairs reporting like *Der Spiegel, Time, L'Express,* etc. Most articles focus on politics, economics, and culture, in Finland and abroad. Each issue includes ample advertising, and articles are illustrated with charts, graphs, statistics, and photos. Issues generally include book reviews. The online version at www.suomenkuvalehti.com provides the full text of articles in all issues since early 2003. Recommended for large public libraries and academic libraries supporting Slavic, Scandinavian, or European Studies.

■ JOURNALISM AND WRITING

Journalism/Writing/Pedagogy

Caroline M. Kent, Head of Research Services, Widener Library, Harvard University, Cambridge, MA 02138; cmkent@fas.harvard.edu

Introduction

Journalism and writing publications are in an interesting state of transition. The web has certainly wrought vast changes in reporting and our expectations of access to news. Journalistic web sites provide breaking news coverage along with in-depth stories: witness the immediate updates from the conflicts in Iraq, including gruesome videos of the killing of hostages. As well, writers and reporters sat at the Democratic and Republican National Conventions in 2004, blogging and e-mailing constantly. Legitimate journalists and writers blog from the front line in Iraq.

These new forms of expression are challenging our conceptions of what journalism, writing, and editing are. At the same time, we're witnessing stunning developments at more traditional institutions: the 2003 scandal at *The New York Times* that involved a young reporter who apparently plagiarized and made up many stories at the country's newspaper of record caused top-level editorial resignations and a fundamental reexamination of journalistic conduct and ethics.

Many of the publications listed in this section concentrate on conventional journalism and writing as we have known them, although you'll find that many of the articles in them explore new global and cooperative venues for self-expression (blogging) and community creation of documents (wikis). The writing journals listed here are directed more to individual practitioners, while the journalism titles tend more toward the academic.

But now, suddenly, it has become important to also include some less traditional forms of expression. E-zines? Well, they are almost passe at this point. Blogging is gaining ground as a significant format. Writers and reporters are taking to the web both to read and report the news and their thoughts, minute by minute, byte by byte.

For the first time, this section has separated out pedagogy as a subheading. More and more titles are appearing in this area, now often going far beyond the little locally produced *how-we-did-it-good* publication. Writing is more pervasive in our society, thanks to the web, and writing programs are beginning to gain some prominence. Once the purview of the diehard true believer, the never-to-be-tenured, teachers of writing are gaining respectability in academia as we are all realizing that our students *cannot* write. So watch for a future increase in this section!

Basic Periodicals

JOURNALISM. Hs: *Communication: Journalism Education Today;* Ga: *AJR: American Journalism Review, Columbia Journalism Review, Editor and Publisher, Online Journalism Review;* Ac: *Columbia Journalism Review, Editor and Publisher, The Harvard International Journal of Press - Politics, Newspaper Research Journal, Online Journalism Review.*

WRITING. Hs: *Writer's Digest;* Ga: *Poets & Writers Magazine, Writer's Block, Writer's Digest;* Ac: *New Writing, Poets & Writers Magazine.*

PEDAGOGY. Ac: *Assessing Writing, Journalism and Mass Communication Educator, The Writing Center Journal.*

Basic Abstracts and Indexes

Communication Abstracts, Humanities Index, MLA International Bibliography, Readers' Guide to Periodical Literature.

Journalism

3729. *American Editor.* Formerly (until 1995): *American Society of Newspaper Editors. Bulletin.* [ISSN: 1083-5210] 1926. 9x/yr. USD 29 domestic; USD 34.50 Canada; USD 44 elsewhere. Ed(s): Craig Branson. American Society of Newspaper Editors, 11690B Sunrise Valley Dr, Reston, VA 20191-1409; asne@asne.org; http://www.asne.org/. Illus. Sample. Circ: 2500. *Indexed:* ABIn. *Bk. rev.:* 1-3, 200-300 words. *Aud.:* Ac, Sa.

This publication of the American Society of Newspaper Editors is designed to convey useful information, to put forward new ideas, and to promote debate among newspaper journalists. Articles report on successes and failures of editors facing challenges from technology, ethics, government regulation, legal cases, management, and social responsibility. A few recent titles include "Editors and Educators on Ethics," "Diversity: Getting the Big Story on Immigration," and "Good Journalism in Dark Days." Brief news items keep editors current on the latest trends and people in the industry. Online access is available to current and noncurrent articles back to 1996. This title will be most useful to libraries that serve prospective and practicing newspaper editors.

3730. *American Journalism.* [ISSN: 0882-1127] 1982. q. Members, USD 35. Ed(s): Jim Martin, Shirley Biagi. American Journalism Historians Association, Department of Communication Studies, California State Univesity at Sacramento, Sacramento, CA 95819-6070; ajha@csus.edu; http://www.berry.edu/ajha/. Adv. Refereed. Circ: 550 Paid. *Indexed:* AmH&L, AmHI, CommAb, HistAb, HumInd, PRA. *Bk. rev.:* 8-10, 500-1,000 words. *Aud.:* Ac.

This small scholarly journal seems to always be packed with fascinating articles—fascinating not just to media historians, but also to anyone interested in cultural history ideas. Some recent article titles include "Breaking Baseball Barriers: The 1953–1954 Negro League and Expansion of Women's Public Roles," "The Soldier Speaks: Yank Coverage of Women and Wartime Work," and "Opposite Extremes: How Two Editors Portrayed a Civil War Atrocity." The writing is livelier than that found in many scholarly journals (perhaps because of the journalistic orientation of many of the authors), but this in no way detracts from the serious, scholarly nature of the journal. Given the fact that its articles cross disciplinary lines, and given that the journal is well indexed, it should be purchased by any university library with serious history programs and by any academic library with media-history collections and programs.

3731. *Columbia Journalism Review.* Incorporates: *More Magazine; Public Interest Alert; Media and Consumer.* [ISSN: 0010-194X] 1961. bi-m. USD 19.95 domestic; USD 27.95 foreign. Ed(s): Michael Hoyt, Brent Cunningham. Columbia University, Graduate School of Journalism, 2950 Broadway, New York, NY 10027; http://www.jrn.columbia.edu/. Illus., index, adv. Sample. Circ: 31000. Vol. ends: No. 6. Microform: PQC. Online: Chadwyck-Healey Inc.; EBSCO Publishing, EBSCO Host;

Florida Center for Library Automation; Gale; LexisNexis; Northern Light Technology, Inc.; OCLC Online Computer Library Center, Inc.; ProQuest K-12 Learning Solutions; ProQuest LLC (Ann Arbor); H.W. Wilson. *Indexed:* ABIn, ABS&EES, AmHI, BRD, BRI, CBRI, CLI, FLI, HumInd, ILP, PAIS, RGPR, SSCI. *Bk. rev.:* 4-6, 100-300 words; 1-2, 1,000-2,000 words. *Aud.:* Hs, Ga, Ac.

This is a wonderfully accessible, well-edited journal full of interesting, well-written articles. It also has an excellent web site on which many of its articles are archived in full text. Its coverage ranges from journalistic practice to articles of both national and international newsworthiness. Some recent titles include "Miami Noir" and "Those Liberal J-Schools." The book review section is a particularly rich one. Each issue not only contains four to six short (100–300 word) "reports" on books, but also one or two extensive and in-depth reviews. Despite its high academic pedigree, this magazine would be a very good choice not only for college and university libraries but also for high school libraries (at an excellent price!). Public libraries that serve populations with high interest in current events should also consider its purchase.

3732. *Editor and Publisher: the newsmagazine of the fourth estate since 1894.* [ISSN: 0013-094X] 1884. m. w. until Jan. 2004. USD 99 domestic; USD 159 combined subscription Canada; USD 320 combined subscription elsewhere. Nielsen Business Publications, 770 Broadway, New York, NY 10003-9595. Illus., index, adv. Sample. Circ: 14700 Paid and controlled. Vol. ends: Dec. Online: EBSCO Publishing, EBSCO Host; Florida Center for Library Automation; Gale; OCLC Online Computer Library Center, Inc.; ProQuest LLC (Ann Arbor); H.W. Wilson. Microform: PQC. *Indexed:* ABIn, AgeL, BPI, LRI. *Aud.:* Ac, Sa.

This magazine lays claim to being "America's oldest journal covering the newspaper industry." Its format is glossy, and its articles are newsy, sometimes rather light, and directed at industry leaders. In keeping with its format as news for executives, there are many short columns and departments. Recent article titles include "Sudoku: A Puzzling Success for Papers" and "Should We Protect Sources That Lie?" University libraries that address the needs of future journalists and editors should consider purchasing this magazine. It would also be appropriate for special industry libraries.

3733. *Ejournalist.* [ISSN: 1444-741X] 2001. irreg. Ed(s): Alan Knight. Central Queensland University, Faculty of Informatics and Communication, Rockhampton Campus, Bruce Highway, North Rockhampton, QLD 4702, Australia; http://www.cqu.edu.au. Refereed. *Aud.:* Ac, Sa.

ejournalist is an open-access, refereed journal published in Australia. What is particularly interesting about this online publication is that it includes English-language articles from a part of the world that many Americans do not read from. Some recent titles include "Framing Ethnic Media: News Broadcasting Policies and Standards in Post September 11 Australia," "Colonials, Bourgeoisies and Media Dynasties: A Case Study of Sri Lankan Media," and "Television as a Catalyst of Democratization in the Arab World." It publishes only a few new articles a year, but they are all substantive and fascinating. Any academic library that serves a journalism program should link to this publication.

3734. *Extra!* [ISSN: 0895-2310] 1987. bi-m. USD 21 domestic; USD 31 foreign. Ed(s): Jim Naureckas. Fairness & Accuracy In Reporting (F.A.I.R.), 112 W. 27th St, New York, NY 10001; fair@fair.org; http://www.fair.org. Circ: 13000. Online: OCLC Online Computer Library Center, Inc.; H.W. Wilson. *Indexed:* AltPI, PRA, RGPR. *Aud.:* Ga, Ac.

FAIR (Fairness and Accuracy In Reporting) is an anti-censorship watch group, working to create balance in media reporting. Its main publication, *Extra!*, is edgy and fascinating and includes actual articles that report on current events as well as discussions on accuracy in news reporting. Recent articles include such titles as "The False Debate Over Broken Borders," "Bush-Hating Nation, Anatomy of an Epithet," and "Wrong on Iraq? Not Everyone." Like most news reporting, it is not scholarly in nature, but the publication should be added to any library collection that serves the needs of journalists or journalism students.

3735. *Grassroots Editor: journal for newspeople.* Formerly: *Grassroots (Carbondale).* [ISSN: 0017-3541] 1960. q. Individuals, USD 25. Ed(s): Richard W Lee. International Society of Weekly Newspaper Editors, Institute of International Studies, Missouri Southern State College, Joplin, MO 64801-1595; leer@ur.sdstate.edu. Illus., index, adv. Sample. Circ: 1000. Vol. ends: Winter. Microform: PQC. Online: EBSCO Publishing, EBSCO Host. *Aud.:* Ac, Sa.

There's always been a special place in this country for the editors of small, local newspapers. Perhaps that place is mythological, but the idea of it remains an important American icon. This thoughtful publication is directed at the editorial and writing staffs of weekly community newspapers in the United States. So recent titles include "The Mansions That Ate Sante Fe: Can Anything Stop the Attack of the Monster Homes" and "Letter Writing Began in the Colonial Period." Public libraries in cities with community newspapers should consider purchasing this inexpensive publication. In addition, academic libraries that support serious journalism programs should buy it.

Index on Censorship. See Civil Liberties/Freedom of Expression and Information section.

3736. *International Journal of Press / Politics.* Formerly (until 2008): *The Harvard International Journal of Press / Politics.* [ISSN: 1940-1612] 1996. q. GBP 242. Ed(s): Alex Jones, Thomas Patterson. Sage Publications, Inc., 2455 Teller Rd, Thousand Oaks, CA 91320; info@sagepub.com; http://www.sagepub.com. Illus., adv. Refereed. Vol. ends: Fall. Online: CSA; EBSCO Publishing, EBSCO Host; Gale; HighWire Press; OCLC Online Computer Library Center, Inc.; OhioLINK; Project MUSE; SAGE Publications, Inc., SAGE Journals Online; SwetsWise Online Content. Reprint: PSC. *Indexed:* CommAb, HRA, IPSA, PAIS, PRA, PSA, SSA, SSCI, SociolAb, V&AA. *Bk. rev.:* 4-6, 100-250 words, signed. *Aud.:* Ac.

This journal, edited and published by Harvard's Kennedy School of Government, strives to address the academic needs of journalists, politicians, and political scientists. It is heavily academic, with well-written, well-referenced, refereed articles. Recent article titles include "Stealthy Wealth: The Untold Story of Welfare Privatization," "Dispelling Late-Night Myths: News Consumption Among Late-Night Comedy Viewers and the Predictors of Exposure to Various Late-Night Shows," and "From Baghdad to Paris: Al-Jazeera and the Veil." In addition to the feature articles, issues often lead off with a substantive interview with a well-known practitioner. Academic libraries in colleges or universities with strong political science, communication, or journalism programs will want this journal.

3737. *Journal of Mass Media Ethics: exploring questions of media morality.* [ISSN: 0890-0523] 1985. q. GBP 321 print & online eds. Ed(s): Jay Black. Lawrence Erlbaum Associates, Inc., 325 Chestnut St, Ste. 800, Philadelphia, PA 19106; journals@erlbaum.com; http://www.leaonline.com. Illus., adv. Sample. Refereed. Microform: PQC. Online: EBSCO Publishing, EBSCO Host; OCLC Online Computer Library Center, Inc.; OhioLINK; SwetsWise Online Content. Reprint: PSC. *Indexed:* AmHI, CommAb, EAA, HumInd, PAIS, PSA, RI-1, RiskAb, SociolAb, V&AA. *Bk. rev.:* Number and length vary. *Aud.:* Ac.

If there was ever a time for a journal like this to exist, it is now. As we watch the growing confusion between reporting and media experts with government sources, we learn quickly that ethical behavior and moral positioning is critical for our journalists. This academic journal does not take positions, but rather includes articles that articulate conflicts and present and define ethical issues. Recent titles include "Mainstream News Media, an Objective Approach, and the March to War in Iraq," "Moral Fables of Public Relations Practice: The Tylenol and Exxon Valdez Cases," and "The Propaganda War on Terrorism." This journal includes a varying number of substantive book reviews. Appropriate for academic libraries that serve communications and journalism departments.

3738. *Journalism and Mass Communication Quarterly: devoted to research and commentary in journalism and mass communication.* Former titles: *Journalism Quarterly;* (until 1928): *Journalism Bulletin.* [ISSN: 1077-6990] 1924. q. USD 140 (Individuals, USD 80). Ed(s): Daniel Riffe. Association for Education in Journalism and Mass Communication, 234 Outlet Pointe Blvd Ste A, Columbia, SC 29210-5667; http://www.aejmc.org. Illus., adv. Sample. Refereed. Circ: 5000 Paid and controlled. Vol. ends: Winter. Microform: PQC. Online: EBSCO Publishing, EBSCO Host; OCLC Online Computer Library Center, Inc.; ProQuest LLC (Ann Arbor); H.W. Wilson. *Indexed:* ABIn, ABS&EES, AgeL, AmH&L, AmHI, ArtHuCI, BAS, BRI, BrHumI, CBRI, CJA, CommAb, EAA, EI, HRA, HistAb, HumInd, IBR, IBSS, IPSA, IndIslam, LISA, LRI, MLA-IB, PAIS, PRA, PSA, RILM, SFSA, SSA, SSCI, SUSA, SociolAb, V&AA. *Bk. rev.:* 12-25, 700-1200 words. *Aud.:* Ac.

This scholarly publication "strives to be the flagship journal of the Association for Education in Journalism and Mass Communication." Its articles develop theory, introduce new ideas, and work to challenge the boundaries of the existing bodies of research. Its issues often contain themes, such as "Advertising Effects," "Copyright Law," and "Research Methodology." Recent articles include "Advertising to Children in China," "Examining the New Influencers: A Self-Presentation Study of A-List Blogs," and "Did Women Listen To News? A Critical Examination of Landmark Radio Audience Research (1935-1948)." This is an interesting journal, filled with thoughtful, well-researched articles. Any library that serves academic programs in communications and journalism should subscribe to this journal.

3739. *Journalism Studies.* [ISSN: 1461-670X] 2000. bi-m. GBP 556 print & online eds. Ed(s): Bob Franklin, Elizabeth L Toth. Routledge, 4 Park Sq, Milton Park, Abingdon, OX14 4RN, United Kingdom; info@routledge.co.uk; http://www.routledge.co.uk. Online: EBSCO Publishing, EBSCO Host; Gale; IngentaConnect; OCLC Online Computer Library Center, Inc.; SwetsWise Online Content. Reprint: PSC. *Indexed:* CommAb, IBSS. *Bk. rev.:* 8-12, 800-1200 words. *Aud.:* Ac.

One of the ongoing complaints about Americans is that we know too little about how our nation and its actions are seen abroad. Certainly the community of journalists is more aware of contemporary foreign opinion, but there is also value in the closer looks given us by authors publishing in journals such as *Journalism Studies.* This British journal, published in association with the European Journalism Training Association, is geared to serious journalists and journalism historians. It contains regular columns such as "Debate," "Reviews," and "Feature Review." Titles of recent feature articles include "Jeffersonian Poetry: An Ideological Analysis of George F. Will's Editorials (2002-2004)," "The Wayward Child: An Ideological Analysis of Sports Contract Holdout Coverage," and "Journalists in Indonesia: Educated But Timid Watchdogs." Yes, this *is* a relatively expensive journal—expensive enough that some academic libraries will decide not to purchase it. But for university libraries that serve strong journalism programs, it is invaluable. Full text is available online.

3740. *News Media and the Law.* Supersedes (in 1977): *Press Censorship Newsletter.* [ISSN: 0149-0737] 1973. 4x/yr. USD 30 domestic; USD 45 foreign. Ed(s): Gregg Leslie. Reporters Committee for Freedom of the Press, 1101 Wilson Blvd. Ste 1100, Arlington, VA 22209-2275; rcfp@rcfp.org; http://www.rcfp.org. Illus., index, adv. Sample. Circ: 3500. Vol. ends: Fall. Microform: PQC. Online: EBSCO Publishing, EBSCO Host; OCLC Online Computer Library Center, Inc.; ProQuest K-12 Learning Solutions; ProQuest LLC (Ann Arbor). *Indexed:* CLI, ILP, LRI. *Aud.:* Sa.

This journal's particular mission is to assist news reporters in understanding their legal rights and professional obligations. It covers particular stories in the news where the media is in court and contains many articles that are educational in nature. Some recent titles include "Nebulous Standards of Secrecy," "Disappearing Dockets," and "Katrina Clampdown." Each issue has departments, such as "News," "Legal Action," and "Legal Defense." This journal is important to any library that addresses the education of journalists, or to those who address the needs of professional journalists.

3741. *Newspaper Research Journal.* [ISSN: 0739-5329] 1979. q. USD 50, Libraries, USD 40 (Individuals, USD 40). Ed(s): Dr. Sandy Utt, Dr. Elinor Grusin. University of Memphis, Department of Journalism, 3711 Veterans, Rm 318, Memphis, TN 38152; cphilpot@memphis.edu. Illus. Refereed. Circ: 900. Vol. ends: Fall. Microform: PQC. Online: EBSCO

Publishing, EBSCO Host; Florida Center for Library Automation; Gale; Northern Light Technology, Inc.; OCLC Online Computer Library Center, Inc.; ProQuest K-12 Learning Solutions; ProQuest LLC (Ann Arbor); H.W. Wilson. *Indexed:* CommAb, PRA, SUSA. *Bk. rev.:* 3-5, 500-750 words. *Aud.:* Ac.

This scholarly journal is intended to address both the needs of the journalism student and the serious media practitioner. Its articles are well written, interesting, and often practical. Sometimes an entire issue will be dedicated to a particular topic, such as a recent one on September 11. In others, there is a wide selection of articles, with titles such as "Plagiarism Persists in News Despite Changing Attitudes" and "Newspaper Coverage Limited For State Supreme Court Cases." Libraries that support serious journalism programs should consider this journal.

3742. Nieman Reports. [ISSN: 0028-9817] 1947. q. USD 20 domestic; USD 30 foreign. Ed(s): Melissa Ludtke. Nieman Foundation, Harvard University, 1 Francis Ave, Cambridge, MA 02138. Illus., index, adv. Circ: 6022. Vol. ends: Dec. CD-ROM: ProQuest LLC (Ann Arbor). Online: EBSCO Publishing, EBSCO Host; Florida Center for Library Automation; Gale; Northern Light Technology, Inc.; OCLC Online Computer Library Center, Inc.; ProQuest LLC (Ann Arbor). *Indexed:* ABIn, BEL&L, RI-1. *Bk. rev.:* 3-6, 700-1,500 words, signed. *Aud.:* Ga, Ac.

This journal publishes substantive articles intended to be thought-provoking discussions for practitioners on current events and issues surrounding the profession of journalism. The breadth of its articles, however, should give it a much wider audience. Some of the recent articles include "A Recurring Image in Art: The Newspaper," "Broadcast News: The Absence of Native Storytellers," and "Attitudes and Mindsets Hinder Journalists in Their Coverage." It contains excellent book reviews and alumni reports for Harvard's Nieman fellows. This journal would be well purchased by academic libraries that serve journalism programs, as well as ones with active public service programs. Public libraries serving well-read audiences should also consider it.

3743. Online Journalism Review. [ISSN: 1522-6883] 1998. w. Ed(s): Joshua S Fouts. Annenberg School for Communication, University Park Campus, Los Angeles, CA 90089; fouts@usc.edu; http://www.ojr.org/. Illus. *Aud.:* Ga, Ac.

Online Journalism Review is produced by the Annenberg School for Communication in Los Angeles. The intended audience is "journalists and anyone interested in where journalism is going in cyberspace," and there aren't many of us who don't fit into the latter category. The site contains columns and sections on business, law, and ethics, to name a few, plus web site reviews. Recent article titles include "Blogging, Wikis, Discussion: How to Write for the Web," "Blogging for Fun...Then Profit," and "E-Mamas Rewrite Parenting Niche." Like many effective online publications, the content shifts quickly, and the site contains some non–journal-like content, such as online forums and blogs. However, material is archived and dated, and web site interactivity is simply part of the newly emerging format. Any academic library, with or without journalism or communications programs, should link to this resource. In addition, many public libraries with technologically savvy patrons should provide a link to it.

3744. Quill (Greencastle): a magazine for the professional journalist. [ISSN: 0033-6475] 1912. 9x/yr. USD 72. Ed(s): Joe Skeel. Society of Professional Journalists, 3909 N Meridian St, Indianapolis, IN 46208; spj@spj.org; http://www.spj.org. Illus., index. Sample. Circ: 11000 Paid. Vol. ends: Dec. Microform: PQC. Online: The Dialog Corporation; EBSCO Publishing, EBSCO Host; Florida Center for Library Automation; Gale; OCLC Online Computer Library Center, Inc.; ProQuest K-12 Learning Solutions; ProQuest LLC (Ann Arbor); H.W. Wilson. *Indexed:* ABIn, AmHI, HumInd. *Aud.:* Sa.

Quill is the official publication of the Society of Professional Journalists. As such, it contains articles and commentary of wide interest, and it has an annual education issue of particular interest to academics. But many of its research articles would be of interest and accessible to any reader. Some recent titles include "Are the watchdogs still watching?," "Asking right questions a key to

minimizing harm," and "Burma among most oppressive for journalists." Academic and special libraries that serve practicing journalists and journalism educators should purchase this title.

Writing

3745. Contentious. 1998. m. Ed(s): Amy Gahran. Contentious, editor@contentious.com; http://blog.contentious.com. *Aud.:* Ac, Sa.

This is *not* an electronic journal or an electronic newsletter! It is a blog, of course, authored and edited by the edgy Amy Gahran, a highly astute journalism consultant whose opinions on modern-day writing are worth reading. (And if you haven't yet read Gahran's opinions, you *really* must!) This title was originally delivered as an e-zine and then morphed into its current format as a blog. But that history in itself stands as an example of what is happening to much modern journalism. Entries contain interesting observations on existing and new forms of online communication and can be used as a good way of getting fast access to brand-new forms (know what "technorati" are?). Some of the recent entries include "My Must-Listen Pod Casts" and "Why News Needs More Collaboration." This title should be pointed to by any academic or special library collection that supports journalism or communication arts populations interested in the newest forms of talking out there in cyberspace.

Creative Screenwriting. See Films section.

3746. E-Media Tidbits: a group weblog by the sharpest minds in online media/journalism/publishing. d. Free. The Poynter Institute, 801 Third St South, St. Petersburg, FL 33701; http://www.poynter.org. *Aud.:* Ac, Sa.

The Poynter Institute, located in St. Petersburg, Florida, has played an increasingly important role in newspaper development in the United States. *E-Media Tidbits* began its electronic life as a newsletter. It has now morphed into a blog, and is an interesting example of how legitimate "self-publishing" can be. Both its past issues and its current entries are archived and available on the web site. Discussions include current events, opinions on web and journalism issues, and interesting observations on the technology used by writers and journalists. Take a look. You will be fascinated! It is now edited by Amy Gahran, which only increases this title's interest. This title should be pointed to by any special or academic collection that supports a news journalism program.

3747. The Internet Writing Journal. [ISSN: 1095-3973] 1997. m. Writers Write, Inc., 8214 Westchester Ste 500, Dallas, TX 75225; journal@writerswrite.com; http://www.writerswrite.com/journal. Illus., adv. *Bk. rev.:* Number varies, 150-200 words. *Aud.:* Ga.

The Internet Writing Journal is billed as "The Online Monthly Magazine for Writers and Book Lovers since 1997." Like many online publications, it is a mix of frequently updated content and static information. The most interesting parts are the frequent interviews with well-known authors, and the now ubiquitous blog "The IWJ Blog: Commentary on books, entertainment and writing." It also includes good book reviews and a number of secondary blogs and columns. There are copious advertisements, some of which appear to be featured sections or at least services recommended by the journal. There are also many classifieds and job listings, as well as information on events and awards. Back issues are archived. This a good site that has cleaned up its presentation and organization in the last two years. Highly recommended for public libraries that serve writing communities.

3748. New Writing: the international journal for the practice and theory of creative writing. [ISSN: 1479-0726] 2004. 3x/yr. EUR 139 (Individuals, EUR 54). Ed(s): Graeme Harper. Multilingual Matters Ltd., Frankfurt Lodge, Clevedon Hall, Clevedon, BS21 7HH, United Kingdom; info@multilingual-matters.com; http://www.multilingual-matters.com. Refereed. *Indexed:* AmHI. *Aud.:* Ac.

This is a fascinating new journal that should probably get a great deal more attention than it has. It is odd that writers, and in particular *creative* writers, frequently do not seem to write about what they do. There are notable exceptions to that, of course. But many creative writers tend to leave how-we-do-it to literature critics who write how-*they*-do-it pieces. This British journal has articles from academics teaching writing, literature critics, and creative writers. Some recent titles include "The Creative Writing Doctorate: Creative Trial or Academic Error?" and "The Nonfiction Impulse in the Beginning Writer." In this era when historians are coming to write fictionalized history, and fiction writers are coming to write on only slivers of reality, this journal fits into an interesting niche. Any academic library that serves either a population of creative writers or those teaching creative writing should consider this journal's purchase.

3749. Poets & Writers Magazine. Formerly (until 1987): *Coda: Poets and Writers Newsletter.* [ISSN: 0891-6136] 1972. bi-m. Ed(s): Therese Eiben. Poets & Writers, Inc., 72 Spring St, New York, NY 10012; http://www.pw.org. Illus., adv. Circ: 71000. Microform: PQC. Online: OCLC Online Computer Library Center, Inc.; ProQuest LLC (Ann Arbor). *Indexed:* AmHI, HumInd. *Aud.:* Ga, Ac.

If a library purchases only one writing journal for creative writers, *Poets & Writers Magazine* should be it. Its content is specifically directed to the interests of poets and writers of serious fiction; each issue contains interviews with important authors, some venerable, some new. There are articles directed at the creative writing process, although this is not a how-to journal for the uninitiated. Some recent articles include "Strangers Meet in Virtual Libraries," "Emily Barton and Gary Shteyngart," and "Since You're Gone: A Profile of Donald Antrim." Regular departments include "News and Trends," "The Literary Life," and "The Practical Writer." There is an extensive and invaluable "Resources" section that includes grants and awards, conferences and residencies, and classifieds. All academic libraries should purchase this journal. Public libraries that serve populations of writers should also consider it.

Scr(i)pt: Where Film Begins. See Films section.

3750. Technical Communication Quarterly. Formerly (until 1992): *Technical Writing Teacher.* [ISSN: 1057-2252] 1973. q. GBP 179 print & online eds. Ed(s): Mark Zachry. Lawrence Erlbaum Associates, Inc., 325 Chestnut St, Ste. 800, Philadelphia, PA 19106; journals@erlbaum.com; http://www.leaonline.com. Illus., adv. Refereed. Circ: 2000. Vol. ends: Fall. Microform: PQC. Online: EBSCO Publishing, EBSCO Host; OCLC Online Computer Library Center, Inc.; OhioLINK; ProQuest LLC (Ann Arbor); SwetsWise Online Content; H.W. Wilson. Reprint: PSC. *Indexed:* ABIn, AbAn, EduInd, LISA, MLA-IB, PsycInfo. *Bk. rev.:* 1-2, 1,000 words. *Aud.:* Ac, Sa.

If you were to include a journal on technical writing in a library collection, this title would probably be a good choice. It purports to publish refereed articles on teaching and research methodologies, historical research, ethics, practical methodologies, digital applications, etc.—all as they relate to technical communication practices. Some recent titles include "Intercultural Rhetoric, Technology Transfer, and Writing in U.S.–Mexico Border Maquilas," "Popularizing Nanoscience: The Public Rhetoric of Nanotechnology, 1986-1999," and "Prediscursive Technical Communication in the Early American Iron Industry." Any academic library that supports a technical writing program should purchase this title.

3751. The Writer. [ISSN: 0043-9517] 1887. m. USD 29 domestic; USD 39 Canada; USD 4.95 newsstand/cover. Ed(s): Elfrieda Abbe. Kalmbach Publishing Co., 21027 Crossroads Circle, PO Box 1612, Waukesha, WI 53187-1612; http://www.kalmbach.com. Illus., index, adv. Circ: 37000 Paid. Vol. ends: Dec. *Indexed:* AmHI, IAPV, MASUSE, RGPR. *Bk. rev.:* Number and length vary. *Aud.:* Hs, Ga, Ac.

This long-established magazine has undergone some major changes, changes that clearly have not negatively affected its high circulation rate. While not as substantive as *Writers Digest* or *Poets and Writers,* this publication is well designed and has high appeal. It contains columns of general interest, such as "Dear Writer" and "How I Write." It contains book reviews and classified ads of interest to writers. Some recent titles include "What Top Fiction Editors Are Looking For" and "How to Promote Your Pod Book." Its primary market is probably beginning writers, and it is therefore best placed in high school, public, and college libraries.

3752. Writer's Block: the Canadian E-zine for the writing trade. [ISSN: 1488-4801] 1995. irreg. Ed(s): Dalya Goldberger. NIVA Inc., 500-1145 Hunt Club Rd, Ottawa, ON K1V 0Y3, Canada; dgoldberger@niva.com; http://www.writersblock.ca/. *Bk. rev.:* 1, 700-1,200 words. *Aud.:* Ga, Sa.

This electronic publication is oriented toward professional writers, editors, and publishers. Recent titles include "Deconstructing the Author Photo" and "Angels and Copy Editors Defend Us!" It contains an extensive writing tips section, covering word choice, grammar, and some aspects of publishing. The archives include all back issues. Although this publication is "aimed at Canadians in the writing trade," most articles are suitable for a wider audience. A good choice for public and special libraries.

3753. The Writer's Chronicle. Formerly (until 1998): *A W P Newsletter.* [ISSN: 1529-5443] 1968. 6x/yr. USD 20 domestic; USD 25 Canada. Ed(s): David W Fenza. Associated Writing Programs, Tallwood House, Mail Stop 1E3, Fairfax, VA 22030; awpchron@mason.gmu.edu; http://awpwriter.org. Illus., adv. Circ: 20000. *Indexed:* AmHI. *Aud.:* Ga, Ac.

The Writer's Chronicle is intended for a broad audience, and contains "information designed to enlighten, inform, and entertain writers, editors, students, and teachers of writing." It contains many interviews and feature articles that have wide appeal, as well as actual fiction and poetry. Some recent titles include "An Interview with Sandra Cisneros," "The Words & the Bees: Advice for Graduating MFA Students in Writing," and "The Lyric Self: Artifice and Authenticity in Recent American Poetry." Any public library that supports a population of creative writers, as well as academic libraries, should consider this journal's purchase.

3754. Writer's Digest. [ISSN: 0043-9525] 1921. m. USD 19.96 domestic; CND 29.96 Canada; USD 58.96 elsewhere. Ed(s): Maria Witte. F + W Publications, Inc., 4700 E Galbraith Rd, Cincinnati, OH 45236; http://www.fwpublications.com. Illus., index, adv. Sample. Circ: 170000 Paid. Vol. ends: Dec. Microform: MIM; PQC. Online: OCLC Online Computer Library Center, Inc.; ProQuest K-12 Learning Solutions; ProQuest LLC (Ann Arbor). *Indexed:* ASIP, IHTDI. *Aud.:* Hs, Ga, Ac.

If a library could purchase only one writing journal, *Writer's Digest* should be it. It contains huge amounts of information on all types of nontechnical writing, interviews, and feature articles on issues of interest to writers, such as book doctoring and copyright. There is market information, sections of classifieds, and advertisements galore. Its format is newsy and glossy, and it is interesting even to the non-writer. All public libraries should purchase this, and academic libraries with writing programs should consider it.

3755. Writing That Works: the business communications report. Formed by the merger of: *Desktop Publishing Users' Report; Communications Concepts;* Which was formerly: *Quick Report; Writing Concepts;* Which incorporates (1990-1995): *Hospital Editors' Idea Exchange;* (in Mar. 1995): *Editors' Forum; Communications Manager;* Which was formerly (until 1990): *Communications Concepts.* 10x/yr. USD 119 in the Americas; USD 128 elsewhere. Ed(s): John De Lellis. Writing that Works, 7481 Huntsman Blvd, Ste 720, Springfield, VA 22153-1648; http://www.writingthatworks.com. *Aud.:* Ga.

Everything that many writers hate about writing for business is clearly outlined as requirements for publication in this journal: quick, easy to read, short sentences, bulleted points. However, there are a large number of people in this country who are responsible for clear communications in a business setting. *Writing That Works* is a small but very useful publication that would fulfill many needs for corporate writers. It specifically outlines (neatly bulleted, of course) the types of articles it publishes: techniques, style issues (editing, grammar, usage), publication management, PR and marketing strategy, and online publishing. Some sample article titles include "Use metaphors to communicate, not decorate" and "For good media relations, treat reporters like customers." For public libraries that serve large business communities.

Written By. See Films section.

Pedagogy

3756. *Across the Disciplines.* Formed by the merger of (1994-2003): *Language and Learning Across the Disciplines;* (2000-2003): *Academic. Writing.* [ISSN: 1554-8244] 2004. irreg. Free to qualified personnel. Ed(s): Sharon Quiroz. W A C Clearinghouse, Dept of English, Eddy hall Rm 359, Fort Collins, CO 80523; Mike.Palmquist@ColoState.edu; http://lamar.colostate.edu/~mp/. Refereed. *Indexed:* MLA-IB. *Bk. rev.:* Occasional, 1,000-1,500 words. *Aud.:* Ac.

"Across the Disciplines, a refereed journal devoted to language, learning, and academic writing, publishes articles relevant to writing and writing pedagogy in all their intellectual, political, social, and technological complexity." Well, despite that mouthful of words, this is an excellent web-based journal that actually is now an amalgam of two former e-journals, *Academic.Writing* and *Language and Learning Across the Disciplines.* Archives for the current and the previous journals are all available online. The content of this interesting journal includes both discussions of academic writing in the academy and pedagogical discussions. It is predominantly a pedagogical publication, but since most academics teach writing in the context of courses, it should have broad appeal. Some titles from recent issues include: "Bridging Disciplinary Divides in Writing Across the Curriculm" and "Teaching Academic Writing to International Students in an Interdisciplinary Writing Context: A Pedagogical Rough Guide." For those of us who live with the complexities of traditional academic language, and who watch our students and faculty struggle to write between conflicting traditions on interdisciplinary topics, this journal fills a significant gap. Any academic library of merit should consider linking to this title.

3757. *Assessing Writing.* [ISSN: 1075-2935] 1994. 3x/yr. EUR 246. Ed(s): L. Hamp-Lyons, W. Condon. Pergamon, The Boulevard, Langford Ln, East Park, Kidlington, OX5 1GB, United Kingdom. Refereed. *Indexed:* L&LBA, LingAb, MLA-IB. *Bk. rev.:* 1-3, 1,000-2,000 words. *Aud.:* Ac. This extremely substantive refereed journal strives to publish articles on writing and teaching writing from an international perspective. It therefore makes it a somewhat more theoretical journal than a "how-to" publication, but that does not detract from its quality. Examples of a few recent titles include "The mediation of technology in ESL writing and its implications for writing assessment," "Self-assessment of writing in independent language learning programs: The value of annotated samples," and "Good academic writing in Hebrew: The perceptions of pre-service teachers and their instructors." Given the cost, many academic libraries will choose not to purchase it. But for those with strong writing programs, this is a good title to consider.

3758. *Communication, Journalism Education Today.* Former titles (until 1997): *C: JET;* (until 1977): *Communication: Journalism Education Today.* [ISSN: 1536-9129] 1967. q. Ed(s): Bradley Wilson. Journalism Education Association, Inc., Kedzie Hall 103, Kansas State University, Manhattan, KS 66506; jea@spub.ksu.edu; http://www.jea.org. Illus., adv. *Aud.:* Hs, Ac.

Communication: Journalism Education Today is published by the Journalism Education Association, which has members ranging from high school through university-level journalism practitioners; but this journal's focus is more at the younger level. It includes some research articles, but also many articles on curriculum development, lesson planning, and tips for teachers and young practitioners. Some titles from recent issues include "We Weren't So Lucky: Hurricane Coverage," "Rodeo, A Photo Essay," and "The Light Show: Indoor Lighting of Sports Facilities, Keep the Light Out of Their Eyes." Recommended for high school libraries without reservation; college-level libraries should evaluate from a sample issue. Some academic libraries with strong teacher-training programs should also consider its purchase.

3759. *Computers and Composition.* [ISSN: 8755-4615] 1983. 4x/yr. EUR 315. Ed(s): Cynthia L Selfe, Dr. Gail E. Hawisher. Elsevier Ltd., The Boulevard, Langford Ln, Oxford, OX5 1GB, United Kingdom. Refereed. Vol. ends: No. 18. *Indexed:* ABIn, CompLI, EduInd, LingAb, MLA-IB, SWA. *Bk. rev.:* 1-4, 2,500-3,000 words. *Aud.:* Ac.

This journal has an interesting charge. It "is devoted to exploring the use of computers in writing classes, writing programs, and writing research." It looks at these issues from pedagogical, psychological, and social points of view. Its articles may discuss legal or ethical issues or interface design. Examples of recent titles are "Paying Attention to Adult Learners Online: The Pedagogy and Politics of Community," "Designing Efficiencies: The Parallel Narratives of Distance Education and Composition Studies," and "Synchronous Online Conference-based Instruction: A Study of Whiteboard Interactions and Student Writing." In keeping with the journal's charge, the editors also maintain an excellent web site that includes not only a complete archive but also supplementary materials and discussions, including blogs on various issues. Any academic library that serves a school of education or writing programs should purchase this title.

3760. *Journalism and Mass Communication Educator.* Formerly: *Journalism Educator.* [ISSN: 1077-6958] 1944. q. USD 90 (Individuals, USD 55; USD 25 newsstand/cover). Ed(s): Jeremy Cohen. Association for Education in Journalism and Mass Communication, 234 Outlet Pointe Blvd Ste A, Columbia, SC 29210-5667; http://www.aejmc.org. Illus., index, adv. Sample. Refereed. Circ: 2500. Vol. ends: Winter. Microform: CIS; PQC. Online: EBSCO Publishing, EBSCO Host; OCLC Online Computer Library Center, Inc.; ProQuest LLC (Ann Arbor); H.W. Wilson. *Indexed:* ABIn, CommAb, EAA, EduInd. *Bk. rev.:* 10-12, 250-500 words. *Aud.:* Ac.

This quarterly focuses on issues of interest to the faculty of communication and journalism programs. Each issue includes research articles, some recent titles of which include "What British Journalism Students Think about Ethics and Journalism," "Examining the Student Newspaper: An Opporutnity to Teach Research Methods," and "Can Scholarly Associations Be Heard Beyond the Academy?" There are also some focused book reviews, often following a theme. Recommended for academic libraries that serve communications and journalism programs.

3761. *The Writing Center Journal.* [ISSN: 0889-6143] 1979. 2x/yr. USD 35 (Individuals, USD 25 includes membership). Ed(s): Beth Boquet, Neal Lerner. International Writing Centers Association, c/o Neal Lerner, Massachusetts Institute of Technology, Writing/Humanistic Studies, Rm 14E-303, Cambridge, MA 02139; nlerner@mit.edu; http://www.writingcenters.org. Adv. Refereed. Circ: 800. *Indexed:* MLA-IB. *Bk. rev.:* 2, 1,200-1,500 words. *Aud.:* Ac.

The Writing Center Journal is the organ publication for the National Writing Centers Association. Thus, its articles address a range of pedagogical, administrative, and association issues. It is fairly particular in its content, but as educators increasingly complain about the quality of student writing, increasing attention should be given to such publications. There is an online index at the association's web site. Some recent articles include "The Idea(s)of an Online Writing Center: In Search of a Conceptual Model" and "Queering the Writing Center." A useful journal for institutions that support writing centers and communities of writers.

■ LABOR AND INDUSTRIAL RELATIONS

See also Business; Disabilities; Economics; and Occupations and Careers sections.

Terence K. Huwe, Director of Library and Information Resources, Institute of Industrial Relations, University of California, Berkeley, 2521 Channing Way, #5555, Berkeley, CA 94720-5555; thuwe@library.berkeley.edu

Lincoln Cushing, Cataloger, Bancroft Library, University of California, Berkeley, 2121 Allston Way, Berkeley, 94720-6000; lcushing@ library.berkeley.edu

Introduction

The traditional name for this discipline, *industrial relations,* conjures up images of the industrial revolution and assembly lines. Yet there are few areas that are more vibrant and interdisciplinary than the study of labor, work, and employment. Labor and industrial relations attracts a large roster of sociologists, economists, business professors, city planners, demographers, anthropologists, engineers (studying occupational safety), public health professors, and historians, simply because work touches most areas of society.

Regardless of how the study of work is named, there is a single common denominator that unites the various approaches: the "employment relationship." The employment relationship is the social (and legal) contract that binds together firms of all sorts and their employees. Labor and industrial relations continues to encompass the study of this pivotal relationship in society, and is enjoying a revival of interest. Particularly since World War II, the workforce has been regarded as a strategic resource, by nations and by corporate firms, and thus the employment relationship attracts much attention from many types of specialists.

Because work touches upon so many related issues, such as immigration, family life, industrial production, and so on, it is tempting to list a very broad range of journals in this section; it is not difficult to find quality research in many surprising places. But despite the growth in the body of literature where articles about work and working life may be found, we have listed only the most central publications here, leaving other intellectual domains, such as migration studies, demographics, and political science, to complement our coverage.

The most important trends in industrial relations are often front-page news. "Globalization" continues to be felt first as an employment issue, with job security, job growth, and protectionism driving international debate. Recent years have seen the emergence of a new and significant trend, "offshoring," which involves the wholesale relocation of job functions to new nations. Yet it is important for the serious researcher to evaluate many perspectives when analyzing such "hot" trends; for example, during 2006, researchers at Case Western University and at the University of California, Berkeley, found that many U.S. companies actually sent work functions to other U.S. firms, not necessarily to other nations. At the same time, experiments in offshoring, both among high-technology firms and heavy industry (such as automobile manufacturing) undergo constant change, and are subject to intangible costs, such as shifting employee travel patterns, varying levels of language fluency, and communications challenges among highly trained engineers working in multiple nations. Offshoring is an excellent example of how a comprehensive information search in labor and industrial relations takes the researcher on a far-reaching journey.

The U.S. labor movement has not been inactive during these turbulent times, and industrial relations literature reflects not only academic interests, but applied and pragmatic agendas as well. American unionists have come to recognize that U.S. employment issues are linked to international forces in the global economy, and they now spend considerable effort reaching out both to new immigrants and to unionists abroad. The overall percentage of unionized workers in the United States has been steadily dropping for years, and labor has been trying new and daring moves to turn the trend around. These include organizing new immigrants, considering "associate membership" for non-union workers, and even the formation of breakaway coalitions within the labor movement. In 2005, a consortium of unions led by the Service Employees International Union (SEIU) formed a coalition called *Change to Win*, with the specific goal of organizing workers, adding new members, and embracing a proactive role within politics and society. *Change to Win* is a new entrant on the political scene, and it remains to be seen whether its long-term prospects will keep it at a distance from the AFL-CIO.

The literature of industrial relations remains stable at its core, while new entrants covering labor and industrial relations often span more than one field, and may even be more properly placed in another discipline (such as migration studies). Cornell's *Industrial and Labor Relations Review* and Berkeley's

Industrial Relations: a journal of economy and society continue in the top two spots as the most prestigious places to publish peer-reviewed literature. *New Labor Forum* (founded in 1997) and *Working USA* take a more populist approach, tackling tough issues in "plain English," challenging the reader to look at everyday working life with new eyes. *Daily Labor Report,* published by the Bureau of National Affairs, is a key practitioner's tool for labor lawyers and human resources professionals. The labor movement has also embraced the Internet, with substantive, content-rich web sites proliferating. In addition, unions now use the Internet as an organizing tool just as political groups have done in recent years.

Collaboration between social movements is another axis on which the area of industrial relations is currently turning. Unions are now very likely to explore ways to partner with nonprofit organizations that provide basic services to new immigrants. They also form coalitions with environmental and public health advocacy groups with an interest in workplace safety. This trend toward broad coalitions is a calculated response to a long, difficult period for unions. "Free market" proponents argue that labor market institutions should be free to evolve without organized labor's input, and many policymakers have embraced this stance. Other pundits argue that the current climate is hostile to organized labor, and that U.S. labor laws have tilted too far in favor of employers.

As a result of the dynamic conditions facing the employment sector and academic research about it, literature searchers are best served by a three-pronged approach in their discovery process. The most effective searches encompass (1) journals; (2) union publications, social advocacy publications, and the general press; and (3) open-web publications from a wide variety of nongovernmental organizations. The latter includes groups like Common Cause, the Economic Policy Institute, LabourStart, and the Brookings Institution, to name a few. In addition, online services such as Alternet and LabourStart cover news that mainstream media do not, and so the web is now rich with historical research about recent employment issues.

Labor and industrial relations are heavily influenced by the law, and employment cases are litigated under the courts and a large number of agencies such as the Equal Employment Opportunity Commission, the National Labor Relations Board, etc. Consequently, there are many high-quality legal publications that are aimed at academics and practitioners. These include *Labor Law Journal, Labor Notes, Employee Benefits Journal,* and *Daily Labor Report.* LaborNet and WorkIndex are very good starting points for a web search. The majority of these titles are available online, although "moving walls" will apply in resources like JSTOR and other vendors with licensing strictures. Many larger aggregators of digital resources, themselves a rapidly evolving breed, offer comprehensive access to the literature of industrial relations.

Finally, the maturation of government information has made some statistics about the workforce much easier to retrieve. The U.S. Bureau of Labor Statistics (www.bls.gov) has paid close attention to its web site, constantly improving it. Search engines on the site are very effective in pinpointing hard-to-find statistics (such as the monthly employment turnover rate). Unionstats.com (www.union-stats.com) has vastly eased the challenge of building a table of data on the workforce, and thus we cite this web service here, under Electronic Sources.

Many factors will govern your library's selection of a vendor, and this core list of titles will serve as a quality test. At the same time, more and more libraries provide finding tools such as web "pathfinders," and the web sites referenced here will lead to the best sources of quality information on the open web.

Although the following two web sites cannot be classified as journals, they are included and described here because they can be very helpful in locating hard-to-find statistics.

UNIONSTATS.COM (http://www.unionstats.com) is the brainchild of two labor relations professors. On an annual basis, they extract union membership information and other data from the Bureau of the Census Current Population Survey. Their Union Membership and Coverage Database provides information on private and public sector union membership, coverage, and density estimates. They employ the U.S. Bureau of Labor Statistics (BLS) methodology, which means that the data found here conforms to the broad standards BLS has championed for many years. The web site provides economy-wide estimates beginning in 1973, and estimates by state, detailed industry, and detailed occupation begin in 1983; estimates by metropolitan statistical region begin in 1986.

UNITED STATES BUREAU OF LABOR STATISTICS. The U.S. Bureau of Labor Statistics (www.bls.gov) has paid close attention to its web site, constantly improving it. Its search help features are particularly well written and ease the retrieval process for statistics (such as the monthly employment turnover rate). The bureau publishes dozens of important news releases and reports, ranging from the Consumer Price Index to the lengthy analyses of the U.S. workforce. Although most government information web sites have improved vastly in the past few years, the BLS site is a standout that will greatly ease the researcher's challenge in finding key data elements about employment.

Basic Periodicals

Hs: *Bulletin of Labour Statistics;* Ga: *America at Work, LaborNet, Labor's Heritage, U.S. Bureau of Labor Statistics. Monthly Labor Review;* Ac: *Bulletin of Labour Statistics, Industrial and Labor Relations Review, Labor History, LaborNet, Workindex, World of Work;* Sa: *Benefits Quarterly, Employee Benefits Journal, Employee Relations Law Journal, Japan Labour Bulletin.*

Basic Abstracts and Indexes

ABI/INFORM, America: History and Life, Business Periodicals Index, PAIS, Econlit, EBSCO Expanded Academic ASAP, Sociological Abstracts, Social Sciences Index.

Academy of Management Journal. See Management, Administration, and Human Resources/General section.

3762. *America at Work.* Formerly (until 1996): *A F L - C I O News.* [ISSN: 1091-594X] 1955. m. Members, USD 14.95. Ed(s): Tula Connell, Tula Cornell. American Federation of Labor - Congress of Industrial Organizations, Public Affairs Department, 815 16th St, NW, Washington, DC 20006; atwork@aflcio.org; http://www.aflcio.org/. Illus. Circ: 55000. Vol. ends: Dec. *Indexed:* MCR. *Bk. rev.:* Occasional, short. *Aud.:* Ga, Ac, Sa.

The successor to the long-term newsletter of the AFL-CIO, *AFL-CIO News,* this publication features short news pieces that reflect the federation's social and political platforms. As an official AFL-CIO publication, it focuses primarily on U.S. labor issues, but it now also covers global labor news. In recent years, more attention has been given not only to workplace issues, but also to family issues such as child care, family leave, and careers. The editors describe their mission as "creating change for working families with ideas, info, and ammo." This publication is suitable as a general labor news source, but it is also useful for libraries with patrons from the labor movement and the related fields of business and economics.

The American Economic Review. See Economics section.

3763. *The American Economic Review (Print Edition).* Formed by the 1911 merger of: *American Economic Association Quarterly; Economic Bulletin.* [ISSN: 0002-8282] 1911. 5x/yr. USD 270. Ed(s): Ben S Bernanke. American Economic Association, 2014 Broadway, Ste 305, Nashville, TN 37203; aeainfo@ctrvax.vanderbilt.edu; http://www.vanderbilt.edu/AEA/. Illus., index, adv. Refereed. Circ:

27000. Vol. ends: Dec. Microform: MIM; PMC; PQC. Online: EBSCO Publishing, EBSCO Host; Gale; IngentaConnect; JSTOR (Web-based Journal Archive); OCLC Online Computer Library Center, Inc.; ProQuest LLC (Ann Arbor). *Indexed:* ABIn, ABS&EES, ATI, AgeL, Agr, AmH&L, ArtHuCI, BAS, BLI, BPI, BRD, BRI, CBRI, EnvAb, ExcerpMed, HistAb, IBR, IBSS, IBZ, IPSA, JEL, LRI, PAIS, RI-1, RRTA, RiskAb, SSCI, SWA, WAE&RSA. *Aud.:* Ac.

This is the scholarly journal of the American Economic Association (AEA), laden with high-level mathematics and statistical models. Though not easily accessible to a lay audience, a sizable portion of the content covers subject matter that affects labor and industrial relations. One issue per year is devoted to papers and proceedings of the annual AEA meeting, while additional volumes contain both full articles and shorter papers. Recent topics include "The Evolution of Managerial Expertise: How Corporate Culture Can Run Amok," "Do Technological Improvements in the Manufacturing Sector Raise or Lower Employment?" and "Do Labor Issues Matter in the Determination of U.S. Trade Policy? An Empirical Reevaluation."

3764. *Benefits Quarterly.* [ISSN: 8756-1263] 1985. q. USD 100; CND 140. Ed(s): Jack L Vanderhei. International Society of Certified Employee Benefit Specialists, Inc., 18700 W. Bluemound Rd., PO Box 209, Brookfield, WI 53008-0209; iscebs@ifebp.org. Illus., index, adv. Sample. Circ: 17000. Vol. ends: Dec. Online: EBSCO Publishing, EBSCO Host; Northern Light Technology, Inc.; OCLC Online Computer Library Center, Inc.; ProQuest LLC (Ann Arbor). *Indexed:* ABIn, AgeL, PAIS. *Bk. rev.:* 6-8, 200-500 words. *Aud.:* Sa.

This journal aims to provide a full-service news resource for all practitioners and students studying benefits and compensation. Articles offer a range of in-depth analyses of employee benefits issues, with effective "pull quotes" and formatting for effective quick scanning. Articles explore breaking trends and new developments and frequently include pragmatic case studies or strategic suggestions for practitioners. The editors also analyze legislative developments and court rulings that effect compensation issues. The column "Review of Current Literature" offers readers a handy guide to new articles that appear in other publications.

3765. *Berkeley Journal of Employment and Labor Law: a continuation of industrial relations law journal.* Formerly (until 1993): *Industrial Relations Law Journal.* [ISSN: 1067-7666] 1976. biennial. USD 47 (Individuals, USD 36). Ed(s): Bridget Smith, Heather Horne. University of California at Berkeley, School of Law, 313 Boalt Hall, Boalt Hall School of Law University of California, Berkeley, CA 94720-7200; kabrams@law.berkeley.edu; http://www.law.berkeley.edu. Illus., index, adv. Sample. Refereed. Circ: 650 Paid. Vol. ends: Dec. Microform: WSH; PQC. Online: EBSCO Publishing, EBSCO Host; Florida Center for Library Automation; William S. Hein & Co., Inc.; LexisNexis. Reprint: WSH. *Indexed:* ABIn, CJA, CLI, ILP, LRI, PAIS, PMA, SSCI. *Bk. rev.:* Various number and length. *Aud.:* Ac, Sa.

This law review has built a reputation for pragmatic writing that is aimed at practicing attorneys who may not be employment law specialists but need quality information on the law, and also at the educated citizen-researcher who is trying to find out more about labor law. Articles cover all aspects of labor law, including "discrimination, traditional labor law, the public sector, international and comparative labor law, benefits, and wrongful termination." The student editors make an effort to address issues in a balanced fashion, with both management and labor perspectives taken into consideration. The journal provides a useful analysis of recent legal developments, a fact that is helpful as a parallel resource to the articles, which often focus on long-term effects of cases that have set legal precedents. Some issues deal with a single topic, such as the impact of NAFTA. The editors survey labor and employment literature and provide abstracts of important articles in other journals, features that further accentuate the journal's role as a key finding tool for developments in employment and labor law.

3766. *British Journal of Industrial Relations.* [ISSN: 0007-1080] 1963. q. GBP 332 print & online eds. Ed(s): Edmund Heery. Blackwell Publishing Ltd., 9600 Garsington Rd, Oxford, OX4 2ZG, United Kingdom; customerservices@blackwellpublishing.com; http://www.blackwellpublishing.com. Illus., index, adv. Refereed. Circ:

2000. Vol. ends: Dec. Online: Blackwell Synergy; EBSCO Publishing, EBSCO Host; Gale; IngentaConnect; OCLC Online Computer Library Center, Inc.; OhioLINK; SwetsWise Online Content. Reprint: PSC. *Indexed:* ABIn, ApEcolAb, ArtHuCI, BAS, BPI, BrHumI, EI, ErgAb, FR, H&SSA, HRA, IBR, IBSS, IBZ, IPSA, JEL, PAIS, PMA, PSA, RiskAb, SSA, SSCI, SociolAb. *Aud.:* Ac, Sa.

This journal addresses a broad spectrum of trends in the field of industrial relations and has changed with the times to reflect the evolving relationship of labor relations. Its articles balance empirical studies and theoretical issues, reflecting the fact that the field of industrial relations is composed of many academic disciplines, chiefly economics, business, and sociology. The editors argue that traditional styles of collective bargaining and trade unions as change agents now compete with "new forms of management, new methods of pay determination, and changes in government policies," and they have broadened the journal's focus in response. Each issue has four or five substantive articles and several shorter features. Most authors provide a myriad of tables and charts to support their arguments. This journal is aimed at academics who have an awareness of the deeper issues in industrial relations, and therefore it may not be easily accessible to the casual reader.

3767. *Bulletin of Labour Statistics: supplementing the annual data presented in the Year Book of Labour Statistics.* [ISSN: 0007-4950] 1965. 4x/yr. CHF 105; USD 84. I L O Publications, PO Box 6, Geneva, 1211, Switzerland. Illus., index. Vol. ends: No. 4. *Indexed:* PAIS. *Aud.:* Ac, Sa.

A tripartite agency of the United Nations, the International Labour Organization (ILO) is governed by a board comprised of management, labor, and government. The ILO is an important source of information about global labor trends, and this bulletin is one of its most important publications. It provides country-level data on employment, unemployment, hours of work, wages, and the consumer price index, and it is one of the few publications that offer meaningful international comparisons of various national workforce issues. Coverage of Eastern European and the former Soviet republics has increased its value as a ready-reference tool for statistics seekers. Each issue features a couple of in-depth articles about statistical data issues, and collection figures largely in the discussion, as most nations collect data by various means. The ILO publishes articles in English, French, and Spanish. This journal is an essential title for academic collections and large public libraries.

3768. *Daily Labor Report.* Former titles: *Daily Economic Reports on Current Trends Affecting Management and Labor; Washington Daily Reporter: Labor Section; Washington Daily Reporter System: Daily Labor Report.* [ISSN: 0418-2693] 1941. d. USD 9264 United States. Ed(s): Susan J Sala. The Bureau of National Affairs, Inc., 1231 25th St, NW, Washington, DC 20037; customercare@bna.com; http://www.bna.com/. Online: Pub.; Thomson West. *Bk. rev.:* short listings of new publications. *Aud.:* Ac, Sa.

The *Daily Labor Report* is published by the Bureau of National Affairs, Inc., a dominant player in labor law publishing. It is published every working day of the year, and is designed to provide labor lawyers, unionists, and government officials with all they need to know about the world of work. It is broken into several separately paginated sections (e.g., A1, B1, C1, etc.) that cover distinct areas of news. These include headlines, legal developments, regulatory developments, new reports and publications of interest, and so on. The editorial direction of this journal has been very active and customer-focused, and as a result, this is a "must have" for labor lawyers. Moreover, it covers the entire United States, with detailed information from the state and local scenes around the country. The *DLR* often publishes the full text of court cases, and when it references groundbreaking new studies that are published by think tanks, it includes URLs, telephone numbers, and names of individuals to contact. Subscriptions include print-only and print-plus-digital, and rates are high, as one expects in the legal market. This publication is essential for lawyers and practitioners, but would also make a very useful addition to a central reference collection.

3769. *Dispute Resolution Journal.* Formerly (until 1993): *Arbitration Journal.* [ISSN: 1074-8105] 1937. q. USD 150. Ed(s): Susan Zuckerman. American Arbitration Association, 1633 Broadway, 10th Fl, New York, NY 10019; http://www.adr.org/. Illus., index, adv. Circ: 3000. Vol. ends:

Dec. Microform: PQC. Online: EBSCO Publishing, EBSCO Host; Northern Light Technology, Inc.; OCLC Online Computer Library Center, Inc.; ProQuest LLC (Ann Arbor); H.W. Wilson. *Indexed:* ABIn, AmH&L, BPI, CLI, HistAb, ILP, LRI, PMA, RiskAb, SSCI. *Aud.:* Ga, Ac, Sa.

Alternative dispute resolution (ADR) has emerged as a viable but contested add-on to the time-honored tradition of going to court. The workplace generates a hefty percentage of all lawsuits, and therefore ADR often applies to workplace litigation and arbitration. The high-quality *Dispute Resolution Journal* highlights new developments in the field and creative strategies for keeping litigants out of court. Articles explore negotiation, mediation, final offer arbitration, and other alternatives to impasse. The journal also explores industrial trends, including developments in construction, technology, commerce, and health care. Since federal law allows for public employees to utilize alternative dispute resolution, public sector issues figure highly in the article mix. Not all contributors are attorneys; expert authors hail from international relations, business, finance, construction, insurance, and technology. The articles are incisive and provide good footnotes that facilitate further research. This title would be an important addition for law libraries, business libraries, and general social science collections.

3770. *Economic and Industrial Democracy: an international journal.* [ISSN: 0143-831X] 1980. q. GBP 462. Ed(s): Jan Ottosson, Lars Magnusson. Sage Publications Ltd., 1 Oliver's Yard, 55 City Rd, London, EC1 1SP, United Kingdom; info@sagepub.co.uk; http://www.sagepub.co.uk. Adv. Refereed. Reprint: PSC. *Indexed:* ABIn, BAS, HRA, IBR, IBSS, IBZ, IPSA, JEL, PMA, PRA, PSA, SSA, SSCI, SWA, SociolAb, V&AA. *Bk. rev.:* Various number and length. *Aud.:* Ga, Ac.

Although this journal is an excellent source of material on European labor issues, its scope is truly international and includes insightful views on U.S. conditions. The prefatory material for each paper includes not only an abstract but a set of keywords as well, facilitating a handy, quick item-level guide (curiously, this feature is absent in the online version). Each issue includes at least one book review. Recent articles include "Employee Ownership and Profit Sharing as Positive Factors in the Reform of Chinese State-Owned Enterprises," "Do Union Mergers Affect the Members? Short- and Long-term Effects on Attitudes and Behaviour," and "Agreements between Labour Unions and Employers' Associations as a Strategy for the Prevention of Repetitive Strain Injury."

3771. *Employee Benefit Plan Review.* Incorporates (in 2002): *Compensation & Benefits Report.* [ISSN: 0013-6808] 1946. m. USD 255. Ed(s): Steve Huth. Aspen Publishers, Inc., 111 Eighth Ave., 7th Fl, New York, NY 10011; customer.service@aspenpubl.com; http://www.aspenpublishers.com. Illus., index. Circ: 2100 Paid. Vol. ends: Jun. Microform: PQC. Online: EBSCO Publishing, EBSCO Host; Northern Light Technology, Inc.; OCLC Online Computer Library Center, Inc.; ProQuest LLC (Ann Arbor). *Indexed:* ABIn, AgeL, BPI, CINAHL, LRI. *Aud.:* Ga, Ac, Sa.

This publication is top-ranked in its area of specialization, and is written both for specialists and generalists. Academics can find useful real-world case studies in its pages, and human resources practitioners can rely upon it to stay current with employee benefits developments. In addition to a strong focus on current practice, the editors include a healthy balance of articles that address new and emerging trends that may not yet have hit the workplace. Issues are organized by topic, and include sections on laws, regulations, and new practices. Short news items serve as ready-reference guides to new developments and news, which can be very important for practitioners who must make sure their firms are compliant with the rapidly changing laws and regulations that govern business. Legal news is aimed at the non-lawyer, but does not oversimplify the nature of the legal issues to a fault. Most contributors are human resources professionals, with some academics contributing "think" pieces now and then. This title is crucial for labor libraries and business and law libraries, but it would also be useful for central reference collections, particularly when county law libraries are not located nearby.

3772. *Employee Benefits Journal.* [ISSN: 0361-4050] 1975. q. USD 80. Ed(s): Mary Jo Brzezinski. International Foundation of Employee Benefit Plans, 18700 W Bluemound Rd, Box 69, Brookfield, WI 53008-0069; books@ifebp.org; http://www.ifebp.org. Illus., index, adv. Circ: 36000. Vol. ends: Dec. *Indexed:* ABIn, AgeL, BPI. *Bk. rev.:* Brief notes. *Aud.:* Ga, Ac, Sa.

This journal offers in-depth articles for practitioners who must stay current with benefits issues and trends. It is pragmatic in tone and focuses on real-world scenarios. Authors analyze trends and major events such as new legislation, but they also report on general news from the field. Some articles are technical in their exploration of increasingly complex issues. Clear writing and good use of graphics make the material as accessible and comprehensible to nonexpert readers as to human resources professionals. Legal aspects of benefits programs are expertly analyzed. The editors also provide a "Literature Review" column, with brief annotations on recent articles and books in the field. This makes a balanced presentation, useful both to academics and practitioners. It would be a worthy addition to large collections that cover labor relations.

3773. *Employee Relations Law Journal.* [ISSN: 0098-8898] 1975. q. USD 385. Ed(s): William Kilberg, Amy McLoughlin. Aspen Publishers, Inc., 111 Eighth Ave., 7th Fl, New York, NY 10011; customer.service@ aspenpubl.com; http://www.aspenpublishers.com. Illus., index. Vol. ends: Spring. Microform: WSH; PMC; PQC. Online: The Dialog Corporation; EBSCO Publishing, EBSCO Host; Florida Center for Library Automation; Gale; Northern Light Technology, Inc.; OCLC Online Computer Library Center, Inc.; ProQuest LLC (Ann Arbor). *Indexed:* ABIn, AgeL, BLI, BPI, CLI, ILP, LRI, PAIS, PMA, SFSA, SSCI. *Aud.:* Ac, Sa.

This journal targets high-level human resources managers, in-house counsel, and employment law specialists, and offers a comprehensive means for them to keep up with the rapid pace of change in workplace issues. Authors strike an analytical and practical note without sinking too far into technical discourse. Well-known professionals contribute signed, short "Literature Review" essays. The journal covers a wide range of "hot" labor issues, including personnel management techniques, legal compliance, and court cases. Recent articles address such topics as the ADA, family medical leave, sexual harassment, age discrimination, and alternative dispute resolution. This is the sort of publication that could be consulted for quick reading and "brushing up," while it offers some real substance for those moments when time allows a more thoughtful perusal. This journal is a top choice for selectors who must make difficult decisions with limited funds.

3774. *European Journal of Industrial Relations.* [ISSN: 0959-6801] 1995. q. GBP 464. Ed(s): Richard Hyman. Sage Publications Ltd., 1 Oliver's Yard, 55 City Rd, London, EC1 1SP, United Kingdom; info@sagepub.co.uk; http://www.sagepub.co.uk. Adv. Refereed. Circ: 900. Reprint: PSC. *Indexed:* HRA, IBSS, JEL, PRA, PSA, RiskAb, SSA, SSCI, SociolAb, V&AA. *Bk. rev.:* Occasional. *Aud.:* Ac.

Scholarly, yet accessible, this journal carries substantive articles on contemporary issues affecting European labor. Recent articles include "The Industrial Determinants of Transnational Solidarity: Global Interunion Politics in Three Sectors," "Pay Developments in Britain and Germany: Collective Bargaining, 'Benchmarking' and 'Mimetic Wages,' and Labour Mobility in Construction." Although there is no conventional book review section, they do carry an occasional "Books Received" section, and from time to time a noteworthy text will get an in-depth review.

3775. *Government Employee Relations Report.* [ISSN: 0017-260X] 1963. w. USD 1479. Ed(s): James F Fitzpatrick, Anthony A Harris. The Bureau of National Affairs, Inc., 1231 25th St, NW, Washington, DC 20037; customercare@bna.com; http://www.bna.com/. Online: Pub.; Thomson West. *Bk. rev.:* Various number and length. *Aud.:* Ac, Sa.

Government Employee Relations Report, another publication of the Bureau of National Affairs, Inc., offers one-stop news and qualitative and quantitative information for government unions and management. It is separately paginated (A1, B1, C1, etc.) by topics, which include legal news, federal news, collective bargaining, feature reports, and more. The editors cover all levels of government, so this publication is a great source for finding out what's happening at the state and local levels in faraway districts. Reporting is balanced between labor and management perspectives. Government information collections, public policy libraries, and law libraries would all benefit from this publication.

3776. *Indian Journal of Industrial Relations.* [ISSN: 0019-5286] 1964. q. INR 600 domestic; USD 100 foreign. Ed(s): Rama J Joshi. Shri Ram Centre for Industrial Relations and Human Resources, 4 Safdar Hashmi Marg, New Delhi, 110 001, India; sricir@yahoo.co.in; http://srcirhr.com. Refereed. Circ: 865 Paid. *Indexed:* BAS, H&SSA, IBSS, PMA, RRTA, SSCI, WAE&RSA. *Bk. rev.:* Various number and length. *Aud.:* Ac, Sa.

A preeminent publishing vehicle for South Asian academics who study the work world, this journal encapsulates the latest research about the workplace in the world's most populous democracy. It includes full-length articles focusing on topics like best practices, collective bargaining, and management strategies, and also provides cases studies and book reviews. The scholarship is solid, and provides a closer look at the conditions of work in the developing world.

3777. *Industrial and Labor Relations Review.* [ISSN: 0019-7939] 1947. q. USD 52 (Individuals, USD 32; Students, USD 16). Ed(s): Tove Hammer. Cornell University, New York State School of Industrial and Labor Relations, 158 Ives Hall, Ithaca, NY 14853-3901; blk5@cornell.edu; http://www.ilr.cornell.edu/depts/ilrrev/. Illus., index, adv. Refereed. Circ: 2500. Vol. ends: Jul. Microform: WSH; PQC. Online: Chadwyck-Healey Inc.; The Dialog Corporation; EBSCO Publishing, EBSCO Host; Florida Center for Library Automation; Gale; JSTOR (Web-based Journal Archive); LexisNexis; OCLC Online Computer Library Center, Inc.; ProQuest K-12 Learning Solutions; ProQuest LLC (Ann Arbor); Thomson West; H.W. Wilson. Reprint: WSH. *Indexed:* ABCPolSci, ABIn, ABS&EES, ASG, AgeL, AmH&L, ArtHuCI, BAS, BPI, BRD, BRI, CBRI, CJA, CLI, CWI, EAA, HRA, HistAb, IBR, IBSS, IBZ, ILP, IPSA, JEL, LRI, PAIS, PMA, PRA, PSA, SSA, SSCI, SUSA, SociolAb, V&AA, WSA. *Bk. rev.:* Various number and length. *Aud.:* Ac, Sa.

This multidisciplinary journal is one of the preeminent scholarly publications in the field of industrial relations. Its empirical studies reflect all aspects of industrial relations, and researchers can rely upon it to guide them to the most important issues of the day. Articles are quantitative, dense, and statistical, which means that a literature search could begin here and move outwards to other journal titles. The content is international in scope. Articles reflect "all aspects of the employment relationship, including collective bargaining, labor law, labor markets, social security and protective labor legislation, management and personnel, human resources, worker participation, workplace health and safety, organizational behavior, comparative industrial relations, and labor history." As is the case with the most scholarly publications in this field, readers will require a commanding knowledge of statistics and economic theory to follow many of the offerings. The book review section offers in-depth, subject-based literature reviews that track the latest publications in the field. This scholarly journal is required for serious academic collections.

3778. *Industrial Relations: a journal of economy and society.* [ISSN: 0019-8676] 1961. q. GBP 221 print & online eds. Ed(s): Daniel J B Mitchell, Trond Petersen. Blackwell Publishing, Inc., Commerce Place, 350 Main St, Malden, MA 02148; customerservices@ blackwellpublishing.com; http://www.blackwellpublishing.com. Illus., index, adv. Refereed. Circ: 2300. Vol. ends: Fall. Microform: PQC. Online: Blackwell Synergy; EBSCO Publishing, EBSCO Host; Gale; IngentaConnect; OCLC Online Computer Library Center, Inc.; OhioLINK; SwetsWise Online Content. Reprint: PSC. *Indexed:* ABIn, AgeL, AltPI, ApEcolAb, BPI, CBCARef, CJA, CLI, EI, ErgAb, H&SSA, HRA, IBR, IBSS, IBZ, IPSA, JEL, LRI, PAIS, PMA, PSA, PsycInfo, RiskAb, SSA, SSCI, SWR&A, SociolAb. *Bk. rev.:* Brief notes. *Aud.:* Ac.

The substantive and wide-ranging articles in this journal deal with all aspects of employee-employer relationships. The publication leans heavily in the direction of economic analysis, and thus requires a deeper knowledge of economic principles in many cases. Many authors address the challenge of how to bring theory into practice, or explore how real-world events may be explained utilizing theory. Each issue has a column on Internet resources and a survey of recent publications. The scope of the articles is international, although most deal with American scenarios. In addition to economics, authors hail from sociology, business administration, psychology, and history. Although the authors are clearly involved in a conversation with each other and not with the average reader, the overall editorial strategy for this publication has balanced "plain English" with complex theory, and therefore readers can expect to find a substantial amount of accessible scholarship here. This journal competes with Cornell's *Industrial and Labor Relations Review* for the top slot as "most frequently cited" journal in the field of industrial relations. This is a valuable journal in the field and should be part of academic collections and large public library collections.

3779. *Industrial Worker.* [ISSN: 0019-8870] 1909. m. USD 20 (Individuals, USD 15). Ed(s): Jon Bekken. Industrial Workers of the World, PO Box 13476, Philadelphia, PA 19101-3476; http://iww.org. Illus. Circ: 4300 Paid. Vol. ends: Dec. Microform: BHP; PQC. Online: ProQuest LLC (Ann Arbor). *Indexed:* AltPI. *Aud.:* Ga, Ac.

This tabloid-style newspaper continues the cause of the Industrial Workers of the World (IWW), and it is unabashedly partisan in its editorial direction. Thus, it receives sustained attention from both labor activists and academics. As one of the most radical labor newspapers in print, it brings an important ideological perspective to any collection, whatever the politics of the region. World labor news is covered in depth, as is news from local unions in the United States. Authors are very much concerned with organizing strategies, the "strike tool," and other longtime labor strategies. Rank-and-file union members are frequent contributors, and the editor is an elected official with a two-year term.

3780. *International Labor and Working-Class History.* Formerly (until 1976): *European Labor and Working Class History Newsletter.* [ISSN: 0147-5479] 1972. s-a. GBP 64. Ed(s): Peter Winn, Victoria Hattam. Cambridge University Press, The Edinburgh Bldg, Shaftesbury Rd, Cambridge, CB2 2RU, United Kingdom; journals@cambridge.org. Illus., index, adv. Refereed. Circ: 1000. *Indexed:* ABS&EES, AltPI, AmH&L, AmHI, ArtHuCI, BAS, HistAb, IBR, IBZ, LeftInd, PSA, SSA, SociolAb. *Bk. rev.:* Number varies; essay length. *Aud.:* Ac.

This journal's essays are dense and scholarly, and generally carry the ideological perspective that "doing history" requires a rethinking of how we look at history itself. The editors argue that it is crucial to "change the character of historical conversation by expanding its scope, enlarging its scope and changing its terms." They attempt to do so by exploring a common subject from a variety of viewpoints, presenting the reader with an array of data from which to draw conclusions. Topics include globalization's impact on workers' rights, social class privilege, unions, and working-class politics. Substantive articles are matched with short reports of work in progress, short features, and critical commentary on material presented in earlier issues. Book reviews are also prominently included. Special-theme issues take one topic, like class struggle throughout history, and provide deep analysis. The journal is globally focused, and significantly, it strives to include the role of family work (such as work performed in the home or away from the traditional workplace), in recognition of the important role of women and underage workers in various societies.

3781. *International Labour Review.* [ISSN: 0020-7780] 1921. q. USD 268 print & onlineeds. Blackwell Publishing Ltd., 9600 Garsington Rd, Oxford, OX4 2ZG, United Kingdom; customerservices@ blackwellpublishing.com; http://www.blackwellpublishing.com. Illus., index, adv. Refereed. Vol. ends: Nov/Dec. Microform: CIS; PMC; PQC. Online: EBSCO Publishing, EBSCO Host; Florida Center for Library Automation; Gale; William S. Hein & Co., Inc.; IngentaConnect; Northern Light Technology, Inc.; OCLC Online Computer Library Center, Inc.; ProQuest LLC (Ann Arbor); SwetsWise Online Content; H.W. Wilson. Reprint: WSH. *Indexed:* ABIn, ASG, ASSIA, AgeL, BAS, BPI, BRI, CABA, CBRI, EIP, ErgAb, FutSurv, HRA, HortAb, IBR, IBSS, IBZ, JEL, MCR, PAIS, PMA, PRA, PSA, RRTA, RiskAb, SFSA, SSA, SSCI, SWA, SociolAb, V&AA, WAE&RSA. *Bk. rev.:* Various number and length. *Aud.:* Ac, Sa.

The International Labour Organization (ILO) is an important publisher that addresses international issues in industrial relations and the trade union movement. The ILO's *Review* focuses heavily on developing countries that do not receive much attention from U.S.- and European-based journals. Contributors include academics, labor leaders, government officials, nongovernmental organization (NGO) leaders, and technical experts. The ILO tracks many

controversial issues such as the worldwide incidence of child labor, and this publication often is the best place to start a search on issues that span national boundaries. The editors publish a literature review, which is unusual in that it provides a means to find international literature. Tables of contents and article abstracts are online from 1996 to the present, and subscribers to the print edition have full online access as well.

3782. *Japan Labour Bulletin.* [ISSN: 0021-4469] 1962. m. JPY 4320 domestic. Ed(s): H. Sakashita. Japan Institute of Labour, Shinjuku Monolith, P.O. Box 7040, Tokyo, 163-0926, Japan; http://www.jil.go.jp. Illus., index. Circ: 3100. Vol. ends: Dec. *Aud.:* Ac, Sa.

Published by the Japan Institute of Labour, a division of the Japanese Ministry of Labour, this concise English-language newsletter covers all aspects of working life in Japan. Its features are short and well written, and report on major topics like labor economy, labor policy, working conditions, and trends in industrial relations. Many issues take one topic and provide an in-depth analysis of it. Recent special topics include labor law and social policy, young workers, social security, and human resource developments. This journal stands alone as the "must have" title for Japanese workplace issues, and you will find it on the shelf in every labor library.

3783. *Journal of Collective Negotiations.* Formerly (until 2006): *Journal of Collective Negotiations in the Public Sector.* 1971. q. USD 324. Ed(s): David A Dilts. Baywood Publishing Co., Inc., 26 Austin Ave, PO Box 337, Amityville, NY 11701-0337; info@baywood.com; http://www.baywood.com. Illus., index, adv. Sample. Refereed. Vol. ends: Dec. *Indexed:* ABIn, BPI, CJA, CLI, EAA, HRA, LRI, PAIS, PMA, PRA, PSA, SSCI. *Aud.:* Ac, Sa.

Public-sector unions are the fastest growing segment of the labor movement, and the interplay between unionized workers and shrinking government budgets means that this area is the frequent subject of analysis. This journal analyzes the challenges of contract negotiations, impasse resolution, strikes and lockouts, grievance issues, and contract administration. It is noteworthy that the overall editorial policy calls for the analysis of public-sector work issues in the greater context of society, legislative developments, and public opinion. Contributors include negotiators, public office holders, and academics. The tone of this journal is active and collaborative, and it seeks to provide a forum for the free exchange of ideas, as rarely happens across the bargaining table. Articles take a pragmatic tone, seeking solutions to complex problems that affect both public policy and employee morale. This is the "one-stop" source for information on public-sector labor issues, and therefore is a necessary addition for any labor or law library. Subscribers have online access to full texts of the entire contents of the journal.

Journal of Economic Perspectives. See Economics section.

3784. *Journal of Human Resources: education, manpower and welfare economics.* [ISSN: 0022-166X] 1966. q. USD 239 print & online eds. (Individuals, USD 70 print & online eds.). Ed(s): William N. Evans. University of Wisconsin Press, Journal Division, 1930 Monroe St, 3rd Fl, Madison, WI 53711-2059; journals@uwpress.wisc.edu; http://www.wisc.edu/wisconsinpress/journals. Illus., index, adv. Refereed. Circ: 2000 Paid. Microform: MIM; PQC. Online: EBSCO Publishing, EBSCO Host; Florida Center for Library Automation; Gale; IngentaConnect; JSTOR (Web-based Journal Archive); OCLC Online Computer Library Center, Inc.; ProQuest LLC (Ann Arbor); H.W. Wilson. Reprint: PSC. *Indexed:* ABIn, ASG, AgeL, CINAHL, CJA, EAA, ERIC, H&SSA, HRA, IBR, IBSS, IBZ, JEL, MCR, PAIS, PMA, PRA, PSA, RiskAb, SFSA, SSA, SSCI, SWA, SWR&A, SociolAb, V&AA, WAE&RSA. *Aud.:* Ac.

This is an academic journal with a strong emphasis on data and statistical analysis. It presents excellent original research on subjects such as "The Role of Permanent Income and Demographics in Black/White Differences in Wealth," "Does Child Labor Decline with Improving Economic Status?" and "Has the Intergenerational Transmission of Economic Status Changed?" The level of methodological rigor and empirical self-critique is remarkable; a typical article,

"The Labor Market Effects of Disability Discrimination Laws," includes eight tables, one of them a 25-page table detailing relevant laws for all states. Library subscription to this journal includes access to the electronic edition available through Ingenta.

3785. *Journal of Labor Economics.* [ISSN: 0734-306X] 1983. q. USD 270 domestic; USD 291.20 Canada; USD 280 elsewhere. Ed(s): Derek A Neal. University of Chicago Press, Journals Division, PO Box 37005, Chicago, IL 60637; subscriptions@press.uchicago.edu; http://www.journals.uchicago.edu. Illus., index, adv. Refereed. Circ: 2000. Vol. ends: Oct. Microform: PQC. Online: EBSCO Publishing, EBSCO Host; Florida Center for Library Automation; Gale; JSTOR (Web-based Journal Archive); OCLC Online Computer Library Center, Inc.; ProQuest LLC (Ann Arbor). Reprint: PSC. *Indexed:* ABIn, AgeL, BPI, H&SSA, IBSS, JEL, PMA, RiskAb, SSCI. *Bk. rev.:* Various number and length. *Aud.:* Ac, Sa.

This journal's editors recognize that the interplay between the economy and social and private behavior is complex and multidisciplinary. Articles are both highly theoretical and applied, as authors explore labor market institutions (such as unions, management, and government) from a variety of perspectives. Topics cover a wide range of labor economics issues, varying from changes in the supply and demand of labor services, the distribution of income, and collective bargaining, to the impact of public-policy decisions. Not a layperson's sourcebook, this journal requires a working knowledge of economic theory. The quality of the scholarship and the diversity of the material covered make this an excellent addition to academic collections.

3786. *Journal of Labor Research.* [ISSN: 0195-3613] 1979. q. EUR 278 print & online eds. Springer New York LLC, 233 Spring St, New York, NY 10013-1578; journals@springer-ny.com; http://www.springer.com. Illus., index, adv. Refereed. Circ: 600. *Indexed:* ABIn, AgeL, CJA, CommAb, H&SSA, HRA, IBSS, JEL, PAIS, PMA, PRA, PSA, RiskAb, SFSA, SSA, SSCI, SociolAb. *Aud.:* Ac, Sa.

This top-ranked journal takes the challenge of exploring the "workplace relationship" very seriously, and offers hard-hitting articles by academics and practitioners. Authors rely heavily on economic theory and statistical analysis, and the lay reader may find this a challenge. Nonetheless, this journal is widely cited and a necessary addition to the labor library. Most issues feature a symposium that brings together several articles presenting a variety of viewpoints on a trend or new policy issue. Recent topics include nonunionized workers, welfare-to-work programs, flexible scheduling, and family leave.

3787. *Labor History.* Formerly: *Labor Historian's Bulletin.* [ISSN: 0023-656X] 1960. q. GBP 220 print & online eds. Ed(s): Gerald Friedman, Craig Phelan. Routledge, 4 Park Sq, Milton Park, Abingdon, OX14 4RN, United Kingdom; info@routledge.co.uk; http://www.routledge.co.uk. Illus., index. Refereed. Circ: 1800 Paid. Vol. ends: Fall. Online: EBSCO Publishing, EBSCO Host; Florida Center for Library Automation; Gale; IngentaConnect; Northern Light Technology, Inc.; OCLC Online Computer Library Center, Inc.; ProQuest K-12 Learning Solutions; ProQuest LLC (Ann Arbor); SwetsWise Online Content. Reprint: PSC. *Indexed:* ABIn, ABS&EES, AltPI, AmH&L, AmHI, ArtHuCI, BPI, CJA, HRA, HistAb, HumInd, IBR, IBSS, IBZ, JEL, LRI, LeftInd, PMA, PRA, PSA, RI-1, RILM, SSA, SSCI, SociolAb, V&AA. *Aud.:* Ac, Sa.

This journal publishes original research about the history of work and how it is represented in literature. It also explores the historical record of labor systems, the social production of labor, occupational culture, and folklore. Authors focus primarily on American labor, but the growing interest in transnational movements is showing up as an additional focus for the editors. This journal is the premier venue for scholars who are interested in presenting new ideas about labor history. The journal's reputation is built on its solid scholarly research and writing, yet it avoids limiting itself to a narrow focus. As the standard journal for this area of study, it belongs in large public libraries and academic collections.

3788. *Labor Law Journal: to promote sound thinking on labor law problems.* [ISSN: 0023-6586] 1949. q. USD 275; USD 42.25 newsstand/ cover per issue. C C H Inc., 2700 Lake Cook Rd, Riverwoods, IL

60015; cust_serv@cch.com; http://www.cch.com. Illus., index. Vol. ends: Dec. Microform: PQC. Online: EBSCO Publishing, EBSCO Host; OCLC Online Computer Library Center, Inc.; ProQuest LLC (Ann Arbor); H.W. Wilson. *Indexed:* ABIn, AgeL, BPI, CLI, IBR, IBZ, ILP, LRI, PAIS, RI-1, SSCI. *Aud.:* Ac, Sa.

This quarterly journal reviews the complex relationship of law, labor, management, and the economy. Their stated editorial purpose is to "promote sound thinking on labor law problems," and they do a good job of it. They offer a middle-of-the-road impartiality, with articles that are useful to lawyers and lay practitioners alike. The content is written by labor experts from management, unions, government, and academia, as well as by consumers, and it covers domestic, foreign, and international labor issues. Although legal material may often seem impenetrable to non-lawyers, the journal's text is jargon-free, and the presentation is easy on the eyes. One special feature is a "Who's What in Labor," publicizing current appointments to positions of interest to government, unions, and management. They also highlight important decisions, regulations, and news developments in the areas of labor-management relations, equal employment opportunity, job safety and health, and employment and training.

3789. *Labor Notes.* [ISSN: 0275-4452] 1979. m. USD 35 (Individuals, USD 24). Ed(s): Chris Kutalik. Labor Education & Research Project, 7435 Michigan Ave, Detroit, MI 48210; labornotes@labornotes.org; http://www.labornotes.org. Illus. Circ: 11000. *Indexed:* AltPI. *Aud.:* Ga, Ac, Sa.

Labor Notes is one of the rock-solid titles in labor news coverage, directed by the slogan "Putting the Movement Back in the Labor Movement." It has carried news and opinion about rank-and-file struggles written by participants and seasoned observers for over 25 years. Although they are heartily on the side of working people, they openly present the contradictions and nuances of the different forces involved in the struggle. The publication is quite independent, and is just as critical of errors within the major unions as it is of greedy management. Their "News Watch" column provides a quick summary of that month's events, and "Resources" is a consistent gem, highlighting new publications, videos, and conferences. As one might expect, there are also controversial op-ed pieces, guest editorials, and a lively letters section. Recent articles include "Unity, Democracy, Militancy: New Trade Union Initiative Launched In India," "SEIU Mega-Mergers in California Move Members To Organize Caucus," and "How Do Unions Defend Pensions When Most People Don't Have One?"

3790. *Labor Relations Bulletin.* Former titles (until 1994): *Discipline and Grievances. White Collar Edition;* (until 1993): *Discipline and Grievances.* [ISSN: 1080-3211] 1950. m. Ed(s): Robert Halprin. Aspen Law & Business, 1185 Ave of the Americas, 37th Fl, New York, NY 10036; customer.service@aspenpubl.com; http://www.aspenpub.com. Illus., index. Online: EBSCO Publishing, EBSCO Host; Florida Center for Library Automation; Gale. *Aud.:* Ac, Sa.

Practical advice and news for employers and union representatives bound by labor contract law. The journal's "Discipline and Grievances" section is a good example, presenting brief studies of actual cases and their decisions. Actual cases are also shared in the "Perspectives on Discipline" section. *LRB* also covers new case law and legislation pertaining to labor relations, NLRB decisions, trends, and emerging concerns in the field. Recent case studies deal with such subjects as insubordination, protected speech, overtime, absenteeism, e-mail use, and enforcement of sexual harassment policy. This title is part of EBSCO's Business Source Premier package, and is appropriate for all academic collections that support a business, labor, or industrial relations program.

3791. *Labor Studies Journal.* [ISSN: 0160-449X] 1976. q. GBP 177. Ed(s): Bruce Nissen. Sage Publications, Inc., 2455 Teller Rd, Thousand Oaks, CA 91320; info@sagepub.com; http://www.sagepub.com. Illus., adv. Refereed. Circ: 800. Vol. ends: Winter. Microform: PQC. Online: EBSCO Publishing, EBSCO Host; Florida Center for Library Automation; Gale; OCLC Online Computer Library Center, Inc.; OhioLINK; Project MUSE; SwetsWise Online Content. Reprint: PSC. *Indexed:* ABIn, ABS&EES, AmH&L, BPI, CJA, HistAb, IBR, IBZ, IPSA, LRI, PAIS, PMA, PSA, RILM, SSA, SociolAb. *Bk. rev.:* 7-12, 400-2,700 words. *Aud.:* Ac, Sa.

This is one of the rare publications that successfully bridges academia and the labor community. Hosted by West Virginia University, it is also the official journal of the United Association for Labor Education (UALE), the major national organization of practitioners in this field. Papers presented at the annual UALE conference are published in *LSJ*. It is a multidisciplinary journal that publishes material based on research about work, workers, labor organizations, labor studies, and worker education in the United States and and internationally. The content covers diverse research methods, both qualitative and quantitative. The articles are directed at a general audience, including union, university, and community-based labor educators, and labor activists and scholars from across the social sciences and humanities. Recent subjects include the relationship of local union organizing in a global economy, a critique of the AFL-CIO's new China policy, and a review of grievance procedures in unionized workplaces. There is also a dynamic "Interactive Forum" for discussion of issues about work and labor, reviews of relevant books, audio-visual and electronic materials, and an unrefereed section highlighting innovations in labor education.

3792. *Labor Watch.* bi-w. Labor Watch, http://www.zmag.org/ LaborWatch.htm. *Aud.:* Ga, Ac, Sa.

Z Magazine has been a standard of leftist labor activism since 1988: Znet is its online forum for a "community of people committed to social change." Znet's *Labor Watch* is the labor segment of this resource, offering links to the most recent Znet/Zmag labor articles. It's a very straightforward offering, posting author/title/date of the most current 30 items. Additional labor links, articles, and even a quote of the day are available on the same screen. Subscribers to *Z Magazine Online* access the full content for the previous five months' issues. The full content of older issues is available to both subscribers and nonsubscribers in the archive.

3793. *LaborNet.* d. LaborNet, http://www.labornet.org. *Aud.:* Ga, Ac, Sa.

LaborNet describes itself as a "global online communication for a democratic, independent labor movement." This site offers a lively source of news, opinions, and resources. The format lists top-level stories with just a headline (such as "SEIU 790 Members and Leaders Launch Decertification Drive," "Retraining Laid-Off Workers, but for What?" and "Comcast Sues City of Oakland over Union Ordinance Allowing Card Check") all linked directly to primary sources. Some of the material is from mainstream publications such as *The Los Angeles Times*, but in addition to independent media sources, the *LaborNet* editorial staff also writes much of the content themselves. Quick sort buttons offer latest news segregated into "U.S. News" and "World News" (with links to other *LaborNet*s in Korea, the United Kingdom, etc.). "Rank 'n File Speak" offers an excellent opinion vehicle, and also hosts links to free forums or conferences, listservs on specific labor topics that generate discussion among practitioners, and a calendar. Unfortunately, the search feature is quite weak, simply returning a list of cryptically titled hyperlinks ("063001/disfun.html") in no particular order.

3794. *Labor's Heritage.* [ISSN: 1041-5904] 1989. q. USD 24 domestic; USD 32 Canada; USD 40 elsewhere. Ed(s): Robert Reynolds. George Meany Center for Labor Studies, 10000 New Hampshire Ave, Silver Spring, MD 20903; breynolds@georgemeany.org; http://www.georgemeany.org. Illus., index. Refereed. Circ: 8000 Paid. Vol. ends: Oct. *Indexed:* AmH&L, HistAb, RILM. *Aud.:* Ga, Ac.

Labor's Heritage is the *National Geographic* of labor history publications. Its high production values, lavish use of color, large-format photographs and illustrations, and engaging text all serve to elevate the status of the field. *LH*'s parent organization, the George Meany Center for Labor Studies, is home to one of the premier labor archives in the country and is also a vital nexus of labor education (through the National Labor College), training programs, and cultural festivals. It is from this vantage point that this magazine is able to attract talented and original scholarship on such topics as Irish immigrants who built the railroads of Central Illinois, the role of the United Farm Workers union in revitalizing California farm labor organizing, the labor origins of the next women's movement, and commemoration of the Bread and Roses strike of 1912. In addition to major articles, the "News" section carries listings of exhibits, collections, research projects, conferences, and other resources in the field of labor history.

3795. *Labour Education.* [ISSN: 0378-5467] 1964. q. CHF 55; USD 44. Ed(s): Clara Foucault Mohammed. I L O Publications, PO Box 6, Geneva, 1211, Switzerland; pubvente@ilo.org; http://www.ilo.org/publns. Illus. Circ: 2500. Vol. ends: No. 4. *Bk. rev.:* Occasional. *Aud.:* Ac, Sa.

Labour Education is published by the Bureau for Workers' Activities (ACTRAV). They are a branch of the International Labour Office, which is the executive secretariat of the International Labour Organization (the only tripartite agency of the United Nations). ACTRAV coordinates all the activities of the office related to workers and their organizations, both at headquarters and in the field. A quarterly review, *Labour Education* is published in three languages (English, Spanish, and French) and devoted to news and analysis of efforts to improve workers' lives. The content is useful to both union and nonunion workers alike, and covers a broad gamut of topics including training and education programs, current events, trade union rights, social justice organizing, and legislation. The publication also includes reviews of relevant resources, such as books, articles, and videos.

3796. *LabourStart.* d. Ed(s): Eric Lee. Labour and Society International, ITF Bldg, Third Fl, 49-60 Borough Rd, London, SE1 1DS, United Kingdom; http://www.labourstart.org. *Aud.:* Ga, Ac, Sa.

This electronic resource is billed as the site "where trade unionists start their day on the net," and it's easy to believe that might be true. They take seriously the task of organizing the workers of the world, aggregating and disseminating labor news in Danish, English, Spanish, Esperanto, French, Italian, Creole, Dutch, Norse, Portuguese, Finnish, Swedish, and Turkish. The site provides a long chronological list of "this week's top stories" listed by country (e.g., "South Africa—Security guard unions reject employer offer, national strike continues," where the country name is a hyperlink to all stories from that nation). A "mail-to" link embedded in the headlines makes the article easy to share with others. Also featured is a "Book of the Day" (*LabourStart* also operates their own online bookstore), a "Photo of the Week," discussion forums, FAQs, and a section of recommended books.

3797. *Monthly Labor Review Online.* [ISSN: 1937-4658] Free. *Bk. rev.:* Occasional. *Aud.:* Ga.

This site not only mirrors its print counterpart, it takes advantage of the power of web publishing. The material posted is well designed and accessible. Abstracts and excerpts of half a dozen articles are provided in html for easy online scanning, with the full-text version available in pdf format. Articles include links to related Bureau of Labor Statistics (BLS) programs and data, and author e-mail links are embedded. "The Editor's Desk," a useful review of new BLS data and research, is updated each business day. The content is informative and neutral, covering current labor statistics, book reviews, publications received (segregated by subject area), and a section called "Labor Month in Review." Content searching is facilitated by an index of articles published in print since 1988, as well as an archive of past issues.

3798. *NATLEX.* 1984. irreg. continuously-updated. International Labour Organization, 4, route des Morillons, Geneva 22, CH-1211, Switzerland; ilo@ilo.org; http://www.ilo.org/. *Aud.:* Ac, Sa.

NATLEX is the database of national labor, social security, and related human rights legislation maintained by the International Labour Organization's (ILO) International Labour Standards Department. This is not as much a "journal" as it is a database portal for foreign and international labor law. The records in *NATLEX* are extensive—over 55,000 records covering over 170 countries and territories—and provide abstracts of legislation and relevant citation information. Each record appears in only one of the three official ILO languages (English/French/Spanish). The data is indexed by keywords and by subject classifications, and viewers may browse for labor legislation by country or by subject. An advanced search feature allows for compound and delimited searching. There is also a summary of new items. Where possible, the full text of the law or a relevant electronic source is linked to the record.

3799. *Negotiation Journal: on the process of dispute settlement.* [ISSN: 0748-4526] 1985. q. GBP 477 print & online eds. Ed(s): Nancy Waters, Michael Wheeler. Blackwell Publishing, Inc., Commerce Place, 350 Main St, Malden, MA 02148; customerservices@ blackwellpublishing.com; http://www.blackwellpublishing.com. Adv.

Refereed. Microform: PQC. Online: Blackwell Synergy; EBSCO Publishing, EBSCO Host; Gale; IngentaConnect; OCLC Online Computer Library Center, Inc.; OhioLINK; ProQuest LLC (Ann Arbor); Springer LINK; SwetsWise Online Content. Reprint: PSC. *Indexed:* ABIn, ABS&EES, AmH&L, ApEcolAb, CJA, HRA, IBR, IBSS, IBZ, IPSA, PAIS, PRA, PSA, PsycInfo, RiskAb, SSA, SSCI, SociolAb. *Aud.:* Ac, Sa.

Organizational dispute resolution can cover a lot of ground, ranging from intense union contract negotiations to daily workplace practice. This is a multidisciplinary publication that offers a very wide view of this field, and covers the full gamut from international to interpersonal dispute resolution. The stated editorial goal of *NJ* is to "encourage the search for and development of better techniques for dealing with differences through the give-and-take of negotiation." Although it does not dwell on issues immediately pertaining to labor and industrial relations, many of the articles are broadly applicable in bargaining and human relations settings. The "Research Digests" section looks at important negotiation-related research that has appeared in other academic and professional journals. Recent full-length articles include "Back-Channel Negotiation: International Bargaining in the Shadows," "Teaching Students How to Use Emotions as They Negotiate," and "Is Teaching Negotiation Too Easy, Too Hard, or Both?"

3800. *New Labor Forum.* [ISSN: 1095-7960] 1997. 3x/yr. GBP 71 print & online eds. Ed(s): Paula Finn. Taylor & Francis Inc., 325 Chestnut St, Ste 800, Philadelphia, PA 19016; orders@taylorandfrancis.com; http://www.taylorandfrancis.com. Illus., adv. Refereed. Circ: 3000. Reprint: PSC. *Indexed:* AltPI, PAIS, PSA, SSA, SociolAb. *Bk. rev.:* Various number and length. *Aud.:* Ga, Ac.

This is the sort of publication that libraries find themselves keeping behind the desk because patrons can't seem to return copies. Subtitled "A Journal of Ideas, Analysis, and Debate," this is where theory and reality duke it out, and the reader wins. Articles from shop-floor organizers mingle with those of tenured faculty. Thorny topics are addressed, from labor union revitalization to the role of unions in a time of war. Fresh ideas abound, such as approaches to considering how globalized distribution can be considered an opportunity for organizing, or questioning "Is the Strike Dead?" They are also good about their support for the role of labor culture, and include poems, cartoons, photographs, and illustrations as well as a whole "Books and the Arts" section.

3801. *New Technology, Work & Employment.* [ISSN: 0268-1072] 1986. 3x/yr. GBP 259 print & online eds. Ed(s): Christopher Baldry. Blackwell Publishing Ltd., 9600 Garsington Rd, Oxford, OX4 2ZG, United Kingdom; customerservices@blackwellpublishing.com; http://www.blackwellpublishing.com. Adv. Refereed. Online: Blackwell Synergy; EBSCO Publishing, EBSCO Host; Gale; IngentaConnect; OCLC Online Computer Library Center, Inc.; OhioLINK; SwetsWise Online Content. Reprint: PSC. *Indexed:* ABIn, ASSIA, ApEcolAb, CompLI, ErgAb, HRA, IBR, IBSS, LISA, PAIS, PMA, RiskAb, SSA, SSCI, SociolAb. *Aud.:* Ga.

It is commonly accepted that technological changes have fundamentally transformed the way most people work, and this internationally edited, interdisciplinary journal delves into the consequences of that paradigm shift. A pleasing blend of academic yet readable articles cover such diverse topics as "Work restructuring in retail distribution," "Teleworking practice in small and medium-sized firms: management style and worker autonomy," and "Teamwork in factories within the French automobile industry."

Occupational Outlook Quarterly. See Occupations and Careers section.

3802. *Our Times Magazine: independent Canadian labour magazine.* [ISSN: 0822-6377] 1981. bi-m. CND 40 (Individuals, CND 25; CND 4.75 newsstand/cover per issue). Ed(s): Lorraine Endicott. Our Times Labour Publishing Inc., 1209 King St W, Ste 201A, Toronto, ON M6K 1G2, Canada; office@ourtimes.ca; http://www.ourtimes.ca. Adv. Circ: 3000. Microform: MML. Online: Micromedia ProQuest; ProQuest LLC (Ann Arbor). *Indexed:* AltPI, CBCARef, CPerI. *Bk. rev.:* Number and length vary. *Aud.:* Ga.

Two-way trade in goods and services between the United States and Canada has surpassed $441 billion, making it the largest trading relationship in the world. Despite that, few labor researchers in this country invest time and effort in studying our neighbor to the north. *Our Times*, subtitled "Canada's Independent Labour Magazine," addresses issues affecting Canadian working people and the organizations that serve them. Articles cover a broad array of topics, including labor history, gender and racial struggles within the labor movement, NAFTA, and occupational safety and health. The magazine is also very good about including labor culture—you'll find poetry, photographs, and illustrations complementing the text. An annual women's issue is also published.

3803. *Relations Industrielles.* [ISSN: 0034-379X] 1945. q. CND 100 (Individuals, CND 50). Ed(s): Sylvie Montreuil. Universite Laval, Department of Industrial Relations, Pavillon DeSeve, bureau 3129, Quebec, PQ G1K 7P4, Canada. Illus., index, adv. Refereed. Circ: 1200. *Indexed:* ABIn, AgeL, AmH&L, CLI, CPerI, HRA, HistAb, IBR, IBSS, IBZ, LRI, PAIS, PMA, PRA, PSA, PdeR, SFSA, SSA, SSCI, SUSA, SociolAb, V&AA. *Bk. rev.:* Number and length vary. *Aud.:* Ac, Sa.

This scholarly journal is published by the industrial relations department of Canada's Universite Laval in Quebec. It bills itself as "the world's first academic journal in industrial relations" and is the only journal of its kind in Canada. *Relations Industrielles* is an interdisciplinary publication that carries articles on all aspects of the world of work. Articles appear in either French or English accompanied by a full summary in the other language and a shorter summary in Spanish. Each issue (numbering over 200 pages) includes reviews of significant books in the field and a bibliography of recent articles published throughout the world. Although predominantly covering Canadian issues, it also ventures into foreign and international topics as well. Recent articles include "Work and Citizenship in Mexico in the Era of Globalization," "Sexual Orientation Provisions in Canadian Collective Agreements," and "Recruitment Strategies and Union Exclusion in Two Australian Call Centres." Tables of contents and abstracts of articles are available back to 1996 on the web site, and full-text access is available online through EBSCO Business Source Premier and Gale Expanded Academic ASAP.

3804. *The Review of Black Political Economy.* [ISSN: 0034-6446] 1970. q. EUR 252 print & online eds. Ed(s): Cecilia Conrad. Springer New York LLC, 233 Spring St, New York, NY 10013-1578; service-ny@springer.com; http://www.springer.com/. Illus., adv. Refereed. Circ: 1000. Microform: PQC. Online: Chadwyck-Healey Inc.; EBSCO Publishing, EBSCO Host; Florida Center for Library Automation; Gale; OCLC Online Computer Library Center, Inc.; OhioLINK; ProQuest LLC (Ann Arbor); SwetsWise Online Content. Reprint: PSC. *Indexed:* ABIn, AgeL, AmH&L, HistAb, IBSS, IIBP, JEL, LRI, PAIS, PSA, RiskAb, SSA, SSCI, SUSA, SociolAb. *Bk. rev.:* Occasional. *Aud.:* Ac.

Unemployment in the United States among blacks is more than double that for whites, 10.8 percent versus 5.2 percent, a gap wider than existed 30 years ago. Although many employed blacks have experienced gains relative to whites, a significant segment of un- and underemployed blacks have fallen further behind. *The Review of Black Political Economy* examines issues related to the economic status of African American and Third World peoples and identifies and analyzes policy prescriptions designed to reduce racial economic inequality. The journal also appraises public and private policies designed to advance economic opportunities. The articles and occasional book reviews cover such ground as inequalities in small business loans, analysis of preferential procurement programs, the impact of structural adjustment in the Caribbean, and the participation of women and people of color in union apprenticeship training programs. Selected full-text coverage is available through EBSCO Business Source Premier and Gale Expanded Academic ASAP.

3805. *Social Policy: organizing for social and economic justice.* [ISSN: 0037-7783] 1970. q. USD 185 (Individuals, USD 45). Ed(s): Michael J Miller. The American Institute for Social Justice, 1024 Elysian Fields, New Orleans, LA 70117. Illus. Circ: 4000 Paid. Vol. ends: Winter. CD-ROM: H.W. Wilson. Microform: PQC. Online: EBSCO Publishing, EBSCO Host; Florida Center for Library Automation; Gale; Northern Light Technology, Inc.; OCLC Online Computer Library Center, Inc.;

H.W. Wilson. *Indexed:* ABCPolSci, ASSIA, AgeL, AltPI, AmH&L, FLI, FutSurv, HistAb, IBSS, IPSA, LeftInd, MCR, PAIS, PRA, PSA, SSA, SSCI, SUSA, SWR&A, SociolAb, V&AA. *Bk. rev.:* Number and length vary. *Aud.:* Ga.

This is an unabashedly partisan magazine, presenting news and analysis on various social change movements. Since labor is a key component of social justice work, each issue carries at least one article on worker organizing. One of the publication's strengths is a broad and balanced view of the role played by conventional unions. An article critical of a particular AFL-CIO policy may sit next to one supportive of a major international union. They are particularly adept at coverage of the intersection between community and labor organizing, especially among communities of color and immigrants. Recent articles include "Building Power in Forty Languages: A Story About Organizing Immigrants in Chicago's Albany Park," "Direct Action for Jobs: The Mission Coalition Hiring Hall," and "Bike Messengers Organize." There was a recent special edition on organizing Wal-Mart, with a follow-up issue featuring Hurricane Katrina and the race, class, and power issues it highlighted and sharpened for so many.

Social Security Bulletin. See Elder Issues section.

3806. *Union Democracy Review.* Supersedes: *Union Democracy in Action.* [ISSN: 1077-5080] 1972. bi-m. USD 15. Ed(s): Herman Benson. Association for Union Democracy, Inc., 104 Montgomery St., Brooklyn, NY 11225-2008; aud@igc.apc.org; http://www.uniondemocracy.com. Circ: 3000. *Indexed:* AltPI. *Aud.:* Ga, Ac, Sa.

The Association for Union Democracy (AUD) is a unique pro-labor, nonprofit organization dedicated to advancing the principles and practices of democratic trade unionism in the North American labor movement. It is a nonpartisan organization and does not support or endorse candidates for union office or particular policies within unions. Rather, AUD supports actions that strengthen the democratic process, promote membership participation, support free speech, and encourage fair elections so that union members can shape and steer the direction of their union. *UDR* is AUD's published voice, and serves as a vital clearinghouse for this movement. It is short (12 pages) but dense, with recent issues including such articles as "The fall of RISE in the Teamsters Union," "The eternal quest for fair hiring in construction," "SEIU pulls plug on 'Future of Labor' discussion online," and "Court forces ironworkers to democratize constitutions." The style is accessible and straightforward, with author contact encouraged.

3807. *U.S. Bureau of Labor Statistics. Monthly Labor Review.* Supersedes: *U.S. Bureau of Labor Statistics. Monthly Review.* [ISSN: 0098-1818] 1915. m. USD 49 domestic; USD 68.60 foreign. Ed(s): Deborah Klein. U.S. Department of Labor, Bureau of Labor Statistics, Postal Square Bldg., 2 Massachusetts Ave, NE, Washington, DC 20212-0001; http://www.bls.gov. Illus., index. Circ: 9000. Vol. ends: Dec. Microform: CIS; PMC. Online: The Dialog Corporation; EBSCO Publishing, EBSCO Host; Florida Center for Library Automation; Gale; William S. Hein & Co., Inc.; Northern Light Technology, Inc.; OCLC Online Computer Library Center, Inc.; ProQuest LLC (Ann Arbor); H.W. Wilson. Reprint: WSH. *Indexed:* ABIn, ASG, ATI, AgeL, AmH&L, AmStI, BPI, BRD, BRI, CBRI, CLI, HistAb, IUSGP, JEL, LRI, MASUSE, PAIS, RGPR, SSCI, SWA, SWR&A, WAE&RSA. *Bk. rev.:* Number and length vary. *Aud.:* Ga, Ac, Sa.

This is the official voice of the Bureau of Labor Statistics (BLS) of the United States Department of Labor, and you can count on it for vast arrays of tabular data. The publication format features several in-depth articles by staff economists and program specialists, along with regular departments that review that month's labor data, describe current labor statistics, and offer lengthy book reviews. It also publishes a calendar of scheduled statistics series releases and occasionally features a focused report on a BLS program. This journal also reports useful labor statistics in various issues, including listings of work stoppages—a useful aid for ready-reference. "Precis" is its short-items section, showcasing news and analysis from outside researchers.

3808. *Work, Employment & Society.* [ISSN: 0950-0170] 1987. q. GBP 238. Ed(s): Helen Rainbird, Michael Rose. Sage Publications Ltd., 1 Oliver's Yard, 55 City Rd, London, EC1 1SP, United Kingdom; info@sagepub.co.uk; http://www.sagepub.co.uk. Adv. Refereed.

Microform: PQC. Online: CSA; EBSCO Publishing, EBSCO Host; HighWire Press; OCLC Online Computer Library Center, Inc.; OhioLINK; SAGE Publications, Inc., SAGE Journals Online; SwetsWise Online Content. Reprint: PSC. *Indexed:* ABIn, ASSIA, ArtHuCI, CJA, H&SSA, HRA, IBR, IBSS, IBZ, PAIS, PMA, PRA, PSA, PsycInfo, SSA, SSCI, SociolAb. *Bk. rev.:* Number and length vary. *Aud.:* Ac.

This British entry is heavily dominated by the sociological study of work, but therein lies its value for labor researchers. It addresses work in the broadest possible sense, and it includes a wide array of articles that explore global and transnational employment trends. This is the sort of journal that union researchers consult to get the big picture, and that academics consult to stay current with what their international colleagues are up to. Recent articles explore management trends with significant impact on workers, such as "total quality management," the impact of technology on work, and disabilities in the workplace. For full-service research collections, this journal is a valuable addition.

3809. *Workforce Management.* Former titles (until 2003): *Workforce (Costa Mesa);* (until 1997): *Personnel Journal;* (until 1927): *Journal of Personnel Research.* [ISSN: 1547-5565] 1922. m. USD 79 domestic; USD 129 Canada; USD 199 elsewhere. Ed(s): Janet Wiscombe. Crain Communications, Inc., 1155 Gratiot Ave, Detroit, MI 48207-2997; http://www.crain.com. Illus., index, adv. Circ: 30000 Paid. Vol. ends: Dec. Online: EBSCO Publishing, EBSCO Host; Florida Center for Library Automation; Gale; OCLC Online Computer Library Center, Inc.; ProQuest K-12 Learning Solutions; ProQuest LLC (Ann Arbor); H.W. Wilson. *Indexed:* ABIn, ASG, AgeL, Agr, BLI, BPI, BRI, CBRI, CWI, EAA, ExcerpMed, PAIS, PMA, SSCI. *Aud.:* Ga.

Workforce Management provides practical information about the impact of current events on human relations. The format is light and enlightened, with snappy graphics, profuse pull-text boxes, and a vibrant letters section. One section covers the trends, problem solving strategies, and resources necessary for action; another covers legal briefings; and a third distills economic data into a usable form for HR professionals. Recent issues cover the case for company child care, a critique of HR practices at Wal-Mart, and the impact of changed overtime pay regulations.

3810. *Workindex.* 1997. d. Ed(s): Michelle Liberatore. Human Resources Executive, 747 Dresher Rd, Horsham, PA 19044; http://www.workindex.com/. Illus. *Bk. rev.:* Number varies, brief. *Aud.:* Ac, Sa.

This is a "gateway to human resource solutions" produced by *Human Resource Executive* magazine. Professionally designed and densely packed, this site is a useful portal to news and resources oriented to the human resources community. Multiple, redundant navigation tools help viewers find what they are looking for, and when all else fails there's a category or keyword search box. In addition to the web site, a free weekly e-newsletter feeds you the top features, such as "EEOC Sees Decline in Discrimination Charges," "Wage-and-Hour Actions Outpace All Other Class Actions," and "FMLA and Infertility Treatments." Cornell's School of Industrial and Labor Relations handles the site indexing, which contributes significantly to the information architecture and ease in retrieving documents. Cornell also grooms the "HR Links" section, a dynamic list of over 5,000 web sites for HR professionals.

3811. *Working U S A: the journal of labor and society.* [ISSN: 1089-7011] 1997. q. GBP 171 print & online eds. Ed(s): Immanuel Ness. Blackwell Publishing, Inc., Commerce Place, 350 Main St, Malden, MA 02148; customerservices@blackwellpublishing.com; http://www.blackwellpublishing.com. Adv. Refereed. Reprint: PSC. *Indexed:* AltPI, JEL, LeftInd, PAIS. *Bk. rev.:* Number and length vary. *Aud.:* Ac, Ga.

This relatively new entry in the field of industrial relations has made waves as a publishing venue of choice for a large number of progressive academics and policymakers. It bills itself as an instrument for studying the workplace with the needs and concerns of "working people" in mind, and this is reflected in the topics it covers. In many cases, authors express partisan viewpoints, in contrast to the colorless, neutral language typically employed by many scholarly journals. Recent article topics include organizing temporary workers, labor education's challenges, and home-care worker issues. Authors are careful to write in plain English, yet offer solid scholarship that is footnoted and enhanced with tables and charts. In just a few short years, this journal has earned a place as a core title both for industrial relations collections and for general business collections.

3812. *World of Work: the magazine of the ILO.* Formerly (until 1992): *I L O Information.* [ISSN: 1020-0010] 1965. 5x/yr. Free. Ed(s): Thomas Netter. International Labour Office, Department of Communication, 4 Route des Morillons, Geneva 22, CH-1211, Switzerland; communication@ilo.org; http://www.ilo.org/communication. Illus. Circ: 50000. Vol. ends: Dec. *Indexed:* BRI, CBRI, ErgAb, FPA, ForAb. *Bk. rev.:* Number and length vary. *Aud.:* Ga.

Although this magazine is published by the International Labour Organization (ILO), its editorial box is careful to note that it is not the ILO's official voice. It does, however, by and large represent the wide range of issues addressed by the ILO. Each issue includes an extensive cover story ("Decent Work for Africa's Development," "World Day Against Child Labor"), numerous general articles, and an extensive selection of brief book reviews. One of the helpful features is the section titled "Planet Work," with brief summaries of major labor news from around the world. *World of Work* has high production values, displaying extensive use of graphics, photos, and color—even the reviewed book covers are shown in full color.

■ LANDSCAPE ARCHITECTURE

Heather Ball, Art and Architecture Library, Virginia Tech, 302 Cowgill Hall, Blacksburg, VA 24062-9001; h.ball@vt.edu

Introduction

Landscape architecture, although a distinct profession, embraces a hybrid approach to design. Contemporary landscape architecture projects incorporate elements of art, design, and science. Additionally, many of these projects show a deep regard for environmental sustainability and an involvement in the historic preservation, reclamation, and conservation of land. Landscape architects often work collaboratively with architects, urban planners, environmental scientists, and artists. A diversity of projects are featured in landscape architecture journals, including urban waterfronts and watersheds, public parks and therapeutic gardens, cemeteries and monuments, university campuses, and green roofs.

Landscape architecture is a global profession and, as a result, many of the titles included here are international in scope. Almost half are published by professional societies. These professionally oriented publications offer up-to-date reports on events and trends related to landscape design, technology, and the environment. Feature articles primarily focus on exemplary designs and are well-illustrated with photographs, plans, and drawings. Other titles in the list are research-oriented, peer-reviewed, and focus on either the history and theory of landscape architecture (e.g., the Dumbarton Oaks Papers from the *Colloquium on the History of Landscape Architecture*) or the scientific analysis of land use and design from the perspectives of environmental studies, land conservation, geography, and planning (e.g., Landscape Research).

All of these selections are well-suited for any library that supports landscape architecture research and professional practice, in particular academic libraries that support landscape architecture curricula. Public librarians might consider purchasing subscriptions to the society publications of their country or region. A subscription to *Topos* would also be a good choice for public libraries, since it provides excellent international coverage of the field.

Basic Periodicals

Ac: *Landscape Architecture, Landscape Journal;* Sa: *Landscape and Urban Planning, Landscape Research, Topos.*

Basic Abstracts and Indexes

Avery Index to Architectural Periodicals; Garden Literature; Geographical Abstracts; ICONDA, International Construction Database.

3813. *Anthos: vierteljahres-Zeitschrift fuer Freiraumgestaltung, Gruen und Landschaftsplanung.* [ISSN: 0003-5424] 1962. q. CHF 89 (Students, CHF 49). Ed(s): Stephanie Perrochet. Bund Schweizer Landschaftsarchitekten und Landschaftsarchitektinnen, Rue du Doubs 32, La Chaux-de-Fonds, 2300, Switzerland; bsla@bsla.ch; http://www.bsla.ch. Illus., adv. Circ: 5000. Vol. ends: Dec. *Indexed:* API, GardL, IBR, IBZ, RRTA, WAE&RSA. *Bk. rev.:* 10. *Aud.:* Ac, Sa.

Anthos is the official publication of Switzerland's society of professional landscape architects, Bund Schweizerischer Landschaftsarchitekten, and is published in German and French, with portions of the news column published in English. Issues are based on themes that cover all facets of landscape architecture, such as conservation of historical gardens, the design of everyday landscapes, and the design of outdoor social spaces. Additional columns feature current events, competitions and awards, book reviews, special events, product and services reviews, and profiles of key individuals in the field. *Anthos* is a good choice for any research collection with an international focus on landscape architecture.

3814. *Colloquium on the History of Landscape Architecture. Papers.* 1972. irreg. Dumbarton Oaks, 1703 32nd St, NW, Washington, DC 20007; http://www.doaks.org/publications.html. Refereed. Circ: 1000. *Aud.:* Ac, Sa.

Each year, Harvard University's Dumbarton Oaks Research Library and Collection sponsors colloquia on three topics: Byzantine Studies, Pre-Columbian Studies, and Garden and Landscape Studies. The Dumbarton Oaks collection of papers on the history of landscape architecture is an exceptional series, solely devoted to an international and in-depth study of both landscape architecture and garden history. Colloquium themes have been as broad in scope as "Environmentalism and Landscape Architecture," and as specific as "Ancient Roman Villa Gardens," but the papers resulting from these colloquia always represent a wide range of study (e.g., cultural geography, sociology, environmental science, architecture, and landscape architecture, art history, and English literature). While most of the contributors to the colloquia are scholars from around the globe who study the social, cultural, or historical aspects of environment, papers by practicing designers and artists are also featured. The papers include sufficient black-and-white illustrative material such as prints, drawings, photographs, and plans. Any landscape architecture or garden history research library should own the complete set.

Fine Gardening. See Gardening section.

Garden History. See Gardening section.

3815. *Garten und Landschaft: Zeitschrift fuer Landschaftsarchitektur.* [ISSN: 0016-4720] 1890. m. Individuals, EUR 118.80; Students, EUR 85.20; EUR 12 newsstand/cover. Ed(s): Robert Schaefer. Callwey Verlag, Streitfeldstr 35, Munich, 81673, Germany; a.hagenkord@callwey.de; http://www.callwey.de. Illus., index, adv. Circ: 6028 Paid and controlled. Vol. ends: Dec. *Indexed:* ExcerpMed, GardL, IBR, IBZ. *Bk. rev.:* 4. *Aud.:* Ac, Sa.

Published by the German Society for Garden Design and Landscape Architecture, issues of *Garten und Landschaft* are thematically based and focus primarily on landscape design and planning in Germany. The layout and content is similar to most society publications, and the journal could be seen as the German cousin to the Danish publication *Landskab* (reviewed below). *Garten und Landschaft* is written primarily in German but features English-language summaries of the main articles. In addition to feature articles about landscape and urban design in Germany, it includes columns that discuss important events, conferences, and competitions, plus book and product reviews and interviews with key people in the field. The authors are practicing landscape architects, designers, scholars, and educators (brief biographical sketches of authors are provided). *Garten und Landschaft* should be considered for any research collection with an international focus on landscape architecture.

3816. *Green Places.* Former titles (Nov. 2003): *Landscape Design;* (until 1971): *Institute of Landscape Architects. Journal.* [ISSN: 1742-3716] 1934. 10x/yr. GBP 39.20 domestic (Students, GBP 28.80 in UK). Ed(s): Chris Young, Diane Millis. Landscape Design Trust, 13a West St,

Reigate, RH2 9BL, United Kingdom; info@landscape.co.uk; http://www.landscape.co.uk. Illus., index, adv. Sample. Circ: 6500. Vol. ends: Jun. *Indexed:* API, ArtInd, GardL, RRTA, WAE&RSA. *Bk. rev.:* 2-6. *Aud.:* Ga, Ac.

Published by the Landscape Design Trust, whose mission is "to foster understanding and awareness of the landscape for the benefit of the environment and the community," *Green Places* showcases public space projects in the United Kingdom with occasional profiles of similar projects in other, mostly European, countries. Each month, the four or five main articles focus on a theme (e.g., tourism and green spaces, public space lighting, waterfront design and planning). The text is supplemented with eye-catching photographs that beautifully evoke the qualities of the places being described. A smattering of plans and technical drawings are also included. The "On Location" section covers public space projects currently in development, and a column called "Forum" presents debates between experts on topics ranging from rural housing and the landscape to the impact of climate change on the development of public spaces. Other columns include an opinion section, news from local community groups "engaged in public space issues," and book reviews. Additionally, an annual issue is devoted to an overview and critique of public space projects and initiatives from the past year. *Green Places* will be a welcome addition to library collections that center on an international and multidisciplinary approach to landscape and public space design and urban planning.

3817. *Landscape: the journal of the Landscape Institute.* [ISSN: 1742-2914] 2004. m. GBP 50 domestic; GBP 79 foreign. Ed(s): Joe Gardiner. Landscape Institute, 33 Great Portland St, London, W1W 8Qg, United Kingdom; mail@landscapeinstitute.org; http://www.landscapeinstitute.org. *Aud.:* Ac, Sa.

A relatively new publication, *Landscape* is published by the Landscape Institute, a professional society of landscape architects in the United Kingdom, and it has a largely U.K. focus. Each issue includes a profile of projects and firms of a particular region within the United Kingdom. A directory of registered practices is provided, organized by region and country. One or two short feature articles are supplemented by regular inspirational columns such as "Perspective," which reviews interesting web sites and publications. Although not yet indexed, *Landscape* is worth considering for inclusion in any comprehensive research collection that has an international focus on landscape architecture.

3818. *Landscape and Urban Planning.* Incorporates (in 1988): *Reclamation and Revegetation Research;* (in 1986): *Urban Ecology;* Formerly (until 1986): *Landscape Planning.* [ISSN: 0169-2046] 1974. 20x/yr. EUR 1711. Ed(s): J R Rodiek. Elsevier BV, Radarweg 29, Amsterdam, 1043 NX, Netherlands; nlinfo-f@elsevier.nl; http://www.elsevier.nl. Illus., index, adv. Refereed. Online: EBSCO Publishing, EBSCO Host; Gale; IngentaConnect; OhioLINK; ScienceDirect; SwetsWise Online Content. *Indexed:* ApEcolAb, BiolAb, CABA, CJA, EngInd, EnvAb, EnvInd, ExcerpMed, FPA, ForAb, GardL, HortAb, M&GPA, PollutAb, RRTA, S&F, SCI, SSCI, SUSA, SWRA, WAE&RSA, ZooRec. *Bk. rev.:* 2-4. *Aud.:* Ac, Sa.

Landscape and Urban Planning is a multidisciplinary and international scholarly journal focused on the "conceptual, scientific, and design approaches to land use." Each volume usually includes a thematic issue (e.g., "Research on the Built and Virtual Environments," "Greenway Planning Around the World," "Ecological Dynamics of Urban and Rural Landscapes in East Asia"). Analysis is from a variety of perspectives, including landscape architecture and planning, environmental conservation, ecology, urban planning, and land management. Black-and-white diagrams, charts, and photographs are of decent quality and adequately illustrate the text. Occasionally, a short book review is included. *Landscape and Urban Planning* should be considered for academic library collections that support research not only in landscape architecture but also in environmental studies, urban planning, and geography.

3819. *Landscape Architecture.* [ISSN: 0023-8031] 1910. 12x/yr. USD 59 domestic; USD 99 foreign. Ed(s): Bill Thompson, Lisa Speckhardt. American Society of Landscape Architects, 636 Eye St, NW, Washington, DC 20001-3736; scahill@asla.org; http://www.asla.org. Illus., index, adv. Sample. Circ: 25000 Paid. Vol. ends: Dec. *Indexed:* API, ArchI, ArtHuCI, ArtInd, EIP, GardL, IBR, IBZ, SSCI. *Bk. rev.:* 4. *Aud.:* Ac, Sa.

Landscape Architecture is the official publication of the American Society of Landscape Architects (ASLA) and as such focuses mainly on projects in the United States, with some coverage of international projects. Feature articles discuss projects that may be considered traditional landscape architecture, but also include projects that reflect the diversity of the profession, crossing over into urban design and planning, and environmental sustainability and planning. The six- to eight-page articles are heavily illustrated. In fact, *Landscape Architecture* is a visual feast, packed with color photographs, illustrations, maps, and plans. Each issue features page-long book reviews, product profiles, and regular columns on the ecological aspect of landscape architecture and professional practice. One issue a year is devoted to the ASLA Annual Awards, presented to professionals and students in a variety of areas including design analysis and planning and research. *Landscape Architecture* is a must for research libraries specializing in landscape architecture, and would be a welcome addition to larger public library collections as well.

3820. *Landscape Architecture Australia.* Formerly (until 2006): *Landscape Australia.* [ISSN: 1833-4814] 1971. q. AUD 48 domestic; AUD 72 in Asia & the Pacific; AUD 81 elsewhere. Ed(s): Kirsty McKenzie. Architecture Media, L3, 4 Princes St, Port Melbourne, VIC 3207, Australia; publisher@archmedia.com.au; http://www.archmedia.com.au. Illus., index, adv. Circ: 2858. Online: RMIT Publishing. *Indexed:* API, GardL. *Bk. rev.:* 2. *Aud.:* Ac.

The official journal of the Australian Institute of Landscape Architects (AILA), *Landscape Architecture Australia* is geared toward a professional audience, but is so visually engaging and readable that anyone interested in designed landscapes will find it appealing. It includes all the features one would expect from a society publication (i.e., book reviews, a calendar of events, in-depth feature articles, brief news and reviews of projects) and annually showcases the AILA National and State Project Awards. The length of the book review section varies, but all reviews are in-depth and explore the latest publications of note. Contributors to *Landscape Architecture Australia* are practicing landscape architects, educators, and historians. Highly recommend for any comprehensive landscape architecture research collection, or any collection focusing on Australia and the region.

3821. *Landscape Journal: design, planning, and management of the land.* [ISSN: 0277-2426] 1981. s-a. USD 198 print & online eds (Individuals, USD 65 print & online eds). Ed(s): M Elen Deming. University of Wisconsin Press, Journal Division, 1930 Monroe St, 3rd Fl, Madison, WI 53711-2059; journals@uwpress.wisc.edu; http://www.wisc.edu/wisconsinpress/journals. Illus., index, adv. Sample. Refereed. Circ: 700. Microform: PQC. Online: EBSCO Publishing, EBSCO Host; Gale; IngentaConnect. Reprint: PSC. *Indexed:* API, Agr, ArtInd, GardL, IBR, IBZ, SUSA. *Bk. rev.:* 8. *Aud.:* Ac.

The official journal of the Council of Educators in Landscape Architecture (CELA), *Landscape Journal* features scholarly articles covering a wide range of perspectives in support of landscape architecture research (e.g., art, planning, geography, architecture, and history). CELA membership is comprised of landscape architecture educators in the United States, Canada, Australia, and New Zealand. The council is "concerned with the content and quality of professional education in landscape architecture," and the content of the journal reflects these interests. Faculty from SUNY, College of Environmental Science and Forestry serve as the main editors, while additional editors and authors reflect the overall membership of CELA. Recent issues each include a feature paper written by prominent landscape architecture scholars and practitioners, in addition to four to six articles, book reviews, and a calendar of events. The publication has black-and-white illustrations, and a few color images were introduced in 2005. *Landscape Journal* is a fine choice for academic collections that support the study of landscape architecture, environmental design, urban planning, and geography.

3822. *Landscape Research.* Formerly (until 1976): *Landscape Research News.* [ISSN: 0142-6397] 1968. q. GBP 479 print & online eds. Ed(s): Dr. Ian Thompson. Routledge, 4 Park Sq, Milton Park, Abingdon, OX14 4RN, United Kingdom; info@routledge.co.uk; http://www.routledge.co.uk. Illus., index, adv. Sample. Circ: 650. Vol. ends: Nov. Online: EBSCO Publishing, EBSCO Host; Gale; IngentaConnect; Northern Light Technology, Inc.; OCLC Online

Computer Library Center, Inc.; ProQuest LLC (Ann Arbor); SwetsWise Online Content. Reprint: PSC. *Indexed:* API, BrArAb, CABA, EnvAb, EnvInd, FLI, ForAb, GardL, HortAb, IBR, IBZ, NumL, RRTA, S&F, SSCI, SWRA, WAE&RSA. *Bk. rev.:* 4, 600-800 words. *Aud.:* Ac, Sa.

The publisher of this journal, the Landscape Research Group, is a nonprofit organization in the United Kingdom dedicated to the advancement of research and education dealing with the general concept and study of landscape. The articles in this journal are international in scope and cover topics as diverse as "environmental design, countryside management, ecology and environmental conservation, land surveying, human and physical geography, behavioral and cultural studies, and archaeology and history." Each year, one or two issues are devoted to a theme (e.g., "Landscape Justice, Morality and the Law of the Land" and "Landscape and Seasonality"). Each article is supplemented with a short abstract and keywords that describe the article. Diagrams, charts, and photographs are reproduced in black and white only, but are of good quality and adequately illustrate the text. Book reviews are succinct and cover an interesting array of international publications. *Landscape Research* is well-suited for academic library collections that support research in landscape architecture, environmental studies, and geography.

3823. ***Landskab: tidsskrift for planlaegning af have og landskab, review for garden and landscape planning.*** Formerly (until 1968): *Havekunst.* [ISSN: 0023-8066] 1920. 8x/yr. DKK 790 domestic; DKK 696 in Europe excl. tax and postage; DKK 766 elsewhere excl. tax and postage. Ed(s): Annemarie Lund. Arkitektens Forlag, Overgaden oven Vandet 10, Copenhagen K, 1415, Denmark; info@arkfo.dk; http://www.arkfo.dk. Illus., index, adv. Sample. Circ: 1627. Vol. ends: Dec. *Indexed:* API. *Bk. rev.:* 2-4. *Aud.:* Ac, Sa.

Landskab is the publication of Danske Landskabsarkitekter, the Association of Danish Landscape Architects. The articles are written in Danish with English-language summaries of feature articles. Articles are heavily illustrated with attractive color photos, sketches, site plans, and details, and cover both historical and contemporary landscape architecture projects mainly in Denmark and in other Scandinavian countries. Occasionally, book reviews are included. *Landskab* should be considered for any landscape architecture collection with an international focus.

Places: a forum of environmental design. See Architecture section.

Studies in History of Gardens & Designed Landscapes. See Gardening section.

3824. ***Topos: European landscape magazine.*** [ISSN: 0942-752X] 1992. q. EUR 115.20 domestic (Students, EUR 81.20). Ed(s): Robert Schaefer. Callwey Verlag, Streitfeldstr 35, Munich, 81673, Germany; a.hagenkord@callwey.de; http://www.callwey.de. Illus., index, adv. Circ: 3746 Paid. *Indexed:* API, IBR, IBZ. *Aud.:* Ac, Sa.

What sets *Topos* apart from other landscape architecture publications on the market today is its consistently international focus. In 2005, the editor of *Topos* announced that the journal's subtitle would be changed from "European landscape magazine" to "international review of landscape architecture and urban design" in order to mark a shift from a largely European focus to an international one, and also to recognize the inclusion of cityscapes. The international scope is evidenced in each issue by the inclusion of a feature article about landscape architecture in a country outside of Europe (e.g., "Landscape Architecture in Argentina," "Landscape Architecture in South Korea," "Landscape Architecture in India"). Previously published in both English and German, *Topos* is now produced only in English. Each issue is thematic (e.g., "Prospective Landscapes," "Urban Design," "Traffic"), and feature articles centering on these themes generally run four to six pages in length. The authors are practicing landscape architects, urban planners, architects, and educators in these fields. *Topos* includes short columns featuring current events, brief interviews with notable designers and planners, announcements of awards, brief reports on the results of relevant competitions internationally, and notices about projects of note recently completed. The layout of *Topos* is contemporary and smartly designed, featuring color photos, plans, and drawings of noteworthy

projects throughout. The book review section is a valuable resource for librarians who want to build international collections in landscape architecture. This publication is highly recommended for any landscape architecture collection.

◼ LATIN AMERICA AND SPAIN

Olivia Olivares, Assistant Librarian, University of Arizona Libraries, 1510 E. University Blvd., Tucson, AZ 85721-0055; olivareso@u.library.arizona.edu; FAX: 520-621-9733.

Joseph R. Diaz, Associate Librarian, University of Arizona Libraries, 1510 E. University Blvd., Tucson, AZ 85721-0055; diazj@u.library.arizona.edu; FAX: 520-621-9733.

Veronica Reyes, Assistant Librarian, University of Arizona Libraries, 1510 E. University Blvd., Tucson AZ 85721-0055; reyesv@u.library.arizona.edu; FAX: 520-621-9733.

Cheryl LaGuardia, Head of Instructional Services, Harvard College Library

Introduction

In this section you will find scholarly and popular journals either about or from Latin America and Spain, published either in English, Spanish, or both languages. These titles, published worldwide, cover immense cultural and geographical areas, and provide ample evidence of the global interest in Latin America.

Several major changes that will affect how librarians decide to include titles in their collections have taken place in publishing for Spanish-speaking audiences in the past couple of years. The first is the widespread availability of free online magazine issues, complete with the full text of articles in the print issues, photo essays, and web exclusives. The web site addresses will be included with each entry when available. Given the availability of full-text, online versions, librarians may choose to forgo traditional print subscriptions for the free online versions. The second is the emergence of Spanish-language versions of old, familiar American titles such as *National Geographic en Espanol, Maxim en Espanol para hombres,* and others. The most popular titles are included here.

Yet another major change is the publication of magazines for Spanish speakers in the United States, rather than in Mexico or other Latin American countries. These American editions will affect the prices of these magazines; with postage and tariffs no longer issues, librarians may find that they can include more in their collections.

This list is not comprehensive; rather, it serves as a guide for developing library collections relevant to this area. We have attempted to include representative titles throughout Latin America, but have emphasized materials readily available in the United States, a situation that has improved with the new, widespread availability of editions of magazines published specifically for the Spanish-speaking market in the United States.

Since ordering titles directly from Latin American publishers can be a slow process, we strongly recommend that selectors of Spanish-language periodicals and other materials find vendors or distributors willing to help identify and provide readily available titles.

The Internet is becoming a more established source of information on Latin America and Latinos in the United States. An increasing number of journals and newspapers are available electronically. Retrieving information about journals and newspapers from the Internet can be a challenging but rewarding undertaking. A vast amount of information is available for those who have access to the technology and are willing to try. One efficient way to search for this information is through mega-sites such as the Latin America information server at the University of Texas at Austin. This site (known as LANIC) provides a gateway to information about Latin America, including information about journals, magazines, and newspapers. Other specialized directories are available as well. What one will find at these sites will vary. For some titles the user will find the full text of the current issue of a magazine or newspaper; other sites will provide only subscription information; still others will offer the tables of contents for current and occasionally for past issues. In general, the titles available on the Internet tend to cover business and current-events themes. Magazines for the general public are in abundance as well. Examples of such mega-sites are the Latin American Network Information Center (LANIC) (lanic.utexas.edu), electronic journals from the WWW Virtual Library (www.edoc.com/ejournal), and the Association of Research Libraries Directory of Electronic Journals, Newsletters, and Academic Discussion Lists (arl.cni.org/scomm/edir/index.html).

Basic Periodicals

Hs: *The Americas, Eres, Geomundo, Tu;* Ga: *The Americas, Buenhogar, Contenido, Hola, Impacto;* Ac: *Historia Mexicana, Review (Americas Society).*

Basic Abstracts and Indexes

Hispanic American Periodicals Index.

3825. *America Indigena.* [ISSN: 0185-1179] 1941. q. USD 75 domestic; USD 80 in Latin America; USD 80 in North America. Instituto Indigenista Interamericano, Ave de las Fuentes 106, Col. Jardines del Pedregal, Mexico City, 01900, Mexico; ininin@data.net.mx; http://www.cdi.gob.mx/conadepi/iii/. Illus., index. *Indexed:* AICP, AmH&L, AnthLit, HAPI, HistAb, IBR, IBSS, IBZ, RI-1, RILM. *Aud.:* Ac.

The stated focus of this long-standing quarterly publication is the "scientific analysis of the problems, processes and tendencies of the native peoples of Latin America." Broad in scope, with articles written in English, Spanish, and Portuguese, this journal covers anthropological, legal, and historical aspects of native culture as well as the relationship between native and non-native societies in Latin America. Recent issues provide extensive coverage of native peoples' legal rights in the Americas, with a heavy emphasis on Central America. The full text of the most recent issues is available online from this magazine's web site. Recommended for academic libraries. (JRD)

3826. *The Americas: a quarterly review of Inter-American cultural history.* [ISSN: 0003-1615] 1944. q. USD 105 (Individuals, USD 40; Students, USD 25 post-secondary only). Ed(s): Donald Fithian Stevens. Academy of American Franciscan History, 1712 Euclid Ave, Berkeley, CA 94709-1208; acadafh@aol.com; http://www.aafh.org. Illus., index, adv. Refereed. Circ: 1000. *Indexed:* ABS&EES, AmH&L, AmHI, ArtHuCI, BRI, CBRI, HAPI, HistAb, HumInd, IBR, IBZ, RILM, SSCI. *Bk. rev.:* 15, 500-700 words. *Aud.:* Ac.

This is a well-established scholarly journal that focuses on the social and cultural history of Latin America and inter-American affairs, with a slant toward the study of the history and influence of the Catholic Church in the Americas. Each issue contains five to ten in-depth articles on very narrow aspects of Latin American sociocultural history, as well as an extensive book review section. A section titled "InterAmerican Notes" highlights upcoming professional conferences, calls for papers, and forthcoming publications. Not to be confused with the Organization of American States magazine by the same title, this refereed journal is intended for academic audiences. (JRD)

3827. *Americas (English Edition).* Formerly: *Pan American Union. Bulletin.* [ISSN: 0379-0940] 1949. bi-m. USD 21 domestic; USD 27 foreign. Ed(s): Maria de los Angeles Ochoa. Organization of American States, Department of Publications, 1889 F St, NW, Washington, DC 20006; rgutierrez@oas.org; http://www.oas.org. Illus. Sample. Circ: 50000 Paid. Microform: PQC. Online: EBSCO Publishing, EBSCO Host; Florida Center for Library Automation; Gale; OCLC Online Computer Library Center, Inc.; ProQuest LLC (Ann Arbor); H.W. Wilson. *Indexed:* AmH&L, AmHI, ArtHuCI, BAS, BRI, HAPI, HistAb, IBR, MASUSE, MLA-IB, PRA, RGPR, RI-1, SSCI. *Bk. rev.:* 2-3, 600-1,200 words. *Aud.:* Hs, Ga, Ac.

A lavishly illustrated bimonthly magazine published by the Organization of American States (OAS), *Americas* is a general-interest periodical that features articles and photo essays on a variety of topics, including art, nature, travel, biography, and cultural anthropology, as well as regular columns on music, food, literature, and dance in Latin America. There is also a column on OAS news, issues, and activities. A staple in the genre of general-interest periodicals

on Latin America since 1949, this colorful and informative publication is available in both English and Spanish. Excerpts from selected articles are available online from the magazine's web site. This journal would make a welcome addition to any high school, public, or academic library collection. (JRD)

Ancient Mesoamerica. See Archaeology section.

3828. *Anuario de Estudios Centroamericanos.* [ISSN: 0377-7316] 1974. 2x/yr. Ed(s): Ronald Solano. Universidad de Costa Rica, Editorial, Sede Rodrigo Facio Brenes, Montes de Oca, San Jose, Costa Rica; direccion@editorial.ucr.ac.cr; http://editorial.ucr.ac.cr. Adv. Circ: 1000. Online: Gale. *Indexed:* AmH&L, HAPI, HistAb, IBR, IBSS, PAIS. *Bk. rev.:* Number and length vary. *Aud.:* Ac.

This refereed scholarly journal, published twice a year, focuses on all aspects of the social sciences. Coverage is limited to the Central American region, with heavy emphasis on the study of the history and culture of Costa Rica. Recent submissions cover such topics as rural development and poverty in Central America in the 1990s, and Spaniards in the City of San Jose, Costa Rica, at the end of the nineteenth century. This is a long-standing publication that belongs in academic libraries with programs in Latin American Studies. (JRD)

Buenhogar. See General Interest–Non-English Language section.

3829. *Caribbean Quarterly.* [ISSN: 0008-6495] 1949. q. Ed(s): Rex Nettleford. University of the West Indies, School of Continuing Studies, PO Box 42, Kingston, 7, Jamaica. Index, adv. Circ: 1500. Microform: PQC. Online: Chadwyck-Healey Inc. Reprint: PSC. *Indexed:* ASSIA, AmH&L, AmHI, BrHumI, HAPI, HistAb, IBR, IBSS, IIBP, IIPA, PAIS, RILM, RRTA, WAE&RSA. *Bk. rev.:* Number and length vary. *Aud.:* Ac.

This journal, published in Jamaica, has been in existence for more than 55 years. Its focus is on the literature, politics, and history of the Caribbean region, and it includes scholarly articles, book reviews, fiction, and poetry. Sample articles focus on the Caribbean as multi-ethnic, as dispossessed, and as independent and attaining selfhood. For academic libraries with programs in Latin American/Caribbean Studies. (JRD)

3830. *Casa y Estilo Internacional.* [ISSN: 1521-8287] bi-m. Ed(s): Alfonso Nino. Linda International Publishing, 12182 SW 128th St, Miami, FL 33186; info@estilonet.com. Adv. *Aud.:* Ga.

This glossy, Spanish-language lifestyle magazine is aimed specifically at the upscale Hispanic market. Topics covered include art design, profiles of custom-made homes and interiors, interviews with trend-setting personalities, a section on cooking, restaurant reviews, and a travel section. This publication is sure to be a winner with those interested in keeping up with the latest styles and trends in interior design and other aspects of "fine living." Recommended for public libraries. (JRD)

3831. *Chasqui: revista de literatura latinoamericano.* [ISSN: 0145-8973] 1972. s-a. USD 25 (Individuals, USD 15). Ed(s): David W Foster. Arizona State University, Languages and Literatures, University Dr & Mill Ave, Tempe, AZ 85287. Illus., adv. Refereed. Circ: 400 Paid. *Indexed:* AmHI, ArtHuCI, HAPI, IBR, MLA-IB, RILM, SSCI. *Bk. rev.:* 25-30, 500-3,000 words. *Aud.:* Ac.

A literary journal with articles published in Spanish, English, and Portuguese, this publication features literary criticism (six to eight articles per issue), bibliographic essays, original works of creative writing, interviews with writers, and plenty of book reviews of works by well-known and lesser-known authors. It encourages the submission of manuscripts that focus on interdisciplinary approaches, the bridging of national and linguistic divisions, subaltern studies, feminism, queer theory, popular culture, and minority topics. One of many in the genre of "revista de literatura latinoamericana," it is appropriate for academic libraries with large Latin American collections. (JRD)

3832. *Colonial Latin American Review.* [ISSN: 1060-9164] 1992. s-a. GBP 220 print & online eds. Ed(s): Frederick Luciani. Routledge, 4 Park Sq, Milton Park, Abingdon, OX14 4RN, United Kingdom; info@routledge.co.uk; http://www.routledge.com. Illus., index. Refereed.

Online: EBSCO Publishing, EBSCO Host; Gale; IngentaConnect; OCLC Online Computer Library Center, Inc.; SwetsWise Online Content. Reprint: PSC. *Indexed:* AICP, AmH&L, AmHI, HAPI, HistAb, L&LBA, MLA-IB, PSA, SociolAb. *Bk. rev.:* Number and length vary. *Aud.:* Ac.

This interdisciplinary journal focuses on the colonial period in Latin America. Included are articles, review essays, research notes, book reviews, conference announcements, and even obituaries in English, Spanish, and Portuguese. *CLAR* is intended to provide a forum for critical analysis and scholarship in the disciplines of art, anthropology, geography, history, and literature, with the goal of fostering dialogue among these disciplines. Articles are from international contributors and are the work of both emerging and established scholars. Recommended for libraries with comprehensive Latin American collections. (JRD)

3833. Contenido. [ISSN: 0010-7581] 1963. m. MXN 220; MXN 20 newsstand/cover per issue; USD 45 foreign. Ed(s): Armando Ayala Anguiano. Editorial Contenido S.A., BUFFON 46, esq. Ejercito Nacional 9o piso, Mexico, Col Anzures, Mexico City, 11590, Mexico; ecsa@data.net.mx; http://www.contenido.com.mx. Illus., adv. Circ: 200000. *Aud.:* Ga.

Very similar in format to *Reader's Digest,* this monthly publication contains many brief, general-interest articles on topics such as health, science, technology, food, recipes, and humor, all from a Mexican perspective. Also included are articles on popular Mexican celebrities and well-known international figures, and features on geography and history. Every issue also contains a condensed book by a well-known Latin American author. Sure to be popular with a variety of readers, this magazine is recommended for public libraries. (JRD)

Cosmopolitan en Espanol. See General Interest: Non–English Language section.

3834. Cristina: la revista. [ISSN: 1067-2575] 1991. m. USD 15 domestic; USD 37.35 foreign. Ed(s): Wanda Negron Cruz. Editorial America, S.A., 6355 NW 36th St, Miami, FL 33166. Adv. *Aud.:* Ga.

Founded in November 1991 and published by Cristina Saralegui, the well-known Latina television talk-show host based in Miami, *Cristina* is a Spanish-language monthly. Each issue contains approximately 80 full-color pages entirely devoted to the Latin world and its people. This periodical includes celebrity news, exclusive interviews, and success stories. Most of the articles are on Latin American actors, musicians, or others who have found fame in the popular arts. Selected articles and columns are available on the magazine's web site. Recommended for public libraries. (JRD)

3835. Critica Hispanica. [ISSN: 0278-7261] 1979. s-a. USD 35 in US & Canada; USD 45 elsewhere. Ed(s): Gregorio C Martin. Critica Hispanica, Department of Modern Language, Duquesne University, Pittsburgh, PA 15282. Illus., adv. Refereed. Circ: 500. *Indexed:* AmHI, ArtHuCI, IBR, MLA-IB, RILM. *Bk. rev.:* 6-10, 400-800 words. *Aud.:* Ac.

This is a scholarly literary and linguistics journal. Each issue is devoted to a specific theme or author, such as the Caribbean character in literature, the Cuban political novel, or Pablo Neruda. Each volume contains nine or ten lengthy articles accompanied by notes and bibliographies, and it may include interviews and book reviews. Articles are in Spanish or English. Recommended for academic libraries that support Latin American literature and literary studies programs. (VR)

3836. Cuadernos Hispanoamericanos: revista mensual de cultura hispanica. [ISSN: 0011-250X] 1948. m. EUR 51.09 domestic; USD 140 in Europe; USD 170 in the Americas. Ed(s): Felix Grande. Agencia Espanola de Cooperacion Internacional (A E C I), Avda Reyes Catolicos 4, Madrid, 28040, Spain; http://www.aeci.es. Illus. Circ: 2000. Reprint: PSC. *Indexed:* AmH&L, ArtHuCI, HAPI, HistAb, IBR, IBZ, MLA-IB, RI-1, RILM, SSCI. *Bk. rev.:* Number and length vary. *Aud.:* Ac.

Cuadernos hispanoamericanos is a fascinating review of current literary and cultural thought from some of Latin America's leading intellectuals. Each issue includes a "Dossier" or collection of essays on a particular aspect of Latin

American culture or the culture of a particular country or geographic region; a "Punto de vista" section with viewpoint essays and occasionally poetry and fiction; and a book review section, "Biblioteca." This journal is recommended for academic libraries. (OO)

3837. Eres. s-m. Editorial Televisa, 6355 NW 36th St, Miami, FL 33166; subscriptions@editorialtelevisa.com. Adv. *Aud.:* Hs, Ga.

Reminiscent of many American teen magazines, *Eres* is full of gossip and glossy photos of the most popular young movie stars, musicians, and other celebrities in the Latin world, although the magazine has recently expanded its coverage to include American celebrities like Hilary Duff. Included in each issue is a photo-filled interview with a popular celebrity such as Marc Antony, an astrology section, and a section on American music. Also included are articles and photos of the latest fashions, and features on topics of concern to teens such as anorexia nervosa, relationships, and personal hygiene. Many of the articles from each issue are available online from the magazine's web site. Sure to appeal to the young-adult crowd. For public libraries. (JRD)

3838. Fem. [ISSN: 0185-4666] 1976. m. MXN 250 domestic; USD 70 in the Americas; USD 82 in Europe. Ed(s): Esperanza Brito de Marti. Difusion Cultural Feminista A.C., Apdo. Postal WTC-289, Del. Beito Juarez, Mexico City, 03812, Mexico; revista@axtel.net. Illus., adv. Circ: 15000. *Indexed:* AltPI, BAS, HAPI, RILM. *Aud.:* Ac, Ga.

Looking for a Latin American counterpart to *Ms.* magazine? *Fem* is it. This progressive news, opinion, and cultural monthly is a refreshing alternative to most Latin American publications for women. Coverage includes features on critical social issues such as AIDS, mental health, child welfare, and abortion, plus articles on Mexican politics written from a feminist perspective. Also included are short stories, poetry, and other creative writing by women. Selected articles are available on the magazine's web site. For public and academic libraries. (JRD)

3839. Feminaria. 1988. s-a. Ed(s): Lea Fletcher. Feminaria Editora, C.C. 402, Buenos Aires, 1000, Argentina; feminaria@fibertel.com.ar; http://www.latbook.com.ar. Refereed. Circ: 1000. *Indexed:* HAPI, MLA-IB. *Bk. rev.:* Number and length vary. *Aud.:* Ac, Sa.

Published in Argentina, this magazine focuses on feminist theory, feminist literary theory, and criticism. While most of the articles are about women and Latin American literature, coverage also includes scholarly works on the social, political, and cultural aspects of modern life. Artwork, interviews, and poetry are also featured, as is a bibliographic section highlighting recent publications from Latin America. Not limiting itself to any one form of feminism, the magazine considers for publication "any work that is not sexist, racist, [or] homophobic or that expresses any other type of discrimination." The full text of each edition is available online. For collections that seek a balance between popular and scholarly reading materials for women in Spanish. (JRD)

3840. Frontera Norte. [ISSN: 0187-7372] 1989. s-a. Ed(s): Erika Moreno. Colegio de la Frontera Norte, Publications Department, Blvd Abelardo L Rodriguez 2925, Zona del Rio, Tijuana, 22350, Mexico; publica@ colef.mx. Illus. Refereed. Circ: 2000. Online: EBSCO Publishing, EBSCO Host; Gale. *Indexed:* Chicano, HAPI, PAIS. *Bk. rev.:* Number and length vary. *Aud.:* Ac.

This primarily Spanish-language scholarly journal publishes extensively researched articles by Mexicans and Americans who specialize in issues confronting the U.S.-Mexico border region. Some articles are in English. Each issue includes five to six articles on political, social, economic, and environmental issues and trends, a section of book reviews, and a position paper, "Nota critica." Articles are extensively researched and annotated. The full text of the articles is available on the journal web site. For academic libraries with border studies collections. (OO)

Furia Musical. See General Interest:Non–English Language section.

3841. Geomundo: la guia practica para explorar tu mundo. [ISSN: 0256-7253] 1977. m. USD 27. Ed(s): Gabriel Gonzalez. Editorial Televisa, 6355 NW 36th St, Miami, FL 33166; subscriptions@ editorialtelevisa.com. Illus., adv. Circ: 116000. *Aud.:* Hs, Ga, Ac.

Very similar in format and content to *National Geographic* magazine, this publication is filled with interesting in-depth articles and beautiful photographs of everything from bugs and plants to art and food to features on exotic peoples and places worldwide. Also included are articles on environmental and social concerns. There is an annual issue that highlights the works of many amateur photographers. Sure to be a popular item, this publication is recommended for all libraries. (JRD)

3842. *Gestos: revista de teoria y practica del teatro hispanico.* [ISSN: 1040-483X] 1986. s-a. USD 45 (Individuals, USD 22.50). Ed(s): Juan Villegas. University of California at Irvine, Department of Spanish and Portuguese, Humanities Hall, Irvine, CA 92697. Illus. Refereed. Circ: 700 Paid. *Indexed:* IBR, MLA-IB. *Bk. rev.:* 8-10, 500-1,000 words. *Aud.:* Ac.

This is an academic publication devoted to the study of Hispanic drama and the theater. Each issue includes six to eight scholarly essays, in English or Spanish, on various aspects of playwriting and the theater, plus interviews with well-known and lesser-known playwrights and reviews of recent dramatic productions. Also contained in each issue is an original play. Coverage includes all of Latin America, Spain, and the United States, making *Gestos* a well-rounded, global source for criticism, interpretation, and news about *el teatro hispano*. For academic libraries. (JRD)

Harper's Bazaar en Espanol. See General Interest: Non–English Language section.

3843. *Hemisphere: a magazine of the Americas.* [ISSN: 0898-3038] 1988. s-a. USD 20 domestic; USD 27 foreign. Ed(s): Eduardo Gamarra. Latin American and Caribbean Center, Florida International University, University Park, Miami, FL 33199; lacc@fiu.edu; http://lacc.fiu.edu/index.php. Illus., adv. Circ: 2000. *Indexed:* ABS&EES, BAS, HAPI, RGPR, RILM. *Aud.:* Ga, Ac.

The masthead of this magazine states that it is "dedicated to provoking debate on the problems, initiatives and achievements of Latin America and the Caribbean." Issues include excellent photo essays as well as articles on government, economics, politics, and social issues. The magazine also features literature reviews and a news-in-brief section. Contributors are from varied backgrounds and include university faculty, intergovernmental agency officials, and relief agency workers. For general audiences and public and academic libraries. (OO)

3844. *Hispamerica: revista de literatura.* [ISSN: 0363-0471] 1972. 3x/yr. USD 36 (Individuals, USD 27). Ed(s): Saul Sosnowski. Hispamerica, c/o Latin American Studies Center, University of Maryland, College Park, MD 20742; SS55@umail.umd.edu; http://www.lasc.umd.edu. Illus., adv. Refereed. Circ: 1000. Vol. ends: Dec. *Indexed:* ArtHuCI, HAPI, IBR, MLA-IB, RILM, SSCI. *Bk. rev.:* 7-15, 300-2,500 words. *Aud.:* Ac.

This Spanish-language journal provides a broad review of issues and perspectives in contemporary Latin American literature. Each issue includes critical essays, short stories and poetry, interviews with Latin American authors, and book reviews. An extensive index is available online. This periodical is of interest primarily to academic libraries that support Latin American literature collections, although public libraries with a large Spanish-speaking clientele might also benefit. (OO)

Hispanic Business Magazine. See Latino Studies section.

3845. *Hispanic Journal (Indiana).* [ISSN: 0271-0986] 1979. s-a. USD 40 (Individuals, USD 20). Ed(s): Jose Carranza. Indiana University of Pennsylvania, Department of Spanish and Classical Languages, 462 Sutton Hall, Indiana, PA 15705; dafoltz@grove.iup.edu; http://www.chss.iup.edu/spanish/. Adv. Refereed. Circ: 450 Paid. *Indexed:* AmHI, HAPI, IBR, IBZ, MLA-IB, RI-1, RILM. *Aud.:* Ac.

The introduction to this excellent scholarly journal states that its purpose is "to publish research and criticism of the highest quality in the areas of Spanish, Portuguese and Catalan literatures, language and linguistics." Articles may be written in English, Spanish, Portuguese, or Catalan. All are annotated and include bibliographies. The tables of contents for recent issues are available online. Recommended for academic libraries. (OO)

Hispanic Journal of Behavioral Sciences. See Psychology section.

3846. *Hispanic Review: a quarterly journal devoted to research in the Hispanic languages and literatures.* [ISSN: 0018-2176] 1933. q. USD 79 (Individuals, USD 47; Students, USD 27). Ed(s): Michael Solomon. University of Pennsylvania Press, 4200 Pine St, Philadelphia, PA 19104-4011; http://www.pennpress.org. Illus., adv. Refereed. Circ: 1600. Vol. ends: Fall. Online: Chadwyck-Healey Inc.; EBSCO Publishing, EBSCO Host; JSTOR (Web-based Journal Archive); Northern Light Technology, Inc.; OCLC Online Computer Library Center, Inc.; Project MUSE; ProQuest K-12 Learning Solutions; ProQuest LLC (Ann Arbor); H.W. Wilson. *Indexed:* AmH&L, AmHI, ArtHuCI, BRI, FR, HAPI, HistAb, HumInd, IBR, IBZ, IndIslam, MASUSE, MLA-IB, RILM, SSCI. *Bk. rev.:* Number and length vary. *Aud.:* Ac.

This scholarly journal's masthead states that it is "devoted to research in the Hispanic languages and literatures." It features articles by noted scholars of literary analysis and criticism. There is a monthly section of book reviews as well. Articles and reviews may be in Spanish or English. The last issue of the year provides a list of articles and book reviews that appeared during the year. In format, content, and style, this journal is quite similar to *Hispanofila, Hispanic Review,* and other university-published literary journals. Recommended for academic libraries that support programs in Spanish language and literature. (OO)

3847. *Hispanofila.* [ISSN: 0018-2206] 1957. 3x/yr. USD 35 (Individuals, USD 25; Students, USD 11). Ed(s): Fred M Clark. University of North Carolina at Chapel Hill, Department of Romance Languages, CB 3170, 238 Dey Hall, Chapel Hill, NC 27599-3170. Illus., index, adv. Refereed. Circ: 500. Vol. ends: May. Microform: PQC. *Indexed:* AmHI, ArtHuCI, IBR, MLA-IB. *Bk. rev.:* Number and length vary. *Aud.:* Ac.

This academic journal publishes research articles and essays by noted scholars on issues in Spanish-language literature and linguistics, although the emphasis is on literature. Articles are footnoted, include bibliographies, and may be written in English or Spanish. Each issue includes an extensive book review section. Recommended for academic libraries. (OO)

3848. *Historia Mexicana.* [ISSN: 0185-0172] 1951. 4x/yr. MXN 300 domestic; USD 120 foreign. Ed(s): Francisco Gomez Rulz. Colegio de Mexico, A.C., Departamento de Publicaciones, Camino al Ajusco 20, Col. Pedregal Santa Teresa, Mexico City, 10740, Mexico; http://www.colmex.mx. Illus., index, adv. Refereed. Circ: 1500. Vol. ends: Jun. *Indexed:* AICP, AmH&L, AmHI, ArtHuCI, BAS, HAPI, HistAb, IBR, IBSS, MLA-IB, PSA, SSCI, SociolAb. *Bk. rev.:* 2-8, 500-2,000 words, signed. *Aud.:* Ac.

Produced by the Centro de Estudios Historicos of the Colegio de Mexico and written in Spanish, this is one of the premier journals in Mexican history. Its contributors include the leading historians working in the field. All articles are extensively footnoted and annotated, and include bibliographies. Each issue also includes a book review section, a section of summaries of recent publications, and a section of English-language abstracts. Recommended for academic libraries that support Latin American Studies programs and history departments with an interest in Mexican or Latin American history. (OO)

3849. *Hola.* [ISSN: 0214-3895] 1944. w. EUR 84 domestic. Ed(s): Eduardo Sanchez Junco. Empresa Editora Hola, S.A., Miguel Angel 1, Madrid, 28010, Spain. Illus., adv. Sample. Circ: 582778. *Aud.:* Ga.

Similar to *People* or *Us* magazines in content and format, *Hola* features articles about the rich and famous of Spain, Europe, and to a lesser extent, the United States. European (mainly Spanish) royalty gets the greatest amount of coverage, followed by the wealthy of Europe, European heads of state, and American movie stars. The articles are lavishly illustrated with large color photographs, and indeed the photographs are more numerous and more prominent than the text. There are also shorter, regular sections on food, beauty, health, and fashion. The full text of this magazine is available online. Of interest to public libraries with Spanish-speaking patrons. (OO)

3850. *Impacto.* [ISSN: 0019-2880] 1950. w. MXN 8 per issue. Ed(s): Carlos Moncada Ochoa. Impacto, Av. Ceylan 517, Apdo. 2986, Mexico City, 23000, Mexico. Illus., adv. Circ: 115000. *Aud.:* Ga.

This large-format Mexican publication is reminiscent of *Life* magazine. It deals largely with political, economic, and social issues in Mexico, with some attention paid to international affairs. Articles cover religion, health, and ecology, as well as the arts and in-depth analysis of Mexican political issues. All articles are in Spanish and are well illustrated. This magazine will appeal to public libraries that serve Spanish-speaking populations. (JRD)

3851. *Journal of Latin American Cultural Studies.* Formerly (until 1995): *Travesia.* [ISSN: 1356-9325] 1992. 3x/yr. GBP 394 print & online eds. Ed(s): Jens Andermann, Catherine Boyle. Routledge, 4 Park Sq, Milton Park, Abingdon, OX14 4RN, United Kingdom; info@routledge.co.uk; http://www.tandf.co.uk/journals. Illus. Vol. ends: Nov. Online: EBSCO Publishing, EBSCO Host; Gale; IngentaConnect; OCLC Online Computer Library Center, Inc.; SwetsWise Online Content. Reprint: PSC. *Indexed:* AmHI, CJA, HAPI, MLA-IB, PSA, SSA, SociolAb. *Bk. rev.:* 3-5, 500-2,000 words. *Aud.:* Ac.

This scholarly journal's primary goals are to stimulate "interdisciplinary work on Latin American culture and cultural history and [to encourage] debate on the teaching and reception of Latin American cultural materials." This well-known title focuses primarily on Latin American culture after 1492, and it covers anthropology, communication, history, and literature. Included in each issue is a section that provides authoritative overviews of the current state of those disciplines that fall within the framework of Latin American cultural studies, including literature, film studies, music, and communication studies. Recent issues include articles on Cuban music and on Miami as portrayed in *telenovelas*. Articles are well written, annotated, and include bibliographies. Recommended for academic libraries, particularly those with a strong Latin American Studies program. (OO)

3852. *Journal of Latin American Studies.* [ISSN: 0022-216X] 1969. q. GBP 192. Ed(s): Paul Cammack. Cambridge University Press, The Edinburgh Bldg, Shaftesbury Rd, Cambridge, CB2 2RU, United Kingdom; journals@cambridge.org; http://www.journals.cambridge.org. Illus., adv. Refereed. Vol. ends: Nov. Microform: PQC. Online: Pub.; EBSCO Publishing, EBSCO Host; Florida Center for Library Automation; Gale; JSTOR (Web-based Journal Archive); OCLC Online Computer Library Center, Inc.; OhioLINK; SwetsWise Online Content. Reprint: PSC. *Indexed:* ABCPolSci, ABIn, AICP, AmH&L, AmHI, AnthLit, ArtHuCI, BrHumI, CABA, ForAb, HAPI, HistAb, IBR, IBSS, IBZ, IPSA, LRI, MLA-IB, PAIS, PRA, PSA, RI-1, S&F, SSA, SSCI, SociolAb, WAE&RSA. *Bk. rev.:* 22-28, 350-2,000 words. *Aud.:* Ga, Ac.

This English-language scholarly journal covers issues and trends in Latin America with an emphasis on sociology, history, anthropology, sociology, economics, and international relations. The articles and reviews are written by leading scholars and researchers. Issues may be dedicated to one particular country or question or may reflect this excellent journal's broad coverage of Latin America. Each issue also includes book reviews. Recommended for academic libraries that support programs in Latin American Studies, political science, and economics, and large public research libraries. (OO)

3853. *Latin American Indian Literatures Journal: a review of American Indian texts and studies.* Supersedes (in 1985): *Latin American Indian Literatures.* [ISSN: 0888-5613] 1977. s-a. USD 49 (Individuals, USD 29; USD 28 per issue). Ed(s): Mary H Preuss. Penn State University, McKeesport, 4000 University Dr, McKeesport, PA 15132-7698; mhp1@psu.edu. Illus., adv. Refereed. Circ: 300 Paid. *Indexed:* AICP, AmHI, AnthLit, ArtHuCI, HAPI, IBR, IBSS, IBZ, MLA-IB, RI-1, RILM. *Bk. rev.:* 3-5, 500-1,500 words. *Aud.:* Ac.

This scholarly journal focuses exclusively on the native aboriginal languages of Latin America. Each issue contains informative and thoroughly researched articles and studies of these languages, as well as book reviews, article abstracts, and bibliographies. Many articles include excerpts of transcriptions of native aboriginal-language poetry or stories in the original, with English-language translations. Some articles include photos of illustrations from codices and other historical documents of interest to linguists and researchers. Highly recommended for academic libraries that support Latin American Studies programs and graduate linguistics programs. (OO)

3854. *Latin American Literary Review.* [ISSN: 0047-4134] 1972. s-a. USD 44 (Individuals, USD 25). Latin American Literary Review Press, PO Box 17660, Pittsburgh, PA 15235; latin@angstrom.net; http://www.lalrp.org. Illus., index, adv. Refereed. Circ: 1500 Paid. Microform: PQC. Online: Northern Light Technology, Inc.; OCLC Online Computer Library Center, Inc.; ProQuest K-12 Learning Solutions; ProQuest LLC (Ann Arbor). *Indexed:* AmHI, ArtHuCI, HAPI, HumInd, IBR, IBZ, MLA-IB. *Bk. rev.:* 4-6, 90-100 words. *Aud.:* Ga, Ac.

This scholarly journal's editorial board includes some of the most prominent Latin American Studies scholars in the United States. Its stated purpose is to publish "scholarly essays and book reviews on the literatures of Spanish America and Brazil." Articles may be in English, Spanish, or Portuguese. The journal's contributors are as illustrious as its editorial board. This publication makes a very important contribution to the understanding of the literature of Latin America. Past issues included excerpts of creative works, but more recent issues have not, with articles in recent issues being of a critical or analytical nature. Highly recommended for academic libraries and large public libraries. (OO)

3855. *Latin American Perspectives: a journal on capitalism and socialism.* [ISSN: 0094-582X] 1974. bi-m. GBP 341. Ed(s): Ronald H Chilcote. Sage Publications, Inc., 2455 Teller Rd, Thousand Oaks, CA 91320; info@sagepub.com; http://www.sagepub.com. Illus., adv. Refereed. Circ: 750 Paid. Microform: PQC. Online: EBSCO Publishing, EBSCO Host; Florida Center for Library Automation; Gale; HighWire Press; JSTOR (Web-based Journal Archive); OCLC Online Computer Library Center, Inc.; SAGE Publications, Inc., SAGE Journals Online; SwetsWise Online Content. Reprint: PSC. *Indexed:* ABCPolSci, ABIn, AltPI, AmH&L, CJA, HAPI, HistAb, IBR, IBSS, IBZ, IPSA, LeftInd, PAIS, PRA, PSA, RILM, SFSA, SSA, SSCI, SUSA, SociolAb, WAE&RSA. *Bk. rev.:* Number and length vary. *Aud.:* Ga, Ac.

Each issue of this scholarly journal offers extensive, well-researched, and annotated articles that discuss a single topic of pressing importance in Latin America. Recent issues have dealt with the civil war in Colombia; the struggle of the indigenous peoples of Chiapas; and political, economic, and social turmoil in Mexico. The articles are written by well-known scholars and researchers and offer diverse perspectives on the issue they treat. Some issues feature excellent book reviews. This journal is highly recommended for academic libraries that support research programs in Latin American Studies, economics, sociology, and political science, as well as large public libraries with a research focus. (OO)

3856. *Latin American Research Review.* [ISSN: 0023-8791] 1965. 3x/yr. USD 180 (Individuals, USD 40). Ed(s): Peter Ward. University of Texas Press, Journals Division, 2100 Comal, Austin, TX 78722; journals@ uts.cc.utexas.edu; http://www.utexas.edu/utpress/journals/journals.html. Illus., index. Sample. Refereed. Circ: 5000 Paid. Microform: PQC. Online: Chadwyck-Healey Inc.; EBSCO Publishing, EBSCO Host; Factiva, Inc.; Florida Center for Library Automation; Gale; JSTOR (Web-based Journal Archive); Northern Light Technology, Inc.; OCLC Online Computer Library Center, Inc.; OhioLINK; Project MUSE; ProQuest K-12 Learning Solutions; ProQuest LLC (Ann Arbor); SwetsWise Online Content; H.W. Wilson. Reprint: PSC. *Indexed:* ABCPolSci, ABS&EES, AmH&L, AmHI, AnthLit, ArtHuCI, CJA, FLI, FR, HAPI, HistAb, IBR, IBSS, IBZ, IIBP, IPSA, PAIS, PRA, PSA, RILM, SSCI, SociolAb, WAE&RSA. *Aud.:* Ga, Ac.

The *Latin American Research Review* was established to achieve "a better understanding and a more systematic communication among individuals and institutions concerned with scholarly studies of Latin America." Each issue includes articles on politics, economics, history, sociology, or culture, all extensively footnoted and with bibliographies appended. There is also an extensive review essay section that examines issues in the light of recently published scholarship. Articles and essays may be in English or Spanish. This journal is highly recommended for large public libraries with a research focus and academic libraries that support Latin American Studies programs. (OO)

Latin American Theatre Review. See Theater section.

Latina (New York). See Fashion and Lifestyle section.

3857. *Letras Femeninas.* [ISSN: 0277-4356] 1974. 2x/yr. USD 50 (Individuals, USD 45). Asociacion de Literatura Femenina Hispanica, c/o Maria Claudia Andre, Dept of Modern and Classical Languages, Holland, MI 49423; andre@hope.edu; http://grafemas.org. Illus., adv. Circ: 600. *Indexed:* HAPI, IAPV, IBR, MLA-IB. *Bk. rev.:* Number and length vary. *Aud.:* Ac.

This journal is dedicated to the study and critique of women's literature in the Hispanic world from a distinctly feminist viewpoint. The journal publishes the work of prominent, established female writers and scholars from Spain, Latin America, and the United States. Articles are in Spanish, English, or Portuguese. Regular sections include review articles, book reviews, interviews, poetry, essays on issues in literature and writing, and news and announcements. Recommended for academic libraries that support women's studies and literature programs. (OO)

3858. *Libros de Mexico.* [ISSN: 0186-2243] 1985. q. USD 40 in the Americas; USD 50 elsewhere. Ed(s): Federico Krafft Vera. Camara Nacional de la Industria Editorial Mexicana, Holanda 13, Col. San Diego Churubusco, Coyoacan, 04120, Mexico; ciecprom@inetcorp.net.mx; http://www.libromex.com.mx. Illus., adv. Circ: 5000. *Indexed:* IBR, IBZ. *Aud.:* Hs, Ga, Ac.

This publication, written completely in Spanish, is an excellent selection tool for librarians in charge of acquiring current material from Mexico. It offers up-to-date information on the Mexican book trade industry. The "Profile" section presents a different publisher in each issue. Additional regular sections include serials, news, interviews, and editorial news. This last section lists new publications by publisher and groups them by Dewey classification number. (JRD)

3859. *Luso - Brazilian Review: devoted to the culture of the Portuguese-speaking world.* [ISSN: 0024-7413] 1963. s-a. USD 172 print & online eds. (Individuals, USD 62 print & online eds.). Ed(s): Severino Albuquerque, Ellen W Sapega. University of Wisconsin Press, Journal Division, 1930 Monroe St, 3rd Fl, Madison, WI 53711-2059; journals@ uwpress.wisc.edu; http://www.wisc.edu/wisconsinpress/journals. Illus., adv. Refereed. Circ: 500. Microform: PQC. Online: EBSCO Publishing, EBSCO Host; OCLC Online Computer Library Center, Inc.; OhioLINK; Project MUSE; SwetsWise Online Content. Reprint: PSC. *Indexed:* AmH&L, AmHI, HAPI, HistAb, IBR, IBZ, L&LBA, MLA-IB, PSA, RILM, SSA, SociolAb. *Bk. rev.:* 5, 700 words. *Aud.:* Ac.

This is an important scholarly journal, published twice a year, that provides a multidimensional look at the Portuguese-speaking world. Includes articles in English or Portuguese on a variety of topics, from studies of immigrant communities in Brazil to a study of slavery in Bahia. A typical issue includes about six articles, a book review section, a list of books received, and segments with announcements, brief contributors' profiles, and a report on research in progress. This publication makes a significant contribution to the understanding of Luso-Brazilian culture. Recommended for academic libraries that support Latin American Studies programs. (JRD)

3860. *Marie Claire en Espanol.* [ISSN: 0188-2724] 1954. m. Ed(s): Louise Gras Mereles. Editorial Televisa, Vasco de Quiroga 2000, Edif E 4o Piso, Mexico City, 01210, Mexico. Illus., adv. Sample. *Aud.:* Ga.

The Spanish edition of the well-known international magazine covers topics considered of interest to women. Like its competitors *Harper's Bazaar* and *Vogue,* it has articles on fashion and beauty and columns dealing with current issues, especially health topics. Interviews with notable figures in the arts,

literature, and music are also frequently included. Each issue devotes several pages to the latest trends in fashion and the culinary arts plus a monthly horoscope. This magazine will find a place in any public library that serves a Spanish-speaking audience. (JRD)

3861. *Mexican Studies.* [ISSN: 0742-9797] 1985. s-a. USD 136 print & online eds. USD 75 newsstand/cover. Ed(s): Jaime E Rodriguez. University of California Press, Journals Division, 2000 Center St, Ste 303, Berkeley, CA 94704-1223; journals@ucpress.edu; http://www.ucpress.edu/journals. Illus., index, adv. Refereed. Circ: 1350 Paid. Microform: PQC. Online: EBSCO Publishing, EBSCO Host; Florida Center for Library Automation; JSTOR (Web-based Journal Archive); OCLC Online Computer Library Center, Inc.; ProQuest LLC (Ann Arbor); SwetsWise Online Content; H.W. Wilson. *Indexed:* AICP, AmH&L, AmHI, ArtHuCI, Chicano, ENW, FLI, HAPI, HRA, HistAb, HumInd, IBR, IBZ, IPSA, PSA, RILM, SSA, SSCI, SociolAb. *Aud.:* Ac.

This interdisciplinary, scholarly publication focuses on research on Mexico and its people. It draws scholars from all disciplines and offers lengthy articles in English or Spanish on cultural, historical, political, social, economic, and scientific factors that affect the country's growth and development. It also offers review essays and sections such as "Other Books Received" and "Notes on Contributors." The journal is a joint effort of the University of California Institute for Mexico and the United States and the Universidad Nacional Autonoma de Mexico. It is now available electronically. Recommended for academic libraries that support teaching and research on Mexico. (VR)

3862. *Mexico Desconocido.* [ISSN: 0187-1560] 1976. m. MXN 240 domestic; USD 60 United States; USD 70 in Europe. Ed(s): Beatriz Quintanar Hinojosa. Editorial Mexico Desconocido S.A.de C.V., Monte Pelvoux 110, Planta Jardin, Lomas de Chapultepec, Mexico City, 11000, Mexico. Illus., index, adv. Circ: 64000. *Aud.:* Ga.

This is a beautifully designed magazine that features articles on the artistry, culture, cuisine, and hidden wonders of Mexico, covering a wide range of geographic areas. Topics have included the artisan work of San Salvador Huixcolotla and hidden caves in Guerrero. Color photographs of natural and architectural design complement the lengthy and informative pieces. Each issue offers eight to ten engaging articles from seven to ten pages in length. Selected articles are available online in Spanish and English versions, although the Spanish version is more expansive than the English. (VR)

3863. *N A C L A Report on the Americas.* Former titles: *Report on the Americas; N A C L A Report on the Americas; N A C L A's Latin America and Empire Report; N A C L A News.* [ISSN: 1071-4839] 1967. bi-m. USD 60 (Individuals, USD 36). Ed(s): Jo Ann Kawell. North American Congress on Latin America, Inc., 38 Greene St, 4th Fl, New York, NY 10013-2505; nacla@nacla.org; http://www.nacla.org. Illus., adv. Refereed. Circ: 11000. Vol. ends: Jul/Jun. Microform: PQC. Online: EBSCO Publishing, EBSCO Host; Florida Center for Library Automation; Gale; OCLC Online Computer Library Center, Inc.; ProQuest LLC (Ann Arbor); H.W. Wilson. *Indexed:* AltPI, HAPI, IBR, LeftInd, PAIS, PRA, RILM. *Bk. rev.:* Number and length vary. *Aud.:* Ga, Ac.

The *NACLA Report* is the primary publication of the North American Congress of Latin America, a non-profit research organization. It provides articles on major trends in Latin America written by scholars, journalists, and others, offering detailed analyses of internal and external political and social developments. Each issue covers a specific topic germane to Latin America. Also included are sections for brief news updates, short book reviews, and research notes. *NACLA Report* offers well-researched news items. The web site contains selected articles from the current issue free of charge, and other articles for a small fee. This is an important magazine for both academic and public libraries. (OO)

3864. *Newsweek en Espanol.* [ISSN: 1091-3416] 1996. w. MXN 875 domestic; USD 100 Canada; USD 150 elsewhere. News for America LLC, Progreso 42, Col Escandon, Mexico City, 11800, Mexico. Illus., adv. Sample. Circ: 70000. *Aud.:* Ga, Ac.

Like its English-language equivalent, this magazine covers international issues such as politics, health, and medicine, science and technology, sports, the world economy, arts, and entertainment. The Spanish-language edition provides the same high-caliber journalism as its English-language counterpart; however, its coverage is geared to a Latin American readership rather than an American audience. For example, the sports section covers baseball teams in Latin America as well as in the United States, and the business pages deal with the economies of Latin American countries. Highly recommended for academic libraries and public libraries that serve Hispanic communities. (OO)

3865. People en Espanol. [ISSN: 1096-5750] 1997. 11x/yr. USD 19.97 domestic; CND 27.95 Canada. Ed(s): Angelo Figueroa. Time, Inc., Time & Life Bldg, Rockefeller Center, 29th Fl, New York, NY 10020-1393; espanol@people.com; http://www.people.com. Adv. Circ: 356000 Paid. Aud.: Ga.

This product of Time, Inc., is closely modeled after its parent publication, *People,* but is in Spanish and is focused on news, people, and events throughout the Latin world. It includes lots of news and information on the arts and entertainment, with a heavy dose of celebrity photographs. Features on many other topics of interest ranging from the literary to the political are also included. A very popular title, this magazine is best suited for public libraries. (JRD)

3866. Planeta.com. Formerly: *El Planeta Platica.* 1994. q. USD 7 newsstand/cover per issue. Ed(s): Ron Mader. Talking Planet, 1511 Twin Springs Ct, Henderson, NV 89014-0320; ron@greenbuilder.com; http://www.planeta.com. Illus., adv. Circ: 90000. *Bk. rev.:* 10-15, 25-50 words. Aud.: Ga.

This online newsletter provides information on the ecological situation in Latin America. The site focuses on environmental news and travel in the Americas and is updated several times a month. It includes sections such as recommended readings, book reviews, and Spanish-language schools in Latin America. *Planeta.com,* as it is now known, has received praise from *The New York Times* and President Vicente Fox. The newsletter also serves as a clearinghouse for other web sites on environmental news and travel in the Americas. Recommended for those interested in current environmental and travel issues in Latin America. (VR)

3867. Problemas del Desarrollo: revista latinoamericana de economia. [ISSN: 0301-7036] 1969. q. MXN 450. Ed(s): Salvador Rodriguez Y Rodriguez. Universidad Nacional Autonoma de Mexico, Instituto de Investigaciones Economicas, Torre II de Humanidades 5o Piso, Ciudad Universitaria, Mexico City, 04510, Mexico; revprode@servidor.unam.mx; http://serpiente.dgsca.unam.mx/iie. Illus., index, adv. Refereed. Circ: 2000. *Indexed:* HAPI, IBR, JEL, PAIS. *Bk. rev.:* 1-10, 800-1,500 words. Aud.: Ac.

This publication offers critical analysis of economic and socio-economic issues that affect Latin America, specifically Mexico. It presents five or six full-length, scholarly articles with research notes and references. Each article is preceded by an abstract in Spanish, English, and French. It also includes a section titled "Conyuntura y dabate," with discussions of such topics as neoliberalism in Mexico and indigenous autonomy. The full text of issues is now available online for free. This journal is recommended for academic libraries with graduate programs in Mexican or Latin American Studies with concentrations in economic or socio-economic development. Also useful for libraries with substantial Latin American collections. (VR)

3868. Proceso: semanario de informacion y analisis. [ISSN: 0185-1632] 1976. w. MXN 660; USD 150 United States; USD 350 in Europe. Ed(s): Rafael Rodriguez Castaneda. Comunicacion e Informacion S.A. de C.V. (CISA), Fresas 13, Col Del Valle, Mexico City, 03100, Mexico; buzon@proceso.com.mx; http://www.proceso.com.mx/. Illus., adv. Sample. Online: Gale. *Indexed:* AltPI. *Bk. rev.:* 1, lengthy. Aud.: Ga, Ac.

Similar in format to *Newsweek* and *Time,* this Spanish-language magazine focuses on current issues in politics, economics, labor, and human rights in Mexico. A section is dedicated to covering international politics with a focus on Latin American countries. This magazine includes color photographs and

political cartoons and regular commentary on theater, culture, art, and music. It belongs in all large public and academic libraries that support Latin American collections and researchers in the area of Latin American politics. The current issue is available online. (VR)

3869. Review (New York, 1968): literature and arts of the Americas. Formerly (until 1987): *Review - Center for Inter-American Relations.* [ISSN: 0890-5762] 1968. 2x/yr. GBP 111 print & online eds. Ed(s): Daniel Shapiro. Routledge, 325 Chestnut St, Ste 800, Philadelphia, PA 19106; journals@routledge.com; http://www.tandf.co.uk/journals. Illus., adv. Sample. Refereed. Circ: 6000. Microform: PQC. Online: EBSCO Publishing, EBSCO Host; Gale; IngentaConnect; OCLC Online Computer Library Center, Inc.; SwetsWise Online Content. Reprint: PSC. *Indexed:* AmHI, ArtHuCI, FLI, HAPI, IBR, IBZ, MLA-IB, RILM. *Bk. rev.:* 9-12, 900-1,200 words. Aud.: Ga, Ac, Sa.

This publication from The Americas Society is dedicated to the arts, culture, and literature of Latin America. Entirely in English, *Review* includes excerpts from literary works such as Vargas Llosa's *La Fiesta del Chivo.* It also features interviews, articles, essays, short fiction, and poetry, as well as art, music, film, and theatre reviews. Often, the magazine focuses on a specific topic, such as Latin American Writing and Music. This is a sophisticated publication that provides access to significant Latin American literary, art, and cultural commentary. Recommended for art and museum libraries and large academic and public libraries. (VR)

3870. Revista Canadiense de Estudios Hispanicos. Former titles (until 1976): *Reflexion Two; Reflexion.* [ISSN: 0384-8167] 1970. 3x/yr. CND 45 (Individuals, CND 30). Ed(s): Richard Young. Revista Canadiense de Estudios Hispanicos, Carleton University, ICLACS, Rm 1423, Dunton Tower, Ottawa, ON K1S 5B6, Canada. Illus., index, adv. Refereed. Circ: 800. Vol. ends: Spring. *Indexed:* HAPI, IBR, IBZ, MLA-IB, RILM. *Bk. rev.:* 10-15, 500-1,500 words. Aud.: Ac.

This publication offers scholarly articles on the study of language, literary criticism, philosophy, and the cultural history of the Spanish-speaking world. Articles are written in Spanish, French, and English, with short abstracts in Spanish. Also offering research notes and an extensive book review section, this is a substantial journal that makes an important contribution to Hispanic and Latin American Studies. Recommended for libraries with strong collections in this subject area. (VR)

3871. Revista de Critica Literaria Latinoamericana. [ISSN: 0252-8843] 1975. s-a. USD 65 (Individuals, USD 35). Ed(s): Raul Bueno. Latinoamericana Editores, 6072 Dartmouth Hall, Dartmouth College, Hanover, NH 03755. Adv. Refereed. Circ: 550 Paid and controlled. *Indexed:* AmHI, ArtHuCI, HAPI, IBR, IBZ, MLA-IB, RILM. *Bk. rev.:* Number and length vary. Aud.: Ac.

First published in 1975 in Lima by founder Antonio Cornejo Polar, this important peer-reviewed publication has been based at the University of Pittsburgh, in Berkeley, and since 1998, at Dartmouth College. The journal has only grown stronger with all of its changes. It is now online, with most articles available in full text from 1999 forward. A general index is in its final stages. *RCLL* includes literary criticism, cultural commentary within its social and historical context, and a substantial book review section. Recommended for academic and public research libraries. (VR)

3872. Revista de Historia de America. [ISSN: 0034-8325] 1938. s-a. MXN 75 domestic; USD 23 in North America; USD 26.50 in South America. Ed(s): Francisco Enriquez Solano. Instituto Panamericano de Geografia e Historia, Ex-Arzobispado 29, Col Observatorio, Mexico City, 11860, Mexico; info@ipgh.org.mx; http://www.ipgh.org.mx/. Illus., adv. Circ: 1500. Microform: PQC. Online: Gale. *Indexed:* AmH&L, ArtHuCI, HAPI, HistAb, IBR, IBZ. *Bk. rev.:* 2-4, 1,500-2,500 words. Aud.: Ac, Sa.

Published by the Instituto Panamericano de Geografia e Historia (IPGH), this journal offers articles in Spanish, Portuguese, or English that cover important issues in the history of Latin America and the Caribbean, specifically from pre-Hispanic occupation through the National period. It includes five to eight scholarly articles with abstracts in English and Spanish. Book reviews are also included. The table of contents and article summaries are available online at the magazine's web site. This is a useful source for students and researchers in Latin American Studies. Recommended for academic libraries and libraries with strong Latin American holdings. (VR)

3873. Revista de Indias. [ISSN: 0034-8341] 1940. 3x/yr. Ed(s): Consuelo Naranjo Orovio. Consejo Superior de Investigaciones Cientificas, Centro de Estudios Historicos, Vitruvio 8, Madrid, 28006, Spain; publ@orgc.csic.es; http://www.csic.es/publica. Illus., index. Circ: 1500. *Indexed:* AICP, AmH&L, ArtHuCI, BAS, HAPI, HistAb, IBR, IBZ, RI-1, RILM, SSCI. *Bk. rev.:* Number and length vary. *Aud.:* Ac.

This well-respected, long-standing journal features articles on everything from pre-Hispanic themes to today's Iberoamerican culture and literature. Its multidisciplinary approach allows for a variety of themes in each volume. One volume a year is dedicated to one or two specific themes, resulting in a sort of monograph or dossier. Each volume offers approximately six full-length articles written in Spanish, English, or Portuguese, each with abstracts in Spanish and English. There is an extensive section for research notes and book reviews. This is an essential journal for academic libraries and collections that focus on Latin American Studies. (VR)

3874. Revista de Occidente. [ISSN: 0034-8635] 1923. m. EUR 74 domestic; EUR 123 in Europe; USD 172 in the Americas. Ed(s): Soledad Ortega. Fundacion Jose Ortega y Gasset, Fortuny 53, Madrid, 28010, Spain; http://www.ortegaygasset.edu/. Illus., index, adv. Circ: 20000. *Indexed:* AmH&L, ArtHuCI, HistAb, IBR, IBZ, MLA-IB, RILM, SSCI. *Bk. rev.:* 1-3, 500-1,250 words. *Aud.:* Ga, Ac.

This journal is widely recognized in academic circles as a forum where intellectuals share their thoughts on the most relevant topics of the time. *Revista de Occidente,* founded by Jose Ortega y Gasset in 1923, offers articles on the social sciences and the humanities. Five or six full-length essays in Spanish on a wide range of topics are accompanied by literary and art criticism. The journal also includes research notes, book reviews, a listing of current publications, and brief profiles for each contributor. Occasionally, an issue is dedicated to a specific theme, such as "Knowledge in the Digital Universe," "Art and Esthetic Thought in France," or "Ortega and European Thought." Recommended for academic libraries and libraries with substantial Latin American collections. (VR)

3875. Revista Iberoamericana. [ISSN: 0034-9631] 1938. q. USD 100 (Individuals, USD 65). Ed(s): Mabel Morana. International Institute of Ibero-American Literature, 1312 C L, University of Pittsburgh, Pittsburgh, PA 15260; iilit@pitt.edu; http://www.pitt.edu/~illi. Illus., adv. Circ: 2000. Microform: PQC. Reprint: PSC. *Indexed:* ArtHuCI, HAPI, IBR, IBZ, MLA-IB, RILM. *Bk. rev.:* 15-20, 500-3,500 words. *Aud.:* Ac.

In publication for more than 65 years, this well-recognized journal has been the vehicle for publishing scholarly studies on Iberoamerican culture and literature. It is often devoted to a single author, such as Ruben Dario, Cesar Vallejo, Vicente Huidobro, Miguel Angel Asturias, Pablo Neruda, or Jorge Luis Borges. There have also been volumes dedicated to the literature of specific countries, such as Brazil, Mexico, Nicaragua, Bolivia, and Colombia. The journal offers essays by scholars, an extensive book review section, and interviews. Articles are published in Spanish and Portuguese. Essential for academic libraries and libraries with extensive Latin American holdings. (VR)

T V y Novelas. See General Interest: Non–English Language section.

3876. Tu. Former titles: *Tu Internacional; Tu.* 1980. m. USD 22.50 domestic; USD 2.50 newsstand/cover per issue. Ed(s): Ana Maria Echevarria. Editorial Televisa, 6355 NW 36th St, Miami, FL 33166; subscriptions@editorialtelevisa.com. Illus., adv. Circ: 190000. *Indexed:* ChemAb. *Aud.:* Ga.

This teen magazine, previously published in Mexico, now publishes an American, Spanish-language edition as well as Argentine and Mexican editions. Each edition dedicates two or three pages to advice for teens from its respective country, as well as additional advice for teens writing to the magazine from all over Latin America. Similar in format to *Seventeen,* this magazine includes regular features on film, music, and videos, and includes celebrity gossip, fashion, health, nutrition, and beauty advice. Three or four articles discuss such

topics as eating disorders, relationships, and peer pressure. Selected articles from each issue are available online on the magazine's web site, where additional items like photo essays can be viewed. Recommended for public and school libraries. (OO)

3877. Vanidades Continental. [ISSN: 0505-0146] 1961. bi-w. USD 29 domestic; USD 84.50 foreign. Ed(s): Sara Castany. Editorial Televisa, 6355 NW 36th St, Miami, FL 33166; info@editorialtelevisa.com; http://www.editorialtelevisa.us/. Illus., adv. Sample. Circ: 89108 Paid. *Aud.:* Ga.

Geared toward educated professional women between the ages of 20 and 40, this magazine features articles on health, beauty, fashion, entertainment, relationship advice, and the workplace. Each issue features a current international personality like Tom Cruise, Nicole Kidman, or Salma Hayek. Recently, this magazine has begun to focus its coverage on Latin American celebrities and Latinos in the United States. It includes short articles on travel, food, home decorating, and a horoscope section. Highly recommended for public libraries. (VR)

■ LATINO STUDIES

Awilda Reyes, Assistant Professor, Government and Maps Librarian, West Chester University, Francis Harvey Green Library, West Chester University, PA 19383; areyes@wcupa.edu; FAX: 610-436-2251

Cheryl LaGuardia, Head of Instructional Services, Harvard College Library

Introduction

In the United States, the term Latino refers loosely to any person of Latin American origin living within U.S. borders. In a U.S. setting, most frequently the term Latino is applied exclusively to immigrants from Hispanophone countries in North and South America and their descendants. The U.S. Census Bureau defines Hispanic or Latino as having a background in a Hispanophone Latin American country or being of direct Spanish ancestry. The Latino population within the United States is comprised mainly of Mexican Americans (or Chicanos), Puerto Ricans, and Cubans; significant numbers of Latinos of Caribbean and Central or South American descent have long been present in the United States as well, and continue to increase.

There is a growing number of library resources pertaining specifically to the study of U.S. Latinos. Resources with the words Latino or Hispanic in their titles often vary in the definition of those words. Magazines from Latin America were not considered for this section (see Latin American section).

Here we are including popular magazines, scholarly journals, and online publication centered on the Latino experience in United States. The publications included do not reflect the total number of serials available.

Some publications in this subject area do not survive for a long period. Librarians need to be alert when looking for new publications.

Getting acquainted with and assessing community interest will provide a better view of the materials needed for the collection. It is common to find publications, newspapers, and newsletters where there is a large concentration of Latinos. The Latino communities' librarians will want to make sure to consult resources that provide adequate and reliable coverage of U.S. Latino groups. Due to the great diversity among Latinos as a group, however, many aspects of U.S. Latino experience and histories have yet to be written.

Basic Periodicals

Aztlan, Hispanic.

Basic Abstracts and Indexes

Alternative Press Index, Chicano Database, Ethnic Newswatch, Hispanic American Periodicals Index.

3878. *El Andar (Online Edition): a Latino magazine for the new millennium.* Formerly (until 2001): *El Andar (Print Edition).* 1998. irreg. Ed(s): Julia Reynolds. El Andar Publications, PO Box 7745, Santa Cruz, CA 95061. *Indexed:* AltPI, ENW. *Aud.:* Hs, Ga, Ac.

El Andar publishes essays, poetry, fiction, artistic and intellectual works, analysis, and debate. Back issues of the print magazine are available online. During its ten-year history, *El Andar* published 93 issues of the free bilingual magazine in Northern California, and they will continue publishing online "whenever we have the time and energy." This is an easy-to-navigate electronic journal. URL: www.elandar.com

3879. *Aztlan: a journal of Chicano studies.* [ISSN: 0005-2604] 1970. s-a. USD 195 (print & online eds.) Individuals, USD 30 in US & Mexico). Ed(s): Chon A Noriega. University of California at Los Angeles, Chicano Studies Research Center Press, 193 Haines Hall, Box 951544, Los Angeles, CA 90095-1544. Illus., adv. Refereed. Circ: 700 Paid. Microform: LIB. *Indexed:* AmH&L, BRI, CBRI, Chicano, ERIC, HAPI, HistAb, IBR, IBZ, L&LBA, MLA-IB, PAIS, PSA, RI-1, RILM, SSA, SociolAb. *Bk. rev.:* 1-7, 350-1,000 words. *Aud.:* Ac.

With artful covers, *Aztlan* is an interdisciplinary, refereed journal dedicated to scholarly research relevant to the Chicano experience. It has remained at the vanguard of its field for over 35 years. It focuses on scholarly essays in the humanities, social sciences, and the arts, but also publishes thematic clusters of shorter articles in its dossier section, an artist's communique, and a review section.

Aztlan brings Chicano Studies into critical dialogue with Latino, ethnic, American, and global studies. Recent issues include a section wherein scholars state their theoretical views and participate in a dialogue by receiving critical feedback from others in their field in subsequent journal issues. This title should find a place in all collections that deal with Chicano/Mexicano Studies.

3880. *Bilingual Research Journal.* Former titles (until 1992): *N A B E Journal;* (until 1979): *N A B E.* [ISSN: 1523-5882] 1975. q. USD 40. Ed(s): Josue Gonzales. National Association for Bilingual Education, 1030 15th St NW, Ste 470, Washington, DC 20005; nabe@nabe.org; http://www.nabe.org. Illus., adv. Refereed. *Indexed:* ABIn, Chicano, ERIC, EduInd, L&LBA, LT&LA, MLA-IB. *Bk. rev.:* 4-6, 80-100 words. *Aud.:* Ga, Ac.

This is a peer-reviewed journal, formerly titled *NABE: Journal of the National Association for Bilingual Education.* Focus is on research articles on bilingual instruction and training, second language learning, bilingualism in society, and language policy in education. There are three sections: research and essays, the traditional formats of scholarly discourse; research in practice, which documents the experience of teachers and other practitioners; and book reviews. A recent article covers "The Navajo Language at a Crossroads: Extinction or Renewal." "*BRJ* editorial policy reflects the intrinsic and inherent value of bilingualism, biliteracy, and linguistic democracy." Recommended for academic and public libraries that serve a bilingual population.

3881. *Bilingual Review.* [ISSN: 0094-5366] 1974. irreg. USD 25. Ed(s): Gary D Keller. Bilingual Review Press, Hispanic Research Center, Arizona State University, Box 875303, Tempe, AZ 85287-5303; brp@asu.edu; http://www.asu.edu/brp. Illus., adv. Refereed. Circ: 1500. Microform: PQC. Online: EBSCO Publishing, EBSCO Host; Gale. *Indexed:* ABIn, AmHI, ArtHuCI, Chicano, ERIC, EduInd, HAPI, IAPV, IBR, L&LBA, MLA-IB, RILM. *Aud.:* Ac.

A literary journal focusing on the linguistics and literature of bilingualism and bilingual education. It publishes scholarly articles, literary criticism, and book reviews as well as creative literature such as poetry, short stories, essays, and short theater pieces. Focused primarily on Chicano, Puerto Rican, and Cuban American literature, it is highly recommended for libraries with Latino literature collections.

3882. *Contacto (Burbank): a magazine for today's Latinos.* 1994. m. Free. Ed(s): Jesus Hernandez Cuellar. Contacto Magazine, 1317 N San Fernado Blvd, PMB 246, Burbank, CA 91504; editor@contactomagazine.com. *Aud.:* Ga.

Offers English/Spanish-language news in-depth. *Contacto* features the subtitle "A Magazine for Today's Latinos (Una Revista para el Latino de Hoy)." This e-journal intends to build bridges among Latinos worldwide through information on politics, the economy, science, technology, business, arts, culture, entertainment, and food. Readers will also enjoy "Un Poco de Humor," a section dedicated to Latino jokes. There is recent coverage of immigration reform issues. The publication is free, and useful for those wanting to be up-to-date on Latino news. An an easy-to-navigate electronic journal. URL: www.contactomagazine.com

3883. *La Herencia: our past, our present, our future.* Formerly: *La Herencia del Norte.* [ISSN: 1531-0442] 1994. q. USD 19.99. Ed(s): Ana Pacheco. Gran Via, Inc., PO Box 22576, Santa Fe, NM 87502. Illus., index, adv. *Bk. rev.:* 2-3, 400-500 words. *Aud.:* Ga, Sa.

La Herencia is an oversized magazine that strives to preserve the Hispanic culture of New Mexico and the region. It is an indispensable resource for anyone interested in borderlands history and the culture of the Southwest. For those interested in the traditions of the area—food, music, religion, customs, culture, and history—this splendid magazine is a must. The publication can be used as a teaching tool in school curricula that include Spanish, history, literature, social studies, and political science. Highly recommended for public libraries, and for collections that focus on Mexican Americans or the Southwest.

3884. *Hispanic: the magazine for and about Hispanics.* [ISSN: 0898-3097] 1988. 10x/yr. USD 18 (Free to qualified personnel). Ed(s): Daniel Eilemberg. Hispanic Publishing Corp., 6355 NW 36th St, Virginia Gardens, FL 33166-7027; http://www.hispaniconline.com. Illus., adv. Circ: 280000. Online: EBSCO Publishing, EBSCO Host; Northern Light Technology, Inc.; OCLC Online Computer Library Center, Inc.; ProQuest K-12 Learning Solutions; ProQuest LLC (Ann Arbor); H.W. Wilson. *Indexed:* AgeL, Chicano, ENW, MASUSE, RGPR. *Bk. rev.:* 1,500 words. *Aud.:* Ga, Ac.

This is a highly popular publication for Hispanic Americans. This English-language magazine targets and reaches upwardly mobile Hispanic professionals, corporate executives, entrepreneurs, members of Hispanic organizations, students, and individuals. The editorial focus is on culture, entertainment, business, careers, and politics, with upbeat, informative, and timely stories on people and issues of interest to Hispanics. It carries news, features, calendar items, statistics, and stories relevant to the community. Past articles have discussed how "Coyotes" openly do business in Mexico. This magazine is highly recommended for public libraries and academic libraries that serve a large Latino student population. URL: www.hispaniconline.com

3885. *Hispanic Business Magazine.* [ISSN: 0199-0349] 1979. m. USD 19.97 domestic; USD 39.97 Mexico; USD 49.97 elsewhere. Ed(s): Todd Cunningham, Judy Erickson. Hispanic Business Inc., 425 Pine Ave, Santa Barbara, CA 93117-3700; hbinfo@hninc.com; http://www.hispanstar.com. Illus., adv. Circ: 245000 Paid and controlled. *Indexed:* BPI, Chicano, PAIS. *Aud.:* Ga, Ac.

This glossy and colorful magazine provides news, popular trends, and information that affect the U.S. Hispanic economic sector. The articles cover successful Hispanic-owned businesses, economic and social trends, politics, careers, marketing strategies, legal matters, travel news, high-tech trends, and consumer products, plus an annual list of top Hispanic businesses. It provides tips for aspiring entrepreneurs and for executives and professionals. Recent issues include a section on the 100 most influential leaders sharing their vision of politics, economic development, diversity, education, and other topics. Highly recommended for public and academic libraries.

3886. *Hispanic Enterprise: the magazine for Latin business and political leaders.* Formerly (until 2007): *Hispanic Trends.* 2002. bi-m. USD 15.80 domestic; USD 38 Canada; USD 45 elsewhere. Ed(s): Joe Vidueira. Hispanic Publishing Corp., 6355 NW 36th St, Virginia Gardens, FL 33166-7027; rperez@hisp.com; http://www.hispaniconline.com. Adv. *Indexed:* ENW. *Aud.:* Ga, Ac.

Hispanic Trends is co-published by the United States Hispanic Chamber of Commerce (USHCC) and Hispanic Publishing Co. It is a how-to publication aimed squarely at the fast-growing business community of Latino entrepreneurs. It is primarily distributed to members of the USHCC, the leading advocate of Hispanic-owned businesses. It reaches today's top Hispanic business and corporate leaders. Sections included in every issue are "Briefcase," which covers trends in businesses with Latino leadership, and "Trends Portfolio," which ranks the stock performance of the top 100 companies with Latino leadership. Recent issues include a section that presents the top 50 corporations for supplier diversity. Highly recommended for academic libraries and public libraries with business and Latino clientele.

3887. *Hispanic Outlook in Higher Education.* [ISSN: 1054-2337] 1990. 25x/yr. USD 29.95. Ed(s): Adalyn Hixson. Hispanic Outlook in Higher Education Publishing Company, Inc., 210 Rt 4 E, Ste 310, Paramus, NJ 07652; outlook@aol.com. Illus., adv. Sample. Refereed. Circ: 28000. Online: Northern Light Technology, Inc.; ProQuest LLC (Ann Arbor). *Indexed:* Chicano, ENW. *Bk. rev.:* Number and length vary. *Aud.:* Ac.

Hispanic Outlook in Higher Education is published 25 times a year. It reaches a broad cultural spectrum of educators, administrators, students, community-based organizations, and corporations. Each edition presents the significance of communication in academic circles, the importance of positive learning experiences, the contributions of both Hispanic and non-Hispanic role models, and constructive observations on policies and procedures in academia. It provides discussion of issues confronted by Hispanics on college campuses and in private industry. Each issue includes employment opportunities, book reviews, and conference information. Past articles have discussed the life of Jaime Escalante, renowned mathematics teacher immortalized in the movie "Stand and Deliver." Recommended for academic libraries.

In Motion Magazine. See Alternatives section.

3888. *L A Ritmo.com: Latin American Rhythm & Sound Magazine.* [ISSN: 1525-853X] 1998. bi-w. Free. Ed(s): Sounni de Fontenay. Tag It, 1837 26th Ave., # 2F, Astoria, NY 11102-3541; info@taggin.com; http://www.laritmo.com. Adv. Circ: 1300. *Aud.:* Ga.

Straight from New York, 'LA'Ritmo.com is an English-language e-magazine that acts as a bridge between the Latino music community and the web. It features interviews of established and up-and-coming artists, top Latino charts, music news, and reviews of the latest releases. It also includes photo galleries, an archive of previous issues, and links to artist's web sites. Useful for anyone who enjoys listening to Latin music. URL: www.laritmo.com

3889. *Latin Beat Magazine: salsa, afro-antillana, latin jazz and more.* [ISSN: 1553-5460] 1991. m. 11/yr. USD 20; USD 35 Canada; USD 50 elsewhere. Latin Beat Magazine, 15900 Crenshaw Blvd, Ste 1-223, Gardena, CA 90249. Adv. *Indexed:* IIMP, MusicInd. *Aud.:* Hs, Ga, Ac.

This magazine is focused on Latin music, with emphasis on salsa, Latin jazz, Latin pop, and afro-world. It is the premier publication in this genre. Through reviews, interviews with established and emerging artists, movie and television news, and concert listings, it offers substantial information to readers. Included are tips on fashion, decorating, family activities, and fabulous contests, all *"con sabor Latino."* Regular features include sections on nightlife, radio news, events, music news, music charts, and music reviews. There is coverage of a national event, the Salsa Congress, the largest in the world. This magazine would fit in any high school or public library that serves a Latino community or in a university with a music program.

3890. *Latin Style: the Latin arts and entertainment magazine.* [ISSN: 1525-7851] 1994. m. 11/yr. USD 24; USD 2.50 newsstand/cover per issue. Ed(s): Walter Martinez. Latin Style Magazine, 244 5th Ave, 2073, New York, NY 10001. Illus., adv. *Aud.:* Ga.

Latin Style is the first major Latin arts and entertainment magazine that targets the English-speaking Hispanic market. It covers the burgeoning Latin culture in the most important cities in the United States and abroad, depicting issues and individuals in the Latin community. The magazine also covers literature, theater, film, politics, and health. A recent issue discusses the "Narcocorrido" narco-trafficker, a traditional song of the U.S.–Mexico border region, and the music of drugs, guns, and guerrillas. Recommended for public libraries.

3891. *Latina Style: a national magazine for the contemporary Hispanic woman.* [ISSN: 1531-0868] 1994. 6x/yr. USD 20 for 2 yrs.; USD 2.95 newsstand/cover. Ed(s): Robert Bard, Rebecca Corvino. Latina Style, Inc., 1730 Rhode Island Ave, NW, Ste 1207, Washington, DC 20036-3102. Illus., adv. Circ: 150000 Paid. *Bk. rev.:* Number and length vary. *Aud.:* Ga.

This colorful, glossy magazine is aimed at contemporary Latina women. Written in English, it has a variety of brief articles covering business, education, politics, beauty, fashion, social events, book reviews, and celebrity gossip. Every issue includes a publisher's message, "Latina Today," "College Beat," "About the Author," "His View," and "Punto Final." A recent article presents photos of White House Latinas with brief synopses of the life and accomplishments of these young women. Recommended for public libraries.

3892. *Latino Leaders: the national magazine of the successful Hispanic American.* [ISSN: 1529-3998] 1999. bi-m. Ed(s): Wendy Pedrero. Ferraez Publications of America, Corp., Invierno 16, Merced Gomez, 01600, Mexico. Circ: 100000. *Aud.:* Ga.

Latino Leaders is a bimonthly publication with national distribution. This glossy and colorful magazine targets an educated and informed white-collar Latino readership. It features interviews with major Latino players in all fields of expertise, focusing on social, political, and business leaders, also covering the rise of influential Hispanics in the entertainment industry and sports. Articles explain who they are and how they got to be where they are today. A recent issue presents the most important Latinos working for the president of the United States. This title should find a place in any public library with a large Latino clientele.

3893. *Latino Studies.* [ISSN: 1476-3435] 2003. q. USD 539 print & online eds. Ed(s): Karen Benita Biegel, Suzanne Oboler. Palgrave Macmillan Ltd., Houndmills, Basingstoke, RG21 6XS, United Kingdom; journalinfo@palgrave.com; http://www.palgrave.com. Illus., index. Sample. Refereed. Reprint: PSC. *Indexed:* HAPI, IBR, IBSS, IBZ, IPSA, L&LBA, PSA, SociolAb. *Bk. rev.:* 2-3. *Aud.:* Ac.

Latino Studies has been published since 2003 and has quickly established itself as a leading, international peer-reviewed journal. As of 2006, it has increased its publishing schedule to four issues per year. The principal aim of the journal is to advance interdisciplinary scholarship about the experiences and struggles of Latinas and Latinos for equity, representation, and social justice. It engages in the study of the local, national, transnational, and hemispheric realities that continue to influence the Latina and Latino presence in the United States. The research articles have extensive bibliographies and notes, and some include photographs in color or black and white. The journal is divided into four sections: scholarly "Articles"; "Vivencias," reports from the field, including description and analysis of local issues, struggles, and debates; "Book Reviews," including media reviews; and "Spanish Abstracts/Resumenes." This journal would be appropriate for any Latino Studies collection.

3894. *Latino Suave.* 2005. bi-m. USD 23. Latino Suave, 1600 Stout St., Ste. 2000, Denver, CO 80202. *Bk. rev.:* Number and length vary. *Aud.:* Ga.

This new, glossy bilingual magazine aims to "inform, inspire, and help transform lives" of its Latino readers. It covers a wide range of issues important to the Latino community—fashion, beauty, arts, culture, sports, business, entrepreneurship, and politics. The magazine includes profiles of successful Hispanic Americans and tries to help members of the community aspire to the American dream. Recommended for public libraries. (AI)

3895. *Latino(a) Research Review.* Formerly (until 2000): *Latino Review of Books.* 1995. q. USD 35 (Individuals, USD 25). State University of New York at Albany, Center for Latino, Latin American, and Caribbean Studies (CELAC), SS 247, Albany, NY 12222; lrr@cnsunix.albany.edu; http://www.albany.edu/celac/docs.lrb. Illus., adv. Refereed. *Indexed:* MLA-IB. *Bk. rev.:* 10-15, 1,000-1,500 words. *Aud.:* Ga, Ac.

This interdisciplinary journal, formerly known as the *Latino Review of Books*, publishes scholarly articles, research notes, review essays, and book reviews on publications, projects, materials, and other issues of interest to scholars and educators in the areas of U.S. Latino and Latin American Studies. "It promotes and pays particular attention to (im)migration and Caribbean regions." Of interest to academic libraries and large public libraries that serve a large Spanish-speaking clientele.

3896. *LatinoLA*. irreg. LatinoCities, Inc., 27 Short Way, South Pasadena, CA 91030; info@latinola.com; http://www.latinola.com/. Adv. *Aud.:* Ga.
This e-magazine includes a considerable amount of information of interest to the Latino community. It focuses on events in the Los Angeles area, but also provides considerable coverage of world news. It includes an arts and entertainment section, a section on careers, and a section called *Expresate* where you can send comments in English or in Spanish. There is an archive of previous articles. You can be creative by e-mailing a story or a poem to the web site. Recent articles include coverage of the movement for migrants' rights. URL: www.latinola.com

Q V Magazine. See Lesbian, Gay, Bisexual, and Transgender section.

3897. *Urban Latino (Long Island City)*. [ISSN: 1531-6602] 1994. bi-m. USD 16 domestic. Ed(s): Rodrigo Salazar. Urban Latino, 44-45 21st St, 3rd Fl, Long Island City, NY 11101. Adv. *Aud.:* Hs, Ga, Ac.
Urban Latino is a contemporary, new-generation, cultural publication geared to bi-cultural Latinos. The magazine focuses on the Latino experience in the United States, viewing all sides of a diverse culture. It reaches young Latinos interested in contemporary music from an East Coast perspective. It includes essays, illustrations, dance clubs, and restaurants, and showcases the achievements of Latino community. Recommended for public and high school libraries in large metropolitan areas.

■ LAW

Donald J. Dunn, Dean & Professor of Law, University of La Verne College of Law, 320 East D Street, Ontario, CA 91764.

Kim Dulin, Associate Librarian for Research Services, Harvard Law School Library, Areeda 526, 1545 Massachusetts Avenue, Cambridge, MA 02138

Introduction

There are over several thousand legal periodicals currently available, and new titles appear with amazing frequency. They tend to fall into four broad categories: (1) law reviews published by law schools and edited by law students, (2) scholarly journals published by professional associations and learned societies, (3) local and national bar association journals focused on news, current events, and the daily practice of law, and (4) commercial publications, supported by advertisements, that are generally practitioner-oriented or focused on a particular legal specialty.

Student-edited law reviews comprise the majority of legal periodical publications. Every law school publishes at least one law review, and some of the larger schools publish many—Harvard Law School recently added its 14th. Serving on a law review gives law students an opportunity to acquire scholarly editing and writing experience, and is considered a prestigious resume-building activity. Although students act as editors and managers, law professors and legal scholars write the lead articles. Law reviews range from general interest (*Yale Law Journal*) to specific focus (*Columbia Journal of Gender and the Law*). A recent feature of many of the top law reviews is a companion online, blog-like component that allows authors to debate issues devolving from articles published in the review's current issues (e.g., *Harvard Law Forum*, or *Northwestern University Law Review Colloquy*).

The proliferation of law reviews results in an overabundance of journals on seemingly every topic, with wide ranges in quality. Professors and scholars seeking to publish their manuscripts in law reviews use a variety of criteria to assess the quality of the law review, including the prestige of the journal and the school that hosts it, the prestige of the authors of lead articles, and the frequency with which others cite the articles included. A useful tool for assessing the

quality of the various law reviews is the Washington and Lee Law Schools' "Law Journals: Submissions and Ranking" web site, http://lawlib.wlu.edu/LJ. This site allows the user to search and rank law reviews by frequency of citation and even price.

The open-access movement continues to be popular with legal scholars. The two largest open-access options are SSRN's Legal Scholarship Network and the BePress Legal Repository. Both add articles and publish new series with increasing frequency. Some law reviews are now adding content on their web sites free of charge, although coverage varies.

A comprehensive source for back issues of law reviews and legal periodicals is HeinOnline, a full-text database that features articles in pdf format, with multiple searching features. Although many journals included in HeinOnline impose an embargo on their most current issues, increasingly more are making their full range of issues available. This may be a good option for libraries that are short on space and only wish to subscribe to a few of the top law reviews and legal periodicals in print.

Basic Periodicals

Ga: *ABA Journal, National Law Journal, The Practical Lawyer, Trial;* Ac: *ABA Journal, Business Lawyer, Columbia Law Review, Harvard Law Review, Law and Contemporary Problems, National Law Journal, University of Chicago Law Review, Yale Law Journal.*

Basic Abstracts and Indexes

Current Law Index, Index to Legal Periodicals, Legal Resource Index, LegalTrac.

3898. *A B A Journal: the lawyer's magazine*. Formerly (until 1984): *American Bar Association Journal*. [ISSN: 0747-0088] 1915. m. USD 120 (Individuals, USD 75). Ed(s): Debra Cassens-Weiss, Danial Kim. American Bar Association, 321 N Clark St, Chicago, IL 60610; abajournal@abanet.org; http://www.abanet.org. Illus., index, adv. Sample. Refereed. Circ: 387632 Paid. Vol. ends: Dec. Microform: WSH; PQC. Online: EBSCO Publishing, EBSCO Host; William S. Hein & Co., Inc.; LexisNexis; OCLC Online Computer Library Center, Inc.; ProQuest LLC (Ann Arbor); Thomson West. Reprint: WSH. *Indexed:* ABIn, ABS&EES, ATI, AgeL, AmH&L, ArtHuCI, BAS, BRI, CBRI, CJA, CJPI, CLI, HistAb, ILP, LRI, PAIS, SSCI. *Bk. rev.:* 2-4, 2,000 words. *Aud.:* Ga, Ac, Sa.
With by far the largest circulation of all the legal publications, due mainly to its distribution to members of the American Bar Association (ABA), this magazine is designed to be of interest to all segments of the legal profession. It can perhaps best be described as *Time* for lawyers. In addition to containing several timely feature articles of four to six pages in length, several "departments" address various aspects of law and law practice. For example, the "President's Message" discusses the ABA president's thinking on major legal concerns; the "Letters" section provides for reader exchanges; the "Substantive Law" department analyzes trends in the law; the "Supreme Court Report" speculates about the outcome of cases not yet decided by the U.S. Supreme Court and reports on recent rulings; and "Practice Strategies" contains information on litigation techniques, solo practice, technology, and other topics of broad interest. From time to time, interviews with prominent legal figures provide insights unavailable elsewhere. The journal's attractive layout, color illustrations, and timeliness contrast remarkably with more traditional, staid legal publications.

3899. *Administrative Law Review (Chicago)*. Formerly (until 1967): *Administrative Law Bulletin*. [ISSN: 0001-8368] 1949. q. Non-members, USD 40. Ed(s): Heather E Kilgore, Carl E Tugberk. American Bar Association, Administrative Law and Regulatory Practice Section, 321 N Clark St, Chicago, IL 60610. Illus., index. Refereed. Circ: 7500 Paid and controlled. Vol. ends: Fall. Microform: WSH. Online: William S. Hein & Co., Inc. Reprint: WSH. *Indexed:* AgeL, CLI, ILP, LRI, SSCI. *Bk. rev.:* Occasional, length varies. *Aud.:* Ac, Sa.
Administrative law is concerned with government authorities other than courts and legislative bodies. Administrative agencies—national, state, and local—promulgate rules and regulations and issue decisions that govern our

daily lives. Consequently, the power wielded by these agencies is often immense. This journal is published jointly by the Section of Administrative Law and Regulatory Practice of the American Bar Association and its student staff members at the Washington College of Law of American University. It discusses all aspects of administrative law, including such topics as consumer protection regulation; administrative rule-making; immigration law; banking and currency regulation; and energy and environmental, insurance, and postal regulations. This title has the widest distribution of all journals devoted to administrative law.

Air & Space Law. See Aeronautics and Space Science section.

3900. *American Business Law Journal.* [ISSN: 0002-7766] 1963. q. GBP 310 print & online eds. Ed(s): Joan T A Gabel. Blackwell Publishing, Inc., Commerce Place, 350 Main St, Malden, MA 02148; customerservices@blackwellpublishing.com; http://www.blackwellpublishing.com. Illus., index, adv. Refereed. Circ: 2000. Vol. ends: Winter. Microform: PQC. Online: Blackwell Synergy; EBSCO Publishing, EBSCO Host; Florida Center for Library Automation; Gale; IngentaConnect; LexisNexis; Northern Light Technology, Inc.; OCLC Online Computer Library Center, Inc.; ProQuest K-12 Learning Solutions; ProQuest LLC (Ann Arbor); SwetsWise Online Content; H.W. Wilson. Reprint: PSC. *Indexed:* ABIn, ATI, BPI, CLI, ILP, LRI, RI-1, RiskAb, SSCI. *Bk. rev.:* Occasional. *Aud.:* Ac, Sa.

The Academy of Legal Studies in Business is a professional organization with a membership that consists primarily of professors who teach in undergraduate and graduate programs. The authors of this journal's articles are usually associated with these types of institutions or programs. A typical issue contains four to six articles. Recent articles address pharmaceutical patents, access to AIDS drugs, and Internet domain-name disputes.

3901. *American Criminal Law Review.* Former titles (until 1971): *American Criminal Law Quarterly;* (until 1963): *Criminal Law Quarterly.* [ISSN: 0164-0364] 1962. q. USD 30 domestic; USD 40 foreign; USD 10 newsstand/cover per issue. Ed(s): Brian C Lewis. Georgetown University Law Center, 600 New Jersey Ave, NW, Washington, DC 20001; http://www.law.gwu.edu. Illus., index, adv. Refereed. Circ: 2153. Vol. ends: No. 4. Microform: WSH; PQC. Online: Florida Center for Library Automation; Gale; LexisNexis; Northern Light Technology, Inc.; OCLC Online Computer Library Center, Inc.; ProQuest LLC (Ann Arbor); Thomson West; H.W. Wilson. Reprint: WSH. *Indexed:* ABS&EES, CJA, CJPI, CLI, ILP, LRI, RiskAb, SSCI. *Bk. rev.:* Occasional, lengthy. *Aud.:* Ac, Sa.

Criminal law is an area that changes frequently, depending upon the political climate and the current membership of the U.S. Supreme Court. This journal, edited by students from the Georgetown University Law Center, includes articles, notes, project reports, and symposia that focus on some of the more complicated issues in the criminal law area. A regular, although not annual, feature is a survey of white-collar crime. Representative articles include "The Useful, Dangerous Fiction of Grand Jury Independence" and "Contradiction, Coherence, and Guided Discretion in the Supreme Court's Capital Sentencing Jurisprudence."

3902. *American Journal of Comparative Law.* [ISSN: 0002-919X] 1952. q. USD 52 domestic; USD 65 in Canada & Mexico; USD 66 elsewhere. Ed(s): George A Bermann. American Society of Comparative Law, University of California, 394 Boalt Hall, Berkeley, CA 94720-7200; http://www.comparativelaw.org. Illus., index, adv. Refereed. Circ: 2100. Vol. ends: Fall. Microform: PQC. Online: William S. Hein & Co., Inc.; JSTOR (Web-based Journal Archive); LexisNexis. Reprint: WSH. *Indexed:* ABCPolSci, ABS&EES, BAS, CJA, CLI, IBR, IBSS, IBZ, ILP, LRI, PAIS, PSA, SSCI. *Bk. rev.:* 6-10, 1,200-5,000 words. *Aud.:* Ac, Sa.

Comparative law, as the topic suggests, compares the laws of one or more nations with those of another or discusses one jurisdiction's law in order for the reader to understand how it might differ from that of the United States or some other country. This widely respected publication features articles by major scholars and comments by law student writers. The diversity of coverage is illustrated by "Company Law Theory—England and France." The annual "Bulletin" section contains the membership list of the American Foreign Law Association and the association president's annual report.

3903. *American Journal of International Law.* [ISSN: 0002-9300] 1907. q. Non-members, USD 200. Ed(s): Michael Reisman, Jonathan Charney. American Society of International Law, 2223 Massachusetts Ave, NW, Washington, DC 20008-2864; http://www.asil.org. Illus., index, adv. Refereed. Circ: 7000. Vol. ends: Oct. Microform: WSH; IDC; PQC. Online: Factiva, Inc.; William S. Hein & Co., Inc.; JSTOR (Web-based Journal Archive); LexisNexis; Northern Light Technology, Inc.; OCLC Online Computer Library Center, Inc.; ProQuest LLC (Ann Arbor). Reprint: WSH. *Indexed:* ABCPolSci, ABS&EES, AmH&L, ArtHuCI, BAS, CLI, HRA, HistAb, IBR, IBSS, IBZ, ILP, IPSA, IndIslam, LRI, PAIS, PRA, PSA, RiskAb, SSCI, SWRA, V&AA. *Bk. rev.:* 15-20. *Aud.:* Ac, Sa.

This highly respected English-language journal, which features a prestigious board of editors, focuses on all aspects of private and public international law. An annual volume averages over 1,000 pages and contains discussions on international organizations, foreign-relations law, and international conventions and protocols. In addition to the major articles and numerous book reviews, the "Current Developments" section addresses major news events, and recent cases are discussed in "International Decisions." This is often the first journal to publish selected treaties and other international documents. "Contemporary Practice of the United States Relating to International Law," which analyzes international issues by subject, is arranged according to the *Annual Digest of United States Practice in International Law,* published by the U.S. Department of State.

3904. *American Journal of Jurisprudence: an international forum for legal philosophy.* Formerly (until 1969): *Natural Law Forum.* [ISSN: 0065-8995] 1956. a. USD 40 (Individuals, USD 25). Ed(s): Gerard V Bradley, John Finnis. University of Notre Dame, Law School, PO Box 780, Notre Dame, IN 46556-0780; http://www.nd.edu. Illus., index, adv. Circ: 1000. Microform: WSH; PMC; PQC. Online: William S. Hein & Co., Inc.; LexisNexis; OCLC Online Computer Library Center, Inc.; H.W. Wilson. Reprint: WSH. *Indexed:* ABCPolSci, CLI, CPL, IBR, IBZ, ILP, LRI, PSA, PhilInd. *Bk. rev.:* 3-5, 2,000-7,000 words. *Aud.:* Ac, Sa.

Jurisprudence, the philosophy of law or the formal science of law, is frequently a "heady" topic, often drawing heavily on the works of such luminaries as Rawls, Hegel, Habermas, Kant, Aquinas, Mill, Kelsen, Unger, Dworkin, and Bentham. However, if one is seeking a broad-based collection—a little of this and a little of that—a publication on jurisprudence fills in a small but important segment of legal scholarship. While jurisprudence articles are frequently found in other journals, this annual volume, published by the Natural Law Institute of the Notre Dame Law School, is the only one in the nation by a law school that is devoted exclusively to legal philosophy. Volume 45 (2000) contains an index to volumes 1–40 (1956–1995). Also published by the school is the *Notre Dame Law Review, The Journal of Legislation, Notre Dame Journal of Law, Ethics & Public Policy,* and *Journal of College and University Law.*

3905. *American Journal of Law & Medicine.* [ISSN: 0098-8588] 1975. q. USD 250 (Individuals, USD 140). Ed(s): Frances Miller. American Society of Law, Medicine & Ethics, 765 Commonwealth Ave, Ste 1634, Boston, MA 02215; info@aslme.org; http://www.aslme.org. Illus., index, adv. Refereed. Circ: 4000. Vol. ends: Winter. Microform: WSH; PMC. Online: EBSCO Publishing, EBSCO Host; Florida Center for Library Automation; Gale; LexisNexis; Northern Light Technology, Inc.; OCLC Online Computer Library Center, Inc.; ProQuest K-12 Learning Solutions; ProQuest LLC (Ann Arbor); Thomson West; H.W. Wilson. Reprint: WSH. *Indexed:* AgeL, CINAHL, CLI, ExcerpMed, H&SSA, ILP, IMFL, LRI, MCR, RI-1, RiskAb, SSA, SSCI. *Bk. rev.:* Occasional. *Aud.:* Ac, Sa.

Published by the American Society of Law, Medicine, and Ethics and affiliated with Boston University School of Law, this publication attempts to foster communication among those in the law and medical fields. This was one of the first interdisciplinary journals to focus on issues affecting the legal and health-care professions, and it continues to be one of the most respected. The journal includes articles from both professionals and students and emphasizes current issues in health law and policy. Its "Recent Developments in Health Law" section includes discussions of recent health law cases. Book reviews are occasional, three at a time, at 600 words each.

3906. American Journal of Legal History. [ISSN: 0002-9319] 1957. q. USD 40 (Individuals, USD 30). Ed(s): Diane Maleson. Temple University, Beasley School of Law, 1719 N Broad St, Philadelphia, PA 19122-6098; http://www2.law.temple.edu/. Illus., index, adv. Refereed. Circ: 1200. Vol. ends: Oct. Microform: WSH. Online: William S. Hein & Co., Inc.; JSTOR (Web-based Journal Archive); Thomson West. Reprint: WSH. *Indexed:* ABCPolSci, AmH&L, ArtHuCI, CJA, CLI, HistAb, IBR, IBZ, ILP, IndIslam, LRI, SSCI. *Bk. rev.:* 7-20, length varies. *Aud.:* Ac, Sa.

Historical underpinnings are often important to an understanding of present-day law. Similarly, a sense of perspective enhances an appreciation of our legal system. Although numerous journals occasionally feature an article on legal history, this journal is devoted exclusively to the topic. Each issue is small, approximately 115 pages, and usually contains three or four feature articles and numerous book appraisals. Historians are important for all disciplines; there is usually at least one legal historian on each law school faculty. This journal provides interesting insights into people, places, and events that have shaped our system of justice and offers a nice respite for students and members of the bar. Temple also publishes *Temple Law Review, Temple Political and Civil Liberties Law Review, Temple Environmental Law and Technology Journal,* and *Temple International and Comparative Law Journal.*

3907. The American Lawyer. [ISSN: 0162-3397] 1979. m. 10/yr. USD 365 domestic; USD 450 foreign. Ed(s): Aric Press. A L M, 345 Park Ave, S, New York, NY 10010; apress@amlaw.com; http://www.alm.com. Illus., index, adv. Circ: 17000. Vol. ends: Dec. *Indexed:* ASIP, CLI, ILP, LRI. *Bk. rev.:* Usually 1. *Aud.:* Ga, Ac, Sa.

When this newspaper first hit the scene, it was often viewed as a legal tabloid and not serious journalism. While its focus is still sometimes sensational, its reputation for investigative reporting has improved. It is a glossy, well-illustrated publication that features bold headlines and snappy captions. In addition to feature articles, there are regular departments including "Headnotes," "Bar Talk," "Big Deals," "Big Suits," "Heavy Hitter," "IP Land," and "In the News." There are frequent special pull-out sections and supplements—for example, an annotated list of the top 100 law firms; corporate mergers and acquisitions; and a legal-recruiters directory. Although this publication may not be prominently displayed in a law firm's waiting room, its large subscription base suggests it is widely read in private.

Animal Law. See Animal Welfare section.

3908. BePress Legal Repository. irreg. Free. Berkeley Electronic Press, 2809 Telegraph Ave, Ste 202, Berkeley, CA 94705; info@bepress.com; http://www.bepress.com. *Aud.:* Ga, Ac, Sa.

Similar to the *Legal Scholarship Network,* this network of law-related research materials is sponsored by Berkeley Electronic Press (BePress). This collection of working papers, articles, and presentations is the product of American law school faculty members and graduate students. Content touches on all areas of the law. Users may search content by keyword or author name and may set up subject-specific e-mail alerts. Content can be downloaded free of charge. BePress also publishes several electronic journals available to libraries for subscription; these include the *Issues in Legal Scholarship, Global Jurist, Review of Law and Economics, International Commentary on Evidence, Theoretical Inquiries in Law,* and the *Muslim World Journal of Human Rights.*

Berkeley Journal of Employment and Labor Law. See Labor and Industrial Relations section.

3909. Berkeley Technology Law Journal. Formerly (until vol.11, 1996): *High Technology Law Journal.* [ISSN: 1086-3818] 1986. q. USD 85 (Individuals, USD 65; USD 27 newsstand/cover per issue). Ed(s): Titi Nguyen, Joe Marra. University of California at Berkeley, School of Law, 587 Simon Hall, Boalt Hall School of Law, Berkeley, CA 94720; kabrams@law.berkeley.edu; http://www.law.berkeley.edu. Illus., index,

adv. Refereed. Circ: 450. Vol. ends: Fall. Microform: WSH; PQC. Online: EBSCO Publishing, EBSCO Host; Florida Center for Library Automation; William S. Hein & Co., Inc.; LexisNexis; H.W. Wilson. Reprint: WSH. *Indexed:* ABIn, CLI, IBSS, ILP, LRI, PAIS, RiskAb. *Bk. rev.:* Occasional, 2,500 words. *Aud.:* Ac, Sa.

Established in 1985 by students at the University of California (Berkeley) School of Law, this journal is devoted to covering issues related to the intersection of law and technology. It is one of the most respected of the law and technology journals, and is a good source for those wanting to keep abreast of the hot topics in this area. Recent articles have addressed cyberanarchy, Internet piracy, and cybercrimes and misdemeanors. One issue a year, the *Annual Review of Law and Technology,* focuses exclusively on the most recent developments in the field.

3910. Boston University Law Review. [ISSN: 0006-8047] 1897. 5x/yr. USD 30 domestic; USD 35 foreign. Ed(s): Howard A. Lipton, Brett Budzinski. Boston University, School of Law, Law Review, 765 Commonwealth Ave, Boston, MA 02215; lawrev@bu.edu; http://www.bu.edu. Illus., index, adv. Refereed. Circ: 3000. Vol. ends: Dec. Microform: WSH. Online: William S. Hein & Co., Inc.; LexisNexis; Thomson West. Reprint: WSH. *Indexed:* CJA, CLI, ILP, LRI, PAIS, SSCI. *Bk. rev.:* Occasional, lengthy. *Aud.:* Ac, Sa.

Among the older law reviews in the country, this student-edited journal is traditional in coverage and format. It features consistently high-quality articles on a wide cross-section of topics by noted authorities, notes by student members of the *Review,* and occasional book reviews. Recent issues cover such diverse topics as impeachment, rape, legal ethics, and trusts. It has one of the highest circulations of all the law school's reviews. An average issue is approximately 250 pages. Boston University School of Law also publishes *The American Journal of Law & Medicine* (jointly with the American Society of Law and Medicine) (see above in this section), *Annual Review of Banking and Financial Law, Boston University International Law Journal, Journal of Science and Technology Law,* and *Public Interest Law Journal.*

3911. Business Lawyer. [ISSN: 0007-6899] 1946. q. Non-members, USD 65. Ed(s): Maury B Poscover. American Bar Association, Section of Business Law, 321 North Clark St, Chicago, IL 60610; businesslaw@ abanet.org; http://www.abanet.org. Illus., index, adv. Circ: 55000. Vol. ends: Aug. Microform: MIM; WSH. Online: Florida Center for Library Automation; Gale; LexisNexis; Northern Light Technology, Inc.; OCLC Online Computer Library Center, Inc.; ProQuest LLC (Ann Arbor); Thomson West. Reprint: WSH. *Indexed:* ABIn, ATI, BLI, CLI, IBR, IBZ, ILP, LRI, PAIS, SSCI. *Bk. rev.:* 1-2, 2,400 words. *Aud.:* Ac, Sa.

This journal's extensive circulation is due in large part to the tremendous number of members in this American Bar Association (ABA) section. A typical issue of this highly esteemed and often-cited publication contains eight to ten articles and 425 pages. A volume includes special reports; surveys, such as the "Survey of the Law of Cyberspace" changes in model acts; and task-force reports. Because the topic "business law" encompasses so many issues—for example, constitutional, banking, commercial, financial institutions, business financing, securities, partnership, bankruptcy, and environmental law—current developments are the principal focus.

3912. California Law Review. [ISSN: 0008-1221] 1912. bi-m. USD 50 USD 11 newsstand/cover per issue. Ed(s): Ted Uno, Daniel L Tristan. University of California at Berkeley, School of Law, 592 Simon Hall, Berkeley, CA 94720. Illus., index, adv. Refereed. Circ: 1650 Paid. Vol. ends: Dec. Microform: WSH; PQC. Online: EBSCO Publishing, EBSCO Host; Florida Center for Library Automation; William S. Hein & Co., Inc.; LexisNexis; Northern Light Technology, Inc. Reprint: WSH. *Indexed:* ABCPolSci, ABIn, ArtHuCI, CJA, CLI, CommAb, ILP, LRI, PAIS, RiskAb, SSCI. *Bk. rev.:* Occasional, length varies. *Aud.:* Ac, Sa.

Consistently ranked among the top ten law reviews, this University of California (Berkeley) publication was the first student-edited law review published west of the Mississippi, and from its inception it included both male and female editors. Each volume includes six issues, and articles cover a wide range of topics, from the International Criminal Court to the admission of DNA evidence to the Chicano fight for justice in Los Angeles. This school also publishes *Berkeley Journal of Gender Law and Justice, Ecology Law Quarterly,* and *Berkeley Technology Law Journal* (for the latter two, see above and below in this section), as well as *Berkeley Journal of African-American Law & Policy, Asian American Law Journal, Berkeley Business Law Journal, Berkeley Journal of Employment and Labor Law, Berkeley Journal of International Law, Berkeley Journal of Criminal Law,* and *Berkeley La Raza Law Journal.*

3913. *The Cambridge Law Journal.* [ISSN: 0008-1973] 1921. 3x/yr. GBP 66. Ed(s): David J Ibbetson. Cambridge University Press, The Edinburgh Bldg, Shaftesbury Rd, Cambridge, CB2 2RU, United Kingdom; journals@cambridge.org; http://www.journals.cambridge.org. Illus., index, adv. Circ: 1600. Vol. ends: Nov. Microform: PQC. Online: Pub.; EBSCO Publishing, EBSCO Host; OCLC Online Computer Library Center, Inc.; OhioLINK; SwetsWise Online Content. Reprint: WSH. *Indexed:* CJPI, CLI, IBR, IBSS, IBZ, ILP, LRI, PSA, SSA, SWR&A, SociolAb. *Bk. rev.:* 30, 1,200-1,500 words. *Aud.:* Ac, Sa.

Considered by most legal scholars to be the best British legal periodical, this publication reverses the format used by its American counterparts—that is, the student case notes and comments precede the longer scholarly articles. The book reviews, both cogent and forceful, serve as excellent aids in collection development for materials from the United Kingdom.

3914. *Chicano - Latino Law Review.* Formerly: *Chicano Law Review.* [ISSN: 1061-8899] 1972. a. USD 25. Ed(s): Salvador Mendoza, Carmen Santana. University of California at Los Angeles, School of Law, 405 Hilgard Ave, Rm 2246, Los Angeles, CA 90024-1476; cllr@lawnet.ucla.edu; http://www.law.ucla.edu. Illus., index, adv. Circ: 600. Microform: LIB. Online: LexisNexis; Thomson West. Reprint: WSH. *Indexed:* CLI, Chicano, ILP, LRI. *Bk. rev.:* Occasional, essay length. *Aud.:* Ac, Sa.

This publication of Chicano-Latino law students at UCLA School of Law, like *Berkeley La Raza Law Journal,* is a law-related publication specifically established to address issues concerning the Mexican American community and the broader-based Latino community. As a forum for an underrepresented minority in the legal community, this publication is important because of its particular perspective. It identifies and analyzes legal issues affecting the Latino community and focuses on how these legal issues have an impact on the political and cultural interaction of the United States and Latin America.

Children's Legal Rights Journal. See Sociology and Social Work/General section.

3915. *Clearinghouse Review: journal of poverty law and policy.* [ISSN: 0009-868X] 1969. bi-m. USD 500 (Individuals, USD 400; USD 250 non-profit organizations). Ed(s): Rita McLennon. National Clearinghouse for Legal Services, Inc., 50 E Washington, Ste 500, Chicago, IL 60602; http://www.povertylaw.org. Illus., index. Circ: 10000. Vol. ends: Apr. Microform: PQC. *Indexed:* AgeL, CLI, ILP, LRI, MCR, PAIS, SWR&A. *Aud.:* Ga, Ac, Sa.

This journal serves the dual purpose of being the professional journal for attorneys who represent low income clients in the Legal Services Corporation (LSC) grantee offices across the country, as well as providing authoritative articles on poverty law for the rest of the legal community. Published by the Sargent Shriver National Center on Poverty Law, this publication includes feature articles on a variety of issues including disability benefits, consumer protection, elder law, civil rights, public housing, and federal and state income assistance programs.

3916. *Clinical Law Review: a journal of lawyering and legal education.* [ISSN: 1079-1159] 1994. s-a. USD 24 domestic; USD 26 foreign; USD 14 newsstand/cover per issue domestic. Ed(s): Randy Hertz. New York University School of Law, 110 W Third St, Subbasement, New York, NY 10012; http://www.law.nyu.edu. Refereed. Reprint: WSH. *Indexed:* CLI, ILP, LRI. *Aud.:* Ac, Sa.

"Practical skills," "hands-on," "lawyering," and "real world" are words that help describe clinical legal education. This journal, jointly sponsored by NYU School of Law, the Clinical Legal Education Association, and the Association of American Law Schools, fills a need by discussing the special forms of academic pedagogy required for successful clinical education experiences.

3917. *Columbia Journal of Gender and the Law.* [ISSN: 1062-6220] 1991. a. USD 65 (Individuals, USD 40; Students, USD 20). Ed(s): Brooke Andrich. Columbia University, School of Law, Jerome Greene Hall, 435 West 116th St, New York, NY 10027; cblr@law.columbia.edu; http://www.columbia.edu/. Illus. Reprint: WSH. *Indexed:* CLI, FemPer, GendWatch, ILP. *Bk. rev.:* Number varies, essay length, signed. *Aud.:* Ac, Sa.

This law review takes an interdisciplinary approach to the interplay between gender and the law. Articles reflect a broad definition of feminism and feminist jurisprudence and address issues affecting all races, ethnicities, classes, sexual orientations, and cultures. Contributors are judges, law professors, law students, and scholars from other disciplines. Recommended for law libraries and academic collections.

3918. *Columbia Journal of Law & the Arts: a quarterly journal of law and the arts, entertainment, communications and intellectual property.* Former titles (until 2001): *Columbia - V L A Journal of Law & the Arts;* (until 1985): *Art and the Law.* [ISSN: 1544-4848] 1974. q. USD 45 in North America; USD 53 elsewhere; USD 12 newsstand/cover per issue in North America. Columbia University, School of Law, Jerome Greene Hall, 435 West 116th St, New York, NY 10027; cblr@law.columbia.edu; http://www.columbia.edu/. Illus., index, adv. Circ: 750. Vol. ends: Summer. Microform: WSH. Online: EBSCO Publishing, EBSCO Host; William S. Hein & Co., Inc.; LexisNexis. Reprint: WSH. *Indexed:* CLI, ILP, LRI, RILM. *Aud.:* Ac, Sa.

As the subtitle of this publication indicates, coverage is sufficiently broad to include a multitude of issues relating to the arts and entertainment industry. The articles in each issue present enlightening, out-of-the-mainstream legal scholarship devoted to the interests of artists and attorneys whose specialty is serving artists. The *Hastings Communications and Entertainment Law Journal* is of the same genre and also worth consideration.

3919. *Columbia Law Review.* [ISSN: 0010-1958] 1901. 8x/yr. USD 54 domestic; USD 70 foreign. Ed(s): Grant Mainland. Columbia Law Review Association, 435 W 116th St, New York, NY 10027; eae@columbialawreview.org. Illus., index, adv. Refereed. Circ: 2000 Paid. Vol. ends: Dec. Microform: WSH. Online: EBSCO Publishing, EBSCO Host; William S. Hein & Co., Inc.; JSTOR (Web-based Journal Archive); LexisNexis; Thomson West. Reprint: WSH. *Indexed:* ABCPolSci, ABIn, ABS&EES, ATI, AgeL, ArtHuCI, BRI, CBRI, CJA, CLI, IBR, IBSS, IBZ, ILP, IPSA, LRI, PAIS, PSA, RiskAb, SSCI. *Bk. rev.:* Occasional, essay length. *Aud.:* Ac, Sa.

A prestigious law review from an equally prestigious law school with a long and distinguished history, this publication follows the traditional model of lead articles by professionals, comments and notes by students, and occasional scholarly book review essays. Recent issues address such diverse topics as taxation, transgender rights, and child pornography. Columbia University School of Law publishes 14 student journals. The others are *American Review of International Arbitration, Columbia Business Law Review, Columbia Human Rights Law Review, Columbia Journal of Environmental Law, Columbia Journal of Law & the Arts* (for the latter, see above in this section), *Columbia Journal of Law and Social Problems, Columbia Journal of Transnational Law, Columbia Journal of Gender and Law, Columbia Journal of Asian Law, Columbia Journal of East European Law, Columbia Science and Technology Law Review, National Black Law Journal,* and *Columbia Journal of European Law.*

Constitutional Commentary. See Civil Liberties/General section.

3920. *Cornell Law Review.* Formerly (until 1967): *Cornell Law Quarterly.* [ISSN: 0010-8847] 1915. 6x/yr. USD 45 domestic; USD 50 foreign; USD 15 Alumni. Ed(s): Dana E Hill. Cornell University, Cornell Law School, 137 Myron Taylor Hall, Ithaca, NY 14850; http://www.law.cornell.edu/. Illus., index, adv. Refereed. Circ: 3500. Vol. ends: No. 6. Microform: WSH. Online: Florida Center for Library Automation; William S. Hein & Co., Inc.; LexisNexis; Thomson West. Reprint: WSH. *Indexed:* ABCPolSci, ATI, ArtHuCI, BLI, CJA, CLI, ILP, LRI, PAIS, SSCI. *Aud.:* Ac, Sa.

Another traditional, student-edited law review that features lengthy, heavily researched articles by preeminent scholars and shorter pieces by student authors, this journal conforms to the law school's mission of preparing lawyers to understand the interactions between legal and social process in service to their clients. Recent articles illustrative of the breadth of coverage include "Separate But Equal and Single Sex Schools" and "Is the President Bound by the Geneva Conventions?" Cornell Law School also publishes the *Cornell International Law Journal* and *Cornell Journal of Law and Public Policy*.

3921. Duke Law Journal. Formerly (until 1957): *Duke Bar Journal.* [ISSN: 0012-7086] 1951. 6x/yr. USD 44 domestic; USD 50 foreign. Duke University, School of Law, PO Box 90364, Durham, NC 27708-0364; http://www.law.duke.edu/. Illus., index, adv. Refereed. Circ: 1400. Vol. ends: Dec. Microform: WSH; PMC. Online: EBSCO Publishing, EBSCO Host; Florida Center for Library Automation; Gale; William S. Hein & Co., Inc.; JSTOR (Web-based Journal Archive); LexisNexis; Thomson West. Reprint: WSH. *Indexed:* CJA, CLI, CommAb, ILP, LRI, RI-1, RiskAb, SSCI. *Bk. rev.:* Occasional, lengthy. *Aud.:* Ac, Sa.

This student-edited review, national in scope, consistently has high-quality articles on a wide range of legal topics. The highly respected "Annual Administrative Law Issue" discusses and evaluates recent developments in administrative law. One symposium issue is generally published every year. The Duke University School of Law provides free online access to all of its law reviews dating back to 1996. Other law reviews published by the school include the influential *Law and Contemporary Problems* (see below in this section), *Duke Journal of Comparative & International Law, Duke Environmental Law & Policy Forum, Duke Journal of Gender Law & Policy, Duke Law & Technology Review,* and the *Alaska Law Review* (because Alaska has no law school, yet has one of the highest numbers of lawyers per capita of any state, an agreement between Duke and the Alaska Bar Association enables this journal to be responsive to the needs of Alaska's diverse legal community).

3922. Ecology Law Quarterly. [ISSN: 0046-1121] 1971. q. USD 60 (Individuals, USD 35). Ed(s): Jasmine Starr, Catrina Fobian. University of California at Berkeley, School of Law, 493 Simon Hall, Boalt Hall School of Law, Berkeley, CA 94720; kabrams@law.berkeley.edu; http://www.law.berkeley.edu. Illus., index, adv. Refereed. Circ: 1150 Paid. Vol. ends: No. 4. Microform: WSH; PMC. Online: EBSCO Publishing, EBSCO Host; Florida Center for Library Automation; William S. Hein & Co., Inc.; LexisNexis. Reprint: WSH. *Indexed:* CLI, EnvAb, EnvInd, ExcerpMed, ILP, LRI, OceAb, PAIS, PollutAb, RI-1, SCI, SSCI, SUSA, SWRA. *Bk. rev.:* Occasional, 500-1,000 words. *Aud.:* Ac, Sa.

When the environment became a major concern following Earth Day in 1970, the law students at Boalt Hall were among the first to address law-related ecological issues via a law review. They are to be commended for their long-standing commitment to these matters. Throughout its history, this journal has featured consistently high-quality pieces by scholars and students that cover such diverse topics as biodiversity, global warming, and wastewater discharge. Consistent with the theme of preserving the environment and its natural beauty and resources, the cover of each issue is enhanced by an Ansel Adams photograph.

3923. The Elder Law Journal. [ISSN: 1070-1478] 1993. s-a. USD 25 domestic; USD 35 foreign. Ed(s): Alexander Chase, Matthew J Meyer. University of Illinois at Urbana-Champaign, College of Law, 244 Law Bldg, 504 East Pennsylvania Ave, Champaign, IL 61820-6996; lrev@law.uiuc.edu; http://www.law.uiuc.edu. Adv. Refereed. Reprint: WSH. *Indexed:* AgeL, CLI, ILP, LRI. *Aud.:* Ac, Sa.

As the baby boomers approach retirement, legal issues affecting the elderly are drawing the attention of the legal academy. This journal, edited by students at the University of Illinois School of Law, is the oldest scholarly law review devoted to issues relating to the elderly. Articles address a wide variety of topics, including estate and financial planning, guardianships, Medicare and Medicaid eligibility, nursing home management, and health law issues. Representative articles include "What Mom Would Have Wanted: Lessons Learned from an Elder Law Clinic About Achieving Clients' Estate Planning Goals" and "Aging of the AIDS Epidemic: Emerging Legal and Public Health Issues for Elderly Persons Living with HIV/AIDS." The school also publishes the *University of Illinois Law Review,* the *University of Illinois Journal of Law, Technology & Policy,* and the *Comparative Labor Law & Policy Journal.*

3924. Emory Law Journal. Formerly (until 1974): *Journal of Public Law.* [ISSN: 0094-4076] 1952. 6x/yr. USD 35 domestic; USD 39 foreign. Ed(s): Christopher Hunber. Emory University, School of Law, 1301 Clifton Rd, Atlanta, GA 30322; http://www.law.emory.edu. Illus., index, adv. Circ: 1100. Vol. ends: No. 4. Microform: WSH; PMC; PQC. Online: EBSCO Publishing, EBSCO Host; William S. Hein & Co., Inc.; LexisNexis; Northern Light Technology, Inc.; OCLC Online Computer Library Center, Inc.; ProQuest LLC (Ann Arbor); Thomson West; H.W. Wilson. Reprint: WSH. *Indexed:* CLI, ILP, LRI, SSCI. *Bk. rev.:* Occasional, lengthy. *Aud.:* Ac, Sa.

The School of Law of Emory University has a national reputation with a national and international focus. Its long-standing primary journal, traditional in nature, reflects the school's scholarly bent. Articles and student notes and occasional review essays address any legal topic. Because this journal is increasingly cited by other reviews, it has an important place on library shelves. Recent symposium issues have been devoted to the future of tort reform and a conference on sovereign debt restructuring. Also published by the school are *Emory International Law Review* and *Emory Bankruptcy Developments Journal.*

Employee Relations Law Journal. See Labor and Industrial Relations section.

3925. Environmental Law (Portland). [ISSN: 0046-2276] 1970. q. USD 40 domestic; USD 48 foreign; USD 10 newsstand/cover per issue domestic. Ed(s): Andrew Graham. Lewis & Clark College, Northwestern School of Law, 10015 SW Terwilliger Blvd, Portland, OR 97219; lclr@lclark.edu; http://www.lclark.edu. Illus., index, adv. Circ: 1100. Vol. ends: Oct. Microform: WSH; PQC. Online: Florida Center for Library Automation; Gale; LexisNexis; Thomson West. Reprint: WSH. *Indexed:* C&ISA, CLI, CerAb, EnvAb, EnvInd, ExcerpMed, IAA, IBSS, ILP, LRI, OceAb, PollutAb, RI-1, SWRA. *Bk. rev.:* Occasional, lengthy. *Aud.:* Ac, Sa.

Environmental law is one of the most rapidly developing and frequently changing areas of the law. The Northwestern University School of Law of Lewis and Clark College has built as its specialty environmental law. Its program is consistently rated at or near the top. The school's journal is consistent with the school's focus, and it is the oldest legal journal devoted exclusively to issues of environmental concern, such as ecosystems, endangered species, and the Clean Water Act. While each issue is hefty, often exceeding 300 pages, it is printed on unbleached, 100 percent recycled, 50 percent post-consumer paper with soy ink. The school also publishes the *Animal Law Review.*

3926. Family Law Quarterly. [ISSN: 0014-729X] 1967. q. Non-members, USD 79.95. American Bar Association, 321 N Clark St, Chicago, IL 60610; abajournal@abanet.org; http://www.abanet.org. Illus., index, adv. Refereed. Circ: 11000. Vol. ends: Winter. Microform: WSH; PMC; PQC. Online: William S. Hein & Co., Inc.; Thomson West. Reprint: WSH. *Indexed:* AgeL, CJA, CJPI, CLI, ILP, LRI, SSCI, V&AA. *Bk. rev.:* Occasional, 500-1,500 words. *Aud.:* Ac, Sa.

The American Bar Association's (ABA) Section of Family Law has as its purpose "to promote the objectives of the American Bar Association by improving the administration of justice in the field of family law by study, conferences, and publication of reports and articles with respect to both legislation and administration." This publication, under editorship of students at Washburn University School of Law, is one of the principal means toward that end. Issues discuss such topics as divorce, parentage, child custody and support, property rights, domestic torts, and adoption. The annotated "Summary of the Year in Family Law" is contained in the Winter issue. *The Family Advocate,* also published by this ABA section, is a more basic magazine that offers practical advice for attorneys practicing family law.

3927. Feminist Legal Studies. [ISSN: 0966-3622] 1993. 3x/yr. EUR 247 print & online eds. Ed(s): Joanne Conaghan. Springer Netherlands, Van Godewijckstraat 30, Dordrecht, 3311 GX, Netherlands;

http://www.springeronline.com. Adv. Refereed. Reprint: PSC. *Indexed:* CLI, FemPer, IBR, IBSS, IBZ, ILP, LRI, PSA, SSA, SWA, SociolAb. *Bk. rev.:* Number and length vary. *Aud.:* Ac, Sa.

This journal provides an international perspective on law, legal theory, and legal practice as they relate to feminist concerns. Contents include articles, review essays, case notes, and book reviews by academics, lawyers, and "authors working outside the academy." Full text is available online for institutional subscriptions. There is a contents-alerting service available from the publisher's web site.

3928. Florida Law Review. Formerly (until 1989): *University of Florida Law Review.* [ISSN: 1045-4241] 1948. 5x/yr. USD 30; USD 8 newsstand/cover per issue. Ed(s): Whitney Carson Harper. University of Florida, Levin College of Law, 115 Holland Hall, PO Box 117637, Gainesville, FL 32611; eic@floridalawreview.org; http://www.law.ufl.edu/ . Illus., index, adv. Circ: 1000. Vol. ends: Dec. Microform: WSH. Online: William S. Hein & Co., Inc.; LexisNexis; Thomson West. Reprint: WSH. *Indexed:* CJA, CLI, ILP, LRI. *Bk. rev.:* Occasional, lengthy. *Aud.:* Ac, Sa.

Founded in 1909, the University of Florida is among the oldest law schools in the South, and so, too, is its primary law review. This publication is traditional in format, with feature articles by scholars and notes and case comments by students. Thus, readers can expect to find contributions on any legal subject. For example, recent issues address nationalism in the age of terrorism, racial segregation in American churches, and insurer insolvency. Students here also publish the *Florida Journal of International Law, Journal of Technology Law & Policy,* and the *Journal of Law & Public Policy.* The *Florida Tax Review* is a faculty-edited publication of the school.

Food and Drug Law Journal. See Food Industry section.

3929. Fordham Law Review. [ISSN: 0015-704X] 1914. bi-m. USD 40 domestic; USD 50 foreign. Ed(s): Deana Kim El-Mallawany. Fordham University, School of Law, Lincoln Center, 140 W 62nd St, New York, NY 10023; lawreview@fordham.edu; http://www.fordham.edu. Adv. Refereed. Circ: 2800. Microform: WSH; PQC. Online: William S. Hein & Co., Inc.; LexisNexis; OCLC Online Computer Library Center, Inc.; Thomson West; H.W. Wilson. Reprint: WSH. *Indexed:* ABS&EES, AgeL, ArtHuCI, BLI, CJA, CLI, ILP, LRI, PSA, SSCI. *Aud.:* Ac, Sa.

Well respected and frequently cited, the *Fordham Law Review* follows a different format than most traditional law reviews. Although feature articles and notes are included, many issues lead with an essay written by a noted scholar, followed by a discussion section with responses to the scholar. Recent essays include "The State Secrets Privilege and the Separation of Powers" and "Euclid Lives: The Uneasy Legacy of Progressivism in Zoning." Fordham also publishes the *Fordham Environmental Law Journal, Fordham Intellectual Property, Media & Entertainment Law Journal, Fordham International Law Journal, Fordham Journal of Corporate and Financial Law, The Common Good,* and *Fordham Urban Law Journal.*

3930. G P Solo. Formerly (until 2000): *General Practice, Solo, and Small Firm Lawyer: The Complete Lawyer;* Which was formed by the merger of (1984-1998): *Compleat Lawyer;* Which was formed by the merger of (1966-1984): *Docket Call;* (1964-1984): *Law Notes for the General Practitioner;* (1997-1998): *Best of A B A Sections. General Practice, Solo & Small Firm Section;* (1997-1998): *Technology and Practice Guide.* [ISSN: 1528-638X] 1998. 8x/yr. USD 48 domestic; USD 72 foreign; USD 9.50 newsstand/cover. Ed(s): Jennifer J Rose, Robert M Salkin. A B A Publishing, 750 N Lake Shore Dr, Chicago, IL 60611; service@abanet.org. Illus., index, adv. Circ: 30000 Paid. *Indexed:* CLI, LRI. *Aud.:* Ga, Ac, Sa.

Although law is becoming more and more specialized, there are still a substantial number of attorneys engaged in general practice. This magazine caters to the needs of the general practitioner by providing timely, concise articles on all aspects of substantive law, news of the American Bar Association (ABA) section and committee activities, and updates relating to legislation,

ethics, taxes, and solo practice. A recent issue focuses exclusively on military law and the legal issues facing those being deployed to Iraq. This publication is a good companion to the ABA's *Law Practice Management* (see below in this section).

3931. George Washington Law Review. [ISSN: 0016-8076] 1932. 6x/yr. USD 40 domestic; USD 44 foreign. Ed(s): Irene Ayzenberg. The George Washington University Law School, 2008 G St, NW, 2nd Fl, Washington, DC 20052; gwlr@gwu.edu; http://www.law.gwu.edu. Illus., index, adv. Refereed. Circ: 2000. Vol. ends: Aug. Microform: WSH; PMC. Online: William S. Hein & Co., Inc.; LexisNexis; Thomson West. Reprint: WSH. *Indexed:* AgeL, ArtHuCI, BAS, CJA, CLI, ILP, LRI, PAIS, PSA, RiskAb, SSA, SSCI, SociolAb. *Bk. rev.:* Occasional, lengthy. *Aud.:* Ac, Sa.

The *Review* tends to contain three or four articles, often with an emphasis on federal law. A review of D.C. Circuit Court opinions is published annually. The school also publishes the *George Washington International Law Review, International Law in Domestic Courts, American Intellectual Property Law Association Quarterly Journal* (with the AIPLA), and the *Public Contact Law Journal* (with the ABA).

3932. Georgetown Journal of International Law. Formerly (until 2003): *Law and Policy in International Business.* [ISSN: 1550-5200] 1969. q. USD 40; USD 12.50 newsstand/cover per issue. Ed(s): Anne B Taylor. Georgetown University Law Center, 600 New Jersey Ave, NW, Washington, DC 20001; jplp@law.georgetown.edu; http://www.law.georgetown.edu. Illus., index, adv. Circ: 861. Vol. ends: Dec. Microform: WSH; PQC. Online: Factiva, Inc.; Florida Center for Library Automation; Gale; William S. Hein & Co., Inc.; LexisNexis; OCLC Online Computer Library Center, Inc.; ProQuest LLC (Ann Arbor); Thomson West; H.W. Wilson. Reprint: WSH. *Indexed:* ABIn, ABS&EES, BAS, CLI, IBR, ILP, LRI, PAIS, PSA, RiskAb. *Bk. rev.:* Occasional, length varies. *Aud.:* Ac, Sa.

This journal, formerly known as the *Journal of Law and Policy in International Business,* is the second-oldest journal at the Georgetown Law Center. It recently expanded its scope to include issues relating to the broader topic of international law. This expansion allowed the journal to solicit articles from a wider range of authors, and reflects the overall emphasis on international law that Georgetown is known for. Recent articles reflecting this expansion of topics include "International Law, American Sovereignty, and the Death Penalty" and "The Process and Prospects for the U.N. Guiding Principles on Internal Displacement to Become Customary International Law: A Preliminary Assessment." The journal continues to include articles on international business law.

3933. Georgetown Journal of Legal Ethics. [ISSN: 1041-5548] 1987. 4x/yr. USD 40; USD 12.50 newsstand/cover per issue. Ed(s): Lauren A Weeman. Georgetown University Law Center, 600 New Jersey Ave, NW, Washington, DC 20001; jplp@law.georgetown.edu; http://www.law.gwu.edu. Illus., index. Refereed. Vol. ends: Spring. Microform: WSH. Online: William S. Hein & Co., Inc.; LexisNexis; OCLC Online Computer Library Center, Inc.; ProQuest LLC (Ann Arbor); H.W. Wilson. Reprint: WSH. *Indexed:* ABIn, CLI, ILP, LRI. *Bk. rev.:* Occasional, lengthy. *Aud.:* Ac, Sa.

Ours is a litigious society, and the bad acts of a few reflect adversely on many in the professional realm. Every law school in the country is required to offer a course in professional responsibility, sometimes called legal ethics. Professional responsibility is a separate requirement on the multistate bar examination. This student-edited journal endeavors to heighten awareness of ethical issues within the legal community by providing scholarly articles, student notes and comments, and other information of interest to members of the bar. Recent writings address such diverse issues as representing children in abuse and neglect cases, civil commitment hearings, and questioning judicial impartiality.

3934. Georgetown Law Journal. [ISSN: 0016-8092] 1912. 6x/yr. USD 45 domestic; USD 55 foreign; USD 15 newsstand/cover per issue. Ed(s): Andrew Ditchfield. Georgetown University Law Center, 600 New Jersey Ave, NW, Washington, DC 20001; jplp@law.georgetown.edu; http://www.law.gwu.edu. Illus., index, adv. Refereed. Circ: 1319.

Microform: WSH. Online: William S. Hein & Co., Inc.; LexisNexis; Northern Light Technology, Inc.; OCLC Online Computer Library Center, Inc.; ProQuest K-12 Learning Solutions; ProQuest LLC (Ann Arbor); Thomson West; H.W. Wilson. Reprint: WSH. *Indexed:* ArtHuCI, BLI, CJA, CLI, CPL, ILP, LRI, PAIS, RiskAb, SSCI. *Aud.:* Ac, Sa.

The Georgetown Law Center, located in our nation's capital, has the largest enrollment and among the highest academic standards of any law school in the country. This journal, the oldest from the District of Columbia law schools, is among ten published by Georgetown and has an outstanding reputation for producing traditional legal scholarship. Articles by noted authorities and student research pieces are lengthy, well documented, and influential. Its "Annual Review of Criminal Procedure"—also known as the "Criminal Procedure Project" and a team effort of the journal staff—is monumental in scope and depth. This journal is among the more frequently cited—by courts and other legal journals—in the country. The school also publishes *American Criminal Law Review, Georgetown Journal of International Law, Georgetown Journal of Legal Ethics,* and *The Tax Lawyer* (for these four, see above and below in this section), as well as *Georgetown Immigration Law Journal, Georgetown International Environmental Law Review, Georgetown Journal of Gender and the Law, Georgetown Journal on Poverty Law & Policy,* and *Georgetown Journal of Law and Public Policy.*

3935. *The Green Bag: an entertaining journal of law.* [ISSN: 1095-5216] 1889. q. USD 35 domestic; USD 50 foreign. Ed(s): Ross E. Davies. The Green Bag, Inc., 6600 Barnaby St., NW, Washington, DC 20015; webmaster@greenbag.org; http://www.greenbag.org. Circ: 1500 Paid. Online: William S. Hein & Co., Inc.; LexisNexis. *Indexed:* ILP, LRI. *Bk. rev.:* 2-4. *Aud.:* Ga, Ac, Sa.

Green bags were once a required accessory for lawyers and law students. The bags, used to carry legal papers and casebooks, were considered the lawyer's "repository of knowledge." From 1889 to 1914, a journal known as *The Green Bag* was published and widely read by members of the bar. It contained short articles penned by scholars, practitioners, and judges discussing legal issues of interest at the time. Many of the articles were light, and some issues even included verse. *The Green Bag* was resurrected in 1997 with the hope of filling the gap in legal publishing between the scholarly law journals and the more practitioner-oriented legal magazines. Its creators describe it as a place for scholars to toss out creative thoughts or make an argument with fewer than 50 footnotes. Contributors to the new version of *The Green Bag* range from famous legal scholars to judges to general practitioners. Articles are varied; some discuss serious legal issues of the day and some are light. All are less than 5,000 words. This is a good, general-purpose legal journal that would be a welcome addition to any type of library. Published in cooperation with the George Mason University School of Law.

Harvard Civil Rights—Civil Liberties Law Review. See Civil Liberties/ General section.

3936. *Harvard Journal of Law & Gender.* Formerly (until 2004): *Harvard Women's Law Journal.* [ISSN: 1558-4356] 1978. s-a. USD 30 domestic; USD 38 Canada; USD 36 elsewhere. Ed(s): Elizabeth Bangs. Harvard University, Law School, Publications Center, 1541 Massachusetts Ave, Cambridge, MA 02138; hlswlj@law.harvard.edu; http://www.harvard.edu/. Adv. Circ: 900. Microform: WSH; PMC. Online: William S. Hein & Co., Inc.; LexisNexis; OCLC Online Computer Library Center, Inc.; Thomson West; H.W. Wilson. Reprint: WSH. *Indexed:* AltPI, CLI, FemPer, ILP, LRI, PAIS, RI-1, SWA, V&AA. *Bk. rev.:* Number and length vary. *Aud.:* Ac, Sa.

This law journal addresses a broad range of gender-related topics. Recent articles have considered paid family leave, women in post-revolutionary Iran, and the integration of women into Harvard Law School's faculty. Contents include academic articles that analyze feminist legal issues and essays based on personal experience. Issues also include case comments, notes on controversial or current topics, and book reviews.

3937. *Harvard Journal of Law and Public Policy.* [ISSN: 0193-4872] 1978. 3x/yr. USD 45 domestic; USD 50 foreign. Ed(s): Amber Taylor. Harvard Society for Law and Public Policy, Inc., Harvard Law School, 1541 Massachusetts Ave, Cambridge, MA 02138;

http://www.law.harvard.edu. Illus., index, adv. Refereed. Circ: 6500 Paid and controlled. Vol. ends: No. 3. Microform: WSH; PMC. Online: EBSCO Publishing, EBSCO Host; Florida Center for Library Automation; Gale; LexisNexis; OCLC Online Computer Library Center, Inc.; ProQuest LLC (Ann Arbor); Thomson West; H.W. Wilson. Reprint: WSH. *Indexed:* ABCPolSci, ArtHuCI, CLI, ILP, LRI, PAIS, RI-1, RiskAb, SSCI. *Bk. rev.:* Occasional. *Aud.:* Ac, Sa.

This journal is published by the the Harvard Society for Law & Public Policy, a conservative and libertarian student group. The journal is one of the most widely circulated student-published law reviews in the country. Articles included reflect the journal's conservative philosophy. Many issues are symposia issues, such as the most recent one titled "Private Law: The New Frontier for Limited Government." Contributors over the years have included conservative politicians and Supreme Court justices. This is a good source for viewpoints that are alternatives to those often found in student-edited law reviews.

3938. *Harvard Journal on Legislation.* [ISSN: 0017-808X] 1964. 2x/yr. USD 30 domestic; USD 38 Canada; USD 36 elsewhere. Ed(s): Alixandra Smith. Harvard University, Law School, Publications Center, 1541 Massachusetts Ave, Cambridge, MA 02138; http://www.law.harvard.edu/. Illus., index, adv. Refereed. Circ: 800. Vol. ends: Summer. Microform: WSH; PQC. Online: EBSCO Publishing, EBSCO Host; William S. Hein & Co., Inc.; LexisNexis; OCLC Online Computer Library Center, Inc.; Thomson West; H.W. Wilson. Reprint: WSH. *Indexed:* ABCPolSci, AgeL, CLI, IBZ, ILP, LRI, PAIS, PSA, RiskAb, SSCI. *Bk. rev.:* Occasional. *Aud.:* Ac, Sa.

This is the second oldest of Harvard Law School's 14 student-edited reviews. According to the journal's publication policy, it specializes in the analysis of legislation and the legislative process by focusing on legislative reform and on organizational and procedural factors that affect the efficacy of legislative decision-making. The journal publishes articles that examine a public-policy problem of nationwide significance and propose legislation to resolve it. A recent symposium is "Hate Speech and Hate Crimes." A section devoted to recent developments provides analysis of recent statutory interpretations and discussions of recent statutory enactments.

3939. *Harvard Law Review.* [ISSN: 0017-811X] 1887. m. 8/yr. USD 200 (Individuals, USD 55). Ed(s): Kenneth Damberger. Harvard Law Review Association, Gannett House, 1511 Massachusetts Ave, Cambridge, MA 02138; articleschair@harvardlawreview.org. Illus., index, adv. Refereed. Circ: 7500. Vol. ends: Jun. Microform: WSH; PQC. Online: EBSCO Publishing, EBSCO Host; Gale; William S. Hein & Co., Inc.; JSTOR (Web-based Journal Archive); LexisNexis; Thomson West. Reprint: WSH. *Indexed:* ABCPolSci, ABIn, ABS&EES, ATI, AgeL, ArtHuCI, BLI, BRI, CBRI, CJA, CLI, IBR, IBSS, IBZ, ILP, IPSA, IndIslam, LRI, PAIS, PSA, PhilInd, RI-1, RiskAb, SSCI. *Bk. rev.:* Occasional, essay length. *Aud.:* Ac, Sa.

When it comes to tradition, Harvard is steeped in it; so, too, is its primary journal. It is by far the most widely subscribed to of all the law school reviews. To be selected for the *Harvard Law Review* is almost always a prediction of greater things to come. Articles are selected from a massive pool of submissions and frequently are in the forefront of legal thinking. A typical volume contains approximately 2,000 pages. Each year, the *Review* publishes an evaluation, complete with charts and statistical analyses, of the U.S. Supreme Court decisions during the recently completed term. The 13 other journals edited by students at the school are *Harvard Journal on Legislation* and *Harvard Journal of Law and Public Policy* (for these two, see above in this section); *Harvard BlackLetter Journal* and *Harvard Civil Rights–Civil Liberties Law Review* (see Civil Liberties section); *Harvard Environmental Law Review; Harvard Human Rights Journal; Harvard International Law Journal; Harvard Journal of Law and Gender; Harvard Journal of Law and Public Policy; Harvard Journal of Law and Technology; Harvard Latino Law Review; Harvard Law Record; Harvard Negotiation Law Review;* and *Unbound.*

3940. *Hastings Law Journal.* Formerly (until 1950): *Hastings Journal.* [ISSN: 0017-8322] 1949. bi-m. USD 33 domestic print & PDF; USD 38 foreign print & PDF. University of California at San Francisco, Hastings College of the Law, 200 McAllister St, San Francisco, CA 94102-4978;

subscriptions@hastingsblg.org; http://www.uchastings.edu. Illus., index, adv. Refereed. Circ: 1400 Paid and controlled. Microform: WSH. Online: William S. Hein & Co., Inc.; LexisNexis; Thomson West. Reprint: WSH. *Indexed:* AgeL, CJA, CLI, HRA, IBR, IBZ, ILP, LRI, PRA, SSCI. *Bk. rev.:* Occasional, essay length. *Aud.:* Ac, Sa.

Established in 1878, Hastings College is the oldest and largest law school in the western United States. Hastings is known for its prestigious "65–Club"—a group of outstanding law professors who have retired from other institutions and now teach at this school. As a result of having this pool of great legal scholars available, the San Francisco location, and the overall quality of the academic program, the school has a student body with some of the best academic credentials in the country. The *Journal* is traditional, having a lengthy major article or two by a prominent scholar followed by student comments and notes. Even the book reviews are highly substantive. This journal is well respected and among the most frequently cited. Hastings also publishes the *Hastings Constitutional Law Quarterly, Hastings Business Law Journal, Hastings International and Comparative Law Review, West–Northwest Journal of Environmental Law and Policy, Hastings Race and Poverty Law Journal, Hastings Communications and Entertainment Law Journal,* and *Hastings Women's Law Journal.*

3941. Hastings Women's Law Journal. [ISSN: 1061-0901] 1989. s-a. USD 28 domestic print & PDF; USD 35 foreign print & PDF. University of California at San Francisco, Hastings College of the Law, 200 McAllister St, San Francisco, CA 94102-4978; subscriptions@hastingsblg.org; http://www.uchastings.edu. Adv. Circ: 600. Microform: WSH. Online: Thomson West. Reprint: WSH. *Indexed:* CLI, ILP, LRI. *Bk. rev.:* 0-1, length varies, signed. *Aud.:* Ac, Sa.

The focus of this journal is on the intersections of gender with race, class, and sexual orientation. It covers a range of topics outside the scope of traditional legal scholarship. Its contents include articles, commentaries, essays, personal narratives, and book reviews. A recent article features a proposal for a private right of action for human trafficking.

3942. Howard Law Journal. [ISSN: 0018-6813] 1955. 3x/yr. USD 28 domestic; USD 35 foreign. Ed(s): Shirlethia V Franklin, Rebecca S Wollensack. Howard University School of Law, 2900 Van Ness St, NW, 311 Notre Dame Hall, Washington, DC 20008; LSoto@law.howard.edu; http://www.law.howard.edu/. Illus., index, adv. Circ: 1100. Vol. ends: No. 3. Microform: WSH; PMC. Online: Chadwyck-Healey Inc.; William S. Hein & Co., Inc.; LexisNexis; Thomson West. Reprint: WSH. *Indexed:* CLI, IIBP, ILP, LRI, PAIS, RiskAb. *Bk. rev.:* 1-2, lengthy. *Aud.:* Ac, Sa.

Howard University is the second oldest law school in our nation's capital, and its student body is predominantly African American. The editors of its *Journal* describe it as dedicated to promoting the civil and human rights of all people, in particular those groups who have been the target of subordination and discrimination, which is identical to the school's mission. A recent symposium issue is devoted to the 50th anniversary of *Brown v. Board of Education.*

Human Rights Quarterly. See Civil Liberties/General section.

3943. International Lawyer. Formerly: *American Bar Association. Section of International and Comparative Law. Journal and Proceedings.* [ISSN: 0020-7810] 1966. q. Free to members; Non-members, USD 60. Ed(s): Christine Szaj. American Bar Association, International Law and Practice Section, 740 15th St, NW, Washington, DC 20005; http://www.abanet.org. Index, adv. Refereed. Circ: 13000. Microform: WSH. Online: LexisNexis; Thomson West. Reprint: WSH. *Indexed:* ABS&EES, BAS, CLI, ILP, LRI, PRA, RiskAb, SSCI, SWRA, WAE&RSA. *Bk. rev.:* Occasional, length varies. *Aud.:* Ac, Sa.

Published under the auspices of the American Bar Association's Section of International Law and Practice, this journal has as its primary focus practical issues that face lawyers engaged in international practice. Topics concerning international trade, licensing, direct investment, finance, taxation, and litigation and dispute resolution are preferred. It provides information on significant current legal developments throughout the world, using articles and recent developments, regional development, and case notes. A recent symposium issue addresses international company and securities laws. Contributions are by professors and practicing attorneys.

3944. Iowa Law Review. [ISSN: 0021-0552] 1915. 5x/yr. USD 45 domestic; USD 52 foreign; USD 10 newsstand/cover per issue. Ed(s): Daniel M Buroker, Dorota Niechwiej. University of Iowa, College of Law, 190 Boyd Law Bldg, Iowa City, IA 52242-1113; http://www.law.uiowa.edu/. Illus., index, adv. Refereed. Circ: 1800. Vol. ends: No. 5. Microform: WSH; PMC. Online: Gale; William S. Hein & Co., Inc.; LexisNexis; Thomson West. Reprint: WSH. *Indexed:* ATI, CJA, CLI, ILP, LRI, PAIS, SSCI. *Bk. rev.:* Occasional, essay length. *Aud.:* Ac, Sa.

It may surprise some to learn that the University of Iowa College of Law, founded in 1865, is the oldest law school west of the Mississippi. The standards used to select the students for the *Review* are among the most rigorous in the country. Due to the College of Law's academic excellence and its longevity, its primary journal has a well-deserved reputation for publishing outstanding legal scholarship. Articles are well researched, heavily documented, and widely cited. Iowa law students also edit the *Journal of Corporation Law, Journal of Gender, Race & Justice,* and *Transnational Law & Contemporary Problems.*

Issues in Law and Medicine. See Civil Liberties/Bioethics: Reproductive Rights, Right-to-Life, and Right-to-Die section.

The Journal of Air Law and Commerce. See Transportation section.

Journal of Criminal Justice. See Criminology and Law Enforcement section.

3945. Journal of Criminal Law & Criminology. Supersedes in part (in 1972): *Journal of Criminal Law, Criminology and Police Science;* Which had former titles (until 1951): *Journal of Criminal Law & Criminology (Chicago, 1931);* (until 1940): *American Institute of Criminal Law and Criminology. Journal.* [ISSN: 0091-4169] 1910. q. USD 50 domestic; USD 60 foreign. Ed(s): Rebecca Stern. Northwestern University, School of Law, 357 E Chicago Ave, Chicago, IL 60611; law-web@law.northwestern.edu; http://www.law.northwestern.edu. Illus., index. Refereed. Circ: 2700. Microform: WSH; PQC. Online: EBSCO Publishing, EBSCO Host; Florida Center for Library Automation; Gale; William S. Hein & Co., Inc.; JSTOR (Web-based Journal Archive); Northern Light Technology, Inc.; OCLC Online Computer Library Center, Inc.; ProQuest LLC (Ann Arbor); Thomson West; H.W. Wilson. Reprint: WSH. *Indexed:* ABCPolSci, CJA, CJPI, CLI, ExcerpMed, IBR, IBSS, IBZ, ILP, IndIslam, LRI, PAIS, PSA, SSA, SSCI, SociolAb. *Bk. rev.:* 0-4, lengthy. *Aud.:* Ac, Sa.

This journal dates back over 80 years and is among the first of the subject-specialty law school reviews. Both its long history and the quality of its content make it a leader in the field and among the most frequently cited legal journals. Edited by students of Northwestern University School of Law, the journal is divided into "Criminal Law" and "Criminology" sections, written by law professionals and social scientists respectively, with a separate section of student-written "Comments." One issue per year contains a highly respected, heavily analytical review of U.S. Supreme Court decisions pertaining to criminal law and criminal procedure.

3946. Journal of Dispute Resolution. Formerly (until 1987): *Missouri Journal of Dispute Resolution.* [ISSN: 1052-2859] 1984. s-a. USD 35 domestic. Ed(s): Jonathan R Bunch. University of Missouri at Columbia, School of Law, 206 Hulston Hall, Columbia, MO 65211; http://www.law.missouri.edu/. Illus., index, adv. Circ: 700 Paid. Vol. ends: No. 2. Microform: WSH. Online: William S. Hein & Co., Inc.; LexisNexis. Reprint: WSH. *Indexed:* CLI, ILP, LRI. *Bk. rev.:* 1, 2,000-4,000 words. *Aud.:* Ac, Sa.

Very few cases actually go to trial. This interdisciplinary journal, published in conjunction with the Center for the Study of Dispute Resolution, fills an important gap in the legal literature in that it discusses the means to avoid the high costs of litigation, such as negotiation, settlement, mediation, and arbitration. Articles, contributed by major legal scholars, address philosophical, practical, and political aspects of dispute processing and at times are the result of empirical research. Some writings relate to the teaching of dispute resolution, while others concern the legal aspects of dispute resolution processes. Comments, case notes, surveys, and studies analyze individual disputes or transactions in detail. The *Missouri Law Review* is also published by the University of Missouri–Columbia School of Law.

3947. *Journal of Health Law.* Former titles: *Journal of Health and Hospital Law;* (until 1988): *Hospital Law.* [ISSN: 1526-2472] 1969. q. Members, USD 125; Non-members, USD 175. American Health Lawyers Association, 1025 Connecticut Ave NW Ste 600, Washington, DC 20036-5405; mbrserv@healthlawyers.org; http://www.healthlawyers.org. Illus. Circ: 3000 Paid. *Indexed:* CLI, ILP, LRI. *Aud.:* Ac, Sa.

Health and the legal issues related to it are one of the most rapidly growing areas of law. A number of journals have emerged that discuss different aspects of health-care law. This journal, a collaborative effort among the American Health Lawyers Association and Saint Louis University School of Law, is the oldest. It is also the most expensive. Other similar publications are *Berkeley Journal of Health Care Law,* Catholic University's *Journal of Contemporary Health Law and Policy,* Duke's *Journal of Health Politics, Policy and Law,* DePaul's *Journal of Health Care Law,* Case Western's *Health Matrix,* and Cleveland State's *Journal of Law and Health.*

3948. *Journal of Law and Economics.* [ISSN: 0022-2186] 1958. q. USD 103 domestic; USD 114.18 Canada; USD 113 elsewhere. Ed(s): Douglas Lichtman, Sam Peltzman. University of Chicago Press, Journals Division, PO Box 37005, Chicago, IL 60637; subscriptions@ press.uchicago.edu; http://www.journals.uchicago.edu. Illus., index, adv. Refereed. Circ: 2800. Vol. ends: Oct. Microform: WSH; PQC. Online: EBSCO Publishing, EBSCO Host; JSTOR (Web-based Journal Archive); LexisNexis; Thomson West. Reprint: PSC; WSH. *Indexed:* ABCPolSci, ABIn, AgeL, AmH&L, BAS, BLI, CJA, CLI, ExcerpMed, HistAb, IBR, IBSS, IBZ, ILP, IPSA, JEL, LRI, PAIS, RiskAb, SSCI. *Aud.:* Ac, Sa.

This highly regarded, widely referenced, interdisciplinary journal is intended for a true specialist who is concerned with the influence of regulation and legal institutions on the operation of economic systems, especially the behavior of markets and the impact of government institutions on markets. Use of charts, graphs, and other forms of statistical analysis is commonplace, and plodding through an article can be quite a chore. Each issue has 8–12 articles, together totaling approximately 300 pages. The University of Chicago Law School is known for its law-and-economics orientation, and this publication is true to the school's mission.

Journal of Law and Policy in International Business. See *Georgetown Journal of International Law.*

Journal of Law and Religion. See Civil Liberties/Freedom of Thought and Belief section.

3949. *Journal of Legal Education.* Formerly (until 1940): *National Journal of Legal Education.* [ISSN: 0022-2208] 1937. q. USD 38 domestic; USD 42 foreign; USD 15 newsstand/cover per issue. Georgetown University Law Center, 600 New Jersey Ave, NW, Washington, DC 20001; http://www.law.gwu.edu. Illus., index, adv. Sample. Refereed. Vol. ends: Dec. Microform: PQC. Online: William S. Hein & Co., Inc. Reprint: WSH. *Indexed:* ABS&EES, CLI, HEA, IBR, IBZ, ILP, LRI, SSCI. *Bk. rev.:* 0-4, 500-10,000 words. *Aud.:* Ac, Sa.

The Association of American Law Schools is a membership organization, and this, its professional journal, is distributed to all law professors in the country. Its primary purpose is to foster a rich interchange of ideas and information about legal education and related matters, including, but not limited to, the legal profession, legal theory, and legal scholarship. The *Journal* features general articles, shorter discussions of developments in legal education, an occasional symposium, and from time to time even a poem or a short story. Because all law professors receive it automatically, it is probably the most widely read of all journals in legal academia.

3950. *The Journal of Legal Studies (Chicago).* [ISSN: 0047-2530] 1972. s-a. USD 83 domestic; USD 91.98 Canada; USD 88 elsewhere. Ed(s): Eric A Posner, Thomas J. Miles. University of Chicago Press, Journals Division, PO Box 37005, Chicago, IL 60637; subscriptions@ press.uchicago.edu; http://www.journals.uchicago.edu. Illus., index, adv. Refereed. Circ: 1600 Paid and free. Vol. ends: Jun. Microform: WSH; PQC. Online: EBSCO Publishing, EBSCO Host; JSTOR (Web-based Journal Archive); LexisNexis. Reprint: PSC; WSH. *Indexed:* AUNI, CJA, CJPI, CLI, IBR, IBSS, IBZ, ILP, IPSA, JEL, LRI, PSA, SSA, SSCI, SociolAb. *Aud.:* Ac, Sa.

Like other law-related publications from the University of Chicago, this title ranks among the most frequently cited of the legal literature. It provides a forum for basic theoretical, empirical, historical, and comparative research into the operation of legal systems and institutions, relying on contributions from economists, political scientists, sociologists, and other social scientists, as well as legal scholars, for its content. Occasionally, an issue is published in two parts or has a special focus. The number and length of articles are consistent with its companion journal, *The Journal of Law & Economics* (see above in this section).

Journal of Maritime Law and Commerce. See Transportation section.

3951. *Journal of Supreme Court History.* Formerly (until 1989): *Supreme Court Historical Society. Yearbook.* [ISSN: 1059-4329] 1976. 3x/yr. GBP 109 print & online eds. Ed(s): Clare Cushman, Melvin I Urofsky. Blackwell Publishing, Inc., Commerce Place, 350 Main St, Malden, MA 02148; customerservices@blackwellpublishing.com; http://www.blackwellpublishing.com. Illus., adv. Refereed. Circ: 5000. Reprint: PSC. *Indexed:* AmH&L, ApEcolAb, CLI, HistAb, ILP, IPSA, LRI, PSA, SociolAb. *Bk. rev.:* 5-7, 500-1,000 words. *Aud.:* Ga.

Established in 1974, the Supreme Court Historical Society is dedicated to the collection and preservation of the history of the Supreme Court of the United States. Its *Journal* reflects this commitment. Initially published as an annual, it expanded to three issues per year in 1999. Articles are brief, historical in nature, and highly illustrated from archival sources, and they discuss all aspects of the court, including justices, cases, and themes. The cost, scope, and interesting coverage make this a nice addition to any type of library collection or even a coffee table.

3952. *Journal of the Legal Profession.* [ISSN: 0196-7487] 1976. a. USD 14. University of Alabama, School of Law, PO Box 870382, University, AL 35487-0382; jolp@law.ua.edu; http://www.law.ua.edu. Illus., index. Microform: WSH. Online: LexisNexis. Reprint: WSH. *Indexed:* CLI, ILP, LRI. *Aud.:* Ac, Sa.

This publication is unique in that it is the only student-edited journal devoted to the legal profession in general. The *Journal* is intended as a forum for the explanation and exposition of the legal profession's problems, shortcomings, and achievements, as well as a legal ethics and law publication for lawyer and judge. The content is clear, concise, and readable enough to be enjoyed by any segment of the legal community. Each annual volume contains an annotated bibliography of law review articles about the legal profession and abstracts of selected ethics opinions. The students at the University of Alabama School of Law also edit the *Alabama Law Review* and *Law and Psychology Review.*

Journal of Transportation Law, Logistics, and Policy. See Transportation section.

3953. *Judicature: journal of the American Judicature Society.* Formerly (until 1966): *American Judicature Society Journal.* [ISSN: 0022-5800] 1917. bi-m. USD 60 USD 11 newsstand/cover per issue domestic. Ed(s): David Richert. American Judicature Society, 2700 University Ave, Des Moines, IA 50311; drichert@ajs.org; http://www.ajs.org. Illus., index, adv. Refereed. Circ: 6000 Paid and controlled. Vol. ends: Apr/May. Microform: PQC. Online: William S. Hein & Co., Inc.; OCLC Online Computer Library Center, Inc.; ProQuest LLC (Ann Arbor); Thomson West; H.W. Wilson. Reprint: WSH. *Indexed:* AmH&L, ArtHuCI, CJA, CJPI, CLI, HistAb, ILP, LRI, PAIS, PSA, SSA, SSCI, SociolAb. *Bk. rev.:* 2-3, 500-5,000 words. *Aud.:* Ga, Ac, Sa.

The American Judicature Society has as its purpose the promotion of the effective administration of justice and is open to all persons interested in working toward court improvement. This publication is intended as a forum for fact and opinion relating to the administration of justice and its improvement. The four to eight articles per issue are short, entertaining, and of current interest. The use of graphics, cartoons, and photographs contributes to overall readability.

3954. *Jurimetrics: journal of law, science and technology.* Former titles (until 1978): *Jurimetrics Journal; Modern Uses of Logic in Law (MULL).* [ISSN: 0897-1277] 1959. q. Members, USD 35; Non-members, USD 40. Sandra Day O'Connor College of Law, McAllister & Orange St, P O Box 877906, Tempe, AZ 85287-7906; http://www.law.asu.edu. Illus., index, adv. Circ: 6200. Vol. ends: Summer. Microform: WSH. Online: William S. Hein & Co., Inc. Reprint: WSH. *Indexed:* CJA, CJPI, CLI, CompR, ILP, LRI. *Bk. rev.:* 1 per issue. *Aud.:* Ac, Sa.

Co-published by the Section of Science and Technology of the American Bar Association and the Arizona State University College of Law, this journal traces its roots to Yale Law School and a previous title. It is the oldest journal of law and science in the United States. Articles relate to computer law; law and medicine; the legal reception of scientific evidence; the legal regulation of science or advanced technology; issues relating to new communications technologies; and the use of technology in the administration of justice. A typical issue will often contain articles, technical notes, and an annotated literature review.

Labor Law Journal. See Labor and Industrial Relations section.

3955. *Labor Lawyer.* [ISSN: 8756-2995] 1985. 3x/yr. Members, USD 40; Non-members, USD 45. Ed(s): Robert J Rabin. American Bar Association, Labor and Employment Law Section, 321 N. Clark St., Ste. 1400, Chicago, IL 60610-7656; abasveetr@abanet.org; http://www.lexis-nexis.com. Illus., index. Circ: 20700. Vol. ends: Fall. Microform: WSH. Online: William S. Hein & Co., Inc. Reprint: WSH. *Indexed:* CLI, ILP, LRI. *Bk. rev.:* Occasional, lengthy. *Aud.:* Ac, Sa.

Another of the many American Bar Association section publications, this journal is devoted to labor and employment law and is intended to provide practitioners, judges, administrators, and the interested public with balanced discussions of topical interest within the parameters of the journal's scope. Each issue contains six to eight articles covering diverse topics, such as sexual harassment, labor unions, and employment law. Most articles are written by those practicing in the field and are practitioner-oriented.

3956. *Law and Contemporary Problems.* [ISSN: 0023-9186] 1933. q. USD 54 domestic; USD 60 foreign; USD 15 newsstand/cover per issue. Ed(s): Theresa N Glover. Duke University, School of Law, Science Dr & Toverview Rd, PO Box 90372, Durham, NC 27708-0372; publications@ law.duke.edu; http://www.law.duke.edu/. Illus., index, adv. Circ: 2100. Vol. ends: Sep. Microform: WSH. Online: EBSCO Publishing, EBSCO Host; Florida Center for Library Automation; Gale; William S. Hein & Co., Inc.; JSTOR (Web-based Journal Archive); LexisNexis; OCLC Online Computer Library Center, Inc.; H.W. Wilson. Reprint: WSH. *Indexed:* ABCPolSci, ATI, BAS, CJA, CLI, CommAb, IBR, IBSS, IBZ, ILP, IPSA, JEL, LRI, PAIS, PSA, RI-1, SSA, SSCI, SociolAb. *Aud.:* Ac, Sa.

If one could select only a few titles from this section, this journal should be among them. Each issue is in a symposium format and devoted to a current legal topic of interest. A special editor for each issue solicits the articles and writes the foreword. Over the years, this publication has earned its well-deserved reputation as among the most distinguished in the country and is generally among the most frequently cited legal publications. A recent symposium was entitled "Who Pays? Who Benefits? Distributional Issues in Health Care." As with other journals published at Duke Law School, this journal's contents are available in full text on the school's web site.

3957. *Law and History Review.* [ISSN: 0738-2480] 1983. 3x/yr. USD 100 print & online eds. Ed(s): David S. Tanenhaus. University of Illinois Press, 1325 S Oak St, Champaign, IL 61820-6903; journals@

uillinois.edu; http://www.press.uillinois.edu. Illus., index, adv. Refereed. Circ: 1200. Microform: WSH; PQC. Online: EBSCO Publishing, EBSCO Host; William S. Hein & Co., Inc.; JSTOR (Web-based Journal Archive); LexisNexis. Reprint: WSH. *Indexed:* AmH&L, CLI, HistAb, ILP, LRI, PSA, SociolAb. *Bk. rev.:* 10-15, 1,000-2,000 words. *Aud.:* Ac, Sa.

This is the official publication of the American Society of Legal History, a membership organization dedicated to further research and writing in the fields of social history of law and the history of its legal ideas and institutions. Articles are scholarly and refereed. Its editorial board consists of preeminent scholars throughout the country. As an interdisciplinary journal, it spans the interplay between law and history.

Law and Human Behavior. See Psychology section.

Law & Inequality: a journal of theory and practice. See Civil Liberties/ General section.

3958. *Law and Literature.* Formerly (until 2002): *Cardozo Studies in Law and Literature.* [ISSN: 1535-685X] 1989. 3x/yr. USD 180 print & online eds. USD 66 newsstand/cover. Ed(s): Peter Goodrich, Mark Sanders. University of California Press, Journals Division, 2000 Center St, Ste 303, Berkeley, CA 94704-1223; journals@ucpress.edu; http://www.ucpress.edu/journals. Illus., index, adv. Refereed. Circ: 446. Vol. ends: Winter. Online: Chadwyck-Healey Inc.; EBSCO Publishing, EBSCO Host; William S. Hein & Co., Inc.; JSTOR (Web-based Journal Archive); LexisNexis; OCLC Online Computer Library Center, Inc.; ProQuest LLC (Ann Arbor); SwetsWise Online Content. Reprint: WSH. *Indexed:* AmHI, CLI, ILP, LRI, MLA-IB, PSA, SociolAb. *Aud.:* Ga, Ac.

Edited by the faculty at the Benjamin N. Cardozo School of Law and a board of international scholars, this journal features contributions by practitioners and scholars, poets and playwrights, artists, and technicians of all kinds. The list of noted contributors is impressive, and the content is a delightful diversion from the traditional, often dry law reviews. A somewhat similar journal is the *Yale Journal of Law & the Humanities* (see below).

Law and Philosophy. See Philosophy section.

3959. *Law and Social Inquiry.* Formerly (until 1988): *American Bar Foundation Journal.* [ISSN: 0897-6546] 1976. q. USD 209 print & online eds. Ed(s): John P Heinz, Christopher Tomlins. Blackwell Publishing, Inc., Commerce Place, 350 Main St, Malden, MA 02148; customerservices@blackwellpublishing.com; http://www.blackwellpublishing.com. Illus., adv. Refereed. Circ: 6700. Vol. ends: Fall. Microform: WSH; PQC. Online: Blackwell Synergy; EBSCO Publishing, EBSCO Host; Gale; William S. Hein & Co., Inc.; JSTOR (Web-based Journal Archive); LexisNexis; ProQuest LLC (Ann Arbor). Reprint: PSC; WSH. *Indexed:* ABS&EES, ArtHuCI, CJA, CJPI, CLI, CommAb, ILP, JEL, LRI, PSA, RI-1, SSA, SSCI, SociolAb. *Aud.:* Ac, Sa.

Empirical research is becoming commonplace in legal scholarship. This journal was among the first to focus on this important trend. The American Bar Foundation is an independent research institute committed to sociolegal research. Its professional journal, a significant contribution to the legal literature, is refereed and its content is empirical and theoretical. The journal is typically divided into three sections: the first contains lengthy articles of an empirical nature directed at legal institutions, lawyers, and law; the second is a series of critical review essays on books that impact on law and society; and the third features shorter book notes. Frequently, an issue or part of an issue will have a particular focus, as illustrated by a symposium in a recent issue on "Violence Between Intimates, Globalization, and the State."

3960. *Law & Society Review.* [ISSN: 0023-9216] 1966. q. GBP 228 print & online eds. Ed(s): Herbert M Kritzer. Blackwell Publishing, Inc., Commerce Place, 350 Main St, Malden, MA 02148; customerservices@ blackwellpublishing.com; http://www.blackwellpublishing.com. Illus., index, adv. Refereed. Circ: 2400. Vol. ends: Dec. Microform: WSH; PQC. Online: Blackwell Synergy; Chadwyck-Healey Inc.; EBSCO Publishing, EBSCO Host; Factiva, Inc.; Gale; IngentaConnect; JSTOR

(Web-based Journal Archive); Northern Light Technology, Inc.; OCLC Online Computer Library Center, Inc.; OhioLINK; ProQuest LLC (Ann Arbor); SwetsWise Online Content; H.W. Wilson. Reprint: PSC; WSH. *Indexed:* ABCPolSci, ASSIA, AgeL, AmH&L, AnthLit, ApEcolAb, ArtHuCI, BAS, CJA, CLI, CommAb, EAA, EI, FR, HRA, HRIS, HistAb, IBR, IBSS, IBZ, ILP, IMFL, IPSA, LRI, PAIS, PRA, PSA, PsycInfo, RI-1, RiskAb, SSA, SSCI, SUSA, SWR&A, SociolAb. *Bk. rev.:* 3-4, essay length. *Aud.:* Ac, Sa.

The Law and Society Association is an international group drawn primarily from the legal and social science professions, whose purpose is the stimulation and support of research and teaching on the cultural, economic, political, psychological, and social aspects of law and legal systems. Contributions are drawn from law professors, sociologists, and political scientists. Big names in these various disciplines are frequent writers for this interdisciplinary, refereed journal.

Law Library Journal. See Library and Information Science section.

3961. *Law Practice: the business of practicing law.* Former titles (until 2004): *Law Practice Management;* (until 1989): *Legal Economics.* [ISSN: 1547-9102] 1975. 8x/yr. Non-members, USD 48. Ed(s): Merrilyn Tarlton, Joan Hamby Feldman. American Bar Association, Law Practice Management Section, 321 N Clark St, Chicago, IL 60610; http://www.lexis-nexis.com/lncc. Illus., index. Sample. Circ: 19000 Paid and free. Vol. ends: Nov. Microform: WSH. Online: LexisNexis; Thomson West. *Indexed:* ABIn, ATI, CLI, LRI, PAIS. *Aud.:* Ac, Sa.

This magazine's purpose is to assist the practicing lawyer in operating and managing the office in an efficient and economical manner. It provides, in an easy-to-read, straightforward style, practical tips and how-to advice on a panoply of topics ranging from how to store files to how to design office space and then plan for the move into it. More and more of the articles pertain to law office computer applications. The advertising highlights the newest in office furniture, equipment, law books, and technology. An occasional cartoon or poem, color illustrations, and notice of events of general interest to the practicing bar contribute to its popularity.

3962. *Legal Scholarship Network.* irreg. Free. Ed(s): A Mitchell Polinsky, Bernard Black. Social Science Research Network (S S R N), Social Science Electronic Publishing, 2171 Monroe Ave, Ste 3, Rochester, NY 14618; sandy_barnes@ssrn.com; http://www.ssrn.com. *Aud.:* Ga, Ac, Sa.

A division of the Social Science Research Network (SSRN), the Legal Scholarship Network (LSN) includes articles related to a wide range of legal interests. Articles are free for downloading in most cases, unless the article author has charged LSN for its inclusion. This increasingly popular web-based legal scholarship network includes working papers and accepted articles for publication from law professors and other legal scholars. Users may search for articles by keyword and author name. LSN also includes over 50 subject-specific journals, such as *Wills, Trusts and Estate Law* or *Family and Children's Law,* that can be accessed and downloaded. LSN is quickly becoming a favorite of legal scholars who seek to avoid maneuvering through the traditional publication process or who seek an efficient way to post their work for distribution and comment.

3963. *Legal Times: law and lobbying in the nation's capital.* Former titles: *Legal Times of Washington;* (until 1982): *Legal Times.* [ISSN: 0732-7536] 1978. w. Mon. USD 199. Ed(s): Richard Barbieri. A L M, 345 Park Ave, S, New York, NY 10010; apress@amlaw.com; http://www.alm.com. Illus., index, adv. Circ: 10000 Paid. Vol. ends: May. Online: Gale; LexisNexis. *Indexed:* BLI, CLI, LRI. *Bk. rev.:* 2-3, length varies. *Aud.:* Ga, Ac, Sa.

This weekly legal newspaper, self-described as covering "law and lobbying in the nation's capital," is frequently national in scope. A typical issue contains from 48 to 80 pages. The staff of editors and reporters write about a host of legal topics, including the U.S. Supreme Court, the federal bureaucracy, major law firms, scandals, and controversial cases. Regular features are especially useful in a variety of ways. For example, "Points of View" is an opinion and commentary section; and "Legal Business" focuses on business issues and law firm mergers. Professional and classified ads are included.

3964. *Litigation (Chicago).* [ISSN: 0097-9813] 1975. q. USD 140. Ed(s): Annemarie Micklo, Joyce S Meyers. American Bar Association, Section of Litigation, 321 N Clark St, Chicago, IL 60610; http://www.abanet.org/litigation/. Illus., index. Sample. Circ: 72000 Paid and controlled. Vol. ends: Summer. Microform: WSH; PMC. Online: William S. Hein & Co., Inc.; Thomson West. Reprint: WSH. *Indexed:* CLI, ILP, LRI. *Bk. rev.:* Occasional, 500-600 words. *Aud.:* Ac, Sa.

This journal is designed for the trial bar and trial judges, with a series of short articles written by members of the practicing bar. Each issue is organized around a theme, such as freedom, burdens, or secrets and lies. Often the articles are argumentative and challenging, typical of the seasoned litigator likely to read this publication. However, articles are also straightforward and entertaining enough to be enjoyed by a much wider audience.

3965. *Marquette Sports Law Review.* Formerly (until 2000): *Marquette Sports Law Journal.* [ISSN: 1533-6484] 1990. s-a. USD 35 domestic; USD 45 foreign; USD 20 newsstand/cover per issue. Ed(s): Lindsay Potrafke. Marquette University, Sensenbrenner Hall, 1103 W Wisconsin Ave, Milwaukee, WI 53233; http://law.marquette.edu. Illus., index, adv. Vol. ends: Spring. Reprint: WSH. *Indexed:* CLI, ILP, LRI, PEI, SD. *Bk. rev.:* Occasional, lengthy. *Aud.:* Ac, Sa.

In response to the growing importance of the relationship between sports and the law, in 1989 Marquette University Law School established the National Sports Law Institute. The institute's principal purpose is "to promote the development of ethical practices in all phases of amateur and professional sports." This journal, a product of the institute, covers a panoply of legal issues in the sports industry and is aimed at attorneys and sports industry professionals. Because sports are so ingrained in the American tradition, this journal provides coverage of an increasingly important area of specialized legal representation. The *Marquette Law Review,* however, is the primary journal of the school.

3966. *Mental and Physical Disability Law Reporter: covers all aspects of handicapped law.* Formerly (until 1984): *Mental Disability Law Reporter.* [ISSN: 0883-7902] 1976. bi-mo. USD 384 (Individuals, USD 324). Ed(s): John W Parry. American Bar Association, Commission on Mental & Physical Disability Law, 740 15th St, NW, Washington, DC 20005-1022; cmpdl@abanet.org; http://www.lexis-nexis.com/lncc/sources/libcont/aba.html. Illus., index, adv. Circ: 1000 Paid. Vol. ends: Nov/Dec. Reprint: WSH. *Indexed:* CJA, CLI, ILP, LRI, PsycInfo. *Aud.:* Ac, Sa.

This publication is quite different from and more expensive than other publications in this section, but its unique subject matter justifies its inclusion. The American Bar Association's Commission on Mental & Physical Disability Law is composed of lawyers, psychiatrists, psychologists, consumer advocates, and mental health administrators who are concerned with promoting multidisciplinary solutions to legal problems of persons with mental and physical disabilities. Each issue starts with a "Directory of Cases & Legislation" that are discussed in that issue. This is followed by "Highlights," "Case Law Developments," "Summary of U.S. Supreme Court Action," and "Legislation and Regulations." A "Special Feature" section appears at the beginning of each issue, discussing a topic of current interest, such as the revised IDEA act or nursing home resident voting rights. There is a "Subject Key" at the end of the publication.

3967. *Michigan Journal of Gender & Law.* [ISSN: 1095-8835] 1994. s-a. USD 30 domestic; USD 35 foreign. University of Michigan, Law School, 801 Monroe St, Ann Arbor, MI 48109-1210; maureena@umich.edu; http://www.law.umich.edu/. Reprint: WSH. *Bk. rev.:* Number and length vary. *Aud.:* Ac.

This feminist publication explores gender issues in the law from diverse viewpoints. Contents include articles, legal briefs, critiques, speeches, and signed book reviews. Topics of recent articles include domestic violence in India and global sex trafficking. Contributors include legal scholars, social scientists, activists, practitioners, students, and others.

3968. *Michigan Law Review.* [ISSN: 0026-2234] 1902. 8x/yr. USD 60 domestic; USD 70 foreign; USD 8 newsstand/cover. Ed(s): Sam T C Erman, Marisa Bono. Michigan Law Review Association, Hutchins Hall, 625 South State St, Ann Arbor, MI 48109-1215; mlr.articles@umich.edu.

Illus., index, adv. Circ: 1865 Paid. Vol. ends: Aug. Microform: WSH. Reprint: WSH. *Indexed:* ABIn, ABS&EES, ATI, AgeL, ArtHuCI, BLI, CJA, CLI, ILP, JEL, LRI, PAIS, SSCI. *Bk. rev.:* Occasional, essay length. *Aud.:* Ac, Sa.

Regardless of which of the numerous ratings of law reviews one might consult, this title is always in the top ten. That recognition is gained from the consistently high-level articles from leading scholars, quality and in-depth student research pieces, and an overall adherence to fine legal scholarship. In publishing lengthy lead articles and student notes, this review is quite traditional. The review features an annual issue devoted to lengthy, critical book reviews that serves as an excellent selection guide. The school also publishes *Michigan Journal of Law Reform, Michigan Journal of Gender & Law* (for the latter, see above in this section), *Michigan Journal of International Law, Michigan Telecommunications and Technology Law Review,* and *Michigan Journal of Race & Law.*

3969. Military Law Review. [ISSN: 0026-4040] 1958. q. USD 17 domestic; USD 21.25 foreign. Ed(s): Jennifer L Crawford. U.S. Army, Judge Advocate General's Legal Center and School, 600 Masie Rd, Charlottesville, VA 22903-1781. Illus., index. Refereed. Circ: 8000. Microform: MIM; PQC. Online: William S. Hein & Co., Inc.; LexisNexis; OCLC Online Computer Library Center, Inc.; Thomson West; H.W. Wilson. Reprint: WSH. *Indexed:* ABCPolSci, ABS&EES, ArtHuCI, CLI, ILP, IUSGP, LRI, PAIS, PRA, PSA, SSCI. *Aud.:* Ac, Sa.

Published at the Judge Advocate General's School, U.S. Army, Charlottesville, Virginia, the *Review* provides a forum for those interested in military law to share the products of their experience and research. It is designed for use by military attorneys in connection with their official duties. Each quarterly issue is a complete, separately numbered volume. One can frequently gain a different insight on issues, as evidenced, for example, by "The Concept of Belligerency in International Law."

3970. Minnesota Law Review. [ISSN: 0026-5535] 1917. 6x/yr. USD 40 domestic; USD 46 foreign; USD 10 newsstand/cover per issue. Ed(s): Amy Bergquist. University of Minnesota, Law School, 229 19th Ave S, Minneapolis, MN 55455; http://www.law.umn.edu. Illus., index, adv. Circ: 1486. Vol. ends: Jun. Microform: WSH; PMC. Online: William S. Hein & Co., Inc.; LexisNexis; OCLC Online Computer Library Center, Inc.; Thomson West; H.W. Wilson. Reprint: WSH. *Indexed:* BLI, CJA, CLI, IBR, ILP, LRI, PAIS, SSCI. *Bk. rev.:* Occasional, length varies. *Aud.:* Ac, Sa.

This is another of the frequently cited traditional law reviews that publish articles and student pieces on a myriad of legal topics. The contents are always thoughtful, heavily documented, and influential. Volumes contain articles representing a wide cross-section of legal thinking that is both provocative and challenging. A recent issue includes articles on "Willful Blindness to Gender-Based Violence Abroad: United States' Implementation of Article Three of the United Nations Convention Against Torture" and "Regulating Oligopoly Conduct Under the Antitrust Laws." *Constitutional Commentary, Law and Inequality: A Journal of Theory and Practice, Crime and Justice, Minnesota Journal of Law, Science & Technology, Minnesota Journal of Business Law & Entrepreneurship, Minnesota Intellectual Property Review,* and *Minnesota Journal of International Law* are also published by this law school.

3971. National Black Law Journal. Formerly (until 1987): *Black Law Journal.* [ISSN: 0896-0194] 1971. 3x/yr. Ed(s): Christopher Owens. Columbia University, School of Law, Jerome Greene Hall, 435 West 116th St, New York, NY 10027; http://www.columbia.edu/. Illus., index, adv. Circ: 650. Vol. ends: No. 3. Microform: WSH; PMC; PQC. Online: Chadwyck-Healey Inc.; Northern Light Technology, Inc.; OCLC Online Computer Library Center, Inc.; ProQuest LLC (Ann Arbor). Reprint: WSH. *Indexed:* CLI, IIBP, ILP, LRI, RI-1, RiskAb. *Bk. rev.:* 2, 600-2,500 words. *Aud.:* Ac, Sa.

This journal is devoted exclusively to discussing and analyzing issues involving the African American community. Issues often have a theme, such as voting rights, affirmative action, or race relations in the South. A recent symposium issue was devoted to the status of African Americans in American legal education. The use of the word *national* in the title is appropriate because law students from a wide variety of schools have contributed to and prepared issues of the *Journal.*

3972. The National Law Journal: the weekly newspaper for the profession. [ISSN: 0162-7325] 1978. w. USD 99 domestic. Ed(s): Rex Bossert. A L M, 345 Park Ave, S, New York, NY 10010; apress@amlaw.com; http://www.alm.com. Illus., index, adv. Circ: 39500. Vol. ends: Aug. Online: Gale; LexisNexis. *Indexed:* ATI, BLI, CLI, EnvAb, LRI. *Aud.:* Ga, Ac, Sa.

This journal has by far the largest subscription base of the several national legal newspapers, and considering its pass-along readership in firms and law libraries, this publication reaches an estimated 200,000 members of the legal community. It offers something for just about everyone involved with law, but its real value is in the timely coverage of people, places, and events. With bureau chiefs in New York, California, Boston, Chicago, and Washington, D.C., and contributors from a host of states, this publication is the best single source for fast-breaking legal developments. Frequently, supplements enhance the publication's overall popularity. The "NLJ Billing Survey" (national billing survey) and a listing of the nation's largest law firms are anxiously awaited.

3973. New York University Law Review (New York, 1950). Former titles (until 1949): *New York University Law Quarterly Review;* (until 1929): *New York University Law Review (New York, 1924).* [ISSN: 0028-7881] 1924. 6x/yr. USD 50 domestic; USD 56 foreign. Ed(s): Carol M Kaplan. New York University School of Law, 110 W Third St, Subbasement, New York, NY 10012; lawreview@nyu.edu; http://www.law.nyu.edu. Illus., index, adv. Refereed. Circ: 2050. Vol. ends: Dec. Microform: WSH. Online: LexisNexis; Thomson West. Reprint: WSH. *Indexed:* ATI, AgeL, CJA, CLI, HRIS, IBR, IBZ, ILP, IPSA, LRI, PAIS, PhilInd, SSCI. *Aud.:* Ac, Sa.

New York University (NYU) School of Law, founded in 1835, is one of the oldest law schools in the United States. This student-edited journal contains in its lead articles some of the finest legal scholarship from some of the best legal minds in the country on just about any legal topic. Student pieces are likewise of high quality. Also published by NYU School of Law are the *Annual Survey of American Law* and *Clinical Law Review* (for the latter, see above in this section), as well as *East European Constitutional Review, International Journal of Constitutional Law, Journal of International Law and Politics, Journal of Law and Liberty, Review of Law & Social Change, Journal on Legislation and Public Policy, Environmental Law Journal,* and the *Tax Law Review* (for the last, see below in this section).

News Media and the Law. See Journalism and Writing/Journalism section.

3974. North Carolina Law Review. [ISSN: 0029-2524] 1922. bi-m. USD 42 domestic; USD 48 foreign; USD 12 newsstand/cover per issue. Ed(s): Mitch Ambruster. North Carolina Law Review Association, University of North Carolina, School of Law, Chapel Hill, NC 27599-3380; http://www.unc.edu/stud. Adv. Refereed. Circ: 950. Microform: BHP; WSH. Online: William S. Hein & Co., Inc.; LexisNexis; Thomson West. Reprint: WSH. *Indexed:* AgeL, CLI, ILP, LRI, PAIS, RiskAb. *Bk. rev.:* Occasional, lengthy. *Aud.:* Ac, Sa.

This school's law review has an 85-year history of publishing quality legal scholarship. The format is traditional, with articles, comments, and notes on any type of topic. One issue per year surveys North Carolina and Fourth Circuit law. Other journals from this school are *First Amendment Law Review, North Carolina Banking Institute Journal, North Carolina Journal of International Law and Commercial Regulation,* and *North Carolina Journal of Law and Technology.*

3975. Northwestern University Law Review. Formerly (until 1952): *Illinois Law Review.* [ISSN: 0029-3571] 1906. q. USD 50 domestic; USD 60 foreign. Ed(s): Alison Buckley. Northwestern University, School of Law, 357 E Chicago Ave, Chicago, IL 60611; http://www.law.northwestern.edu. Illus., index, adv. Refereed. Circ: 1200. Vol. ends: No. 4. Microform: BHP; WSH; PQC. Online: EBSCO Publishing, EBSCO Host; William S. Hein & Co., Inc.; LexisNexis; ProQuest LLC (Ann Arbor); Thomson West. Reprint: WSH. *Indexed:* ABCPolSci, CJA, CLI, ILP, LRI, PAIS, RI-1, SSCI. *Bk. rev.:* Occasional, length varies. *Aud.:* Ac, Sa.

This law review is more than a century old and is well respected. Articles are generally submitted by leading scholars and are varied and thought-provoking. Recent symposium issues have covered the Rehnquist Court and personal jurisdiction in the Internet age. Student comments and notes and lengthy book review essays are also included. The prestigious *Journal of Criminal Law and Criminology* (see above in this section), the *Journal of International Law & Business*, the *Northwestern Journal of Technology and Intellectual Property*, the *Journal of Law and Social Policy*, and the *Journal of International Human Rights* are the other review-type publications of this law school.

3976. *The Practical Lawyer.* [ISSN: 0032-6429] 1955. bi-m. 8/yr. until 2002. USD 65; USD 99 combined subscription print & online eds. Ed(s): Mark T Carroll. American Law Institute - American Bar Association, Committee on Continuing Professional Education, 4025 Chestnut St, Philadelphia, PA 19104-3099; publications@ali-aba.org; http://www.ali-aba.org. Illus., index. Circ: 3500 Paid. Vol. ends: Dec. Microform: WSH; PQC. Online: Northern Light Technology, Inc.; ProQuest LLC (Ann Arbor). *Indexed:* ATI, AgeL, BLI, CLI, ILP, LRI. *Aud.:* Ga, Ac, Sa.

This wonderful little magazine provides a nuts-and-bolts approach to the practice of law with information about continuing legal education programs. Articles are practical, as the title suggests. Articles are accompanied by practice checklists to be used to ensure that the germane matters are covered. A regular column on writing and style, "The Grammatical Lawyer," has been compiled and published as a book. Newer titles by the same publisher, but subject-specific, are *The Practical Real Estate Lawyer, The Practical Tax Lawyer,* and *The Practical Litigator.*

3977. *Preview of United States Supreme Court Cases.* [ISSN: 0363-0048] 1963. 8x/yr. USD 130 (Members, USD 105; Non-members, USD 115). Ed(s): Charles Williams. American Bar Association, Public Education Division, 541 N Fairbanks Ct, Chicago, IL 60611-3314; http://www.lexis-nexis.com/lncc/sources/libcont/aba.html. Illus. Sample. Circ: 3000. Vol. ends: May. Online: Thomson West. *Indexed:* CJPI. *Aud.:* Ga, Ac, Sa.

This publication is a departure from other titles described in this section. As its title indicates, each issue, monthly during the U.S. Supreme Court term, provides a discussion of cases soon to be decided by the court. After a case is calendared for oral argument, but before a decision is rendered, a legal professional in the subject field of the case presents the issues, gives the facts, analyzes the background and significance of the case, lists the counsel for each side and their legal arguments, and indicates the parties who have filed *amicus* briefs. The advisory board is composed of heavyweights; and 20 legal scholars write the "previews." For those interested in some advance warning about what the nation's Supreme Court is considering, this current-awareness source serves this important purpose exceedingly well.

3978. *Real Property, Probate and Trust Journal.* Incorporated: *American Bar Association. Section of Real Property, Probate and Trust Law. Newsletter; American Bar Association. Section of Real Property, Probate, and Trust Law. Proceedings; Probate and Trust Legislation.* [ISSN: 0034-0855] 1966. q. Members, USD 50; Non-members, USD 60. Ed(s): Amy Morris Hess. American Bar Association, Real Property, Probate and Trust Law Section, 321 N Clark St, Chicago, IL 60611; http://www.abanet.org. Illus., index. Circ: 37970. Vol. ends: Winter. Microform: WSH. Online: Factiva, Inc.; William S. Hein & Co., Inc.; ProQuest LLC (Ann Arbor); Thomson West. Reprint: WSH. *Indexed:* ATI, AgeL, CLI, ILP, LRI, SSCI. *Bk. rev.:* Occasional, lengthy. *Aud.:* Ac, Sa.

This journal's focus is principally scholarly, and it is edited by law students at the University of South Carolina School of Law. Each issue contains four to six heavily researched, substantive articles. Recent articles have ranged from a discussion of the property interests in tissues, cells, and gametes to premarital agreements. Much of the section materials once found in this publication, as well as shorter, more practice-oriented articles, are contained in *Probate & Property,* published by the same ABA section.

3979. *Scribes Journal of Legal Writing.* [ISSN: 1049-5177] 1990. a. USD 50 per vol. Ed(s): Glen-Peter Ahlers, Sr. American Society of Writers on Legal Subjects, Scribes Administrative Office, Barry University School of Law, Orlando, FL 32807-3650; stockmen@cooley.edu;

http://www.scribes.org. Illus. Circ: 3900 Controlled. Online: William S. Hein & Co., Inc.; LexisNexis; OCLC Online Computer Library Center, Inc.; H.W. Wilson. Reprint: WSH. *Indexed:* CLI, ILP, LRI. *Bk. rev.:* 5, 1,500-3,000 words. *Aud.:* Ac, Sa.

After years of criticism of lawyers' use of "legalese," this scholarly journal seeks to promote better legal writing within the legal community. Its goals are refreshing. It advocates "lucidity, concision, and felicity of expression" and hopes "to spread the growing scorn for whatever is turgid, obscure, or needlessly dull." Leading legal scholars who are equally good writers and grammarians contribute up to a dozen 6- to 20-page articles in each issue. Student essays are published, and all contributions are first-rate. Also included is a section titled "Notes and Queries" that contains brief (approximately 1,500 words) attempts to correct common mistakes in, or misjudgments about, legal writing. Membership in Scribes, the American Society of Writers on Legal Subjects, is open to members of the legal profession who are authors of a book or two or more articles, or who have served as editor of a legal journal, and to judges who have written opinions published in an official reporter.

3980. *Southern California Law Review.* [ISSN: 0038-3910] 1927. bi-m. USD 36 domestic; USD 45 foreign. Ed(s): Kimberly D Encinas, Damian Moos. University of Southern California, Gould School of Law, University Park, Los Angeles, CA 90089-0071; rlawsarticlesubmissions@yahoo.com; http://lawweb.usc.edu. Illus., index, adv. Refereed. Circ: 1500. Vol. ends: No. 6. Microform: WSH; PMC. Online: William S. Hein & Co., Inc.; LexisNexis. Reprint: WSH. *Indexed:* AgeL, BAS, CJA, CLI, ILP, IPSA, LRI, PSA, SSCI, SUSA. *Aud.:* Ac, Sa.

This small, highly selective law school produces another of the well-respected law reviews emanating from California. The review is traditional in format, with two or three feature articles per issue, along with student notes. Feature articles are timely and probing; an example is a recent article titled "Cookies and the Common Law: Are Internet Advertisers Trespassing on Our Computers?" University of Southern California law students also publish the *Southern California Interdisciplinary Law Journal* and *Southern California Review of Law and Social Justice* (for the latter, see below in this section).

3981. *Southern California Review of Law and Social Justice.* Formerly (until 2006): *Southern California Review of Law and Women's Studies.* [ISSN: 1935-2778] 1991. s-a. USD 25. Ed(s): Kimberley Baker, Ivy Tseng. University of Southern California, Gould School of Law, University Park, Los Angeles, CA 90089-0071; rlawsarticlesubmissions@yahoo.com; http://lawweb.usc.edu. Microform: WSH. Online: William S. Hein & Co., Inc. Reprint: WSH. *Indexed:* ABS&EES, CLI, ILP, LRI, SSA. *Bk. rev.:* 0-1, length varies, signed. *Aud.:* Ac, Sa.

This journal from the University of Southern California Law School examines the relationship between gender and the law from an interdisciplinary and multicultural perspective. Contents include articles, essays, legal notes, and briefs. Special issues publish symposium papers on a single theme. Tables of contents are available online at the journal's web site. Useful for law libraries and larger academic collections.

3982. *Stanford Law Review.* Formerly: *Stanford Intramural Law Review.* [ISSN: 0038-9765] 1948. bi-m. USD 42 domestic; USD 47 foreign; USD 16 newsstand/cover. Stanford University, Stanford Law School, Crown Quadrangle, 559 Nathan Abbott Way, Stanford, CA 94305-8610; http://www.law.stanford.edu. Illus., index, adv. Refereed. Vol. ends: Jul. Microform: WSH. Online: Florida Center for Library Automation; Gale; William S. Hein & Co., Inc.; JSTOR (Web-based Journal Archive); LexisNexis; ProQuest LLC (Ann Arbor); Thomson West. Reprint: WSH. *Indexed:* ABCPolSci, ATI, AgeL, ArtHuCI, BAS, CJA, CLI, ILP, LRI, PAIS, SSCI. *Bk. rev.:* 1-2, 4,000-8,000 words. *Aud.:* Ac, Sa.

No self-respecting library, even one seeking to have only a minimal legal collection, would be without this publication. Stanford's admission requirements are among the highest in the nation, and its faculty members are among the most prestigious. Its *Review* reflects the overall quality of the institution. Articles can be broad, such as "The First Amendment's Purpose." Occasional essays examine a legal issue of current interest, often in response to an earlier piece in the *Review*. Student notes and lengthy book-review essays round out an issue. Students also edit the *Stanford Environmental Law Journal*,

Stanford Journal of Civil Rights and Civil Liberties, Stanford Journal of International Law, Stanford Journal of Legal Studies, Stanford Law & Policy Review, Stanford Journal of Law, Business, and Finance, and *Stanford Technology Law Review.*

3983. Student Lawyer (Chicago). Supersedes: *Student Lawyer Journal.* [ISSN: 0039-274X] 1972. m. Membership, USD 20. Ed(s): Ira Pilchen. American Bar Association, Law Student Division, 321 N Clark St, Chicago, IL 60610; abalsd@abanet.org; http://www.abanet.org. Illus., index, adv. Sample. Circ: 39000 Paid. Vol. ends: May. Microform: WSH. *Indexed:* CLI, LRI. *Aud.:* Ga, Ac, Sa.

All law students who are attending American Bar Association (ABA)–accredited law schools are eligible for membership in the ABA's Law Student Division. Relevant, lively, and informative articles on legal education, social/legal issues, careers, the practice of law, and news of the Law Student Division comprise the contents of this popular magazine. Often it presents a "what's on my mind" article from a law student's point of view or provides entertaining anecdotes, and sometimes "survival techniques," for the study-weary student. There is advertising, information on bar review courses, an annual guide to summer-abroad law programs, and miscellaneous tidbits for students, prospective students, and the general reader.

3984. Tax Law Review. [ISSN: 0040-0041] 1945. q. USD 110 domestic; USD 133 foreign. Ed(s): Deborah Schenk. New York University School of Law, Tax Law Office, 245 Sullivan St, 4th Fl, New York, NY 10012-1099; law.jlpp@nyu.edu; http://www.law.nyu.edu. Illus., index, adv. Vol. ends: Summer. Microform: WSH. Online: William S. Hein & Co., Inc.; ProQuest LLC (Ann Arbor); Thomson West. Reprint: WSH. *Indexed:* ABIn, ATI, BLI, CLI, ILP, LRI, PAIS. *Aud.:* Ac, Sa.

This faculty-edited publication of the New York University School of Law is widely regarded as the most prestigious scholarly publication in the field of taxation. The review publishes four issues annually; one is devoted to a discussion of tax policy. Libraries that seek materials on taxation would certainly want to acquire this publication.

3985. The Tax Lawyer. Former titles (until 1967): *American Bar Association. Tax Section. Bulletin.* [ISSN: 0040-005X] 1947. q. USD 83 non-members (Individuals, USD 24 non-members; Members, USD 60). Ed(s): Jerald Davis August. Georgetown University Law Center, 600 New Jersey Ave, NW, Washington, DC 20001; http://www.law.georgetown.edu. Illus., index, adv. Refereed. Circ: 24000. Vol. ends: Summer. Microform: WSH; PQC. Online: Thomson West. Reprint: WSH. *Indexed:* ABIn, ATI, BLI, CLI, ILP, LRI. *Aud.:* Ac, Sa.

This is a joint publishing endeavor of the American Bar Association's Section of Taxation and the students at the Georgetown University Law Center. The section's editorial board is responsible for the scholarly articles—typically three or four of approximately 35 pages each in each issue. A student editorial board is responsible for student notes. The articles and notes are of high quality and run the gamut of issues involving taxation.

3986. Texas Law Review. [ISSN: 0040-4411] 1922. 7x/yr. USD 47 domestic; USD 55 foreign. Ed(s): Paul Goldman. University of Texas at Austin, School of Law Publications, 727 E 26th St, Austin, TX 78705-3299; publications@mail.utexas.edu; http://www.texaslawpublications.com. Illus., index, adv. Refereed. Circ: 1200 Paid. Vol. ends: Jun. Microform: WSH. Online: EBSCO Publishing, EBSCO Host; Factiva, Inc.; William S. Hein & Co., Inc.; LexisNexis; Northern Light Technology, Inc.; OCLC Online Computer Library Center, Inc.; ProQuest K-12 Learning Solutions; ProQuest LLC (Ann Arbor); H.W. Wilson. Reprint: WSH. *Indexed:* ABCPolSci, ABIn, ArtHuCI, CJA, CLI, IBR, IBZ, ILP, LRI, SSCI. *Bk. rev.:* Occasional, lengthy. *Aud.:* Ac, Sa.

There is the South, North, East, and West, and then there is Texas. The University of Texas, with its 50,000-member student body and capital-city Austin location, is considered to have one of the finest law schools and law reviews in the nation. Like other student-edited law school publications, this one contains two or three major articles by legal scholars on an array of legal topics; student notes relating to recent legislation or cases; and essay-length

book reviews. Other publications by University of Texas law students are the *American Journal of Criminal Law, Texas Journal on Civil Liberties & Civil Rights, Texas Hispanic Journal of Law and Policy, The Review of Litigation, Texas Environmental Law Journal, Texas Intellectual Property Law Journal, Texas International Law Journal, Texas Journal of Oil, Gas and Energy Law, Texas Review of Entertainment and Sports Law, Texas Review of Law & Politics,* and *Texas Journal of Women and the Law.*

3987. Tort Trial & Insurance Practice Law Journal. Former titles (until 2003): *Tort & Insurance Law Journal;* (until 1985): *Forum (Chicago, 1965).* [ISSN: 1543-3234] 1965. q. Members, USD 43; Non-members, USD 50. Ed(s): Richard C Mason. American Bar Association, 321 N Clark St, Chicago, IL 60610; http://www.abanet.org. Illus., index. Circ: 30000. Vol. ends: Summer. Microform: WSH; PQC. Online: William S. Hein & Co., Inc.; LexisNexis; Thomson West. Reprint: WSH. *Indexed:* CLI, ILP, LRI, PAIS. *Aud.:* Ac, Sa.

Because of the myriad of issues associated with tort law and insurance law, this is one of the largest sections of the American Bar Association. This publication mirrors the interests of the section, which spans 33 general substantive and procedural areas involved in or affecting the law of torts and insurance. An issue will typically contain six or seven articles of approximately 20 pages each, which address such topics as product liability, automotive law, aviation and space law, workers' compensation, media and defamation torts, health and life insurance, medicine, damages, and commercial torts. Once a year, an entire issue is devoted to a survey of tort trial and insurance practice law. Because both torts and insurance cut across all disciplines and impact on our daily lives, this is an especially important publication.

Transportation Law Journal. See Transportation section.

3988. Trial. Formerly: *National Legal Magazine.* [ISSN: 0041-2538] 1965. m. Members, USD 50; Non-members, USD 40. Ed(s): Julia Gannon Shoop. Association of Trial Lawyers of America, The Leonard M. Ring Law Center, 1050 31st St, NW, Washington, DC 20007-4499; http://www.atla.org. Illus., index, adv. Circ: 55000 Paid and controlled. Vol. ends: Dec. Microform: WSH; PQC. Online: Florida Center for Library Automation; Gale; Northern Light Technology, Inc.; OCLC Online Computer Library Center, Inc. *Indexed:* AgeL, CJA, CJPI, CLI, HRIS, ILP, LRI, RiskAb, SSCI. *Bk. rev.:* 2-7, 300-1,500 words. *Aud.:* Ga, Ac, Sa.

The purpose of this attractive magazine is to provide information that is timely, practical, and readable and that will serve the large membership of the American Trial Lawyers Association. Approximately a dozen articles appear in each issue, and most are how-to in nature. A recent issue focuses on pharmacology for lawyers. Certain regular columns offer practical information. Other sections are intended for current awareness and for professional-services advertising.

3989. Trusts and Estates. [ISSN: 0041-3682] 1904. m. USD 199 domestic; USD 212 Canada; USD 231 elsewhere. Ed(s): Rorie Sherman. Prism Business Media, 249 W 17th St, New York, NY 10011; inquiries@ prismb2b.com; http://www.prismbusinessmedia.com. Illus., index, adv. Circ: 14597 Paid. Vol. ends: Dec. Microform: CIS; PQC. Online: Florida Center for Library Automation; OCLC Online Computer Library Center, Inc.; ProQuest LLC (Ann Arbor); H.W. Wilson. *Indexed:* ABIn, ATI, AgeL, BLI, BPI, CLI, ILP, LRI, PAIS. *Aud.:* Ga, Ac, Sa.

Planning for one's death during life, dealing with the myriad issues that arise after death, and capitalizing on the available options to maximize tax benefits during one's lifetime are the principal focuses of this publication. Prudent tax planning, wise use of trusts, insurance options, and issues involving divorce and separation are examples of the type of coverage. While this title is intended for lawyers, trust officers, and others involved in estate planning and administration, there is sufficient information, presented clearly and concisely, to warrant a far wider readership. As the population ages, this publication will undoubtedly grow in popularity.

3990. U C L A Law Review. Formerly (until 1953): *U C L A Intramural Law Review.* [ISSN: 0041-5650] 1952. bi-m. USD 40 domestic; USD 52 foreign. Ed(s): Ryan D White. University of California at Los Angeles,

School of Law, 405 Hilgard Ave, Rm 2410, PO Box 951476, Los Angeles, CA 90095-1476; http://www.law.ucla.edu. Illus., index, adv. Refereed. Circ: 1000. Vol. ends: Aug. Microform: WSH. Online: William S. Hein & Co., Inc.; LexisNexis; Thomson West. Reprint: WSH. *Indexed:* ABIn, CJA, CLI, CommAb, ILP, LRI, PAIS, SSCI. *Aud.:* Ac, Sa.

Located on the university campus in the foothills of the Santa Monica Mountains, this law school recruits one of the finest student bodies in the country. Its primary journal reflects the same high qualities. One to three lead articles on any legal topic, some exceeding 100 pages in length, are written by legal professionals. Student comments frequently examine cutting-edge issues in the law. Student notes on recent cases are rare. The UCLA law students also edit *Chicano-Latino Law Review* (see above in this section), *Indigenous Peoples Journal of Law, Culture and Resistance, The Durkeminier Awards: Best Sexual Orientation Law Review Articles, UCLA Pacific Basin Law Journal, UCLA Women's Law Journal, UCLA Asian Pacific American Law Journal, UCLA Journal of International Law and Foreign Affairs, Journal of Law and Technology, Entertainment Law Review, UCLA Journal of Islamic and Near Eastern Law,* and *UCLA Journal of Environmental Law and Policy.*

3991. University of Chicago Law Review. [ISSN: 0041-9494] 1933. q. USD 45 domestic; USD 48 in Canada & Mexico; USD 51 elsewhere. Ed(s): Felicia Ellsworth, Linda Friedrich. University of Chicago, Law School, 1111 E 60th St, Chicago, IL 60637-2786; http://www.law.uchicago.edu. Illus., index, adv. Refereed. Circ: 2400. Vol. ends: Fall. Microform: WSH; PMC; PQC. Online: Chadwyck-Healey Inc.; Factiva, Inc.; William S. Hein & Co., Inc.; JSTOR (Web-based Journal Archive); LexisNexis; Northern Light Technology, Inc.; OCLC Online Computer Library Center, Inc.; ProQuest LLC (Ann Arbor). Reprint: WSH. *Indexed:* ABCPolSci, ABIn, ArtHuCI, BLI, CJA, CLI, ILP, LRI, SSCI. *Bk. rev.:* 1-2, essay length. *Aud.:* Ac, Sa.

The University of Chicago Law School's curriculum stresses the interdependence of legal and social studies in the training of lawyers. A significant fraction of the faculty represent disciplines other than law, including economics, history, sociology, philosophy, and political science. Certainly the *Review,* which at times reaches more than 1,500 pages, is among the most highly respected and most often cited of all legal periodicals. A representative issue contains a major article or two; student comments; and essay-length book reviews. The school is also the home of the *Supreme Court Review, Journal of Law & Economics,* and *Journal of Legal Studies* (for the latter two, see above in this section). The school also publishes the *University of Chicago Legal Forum* and the *Chicago Journal of International Law.*

3992. University of Michigan Journal of Law Reform. Former titles (until 1972): *Journal of Law Reform; Prospectus.* [ISSN: 0363-602X] 1968. q. USD 35 domestic vol.40; USD 40 foreign vol.40; USD 15 newsstand/cover per issue. University of Michigan, Law School, 801 Monroe St, Ann Arbor, MI 48109-1210; http://www.law.umich.edu/. Illus., index, adv. Microform: WSH; PMC. Online: William S. Hein & Co., Inc.; LexisNexis. Reprint: WSH. *Indexed:* CJA, CLI, ILP, LRI, PAIS. *Aud.:* Ac, Sa.

This journal seeks to improve the law and its administration by providing a forum for discussion that identifies contemporary issues for reform efforts, proposes concrete means to accomplish change, and evaluates the impact of law reform. Faculty members and other legal professionals contribute the articles; students write the comments and notes.

3993. University of Pennsylvania Law Review. Former titles (until 1944): *University of Pennsylvania Law Review and American Law Register;* (until 1907): *American Law Register (Philadelphia, 1898);* (until 1897): *American Law Register and Review;* (until 1891): *American Law Register (Philadelphia, 1852);* (until 1852): *American Law Journal;* (until 1848): *Pennsylvania Law Journal.* [ISSN: 0041-9907] 1842. bi-m. USD 47 domestic; USD 57 foreign; USD 10 newsstand/cover per issue. Ed(s): Ellen London, Katherine C Hayes. University of Pennsylvania, Law School, 3400 Chestnut St, Philadelphia, PA 19104-6204; jlelsubs@ law.upenn.edu; http://www.law.upenn.edu/. Illus., index, adv. Refereed.

Circ: 1850. Vol. ends: Jun. Microform: WSH. Online: EBSCO Publishing, EBSCO Host; William S. Hein & Co., Inc.; LexisNexis; Thomson West. Reprint: WSH. *Indexed:* ABCPolSci, CJA, CLI, IBZ, ILP, LRI, PAIS, PSA, PhilInd, SSCI. *Bk. rev.:* Occasional, essay length. *Aud.:* Ac, Sa.

This is one of the oldest law reviews in the nation, dating from 1886; and if tracked to its lineal successor (the *American Law Register,* which originated in 1852), the *University of Pennsylvania Law Review* has the highest volume number of all existing reviews. It is influential, traditional in format, diverse in the type of subjects discussed, and edited by a student board of editors with first-rate academic credentials. Contributions concentrate mainly on everyday issues such as bankruptcy, constitutional law, intellectual property, and criminal law. Other journals edited by the law students at the University of Pennsylvania are the *University of Pennsylvania Journal of Business and Employment Law, University of Pennsylvania Journal of Constitutional Law, University of Pennsylvania Journal of Law and Social Change,* and the *University of Pennsylvania Journal of International Law.*

3994. University of Toronto Law Journal. [ISSN: 0042-0220] 1937. q. CND 115. Ed(s): Karen Knop. University of Toronto Press, Journals Division, 5201 Dufferin St, Toronto, ON M3H 5T8, Canada; journals@ utpress.utoronto.ca; http://www.utpjournals.com. Illus., index, adv. Sample. Refereed. Circ: 700. Vol. ends: Fall. Microform: MML; PQC. Online: EBSCO Publishing, EBSCO Host; William S. Hein & Co., Inc.; JSTOR (Web-based Journal Archive); LexisNexis; OCLC Online Computer Library Center, Inc.; OhioLINK; Project MUSE. Reprint: PSC; WSH. *Indexed:* CBCARef, CLI, CPerI, IBR, IBZ, ILP, LRI, PAIS, PSA, SSA, SSCI, SociolAb. *Bk. rev.:* Occasional, lengthy. *Aud.:* Ac, Sa.

Our neighbor to the north deserves to have some representation in this law listing. That distinction goes to this highly regarded journal. Edited by members of the prestigious University of Toronto Faculty of Law, the *Journal* provides a heavy dose of analysis of Canadian law and Canadian legal history. Unlike in the United States, where faculty members prefer to publish anywhere but in their own review, most articles in this publication are by faculty members from the law school. Student pieces are published in a separate journal, the semi-annual *University of Toronto Faculty of Law Review.* Libraries with a special interest in Canadian materials would certainly want to consider either or both of these titles. For libraries that seek materials on the relationship between the United States and Canada, the *Canada–United States Law Journal,* published annually by law students at Case Western Reserve University, is a better choice.

3995. The Urban Lawyer: the national quarterly on state and local government law. [ISSN: 0042-0905] 1969. q. USD 130 (Individuals, USD 69 non-member; Individual members, USD 35). Ed(s): Julie M Cheslik, Robert M Vercruck. A B A Publishing, 750 N Lake Shore Dr, Chicago, IL 60611; service@abanet.org; http://www.abanet.org. Illus., index. Refereed. Circ: 6000. Vol. ends: Fall. Microform: WSH; PMC. Reprint: WSH. *Indexed:* ABS&EES, AgeL, ArtHuCI, CJA, CLI, HRIS, ILP, LRI, SSCI, SUSA. *Bk. rev.:* Number and length vary. *Aud.:* Ac, Sa.

Local government law is wide-ranging and far-reaching. This publication of the American Bar Association's Section of Urban, State, and Local Government Law has a student editorial board based at the University of Missouri–Kansas City School of Law. Articles run the gamut represented by the section's scope, and cover such issues as gerrymandering, Superfund cleanups, sales tax incentive programs, governmental tort liability, airports, land use planning and zoning, labor relations, and HUD housing. Each issue contains four or five articles; a section discussing cases, statutes, and recent developments; and book reviews. The entire Fall issue discusses developing issues in urban, state, and local government law and contains a section directory.

3996. Vanderbilt Law Review. [ISSN: 0042-2533] 1947. 6x/yr. USD 42 domestic; USD 48 foreign. Ed(s): Kellie Lynn Branson. Vanderbilt University, Law School, 131 21st Ave South, Nashville, TN 37203-1181; mwaggone@law.vanderbilt.edu. Index, adv. Refereed. Circ: 1300. Microform: WSH; PMC; PQC. Online: Factiva, Inc.; William S. Hein & Co., Inc.; LexisNexis; Northern Light Technology, Inc.; OCLC Online

Computer Library Center, Inc.; ProQuest LLC (Ann Arbor); Thomson West; H.W. Wilson. Reprint: WSH. *Indexed:* ABIn, ATI, ArtHuCI, CJA, CLI, CommAb, ILP, LRI, SSCI. *Aud.:* Ac, Sa.

The Vanderbilt University School of Law is among the most respected in the nation, and its review enjoys the same reputation. Articles and student notes cover the gamut of legal scholarship, with recent issues addressing shareholder liability, field tariffs, the regulation of lawyers, and wrongful death. Other Vanderbilt legal journals are *Vanderbilt Journal of Entertainment and Technology Law* and *Vanderbilt Journal of Transnational Law.*

3997. *Virginia Law Review.* Incorporates (1895-1928): *Virginia Law Register.* [ISSN: 0042-6601] 1913. 8x/yr. USD 52 in US & Canada; USD 63 elsewhere. Ed(s): Daniel Bress, Carrie Apfel. Virginia Law Review Association, University of Virginia, School of Law, 580 Massie Rd, Charlottesville, VA 22903-1789. Illus., index, adv. Refereed. Circ: 2200 Paid. Vol. ends: Nov. Microform: WSH. Online: William S. Hein & Co., Inc.; JSTOR (Web-based Journal Archive); LexisNexis; Thomson West. Reprint: WSH. *Indexed:* ABIn, ATI, AgeL, AmH&L, ArtHuCI, CJA, CLI, HistAb, ILP, LRI, PAIS, RiskAb, SSCI. *Bk. rev.:* Occasional, essay length. *Aud.:* Ac, Sa.

The University of Virginia School of Law has produced many of the great lawyers of this country. It is an institution rich in tradition, and its *Review* ranks among the best of all those published. With the standard professional articles and student notes and comments, this publication is as widely regarded for the content of the articles as it is for the contributors. Other journals published by University of Virginia law students are *Virginia Journal of International Law, Virginia Environmental Law Journal, Virginia Law & Business Review, Virginia Journal of Law and Technology, Virginia Sports and Entertainment Law Journal, Journal of Law and Politics, Virginia Journal of Social Policy & the Law,* and *Virginia Tax Review.*

3998. *Washington and Lee Law Review.* [ISSN: 0043-0463] 1939. 4x/yr. USD 35 per vol. domestic; USD 39 per vol. foreign. Ed(s): Brian Williams, Carter Williams. Washington and Lee University, School of Law, Lewis Hall, Lexington, VA 24450-1799; http://law.wlu.edu. Illus., index, adv. Circ: 1100. Vol. ends: No. 4. Microform: WSH. Online: Factiva, Inc.; William S. Hein & Co., Inc.; LexisNexis; OCLC Online Computer Library Center, Inc.; ProQuest LLC (Ann Arbor); Thomson West; H.W. Wilson. Reprint: WSH. *Indexed:* ATI, BLI, CLI, ILP, LRI. *Bk. rev.:* Occasional, essay length. *Aud.:* Ac, Sa.

With one of the smallest enrollments and lowest student–faculty ratios of any law school in the country, this delightful little school produces a national journal that discusses important legal problems. Special funding enables the school to attract outstanding scholars for lectures, and their papers often appear in the *Review.* Often an issue will focus on a special topic, such as a recent symposium on "Critical Race Theory: The Next Frontier."

3999. *Washington Law Review.* Former titles (until 1967): *University of Washington Law Review;* (until 1966): *Washington Law Review;* (until 1961): *Washington Law Review and State Bar Journal;* Which was formed by the merger of: *Washington Law Review (Seattle, 1925); State Bar Review.* [ISSN: 0043-0617] 1925. 4x/yr. USD 32 domestic; USD 38 foreign; USD 12 newsstand/cover per issue. Ed(s): Rebecca Harrison. University of Washington, School of Law, William H. Gates Hall, PO Box 353020, Seattle, WA 98195-3020; pacrim@u.washington.edu; http://www.law.washington.edu. Illus., adv. Refereed. Circ: 1300 Paid. Vol. ends: Sep. Microform: WSH. Online: LexisNexis; Thomson West. Reprint: WSH. *Indexed:* ATI, AgeL, CJA, CLI, CommAb, ILP, LRI, RiskAb, SSCI. *Bk. rev.:* Occasional, lengthy. *Aud.:* Ac, Sa.

Established in 1899, the University of Washington in Seattle is one of the oldest West Coast law schools. The school has a relatively small but highly diverse student enrollment and an excellent student–faculty ratio. Its law review is traditional in nature, organized around lead articles and student notes and comments, and national in scope. An example of a representative article is "Recognizing the Societal Value in Information Privacy." The school also publishes the *Pacific Rim Law & Policy Review* and the *Shidler Journal of Law, Commerce & Technology.*

4000. *Washington University Law Review.* Former titles (until 2006): *Washington University Law Quarterly;* (until 1936): *St. Louis Law Review.* 1915. bi-m. USD 60 domestic; USD 72 foreign; USD 10 newsstand/cover per issue domestic. Ed(s): Georgia Garthwaite, Rebecca K Schendel. Washington University, School of Law, 1 Brookings Dr, Campus Box 1120, St Louis, MO 63130-4899; http://law.wustl.edu. Adv. Circ: 800. Microform: WSH; PMC. Online: William S. Hein & Co., Inc.; LexisNexis; OCLC Online Computer Library Center, Inc.; Thomson West; H.W. Wilson. Reprint: WSH. *Indexed:* CLI, ILP, LRI, PhilInd. *Aud.:* Ac, Sa.

This review and its law school have a long-standing and well-deserved standard of excellence. The facility is outstanding thanks to a significant contribution by Anheuser-Busch. The journal is traditional, with articles, notes, and discussions of recent developments. Other journals prepared by students at this school are *Washington University Journal of Law and Policy* and *Washington University Global Studies Law Review.*

4001. *Wisconsin Law Review.* [ISSN: 0043-650X] 1920. 6x/yr. USD 36 domestic; USD 40 foreign. Ed(s): Lola Velazquez-Aguilu. University of Wisconsin at Madison, Law School, 975 Bascom Mall, Madison, WI 53706-1399; http://www.law.wisc.edu/. Illus., index, adv. Refereed. Circ: 2150 Paid. Vol. ends: No. 6. Microform: WSH; PQC. Online: William S. Hein & Co., Inc.; LexisNexis; OCLC Online Computer Library Center, Inc.; Thomson West; H.W. Wilson. Reprint: WSH. *Indexed:* AgeL, ArtHuCI, CJA, CLI, ILP, LRI, PAIS, PSA, RiskAb, SSA, SSCI, SociolAb. *Bk. rev.:* 1, length varies. *Aud.:* Ac, Sa.

This outstanding law school was a pioneer in articulating the view that law must be studied in its relationship to society, often in its historical context. Some of the major national social legislation has originated with Wisconsin law professors. While the *Review* carries articles by law professionals on any legal topic, it also remains true to the school's social concerns by publishing such articles as "Battered Women and the State: The Struggle for the Future of Domestic Violence Policy." Student notes and comments are likewise eclectic, with the notes focusing more on Wisconsin law. Remaining true to its mission, the law school also publishes the *Wisconsin Women's Law Journal, Praxis,* and the *Wisconsin International Law Journal.*

4002. *Women's Rights Law Reporter.* [ISSN: 0085-8269] 1970. 3x/yr. USD 40 (Individuals, USD 20; Students, USD 15). Ed(s): Lauren V Pyleski, Kerry Roach. Women's Rights Law Reporter, Rutgers University School of Law, 123 Washington St, Newark, NJ 07102; wrlr@pegasus.rutgers.edu; http://info.rutgers.edu/. Illus., index, adv. Circ: 2000. Vol. ends: No. 3. Microform: WSH; PMC; PQC. Online: William S. Hein & Co., Inc.; LexisNexis. Reprint: WSH. *Indexed:* AltPI, CJA, CLI, FemPer, ILP, LRI, PAIS, RI-1, SSA, SWA, WSA. *Bk. rev.:* Number and length vary. *Aud.:* Hs, Ga, Ac, Sa.

This journal focuses exclusively on women's rights law and related areas of law or public policy. Contents include articles, reports, notes on current topics, and book reviews. Recent articles have looked at the status of women in Chile and the importance of the traditional family in law. Contents pages are available on the journal's web site. Recommended for law libraries, academic libraries, and larger public libraries.

4003. *Yale Journal of Law & the Humanities.* [ISSN: 1041-6374] 1988. s-a. USD 34 (Individuals, USD 18). Yale University, Law School, PO Box 208215, New Haven, CT 06520-8215; yhrdlj@yale.edu; http://www.law.yale.edu. Illus., index, adv. Sample. Circ: 525. Vol. ends: No. 2. Microform: WSH. Online: William S. Hein & Co., Inc.; LexisNexis; OCLC Online Computer Library Center, Inc.; H.W. Wilson. Reprint: WSH. *Indexed:* AmH&L, CLI, HistAb, ILP, LRI, MLA-IB, RILM. *Bk. rev.:* Occasional, essay length. *Aud.:* Ga, Ac, Sa.

Just when it seemed that all law reviews were drab and boring, here is one that intertwines the law and the liberal arts. Perhaps reacting to the law and economics focus prevalent at Yale, this journal eschews the scientific and embraces philosophy, literature, anthropology, social and political science, and the fine arts. Boasting an outstanding, nationally drawn editorial advisory board and an equally well-recognized group of writers, the *Journal* is a welcome and important departure from traditional legal scholarship. A recent issue includes

"Blaming Culture for Bad Behavior." The semi-annual *Cardozo Studies in Law and Literature,* launched in the same year as this publication, has a similar focus. Let us hope there are more to come.

4004. *Yale Law Journal.* [ISSN: 0044-0094] 1891. 8x/yr. USD 55 domestic; USD 65 foreign. Yale Journal Co. Inc., 127 Wall St, PO Box 208215, New Haven, CT 06520-8215; yjil@yale.edu; http://www.yale.edu. Illus., index, adv. Circ: 4500. Vol. ends: Jul. Microform: WSH. Online: Florida Center for Library Automation; Gale; JSTOR (Web-based Journal Archive); LexisNexis; Northern Light Technology, Inc.; OCLC Online Computer Library Center, Inc.; ProQuest LLC (Ann Arbor). Reprint: WSH. *Indexed:* ABCPolSci, ABIn, ATI, AgeL, ArtHuCI, BAS, BLI, BRI, CBRI, CJA, CLI, IBR, IBSS, IBZ, ILP, IPSA, JEL, LRI, PAIS, PhilInd, RiskAb, SSCI. *Bk. rev.:* Occasional, essay length. *Aud.:* Ac, Sa.

Regardless of whom one asks or what survey one reads, the *Yale Law Journal* will always be among the very first law reviews mentioned for outstanding legal scholarship and influential content. It is simply among the best there is, and its importance cannot be overstated. Yale sees the study of law as interrelated with other intellectual disciplines and includes prominent scholars from economics, philosophy, and psychoanalysis among its faculty. Recent issues include articles on fair use, the right to destroy one's own property, and the future of disability law. Six other journals are edited by the Yale law students: *Yale Law & Policy Review; Yale Journal of Law & the Humanities* (for the latter, see above in this section); *Yale Journal of International Law; Yale Journal of Law & Feminism; Yale Journal of Health Policy, Law, and Ethics;* and *Yale Journal on Regulation.* There are also *Yale Human Rights & Development Law Journal* and *Yale Journal of Law and Technology.*

■ LIBRARY AND INFORMATION SCIENCE

See also Archives and Manuscripts; Bibliography; Books and Book Reviews; Printing and Graphic Arts; and Serials sections.

Amy Jackson, Metadata and Digital Initiatives Librarian, Indiana State University Library, Cunningham Memorial Library, Terre Haute, IN 47809

Introduction

In order for librarians to remain informed on current trends and issues in the field of library and information science, it is important that they have access to professional literature. Library journals serve as a means of communication between librarians, and offer perspectives, advice, current events, and literature reviews from other librarians in similar positions.

This section presents basic titles recommended for various library collections. Although some library journals address general librarianship, many titles are devoted to specialized topics. These topics include reference, technical services, systems, digital libraries, administration, children's services, and various subject specialties. When one is determining journals for a collection, each title should be evaluated for its ability to meet the needs of the individual library and the patrons it serves.

Only English-language publications are included, and local and in-house publications are excluded. Although a few publications originate from outside of the United States, most of the reviewed journals are published in the United States.

Basic Periodicals

Ems: *Children and libraries, Library media connection, School library journal, School library media research, Teacher librarian;* Hs: *School library journal, Young Adult library services, Teacher librarian;* Ga: *American Libraries, Library journal;* Ac: *College & Research libraries, Journal of Academic Librarianship.*

Basic Abstracts and Indexes

Information Science Abstracts, Library and Information Science Abstracts, Library Literature.

4005. *A L A W O N.* [ISSN: 1069-7799] 1992. irreg. Free. American Library Association, Washington Office, 1301 Pennsylvania Ave, NW, Ste 403, Washington, DC 20004; alawash@alawash.org; http://www.ala.org/washoff/publics.html. *Aud.:* Ga, Ac, Sa.

This is the American Library Association Washington Office's free online publication, and it provides timely reports on federal issues affecting libraries. Recent newsletters report on copyright, the Patriot Act, hurricane recovery funds, and government grants. Recommended for all professional librarians.

4006. *A L C T S Newsletter Online.* Supersedes (in Dec. 1998): *A L C T S Newsletter;* Which was formerly (until 1990): *R T S D Newsletter (Resources and Technical Services Division).* [ISSN: 1523-018X] 1976. 6x/yr. Free. Ed(s): Miriam Palm. American Library Association, 50 E Huron St, Chicago, IL 60611-2795; http://www.ala.org. Illus. Online: OCLC Online Computer Library Center, Inc.; H.W. Wilson. *Indexed:* LibLit. *Aud.:* Ac, Sa.

The primary focus of this newsletter, published by the Association for Library Collections & Technical Services, is to keep members informed on news and activities of the association. Issues contain conference reports, announcements, information about new publications, calendars, and articles discussing new standards and best practices. Highly recommended for librarians in technical services and related fields.

4007. *A R L: a bimonthly report on research library issues and actions.* Formerly (until 1990): *A R L Newsletter.* [ISSN: 1050-6098] 1965. bi-m. Members, USD 25; Non-members, USD 50. Ed(s): Kaylyn Hipps, Jaia Barrett. Association of Research Libraries, 21 Dupont Circle, Ste 800, Washington, DC 20036; pubs@arl.org; http://www.arl.org/newsltr. Illus. Circ: 1000. Online: OCLC Online Computer Library Center, Inc.; H.W. Wilson. *Indexed:* LibLit, PAIS. *Aud.:* Ac, Sa.

A monthly report from the Association of Research Libraries (ARL), the Coalition of Networked Information (CNI), and the Scholarly Publishing and Academic Resources Coalition (SPARC), this publication addresses the activities and issues of the contributing organizations. Articles cover a broad range of topics including copyright, digital libraries, salaries, federal relations, collection management, and institutional repositories. Recommended for academic and special libraries.

4008. *The Acquisitions Librarian.* [ISSN: 0896-3576] 1989. 4x/yr. USD 390 print & online eds. Ed(s): Bill Katz. Haworth Press, Inc., 10 Alice St, Binghamton, NY 13904-1580. Illus., index, adv. Sample. Refereed. Circ: 345 Paid. Microform: PQC. Online: EBSCO Publishing, EBSCO Host; OCLC Online Computer Library Center, Inc.; SwetsWise Online Content. Reprint: HAW. *Indexed:* C&ISA, CerAb, ChemAb, FR, IAA, IBR, IBZ, ISTA, LISA, RILM. *Aud.:* Ga, Ac, Sa.

Devoting each issue to a single topic, this biannual publication for acquisition librarians also addresses issues related to the broader field of librarianship. Articles are practical and up-to-date, and include general articles, case studies, and policies. Recent topics include integrating print and digital resources, managing digital resources in libraries, balancing university literature collections, and maintaining up-to-date collections and policies. Essential reading for all acquisition librarians.

4009. *Against the Grain: linking publishers, vendors and librarians.* [ISSN: 1043-2094] 1989. bi-m. USD 45 domestic; USD 55 Canada; USD 75 elsewhere. Ed(s): Katina Strauch. Against the Grain, LLC, 209 Richardson Ave., MSC 98, The Citadel, Charleston, SC 29409; strauchk@earthlink.net. Illus., adv. Sample. Circ: 2100. Vol. ends: Dec/Jan. *Indexed:* ISTA, LISA, LibLit. *Bk. rev.:* 10-20, 100-500 words. *Aud.:* Ga, Ac, Sa.

This bimonthly publication provides information relevant to librarians, publishers, vendors, book jobbers, and subscription agents. Each issue contains news, articles, interviews, book reviews, technology issues, legal issues, and current information from the publishing and bookselling fields. Recent articles explore collecting, electronic journals and books, and user behaviors. This publication is highly recommended for acquisition librarians, publishers, and booksellers.

4010. *American Libraries.* Former titles (until 1970): *A L A Bulletin;* (until 1939): *American Library Association. Bulletin.* [ISSN: 0002-9769] 1907. m. 11/yr. USD 60 in North America; USD 70 elsewhere. Ed(s): Gordon Flagg, Leonard Kniffel. American Library Association, 50 E Huron St, Chicago, IL 60611-2795; http://www.ala.org. Illus., index, adv. Circ: 58475 Paid. Vol. ends: Jan. Microform: NBI; PMC; PQC. Online: The Dialog Corporation; EBSCO Publishing, EBSCO Host; Florida Center for Library Automation; Gale; OCLC Online Computer Library Center, Inc.; ProQuest K-12 Learning Solutions; ProQuest LLC (Ann Arbor); H.W. Wilson. *Indexed:* ABIn, ABS&EES, ASIP, AgeL, BEL&L, BRI, CBRI, CINAHL, EduInd, FLI, IBR, IBZ, ISTA, LISA, LRI, LibLit, MASUSE, MRD, PAIS, RI-1, RILM. *Aud.:* Ga, Ac, Sa.

This monthly publication is the official journal of the American Library Association. It reports on the activities, purposes, and goals of the association, as well as broader library-related topics. Regular sections include job postings, national and international library news, continuing education, and information technology. Featured articles cover a broad range of library-related topics, including collection development, management, strategic planning, children's services, digital libraries, reference, and technical services. Essential reading for all librarians, and highly recommended for all libraries.

4011. *American Society for Information Science and Technology.* **Bulletin.** Former titles (until 2001): *American Society for Information Science. Bulletin;* (until 1974): *A S I S Newsletter;* (until 1971): *American Society for Information Science. Newsletter;* (until 1968): *American Documentation Institute. Newsletter.* [ISSN: 1931-6550] 1961. bi-m. Members, USD 19; Non-members, USD 60; USD 10 newsstand/ cover. Ed(s): Irene Travis. American Society for Information Science & Technology, 1320 Fenwick Ln, Ste 510, Silver Spring, MD 20910; asis@asis.org; http://www.asis.org. Illus., adv. Circ: 4500. Microform: PQC. Online: EBSCO Publishing, EBSCO Host; OCLC Online Computer Library Center, Inc.; ProQuest LLC (Ann Arbor); Wiley InterScience. *Indexed:* ABIn, ABS&EES, CINAHL, CompLI, EngInd, ISTA, LISA, LRI, LibLit, PAIS, SSCI, SWR&A. *Aud.:* Ga, Ac, Sa.

This publication is the newsmagazine of the American Society for Information Science and Technology. Its primary purpose is to communicate with society members and other information science professionals. In addition to pragmatic, non-research articles, the publication also contains opinion columns and news regarding the members and events of the society. Recent articles include discussions regarding information seekers, open source software, intellectual property, social informatics, and digital publishing. This is an important title for information science professionals and other librarians interested in information technology.

4012. *American Society for Information Science and Technology.* **Journal.** Former titles (until 2000): *American Society for Information Science. Journal;* (until 1970): *American Documentation;* (until 1942): *Journal of Documentary Reproduction.* [ISSN: 1532-2882] 1938. 14x/yr. USD 1999. Ed(s): Donald H Kraft. John Wiley & Sons, Inc., 111 River St, Hoboken, NJ 07030-5774; uscs-wis@wiley.com; http://www.wiley.com. Illus., index, adv. Refereed. Circ: 4800. Microform: PQC. Online: EBSCO Publishing, EBSCO Host; OhioLINK; ProQuest LLC (Ann Arbor); SwetsWise Online Content; Wiley InterScience. Reprint: PSC. *Indexed:* ABIn, ABS&EES, AgeL, AmH&L, C&ISA, CINAHL, CJA, CerAb, ChemAb, CompLI, CompR, EngInd, ExcerpMed, FR, HistAb, IAA, ISTA, LISA, LibLit, MLA-IB, PAIS, PollutAb, RILM, SCI, SSCI, SWR&A. *Bk. rev.:* Number and length vary. *Aud.:* Ga, Ac, Sa.

As the scholarly journal of the American Society for Information Science and Technology, this publication reports new research in the field of information transfer and communication processes within the context of recorded knowledge. Recent article topics include information retrieval, multilingual searching, thesaurus development, web design, and distance-learning environments. Recent themed issues include knowledge management in Asia,

multilingual information systems, search user interfaces, and soft approaches to information retrieval and information access on the web. This publication also includes book reviews, calls for papers, best student papers, and brief communications. Recommended for information science and technology professionals.

4013. *Art Documentation: bulletin of the Art Libraries Society of North America.* Supersedes (in 1981): *A R L I S - N A Newsletter.* [ISSN: 0730-7187] 1972. s-a. USD 5 per issue. Ed(s): Judy Dyki, Kathy Zimon. Art Libraries Society of North America, 329 March Rd., Ste 232, Box 11, Kanata, ON K2K 2E1, Canada; arlisna@igs.net; http://www.arlisna.org. Illus., adv. Refereed. Circ: 1400. Microform: PQC. Online: OCLC Online Computer Library Center, Inc.; H.W. Wilson. *Indexed:* ABM, DAAI, LISA, LibLit. *Bk. rev.:* Number and length vary. *Aud.:* Ga, Ac, Sa.

This peer-reviewed publication is the official bulletin of the Art Libraries Society of North America. Articles discuss recent developments in the field of art librarianship and visual resource curatorship as well as news and events of the society. Recent article topics include image transition from analog to digital, image cataloging, artists' books, and art library collections. Each issue also includes extensive book review sections. An essential publication for all art libraries and visual resource centers.

4014. *The Bottom Line: managing library finances.* [ISSN: 0888-045X] q. EUR 1339 combined subscription in Europe print & online eds.; USD 1499 combined subscription in North America print & online eds.; AUD 1889 combined subscription in Australasia print & online eds. Ed(s): Bradford Lee Eden. Emerald Group Publishing Limited, Howard House, Wagon Ln, Bingley, BD16 1WA, United Kingdom; information@ emeraldinsight.com; http://www.emeraldinsight.com. Sample. Refereed. Online: Pub.; EBSCO Publishing, EBSCO Host; Gale; IngentaConnect; Northern Light Technology, Inc.; OCLC Online Computer Library Center, Inc.; OhioLINK; ProQuest LLC (Ann Arbor); SwetsWise Online Content. Reprint: PSC. *Indexed:* ABIn, ATI, C&ISA, CerAb, IAA, ISTA, LISA, LibLit. *Bk. rev.:* Number and length vary. *Aud.:* Ga, Ac, Sa.

Directed at individuals responsible for financial decisions in libraries, this publication discusses managing library finances and other broad issues affecting libraries. Recent finance-related article topics include international libraries, library funding, and fundraising. Broader topics include collection management, preservation, digital libraries, and disaster plans. Issues also include news, opinion columns, and book reviews. Highly recommended for library administrators in all types of libraries.

4015. *The Charleston Advisor: critical reviews of Web products for information professionals.* [ISSN: 1525-4011] 1999. q. USD 295 (Individuals, USD 295; USD 495 others). Ed(s): Rebecca T Lenzini. The Charleston Company, 618 South Monroe Way, Denver, CO 80209; rlenzini@charlestonco.com; http://www.charlestonco.com. Adv. Sample. Circ: 750 Paid. Online: EBSCO Publishing, EBSCO Host. *Indexed:* ISTA. *Aud.:* Ga, Ac, Sa.

The Charleston Advisor is the leading source of reviews for Internet-accessible electronic resources available to libraries. Each resource is rated on content, searchability, price, and contract terms. In addition to the written review, each resource is given a score from one to five, and the online edition lists all products reviewed and their scores. The formal reviews are all refereed. In addition to formal reviews, each issue of the publication also contains comparative reviews, articles, press releases, editorials, and news. An essential publication for all librarians responsible for purchasing electronic resources.

4016. *Children and Libraries.* [ISSN: 1542-9806] 2003. 3x/yr. USD 40 domestic; USD 50 foreign; USD 12 per issue. Ed(s): Sharon Verbeten. American Library Association, Association for Library Service to Children, 50 E Huron St, Chicago, IL 60611; alsc@ala.org; http://www.ala.org/alsc. Adv. Refereed. Circ: 4200 Paid. Online: EBSCO Publishing, EBSCO Host; OCLC Online Computer Library Center, Inc.; H.W. Wilson. *Indexed:* LISA, LibLit. *Bk. rev.:* Number and length vary. *Aud.:* Ems, Hs.

Children and Libraries is the official publication of the Association for Library Services to Children, a division of the American Library Association. Articles address all aspects of library services for children, including technology, collection development, cataloging, information literacy, and programming. Issues also include book reviews, association news, and recommended titles. An essential title for libraries providing services to children.

4017. *Collection Building*. [ISSN: 0160-4953] 1978. q. EUR 1339 combined subscription in Europe print & online eds.; USD 1499 combined subscription in North America print & online eds.; AUD 1889 combined subscription in Australasia print & online eds. Ed(s): Eileen Breen, Kay Ann Cassell. Emerald Group Publishing Limited, Howard House, Wagon Ln, Bingley, BD16 1WA, United Kingdom; information@emeraldinsight.com; http://www.emeraldinsight.com. Refereed. Online: Pub.; EBSCO Publishing, EBSCO Host; Gale; IngentaConnect; OCLC Online Computer Library Center, Inc.; OhioLINK; ProQuest LLC (Ann Arbor); SwetsWise Online Content. Reprint: PSC. *Indexed:* C&ISA, CerAb, FR, IAA, ISTA, LISA, LibLit. *Bk. rev.:* Number and length vary. *Aud.:* Ems, Hs, Ga, Ac, Sa.

This publication offers practical and theoretical articles that discuss collection building and management. International in scope, the articles discuss academic, public, and school library collections. Recent articles examine government documents, children's collections, electronic journals, and the digital divide. Issues also include library collection news and trends, book reviews, and editorials. Recommended for librarians responsible for building collections.

4018. *College & Research Libraries*. [ISSN: 0010-0870] 1939. bi-m. Members, USD 25; Non-members, USD 70. Ed(s): Dawn Mueller, William Gray Potter. Association of College and Research Libraries, 50 E Huron St, Chicago, IL 60611; acrl@ala.org; http://www.ala.org/acrl. Illus., index, adv. Sample. Refereed. Circ: 13000. Vol. ends: Nov. Microform: PQC. Online: OCLC Online Computer Library Center, Inc.; H.W. Wilson. *Indexed:* ABIn, AmH&L, ArtHuCI, BEL&L, BRD, BRI, CBRI, ChemAb, EduInd, FR, HEA, HistAb, IBR, IBZ, ISTA, LISA, LibLit, LingAb, MLA-IB, MusicInd, PAIS, SCI, SSCI. *Bk. rev.:* 6 per issue; length varies. *Aud.:* Ac, Sa.

This publication is a scholarly research journal published by the Association of College & Research Libraries, a division of the American Library Association. Articles reflect trends and developments that impact academic librarians and research libraries. Recent article subjects include interlibrary loan, information literacy, controlled vocabularies, and the open access movement. Articles are supported with appropriate tables, figures, and surveys, and each issue includes book reviews. Highly recommended for academic and research libraries.

4019. *College & Research Libraries News*. [ISSN: 0099-0086] 1966. 11x/yr. Free to members; Non-members, USD 46; USD 6.50 per issue. Ed(s): Stephanie Orphan. Association of College and Research Libraries, 50 E Huron St, Chicago, IL 60611; acrl@ala.org; http://www.ala.org/acrl. Illus., adv. Sample. Circ: 13000 Paid. Vol. ends: Dec. Online: OCLC Online Computer Library Center, Inc.; H.W. Wilson. *Indexed:* A&ATA, ABS&EES, FR, IBR, ISTA, LISA, LibLit, PAIS, RI-1, SCI, SWA. *Bk. rev.:* Number and length vary. *Aud.:* Ac, Sa.

The official newsmagazine and publication of record for the Association of College & Research Libraries, this publication communicates current news and trends that affect academic and research libraries. Regular columns include Internet Resources, Internet Reviews, Preservation News, Washington Hotline, Grants and Acquisitions, People in the News, and New Publications. Recent articles address bibliographic instruction, international libraries, technology, and tenure for librarians. Highly recommended for academic and research libraries.

4020. *Computers in Libraries: complete coverage of library information technology*. Formerly (until 1989): *Small Computers in Libraries;* Which incorporated (1986-1988): *Systems Librarian and Automation Review;* (1985-1987): *Bulletin Board Systems;* And (1986-1987): *Public Computing.* [ISSN: 1041-7915] 1981. 10x/yr. USD 99.95 (Individuals, USD 67.95). Ed(s): Kathy Dempsey. Information Today, Inc., 143 Old Marlton Pike, Medford, NJ 08055-8750; custserv@infotoday.com; http://www.infotoday.com. Illus., index. Circ: 6000. Vol. ends: Dec.

Online: EBSCO Publishing, EBSCO Host; Florida Center for Library Automation; Gale; Northern Light Technology, Inc.; OCLC Online Computer Library Center, Inc.; ProQuest K-12 Learning Solutions; ProQuest LLC (Ann Arbor); H.W. Wilson. *Indexed:* ABIn, CINAHL, CLI, CompR, ERIC, FR, IBR, IBZ, ILP, ISTA, LISA, LibLit, MRD, MicrocompInd. *Aud.:* Ems, Hs, Ga, Ac, Sa.

This monthly publication covers news and trends affecting technology in all types of libraries. Articles provide practical advice, and technical jargon is kept to a minimum. Recent articles address wireless technology, portable devices, RSS feeds, networks, and security. Recommended for librarians who are interested in technology and its use in libraries.

4021. *Current Cites*. [ISSN: 1060-2356] 1990. m. University of California at Berkeley, School Library, Berkeley, CA 94720; http://sunsite.berkeley.edu/currentcites/. *Aud.:* Ac, Sa.

This electronic publication serves as a bibliography of current news in the field of information science. Each of the monthly newsletters contains 8 to 12 annotated citations of current literature in prominent library and information science sources. An excellent resource for all librarians.

4022. *D T T P*. Formerly (until 1974): *Documents to the People.* [ISSN: 0091-2085] 1972. q. USD 44 domestic; USD 50 Canada; USD 55 elsewhere. Ed(s): Andrea Sevetson. American Library Association, 50 E Huron St, Chicago, IL 60611-2795; http://www.ala.org. Illus., adv. Circ: 2000. Vol. ends: Dec. Online: OCLC Online Computer Library Center, Inc.; ProQuest LLC (Ann Arbor); H.W. Wilson. *Indexed:* LibLit. *Bk. rev.:* Number and length vary. *Aud.:* Ac, Sa.

This quarterly publication is the official journal of the Government Documents Round Table (GODORT) of the American Library Association. *DTTP* covers the news and activities of the round table, as well as local, state, national, and international government information and activities. Recent articles discuss preservation of born-digital documents, blogs, map librarians, and United Nations depository libraries. Issues also include book reviews and columns by GODORT officers. An essential publication for government document librarians.

4023. *The Indexer: the international journal of indexing*. [ISSN: 0019-4131] 1958. s-a. GBP 50; USD 85. Ed(s): Christine MacGlashan. Society of Indexers, Blades Enterprise Centre, John St, Sheffield, S2 4SU, United Kingdom; admin@indexers.org.uk; http://www.socind.demon.co.uk. Illus., adv. Refereed. Circ: 2500. *Indexed:* BRI, BrArAb, CBRI, ChemAb, FR, ISTA, IndIslam, LISA, LibLit, NumL, RI-1, SWR&A. *Bk. rev.:* Number and length vary. *Aud.:* Ac, Sa.

Published by the Society of Indexers, this semi-annual, peer-reviewed publication informs readers on the trends and developments in the international indexing community. Articles address practical, theoretical, and historical aspects of indexing. Recent article topics include how to start in the indexing field, subheadings, controlled vocabularies, indexing in an XML context, and Canadian indexing activities. Articles highlighting the activities of the society are included in each issue, as well as review of books and electronic resources. The column "Indexes reviewed" provides reviews of indexes in current publications. An essential journal for all indexers and librarians interested in the field of indexing.

4024. *Information Outlook*. Formed by the merger of (1910-1997): *Special Libraries;* (1980-1997): *SpeciaList.* [ISSN: 1091-0808] 1997. m. USD 125. Ed(s): John T Adams, III. Special Libraries Association, 331 S Patrick St, Alexandria, VA 22314-3501; http://www.sla.org. Illus., index, adv. Circ: 16000. Microform: PQC. Online: EBSCO Publishing, EBSCO Host; Florida Center for Library Automation; Gale; Northern Light Technology, Inc.; OCLC Online Computer Library Center, Inc.; ProQuest K-12 Learning Solutions; ProQuest LLC (Ann Arbor). *Indexed:* ABIn, AmH&L, BAS, BRI, C&ISA, CBRI, CINAHL, CerAb, FR, HistAb, IAA, IBR, IBZ, ISTA, LISA, LibLit, MicrocompInd, PAIS, SCI, SSCI. *Aud.:* Sa.

This is the monthly professional journal of the Special Libraries Association. The practical articles in this publication are directed toward information professionals working in special libraries of all sizes. Recent topics include career development, management, knowledge management, and internal marketing. Case studies are common, and regular features include web site reviews, copyright issues, and news and events of the association. Recommended for all information professionals in special libraries.

4025. Information Technology and Libraries. Formerly (until 1982): *Journal of Library Automation;* Which incorporated (1969-1972): *J O L A Technical Communications.* [ISSN: 0730-9295] 1968. q. Non-members, USD 60. Ed(s): Dan Marmion. American Library Association, 50 E Huron St, Chicago, IL 60611-2795; http://www.ala.org. Illus., index, adv. Refereed. Circ: 7000 Controlled. Vol. ends: Mar. Microform: PQC. Online: EBSCO Publishing, EBSCO Host; Florida Center for Library Automation; Gale; OCLC Online Computer Library Center, Inc.; ProQuest K-12 Learning Solutions; ProQuest LLC (Ann Arbor); H.W. Wilson. *Indexed:* ABIn, ABS&EES, ArtHuCI, CINAHL, ChemAb, CompLI, CompR, FR, IBR, IBZ, ISTA, LISA, LibLit, PAIS, RILM, SCI, SSCI. *Aud.:* Ac, Sa.

This publication is the refereed journal of the Library and Information Technology Association, a division of the American Library Association. Articles address all aspects of information technology relevant to libraries, including digital libraries, online catalogs, software engineering, electronic publishing, and metadata. Each issue includes a "President's column," editorials, and feature articles. Recent article topics include cataloging, library web pages, RFID, wikis, and digital libraries. Highly recommended for all librarians interested in technology and its use in libraries.

4026. Issues in Science and Technology Librarianship: a quarterly publication of the Science and Technology Section, Association of College and Research Libraries. [ISSN: 1092-1206] 1991. q. Free. Ed(s): Andrea Duda. Association of College and Research Libraries, Science and Technology Section, 50 E Huron St, Chicago, IL 60611-2795. Illus. Refereed. *Indexed:* ISTA, LISA, LibLit. *Bk. rev.:* 350-500 words; number varies. *Aud.:* Ac, Sa.

This quarterly, electronic publication offers materials of interest to science and technology librarians. Each issue contains themed articles, refereed articles, database reviews, Internet sources, viewpoints, and book reviews. Recent themes address outreach and marketing, facilities, and open access journals. Other articles have explored collection development, library reorganization, and GIS implementation. Highly recommended for science and technology librarians.

4027. The Journal of Academic Librarianship. [ISSN: 0099-1333] 1975. 6x/yr. EUR 285. Pergamon, The Boulevard, Langford Ln, East Park, Kidlington, OX5 1GB, United Kingdom; nlinfo-f@elsevier.nl; http://www.elsevier.nl. Illus., index, adv. Refereed. Circ: 3000. Vol. ends: Nov. Microform: PQC. Online: EBSCO Publishing, EBSCO Host; Gale; IngentaConnect; OCLC Online Computer Library Center, Inc.; OhioLINK; ScienceDirect; SwetsWise Online Content; H.W. Wilson. *Indexed:* ABIn, ABS&EES, AgeL, ArtHuCI, BRI, CBRI, ERIC, EduInd, FR, IBR, IBZ, ISTA, LISA, LibLit, SSCI. *Bk. rev.:* approx. 500 words, number varies. *Aud.:* Ac, Sa.

The Journal of Academic Librarianship, published six times each year, is a refereed journal with international contributions and readership. The journal serves as a forum for authors to communicate research findings and case studies, analyze policies and procedures, and review books relevant to the library profession. Recent article topics include undergraduate citation behavior, information literacy instruction, digital libraries, international libraries, and unicode. Highly recommended for academic libraries.

4028. Journal of Information Ethics. [ISSN: 1061-9321] 1992. s-a. USD 120 (Individuals, USD 40). Ed(s): Robert Hauptman. McFarland & Company, Inc., 960 NC Hwy 88 W, PO Box 611, Jefferson, NC 28640; info@mcfarlandpub.com; http://www.mcfarlandpub.com. Illus., adv. Refereed. *Indexed:* FR, IBR, IBZ, ISTA, LISA, LibLit, PhilInd, RI-1, SSCI. *Bk. rev.:* Number varies, 800-1,200 words, signed. *Aud.:* Ac, Sa.

This semi-annual publication features peer-reviewed articles discussing information ethics. Issues include book reviews, web site reviews, and feature articles. Recent articles discuss plagiarism, wireless campuses, intellectual property, and online consumers' privacy. Recommended for all library science collections.

4029. Law Library Journal. [ISSN: 0023-9283] 1908. q. Free to members; Non-members, USD 110. Ed(s): Frank Houdek. American Association of Law Libraries, 53 W Jackson Blvd, Ste 940, Chicago, IL 60604; orders@aall.org; http://www.aallnet.org. Illus., index, adv. Refereed. Circ: 5400 Paid. Vol. ends: Fall. Microform: PMC. Online: William S. Hein & Co., Inc.; LexisNexis; OCLC Online Computer Library Center, Inc.; H.W. Wilson. Reprint: WSH. *Indexed:* ArtHuCI, CJA, CLI, IBR, IBZ, ILP, ISTA, LISA, LRI, LibLit, SSCI. *Bk. rev.:* Number and length vary. *Aud.:* Ac, Sa.

Law Library Journal has been the official publication of the American Association of Law Libraries since 1908. This quarterly journal communicates news and events of the association, as well as articles related to law, legal materials, and librarianship. Issues include book reviews, proceedings and reports of the association, annotated bibliographies, and obituaries. Recent article topics include government information, the future of law librarianship, standards for law libraries, persistent identifiers for electronic resources, and law library management. Essential reading for all law librarians and providers of legal reference services.

4030. Libraries & the Cultural Record: exploring the history of collections of recorded knowledge. Former titles (until 2006): *Libraries & Culture;* (until 1987): *Journal of Library History;* (until 1973): *Journal of Library History, Philosophy, and Comparative Librarianship;* (until 1972): *Journal of Library History.* [ISSN: 1932-4855] 1966. q. USD 114 (Individuals, USD 44). Ed(s): David B. Gracy, II. University of Texas Press, Journals Division, 2100 Comal, Austin, TX 78722; journals@uts.cc.utexas.edu; http://www.utexas.edu/utpress/journals/journals.html. Illus., index, adv. Refereed. Circ: 530. Vol. ends: Nov. Microform: PQC. Online: EBSCO Publishing, EBSCO Host; Florida Center for Library Automation; Gale; OCLC Online Computer Library Center, Inc.; OhioLINK; Project MUSE; ProQuest LLC (Ann Arbor); SwetsWise Online Content; H.W. Wilson. Reprint: PSC. *Indexed:* ABS&EES, AmH&L, AmHI, ArtHuCI, BRI, CBRI, FR, HistAb, IBR, IBZ, LISA, LibLit, MLA-IB, RI-1, SSCI. *Bk. rev.:* 11-20, 500-1,200 words, signed. *Aud.:* Ac, Sa.

In 2006 the focus of this publication has shifted from the history of libraries to the history of collections of recorded knowledge. The peer-reviewed articles in this interdisciplinary publication examine the social and cultural context of these collections. Recent article topics include the New York Society Library, library history in the LIS curriculum, library history research, and international libraries. A recent special issue examines the Woman's Building Library of the World's Columbian Exposition in 1893. Books selected for review discuss the history of libraries, archives, museums, and preservation of collections. Highly recommended for library and information science collections and others interested in the history of recorded knowledge.

4031. Library Administration and Management. Former titles (until 1986): *L A M A Newsletter; L A D Newsletter.* [ISSN: 0888-4463] 1975. q. USD 65 domestic; USD 75 foreign; USD 17 per issue. Ed(s): Lorraine Olley, Robert Moran. American Library Association, 50 E Huron St, Chicago, IL 60611-2795; http://www.ala.org. Illus., adv. Circ: 6000 Paid. Vol. ends: Winter. Microform: PQC. Online: OCLC Online Computer Library Center, Inc.; ProQuest LLC (Ann Arbor); H.W. Wilson. *Indexed:* ABIn, ISTA, LISA, LibLit. *Aud.:* Ac, Sa.

This journal is the official publication of the Library Administration and Management Association, a division of the American Library Association. With an audience of library managers at all levels, articles explore issues and methodologies of library management in a practical manner. Articles and columns include case studies, interviews, feature articles, and news of the association. Recent article topics include fund raising, the PATRIOT Act, and mentoring new librarians. An essential publication for all library administrators and managers.

4032. *Library Hi Tech.* [ISSN: 0737-8831] 1983. q. EUR 409 combined subscription in Europe print & online eds.; USD 429 combined subscription in North America print & online eds.; AUD 609 combined subscription in Australasia print & online eds. Ed(s): Dr. Michael Seadle. Emerald Group Publishing Limited, Howard House, Wagon Ln, Bingley, BD16 1WA, United Kingdom; information@emeraldinsight.com; http://www.emeraldinsight.com. Illus., index, adv. Sample. Refereed. Circ: 2600. Microform: PQC. Online: Pub.; EBSCO Publishing, EBSCO Host; Gale; IngentaConnect; OCLC Online Computer Library Center, Inc.; OhioLINK; ProQuest LLC (Ann Arbor); SwetsWise Online Content. Reprint: PSC. *Indexed:* ABIn, BRI, C&ISA, CBRI, CINAHL, CerAb, CompLI, ConsI, FR, IAA, ISTA, IndIslam, LISA, LibLit, MicrocompInd, SSCI. *Bk. rev.:* Number and length vary. *Aud.:* Ga, Ac, Sa.

Library Hi-Tech, a quarterly, peer-reviewed journal, focuses on all types of technology used in the international library community. The majority of issues focus on specific topics; recent topics include content management systems, open source software, IMLS National Leadership Grants, and metadata. Article formats include case studies, general articles, research papers, technical papers, and conceptual papers. Recommended for academic libraries.

4033. *Library Hotline: breaking news for library and information decisions makers.* Formerly (until 1983): *L J - S L J Hot Line (Library Journal - School Library Journal).* [ISSN: 0740-736X] 1972. w. except last 2 weeks of yr. USD 115 domestic; USD 147 in Canada & Mexico; USD 158 elsewhere. Ed(s): Susan DiMattia. Reed Business Information, 360 Park Ave South, New York, NY 10010; http://www.reedbusiness.com. Illus., adv. Circ: 3500. Vol. ends: Dec. *Aud.:* Ga, Ac, Sa.

This weekly newsletter from Library Journal and School Library Journal provides updates and current news from the library community. In addition to short articles focusing on current events, each issue also features people in the news, company announcements, money matters, news, and a classified section listing career opportunities. An excellent source for current information, this newsletter is recommended for library science collections.

4034. *Library Journal.* Former titles (until 1976): *L J (Library Journal);* (until 1974): *Library Journal.* [ISSN: 0363-0277] 1876. 22x/yr. USD 149.99 domestic; USD 199.99 Canada; USD 259.99 elsewhere. Ed(s): John Berry, Bette-Lee Fox. Reed Business Information, 360 Park Ave South, New York, NY 10010; http://www.reedbusiness.com. Illus., index, adv. Sample. Refereed. Circ: 19510 Paid. Vol. ends: Dec. Microform: CIS; NBI; RPI; PMC. Online: EBSCO Publishing, EBSCO Host; Factiva, Inc.; Florida Center for Library Automation; Gale; LexisNexis; OCLC Online Computer Library Center, Inc.; ProQuest LLC (Ann Arbor); H.W. Wilson. *Indexed:* ABIn, ABS&EES, ASIP, AgeL, AmHI, ArtHuCI, BAS, BRD, BRI, CINAHL, CWI, ERIC, EduInd, GardL, ISTA, LISA, LRI, LibLit, MASUSE, MLA-IB, MRD, PAIS, PRA, RI-1, RILM, SSCI. *Bk. rev.:* 175-200 words, number varies. *Aud.:* Ga, Ac, Sa.

Library Journal's mission is to be a "one-stop source" for the information needs of all librarians. Each issue contains letters to the editor, opinion pieces, library news, feature articles, interviews, and reviews of books, DVDs, and software. Recent articles address the PATRIOT Act, digital libraries, technology, and international libraries. Recommended for all library professionals.

4035. *Library Management.* Incorporates: *Librarian Career Development;* Formerly: *Library Research Occasional Paper.* [ISSN: 0143-5124] 1976. 9x/yr. EUR 11149 combined subscription in Europe print & online eds.; USD 11899 combined subscription in North America print & online eds.; AUD 14679 combined subscription in Australasia print & online eds. Ed(s): Stephen O'Connor. Emerald Group Publishing Limited, Howard House, Wagon Ln, Bingley, BD16 1WA, United Kingdom; information@emeraldinsight.com; http://www.emeraldinsight.com. Refereed. Online: Pub.; EBSCO Publishing, EBSCO Host; Gale; IngentaConnect; OCLC Online Computer Library Center, Inc.; OhioLINK; ProQuest LLC (Ann Arbor); SwetsWise Online Content. Reprint: PSC. *Indexed:* ABIn, C&ISA, CerAb, FR, IAA, ISTA, LISA, LibLit. *Bk. rev.:* Number and length vary. *Aud.:* Ac, Sa.

Library Management seeks to provide international perspectives on library management issues. Articles provide practical implications of management theories through case studies, research papers, and general papers. Recent themed issues include the semantic web and repository print libraries, and other articles discuss retrospective conversion, team environments, and mentoring. Highly recommended for library managers.

4036. *Library Media Connection: magazine for secondary school library media and technology specialists.* Incorporates: *The Book Report; Library Talk.* [ISSN: 1542-4715] 1982. 7x/yr. USD 69 domestic; USD 91 Canada. Ed(s): Carol Simpson. Linworth Publishing, Inc., 480 E Wilson Bridge Rd, Ste L, Worthington, OH 43085; linworth@linworthpublishing.com; http://www.linworth.com. Illus., adv. Circ: 20000 Paid. Vol. ends: May. Microform: PQC. Online: EBSCO Publishing, EBSCO Host; Gale; OCLC Online Computer Library Center, Inc.; H.W. Wilson. *Indexed:* ABIn, BRI, CBRI, ERIC, EduInd, LibLit, MASUSE, MRD. *Bk. rev.:* 25-50 words, number varies. *Aud.:* Ems, Hs.

As a professional journal for school library media and technology specialists, *Library Media Connection* provides reviews, professional development, and practical articles for its readers. Recent article topics include teaching information literacy, library helper programs, copyright, collaboration, and technology. Each issue also features evaluations of children's books, software, and online resources. Essential reading for all school library media and technology professionals.

4037. *The Library Quarterly.* [ISSN: 0024-2519] 1931. q. USD 150 domestic; USD 164 Canada; USD 157 elsewhere. Ed(s): John C Bertot, Wayne A Wiegand. University of Chicago Press, Journals Division, PO Box 37005, Chicago, IL 60637; subscriptions@press.uchicago.edu; http://www.journals.uchicago.edu. Illus., index, adv. Refereed. Circ: 1300 Paid. Vol. ends: Oct. Microform: MIM; PMC; PQC. Online: EBSCO Publishing, EBSCO Host; Florida Center for Library Automation; Gale; OCLC Online Computer Library Center, Inc.; ProQuest K-12 Learning Solutions; ProQuest LLC (Ann Arbor). Reprint: PSC. *Indexed:* ABS&EES, AgeL, AmH&L, ArtHuCI, BAS, BRD, BRI, CBRI, ChemAb, FLI, FR, HistAb, IBR, IBZ, ISTA, IndIslam, LISA, LibLit, PAIS, RI-1, RILM, SSCI. *Bk. rev.:* 4-5, 900-1,300 words. *Aud.:* Ac, Sa.

This refereed, quarterly journal seeks to inform its readership of research in all aspects of librarianship. Each issue includes book reviews and articles discussing topics such as digital libraries, collaboration, career satisfaction, and the history of individual libraries. Recommended for academic and special libraries.

4038. *Library Review.* [ISSN: 0024-2535] 1927. 9x/yr. EUR 8709 combined subscription in Europe print & online eds.; USD 10259 combined subscription in North America print & online eds.; AUD 11329 combined subscription in Australasia print & online eds. Ed(s): David McMenemy, Nicholas Joint. Emerald Group Publishing Limited, Howard House, Wagon Ln, Bingley, BD16 1WA, United Kingdom; information@emeraldinsight.com; http://www.emeraldinsight.com. Refereed. Online: Pub.; EBSCO Publishing, EBSCO Host; Gale; IngentaConnect; OCLC Online Computer Library Center, Inc.; OhioLINK; ProQuest LLC (Ann Arbor); SwetsWise Online Content. Reprint: PSC. *Indexed:* AmH&L, AmHI, BRI, C&ISA, CBRI, CerAb, FR, HistAb, IAA, IBR, IBZ, ISTA, LISA, LibLit. *Bk. rev.:* 2-6, length varies. *Aud.:* Ga, Ac, Sa.

Library Review provides librarians, educators, and researchers with information from libraries around the world. Articles are written by librarians with diverse backgrounds, and recent topics explore digital libraries, public library management, international libraries, and professional development for librarians. Recent themed issues consider disability issues and libraries in Scotland, information and IT literacy, and restructuring LIS education. Each issue also includes reviews of recent library and information science publications. Recommended for all library collections.

4039. *Library Technology Reports: expert guides to library systems and services.* [ISSN: 0024-2586] 1965. 6x/yr. USD 325 in North America; USD 370 elsewhere; USD 63 per issue. Ed(s): Nicole Waller. American Library Association, 50 E Huron St, Chicago, IL 60611-2795;

http://www.ala.org. Illus., index, adv. Refereed. Circ: 1900. Vol. ends: Jan. Online: EBSCO Publishing, EBSCO Host; Florida Center for Library Automation; Gale; Northern Light Technology, Inc.; OCLC Online Computer Library Center, Inc.; ProQuest K-12 Learning Solutions; ProQuest LLC (Ann Arbor). *Indexed:* ISTA, LibLit. *Aud.:* Ac, Sa.

Published by the American Library Association, this journal explores new and emerging technology in the library and information science field. Each issue is devoted to a single topic; topics for 2006 consider "Linking and the OpenURL," "Electronic-Resource Management: Staffing, Services, and Systems," "Web Services and the Service-Oriented Architecture," and "Gaming and Libraries: Intersection of Services." Most issues also include bibliographies of related materials for additional reading. Highly recommended for managers of technology in libraries.

4040. Library Trends. [ISSN: 0024-2594] 1952. q. USD 128. Ed(s): John Unsworth, Boyd Rayward. The Johns Hopkins University Press, 2715 N Charles St, Baltimore, MD 21218-4363; http://muse.jhu.edu. Illus., index. Refereed. Circ: 2000 Paid. Microform: MIM; PQC. Online: EBSCO Publishing, EBSCO Host; Florida Center for Library Automation; Gale; Northern Light Technology, Inc.; OCLC Online Computer Library Center, Inc.; Project MUSE; ProQuest K-12 Learning Solutions; ProQuest LLC (Ann Arbor); SwetsWise Online Content; H.W. Wilson. Reprint: PSC. *Indexed:* AgeL, FR, IBR, IBZ, ISTA, LISA, LibLit, PAIS, RILM, SCI, SSCI. *Aud.:* Ga, Ac, Sa.

This quarterly publication examines new and emerging trends in the field of library and information science. Each themed issue examines all aspects of a topic and its impact on libraries. Recent issue titles include "Library Resource Sharing Networks," "Children's Access and Use of Digital Resources," "Digital Preservation: Finding Balance," and "The Commercialized Web: Challenges for Libraries and Democracy." Articles address the impact of the topic on all library departments, including reference, technical services, administration, and systems. Recommended reading for all librarians.

4041. Medical Reference Services Quarterly. [ISSN: 0276-3869] 1982. q. USD 385 print & online eds. Ed(s): Sandra M Wood. Haworth Information Press, 10 Alice St, Binghamton, NY 13904; getinfo@ haworthpress.com; http://www.haworthpress.com. Illus., adv. Sample. Refereed. Circ: 721 Paid. Microform: PQC. Online: EBSCO Publishing, EBSCO Host; OCLC Online Computer Library Center, Inc.; SwetsWise Online Content. Reprint: HAW. *Indexed:* BiolAb, CINAHL, ExcerpMed, IBR, IBZ, ISTA, LISA, LibLit. *Bk. rev.:* 8-12, 500-800 words. *Aud.:* Ac, Sa.

Medical Reference Services Quarterly is a peer-reviewed publication for an audience of medical and health sciences librarians who provide reference services in the educational, clinical, and research environments. Articles provide practical information on such topics as postgraduate medical training programs, citation formats, guides to medical information resources, and Internet medical resources. Each issue also includes book reviews and reviews of articles in related publications. Essential for all medical and health-sciences reference librarians.

4042. Public Libraries. Former titles: *P L A Newsletter;* (until 1969): *Just Between Ourselves.* [ISSN: 0163-5506] 1962. 6x/yr. USD 50 domestic; USD 60 foreign; USD 10 per issue. Ed(s): Kathleen Hughes. American Library Association, 50 E Huron St, Chicago, IL 60611-2795; http://www.ala.org. Illus., index, adv. Circ: 10566. Microform: PQC. Online: OCLC Online Computer Library Center, Inc.; ProQuest K-12 Learning Solutions; ProQuest LLC (Ann Arbor); H.W. Wilson. *Indexed:* LibLit. *Bk. rev.:* Number and length vary. *Aud.:* Ga, Ac, Sa.

This journal is the official publication of the Public Library Association, a division of the American Library Association. Articles and columns examine industry news, association updates, professional development, literature reviews, and ideas and strategies for providing library services to the public. Recent articles explore self-checkout, fund-raising, programming, copyright, and recruitment and retention of librarians. Essential reading for all public librarians.

4043. Reference and User Services Quarterly. Formerly (until 1997): *R Q.* [ISSN: 1094-9054] 1960. q. USD 65 domestic; USD 70 in Canada & Mexico; USD 75 elsewhere. Ed(s): Diane Zabel. American Library Association, 50 E Huron St, Chicago, IL 60611-2795; http://www.ala.org. Illus., index, adv. Sample. Refereed. Circ: 6800. Vol. ends: Fall. Microform: PQC. Online: EBSCO Publishing, EBSCO Host; Factiva, Inc.; Florida Center for Library Automation; Gale; OCLC Online Computer Library Center, Inc.; ProQuest LLC (Ann Arbor); H.W. Wilson. *Indexed:* AgeL, AmH&L, ArtHuCI, BRI, CBRI, FR, HistAb, ISTA, IndIslam, LISA, LibLit, PAIS, RI-1, SSCI. *Bk. rev.:* 18-25; length varies. *Aud.:* Ga, Ac, Sa.

As the official publication of the Reference and User Services Association of the American Library Association, this journal communicates information regarding user-oriented library services to librarians in special, public, and academic libraries. In addition to reference trends and resources, articles also address news of the association, professional development, and literature reviews. Recent articles examine visual images, readers' advisory services, information seeking behavior, and Wikipedia as a reference resource. A basic title for all library collections.

4044. The Reference Librarian. [ISSN: 0276-3877] 1981. s-a. in 2 vols. USD 470 print & online eds. Ed(s): Bill Katz. Haworth Press, Inc., 10 Alice St, Binghamton, NY 13904-1580; getinfo@haworthpress.com; http://www.haworthpress.com. Illus., index, adv. Sample. Refereed. Circ: 636 Paid. Microform: PQC. Online: EBSCO Publishing, EBSCO Host; OCLC Online Computer Library Center, Inc.; SwetsWise Online Content. Reprint: HAW. *Indexed:* C&ISA, CerAb, ExcerpMed, FR, IAA, IBR, IBZ, ISTA, LISA, LibLit. *Aud.:* Ac, Sa.

This semi-annual publication addresses new trends and developments in the field of reference librarianship. Articles are appropriate for professional librarians and graduate students enrolled in reference and user services courses. Recent articles discuss virtual depositories, government documents, virtual reference, and copyright. Recommended reading for all reference librarians.

4045. Reference Services Review. [ISSN: 0090-7324] 1972. q. EUR 409 combined subscription in Europe print & online eds.; USD 459 combined subscription in North America print & online eds.; AUD 609 combined subscription in Australasia print & online eds. Ed(s): Eleanor Mitchell, Sarah Barbara Watstein. Emerald Group Publishing Limited, Howard House, Wagon Ln, Bingley, BD16 1WA, United Kingdom; information@emeraldinsight.com; http://www.emeraldinsight.com. Illus., index, adv. Sample. Refereed. Circ: 2000. Reprint: PSC. *Indexed:* AgeL, BRI, C&ISA, CBRI, CINAHL, CerAb, FR, HistAb, IAA, ISTA, LISA, LibLit, RI-1, RILM. *Aud.:* Ac, Sa.

Reference Services Review is a quarterly, peer-reviewed publication that examines all aspects of reference services. Recent themed issues examine institutional repositories, LOEX-of-the-West 2004, and emerging roles of health-sciences librarians. Articles include research papers, viewpoints, case studies, and literature reviews, and recent topics explore information literacy, public computing, the Internet as a research source, library instruction, and reference and digital projects. Recommended for all library collections.

4046. Reforma Newsletter: national association to promote library and information services to Latinos and the Spanish-speaking. [ISSN: 0891-8880] 1971. q. USD 35 (Individuals, USD 20). Ed(s): Denice Adkins. Reforma, PO Box 832, Anaheim, CA 92815-0832; denice@webpan.com; http://www.reforma.org. Illus., adv. Circ: 900. Vol. ends: Winter. *Bk. rev.:* 10-15; 100-250 words. *Aud.:* Ga, Ac, Sa.

Reforma Newsletter, published by the National Association to Promote Library and Information Services to Latinos and the Spanish-Speaking, serves as a platform to encourage the development of Spanish-speaking and bilingual library services, as well as the recruitment of Hispanic and bicultural librarians. Each issue includes articles, news, people in the news, and book reviews. Recent articles discuss international book fairs, bilingual story hour, and banned books. An excellent tool for promoting diversity in the library profession, this newsletter is essential for any library that serves Hispanic or Spanish-speaking populations.

4047. *School Library Journal: the magazine of children, young adults & school librarians.* Formerly: *Junior Libraries.* [ISSN: 0362-8930] 1954. m. USD 124 domestic; USD 170 in North America; USD 182 elsewhere. Ed(s): Brian Kenney, Lu Ann Toth. Reed Business Information, 360 Park Ave South, New York, NY 10010; http://www.reedbusiness.com. Illus., index, adv. Sample. Circ: 39500 Paid. Vol. ends: Aug. Microform: NBI; PQC. Online: EBSCO Publishing, EBSCO Host; Factiva, Inc.; Florida Center for Library Automation; Gale; LexisNexis; OCLC Online Computer Library Center, Inc.; ProQuest K-12 Learning Solutions; ProQuest LLC (Ann Arbor); H.W. Wilson. *Indexed:* ABIn, ABS&EES, ASIP, BRD, BRI, CBRI, ERIC, EduInd, LISA, LibLit, MASUSE, MRD. *Bk. rev.:* 50-100 words; number varies. *Aud.:* Ems, Hs, Ga.

This monthly publication contains news, trends, and literature reviews relevant to librarians who provide services for children and young adults. Recent articles discuss the PATRIOT Act, school dropout rates, technology, and the role of the school librarian. Each issue also includes book reviews. Essential reading for all librarians who provide services to young adults and children.

4048. *School Library Media Activities Monthly.* [ISSN: 0889-9371] 1984. m. 10/yr. USD 55 domestic; USD 68 foreign. Ed(s): Deborah D. Levitov. Libraries Unlimited, Inc., 88 Post Road W, Westport, CT 06881; lu-books@lu.com; http://www.lu.com/. Illus., index, adv. Sample. Circ: 14000 Paid. *Indexed:* ABIn, ABS&EES, ERIC, EduInd, LibLit. *Bk. rev.:* Number and length vary. *Aud.:* Ems, Hs.

This monthly publication for K-8 school library media specialists addresses collaboration with teachers, current reference sources, technology, and information literacy. Recent articles explore certification of school library media specialists, collection development, budgets, blogs, and digital libraries. Issues also review current literature and web sites for children and young adults. Highly recommended for all K-8 school library media specialists.

4049. *School Library Media Research.* Formerly (until 1998): *School Library Media Quarterly Online;* Which superseded in part (in 1997): *School Library Media Quarterly;* Which was formerly (until 1981): *School Media Quarterly;* (until 1972): *School Libraries;* (until 1952): *American Association of School Librarians. Newsletter.* [ISSN: 1523-4320] 1951. 5x/yr. Free. Ed(s): Daniel Callison. American Library Association, 50 E Huron St, Chicago, IL 60611-2795; http://www.ala.org. Illus. Refereed. *Indexed:* EduInd, LibLit. *Aud.:* Ems, Hs.

This refereed publication of the American Association of School Librarians, a division of the American Library Association, publishes high-quality research papers concerning the management and utilization of school library media programs. Articles emphasize evaluation, teaching methods, and instructional theory. Recent article topics include collaboration between teachers and librarians, international libraries, and education reform. Volumes also include editor's choice articles and best of ERIC articles. A valuable resource for school library media professionals.

4050. *Teacher Librarian: the journal for school library professionals.* Formerly (until 1998): *Emergency Librarian.* [ISSN: 1481-1782] 1973. 5x/yr. USD 54. Ed(s): Esther Rosenfeld, David Loertscher. Scarecrow Press, Inc., 15200 NBN Way, Blue Ridge Summit, PA 17214. Illus., adv. Sample. Refereed. Circ: 10000 Paid. Vol. ends: Jun. Microform: MML; PQC. Online: EBSCO Publishing, EBSCO Host; Florida Center for Library Automation; Gale; Micromedia ProQuest; OCLC Online Computer Library Center, Inc.; ProQuest K-12 Learning Solutions; ProQuest LLC (Ann Arbor); H.W. Wilson. *Indexed:* ABIn, BRI, CBCARef, CBRI, CEI, CPerI, ERIC, EduInd, ISTA, LISA, LibLit. *Bk. rev.:* Number and length vary. *Aud.:* Ems, Hs, Ac.

Published five times each year, *Teacher Librarian* provides information for professional librarians working with children and young adults. Regular features include reviews of profession literature, Internet resources, and new books for children, as well as articles discussing information technology and school library management. Recent article topics include literacy, storytelling, professional development, and collaboration. Highly recommended for school librarians and library media specialists.

4051. *The Unabashed Librarian: the "how I run my library good" letter.* [ISSN: 0049-514X] 1971. 4x/yr. USD 65.50 domestic; USD 73.50 foreign. Maurice J. Freedman, Ed. & Pub., PO Box 325, Mount Kisco, NY 10549. *Indexed:* LISA, LibLit. *Bk. rev.:* Number and length vary. *Aud.:* Ga, Ac, Sa.

The Unabashed Librarian offers an eclectic collection of library news and opinions in each of its quarterly newsletters. Articles range from opinion pieces and current events to practical information about library management, and each issue includes book, movie, and web site reviews. The last page of each issue features a crossword puzzle with literary clues. Recommended for all collections.

4052. *Young Adult Library Services.* [ISSN: 1541-4302] 2002. s-a. USD 40 domestic; USD 50 foreign; USD 12 per issue. American Library Association, 50 E Huron St, Chicago, IL 60611-2795; http://www.ala.org. Adv. Circ: 3766 Paid and free. *Indexed:* LISA, LibLit. *Aud.:* Ems, Hs, Ga.

As the official publication of the Young Adult Library Services Association (YALSA), a division of the American Library Association, this journal publishes news and articles relevant to providers of teen library services. Recent articles explore library programming, the future of library services to children, and collaboration and partnerships. Other features include bibliographies, association news, and announcements of awards. Essential reading for all professionals who provide library services to young adults.

■ LINGUISTICS

See also Anthropology; Classical Studies; Education; Literature; Psychology; and Sociology sections.

Margie Ruppel, Reference & Interlibrary Loan Librarian, David L. Rice Library, University of Southern Indiana, Evansville, IN, mdruppel@ usi.edu

Introduction

Hundreds of linguistics topics routinely combine and diverge to form very interesting research studies, and hence both general and interdisciplinary journals for the field. *American Speech* is the oldest and most fundamental journal devoted to the field, while a newer journal, *Intercultural Pragmatics*, zeroes in on the conversations between people of differing languages.

Titles range from general to applied, monolingual to multilingual, regional to international, historical to contemporary, research to theory, quantitative to qualitative, to a combination of all of these, with an eye toward a certain geographic region or language. Linguistics journals also differ according to the discipline's many subtopics, such as morphology, language usage, phonetics, grammar, syntax, semantics, pragmatics, dialectology, phonology, and phonetics. An interesting article that illustrates the convergence of disciplines was published in *Language Variation and Change*, titled, " 'Mam, my trousers is fa'in doon!': Community, caregiver, and child in the acquisition of variation in a Scottish dialect."

My main goal is to provide librarians with a list of the highest-quality peer-reviewed journals in three areas: (1) general linguistics, (2) theoretical linguistics, and (3) interdisciplinary linguistics. Academic libraries' collection development goals definitely differ by size, academic programs offered, and institutional mission. My strategy with this section of *Magazines for Libraries*, however, is to review the types of journals in which academic libraries are most interested: general, theoretical, and interdisciplinary, in that order.

Missing from this edition are most of the journals devoted to specific lesser-known languages. I included these types of journals in the previous edition. *Australian Journal of Linguistics* and *Belgian Journal of Linguistics* are two examples of the journals excluded from the current edition. These publications remain high-quality journals, but they are not core for many academic collections. See the 15th edition of *Magazines for Libraries* for reviews of many of these journals.

The selection of general linguistics journals are a result of reading *Linguistics: A Guide to the Reference Literature*, by Anna L. DeMiller (Libraries Unlimited, 2000), and "Quality Judgments of Journals as Indicators of Research Performance in the Humanities and the Social and Behavioral Sciences," by A. J. Nederhof and R. A. Zwaan (*Journal of the American Society for Information Science*, vol. 42, no. 5, pp. 332–340). Both sources list core general linguistics journals, with the latter based on opinions of professional linguists. *Language, Linguistic Inquiry* and *Journal of Linguistics* are examples of core general linguistics journals.

I employed similar methods to choose the theoretical linguistics journals, with the exception of the Nederhof article. In its place, I used a study on core theoretical linguistics journals: "Some Aspects of Scholarly Communication in Linguistics: An empirical study" (*Language*, vol. 66, no. 3, pp. 553–557). These considerations led to an overall recommendation of "core journal" in the entries. Examples of core theoretical linguistics journals are *Linguistic Analysis* and *The Linguistic Review*.

The selection of interdisciplinary linguistics journals is more subjective. I searched the *MLA Directory of Periodicals* for peer-reviewed journals with "linguistics" as a subject keyword. While this resulted in over 300 results, I scanned the titles and chose some of the more interesting ones. Then I evaluated the journals, using their official web sites. *Linguistics and Philosophy* and *Intercultural Pragmatics* are two of the interdisciplinary titles that made the final list. I had hoped to find some peer-reviewed, open-access linguistics journals, but currently only newsletter-type linguistics publications exist in electronic-only format.

In order to get a better idea of which journals are most useful to those interested in linguistics, I completed a citation analysis in the Institute for Scientific Information's Journal Performance Indicators database. A few of the highest-ranked journals (in the 90th, 80th, and 70th percentile brackets) include *Linguistic Inquiry, Language,* and *Natural Language & Linguistic Theory*. I have labeled them "highly cited" in the reviews. Journals in a lower percentile bracket (60th and below) are "moderately cited," "often cited," or "rarely cited" in the reviews. Many linguistics journals are not in the ISI database.

To identify additional linguistics journals, the best source is *The Linguist List* (http://linguist.emich.edu), maintained by Eastern Michigan University and Wayne State University. You may also want to consult the Linguistic Society of America's list of publications (www.lsadc.org), or *The Fifth Directory of Periodicals: Publishing articles on American and English language and literature, criticism and theory, film, American studies, poetry, and fiction*, by Richard Barlow (Ohio University Press, 1992).

Basic Periodicals

Ac: *American Speech, Applied Linguistics, Journal of English Linguistics, Journal of Linguistics, Journal of Phonetics, Language, Language in Society, Linguistic Inquiry, The Linguistic Review, Linguistics, Linguistics and Education, Modern Language Journal, Natural Language and Linguistic Theory.*

Basic Abstracts and Indexes

Language Teaching, Linguistics Abstracts, Linguistics and Language Behavior Abstracts, MLA International Bibliography, Social Sciences Citation Index, Sociological Abstracts.

American Journal of Philology. See Classical Studies section.

4053. *American Speech: a quarterly of linguistic usage.* [ISSN: 0003-1283] 1925. q. USD 132 (Individuals, USD 50). Ed(s): Michael Adams. Duke University Press, 905 W Main St, Ste 18 B, Durham, NC 27701; subscriptions@dukeupress.edu; http://www.dukeupress.edu. Illus., adv. Sample. Refereed. Circ: 1500 Paid. Vol. ends: Winter. Microform: PQC. Online: EBSCO Publishing, EBSCO Host; Gale; HighWire Press; JSTOR (Web-based Journal Archive); Northern Light Technology, Inc.; OCLC Online Computer Library Center, Inc.; OhioLINK; Project MUSE; SwetsWise Online Content. Reprint: PSC. *Indexed:* AmH&L, AmHI, ArtHuCI, BEL&L, FR, HistAb, HumInd, IBR, IBZ, L&LBA, LRI, LT&LA, LingAb, MLA-IB, RILM. *Bk. rev.:* 1-2, 2-6 pages. *Aud.:* Ga, Ac.

As one might guess from the title, this journal focuses on the English language in the Western hemisphere, especially "current usage, dialectology, and the history and structure of English." Some of the content covers English in other countries; languages that influence English; and languages influenced by English. A recent article maintains the editors' mission of appealing to a wide readership: "Correctness, Pleasantness, and Degree of Difference Ratings across Regions." *American Speech* subscribers also receive its monographic supplement *Publication of the American Dialect Society*. Number 91 in this annual is *English on the Bonin (Ogasawara) Islands*. "Among the New Words" is a particularly noteworthy section. This regular feature discusses words and phrases new to English, covering their etymology, intended meaning, and published examples of usage. The fall 2006 issue lists the top words of the year, such as "Brangelina" and "Cyber Monday." *American Speech* is recommended for all academic linguistics collections because of its general nature, orientation to English in the Western hemisphere, and high citation rate. See also *International Journal of American Linguistics*.

4054. *Anthropological Linguistics.* [ISSN: 0003-5483] 1959. q. USD 150 (Individuals, USD 50). Ed(s): Douglas R Parks. Indiana University, Anthropology Department, Student Bldg 130, 701 E Kirkwood Ave, Bloomington, IN 47405; anthling@indiana.edu; http://www.indiana.edu/~anthling. Illus., index, adv. Sample. Refereed. Circ: 800 Paid. Microform: PQC. *Indexed:* ABS&EES, AICP, AbAn, AmHI, AnthLit, BAS, BEL&L, EI, FR, HumInd, IBR, IBSS, IBZ, IndIslam, L&LBA, LingAb, MLA-IB, RILM, SSCI. *Bk. rev.:* 5-12, 2-12 pages. *Aud.:* Ac.

Cultural, historical, and philological aspects of linguistics are the focus of this publication. Specific topics include psycholinguistics, sociolinguistics, historical linguistics, semantics, descriptive linguistics, Native American languages, linguistic prehistory, archival materials, historical documents, analyses of texts and discourse, semantic systems and cultural classifications, and ethnohistory. The journal's general mission is to cover the "full range of scholarly study of the languages and cultures of the peoples of the world, especially the native peoples of the Americas," recently manifested in the article "Recovering Sociolinguistic Context from Early Sources: The Case of Northwestern California." Published jointly by the Department of Anthropology and the American Indian Research Institute at Indiana University. Most useful for institutions that offer a combination of linguistics, anthropology, and Native American programs.

4055. *Applied Linguistics.* [ISSN: 0142-6001] 1980. q. EUR 272 print or online ed. Ed(s): Gabriele Kasper, Guy Cook. Oxford University Press, Great Clarendon St, Oxford, OX2 6DP, United Kingdom; jnl.orders@oup.co.uk; http://www.oxfordjournals.org. Illus., adv. Sample. Refereed. Circ: 2050. Vol. ends: Dec. Online: Chadwyck-Healey Inc.; EBSCO Publishing, EBSCO Host; Gale; HighWire Press; IngentaConnect; OCLC Online Computer Library Center, Inc.; OhioLINK; Oxford Journals; ProQuest LLC (Ann Arbor); SwetsWise Online Content. Reprint: PSC. *Indexed:* ArtHuCI, BrEdI, ERIC, FR, IBR, IBSS, IBZ, L&LBA, LT&LA, LingAb, MLA-IB, PsycInfo, SSCI, SWA. *Bk. rev.:* 4-5, 1-3 pages. *Aud.:* Ac.

The mission of *Applied Linguistics* is evidenced in the 2005 special issue on "Applied Linguistics and Real-World Issues." By "real-world issues," it means "specific situations in which people use and learn languages." Recent articles are "Applied Linguists and Institutions of Opinion" and "The Emergence of Metaphor in Discourse." Published as a joint effort between three associations (the American Association for Applied Linguistics, the International Association of Applied Linguistics, and the British Association for Applied Linguistics), the journal is more interested in the handling of language problems in a principled, applied, theoretical manner, as opposed to ad hoc "how I did it" solutions. This journal is recommended for all institutions where linguistics degrees are granted because it is heavily cited in the linguistics literature, and because it bridges the gap between theory and practice.

C L A Journal. See African American section.

4056. *Canadian Journal of Linguistics.* Formerly (until 1961): *Canadian Linguistic Association. Journal.* [ISSN: 0008-4131] 1954. 3x/yr. CND 65 domestic; USD 65 foreign. Ed(s): Rose-Marie Dechaine. University of Toronto Press, Journals Division, 5201 Dufferin St, Toronto, ON M3H 5T8, Canada; journals@utpress.utoronto.ca; http://www.utpjournals.com. Illus., index, adv. Sample. Refereed. Circ: 750 Paid. Vol. ends: Nov. Microform: PQC. Online: EBSCO Publishing, EBSCO Host; OCLC

Online Computer Library Center, Inc.; OhioLINK; Project MUSE; SwetsWise Online Content. *Indexed:* AbAn, ArtHuCI, BAS, CBCARef, CEI, FR, IBR, IBSS, IBZ, L&LBA, LT&LA, LingAb, MLA-IB, SSCI. *Bk. rev.:* 5-15, 1,000 words. *Aud.:* Ac.

CJL is cited fairly often in the linguistics literature, owing to the fact that it is a core journal for general and theoretical linguistics. As the official journal of the Canadian Linguistic Association (www.chass.utoronto.ca/~cla-acl), the journal's main goal is "to promote the study of linguistics in Canada," particularly the theoretical aspect of linguistics. To this end, recent articles have been about vowel production in Winnipeg, St. John's English, and Southeastern French nasal vowels. A special issue was dedicated to Canadian English in a global context. Supplemental academic purchase only.

4057. Cognitive Linguistics: an interdisciplinary journal of cognitive science. [ISSN: 0936-5907] 1989. q. EUR 341; EUR 392 combined subscription print & online eds.; EUR 85 per issue. Ed(s): Ewa Dabrowska. Mouton de Gruyter, Genthiner Str 13, Berlin, 10785, Germany; mouton@degruyter.de; http://www.degruyter.de. Illus., index, adv. Sample. Refereed. Reprint: PSC. *Indexed:* ArtHuCI, IBR, IBSS, IBZ, L&LBA, LingAb, MLA-IB, PsycInfo. *Bk. rev.:* 0-5, 5-15 pages. *Aud.:* Ac, Sa.

Cognitive linguistics refers to the creation, learning, and usage of language. The journal *Cognitive Linguistics* publishes research on "language as an instrument for organizing, processing and conveying information." More specifically, the journal contains pieces on topics such as natural language categorization, linguistic organization, language-in-use, and the relationship between language and thought. "Naming Motion Events in Spanish and English" is the title of a recent article. The Squib section contains short notes on facts, principles, research topics, problems, puzzles, and commentary. Beginning in 2007, the first issue of each print volume will have a Cognitive Linguistics Bibliography on CD-ROM, also available as an online subscription. The bibliography is a searchable database of abstracts of cognitive linguistics publications. Publications cover pragmatics, poetics, sociolinguistics, anthropology, literary studies, and applied linguistics. The journal's web site states that it plans to add 1,000 entries to the bibliography each year. A subscription to the journal comes with membership in the International Cognitive Linguistics Association (www.cognitivelinguistics.org). Recommended for specialized academic linguistics collections.

4058. Corpora: corpus-based language learning, language processing and linguistics. [ISSN: 1749-5032] 2006. s-a. GBP 60 (Individuals, GBP 30). Ed(s): Tony McEnery. Edinburgh University Press, 22 George Sq, Edinburgh, EH8 9LF, United Kingdom; journals@eup.ed.ac.uk; http://www.eup.ed.ac.uk. *Indexed:* MLA-IB. *Bk. rev.:* 0-2; 3-5 pages. *Aud.:* Ac.

This journal is a valuable addition to many academic linguistics collections because it covers all languages and because it is interdisciplinary. *Corpora* does not limit itself to English and European languages. Recent articles discuss Spanish, Arabic, Mandarin Chinese, American English, and New Zealand English. In addition, it seeks to include research on all areas of linguistics, as well as many disciplines such as history, literature, and cultural studies "in the belief that these areas have something to offer each other through their common focus on corpus data," as well as corpus-based theory and methodology. Corpus data is derived from corpora, large sets of texts, either monolingual or multilingual. The main thrust of the journal is the uses of corpora, such as corpora building, corpus tool construction, and corpus annotation. While several articles are based on corpora, collections of language or texts used to study linguistics, the editorial focus favors "papers which contribute to corpus-based theory or methodology (e.g., building, annotation, tools, analysis, etc.)." See also *International Journal of Corpus Linguistics.*

4059. E L T Journal: an international journal for teachers of English to speakers of other languages. Former titles (until 1981): *English Language Teaching Journal;* (until 1973): *English Language Teaching.* [ISSN: 0951-0893] 1946. q. EUR 165 print or online ed. Ed(s): Keith Morrow. Oxford University Press, Great Clarendon St, Oxford, OX2 6DP, United Kingdom; jnl.orders@oup.co.uk; http://www.oxfordjournals.org. Illus., index, adv. Sample. Refereed. Circ: 3850. Vol. ends: Oct. Microform: PQC. Online: EBSCO Publishing,

EBSCO Host; Gale; HighWire Press; IngentaConnect; OCLC Online Computer Library Center, Inc.; OhioLINK; Oxford Journals; ProQuest LLC (Ann Arbor); SwetsWise Online Content; H.W. Wilson. Reprint: PSC. *Indexed:* ABIn, BrEdI, ERIC, EduInd, IBR, IBZ, L&LBA, LT&LA, LingAb, MLA-IB. *Bk. rev.:* 2-10, 1-15 pages. *Aud.:* Hs, Ga, Ac.

As the title implies, *ELT Journal*'s audience is everyone involved in teaching English as a second or foreign language, whether they are in education, psychology, linguistics, or sociology. Its aim is to bridge the gap between these disciplines and practical day-to-day concerns, focusing on how English is taught and learned throughout the world. Authors who published in the last two issues are from Japan, Russia, Taiwan, the United Kingdom, Spain, Korea, Netherlands, China, Bangladesh, Canada, New Zealand, and the United States. A recent article is titled "Teaching gender usage in modern English." A recent issue also contains a review of recent business English publications and a column about web sites with teaching videos. It is published in conjunction with the International Association of Teachers of English as a Foreign Language (www.iatefl.org). Most academic libraries will probably need to choose between this journal and *English World-Wide*, as they have similar scopes. See also *TESOL Quarterly; Modern Language Journal;* and *Studies in Second Language Acquisition.*

4060. English World-Wide: a journal of varieties of English. [ISSN: 0172-8865] 1980. 3x/yr. EUR 268 combined subscription print & online eds. Ed(s): Edgar W Schneider. John Benjamins Publishing Co., PO Box 36224, Amsterdam, 1020 ME, Netherlands; subscription@benjamins.nl; http://www.benjamins.com. Illus., adv. Sample. Refereed. Circ: 600. Online: EBSCO Publishing, EBSCO Host; Gale; IngentaConnect; SwetsWise Online Content. *Indexed:* BEL&L, FR, IBR, IBSS, IBZ, L&LBA, LingAb, MLA-IB, RILM, SSA, SociolAb. *Bk. rev.:* 3-5, 1-5 pages. *Aud.:* Ac.

Articles in this journal are empirical, descriptive, or theoretical, or a combination of these approaches. Its main focus is "New Englishes" such as those in Africa, Asia, the Pacific, and the Caribbean, while its secondary focus is on the "social and regional variation of English-speaking countries in Europe, North America, and the Southern hemisphere." Short annotated texts, bibliographies, review essays, and other regular reviews are also published. Recent articles cover Scottish Standard English, American English, Indian English, Australian English, Brunei English, Canadian English, Singaporean English, and African American English. Recent contributors are from New Zealand, Singapore, the United States, and Canada, but submissions from all countries are welcome. Although this journal is not a core selection for linguistics collections, the topic of English dialects and sociolects are of interest to most linguistics researchers.

4061. Folia Linguistica: acta societatis linguisticae Europaeae. [ISSN: 0165-4004] 1967. s-a. EUR 220; EUR 253 combined subscription print & online eds.; EUR 110 newsstand/cover. Ed(s): Wolfgang Dressler. Mouton de Gruyter, Genthiner Str 13, Berlin, 10785, Germany; mouton@degruyter.de; http://www.degruyter.de. Illus., index, adv. Sample. Refereed. Reprint: SCH. *Indexed:* ABS&EES, AmH&L, ArtHuCI, BAS, FR, HistAb, IBR, IBSS, IBZ, L&LBA, LT&LA, LingAb, MLA-IB, PsycInfo. *Bk. rev.:* 0-1, 1,000 words. *Aud.:* Ac, Sa.

Each issue of *Folia Linguistica* offers research and information on general and comparative linguistics, and occasionally publishes overviews of European linguistics research areas. Its official mission is to cover "all non-historical areas in the traditional disciplines of general linguistics (phonology, morphology, syntax, semantics, pragmatics), and also sociological, discoursal, computational and psychological aspects of language and linguistic theory." A typical article in this journal is "Case before Gender in the Acquisition of German." Each volume consists of two issues, plus a supplementary issue of *Folia Linguistica Historica*. Special issues are periodically published, as in the recent thematic issue on natural morphology. Subscribing libraries will want to meet three criteria: (1) their institution's linguistics students often study European languages, (2) it is imperative to have all major journals for general linguistics, and (3) their funds permit subscribing to this fairly expensive journal.

4062. *Intercultural Pragmatics.* [ISSN: 1612-295X] 2004. q. EUR 164; EUR 189 combined subscription print & online eds.; EUR 41 newsstand/cover. Ed(s): Istvan Kecskes. Mouton de Gruyter, Genthiner Str 13, Berlin, 10785, Germany; mouton@degruyter.de; http://www.degruyter.de. Refereed. *Indexed:* IBR, IBZ, L&LBA, MLA-IB. *Bk. rev.:* 2 reviews; 5-9 pages. *Aud.:* Ac, Sa.

Pragmatics is the branch of linguistics that is most concerned with language usage, understanding, and appropriateness. Combined with the concept "intercultural," this involves politeness, speech acts, presuppositions, and analysis of discourse and conversation between cultures. Officially, the journal's goal is to "promote the understanding of intercultural competence by focusing on theoretical and applied pragmatics research that involves more than one language." Because of the subject's nature, many of the articles cross the disciplines of anthropology, theoretical and applied linguistics, psychology, communication, sociolinguistics, second language acquisition, and bi- and multilingualism. As evidence of the interdisciplinary nature of the journal, a recent article combines communication and pragmatics: "A Pragmatic Analysis of Children's Interlanguage in EFL Preschool Contexts." A recent special issue focuses on French pragmatics. The most significant characteristic of this journal is stated in the mission: "The editors, editorial board members, and the publisher are all committed to producing a journal that is non-mainstream, intriguing, and open to new ideas." *Intercultural Pragmatics* is a new scholarly journal (2004-), published by the company synonymous with linguistics journals (Mouton de Gruyter), but is not an essential selection for most academic linguistics collections.

4063. *International Journal of American Linguistics.* [ISSN: 0020-7071] 1917. q. USD 229 domestic; USD 247.74 Canada; USD 235 elsewhere. Ed(s): Keren Rice. University of Chicago Press, Journals Division, PO Box 37005, Chicago, IL 60637; subscriptions@press.uchicago.edu; http://www.journals.uchicago.edu. Illus., index, adv. Sample. Refereed. Circ: 1000 Paid. Vol. ends: Oct. Microform: PMC; PQC. Online: EBSCO Publishing, EBSCO Host; Florida Center for Library Automation; Gale; JSTOR (Web-based Journal Archive); OCLC Online Computer Library Center, Inc.; ProQuest K-12 Learning Solutions; ProQuest LLC (Ann Arbor). Reprint: PSC. *Indexed:* AICP, AbAn, AmH&L, AmHI, AnthLit, ArtHuCI, FR, HAPI, HumInd, IBR, IBSS, IBZ, IndIslam, L&LBA, LT&LA, LingAb, MLA-IB, SSCI. *Bk. rev.:* 2-5, 2-4 pages. *Aud.:* Ac, Sa.

This publication is associated with, but not published by, the Society for the Study of the Indigenous Languages of the Americas (http://linguistics.buffalo.edu/ssila/index.htm), which explains its scope: all languages native to North, Central, and South America, including Native American, Creole, Eskimo-Aleut, North American, Pidgin, and South American, and in general, linguistics in the Western hemisphere. One of the native languages is Navajo, the subject of a recent article: "Time in Navajo: Direct and Indirect Interpretation." Another recent article is about the Ch'olan branch of the Mayan language. *IJAL* began in 1917 and focuses on the "presentation of grammatical fragments and other documents relevant to Amerindian languages." It is moderately cited in the literature, and is a primary selection for academic linguistics collections. See also *American Speech.*

4064. *International Journal of Corpus Linguistics.* [ISSN: 1384-6655] 1996. 4x/yr. EUR 345 combined subscription print & online eds. Ed(s): Michaela Mahlberg. John Benjamins Publishing Co., PO Box 36224, Amsterdam, 1020 ME, Netherlands; subscription@benjamins.nl; http://www.benjamins.com. Illus., index. Sample. Refereed. *Indexed:* FR, IBR, IBZ, L&LBA, LingAb, MLA-IB. *Bk. rev.:* 3-5, 3-15 pages. *Aud.:* Ac, Sa.

Linguistic description. Sociolinguistics. Empirical investigation. Natural language processing. Computational methods. Linguistic data. All of these phrases fit into this journal's mission: (1) using authentic spoken texts to study language as a social phenomenon, and (2) "conciliate the expectations of language industry with the goals of academic linguistics research." Corpus refers to a body of language (textual or oral) that can be analyzed in linguistics research. Corpus linguistics is important because it develops lexicons to be used in natural language processing applications and electronic dictionaries. For example, this article used both spoken and written American English corpora as its basis: "Definite article usage before Last/Next Time in spoken and written

American English." The best thing about this journal is that its research articles are empirical. Its scope, however, makes it a supplementary purchase for academic library collections. See also *Corpora.*

4065. *Journal of English Linguistics.* [ISSN: 0075-4242] 1967. q. GBP 292. Ed(s): Robin Quinn, Anne Curzan. Sage Publications, Inc., 2455 Teller Rd, Thousand Oaks, CA 91320; info@sagepub.com; http://www.sagepub.com. Illus., index, adv. Sample. Refereed. Circ: 600. Vol. ends: Dec. Online: EBSCO Publishing, EBSCO Host; Gale; HighWire Press; OCLC Online Computer Library Center, Inc.; SAGE Publications, Inc., SAGE Journals Online; SwetsWise Online Content. Reprint: PSC. *Indexed:* AmHI, ArtHuCI, CommAb, EAA, FR, IBR, IBZ, L&LBA, LingAb, MLA-IB. *Bk. rev.:* 1-5, 4-6 pages. *Aud.:* Ac, Sa.

The recent article, "Tense Variation in Preadolescent Narratives," hints at this journal's scope: subjects from Old and Middle English to modern English grammar, corpus linguistics, and dialectology. A recent special issue on the "range of English linguistics" covers American dialectology, the history of English research, and narrative analysis. The journal also publishes pieces about other topics such as language contact, pidgins and creoles, and stylistics, if they focus on the English language. Add this to basic undergraduate- and graduate-level linguistics collections if funds permit.

4066. *Journal of Germanic Linguistics.* Formerly (until 2000): *American Journal of Germanic Linguistics and Literatures.* [ISSN: 1470-5427] 1989. q. GBP 122. Ed(s): Robert W Murray. Cambridge University Press, The Edinburgh Bldg, Shaftesbury Rd, Cambridge, CB2 2RU, United Kingdom; information@cambridge.org; http://www.cup.cam.ac.uk/. Illus., index, adv. Sample. Refereed. Circ: 350. *Indexed:* L&LBA, LingAb, MLA-IB. *Bk. rev.:* 1-5, 4-6 pages. *Aud.:* Ac, Sa.

While this journal may only be of interest to institutions that offer German and linguistics majors, it targets general issues such as formal theory, sociolinguistics, and psycholinguistics. It is specifically concerned with the phonology, morphology, syntax, semantics, and historical development of "Germanic languages and dialects from the earliest phases to the present, including English (to 1500) and the extraterritorial varieties." Articles are usually published in English, but occasionally in German. Published by the Society for Germanic Linguistics (http://german.lss.wisc.edu/~sgl).

4067. *Journal of Linguistics.* [ISSN: 0022-2267] 1965. 3x/yr. GBP 137. Ed(s): Robert Borsley, Maggie Tallerman. Cambridge University Press, The Edinburgh Bldg, Shaftesbury Rd, Cambridge, CB2 2RU, United Kingdom; journals@cambridge.org; http://www.journals.cambridge.org. Illus., index, adv. Sample. Refereed. Vol. ends: Nov. Microform: PQC. Online: Pub.; EBSCO Publishing, EBSCO Host; OCLC Online Computer Library Center, Inc.; OhioLINK; SwetsWise Online Content. Reprint: PSC. *Indexed:* AbAn, AmHI, ArtHuCI, BAS, FR, HumInd, IBR, IBSS, IBZ, L&LBA, LT&LA, LingAb, MLA-IB, SSCI. *Bk. rev.:* 10-12, 3-6 pages. *Aud.:* Ac, Sa.

Journal of Linguistics aims to cover mainly theoretical linguistics and phonetics, as in the recent article, "Ing forms and the progressive puzzle: a construction-based approach to English progressives." Articles are written in English, but can cover other languages. For example, this article is not about English: "Case and word order in Lithuanian." Published for the Linguistics Association of Great Britain (www.lagb.org.uk), this journal is often cited in the literature and makes a good selection for basic linguistics collections because it covers the broad topic of linguistics.

4068. *Journal of Phonetics.* [ISSN: 0095-4470] 1973. 4x/yr. EUR 655. Ed(s): G. Docherty. Academic Press, Harcourt Pl, 32 Jamestown Rd, London, NW1 7BY, United Kingdom; apsubs@acad.com; http://www.elsevier.com/. Adv. Refereed. Reprint: PSC. *Indexed:* AbAn, ArtHuCI, BEL&L, IBR, IBSS, IBZ, L&LBA, LT&LA, LingAb, MLA-IB, PsycInfo, SSCI. *Bk. rev.:* 0-3, length varies. *Aud.:* Ac, Sa.

Journal of Phonetics is another core selection for linguistics collections because of phonetics' importance in the field of linguistics. Phonetics is the study of the sounds of human speech. A unique feature of the journal is that it publishes only manuscripts that are experimental or theoretical in nature. Generally, the journal's articles deal with the "phonetic aspects of language and linguistic communication processes." Specifically, this can include phonetics as it relates to speech production and acoustics, psycholinguistics, phonology, automated speech recognition and production, vocal fold functioning, and language acquisition. Recently, the journal published an article titled "Free classification of regional dialects of American English."

4069. Journal of Semantics. [ISSN: 0167-5133] 1982. q. EUR 249 print or online ed. Ed(s): Bart Geurts. Oxford University Press, Great Clarendon St, Oxford, OX2 6DP, United Kingdom; jnl.orders@oup.co.uk; http://www.oxfordjournals.org. Adv. Refereed. Circ: 530. Reprint: PSC. *Indexed:* AmHI, BEL&L, FR, HumInd, IBSS, L&LBA, LT&LA, LingAb, MLA-IB, PhilInd. *Bk. rev.:* 0-1, length varies. *Aud.:* Ac, Sa.

Natural language semantics is at the heart of this scholarly publication. Semantics is the study of meaning in language. This journal's scope extends beyond semantics, and is "explicitly interdisciplinary, in that it aims at an integration of philosophical, psychological, and linguistic semantics as well as semantic work done in logic, artificial intelligence, and anthropology." Only original research is accepted, "relating to questions of comprehension and interpretation of sentences, texts, or discourse in natural language." A recent article is titled "On the Semantics of Comparative Correlatives in Mandarin Chinese," illustrating the journal's international inclusiveness. *Journal of Semantics* is a core selection for basic and specialized academic linguistics collections because of its acceptance standards and because semantics is a major branch of linguistics.

Journal of Slavic Linguistics. See Slavic Studies section.

4070. Language and Education: an international journal. [ISSN: 0950-0782] 1987. q. will be 6/yr from 2003. EUR 559 print & online eds. (Individuals, EUR 99 print & online eds.). Ed(s): Viv Edwards. Multilingual Matters Ltd., Frankfurt Lodge, Clevedon Hall, Clevedon, BS21 7HH, United Kingdom; info@multilingual-matters.com; http://www.multilingual-matters.com. Illus., index, adv. Sample. Refereed. Online: EBSCO Publishing, EBSCO Host; Gale; SwetsWise Online Content. *Indexed:* BrEdI, ERIC, IBR, IBZ, L&LBA, LT&LA, LingAb. *Bk. rev.:* 1-4, 2-5 pages, signed. *Aud.:* Ac.

Topics such as team teaching and media literacy, combined with the study of language, comprise this journal. The content of *Language and Education* is two-fold; not only does it cover the curriculum, pedagogy, and evaluation aspects of education theory, it also includes "all aspects of mother tongue and second language education." To this end, two recent articles are "Writing in English in Malaysian High Schools" and "Teaching Children How to Use Language to Solve Math Problems." This journal, however, does not cover foreign-language teaching or English as a foreign language. Language specialists, especially those who are interested in the theory behind teaching it, would benefit from reading this journal. Although the journal has an international scope, most of its recent articles contain research from Australia and the United Kingdom. Two sample issues reviewed also contain one article from South Africa and one each from Hong Kong, Malaysia, and the United States. While *Language and Education* is a high-quality, peer-reviewed journal, its scope makes it a marginal purchase for most academic linguistics and education collections.

4071. Language and Literature. [ISSN: 0963-9470] 1992. q. GBP 392. Ed(s): Paul Simpson. Sage Publications Ltd., 1 Oliver's Yard, 55 City Rd, London, EC1 1SP, United Kingdom; info@sagepub.co.uk; http://www.sagepub.co.uk. Adv. Refereed. Circ: 800. Online: EBSCO Publishing, EBSCO Host; Gale; HighWire Press; OCLC Online Computer Library Center, Inc.; SAGE Publications, Inc., SAGE Journals Online; SwetsWise Online Content. Reprint: PSC. *Indexed:* CommAb, L&LBA, LingAb, MLA-IB, RILM. *Bk. rev.:* 1-4, 2-5 pages. *Aud.:* Ac.

The article "A stylistic analysis of Saul Bellow's *Herzog*: a mode of 'postmodern polyphony'" points to the overall goal of this journal: to publish research relevant to stylistics. Stylistics refers to the linguistic analysis of literature and related areas. The journal is the official publication of PALA (Poetics and Linguistics Association). PALA (www.pala.ac.uk) is based in the United Kingdom, but the journal has international coverage. One of its special topic issues focuses on foregrounding in poetics and linguistics. Specific areas

of research also include the connection between "stylistics, critical theory, linguistics and literary criticism, and their applications in teaching to native and non-native speaking students." Due to its quite specific focus, this journal is a supplementary purchase for most linguistics collections.

4072. Language in Society. [ISSN: 0047-4045] 1972. 5x/yr. GBP 196. Ed(s): Barbara Johnstone. Cambridge University Press, The Edinburgh Bldg, Shaftesbury Rd, Cambridge, CB2 2RU, United Kingdom; journals@cambridge.org; http://www.journals.cambridge.org. Illus., adv. Sample. Refereed. Vol. ends: Dec. Microform: PQC. Online: Pub.; EBSCO Publishing, EBSCO Host; OCLC Online Computer Library Center, Inc.; OhioLINK; SwetsWise Online Content. Reprint: PSC. *Indexed:* ASSIA, AbAn, AgeL, AmHI, AnthLit, ArtHuCI, BAS, BEL&L, BRI, BrEdI, CBRI, CommAb, EI, HumInd, IBR, IBSS, IBZ, L&LBA, LT&LA, LingAb, MLA-IB, PsycInfo, RILM, SSA, SSCI, SociolAb. *Bk. rev.:* 10-15, 2-4 pages, signed. *Aud.:* Ac.

Recent pieces about children's conversation, story initiation, ethnolect study, urban vernaculars, the word "elderly," retail encounters, metalinguistic labor, inquiry testimony, London adolescents, and Bible translation illustrate this journal's focus on "all branches of the study of speech and language as aspects of social life." Within this focus, preference is given to manuscripts that combine empirical studies with theory or methodological interest. A core journal in applied linguistics, *Language in Society* is recommended for all academic library collections for many reasons: It is heavily cited in linguistics literature; it is the premier journal for sociolinguistics; and it balances empirical studies with linguistic theory.

4073. Language Variation and Change. [ISSN: 0954-3945] 1989. 3x/yr. GBP 103. Ed(s): Anthony Kroch, William Labov. Cambridge University Press, The Edinburgh Bldg, Shaftesbury Rd, Cambridge, CB2 2RU, United Kingdom; journals@cambridge.org; http://www.journals.cambridge.org. Illus., adv. Sample. Refereed. Microform: PQC. Online: Pub.; EBSCO Publishing, EBSCO Host; OCLC Online Computer Library Center, Inc.; OhioLINK; SwetsWise Online Content. Reprint: PSC. *Indexed:* AnthLit, L&LBA, LT&LA, LingAb, MLA-IB. *Aud.:* Ac.

"'Mam, my trousers is fa'in doon!': Community, caregiver, and child in the acquisition of variation in a Scottish dialect" is a recent contribution to this journal, which has as its mission to publish work "dedicated to the description and understanding of variability and change at the levels of the speaker/hearer and the speech community." A prominent feature of the journal is that its articles contain quantitative language data that have been systematically analyzed. Libraries looking for an inexpensive supplement to general linguistics collections will want to consider this journal.

4074. Language (Washington). [ISSN: 0097-8507] 1925. q. USD 135 (Individuals, USD 75; Students, USD 30). Ed(s): Stanley Dubinsky, Brian D Joseph. Linguistic Society of America, 1325 18th St., N.W., Ste. 211, Washington, DC 20036; lsa@lsadc.org; http://www.lsadc.org. Illus., adv. Sample. Refereed. Circ: 6000 Paid. Vol. ends: Dec. Online: EBSCO Publishing, EBSCO Host; JSTOR (Web-based Journal Archive); OCLC Online Computer Library Center, Inc.; OhioLINK; Project MUSE; SwetsWise Online Content. Reprint: PSC. *Indexed:* ABS&EES, AICP, AmHI, AnthLit, ArtHuCI, BEL&L, FR, HumInd, IBR, IBSS, IBZ, IndIslam, L&LBA, LT&LA, LingAb, MLA-IB, PhilInd, SSCI. *Bk. rev.:* 5-9, 1-4 pages. *Aud.:* Ac.

Language, the journal of the Linguistic Society of America (LSA), is a primary example of a scholarly linguistics journal. If a library had to choose one journal to have for its linguistics collection, this is the one, because of its scope and how heavily cited it is in the linguistics literature. In general, the journal publishes technical articles on problems in linguistics science. Specifically, recent articles cover English binomials, Spanish verbs, properhood, evolutionary game theory and typology, and prefix ordering in the Chintang language. Letters to the editor, not usually featured in linguistics journals, serve as a space for commentary among linguistics researchers and practitioners. At least one author of each article must be a member of the LSA (www.lsadc.org). Highly recommended for academic linguistics collections of all sizes and scopes.

4075. Languages in Contrast: international journal for contrastive linguistics. [ISSN: 1387-6759] 1998. s-a. EUR 165 combined subscription print & online eds. Ed(s): Silvia Bernardini, Hilde Hasselgaard. John Benjamins Publishing Co., PO Box 36224, Amsterdam, 1020 ME, Netherlands; subscription@benjamins.nl; http://www.benjamins.com. *Indexed:* FR, IBR, IBZ, L&LBA, LingAb, MLA-IB. *Aud.:* Ac, Sa.

Contrastive studies of two or more languages prevail in this journal, but interdisciplinary studies are also welcome, "particularly those that make links between contrastive linguistics and translation, lexicography, computational linguistics, language teaching, literary and linguistic computing, literary studies and cultural studies." One recent article studies medical discourse in English/Spanish translation, while another focuses on combining clauses in English/French translation. All research articles are corpus based, meaning they gather data from a large set of texts. An article on British English and Mandarin Chinese uses both written and spoken corpora. In addition, any aspect of the languages can be covered: vocabulary, phonology, sociolinguistics, etc. A high-quality, supplemental purchase for most academic linguistics collections.

4076. Lingua. [ISSN: 0024-3841] 1947. 12x/yr. EUR 1093. Ed(s): J Rooryck. Elsevier BV, North-Holland, Sara Burgerhartstraat 25, Amsterdam, 1055 KV, Netherlands; nlinfo-f@elsevier.nl; http://www.elsevier.nl. Illus., index, adv. Sample. Refereed. Circ: 1078. Microform: PQC. Online: EBSCO Publishing, EBSCO Host; Gale; IngentaConnect; OhioLINK; ScienceDirect; SwetsWise Online Content. *Indexed:* AbAn, AmHI, ArtHuCI, BAS, EI, FR, IBR, IBZ, IndIslam, L&LBA, LT&LA, LingAb, MLA-IB, SSCI. *Bk. rev.:* 0-3, 5-10 pages. *Aud.:* Ac, Sa.

Lingua is an essential selection for both general and theoretical academic linguistics collections because of its general interest level and high citation rate. It covers problems in all areas of general linguistics, and publishes only articles of interest to all linguists regardless of their area of expertise. "Scientific quality and scholarly standing" are the two main criteria for publication. Recent contributions include "Observations on embedding verbs, evidentiality, and presupposition" and "The independence of phonology and morphology: The Celtic mutations." One volume is dedicated to the topic of sign language around the world. This journal also "has the facility to publish supplementary material online, for example, audio and video files."

4077. Linguistic Analysis. [ISSN: 0098-9053] 1975. 2x/yr. USD 134 (Individuals, USD 58). Ed(s): Michael K Brame. Linguistic Analysis, PO Box 2418, Vashon, WA 98070; Info@linguisticanlysis.com. Illus., index, adv. Sample. Refereed. Circ: 1000. Microform: PQC. *Indexed:* ABS&EES, AbAn, ArtHuCI, BAS, CompR, IBR, IBZ, LT&LA, LingAb, MLA-IB, SSCI. *Aud.:* Ac, Sa.

This journal's mission is to publish high-quality articles about formal phonology, morphology, syntax, and semantics. Recent interesting articles include "The Dynamics of Islands: Speculations on the locality of movement" and "Interpreting Uninterpretable Features." Occasional special double issues are published. For example, issues 1–2 and 3–4 for 2003 are comprised of two parts on "Dynamic Interfaces." *Linguistic Analysis* is a highly cited journal, and serves as a core journal for both general and theoretical linguistics. Consider for medium and large academic linguistics collections.

4078. Linguistic Inquiry. [ISSN: 0024-3892] 1970. q. USD 320 print & online eds. (Individuals, USD 68 print & online eds.). Ed(s): Samuel Jay Keyser. M I T Press, 238 Main St., Ste. 500, Cambridge, MA 02142; journals-info@mit.edu; http://mitpress.mit.edu. Illus., index, adv. Refereed. Circ: 3200. Microform: PQC. Online: EBSCO Publishing, EBSCO Host; Gale; IngentaConnect; OCLC Online Computer Library Center, Inc.; OhioLINK; Project MUSE; SwetsWise Online Content. Reprint: SCH. *Indexed:* ABS&EES, AbAn, ArtHuCI, BAS, FR, IBR, IBSS, IBZ, L&LBA, LT&LA, LingAb, MLA-IB, PhilInd, SSCI. *Aud.:* Ac.

The scope of this journal is international and theoretical, as evidenced in the recent article titled "V-Raising and Grammar Competition in Korean." Other recent topics are Mandarin Chinese, Polish, Russian, "Rightward Scrambling as Rightward Remnant Movement," and the "nature of long-distance anaphors." Its web site states that its mission is to cover "new theoretical developments based on the latest international discoveries." While *Linguistic Inquiry* is heavily cited and considered a core linguistics journal, it is most useful to experts in the field. Recommended as a supplementary purchase for academic collections.

4079. The Linguistic Review. [ISSN: 0167-6318] 1981. q. EUR 233; EUR 268 combined subscription print & online eds.; EUR 58 per issue. Ed(s): Harry van der Hulst. Mouton de Gruyter, Genthiner Str 13, Berlin, 10785, Germany; mouton@degruyter.de; http://www.degruyter.de. Illus., adv. Sample. Refereed. Reprint: PSC. *Indexed:* ArtHuCI, BAS, BEL&L, FR, IBR, IBSS, IBZ, L&LBA, LT&LA, LingAb, MLA-IB, PsycInfo. *Bk. rev.:* 0-1. *Aud.:* Ac.

The scope of this journal can best be described as theory of formal grammar, including syntax, semantics, phonology, and morphology. Formal grammar, or "generative grammar," is a set of rules that generate the expressions in a natural language. A second goal of the journal is to discuss theoretical linguistics as a branch of cognitive psychology, defined as the branch of psychology that examines mental processes such as problem solving, memory, and language. Some of the latest articles are "Another look at li placement in Bulgarian" and "Functional organization of speech across the life span: a critique of generative phonology." *The Linguistic Review* is recommended for most general academic linguistics collections because it is cited fairly often and because it contains good coverage of general and theoretical linguistics.

4080. Linguistics: an interdisciplinary journal of the language sciences. [ISSN: 0024-3949] 1963. bi-m. EUR 432; EUR 497 combined subscription print & online eds.; EUR 72 per issue. Ed(s): Johan van der Auwera. Mouton de Gruyter, Genthiner Str 13, Berlin, 10785, Germany; mouton@degruyter.de; http://www.degruyter.de. Illus., adv. Sample. Refereed. Microform: SWZ. Online: EBSCO Publishing, EBSCO Host; Florida Center for Library Automation; Gale; OCLC Online Computer Library Center, Inc.; SwetsWise Online Content. Reprint: PSC. *Indexed:* AbAn, AmHI, ArtHuCI, BAS, FR, HumInd, IBR, IBSS, IBZ, L&LBA, LT&LA, LingAb, MLA-IB, PsycInfo, RILM, SSCI. *Bk. rev.:* 3-4, 3-7 pages. *Aud.:* Ac.

Conventional linguistics disciplines, including pragmatics, semantics, syntax, morphology, phonology, encompass most of this journal's content. Related disciplines are included if they are "deemed to be of interest to linguists and other students of natural language." A traditional topic is covered in the recent article "Cognitive factors in the perception of Spanish stress placement: implications for a model of speech perception." "Dutch collective nouns and conceptual profiling" is another recent article. Overall, this journal covers linguistics, language acquisition, morphology, neurolinguistics, phonology, psycholinguistics, semantics, syntax, pragmatics, and phonetics. Many issues have thematic content. An essential purchase for academic linguistics collections.

4081. Linguistics and Philosophy: a journal of natural language syntax, semantics, logic, pragmatics, and processing. [ISSN: 0165-0157] 1977. bi-m. EUR 707 print & online eds. Ed(s): Pauline Jacobson. Springer Netherlands, Van Godewijckstraat 30, Dordrecht, 3311 GX, Netherlands; http://www.springeronline.com. Illus., index, adv. Sample. Refereed. Vol. ends: No. 6. Microform: PQC. Online: EBSCO Publishing, EBSCO Host; Gale; IngentaConnect; OCLC Online Computer Library Center, Inc.; OhioLINK; Springer LINK; SwetsWise Online Content. Reprint: PSC. *Indexed:* AmHI, ArtHuCI, FR, IBR, IBSS, IBZ, IPB, L&LBA, LT&LA, LingAb, MLA-IB, PhilInd, SSCI. *Aud.:* Ac, Sa.

Two concrete examples of the research published in this journal are the recent articles "The universal density of measurement" and "Vagueness and grammar: The semantics of relative and absolute gradable adjectives." The articles illustrate the journal's mission: to publish research and discussions of "structure and meaning in natural language, as addressed in the philosophy of language, linguistic semantics, syntax and related disciplines." More specific topics include the philosophical theories of meaning and truth, reference, description, entailment; theories of semantic interpretation; lexical semantics; psycholinguistic theories; and issues of the processing and acquisition of natural language. Subscribing to *Linguistics and Philosophy* is a good strategy for adding value to (or rounding out) an academic linguistics collection.

4082. *Modern Language Journal: devoted to research and discussion about the learning and teaching of foreign and second languages.* [ISSN: 0026-7902] 1916. q. GBP 119 print & online eds. Ed(s): Sally Sieloff Magnan. Blackwell Publishing, Inc., Commerce Place, 350 Main St, Malden, MA 02148; customerservices@blackwellpublishing.com; http://www.blackwellpublishing.com. Illus., index, adv. Refereed. Circ: 7000. Vol. ends: Dec. Microform: PMC; PQC. Online: Blackwell Synergy; EBSCO Publishing, EBSCO Host; Gale; IngentaConnect; JSTOR (Web-based Journal Archive); OCLC Online Computer Library Center, Inc.; OhioLINK; SwetsWise Online Content; H.W. Wilson. Reprint: PSC. *Indexed:* ABIn, ABS&EES, AmH&L, ApEcolAb, ArtHuCI, BEL&L, BRD, BRI, CBRI, ERIC, EduInd, IBR, IBZ, L&LBA, LT&LA, LingAb, MLA-IB, MRD, PsycInfo, SSCI. *Bk. rev.:* 20-30, 1-2 pages. *Aud.:* Hs, Ga, Ac.

MLJ is published for the National Federation of Modern Language Teachers Associations, whose mission is the "expansion, promotion, and improvement of the teaching of languages, literatures, and cultures throughout the United States." As a highly cited, comprehensive scholarly publication with a 10 percent acceptance rate, *MLJ* is a core selection for academic periodical collections. It contains articles, research studies, editorials, reports, book reviews, and professional news about modern languages, focusing on "research and discussion about the learning and teaching of foreign and second languages." In addition to articles such as "Negotiation of Meaning and Noticing in Text-Based Online Chat," the journal has sections on upcoming conferences, calls for papers, new degree programs, research projects, legislative news, and lists of relevant articles published in other journals. Considering the high-quality articles, commentary, discussion, and other features that add value, *MLJ* has a wealth of information about learning and teaching languages. See also *TESOL Quarterly; ELT Journal;* and *Studies in Second Language Acquisition.*

4083. *Morphology.* Formerly (until 2006): *Yearbook of Morphology.* [ISSN: 1871-5621] 1988. 2x/yr. EUR 161 print & online eds. Ed(s): Jaap van Marle, Geert Booij. Springer Netherlands, Van Godewijckstraat 30, Dordrecht, 3311 GX, Netherlands; http://www.springeronline.com. Refereed. Reprint: PSC. *Indexed:* BEL&L, L&LBA, MLA-IB. *Aud.:* Ac.

This journal was formerly titled *Yearbook of Morphology. Morphology* is the study of the structure or forms of words. While only one issue (2006) is posted online, the journal sounds promising and useful to linguists because of its content. Relevant to both theoretical linguistics and morphological theory, contents can include "grammatical descriptions, corpora of data concerning language use and other naturalistic data, and experiments; interaction of morphology with other areas of linguistics; nature of the mental lexicon; morphological variation and change; the range and limits of variation in natural languages; and the evolution and change of language." An article from its first issue is titled "Semitic Morphology: Root-based or word-based?" Because this is the only journal devoted to morphology, many academic libraries should consider it for their collections.

4084. *Natural Language and Linguistic Theory.* [ISSN: 0167-806X] 1983. q. EUR 764 print & online eds. Ed(s): Joan Maling. Springer Netherlands, Van Godewijckstraat 30, Dordrecht, 3311 GX, Netherlands; http://www.springeronline.com. Illus., adv. Sample. Refereed. Vol. ends: Nov. Microform: PQC. Online: Chadwyck-Healey Inc.; EBSCO Publishing, EBSCO Host; Gale; IngentaConnect; OCLC Online Computer Library Center, Inc.; OhioLINK; ProQuest LLC (Ann Arbor); Springer LINK; SwetsWise Online Content. Reprint: PSC. *Indexed:* AbAn, AmHI, ArtHuCI, BEL&L, CommAb, FR, IBR, IBZ, L&LBA, LT&LA, LingAb, MLA-IB, SSCI. *Bk. rev.:* 0-1, 5,000 words. *Aud.:* Ac.

"Strategies of Relativization in Italian Sign Language" is a recent article from this journal, whose mission is to bring together linguistic phenomena and theoretical research. The theoretical side of the journal's content presents articles on the syntax, semantics, phonology, and lexicon of the natural language. One of the journal's goals is to "encourage work which makes complex language data accessible to those unfamiliar with the language area being studied, and work which makes complex theoretical positions more accessible to those working outside the theoretical framework under review."

This goal is evident in the fact that they wish to publish articles that "facilitate accessibility for a graduate student readership." A supplemental purchase for academic linguistics collections.

4085. *Probus: international journal of Latin and Romance linguistics.* [ISSN: 0921-4771] 1989. s-a. EUR 182; EUR 209 combined subscription print & online eds.; EUR 91 newsstand/cover. Ed(s): W. Leo Wetzels. Mouton de Gruyter, Genthiner Str 13, Berlin, 10785, Germany; mouton@degruyter.de; http://www.degruyter.de. Adv. Refereed. Reprint: PSC. *Indexed:* AmHI, ArtHuCI, IBR, IBSS, IBZ, L&LBA, LingAb, MLA-IB. *Aud.:* Ac.

Probus contains "discussion of historical and synchronic research in the field of Latin and Romance linguistics, with special emphasis on phonology, morphology, syntax, lexicon and sociolinguistics." The journal's web site says it covers ideas, explanations, and solutions related to the Romance languages. One such solution is contained in the recent article titled "An analogical solution for Spanish soy, doy, voy, and estoy." An explanation is given in the article "The internal syntactic structure of relational adjectives." Another recent article, "On the licensing of overt subjects in Spanish infinitival clauses," discusses a linguistic idea. This journal is not an essential purchase for general linguistics collections, but it is a scholarly journal that should be considered for larger collections.

Scandinavian Studies. See Europe/General section.

Slavic and East European Journal. See Slavic Studies section.

4086. *Studies in Second Language Acquisition.* [ISSN: 0272-2631] 1977. q. GBP 145. Ed(s): Albert Valdman. Cambridge University Press, The Edinburgh Bldg, Shaftesbury Rd, Cambridge, CB2 2RU, United Kingdom; journals@cambridge.org; http://www.journals.cambridge.org. Illus., adv. Sample. Refereed. Vol. ends: Dec. Microform: PQC. Online: Pub.; EBSCO Publishing, EBSCO Host; OCLC Online Computer Library Center, Inc.; OhioLINK; SwetsWise Online Content. Reprint: PSC. *Indexed:* ABIn, BAS, EduInd, IBR, IBZ, L&LBA, LT&LA, LingAb, MLA-IB, PsycInfo, SSCI. *Bk. rev.:* 5-12, 1-2 pages. *Aud.:* Ac.

SSLA publishes mainly theory-based articles about issues related to second- and foreign-language acquisition of any language, and occasionally accepts "empirical investigations of the interface between SLA and language pedagogy." The journal welcomes all unsolicited submissions, but only 10–20 percent are accepted. In addition, thematic issues, point and counterpoint articles, responses, book reviews, and "state of the art" pieces are commissioned by the editors. A current special issue focuses on the acquisition of relative clauses and the noun phrase accessibility hierarchy, and an article from another issue is titled "Transitivity Alternations and Sequence Learning: Insights from L2 Spanish Production Data." Recommended for academic libraries with specializations in linguistics and teaching second and foreign languages. See also *ELT Journal; Modern Language Journal;* and *TESOL Quarterly.*

4087. *T E S O L Quarterly: a journal for teachers of English to speakers of other languages and of standard English as a second dialect.* [ISSN: 0039-8322] 1967. q. USD 360 (Individual members, USD 45). Ed(s): Suresh A Canagarajah. Teachers of English to Speakers of Other Languages, 700 S Washington St, Ste 200, Alexandria, VA 22314; tesol@tesol.edu; http://www.tesol.org. Illus., adv. Sample. Refereed. Circ: 12000. Vol. ends: Winter. Microform: PQC. Online: EBSCO Publishing, EBSCO Host; Gale; IngentaConnect. *Indexed:* ABIn, EAA, EduInd, IBR, IBZ, L&LBA, LT&LA, MLA-IB, SSCI. *Bk. rev.:* 4-6, 3-5 pages. *Aud.:* Hs, Ac, Sa.

This exceptional journal's mission, similar to TESOL's (www.tesol.org) organizational mission, is to "foster inquiry into the teaching and learning of English to speakers of other languages by providing a forum for TESOL professionals to share their research findings and explore the ideas and relationships within second language teaching and learning." TESOL produces professional standards, continuing education, student programs, and encourages communication among ESL professionals or English as a second dialect. *TESOL Quarterly*'s articles focus on combining theory and practice, thereby producing useful contributions for the readership. Topics include the psychology and sociology of language learning and language teaching, curriculum design, pedagogy, testing and evaluation, professional preparation/ standards, language planning, and research methodology. A recent article illustrates the journal's mission: "Teachers' and Learners' Reactions to a Task-Based EFL Course in Thailand." Special issues are published once per volume. In addition to the articles, readers learn about new research, research issues, teaching issues, and new books, and can read or contribute to commentary on related issues. This journal is recommended for high school libraries where ESL is important, and academic institutions supporting teacher education programs. See also *ELT Journal; Modern Language Journal;* and *Studies in Second Language Acquisition.*

Visible Language. See Printing and Graphic Arts section.

■ LITERARY REVIEWS

See also Fiction; Literature; Little Magazines; and News and Opinion sections.

Mary Beth Clack, Research Librarian, Widener Library, Harvard University, Cambridge, MA 02138; mclack@fas.harvard.edu.

Laura Farwell Blake, Research Librarian, Widener Library, Harvard University, Cambridge, MA 02138; farwell@fas.harvard.edu

Introduction

It continues to be a pleasure to read new work from familiar and emerging writers, discover new publications, and revel in well-known titles. We watch the emergence of new forms, as sites aggregate reviews and merge print with new media, and traditional literary reviews engage with their readers on the web. There is a wide range of voices, forms, media, and perspectives in this small set of titles.

We have included information on the web presences of journals, both those of long standing and those new to readers, since these digital editions are now integral to the reading of the literary public.

We stand by our statement in the last edition of *MFL*: The publications here all demand to be read and, in the case of some web publications, to be heard; these short stories, essays, poems, novellas, works of art, and thoughtful prose have the power to provoke, to inspire, to clarify, to create new forms of literary expression, and to exemplify the best of the traditional.

Basic Periodicals

Ga, Ac: *The Georgia Review, Hudson Review, The Iowa Review, The Kenyon Review, The North American Review, Ontario Review, The Paris Review, Prairie Schooner, Sewanee Review, TriQuarterly, Virginia Quarterly Review, Web del Sol, The Yale Review.*

Basic Abstracts and Indexes

American Humanities Index, Annual Bibliography of English Language and Literature, Humanities Index, Index of American Periodical Verse, MLA International Bibliography of Books and Articles on the Modern Languages and Literatures.

4088. *Agni.* Formerly (until 1988): Agni Review. [ISSN: 1046-218X] 1972. 2x/yr. USD 17 domestic; USD 20 Canada; USD 23 elsewhere. Ed(s): Sven Birkerts. Agni Review, Inc., 236 Bay State Rd, Boston, MA 02215-1403. Adv. Circ: 3000. *Indexed:* AmHI, HumInd, IAPV, MLA-IB. *Aud.:* Ga, Ac.

Agni's online edition features interviews and miscellany, as well as selections of poetry, short fiction, essays, art, and reviews from the print issues. The online archive of Essays/Reviews is extensive. International authors continue to be included, along with elegant *Editor's Notes* by Sven Birkerts.

4089. *Alaska Quarterly Review.* [ISSN: 0737-268X] 1982. s-a. USD 10 domestic; USD 14 foreign. Ed(s): Ronald Spatz. University of Alaska at Anchorage, College of Arts and Sciences, 3211 Providence Dr, Anchorage, AK 99508; AYAQR@uaa.alaska.edu; http://www.uaa.alaska.edu/aqr/. Illus. Circ: 2200. Vol. ends: Fall/Winter. Microform: PQC. *Indexed:* AmHI. *Aud.:* Ga, Ac.

"Contemporary literary art" in fiction, short plays, poetry, and nonfiction in traditional and experimental styles is presented in this journal. The strong sense of the "True North" in its pages, emphasizing Alaskan subjects and motifs, come alive in the recent issue on "Hidden Alaska: Poetry & Prose." Thirty-three Alaskan writers are featured. Editor Ronald Spatz looks for "freshness, honesty, and a compelling subject" in selecting works for inclusion in *AQR.*

4090. *Antioch Review.* [ISSN: 0003-5769] 1941. q. USD 76 (Individuals, USD 40; USD 8 newsstand/cover per issue domestic). Ed(s): Robert S Fogarty. Antioch Review, Inc., PO Box 148, Yellow Springs, OH 45387; review@antioch.edu. Illus., index, adv. Circ: 3000. Vol. ends: Fall. Microform: MIM; PMC; PQC. Online: Chadwyck-Healey Inc.; EBSCO Publishing, EBSCO Host; Florida Center for Library Automation; Gale; Northern Light Technology, Inc.; OCLC Online Computer Library Center, Inc.; ProQuest K-12 Learning Solutions; ProQuest LLC (Ann Arbor); H.W. Wilson. *Indexed:* ABS&EES, AgeL, AmH&L, AmHI, ArtHuCI, BAS, BRD, BRI, CBRI, FLI, HistAb, HumInd, IAPV, IBR, IBZ, MLA-IB, PAIS, PhilInd, RILM, SFSA, SSCI. *Bk. rev.:* 15-30, 300 words. *Aud.:* Ga, Ac.

The *Antioch Review,* now in its 67th year, takes pride in being one of the oldest continuously published literary reviews in the United States. Its advisory board is notably distinguished, and currently includes Daniel Bell, T. Coraghessan Boyle, Gordon Lish, and Mark Strand, among others. In recent years, the review has increased the amount of space devoted to poetry and reviews, in addition to essays of remarkable cogency and timeliness. In addition to its blockbuster theme issue on jazz, special issues on poetry and new writing across the genres have been featured. As Gordon Lish observed, the review "freely serves the mind and heart of the free reader."

4091. *Artful Dodge.* [ISSN: 0196-691X] 1979. s-a. USD 20 (Individuals, USD 14). Ed(s): Daniel Bourne. Artful Dodge Publications, Department of English, The College of Wooster, Wooster, OH 44691; http://www.cais.com/gesir/viction/ardodge. Illus., adv. Circ: 1000. *Indexed:* AmHI, IAPV. *Bk. rev.:* Number and length vary. *Aud.:* Ga, Ac.

Ohio-based literary magazine *Artful Dodge* is supported by the Ohio Arts Council and offers a wide selection of American literature. The editors also look for contributions from outside the United States and have an abiding interest in translation, especially from Eastern Europe and Third World. Regularly featured are poets in tranlation, along with special sections on subjects such as poetry from the Polish underground and the Middle East. The web site has links to poets as translators, poets as expatriates, past selections, interviews, making introductions, and forged letters.

4092. *Bellevue Literary Review: a journal of humanity and human experience.* [ISSN: 1537-5048] 2001. s-a. USD 18 (Individuals, USD 12). Ed(s): Dr. Danielle Ofri. New York University School of Medicine, 550 First Ave, New York, NY 10016. *Indexed:* AmHI, IAPV. *Aud.:* Ga, Ac.

Emanating from Bellevue Hospital and New York University's Department of Medicine, the *Bellevue Literary Review* is a "journal of humanity and human experience." Since its inception in 2000, submissions of fiction, creative nonfiction, poetry, and critical essays have risen steadily. *JAMA* called the review a "kaleidoscope of creativity contained within a theme that concerns the general reader but which also informs the minds of patients and healers." Its acclaimed editorial staff includes Editor-in-Chief Danielle Ofri, whose work has been featured in the Poetry Foundation's archive.

4093. *The Blue Moon Review.* 1994. irreg. Ed(s): Doug Lawson. The Blue Moon Review, http://thebluemoon.com. *Aud.:* Ga, Ac.

Fiction, poetry, commentary, essays, and creative nonfiction, both in text and audio, are accompanied by a "Workshop" and "Cafe Blue" in this online journal. The workshop and cafe provide a forum and a discussion list, respectively. The fiction and poetry are a mixed bag in interest, content, and style; much is by very new writers. There are some interesting uses of hypertext within the context of traditional narrative.

4094. *Boulevard: journal of contemporary writing.* [ISSN: 0885-9337] 1986. 3x/yr. USD 15; USD 8 newsstand/cover per issue; USD 21 foreign. Ed(s): Richard Burgin. St. Louis University, St. Louis, MO 63108-2103. Illus., adv. Sample. Circ: 4000. Online: EBSCO Publishing, EBSCO Host. *Indexed:* AmHI, IAPV. *Aud.:* Ga, Ac.

Published at St. Louis University, *Boulevard*'s innovative contributions include short fiction, criticism, essays, poetry, and artwork. The review often includes special sections on such topics. Most recently, two special sections were featured: a symposium on the current status and value of literary awards and prizes (Spring 2007) and a symposium on reviewing contemporary literature (Fall 2006). This journal's illustrious board includes Francine Prose, James Tate, and David Mamet. Found in its pages is the work of Alice Adams, John Ashbery, John Barth, Ann Beattie, Robert Bly, Donald Hall, Philip Levine, David Mamet, Joyce Carol Oates, Francine Prose, and other notables.

4095. *Brick: a literary journal.* [ISSN: 0382-8565] 1977. 3x/yr. Individuals, CND 38; CND 12 per issue domestic. Ed(s): Michael Redhill. Brick, P O Box 537, Toronto, ON M4T 2M5, Canada. Illus. Circ: 1200. *Indexed:* CBCARef, CPerI. *Bk. rev.:* Number and length vary. *Aud.:* Ga, Ac.

Brick incorporates some of the finest and freshest writing published today, including essays, letters, interviews, and photos along with the usual literary fare of fiction, poetry, and essays. Ariel Dorfman's characterization of this established Canadian review is found on its web site: "so many adventuresome and courageous incursions and crossings of another sort, into stories and thoughts and poems that one could find nowhere else. This is a brick that needs to be heaved right through the windows of every reading mind on the continent." It is acclaimed by critics for its humor, clarity, flair, and international scope, and recent authors have included Carolyn Forche, Vikram Seth, Oliver Sacks, Leonard Cohen, and Toni Morrison. Touching portraits of Jan Morris and John Fante appear in a recent issue.

Canadian Fiction. See Fiction: General/Mystery and Detective/General section.

4096. *Chicago Review.* [ISSN: 0009-3696] 1946. q. USD 18 domestic; USD 28 in Canada & Mexico; USD 38 elsewhere. Ed(s): Eirik Steinhoff. Chicago Review, 5801 S Kenwood Ave, Chicago, IL 60637-1794; org_crev@orgmail.uchicago.edu. Illus., adv. Refereed. Circ: 2800 Paid. Microform: PQC. Online: Chadwyck-Healey Inc.; EBSCO Publishing, EBSCO Host; Factiva, Inc.; Florida Center for Library Automation; Gale; Northern Light Technology, Inc.; OCLC Online Computer Library Center, Inc.; ProQuest K-12 Learning Solutions; ProQuest LLC (Ann Arbor); H.W. Wilson. *Indexed:* ABS&EES, AmHI, ArtHuCI, BAS, HumInd, IAPV, MLA-IB, RILM. *Bk. rev.:* 4-9, 2-6 pages, signed. *Aud.:* Ga, Ac.

The *Chicago Review* includes fiction, poetry, essays, criticism, and photography. In keeping with its intent to be an "international journal of writing and cultural exchange," the review features poetry and prose in a wide variety of countries and works not represented in English translations. Special issues are particularly rich in content. The British poetry issue appeared in Spring 2007, and the 60th anniversary issue (Autumn 2006) was devoted to "Kenneth Rexroth: A Centenary Portfolio." The web edition's online archives include memoirs by the staff and selections from 1946 onward.

4097. *Colorado Review: a journal of contemporary literature.* Formerly (until 1965): *Colorado State Review.* [ISSN: 1046-3348] 1955. 3x/yr. USD 34 (Individuals, USD 24). Ed(s): Stephanie G'Schwind. Colorado State University, English Department, Colorado Review, Fort Collins, CO 80523; creview@colostate.edu; http://coloradoreview.colostate.edu. Adv. Circ: 1500. *Indexed:* AmHI, IAPV. *Bk. rev.:* Number and length vary. *Aud.:* Ga, Ac, Sa.

Hailing from the Center for Literary Publishing at Colorado State University, the *Colorado Review* is committed to publishing serious poetry, fiction, and nonfiction. The review is eclectic, including new writing and a diverse group of writers, with more fiction and creative nonfiction accompanied by poetry, interviews, and book reviews. Aiming to provide a greater literary awareness in Colorado and beyond, and to promote new writers, the center is staffed with interns who are graduate students from its creative writing program.

4098. *Conjunctions.* [ISSN: 0278-2324] 1981. s-a. USD 18 domestic; USD 25 foreign. Ed(s): Bradford Morrow. Bard College, Publication Department, PO Box 5000, Annandale On Hudson, NY 12504-5000; http://www.conjunctions.com. Adv. Circ: 7500. *Indexed:* AmHI, IAPV, RILM. *Aud.:* Ga, Ac.

Conjunctions' collaborative editorial process selects "writers and artists whose work challenges accepted forms and modes of expression, experiments with language and thought, and is fully realized art." The skillfully designed electronic version of the journal presents a "living notebook" of innovative fiction, poetry, criticism, drama, art, and interviews. The web site is searchable and includes an author index for issues 1–47. *Web Conjunctions* includes frequent updates (often several per month) and special online supplements.

4099. *The Cortland Review: an online literary magazine.* [ISSN: 1524-6744] 1997. q. Free. Ed(s): Guy Shahar. Cortland Review, 527 Third Ave #279, New York, NY 10016. *Aud.:* Ga, Ac.

Subtitled "an online literary magazine in Real Audio," *The Cortland Review* has included recorded poetry and fiction, and the site now features an audio host on the homepage. Innovative features accompany the regular issues. Topics have included "A Manifesto on the Contemporary Sonnet," "Language-driven poetry," and "Stephen Dobyns on Poetry" for National Poetry Month. Essays and reviews round out each new issue. The site gives news and book recommendations. Full text and audio are available for all issues since Issue 3, and all features since March 1998.

4100. *Critical Quarterly.* [ISSN: 0011-1562] 1959. q. GBP 190 print & online eds. Ed(s): Colin MacCabe. Blackwell Publishing Ltd., 9600 Garsington Rd, Oxford, OX4 2ZG, United Kingdom; customerservices@blackwellpublishing.com; http://www.blackwellpublishing.com. Illus., adv. Sample. Refereed. Circ: 2200. Vol. ends: Dec. Online: Blackwell Synergy; EBSCO Publishing, EBSCO Host; Gale; IngentaConnect; OCLC Online Computer Library Center, Inc.; OhioLINK; SwetsWise Online Content. Reprint: PSC. *Indexed:* AmHI, ApEcolAb, ArtHuCI, BEL&L, BRI, BrHumI, CBRI, FLI, HumInd, IBR, IBZ, L&LBA, LRI, MLA-IB, RI-1, RILM, SSA, SSCI, SociolAb. *Aud.:* Ga, Ac.

Critical Quarterly provides a forum for contemporary poetry, fiction, and criticism and a full range of cultural forms, from commentary on the literary canon to debate and discussion of cinema, television, and other aspects of cultural life and studies. At the forefront of literary discourse, this influential journal recently began discussing the possibility of a "new Philology," examining, in editor Colin MacCabe's words, "questions of genre, register, stereotype and audience [that] develop what is understood as the material of language" (Spring 2007). Each issue also includes a regular section on current issues in language, education, and politics. Stanley Fish, Malcolm Bradbury, A. S. Byatt, Anthony Smith, and Cornel West have been counted among its illustrious contributors.

4101. *The Dalhousie Review: a Canadian journal of literature and opinion.* [ISSN: 0011-5827] 1921. 3x/yr. CND 33.50 (Individuals, CND 22.50). Ed(s): Ronald Huebert. Dalhousie University Press, Ltd., Dalhousie University, Halifax, NS B3H 3J5, Canada. Illus., index, adv. Refereed. Circ: 800. Vol. ends: Winter. Microform: MML. *Indexed:* ABS&EES, AmH&L, AmHI, ArtHuCI, BAS, BEL&L, BRI, CBCARef, CBRI, CPerI, HistAb, HumInd, IBR, MLA-IB, PAIS, PhilInd, RILM, SSCI. *Bk. rev.:* 2-8, 2-3 pages signed. *Aud.:* Ga, Ac.

An important and established Canadian literary journal, *The Dalhousie Review* regularly presents fiction, poetry, essays, and book reviews. An increasing number of short stories have been published recently that reflect the growth in genre submissions and the vitality of creative writing programs. The review is known for its treatment of a wide range of intellectual interests and for a scholarly orientation. Recent themes include location and rooting in a place or culture, featuring "located stories" of assimilation and the immigrant experience. In the past few years, the journal has been redesigned to give it a more contemporary look, including cover motifs that suggest the diverse "windows" of intellectual observation.

4102. Denver Quarterly. Formerly (until 1976): *The University of Denver Quarterly.* [ISSN: 0011-8869] 1966. q. USD 29 (Individuals, USD 20; USD 6 per issue). Ed(s): Bin Ramke. University of Denver, Department of English, 2000 E. Ashbury, Denver, CO 80208; kkelsey@du.edu; http://www.ud.edu/. Illus., index, adv. Circ: 1500. Vol. ends: Dec. Microform: PQC. *Indexed:* AmHI, IAPV, IBR, IBZ, MLA-IB. *Bk. rev.:* 0-3, 3-13 pages, signed. *Aud.:* Ga, Ac.

The *Denver Quarterly* is housed at the University of Denver's Department of English, and its editors publish new and experimental forms of literature. Reflecting the editors' interests, many prose-poetry offerings are included. Reviews and interviews appear along with translations, which are held in high esteem by the review as an "art form in itself." Featured recently has been the work of Srikanth Reddy, Peter Grandbois on Juan Goytisolo, and Rene Char translated by Nancy Naomi Carlson.

4103. DoubleTake. [ISSN: 1080-7241] 1995. q. USD 32 domestic; USD 42 Canada; USD 47 elsewhere. Ed(s): Randy Testa, Robert Coles. Doubletake Community Service Corp, 55 Davis Sq, Somerville, MA 02144-2908; dtmag@doubletakemagazine.org; http://www.doubletakemagazine.org. Illus., adv. Circ: 45000 Paid. Vol. ends: Fall. *Indexed:* RGPR. *Bk. rev.:* 3-5, 2-3 pages, signed. *Aud.:* Ga, Ac.

DoubleTake radiates energy, containing a mix of fiction, poetry, essays, and photography. The editors describe much of the content as accounts of "what it means to have a life in a particular place and time." Highlighting events of the times, articles have focused on women in prison, with penetrating photographs, narratives, diary entries, and letters describing women's experiences of life in prison, with interviews included. The web site has been expanded to include more initiatives in the education section (including the participation of Robert Coles and Ken Burns in the Summer Documentary Institute) and an online archive. The "Classroom Companion" section continues to be very useful for secondary-education applications, presenting units of study and creative ways to use *DoubleTake*'s articles to enhance high school curricula. Themes include a sense of place, work in America, a sense of identity, and political ideology. The site also gives suggestions for activities that develop students' problem solving, creative writing, and visual literacy skills in each of these areas.

4104. Evergreen Review (Online Edition). Formerly (until 1984): *Evergreen Review (Print Edition).* 1957. irreg. Free. Ed(s): Barney Rosset. Evergreen Review, 61 Fourth Ave, New York, NY 10003; http://www.evergreenreview.com. Illus. *Bk. rev.:* 1-2, 300-500 words, signed. *Aud.:* Ga, Ac.

This is the digital child of the venerated counterculture journal of the same title founded by Barney Rosset. It is as important a contribution as the print journal was, and it maintains the attitude of its print parent while it uses technology to full effect, featuring photo and textual essays, video articles, and "hyperfiction," as well as traditional fiction, satire, and prose-poetry. Memoirs and a photo gallery have appeared in recent issues. Notably, original reviews from number 1 to number 20 (1957—1961) are available for download from the web site.

4105. Exquisite Corpse: a journal of letters and life. Formerly (until 1997): *Exquisite Corpse (Print).* 1981. 6x/yr. USD 30; USD 5 newsstand/cover per issue. Exquisite Corpse, c/o Andrei Codrescu, PO Box 25051, Baton Rouge, LA 70894; http://www.corpse.org. Illus. Refereed. Circ: 3500 Paid. *Aud.:* Ga, Ac.

This lively, witty, and interestingly edgy journal is edited by Andrei Codrescu. It has an international scope and feel and publishes multimedia works. Also provided here are poetry, fiction, reviews, serials, commentary on culture, literature, performance, opinion pieces on public affairs, and online communities (including the "Corpse Cafe'").

4106. Fence. [ISSN: 1097-9980] 1998. s-a. USD 17; USD 10 per issue. Ed(s): Rebecca Wolff. Fence Magazine, Inc., 14 Fifth Ave, 1A, New York, NY 10011. Adv. Circ: 12000. *Aud.:* Ga, Ac.

Fence's stated goal is to publish work by "fence-sitters," and to explore the boundaries between experiment and tradition, and between countries and languages and social strata. Its contents include poetry, fiction, nonfiction, photographs, original artwork, and recent essays on cinema verite. It has weathered adversity in its first nine years, but its editor, Rebecca Wolff, has persevered, and *Fence* continues to publish idiosyncratic and eccentric voices in the literary field. The web site features current and back issues, selected full text, and an events section.

Fiction. See Fiction: General/Mystery and Detective/General section.

4107. Field: contemporary poetry and poetics. [ISSN: 0015-0657] 1969. s-a. USD 14. Ed(s): David Young, Martha Collins. Oberlin College Press, 50 N Professor St, Oberlin, OH 44074; oc.press@oberlin.edu; http://www.oberlin.edu/ocpress/. Adv. Circ: 1500 Paid. Microform: PQC. *Indexed:* ABS&EES, AmHI, BEL&L, IAPV, MLA-IB. *Bk. rev.:* Number and length vary. *Aud.:* Ac, Sa.

Published by the Oberlin College Press, *Field* is dedicated to contemporary poetry and poetics, with fiction, essays, poetry, and book reviews gracing its pages. Regular symposia are dedicated to close readings of the work of Hart Crane, Jean Valentine, and Paul Celan. The review features notable translations, with writers such as Sor Juana Inez de la Cruz, Tomaz Salamun, Tomas Transtromer, Venus Khoury-Ghata, and Luciano Erba.

4108. Fulcrum (Cambridge): an annual of poetry and aesthetics. [ISSN: 1534-7877] 2002. a. USD 42. Ed(s): Katia Kapovich, Philip Nikolayev. Fulcrum Poetry Press, Inc., 33 Harvard St, Ste D-2, Cambridge, MA 02139. *Aud.:* Ga, Ac.

Launched in 2002, *Fulcrum* is an international annual that presents poetry; critical and philosophical essays on poetry; debates; and visual art. Hailed as hospitable to a range of poetic practices and a wider range of philosophical interests than most poetry journals, this review is fresh, exciting, and promising. Its mission is to generate a "greater self-knowledge gained from genuine conversations across geographical and aesthetic space." The recent issue hosts translations and theme essays on "Poets and Philosophers," interspersed with the poetic offerings. A special section is devoted to "Poetry & Harvard in the 1920s," providing an interesting historical perspective.

4109. The Georgia Review. [ISSN: 0016-8386] 1947. q. USD 24 domestic; USD 30 foreign. Ed(s): T R Hummer. University of Georgia, Georgia Review, Athens, GA 30602-9009; http://www.ugd.edu/garev. Illus., index, adv. Sample. Circ: 5000. Vol. ends: Winter. Microform: PQC. *Indexed:* AmH&L, AmHI, ArtHuCI, BEL&L, BRI, CBRI, FLI, HistAb, HumInd, IAPV, IBR, IBZ, MLA-IB, PhilInd, RILM. *Bk. rev.:* 4-11, 1-25 pages, signed. *Aud.:* Ga, Ac.

The renowned *Georgia Review,* winner of a 2007 Georgia Governor's Award in the Humanities, is an eclectic mix of essays, fiction, drama, poetry, art, and color photography. Book reviews and book briefs appear in each issue. To commemorate the seminal contributions of long-time editor Stanley W. Lindberg, the Spring 2007 issue includes "The Commerce between Us: Correspondence from the Archives of the *Georgia Review,* 1977-2000." In the Fall/Winter 2006 issue, the 1947–76 archives were similarly published. Work by Philip Levine, Wole Soyinka, Rita Dove, and John Updike has been featured. The web site now has news, the *GR* blog, and two complete indexes (by author and by issue).

4110. The Gettysburg Review. [ISSN: 0898-4557] 1988. q. USD 24 domestic; USD 32 foreign; USD 7 per issue. Ed(s): Kim Dana Kupperman, Peter Stitt. Gettysburg College, 300 N Washington St, Gettysburg, PA 17325-1491; http://www.gettysburg.edu. Illus., index, adv. Circ: 4500 Paid. Vol. ends: Winter. *Indexed:* AmH&L, AmHI, HistAb, HumInd, IAPV, MLA-IB, RILM. *Aud.:* Ga, Ac.

The Gettysburg Review is known for its award-winning fiction, poetry, essays, and essay-reviews, and for capturing numerous design awards for the impact of its graphics and artwork. Paintings are showcased in each issue. The award-winning critic of contemporary literature, Peter Stitt, continues to edit the review. Charles Simic, D.R. Cruikshank, Donald Hall, Robert Bly, and Billy Collins have had their work appear in recent issues. The web site has been more fully developed to include current selections, contents for some back issues, and news on authors and awards.

4111. The Harvard Review. [ISSN: 1077-2901] 1992. s-a. USD 24 (Individuals, USD 16). Ed(s): Christina Thompson. Harvard University, Lamont Library, Cambridge, MA 02138; http://www.hcs.harvard.edu. Illus., adv. Circ: 3000 Paid. *Indexed:* ABS&EES, AmHI, BRD, HumInd, IAPV, MLA-IB. *Bk. rev.:* Number and length vary. *Aud.:* Ga, Ac.

Published at Harvard University, The Harvard Review presents two hefty tomes per year of poetry, fiction, nonfiction, and a substantial book review section, along with memoirs, visual arts, drama, translations, and graphics. Under the editorship of Christina Thompson, the *Review* has continued to offer the work of newer writers and a mix of styles and traditions. Its lively cover designs were featured in the AIGA BoNE (Best of New England) Show in summer 2007. Its web site now publishes news, accolades of note, and links to the "Harvard Review in the Press."

4112. Hudson Review: a magazine of literature and the arts. [ISSN: 0018-702X] 1948. q. USD 38 (Individuals, USD 32; USD 9 newsstand/ cover). Ed(s): Paula Deitz. Hudson Review, Inc., 684 Park Ave, New York, NY 10021; hudsonreview@erols.com. Illus., index, adv. Circ: 4500. Vol. ends: Winter. Microform: MIM; PQC. Online: Chadwyck-Healey Inc.; EBSCO Publishing, EBSCO Host; Factiva, Inc.; OCLC Online Computer Library Center, Inc.; ProQuest LLC (Ann Arbor); H.W. Wilson. *Indexed:* ABS&EES, AmHI, ArtHuCI, BAS, BRI, CBRI, FLI, HumInd, IAPV, IBR, IBZ, MLA-IB, RILM. *Bk. rev.:* 5-7, 2-11 pages, signed. *Aud.:* Ga, Ac.

Marking its 58th year in 2007, Hudson Review offers essays, memoirs, fiction, poetry, and reviews. With an emphasis on the arts, the review's signature "Chronicles" section explores current film, theater, art, music, and dance in depth. To commemorate its 55th anniversary year, the *Review* published a companion CD with poets reading works from the review's inception. The web site includes a page with links to prominent essays and poems (audio) titled "Hudson Review Poets and Critics Online."

4113. The Iowa Review. [ISSN: 0021-065X] 1970. 3x/yr. Individuals, USD 20. Ed(s): Mary Hussman, David Hamilton. University of Iowa, Department of English, English-Philosophy Bldg, Iowa City, IA 52242-1492; english@uiowa.edu; http://www.iowa.edu/. Illus., index, adv. Circ: 1500. Microform: PQC. Online: Chadwyck-Healey Inc. *Indexed:* ABS&EES, ASIP, AmHI, BEL&L, HumInd, IAPV, ILP, MLA-IB, RILM. *Bk. rev.:* 2, 2-4 pages, signed. *Aud.:* Ga, Ac.

Described by one of its readers as "stately and experimental," The Iowa Review's mission has been "nudging along American literature" by presenting new and compelling writers to a larger audience. It publishes fiction, essays, interviews, poems, reviews, and the Human Rights Index. Recent special issues include the "Sound Issue" and "Place & Space in New Media." The print review is complemented by TIR Web, in which electronic literature and other varieties of experimental writing and art are hosted. Redesigned in 2005, the web site adds new work every three months.

4114. Jacket: international poetry and prose magazine. [ISSN: 1440-4737] 1997. 3x/yr. Ed(s): John Tranter. Australian Literary Management, 2-A Booth St, Balmain, NSW 2041, Australia. *Aud.:* Ga, Ac, Sa.

Called an "Internet cafe for postmodernists" by *Time* magazine, *Jacket* is lively and inventive, hosting new writing, and with poetry, creative prose, interviews, reviews, and informative feature articles. The site explains that the site is actively constructed: current numbers are posted piece by piece until full, and future issues are posted as works-in-progress. Most of the pieces are original, but occasionally material is excerpted from "hard-to-get books or magazines" to increase these publications' readership. The site is searchable by keyword and also contains links to over 500 book reviews. Readers may request a text-only newsletter of news and announcements that appears about six times a year.

4115. Jewish Quarterly. [ISSN: 0449-010X] 1953. q. GBP 25 in Europe; GBP 35 elsewhere. Ed(s): Matthew Reisz. Jewish Literary Trust Ltd., PO Box 35042, London, NW1 7XH, United Kingdom; http://www.jewishquarterly.org/. Illus., index, adv. Circ: 3000 Controlled. Microform: PQC. *Indexed:* IBR, IJP, RILM. *Aud.:* Ga, Ac.

Highly praised in Europe, the lively Jewish Quarterly includes fiction, nonfiction, art, and letters from its active readership, along with poetry, interviews, and memoirs. There is increasing emphasis on the visual arts, literature, and cinema. Its "Regulars" section features lively commentary from Sasha Frieze, Corinne Pearlman, Vivian Eden, and David Katz, among others. Recently, the review's pages have treated the renewed conflict between religion and science, the war in Lebanon, Israeli politics and culture, the condition of French Jews today, and other international topics. The web site presents full text for several back years.

4116. The Kenyon Review: an international journal of literature, culture, and the arts. [ISSN: 0163-075X] 1939. q. USD 35 (Individuals, USD 30). Ed(s): Meg Galipault, David H Lynn. The Kenyon Review, Walton House, Kenyon College, Gambier, OH 43022-9623; http://www.kenyon.edu. Illus., index, adv. Refereed. Circ: 5000 Paid. Online: Chadwyck-Healey Inc.; EBSCO Publishing, EBSCO Host; Gale; Northern Light Technology, Inc.; OCLC Online Computer Library Center, Inc.; ProQuest K-12 Learning Solutions; ProQuest LLC (Ann Arbor); H.W. Wilson. *Indexed:* AmHI, ArtHuCI, BRD, BRI, CBRI, HumInd, IAPV, IBR, IBZ, MLA-IB, PhilInd, RILM. *Bk. rev.:* 1-2, 7-11 pages, signed. *Aud.:* Ga, Ac.

Founded by influential critic and poet John Crowe Ransom, The Kenyon Review has had a reputation for high-quality writing and has recently featured work by Roger Rosenblatt, T.C. Boyle, Jay Parini, Lawrence Joseph, and Joyce Carol Oates. As a result of a recent editorial decision, fewer special or thematically defined issues will be published, in the interest of offering more of the best in new writing. Redesign of the print edition a few years ago, including stunning cover photographs, has been complemented by a redesign of the web site. The handsome site's news, readings, and literary links sections are joined by podcasts, the newest of which is an interview with Ian MacEwan, recipient of the journal's award for literary achievement. Other podcasts offer readings by Rebecca McClanahan, Brad Kessler, and David Goodwillie, as well as interviews with Jason Schneiderman, Fiona McCrae, Mark Strand, and Dana Roeser.

4117. The Literary Review: an international journal of contemporary writing. [ISSN: 0024-4589] 1957. q. USD 18 domestic; USD 21 foreign. Ed(s): Walter Cummins. Fairleigh Dickinson University, Literary Review, 285 Madison Ave, Madison, NJ 07940. Refereed. Circ: 2000 Paid and free. Microform: MIM; PQC. Online: Chadwyck-Healey Inc.; EBSCO Publishing, EBSCO Host; Florida Center for Library Automation; Gale; Northern Light Technology, Inc.; OCLC Online Computer Library Center, Inc.; ProQuest K-12 Learning Solutions; ProQuest LLC (Ann Arbor); H.W. Wilson. *Indexed:* ABS&EES, AmHI, ArtHuCI, HumInd, IAPV, IBR, IBZ, MASUSE, MLA-IB, RILM. *Bk. rev.:* 4-5. *Aud.:* Ga, Ac.

TLR, as it is known, publishes fiction, poetry, essays on contemporary literature, and reviews from writers around the globe. The editors note that "preference is given to essays and reviews on authors who have not received wide coverage in other magazines. We are especially interested in introducing writers from many nations to our readers." The Fall 2006 50th-anniversary issue presents the winners of the competitive PEN translation Fund Grants, with an elegant lead article by Robert Pinsky on the values and perils of translation. The web site,

TLR Web, has been redesigned, offering "Editors' Choice" reviews, the "Writer's Choice" feature highlighting proising new talent, a listing of international issues, web chapbooks, and material added on an ongoing basis, supplementing the print review.

Manoa. See Little Magazines section.

4118. *Massachusetts Review: a quarterly of literature, arts and public affairs.* [ISSN: 0025-4878] 1959. q. USD 30 (Individuals, USD 22; USD 9 per issue). Ed(s): Corwin Dore Ericson, David Lenson. Massachusetts Review, Inc., South College, University of Massachusetts, Amherst, MA 01003. Illus., index, adv. Refereed. Circ: 1500. Microform: PQC. Online: Chadwyck-Healey Inc.; EBSCO Publishing, EBSCO Host; Northern Light Technology, Inc.; OCLC Online Computer Library Center, Inc.; ProQuest LLC (Ann Arbor); H.W. Wilson. *Indexed:* ABS&EES, AmH&L, AmHI, ArtHuCI, FLI, HistAb, HumInd, IAPV, IBR, MLA-IB, PhilInd, RI-1, RILM. *Aud.:* Ga, Ac.

Supported by Five Colleges, Inc., the *Massachusetts Review* adds public affairs and social and historical commentary to its literary and arts offerings. Although based in New England, it appeals to a wider audience because of its significant writing on race and culture. Pieces by Julia Alvarez, Stephen Dobyns, Toni Morrison, and Chinua Achebe have appeared in its pages. Other theme issues have concentrated on the performing arts, diversity, and a tribute to Allen Ginsburg and American poetry. There is a companion program, MR2, the "audio extension of the journal."

4119. *Michigan Quarterly Review.* [ISSN: 0026-2420] 1962. q. USD 25 domestic; USD 30 foreign. Ed(s): Laurence Goldstein. University of Michigan, Law School, 625 South State St, Ann Arbor, MI 48109-1215; http://www.law.umich.edu. Illus., index, adv. Refereed. Circ: 1500 Paid. Vol. ends: Fall. Microform: PQC. Online: Chadwyck-Healey Inc.; OCLC Online Computer Library Center, Inc.; ProQuest LLC (Ann Arbor); H.W. Wilson. *Indexed:* ABS&EES, AmH&L, AmHI, ArtHuCI, BAS, BEL&L, BRI, CBRI, FLI, HistAb, HumInd, IAPV, MLA-IB, PAIS, PhilInd, RI-1, RILM, SSCI. *Bk. rev.:* 1-3, 5-16 pages, signed. *Aud.:* Ga, Ac.

Called the University of Michigan's flagship journal, *Michigan Quarterly* has published only special theme issues since 1979. The review's fiction, poetry, prose poetry, book reviews, and criticism are expertly edited and assembled. In a recent issue, Toni Morrison leads off with an article on values in the university. Other notable contributors to the two issues on "Secret Spaces and Childhood" include John Stilgoe, Edmund Wilson, Robert Coles, and Diana Ackerman. A two-part issue, "Jewish in America," has been published along with a special issue on "Vietnam: Beyond the Frame" and a tribute to Arthur Miller. The searchable, browsable web site contains abstracts for contents of the past several issues.

4120. *Minnesota Review: a journal of committed writing; fiction, poetry, essays, reviews.* [ISSN: 0026-5667] 1960. s-a. USD 52 (Individuals, USD 30). Ed(s): Jeffrey Williams. University of Missouri - Columbia, Department of English, 110 Tate Hall, Columbia, MO 65211. Illus., adv. Circ: 1500. Microform: PQC. Online: Chadwyck-Healey Inc.; OCLC Online Computer Library Center, Inc.; ProQuest LLC (Ann Arbor). *Indexed:* AmHI, ArtHuCI, BRI, CBRI, FLI, IAPV, IBR, IBZ, MLA-IB, SSCI. *Bk. rev.:* 7, 6-16 pages, signed. *Aud.:* Ga, Ac.

Calling itself a "journal of committed writing," the *Minnesota Review* energetically presents a mix of literature and political commentary. In addition to poetry, fiction, and reviews, much of the content examines issues of interest to academics. Recently, the productive tension between activism and the academy is explored in a collection of articles first written for a conference on the future of graduate education. Sections of interest include "Surveying the Field," with current critical commentary on cutting-edge subjects, and a special section highlighting "Fifties Culture." Theme issues of late include "Smart Kids" and poetry of the absurd. The "Surveying the Field" section features articles on timely topics in literary theory and about the canon, textuality, and alterity.

4121. *The Missouri Review.* [ISSN: 0191-1961] 1978. 3x/yr. USD 22. Ed(s): Speer Morgan. University of Missouri at Columbia, 1507 Hillcrest Hall, 3rd Fl -D, Columbia, MO 65211. Illus., index, adv. Circ: 6500. *Indexed:* AmHI, IAPV, MLA-IB, RILM. *Bk. rev.:* 11-18, 1-5 pages, signed. *Aud.:* Ga, Ac.

The Missouri Review features fiction, poetry, essays, interviews, and book reviews; literary criticism is excluded. Theme issues are not determined in advance; rather, they flow from writers' submissions. The editors' creativity is evidenced in two special departments. The "Found Text Feature" presents never-before-published works, such as Knopf's selection decisions and famous rejection letters. In the 25th anniversary issue, this section includes production memos and photos from David Selznick. In "History as Literature," seminal primary materials, such as the previously unpublished letters of Neal Cassidy to Jack Kerouac, are included. The web site's redesign provides a reader-friendly sidebar for easy navigation of editorials, features, poetry, fiction, nonfiction, interviews, book reviews, and other content.

4122. *New Letters: a magazine of writing and art.* Former titles (until vol.37, 1971): *University Review;* (until vol.30, 1964): *University of Kansas City Review;* (until vol.8, 1942): *University Review.* [ISSN: 0146-4930] 1934. q. USD 30 (Individuals, USD 22). Ed(s): Robert Stewart. University of Missouri at Kansas City, 5100 Rockhill Rd, Kansas City, MO 64110; mckinley@umkc.edu. Illus., adv. Circ: 1500. *Indexed:* AmHI, ArtHuCI, HumInd, IAPV, MLA-IB. *Aud.:* Ga, Ac.

Affiliated with the University of Missouri at Kansas City, the rubric for *New Letters,* "an international magazine of writing and art: in print and on the air," signals its unique strengths. Artwork figures prominently in the print review, along with poetry, fiction, and essays. The web site features a description of the radio companion to the literary quarterly, "New Letters on the Air," which began broadcasting in 1977. Distributed via public radio, the weekly program is devoted to an author's reading from his or her work and an interview with host Angela Elam. Over 800 programs, available on cassette, are listed in the "On the Air" section.

4123. *New Millennium Writings.* [ISSN: 1086-7678] 1996. a. USD 10 per issue. Ed(s): Don Williams. New Messenger Writing and Publishing, NMW Room M2, PO Box 2463, Knoxville, TN 37901. Illus., adv. Sample. Circ: 3300 Controlled. *Aud.:* Ga.

Appealing to a general audience as well as to academics, *New Millennium Writings* considers itself vibrant and adventurous. The introduction to its first issue states: "[I]f it . . . *oscillates*, we will publish it." In addition to poetry, nonfiction, interviews, and artwork, the review has numerous departments, including "Humor," "The Writing Well," "Observations" (usually by editor Don Williams), "Millennial Moments," and the "Janus File" (containing tributes to well-known authors). Number 11 (vol. 6, no. 1) showcases the "best of the best" interviews and profiles from 1996 to 2001. The web site has selected links to full texts from the issues published thus far. The pages for describing the contents of each issue have contributors' photos and quoted text from their works in the "Featured Writers" section. Each issue also presents the winners of the *New Millennium* Awards.

4124. *The New Renaissance: an international magazine of ideas and opinions, emphasizing literature & the arts.* [ISSN: 0028-6575] 1968. s-a. USD 20 domestic; USD 21.60 Canada; USD 25.33 elsewhere. Ed(s): Louise T Reynolds. Friends of the new renaissance, Inc., 26 Heath Rd, 11, Arlington, MA 02474-3645; svanden@spfldcol.edu; http://www.tnrlitmag.net. Illus., index. Circ: 1100 Paid. *Indexed:* AltPI, AmHI, IAPV. *Bk. rev.:* 0-2, 5-7 pages, signed. *Aud.:* Ga, Ac.

Unlike many literary reviews that are published by an academic department or writing program, *The New Renaissance* is funded by a grant from the Massachusetts Cultural Council. Its lead articles present ideas and opinions on a range of current-interest topics, such as genetic engineering, childhood immunization, ecology, future studies, and animal rights. Fiction, poetry, essays, and reviews are accompanied by compelling artwork, photos, drawings, and other illustrations. The "Catching Up" department gives updates on prizes, exhibits, editorships, and new publications. Lively exchanges appear in the reader correspondence section.

4125. *News from the Republic of Letters.* [ISSN: 1095-1644] 1997. s-a. USD 35. Ed(s): Keith Botsford. The Toby Press LLC, 2 Great Pasture Rd, Danbury, CT 06810; toby@tobypress.com; http://www.tobypress.com. Illus., adv. Circ: 2000 Paid. *Bk. rev.:* 1-2, length varies. *Aud.:* Ga, Ac.

News from the Republic of Letters is an independent review of literature and the arts founded by Nobel Prize–winner Saul Bellow and current editor Keith Botsford. Tabloid in format for issues 1–11, it offers a lively collection of essays, poems, reviews, and timely "Arias" on major topics of the day. "Among the tasks which the editors consider important is that of bringing attention to important or neglected books" (vol. 1, no. 1, May 1997), including work by gifted writers who are not well known. "Lives" (memoirs, biography, correspondence) and "Texts" (fiction and nonfiction of any length in any language) are published. The web site contains excerpts from numbers 1 to 10 (or beyond), and since issue 12 the review has become a biannual issued in paperback.

4126. *The North American Review.* [ISSN: 0029-2397] 1815. bi-m. USD 22 domestic; USD 29 Canada; USD 32 elsewhere. Ed(s): Grant Tracey, Vince Gotera. North American Review, University of Northern Iowa, 1222 W 27th St, Cedar Falls, IA 50614-0516; vince.gotera@uni.edu. Illus., index, adv. Sample. Refereed. Circ: 4700. Microform: PMC; PQC. Online: Chadwyck-Healey Inc.; Florida Center for Library Automation; Gale; Northern Light Technology, Inc.; OCLC Online Computer Library Center, Inc.; H.W. Wilson. *Indexed:* AmH&L, AmHI, ArtHuCI, BEL&L, BRI, CBRI, HistAb, HumInd, IAPV, RILM. *Bk. rev.:* 0-1, 3 pages, signed. *Aud.:* Ga, Ac.

Dating from 1815, with a hiatus in the late 1870s, *The North American Review* has long been considered an important literary journal. The *Review*'s history notes that its originally "British flavor" has diminished over the years; it takes pride in having published, among others, Walt Whitman, Henry James, and Joseph Conrad. Recent issues include emerging as well as established writers. Over time, its content has been expanded to include current affairs and politics as well as literature. The editors aim to take a "broad view of current North American preoccupations—especially the problems of the environment." The journal contains the regular departments "Natural Orders," "Foreign Correspondence," "Kasper," and "Synecdoche." The *Review* has received commendations for its design, illustrations, and award-winning covers. The web site's introductory page lists this celebrated journal's numerous awards, and the online archives house seven web issues.

4127. *North Dakota Quarterly.* Formerly (until 1956): *Quarterly of the University of North Dakota.* [ISSN: 0029-277X] 1911. q. USD 30 (Individuals, USD 25). Ed(s): Robert W Lewis. University of North Dakota, PO Box 7209, Grand Forks, ND 58202; http://www.und.nodak.edu. Adv. Refereed. Circ: 400 Paid. *Indexed:* ABS&EES, AmH&L, AmHI, FLI, HistAb, IAPV, IBR, IBZ, MLA-IB, RILM. *Bk. rev.:* 3-8, 2-8 pages, signed. *Aud.:* Ga, Ac.

Emphasis on the Northern Plains characterizes the *North Dakota Quarterly*, and special issues alternate with general-interest issues. Articles and literary pieces (stories, poems, reviews) on such subjects as the language of mountains and American Indian studies have been featured. Many illustrations appeared throughout the American Indian issue, along with articles treating forgotten authors, the revival of Indian languages, and the unique aspects of reservation life. The review also seeks to publish personal essays about "books that mattered," especially on ecological themes. The editor's news notes close each issue.

4128. *Notre Dame Review.* [ISSN: 1082-1864] 1995. s-a. USD 20 (Individuals, USD 15; USD 8 newsstand/cover per issue). Ed(s): John Matthias, William O'Rourke. University of Notre Dame, Creative Writing Program, 356 O'Shaughnessy Hall, Notre Dame, IN 46556; english.ndreview.1@nd.edu; http://www.nd.edu/~ndr/review.htm. Illus., adv. Circ: 2000. *Indexed:* AmHI. *Bk. rev.:* 13-18, 50-350 words, signed. *Aud.:* Ga, Ac.

Seeking to provide a "panoramic view" of contemporary American and international writing, the *Notre Dame Review* contains short stories, poetry, reviews, criticism, art, and interviews. The *Review*'s stated goal is to showcase many styles and work that "takes on issues by making the invisible seen." The

special web version, "nd[re]view," complements the print journal with special features: interviews, critique and commentary, and sometimes color images and audio related to the authors and artists in the printed review. The print journal and the web site are described as constituting a hybrid print-and-electronic magazine that "engages readers as a community centered in literary concerns." An online discussion group for readers and authors to exchange views was planned as well.

4129. *Ontario Review.* [ISSN: 0316-4055] 1974. s-a. USD 16 domestic; USD 20 foreign. Ed(s): Raymond J Smith. Ontario Review, Inc., 9 Honey Brook Dr, Princeton, NJ 08540; http://www.ontarioreviewpress.com. Illus., index. Sample. Circ: 1200 Paid. Microform: MML. *Indexed:* AmHI, IAPV, MLA-IB. *Aud.:* Ga, Ac.

Handsome and thoughtfully designed, *Ontario Review* includes "original fiction, poetry, personal essays, drama, photographs, graphics, and interviews with prominent contemporary authors." Although the journal's focus has broadened over time, editor Raymond Smith and associate editor Joyce Carol Oates established the *Ontario Review* in 1974 to bridge the gap between Canadian and American arts and literatures. Nurturing young writers is one of the editors' goals. Issues offer a blend of well-known writers with promising new poets and storytellers. Over 400 well-known writers, including Maxine Kumin, Doris Lessing, Reynolds Price, Margaret Atwood, and John Updike, have been published here. The web site (www.ontarioreviewpress.com) features the current issue, back issues (tables of contents and full text of selected pieces from issue 44 onward), and a description of and excerpts from the forthcoming issue.

Other Voices. See Fiction: General/Mystery and Detective/General section.

Parabola. See General Editorial/General section.

4130. *The Paris Review: the international literary quarterly.* [ISSN: 0031-2037] 1953. q. USD 40 domestic; USD 45 Canada; USD 50 elsewhere. Ed(s): Philip A Gourevitch. The Paris Review Foundation, Inc., 62 White St., New York, NY 10013-3593; postmaster@theparisreview.com; http://www.theparisreview.com. Illus., index, adv. Circ: 14000. Microform: PQC. Online: Chadwyck-Healey Inc.; Northern Light Technology, Inc.; OCLC Online Computer Library Center, Inc.; ProQuest LLC (Ann Arbor). *Indexed:* AmHI, ArtHuCI, BEL&L, HumInd, IAPV, RILM, SSCI. *Aud.:* Ga, Ac.

Founded in 1953, this elegant journal is guided by the principle that creative writing ought to reside at the center of the literary review. It examines all aspects of the creative process in literature. Each issue is substantial in length and includes fiction, essays, poetry, and, notably, interviews with writers on writing. Jack Kerouac, Philip Roth, and V.S. Naipaul were first published here. Selections from current issues are available on the web site, www.theparisreview.org, as are summaries and tables of contents for past issues. It further includes "Look, Listen, and Read" features and an archive of interviews, as well as an "Audio" section with writers reading from their works.

4131. *Prairie Schooner.* [ISSN: 0032-6682] 1926. q. USD 26. Ed(s): Hilda Raz. University of Nebraska at Lincoln, 201 Andrews Hall, Lincoln, NE 68588-0334; http://www.unl.edu/schooner/psmain.htm. Index, adv. Circ: 3200. Vol. ends: Winter. Microform: PQC. Online: Chadwyck-Healey Inc.; EBSCO Publishing, EBSCO Host; Florida Center for Library Automation; Gale; OCLC Online Computer Library Center, Inc.; OhioLINK; Project MUSE; SwetsWise Online Content. Reprint: PSC. *Indexed:* ABS&EES, AmHI, ArtHuCI, BRI, CBRI, HumInd, IAPV, MLA-IB. *Bk. rev.:* 0-7, 1-8 words, signed. *Aud.:* Ga, Ac.

Prairie Schooner, now in its 81st year, continues to publish poetry, fiction, essays, reviews, and works in translation—by both new and established writers. It is sponsored by the University of Nebraska–Lincoln, and its distinguished contributors have included Willa Cather, Tennessee Williams, and Raymond Carver. The journal's web site offers excerpts from the current issue and links to tables of contents of past issues.

4132. *Salmagundi: a quarterly of the humanities & social sciences.*
[ISSN: 0036-3529] 1965. q. USD 32 (Individuals, USD 20). Ed(s):
Robert Boyers, Peggy Boyers. Skidmore College, 815 North Broadway,
Saratoga Springs, NY 12866; pboyers@skidmore.edu;
http://www.skidmore.edu/. Illus., index, adv. Sample. Refereed. Circ:
4800. Microform: PQC. Online: Chadwyck-Healey Inc.; Northern Light
Technology, Inc.; OCLC Online Computer Library Center, Inc.;
ProQuest LLC (Ann Arbor); H.W. Wilson. *Indexed:* ABS&EES,
AmH&L, AmHI, ArtHuCI, BAS, BRI, CBRI, FLI, HistAb, HumInd,
IAPV, L&LBA, MLA-IB, PhilInd, RILM, SSA, SSCI. *Bk. rev.:* 0-5, 5-23
pages, signed. *Aud.:* Ga, Ac.

Published by Skidmore College, *Salmagundi* is subtitled "a quarterly of the
Humanities and Social Sciences," and its scope is, indeed, that expansive. The
journal addresses itself to the "general" reader, rather than to academicians, and
publishes "essays, reviews, interviews, fiction, poetry, regular columns,
polemics, debates and symposia." With regular and special columns—including
commentary on art, fiction, and international politics, and poetry—the journal
ranges widely and deeply through literature and culture. It features such writers
as Lynn Sharon Schwartz, George Steiner, Christopher Hitchens, Carolyn
Forche, and Louise Gluck.

4133. *The Sewanee Review.* [ISSN: 0037-3052] 1892. q. USD 38. Ed(s):
George Core. The Johns Hopkins University Press, 2715 N Charles St,
Baltimore, MD 21218-4363; myq@press.jhu.edu;
http://www.press.jhu.edu. Illus., index, adv. Circ: 2848 Paid and free.
Vol. ends: Oct. Microform: PQC. Online: Chadwyck-Healey Inc.;
EBSCO Publishing, EBSCO Host. *Indexed:* AmHI, ArtHuCI, BEL&L,
BRD, BRI, CBRI, HumInd, IAPV, IBR, IBZ, MLA-IB, PhilInd, RI-1,
RILM. *Bk. rev.:* 6-10, 2-6 pages, signed. *Aud.:* Ga, Ac.

The University of the South, in Sewanee, Tennessee, is the home of this
venerable journal, begun in 1892. It is a distinguished, traditional literary
magazine devoted to British and American fiction, poetry, essays, reviews, and
criticism. Poets published in its pages have included T.S. Eliot, Dylan Thomas,
Wallace Stevens, and Howard Nemerov. At "115 years young," it describes
itself as "old school in the best way possible."

4134. *Shenandoah.* [ISSN: 0037-3583] 1950. q. USD 25 (Individuals, USD
22; USD 8 newsstand/cover per issue). Ed(s): Lynn Leech, R T Smith.
Washington and Lee University, Shenandoah, Troubadour Theater, 2nd
Fl, Lexington, VA 24450-0303. Illus., index, adv. Circ: 1400 Paid. Vol.
ends: Winter. *Indexed:* AmHI, ArtHuCI, BRI, CBRI, IAPV, IBR, IBZ,
MLA-IB. *Bk. rev.:* 0-7, 1-3 pages. *Aud.:* Ga, Ac.

This review was founded in 1950 by students and faculty at Washington and
Lee—one of their number Tom Wolfe, to whom a section of a recent issue has
been devoted. Cover art and graphics are elegant. Short stories and poems
accompany interviews, literary essays, brief reviews, and personal essays.
Annual prizes are awarded for the best story, poem, and essay published in each
volume. The review's web site includes a sampler of verse and prose and a table
of contents for the current issue. A well-established and thoughtful review, with
a subtle and modest editorial wit.

Short Story. See Fiction: General/Mystery and Detective/General section.

4135. *South Carolina Review.* [ISSN: 0038-3163] 1968. 2x/yr. USD 27
(Individuals, USD 22). Clemson University, Department of English, 801
Strode Tower, PO Box 340523, Clemson, SC 29634-0523. Illus., adv.
Circ: 600. *Indexed:* AmH&L, AmHI, BRI, CBRI, HistAb, HumInd,
IAPV, MLA-IB. *Bk. rev.:* Number and length vary. *Aud.:* Ga, Ac.

From its home at Clemson University, this review emphasizes Southern and
American literature, but its focus is wide, including essays, scholarly criticism,
poetry, book reviews, and stories of all sorts. Special issues have focused on
writers such as Robert Frost, Mary Gordon, Walker Percy, and James Dickey.
The South Caroline Review online library (SCROLL) is also published on the
web at www.clemson.edu/caah/cedp/SCR_CurrIss.htm.

4136. *The Southern Review.* [ISSN: 0038-4534] 1935. q. USD 50
(Individuals, USD 25). Ed(s): Bret Lott, James Olney. Louisiana State
University, 43 Allen Hall, Baton Rouge, LA 70803-5005;

http://www.lsu.edu. Index, adv. Sample. Circ: 3140. Vol. ends: Oct.
Microform: PQC. Online: Chadwyck-Healey Inc.; EBSCO Publishing,
EBSCO Host; Florida Center for Library Automation; Gale; Northern
Light Technology, Inc.; OCLC Online Computer Library Center, Inc.;
ProQuest K-12 Learning Solutions; ProQuest LLC (Ann Arbor); H.W.
Wilson. *Indexed:* AmH&L, AmHI, ArtHuCI, BRI, CBRI, HistAb,
HumInd, IAPV, IBR, IBZ, MLA-IB, RI-1, RILM. *Bk. rev.:* 1, 4-6 pages,
signed. *Aud.:* Ga, Ac.

Louisiana State University publishes this quarterly journal. Its scope is
contemporary literature from the United States and abroad, with an emphasis on
Southern history and culture. Poems, short stories, excerpts from novels in
progress, reviews, essays, and interviews comprise its contents. The editors note
that they emphasize the importance of craftmanship and seriousness of subject
matter and eschew sensationalism. Bret Lott has been editor since 2004. It was
awarded Best Journal Design in 2006 by the Council of Editors of Learned
Journals.

4137. *The Southwest Review.* Incorporates (1921-1925): *The Reviewer.*
[ISSN: 0038-4712] 1915. q. USD 24 domestic; USD 29 foreign. Ed(s):
Willard Spiegelman. Southern Methodist University, 307 Fondren Library
W, Box 374, Dallas, TX 75275; swr@mail.smu.edu; http://www.smu.edu.
Illus., index, adv. Sample. Circ: 1500 Paid. Microform: PQC. Online:
EBSCO Publishing, EBSCO Host; Florida Center for Library
Automation; Gale; Northern Light Technology, Inc.; OCLC Online
Computer Library Center, Inc.; ProQuest K-12 Learning Solutions;
ProQuest LLC (Ann Arbor); H.W. Wilson. *Indexed:* AmH&L, AmHI,
BEL&L, BRI, CBRI, HistAb, HumInd, IAPV, IBR, IBZ, MLA-IB. *Aud.:*
Ga, Ac.

This Texas-based journal (from Southern Methodist University) of long
standing has an esteemed editorial advisory board that includes Joyce Carol
Oates, Helen Vendler, and John Hollander. Works of fiction, poetry, and literary
and personal essays, as well as writing on the arts and culture, travel, and
political subjects, are published. Recent contributors include Naguib Mahfouz,
Dana Gioia, and Annie Dillard.

4138. *The Threepenny Review.* [ISSN: 0275-1410] 1980. q. USD 25; USD
7 newsstand/cover. Ed(s): Wendy Lesser. Threepenny Review, PO Box
9131, Berkeley, CA 94709. Adv. Circ: 9000 Paid. Microform: PQC.
Indexed: AltPI, AmHI, BRI, CBRI, IAPV. *Bk. rev.:* 0-7. *Aud.:* Ga, Ac.

The Threepenny Review is a lively presence on the literary landscape. It reliably
delivers a varied collection of short fiction; memoirs; reviews of books, film,
dance, music, and theater; and essays on such topics as architecture, television,
and politics. It is guided by editor Wendy Lesser, who is aided by consulting
editors including John Berger, Anne Carson, Elizabeth Hardwick, and Gore
Vidal. This well-designed journal has beautiful cover art on each issue. Their
mature and well-developed web site includes a link to their blog, tables of
contents for current and past issues, a "Reading Room," and a "Gallery" of
cover art. URL: www.threepennyreview.com.

4139. *TriQuarterly.* [ISSN: 0041-3097] 1964. 3x/yr. USD 36 (Individuals,
USD 24; USD 11.95 per issue). Ed(s): Susan Firestone Hahn. Northwest-
ern University Press, 625 Colfax St, Evanston, IL 60208-4210; nupress@
northwestern.edu; http://nupress.northwestern.edu. Illus., index, adv.
Sample. Circ: 5000 Paid. Microform: PQC. Online: Chadwyck-Healey
Inc.; Florida Center for Library Automation; Gale; Northern Light
Technology, Inc.; OCLC Online Computer Library Center, Inc.;
ProQuest K-12 Learning Solutions; ProQuest LLC (Ann Arbor); H.W.
Wilson. *Indexed:* ABS&EES, AmH&L, AmHI, ArtHuCI, BRI, CBRI,
HistAb, HumInd, IAPV, MLA-IB, RILM, SSCI. *Bk. rev.:* 1, lengthy,
signed. *Aud.:* Ga, Ac.

Founded in 1958, and consistently excellent, this preeminent "international
journal of writing, art, and cultural inquiry" has among its contributing editors
Rita Dove, Robert Pinsky, and Richard Ford. It is a vibrant publication, sophisticated and energetic, with poetry and novellas and novel excerpts alongside short
stories and essays; and its length (more than 300 pages) allows a full, varied list
of contributors. Northwestern University Press is its publisher.

4140. *Virginia Quarterly Review: a national journal of literature and discussion.* [ISSN: 0042-675X] 1925. q. USD 28 (Individuals, USD 25). Ed(s): Staige D Blackford. University of Virginia, 1 West Range, PO Box 400223, Charlottesville, VA 22904-4423; http://www.virginia.edu. Illus., index, adv. Circ: 4200. Vol. ends: Oct. Microform: PMC; PQC. Online: Chadwyck-Healey Inc.; EBSCO Publishing, EBSCO Host; Northern Light Technology, Inc.; OCLC Online Computer Library Center, Inc.; ProQuest K-12 Learning Solutions; ProQuest LLC (Ann Arbor); H.W. Wilson. *Indexed:* ABS&EES, AmH&L, AmHI, ArtHuCI, BAS, BRD, BRI, CBRI, FutSurv, HistAb, HumInd, IAPV, IBR, IBZ, MLA-IB, PAIS, RILM, SSCI. *Bk. rev.:* 90-100, 40-2,000 words, signed. *Aud.:* Ga, Ac.

This important journal, which began publication in 1925, includes work on public affairs, the arts, history, literary essays, fiction, and poetry. It describes itself as a national journal of literature and discussion. A recent issue includes a special section on the war in Iraq. The review section is substantial, including in-depth reviews as well as briefer notes on works recently published. Its well-designed and elegant online presence at www.virginia.edu/vqr includes searchable archives for issues back to 1999, with selected pieces available, web exclusives, and a blog.

4141. *Web del Sol.* 1994. m. Ed(s): Mike Neff. Web del Sol, 2915 Fairmont St., Falls Church, VA 22042; http://webdelsol.com. *Aud.:* Ga, Ac.

This digital publication has grown more engaging with time. It describes itself as "the Locus of the New Literary Art." It hosts new and well-established literary publications (some of which are also issued in print), publishes its own online journal (*Del Sol*), and provides reviews and essays. It also offers links to arts and literary resources of interest, opportunities to see hypermedia via a "new media portal," and interactive online communities devoted to literature and poetry writing. It also features a section with chapbook pages for writers including Holly Iglesias, Madison Smartt Bell, and David Ignatow. "House of Blogs" and "Jazz Alley," together with sections devoted to film and a range of other literary topics, create a jam-packed reading, listening, viewing experience.

4142. *Witness (Farmington Hills).* [ISSN: 0891-1371] 1987. 2x/yr. USD 22 (Individuals, USD 15). Ed(s): Peter Stine. Oakland Community College, 27055 Orchard Lake Rd, Farmington, MI 48334; http://www.occ.cc.mi.us. Illus., adv. Sample. Refereed. Circ: 1500 Paid. *Indexed:* AmHI, IAPV. *Aud.:* Ga, Ac.

Witness is a consistently interesting read, containing short stories, poetry, literary essays, memoirs, and photography. The review bears literary witness to social issues and subjects ranging from war to civil rights, from work to rural life. Annual special issues have included "Aging in America," "Animals in America," and "Ethnic America."

4143. *The Yale Review.* [ISSN: 0044-0124] 1911. q. GBP 100 print & online eds. Ed(s): Susan Bianconi, J D McClatchy. Blackwell Publishing, Inc., Commerce Place, 350 Main St, Malden, MA 02148; customerservices@blackwellpublishing.com; http://www.blackwellpublishing.com. Illus., index, adv. Sample. Circ: 6000 Paid. Vol. ends: Oct. Microform: PMC; PQC. Online: Blackwell Synergy; EBSCO Publishing, EBSCO Host; Gale; OCLC Online Computer Library Center, Inc.; OhioLINK. *Indexed:* ABS&EES, AmH&L, AmHI, ArtHuCI, BAS, BEL&L, BRD, BRI, CBRI, FLI, HistAb, HumInd, IAPV, IBR, IBZ, IPSA, MLA-IB, PAIS, PhilInd, RILM. *Bk. rev.:* 4-5, 6-22 pages, signed. *Aud.:* Ga, Ac.

The Yale Review, an influential presence in the world of literary magazines, has been published since 1911. Appearing here are short stories, poetry, personal and literary essays, reviews, and articles discussing history and culture. The journal's long list of major writers includes Robert Penn Warren, Theodore Roethke, Anne Sexton, and, more recently, Richard Wilbur, Anita Brookner, Cynthia Ozick, and Haruki Murakami. This review, edited by J.D. McClatchy, balances academic discipline and issues of social interest, ranging over topics from Wharton to war.

■ LITERATURE

See also Africa; African American; China; Classical Studies; Europe; Fiction; Latin American; Gay, Lesbian, Bisexual, and Transgender; Literary Reviews; Little Magazines; and Theater sections.

Susan Metcalf, Instructional Services Librarian, Rice Library, University of Southern Indiana, 8600 University Blvd., Evansville, IN 47712; smetcalf@usi.edu.

V. Blue Lemay, PhD., Instructor, Humanities Department, University of Southern Indiana, 8600 University Blvd., Evansville, IN 47712; vlemay@usi.edu

Introduction

The journals in this section focus on literature and literary criticism, including American, English, and European, spanning periods from the ancient to the contemporary, and offering an assortment of approaches from reception theory to cultural materialism. Journals are essential forums and instrumental resources for the scholarly and public communities to communicate. Because they function to address a diversity of audiences, we have chosen journals that are necessarily varied, ranging from *Notes and Queries,* which provides rigorous close textual analysis, to *Postcolonial Text,* an electronic journal that explores various epistemological, cultural, social, and political links between texts for international readers.

The majority of the journals we have selected are primarily academic and highly respected, and customarily they have an extensive readership. Many of these journals fill a distinctive niche, set high standards, and guarantee originality. We provide libraries with information on these literary and cultural journals by concisely isolating the aims or agendas of each journal, summarizing content and calculating the length of articles and reviews. We also call explicit attention to special features or issues of particular journals. We have updated the list of journals, and especially have added new electronic or innovative journals or attended to new features such as redesigned web sites or options for RSS feeds.

Basic Periodicals

Ac: *American Literature, Comparative Literature, Contemporary Literature, Essays in Criticism, Modern Fiction Studies, Nineteenth-Century Literature, PMLA, The Review of Contemporary Fiction, Speculum, Studies in English Literature 1500–1900, Victorian Studies, World Literature Today.*

Basic Abstracts and Indexes

American Humanities Index, Annual Bibliography of English Language and Literature, Arts & Humanities Citation Index, Humanities Index, MLA International Bibliography.

4144. *A N Q: A Quarterly Journal of Short Articles, Notes and Reviews.* Formerly (until 1986): *American Notes and Queries.* [ISSN: 0895-769X] 1962. q. USD 134 (Individuals, USD 63 print & online eds.). Heldref Publications, 1319 18th St, NW, Washington, DC 20036-1802; subscribe@heldref.org; http://www.heldref.org. Index. Refereed. Circ: 425 Paid. Microform: PQC. Online: Chadwyck-Healey Inc.; EBSCO Publishing, EBSCO Host; Florida Center for Library Automation; Gale; OCLC Online Computer Library Center, Inc.; ProQuest K-12 Learning Solutions; ProQuest LLC (Ann Arbor); H.W. Wilson. Reprint: PSC. *Indexed:* AmHI, ArtHuCI, BRI, CBRI, HumInd, IBR, MLA-IB, RILM. *Bk. rev.:* 1-7, 2-4 pages, signed. *Aud.:* Ac.

Filling a unique niche, this literary journal provides brief yet incisive research-based essays on the literature of the English-speaking world. It includes 10–14 essays, ranging from two to ten pages each, that cover discussions and explanations of "obscure allusions, sources and analogues...textual emendations, and rare correspondence from neglected archives." Authors discussed in the more recent issues include William Collins, Ben Jonson, Keats, Fitzgerald, and Housman. Recent essays include "The Syntactic Analysis of the Opening Verses in Beowulf," "The Elder Henry James to a Collector: An

Unpublished Letter," and "Old Testament Sourcing in Edith Wharton's 'All Souls.'" The journal's web site provides the table of contents from 2004 to present. Recommended for large academic and public libraries with strong literature collections.

4145. A R I E L. Formerly (until 1967): *Review of English Literature.* [ISSN: 0004-1327] 1960. q. CND 70 (Individuals, CND 28). Ed(s): Pamela J McCallum. University of Calgary Press, University of Calgary, 2500 University Dr NW, Calgary, AB T2N 1N4, Canada; http://www.uofcpress.com. Illus., index, adv. Refereed. Circ: 900 Paid and free. Vol. ends: Oct. *Indexed:* AmHI, ArtHuCI, CBCARef, CPerI, HumInd, IBR, IBZ, MLA-IB, RILM. *Bk. rev.:* 4-7, 2-3 pages, signed. *Aud.:* Ac.

ARIEL: a review of international English literature focuses primarily on the "configurations of colonial power and discourses, resistances to colonization and its effects and inter-relations among literatures." *ARIEL* publishes articles, book reviews, poems, and more recently a "special clusters" section of three thematic essays, most recently essays that address issues of "Post-Colonial Rewritings" and "Writing America." Previous content has included interviews as well. Typically articles are 20 or so pages in length, and most recent content has included articles on Chadha, Goodison, Selvon, Achebe, and others. Recent articles include "Racial Fantasy in Joseph Conrad's 'Nigger of the *Narcissus*'" and "Of Houses and Canons: Reading the Novels of Shashi Deshpande." The journal's web site provides a table of contents from 2002 to present. Recommended for academic libraries.

4146. American Literary History. [ISSN: 0896-7148] 1989. q. USD 198 print or online ed. Ed(s): Gordon Hutner. Oxford University Press, 2001 Evans Rd, Cary, NC 27513; http://www.us.oup.com. Illus., adv. Refereed. Circ: 1350. Vol. ends: Dec. Online: Chadwyck-Healey Inc.; EBSCO Publishing, EBSCO Host; Gale; HighWire Press; IngentaConnect; JSTOR (Web-based Journal Archive); OCLC Online Computer Library Center, Inc.; OhioLINK; Oxford Journals; Project MUSE; ProQuest LLC (Ann Arbor); SwetsWise Online Content; H.W. Wilson. Reprint: PSC. *Indexed:* AmH&L, AmHI, ArtHuCI, HistAb, HumInd, IBR, MLA-IB, RILM. *Bk. rev.:* 3-5, 8-16 pages, signed. *Aud.:* Ac.

Published by Oxford University Press, this journal promotes a "much-needed forum for the various, often competing voices of contemporary literary inquiry" in American literature by encouraging a diversity of "rich and varied criticism" on interdisciplinary topics by informed and insightful authors. Edited by Gordon Hunter, this refereed journal publishes articles that are sophisticated in content but accessible and engaging to a number of scholarly readers of varying backgrounds, especially those interested in the full range of the American experience, from its origins in the colonial period to its contemporary cultural refractions. This quarterly journal often contains articles 23–25 pages long, and features essays, critical exchanges, commentaries, and reviews. It typically covers not only social, economic, political, historical, and theoretical interests but also raises relevant concerns of literary studies such as the definition of genre, the uses of periodicity, and the value of canon formation. Recent articles include "Thinking with Rhetorical Figures: Performing Racial and Disciplinary Identities in Late-Nineteenth-Century America," "What is a Black Author?: A Review of Recent Charles Chestnut Studies," and "Women and Dixie: The Feminization of Southern Women's History and Culture." Two RSS feeds for tables of contents and abstracts of recent issues are available at http://alh.oxfordjournals.org/rss/index.dtl. Through Oxford Open initiative, authors may pay extra to have their essay made available for free online at www.oxfordjournals.org/oxfordopen. (VBL)

4147. American Literary Realism. Formerly (until 1999): *American Literary Realism, 1870-1910.* [ISSN: 1540-3084] 1967. 3x/yr. USD 48 print & online eds. (Individuals, USD 35 print & online eds.). Ed(s): Gary Scharnhorst. University of Illinois Press, 1325 S Oak St, Champaign, IL 61820-6903; journals@uillinois.edu; http://www.press.uillinois.edu. Illus., index, adv. Refereed. Circ: 700. *Indexed:* AmH&L, AmHI, ArtHuCI, BEL&L, HistAb, HumInd, IBR, IBZ, MLA-IB, RILM, SSCI. *Bk. rev.:* 3-7, 1-2 pages, signed. *Aud.:* Ac.

American Literary Realism publishes critical essays on American literature, notes and documents, and book reviews. A typical essay ranges between 10 and 20 pages in length, and recent issues have included essays on Chopin, Dreiser,

Twain, Wharton, and Howells. Most recent content includes "Searching for 'Common Ground': Class, Sympathy, and Perspective in Howells' Social Fiction," "Sarah Orne Jewett and (Maritime) Literary Tradition: Coastal and Narrative Navigations in *The Country of the Pointed Firs*," and "A River 'Ready For Business': Life Down the Mississippi as a Main Undercurrent in Mark Twain's *Pudd'nhead Wilson*." The journal's web site provides the table of contents from 1999 to present. Recommended for medium and large academic libraries.

4148. American Literature: a journal of literary history, criticism, and bibliography. [ISSN: 0002-9831] 1929. q. USD 235 (Individuals, USD 45). Ed(s): Priscilla B Wald. Duke University Press, 905 W Main St, Ste 18 B, Durham, NC 27701; http://www.dukeupress.edu. Illus., index, adv. Refereed. Circ: 2607. Vol. ends: Dec. Microform: MIM; PQC. Online: EBSCO Publishing, EBSCO Host; Gale; HighWire Press; JSTOR (Web-based Journal Archive); Northern Light Technology, Inc.; OCLC Online Computer Library Center, Inc.; OhioLINK; Project MUSE; ProQuest K-12 Learning Solutions; ProQuest LLC (Ann Arbor); SwetsWise Online Content. Reprint: PSC. *Indexed:* AmH&L, AmHI, ArtHuCI, BEL&L, BRD, BRI, CBRI, HistAb, HumInd, IBR, IBZ, MLA-IB, RI-1, RILM, SSCI. *Bk. rev.:* 25-40, 1-2 pages, signed. *Aud.:* Ac.

Published in cooperation with the American Literature Section of the Modern Language Association, *American Literature* is considered to be one of the premier journals in its field. Journal content covers American authors from colonial times to the present. Content includes articles, review essays, and book reviews. Examples of special past issues include "Global Contexts, Local Literatures: The New Southern Studies," "Erasing the Commas: RaceGender-ClassSexualityRegion," "Literature and Science: Cultural Forms, Conceptual Exchanges," "Violence, the Body, and 'The South,'" and "Unsettling Blackness." A searchable table of contents back to 2000 is available on the journal's web site. A core-collections title for academic as well as public libraries with strong literature collections.

4149. Arizona Quarterly: a journal of American literature, culture and theory. [ISSN: 0004-1610] 1945. q. USD 25 (Individuals, USD 20; USD 29 foreign). Ed(s): Edgar A Dryden. University of Arizona, Arizona Board of Regents, 1731 E Second St, Tucson, AZ 85721-0014; azq@u.arizona.edu; http://www.u.arizona.edu. Illus., index, adv. Sample. Refereed. Circ: 600. Vol. ends: Winter. Microform: PQC. Online: Chadwyck-Healey Inc.; OCLC Online Computer Library Center, Inc.; Project MUSE; ProQuest LLC (Ann Arbor). Reprint: PSC. *Indexed:* AmH&L, AmHI, HistAb, HumInd, IBR, IBZ, MLA-IB, RILM. *Aud.:* Ac.

Arizona Quarterly publishes articles of theoretical, historical, and cultural interest on canonical and non-canonical works of American literature and film. From its web site: "Our essays are selected for their solid scholarship, tight argument, contextual awareness, and a style demonstrating clarity and grace. It does not consider poetry, fiction, or unsolicited review articles." The most recent issues contain six essays that range from 20 to 30 pages in length followed by a list of contributors. Recent content includes "'The Man He Almost Is': Jerry Maguire and Judith Butler," "A Public History of the Dividing Line: H.D., the Bomb, and the Roots of the Postmodern," and "Slave life; freed life—every day was a test and trial: Identity and memory in *Beloved*." Appropriate for libraries that support academic programs in American literature.

4150. Australian Literary Studies. [ISSN: 0004-9697] 1963. s-a. AUD 85 (Individuals, AUD 45). Ed(s): Leigh Dale. University of Queensland Press, PO Box 6042, St Lucia, QLD 4067, Australia; uqp@uqp.uq.edu.au; http://www.uqp.uq.edu.au/. Illus., index, adv. Refereed. Circ: 1000. Microform: PQC. Online: EBSCO Publishing, EBSCO Host; Florida Center for Library Automation; Gale; RMIT Publishing. *Indexed:* AmHI, ArtHuCI, HumInd, IBR, IBZ, MLA-IB, SSCI. *Bk. rev.:* 6-8, 2-5, signed. *Aud.:* Ac.

Australian Literary Studies features critical essays and reviews on Australian literature. Issues contain eight to ten articles of 10–20 pages in length, and more recent content has included "'Unexpected Effects': Marked Men in Contemporary Australian Women's Fiction," "Burglary in Shady Hill and Sarsaparilla: The Politics of Conformity in White and Cheever," and "First Steps toward a

History of the Mid-Victorian Novel in Colonial Australia." The journal also produces an annual bibliography of scholarly books, articles, and reviews pertaining to Australian literature and language. Recommended for large academic libraries that support comprehensive literature collections and large public libraries that support collections in Australian Studies.

4151. Boundary 2: an international journal of literature and culture.
[ISSN: 0190-3659] 1972. 3x/yr. USD 176 (Individuals, USD 33). Ed(s): Paul A Bove. Duke University Press, 905 W Main St, Ste 18 B, Durham, NC 27701; subscriptions@dukeupress.edu; http://www.dukeupress.edu. Illus., index, adv. Sample. Refereed. Circ: 430. Vol. ends: Fall. Online: EBSCO Publishing, EBSCO Host; Gale; HighWire Press; JSTOR (Web-based Journal Archive); Northern Light Technology, Inc.; OCLC Online Computer Library Center, Inc.; OhioLINK; Project MUSE; ProQuest K-12 Learning Solutions; ProQuest LLC (Ann Arbor); SwetsWise Online Content. Reprint: PSC. *Indexed:* ABS&EES, AmHI, AnthLit, ArtHuCI, FLI, HumInd, IAPV, IBR, IBZ, LRI, MLA-IB, PSA, PhilInd, RILM, SSCI, SociolAb. *Bk. rev.:* Number and length vary. *Aud.:* Ac.

Published by Duke University, this strident journal is dedicated to "understanding the present" by approaching problems from a "number of politically, historically, and theoretically informed perspectives." This international journal of literature and culture often opens with a section on specific authors and an examination of their ideas, such as "dossier on de Man" or "dossier on Leo Strauss." The next section is dedicated to six or seven articles, 15–30 pages in length, that deal with the study of national and international culture and politics: "Representing the Cherokee Nation: Subaltern Studies and Native American Sovereignty," "Cursing Time: Race and Religious Rhetoric in *Light in August*," and "Closet, Coup, and Cold War: F. O. Matthiessen's *From the Heart of Europe*." The journal also offers special issues concerned with rethinking customary views on a given subject or author; the latest of these issues have been "Problems of Comparability/Possibilities for Comparative Studies" and "Critical Secularism." The editors, who will not accept unsolicited manuscripts, have announced that they are only interested in articles "that identify and analyze the tyrannies of thought and action spreading around the world and that suggest alternatives to these emerging configurations of power." Individual subscribers and institutions with electronic access can view issues of the journal online. Recommended for academic libraries. (VBL)

4152. Calyx: a journal of art & literature by women. [ISSN: 0147-1627] 1976. 2x/yr. USD 27 (Individuals, USD 21; USD 38 per vol. in Canada & Mexico). Ed(s): Beverly McFarland, Micki Reaman. Calyx, Inc., PO Box B, Corvallis, OR 97339-0539; calyx@proaxis.com; http://www.proaxis.com/~calyx. Illus., adv. Circ: 4500. Vol. ends: No. 3. *Indexed:* ABS&EES, AmHI, FemPer, HumInd, IAPV, SWA. *Bk. rev.:* 5-12, 1-3 pages. *Aud.:* Ga, Ac.

CALYX, A Journal of Art and Literature by Women is a forum for women's creative literary works, including new poetry, short stories, essays, and reviews, as well as artwork and photography. Previous authors that have been newly discovered through this publication include Julia Alvarez, Paula Gunn Allen, Barbara Kingsolver, and Nobel laureate Wislawa Szymborska. *CALYX* was also the first U.S. publisher to reproduce in color the work of Frida Kahlo. The journal has received a number of literary awards, including the Oregon Governor's Arts Award, Pushcart Prizes, and American Literary Magazine Awards. Recommended for academic libraries and libraries that support collections in women's studies.

4153. The Cambridge Quarterly. [ISSN: 0008-199X] 1964. q. EUR 209 print or online ed. (Individuals, EUR 60 print & online eds.). Ed(s): David C. Gervais, Ann Newton. Oxford University Press, Great Clarendon St, Oxford, OX2 6DP, United Kingdom; jnl.orders@ oup.co.uk; http://www.oxfordjournals.org. Illus., index, adv. Refereed. Circ: 2164. Reprint: PSC. *Indexed:* AmHI, ArtHuCI, BEL&L, BrHumI, FLI, HumInd, MLA-IB. *Bk. rev.:* 4-7 reviews, 4-13 pages. *Aud.:* Ac.

The focus of this Oxford University journal is primarily literary criticism and its "fundamental aim to take a critical look at accepted views." Recent articles have covered an assortment of literary interests that range from English, American, and European texts of many periods and pursued an array of aesthetic subjects including music, cinema, sculpture, and painting: for example, "Cezanne's

Nudes and Balzac," "Lancelot Andrewes's Sacramental Wordplay," "Cruelty in Nabokov," and "Remaking Yeats in *Ulysses*." Generally, the journal contains three to four essays, includes between 15 and 26 pages, and written by experienced authors with multifaceted and careful interpretations. In addition, once a year the journal endows a prize for, and publishes, the best dissertation submitted for the final Cambridge University English Honours examination. One such essay is entitled "The Pockets of Henry Fielding's Writing." This quarterly journal usually contains four to seven book reviews and also offers XML RSS feed. The RSS feeds provide table of contents and abstract information for recent and current issues of each journal. (VBL)

4154. Canadian Literature: a quarterly of criticism and review. [ISSN: 0008-4360] 1959. q. CND 69 (Individuals, CND 49). Ed(s): Laurie Ricou. University of British Columbia, Buchanan E162, 1866 Main Mall, Vancouver, BC V6T 1Z1, Canada. Illus., adv. Refereed. Circ: 1000. Vol. ends: Winter. Microform: PQC. Online: Chadwyck-Healey Inc.; EBSCO Publishing, EBSCO Host; Micromedia ProQuest; OCLC Online Computer Library Center, Inc.; ProQuest K-12 Learning Solutions; ProQuest LLC (Ann Arbor). *Indexed:* AmHI, ArtHuCI, BEL&L, BRD, BRI, CBCARef, CBRI, CPerI, FR, HumInd, IAPV, IBR, IBZ, LRI, MLA-IB, RILM, SSCI. *Bk. rev.:* 30-46, 1-2 pages, signed. *Aud.:* Ac.

Canada's oldest and most notable literary journal, *Canadian Literature* publishes critical essays, poems, interviews, books in review, opinions, and notes. While much of the content is published in English, some material appears in French. Each issue contains a guest editorial, four to six articles or interviews, over 100 books in review, one or two "Opinions and Notes," and a brief "Last Pages" section. Interspersed throughout the journal are several previously unpublished poems by Canadian writers. This journal does not publish fiction. Some issues are dedicated to a particular theme such as "Litterature francophone hors-Quebec/Francophone Writing Outside Quebec" (Winter 2005); "The Literature of Atlantic Canada" (Summer 2006); "South Asian Diaspora" (Autumn 2006); and the Spring 2007 special issue on Gabrielle Roy. The journal's web site has been redesigned and includes static content in both English and French, updated lists of Canadian literary journals and publishers, links to Canadian Literary Awards sites and related blogs, and an RSS feed at www.canlit.ca/feeds/canlit.rss. Under "Resources," one will also find a new online "Letters" section for posting responses to published content. The journal is searchable from 1959 to present and includes full text to books in review from Autumn 1997. This title is essential for libraries that support research in Canadian literature and appropriate for other libraries that support large literature collections.

4155. Ciberletras: revista de critica literaria y de cultura - journal of literary criticism and culture. [ISSN: 1523-1720] 1999. s-a. Free. Ed(s): Susana Haydu, Cristina Arambel-Guinazu. Lehman College, City University of New York, Department of Languages and Literatures, 250 Bedford Park Blvd W, Bronx, NY 10468. Refereed. *Indexed:* AmHI, MLA-IB. *Bk. rev.:* 2-3, signed. *Aud.:* Ac.

Funded chiefly by Lehman College, City University of New York, *CiberLetras* publishes articles, book reviews, interviews, and notes in English or Spanish on the literatures of Spain and Latin America. The advisory committee is made up of scholars from Yale, La Universidad Nacional Autonoma de Mexico, and La Universidad de Buenos Aires, along with an editorial committee of 25 scholars who represent institutions throughout the United States and Europe. Examples of past special issues featured "Erotismo y violencia en la narrativa hispana de los ultimos veinte anos," "La novela policial hispanica actual," and the poetry of Latin America over the past 25 years. The web site maintains an archive back to 1999. Approximately 300 articles are indexed in the MLA International Bibliography database.

4156. College Literature. [ISSN: 0093-3139] 1974. q. USD 80 (Individuals, USD 40). Ed(s): Dr. Kostas Myrsiades. West Chester University, 210 East Rosedale Ave, West Chester, PA 19383; collit@wcupa.edu; http://www.collegeliterature.org. Illus., index, adv. Refereed. Circ: 1000 Paid. Vol. ends: Oct. Online: Chadwyck-Healey Inc.; EBSCO Publishing, EBSCO Host; Florida Center for Library Automation; Gale; Northern Light Technology, Inc.; OCLC Online Computer Library Center, Inc.;

OhioLINK; Project MUSE; ProQuest K-12 Learning Solutions; ProQuest LLC (Ann Arbor); SwetsWise Online Content; H.W. Wilson. *Indexed:* ABIn, ABS&EES, AmHI, ArtHuCI, BEL&L, BRI, CBRI, EduInd, HumInd, L&LBA, MLA-IB, RILM, SSCI. *Bk. rev.:* 4-5, 3-5 pages. *Aud.:* Ac.

This innovative journal, both practical and theoretical in nature, serves college and university teachers by providing "usable, readable, and timely material designed to keep its readers abreast of new developments and shifts" in English, American, European, Eastern, and Third World literatures. This interdisciplinary and comparative journal offers general and special issues. General issues typically include abstracts; review essays; and at least seven articles, which are often bold and persuasive in conceptual effect, varying in length from 18 to 25 pages. Special issues such as the call for "Reading Homer in the 21st Century" or "Cognitive Shakespeare: Criticism and Theory in the Age of Neuroscience" blend textual analysis, literary theory, and pedagogy for "studying and teaching new bodies of literature and experiencing old literatures in new ways." The special issue on Shakespeare concentrates on sections "Theorizing Cognition: Understanding Shakespearean Patterns," "Historicizing Cognition: Interpreting Individuals Plays," "Using Cognition: Performing and Adapting Shakespeare Today." The journal is available online and is recommended for all academic libraries. (VBL)

4157. *Comparative Critical Studies.* Formed by the merger of (1979-2004): *Comparative Criticism; New Comparisons.* [ISSN: 1744-1854] 2004. 3x/yr. GBP 70.50. Ed(s): Robert Weninger. Edinburgh University Press, 22 George Sq, Edinburgh, EH8 9LF, United Kingdom; journals@eup.ed.ac.uk; http://www.eup.ed.ac.uk. *Indexed:* AmHI. *Bk. rev.:* 0-9; 2-4 pages. *Aud.:* Ac.

This new journal, starting in 2004, replaces *Comparative Criticism* and *New Comparison,* which are now discontinued. Published by the Edinburgh University Press and allied with the British Comparative Literature Association, this tri-annual journal is "concerned with comparative literary and critical studies internationally and in the U.K., from whatever standpoint." Special issues on current topics or thematic clusters such as "Reception Studies," "Diaspora and Empire," "Novelization in the Literatures of the Islamic World," and "Gender" will be forthcoming. Recent articles have centered on "Comparative Literature at a Crossroads?," in which seven authors reflected on comparative literature in the twenty-first century and in the future as well as its shape in the international contexts of Europe, U.K., France, Germany, and China. This journal may feature book reviews, averaging from six to eight, and may also publish selected papers from the international and workshop conferences of the British Comparative Literature Association. This journal is to cover new developments in the field through reviews and bibliographies. Lastly, it also may publish the winners of the annual "John Dryden Translation Competition," in which the first prize recently went to "Love of Marie," translated from the French, and the second prize went to "The Happiness of Kati," translated from the Thai. This publication will appeal to academic libraries with English and Comparative Literature programs. (VBL)

4158. *Comparative Literature.* [ISSN: 0010-4124] 1949. q. USD 60 (Individuals, USD 35). Ed(s): George Rowe. University of Oregon, Comparative Literature, 1249 University of Oregon, Eugene, OR 97403-1249; http://www.uoregon.edu. Illus., index. Refereed. Circ: 2400. Vol. ends: Nov. Microform: PQC. Online: Chadwyck-Healey Inc.; EBSCO Publishing, EBSCO Host; JSTOR (Web-based Journal Archive); Northern Light Technology, Inc.; OCLC Online Computer Library Center, Inc.; ProQuest K-12 Learning Solutions; ProQuest LLC (Ann Arbor); H.W. Wilson. *Indexed:* ABS&EES, AmHI, ArtHuCI, BAS, BRI, CBRI, HumInd, IBR, IBZ, IndIslam, MLA-IB, PhilInd, RI-1, RILM. *Bk. rev.:* 4-7, 2-3 pages, signed. *Aud.:* Ac.

Under the direction of the University of Oregon and selected as the official journal of the American Literature Association, *Comparative Literature* has 2,400 subscribers, an important portion of which are located outside the United States. The editor, George E. Rowe, and the editorial board are "sympathetic to a broad range of theoretical and critical approaches" and are "not confined to a single national literature." Proud of its designation as "the oldest U.S. journal in its field," the journal has expanded to reflect the changes in literary criticism. Its most recent articles, averaging three to six per issue, and of approximately 15–20 pages in length, exemplify its outlook: "Vidal in Furs: Lyric Poetry,

Narrative, and Masoch(ism)," "Neobaroque: Latin America's Alternative Modernity," and "The Fanatic: Philip Roth and Hanif Kureishi Confront Success." This comparative journal contains at least four to six brief book reviews, and an occasional review essay. (VBL)

4159. *Comparative Literature Studies.* [ISSN: 0010-4132] 1963. q. USD 68. Ed(s): Thomas O Beebee. Pennsylvania State University Press, 820 N University Dr, USB-1, Ste C, University Park, PA 16802-1003; pspjournals@psu.edu; http://www.psupress.org. Illus., index, adv. Sample. Refereed. Circ: 1792 Paid. Microform: PQC. Online: EBSCO Publishing, EBSCO Host; OCLC Online Computer Library Center, Inc.; OhioLINK; Project MUSE; SwetsWise Online Content. Reprint: PSC. *Indexed:* ABS&EES, AmHI, ArtHuCI, BAS, BEL&L, BRI, CBRI, FR, HumInd, IBR, IBZ, IndIslam, MLA-IB, RI-1. *Bk. rev.:* 4-16, 2-4 pages, signed. *Aud.:* Ac.

The editor, Thomas O. Beebee, and the editorial board welcome "comparative articles in literary history, the history of ideas, critical theory, studies between authors, and literary relations with and beyond the Western tradition." Published by the Comparative Department at Penn State University, *CLS* has recently published the following articles: "Representing the Other: Ercilla's *La Araucana,* Virgil's *Aeneid,* and the New World Encounter," "Performance of Negation, Negation of Performance: Death and Desire in Kojeve, Bataille, and Girard," and "Nayama and Heka: African Concepts of the Word." This comparative journal contains at least five to seven book reviews, and it often announces forthcoming special issues, lately concerning intra-national comparisons, comparative cultural studies, or globalization and world literature. Every two years, the journal is dedicated to East–West relationships, edited in conjunction with the College of International Relations at Nihon University. Appropriate for academic and larger public libraries. (VBL)

4160. *Contemporary Literature.* Formerly (until 1967): *Wisconsin Studies in Contemporary Literature.* [ISSN: 0010-7484] 1960. q. USD 160 print & online eds. (Individuals, USD 49 print & online eds.). Ed(s): Thomas Schaub. University of Wisconsin Press, Journal Division, 1930 Monroe St, 3rd Fl, Madison, WI 53711-2059; journals@uwpress.wisc.edu; http://www.wisc.edu/wisconsinpress/journals. Illus., index, adv. Refereed. Circ: 1800. Microform: PQC. Online: EBSCO Publishing, EBSCO Host; Florida Center for Library Automation; Gale; JSTOR (Web-based Journal Archive); Northern Light Technology, Inc.; OCLC Online Computer Library Center, Inc.; OhioLINK; Project MUSE; ProQuest LLC (Ann Arbor); SwetsWise Online Content; H.W. Wilson. Reprint: PSC. *Indexed:* ABS&EES, AmHI, ArtHuCI, BEL&L, HumInd, IBR, IBZ, MLA-IB, RILM. *Bk. rev.:* 0-3, 5-10 pages, signed. *Aud.:* Ac.

This journal, presenting articles and reviews by leaders in the field, "covers the whole range of critical practices, and brings new vitality and perspective to contemporary literary studies." This quarterly journal, focusing on both established and emerging writing in English, emphasizes the relationships of text to cultural, historical, and theoretical contexts of contemporary writing; for example, one issue concentrates on "Immigrant Fictions: Contemporary Literature in an Age of Globalization." Generally speaking, each issue contains an engaging interview by an established author, most recently Iva Pekarkova, and in the past interviews have included Pat Barker, Alice McDermott, Medbh Mcguckian, Joseph O'Connor, and Susan Wheeler. Some of the journal's articles, approximately 30 pages in length, and numbering three or four to each issue, have included "Carry on, England: Tom Raworth's 'West Wind,' Intuition, and Neo-Avant-Garde Poetics," "From the Ground Up: The Evolution of the South-West Africa Chapter in Pynchon's *V,*" and "James Merrill's Polyphonic Muse." There are roughly three or four reviews, varying in length from four to ten pages. Recommended for academic and larger public libraries. (VBL)

Critical Inquiry. See Cultural Studies section.

4161. *Criticism: a quarterly for literature and the arts.* [ISSN: 0011-1589] 1959. q. USD 95 (Individuals, USD 42). Ed(s): Cannon Schmitt. Wayne State University Press, The Leonard N Simons Bldg, 4809 Woodward Ave, Detroit, MI 48201-1309; http://wsupress.wayne.edu/. Illus., index, adv. Refereed. Circ: 1175 Paid. Microform: PQC. Online: Chadwyck-Healey Inc.; EBSCO Publishing, EBSCO Host; Florida Center for

Library Automation; Gale; Northern Light Technology, Inc.; OCLC Online Computer Library Center, Inc.; OhioLINK; Project MUSE; ProQuest K-12 Learning Solutions; ProQuest LLC (Ann Arbor); SwetsWise Online Content; H.W. Wilson. *Indexed:* ABS&EES, AmHI, ArtHuCI, BRI, CBRI, FLI, HumInd, IBR, IBZ, MLA-IB, PhilInd, RI-1, RILM, SSCI. *Bk. rev.:* 0-4, 2-6 pages, signed. *Aud.:* Ac.

Originating from Wayne State University, this innovative journal for literature and the arts canvasses "a wide range of textual, visual, and performative practices" and "explores the limits of disciplinarity." This quarterly journal publishes articles that are forcefully convincing and acutely perceptive, often ranging from 15 to 25 pages. Recent articles include "Theology and Economics in the Writing of Robert Crowley," "Reading Shakespeare's Cupid," and "Derek Jarman's Carravagio: The Screenplay as Book." Like the articles, the reviews of the journal, often four or five in number, are "dedicated to the futures of the critical enterprise," and the latest focused on Alan Liu's *The Laws of Cool,* a book which, according to the reviewer, "brilliantly analyzes the pop literature of business culture to expose and dissect its ideology." (VBL)

4162. *Critique (Washington): studies in contemporary fiction.* [ISSN: 0011-1619] 1958. q. USD 129 (Individuals, USD 59 print & online eds.; USD 31 newsstand/cover). Ed(s): Helen Strang. Heldref Publications, 1319 18th St, NW, Washington, DC 20036-1802; subscribe@heldref.org; http://www.heldref.org. Illus., index, adv. Refereed. Circ: 1118 Paid. Vol. ends: Fall. CD-ROM: ProQuest LLC (Ann Arbor). Online: Chadwyck-Healey Inc.; EBSCO Publishing, EBSCO Host; Florida Center for Library Automation; Gale; OCLC Online Computer Library Center, Inc.; ProQuest K-12 Learning Solutions; ProQuest LLC (Ann Arbor); H.W. Wilson. Reprint: PSC. *Indexed:* AmHI, ArtHuCI, BRI, CBRI, HumInd, IBR, IBZ, MLA-IB. *Aud.:* Ac.

This journal, authoritative and discriminating in nature, has "consistently identified the most notable novelists of our time," including Pynchon and Vonnegut in the '70s; Atwood and Morrison in the '80s; Amy Tan and Nurrudin Farah in the '90s; and Lorrie Moore and Mark Danielewski in the twentieth century. Recent articles, both astute and refined, on contemporary fiction and emerging writers have included "The Faithful Trace of Misgiving in W. G. Sebald's *The Emigrants,*" "Quantum Mechanics as Critical Model: Reading Nicholas Mosley's *Hopeful Monsters,*" and "Beyond the Boundaries of the Blues: Diane McKinney-Whetstone's *Blues Dancing* as Middle-Class Blues Narrative." Typically, there are five to eight essays of moderate length in each issue. Recommended for large public and academic libraries. (VBL)

4163. *E L H.* [ISSN: 0013-8304] 1934. q. USD 175. Ed(s): Frances Ferguson. The Johns Hopkins University Press, 2715 N Charles St, Baltimore, MD 21218-4363; http://muse.jhu.edu. Illus., adv. Refereed. Circ: 1464. Vol. ends: Winter. Microform: PQC. Online: Chadwyck-Healey Inc.; EBSCO Publishing, EBSCO Host; Florida Center for Library Automation; Gale; JSTOR (Web-based Journal Archive); OCLC Online Computer Library Center, Inc.; OhioLINK; Project MUSE; ProQuest LLC (Ann Arbor); SwetsWise Online Content. Reprint: PSC. *Indexed:* AmH&L, AmHI, ArtHuCI, BEL&L, HistAb, HumInd, IBR, IBZ, MLA-IB, RILM, SSCI. *Aud.:* Ac.

Published by Johns Hopkins University Press, *ELH* is a recognized journal that concentrates on English and American literature, highlighting works from the Renaissance to the nineteenth century. The journal is supported by an impressive editorial board and knowledgeable scholars who maintain high standards when reading and accepting submissions. For more than 70 years, this quarterly journal, rather than seeking "to sponsor particular methods or aims," consistently publishes articles "with an intelligent mix of historical, critical, and theoretical concerns." Some recent articles have focused on Hazlitt, Keats, Rosetti, Hawthorne, and Addison, and have concerned pleasure, agency, theories of cultural reproduction, domestic fiction, gothic violence, and even sexual and consumer desire. It is truly "an indispensable, if traditional, journal for academic and larger public libraries." XML/RSS is also available. (VBL)

4164. *Early American Literature.* Formerly (until 1967): *Early American Literature Newsletter.* [ISSN: 0012-8163] 1966. 3x/yr. USD 52.50 (Individuals, USD 33). Ed(s): David S Shields. University of North Carolina Press, 116 S. Boundary St, Chapel Hill, NC 27514-3808; uncpress_journals@unc.edu; http://www.uncpress.unc.edu. Illus., index,

adv. Refereed. Circ: 600 Paid and controlled. Online: Chadwyck-Healey Inc.; EBSCO Publishing, EBSCO Host; Florida Center for Library Automation; Gale; Northern Light Technology, Inc.; OCLC Online Computer Library Center, Inc.; OhioLINK; Project MUSE; ProQuest K-12 Learning Solutions; ProQuest LLC (Ann Arbor); SwetsWise Online Content; H.W. Wilson. *Indexed:* AmH&L, AmHI, ArtHuCI, BEL&L, HistAb, HumInd, IBR, IBZ, MASUSE, MLA-IB, RI-1, RILM. *Bk. rev.:* 3-4, 3-5 pages, signed. *Aud.:* Ac.

Early American Literature specializes in articles on American literature through 1830, include Native American, Ibero-American, American Francophone, and Dutch and German American colonial literature. The journal publishes one review essay, five to six articles of 20–30 or more pages in length, and book reviews typically of five to seven pages, with some substantially longer. Examples of current content include "Mary Rowlandson and the Invention of the Secular" and "The Role of Native American Voices in Rethinking Early American Literary Studies." Other recent articles have provided criticism of Anne Bradstreet's poem "Contemplations," J. Hector St. John de Crevecoeur's *Letters from an American Farmer,* and Thomas Morton's *New English Canaan.* This journal has recently moved from the University of North Carolina at Chapel Hill to the Citadel. Recommended for large academic research libraries.

4165. *Early Modern Literary Studies: a journal of sixteenth- and seventeenth-century English literature.* [ISSN: 1201-2459] 1995. 3x/yr. Free. Ed(s): Dr. Lisa Hopkins. Sheffield Hallam University, Department of English, School of Cultural Studies, c/o Dr. Lisa Hopkins, Ed., Collegiate Crescent Campus, Sheffield, S10 2BP, United Kingdom. Illus. Refereed. Vol. ends: Dec. *Indexed:* AmHI, BRI, CBCARef, CBRI, MLA-IB. *Bk. rev.:* 8-11, signed. *Aud.:* Ac.

Centered on the sixteenth and seventeenth centuries, this refereed journal is free online and serves an academic audience. Articles in *EMLS,* which may be interdisciplinary, examine English literature, literary culture, and language. Two recent articles, for example, exemplify the aim of the journal; one is "The School of the World: Trading on Wit in Middleton's *Trick to Catch the Old One,*" in which the author argues that "Middleton seeks an epistemologically practical route through which to negotiate the social change that markets promote." In the other article, "'Headdie Ryots' as Reformations: Marlowe's Libertine Poetics," the author claims, "While Marlowe's drama has frequently been discussed in terms of the playwright's engagement with early modern theology and religious politics, his erotic poetry is not usually read with questions about religion in late-Elizabethan England in mind." The journal also has special issues that are concerned with selected, in-depth essays on topics such as Margaret Cavendish, constructions of early modern subjectivity, or Shakespeare on the screen. In addition to book reviews (approximately ten an issue), this journal offers the unique "theatre review," which evaluates performances such as *As You Like It* at the Crucible Theatre, Sheffield, 31 January-24 March 2007." Lastly, this journal is electronic: its web site is clear and informative; and it also maintains "links to the most useful and comprehensive Internet resources for Renaissance scholars, including archives, electronic texts, discussion groups, and beyond." (VBL)

4166. *EHumanista: journal of Iberian studies.* [ISSN: 1540-5877] 2001. s-a. Free. Ed(s): Antonio Cortijo Ocana. University Of California, Santa Barbara, Department of Spanish & Portuguese, Phelps Hall 4206, Santa Barbara, CA 93106-4150; http://www.spanport.ucsb.edu. Refereed. *Indexed:* MLA-IB. *Bk. rev.:* 6-8, signed. *Aud.:* Ac.

eHumanistica: Journal of Iberian Studies is published by the University of California, Santa Barbara, Department of Spanish and Portuguese. Effective 2007, this peer-reviewed journal became freely available online, providing a readily accessible forum for original research in Spanish and Portuguese Medieval and Early Modern Literatures and Cultures. Because of the cross-cultural nature of this publication, it publishes essays in a number of different languages, including Spanish, Portuguese, English, Catalan, Galician, and Euskera. The journal is specifically interested in providing access to manuscripts that are currently only available in special collections or on microform. The online format allows for the acceptance of content of varying lengths and in diverse formats, including visual, audio, and/or interactive material. The majority of content is retrievable in pdf format. The journal is indexed in the MLA International Bibliography database (from 2001).

4167. *Eighteenth-Century Fiction.* [ISSN: 0840-6286] 1988. q. CND 105 domestic; USD 105 United States; USD 125 elsewhere. Ed(s): Jacqueline Languille, Julie Park. McMaster University, Faculty of Humanities, 1280 Main St West, Hamilton, ON L8S 4L9, Canada. Illus. Sample. Refereed. Circ: 650 Paid. *Indexed:* AmH&L, AmHI, CBCARef, CPerI, HistAb, HumInd, IBR, IBZ, LRI, MLA-IB. *Bk. rev.:* 14-25, 1-4 pages, signed. *Aud.:* Ac.

Eighteenth-Century Fiction publishes essays on "all aspects of imaginative prose" that was published during the long eighteenth century, the period of 1660–1832. The most recent issues included four or five articles and 8–14 book reviews, three or four pages long. A list of contributors is also provided. The languages of the journal are English and French. A most recent special issue was on war and included articles on the technologies of war and narration, allegory and critique, and men of war. The *ECF* web site provides the table of contents from 1988 to present. Selected full text is also provided for volumes 1–10, with additional articles being added as author permission is obtained. Recommended for large academic libraries.

4168. *The Eighteenth-Century Novel.* [ISSN: 1528-3631] 2001. a. USD 112.50. Ed(s): Albert J Rivero, George Justice. A M S Press, Inc., Brooklyn Navy Yard, 63 Flushing Ave., Bldg.292, Ste 417, Brooklyn, NY 11205-1005; queries@amspressinc.com; http://www.amspressinc.com. Illus., index. Refereed. *Indexed:* MLA-IB. *Bk. rev.:* 3-6, 2-3 pages each, signed. *Aud.:* Ac.

One of the relatively new AMS Annuals, *The Eighteenth-Century Novel* covers the long eighteenth century (i.e., 1660–1815) and publishes new research on the Anglophone novel. The two most recent volumes include 8–11 articles each, averaging 20–30 pages in length, and 5–14 book reviews of three to five pages each. The content spans a wide range of topics and includes a section on pedagogy, specifically an essay exploring Samuel Johnson's *Rasselas*. Recent articles include "Accounting for Crusoe's Struggles with Sexuality," "The Fantomina Phenomenon: Eliza Haywood and the Formation of a Heroine," "Allegories of Mentoring: Johnson and Frances Burney's Cecilia," and "Reading Quixotes and Quixotic Readers: Teaching Lennox's Female Quixote." Appropriate for large university libraries.

4169. *English Language Notes.* [ISSN: 0013-8282] 1963. s-a. USD 65 (Individuals, USD 40). Ed(s): Karen Jacobs, John-Michael Rivera. University of Colorado at Boulder, English Language Notes, Campus Box 226, Boulder, CO 80309-0226; http://www.colorado.edu/. Illus., index, adv. Refereed. Circ: 1000. Vol. ends: Dec. *Indexed:* AmHI, ArtHuCI, BEL&L, HumInd, IBR, IBZ, MLA-IB, RI-1, RILM. *Bk. rev.:* 1-3, 2-3 pages, signed. *Aud.:* Ac.

This innovative journal has "undergone a change in editorship and an extensive makeover as a biannual journal devoted exclusively to special topics in all fields of literary and cultural studies." The new *ELN*, committed to three to four pages of length for each contributor, seeks to "provide a unique forum for cutting-edge scholarly debate and exchange in the humanities." Indeed, a recent issue has centered on "Literary History and the Religious Turn," and assembled a striking collection of notes by prominent scholars, some of which are entitled "The Religious Turn (to Theory) in Shakespeare Studies," "Reconstructing the Sacred: Latina Feminist Theology in Sandra Cisneros's *Woman Hollering Creek*," and "Mel Gibson's *The Passion of the Christ* and the Politics of Resurrection." Other special topics have included "Photography and Literature," which includes sections on critical notes and interventions, photo-text collaborations, conversation on digital photography, forums on race, narrating trauma, and photo-poetics. Especially attractive to academic libraries, *ELN* pursues refreshing and energizing perspectives on texts by utilizing a number of theoretical, creative, and cultural approaches. (VBL)

4170. *English Literary Renaissance.* [ISSN: 0013-8312] 1971. 3x/yr. GBP 112 print & online eds. Ed(s): Arthur F Kinney, Kirby Farrell. Blackwell Publishing Ltd., 9600 Garsington Rd, Oxford, OX4 2ZG, United Kingdom; customerservices@blackwellpublishing.com; http://www.blackwellpublishing.com. Illus., index, adv. Refereed. Circ: 1065. Vol. ends: No. 3. *Indexed:* AmH&L, AmHI, ArtHuCI, BEL&L, HistAb, HumInd, IBR, IBZ, MLA-IB, RI-1, RILM. *Aud.:* Ac.

This respected journal, edited by Arthur F. Kinney and published by Blackwell Publishing, attends to "current criticism and scholarship of Tudor and early Stuart English literature, 1485-1665," and privileges works by Shakespeare, Donne, and Milton. However, this tri-quarterly journal also has considerable interest in the "intellectual context and literary achievement" of numerous writers and poets of this innovative and productive time period, especially the artistic endeavors of Spenser, Sidney, Donne, and Herbert, as well as the lesser known works by authors such as Anne Askew, Margaret Cavendish, William Lambarde, and Jane Seager. The journal often features "rare texts and newly discovered manuscripts" and utilizes illustrations of "woodcuts and engravings." Each article, the length of 15–20 pages, entails distinctive interpretations: one essay considers the politics of cooking and the gendering of cooks in Jonson's *Bartholomew Fair* and Massinger's *A New Way to Pay Old Debts*; another concerns how *A Mirror for Magistrates* has implications for the study of autobiographical writings and theories of subjectivity. Yet another essay focuses on how the image of the garden represents the intersection between the human body and the body of the nation state in Shakespeare's *Winter's Tale*. (VBL)

4171. *English Literature in Transition, 1880-1920.* Formerly (until 1963): *English Fiction in Transition, 1880-1920.* [ISSN: 0013-8339] 1957. q. USD 32 (Individuals, USD 18; USD 10 newsstand/cover). Ed(s): Robert Langenfeld. E L T Press, Department of English, PO Box 26170, Greensboro, NC 27402-6170. Illus., index, adv. Sample. Refereed. Circ: 700. Vol. ends: No. 4. Microform: PQC. Online: Chadwyck-Healey Inc.; EBSCO Publishing, EBSCO Host; Florida Center for Library Automation; Gale. *Indexed:* AmHI, ArtHuCI, BRI, CBRI, HumInd, IBR, IBZ, MLA-IB, RILM, SSCI. *Bk. rev.:* 9-15; 2-5 pages. *Aud.:* Ac.

In 2007, *ELT* celebrated its 50th anniversary. The journal continues to publish essays on fiction, poetry, drama, and related topics pertaining to the 1880–1920 era in British literature. Typically, issues contain four articles ranging from 7 to 25 or more pages, with an additional 10–15 book reviews. While the journal may publish review articles on major writers, the discussion should be linked to less-prominent authors of the time. Examples of recent articles include "Frances Power Cobbe's Life and the Rules for Women's Autobiography," "Kipling's 'The White Man's Burden' and Its Afterlives," and "Wilde Women and The Yellow Book: The Sexual Politics of Aestheticism and Decadence." Volumes 26–50 (1983–2007) are indexed on *ELT*'s web site. Appropriate for large academic libraries and large public libraries that support collections in literature.

4172. *Essays in Criticism: a quarterly journal of literary criticism.* [ISSN: 0014-0856] 1951. q. EUR 185 print or online ed. Ed(s): Dr. Seamus Perry, Stephen Wall. Oxford University Press, Great Clarendon St, Oxford, OX2 6DP, United Kingdom; jnl.orders@oup.co.uk; http://www.oxfordjournals.org. Illus., index, adv. Refereed. Circ: 1700. Vol. ends: Oct. Microform: MIM; PQC. Online: EBSCO Publishing, EBSCO Host; Florida Center for Library Automation; Gale; HighWire Press; IngentaConnect; Northern Light Technology, Inc.; OCLC Online Computer Library Center, Inc.; OhioLINK; Oxford Journals; SwetsWise Online Content; H.W. Wilson. Reprint: PSC. *Indexed:* AmHI, ArtHuCI, BEL&L, BrHumI, HumInd, IBR, IBZ, MLA-IB, RI-1. *Bk. rev.:* 3-4; 6-8 pages. *Aud.:* Ac.

This distinguished quarterly journal of literary criticism, founded in 1951 and published by Oxford University Press, covers English literature from the time of Chaucer to the present day, and has achieved its notable excellence by its "originality in interpretation," which is "allied to the best scholarly standards." The journal contains two to five articles, which are typically both erudite and perspicacious in content, are usually 15–19 pages in length, and showcase contributors from both the United States and the United Kingdom. Special features of the journal are the "Critical Opinion" section, which "offers topical discussion on a wide range of literary issues," and the "New Impressions" essays, which examine works of literary criticism that have remained almost continually in print. Concluding the journal is a book review section; and each April, the journal publishes the F. W. Bateson Memorial Lecture, an Oxford address that has been delivered in recent times by a number of outstanding scholars. This refereed journal is suitable for academic and large public libraries, offers XML RSS feed, and has online, full-text availability. (VBL)

4173. Exemplaria: a journal of theory in medieval and Renaissance studies. [ISSN: 1041-2573] 1989. q. USD 118. Ed(s): Judith Shoaf, R Allen Shoaf. Maney Publishing, Ste. 1C, Joseph's Well, Hanover Walk, Leeds, LS3 1AB, United Kingdom; maney@maney.co.uk; http://www.maney.co.uk. Illus., adv. Sample. Refereed. Circ: 405. Indexed: AmHI, ArtHuCI, BEL&L, MLA-IB. Aud.: Ac.

"One of the most consistently interesting and challenging journals devoted to Medieval and Renaissance studies," Exemplaria deserves its admiration for being a scholarly endeavor that "breaks into new territory, while never compromising on scholarly quality." This journal has included symposia and special issues on teaching Chaucer, women, history and literature, rhetoric, medieval noise, and Jewish medieval studies and literary theory. Most recently, however, it has focused on "King Oswald's Holy Hands: Metonymy and the Making of a Saint in Bede's Ecclesiastical History," "The Heart of Guillem de Cabestaing: Courtly Lovers, Cannibals, Early Modern Subjects," and "The Mystical Language of Daily Life: Vernacular Sufi Poetry and The Songs of Abu al-Hasan al-Shushtari." A special issue on "Movie Medievalism" has received high recognition from the Society for Medieval Feminist Scholarship. Recommended for academic libraries, especially those with graduate programs in Medieval Studies. (VBL)

4174. The Explicator. [ISSN: 0014-4940] 1942. q. USD 128 (Individuals, USD 59 print & online eds.; USD 31 newsstand/cover). Ed(s): Paul Haynos. Heldref Publications, 1319 18th St, NW, Washington, DC 20036-1802; subscribe@heldref.org; http://www.heldref.org. Illus., index, adv. Refereed. Circ: 1575 Paid. Vol. ends: No. 4. CD-ROM: ProQuest LLC (Ann Arbor). Online: Chadwyck-Healey Inc.; EBSCO Publishing, EBSCO Host; Florida Center for Library Automation; Gale; Northern Light Technology, Inc.; OCLC Online Computer Library Center, Inc.; ProQuest K-12 Learning Solutions; ProQuest LLC (Ann Arbor); H.W. Wilson. Reprint: PSC. Indexed: AmHI, ArtHuCI, HumInd, IBR, IBZ, MASUSE, MLA-IB, RILM. Aud.: Ac.

The cover of The Explicator employs a quotation by Dryden—"The last verse...is not yet sufficiently explicated"—in order to announce its unique specialization in text-based criticism. This is an approach that offers concise and precise explications of short, selected passages in poetry and prose. "Concentrating on works that are frequently anthologized and studied in college classrooms," this well-established journal, containing about 25–30 brief essays, offers distinctive interpretive forays into both English and American literature as well as world literature that is "from ancient Greek and Roman times to our own." This quarterly and refereed journal acts as a handy resource for teachers and students of literature, especially undergraduates, because its clarity of thought and utilization of many critical approaches elucidates a variety of authors who range from Shakespeare to Poe and Wordsworth to Coetzee. (VBL)

The Horn Book Magazine. See Books and Book Reviews section.

4175. Journal of Commonwealth Literature. [ISSN: 0021-9894] 1965. q. GBP 315. Ed(s): John Thieme. Sage Publications Ltd., 1 Oliver's Yard, 55 City Rd, London, EC1 1SP, United Kingdom; info@sagepub.co.uk; http://www.sagepub.co.uk. Adv. Sample. Refereed. Circ: 750. Reprint: PSC. Indexed: AmHI, ArtHuCI, BAS, BEL&L, BrHumI, HumInd, IBR, IBZ, MLA-IB. Bk. rev.: 20, brief, unsigned. Aud.: Ac.

This journal covers the literature of former and current British colonies or territories, including but not limited to Australia, Canada, The Caribbean, Central and East Africa, India, Malaysia, Pakistan, South Africa, and Sri Lanka. Journal of Commonwealth Literature publishes material that focuses on Commonwealth Literature, Postcolonial Literature, and new Literatures in English. The seven to ten articles per issue range from 15 to 20 pages in length. Recent content includes "From Forked Tongue to Forked Tongue: Rushdie and Milton in the Postcolonial Conversation," "Voicing the 'Great Australian Silence': Kate Grenville's Narrative of Settlement in The Secret River," "Shattering the Word-Mirror in Elizabeth Costello: J. M. Coetzee's Deconstructive Experiment," and "Writing Singapore Gay Identities: Queering the Nation in Johann S. Lee's Peculiar Chris and Andrew Koh's Glass Cathedral." Interviews and brief reviews of books received are also included. Each year the last volume consists of an annual bibliography and covers several regions of the

Commonwealth. The journal's web site provides an index from 1966 to present, with abstracts since 2006. Links to two RRS feeds are also available. Suitable for large academic libraries.

4176. Journal of English and Germanic Philology. Former titles: Journal of English and Germanic Philology; Journal of Germanic Philology. [ISSN: 0363-6941] 1897. q. USD 123 print & online eds. (Individuals, USD 56 print & online eds.). Ed(s): Stephen Jaeger, C Wright. University of Illinois Press, 1325 S Oak St, Champaign, IL 61820-6903; journals@uillinois.edu; http://www.press.uillinois.edu. Adv. Refereed. Circ: 1200. Microform: MIM; IDC; PMC; PQC. Online: Florida Center for Library Automation; Gale; OCLC Online Computer Library Center, Inc.; ProQuest LLC (Ann Arbor). Indexed: AmHI, ArtHuCI, BRI, CBRI, HumInd, IBR, IBZ, L&LBA, MLA-IB, RILM, SSCI. Bk. rev.: 6-7, 1-4 pages. Aud.: Ac.

First published in 1897, and one of the most prestigious journals in its field, the Journal of English and Germanic Philology has recently shifted its focus to "Northern European cultures of the Middle Ages, covering Medieval English, Germanic, and Celtic Studies." According to its web site, the journal specializes in the "literatures and cultures of the early and high Middle Ages in Britain, Ireland, Germany, and Scandinavia; and any continuities and transitions linking the medieval and post-medieval eras, including modern 'medievalisms' and the history of Medieval Studies." Typically, issues include three to five major essays ranging from 20 to 30 pages, and 15–20 book reviews (one to three pages each). The October issue includes an index for the year. A recent special issue focuses on the "Master Narratives of the Middle Ages," and an upcoming special issue will address "The State of Medieval Studies." A new JEGP online archive provides abstracts of both articles and book reviews from volume 102, 2003 to the present. Recommended for medium and large academic libraries.

4177. Journal of Modern Literature. [ISSN: 0022-281X] 1970. 4x/yr. USD 117 (Individuals, USD 42). Ed(s): Jean-Michel Rabate, Rachel Blau DuPlessis. Indiana University Press, 601 N Morton St, Bloomington, IN 47404. Illus., index, adv. Sample. Refereed. Circ: 1000. Vol. ends: Nov. Microform: PQC. Online: Chadwyck-Healey Inc.; EBSCO Publishing, EBSCO Host; Florida Center for Library Automation; Gale; OCLC Online Computer Library Center, Inc.; OhioLINK; Project MUSE; ProQuest LLC (Ann Arbor); SwetsWise Online Content; H.W. Wilson. Reprint: PSC. Indexed: ABS&EES, AmHI, ArtHuCI, FLI, HumInd, IBR, IBZ, MLA-IB, RILM. Aud.: Ac.

Published by Indiana University, this quarterly and international journal "emphasizes scholarly studies of literature in all languages, as well as related arts and cultural artifacts, from 1900 to the present." Contributors include scholars from Australia, England, France, Italy, Nigeria, Saudi Arabia, South Africa, and Spain. Containing 9–14 articles per issue, this journal's most recent articles have included "Modernist Anti-Philosophicalism and Virginia Woolf's Critique of Philosophy," "Seafarer Socialism: Pound, The New Age, and Anglo-Medieval Radicalism," and "Acts of Containment: Marianne Moore, Joseph Cornell, and the Poetics of Enclosure." A special issue slated for publication in 2008 is dedicated to "Contemporary Opera and Modern Literature." In some issues, this journal also contains reviews from four to six pages in length. (VBL)

4178. Journal of Postcolonial Writing. Former titles (until 2005): World Literature Written in English; (until 1972): World Literature Written in English Newsletter; (until 1971): W L W E Newsletter. [ISSN: 1744-9855] 1967. s-a. GBP 192 print & online eds. Ed(s): Janet Wilson, Sarah Lawson Welsh. Routledge, 4 Park Sq, Milton Park, Abingdon, OX14 4RN, United Kingdom; journals@routledge.com; http://www.routledge.com. Refereed. Microform: MML. Online: EBSCO Publishing, EBSCO Host; SwetsWise Online Content. Reprint: PSC. Indexed: AmHI, CBCARef, MLA-IB. Aud.: Ac.

Formerly known in 2005 as World Literature Written in English, it is now called Journal of Postcolonial Writing, although it continues to focus on world literature, especially addressing new perspectives on the "postcolonial in its relation to the global." Its aim is to interrogate nationalism and national boundaries, new ethnicities, global technologies, and diasporic voices, as well as "the economic forces of production which increasingly commodify culture." Recently, some of the critical and theoretical articles, typically six or seven in each issue and averaging 14 pages in length, concern the operatic allusions in Witi Ihimaera's *The Dream Swimmer*; migration and identity in Kapka Kassabova's *Reconnaissance*; and language and the role of the artist in Janet Frames's *Living in the Maniototo*. This Routledge journal contains notable interviews, informative profiles of postcolonial writers and theorists, concise reviews of critical studies of contemporary writing, and even brief selections of poetry and short prose fiction. Recommended for academic libraries with graduates interested in the postcolonial. (VBL)

4179. *Kalliope: a journal of women's literature & art.* [ISSN: 0735-7885] 1979. s-a. USD 35 (Individuals, USD 20). Ed(s): Margaret Clark. Florida Community College at Jacksonville, Kalliope Writers' Collective, 11901 Beach Blvd, Jacksonville, FL 32246; http://www.fccj.org/kalliope. Illus. Refereed. Circ: 1600. Microform: PQC. *Indexed:* AmHI, FemPer, IAPV. *Bk. rev.:* 4, 150-400 words, signed. *Aud.:* Ga, Ac.

The year 2007 marks *Kalliope's* 27th anniversary, making this women's literary journal one of the oldest in the United States. Run by the Kalliope Women Writers' Collective, the journal publishes poetry, short fiction, interviews, reviews, and visual art (black-and-white) by women who are established as well as emerging writers and visual artists. In 2006, the journal sponsored its First Annual Kalliope Short Fiction Contest. Recommended for both general readers and academic libraries.

4180. *Kritika Kultura.* [ISSN: 1656-152X] 2002. s-a. Free. Ed(s): Maria Luisa Torres Reyes. Ateneo de Manila University, Department of English, Loyola Heights, Quezon City, 1108, Philippines; kritikakultura@admu.edu.ph. *Aud.:* Ac.

Kritika Kultura: Journal of language and literary and cultural studies in the Philippines is a refereed electronic journal published in the Philippines by the Department of English at Ateneo de Manila University. This journal focuses on the political economy of language, literature, and culture; the production of cultural texts; audience reception; the history and dynamics of canon formation; identity politics; gender and sexuality; ethnicity; diaspora; nationalism; and post-colonialism. Content includes essays, poetry, interviews, and reviews. This cross-cultural and interdisciplinary journal publishes a variety of content, including articles related to theatre, film, and linguistics as well as to literature and language.

Literature and Theology. See Religion section.

4181. *M E L U S.* [ISSN: 0163-755X] 1974. q. Institutional members, USD 80; Individual members, USD 50. Ed(s): Martha J Cutter. Society for the Study of the Multi-Ethnic Literature of the United States, 215 Glenbrook Rd U-4025, Department of English, Storrs, CT 06269-4025; rodier@marshall.edu; http://english.boisestate.edu/melus/index.htm. Illus., index, adv. Refereed. Circ: 950 Paid. Vol. ends: Winter. Microform: PQC. Online: Chadwyck-Healey Inc.; EBSCO Publishing, EBSCO Host; Florida Center for Library Automation; Gale; JSTOR (Web-based Journal Archive); OCLC Online Computer Library Center, Inc.; ProQuest K-12 Learning Solutions; ProQuest LLC (Ann Arbor); H.W. Wilson. *Indexed:* ABS&EES, AbAn, AmHI, ArtHuCI, Chicano, HumInd, IBR, IBZ, IIBP, MLA-IB. *Bk. rev.:* 0-7, 2-4 pages, signed. *Aud.:* Ac.

Founded in 1973, this exceptional journal features articles, interviews, and reviews that are committed to expanding the "definition of American literature through the study and teaching of Latino American, Native American, African American, Asian and Pacific American, and ethnically specific Euro-American literary works, their authors, and their cultural contexts." This journal is thematically organized, and its most recent articles, some by American and some by international authors, have included "Ethnographies of Transnational Migration in Ruben Martinez's *Crossing Over,*" "Authorship and the Written Word in Amy Tan's Novels," and "Disability and Trauma in *The Farming of Bones.*" This quarterly and refereed journal, usually containing eight to ten articles and at least five reviews, moves over a diverse range of topics and is open "to all scholarly methods and theoretical approaches." (VBL)

4182. *M L N.* Formerly (until 1962): *Modern Language Notes.* [ISSN: 0026-7910] 1886. 5x/yr. USD 175. Ed(s): Rainer Nagele. The Johns Hopkins University Press, 2715 N Charles St, Baltimore, MD

21218-4363; http://muse.jhu.edu. Illus., index, adv. Refereed. Circ: 1062. Vol. ends: Dec. Microform: IDC; PMC; PQC. Online: Chadwyck-Healey Inc.; EBSCO Publishing, EBSCO Host; Florida Center for Library Automation; Gale; JSTOR (Web-based Journal Archive); OCLC Online Computer Library Center, Inc.; OhioLINK; Project MUSE; ProQuest LLC (Ann Arbor); SwetsWise Online Content. Reprint: PSC. *Indexed:* ABS&EES, AmHI, ArtHuCI, BRI, CBRI, FLI, HumInd, IBR, IBZ, L&LBA, MLA-IB, PhilInd, RILM, SSCI. *Bk. rev.:* 1-7; 1-3 pages, signed. *Aud.:* Ac.

Founded in 1886, this journal, published five times a year, was one of those that pioneered the introduction of contemporary continental criticism into American scholarship. "Critical studies in the modern languages (Italian, Hispanic, German, French) and recent work in comparative literature are the basis for the articles and notes in *MLN.*" Each issue, containing eight to ten articles, varying in length from 8 to 20 pages, is often written by contributors in international settings and well-known for their scholarship. Articles may occasionally be written in a language other than English—for instance, in French, German, Spanish, or Italian. Focused on contemporary European literature, each issue is specialized; the first issue of every volume focuses on works in Italian, the second on works in Spanish, the third on works in German, and the fourth on works in French. The fifth issue of every volume covers comparative literature and includes an index to the entire volume. Recently, the French issue, dedicated to the philosopher Jacques Derrida, included articles on "Derrida da capo" by Jean-Luc Nancy, "Ce qui a l'air de quoi" by Helene Cixous, and "Composition Displacement" by Peggy Kamuf. Full-text sample articles on the homepage of the journal are available as well as XML/RSS syndication. (VBL)

4183. *Medium Aevum.* Formerly (until 1932): *Arthuriana (Oxford).* [ISSN: 0025-8385] 1928. s-a. GBP 24 domestic; GBP 30.50 foreign; USD 60 foreign. Ed(s): Jane Taylor, Nigel Palmer. Society for the Study of Mediaeval Languages and Literature, c/o Dr. D.G. Pattison, Hon Treas., Magdalen College, Oxford, OX1 4AU, United Kingdom. Illus., index, adv. Refereed. Circ: 850. Vol. ends: No. 2. Online: Chadwyck-Healey Inc.; EBSCO Publishing, EBSCO Host; Florida Center for Library Automation; Gale; Northern Light Technology, Inc.; OCLC Online Computer Library Center, Inc.; ProQuest LLC (Ann Arbor); H.W. Wilson. *Indexed:* AmHI, ArtHuCI, BEL&L, BrHumI, FR, HumInd, IBR, IBZ, LRI, MLA-IB, RILM. *Bk. rev.:* 16-82, 1-2 pages, signed. *Aud.:* Ac.

Published twice-yearly by the Society for the Study of Mediaeval Languages and Literature, *Medium Aevum* publishes articles, notes, and reviews on medieval literature and languages. Although primarily in English, the journal publishes articles in all major European languages. Typically articles range from 10 to 25 pages in length. Recent issues have analyzed the travel narratives of Jean Mandeville; the concept of holy war and the crusades based on the Old French chanson de geste, "Charroi de Nimes"; and the Arthurian legendary texts of "Conte del Graal," by Chretien de Troyes, and Wace's "Roman de Brut." Recommended for large research libraries.

4184. *Modern Fiction Studies.* [ISSN: 0026-7724] 1955. q. USD 135. Ed(s): John N Duvall. The Johns Hopkins University Press, 2715 N Charles St, Baltimore, MD 21218-4363; http://muse.jhu.edu. Illus., adv. Refereed. Circ: 2000. Vol. ends: Winter. Microform: PQC. Online: Chadwyck-Healey Inc.; EBSCO Publishing, EBSCO Host; OCLC Online Computer Library Center, Inc.; OhioLINK; Project MUSE; ProQuest LLC (Ann Arbor); SwetsWise Online Content. Reprint: PSC. *Indexed:* ABS&EES, AmHI, ArtHuCI, BRI, CBRI, HumInd, IBR, IBZ, MLA-IB, RILM, SSCI. *Bk. rev.:* 0-40, 1-3 pages, signed. *Aud.:* Ac.

Published by Johns Hopkins University Press, this widely circulated journal publishes essays on modern and contemporary fiction of both canonical and emergent works, welcoming "historical, interdisciplinary, theoretical, and cultural approaches to modern and contemporary narrative." *MFS*, originating from the Purdue English Department, publishes two general issues and two special issues each year. General issues include five or six essays, all of which are vivid and refreshing in thought, usually of 13–20 pages in length. The latest essays focus on speech, silence, and discourse in J. M. Coetzee's *Foe*, the scopic drive and visual projection in *Heart of Darkness,* and the problem of feminist futurity. Special issues are devoted to announced topics; the most recent focuses on the fiction of Muriel Spark. But, previously, the highlight was Toni Morrison, which featured well-grounded sections on *Paradise,* gender and justice, music, and memory in her texts. The general issue of the journal also includes about 40 reviews of recent books on modern fiction and theory, reviews that are sometimes neatly divided into "The Americas," "British, Irish, and Postcolonial Literatures," and "Theory and Cultural Studies." (VBL)

4185. *Modern Language Quarterly: a journal of literary history.* [ISSN: 0026-7929] 1940. q. USD 183 (Individuals, USD 35). Ed(s): Marshall Brown. Duke University Press, 905 W Main St, Ste 18 B, Durham, NC 27701; subscriptions@dukeupress.edu; http://www.dukeupress.edu. Illus., index, adv. Refereed. Circ: 789 Paid and controlled. Vol. ends: Dec. Microform: MIM; PMC; PQC. Online: EBSCO Publishing, EBSCO Host; Florida Center for Library Automation; Gale; HighWire Press; Northern Light Technology, Inc.; OCLC Online Computer Library Center, Inc.; OhioLINK; Project MUSE; ProQuest K-12 Learning Solutions; ProQuest LLC (Ann Arbor); SwetsWise Online Content. Reprint: PSC. *Indexed:* ABS&EES, AmHI, ArtHuCI, HumInd, IBR, IBZ, MLA-IB, SSCI. *Bk. rev.:* 0-6, 2-6 pages, signed. *Aud.:* Ac.

In 1993, this journal acquired the subtitle, "a journal of literary history," in order to emphasize all the multifarious aspects of change in literary history within American and European literature. Now the journal incorporates not only approaches centered on sources and influences, authorial intention, and the history of ideas, but also contemporary approaches on cultural representation and critique. The journal is interested in judicious articles "on periods, on the development of modes, genres, and motifs, on influence, on reception, on causation and invention, on the production and dissemination of ideologies and the production and destiny of texts, on the historical dimensions of semiotics, hermeneutics, and deconstruction." It is also interested in "historicism in relation to feminism, ethnic studies, cultural materialism, [and] discourse analysis." Most recent articles, averaging between 20 and 30 pages, include "Milton, the Gunpowder Plot, and the Mythography of Terror," "Henry Mackenzie's *Report on Ossian*: Cultural Authority in Transition," and "'A very knowing American': The Inca Garcilaso de la Vega and Swift's *A Modest Proposal.*" Periodically, special issues cover sizable and multifaceted topics such as "Genre and History." Typically, reviews number four to an issue, averaging three pages in length. Recommended for academic libraries with literature collections. (VBL)

4186. *Modern Language Review.* [ISSN: 0026-7937] 1905. q. GBP 122. Maney Publishing, Ste. 1C, Joseph's Well, Hanover Walk, Leeds, LS3 1AB, United Kingdom; maney@maney.co.uk; http://www.maney.co.uk. Illus. Refereed. Circ: 1800. Vol. ends: Oct. Microform: BHP; PMC. Online: Chadwyck-Healey Inc.; EBSCO Publishing, EBSCO Host; Gale; IngentaConnect. Reprint: PSC. *Indexed:* AmHI, ArtHuCI, BEL&L, BRI, BrHumI, CBRI, FLI, HumInd, IBR, IBZ, MLA-IB, RI-1, RILM, SSCI. *Bk. rev.:* approx. 115, 1-4 pages, signed. *Aud.:* Ac.

This quarterly journal, started in 1905 and connected to the Modern Humanities Research Association, invites articles "predominantly on medieval and modern literature, in the languages of continental Europe, together with English (including the United States and the Commonwealth), Francophone Africa and Canada, and Latin America." Recent articles, nine or ten to an issue, have concerned "Baudelaire, Degeneration Theory, and Literary Criticism in *Fin de siecle* Spain," "Transforming the Horizon: Reverdy's World War I," and "Ovid and the 'free play of signs' in Thomas Nashe's *The Unfortunate Traveller.*" A substantial bulk of the journal, however, concentrates on reviews, including book reviews in English, French, Italian, Spanish, German, and Dutch, and Scandinavian languages as well as Slavonic and other Eastern European languages. These prodigious reviews, sometimes verging on 100 in a single issue and covering over 500 books in a year, are brief and decisive, of two pages in length. Recommended for academic and large public libraries. (VBL)

4187. *Modern Philology: critical and historical studies in postclassical literature.* [ISSN: 0026-8232] 1903. q. USD 166 domestic; USD 181.96 Canada; USD 173 elsewhere. Ed(s): Richard A Strier. University of Chicago Press, Journals Division, PO Box 37005, Chicago, IL 60637; subscriptions@press.uchicago.edu; http://www.journals.uchicago.edu. Illus., index, adv. Refereed. Circ: 1100 Paid. Vol. ends: May. Microform: IDC; PMC; PQC. Online: EBSCO Publishing, EBSCO Host; Florida Center for Library Automation; Gale; JSTOR (Web-based Journal Archive); OCLC Online Computer Library Center, Inc.; ProQuest LLC (Ann Arbor). Reprint: PSC. *Indexed:* ABS&EES, AmHI, ArtHuCI, BEL&L, BRD, BRI, CBRI, HumInd, IBR, IBZ, L&LBA, MLA-IB, RI-1, RILM. *Bk. rev.:* 10-15, 2-4 pages, signed. *Aud.:* Ac.

Editor Richard Strier, an accomplished and well-known scholar of English literature, states that the aim of the journal is "to publish literary criticism and scholarship that does its work, whether of appreciation, understanding, or critique, through close attention to the language and details of texts" and by utilizing a keen sense of "historical awareness." Although its coverage typically ranges through literature of English and European languages from the medieval period to the present, the journal has recently welcomed "contributions on literature in non-European languages and contributions that productively compare texts or traditions from European and non-European literatures." Recent articles, 30–50 pages in length and accessible to a wide audience, have concerned "Donne's Epigrams, A Sequential Reading," "The Nation and the Renaissance Body in Thomas Nashe's *The Unfortunate Traveller*," and "Typological Aporias in *Paradise Lost.*" This journal, recommended for academic libraries, is dedicated to scholarly book reviews and also offers RSS feeds and TOC alerts. (VBL)

4188. *Mosaic (Winnipeg, 1967): a journal for the interdisciplinary study of literature.* Formerly (until 1978): *Journal for the Comparative Study of Literature and Ideas.* [ISSN: 0027-1276] 1967. q. USD 75 (Individuals, USD 48; Students, USD 32). Ed(s): Dr. Dawne McCance. University of Manitoba, Tier Bldg, Rm 208, Winnipeg, MB R3T 2N2, Canada; mosaic_journal@umanitoba.ca; http://www.umanitoba.ca/publications/mosaic. Illus., index, adv. Sample. Refereed. Circ: 800. Vol. ends: Fall. Microform: PQC. Online: Chadwyck-Healey Inc.; Florida Center for Library Automation; Gale; Micromedia ProQuest; OCLC Online Computer Library Center, Inc.; ProQuest K-12 Learning Solutions; ProQuest LLC (Ann Arbor). *Indexed:* AmHI, ArtHuCI, BAS, BEL&L, CBCARef, CPerI, FLI, HumInd, IBR, IBZ, MLA-IB, RI-1, RILM. *Aud.:* Ac.

Mosaic, an award-winning journal that is strikingly intrepid and widely circulated, "is an interdisciplinary journal devoted to publishing the very best critical work in literature and theory. The journal brings insights from a wide variety of disciplines to bear on literary texts, cultural climates, topical issues, divergent art forms and modes of creative activity." Recent essays have concerned theories of mourning in the postcolonial romance and ghost story of Makeda Silvera's *The Heart Does Not Bend,* the interconnection between terrorism and art in Don DeLillo and Baudrillard, and the dynamics of reproduction and evolutionary discourse in John von Neumann's "Theory of Self Reproducing Automata" and Richard Powers's novel *Galatea.* These rigorous essays, usually numbering from eight to ten in each volume and written by contributors from around the world, tend to be 16 pages in length and predominantly deal "with cutting-edge exploration of theory." This quarterly journal is recommended for larger academic libraries that serve advanced undergraduate and graduate programs in literature. (VBL)

4189. *Narrative.* [ISSN: 1063-3685] 1993. 3x/yr. USD 60. Ed(s): James Phelan. Ohio State University Press, 180 Pressey Hall, 1070 Carmack Rd, Columbus, OH 43210-1002; ohiostatepress@osu.edu; http://www.ohiostatepress.org. Refereed. Circ: 1000 Paid. Microform: PQC. Online: EBSCO Publishing, EBSCO Host; Florida Center for Library Automation; Gale; Northern Light Technology, Inc.; OCLC Online Computer Library Center, Inc.; OhioLINK; Project MUSE; SwetsWise Online Content. *Indexed:* AmHI, ArtHuCI, HumInd, MLA-IB, RILM. *Aud.:* Ac.

Appealing to a diverse audience, which is composed in part of non-specialists, this triannual journal is "dedicated to the investigation of narrative, its elements, techniques, and forms; its relation to other modes of discourse; its power and influence in cultures past and present." The journal, focused on English, American, and European texts, defines narrative in general terms, and includes study of the novel, epic poetry, biography, film, music, performance, and even medical case histories. This journal usually contains six to ten articles and highly values the intersection of theoretical investigation and practical criticism. It has included the following recent articles: "Romance and the

Courtship Plot in Jane Austen," "The Story Was Already Written: Narrative Theory in *The Lord of the Rings*," and "Theory of Fiction: A Non-Western Narrative Tradition." (VBL)

4190. *New Literary History: a journal of theory and interpretation.*
[ISSN: 0028-6087] 1969. q. USD 165. Ed(s): Ralph Cohen. The Johns Hopkins University Press, 2715 N Charles St, Baltimore, MD 21218-4363; http://muse.jhu.edu. Illus., index, adv. Refereed. Circ: 1009 Controlled. Vol. ends: Nov. Microform: PQC. Online: Chadwyck-Healey Inc.; EBSCO Publishing, EBSCO Host; Florida Center for Library Automation; Gale; JSTOR (Web-based Journal Archive); OCLC Online Computer Library Center, Inc.; OhioLINK; Project MUSE; ProQuest LLC (Ann Arbor); SwetsWise Online Content. Reprint: PSC. *Indexed:* ABS&EES, AmH&L, AmHI, ArtHuCI, BAS, BEL&L, FLI, HistAb, HumInd, IBR, IBZ, L&LBA, LRI, MLA-IB, PSA, PhilInd, RILM, SSA, SSCI, SociolAb. *Aud.:* Ac.

A quotation by Samuel Johnson opens this journal: "Literary history is an account of the state of learning...." This statement accurately reflects this journal's continued interest in "practical criticism" and practical learning. It examines the "relation between past works and present critical and theoretical needs" and has proudly "resisted short-lived trends and subsuming ideologies." Originating out of Johns Hopkins University Press, *NLH* has an impressive editorial board of some of the finest scholars, such as Fredric R. Jameson, Toril Moi, Martha C. Nussbaum, and Hayden White. The journal invites theoretical and interdisciplinary articles that deal with all facets of literary history and its change, definition, interpretation, or problems. Thus, there is a focus on the idea and uses of literary history, including the nature and aims of literary theory, the reading process, hermeneutics, definition of periods, the relation of linguistics to literature, and the evolution of styles, conventions, and genres. Each issue has a unique focus: the Spring issue focused on "Critical Inquiries," Summer on "Reading and Healing," and Autumn on "Attending to Media." The latter contained articles on "The Black Arts Movement and the Genealogy of Multimedia," "Moving Tales: Narrative Drift in Oral Culture and Scripted Theater," and "Childhood and the Evocation of the Past in Two European 'Heritage' Films." This journal offers XML/RSS syndication and is recommended for academic and large public libraries. (VBL)

4191. *Nineteenth-Century Literature (Berkeley).* Former titles: *Nineteenth-Century Fiction;* (until 1949): *The Trollopian.* [ISSN: 0891-9356] 1945. q. USD 142 print & online eds. USD 39 newsstand/cover. Ed(s): Tom Wortham, Joseph Bristow. University of California Press, Journals Division, 2000 Center St, Ste 303, Berkeley, CA 94704-1223; journals@ucpress.edu; http://www.ucpress.edu/journals. Illus., index, adv. Sample. Refereed. Circ: 1900 Paid. Vol. ends: Mar. Microform: PQC. Online: Chadwyck-Healey Inc.; EBSCO Publishing, EBSCO Host; Florida Center for Library Automation; Gale; JSTOR (Web-based Journal Archive); OCLC Online Computer Library Center, Inc.; ProQuest LLC (Ann Arbor); SwetsWise Online Content; H.W. Wilson. *Indexed:* AmH&L, AmHI, ArtHuCI, BRI, CBRI, HistAb, HumInd, IBR, IBZ, MLA-IB, RI-1. *Bk. rev.:* 5-10, 2-4 pages, signed. *Aud.:* Ac.

This interdisciplinary journal publishes articles on the nineteenth-century literature of the United States, Britain, the British Empire, and Europe and explores a number of issues including gender, history, and psychology, as well as cultural, military, and urban studies. Typical articles range from 25 to 30 pages in length. Recent articles have included "'The Actual Sky Is a Horror': Thomas Hardy and the Arnoldian Conception of Science," "The Return of the 'Unnative': The Transnational Politics of Elizabeth Gaskell's *North and South*," and "Policing and Performing Liberal Individuality in Anthony Trollope's *The Warden*." Five or six books reviews are also included. The journal's web site provides a searchable table of contents with abstracts, as well as an RSS citation alert option. Recommended for all academic libraries and large libraries that support strong collections in literature.

4192. *Notes and Queries: for readers and writers, collectors and librarians.* [ISSN: 0029-3970] 1849. q. EUR 216 print or online ed. Ed(s): L G Black, Bernard J O' Donoghue. Oxford University Press, Great Clarendon St, Oxford, OX2 6DP, United Kingdom; jnl.orders@oup.co.uk; http://www.oxfordjournals.org. Adv. Refereed. Circ: 1100. Microform: PMC; PQC. Online: Chadwyck-Healey Inc.; EBSCO

Publishing, EBSCO Host; Factiva, Inc.; Florida Center for Library Automation; Gale; HighWire Press; IngentaConnect; OCLC Online Computer Library Center, Inc.; OhioLINK; Oxford Journals; ProQuest LLC (Ann Arbor); SwetsWise Online Content; H.W. Wilson. Reprint: PSC. *Indexed:* AmH&L, AmHI, ArtHuCI, BEL&L, BrArAb, BrHumI, HistAb, HumInd, IBR, IBZ, L&LBA, MLA-IB, RILM, SSCI. *Bk. rev.:* 17-30, 1-2 pages, signed. *Aud.:* Ac, Sa.

The title of *Notes and Queries* accurately reflects its purpose, namely the "asking and answering of readers' questions. It is devoted principally to English language and literature, lexicography, history and scholarly antiquarianism." The journal specializes in the activity of collecting both interesting facts and meticulous details about specific words or selected passages in literature, ranging mostly from the Medieval to the early twentieth-century. Some of the most recent, succinct, and concise notes concern "Form and Function of Demonstratives in the Middle English Southern Texts and Speculation on the Origin of *TH*-Type Third Person Plural Pronouns in the North and South," "An Unpublished Letter from Lord Byron to Lady Caroline Lamb," and "A New Source for *The Waste Land*." This quarterly journal, originating from the Oxford University Press, contains reviews, a list of books received, and occasionally a special section on "Readers' Replies," which replies to previous entries in the journal. This refereed journal predominantly appeals to large academic libraries, offers XML RSS feed, and has online, full-text availability. (VBL)

4193. *Novel: A Forum on Fiction.* [ISSN: 0029-5132] 1967. 3x/yr. USD 40 (Individuals, USD 30). Ed(s): Nancy Armstrong. Brown University, Department of Literature, PO Box 1984, Providence, RI 02912; http://www.brown.edu/. Illus., index, adv. Refereed. Circ: 1500. Vol. ends: Spring. Microform: PQC. Online: Chadwyck-Healey Inc.; EBSCO Publishing, EBSCO Host; JSTOR (Web-based Journal Archive); Northern Light Technology, Inc.; OCLC Online Computer Library Center, Inc.; ProQuest LLC (Ann Arbor); H.W. Wilson. *Indexed:* ABS&EES, AmHI, ArtHuCI, HumInd, IBR, IBZ, MASUSE, MLA-IB. *Bk. rev.:* 6-9, 2-4 pages, signed. *Aud.:* Ac.

Fall 2007 marks the 40th anniversary of *The Novel: A Forum on Fiction*. This reputable journal publishes on "theories of the novel, the novel in an international context, fictions of nationalism and globalism, narratives of race and ethnicity, the novel and the history of sexuality, fiction and the culture concept, the novel and mass media, aesthetic theory and the genres and forms of the novel, fiction and the sciences, agency in or of the novel." A typical issue contains five essays, of 15–20 pages in length, along with five to ten book reviews. Recent articles explore aspects of works by Sylvia Plath, Nadine Gordimer, Nathanael West, George Eliot, and Thomas Hardy. Topics of recent and forthcoming special issues include "The Early American Novel," "Ishiguro," and "The Contemporary African Novel." Recommended for large public libraries that support research collections as well as academic libraries.

4194. *P M L A.* [ISSN: 0030-8129] 1884. 6x/yr. USD 150 Free to members. Ed(s): Judy Goulding, Patricia Yaeger. Modern Language Association of America, 26 Broadway, 3rd Fl, New York, NY 10004-1789; http://www.mla.org. Illus., index, adv. Sample. Refereed. Circ: 32500 Paid and controlled. Vol. ends: Nov. Microform: PQC. Online: EBSCO Publishing, EBSCO Host; Gale; IngentaConnect; JSTOR (Web-based Journal Archive); OCLC Online Computer Library Center, Inc.; ProQuest LLC (Ann Arbor). Reprint: PSC. *Indexed:* ABS&EES, AmHI, ArtHuCI, FLI, HumInd, IBR, IBZ, MLA-IB, RILM. *Aud.:* Ac.

This journal, originating from the Modern Language Association of America, publishes articles by its members, and targets scholars and teachers of language and literature. The journal is self-described as "receptive to a variety of topics, whether general or specific, and to all scholarly methods and theoretical perspectives." The main articles may number from 8 to 12 in any given issue, and they not only range over topics from Cartesian corporeality to transnationalism, but also range over texts from Frederick Douglass to Ezra Pound. This journal, issued six times a year, offers sections on timely special topics, on the changing characteristics of the profession, on little-known documents, and on the commemoration of distinguished scholars. Widely circulated and frequently cited, the journal does provide a forum for members to briefly comment on articles in previous issues; but it does not publish book reviews or new works of fiction. The November issue, in particular, is the program for the association's annual convention; but the web site, updated twice a month, includes information of general interest that can not be found in the journal. *"PMLA* is a core journal and is recommended for all libraries."* (VBL)

4195. *Papers on Language and Literature: a journal for scholars and critics of language and literature.* [ISSN: 0031-1294] 1965. q. USD 60 (Individuals, USD 24). Ed(s): Brian Abel Ragen. Southern Illinois University at Edwardsville, SIUE Campus Box 1167, Edwardsville, IL 62026; http://www.siue.edu. Illus., index, adv. Refereed. Circ: 550. Vol. ends: Fall. Microform: PQC. Online: Chadwyck-Healey Inc.; EBSCO Publishing, EBSCO Host; Florida Center for Library Automation; Gale; OCLC Online Computer Library Center, Inc.; ProQuest LLC (Ann Arbor); H.W. Wilson. *Indexed:* ABS&EES, AmHI, ArtHuCI, BEL&L, HumInd, IBR, IBZ, L&LBA, MLA-IB, RILM. *Bk. rev.:* 0-3, 4-6 pages, signed. *Aud.:* Ac.

The focus of *Papers on Language & Literature* (*PLL*) is broad-ranging, covering material across all national literatures and time periods, although it publishes primarily articles on English and American literature. The journal also publishes primary sources such as letters, journals, diaries, and memoirs. Typically, five articles of 15–20 pages appear in each issue, addressing topics of literary theory, criticism, and history. Recent content includes "Lion and Ha Jin's Tiger: The Interplay of Imagination and Reality," "Law and Self-Interest in *The Merchant of Venice*," and "Panopticism and the Construction of Power in Franz Kafka's *The Castle*," and "Nuclear Cassandra: Prophecy in Doris Lessing's *The Golden Notebook*." Forthcoming articles include "Elijah and the Beginning of Evelyn Waugh's *Men at Arms*," "Cather and Woolf in Dialogue: *The Professor's House* and *To the Lighthouse*," and "The Heroism of Heurodis: Self-Mutilation and Restoration in *Sir Orfeo*." This accessible journal is recommended for medium to large academic libraries.

4196. *Postcolonial Text.* [ISSN: 1705-9100] 2004. s-a. Free. Ed(s): Ranjini Mendis. Postcolonial Text, c/o Ranjini Mendis, Dept of English, Kwantlen University College, Surrey, BC V3W 2M8, Canada. Refereed. *Aud.:* Ac.

This electronic and refereed journal specializes in "postcolonial, transnational, and indigenous themes." Offering a genuine space on the Internet for an international forum, this journal promotes critical discussions for "negotiating the various epistemological, cultural, social, and political links and disjunctures between postcolonial, western, and diasporic communities of writers, readers, and academics." The web site is incredibly clear, informative, and easy to navigate. A reader may click on abstracts or the pdf in order to access articles, which normally range from 11 to 21 pages. Recent articles on postcolonial literature, culture, and theory have been "Unspeakable Outrages and Unbearable Defilements: Rape Narratives in the Literature of Colonial India," "Performing (R)evolution: The Story of El Teatro Campesino," and "Desiring the Metropolis: The Anti-Aesthetic and Semicolonial Modernism." In addition to substantial articles, this journal often offers remarkable interviews with known and emerging authors, editorial essays, relevant book reviews, and attention-getting fiction and poetry. There are also clusters of papers on special topics that have thoughtful and authentic discussions, one of which was a discussion concerning J. Edward Chamberlin's "If This Is Your Land, Where Are Your Stories?" This journal is highly recommended for academic libraries with strong collections in literature. (VBL)

Postmodern Culture: an electronic journal of interdisciplinary criticism. See Cultural Studies section.

4197. *Qui Parle: a journal of literary studies.* [ISSN: 1041-8385] 1986. s-a. USD 30 (Individuals, USD 20). Ed(s): Jim Hinch. University of California at Berkeley, Doreen B. Townsend Center for the Humanities, 220 Stephens Hall #2340, Berkeley, CA 94720-2340; http://ls.berkeley.edu/dept/townsend/dept.html. Adv. Refereed. Circ: 1000. *Indexed:* MLA-IB. *Aud.:* Ac.

Founded in 1986 by an editorial board from the University of California at Berkeley, this biannual journal is intensely provocative, rigorous, and innovative, having published articles by some of the most pioneering scholars in literary criticism, theory, and cultural studies, such as Jacques Derrida, Judith Butler, Jane Gallop, Jean-Joseph Goux, Peggy Kamuf, Thomas Laqueur, Jean-Luc Nancy, and Slavoj Zizek. This journal publishes "interdisciplinary

articles covering a range of outstanding theoretical and critical work in the humanities" and seeks to encourage dialogues "which challenge conventional understandings of reading and scholarship in academia." In the past it has featured subjects on "aural Aesthetics," "Digitality," "Heidegger & Company," "Nation and Fantasy," and "Bodies and Disgust." Recent articles have concerned "Frederick Douglass' Differing Opinions on the Pro-Slavery Character of the American Union," "Disaster as a Place of Morality: The Sovereign, the Humanitarian, and the Terrorist," and "Elsewheres: Radical Relativism and the Frontiers of Empire." Recommended for academic libraries with advanced graduate programs. (VBL)

4198. *Religion and Literature.* Formerly (until 1984): *Notre Dame English Journal.* [ISSN: 0888-3769] 1957. 3x/yr. Individuals, USD 25. Ed(s): Sian White, Kevin Hart. University of Notre Dame, Department of English, 356 O'Shaughnessy Hall, Notre Dame, IN 46556. Adv. Refereed. Circ: 500 Paid. *Indexed:* AmHI, ArtHuCI, CPL, FR, IBR, IBZ, MLA-IB, NTA, R&TA, RI-1. *Bk. rev.:* 3-5, 5 pages, signed. *Aud.:* Ac.

Having published works by outstanding and innovative scholars—such as M. H. Abrams, Paula Gunn Allen, Thomas J. J. Altizer, Rene Girard, Terry Eagleton, John Milbank, Regina M. Schwartz, etc.—this journal is also edited by Kevin Hart, a well-known scholar himself, writing on the intersection of religion and literary forms. Indeed, this formidable journal is devoted to the discussion of "two crucial human concerns, the religious impulse and the literary forms of any era, place, or language." In the past, it has focused on gift and narrative, iconicity, hesychasm, mystical writings, and dramatic texts. It also has dealt with a wide range of texts by Samuel Beckett, Christopher Marlowe, Margaret Thorpe, and Mechtild of Hackeborn. More recently, this journal, published three times a year, centered on American literature's relation to religion, featuring at least one article on "How the Church Became Invisible: A Christian Reading of American Literary Tradition." It also publishes review essays and book reviews. Recommended for all libraries, especially those with a religious studies program or a general interest in religion and literature. (VBL)

4199. *Renaissance Forum: an electronic journal of early-modern literary and historical studies.* [ISSN: 1362-1149] 1996. 2x/yr. Free. Ed(s): Glenn Burgess, Robin Headlam-Wells. University of Hull, Department of History, University Of Hull, Cottingham Rd, Hull, HU6 7RX, United Kingdom. Illus. Refereed. Vol. ends: Sep. *Indexed:* MLA-IB. *Bk. rev.:* 8-10, signed. *Aud.:* Ac.

This electronic journal specializes in early modern English literary and historical scholarship. It especially provides a "forum for scholarly and theoretical debate of a kind that is not possible in most conventional journals." Edited at the University of Hull, this journal has been published biannually online since 1996. Unfortunately, it has not been updated since 2004. (VBL)

Research in African Literatures. See Africa section.

4200. *The Review of Contemporary Fiction.* [ISSN: 0276-0045] 1981. 3x/yr. USD 26 (Individuals, USD 17; USD 8 newsstand/cover). Ed(s): Danielle Dutton. Center for Book Culture, Inc., ISU Campus 8905, Normal, IL 61790-8905; contact@centerforbookculture.org; http://www.centerforbookculture.org. Illus., index, adv. Circ: 2955 Paid and free. Vol. ends: Fall. Microform: PQC. Online: Chadwyck-Healey Inc.; EBSCO Publishing, EBSCO Host; Florida Center for Library Automation; Gale; Northern Light Technology, Inc.; OCLC Online Computer Library Center, Inc.; ProQuest K-12 Learning Solutions; ProQuest LLC (Ann Arbor); H.W. Wilson. *Indexed:* ABS&EES, AmHI, BEL&L, BRI, CBRI, HumInd, IBR, IBZ, MLA-IB, RILM. *Bk. rev.:* 8-50, 1/2-1 page, signed. *Aud.:* Ac.

The Review of Contemporary Fiction "features critical essays on fiction writers whose work resists convention and easy categorization." The journal's focus is varied, from postmodern to experimental and avant-garde, to metafictional and subversive, and it covers works by established or new or previously unchampioned writers from the United States as well as from abroad. Each issue focuses on an author, a group of authors or a particular theme. Recent articles have featured William Eastlake, Julieta Campos, and Jane Bowles. The Spring 2006 issue was devoted to the work of Steven Millhauser, and the most recent issue features articles on New Cuban fiction. Articles can range from 5 to 70 pages, with book reviews being one or two paragraphs in length. Interviews are also sometimes included and may be accessible full-text from the journal's web site along with the journal's table of contents (1981 to present). This journal would serve a wide audience and is recommended for both academic and public libraries.

4201. The Review of English Studies: a quarterly journal of English literature and the English language. [ISSN: 0034-6551] 1925. 5x/yr. EUR 291 print or online ed. Ed(s): David Bradshaw, Gordon Campbell. Oxford University Press, Great Clarendon St, Oxford, OX2 6DP, United Kingdom; jnl.orders@oup.co.uk; http://www.oxfordjournals.org. Illus., index, adv. Refereed. Circ: 2050. Vol. ends: Nov. Microform: PQC. Online: Chadwyck-Healey Inc.; EBSCO Publishing, EBSCO Host; Florida Center for Library Automation; Gale; HighWire Press; IngentaConnect; JSTOR (Web-based Journal Archive); Northern Light Technology, Inc.; OCLC Online Computer Library Center, Inc.; OhioLINK; Oxford Journals; ProQuest LLC (Ann Arbor); SwetsWise Online Content; H.W. Wilson. Reprint: PSC. *Indexed:* AmHI, ArtHuCI, BEL&L, BRI, BrHumI, CBRI, HumInd, IBR, IBZ, L&LBA, MLA-IB. *Bk. rev.:* 7-22, 1-2 pages, signed. *Aud.:* Ac.

The Review of English Studies publishes articles on English literature and the English language. While it focuses more on historical scholarship than on interpretive criticism, this journal will also consider "fresh readings of authors and texts...offered in light of newly discovered sources or new interpretation of known material." Since 1999, this journal has sponsored the RES Essay Prize and encouraged the scholarly efforts of postgraduate researchers. The most recent prize was awarded for "Like a Hand in the Margine of a Booke: William Blount's *Marginalia* and the Politics of Sidney's *Arcadia*." Recent issues have contained five articles of 20–25 pages in length, followed by 7–20 or so book reviews. Examples of recent content include "The 'Stupid' Final Lines of *Titus Andronicus*," "Thomas Middleton's View of Public Utility," and "The Faerie King's Kunstkammer: Imperial Discourse and the Wondrous in *Sir Orfeo*." The journal's web site provides a searchable table of contents with abstracts from 1925 to present as well as alerting services for eTOCs and an RSS feed. Recommended for large academic research libraries.

4202. Romanticism: the journal of romantic culture and criticism. [ISSN: 1354-991X] 1995. 3x/yr. GBP 115. Ed(s): Drummond Bone, Timothy Webb. Edinburgh University Press, 22 George Sq, Edinburgh, EH8 9LF, United Kingdom; http://www.eup.ed.ac.uk. Illus., adv. Online: EBSCO Publishing, EBSCO Host. *Indexed:* AmHI, MLA-IB. *Bk. rev.:* 10-15, 2-4 pages, signed. *Aud.:* Ac.

Romanticism provides a forum for romantic studies, covers 1750–1850, and publishes critical, historical, textual, and bibliographical essays. Issues contain six or seven articles of 10–15 pages with a few substantially longer in length, followed by three to five book reviews. Recent thematic issues feature "Rebels and Mutineers" and "John Keats and his Circle." Recent essays include "The Suppression of Samuel Bamford's Peterloo Poems," "Night and Gothic Grandeur: Politics and Antiquarianism in Wordsworth's *Salisbury Plain*," "'Oriental' and 'Orientalist' Poetry: The Debate in Literary Criticism in the Romantic Period," and "Inuit Diasporas: Frankenstein and the Inuit in England." The journal's web site provides a table of contents back to 2001. Recommended for academic libraries that support advanced literature studies.

4203. Romanticism on the Net. [ISSN: 1467-1255] 1996. q. Free. Ed(s): Michael Eberle-Sinatra. St. Catherine's College, Oxford, OX1 3UJ, United Kingdom; michael.laplace-sinatra@stcatz.ox.ac.uk; http://users.ox.ac.uk/~scat0385/. Refereed. *Indexed:* MLA-IB. *Bk. rev.:* 5-10, signed. *Aud.:* Ac.

Romanticism on the Net is an international refereed journal devoted to studies in British Romanticism. In 2006, *RoN* celebrated its tenth year of publishing online. Recent content has featured 7–14 articles and four to six book reviews, all in English. Recent special issues have addressed the topics of "Transatlantic Romanticism," "Lord Byron's Canons," and "The Gothic: From Ann Radcliffe to Anne Rice." Content is currently fully searchable online, but for now only in French. The web site also lists related journal titles, associations, web sites, and upcoming conferences. URL: www.ron.umontreal.ca.

4204. Room. Formerly (until 2007): *Room of One's Own.* [ISSN: 1914-4083] 1975. q. CND 36 (Individuals, CND 27). Growing Room Collective, P O Box 46160, Vancouver, BC V6J 5G5, Canada; http://www.islandnet.com/room/enter. Adv. Circ: 1000 Paid. Microform: MML; PQC. *Indexed:* AmHI, CBCARef, CPerI, FemPer, MLA-IB, SWA. *Bk. rev.:* 0-3; 1-2 pages, signed. *Aud.:* Ga, Ac.

This magazine turned 30 recently and has broadened its focus and shortened its name to *Room*. A literary magazine of women's writing and art, the journal continues to publish fiction, poetry, reviews, art work, and interviews, and has added several new editorial features including letters in "The FrontRoom," topical Q&As in "The BackRoom," and a reader profiles in "Roommate." *Room* also sponsored an annual Fiction and Poetry Contest. Some full text to back issues is available on their web site.

4205. Southern Literary Journal. [ISSN: 0038-4291] 1968. s-a. USD 45 (Individuals, USD 28). Ed(s): Kristina Bubo, Minrose Gwin. University of North Carolina Press, 116 S. Boundary St, Chapel Hill, NC 27514-3808; uncpress_journals@unc.edu; http://www.uncpress.unc.edu. Illus., index. Refereed. Circ: 500 Paid and free. Microform: PQC. Online: Chadwyck-Healey Inc.; EBSCO Publishing, EBSCO Host; Florida Center for Library Automation; Gale; Northern Light Technology, Inc.; OCLC Online Computer Library Center, Inc.; OhioLINK; Project MUSE; ProQuest K-12 Learning Solutions; ProQuest LLC (Ann Arbor); SwetsWise Online Content; H.W. Wilson. Reprint: PSC. *Indexed:* AmH&L, AmHI, ArtHuCI, HistAb, HumInd, MLA-IB, RI-1, RILM. *Bk. rev.:* 3-5, 3-4 pages, signed. *Aud.:* Ac.

Southern Literary Journal publishes articles and reviews on the literature of the southern United States from literary, historical, and cultural perspectives. Typically articles range from 15 to 20 pages followed by three to five substantial book reviews. Recent articles have analyzed Booker T. Washington's "Up from Slavery," Ellen Glasgow's "The Battle-Ground," and Olive Tilford Dargan's "Call Home the Heart" and "A Stone Came Rolling." Recommended for medium to large academic libraries and public libraries that support Southern literature collections.

4206. Speculum: a journal of Medieval studies. [ISSN: 0038-7134] 1926. q. USD 100. Ed(s): Paul E Szarmach. Medieval Academy of America, 104 Mount Auburn St., 5th fl, Cambridge, MA 02138-5019; speculum@medievalacademy.org; http://www.medievalacademy.org. Illus., index, adv. Refereed. Circ: 6500. Vol. ends: Oct. Microform: MIM; PQC. Online: JSTOR (Web-based Journal Archive). *Indexed:* ABS&EES, AmHI, ArtHuCI, ArtInd, BEL&L, BRI, BrArAb, CBRI, FR, HumInd, IBR, IBZ, IPB, IndIslam, IndVet, MLA-IB, NumL, PhilInd, RI-1, RILM, SSCI, VB. *Bk. rev.:* 80-90, 2 pages, signed. *Aud.:* Ac.

This respected journal, sponsored by the Medieval Academy of America, is dedicated exclusively to the Middle Ages of Western Europe, ranging between the years 500 and 1500. The journal welcomes submissions that "tackle large interpretative questions, undertake the synthetic analysis of major methodologies, or consider newer theoretical approaches to medieval studies." Recent articles have included "Monks, Kings and the Transformation of Sanctity: Jonas of Bobbio and the End of the Holy Man" and "Chess and Courtly Culture in Medieval Castile: The Libro de Ajedrez of Alfonso X, el Sabio." Because the journal may also include Arabic, Byzantine, Hebrew, and Slavic Studies, articles such as "Concern about Judaizing in Academic Treatises on the Law, c. 1130–1230" are also published. Recommended for academic libraries with Medieval studies programs. (VBL)

4207. Studies in American Fiction. [ISSN: 0091-8083] 1973. s-a. USD 18 (Individuals, USD 12). Ed(s): Mary Loeffelholz. Northeastern University, Department of English, 406 Holmes Hall, 360 Huntington Ave., Boston, MA 02115; http://www.northeastern.edu. Illus., adv. Refereed. Circ: 900. Vol. ends: Fall. Online: Chadwyck-Healey Inc.; Florida Center for Library Automation; Gale; Northern Light Technology, Inc.; OCLC Online Computer Library Center, Inc.; H.W. Wilson. Reprint: PSC. *Indexed:* AmHI, ArtHuCI, BEL&L, HumInd, IBR, IBZ, MLA-IB. *Bk. rev.:* 2-5, 1-2 pages, signed. *Aud.:* Ac.

Studies in American Fiction publishes articles and reviews on the prose fiction of the United States. Covering colonial times to the present, the journal features both canonical and emergent writers. The most recent issues available (2006) include the following articles: "Naming the Trees: Literary Onomastics in Susan Warner's *The Wide, Wide World*," "Sympathetic Listening in Frederick Douglass's 'The Heroic Slave' and 'My Bondage and My Freedom,'" "Two Samuels of Hartford: Clemens, Colt, and the Unification of a Disjointed Mysterious Ending," and "'It Could Have Been Any Street': Ann Petry, Stephen Crane, and the Fate of Naturalism." The journal's web site currently offers the table of contents from 1973 to 2003. Recommended for medium and large academic libraries.

4208. Studies in English Literature 1500-1900. [ISSN: 0039-3657] 1961. q. USD 108. Ed(s): Logan Browning. The Johns Hopkins University Press, 2715 N Charles St, Baltimore, MD 21218-4363; http://muse.jhu.edu. Illus., adv. Refereed. Circ: 1062. Microform: PQC. Online: Chadwyck-Healey Inc.; EBSCO Publishing, EBSCO Host; Gale; JSTOR (Web-based Journal Archive); OCLC Online Computer Library Center, Inc.; OhioLINK; Project MUSE; ProQuest LLC (Ann Arbor); SwetsWise Online Content; H.W. Wilson. Reprint: PSC. *Indexed:* AmH&L, AmHI, ArtHuCI, HistAb, HumInd, IBR, IBZ, L&LBA, MASUSE, MLA-IB, RILM. *Aud.:* Ac.

Offering historical and critical essays on literature published between 1500 and 1900, this quarterly journal is divided into numbers, each of which conveniently specializes in specific time periods of British literature: "English Renaissance," "Tudor and Stuart Drama," "Restoration and Eighteenth Century," and "Nineteenth Century." Edited by Robert L. Patten and supported by a remarkable editorial board, this journal offers mixed-audience essays with lucid, thorough, and sharp analyses of major and minor works of specific periods. Some articles, usually eight to ten in an issue and of moderate length, have concerned Mary Cary as a radical religious exegete and visionary poet; the influence of Victorian debates about aesthetic education on Thomas Hardy; and the inadequacies of modern sexual taxonomies for understanding the nature of premodern intimacy. The journal also offers an informative overview by a seasoned scholar of recent studies in the field. XML/RSS syndication is offered. (VBL)

4209. Studies in Philology. [ISSN: 0039-3738] 1903. 4x/yr. USD 52.50 (Individuals, USD 33). Ed(s): Don Kennedy. University of North Carolina Press, 116 S. Boundary St, Chapel Hill, NC 27514-3808; uncpress_journals@unc.edu; http://www.uncpress.unc.edu. Adv. Refereed. Circ: 1500. Microform: MIM; IDC; PMC; PQC. Online: Chadwyck-Healey Inc.; EBSCO Publishing, EBSCO Host; Northern Light Technology, Inc.; OCLC Online Computer Library Center, Inc.; OhioLINK; Project MUSE; ProQuest K-12 Learning Solutions; ProQuest LLC (Ann Arbor); SwetsWise Online Content; H.W. Wilson. Reprint: PSC. *Indexed:* AmHI, ArtHuCI, BEL&L, HumInd, IBR, IBZ, MLA-IB, NTA, RI-1, RILM. *Aud.:* Ac.

Edited by Edward Donald Kennedy and published by the University of North Carolina at Chapel Hill, this quarterly journal "publishes articles on all aspects of British literature from the Middle Ages to 1900, and also, articles on relations between British literature and works in the classical, Romance, and Germanic languages." Circulating to 900 subscribers, mostly scholars and students of English and comparative literature, history, religion, classics, and philosophy, this journal, one of the first in literary criticism in the United States, averages about five articles of 15 to 20 pages in length. Recent articles, focusing on close textual details, have concerned emendations in *Beowulf*, religion and ideology of warfare in *Henry V*, and rhyme distribution chronology in John Gower's Latin Poetry. Recommended for academic libraries with graduate populations in English. (VBL)

4210. Studies in Romanticism. [ISSN: 0039-3762] 1961. q. USD 60 (Individuals, USD 23). Ed(s): David Wagenknecht. Boston University, Graduate School, 236 Bay State Rd, Boston, MA 02215; http://www.bu.edu/. Illus., index, adv. Refereed. Circ: 1400. Vol. ends: Winter. Microform: PQC. Online: Chadwyck-Healey Inc.; Florida Center for Library Automation; Gale; Northern Light Technology, Inc.; OCLC Online Computer Library Center, Inc.; ProQuest K-12 Learning Solutions; ProQuest LLC (Ann Arbor); H.W. Wilson. *Indexed:* AmH&L, AmHI, ArtHuCI, BEL&L, HistAb, HumInd, IBR, IBZ, MLA-IB, MusicInd, RILM. *Bk. rev.:* 4-6, 2-6 pages, signed. *Aud.:* Ac.

The leading journal on the Romantic movement, *Studies in Romanticism* publishes essays on literature, arts, and culture. While covering both Europe and the United States, the journal tends to focus primarily on English literature. A typical issue contains six articles that range from 15 to 20 pages, with a few essays substantially longer. Each issue includes four to six book reviews. Recent content includes "Caliban to the Audience: Auden's Revision of Wordsworth's Sublime," "Antiquarian Authorship: D'Israeli's Miscellany of Literary Curiosity and the Question of Secondary Genres," and "Colonial Desires: The Fantasy of Empire and Elizabeth Hamilton's 'Translations of the Letters of a Hindoo Rajah.'" At this time, no web site is maintained for this journal. Recommended for medium to large academic libraries that support advanced studies in literature.

4211. Studies in the Novel. [ISSN: 0039-3827] 1969. q. USD 45 (Individuals, USD 30; USD 55 foreign). Ed(s): Jacqueline Foertsch. University of North Texas, English Department, PO Box 311307, Denton, TX 76203-1307; jamest@unt.edu; http://www.engl.unt.edu. Illus., index. Refereed. Circ: 1700. Vol. ends: No. 4. Microform: PQC. Online: Chadwyck-Healey Inc.; EBSCO Publishing, EBSCO Host; Florida Center for Library Automation; Gale; Northern Light Technology, Inc.; OCLC Online Computer Library Center, Inc.; ProQuest K-12 Learning Solutions; ProQuest LLC (Ann Arbor); H.W. Wilson. *Indexed:* ABS&EES, AmHI, ArtHuCI, BEL&L, HumInd, IBR, IBZ, MLA-IB. *Bk. rev.:* 0-7, 1-2 pages, signed. *Aud.:* Ac.

Studies in the Novel publishes criticism on the novel in all times and places and considers all interpretive methods. The typical issue includes five articles of 15–20 pages in length, seven to ten book reviews, and occasionally an essay-review. Recent issues have covered Cather, Dickens, Gaskell, Green, Wells, and Wharton. The most recent issue included essays on Aphra Behn's *Oroonoko*, Caleb Williams and politics of the Gothic, and violence in D. H. Lawrence. Approximately once per year, a special issue is released; the most recent was on Joyce Carol Oates (Winter 2006). The web site provides a cumulative index by subject from 1969 to present, along with abstracts to the articles in the current issue. Recommended for all academic libraries and large public libraries.

4212. Studies in Twentieth and Twenty-First Century Literature. Formerly (until 2004): *Studies in Twentieth Century Literature.* [ISSN: 1555-7839] 1976. s-a. USD 30 (Individuals, USD 25). Ed(s): Jordan Stump, Silvia Sauter. Kansas State University, Department of Modern Languages, Eisenhower Hall, Manhattan, KS 66506-1003. Illus., index, adv. Refereed. Circ: 500. *Indexed:* ABS&EES, AmHI, ArtHuCI, HumInd, IBR, IBZ, MLA-IB. *Bk. rev.:* 0-13, 2-3 pages, signed. *Aud.:* Ac.

This twice-yearly journal publishes articles in English on twentieth- and twenty-first-century literature written in French, German, Russian, and Spanish (including Hispanic American). The content is wide-ranging from poetry to prose, drama, and literary theory. Typically issues include seven to nine essays, and one volume per year is devoted to a particular theme. The most recent volume (Winter 2006) is a special issue titled "Rethinking Spain from Across the Seas." The journal's web site currently lists the table of contents from 1976 to 2003 and includes links to abstracts from 1995 onward. Recommended for medium to large academic libraries.

4213. Style (DeKalb). [ISSN: 0039-4238] 1967. q. USD 50 (Individuals, USD 35). Ed(s): John V Knapp. Northern Illinois University, Department of English, Dekalb, IL 60115; lwatson@niu.edu. Adv. Refereed. Circ: 420 Paid. Online: Chadwyck-Healey Inc.; EBSCO Publishing, EBSCO Host; Florida Center for Library Automation; Gale; OCLC Online Computer Library Center, Inc.; ProQuest K-12 Learning Solutions; ProQuest LLC (Ann Arbor); H.W. Wilson. Reprint: PSC. *Indexed:* ABS&EES, AmHI, ArtHuCI, FLI, HumInd, IBR, IBZ, L&LBA, LingAb, MLA-IB, RILM. *Bk. rev.:* 0-2, 2-3 pages, signed. *Aud.:* Ac.

This interdisciplinary journal focuses on "questions of style, stylistics, and poetics, including research and theory in discourse analysis, literary and nonliterary genres, narrative, figuration, metrics, rhetorical analysis, and the pedagogy of style." It addresses issues of literary criticism, critical theory, computational linguistics, cognitive linguistics, and philosophy of language, as well as rhetoric and writing studies. *Style* publishes reviews, review-essays, surveys, interviews, translations, and enumerative and annotated bibliographies, as well as reports on conferences, web sites, and software. Recent articles have dealt with the topics of linguistics, poetry, and poetics. A recent volume (Fall 2006) is a special issue on "Czech Fictional Worlds." Their web site provides a table of contents from 1991 (volume 25) to the present issue, with working links to abstracts from 1996 onward. Recommended for academic research libraries.

4214. *Texas Studies in Literature and Language.* [ISSN: 0040-4691] 1959. q. USD 110 (Individuals, USD 38). Ed(s): John Rumrich, Tony Hilfer. University of Texas Press, Journals Division, 2100 Comal, Austin, TX 78722; journals@uts.cc.utexas.edu; http://www.utexas.edu/utpress/journals/journals.html. Illus., index, adv. Refereed. Circ: 600. Vol. ends: Winter. Microform: PQC. Online: Chadwyck-Healey Inc.; EBSCO Publishing, EBSCO Host; Florida Center for Library Automation; Gale; OCLC Online Computer Library Center, Inc.; OhioLINK; Project MUSE; ProQuest LLC (Ann Arbor); SwetsWise Online Content; H.W. Wilson. Reprint: PSC. *Indexed:* ABS&EES, AmHI, ArtHuCI, BEL&L, FR, HumInd, IBR, IBZ, L&LBA, MLA-IB, PhilInd, RILM. *Aud.:* Ac.

Edited by Tony Hilfer and John Rumrich, from the University of Texas at Austin, this quarterly journal invites essays that are both "stylistically precise" and "critically contextualized" in order to "contribute to our understanding of a significant subject." These essays deal with all periods of literary history, and most often address British and American literature. Recent articles have included "The Polis's Different Voices: Narrating England's Progress in Dickens' *Bleak House*," "Dissonant Voices in Richard Rodriguez's *Hunger of Memory*" and Luce Irigaray's *This Sex Which Is Not One*," and "Faithful Likeness: Lists of Similes in Milton, Shelley, and Rossetti." Recommended for academic and large public libraries, this journal also has an updated web site and offers RSS feeds. (VBL)

4215. *Textual Practice: an international journal of radical literary studies.* [ISSN: 0950-236X] 1987. q. GBP 349 print & online eds. Ed(s): Peter Nicholls. Routledge, 4 Park Sq, Milton Park, Abingdon, OX14 4RN, United Kingdom; http://www.routledge.co.uk. Illus., adv. Refereed. Circ: 900. Vol. ends: Winter. Online: EBSCO Publishing, EBSCO Host; Gale; IngentaConnect; OCLC Online Computer Library Center, Inc.; SwetsWise Online Content. Reprint: PSC. *Indexed:* AmHI, ArtHuCI, BrHumI, HumInd, MLA-IB. *Bk. rev.:* 8-15, 3-7 pages, signed. *Aud.:* Ac.

The article "Appropriating Primal Indeterminacy: Language, Landscape and Postmodern Poetics in Susan Howe's *Thorow*" exemplifies how *Textual Practice* is a journal dedicated to "radical literary studies, continually pressing theory into new engagements." Published by Routledge, this intriguing journal often contains at least seven articles, averaging about 20 pages in length, dealing with the "turning points of theory with politics, history and texts." Recent articles include "The Persistence of Irony: Interfering with Surrealist Black Humour" and "On Tensions in Kant's Account of Reason in Politics." Started in 1987 and currently edited by Peter Nicholls of the University of Sussex, this journal also offers (at the very least) four to eight insightful book reviews, and it has been Britain's principal international journal. It is recommended for academic libraries with large research and literature collections. (VBL)

4216. *Tulsa Studies in Women's Literature.* [ISSN: 0732-7730] 1982. s-a. USD 17 (Individuals, USD 15; Students, USD 13). Ed(s): Laura Stevens, Holly A Laird. University of Tulsa, 600 S College Ave, Tulsa, OK 74104-3189. Illus., index, adv. Refereed. Circ: 600. Microform: PQC. Online: JSTOR (Web-based Journal Archive). *Indexed:* AmH&L, AmHI, ArtHuCI, BRI, CBRI, FemPer, HistAb, HumInd, IBR, MLA-IB, SSCI, SWA, WSA. *Bk. rev.:* 7-9; 1-4 pages. *Aud.:* Ac.

Tulsa Studies in Women's Literature is celebrating its 25th year of publishing articles and reviews that focus on women's literature and feminist criticism. Covering all time periods, *TSWL* includes poetry, prose, drama, memoirs, and diaries. The Jubilee Issue (June 2007) contains essays by leading feminist literary scholars, including "Professionalizing Feminism: What A Long, Strange Journey It Has Been," "Writing Women in Early American Studies: On Canons, Feminist Critique, and the Work of Writing Women into History," "Medieval Feminism in Middle English Studies: A Retrospective," and "Ancient Roman Women's Writings Sub Specie XXV Annorum." *TSWL*'s web site includes the

current issue's table of contents and an index to previous content from volumes 1 through 22.1 (1982–2003). Full text is available through JSTOR. Recommended for medium to large academic libraries.

4217. *Twentieth Century Literature: a scholarly and critical journal.* [ISSN: 0041-462X] 1955. q. USD 90 (Individuals, USD 40). Ed(s): Lee Zimmerman. Hofstra University, 107 Hofstra University, Hempstead, NY 11549-1070; http://www.hofstra.edu/. Illus., index, adv. Refereed. Circ: 3000 Paid and controlled. Vol. ends: No. 4. Microform: MIM; PQC. Online: Chadwyck-Healey Inc.; EBSCO Publishing, EBSCO Host; Florida Center for Library Automation; Gale; JSTOR (Web-based Journal Archive); Northern Light Technology, Inc.; OCLC Online Computer Library Center, Inc.; ProQuest K-12 Learning Solutions; ProQuest LLC (Ann Arbor); H.W. Wilson. *Indexed:* AmHI, ArtHuCI, BEL&L, HumInd, IBR, IBZ, MASUSE, MLA-IB, RILM. *Bk. rev.:* 3-4, 4-10 pages. *Aud.:* Ac.

Twentieth-Century Literature publishes essays on all aspects of contemporary literature written between 1900 and 1999, including essays in English on works in other languages. Typically issues include four essays, 15–20 pages each, followed by three substantial book reviews. Recent essays in the journal have examined *A Farewell to Arms*, *The Handmaid's Tale*, and *Waiting for the Barbarians*. The journal's Andrew J. Kappel Prize in Literary Criticism for 2006 was awarded to Frances Dickey's essay on one painting and two poems: "Parrot's Eye: A Portrait by Manet and Two by T. S. Eliot." This journal is a core collections title for academic as well as public libraries with significant literature collections.

4218. *University of Toronto Quarterly: a Canadian journal of the humanities.* [ISSN: 0042-0247] 1931. q. CND 140 domestic; USD 140 United States; USD 160 elsewhere. Ed(s): Brian Corman. University of Toronto Press, Journals Division, 5201 Dufferin St, Toronto, ON M3H 5T8, Canada; journals@utpress.utoronto.ca; http://www.utpjournals.com. Adv. Circ: 900. Microform: MML; PQC. Online: EBSCO Publishing, EBSCO Host; Micromedia ProQuest; OCLC Online Computer Library Center, Inc.; Project MUSE; SwetsWise Online Content. Reprint: PSC. *Indexed:* ABS&EES, AmH&L, AmHI, ArtHuCI, BEL&L, CBCARef, CPerI, HistAb, HumInd, IBR, IBZ, IndIslam, MLA-IB, RILM. *Bk. rev.:* Number and length vary. *Aud.:* Ac.

University of Toronto Quarterly publishes critical essays and reviews across the humanities, with articles that pertain to English literature being the most prominent. Articles range in length from 10 to over 25 pages, with "Review Articles" tending to be much shorter (five to ten pages). Each issue includes three to five articles and five or six review articles. The journal does not publish fiction or poetry. Recently published articles include "Presence, Deixis, and the Making of Meaning in Gertrude Stein's *Tender Buttons*," "Rethinking Sexuality and Class in *Twelfth Night*," and "'Just a Backlash': Margaret Atwood, Feminism and *The Handmaid's Tale*." The winter "Letters in Canada" issue (650+ pages, with over 350 contributors) contains reviews of the previous year's work in Canadian fiction, poetry, drama, translations/transductions, and works in the humanities. Book reviews are signed. Publishes in both English and French. Recommended for all libraries that support programs in Canadian Studies.

4219. *Victorian Poetry.* [ISSN: 0042-5206] 1963. q. USD 60 (Individuals, USD 45). Ed(s): John B Lamb. West Virginia University Press, Victorian Poetry Office, Department of English, PO Box 6296, Morgantown, WV 26506; hattfiel@wvu.edu; http://www.wvu.edu/. Illus., index. Sample. Refereed. Circ: 750 Paid. Vol. ends: Winter. Microform: PQC. Online: Chadwyck-Healey Inc.; EBSCO Publishing, EBSCO Host; Florida Center for Library Automation; Gale; OCLC Online Computer Library Center, Inc.; OhioLINK; Project MUSE; SwetsWise Online Content; H.W. Wilson. Reprint: PSC. *Indexed:* AmHI, ArtHuCI, HumInd, IBR, IBZ, MLA-IB, RILM. *Aud.:* Ac.

Victorian Poetry publishes essays on poetry, and occasionally prose, of the Victorian era in Britain, which spans 1830 to 1914. Content focuses on British and other English-language literatures, sometimes in relation to other texts of other times and places, and covers a wide range of perspectives, including feminist and new historicist. As stated on the journal's web page, the journal has more recently "expanded its purview from the major figures of Victorian

England (Tennyson, Browning, the Rossettis, etc.) to a wider compass of poets of all classes and gender identifications in nineteenth-century Britain and the Commonwealth." A recent special issue features Elizabeth Barrett Browning, and the journal is planning to feature Tennyson in the Spring 2009. Recommended for medium and larger academic libraries that support Victorian studies.

4220. Victorian Studies: a journal of the humanities, arts and sciences. [ISSN: 0042-5222] 1957. q. USD 112 (Individuals, USD 42.50). Ed(s): Ivan Kreilkamp, Andrew H Miller. Indiana University Press, 601 N Morton St, Bloomington, IN 47404. Illus., index, adv. Refereed. Circ: 3000. Microform: PQC. Online: Chadwyck-Healey Inc.; EBSCO Publishing, EBSCO Host; Gale; IngentaConnect; OCLC Online Computer Library Center, Inc.; OhioLINK; Project MUSE; ProQuest K-12 Learning Solutions; ProQuest LLC (Ann Arbor); SwetsWise Online Content; H.W. Wilson. Reprint: PSC. *Indexed:* AmH&L, AmHI, ArtHuCI, BAS, BEL&L, BRI, CBRI, HistAb, HumInd, IBR, IBZ, LRI, MLA-IB, MSN, RILM, SSCI. *Bk. rev.:* 32-34, 1-3 pages, signed. *Aud.:* Ac.

Victorian Studies publishes articles, review essays, book reviews, comments, and queries, and focuses on the Victorian age in Britain. The journal has recently changed its subtitle to "Interdisciplinary Journal of Social, Political, and Cultural Studies." Issues tend to contain three articles (20–35 pages), occasionally one or two review essays, and an extensive book review section. Recent content includes "'A Something-Nothing Out of Its Very Contrary': The Photography of Coleridge," "Displaced Memories in Victorian Fiction and Psychology," and "Black Ireland's Race: Thomas Carlyle and the Young Ireland Movement." As of December 2006, the journal was no longer to be available through *Ingenta*, but instead through *Inscribe*. Recommended for all academic and larger public libraries.

4221. Western American Literature. [ISSN: 0043-3462] 1966. q. USD 65 (Individuals, USD 22). Ed(s): Melody Graulich. Western Literature Association, Utah State University, English Department, Logan, UT 84322-3200; wal@cc.usu.edu; http://www.usu.edu/~westlit. Adv. Refereed. Circ: 1200. Microform: PQC. *Indexed:* AmH&L, AmHI, ArtHuCI, BRI, CBRI, FLI, HistAb, IBR, IBZ, MLA-IB, SSCI. *Bk. rev.:* 14-22, 1-2 pages, signed. *Aud.:* Ac, Sa.

Western American Literature publishes primarily essays on any aspect of the literature of the American West. In recent issues the journal has started to focus broadly on Western culture in order to provide more of a cultural context for the essays. Typical issues include three essays followed by 10–15 short book reviews. New content includes images of "paintings, photography, film stills, botanical and survey drawings, maps, murals." Contributions cover topics from cultural geography to ecocriticism and environmental writing, and from new Western history to traditional favorites of Western literature such as Edward Abbey, John Muir, and Terry Tempest Williams. The journal's web site posts the table of contents from 1966 to present, and lists bibliographies of related research as well as M.A. theses and doctoral dissertations (1997–2003). It also provides additional links to related web sites. Recommended for medium to large academic libraries and public libraries that support large literature collections.

4222. Women's Writing. [ISSN: 0969-9082] 1994. 3x/yr. GBP 295 print & online eds. Ed(s): Marie Mulvey-Roberts. Routledge, 4 Park Sq, Milton Park, Abingdon, OX14 4RN, United Kingdom; info@routledge.co.uk; http://www.routledge.co.uk. Illus., index. Sample. Refereed. Vol. ends: Dec. Reprint: PSC. *Indexed:* AmH&L, AmHI, BrHumI, FemPer, HistAb, HumInd, IBR, IBZ, MLA-IB, SWA. *Bk. rev.:* 0-4, 1,000 words, signed. *Aud.:* Ac.

Women's Writing is an international journal and focuses on issues of gender, race, class, and culture in women's writing prior to 1900, with a primary focus on Elizabethan and Victorian literature. Forthcoming special issues include "Revisiting the Brontes," "Still Kissing the Rod: Early Modern Women's Writing," "Transgressive Women," and "Charlotte Smith: The Bicentennial." The journal's web site provides the table of contents and abstracts from 1994 to present, along with options for RSS feeds. Recommended for large academic libraries.

4223. World Literature Today: a literary bimonthly of the University of Oklahoma. Incorporates (2001-2004): *W L T Magazine;* Which was formerly (until 1977): *Books Abroad.* [ISSN: 0196-3570] 1927. bi-m. USD 118 (Individuals, USD 25). Ed(s): Daniel Simon, David Draper Clark. University of Oklahoma, 630 Parrington Oval, Ste 110, Norman, OK 73019-4033; http://www.ou.edu/worldlit/. Illus., index, adv. Refereed. Circ: 7000. Microform: PQC. Online: Chadwyck-Healey Inc.; EBSCO Publishing, EBSCO Host; Florida Center for Library Automation; Gale; Northern Light Technology, Inc.; OCLC Online Computer Library Center, Inc.; ProQuest K-12 Learning Solutions; ProQuest LLC (Ann Arbor); H.W. Wilson. Reprint: PSC. *Indexed:* ABS&EES, AmHI, ArtHuCI, BAS, BEL&L, BRD, BRI, CBRI, HAPI, HumInd, IBR, IBZ, MASUSE, MLA-IB, RILM, SSCI. *Bk. rev.:* 150-250, 1/2-1 page, signed. *Aud.:* Ac.

This very accessible bimonthly journal is surely the best in its field, covering contemporary literature from around the world. Contents include interviews, poetry, fiction, essays on writers and trends, author profiles, travel writing, and a column on children's literature. The journal is interdisciplinary as well and covers the arts, culture, and politics as these issues relate to world literature. Special issues are frequent, recently featuring "Graphic Literature" and "Inside China." A section of outstanding world literature in review provides 20 or more pages of informative book reviews, covering more than 60 languages. A new partnership between the "NewsHour with Jim Lehrer" and *WLT* will promote world literature on public television. The journal's web site will give you a good sense of the print publication, and it also provides online indexes back to 2002. Coming in 2008 the journal should be available through JSTOR (1927–2005). Recommended for general readers as well as all academic libraries and public libraries.

■ LITTLE MAGAZINES

See also Alternatives; Literary Reviews; and Literature sections.

Anne R. Armstrong, Assistant Librarian and Assistant Professor, University of Illinois at Chicago

Introduction

While "little magazines" cannot be succinctly defined, they generally publish the poetry, fiction, nonfiction, and artwork of newly emerging and established authors and artists. Authors who have not yet attained critical or commercial success through mainstream publications frequently begin their careers by publishing in little magazines, and are more likely motivated by a desire to attain recognition within literary circles than by financial reward. Of the thousands of writers to publish in little magazines in a given year, some go on to win prestigious literary awards such as the Pushcart Prize or the O. Henry Awards or gain publication in Best American Short Stories or Best American Poetry. Authors including Ernest Hemingway, Marianne Moore, and William Carlos Williams published their work in little magazines before breaking into mainstream publications.

The format and content of little magazines varies greatly; characteristics such as size and physical appearance frequently depend upon the level and source of funding and advertising of a given publication. Universities and colleges sponsor some little magazines, while independent organizations and individual benefactors sponsor others. Smaller publications can be fewer than 50 staple-bound pages, while highly subsidized publications have a sleek, professionally bound appearance. The recent proliferation of electronically available little magazines has broadened the scope of audiences and diversified the content of this Little Magazines section. Electronic publications increasingly capitalize on interactive web technologies such as blogs, flash animation, sound, and video.

Regardless of the size or notoriety of their publications, the editors of little magazines share a commitment to exposing the work of emerging and established authors and artists. The writing in little magazines is often experimental in nature, thus less openly received by the mainstream press. In addition to publishing fiction, poetry, and art, little magazines also feature creative nonfiction, book reviews, and essays reflecting a wide range of political, sociological, and aesthetic issues.

Basic Periodicals

Hs: *Five Points, Louisville Review;* Ga: *Doubletake, Five Points, Paris Review, Poetry;* Ac: *Paris Review, Poetry.*

Basic Abstracts and Indexes

American Humanities Index, Index of American Periodical Verse.

4224. 3rd Bed. [ISSN: 1523-6773] s-a. USD 16 (Individuals, USD 14; USD 18 foreign). Ed(s): Vincent Standley. 3rd Bed, 131 Clay St, Central Falls, RI 02863. *Indexed:* AmHI. *Aud.:* Ga, Ac.

Founded in response to a "lack of openness" to new writers by more established literary magazines, *3rd Bed* includes poetry, prose, and artwork from newly established writers and artists. The magazine contains original artwork by up-and-coming artists such as Laylah Ali.

Agni. See Literary Reviews section.

Antioch Review. See Literary Reviews section.

4225. Archipelago. 1996. 4x/yr. Ed(s): Katherine McNamara. Archipelago, PO Box 2485, Charlottesville, VA 22902; editor@archipelago.org; http://archipelago.org. Illus. *Aud.:* Ga, Ac.

Published in Charlottesville, Virginia, *Archipelago* features poetry, fiction, nonfiction, essays, interviews, and translations in a simple, large-print layout. Recent issues have also included animated artwork. Readers may download issues in pdf format or subscribe to the journal via e-mail in addition to reading the html version. The web site contains a searchable archive of past issues.

4226. The Baltimore Review. [ISSN: 1092-5716] 1996. s-a. USD 15. Ed(s): Barbara Westwood Diehl. Baltimore Review, PO Box 410, Riderwood, MD 21139; hdiehl@bcpl.net; http://www.bcpl.net. Illus. Sample. Refereed. *Aud.:* Ga.

The Baltimore Review is a national journal of poetry, fiction, and creative nonfiction featuring writers from the Baltimore area and beyond. The publication was founded by the Baltimore Writers' Alliance in 1980 to promote the growth of writers in the greater Baltimore area. The magazine has a clean, simple layout and focuses exclusively on the written word, with the exception of cover photography.

4227. Beloit Poetry Journal. [ISSN: 0005-8661] 1950. q. USD 23 (Individuals, USD 18). Ed(s): John Rosenwald, Lee W Sharkey. Beloit Poetry Journal Foundation, Inc., PO Box 151, Farmington, ME 04938; http://www.bpj.org. Refereed. Circ: 770 Paid. *Indexed:* AmHI, ArtHuCI, IAPV. *Bk. rev.:* Number and length vary. *Aud.:* Hs, Ga, Ac.

Founded in 1950, the *Beloit Poetry Journal* (*BPJ*) was originally affiliated with Beloit College but declared editorial and financial independence in 1958 after an issue devoted to the British "Movement" and the American "Underground" offended college faculty and trustees. *BPJ* was among the first magazines to feature the work of Anne Sexton, Gwendolyn Brooks, Charles Bukowski, and Sherman Alexie. The format of issues is consistently simple, relatively brief (usually no more than 50 pages long), and entirely comprised of poetry, with the exception of occasional reviews of poetry books.

4228. Black Warrior Review. [ISSN: 0193-6301] 1974. s-a. USD 20 (Individuals, USD 16). Ed(s): Dan Kaplan, Aaron Welborn. Black Warrior Review, PO Box 862936, Tuscaloosa, AL 35486. Adv. Circ: 1800. *Indexed:* AmHI, BRI, CBRI, IAPV, MLA-IB. *Bk. rev.:* Number and length vary. *Aud.:* Ac.

Black Warrior Review features the poetry, short fiction, and nonfiction of established and newly emerging writers. While the bulk of the publication is comprised of poetry and short stories, interviews, reviews of small-press fiction, and poetry and essays are also included. Every issue contains a 6- to 12-page insert of color plates featuring the portfolio of a particular artist. As a part of the "chapbook series," each issue contains a writer's chapbook. This unique series offers readers a comprehensive view of a particular author's style.

Callaloo. See African American section.

Calyx. See Literature section.

4229. The Chattahoochee Review. [ISSN: 0741-9155] 1980. q. USD 20; USD 6 per issue. Ed(s): Jo Ann Yeager Adkins, Marc Fitten. Georgia Perimeter College, 2101 Womack Rd., Dunwoody, GA 30338-4497; http://www.gpc.peachnet.edu/~twadley/cr/index.htm. Index, adv. Circ: 1250. Microform: PQC. Online: EBSCO Publishing, EBSCO Host. *Indexed:* AmHI, IAPV. *Bk. rev.:* 3. *Aud.:* Ga.

Sponsored by Georgia Perimeter College, a two-year liberal arts college serving the Atlanta metropolitan area, *The Chattahoochee Review* publishes poetry, fiction, nonfiction, interviews, and art geared toward an audience characterized as "the educated general public." While the magazine frequently features Southern authors, contributions are drawn from an international pool of both recognized and emerging writers.

Chicago Review. See Literary Reviews section.

4230. Clackamas Literary Review. [ISSN: 1088-3665] 1997. s-a. USD 10; USD 6 newsstand/cover per issue. Ed(s): Kate Gray, Bradley J Stiles. Clackamas Community College, 19600 South Molalla Ave, Oregon City, OR 97045; http://www.clackamas.cc.or.us/clr. Adv. *Indexed:* IAPV, MLA-IB. *Bk. rev.:* 1-2. *Aud.:* Ga, Ac.

Edited and published at Clackamas Community College in Oregon City, Oregon, the *Clackamas Literary Review* publishes poetry, fiction, and creative nonfiction of new and established writers. Nonfiction material includes essays and interviews. The cover features original artwork.

Conjunctions. See Literary Reviews section.

4231. Cream City Review. [ISSN: 0884-3457] 1975. s-a. USD 22; USD 12 newsstand/cover per issue. Ed(s): Jay Johnson, Drew Blanchard. University of Wisconsin at Milwaukee, English Department, PO Box 413, Milwaukee, WI 53201. Adv. Refereed. Circ: 1000 Paid. *Indexed:* AmHI, IAPV. *Bk. rev.:* 1-3. *Aud.:* Ga, Ac.

Founded in 1975, *The Cream City Review* is operated by students at the University of Wisconsin–Milwaukee in association with the creative writing concentration of the English department. The expression "cream city" refers to the cream-colored bricks that Milwaukee was once known for. Each issue contains a mixture of poetry, short stories, essays, book reviews, and visual art by established and previously unpublished writers and artists. Reviews center on literature, film, theater, and art.

4232. CutBank. [ISSN: 0734-9963] 1973. s-a. USD 12. University Of Montana, Department of English, Missoula, MT 59812. Illus., adv. Refereed. Circ: 400. *Indexed:* ASIP, AmHI, IAPV. *Aud.:* Ga, Ac.

CutBank features poetry, fiction, and art of "high quality and serious intent." Featured authors are both previously unpublished and well known. Black-and-white photographs and artwork are included in each issue.

4233. The Drunken Boat (Farmington). [ISSN: 1530-7646] 2000. q. Ed(s): Rebecca Seiferle. The Drunken Boat, 5602 Tarry Terrace, Farmington, NM 87402. *Aud.:* Ga.

Drunken Boat is an innovative online journal taking full advantage of the interactive, audiovisual capabilities of the web. Issues feature poetry, prose, translations, web art, photos, sound, and video. Poems are frequently accompanied by audio recordings of authors reading their own work. Visual pieces often incorporate flash animation. To fully enjoy the unique sound and video entries, readers of *Drunken Boat* should access the publication from computers with up-to-date audio and video players.

Fence. See Literary Reviews section.

4234. Fiddlehead. [ISSN: 0015-0630] 1945. q. USD 30. Ed(s): Ross Leckie. University of New Brunswick, Campus House, P.O. Box 4400, Fredericton, NB E3B 5A3, Canada. Circ: 1000. Microform: MML; PQC. Online: LexisNexis; Micromedia ProQuest. *Indexed:* AmHI, ArtHuCI, CBCARef, CPerI. *Bk. rev.:* 6-7. *Aud.:* Ga.

Fiddlehead: Atlantic Canada's International Literary Journal is published by the University of New Brunswick. Founded in 1945, it features poetry, short stories, essays, excerpts of novels, plays, and book reviews. Many contributions are by Canadian authors, including the cover artwork, which features the work of New Brunswick artists.

4235. Five Fingers Review. [ISSN: 0898-0233] 1984. a. USD 30 (Individuals, USD 23). Ed(s): Jaime Robles. Five Fingers Press, PO Box 4, San Leandro, CA 94577-0100. Illus. Refereed. Circ: 1500. *Indexed:* AmHI. *Aud.:* Ga, Ac.

Five Fingers Review (5FR) aims to publish "the best non-commercial writing by both emerging and established writers from the United States and abroad." The review features poetry, fiction, essays, interviews, translations, and visual art. Visual and verbal work featured is frequently experimental in nature. Each annual issue of *5FR* is approximately 200 pages in length, and centered on a social or aesthetic theme such as "Darkness: Shade and Shadow," "Skin," or "Gardens in the Urban Jungle."

4236. Five Points: a journal of literature and art. [ISSN: 1088-8500] 1996. 3x/yr. USD 20; USD 7 per issue. Ed(s): Megan Sexton, David Bottoms. Georgia State University, Department of English, MSC 8R0322, 33 Gilmer Street SE, Unit 8, Atlanta, GA 30303-3088; bburmester@gsu.edu; http://www.gsu.edu/~wwweng. Illus., adv. Sample. Refereed. Circ: 2000. *Indexed:* AmHI, IAPV, IBR, IBZ, MLA-IB. *Aud.:* Hs, Ga, Ac.

An award-winning journal with a polished design, *Five Points* features poetry, fiction, essays, and interviews of well-known authors as well as lesser known, newly emerging authors. Recent contributors include Alice Hoffman, Philip Levine, and Ann Beattie. Each issue contains an insert of plates featuring photography or artwork.

4237. Geist: Canadian ideas, Canadian culture. [ISSN: 1181-6554] 1990. q. CND 40 for 3 yrs. domestic; USD 40 for 3 yrs. United States. Ed(s): Stephen Osborne. Geist Foundation, 103 1014 Homer St, Vancouver, BC V6B 2W9, Canada; geist@geist.com; http://www.geist.com. Illus., adv. Circ: 6000 Paid. *Indexed:* CBCARef. *Aud.:* Ga, Ac.

Geist is a literary magazine of ideas and culture published by the Geist Foundation, an organization established "to organize and encourage cultural activities that bring the work of Canadian writers and artists to public attention, explore the lines between fiction and nonfiction, and present new views of the connective tissues of this place Canada." In addition to publishing poetry, fiction, and nonfiction, this full-size magazine features "nontraditional" and entertaining material such as maps, cartoons, and crossword puzzles.

4238. Guernica: a magazine of art and politics. 2004. irreg. Guernica Magazine, c/o English Department, City College, New York, NY 10031. *Aud.:* Ga.

Guernica places equal weight on poetry, fiction, social commentary, and art. Entries are posted in a blog format, in which the most recent entries are published on the home page and all previous entries are archived. RSS feeds are available to readers. *Guernica* is named after the famous Picasso painting as well as a now-defunct bar that formerly featured poetry and fiction readings.

4239. Image (Seattle): art faith mystery. [ISSN: 1087-3503] 1989. q. USD 39.95 domestic; USD 59.95 foreign. Ed(s): Gregory Wolfe. Center for Religious Humanism, 3307 3d Ave W, Seattle, WA 98119-1997; image@imagejournal.org; http://www.imagejournal.org. Adv. Circ: 4000 Paid and controlled. *Indexed:* AmHI, ChrPI, IAPV, MLA-IB, R&TA, RI-1, RILM. *Bk. rev.:* Number and length vary. *Aud.:* Ga, Ac.

Image is a quarterly journal featuring interviews, memoirs, essays, and book reviews exploring the relationship between art and the Judeo-Christian faith. Entries encompass a broad spectrum of the arts, including fiction, poetry, painting, film, sculpture, music, dance, and architecture. Color-plate inserts containing reproductions of visual art by multiple artists are included in each issue. Past contributors have included Annie Dillard, Madeline L'Engle, Elie Wiesel, and Bill Viola.

4240. Indiana Review. Formerly (until 1982): *Indiana Writes.* [ISSN: 0738-386X] 1976. s-a. USD 17. Ed(s): Esther Lee. Indiana Review, Indiana University, Ballantine Hall 465, 1020 E Kirkwood, Bloomington, IN 47405-7103. Illus., adv. Refereed. Circ: 2000. Microform: PQC. Online: Chadwyck-Healey Inc.; EBSCO Publishing, EBSCO Host; ProQuest LLC (Ann Arbor). *Indexed:* AmHI, IAPV, MLA-IB. *Bk. rev.:* 3-6. *Aud.:* Ga, Ac.

The mission of the *Indiana Review* is "to offer the highest quality writing within a wide aesthetic." This nonprofit, award-winning literary magazine is managed entirely by graduate students at Indiana University and was selected as the first-place winner of the American Literary Magazine Award in 1996. Each issue contains an extensive collection of poetry, short stories, nonfiction, and reviews. Occasional issues are themed, such as a recent "Collaboration and Collage" issue. Past issues have featured the work of such prestigious writers as Sherman Alexie, Raymond Carver, Andre Dubus, Stuart Dybek, Ha Jin, and Anne Packer.

4241. The Journal (Columbus). Formerly (until 1987): *Ohio Journal.* [ISSN: 1045-084X] 1972. s-a. USD 12; USD 7 newsstand/cover per issue. Ed(s): Michelle Herman, Kathy Fagan. Ohio State University, Department of English, 421 Denney Hall, 164 W 17th Ave, Columbus, OH 43210. Illus., adv. Circ: 1200 Paid. *Indexed:* AmHI, IAPV. *Bk. rev.:* 1-2. *Aud.:* Ga, Ac.

Originally called "The Ohio Journal," *The Journal* was established in 1973 at Ohio State University. *The Journal* publishes material from a broad range of genres by established and emerging writers from Ohio and beyond. It features poetry, short stories, excerpts from novels, book reviews, and "and other daring or wholly original pieces."

Kalliope. See Literature section.

4242. Louisville Review. [ISSN: 0148-3250] 1976. s-a. USD 14. Ed(s): Sena Jeter Naslund. Louisville Review Corporation, Spalding University, 851 S 4th St, Louisville, KY 40203. Circ: 500 Paid and controlled. *Indexed:* AmHI. *Aud.:* Ems, Hs, Ga, Ac.

Established in 1976, the *Louisville Review* aspires "to import the best writing to local readers, to juxtapose the work of established writers with new writers, and to export the best local writers to a national readership." Past contributors include Louise Erdrich, Ursula Hegi, and Alberto Rios. The magazine publishes poetry, fiction, nonfiction, and drama.

4243. The Malahat Review. [ISSN: 0025-1216] 1967. q. CND 35 domestic; USD 35 foreign; CND 15 newsstand/cover. Ed(s): John Barton. The Malahat Review, PO Box 1700, Victoria, BC V8W 2Y2, Canada. Illus., adv. Refereed. Circ: 1000 Paid. Microform: MML. *Indexed:* ABS&EES, AmHI, ArtHuCI, BAS, BEL&L, CBCARef, CPerI, IAPV, MLA-IB. *Bk. rev.:* 5-6. *Aud.:* Ga, Ac.

The Malahat Review is a literary magazine featuring the poetry and fiction of writers from Canada and around the world. In support of a mission to bring Canadian authors to the forefront, book reviews of works by Canadian authors are included in each issue. While most issues are comprised of fiction, poetry, and reviews, a recent special issue focuses entirely on the process and implications of writing reviews.

4244. Manoa: a Pacific journal of international writing. [ISSN: 1045-7909] 1988. s-a. USD 40 (Individuals, USD 22; USD 20 per issue). Ed(s): Frank Stewart. University of Hawaii Press, Journals Department, 2840 Kolowalu St, Honolulu, HI 96822-1888; uhpjourn@hawaii.edu; http://www.uhpress.hawaii.edu/. Illus., adv. Sample. Refereed. Circ: 750. Online: EBSCO Publishing, EBSCO Host; OCLC Online Computer Library Center, Inc.; OhioLINK; Project MUSE; SwetsWise Online Content. Reprint: PSC. *Indexed:* AmHI, IAPV, L&LBA, MLA-IB. *Bk. rev.:* 6-12, length varies. *Aud.:* Ga, Ac.

Founded in 1989, *MANOA* is a journal published by the University of Hawaii that aims to bring the literature of Asia and the Pacific to the United States and to bring American writing to Asian and Pacific readers. The journal contains poetry, fiction, artwork, and essays from places such as the People's Republic of China, Tibet, Nepal, Taiwan, Japan, Korea, and more. All issues have guest editors and a unique focus or theme, such as contemporary writing from Cambodia or contemporary poetry from Taiwan. The journal regularly includes original translations and book reviews.

4245. *Many Mountains Moving: a literary journal of diverse contemporary voices.* [ISSN: 1080-6474] 1994. s-a. USD 16 domestic; USD 9 newsstand/cover per issue domestic; USD 12 newsstand/cover per issue elsewhere. Ed(s): Naomi Horii. Many Mountains Moving, 420 22nd St, Boulder, CO 80302; http://www.mmminc.org. Illus., adv. Sample. Refereed. Circ: 2500. *Indexed:* AmHI, IAPV. *Aud.:* Ga, Ac.

Many Mountains Moving is "a literary journal of diverse contemporary voices." It seeks to promote the appreciation of diverse cultures through literature and art, to support established and emerging writers and artists, and to provide a literary space for writers of diverse backgrounds. Issues are substantial in length (usually over 300 pages), and include poetry, fiction, essays, and art. Issues are often theme based. Past themes have included matters of the heart, science and literature, and cybernetics.

4246. *The Marlboro Review.* [ISSN: 1084-452X] 1995. s-a. USD 20 (Individuals, USD 16). Ed(s): Ellen Dudley. The Marlboro Review Inc., PO Box 243, Marlboro, VT 05344; dudley@sover.net; http://www.marlbororeview.com. Illus., adv. Sample. Refereed. Circ: 300. *Indexed:* AmHI. *Bk. rev.:* 3. *Aud.:* Ga, Ac.

Based in Marlboro, Vermont, *The Marlboro Review* includes contemporary fiction, poetry, translations, and essays. Essays address cultural, scientific, and philosophical issues.

4247. *Memorious: a forum for new verse and poetics.* 2004. irreg. Ed(s): Robert Arnold, Brian Green. Memorious, http://www.memorious.org. *Aud.:* Ga.

Each issue of *Memorious: A Forum for New Verse and Poetics* features original prose, verse, and artwork, as well as "views," which are essays examining the craft of writing. *Memorious* is a member of the Council of Literary Magazines and Presses.

Meridians. See Gender Studies section.

Michigan Quarterly Review. See Literary Reviews section.

4248. *Mudlark: an[e]lectronic journal of poetry & poetics.* [ISSN: 1081-3500] 1995. irreg. Free. Ed(s): William Slaughter. Mudlark, c/o William Slaughter, Department of English & Foreign Languages, Jacksonville, FL 32224-2645; mudlark@unf.edu; http://www.unf.edu/mudlark/. *Aud.:* Ga, Ac.

Mudlark is an online poetry journal containing three types of documents, or formats: "issues" are the electronic equivalent of print chapbooks; "posters" are the electronic equivalent of print broadsides; and "flash" poems are poems that have news in them and are relevant to current events. *Mudlark* is primarily text based to ensure a fast download and maintain a focus on poetry.

4249. *New England Review.* Former titles (until 1990): *New England Review and Bread Loaf Quarterly;* (until 1982): *New England Review.* [ISSN: 1053-1297] 1978. q. USD 40 (Individuals, USD 25; USD 8 newsstand/cover per issue). Middlebury College, Middlebury, VT 05759. Adv. Circ: 3000. Microform: PQC. Online: Chadwyck-Healey Inc.; EBSCO Publishing, EBSCO Host; Northern Light Technology, Inc.; OCLC Online Computer Library Center, Inc.; ProQuest K-12 Learning Solutions; ProQuest LLC (Ann Arbor); H.W. Wilson. *Indexed:* ABS&EES, AmHI, ArtHuCI, BEL&L, BRI, CBRI, HumInd, IAPV, MLA-IB, RILM. *Bk. rev.:* 1. *Aud.:* Ga, Ac.

The *New England Review* is a literary quarterly featuring poetry, art, fiction, literary nonfiction, interviews, essays, book reviews, drama and screenplays, translations, and more. In addition to "Poetry" and "Fiction," the occurrence of section headings such as "Literary Lives," "Recollections," "Reader's Notebook," "Classics Revisited," and "Rediscoveries" reflects a diversity in content and form.

New Letters. See Literary Reviews section.

New Millennium Writings. See Literary Reviews section.

4250. *Nimrod International Journal.* Formerly (until Fall-Win. 1998): *Nimrod.* [ISSN: 1931-1214] 1956. s-a. Awards Issue (Fall Publication); Thematic Issue (Spring Publication). USD 25 (Individuals, USD 17.50). Ed(s): Francine Ringold. Nimrod, University of Tulsa, 600 S College Ave, Tulsa, OK 74104-3189. Illus., adv. Refereed. Circ: 4000 Paid. *Indexed:* AmHI, IAPV. *Aud.:* Ga, Ac.

Nimrod International Journal highlights the poetry and fiction of new writers, writers in translation, and established authors publishing new work. Each issue includes traditional and experimental poetry, prose, and artwork. Many issues have a theme. Past themes include "Metamorphoses: The Power of Change" and "Vietnam Revisited."

Ontario Review. See Literary Reviews section.

The Paris Review. See Literary Reviews section.

4251. *Pleiades: a journal of new writing.* [ISSN: 1063-3391] 1991. s-a. USD 12. Ed(s): Kevin Prufer. Pleiades Press, Dept of English, Central Missouri State University, Warrensburg, MO 64093. Adv. Circ: 2500. *Indexed:* AmHI, MLA-IB. *Bk. rev.:* 5-7. *Aud.:* Ga, Ac.

Pleiades is a "journal of new writing" that features poetry, short fiction, essays, and book reviews by new and established writers. New writers are frequently introduced by more established writers in a unique "Introducing" feature. Essays cover a range of subjects, but primarily focus on literary topics such as poetry and religion, the portrayal of poets in film, or the study of literature. Each issue concludes with book reviews that offer in-depth analysis of newly published poetry, fiction, and literary nonfiction from small, university, and mainstream presses.

4252. *Poetry (Chicago).* [ISSN: 0032-2032] 1912. m. except bimonthly Oct.-Nov. USD 35 domestic; USD 46 foreign; USD 5 newsstand/cover per issue. Ed(s): Joseph Parisi. The Poetry Foundation, 1030 N Clark St., Ste 420, Chicago, IL 60610; http://www.poetrymagazine.org. Adv. Circ: 10000. Vol. ends: Oct/Sep. Microform: PMC; PQC. Online: Chadwyck-Healey Inc.; EBSCO Publishing, EBSCO Host; Florida Center for Library Automation; Gale; OCLC Online Computer Library Center, Inc.; ProQuest K-12 Learning Solutions; ProQuest LLC (Ann Arbor); H.W. Wilson. *Indexed:* ASIP, AmHI, ArtHuCI, BRD, BRI, CBRI, HumInd, IAPV, MASUSE. *Bk. rev.:* 2-11. *Aud.:* Ga, Ac.

Since its founding in 1912, *Poetry*'s mission has been "to print the best poetry written today, in whatever style, genre, or approach." The magazine was among the first to publish Carl Sandburg and William Carlos Williams, among other now-classic poets. Independent and unaffiliated with any one aesthetic school, *Poetry* is generally regarded as the premier journal of verse, and is recommended for all collections with an interest in poetry. Also includes book reviews and occasional essays.

4253. *Poetry Daily.* 1997. d. Ed(s): Don Selby, Diane Boller. Daily Poetry Association, PO Box 1306, Charlottesville, VA 22902-1306; http://www.poems.com. *Aud.:* Ga, Ac.

Poetry Daily is an online anthology of contemporary poetry aspiring "to make it easier for people to find poets and poetry they like and to help publishers bring news of their books, magazines and journals to more people." The magazine features a different poet every day, in addition to information about the poet and attribution of the poem's source (poems are selected from books, magazines, and journals). The magazine features both established and newly emerging poets. Past features and daily poems are archived for one year and indexed by poet, title, and date.

4254. Poetry Magazines. 2003. unknown. Poetry Library, Royal Festival Hall, London, SE1 8XX, United Kingdom; info@poetrymagazines.org.uk; http://www.poetrylibrary.org.uk/poetry/. *Aud.:* Ga, Ac.

Funded by the Arts Council of England, this online archive provides selected full-text coverage of over 20 twentieth- and twenty-first-century British poetry magazines. The web site allows readers to browse publications by title, or to search by keyword for full-text items in the archive. Featured magazines include poems, prose, articles, and artwork. Advertising and listings are not included.

4255. Poets & Writers Online. Poets & Writers, Inc., 72 Spring St, New York, NY 10012; http://www.pw.org. *Aud.:* Hs, Ga, Ac.

This web site complements the print publication *Poets & Writers*, a magazine for writers featuring essays, interviews, and practical articles for new and established writers about the craft and industry of writing. While the web site lists tables of contents and exerpts from the print publication, it does not provide the full text of most articles. The web site features teaching guides, reading lists, industry shorts, and quotations.

Prairie Schooner. See Literary Reviews section.

4256. Prism International: contemporary writing from Canada and around the world. [ISSN: 0032-8790] 1959. q. USD 32 (Individuals, USD 25). Ed(s): Billeh Nickerson. University of British Columbia, Faculty of Arts, Creative Writing Program, E462 1866 Main Mall, Vancouver, BC V6T 1Z1, Canada; prism@interchange.ubc.ca; http://www.arts.ubc.ca/. Adv. Refereed. Circ: 1100 Paid. Microform: MML; PQC. *Indexed:* ABS&EES, AmHI, ArtHuCI, CBCARef. *Aud.:* Ga, Ac.

PRISM International is a quarterly journal based in Vancouver, British Columbia, publishing poetry, short fiction, creative nonfiction, and drama by Canadian and international authors. The poetry and fiction in *PRISM International* are often humorous in tone. This journal features the work of emerging and established writers. Margaret Atwood, Jorge Luis Borges, and Michael Ondaatje have contributed to past issues.

4257. River Styx. [ISSN: 0149-8851] 1975. 3x/yr. Individuals, USD 20; USD 7 newsstand/cover per issue. Ed(s): Richard Newman. Big River Association, 3547 Olive St, Ste 107, St. Louis, MO 63103-1002. Illus., adv. Circ: 2300. *Indexed:* AmHI, HumInd, IAPV. *Aud.:* Ga, Ac.

The title page of each issue of *River Styx* contains the slogan "Multicultural Literary Explorers Since 1975." This award-winning journal, founded by a collective of St. Louis writers and musicians, features contemporary poetry, fiction, essays, interviews, and art. Rita Dove, Robert Haas, and Derek Walcott are among the notable authors published in past issues.

Room of One's Own. See Literature section.

4258. Rosebud: the magazine for people who enjoy good writing. [ISSN: 1072-1681] 1993. 3x/yr. USD 24 domestic; USD 35 foreign; USD 7.95 newsstand/cover per issue. Ed(s): J Rod Clark. Rosebud, Inc., PO Box 459, Cambridge, WI 53523; jrodclark@smallbytes.net; http://www.itis.com/rosebud. Illus., adv. Sample. Circ: 6000 Paid. *Indexed:* AmHI, IAPV. *Aud.:* Ga.

Rosebud, "the magazine for people who enjoy good writing," publishes poetry, creative prose, and visual art. Issues regularly contain features such as literary crossword puzzles, comics, and the "Rosebud Roundtable," a series of discussions pertaining to literature and art hosted by *Rosebud*'s editors. The magazine features the work of new artists and authors as well as renowned authors and artists such as R. Crumb, Ray Bradbury, Sandra Cisneros, and Diane Wakoski.

Small Press Review. See Books and Book Reviews section.

The Southern Review. See Literary Reviews section.

4259. Stand Magazine. Formerly: *Stand*. [ISSN: 0952-648X] 1952. q. GBP 35 (Individuals, GBP 25). Ed(s): Michael Hulce, John Kinsella. Stand Magazine Ltd., c/o School of English, University of Leeds, Leeds, LS2 9JT, United Kingdom; stand@english.novell.leeds.ac.uk. Illus., adv. Circ: 3000 Paid. Vol. ends: Dec. *Indexed:* AmHI, ArtHuCI, BRI, CBRI, IAPV. *Bk. rev.:* 10. *Aud.:* Ac.

Founded in Leeds, England, in 1952, *Stand Magazine* is a quarterly literary magazine featuring poetry, short fiction, and reviews. Although it is published in England, its authors are international in scope. Some issues have a theme, such as past issues on Nobel laureates and a translation issue.

4260. StoryQuarterly. [ISSN: 1041-0708] 1975. a. USD 9 per issue. Ed(s): M M Hayes. StoryQuarterly, Inc., PO Box 1416, Northbrook, IL 60065; storyquarterly@yahoo.com; http://www.storyquarterly.com. Illus., adv. Sample. Circ: 2500. *Indexed:* AmHI, HumInd. *Aud.:* Ga, Ac.

Established in 1975, *StoryQuarterly* is an annual magazine that publishes high-quality short stories by American and international authors. Many stories featured in this publication have gained recognition in *Best American Short Stories*, *O. Henry Prize Stories*, and *The Pushcart Prize* issues. Past authors have included T. Coraghessan Boyle, J. M. Coetzee, Stuart Dybek, Gail Godwin, and Alice Hoffman.

4261. Tin House. [ISSN: 1541-521X] 1999. q. USD 19.95 domestic; USD 35.95 Canada; USD 49.95 elsewhere. Ed(s): Win McCormack. Tin House, PO Box 10500, Portland, OR 97296-0500; tinhouse@pcspublink.com; http://www.tinhouse.com. Illus., adv. *Indexed:* AmHI. *Aud.:* Ga.

Tin House aims to "feature the best writers writing about what they are most passionate about, be it in the form of fiction, poetry, or essay, regardless of fashion or timeliness." The magazine features unknown authors as well as widely recognized authors such as David Foster Wallace, Jonathan Lethem, and Derek Walcott. Recurring features include a "New Voices" section, a "Lost and Found" section, and interviews.

TriQuarterly. See Literary Reviews section.

4262. Two Lines: a journal of translation. [ISSN: 1525-5204] 1995. a. USD 13 domestic; USD 13.50 in Canada & Mexico; USD 15 elsewhere. Ed(s): Olivia E Sears. Two Lines, 35 Stillman St., Ste. 201, San Francisco, CA 94107-1364. Illus. Circ: 500. *Aud.:* Ga, Ac.

Founded by the Center for Art in Translation in 1994, *Two Lines* has published original English translations of poetry, fiction, essays, religious and historical texts, and letters from more than 50 countries. English translations of all material are printed side by side with the original language, and each entry is preceded by an introduction placing the author within the literary tradition of his or her country or region. Issues have themes, such as "Masks," "Bodies," and "Parties."

4263. Two Rivers Review. [ISSN: 1524-2749] 1998. s-a. USD 10. Two Rivers Review, 300, Clinton, NY 13323-0300; tworiversreview@juno.com; http://www.trrpoetry.tripod.com. Adv. Circ: 350. *Bk. rev.:* 1-2. *Aud.:* Ga.

Two Rivers Review is a biannual publication featuring poetry, a small amount of short fiction, and occasional translations. It publishes two poetry chapbooks per year. Issues are simply designed and relatively short (no more than 50 pages).

Virginia Quarterly Review. See Literary Reviews section.

4264. *X C P: Cross-Cultural Poetics.* Former titles (until 1997): *Cross-Cultural Poetics;* (until 1996): *North American Ideophonics.* [ISSN: 1086-9611] 1989. s-a. USD 40 (Individuals, USD 18; USD 10 newsstand/cover per issue). Ed(s): Mark Nowak. College of St. Catherine - Minneapolis, 601 25th Ave S, Minneapolis, MN 55454; manowak@ stkate.edu; http://bfn.org/~xcp. Illus. Circ: 750. *Indexed:* AltPI, AmHI, BRI, CBRI, IAPV, MLA-IB. *Bk. rev.:* 10-12. *Aud.:* Ac.

XCP: Cross Cultural Poetics features academic essays, poetry, short fiction, plays, interviews, and reviews. While articles and essays cover a broad range of topics, they are generally academic and theoretical, and often address politics, gender, and ethnicity. Each issue concludes with a sizable section of reviews of literary and academic works published by university and small presses. Recent contributors to *XCP* include Adrienne Rich and Amiri Baraka.

Zoetrope. See Fiction: General/Mystery and Detective/General section.

4265. *Zyzzyva: the last word: west coast writers and artists.* [ISSN: 8756-5633] 1985. 3x/yr. USD 44 domestic; USD 64 foreign. Ed(s): Howard Junker. Zyzzyva, Inc., PO Box 590069, San Francisco, CA 94159-0069; editor@zyzzyva.org; http://www.zyzzyva.org. Illus., index, adv. Sample. Circ: 4000. Vol. ends: Winter. *Indexed:* AmHI, IAPV. *Aud.:* Ac.

Zyzzyva is an independent magazine featuring the work of writers and artists living in the West Coast states of Alaska, California, Hawaii, Oregon, and Washington. Each issue contains a mix of poetry, fiction, essays, and original black-and-white images. Issues contain the work of established writers as well as previously unpublished writers who are featured in a special "First Time in Print" section.

■ MANAGEMENT, ADMINISTRATION, AND HUMAN RESOURCES

General/Functional Management/Human Resources/Management Education/Operations Research and Management Science/Organizational Behavior and Studies/Strategic Analysis

See also Business; Finance; Labor and Industrial Relations; and Systems sections.

Peggy Tyler, Reference Librarian, Clemson University Libraries, Clemson, SC 29634; ptyler@clemson.edu

Meredith Futral, Reference Librarian, Clemson University Libraries, Clemson, SC 29634; mfutral@clemson.edu

Enrique Diaz, Designer/Multimedia Specialist, Harvard College Library, Harvard University, Cambridge, MA

Cheryl LaGuardia, Head of Instructional Services for the Harvard College Library, Widener Library, Research Services, Harvard University, Cambridge, MA 02138; claguard@fas.harvard.edu

Introduction

Management is an applied practice; it is the profession of almost 3,000,000 Americans, according to the 2000 census. It is also the process by which organizations administer resources to achieve collective goals. The huge population of practicing managers and the associated academic community of scholars and students studying the field foster and support thousands of management magazines and journals. This section provides core listings of titles for management collections, based on a combination of the quality of the publications, their wide indexing, and patron demand.

Most of the journals here state that their mission is to present empirical academic research that is scholarly, but still of direct interest and use to those in organizational practice. Even the most theoretical articles usually try to provide a discussion of applications and research implications for working managers. There are also other journals and magazines that provide news and reports of research and trends in the profession—examples of all of these are

provided below. An even larger number of journals are bypassing print entirely and are publishing only on the web than was the case in the last edition of *Magazines for Libraries,* so web addresses are included whenever available.

Basic Periodicals

Ac: *Academy of Management Journal, Academy of Management Review, Administrative Science Quarterly, European Management Journal, HRFocus, MIT Sloan Management Review, Personnel Psychology, Training.*

Basic Abstracts and Indexes

ABI/INFORM, Business Source Premier, Factiva, Psychological Abstracts, SSRN Management Research Network, Wilson Business Full Text.

General

4266. *Academy of Management Journal.* Formerly (until 1962): *The Journal of the Academy of Management.* [ISSN: 0001-4273] 1958. bi-m. USD 140 domestic individuals & academic libraries (Corporations, USD 170). Ed(s): Amme Tsui. Academy of Management, 235 Elm Rd, P O Box 3020, Briarcliff Manor, NY 10510-3020; academy@pace.edu; http://www.aomonline.org. Illus., index, adv. Refereed. Circ: 11500. Vol. ends: Dec. Microform: PQC. Online: EBSCO Publishing, EBSCO Host; JSTOR (Web-based Journal Archive); OCLC Online Computer Library Center, Inc.; ProQuest LLC (Ann Arbor). *Indexed:* ABIn, AgeL, BAS, BPI, CINAHL, CommAb, ErgAb, IBSS, PsycInfo, SSCI. *Bk. rev.:* Various number and length. *Aud.:* Ac, Sa.

AMJ is considered the premier experimental research journal for management science. Articles present the results of empirical studies of a wide range of current management practices and theories written by university researchers (primarily in the United States). A strong background in statistical analysis is recommended for readers of the studies' methods and results, but each article concludes with a discussion of how its findings might affect management theory and practice. A must for any academic library supporting a management curriculum. URL: http://aom.pace.edu/amjnew

4267. *The Academy of Management Perspectives.* Former titles (until Feb. 2006): *Academy of Management Executive;* (until 1993): *Executive;* (until 1989): *Academy of Management Executive.* [ISSN: 1558-9080] 1987. q. USD 110 (Individuals, USD 70; Corporations, USD 150). Ed(s): Dr. Robert C. Ford. Academy of Management, 235 Elm Rd, P O Box 3020, Briarcliff Manor, NY 10510-3020; http://www.aomonline.org. Illus., adv. Refereed. Circ: 13700. Online: EBSCO Publishing, EBSCO Host; Northern Light Technology, Inc.; OCLC Online Computer Library Center, Inc.; ProQuest LLC (Ann Arbor). *Indexed:* ABIn, ABS&EES, AgeL, BPI, IBSS, PsycInfo, SSCI. *Bk. rev.:* 4-8. *Aud.:* Ac, Sa.

This is the practitioner publication from the Academy of Management, for "'thought leaders' who shape the views of practicing managers—consultants, business writers, and, most importantly, academics in their role as educators." Peer-reviewed articles provide accessible organizational applications of academic research in management theory. Under new editorial direction, the magazine addresses a variety of management topics, but some issues are devoted to a single theme (decision making or global transfer of knowledge). Recommended for corporate libraries and all academic business libraries. URL: http://journals.aomonline.org/amp

4268. *Academy of Management Review.* [ISSN: 0363-7425] 1976. q. USD 99 domestic individuals & academic libraries (Corporations, USD 135). Ed(s): Richard J Klimoski. Academy of Management, 235 Elm Rd, P O Box 3020, Briarcliff Manor, NY 10510-3020; academy@pace.edu; http://www.aomonline.org. Illus., index, adv. Refereed. Circ: 11500. Vol. ends: Oct. Microform: PQC. Online: EBSCO Publishing, EBSCO Host; JSTOR (Web-based Journal Archive); Northern Light Technology, Inc.; OCLC Online Computer Library Center, Inc.; ProQuest LLC (Ann Arbor); H.W. Wilson. *Indexed:* ABIn, AgeL, BPI, IBSS, PsycInfo, SSCI. *Bk. rev.:* 4-5, 1,200 words, signed. *Aud.:* Ac, Sa.

Management theory, not professional practice, is the focus of this scholarly journal. Philosophical and analytical essays, critical discussions and debates of new and old theories and methods, and reflective literature reviews are the most common formats for "conceptual articles" aimed at developing new hypotheses for research and broad ideas for managerial practice. Along with four or five book reviews, each issue includes a few pages listing recent business books received by the academy and a number of book advertisement pages useful for collection development. One of the most heavily cited journals in the discipline, and highly recommended for academic libraries. URL: http://aom.pace.edu/amr

4269. Administrative Science Quarterly. [ISSN: 0001-8392] 1956. q. USD 190 (Individuals, USD 70; Students, USD 30). Ed(s): Donald A Palmer. Cornell University, Johnson Graduate School of Management, 20 Thornwood Dr., Ste. 100, Ithaca, NY 14850-1265; asq_journal@ cornell.edu; http://www.johnson.cornell.edu/. Illus., index, adv. Refereed. Circ: 4484 Paid. Vol. ends: Dec. Microform: PQC. Online: The Dialog Corporation; EBSCO Publishing, EBSCO Host; Florida Center for Library Automation; Gale; JSTOR (Web-based Journal Archive); Northern Light Technology, Inc.; OCLC Online Computer Library Center, Inc.; ProQuest LLC (Ann Arbor); H.W. Wilson. *Indexed:* ABCPolSci, ABIn, ATI, AmH&L, ArtHuCI, BAS, BPI, CINAHL, CommAb, EAA, EI, HRA, HistAb, IBR, IBSS, IBZ, IPSA, MCR, PAIS, PMA, PRA, PSA, PsycInfo, SFSA, SSA, SSCI, SUSA, SWR&A, SociolAb, V&AA. *Bk. rev.:* 10-12, 600-1,200 words, signed. *Aud.:* Ac, Sa.

This is a very modern (and very influential) organizational studies journal. *ASQ* hides its big brain behind serene covers with scenic color photographs and off-white pages with unusual margins, layout, and typography. This inviting package contains scholarly articles both experimental and theoretical on topics as wide-ranging as the organizational effects of managers' career mobility and the role of social networks in team building. A significant portion of each issue is dedicated to a dozen or more book reviews and a list of publications received. This is a core title for management collections that librarians should pick up and browse on a regular basis. URL: www.johnson.cornell.edu/publications/ASQ

4270. Association Now. Former titles (until 2005): *Association Management; American Society of Association Executives. Journal.* [ISSN: 1557-7562] 1949. m. Members, USD 24; Non-members, USD 60. Ed(s): Scott Briscoe, Keith C Skillman. American Society of Association Executives, The Center for Association Leadership, 1575 Eye St, NW, Washington, DC 20005-1168; editorial@asaenet.org; http://www.asaenet.org. Illus., index, adv. Circ: 24000 Paid. Vol. ends: Dec. Microform: PQC. Online: EBSCO Publishing, EBSCO Host; Florida Center for Library Automation; Gale; Northern Light Technology, Inc.; OCLC Online Computer Library Center, Inc.; ProQuest LLC (Ann Arbor); H.W. Wilson. *Indexed:* ABIn, ATI, AgeL, BPI, CWI, LRI, PAIS, PMA. *Aud.:* Sa.

If you run an association, this is the trade publication that comes with your membership in the American Society of Association Executives. This glossy, heavily illustrated monthly is full of how-to articles and tips for managing nonprofit organizations. Since it is indexed in most of the basic business abstracts and indexes, demand for articles might be worth the low subscription price, even in libraries where association executives are not commonly found. URL: http://www.asaecenter.org/publicationsresources/ AnowMagCurrentIssueTOC.cfm?navItemNumber=14971

4271. C M A Management: for strategic business ideas. Former titles: *Management for Strategic Business Ideas;* (until 1999): *C M A Magazine;* (until 1995): *C M A. Certified Management Accountant;* (until 1985): *Cost and Management.* [ISSN: 1490-4225] 1926. 10x/yr. CND 15. Ed(s): Rob Colman. Society of Management Accountants of Canada, Mississauga Executive Centre, One Robert Speck Pkwy, Ste 1400, Mississauga, ON L4Z 3M3, Canada; info@cma-canada.org; http://www.cma-canada.org/cmacan/. Illus., index, adv. Circ: 72336. Vol. ends: Dec/Jan. Microform: MML; PQC. Online: EBSCO Publishing, EBSCO Host; Gale; Micromedia ProQuest; OCLC Online Computer Library Center, Inc.; ProQuest LLC (Ann Arbor). *Indexed:* ABIn, ATI, CBCARef, CPerI, CWI, PMA, SSCI. *Bk. rev.:* 3. *Aud.:* Sa.

A Canadian magazine for management professionals, *CMA* is published in both English and French versions. Professional business writers and practicing executives/managers author the feature articles on such topics as transfer pricing and other cross-border business concerns, creative leadership, and e-commerce. Each issue also contains a large number of columns and news items. The magazine's web site provides access to a large number of full-text pages for each current issue and back issues through 2002. Recommended for Canadian business library collections and academic libraries where there is an interest beyond the free coverage provided online. URL: http://www.managementmag.com

4272. Corporate Board. Formerly (until 1983): *Corporate Director.* [ISSN: 0746-8652] 1980. bi-m. Individuals, USD 520; Corporations, USD 2900. Ed(s): Ralph D Ward. Vanguard Publications, Inc., 4440 Hagadorn Rd, Okemos, MI 48864-2414; info@corporateboard.com; http://www.corporateboard.com. Index, adv. Sample. Circ: 4000 Paid. Online: EBSCO Publishing, EBSCO Host; Florida Center for Library Automation; Gale. *Aud.:* Sa.

This journal is published to provide corporation officers and board members the latest information on corporate governance. Published six times a year, a typical issue contains five feature articles about oversight of corporate activities, a review of recent governmental regulations and corporate surveys, an interview with one prominent corporate board member, and extended quotes from speeches and articles written by others. A list of recent corporate board elections results is also included. Expensive and narrowly focused, this journal is only recommended for corporate libraries and universities with executive MBA programs. URL: www.corporateboard.com

4273. Director. [ISSN: 0012-3242] 1947. m. GBP 42 domestic; GBP 57 in Europe; GBP 73 elsewhere. Ed(s): Tom Nash. Director Publications Ltd., 116 Pall Mall, London, SW1Y 5EA, United Kingdom; enquiries@ iod.com; http://www.iod.com/. Illus. Circ: 58441. Microform: PQC. Online: EBSCO Publishing, EBSCO Host; Northern Light Technology, Inc.; OCLC Online Computer Library Center, Inc.; ProQuest LLC (Ann Arbor). *Indexed:* ABIn, PAIS. *Bk. rev.:* 3-4, 100-300 words, signed. *Aud.:* Sa.

Director is an attractive British monthly magazine that provides insight into the current interests of executive officers in the United Kingdom (the euro, entrepreneurship, cost cutting, hiring consultants) and profiles of successful and struggling corporations, along with lighter pieces about executive hobbies and travel. Each issue includes three or four short book reviews. Recommended for large academic libraries with an interest in international business. URL: www.iod.com

4274. Directors & Boards: thought leadership in governance since 1976. [ISSN: 0364-9156] 1976. q. USD 325 domestic; USD 350 foreign. Ed(s): Barbara Wenger. Directors & Boards, 1845 Walnut St, 9th Fl, Philadelphia, PA 19103-4709; jkristie@directorsandboards.com; http://www.directorsandboards.com. Illus., index, adv. Circ: 5000. Vol. ends: Summer. Microform: PQC. Online: Florida Center for Library Automation; Gale; OCLC Online Computer Library Center, Inc. *Indexed:* ABIn, ATI, BLI, CLI, LRI, PAIS, PMA. *Bk. rev.:* 1-2 signed, 500 words each. *Aud.:* Sa.

Positioning itself as a journal "written by and for the board elite," this publication still has plenty of useful content for the business student who aspires to corporate governance or simply wants to know what published conversations directors are engaging in. Once each quarter, *Directors & Boards* publishes profiles and interviews with directors, several articles (very applied, about topics such as compensation, liability, performance evaluation, and financial controls), and a number of columns, including a roster of new board directors and book review or two. The web site provides weekly and monthly articles and briefings that supplement the print contents. Recommended for academic libraries that support business programs. URL: www.directorsandboards.com

4275. European Management Journal. [ISSN: 0263-2373] 1983. 6x/yr. EUR 761. Ed(s): Paul Stonham. Pergamon, The Boulevard, Langford Ln, East Park, Kidlington, OX5 1GB, United Kingdom. Illus., index, adv. Refereed. Circ: 1000. Vol. ends: Dec. Microform: PQC. Online: EBSCO

Publishing, EBSCO Host; Gale; IngentaConnect; OCLC Online Computer Library Center, Inc.; OhioLINK; ScienceDirect; SwetsWise Online Content. *Indexed:* ABIn, BPI, IBSS, PAIS, PsycInfo. *Bk. rev.:* 2-5, 300-800 words. *Aud.:* Ac, Sa.

Scholarly yet readable articles on management issues in European Union countries are featured—academic research articles by authors throughout the English-speaking world, case studies, interviews, and "Executive Briefings." This is an exceptionally content-rich source for readers interested in a high level of discourse about European business. Expect two to five substantial reviews in the "Books for Managers" section. Highly recommended for academic libraries supporting business students and faculty. URL: www.elsevier.com/locate/emj

Harvard Business Review. See Business/General section.

4276. *International Journal of Cross Cultural Management.* [ISSN: 1470-5958] 2001. 3x/yr. GBP 268. Ed(s): Terence Jackson, Zeynep Aycan. Sage Publications Ltd., 1 Oliver's Yard, 55 City Rd, London, EC1 1SP, United Kingdom; info@sagepub.co.uk; http://www.sagepub.co.uk. Adv. Refereed. Online: CSA; EBSCO Publishing, EBSCO Host; HighWire Press; OCLC Online Computer Library Center, Inc.; ProQuest LLC (Ann Arbor); SAGE Publications, Inc., SAGE Journals Online; SwetsWise Online Content. Reprint: PSC. *Indexed:* ABIn, CommAb, HRA, IBR, IBSS, IBZ, IndIslam, PsycInfo. *Aud.:* Ac, Sa.

The editorial board of this scholarly journal covers six continents. The focus of their publication is to contribute to an "understanding of the issues, problems, and practices of managing, working, and organizing across cultures." Its research articles are aimed at students and scholars in international management programs, and have included studies on such topics as leadership preferences across cultures, multinational perspectives of work values, and the influence of Confucian ideology in Chinese. The international focus is reinforced by the inclusion of abstracts in French and Chinese at the end of each article. Highly recommended for any academic library serving an international business program. URL: http://ccm.sagepub.com

4277. *Ivey Business Journal (Online Edition): improving the practice of management.* Former titles (until 2002): *Ivey Business Journal (Print Edition);* (until 1999): *Ivey Business Quarterly;* (until 1997): *Business Quarterly;* (until 1950): *Quarterly Review of Commerce.* 1933. bi-m. CND 44.94 domestic; CND 48.30 Atlantic; USD 42 United States. Ed(s): Stephen Bernhut. Ivey Management Services, 179 John St, Ste 501, Toronto, ON M5T 1X4, Canada; ibj@ivey.uwo.ca; http://www.ivey.uwo.ca/publications/bq. Illus., adv. Circ: 9123 Paid. Microform: MIM; MML; PQC. Online: The Dialog Corporation; EBSCO Publishing, EBSCO Host; Factiva, Inc.; Florida Center for Library Automation; Gale; LexisNexis; Micromedia ProQuest; OCLC Online Computer Library Center, Inc.; ProQuest LLC (Ann Arbor); H.W. Wilson. *Indexed:* ABIn, BPI, CBCARef, CPerI, PAIS, SSCI. *Aud.:* Ac, Sa.

The Richard Ivey School of Business at the University of Western Ontario publishes yet another example of a good popular management journal written by academics and practicing managers for a primarily corporate audience. Each issue has an overriding theme—work-life balance, global business, leadership, innovation—with a Canadian focus that is useful for any business readership. The online version provides tables of contents and abstracts for all, and full text for subscribers. Recommended as another global voice on management issues for academic business collections. URL: www.iveybusinessjournal.com

4278. *Journal of General Management.* Formed by the merger of (1969-1973): *Journal of Business Finance;* (19??-1973): *Journal of Business Policy.* [ISSN: 0306-3070] 1973. q. GBP 173 combined subscription print & online; USD 367.50 combined subscription print & online; GBP 41.25 per issue. Ed(s): Dr. Kevin Money. Braybrooke Press Ltd., Remenham House, Remenham Hill, Henley-on-Thames, RG9 3EP, United Kingdom; http://www.braybrooke.co.uk. Illus., index, adv. Circ: 1000. Vol. ends: Summer. *Indexed:* ABIn, AgeL, ExcerpMed, IBSS, PAIS, SSCI. *Bk. rev.:* 1 signed, 500 words. *Aud.:* Ac, Sa.

This management journal offers five or six lengthy review or research articles and one book review per issue. Written by academic faculty worldwide, these wide-ranging, scholarly articles might be on any subject of interest to its manager audience—sport sponsorship, e-business, emotional intelligence, and cross-cultual management have been recent topics. The global focus, wide indexing, and inexpensive price make it a good addition to academic collections. URL: www.braybrooke.co.uk/jogm

4279. *Journal of Management.* [ISSN: 0149-2063] 1975. bi-m. GBP 330. Ed(s): David C Feldman. Sage Publications, Inc., 2455 Teller Rd, Thousand Oaks, CA 91320; info@sagepub.com; http://www.sagepub.com. Illus., index, adv. Refereed. Circ: 2000. Vol. ends: No. 6. Microform: PQC. Online: CSA; EBSCO Publishing, EBSCO Host; Florida Center for Library Automation; Gale; HighWire Press; IngentaConnect; Northern Light Technology, Inc.; OCLC Online Computer Library Center, Inc.; OhioLINK; SAGE Publications, Inc., SAGE Journals Online; ScienceDirect; SwetsWise Online Content; H.W. Wilson. Reprint: PSC. *Indexed:* ABIn, BPI, PAIS, PMA, PsycInfo, SSCI. *Aud.:* Ac, Sa.

The *Journal of Management* is published by the Southern regional division of the Academy of Management. It publishes the same type of articles one would find in the Academy of Management's *Journal* or *Review*—high-quality theoretical and empirical scholarship covering a very broad scope of management science topics. There are five to seven scholarly articles every two months, with an annual review (influential in the management discipline) published as the last issue of every year. Very highly recommended for academic libraries, as are all Academy of Management publications. URL: http://jom.sagepub.com

4280. *Journal of Management Studies.* [ISSN: 0022-2380] 1964. 8x/yr. GBP 844 print & online eds. Ed(s): Steven W Floyd, Mike Wright. Blackwell Publishing Ltd., 9600 Garsington Rd, Oxford, OX4 2ZG, United Kingdom; customerservices@blackwellpublishing.com; http://www.blackwellpublishing.com. Illus., index, adv. Refereed. Circ: 1600. Vol. ends: Nov. Online: Blackwell Synergy; EBSCO Publishing, EBSCO Host; Gale; IngentaConnect; OCLC Online Computer Library Center, Inc.; OhioLINK; SwetsWise Online Content. Reprint: PSC. *Indexed:* ABIn, BPI, EAA, ErgAb, IBR, IBSS, IBZ, IPSA, PMA, PsycInfo, SSCI. *Bk. rev.:* 5-7, 800-1,000 words (not in every issue). *Aud.:* Ac, Sa.

The eight yearly issues of this scholarly journal have six to nine articles on theoretical or highly applied topics in business management. Topics as far-ranging as the role of authenticity in "cultural industries," emotional exhaustion in the workplace, multiple loyalties, organizational learning, and disciplining professional employees appear in the journal contents. An occasional special issue focuses on a single theme ("the dynamics of voice and silence in organizations," "micro-strategy and strategizing," "the changing multinational firm"). The journal has a strong international and cross-cultural focus. Highly recommended for academic libraries serving graduate business schools. URL: www.blackwellpublishing.com/journal.asp?ref=0022-2380&site=1

4281. *Journal of Managerial Issues.* [ISSN: 1045-3695] 1989. q. USD 90 (Individuals, USD 60). Ed(s): Dr. Charles C Fischer. Pittsburg State University, Department of Economics, Finance & Banking, 1701 South Broadway, Pittsburg, KS 66762-7533; chuck@pittstate.edu; http://www.pittstate.edu/econ/jmi.html. Illus., index. Sample. Refereed. Circ: 1000 Paid. Microform: PQC. Online: EBSCO Publishing, EBSCO Host; Florida Center for Library Automation; Gale; Northern Light Technology, Inc.; OCLC Online Computer Library Center, Inc.; ProQuest LLC (Ann Arbor). *Indexed:* ABIn, CommAb, HRA, IPSA, ISTA, PAIS, PRA, PsycInfo, RiskAb. *Aud.:* Ac, Sa.

One of the many academic journals that claim a spot on the bridge providing scholarly research and topical literature reviews to both scholastic and business readership (although the dense statistical nature of most of the articles strongly skew this title to the academic side). Its articles range broadly from finance to human resources to decision-making to CEO pay structures. A manager or student is unlikely to be leafing though its seven or eight quarterly articles, but the large number of indexing and abstracting services that include this title will send many scholars and even practitioners to the shelf to find an article of interest. Recommended for the academic business collection. URL: www.pittstate.edu/econ/jmi.html

Journal of Small Business Management. See Business/Small Business section.

4282. *M I T Sloan Management Review.* Former titles (until 2001): *Sloan Management Review;* (until 1970): *Industrial Management Review.* [ISSN: 1532-9194] 1960. q. Individuals, USD 89. Ed(s): Beth Maqura, Jane Gebhart. Massachusetts Institute of Technology, 77 Massachusetts Ave, Room E60-100, Cambridge, MA 02139-4307. Illus., index. Refereed. Circ: 25000. Vol. ends: Summer. Microform: PQC. Online: Chadwyck-Healey Inc.; EBSCO Publishing, EBSCO Host; Florida Center for Library Automation; Gale; Northern Light Technology, Inc.; OCLC Online Computer Library Center, Inc.; ProQuest K-12 Learning Solutions; ProQuest LLC (Ann Arbor); H.W. Wilson. *Indexed:* ABIn, AgeL, BLI, BPI, EAA, EnvAb, JEL, LogistBibl, PAIS, PMA, SSCI. *Bk. rev.:* 6-12, 200-2,000 words. *Aud.:* Ac, Sa.

A scholarly journal that is truly focused on business readers, *SMR* is a crisp, readable, four-color illustrated publication that looks and reads enough like a business magazine to keep its research-based contributions from intimidating its audience. Its level is also accessible to undergraduate business students beginning to read research-based business literature. Every issue has a number of single-page "Research Briefs" that provide overviews of recently published or forthcoming studies, eight to ten articles primarily reporting studies involving "corporate strategy, leadership, and management of technology and innovation," followed by a couple of short opinion pieces. This is a must-have title for both academic libraries and large public libraries with a substantial business clientele. URL: http://web.mit.edu/smr

4283. *Office Solutions: the magazine for office professionals.* Formerly (until 2000): *Office Systems (Year);* Incorporates: *Managing Office Technology;* Which was formerly (until June 1993): *Modern Office Technology;* (1956-1983): *Modern Office Procedures.* [ISSN: 1529-1804] 1984. 6x/yr. USD 36 (Free to qualified personnel). Ed(s): Scott Cullen. OfficeVision, Inc., 252 N Main St, Ste 200, Mt Airy, NC 27030. Illus., adv. Circ: 81250 Paid and controlled. Vol. ends: Dec. Microform: PQC. Online: EBSCO Publishing, EBSCO Host; Florida Center for Library Automation; Gale; OCLC Online Computer Library Center, Inc.; ProQuest LLC (Ann Arbor); H.W. Wilson. *Indexed:* ABIn, BPI, CWI, ConsI, MicrocompInd. *Bk. rev.:* Number and length vary. *Aud.:* Ga, Ac, Sa.

This publication is geared toward those working in the office management field, and it covers the wide variety of issues facing office managers and office workers today. Topics include privacy issues, telecommuting, workplace styles, and the impact of technology on office work. Also included are product reviews, product announcements, and book reviews. Recommended. URL: www.os-od.com

4284. *Public Performance and Management Review.* Former titles (until 2000): *Public Productivity and Management Review;* (until 1990): *Public Productivity Review.* [ISSN: 1530-9576] 1975. q. USD 479 print & online eds. Ed(s): Marc Holzer. M.E. Sharpe, Inc., 80 Business Park Dr, Armonk, NY 10504; custserv@mesharpe.com; http://www.mesharpe.com. Illus., index, adv. Refereed. Circ: 1450. Vol. ends: Jun. Microform: PQC. Online: EBSCO Publishing, EBSCO Host; OCLC Online Computer Library Center, Inc.; SwetsWise Online Content; H.W. Wilson. *Indexed:* ABIn, BPI, CINAHL, PAIS, PMA, PSA, SUSA. *Bk. rev.:* Number and length vary. *Aud.:* Ac, Sa.

Managers in the public sector and academics are the intended audience for this scholarly journal "dedicated to creative problem solving." Each issue provides four or five articles on a single topic in public administration (outsourcing, budgeting, personnel management, training) with a broad international scope. Additional articles report on current research, discuss the application of corporate management techniques to the public sector, or provide a case study that is then commented on by one or more public sector professionals or academic researchers. There are frequently substantial book reviews. Recommended for special libraries in the public sector and academic libraries supporting nonprofit management coursework and research. URL: www.mesharpe.com/journals.asp

4285. *S A M Advanced Management Journal.* Former titles (1975-1984): *Advanced Management Journal;* (1969-1974): *S A M Advanced Management Journal.* [ISSN: 0749-7075] 1935. q. USD 54 domestic; USD 69 foreign. Ed(s): Moustafa H Abdelsamad. Society for Advancement of Management, Texas A&M University Corpus Christi, College of Business, Corpus Christi, TX 78412; moustafa@falcon.tamucc.edu; http://www.enterprise.tamucc.edu/sam. Illus., index, adv. Circ: 5000. Vol. ends: Autumn. Microform: PQC. Online: EBSCO Publishing, EBSCO Host; Gale; OCLC Online Computer Library Center, Inc.; ProQuest LLC (Ann Arbor); H.W. Wilson. *Indexed:* ABIn, ATI, AgeL, BPI, PMA. *Aud.:* Ac, Sa.

This slim journal from the Society for Advancement of Management is a quarterly conduit for academics and practicing managers to share research on a very wide range of management topics. The shorter length of articles and less complex language and statistical analysis make this journal a useful title for undergraduates looking for readable primary research; the practical focus of articles make this title useful for managers in the field. Recommended for undergraduate academic collections. URL: www.cob.tamucc.edu/sam/amj

Workforce Management. See Labor and Industrial Relations section.

Functional Management

There are hundreds of functional management magazines and journals that provide managers with specific job responsibilities or in specific industries with research reports, news, or overviews of new practices. Among the many topic areas are inventory control, production, product development, supply chain management, information technology, purchasing, research & development, and project management; each of these functions might then have several industry-specific journals within the category (automotive, food and beverage, textile, computing, etc.) The titles mentioned below are a few of the most widely used publications in some of these areas.

4286. *A P I C S - The Performance Advantage.* [ISSN: 1056-0017] 1991. 10x/yr. Non-members, USD 65. Ed(s): Doug Kelly. A P I C S - The Educational Society for Resource Management, 5301 Shawnee Rd, Alexandria, VA 22312-2317; service@apicshq.org; http://www.apics.org. Illus., index, adv. Circ: 72153. *Indexed:* LogistBibl. *Bk. rev.:* 0-2, signed, 1 page each. *Aud.:* Sa.

This is the member magazine of APICS, the Association for Operations Management. The magazine contains feature articles, case studies, and news on production and inventory, supply chain management, enterprise management, and warehousing and logistics management. The magazine encourages authors to focus on including implementation strategies within the articles. It is also very much a showcase for manufacturing and service advertisers. Selected full text is available for nonmembers at the association web site. This magazine will be read by practicing supply chain managers and would be of interest to undergraduates considering a career in the field. URL: www.apics.org/Magazine

4287. *Industrial Engineer: engineering & management solutions at work.* Former titles (until 2003): *I I E Solutions;* (until 1995): *Industrial Engineering;* (until 1969): *The Journal of Industrial Engineering.* [ISSN: 1542-894X] 1949. m. USD 87 domestic; USD 108 foreign; USD 7 newsstand/cover. Ed(s): Jane Gaboury. Institute of Industrial Engineers, 3577 Parkway Ln, Ste 200, Norcross, GA 30092; cs@iienet.org; http://www.iienet.org. Illus., index, adv. Circ: 17000 Paid and free. Microform: PQC. Online: The Dialog Corporation; EBSCO Publishing, EBSCO Host; Gale; OCLC Online Computer Library Center, Inc.; ProQuest K-12 Learning Solutions; ProQuest LLC (Ann Arbor); H.W. Wilson. *Indexed:* ABIn, AS&TI, ApMecR, CWI, CompLI, EngInd, ErgAb, ExcerpMed, MathR, SCI. *Aud.:* Sa.

An official magazine of the Institute of Industrial Engineers designed specifically for managers and engineers in business, industry, and government. Feature articles cover a broad range of practical industry topics such as simulation; quality, production and inventory control; ergonomics and worker safety; and material handling, supply chains, and logistics. Recurring columns include news, trends, profiles of individuals, product and software reviews, association events and activities, and executive summaries of research published concurrently in its sister publication *IIE Transactions*. Online access at www.iienet.org/magazine is limited to members of the institute and print subscribers.

4288. *Industrial Management*. [ISSN: 0019-8471] 1952. bi-m. Non-members, USD 59. Institute of Industrial Engineers, Society for Engineering and Management Systems, 3577 Pkwy Ln Ste 200, Norcross, GA 30092; http://www.iienet.org/public/articles/index.cfm?Cat=200. Illus., index. Circ: 3000. Online: EBSCO Publishing, EBSCO Host; Florida Center for Library Automation; Gale; Northern Light Technology, Inc.; OCLC Online Computer Library Center, Inc.; ProQuest LLC (Ann Arbor); H.W. Wilson. *Indexed:* ABIn, BPI, EngInd, LRI, LogistBibl. *Aud.:* Sa.

This is a practical journal offering professional, prescriptive advice to operating managers and industrial engineers in management positions. There are profiles of successful managers and feature articles on current management issues. Readers will find four to six articles on such topics as change management, human resource issues, production control, and strategic planning. Recommended for undergraduate reading. URL: http://im.iienet.org

4289. *The International Journal of Logistics Management*. [ISSN: 0957-4093] 1990. 2x/yr. EUR 369 combined subscription in Europe print & online eds.; USD 439 combined subscription in North America print & online eds.; AUD 599 combined subscription in Australasia print & online eds. Ed(s): Douglas Lambert, Martin Christopher. Emerald Group Publishing Limited, Howard House, Wagon Ln, Bingley, BD16 1WA, United Kingdom; information@emeraldinsight.com; http://www.emeraldinsight.com. Illus., adv. Refereed. Circ: 2000 Paid. Vol. ends: No. 2. Reprint: PSC. *Indexed:* ABIn, HRIS, LogistBibl. *Aud.:* Ac, Sa.

This journal includes both scholarly research and practical case histories for managers, researchers, teachers, and students. There are seven to nine articles providing readers with new ideas and practices and current developments in the field of logistics management and supply chain management. Coverage is international (authors and articles). Recommended for academic business libraries where international business is of interest. URL: www.logisticssupply-chain.org

4290. *International Journal of Physical Distribution & Logistics Management*. Former titles (until 1990): *International Journal of Physical Distribution and Materials Management*; (until 1977): *International Journal of Physical Distribution*; Which incorporated (in 1975): *International Journal of Physical Distribution Monograph*; Which was formerly (1970-1974): *P D M. Physical Distribution Monograph*. [ISSN: 0960-0035] 1970. 10x/yr. EUR 12189 combined subscription in Europe print & online eds.; USD 13099 combined subscription in North America print & online eds.; AUD 16069 combined subscription in Australasia print & online eds. Ed(s): Richard F Poist, Jr., Michael R Crum. Emerald Group Publishing Limited, Howard House, Wagon Ln, Bingley, BD16 1WA, United Kingdom; information@emeraldinsight.com; http://www.emeraldinsight.com. Illus., index. Refereed. Online: Pub.; EBSCO Publishing, EBSCO Host; Florida Center for Library Automation; Gale; IngentaConnect; OCLC Online Computer Library Center, Inc.; OhioLINK; ProQuest LLC (Ann Arbor); SwetsWise Online Content. Reprint: PSC. *Indexed:* ABIn, C&ISA, CerAb, ExcerpMed, IAA, LogistBibl, PAIS, SSCI. *Aud.:* Ac, Sa.

This is the self-proclaimed leader in the field of logistics, but the high cost of this scholarly journal makes it out of reach for most libraries. Combining the practical and scholarly in the latest developments of distribution and logistics management, *IJPDLM* offers four articles in each issue. Special issues are occasionally thematic, e.g., logistics and supply chain risk and uncertainty. Targeted at both business planners and researchers, it is appropriate for larger research institutions only.

4291. *International Journal of Production Research*. [ISSN: 0020-7543] 1961. s-m. GBP 4902 print & online eds. Ed(s): J E Middle. Taylor & Francis Ltd., 4 Park Sq, Milton Park, Abingdon, OX14 4RN, United Kingdom; info@tandf.co.uk; http://www.tandf.co.uk/journals. Illus., index, adv. Refereed. Microform: MIM; PQC. Online: EBSCO Publishing, EBSCO Host; Gale; IngentaConnect; OCLC Online Computer Library Center, Inc.; SwetsWise Online Content. Reprint: PSC. *Indexed:* ABIn, C&ISA, CerAb, EngInd, ErgAb, IAA, SCI, SSCI. *Aud.:* Ac, Sa.

Official journal of the International Foundation for Production Research, *IJPR* is one of the top-ranked journals in the field of operations management. Each bi-weekly issue contains approximately 10 articles, 15 to 25 pages in length. Manufacturing strategy, policy formulation and evaluation, and the contribution of technological innovation are major concerns. Techniques developed in computer and mathematical sciences used in the design, measurement, or operation of production systems are also considered. Aimed at research engineers and industrial practitioners, academic libraries will find this title important to support advanced business administration degree programs.

4292. *Journal of Product Innovation Management*. [ISSN: 0737-6782] 1984. bi-m. GBP 541 print & online eds. Ed(s): C Anthony Di Benedetto. Blackwell Publishing, Inc., Commerce Place, 350 Main St, Malden, MA 02148; customerservices@blackwellpublishing.com; http://www.blackwellpublishing.com. Illus., index, adv. Sample. Refereed. Circ: 2500. Vol. ends: Nov. Online: Blackwell Synergy; EBSCO Publishing, EBSCO Host; Gale; IngentaConnect; OCLC Online Computer Library Center, Inc.; OhioLINK; ScienceDirect; SwetsWise Online Content. Reprint: PSC. *Indexed:* ABIn, C&ISA, CerAb, CommAb, EngInd, IAA, RiskAb, SCI, SSCI. *Bk. rev.:* 3-13, 400-1,700 words. *Aud.:* Ac, Sa.

The Product Development and Management Association intends this journal to cast a wide net into the theoretical and empirical academic research in product design and manufacturing processes and the work of students and professionals in every part of product development process. The journal presents scholarly research articles along with case histories and conceptual reviews from management, engineering, and the sciences, with an international and cross-cultural scope. Book reviews and abstracts of articles in other journals are featured in each issue. Highly recommended for academic libraries. URL: www.pdma.org/journal

4293. *Journal of Productivity Analysis*. [ISSN: 0895-562X] 1989. bi-m. EUR 727 print & online eds. Ed(s): Robin C Sickles. Springer New York LLC, 233 Spring St, New York, NY 10013-1578; service-ny@springer.com; http://www.springer.com/. Illus., index, adv. Sample. Refereed. Vol. ends: No. 4. Online: EBSCO Publishing, EBSCO Host; Gale; IngentaConnect; OCLC Online Computer Library Center, Inc.; OhioLINK; ProQuest LLC (Ann Arbor); Springer LINK; SwetsWise Online Content. Reprint: PSC. *Indexed:* ABIn, CABA, DSA, JEL, RRTA, SSCI, WAE&RSA. *Aud.:* Ac, Sa.

Encompasses productivity-related developments spanning the disciplines of economics, the management sciences, operations research, and business and public administration. Topics covered can include productivity theory, organizational design, index number theory, and related foundations of productivity analysis. The journal also publishes research on computational methods that are employed in productivity analysis, including econometric and mathematical programming techniques and empirical research. Article titles frequently indicate the use of decision-making models and data envelopment analysis(DEA). Appropriate for scholars and practitioners in the fields of productivity and quality management.

4294. *Journal of Supply Chain Management: a global review of purchasing and supply*. Former titles (until 1999): *International Journal of Purchasing & Materials Management*; (until 1991): *Journal of Purchasing and Materials Management*; *Journal of Purchasing*. [ISSN: 1523-2409] 1965. q. GBP 142 print & online eds. Ed(s): Alvin Williams. Blackwell Publishing, Inc., Commerce Place, 350 Main St, Malden, MA

02148; customerservices@blackwellpublishing.com; http://www.blackwellpublishing.com. Illus., index, adv. Refereed. Circ: 3000. Vol. ends: Nov (No. 4). Microform: PQC. Online: Blackwell Synergy; The Dialog Corporation; EBSCO Publishing, EBSCO Host; Florida Center for Library Automation; Gale; OCLC Online Computer Library Center, Inc.; ProQuest LLC (Ann Arbor); SwetsWise Online Content; H.W. Wilson. Reprint: PSC. *Indexed:* ABIn, BPI, LogistBibl. *Bk. rev.:* Number and length vary. *Aud.:* Ac, Sa.

This is a thin publication with an attractive two-color design and writing style that serves its mission as a provider of information about purchasing, materials, and supply to academics and management professionals. Articles are high quality and written at a level accessible to anyone with an interest in the topic. Four articles each quarter analyze the principles and applications of supply management, supply chain management, and purchasing strategies. Each issue also includes an interview with a supply management professional from a major company (American Express, AstraZeneca Pharmaceuticals, Honeywell). Recommended for undergraduate and graduate collections. URL: www.napm.org/Pubs/journalscm

4295. *M I S Quarterly.* [ISSN: 0276-7783] 1977. q. USD 150 (Individuals, USD 85). Ed(s): Carol Saunders. M I S Research Center, University of Minnesota, Carlson School of Management, Minneapolis, MN 55455. Illus., index, adv. Refereed. Circ: 3000. Vol. ends: Dec. Online: EBSCO Publishing, EBSCO Host; Florida Center for Library Automation; Gale; JSTOR (Web-based Journal Archive); OCLC Online Computer Library Center, Inc.; ProQuest LLC (Ann Arbor); H.W. Wilson. *Indexed:* ABIn, BPI, CompLI, EngInd, ISTA, SCI, SSCI. *Aud.:* Ac, Sa.

This journal has recently undergone a change in its mission statement. It is now publishing research articles about the development of IT-based services, the management of IT resources, and the economics and use of IT with managerial and organizational implications. Along with these longer research articles, there are sections of "Research Notes" and "Issues and Opinions" that provide forums for dialogue about recent articles or current issues in the MIS world. Highly recommended for academic libraries. (A related publication is *MIS Quarterly Executive* [www.misqu.org], the Society for Information Management's publication for practicing managers with a more case-based focus.) URL: www.misq.org

4296. *Manufacturing and Service Operations Management.* [ISSN: 1523-4614] 1999. bi-m. Non-members, USD 136. Ed(s): Gerard Cachon. I N F O R M S, 7240 Parkway Dr, Ste 310, Hanover, MD 21076-1344; informs@informs.org; http://www.informs.org. Illus., adv. Refereed. Circ: 1000 Paid and controlled. Online: EBSCO Publishing, EBSCO Host; Gale; HighWire Press; OCLC Online Computer Library Center, Inc.; ProQuest LLC (Ann Arbor); SwetsWise Online Content. *Indexed:* ABIn, EngInd, SCI, SSCI. *Aud.:* Ac, Sa.

This is a highly technical and applied journal that contains articles that have been written using a variety of methodological approaches. The articles are based on disciplinary areas (economics, operations research, organizational behavior, psychology, statistics) that can be used as a lens through which to view the functional operations of an organization. Recent topics include "Sale Timing in a Supply Chain," "Inventory Management," and "Inventory and the Stock Market." Recommended for graduate academic collections. URL: www.msom.org

4297. *Production Planning & Control.* [ISSN: 0953-7287] 1990. 8x/yr. GBP 615 print & online eds. Ed(s): Dr. Stephen J Childe. Taylor & Francis Ltd., 4 Park Sq, Milton Park, Abingdon, OX14 4RN, United Kingdom; info@tandf.co.uk; http://www.tandf.co.uk/journals. Adv. Sample. Refereed. Online: EBSCO Publishing, EBSCO Host; Gale; IngentaConnect; OCLC Online Computer Library Center, Inc.; SwetsWise Online Content. Reprint: PSC. *Indexed:* ABIn, C&ISA, CerAb, EngInd, ErgAb, IAA, SCI. *Bk. rev.:* 1-2, signed. *Aud.:* Ac, Sa.

The field of production planning supports several good publications where academics and managers can share research developments and industry practices. This is yet another of those journals, with a more European focus. Information is provided in a variety of article types—invited keynote papers,

research reports, review articles, case studies, field reports, conference notes, and book reviews. Recommended for academic libraries interested in a wider range of journals on this topic. URL: www.tandf.co.uk/journals

4298. *Project Management Journal.* Formerly (until 1984): *Project Management Quarterly.* [ISSN: 8756-9728] 1970. q. USD 145 Free to members. Ed(s): Parviz F Rad. Project Management Institute, 4 Campus Blvd, Newtown Square, PA 19073-3299; pmihq@pmi.org; http://www.pmi.org. Adv. Refereed. Circ: 85000 Paid. Vol. ends: Dec. *Indexed:* ABIn, BPI, RiskAb. *Bk. rev.:* 0-2, 400 words. *Aud.:* Ac, Sa.

The refereed journal of the Project Management Institute (PMI), this publication provides a good balance of research and applied articles of interest to academics and practitioners. Articles provide a broad view of project management including advanced state-of-the-art project management techniques, research, theories, and applications. Recent topics include "Decision Making for Successful Product Development" and "Managing Complex Outsourced Projects." Short news and advice pieces are left to PMI's magazine, *PMNetwork.* Recommended for academic collections. URL: www.pmi.org/info/PIR_PMJournal.asp

4299. *Purchasing (Newton): the magazine for chief procurement officers and supply chain executives.* [ISSN: 0033-4448] 1936. 19x/yr. USD 109.90 domestic (Free to qualified personnel). Ed(s): Doug Smock, Paul Teague. Reed Business Information, 275 Washington St, Newton, MA 02458; http://www.reedbusiness.com. Illus., index, adv. Circ: 97097 Paid and controlled. Vol. ends: Jun/Dec. Online: EBSCO Publishing, EBSCO Host; Factiva, Inc.; Florida Center for Library Automation; Gale; OCLC Online Computer Library Center, Inc.; ProQuest LLC (Ann Arbor); H.W. Wilson. *Indexed:* ABIn, BPI, C&ISA, CerAb, IAA, LRI, LogistBibl. *Bk. rev.:* Various number and length. *Aud.:* Ac, Sa.

A glossy, cluttered newsmagazine for purchasing and supply chain management professionals (with an equally glossy and cluttered web site), *Purchasing* currently focuses its biweekly content on specific industries, currently alternating among a metals edition, an electronics and technology edition, and a chemicals edition. There are short, punchy pieces, many with graphs and tables ranking companies, reporting and forecasting trends, and revealing survey results. Subscribers also receive buyer's guides for chemicals, metals, and "e-procurement." URL: www.purchasing.com

4300. *Quality Management Journal.* [ISSN: 1068-6967] 1993. q. USD 130 (Individuals, USD 75). Ed(s): Barbara Flynn. American Society for Quality, 600 N Plankinton Ave, P O Box 3005, Milwaukee, WI 53203-2914; help@asq.org; http://www.asq.org. Illus., adv. Circ: 14000. Vol. ends: Jul (No. 4). *Indexed:* ABIn. *Bk. rev.:* 4-7 500-1000 words. *Aud.:* Ac, Sa.

Quality Management Journal is dedicated to the broad topic of the pursuit of quality operations and products, with presentation and discussion of current research on subjects such as "A Model of Web Site Quality Assessment" and several reviews of recent quality management books. The journal's web site is an excellent supplement, providing access to full sample issues plus a selected full-text article from every issue, long abstracts or full text from the executive briefs of the research articles, and the text of most book reviews. This publication provides a scholarly yet applied view of the topic and is recommended for academic libraries serving management faculty and students. URL: www.asq.org/pub/qmj

Quality Progress. See Engineering and Technology/Manufacturing Engineering section.

4301. *R & D Management.* [ISSN: 0033-6807] 1970. 5x/yr. GBP 721 print & online eds. Ed(s): Jeff Butler, Alan W Pearson. Blackwell Publishing Ltd., 9600 Garsington Rd, Oxford, OX4 2ZG, United Kingdom; customerservices@blackwellpublishing.com; http://www.blackwellpublishing.com. Illus., adv. Refereed. Circ: 1150. Vol. ends: Oct (No. 4). Online: Blackwell Synergy; EBSCO Publishing,

EBSCO Host; Gale; IngentaConnect; OCLC Online Computer Library Center, Inc.; OhioLINK; SwetsWise Online Content. Reprint: PSC. *Indexed:* ABIn, BPI, CABA, IBR, IBZ, PAIS, RiskAb, SSCI, WAE&RSA. *Bk. rev.:* 2-4, 750-1,000 words. *Aud.:* Ac, Sa.

This journal focuses on the issues managers deal with in organizations or work units developing innovative processes and products, including such topics as "research, development, design and innovation, and related strategic and human resource issues." There are seven to nine well-written and well-edited articles per issue. Some issues also have two to four book reviews. This publication would be of interest to engineering and design students and faculty as well as management and organizational psychology departments. Highly recommended. URL: www.blackwellpublishing.com

4302. *Research Technology Management: international journal of research management.* Formerly: *Research Management.* [ISSN: 0895-6308] 1958. bi-m. USD 205 (Individuals, USD 105). Ed(s): Michael F Wolff. Industrial Research Institute, 2200 Clarendon Blvd, Arlington, VA 22201; http://www.iriinc.org. Illus., index. Refereed. Circ: 3000 Paid. Vol. ends: Nov/Dec. Microform: PQC. Online: EBSCO Publishing, EBSCO Host; Florida Center for Library Automation; Gale; IngentaConnect; OCLC Online Computer Library Center, Inc.; ProQuest K-12 Learning Solutions; ProQuest LLC (Ann Arbor); SwetsWise Online Content; H.W. Wilson. *Indexed:* ABIn, ABS&EES, BPI, EngInd, EnvAb, H&SSA, IUSGP, PAIS, RiskAb, SCI, SSCI, WRCInf. *Bk. rev.:* 4-6, 75-300 words. *Aud.:* Ac, Sa.

This publication is typographically cluttered and graphically overstimulated, but the content has excellent value—lots of well-written, applied, "how to do it in your organization" pieces about a wide range of managerial and technological topics. Issues contain news briefs, feature articles, research reports, interviews, commentary, case studies, and brief reviews of new books and important papers in the field. R&D managers working in high-tech organizations would find a great deal of advice and inspiration. Articles would also be useful and interesting for undergraduates. Recommended for academic libraries. URL: www.iriinc.org

Risk Management. See Finance/Trade Journals section.

4303. *Supply Chain Management: an international journal.* [ISSN: 1359-8546] 1996. 5x/yr. EUR 2299 combined subscription in Europe print & online eds.; USD 2519 combined subscription in North America print & online eds.; AUD 3149 combined subscription in Australasia print & online eds. Ed(s): Andrew Fearne. Emerald Group Publishing Limited, Howard House, Wagon Ln, Bingley, BD16 1WA, United Kingdom; information@emeraldinsight.com; http://www.emeraldinsight.com. Refereed. Reprint: PSC. *Indexed:* ABIn, C&ISA, CABA, CerAb, HortAb, IAA, LogistBibl, SSCI. *Aud.:* Ac, Sa.

The supply chain is the topic of many functional management journals. What makes this title stand out are its broadly international articles (research applications and case studies are routinely provided beyond North America and Europe) and its high level of scholarship. The journal connects practitioners and academics in the area of supply chain management. Recent special issues contain articles related to "Exploring SCM in the Creative Industries" and "E-supply Chain." Recommended for graduate-level academic collections. URL: www.emeraldinsight.com/journals

Human Resources

Human resources publications tend to concentrate on the applied practice of employee recruitment, selection, training, evaluation, compensation, and development. These titles are very closely related to those in the Organizational Behavior and Studies subdivision, but tend to be practitioner journals for managers and executives overseeing HR functions.

Benefits Quarterly. See Labor and Industrial Relations section.

4304. *Compensation and Benefits Review: the journal of total compensation strategies.* Formerly (until 1985): *Compensation Review.* [ISSN: 0886-3687] 1969. bi-m. GBP 300. Ed(s): Fay Hansen. Sage Publications, Inc., 2455 Teller Rd, Thousand Oaks, CA 91320; info@sagepub.com; http://www.sagepub.com. Illus., index, adv. Circ: 1027 Paid. Vol. ends: Nov/Dec. Microform: PQC. Online: CSA; The Dialog Corporation; EBSCO Publishing, EBSCO Host; HighWire Press; OCLC Online Computer Library Center, Inc.; OhioLINK; ProQuest LLC (Ann Arbor); SAGE Publications, Inc., SAGE Journals Online; SwetsWise Online Content; H.W. Wilson. Reprint: PSC. *Indexed:* ABIn, ABS&EES, AgeL, BPI, PAIS, PMA, SSCI. *Bk. rev.:* 1-8, 250-700 words. *Aud.:* Sa.

Although the title might sound like the annual booklet of tables and lists your employer sends you about your retirement and health coverage, this is a professional journal that would be right at home in the strategic management section. Its articles are written by corporate compensation managers who present analyses of pay and benefits issues for organizational decision makers. The journal is published in the United Kingdom, but it has a U.S. focus; the laws and regulations discussed (Section 529, Fair Labor Standards Act) are for U.S. managers. Not all articles have a legal focus; recent topics include the graying of the workforce, executive compensation, and prescription drug costs. The journal also provides surveys, statistical summaries, and tables to support the content. This is a niche title aimed at practicing HR managers, but it would be a good addition to larger academic collections. URL: www.sagepub.com/journal.aspx?pid=68

4305. *Employee Responsibilities and Rights Journal.* [ISSN: 0892-7545] 1988. q. EUR 425 print & online eds. Ed(s): John P Keenan. Springer New York LLC, 233 Spring St, New York, NY 10013-1578; service-ny@springer.com; http://www.springer.com/. Illus., adv. Refereed. Microform: PQC. Online: EBSCO Publishing, EBSCO Host; Gale; IngentaConnect; OCLC Online Computer Library Center, Inc.; OhioLINK; ProQuest LLC (Ann Arbor); Springer LINK; SwetsWise Online Content. Reprint: PSC. *Indexed:* ABIn, IMFL, IPSA, PAIS, PMA, PsycInfo, SSA. *Bk. rev.:* 4-6, 2,500-4,000 words. *Aud.:* Ac, Sa.

The title of this publication sounds more like an HR manual than the scholarly journal that it is. Each issue has four or five articles written primarily by academic faculty about the legal, ethical, psychological, economic, and social impacts of worker-employer relationships. Article formats very widely from summaries of focus groups to meta-analyses, experimental research, topical reviews, and case studies, among others. Topical coverage is equally broad: recent article topics include working mothers whose children have chronic illnesses, organizational justice and salary inequities, self-directed work teams, and sexual harassment. Recommended for practitioners and graduate HR or organizational psychology collections. URL: http://springerlink.metapress.com/openurl.asp?genre=journal&issn=0892-7545

4306. *H R Magazine: the business of people.* Former titles: *Personnel Administrator;* (until 1954): *Personnel News.* [ISSN: 1047-3149] 1950. m. Non-members, USD 70. Ed(s): Leon Rubis, Patrick Mirza. Society for Human Resource Management, 1800 Duke St, Alexandria, VA 22314-3499; shrm@shrm.org; http://www.shrm.org. Illus., index, adv. Circ: 195000. Vol. ends: Dec. Online: EBSCO Publishing, EBSCO Host; Florida Center for Library Automation; Gale; OCLC Online Computer Library Center, Inc.; ProQuest LLC (Ann Arbor); H.W. Wilson. *Indexed:* ABIn, AgeL, BPI, BRI, CBRI, EAA, LRI, PAIS, PMA. *Bk. rev.:* 1, 600 words. *Aud.:* Ac, Sa.

The Society for Human Resource Management (SHRM) is the primary organization of HR professionals (and students), and its monthly magazine is the society's traditional voice, especially in libraries (although members may access a number of other electronic publications at the SHRM web site). Each issue has substantial feature articles and at least a dozen shorter columns and regular departments covering current HR practices and the larger organizational role of human resources. Most issues have a "Special Report" section on a single topic—recent sections include relocation, outsourcing, benefits, and best companies to work for. This core HR publication is very widely indexed and will be in demand by undergraduate students. URL: www.shrm.org/hrmagazine

4307. *HRfocus: the hands-on tool for human resources professionals.* Formerly (until 1991): *Personnel.* [ISSN: 1059-6038] 1919. m. USD 376.95 combined subscription in US & Canada print & online eds.; USD 394 combined subscription elsewhere print & online eds. Ed(s): Sue Sandler. Institute of Management & Administration, Inc., 3 Park Ave, New York, NY 10016-5902; subserve@ioma.com; http://www.ioma.com. Illus., index, adv. Circ: 8000 Controlled. Vol. ends: Dec. Microform: PQC. Online: EBSCO Publishing, EBSCO Host; Factiva, Inc.; Florida Center for Library Automation; Gale; OCLC Online Computer Library Center, Inc.; ProQuest LLC (Ann Arbor); H.W. Wilson. *Indexed:* ABIn, ATI, BPI, CWI, EAA, ExcerpMed, PMA, SSCI. *Aud.:* Sa.

Despite its unassuming appearance as a three-hole-punched, 16-page newsletter, *HRfocus* is one of the most widely recognized titles in the field. Articles are short, unsigned, and provide legal and regulatory updates, topical advice, and news briefs of recently issued surveys and reports. Every third issue has four-page, special-report insert on a single topic—outsourcing, change management, and workplace violence have been featured recently. This publication is focused entirely toward HR management professionals, but it should still be purchased by academic libraries. URL: www.ioma.com/issues/HRF

4308. *Human Resource Management.* Formerly (until 1971): *Management of Personnel Quarterly.* [ISSN: 0090-4848] 1961. q. USD 779. Ed(s): Mark Huselid. John Wiley & Sons, Inc., 111 River St, Hoboken, NJ 07030-5774; uscs-wis@wiley.com; http://www.wiley.com. Illus., index, adv. Refereed. Vol. ends: Winter. Microform: PQC. Online: Chadwyck-Healey Inc.; EBSCO Publishing, EBSCO Host; OhioLINK; ProQuest LLC (Ann Arbor); SwetsWise Online Content; Wiley InterScience. Reprint: PSC. *Indexed:* ABIn, AgeL, BPI, CINAHL, EAA, H&SSA, HRA, PAIS, PMA, PsycInfo, SSCI. *Bk. rev.:* 1, 1,500 words. *Aud.:* Ac, Sa.

This is a scholarly HR journal, with articles ranging from theory testing in academic settings to field/case studies and experiments to overviews of best practices. Topics cover an enormously wide range of all "people management" issues (including occasional special issues on a single topic, such as the future of HR or e-HR), and are written in a style applied enough to be of direct use to practitioners. A few substantial book reviews end some issues. Recommended for academic collections. URL: www.wiley.com/WileyCDA/WileyTitle/productCd-HRM.html

4309. *Human Resource Planning.* [ISSN: 0199-8986] 1978. q. Free to members; Non-members, USD 150. Ed(s): Richard Vosburgh, Lisa Boyd. Human Resource Planning Society, 317 Madison Ave, Ste 1509, New York, NY 10017; info@hrps.org; http://www.hrps.org. Illus., index, adv. Circ: 3500 Paid. Vol. ends: No. 4. Online: EBSCO Publishing, EBSCO Host; Florida Center for Library Automation; Gale; Northern Light Technology, Inc.; OCLC Online Computer Library Center, Inc.; ProQuest LLC (Ann Arbor); H.W. Wilson. *Indexed:* ABIn, BPI. *Bk. rev.:* 2, 1,000 words. *Aud.:* Ac, Sa.

The Human Resource Planning Society is a nonprofit organization of high-level practitioners who "function as business partners in the application of strategic human resource management practices to their organizations." Their publication therefore focuses on planning and management strategy more than the traditional administrative role of HR. The front half of this slim, well-laid-out journal contains short overviews of the "Current Practices" of HR executives and an editorial piece; the second half has three or four articles, mostly by consultants and researchers on decision-making topics such as executive coaching, turf battles, or evaluation metrics. Recommended for graduate-level academic collections. URL: www.hrps.org/publications_journal.html

Journal of Human Resources. See Labor and Industrial Relations section.

4310. *Public Personnel Management.* Formerly (until 1973): *Personnel Administration and Public Personnel Review;* Which was formed by the merger of (1940-1972): *Public Personnel Review;* (1938-1972): *Personnel Administration.* [ISSN: 0091-0260] 1972. q. USD 130 domestic (Members, USD 40; Non-members, USD 50). Ed(s): Elizabeth

Kirkland. International Personnel Management Association, 1617 Duke St, Alexandria, VA 22314; publications@ipma-hr.org; http://www.ipma-hr.org. Illus., index, adv. Refereed. Circ: 8000 Paid. Vol. ends: Winter. Microform: MIM; PQC. Online: EBSCO Publishing, EBSCO Host; Florida Center for Library Automation; Gale; Northern Light Technology, Inc.; OCLC Online Computer Library Center, Inc.; ProQuest K-12 Learning Solutions; ProQuest LLC (Ann Arbor); H.W. Wilson. Reprint: PSC. *Indexed:* ABCPolSci, ABIn, ATI, AgeL, BPI, BRI, CBRI, CINAHL, CJA, EAA, HRA, PAIS, PMA, PsycInfo, SSCI. *Aud.:* Sa.

This is a traditional-looking academic journal whose audience is primarily personnel managers in the public sector. The contents are mostly review articles and cases written by both practitioners and academics, with some empirical studies. There are nine or ten articles each quarter on a very wide range of HR topics. Articles do not tend to have a narrow public administration focus, so libraries beyond those with MPA programs may want to consider subscribing to this intelligent (and inexpensive) publication. URL: www.ipma-hr.org

4311. *Training: the magazine covering the human side of business.* Formerly: *Training in Business and Industry.* [ISSN: 0095-5892] 1964. m. USD 78 domestic; USD 88 Canada; USD 154 elsewhere. Ed(s): Martin Delahoussaye, Tammy Gordon. Nielsen Business Publications, 50 S Ninth St, Minneapolis, MN 55402; bmcomm@vnuinc.com; http://www.nielsenbusinessmedia.com. Illus., index, adv. Circ: 50000 Paid. Vol. ends: Dec. Microform: PQC. Online: EBSCO Publishing, EBSCO Host; Florida Center for Library Automation; Gale; OCLC Online Computer Library Center, Inc.; ProQuest K-12 Learning Solutions; ProQuest LLC (Ann Arbor); H.W. Wilson. *Indexed:* ABIn, AgeL, Agr, BPI, SFSA. *Bk. rev.:* 1-3, 750 words. *Aud.:* Sa.

It's skinny and very glossy, but *Training* is a must-have title for HR collections due to its wide circulation in corporate training departments and its inclusion in most basic business indexes. Its annual "Top 100" issue ranking "organizations that excel at human capital development" is also influential. There are short, well-written news reports and features about current trends and issues in employee training, discussions of best practices, company profiles and surveys, and short book reviews. The magazine's web site provides additional content for subscribers. URL: www.trainingmag.com

Management Education

4312. *Academy of Management Learning and Education.* [ISSN: 1537-260X] 2002. 4x/yr. USD 99 domestic individuals & academic libraries (Corporations, USD 135). Academy of Management, 235 Elm Rd, P O Box 3020, Briarcliff Manor, NY 10510-3020; academy@pace.edu; http://www.aomonline.org. Refereed. Online: EBSCO Publishing, EBSCO Host. *Indexed:* ABIn, PsycInfo, SSCI. *Bk. rev.:* 4-5. *Aud.:* Ac, Sa.

Another Academy of Management title, this publication focuses on learning and teaching in both higher education and in corporate training settings. It includes articles in an appealing range of styles—two or three scholarly articles (both theoretical and experimental) and essays and interviews on current topics such as "9-11 and management education" or "the darker side of power in the Office of the Dean." Rounding out each issue are "Exemplary Contributions," invited articles by distinguished scholars and practitioners, and "Resource Reviews," a section of four or five assigned reviews of books and other instructional media. Essential for academic libraries supporting business departments. URL: www.aom.pace.edu/amle

4313. *Journal of Management Education.* Former titles (until 1977): *Organizational Behavior Teaching Review; Exchange - The Organizational Behavior Teaching Journal; Teaching Organization Behavior; Teaching of Organization Behavior.* [ISSN: 1052-5629] 1975. bi-m. GBP 302. Ed(s): Jane Schmidt-Wilk, Susan J Herman. Sage Publications, Inc., 2455 Teller Rd, Thousand Oaks, CA 91320; info@sagepub.com; http://www.sagepub.com. Illus., adv. Refereed. Circ: 950 Paid. Vol. ends: Nov (No. 4). Reprint: PSC. *Indexed:* ABIn, FR, HRA, PMA. *Aud.:* Ac.

The *Journal of Management Education* is a forum for educators to share ideas and strategies for teaching management classes, offering specific exercises and assignments along with broader discussions about issues such as gender and cultural stereotyping in the classroom or the benefits and disadvantages of group work. Both theories and applied experiences with teaching tools such case methods, role playing, and writing to learn are included, with occasional thematic issues such as teaching about the natural environment and business. Academic libraries at institutions interested in developing faculty teaching should subscribe. URL: http://jme.sagepub.com

Operations Research and Management Science

This discipline focuses on using computational models to analyze and improve management decision-making. Academic researchers and practitioners all use a high level of statistical and programming skills to work in this area, so the literature of the field is more often than not mathematically dense.

4314. Decision Sciences. [ISSN: 0011-7315] 1970. q. GBP 251 print & online eds. Ed(s): Jeanne Elliott, Vicki Smith-Daniels. Blackwell Publishing, Inc., Commerce Place, 350 Main St, Malden, MA 02148; customerservices@blackwellpublishing.com; http://www.blackwellpublishing.com. Illus., adv. Refereed. Circ: 4000. Vol. ends: Fall. Microform: PQC. Online: Blackwell Synergy; EBSCO Publishing, EBSCO Host; Gale; IngentaConnect; Northern Light Technology, Inc.; OCLC Online Computer Library Center, Inc.; OhioLINK; ProQuest K-12 Learning Solutions; ProQuest LLC (Ann Arbor); SwetsWise Online Content. Reprint: PSC. *Indexed:* ABIn, ATI, BPI, ExcerpMed, PsycInfo, SSCI. *Aud.:* Ac, Sa.

Despite its broad title, this is not a publication on the general science of how people make decisions, but an applied research journal looking at decision points and processes in business operations and supply chains. Using theoretical, empirical, and analytical research methods, academic researchers address specific decision problems in organizations. There are six to eight articles each quarter, with occasional technical notes also included. Recommended for academic collections. URL: www.decisionsciences.org/dsj

4315. European Journal of Operational Research. [ISSN: 0377-2217] 1977. 24x/yr. EUR 4949. Ed(s): R. Slowinski, Jean-Charles Billaut. Elsevier BV, North-Holland, Sara Burgerhartstraat 25, Amsterdam, 1055 KV, Netherlands; nlinfo-f@elsevier.nl; http://www.elsevier.nl. Illus. Refereed. Microform: PQC. Online: EBSCO Publishing, EBSCO Host; Gale; IngentaConnect; OhioLINK; ScienceDirect; SwetsWise Online Content. *Indexed:* ABIn, C&ISA, CCMJ, CJA, CompLI, EngInd, ExcerpMed, MSN, MathR, RiskAb, SCI, SSCI. *Bk. rev.:* 6, 100 words. *Aud.:* Ac.

Submissions are primarily invited by the Association of European Operational Research Societies. Emphasis is placed on theoretical developments and the role computers play in operations research and the practice of decision making. Theory and methodology papers, society communications, software reviews, and book reviews fill out each issue. Targeted to scientists and researchers at a postgraduate level, this title will find a limited audience due to its high cost. Strictly of interest to larger academic institutions.

4316. I N F O R Journal: information systems and operational research/ systemes d'information et recherche operationnelle. Formerly (until 1970): *Canadian Operational Research Society Journal.* [ISSN: 0315-5986] 1963. q. CND 95 domestic; USD 95 United States; USD 115 elsewhere. Ed(s): Bernard Gendron. University of Toronto Press, Journals Division, 5201 Dufferin St, Toronto, ON M3H 5T8, Canada; journals@ utpress.utoronto.ca; http://www.utpjournals.com. Illus., index, adv. Sample. Refereed. Circ: 400. Online: EBSCO Publishing, EBSCO Host; Micromedia ProQuest; OCLC Online Computer Library Center, Inc.; ProQuest LLC (Ann Arbor). *Indexed:* ABIn, CBCARef, CCMJ, CompR, EngInd, MSN, MathR, SCI. *Aud.:* Ac, Sa.

Published by the Canadian Operational Research Society whose aim is to integrate the concepts of both operations research (OR) and information systems (IS) to allow for communication between theoreticians and practitioners. Highly technical in nature, each issue includes a few contributed papers by international scholars and five or six invited articles on practical applications, including case studies, that combine elements of OR and IS. More theoretical papers are also welcome when authors clearly demonstrate the relevance of the

results in terms of applications. Most articles are written in English, occasionally in French; abstracts appear in both languages. Recommended for academic collections supporting advanced degree programs.

4317. Interfaces (Linthicum). Formerly: *Institute of Management Sciences Bulletin.* [ISSN: 0092-2102] 1971. bi-m. USD 300 print & online eds. (Individuals, USD 189 print & online eds.). Ed(s): Jeffrey D Cam. I N F O R M S, 7240 Parkway Dr, Ste 310, Hanover, MD 21076-1344; informs@informs.org; http://www.informs.org. Illus., index, adv. Sample. Refereed. Circ: 4000 Paid and controlled. Microform: PQC. Online: EBSCO Publishing, EBSCO Host; Factiva, Inc.; Gale; HighWire Press; OCLC Online Computer Library Center, Inc.; ProQuest LLC (Ann Arbor); SwetsWise Online Content. *Indexed:* ABIn, AS&TI, AgeL, BPI, CompR, ErgAb, ExcerpMed, IBR, IBSS, IBZ, LT&LA, PMA, SCI, SSCI. *Bk. rev.:* 2-4, signed, essay length. *Aud.:* Ac, Sa.

Interfaces is case based, with six to eight articles written by managers, consultants, and academics reporting on the results of the "practice and implementation of operations research and management science in commerce, industry, government, or education." Along with these very readable and straightforward application studies, there are usually "Practice Abstracts" (much shorter reports of these same types of projects) and several substantial book reviews (as well as a list of received books that were not reviewed). The first issue of each volume is a special issue that includes the finalists and winners of the Franz Edelman Award for Achievement in Operations Research and the Management Sciences. Highly recommended for all academic business collections. URL: http://interfaces.pubs.informs.org

4318. International Journal of Operations and Production Management. [ISSN: 0144-3577] 1980. m. EUR 9809 combined subscription in Europe print & online eds.; USD 10579 combined subscription in North America print & online eds.; AUD 12979 combined subscription in Australasia print & online eds. Ed(s): Dr. Margaret Taylor, Dr. Andrew Taylor. Emerald Group Publishing Limited, Howard House, Wagon Ln, Bingley, BD16 1WA, United Kingdom; information@emeraldinsight.com; http://www.emeraldinsight.com. Illus., index. Refereed. Online: Pub.; EBSCO Publishing, EBSCO Host; Florida Center for Library Automation; Gale; IngentaConnect; OCLC Online Computer Library Center, Inc.; OhioLINK; ProQuest LLC (Ann Arbor); SwetsWise Online Content. Reprint: PSC. *Indexed:* ABIn, C&ISA, CerAb, ErgAb, IAA, SSCI. *Aud.:* Ac, Sa.

Associated with the European Operations Management Association, this scholarly title is aimed at academic scholars, managers, and consultants. Lengthy articles focus on management versus technical content, blending theory and application in the development and implemention of operation systems. Topics covered include operational strategy, industrial engineering, performance measurement, and computer applications in both service and manufacturing sectors. Prohibitively expensive for most libraries, this title is appropriate for larger research institutions.

4319. Journal of Operations Management. [ISSN: 0272-6963] 1980. 6x/yr. EUR 536. Ed(s): R. B. Handfield. Elsevier BV, Radarweg 29, Amsterdam, 1043 NX, Netherlands; nlinfo-f@elsevier.nl; http://www.elsevier.nl. Illus., index, adv. Sample. Refereed. Circ: 1000. Vol. ends: Nov. Microform: PQC. Online: EBSCO Publishing, EBSCO Host; Gale; IngentaConnect; OhioLINK; ScienceDirect; SwetsWise Online Content. *Indexed:* ABIn, C&ISA, EngInd, RiskAb, SCI, SSCI. *Aud.:* Ac, Sa.

Every component in the management of business operations is open for examination in this journal—technology management, project management, purchasing systems, quality management, and many, many more. The one unifying theme for these topics is that they are all examined using the rigorous analytical methods of operations management research. However, the concepts, theories, and discussions of each article topic are presented in an understandable way to students and practitioners who may not have complete mastery of the computations. Each journal issue typically contains five or six long research articles (15–20 pages). Recommended for academic libraries. URL: www.elsevier.com

4320. *Management.* [ISSN: 1286-4692] 1998. irreg. Free. Ed(s): Martin Evans, Bernard Forgues. D M S P Research Center, Paris-Dauphine University, Paris, 75775 Cedex 16, France; management@dauphine.fr; http://www.dmsp.dauphine.fr/MANAGEMENT/ . Refereed. *Bk. rev.:* Number and length vary. *Aud.:* Ac, Sa.

This e-journal of peer-reviewed research articles on "management research, strategy, and organizational theory" encourages diversity—in the broad range of research methods and topics used by its authors, and in the truly international scope of its coverage. Its advisory and editorial boards consist of research faculty worldwide, and articles are published in the authors' own languages (most are in English). The site also includes book reviews and an open forum for debate. Updating is irregular—articles are published as soon as they are accepted—but the journal occasionally puts together a special issue on a single topic. Recommended for academic libraries. URL: www.dmsp.dauphine.fr/management

4321. *Management Science.* Incorporates: *Management Technology: Monograph of the Institute of Management Science.* [ISSN: 0025-1909] 1954. m. USD 593 print or online eds. (Individuals, USD 213 print & online eds.). Ed(s): Elizabeth Martin, Wallace J Hopp. I N F O R M S, 7240 Parkway Dr, Ste 310, Hanover, MD 21076-1344; informs@informs.org; http://www.informs.org. Illus., index, adv. Refereed. Circ: 5000 Paid. Vol. ends: Dec. Online: EBSCO Publishing, EBSCO Host; Gale; HighWire Press; JSTOR (Web-based Journal Archive); OCLC Online Computer Library Center, Inc.; ProQuest LLC (Ann Arbor); SwetsWise Online Content. *Indexed:* ABIn, ATI, AgeL, ArtHuCI, BPI, C&ISA, CJA, CompR, EAA, EngInd, HRIS, IAA, IBSS, MathR, PsycInfo, SCI, SSCI. *Aud.:* Ac, Sa.

This journal pulls theory-based mathematical models from a diverse range of fields within and beyond the traditional scope of business scholarship—psychology, engineering, economics, accounting, political science—to analyze organizational and operational problems of interest to managers. The focus of the articles in each issue is "to reveal novel concepts of broad interest to the management research community." All business activities are (or could be) addressed by *Management Science* articles; a sample of topics includes data shuffling, risk management with benchmarking, improving preference assessment, and the personal computer and entrepreneurship. This is an important journal for academic collections. URL: http://mansci.pubs.informs.org

4322. *Managerial and Decision Economics: the international journal of research and progress in management economics.* [ISSN: 0143-6570] 1980. 8x/yr. USD 1720 print or online ed. Ed(s): Paul Rubin. John Wiley & Sons Ltd., The Atrium, Southern Gate, Chichester, PO19 8SQ, United Kingdom; customer@wiley.co.uk; http://www.wiley.co.uk. Illus., adv. Refereed. Circ: 700. Microform: PQC. Online: EBSCO Publishing, EBSCO Host; JSTOR (Web-based Journal Archive); OhioLINK; ProQuest LLC (Ann Arbor); SwetsWise Online Content; Wiley InterScience. Reprint: PSC. *Indexed:* ABIn, C&ISA, CJA, CerAb, IAA, IBSS, JEL, PAIS, PsycInfo, RiskAb. *Bk. rev.:* 2-3 about 2,000 words. *Aud.:* Ac, Sa.

This is listed as a management title rather than an economics title because of its applied focus on research "useful for managerial decision-making and management strategy." Economic theory is used to examine an incredibly wide range of organizational topics. For instance, in one issue alone, article topics included industry clustering of initial public offerings, the international drivers of domestic airline mergers in 20 nations, and optimal response to a next-generation new product introduction. Highly recommended for management and economic collections. URL: www.interscience.wiley.com/jpages/0143-6570

4323. *Omega.* [ISSN: 0305-0483] 1973. 6x/yr. EUR 1146. Ed(s): B Lev. Pergamon, The Boulevard, Langford Ln, East Park, Kidlington, OX5 1GB, United Kingdom. Illus., index, adv. Refereed. Circ: 1400. Vol. ends: Dec (No. 29). Microform: PQC. Online: EBSCO Publishing, EBSCO Host; Florida Center for Library Automation; Gale; IngentaConnect; OhioLINK; ScienceDirect; SwetsWise Online Content. *Indexed:* ABIn, ApMecR, CJA, ExcerpMed, IMFL, SCI, SSCI. *Aud.:* Ac, Sa.

Omega offers research articles of a highly mathematical nature that review and assess both cutting-edge and traditional management science models and theories, or analyze applications of management techniques in specific settings (manufacturing, service, and educational organizations are all included in its coverage). Longer research articles are sometimes supplemented by shorter critical assessments of management techniques, memoranda, and feedback. This is a very scholarly journal that is recommended to support graduate management education. URL: www.elsevier.com

4324. *Operational Research Society. Journal.* Former titles (until vol.29, 1978): *Operational Research Quarterly;* (until 1970): *O R;* (until 1953): *Operational Research Quarterly.* [ISSN: 0160-5682] 1950. m. USD 1693 print & online eds. Ed(s): Terry Williams, John Wilson. Palgrave Macmillan Ltd., Houndmills, Basingstoke, RG21 6XS, United Kingdom; http://www.palgrave.com. Illus., index, adv. Vol. ends: Dec. Online: EBSCO Publishing, EBSCO Host; Gale; IngentaConnect; JSTOR (Web-based Journal Archive); OCLC Online Computer Library Center, Inc.; ProQuest LLC (Ann Arbor); SwetsWise Online Content. Reprint: PSC. *Indexed:* ABIn, AgeL, ApMecR, BPI, C&ISA, CJA, CompLI, EngInd, ExcerpMed, HRIS, IBR, IBZ, RRTA, RiskAb, SCI, SSCI, WAE&RSA. *Bk. rev.:* 4-6, 300-500 words. *Aud.:* Ac, Sa.

Publishes scholarly articles in the field of operations research. Each issue contains case-oriented papers, theoretical papers (often based on mathematical models), technical notes, and book reviews. Papers cover a wide range of topics including community operations research, decision support systems, and scheduling. Recommended for academic libraries. URL: www.palgrave-journals.com/jors

4325. *Production and Operations Management.* [ISSN: 1059-1478] 1992. q. USD 200 domestic; USD 210 foreign. Ed(s): Kalyan Singhal. Production and Operations Management Society, College of Engineering, Florida International University, Miami, FL 33174; poms@fiu.edu; http://www.poms.org. Illus., adv. Refereed. Circ: 1200 Paid. Vol. ends: Winter. *Indexed:* ABIn, SCI. *Aud.:* Ac, Sa.

This is the journal of the Production and Operations Management Society. The operations management research presented in the journal has a decided focus on manufacturing and services industries. Academics and managers who are interested in product and process design, operations, and supply chains are the intended audience for this scholarly journal. There is a healthy mix of applied and theoretical research and reviews of current topics in the field. Recommended for academic collections, particularly those that support graduate business and industrial engineering studies. URL: www.poms.org/Journal.html

Organizational Behavior and Studies

The journals listed here provide more primary scholarly research than the typical titles in the Human Resources section. These publications involve theory development and testing, program and test development and evaluation, and systematic problem solving in the personnel and organizational arena of business and industry.

4326. *Global Business and Organizational Excellence: a review of research & best practices.* Former titles (until Nov/Dec.2006): *Journal of Organizational Excellence;* (until 2000): *National Productivity Review;* Incorporates (19??-2001): *Competitive Intelligence Review;* Which was formerly (until 1990): *Competitive Intelligencer.* [ISSN: 1932-2054] 1981. bi-m. USD 639. Ed(s): Jane G Bensahel, Dr. Yahia H Zoubir. John Wiley & Sons, Inc., 111 River St, Hoboken, NJ 07030-5774; uscs-wis@wiley.com; http://www.wiley.com. Illus., adv. Circ: 500 Paid and controlled. Vol. ends: Fall. Microform: PQC. Online: EBSCO Publishing, EBSCO Host; Gale; Northern Light Technology, Inc.; OCLC Online Computer Library Center, Inc.; OhioLINK; ProQuest LLC (Ann Arbor); SwetsWise Online Content; Wiley InterScience. *Indexed:* ABIn, BPI, PAIS, PMA. *Bk. rev.:* 8-10, 300-500 words. *Aud.:* Ac, Sa.

The title should tip you off that this journal is aimed at executives and consultants looking for the latest tools and strategies to most effectively manage their "human capital" for organizational success. The publication very effectively carries out its applied mission; its descriptive/prescriptive articles provide overviews and corporate case studies about topics such as corporate concierges, using nonprofit consulting as a corporate marketing tool, and changes in sales force compensation to reflect economic changes. There are also book reviews and short surveys of current articles written in the field. Recommended for academic business collections, especially those that serve MBA programs. URL: www.interscience.wiley.com/jpages/1531-1864

4327. Organization Science. [ISSN: 1047-7039] 1990. q. Non-members, USD 146. Ed(s): Claudia Bird Schoonhoven. I N F O R M S, 7240 Parkway Dr, Ste 310, Hanover, MD 21076-1344; informs@informs.org; http://www.informs.org. Illus., adv. Refereed. Circ: 1900. Vol. ends: Nov/Dec. Online: EBSCO Publishing, EBSCO Host; Gale; HighWire Press; JSTOR (Web-based Journal Archive); ProQuest LLC (Ann Arbor); SwetsWise Online Content. *Indexed:* ABIn, IBSS, PsycInfo, SSCI. *Aud.:* Ac.

This scholarly journal falls among those using empirical studies (and the occasional case history) to look at organizational functions. Authors from throughout the social sciences and management provide five to seven long articles in each issue, primarily examining work systems, with a strong focus on learning and information and communication processes. Recent article topics range from "the origin and transformation of Branson, Missouri's musical theaters" to "time, culture, and behavioral sequences in negotiation." Highly recommended for academic collections—its interdisciplinary nature does not limit it to business libraries. URL: http://web.gsm.uci.edu/orgsci

4328. Organizational Dynamics. [ISSN: 0090-2616] 1972. 4x/yr. EUR 187. Ed(s): Fred Luthans. Pergamon, The Boulevard, Langford Ln, East Park, Kidlington, OX5 1GB, United Kingdom. Illus., index. Circ: 4000. Vol. ends: Spring. Microform: PQC. Online: EBSCO Publishing, EBSCO Host; Florida Center for Library Automation; Gale; IngentaConnect; Northern Light Technology, Inc.; OCLC Online Computer Library Center, Inc.; OhioLINK; ScienceDirect; SwetsWise Online Content; H.W. Wilson. *Indexed:* ABIn, AgeL, BPI, PMA, PsycInfo, SSCI. *Bk. rev.:* 2-6, 700-900 words. *Aud.:* Ac, Sa.

The journal is relatively thin compared to many others in the category, but a typical issue has seven substantial scholarly articles. Recent topics include a positive psychology approach to the value of older workers, displaying competence during crisis, and promoting organizational justice in the workplace. There is empirical research mixed with case studies, theoretical overviews, and interviews. Professional managers are the primary audience, and the articles provided are appropriately balanced among inquiry, overviews, and applications. Highly recommended for undergraduate and graduate collections. URL: www.elsevier.com/locate/issn/00902616

4329. Personnel Psychology: a journal of applied research. [ISSN: 0031-5826] 1948. q. GBP 224 print & online eds. Ed(s): Ann Marie Ryan. Blackwell Publishing, Inc., Commerce Place, 350 Main St, Malden, MA 02148; http://www.blackwellpublishing.com. Illus., index, adv. Sample. Refereed. Circ: 2800. Vol. ends: Winter. Microform: PQC. Online: Blackwell Synergy; EBSCO Publishing, EBSCO Host; Florida Center for Library Automation; Gale; IngentaConnect; Northern Light Technology, Inc.; OCLC Online Computer Library Center, Inc.; ProQuest LLC (Ann Arbor); SwetsWise Online Content. Reprint: PSC. *Indexed:* ABIn, AgeL, BPI, BRI, CBRI, CommAb, EAA, HRA, PMA, PsycInfo, RiskAb, SSCI. *Bk. rev.:* 15-20, 1,000-1,500 words. *Aud.:* Ac, Sa.

Personnel Psychology is a core scholarly journal in this field; every academic library whose schools offer management and applied psychology classes should subscribe. It is empirical, with each issue offering six or seven studies examining variables in workplace selection, performance, and evaluation. Recent topics include performance effects of 360-degree feedback systems, predictors of objective and subjective career success, and the impact of poor performers on team success. After the research articles, there is a "Scientist-Practitioner Forum" piece focused on addressing a problem or issue facing personnel practitioners (such as putting personnel surveys on the web or use of a specific job-analysis model). Each issue also has a book review section in the back where 15–20 books receive substantial reviews, followed by a list of

unreviewed material received by their editorial office. The journal is one of the best library collection development tools in this discipline. URL: www.blackwellpublishing.com/journals/PEPS

Strategic Analysis

These journals cover a specific managerial process involving both industry research and the study of changes in organizational strategies for competitive advantage.

4330. Business Strategy and the Environment. Incorporates: *Greening of Industry Newsletter.* [ISSN: 0964-4733] 1992. 8x/yr. USD 1177 print or online ed. Ed(s): Dr. Richard Welford. John Wiley & Sons Ltd., The Atrium, Southern Gate, Chichester, PO19 8SQ, United Kingdom; customer@wiley.co.uk; http://www.wiley.co.uk. Illus., adv. Refereed. Vol. ends: Dec. Reprint: PSC. *Indexed:* ABIn, C&ISA, CerAb, EnvAb, EnvInd, IAA, IBSS, PollutAb, PsycInfo. *Bk. rev.:* Signed, number and length vary. *Aud.:* Ac, Sa.

This scholarly journal is concerned with both the business environment and the earth's environment. The focus of the technical research articles and shorter research reports called "BSE Briefings" is to provide an "understanding of business responses to improving environmental performance." There are occasional special issues (most about aspects of sustainability), and issues often have book reviews and lists of books and publications received. Recommended for academic business and environmental collections. URL: www.interscience.wiley.com/jpages/0964-4733

4331. Business Strategy Review. [ISSN: 0955-6419] 1990. q. GBP 202 print & online eds. Ed(s): Stuart Crainer. Blackwell Publishing Ltd., 9600 Garsington Rd, Oxford, OX4 2ZG, United Kingdom; customerservices@blackwellpublishing.com; http://www.blackwellpublishing.com. Circ: 1200. Online: Blackwell Synergy; EBSCO Publishing, EBSCO Host; Florida Center for Library Automation; Gale; IngentaConnect; OCLC Online Computer Library Center, Inc.; OhioLINK; SwetsWise Online Content. Reprint: PSC. *Indexed:* ABIn, ApEcolAb. *Bk. rev.:* Several books on a theme reviewed together; signed. *Aud.:* Ac, Sa.

Business Strategy Review is sponsored by the London Business School, and offers a global view on current business decision-making. Each issue combines articles of original research, global case studies, and corporate profiles; all the pieces are written in a very accessible style. Issues also include company histories, interviews, and, often, a set of book reviews around a single theme. Highly recommended. URL: www.blackwellpublishing.com/journal.asp?ref=0955-6419

4332. Journal of Business Strategy. Incorporates (1975-1995): *Small Business Reports;* Incorporates (1989-1994): *Journal of European Business;* Which incorporated (1990-1991): *Journal of Pricing Management.* [ISSN: 0275-6668] 1980. bi-m. EUR 439 combined subscription in Europe print & online eds.; USD 499 combined subscription in North America print & online eds.; AUD 869 combined subscription in Australasia print & online eds. Ed(s): Nanci Healy. Emerald Group Publishing Limited, Howard House, Wagon Ln, Bingley, BD16 1WA, United Kingdom; information@emeraldinsight.com; http://www.emeraldinsight.com. Illus. Vol. ends: Dec. Microform: PQC. Online: Pub.; EBSCO Publishing, EBSCO Host; Factiva, Inc.; Florida Center for Library Automation; Gale; IngentaConnect; Northern Light Technology, Inc.; OCLC Online Computer Library Center, Inc.; ProQuest LLC (Ann Arbor); SwetsWise Online Content. Reprint: PSC. *Indexed:* ABIn, ABS&EES, Agr, BPI, CWI, LRI, LogistBibl, PAIS, SUSA. *Bk. rev.:* 5-7 mid-length. *Aud.:* Ac, Sa.

This journal provides five or six practical articles related to business theory and real life situations. The content is meant to help readers develop successful business strategies. Recent topics include corporate entrepreneurship, strategic account management, and practical strategy development. The journal is a source for undergraduate papers and presentations. Recommended for academic libraries. URL: www.emeraldinsight.com/journals

4333. *Long Range Planning.* [ISSN: 0024-6301] 1968. 6x/yr. EUR 1497. Ed(s): C. Baden-Fuller. Pergamon, The Boulevard, Langford Ln, East Park, Kidlington, OX5 1GB, United Kingdom. Illus., index, adv. Refereed. Circ: 4700. Vol. ends: Dec. Microform: MIM; PQC. Online: EBSCO Publishing, EBSCO Host; Gale; IngentaConnect; OhioLINK; ScienceDirect; SwetsWise Online Content. *Indexed:* ABIn, AgeL, BPI, EngInd, EnvAb, ExcerpMed, FutSurv, PAIS, PsycInfo, SSCI, SUSA. *Bk. rev.:* 4-7, 400-2,000 words. *Aud.:* Ac, Sa.

The focus here is on management goal setting, planning, and strategy, with topics such as strategic renewal, alliance management, and boundaries and innovation. Executive summaries are provided for the scholarly research articles in each issue, and there are usually three or four book reviews followed by several pages of very short abstracts of books on business strategy. This title is recommended for purchase only if demand from its inclusion in most business/management indexes calls for a subscription in your library. URL: www.elsevier.com/inca/publications/store/3/5/8/index.htt

4334. *Strategic Change.* Formerly (until 1996): *Journal of Strategic Change.* [ISSN: 1086-1718] 1992. 8x/yr. USD 785 print or online ed. Ed(s): Graham Beaver. John Wiley & Sons Ltd., The Atrium, Southern Gate, Chichester, PO19 8SQ, United Kingdom; customer@wiley.co.uk; http://www.wiley.co.uk. Illus., adv. Refereed. Circ: 450. Vol. ends: Nov/Dec. Microform: PQC. Online: EBSCO Publishing, EBSCO Host; OhioLINK; ProQuest LLC (Ann Arbor); SwetsWise Online Content; Wiley InterScience. Reprint: PSC. *Indexed:* ABIn, PsycInfo. *Bk. rev.:* 3, 300-400 words. *Aud.:* Ac, Sa.

A thin journal with four or five articles in each of its eight yearly issues, *Strategic Change* offers a scholarly, yet applied, view of the management of change in corporations and their operating environment. The article coverage is international and very well selected, with topical research articles (survivor syndrome, organization culture, corporate social responsibility) and case studies. This is an important topic handled very well, and the journal is recommended for academic business collections. URL: www.interscience.wiley.com/jpages/1086-1718

4335. *Strategic Management Journal.* [ISSN: 0143-2095] 1979. 13x/yr. USD 1917 print or online ed. Ed(s): Dan Schendel. John Wiley & Sons Ltd., The Atrium, Southern Gate, Chichester, PO19 8SQ, United Kingdom; customer@wiley.co.uk; http://www.wiley.co.uk. Illus., index, adv. Refereed. Circ: 4000. Vol. ends: Dec. Microform: PQC. Online: EBSCO Publishing, EBSCO Host; JSTOR (Web-based Journal Archive); OCLC Online Computer Library Center, Inc.; OhioLINK; ProQuest LLC (Ann Arbor); SwetsWise Online Content; Wiley InterScience. Reprint: PSC. *Indexed:* ABIn, ArtHuCI, BAS, BPI, CJA, EngInd, IBSS, PsycInfo, RiskAb, SSCI. *Aud.:* Ac, Sa.

Skimming the articles of several issues of this journal is like following an ongoing high-level discussion among academics and practitioners in strategic management. This journal covers all areas of the theory and practice of strategic management. There are presentations of scholarly research and shorter "research notes" hitting the highlights of other studies, interspersed with some commentary and editorial opinion. The topics, although treated in a very scholarly manner, are usually practical in nature ("is speed of integration really a success factor of mergers and acquisitions?" or "the effects of top management backgrounds on investor decisions"). Recommended for academic collections supporting graduate business programs. URL: www.interscience.wiley.com/jpages/0143-2095

4336. *Strategy + Business.* [ISSN: 1083-706X] 1995. q. USD 38 domestic; USD 48 foreign. Ed(s): Art Kleiner. Booz, Allen & Hamilton, Inc., 101 Park Ave, New York, NY 10178. Adv. Circ: 52343 Paid. *Indexed:* C&ISA, CerAb, IAA, LogistBibl. *Aud.:* Ac, Sa.

This magazine provides information about trends and innovations in strategic management. The contents include reports of academic research studies, interviews with top managers, case studies and personal narratives, news articles, and many essays/reviews about business books. The publisher is Booz Allen Hamilton, a major management consulting firm, but contributors come from throughout the business and scholarly world. Although aimed at executives, the topic coverage would be of interest to business students or

investors. Free registration at the magazine's web site provides access to the text of most of the magazine's pages published since 1995; print subscriptions are also available. URL: www.strategy-business.com/magazine

4337. *Strategy & Leadership.* Incorporates (1996-2001): *The Antidote;* Formerly (until 1996): *Planning Review;* Which superseded (in 1985): *Managerial Planning;* Which was formerly: *Budgeting.* [ISSN: 1087-8572] 1972. bi-m. EUR 1399 combined subscription in Europe print & online eds.; USD 869 combined subscription in North America print & online eds.; AUD 2509 combined subscription in Australasia print & online eds. Ed(s): Mr. Robert Randall. Emerald Group Publishing Limited, Howard House, Wagon Ln, Bingley, BD16 1WA, United Kingdom; information@emeraldinsight.com; http://www.emeraldinsight.com. Illus., adv. Refereed. Vol. ends: Nov/Dec. Reprint: PSC. *Indexed:* ABIn, ATI, BPI, PAIS. *Bk. rev.:* Number and length vary. *Aud.:* Ac, Sa.

This very attractive, modern, streamlined journal publishes several of its six yearly issues on a single theme—"creating value with customers," "innovation," or "special report on nonprofit leadership." The four to six "special report articles" on each theme discuss specific areas of strategy development and application or describe case studies, supplemented by CEO advisories and book reviews. At the end of each issue are "Quick Takes," listing the "key points and action steps" from each of the feature articles. This readable title is recommended for academic libraries. URL: www.emeraldinsight.com/journals

■ MARINE SCIENCE AND TECHNOLOGY

Janet G. Webster, Associate Professor/Librarian, Hatfield Marine Science Center, Oregon State University, Newport, OR 97365

Barbara A. Butler, Associate Professor/Librarian, Oregon Institute of Marine Biology, University of Oregon, Charleston, OR 97420

Introduction

The world's oceans and estuaries fascinate many—from oceanographers studying the deep seas to resource managers regulating fishing seasons to children finding their first seashell on the beach. The complexity of the marine environment is reflected in the specialized and interdisciplinary journals covering marine science. Journals can focus on particular flora or fauna, a certain subdiscipline, or on one ocean basin. Specialized scientific publications address particular aspects of the system including its physical dynamics and its chemistry, geology, and biology. There are journals devoted to the technology used to explore the oceans and estuaries, advising engineers how to manage and harness the dynamic environment. Policy and management journals address the complexity of human interaction with the sea and aid planners who need to translate research into practice. Maritime titles cover transportation and law of the sea.

The breadth of the field challenges a librarian shaping a collection. A comprehensive research collection is difficult to maintain given the vastness of the subject and the number of related titles. The classic subfields of oceanography—physical, biological, chemical, and geological—each have specific journals in addition to those covering all aspects. Studying the marine realm on a global scale often involves remote-sensing technology, a topic not covered in this section. Also, other special technical and engineering journals are important to marine science research, and should be part of a strong academic collection. Marine policy is crafted on scientific foundations; so collections involved with environmental planning and management need the scientific and the social science titles as well.

For those collecting for a nonacademic audience, few marine titles are aimed at the general public, yet the subject is well covered in *National Geographic, Scientific American,* and other general science and environment periodicals in addition to the ones mentioned below. Librarians selecting journals in the marine sciences should know the interests and needs of their audience and make choices accordingly.

Identifying marine science information is also challenging because it is so multidisciplinary. Not one index covers the field comprehensively. *Web of*

Science provides adequate general access. For the subfields of oceanography, the librarian will need access to resources such as *SciFinder Scholar* (*Chemical Abstracts*) or *GeoRef* depending on the research question. *Biosis* and *Zoological Record* cover the biological aspects well. *Aquatic Science and Fisheries Abstracts* (*ASFA*) is an essential resource for the applied science of the marine and estuarine environments. Marine policy and management information remains more difficult to access and requires multiple indexes including *ASFA* and relevant social sciences databases. For general public and basic academic collections, an index such as EBSCO's *Academic Search Premier* is adequate for both the science and management elements of the field.

Basic Periodicals

Hs, Ga: *California Wild, Cousteau Kids, Currents, Explorations, Oceanus*; Ac: *Advances in Marine Biology, Deep-Sea Research, Parts 1 and 2, Journal of Experimental Marine Biology and Ecology, Journal of Marine Research, Journal of Physical Oceanography, Limnology and Oceanography, Marine Biology, Marine Ecology Progress Series, Marine Geology, Marine Mammal Science, Oceanography, Oceanography and Marine Biology, Progress in Oceanography*.

Basic Abstracts and Indexes

Aquatic Sciences and Fisheries Abstracts, BIOSIS, Web of Science, National Sea Grant Library Database (http://nsgl.gso.uri.edu).

4338. *Advances in Marine Biology.* [ISSN: 0065-2881] 1963. irreg. Ed(s): Craig Young, Alan Southward. Academic Press, 525 B St, Ste 1900, San Diego, CA 92101-4495; apsubs@acad.com; http://www.elsevier.com/. Index. Refereed. *Indexed:* ApEcolAb, B&AI, ChemAb, OceAb, SCI, ZooRec. *Aud.:* Ac.

Provides in-depth, timely reviews on a wide range of topics in marine biology, fisheries science, ecology, zoology, and oceanography. One to three volumes are published annually with some volumes containing several review articles while others focus on a theme such as aquatic geomicrobiology or biogeography of the oceans. Essential to both academic and research libraries

American Fisheries Society. Transactions. See Fish, Fisheries, and Aquaculture section.

4339. *Applied Ocean Research.* [ISSN: 0141-1187] 1979. 6x/yr. EUR 978. Ed(s): S K Chakrabarti, M. Ohkusu. Pergamon, The Boulevard, Langford Ln, East Park, Kidlington, OX5 1GB, United Kingdom; http://www.elsevier.nl. Adv. Refereed. Microform: PQC. Online: EBSCO Publishing, EBSCO Host; Gale; IngentaConnect; OhioLINK; ScienceDirect; SwetsWise Online Content. *Indexed:* ApMecR, EngInd, M&GPA, OceAb, PetrolAb, SCI, SWRA. *Aud.:* Ac, Sa.

Ocean engineering is a very specialized discipline with a limited readership. This title provides solid research articles on topics ranging from mooring systems to wave dynamics. Only useful for specialized research collections with engineering interests in the marine environment.

4340. *Aquatic Botany.* [ISSN: 0304-3770] 1975. 8x/yr. EUR 1369. Ed(s): Jan Vermaat, Dr. G Bowes. Elsevier BV, Radarweg 29, Amsterdam, 1043 NX, Netherlands; nlinfo-f@elsevier.nl; http://www.elsevier.nl. Illus., index, adv. Refereed. Vol. ends: No. 4. Microform: PQC. Online: EBSCO Publishing, EBSCO Host; Gale; IngentaConnect; OhioLINK; ScienceDirect; SwetsWise Online Content. *Indexed:* ApEcolAb, BiolAb, CABA, ChemAb, EnvAb, EnvInd, ExcerpMed, ForAb, HortAb, IndVet, OceAb, RRTA, S&F, SCI, SWRA, VB. *Bk. rev.:* 1-2, 1,000-3,000 words, signed. *Aud.:* Ac, Sa.

This title satisfies the need for a research outlet on aquatic plant communities, not just marine. Coverage is fairly evenly split between freshwater and saltwater/brackish with a strong interest in various types of wetlands. Articles examine community dynamics as well as basic structure and function. While highly specialized, recommended for academic collections supporting botany and environmental studies.

4341. *Aquatic Conservation: marine and freshwater ecosystems.* [ISSN: 1052-7613] 1991. 7x/yr. USD 1156 print or online ed. Ed(s): Philip Boon. John Wiley & Sons Ltd., The Atrium, Southern Gate, Chichester, PO19 8SQ, United Kingdom; customer@wiley.co.uk; http://www.wiley.co.uk. Illus., adv. Refereed. Circ: 500. Vol. ends: No. 4. Microform: PQC. Online: EBSCO Publishing, EBSCO Host; OhioLINK; SwetsWise Online Content; Wiley InterScience. Reprint: PSC. *Indexed:* ApEcolAb, BiolAb, CABA, EnvInd, FPA, ForAb, HortAb, IndVet, OceAb, PollutAb, RRTA, S&F, SCI, SWRA, VB, WAE&RSA, WRCInf, ZooRec. *Bk. rev.:* 3, 500-1,000 words. *Aud.:* Ac, Sa.

Conservation of aquatic resources in freshwater, brackish and saltwater environments is examined by the contributors to this journal. Practical management issues as well as more basic considerations of biology and ecology are included. Topics range from the effect of invasive species on habitats, to the relationship of land/water use, to species distribution, to habitat modeling for conservation ends. Special issues appear annually, usually as supplements, and address issues such as pond biodiversity. Recommended for academic collections with aquatic, conservation, and resource management interests.

4342. *Aquatic Living Resources: international journal devoted to aquatic resources.* Incorporates: *Revue des Travaux de l'Institut des Peches Maritimes;* Formerly (until 1987): *Aquatic Living; I F R E M E R. Revue des Travaux.* [ISSN: 0990-7440] 1928. q. EUR 372 combined subscription domestic print & online eds.; EUR 384 combined subscription in the European Union print & online eds.; USD 417 combined subscription elsewhere print & online eds. E D P Sciences, 17 Ave du Hoggar, Parc d'Activites de Courtaboeuf, BP 112, Les Ulis, F-91944, France; subscribers@edpsciences.org; http://www.edpsciences.org. Illus. Refereed. Circ: 950. Online: EBSCO Publishing, EBSCO Host; Gale; IngentaConnect; OhioLINK; ScienceDirect; SwetsWise Online Content. *Indexed:* BiolAb, C&ISA, CABA, CerAb, ForAb, HortAb, IAA, IndVet, OceAb, RRTA, S&F, SCI, SWRA, VB, WAE&RSA, ZooRec. *Aud.:* Ac.

Applied research on the living resources in aquatic habitats, from freshwater to marine, is the primary focus of this title. Coverage is worldwide with a non-North American bias. Research papers and shorter notes address resource biology as it relates to management and exploitation of those resources. Typically, one of the four issues is dedicated to a special issue such as common carp genetics or cephalopod life history and fisheries. Appropriate for academic collections with a strong marine and fisheries focus.

4343. *Aquatic Mammals.* [ISSN: 0167-5427] 1972. 3x/yr. USD 190 (Individuals, USD 95). Ed(s): Jeanette Thomas. Western Illinois University Regional Center, 3561 60th St, Moline, IL 61265. Illus. Refereed. Circ: 300. Vol. ends: No. 3. *Indexed:* BiolAb, IndVet, OceAb, VB, ZooRec. *Bk. rev.:* 1, 1,000 words. *Aud.:* Ac, Sa.

The European Association for Aquatic Mammals has a strong interest in the care and conservation of aquatic mammals. Articles published here reflect this, covering health issues and human interaction as well as basic life history of various species. They vary in length from brief observations of behavior to in-depth descriptions of disease. The journal focuses more on medicine and care than *Marine Mammal Science*, another of the few titles addressing marine mammals. Appropriate for academic collections with marine mammal research and veterinary schools.

Biological Bulletin. See Zoology section.

4344. *Botanica Marina.* [ISSN: 0006-8055] 1957. bi-m. EUR 1113 EUR 204 newsstand/cover. Ed(s): A R O Chapman. Walter de Gruyter GmbH & Co. KG, Genthiner Str 13, Berlin, 10785, Germany; bot.mar.editorial@degruyter.de; http://www.degruyter.com/journals/bm. Illus., index, adv. Sample. Refereed. Circ: 450 Paid. Online: EBSCO Publishing, EBSCO Host; OCLC Online Computer Library Center, Inc.; SwetsWise Online Content. Reprint: PSC. *Indexed:* BiolAb, CABA, ChemAb, DSA, FPA, ForAb, HortAb, OceAb, S&F, SCI, SWRA, WAE&RSA, ZooRec. *Aud.:* Ac, Sa.

This journal covers all aspects of marine algae and marine angiosperms: systematics, floristics, biogeography, biochemistry, molecular biology, genetics, chemistry, mycology, and microbiology. It is global in scope, focuses on the utilization of marine plants and algae, and differs from *Aquatic Botany*, which focuses on aquatic plant communities. *Botanica Marina* is accredited with the International Association for Plant Taxonomy for the registration of new names of algae and fungi (including fossils). Recommended for academic collections, especially those with an interest in resource utilization.

4345. Bulletin of Marine Science. Formerly (until 1964): *Bulletin of Marine Science of the Gulf and Caribbean.* [ISSN: 0007-4977] 1951. bi-m. USD 370 print & online eds. (Individuals, USD 155 print & online eds.). Ed(s): Samuel C Snedaker. Rosenstiel School of Marine and Atmospheric Science, 4600 Rickenbacker Causeway, Miami, FL 33149-1098; bms@rsmas.miami.edu; http://www.rsmas.miami.edu/bms/. Refereed. Circ: 1000 Paid. *Indexed:* AnBeAb, ApEcolAb, B&AI, BiolAb, CABA, ChemAb, EnvInd, ExcerpMed, ForAb, HortAb, IBR, IndVet, M&GPA, OceAb, PetrolAb, PollutAb, RRTA, S&F, SCI, SWRA, VB, WAE&RSA, ZooRec. *Bk. rev.:* 3, 300 words, signed. *Aud.:* Ac.

Contributions include all aspects of marine biological research conducted in tropical and subtropical oceans: marine biology, biological oceanography, fisheries, marine affairs, applied marine physics, marine geology and geophysics, marine and atmospheric chemistry, and meteorology and physical oceanography. Of interest to those in tropical and subtropical settings or those academic institutions with a global interest in marine biology.

4346. Cahiers de Biologie Marine. [ISSN: 0007-9723] 1960. q. EUR 226.89 domestic; EUR 222.22 foreign. Ed(s): Claude Jouin Toulmond. Station Biologique de Roscoff, Place Georges Teissier, BP 74, Roscoff, Cedex 29682, France; jouin@sb-roscoff.fr; http://www.sb-roscoff.fr/ cbmintro_eng.html. Illus., adv. Refereed. Circ: 400. *Indexed:* BiolAb, CABA, ChemAb, FPA, ForAb, HortAb, IndVet, OceAb, PollutAb, S&F, SCI, SWRA, WAE&RSA, ZooRec. *Aud.:* Ac.

Includes papers on all aspects of biological oceanography and the biology of marine organisms: benthic and planktonic ecology, ecophysiology, population dynamics, population genetics, food webs, systematics, and phylogeny. This title is decidedly worldwide in scope. Appropriate for academic institutions supporting a marine biology curriculum or marine biology research.

4347. California Wild: natural sciences for thinking animals. Formerly (until 1997): *Pacific Discovery.* [ISSN: 1094-365X] 1948. q. USD 12.95 domestic; USD 22 foreign. Ed(s): Kathleen Wong. California Academy of Sciences, 875 Howard St, San Francisco, CA 94103. Illus., adv. Circ: 30000. Microform: PQC. *Indexed:* BiolDig. *Bk. rev.:* 4, 300 words, signed. *Aud.:* Hs, Ga.

The California Academy of Science publishes this quarterly magazine for those interested in the natural history of the western United States. While focused on the West, it covers marine and desert topics, astronomy, and general issues in science. Book reviews, seasonal observations, and reports from various departments in the academy round out an issue. The online version does not contain all the content or replicate the strong visuals of the print edition. Useful for collections with students and readers intrigued by natural history.

Canadian Journal of Fisheries and Aquatic Sciences. See Fish, Fisheries, and Aquaculture section.

4348. Coastal Engineering. [ISSN: 0378-3839] 1977. 12x/yr. EUR 1636. Ed(s): H F Burcharth. Elsevier BV, Radarweg 29, Amsterdam, 1043 NX, Netherlands; nlinfo-f@elsevier.nl; http://www.elsevier.nl. Refereed. Microform: PQC. Online: EBSCO Publishing, EBSCO Host; Gale; IngentaConnect; OhioLINK; ScienceDirect; SwetsWise Online Content. *Indexed:* ApMecR, C&ISA, EngInd, EnvAb, M&GPA, OceAb, PetrolAb, PollutAb, SCI, SWRA, WRCInf. *Aud.:* Ac, Sa.

Another example of a highly specialized title, *Coastal Engineering* is a sister journal to *Applied Ocean Research.* The focus here is on near-shore engineering issues with particular interest in coastal structures (breakwaters and jetties) and wave dynamics of this environment. One volume annually is usually devoted to special topics such as morphodynamics. Only relevant for specialized research collections with engineering interests in the marine environment.

4349. Coastal Services: the magazine that links people, resources and information. 1998. bi-m. National Oceanic and Atmospheric Administration (N O A A), Coastal Services Center, 2234 South Hobson Ave, Charleston, SC 29405-2413. *Indexed:* SWRA. *Aud.:* Hs, Ac, Sa.

This newsletter provides useful information for coastal resource managers and others interested in coastal issues. Produced by the U.S. National Oceanic and Atmospheric Administration's Coastal Services Center, it highlights projects throughout the country and solutions or strategies to address real issues. The print version is more attractive than the online edition, yet the latter is convenient for the links to other resources. Appropriate for public and academic collections with an audience interested in coastal issues and policy.

4350. Continental Shelf Research. [ISSN: 0278-4343] 1982. 20x/yr. EUR 2230. Ed(s): Richard W Sternberg, Michael B Collins. Pergamon, The Boulevard, Langford Ln, East Park, Kidlington, OX5 1GB, United Kingdom. Refereed. Vol. ends: No. 21. Microform: PQC. Online: EBSCO Publishing, EBSCO Host; Gale; IngentaConnect; OhioLINK; ScienceDirect; SwetsWise Online Content. *Indexed:* CABA, DSA, ForAb, IndVet, M&GPA, OceAb, PollutAb, S&F, SCI, SWRA, VB, WRCInf, ZooRec. *Aud.:* Ac, Sa.

This journal focuses on the shallow marine environment defined as the coast to the continental shelf break. All aspects of marine science are covered, with an emphasis on processes and innovative techniques applied in this environment. Two to four issues every year address special topics such as physical oceanographic modeling and sediment transport. A core title for oceanography collections, although less important for biologically focused collections.

4351. Coral Reefs. Formerly: *International Society for Reef Studies. Journal.* [ISSN: 0722-4028] 1982. 4x/yr. EUR 989 print & online eds. Ed(s): Dr. Peter K Swart, Dr. Richard E Dodge. Springer, Tiergartenstr 17, Heidelberg, 69121, Germany. Adv. Refereed. Microform: PQC. Online: EBSCO Publishing, EBSCO Host; OhioLINK; Springer LINK; SwetsWise Online Content. Reprint: PSC. *Indexed:* BiolAb, OceAb, PollutAb, SCI, SWRA, ZooRec. *Aud.:* Ac, Sa.

As the title suggests, this publication of the International Society for Reef Studies provides a focal point for all aspects of reef-related research: ecology of reef organisms, nutrient flows, reef structure and morphology, evolutionary ecology of reef biota, and the science behind reef management. One aim of the journal is to emphasize the importance of experimentation, modeling, quantification, and applied science in reef studies. Appropriate for academic institutions, it contains articles of interest to those in environmental studies.

4352 *Aud.:* Ems, Hs, Ga. .

As the title suggests, this publication from the Cousteau Society is geared toward a young audience. Typical issues include stories on expeditions and marine organisms, while conveying the societal goal of educating the public to the importance of the world's oceans. Useful for public and school libraries.

4353. Current: the journal of marine education. [ISSN: 0889-5546] 1976. q. Membership, USD 40. Ed(s): Lisa Tooker. National Marine Educators Association, David Niebuhr, Mote Marine Laboratory, Sarasota, FL 34236; http://www.marine-ed.org. Illus., adv. Refereed. Circ: 1500. *Aud.:* Ac, Sa.

While its audience is ostensibly science teachers, this title provides well-written, scientifically accurate articles of interest to students and the general reader. Each issue focuses on a single topic (e.g., hydrothermal vents, invasive species) providing a variety of articles, classroom activities, and additional resources. Especially useful for public and academic collections involved with teachers, home-schoolers, aquarium volunteers, et al.

4354. Deep-Sea Research. Part 1: Oceanographic Research Papers. Supersedes in part (until 1993): *Deep-Sea Research. Part A: Oceanographic Research Papers;* Which had former titles (until 1979): *Deep-Sea Research (New York, 1977); (until 1977): Deep-Sea Research and Oceanographic Abstracts; (until 1961): Deep-Sea Research (New York, 1953).* [ISSN: 0967-0637] 1953. 12x/yr. EUR 2589. Ed(s): M Bacon. Pergamon, The Boulevard, Langford Ln, East Park, Kidlington, OX5 1GB, United Kingdom. Illus., index, adv. Refereed. Vol. ends: No.

10. Microform: PQC. Online: EBSCO Publishing, EBSCO Host; Gale; IngentaConnect; OhioLINK; ScienceDirect; SwetsWise Online Content. *Indexed:* BiolAb, CABA, ChemAb, EngInd, ExcerpMed, M&GPA, OceAb, PetrolAb, SCI, SWRA, ZooRec. *Aud.:* Ac, Sa.

This journal publishes articles on all aspects of oceanographic research including geological, physical, chemical, and biological aspects of the ocean, sea floor, and air-sea interface. As the title suggests, this publication deals with the deep sea, which is defined as being beyond the continental shelf. An essential journal for any institution with a marine biology or oceanography program.

4355. *Deep-Sea Research. Part 2: Topical Studies in Oceanography.* Supersedes in part (in 1993): *Deep-Sea Research. Part A, Oceanographic Research Papers;* Which was formerly (until 1978): *Deep-Sea Research (New York, 1977);* (until 1976): *Deep-Sea Research and Oceanographic Abstracts;* (until 1961): *Deep-Sea Research (New York, 1953).* [ISSN: 0967-0645] 1993. 26x/yr. EUR 3483. Ed(s): John Milliman. Pergamon, The Boulevard, Langford Ln, East Park, Kidlington, OX5 1GB, United Kingdom. Refereed. Microform: PQC. Online: EBSCO Publishing, EBSCO Host; Gale; IngentaConnect; OhioLINK; ScienceDirect; SwetsWise Online Content. *Indexed:* CABA, ChemAb, EngInd, M&GPA, OceAb, S&F, SCI, ZooRec. *Aud.:* Ac, Sa.

Topical issues include results of international or interdisciplinary projects and collections of conference papers. Issues frequently have nontext supporting materials (numerical data, images, and video) that are made available electronically. Along with its companion journal *Deep-Sea Research Part 1: Oceanographic Research Papers*, this title is essential for any institution with a marine biology or oceanography program.

Dynamics of Atmospheres and Oceans. See Atmospheric Sciences section.

Earth Interactions. See Atmospheric Sciences section.

4356. *Estuaries and Coasts.* Former titles (until Feb. 2006): *Estuaries; Chesapeake Science.* [ISSN: 1559-2723] 1978. bi-m. EUR 550 print & online eds. Ed(s): Carlos Duarte, Dr. Stephen Threlkeld. Springer New York LLC, 233 Spring St, New York, NY 10013-1578; journals@ springer-ny.com; http://www.springer.com. Illus., index, adv. Refereed. Circ: 1800. Vol. ends: No. 4. Microform: MIM; PMC; PQC. Online: EBSCO Publishing, EBSCO Host; JSTOR (Web-based Journal Archive). *Indexed:* Agr, AnBeAb, ApEcolAb, BiolAb, CABA, ChemAb, ExcerpMed, ForAb, HortAb, M&GPA, OceAb, PollutAb, RRTA, S&F, SCI, SWRA, WAE&RSA, WRCInf, ZooRec. *Bk. rev.:* 2, 500 words. *Aud.:* Ac.

More limited than *Estuarine, Coastal and Shelf Science, Estuaries and Coasts* (formerly *Estuaries*) focuses on the ecology, dynamics, and habitats within the ocean/land interface. Many of the articles describe eastern U.S. projects, with a handful on the Pacific coast and other parts of the world. Recent articles explore the evolution of tidal creeks and wetlands, restoration models, and food resources for sturgeon. As a society-published journal, it is reasonably priced and of consistent quality. Appropriate for academic collections with a nearshore focus or interest in environmental change.

4357. *Estuarine, Coastal and Shelf Science.* Formerly (until 1982): *Estuarine and Coastal Marine Science.* [ISSN: 0272-7714] 1973. 20x/yr. EUR 3042. Ed(s): D. S. McLusky, E. Wolanski. Academic Press, Harcourt Pl, 32 Jamestown Rd, London, NW1 7BY, United Kingdom; apsubs@acad.com; http://www.elsevier.com/. Illus., index, adv. Refereed. Vol. ends: No. 6. Online: EBSCO Publishing, EBSCO Host; Gale; IngentaConnect; OCLC Online Computer Library Center, Inc.; OhioLINK; ScienceDirect; SwetsWise Online Content. *Indexed:* BiolAb, CABA, ChemAb, EnvAb, EnvInd, ExcerpMed, FPA, ForAb, HortAb, IndVet, M&GPA, OceAb, PetrolAb, PollutAb, RRTA, S&F, SCI, SWRA, VB, WAE&RSA, WRCInf, ZooRec. *Aud.:* Ac.

This title provides a focused forum dealing with the study of estuaries, coastal zones, and continental shelf seas. *Estuarine, Coastal and Shelf Science* is both international and multidisciplinary, and presents research conducted from the

upper limits of the tidal zone to the outer edge of the continental shelf. The scope of this journal includes research on the wide range of biological, anthropogenic, physical, and meteorological influences that come to play within estuaries and coasts. An important part of any marine science collection.

European Journal of Phycology See Botany section.

4358. *Explorations (La Jolla): global discoveries for tomorrow's world.* Incorporates (in 1994): *Scripps Institution of Oceanography. Annual Report;* Which was formerly (until 1984): *Scripps Institution of Oceanography (Year);* (until 1978): *S I O Scripps Institution of Oceanography;* (until 1976): *Scripps Institution of Oceanography. Annual Report;* (until 1972): *S I O: A Report on the Work and Programs of Scripps Institution of Oceanography.* [ISSN: 1075-2560] 1994. q. Ed(s): Nan P Criqui. Scripps Institution of Oceanography, Technical Publications Office, University of California at San Diego, 9500 Gilman Dr, La Jolla, CA 92093-0233; techpubs@sio.uscd.edu. Illus. Circ: 18000. *Aud.:* Ems, Hs, Ga.

The research of the Scripps Institution of Oceanography is reported in feature articles, short highlights, and profiles of scientists. The magazine well serves its purpose as an outreach tool to the public and those interested in the Scripps Institution. The content reflects the breadth of Scripps marine research both geographically and topically. A special section, "Voyager," targets school age children and has an excellent web counterpart. The winter issue is a DVD, and the other three issues are print. Appropriate for middle school audiences and academic collections with a strong undergraduate marine program.

Fisheries. See Fish, Fisheries, and Aquaculture section.

Fishery Bulletin. See Fish, Fisheries, and Aquaculture section.

G3: Geochemistry, Geophysics, Geosystems. See Earth Sciences section.

4359. *Global and Planetary Change.* [ISSN: 0921-8181] 1988. 20x/yr. EUR 1631. Ed(s): S. Cloetingh, K McGuffie. Elsevier BV, Radarweg 29, Amsterdam, 1043 NX, Netherlands; nlinfo-f@elsevier.nl; http://www.elsevier.nl. Illus., index, adv. Refereed. Vol. ends: No. 6. Microform: PQC. Online: EBSCO Publishing, EBSCO Host; Gale; IngentaConnect; OhioLINK; ScienceDirect; SwetsWise Online Content. *Indexed:* CABA, EnvAb, EnvInd, FR, ForAb, M&GPA, MinerAb, OceAb, PollutAb, S&F, SCI, SSCI, SWRA, WAE&RSA, ZooRec. *Aud.:* Ac, Sa.

This journal is of interest to earth scientists, oceanographers, and biologists. It focuses on the record of change in the earth's history and presents multidisciplinary analysis of recent and future changes. Topics include changes in the chemical composition of the oceans and atmosphere, climate change, sea level variations, human geography, global geophysics and tectonics, global ecology, and biogeography. Useful for a wide variety of academic institutions, particularly those with environmental studies and oceanography programs.

4360. *Global Biogeochemical Cycles: an international journal of global change.* [ISSN: 0886-6236] 1987. q. USD 604. Ed(s): Meinrat O. Andreae. American Geophysical Union, 2000 Florida Ave, NW, Washington, DC 20009-1277; http://www.agu.org. Illus., adv. Refereed. Vol. ends: No. 4. Online: EBSCO Publishing, EBSCO Host. *Indexed:* Agr, ApEcolAb, CABA, ChemAb, FPA, ForAb, HortAb, M&GPA, OceAb, PollutAb, S&F, SCI, SWRA, WAE&RSA. *Aud.:* Ac, Sa.

This is a very important journal within environmental science, geoscience, meteorology, and atmospheric science. Articles include research on geosphere and biosphere changes resulting from marine, hydrologic, atmospheric, extraterrestrial, geologic, and human causes over time scales large and small. An essential part of academic library collections supporting oceanography and environmental studies programs.

4361. *Harmful Algae.* [ISSN: 1568-9883] 2002. 6x/yr. EUR 357. Ed(s): Theodore Smayda, Dr. Sandra E. Shumway. Elsevier BV, Radarweg 29, Amsterdam, 1043 NX, Netherlands; nlinfo-f@elsevier.nl; http://www.elsevier.nl. *Indexed:* BiolAb, CABA, FS&TA, HortAb, IndVet, OceAb, RRTA, S&F, SCI, VB, ZooRec. *Aud.:* Sa.

This title provides a forum for information on harmful microalgae and cyanobacteria in both fresh and marine waters. It focuses on the life histories, physiology, toxicology, monitoring, and management of blooms, and includes both original research and reviews. Appropriate for libraries supporting research in this area and those serving an extensive environmental studies program.

4362. *I C E S Journal of Marine Science: journal du conseil.* Former titles (until 1991): *Conseil International pour l'Exploration de la Mer. Journal;* (until 1968): *Conseil Permanent International pour l'Exploration de la Mer. Journal.* [ISSN: 1054-3139] 1926. 9x/yr. EUR 899 print or online ed. Ed(s): A I L Payne. Oxford University Press, Great Clarendon St, Oxford, OX2 6DP, United Kingdom; enquiry@oup.co.uk; http://www.oxfordjournals.org. Adv. Refereed. Circ: 1000. Online: EBSCO Publishing, EBSCO Host; Gale; HighWire Press; IngentaConnect; OCLC Online Computer Library Center, Inc.; OhioLINK; ScienceDirect; SwetsWise Online Content. Reprint: PSC. *Indexed:* BiolAb, CABA, ChemAb, EnvAb, EnvInd, HortAb, IndVet, OceAb, PollutAb, RRTA, S&F, SCI, SWRA, VB, WAE&RSA, ZooRec. *Aud.:* Ac.

The International Council for the Exploration of the Sea (ICES) coordinates and promotes applied research in the North Atlantic. Its journal is an outlet for that research as well as for other information contributing to a broad understanding of all marine systems, their resources, and the effects of human activity on both. Articles address management and conservation issues through biology and ecology, fishing and other human activities, climate change, and changes in technology. Typically, one or two issues of the eight per year are symposium proceedings; ICES offers these as a separate series, but it is more efficient to purchase through the journal subscription. An essential title for marine science research collections.

4363. *IEEE Journal of Oceanic Engineering.* [ISSN: 0364-9059] 1976. q. USD 285. Ed(s): James F Lynch. IEEE, 445 Hoes Ln, Piscataway, NJ 08854-1331; subscription-service@ieee.org; http://www.ieee.org. Illus., index, adv. Refereed. Vol. ends: No. 4. Online: Pub.; EBSCO Publishing, EBSCO Host. *Indexed:* AS&TI, C&ISA, CerAb, EngInd, H&SSA, IAA, M&GPA, OceAb, PetrolAb, SCI. *Aud.:* Ac, Sa.

The IEEE Oceanic Engineering Society encourages articles and technical communications that apply electrical, electronics, and instrumentation engineering to the marine environment. Topics vary from specific design of new instruments for marine research, such as satellite tags, to investigation of ambient noise. More important than *Ocean Engineering* to both engineering and oceanographic collections.

Journal of Atmospheric and Oceanic Technology. See Atmospheric Sciences section.

4364. *The Journal of Cetacean Research and Management.* [ISSN: 1561-0713] 1999. 3x/yr. GBP 110 (Individuals, GBP 75; GBP 25 per issue). Ed(s): G P Donovan. International Whaling Commission, The Red House,135 Station Rd, Impington, CB4 9NP, United Kingdom; secretariat@iwcoffice.org; http://www.iwcoffice.org. Refereed. *Indexed:* BiolAb, OceAb, ZooRec. *Aud.:* Ac, Sa.

This title replaces the scientific section of *Reports of the International Whaling Commission* (IWC) and publishes peer-reviewed papers important to the conservation and management of cetaceans. The focus tends toward population abundance and distribution, and the affects of harvest and other human interactions, with occasional notes on unusual sightings or behavior. An annual supplement includes the *Reports of the IWC Scientific Committee,* containing population trends, discussion of issues and concerns, and management updates. Appropriate for research collections with strong marine mammal programs.

4365. *Journal of Coastal Research: an international forum for the littoral sciences.* Formerly (until 1984): *Litoralia.* [ISSN: 0749-0208] 1985. q. Individuals, USD 125 print & online eds. Ed(s): Charles W Finkl, Jr. Coastal Education & Research Foundation, Inc., PO Box 210187, Royal Palm Beach, FL 33421-0187; cfinkl@gate.net; http://www.cerf-jcr.com. Illus., index, adv. Refereed. Circ: 1500. Vol. ends: No. 4. *Indexed:* AS&TI, BiolAb, BiolDig, C&ISA, CABA, CerAb, ExcerpMed, ForAb, HortAb, IAA, M&GPA, OceAb, PollutAb, RRTA, S&F, SCI, SSCI, SWRA, WAE&RSA, ZooRec. *Bk. rev.:* 2, 1,000 words, signed. *Aud.:* Ac.

This title provides "an international forum for the littoral sciences," and it covers the coastal zone in-depth and internationally. Research topics range from validating surf observations to sediment transport patterns to seabed geomorphology. Several issues each year have a thematic section addressing a geographic area or topic of interest. The quality of the illustrations is excellent. A solid choice for libraries with marine and geoscience collections.

4366. *Journal of Experimental Marine Biology and Ecology.* [ISSN: 0022-0981] 1967. 28x/yr. EUR 4716. Ed(s): Dr. Sandra E. Shumway, R Hughes. Elsevier BV, Radarweg 29, Amsterdam, 1043 NX, Netherlands; nlinfo-f@elsevier.nl; http://www.elsevier.nl. Illus., index, adv. Refereed. Vol. ends: No. 2. Microform: PQC. Online: EBSCO Publishing, EBSCO Host; Gale; IngentaConnect; OhioLINK; ScienceDirect; SwetsWise Online Content. *Indexed:* ApEcolAb, B&AI, BiolAb, CABA, ChemAb, EnvAb, EnvInd, ExcerpMed, ForAb, HortAb, IndVet, OceAb, PollutAb, RRTA, S&F, SCI, SSCI, SWRA, VB, ZooRec. *Bk. rev.:* 1, 1,000 words, signed. *Aud.:* Ac.

The focus of this journal is laboratory and field experimental study, and its scope includes biochemistry, physiology, behavior, genetics, ecosystems, and ecological modeling. Of interest to marine ecologists, physiologists, and biochemists, this title is appropriate for academic institutions with marine biology, oceanography, and ecology programs.

Journal of Geophysical Research. See Earth Sciences section.

4367. *Journal of Marine Research.* [ISSN: 0022-2402] 1937. bi-m. USD 150 (Individuals, USD 50). Ed(s): George Veronis. Sears Foundation for Marine Research, Kline Geology Laboratory, Yale University, New Haven, CT 06520-8109; jmr@yale.edu. Illus., index. Refereed. Circ: 1000. Vol. ends: No. 6. Microform: PMC; PQC. Online: EBSCO Publishing, EBSCO Host; Gale; IngentaConnect. *Indexed:* ApMecR, B&AI, BiolAb, ChemAb, ExcerpMed, GSI, M&GPA, OceAb, PetrolAb, PollutAb, SCI, SWRA, ZooRec. *Aud.:* Ac.

The scope of this journal, from the Sears Foundation for Marine Research of Yale University, includes physical, biological, and chemical oceanography, and a preference is given to articles that report on a combination and interaction of ecological and physical processes. This publication is global in scope and affordably priced. Essential to all marine science collections.

4368. *Journal of Marine Science and Technology.* [ISSN: 0948-4280] 1996. q. EUR 207 print & online eds. Ed(s): Hideaki Miyata. Springer Japan KK, No 2 Funato Bldg, 1-11-11 Kudan-kita, Tokyo, 102-0073, Japan; http://www.springer.jp. Refereed. Reprint: PSC. *Indexed:* EngInd, OceAb, SCI. *Aud.:* Ac, Sa.

The title of this journal suggests a broader subject coverage than in reality. The narrow focus on marine engineering and naval architecture includes articles on hull design, stability modeling, and material strength; important to the field, but not terribly relevant to others in marine science. Appropriate only for libraries supporting marine engineering studies.

4369. *Journal of Marine Systems.* [ISSN: 0924-7963] 1990. 20x/yr. EUR 2426. Ed(s): J L Largier, W Fennel. Elsevier BV, Radarweg 29, Amsterdam, 1043 NX, Netherlands; nlinfo-f@elsevier.nl; http://www.elsevier.nl. Illus., adv. Refereed. Vol. ends: No. 4. Microform: PQC. Online: EBSCO Publishing, EBSCO Host; Gale; IngentaConnect; OhioLINK; ScienceDirect; SwetsWise Online Content. *Indexed:* CABA, EngInd, EnvAb, M&GPA, OceAb, PollutAb, S&F, SCI, SWRA, ZooRec. *Aud.:* Ac, Sa.

As implied in its title, this journal examines interdisciplinary, system-driven questions in the marine environment. Scale ranges from lagoons to ocean basins, all with a focus on how the marine system shapes the biological, chemical, and physical environment. Coverage is international. Appropriate for research oceanography collections, especially those with a physical emphasis.

4370. *Journal of Oceanography.* Supersedes in part (in 1992): *Oceanographical Society of Japan. Journal.* [ISSN: 0916-8370] 1941. bi-m. EUR 1008 print & online eds. Ed(s): K Hanawa. Springer Netherlands, Van Godewijckstraat 30, Dordrecht, 3311 GX, Netherlands; http://www.springeronline.com. Illus., adv. Refereed. Circ: 2100. *Indexed:* ChemAb, M&GPA, OceAb, PollutAb, SCI, SWRA, ZooRec. *Aud.:* Ac, Sa.

Originally published as the outlet for the Oceanographic Society of Japan, this journal continues to be biased towards basic oceanographic research in the Pacific Basin. Relevant topics include current dynamics, chemical fluxes, and occasional biological phenomena. Most useful for oceanography collections supporting research in the Pacific.

Journal of Phycology. See Botany section.

4371. *Journal of Physical Oceanography.* [ISSN: 0022-3670] 1971. m. USD 428. Ed(s): Peter Muller. American Meteorological Society, 45 Beacon St, Boston, MA 02108; amsinfo@ametsoc.org; http://ams.allenpress.com. Illus., index, adv. Refereed. Circ: 1397. Vol. ends: No. 12. Online: Allen Press Inc.; EBSCO Publishing, EBSCO Host; Northern Light Technology, Inc.; OCLC Online Computer Library Center, Inc.; ProQuest K-12 Learning Solutions; ProQuest LLC (Ann Arbor). *Indexed:* ApMecR, BiolDig, CCMJ, ChemAb, EngInd, IAA, M&GPA, MSN, MathR, OceAb, PetrolAb, SCI, SWRA. *Aud.:* Ac, Sa.

The American Meteorological Society publishes this journal relating to the physics of the ocean and the processes that operate at its boundaries. The primary aim of the journal is to promote understanding of the ocean and its role within the earth system. Typical articles address surface phenomena, oceanography (large and small scale), circulation, and modeling. A core journal for all academic libraries serving an oceanography program.

4372. *Journal of Plankton Research.* [ISSN: 0142-7873] 1979. 13x/yr. EUR 843 print or online ed. Ed(s): Kevin J Flynn. Oxford University Press, Great Clarendon St, Oxford, OX2 6DP, United Kingdom; jnl.orders@oup.co.uk; http://www.oxfordjournals.org. Illus., index, adv. Refereed. Circ: 620. Vol. ends: No. 3. Online: EBSCO Publishing, EBSCO Host; Gale; HighWire Press; IngentaConnect; OCLC Online Computer Library Center, Inc.; OhioLINK; Ovid Technologies, Inc.; Oxford Journals; ProQuest LLC (Ann Arbor); SwetsWise Online Content. Reprint: PSC. *Indexed:* AnBeAb, ApEcolAb, ArtHuCI, B&AI, BiolAb, CABA, ChemAb, FPA, ForAb, IndVet, OceAb, PollutAb, RRTA, S&F, SCI, SWRA, ZooRec. *Bk. rev.:* 1, 500 words, signed. *Aud.:* Ac, Sa.

Ecology, physiology, taxonomy, and behavior of plankton are covered in this journal, with a majority of articles describing marine environments. Contributors address these drifting organisms, zooplankton, and phytoplankton with research articles and short communications. Occasional "horizon" pieces challenge traditional views or review current trends. An essential title for biological oceanography research collections.

4373. *Journal of Sea Research.* Formerly (until vol.35, 1996): *Netherlands Journal of Sea Research.* [ISSN: 1385-1101] 1961. 8x/yr. EUR 608. Ed(s): J J Beukema, C. J.M. Philippart. Elsevier BV, Radarweg 29, Amsterdam, 1043 NX, Netherlands; nlinfo-f@elsevier.nl; http://www.elsevier.nl. Refereed. Circ: 600. Online: EBSCO Publishing, EBSCO Host; Gale; IngentaConnect; OhioLINK; ScienceDirect; SwetsWise Online Content. *Indexed:* BiolAb, CABA, ChemAb, EnvAb, EnvInd, ExcerpMed, M&GPA, OceAb, S&F, SCI, ZooRec. *Aud.:* Ac, Sa.

Another of the many titles examining coastal and shelf ecosystems, this journal has a northern European bias, yet covers topics of interest to coastal scientists everywhere. Appropriate for research collections in the marine sciences.

4374. *Journal of Waterway, Port, Coastal, and Ocean Engineering.* Former titles (until 1982): *American Society of Civil Engineers. Waterway, Port, Coastal and Ocean Division. Journal;* (until 1977): *American Society of Civil Engineers. Waterways, Harbors, and Coastal Engineering Division. Journal;* (until 1973): *American Society of Civil Engineers. Waterways and Harbors Division. Journal.* [ISSN: 0733-950X] 1956. bi-m. USD 374. Ed(s): Vijay Panchang. American Society of Civil Engineers, 1801 Alexander Bell Dr, Reston, VA 20191-4400; http://www.asce.org. Illus. Refereed. Circ: 2000. Microform: PQC. Online: American Institute of Physics, Scitation; EBSCO Publishing, EBSCO Host; SwetsWise Online Content. *Indexed:* AS&TI, C&ISA, CerAb, EngInd, EnvInd, H&SSA, HRIS, IAA, M&GPA, OceAb, PetrolAb, PollutAb, SCI, SWRA, WRCInf. *Aud.:* Ac, Sa.

This international journal focuses on the applied issues of civil engineering in the aquatic environment, from bridge construction to wave action on breakwaters to forcing action in open waters. Sponsored by the American Society of Civil Engineers, the technical papers, notes, and discussion items address issues of interest globally while describing local solutions. Essential for engineering collections with interest in the marine and aquatic environments.

4375. *Limnology and Oceanography.* [ISSN: 0024-3590] 1956. 8x/yr. USD 378. American Society of Limnology and Oceanography, Inc., 1444 Eye St. NW #200, Washington, DC 20005; business@aslo.org; http://www.aslo.org. Illus., index. Refereed. Circ: 5300 Paid. Vol. ends: No. 8. *Indexed:* AnBeAb, ApEcolAb, B&AI, BiolAb, CABA, ChemAb, EnvAb, EnvInd, ExcerpMed, ForAb, GSI, IndVet, M&GPA, OceAb, PollutAb, S&F, SCI, SWRA, VB, WRCInf, ZooRec. *Bk. rev.:* 2, 750 words, signed. *Aud.:* Ac, Sa.

This journal is published by the American Society of Limnology and Oceanography, but it is not limited to North America in geographic scope. Unfortunately, the print publication is bundled with electronic access and is now only available as part of a package that also includes the more specialized partner journal *Limnology and Oceanography: Methods* (electronic-only) and the society's *Bulletin.* The focus of this journal is aquatic ecosystems and includes original research articles on all aspects of limnology and oceanography. An essential journal for any academic institution with a marine biology or oceanography program, but it will also result in a subscription to the more specialized *Methods* journal and the society's news bulletin.

4376. *Marine and Freshwater Research.* Formerly (until 1995): *Australian Journal of Marine and Freshwater Research.* [ISSN: 1323-1650] 1950. 8x/yr. AUD 1540 print & online eds. (Individuals, AUD 200 print & online eds.). Ed(s): Dugald McGlashan. C S I R O Publishing, 150 Oxford St, PO Box 1139, Collingwood, VIC 3066, Australia; publishing@csiro.au; http://www.publish.csiro.au/. Illus., index, adv. Refereed. Circ: 700. Vol. ends: No. 8. Microform: PQC. Online: EBSCO Publishing, EBSCO Host; Gale; OCLC Online Computer Library Center, Inc.; SwetsWise Online Content. *Indexed:* AnBeAb, ApEcolAb, BiolAb, C&ISA, CABA, CerAb, ChemAb, EnvAb, EnvInd, ExcerpMed, FPA, FS&TA, ForAb, HortAb, IAA, IndVet, M&GPA, OceAb, PollutAb, RRTA, S&F, SCI, SWRA, VB, WAE&RSA, ZooRec. *Aud.:* Ac, Sa.

This journal, published by the Commonwealth Scientific and Industrial Research Organization and the Australian Academy of Science, includes a broad range of interdisciplinary research in ecology, hydrology, biogeochemistry, and oceanography with the overarching goal of highlighting the interconnectedness of aquatic environments, processes, and management applications. Specific subjects can include fisheries science, biogeochemistry, physiology, genetics, biogeography, and toxicology. Although published in Australia, this journal is global in scope. Recommended for academic libraries supporting marine or aquatic-based programs.

4377. *Marine Biological Association of the United Kingdom. Journal.* [ISSN: 0025-3154] 1887. bi-m. GBP 688. Ed(s): P E Gibbs, John A Raven. Cambridge University Press, The Edinburgh Bldg, Shaftesbury Rd, Cambridge, CB2 2RU, United Kingdom; journals@cambridge.org; http://www.journals.cambridge.org. Illus., index, adv. Refereed. Vol. ends: No. 4. Microform: BHP; PQC. Online: Pub.; EBSCO Publishing,

EBSCO Host; OCLC Online Computer Library Center, Inc.; OhioLINK; SwetsWise Online Content. *Indexed:* B&AI, BiolAb, CABA, ChemAb, ForAb, HortAb, IndVet, OceAb, PollutAb, S&F, SCI, VB, WRCInf, ZooRec. *Aud.:* Ac, Sa.

This journal, produced by the Marine Biological Association of the United Kingdom, is international in scope. It publishes on all aspects of marine biology, including ecological surveys and population studies of oceanic, coastal, and shore communities; physiology and experimental biology; taxonomy, morphology, and life history of marine animals and plants; and chemical and physical oceanographic work that relates closely to the biological environment. Appropriate for all academic research libraries with a marine biology program.

4378. Marine Biology: international journal on life in oceans and coastal waters. [ISSN: 0025-3162] 1967. m. EUR 5598 print & online eds. Ed(s): Otto Kinne. Springer, Tiergartenstr 17, Heidelberg, 69121, Germany. Illus., adv. Sample. Refereed. Vol. ends: No. 4. Microform: PQC. Online: EBSCO Publishing, EBSCO Host; OhioLINK; ProQuest LLC (Ann Arbor); Springer LINK; SwetsWise Online Content. Reprint: PSC. *Indexed:* AnBeAb, ApEcolAb, B&AI, BiolAb, CABA, ChemAb, DSA, EnvInd, ExcerpMed, FS&TA, ForAb, HortAb, IBR, IndVet, OceAb, S&F, SCI, SWRA, VB, ZooRec. *Aud.:* Ac, Sa.

This journal is very broad in scope, including research on all aspects of plankton research, biological and biochemical oceanography, environment-organism interrelationships, experimental biology, metabolic rates and routes, biochemical research on marine organisms, biosystem research, energy budgets, dynamics and structures of communities, use of marine resources, anthropogenic influences on marine environments, evolution, modeling, and scientific apparatus and techniques. A broadly focused journal essential to every marine science collection.

4379. Marine Biology Research. Formed by the merger of (1961-2005): *Sarsia;* (1964-2005): *Ophelia.* [ISSN: 1745-1000] 2005. bi-m. GBP 223 print & online eds. Ed(s): Tom Fenchel, Tore Hoisaeter. Taylor & Francis Ltd., 4 Park Sq, Milton Park, Abingdon, OX14 4RN, United Kingdom; info@tandf.co.uk; http://www.tandf.co.uk/journals. *Indexed:* ApEcolAb, BiolAb, CABA, HortAb, IndVet, OceAb, SCI, VB, ZooRec. *Aud.:* Ac, Sa.

This new journal came about as a merger of the long-standing core titles *Sarsia* and *Ophelia.* It aims to provide an international forum for all areas of marine biology and oceanography, including ecology, behavior, taxonomy, environment, and evolution. Articles on applied research that contribute to general biological insight are also included. Core to academic and research institutions with marine biology or oceanography collections.

4380. Marine Biotechnology. Formed by the merger of (1992-1998): *Molecular Marine Biology and Biotechnology;* (1993-1998): *Journal of Marine Biotechnology.* [ISSN: 1436-2228] 1998. bi-m. EUR 718 print & online eds. Ed(s): Thomas T Chen, Shigetoh Miyachi. Springer New York LLC, 233 Spring St, New York, NY 10013-1578; journals@springer-ny.com; http://www.springer.com/. Illus., adv. Refereed. Vol. ends: No. 4. Online: EBSCO Publishing, EBSCO Host; OhioLINK; Springer LINK; SwetsWise Online Content. Reprint: PSC. *Indexed:* BioEngAb, BiolAb, CABA, ChemAb, DSA, EngInd, FS&TA, ForAb, HortAb, IndVet, OceAb, PollutAb, S&F, SCI, VB, ZooRec. *Aud.:* Ac, Sa.

This title is the official journal of the European Society for Marine Biotechnology and the Japanese Society for Marine Biotechnology, and is global in scope. Typical topics will include molecular biology, genomics, proteomics, cell biology, and biochemistry, and will be focused on the biotechnology of sea organisms involved. Notably excluded from the journal are articles on genomic or microsatellite sequences or expressed sequence tags unless this research addresses a larger biological issue. Appropriate in libraries supporting marine biology and molecular biology research and advanced undergraduate studies.

4381. Marine Chemistry. [ISSN: 0304-4203] 1972. 20x/yr. EUR 2266. Ed(s): Frank J Millero. Elsevier BV, Radarweg 29, Amsterdam, 1043 NX, Netherlands; nlinfo-f@elsevier.nl; http://www.elsevier.nl. Illus., adv. Refereed. Vol. ends: No. 4. Microform: PQC. Online: EBSCO Publish-

ing, EBSCO Host; Gale; IngentaConnect; OhioLINK; ScienceDirect; SwetsWise Online Content. *Indexed:* BiolAb, ChemAb, ExcerpMed, M&GPA, OceAb, PetrolAb, PollutAb, SCI, SWRA, WRCInf. *Aud.:* Ac, Sa.

This title includes original research and occasional reviews addressing chemistry of the marine environment, with an emphasis on dynamics. It is an international forum, and will be of interest to marine chemists, chemical oceanographers, and geochemists. Appropriate for academic collections supporting a research program in marine chemistry or oceanography.

4382. Marine Ecology - Progress Series. [ISSN: 0171-8630] 1979. 25x/yr. EUR 4950 combined subscription domestic print & online eds.; EUR 5100 combined subscription foreign print & online eds. Ed(s): Otto Kinne. Inter-Research, Nordbuente 23, Oldendorf, 21385, Germany; ir@int-res.com; http://www.int-res.com. Illus., index, adv. Refereed. Circ: 1000. Vol. ends: No. 3. *Indexed:* AnBeAb, ApEcolAb, BiolAb, CABA, ChemAb, DSA, ForAb, HortAb, IBR, IndVet, M&GPA, OceAb, PollutAb, RRTA, S&F, SCI, SWRA, VB, ZooRec. *Aud.:* Ac, Sa.

This journal includes research articles, reviews, invited reviews, and notes on topics both fundamental and applied in marine ecology. Topics include botany, zoology, ecological aspects of fisheries and aquaculture, resource management, and ecosystem research. Occasional "theme" sections will synthesize information on a topic by a multi-author team. A core title for libraries supporting teaching and research in environmental studies and marine biology.

4383. Marine Environmental Research. Incorporates (in 1991): *Oil and Chemical Pollution;* Which was formerly (until 1982): *Journal of Oil and Petrochemical Pollution.* [ISSN: 0141-1136] 1978. 10x/yr. EUR 1625. Ed(s): Dr. R. Spies, Dr. John Widdows. Elsevier Ltd., The Boulevard, Langford Ln, Oxford, OX5 1GB, United Kingdom. Illus., index, adv. Refereed. Vol. ends: No. 5. Microform: PQC. Online: EBSCO Publishing, EBSCO Host; Gale; IngentaConnect; OhioLINK; ScienceDirect; SwetsWise Online Content. *Indexed:* BiolAb, CABA, ChemAb, DSA, EngInd, EnvAb, EnvInd, ExcerpMed, FPA, FS&TA, ForAb, HortAb, IndVet, OceAb, PetrolAb, PollutAb, RRTA, S&F, SCI, SWRA, VB, WAE&RSA, WRCInf, ZooRec. *Aud.:* Ac, Sa.

Environmental is the key concept for this journal, with its focus on chemical, physical, and biological interactions within the marine realm. Articles examine processes and environmental change with an eye toward understanding systems to facilitate more informed management. The international scope enhances the sharing of information on marine environmental science. Useful for extensive marine science collections.

Marine Fisheries Review. See Fish, Fisheries, and Aquaculture section.

4384. Marine Geodesy: an international journal of ocean surveys, mapping and sensing. [ISSN: 0149-0419] 1977. q. GBP 329 print & online eds. Ed(s): Dr. Narendra K Saxena. Taylor & Francis Inc., 325 Chestnut St, Ste 800, Philadelphia, PA 19016; orders@taylorandfrancis.com; http://www.taylorandfrancis.com. Illus. Refereed. Vol. ends: No. 4. Online: EBSCO Publishing, EBSCO Host; Gale; IngentaConnect; OCLC Online Computer Library Center, Inc.; SwetsWise Online Content. Reprint: PSC. *Indexed:* EnvAb, EnvInd, IBR, M&GPA, OceAb, SSCI. *Bk. rev.:* 3, 500 words. *Aud.:* Ac, Sa.

This international journal covers a highly specialized field of marine studies—the science of measuring and monitoring the ocean. Articles describe instrument bias and calibration challenges, boundary datum, and use of remote sensing. A relevant, yet probably underutilized addition to research collections supporting field-based oceanography programs.

4385. Marine Geology. [ISSN: 0025-3227] 1964. 44x/yr. EUR 3727. Ed(s): John T Wells, G de Lange. Elsevier BV, Radarweg 29, Amsterdam, 1043 NX, Netherlands; nlinfo-f@elsevier.nl; http://www.elsevier.nl. Illus., index, adv. Refereed. Vol. ends: No. 4. Microform: PQC. Online: EBSCO Publishing, EBSCO Host; Gale; IngentaConnect; OhioLINK; ScienceDirect; SwetsWise Online Content. *Indexed:* ChemAb, EngInd, M&GPA, OceAb, PetrolAb, PollutAb, SCI. *Aud.:* Ac, Sa.

Along with *Journal of Geophysical Research*, this title provides geologists a venue for discussing rocks and sediments in the marine realm. Its focus is on the science of marine geology, not its management or hydrodynamics. Multiple volumes are published annually, with one or two addressing a special topic such as prodelta systems or linkages of ocean chemistry to geological processes. A core title for geologic oceanography collections.

4386. *Marine Geophysical Researches: an international journal for the study of the earth beneath the sea.* [ISSN: 0025-3235] 1970. q. EUR 640 print & online eds. Ed(s): Peter Clift, Y John Chen. Springer Netherlands, Van Godewijckstraat 30, Dordrecht, 3311 GX, Netherlands; http://www.springeronline.com. Illus., adv. Refereed. Microform: PQC. Online: EBSCO Publishing, EBSCO Host; Gale; IngentaConnect; OCLC Online Computer Library Center, Inc.; OhioLINK; Ovid Technologies, Inc.; Springer LINK; SwetsWise Online Content. Reprint: PSC. *Indexed:* ChemAb, EngInd, M&GPA, OceAb, PetrolAb, SCI. *Aud.:* Ac, Sa.

This publication has traditionally dealt with data on the deep ocean basins, but recently has focused content on understanding the global mid-ocean ridge system. Typical articles may address studies of continental margins, as well as techniques and tools for deep sea floor imaging and measuring. This publication will be of interest to geologists and oceanographers. Recommended for academic and research libraries supporting these types of programs.

4387. *Marine Georesources and Geotechnology.* Formed by the merger of (1975-1993): *Marine Geotechnology;* (1977-1993): *Marine Mining.* [ISSN: 1064-119X] 1993. q. GBP 291 print & online eds. Ed(s): Michael J Cruickshank, Ronald C Chaney. Taylor & Francis Inc., 325 Chestnut St, Ste 800, Philadelphia, PA 19016; orders@taylorandfrancis.com; http://www.taylorandfrancis.com. Illus., index, adv. Refereed. Circ: 260. Vol. ends: No. 4. Microform: PQC. Online: EBSCO Publishing, EBSCO Host; Gale; IngentaConnect; OCLC Online Computer Library Center, Inc.; SwetsWise Online Content. Reprint: PSC. *Indexed:* AS&TI, BiolAb, C&ISA, CerAb, ChemAb, EngInd, EnvAb, IAA, MinerAb, OceAb, PetrolAb, PollutAb, SCI, SWRA. *Aud.:* Ac, Sa.

A companion title to *Marine Geology*, this journal focuses on applied aspects of seafloor sediments and rocks as well as their use. Topics addressed range from characterizations of dredged materials to restoration of marine macrofauna to the effect of nodule mining. Useful for academic collections with marine engineering and applied geology programs.

4388. *Marine Mammal Science.* [ISSN: 0824-0469] 1985. q. USD 248 print & online eds. Ed(s): James Estes. Blackwell Publishing, Inc., Commerce Place, 350 Main St, Malden, MA 02148; customerservices@ blackwellpublishing.com; http://www.blackwellpublishing.com. Illus., adv. Refereed. Reprint: PSC. *Indexed:* AnBeAb, ApEcolAb, BiolAb, CABA, DSA, ForAb, IndVet, OceAb, RRTA, SCI, VB, ZooRec. *Bk. rev.:* 3, 2,000 words. *Aud.:* Ac, Sa.

This journal is published by the Society for Marine Mammalogy. Typical articles address form and function, evolution, systematics, physiology, biochemistry, behavior, population biology, life history, genetics, ecology, and conservation. Articles, review articles, notes, opinions, and letters are all included, and editorial staff screen articles for appropriate experimental procedures involving these often-protected species. A core title for libraries serving a marine biology major.

4389. *Marine Policy.* [ISSN: 0308-597X] 1977. 6x/yr. EUR 981. Ed(s): E D Brown. Pergamon, The Boulevard, Langford Ln, East Park, Kidlington, OX5 1GB, United Kingdom. Illus., index, adv. Refereed. Vol. ends: No. 6. Microform: PQC. Online: EBSCO Publishing, EBSCO Host; Gale; IngentaConnect; OhioLINK; ScienceDirect; SwetsWise Online Content. *Indexed:* CJA, EnvAb, EnvInd, ExcerpMed, FutSurv, IBSS, OceAb, PAIS, PollutAb, SSCI, WAE&RSA. *Aud.:* Ac, Sa.

Specialists in marine affairs contribute articles relevant to policy formulation and analysis. The audience includes lawyers, marine resource managers, economists, political scientists, and other social scientists. Recent volumes have an increased focus on fisheries policy although maritime issues and marine management tools are also covered. Occasionally, issues address a special topic giving a historical overview or discussing emerging trends. A core title for academic collections with a marine policy or management component.

4390. *Marine Pollution Bulletin.* [ISSN: 0025-326X] 1970. 24x/yr. EUR 1396. Ed(s): J Pearce, Charles Sheppard. Pergamon, The Boulevard, Langford Ln, East Park, Kidlington, OX5 1GB, United Kingdom. Illus., index, adv. Refereed. Circ: 2000 Paid. Vol. ends: No. 12. Microform: PQC. Online: EBSCO Publishing, EBSCO Host; Gale; IngentaConnect; OhioLINK; ScienceDirect; SwetsWise Online Content. *Indexed:* ApEcolAb, BiolAb, CABA, ChemAb, DSA, EngInd, EnvAb, EnvInd, ExcerpMed, FPA, FS&TA, ForAb, HortAb, IndVet, M&GPA, OceAb, PetrolAb, PollutAb, RRTA, S&F, SCI, SSCI, SWRA, VB, WAE&RSA, WRCInf, ZooRec. *Bk. rev.:* 2, 500 words. *Aud.:* Ac, Sa.

Readers will find an inclusive and rigorous approach to the condition of the marine environment in this journal. Using a variety of features, it documents marine conditions, effects of human activity, and measurements of and responses to pollutants. Brief news items cover pollution activities and events around the globe. The editorials and invited reviews offer in-depth insight into marine environmental issues. In addition to the monthly issues, special issues focus on conferences or topics such as water quality in a geographic region. A core title for academic and research collections supporting environmental science, marine management, and biological oceanography programs.

4391. *Marine Technology Society Journal: the international, interdisciplinary society devoted to ocean and marine engineering, science and policy.* Formerly (until 1968): *Journal of Ocean Technology;* Incorporated: *Ocean Soundings.* [ISSN: 0025-3324] 1966. q. USD 120 domestic; USD 135 foreign. Ed(s): Dan Walker. Marine Technology Society, 5565 Sterrett Pl, Ste 108, Columbia, MD 21044; mtspubs@erols.com; http://www.mtsociety.org. Illus., index, adv. Refereed. Circ: 3200. Vol. ends: No. 4. Online: Northern Light Technology, Inc.; OCLC Online Computer Library Center, Inc.; ProQuest LLC (Ann Arbor); H.W. Wilson. *Indexed:* AS&TI, B&AI, ChemAb, EngInd, EnvAb, EnvInd, ExcerpMed, HRIS, M&GPA, OceAb, PetrolAb, PollutAb, SCI, SSCI, SWRA, ZooRec. *Bk. rev.:* 1-3, 500 words. *Aud.:* Ga, Ac, Sa.

The Marine Technology Society is open to all those interested in marine technology—how it works, how to use it in science, how it affects society. Its journal is the vehicle for communicating these varied perspectives to a wide audience and hence often presents material in a more popular style. The regular issues focus on uses of technology in marine sciences with articles written by both scientists and industry researchers. Special issues address such topics as acoustic tracking of fish, ocean education, and marine sanctuary management. A useful title for general collections serving an audience with marine interests as well as academic collections supporting broad marine programs.

4392. *Mariners Weather Log: a climatic review of North Atlantic and North Pacific Ocean and Great Lake areas.* [ISSN: 0025-3367] 1957. s-a. USD 13 domestic; USD 18.20 foreign. Ed(s): Robert A Luke. U.S. Department of Commerce, National Oceanic and Atmospheric Administration, National Weather Service, 1325 East West Hwy, Silver Spring, MD 20910; http://www.nws.noaa.gov. Illus., index, adv. Circ: 8100. Vol. ends: Dec. *Indexed:* AmStI, IUSGP, M&GPA, OceAb. *Aud.:* Ga, Sa.

This inexpensive print publication from the National Weather Service (NWS) is freely available online. Articles address weather forecasting, marine weather phenomena, and news from over 10,000 ships involved in the NWS Voluntary Observing Program. The meteorological content will be of interest to the maritime community, including marine institutions, scientists, and educational and research facilities. Not a core title, but a nice addition to both public and academic libraries.

4393. *Ocean & Coastal Management.* Formerly (until 1992): *Ocean and Shoreline Management;* Which was formed by the merger of (1973-1986): *Ocean Management;* (1985-1987): *Journal of Shoreline Management.* [ISSN: 0964-5691] 1973. 12x/yr. EUR 1545. Ed(s): B Cicin-Sain. Pergamon, The Boulevard, Langford Ln, East Park, Kidlington, OX5 1GB, United Kingdom. Illus., adv. Refereed. Vol. ends: No. 44. Microform: PQC. Online: EBSCO Publishing, EBSCO Host;

Gale; IngentaConnect; OhioLINK; ScienceDirect; SwetsWise Online Content. *Indexed:* EngInd, EnvAb, EnvInd, ExcerpMed, IPSA, M&GPA, OceAb, PAIS, PollutAb, SCI, SSCI, SWRA, WAE&RSA, ZooRec. *Bk. rev.:* 1-2, 300-600 words. *Aud.:* Ac, Sa.

This multidisciplinary, international journal covers many management issues with a focus on near shore and coastal ones. Authors are encouraged to address improvement of management practices or approaches as part of their communication. Topics include coastal zone management throughout the world, use of GIS as a management tool, and application of precautionary fisheries management. One or two issues of the six annually are dedicated to special topics on coastal management. A core title for academic collections with marine policy and management aspects.

4394. *Ocean Development and International Law.* Formerly (until 1973): *Ocean Development and International Law Journal.* [ISSN: 0090-8320] 1973. q. GBP 408 print & online eds. Ed(s): Ted L McDorman. Taylor & Francis Inc., 325 Chestnut St, Ste 800, Philadelphia, PA 19016; orders@taylorandfrancis.com; http://www.taylorandfrancis.com. Adv. Refereed. Microform: WSH. Online: EBSCO Publishing, EBSCO Host; Gale; IngentaConnect; OCLC Online Computer Library Center, Inc.; SwetsWise Online Content. Reprint: PSC. *Indexed:* ABS&EES, C&ISA, CJA, CLI, CerAb, EnvAb, EnvInd, IAA, IBSS, ILP, IPSA, IndIslam, JEL, LRI, OceAb, PAIS, PRA, PSA, SSCI. *Aud.:* Sa.

Less specialized than *Marine Policy*, this journal contains articles on law of the sea, comparative domestic ocean law, shipping, ocean engineering, marine economics, and marine science that will be of interest to those involved in the management or utilization of ocean resources. Appropriate for libraries supporting programs in aquaculture, resource management, and environmental law.

4395. *Ocean Engineering.* [ISSN: 0029-8018] 1968. 18x/yr. EUR 2634. Ed(s): Rameswar Bhattacharyya, Michael E McCormick. Pergamon, The Boulevard, Langford Ln, East Park, Kidlington, OX5 1GB, United Kingdom. Illus., index, adv. Refereed. Circ: 1200. Vol. ends: No. 28. Microform: PQC. Online: EBSCO Publishing, EBSCO Host; Gale; IngentaConnect; OhioLINK; ScienceDirect; SwetsWise Online Content. *Indexed:* AS&TI, ApMecR, C&ISA, ChemAb, EngInd, ExcerpMed, H&SSA, OceAb, PetrolAb, SCI, SWRA. *Aud.:* Ac, Sa.

This highly specialized journal covers marine engineering from ships to structures to instrumentation. Aimed at engineers, research articles range from tanker design issues to estimating breakwater damage. Issues often carry short communications on recent field work, instrument modeling, and testing. Appropriate for specialized marine and engineering collections.

4396. *Oceanography: serving ocean science and its applications.* [ISSN: 1042-8275] 1988. q. Free to members. Ed(s): Larry Atkinson. Oceanography Society, 1931, Rockville, MD 20849-1931; anne@ccpo.odu.edu; http://tos.org/. Illus., adv. Refereed. Circ: 2000 Paid. Vol. ends: No. 4. *Indexed:* M&GPA, OceAb, ZooRec. *Bk. rev.:* 2, 1,000 words, signed. *Aud.:* Ga, Ac, Sa.

This title presents a range of research, technological developments, book reviews, and current events of interest to the broad community of scientists and managers involved with ocean science. It is written for an informed and knowledgeable audience yet is highly readable with strong supporting illustrations. Issues frequently focus on a special topic such as the Indonesian seas or women in oceanography. Selected articles and features are freely available at the Oceanography Society's web site. An excellent choice for a college or public library for its general science collection.

4397. *Oceanography and Marine Biology: an annual review.* [ISSN: 0078-3218] 1963. a. Ed(s): Margaret Barnes, R J A Atkinson. Taylor & Francis Ltd., 4 Park Sq, Milton Park, Abingdon, OX14 4RN, United Kingdom; http://www.tandf.co.uk/books/. *Indexed:* ChemAb, M&GPA, OceAb, SCI, ZooRec. *Aud.:* Ac.

These authoritative review articles are appropriate introductory material for students and are also useful for researchers keeping abreast of topics beyond their own field of research. The comprehensive reference lists included also serve to enhance the value of the review articles. Sample topics from a recent issue include analysis of cold seep sediments, ecology of rafting in marine ecosystems, and biofouling. An essential element in any library supporting marine biology or environmental studies undergraduate education.

4398. *Oceanus: reports on research at the Woods Hole Oceanographic Institution.* Incorporates in 1994: *Woods Hole Oceanographic Institution. Reports on Research.* [ISSN: 0029-8182] 1952. s-a. USD 15 domestic; USD 18 Canada; USD 25 elsewhere. Ed(s): Laurence Lippsett. Woods Hole Oceanographic Institution, Mail Stop 5, Woods Hole, MA 02543-1050; http://www.whoi.edu/oceanus. Illus., index, adv. Refereed. Circ: 6000. Vol. ends: No. 2. Microform: PQC. Online: EBSCO Publishing, EBSCO Host; Florida Center for Library Automation; Gale; Northern Light Technology, Inc.; OCLC Online Computer Library Center, Inc.; ProQuest LLC (Ann Arbor); H.W. Wilson. *Indexed:* AS&TI, B&AI, BiolDig, ChemAb, EnvInd, ExcerpMed, FutSurv, GSI, M&GPA, MASUSE, OceAb, PollutAb, RGPR, SCI, SSCI. *Aud.:* Hs, Ga, Ac, Sa.

The Woods Hole Oceanographic Institute (WHOI), one of the world's premier marine research organizations, resumed publication of this title in 2004 both in print and online. The articles by WHOI scientists and science writers report on current research, expeditions, and marine issues covering topics from intertidal animals to new instrumentation to detect tsunamis. Short news items are interspersed with two- or three-page articles. All are profusely illustrated. The online version has additional features such as video and digital photos. Very useful for general public collections as well as high schools and academic institutions.

4399. *Progress in Oceanography.* [ISSN: 0079-6611] 1963. 16x/yr. EUR 2661. Ed(s): Detlef R. Quadfasel, Charles B. Miller. Pergamon, The Boulevard, Langford Ln, East Park, Kidlington, OX5 1GB, United Kingdom. Illus., index, adv. Refereed. Vol. ends: No. 4. Microform: PQC. Online: EBSCO Publishing, EBSCO Host; Gale; IngentaConnect; OhioLINK; ScienceDirect; SwetsWise Online Content. *Indexed:* ApMecR, ChemAb, EngInd, M&GPA, OceAb, PollutAb, SCI, SWRA, ZooRec. *Aud.:* Ac, Sa.

Many consider this publication to be essential reading for oceanographers. A highlight of this publication is longer, comprehensive articles that review an aspect of oceanography or offer a treatise on a developing aspect of oceanographic research. Some volumes include collections of papers and conference proceedings. This title belongs in libraries supporting oceanography programs, and will be of interest to physical and chemical oceanographers as well as marine biologists

Remote Sensing of Environment. See Environment and Conservation section.

4400. *Sea Technology: for design engineering and application of equipment and services in the global ocean community.* Formerly (until 1973): *Undersea Technology and Oceanology International & Offshore Technology;* Which was formed by the merger of (1961-1972): *Undersea Technology;* (1971-1972): *Oceanology International Offshore Technology.* [ISSN: 0093-3651] 1960. m. USD 50 domestic; USD 60 foreign; USD 4.50 per issue. Ed(s): Michele B. Umansky. Compass Publications, Inc. (Arlington), 1501 Wilson Blvd, Ste 1001, Arlington, VA 22209-2403. Illus., index, adv. Circ: 16000 Controlled. Vol. ends: No. 12. Microform: PQC. Online: Northern Light Technology, Inc.; OCLC Online Computer Library Center, Inc.; ProQuest K-12 Learning Solutions; ProQuest LLC (Ann Arbor); H.W. Wilson. *Indexed:* AS&TI, ApMecR, BiolDig, C&ISA, CerAb, EngInd, ExcerpMed, H&SSA, HRIS, IAA, M&GPA, OceAb, PetrolAb, PollutAb, SCI, SWRA. *Aud.:* Sa.

The monthly trade journal for marine technology and engineering combines short articles on issues and new developments with product reviews and news from the industry and the U.S. government. Articles address such topics as homeland security, toxicity sensors, and remotely operated vehicles. Appropriate for a general audience with technical and engineering interests.

Tellus. See Atmospheric Science section.

■ MARRIAGE AND DIVORCE

Joan Giglierano, Reference and Instruction Librarian, Roesch Library, University of Dayton, 300 College Park, Dayton, OH 45459-1360; joan.giglierano@notes.udayton.edu

Introduction

No one planning to marry expects their marriage to end in divorce. Although the overall divorce rate in the United States has declined since a peak in the early 1980s, the probability of divorce or separation for the average couple marrying for the first time remains between 40 and 50 percent (National Marriage Project, *The State of Our Unions: 2006*).

Factors contributing to marital stability include median age of first marriage, which increased from 20 in 1960 to 26 in 2005 for women, and from 23 to 27 for men. The Tax Foundation reported in October 2005 that the prevalence of dual incomes among married couples had increased by 31 percent between 1980 and 2003, enhancing financial security. Education levels, too, had a positive effect on marriage. Steven P. Martin in a 2004 paper titled "Growing Evidence for a 'Divorce Divide'? Education, Race, and Marital Dissolution Rates in the U.S. since the 1970s," found rates of marital dissolution had decreased by almost half from the 1970s to the 1990s among four-year college graduates.

For couples wishing to end their marriages, however, the process of obtaining divorces or dissolutions has eased over the last several decades, and the stigma once associated with doing so has lessened. No-fault divorce laws are on the books in all 50 states. A booming industry of lawyers, mental health experts, and self-help media stands ready to serve those who decide to dissolve their marriages.

The literature of marriage and divorce includes publications that focus on nurturing marriages, plus a few that offer support and information for people who divorce; journals concerned with family, marital, sexual, and relationship counseling; and those that report current research findings on the sociology and history of marriage and divorce. Many magazines and journals that include articles on marriage and divorce topics will be found in the Family section, since the dynamic of the marital relationship is so profoundly interwoven with that of the resulting family unit. For listings of professionals such as lawyers, counselors, and financial planners, as well as for state-specific information on divorce, individuals will find up-to-date resources on web sites such as DivorceNet (www.divorcenet.com) and Divorce Online (www.divorceonline.com).

Basic Periodicals

Journal of Couple & Relationship Therapy, Journal of Sex & Marital Therapy.

Basic Abstracts and Indexes

Family & Society Studies Worldwide, Family Index, PsycINFO, Sage Family Studies Abstracts, Social Sciences Abstracts, Social Work Abstracts, Sociological Abstracts, Studies on Women and Gender Abstracts.

Bride's. See Weddings section.

Contemporary Family Therapy: an international journal. See Family section.

The Family Journal. See Family section.

Family Law Quarterly. See Law section.

Fathering Magazine. See Parenting section.

4401. *Journal of Couple & Relationship Therapy.* Formerly (until 2002): *Journal of Couples Therapy.* [ISSN: 1533-2691] 2001. q. USD 440 print & online eds. Ed(s): Joseph L. Wetchler. Haworth Press, Inc., 10 Alice St, Binghamton, NY 13904-1580; getinfo@haworthpress.com;

http://www.haworthpress.com. Adv. Sample. Refereed. Circ: 161 Paid. Reprint: HAW. *Indexed:* CINAHL, CJA, CWI, IBR, IBZ, IMFL, SFSA, SSA, SWA, SWR&A, V&AA. *Bk. rev.:* Number and length vary. *Aud.:* Ac.

Written by expert practitioners and researchers in marriage and family therapy and services, *Journal of Couple & Relationship Therapy* "promotes a better understanding of what contributes to healthy adult relationships and how therapy facilitates the process." Its clinical, theoretical, and research articles discuss issues for which heterosexual or same-sex couples seek the help of premarital, marital, sex, divorce, and/or re-marital therapists. Among recently published articles are "Areas of Desired Change Among Married Midlife Individuals," "Conflict Resolution Styles Among Latino Couples," "Mandated Premarital Therapy and Early Marital Adjustment: Implications for Therapy," "Online Infidelity Evaluation and Treatment Implications," and "Broken Bonds: An Emotionally Focused Approach to Infidelity." A regular feature, "Journal File," summarizes studies, findings, or the latest news on relevant topics, for example, "Current Research on the Relationship Between Work and Marriage." Recommended for libraries serving mental health professionals.

4402. *Journal of Divorce & Remarriage: research and clinical studies in family theory, family law, family mediation and family therapy.* Formerly (until 1990): *Journal of Divorce.* [ISSN: 1050-2556] 1977. q. in 2 vols. USD 720 print & online eds. Ed(s): Craig A Everett. The Haworth Clinical Practice Press, 10 Alice St, Binghamton, NY 13904; getinfo@haworthpress.com; http://www.haworthpress.com/. Illus., index, adv. Sample. Refereed. Circ: 379 Paid. Vol. ends: No. 4. Microform: PQC. Online: EBSCO Publishing, EBSCO Host; OCLC Online Computer Library Center, Inc.; ProQuest LLC (Ann Arbor); SwetsWise Online Content. Reprint: HAW. *Indexed:* ASG, ASSIA, AgeL, CJA, CWI, GendWatch, HRA, IBR, IBZ, IMFL, PsycInfo, RI-1, SFSA, SSA, SSCI, SWA, SWR&A, SociolAb, V&AA. *Bk. rev.:* Number and length vary. *Aud.:* Ac, Sa.

Journal of Divorce & Remarriage publishes peer-reviewed clinical research articles on "all aspects of divorce, including predivorce marital and family treatment, marital separation and dissolution, children's responses to divorce and separation, single parenting, remarriage, and stepfamilies." Its intended audience includes counselors, social workers, family therapists, and lawyers involved in family law. Recent articles include "From Divorce to Remarriage: Financial Management and Security Among Remarried Women," "Post-Divorce Adjustment and Social Relationships: A Meta-Analytic Review," "Does the Rebound Effect Exist? Time to Remarriage and Subsequent Union Stability," and "Parents' and Adolescents' Communication with Each Other About Divorce-Related Stressors and its Impact on Their Ability to Cope Positively with the Divorce." The journal is interdisciplinary in focus, and most issues include articles about divorce in countries outside the United States, for example, "Attractors and Barriers to Divorce: A Retrospective Study in Three European Countries." Recommended for academic and special libraries.

Journal of Marital and Family Therapy. See Family section.

Journal of Marriage and Family. See Family section.

4403. *Journal of Sex & Marital Therapy.* [ISSN: 0092-623X] 1974. 5x/yr. GBP 218 print & online eds. Ed(s): Dr. R Taylor Segraves. Routledge, 325 Chestnut St, Ste 800, Philadelphia, PA 19106; journals@routledge.com; http://www.routledge.com. Illus., index, adv. Refereed. Circ: 2000. Vol. ends: Oct/Dec. Microform: PQC. Online: EBSCO Publishing, EBSCO Host; Gale; IngentaConnect; OCLC Online Computer Library Center, Inc.; SwetsWise Online Content. Reprint: PSC. *Indexed:* ASG, AgeL, CJA, ExcerpMed, FR, PsycInfo, SFSA, SSA, SSCI, SWA, SociolAb, V&AA. *Bk. rev.:* Number and length vary. *Aud.:* Ac, Sa.

The focus of this journal is the biological and psychological treatment of sexual and marital disorders, and its audience includes sex therapists, marriage and family therapists, psychiatrists, psychologists, clinical social workers, physicians, nurses, clergy practitioners, and pastoral counselors. The clinical and research articles address marital relationships, special clinical and medical problems, therapeutic techniques and their outcomes, and the theoretical parameters of sexual functioning. Hormonal contraception and sexual desire, sexual dysfunction and chronic illness, behavioral assessment of couples' communication in female orgasmic disorders, treatments for erectile dysfunction, and persistent sexual arousal syndrome are among the topics in recent issues. The *Journal of Sex & Marital Therapy* is widely available in academic and medical library collections due to its broad readership, its high-quality articles, and its low cost. Other leading journals in the area of sex research are the *Journal of Sex Research* and the *Archives of Sexual Behavior*. The *Journal of Sex & Marital Therapy* is highly recommended for academic libraries.

Marriage & Family Review. See Family section.

4404. *Marriage Magazine: celebrating committed couples.* Formerly: *Marriage Encounter.* [ISSN: 1063-1054] 1971. bi-m. USD 19.95 domestic; USD 24.95 foreign; USD 3.50 newsstand/cover per issue. Ed(s): Krysta Eryn Kavenaugh. International Marriage Encounter, Inc., 955 Lake Dr., St. Paul, MN 55120-1497; marriagem@aol.com. Adv. Circ: 11000 Paid. *Bk. rev.:* Number and length vary. *Aud.:* Ga.

According to its web site, *Marriage Magazine* originated in the Marriage Encounter movement, though there is no longer any formal affiliation. It strives "to help change the statistics on marriage in the new millennium . . . by offering role models for long-term, happy, healthy marriages, influencing family policy, and reversing the trend toward the dissolution of marriages." Each issue offers practical ideas to help with the "day-to-day" of married life. Sample topics of recent articles include financial compatibility, nurturing marriage when couples have children, issues to consider when thinking about remarriage, and balancing the need for time together vs. money. Regular features include spotlighted couples, tips to make marriage work, and couples prayers. The magazine's web site offers selected articles. Subscribed to by church, seminary, and Christian academic libraries, *Marriage* will also find an audience in public libraries.

4405. *Marriage Partnership.* Formerly (until 1987): *Partnership.* [ISSN: 0897-5469] 1984. q. USD 19.95 domestic; USD 29.90 foreign; USD 5 per issue. Ed(s): Harold B. Smith, Ginger Kolbaba. Christianity Today International, 465 Gundersen Dr, Carol Stream, IL 60188; http://www.christianitytoday.com. Illus., adv. Circ: 60000 Controlled. Vol. ends: Winter. Online: EBSCO Publishing, EBSCO Host; Gale. *Indexed:* CWI, ChrPI. *Bk. rev.:* Number and length vary. *Aud.:* Ga.

Marriage Partnership, a self-help magazine, offers practical and biblical advice from an evangelical perspective on issues couples face in day-to-day life. Its audience is those wishing to achieve a healthy Christian marriage. Regular columns include "24/7," "Real Sex," "The Early Years," (written by couples married five years or less) and "Ever After" (about making love last a lifetime). Each issue includes how-to pieces, expert interviews, couple profiles, humorous articles, and true-life stories, plus articles on topics such as communication, spirituality, keeping romance alive, and financial issues. Selected articles are available on the magazine's web site. *Marriage Partnership* is available in church, seminary, and Christian academic libraries, as well as in some public libraries.

Modern Bride. See Weddings section.

Sexual and Relationship Therapy. See Sexuality section.

■ MATHEMATICS

General/Research Journals

J. Parker Ladwig, Mathematics Library, University of Notre Dame, 009 Hayes-Healy Center, Notre Dame, IN 46556-5641; 574-631-3617; FAX: 574-631-9660; ladwig.1@nd.edu

Introduction

"Today's world demands a mathematically literate citizenry, well prepared for ever-changing technology and growing global competition, and led by a new generation of mathematics and science professionals" (*Position Statement,*

National Council of Teachers of Mathematics, August 2006). Mathematics can invoke a sense of dread, mystery, or logical precision. It is loved for a variety of reasons: its elegant formulas, its definite answers, its proofs that are a model of philosophical demonstration, or its discipline of abstraction. It is also a subject that builds upon itself so carefully that most advanced mathematics is inaccessible to those who have not spent years in its study.

Librarians can encourage mathematical literacy by fostering and supporting an interest in mathematics. This section is divided into two parts: magazines other than research journals, and research journals. The first part draws attention to those titles that support mathematical literacy. They should be considered for *every* library. The second part covers research journals, i.e., those that promote research, not just literacy. Some of the largest public libraries may also find this part of interest. Most mathematics journals are now available electronically, generally in full text, but at least with tables of contents.

In crafting this list of journals, several factors were considered: a journal's consistent presence in *Magazines for Libraries*, its appeal to students of mathematics (not just teachers), its reputation among mathematicians and librarians, its subscription price and price per page, and finally its ability to fill a niche unfilled by other titles. Several venerable, but pricey, research journals are included. They may not be the best value, but librarians should be aware of them. Specialized research journals have been excluded in order to concentrate on those titles with the broadest interest. Finally, librarians (and mathematicians interested in libraries) should be aware of the professional association for mathematics librarians: the Physics-Astronomy-Mathematics (PAM) Division of the Special Libraries Association. The PAM web site is at www.sla.org/division/dpam, and PAM members are always willing to help.

Basic Periodicals

Ems: *Teaching Children Mathematics, Mathematics Teaching in the Middle School*; Hs: *Mathematics Teacher*; Ga: *Journal of Recreational Mathematics, Math Horizons*; Ac: *American Mathematical Monthly, Bulletin of the American Mathematical Society, The Mathematical Intelligencer, SIAM Review.*

Basic Abstracts and Indexes

MathSciNet.

General

Chance. See Statistics section.

4406. *Journal of Recreational Mathematics.* [ISSN: 0022-412X] 1968. q. USD 225. Ed(s): Lamarr Widmer, Charles Ashbacher. Baywood Publishing Co., Inc., 26 Austin Ave, PO Box 337, Amityville, NY 11701-0337; info@baywood.com; http://www.baywood.com. Illus. Sample. Refereed. Vol. ends: No. 4. *Indexed:* GSI, MathR. *Bk. rev.:* 3-6, 300-600 words, signed. *Aud.:* Hs, Ga, Ac.

The *Journal of Recreational Mathematics* is "uniquely devoted to the lighter side of mathematics. No special mathematical training is required. You will find such things as number curiosities and tricks, paper-folding creations, chess and checker brain-teasers, articles about mathematics and mathematicians, and discussion of some higher mathematics and their applications to everyday life and to puzzle-solving. It includes some occasional word games and cryptography, a lot to do with magic squares, map-coloring, geometric dissections, games with a mathematical flavor, and many other topics generally included in the fields of puzzles and recreational mathematics." Its non-textbook approach will clarify in a recreational form many of the abstract concepts wrestled with in formal classroom situations. There are several medium-length, signed book reviews in each issue. It is one of the few mathematics journals with neither the full text nor tables of contents available online. Because it makes mathematics accessible to general adult readers, though, it is a basic resource for public libraries. It may also be suitable for high school and college libraries.

4407. *Math Horizons.* [ISSN: 1072-4117] 1993. q. Members, USD 25; Non-members, USD 35. Mathematical Association of America, 1529 18th St, NW, Washington, DC 20036. *Aud.:* Hs, Ga.

Math Horizons is published by the MAA (see *American Mathematical Monthly*). It is a glossy, popular magazine intended "to introduce [undergraduate] students to the world of mathematics outside the classroom." There are no book reviews. Tables of contents are available online at www.maa.org/mathhorizons. Of all the journals covering mathematics, this is probably the most accessible to a general adult audience (see also *Journal of Recreational Mathematics*). It is a basic resource for public libraries and recommended for college and academic libraries. It may also be suitable for some high school libraries.

4408. *Mathematical Gazette.* [ISSN: 0025-5572] 1894. 3x/yr. GBP 55 domestic; GBP 59 foreign. Ed(s): Gerry Leversha. Mathematical Association, 259 London Rd, Leicester, LE2 3BE, United Kingdom; office@m-a.org.uk; http://www.m-a.org.uk. Illus., index, adv. Circ: 3000. Vol. ends: No. 3. *Indexed:* IndIslam, MathR. *Bk. rev.:* 25-35, 600-1,500 words, signed; 10-15, 100-300 words, signed. *Aud.:* Hs, Ac, Sa.

The *Mathematical Gazette* is now over a century old. It is the chief publication (among seven) of the United Kingdom's Mathematical Association (www.m-a.org.uk), founded in 1871 to improve education in mathematics. In addition to its expository articles, the *Gazette* contains regular sections for letters, problems, and extensive medium-length and short, signed book reviews. The focus is on the teaching and learning of mathematics for audiences 15–20 years old. The tables of contents are available online at www.m-a.org.uk/resources/periodicals/the_mathematical_gazette. It is recommended for high school and academic libraries, especially because it gives a British perspective on mathematics education.

4409. *Mathematics Magazine.* Incorporates (in 1976): *Delta (Washington);* Which was formerly (until 1946): *National Mathematics Magazine;* (until 1934): *Mathematics News Letter.* [ISSN: 0025-570X] 1926. 5x/yr. USD 99. Ed(s): Frank A Farris. Mathematical Association of America, 1529 18th St, NW, Washington, DC 20036; http://www.maa.org. Illus., index, adv. Refereed. Circ: 14000. Microform: PQC. Online: JSTOR (Web-based Journal Archive); Northern Light Technology, Inc.; OCLC Online Computer Library Center, Inc.; ProQuest K-12 Learning Solutions; ProQuest LLC (Ann Arbor). *Indexed:* CCMJ, GSI, MASUSE, MSN, MathR. *Bk. rev.:* 3-5, 300-750 words. *Aud.:* Hs, Ga, Ac, Sa.

Mathematics Magazine is a journal of the MAA (see *American Mathematical Monthly*) and "aims to provide lively and appealing mathematical expositions . . . accessible to undergraduates." It is divided into five sections: "Articles," "Notes" (e.g., "Using Tangent Lines to Define Means"), "Problems," "Reviews," and "News and Letters." There are several medium-length, unsigned book reviews in each issue. Tables of contents are available online at www.maa.org/pubs/mathmag.html. The full text of volumes 1–76 is available electronically from JSTOR at www.jstor.org. This journal is a basic resource for academic libraries and may be suitable for some public and high school libraries.

4410. *Mathematics Teacher.* [ISSN: 0025-5769] 1908. 9x/yr. Institutional members, USD 99; Individual members, USD 76. Ed(s): Sandy Berger, Nancy Blue Williams. National Council of Teachers of Mathematics, 1906 Association Dr, Reston, VA 20191-1502; nctm@nctm.org; http://www.nctm.org. Illus., adv. Refereed. Circ: 37274 Paid. Microform: PQC. Online: Northern Light Technology, Inc.; OCLC Online Computer Library Center, Inc.; ProQuest LLC (Ann Arbor); H.W. Wilson. *Indexed:* ABIn, BRI, CBRI, ECER, ERIC, EduInd, MRD, MathR. *Bk. rev.:* 5-8, 100-300 words, signed. *Aud.:* Ems, Hs, Ac, Sa.

Mathematics Teacher is the oldest journal published by the National Council of Teachers of Mathematics (NCTM). In fact, the NCTM was founded in 1920, 12 years after the first issue. The NCTM is the world's largest organization for teaching mathematics and includes members from the United States and Canada. Its mission is "to provide the vision and leadership necessary to ensure a mathematics education of the highest quality for all students." It is well known for its *Principles and Standards for School Mathematics,* and those selecting NCTM journals should be aware that the NCTM was involved in what came to be known as the "Math Wars." *Mathematics Teacher* is "devoted to improving mathematics instruction in grade 8 through two-year and teacher-education colleges." "It offers activities, lesson ideas, teaching strategies, and problems through in-depth articles, departments, and features, [and includes] great

resources for secondary teachers, preservice teachers, and teacher educators." Each issue has several short, signed book reviews. It is available online at http://my.nctm.org/eresources/journal_home.asp?journal_id=2. Although it does not directly address high school students, it does focus on their teachers. It is a basic journal for high school libraries. It may also be of interest to some middle school and public libraries and to those academic libraries that serve educators.

4411. *Mathematics Teaching: incorporating Micromath.* Incorporates (1985-2006): *Micromath.* [ISSN: 0025-5785] 1956. q. GBP 75 schools (Individual members, GBP 55; Students, GBP 25). Ed(s): Jeoff Dunn. Association of Teachers of Mathematics, Unit 7 Prime Industrial Park, Shaftesbury St, Derby, DE23 8YB, United Kingdom; admin@atm.org.uk; http://www.atm.org.uk. Illus., index, adv. Circ: 3800 Controlled. Vol. ends: Dec. Microform: PQC. Online: EBSCO Publishing, EBSCO Host; OCLC Online Computer Library Center, Inc.; ProQuest LLC (Ann Arbor); H.W. Wilson. *Indexed:* ABIn, BrEdI, ERIC, EduInd. *Aud.:* Ems, Hs, Sa.

Mathematics Teaching is a publication of the United Kingdom's Association of Teachers of Mathematics (ATM), founded in 1950, which aims to "support the teaching and learning of mathematics" and by working for change "to relate mathematical education more closely to the powers and needs of the learner." It is "a journal for the teachers and learners of mathematics of all ages. It sets out to air the complexities of teaching and learning—rather than the complexities of mathematics—by describing the classroom through the eyes of both teachers and pupils." It includes cover articles like "On rebecoming unfamiliar," discussions of classroom activities, research papers, information on the annual ATM conference, and, on its web site, occasional extras in pdf format. There are no book reviews. Tables of contents and "extras" are available online at www.atm.org.uk/mt/index.html. Recommended for those elementary, middle, and high school libraries interested in a British perspective on mathematics teaching.

4412. *Mathematics Teaching in the Middle School.* [ISSN: 1072-0839] 1994. 9x/yr. USD 99 (Individuals, USD 76). Ed(s): Kathleen Lay, Dolores Pesek. National Council of Teachers of Mathematics, 1906 Association Dr, Reston, VA 20191-1502; nctm@nctm.org; http://www.nctm.org. Illus., index. Sample. Refereed. Circ: 28026 Paid. Vol. ends: May. *Indexed:* ABIn, EduInd, MRD. *Bk. rev.:* 5-8, 100-300 words, signed. *Aud.:* Ems, Hs, Ga, Ac, Sa.

Mathematics Teaching in the Middle School is a publication of the NCTM (see *Mathematics Teacher*). It is "intended as a resource for middle school students, teachers, and teacher educators. The focus of the journal is on intuitive, exploratory investigations that use informal reasoning to help students develop a strong conceptual basis that leads to greater mathematical abstraction." This journal includes several short to medium-length, signed book reviews per issue. It is available online at http://my.nctm.org/eresources/journal_home.asp?journal_id=3. Although it does not directly address middle school students, it does focus on their teachers. It is a basic magazine for middle school libraries. It may also be of interest to some high school and public libraries and to those academic libraries that serve educators.

4413. *Pi Mu Epsilon Journal.* [ISSN: 0031-952X] 1949. s-a. USD 20 for 2 yrs. domestic; USD 25 for 2 yrs. foreign. Ed(s): Brigitte Servatius. Pi Mu Epsilon, Inc, c/o Michelle Schultz, Dept of Mathematical Sciences, Las Vegas, NV 89154-4020; http://www.pme-math.org. Illus., adv. Refereed. Circ: 3500 Paid. Microform: PQC. *Indexed:* MathR. *Aud.:* Hs, Ac, Sa.

The *Pi Mu Epsilon Journal* is the official publication of the Pi Mu Epsilon National Honorary Mathematics Society (PME) (www.pme-math.org). PME was founded in 1914 at Syracuse University and currently has over 300 chapters at colleges and universities throughout the United States. "In its quest to promote mathematics, Pi Mu Epsilon sponsors a journal devoted to topics in mathematics accessible to undergraduate students." In addition to its articles, many written by undergraduates, there are sections for problems and puzzles. There are no book reviews. Of the journals written for undergraduates, this one tends to focus the most on pure mathematics. Neither the full text nor the tables of contents are available online. It is recommended for academic libraries that serve undergraduate mathematics majors and may also be of interest to some high school and public libraries.

4414. *Teaching Children Mathematics.* Formerly (until May 1994): *Arithmetic Teacher.* [ISSN: 1073-5836] 1954. m. Sep.-May. Institutional members, USD 99; Individual members, USD 76. National Council of Teachers of Mathematics, 1906 Association Dr, Reston, VA 20191-1502; nctm@nctm.org; http://www.nctm.org. Illus., index, adv. Sample. Refereed. Circ: 45000 Paid. Vol. ends: May. Microform: PQC. Online: Florida Center for Library Automation; Gale; Northern Light Technology, Inc.; OCLC Online Computer Library Center, Inc.; ProQuest LLC (Ann Arbor); H.W. Wilson. *Indexed:* ABIn, BRI, ECER, ERIC, EduInd, MRD. *Bk. rev.:* 3-5, 100-300 words, signed. *Aud.:* Ems, Hs, Ga, Ac, Sa.

Teaching Children Mathematics is another publication of the NCTM (see *Mathematics Teacher*). It is a "forum for the exchange of ideas and a source of activities and pedagogical strategies for mathematics education pre-K–6. It presents new developments in curriculum, instruction, learning, and teacher education; interprets the results of research; and in general provides information on any aspect of the broad spectrum of mathematics education appropriate for preservice and in-service teachers." It also includes several short to medium-length, signed book reviews per issue. It is available online at http://my.nctm.org/eresources/journal_home.asp?journal_id=4. Although it does not directly address elementary school students, it does focus on their teachers. It is a basic magazine for elementary school libraries. It may also be of interest to some high school and public libraries and to those academic libraries serving educators.

4415. *U M A P Journal.* [ISSN: 0197-3622] 1980. q. Membership, USD 99. Ed(s): P J Campbell. Consortium for Mathematics and Its Applications, 57 Bedford St, Ste 210, Lexington, MA 02420-4428; info@comap.com; http://www.comap.com/. Illus., index, adv. Circ: 1500. Vol. ends: No. 4. *Indexed:* ABIn, EduInd. *Bk. rev.:* 3-10, 250-1,500 words. *Aud.:* Hs, Ga, Ac, Sa.

The *UMAP Journal* is published by the Consortium for Mathematics and Its Applications (COMAP) (www.comap.com). COMAP was founded in 1980 and is a nonprofit organization whose mission is to improve mathematics education for students of all ages. It "works with teachers, students, and business people to create learning environments where mathematics is used to investigate and model real issues in our world." Some of its partners include the National Science Foundation, the Mathematical Association of America, the National Council of Teachers of Mathematics, and the Society for Industrial and Applied Mathematics. COMAP also publishes magazines of interest to elementary and high schools. *UMAP* "blends contemporary teaching modules with commentaries and articles to create a boldly different periodical. Each issue puts several real-world problems under a mathematical lens, and demonstrates how real people are using mathematics in their jobs and lives." It includes medium-length, signed book reviews. Of the undergraduate journals listed in this section, *UMAP* is the one most focused on applied mathematics. The most recent issue's table of contents is available at www.comap.com/product/periodicals/index.html. This journal is recommended for academic libraries and may also be suitable for some high school and public libraries.

Research Journals

4416. *Acta Mathematica.* [ISSN: 0001-5962] 1882. q. 2 vols/yr. EUR 310 print & online eds. Ed(s): Uffe Haagerup. Springer Netherlands, Van Godewijckstraat 30, Dordrecht, 3311 GX, Netherlands; http://springerlink.com. Illus., index. Refereed. Vol. ends: No. 2. Reprint: PSC. *Indexed:* CCMJ, MSN, MathR, SCI. *Aud.:* Ac, Sa.

Acta Mathematica is an official journal of the Royal Swedish Academy of Sciences (see www.kva.se). The academy was founded in 1739 and was "modelled on the pattern of the Royal Society of London." *Acta Mathematica* is sometimes referred to as *Acta Mathematica-Djursholm,* after its city of publication, to distinguish it from other journals of the same title. It contains research papers in all fields of mathematics. Most of the papers are in English, but some are in French or German. Although more than 600 pages are published annually, there are only about 10–15 articles. These tend to be papers that are

highly cited and of lasting importance. There are no book reviews. As of January 2006, the journal became available online at www.springerlink.com/content/1871-2509. It is highly recommended for all academic libraries.

4417. *American Journal of Mathematics.* [ISSN: 0002-9327] 1878. bi-m. USD 340. Ed(s): Christopher Sogge. The Johns Hopkins University Press, 2715 N Charles St, Baltimore, MD 21218-4363; http://muse.jhu.edu. Illus., index, adv. Refereed. Circ: 1022 Paid. Vol. ends: No. 6. Microform: PMC; PQC. Online: EBSCO Publishing, EBSCO Host; Florida Center for Library Automation; Gale; JSTOR (Web-based Journal Archive); OCLC Online Computer Library Center, Inc.; OhioLINK; Project MUSE; ProQuest K-12 Learning Solutions; ProQuest LLC (Ann Arbor); SwetsWise Online Content. Reprint: PSC. *Indexed:* CCMJ, GSI, MSN, MathR, SCI, SSCI. *Aud.:* Ac, Sa.

The *American Journal of Mathematics,* published by Johns Hopkins University Press, is "the oldest mathematics journal in the Western Hemisphere in continuous publication . . . and ranks as one of the most respected and celebrated journals in the field." The journal "does not specialize, but instead publishes articles of broad appeal covering the major areas of contemporary mathematics." Each year, there are 40–50 articles totaling about 1,400 pages. There are no book reviews. The journal is available online through Project Muse, http://muse.jhu.edu/journals/american_journal_of_mathematics. Recommended for most research libraries.

4418. *American Mathematical Monthly.* [ISSN: 0002-9890] 1894. 10x/yr. USD 177. Ed(s): John H Ewing, Bruce Palka. Mathematical Association of America, 1529 18th St, NW, Washington, DC 20036; http://www.maa.org. Illus., index, adv. Refereed. Circ: 18000. Vol. ends: No. 10. Microform: PQC. Online: JSTOR (Web-based Journal Archive); Northern Light Technology, Inc.; OCLC Online Computer Library Center, Inc.; ProQuest K-12 Learning Solutions; ProQuest LLC (Ann Arbor). *Indexed:* CCMJ, GSI, IndIslam, MSN, MathR, SCI. *Bk. rev.:* 1-4, 1,200-2,000 words, signed. *Aud.:* Hs, Ga, Ac, Sa.

American Mathematical Monthly is a distinguished publication of the Mathematical Association of America (MAA) (www.maa.org). The MAA was founded in 1915 and is the "largest professional society that focuses on undergraduate mathematics education." The society publishes several other journals, some of which are included in this section. The *Monthly*'s articles "inform, stimulate, challenge, enlighten, and even entertain.... They may be expositions of old or new results, historical or biographical essays, speculations or definitive treatments, broad developments, or explorations of a single application. Novelty and generality are far less important than clarity of exposition and broad appeal." The *Monthly* is divided into four sections: "Articles," "Notes" (e.g., "The Right-Hand Derivative of an Integral"), "Problems and Solutions," and "Reviews." Other sections are occasionally added, for example, "Editor's Endnotes." There are a few lengthy, signed book reviews and sometimes a section called "Telegraphic Reviews." These are short and "designed to alert readers...to new books appropriate to mathematics teaching and research." The tables of contents and abstracts are available online at www.maa.org/pubs/monthly.html. The full text for volumes 1–110 are available electronically via JSTOR (www.jstor.org). The *Monthly* is a basic resource for academic libraries and may be of interest to some high school and public libraries.

4419. *American Mathematical Society. Bulletin. New Series.* Formerly (until 1979): *American Mathematical Society. Bulletin.* [ISSN: 0273-0979] 1894. q. Institutional members, USD 348; Individual members, USD 261; Non-members, USD 435. Ed(s): Susan Friedlander. American Mathematical Society, 201 Charles St, Providence, RI 02904-2294; ams@ams.org; http://www.ams.org. Refereed. Circ: 27000. Microform: PMC; PQC. Online: EBSCO Publishing, EBSCO Host; OCLC Online Computer Library Center, Inc.; SwetsWise Online Content; H.W. Wilson. *Indexed:* CCMJ, GSI, MSN, MathR, SCI, SSCI. *Bk. rev.:* 4-8, 3,000-5,000 words, signed. *Aud.:* Ac, Sa.

The *Bulletin* is the oldest and one of the most important publications of the American Mathematical Society (AMS) (www.ams.org). The AMS was founded in 1888 to "further the interests of mathematical research and scholarship" and is one of the most important mathematical societies in the world. It publishes and distributes a number of journals. Those with the broadest focus and most importance are included in this section, but see also www.ams.org/journals for more information. The *Bulletin* contains articles of two types: "papers that present a clear and insightful exposition of significant aspects of contemporary mathematical research...; and brief, timely reports on important mathematical developments." It also contains four to eight long, signed book reviews per issue (3,000–5,000 words). It is available electronically at www.ams.org/bull. This is a basic resource for academic libraries.

4420. American Mathematical Society. Journal. [ISSN: 0894-0347] 1988. 4x/yr. Institutional members, USD 238 print & online eds.; Individual members, USD 179 print & online eds.; Non-members, USD 298 print & online eds. Ed(s): John W Morgan, Weinan E. American Mathematical Society, 201 Charles St, Providence, RI 02904-2294; ams@ams.org; http://www.ams.org. Refereed. Circ: 1000. Online: EBSCO Publishing, EBSCO Host; JSTOR (Web-based Journal Archive); OCLC Online Computer Library Center, Inc.; SwetsWise Online Content. *Indexed:* CCMJ, GSI, MSN, MathR, SCI. *Aud.:* Ac, Sa.

The *Journal* is highly cited, even though it is one of the AMS's newest journals (see also *American Mathematical Society. Bulletin*). It is "devoted to research articles of the highest quality in all areas of pure and applied mathematics"—the AMS's most significant research articles. There are 25–30 articles per year, totaling about 1,000 pages, but no book reviews. It is available online at www.ams.org/jams. Volumes 1—14 are available electronically from JSTOR at www.jstor.org. Highly recommended for academic libraries that serve research mathematicians.

4421. American Mathematical Society. Memoirs. [ISSN: 0065-9266] 1950. bi-m. Institutional members, USD 540; Non-members, USD 675. Ed(s): Robert Guralnick. American Mathematical Society, 201 Charles St, Providence, RI 02904-2294; ams@ams.org; http://www.ams.org. Refereed. Circ: 1200. *Indexed:* CCMJ, MSN, MathR, SCI. *Aud.:* Ac, Sa.

Memoirs may be subscribed to as a journal, but it is more like a monographic series. There are six mailings per year, but each mailing contains more than one volume. "Memoirs is a series devoted to the publication of research in all areas of pure and applied mathematics. Manuscripts accepted for publication are similar to those published in *Transactions*.... Each issue contains either a single monograph or a group of related papers." There are about 30 articles published per year, totaling about 3,000 pages, and no book reviews. It is comparable to *Transactions* (see below in this section) in its importance. A list of volumes, with tables of contents and abstracts, is online at www.ams.org/bookstore/memoseries. Highly recommended for academic libraries serving research mathematicians.

4422. American Mathematical Society. Transactions. [ISSN: 0002-9947] 1900. m. Institutional members, USD 1451 print & onlne eds.; Non-members, USD 1814 print & online eds. Ed(s): Robert Guralnick. American Mathematical Society, 201 Charles St, Providence, RI 02904-2294; ams@ams.org; http://www.ams.org. Refereed. Circ: 1231 Paid. Microform: PMC; PQC. Online: EBSCO Publishing, EBSCO Host; JSTOR (Web-based Journal Archive); OCLC Online Computer Library Center, Inc.; SwetsWise Online Content. *Indexed:* CCMJ, MSN, MathR, SCI. *Aud.:* Ac, Sa.

Transactions is one of the oldest, most highly cited, and most important of AMS journals (see *American Mathematical Society. Bulletin.*). It is "devoted to research articles in all areas of pure and applied mathematics," and papers are longer than ten pages. There are roughly 250–300 articles per year in more than 5,000 pages. There are no book reviews. It is available online at www.ams.org/tran. Volumes 1–353 are available electronically from JSTOR at www.jstor.org. Although it is expensive, it is a good value and strongly recommended for academic libraries.

4423. Annals of Mathematics. Formerly (until 1884): *The Analyst*. [ISSN: 0003-486X] 1874. bi-m. USD 265. The Johns Hopkins University Press, 2715 N Charles St, Baltimore, MD 21218-4363; http://www.press.jhu.edu. Illus., index. Refereed. Circ: 1585. Vol. ends: No. 3. Microform: PMC; PQC. Online: EBSCO Publishing, EBSCO Host; JSTOR (Web-based Journal Archive). *Indexed:* CCMJ, MSN, MathR, SCI. *Aud.:* Ga, Ac, Sa.

The *Annals of Mathematics* (http://annals.princeton.edu) is one of the most highly respected mathematics journals. It is an inexpensive university press journal published with the cooperation of Princeton University and the Institute for Advanced Study (IAS) (www.ias.edu). The IAS was founded in 1930 and "over the past seventy-two years...has been home to some of the most highly regarded thinkers of the twentieth century," including Albert Einstein and Andrew Wiles. *Annals* publishes articles in all areas of mathematics research. Volumes 1–154 are available electronically from JSTOR (www.jstor.org). Volumes 148–present are available electronically from Project Euclid (http://projecteuclid.org), a Scholarly Publishing and Academic Resources Coalition (SPARC) Scientific Communities Partner. There are 35–45 articles published per year, totaling about 1,600 pages. There are no book reviews. Strongly recommended for all academic libraries.

Annals of Probability. See Statistics section.

Annals of Statistics. See Statistics section.

Applied Statistics. See *Royal Statistical Society. Journal. Series C. Applied Statistics* in the Statistics section.

4424. Cambridge Philosophical Society. Mathematical Proceedings. Formerly: *Cambridge Philosophical Society. Proceedings. Mathematical and Physical Sciences*. [ISSN: 0305-0041] 1843. bi-m. GBP 445. Ed(s): G P Paternain. Cambridge University Press, The Edinburgh Bldg, Shaftesbury Rd, Cambridge, CB2 2RU, United Kingdom; journals@cambridge.org; http://www.journals.cambridge.org. Illus., index, adv. Refereed. Vol. ends: No. 3. Microform: PMC; PQC. Online: Pub.; EBSCO Publishing, EBSCO Host; OCLC Online Computer Library Center, Inc.; OhioLINK; SwetsWise Online Content. *Indexed:* ApMecR, CCMJ, ChemAb, MSN, MathR, SCI. *Aud.:* Ac, Sa.

The *Mathematical Proceedings of the Cambridge Philosophical Society* is an important journal published by Cambridge University Press (compare it to *Annals of Mathematics* and *American Journal of Mathematics*). Begun in the mid-nineteenth century, it "covers the whole range of pure and applied mathematics, theoretical physics and statistics." There are 70–80 articles published each year in about 600 pages. There are no book reviews. It is available electronically at www.cambridge.org/uk/journals. Recommended for academic libraries.

4425. Canadian Journal of Mathematics. [ISSN: 0008-414X] 1945. bi-m. CND 696 combined subscription domestic print & online eds.; USD 696 combined subscription foreign print & online eds. Ed(s): Nassif Ghoussoub, James B Carrell. Canadian Mathematical Society, 577 King Edward, Ste 109, P O Box 450, Ottawa, ON K1N 6N5, Canada; publications@cms.math.ca; http://www.cms.math.ca. Illus., adv. Refereed. Circ: 1400. Vol. ends: No. 6. Microform: PQC. Online: EBSCO Publishing, EBSCO Host. *Indexed:* CCMJ, MSN, MathR, SCI. *Aud.:* Ac, Sa.

The *Canadian Journal of Mathematics* (*CJM*) is an official publication of the Canadian Mathematical Society (www.cms.math.ca). The society was founded in 1945 as the Canadian Mathematical Congress, and "the founding members hoped that this congress [would] be the beginning of important mathematical development in Canada." Longer articles are included in the *CJM,* and shorter articles are published in the *Canadian Mathematical Bulletin* (not listed in this section). To be included in the *CJM,* "papers must treat new mathematical research, be well written, and be of interest to a reasonable segment of the mathematical community." There are no book reviews. Papers are generally in English, but may also be in French. There are 40–50 articles per year for a total of about 1,400 pages. It is available electronically at http://journals.cms.math.ca/CJM. Recommended for most academic libraries.

4426. College Mathematics Journal. Formerly (until 1983): *Two-Year College Mathematics Journal*. [ISSN: 0746-8342] 1970. 5x/yr. USD 97. Ed(s): Bart Braden. Mathematical Association of America, 1529 18th St, NW, Washington, DC 20036; http://www.maa.org. Illus., index, adv. Refereed. Circ: 10000. Vol. ends: No. 5. Microform: PQC. Online:

JSTOR (Web-based Journal Archive); Northern Light Technology, Inc.; OCLC Online Computer Library Center, Inc.; ProQuest K-12 Learning Solutions; ProQuest LLC (Ann Arbor). *Indexed:* ABIn, CCMJ, EduInd, GSI, MSN, MathR. *Bk. rev.:* 15-20, 300-500 words, signed. *Aud.:* Hs, Ga, Ac, Sa.

The *College Mathematics Journal* is a publication of the MAA (see *American Mathematical Monthly*) and provides "articles that...enrich undergraduate instruction and enhance classroom learning." The articles cover a mix of mathematics education and pure, applied, and recreational mathematics (see also *Journal for Research in Mathematics Education*). There are 15–20 short- to medium-length, signed book reviews. Tables of contents and abstracts are available online at www.maa.org/pubs/cmj.html. Volumes 1–34 are available electronically from JSTOR (www.jstor.org). It is strongly recommended for academic libraries and may be suitable for some high school and public libraries.

4427. *Duke Mathematical Journal.* [ISSN: 0012-7094] 1935. 15x/yr. USD 1565 (Individuals, USD 800). Ed(s): Jonathan Wahl, Phillip A Griffiths. Duke University Press, 905 W Main St, Ste 18 B, Durham, NC 27701; subscriptions@dukeupress.edu; http://www.dukeupress.edu. Illus., index, adv. Refereed. Circ: 915 Paid. Vol. ends: No. 3. Microform: MIM; PQC. Online: EBSCO Publishing, EBSCO Host. Reprint: PSC. *Indexed:* CCMJ, MSN, MathR, SCI. *Aud.:* Ac, Sa.

The *Duke Mathematical Journal* (*DMJ*) is one of the more important university press journals (compare it to *Annals of Mathematics* and *American Journal of Mathematics*). Unfortunately, it is also one of the journals most like the largest commercial publishers in terms of its price. *DMJ* focuses on pure mathematics and publishes 90–100 articles per year in about 2,500 pages. There are no book reviews. Volumes 1–present are available electronically from Project Euclid (http://projecteuclid.org). Highly recommended for academic libraries.

4428. *Historia Mathematica.* [ISSN: 0315-0860] 1974. 4x/yr. EUR 439. Ed(s): C. Fraser, U. Bottazzini. Academic Press, 525 B St, Ste 1900, San Diego, CA 92101-4495; apsubs@acad.com; http://www.elsevier.com/. Illus., adv. Refereed. Online: EBSCO Publishing, EBSCO Host; Gale; IngentaConnect; OCLC Online Computer Library Center, Inc.; OhioLINK; ScienceDirect; SwetsWise Online Content. *Indexed:* AmH&L, ArtHuCI, CCMJ, HistAb, IBZ, IndIslam, MSN, MathR, SCI, SSCI. *Bk. rev.:* 1-2, 1,000-1,500 words, signed; 1-2, 500-600 words, signed; 18-22 pages of 50- to 100-word abstracts. *Aud.:* Ga, Ac, Sa.

Historia Mathematica is the most important journal covering the history and sometimes the philosophy of mathematics. It is an official publication of the International Commission for the History of Mathematics (www.unizar.es/ichm). It "publishes historical scholarship on mathematics and its development in all cultures and time periods," and while most of the articles are in English, some are in French or German. Besides research articles, each issue includes one or two lengthy, signed book reviews and many pages of abstracts for recent publications. These reviews and abstracts try to cover everything published about the history of mathematics. Each year, there are about 15 research articles in the 500 pages published. Tables of contents and most of the full text is available online at www.sciencedirect.com/science/journal/03150860. It is highly recommended for academic libraries and may be suitable for public libraries with strong science collections.

4429. *I M A Journal of Applied Mathematics.* Supersedes in part (in 1981): *Institute of Mathematics and Its Applications. Journal.* [ISSN: 0272-4960] 1981. bi-m. EUR 731. Ed(s): David J. Needham, Yibin Fu. Oxford University Press, Great Clarendon St, Oxford, OX2 6DP, United Kingdom; jnl.orders@oup.co.uk; http://www.oxfordjournals.org. Illus., adv. Sample. Refereed. Circ: 580. Vol. ends: No. 6. Online: EBSCO Publishing, EBSCO Host; Gale; HighWire Press; IngentaConnect; OCLC Online Computer Library Center, Inc.; OhioLINK; Oxford Journals; ProQuest LLC (Ann Arbor); SwetsWise Online Content. Reprint: PSC. *Indexed:* ApMecR, C&ISA, CCMJ, ChemAb, EngInd, ExcerpMed, IAA, MSN, MathR, SCI. *Aud.:* Ac, Sa.

The *IMA Journal of Applied Mathematics* is published for the Institute of Mathematics and its Applications (IMA) (www.ima.org.uk). The IMA was founded in the United Kingdom in 1964 and is "the professional and learned society for qualified and practising mathematicians. Its mission is to promote

mathematics in industry, business, the public sector, education and research." The IMA publishes five other journals, including the highly cited (but more specialized) *IMA Journal of Numerical Analysis* (not listed in this section). The *IMA Journal of Applied Mathematics* concentrates on "all areas of the application of mathematics. It also seeks to publish papers on new developments of existing mathematical methods.... Longer papers that survey recent progress in topical fields of mathematics and its applications are also published." There are about 30 articles per year in 600 pages, but there are no book reviews. It is available electronically at http://imamat.oxfordjournals.org. Recommended for academic libraries.

4430. *Indiana University Mathematics Journal.* Former titles (until 1970): *Journal of Mathematics and Mechanics;* (until 1956): *Journal of Rational Mechanics and Mathematics.* [ISSN: 0022-2518] 1952. 6x/yr. USD 320 (Individuals, USD 100). Ed(s): Peter Sternberg. Indiana University, Department of Mathematics, 831 East Third St, Indiana University, Bloomington, IN 47405-7106. Illus., index. Refereed. Circ: 675 Paid. Online: EBSCO Publishing, EBSCO Host. *Indexed:* CCMJ, IAA, MSN, MathR, SCI. *Aud.:* Ac, Sa.

The *Indiana University Mathematics Journal* is an important university press journal (compare *Annals of Mathematics* and *American Journal of Mathematics*). It focuses on "significant research articles in both pure and applied mathematics" even though its former title suggests a more applied emphasis. Each year, there are about 40–50 articles in about 2,000 pages. There are no book reviews. Volumes 1–present are available online at www.iumj.indiana.edu/IUMJ. Recommended for academic libraries.

4431. *Institut des Hautes Etudes Scientifiques, Paris. Publications Mathematiques.* [ISSN: 0073-8301] 1959. s-a. EUR 425 print & online eds. Ed(s): E Ghys. Springer, Tiergartenstr 17, Heidelberg, 69121, Germany. Illus., adv. Sample. Refereed. *Indexed:* CCMJ, MSN, MathR, SCI. *Aud.:* Ac, Sa.

Publications Mathematiques de l'IHES is one of the most important European mathematics journals. Many articles are published in English, the rest in French or German. It is sponsored by the Institut des Hautes Etudes Scientifiques in France (www.ihes.fr), "an institute of advanced research in mathematics and theoretical physics with an interest in epistemology and the history of science." The IHES was founded in 1958 and is the European counterpart of the Institute for Advanced Study (see *Annals of Mathematics*). *Publications Mathematiques* is simply described as "an international journal publishing papers of the highest scientific level." There are about ten articles per year totaling about 500 pages, but no book reviews. Current issues are available electronically at www.springerlink.com/content/1618-1913. Older volumes are freely available online from NUMDAM (www.numdam.org/?lang=en), a program instituted on behalf of the French National Center for Scientific Research (CNRS), which "addresses the retro-digitization of mathematics documents published in France." Strongly recommended for most academic libraries.

4432. *Inventiones Mathematicae.* [ISSN: 0020-9910] 1966. m. EUR 2778 print & online eds. Ed(s): G Faltings, J-M Bismut. Springer, Tiergartenstr 17, Heidelberg, 69121, Germany. Illus., adv. Sample. Refereed. Vol. ends: No. 3. Microform: PQC. Online: EBSCO Publishing, EBSCO Host; OhioLINK; Springer LINK; SwetsWise Online Content. Reprint: PSC. *Indexed:* CCMJ, MSN, MathR, SCI. *Aud.:* Ac, Sa.

Inventiones Mathematicae was founded in 1966 by Springer-Verlag and is one of the most prestigious journals for pure mathematics. Its purpose is modestly stated: "to bring out new contributions to mathematics." Some of the articles are in German or French. It publishes about 75–80 articles per year in 2,100 pages. There are no book reviews. It is available electronically at www.springerlink.com/content/1432-1297. Volumes from 1966 to 1996 are freely available online from the EMANI Project (Electronic Mathematics Archives Network Initiative; http://dz1.gdz-cms.de). Though it is the most expensive journal in this section, Springer has kept price increases at a modest level. Strongly recommended for most academic libraries.

4433. *Journal for Research in Mathematics Education.* [ISSN: 0021-8251] 1970. 5x/yr. Institutional members, USD 156; Individual members, USD 100. Ed(s): Edward T Silver, Sandy Berger. National Council of Teachers of Mathematics, 1906 Association Dr, Reston, VA

20191-1502; nctm@nctm.org; http://www.nctm.org. Illus., index, adv. Refereed. Circ: 7000 Paid. Vol. ends: Jul. Microform: PQC. Online: EBSCO Publishing, EBSCO Host; JSTOR (Web-based Journal Archive); Northern Light Technology, Inc.; OCLC Online Computer Library Center, Inc.; ProQuest LLC (Ann Arbor); H.W. Wilson. *Indexed:* ABIn, EduInd, PsycInfo, SSCI. *Bk. rev.:* 3-5, 500-1,000 words, signed. *Aud.:* Ga, Ac, Sa.

The *Journal for Research in Mathematics Education* is an official journal of the NCTM (see *Mathematics Teacher*). It is "devoted to the interests of teachers of mathematics and mathematics education at all levels—preschool through adult. It is a forum for disciplined inquiry into the teaching and learning of mathematics." It includes articles, brief reports, and commentaries on research, and a few lengthy, signed book reviews (see also *College Mathematics Journal* and *American Mathematical Monthly*). It is available electronically at http://my.nctm.org/eresources/journal_home.asp?journal_id=1. It is recommended for academic libraries and may be of interest to some high school and public libraries.

4434. Journal fuer die Reine und Angewandte Mathematik: Crelle's journal. [ISSN: 0075-4102] 1826. m. EUR 2400; EUR 2600 combined subscription print & online eds.; EUR 216 newsstand/cover. Ed(s): Rainer Weissauer, Yuri I Manin. Walter de Gruyter GmbH & Co. KG, Genthiner Str 13, Berlin, 10785, Germany; wdg-info@degruyter.de; http://www.degruyter.de. Adv. Refereed. Circ: 800 Paid and controlled. Microform: PMC; PQC. Online: EBSCO Publishing, EBSCO Host; OCLC Online Computer Library Center, Inc.; SwetsWise Online Content. Reprint: PSC. *Indexed:* CCMJ, MSN, MathR, SCI. *Aud.:* Ac, Sa.

The *Journal fuer die reine und angewandte Mathematik* is a distinguished European journal, the oldest mathematics journal still in publication. It was founded in 1826 by August Leopold Crelle and has come to be known as *Crelle's Journal*. Many articles are in English, the remainder in German or French. As its name indicates, it publishes significant articles in both pure and applied mathematics. There are about 90–100 articles per year in some 3,000 pages. Current volumes are available electronically at www.degruyter.de/rs/278_3127_ENU_h.htm. Because of its price, it is not the best value, but it is still worth considering for many academic libraries.

Journal of Symbolic Logic. See Philosophy section.

4435. London Mathematical Society. Proceedings. [ISSN: 0024-6115] 1865. bi-m. EUR 881. Ed(s): Dr. Constatin Teleman, Burt Totaro. Oxford University Press, Great Clarendon St, Oxford, OX2 6DP, United Kingdom; enquiry@oup.co.uk; http://www.oxfordjournals.org. Illus., index, adv. Refereed. Circ: 1400. Vol. ends: No. 3. Microform: PMC; PQC. Online: Cambridge University Press; EBSCO Publishing, EBSCO Host; OCLC Online Computer Library Center, Inc.; OhioLINK; SwetsWise Online Content. *Indexed:* ApMecR, CCMJ, MSN, MathR, SCI. *Aud.:* Ac, Sa.

The *Proceedings* is the flagship publication of the London Mathematical Society (LMS) (www.lms.ac.uk). The LMS was founded in 1865 and is the major British learned society for mathematics. The *Proceedings* covers a broad spectrum of advanced mathematics, including some applied areas. There are no book reviews. It is available online at http://plms.oxfordjournals.org and is recommended for most academic libraries. The LMS publishes other journals, including the *Bulletin of the LMS* ([ISSN: 0024-6093] 1969. 6/yr. $475) and the *Journal of the LMS* ([ISSN: 0024-6107] 1926. 6/yr. $1,048).

4436. The Mathematical Intelligencer. [ISSN: 0343-6993] 1978. q. EUR 96 print & online eds. Ed(s): Chandler Davis. Springer New York LLC, 233 Spring St, New York, NY 10013-1578; journals@springer-ny.com; http://www.springer.com/. Illus., index, adv. Refereed. Vol. ends: No. 4. Microform: PQC. Online: EBSCO Publishing, EBSCO Host. Reprint: PSC. *Indexed:* CCMJ, GSI, MASUSE, MSN, MathR, SCI, SSCI. *Bk. rev.:* 2-5, 1,000-2,000 words, signed. *Aud.:* Hs, Ga, Ac, Sa.

The Mathematical Intelligencer is what mathematicians read for enjoyment. It "publishes articles about mathematics, about mathematicians, and about the history and culture of mathematics. Articles...inform and entertain a broad audience of mathematicians, including many mathematicians who are not

specialists in the subject of the article. Articles might discuss a current fad or a past trend, theorems or people, history or philosophy, applications or theory." Articles are written in a casual style, often with humor or controversy, and there are a number of pictures and graphics. There are a few medium-length to long, signed book reviews. Neither the full text nor tables of contents are available electronically. Because it avoids specialization, it is recommended as a basic resource for every college or academic library that serves mathematicians. Some public and high school libraries may also find it of interest.

4437. S I A M Journal on Applied Mathematics. Formerly (until 1965): *Society for Industrial and Applied Mathematics. Journal.* [ISSN: 0036-1399] 1953. bi-m. USD 498 print & online eds. (Individuals, USD 96 print & online eds.). Ed(s): Li Pamela Cook. Society for Industrial and Applied Mathematics, 3600 University City Science Center, Philadelphia, PA 19104-2688; siam@siam.org; http://www.siam.org. Adv. Refereed. Circ: 2164. Online: EBSCO Publishing, EBSCO Host; JSTOR (Web-based Journal Archive); SwetsWise Online Content. *Indexed:* AS&TI, ApMecR, CCMJ, ChemAb, CompR, EngInd, IAA, MSN, MathR, SCI. *Aud.:* Ac, Sa.

The *SIAM Journal on Applied Mathematics* was the first journal published by the Society for Industrial and Applied Mathematics (SIAM) (www.siam.org). SIAM was founded in the 1950s, and its goal is "to ensure the strongest interactions between mathematics and other scientific and technological communities." The *Journal* "publishes research articles that treat scientific problems using methods that are of mathematical interest. Appropriate subject areas include the physical, engineering, financial, and life sciences." It includes 80–120 articles in 2,200 pages. There are no book reviews. It is available online at http://epubs.siam.org/SIAP/siap_toc.html. Volumes from 1953 to 2002 are available via JSTOR at www.jstor.org. Strongly recommended for most academic libraries.

4438. S I A M Review. [ISSN: 0036-1445] 1959. q. USD 282. Ed(s): Margaret H Wright. Society for Industrial and Applied Mathematics, 3600 University City Science Center, Philadelphia, PA 19104-2688; http://www.epubs.siam.org. Illus., index, adv. Refereed. Circ: 10223. Vol. ends: No. 4. Online: EBSCO Publishing, EBSCO Host; JSTOR (Web-based Journal Archive); SwetsWise Online Content. *Indexed:* ABIn, AS&TI, ApMecR, BRI, C&ISA, CBRI, CCMJ, CompLI, CompR, EngInd, MSN, MathR, SCI, SSCI. *Bk. rev.:* 10-25, 300-1,500 words, signed. *Aud.:* Ga, Ac, Sa.

The *SIAM Review* is an official publication of the Society for Industrial and Applied Mathematics (SIAM) (www.siam.org). In addition to the *SIAM Review* and the *SIAM Journal on Applied Mathematics* (see in this section), SIAM publishes 11 other journals (see http://epubs.siam.org). Many of these are the most important journals in their fields. Each issue of the *Review* has five sections: "Survey and Review," "Problems and Techniques," "SIGEST," "Education," and "Book Reviews." The Survey and Review section "features papers with a deliberately integrative and up-to-date perspective on a major topic in applied or computational mathematics or scientific computing." Problems and Techniques "contains focused, specialized papers...informing readers about interesting problems, techniques and tools." SIGEST includes "digested versions of selected papers from SIAM's [other] journals." The Education section "contains articles for students, not faculty, that might be interesting enough to include in courses, but are not typically in textbooks." The Book Reviews section contains a featured review or two and a number of other medium-length, signed reviews. This journal is available electronically at http://epubs.siam.org/SIREV/sirev_toc.html. Back volumes are available from JSTOR at www.jstor.org. The *Review* is a basic resource for academic libraries and should also be considered for some public and high school libraries.

4439. Studies in Applied Mathematics (Malden). Formerly (until 1968): *Journal of Mathematics and Physics.* [ISSN: 0022-2526] 1922. 8x/yr. GBP 905 print & online eds. Ed(s): David Benney. Blackwell Publishing, Inc., Commerce Place, 350 Main St, Malden, MA 02148; customerservices@blackwellpublishing.com; http://www.blackwellpublishing.com. Illus., adv. Refereed. Vol. ends: No. 3. Microform: PQC. Online: Blackwell Synergy; EBSCO Publishing,

EBSCO Host; Gale; IngentaConnect; OCLC Online Computer Library Center, Inc.; OhioLINK; SwetsWise Online Content. Reprint: PSC. *Indexed:* ABIn, ApMecR, CCMJ, MSN, MathR, SCI. *Aud.:* Ac, Sa.

Studies in Applied Mathematics is an important university journal published for the Massachusetts Institute of Technology (compare *Annals of Mathematics* and *American Journal of Mathematics*). It "reports research results involving the core concepts of applied mathematics research.... The domain...is the interplay between mathematics and applied disciplines." There are about 30–35 articles published each year in roughly 800–900 pages. There are no book reviews. It is available online at www.blackwellpublishing.com/journal.asp?ref=0022-2526. Recommended for academic libraries.

■ MEDIA AND AV

See also Communication; Education; Films; and Television, Video, and Radio sections.

Xiaochang Yu, Systems Librarian, VCU Libraries, Virginia Commonwealth University, Richmond, VA 23284-2033; FAX: 804-828-0151; xyu@vcu.edu

Introduction

Most magazines listed in this section are research-oriented journals whose primary audiences are professors and researchers in educational and instructional technology. Many essays in these journals discuss theoretical and methodological issues in the field. Others are popular magazines intended mainly for media specialists and other practitioners in schools, colleges, and business and industry sectors. Many articles in these popular magazines offer hands-on descriptions of applying technology to media services and provide critical evaluations of new technology and products. All of the titles in this section have some web presence.

Like many other fields, audiovisual and media technology have become increasingly computer integrated and web integrated. Computer-assisted animation, multimedia presentation, web video technology, mobile technology, etc., are widely discussed topics in the field these days. Therefore, readers may also consult computer-related sections in this volume as well as sections referred to in cross-references in this section.

Basic Periodicals

Educational Technology Research and Development, Innovations in Education and Teaching International, International Journal of Instructional Media, Presentations, TechTrends.

Basic Abstracts and Indexes

Current Index to Journals in Education, Education Index, ERIC.

4440. *British Journal of Educational Technology.* Formerly: *Journal of Eductional Technology.* [ISSN: 0007-1013] 1970. bi-m. GBP 523 print & online eds. Ed(s): Nick Rushby. Blackwell Publishing Ltd., 9600 Garsington Rd, Oxford, OX4 2ZG, United Kingdom; customerservices@ blackwellpublishing.com; http://www.blackwellpublishing.com. Illus., index, adv. Refereed. Circ: 1200. Vol. ends: Sep. Microform: PQC. Online: Blackwell Synergy; EBSCO Publishing, EBSCO Host; Gale; IngentaConnect; OCLC Online Computer Library Center, Inc.; OhioLINK; SwetsWise Online Content; H.W. Wilson. Reprint: PSC. *Indexed:* ABIn, ApEcolAb, BrEdI, CompLI, EAA, ERIC, EduInd, EngInd, ErgAb, FR, IBR, IBZ, L&LBA, PsycInfo, SSCI. *Bk. rev.:* 10, 150-500 words. *Aud.:* Ac.

This journal addresses theory, development, and applications of technologies in education, training, and communications with such specific topics as computer-assisted instruction, information technology for people with special needs, and the design and production of educational materials. Each issue contains articles, colloquium reports, and reviews. Articles are refereed and tend to be analytical

and research oriented. Colloquium reports have a conversational style and may include sections such as short think-pieces, reactions to previous contributions, and so forth. The journal has more book reviews than any other magazine covered in this section.

Educational and Training Technology International. See *Innovations in Education and Training International.*

4441. *Educational Media International.* Former titles (until 1986): *Educational Media International;* (until 1971): *Audio-Visual Media.* [ISSN: 0952-3987] 1961. q. GBP 289 print & online eds. Ed(s): John Hedberg. Routledge, 4 Park Square, Milton Park, Abingdon, OX14 4RN, United Kingdom; http://www.routledge.co.uk. Illus., adv. Refereed. Circ: 500. Microform: PQC. Online: EBSCO Publishing, EBSCO Host; Gale; IngentaConnect; OCLC Online Computer Library Center, Inc.; SwetsWise Online Content. Reprint: PSC. *Indexed:* ABIn, BrEdI, CommAb, ERIC, EduInd, ExcerpMed, FLI, SWA. *Bk. rev.:* 2-3, 500 words. *Aud.:* Ac.

This journal focuses on innovations in educational technology. A typical issue begins with an editorial that summarizes 7–12 short articles included in the issue. Each article begins with abstracts in three languages: English, French, and Dutch. Articles are easy to read. Some of them are basically empirical studies reporting practices in specific regions or countries. Because *Educational Media International* is the official journal of the International Council for Educational Media, whose membership list consists of 27 countries, both its authors and audience are worldwide. Also covered are association activities. The journal provides a valuable forum for the exchange of ideas and experiences among media professionals in different countries.

Educational Technology. See Education/Specific Subjects and Teaching Methods: Technology section.

Educational Technology Research & Development. See Education/ Specific Subjects and Teaching Methods: Technology section.

4442. *Electronic Journal of E-Learning.* [ISSN: 1479-4403] 2003. s-a. Free. Management Centre International Ltd., Curtis Farm, Kidmore End, Near Reading, RG4 9AY, United Kingdom; submissions@ejel.org; http://www.ejel.org. *Bk. rev.:* Number and length vary. *Aud.:* Ac.

This electronic journal includes research papers, case studies, conference reports, and book reviews relevant to the study, implementation, and management of e-learning initiatives. E-learning can be defined as learning through electronic applications and processes, such as Internet-based learning, computer-based learning, virtual classrooms, and digital collaboration. The journal is currently published semiannually with a general issue and a special issue. The general issue contains papers submitted in response to a call for papers, and the special issue contains papers selected from its sister conference, the European Conference on e-Learning. The contributors are mostly college professors in European countries. This is a very decent publication covering the new developments in e-learning, an increasingly important area of education. URL: www.ejel.org.

4443. *Innovations in Education and Teaching International (Print Edition).* Former titles (until 2000): *Innovations in Education and Training International (Print Edition);* (until 1995): *Educational and Training Technology International;* (until 1989): *Programmed Learning and Educational Technology; Programmed Learning.* [ISSN: 1470-3297] 1964. q. GBP 300 print & online eds. Ed(s): Philip Barker, Gina Wisker. Routledge, 4 Park Sq, Milton Park, Abingdon, OX14 4RN, United Kingdom; info@routledge.co.uk; http://www.routledge.co.uk. Illus., adv. Refereed. Circ: 1200. Vol. ends: Nov. Microform: PQC. Online: EBSCO Publishing, EBSCO Host; Gale; IngentaConnect; OCLC Online Computer Library Center, Inc.; ProQuest LLC (Ann Arbor); SwetsWise Online Content. Reprint: PSC. *Indexed:* AgeL, BrEdI, EAA, ERIC, FR, IBR, IBZ, PsycInfo, SSCI. *Bk. rev.:* 2-4, 750-1,000 words. *Aud.:* Ac.

This quarterly publication of the Staff and Educational Development Association covers various topics in education and training. Its scope is much broader than that of most other journals listed in this section. Besides instructional technology, the journal also covers such topics as the self-evident nature of teaching, online professional development for academic staff, and motivation theories. The types of publications include papers, case studies, and opinions. Papers are well researched and case studies are focused. The contributors are educators from all over the world. This journal takes a more theoretical approach than *Educational Media International,* another publication from Routledge (above in this section). Recommended for academic libraries.

4444. *Instructional Science: an international journal of learning and cognition.* [ISSN: 0020-4277] 1971. bi-m. EUR 629 print & online eds. Ed(s): Patricia A Alexander, Peter Goodyear. Springer Netherlands, Van Godewijckstraat 30, Dordrecht, 3311 GX, Netherlands; http://www.springeronline.com. Illus., index, adv. Sample. Refereed. Vol. ends: Nov. Microform: PQC. Online: EBSCO Publishing, EBSCO Host; Gale; IngentaConnect; OCLC Online Computer Library Center, Inc.; OhioLINK; Ovid Technologies, Inc.; Springer LINK; SwetsWise Online Content. Reprint: PSC. *Indexed:* ABIn, BrEdI, CommAb, CompR, EAA, ERIC, EduInd, HEA, IBR, IBSS, IBZ, L&LBA, PsycInfo, SSCI. *Bk. rev.:* 2-3, length varies. *Aud.:* Ac.

A typical issue of this scholarly journal consists of two to four in-depth articles. Although many articles deal with instructional technology, the journal covers a wide range of disciplines in education. The focus is on promoting a deeper understanding of the nature and theory of the teaching and learning process. Thus, the approach is highly academic. Recent topics include educational use of communication technologies, networked learning, and artificial intelligence in education. Articles are written by experts worldwide, and many articles require some background knowledge.

4445. *International Journal of Instructional Media.* [ISSN: 0092-1815] 1973. q. USD 186 domestic; USD 196 foreign. Ed(s): Phillip J Sleeman. Westwood Press, Inc., 116 E 16th St, New York, NY 10003-2112. Illus., index. Refereed. Circ: 500. Vol. ends: No. 4. *Indexed:* ABIn, CompLI, ERIC, EduInd, IBR, IBZ, RILM. *Bk. rev.:* 2-3, 2-21 pages. *Aud.:* Ac.

This journal contains original articles concerning rising issues in instructional media in particular and educational technology in general. Areas of research include computer technology, telecommunications, distance-teaching technology, instructional media and technology, interactive video, software applications, and instructional-media management. Articles are well researched, and most of them take conceptual approaches to the process of applying instructional technology to teaching and learning. Also discussed are advantages and disadvantages of various applications of educational techniques. Recommended for academic libraries.

4446. *Journal of Educational Multimedia and Hypermedia.* [ISSN: 1055-8896] 1992. q. USD 165 (Members, USD 55; USD 40 student members). Ed(s): Gary H Marks. Association for the Advancement of Computing in Education, PO Box 1545, Chesapeake, VA 23327-1545; info@aace.org; http://www.aace.org. Adv. Refereed. Online: EBSCO Publishing, EBSCO Host; Florida Center for Library Automation; Gale; OCLC Online Computer Library Center, Inc.; ProQuest LLC (Ann Arbor); H.W. Wilson. *Indexed:* ABIn, CommAb, CompLI, CompR, EAA, ERIC, EduInd, ErgAb, LISA, MicrocompInd, PsycInfo, SWA. *Aud.:* Ac.

JEMH is published by Association for the Advancement of Computing in Education (AACE). It is designed to provide a multidisciplinary forum to present and discuss research, development, and applications of multimedia and hypermedia in teaching and learning. Recent articles include topics such as mobile technology in education and people's emotional responses to computers. The online version of the journal is searchable as part of the AACE Digital Library. JEMH is one of few journals that is fully devoted to educational multimedia and hypermedia.

4447. *Journal of Educational Technology Systems.* Formerly: *Journal of Educational Instrumentation.* [ISSN: 0047-2395] 1972. q. USD 324. Ed(s): David C Miller. Baywood Publishing Co., Inc., 26 Austin Ave, PO Box 337, Amityville, NY 11701-0337; info@baywood.com; http://www.baywood.com. Illus., index, adv. Sample. Refereed. *Indexed:* ABIn, C&ISA, CerAb, CompLI, EAA, ERIC, EduInd, IAA, IBR, IBZ, ISTA, L&LBA, MicrocompInd, RiskAb. *Aud.:* Ac.

Journal of Educational Technology Systems is the official publication of the Society for Applied Learning Technology. It "deals with systems in which technology and education interface and is designed to inform educators who are interested in making optimum use of technology." Most of the articles are focused on education-related computer technology and its impacts on teaching and learning. Each issue starts with an editorial overview that summarizes all the articles in the issue. Articles are generally research oriented and accompanied by abstracts. Most of the pieces are by college professors. It is an established, peer-reviewed publication and belongs in libraries that offer resources on educational technology.

4448. *Media & Methods: educational products, technologies & programs for schools & universities.* Formerly (until 1969): *Educators Guide to Media and Methods.* [ISSN: 0025-6897] 1964. 5x/yr. USD 35 domestic; USD 51.50 foreign. Ed(s): Christine Weiser. American Society of Educators, 1429 Walnut St, Philadelphia, PA 19102; michelesok@aol.com; http://www.media-methods.com. Illus., index, adv. Circ: 14659 Controlled. Vol. ends: May/Jun. Microform: PQC. Online: EBSCO Publishing, EBSCO Host; OCLC Online Computer Library Center, Inc.; ProQuest LLC (Ann Arbor); H.W. Wilson. *Indexed:* ABIn, ConsI, ERIC, EduInd, FLI, ISTA, MRD, MicrocompInd. *Bk. rev.:* 4-5, 150-200 words. *Aud.:* Ems, Hs, Ac.

Each issue has feature articles and departments. Articles are easy to read and provide hands-on experiences to meet the practical needs of media specialists and school librarians. Because media and school library services have become increasingly computer dependent, it is not surprising that many articles deal with computer-related technologies. Readers will also find valuable information on selection and evaluation of various media products, including laptops, digital cameras, DVD players, multimedia projectors, multimedia TV, and visual presenters.

4449. *Media History Monographs.* 1997. q. Free. Ed(s): Patrick S Washburn, David Copeland. Ohio University, E. W. Scripps School of Journalism, Athens, OH 45701-2979; http://www.scripps.ohiou.edu. Refereed. *Indexed:* AmH&L, HistAb. *Aud.:* Ac.

Too long for most journals, but too short for most books. Faced with this dilemma, the editors of the monographs have decided to publish such scholarship in journal form online. The subject is journalism and mass communications, primarily concerning history with some attention to ongoing activities.

4450. *Presentations: technology and techniques for effective communication.* Former titles (until 1993): *Presentation Products;* (until 1992): *Presentation Products Magazine.* [ISSN: 1072-7531] 1988. m. USD 69 domestic (Free to qualified personnel). Ed(s): Tad Simons, Julie Hill. Nielsen Business Publications, 50 S Ninth St, Minneapolis, MN 55402; bmcomm@vnuinc.com; http://www.nielsenbusinessmedia.com. Illus., adv. Circ: 75000 Controlled. Vol. ends: Dec. Microform: PQC. Online: EBSCO Publishing, EBSCO Host; Gale; Northern Light Technology, Inc.; OCLC Online Computer Library Center, Inc.; ProQuest LLC (Ann Arbor). *Indexed:* ABIn, C&ISA, CerAb, IAA, ISTA, MicrocompInd. *Aud.:* Ac, Sa.

This illustrated publication contains updated information on presentation products, which range from overhead projectors to multimedia notebooks to computer-graphics creation tools. Articles are most valuable for audiovisual and media professionals seeking advice and tips about selecting and using new presentation equipment. Among the useful special features is the annual "Buyers Guide to Presentation Products," which appears in the December issue. Recommended for libraries with strong media departments.

4451. *Public Broadcasting Report: the authoritative news service for public broadcasting and allied fields.* Incorporates (1967-1997): *E T V Newsletter (Educational Television).* [ISSN: 0193-3663] 1978. bi-w. USD 680. Ed(s): Michael Feazel. Warren Communications News, Inc., 2115 Ward Ct, NW, Washington, DC 20037; info@warren-news.com; http://www.warren-news.com. Illus., index. Sample. Vol. ends: Dec. Online: Gale; LexisNexis; Northern Light Technology, Inc.; ProQuest K-12 Learning Solutions. *Aud.:* Sa.

Public Broadcasting Report covers a broader range of areas than its predecessor, *ETV Newsletter.* This newsletter provides timely news on happenings in the public-broadcasting business, which includes PBS, NPR, CPB, ETV, and ITV. Many of the reports can be called inside stories, for example, reports on government policy issues in public broadcasting. Coverage also includes educational training programs, awards, grants, and personnel issues. The publication has earned its reputation of providing authoritative news on public broadcasting. However, the price for this biweekly newsletter may intimidate some potential subscribers.

School Library Media Research. See Library and Information Science section.

4452. *Studio/Monthly: shoot post deliver.* Formerly (until 2005): *A V Video & Multimedia Producer;* Which was formed by the merger of (1995-1996): *Multimedia Producer;* (1978-1996): *A V Video;* Which incorporated (19??-1990): *Video Management;* Which was formerly (until 1989): *Video Manager;* (until 1984): *Video User;* (until 1980): *V U Marketplace;* A V Video was formerly (until 1984): *Audio Visual Directions;* (until 1980): *Audio Visual Product News.* [ISSN: 1554-3412] 1996. m. USD 89 (Free to qualified personnel). Ed(s): Beth Marchant, Linda Romanello. Access Intelligence, LLC, 4 Choke Cherry Rd, 2nd Fl, Rockville, MD 20850; clientservices@accessintel.com; http://www.accessintel.com. Illus., adv. Circ: 80000 Paid and controlled. Vol. ends: Dec. Online: Gale. *Aud.:* Ac, Sa.

In late 1996, *AV Video* and *Multimedia Producer* were combined into *AV Video & Multimedia Producer.* The combination reflects the fact that audiovisual services and multimedia services have become increasingly integrated. Since 2000, the magazine has focused more on the producer side of multimedia products. The publication continues to feature significant changes in audiovisual and multimedia production and presentation technology. Each issue has two major parts: feature articles and departments. Feature articles offer in-depth coverage of new technologies and stories of applying technology in media services. Departments provide easily located information on a variety of interesting topics. In its "Test Patterns" section, for instance, hands-on reviews of new technology and products are offered. The publication includes extensive advertising and a valuable advertisers' index.

4453. *TechTrends: for leaders in education and training.* Former titles (until 1985): *Instructional Innovator; Audiovisual Instruction with Instructional Resources; Audiovisual Instruction.* [ISSN: 8756-3894] 1956. bi-m. EUR 88 print & online eds. Ed(s): Sharon Smaldino. Springer New York LLC, 233 Spring St, New York, NY 10013-1578; service-ny@springer.com; http://www.springer.com/. Illus., index, adv. Circ: 6400 Paid and free. Vol. ends: Nov. Reprint: PSC. *Indexed:* ABIn, ERIC, EduInd, FLI, ISTA, MRD, MicrocompInd. *Aud.:* Ems, Hs, Ac.

This peer-reviewed magazine is the official publication of the Association for Educational Communications and Technology. It provides school media specialists and other educators a forum for exchanging personal experiences of applying technology in education and training. Emphasis is on new and practical ideas and firsthand experience. Articles have a conversational style and are easy to follow. Regular columns and departments are of popular interest. Recommended.

■ MEDICINE

See also Family Planning; Health and Fitness; Health Care Administration; Health Professions; Nursing; and Public Health sections.

Stephanie N. Aude (SNA), Oliver Wendell Holmes Library, Phillips Academy, Andover, MA 01810; saude@andover.edu

Sara Ciaburri (SLC), Oliver Wendell Holmes Library, Phillips Academy, Andover, MA 01810; sciaburri@andover.edu

Introduction

Improved health is the goal of nearly all medical research, whether done by patients, caregivers, physicians, or scholars. Indeed, medical questions continue to be among the most common reference questions at public libraries, and medical searches are thought to be among the most popular web searches. The vast proliferation of medical information on the Internet has arguably sent researchers of all skill levels in two directions: back to more online content and on to both new and venerable print publications. In other words, even in the fast-paced medical research world, print is very much alive and well. The goal of this section is to highlight useful and accessible medical publications and to advance health care overall.

This section evaluates selected medical periodicals that appeal to a variety of health practitioners, scholars as well as the general public. Most print publications reviewed here also have some level of online content. Free content frequently includes an index or table of contents and selected full text from recent issues. Most titles make full text available to print subscribers.

At this time, nearly 5,000 medical journals are indexed in Medline, the National Library of Medicine (NLM) bibliographic database covering the fields of medicine, nursing, dentistry, veterinary medicine, the health care system, and the preclinical sciences. Abstracts and indexes are freely available on the NLM web site. Full text of Medline content is available through the NLM's document delivery service as well as several online content vendors such as EBSCO, Ovid, and ScienceDirect.

Basic Periodicals

JAMA: The Journal of the American Medical Association, Journal of Immunology, The Lancet, National Medical Association Journal, The New England Journal of Medicine.

Basic Abstracts and Indexes

Cumulative Index to Nursing and Allied Health Literature, MEDLINE.

4454. *AIDS Patient Care and S T Ds.* Formerly (until 1996): *AIDS Patient Care.* [ISSN: 1087-2914] 1987. m. USD 628. Ed(s): Jeffrey Laurence. Mary Ann Liebert, Inc. Publishers, 140 Huguenot St, 3rd Fl, New Rochelle, NY 10801-5215; info@liebertpub.com; http://www.liebertpub.com. Illus., adv. Sample. Refereed. Vol. ends: Dec. Online: EBSCO Publishing, EBSCO Host; Gale; OCLC Online Computer Library Center, Inc.; Ovid Technologies, Inc.; SwetsWise Online Content. Reprint: PSC. *Indexed:* CINAHL, ExcerpMed, H&SSA, PsycInfo, RiskAb, SCI, SSCI. *Aud.:* Ga, Ac, Sa.

AIDS Patient Care and STDs is a monthly, peer-reviewed scholarly journal that focuses on the latest developments in AIDS research, patient care, complications, and medications. The approximately eight articles in each issue discuss topics including HIV testing, beliefs among those with the HIV virus, and patient symptoms and treatments. While the intended audience for this journal is health care professionals, it is not extremely technical and would be appropriate for hospital libraries that serve both doctors and patients. www.liebertpub.com/publication.aspx?pub_id=1 (SLC)

Alternative Medicine Magazine. See Health and Fitness section.

4455. *American Journal of Health Behavior.* Formerly (until 1996): *Health Values.* [ISSN: 1087-3244] 1977. bi-m. USD 167 (Individuals, USD 90). Ed(s): Elbert D Glover. P N G Publications, PO Box 4593, Star City, WV 26504-4593; pglover@wvu.edu; http://www.ajhb.org.

Illus., index, adv. Refereed. Circ: 2000 Paid. Microform: PQC. Online: EBSCO Publishing, EBSCO Host; ProQuest K-12 Learning Solutions; ProQuest LLC (Ann Arbor); SwetsWise Online Content. *Indexed:* ASSIA, AgeL, CABA, CINAHL, CJA, DSA, EAA, ERIC, PEI, PsycInfo, RRTA, RiskAb, S&F, SFSA, SSA, SSCI, SWA, SociolAb, V&AA. *Aud.:* Ac, Sa.

The American Journal of Health Behavior (www.ajhb.org) is the official publication of the American Academy of Health Behavior. Focusing on "the impact of personal attributes, personality characteristics, behavior patterns, social structure, and processes on health maintenance, health restoration, and health improvement," this journal discusses patient behavior with regard to the diseases, disorders, and other health-related issues that they suffer. Topics include but are not limited to HIV/AIDS, smoking, childhood obesity, and reproductive health. This is a peer-reviewed, scholarly journal that would be appropriate in any hospital or medical school library. (SLC)

4456. *Arthritis Practitioner.* [ISSN: 1557-2544] 2005. bi-m. Free. Ed(s): Jeff Hall. H M P Communications, LLC, 83 General Warren Blvd, Ste 100, Malvern, PA 19355-1245; http://www.hmpcommunications.com. Adv. *Aud.:* Ac, Sa.

Arthritis Practitioner is a bimonthly publication aimed at nurse practitioners and physician assistants, focusing on the broad area of arthritis and musculoskeletal conditions. New developments in treatment, diagnosis, and medication are discussed. The section titled "Diagnostic Dilemmas" attempts to help nurse practitioners properly diagnose what seem to be common ailments but are actually more complicated conditions. An index to advertisers is also included. This publication is recommended for any library with a consumer health focus. www.arthritispractitioner.com (SLC)

Autism Spectrum Quarterly. See Disabilities section.

4457. *B E T A.* [ISSN: 1058-708X] 1989. s-a. Free. Ed(s): Reilly O'Neal. San Francisco AIDS Foundation, PO Box 426182, San Francisco, CA 94142-6182; http://www.sfaf.org. *Aud.:* Ac, Sa.

BETA is a free quarterly publication on the topic of HIV/AIDS treatment and research advances. Published by the San Francisco AIDS Foundation, this publication includes contributions from scientists, health practitioners, and AIDS activists. Regular features include "News Briefs," "Open Clinical Trials," and "Women and HIV." Both Spanish and English editions are available. A full pdf version of *BETA* is available at www.sfaf.org/beta. This accessible periodical is highly recommended for public, academic, and hospital libraries. (SNA)

4458. *Bulletin of the History of Medicine.* [ISSN: 0007-5140] 1933. q. USD 150. Ed(s): Randall M Packard, Mary E Fissell. The Johns Hopkins University Press, 2715 N Charles St, Baltimore, MD 21218-4363; http://www.press.jhu.edu. Illus., adv. Refereed. Circ: 1910 Paid. Microform: PMC; PQC. Online: Chadwyck-Healey Inc.; EBSCO Publishing, EBSCO Host; OCLC Online Computer Library Center, Inc.; OhioLINK; Project MUSE; ProQuest LLC (Ann Arbor); SwetsWise Online Content. Reprint: PSC. *Indexed:* ABS&EES, AmH&L, ArtHuCI, BAS, BiolAb, BrArAb, CABA, ChemAb, ExcerpMed, FR, GSI, HistAb, IBR, IBZ, IndIslam, NumL, SCI, SSA, SSCI. *Bk. rev.:* Number and length vary. *Aud.:* Ga, Ac.

The American Association for the History of Medicine and the Johns Hopkins Institute of the History of Medicine produce this hefty quarterly journal. The social, cultural, and scientific aspects of the history of medicine are addressed in such articles as "The Making of the Truth Serum," "Personalizing Illness and Modernity," and "The Retreat of Plague from Central Europe 1640–1720: A Geomedical Approach." This journal appeals to historians, medical professionals, and archivists in the history of health sciences and is a very appropriate choice for academic libraries. Book reviews are regularly featured. Abstracts and tables of content may be accessed free of charge from the journal's JSTOR web site. (SNA)

4459. *Caring (Washington).* Supersedes: *Home Health Review.* [ISSN: 0738-467X] 1982. m. USD 120 (Individuals, USD 49). Ed(s): Val Halamandaris. National Association for Home Care, 228 Seventh St, S E, Washington, DC 20003-4306; pubs@nahc.org; http://www.nahc.org. Illus., index, adv. Sample. Circ: 5927. Vol. ends: Dec. *Indexed:* ASG, AgeL, CINAHL. *Aud.:* Ac, Sa.

Caring (www.caringmagazine.com) is a monthly publication from the National Association for Homecare and Hospice. Each issue revolves around a specific theme and includes approximately ten feature articles on that topic. Recent issues focus on "Hospice and Home Care in Rural Areas" and "Legal Issues in Hospice and Home Care." Information about the industry, marketing, and leadership is also included. *Caring* has a wide audience including patients, caregivers, and physicians. It is recommended for hospital libraries. (SLC)

4460. *Chronic Illness.* [ISSN: 1742-3953] 2005. q. GBP 293. Ed(s): Christopher Dowrick. Sage Publications Ltd., 1 Oliver's Yard, 55 City Rd, London, EC1 1SP, United Kingdom; info@sagepub.co.uk; http://www.sagepub.co.uk. *Indexed:* CINAHL, ExcerpMed, PsycInfo. *Aud.:* Ac, Sa.

Chronic Illness is a new scholarly journal that aims to inform medical professionals and patients of the latest research, practices, and policies in treating all forms of chronic illness. Each issue contains news and viewpoints, a critical essay, commentaries, research papers, and a short report on illnesses such as asthma, HIV/AIDS, sickle cell disease, and heart disease. The focus of the articles is on patients with chronic illness and how it is managed. This journal is recommended for hospital or medical school libraries. www.maney.co.uk/search?fwaction=show&fwid=425 (SLC)

4461. *Coping with Cancer.* Formerly: *Coping.* [ISSN: 1544-5488] 1986. bi-m. USD 19 domestic; USD 25 foreign. Ed(s): Laura Shipp, Kay Thomas. Media America, Inc., PO Box 682268, Franklin, TN 37068-2268; copingmag@aol.com; http://www.copingmag.com. Illus., adv. Sample. Circ: 90000 Paid and controlled. Vol. ends: Dec. *Aud.:* Ga, Sa.

This cheerful, glossy consumer magazine aims to motivate cancer patients and their loved ones to live well. Personal survival stories including celebrity profiles are some of the main features of this publication. Readers will not find alarming statistical reports, eulogies, or stories of grief. Rather, the magazine presents a very strong editorial focus on the human capacity to respond to cancer with a high degree of self-efficacy. Regular departments include inspirational poems, cancer research news, and support network information. The magazine's web site, www.copingmag.com, does not offer content, only subscription information. An excellent choice for public libraries. (SNA)

4462. *Diabetes Care.* [ISSN: 0149-5992] 1978. m. USD 700 (Individuals, USD 350). Ed(s): Mayer B Davidson, Aime M Ballard. American Diabetes Association, 1701 N Beauregard St, Alexandria, VA 22311-1717; customerservice@diabetes.org; http://www.diabetes.org. Illus., adv. Refereed. Circ: 13000 Paid. CD-ROM: Ovid Technologies, Inc. Microform: PQC. Online: EBSCO Publishing, EBSCO Host; Florida Center for Library Automation; Gale; HighWire Press; Northern Light Technology, Inc.; Ovid Technologies, Inc.; ProQuest K-12 Learning Solutions; ProQuest LLC (Ann Arbor). *Indexed:* Agr, CABA, CINAHL, ChemAb, DSA, ExcerpMed, HortAb, RRTA, SCI, SSCI. *Aud.:* Ga, Ac, Sa.

Diabetes Care, published by the American Diabetes Association, is geared toward an audience of health care professionals who focus on diabetes treatment and care. Each monthly issue is comprised of mainly original research in such topics as Clinical Care/Education/Nutrition, Epidemiology/Health Services/Psychosocial Research, Emerging Treatments and Technologies, Pathophysiology/Complications, and Cardiovascular and Metabolic Risk. Brief reports, letters, and reviews are also included. The full text and abstracts of each article from 2001–2006 is available on the journal's web site (http://care.diabetesjournals.org). (SLC)

4463. *Diabetes Forecast: the healthy living magazine of the American Diabetes Association for more than 50 years.* Formerly: *A.D.A. Forecast.* [ISSN: 0095-8301] 1948. m. Membership, USD 28. Ed(s):

Andrew Keegan. American Diabetes Association, 1701 N Beauregard St, Alexandria, VA 22311-1717; customerservice@diabetes.org; http://www.diabetes.org. Illus. Sample. Circ: 360000 Paid. Vol. ends: Dec. Online: Florida Center for Library Automation; Gale; Northern Light Technology, Inc.; OCLC Online Computer Library Center, Inc.; ProQuest K-12 Learning Solutions; ProQuest LLC (Ann Arbor). *Indexed:* Agr, CINAHL. *Aud.:* Hs, Ga, Ac, Sa.

Diabetes Forecast, published by the American Diabetes Association since 1948, is a colorful, patient-focused publication that aims to give advice to those who suffer with type I and type II diabetes. Letters from readers, articles on current research, recipe suggestions, and a shopper's guide to diabetes supplies are included. A section titled "Making Friends" allows patients to tell their personal stories and include contact information so that they can meet people in their area who also suffer from the disease. American Diabetes Association contacts are also included. This magazine is highly recommended for any library that focuses on consumer health and patient care. www.diabetes.org/diabetes-forecast.jsp (SLC)

4464. *Diabetes Self-Management.* [ISSN: 0741-6253] 1983. bi-m. USD 18. Ed(s): James Hazlett. R.A. Rapaport Publishing, Inc., 150 W 22nd St, New York, NY 10011; staff@rapaportpublishing.com. Illus., adv. Sample. Circ: 470000 Paid. Vol. ends: Nov/Dec. *Indexed:* CINAHL. *Aud.:* Hs, Ga, Sa.

Because there are over 20 million American diabetics, this colorful bimonthly magazine will have wide appeal for most public libraries and some academic libraries. The cheerful and accessible editorial tone (headlines include "Take a Bite out of Hypoglycemia" and "Three Clucks for Poultry") does not undermine the importance of the diabetes research news and self-help information that are the focus of the magazine. Regular sections include "Diabetes Definitions," a brief tutorial on core knowledge, and "Diabetes Resources," a column spotlighting new devices and methods for managing the disease. This magazine does not publish personal stories. (SNA)

4465. *Epilepsy U S A.* Formerly (until 1991): *National Spokesman.* [ISSN: 1060-9369] 1972. 8x/yr. USD 25. Ed(s): Karina Barrentine. Epilepsy Foundation of America, 8301 Professional Pl, Landover, MD 20785; postmaster@efa.org; http://www.epilepsyfoundation.org/. Illus. Sample. Circ: 23000. Vol. ends: Dec. *Aud.:* Ga, Sa.

This friendly, inspirational magazine presents a contemporary medical, biographical, and policy portrait of epilepsy, a neurological disorder that affects 2.7 million Americans of all ages. News briefs, a regular feature, include research and funding news as well as mentions of outstanding personal achievement. Epilepsy drugs and adaptive merchandise such as headgear are frequently spotlighted. Although this publication does not include advertising, it regularly features information funded by pharmaceutical companies. Full-text articles are available free on the web site (www.epilepsyfoundation.org/epilepsyusa). A good selection for public libraries. (SNA)

4466. *Families of Loved Ones.* [ISSN: 1559-9981] 2005. q. USD 12. Ed(s): Rene Cantwell. Cantwell Media, LLC, 310 Grant Ave, Dumont, NJ 07628; http://www.cantwellmedia.com. Adv. *Aud.:* Ga, Sa.

This slim and accessible quarterly magazine explains caregiving options and resources for a variety of settings and patient abilities. Although this new publication seems to focus on specific services in the New Jersey area, it is well written and presents issues that are pertinent to anyone caring for and making decisions for an incapacitated loved one. Feature topics have included health care proxies, choosing nursing homes, hospice care, and adult day care. Most content is written by clinicians from the allied health professions. Inspirational mini-articles such as "Ten Things Every Caregiver Should Know" and "Lessons in Grace" represent contributions from caregivers themselves. This upbeat magazine, appropriate for public libraries, serves as a community in print for an often overworked and isolated audience in need of practical health and legal information. (SNA)

4467. *Gender Medicine.* [ISSN: 1550-8579] 2004. 4x/yr. USD 209. Ed(s): Cindy H Jablonowski, Marianne J Legato. Excerpta Medica, Inc., 685 Rte 202/206, Bridgewater, NJ 08807; http://www.excerptamedica.com/. Refereed. *Indexed:* ExcerpMed. *Aud.:* Ac, Sa.

Gender Medicine is a peer-reviewed quarterly that covers a wide range of issues in patient care, focusing on the differences between the sexes with regard to diagnosis and treatment. Each issue includes a review article, an editorial on a hot issue in gender medicine, and two or three original research articles. A selection of the broad topics covered includes cardiovascular disease, menopause, and sex differences in viral infection. This title is highly recommended for hospital or medical school libraries. The web site (www.gendermedjournal.com) includes an archive of issues from 2004–2005 with electronic versions of some articles available at no charge. (SLC)

4468. *Grapevine (New York): the international monthly journal of Alcoholics Anonymous.* [ISSN: 0362-2584] 1944. m. USD 15 domestic; USD 23 foreign. Ed(s): Ames Sweet. Alcoholics Anonymous Grapevine, Inc., PO Box 1980, New York, NY 10163-1980; gveditorial@aagrapevine.org; http://www.aagrapevine/@org. *Aud.:* Sa.

Written, edited, and illustrated by Alcoholics Anonymous members and affiliates, *AA Grapevine* aims to put alcoholics in touch with one another. Known as "a meeting in print," this is a no-nonsense, black-and-white, digest-style publication with a broad acceptance of individual approaches to the program. Addiction humor (the regular "Ham on Wry" page—personal maxims and jokes) and personal addiction and recovery stories make up the content of the journal. AA conferences and retreats are listed in a regular events calendar. Downloadable audio editions and pdf versions of *AA Grapevine* are available via the Alcoholics Anonymous web site (www.alcoholics-anonymous.org). (SNA)

Harvard Men's Health Watch. See Health and Fitness section.

4469. *Health Care for Women International.* Formerly (until 1983): *Issues in Health Care of Women.* [ISSN: 0739-9332] 1979. 10x/yr. GBP 503 print & online eds. Ed(s): Dr. Eleanor Krassen Covan. Taylor & Francis Inc., 325 Chestnut St, Ste 800, Philadelphia, PA 19016; orders@taylorandfrancis.com; http://www.taylorandfrancis.com. Illus., index, adv. Sample. Refereed. Circ: 400. Vol. ends: Nov/Dec (No. 6). Online: EBSCO Publishing, EBSCO Host; Gale; IngentaConnect; OCLC Online Computer Library Center, Inc.; SwetsWise Online Content. Reprint: PSC. *Indexed:* CINAHL, CJA, FemPer, GSI, IBSS, PsycInfo, SFSA, SSA, SWA, SociolAb. *Bk. rev.:* 0-1, length varies, signed. *Aud.:* Ac, Sa.

Produced by the International Council on Women's Health Issues, this peer-reviewed journal should have wide appeal for academic libraries serving a range of social and natural science disciplines. Recent issues focus on women and cancer and factors affecting women in middle age. An e-mail contents alert service is available on the publisher's web site, as are the table of contents from recent issues. Refereed articles assess socio-economics, biology, politics, and spirituality as they are inextricably linked to women's health. A new feature in this journal is a discussion and letters section inviting readers to comment on papers. (SNA)

4470. *J A M A: The Journal of the American Medical Association.* Former titles (until 1960): *American Medical Association. Journal;* Which superseded (1848-1882): *American Medical Association. Transactions.* [ISSN: 0098-7484] 1883. w. 48/yr. USD 555 print & online eds. Ed(s): Dr. Catherine D DeAngelis. American Medical Association, 515 N State St, Chicago, IL 60610-0946; http://www.ama-assn.org. Illus., index, adv. Sample. Refereed. Circ: 332337 Paid. Vol. ends: Jun/Dec. Microform: PMC; PQC. Online: The Dialog Corporation; EBSCO Publishing, EBSCO Host; Florida Center for Library Automation; Gale; HighWire Press; Ovid Technologies, Inc.; ProQuest K-12 Learning Solutions. *Indexed:* ABS&EES, AbAn, AgeL, Agr, BiolAb, BiolDig, CABA, CINAHL, CJA, DSA, EnvAb, ExcerpMed, FS&TA, GSI, H&SSA, HortAb, IndIslam, IndVet, LRI, MLA-IB, PEI, PRA, PsycInfo, RILM, RRTA, RiskAb, S&F, SCI, SUSA, SWA, V&AA, VB, WAE&RSA. *Bk. rev.:* Number and length vary. *Aud.:* Ac, Sa.

A weekly, international, peer-reviewed publication, *JAMA* is one of the most highly esteemed and cited medical journals in existence. The content reflects a very broad picture of modern medicine including original contributions about disease prevention, research advances, and medical ethics. Book and media reviews are included in each issue as are editorials and continuing medical education information. Dedicated to exploring "the art and science" of medicine, *JAMA* includes a humanities department each week exploring medical history, poetry and medicine, and the journal's cover art. Full-text online content is provided free of charge to institutions in developing countries. The web site, www.jama.com, provides selected free content and full text to subscribers. Bonus audio content summarizing the weekly issues is available free of charge. This journal belongs in all academic and medical libraries and large public libraries. (SNA)

4471. Journal of Immunology. Former titles (until 1950): *Journal of Immunology, Virus-Research & Experimental Chemotherapy;* (until 1943): *Journal of Immunology.* [ISSN: 0022-1767] 1916. 2x/m. USD 700 (Individuals, USD 355). Ed(s): Dr. Robert Rich, M. Michele Hogan. American Association of Immunologists, 9650 Rockville Pike, Bethesda, MD 20814; infoji@faseb.org; http://www.jimmunol.org. Illus., index, adv. Refereed. Circ: 9500 Paid. Microform: PQC. Online: EBSCO Publishing, EBSCO Host; HighWire Press. *Indexed:* B&AI, BiolAb, CABA, ChemAb, DSA, ExcerpMed, FPA, ForAb, HortAb, IAA, IndVet, SCI, VB. *Aud.:* Ac, Sa.

Journal of Immunology, the most-cited journal in the subject area, is peer-reviewed and published twice a month by the American Association of Immunologists. Each issue contains approximately 65 articles detailing current research on all areas of immunology. Broad topics include Cellular Immunology and Immune Regulation, Molecular and Structural Immunology, and Immunogenetics. The section titled "Cutting Edge" focuses on the more experimental research being done in the field. Full text of the articles in each issue from 1998 to the present can be downloaded in pdf format from the journal's web site (www.jimmunol.org). (SLC)

4472. The Lancet (North American Edition). [ISSN: 0099-5355] 1966. 52x/yr. USD 969. Ed(s): Stephanie Clark, Dr. Richard Horton. The Lancet Publishing Group, 84 Theobald's Rd, London, WC1X 8RR, United Kingdom; http://www.thelancet.com. Illus., index, adv. Sample. Refereed. Circ: 18000. Vol. ends: Jun/Dec. Microform: PQC. Online: EBSCO Publishing, EBSCO Host; Florida Center for Library Automation; Gale; LexisNexis; OCLC Online Computer Library Center, Inc.; ProQuest LLC (Ann Arbor). *Indexed:* AgeL, Agr, BiolDig, CINAHL, DSA, GSI, H&SSA, IndIslam, IndVet, LRI, RILM, RiskAb, WRCInf. *Bk. rev.:* Number and length vary. *Aud.:* Ga, Ac, Sa.

Founded in 1823, this prestigious international medical journal is not affiliated with any medical or scientific institutions. *The Lancet* aims to impact global medicine with its weekly presentation of peer-reviewed medical research articles, compelling exchanges (the "Comment and Correspondence" section), and its respected editorial opinions. *The Lancet* is an essential purchase for academic libraries as scholars and news media alike frequently cite its content. The web site (www.thelancet.com) contains audio content. (SNA)

4473. Mamm: women, cancer and community. [ISSN: 1099-5633] 1997. 10x/yr. USD 19.95. Ed(s): Gwen Darien. MAMM LLC, 54 W 22nd St, 4th Flr, New York, NY 10010; elsieh@mamm.com. Adv. *Indexed:* CINAHL, FemPer. *Bk. rev.:* 1-2, 250 words. *Aud.:* Ga, Sa.

Medical and lifestyle decisions for women with breast and gynecologic cancers are the focus of this accessible, upbeat, and glossy color publication. Articles cover a broad range of issues from intercourse after mastectomy to current clinical trials. Cancer patients and survivors regularly contribute stories detailing how cancer touches not just health but careers, families, and sexuality. Research updates and new drug information make up the core content of every issue. A humorous "Cancer Girl" column pokes fun at the rigidly clinical directives women often receive from the medical establishment. The web site, www.mamm.com, provides selected full-text access to current and back issues. (SNA)

4474. Medical Care Research and Review. Former titles (until Mar. 1995): *Medical Care Review; Public Health Economics and Medical Care Abstracts.* [ISSN: 1077-5587] 1944. bi-m. GBP 482. Ed(s): Jeffrey Alexander. Sage Publications, Inc., 2455 Teller Rd, Thousand Oaks, CA 91320; info@sagepub.com; http://www.sagepub.com. Illus., adv. Sample. Refereed. Circ: 185 Paid. Vol. ends: Dec. Microform: PQC. Online: CSA; EBSCO Publishing, EBSCO Host; HighWire Press; OCLC Online

Computer Library Center, Inc.; SAGE Publications, Inc., SAGE Journals Online; SwetsWise Online Content. Reprint: PSC. *Indexed:* ASG, ASSIA, AgeL, CINAHL, ExcerpMed, HRA, MCR, PAIS, PsycInfo, SCI, SSCI, V&AA. *Bk. rev.:* 2-3, 200-300 words. *Aud.:* Ac, Sa.

Current multidisciplinary health services research is the focus of this peer-reviewed bimonthly. Medical policy, management, and practice findings are covered from fields including finance, social work, statistics, and organizational behavior. This publication regularly offers literature reviews, empirical research, and what are called "data and trends" articles. Timely topics such as Medicaid reimbursement and doctor's perceptions of managed care are samples of the research topics in the journal. An annual print index is found at the end of each volume, and the publisher's web site (http://mcr.sagepub.com) offers a database indexing issues back to 1999. Academic and special libraries serving researchers and professionals in business, the natural sciences, and the social sciences will want to add this broadly focused journal to their collections. (SNA)

4475. National Medical Association. Journal. [ISSN: 0027-9684] 1908. m. USD 205 (Individuals, USD 120; USD 20 newsstand/cover). Ed(s): Eddie Hoover. National Medical Association, 1012 Tenth St, NW, Washington, DC 20001; ktaylor@nmanet.org; http://www.nmanet.org. Illus., index, adv. Sample. Refereed. Circ: 40000 Paid and controlled. Vol. ends: Dec. Online: EBSCO Publishing, EBSCO Host; ProQuest K-12 Learning Solutions; ProQuest LLC (Ann Arbor). *Indexed:* AgeL, BiolAb, CABA, CJA, ChemAb, DSA, ExcerpMed, H&SSA, MCR, PsycInfo, RRTA, SCI, WAE&RSA. *Aud.:* Ac, Sa.

This venerable scholarly journal presents a very broad spectrum of medicine. Published monthly, it reports original, empirical research findings in all areas of traditional medical practice, public health, and relevant basic science. Regular sections include book and movie reviews and "Health Tidbits," a newsy page with updates on research, study funding, and public policy. Selected full text is available for free at the journal's web site, www.nmanet.org. A must for large academic libraries and medical libraries of all types. (SNA)

4476. New England Journal of Medicine. Formerly (until 1928): *Boston Medical and Surgical Journal.* [ISSN: 0028-4793] 1812. w. USD 209 print & online eds. (Individuals, USD 149 print & online eds.). Ed(s): Dr. Jeffrey M Drazen. Massachusetts Medical Society, 860 Winter St, Waltham, MA 02451-1411; http://www.massmed.org. Illus., index, adv. Sample. Refereed. Circ: 231126 Paid. Vol. ends: Jun/Dec. CD-ROM: Ovid Technologies, Inc. Microform: PMC; PQC. Online: EBSCO Publishing, EBSCO Host; HighWire Press; Ovid Technologies, Inc.; ProQuest LLC (Ann Arbor). *Indexed:* ASG, AbAn, AgeL, Agr, BiolAb, BiolDig, CABA, CINAHL, CJA, ChemAb, DSA, EnvAb, EnvInd, ExcerpMed, FS&TA, FutSurv, GSI, H&SSA, HortAb, IndVet, LRI, MCR, PsycInfo, RILM, RRTA, RiskAb, S&F, SCI, SSCI, SWR&A, V&AA, VB, WAE&RSA. *Bk. rev.:* Number and length vary. *Aud.:* Ac, Sa.

The *New England Journal of Medicine* has published original medical research, case studies, and review articles since 1812. This esteemed journal is one of the most cited of any scientific or medical periodical. The journal's web site (www.nejm.org) features free access to the full text of its content six months after publication. Other features of the web site include downloadable podcasts summarizing the print editions and interviews with leading physicians and researchers. This core medical journal belongs in academic libraries, large public libraries, and appropriate special research settings such as hospital libraries. (SNA)

4477. Obesity Management. [ISSN: 1545-1712] 2004. bi-m. USD 264. Ed(s): Dr. James O Hill. Mary Ann Liebert, Inc. Publishers, 2 Madison Ave, Larchmont, NY 10538; info@liebertpub.com; http://www.liebertpub.com. Refereed. *Indexed:* ExcerpMed. *Bk. rev.:* Number and length vary. *Aud.:* Ga, Ac, Sa.

Obesity Management is a bimonthly, peer-reviewed publication focusing on obesity treatment, the care of obese patients, and health risks associated with obesity. The majority of the articles included in each issue are geared toward physicians, however many articles would be of great interest to patients, too. Each issue features an editorial from an expert physician, articles detailing strategies for managing obesity, book reviews, and a section titled "Web Watch," which reviews five to eight free web resources related to obesity and other ailments that are common among obese people. www.liebertpub.com/publication.aspx?pub_id=123 (SLC)

4478. Quest (Tucson). Former titles (until 1994): *M D A Reports;* (until 1992): *M D A Newsmagazine; M D A News - Muscular Dystrophy Association; Muscular Dystrophy News.* [ISSN: 1087-1578] 1950. bi-m. USD 22 (Individuals, USD 14; Free to qualified personnel). Ed(s): Carol Sowell. Muscular Dystrophy Association, Inc., 3300 E Sunrise Dr, Tucson, AZ 85718-3299; http://www.mdausa.org. Illus., adv. Sample. Circ: 115000 Paid and controlled. Vol. ends: Fall. *Bk. rev.:* 1-2, 150 words. *Aud.:* Ga, Sa.

Quest, the bimonthly trade publication of the Muscular Dystrophy Association (MDA), is distributed to all individuals and institutions affiliated with the association. The six feature articles in each issue focus on patient concerns, new trends in treatments, and how to cope with muscular dystrophy. The section called "MDA Matters" lists MDA events and announcements, and a "Pen Pals" section is included to help patients connect with one another. Numerous advertisements for products related to the treatment of muscular dystrophy are prevalent throughout each issue. This title is recommended for hospital libraries or public libraries with a focus on consumer health information. www.mdausa.org/publications/Quest/q-curr.cfm (SLC)

4479. The Spine Journal. [ISSN: 1529-9430] 2001. 6x/yr. USD 295. Ed(s): Charles L Branch, Jr. Elsevier BV, Radarweg 29, Amsterdam, 1043 NX, Netherlands; nlinfo-f@elsevier.nl; http://www.elsevier.nl. Adv. Circ: 3401. Online: EBSCO Publishing, EBSCO Host; Gale; IngentaConnect; OhioLINK; ScienceDirect; SwetsWise Online Content. *Indexed:* ExcerpMed. *Aud.:* Ac, Sa.

This multidisciplinary, peer-reviewed journal is an illustrated, black-and-white bimonthly presenting original research and clinical cases on spine conditions and treatment. It is the official publication of the North American Spine Society, whose mission is to advance spine care through education, research, and advocacy. Technical notes, editorials, and special features are regular departments in this journal. Full text is available free to society members on the web site (www.spine.org/tsj.cfm). This publication is appropriate for academic, medical, and hospital libraries. (SNA)

4480. Take Charge (Email Edition). Former titles: *Take Charge (Print Edition);* (until 2006): *Foundation Focus.* 1977. 3x/yr. Free. Crohn's & Colitis Foundation of America, Inc., 386 Park Ave S, 17th Fl, New York, NY 10016-8804; info@ccfa.org; http://www.ccfa.org. Adv. Circ: 65000. *Aud.:* Sa.

Formerly called *Foundation Focus*, *Take Charge* discusses the two main forms of irritable bowel syndrome (IBS)—Crohn's disease and colitis. The articles focus on maintenance of IBS and current therapies and treatments. Features include interviews with diagnosed celebrities and discussions about drug therapies and diet suggestions. Books that focus on IBD are reviewed and advice from doctors and nutritionists is also included. This magazine is geared toward IBD patients and their families and is highly recommended for hospital libraries or public libraries that provide consumer health information. www.ccfa.org/myccfa/takecharge (SLC)

■ MENOPAUSE/ANDROPAUSE

Miriam Leigh, Staff Assistant, Widener Library, Harvard University, Cambridge, MA 02138

Introduction

In recent years, the human aging process, particularly menopause and andropause (a drop in testosterone in older men), has become the subject of intense study, due in part to the aging baby boomer population. They and subsequent generations have grown up in a time where physical decline ceased to be inevitable, and their desire to maintain their health as they age has driven both a highly lucrative consumer industry and a fast-moving research industry.

In addition to information geared toward the lay consumer available in the popular media, the volume of material generated by and for the medical community on the topics of menopause and andropause has increased in the last 15 years, from just one periodical prior to 1991 to six today. The publications listed in this section are scholarly journals, primarily directed toward researchers and physicians, and all are published under the purview of medical societies.

Basic Periodicals

Ac, Sa: *Maturitas, Menopause Management.*

Basic Abstracts and Indexes

EMBASE/Excerpta Medica, Index Medicus/MEDLINE, Science Citation Index, Current Contents/Clinical Medicine, SciSearch.

The Aging Male. See Geriatrics and Gerontological Studies section.

4481. Climacteric. [ISSN: 1369-7137] 1998. bi-m. GBP 232 print & online eds. Ed(s): David W Sturdee, Alastair H MacLennan. Informa Healthcare, Mortimer House, 37-41 Mortimer St, London, W1T 3JM, United Kingdom; healthcare.enquiries@informa.com; http://www.tandf.co.uk/journals/. Illus., index, adv. Refereed. Circ: 800 Paid. Vol. ends: Dec (No. 4). Online: EBSCO Publishing, EBSCO Host; Gale; IngentaConnect; OCLC Online Computer Library Center, Inc.; ProQuest LLC (Ann Arbor); SwetsWise Online Content. Reprint: PSC. *Indexed:* ExcerpMed, SCI. *Aud.:* Ac, Sa.

Climacteric is published six times annually as the mouthpiece of the International Menopause Society. It offers literature reviews, editorials, letters to the editor, and Society meeting details, in addition to peer-reviewed research articles. Although it claims to report on "all aspects of aging in men and women," *Climacteric*'s articles appear to focus exclusively on women's health concerns. The content covers "underlying endocrinological changes, treatment of the symptoms of the menopause and other age-related changes, hormone replacement therapies, alternative therapies, effective life-style modifications, non-hormonal midlife changes, and the counselling and education of perimenopausal and postmenopausal patients." Its articles are largely technical in nature, though there are many that would also appeal to practicing physicians. Recommended for academic and medical libraries.

4482. Maturitas. Incorporates (1994-1998): *European Menopause Journal.* [ISSN: 0378-5122] 1978. 12x/yr. EUR 1401. Ed(s): P. Kenemans, J. H.H. Thijssen. Elsevier Ireland Ltd, Elsevier House, Brookvale Plaza, E. Park, Shannon, Ireland. Refereed. Microform: PQC. Online: EBSCO Publishing, EBSCO Host; Gale; IngentaConnect; OhioLINK; ScienceDirect; SwetsWise Online Content. *Indexed:* ASG, BiolAb, CABA, ChemAb, DSA, ExcerpMed, HortAb, IndVet, PsycInfo, RRTA, SCI, SSCI, VB. *Bk. rev.:* Number and length vary. *Aud.:* Ac, Sa.

Maturitas, a peer-reviewed monthly journal, is published as the official journal of the European Menopause and Andropause Society. As such, it does not merely focus on midlife changes for women, but rather "the medical, sociological and psychological aspects of life in the middle years and beyond" for both men and women. It is international in scope, and comprises primarily original research articles, although it does also feature book reviews and letters to the editor as appropriate. This journal also publishes notices of conferences and other announcements. This technical periodical would be a good fit for an academic or medical research library.

4483. Menopause. [ISSN: 1072-3714] 1994. bi-m. USD 499 (Individuals, USD 292). Ed(s): Isaac Schiff, Diane Graham. Lippincott Williams & Wilkins, 530 Walnut St, Philadelphia, PA 19106-3621; custserv@lww.com; http://www.lww.com. Illus., adv. Refereed. Circ: 2584 Paid. Microform: PQC. Online: EBSCO Publishing, EBSCO Host; Ovid Technologies, Inc.; SwetsWise Online Content. *Indexed:* CABA, CINAHL, DSA, ExcerpMed, FPA, ForAb, HortAb, RRTA, SCI. *Aud.:* Ac, Sa.

Menopause, launched in 1994, is a peer-reviewed journal geared to providing "a forum for new research, applied basic science, and clinical guidelines on all aspects of menopause." It includes a variety of article formats, including editorials, original research articles, review articles, and letters to the editor. *Menopause* encompasses far more than simply the immediate gynecological aspects of menopause, and explores cancer risk, sociological and anthropological trends, cognitive concerns, nutrition, alternative therapies, and more. Doctors looking for continuing medical education credits will be pleased to find opportunities offered in selected issues. Published for the North American Menopause Society, this journal is also used as a forum for NAMS to explore its role in the menopause research community. This publication would be appropriate for academic and research libraries that support practicing physicians and medical researchers.

4484. *Menopause International (Print Edition).* Formerly (until 2007): *British Menopause Society. Journal (Print Edition).* [ISSN: 1754-0453] 1995. s-a. GBP 147 print & online eds (Individuals, GBP 64 print & online eds). Ed(s): Margaret Rees. Royal Society of Medicine Press Ltd., 1 Wimpole St, London, W1M 8AE, United Kingdom; publishing@ rsm.ac.uk; http://www.rsmpress.co.uk. *Indexed:* ExcerpMed. *Bk. rev.:* Number and length vary. *Aud.:* Ac, Sa.

This readable journal, published quarterly, focuses heavily on subjects most relevant to practicing doctors. *Menopause International* "features original research and review articles, clinical case histories as well as opinions and debates on topical issues," all dealing with subjects relating to menopause or postmenopausal health concerns in women. In addition to research articles, the journal offers news briefs, British Menopause Society reports and meeting proceedings, book reviews, and literature reviews of relevant articles in other journals. Most issues are available by subscription or single issue purchase only; however, selected back issues of the *Journal of the British Menopause Society* are available at no cost through IngentaConnect. This journal would be most appropriate in a library that supports practicing physicians.

4485. *Menopause Management.* [ISSN: 1062-7332] 1992. bi-m. USD 95 domestic; USD 129 foreign. Ed(s): Wulf H Utian. HealthCom Media, 4259 W Swamp Rd, Ste 408, Doylestown, PA 18901. Adv. Refereed. Circ: 33000. *Aud.:* Ac, Sa.

Geared toward health-care providers focused on the health of midlife women, *Menopause Management* publishes highly informative articles regarding clinical management of menopause and its effects. It also contains opinion pieces on current trends and issues written by the editor, and a forum where physicians can write in with questions, regarding which members of the Editorial Advisory Board will discuss options. This journal also offers continuing medical education credits in its supplement issues. This publication "combines an authoritative voice with a highly focused clinical and practical editorial format to create an ideal medium for promoting clinical products for the mature woman." As such, it tends to be a more popular-style journal. Each issue is brief, allowing the reader to absorb pertinent information in a short period of time. It would be best placed in a library that serves the clinical medical community.

■ MIDDLE EAST

Donald Altschiller, History and Government Documents Bibliographer, Mugar Memorial Library, Boston University, Boston, MA 02215

Introduction

In a recent Pew Research Center poll, almost 40 percent of Americans said that they didn't understand the political situation in the Middle East. This is an astonishing statistic considering the enormous political, economic, and military involvement of the United States in this region. The term "Middle East" often connotes to many Americans a few immediate associations: the war in Iraq, the growing nuclear threat from Iran, the Arab–Israeli conflict, and American dependence on Arab oil. Yet our knowledge of this area, once known as the "cradle of civilization"—the birthplace of three world religions and our system of writing and agriculture—suffers from several misconceptions about its ethnic and religious diversity.

The region is inhabited not only by Arab Muslims and Israeli Jews but by many other peoples: non-Arab Muslims (Berbers, Kurds, Turks, Iranians), Jews from Arab countries (Morocco, Egypt, Iraq, Syria, Yemen), religions and religious sects arising before and after the Prophet Mohammed (Alawites, Baha'is, Druze, Zoroastrians), and a wide range of Christians (Assyrians, Coptics, Melkites, Armenians, Maronites, Eastern Orthodox, and Roman Catholics). Since the U.S.-led overthrow of the regime of Iraqi dictator Saddam Hussein, television viewers and newspaper readers are constantly hearing and reading about the conflicts in Iraq among the Kurds, Shi'ites, Sunnis, and Assyrians. Yet most Americans are ignorant of these different communities and their growing impact on world affairs.

To better understand the historical background and the religious and ethnic complexity of the region, one needs to go beyond the popular press and look at the eclectic range of journals focusing on the Middle East. This section is a significant revision of that of the 15th edition and enlarges the topical range of publications. Unfortunately, a few journals have become defunct since the last edition. I hope the inclusion of several lesser-known periodicals will better inform librarians about important Middle East communities and cultures that are too often ignored.

Current Contents of Periodicals on the Middle East is an outstanding source for recent articles that appear in a wide variety of both general and specialized journals. (See entry on the MERIA Journal: http://meria.idc.ac.il/currentcontents/currentcontents.html.)

Basic Periodicals

International Journal of Middle East Studies, Jerusalem Report, Middle East Journal, Middle East Quarterly, Middle Eastern Studies.

Basic Abstracts and Indexes

Historical Abstracts, Index Islamicus, Index to Jewish Periodicals, Middle East: Abstracts and Index, PAIS International in Print, ATLA.

4486. *Arab Studies Journal.* [ISSN: 1083-4753] 1993. 2x/yr. USD 40 (Individuals, USD 25). Ed(s): Amber Concepcion, Bassam S A Haddad. Georgetown University, Center for Contemporary Arab Studies, ICC 241, Washington, DC 20057. Refereed. *Indexed:* IBSS, IndIslam. *Bk. rev.:* Number and length vary. *Aud.:* Ac.

Published by graduate students affiliated with the Georgetown University Center for Contemporary Arab Studies and the New York University Hagop Kevorkian Center for Near Eastern Studies, this journal includes multidisciplinary articles on Arab and Middle East Studies. It has published special issues on Islamic Law and Society, Language and Culture, and Middle East Exceptionalism. Each issue includes a large number of book reviews and also contains a cumulative author/book review index covering the contents of the journal since it was established in 1993.

4487. *Assyrian Star.* [ISSN: 0004-6051] 1952. q. USD 55. Ed(s): Sam Darmo. Assyrian-American National Federation, PO Box 2804, Worcester, MA 01613-2804. Illus., adv. Circ: 1500 Controlled. *Bk. rev.:* Number and length vary. *Aud.:* Ga, Ac.

This 55-year-old publication is the official voice of the Assyrian American National Federation and contains an eclectic range of articles on Assyrian culture and history (including the only Assyrian on the *Titanic*!). The journal contains announcements and news about community activities in the United States, profiles of notable Assyrian-Americans, and book reviews (and notices), but it also publishes articles on present-day Assyrian communities and their current plight in Iraq. Published in English, Assyrian, and Arabic, this quarterly publication has featured special issues on music, political parties and organizations, and the Assyrian language and calligraphy.

4488. *Azure: ideas for the Jewish nation.* [ISSN: 0793-6664] 1996. s-a. USD 26. Ed(s): Daniel Polisar. The Shalem Center, 22A Hatzfira St., Jerusalem, Israel; shalem@shalem.org.il; http://www.shalem.org.il/azure.htm. Adv. Refereed. *Indexed:* IJP. *Bk. rev.:* 2-3. *Aud.:* Ga, Ac.

Published by a political think tank in Israel, this journal contains articles offering politically conservative perspectives on Jewish nationalism and Israeli history and culture. Critical of some left-wing writings by Israeli historians, the journal provides an alternative perspective to the prevailing historiography found in some Israel-oriented journals. A recent article by Yehoshua Porath, the eminent historian of Palestinian nationalism, debunks many myths held by

Israeli historical revisionists about the War of Independence. Other articles include an examination of the inflation of Palestinian population statistics and a philo-Semitic essay by a French Huguenot Protestant.

4489. *The Cyprus Review: a journal of social, economic and political issues.* [ISSN: 1015-2881] 1989. s-a. USD 60 (Individuals, USD 40). Ed(s): Nicos Peristianis. Intercollege - Research and Development Center, PO Box 4005, Nicosia, 1700, Cyprus; antoniad@intercol.edu. Adv. Circ: 150. Online: DataStar; The Dialog Corporation. *Indexed:* IBR, IBSS, IBZ, IPSA, JEL, LingAb, PAIS, PRA, PSA, SSA, SociolAb. *Bk. rev.:* Number and length vary. *Aud.:* Ac.

This semi-annual English-language journal publishes articles on a wide range of social science issues pertaining to Cyprus, including matters of anthropology, economics, history, international relations, and politics, among other topics. Recent articles have covered Cyprus culinary culture, proposed European solutions to the Cyprus conflict, and the early historical conflicts between the Greek and Turkish Cypriot communities.

4490. *Egypt Today.* 1979. m. EGP 238 domestic; USD 70 United States; EGP 9 newsstand/cover per issue. Ed(s): Lyla Allan. International Business Associates, 1079 Corniche el-Nil, Garden City,, Cairo, Egypt (Arab Republic of Egypt); editor@egypttoday.com; http://www.egypttoday.com. Adv. Circ: 20000. *Aud.:* Ga.

Resembling consumer-oriented U.S. city magazines, this glossy publication features articles on popular culture, personalities, and local and regional politics. Interspersed with the articles are numerous advertisements for fancy hotels, expensive cars, and other upscale products aimed at tourists and business travelers. This monthly also provides extensive event listings for music, theater, and movies in Cairo, Alexandria, and other Egyptian cities.

4491. *I A J E Newsletter.* [ISSN: 1545-1690] 1999. irreg. USD 30. Ed(s): Victor Sanua. International Association of Jews from Egypt (I A J E), 2416 Quentin Rd, Brooklyn, NY 11229. *Bk. rev.:* Number and length vary. *Aud.:* Ga.

This interesting newsletter provides a forum for Egyptian-born Jews, a once-thriving community of more than 80,000 before 1948. Since most members of the community and their descendants now live in the United States, France, Israel, South America, and elsewhere around the world, this publication aims to help readers re-establish contact with their former countrymen and also to share stories about their homeland experiences. A charmingly informal publication written in both English and French, this illustrated newsletter contains historical notes, book reviews, information queries, and many reminiscences. Although the journal was published semi-annually until 2003, it apparently is no longer published regularly. The website, however, contains mostly full-text pdf versions of almost all the newsletters. URL: www.iajegypt.org/newsletter.shtml

4492. *International Journal of Kurdish Studies.* Former titles (until 1993): *Kurdish Studies;* (until 1991): *Kurdish Times.* [ISSN: 1073-6697] 1986. s-a. USD 65 (Individuals, USD 40; Students, USD 30). Ed(s): Vera Beaudin Saeedpour. Kurdish Library, 345 Park Pl, Brooklyn, NY 11238; kurdishlib@aol.com; http://www.kurdistanica.com/english/biblio/library/ny-library.html. Illus., adv. Refereed. Circ: 500. Vol. ends: Dec. *Indexed:* IBSS, IndIslam, PAIS. *Aud.:* Ga, Ac.

Published by the Kurdish Library, a unique repository of journals, reports, maps, clippings, and visual materials, this journal covers Kurdish history, culture, and contemporary affairs. Although there are an estimated 20 million Kurds scattered mostly in four Middle Eastern countries—the largest stateless ethnic group in the world—there has been insufficient attention devoted to this non-Arab, mostly Muslim ethnic group. A helpful annotated index to the contents of this journal from 1986 to 2002 appears in volume 17. The 20th anniversary issue features an eclectic range of articles on Kurdish cities, the first Kurdish periodical in Iran and some book chapter reprints written by travelers and scholars during the 19th and early 20th century.

4493. *International Journal of Middle East Studies.* [ISSN: 0020-7438] 1970. q. plus two bulletins. GBP 217. Ed(s): Judith Tucker. Cambridge University Press, The Edinburgh Bldg, Shaftesbury Rd, Cambridge, CB2 2RU, United Kingdom; journals@cambridge.org; http://www.journals.cambridge.org. Illus., adv. Refereed. Vol. ends: Spring. Microform: PQC. Online: Pub.; EBSCO Publishing, EBSCO Host; JSTOR (Web-based Journal Archive); OCLC Online Computer Library Center, Inc.; OhioLINK; SwetsWise Online Content. Reprint: PSC. *Indexed:* ABCPolSci, AICP, AbAn, AmH&L, ArtHuCI, BRI, CABA, CJA, CommAb, HistAb, IBR, IBSS, IBZ, IPSA, IndIslam, L&LBA, MLA-IB, PAIS, PRA, PSA, PhilInd, RRTA, SSA, SSCI, SociolAb, WAE&RSA. *Bk. rev.:* Number and length vary. *Aud.:* Ac.

Published under the auspices of the Middle East Studies Association of North America, this quarterly journal publishes articles and book reviews on the Arab world, Israel, Iran, Afghanistan, Turkey, the Caucasus, and Muslim South Asia from the seventh century to the present time. The articles are multidisciplinary, covering history, political science, international relations, economics, anthropology, sociology, and related humanities disciplines, including literature, religion, and philosophy. This journal is primarily geared toward scholars and academic specialists. Starting in 2007, the journal inaugurated "Quick Studies," an interesting new front section. These short articles aim at initiating discussion on current research of primary sources including texts (court cases, manuscripts), visual materials (photographs, paintings), and data (charts and graphs).

4494. *Iranian Studies.* [ISSN: 0021-0862] 1968. q. GBP 235 print & online eds. Ed(s): Homa Katouzian. Routledge, 4 Park Sq, Milton Park, Abingdon, OX14 4RN, United Kingdom; info@routledge.co.uk; http://www.routledge.co.uk. Illus., index, adv. Sample. Refereed. Circ: 600. Online: EBSCO Publishing, EBSCO Host; Gale; IngentaConnect; OCLC Online Computer Library Center, Inc.; SwetsWise Online Content. Reprint: PSC. *Indexed:* AmH&L, AmHI, AnthLit, BrHumI, HistAb, IBR, IBZ, IPSA, IndIslam, MLA-IB, PSA, RILM, SSA, SociolAb. *Bk. rev.:* Number and length vary. *Aud.:* Ac.

This academic journal contains articles on the "Persian or Iranian legacy" in the fields of history, literature, politics, and culture. Coverage geographically spans a wide area that includes Iran, Afghanistan, Central Asia, the Caucasus, and northern India.

4495. *Israel Affairs.* [ISSN: 1353-7121] 1994. q. GBP 338 print & online eds. Ed(s): Efraim Karsh. Routledge, 4 Park Sq, Milton Park, Abingdon, OX14 4RN, United Kingdom; info@routledge.co.uk; http://www.routledge.co.uk. Adv. Sample. Refereed. Reprint: PSC. *Indexed:* IBSS, IJP, IPSA, PSA, RiskAb, SSA, SociolAb. *Aud.:* Ac.

This journal covers an eclectic range of subjects including Israeli history, politics, literature, economics, law, military and strategic issues, and of course, the Arab–Israeli conflict. Article abstracts provide helpful summaries. The editor, Efraim Karsh, is an eminent Middle East scholar and researcher.

4496. *Israel Studies.* [ISSN: 1084-9513] 1996. 3x/yr. USD 92 (Individuals, USD 37.50). Ed(s): Dr. S Ilan Troen. Indiana University Press, 601 N Morton St, Bloomington, IN 47404. Adv. Refereed. Circ: 500. Online: EBSCO Publishing, EBSCO Host; Florida Center for Library Automation; Gale; OCLC Online Computer Library Center, Inc.; OhioLINK; Project MUSE; ProQuest K-12 Learning Solutions; ProQuest LLC (Ann Arbor); SwetsWise Online Content; H.W. Wilson. Reprint: PSC. *Indexed:* AmH&L, ENW, HistAb, IJP, IPSA, MLA-IB, PAIS, PRA, PSA, SociolAb. *Aud.:* Ac.

Edited by a distinguished Israeli historian at Ben-Gurion University, this journal publishes an eclectic range of articles on Israeli history, politics, and culture. A recent special issue is devoted to critical perspectives on the changing role of the Israeli military and Ministry of Defense. The journal occasionally publishes useful primary source documents. Nicely designed, the journal also includes photographs and illustrations.

4497. *The Jerusalem Report.* [ISSN: 0792-6049] 1990. bi-w. ILS 240 domestic; USD 69 in US & Canada; USD 79.97 elsewhere. Ed(s): David Horovitz. Jerusalem Report, PO Box 1805, Jerusalem, 91017, Israel. Illus., adv. Online: LexisNexis; ProQuest LLC (Ann Arbor). *Indexed:* IJP, NTA. *Aud.:* Ga.

Although this news magazine mainly covers Israel and the Jewish diaspora, it also provides outstanding coverage of the Middle East and the larger Muslim world. While the cover stories frequently focus on very recent events, the reporting and analysis provide much insightful and in-depth coverage. The magazine has earned much respect throughout the region for its hard-hitting articles on political developments in Israel and also the Arab world. An outstanding publication for both public and academic libraries.

4498. *The Journal of Israeli History: studies in Zionism and statehood.*
Formerly (until Spring 1993): *Studies in Zionism;* Which superseded (in 1982): *Zionism: Studies in the History of the Zionist Movement and of the Jews in Palestine - Ha-Tsiyonut.* [ISSN: 1353-1042] 1980. s-a. GBP 191 print & online eds. Ed(s): Derek J Penslar, Anita Shapira. Routledge, 4 Park Sq, Milton Park, Abingdon, OX14 4RN, United Kingdom; info@routledge.co.uk; http://www.routledge.co.uk. Illus., adv. Sample. Refereed. Vol. ends: Fall. Reprint: PSC. *Indexed:* AmH&L, AmHI, HistAb, IBR, IBSS, IBZ, IJP, PSA, R&TA, RI-1, SociolAb. *Bk. rev.:* Number and length vary. *Aud.:* Ac, Sa.

Previously published under different titles, this fine historical journal has expanded its coverage from the pre-state period and the study of Zionism to a multidisciplinary study of the State of Israel, the Israeli–Palestinian conflict, and Israel's relation with the Jewish diaspora. A recent special issue contains papers given at a Brandeis University conference entitled "Convergence and Divergence: Anti-Semitism and Anti-Zionism in Historical Perspective." Edited by two major scholars of Zionism, this journal provides an important forum for current research on the history and culture of the Jewish state.

4499. *Journal of Muslim Minority Affairs.* Formerly: *Institute of Muslim Minority Affairs. Journal.* [ISSN: 1360-2004] 1979. 3x/yr. GBP 319 print & online eds. Ed(s): Saleha S Mahmood. Routledge, 4 Park Sq, Milton Park, Abingdon, OX14 4RN, United Kingdom; info@routledge.co.uk; http://www.routledge.co.uk. Adv. Refereed. Online: EBSCO Publishing, EBSCO Host; Gale; IngentaConnect; Northern Light Technology, Inc.; OCLC Online Computer Library Center, Inc.; ProQuest K-12 Learning Solutions; ProQuest LLC (Ann Arbor); SwetsWise Online Content. Reprint: PSC. *Indexed:* AmH&L, BAS, HistAb, IBR, IBSS, IBZ, IPSA, IndIslam, PAIS, PSA, RI-1, SSA, SociolAb. *Aud.:* Ac, Sa.

Published three times a year, this journal is solely devoted to a "frank but responsible" discussion of Muslim communities in non-Muslim societies. Although Muslims are the largest religious group in the Middle East, this journal has also explored the interactions between Maronite Christians and Muslims in Lebanon and Christian identity in the Jordanian Arab culture. Other issues have covered the situation of Middle East Muslims in Europe, the occasionally strained relations between African American Muslims and Muslim immigrants in the United States, Kurdish activism, the Turkish diaspora, and Islam in Turkey.

4500. *Journal of Near Eastern Studies.* Former titles (until 1941): *American Journal of Semitic Languages and Literatures;* (until 1895): *Hebraica.* [ISSN: 0022-2968] 1884. q. USD 186 domestic; USD 201.16 Canada; USD 191 elsewhere. Ed(s): Wadad Kadi. University of Chicago Press, Journals Division, PO Box 37005, Chicago, IL 60637; subscriptions@press.uchicago.edu; http://www.journals.uchicago.edu. Illus., index, adv. Refereed. Circ: 1410 Paid. Vol. ends: Oct. Microform: MIM; PMC; PQC. Online: The Dialog Corporation; EBSCO Publishing, EBSCO Host; Florida Center for Library Automation; Gale; JSTOR (Web-based Journal Archive); OCLC Online Computer Library Center, Inc.; ProQuest K-12 Learning Solutions; ProQuest LLC (Ann Arbor). Reprint: PSC. *Indexed:* A&ATA, AbAn, AmH&L, AmHI, AnthLit, ArtHuCI, BAS, BRI, FR, HumInd, IBR, IBSS, IBZ, IndIslam, L&LBA, MLA-IB, NTA, OTA, PRA, R&TA, RI-1, SSCI. *Aud.:* Ac.

While the other journals in this section mostly cover the modern Middle East, this venerable academic periodical, first published in 1884, is largely devoted to ancient and medieval cultures of the region. Written by scholars, the articles cover archaeology, art, history, linguistics, religion, law, science, the Hebrew Bible, and Islamic Studies, among other topics. An eminent journal for larger academic libraries.

4501. *Journal of Palestine Studies: a quarterly on Palestinian affairs and the Arab-Israeli conflict.* [ISSN: 0377-919X] 1971. q. USD 175 print & online eds. USD 48 newsstand/cover. Ed(s): Rashid I Khalidi. University of California Press, Journals Division, 2000 Center St, Ste 303, Berkeley, CA 94704-1223; journals@ucpress.edu; http://www.ucpress.edu/journals. Illus., index, adv. Refereed. Circ: 2965. Microform: PQC. Online: EBSCO Publishing, EBSCO Host; JSTOR (Web-based Journal Archive); Northern Light Technology, Inc.; OCLC Online Computer Library Center, Inc.; ProQuest LLC (Ann Arbor); SwetsWise Online Content. *Indexed:* ABCPolSci, AltPI, AmH&L, ArtHuCI, ENW, HistAb, IBR, IBSS, IBZ, IPSA, PAIS, PSA, SSA, SSCI, SociolAb. *Aud.:* Ac, Sa.

Published by the University of California Press for the Washington, D.C.–based Institute for Palestine Studies, this journal is the preeminent English-language academic publication devoted to Palestinian Arab history and the Arab–Israeli conflict. Although it publishes partisan articles on this long-festering conflict, the journal also includes a documents section that provides reference material that is not easily accessible elsewhere. The "Bibliography of Periodical Literature" contains many useful citations and the quarterly chronology lists significant news events.

Journal of South Asian and Middle Eastern Studies. See Asia and the Pacific/South Asia section.

4502. *M E R I A Journal.* 1997. q. Free. Ed(s): Barry Rubin. Global Research in International Affairs, Interdisciplinary Center, Herzliya, Israel; gloria@idc.ac.il; http://gloria.idc.ac.il. Refereed. Circ: 10065 Controlled. *Aud.:* Ga, Ac, Sa.

MERIA, the Middle East Review of International Affairs, is an outstanding gateway to important web sites on the Middle East. It provides access to *MERIA Journal*, an electronic publication that reaches a reported 22,000 readers, including leading policy-makers and academics. The site contains *MERIA News*, a monthly magazine containing shorter analytical articles and announcements, and the invaluable *Current Contents of Periodicals on the Middle East*. Especially useful are the *MERIA Research Guides*, which offer bibliographies and web resources compiled by country experts. *MERIA Books* contains collections of articles from the *Journal, MERIA News*, and other sources. *MERIA* is a major resource for both scholars and general readers.

4503. *Middle East Journal.* [ISSN: 0026-3141] 1947. q. USD 48 (Individuals, USD 36). Ed(s): Michael Dunn. Middle East Institute, 1761 N St, NW, Washington, DC 20036; mideasti@mideasti.org; http://www.mideasti.org/. Illus., adv. Refereed. Circ: 4500. Vol. ends: Fall. Microform: PQC. Online: Chadwyck-Healey Inc.; Florida Center for Library Automation; Gale; Northern Light Technology, Inc.; OCLC Online Computer Library Center, Inc.; ProQuest K-12 Learning Solutions; ProQuest LLC (Ann Arbor). *Indexed:* ABCPolSci, ABS&EES, AICP, AmH&L, ArtHuCI, BAS, BRD, BRI, CBRI, FR, HistAb, IBR, IBSS, IBZ, IPSA, IndIslam, JEL, PAIS, PRA, PSA, RI-1, RRTA, RiskAb, SSCI, SociolAb. *Bk. rev.:* Number and length vary. *Aud.:* Ga, Ac.

Published by the oldest Middle East institute in the United States that is not affiliated with a university, this journal covers the history, politics, and economy of nations from North Africa to Pakistan, the newly emerging nations of Central Asia, and the Caucasus. Written mostly by scholars, the journal publishes accessible articles that may interest fellow academics and also serious lay readers. The book review section listing for "Recent Publications" should alert acquisition librarians to many titles not generally cited elsewhere.

4504. *Middle East Media Research Institute.* 1998. d. Middle East Media Research Institute, PO Box 27837, Washington, DC 20038-7837. *Aud.:* Ga, Ac, Sa.

Following the 9/11 attacks, many Americans have engaged in public self-criticism about their lack of knowledge of the Arab and Muslim world. This web site is an essential source for acquiring a deeper understanding and knowledge of current Middle East affairs and viewpoints. The MEMRI site provides translations of the Arabic-, Farsi-, and Turkish-language media. The topics covered are remarkably broad: the United States and the Middle East, inter-Arab relations, the Arab–Israeli conflict, economic studies, jihad and terrorism, and reform in the Arab and Muslim world. The translations are often unique, providing an opportunity to read the same material that is published or broadcast throughout the region. Translations are verbatim, and the editors offer no commentary. In recent years, several news stories about the Middle East received international coverage after appearing on MEMRI. The site has recently added videotapes from noteworthy Arab and Iranian television programs. Some Middle East scholars have called this site the preeminent source for current information on the Middle East. URL: www.memri.org

4505. Middle East Quarterly. [ISSN: 1073-9467] 1994. q. USD 65 (Individuals, USD 40; Students, USD 27). Ed(s): Michael Rubin. Middle East Forum, 1500 Walnut St, Ste 1050, Philadelphia, PA 19103-4624; mideastq@aol.com; http://www.meforum.org. Illus., adv. Circ: 2100 Paid. Online: EBSCO Publishing, EBSCO Host; Florida Center for Library Automation; Gale. Reprint: PSC. *Indexed:* BRI, CBRI, IBSS, IJP, IPSA, IndIslam, PAIS, PSA, SSA, SociolAb. *Bk. rev.:* Number and length vary. *Aud.:* Ga, Ac.

Several years before the 9/11 terrorist attacks, this journal, probably alone among all Middle East publications, published articles warning about the imminent dangers posed by Islamic extremists and Osama bin Laden. An *MEQ* article predicted that terrorists would hijack airplanes and crash them into skyscrapers. Unapologetically asserting that its goal is to "define and promote American interests in the Middle East," this journal has published essays on the United States and the Arab world, the Arab–Israeli and other regional conflicts, and the rise of terrorism. This quarterly has published interviews with highly knowledgeable but lesser-known government officials and scholars, and also contains a "Dissident Watch" section. A recent issue examines the disturbing confluence of views among right-wing extremists, including neo-Nazis and the Iranian president, Mahmoud Ahmadinejad. The articles are enhanced by sidebars that offer unusual and occasionally amusing tidbits about contemporary affairs. Except for the most recent issues, the text of almost all back issues is available at their web site.

4506. Middle East Studies Association Bulletin. [ISSN: 0026-3184] 1967. s-a. June & Dec. Membership, USD 90. Ed(s): John VenderLippe. Middle East Studies Association of North America, Inc., SUNY New Paltz, Department of History, New Paltz, NY 12561; bulletin@newpaltz.edu. Illus., index, adv. Circ: 2200 Paid. Vol. ends: Dec. *Indexed:* ABS&EES, AICP, AmH&L, AmHI, CABA, HistAb, HumInd, IBR, IBSS, IBZ, IPSA, IndIslam, L&LBA, PSA, RI-1, RILM, RRTA. *Bk. rev.:* Number and length vary. *Aud.:* Ac.

Published by the largest U.S. academic association devoted to the study of the Middle East, this journal contains a very large book review section but also features essays on diverse Middle East topics. In addition, it occasionally publishes lists of recent doctoral degree recipients, conference programs, and film and music reviews. The web site provides access to selected articles.

4507. Middle Eastern Studies. [ISSN: 0026-3206] 1964. 6x/yr. GBP 475 print & online eds. Ed(s): Sylvia Kedourie, Elie Kedourie. Routledge, 4 Park Sq, Milton Park, Abingdon, OX14 4RN, United Kingdom; info@routledge.co.uk; http://www.routledge.co.uk. Illus., adv. Sample. Refereed. Microform: PQC. Online: EBSCO Publishing, EBSCO Host; Florida Center for Library Automation; Gale; IngentaConnect; Northern Light Technology, Inc.; OCLC Online Computer Library Center, Inc.; ProQuest LLC (Ann Arbor); SwetsWise Online Content. Reprint: PSC. *Indexed:* ABCPolSci, AbAn, AmH&L, AmHI, ArtHuCI, BrHumI, FR, HistAb, IBR, IBSS, IBZ, IPSA, IndIslam, PSA, RiskAb, SSA, SSCI, SociolAb. *Bk. rev.:* Number and length vary. *Aud.:* Ac, Sa.

Founded by the late, Iraqi-born scholar Elie Kedourie and now edited by his wife Sylvia Kedourie, this journal publishes articles "on the history and politics of the Arabic-speaking countries in the Middle East and North Africa as well as on Turkey, Iran and Israel." A demanding scholar, Professor Kedourie established a possibly unique policy among academic journals: no biographical notes on contributors. He said, "I want articles to be judged on their merit and not with reference to the author's background." This 43-year-old publication still maintains its scholarly integrity and is one of the major academic journals covering the Middle East.

4508. New Perspectives on Turkey. [ISSN: 0896-6346] 1987. s-a. Tarih Vakfi Binalari, Vali Konagi Cad, Samsun apt 57, Istanbul, 80200, Turkey; tarihvakfi@tarihvakfi.org.tr; http://www.tarihvakfi.org.tr. Refereed. *Indexed:* AmH&L, HistAb, IBSS, PSA, SociolAb. *Bk. rev.:* 2-3, length varies. *Aud.:* Ac, Sa.

This journal claims to be the sole English-language, refereed academic journal published in Turkey. A semi-annual publication, it contains articles on the country's history, society, economy, politics, and culture, with special emphasis on comparative studies. Recent special issues feature articles on the Kurdish Question and a comparison of Japanese and Turkish modernization. Each issue contains about two or three book reviews.

4509. Nineveh. [ISSN: 0749-5919] 1978. 3x/yr. USD 20 domestic; USD 25 Canada; USD 30 elsewhere. Ed(s): Robert Karoukian. Assyrian Foundation of America, PO Box 2660, Berkeley, CA 94702; sargonmichael@yahoo.com; http://www.assyrianfoundation.org. *Bk. rev.:* 5-10, length varies. *Aud.:* Ga, Ac, Sa.

This eclectic publication features articles on Assyrians, the indigenous people of Iraq, southwest Turkey, and parts of Syria and Iran. Despite persecution, this remarkable community has been able to maintain its distinct culture, literature, and language. This magazine publishes a veritable smorgasbord of items on this ancient Christian group: memoirs of immigrants, organizational news, excerpts from scholarly journals, book reviews, discussion of artifacts and archaeology, sport news, poetry, and recipes. Published in English and Assyrian, this illustrated journal has reproduced documents captured during the 1991 Gulf War about the Iraqi persecution of Assyrian Christians. In addition, recent issues cover the current plight of their coreligionists in this war-torn nation and the cultural and educational activities of Assyrian-Americans.

4510. Palestine - Israel Journal of Politics, Economics and Culture. [ISSN: 0793-1395] 1994. q. USD 60 (Individuals, USD 50). Ed(s): Daniel Bar-Tal, Ziad Abu Zayyad. Palestine - Israel Journal of Politics, Economics and Culture, 4 El Hariri St., Jerusalem, Israel; pij@palnet.com; http://www.pij.org. Index, adv. Sample. Refereed. *Indexed:* ABIn, AltPI, ENW, IBSS, IJP, IPSA, IndIslam, PAIS. *Aud.:* Hs, Ga, Ac, Sa.

Written and edited by Israeli Jews and Palestinian Arabs, this unique English-language journal provides varying perspectives on their historical conflict, mostly from a leftist perspective. The journal has an admirable aim: "to promote rapprochement and better understanding between peoples, and [to strive] to discuss all issues without prejudice and without taboos." Recent issues include articles on the concept of a truce (*hudna*) in Islamic sources and unilateralism versus negotiations. A chronology of events and a documents section are useful reference features.

4511. Persian Heritage. [ISSN: 1094-494X] 1996. q. USD 20. Ed(s): Shahrokh Ahkami. Persian Heritage, Inc., 1110 Passaic Ave, Passaic, NJ 07055. *Bk. rev.:* Number and length vary. *Aud.:* Ga, Sa.

Written in both English and Farsi, this quarterly magazine claims to be the "most widely circulated" bilingual Iranian publication outside Iran. Mostly aimed at Iranian expatriates but also covering topics for other readers interested in Iran, this magazine contains articles on politics, culture, arts, and news. Recent issues include a discussion of the controversy over the name "Persian Gulf," which many Iranians feel has been unhistorically termed the "Arab Gulf"; a biography of a prominent Iranian sculptor; and a commentary by a second-generation Iranian-American.

4512. Turkish Policy Quarterly. q. TRL 135 (Individuals, TRL 60; TRL 155 combined subscription print & online eds.). Ed(s): Nigar Goksel. Turkish Policy Quarterly, Ayazaga Ticaret Merkezi, Tahiraga Cesme Cad. No:1, B Blok, 7th Fl, Istanbul, 80670, Turkey; subscriptions@turkishpolicy.com; http://www.turkishpolicy.com. *Aud.:* Ac, Sa.

Although Turkey is the largest country in the Middle East, it appears to receive much less media attention than its less populous neighbors. Published by the ARI Movement, an independent Turkish public policy group, this journal aims to "promote informed debate about Turkish policies in the international area." Handsomely designed, this quarterly publishes articles by scholars of Turkey and Turkish government officials. Recent issues feature articles on the European Union and Turkey, Turkish–Kurdish relations, the role of religion in Turkish politics, and the relations among bordering nations in the Black Sea region.

4513. *Turkish Studies.* [ISSN: 1468-3849] 2000. 3x/yr. GBP 161 print & online eds. Ed(s): Barry Rubin. Routledge, 4 Park Sq, Milton Park, Abingdon, OX14 4RN, United Kingdom; journals@routledge.com; http://www.routledge.co.uk. Adv. Sample. Refereed. Vol. ends: Fall. Reprint: PSC. *Indexed:* AmH&L, HistAb, IBR, IBSS, IBZ, IPSA, IndIslam, PSA, SociolAb. *Bk. rev.:* Number and length vary. *Aud.:* Ac.

Edited by the erudite and prolific Middle East scholar Barry Rubin, this important journal publishes a wide range of articles by scholars from Turkey, Israel, Europe, and elsewhere. Started by the Global Research Institute in International Affairs (GLORIA), this publication is produced by its Turkish Studies Institute (gloria@idc.ac.il), which also sends out a regular Internet bulletin offering news and announcements about scholarship on modern Turkey. Special issues have covered political parties in Turkey and Turkish–European Union and Turkish–Russian relations. The journal has an excellent book review section.

4514. *Yale Israel Journal: exploring the history, politics and culture of Israel.* 2003. s-a. USD 12. Yale Israel Journal, PO Box 204669, New Haven, CT 06520. *Bk. rev.:* Number and length vary. *Aud.:* Ga, Ac.

Published by Yale students, this independent journal publishes essays, interviews, and book reviews. Recent issues have included articles on the status and rights of gays in Palestinian society, an interview with a retired Israeli brigadier general who serves in the Knesset, and an essay on the Jews of Kurdistan.

■ MILITARY

Kathleen M. Conley, Head, General Reference and Documents; Rare Books and Special Collections Librarian; Milner Library, Illinois State University, Normal, IL 61790-8900 kcconle@ilstu.edu

Cheryl LaGuardia, Head of Instructional Services for the Harvard College Library, Widener Library, Research Services, Harvard University, Cambridge, MA 02138; claguard@fas.harvard.edu

Introduction

It would appear that there are publications for every specialty or niche in the armed services; many are showcases for the newest in training, operations, weaponry, technology, or tactics. Over and over again in recent publications, "effects-based operations" appears to be a common thread. It is defined in one publication as "operations that are planned, executed, assessed and adopted based on a holistic understanding of the operational environment in order to influence or change system behavior or capabilities using the integrated application of selected instances of power to achieve directed policy aims." In other words, the effectiveness of the mission is as important as its success. Many of the publications included recognize that civil-military relations and cultural sensitivities are crucial to the success of today's forces. Writings in some journals acknowledge that successful strategies must recognize the interdependency of military, political, economic, religious, and historical factors. The opinions of psychologists, sociologists, historians, teachers, and even peacekeepers are sought out and incorporated into planning.

Regardless of one's political leanings, it is incumbent upon citizens to take advantage of the wealth and depth of information presented in these publications in order to be informed about the objectives and analyses of operations in which the United States is heavily involved. Newsmagazines, radio or television talk shows, or even the daily papers do not cover the military in-depth from diverse angles; what they do cover is often only the most urgent, the most sensational, or the story that can be conveyed in a short amount of time and still be understandable to the general public. Although many current issues of these serials are available on the Internet, there are very few substantive electronic-only publications. Several of these journals are classified as government publications and should be widely available in depository libraries.

A great strength of these magazines and journals is the extensive inclusion of book reviews. The message seems to be that wide and deep reading will be of great benefit to policymakers, members of the armed forces, or anyone else who picks up these journals. Libraries can facilitate discourse on the very important and timely topics that are included in these military publications by acquiring a few core titles.

Basic Periodicals

Hs: *Aviation History, Marines, Military History Quarterly, Soldiers* Ga: *Air Force Magazine, Armed Forces Journal International, Army, Aviation History, Defense Monitor, Leatherneck, Military History, Military History Quarterly, National Guard, Naval History, World War II* Ac: *The Air & Space Power Journal, AirForces Monthly, Armed Forces and Society, Armed Forces Journal International, Army, Defense Monitor, Joint Force Quarterly, Journal of Military History, The Journal of Slavic Military Studies, The Journal of Strategic Studies, Military Review, Naval War College Review, Survival: The IISS Quarterly, U S Naval Institute Proceedings.*

Basic Abstracts and Indexes

Air University Library Index to Military Periodicals.

4515. *The Air & Space Power Journal.* Former titles (until 2002): *The Aerospace Power Journal;* (until 1999): *Airpower Journal;* (until 1987): *Air University Review.* [ISSN: 1555-385X] 1947. q. USD 32 domestic; USD 44.80 foreign. Ed(s): Lt.Col. Paul D Berg. U.S. Air Force, Air University, Maxwell Air Force Base, 401 Chennault Cir, Montgomery, AL 36112-6428; apj@maxwell.af.mil; http://www.airpower.maxwell.af.mil. Illus., index. Sample. Refereed. Circ: 20000 Paid and controlled. Vol. ends: Winter. Microform: PQC. Online: EBSCO Publishing, EBSCO Host; Gale; Northern Light Technology, Inc.; OCLC Online Computer Library Center, Inc.; ProQuest K-12 Learning Solutions. *Indexed:* ABS&EES, AUNI, AmH&L, BAS, BRI, C&ISA, CerAb, HistAb, IAA, IBR, IBZ, IUSGP, PAIS, PRA. *Bk. rev.:* Number varies, 200–500 words. *Aud.:* Ac. Sa.

This professional flagship journal aims to present the latest thinking about military doctrine, tactics, strategy, readiness, and other issues relating to national defense, focusing on air and space power issues of concern to today's Air Force. Several feature articles explore such current topics as the impact of the Internet on collecting open source intelligence, the necessity of teaching military virtue, or the outlook for oil and America. The thought-provoking, intelligent articles are written by scholars and high-ranking military personnel and could add immeasurably to the layperson's understanding of current global and military issues. Fifteen to twenty substantial reviews cover books primarily related to military airpower, but encompass all relevant historical periods. A new section, "The Merge," presents contending ideas and invites reader response. This journal is published in English, Spanish, Portuguese, Arabic, and, recently, French to reach French-speaking militaries in Africa. An online companion, Chronicles Online Journal, has a broader editorial focus. Highly recommended for academic libraries.

4516. *Air Force Magazine: the force behind the force.* Former titles (until 1971): *Air Force and Space Digest;* (until 1959): *Air Force.* [ISSN: 0730-6784] 1942. m. USD 36 domestic; USD 46 in Canada & Mexico; USD 65 elsewhere. Ed(s): Robert S Dudney, John Tirpak. Air Force Association, 1501 Lee Hwy, Arlington, VA 22209-1198; http://www.afa.org. Illus., adv. Circ: 200000 Paid. Vol. ends: Dec. *Indexed:* ABS&EES, AUNI, AmH&L, C&ISA, CerAb, HistAb, IAA, PRA. *Bk. rev.:* 5, 150–200 words. *Aud.:* Ga, Ac.

Air Force Magazine is a monthly published by the Air Force Association, "an independent, nonprofit, civilian education organization promoting public understanding of aerospace power and the pivotal role it plays in the security of the nation." This publication provides an excellent snapshot of current events through its "Washington Watch," "Action in Congress," and annual "Almanac." The latter, which appears in the May issue, is a useful feature that includes primarily statistical material about the Air Force, including its budget, people, equipment, funding, bases, and heroes; it provides excellent data for comparison and charting trends. Feature articles portray prominent Air Force personnel, programs, and operations, and provide authoritative background information, news, and developments. The web site features a "Daily Digest" that comments on relevant news stories, posts in-depth reports, and past features from the magazine. Public and academic libraries would find much of interest here.

4517. *AirForces Monthly: the world's leading military aviation magazine.* [ISSN: 0955-7091] 1988. m. GBP 36 domestic; EUR 64.20 in Europe eurozone; GBP 42.80 in Europe non eurozone. Ed(s): Alan Warnes. Key Publishing Ltd., PO Box 300, Stamford, PE9 1NA, United Kingdom; ann.saundry@keypublishing.com; http://www.keypublishing.com. Illus., adv. Circ: 25787. *Aud.:* Ga, Ac.

This publication is visually appealing and touts itself as the "world's leading aviation magazine." It covers aviation from a global perspective, looking at air forces around the world, military conflicts, weaponry, and, of course, insights into the latest technology. Readers who are interested in global conflicts and the airpower that is employed to strike or defend would find this publication of interest. Because the articles are accessible, general-aviation buffs might also find this publication of interest. An intriguing feature of the web site is the online forum that allows readers to discuss military aviation around the world. Because of its format, the magazine would probably appeal to readers in public libraries, and because of its breadth of coverage, it should also be acquired by academic libraries.

4518. *The American Legion.* Formerly (until 1981): *American Legion Magazine.* [ISSN: 0886-1234] 1920. m. Non-members, USD 15. Ed(s): John B Raughter, Jeff Stoffer. American Legion Magazine, PO Box 1055, Indianapolis, IN 46206; http://www.legion.org. Illus., adv. Circ: 2550000 Paid. Vol. ends: Jun/Dec. Online: OCLC Online Computer Library Center, Inc. *Indexed:* HRIS, LRI, PAIS. *Aud.:* Ga.

This publication is a politically conservative voice that strongly expresses the ideals of patriotism, support for our troops, preservation of the memories of wars in which Americans have fought, and, of course, a strong national defense. Mutual help and a commitment to the welfare of veterans and their widows and orphans are also tenets of the American Legion. The reader can find in this magazine points of view not espoused widely in the mainstream media. For example, in a recent issue, "By the Numbers" shows evidence of improvement in the quality of life for Iraqi citizens. Another article details the reasons that 9/11 and the war in Iraq are linked. A special feature presents opposing viewpoints on a national issue by two legislators. This is an excellent general-interest source on veterans' issues, and should be available in public libraries.

4519. *Armed Forces and Society: an interdisciplinary journal on military institutions, civil-military relations, arms control and peacekeeping, and conflict management.* [ISSN: 0095-327X] 1972. q. GBP 239. Ed(s): Patricia M Shields. Sage Publications, Inc., 2455 Teller Rd, Thousand Oaks, CA 91320; info@sagepub.com; http://www.sagepub.com. Illus., index, adv. Refereed. Circ: 1700. Vol. ends: Summer. Microform: PQC. Online: EBSCO Publishing, EBSCO Host; Florida Center for Library Automation; Gale; HighWire Press; OCLC Online Computer Library Center, Inc.; OhioLINK; ProQuest LLC (Ann Arbor); SwetsWise Online Content. Reprint: PSC. *Indexed:* ABCPolSci, ABS&EES, AUNI, AgeL, AmH&L, BAS, BRI, CBRI, CJA, HistAb, IBR, IBSS, IBZ, IPSA, PAIS, PRA, PSA, RI-1, SSA, SSCI, SociolAb. *Bk. rev.:* 5–10, 300–500 words. *Aud.:* Ac.

This interdisciplinary publication, issued by the Inter-University Seminar on Armed Forces and Society, is "a forum for the interchange and assessment of research and scholarship in the social and behavioral sciences dealing with the military establishment and civil-military relations." In addition to military strategists, contributors include anthropologists, political scientists, historians, and psychologists. The several articles are analyses of "military professionalism, civil-military relations, social composition of the armed forces, organizational change within armed forces, public policy on defense issues, peacekeeping, arms control, and conflict resolution" supported and sustained by objective research. This research is touted as making an invaluable contribution to the education of citizens about the armed forces. Several articles, research notes, review essays, and book reviews present historical perspectives, qualitative or quantitative research, and policy-shaping or theoretical themes with an international focus, all reaching a high standard of scholarship and argument. A valuable contribution to military scholarship in part by those in the humanities and social sciences, this journal is recommended for academic libraries.

4520. *Armed Forces Journal.* Former titles (until Dec. 2002): *Armed Forces Journal International;* (until 1973): *Armed Forces Journal.* [ISSN: 1559-162X] 1863. m. USD 60 in US & Canada (Free to qualified personnel). Ed(s): John G Roos. Defense News Media Group, 6883 Commercial Dr, Springfield, VA 22159; custserv@defensenews.com. Illus., adv. Sample. Circ: 27000 Controlled. Vol. ends: Dec. Microform: PQC. *Indexed:* ABS&EES, AUNI. *Aud.:* Ga, Ac.

AFJ proclaims itself the "premier magazine for military leadership," but its newsy style, intelligent review and analysis of current political issues, as well as excellent coverage of military technology, strategy, doctrine, and tactics ensure a wider readership. A recent issue relates strategic successes of the emerging partnership between the Bush administration and India, a debate on the efficacy of "effects-based operations," and a look at the daily challenges Iraqi citizens face. "Blogs of War" highlights important emerging sources of information such as web sites offering the most recent and best information on Indian military strategy; another looks at the Afghan blogosphere. "Inside the Beltway" surveys political and administrative views and actions on military or national security affairs. A lighthearted look at military jargon is found in the "Non-Word of the Month," and has included "warlordism" and "unwatering." This title is thoroughly engaging, thought-provoking, and a must for citizens who want to be informed on military issues. Recommended for public and academic libraries.

4521. *Armor: the magazine of mobile warfare.* [ISSN: 0004-2420] 1888. bi-m. Members, USD 22; Non-members, USD 26. Ed(s): Christy Bourgeois, Lt.Col. Shane Lee. U.S. Army Armor Center, 201 6th Ave, Ste 373, Bldg 1109 A, Ft. Knox, KY 40121-; knox.armormag@conus.army.mil; http://www.knox.army.mil/. Illus., index, adv. Circ: 13000 Paid and controlled. Online: Gale; Northern Light Technology, Inc.; OCLC Online Computer Library Center, Inc.; ProQuest K-12 Learning Solutions; ProQuest LLC (Ann Arbor). *Indexed:* ABS&EES, AUNI, IUSGP. *Bk. rev.:* 5-9, 500-1000 words. *Aud.:* Ac.

This is the professional journal of the U. S. Army's Armor branch and one of the oldest professional military journals. It originally was published to provide a forum for cavalry officers often separated by great distances on the American frontier to discuss doctrine, equipment needs, and tactics. Now, of course, the focus is on armored fighting vehicles. The stated purpose of the bulletin "is not to reinforce official positions, or to act as a command information conduit, but to surface controversy and debate among professionals in the force." It aims to bridge the gap between practical experience and doctrine by publishing articles on training; history, especially if it details successful counterinsurgencies; tactics and techniques; the future as it relates to combat systems; tactical vignettes; or other issues that face soldiers as they fight. Photographs, charts, and exquisitely drawn pencil sketches illustrate the articles. There are several book reviews that focus on conflicts of the last few years, but not exclusively so. This publication is recommended for academic libraries, especially those that support military science studies.

4522. *Army.* Former titles (until 1956): *The Army Combat Forces Journal;* (until 1954): *United States Army Combat Forces Journal.* [ISSN: 0004-2455] 1950. m. Free to members; Non-members, USD 33; USD 3 newsstand/cover. Ed(s): Larry Moffi, Mary Blake French. Association of the U.S. Army, 2425 Wilson Blvd, Arlington, VA 22201-3326; armymag@ausa.org; http://www.ausa.org. Illus., adv. Circ: 85000 Paid. Vol. ends: Dec. *Indexed:* ABS&EES, AUNI. *Bk. rev.:* 2–3, 500 words. *Aud.:* Ga, Ac.

This attractive magazine is reminiscent of a newsmagazine in its format, layout, and evocative photographs. There is an emphasis on current events, which of course means operations in Afghanistan and Iraq, although the articles also look at past issues in army landpower and pinpoint what future trends in military art and science might be. "Company Command: Building Combat-Ready Teams" has addressed the training of Iraqi forces or air-ground integration in recent issues. "Washington Report" notes how the Executive Branch and Congress address current defense issues. Often, articles are appended by a list of recommended reading. Additionally, several book reviews are accompanied by Amazon.com–like thumbnails of the book jackets. This magazine is interesting, appealing, and should be considered by academic and public libraries.

4523. *Aviation History.* Former titles (until 1994): *Aviation;* (until 1993): *Aviation Heritage.* [ISSN: 1076-8858] 1990. bi-m. USD 29.95; USD 4.99 newsstand/cover. Ed(s): Carl von Wodke. Weider History Group, 741 Miller Dr, S E, Ste D-2, Leesburg, VA 20175. Illus., adv. Circ: 51000 Paid. *Indexed:* MASUSE. *Bk. rev.:* 2-5 500-750 words. *Aud.:* Ga.

Aviation History is a general-interest publication, albeit one that would appeal to readers with a strong interest in aviation. Articles cover commercial, experimental, and high-performance aircraft in addition to military airpower. This magazine is profusely illustrated and appealing. Some articles cover subjects not easily found elsewhere, such as "Hitler's Female Test Pilot." Pioneers of or outstanding contributors to aviation are featured. Computer games and books are reviewed, and there is a calendar of events. This publication should be evaluated for secondary school and public libraries.

4524. *Blue & Gray Magazine: for those who still hear the guns.* [ISSN: 0741-2207] 1983. bi-m. USD 19.95 domestic; USD 29.95 foreign. Ed(s): Michael Bergman. Blue & Gray, 522 Norton Road, Columbus, OH 43228. *Bk. rev.:* 2-6 250 words. *Aud.:* Ga, Ac.

This publication is for Civil War buffs and scholars alike, but unlike other popular magazines on the Civil War, this one concentrates solely on campaigns, battles, and leaders. The articles are written by licensed battlefield guides or, often, by historians who are qualified though not necessarily credentialed. A special feature in every issue, "The General's Tour," provides a tramp across battlefields from the comforts of one's easy chair and includes maps, period and modern photographs, and other points and persons of interest. Several short book reviews cover books that deal almost exclusively with the military aspects of the war. The web site carries endorsements for the magazine from such esteemed historians as James McPherson, Edward Bearss, and Gary W. Gallagher. This public is recommended for both public and academic libraries.

4525. *Civil Wars.* [ISSN: 1369-8249] 1998. q. GBP 237 print & online eds. Ed(s): Caroline Kennedy-Pipe, David M Keithly. Routledge, 4 Park Sq, Milton Park, Abingdon, OX14 4RN, United Kingdom; info@routledge.co.uk; http://www.routledge.com. Illus., index, adv. Sample. Refereed. Vol. ends: Winter. Reprint: PSC. *Indexed:* AmH&L, HistAb, IBSS, IPSA, PSA, SociolAb. *Aud.:* Ac.

Articles in this journal explore the diverse reasons and complicated situations that result in civil wars around the globe. Broadly stated, topics include state building, ethnic conflicts that escalate, the ethics of intervention, and resource implications. Peacekeeping processes are also explored. Although the end result is often military, economics, politics, and religion are often mitigating factors. Recent articles include "Abdicated and Assumed Responsibilities? The Multiple Roles of Political Leadership During the Northern Ireland Peace Process" and "Managing Ethnic Civil Wars: Assessing the Determinants of Successful Mediation." Occasionally, an entire issue will be devoted to the conflicts and attempts at resolution in one country. This journal is cross-disciplinary and could be used by students of sociology, politics, government, or international relations. It is definitely recommended for academic libraries.

4526. *Defense Monitor.* [ISSN: 0195-6450] 1972. 10x/yr. USD 45. Ed(s): Col. Daniel Smith. Center for Defense Information, 1779 Massachusetts Ave, NW, Washington, DC 20036-2109; cdi@igc.apc.org; http://www.cdi.org. Illus. Circ: 35000. Vol. ends: Dec. *Indexed:* AUNI, PRA. *Aud.:* Ga, Ac.

This eight-page newsletter provides intriguing and informed short pieces on military matters that provide the reader with information not usually found in the mainstream media. *Defense Monitor* presents a respectable independent voice that unflinchingly looks at the foibles, follies, and, sometimes, failures of Congress and the Executive Branch with regard to military affairs. For example, "Congressional Pork in the Defense Budget—A Tutorial" and "Our Soldiers' Unmet Needs" are eye-opening reading. The newsletter is a product of the

Center for Defense Information, a Washington think tank. This title belongs in academic libraries where it could be used as a jumping-off point for further discourse, and it should also be considered for public libraries.

4527. *Defense News.* [ISSN: 0884-139X] 1986. w. Mon. USD 129 domestic; USD 169 Canada; USD 199 elsewhere. Defense News Media Group, 6883 Commercial Dr, Springfield, VA 22159; custserv@ defensenews.com. Adv. Circ: 40000. *Aud.:* Ac, Sa.

This weekly, in tabloid format, presents an international perspective on defense issues including worldwide markets for defense technology, military budgets, new products and technology, defense programs and tactics, interviews with defense leaders, and the politics of defense, among others. Two recent lengthy reports focus on the global naval forecast and the latest in helicopter design and technology. Every other page is a full-color ad for military equipment or technology. *Defense News* prides itself on accuracy, credibility, and timeliness in defense reporting. The audience for this publication includes decision-makers or stakeholders in the military or those who supply the military. Special or academic libraries that support programs in international relations would find this publication useful.

4528. *Fortitudine: bulletin of the Marine Corps historical program.* Formerly: *Harumfrodite.* [ISSN: 0362-9910] 1970. q. USD 15 domestic; USD 21 foreign. U.S. Marine Corps, History and Museums Division, Marine Corps Historical Center, 1254 Charles Morris St. SE, Washington Navy Yard, DC 20374-5040; http://hqinet001.hqmc.usmc.mil/HD/. Illus. Circ: 18000. *Indexed:* IUSGP. *Bk. rev.:* 7-10, 75w. *Aud.:* Ga, Sa.

This unusually named publication refers to the motto of the United States Marine Corps in the 1812 era. The purpose of this bulletin of the Marine Corps Historical Program is to "provide education and training in the uses of military and Marine Corps history," but it is not a journal of Marine Corps history. Each issue has a theme such as urban warfare, Parris Island, or the build-up in Vietnam. Sections in each bulletin, such as "Marine Corps Chronology," "History Writing," "Ordnance Collection," "Oral History," "Combat Art," and "Field History" illustrate those themes. Covers for this attractive publication feature, in most cases, original artwork held in the division's art collection. This publication should appeal to those civilians interested in Marine Corps history, and is recommended for public libraries.

4529. *Infantry: a professional bulletin for the U.S. Army infantryman.* Formerly (until 1957): *U.S. Army Infantry School Quarterly.* [ISSN: 0019-9532] 1921. bi-m. USD 15 domestic; USD 30 foreign. Ed(s): Russell A Eno. U.S. Army Infantry School, PO Box 52005, Ft. Benning, GA 31995-2005; http://www.infantry.army.mil/infantry/index.asp. Circ: 13000 Paid. Microform: PQC. Online: EBSCO Publishing, EBSCO Host; Gale; Northern Light Technology, Inc.; OCLC Online Computer Library Center, Inc.; ProQuest K-12 Learning Solutions; ProQuest LLC (Ann Arbor). *Indexed:* AUNI, IUSGP. *Bk. rev.:* two per issue. *Aud.:* Ac, Sa.

This professional bulletin is published by the Army Infantry School at Fort Benning, Georgia, and directed to infantrymen. Several feature articles examine organization, tactics, weapons, and equipment with a heavy emphasis on training. The focus is overwhelmingly on current engagements. The bulletin is definitely for those familiar with army jargon because the straightforward text is sprinkled liberally with military acronyms. The few historical articles are included because they proffer "lessons for today" or look at places that remain areas of interest in the ongoing war on terrorism. Because this is a government publication, it is likely to find a home in academic depository libraries or at institutions that offer military studies.

4530. *International Journal of Intelligence and Counterintelligence.* [ISSN: 0885-0607] 1986. q. GBP 178 print & online eds. Ed(s): Richard R Valcourt. Taylor & Francis Inc., 325 Chestnut St, Ste 800, Philadelphia, PA 19016; orders@taylorandfrancis.com; http://www.taylorandfrancis.com. Illus. Refereed. Online: EBSCO Publishing, EBSCO Host; Gale; IngentaConnect; OCLC Online Computer Library Center, Inc.; SwetsWise Online Content. Reprint: PSC. *Indexed:* AmH&L, HistAb, PAIS, PSA, RiskAb. *Bk. rev.:* 4 per issue. *Aud.:* Ac, Sa.

Planning and execution of military operations are guided and girded by intelligence decisions and policy formulated by government and business entities. This scholarly publication brings together informed discussion by scholars and professionals on national security issues past and current. This journal is nonpartisan, exposing readers to diverse points of view. Recent articles discuss foreign intelligence liaison in the wake of 9/11, problems with U.S. intelligence reform, the Chekist takeover of the Russian state, and the use of financial intelligence against the funding of terrorism. Several lengthy book reviews in each issue discuss all aspects of national security. This publication is appropriate for academic libraries, especially those that support programs that emphasize intelligence studies and foreign policy.

4531. Joint Force Quarterly. [ISSN: 1070-0692] 1993. q. USD 20 domestic; USD 28 foreign. Ed(s): Col. Merrick E Krause. National Defense University, Fort Lesley J McNair, Washington, DC 20319-5066; http://www.ndu.edu. Illus., index. Sample. Circ: 36622. Online: EBSCO Publishing, EBSCO Host; Florida Center for Library Automation; Gale; ProQuest LLC (Ann Arbor). *Indexed:* ABS&EES, AUNI, PAIS. *Bk. rev.:* 4, 500 words. *Aud.:* Ac.

Published by the Institute for National Strategic Studies, National Defense University, *JFQ* has traditionally focused on "joint doctrine, coalition warfare, contingency planning, combat operations conducted by the unified commands, and joint force development." Its status as an official voice of the United States military is evinced by the fact that it is delivered to every general and flag officer in the Department of Defense and key members of the Executive Branch. An emphasis introduced in 2005 is "integrated operations," a realization that all branches of the military must partner with international, private sector, nongovernmental, industrial, and charitable entities to accomplish security objectives successfully. This publication is profusely illustrated, and the articles are readable, reasoned, and written by scholars in the field. Truly educational, this journal should find a place in academic or large pubic libraries.

Joint Force Quarterly: a professional military journal. See Government Periodicals—Federal section.

4532. Journal of Military History. Former titles (until vol.52): *Military Affairs;* (until 1940): *American Military Institute. Journal;* (until 1938): *American Military History Foundation. Journal.* [ISSN: 0899-3718] 1937. q. USD 75 in North America; USD 85 elsewhere. Ed(s): Larry Bland, Bruce Vandervort. Society for Military History, George C Marshall Library, Virginia Military Institute, Lexington, VA 24450-1600; jmsmh@vmi.edu; http://www.smh-hq.org. Illus., index, adv. Sample. Refereed. Circ: 3200 Paid. Vol. ends: Oct. Microform: PQC. Online: Chadwyck-Healey Inc.; EBSCO Publishing, EBSCO Host; JSTOR (Web-based Journal Archive); Northern Light Technology, Inc.; OCLC Online Computer Library Center, Inc.; OhioLINK; Project MUSE; ProQuest LLC (Ann Arbor); SwetsWise Online Content. *Indexed:* ABS&EES, AUNI, AmH&L, AmHI, ArtHuCI, BAS, BRI, CBRI, HistAb, HumInd, IBR, IBZ, SSCI. *Bk. rev.:* Number varies, 200-300 words. *Aud.:* Ga, Ac.

This scholarly, refereed journal is published by the Society for Military History, one of the most prestigious organizations for military historians. All eras of warfare and geographical areas are covered by the six lengthy, extensively researched articles. Academic credentials and current assignments are given for all authors. In addition to the feature articles, each issue has between 50 and 60 book reviews. Another useful feature is the listing of recent journal articles from other publications, classified by time period. This esteemed journal should be part of every academic library and considered by large public libraries.

4533. The Journal of Strategic Studies. [ISSN: 0140-2390] 1978. bi-m. GBP 466 print & online eds. Ed(s): Joe A Maiolo, Thomas G Mahnken. Routledge, 4 Park Sq, Milton Park, Abingdon, OX14 4RN, United Kingdom; info@routledge.co.uk; http://www.routledge.co.uk. Illus., index, adv. Sample. Refereed. Microform: PQC. Online: EBSCO Publishing, EBSCO Host; Gale; IngentaConnect; OCLC Online Computer Library Center, Inc.; SwetsWise Online Content. Reprint: PSC. *Indexed:* AmH&L, AmHI, ArtHuCI, BAS, BrHumI, HistAb, IBR, IBSS, IBZ, IPSA, IndIslam, PSA, SociolAb. *Bk. rev.:* 3-4 500w. *Aud.:* Ac.

Confluences of national politics and increasingly complex and innovative technologies with which to wage wars have necessitated sophisticated strategic planning and subsequent implementation. Articles in this journal underscore the importance of interdisciplinary studies to the field of military policy. In 2005, the journal began publishing collections of essays that deal with significant books in the field and also began featuring articles that explore the field of strategic studies itself. Three or four book reviews on historical or theoretical strategic issues appear in each issue. Because of the scholarly nature of the discourse, this journal is suitable for college or university libraries.

4534. Leatherneck: magazine of the Marines. [ISSN: 0023-981X] 1917. m. USD 21 enlisted member; USD 32 officers. Ed(s): Walter G Ford. Marine Corps Association, 715 Broadway St, PO Boox 1775, Quantico, VA 22134; http://www.mca-marines.org. Illus., index, adv. Sample. Circ: 94000 Paid. Vol. ends: Dec. Microform: PQC. Online: Northern Light Technology, Inc.; ProQuest K-12 Learning Solutions; ProQuest LLC (Ann Arbor). *Bk. rev.:* 5, 200 words. *Aud.:* Hs, Ga.

Leatherneck is simply *the* magazine of the Marine Corps—past, present, and future. The origin of the title, synonymous with "Marine," is of uncertain origin, but has been in use since the eighteenth century. This publication began in 1917 as a newsletter for Marines stationed at Quantico, Virginia, and continues to support the Marine Corps around the world with feature stories, photographs, and illustrations that unabashedly support the strong traditions and history of the U.S. Marine Corps. Content focuses on contemporary issues, such as the war on terrorism, larger-than-life personalities, state-of-the-art tactical equipment, and personal stories from past conflicts such as Korea and Vietnam. This magazine also publishes poetry about the "world's finest," a "final salute" to those who have passed on, and provides a venue for readers to "sound off." Appealing primarily, although not exclusively, to those who have a Marine Corps connection, this publication could find a home in public or high school libraries.

4535. M H Q: the quarterly journal of military history. [ISSN: 1040-5992] 1988. q. USD 39.95 domestic; USD 49.95 Canada; USD 59.95 elsewhere. Weider History Group, 741 Miller Dr, S E, Ste D-2, Leesburg, VA 20175. Illus., index, adv. Circ: 39733 Paid and controlled. Vol. ends: Summer. *Indexed:* AmH&L, HistAb, RGPR. *Bk. rev.:* 2-4, 200-300 words. *Aud.:* Hs, Ga.

Lavishly and liberally illustrated with maps, drawings, and photographs, this wonderfully appealing publication is written for the general public, but that is not to say that the articles merit derision from academics and scholar-historians. The articles are written by professors, military or other experts associated with military or historical agencies, as well as freelance writers and staff of *MHQ*, and cover all time periods and nations. Sources consulted in compiling the research are not listed, however. Well-written and accessible, the articles are devoid of military jargon. Special features include "Terms from Military History," which looks at the origins of common expressions, substantial book reviews, and artist's depictions of war. This magazine would be an excellent choice for public or high school libraries.

4536. Marine Corps Gazette: the professional journal for United States Marines. [ISSN: 0025-3170] 1916. m. USD 32 (Free to qualified personnel). Ed(s): Col. John P Glasgow. Marine Corps Association, 715 Broadway St, PO Boox 1775, Quantico, VA 22134; http://www.mca-marines.org. Illus., index, adv. Sample. Circ: 30886 Paid and free. Vol. ends: Dec. Microform: PQC. Online: Northern Light Technology, Inc.; OCLC Online Computer Library Center, Inc.; ProQuest K-12 Learning Solutions; ProQuest LLC (Ann Arbor). *Indexed:* AUNI, AmH&L, BRI, CBRI, HistAb, PAIS. *Bk. rev.:* 6, 300–750 words. *Aud.:* Ga, Ac.

This publication is the professional journal of the U.S. Marine Corps. The avowed purpose of the *Gazette* is to "express new ideas, discard old dogma, and even—on occasion—to air grievances," with the idea of the moving the Marine Corps forward and adapting to the complexities of the modern world. Each issue has a focus, such as Marine aviation. "Ideas and Issues" classifies material under public or private affairs, intelligence, leadership, commentary, technology, and concepts. Additionally, there are several feature articles. This magazine is written by Marines for Marines, but there is enough of interest to the general public for public libraries to consider.

4537. *Military Collector & Historian.* [ISSN: 0026-3966] 1951. q. Non-members, USD 30. Ed(s): Fred Gaede. Company of Military Historians HQ and Museum, N Main St, Westbrook, CT 06498. Illus., adv. Circ: 4200. Microform: PQC. *Indexed:* AmH&L, HistAb, RILM. *Bk. rev.:* 3-6 250-750 words. *Aud.:* Ac, Sa.

The Company of Military Historians was founded in 1949 "as an educational, scientific, and literary institution devoted to the study and dissemination of information on the uniforms, equipment, history, and traditions of members of the Armed Forces of the United States worldwide and other nations serving in the Western Hemisphere." Contributors to *Military Collector & Historian* include historians, artists, military personnel, librarians, and teachers. Content describes weapons, uniforms, accoutrements, colors, and standards. Information on military organizations, unit histories, military art and artists, and also activities of the organization is included. The identification, dissemination of information about, and preservation of military material culture is a common thread among the features. Several books are reviewed. Of note are the beautifully detailed and historically accurate color and black-and-white plates that appear in each issue. This publication is recommended for academic libraries that support strong history or military science programs and for libraries of appropriate museums and historical societies.

4538. *Military History.* [ISSN: 0889-7328] 1984. 10x/yr. USD 24.95 domestic; USD 36.95 foreign; USD 4.99 newsstand/cover. Ed(s): Mike Robbins. Weider History Group, 741 Miller Dr, S E, Ste D-2, Leesburg, VA 20175. Adv. Circ: 176000 Paid. *Indexed:* AUNI, AmH&L, HistAb, MASUSE. *Bk. rev.:* 3-5, 250-700 words. *Aud.:* Ga.

This magazine is for the military history generalist, so the Civil War or Korean War buff will probably not find enough of interest. However, since its scope is so broad, it fills a niche in the military magazine market. One can find articles on ancient wars through present-day conflicts. Much of the content focuses on prominent battles or famous participants, but there are articles on less recognizable players such "Nadezhda Durova: Cavalry Maiden in the Tsar's Service" or "Mad Mahdi" to pique one's interest. Occasionally, sidebars on war such as military music or the role women played in certain conflicts are featured. Each issue examines a particular weapon or tool of war, and book reviews are also included. Interviews with or narrative accounts of memorable characters in particular military actions make for engrossing reading. The magazine is profusely illustrated, appealing, and written for the general public.

4539. *Military Review (English Edition): the professional journal of the United States Army.* [ISSN: 0026-4148] 1922. bi-m. USD 42 domestic; USD 58.80 foreign. Ed(s): Lt.Col. William M Darley, Lt.Col. George Chandler. U.S. Army Combined Arms Center, 290 Grant Ave, Bldg 77, Fort Leavenworth, KS 66027-1254. Illus., index. Sample. Circ: 27000 Paid and controlled. Vol. ends: Dec. Microform: PQC. Online: EBSCO Publishing, EBSCO Host; Gale; Northern Light Technology, Inc.; OCLC Online Computer Library Center, Inc.; ProQuest K-12 Learning Solutions; ProQuest LLC (Ann Arbor). *Indexed:* ABS&EES, AUNI, AmH&L, BAS, HistAb, IBR, IBZ, IPSA, IUSGP, PAIS, PRA, RiskAb. *Bk. rev.:* 6–11, 200–300 words. *Aud.:* Ac, Ga.

This professional journal focuses on "research and analysis of the concepts, doctrine and principles of warfighting between the tactical and operational levels of war." Its articles include both tactical and strategic matters; recent issues discuss leader education and development, the importance of cultural education, and best practices in counterinsurgency or surveillance activities. Several articles highlighting specific historical engagements with an emphasis on what worked and what could have been done differently encourage lessons to be learned. Some of the articles look at military forces or strategies in foreign countries. This journal encourages original thought and debate, and the understandable, jargon-free articles are written by military officers and credentialed scholars. A strength of this publication is the many book reviews, from essay length to shorter, but still substantial, which cover many subjects and time periods. Recent issues review a biography of U.S. Grant, memoirs of a Syrian defense minister, underground G.I. newspapers in Vietnam, and the last days of the Third Reich. Available online at http://usacac.leavenworth.army.mil/CAC/milreview. *Miltary Review* is published in English, Spanish, Portuguese, and Arabic. This title is highly recommended for academic and large public libraries.

4540. *National Guard.* Former titles (until 1978): *Guardsman;* (until 1975): *National Guardsman.* [ISSN: 0163-3945] 1947. m. Non-members, USD 25. Ed(s): Pamela Kane. National Guard Association of the United States, One Massachusetts Ave, NW, Washington, DC 20001; http://www.ngaus.org. Illus., adv. Circ: 70000. Vol. ends: Dec. Microform: PQC. Online: Northern Light Technology, Inc.; OCLC Online Computer Library Center, Inc.; ProQuest K-12 Learning Solutions; ProQuest LLC (Ann Arbor). *Indexed:* AUNI. *Aud.:* Ga.

This monthly publication of the National Guard Association of the United States surveys activities of the guard worldwide, showcases association news, and includes a message from the chairman of the board. Much of the content assesses the political and budgetary defense climate in Washington and the rightful place of the guard in the nation's military planning and operations. Because the National Guard has played such a prominent role in Operations Enduring Freedom and Iraqi Freedom, this publication should be of interest to contemporary readers. Recommended for public libraries.

4541. *Naval History.* [ISSN: 1042-1920] 1987. bi-m. Members, USD 20; Non-members, USD 27; USD 3.95 newsstand/cover per issue. Ed(s): Richard G Latture, Julianne Olver. U S Naval Institute, 291 Wood Rd, Annapolis, MD 21401; http://www.usni.org. Illus., adv. Circ: 28000 Paid. *Indexed:* ABS&EES, AmH&L, HistAb. *Bk. rev.:* 1-2; 250-500 words. *Aud.:* Ga, Ac.

Attractive, interesting, and appealing to the general reader, *Naval History* is the second publication, along with the *Proceedings* of the U.S. Naval Institute. Key features include excellent photography and artistic depictions of maritime history. The articles encompass interviews with important naval personnel, scholarly analyses, book reviews, profiles of historic ships and aircraft, and "firsthand accounts by the people who participated in our naval triumphs and tragedies." Some issues have themes; a recent one focuses on riverine operations in the Civil War. The articles are authoritative and well written and cover an important arena of military history. This title would be a good addition for public libraries, but it should not be overlooked by academic libraries.

4542. *Naval War College Review.* [ISSN: 0028-1484] 1948. q. Free to qualified personnel. Ed(s): Pelham G Boyer. U.S. Naval War College, 686 Cushing Rd, Code 32, Newport, RI 02841-1207; http://www.nwc.navy.mil. Illus., index. Sample. Circ: 9500 Controlled. Microform: BHP; MIM; PQC. Online: EBSCO Publishing, EBSCO Host; Gale; Northern Light Technology, Inc.; OCLC Online Computer Library Center, Inc.; ProQuest K-12 Learning Solutions; ProQuest LLC (Ann Arbor). *Indexed:* ABS&EES, AUNI, AmH&L, BAS, BRI, CBRI, HistAb, IBR, IBZ, IPSA, IUSGP, PRA, PSA. *Bk. rev.:* 20–25, 300–500 words. *Aud.:* Ac.

This refereed journal is the government publication most cited in the area of foreign affairs. The several articles that deal with current, timely public-policy issues in the areas of national security and maritime affairs are reflective of the academic and professional interests of the Naval War College and, while they appeal primarily to those with an interest in maritime issues, should appeal to a broader audience. Recent articles discuss the Iranian nuclear issue and the differing perspectives on domestic security in Washington and in European capitals, subjects that should engage the thoughtful reader. There are several lengthy book reviews in each issue, and most cover military topics, but occasional titles such as Jared Diamond's *Collapse: How Societies Choose to Fail or Succeed* and Malcolm Gladwell's *Blink: The Power of Thinking Without Thinking* are included. The *Naval War College Review* web site has an author and subject index for all articles published since 1948. This esteemed publication should be a core title for academic libraries.

4543. *Parameters (Carlisle): the United States army's senior professional journal.* [ISSN: 0031-1723] 1971. q. USD 26 domestic; USD 36.40 foreign. Ed(s): Col. Robert Taylor. U.S. Army, War College, Attn: Parameters, 122 Forbes Ave, Carlisle, PA 17013-5238. Illus., index. Sample. Refereed. Circ: 13500. Vol. ends: Winter. Microform: PQC. Online: EBSCO Publishing, EBSCO Host; Florida Center for Library Automation; Gale; OCLC Online Computer Library Center, Inc.; ProQuest LLC (Ann Arbor); H.W. Wilson. *Indexed:* ABCPolSci, ABS&EES, AUNI, AmH&L, BRD, BRI, CBRI, HistAb, IBR, IBZ, IUSGP, PAIS, PSA. *Bk. rev.:* 4–13, 500–1,000 words. *Aud.:* Ac.

This important refereed journal presents diverse ideas and issues, and "provides a forum for mature thought on the art and science of land warfare, joint and combined matters, national and international security affairs, military strategy, military leadership and management, military history, and ethics." Its primary audiences are members of the U.S. Army and the Department of Defense, and it aims to provide important continuing education and professional development for the graduates of the U.S. Army War College as well as other military personnel and academicians. Each issue carries several feature articles as well as two or three articles with a particular focus, such as "The Conduct of War," "Countering Insurgents," and "Rebuilding and Renewal." The articles are thought-provoking, relevant to today's defense and policy issues, well written, accessible, and thoroughly researched. "Commentary and Reply" affords readers the opportunity to comment in-depth on previous articles and the authors to respond. As many as 15 lengthy book reviews covering international or historical as well as contemporary topics enlighten each issue. This is a core title and should find a place in most academic libraries.

4544. Sea Power. Formerly: *Navy - the Magazine of Sea Power.* [ISSN: 0199-1337] 1958. m. USD 48. Ed(s): Rick Bernard, Richard R. Burgess. Navy League of the United States, 2300 Wilson Blvd, Arlington, VA 22201-3308; mail@navyleague.org; http://www.navyleague.org. Illus., adv. Circ: 68468 Paid. Vol. ends: Dec. Microform: PQC. Online: EBSCO Publishing, EBSCO Host; Northern Light Technology, Inc.; OCLC Online Computer Library Center, Inc.; ProQuest K-12 Learning Solutions; ProQuest LLC (Ann Arbor). *Indexed:* ABS&EES, AUNI, AmH&L, HistAb. *Aud.:* Ga, Ac.

Published by the Navy League, a civilian organization that presents citizens' voices in support of maritime services, this attractive monthly is the only magazine to focus on the United States' maritime defense. Current issues discuss with clarity and intelligence such timely topics as the impact of higher fuel costs on shipping or the state of port security. Special reports such as "Intelligence, Surveillance and Reconnaissance" or "NetCentric Warfare" afford in-depth coverage of relevant current issues. The aim of this publication is to educate citizens as well as the armed forces and other policymakers as to the conditions and capabilities of naval and maritime forces. An almanac, published as the January issue of *Sea Power,* gives the missions and organizational overviews of the Coast Guard, Navy, Marine Corps, Maritime Administration, and officer training programs, and snapshots of the maritime academies for the previous year. Because of the uniquely gathered information here, this publication should find a home in academic, public, and appropriate corporate libraries.

4545. Soldiers. Formerly: *Army Digest.* [ISSN: 0093-8440] 1946. m. USD 46 domestic; USD 64 foreign. Ed(s): Gil High. U.S. Department of the Army, 9325 Gunston Rd., Ste S108, Ft. Belvoir, VA 22060-5581. Illus., index. Circ: 1000000 Controlled. Microform: PQC. Online: EBSCO Publishing, EBSCO Host; Gale; Northern Light Technology, Inc.; OCLC Online Computer Library Center, Inc.; ProQuest K-12 Learning Solutions; ProQuest LLC (Ann Arbor). *Indexed:* ABS&EES, AUNI, BAS, IUSGP, PAIS. *Aud.:* Ga, Ac, Sa.

This glossy, award-winning magazine is the official publication of the United States Army. Its features cover army leaders, trends, practical applications, equipment, and current events. Some issues are theme-based, spotlighting recruitment and retention, medical care, or Earth Day, for example. Some issues have pull-out posters or pull-out "Hot Topics" sections. The latter includes identity theft, alcohol abuse, and family violence. The articles are short, practical, and informative, giving an upbeat, holistic portrait of today's soldier. This publication should be of interest to public library users or high school libraries in areas where many young men and women enlist after graduation, in addition to its obvious military audience.

Soldiers. See Government Periodicals—Federal section.

4546. Special Warfare. [ISSN: 1058-0123] 1988. q. USD 18 domestic; USD 22.50 foreign. Ed(s): Jerry D Steelman. John F. Kennedy Special Warfare Center and School, Attn: AOJK-DT-DM, USAJFKSWCS, Ft. Bragg, NC 28310; steelman@soc.mil. Circ: 10000 Paid and controlled. *Indexed:* ABS&EES, AUNI. *Bk. rev.:* 2; 750-1000 words. *Aud.:* Ac, Sa.

Special-operations forces are the elite branch of the U.S. Army, and this publication, directed to special-ops forces, offers a fascinating look at ever-evolving training and core philosophies. Special-ops forces are involved in intelligence, logistics, fire-support coordination, direct action, special reconnaissance, and other critical activities. The mission of *Special Warfare* is "to promote the professional development of special-operations forces by providing a forum for the examination of established doctrine and new ideas." The publication is visually appealing with many color photographs, tables, and charts. Content focuses on lessons learned and analyses, as well as news about the Army's special-operations university. A recent issue includes several articles on the transformation of SERE, the Survival, Evasion, Resistance, and Escape course mandated by the current operational environment. Of late, the journal has moved away from longer academic papers to shorter and more easily read articles, often, but certainly not exclusively, written by members of the staff. In fact, qualified members of the Armed Forces, security-policy decision-makers, defense analysts, and academic researchers are encouraged to submit articles. This publication is recommended for academic libraries.

4547. Survival (Abingdon). [ISSN: 0039-6338] 1959. q. GBP 175 print & online eds. Ed(s): Dana H Allin. Taylor & Francis Ltd., 4 Park Sq, Milton Park, Abingdon, OX14 4RN, United Kingdom; info@tandf.co.uk; http://www.tandf.co.uk/journals. Adv. Refereed. Circ: 4800. Microform: PQC. Online: Chadwyck-Healey Inc.; EBSCO Publishing, EBSCO Host; Gale; HighWire Press; IngentaConnect; OCLC Online Computer Library Center, Inc.; OhioLINK; ProQuest LLC (Ann Arbor); SwetsWise Online Content. Reprint: PSC. *Indexed:* AUNI, AmH&L, BAS, HistAb, IBR, IBSS, IBZ, IPSA, PAIS, PRA, PSA, SSCI, SociolAb. *Bk. rev.:* 1-5 per issue. *Aud.:* Ac.

Thoughtful discussion of strategic issues and how they affect military and political policy in the post–Cold War world inform readers of this scholarly publication issued by the International Institute for Strategic Studies. The independent institute is a center for "research, information and debate on the problems of conflict, however caused, that have, or potentially have, an important military content." Articles such as "Jihad in Europe" and "Terms of Estrangement: French-American Relations in Perspective" discuss current issues of importance beyond their immediate context to their potential global significance. Presciently, an article in *Survival* 18 months prior to September 11, 2001, warned that the new face of terrorism was Osama bin Laden and that he and his operatives were planning to inflict damage on a large scale. The articles are stimulating, well written, and well argued. One to five book reviews and a longer review essay are included in each issue. Highly recommended for academic libraries.

4548. U S Naval Institute. Proceedings. [ISSN: 0041-798X] 1874. m. Membership, USD 39. Ed(s): Robert Timberg, Brendan Greeley, Jr. U S Naval Institute, 291 Wood Rd, Annapolis, MD 21401; http://www.usni.org. Illus., index, adv. Circ: 90000 Paid. Vol. ends: Dec. Microform: PQC. Online: EBSCO Publishing, EBSCO Host; OCLC Online Computer Library Center, Inc.; ProQuest LLC (Ann Arbor). *Indexed:* ABS&EES, AUNI, AmH&L, BAS, ChemAb, HistAb, PAIS. *Bk. rev.:* 3, 500–1,000 words. *Aud.:* Ga, Ac.

The United States Naval Institute is an "independent forum on the sea services and national defense." The institute supports the professional development of maritime personnel, honors the heritage of sea services, promotes national defense, and encourages critical debate on defense issues. This content is reflected in the *Proceedings,* which offers articles by military or civilian experts, interviews with military leaders and strategists, spirited reader commentary, book reviews, and much color photography. The May issue carries a year-in-review of the Navy, Marine Corps, Merchant Marines, and Coast Guard. This publication is considered *de rigueur* for those wanting to be apprised of current naval thinking. This title is recommended for academic libraries.

4549. War in History. [ISSN: 0968-3445] 1994. q. GBP 260. Ed(s): Dennis Showalter, Hew Strachan. Sage Publications Ltd., 1 Oliver's Yard, 55 City Rd, London, EC1 1SP, United Kingdom; info@sagepub.co.uk; http://www.sagepub.co.uk. Illus., adv. Sample. Refereed. Circ: 600. Online: EBSCO Publishing, EBSCO Host; Gale; HighWire Press;

IngentaConnect; OCLC Online Computer Library Center, Inc.; OhioLINK; ProQuest LLC (Ann Arbor); SwetsWise Online Content. Reprint: PSC. *Indexed:* AmH&L, AmHI, ArtHuCI, HistAb, IBR, IBZ. *Bk. rev.:* 15-35 per issue. *Aud.:* Ac.

This journal places military history in a broader context that includes historical, economic, political, and social narratives. It welcomes articles that make new factual or interpretive contributions that cover all periods of history and types of warfare. The articles are scholarly and focused and written for the historian or expert; the emphasis is decidedly on non-North American activities. Recent article titles include "Some Observations on Administration and Logistics of the Siege of Nicaea," "Conscription in the French Restoration: The 1818 Debate on Military Service," and "Standardized Numbers in the Byzantine Army." A strength of this publication is the book reviews. Each issue reviews anywhere from 15 to 35 titles covering all periods and places of historical warfare. Although this title is not a core military title, it should be considered by academic libraries.

4550. *World War II.* [ISSN: 0898-4204] 1986. 10x/yr. USD 24.95 domestic; USD 36.95 foreign; USD 5 newsstand/cover. Weider History Group, 741 Miller Dr, S E, Ste D-2, Leesburg, VA 20175. Adv. Circ: 200000 Paid. *Indexed:* ABS&EES, MASUSE. *Bk. rev.:* Number and length vary. *Aud.:* Ga.

This magazine aimed at the general reader features articles on battles, leaders, fighting men, weapons, and tactics. Many of the articles tell a particular story, and personalities from both the European and Pacific theaters of operations find a voice here. Individual acts of heroism are spotlighted in "One Man's War." Often unusual facts and incidents are profiled. Editorial staff often contributes to articles or reviews the several books featured in each issue. Articles are signed, but little if any background information is provided on the authors; however, the articles are accessible and interestingly written. This publication is lavishly illustrated with artistic renderings, maps, and plenty of photographs. Public libraries should find this magazine of interest, especially those that serve an older demographic.

■ MODEL MAKING

General/Model Railroads/Model Aircraft/Model Automobiles/Model Ships

Brian C. Greene, Assistant Head Librarian, Access Services Dept., Northeastern University Libraries, 360 Huntington Ave., Boston, MA 02115; br.greene@neu.edu

Introduction

Model making encompass a wide variety of subject specialties and skill levels that reflect an equally broad range of interests and abilities found among model enthusiasts. For instance, there are specialty magazines devoted to such subjects as model aircraft, model railroads, model ships, and model automobiles, as well as military and science fiction models.

Models run the gamut from static, highly detailed matchstick models to operational radio-controlled flyers and engine-powered locomotives. Models may be realistic historical-era or commercial replicas, or they may depict ships and vehicles from a fantasy world.

Models are made of various material types, including wood, plastic, and metal. Some are assembled from kits, while others are built from scratch. Many models are designed according to scale. Some of these are small enough to fit onto a desktop display stand, while larger ones are known as "garage models."

In general, this section will focus on the building and collecting of models, and not on the operational aspects of modeling, such as flying, racing, or competing. Additionally, antique and modern doll, miniature, figurine, and toy collecting will not be covered in this section, as they fall outside its scope.

Finally, this section is not meant to be an exhaustive or comprehensive list of all the periodicals that touch on modeling as a hobby. Instead, this section focuses only on what is recommended for public libraries to purchase for their collections. Most of the magazines listed here are aimed at an adult audience, but some will be suitable for older children as well.

Basic Periodicals

Ga: *FineScale Modeler, Model Railroader, Model Airplane News, Scale Auto, Seaways' Ships in Scale.*

Basic Abstracts and Indexes

Readers' Guide to Periodical Literature.

General

4551. *FineScale Modeler.* [ISSN: 0277-979X] 1981. 10x/yr. USD 39.95 domestic; USD 50 foreign; USD 4.95 newsstand/cover. Ed(s): Mark Thompson. Kalmbach Publishing Co., 21027 Crossroads Circle, PO Box 1612, Waukesha, WI 53187-1612; customerservice@kalmbach.com; http://www.kalmbach.com. Illus., index, adv. Sample. Circ: 61000 Paid. Vol. ends: Dec. *Indexed:* BRI, IHTDI. *Bk. rev.:* 3-30, 50-150 words. *Aud.:* Ga.

FineScale Modeler is the best-known plastic scale modeling magazine in the world. Feature articles help readers build better modeling skills via the construction of specific projects. *FSM* offers expert tips and techniques, especially with regard to kit assembly and modification. Although many of the models featured in the magazine carry military themes, this is not a military modeling publication. Regular columns include a "Reader Gallery and Showcase" section, and updates and reviews of new product kits and prototype information. One of the magazine's highlights is its "Great Scale Modeling" annual issue, which features some of the best models from around the world, including highlights from various model shows.

Model Railroads

4552. *Model Railroader.* [ISSN: 0026-7341] 1934. m. USD 39.95 domestic; USD 50 foreign; USD 4.95 newsstand/cover domestic. Ed(s): Terry Thompson. Kalmbach Publishing Co., 21027 Crossroads Circle, PO Box 1612, Waukesha, WI 53187-1612; customerservice@ kalmbach.com; http://www.kalmbach.com. Illus., index, adv. Sample. Circ: 176000 Paid. Vol. ends: Dec. Microform: PQC. Online: EBSCO Publishing, EBSCO Host; Gale; Micromedia ProQuest; Northern Light Technology, Inc.; OCLC Online Computer Library Center, Inc.; ProQuest K-12 Learning Solutions; ProQuest LLC (Ann Arbor); H.W. Wilson. *Indexed:* BRI, CBCARef, CBRI, ConsI, IHTDI, MASUSE, RGPR. *Bk. rev.:* 100-400 words. *Aud.:* Ga.

Model Railroader stands apart from all other railroad enthusiast magazines due to its extraordinarily high circulation and its focus on creating railroad layouts. Whereas other magazines focus only on model trains and their operation, *Model Railroader* places a strong emphasis on creating realistic environments for operating trains. Regular columns include industry news, event coverage, step-by-step projects, and expert advice. Articles feature outstanding projects, complete with instructions. This attractive, full-color magazine includes an advertising index and a directory of retailers by state. This is one publication not to be missed.

4553. *Railroad Model Craftsman.* Formerly: *Model Railroad Craftsman.* [ISSN: 0033-877X] 1933. m. USD 34.95 domestic; USD 45 foreign; USD 4.50 newsstand/cover. Ed(s): William Schaumburg. Carstens Publications, Inc., 108 Phil Hardin Rd, Newton, NJ 07860-0777; carstens@carstens-publications.com; http://www.carstens-publications.com. Illus., index, adv. Sample. Circ: 94000 Paid. Vol. ends: May. *Bk. rev.:* 100-400 words. *Aud.:* Ga.

Railroad Model Craftsman is the second leading magazine in the railroad hobby industry. It features high-quality articles, photographs, and prototype drawings, and critical product reviews. It even includes reviews of new books and DVDs on the topic of model railroading. This full-color glossy magazine features outstanding projects, how-to-do-it articles, and an event calendar.

4554. *Train Collectors Quarterly.* [ISSN: 0041-0829] 1955. q. USD 14. Ed(s): Bruce D Manson, Jr. Train Collectors Association, 300 Paradise Ln, PO Box 248, Strasburg, PA 17579-0248; http://www.traincollectors.org/. Illus., index. Sample. Circ: 29000 Controlled. Vol. ends: Oct. *Bk. rev.:* Number and length vary. *Aud.:* Ga.

Train Collectors Quarterly is a unique scholarly publication, focusing on the history of toy train collecting. Feature articles are highly detailed and speak with surprising authority. The *TCQ* is the official publication of the Train Collectors Association, the largest such society in the U.S. Regular columns provide coverage of the association's activities and feature the collections of its members. This journal does not include advertisements.

Model Aircraft

4555. *Backyard Flyer.* [ISSN: 1542-2135] 2001. bi-m. USD 19.95 domestic; USD 29.95 Canada; USD 34.95 elsewhere. Ed(s): Jon Chappell. Air Age Media, 100 E Ridge, Ridgefield, CT 06877-4606; http://www.airage.com. Illus., adv. *Indexed:* MASUSE. *Aud.:* Ems, Hs, Ga.

Backyard Flyer is a popular new magazine aimed at beginning hobbyists and children interested in radio-controlled miniature aircraft. Developments in radio control technology allow these model airplanes to be small and silent, enough so that they may be operated in backyards and parks, eliminating the need for liability insurance. The magazine includes tips for proper plane assembly, first-flight success, and troubleshooting. Articles feature product reviews and a buyers' guide to the best ready-to-fly aircraft.

4556. *Flying Models: the model builder's how-to-do-it magazine.* [ISSN: 0015-4849] 1927. m. USD 34.95 domestic; USD 45 Canada; USD 4.50 newsstand/cover. Ed(s): Frank Fanelli. Carstens Publications, Inc., 108 Phil Hardin Rd, Newton, NJ 07860-0777; carstens@carstens-publications.com; http://www.carstens-publications.com. Illus., adv. Sample. Circ: 33710 Paid. Vol. ends: Dec. *Aud.:* Ga.

Flying Models is the oldest U.S. flying-model magazine, and one of the oldest model-making magazines in the world. Unlike some of the newer publications, *FM* devotes space to traditional models as well as to new trends. Contents include columns on new developments in the hobby, model construction, product reviews, and advice for new hobbyists. *Flying Models* also maintains a plans directory service for full-size drawings of projects that have appeared as articles.

4557. *Model Airplane News.* Formerly: *Air Age Publishing.* [ISSN: 0026-7295] 1929. m. USD 29.95 domestic; USD 44.95 Canada; USD 54.95 elsewhere. Air Age Media, 100 E Ridge, Ridgefield, CT 06877-4606; http://www.airage.com. Illus., adv. Sample. Circ: 80000 Paid. Vol. ends: Dec. Microform: PQC. Online: EBSCO Publishing, EBSCO Host; Micromedia ProQuest; Northern Light Technology, Inc.; OCLC Online Computer Library Center, Inc.; ProQuest K-12 Learning Solutions; ProQuest LLC (Ann Arbor). *Indexed:* CBCARef, ConsI, MASUSE. *Aud.:* Ga.

Model Airplane News is one of the oldest and most popular magazines dedicated to the building and flying of radio-controlled airplanes. Regular content focuses on the construction of planes and engines, flight tests, product reviews, project descriptions, and tips and advice for beginners. Monthly issues feature various themes such as model helicopters. This attractive, full-color title is the model airplane magazine of choice for most public libraries.

Model Automobiles

4558. *Model Cars Magazine.* Formerly (until 1998): *Plastic Fanatic.* [ISSN: 1527-4608] 1985. 9x/yr. USD 29 domestic; USD 39 foreign. Ed(s): Gregg Hutchings. Golden Bell Press Inc., 2403 Champa St, Denver, CO 80205; print@goldenbellpress.com; http://www.goldenbellpress.com. Illus. *Bk. rev.:* Number and length vary. *Aud.:* Ga.

Model Cars Magazine is dedicated to the building and customizing of static scale models of automobiles. Issues feature reviews of kits and how-to-do-it articles, clearly illustrated with step-by-step photographs. The magazine devotes a great deal of space to contests and outstanding modelers and their work. The accompanying web site also sponsors an online forum for readers.

4559. *Scale Auto.* Formerly (until 2002): *Scale Auto Enthusiast.* [ISSN: 1550-5251] 1979. bi-m. USD 24.95 domestic; USD 33 foreign; USD 4.50 newsstand/cover. Ed(s): Jim Haught. Kalmbach Publishing Co., 21027 Crossroads Circle, PO Box 1612, Waukesha, WI 53187-1612; http://www.kalmbach.com. Illus., adv. Sample. Circ: 30820 Paid. Vol. ends: Apr. *Aud.:* Ga.

Scale Auto is the leading publication on building and collecting static automotive models, including muscle cars, stock cars, street rods, lowriders, and trucks. Regular columns highlight industry news and product and kit reviews, as well as coverage of events. Articles feature readers' outstanding projects, including kit construction, superdetailing, modification, and painting, complete with full-color photographs. If a library can only afford one automotive modeling magazine, this is the one to buy.

Model Ships

4560. *Seaways' Ships in Scale.* Formerly (until 1992): *Seaways.* [ISSN: 1065-8904] 1990. bi-m. USD 26.95 domestic; USD 29.95 in Canada & Mexico; USD 38 elsewhere. Seaways Publishing, Inc., 5655 Silver Creek Valley Rd, No 242, San Jose, CA 95138-2473. Illus., index, adv. Circ: 6000 Paid. Vol. ends: Nov/Dec. *Indexed:* AmH&L, HistAb. *Bk. rev.:* 1, 200-500 words. *Aud.:* Ga, Sa.

Seaways' Ships in Scale is the only publication of its kind, a specialized workshop and research magazine for ship model builders. Articles feature how-to instructions that cover a wide variety of ship models from all historical eras, spanning a broad range of construction materials, including both wood and steel. The magazine is aimed at readers of all levels of modeling experience, although readers should be aware of the challenging aspects of the hobby. The publication's web site serves as a gateway to nautical research and ship modeling information, and hosts a listserv dedicated to the hobby.

■ MUSIC

General/Popular

See also Music Reviews section.

Esther Gillie, User Services Coordinator of the Music Library, University of Illinois–Urbana Champaign, 1114 Nevada St., Urbana, IL 61801; gillie@uiuc.edu (General subsection)

Ralph Montilio, Public Services Assistant of Tozzer Library, Harvard University, 21 Divinity Ave., Cambridge, MA 02138; montilio@ fas.harvard.edu (General subsection)

Beth Flood, Music and Media Cataloger, Loeb Music Library, Harvard University, Music Building, North Yard, Cambridge, MA 02138; eflood@fas.harvard.edu (Popular subsection)

Liza Vick, Music Reference and Research Services Librarian, Loeb Music Library, Harvard University, Music Building, North Yard, Cambridge, MA 02138; lizavick@fas.harvard.edu (General and Popular subsections)

Introduction

In this section, the General subsection lists titles of scholarly periodicals that are published mainly in the United States and Europe. Coverage includes performance areas such as instrumental, vocal, and choral music; genres such as opera and chamber music; disciplines such as musicology, music theory, composition, music education, and ethnomusicology; and areas of interest such as historical eras, physical and psychological aspects of making and listening to music, music technology, and the intersection of music with other fields in contemporary art and culture. Journals that focus on a single composer or instrument (with the exception of keyboard instruments) are not included.

The Popular subsection includes periodical titles that cover many genres, including jazz, rock, heavy metal, reggae, folk, bluegrass, country, and other popular and world musics. These magazines are published mainly in the United States or Great Britain, and many consist primarily of interviews and artist biographies, news, and recordings and media reviews. These titles also cover the scholarly study of popular music, general pop culture as it pertains to music, and specific instruments and equipment.

Basic Periodicals

GENERAL. Hs: *American Music Teacher, Choral Journal, Instrumentalist, Music Educators Journal;* Ga: *American Music, Ethnomusicology, The Musical Quarterly, Opera News;* Ac: *Journal of Music Theory, Journal of Research in Music Education, American Musicological Society. Journal.*

POPULAR. Hs, Ga, Ac: *Rolling Stone.* Select others as needed.

Basic Abstracts and Indexes

International Index to Music Periodicals, Music Index, RILM Abstracts of Music Literature.

General

4561. *Acta Musicologica.* Formerly (until 1931): *Internationale Gesellschaft fuer Musikwissenschaft. Mitteilungen.* [ISSN: 0001-6241] 1928. 2x/yr. EUR 85. Ed(s): Philippe Vendrix. Baerenreiter Verlag, Heinrich-Schuetz-Allee 35, Kassel, 34131, Germany; order@baerenreiter.com; http://www.baerenreiter.com. Illus., index, adv. Refereed. Circ: 1900 Paid and controlled. Vol. ends: Dec. *Indexed:* ArtHuCI, FR, IBR, IBZ, IIMP, MusicInd, RILM. *Aud.:* Ac, Sa.

Acta Musicologica (published by the International Musicological Society) presents scholarly articles in the fields of musicology and ethnomusicology, from contributors worldwide. The journal covers a wide variety of time periods, composers, and research methodologies; it also includes tributes to eminent musicologists and information on upcoming conferences. Articles appear in numerous languages, including English, French, German, Italian, and Spanish. Of great interest to musicologists, it is recommended for academic music libraries.

4562. *Amazing Sounds: the alternative music e-magazine.* 1996. irreg. Amazing Sounds, http://www.amazings.com/ingles.html. *Aud.:* Hs, Ga, Ac.

This online magazine focuses on electronic, ambient, avant-garde, new age, and other contemporary music genres around the world (including such artists as Peter Gabriel and Kaija Saariaho). It focuses on the musicians and their musical styles, and includes biographical articles, numerous recording reviews, and interviews with musicians (some contain photographs, album covers, CV-style works lists, or other images). Other sections include news, an artists gallery that lists musicians and their essential works, and links to other web resources, including mail-order service (locating recordings). Content is in both English and Spanish; useful for anyone interested in contemporary music.

4563. *American Music.* [ISSN: 0734-4392] 1983. q. USD 79 (Individuals, USD 45). Ed(s): Michael Hicks. University of Illinois Press, 1325 S Oak St, Champaign, IL 61820-6903; journals@uillinois.edu; http://www.press.uillinois.edu. Illus., adv. Sample. Refereed. Circ: 1650 Paid. Microform: PQC. Online: Chadwyck-Healey Inc.; Florida Center for Library Automation; Gale; JSTOR (Web-based Journal Archive); Northern Light Technology, Inc.; OCLC Online Computer Library Center, Inc.; ProQuest K-12 Learning Solutions; ProQuest LLC (Ann Arbor). *Indexed:* ABS&EES, AmHI, ArtHuCI, BRI, CBRI, HumInd, IBR, IBZ, IIMP, MusicInd, RILM. *Bk. rev.:* 10-12, 1,000 words, signed. *Aud.:* Ga, Ac, Sa.

American Music is devoted to all aspects of music history and contemporary music in America. Articles cover American composers, performers, publishers, institutions, and events, and the American music industry. Musical genres include jazz, folk, dance, theater, blues, popular, and classical. Book, recording, multimedia, and web site reviews, bibliographies, and discographies are included. Some content is available online at the publisher's web site. This is one of the premier journals in its subject area and is of interest to performers and scholars of American music. Recommended for academic and public libraries with any American music focus. A related title is the *Journal of the Society for American Music.*

4564. *American Music Research Center Journal.* [ISSN: 1058-3572] 1991. a. USD 14.50 domestic; USD 16.50 foreign. Ed(s): Thomas L Riis. American Music Research Center, Univ of Colorado at Boulder, College of Music, Boulder, CO 80309. Sample. Refereed. Circ: 300 Paid. *Indexed:* IIMP, MusicInd, RILM. *Bk. rev.:* 1, 500 words, signed. *Aud.:* Ac.

American Music Research Center Journal is dedicated to publishing articles of general interest about American music, particularly in subject areas relevant to its collections. Submissions of articles and proposals from the scholarly community are welcomed.

4565. *American Music Teacher.* [ISSN: 0003-0112] 1951. bi-m. USD 24 (Non-members, USD 30; USD 6 per issue domestic). Ed(s): Marcie G Lindsey. Music Teachers National Association, 441 Vine St, Ste 505, Cincinnati, OH 45202-2811; mtnanet@mtna.org; http://www.mtna.org. Illus., adv. Circ: 25000 Paid. Vol. ends: Jun/Jul. Online: Chadwyck-Healey Inc.; EBSCO Publishing, EBSCO Host; Florida Center for Library Automation; Gale; Northern Light Technology, Inc.; OCLC Online Computer Library Center, Inc.; ProQuest LLC (Ann Arbor); H.W. Wilson. *Indexed:* ABIn, BRI, CBRI, EduInd, IBR, IBZ, IIMP, MusicInd, RILM. *Bk. rev.:* 5-7, 500 words, signed. *Aud.:* Ac, Sa.

The purpose of *American Music Teacher,* the official publication of the Music Teachers National Association (MTNA), is to provide articles, reviews, and regular columns that inform, educate, and challenge music teachers and foster excellence in the music teaching profession. Issues include articles and columns that reflect the interests of the broad spectrum of teachers served by MTNA; announcements of national, state, and local news and competitions; opportunities for professional enrichment and opportunities for students; and discussions of issues and trends in the music field. Of interest to private and collegiate music teachers, it is recommended for academic and large public libraries.

4566. *American Musicological Society. Journal.* Formerly: *American Musicological Society. Bulletin.* [ISSN: 0003-0139] 1948. 3x/yr. USD 119 print & online eds. USD 44 newsstand/cover. Ed(s): Bruce Alan Brown. University of California Press, Journals Division, 2000 Center St, Ste 303, Berkeley, CA 94704-1223; journals@ucpress.edu; http://www.ucpress.edu/journals. Illus., index, adv. Refereed. Circ: 3045. *Indexed:* ABS&EES, AmHI, ArtHuCI, BAS, HumInd, IBR, IBZ, IIMP, IndIslam, MLA-IB, MusicInd, RI-1, RILM. *Bk. rev.:* 3-5, 3,000 words, signed. *Aud.:* Ac, Sa.

The *American Musicological Society. Journal* (JAMS) is arguably the premier journal for historical musicology, publishing refereed articles in music history, theory, criticism, analysis, aesthetics, iconography and organology, performance practice, aesthetics, and hermeneutics. Primary focus is the history of Western art music, but articles addressing ethnomusicology, gender and sexuality, popular music and cultural studies also appear (this information is present on the journal web site). A typical issue includes three extensive articles (with abstracts), signed book reviews, communications, and a list of publications received that includes books and scholarly editions of music. The journal's web site contains tables of contents with abstracts from 2000 to the present, and full text is available online to subscribers. Highly recommended for academic libraries; necessary for music libraries that support research programs.

4567. *Cambridge Opera Journal.* [ISSN: 0954-5867] 1989. 3x/yr. GBP 109. Ed(s): Mary Ann Smart, Emanuelle Senici. Cambridge University Press, The Edinburgh Bldg, Shaftesbury Rd, Cambridge, CB2 2RU, United Kingdom; journals@cambridge.org;

http://www.journals.cambridge.org. Illus., adv. Refereed. Vol. ends: Nov. Reprint: PSC. *Indexed:* AmHI, BrHumI, IIMP, IIPA, MusicInd, RILM. *Bk. rev.:* 1-2, 6-10 pages, signed. *Aud.:* Ac, Sa.

A highly reputable scholarly publication, the *Cambridge Opera Journal* is a preeminent forum for all aspects of the European operatic canon, as well as American opera, musical theater, theory, historiography, and contemporary operas. Articles provide information on topics such as form, style, composers and singers, eras, staging, gender studies, literature, ballet, history, and other related topics. Issues include illustrations, musical examples, and reviews of recent publications of importance in the field. Crucial to performers and scholars, it is recommended for academic and large public libraries; essential for those that support musicology or opera programs.

4568. Chamber Music. Former titles (until 1986): *Chamber Music Magazine;* (until 1983): *American Ensemble.* [ISSN: 1071-1791] 1978. bi-m. USD 28. Ed(s): Ellen Goldenshn. Chamber Music America, 305 Seventh Ave, 5th Fl, New York, NY 10001-6008. Adv. Circ: 13000. *Indexed:* IIMP, MusicInd, RILM. *Bk. rev.:* 2-3, 500-1,000 words, signed. *Aud.:* Ac, Sa.

Chamber Music is the official publication of Chamber Music America, an organization committed to promoting artistic excellence and economic stability within the profession and to ensuring that chamber music is a vital part of American life. Complete with color photos, articles feature interviews with various chamber ensembles; information on conferences, workshops, and festivals; strategies for economic planning; and guidance regarding technological concerns. Styles discussed range from classical to jazz to popular music. The table of contents is available online. Of interest to performers, educators, students, and chamber music aficionados, it is recommended for academic and large public libraries.

4569. Choir & Organ. [ISSN: 0968-7262] 1993. bi-m. GBP 21.30 UK & Ireland; EUR 42.20 in Europe; USD 48.25 in US & Canada. Ed(s): Matthew Power. Orpheus Publications Ltd., 30 Cannon St, London, EC4M 6YJ, United Kingdom; info@orpheuspublications.com; http://www.orphpl.com/home.asp?id=co3. Illus., adv. Circ: 8000 Paid. Vol. ends: Jul/Aug. Online: EBSCO Publishing, EBSCO Host. *Indexed:* AmHI, BrHumI, IBR, IBZ, IIMP, MASUSE, MusicInd, RILM. *Aud.:* Ac, Sa.

Choir & Organ is a classical music magazine for organists, choir and choral directors, singers, organ builders, and lovers of choral and organ music. Articles provide insights into the careers of leading musicians, organists, and choral conductors; describe important instruments, composers, and compositions; and provide comprehensive news and reviews of new publications, recordings, DVDs, festivals, and events. Many color photos of organs are included in each issue. Recommended for academic and public libraries.

4570. Choral Journal. [ISSN: 0009-5028] 1959. m. Aug.-July. USD 35. Ed(s): Carroll Gonzo. American Choral Directors Association, PO Box 2720, Oklahoma City, OK 73101; chojo@sirinet.net; http://www.choralnet.org/. Illus., index, adv. Refereed. Circ: 21000 Paid. Vol. ends: Jul. Microform: PQC. Online: Chadwyck-Healey Inc. *Indexed:* ABS&EES, IIMP, MusicInd, RILM. *Bk. rev.:* 3-5, 200-500 words, signed. *Aud.:* Hs, Ac, Sa.

The American Choral Directors Association publishes *Choral Journal* to provide its members with practical and scholarly information about choral music and its performance. Articles and columns cover topics such as rehearsal techniques, composers, history, form and style of choral music, interviews with eminent conductors and composers, performance practice, vocal pedagogy, and educational techniques and philosophies. Issues include association news, convention information (in the January issue), and reviews of recordings, music, and books. Recommended for academic, public, and high school libraries. The web site features selective online content.

4571. Clavier: a magazine for pianists and organists. Formerly (until 1966): *Piano Teacher.* [ISSN: 0009-854X] 1962. 10x/yr. USD 19. Ed(s): Judy Nelson. The Instrumentalist Co., 200 Northfield Rd, Northfield, IL 60093-3390. Illus., index, adv. Circ: 16000. Vol. ends: Dec. *Indexed:* ABIn, ABS&EES, ArtHuCI, EduInd, IIMP, MusicInd, RILM, SSCI. *Aud.:* Hs, Ac, Sa.

Clavier is published for piano teachers and students and offers practical information and innovative ideas for educators, students, and performers. Articles are written by veteran teachers and performers who share their experience in working with all levels of students. Leading educators discuss new ideas and advice for piano teachers, including teaching and repertoire suggestions. Issues include interviews and profiles of teachers and artists, articles on the business side of teaching, new music reviews, competition information, and ideas for rekindling the interest and enthusiasm of students. Recommended for academic, public, and high school libraries.

4572. Computer Music Journal. [ISSN: 0148-9267] 1977. q. USD 272 print & online eds. (Individuals, USD 58 print & online eds.). Ed(s): Douglas Keislar. M I T Press, 238 Main St., Ste. 500, Cambridge, MA 02142; journals-info@mit.edu; http://mitpress.mit.edu. Illus., adv. Refereed. Circ: 4000. Vol. ends: Winter. Microform: PQC. Online: EBSCO Publishing, EBSCO Host; Florida Center for Library Automation; Gale; IngentaConnect; OCLC Online Computer Library Center, Inc.; OhioLINK; Project MUSE; SwetsWise Online Content. *Indexed:* ArtHuCI, C&ISA, CerAb, CompLI, CompR, EngInd, IAA, IBR, IBZ, IIMP, ISTA, LISA, MusicInd, RILM, SCI. *Bk. rev.:* 2-3, 1,500 words, signed. *Aud.:* Ac, Sa.

Computer Music Journal (*CMJ*) covers topics related to digital audio signal processing and electroacoustic music. Resources are aimed at musicians, composers, scientists, engineers, computer enthusiasts, and anyone else interested in computer-generated sound. Issues include articles (and multimedia material) on the skills, technologies, and future of digital sound and musical applications on computers. Generally included are several feature articles, announcements of competitions, conferences, symposia, and numerous reviews of events, publications, multimedia, recordings, and products. It is also available online. Recommended for academic libraries; highly recommended for those that serve music programs with an emphasis in digital technology.

4573. Conductors Guild. Journal. [ISSN: 0734-1032] 1980. s-a. Free to members. Ed(s): Anna Reguero. Conductors Guild, Inc., 5300 Glenside Dr, Ste 2207, Richmond, VA 23228; guild@conductorsguild.net; http://www.conductorsguild.net. Illus., adv. Circ: 1800. Vol. ends: Summer/Fall. *Indexed:* RILM. *Bk. rev.:* 5-8, 1,000-1,500 words, signed. *Aud.:* Hs, Ac, Sa.

The *Journal of the Conductors Guild* aims to be a resource for conductors by publishing articles that serve conductors' needs and interests. The scope of articles ranges from world-famous orchestras to community orchestras; topics include the history of conducting and its practitioners, particular aspects of orchestral works (e.g., metronome markings in Beethoven symphonies), and guides to the performance of specific pieces (e.g., a guide to Bruckner's E-minor symphony). Other contents of this journal include transcripts of sessions from Conductors Guild conferences and seminars, and lists of errata in musical scores. A typical issue will contain five to seven articles and several substantive book reviews. The journal's web site provides indices of articles by volume, author, and title. Recommended for academic, large public, and large high school libraries.

4574. Contemporary Music Review. [ISSN: 0749-4467] 1984. bi-m. GBP 625 print & online eds. Ed(s): Joshua Fineberg, Peter Nelson. Routledge, 4 Park Sq, Milton Park, Abingdon, OX14 4RN, United Kingdom; journals@routledge.com; http://www.routledge.co.uk. Refereed. Online: EBSCO Publishing, EBSCO Host; IngentaConnect; OCLC Online Computer Library Center, Inc.; SwetsWise Online Content. Reprint: PSC. *Indexed:* AmHI, BrHumI, HumInd, IIMP, MusicInd, RILM. *Bk. rev.:* Number and length vary. *Aud.:* Ga, Ac.

Contemporary Music Review is a contemporary music journal that provides a forum for discussion of issues in composition. Each issue focuses on a specific topic, covering composition in many aspects—techniques, aesthetics, and technology—and its relationship with other disciplines and currents of thought.

The publication may sometimes serve as a vehicle to communicate actual musical materials. It also includes interviews (musicians discussing their craft) and themes (such as "Performers on Performance"). Some issues focus on a particular composer. Articles are often understandable to readers with a nonprofessional interest in music. Each issue contains four to ten articles of 10–30 pages each. Articles begin with abstracts and a list of keywords and often contain a discography. Some articles provide notes and references, and some issues offer indexes. Book reviews appear only occasionally. Recommended for academic and large public libraries.

4575. Council for Research in Music Education. Bulletin. [ISSN: 0010-9894] 1963. q. USD 45 (Individuals, USD 35). Ed(s): Gregory Denardo. University of Illinois at Urbana-Champaign, School of Music, 1114 W Nevada St., Urbana, IL 61801; musadm@music.uiuc.edu; http://www.music.uiuc.eduml. Illus., index. Refereed. Circ: 2000. Microform: PQC. *Indexed:* ABIn, ArtHuCI, EduInd, IBR, IBZ, IIMP, MusicInd, RILM, SSCI. *Bk. rev.:* 5-10, 750-1,000 words, signed. *Aud.:* Ac, Sa.

Published as a service to music educators at all levels, this official bulletin of the Council for Research in Music Education (CRME) disseminates scholarly research in the field. Article topics include teaching methodologies, repertoire lists, assessments, motivation, music perception, cognition, stress, etc. Issues include articles of interest (five or six), dissertation and book reviews in the field of music education, and reports of research in progress. It also includes reports from seminars and conferences that are sponsored by other organizations, such as the International Society for Music Education. Of particular interest to music teachers, the *Bulletin* is recommended for academic and large public libraries.

4576. Current Musicology. [ISSN: 0011-3735] 1965. 2x/yr. USD 36 (Individuals, USD 25; Students, USD 18). Ed(s): Katherine Dacey-Tsuei. Columbia University, Department of Music, 614 Dodge Hall, Mail Code 1812, New York, NY 10027-7004; current-musicology@columbia.edu; http://www.columbia.edu/~ds193/cm.html. Illus., index, adv. Circ: 1500 Paid. Microform: PQC. Online: Chadwyck-Healey Inc.; OCLC Online Computer Library Center, Inc.; ProQuest K-12 Learning Solutions; ProQuest LLC (Ann Arbor). *Indexed:* ABS&EES, AmHI, ArtHuCI, HumInd, IBR, IBZ, IIMP, MusicInd, PhilInd, RILM. *Bk. rev.:* 3-4, 8-10 pages, signed. *Aud.:* Ac, Sa.

Published by the Department of Music at Columbia University (and founded by graduate students), *Current Musicology* serves as an international forum for scholarly music research. It seeks to reflect the forefront of thought in historical musicology, ethnomusicology, music theory, music cognition, philosophy of music, and interdisciplinary studies (musicology understood broadly). According to the journal web site, its goal is to "serve the needs of musicologists who are about to undertake, are presently engaged in, or have recently completed their graduate studies. From its inception, the aim of the journal was to publish short articles of research, criticism, and opinion, predominantly by younger authors." Special sections are devoted to this intended audience, such as teaching music survey courses, music theory, computer music, and composers. Reviews of collections, in-depth discussions of recent publications, and book reviews are included in each issue. Recommended for academic libraries, especially those that support musicology studies.

4577. Early Music. [ISSN: 0306-1078] 1973. q. EUR 215 print or online ed. Ed(s): Tess Knighton. Oxford University Press, Great Clarendon St, Oxford, OX2 6DP, United Kingdom; jnl.orders@oup.co.uk; http://www.oxfordjournals.org. Illus., adv. Refereed. Circ: 3500. Vol. ends: Nov. Microform: PQC. Online: Chadwyck-Healey Inc.; EBSCO Publishing, EBSCO Host; Florida Center for Library Automation; Gale; HighWire Press; IngentaConnect; JSTOR (Web-based Journal Archive); Northern Light Technology, Inc.; OCLC Online Computer Library Center, Inc.; Oxford Journals; Project MUSE; ProQuest LLC (Ann Arbor); SwetsWise Online Content; H.W. Wilson. Reprint: PSC. *Indexed:* AmH&L, AmHI, ArtHuCI, BrHumI, HistAb, HumInd, IBR, IBZ, IIMP, MusicInd, RILM. *Bk. rev.:* 2-4, 750-1,000 words, signed. *Aud.:* Ac, Sa.

Early Music is an important journal for anyone interested in early music and its interpretation. Contributions from scholars and performers of international standing explore every aspect of earlier musical repertoires, present new

evidence for our understanding of the music of the past, and tackle controversial issues of performance practice. Articles also discuss topics such as period instruments, performance practice, notation, iconography, and historical contexts. Some issues are dedicated to a particular theme to mark the anniversary of a composer or to explore areas such as the music of the New World or the early musical traditions of non-Western cultures. Each issue also contains numerous book, music, and recording reviews, as well as announcements of festivals and workshops. Also available online, it is highly recommended to anyone studying early music and highly recommended for academic libraries that support performance practice.

4578. Early Music History: studies in medieval and early modern music. [ISSN: 0261-1279] 1982. a. GBP 102. Ed(s): Iain Fenlon. Cambridge University Press, The Edinburgh Bldg, Shaftesbury Rd, Cambridge, CB2 2RU, United Kingdom; journals@cambridge.org; http://www.cup.cam.ac.uk/. Illus., adv. Refereed. Microform: PQC. Online: Pub.; EBSCO Publishing, EBSCO Host; JSTOR (Web-based Journal Archive); OCLC Online Computer Library Center, Inc.; OhioLINK; SwetsWise Online Content. *Indexed:* AmH&L, AmHI, ArtHuCI, HistAb, IBR, IBZ, IIMP, MusicInd, RILM. *Bk. rev.:* 2, 2,500 words, signed. *Aud.:* Ac, Sa.

Early Music History specializes in study of music from the early Middle Ages to the end of the seventeenth century. It prioritizes studies using interdisciplinary approaches and developing new methodologies. The scope includes manuscript studies, textual criticism, iconography, studies of the relationship between words and music, and the relationship between music and society. Published annually, it focuses on the music of Britain, America, and Europe. Several book reviews are included in each issue. Recommended for academic libraries, especially those that support early music studies and/or musicology.

4579. Echo (Los Angeles): a music-centered journal. [ISSN: 1535-1807] 1999. biennial. Free. Ed(s): Jonathan Greenberg, Philip Gentry. University of California at Los Angeles, Department of Musicology, PO Box 951623, Los Angeles, CA 90095-1623. Illus. Refereed. Vol. ends: Fall. *Bk. rev.:* 2-3, 5-7 pp. *Aud.:* Ac, Sa.

Echo: a music-centered journal is an interdisciplinary, peer-reviewed publication created and edited by graduate students at the Department of Musicology at the University of California, Los Angeles (with a distinguished editorial board). It is entirely web-based, and can be accessed free of charge by anyone online. *Echo*'s stated purpose is to create a forum for discussion about music and culture that includes voices from diverse backgrounds. Editorial purpose is to make all work accessible to readers without formal musical training. Use of sound and film clips enables authors to discuss nuances of performance without relying solely on music notation. Topics address music in social contexts, and are not confined to any geographically, historically, or methodologically limited genre. The design presents articles in an attractive and visually stimulating layout that complements the ideas and subject matter discussed in the text. Articles span musicology, ethnomusicology, technology, popular music, education, and cultural theory. Recommended for academic libraries.

4580. Eighteenth Century Music. [ISSN: 1478-5706] 2004. s-a. GBP 73. Ed(s): W Dean Sutcliffe, Cliff Eisen. Cambridge University Press, The Edinburgh Bldg, Shaftesbury Rd, Cambridge, CB2 2RU, United Kingdom; journals@cambridge.org; http://www.cup.cam.ac.uk/. Refereed. Reprint: PSC. *Indexed:* IIMP, MusicInd. *Bk. rev.:* Number and length vary. *Aud.:* Ac, Sa.

Eighteenth Century Music began publishing in 2004 "to offer a natural home for research and commentary on music of the eighteenth century." Its content focuses on music c. 1660 to 1830, with topics ranging from musical analyses of compositions, analyses of performance methods, critiques, and interdisciplinary studies of the music in its cultural and social contexts. Issues include many book, music, and recording reviews, and reports of current news and events. Recommended for academic collections.

4581. Ethnomusicology. [ISSN: 0014-1836] 1953. 3x/yr. Free to members. Ed(s): Timothy Cooley. University of Illinois Press, 1325 S Oak St, Champaign, IL 61820-6903; journals@uillinois.edu; http://www.press.uillinois.edu. Illus., index, adv. Refereed. Circ: 2000.

Vol. ends: Fall. Microform: PQC. Online: Chadwyck-Healey Inc.; JSTOR (Web-based Journal Archive); Northern Light Technology, Inc.; OCLC Online Computer Library Center, Inc.; ProQuest LLC (Ann Arbor). *Indexed:* ABS&EES, AICP, AbAn, AmH&L, AmHI, AnthLit, ArtHuCI, BAS, FR, HumInd, IBR, IBSS, IBZ, IIMP, IndIslam, MLA-IB, MusicInd, RI-1, RILM, SSCI. *Bk. rev.:* 6-8, 500-1,000 words, signed. *Aud.:* Ac, Sa.

This journal is the official organ of the Society for Ethnomusicology. It features scholarly articles that represent theoretical perspectives and research in ethnomusicology and related fields from an international perspective. Concepts discussed are multidisciplinary and worldwide in scope, and are aimed at a diverse audience of musicians, musicologists, folklorists, popular culture scholars, and cultural anthropologists. Recent article topics include Hasidic and Tamil music, commodification, and profiles of prominent ethnomusicologists. There are reviews of books, recordings, and multimedia. Most issues also include a current bibliography, discography, and list of recent films and videos. The table of contents is also available online, back issues in JSTOR. Recommended for academic and large public libraries; essential for those that support ethnomusicology programs.

4582. *Ethnomusicology Online.* [ISSN: 1092-7336] 1995. a. Free. Ed(s): Karl Signell. Ethnomusicology Online, University of Maryland, Music Dept., Baltimore, MD 21228; signell@umbc.edu; http://umbc.edu/eol. Refereed. *Indexed:* MLA-IB, RILM. *Bk. rev.:* Number and length vary. *Aud.:* Ac, Sa.

This annual e-journal provides information on ethnomusicology resources worldwide. Issues can include reviews of books, journals, articles, recordings, visual media, dissertations, software, and web sites, complete with graphics and audio examples. Memorials and obituaries are occasionally listed, and there is a list of links to other online resources relevant to ethnomusicology, such as institutions, publications, books, teachers, and other world music sites. A table of contents to each issue provides easy access, and the index to multimedia reviews is searchable by author, by geographic area, and by map location. Of interest to performers, musicologists, ethnomusicologists, and students, it is recommended for academic and public libraries.

4583. *Eunomios.* 2000. s-a. Ed(s): Paolo Rosato, Michele Ignelzi. Eunomios, staff@eunomios.org; http://www.eunomios.org/. *Aud.:* Ac, Sa.

Eunomios is an open online journal devoted to the theory, analysis, and semiotics of music. It hosts user-contributed papers, and publication on the web site occurs almost immediately, without editing or peer review. A forum for discussion and debating issues related to the articles published is an interesting feature. There is a very useful list of links to electronic journals, institutes, and other resources. Recent contributions include articles on musical creativity, dramaturgy, and jazz improvisation. Recommended for academic libraries with interest in theory or semiotics.

4584. *Fontes Artis Musicae.* [ISSN: 0015-6191] 1953. q. Free to members. Ed(s): Maureen Buja. International Association of Music Libraries, Archives and Documentation Centres (U.S.), 8551 Research Way, Ste 180, Middleton, WI 53562; http://www.areditions.com/. Illus., index, adv. Circ: 2200 Paid. Vol. ends: Dec. *Indexed:* ArtHuCI, BrHumI, FR, IIMP, LISA, LibLit, MusicInd, RILM, SSCI. *Bk. rev.:* 4-6, 500-750 words, signed. *Aud.:* Ac, Sa.

Fontes Artis Musicae is published by the International Association of Music Libraries, Archives and Documentation Centres (IAML). Issues include reports from IAML committees, working groups, branches, and officers; memorials; reviews of music resources; and announcements of upcoming events. Articles focus on music bibliography, music librarianship, and musicological research, and may be written in French, English, or German. Tables of contents back to September 1994 are available at the journal's web site (www.iaml.info/en/fontes). Of interest mainly to music librarians, archivists, bibliographers, and musicologists, it is recommended for academic libraries.

4585. *Instrumentalist: a magazine for school and college band and orchestra directors, professional instrumentalists, teacher-training specialists in instrumental music education and instrumental teachers.* [ISSN: 0020-4331] 1946. m. USD 21. Ed(s): Floyd Hendricks. The

Instrumentalist Co., 200 Northfield Rd, Northfield, IL 60093-3390. Illus., index, adv. Circ: 19200 Paid. Vol. ends: Jul. *Indexed:* ABIn, EduInd, IIMP, MusicInd, RILM. *Aud.:* Hs, Ga, Ac, Sa.

Instrumentalist is a commercial publication that targets high school and academic band and orchestra directors. The articles, written by experienced directors and performers, cover topics such as rehearsal techniques, conducting tips, programming ideas, instrument clinics, master classes, repertoire analyses, and interviews with composers, performers, conductors, and teachers. Monthly new music reviews, numerous color photos, job guides, summer camp directories, and announcements of upcoming festivals are included. Of interest to school band and orchestra directors, it is recommended for academic, large public, and high school libraries.

4586. *International Journal of Music Education.* Formerly (until 1983): *Australian Journal of Music Education.* [ISSN: 0255-7614] 1967. q. GBP 311. Ed(s): Jane Cheung, Timothy Brophy. Sage Publications Ltd., 1 Oliver's Yard, 55 City Rd, London, EC1 1SP, United Kingdom; info@sagepub.co.uk; http://www.sagepub.co.uk. Illus., adv. Refereed. Circ: 2000. Microform: PQC. Online: CSA; Chadwyck-Healey Inc.; EBSCO Publishing, EBSCO Host; HighWire Press; SAGE Publications, Inc., SAGE Journals Online; SwetsWise Online Content. Reprint: PSC. *Indexed:* ArtHuCI, BrEdI, IBR, IBZ, IIMP, MusicInd, PsycInfo, RILM. *Aud.:* Ac, Sa.

This journal is published by the International Society for Music Education. Articles concern the teaching and learning of music, and particularly target international audiences and issues. Topics such as culture, heritage, innovations in music education, preservation, popular music, aesthetics, philosophy, and other concerns are discussed. While the articles are printed in English, abstracts in French, German, and Spanish are included. Of interest to teachers of all levels of students, it is recommended for academic libraries.

4587. *International Musician.* [ISSN: 0020-8051] 1901. m. USD 39 domestic; USD 54 Canada. Ed(s): Antoinette Follett, Tom Lee. American Federation of Musicians of the United States and Canada, 1501 Broadway, New York, NY 10036; http://www.afm.org. Illus., adv. Circ: 110000 Paid. Vol. ends: Jun. Microform: PQC. Online: Chadwyck-Healey Inc. *Indexed:* IIMP, MusicInd. *Aud.:* Ga, Ac, Sa.

International Musician is received by all members of the American Federation of Musicians and is a primary source for union information and communication. Covering all genres of music, this publication reports on union accomplishments, events and developments in the music business, and benefits for union members. Information is given on planning for the future, legal advice, resources for self-improvement, and health advice. Each issue contains a cover story on a successful musician or group, short articles on member anniversaries and achievements, a section on marketing oneself, and editorials. Also includes classified advertising with categories for auditions, items for sale, items wanted, and lost or stolen instruments. Recommended for public and academic libraries.

4588. *Journal of Music Theory.* [ISSN: 0022-2909] 1957. s-a. USD 45 (Individuals, USD 30). Ed(s): Ian Quinn. Yale University, School of Music, PO Box 208310, New Haven, CT 06520; http://www.yale.edu/. Illus., index, adv. Refereed. Circ: 1700. Vol. ends: Fall. Microform: MIM; PQC. Online: JSTOR (Web-based Journal Archive). Reprint: PSC. *Indexed:* ArtHuCI, IBR, IBZ, IIMP, MusicInd, RILM, SSCI. *Bk. rev.:* 2-3, 3-6 pages, signed. *Aud.:* Ac.

Founded in 1957 at the Yale School of Music, the *Journal of Music Theory* publishes peer-reviewed scholarly articles on theoretical and technical aspects of music composition, both historical and contemporary. Examples of articles are "A Cognitive Theory of Musical Meaning," and "Counterpoint and Analysis in Fourteenth-Century Song." Each issue contains at least two book reviews of three to six pages each. The second number of each volume contains an index to the volume. Recommended for academic libraries.

4589. *Journal of Music Therapy.* [ISSN: 0022-2917] 1964. q. USD 135 domestic; USD 144 foreign. Ed(s): Jayne Standley. American Music Therapy Association, 8455 Colesville Rd, Ste 1000, Silver Spring, MD 20910-3392; subscribe@musictherapy.org; http://www.musictherapy.org. Illus., index. Refereed. Circ: 6000. Vol. ends: Winter. Microform: PQC.

Online: Chadwyck-Healey Inc.; OCLC Online Computer Library Center, Inc.; ProQuest K-12 Learning Solutions; ProQuest LLC (Ann Arbor); H.W. Wilson. *Indexed:* ABIn, AgeL, ArtHuCI, ECER, EduInd, IBR, IBZ, IIMP, MusicInd, PsycInfo, RILM, SSCI. *Aud.:* Ac, Sa.

The *Journal of Music Therapy,* published by the American Music Therapy Association, presents scholarly articles for music therapists, psychologists, psychiatrists, and others in related fields. Articles document both theoretical and experimental studies on the effects of music on physiological, emotional, and mental states, such as relaxation, attention, and memory. Aspects of music therapy education and problems for students in the field are also considered. Each issue contains three to five articles with abstracts and references. Examples of articles are "The Use of Music to Enhance Reading Skills of Second Grade Students and Students with Reading Disabilities" and "Talking with Music Teachers about Inclusion: Perceptions, Opinions and Experiences." An index appears in the last issue of each volume. Contents of issues can be found at the journal's web site. Recommended for academic libraries.

4590. *Journal of Musicology: a quarterly review of music history, criticism, analysis, and performance practice.* [ISSN: 0277-9269] 1982. q. USD 163 print & online eds. USD 45 newsstand/cover. Ed(s): John Nadas. University of California Press, Journals Division, 2000 Center St, Ste 303, Berkeley, CA 94704-1223; journals@ucpress.edu; http://www.ucpress.edu/journals. Illus., adv. Refereed. Circ: 651. Microform: PQC. Online: EBSCO Publishing, EBSCO Host; Florida Center for Library Automation; JSTOR (Web-based Journal Archive); Northern Light Technology, Inc.; OCLC Online Computer Library Center, Inc.; ProQuest LLC (Ann Arbor); SwetsWise Online Content; H.W. Wilson. *Indexed:* ABS&EES, AmH&L, AmHI, ArtHuCI, HistAb, HumInd, IBR, IBZ, IIMP, MusicInd, RILM, SSCI. *Aud.:* Ac, Sa.

The *Journal of Musicology* provides a forum for peer-reviewed articles on topics in all areas of musical scholarship, including history, criticism, analysis, performance, and research. Articles and review essays treat music from a variety of perspectives for scholars, musicians, and other students of music. Each issue contains four to five articles, with abstracts appearing at the end of articles. The journal's web site, www.journalofmusicology.org, has links to issues and abstracts back to the summer of 2001. Recommended for academic and large public libraries.

4591. *Journal of Research in Music Education.* [ISSN: 0022-4294] 1953. q. GBP 77. Sage Publications, Inc., 2455 Teller Rd, Thousand Oaks, CA 91320; info@sagepub.com; http://www.sagepub.com. Illus. Refereed. Circ: 3300. Vol. ends: Winter. Microform: PQC. Online: Chadwyck-Healey Inc.; EBSCO Publishing, EBSCO Host; Florida Center for Library Automation; Gale; OCLC Online Computer Library Center, Inc.; ProQuest K-12 Learning Solutions; ProQuest LLC (Ann Arbor); H.W. Wilson. *Indexed:* ABIn, ArtHuCI, ERIC, EduInd, IBR, IBZ, IIMP, MusicInd, PsycInfo, RILM, SSCI, SWA. *Aud.:* Ac, Sa.

The *Journal of Research in Music Education* publishes articles on historical, philosophical, descriptive, and experimental research in music education. Articles are critiqued by an editorial committee of scholars and published for researchers and music teachers in all settings. Each issue contains approximately six articles written by professional educators and announcements that often include calls for papers. Issues begin with a short "Forum," written by the editor, that gives an introduction to that issue's contents and comments on topics or contributors. Examples of articles include "Undergraduate Instrumental Music Education Majors' Approaches to Score Study in Various Musical Contexts" and "Musicians' Cognitive Processing of Imagery-Based Instructions for Expressive Performance." Recommended for academic, high school, and large public libraries.

4592. *Journal of Seventeenth Century Music.* [ISSN: 1089-747X] 1995. irreg. Free. Ed(s): Bruce Gustafson. Society for Seventeenth - Century Music, 337 W James St, Lancaster, PA 17603. Illus. Refereed. *Indexed:* RILM. *Bk. rev.:* Number and length vary. *Aud.:* Ac, Sa.

The *Journal of Seventeenth-Century Music* is published by the Society for Seventeenth-Century Music, in arrangement with the University of Illinois Press. Refereed articles and essays approach the musical cultures of the seventeenth century from the perspectives of history, theory, aesthetics, performance, dance, and theater. Articles often contain links to notes and references; authors are encouraged to include additional reference material, appendices, texts of archival documents, etc., and sometimes digital illustrations or sound files. Issues also contain a note from the editor, responses from readers, and an occasional review. Recommended for academic libraries. URL: http://sscm-jscm.press.uiuc.edu/jscm

4593. *Journal of Singing.* Former titles (until Sep. 1995): *N A T S Journal;* (until May 1985): *N A T S Bulletin.* [ISSN: 1086-7732] 1944. 5x/yr. USD 50 (Individuals, USD 45). Ed(s): Richard Sjoerdsma. National Association of Teachers of Singing (N A T S), 9957 Moorings Dr, Ste 401, Jacksonville, FL 32257; info@nats.org; http://www.nats.org. Illus., index, adv. Refereed. Circ: 7000 Paid. Microform: PQC. Online: Chadwyck-Healey Inc.; H.W. Wilson. *Indexed:* ABS&EES, CINAHL, EduInd, IIMP, MusicInd, RILM. *Bk. rev.:* 1-2, 300-500 words, signed. *Aud.:* Ac, Sa.

The National Association of Teachers of Singing publishes this journal for students and teachers of singing in all countries. Articles present information on topics such as repertoire, vocal techniques, standards, care of the voice, teaching methodologies, and singing as physical therapy. Issues include announcements of upcoming events, conferences, and workshops; reviews of books, music, and recordings; and organizational information. Of interest to singers, vocal coaches, and choral conductors, it is recommended for academic and large public libraries.

4594. *Leonardo Music Journal.* [ISSN: 0961-1215] 1991. a. USD 68 print & online eds. (Individuals, USD 34 print & online eds.). Ed(s): Nicolas Collins. M I T Press, 238 Main St., Ste. 500, Cambridge, MA 02142; journals-info@mit.edu; http://mitpress.mit.edu. Refereed. *Indexed:* ABM, AmHI, ArtHuCI, HumInd, IBR, IBZ, MusicInd, RILM. *Aud.:* Ac, Sa.

Leonardo Music Journal publishes peer-reviewed articles on the efforts of musicians and multimedia artists as they use science and technology in the creation of new music. Areas covered include analyses of new music compositions and presentation, the use of scientific methods for insight into the comprehension of music, and the documentation of new sound and interactive works of art. The journal's audience includes musicians, composers, sound artists, scientists, theoreticians, and instrument makers. Each annual issue contains approximately ten articles, and it comes with a CD that contains musical examples related to that issue's topic. The journal's web site contains selected articles, contents and abstracts of current and previous issues, and contents of previous CDs. Recommended for academic libraries.

4595. *MandoZine.* 1996. bi-m. Ed(s): John Baxter. MandoZine, http://www.mandozine.com. *Aud.:* Hs, Ga.

This publication is an excellent resource for mandolin music. It includes extensive information of general interest, as well as instructional resources intended for beginning mandolin players. Sections of the zine contain histories of many different mandolin models, practice music in TablEdit, ABC, and pdf formats, and an extensive listing of different techniques with instructions. There is also a link to the auxiliary site MandoTunes, which includes audio and video files.

4596. *Medical Problems of Performing Artists.* [ISSN: 0885-1158] 1986. q. USD 98 (Individuals, USD 60). Ed(s): Dr. Ralph A Manchester. Science & Medicine, PO Box 313, Narberth, PA 19072. Illus., index, adv. Refereed. Circ: 1000. *Indexed:* ArtHuCI, BiolAb, CINAHL, ExcerpMed, IIMP, IIPA, MusicInd, RILM, SCI, SSCI. *Bk. rev.:* 1, 250 words, signed. *Aud.:* Ac, Sa.

Medical Problems of Performing Artists publishes peer-reviewed articles that focus on the origin, diagnoses, and treatment of medical problems encountered by performing artists. These include muscular and neurological disorders, anxieties, stress, voice and hearing disorders, repetitive stress injuries, substance abuse, etc. As the official journal of the Performing Arts Medicine Association, this journal acts as a forum for medical and academic professionals to communicate their research findings and practices. Each issue contains approximately six articles with abstracts, abstracts of relevant articles in other journals, and occasional book reviews. Tables of contents and abstracts are available for back issues at www.sciandmed.com/mppa. Recommended for academic and large public libraries.

4597. *Music and Letters.* [ISSN: 0027-4224] 1920. q. EUR 200 print or online ed. Ed(s): Nigel Fortune, Daniel Grimley. Oxford University Press, Great Clarendon St, Oxford, OX2 6DP, United Kingdom; jnl.orders@oup.co.uk; http://www.oxfordjournals.org. Illus., index, adv. Refereed. Circ: 1250. Vol. ends: Nov. Microform: PQC. Online: Chadwyck-Healey Inc.; EBSCO Publishing, EBSCO Host; Florida Center for Library Automation; Gale; HighWire Press; IngentaConnect; JSTOR (Web-based Journal Archive); OCLC Online Computer Library Center, Inc.; OhioLINK; Oxford Journals; Project MUSE; ProQuest LLC (Ann Arbor); SwetsWise Online Content; H.W. Wilson. Reprint: PSC. *Indexed:* AmH&L, AmHI, ArtHuCI, BrHumI, HistAb, HumInd, IBR, IBZ, IIMP, MLA-IB, MusicInd, RILM, SSCI. *Bk. rev.:* 25, 500-1,000 words, signed. *Aud.:* Ac, Sa.

Music and Letters publishes articles on historical, analytical, and critical musicology that cover all musical periods. Topics may focus on letters, documents, reminiscences, and other written records that relate to musicians and their compositions, e.g., memories of Beethoven by his contemporaries, or the influence of French poetic rhythm on Verdi's operas. A typical issue contains three or four articles and a large number book reviews, as well as occasional music reviews. The journal's web site contains tables of contents and abstracts back to 1920. Searching capability by author, title, citation, and keyword is provided. Recommended for academic libraries.

4598. *Music Educators Journal.* Former titles (until 1934): *Music Supervisors' Journal;* (until 1915): *Music Supervisors' Bulletin.* [ISSN: 0027-4321] 1914. 5x/yr. Free to members; USD 90 combined subscription domestic includes Teaching Music. Ed(s): Dorothy Wagener. M E N C: National Association for Music Education, 1806 Robert Fulton Dr, Reston, VA 20191-4348; http://www.menc.org. Illus., index. Refereed. Circ: 80000. Vol. ends: May. Microform: PQC. Online: Chadwyck-Healey Inc.; EBSCO Publishing, EBSCO Host; Gale; OCLC Online Computer Library Center, Inc.; ProQuest LLC (Ann Arbor); H.W. Wilson. *Indexed:* ABIn, AgeL, ArtHuCI, BAS, BRI, CBRI, ECER, ERIC, EduInd, IBR, IBZ, IIMP, MusicInd, RILM. *Bk. rev.:* 8, 150-200 words, signed. *Aud.:* Ems, Hs, Ga, Ac, Sa.

As the official magazine of the Music Educators National Conference (MENC), this journal focuses on the approaches and methods used for teaching music in schools, colleges, community orchestras, and other education environments. Examples of topics covered include a report on the interaction of music teachers and music therapists in helping children, techniques for assisting developing singers, and how to manage time effectively in rehearsals. Each issue contains five to six articles, approximately eight short book reviews, and video reviews. "Samplings" provides abstracts of articles published in other MENC journals. Recommended for all libraries and music teachers.

4599. *Music Library Association. Notes: quarterly journal of the music library association.* [ISSN: 0027-4380] 1942. q. USD 100 (Individuals, USD 85). Ed(s): James P Cassaro. Music Library Association, 8551 Research Way, Suite 180, Middleton, WI 53562; mla@areditions.com; http://www.musiclibraryassoc.org. Illus., index, adv. Refereed. Circ: 2900 Paid and controlled. Vol. ends: Jun. Microform: PQC. Online: Chadwyck-Healey Inc.; EBSCO Publishing, EBSCO Host; Factiva, Inc.; Florida Center for Library Automation; Gale; JSTOR (Web-based Journal Archive); OCLC Online Computer Library Center, Inc.; Project MUSE; ProQuest LLC (Ann Arbor); SwetsWise Online Content; H.W. Wilson. *Indexed:* ABS&EES, AmHI, ArtHuCI, BRD, BRI, BrHumI, CBRI, HumInd, IBR, IBZ, IIMP, LISA, LibLit, LingAb, MusicInd, RILM. *Bk. rev.:* 40-50, 250-500 words, signed. *Aud.:* Ac, Sa.

Notes, the quarterly journal of the Music Library Association (MLA), publishes articles on contemporary and historical issues in music librarianship, music bibliography, and music publishing. Each issue contains two to four articles, but the main body of the journal is an extensive section of signed book reviews with subheadings for popular music, ethnomusicology, composers, reference books, instruments, and music reviews. Issues also contain reviews of sound recordings, digital media and software, a long list of books recently published, and lists of music and music publishers' catalogs received. Highly recommended for all music librarians and bibliographers.

4600. *Music Perception.* [ISSN: 0730-7829] 1983. 5x/yr. USD 329 print & online eds. USD 72 newsstand/cover. Ed(s): Lola L Cuddy. University of California Press, Journals Division, 2000 Center St, Ste 303, Berkeley, CA 94704-1223; journals@ucpress.edu; http://www.ucpress.edu/journals. Illus., index, adv. Refereed. Circ: 699. Vol. ends: Summer. Microform: PQC. Online: Chadwyck-Healey Inc.; EBSCO Publishing, EBSCO Host; Florida Center for Library Automation; OCLC Online Computer Library Center, Inc.; ProQuest LLC (Ann Arbor); SwetsWise Online Content. *Indexed:* ArtHuCI, IBR, IBZ, IIMP, L&LBA, MusicInd, PsycInfo, RILM, SSCI. *Bk. rev.:* 2, 2,000-3,500 words, signed. *Aud.:* Ac, Sa.

Music Perception publishes refereed articles on the continuing research into how music is experienced and interpreted. Contributors are scientists and musicians, using critical, methodological, theoretical, and empirical approaches to analyze music. These approaches come from disciplines such as psychology, neurology, linguistics, acoustics, artificial intelligence, music theory, and others. Examples of articles are "Tapping to a Very Slow Beat: A Comparison of Musicians and Nonmusicians" and "Learning *Clair de Lune*: Retrieval Practice and Expert Memorization." Each issue contains three to five articles, occasional book reviews, and announcements of future conferences and meetings. For subscribers, the web site provides tables of contents from 2001 forward. Recommended for academic libraries.

4601. *Music Theory Spectrum.* [ISSN: 0195-6167] 1979. s-a. USD 129 print & online eds. USD 71 newsstand/cover. Ed(s): Henry Klumpenhouwer. University of California Press, Journals Division, 2000 Center St, Ste 303, Berkeley, CA 94704-1223; journals@ucpress.edu; http://www.ucpress.edu/journals. Adv. Refereed. Circ: 1458. *Indexed:* ArtHuCI, IBR, IBZ, IIMP, MusicInd, RILM. *Bk. rev.:* Number and length vary. *Aud.:* Ac.

The official print journal of the Society for Music Theory, *Music Theory Spectrum* reports on topics relating to music theory and analysis. Topics include critical theory, history of theory, aesthetics, and cognition, with occasional special issues that focus on a specific subject. Issues generally contain four or more articles, and extensive book reviews. Some issues also contain announcements for new books and sections for reader response. Subscriptions are included with membership in the society. Currently available online for libraries. Recommended for academic libraries.

4602. *Musical America International Directory of the Performing Arts.* Formerly (until 1968): *Musical America Annual Directory Issue.* [ISSN: 0735-7788] 1960. a. USD 135. Commonwealth Business Media, Inc., 400 Windsor Corporate Ctr, 50 Millstone Rd, Ste 200, East Windsor, NJ 08520-1415; customerservice@cbizmedia.com; http://www.cbizmedia.com. Illus., index, adv. Circ: 15000 Paid and controlled. *Aud.:* Hs, Ga, Ac.

Musical America International Directory of the Performing Arts provides a broad range of over 14,000 listings of arts organizations worldwide. The directory contains a categorical and alphabetical index of the more than 10,000 advertisers that appear in this annual publication. It also contains articles on the "Musician of the Year" in the categories of ensemble, composer, conductor, instrumentalist, and vocalist, and reports by artists' managers on their artists achievements of the past year. Directory listings are divided into "United States and Canada" and "International" listings, with each of these categories subdivided into orchestras, opera companies, choral groups, dance companies, festivals, music schools and departments, record companies, magazines, and radio stations. The directory's web site contains (for subscribers only) access to industry news, readers' comments, and full searching of listings. Access to a calendar of events, career center, some directory articles, industry links, press releases, and limited searching are free. Recommended for all collections that serve musicians and music users.

4603. *The Musical Quarterly.* [ISSN: 0027-4631] 1915. q. USD 162 print or online ed. Ed(s): Irene Zedlacher, Leon Botstein. Oxford University Press, 2001 Evans Rd, Cary, NC 27513; jnlorders@oup-usa.org; http://www.us.oup.com. Illus., index, adv. Refereed. Circ: 2500 Paid. Vol. ends: Winter. Microform: PMC; PQC. Online: Chadwyck-Healey Inc.; EBSCO Publishing, EBSCO Host; Gale; HighWire Press; IngentaConnect; JSTOR (Web-based Journal Archive); OCLC Online

Computer Library Center, Inc.; Oxford Journals; ProQuest LLC (Ann Arbor); SwetsWise Online Content; H.W. Wilson. Reprint: PSC. *Indexed:* ABS&EES, AmHI, ArtHuCI, BRD, BRI, BrHumI, CBRI, FLI, HumInd, IBR, IBZ, IIMP, MLA-IB, MusicInd, RILM. *Aud.:* Ga, Ac.

The Musical Quarterly publishes peer-reviewed articles that focus on the contemporary study of music from the perspective of, and in combination with, other scholarly disciplines. Regular sections include "American Musics," "Music and Culture," and "Institutions, Industries, Technologies." Each issue contains between seven and nine articles with notes. The last issue of each volume contains a subject and author index to the volume. The web site contains links to tables of contents of issues from 1915 forward, and search functions by author, title, citation, and keyword. Recommended for public and academic libraries.

4604. *Nineteenth Century Music.* [ISSN: 0148-2076] 1977. 3x/yr. USD 170 print & online eds. USD 62 newsstand/cover. Ed(s): Lawrence Kramer. University of California Press, Journals Division, 2000 Center St, Ste 303, Berkeley, CA 94704-1223; journals@ucpress.edu; http://www.ucpress.edu/journals. Illus., index, adv. Refereed. Circ: 1326 Paid. Vol. ends: Spring. Online: Chadwyck-Healey Inc.; EBSCO Publishing, EBSCO Host; Florida Center for Library Automation; JSTOR (Web-based Journal Archive); OCLC Online Computer Library Center, Inc.; ProQuest LLC (Ann Arbor); SwetsWise Online Content; H.W. Wilson. *Indexed:* ABS&EES, AmH&L, AmHI, ArtHuCI, HistAb, HumInd, IBR, IBZ, IIMP, MusicInd, RILM. *Bk. rev.:* 1, 4,000 words, signed. *Aud.:* Ac, Sa.

Nineteenth Century Music publishes refereed articles on the musical environment from 1780 to 1920, as it related to, and interacted with, that era's cultural and social environments. Topics include music composition, theory, analysis, performance, aesthetics, social and cultural contexts, history, historiography, and gender studies. It contains occasional reviews of books, articles, and performances. Available online. Recommended for academic libraries.

4605. *Opera News.* [ISSN: 0030-3607] 1936. m. USD 30 domestic. Ed(s): F. Paul Driscoll. Metropolitan Opera Guild, Inc., 70 Lincoln Center Plaza, New York, NY 10023; http://www.metguild.org/. Illus., index, adv. Circ: 100000 Paid. Vol. ends: Jun/Jun. Microform: PQC. Online: Chadwyck-Healey Inc.; EBSCO Publishing, EBSCO Host; Florida Center for Library Automation; Gale; Northern Light Technology, Inc.; OCLC Online Computer Library Center, Inc.; ProQuest K-12 Learning Solutions; ProQuest LLC (Ann Arbor); H.W. Wilson. *Indexed:* ABS&EES, AmHI, ArtHuCI, BRI, CBRI, FLI, HumInd, IIMP, IIPA, MASUSE, MusicInd, RGPR, RILM. *Bk. rev.:* 1-3, 500 words, signed. *Aud.:* Ga, Ac.

Published by the Metropolitan Opera Guild, *Opera News* provides fans with the latest news and information on the Metropolitan Opera company and opera around the world. Each glossy issue contains approximately seven articles that provide history and analysis of selected works, and profiles of artists and composers. A section of the magazine offers information on upcoming Metropolitan Opera broadcasts with lists of cast members, synopses of plots, and references to further information on each opera. Also included in each issue is the latest opera and opera-related news, concert reviews arranged by countries and cities, CD and video reviews, and occasional book reviews. A two-page "Dateline" section lists upcoming performances worldwide. Recommended for public and academic libraries.

4606. *The Opera Quarterly.* [ISSN: 0736-0053] 1983. q. USD 203 print or online ed. Ed(s): David J Levin. Oxford University Press, 2001 Evans Rd, Cary, NC 27513; jnlorders@oup-usa.edu; http://www.us.oup.com. Illus., adv. Refereed. Circ: 5800 Paid and controlled. Vol. ends: Fall. Online: Chadwyck-Healey Inc.; EBSCO Publishing, EBSCO Host; Gale; HighWire Press; IngentaConnect; OCLC Online Computer Library Center, Inc.; OhioLINK; Oxford Journals; Project MUSE; ProQuest LLC (Ann Arbor); SwetsWise Online Content; H.W. Wilson. Reprint: PSC. *Indexed:* ABS&EES, AmH&L, AmHI, ArtHuCI, HistAb, HumInd, IBR, IBZ, IIMP, IIPA, MusicInd, RILM. *Bk. rev.:* 4-5, 1,000-1,500 words, signed. *Aud.:* Ga, Ac.

The Opera Quarterly publishes articles on opera performers, opera history, and analyses of works, as well as interviews and remembrances of major vocalists. The journal's summer issue commemorates a special composer, singer, or topic (e.g., Wagner's *Der fliegender Hollander*). Each issue contains approximately six articles (with illustrations), as well as book, CD, and video reviews. Also listed are books and CDs received. Tables of contents from 1983 to the present are available at the journal's web site. Recommended for large public and academic libraries.

4607. *The Orff Echo.* [ISSN: 0095-2613] 1968. 4x/yr. Membership, USD 70. Ed(s): Caprice Lawless. American Orff-Schulwerk Association, 3105 Lincoln Blvd, Cleveland, OH 44118-2035; bxfn94b@prodigy.com. Adv. Refereed. Circ: 5100. *Indexed:* MusicInd. *Bk. rev.:* Number and length vary. *Aud.:* Ems, Hs, Ga, Ac, Sa.

This is the official publication of the American Orff-Schulwerk Association, an organization dedicated to the creative teaching approach developed by Carl Orff and Gunild Keetman. Their mission is "to demonstrate and promote the value of Orff Schulwerk, to support professional development opportunities, and to align applications of the Orff Schulwerk approach with the changing needs of American society." Articles cover such topics as the lifelong learner, building musical skills, music as therapy, musical process, and the inner voice of music. Issues include book, recording, and video reviews, study listings, teaching tips, and information on recent research. Of interest to music teachers of all levels, it is recommended for elementary, high school, academic, and public libraries.

4608. *Perspectives of New Music.* [ISSN: 0031-6016] 1962. s-a. USD 44 domestic; USD 54 foreign. Ed(s): Benjamin Boretz, Robert Morris. Perspectives of New Music, Inc., University of Washington, Music, Box 353450, Seattle, WA 98195-3450; pnm@u.washington.edu; http://www.perspectiveofnewmusic.org/. Illus., index, adv. Refereed. Circ: 1350 Paid. Vol. ends: Summer. Microform: PQC. Online: Chadwyck-Healey Inc.; Florida Center for Library Automation; Gale; JSTOR (Web-based Journal Archive); Northern Light Technology, Inc.; OCLC Online Computer Library Center, Inc.; ProQuest K-12 Learning Solutions; ProQuest LLC (Ann Arbor); H.W. Wilson. *Indexed:* ABS&EES, AmHI, ArtHuCI, HumInd, IBR, IBZ, IIMP, MusicInd, RILM. *Aud.:* Ac, Sa.

Perspectives of New Music publishes articles on musicians and developments in contemporary music and is aimed at composers, performers, and scholars. Articles contain research and analyses of new music theory and composition, sociological and philosophical studies, interviews, reviews, and occasional excerpts from musical scores. Some issues focus on an important musician. Issues generally contain seven to nine articles with musical diagrams and notation. Tables of contents of the latest four years can be viewed on the journal's web site. Recommended for academic libraries.

4609. *Philosophy of Music Education Review.* [ISSN: 1063-5734] 1993. s-a. USD 55 (Individuals, USD 27.50). Ed(s): Estelle R. Jorgensen. Indiana University Press, 601 N Morton St, Bloomington, IN 47404. Refereed. *Indexed:* ABIn, ERIC, EduInd, IIMP, MusicInd, PhilInd, RILM. *Bk. rev.:* 1, 500-1,000 words. *Aud.:* Ac, Sa.

Philosophy of Music Education Review provides an international forum for articles that present research on philosophical and theoretical aspects of music education. Authors and readership include scholars, teachers, and artists. Topics include educational methods and research findings on music's influence and application to other educational disciplines. Examples of topics are "The Significance of Music for the Promotion of Moral and Spiritual Value" and "Justifying the Right to Music Education." Each issue typically contains discussions of articles and a book review. Recommended for academic libraries. Available online through Project Muse.

4610. *Psychology of Music.* [ISSN: 0305-7356] 1973. q. GBP 284. Ed(s): Raymond A R Macdonald. Sage Publications Ltd., 1 Oliver's Yard, 55 City Rd, London, EC1 1SP, United Kingdom; info@sagepub.co.uk; http://www.sagepub.co.uk. Illus., index, adv. Refereed. Circ: 700. Online: CSA; Chadwyck-Healey Inc.; EBSCO Publishing, EBSCO Host;

HighWire Press; OCLC Online Computer Library Center, Inc.; OhioLINK; SAGE Publications, Inc., SAGE Journals Online; SwetsWise Online Content. Reprint: PSC. *Indexed:* BrEdI, IBR, IBZ, IIMP, MusicInd, PsycInfo, RILM. *Bk. rev.:* 2, 1,000 words, signed. *Aud.:* Ac, Sa.

The aim of the Society for Education, Music and Psychology Research (formerly, Society for Research in Psychology of Music and Music Education) is to provide an international forum for the research of psychological aspects in music and music education, and to publish current research findings in this field. The journal *Psychology of Music* publishes peer-reviewed articles on topics such as the interaction of music and social behavior, the cognitive processes involved in music composition and education, group dynamics, and the effect of music on perception and emotion. Issues include book reviews. Also available electronically by subscription. Tables of contents of past issues can be viewed on the journal's web site. Of interest to performers, teachers, and scholars, it is recommended for academic libraries.

4611. *Psychomusicology: a journal of research in music cognition.* [ISSN: 0275-3987] 1981. s-a. Ed(s): Jack A Taylor. Music and Arts Publications, 1211 Brandt Dr, Tallahassee, FL 32308-5210. Refereed. Circ: 300. *Indexed:* IIMP, MusicInd, PsycInfo, RILM. *Aud.:* Ac, Sa.

Psychomusicology presents research that concerns all aspects of music cognition (music performance, pitch and scale recognition, tonality, rhythm, melody, composition, improvisation, musical development, music emotions, neurology of music, etc.). Issues include reports of experimental research, reviews of extended research works, theoretical papers that are based on experimental research, and brief reports of research in progress, replications, commentaries on trends in psychomusicology, and brief notes on research methodology and instrumentation. Of interest to teachers, performers, and scholars, it is recommended for academic libraries.

4612. *Society for American Music. Journal.* [ISSN: 1752-1963] 2007. q. GBP 88 print & online eds. Ed(s): Ellie M Hisama. Cambridge University Press, The Edinburgh Bldg, Shaftesbury Rd, Cambridge, CB2 2RU, United Kingdom; information@cambridge.org; http://www.journals.cambridge.org. Refereed. *Bk. rev.:* 2-5 pp., 600-1,000 words. *Aud.:* Ac, Sa.

Journal of the Society for American Music (*JSAM*) is an international, peer-reviewed journal that deals with all aspects of American music and music in the Americas. Research focus is on interdisciplinary studies in fields such as historical musicology, music theory, ethnomusicology, cultural theory, identity studies, and American studies. Each issue features articles, reviews of books, recordings, and multimedia items. *JSAM* welcomes papers on cultural hierarchy; social, political, economic, gender, race, ethnicity, and sexuality issues; the impact and role of the media; sacred, secular, and popular traditions; geographical and historical patterns; composers, performers, and audiences; historiography and reception history; and problems of research, analysis, criticism, and aesthetics). *JSAM* is the official organ of the Society for American Music and is highly recommended for libraries that support American Studies or the academic study of popular music.

The Source. See African American section.

4613. *The Strad: a monthly journal for professionals and amateurs of all stringed instruments played with the bow.* [ISSN: 0039-2049] 1890. m. GBP 44.05 domestic & Ireland; GBP 64 in Europe; GBP 54 in US & Canada. Ed(s): Ariane Todes. Orpheus Publications Ltd., 30 Cannon St, London, EC4M 6YJ, United Kingdom; info@orpheuspublications.com; http://www.orphpl.com/home.asp?id=co3. Illus., adv. Sample. Circ: 17000 Paid. Microform: PQC; WMP. Online: EBSCO Publishing, EBSCO Host. *Indexed:* AmHI, ArtHuCI, BrHumI, IBR, IBZ, IIMP, MusicInd, RILM. *Bk. rev.:* 3-5, length varies. *Aud.:* Ac, Sa.

The Strad focuses on all people and things related to the most popular classical string instruments (violin, viola, cello). Topics of articles include profiles of orchestras, ensembles, performers, luthiers, teachers and explication of their

methods, instruction on playing technique, a focus on special instruments, etc. Issues also contain book, CD, and concert reviews. The magazine's web site provides partial access to the tables of contents of back issues. Recommended for public and academic libraries.

4614. *Strings: the magazine for players and makers of bowed instruments.* [ISSN: 0888-3106] 1986. 10x/yr. USD 36.95 domestic; USD 49.95 Canada; USD 61.95 elsewhere. String Letter Publishing, 255 West End Ave, San Rafael, CA 94901; http://www.stringletter.com. Adv. Circ: 13957 Paid. *Indexed:* IIMP, MusicInd, RILM. *Bk. rev.:* Number and length vary. *Aud.:* Ac, Sa.

Strings is a commercial magazine devoted to all aspects of stringed instruments played with a bow, including violin, viola, violoncello, and double bass. Articles feature topics such as instrument care and repair, repertoire, performance issues, interviews with players and composers, information about various violin makers, and materials used in creating stringed instruments. Also includes news of events, a concert calendar, information on contests and workshops, and reviews of recordings, books, and music. Special issues include a summer study guide and a music school directory. The journal's web site provides access to the tables of contents of back issues. Of interest to string players, teachers, and stringed instrument makers and repair persons, it is recommended for academic and public libraries.

4615. *Tempo (London, 1939): a quarterly review of modern music.* [ISSN: 0040-2982] 1939. q. GBP 60. Ed(s): Calum MacDonald. Cambridge University Press, The Edinburgh Bldg, Shaftesbury Rd, Cambridge, CB2 2RU, United Kingdom; journals@cambridge.org; http://www.cup.cam.ac.uk/. Illus., adv. Reprint: PSC. *Indexed:* AmHI, ArtHuCI, BrHumI, IIMP, MusicInd, RILM. *Bk. rev.:* 2-4, 1,500 words, signed. *Aud.:* Ac, Sa.

Tempo publishes articles on twentieth-century and contemporary concert music that include profiles of composers and musicians, interviews, aesthetic studies, and historical and analytical studies of composers' works. Articles are international in scope. A typical issue contains four research articles, reviews of books and CDs, and reviews of world premieres. A "News" section lists premieres of new compositions, new books received, and appointments. The journal's web page lists contents of issues of the last five years. Recommended for academic libraries.

4616. *Twentieth Century Music.* [ISSN: 1478-5722] 2004. s-a. GBP 69. Ed(s): Allan Moore, Christopher Mark. Cambridge University Press, The Edinburgh Bldg, Shaftesbury Rd, Cambridge, CB2 2RU, United Kingdom; journals@cambridge.org; http://www.cup.cam.ac.uk/. Refereed. Reprint: PSC. *Indexed:* MusicInd, RILM. *Bk. rev.:* Number and length vary. *Aud.:* Ac.

Twentieth Century Music represents a forum for ideas and exchange on all aspects of music from the late nineteenth century to the present. One of the goals of the journal is to find new approaches for appreciation and study of the music. Topics include music from Western and non-Western traditions, as well as popular music, jazz, improvised music, film music. Each issue includes several extensive book reviews. Recommended for academic libraries.

4617. *Women and Music: a journal of gender and culture.* [ISSN: 1090-7505] 1997. a. USD 70. Ed(s): Suzanne G Cusick. University of Nebraska Press, 1111 Lincoln Mall, Lincoln, NE 68588-0630; journals@unlnotes.unl.edu; http://www.nebraskapress.unl.edu. Adv. Refereed. Circ: 500. Online: Chadwyck-Healey Inc.; EBSCO Publishing, EBSCO Host; Florida Center for Library Automation; Gale; OCLC Online Computer Library Center, Inc.; Project MUSE; ProQuest LLC (Ann Arbor); SwetsWise Online Content. *Indexed:* CWI, FemPer, GendWatch, IBR, IBZ, IIMP, MusicInd, RILM. *Bk. rev.:* 10, essay length, signed. *Aud.:* Ac, Sa.

Women and Music is an annual publication of the International Alliance for Women in Music (IAWM) that contains refereed articles that describe and analyze relationships of music, gender, and culture. Topics are international in scope and deal with various cultures and periods of time from the perspective of a variety of disciplines. Articles may discuss issues relating to women composers, performers, teachers, etc. Contains review essays and book reviews. Recommended for academic collections.

4618. *The World of Music*. [ISSN: 0043-8774] 1959. 3x/yr. EUR 58 domestic; EUR 70 foreign; EUR 22 newsstand/cover. Ed(s): Max Peter Baumann. V W B - Verlag fuer Wissenschaft und Bildung, Postfach 110368, Berlin, 10833, Germany; info@vwb-verlag.com; http://www.vwb-verlag.com. Illus., adv. Refereed. Circ: 1200. *Indexed:* ArtHuCI, BAS, FR, IBR, IBSS, IBZ, IIMP, MLA-IB, MusicInd, RILM, SSCI. *Bk. rev.:* 5, 750-1,000 words, signed. *Aud.:* Ac, Sa.

The World of Music publishes the results of ethnomusicological research in music histories and traditions, and music-related arts. Issues may focus on a specified topic, e.g., "Music and Childhood," or a geographic region, e.g., "Japanese Musical Traditions." A typical issue contains six to eight articles and several book and CD reviews. Articles vary in length from 5 to 20 pages and often include notes and bibliographies. Issues include photographs and musical examples. Both the publisher's web site and the journal's web site (http://the-world-of-music-journal.blogspot.com) list tables of contents; the journal's site also displays abstracts of articles from 1997 to the present, as well as a bibliography arranged alphabetically by author. Recommended for academic libraries.

Popular

4619. *Alternative Press*. [ISSN: 1065-1667] 1969. m. USD 12 domestic; USD 36 in Canada & Mexico; USD 60 elsewhere. Ed(s): Leslie Simon, Aaron Burgess. Alternative Press Magazine, Inc., 1305 W 80th St, Ste 2 F, Cleveland, OH 44102-1996; http://www.altpress.com. Illus., adv. Circ: 100000 Paid. *Indexed:* IIMP. *Aud.:* Ga.

An important source of information about performers in various styles of alternative music, including metal, punk, ska, emo pop, indie pop, and others. It features interviews with band members, as well as actors, fashion designers, and other popular figures. It also contains videogame, DVD, and movie reviews, and a daily calendar listing new releases. Special issues include features such as the top 100 bands of the year. A particularly useful section is the "AP Record Store," which includes reviews and recommendations for upwards of 60 new albums per issue.

4620. *The Beat (Los Angeles): reggae, African, Caribbean, world music*. Formerly: *Reggae and African Beat*. [ISSN: 1063-5319] 1982. 5x/yr. USD 20 domestic; USD 25 in Canada & Mexico; USD 40 elsewhere. Ed(s): C C Smith. Bongo Productions, PO Box 65856, Los Angeles, CA 90065; getthebeat@aol.com. Illus., adv. Circ: 10000 Paid. *Indexed:* RILM. *Bk. rev.:* Number and length vary. *Aud.:* Ga.

This publication covers reggae and African popular music, as well as genres such as Brazilian music, Afro-Cuban jazz, traditional Maori music, and New Zealand reggae. It focuses on reviews of recordings and includes brief descriptions, world music news, ratings, and longer analysis. It also contains a few reviews of books specifically about African or Caribbean music or musicians and new release lists. Summaries of articles in the current issue are available at the publisher's web site. Highly readable and informative for performers and enthusiasts alike.

4621. *Billboard (New York): the international newsweekly of music, video, and home entertainment*. [ISSN: 0006-2510] 1894. w. 51/yr. USD 299 in US & Canada; USD 450 in Europe; USD 925 Japan. Ed(s): Tamara Conniff. Nielsen Business Publications, 770 Broadway, New York, NY 10003-9595; bmcomm@vnuinc.com; http://www.nielsenbusinessmedia.com. Illus., adv. Circ: 40000 Paid. Microform: BHP; PQC. Online: Chadwyck-Healey Inc.; The Dialog Corporation; EBSCO Publishing, EBSCO Host; Florida Center for Library Automation; Gale; LexisNexis; OCLC Online Computer Library Center, Inc.; ProQuest K-12 Learning Solutions; ProQuest LLC (Ann Arbor); H.W. Wilson. *Indexed:* ABIn, ArtHuCI, BPI, CBRI, CWI, CommAb, IIMP, IIPA, LRI, MASUSE, MusicInd, RILM, SFSA, SSCI. *Aud.:* Ga.

Well known for its charts of best-selling titles and artists, *Billboard* is an essential publication for news and information about the music industry. It includes reports on such topics as copyright, digital sales, peer-to-peer file sharing, and other trends and current technologies. Articles cover artists and bands in all styles of music. Also included is information on top-selling concerts and touring awards, as well as reviews of new releases. Related annual publications include the *Billboard History of Rock 'n' Roll, Billboard's International Buyer's Guide of the Music-Record-Tape Industry, Billboard's International Talent and Touring Directory,* and *Billboard*'s year-end awards issues.

4622. *Black Beat*. Formerly (until 1983): *Soul Teen*. [ISSN: 0745-8649] 1974. bi-m. USD 19.94 domestic; USD 29.94 foreign; USD 4.99 newsstand/cover per issue domestic. Ed(s): Danica Damiel. Dorchester Media, 200 Madison Ave, Ste 2000, New York, NY 10016; info@dorchestermedia.com; http://www.dorchestermedia.com. Illus., adv. *Aud.:* Hs.

Designed for an African American teenage audience, this magazine includes biographies of popular artists, pin-up posters, interviews, and regular columns on TV, video, and fashion news. It features many full-color photographs. Also included are reviews of hip-hop, rap, and R&B recordings, as well as news of stage productions and new music acts. Covers American performers, as well as some international figures.

4623. *Bluegrass Unlimited*. [ISSN: 0006-5137] 1966. m. USD 25 domestic; USD 36 Canada; USD 39 elsewhere. Ed(s): Sharon K McGraw, Peter V Kuykendall. Bluegrass Unlimited Inc., PO Box 771, Warrenton, VA 20188-0771; info@bluegrassmusic.com. Illus., adv. Circ: 26839 Paid. *Indexed:* IIMP, MLA-IB, MusicInd, RILM. *Bk. rev.:* Number and length vary. *Aud.:* Ga.

According to its official web site, this magazine is "dedicated to the furtherance of bluegrass and old-time country musicians, devotees, and associates." Special issues focus on topics such as instruments and festivals, and the scope includes the United States as well as a small number of worldwide performances and events. The many ads for festivals and instruments are helpful, as are the many reviews (recordings, DVDs, and books [new and reissued]). There are also a list of new releases, a survey of top songs and albums, and a calendar of personal appearances organized by date. The prose is aimed at a general audience, informative to both performers and interested public.

4624. *C C M Magazine*. Former titles (until 1998): *Contemporary Christian Music*; (until 1986): *Contemporary Christian*; (until 1983): *Contemporary Christian Music*. [ISSN: 1524-7848] 1978. m. USD 19.95 domestic; USD 27.95 Canada; USD 33.95 elsewhere. Salem Publishing, 104 Woodmont Blvd, Ste 300, Nashville, TN 37205. Illus., adv. Circ: 70000 Paid. *Indexed:* ChrPI, IIMP, MusicInd. *Bk. rev.:* Number and length vary. *Aud.:* Ga.

The coverage of this publication includes several genres of Christian music, as well as Christian living and lifestyle. The magazine includes interviews, reviews of concerts and new books, plays, films, and music releases, and a calendar of artist birthdays, concert dates, and other events. Also included are such features as a list of top-selling Christian rock, adult contemporary, R&B, hip-hop, and praise and worship albums. Some articles present special topics such as an overview of Christian colleges in the United States. Limited content online.

4625. *Circus: america's rock magazine*. Former titles (until 1979): *Circus Weekly*; (until 1978): *Circus*. [ISSN: 0009-7365] 1969. m. USD 13.99; USD 6.99 newsstand/cover per issue. Ed(s): Gerald Rothberg, Gerald Rothberg. Circus Enterprises Corp., 6 W 18th St, New York, NY 10011. Illus., adv. Circ: 100000 Paid. *Aud.:* Hs, Ga.

Covering contemporary heavy metal and hard rock, this publication features interviews and biographical articles about bands, interspersed with full-color photographs. It also includes other pop culture news. Intended for teen readers.

4626. *D J Times: the international magazine for the professional mobile & club DJ.* [ISSN: 1045-9693] 1988. m. USD 30 domestic; USD 40 in Canada & Mexico; USD 55 elsewhere. Ed(s): Jim Tremayne. Testa Communications, Inc., 25 Willowdale Ave, Port Washington, NY 11050; djtimes@testa.com; http://www.djtimes.com. Illus., adv. *Indexed:* IIMP. *Aud.:* Ga, Sa.

This publication focuses on DJs as performers, with feature articles that discuss albums, equipment, musical techniques, and tips on promoting a DJ business. It includes reviews of new equipment, artists, and techniques, as well as interviews, charts (club hits), and biographical sketches. Styles covered in the recordings review section include techno, house, indie rock, disco, hip-hop, and other genres, as well as compilations. Full text is available on the publisher's web site.

4627. *Down Beat: jazz, blues, and beyond.* [ISSN: 0012-5768] 1934. m. USD 24.95 domestic; USD 34.95 Canada; USD 46.95 foreign. Ed(s): Jason Koransky. Maher Publications, 102 North Haven Rd, Elmhurst, IL 60126; jasonk@downbeatjazz.com; http://www.downbeat.com. Illus., adv. Circ: 92000 Paid. Microform: PQC. Online: Chadwyck-Healey Inc.; Florida Center for Library Automation; Gale; OCLC Online Computer Library Center, Inc.; ProQuest LLC (Ann Arbor). *Indexed:* AmHI, ArtHuCI, BRI, CBRI, IIMP, MASUSE, MusicInd, RGPR, RILM. *Bk. rev.:* 25-35, 500-1,000 words. *Aud.:* Ga.

A well-known jazz publication appropriate for a general audience, *Downbeat* contains interviews and biographical articles that feature current and historic jazz figures. It includes coverage of international artists while focusing primarily on American bands and musicians. Its features include news on forthcoming releases, articles and buying guides on equipment and instruments, advertisements for new recordings, play-along scores, transcriptions, and instructional material. There are also reviews of jazz, blues, and reissue recordings, and of jazz-related books. Selections from current and past issues are available on the publisher's web site. Intended for aficionados and anyone interested in jazz. Essential for public libraries and academic libraries that support jazz studies.

4628. *Goldmine: the collector's record and compact disc marketplace.* Former titles (until 1985): *Record Collectors Goldmine; Goldmine.* [ISSN: 1055-2685] 1974. bi-w. USD 39.95 domestic; USD 62 Canada; USD 86.95 foreign. Ed(s): Brian Earnest. Krause Publications, Inc., 700 E State St, Iola, WI 54990-0001; info@krause.com; http://www.krause.com. Illus., adv. Circ: 17026 Paid and free. Microform: PQC. Online: Chadwyck-Healey Inc. *Indexed:* IIMP, MusicInd. *Aud.:* Ga.

Goldmine is a major source of information about the collecting of records and other music memorabilia. Each issue features interviews and articles about artists and groups in genres from rock, folk, and country to classical, and the articles often include extensive discographies. Feature columns discuss new releases, reissues, and specific recordings. Valuable inclusions in the magazine are the full-page advertisements for vintage recordings, information on collecting conventions, auction inventories, and set sales. Selected issues are available online to subscribers.

4629. *Guitar One: the magazine you can play.* Former titles (until 1995): *Guitar Magazine; Guitar for the Practicing Musician.* [ISSN: 1089-6406] 1983. m. USD 24.95 domestic; USD 39.95 Canada; USD 54.95 elsewhere. Ed(s): Michael Mueller. Future U S, Inc., 4000 Shoreline Court, Ste. 400, South San Francisco, CA 94080; http://www.futureus-inc.com. Illus., adv. Circ: 150000 Paid. *Aud.:* Ga.

Focusing on playing technique in styles ranging from rock and blues to jazz, this magazine also includes the biographical journeys of various guitarists, news and reviews of equipment, and many musical examples of riffs as well as full transcriptions of classic songs. It regularly comes with an accompanying CD-ROM, which includes audio tracks of the printed musical examples, music to accompany feature stories, lesson tracks, play-along tracks, and gear reviews. Selected back issues are available online.

4630. *Guitar Player: for professional and amateur guitarists.* [ISSN: 0017-5463] 1967. m. USD 11.99. NewBay Media, LLC, 810 Seventh Ave, 27th Fl, New York, NY 10019; http://www.nbmedia.com. Illus., adv. Circ: 155000. *Indexed:* IIMP, LRI, MASUSE, MusicInd, RILM. *Aud.:* Ga.

Guitar Player encompasses a wide range of styles of guitar music, including jazz, classical, progressive rock, and metal. While heavy on advertisements, the magazine includes interviews with artists, lessons, recording reviews, instructions for sheet music downloads, and gear reviews. Each issue also includes short musical figures by famous players. Selected issues are available online.

4631. *Guitar World.* [ISSN: 1045-6295] 1980. m. USD 14.95 domestic; USD 27 Canada; USD 47 elsewhere. Ed(s): Brad Tolinski. Future U S, Inc., 4000 Shoreline Court, Ste. 400, South San Francisco, CA 94080; http://www.futureus-inc.com. Illus., adv. Circ: 200000 Paid. *Indexed:* MusicInd. *Aud.:* Ga.

With a more popular than technical slant, *Guitar World* is recommended for beginning guitarists and fans. Interviews and feature stories cover performers and styles such as metal and thrash. It includes many musical figures as well as performance instructions for and transcriptions of popular rock songs. Each issue also features equipment reviews and technical advice about gear. Selective content is online.

4632. *Jazz Education Journal.* Former titles (until 2001): *Jazz Educators Journal; National Association of Jazz Educators. Newsletter; N A J E Educator.* [ISSN: 1540-2886] 1968. bi-m. USD 36 domestic; USD 46 foreign. Ed(s): Leslie Sabina. International Association of Jazz Educators, PO Box 724, Manhattan, KS 66505-0724; info@iaje.org. Illus., adv. Refereed. Circ: 7500. Online: Chadwyck-Healey Inc. *Indexed:* IIMP, MusicInd, RILM. *Aud.:* Ac.

This professional journal of the International Association of Jazz Educators (IAJE) includes feature articles that report success stories of specific elementary, high school, and college jazz programs and groups. It also presents interviews with specific educators. It also contains useful information such as surveys of new teaching materials and reviews of printed music and sound recordings. Column topics include global jazz, legal issues in jazz, annual CD awards, and question-and-answer sections. A directory of IAJE members is included in each August issue. Selected full text is available on publisher's web site.

4633. *Jazz Perspectives.* [ISSN: 1749-4060] 2007. s-a. GBP 117 print & online eds. Ed(s): John Howland, Lewis Porter. Routledge, 4 Park Sq, Milton Park, Abingdon, OX14 4RN, United Kingdom; info@routledge.co.uk; http://www.tandf.co.uk/journals. Refereed. *Bk. rev.:* 5-7 pp., 600-1,000 words. *Aud.:* Ac, Sa.

Jazz Perspectives is an international peer-reviewed journal devoted to jazz scholarship. This journal intends to bridge the gap between the jazz-as-music and jazz-as-culture sides of contemporary jazz studies. It promotes broader international perspectives on the jazz tradition and its legacy. Issues focus on interdisciplinary studies, featuring articles that address original research and analysis (musical, historical, and cultural). There are also book and media reviews and essays on significant recent literature (education, performers, recording history), as well as new recordings and media. Highly recommended for libraries that support jazz studies or with clientele interested in academic jazz study.

4634. *The Jazz Report: voice of the artist.* [ISSN: 0843-3151] 1987. q. CND 18 domestic; USD 20 elsewhere. Ed(s): Greg Sutherland. King Sutherland Productions, 592 Markham St, Ste 7, Toronto, ON M6G 2L8, Canada. Illus., adv. *Aud.:* Ga, Sa.

Presents interviews and biographical articles about jazz and blues artists, as well as current news. Also included are reviews of recordings and equipment. This publication is intended for both specialized and general audiences.

4635. *JAZZed: the jazz educator's magazine.* 2006. bi-m. USD 24 domestic; USD 36 Canada; USD 48 elsewhere. Symphony Publishing LLC, 210 Boylston St, Chestnut Hill, MA 02167; http://www.symphonypublishing.com. Circ: 13000. *Aud.:* Ems, Hs, Ga, Ac.

JAZZed is a glossy magazine for jazz music professionals and others involved in teaching jazz musicians. Articles include interviews with musicians, music industry professionals, and others employed in the business of producing materials for teaching jazz music. Topics covered include instrumental techniques, improvisation, music theory, and issues and challenges encountered in teaching jazz. Also included are sections of announcements, news, recordings released, and classifieds. Limited content is available at http://www.jazzedmagazine.com.

4636. *Jazziz.* [ISSN: 0741-5885] 1983. m. USD 69.95 domestic; USD 79.95 in Canada & Mexico; USD 99.95 elsewhere. Ed(s): Mike Koretzky, Fernando Gonzales. Jazziz Magazine, Inc., 3620 NW 43rd St Ste D, Gainesville, FL 32606; jazziz@sprintmail.com; http://www.jazziz.com. Illus., adv. Circ: 110000 Paid. *Indexed:* IIMP, MusicInd, RILM. *Aud.:* Ga.

This publication focuses on new trends in jazz and on broadening listeners' understanding of jazz music, providing thoughtful observations on jazz and its evolution. Articles concentrate on the music and musicians, including international artists and styles. Included are reviews, news, and a jazz festival guide. Each issue comes with a compilation CD of tracks selected to complement the theme of the issue. Recent themes include global jazz, New Orleans jazz, European jazz pianists, and the jazz-blues overlap. The table of contents and some articles are available on the publisher's web site.

4637. *JazzTimes: America's jazz magazine.* Supersedes: *Radio Free Jazz.* [ISSN: 0272-572X] 1972. 10x/yr. USD 23.95 domestic; USD 35.95 Canada; USD 59.95 elsewhere. Ed(s): Lee Mergner. Jazz Times Inc., 8737 Colesvlle Rd, 9th Fl, Silver Spring, MD 20910-3921. Illus., adv. Circ: 100000 Paid. Microform: PQC. *Indexed:* IIMP, MusicInd, RILM. *Aud.:* Ga.

Features biographical articles on contemporary and historic jazz figures and their styles of playing and living. Included are unique columns on albums, gigs, news, electronic equipment, and the column "Before & After," which features artists' reactions while listening to specific recordings. A particularly useful aspect of this publication is the extensive reviews section for new recordings, which contains upwards of 100 titles per issue. Some issues also include recommendations on summer jazz programs, education programs, and music festivals.

4638. *Journal of Country Music.* Formerly: *Country Music Foundation News Letter.* [ISSN: 0092-0517] 1970. 3x/yr. USD 23.85. Ed(s): Jeremy Tepper. Country Music Foundation, Inc., 222 5th Ave., S, Nashville, TN 37203-4206. Illus., adv. Circ: 4000. *Indexed:* ArtHuCI, IIMP, MLA-IB, MusicInd, RILM. *Bk. rev.:* Number and length vary. *Aud.:* Ac.

Published by the Country Music Foundation, this journal contains musicological articles that cover different styles of country music, as well as interviews and biographies of performers and discussions of their music. Also includes a helpful reviews section for books and recordings.

4639. *Keyboard: the world's leading music technology magazine.* Formerly (until 1981): *Contemporary Keyboard.* [ISSN: 0730-0158] 1975. m. USD 12 domestic; USD 34 in Canada & Mexico; USD 44 elsewhere. Ed(s): Ernie Rideout, Debbie Greenberg. NewBay Media, LLC, 1111 Bayhill Dr, Ste 125, San Bruno, CA 94066; http://www.nbmedia.com. Illus., adv. Circ: 70000 Paid. Microform: PQC. Online: Chadwyck-Healey Inc.; Gale; ProQuest K-12 Learning Solutions; ProQuest LLC (Ann Arbor). *Indexed:* IIMP, MusicInd, RILM. *Aud.:* Ga.

This publication focuses on electronic keyboard equipment and how to use it. Articles cover band members and the keyboards and gear they use, while musical styles covered include rock, hip-hop, jazz, and others. Included are short lessons and musical examples for beginning and intermediate players, as well as a full song. Columns cover various techniques such as sampling or incorporating video clips into performance, as well as instruction on how to use featured technological equipment. Also contains reviews of recordings and extensive reviews of keyboard gear. Selections from the current issue are available online.

4640. *Living Blues: the magazine of the African American blues tradition.* Incorporates: *Living Bluesletter.* [ISSN: 0024-5232] 1970. bi-m. USD 23.95 domestic; USD 29.95 Canada; USD 39.95 elsewhere. Ed(s): Scott Barretta. University of Mississippi, Center for the Study of Southern Culture, Barnard Observatory, PO Box 1848, University, MS 38677-1848; LivingBlues@LivingBluesOnline.com; http://www.LivingBluesOnline.com. Illus., adv. Circ: 25000. Microform: PQC. *Indexed:* IIBP, IIMP, MLA-IB, MusicInd, RILM. *Aud.:* Ga, Ac.

Presents a historical and biographical approach to documenting blues music, through excellent articles and photographs. Included are interviews (current and historic), book excerpts, and reviews of new recordings, DVDs, books, and reissues. Also includes a blues festival guide and radio charts. This scholarly publication provides an oral history approach that is both informative and captivating.

4641. *Metal Edge.* Former titles (until 199?): *T V Picture Life, Metal Edge;* (until 1984): *T V Picture Life.* [ISSN: 1068-2872] 1957. m. USD 29.95 domestic; USD 35.95 Canada; USD 37.95 elsewhere. Ed(s): Cathy Stodder. Zenbu Media, Llc., 104 W 29th St Rm 1101, New York, NY 10001-5310. Illus., adv. Circ: 150000 Paid. *Aud.:* Ga.

This magazine is about the music and musicians involved in heavy metal and hard rock. It includes extensive interviews, biographies, advertisements for new albums, recording reviews, editorials, and tour and concert schedules. Some issues focus on special topics such as women in rock, and many articles incorporate the history of certain groups and artists.

4642. *Music Technology Buyer's Guide.* a. USD 6.95 newsstand/cover per issue. NewBay Media, LLC, 810 Seventh Ave, 27th Fl, New York, NY 10019; http://www.nbmedia.com. *Aud.:* Hs, Ga.

Previously issued as the December issue of *Keyboard* magazine, this publication includes extensive reviews of equipment and gear for keyboard players, guitarists, and other musicians. Featured equipment includes audio interfaces, hardware recorders, instruments, microphones, midi hardware, mixers, signal processors, and more.

4643. *New Musical Express.* Incorporates (1926-2000): *Melody Maker.* [ISSN: 0028-6362] 1952. w. GBP 98. Ed(s): Conor McNicholas. I P C ignite! Ltd., King's Reach Tower, Stamford St, London, SE1 9LS, United Kingdom; http://www.ipcmedia.com/. Illus., adv. Circ: 90763. Microform: RPI. *Indexed:* IIMP. *Aud.:* Ga.

This tabloid-sized British magazine contains descriptions of bands and their music and antics, as well as reviews of many albums and singles. It covers British, Canadian, and American groups, in genres including indie rock and pop, punk, post-punk, R&B, and dance music. Also included are news, classifieds, British concert listings, reviews of music videos, and advertisements for new releases. Table of contents and audio clips are available on publisher's web site.

4644. *Popular Music.* [ISSN: 0261-1430] 1982. 3x/yr. GBP 136. Ed(s): John Street, Keith Negus. Cambridge University Press, The Edinburgh Bldg, Shaftesbury Rd, Cambridge, CB2 2RU, United Kingdom; journals@cambridge.org; http://www.journals.cambridge.org. Illus., adv. Refereed. Microform: PQC. Online: Pub.; EBSCO Publishing, EBSCO Host; JSTOR (Web-based Journal Archive); OCLC Online Computer Library Center, Inc.; OhioLINK; SwetsWise Online Content. Reprint: PSC. *Indexed:* AmHI, ArtHuCI, BrHumI, HumInd, IIMP, MusicInd, RILM. *Bk. rev.:* Number and length vary. *Aud.:* Ac.

A primary journal for academic study that encompasses all genres of popular music. Covers popular music through a musicological and ethnomusicological approach, influenced by other areas of study. Each issue includes scholarly articles and in-depth book reviews. The annotated list of new books in each October issue is a particularly valuable part of the publication. Full text is available online.

4645. *Popular Music & Society.* [ISSN: 0300-7766] 1972. 5x/yr. GBP 148 print & online eds. Ed(s): Gary Burns. Routledge, 4 Park Square, Milton Park, Abingdon, OX14 4RN, United Kingdom; http://www.routledge.co.uk. Illus., index, adv. Refereed. Circ: 1000. Microform: PQC. Online: Chadwyck-Healey Inc.; EBSCO Publishing, EBSCO Host; Florida Center for Library Automation; Gale; IngentaConnect; Northern Light Technology, Inc.; OCLC Online Computer Library Center, Inc.; ProQuest K-12 Learning Solutions; ProQuest LLC (Ann Arbor); SwetsWise Online Content; H.W. Wilson. Reprint: PSC. *Indexed:* AmH&L, AmHI, ArtHuCI, BRI, BrHumI, CBRI, CommAb, HistAb, HumInd, IBR, IBSS, IBZ, IIMP, MRD, MusicInd, PRA, RILM, SFSA, SSCI. *Bk. rev.:* Number and length vary. *Aud.:* Ac.

This journal presents the academic study of popular music through the orientations of related disciplines, including anthropology, sociology, and gender studies. Also included are scholarly reviews of new popular music recordings and of books about popular music. Full text is available online.

4646. *Roctober.* 1992. 3x/yr. USD 10 domestic; USD 15 in Canada & Mexico; USD 20 elsewhere. Ed(s): Jake A Austen. Roctober, 1507 E 53rd St, 617, Chicago, IL 60615. Illus., adv. Circ: 3500. *Bk. rev.:* 10, 200 words. *Aud.:* Ga.

This publication presents an offbeat, eccentric collection of lengthy interviews with various bands and musicians, reviews of recordings and other media, and peculiar comics. Articles are eclectic, covering topics like Beach Boys trivia or presenting information such as an extensive listing of TV celebrities and recordings with which they were involved. Styles of music covered include psychedelic rock, punk, soul, and more. Tables of contents and some articles are available online.

4647. *Rolling Stone.* [ISSN: 0035-791X] 1967. bi-w. USD 19.95 domestic; USD 38 Canada; USD 65 elsewhere. Ed(s): Will Dana, Jann S Wenner. Rolling Stone LLC, 1290 Ave. of the Americas, 2nd Fl, New York, NY 10104. Illus., adv. Circ: 1200000 Paid. CD-ROM: ProQuest LLC (Ann Arbor). Microform: PQC. Online: Chadwyck-Healey Inc.; EBSCO Publishing, EBSCO Host; Florida Center for Library Automation; Micromedia ProQuest; Northern Light Technology, Inc.; OCLC Online Computer Library Center, Inc.; ProQuest K-12 Learning Solutions; ProQuest LLC (Ann Arbor). *Indexed:* BRI, CBCARef, CBRI, CPerI, FLI, IIMP, IIPA, MASUSE, MRD, MusicInd, RGPR, RI-1, RILM. *Bk. rev.:* Number and length vary. *Aud.:* Ga.

This magazine represents one of the more important sources of information and news about musicians, actors, pop stars, political figures, and other popular culture favorites. It includes well-written columns that provide social commentary and address current news stories, music, and movies. It features lengthy biographical articles and interviews, politically inspired pieces, and reviews of recordings, books, and movies. Full text is available online.

4648. *Sing Out!: folk music & folk songs.* [ISSN: 0037-5624] 1950. q. USD 25 domestic; USD 30 Canada; USD 43 elsewhere. Ed(s): Scott Atkinson, Mark D Moss. Sing Out Corp., PO Box 5460, Bethlehem, PA 18015-0460. Illus., adv. Circ: 13500. Microform: PQC. Online: Chadwyck-Healey Inc.; Gale. *Indexed:* ASIP, AltPI, IIMP, MLA-IB, MusicInd, RILM. *Bk. rev.:* Number and length vary. *Aud.:* Ga.

A primary source of information about folk music of all styles from North America and abroad. Each issue provides printed music for more than 20 songs, with midi files available on the publisher's web site. It also includes interviews, teach-ins featuring instruction on various folk instruments, and a lengthy festival and camp guide. Columns include reviews of books and printed music, videos, and an extensive section of recordings reviews, along with an annotated list of new publications.

4649. *Spin.* [ISSN: 0886-3032] 1985. m. USD 11.95 domestic; USD 24 Canada; USD 40 elsewhere. Hartle Media Ventures LLC, 59 Grant Ave, 4th Fl, San Francisco, CA 94108; http://hartlemedia.com/. Illus., adv. Circ: 350000 Paid. Microform: PQC. *Indexed:* ASIP, IIMP, IIPA, MusicInd, RILM. *Aud.:* Hs, Ga.

Encompassing popular music and pop culture, this magazine features articles on musicians, actors, and other pop culture icons, as well as reviews of CDs, games, DVDs, and books, plus many advertisements. Music sections cover several genres, including rock, pop, rap, hip-hop, and more. There are also recommendations for music downloads and podcasts. The magazine is intended for teen and young adult audiences. Selections from the current issue are available online.

Vibe Vixen. See African American section.

■ MUSIC REVIEWS

General/Audio Equipment

Erica Lynn Coe, Head, Instruction Services, University of Washington Tacoma Library, 1900 Commerce Street, Tacoma, WA 98402; elcoe@u.washington.edu

Introduction

With the proliferation of MP3 devices, satellite radio, and streaming media, music is all around us. Today, consumers are more selective about the music they buy, which makes this section very relevant. The section is devoted to magazines published in the United States and the United Kingdom that focus primarily on reviews of music and audio equipment. The majority of these titles cover classical music. Many magazines for popular genres such as rock and pop tend to focus on the culture, lifestyle, and fashion surrounding the music, rather than reviews. Please refer to the Music section to find magazines in a wider array of genres. The magazines in the Audio Equipment subsection focus primarily on product reviews. Additional product review magazines may be found in the Television, Video, and Radio section.

There are, of course, numerous web sites that provide music reviews. Two noteworthy sites not included below are *Classical CD Review: a site for the serious collector* (http://classicalcdreview.com), with reviews by well-established reviewers, and *Classical Net* (www.classical.net) with over 3,200 CD, DVD, and book reviews. There are also web sites that provide collections of reviews from magazines, newspapers, or web sites. Two notable sites are *Rock's Backpages* (www.rocksbackpages.com) and *Metacritic* (www.metacritic.com). Additional web sites can be found by using the online directories of Google (http://directory.google.com) and Yahoo! (http://dir.yahoo.com).

Basic Periodicals

Ga: *Absolute Sound, American Record Guide, BBC Music Magazine, Gramophone, Sensible Sound, Stereophile;* Ac: *American Record Guide, BBC Music Magazine, Fanfare, Gramophone, Stereophile.*

Basic Abstracts and Indexes

Music Article Guide, Music Index, RILM Abstracts of Music Literature.

General

4650. *All About Jazz.* irreg. Ed(s): Nils Jacobson, Chris Slawecki. All About Jazz, 761 Sproul Road, #211, Springfield, PA 19064; http://www.allaboutjazz.com/. Adv. *Bk. rev.:* Various number and length. *Aud.:* Ga, Ac.

All About Jazz (www.allaboutjazz.com) boasts that it is "a site produced by jazz fans for jazz fans," and it aims to cover the past, present, and future of jazz from an international perspective. At the time of this writing, the Reviews section included 19,520 searchable CD reviews, with more reviews posted daily. The most recent 200 reviews are displayed by date in reverse chronological order. Users can search by artist name, album title, record label, author of review, and style. There are 18 styles to choose from, and they include Classical, Blues, Ambient, Funk/Groove, and the mashed-together Mainstream/Bop/Hard Bop/Cool. Reviews are written in a conversational style and range from 200 to 500 words. The focus of the review is on the music and performance. Many reviews begin with a brief background of the artist or group to place the recording in context. Reviews include track listings, personnel, and artist's web site, as well as internal links to pages about the artist and music label. The Articles section includes interviews, artist profiles, and reviews of books, concert/festival/event, and DVD/video/film. The web site has undergone extensive reorganization and updating in the past year. RSS feeds are now available for CD reviews, articles, and general news. A new personalization feature allows users to select favorite genres, columns, and writers to create a page with quick links to desired content. Users will also be notified about updates based on these favorites. Once registered, users can also view local calendars and submit events, access free MP3 downloads, and participate in the discussion forums. Recommended for both neophytes and serious jazz aficionados.

4651. *Allmusic.* Formerly (until 2005): *All-Music Guide.* 1994. m. All Media Guide, 1168 Oak Valley Dr, Ann Arbor, MI 48108; http://www.allmusic.com. *Aud.:* Hs, Ga, Ac.

Allmusic (www.allmusic.com) provides extensive information on genres and styles, artists, albums, and songs. The site can be browsed by genre, instrument, country, mood, and theme. Searching is available by artist/group, album, song, and classical work. At the time of writing, there were well over a million albums and over 300,000 of these included reviews. In addition to reviews, the album pages provide ratings, track lists, releases and editions, credits, Billboard charts and Grammy awards, and buying information. The conversational reviews range in length from 150 to 400 words and discuss the music in relation to previous albums by the same artist/group. The five-star rating system also scores the album within the scope of the artist/group's repertoire. Reviews for classical works discuss both the performance and musical quality on the one hand and the sound quality on the other, with separate ratings for each. These ratings are not dependent on the artist's repertoire since there are often multiple artists or groups involved. Album pages can be accessed by either browsing or searching. The Advanced Search page allows users to search by style and year of release; style and rating; awards; or chart by year and chart position. The site menu on the home page provides links to New Releases, Editor's Choice, and Classical Reviews. The Editor's Choice column provides the best of the new releases from the past three months. The Whole Note section also has a regular Review Roundup column along with interviews and the Editor's Choice Playlist. Other content includes artist/group biographies, song reviews, and music videos and samples. Free registration is supposed to provide access to "premium content," but this reviewer did not notice any difference in site navigation or content. With styles ranging from children's sing-along to urban, this site is highly recommended for all music lovers.

4652. *American Record Guide: classical recordings and music in concert.* Formerly: *American Music Lover.* [ISSN: 0003-0716] 1935. bi-m. USD 50 (Individuals, USD 39; USD 7.99 newsstand/cover per issue). Ed(s): Donald R Vroon. Record Guide Productions, 4412 Braddock St, Cincinnati, OH 45204. Illus., index, adv. Sample. Circ: 6100 Paid and free. Vol. ends: Dec. Online: Chadwyck-Healey Inc.; EBSCO Publishing, EBSCO Host; Gale; Northern Light Technology, Inc.; OCLC Online Computer Library Center, Inc.; ProQuest K-12 Learning Solutions; ProQuest LLC (Ann Arbor). *Indexed:* ASIP, BRI, CBRI, IIMP, MASUSE, MusicInd. *Bk. rev.:* Various number and length. *Aud.:* Ga, Ac.

American Record Guide, "America's oldest classical music review magazine," aims to remain free of advertiser influence. This results in a high-quality, robust magazine with few ads and over 150 pages of straightforward, critical recording reviews. The Guide to Records and Collections section of each issue include around 400 reviews of music releases. The engaging and personal reviews, ranging from 250 to 500 words, often begin with a history of the composer, performer, or work to place the recording in context, and most end with a recommendation. All aspects of the recording are up for scrutiny, including vocal and instrumental performance, listenability, interpretation of classics, song selection in collections, recording quality, and even CD packaging with regard to liner notes and accompanying texts. Reviews can also be found in The Newest Music section, where several new recordings are reviewed in one article. Most issues contain an Overview article that provides an extensive review of recordings by one composer, or from one area of the repertoire such as Russian music. The magazine also includes video and live-performance reviews, as well as articles on current events in the classical music world. The

web site (www.americanrecordguide.com) gives basic information and subscription rates, and subscribers can log in to access additional features. The large number of reviews makes this an excellent magazine for public and academic libraries.

4653. *B B C Music Magazine: the complete monthly guide to classical music.* [ISSN: 0966-7180] 1992. m. GBP 38; GBP 3.99 newsstand/cover. B B C Worldwide Ltd., 80 Wood Ln, London, W12 0TT, United Kingdom; bbcworldwide@bbc.co.uk; http://www.bbcmagazines.com. Illus., index, adv. Circ: 68104. Vol. ends: Aug. *Indexed:* IIMP, IIPA, MusicInd, RILM. *Bk. rev.:* Various number and length. *Aud.:* Ga, Ac.

BBC Music Magazine, "the world's best-selling classical music magazine," provides feature articles, news, interviews, and reviews of CDs, books, and DVDs. The North American edition also includes U.S.- and Canada-focused news, interviews, features, and reviews. The review section is divided into categories covering orchestral, opera, choral and song, chamber, instrumental, world music, and jazz. Reviews average 200–300 words and often cover the background of the work or artist, performance and sound quality, and comparison to other recordings with a benchmark version. A five-star rating system is applied to both performance and sound quality. A CD of a full-length work or works accompanies each issue with a listening guide providing a description of each track. The web site (www.bbcmusicmagazine.com) includes tables of contents for current and back issues, subscription information, and concert listings. Free registration provides access to a searchable, full-text database of over 18,000 CD and DVD reviews. The keyword-only search can be limited to type (CD or DVD) and genre, but unfortunately, there is no browse option. With readable, intelligent reviews, *BBC Music Magazine* is recommended for general and academic libraries.

4654. *C D Hotlist.* 1999. m. Ed(s): Rick Anderson. CD Hotlist, Electronic Resources/Serials Coordinator, The University Libraries, University of Reno, Reno, NV 89557; rickand@unr.edu; http://www2.library.unr.edu/anderson/cdhl/index.htm. *Aud.:* Ga, Ac.

CD Hotlist is a monthly recommendation service written by librarians for librarians. This service is now offered exclusively by Baker & Taylor. The monthly lists are divided by genre including classical, country/folk, jazz, rock/pop, and world/ethnic. The majority of the recommendations fall in the classical and jazz categories. Entries include the recording information, genre, release type (new, reissue, compilation, box set, etc.), list price from B&T with a link to buy, and comments. A gold star indicates that the album is highly recommended by the editor. The comments are succinct, ranging from 50 to 150 words, and focus on the performance and musical quality with an occasional mention of the packaging or sonics. Archived lists are available back to January 2003. Highly recommended for all libraries purchasing music.

4655. *Classics Today: your online guide to classical music.* 1999. d. Ed(s): David Hurwitz, David Vernier. Classics Today, dvernier@classicstoday.com; http://www.classicstoday.com. *Aud.:* Ga, Ac.

The purpose of *Classics Today* (www.classicstoday.com) is to "enable you to find the music and recordings that suit your personal taste." The site provides feature articles, news, and reviews of CDs, DVDs, and SACDs. CD reviews generally range from 100 to 300 words but some are twice that long. Ratings are based on a one to ten scale, with one being unacceptable with no redeeming qualities and ten being superior with qualities of unusual merit. The review search feature covers title of work/album, genre, composer, label, medium, date range, and rating scale. Reviews can also be accessed under current 10/10 reviews, 30-day review summary, and today's new reviews. Special, selected CDs are classified as Discs of the Month. The Classical Gourmet section provides five recipes with recommended recordings. The Music for Skaters and Athletes service provides recommendations for program music for a fee. Recommended for both neophytes and classical aficionados.

4656. *Dirty Linen: folk & world music.* [ISSN: 1047-4315] 1988. bi-m. USD 22 domestic; USD 30 Canada; USD 40 elsewhere. Ed(s): Paul Hartman. Dirty Linen, Ltd., PO Box 66600, Baltimore, MD 21239-6600; editor@dirtylinen.com; http://www.dirtylinen.com. Illus., adv. Circ: 12400 Paid. Vol. ends: Jun/Jul. Online: Chadwyck-Healey Inc. *Indexed:* IIMP, MusicInd. *Bk. rev.:* Various number and length. *Aud.:* Ga, Ac.

Dirty Linen celebrates folk, roots, traditional, blues, bluegrass, and world music with feature articles, interviews and profiles, news, and reviews of albums, concerts, books, and videos. The Recordings section has reviews ranging from 300 to 500 words while Linen Shorts provides shorter reviews. Other review sections cover small-label British and Celtic music releases and children's music. The December/January issues include holiday recording reviews. Reviews are straightforward and thoughtful and often include discussion of individual songs from the album. Albums or songs are often compared to the artist's other works or even works from other artists in the genre. The web site (www.dirtylinen.com) includes tables of contents for current and back issues with excerpts and sample reviews. Subscription information and a tour guide are also available. This highly readable magazine is recommended for all libraries serving users interested in folk and world music.

Down Beat. See Music/Popular section.

4657. *Fanfare (Tenafly): the magazine for serious record collectors.*
[ISSN: 0148-9364] 1977. bi-m. USD 39 domestic; USD 54 foreign; USD 7 newsstand/cover per issue. Ed(s): Joel Flegler. Fanfare, Inc., 273 Woodland St, Tenafly, NJ 07670. Illus., adv. Sample. Circ: 26000 Paid and free. Vol. ends: Jul/Aug. Online: Chadwyck-Healey Inc. *Indexed:* BRI, CBRI, IIMP, MusicInd, RILM. *Bk. rev.:* Various number and length. *Aud.:* Ga, Ac.

Since its inception, *Fanfare* was intended to provide informative reviews without being "stuffy and academic," and this is still the case. Reviews are written in an easy-to-read, descriptive, and informal style. Each issue includes over 250 reviews of mostly classical recordings and collections, with most reviews ranging from 400 to 500 words. Reviews might cover the background of the artist or work, the performance quality, and comparisons with other recordings. The magazine also includes interviews with performers and composers, label profiles, industry articles, and book and DVD reviews. Additional review columns include Jazz, Hall of Fame, and Bollywood and Beyond. The web site (www.fanfaremag.com) includes samples of current reviews intermixed with ads, lists of feature articles from the current issue, and subscription information. The newly introduced Fanfare Archive is in "phase one" and provides an index to the contents of issues back to volume 26 with full text available to magazine subscribers. Browsing is made easier by multiple indexes that include issues, columns, conductors, performers, instruments, and composers and works. Completion of phase two will provide the entire contents back to volume one. With numerous and lengthy reviews, this magazine is very highly recommended for public and academic libraries.

4658. *Gramophone: your guide to the best in recorded classical music.*
[ISSN: 0017-310X] 1923. 13x/yr. GBP 45.76 domestic; GBP 62 in Europe; USD 87.23 in North America. Haymarket Publishing Ltd., 174 Hammersmith Rd, London, W6 7JP, United Kingdom; hpg@haymarketgroup.com; http://www.haymarketgroup.co.uk. Illus., index, adv. Sample. Circ: 53000 Paid. Vol. ends: May. *Indexed:* IIMP, MusicInd. *Aud.:* Ga, Ac.

Gramophone: The Classical Music Magazine includes profiles, interviews, news, obituaries, city profiles, music reviews, book and DVD reviews, and a small product-review section. The "Editor's Choice" CD included with each issue includes tracks from the top ten CDs of the month. The first section in the magazine includes brief overviews by the editor of the tracks, and the full CDs are reviewed in the music review section. The review section has 150–200 reviews per issue and is divided by genre (orchestral, chamber, vocal, etc.). Easy to read and straightforward, the reviews focus on the music and performance. A review index is included in each issue. The Audio section includes a news section that provides brief reviews of the best in audio and new technology. Longer reviews covering product overviews and performance evaluations are provided for a few products. A sidebar includes price, dimensions, and manufacturer information. A list is also provided of new releases on CD, SACD, and DVD. An index is published annually, and it includes features, composers, and artists. The online version includes selected news and features, a section devoted to their annual awards, excerpts from the current issue, and details of *Gramophone* publications. Free registration allows users to search a database that includes over 30,000 classical reviews from the magazine back to 1983, with hundreds more being added each month. Some reviews from "GramoFile" are available without registration via the monthly "Editor's Choice Top 10

Recordings" and the "Recommended Recordings" based on the *Classical Good CD Guide*. The Audio News link connects to another Haymarket publication, *What Hi-Fi? Sound and Vision*, which covers sound systems and home cinema products. The web site also provides free access to the *Grove Concise Dictionary of Music*. Highly recommended for public and academic libraries.

4659. *In Music We Trust.* 1997. m. Ed(s): Alex Steininger. In Music We Trust, Inc., 15213 SE Bevington Ave, Portland, OR 97267. Adv. Circ: 25000. *Aud.:* Hs, Ga, Ac.

In Music We Trust (www.inmusicwetrust.com) covers rock/pop, punk/hardcore, metal/hard rock, country/bluegrass, electronic/gothic, rap/r&b, and ska/swing/jazz. Each month, over 100 reviews are added. Reviews vary in length, but all are well written and provide an overall impression of the album. The site also includes feature articles, interviews, show reviews, and DVD reviews. Every issue back to 1997 is archived. This easy-to-navigate site is recommended for anyone looking for music that might not be reviewed elsewhere.

4660. *jazzreview.com.* d. Ed(s): Samira Elkouh. JazzReview.com, 10033 W. Ruby Ave., Milwaukee, WI 53225; morrice@jazzreview.com. *Bk. rev.:* Various number and length. *Aud.:* Hs, Ga, Ac.

jazzreview.com (www.jazzreview.com) is a virtual Mecca for the jazz lover with interviews, news, biographies, a concert search, a discussion forum, and reviews of CDs, books, and concerts. The database includes over 5,000 reviews that can be sorted by artist, year, or style. There are 28 styles covered, including acid, ambient, bebop, big band, blues, folk jazz, fusion, gospel, Latin jazz/funk, soul/funk, and world music. The search tab links to a review search covering artist/group name, musicians (sidemen) or intruments, CD title, label, year, critic, or style. Well-written reviews focus on the music and performance and sometimes mention the background of the artist or work. This easy-to-use web site is recommended for all libraries serving jazz lovers.

JazzTimes. See Music/Popular section.

4661. *Songlines.* [ISSN: 1464-8113] 1999. 6x/yr. GBP 24.90 domestic; GBP 31 in Europe; GBP 38 elsewhere. Ed(s): Simon Broughton. Songlines, PO Box 54209, London, W14 0WU, United Kingdom. Adv. *Indexed:* MusicInd. *Aud.:* Hs, Ga.

Songlines covers music on an international scope, with news; interviews; world music guides; festival and tour guides; and reviews of CDs, DVDs, and world cinema, live concerts, and books. Music reviews are categorized by region with an additional section on "Fusion." Reviews are insightful and well written, focusing on the music and performance and often placing the artist/group and album in the context of the genre. Ratings are based on a five-star system. The ten "Top of the World" choices, one for each category, are chosen for high quality, broad appeal, and ready availability in the United Kingdom. The web site (www.songlines.co.uk) provides news, subscription information, an overview of the current issue, Top of the World reviews, festivals/events, tours, and gigs. The Archive features include Beginners' Guides for legendary artists, City Guides, and Festival Profiles. The international scope makes this highly recommended for all libraries serving diverse populations or those interested in world music.

Sound & Vision. See Television, Video, and Radio section.

4662. *SoundStage.* 1995. m. Free. Ed(s): Marc Mickelson. Schneider Publishing, 390 Rideau St, Box 20068, Ottawa, ON K1N 9N5, Canada; feedback@soundstage.com; http://www.sstage.com. *Aud.:* Ga, Ac.

SoundStage (www.soundstage.com) focuses on high-end audio and music, providing columns, factory-tour articles, and reviews of equipment and music. Equipment reviews cover physical attributes, performance quality, comparisons to similar products, and testing processes including recordings used. Most reviews include a sidebar with a helpful summary highlighting sound, features, use, and value. Associated equipment is also listed in a sidebar when applicable. Reviews are provided on the site for four months with archived reports available from *SoundStageAV.com*, which features the equipment review archives for all the *SoundStage! Network* sites. Other sites in the network are HomeTheater-Sound.com, UltraAudio.com, GoodSound.com, onhifi.com, and onhometheater.com. Music is rated on musical performance, recording quality, and overall enjoyment, with each discussed in the review. DVD reviews also include a rating for image quality. Archived music reviews are categorized by pop/rock/rap/alternative, folk/country/gospel, progressive/world, jazz/blues, classical, and remasters/reissues. Additional categories are provided for DVD-V and multichannel and stereo SACD, DVD-A, and DualDisc. Best Recordings are also provided back to 1999. Recommended for all libraries serving audiophiles.

Audio Equipment

4663. *The Absolute Sound: the high end journal of audio & music.* [ISSN: 0097-1138] 1973. 6x/yr. USD 36 domestic; USD 39 Canada; USD 65 elsewhere. Ed(s): Harry Pearson. Absolute Multimedia Inc., 8121 Bee Caves Rd., Ste. 100, Austin, TX 78746-4938; info@avguide.com; http://www.theabsolutesound.com. Illus., index, adv. Sample. Circ: 33000. Vol. ends: Dec/Jan. Microform: PQC. *Aud.:* Ga, Ac.

The Absolute Sound "explores music and the reproduction of music in the home" by providing columns, reports, and reviews of audio equipment and music recordings. Equipment reports include physical attributes, performance quality, comparisons to similar products and discussion of the testing process and recordings used. A sidebar highlights specifications, manufacturer information, and a list of associated equipment when appropriate. The music review section is divided by genre and covers rock (which replaced popular), classical, and jazz. Ratings are provided for music and sonics based on a scale of one to five with one being poor and five extraordinary. Reviews, averaging between 250 and 400 words, generally begin with a brief background of the artist, group, or album, followed by discussion of music quality, and wrap up with production quality. At the end of the review are recommendations of albums by other groups for further listening. The best box sets are reviewed in January. The February issue covers the best albums of the previous year with Top Ten albums by genre and the Gold Ear Music Awards for writers' top three favorite albums. The web site (www.theabsolutesound.com) provides the table of contents for the current issue, subscription information, and review lists for back issues. The entire current issue is available to download for USD 10, and back issues cost USD 7. Reviews, news, forums, a blog, tech briefings, and buyers' and how-to guides are available. Users must log in with their e-mail address to download PDF files. The music section also provides artist profiles/interviews, genre overviews, and awards and recommendations. With well-written reviews and extensive content, this magazine and web site are highly recommended for public and academic libraries.

4664. *Hi-Fi News: pure audio excellence.* Formerly (until 2000): *Hi-Fi News and Record Review;* Which was formed by the merger of (1956-1971): *Hi-Fi News;* (1970-1971): *Record Review.* [ISSN: 1472-2569] 1971. m. GBP 34.56 domestic; USD 98.16 United States. Ed(s): Paul Miller. I P C Country & Leisure Media Ltd., King's Reach Tower, Stamford St, London, SE1 9LS, United Kingdom; http://www.ipcmedia.com. Illus., index, adv. Sample. Circ: 21196. Vol. ends: Dec. Microform: PQC. *Indexed:* BrTechI, C&ISA, CerAb, IAA. *Aud.:* Ga, Ac.

Hi-Fi News provides news, feature articles, and product tests for audio equipment with a few album reviews thrown into the mix. The On Test section provides reviews and ratings for a wide range of products including turntables, CD/SACD/DVD-A players, receivers, speakers, processors, and systems. The ratings system uses a one to five scale for each of four categories: features, sound quality, build quality, and value for money. This results in a possible score of 20/20 with 19/20 being "Pure Audio Gold." The reviews cover each of the rating categories in depth and provide a summary verdict, review system breakdown, U.K. contact numbers, and lab report with graphs and specifications. The music reviews are low in number, around 20 an issue, and very brief, averaging from 50 to 70 words with ratings given for recording and performance. The online version (www.hifinews.co.uk) includes the current issue's table of contents, a preview of the next issue, and subscription information. In the left navigation column under Equipment, one can browse the article index, Hot 100, tests, and books of reviews to purchase. A new digital reprint service was launched to allow users to purchase PDF downloads of product tests, features, and show reports from January 2004 issue forward, but presently the browse options and search function are not working properly. From the "Buy a Test" page, the Purchase Reviews link in the left navigation

column links to a site that makes it easier to browse and search reviews and articles (www.testreports.co.uk/music/hifi). Lab results to accompany reviews are also available from yet another site, Miller Audio Research (www.milleraudioresearch.com/avtech/index.html), which was founded by Paul Miller, the current editor of *Hi-Fi News.* The files are available for free with registration as HTML or downloadable zip files starting in 2005, with 2007 being added soon. Sample test files from 2003 and 2004 are currently available without registration. Music reviews are not available. The easy-to-read reviews and extent of product coverage make this magazine highly recommended for public and academic libraries.

4665. *Sensible Sound: helping audiophiles and music lovers to spend less and get more.* [ISSN: 0199-4654] 1977. bi-m. USD 29; USD 7 newsstand/cover. Ed(s): Karl A Nehring. Sensible Sound, Inc., 403 Darwin Dr., Snyder, NY 14226; advertising@sensiblesound.com. Illus., adv. Sample. Circ: 17000 Paid and free. Vol. ends: Winter. *Aud.:* Ga, Ac.

The goal of *Sensible Sound* is to provide readers with reviews of audio equipment that they can actually afford to buy. Reviews cover specifications, design, set-up procedure, testing procedures, performance quality, and comparisons to similar products. Some reviews also include graphs charting various performance specifications. Review columns include "More Jazz Than Not," written by the editor; "Double Double," comparing two recordings of the same work; "Carousel Corner," reviewing vinyl albums; "Reissue Roundup," focusing on reissued recordings; and "John Puccio Reviews," covering classical music. The reviews are easy to read and discuss performance and sound quality. The annual list of the staff's "Recommended Recordings" from the previous year is typically in the second issue of the year. The web site (www.sensible-sound.com) provides subscription and advertising information with a general overview of the current issue. Highly recommended for public and academic libraries serving budget-minded audiophiles.

4666. *Stereophile.* [ISSN: 0585-2544] 1962. m. USD 12.97. Ed(s): John Atkinson. Source Interlink Companies, 261 Madison Ave., New York, NY 10016; edisupport@sourceinterlink.com; http://www.sourceinterlink.com. Illus., index, adv. Circ: 80000 Paid. Vol. ends: Dec. *Indexed:* RILM. *Aud.:* Ga, Ac.

Stereophile focuses on getting the best quality from high-end audio equipment with feature columns, show reports, interviews, industry news, and reviews of music and audio equipment. The equipment reports cover the physical attributes, performance quality, comparisons, and testing process including the recordings used. Some reviews also include graphs charting various performance specifications. Sidebars give manufacturer information, price, specifications, measurements, and associated equipment when applicable. Follow-up articles take a new look at a product previously reviewed. Record reviews feature a recording of the month, with other reviews listed under classical, rock/pop, and jazz. The music and performance are the main focus, with some reviews mentioning sound quality. A five-star rating system is used for both performance and sonics. Annual recommendation lists include Recommended Components in April and October, Products of the Year in December, and Records to Die For in February. The web site (www.stereophile.com) provides news, forums, blogs, and eNewsletters. Full text is available for columns, interviews, show reports, select equipment reviews, recording of the month, and annual recommendation lists from previous editions. Written by *Stereophile* writers, the "Face the Music" section provides record reviews in a blog format, allowing comments from readers. Unfortunately, the section is not updated very often and a rating system is not used. The music reviews published in the magazine are not available on the web site. The extensive coverage of both audio equipment and music makes this a must-have for libraries serving both neophyte and serious audiophiles.

■ NATIVE AMERICANS

Robert C. Johnston, Associate Dean, Libraries & Learning Technologies, American University in Cairo, 113 Kasr el Aini St., Cairo, Egypt; johnston@aucegypt.edu

Introduction

Titles reviewed in this section fall into three categories, scholarly works about Native Americans, popular magazines aimed at general and specialized audiences (native and/or non-native) and newspapers mostly serving specific Native American communities. Some of these publications do overlap. As with most area studies, the academic journals such as the newly added *Native Studies Review* tend to be interdisciplinary, although there are some specialized publications such as the *Canadian Journal of Native Education* and *Studies in American Indian Literatures*. In addition, while the geographical scope of these publications tend to focus on the United States and Canada, some also include works on aboriginal peoples from outside of North America and one, *The European Review of Native American Studies*, provides its own unique perspective of the field. The publications aimed at general and specialized audiences cover a wide range of areas, from the arts (*American Indian Art Magazine* and *Inuit Art Quarterly*), to news (*American Indian Report*), to education (*Tribal College* and *Winds of Change*), to Native American culture and history (*Native Peoples* and *American Indian*), and public affairs/law (*Native American Law Report* and *Indian Affairs*). This group of publications was further reduced this year by the cessation of the highly regarded *Native Americas* and problems in obtaining review issues of *The Circle*, *Tribal Justice Today*, *The Journal of Chickasaw History and Culture*, and others. Some of these publications, such as *Native Peoples* and *American Indian*, would be a worthwhile addition to any public or school library, while *Tribal College* and *Winds of Change* should be in any high school library serving native student populations. The last group of publications, newspapers, almost exclusively serves specific tribal communities. These are well represented by *Navajo Times*, *Cherokee Observer*, and *TheEastern Door* (Canadian Mohawk). These would obviously have a more limited audience. However, two publications, *Indian Country Today* and the newly added *Windspeaker*, both qualify as "national" Native American newspapers, the latter serving Canada. *American Indian and Alaska Native Mental Health Research* continues to be the only identified strictly online publication, although most of the publications do have web sites with at least selected articles and in a few cases complete archives available. The good news is that more publications, such as the newly added *Windspeaker* and its associated publications, are showing up in full-text databases (Ethnic Newswatch), and some of the academic journals are available in full text in Project Muse, Academic Search Premier, ProQuest 5000, and Wilson's Omnifile.

Basic Periodicals

Hs: *Native Peoples, Tribal College, Winds of Change;* Ga: *American Indian, American Indian Report, Indian Country Today, Native Peoples, Windspeaker;* Ac: *American Indian Quarterly, European Review of Native American Studies, Native American Studies, Studies in American Indian Literatures, Wicazo Sa Review.*

Basic Abstracts and Indexes

Abstracts in Anthropology, Alternative Press Index, America: History and Life, Anthropological Literature, Current Index to Journals in Education, Historical Abstracts, Ethnic NewsWatch, Project Muse, Academic Search Premier, Wilson Omnifile.

4667. *American Indian.* [ISSN: 1528-0640] 2000. q. Free to members. National Museum of the American Indian, 4220 Silver Hill Rd, Suitland, MD 20746; http://www.nmai.si.edu/. *Aud.:* Hs, Ga.

American Indian is a highly illustrated magazine published by the Smithsonian National Museum of the American Indian (NMAI). It is beautifully produced, full of color illustrations and advertisements, mostly for Native American art galleries and foundations. Each of the issues reviewed contained five feature articles and a quarterly calendar of NMAI exhibitions, programs, and screenings at their facilities in both Washington, D.C., and New York City. Feature articles

focus primarily on Native American arts, culture, and traditions. Recent issues contain articles on various tribal honoring traditions; a tribute to Vine Deloria, Jr., noted theologian, historian, and activist; and contemporary arctic artists. This magazine will have a broad appeal to public libraries.

4668. *American Indian and Alaska Native Mental Health Research (Online Edition).* [ISSN: 1533-7731] 1998. irreg. Free. Ed(s): Spero Manson. National Center for American Indian Mental Health Research, University of Colorado Health Sciences Center, Department of Psychiatry, PO Box 6508, Aurora, CO 80045-0508; billie.greene@uchsc.edu; http://www.uchsc.edu/ai/ncaianmhr. Refereed. *Indexed:* ERIC. *Aud.:* Ac, Sa.

AIANMHR is the sole electronic-only publication in this list. It is free, and current issues and the table of contents for all backfiles are available on the web site. They are in the process of loading pdf copies of the complete backfiles on to the site, and currently have Vol. 8 (1998) through the current issue loaded. It is a peer-reviewed scientific/medical journal focusing on current mental health issues and concerns of Native Americans. As stated, its target audience includes mental and public health providers and administrators, tribal health program staff, social workers, and those who work within the court systems for evaluating service delivery. The journal includes research articles, case studies, program reviews in the fields of psychology, psychiatry, nursing, sociology, anthropology, social work, and specific areas of education, medicine, history, and law. Recent articles include "Alcohol Problems in Alaska Natives: Lessons from the Inuit," "Culturally Competent Research with American Indians and Alaska Natives: Findings and Recommendations of the First Symposium of the Work Group on American Indian Research and Program Evaluation Methodology," and "Commentary: Disparities in Data for American Indians and Alaska Natives." This title is recommended for medical libraries and libraries supporting programs in social work, psychology, mental health, and Native American Studies.

4669. *American Indian Art Magazine.* Formerly (until 1977): *American Indian Art.* [ISSN: 0192-9968] 1975. q. USD 20 domestic; USD 24 Canada; USD 56 elsewhere. Ed(s): Roanne P. Goldfein. American Indian Art, Inc., 7314 E Osborn Dr, Scottsdale, AZ 85251. Illus., index, adv. Circ: 30000 Paid and controlled. Vol. ends: Nov. *Indexed:* ABM, AICP, AbAn, AmH&L, AnthLit, ArtInd, FR, HistAb, RILM. *Bk. rev.:* 1-30, 75-1,500 words. *Aud.:* Ac, Sa.

American Indian Art Magazine is primarily of interest to Native American art collectors and aficionados, and would also interest museum professionals. It is highly illustrated and has numerous advertisements. Each of the issues reviewed contain four feature articles, a directory of museums, a three-month calendar of events, and a column titled "Legal Briefs" The two columns reviewed were on repatriation of artifacts and issues related to evaluation of artifacts for tax purposes. Each issue also includes a book review section. These range from a single bibliographic essay of 1,500 words to a list of 30 titles with brief (75-word) annotations. Recent feature articles include a historical survey of Santa Ana Pueblo pottery, Chemehuevi coiled baskets, and Arikara story drawings. While articles are in-depth and include footnotes and brief biographies, the prolific color illustrations and writing make it accessible to a general audience. This magazine is recommended to academic institutions with American Studies and Native Studies programs, and to art and anthropology departments with an interest in Native Americans. It is also recommended for public libraries serving communities with an interest in Native American art.

4670. *American Indian Quarterly.* [ISSN: 0095-182X] 1974. q. USD 125 (Individuals, USD 42). Ed(s): Amanda Cobb. University of Nebraska Press, 1111 Lincoln Mall, Lincoln, NE 68588-0630; journals@ unlnotes.unl.edu; http://www.nebraskapress.unl.edu. Illus., index, adv. Sample. Refereed. Circ: 400. Microform: PQC. Online: Chadwyck-Healey Inc.; EBSCO Publishing, EBSCO Host; Factiva, Inc.; Florida Center for Library Automation; Gale; JSTOR (Web-based Journal Archive); Northern Light Technology, Inc.; OCLC Online Computer Library Center, Inc.; OhioLINK; Project MUSE; ProQuest K-12 Learning Solutions; ProQuest LLC (Ann Arbor); SwetsWise Online Content; H.W. Wilson. Reprint: PSC. *Indexed:* AICP, AbAn, AmH&L,

AmHI, AnthLit, BRI, CBRI, ENW, ERIC, HistAb, HumInd, IBR, IBZ, L&LBA, LRI, MASUSE, MLA-IB, PAIS, RI-1, RILM, SSA, SociolAb. *Bk. rev.:* 6-30, 400-800 words. *Aud.:* Ac, Sa.

While this weighty interdisciplinary journal states that it focuses on the histories, anthropologies, literatures, religions, and arts of North America, the lead article in a recent special issue on Indigenous Languages and Indigenous Literatures discusses "Indigenous Maori and Tongan Language and Culture." Other articles in the issue include "Rethinking Native American Language Revitalization" and "Alaskan Haida Stories of Language Growth and Regeneration." The special issue on the National Museum of the American Indian features articles on its philosophy and role, exhibition development, and critiques of the museum's work. Both issues also include interviews and additional articles on "Moral Minimalism in American Indian Land Claims" and "Havasu Poetry." All articles are well researched and documented. Also included are over a dozen detailed book reviews and a compilation of recent dissertations. The publication seems to have overcome its previously irregular publishing schedule by combining Winter/Spring and Summer/Fall issues to become a semi-annual publication. Full text of the journal is available in EBSCO's Academic Search Premier (1990-) and Project Muse from 2001. The quality of this peer-reviewed journal strongly recommends it to academic libraries.

4671. *American Indian Report.* [ISSN: 0894-4040] 1985. m. USD 29.95 domestic; USD 44.95 Canada; USD 80 elsewhere. Ed(s): Marguerite Carroll. Falmouth Institute, Inc., 3702 Pender Dr, Ste 300, Fairfax, VA 22030-6066; http://www.falmouthinstitute.com. Adv. Sample. Circ: 8000 Paid. *Aud.:* Hs, Ga.

American Indian Report is the monthly newsmagazine serving Native Americans across the United States and to a lesser extent Canada. In addition to regular monthly columns highlighting federal legislation, recent Native American news events, business topics, and tribal news, well-written feature articles cover such current topics such as Native women and domestic violence, Native American housing needs, Native banking, Native education, and Native Americans in national politics. This publication is strongly recommended for any public library serving populations with an interest in current Native American issues.

4672. *Canadian Journal of Native Education.* Formerly: *Indian-Ed.* [ISSN: 0710-1481] 1973. q. Individuals, CND 26.75. University of Alberta, Educational Policy Studies, 7 104 Education Centre North, Edmonton, AB T6G 2G5, Canada; naomi@phys.ualberta.ca. Illus., adv. Sample. Refereed. Circ: 700 Paid. Vol. ends: Dec (No. 2). Microform: MML. Online: Micromedia ProQuest; Northern Light Technology, Inc.; OCLC Online Computer Library Center, Inc.; ProQuest LLC (Ann Arbor). *Indexed:* CEI, L&LBA, SSA. *Bk. rev.:* 10, 750-1,250 words. *Aud.:* Ac, Sa.

This semi-annual journal accepts manuscripts from practitioners, scholars, and researchers in Native American education. It also specifically encourages submissions from indigenous scholars. The Spring/Summer issue is thematic, with a general edition published for Fall/Winter. In addition to articles on research and discussion and review of educational theory and practice, the journal also includes a forum for teaching stories and essays. Each issue includes 7-12 peer-reviewed articles, in addition to editorials and book reviews. There is no advertising. Recent articles include "Progressing toward an indigenous research paradigm in Canada and Australia," "The path to education in a Canadian aboriginal context," and "Traditional plant knowledge of the Tsimshian curriculum: Keeping knowledge in the community." Full text is available (1998-) in the ProQuest 5000 and Education Complete databases. Recommended for libraries serving Native American Studies programs or education programs with a global perspective.

4673. *Cherokee Observer: the only independent Cherokee newspaper.* [ISSN: 1077-0968] 1993. m. USD 20 domestic; USD 41.50 foreign. Ed(s): Franklin McLain, Sr. Cherokee Observer Inc., P.O.Box 487, Blackwell, OK 74631-0487; cwyob@accesscc.com; http://www.cherokeeobserver.org. Illus., adv. Sample. Circ: 3000 Paid. Vol. ends: Dec (No. 12). *Indexed:* ENW. *Aud.:* Ga.

This monthly newspaper, available both in print and selectively via its web site (www.cherokeeobserver.org) focuses primarily on the political landscape of the Cherokee nation, from tribal council controversies to land claim issues and judicial actions. The articles do often reflect a highly politicized perspective. In addition, the paper advocates preservation of Cherokee culture and language through articles and by promoting the study and use of the Cherokee language. A small portion of the paper is printed in Cherokee, and there are numerous ads for instruction and publications in the Cherokee language. Recommended for libraries serving Cherokee populations.

4674. *Confederated Umatilla Journal.* 1995. m. USD 12. Ed(s): Wil Phinney. Confederated Tribes of the Umatilla Indian Reservations, PO Box 638, Pendleton, OR 07801; info@ctuir.com; http://www.umatilla.nsn.us. Adv. Circ: 6800 Paid and controlled. *Indexed:* ENW. *Aud.:* Hs, Ga, Sa.

This outstanding monthly newspaper serves the confederated tribes of the Umatilla Indian Reservation in Oregon. In addition to numerous well-written feature articles on such issues as economic development, repatriation of cultural artifacts, Native health issues, and tribal government activities, there are regular columns covering local education, sports, local history, and youth events. This is one of the best examples of a tribal/regional newspaper, and is highly recommended for libraries serving the Pacific Northwest.

4675. *The Eastern Door: Kanien'keha:ka Na'kon:ke Rontehnhohanonhnha.* [ISSN: 1193-8374] 1992. w. CND 62; USD 68 United States; CND 118 elsewhere. Ed(s): Kenneth Deer. Kahnawake Mohawk Territory Newspaper, P O Box 1170, Kahnawake, PQ J0L 1B0, Canada; easterndoor@axess.com; http://www.easterndoor.com. Illus., adv. Sample. Circ: 2200 Paid. Vol. ends: Jan. *Bk. rev.:* 1-2, 500 words. *Aud.:* Hs, Ga.

A Canadian publication, *The Eastern Door* is a community-based weekly newspaper serving the Kahnawake Mohawk Territory. As such, its coverage is strictly local in nature. Front-page stories from recent issues include controversy over the removal of a local council official, council meetings with provincial and federal government over the local tobacco industry, a school library read-a-thon, and a local citizen's claimed assault by a Peacekeeper (territorial police). Regular sections also include extensive sports coverage, editorial commentary, classifieds, obituaries, and entertainment. Much of the content is available on the publication's web site on a delayed basis. Recommended primarily for the local audience or academic institutions with research interests in current Native American communities.

4676. *European Review of Native American Studies.* [ISSN: 0238-1486] 1987. s-a. EUR 20.45; USD 29. Ed(s): Christian Feest. European Review of Native American Studies, c/o Christian Feest, Ed., Linzerstr. 281/1/17, Vienna, 140, Austria; cff.ssk@t-online.de. Illus., adv. Sample. Refereed. Circ: 600. Vol. ends: No. 2. *Indexed:* AICP, AmH&L, AnthLit, HistAb, IBR, IBZ, MLA-IB, RILM. *Bk. rev.:* 3-6, 400-1,200 words. *Aud.:* Ac, Sa.

European Review of Native American Studies provides a much-needed European perspective for both Native American and American Studies. Each juried semi-annual issue offers five to ten well-researched articles on a wide range of disciplines, by authors from Europe as well as North America. Recent articles include "I am a 'Redskin': The adoption of a Native American expression (1769-1826)," "'Growing up it seemed I lived in two worlds': American Indian responses to government boarding schools, 1890–1940," "Native Americans in higher education: The complex mission of a Native American Studies program in an Ivy League school," and "Marketing Native North America: The promotion and state of art and design." Each issue also includes "The American Indian Workshop Newsletter," which contains conference and workshop reports, editorial essays, a classified listing of European publications relating to Native Americans, and substantial reviews of recent books. This journal is strongly recommended for any academic library serving Native American or American Studies programs.

4677. *Indian Affairs.* [ISSN: 0046-8967] 1949. 3x/yr. USD 10. Ed(s): Merrill O'Connor. Association on American Indian Affairs, Inc., Executive Office, 966 Hungerford Dr, Rockville, MD 20850; aaia@sbtc.net; http://www.indian-affairs.org/index.htm. Circ: 40000. *Indexed:* AnthLit. *Aud.:* Ac, Ga, Sa.

Indian Affairs is the official semi-annual publication of the Association on American Indian Affairs (AAIA). Its staff and board of directors is predominantly Native American. AAIA is the oldest independent, national, grassroots Indian advocacy organization, working to preserve native languages, provide legal support to protect sacred places, assist in the repatriation of Indian artifacts, and promote Indian child welfare. The newsletter generally includes brief articles about successes such as the return of Tlingit ceremonial headdresses, a joint program with the American Indian Ritual Object Repatriation Foundation, development threats to the Bear Butte sacred site, and the use of translated rap music to help teach Native language. It also publicizes scholarship and youth summer camp information. This publication is an excellent source of public advocacy information for Native Americans, and is recommended for libraries serving Native American communities and supporting Native Studies programs.

4678. *Indian Country Today.* Which was formed by the merger of: *Indian Country Today (Southwest Edition); Indian Country Today (Northern Plains Edition); Both of which superseded (in 1994): Indian Country Today; Formerly (until 1992): Lakota Times.* 1981. w. Wed. USD 48 domestic; USD 83 in Canada & Mexico; USD 227 elsewhere. Four Directions Media, 3059 Seneca Tpk., Canastota, NY 13032; http://www.fourdirectionsmedia.com/. Illus., adv. Sample. Circ: 22000. *Indexed:* ENW. *Aud.:* Hs, Ga, Ac.

The weekly *Indian Country Today* is the best example of a national Native American newspaper. The scope of coverage is truly universal. Front-page articles often focus on U.S. federal government topics such as "Senate committee agrees to refine gambling oversight," "An early look into the 109th congressional session," and "Bill introduced to assist suicide prevention services." Each issue includes a national survey of specific tribal news in "News from the Nations," significant business news in "Trade and Commerce," and a classified section. There are also irregular sections on health and cooking, and a regular monthly section on education. The importance of education is further emphasized by an annual glossy supplement produced in September and included as part of a subscription. The editorial/perspective section contains excellent pieces on such issues as the need for more balanced coverage in the Anglo press and the broader impact of the Abramoff scandal on Native American issues. Selected articles are also available on the publication's web site. This newspaper is definitely recommended to public, school, and academic libraries.

4679. *Inuit Art Quarterly.* [ISSN: 0831-6708] 1986. q. CND 26.75 domestic; USD 25 United States; CND 39 elsewhere. Ed(s): Marybelle Mitchell. Inuit Art Foundation, 2081 Merivale Rd, Nepean, ON K2G 1G9, Canada; http://www.inuitart.org. Illus., index, adv. Circ: 1923 Paid. Vol. ends: Winter. *Indexed:* ABM, AICP, AbAn, ArtInd, CBCARef, IBR, IBZ. *Bk. rev.:* 1-2, 500-1,000 words. *Aud.:* Ga, Ac, Sa.

This beautifully illustrated publication well serves the Inuit Art Foundation in its mission to "assist Inuit in the development of their professional skills and marketing of their art." Each issue contains two or three feature articles on specific regional motifs, art forms, or artists, describing and illustrating the philosophy, techniques, and symbolic elements. Regular columns are also included on museum and gallery exhibits, a calendar of events, obituaries of Inuit artists, and book reviews. Each issue also contains numerous ads for galleries and/or specific artists. The magazine is recommended for collectors and libraries or museums with an interest in Native American or Inuit art.

4680. *Journal of American Indian Education.* [ISSN: 0021-8731] 1961. 3x/yr. USD 45 (Individuals, USD 20; USD 8 newsstand/cover per issue). Ed(s): Denis F Viri. Arizona State University, Center for Indian Education, College of Education, PO Box 871311, Tempe, AZ 85287-1311; http://coe.asu.edu/cie. Illus., index. Refereed. Circ: 1000.

Vol. ends: Spring (No. 3). Microform: PQC. Online: OCLC Online Computer Library Center, Inc.; H.W. Wilson. *Indexed:* ABIn, AbAn, ERIC, EduInd, HEA, L&LBA, SSA, SociolAb. *Bk. rev.:* Number and length vary. *Aud.:* Ac, Sa.

This refereed journal, published by the Arizona State University Center for Indian Education, primarily seeks papers related to the education of American Indian/Alaska Natives, although they also invite articles pertaining to other native peoples of the world. Each issue contains two or three research-based practitioner and analytical articles. Detailed book reviews are also included on a regular basis. Recent articles include a historical analysis of Hopi attendance at California boarding school from 1906 to 1909, analysis of the performance gap between American Indian and Anglo students in New York, and a case study of nursing education for American Indians from the plateau tribes. Back issues are archived on the publication's web site. Recommended for libraries serving Native American Studies and education programs.

4681. *Mazina'igan: a chronicle of the Lake Superior Ojibwe.* 1984. q. Free. Ed(s): Sue Erickson. Great Lakes Indian Fish & Wildlife Commission, 100 Maple St., Odanah, WI 54861. Illus. Sample. Circ: 13500. *Aud.:* Hs, Ga, Sa.

Mazina'igan is a free quarterly newspaper published by the Great Lakes Indian Fish and Wildlife Commission representing the Ojibwe tribes of Michigan, Minnesota, and Wisconsin. Issues back to 1999 are available on their web site (www.glifwc.org/pub/mazinaigan.htm). The paper's main focus is issues relating to fish, wildlife, and land use management in the upper Great Lakes region. Each highly illustrated issue contains numerous articles on policy issues, wildlife studies, and environmental and cultural education. Recent major articles have appeared on the Madeline Island Historical Museum, aquatic invasive species (AIS), and the marketing of Lake Superior fish. Each issue also contains a children's page on one of the issue's major topics. This publication is recommended to any library in the region serving communities with a stake in water and resource management.

4682. *Native American Law Report.* [ISSN: 1543-9526] 2003. m. USD 277; USD 307 combined subscription print & email eds. Ed(s): Susan Hsu. Business Publishers, Inc., 2272 Airport Rd S, Naples, FL 34112. *Aud.:* Ac, Sa.

Native American Law Report is a monthly review of legal cases, decisions, and issues relating to Native Americans. It can be received in either print or pdf format. Significant issues are discussed in the lead articles, followed by a digest of column-length reviews of specific court cases in progress or recently decided. Each issue ends with a special supplement such as "Helping Handouts: News you can use for the Native American community," or announcements of special reports available on topics ranging from "Casino and gaming issues for Native Americans" to "Federal agency funding for Native American tribes." This publication is recommended for any law school or law libraries in regions with Native American populations.

4683. *Native American Times.* Formerly (until 2001): *Oklahoma Indian Times.* [ISSN: 1542-4928] 1995. w. Thu. USD 39. Ed(s): Sam Lewis. Oklahoma Indian Times Inc., Box 692050, Tulsa, OK 74169; http://www.okit.com/. Illus., adv. Circ: 80000. *Indexed:* ENW. *Bk. rev.:* Occasional. *Aud.:* Hs, Ga.

Native American Times is now a weekly publication. Although it does provide very good coverage of national issues, it still focuses on the Oklahoma region. In addition to the commentary and classified sections in every issue, there are also regular sections on health and education, arts and entertainment, and calendar and information. There are also periodic supplements such as the "2006 Pow Wow Guide, Spring & Summer." Recent lead stories have included "Lawmakers seek to save urban Indian health care centers," "Idaho governor picked as next Secretary of the Interior," and "Sacred Run 2006 comes to Oklahoma." This is definitely a regional publication with excellent national coverage. Recommended for regional public libraries.

4684. *Native Peoples: arts and lifeways.* Incorporates: *Native Artists.* [ISSN: 0895-7606] 1987. bi-m. USD 20 domestic; USD 28 Canada; USD 40 elsewhere. Ed(s): Dan Gibson. Media Concepts Group, Inc.,

5333 N Seventh St, Ste C 224, Phoenix, AZ 85014. Illus., index, adv. Circ: 50000 Paid. Vol. ends: Summer (No. 4). *Indexed:* ArtInd, BRI, CBRI. *Bk. rev.:* 2-3, 650-850 words. *Aud.:* Hs, Ga.

Native Peoples is probably the single best publication available for the general public interested in Native American culture and life. Its writing and graphics are extremely high quality. It is well laid out and offers very broad coverage of Native American topics. In addition to five or six highly readable feature articles, there are regular essays/opinion columns, letters, news, upcoming events, gallery reviews, collections, history, touring highlights, and book reviews. Recent articles include interviews with veteran actress Tantoo Cardinal and newcomer Q'Orianka Kilcher, an ongoing series on the Lewis and Clark expedition, well-illustrated articles on Indian antique arts, cooking techniques (complete with recipes) of the Cuba-Ciboney people, and a survey of exceptional artists from the Santa Fe Indian Market. The publication's web site provides access to the current issue's table of contents as well as a calendar of events and links to other web resources. Highly recommended for any library.

4685. Native Studies Review. [ISSN: 0831-585X] 1985. s-a. CND 45 (Individuals, CND 30; Students, CND 20). Ed(s): Laurie Meijer Drees. University of Saskatchewan, Native Studies Department, 121 McLean Hall, 106 Wiggins Rd, Saskatoon, SK S7N 5E6, Canada; macdoug@ duke.usask.ca; http://www.usask.ca/native_studies. Illus., adv. Refereed. *Indexed:* AmH&L, CBCARef, HistAb. *Bk. rev.:* 1-2, 1000-1500 words. *Aud.:* Ac, Sa.

Although not included in earlier editions of this volume, *Native Studies Review* has been published by the Native Studies department of the University of Saskatchewan since 1984. Its mission as a multidisciplinary, social science–based journal is to feature original scholarly research by established scholars as well as graduate students "on aboriginal perspectives and issues in contemporary and historical contexts." While its primary focus is Canadian, it does accept works of a more global nature. Each of the semi-annual issues generally includes four or five refereed articles and two lengthy book reviews. Issues are occasionally filled out by forum contributions appraising a key topic or publication. There are also occasional thematic issues, such as one reviewed on "Native-Newcomer Relations: Comparative Perspectives." It has been available in full text in EBSCO's Academic Search Premier since 2003. It is recommended as a core publication for libraries supporting Native American Studies programs.

4686. Navajo Times. Former titles (until 1987): *Navajo Times Today;* (until 1984): *Navajo Times.* 1957. w. Thu. USD 0.75 newsstand/cover per issue; USD 65; USD 250 foreign. Ed(s): Duane A. Beyal. Navajo Times Company, Hwy 264, Rte. 12, Window Rock, AZ 86515. Adv. Circ: 17200 Paid. Microform: LIB. *Indexed:* ENW. *Aud.:* Ga, Sa.

The *Navajo Times* covers national news relating to the Navajo Nation, as well as detailed coverage of local news and issues. Recent feature articles include in-depth coverage of the Third Annual Lori Piestewa Memorial Day commemoration, a ballot initiative regarding the tribe's permanent trust fund, and a review of the Navajo Nation's tribal education program. The main section of the paper also includes a lively editorial/opinion/letters to the editor page. Other regular sections cover sports, entertainment including arts and culture, education, and classified ads. The web site provides full-text access to selected articles for the past year. This publication is recommended for all public libraries serving the region and those academic libraries serving programs with research interests in modern Native American society.

4687. News from Native California: an inside view of the California Indian world. [ISSN: 1040-5437] 1987. q. USD 19 domestic; USD 34 foreign. Ed(s): Margaret Dubin. Clapperstick Institute, PO Box 9145, Berkeley, CA 94709; nnc@heydaybooks.com; http://www.heydaybooks.com/news. Illus., index, adv. Circ: 4500 Paid. Vol. ends: No. 4. *Indexed:* AICP, AltPI, ENW, MASUSE. *Bk. rev.:* 1, 500-1,200 words. *Aud.:* Hs, Ga, Sa.

Initially conceived in 1987 as simply a quarterly "Calendar of Events," *News From Native California* quickly became a highly regarded review of the arts, history, literature, culture, and politics of all of California's Native American communities. Recent feature articles include such titles as "Photographs Link Ohlone Past and Present," "Voices of the Flute: Songs of Three Southern California Indian Nations," "Echoes from the Road: A Journey Through

California's Indian Country," and "Woven Legacy: A Collection of Dat-so-la-lee Works, 1900–1921." Regular columns include the originally intended "Calendar of Events," a quarterly review of contemporary arts, and well-written, insightful book reviews. The web site provides access to tables of contents, the calendar of events, and selected articles. This publication is recommended for any public, high school, or academic library in California, as well as academic libraries outside of California supporting Native American Studies programs.

4688. Studies in American Indian Literatures. Formerly (until 1980): *Association for Study of American Indian Literatures. Newsletter.* [ISSN: 0730-3238] 1977. q. USD 90 (Individuals, USD 37). Ed(s): Malea Powell. University of Nebraska Press, 1111 Lincoln Mall, Lincoln, NE 68588-0630; journals@unlnotes.unl.edu; http://www.nebraskapress.unl.edu. Illus., adv. Refereed. Circ: 400. Vol. ends: Winter. *Indexed:* AICP, ArtHuCI, IBR, IBZ, MLA-IB. *Bk. rev.:* 10, 1,000-2,400 words. *Aud.:* Ac, Sa.

Studies in American Indian Literature is a refereed journal, published by the University of Nebraska Press. It primarily publishes scholarly, critical, pedagogical, and theoretical articles on a American Indian literatures, as well as interviews, literature reviews, and bibliographic essays. In addition, it also accepts works of poetry, short fiction, and book reviews. Special issues are occasionally published, such as one reviewed honoring the dean of Native American literary studies, A. Lavonne Brown Ruoff. A sample issue contained five scholarly articles, two creative submissions, and five book reviews. Each issue includes a directory of major tribes and bands mentioned including contact information and web sites if available. Full text is available on Project Muse beginning in 2004. It is strongly recommended for libraries supporting American literature, Native American and American Studies programs.

4689. Tribal College: journal of American Indian higher education. [ISSN: 1052-5505] 1989. q. USD 34 (Individuals, USD 24). Ed(s): Marjane Ambler. American Indian Higher Education Consortium, PO Box 720, Mancos, CO 81328; info@tribalcollegejournal.org. Illus., index, adv. Sample. Vol. ends: Summer (No. 4). *Indexed:* ABIn, ENW, ERIC, EduInd, HEA. *Bk. rev.:* 2, 300 words. *Aud.:* Ga, Ac, Sa.

Tribal College Journal is a publication of the American Indian Higher Education Consortium (AIHEC), whose mission is to provide information for anyone interested in Indian higher education. It does so by providing scholarly and journalistic articles and a one-stop source of information about the 37 Indian-controlled colleges in the United States and Canada. There are also numerous ads from other educational institutions and employers who wish to recruit Native American students. A typical issue includes two or three feature articles such as "The Future Is Green: Tribal colleges saving water, electricity and money" and "Historical Trauma: Holocaust victims, American Indians recovering from abuses of the past." In addition, there are regular columns including a "Resource Guide" to information sources relating to the feature articles, "Profiles" of educational leaders and campus programs, "Media Reviews" of print and audiovisual resources, and a directory of all AIHEC colleges. Full text is available in EBSCO's Academic Search Premier from 2000 on. This publication is an absolute must for any library serving Native American populations and Native American Studies programs.

4690. Whispering Wind: American Indian: past & present. [ISSN: 0300-6565] 1967. bi-m. USD 21 domestic; USD 37 foreign. Jack Heriard, Ed. & Pub., PO Box 1390, Folsom, LA 70437-1390; whiswind@i-55.com; http://www.writtenheritage.com/. Illus., index, adv. Sample. Refereed. Circ: 24000. Vol. ends: No. 6. *Indexed:* AICP, ENW. *Bk. rev.:* 4-6, 300-500 words. *Aud.:* Hs, Sa.

Whispering Wind is a popular magazine aimed at preserving Native American culture and traditions through historical and practical articles on traditional Native American arts, crafts, design, practices, music, dance, and dress. Each bimonthly issue is packed with detailed and well-illustrated articles such as "Ten Tips for Perfect Ribbon Work," "German Silver Crosses in Lakota Attire," "Cutting and Stringing Buckskin Thong," and "Pawnee Men: Late 1860s and 1870s," an analysis of photographs taken by William Henry Jackson. Each issue also contains regular columns of music and book reviews, a calendar of pow-wow dates, and classified ads for books, clothing, and sources of craft supplies, plus significant color advertising. This magazine is recommended for any public library, but especially those serving Native American populations.

4691. *Wicazo Sa Review: a journal of Native American studies.* [ISSN: 0749-6427] 1985. s-a. USD 50 (Individuals, USD 20). Ed(s): James Riding In. University of Minnesota Press, 111 Third Ave S, Ste 290, Minneapolis, MN 55401-2520; ump@umn.edu; http://www.upress.umn.edu. Illus., adv. Sample. Refereed. Circ: 400. Vol. ends: No. 2. *Indexed:* AICP, AltPI, AmH&L, AmHI, HistAb, HumInd, MLA-IB, RILM. *Bk. rev.:* 1-2, 800 words. *Aud.:* Ac.

Wicazo Sa Review is probably one of the most serious and important journals in Native American Studies. Over the past 20 years, it has helped shape the development of Native American Studies as a discipline by providing indigenous peoples of the Americas with a vehicle to "take possession of their own intellectual and creative pursuits" and "define the cultural, religious, legal and historical parameters of scholarship and the process of decolonization." Each semi-annual issue contains insightful and challenging editorials and essays, five to seven well-written, interdisciplinary articles, and several excellent book reviews. In addition, there is a review of the Annual American Indian Studies Consortium meeting. Recent articles include "Spiritual Appropriation as Sexual Violence," "Changing the Subject: Individual versus Collective Interests in Indian Country Research," and "The Native American Graves Protection and Repatriation Act (1990): Where the Native Voice is Missing." The journal is indexed in America: History and Life, MLA International Bibliography, and full text is available in Project Muse and Arts & Humanities from 2000. This title is absolutely necessary for academic institutions with Native American and American Studies programs, and is highly recommended for all academic institutions.

4692. *Winds of Change: American Indian education & opportunity.* [ISSN: 0888-8612] 1986. q. Non-members, USD 24. Ed(s): James R Weidlein. A I S E S Publishing, 4450 Arapahoe Ave Ste 100, Boulder, CO 80303-9102; woc@indra.com; http://www.aises.uthscsa.edu. Illus., index, adv. Sample. Circ: 60000 Paid. Vol. ends: Fall. *Bk. rev.:* 2-10, 250-600 words. *Aud.:* Hs, Ac, Sa.

Published by the American Indian Science and Engineering Society (AISES), *Winds of Change*'s mission is to encourage young Native American students to pursue education and careers in science and engineering. Each colorfully illustrated issue contains professionally written articles about career opportunities, success stories, and Native American contributions in the areas of health, science, technology, and engineering. Each article also contains links to additional sources of information. Regular columns on summer internships and educational opportunities, book reviews, classified ads, and AISES news are also included. There are also numerous color ads recruiting young Native Americans to employment and educational opportunities. This publication is essential for school and public libraries serving Native American populations.

4693. *Windspeaker.* Formerly (until 1986): *A M M S A.* [ISSN: 0834-177X] 1983. m. CND 40 domestic; CND 52 United States; CND 60 elsewhere. Ed(s): Debora Lockyer. Aboriginal Multi-Media Society of Alberta, 15001 112 Ave, NW, Edmonton, AB T5M 2V6, Canada; http://www.ammsa.com/. Illus., adv. Circ: 12000 Paid. Microform: MML. Online: EBSCO Publishing, EBSCO Host; Gale; Micromedia ProQuest; ProQuest K-12 Learning Solutions; ProQuest LLC (Ann Arbor). *Indexed:* CBCARef, CPerI, ENW. *Aud.:* Ga, Sa.

Windspeaker is the flagship publication of the Aboriginal Multi-Media Society of Alberta. As such, its mission is to serve as "Canada's National Aboriginal news source." The publisher also produces four other monthly newspapers covering specific provinces: *Alberta Sweetgrass, Saskatchewan Sage, BC Raven's Eye,* and *Ontario Birchbark.* The last two are free with a subscription to *Windspeaker,* and the first two are an additional $15 each. In addition to well-written feature articles, *Windspeaker* also contains regular columns such as "Rants and Raves" (editorial/letters), "What's Happening" (news summary), "Radio's Most Active" (entertainment), "Strictly Speaking" (essays), and "Footprints" (tributes). While there is no classified section, there are ads throughout the publication. There are also occasional special supplements

devoted to topics such as aboriginal businesses. These publications are recommended for libraries serving First Nation populations across Canada and in the appropriate provinces.

■ NEWS AND OPINION

See also Alternatives; General Interest; and Newspapers sections.

Holly A. Wilson, Research & Instruction Librarian, Assistant Professor, Pratt Institute, 200 Willoughby Ave., Brooklyn, NY 11205; hwilson5@pratt.edu

Introduction

In this time of globalization and information overload, it is vitally important to have access to reliable and credible sources of news and opinion. It is not enough these days to rely on television news to achieve any sort of in-depth understanding of current events and issues. This section gives examples of publications that cover news, current events, politics, and culture from a range of viewpoints. This is by no means an exhaustive resource, but should serve to give libraries some guidance in the development of a collection in the area of news and opinion. Most of the publications are suited for both public and academic libraries; a few, like the standard newsweeklies (specifically *Time* and *Newsweek*), are also appropriate and highly recommended for high schools.

The three primary newsweeklies in the United States, *Newsweek, Time,* and *U.S. News & World Report,* are all discussed in this section and are recommended for any library collection as standard subscriptions. To expand somewhat internationally, the British counterparts, namely *New Statesman* and *The Spectator,* would serve that purpose well. Other titles in this section are included to facilitate a well-rounded balance of opinions.

Since the publication of the previous edition of *Magazines for Libraries,* the most significant change relates to the online content available through a majority of the magazines' web sites. Often there is online-only content (frequently daily news updates) or RSS feeds and blogs that would be of interest to users wanting updates for topics and subjects of interest. This additional content is included within the discussion of particular titles.

The following web sites provide news, but they are not set up as "serials." They are updated frequently, include multimedia, often provide RSS feeds, and tend not to be archived.

BBC News. BBC News. news.bbc.co.uk.

CNN Interactive. CNN Network. www.cnn.com.

FoxNews. Fox News Network. www.foxnews.com.

MSNBC. NBC Network and Microsoft Corporation. www.msnbc.com.

NPR News. National Public Radio. www.npr.org/news.

Basic Periodicals

Hs: *New Perspectives Quarterly, Newsweek, Time;* Ga, Ac: *The Nation, National Review, New Perspectives Quarterly, The New Republic, Newsweek, Time, U.S. News & World Report.*

Basic Abstracts and Indexes

Alternative Press Index, PAIS International, Periodical Abstracts, Readers' Guide to Periodical Literature.

4694. *The American Spectator.* Former titles (until 1976): *Alternative; an American Spectator; Alternative.* [ISSN: 0148-8414] 1967. 10x/yr. USD 39 domestic; USD 59 foreign. Ed(s): R Emmett Tyrrell, Jr. The American Spectator, 1611 N Kent St, Ste 901, Arlington, VA 22209; editor@spectator.org; http://www.spectator.org. Illus., index, adv. Sample. Circ: 139000 Paid. Vol. ends: Dec. Microform: BHP; PQC. Online: EBSCO Publishing, EBSCO Host; Florida Center for Library Automation; Gale; LexisNexis; Northern Light Technology, Inc.;

OCLC Online Computer Library Center, Inc.; ProQuest K-12 Learning Solutions; ProQuest LLC (Ann Arbor); H.W. Wilson. *Indexed:* ABS&EES, ASIP, BRI, CBRI, MASUSE, PAIS, RGPR, SUSA. *Bk. rev.:* 3-4, 1,500 words, signed. *Aud.:* Ga, Ac.

The American Spectator has as its mission "to provide its unique view of American conservative politics, with a keen sense of irreverence." There is often a somewhat humorous bent to the writing, and regular pieces, such as "Enemy of the Week" and "Ben Stein's Diary," are only a few of the perks that subscribers experience. At the time of this writing, the web site seems to be undergoing a revision, since many of the areas are listed as "coming soon." There is, however, some content available on the site, including "Editor's Desk," "Washington Prowler," and the "AmSpecBlog." This magazine would serve to bolster a balanced collection in any public or academic library.

4695. The American (Washington, D.C.). Formerly (until Nov.2006): *American Enterprise;* Which was formed by the merger of (1978-1989): *Public Opinion (Washington);* (197?-1989): *The A E I Ecomomist.* [ISSN: 1932-8117] 1990. bi-m. USD 40 domestic; USD 50 Canada; USD 60 elsewhere. Ed(s): James K Glassman. American Enterprise Institute for Public Policy Research, 1150 17th St NW, Washington, DC 20036; http://www.aei.org/. Illus., adv. Circ: 31000 Paid and free. Vol. ends: Nov/Dec. Microform: NBI. Online: EBSCO Publishing, EBSCO Host; Florida Center for Library Automation; Gale; Northern Light Technology, Inc.; OCLC Online Computer Library Center, Inc.; ProQuest K-12 Learning Solutions; ProQuest LLC (Ann Arbor); H.W. Wilson. *Indexed:* ABCPolSci, ABS&EES, AgeL, IPSA, JEL, LRI, MASUSE, PAIS. *Bk. rev.:* 3, length varies, signed. *Aud.:* Ga, Ac.

The American has a focus on business and economics, but does so with a broad scope. Areas such as fashion, sports, and art, to name a few, are discussed within a business perspective. Regular columns include "Young Economist," "American Interview," and "Techno-Ideas." The content is available free via their web site, which includes additional content that the print version directs the reader to. When articles are viewed on the web site, a list of related articles appears to facilitate further reading. Topical RSS feeds and podcasts are available in the "Online Extras" section. The online Archive is accessible either by issue or by topic. This publication is a good choice for libraries wishing to provide a holistic view of business and economics related to our everyday lives. Articles are well written and suitable for a general audience.

Briarpatch. See Alternatives section.

Business Week. See Business/General section.

4696. Commentary: journal of significant thought and opinion on contemporary issues. Formerly (until 1945): *Contemporary Jewish Record.* [ISSN: 0010-2601] 1938. 11x/yr. Members, USD 42; Non-members, USD 45; USD 4.50 per issue. Ed(s): Gary Rosen, Neal Kozodoy. American Jewish Committee, 165 E 56th St, New York, NY 10022; pr@ajc.org; http://www.ajc.org. Index, adv. Sample. Circ: 35000 Paid. Vol. ends: Jun/Dec. Online: Chadwyck-Healey Inc.; EBSCO Publishing, EBSCO Host; Florida Center for Library Automation; Gale; Northern Light Technology, Inc.; OCLC Online Computer Library Center, Inc.; ProQuest LLC (Ann Arbor); H.W. Wilson. *Indexed:* ABCPolSci, ABS&EES, AmH&L, AmHI, ArtHuCI, BAS, BEL&L, BRD, BRI, CBRI, CPerI, CWI, FLI, FutSurv, HistAb, HumInd, IBR, IBSS, IBZ, IJP, IPSA, LRI, MASUSE, MLA-IB, MRD, NTA, PAIS, PRA, RGPR, RI-1, RILM, SSCI. *Bk. rev.:* 5, 1,500-2,000 words, signed. *Aud.:* Ga, Ac.

As stated in the "About Us" section of the web site, *Commentary* is "America's premier monthly magazine of opinion and a pivotal voice in American intellectual life. Since its inception in 1945, and increasingly after it emerged as the flagship of neoconservatism in the 1970's, the magazine has been consistently engaged with several large, interrelated questions: the fate of democracy and of democratic ideas in a world threatened by totalitarian ideologies; the state of American and Western security; the future of the Jews, Judaism, and Jewish culture in Israel, the United States, and around the world; and the preservation of high culture in an age of political correctness and the collapse of critical standards." Several articles are available online, including some recent content.

Subscribers can access all archived content dating back to 1945. Tables of contents and often abstracts of articles are freely available. The publication is a good addition to a range of viewpoints and is suited for a public or academic library.

Commonweal. See Religion section.

4697. The Contemporary Review. Incorporates: *Fortnightly.* [ISSN: 0010-7565] 1866. m. GBP 47 domestic; GBP 52.40 in Europe; USD 184 in US & Canada. Ed(s): Dr. Alex Kerr, Richard Mullen. Contemporary Review Co. Ltd., PO Box 1242, Oxford, OX1 4FJ, United Kingdom. Illus., index, adv. Sample. Circ: 680000. Vol. ends: Jun/Dec. Microform: PMC; PQC. Online: Chadwyck-Healey Inc.; EBSCO Publishing, EBSCO Host; Florida Center for Library Automation; Gale; Northern Light Technology, Inc.; OCLC Online Computer Library Center, Inc.; ProQuest K-12 Learning Solutions; ProQuest LLC (Ann Arbor); H.W. Wilson. *Indexed:* AmH&L, AmHI, BAS, BRI, CBRI, FLI, HistAb, HumInd, IBR, IBZ, MLA-IB, RI-1, RILM. *Bk. rev.:* Various number and length, signed. *Aud.:* Ga, Ac.

Founded in 1866, *The Contemporary Review* is "a forum for discussion of a broad spectrum of topics including International Affairs, Politics, Literature, and the Arts." This quarterly publication remains advertising-free and editorially independent. "Our aim remains to provide a platform where experts in one field may address intelligent people in other fields." The notable point about this is that the articles are written so that they cater to those in other fields than the authors', thereby making them available to a broader readership. Each issue is 136 pages, with 36 of those being dedicated to reviews. The content is largely objective and accessible to most readers. It is recommended for most libraries; a must for those that serve an intellectually curious population.

4698. Current (Washington, 1960). [ISSN: 0011-3131] 1960. m. except Mar.-Apr., Jul.-Aug. combined. USD 117 (Individuals, USD 47; USD 11 newsstand/cover). Ed(s): Chelsea Jennings. Heldref Publications, 1319 18th St, NW, Washington, DC 20036-1802; subscribe@heldref.org; http://www.heldref.org. Illus., index, adv. Refereed. Circ: 1041 Paid. Vol. ends: Jan. CD-ROM: ProQuest LLC (Ann Arbor). Online: OCLC Online Computer Library Center, Inc. Reprint: PSC. *Indexed:* ABS&EES, AmH&L, ArtHuCI, HRA, IBR, IBZ, LRI, RGPR, SSCI. *Aud.:* Hs, Ga, Ac.

"A journal of reprints, *Current* publishes provocative articles, essays, and reviews selected from the nation's most respected sources." While the articles are definitely of high quality and worth reading, it is unclear how *Current* goes about selecting items for inclusion. Issues are not thematic or topical, so it is difficult to determine the benefit of this magazine. Many large libraries may already subscribe to the original source journals that the articles were first published in. However, this journal may be a way to increase the collection of a smaller library, since it pulls from a broad range of source material.

4699. Dissent (New York). [ISSN: 0012-3846] 1954. q. USD 24. Ed(s): Michael Walzer, Mitchell Cohen. Foundation for the Study of Independent Social Ideas, Inc., 310 Riverside Dr., Apt. 2008, New York, NY 10025-4129; advertise@dissentmagazine.org; http://www.dissentmagazine.org. Illus., index, adv. Sample. Circ: 10000 Paid. Vol. ends: Fall (No. 4). Microform: PQC. Online: EBSCO Publishing, EBSCO Host; OCLC Online Computer Library Center, Inc.; ProQuest K-12 Learning Solutions; ProQuest LLC (Ann Arbor); H.W. Wilson. *Indexed:* ABCPolSci, ABS&EES, AltPI, AmH&L, AmHI, BAS, BRI, CBRI, FLI, FutSurv, HistAb, IBR, IBZ, IPSA, IndIslam, LRI, LeftInd, PAIS, PSA, RILM, SSA, SSCI, SWR&A, SociolAb. *Bk. rev.:* 5, 2,000 words, signed. *Aud.:* Ga, Ac.

To quote the *Dissent* web site: " . . . a magazine of independent minds. A magazine . . . that welcomes the clash of strong opinions. Each issue features reflective articles about politics in the U.S., incisive social and cultural commentary, plus the most sophisticated coverage of European politics you'll find anywhere outside of Europe." As the *Utne Reader* says, "Politics, economics, and culture come together in every article, giving the entire publication a balance most political journals lack." This is a quarterly publication and, while it is decidedly liberal, it is not forceful or heavy-handed in its opinions. It is notable for a global perspective, since each issue has a

"Politics Abroad" section. There are a good number of feature articles, all well written and insightful. The web site provides access to several articles in the current issue as well as full access to articles in back issues, all for free. This is a good publication that would be a worthwhile addition to any public or academic library collection.

The Economist. See Economics section.

Foreign Affairs. See Political Science/International Relations section.

The Guardian. See Newspapers/General section.

4700. Human Events: the national conservative weekly. [ISSN: 0018-7194] 1944. w. Fri. USD 35.95 for 35 wks.; USD 69.95 for 70 wks. Ed(s): Thomas S. Winter, Christopher Field. Eagle Publishing, Inc., One Massachusetts Ave, NW, Washington, DC 20001; http://www.phillips.com. Illus., index, adv. Sample. Circ: 78000 Paid. Vol. ends: Dec. Microform: BHP; PQC. Online: Chadwyck-Healey Inc.; EBSCO Publishing, EBSCO Host; Northern Light Technology, Inc.; ProQuest K-12 Learning Solutions; ProQuest LLC (Ann Arbor). *Indexed:* AmH&L, BRI, CBRI, MASUSE. *Bk. rev.:* Various number and length, signed. *Aud.:* Ga, Ac.

Human Events is one of the leading conservative magazines and has been "Leading the Conservative Movement since 1944." The content is decidedly partisan, including regular columns called "Hillary Watch" and "Jihad Watch." The roster of contributors reveals a strong showing of conservative heavy-hitters, including Pat Buchanan, Ann Coulter, and Newt Gingrich, to name a few. Much of the content is available online, including an RSS feed. There is a subject breakdown as well as the ability to select a contributor to search articles. *Human Events* would be a good choice for most public and academic collections, particularly those looking for a balance of viewpoints.

4701. In These Times. [ISSN: 0160-5992] 1976. bi-w. Individuals, USD 24.95. Ed(s): Joel Bleifuss. Institute for Public Affairs, 2040 N Milwaukee Ave, Chicago, IL 60647-4002. Illus., adv. Circ: 14891. Vol. ends: Nov. Microform: PQC. Online: LexisNexis. *Indexed:* ASIP, AltPI, LeftInd, PAIS, PRA. *Bk. rev.:* Various number and length. *Aud.:* Ga, Ac.

"*In These Times* is dedicated to informing and analyzing popular movements for social, environmental and economic justice; to providing a forum for discussing the politics that shape our lives; and to producing a magazine that is read by the broadest and most diverse audience possible." This monthly news and political opinion magazine has just passed its 30th anniversary. It fearlessly covers topics that mainstream media and powerful corporate concerns may wish to remain undiscussed. This is a recommended title for public and academic libraries that would like to offer more than the mainstream to their patrons. The online archive offers access to content dating back to 2000 and can be keyword-searched easily on the main page.

4702. Interview (New York). Formerly (until 1989): *Andy Warhol's Interview.* [ISSN: 0149-8932] 1969. m. USD 14.97 domestic; USD 37.50 Canada; USD 45 elsewhere. Ed(s): Ingrid Sischy. Brant Publications, Inc., 575 Broadway, 5th Fl, New York, NY 10012. Illus., adv. Circ: 155803 Paid. Vol. ends: Dec (No. 12). Microform: PQC. Online: Chadwyck-Healey Inc.; EBSCO Publishing, EBSCO Host; Gale; OCLC Online Computer Library Center, Inc.; ProQuest K-12 Learning Solutions; ProQuest LLC (Ann Arbor); H.W. Wilson. *Indexed:* ABS&EES, ASIP, FLI, IIFP, IIPA, MASUSE, MRD, RGPR. *Bk. rev.:* Various number and length. *Aud.:* Ga, Ac.

Interview magazine is a source for interviews and articles pertaining to news and popular culture. Contributors are often well-known popular culture figures themselves. There are several reviews of books, music, and film in addition to the articles and interviews. For libraries with an interest in popular culture, this is a recommended title.

Le Monde Diplomatique. See Europe section.

4703. Monthly Review: an independent socialist magazine. [ISSN: 0027-0520] 1949. m. Jul.-Aug. comb. USD 48 (Individuals, USD 29). Ed(s): Harry Magdoff, John Bellamy Foster. Monthly Review Foundation, 122 W 27th St, 10th fl, New York, NY 10001; mrmag@monthlyreview.org; http://www.monthlyreview.org. Illus., index, adv. Refereed. Circ: 6000 Paid. Vol. ends: Dec. Microform: PQC. Online: EBSCO Publishing, EBSCO Host; Florida Center for Library Automation; Gale; Northern Light Technology, Inc.; OCLC Online Computer Library Center, Inc.; ProQuest LLC (Ann Arbor); H.W. Wilson. *Indexed:* ABS&EES, AltPI, AmH&L, BAS, HistAb, IBR, IBZ, LeftInd, PAIS, PRA, PSA, RRTA, SSA, SSCI, SociolAb, WAE&RSA. *Bk. rev.:* Various number and length, signed. *Aud.:* Ga, Ac.

Monthly Review is billed as "an independent socialist magazine" and in that spirit offers all content free on the publication's web site. Subscriptions are encouraged for those who can afford it, but they are committed to getting their message out to everyone. The articles are well written and scholarly, with three to six lengthy articles per issue written by notable contributors to their fields. In addition, there are a few book reviews in each issue as well as a partial-page "Monthly Review Fifty Years Ago" reflective piece. For an adult-level collection looking to round out its viewpoints, this title would be an excellent choice.

Mother Jones. See General Editorial/General section.

4704. Ms. [ISSN: 0047-8318] 1972. q. USD 25 domestic; USD 42 Canada; USD 78 elsewhere. Ed(s): Katherine Spillar, Michel Cicero. Liberty Media for Women, L.L.C., 1600 Wilson Blvd, Ste 801, Arlington, VA 22209; info@msmagazine.com; http://www.msmagazine.com. Illus., adv. Circ: 110000 Paid. Vol. ends: Nov/Dec. Microform: PQC. Online: OCLC Online Computer Library Center, Inc.; ProQuest K-12 Learning Solutions; ProQuest LLC (Ann Arbor). *Indexed:* ABS&EES, BEL&L, BRD, BRI, CBRI, CWI, ConsI, FLI, FemPer, LRI, MASUSE, MRD, PAIS, RGPR, RI-1, RILM, SWA, WSA. *Bk. rev.:* 8, 124-300 words, signed. *Aud.:* Hs, Ga, Ac.

Ms. provides thought-provoking and insightful articles on issues and concerns of feminism and humanitarianism. Their focus on inspiring people to activism is evident on the banner of the publication's web site: "More than a magazine—a movement." Each issue covers a variety of topics, such as environmental issues, humanitarian causes, and profiles of prominent feminists. Also covered are the arts and culture, including fiction and poetry. There are several in-depth book reviews as well as brief snapshot book reports in each issue. The web site offers full access to selected current articles. Full back issues are available for purchase, but a few articles from each issue are available for free. *Ms.* would be a good title to include for most public and academic libraries.

4705. The Nation. [ISSN: 0027-8378] 1865. w. except the second week in Jan.; bi-w. in July & Aug. USD 29.97 domestic; USD 61.97 Canada; USD 94.97 elsewhere. Ed(s): Karen Rothmyer, Katrina Vanden Heuvel. The Nation Company, L.P., 33 Irving Pl, 8th Fl, New York, NY 10003. Illus., index, adv. Sample. Circ: 127712 Paid. Vol. ends: Jun/Dec. CD-ROM: ProQuest LLC (Ann Arbor). Microform: PMC; PQC. Online: EBSCO Publishing, EBSCO Host; Florida Center for Library Automation; Gale; Northern Light Technology, Inc.; OCLC Online Computer Library Center, Inc.; ProQuest K-12 Learning Solutions; ProQuest LLC (Ann Arbor); H.W. Wilson. *Indexed:* ABS&EES, AgeL, AltPI, ArtHuCI, BRD, BRI, CBRI, CWI, FLI, FutSurv, IAPV, LRI, MASUSE, MRD, PAIS, PRA, RGPR, SSCI. *Bk. rev.:* 4, 1,000 words, signed. *Aud.:* Ga, Ac.

The Nation is a decidedly liberal publication. A number of letters and editorials open each issue. Topics covered include, but are not limited to, politics, the arts, and economics. Articles are direct and concise, averaging about three pages each. Much content is available on the web site. Currently *The Nation* archive has a searchable index and page images of every issue published from 1865 to the present. Articles are available for a fee. There are services for libraries, but content is also available through other database products, such as Academic Search Premier. The web site includes blogs, RSS feeds, and a free MP3 download of each week's "RadioNation" program.

National Journal. See Political Science/Comparative and American Politics section.

4706. *National Review: a journal of fact and opinion.* [ISSN: 0028-0038] 1955. bi-w. USD 29.50. Ed(s): Jay Nordlinger, Richard Lowry. National Review, Inc., 215 Lexington Ave, New York, NY 10016; nronline@nationalreview.com. Illus., index, adv. Circ: 270000 Paid. Vol. ends: No. 25. CD-ROM: ProQuest LLC (Ann Arbor). Microform: NBI; PQC. Online: The Dialog Corporation; EBSCO Publishing, EBSCO Host; Florida Center for Library Automation; Gale; LexisNexis; Northern Light Technology, Inc.; OCLC Online Computer Library Center, Inc.; ProQuest K-12 Learning Solutions; ProQuest LLC (Ann Arbor); H.W. Wilson. *Indexed:* ABS&EES, AgeL, BAS, BRD, BRI, CBRI, CWI, FLI, FutSurv, LRI, MASUSE, MRD, PRA, RGPR, RI-1, SWR&A. *Bk. rev.:* 4, 1,000 words, signed. *Aud.:* Ga, Ac.

National Review is most certainly a conservative voice on current issues and news. Each issue begins with a multiple-page spread that offers a wide range of brief news pieces, primarily political in nature; these tend to be somewhat like rants in several instances. Each issue also has a long cover story and several regular columns. There are book reviews and political cartoons as well. This title should be included in library collections covering issues from a variety of viewpoints and is highly recommended for public and academic libraries. The web site, while related to the publication, stands on its own and features "Blog Row," which allows the user to choose a variety of blogs based on a particular topic or writer.

4707. *The New American (Appleton).* Formed by the merger of (1958-1985): *American Opinion;* (1965-1985): *Review of the News.* [ISSN: 0885-6540] 1985. bi-w. USD 39 domestic; USD 48 Canada; USD 66 elsewhere. Ed(s): Gary Benoit. American Opinion Publishing Inc., PO Box 8040, Appleton, WI 54912. Illus. Sample. Circ: 50000 Paid. Vol. ends: Dec. Microform: PQC. Online: Gale; OCLC Online Computer Library Center, Inc.; ProQuest K-12 Learning Solutions; ProQuest LLC (Ann Arbor). *Bk. rev.:* Various number and length, signed. *Aud.:* Ga, Ac.

The New American is decidedly more opinion than news. It is a publication of the John Birch Society, and the viewpoints are from a fundamentalist Christian perspective. Selected content is available through the web site, but much of the site is dedicated to educating about the society and its mission. For a library collection seeking to expand the range of viewpoints, this would be a good addition for a conservative voice.

New Criterion. See Art/General section.

New Left Review See Political Science section.

4708. *New Perspectives Quarterly: a journal of social and political thought.* Formerly (until 1986): *Center for the Study of Democratic Institutions. Center Magazine;* (until 1967): *Center for the Study of Democratic Institutions. Center Diary.* [ISSN: 0893-7850] 1963. q. GBP 267 print & online eds. Ed(s): Nathan Gardels. Blackwell Publishing, Inc., Commerce Place, 350 Main St, Malden, MA 02148; customerservices@blackwellpublishing.com; http://www.blackwellpublishing.com. Illus., adv. Sample. Refereed. Circ: 15000. Vol. ends: No. 5. Microform: PQC. Online: Blackwell Synergy; EBSCO Publishing, EBSCO Host; Gale; Northern Light Technology, Inc.; OCLC Online Computer Library Center, Inc.; OhioLINK; ProQuest K-12 Learning Solutions; SwetsWise Online Content; H.W. Wilson. Reprint: PSC. *Indexed:* ABS&EES, ApEcolAb, BAS, IBR, IBZ, IPSA, MASUSE, PAIS, PRA, PSA, RGPR. *Bk. rev.:* Various number and length. *Aud.:* Hs, Ga, Ac.

New Perspectives Quarterly, commonly known as *NPQ,* is a significant publication in the way it is organized. Each issue covers a number of specific topics. Expert contributors each discuss the topic from his or her own particular viewpoint. Generally the reader is left with a well-rounded understanding of the issue rather than a singular perspective. For this alone, it is a worthy addition to most library collections; the writing from world-class contributors is a bonus. Content is also available online, accessed by the topic as it appeared in the journal.

4709. *The New Republic: a journal of politics and the arts.* [ISSN: 0028-6583] 1914. w. USD 39.97; USD 3.95 newsstand/cover. Ed(s): Martin Peretz, Peter Beinart. New Republic, 1331 H St NW, Ste 700, Washington, DC 20005-4737. Illus., index, adv. Circ: 100000 Paid. Vol. ends: Jun/Dec. CD-ROM: ProQuest LLC (Ann Arbor). Microform: NBI; PMC; PQC. Online: The Dialog Corporation; EBSCO Publishing, EBSCO Host; Florida Center for Library Automation; Gale; LexisNexis; Northern Light Technology, Inc.; OCLC Online Computer Library Center, Inc.; ProQuest LLC (Ann Arbor); H.W. Wilson. *Indexed:* ABIn, ABS&EES, AgeL, AmH&L, ArtHuCI, BAS, BEL&L, BRD, BRI, CBRI, CPerI, CWI, EnvAb, FLI, FutSurv, HistAb, IAPV, LRI, MASUSE, MRD, NTA, PRA, RGPR, RI-1, RILM, SSCI. *Bk. rev.:* Various number and length. *Aud.:* Ga, Ac.

The New Republic is pretty much the closest you can come to objective coverage of Washington from an insider's perspective. In the "About Us" section of the web site, it states that since its founding in 1914, "its mission was to provide its readers with an intelligent, stimulating and rigorous examination of American politics, foreign policy and culture. It has brilliantly maintained its mission for ninety years." Not necessarily modest, but it does hold true. Subscribers have access to the online archives where full issues back to 2003 can be downloaded in pdf format. In addition to the regular magazine content, subscribers to the print version also have access to daily online content that gives in-depth analysis of current issues. Only the beginning of each article is viewable for nonsubscribers. The objective voice would make this a solid addition to any collection.

4710. *New Statesman.* Formerly (until 1996): *New Statesman & Society;* Which was formed by the merger of (1962-1988): *New Society;* (1931-1988): *New Statesman;* Which was formerly (until 1957): *New Statesman & Nation;* Which was formed by the merger of: *New Statesman; Nation.* [ISSN: 1364-7431] 1988. w. GBP 140 (Individuals, GBP 115). Ed(s): Peter Wilby. New Statesman Ltd., 52 Grosvenor Gardens, 3rd Fl, London, SW1W 0AU, United Kingdom; sbrasher@newstatesman.co.uk. Illus., index, adv. Circ: 21000. Vol. ends: Jun/Dec. Microform: PMC; PQC. Online: EBSCO Publishing, EBSCO Host; Florida Center for Library Automation; Gale; LexisNexis; Northern Light Technology, Inc.; OCLC Online Computer Library Center, Inc.; ProQuest K-12 Learning Solutions; ProQuest LLC (Ann Arbor); SwetsWise Online Content; H.W. Wilson. *Indexed:* ABIn, AmHI, BRD, BRI, BrHumI, CBRI, FLI, HRIS, LRI, MASUSE, MRD, RILM, SSCI, SWA. *Bk. rev.:* Long and brief reviews in each issue, signed. *Aud.:* Ga, Ac.

New Statesman is an award-winning British weekly focusing on items related to news and culture. Each issue contains a number of feature articles, an "Arts & Culture" section, several regular columns, and a handful of book reviews. The viewpoint is somewhat socialist, but not overly so. Articles are well written and cover a wide range of topics, as would be expected from one of the key newsweeklies in Britain. Online content now features quite a number of blogs as well as access to specific columns. Many articles and book reviews are additionally available as audio files. RSS feeds and podcasts are also online. The archives are now freely accessible for all content starting in 1998. Recommended for large public and academic library collections. This title should be included for libraries that also subscribe to *The Spectator.*

4711. *Newsweek.* Incorporates (in 1933): *Today.* [ISSN: 0028-9604] 1933. w. USD 20 domestic; USD 64.26 Canada; USD 3.95 newsstand/cover. Ed(s): Richard M, Smith, Richard M Smith. Newsweek, Inc., 251 W 57th St, New York, NY 10019-1894; customer.care@newsweek.com. Illus., index, adv. Circ: 3100000 Paid. Vol. ends: Jun. Microform: NBI; PMC; PQC. Online: EBSCO Publishing, EBSCO Host; Factiva, Inc.; Florida Center for Library Automation; Gale; LexisNexis; Micromedia ProQuest; OCLC Online Computer Library Center, Inc.; ProQuest LLC (Ann Arbor); H.W. Wilson. *Indexed:* ABIn, AgeL, BLI, BRD, BRI, BiolDig, CBCARef, CBRI, CINAHL, CPerI, EnvAb, EnvInd, FLI, FutSurv, IIPA, LRI, MASUSE, MRD, NTA, RGPR, RI-1, RILM. *Bk. rev.:* 2-5, 500-1,300 words, signed. *Aud.:* Hs, Ga, Ac.

Newsweek is one of three newsweeklies that dominate the American market. The others are *Time* and *U.S. News and World Report.* These three publications are a standard recommendation for all libraries, in general. Articles range from news and politics to reviews of new movies. Articles vary in length from a page to a few pages and are good for skimming to summarize a week's happenings. The web site is in partnership with MSNBC.com, but it is somewhat difficult to navigate. Subjects are listed on the left side and link to a few selected current articles. The archives are searchable for free, but content is only available to subscribers or for a per-item fee.

4712. People. Formerly: *People Weekly.* [ISSN: 0093-7673] 1974. w. USD 113.88; USD 3.49 newsstand/cover per issue. Ed(s): Norman Pearlstine, Larry Hackett. Time, Inc., Time & Life Bldg, Rockefeller Center, 29th Fl, New York, NY 10020-1393; http://www.timeinc.com. Illus., adv. Circ: 3350000 Paid. Vol. ends: Jun/Dec. Microform: PQC. Online: EBSCO Publishing, EBSCO Host; Florida Center for Library Automation; Gale; LexisNexis; OCLC Online Computer Library Center, Inc.; H.W. Wilson. *Indexed:* BRI, CBRI, CPerI, MASUSE, MusicInd, RGPR. *Bk. rev.:* 5-7, 150-250 words. *Aud.:* Ga.

People is all about, well, people. In spite of a few longer articles, it's not really a news source as much as it is a place to go for celebrity updates and to see who's wearing what this week. The web site offers all content for subscribers and select content to nonsubscribers, such as photos, news, and a stylewatch. The site is busy and not terribly easy to navigate. This is a title to be added for leisure reading, not as a source for serious news.

4713. The Progressive (Madison). [ISSN: 0033-0736] 1909. m. USD 50 (Individuals, USD 32; USD 58 foreign). Ed(s): Amitabh Pal, Matthew Rothschild. The Progressive, Inc., 409 E. Main St., Madison, WI 53703-2899; circ@progressive.org; http://www.progressive.org. Illus., index, adv. Sample. Circ: 60000 Paid. Microform: PQC. Online: EBSCO Publishing, EBSCO Host; Florida Center for Library Automation; Gale; OCLC Online Computer Library Center, Inc.; ProQuest K-12 Learning Solutions; ProQuest LLC (Ann Arbor); H.W. Wilson. *Indexed:* ABS&EES, AgeL, AltPI, BAS, BRI, CBRI, CWI, FutSurv, LRI, MASUSE, MRD, PAIS, PRA, RGPR. *Bk. rev.:* 2, 1,200 words, signed. *Aud.:* Ga, Ac.

From the web site: *"The Progressive, a monthly since 1948, has steadfastly stood against militarism, the concentration of power in corporate hands, and the disenfranchisement of the citizenry. It has continued to champion peace, social and economic justice, civil rights, civil liberties, human rights, a preserved environment, and a reinvigorated democracy. Its bedrock values remain nonviolence and freedom of speech."* The articles contained in each issue are to the point and average two or three pages each. There are interviews with prominent figures and a variety of book reviews too. The web site permits access to the full text of a few articles from current and past issues. The site is updated daily with a "This Just In" section, and it also has an ongoing "McCarthyism Watch" that is freely available. Also of interest is the Progressive Radio Show, which is a half-hour weekly program hosted by the editor, and a Progressive Point of View, which is a daily two-minute commentary that is available as an audio file download from the site. This would make a good addition to achieve a balanced collection in many public and academic libraries.

Progressive Review See Zines section.

Reason. See Civil Liberties/Political-Economic Rights section.

4714. Slate. [ISSN: 1091-2339] 1996. d. Free. Washington Post Co., 1150 15th St, NW, Washington, DC 20071. Illus., adv. Online: LexisNexis. *Indexed:* ABS&EES. *Aud.:* Ga, Ac.

Slate is a free online daily magazine (the site is owned by the Washington Post Company) that covers topics of general interest with focus on "analysis and commentary about politics, news, and culture." *Slate* has won several awards, including the National Magazine Award for General Excellence Online. Content is categorized into several sections, including "News & Politics," "Arts & Life," "Business & Tech," and "Health & Science." Aside from the categories and links to the daily issues and search feature of the site, it can be a bit difficult to navigate. When full articles are accessed, links to related articles are given. *Slate.com* is a good source of opinion pieces in a variety of subject areas and should be available in most public and academic libraries.

Social Policy. See Labor and Industrial Relations section.

4715. The Spectator. [ISSN: 0038-6952] 1828. w. GBP 103 domestic; GBP 125 in Europe; GBP 115 United States. The Spectator (1828) Ltd., 56 Doughty St, London, WC1N 2LL, United Kingdom. Illus., index, adv. Circ: 46400. Microform: PMC; PQC. Online: Florida Center for Library Automation; Gale; LexisNexis; Northern Light Technology, Inc.; OCLC Online Computer Library Center, Inc.; ProQuest K-12 Learning Solutions; ProQuest LLC (Ann Arbor). *Indexed:* ABS&EES, BRI, CBRI, RILM. *Bk. rev.:* Various number and length, signed. *Aud.:* Ga, Ac.

The Spectator boasts that it is the "oldest continuously published magazine in the English language," having begun publication in 1828. One of the two major British newsweeklies (*New Statesman* is the other), the coverage ranges from news and regular weekly columns to "Arts," "Life," "Style & Travel," and several book reviews per issue. Political cartoons and a British sense of humor make this an interesting read that is recommended for large public and academic libraries. A must for libraries subscribing to *New Statesman.* The online archives permit free access to content dating back to 2000. Their "exclusive online" content includes a blog, features, "Irregulars," and a monthly wine discussion.

4716. Tikkun Magazine: a bi-monthly Jewish critique of politics, culture and society. [ISSN: 0887-9982] 1986. bi-m. USD 29 domestic; USD 39 in Canada & Mexico; USD 43 elsewhere. Ed(s): Michael Lerner. Institute for Labor & Mental Health, 2342 Shattuck Ave, Ste 1200, Berkeley, CA 94704; magazine@tikkun.org; http://www.tikkun.org. Illus., adv. Sample. Circ: 40000. Vol. ends: Nov/Dec. Online: EBSCO Publishing, EBSCO Host; Florida Center for Library Automation; Gale; OCLC Online Computer Library Center, Inc.; ProQuest K-12 Learning Solutions; ProQuest LLC (Ann Arbor); H.W. Wilson. *Indexed:* ABS&EES, AltPI, AmHI, BRI, CBRI, ENW, HumInd, IJP, LeftInd, NTA, RI-1, RILM. *Bk. rev.:* Various number and length. *Aud.:* Ga, Ac.

Tikkun is a liberal Jewish magazine but also has an interfaith organizational component (a side project is the Network of Spiritual Progressives). It is accessible and relevant to all faiths, and the magazine's philosophy is that a spiritual consciousness is necessary in addition to a political consciousness to heal the world. The writing is high quality and often attracts notable contributors. There is also a strong component of art and culture. The online article archive, which boasts over 2,600 articles and dates back to 1993, can be accessed for a fee of $10 per year. There are a few exclusively online articles as well as several blogs. This title would make an excellent addition to any academic or public library.

4717. Time. [ISSN: 0040-781X] 1923. w. USD 29.95 domestic; USD 39.95 Canada; USD 3.95 newsstand/cover. Ed(s): Norman Pearlstine, Adi Ignatius. Time, Inc., Time & Life Bldg, Rockefeller Center, 29th Fl, New York, NY 10020-1393; http://www.time.com/. Illus., index, adv. Circ: 3250000 Paid. Vol. ends: Jun. CD-ROM: ProQuest LLC (Ann Arbor). Microform: PQC. Online: EBSCO Publishing, EBSCO Host; Gale; LexisNexis; OCLC Online Computer Library Center, Inc.; ProQuest K-12 Learning Solutions; ProQuest LLC (Ann Arbor); H.W. Wilson. Online: Florida Center for Library Automation. *Indexed:* ABIn, AgeL, BEL&L, BLI, BRD, BRI, BiolDig, CBRI, CINAHL, CPerI, EnvAb, EnvInd, FLI, FutSurv, IIPA, LRI, MASUSE, MRD, NTA, PRA, RGPR, RI-1, RILM. *Bk. rev.:* Various number and length, signed. *Aud.:* Hs, Ga, Ac.

Time is one of the three primary newsweeklies in the United States (the other two are *Newsweek* and *U.S. News and World Report*). Coverage is on news, current events, popular culture, and other areas of general interest. There is a predominance of softer news items in *Time,* such as celebrity doings, but it should still be considered a standard item for most libraries. The web site, now in partnership with CNN.com, breaks content into several sections, including "U.S.," "World," "Business & Tech," and "Health & Science." The site is not the easiest to navigate, but the keyword searching is helpful for locating articles. The archives are available free and are searchable through the main page of the site.

4718. U S A Today (Valley Stream). Former titles (until 1978): *Intellect;* (until 1972): *School and Society;* Which incorporated: *Educational Review.* [ISSN: 0161-7389] 1915. m. USD 29 domestic; USD 35 Canada; USD 9.50 newsstand/cover per issue. Ed(s): Wayne Barrett, Robert Rothenberg. S A E Inc., 500 Bi County Blvd, Ste. 203,

Farmingdale, NY 11735-3931. Illus., index, adv. Circ: 257000. Microform: PMC; PQC. Online: The Dialog Corporation; EBSCO Publishing, EBSCO Host; Florida Center for Library Automation; Gale; OCLC Online Computer Library Center, Inc.; ProQuest LLC (Ann Arbor); H.W. Wilson. *Indexed:* ABS&EES, BRI, BiolDig, CBRI, EAA, FLI, HEA, LRI, MASUSE, NewsAb, PhilInd, RGPR, SSCI, WSA. *Bk. rev.:* 2-4, 200-750 words, signed. *Aud.:* Ga, Ac.

USA Today, not to be confused with the daily Gannett newpaper, is a monthly newsmagazine that shares similar formatting to *Newsweek* and publications of that ilk. Coverage can be any area of current interest, but as a monthly, it tends to be more analytical than the newsweeklies often are. This should be added to collections that subscribe to the newsweeklies and are looking for supplementary titles to provide greater depth.

4719. U S News & World Report. Formed by the merger of (1946-1948): *World Report;* (1933-1948): *United States News;* Which was formerly (until 1933): *The United States Daily.* [ISSN: 0041-5537] 1933. w. USD 29.97 domestic. Ed(s): Mortimer B Zuckerman, Victoria Pope. U S News & World Report Inc., 1050 Thomas Jefferson St, NW, Washington, DC 20007; letters@usnews.com; http://www.usnews.com. Illus., adv. Circ: 2351313 Paid. Vol. ends: Jun. Online: The Dialog Corporation; EBSCO Publishing, EBSCO Host; Factiva, Inc.; Florida Center for Library Automation; Gale; LexisNexis; Micromedia ProQuest; OCLC Online Computer Library Center, Inc.; ProQuest K-12 Learning Solutions; ProQuest LLC (Ann Arbor); H.W. Wilson. *Indexed:* AgeL, BRI, BiolDig, CBCARef, CINAHL, CPerI, EnvAb, EnvInd, FLI, FutSurv, HRIS, LRI, MASUSE, PAIS, RGPR, RI-1, RILM. *Aud.:* Hs, Ga, Ac.

U.S. News & World Report, Time, and *Newsweek* are the three key newsweekly publications in the United States. *U.S. News* should be a standard for all libraries for that reason. This title is generally said to be more objective than the other two, but also somewhat more conservative. There is a greater emphasis on journalism, and it contains less of the "soft news" that is often included in the others. Articles can span several pages and are well reasoned. The web site is divided into categories, including "Nation & World," "Money & Business," and "Education." Each of these sections breaks down into more specific subsections, which provides some ease of navigation. There is also a section for photos and video clips, which include daily and weekly galleries. RSS feeds and mobile device feeds are available for a variety of topics. Of key interest to *U.S. News & World Report* subscribers are the various special issues that are released throughout the year. Best known among these are the rankings of institutions of higher education. Most of the content is freely available online, but only subscribers get access to the detailed rankings information. For these issues and features alone, the title is required for most libraries.

4720. The Washington Monthly. [ISSN: 0043-0633] 1969. 10x/yr. USD 29.95 domestic; USD 39.95 foreign. Ed(s): Paul Glastris. Washington Monthly LLC, 733 15th St, Washington, DC 2005; editors@ washingtonmonthly.com; http://www.washingtonmonthly.com. Illus., adv. Sample. Circ: 33000. Vol. ends: Feb. Microform: PQC. Online: The Dialog Corporation; EBSCO Publishing, EBSCO Host; Florida Center for Library Automation; Gale; Northern Light Technology, Inc.; OCLC Online Computer Library Center, Inc.; ProQuest LLC (Ann Arbor); H.W. Wilson. *Indexed:* ABS&EES, AgeL, AmH&L, BRI, CBRI, FutSurv, HistAb, IPSA, LRI, MASUSE, PAIS, PRA, RGPR, RI-1. *Bk. rev.:* Various number and length, signed. *Aud.:* Ga, Ac.

According to its mission, *The Washington Monthly* is "an independent voice, listened to by insiders and willing to take on sacred cows—liberal and conservative." They offer in-depth, nonpartisan coverage of issues and politics. The articles are well written and interesting, with several reviews of books on politics included in each issue. A small feature that appears monthly is the "Monthly Journalism Award" in which the editors highlight a journalistic accomplishment from the previous month. Selected content is available on the web site, and full back issues are available for purchase. Because of the balanced and well-reasoned nature of the content, *The Washington Monthly* is recommended for most library collections.

The Week. See General Interest section.

World Policy Journal. See Political Science/International Relations section.

4721. Z Magazine. Formerly: *Zeta Magazine.* [ISSN: 1056-5507] 1988. m. USD 40 (Individuals, USD 30). Ed(s): Eric Sargent, Lydia Sargent. ZCommunications, 18 Millfield St, Woods Hole, MA 02543; lydia.sargent@zmag.org; http://www.zmag.org. Illus. Sample. Circ: 26000. Vol. ends: Dec. *Indexed:* ABS&EES, AltPI, PAIS. *Bk. rev.:* Various number and length. *Aud.:* Ga, Ac.

As the publication's mission states, "Z is an independent monthly magazine dedicated to resisting injustice, defending against repression, and creating liberty. It sees the racial, gender, class, and political dimensions of personal life as fundamental to understanding and improving contemporary circumstances; and it aims to assist activist efforts for a better future." To this end, *Z Magazine* divides its content into four categories: "Commentary," "Activism," "Features," and "Culture." The "Commentary" section is labeled by topic ("Conservative Watch," "Media Beat," and "Reproductive Rights" are a few that have appeared in recent issues). Several political cartoons are interspersed throughout each issue. This would be a strong addition to most library collections. Several articles are available online through the web site, and a few articles from each issue are immediately accessible even to nonsubscribers. Subscribers have access to all articles online; after five months, all content is free online and accessed by table of contents for each issue, or indexed by author and topic.

■ NEWSPAPERS

General/Commercial Web News Systems

See also newspapers in other sections (Latin America, Europe, etc.) and check the index for specific titles not included here.

Jim Ronningen, Associate Librarian, Social Sciences, 218 Doe Library, University of California, Berkeley, CA 94720-6000; jronning@ library.berkeley.edu; FAX 510-642-6830

Introduction

The librarian's job in choosing newspapers can be helped by thinking of the print version as a cross-section of the flow of news frozen at a point in time daily. Separate from the many other ways to receive the news now, this format can be chosen based upon library patron demand and the necessity to include local titles and obvious stalwarts like *The New York Times.*

The entries here always link to the paper's web site and describe it, but once that web site is explored—well, for the older reader used to newsprint, that way madness lies. It's incumbent upon us to help reluctant patrons explore what's available digitally, but it may just come down to how much one can stand. The availability of multimedia through news publisher partnerships, not to mention new avenues for readers and citizen journalists to contribute, can lead to an overwhelming experience.

Newspapers are indeed struggling, and measures are being taken to cut costs. Sometimes it means a format change that allows for a smaller paper that requires less raw newsprint; sometimes it means layoffs. I can't say, as I did in previous editions, that newspapers aren't going away any time soon. No one knows how much longer some publishers will continue with print. On the one hand, the tradition of newspaper publishing makes quitting print almost unthinkable, but on the other, economics forces the thought. They are still an efficient way of getting a daily digest of information in a format that makes sense for many people—easily portable, won't break if dropped, and no peripheral technology needed, except for maybe a pair of reading glasses. However, the draining away of advertising revenue to other media continues.

To further our mission as information providers, small local papers or ones with a particular focus—health, homelessness, skateboarding, what have you—deserve our particular attention. Their value lies where the major newspapers' macro view overlooks what they cover. Those smaller titles may or may not have web sites, and they could be the only way to hear voices that have no other outlet.

Basic Periodicals

All libraries should have: every local newspaper, including those that provide news and viewpoints that may not be reflected in the mass-circulation dailies; state and regional newspapers for their broader scope; at least one national newspaper of quality that offers comprehensive, in-depth reporting on national and international events; and foreign newspapers, if possible, because they can broaden horizons and have the eye-opening effect of revealing how often mainstream U.S. newspapers share a homogeneous point of view.

Basic Abstracts and Indexes

Depending on your library's budget and focus, the possibilities here are numerous. Collecting title-specific indexes for the newspaper titles you subscribe to is an obvious choice; they may be available in print or online. This may be unnecessary if you have access to an aggregator that indexes your titles and may provide article content as well — and this is certainly the trend we are seeing in the increasingly online environment.

General

4722. *The Atlanta Journal - Constitution.* Formed by the merger of (1868-2001): *Atlanta Journal;* (1868-2001): *Constitution (Atlanta).* [ISSN: 1539-7459] 2001. d. USD 0.50 newsstand/cover; USD 2 newsstand/cover Sun.; USD 120 subscr - carrier delivery in city. Ed(s): Hank Klibanoff, Julia Wallace. Cox Newspapers, Inc., 6205 Peachtree Dunwoody Rd., Atlanta, GA 30328. Circ: 382421. Online: OCLC Online Computer Library Center, Inc.; ProQuest LLC (Ann Arbor). *Aud.:* Ga.

The *AJC*, as it's commonly known, is the result of a merger of the *Constitution* and the *Journal* which began in 1982, with separate morning and afternoon deliveries phased out by 2001. The flagship of Cox Enterprises, the seven-day-a-week, mornings-only newspaper is the major regional newspaper for the South. The editorial stance generally leans liberal, sometimes contrasting with public opinion within the region. Since 2003, it has included a weekly entertainment tabloid, *Access Atlanta,* which competes with the rather "alternative" *Creative Loafing.* In 2006, Mike Luckovich won a Pulitzer for editorial cartooning, and in 2007 columnist Cynthia Tucker won for commentary. The web version is at www.ajc.com. The archives are searchable for free, but payment is required for complete article content. Photos and graphics are not included in the archives.

4723. *The Boston Globe.* [ISSN: 0743-1791] 1872. d. USD 540. Ed(s): Helen Donovan, Martin Baron. New York Times Company, 135 Morrissey Blvd., Boston, MA 02107. Circ: 450538. *Indexed:* CWI. *Aud.:* Ga.

The *Globe* was already the most respected news source in New England before it joined the New York Times Corporation in 1993, which only increased its resources and reach—but that doesn't mean the print edition is saved from the same pressures affecting all newspapers. The company has over recent years made the successful transition to the web site's being the home base, where readers access the full range of information sources available today, and it's generally clear which items are updating stories that appeared earlier in print. The site, at www.boston.com, is a gateway to regional resources and is in my opinion one of the most successful web presences for a news publisher. A Pulitzer for national reporting was awarded to Charlie Savage in 2007. Archival access is available in a variety of arrangements, including some free content; there is a gap in the archives between 1924 and 1979.

4724. *Chicago Tribune.* [ISSN: 1085-6706] 1847. d. USD 0.50 newsstand/ cover; USD 1.75 newsstand/cover Sun.; USD 2.25 subscr - home delivery per week. Ed(s): Ann Marie Lipinski. Tribune Company, 435 N. Michigan Ave., Chicago, IL 60611-4066. Circ: 600988 Paid. *Indexed:* RI-1, RILM. *Aud.:* Ga.

The *Tribune* is the farthest-reaching source for Midwest regional news and the largest-circulation paper in Chicago itself. (The *Chicago Sun-Times* doesn't lag that far behind, however, and Chicagoans are lucky to have a choice between the *Tribune* and the more populist voice of the *Sun-Times.*) The paper is the flagship

of the Tribune Company, a large empire with holdings in a variety of media. It has the resources for staff coverage of national and international events, and has a long history of awards, from Pulitzers to local press association kudos. For libraries in the Chicagoland area, a subscription is a no-brainer, but the diversity and complexity of the region would demand inclusion of other titles that reflect racial, ethnic, neighborhood, labor, and other interests. The web site is at www.chicagotribune.com. Archives available in a variety of pricing schemes are text-only from 1985 forward; 1852–1984 is a database of article image files.

4725. *The Christian Science Monitor.* Formerly (until 1925): *Christian Science Monitor.* [ISSN: 0882-7729] 1908. d. Mon.-Fri. USD 219. Ed(s): Mary Trammel, Marshall Ingwerson. The Christian Science Publishing Society, One Norway St, Boston, MA 02115-3122; http://www.csmonitor.com. Illus., adv. Circ: 71924 Paid. Microform: PQC. Online: The Dialog Corporation; EBSCO Publishing, EBSCO Host; Gale; LexisNexis; Newsbank, Inc.; Northern Light Technology, Inc.; OCLC Online Computer Library Center, Inc.; ProQuest K-12 Learning Solutions; ProQuest LLC (Ann Arbor). *Indexed:* ATI, BRD, BRI, CBRI, LRI, MASUSE, MusicInd, NewsAb, NumL, RI-1. *Aud.:* Ga.

This paper, started as an alternative to commercial newspapers, has had the freedom to examine its subjects in depth and has done that very well for almost a century. It does feature the regular topical sections that one would expect to find in a daily newspaper, and these generally carry out the mission of exploring further than do most other papers. It avoids sensational subjects, so there's no parade of celebrities heading off to rehab, but that does mean that one's appetite for popular culture may need to be satisfied elsewhere. Libraries with small budgets that can afford only one newspaper to bring national and international scope to their readers could look to this inexpensive subscription. The web site, at www.csmonitor.com, was an early adopter of features such as RSS feeds; the need to show a profit has resulted in the addition of advertising. There is a fee-based historic archive for articles from 1908 to 1980; after that, article content is apparently free (although an easily findable, clear statement about that would be appreciated).

4726. *Financial Times (North American Edition).* [ISSN: 0884-6782] 1985. d. Mon.-Sat. USD 298 domestic; CND 498 Canada. Ed(s): Lionel Barber. The Financial Times Inc., 1330 Ave of the Americas, New York, NY 10019; http://www.ft.com. Illus., adv. Circ: 107973. CD-ROM: Chadwyck-Healey Inc. Microform: RPI. Online: Gale; OCLC Online Computer Library Center, Inc. *Indexed:* ChemAb. *Aud.:* Ga.

For readers who are looking for a tighter focus on business news than is found in the more all-encompassing *Wall Street Journal,* the *Financial Times* may be preferred. It is what it claims to be, a "world business newspaper," with a global network and bureaus in the money capitals of the world. In 2007 the redesign of the print version was unveiled, with new typeface and changed layout that increases space for news content in some categories, but no reduction in paper size. Noteworthy are the special reports, over 200 yearly, which give lengthier treatment to selected topics and rival *The Economist* for depth. For those of us who associate the world of finance with a somewhat hidebound attitude of tight control, the fluid, multifaceted web site, www.ft.com, comes as a surprise. It exploits all current web functions, including the more "2.0" features such as blogging and discussion forums. Archived material, special reports, and financial data are available to subscribers.

4727. *The Globe and Mail.* Formed by the 1936 merger of: *Globe (Toronto); Mail and Empire;* Which was formerly (until 1929): *Daily Mail and Empire;* Which was formed by the 1895 merger of: *Empire; Toronto Daily Mail;* Which was formerly (1872-1880): *Mail (Toronto).* [ISSN: 0319-0714] 1844. d. Mon.-Sat. CND 310.92. Ed(s): Edward Greenspon. Globe and Mail Publishing, 444 Front St W, Toronto, ON M5V 2S9, Canada; http://www.globeandmail.com. Illus., adv. Circ: 381783 Paid. Microform: PQC. Online: Gale; LexisNexis. *Indexed:* BRI, CBCARef, CBRI, CPerI. *Bk. rev.:* Number and length vary. *Aud.:* Ga.

The Globe and Mail is a nationally distributed, Toronto-based newspaper with the largest circulation in Canada. This results in the macro view that one would expect. The paper has the wherewithal for good provincial, national, and international reportage, but it sometimes leaves one wanting supplemental news sources about Toronto itself. Politics and business coverage are particularly thorough, including the "Report on Business" magazine. The web site features considerable multimedia, unsurprising considering *The Globe and Mail* is a piece of CTVglobemedia. Archives only go back to January 2000, with some content subscriber-only or fee-based.

4728. *The Guardian.* Formerly (until 1959): *Manchester Guardian.* [ISSN: 0261-3077] 1821. d. Mon.-Sat. GBP 10.79 per month in British Isles. Ed(s): Alan Rusbridger. Guardian Newspapers Ltd., 164 Deansgate, Guardian Newspapers Ltd, Manchester, M60 2RR, United Kingdom; http://www.guardian.co.uk. Illus., adv. Circ: 378516. CD-ROM: Chadwyck-Healey Inc. Microform: PQC. Online: LexisNexis; Newsbank, Inc.; ProQuest K-12 Learning Solutions; ProQuest LLC (Ann Arbor). *Indexed:* AmHI, BAS, BrHumI, NewsAb, RILM. *Bk. rev.:* Number and length vary. *Aud.:* Ga.

The Guardian and the related Sundays-only *Observer* provide an opportunity to get news and opinion with the rough edges unsmoothed. Independently financed through the Scott Trust, they are not overseen by a larger corporate parent watching the bottom line as so many contemporary news sources are, and this publication can make one wonder what the others are glossing over or leaving out entirely. Topics of the greatest importance such as politics and economic policy receive scrutiny from uncompromising writers who won't "go along to get along." The paper is an award-winner with high standards and excellent coverage of the United Kingdom and the world, and both print and web versions have minimal space given over to consumerism. Most content is freely available through the *GuardianUnlimited* web site, www.guardian.co.uk, with byproducts such as digital versions of the print papers available by subscription. Free archives for articles published since 1999.

4729. *Los Angeles Times.* Formerly: *Los Angeles Daily Times.* [ISSN: 0458-3035] 1886. d. USD 0.50 newsstand/cover; USD 1.50 newsstand/ cover. Ed(s): Dean Baquet. Times Mirror Company, Times Mirror Square, Los Angeles, CA 90053; letters@news.latimes.com. Circ: 955211. *Indexed:* CINAHL. *Bk. rev.:* Number and length vary. *Aud.:* Ga.

Knowing that a paper is locally owned can make a huge difference for the careful reader. For *The Los Angeles Times,* when the powerful Chandler family owned it, one had a much better sense of how it shaped and reflected the character of Los Angeles. Like it or not, it was a very establishment organ with deep roots and vast influence. Since the Tribune chain bought it in 2000, it has joined that category of papers that seem like they could come from just about any major American city. Fourteen special community sections were axed. More recently, corporate reaction to loss of profits resulted in April 2007 layoffs, including 70 people from the newsroom. Stories with larger scope are still well represented, and excellent work by the remaining reporting staff continues. It remains the single most important newspaper for the southwestern United States, but libraries offering it will want to supplement it with other titles that reflect the diversity of their communities. The web site, www.latimes.com, has text-only archives available from January 1985, with the latest week free; 1881–1984 are article image files.

4730. *The Miami Herald.* [ISSN: 0898-865X] 1910. d. USD 0.35 newsstand/cover; USD 1 newsstand/cover Sun.; USD 90.69. Ed(s): Anders Gyllenhaal, Dave Wilson. Circ: 280496 Paid. Online: Newsbank, Inc. *Aud.:* Ga.

Readers value *The Miami Herald* as the principal news source from a very interesting spot, where North American, Caribbean, and Latin American cultures come together. It responded to demographic change early on by teaming up with a sister newspaper, *El Nuevo Herald,* for South Florida's large Spanish-speaking population. *El Nuevo* is no longer just a version of the English-language paper, but a very different animal with its own staff and editorial choices. The *Herald* is home to humorist Dave Barry and the recipient of many awards. The latest Pulitzer went to Debbie Cenziper in 2007, for her expose on the mismanagement of a housing agency. Their overstuffed web site at www.miamiherald.com offers a wealth of information, if you can navigate it; this is partially due to the increasingly common partnership between newspapers and other media outlets. The fee-based archives date from 1982 forward.

4731. *The New York Times.* Formerly (until 1857): *New-York Daily Times.* [ISSN: 0362-4331] 1851. d. USD 425.80; USD 218.80 Mon.-Fri.; USD 220.80 Sat.-Sun. Ed(s): Bill Keller, Gail Collins. New York Times Company, 229 W 43rd St, New York, NY 10036; 1-800@nytimes.com. Illus., adv. Circ: 1118565. CD-ROM: ProQuest LLC (Ann Arbor). Microform: PQC. Online: The Dialog Corporation; Gale; LexisNexis; Newsbank, Inc.; OCLC Online Computer Library Center, Inc.; ProQuest LLC (Ann Arbor). *Indexed:* Agr, BLI, BPI, BRD, BRI, BiolDig, CBRI, CWI, ChemAb, EnvAb, FLI, FutSurv, GSI, IIMP, IIPA, LRI, MRD, MicrocompInd, MusicInd, NewsAb, PRA, RGPR, RI-1, RILM. *Bk. rev.:* Number and length vary. *Aud.:* Ga.

For libraries that can subscribe to only one national newspaper, this is the obvious choice. Through comprehensive coverage of national and international events (with state and local news remaining strong in New York editions), *The New York Times* simply provides far more information than a competitor like *USA Today.* The writing and editing are regularly excellent; rarely does one finish reading a *NYT* article with relevant questions left unanswered. Trust in its credibility is still high despite the few high-profile cases of reporters who fictionalized their work. (One longstanding critique that is harder to shake off is that the management and some editors and reporters are too clubby with the influential people that the *Times* covers.) The web site at www.nytimes.com is a case study of a news publisher's need to incorporate new platforms, and functions while trying to satisfy traditionalists. At this writing the "Times Reader" version is just out, and it compares with the electronic edition already in place in that it adjusts to screen size (including tablets) and is closer in other ways to the experience of reading the print version. The fee-based searchable archives are available from 1851 forward in a variety of arrangements.

4732. *San Francisco Chronicle.* 1865. d. USD 0.25 newsstand/cover; USD 1 newsstand/cover Sun.; USD 15.80 subscr - home delivery per month. Ed(s): Narda Zacchino, Kenn Altine. Circ: 512000 Paid. *Indexed:* BRI. *Bk. rev.:* Number and length vary. *Aud.:* Ga.

The print *San Francisco Chronicle* has been showing signs of an identity crisis, trying to hold on to traditional newspaper readers while appealing to the younger demographic. Attempts have included emphasizing local relevance (resulting in mistakes like banner headlines that revealed that people do cheat on their bus fares) and hiring arts critics who are 99 percent attitude and one percent criticism. But it's still worthwhile because it continues to be very much of its place in a way that eludes large metropolitan dailies of a more "absentee" corporate provenance. And what a weird place that can be: the *Chron* faces covering the very culturally diverse San Francisco Bay Area. Cost-cutting will only hurt that effort—layoffs of up to 25 percent were set for 2007 (resulting in the resignation of managing editor Robert Rosenthal). The web site for the paper and its media partners is at www.sfgate.com. Free archives are available from 1995 forward.

4733. *Seattle Times.* [ISSN: 0745-9696] 1896. d. USD 0.25 newsstand/ cover; USD 1.50 newsstand/cover Sun.; USD 3.55 subscr - carrier delivery per week. Ed(s): Michael Fancher, Stanley Farrar. Blethen Co., 1120 John St, Seattle, WA 98109; opinion@seattletimes.com. Adv. Circ: 215000 Paid. *Indexed:* RILM. *Aud.:* Ga.

The Seattle Times edges out *The Seattle Post-Intelligencer* as the most important news source in the Pacific Northwest because it tends to have more complete local and regional coverage, while both papers pull in most of their national and international content from outside news services. In April 2007, a settlement was reached regarding the joint operating agreement between the two titles, buying the *PI* nine more years of life. Both papers face the same problem that others do in regions known for high-tech industry and younger workforces: a higher concentration of people likely to find their news digitally. Their web sites (seattletimes.nwsource.com/html/home and seattlepi.nwsource.com), have searchable archives with recent years of free content.

4734. *The Sun.* [ISSN: 1930-8965] 1837. d. USD 0.50 newsstand/cover; USD 1.66 Sun.; USD 14.76 subscr - carrier delivery per month. Ed(s): Anthony Barbieri, Sheila McCauley. Circ: 321165 Paid. *Bk. rev.:* Number and length vary. *Aud.:* Ga.

The *Baltimore Sun* has a well-deserved reputation for attracting top talent, and the quality of the reporting still reflects it. It's recommended here for that reason, although regional competition with the *Washington Post* has prompted cost-cutting measures, including staff reduction since 2000, when the paper became part of the *Tribune* chain. In 2002, a cable television executive lacking a journalism background took over as publisher, which raised some eyebrows among the paper's devotees. The paper's history of award-winning reporting includes a Pulitzer for beat reporting in 2003 and another beat reporting award from the Education Writers of America in 2004. The web site at www.baltimore-sun.com includes an archive dating back to 1990; the latest two weeks are free.

4735. The Times. Formerly (until 1788): *Daily Universal Register.* [ISSN: 0140-0460] 1785. d. Mon.-Sat. GBP 550 domestic; GBP 770 in Europe; GBP 500 United States. Times Newspapers Ltd., 1 Pennington St, London, E98 1ST, United Kingdom; http://www.thetimes.co.uk/. Illus., index, adv. Circ: 619682. CD-ROM: Chadwyck-Healey Inc. Microform: RPI. Online: Gale; LexisNexis; ProQuest LLC (Ann Arbor). *Indexed:* BrHumI, BrTechI, LRI, RILM. *Bk. rev.:* Number and length vary. *Aud.:* Ga, Ac.

The Times—or *The London Times* as it is sometimes referred to—is arguably the world's most famous newspaper. Published uninterruptedly since 1785, it is the standard source for British political, legal, business, cultural, and social news. *The Sunday Times* is equally well known for its in-depth, award-winning news coverage and commentary, as well as its literary section. The web site, www.timesonline.co.uk, has a wonderfully clear, user-friendly layout. Reader comments are solicited frequently. Highly recommended for all libraries that cover international news; indispensable for research libraries and large public libraries. Online archives are available, with much recent content free.

4736. Wall Street Journal (Eastern Edition). Supersedes (in 1959): *Wall Street Journal.* [ISSN: 0099-9660] 1889. d. Mon.-Fri. USD 99 combined subscription print & online edition; USD 1 newsstand/cover. Ed(s): Paul E. Steiger, Bill Grueskin. Dow Jones & Company, 200 Liberty St, New York, NY 10281; wsj.service@dowjones.com; http://www.wsj.com. Illus., adv. Circ: 1857050 Paid. Online: Factiva, Inc.; OCLC Online Computer Library Center, Inc.; ProQuest K-12 Learning Solutions; ProQuest LLC (Ann Arbor). *Indexed:* ABIn, ATI, Agr, BLI, BPI, BRI, CBRI, CWI, ChemAb, FutSurv, GardL, LogistBibl, MCR, NewsAb, PAIS, RI-1. *Aud.:* Ga.

The expansion of the *Wall Street Journal*'s scope from finance to general news is linked to its growth into a mass-circulation newspaper. It's clear that there was a market for it; the *WSJ* is the second-best-selling newspaper in the United States, after *USA Today*. The financial data and reportage are still top priority, of course, but they share space with national and international events. A print subscription will be a necessity for any library with patrons who follow the markets, especially older readers who aren't used to going online for the latest news and numbers. It revamped its format to shrink the size of the paper, but not in a way that will ruffle any feathers. In 2007 it received staff Pulitzers for public service and international reporting. The web site is at online.wsj.com/public/us, but it is one of the most restrictive titles in print and web, requiring subscription for much current and archival material.

4737. The Washington Post. [ISSN: 0190-8286] 1877. d. USD 0.35 newsstand/cover; USD 1.50 newsstand/cover Sun.; USD 187.20 subscr - home delivery. Ed(s): Steve Coll, Leonard Downie, Jr. Washington Post Co., 1150 15th St, NW, Washington, DC 20071. Circ: 732872. *Indexed:* Agr, IIMP, IIPA. *Bk. rev.:* Number and length vary. *Aud.:* Ga.

The Washington Post is the preeminent newspaper for analysis of federal politics; post-Watergate, the national spotlight on it has never wavered. It's known for aggressive investigative reporting, as well as for being a part of the very power structure it reports on, in the sense that there have been close "inside the Beltway" relationships that outsiders were not privy to. Its opinion pages are, unsurprisingly, very influential. Not a national newspaper in the sense of expanded focus for nationwide distribution, it still has great coverage of issues around the country as well as those at a national and international level, and it has by no means neglected its coverage of the D.C. region. The web site, www.washingtonpost.com, has fee-based archives back to 1877; the most recent two weeks are free.

Commercial Web News Systems

The market in web news systems changes very rapidly: most news-producing vendors offer some kind of electronic option, with some text available immediately online. News files are often incorporated into other electronic products, too, and recent years have seen small companies engulfed by larger publishers and information aggregators. The good news is that these online infobases give researchers ready access to sources previously available to only the most determined and mobile scholars. Some sources offer added value by including news feeds from newswires, but free news sources that are now established on the web are superseding the necessity of incorporating such feeds.

Accessible Archives. Accessible Archives Inc., 697 Sugartown Rd., Malvern, PA 19355. www.accessible.com. Provides full-text primary source materials from eighteenth- and nineteenth-century newspapers and magazines, through databases such as *The Pennsylvania Gazette 1728–1800, The Civil War: A Newspaper Perspective, African American Newspapers: The 19th Century,* and *Godey's Lady's Book.*

Alt-Press Watch. ProQuest, 300 North Zeeb Rd., P.O. Box 1346, Ann Arbor, MI 48106-1346. www.il.proquest.com. The description of this database calls its sources "the alternative and independent press," which may still leave one wondering. Scanning the title list, a mix of newspapers and magazines, is the best method for getting it. Some examples: *The Advocate, Auto-Free Times, Creative Loafing* (in four Southern cities), *Industrial Worker, Miami New Times, SF Weekly, Youth Today.*

Canadian Business & Current Affairs (CBCA). ProQuest Information and Learning, 300 North Zeeb Rd., P.O. Box 1346, Ann Arbor, MI 48106-1346. www.il.proquest.com. Full text for over 300 serials, indexing for over 700, *CBCA* covers *The Globe and Mail* and other major Canadian papers. The successor to *Canadian Index.* A related ProQuest product, *Paper of Record,* is an online historic newspaper archive for Canada, with some source material dating back as far as 1752.

Custom Newspapers. Infotrac/Gale/Thomson, 27500 Drake Rd., Farmington Hills, MI 48331. www.gale.com. This product replaces *British Newspaper Index* and goes well beyond it. Titles can be chosen from an extensive list of British and American papers. The earliest start date, which applies to many entries on the *Custom Newspapers* source list, is January 1996. Allows setting up a customized source list and search parameters, letting users create their own electronic edition.

Ethnic NewsWatch. ProQuest Information and Learning, 300 North Zeeb Road, P.O. Box 1346, Ann Arbor, MI 48106-1346. www.il.proquest.com. *Ethnic NewsWatch* is a full-text database of over 200 newspapers and magazines "of the ethnic, minority and native press," in English and Spanish. The search interface is available in Spanish as well as English. Sources range from small to relatively large circulation publications, with titles like the *New York Amsterdam News,* the *Navajo Times,* the *Armenian Reporter, El Sol de Texas,* and *AsianWeek.*

Factiva. Dow Jones Reuters Business Interactive Ltd., 105 Madison Ave., 10th floor, New York, NY 10016. www.factiva.com. Succeeds *Dow Jones Interactive. Factiva* is a large full-text database with a focus on business research, drawing upon newspapers, newswires, trade journals, newsletters, magazines, and transcripts. A simple company name search can yield a very complete picture of relevant recent events.

FACTS.com. Facts on File News Services, 512 Seventh Ave., 22nd floor, New York, NY 10018. www.facts.com/online-fdc.htm. This five-part reference suite includes the *Facts on File World News Digest,* which features reworked news source material. The format is useful in environments where prepackaged topic searches are appropriate; not the place to go for large databases of verbatim news articles. Other files in the suite are almanacs, selected current issues, or science-oriented.

Global NewsBank. NewsBank Inc., 5020 Tamiami Trail N., Suite 110, Naples, FL 34103. www.newsbank.com. *Global NewsBank* is an online information system that offers grouped, topic-oriented links that are helpful for the less-experienced researcher. The worldwide resources include transcribed broadcasts. Excellent for students researching the varying perspectives on international issues.

Historical Newspapers. ProQuest, 300 North Zeeb Rd., P.O. Box 1346, Ann Arbor, MI 48106-1346. www.proquestcompany.com. *Historical Newspapers Online* contains four major historical resources: *Palmer's Index to the Times,* covering the period from 1790 to 1905 in *The Times*; *The Official Index to the Times*, which takes the coverage forward from 1906 to 1980; *The Historical Index to the New York Times*, which covers *The New York Times* from 1851 to September 1922; *Palmer's Full Text Online 1785–1870*, providing access to the full-text articles referenced in *Palmer's Index to the Times*.

LEXIS-NEXIS Academic Universe. Reed Elsevier plc, 25 Victoria St., London SW1H 0EX, UK. www.lexis-nexis.com. *LexisNexis Academic Universe* is the simplified, user-friendly package derived from the huge Lexis-Nexis database of news text. Full text from almost all major U.S. newspapers is here, with the notable exception being the *Wall Street Journal*'s abstracts only. The database provides news, financial, medical, and legal text from newspapers, broadcasts, wire services, government documents, and other categories. Images and graphics are not included. Of (probably long-term) interest is the 2003 addition of translated transcripts from *Al-Jazeera*. International resources in Dutch, French, German, Italian, Portuguese, and Spanish are also included.

NewsBank Full-Text Newspapers; NewsBank Libraries can customize a subscription to create a list of local titles. The community-level information can be a valuable resource for public libraries, and is often under the radar screen of other aggregators with a more macro level of coverage.

Newspaper Source. EBSCO Publishing, 10 Estes St., Ipswich, MA 01938. www.epnet.com. The patchwork quilt of full text, indexing, and abstracting in this online source (also available on CD-ROM) can be valuable, but pay close attention to coverage details. *The Christian Science Monitor* is here cover-to-cover back to January 1995, but with other titles there's partial coverage with too many exceptions to list.

World News Connection. National Technical Information Service, U.S. Department of Commerce, Springfield, VA 22161. http://wnc.fedworld.gov/description.html. Distributed by the National Technical Information Service, U.S. Department of Commerce, *WNC* provides web access to full-text, English translations of current non-U.S. media sources beginning in 1996. A derivative of intelligence-gathering efforts begun over 60 years ago, there are sources here that you won't find transcribed in other full-text databases, such as local radio broadcasts of government statements. This is the online continuation of the *FBIS* and *JPRS* index and content microform systems.

■ NUMISMATICS

David Van de Streek, Library Director, York Campus, Penn State University, Lee R. Glatfelter Library, 1031 Edgecomb Ave., York, PA 17403; SDV1@PSU.EDU

Introduction

Numismatics is commonly thought of as coin collecting, but is more broadly the study and collecting of coins, paper money, tokens, medals, and associated areas. Coin collecting is easily the largest segment of numismatics and presently is riding a very large wave of collector interest and market activity. Estimates are that within the United States many millions of people are involved in some fashion with numismatics.

Even with this wide interest, however, there exists only a handful of numismatic publications that broadly address the interests and needs of most collectors. Numerous other publications are available in the genre, but most are highly specialized in focus and have limited readership potential, limiting their usefulness for library collections. Of the periodicals listed in this section, six (*CoinWorld, Coinage, Coins, Numismatist, Numismatic News, World Coin News*) have broad enough coverage that they can be thought of as general numismatic resources, even though a high proportion of their material is specifically about coins. Each contains enough about paper money, tokens, and some of the very specialized areas of numismatics that these will be useful to a wide audience of collectors and specialists.

Numismatic periodicals are liberally filled with dealer advertising and inventory lists, which should not be used as a yardstick to guage the quality of the publication. To most readers this can be useful and interesting information, as they may refer to these ads and listings either to make purchases or to help them approximate the value of their own collections.

Librarians looking for one representative numismatic periodical should strongly consider *Coin World*. This weekly has long been highly respected within the field, and its high circulation is certainly an indicator of its wide acceptance and authority within numismatics.

Basic Periodicals

Hs: *Coins;* Ga: *Coin World, Coinage, Coins, Numismatist;*

Basic Abstracts and Indexes

Numismatic Literature.

4738. ***A N A Journal: advanced studies in numismatics.*** [ISSN: 1930-3270] 2006. q. Members, USD 65.95; Non-members, USD 85.98; USD 21.95 per issue. American Numismatic Association, 818 N Cascade Ave, Colorado Springs, CO 80903-3279; http://www.money.org. Refereed. *Aud.:* Ga, Ac.

Newly launched as a companion to the American Numismatic Association's signature publication *Numismatist*, this is intended as a scholarly resource that examines numismatics as it interrelates with the broader spheres of "culture, art, science, and history." Its material reaches into all areas of numismatics, including international coinage and that of antiquity. Peer-reviewed articles are contributed by notable numismatists, and are thorough, comprehensive, well written, and well researched. These are largely historical overviews of a numismatic topic, typically set within a broader cultural and fiscal context, illustrating the interplay of money and such things as economic issues, banking history, and public opinion. This is tastefully done, with nice graphics, and has the promise of providing a scholarly approach to numismatics while still being interesting and accessible to collectors. This is a good fit for research-oriented collections.

4739. ***Bank Note Reporter: complete monthly guide for paper money collectors.*** [ISSN: 0164-0828] 1973. m. USD 30 domestic; USD 45.98 Canada; USD 55.98 elsewhere. Ed(s): Dave Harper. Krause Publications, Inc., 700 E State St, Iola, WI 54990-0001; info@krause.com; http://www.krause.com. Illus., adv. Sample. Circ: 8072 Paid and free. Vol. ends: Dec. *Indexed:* NumL. *Bk. rev.:* Occasional, 200-400 words. *Aud.:* Ga, Sa.

This tabloid-sized newspaper broadly covers the collecting of paper money and related items, such as stock certificates and military payment coupons. Focusing mainly on U.S. currency, this provides both current information about the hobby and the collector's market, as well as interesting and informative feature material. Features typically are about a specific piece of currency or a group of related currencies, and usually provide historical overviews of monetary events and other significant events relating to that currency. A standard feature is a price guide that represents approximate retail prices for most U.S. paper money issues. The web site has one article from the current issue and several archived ones from recent issues. Subcribers have access to online issues. This is a very complete resource for paper money collectors.

4740. ***Coin Prices.*** [ISSN: 0010-0412] 1967. bi-m. USD 18.98 domestic; USD 29.98 foreign; USD 4.25 per issue. Ed(s): Bob Van Ryzin. Krause Publications, Inc., 700 E State St, Iola, WI 54990-0001; info@krause.com; http://www.krause.com. Illus., adv. Sample. Circ: 56611 Paid and free. Microform: MIM; PMC; PQC. *Aud.:* Ga.

Virtually the entire content of this magazine is a price guide for all regularly issued United States coins, dating 1793 to the present. Prices reflect an average retail cost, approximating what a buyer would pay to acquire a coin. Each listed coin has a range of prices that correspond with selected quality grades for that coin, spanning heavily circulated to uncirculated. Rotating issues of the magazine also have an additional pricing section for areas of numismatics in lesser demand, such as Mexican and Canadian coinage. As a gauge for frequently changing market conditions, this can be a useful collector tool. Print subscribers also have access to an online version of this price guide.

4741. ***Coin World.*** Formerly: *Numismatic Scrapbook*. [ISSN: 0010-0447] 1960. w. Tue. USD 41.95 domestic; USD 119.95 Canada; USD 176.95 elsewhere. Ed(s): Beth Deisher. Amos Press Inc., P O Box 29, Sidney,

OH 45365; cweditor@amospress.com; http://www.amospress.com. Illus., adv. Sample. Circ: 87000. Vol. ends: Dec. Microform: PQC. *Indexed:* BRI, NumL. *Bk. rev.:* 1-3, 200-400 words. *Aud.:* Hs, Ga.

This is one of the most highly respected and widely read of all numismatic publications. A weekly, tabloid-sized newspaper, it covers a broad range of numismatic interests and topics, mixing current news items with feature material. Regular articles and contributed features are often written by specialists or acknowledged experts in that field, most of whom are highly regarded within numismatics. Coverage extends to virtually all areas of numismatics, including international coinage, and includes numerous items that can be very useful for collectors in enhancing their knowledge and collecting skills. The web site has a table of contents listing of the most current issue, as well as a keyword searchable archive of full-text articles since 2001. Subcriptions may be bundled with *Coin World's Coin Values*. This is an informative, instructional, and comprehensive publication, with quality features and departments, and it should be a primary resource for most libraries.

4742. *Coin World's Coin Values.* [ISSN: 1545-5319] 2003. m. USD 29.95 domestic; USD 44.95 Canada; USD 59.95 elsewhere. Ed(s): Beth Deisher. Amos Press Inc., P O Box 29, Sidney, OH 45365; http://www.amospress.com. Adv. *Aud.:* Ga.

This is a highly useful publication for collectors of U.S. coinage, serving primarily as a price guide and additionally as a collector's resource. The price guide is the most thorough and most comprehensive one available to collectors, with listings for every regularly issued U.S. coin throughout a very expansive range of grading levels. As part of its feature material, a standout continuing series on coin grading examines each different coin denomination and minting style, providing detailed descriptions and illustrative photos of successive grading levels from heavily worn examples through strictly uncirculated ones. Regular columns address hot and cold areas of the coin market plus those that are affordable and collectible. Subscribers have access to an online version of the price guide. This tastefully done, high-quality publication may be bundled with a subscription to *Coin World*.

4743. *Coin World's Paper Money Values.* [ISSN: 1556-0317] 2005. bi-m. USD 19.97 domestic; USD 27.47 Canada; USD 34.97 elsewhere. Ed(s): Beth Deisher. Amos Press Inc., P O Box 29, Sidney, OH 45365; http://www.amospress.com. Adv. *Aud.:* Ga.

A recently launched publication, this is both a very comprehensive pricing resource for every U.S. currency issue since 1861, as well as being a source of interesting feature material about paper money. The price guide is the most expansive one commonly available and lists approximate retail costs for several levels of grading quality for each specific money issue. Feature material is contributed by notables in the field, focusing mostly on design elements or motifs in printed money, as well as the history or usage of specific currency issues. This is a quality production, with excellent color plates and graphics, and promises to be a reliable pricing guide for paper money enthusiasts.

4744. *Coinage.* [ISSN: 0010-0455] 1964. m. USD 24; USD 4.99 per issue. Ed(s): Marcy Gibbel, Ed Reiter. Miller Magazines, Inc, 290 Maple Ct, # 232, Ventura, CA 93003-3517. Illus., adv. Sample. Circ: 150000 Paid. Vol. ends: Dec. Microform: PQC. *Indexed:* NumL. *Aud.:* Ga.

This is a good general-interest magazine that covers a wide variety of numismatic topics. Feature articles focus most often on currently significant numismatic topics, but also range from historically based material to informative items on both collecting and the coin market. An interesting regular feature is "Coin Capsule," which highlights the coinage or significant numismatic events of a random year, along with the perspective of that year's noteworthy historical, political, and cultural events. The magazine has good writing, is generally well produced, and has excellent close-up color photos of coins and paper money. The magazine's web site has a table of contents listing for the current issue, but has no archive and no full-text material. Because its general content and broad coverage can appeal to both beginning and experienced collectors, this should be considered as part of a basic collection.

4745. *CoinLink.com: numismatic news and resources.* 1995. irreg. CoinLink, PO Box 916909, Longwood, FL 32791-6909. *Aud.:* Ga.

This is an excellent source of current information that addresses both collecting and marketplace issues in numismatics. Updated daily, this offers a very large representative selection of news articles and opinion pieces culled from a variety of newswires and numismatic publications. Coverage is expansive, with material present for virtually every interest sector within numismatics. An extensive archive of news items and articles is available, aggregated monthly, but it is not searchable, making it not as useful as it could potentially be. The site has numerous links to other collector resources, both informational and commercial. This is a very comprehensive and useful site for almost anyone having an interest in numismatics. URL: www.coinlink.com.

4746. *Coins.* [ISSN: 0010-0471] 1955. m. USD 28.98 combined subscription domestic print& online eds.; USD 4.99 per issue. Ed(s): Bob Van Ryzin. Krause Publications, Inc., 700 E State St, Iola, WI 54990-0001; info@krause.com; http://www.krause.com. Illus., adv. Sample. Circ: 52660 Paid and free. Vol. ends: Dec. Microform: PMC; PQC. *Indexed:* NumL. *Bk. rev.:* Occasional, 600-800 words. *Aud.:* Hs, Ga.

This general-interest magazine is one of the standards in the field, covering most areas of numismatics with enough breadth to appeal to most collectors. Each issue is usually built around a specific collecting theme, such as silver dollars, and has four to six lengthy feature articles devoted to that topic. It is then rounded out with additional features, news items, and regularly appearing columns. A regular feature is a price guide to retail coin values, but this is less comprehensive than those in other sources, listing only the most frequently traded U.S. coins. It also has a very thorough paper money price guide. One detracting element of the publication is its use of newsprint-quality paper and black-and-white graphics in two-thirds of the magazine. The web site has one full-text article from the most recent issue and a few others from recent issues. Print subscribers are also able to access online content. This magazine can be used either as part of a basic collection or as a complement to one.

4747. *Numismatic News: the complete information source for coin collectors.* [ISSN: 0029-604X] 1952. w. USD 24.99 domestic; USD 151.98 foreign. Ed(s): David Kranz, David Harper. Krause Publications, Inc., 700 E State St, Iola, WI 54990-0001; info@krause.com; http://www.krause.com. Illus., adv. Sample. Circ: 34392 Paid and free. Vol. ends: Dec. Microform: PMC; PQC. *Indexed:* NumL. *Bk. rev.:* Occasional, 100-300 words. *Aud.:* Ga.

A tabloid-sized newsweekly that broadly covers the major areas of numismatics, this is primarily a source of current news and events, often with a focus on how these affect collectors or conditions within the coin market. Its features and regular columns are a mix of general interest and historical pieces, along with those aimed at improving collector knowledge. These sometimes feature lesser known and less popular areas of collecting, which can serve as good introductions to those fields. This has a monthly pull-out supplement, a price guide that lists approximate retail prices for all but a few U.S. coins in their respective grading levels of quality. The web site has one full-text article from the most recent issue, plus many others from recent issues. Subscribers have access to online issues of the publication.

4748. *Numismatist: for collectors of coins, medals, tokens and paper money.* Incorporates (1987-1994): *First Strike;* (1951-1981): *A N A Club Bulletin.* [ISSN: 0029-6090] 1888. m. Non-members, USD 35; USD 5 per issue. Ed(s): Barbara J Gregory. American Numismatic Association, 818 N Cascade Ave, Colorado Springs, CO 80903-3279; http://www.money.org. Illus., index, adv. Sample. Circ: 30000 Controlled. Vol. ends: Dec. *Indexed:* ABS&EES, NumL. *Bk. rev.:* 1-3, 50-200 words. *Aud.:* Ga, Ac.

This is the membership publication of the American Numismatic Association, which is the premier collecting and leadership society in American numismatics. The magazine is the oldest continuously published magazine in the field and is a wide-ranging resource that combines news and informational articles with comprehensive feature material. Articles and feature material are consistently well written, with many being contributed by some of the most knowledgeable and significant figures in numismatics. Its content is usually interesting and informative, and can touch on almost any numismatic topic, making this potentially interesting to a wide swath of collectors. The web site has a table of contents, events calendar, and several full-text articles from the most recent issue, as well as from each issue of the last several years. This is a very inclusive publication that should be considered as a part of almost any basic collection.

4749. *Paper Money: official journal of The Society of Paper Money Collectors.* [ISSN: 0031-1162] 1962. bi-m. USD 6 per issue. Ed(s): Fred Reed. Society of Paper Money Collectors, Inc., PO Box 117060, Carrollton, TX 75011. Illus., index, adv. Sample. Circ: 2500. Vol. ends: Nov/Dec. *Indexed:* NumL. *Bk. rev.:* 1, 250 words. *Aud.:* Ga, Sa.

This is the membership journal of the Society of Paper Money Collectors, which, in addition to its member news, provides often lengthy articles about all forms of paper money and fiscal paper. Feature articles are primarily historical treatments of monetary events or specific issues of money, and these are typically set in a broader framework that includes information about national monetary policies and specific banks or other financial institutions. Some issues of the magazine are topically oriented, with all feature material focusing on specific currency, such as Civil War money. Articles are frequently contributed by acknowledged paper money experts, adding to the authority of the publication. Generally scholarly in approach, the overall appeal and usefulness of this journal has been enhanced both by an increased page count and also by recent stylistic changes. The web site has a table of contents list for the current issue and more than two years of prior issues, but no full-text material is available. This should have strong appeal for readers interested in the historical context of paper money, and may be useful in the broader arena of history or American Studies as well.

4750. *World Coin News.* [ISSN: 0145-9090] 1973. m. USD 25.99 domestic; USD 41.99 Canada; USD 53.99 elsewhere. Ed(s): Dave Harper. Krause Publications, Inc., 700 E State St, Iola, WI 54990-0001; info@krause.com; http://www.krause.com. Illus., adv. Sample. Circ: 8729 Paid and free. Vol. ends: Dec. Microform: PMC. *Indexed:* NumL. *Aud.:* Ga.

This is the only comprehensive numismatic publication that deals exclusively with international coinage. A tabloid-sized newspaper, it mixes current news articles with feature material on coins and occasionally paper money. Feature material is usually informative, often including the historical or political context of the described coins or numismatic events. Some of its material is also useful in helping collectors develop or refine their collecting knowledge and skills. The web site has one full-text article from the most recent issue plus a few archived articles. Print subscribers also have access to online issues of the publication. Collecting world coinage is not nearly as popular as collecting U.S. coinage, limiting the potential audience for this publication, but for those collecting world coins, this is still a useful periodical that can serve as a nice supplement for core numismatic titles.

■ NURSING

See also Health Care Administration; and Medicine sections.

Laura Burkhart, MLIS, University of Pittsburgh; Redwood City, CA 94062

Introduction

The titles in this section have been chosen for their ability to cover a broad spectrum of areas related to nursing. The included titles contain professional and practical information for nurses, and represent areas of nursing education, research, and theory. An attempt has also been made to provide information relevant to various types of nurses, including nurse practitioners, licensed practical nurses, and registered nurses. No attempt has been made in this section to cover nursing at the level of medical specialty. The titles are almost wholly geared to special and academic libraries, suitable for the specific audience this section supports.

Basic Periodicals

Hs: *Imprint;* Ac: *American Journal of Nursing, International Nursing Review;* Sa: *Nurse Practitioner, Nursing, R N.*

Basic Abstracts and Indexes

Cumulative Index to Nursing and Allied Health Literature.

4751. *American Journal of Nursing.* [ISSN: 0002-936X] 1900. m. USD 234.95 (Individuals, USD 34.90). Ed(s): Diana J Mason. Lippincott Williams & Wilkins, 333 7th Ave, 19th Fl, New York, NY 10001; custserv@lww.com; http://www.lww.com. Illus., index, adv. Sample. Refereed. Circ: 144000 Paid. Vol. ends: Dec. CD-ROM: Ovid Technologies, Inc. Microform: PMC; PQC. Online: EBSCO Publishing, EBSCO Host; OCLC Online Computer Library Center, Inc.; Ovid Technologies, Inc.; SwetsWise Online Content. *Indexed:* ASG, ASSIA, AgeL, BRI, CBRI, CINAHL, ChemAb, ECER, GSI, H&SSA, IMFL, MCR, PAIS, SCI, SSCI, SWA, SWR&A. *Bk. rev.:* Number and length vary. *Aud.:* Ac, Sa.

The official journal of the American Nurses Association, *AJN* is a peer-reviewed title that is a must for any nursing library, whether academic or clinical. The articles are clearly written, well illustrated, and fully referenced. Continuing education credits are available in each issue, with online, mail-in, or fax options. Topics related to all areas of nursing are explored, with such regular sections as "Drug Watch," "Health & Safety," and "The Politics of Caring." Recent article topics include care for older adults with dementia, and postpartum depression. Table of contents information is available at http://ajnonline.com.

4752. *Home Healthcare Nurse.* Incorporates (1979-1983): *Nephrology Nurse.* [ISSN: 0884-741X] 1983. m. USD 255 (Individuals, USD 52.95). Ed(s): Tina M Marrelli. Lippincott Williams & Wilkins, 530 Walnut St, Philadelphia, PA 19106-3621; http://www.lww.com. Illus., adv. Sample. Refereed. Circ: 8192 Paid. *Indexed:* AgeL, CINAHL. *Bk. rev.:* Number and length vary. *Aud.:* Sa, Ac.

This is the official journal of the Home Healthcare Nurses Association. It provides access to evidence-based research and professional information through peer-reviewed articles. Departments in each issue include "Clipboard," "Patient Education," and "Commentary." Articles are well referenced and illustrated, and recent topics include end-stage COPD, caring for self-neglecting seniors, and effective communication among healthcare providers. Continuing education credits are available in each issue. This title is recommended for clinical libraries and large academic collections.

4753. *Imprint (New York): the professional magazine of nursing students.* Formerly: *N S N A Newsletter.* [ISSN: 0019-3062] 1968. 5x/yr. USD 36 (Individuals, USD 18). Ed(s): Larisa C Mendez. National Student Nurses' Association, 45 Main St, Ste 606, Brooklyn, NY 11201-1075; nsna@nsna.org; http://www.nsna.org. Illus., index, adv. Sample. Circ: 50000. Vol. ends: Dec/Jan. *Indexed:* CINAHL. *Aud.:* Hs, Ac.

The official publication of the National Student Nurses Association (NSNA), *Imprint* contains articles and information specifically geared to the nursing student. Recent articles feature information on areas of speciality like geriatrics or perioperative nursing, study tips, the first year after qualification, counterfeit medications, and global health issues. NSNA activity information, conference previews, and profiles of working nurses in various fields are also included. Selected full text is available at the *Imprint* web site (www.nsna.org/pubs/periodicals) for current and some previous issues. This title belongs in academic libraries and hospital libraries affiliated with nursing programs.

4754. *International Nursing Review.* Former titles (until 1945): *International Nursing Bulletin; International Nursing Review.* [ISSN: 0020-8132] 1926. q. GBP 163 print & online eds. Ed(s): Dr. Jane Robinson. Blackwell Publishing Ltd., 9600 Garsington Rd, Oxford, OX4 2ZG, United Kingdom; customerservices@blackwellpublishing.com; http://www.blackwellpublishing.com. Illus., adv. Sample. Refereed. Circ: 3500. Vol. ends: Nov/Dec. Microform: PQC. Online: Blackwell Synergy; EBSCO Publishing, EBSCO Host; Gale; IngentaConnect; OCLC Online Computer Library Center, Inc.; OhioLINK; Ovid Technologies, Inc.; SwetsWise Online Content. Reprint: PSC. *Indexed:* ASSIA, ApEcolAb, CINAHL, H&SSA, PsycInfo, SCI, SSCI. *Bk. rev.:* Number and length vary. *Aud.:* Ac, Sa.

This is the official journal of the International Council of Nurses. Each issue contains articles of clinical and professional interest to nurses. The international point of view in the refereed journal provides a unique counterpoint to other nursing titles. Each issue contains the departments "International Perspectives," "Inside View," "Experiences from the Field," and "Original Articles." The departments cover diverse topics, including ethics, patient safety, education, globalization, and technology. Recent articles cover nurses at the forefront of innovation, detection of eating difficulty after stroke, cultural competency and nursing care, and use of traditional healers. Table of contents information is available at the *INR* web site, www.blackwellpublishing.com/ads.asp?ref= 0020-8132&site=1. This title is a fundamental part of any nursing collection.

4755. Journal of Practical Nursing. [ISSN: 0022-3867] 1951. q. USD 25 domestic; USD 40 foreign. Ed(s): Patrick Mahan. National Association for Practical Nurse Education and Service, Inc., PO Box 25647, Alexandria, VA 22313; http://www.napnes.org. Illus., index, adv. Sample. Refereed. Circ: 7000 Paid and controlled. Vol. ends: Dec. Microform: PQC. Online: ProQuest LLC (Ann Arbor). *Indexed:* AgeL, CINAHL. *Aud.:* Ga, Ac, Sa.

This refereed journal speaks to the needs of licensed practical nurses. Each issue provides articles related to the physical and emotional needs of patients, as well as continuing education, educational training programs, and personal experiences. Clinical articles are well referenced and illustrated. Topics covered in recent issues include an examination of infant mortality, students as nursing leaders for the next generation, hand washing in infection control, and reducing stress in patients being relocated to long-term care facilities. *JPN* is a valuable title for academic programs supporting LPNs.

L P N 2006. See Health Professions section.

Men in Nursing. See Health Professions section.

Minority Nurse. See Health Professions section.

4756. The Nurse Practitioner: the American journal of primary health care. [ISSN: 0361-1817] 1975. m. USD 190 (Individuals, USD 55). Ed(s): Jamesetta A Newland. Lippincott Williams & Wilkins, 323 Norristown Rd, Ste 200, Ambler, PA 19002; custserv@lww.com; http://www.lww.com. Illus., index, adv. Sample. Refereed. Circ: 24653. Vol. ends: Dec. Microform: PQC. Online: EBSCO Publishing, EBSCO Host; Northern Light Technology, Inc.; OhioLINK; Ovid Technologies, Inc.; ProQuest LLC (Ann Arbor); SwetsWise Online Content. *Indexed:* AgeL, CINAHL. *Bk. rev.:* Number and length vary. *Aud.:* Ac, Sa.

Nurse practitioners are the focus of this peer-reviewed title intended to present cutting-edge professional information. Articles provide access to current clinical information in a practical and easy-to-understand manner. References and photographs, illustrations, and charts and tables are included. Continuing education opportunities are available in each issue. "Medication Update" and "Literature Review" are two recurring departments, with the reviews covering several areas of practice in each issue. This is an excellent title for both academic and special libraries with clinical collections.

4757. Nursing Education Perspectives. Former titles: *Nursing and Health Care Perspectives; N and H C Perspectives on Community;* (until 1995): *Nursing and Health Care;* Which superseded (in 1980): *N L N News.* [ISSN: 1536-5026] 1952. bi-m. USD 137 (Individuals, USD 70; Individual members, USD 40). Ed(s): Leslie Block, Joyce J Fitzpatrick. National League for Nursing, 61 Broadway, 33rd fl, New York, NY 10006-2701; nlnweb@nln.org; http://www.nln.org. Illus., adv. Sample. Refereed. Circ: 9000 Paid. CD-ROM: Ovid Technologies, Inc. *Indexed:* AgeL, CINAHL, MCR, SSCI. *Bk. rev.:* 0-7, length varies. *Aud.:* Ac, Sa.

This peer-reviewed title is the official publication of the National League of Nursing. The journal focuses on nursing education, including the implementation and design of nursing programs, ethics, and faculty concerns. Regular departments include "Faculty Matters," "Emerging Technologies Center," and

"Bookends." Recent article topics cover new technologies and the evolution of nursing education, disaster response education, and accelerated nursing programs. This is a highly recommended title for academic and hospital libraries with nursing programs.

Nursing Forum. See Health Professions section.

4758. Nursing Management. Formerly (until 1981): *Supervisor Nurse;* Incorporates (1994-1999): *Recruitment, Retention & Restructuring Report;* Which was formerly (1988-1994): *Recruitment & Retention Report.* [ISSN: 0744-6314] 1970. m. USD 244 (Individuals, USD 53.95). Ed(s): Richard Hader. Lippincott Williams & Wilkins, 323 Norristown Rd, Ste 200, Ambler, PA 19002; custserv@lww.com; http://www.lww.com. Illus., adv. Sample. Circ: 110000 Paid. Vol. ends: Dec. Microform: PQC. Online: EBSCO Publishing, EBSCO Host; Northern Light Technology, Inc.; OCLC Online Computer Library Center, Inc.; ProQuest LLC (Ann Arbor); SwetsWise Online Content. *Indexed:* ABIn, AgeL, CINAHL. *Bk. rev.:* 0-2, length varies. *Aud.:* Ac, Sa.

Although primarily focused on the management and supervision areas of nursing, *Nursing Management* also contains clinical articles and continuing education that is suitable for all nurses. Articles covering staff retention, staffing ratios, implementing a lift team policy, vascular site infection, and hand hygiene have all been featured recently. Table of contents information for current and some past issues is available at the *NM* web site (www.nursingmanagement-.com). This is a good title to have on hand in academic and other nursing collections.

Nursing Outlook. See Health Professions section.

4759. Nursing (Year): the voice and vision of nursing. [ISSN: 0360-4039] 1971. m. USD 189 (Individuals, USD 33.90). Ed(s): Anne Woods. Lippincott Williams & Wilkins, 323 Norristown Rd, Ste 200, Ambler, PA 19002; http://www.lww.com. Illus., index, adv. Sample. Circ: 300424 Paid. Vol. ends: Dec. Microform: PQC. Online: EBSCO Publishing, EBSCO Host; Gale; OCLC Online Computer Library Center, Inc.; Ovid Technologies, Inc.; ProQuest K-12 Learning Solutions; ProQuest LLC (Ann Arbor); SwetsWise Online Content. *Indexed:* AgeL, CINAHL, GSI. *Bk. rev.:* Number and length vary, some signed. *Aud.:* Ac, Sa.

This monthly peer-reviewed journal provides articles focused on practical patient care. The communicative and personal style of the articles facilitates understanding and quick, hands-on implementation. Each issue contains continuing education credits, along with the featured sections "Action STAT," "Ethical Problems," "Legal Questions," "Medication Errors," and "Clinical Rounds." Table of contents information is available at the *Nursing* web site (www.nursing2006.com) for current and some archived issues. This title is recommended for clinical settings and libraries supporting academic nursing programs.

Policy, Politics & Nursing Practice. See Health Professions section.

4760. R N. Formerly: *R N: National Magazine For Registered Nurses.* [ISSN: 0033-7021] 1937. m. USD 39 domestic; USD 54 foreign; USD 11 per issue domestic. Ed(s): Helen Lippman, Marya Ostrowski. Advanstar Medical Economics Healthcare Communications, 5 Paragon Dr, Montvale, NJ 07645-1742; http://www.advanstarhealthcare.com/hcg. Illus., index, adv. Sample. Circ: 237615 Paid. Vol. ends: Dec. CD-ROM: Ovid Technologies, Inc. Microform: RPI; PQC. Online: EBSCO Publishing, EBSCO Host; Florida Center for Library Automation; Gale; OCLC Online Computer Library Center, Inc.; H.W. Wilson. *Indexed:* AgeL, CINAHL, GSI, LRI. *Aud.:* Ac, Sa.

A refereed journal, *RN* contains well-referenced articles with a clinical focus. Four articles in each issue provide continuing education credits and readers may enroll in a home study program. Up-to-date articles are presented in a clear manner with an emphasis on practical information. Regularly featured sections include "Consult Stat," "Professional Update," "Clinical Highlights," and "In the Public Eye." A conference planner for upcoming events and "CareerSearch" information are also provided. *RN* (www.rnweb.com) provides table of contents information for all users. This easy-to-read and informative journal is recommended for clinical settings and academic libraries with nursing programs.

■ OCCUPATIONS AND CAREERS

See also Education; and Labor and Industrial Relations sections.

Jan A. Maas, Division Chief, Education & Job Information Center, Brooklyn Public Library, Grand Army Plaza, Brooklyn, NY 11238; j.maas@brooklynpubliclibrary.org

Introduction

Job hunters at all stages of their careers often turn to libraries for guidance and assistance. The Occupations and Careers section presents an array of standard magazines, available for your patrons in paper format, and electronic journals and job-hunting sites, available anywhere via the World Wide Web.

The list of standard magazines includes journals that feature employment advertisements and other practical information for job-seekers: career profiles, resume-writing tips, and interview coaching. Also on the list are research journals for counselors and human-resources personnel, as well as periodicals that emphasize data and statistical analysis or reports on theoretical and practical approaches to counseling and employee development.

In all, this section offers a broad array of magazines and electronic journals that serve differing publics: from high school students, adult job-seekers, or midlife career-changers, to employment counselors, policy researchers, or persons with disabilities or special needs.

To accommodate the typical job hunter, eager for employment, here are several Internet job-hunting sites, offering job-search engines and a place to post a resume.

CareerJournal.com. www.careerjournal.com. This web site is the electronic heir to the popular *National Employment Business Weekly,* formerly published by *The Wall Street Journal* and now ceased. It features current articles from *The Wall Street Journal* that relate to careers and employment opportunities. A vast array of columns is available at the click of a mouse, from salary and hiring information to job hunting advice, to tips on managing a career. Searchers can look for jobs via keyword search or location. Although the site's job ads are aimed at a business audience, the features are worthwhile for anyone trying to navigate today's job-hunting waters.

JobWeb. www.jobweb.com. Maintained by the National Association of Colleges and Employers, *JobWeb* (www.jobweb.com) is an electronic gateway to career planning and employment information. While primarily designed as a connection between employers and recent college graduates, it is also valuable for any college-educated member of the public. The site includes information about many employers and how-to articles on resume writing and interview skills, plus career and salary guides.

Monster.com. www.monster.com. More than a site for posting resumes, *Monster.com* also includes listings for U.S. and international job openings. It provides a free search service called "My Monster," which takes one's resume and ideal job specifications and searches continually for matching employment ads on the Internet.

The Riley Guide. www.rileyguide.com. For more than 13 years, *The Riley Guide* has been the first place to turn for accurate, ad-free employment information on the web. Margaret F. (Riley) Dikel, a former librarian, maintains numerous links to job-information sites, career-planning services, and research resources at this easy-to-use site. She also includes sections on general recruiters and job banks in most areas of the country and around the world, and highlights career resources for women, minorities, and other groups. The site features an alphabetical index that is particularly useful for finding niche sites in scores of fields, including agriculture, government, health care, legal services, the natural sciences, nonprofits, and many more. Also included are links to resume-writing and interviewing guides. *The Riley Guide* has been cited for excellence by *Yahoo! Internet World* and by Richard Bolles, author of *What Color Is Your Parachute? The Internet Guide.*

Basic Periodicals

Hs: *Career Opportunities News, Career World, Occupational Outlook Quarterly;* Ga: *Affirmative Action Register, Career Opportunities News, Occupational Outlook Quarterly;* Ac: *Career Opportunities News, Journal of Career Development, Occupational Outlook Quarterly;* Sa: *Careers and the Disabled, Journal of Employment Counseling, Journal of Volunteer Administration.*

Basic Abstracts and Indexes

Current Index to Journals in Education.

4761. ***Affirmative Action Register: for effective equal opportunity recruitment.*** [ISSN: 0146-2113] 1974. m. except July. Individuals, USD 15; Free to qualified personnel. Ed(s): Joyce R Green. Affirmative Action Register, 8356 Olive Blvd., St. Louis, MO 63132. Illus., adv. Sample. Circ: 60000 Controlled. Vol. ends: Feb/Aug. *Aud.:* Ga, Ac.

This publication is a copious collection of job ads for qualified minorities, women, veterans, and the disabled. Most ads are large, covering a quarter-page or more, and include complete job description, qualifications, and instructions for submission of resumes. Although most advertisers are colleges and universities seeking faculty or administrators, some government and social agencies also submit ads. An index lists the advertising institutions by name. The online version (www.aar-eeo.com) lists positions by category. An important resource for any library that serves job-seekers.

4762. ***ArtSearch: the national employment bulletin for the performing arts.*** [ISSN: 0730-9023] 1981. s-m. 23/yr. USD 150 print & online (Individuals, USD 60 print & online). Ed(s): Carol Van Keuren. Theatre Communications Group, Inc., 520 Eighth Ave, 24th Fl, New York, NY 10018; tcg@tcg.org; http://www.tcg.org. Sample. Circ: 6200. *Aud.:* Ga, Ac.

ArtSearch is a popular job placement bulletin for the performing arts, including arts administration. Each edition contains about 300 advertisements. Administrative positions are listed for executive managers as well as artistic directors. Other jobs are listed for the fields of production and design, career development, and education. An online version of *ArtSearch* is also available by subscription.

The Black Collegian. See African American section.

Black Enterprise. See African American section.

Career Development for Exceptional Individuals. See Disabilities section.

4763. ***The Career Development Quarterly.*** Formerly (until 1986): *Vocational Guidance Quarterly.* [ISSN: 0889-4019] 1952. q. USD 100. Ed(s): Mark Pope. American Counseling Association, 5999 Stevenson Ave, Alexandria, VA 22304-3300; http://www.counseling.org. Illus., index, adv. Sample. Refereed. Circ: 5900. Vol. ends: Jun. *Indexed:* ABIn, ABS&EES, AgeL, ERIC, EduInd, HEA, PsycInfo, SSCI, SWA, SWR&A. *Aud.:* Ac, Sa.

This professional and scholarly journal publishes research on the theory and practice of all aspects of career development, including counseling, occupational resources, labor market dynamics, and career education. This research seeks to address career development issues among a broad range of populations, including women, minorities, the aging, and youth at risk. As a result, it usually features case studies that present problems and practical solutions, along with more theoretical studies. A year-end review summarizes career and counseling research from other publications.

4764. ***Career Opportunities News.*** [ISSN: 0739-5043] 1983. 6x/yr. USD 75. Ferguson Publishing Co., c/o Facts On File, Inc., 132 W 31st St, 17th Fl, New York, NY 10001; CustServ@factsonfile.com; http://www.fergpubco.com/. Index. Vol. ends: May/Jun. *Bk. rev.:* 1-8, 75 words. *Aud.:* Hs, Ga, Ac.

This bimonthly surveys trends in the professions, government employment, and the general U.S. labor market. It offers well-documented facts and figures gleaned from reports by government agencies, private associations, and academic foundations, presented in short, easy-to-read articles. There are special columns for women and minorities. This journal is a valuable tool for career counselors, college students, and job seekers at all levels and deserves a place in college and public library collections.

4765. *Career World.* Formed by the merger of (1977-1981): *Career World 1;* (1977-1981): *Career World 2;* Which was formerly (1972-1977): *Career World;* Incorporates: *Real World.* [ISSN: 0744-1002] 1981. 6x/yr. USD 22.95 per academic year; USD 5.08 per academic year 10 or more subscriptions. Ed(s): Charles Piddock. Weekly Reader Corp., 200 First Stamford Pl, PO Box 120023, Stamford, CT 06912-0023; science@ weeklyreader.com; http://www.weeklyreader.com. Illus., index. Sample. Circ: 120000 Paid. Vol. ends: May. Online: EBSCO Publishing, EBSCO Host; Florida Center for Library Automation; Gale; Northern Light Technology, Inc.; OCLC Online Computer Library Center, Inc.; ProQuest K-12 Learning Solutions; ProQuest LLC (Ann Arbor); H.W. Wilson. *Indexed:* ICM, MASUSE, RGPR. *Aud.:* Ems, Hs.

This magazine is especially useful for students in grades 7–12 as they begin to explore career paths and educational options, and for teachers as they guide them toward the future. Each issue is filled with articles on career trends (including salary scales) and practical tips for job hunting or starting one's own business. Students can also read about colleges and scholarships, vocational training, and job interview skills. The overall approach of this clearly written, brightly illustrated publication is geared to realistic expectations and the hard work involved in making one's life a success. Teachers get a special edition that includes lesson plans and discussion aids. Highly recommended for school or public libraries.

4766. *Careers and the Disabled.* Formerly: *Careers and the Handicapped.* [ISSN: 1056-277X] 1986. 6x/yr. USD 13. Ed(s): James Schneider. Equal Opportunity Publications, Inc., 445 Broad Hollow Rd, Ste 425, Melville, NY 11747; info@eop.com; http://www.eop.com. Illus., adv. Sample. Circ: 10000 Paid. *Indexed:* BRI. *Bk. rev.:* 3-5, 150 words. *Aud.:* Ac, Sa.

People living with disabilities—in sight, hearing, or motor activity, for example—will value this magazine for its excellent coverage of issues that concern the disabled and the employment opportunities available to them. In addition to giving general job-hunting advice on resume writing and interviewing, this publication focuses on careers and occupational fields suitable for the disabled. Many articles take the form of personality profiles of people with disabilities who are achieving their career goals. Others report on legal issues such as the Americans with Disabilities Act (ADA) or on steps that can be taken to improve accessibility in various environments. A unique feature is a page in Braille featuring information for the blind. Also included is a career directory that acknowledges companies that are committed to recruiting entry-level and professional people with disabilities. This magazine deserves a place in any library that serves a significant number of people with disabilities.

The Chronicle of Higher Education. See Education/Higher Education section.

Entrepreneur. See Business/Small Business section.

4767. *Equal Opportunity: the career magazine for minority graduates.* [ISSN: 0071-1039] 1968. 3x/yr. USD 13; USD 5 newsstand/cover per issue. Ed(s): James Schneider. Equal Opportunity Publications, Inc., 445 Broad Hollow Rd, Ste 425, Melville, NY 11747; info@eop.com; http://www.eop.com. Illus., adv. Sample. Circ: 10000 Paid. Vol. ends: Spring. *Indexed:* BRI. *Bk. rev.:* 3-6, 100-150 words. *Aud.:* Ga, Ac.

Subtitled "the career magazine for minority graduates," this publication focuses on the needs of African Americans, Hispanics, Asians, and Native Americans. Articles emphasize careers with potential for minorities, or tell the stories of people who have achieved success in industry, government, or the professions. Other articles present general tips on interviewing, job hunting, or getting along in the corporate environment. Although this advice is addressed to members of minority groups, it would be equally useful to anyone trying to find a job. Also

included is an affirmative-action career directory, listing companies that are committed to recruiting "members of minority groups who are entry-level graduates and professionals." The list gives the addresses of human resources departments and, in some cases, the names of contacts within companies or organizations. Highly recommended for libraries that serve minority populations.

4768. *Federal Career Opportunities.* [ISSN: 0279-2230] 1974. bi-w. USD 175; USD 19.97 per month online. Ed(s): Judelle A McArdle. Federal Research Service, Inc., PO Box 1708, Annandale, VA 22003-1708; http://www.fedjobs.com. Illus., adv. Vol. ends: Dec. *Aud.:* Hs, Ga, Ac.

Anyone interested in a job with the federal government should make a habit of reviewing biweekly issues of this publication, because it lists thousands of government jobs—in the United States and around the world. *Federal Career Opportunities* (*FCO*) is basically a list, and is not graphically designed to be anything else, but careful study will reveal that everything a job hunter needs is here: position titles, series and grade numbers, announcement numbers, closing dates, and application addresses. The publisher, a private company not affiliated with any government agency, also produces a fee-based electronic version of government job listings through its web site (www.fedjobs.com). This is updated every weekday. Highly recommended for college libraries and job information centers of public libraries.

4769. *Federal Jobs Digest.* [ISSN: 0739-1684] 1977. bi-w. USD 112.50 (Individuals, USD 125). Ed(s): Peter E Ognibene. Federal Jobs Digest, 326 Main St, Emmaus, PA 18049. Illus., adv. Circ: 3500 Paid. *Aud.:* Ga.

This biweekly newspaper lists more than 13,000 current federal job openings throughout the nation and overseas. It also features articles on trends in federal hiring needs and detailed advice on how to apply for a federal job. At www.jobsfed.com, registered users may view jobs and post a resume; some fees may be involved. Highly recommended for public library job information centers.

4770. *Journal of Career Development.* Formerly (until 1984): *Journal of Career Education.* [ISSN: 0894-8453] 1972. q. GBP 315. Ed(s): Mark Pope. Sage Publications, Inc., 2455 Teller Rd, Thousand Oaks, CA 91320; info@sagepub.com; http://www.sagepub.com. Illus., index, adv. Sample. Refereed. Vol. ends: Summer (No. 4). Microform: PQC. Online: EBSCO Publishing, EBSCO Host; Gale; HighWire Press; IngentaConnect; OCLC Online Computer Library Center, Inc.; OhioLINK; ProQuest LLC (Ann Arbor); Springer LINK; SwetsWise Online Content. Reprint: PSC. *Indexed:* ABIn, ABS&EES, EAA, ERIC, EduInd, HEA, HRA, IBR, PsycInfo, SSCI, SWR&A. *Aud.:* Ac, Sa.

Scholarly articles in this quarterly present research in the theory and practice of the field of career education and development, with a focus on how research can influence practice. The populations studied are diverse: adults and adolescents, people with special needs, the gifted, minorities, and families. Counselors and clinicians, as well as social scientists and policymakers, will find rich material in this periodical. This is highly suitable for academic and specialized libraries. Contents are available online at the publisher's web site (http://jcd.sagepub.com).

4771. *Journal of Employment Counseling.* [ISSN: 0022-0787] 1965. q. USD 50. Ed(s): Norman E Amundson. American Counseling Association, 5999 Stevenson Ave, Alexandria, VA 22304-3300; http://www.counseling.org. Illus., index, adv. Sample. Refereed. Circ: 1500. Vol. ends: Dec. Microform: PQC. Online: EBSCO Publishing, EBSCO Host; Florida Center for Library Automation; Gale; Northern Light Technology, Inc.; OCLC Online Computer Library Center, Inc.; ProQuest K-12 Learning Solutions; ProQuest LLC (Ann Arbor); H.W. Wilson. Reprint: PSC. *Indexed:* ABIn, ASSIA, AgeL, ERIC, EduInd, HEA, HRA, PsycInfo, SFSA, SSCI, SWR&A. *Aud.:* Ac, Sa.

Addressed to professional employment counselors, this quarterly presents scholarly research that seeks to illuminate the practice and theory of the field. Well-documented articles report on such topics as psychological stress, older women workers, and the role of paraprofessionals in the employment counseling field. The emphasis is on theory that might make a practical difference in a professional counseling situation. This is a periodical of high interest and value to those in the field, deserving a place in an academic or professional library.

4772. Journal of Volunteer Administration. Formerly (until 1982): *Volunteer Administration.* [ISSN: 0733-6535] 1967. q. USD 45 domestic; USD 55 in Canada & Mexico. Ed(s): Mary Merrill. Association for Volunteer Administration, PO Box 32092, Richmond, VA 23294-2092; avaintl@mindspring.com. Illus., index, adv. Sample. Refereed. Circ: 1300 Paid. Vol. ends: Fall. *Indexed:* AgeL, PAIS. *Aud.:* Ac, Sa.

This quarterly is a forum for those involved in volunteer administration, a subject that essentially covers anything related to volunteers themselves, volunteer programs, or volunteer management. Articles follow a scholarly style; they emphasize data and research into the theory and practice of volunteerism, including the history and philosophy of the field. Occasional articles also report on training designs and other practical measures to increase the effectiveness of volunteers. The magazine deserves a place in any academic library that serves students of education and other social sciences, and could be useful to administrators of social agencies that use volunteer help.

Monthly Labor Review. See *U.S. Bureau of Labor Statistics. Monthly Labor Review* in the Labor and Industrial Relations section.

4773. N A C E Journal: the international magazine of placement and recruitment. Former titles (until 2002): *Journal of Career Planning & Employment;* (until 1985): *Journal of College Placement;* (until 1951): *School and College Placement.* [ISSN: 1542-2046] 1940. q. Free to members; Non-members, USD 72. Ed(s): Jerry Bohovich. National Association of Colleges and Employers, 62 Highland Ave, Bethlehem, PA 18017-9085; info@naceweb.org; http://www.naceweb.org. Illus., index, adv. Sample. Circ: 4314 Paid. Vol. ends: May. Microform: PQC. Online: OCLC Online Computer Library Center, Inc.; ProQuest LLC (Ann Arbor). *Indexed:* ABIn, ATI, BRI, CBRI, EduInd, HEA, PAIS, PMA. *Bk. rev.:* 10-12, 100-250 words. *Aud.:* Ac.

This quarterly, the journal for placement officers, employment counselors, and other members of the National Association of Colleges and Employers, focuses on major trends in the human relations field. Regular features include "Legal Q&A" and "Resources Reviews." Articles cover such topics as diversity, internships, campus recruitment, and changing employment markets. This journal also features news about people in the field, industries and individual companies, conferences and awards, and upcoming career fairs and other events. The web site (www.naceweb.org) features employment listings in its "Jobwire."

The New Social Worker. See Sociology an Social Work/Social Work and Social Welfare section.

4774. Occupational Outlook Quarterly. [ISSN: 0199-4786] 1957. q. Sep.-June. USD 15 domestic; USD 21 foreign; USD 6 newsstand/cover per issue domestic. Ed(s): Kathleen Green. U.S. Department of Labor, Bureau of Labor Statistics, Postal Square Bldg., 2 Massachusetts Ave, NE, Washington, DC 20212-0001; blsdata_staff@bls.gov; http://www.bls.gov. Illus., index. Sample. Circ: 15000. Vol. ends: Winter. Microform: CIS; NBI; PQC. Online: EBSCO Publishing, EBSCO Host; Florida Center for Library Automation; Gale; Northern Light Technology, Inc.; OCLC Online Computer Library Center, Inc.; ProQuest K-12 Learning Solutions; ProQuest LLC (Ann Arbor); H.W. Wilson. *Indexed:* ABIn, ASG, AgeL, AmStI, BPI, EduInd, IUSGP, MASUSE, PAIS, RGPR. *Aud.:* Hs, Ga, Ac.

At least one major article in each issue focuses on a particular career while other pieces cover various aspects of the labor market or highlight jobs with a strong potential for growth. This publication always contains a wealth of data, including projections about the future of the labor force, industry, and a large variety of occupations. The magazine's attractive graphics and easy-to-read style have made it a favorite among high school and college students research-

ing careers. It may be of equal value to midlife career-changers who are assessing new employment opportunities. Highly recommended for school, academic, and public libraries. An online version is available at www.bls.gov/opub/ooq/ooqhome.htm.

Techniques. See Education/Specific Subjects and Teaching Methods: Technology section.

Training. See Management, Administration, and Human Resources/Human Resources section.

Work and Occupations. See Sociology and Social Work/General section.

Working Mother. See Fashion and Lifestyle section.

■ PALEONTOLOGY

See also Biological Sciences; and Earth Sciences sections.

Brian C. Greene, Assistant Head Librarian, Access Services Dept., Northeastern University Libraries, 360 Huntington Ave., Boston, Massachusetts 02115; br.greene@neu.edu

Introduction

Paleontology, or the scientific study of fossils, is among the broadest of the sciences, and necessarily so, since it examines the history of life on Earth. Interdisciplinary in nature, paleontology requires expertise in both biology and geology, since its focus is the study of biological objects (fossils) in a geological context (sediment). By investigating the fossil record, paleontologists are able to identify prehistoric species of organisms, trace their evolutionary relationships, and reconstruct their biology, behavior, and ecological habitats. Like many scientific disciplines, paleontology is split along a principal dichotomy: pure science versus applied science.

Pure paleontology is paleontology in the classic sense, which consists of taxonomy and systematics. Taxonomy is the process by which fossils are identified, described, and classified. Systematics compares the fossilized species, analyzes the relationships between them, and reconstructs their evolutionary history. Systematic paleontology often subdivides according to the type of fossilized organism that is considered. For instance, vertebrate paleontologists study the fossilized remains of extinct animals with backbones, whereas invertebrate paleontologists study the fossilized remains of extinct animals without backbones. Paleobotanists examine the remains of ancient plant life, while micropaleontologists investigate the remains of ancient microscopic organisms, such as bacteria, protozoa, and other single-celled organisms. Journals devoted to systematic paleontology typically feature high-quality illustrations and carefully detailed descriptions of such fossils.

Building upon systematic paleontology is applied paleontology, which consists of two major subdisciplines: biostratigraphy and paleobiology. Biostratigraphy is the study of the temporal and spatial distribution of fossil organisms, or in simpler terms, why does a fossil occur when and where it does in the Earth's sediment? Paleobiology analyzes and interprets the relationships of fossils to the evolution of life on Earth, as well as to the environment. Paleobiology interfaces with a wide variety of scientific disciplines such as ecology, climatology, evolutionary biology, and environmental science, to form new subdisciplines such as paleobiogeography, paleoecology, and paleoclimatology. Journals devoted to applied paleontology tend to be highly interdisciplinary in nature, covering a wide range of biological, ecological and environmental topics, often with an eye to the broader implications of each. And as the gap between biostratigraphy and paleobiology continues to narrow, since both are placing greater emphasis on the biological and environmental aspects of the discipline, these journals will be attractive not only to paleontologists, but to biologists, geologists, and environmental scientists working in the field.

Because paleontology is first and foremost an academic discipline, the journal titles listed here will be most appropriate for academic and research libraries. However, a few titles will be suitable for a general audience of interested nonprofessionals. Additionally, a number of these journals have important applications in the energy industry and business sector, and these titles should be considered for purchase by any corporate or public library serving these interests. This list is not intended to serve as a comprehensive or exhaustive file of all such titles in the field, but is instead a representative cross-section that aims to strike a balance between the classic study of systematic paleontology and the newer, burgeoning fields of applied paleontology.

Basic Periodicals

Journal of Paleontology, Lethaia, Palaeontology, Journal of Vertebrate Paleontology, Paleoceanography, Paleobiology, Palaeogeography, Palaeoclimatology, Palaeoecology, Palaios.

Basic Abstracts and Indexes

BioOne, BIOSIS, GeoRef, Zoological Record.

4775. Acta Palaeontologica Polonica. [ISSN: 0567-7920] 1956. q. EUR 194 foreign. Ed(s): Zofia Kielan-Jaworowska. Polska Akademia Nauk, Instytut Paleobiologii, ul Twarda 51-55, Warsaw, 00-818, Poland. Illus., adv. Refereed. Circ: 500. *Indexed:* BiolAb, IBR, PetrolAb, SCI, VB, ZooRec. *Bk. rev.:* 0-1; 500-1,200 words. *Aud.:* Ac, Sa.

Acta Palaeontologica Polonica is a quarterly journal published by the Institute of Paleobiology of the Polish Academy of Sciences. International in scope, this highly respected journal covers all areas of paleontology, placing particular emphasis on the biologically-oriented aspects of the discipline. English is the exclusive language of this peer-reviewed publication. Appropriate for academic and research collections.

4776. Alcheringa: an Australian journal of palaeontology. [ISSN: 0311-5518] 1975. s-a. GBP 105 print & online eds. Ed(s): Dr. Stephen McLoughlin. Taylor & Francis Ltd., 4 Park Sq, Milton Park, Abingdon, OX14 4RN, United Kingdom; info@tandf.co.uk; http://www.tandf.co.uk/journals. Illus. Refereed. Circ: 600. Vol. ends: No. 4. Reprint: PSC. *Indexed:* PetrolAb, SCI, ZooRec. *Aud.:* Ac, Sa.

Published quarterly by the Association of Australasian Palaeontologists of the Geological Society of Australia, this journal covers all aspects of paleontology and its ramifications for the earth and biological sciences, including taxonomy, biostratigraphy, micropaleontology, vertebrate paleontology, paleobotany, palynology, paleobiology, paleoanatomy, paleoecology, biostratinomy, biogeography, chronobiology, biogeochemistry, and palichnology. High-quality illustrations, including line drawings and photographs, are an important feature of this scholarly journal. Author distribution is evenly split among Australian and international researchers. Recommended for comprehensive university library collections.

4777. American Paleontologist: a newsmagazine of earth sciences. [ISSN: 1066-8772] 1992. q. Membership, USD 30. Ed(s): Warren D Allmon. Paleontological Research Institution, 1259 Trumansburg Rd, Ithaca, NY 14850-1398; http://www.englib.cornell.edu/pri/. Illus., adv. *Indexed:* ZooRec. *Aud.:* Hs, Ga.

A publication of the Paleontological Research Institute, *American Paleontologist* is the one fossil magazine specifically designed for the interested nonspecialist. The short, highly readable articles address such topics as dinosaurs, amateur paleontology, and active areas of research from clams to mammals. Recommended for high school, public, and undergraduate libraries.

4778. Bulletins of American Paleontology. [ISSN: 0007-5779] 1895. 2x/yr. Ed(s): Warren D Allmon. Paleontological Research Institution, 1259 Trumansburg Rd, Ithaca, NY 14850-1398; http://www.englib.cornell.edu/pri/. Illus., adv. Refereed. Reprint: PSC. *Indexed:* BiolAb, PetrolAb, ZooRec. *Aud.:* Ac, Sa.

Bulletins of American Paleontology is the oldest paleontological journal in the Western Hemisphere. Published by the Paleontological Research Institution (PRI) since 1895, *BAP* offers paleontological researchers an outlet for their significant, longer articles and monographs (50–200 pages) in any area of paleontology, but most especially descriptive systematics requiring high-quality photographic illustrations. *BAP* publishes two or three peer-reviewed issues per year, each issue consisting of a separate monograph. Recommended for university libraries affiliated with paleontology departments or research programs.

4779. Geobios. [ISSN: 0016-6995] 1968. 6x/yr. EUR 206. Ed(s): Serge Legendre. Elsevier France, Editions Scientifiques et Medicales, 23 Rue Linois, Paris, 75724, France; http://www.elsevier.fr. Illus., index, adv. Refereed. Circ: 850. Vol. ends: Dec (No. 6). *Indexed:* BiolAb, PetrolAb, SCI, SSCI, ZooRec. *Bk. rev.:* 0-5, 1,500-2,000 words. *Aud.:* Ac, Sa.

Geobios is the official organ of the European Paleontological Association (EPA). The journal features articles on biodiversity, evolution, biostratigraphy, stratigraphy, paleogeography, and paleobiology, provided they are of interest to the international scientific community. Six issues are published annually, with occasional supplements devoted to one specific theme, in order to accommodate longer contributions. *Geobios* publishes original papers in French or English, with abstracts and keywords appearing in both languages. Despite its French editorial orientation, this journal maintains an international scope in contributions, editors, and topics. Recommended for research libraries.

4780. Historical Biology: an international journal of paleobiology. [ISSN: 0891-2963] 1988. a. GBP 737 print & online eds. Ed(s): Gareth Dyke. Taylor & Francis Ltd., 4 Park Sq, Milton Park, Abingdon, OX14 4RN, United Kingdom; info@tandf.co.uk; http://www.tandf.co.uk/journals. Illus. Refereed. Vol. ends: No. 4. Online: EBSCO Publishing, EBSCO Host; Gale; IngentaConnect; OCLC Online Computer Library Center, Inc.; SwetsWise Online Content. Reprint: PSC. *Indexed:* AnBeAb, ApEcolAb, GSI, ZooRec. *Bk. rev.:* 2,000-2,500 words. *Aud.:* Ac, Sa.

Historical Biology is an international outlet for high-quality papers in systematics and evolutionary trends within animal and plant groups that have both living and fossil representatives. Peer-reviewed articles from all areas of paleontology, evolutionary biology, and systematics are represented here, as well as longer, monographic works on historical animal and plant systematics. The journal publishes four online issues and one print archival volume annually. Recommended for large university and research collections.

4781. Journal of Foraminiferal Research. Former titles (until 1970): *Cushman Foundation for Foraminiferal Research. Contributions;* (until 1949): *Contributions from the Cushman Laboratory for Foraminiferal Research.* [ISSN: 0096-1191] 1925. q. USD 90 (Members, USD 40). Ed(s): Ronald E Martin. Cushman Foundation for Foraminiferal Research, MRC 121 NMNH, Smithsonian Institution, Washington, DC 20560; http://cushforams.niu.edu. Illus., index, adv. Sample. Refereed. Circ: 800. Vol. ends: No. 4. *Indexed:* BiolAb, PetrolAb, SCI, SWRA, ZooRec. *Aud.:* Ac, Sa.

The *Journal of Foraminiferal Research* is the official publication of the Cushman Foundation for Foraminiferal Research. *JFR* publishes original papers of international interest that deal with all aspects of the Order Foraminiferida (single-cell protists with shells). Papers that deal with foraminifera as part of stratigraphic or ecologic studies with allied organisms are also included. All papers are in English and feature high-quality photographic illustrations. Each issue includes citations and abstracts of recently published literature in the field. This scholarly journal is appropriate for specialized academic collections.

4782. Journal of Paleontology. [ISSN: 0022-3360] 1927. bi-m. Ed(s): Brian J Witzke, Julia Golden. Paleontological Society, PO Box 1897, Lawrence, KS 66044-8897; http://www.paleosoc.org/. Illus., index, adv. Refereed. Circ: 3500. Vol. ends: Nov (No. 6). Microform: PQC. Online: Allen Press Inc.; BioOne; CSA; EBSCO Publishing, EBSCO Host; HighWire Press; JSTOR (Web-based Journal Archive); Northern Light Technology, Inc.; OCLC Online Computer Library Center, Inc.; OhioLINK; ProQuest K-12 Learning Solutions; ProQuest LLC (Ann Arbor). *Indexed:* AbAn, B&AI, BiolAb, IBR, OceAb, PetrolAb, SCI, SSCI, ZooRec. *Bk. rev.:* 4, 500 words. *Aud.:* Ac, Sa.

The *Journal of Paleontology* publishes original articles and notes on the systematics, phylogeny, paleoecology, paleogeography, and evolution of fossil organisms. It emphasizes specimen-based research and features high-quality illustrations. All taxonomic groups are treated, including invertebrates, microfossils, plants, and vertebrates. Though sponsored by the U.S.-based Paleontological Society, this journal is international in scope, and is a must for the core collection of every academic and research library.

Journal of Quaternary Science. See Earth Sciences and Geology section.

4783. *Journal of Systematic Palaeontology.* Former titles (until 2003): *Natural History Museum. Bulletin. Geology;* (until 1994): *British Museum (Natural History). Bulletin. Geology;* Which incorporated (1950-1974): *British Museum (Natural History). Bulletin. Mineralogy.* [ISSN: 1477-2019] 2003. q. GBP 171. Ed(s): Dr. Andrew B Smith. Cambridge University Press, The Edinburgh Bldg, Shaftesbury Rd, Cambridge, CB2 2RU, United Kingdom; journals@cambridge.org; http://www.journals.cambridge.org. Illus., index. Refereed. Circ: 750. *Indexed:* BiolAb, ChemAb, PetrolAb, SCI, ZooRec. *Aud.:* Ac, Sa.

The *Journal of Systematic Palaeontology* publishes major papers describing new or poorly understood fauna and flora, as well as papers that use systematics in ways that significantly advance the current understanding of paleogeography, paleobiology, functional morphology, paleoecology, biostratigraphy, and phylogenetic relationships. The journal aims to demonstrate and strengthen the fundamental contributions that systematics and collection-based data make to evolutionary paleontology. *JSP* is sponsored by the Natural History Museum of London and is a direct successor to the *Bulletin of the Natural History Museum*. Highly recommended for academic and research libraries that are affiliated with paleontology departments.

4784. *Journal of Vertebrate Paleontology.* [ISSN: 0272-4634] 1981. q. USD 270 domestic; USD 300 foreign. Ed(s): Mark V H Wilson. Society of Vertebrate Paleontology, 60 Revere Dr, Ste 500, Northbrook, IL 60062; svp@vertpaleo.org; http://www.vertpaleo.org. Illus., index, adv. Refereed. Vol. ends: Dec (No. 4). *Indexed:* BiolAb, SCI, ZooRec. *Bk. rev.:* 0-4, 1,000-2,000 words. *Aud.:* Ac, Sa.

Published by the U.S.-based Society of Vertebrate Paleontology, *JVP* features articles on vertebrate origins, evolution, functional morphology, taxonomy, biostratigraphy, paleoecology, paleobiogeography, and paleoanthropology. The central focus of the journal is the history, evolution, comparative anatomy, and taxonomy of vertebrate animals, as well as the occurrence, collection, and study of fossil vertebrates and the stratigraphy of the beds in which they are found. Issues generally contain 15–18 papers, ranging anywhere from 8 to 20 pages in length. Shorter manuscripts are published as "notes." Book reviews appear occasionally. A leading journal in the field of systematic paleontology, this title is a must for the core collection of any academic or research library.

4785. *Lethaia: an international journal of palaeontology and stratigraphy.* [ISSN: 0024-1164] 1968. q. USD 324 print & online eds. Ed(s): Svend Stouge. Blackwell Publishing Ltd., 9600 Garsington Rd, Oxford, OX4 2ZG, United Kingdom; customerservices@blackwellpublishing.com; http://www.blackwellpublishing.com. Illus., index, adv. Refereed. Circ: 1000. Vol. ends: No. 4. Microform: PQC. Online: EBSCO Publishing, EBSCO Host; Gale; IngentaConnect; OCLC Online Computer Library Center, Inc.; SwetsWise Online Content. Reprint: PSC. *Indexed:* AbAn, BiolAb, IBR, PetrolAb, SCI, ZooRec. *Bk. rev.:* 1,700 words. *Aud.:* Ac, Sa.

Lethaia is a leading international journal that emphasizes new developments and discoveries in paleobiology and biostratigraphy. A formal publication outlet for the International Palaeontological Association (IPA) and the International Commission on Stratigraphy (ICS), articles concentrate on the development of new ideas and methods of wide significance pertaining to the two core topics of paleobiology and ecostratigraphy. In addition to articles, *Lethaia* contains shorter contributions in the form of discussions, presentations of current scientific activities, reviews and editorials. Each issue contains 10–12 papers that are international in scope. Occasionally, issues will include discussions of previously published papers, short notes on current paleontological research, and literature reviews. *Lethaia* is a recommended addition to the core collection for most academic and research libraries.

4786. *Marine Micropaleontology.* [ISSN: 0377-8398] 1976. 16x/yr. EUR 1432. Ed(s): E Thomas, A. Mackensen. Elsevier BV, Radarweg 29, Amsterdam, 1043 NX, Netherlands; nlinfo-f@elsevier.nl; http://www.elsevier.nl. Illus. Sample. Refereed. Vol. ends: Nov (No. 4). Microform: PQC. Online: EBSCO Publishing, EBSCO Host; Gale; IngentaConnect; OhioLINK; ScienceDirect; SwetsWise Online Content. *Indexed:* BiolAb, M&GPA, OceAb, PetrolAb, SCI, ZooRec. *Bk. rev.:* 0-1, 3,000 words. *Aud.:* Ac, Sa.

Marine Micropaleontology is an international journal that publishes the results of research in all fields of marine micropaleontology relating to the ocean basins and continents. These fields include paleoceanography, evolution, ecology, paleoecology, biology, paleobiology, paleoclimatology, biochronology, taphonomy, and the systematic relationships of higher taxa. Featured articles focus on the use of marine micropaleontology to solve geological and biological problems, and tend to promote innovative, provocative, and controversial ideas. All articles are in English, and the international orientation of this journal is reflected in its papers and editorial board. Although the price may be prohibitive for some, this publication is a first choice for any academic or corporate library supporting marine micropaleontology or oil research.

4787. *Micropaleontology.* Formerly (until 1955): *The Micropaleontologist.* [ISSN: 0026-2803] 1947. 6x/yr. USD 640 (Members, USD 320). Ed(s): John A Van Couvering. American Museum of Natural History, Central Park West at 79th St, New York, NY 10024-5192; scipubs@amnh.org; http://www.amnh.org. Illus. Refereed. Circ: 900. Vol. ends: No. 4. Microform: MIM; PQC. Online: BioOne; CSA; HighWire Press; JSTOR (Web-based Journal Archive); OCLC Online Computer Library Center, Inc.; OhioLINK. *Indexed:* BiolAb, ChemAb, IBR, M&GPA, OceAb, PetrolAb, SCI, ZooRec. *Bk. rev.:* 0-1, 200-1,000 words. *Aud.:* Ac, Sa.

Micropaleontology is a specialized journal which publishes original research in the paleobiology and systematics of animal, plant, and protist microfossils. This international, peer-reviewed journal is sponsored by the Micropaleontology Project, which publishes six issues per year, including theme issues and monographs. Approximately four to six papers appear in each issue, alongside professional notes, book reviews, biographies, and letters. Recommended for comprehensive research collections.

4788. *Palaeogeography, Palaeoclimatology, Palaeoecology.* [ISSN: 0031-0182] 1965. 56x/yr. EUR 3946. Ed(s): D. J. Bottjer, T Correge. Elsevier BV, Radarweg 29, Amsterdam, 1043 NX, Netherlands; nlinfo-f@elsevier.nl; http://www.elsevier.nl. Illus., index, adv. Sample. Refereed. Microform: PQC. Online: EBSCO Publishing, EBSCO Host; Gale; IngentaConnect; OhioLINK; ScienceDirect; SwetsWise Online Content. *Indexed:* AbAn, ApEcolAb, BiolAb, BrArAb, CABA, ChemAb, EnvAb, FPA, ForAb, IBR, M&GPA, OceAb, PetrolAb, S&F, SCI, SSCI, SWRA, ZooRec. *Bk. rev.:* 3-5, 1,500-2,000 words. *Aud.:* Ac, Sa.

Palaeogeography, Palaeoclimatology, Palaeoecology is an international journal consisting of high-quality, multidisciplinary studies in the field of paleoenvironmental geology. Articles combine paleontological research with data gathered from many other disciplines, all with global implications, in order to understand ancient and recent Earth environments. According to the 2005 Journal Citation Reports, *Palaeo 3* is the most cited journal in the field of paleontology. Often bundled with *Global and Planetary Change* (ISSN: 0921-8181), this journal is highly recommended as a core title for all collections that serve researchers in the geosciences.

4789. *Palaeontographical Society. Monographs (London).* Formerly: *Monographs of the Palaeontological Society.* [ISSN: 0269-3445] 1848. a. GBP 90 (Individuals, GBP 33). Ed(s): A W A Rushton, M Williams. Palaeontographical Society, Department of Paleontology, Natural History Museum, Cromwell Rd, London, SW7 5BD, United Kingdom. Illus., index. Refereed. Circ: 368. *Indexed:* BiolAb, ZooRec. *Aud.:* Ac, Sa.

The Palaeontographical Society (London) exists for the sole purpose of figuring and describing British fossils through a series of monographs. This periodical is issued as an annual volume of serially numbered publications, and each publication may be a single complete monograph or part of a continuing monograph. Each monograph features full taxonomic treatment, presentation, and illustration of each fossil group. Recommended for college and university libraries supporting systematic paleontology.

4790. *Palaeontologia Electronica.* [ISSN: 1094-8074] 1998. s-a. Free. Ed(s): Jennifer Rumford. Coquina Press, PO Box 369, Calvert, TX 77837. Refereed. *Indexed:* SCI, ZooRec. *Bk. rev.:* 0-3, 1,000-1,500 words. *Aud.:* Ga, Ac, Sa.

Palaeontologia Electronica, the first open-access journal in paleontology (http://palaeo-electronica.org), is sponsored by the Palaeontological Association, the Paleontological Society, and the Society of Vertebrate Paleontology. This peer-reviewed journal covers all branches of paleontology, including micropaleontology, palynology, invertebrate paleontology, paleobotany, vertebrate paleontology, and related disciplines. The journal is highly graphical—research articles feature animations, 2-D and 3-D modeling techniques, and high-resolution digital images. Archived issues are available online back to 1998. *PE* is an important resource that is freely available to all library collections.

4791. *Palaeontology.* [ISSN: 0031-0239] 1957. bi-m. GBP 508 print & online eds. Ed(s): D J Batten. Blackwell Publishing Ltd., 9600 Garsington Rd, Oxford, OX4 2ZG, United Kingdom; customerservices@ blackwellpublishing.com; http://www.blackwellpublishing.com. Illus., index. Refereed. Circ: 2000. Vol. ends: No. 6. Reprint: PSC. *Indexed:* BiolAb, OceAb, PetrolAb, SCI, ZooRec. *Aud.:* Ac, Sa.

Sponsored by the Palaeontological Association (London), *Palaeontology* publishes research papers on all aspects of paleontology, including paleozoology, paleobotany, systematic studies, paleoecology, micropaleontology, paleobiogeography, functional morphology, stratigraphy, taxonomy, taphonomy, paleoenvironmental reconstruction, paleoclimate analysis, and biomineralization studies. A high standard of illustration is an important feature of the journal. Six issues are published annually, each consisting of 10–12 research articles. The journal provides free, open access to all reviews, and to content that is over seven years old. Free online access to the journal is available to institutions in the developing world through the OARE Initiative (Online Access to Research in the Environment) in conjunction with UNEP, the United Nations Environment Programme. A primary research journal in the field, this title is a must for the core collection of academic libraries.

4792. *Palaios.* [ISSN: 0883-1351] 1986. bi-m. USD 300 (Members, USD 85). Ed(s): Christopher G Maples. S E P M - Society for Sedimentary Geology, 6128 E. 38th St., Ste. 308, Tulsa, OK 74135-5814; orders@allanepress.com; http://www.sepm.org. Illus., index, adv. Refereed. Circ: 1300. Vol. ends: No. 6. *Indexed:* ApEcolAb, BiolAb, M&GPA, PetrolAb, SCI, ZooRec. *Bk. rev.:* 1-3, 300-800 words. *Aud.:* Ac, Sa.

Palaios publishes research articles that focus on the impact of life on Earth's history as recorded in the paleontological and sedimentological records, with a special emphasis on the application of paleontology to solving geologic problems. Articles cover a broad range of areas, such as biogeochemistry, ichnology, paleoclimatology, paleoecology, paleoceanography, sedimentology, and stratigraphy, with an eye toward the broader implications of each. Each issue features several comprehensive research articles as well as shorter papers, book reviews, news updates, and announcements. Because of its broad, interdisciplinary scope, this journal is highly recommended for the core collections of college and university libraries.

4793. *Paleobiology.* [ISSN: 0094-8373] 1975. q. USD 90 (Individuals, USD 46; Members, USD 41). Ed(s): William M DiMichele, John M Pandolfi. Paleontological Society, PO Box 1897, Lawrence, KS 66044-8897; ps@allenpress.com. Illus., index, adv. Refereed. Circ: 2400. Vol. ends: Fall (No. 4). Microform: PQC. Online: Allen Press Inc.; BioOne; CSA; HighWire Press; JSTOR (Web-based Journal Archive); OCLC Online Computer Library Center, Inc.; OhioLINK; ProQuest LLC (Ann Arbor). *Indexed:* AbAn, ApEcolAb, BiolAb, BrArAb, CABA, FPA, ForAb, PetrolAb, S&F, SCI, ZooRec. *Bk. rev.:* 1, 1,500-2,000 words. *Aud.:* Ac, Sa.

Published by the Paleontological Society (U.S.), *Paleobiology* is a peer-reviewed, international journal which publishes original contributions emphasizing various aspects of biological paleontology. These may include such topics as speciation, extinction, development of individuals and colonies, natural selection, evolution, patterns of variation, abundance, and the distribution of organisms in space and time. Papers are included only if they have significant and broad applications, as the journal aims to attract readers from more than one specialty. A "Matters of the Record" section features up-to-date discussions of new discoveries, reviews of recent conceptual advances, and brief syntheses of important topics. A highly respected and reasonably priced journal, it is enthusiastically recommended for the core collection of academic and research libraries. According to the 2005 Journal Citation Reports, ;Paleobiology ranked second among all paleontology journals according to Impact Factor.

4794. *Paleoceanography.* [ISSN: 0883-8305] 1986. q. USD 490. Ed(s): Lisa Sloan, Larry Peterson. American Geophysical Union, 2000 Florida Ave, NW, Washington, DC 20009-1277; http://www.agu.org. Illus., index. Sample. Refereed. Vol. ends: Dec (No. 6). Online: EBSCO Publishing, EBSCO Host. *Indexed:* M&GPA, OceAb, PetrolAb, SCI, ZooRec. *Aud.:* Ac, Sa.

Published by the American Geophysical Union, this journal features original contributions that deal with reconstructions of past conditions and processes of change as recorded in sediments deposited in water. This especially includes marine sediments, but may also extend to sediments from freshwater environments. Approaches to past reconstruction include sedimentology, geochemistry, paleontology, oceanography, geophysics, and modeling. Contributions are global and regional in scope, and cover all ages (Precambrian to the Quaternary, including modern analogs). According to the 2005 Journal Citation Reports, *Paleoceanography* ranked number one of 35 titles in paleontology according to Impact Factor. This title is strongly recommended for all specialized academic and research collections.

4795. *Paleontological Journal.* [ISSN: 0031-0301] 1959. bi-m. EUR 3888 print & online eds. Ed(s): A Y Rozanov. M A I K Nauka - Interperiodica, Profsoyuznaya ul 90, Moscow, 117997, Russian Federation; compmg@maik.ru; http://www.maik.ru. Illus., adv. Refereed. Circ: 425. Vol. ends: Dec (No. 6). Microform: PQC. Online: Springer LINK; SwetsWise Online Content. *Indexed:* BiolAb, SCI, SWRA. *Bk. rev.:* 0-1, 1,500-3,000 words. *Aud.:* Ac, Sa.

Paleontological Journal (Paleontoloicheskii Zhurnal) is the principal Russian periodical in paleontology. The journal publishes original work on the anatomy, morphology, and taxonomy of fossil organisms, as well as their distribution, ecology, and origin. It also publishes studies on the evolution of organisms, ecosystems, and the biosphere, and provides information on global biostratigraphy, with an emphasis on Eastern Europe and Asia. Due to the high cost, this title is recommended only for comprehensive research collections.

4796. *Paleontological Research.* Formerly (until 1996): *Nihon Koseibutsu Gakkai Hokoku, Kiji/Paleontological Society of Japan. Transactions and Proceedings.* [ISSN: 1342-8144] 1935. q. USD 75 (Individuals, JPY 6000). Ed(s): Kenshiro Ogasawara. The Paleontological Society of Japan, TohShin Bldg. 3F, Hongo 2-27-2, Tokyo, 113-0033, Japan; psj-office@ world.ocn.ne.jp; http://ammo.kueps.kyoto-u.ac.jp/palaeont/. Illus. Refereed. Circ: 1200. *Indexed:* BiolAb, PetrolAb, ZooRec. *Aud.:* Ac, Sa.

Published by the Palaeontological Society of Japan, *PR* is an international, peer-reviewed journal focusing on all areas of paleontological research, including the evolutionary history of life, the origin of biodiversity, mass extinctions and their aftermath, Earth's environmental changes, and applications of paleontology to Earth and planetary sciences and technologies. Articles are in English. Recommended for academic libraries and comprehensive research collections.

4797. *Palynology.* Supersedes (in 1977): *Geoscience and Man;* Incorporates (1970-1976): *American Association of Stratigraphic Palynologists. Proceedings of the Annual Meeting.* [ISSN: 0191-6122] 1975. a. Institutional members, USD 100. Ed(s): James B Riding. American Association of Stratigraphic Palynologists Foundation, c/o Vaughn M

Bryant, Jr, Palynology Laboratory, Texas A & M Univ, College Station, TX 77843-4352; vbryant@tamu.edu; http://www.palynology.org. Illus., index. Circ: 980 Paid. Online: BioOne; CSA; HighWire Press. *Indexed:* AnthLit, BiolAb, PetrolAb, SCI, ZooRec. *Aud.:* Ac, Sa.

Palynology is the principal publication of the American Association of Stratigraphic Palynologists. The journal publishes manuscripts on all aspects of palynology, or the study of palynomorphs, which are microscopic fossils and their modern counterparts that are made of organic material and are resistant to acid processing treatments. These include acritarchs, dinoflagellate cysts, chitinozoa, fungal spores, green/blue algae, plant spores, pollen grains, and scolecodonts. Strong emphasis is placed on stratigraphic applications and biostratigraphy. Volumes are published annually and feature seven or eight research articles as well as the abstracts of the proceedings of the association's annual meeting. Recommended for specialized academic collections in paleontology, as well as for libraries supporting research in the oil and gas industries.

4798. *Quaternary Science Reviews.* [ISSN: 0277-3791] 1982. 24x/yr. EUR 1918. Ed(s): Jim Rose, D H Keen. Pergamon, The Boulevard, Langford Ln, East Park, Kidlington, OX5 1GB, United Kingdom. Refereed. Microform: PQC. Online: EBSCO Publishing, EBSCO Host; Gale; IngentaConnect; OhioLINK; ScienceDirect; SwetsWise Online Content. *Indexed:* AbAn, AnthLit, BrArAb, ChemAb, EngInd, M&GPA, NumL, OceAb, SCI, SWRA, ZooRec. *Bk. rev.:* Number and length vary. *Aud.:* Ac, Sa.

Quaternary Science Reviews publishes review papers covering all aspects of Quaternary science. These aspects include geology, geomorphology, geography, archaeology, soil science, paleobotany, paleontology, paleoclimatology, and the full range of applicable dating methods. *QSR* helps readers stay current on new developments in this rapidly changing field. Occasionally, a single issue will be devoted to an entire theme that arises from a recently held scientific meeting, or is a response to a significant change in Quaternary subject matter. Recommended for academic and research libraries that support paleontology and/or geology departments.

4799. *Review of Palaeobotany and Palynology.* [ISSN: 0034-6667] 1967. 20x/yr. EUR 2340. Ed(s): H Visscher, H. Kerp. Elsevier BV, Radarweg 29, Amsterdam, 1043 NX, Netherlands; nlinfo-f@elsevier.nl; http://www.elsevier.nl. Illus., index, adv. Refereed. Microform: PQC. Online: EBSCO Publishing, EBSCO Host; Gale; IngentaConnect; OhioLINK; ScienceDirect; SwetsWise Online Content. *Indexed:* AbAn, Agr, BiolAb, CABA, FPA, ForAb, HortAb, PetrolAb, S&F, SCI, SWRA, ZooRec. *Aud.:* Ac, Sa.

The *Review of Palaeobotany and Palynology* is an international journal that covers all fields of paleobotany and palynology, including all groups ranging from marine palynomorphs to higher land plants. Typical topics are systematics, evolution, paleobiology, paleoecology, biostratigraphy, biochronology, paleoclimatology, paleogeography, taphonomy, paleoenvironmental reconstructions, vegetation history, and the practical applications of paleobotany and palynology, such as coal and petroleum geology and archaeology. Special emphasis is placed on the applications of paleobotany and palynology in solving fundamental geological and biological problems using innovative and interdisciplinary approaches. The high cost of the title will test many libraries' budgets, but the journal is strongly recommended for both academic collections and research libraries that support the coal and oil industries.

■ PARAPSYCHOLOGY

Christianne L. Casper, Instruction Coordinator, Broward Community College, South Campus Library, 7200 Pines Blvd., Pembroke Pines, FL 33024; a012724t@bcfreenet.seflin.lib.fl.us

Introduction

There have been accounts of paranormal experiences throughout history and across all cultures. These events are described as unusual experiences that appear to be unexplainable through known scientific principles. Parapsychology is the study of such paranormal phenomena.

There are those who study parapsychology with total belief that they will prove the existence of paranormal phenomena, while others are completely skeptical, working aggressively to explain such phenomena in known scientific terms. Then there are those who fall in the middle, who are open to all possibilities but believe that the burden of proof lies with those who make paranormal claims. Popular interest in parapsychology has steadily increased, and this has produced a growing number of journals to inform and promote parapsychological research.

Two of the oldest and most prominent journals published are from the American Society for Psychical Research and the Society for Psychical Research (British). They are both core journals for any parapsychological collection. The *Journal of Parapsychology* and the *Journal of Religion and Psychical Research* provide a professional forum for psychical research.

There are other journals that simply seek to provide information on paranormal and strange phenomena. These include the *Fortean Times* (British) and *Nexus Magazine* (Australian). Then there are those journals that take on the role of skepticism, investigating paranormal claims in order to separate scientific findings from media sensationalism. These include *Skeptical Inquirer* and *Skeptic*.

The journals reviewed here reflect multiple viewpoints, providing as reliable and authoritative information as is scientifically possible.

Basic Periodicals

Ga, Ac: *American Society for Psychical Research. Journal, Journal of Parapsychology, Journal of Religion & Psychical Research, Skeptic, Skeptical Inquirer;* Sa: *American Society for Psychical Research. Journal, Journal of Parapsychology, Journal of Religion and Psychical Research, Skeptical Inquirer, Society for Psychical Research. Journal.*

Basic Abstracts and Indexes

Exceptional Human Experience.

4800. *American Society for Psychical Research. Journal.* [ISSN: 0003-1070] 1907. q. USD 100 (Individuals, USD 70; Students, USD 45). Ed(s): Rhea A White. American Society for Psychical Research, Inc., 5 W 73rd St, New York, NY 10023. Illus., index. Sample. Refereed. Circ: 2000. Vol. ends: Oct. Microform: PQC. *Indexed:* IBR, PhilInd, PsycInfo, SSCI. *Bk. rev.:* 3-4. *Aud.:* Ac, Sa.

The American Society for Psychical Research was founded in 1885 and is the oldest psychic research organization in the United States. Its journal is known for its informative, scholarly coverage of topics including, but not limited to, ESP, precognition, psychokinesis, and psychic healing. The journal includes scholarly reports, research, and field studies focusing on firsthand reports of paranormal phenomena. Issues average about four articles, with tables/graphs, footnotes, and references. Some issues include a correspondence column and a book review section. The society's web site, www.aspr.com, includes sample articles.

4801. *The Anomalist (Online Edition).* Formerly (until 2002): *The Anomalist (Print).* 1994. irreg. Ed(s): Patrick Huyghe. The Anomalist, PO Box 577, Jefferson Valley, NY 10535. *Bk. rev.:* Number and length vary. *Aud.:* Ga.

The Anomalist at www.anomalist.com explores the unexplained mysteries of science, nature, and history. In fall 2002, *The Anomalist* combined its print and web editions to create one online journal. This journal includes news from around the world that is updated daily, as well as original articles, commentaries, and book reviews. In addition, under Site Archives, there are the "High Strangeness Reports," the "A Files," and "Quotable Fort" (quotations from Charles Fort). Article archives are also available.

4802. *European Journal of Parapsychology.* [ISSN: 0168-7263] 1974. s-a. GBP 70. Ed(s): Paul Stevens. Koestler Chair of Parapsychology, Dept. of Psychology, Univ. of Edinburgh, Edinburgh, EH8 9JZ, United Kingdom; http://moebius.psy.ed.ac.uk/ejp.html. Refereed. Circ: 250. *Indexed:* PsycInfo. *Bk. rev.:* 2-4 per issue. *Aud.:* Ac, Sa.

The *European Journal of Parapsychology* is a scholarly journal that focuses on enhancing research in parapsychology, especially in Europe. It provides original papers that communicate empirical, theoretical, historical, and sociological research results as they relate to parapsychology. There are five to nine articles per issue, and each article includes an abstract, charts/statistics, and extensive references. "Research Notes" and book reviews are also included. The journal's web site (http://ejp.org.uk) includes a back-issue index as well as the table of contents for the current issue.

4803. *Fortean Times: the journal of strange phenomena.* [ISSN: 0308-5899] 1973. m. GBP 30 domestic; GBP 37.50 in Europe; GBP 45 elsewhere. Ed(s): David Sutton. John Brown Citrus Publishing, The New Boathouse, 136-142, Bramley Rd, London, W10 6SR, United Kingdom; ft@johnbrown.co.uk; http://www.forteantimes.com. Illus., adv. Circ: 60193 Paid. *Bk. rev.:* 7-9. *Aud.:* Ga, Ac, Sa.

Fortean Times was founded to continue the investigative research of Charles Fort (1874–1932), one of the first UFOlogists and a skeptical investigator of the bizarre and unusual. This publication provides news; reviews; research on strange phenomena, psychic experiences, and prodigies; and portents from around the world. While the publication maintains a humorous air, its goal is to provide thought-provoking, educational information. The articles provide resources that usually include recommended readings, surfings, and/or notes. In addition to articles, each issue includes book and media reviews, "Strange Days," and "Forum." The online edition includes the table of contents for the current issue, brief book and media reviews, an article archive, breaking news, a gallery, and exclusive features.

4804. *Journal of Parapsychology.* [ISSN: 0022-3387] 1937. s-a. USD 75 (Individuals, USD 65; USD 85 foreign). Ed(s): John A. Palmer. Rhine Research Center, 2741 Campus Walk Ave., Bldg. 500, Durham, NC 27705; http://www.rhine.org. Illus., index, adv. Sample. Refereed. Circ: 500 Paid. Vol. ends: Dec. Microform: PQC. Online: EBSCO Publishing, EBSCO Host; Florida Center for Library Automation; Gale; Northern Light Technology, Inc.; OCLC Online Computer Library Center, Inc.; ProQuest K-12 Learning Solutions; ProQuest LLC (Ann Arbor); H.W. Wilson. *Indexed:* BRI, CBRI, ExcerpMed, IBR, IBZ, PsycInfo, SSCI. *Bk. rev.:* 3-5. *Aud.:* Ac, Sa.

The *Journal of Parapsychology,* founded by J.B. Rhine, was one of the first scholarly parapsychology journals published. Its primary focus is to provide a professional forum for original research reports on experimental parapsychology. In addition to the technical experimental reports, the journal averages six to eight articles and includes surveys of literature, book reviews, and correspondence. Tables of contents for previous issues are available online at www.rhine.org.

4805. *Journal of Spirituality and Paranormal Studies.* Former titles (until 2006): *Journal of Religion & Psychical Research;* (until 1980): *Academy of Religion and Psychical Research. Journal.* 1979. q. Ed(s): Dr. Donald R Morse. Academy of Religion and Psychical Research, PO Box 614, Bloomfield, CT 06002-0614. Index. Sample. Circ: 200. Vol. ends: Oct. *Indexed:* RI-1. *Bk. rev.:* 3-5. *Aud.:* Ac, Sa.

This journal was established to provide a forum among clergy, academics, and researchers concerning religion, philosophy, and psychical research. There are about five articles in each issue, some with references. In addition, there are research proposals, abstracts of completed research, views and comments, book reviews, and correspondence. Recommended for religion or parapsychology collections. An index to the publishing organization's journals and some samples of journal articles are available at www.lightlink.com/arpr.

4806. *Nexus Magazine.* [ISSN: 1039-0170] 1987. bi-m. AUD 33 domestic; USD 24.95 United States. Ed(s): Duncan M Roads. Nexus Magazine Pty Ltd., PO Box 30, Mapleton, QLD 4560, Australia; editor@nexusmagazine.com; http://www.nexusmagazine.com/. Illus., adv. Circ: 45000 Paid. Vol. ends: Nov/Dec (No. 6). *Bk. rev.:* 10-14. *Aud.:* Ga.

Nexus Magazine is an international periodical that looks at global issues and science news dealing with controversial phenomena and the unexplained. Each issue includes "Global News," "Science News," "The Twilight Zone," and five to seven articles. In addition, there is a large selection of book reviews as well

as video and music reviews. The online version includes the table of contents for the current issue and previously published articles. There is a catalogue of books and materials published by Nexus and a list of web sites of interest.

4807. *Skeptic.* [ISSN: 1063-9330] 1992. q. USD 30 domestic; USD 40 in Canada & Mexico; USD 50 elsewhere. Ed(s): Michael Shermer. Millenium Press, 2761 N Marengo Ave, Altadena, CA 91001; arcie@netcom.com; http://www.skeptic.com. Illus., index, adv. Sample. Refereed. Circ: 10000 Paid. Vol. ends: Nov. Online: EBSCO Publishing, EBSCO Host; Florida Center for Library Automation; Gale; Northern Light Technology, Inc.; OCLC Online Computer Library Center, Inc.; ProQuest LLC (Ann Arbor); H.W. Wilson. *Indexed:* ASIP, AmHI, BRI, CBRI, GSI, RI-1. *Bk. rev.:* 5-7. *Aud.:* Ga, Ac.

Skeptic promotes scientific and critical thinking while investigating claims made on a variety of topics, including pseudoscience, pseudohistory, the paranormal, magic, superstition, fringe claims, and revolutionary science. The features included in every issue are "Articles," "News," "Forum," "Reviews," and "Junior Skeptic." Some issues of *Skeptic* also include movie and audio reviews. The online version provides the table of contents for the current issue, archives, book reviews, a reading room (resources and forum) and "Junior Skeptic."

4808. *Skeptical Inquirer: the magazine for science and reason.* Formerly (until 1977): *Zetetic.* [ISSN: 0194-6730] 1976. bi-m. USD 35 domestic. Ed(s): Ken Frazier. Committee for the Scientific Investigation of Claims of the Paranormal, PO Box 703, Buffalo, NY 14226-0703; info@csicop.org; http://www.csicop.org. Illus., index. Circ: 50000. Online: Factiva, Inc.; Florida Center for Library Automation; Gale; Northern Light Technology, Inc.; OCLC Online Computer Library Center, Inc.; ProQuest K-12 Learning Solutions; ProQuest LLC (Ann Arbor). *Indexed:* RGPR, RI-1. *Bk. rev.:* 2-4. *Aud.:* Ga, Ac, Sa.

Skeptical Inquirer focuses on what the scientific community knows about claims of the paranormal, as opposed to media sensationalism. The journal promotes scientific research, critical thinking, and science education. Standard features include "News and Comment," "Notes on a Strange World," "Forum," "Articles," "New Books," and "Letters to the Editor." In addition to parapsychology, topics investigated include UFOs, alternative therapy, psychic claims, astrology, skepticism in general, and other paranormal experiences. The online version includes an index of articles, special features, and online articles.

4809. *Society for Psychical Research. Journal.* [ISSN: 0037-9751] 1884. q. GBP 40; USD 80. Ed(s): Zofia Weaver. Society for Psychical Research, 49 Marloes Rd, Kensington, London, W8 6LA, United Kingdom; http://www.spr.ac.uk/. Illus., index, adv. Sample. Vol. ends: Oct. *Indexed:* IBR, IBZ, PsycInfo. *Bk. rev.:* Occasional. *Aud.:* Sa.

The journal of the Society for Psychical Research is one of the oldest parapsychological publications. It aims to objectively examine paranormal experiences and reports that appear to be otherwise inexplicable. The journal publishes field and case studies, experimental reports, book reviews, and historical and theoretical papers. All papers are strictly peer-reviewed. There are approximately five articles per issue, complete with tables, graphs, and references. The contents of approximately 120 years' worth of journals, proceedings, and abstracts are available online to members only.

■ PARENTING

Caroline M. Kent, Head of Research Services, Widener Library, Harvard University, Cambridge, MA 02138

Introduction

Are there publications that can actually help a new (or even experienced) parent?! It is certainly the case that new parents are always desperate for information and help, and that there is therefore a market for such publications. This is particularly so in this era when many parenting individuals are separated from the older generations of their families—generations that carry parenting wisdom and experience.

It is also arguable that parenting is now more complicated in this era of dual-career families, single and divorced parents, and alternative families of all sorts. Even those families practicing a more traditional family form, with a stay-at-home mom, may find the lack of neighborhoods and extended family daunting. The modern reality is that there aren't too many parents who don't feel that they need all the help they can get!

Parenting magazines really fall neatly into two categories: magazines that are general enough to contain articles of interest to a wide range of families; and magazines that contain articles interesting to particular parents, such as adoptive or single parents. It should also be acknowledged that there are many national parenting web sites that do not easily fall into the category of e-zines. There is content on these sites that is serial in nature, but a substantial portion of the site may actually be guided (or unguided) message boarding. Because of the nature of these sites, they are not included in this list. However, libraries wishing to create robust resource link pages must consider them. One large and impressive example of sources in this category is ParentSoup (www.parentsoup.com). Beyond message boarding, of course, looms blogging—not something to be dealt with here, but it is a serial-style format that we must all watch carefully.

Another note on format: This section must necessarily be more tolerant of the newsletter format, since parents often have little time for prolonged reading. There are some very thoughtful newsletters that address niche-need (e.g., *Different Kind of Parenting*), and these should be evaluated carefully.

There aren't many journals in this section that would appeal to the clientele at most college and university libraries. The exception to that would be any school that has an active child development or family therapeutic program.

In addition to the titles listed here, there are a large number of excellent local parenting magazines (such as *Boston Parents' Paper* and *Black Parenting Today: Information and Resources for Greater Philadelphia Families*). Public libraries should identify such publications for their areas and include them in current collections.

Basic Periodicals

Ga: *American Baby, Baby Talk, Child, FamilyFun, Parent & Child, Parenting, Parents*.

Basic Abstracts and Indexes

Education Index, ERIC, Exceptional Child Education Resources, Psychological Abstracts, Readers' Guide to Periodical Literature.

4810. *Adoption Today.* Formerly (until 2000): *Chosen Child.* [ISSN: 1527-8522] 1998. bi-m. USD 24 domestic; USD 29.50 Canada; USD 42 elsewhere. Louis & Company Publishing, 541 E Garden Dr, Unit N, Windsor, CO 80550-3150. *Bk. rev.:* 3-4, 50-100 words. *Aud.:* Ga, Sa.

Unlike the softer, more adoptive-parent–oriented *Adoptive Families, Adoption Today* pulls few punches. It more clearly represents all voices in adoption, that is, the voices of adoptees, birth parents, and adoption professionals, as well as those of adoptive parents. The result is an interesting magazine that seeks to illuminate those adoption issues that are often hard to face. Its articles and editorials are edgy and interesting, often authored by controversial adoption advocates such as Marley Greiner ("The Bastard Nation") and Trish Maskew ("Ethica"). Some recent articles include "When the Headlines Are Unsettling," "Adoption of Children with Prenatal Alcohol Exposure," and "Why Open International Adoption?" Any public library that serves a large adoption community should consider its purchase, as well as any academic or special library that serves the needs of social work students or adoption professionals.

4811. *Adoptive Families.* Formerly (until 1994): *Ours (Minneapolis).* [ISSN: 1076-1020] 1967. bi-m. USD 24.95 domestic; USD 32.95 Canada; USD 36.95 elsewhere. Ed(s): Susan Caughman. Adoptive Families Magazine, 39 W 37th Str, 15th fl, New York, NY 10018. Illus., adv. Sample. Circ: 25000. *Bk. rev.:* 3-8, 50 words. *Aud.:* Ga, Sa.

This glossy, family-oriented magazine is considered the standard publication by the adoptive family community. The editor, Susan Caughman, has done much to broaden the editorial perspective from the magazine's earlier version: There are now regular columns contributed by birth parents, adoption lawyers, doctors, and adoption experts, such as Lois Melina, etc. The magazine still maintains its family orientation, with pictures of subscribing families and

feature articles of general interest. Recent examples of articles include "Adopting an Older Child?," "Parenting Transracially," and "China Ghosts." *Adoptive Families* has a slightly softer, more cheerful take on adoption than the harder *Adoption Today*, but it remains a central and important magazine for the adoption community. American adoption has become less secret and more of a topic for public discussion. For that reason, any public library that serves growing families should consider purchasing this magazine, as should academic or special collections that serve adoption professionals.

4812. *American Baby: for expectant and new parents.* Formerly: *Mothers-to-Be - American Baby.* [ISSN: 0044-7544] 1938. m. USD 12 domestic (Free to qualified personnel). Ed(s): Judith Nolte. Meredith Corp., 125 Park Ave, 19th Fl, New York, NY 10017; http://www.meredith.com. Illus., adv. Sample. Circ: 2000000 Controlled. *Indexed:* Agr, CINAHL. *Aud.:* Ga.

There aren't too many American families with young children who don't read or at least receive issues of this magazine. Expectant parents can get it free for several months. It is the oldest and most reliable of the commercial baby-parenting magazines, containing a wide range of short, easy-to-read articles on baby and parent health issues, developmental discussions, baby care, and family issues. In addition to the huge number of advertisements for baby-related products, it also contains discussion and reviews of new products. There are advice columns that cover everything from behavior to health and nutrition. The magazine also has a healthy and well-maintained web site that is updated frequently. All public libraries should should invest in this.

4813. *At-Home Dad: promoting the home-based father.* [ISSN: 1081-5767] 1994. q. USD 15. Ed(s): Peter Baylies. At-Home Dad, 61 Brightwood Ave, North Andover, MA 01845; athomedad@aol.com; http://www.athomedad.com. Illus., adv. Circ: 1000. Online: ProQuest LLC (Ann Arbor). *Indexed:* GendWatch. *Aud.:* Ga, Sa.

At-Home Dad is an appealing mix of fun, facts, suggestions, and inspiration for men who are primary caregivers for their children. Articles cover every facet of parenting and child-rearing from swimming lessons to dealing with "down" times when the children are away from home. Columns offer advice on raising children and sources of information and help in meeting the challenge. The "At-Home Dad Network," a section that appears in each issue of the newsletter, provides news of the Dad-to-Dad support group. *At-Home Dad* is an excellent selection for most public libraries.

4814. *Baby Talk.* Former titles (until 2000): *Parenting's Baby Talk;* (until 199?): *Baby Talk Magazine;* (until 1977): *New Baby Talk;* (until 1976): *Baby Talk.* [ISSN: 1529-5389] 1935. 10x/yr. USD 19.95 (Free to qualified personnel). Time - Warner Inc., 530 5th Ave, New York, NY 10036. Illus., adv. Sample. Circ: 1800000. Vol. ends: Nov. *Indexed:* RGPR. *Bk. rev.:* 2-3. *Aud.:* Ga.

Baby Talk, one of the oldest continuing parenting magazines, is targeted to the needs of expectant mothers and parents of newborns. For these readers, it is even free for the asking. Packed with short, informative articles on baby care, health, developmental concerns, family issues, and product discussions, it also has regular columns, many of them based on readers' questions (such as "Wit and Wisdom" and "Ask Dr. Mom"). Every public library should consider this publication.

4815. *Brain, Child: the magazine for thinking mothers.* [ISSN: 1528-5170] q. USD 19.95 domestic; USD 26 Canada; USD 34 elsewhere. Ed(s): Jennifer Niesslein, Stephanie Wilkinson. March Press, LLC, Box 714, Lexington, VA 24450; publisher@brainchildmag.com. Adv. Vol. ends: Winter. *Bk. rev.:* 2-4. *Aud.:* Ga, Ac.

How can we resist a journal that says in its mission statement that "motherhood is worthy of literature"? Or that this "isn't your typical magazine. We couldn't cupcake-decorate our way out of a paper bag." This journal is totally irresistible! Each issue contains a mix of intriguing essays, feature articles, humor, fiction, and art—some of which has some powerful names attached, such as Barbara Kingsolver, Perri Klass, Mary Gordon, and Alice Hoffman (all mothers themselves). This isn't a how-to magazine; rather, it is a why-do-we-do-it-at-all magazine. Recent essays include "We (Don't) All Sleep Alone," "Are Kids' Consumer Trends Worth Fighting For," and "Slide: A Different Species of

Playground Prowler." There's a great humor column ("MotherWit") and a book review section that is thoughtful without taking itself too seriously. Funny, thought-provoking, and full of terrific reads, this magazine should be considered by any college library with a writing program and any public library with the right constituency.

Child & Family Behavior Therapy. See Family section.

4816. ***Cookie: a lifestyle magazine for sophisticated parents.*** [ISSN: 1556-410X] 2005. 6x/yr. Ed(s): Pilar Guzman. Fairchild Publications, Inc., 7 W 34th St, New York, NY 10001-8191; customerservice@fairchildpub.com; http://www.fairchildpub.com. Adv. Circ: 300000. *Aud.:* Ga.

"*Cookie* showcases all the best for your family, featuring fashion, home, travel, entertainment and health for parents and their children. With a clean, stylish design aesthetic, *Cookie* believes that being a good parent and maintaining your sense of style are not mutually exclusive." Now, that mission statement pretty much sums up what this new, glossy magazine's intent is. If you can make it past that statement, and the magazine's subtitle, you will in fact find an attractive, well-written magazine that has many articles that are interesting and have wide appeal. For public libraries that serve populations of new parents with good incomes.

4817. ***DadMag.com.*** irreg. DADMAG.com, LLC, 1333 N Kingsbury, Ste 100, Chicago, IL 60622; InfoCenter@Dadmag.com; http://www.dadmag.com/. *Bk. rev.:* 10, 200 words. *Aud.:* Ga, Sa.

An online journal that celebrates fatherhood, *Dadmag.com* looks at topics from single fatherhood to rearing teens. Feature articles, editorials, reviews, and reader opinion are all included. The writing is excellent. Some recent article titles include "Coping at Home After Losing a Job" and "Why Dads Matter." All public libraries should consider this title.

4818. ***Daughters: for parents of girls.*** [ISSN: 1521-4273] 1996. bi-m. USD 27.99. Ed(s): Helen Cordes. New Moon Publishing, 2 W First St, Ste 101, Duluth, MN 55802; newmoon@newmoon.org; http://www.newmoon.org. *Indexed:* CWI, GendWatch. *Aud.:* Ga.

My only complaint about *Daughters* is that there is no corresponding publication entitled *Sons*. Anyone who parents both boys and girls knows that although the two might be equal, they are far from alike. This small and interesting publication's whole focus is on the parenting of girls: the psychological, social, and spiritual issues that arise in the lives of young women. Examples of recent titles include "Journaling Toward Body Love," "Let's Talk: Lifting the Weight Over Size," and "Positive Parenting Power and Sports." Each issue may include interviews, Internet resource lists, links for dads, and news. An excellent choice for any public library.

4819. ***Different Kind of Parenting: a 'zine for parents whose children have died.*** [ISSN: 1533-8886] 2001. q. USD 8 newsstand/cover per issue. Ed(s): Kara L C Jones. Kota Press, PO Box 514, Vashon Island, WA 98070; http://www.kotapress.com. *Aud.:* Ga.

Would that such a publication were not necessary. Its origins are the grief writings of the poet Kara Jones. It remains a small publication, more a newsletter than a magazine. While this title might seem macabre to some, journaling and grief writing are regarded as an important healing mechanism. Some titles of recent essays include "Mothers Day & Fathers Day," "Write Rite Right," and "What Pema Chodron Taught Me." Although this calls itself a zine, in reality it is a newsletter. Large public libraries should consider this; further, hospital libraries with patient collections should consider its purchase.

Exceptional Parent. See Family section.

4820. ***Family Matters!: parenting magazine.*** [ISSN: 1529-2673] 1999. m. Free. Ed(s): Laura Ramirez. Kokopellis Treasures, 5231 Rosehill Ct, Reno, NV 89502-7785; lauraramirez@charter.net. Circ: 5573. *Bk. rev.:* 2-4. *Aud.:* Ga.

Family Matters! is a very thoughtful and vital online magazine. The brainchild of psychologist Laura Ramirez, it focuses on the psychology of parenting and ethics and values in families. Any public library that serves families should consider linking to this site: www.familymatters.tv.

4821. ***FamilyFun.*** [ISSN: 1056-6333] 1991. 10x/yr. USD 10 domestic; USD 22 Canada; USD 30 elsewhere. Ed(s): Barbara Findlen, Ann Hallock. Family and Children's Magazine Group, 114 5th Ave, New York, NY 10011; fafcustserv@cdsfulfillment.com; http://www.familyfun.com. Illus., adv. Circ: 1700000 Paid. *Bk. rev.:* 5-6, 75-100 words. *Aud.:* Ga.

Well, okay, so it's Disney, or a branch of Disney, that publishes this magazine. But if there's one thing that the Disney magicians are good at conjuring up, it's fun, right? The format is nice, with great photographs of kids and their families—all having fun! There are craft activities, rainy-day-fun ideas, traveling-with-the-kids ideas, and party ideas of all kinds, as well as reviews of toys and games, books, and videos. This is actually a wonderful magazine, jam-packed with ideas for even the most creative of parents. It is really the only magazine that has family activities as its total focus; therefore, it is an invaluable addition to any parenting magazine collection. Any public library not located in a retirement home should purchase this. Very highly recommended.

4822. ***Fathering Magazine: the online magazine for men with families.*** [ISSN: 1091-5516] 1995. m. Free. Ed(s): Alexander Sheldon. Fathering Enterprises, Inc., PO Box 231891, Houston, TX 77223; sheldon@fathermag.com; http://www.fathermag.com/. Illus., adv. Circ: 1000000. *Aud.:* Ga, Sa.

This substantive online journal is intended for teachers, students, and practitioners, as well as dads themselves. It includes research and practice-based articles on all aspects of fatherhood and males in the role of parent. Issues covered include parenting, father/child relationships, divorce, stepfathers, child custody, and more. *Fathering Magazine* is a title that academic and research librarians should be aware of and recommend when appropriate. All public libraries should consider it.

4823. ***Fostering Families Today.*** [ISSN: 1531-409X] 2001. bi-m. USD 24 domestic; USD 29 Canada. Louis & Company Publishing, 541 E Garden Dr, Unit N, Windsor, CO 80550-3150. *Aud.:* Ga, Sa.

Thank goodness! We have needed this magazine for so long, and finally, here it is. The foster parent community clearly deals with many of the same issues as adoptive parents and people parenting their birth children; but there is a deep range of social, legal, medical, and psychological issues that are particular to their interests. This glossy new magazine strives to service those interests and includes recent articles such as "Laughter, Bonding & Adopting the Older Child," "New Law Strengthens Role of Foster Parents in Court," and "Making the Relationship Work for Children." There are also regular columns, such as "Washington Beat" and "Family Talk," which keep an eye on important legislative and medical issues relevant to fostering. Given the number of children in care in the United States, any medium to large public library should purchase this magazine. In addition, any special or academic library that serves social workers or social work students should consider its purchase.

4824. ***Gay Parent.*** [ISSN: 1545-6714] 1998. bi-m. USD 20 domestic; USD 30 foreign. Ed(s): Angeline Acain. Gay Parent, PO Box 750852, Forest Hills, NY 11375-0852. Adv. Sample. *Bk. rev.:* 1, 150 words, signed. *Aud.:* Ga.

Gay Parent is one of the more thoughtful parenting magazines in print. It assumes that its readership is interested in substantive book reviews, extensive interviews, and legislative information. It periodically publishes lists of gay-friendly private schools and camps, and articles on adoption and foster care. Subscribers may elect to get the full text of the magazine online for a reduced subscription rate. This magazine will be well placed in any public library with a parent population interested in diverse family structures.

4825. ***Gifted Child Today Magazine: the nation's leading resource for nurturing talented children.*** Former titles (until 1993): *Gifted Child Today; G C T (Gifted, Creative, Talented Children).* [ISSN: 1076-2175] 1978. q. USD 35 domestic; USD 45 foreign. Ed(s): Susan Johnsen.

Prufrock Press Inc., PO Box 8813, Waco, TX 76714-8813; info@prufrock.com; http://www.prufrock.com. Illus., adv. Sample. Circ: 20000. *Indexed:* ABIn, ECER, ERIC, EduInd, RILM. *Bk. rev.:* 3-5, 100 words. *Aud.:* Ga, Sa.

This magazine is intended to support both teachers and parents of gifted children. It is full of articles not only on the educational theory of the teaching of the gifted but also on ideas for both curriculum development and learning plans for home. Recent articles include "Cultural Diversity in Gifted Education," "Teaching Science to Gifted Children in the Primary Grades," and "Underachievement Among Gifted Children." Recommended for school libraries, academic libraries that support education programs, and large public libraries.

4826. The Informed Parent: the weekly internet magazine of the 21st century. m. Ed(s): John H Samson. Intermag Productions, 23546 Coyote Springs Dr, Diamond Bar, CA 91765; http://www.informedparent.com. *Aud.:* Ga.

The Informed Parent is published by the Pediatric Medical Center of Long Beach, California. Articles are written by staff and other experts in the fields of education, social work, and psychology. Titles of recent features include "Snoring in a Two-Year Old—A Problem or Not?," "Risperdal and Autism," and "A Refresher on Jaundice." The articles are well written and informative, and a loosely indexed online archive is maintained. Further, the site offers a list of both children's and adult books on health topics that is linked to Amazon.com. This is a clear, well-developed site that all public libraries that serve families should consider.

4827. Main Street Mom. w. Ed(s): Mia Cronan. Word Results, Co., PO Box 264, Hudson, OH 44236-0264; subscribeme@mainstreetmom.com; http://www.mainstreetmom.com/. *Bk. rev.:* Number and length vary. *Aud.:* Ga.

In years past, it was assumed by publishers that the readers of such magazines as *Good Housekeeping* and *Redbook* were women who were keeping house and being stay-at-home moms. Not so anymore. But women who do choose to stay at home and parent often find themselves alone, without the traditional neighborhood and family supports that they once had. This online publication is intended to fill this gap. It contains a wide range of feature articles, some on parenting but also some on cooking, crafts, and family issues. Recent article titles include "10 Ways to Get Your Kids to Talk to You," "How Do You Want to Spend the Rest of Your Life," and "Battle of the Generations, Round One." One interesting feature that goes beyond formal articles is the hosted message boards that offer help on an ever-changing and wide variety of topics. And these online discussions are attended by an international group of moms: while I was on for five minutes, there were women from Tupelo, Mississippi; New York City; Melbourne, Australia; Ontario; and Tasmania engaged in active discussion—a truly global neighborhood! Any public library that serves a large population of stay-at-home parents should consider linking to this resource.

4828. Mothering: the magazine of natural family living. [ISSN: 0733-3013] 1976. bi-m. USD 22.95 domestic; USD 27.95 Canada; USD 32.95 elsewhere. Ed(s): Peggy O'Mara. Mothering Magazine, 1807 2nd St #100, Santa Fe, NM 87505. Illus., index, adv. Sample. Circ: 78000 Paid. Microform: PQC. Online: EBSCO Publishing, EBSCO Host; Gale; Northern Light Technology, Inc.; OCLC Online Computer Library Center, Inc. *Indexed:* AltPI, CWI. *Aud.:* Ga.

Ads for cloth diapers, baby slings, and wooden toys should give the reader a good indication of this magazine's editorial position. Although it covers parenting issues beyond pregnancy and childbirth, we include this magazine here as an alternative to the other conventional, consumer-oriented pregnancy magazines. The news section takes a critical look at health issues related to pregnancy and childbirth, and it reviews studies and legislation on issues such as mercury in vaccines and how C-sections affect breast-milk intake. Features are written by experts or advocates in the field, rather than staff reporters, and include extensive bibliographic notes. *Mothering* has a boldly activist agenda. Its web site (www.mothering.com) includes an "Action Alert" section, which lists key issues and how readers can participate. Recommended for public libraries and academic libraries that support programs in child development and, possibly, women's studies.

4829. Parent & Child: the learning link between home & school. [ISSN: 1070-0552] 1993. 8x/yr. USD 9.97. Ed(s): Stephanie Izarek. Scholastic Inc., 557 Broadway, New York, NY 10012; http://www.scholastic.com. Adv. Circ: 1200000 Paid. *Bk. rev.:* 3-4, 25 words. *Aud.:* Ga, Sa.

Parent & Child has an interesting life: first, it is a printed magazine that covers learning issues from birth to about six years, happening to be part of Scholastic's larger web presence, which not only includes this magazine's content. But also, it takes the reader further through middle school. Not surprisingly, Scholastic has collected an advisory board for the magazine that includes several national early childhood experts. The articles are short and informative and are intended to bridge a child's preschool learning experience with its learning life at home. The magazine presents learning and health issues, behavioral and developmental information, and lots of activities for parents to use at home. All public libraries should consider this magazine; also, learning resource centers at schools that train early childhood staff should purchase it.

4830. Parenting. [ISSN: 0890-247X] 1987. 11x/yr. USD 12 domestic; USD 22 Canada; USD 3.99 per issue. Time Publishing Ventures, 1325 Ave of the Americas, 27th Fl, New York, NY 10019; http://www.parenting.com. Illus., adv. Circ: 1300000 Paid and controlled. Online: EBSCO Publishing, EBSCO Host; Gale; LexisNexis; OCLC Online Computer Library Center, Inc.; ProQuest LLC (Ann Arbor); H.W. Wilson. *Indexed:* RGPR. *Bk. rev.:* 4-6, 40-50 words. *Aud.:* Ga.

Parenting is jam-packed with information for parents, particularly new parents. As with many parenting publications, its articles diminish in number and usefulness as the child becomes older (perhaps this is based on the assumption that only new parents need help!). There are many columns and departments, such as "Your Health" and "Reviews," as well as quizzes, recipes, feature articles, and product reviews—all packaged in short, quick-read columns, certainly a necessary length for new parents. The ads alone make this magazine extremely useful. The associated web site has related, complementary information, also packaged neatly and effectively. This useful and reliable magazine is highly recommended for any public library that serves families.

4831. Parents: on rearing children from crib to college. Former titles (until 1993): *Parents' Magazine;* (until 1985): *Parents;* (until 1978): *Parents' Magazine;* (until 1977): *Parents' Magazine and Better Homemaking; Parents' Magazine and Better Family Living;* Incorporates (1976-1981): *Parents Home;* Which was formerly (until 19??): *Handy Andy Magazine.* [ISSN: 1083-6373] 1926. m. USD 9.97 domestic; USD 29.97 Canada. Meredith Corp., 1716 Locust St, Des Moines, IA 50309-3023; http://www.meredith.com. Illus., adv. Circ: 2200000 Paid and controlled. CD-ROM: ProQuest LLC (Ann Arbor). Online: OCLC Online Computer Library Center, Inc.; ProQuest LLC (Ann Arbor); H.W. Wilson. *Indexed:* BRI, CBRI, CINAHL, ConsI, IHTDI, PdeR, RGPR. *Bk. rev.:* 4-5, 50 words. *Aud.:* Ga.

Parents has in many ways become the industry standard for parenting magazines. As with many others, its focus tends to be on early childhood development and health topics rather than on issues associated with older children. There are many regular columns on child development and health, and on maternal and parental health—often focused on readers' questions. Current columns include "What's It Really Like?," "Work & Family," and "Good Manners." Feature articles include many short pieces on family life, home style, fun time, and health and safety, to name just a few departments. Recent article titles include "57 Cool Things to Do with Your Baby This Year," "Sugar Shocker," and "Disney: Stuff They Don't Tell You in a Guidebook." Highly recommended for any public library that addresses the needs of families.

4832. Pediatrics for Parents: the newsletter for anyone who cares for a child. [ISSN: 0730-6725] 1980. m. USD 20 domestic; USD 26 Canada; USD 35 elsewhere. Ed(s): Dr. Richard J Sagall. Pediatrics for Parents, Inc., 63716, Philadelphia, PA 19147-7516; pediatricsforparents@pobox.com; http://www.moms-refuge.com/. Adv. Sample. Circ: 80000 Paid. Microform: PQC. Online: EBSCO Publishing, EBSCO Host; Gale; Northern Light Technology, Inc.; ProQuest K-12 Learning Solutions; ProQuest LLC (Ann Arbor). *Aud.:* Ga.

This is similar to many other health newsletters now widely available, although it is the only one that specifically addresses children's health issues. It has a loose-leaf format (and libraries should be prepared for the storage and retention issues associated with that). Articles are clear and highly informative. Although some of these topics are periodically covered in more general parenting titles, *Pediatrics for Parents* contains much information otherwise unavailable to lay people. The online version of the newsletter allows subscribers to access pdf versions of articles significantly before the print version is mailed out. Any public library that serves parents should consider purchasing this title.

Topics in Early Childhood Special Education. See Disabilities section.

4833. *Twins: the magazine for parents of multiples.* [ISSN: 0890-3077] 1984. bi-m. USD 25.95 domestic; USD 31.95 Canada; USD 35.95 elsewhere. Ed(s): Susan J. Alt. Business Word, Inc., 11211 E Arapahoe Rd, Ste 101, Centennial, CO 80112-3851. Illus. Sample. Circ: 20000 Paid and controlled. Vol. ends: Nov/Dec. *Bk. rev.:* 2-3, 50 words. *Aud.:* Ga.

Oh, my. Double the joy—and double the trials of parenthood! Although there probably isn't a parent of twins (or triplets) who would have it any other way, there's no question that there are particular issues, both logistical and psychological, of handling the children of multiple birth. With fertility technologies increasing in use and sophistication, twinning (and beyond!) is much more common than it once was, so a cheerful, helpful magazine like *Twins* is welcome. It contains product reviews, feature articles, developmental discussions, and more. Articles are thoughtful, often highly personal discussions of issues and successes. Recommended for public libraries.

4834. *Wonder Time: celebrate your child's love of learning.* [ISSN: 1558-7495] 2006. q. USD 10 domestic; USD 22 Canada; USD 4.95 newsstand/cover per issue domestic. Ed(s): Lisa Stiepock. Buena Vista Magazines, Inc., 114 5th Ave, New York, NY 10011. Adv. *Aud.:* Ga.

Of all the new parenting magazines that have come out in recent years, this by far has the greatest appeal and most clearly fills an unmet need. Modern parenting and the education of children is very complicated in the face of raised expectations by state education departments, dual-career families, and increased pressure on children's time from electronics (which is both good and bad). This glossy elegant journal addresses these complexities nicely, and includes articles on play, education, childhood development, and the inevitable desperation of parenthood. The online version is also excellent, containing extra material, such as a "stay-at-home dad" blog. For all public libraries that address the needs of parents.

Working Mother See Fashion and Lifestyle section.

■ PEACE AND CONFLICT STUDIES

Suhasini L. Kumar, Coordinator Information Services, Carlson Library, The University of Toledo, 2801 W. Bancroft St., Toledo, OH 43606; Skumar@utnet.utoledo.edu

Introduction

More than 20 years ago, Nobel Peace Prize winner Elie Wiesel said in his acceptance lecture, "Mankind needs peace more than ever, for our entire planet, threatened by nuclear war, is in danger of total destruction. A destruction only man can provoke, only man can prevent." In 2005, the double Peace Prize was awarded to the International Atomic Energy Agency (IAEA) and its Director-General Mohamed ElBaradei. The IAEA had worked relentlessly to curb the proliferation of nuclear weapons and to promote the safe and peaceful use of nuclear technology, but there is still a grave need to make increasingly significant advancement on the issue of nuclear nonproliferation and disarmament. Elie Wiesel concluded his lecture with these profound words: "Peace is not God's gift to us but our gift to each other." Mankind is wholly responsible for the state of peace, our present condition, however, invokes one to lament with the poet William Wordsworth, "Much it grieves my heart to think what man has made of man."

Although the world presents a dismal picture with what appears to be insurmountable deterrents to peace, many of these problems can be resolved by cultivating a sense of responsibility for all mankind, and by consciously working toward creating an environment of peace.

There are several organizations, societies, and associations that are committed to peace and that strive to eliminate war. They consider it to be of vital importance that people be taught the basic tenets of peaceful coexistence and be inculcated with a strong desire for a culture of peace. These organizations publish books, journals, and newsletters in order to keep people informed about every aspect of peace and explore every event and incident that might threaten to explode into a dispute, and they provide in-depth analysis of various conditions and offer possible solutions to these controversial situations.

Peace associations such as the Canadian Peace Research and Education Association, the International Peace Research Association, and the Peace Science Society (International) usually publish scholarly journals with well-researched articles that include statistical information and empirical tests with results. Journals such as the *Journal of Peace Research, The Journal of Conflict Resolution,* and *Conflict Management and Peace Science* are some that fall into this category. There are also newsletters and grassroots publications that ardently support peace and provide news and articles that would be of interest to people from every stratum of society and encourage readers to voice their opinions freely. *Peace Magazine* is an example of this type of publication.

There has been a remarkable increase in the number of peace journals available on the Internet, and many publishers are also trying to offer access to archival information. There are several journals and newsletters that are available both in print and online. Although a subscription is usually required for Internet access to these publications, some of them, such as the newsletter *Peace Watch,* are free.

The periodicals selected for this section represent a broad array of journals, magazines, and newsletters that are committed to the pursuit of peace. The authors and editors of these publications are international contributors who are passionately involved with peace efforts. These publications have proven to be a valuable source of information to academicians, researchers, peace activists, and other advocates of peace.

Basic Periodicals

Hs: *Arms Control Today, Fellowship, Peace Review;* Ac: *Arms Control Today, Bulletin of the Atomic Scientists, Conflict Management and Peace Science, Journal of Conflict Resolution, Journal of Peace Research, Peace & Change, Peace Review.*

Basic Abstracts and Indexes

Alternative Press Index, Peace Research Abstracts Journal.

4835. *Action Report.* Former titles: *Peace Action;* (until 1993): *SANE - Freeze News;* (until 1990): *SANE World - Freeze Focus.* 1961. 4x/yr. USD 28. Ed(s): Gordon Clark. Peace Action, 1100 Wayne Ave., Ste. 1020, Silver Spring, MD 20910-5643; paprog@igc.apc.org; http://www.webcom.com/peaceact/. Illus. Circ: 38000. Vol. ends: Winter. Microform: PQC. *Aud.:* Ga.

The newsletter *Action Report,* which was formerly known as *Peace Action* and *Sane/Freeze News,* is a quarterly publication of Peace Action, one of the largest grassroots peace and justice organizations. Peace Action communicates important news and issues on the peace movement to its members and supporters of Peace Action and Peace Action Education through this newsletter. This publication encourages supporters to act on important peace and nonviolence-related issues and can be a source of inspiration to both peace activists and educators.

4836. *Arms Control Today.* [ISSN: 0196-125X] 1971. m. USD 80 (Individuals, USD 60). Ed(s): Miles A Pomper. Arms Control Association, 1150 Connecticut Ave, NW, Ste 620, Washington, DC 20036; aca@armscontrol.org; http://www.armscontrol.org. Illus., index, adv. Sample. Circ: 3000. Vol. ends: Dec. Microform: PQC. Online: EBSCO

Publishing, EBSCO Host; Florida Center for Library Automation; Gale; Northern Light Technology, Inc.; OCLC Online Computer Library Center, Inc.; ProQuest K-12 Learning Solutions; ProQuest LLC (Ann Arbor). *Indexed:* PAIS, PRA. *Bk. rev.:* 1, 800-1,200 words. *Aud.:* Ac.

The Arms Control Association, through its magazine *Arms Control Today,* provides policy makers, the press, and the interested public with authoritative information, analysis, and commentary on arms control proposals, treaties, negotiations and agreements, and related national security issues. It emphasizes arms control and is dedicated to promoting a better understanding of topics that concern arms control. The magazine offers comprehensive data and intelligence on national security issues. Each issue begins with a "Focus" essay that highlights an important issue related to arms control. In an article in the June 2006 issue, "Small Arms, Large Problem: The International Threat of Small Arms Proliferation and Misuse," the author talks about illegal proliferation of small arms and light weapons and considers this to be one of the most urgent security threats we face today. Interviews with important decision makers in the arms control arena are also conducted and well documented. There are also several feature articles. The "News and Negotiations" section has articles such as "U.S. Offers Iran Direct Talks" and "U.S.-Indian Nuclear Deal Simmers." A bibliography with citations to current literature on topics relevant to the subject being discussed is found in each issue. Each issue ends with news briefs. An excellent resource for academic libraries and research centers.

4837. *Bulletin of the Atomic Scientists.* Formerly (until 1946): *Bulletin of the Atomic Scientists of Chicago.* [ISSN: 0096-3402] 1945. bi-m. USD 28; USD 6 newsstand/cover domestic; USD 8 newsstand/cover Canada. Ed(s): John Rezek, Mark Strauss. Educational Foundation for Nuclear Science, 6042 S Kimbark Ave, Chicago, IL 60637; schwartz@ thebulletin.org. Illus., index, adv. Refereed. Circ: 11000 Paid and controlled. CD-ROM: ProQuest LLC (Ann Arbor). Microform: MIM; NBI; PQC. Online: EBSCO Publishing, EBSCO Host; Florida Center for Library Automation; Gale; Northern Light Technology, Inc.; OCLC Online Computer Library Center, Inc.; ProQuest K-12 Learning Solutions; ProQuest LLC (Ann Arbor); H.W. Wilson. *Indexed:* ABCPolSci, ABS&EES, AltPI, AmH&L, BAS, BRD, BRI, BiolDig, CBRI, ChemAb, EnvInd, ExcerpMed, FutSurv, GSI, H&SSA, HistAb, MASUSE, MRD, PAIS, PRA, RGPR, RI-1, RiskAb, SCI, SSCI. *Bk. rev.:* Number and length vary. *Aud.:* Ga, Ac, Sa.

Published by the Educational Foundation for Nuclear Science, the bulletin of the atomic scientists' mission is to educate citizens about global security concerns, especially the continuing dangers posed by nuclear and other weapons of mass destruction. Founded in 1945 by two atomic scientists, Eugene Rabinowitch and Hyman Goldsmith, this journal has faithfully adhered to its mission. A recent cover story is titled "When Could Iran Get the Bomb?" Feature articles cover such topics as the international weapons trade, analysis of the causes of world conflict, prescriptions for survival, and nuclear weapon statistics. It provides the general public, policy makers, scientists, and journalists with nontechnical, scientifically sound, policy-relevant information about nuclear weapons and other global security issues. Available online.

4838. *Conflict Management and Peace Science.* Formerly (until 1981): *Journal of Peace Science.* [ISSN: 0738-8942] 1974. q. GBP 146 print & online eds. Ed(s): Glen Palmer. Taylor & Francis Inc., 325 Chestnut St, Ste 800, Philadelphia, PA 19016; orders@taylorandfrancis.com; http://www.taylorandfrancis.com. Illus. Refereed. Circ: 1000. Vol. ends: No. 2. Reprint: PSC. *Indexed:* ABCPolSci, AmH&L, HistAb, JEL, PAIS, PRA, PSA, RiskAb, SSCI. *Bk. rev.:* 1, 1,200 words. *Aud.:* Ac.

Devoted to the scientific study of conflict and conflict analysis, *Conflict Management and Peace Science* is published by the Peace Science Society (International) at Pennsylvania State University. This society's main objective is to encourage the exchange of ideas and promote studies on peace analysis using scientific methods. Scholars and an international group of experts who specialize in diverse fields contribute articles to this journal. The most recent issue focuses on the subject of deterrence, with articles such as "Deterrence Is Dead. Long Live Deterrence" and "Sequential Analysis of Deterrence Games with a Declining Status Quo." Research articles provide empirical results based on statistical tests. Each issue includes five or six articles, each preceded by an

abstract. A list of references provides the researcher with further readings. Primarily written for a scholarly clientele, the journal will be useful in academic and research libraries.

4839. *Fellowship.* Formerly (until 1935): *The World Tomorrow.* [ISSN: 0014-9810] 1918. bi-m. USD 25 domestic; USD 35 Canada; USD 40 elsewhere. Ed(s): Ethan Vesely-Flad. Fellowship of Reconciliation, 521 N Broadway, Box 271, Nyack, NY 10960; http://www.forusa.org. Illus., index, adv. Sample. Refereed. Circ: 9000 Paid. Vol. ends: Nov/Dec. Microform: PQC. Online: ProQuest LLC (Ann Arbor). *Indexed:* AltPI, MRD, PAIS, PRA, RI-1. *Bk. rev.:* 6, 350 words. *Aud.:* Hs, Ga, Ac.

Fellowship is an important multi-faith, multicultural magazine committed to justice and peace. It is published by the organization Fellowship of Reconciliation (FOR), and it is one of the longest-running peace journals in the United States. Published since 1935, it follows its predecessor, *The World Tomorrow,* which began in 1918. Committed to active nonviolence as a way of life, *Fellowship* serves FOR's mission and strives for an ideal world of peace. A recent feature story, "Seeds of Reconciliation Sprout in the Shadow of Genocide," describes how the Bosnian Student Project (BSP) helped get out of the war zone Bosniak Muslim, mixed ethnic, and other students who were unable to continue their education because of "ethnic cleansing" and the creative role that BSP graduates are still playing in promoting healing and reconciliation in their country. *Fellowship* provides interesting reading with feature articles, interviews, poems, and news briefs. Philosophical and reflective, *Fellowship* is concerned with conflict resolution through the united effort of all peoples. A very useful resource for public and academic libraries.

4840. *International Journal on World Peace.* [ISSN: 0742-3640] 1984. q. USD 30 (Individuals, USD 20; Students, USD 10). Ed(s): Gordon L Anderson. Professors World Peace Academy, 1925 Oakcrest Ave., Ste. 7, Saint Paul, MN 55113-2619; ijwp@pwpa.org; http://www.pwpa.org. Illus., index, adv. Sample. Refereed. Circ: 10000. Vol. ends: Dec. Microform: PQC. Online: EBSCO Publishing, EBSCO Host; Florida Center for Library Automation; Gale; Northern Light Technology, Inc.; OCLC Online Computer Library Center, Inc.; ProQuest K-12 Learning Solutions; ProQuest LLC (Ann Arbor). *Indexed:* CJA, CWI, IBR, IBZ, IPSA, PAIS, PRA, PSA, SSA, SSCI, SWR&A, SociolAb. *Bk. rev.:* 6, 150-1,100 words. *Aud.:* Ga, Ac.

International Journal on World Peace is a scholarly publication committed to peace and cuts across all disciplines, politics, and philosophies. It is published by the Professors World Peace Academy, and its editorial board consists of scholars from several countries ranging from Australia and the United States to Norway and India. Recent issues provide such articles as "Empowering the Human Security Debate: Making it Coherent and Meaningful" and "A Conspiracy Theory of America's Mideast Policy." The authors include a diverse group of international scholars. A news section and book reviews follow feature articles. The journal should provide interesting reading to patrons in both public and academic libraries.

4841. *International Peacekeeping.* [ISSN: 1353-3312] 1994. q. GBP 362 print & online eds. Ed(s): Michael Pugh. Taylor & Francis Ltd., 4 Park Sq, Milton Park, Abingdon, OX14 4RN, United Kingdom; info@tandf.co.uk; http://www.tandf.co.uk/journals. Illus., adv. Sample. Refereed. Vol. ends: Winter. Reprint: PSC. *Indexed:* AmH&L, HistAb, IBSS, IPSA, PSA, RiskAb, SociolAb. *Bk. rev.:* 4-6. *Aud.:* Ac.

International Peacekeeping fundamentally examines the theory and practice of peacekeeping. It propagates the theory that peacekeeping is primarily a political act. This refereed journal analyzes peacekeeping concepts and operations and provides in-depth research on peace and conflict resolution. It provides debates and articles on sanction enforcements; international policing; and the relationship between peacekeepers, state authorities, rival factions, civilians, and governmental organizations. There is an interesting section devoted to eyewitness accounts and a "Digest of Operations" section. A recent article, "Taming chaos: A Foucauldian view of U.N. peacekeeping, democracy and normalization," addresses U.N. peacekeeping attempts at maintaining order by normalizing the international arena. Another article, titled "Promoting norms through peacekeeping: UNPREDEP and conflict prevention," investigates the preventive peacekeeping mission to the former Yugoslav Republic of Macedonia from a social constructivist point of view. This is an important resource for academic and research institutions that promote peace studies.

4842. *International Security.* [ISSN: 0162-2889] 1976. q. USD 208 print & online eds. (Individuals, USD 50 print & online eds.). Ed(s): Steven E Miller. M I T Press, 238 Main St., Ste. 500, Cambridge, MA 02142; journals-info@mit.edu; http://mitpress.mit.edu. Illus., index, adv. Refereed. Circ: 5530. Vol. ends: Winter. Microform: PQC. Online: EBSCO Publishing, EBSCO Host; Florida Center for Library Automation; Gale; IngentaConnect; JSTOR (Web-based Journal Archive); OCLC Online Computer Library Center, Inc.; OhioLINK; Project MUSE; SwetsWise Online Content; H.W. Wilson. Reprint: PSC. *Indexed:* ABCPolSci, ABS&EES, AUNI, AmH&L, ArtHuCI, BAS, FutSurv, HistAb, IBR, IBSS, IBZ, IPSA, PAIS, PRA, PSA, RiskAb, SSCI. *Aud.:* Ac.

International Security is primarily concerned with international peacekeeping. It is published by the Belfer Center for Science and International Affairs at Harvard University. Scholarly, well-researched articles analyze all aspects of international security and are contributed by experts in the theory and practice of peacekeeping. The publication is committed to "timely analysis" of security issues. It provides information on new developments in the areas of causes and prevention of war; ethnic conflict and peacekeeping; post–Cold War security problems; European, Asian, and regional security; nuclear forces and strategy; arms control and weapons proliferation; and post-Soviet security issues and diplomatic and military history. "Symbolic Politics or Rational Choice? Testing Theories of Extreme Ethnic Violence" and "Building a Republican Peace: Stabilizing States after War" are some of the articles found in the most recent issue. The "Editor's Note" provides an introduction to essays in the journal. This is a valuable resource for academic and research libraries that promote peace and international studies.

4843. *Journal of Conflict Resolution: research on war and peace between and within nations.* Formerly: *Conflict Resolution.* [ISSN: 0022-0027] 1957. bi-m. GBP 554. Ed(s): Bruce M Russett. Sage Publications, Inc., 2455 Teller Rd, Thousand Oaks, CA 91320; info@sagepub.com; http://www.sagepub.com. Illus., index, adv. Refereed. Circ: 2200. Vol. ends: Dec. Microform: PQC. Online: CSA; EBSCO Publishing, EBSCO Host; Florida Center for Library Automation; Gale; HighWire Press; JSTOR (Web-based Journal Archive); OCLC Online Computer Library Center, Inc.; OhioLINK; ProQuest LLC (Ann Arbor); SAGE Publications, Inc., SAGE Journals Online; SwetsWise Online Content. Reprint: PSC. *Indexed:* ABCPolSci, ABIn, ABS&EES, AmH&L, BAS, CJA, CommAb, EAA, EI, HistAb, IBR, IBSS, IBZ, IPSA, IndIslam, JEL, PAIS, PRA, PSA, PsycInfo, RiskAb, SSA, SSCI, SWR&A, SociolAb. *Aud.:* Ac.

The *Journal of Conflict Resolution* is a scholarly journal that focuses on international conflict. It provides articles and research reports on intergroup conflicts within and between nations and promotes a better understanding of war and peace. It is the official publication of the Peace Science Society (International). The editorial board members belong to universities and colleges from all over the world. This scholarly journal is mainly directed toward academicians and researchers, and is described as "an inter-disciplinary journal of social scientific theory and research on human conflict." The journal usually contains six to eight articles that focus on solid, measurable facts and carefully reasoned arguments. *JCR* provides the latest ideas, approaches, and processes in conflict resolution. It offers theoretical and empirical results that intend to provide a better understanding of military strategy and war. Detailed research projects provide statistics, tables, charts, graphs, and results of case studies. Articles include abstracts and references. A recent article examines major theoretical assumptions about forgiveness by victims of human rights abuses: "Forgiveness and Transitional Justice in the Czech Republic." This journal is an excellent resource for academic libraries that focus on peace studies. It is also available online.

4844. *Journal of Peace Research: an interdisciplinary and international quarterly of scholarly work in peace research.* [ISSN: 0022-3433] 1964. bi-m. GBP 640. Ed(s): Nils Petter Gleditsch. Sage Publications Ltd., 1 Oliver's Yard, 55 City Rd, London, EC1 1SP, United Kingdom;

info@sagepub.co.uk; http://www.sagepub.co.uk. Illus., index, adv. Refereed. Circ: 1550. Vol. ends: Nov. Microform: PQC. Online: CSA; EBSCO Publishing, EBSCO Host; HighWire Press; JSTOR (Web-based Journal Archive); OCLC Online Computer Library Center, Inc.; OhioLINK; SAGE Publications, Inc., SAGE Journals Online; SwetsWise Online Content. Reprint: PSC. *Indexed:* ABCPolSci, AmH&L, AmHI, ArtHuCI, BRI, BrHumI, CBRI, CJA, CommAb, FutSurv, HRA, HistAb, IBR, IBSS, IBZ, IPSA, JEL, PAIS, PRA, PSA, RiskAb, SFSA, SSA, SSCI, SUSA, SWA, SWR&A, SociolAb. *Bk. rev.:* 15-20, 150-450 words. *Aud.:* Ga, Ac.

Journal of Peace Research is published by the International Peace Research Association. Edited at the Peace Research Institute, it is supported by the Nordic Publishing Board in Social Sciences. It is an interdisciplinary, international quarterly that provides empirical, theoretical, and timely articles on global security and peace. It addresses the causes of violence, methods of conflict resolution, and ways of sustaining peace. An article in a recent issue, "Interdependence and the Duration of Militarized Conflict," discusses the effects of interdependence once actual conflict has started. Authors from over 50 countries have published in this journal. Each issue includes an extensive review section that presents and evaluates leading books in the field of peace research. This journal keeps the reader abreast of the latest developments in the area of peace studies, and it will be appreciated in academic libraries and peace research centers.

4845. *Nonviolent Activist.* Formerly (until 1984): *W R L News.* [ISSN: 8755-7428] 1945. bi-m. Free. Ed(s): Judith Mahoney Pasternak. War Resisters League, 339 Lafayette St, New York, NY 10012-2782; wrl@igc.org; http://www.nonviolence.org/wrl. Illus., index, adv. Sample. Circ: 10000. Vol. ends: Nov/Dec. Microform: PQC. *Indexed:* AltPI, PRA. *Bk. rev.:* 1-3, 300-500 words. *Aud.:* Ga, Ac.

Nonviolent Activist, a notable grassroots publication, is the official magazine of one of the most important American peace organizations, the War Resisters League (WRL). The WRL affirms that all war is a crime against humanity and is determined not to support any kind of war, international or civil, and it strives nonviolently for the removal of all causes of war. *Nonviolent Activist* reflects the ideals of the WRL. It publishes articles related to peace and social justice issues. There are sections for book reviews, letters, activists' news, and WRL news. A very good resource for peace activists and researchers interested in world peace.

4846. *Peace & Change: a journal of peace research.* [ISSN: 0149-0508] 1972. q. GBP 322 print & online eds. Ed(s): Robbie Leiberman, Barry L Gan. Blackwell Publishing, Inc., Commerce Place, 350 Main St, Malden, MA 02148; customerservices@blackwellpublishing.com; http://www.blackwellpublishing.com. Illus., index, adv. Refereed. Circ: 1300. Vol. ends: Oct. Online: Blackwell Synergy; EBSCO Publishing, EBSCO Host; Gale; IngentaConnect; OCLC Online Computer Library Center, Inc.; OhioLINK; SwetsWise Online Content. *Indexed:* ABS&EES, AmH&L, ApEcolAb, HistAb, IPSA, PAIS, PRA, PSA, RILM, RiskAb, SUSA, SociolAb. *Bk. rev.:* 3-4, essay length. *Aud.:* Ga, Ac.

Published on behalf of the Peace History Society and the Peace and Justice Studies Association, this scholarly journal consists of analytical and deductive articles on peace and conflict resolution. It addresses a wide variety of topics concerning nonviolence, peace movements and activists, conflict resolution, race and gender issues, cross-cultural studies, international conflict, and post–Cold War concerns. The journal attempts to transcend national, disciplinary, and other arbitrary boundaries while trying to link peace research, education, and activism. Each issue has four or five feature articles, a review essay, book reviews, and a notes section with short biographical information about each author. Recent articles include "Enemy Combatants and Guantanamo: The Rule of Law and Law of War of Post 9/11" and "Evaluating the Legacy of Nonviolence in South Africa." This journal would be useful in an academic library or research center.

4847. *Peace and Conflict: journal of peace psychology.* [ISSN: 1078-1919] 1995. q. GBP 286 print & online eds. Ed(s): Richard Wagner. Lawrence Erlbaum Associates, Inc., 325 Chestnut St, Ste. 800, Philadelphia, PA

19106; journals@erlbaum.com; http://www.leaonline.com. Illus., index, adv. Refereed. Vol. ends: Dec. Reprint: PSC. *Indexed:* IBSS, IPSA, PAIS, PRA, PSA, PsycInfo, RiskAb, SSA, SociolAb. *Bk. rev.:* 4, 500-600 words. *Aud.:* Ac.

Peace and Conflict: Journal of Peace Psychology is published by the American Psychological Association's Division of Peace Psychology. The journal strives to support the ideals of the division and helps advance psychological knowledge that would build "peace in the world at large and within nations, communities, and families." The journal tries to apply information gathered from various areas in the field of psychology to solving issues relating to peace. It advocates equity, social justice, and protection of the environment, which it considers to be the hallmark of world order and peace. The journal publishes clinical, research-oriented articles; historical work; policy analysis; case studies; essays; interviews; and book reviews. A recent article, "Therapeutic Work with Victims of Sexual Violence in War and Postwar: A Discourse Analysis of Bosnian Experiences," is an analysis of information from interviews with 23 local Bosnian health workers who had worked with victims of sexual violence in the Bosnian war and postwar settings. This journal would be a fine addition to peace research centers and academic libraries.

4848. Peace, Conflict & Development: an interdisciplinary journal. [ISSN: 1742-0601] 2002. s-a. Free. Ed(s): Kelly Rhys. University of Bradford, Department of Peace Studies, Richmond Rd, Bradford, BD7 1DP, United Kingdom; editor@peacestudiesjournal.org.uk. Refereed. *Indexed:* PSA. *Bk. rev.:* Number and length vary. *Aud.:* Ac.

This is a new, open-access journal that focuses on contemporary issues in conflict and peace studies. The journal is managed and edited by doctoral students at the University of Bradford's Department of Peace Studies, with the support of a part-time paid coordinator and academic staff. Its main purpose is to publish innovative articles on a wide range of topics including human rights issues, democracy, conflict resolution, security, war, and the peace process. The journal consists of academic essays, fieldwork reports from researchers and practitioners, and book reviews. A recent issue includes an essay titled "The War on Terror: An Assessment" and articles such as "Questioning the Concept of New Terrorism." A good online resource for academic libraries.

4849. Peace Magazine. [ISSN: 0826-9521] 1985. bi-m. CND 17.50 domestic; CND 20 foreign. Ed(s): Metta Spencer. Canadian Disarmament Information Service (CANDIS), Peace Magazine, PO Box 248, Toronto, ON M5S 2S7, Canada. Illus., index, adv. Sample. Circ: 2666 Paid. Vol. ends: Nov/Dec. Microform: MML. Online: Gale; Micromedia ProQuest. *Indexed:* ABS&EES, AltPI, CBCARef, CPerI, PRA. *Bk. rev.:* 3-4, 250-600 words. *Aud.:* Hs, Ga, Ac.

Peace Magazine is a quarterly that consists of articles, news stories, book and film reviews, letters, and a calendar of events focusing on peace issues. It is published by the Canadian Disarmament Information Service, a group of people dedicated to educating the public on every aspect of peace. Articles deal with subjects related to the terrible effect that wars have on people, their minds, and the minds of their children. They address human rights abuses, inequity, corrupt governance, and intolerance of diversity. Articles are written by activists, journalists, and scholars. This illustrated, 32-page magazine includes an eight-page section produced in collaboration with Science for Peace. The "Our Readers Write" section encourages readers to voice their opinions on issues that concern them; readers also offer their comments on articles from previous issues. There is a book review section and a news section, "Newsworthy," which highlights peace issues. A good resource for public, high school, and academic libraries.

4850. Peace Research: the Canadian journal of peace studies. [ISSN: 0008-4697] 1969. 2x/yr. CND 73 (Individuals, CND 36). Ed(s): Dr. M V Naidu. M.V. Naidu, Ed. & Pub., c/o Brandon University, 270 18th St, Brandon, MB R7A 6A9, Canada; naidu@brandonu.ca. Illus., index, adv. Refereed. Circ: 1000. Vol. ends: Nov. Microform: MML. Online: LexisNexis; Micromedia ProQuest; ProQuest LLC (Ann Arbor). *Indexed:* ABS&EES, CBCARef, CPerI, IBR, IBZ, PRA, SFSA, V&AA. *Bk. rev.:* 1-2, 500-1,000 words. *Aud.:* Ga, Ac.

This journal focuses on studies in peace education, peace research, and peace movements. Deeply committed to the eradication of violence, armament, and war, it advocates nonviolence, disarmament, and peaceful settlement of disputes. Articles address human rights issues relating to equality, liberty, justice, economic development, environmental protection, cultural advancement, feminism, and humanism. Published under the auspices of the Canadian Peace Research and Education Association (CPREA), the journal concludes with the CPREA newsletter. Recent articles include "Critical Analysis of the Concept of Peace" and "Is the Islamic Bomb a Reality?" Academicians and researchers from all over the world contribute articles. Academic libraries and peace research centers will find this journal a useful resource.

4851. Peace Research Reviews. [ISSN: 0553-4283] 1967. irreg. approx. 3/yr. CND 72 for 2 yrs. Ed(s): Hanna Newcombe. Peace Research Institute-Dundas, 25 Dundana Ave, Dundas, ON L9H 4E5, Canada; info@prid.on.ca; http://www.prid.on.ca. Illus., adv. Circ: 400. Vol. ends: No. 6. *Indexed:* ABCPolSci, AmH&L, HistAb. *Aud.:* Ac.

This learned journal from the Peace Research Institute, Dundas, Ontario, provides in-depth scholarly articles on topics related to peace. *Peace Research Reviews* is dedicated to the study of peace, with each volume exclusively devoted to one major theme. The journal has a bibliography and a brief biography of each author. The editor, Hanna Newcombe, is also the editor of *Peace Research Abstracts Journal. Peace Research Reviews* would be a valuable addition to any research collection concerned with peace studies.

4852. Peace Review: a journal of social justice. [ISSN: 1040-2659] 1989. q. GBP 377 print & online eds. Ed(s): Robert Elias. Routledge, 4 Park Sq, Milton Park, Abingdon, OX14 4RN, United Kingdom; info@routledge.co.uk; http://www.routledge.co.uk. Illus., index, adv. Sample. Refereed. Circ: 500. Vol. ends: Dec. Reprint: PSC. *Indexed:* AltPI, CJA, IBR, IBZ, IPSA, PAIS, PRA, PSA, SSA, SociolAb. *Bk. rev.:* 2-3, 1,000-1,500 words. *Aud.:* Ga, Ac.

Peace Review is a multidisciplinary, transnational journal that focuses on research and analysis and is directed toward important issues and controversies that hinder the maintenance of peace. The journal publishes articles related to peace research and may include human rights issues, conflict resolution, protection of the environment, and anything else concerned with peace. The journal's aim is to present the results of this research in short, informative essays. Each issue generally revolves around a particular theme; sometimes essays relating to other topics are also published in the same issue. Contributors include journalists, political scientists, teachers, activists, theologians, and peace enthusiasts. In addition to articles and other features, there is a separate section on recommended books and videos.

Peace Watch. See Government Periodicals—Federal section.

4853. Security Dialogue. Formerly (until 1992): *Bulletin of Peace Proposals.* [ISSN: 0967-0106] 1970. bi-m. GBP 506. Ed(s): J Peter Burgess. Sage Publications Ltd., 1 Oliver's Yard, 55 City Rd, London, EC1 1SP, United Kingdom; info@sagepub.co.uk; http://www.sagepub.co.uk. Illus., index, adv. Microform: PQC. Online: CSA; EBSCO Publishing, EBSCO Host; HighWire Press; OCLC Online Computer Library Center, Inc.; OhioLINK; SAGE Publications, Inc., SAGE Journals Online; SwetsWise Online Content. Reprint: PSC. *Indexed:* AmH&L, BAS, HistAb, IBR, IBSS, IBZ, IPSA, PAIS, PRA, PSA, RiskAb, SSA, SSCI, SociolAb, V&AA. *Aud.:* Ac.

Security Dialogue provides the most current information on global peace and security. It offers new ideas on important issues concerning peace and security. It intends to provoke thought and reflection through "interregional dialogue" on issues concerning international security. An article in a recent issue, "Surveillance Strategies and Populations at Risk: Biopolitical Governance in Canada's National Security Policy," uses Foucauldian analysis to establish the connection between biopolitics and security. The journal provides expert coverage on such topics as the role of the United Nations, conflict prevention, mediation, sovereignty, and intervention. This journal would prove to be a very useful resource in academic or research libraries that specialize in peace research.

■ PETS

Associations

See also Animal Welfare; Birds; Horses; Sports; and Veterinary Science sections.

Camille McCutcheon, Coordinator of Library Instruction/Associate Librarian, University of South Carolina Upstate, 800 University Way, Spartanburg, SC 29303, CMcCutcheon@uscupstate.edu, FAX: 864-503-5601

Introduction

Most of the pet magazines that are published focus exclusively on either dogs, cats, birds, ferrets, reptiles, or fish. *Dog Fancy, Cats & Kittens, Reptile Care,* and *Tropical Fish Hobbyist* are just a few examples. Currently, there are very few general pet magazines available. *Pets Magazine* and *Pets Quarterly* both contain articles on various kinds of pets, including dogs, cats, birds, and fish. Articles concerning health, nutrition, care, behavior, communication, grooming, training, the human/animal bond, and heartwarming stories of actual animals are commonly featured in many of the magazines noted in this section.

During the past several years, there has been an increase in the number of titles that are part lifestyle magazine, part pet publication. Many of these magazines contain articles on fashion, beauty, design, travel, and profiles of and interviews with celebrity pet owners. As a reflection of this publishing trend, several of these hybrid titles are included in this chapter.

One of the leading publishers of pet and animal magazines is BowTie Magazines, which publishes titles such as *Aquarium Fish Magazine, Dog Fancy, Cat Fancy,* and *Bird Talk.* BowTie Magazines also produces a line of annual titles such as *Ferrets USA* and *Birds USA,* which contain relevant information for new or prospective pet owners. These annual editions are mentioned throughout the section. Two noteworthy annual publications that do not have monthly or bimonthly counterparts are *Rabbits USA* and *Critters USA,* which contains information on small mammals such as gerbils, rats, mice, guinea pigs, hamsters, and sugar gliders.

Most of the magazines noted in this section have web sites, where visitors can locate subscription information, scan the table of contents, and view a photograph of the cover for the current issue. Other sites are more extensive and allow visitors to read selected articles from current and previous issues, participate in online forums, and pose questions online to veterinarians and other pet experts.

The Electronic Journals subsection contains titles of pet publications that are only available online. Unfortunately, the quality of online pet magazines varies. Although there are numerous electronic pet serials available on the Internet, in most cases it is difficult, if not impossible, to discern when articles and other information posted to these web sites were last updated.

Basic Periodicals

Hs: *Cat Fancy, Dog Fancy;* Ga: *A.F.A. Watchbird, Cat Fancy, Dog Fancy;* Ac: *Anthrozoos.*

4854. *The A F A Watchbird: journal of the American Federation of Aviculture.* [ISSN: 0199-543X] 1974. q. Members, USD 40. Ed(s): Stephanie Bledsoe. American Federation of Aviculture, PO Box 7312, Kansas City, MO 64116-0012; afaoffice@aol.com; http://www.afabirds.org/. Illus., adv. Circ: 5000. Vol. ends: Nov/Dec. *Aud.:* Hs, Ga, Ac.

The AFA Watchbird is the official publication of the American Federation of Aviculture. The AFA is dedicated to promoting aviculture and to informing the "public about keeping and breeding birds in captivity." The magazine's color photography is beautiful. The articles are detailed and informative, and some of them contain a list of references. Contributors include aviculturists, veterinarians, avian scientists, and avian biologists. Profiles of bird species, as well as articles on bird breeding, the health and welfare of birds, and the activities of the AFA, are featured. The web site for the American Federation of Aviculture contains information on the *AFA Watchbird,* including the table of contents and a photograph of the cover of the current issue.

4855. *A K C Family Dog: all the best for your purebred pet.* [ISSN: 1559-5072] 2003. bi-m. USD 9.95 domestic. Ed(s): Erika Mansourian. American Kennel Club, Inc., 260 Madison Ave, New York, NY 10016; ejm@akc.org; http://www.akc.org. Illus. Sample. Circ: 175000. *Aud.:* Ga.

AKC Family Dog is an informative magazine for owners of purebred dogs and for dog enthusiasts. Each issue contains feature articles on topics such as canine health and behavior, along with regular columns on training, behavior, grooming, and fun facts about various breeds. Contributors include veterinarians, professional dog trainers, and authors of books on dogs. Topics of recent articles include new medical treatments for dogs with arthritis, the use of dogs in pet therapy, and canine body language. The web site is extensive and includes general information about the magazine along with the table of contents and a photograph of the cover of the current issue. Information about breeds, breeders, AKC events, and an online store are all available from the web site.

4856. *A K C Gazette: the official journal for the sport of purebred dogs.* Formerly (until 1995): *Pure-Bred Dogs, American Kennel Gazette.* [ISSN: 1086-0940] 1889. m. USD 31.95 domestic; USD 51.95 foreign. Ed(s): Erika Mansourian, Tanya Bielski-Braham. American Kennel Club, Inc., 260 Madison Ave, New York, NY 10016; ejm@akc.org; http://www.akc.org. Illus., index, adv. Circ: 45000 Paid. Vol. ends: Dec. Microform: PQC. Online: ProQuest LLC (Ann Arbor). *Aud.:* Ga, Sa.

AKC Gazette is the official publication of the American Kennel Club (AKC). The detailed information found in this magazine will be of interest both to general dog owners and to those who own and work with purebred dogs. Each issue contains an in-depth breed profile and feature articles on canine health and on the activities of the AKC. Contributors include AKC judges, breeders, dog photographers, trainers, veterinarians, and exhibitors. "Better Breeding," "The Judge's Eye," and "Healthy Dog" are just some of the monthly columns and departments. There are also columns that contain information and insights about specific breeds. The web site is extensive and includes general information about the magazine, along with the table of contents and a photograph of the cover of the current issue. Information about breeds, breeders, AKC events, and an online store are all available from the web site.

4857. *Animal Fair: a lifestyle magazine for animal lovers.* [ISSN: 1525-3309] 1999. q. USD 19.99 for 2 yrs. domestic; USD 29.99 for 2 yrs. Canada. Ed(s): Wendy Diamond. Animal Fair Media, Inc., 545 8th Ave, Ste 401, New York, NY 10018; info@animalfair.com; http://www.animalfair.com. Illus. Sample. Circ: 200000. *Aud.:* Ga.

Animal Fair is a lifestyle magazine for animal lovers. *Animal Fair* has theme-related issues: design/home, holiday, travel, and health/fitness. In addition to the theme-related feature articles, there are also interviews with celebrity pet owners and new product announcements. The web site for *Animal Fair* contains general information about the magazine, along with a photograph of the cover of the current issue. Back issues also can be purchased online. Recommended for large public library collections.

4858. *Animal Wellness Magazine: for a long, healthy life!* Formerly (until 2000): *Animal.* [ISSN: 1710-1190] 2000. bi-m. USD 19.95 domestic; USD 24.95 Canada. Ed(s): Dana Cox. Redstone Media Group Inc., 164 Hunter St., West, Peterborough, ON K9H 2L2, Canada; submissions@ animalanimal.com; http://animalwellnessmagazine.com/. Illus. Sample. Circ: 20000. *Bk. rev.:* 2; 100-150 words. *Aud.:* Hs, Ga.

The purpose of *Animal Wellness Magazine* is to provide owners of companion animals, such as cats, dogs, and horses, with the information needed to improve the quality of life for their animals. The magazine's motto is "living pawsitive!" It is an attractive publication that has many color photographs and well-written and interesting articles. It offers information on holistic and natural alternatives to Western medicine. There are also feature articles regarding nutrition, health, behavior, and social and activism issues. Contributors include veterinarians who practice holistic veterinary medicine, psychologists, authors of books on holistic and natural medicine for animals, animal behaviorists, and natural horse-care consultants. Topics of recent articles include Lyme disease, toxoplasmosis, cat training, animal-friendly lawn care, and controlling equine parasites. Regularly featured columns and departments include a holistic veterinary question-and-answer section, new pet products, a wellness resource guide, pet products endorsed by *Animal Wellness Magazine,* book reviews that average 150–200 words in length, and a classified ads section. The web site for the magazine is extensive. It provides subscription information and the table of contents and photographs of the covers for the most recent issues. Back issues can be purchased online. Visitors can read selected articles from these issues and also can use locators to find holistic veterinarians and pet shelters.

4859. *Anthrozoos: a multidisciplinary journal of the interactions of people and animals.* Formerly (until 1985): *Delta Society. Journal.* [ISSN: 0892-7936] 1984. q. GBP 90 (Individuals, GBP 45; GBP 30 per issue domestic). Ed(s): Joanne Swabe, Anthony Podberscek. Berg Publishers, Angel Court, 1st Fl, 81 St Clements St, Oxford, OX4 1AW, United Kingdom; enquiry@bergpublishers.com; http://www.bergpublishers.com/. Illus., index, adv. Sample. Refereed. Circ: 450. Vol. ends: No. 4. *Indexed:* AgeL, Agr, ArtHuCI, CABA, DSA, EnvInd, FoVS&M, IndVet, PsycInfo, RI-1, RRTA, SCI, SSCI, VB. *Bk. rev.:* 1-4; words, 1,000 to 3,000 words in length. *Aud.:* Ac.

Anthrozoos is the official journal of the International Society for Anthrozoology. It is a multidisciplinary, refereed journal that is published by Purdue University Press in cooperation with the Humane Society of the United States and the International Association of Human-Animal Interaction Organizations. The journal contains little academic jargon and would appeal to individuals interested in animals and society and in human/animal interactions. Some of the fields covered include psychology, sociology, ethics, health, and veterinary medicine. One of the primary components of this publication is the "Reviews and Research Reports" section, which describes studies and the results of research on human/animal interactions. There are meeting announcements and in-depth book reviews that are 1,000–3,000 words in length. This publication is recommended for academic and large public library collections. The web site contains general information about *Anthrozoos*, including sample article titles that were published in past issues of the journal.

4860. *Aquarium Fish Magazine: America's favorite fishkeeping magazine.* [ISSN: 0899-045X] 1988. m. USD 14.99 domestic; USD 32.99 foreign. Ed(s): Russ Case. BowTie, Inc., 2401 Beverly Blvd, PO Box 57900, Los Angeles, CA 90057; http://www.bowtieinc.com/. Illus., adv. Circ: 47115 Paid. Vol. ends: Dec. *Aud.:* Hs, Ga.

Aquarium Fish Magazine is a practical, in-depth resource for fishkeepers. The color photography is beautiful, the layout is very attractive, and the articles are well written. Some of the articles even contain a list of references. Contributors include aquarium hobbyists, marine hobbyists, aquarium biologists, and authors of books on fish and reefkeeping. Topics of recent articles include aquascaping aquariums, changing tank water, ponds for apartment dwellers, and the dance rituals of courting sea horses. A different species of fish is profiled each month. There are numerous question-and-answer sections, such as the "Cichlid Forum," the "Reef Aquarist," "Freshwater Q&A," and the "Aquabotanist." There is even a question-and-answer section for young fishkeepers called "FishKidz." A showcase of new products and a classified ads section are included in every issue. Bowtie Magazines also has several annual titles that would be of interest to fishkeeping enthusiasts. The titles are *Aquarium USA,* which is a guide to fishkeeping, *Marine Fish and Reef USA,* which a guide to saltwater habitats, and *Koi World and Water Gardens,* which is a guide to keeping a koi pond and water garden. The *Aquarium Fish Magazine* web site is very informative, attractive, and user-friendly. The table of contents and a photograph of the cover for the current issue are featured. Also included are species profiles; *Aquarium Fish Magazine* article indexes for the previous few years; resources for ponds and for pond, freshwater, and saltwater fish; online forums; a photo gallery; subscription information; and classified ads.

4861. *The Bark: dog is my co-pilot.* [ISSN: 1535-1734] 1997. bi-m. USD 18 domestic; USD 39 Canada; USD 48 elsewhere. Ed(s): Claudia Kawczynska. The Bark, Inc., 2810 8th St, Berkeley, CA 94710; editor@thebark.com. Illus., adv. Sample. Circ: 100000 Paid and controlled. *Bk. rev.:* 7-9; average 500 words. *Aud.:* Ga.

The Bark is an upscale and intelligent publication about modern dog culture. The magazine's motto is "Dog is my co-pilot." The layout is very attractive, and the color photography is impressive. Focusing on the human–canine bond, *The Bark* offers a variety of interesting and well-written articles on health, behavior, art, literature, travel, recreation, and social and activism issues. There are also interviews, essays, stories, poetry, and book reviews, which average about 500 words in length. The magazine's web site is called *The Bark Unleashed.* It

provides subscription information, tables of contents and photographs of the covers for the current and previous issues. Back issues can be purchased online. *The Bark Unleashed* also offers a blog and an e-zine, which contains interviews, special features, and commentary, as well as articles on health, behavior, travel, and training.

4862. *Best Friends: all the good news about animals, wildlife, and the earth.* 1992. bi-m. USD 25 donation. Ed(s): Michael Mountain. Best Friends Animal Society, 5001 Angel Canyon Dr, Kanab, UT 84741. Illus., adv. Sample. Circ: 250000. *Bk. rev.:* 3- 5; 100-200 words. *Aud.:* Hs, Ga.

Best Friends is published by the Best Friends Animal Society, which runs the largest sanctuary in the United States for abused and abandoned animals. It is a perfect magazine for people who love animals. News and articles about animals and wildlife; Best Friends Animal Sanctuary stories and special adoptions; information about pet health and behavior; "No More Homeless Pets News"; and humorous animal stories are some of the features of the magazine. *Best Friends* also contains book reviews that average about 100–200 words in length. The Best Friends Animal Society offers an extensive and informative web site. Visitors can download the current and recent back issues without advertisements. A weekly news report from the sanctuary, subscription information, and online forums also are accessible from the web site.

4863. *Bird Talk: dedicated to better care for pet birds.* Formerly (until 198?): *International Bird Talk;* Incorporates (1978-1995): *Bird World;* (1928-1950): *American Canary Magazine.* [ISSN: 0891-771X] 1982. m. USD 27.97 domestic; USD 45.97 foreign. Ed(s): Laura Doering, Melissa Kauffman. BowTie, Inc., 2401 Beverly Blvd, PO Box 57900, Los Angeles, CA 90057; http://www.animalnetwork.com/. Illus., index, adv. Circ: 94790 Paid. Vol. ends: Dec. *Aud.:* Hs, Ga.

Bird Talk is a superb resource for bird owners. This attractive publication contains many excellent color photographs and well-written and informative articles on topics ranging from profiles of bird species to bird psychology and health. Contributors include avian behaviorists, avian veterinarians, authors of books on birds, parrot behavior consultants, avian technicians, and bird breeders. Topics of recent articles include popular bird names, weaning, ecotours, the link between inflammatory skin diseases and feather-damaging behavior, and profiles of African Grey parrots and strawberry finches. "Causes & Cures," which provides information on avian health and welfare, and "Small Birds," which provides information on small bird care and training, are just a few of the question-and-answer sections found in *Bird Talk.* Some of the columns include "Heart to Heart," which concerns the human-avian experience, and "Parrot Psychology," which provides information about bird behavior. The section *"BT* Style" contains tips for diet and housing, new and innovative products, and home and fashion hints. A calendar of avian conventions and seminars; a breeders' directory for large and small birds; bird photographs submitted by readers; and a classified ads section are some of the regular features of *Bird Talk.* The annual publication, *Birds USA,* is a guide to buying and keeping pet birds and would be an excellent resource for new or prospective bird owners. The *Bird Talk* web site is also a terrific resource. It is user-friendly and very attractive. The table of contents and a photograph of the cover for the current issue are featured. Also included are species profiles; subscription information; expert bird care tips on behavior, training, breeding, health, and nutrition; a breeder locator; online reader surveys and contests; online forums; and a photo gallery.

4864. *Bird Times: the magazine of the best about birds.* Formerly: *Caged Bird Hobbyist.* [ISSN: 1096-7923] 1992. bi-m. USD 19.97 domestic; USD 25.97 Canada; USD 31.97 elsewhere. Ed(s): Rita Davis. Pet Publishing, Inc., 7-L Dundas Circle, Greensboro, NC 27407; editorial@ petpublishing.com; http://www.petpublishing.com. Illus., adv. Sample. Circ: 20000. *Bk. rev.:* 3-5; 50-100 words. *Aud.:* Hs, Ga.

Bird Times is a wonderful resource for bird owners. The style, content, and color photography are terrific. The articles are informative and well-written, and contributors include aviculturalists, ornithologists, professional bird trainers, authors of books on birds, and avian care specialists. There are species profiles, along with regular features on companion birds such as budgerigars, canaries and finches, cockatiels, parrots, and pigeons and doves. There are also stories of actual birds, along with information on general care, diet, health, breeding, training, and behavior. There are reviews of bird books and videos that average about 50–100 words in length. There is also a breeder locator and a showcase of bird products. The *Bird Times* web site is attractive and contains general information about the magazine, news and articles about birds, profiles of bird species, a listing of bird breeders, bird stories submitted by readers, and links to other avian-related web sites. Back issues of the magazine also can be ordered online.

4865. Cat Fancy: cat care for the responsible owner. Supersedes (in 1986): *International Cat Fancy*. [ISSN: 0892-6514] 1965. m. USD 22.97 domestic; USD 45.97 foreign. Ed(s): Sandy Meyer, Susan Logan. BowTie, Inc., 2401 Beverly Blvd, PO Box 57900, Los Angeles, CA 90057; http://www.bowtieinc.com/. Illus., index, adv. Circ: 238123 Paid and controlled. Vol. ends: Dec. *Indexed:* BRI. *Bk. rev.:* Number and length vary; 20- 30 words. *Aud.:* Hs, Ga.

Cat Fancy is a terrific resource for cat owners. The articles are informative and practical, with topics ranging from profiles of breeds to features on cat health, behavior, grooming, and training. The magazine has an attractive layout and contains many color photographs. Some of the magazine's contributors are veterinarians. Topics of recent articles include maintaining a cat-friendly home, cats and outdoor enclosures, parasites and cats, and leash-training kittens. Some of the regularly featured departments include "Purrs and Hisses," which contains letters to the editor; "What's New Pussycat?," which showcases new products for cats; and "Humane Matters," which profiles shelter cats that have found forever homes. There is a section for young cat fanciers called "Cats for Kids," where kids can submit poetry, jokes, and drawings of cats. There is also an "Ask the Vet" section. Other departments include topics of articles featured in the upcoming issue, a calendar of cat club meetings, a breeder directory, a classified ads section, and a gallery of photographs that have been submitted by readers. Some of the issues have book reviews that average about 30 words in length. BowTie Magazines also has annual publications about cats. *Kittens USA* is a guide to adopting and caring for kittens, whereas *Cats USA* is a guide to buying and caring for purebred kittens. The *Cat Fancy* web site is very informative and extensive. The table of contents and photographs of the covers for the current and recent back issues are featured. Also included are breed profiles; resources on kittens, behavior, health care, nutrition, and adoption; an online store for purchasing cat books; a breeder locator; online forums; a photo gallery; subscription information; and classified ads. Finally, there is an "Ask the Experts" section, where visitors can pose questions to a veterinarian.

4866. Catnip: the newsletter for caring cat owners. [ISSN: 1069-6687] 1993. m. USD 29 domestic; CND 39 Canada. Ed(s): Arden Moore, John Berg. Tufts University, Cummings School of Veterinary Medicine, Tufts Media, 200 Bosto Ave, Ste 3500, Medford, MA 02155; vetadmissions@ tufts.edu; http://www.tufts.edu. Illus. Sample. Circ: 45000. *Aud.:* Ga.

Catnip is a monthly newsletter published by Tufts Media in cooperation with the Cummings School of Veterinary Medicine at Tufts University. Twenty-four pages in length, *Catnip* provides information on treatment and health care for cats and does not accept commercial advertising. Many of the contributors are veterinarians. This newsletter contains numerous black-and-white photographs. The articles are informative and would be of interest to cat owners. *Catnip* has articles on cat medicine, health, behavior, feline diseases, cat product comparisons, stories of actual cats, and a feline health care question-and-answer section. Topics of recent issues include the connection between humans and felines, the sport of feline agility, and advances in anesthesia. *Catnip's* web site provides general information about the newsletter, including subscription rates, and highlights some of the titles of articles from recent issues. Visitors can also read sample articles from the newsletter.

4867. Cats & Kittens. [ISSN: 1079-8285] 1995. bi-m. USD 19.97 domestic; USD 25.97 Canada; USD 31.97 elsewhere. Ed(s): Rita Davis. Pet Publishing, Inc., 7-L Dundas Circle, Greensboro, NC 27407; editorial@ petpublishing.com; http://www.petpublishing.com. Illus., adv. Sample. Circ: 50000. *Bk. rev.:* 4-6; 100 words. *Aud.:* Hs, Ga.

Cats & Kittens is a wonderful magazine for cat owners and enthusiasts. It is an attractive publication that has many color photographs and well-written and interesting articles. Topics range from stories of actual cats, to profiles of breeds, to special reports on cat health, to information on cat training. Topics of recent articles include kitty playtime, congenital heart disease, feline fine art, and

profiles of the Bengal and the Toyger cat breeds. Some of the regular features include humor columns and reviews of cat books and videos. The reviews average about 100 words in length. Other departments include profiles of new products and a breeder locator. The *Cats & Kittens* web site is attractive and contains general information about the magazine; news and articles about cats and kittens; cat stories submitted by readers; and links to cat associations and other feline-related web sites. Back issues of the magazine also can be ordered online. Finally, profiles of cat breeds and a listing of breeders are included.

4868. Dog & Kennel. [ISSN: 1079-8277] 1997. bi-m. USD 19.97 domestic; USD 25.97 Canada; USD 31.97 elsewhere. Ed(s): Rita Davis. Pet Publishing, Inc., 7-L Dundas Circle, Greensboro, NC 27407; editorial@ petpublishing.com; http://www.petpublishing.com. Illus., adv. Sample. Circ: 50000. *Bk. rev.:* 6-8; 100 words. *Aud.:* Hs, Ga.

Dog & Kennel is terrific magazine for dog owners and enthusiasts. It is an attractive publication that has many color photographs and well-written and interesting articles. Topics range from dog stories to profiles of breeds, to special reports on canine health, to information on dog training and grooming. Topics of recent articles include canine sports medicine, nail cutting techniques, solutions for gall bladder trouble, and profiles of Tibetan Terriers and Kerry Blue Terriers. Some of the regular features include profiles of new products, a breeder locator, and reviews of dog books and videos. The reviews average about 100 words in length. The *Dog & Kennel* web site is attractive and has general information about the magazine; news and articles about dogs; dog stories submitted by readers; and links to canine associations and to other dog-related web sites. Back issues of the magazine also can be ordered online. Finally, profiles of dog breeds and a listing of breeders are accessible from the web site.

4869. Dog Fancy: the world's most widely read dog magazine. Former titles (until 1986): *International Dog Fancy; Dog Fancy*. [ISSN: 0892-6522] 1970. m. USD 27.97 domestic; USD 45.97 foreign. Ed(s): Allan Reznik, Susan Chaney. BowTie, Inc., 2401 Beverly Blvd, PO Box 57900, Los Angeles, CA 90057; editor@animalnetwork.com; http://www.animalnetwork.com/. Illus., index, adv. Circ: 245614 Paid and controlled. *Indexed:* BRI. *Bk. rev.:* number and length vary. *Aud.:* Hs, Ga.

Dog Fancy is an excellent publication for dog owners and enthusiasts. The layout is attractive, and the magazine contains many color photographs and informative and well-written articles. Contributors include certified pet dog trainers, authors of books about dogs, and veterinarians. There are profiles of breeds and feature articles on topics such as canine nutrition, health and welfare, behavior, and living with dogs. Topics of recent articles include profiles of Italian Greyhounds, Yorkshire Terriers, and American Bulldogs; puppy training secrets; health dangers of fleas and ticks; and holistic health care. Some of the monthly sections and columns include "Readers Bark Back," which consists of letters to the editor and dog photographs submitted by readers; "Newshound," which includes dog news, tips, and trends; "Best Behavior," which offers advice on dog training and behavior; and "Checkup," which includes articles on health and science. There is also a "Help & Advice" section, where readers can pose questions to a dog trainer and to a veterinarian. Other departments include "Canine Traveler," which profiles dog-friendly vacation spots; and "K9 Kids," which contains drawings, stories, poems, and riddles about dogs submitted by young dog owners. *Dog Fancy* also contains a directory of breeders and a classified ads section. BowTie Magazines has annual publications about dogs. *Puppies USA* is a guide to adopting and caring for puppies, whereas *Dogs USA* is a guide to buying and owning purebred puppies. The *Dog Fancy* web site is very informative and extensive. The table of contents and photographs of the covers for the current and recent back issues are featured. Back issues can be purchased online. There are also breed profiles; resources on puppies, adoption, holistic care, behavior, health care, and nutrition; an online store for purchasing dog books; a breeder locator; online reader surveys and contests; online forums; a photo gallery; subscription information; and classified ads.

4870. Dog World: active dogs, active people. [ISSN: 0012-4893] 1916. m. USD 14.99 domestic; USD 32.99 foreign. Ed(s): Allan Reznik, David Greenwald. BowTie, Inc., 2401 Beverly Blvd, PO Box 57900, Los Angeles, CA 90057; editor@animalnetwork.com;

http://www.animalnetwork.com/. Illus., index, adv. Circ: 40263 Paid. Vol. ends: Dec. Microform: PQC. Online: EBSCO Publishing, EBSCO Host; OCLC Online Computer Library Center, Inc. *Indexed:* MASUSE. *Bk. rev.:* Number and length vary. *Aud.:* Ga, Sa.

Loaded with color photographs and well-written and in-depth articles, *Dog World* is an excellent publication for dog owners, trainers, and breeders. There are feature articles on breeds, shows, health, training, showing, and breeding. *Dog World* even has a monthly profile of rare dog breeds. Contributors include veterinarians, agility trainers, exhibitors, breeders, handlers, and authors of books on dogs. *Dog World* contains numerous columns such as "Showstoppers," "About Agility," "Judge's Perspective," and "Breeder's Notebook," which are featured in every issue. Monthly departments include dogs in the news, new products for dogs and their owners, a directory of breeders, and a classified ads section. There is also a calendar for conformation and performance events. Reviews of books for the dog enthusiast average about 300–400 words in length. *Dog World* features a department called "The Way We Were," which offers a glimpse at the cover and a page from an older issue of the magazine that was published decades ago. The *Dog World* web site is very informative and extensive. The table of contents and photographs of the covers for the current and some of the back issues are featured. Back issues can be purchased online. There are breed profiles; resources on puppies, adoption, holistic care, behavior, health care, and nutrition; an online store for purchasing dog books; a breeder locator; online reader surveys and contests; online forums; a photo gallery; subscription information; and classified ads.

4871. *Dogs in Canada: devoted to Canadians and their dogs.* Incorporates (1975-1976): *Dogs Annual;* Which was formerly (until 1974): *Kennel Directory.* [ISSN: 0012-4915] 1889. m. CND 39 domestic; USD 57 United States; USD 92 elsewhere. Ed(s): Beth Marley, Kelly Caldwell. Apex Publishing Ltd., 89 Skyway Ave, Ste 200, Etobicoke, ON M9W 6R4, Canada; info@dogsincanada.com; http://www.dogsincanada.com. Illus., adv. Sample. Circ: 41390. *Indexed:* CBCARef. *Bk. rev.:* various number and length. *Aud.:* Ga, Sa.

Dogs in Canada is a publication for members of the Canadian Kennel Club and for other dog enthusiasts. There are feature articles on breeds, breeding, showing, training, obedience, and health. Contributors include trainers, veterinarians, breeders, exhibitors, professional dog groomers, and authors of books on dogs. Canine urban legends, animal hording, and veterinarians and vaccines are topics of recently featured articles. Several of the magazine's columns and departments provide tips on obedience, behavior, and health. "Breedlines," contains information, issues, and trends for various dog breeds, while "Looking Back," offers a glimpse at the cover and a page from an older issue of the magazine that was published decades ago. There is also a directory of kennel clubs as well as a calendar of upcoming clinics, seminars, sanction matches, and other events. *Dogs in Canada Annual* contains the basics of dog ownership, information about breeds, and a directory of breeders. There is also a cat section in this annual publication, which has information about nutrition, behavior and health, and a directory of purebred cat breeders. The web site for *Dogs in Canada* has an index to breeds and breeders, subscription information, and a selection of articles that have appeared in previous issues of the magazine.

4872. *Fanc-e-Mews.* bi-m. Free. The Cat Fancier's Association, cfa@cfa.org; http://www.cfainc.org. *Bk. rev.:* Number and length vary. *Aud.:* Ga.

Published by the Cat Fanciers' Association, *Fanc-E-Mews* is a wonderful online magazine for cat owners and enthusiasts. Regular features include profiles of cat breeds and articles on health, care, and training. There are also book reviews, information about pet legislation, a calendar of upcoming cat shows, and classified ads.

4873. *Ferrets: the ultimate guide for today's ferret owner.* [ISSN: 1528-9826] 1997. bi-m. USD 19.95 domestic; USD 28.95 foreign; USD 3.99 newsstand/cover per issue. Ed(s): Marylou Zarbock. BowTie, Inc., 2401 Beverly Blvd, PO Box 57900, Los Angeles, CA 90057; http://www.animalnetwork.com/. Illus., adv. Circ: 20729 Paid and controlled. *Aud.:* Hs, Ga.

Ferrets magazine is a terrific resource for ferret owners. The articles are well-written and interesting. Contributors include veterinarians, ferret owners, small animal specialists, and authors of books on ferrets. Topics of recent articles include ferret-specific shelters, feng shui and ferrets, and Disseminated Idiopathic Myositis (DIM), a new killer disease that affects young ferrets. "Vet Q&A" and an "Acting Up Q&A," are regular features that contain questions submitted by readers concerning the health and behavior of their pets. Departments in each issue consist of letters to the editor, the latest ferret community news, a calendar of upcoming events, new products for ferrets and their owners, and a classified ads section. There is also an annual publication called *Ferrets USA*, which is an excellent resource for new or prospective ferret owners. The web site for *Ferrets* magazine is very informative and user-friendly. The table of contents and a photograph of the cover for the current issue are featured. Also included are resources for behavior, care, health, and nutrition of ferrets; a breeder locator; online forums, contests and surveys; a photo gallery; subscription information; and classified ads.

4874. *Fido Friendly: the travel magazine for you & your dog.* 2001. q. USD 12 domestic; USD 24 Canada; USD 32 elsewhere. Ed(s): Nick Sveslovsky. Fido Friendly, 10219, Costa Mesa, CA 92627-0083; inquiries@fidofriendly.com. Illus., adv. Sample. Circ: 30000. *Aud.:* Hs, Ga.

Fido Friendly is a travel magazine for dogs and their owners, and its motto is "Leave no dog behind." This magazine profiles cities and states that are dog-friendly and provides tips for traveling with dogs. It also has a directory that contains *Fido Friendly* accommodations and restaurants, dog parks, and camping/RV sites in the United States and Canada. A quarterly publication, *Fido Friendly* has theme-related issues on spring fashion, camping and hiking, a holiday gift guide, and an annual car buying guide with Fido in mind. Visitors to the *Fido Friendly* web site can view the table of contents and a photograph of the cover for the current issue as well as information regarding some of the recent back issues. Tips for traveling with dogs, along with links to travel accommodations, also are accessible from the web site.

4875. *Freshwater and Marine Aquarium: dedicated to tropical fish enthusiasts since 1978.* [ISSN: 0160-4317] 1978. m. USD 25 domestic; USD 43 foreign. Ed(s): Clay Jackson, Russ Case. BowTie, Inc., 3 Burroughs, Irvine, CA 92618-2804; editor@animalnetwork.com; http://www.animalnetwork.com/. Illus., adv. Circ: 7237. Vol. ends: Dec. *Indexed:* ZooRec. *Aud.:* Ga, Sa.

Freshwater and Marine Aquarium (*FAMA*) caters to the tropical fish enthusiast. The articles are interesting, in-depth, and well written. Topics of recent feature articles include fish health and nutrition, a profile of North Carolina?s aquarium at Roanoke Island, lionfish, and green terrors, which are South American cichlids. *FAMA* has many informative columns, several of which have a question-and-answer format, such as "Freshwater Forum," which is a column for the freshwater hobbyist, and "Horse Forum," which is a column for hobbyists interested in seahorses. Other columns include "Conservation Corner," "The Fishy Quiz," and "Bettas...And More." Visitors to *FAMA*'s web site can obtain subscription information and view the table of contents and a photograph of the cover for the current issue.

4876. *I Love Cats.* [ISSN: 0899-9570] 1988. bi-m. USD 36 domestic; USD 46 Canada; USD 56 elsewhere. Ed(s): Lisa Allmendiger. Redon Publishing, 16 Meadow Hill Ln, Armonk, NY 10504. Illus., adv. Sample. Circ: 25000. *Bk. rev.:* 1-4; 100 words. *Aud.:* Hs, Ga.

I Love Cats is a publication that contains entertaining and useful information for cat lovers. Article topics range from stories of actual cats, to health concerns, to how animals communicate. Topics of recent articles include curbing nocturnal behavior, pet disaster preparedness, and setting up a pet trust. Other regular features generally found in *I Love Cats* include an ask-the-vet section and book reviews that average about 100 words in length. The *I Love Cats* web site contains subscription information, an online store, and practical tips for cat owners.

4877. *Modern Dog: the lifestyle magazine for urban dogs and their companions.* [ISSN: 1703-812X] 2002. q. CND 18 domestic; USD 15 United States; USD 45 elsewhere. Ed(s): Connie Wilson. Modern Dog, 343 Railway St, Ste 202, Vancouver, BC V6A 1A4, Canada; connie@moderndog.ca. Illus., adv. Sample. Circ: 50000. *Aud.:* Ga.

According to this publication's web site, "a large part of *Modern Dog*'s mission is to support the efforts of organizations that work tirelessly to assist abused, neglected or homeless dogs." Published in Canada, this magazine is a glossy haute couture publication for dogs and their companions. It contains a breed profile, articles on fashion, dog accessories, dog-lore, dog psychology, fashion photography, interviews with celebrity pet owners, and queries posed by readers to vets and dog trainers. Topics of recent articles include cloning dogs, popular dog names, a puppy mill expose, and flying with dogs. The web site for *Modern Dog* has a partial table of contents and photographs of the current and previous covers. Back issues of *Modern Dog* can be ordered online. Subscription information and a resource directory of links to other canine-related web sites are also included. This magazine is recommended for large public library collections.

4878. *Our Animals.* [ISSN: 0030-6789] 1906. q. USD 15 in US & Canada. Ed(s): Paul M Glassner. San Francisco Society for the Prevention of Cruelty to Animals, 2500 16th St, San Francisco, CA 94103; ouranimals@sfspca.org; http://www.sfspca.org. Illus., adv. Sample. Circ: 30000. Vol. ends: No. 4. *Aud.:* Hs, Ga.

Our Animals is the award-winning publication of the San Francisco Society for the Prevention of Cruelty to Animals. Full of color photographs, *Our Animals* contains heartwarming stories about SF/SPCA's animals finding "forever" homes and about some of the many special programs sponsored by the organization, such as the foster program, the pet loss support group, the hearing dog program, and Maddie's Pet Adoption Center, which is a recognized model for animal shelters. The web site contains information about the SF/SPCA and its programs, along with general information about *Our Animals*, including a photograph of the cover for the current issue. Visitors can also read selected articles from recent issues.

4879. *Parrot Chronicles.com: the online magazine for parrot lovers.* bi-m. Free. Parrot Chronicles.com. *Aud.:* Ga.

ParrotChronicles.com contains a wealth of information for parrot owners. There are feature articles, stories of parrots in the news, basic information about different parrot species, and a FAQ about owning and caring for parrots. There are contests, classified ads, and question-and-answer sections where readers can pose questions to a veterinarian and to a companion parrot behavior consultant. Articles from previous issues of *ParrotChronicles.com* are listed alphabetically and by topic. There also are links to bird clubs, bird rescue groups, and a site where visitors can search for local avian veterinarians.

4880. *Pets Magazine: exploring the human-animal bond.* Former titles (until 1985): *Pets;* (until 1983): *Pets Magazine.* [ISSN: 0831-2621] 1983. bi-m. CND 24 domestic; USD 30 United States; USD 55 elsewhere. Ed(s): Blair Adams. Kenilworth Media Inc., 15 Wertheim Court, Ste 710, Richmond Hill, ON L4B 3H7, Canada; publisher@kenilworth.com; http://www.kenilworth.com. Illus., adv. Sample. Circ: 34500. Online: LexisNexis. *Indexed:* CBCARef, CPerI. *Aud.:* Hs, Ga.

The Canadian publication *Pets Magazine* explores the bond between humans and animals. Distributed by participating Canadian veterinary clinics and hospitals, this excellent resource contains the latest pet news from across Canada and from around the world; feature articles on caring for puppies, dogs, kittens, cats, birds, fish, ferrets, rabbits, and older pets; and up-to-date medical advancements in pet health. The articles are informative, well-written, and very readable. *Pets Magazine* has numerous photographs, and the layout is very attractive. Many of the contributors are veterinarians. The web site for *Pets Magazine* provides general information about the publication, along with the table of contents and a photograph of the cover for the current issue. Visitors also can read selected articles from previous issues.

4881. *Pets Quarterly.* Formerly (until 1996): *Pets Quarterly.* [ISSN: 1207-2222] 1995. q. CND 12.95 domestic; USD 12.95 United States. Canadian Association Publishers, PO Box 90510, Scarborough, ON M1J 3N7, Canada; info@capmagazines.ca; http://www.capmagazines.ca/. Illus., adv. Sample. Circ: 20000. *Aud.:* Hs, Ga.

Published in Canada, *Pets Quarterly* focuses on pet health, care, and nutrition. This magazine is distributed by veterinarians and through the adoption kits of the Canadian Societies for the Prevention of Cruelty to Animals and the

Humane Societies of Canada. Topics of recent articles include tips for hiking with dogs, handling feral cats, and cancer in cats and dogs. Each issue also contains articles on fish and birds called "Wet Pets" and "On the Fly," respectively. Some departments in each issue include pet news from across Canada and from around the world; information on new pet products; titles and descriptions of recently published pet books; and news from the Canadian Federation of Human Societies and from the Canadian Veterinary Medical Association. *Pets Quarterly* also contains a question-and-answer section, where readers can pose questions to veterinarians about cats, dogs, birds, and exotic animals. The articles are well-written and informative. The web site for *Pets Quarterly* has general information about the magazine, the table of contents and a photograph of the cover for the current issue, and links to other pet web sites.

4882. *Rare Breeds Journal.* Incorporates (in 2003): *Animals Exotic and Small;* Incorporates in part: *The Jumping Pouch.* [ISSN: 1048-986X] 1987. bi-m. USD 30 domestic; USD 35 in Canada & Mexico; USD 50 elsewhere. Ed(s): Maureen Neidhardt. Rare Breeds Journal, PO Box 66, Crawford, NE 69339; http://www.ckcusa.com/webads/exotics/rarebre.htm. Illus., adv. Sample. Circ: 4000 Paid. Vol. ends: Jan/Feb. *Bk. rev.:* various number and length. *Aud.:* Sa.

Rare Breeds Journal (*RBJ*) contains information on alternative livestock, wildlife, animals, and pets and is a resource for enthusiasts of unique animals and minor breeds. Its motto is "animals develop principles that develop character in people." Some of *RBJ*'s features include interviews with ranchers and breeders; news from registries and associations; and articles on the housing, breeding, care, and health of animals. Contributors include breeders, owners, and trainers. *RBJ* is printed on newsprint and contains a mixture of color and black-and-white photography. Its coverage is international in scope. Exotic animals featured in this magazine include miniature horses, Texas Longhorns, rare horse breeds, camels, Babydoll sheep, emus, Pygmy goats, wallabies, kangaroos, yaks, and miniature Zebu cattle. *RBJ* also has book reviews, a classified ads section, a directory of breeders, and listings of associations, registries, and organizations. The *RBJ* web site contains general information about the publication and a directory of breeders and associations. *RBJ* is recommended for library collections that serve individuals interested in the breeding, raising, and selling of unique animals and minor breeds.

4883. *Reptile Care.* [ISSN: 1741-2390] 2003. bi-m. USD 35 United States; USD 45 Canada. Mulberry Publications Ltd., Wellington House, Ste 209, Butt Rd, Colchester, CO3 3DA, United Kingdom. Illus. Sample. Circ: 41000. *Aud.:* Ga.

Published in the United Kingdom, *Reptile Care* is an excellent resource for reptile and amphibian enthusiasts. The layout is very attractive, the photography is stunning, and the articles are informative, well-written, and in-depth. Topics of recent feature articles including coping with iguana stress, an interview with a well-known python breeder, and profiles of Rainbow boas, Mata Mata turtles, Giant African Land snails, and Vietnamese Mossy frogs. Regular features of *Reptile Care* include reptile news from around the globe, readers' queries answered by a panel of experts, recent herpetological news from scientific publications, and a gallery of photos submitted by readers. There is also a listing of reptile events and a classified ads section. The web site contains general information about the magazine. Visitors to the site can pose questions to leading reptile experts. There are also links to reptile events, clubs, and societies.

4884. *Reptiles: the world's leading reptile magazine.* [ISSN: 1068-1965] 1993. m. USD 27.97 domestic; USD 45.97 foreign. Ed(s): Russ Case. BowTie, Inc., 2401 Beverly Blvd, PO Box 57900, Los Angeles, CA 90057; http://www.animalnetwork.com/. Illus., index, adv. Circ: 41406 Paid and controlled. Vol. ends: Dec. *Indexed:* ZooRec. *Aud.:* Ga.

Loaded with stunning photographs, *Reptiles* contains articles on both reptiles and amphibians. Topics of recent feature articles include the best national parks for herping, constructing an in-ground turtle pen, raising fruit flies for herp consumption, and profiles of yellow-footed tortoises, Tokay geckos, and fire skinks. The articles are well-written, in-depth, and informative, and the magazine's layout is attractive. Some of the articles even include a list of references. There is a section profiling the magazine's contributors, which include herpetologists, herpetoculturists, biologists, veterinarians, and entomologists. *Reptiles Magazine* also has reptile news and trivia, "Ssstuff," which features herp books, a listing of reptile events entitled "Herp Happenings," and a "Veterinarian Q&A." Each issue also has a breeder directory and a classified ads section. BowTie Magazines has an annual publication called *Reptiles USA*, which is a guide to buying and caring for reptiles and amphibians. New and prospective owners of reptiles and amphibians would find *Reptiles USA* very informative. The web site for *Reptiles* is extensive and filled with useful information about reptiles and amphibians. It contains the table of contents and a photograph of the cover for the current issue. Other features include subscription rates, the latest herp news, an "Ask the Vet" section, species profiles, a photo gallery, online forums, and a breeder locator section.

4885. *Tropical Fish Hobbyist.* [ISSN: 0041-3259] 1952. m. USD 28 domestic; USD 39 in Canada & Mexico; USD 48 elsewhere. Ed(s): David Boruchowitz, Albert Connelly, Jr. T.F.H. Publications, Inc., One TFH Plaza, Third and Union Aves, Neptune, NJ 07753; info@tfh.com; http://www.tfh.com. Illus., index, adv. Sample. Circ: 35000. Vol. ends: Aug. *Indexed:* BRI, ZooRec. *Aud.:* Ga, Sa.

Tropical Fish Hobbyist (*TFH*) is an excellent resource for the tropical fish enthusiast. The color photography is beautiful, the layout is attractive, and the articles are in-depth and well-written. Some of the articles even have lists of references. Contributors include biologists; aquarium hobbyists; breeders; freshwater, marine, and reef aquarists; and authors of works on marine aquariums. Topics of recent articles include clownfish and anemone compatibility, tips for establishing a garden pond, selecting fish for the nature aquarium, and a guide to wild swordtails. There are several question-and-answer sections in which readers can submit questions and problems related to discus and to freshwater and saltwater aquariums. "Fish of the Month," "Marine Invert of the Month," a product spotlight section, a calendar of events for aquarium and tropical fish club meetings, and a classified ads section are also included in each issue. The January issue contains an annual index to *TFH*. *TFH*'s web site is informative, easy to navigate, and contains general information about the magazine. Photographs of the covers along with the tables of contents for the current and the next month's issues are featured.

4886. *Whole Dog Journal: a monthly guide to natural dog care & training.* [ISSN: 1097-5322] 1998. m. USD 39 in US & Canada; USD 48 elsewhere. Ed(s): Nancy Kerns. Belvoir Media Group, LLC, 800 Connecticut Ave, Norwalk, CT 06854-1631; customer_service@belvoir.com; http://www.belvoir.com. Illus., adv. Sample. Circ: 5000. Vol. ends: Dec. *Aud.:* Ga, Sa.

Whole Dog Journal offers dog owners in-depth information and advice on holistic health care and nonviolent training. There are feature articles on herbal remedies, adoption, neutering, behavior, training, product reviews, diet, and care, as well as information on complementary therapies such as chiropractic, massage, acupuncture, and homeopathy. Topics of recent articles include treatment for heartworm infections, recognizing and reducing signs of stress in dogs, frozen commercial diets, and a hospice how-to. *Whole Dog Journal* does not accept commercial advertising and conducts its own tests, reviewing, and evaluation of products. Contributors include veterinary herbalists, authors of books on natural pet care, and certified pet dog trainers. Visitors to the web site can view sample articles and a partial table of contents for the current issue. There is a subscriber side to the web site. Magazine subscribers can log in and access articles from the current and previous issues.

4887. *Your Cat.* [ISSN: 1353-260X] 1994. m. GBP 48 in Europe; GBP 58 elsewhere. Ed(s): Sue Parslow. Bourne Publishing Group Ltd. (B P G), Roebuck House, 33 Broad St, Stamford, PE9 1RB, United Kingdom. Illus., adv. Sample. Circ: 26000. *Aud.:* Hs, Ga.

Published in the United Kingdom, *Your Cat* is a terrific resource for cat owners and enthusiasts. The articles in *Your Cat* are well-written and extremely informative. The magazine's layout is very attractive, and it contains many color photographs. Contributors include veterinarians, cat nutrition specialists, homeopathic veterinary surgeons, counseling psychologists, and authors of books on cats. Topics of articles range from health and welfare, to personality and behavior, to profiles of breeds, to the human-feline bond. Topics of recent articles include how to live with a possessive cat, cancer and cats, skin and coat care, and profiles of the Cornish Rex and Singapura breeds. One of the features of *Your Cat* is a question-and-answer section where readers pose questions to a

panel of experts. Overall topics of these Q&A sections include general cat care, showing and breeding, behavior, veterinary, and nutrition. Other regular features and columns of *Your Cat* include fictional stories about cats, cats in the news, a breeder directory, a preview of the upcoming issue of the magazine, cat photos submitted by readers, and a classified ads section. The web site for *Your Cat* is attractive, easy to navigate, and features information about the current issue. Visitors can read sample questions-and-answers that readers have posed to the magazine's panel of experts. The site also includes general information about *Your Cat* and links to cat organizations in the United Kingdom. Back issues of *Your Cat* also can be purchased online.

4888. *Your Dog.* [ISSN: 1078-0343] 1994. m. USD 39 domestic; USD 72 foreign. Ed(s): Betty Liddick, John Berg. Tufts University, Cummings School of Veterinary Medicine, Tufts Media, 200 Bosto Ave, Ste 3500, Medford, MA 02155; vetadmissions@tufts.edu. Illus. Sample. Circ: 45000. *Aud.:* Ga.

Your Dog is a monthly newsletter published by Tufts Media in cooperation with the Cummings School of Veterinary Medicine at Tufts University. Twenty-four pages in length, *Your Dog* provides information on treatment and health care for dogs. *Your Dog* does not accept commercial advertising. Many of the contributors are veterinarians. This newsletter contains numerous black-and-white photographs. The articles are informative and would be of interest to dog owners. *Your Dog* has articles on canine behavior, medicine, health, animal welfare, disease, and a dog health care question-and-answer section. Topics of recent articles include dogs and airborne allergies, problem barking, canine epilepsy, and choking and dogs. *Your Dog*'s web site provides general information about the newsletter and highlights some of the article titles from the current issue. Visitors can also read sample articles from the newsletter.

4889. *Your Dog.* [ISSN: 1355-7386] 1995. m. GBP 48 in Europe; GBP 58 elsewhere. Ed(s): Sarah Wright. Bourne Publishing Group Ltd. (B P G), Roebuck House, 33 Broad St, Stamford, PE9 1RB, United Kingdom. Illus., adv. Sample. Circ: 28044. *Aud.:* Ga.

Published in the United Kingdom, *Your Dog* is a terrific resource for dog owners and enthusiasts. The articles in *Your Dog* are well-written and extremely informative. The magazine's layout is very attractive, and it contains lots of color photographs. Contributors include veterinarians, breeds experts, show judges, professional groomers, canine behaviorists, animal nutrition specialists, trainers, homeopathic veterinarians, and authors of books on dogs. Topics of articles range from health and welfare, to personality and behavior, to breed profiles, to the human–canine bond. Topics of recent articles include steps to a healthy pet, grooming, acupuncture, dogs and hydrotherapy, and profiles of English Toy Terriers and Sealyham Terriers. One of the features of *Your Dog* is a question-and-answer section in which readers pose questions to a panel of experts. Topics of these Q&A sections include grooming and showing, behavior, health, training, and breeds. Other regular features of *Your Dog* include dog news, dog photos submitted by readers, and a classified ads section. Currently, the web site for *Your Dog* only contains a link to subscription information for this magazine.

Associations

American Aquarist Society, Inc., Box 100, 3901 Hatch Blvd., Sheffield, AL 35660.

American Cat Fanciers Association, P.O. Box 1949, Nixa, MO 65714-1949, www.acfacats.com, mcats@bellsouth.com.

American Cichlid Association, 43081 Bond Court, Sterling Heights, MI 48313, www.cichlid.org, acawebmaster@cichlid.org.

American Federation of Aviculture, P.O. Box 7312, N. Kansas City, MO 64116, www.afabirds.org, afaoffice@aol.com.

American Fancy Rat and Mouse Association, 9230 64th Street, Riverside, CA 92509-5924, www.afrma.org, rattusrat@hotmail.com.

American Ferret Association Inc., PMB 255 626-C Admiral Dr., Annapolis, MD 21401, www.ferret.org, afa@ferret.org.

American Gerbil Society, Inc., 18893 Lawrence 2100 Mt Vernon, Mo 65712, www.agsgerbils.org, mountash@mfx.net.

American Kennel Club, 260 Madison Ave, New York, NY 10016, www.akc.org.

Canadian Kennel Club, 89 Skyway Avenue, Suite 100 Etobicoke, Ontario M9W 6R4, www.ckc.ca, information@ckc.ca.

Cat Fanciers' Association, Inc., P.O. Box 1005, Manasquan, NJ 08736-0805, www.cfainc.org, cfa@cfa.org.

American Society for the Prevention of Cruelty to Animals, 424 E. 92nd St., New York, NY 10128-6804, www.aspca.org.

Canadian Cat Association, 289 Rutherford Road, S #18, Brampton, ON, L6W 3R9, www.cca-afc.com, office@cca-afc.com.

Goldfish Society of America, P.O. Box 551373, Fort Lauderdale, FL 33355, www.goldfishsociety.org, info@goldfishsociety.org.

House Rabbit Society, 148 Broadway, Richmond, CA 94804, www.rabbit.org, mec@rabbit.org.

Humane Society of the United States, 2100 L St., NW, Washinton, DC 20037, www.hsus.org.

Rat, Mouse, and Hamster Fanciers, 783 Solana Dr., Lafayette, CA 94549, www.ratmousehamster.com.

■ PHILATELY

Joe Bourneuf, Head of Reference and Information Services, Widener Library, Harvard University, Cambridge, MA 02138

Introduction

Although sticklers may insist that philately applies only to the study of stamps and related postal articles rather than the hobby or business of collecting them, most take the word to encompass both activities. The first postage stamps, representing the pre-payment of postal fees, were issued on May 1, 1840. These were known as the "one-penny black" and the "two-penny blue." The United States issued postal stamps beginning in 1847. Collecting stamps caught on almost immediately and soon gained such a numerous and devoted following that within a few years it was ridiculed as a silly fad in the press of the time.

Today there are an estimated two million stamp collectors in the United States alone. Stamps are collected by country, topic, or format. The most popular type of collecting is by country of issuance or geographic region. The topical collector collects stamps dealing with a certain subject or theme, such as Judaica, space, medicine, or women on stamps. The format collector is interested in philatelic materials selected by type of postal service rendered, such as airmail, first-day covers, booklets, postmarks, pre-cancels, and postal stationery (to name a few). Most stamp magazines are highly specialized. Although many of these enjoy a considerable audience, they are not reviewed here because of their narrow focus. The emphasis here is on general English-language stamp publications that deal with stamps worldwide, or that focus on the United States, Canada, and Great Britain, nations whose philately is of most interest to American collectors.

In the last few years, the number of philatelic web sites has grown exponentially, but most are vendor sites or auction sites, which are not appropriate for review because they are not electronic journals, magazines, or newletters. There are web sites affiliated with many of the recommended print philatelic magazines, but there is only one purely electronic philatelic journal: *Stamps.Net: the Internet magazine for stamp collectors.*

Basic Periodicals

Ems: *American Philatelist, Canadian Philatelist, Gibbon's Stamp Monthly, Global Stamp News, Linn's Stamp News, Meekel's and stamps magazine, Philatelic Literature Review, Postal History Journal, Scott Stamp Monthly, Stamp Magazine, Stamps.Net, Topical Time.*

4890. *American Philatelist.* [ISSN: 0003-0473] 1887. m. USD 48 domestic; USD 43 in Canada & Mexico; USD 50 elsewhere. Ed(s): Barbara Boal. American Philatelic Society, Inc., 100 Match Factory Pl, Bellefonte, PA 16823; flsente@stamps.org; http://www.philately.com/philately/aps.htm. Illus., index, adv. Sample. Circ: 48000 Paid. Vol. ends: Dec. *Indexed:* A&ATA, ABS&EES, BRI, CBRI. *Bk. rev.:* 50-300 words. *Aud.:* Ga, Ac.

American Philatelist is the oldest philatelic journal still in publication in the world and is the official publication of the American Philatelic Society (APS), the leading philatelic organization in the United States. Despite the title, this magazine is worldwide in scope and covers all aspects of stamp collecting. Articles address contemporary philatelic themes as well as historical issues and are supplemented with color illustrations of stamps and postal documents. Each issue features a "Sales Talk" giving news, resources, and sources for stamp buying and selling, and "Show Time" offering a calendar of stamp shows and exhibitions. This journal also offers its members news on the society's activities as well as classified ads. An annual author and subject index to the previous year is available on the society's web site: www.stamps.org. This high-quality journal is essential for all general collections.

4891. *Canadian Philatelist.* [ISSN: 0045-5253] 1950. bi-m. Members, CND 25; Non-members, CND 30. Ed(s): Tony Shaman. Philaprint Ltd., 10 Summerhill Ave, Toronto, ON M4T 1AB, Canada. Illus., index, adv. Circ: 3000 Controlled. Vol. ends: Nov/Dec. Microform: MML. *Indexed:* CBCARef. *Bk. rev.:* 7-10, 350 words. *Aud.:* Ga, Ac.

Canadian Philatelist publishes articles in English and French primarily on the stamps and postal history of Canada. Regular columns include an auction and events calendar, news from the Canadian Postal Service, vignettes of early British North American postal history, letters to the editor, and a listing of recently issued Canadian stamps. It is the official publication of the Royal Philatelic Society of Canada, the leading philatelic organization in the country. Its web site, www.rpsc.org/tcp/index.php, allows topic, author, and title searching of this publication from 1950 to the present. Images of each issue excluding the last five years are available in pdf, as are the issues of four earlier publications of the society dating back to 1891.

4892. *Gibbons Stamp Monthly.* Formerly (until 1977): *Stamp Monthly.* [ISSN: 0954-8084] 1890. m. GBP 39 domestic; GBP 64 foreign. Ed(s): Hugh Jefferies. Stanley Gibbons Publications Ltd., 5 Parkside, Christchurch Rd, Ringwood, BH24 3SH, United Kingdom; info@stanleygibbons.co.uk; http://www.stanleygibbons.com. Illus., index, adv. Sample. Circ: 25000 Paid. Vol. ends: May. *Bk. rev.:* 5-10, 50-100 words. *Aud.:* Ga.

This glossy British magazine offers articles and news of interest to collectors of stamps and other postal materials issued in the United Kingdom and the Commonwealth. It enjoys a wide circulation, especially within the British Isles, due to its readable, popular articles. There are also more erudite pieces intended for the serious philatelist. Regular features include catalogue price updates, issuance of first-day covers, varieties, auctions, fairs, and competitions. Each issue also contains the most recent new-issue supplement to the *Stanley Gibbons Stamp Catalogue,* the most popular stamp catalogue published in Great Britain.

4893. *Global Stamp News.* [ISSN: 1060-0361] 1990. m. USD 10.95. Ed(s): Jan Brandewie. Brandewie Inc., 110 N Ohio Ave, Box 97, Sidney, OH 45365. Illus., adv. Sample. Circ: 33000 Controlled. *Bk. rev.:* 1-4, 100-900 words. *Aud.:* Hs, Ga.

Advertisers cover most of the expenses of publishing this tabloid, making it one of the best values in stamp publishing. *Global Stamp News* is an informative publication, with more than 50 pages in each monthly issue. Numerous advertisements are interspersed with short articles, many of which are submitted by readers. These informative articles represent a wide variety of worldwide collecting interests and evidence a shared fascination with stamps.

4894. *Linn's Stamp News.* Formerly: *Linn's Weekly Stamp News.* [ISSN: 0161-6234] 1928. w. USD 45.95 domestic; USD 90.95 Canada; USD 120.95 elsewhere. Ed(s): Michael Schreiber. Amos Press Inc., P O Box 29, Sidney, OH 45365; http://www.amospress.com. Illus., adv. Sample. Circ: 40000 Paid. Vol. ends: Dec. Microform: PQC. *Bk. rev.:* 1-5, 50-400 words. *Aud.:* Ga.

This tabloid is the world's highest-circulation weekly philatelic newspaper. Articles cover all aspects of stamp collecting worldwide, with a special emphasis on the United States and Canada. *Linn's* has a particular appeal for those collectors and stamp dealers who actively buy and sell stamps, as it strives to provide accurate and timely information on the stamp market. An extensive classified section, regular columns and news articles on stamp market tips and trends, and numerous advertisements form the basis of a stamp marketplace for the buying, selling, and exchanging of all varieties of philatelic materials. News and information are provided on stamp societies, stamp events, show awards, auction calendars, new worldwide issues, the U.S. stamp program, postmarks, forgeries, cachets, and covers. *Linn's Stamp News* is also available online (www.linns.com). This dynamic web site is keyword-searchable and includes links to several of the feature articles in the current weekly issue, current information on the price performance of U.S. stamps, a stamp show calendar searchable by month or by state, and weekly updates on the U.S., U.N., and Canadian stamp programs. There is a reference section (with hyperlinks) that includes a glossary of philatelic terms, listings of the world's postal administrations and postal history societies, and a tutorial of stamp collecting basics.

4895. *Mekeel's and Stamps Magazine.* Formed by the merger of (1891-1995): *Mekeel's Stamp News; Stamp Auction News.* [ISSN: 1095-0443] 1995. w. USD 32.50 for 2 yrs. Ed(s): John L Leszak. Philatelic Communications Corp., PO Box 5050, White Plains, NY 10602; stampnews@mindspring.com. Illus., adv. Sample. Circ: 8000. *Bk. rev.:* Occasional. *Aud.:* Ga.

Founded in 1891 by Charles H. Mekeel, *Mekeel's* is said to be the oldest continuing weekly philatelic journal published in the world. The latest issue seen as of this writing is number 6,067. Each issue offers the latest philatelic news, articles on all aspects of stamp collecting, numerous auction and show calendars, and a plethora of advertisements.

4896. *Philatelic Literature Review.* [ISSN: 0270-1707] 1942. q. USD 30 (Individuals, USD 18). Ed(s): Barbara Boal. American Philatelic Research Library, 100 Match Factory Place, Bellefonte, PA 16823; plr@stamps.org; http://www.stamps.org/TheLibrary/lib_TAP.htm. Illus., index, adv. Sample. Circ: 2750. Vol. ends: Dec. *Indexed:* BRI, CBRI. *Bk. rev.:* 10-20, 100-750 words. *Aud.:* Ac, Sa.

Philatelic Literature Review is published by the American Philatelic Research Library, the largest public philatelic library in the United States. This library is under the aegis of the American Philatelic Society, which also publishes the *American Philatelist.* The value of this periodical as a reference tool is threefold: knowledgeable, in-depth book reviews written by specialists in the field; biographical and research articles on the history of philately; and original, comprehensive indexes and bibliographies on all aspects of stamp collecting. Each issue also features market information, news from the American Philatelic Research Library, a directory of dealers, and a philatelic literature clearinghouse where members list philatelic literature for sale or wanted for purchase. This is essential for any collection that supports research in the field.

4897. *Postal History Journal.* [ISSN: 0032-5341] 1957. 3x/yr. USD 30 domestic; USD 35 in Canada & Mexico; USD 40 elsewhere. Ed(s): Diane F DeBlois, Robert Dalton Harris. Postal History Society, Inc., 869 Bridgewater Dr, New Oxford, PA 17350. Illus., index, adv. Vol. ends: Oct. Microform: PQC. *Bk. rev.:* 2-5, 100-400 words. *Aud.:* Ac, Sa.

This journal is renowned for its scholarly, well-researched articles and commentaries on all aspects of postal history worldwide. Recent issues feature articles on such diverse subjects as a "Survey of Siamese Postal Affairs to 1908" and "Stamp Positions on Covers: from romance to political protest." Annotated bibliographies of American and foreign postal-history articles published in other journals can be found in each issue, as well as news and information for members of the Postal History Society. Recommended for all comprehensive collections.

4898. *Scott Stamp Monthly.* Supersedes in part (until 1982): *Scott's Monthly Stamp Journal;* Which was formerly: *Scott's Monthly Journal.* [ISSN: 0737-0741] 1920. m. USD 31.97 domestic; USD 46.97 Canada; USD 61.97 elsewhere. Ed(s): Michael Baadke. Scott Publishing Company, 911 Vandemark Rd, PO Box 828, Sidney, OH 45365; http://www.scottonline.com. Illus., index, adv. Sample. Circ: 28000 Paid. Vol. ends: Dec. *Bk. rev.:* 1-3, length varies. *Aud.:* Hs, Ga.

This magazine, which is held by more libraries than any other philatelic title, is published by the Scott Publishing Company, a division of Amos Hobby Publishing, which is also the publisher of *Linn's Stamp News* and of the annual

Scott Standard Postage Stamp Catalogue, the philatelist's bible. A key part of each issue is an update to the annual *Catalogue,* giving revised valuations on a timely basis. The online edition of *Scott Stamp Monthly,* www.scottonline.com, offers even more immediate access to this key information. Each issue also provides general-interest articles on stamps worldwide, with color illustrations, appealing to philatelists of all ages. Monthly columns provide articles that recreate popular historical subjects through stamps, give tips for working with stamps, and discuss postal errors and postal history. Each issue also features a full-color comic titled "Amazing Stamp Stories," puzzles, an auction calendar, and a listing by date of issue of the most recent stamps issued by the United States, Canada, and the United Nations. This magazine is highly recommended for all public libraries.

4899. *Stamps.Net: the Internet magazine for stamp collectors.* 1998. irreg. Ed(s): Randy L Neil. Champion Stamp Company Inc., 432 W 54th St, New York, NY 10019; http://www.stamps.net. *Aud.:* Hs, Ga.

Stamps.Net appears to be the sole general-interest stamp e-journal without a print counterpart. It provides up-to-the-minute philatelic news via several short featured stories, updated on a continuing basis, and an archive of previous articles. *Stamps.Net* provides links to philatelic societies, clubs, and stamp show web sites. A link is also provided to *StampFinder,* a global stamp exchange web site offering one-stop shopping for more than 800,000 stamps from numerous dealers, plus links to dealer web sites, and voluminous classified advertisements.

4900. *Topical Time.* [ISSN: 0040-9332] 1949. bi-m. USD 20 domestic; USD 30 foreign. Ed(s): George Griffenhagen. American Topical Association, Inc., 411 Lillard Rd, Arlington, TX 76012; americantopical@ msn.com; http://www.americantopicalassn.org. Illus., index, adv. Circ: 3500 Paid. Vol. ends: Nov/Dec. *Bk. rev.:* 5-10, 100-500 words. *Aud.:* Ga, Sa.

Many collect stamps that are focused on a subject or theme rather than on a nation or a philatelic format such as first-day covers. *Topical Time* is the only English-language philatelic magazine solely devoted to the interests of topical stamp collectors. Each issue contains several articles on specific topics or themes being collected. For example, a recent issue carries a piece on stamps depicting characters and scenes from Shakespeare's tragedies and another on stamps relating to the tarantella folk dance. A regular feature is the index to topical periodical articles that have appeared in other stamp magazines. As the official publication of the American Topical Association, it offers society news, including a monthly update on the activities of study groups focusing on a particular topic. Members are encouraged to join one or more groups, and to submit articles to *Topical Time.*

■ PHILOSOPHY

R. Scott Harnsberger, Government Documents Librarian, Newton Gresham Library, Sam Houston State University, Huntsville, TX 77341-2179; lib_rsh@shsu.edu; FAX: 936-294-3780

Introduction

Librarians and researchers need to be aware that an important and often overlooked aspect of philosophy periodicals is their potential to support research in a broad range of scholarly inquiry in fields as diverse as art, education, law, linguistics, literature, politics, psychology, religion, science, and sociology, to name a few. The editors of the journals in this section endeavor to present scholarship that exemplifies depth of philosophical insight, mastery of the relevant philosophical literature, originality of thought, rigor of argumentation, and clarity of presentation.

Philosophy journals have become increasingly specialized since the 1950s. Most major subdivisions of the field, as well as many prominent philosophers, have publications devoted to them. Several journals have been founded in recent years with the goal of promoting a dialogue either between Anglo-American and continental European philosophers or philosophers working within the European community itself.

It seems likely that as the international geopolitical atmosphere becomes increasingly turbulent, articles that analyze and explicate philosophical concepts and issues surrounding war, terrorism and political violence, civil and human rights, national reconciliation, restorative justice, racism, pacifism, etc., will have an increasingly important role to play in public policy debates.

Indexing coverage is improving for philosophy periodicals published in an electronic-only format, which should begin to bolster their readership and impact on the field.

Basic Periodicals

Ac: *Ethics, The Journal of Philosophy, Journal of the History of Philosophy, Mind, Nous, Philosophical Studies, Philosophy and Public Affairs, Philosophy of Science;* Sa: *The Journal of Symbolic Logic.*

Basic Abstracts and Indexes

Arts and Humanities Citation Index, Humanities Index, The Philosopher's Index, Repertoire Bibliographique de la Philosophie.

4901. *Acta Analytica.* [ISSN: 0353-5150] 1986. q. EUR 218 print & online eds. Ed(s): Danilo Suster. Springer Netherlands, Van Godewijckstraat 30, Dordrecht, 3311 GX, Netherlands; http://www.springeronline.com. Adv. *Indexed:* IPB, PhilInd. *Aud.:* Ac.

Acta Analytica is an English-language Slovenian journal that publishes thematic issues in the analytic tradition, chiefly centering around topics in metaphysics, epistemology, philosophical logic, philosophy of language, cognitive science, and practical ethics. Contributions explicating issues surrounding contextualism have been particularly noteworthy. URL: http://rcum.uni-mb.si/~actaana

4902. *American Philosophical Quarterly.* [ISSN: 0003-0481] 1964. q. USD 270 (Individuals, USD 55). Ed(s): Neil Tennant. University of Illinois Press, 1325 S Oak St, Champaign, IL 61820-6903; journals@uillinois.edu; http://www.press.uillinois.edu. Illus., index. Sample. Refereed. Circ: 1800. *Indexed:* AmHI, ArtHuCI, FR, HumInd, IBR, IBSS, IBZ, IPB, PhilInd, RI-1, RILM, SSCI. *Aud.:* Ac.

This is an excellent general philosophy journal that publishes technical, critical essays on specific problems, arguments, and issues in the areas of metaphysics, epistemology, philosophy of mind, ethics, philosophy of language, and action theory. The "Recent Work" series appears occasionally and provides an overview of scholarly work on selected philosophers or philosophical topics. URL: www.press.uillinois.edu/journals/apq.html

4903. *Analysis.* [ISSN: 0003-2638] 1933. q. GBP 45 print & online eds. Ed(s): Michael Clark. Blackwell Publishing Ltd., 9600 Garsington Rd, Oxford, OX4 2ZG, United Kingdom; customerservices@blackwellpublishing.com; http://www.blackwellpublishing.com. Illus., index, adv. Refereed. Circ: 1350. Vol. ends: No. 4. Online: Blackwell Synergy; EBSCO Publishing, EBSCO Host; Gale; IngentaConnect; OCLC Online Computer Library Center, Inc.; OhioLINK; SwetsWise Online Content. Reprint: PSC. *Indexed:* AmHI, ApEcolAb, ArtHuCI, CCMJ, IBR, IBSS, IBZ, IPB, L&LBA, MSN, MathR, PhilInd. *Aud.:* Ac.

Analysis publishes relatively short articles that either advance or critique precisely defined arguments or positions in contemporary analytic philosophy, chiefly in the areas of metaphysics, philosophical logic, philosophy of language, philosophy of mind, epistemology, and ethics. URL: www.nottingham.ac.uk/journals/analysis

4904. *Ancient Philosophy.* [ISSN: 0740-2007] 1980. s-a. USD 70 (Individuals, USD 32). Ed(s): Dr. Ronald Polansky. Duquesne University, Department of Philosophy, 600 Forbes Ave, Pittsburgh, PA 15282. Illus., adv. Refereed. Circ: 750. Vol. ends: No. 2. Reprint: PSC. *Indexed:* AmHI, HumInd, IBR, IBZ, IPB, PhilInd, RI-1. *Bk. rev.:* 15-20, 1,000-2,000 words, signed. *Aud.:* Ac.

The articles in this journal are principally on Plato and Aristotle, although others deal with their contemporaries, the Presocratics, the Neoplatonists, and medieval commentators on Aristotle. Each issue averages eight to ten articles (all of which are extensively footnoted and accompanied by bibliographies) and

two to four discussion papers. This journal is a good supplement to *Phronesis* (below in this section) for larger academic collections where ancient philosophy is emphasized. URL: www.ancientphilosophy.com

4905. *Archiv fuer Geschichte der Philosophie.* [ISSN: 0003-9101] 1976. 3x/yr. EUR 164; EUR 189 combined subscription print & online eds.; EUR 61 newsstand/cover. Ed(s): Christoph Horn, Wolfgang Bartuschat. Walter de Gruyter GmbH & Co. KG, Genthiner Str 13, Berlin, 10785, Germany; wdg-info@degruyter.de; http://www.degruyter.de. Illus., index, adv. Refereed. Circ: 750 Paid. Vol. ends: No. 3. Reprint: SCH. *Indexed:* AmHI, ArtHuCI, FR, IBR, IBZ, IPB, MLA-IB, PhilInd. *Bk. rev.:* 5-10, 500-1,000 words. *Aud.:* Ac.

This journal features a broad base of international scholarship on the history of philosophy, with articles in both English and German. The articles address specific problems and issues in the writings of the major philosophers from antiquity to the early twentieth century. The journal occasionaly features the first publication of short historical primary texts. URL: www.degruyter.de/rs/282_697_ENU_h.htm

4906. *Aristotelian Society. Proceedings. Supplementary Volume.* [ISSN: 0309-7013] 1887. a. GBP 79 print & online eds. Ed(s): Dr. Mark Eli Kalderon. Aristotelian Society, c/o Georgia Testa, Rm 260, Senate House, London, WC1E 7HU, United Kingdom; mail@aristoteliansociety.org.uk; http://www.sas.ac.uk/aristotelian_society/. Illus. Sample. Refereed. Online: Blackwell Synergy; EBSCO Publishing, EBSCO Host; Gale; IngentaConnect; OCLC Online Computer Library Center, Inc.; OhioLINK; SwetsWise Online Content. Reprint: PSC. *Indexed:* PhilInd. *Aud.:* Ac.

The Aristotelian Society is one of the oldest and most distinguished organizations for Anglo-American philosophers. The annual proceedings, published in June as a supplementary volume to the quarterly journal, contain papers read at the annual joint sessions of the Aristotelian Society and the Mind Association, leading off with the presidential address. This publication invariably represents exemplary standards of scholarship, and it is highly recommended for all collections. URL: www.blackwellpublishing.com/journal.asp?ref=0309-7013&site=1

4907. *Australasian Journal of Logic.* [ISSN: 1448-5052] 2003. irreg. Free. Australasian Association for Logic. Refereed. *Indexed:* CCMJ, MSN, MathR. *Aud.:* Ac, Sa.

Sponsored by the Australasian Association for Logic, this journal publishes articles of interest to logicians that further research in core areas of pure logic and their application to related fields such as mathematics, computer science, and linguistics. URL: www.philosophy.unimelb.edu.au/ajl/index.html

4908. *Australasian Journal of Philosophy.* Formerly (until 1947): *Australasian Journal of Psychology and Philosophy.* [ISSN: 0004-8402] 1923. q. GBP 104 print & online eds. Ed(s): Marice Goldsmith. Routledge, 4 Park Sq, Milton Park, Abingdon, OX14 4RN, United Kingdom; journals@routledge.com; http://www.routledge.com. Illus., index, adv. Sample. Refereed. Circ: 1225 Paid. Vol. ends: No. 4. Microform: MIM. Online: Chadwyck-Healey Inc.; EBSCO Publishing, EBSCO Host; Gale; IngentaConnect; OCLC Online Computer Library Center, Inc.; OhioLINK; ProQuest LLC (Ann Arbor); SwetsWise Online Content. Reprint: PSC. *Indexed:* AmH&L, AmHI, ArtHuCI, BrHumI, HistAb, IBR, IBZ, IPB, PhilInd, SSCI. *Bk. rev.:* 5-10, 750-1,000 words, signed. *Aud.:* Ac.

This is Australia's oldest continuously published philosophy journal and the official publication of the Australasian Association of Philosophy. It will therefore be of special interest to philosophers in that region. Many of the contributors are Australian, although others are from North America and Europe. A majority of the articles deal with contemporary issues in metaphysics, epistemology, philosophy of science, and ethics. Short critiques of arguments that have appeared in recently published articles and books—as well as replies—are gathered in the "Discussions" section. One book is often singled out and given an extended review under "Critical Notice." The work of David

Lewis and David Armstrong have been the focus of recent special issues. This is a good general publication for larger collections needing journals in the analytic tradition. URL: www.tandf.co.uk/journals/titles/00048402.asp

4909. Bibliographie de la Philosophie. [ISSN: 0006-1352] 1937. q. USD 135. Ed(s): Jean Pierre Cotten. International Institute of Philosophy, 8 rue Jean Calvin, Paris, 75005, France. Index, adv. Circ: 1100. Vol. ends: No. 4. *Aud.:* Ac.

This classified bibliography is published by the International Institute of Philosophy with the aid of UNESCO, the French National Centre for Scientific Research, and the Centre of Documentation and Philosophical Bibliography of the University of Franche Comte. Each issue contains brief descriptive summaries (averaging 100–250 words) of approximately 450 philosophy books published worldwide. The abstracts are authored by scholars representing "national centers" in more than 50 countries and are generally written in English, French, German, Italian, and Spanish. The fourth number of each volume contains an author/title index. Although not a source for critical evaluations, this is a good companion to *Philosophical Books* (below in this section) for collection development purposes. URL: www.umr8547.ens.fr/Productions/iip-Publications.html

Bioethics. See Civil Liberties/Bioethics: Reproductive Rights, Right-to-Life, and Right-to-Die section.

4910. British Journal for the History of Philosophy. [ISSN: 0960-8788] 1993. q. GBP 326 print & online eds. Ed(s): G A J Rogers. Routledge, 4 Park Square, Milton Park, Abingdon, OX14 4RN, United Kingdom; info@routledge.co.uk; http://www.routledge.com. Illus., index, adv. Sample. Refereed. Circ: 400. Vol. ends: No. 3. Reprint: PSC. *Indexed:* AmH&L, AmHI, BrHumI, FR, HistAb, HumInd, IPB, PhilInd. *Bk. rev.:* 10-15, 1,500-2,000 words, signed. *Aud.:* Ac.

This publication, sponsored by the British Society for the History of Philosophy, emphasizes the context—intellectual, political, and social—in which philosophical texts were created. Articles are also published on historical topics in the natural and social sciences and theology when they bear on philosophical problems. The focus is mainly on European philosophy, especially British, during the period from the Renaissance to the 1940s. URL: www.tandf.co.uk/journals/titles/09608788.asp

4911. The British Journal for the Philosophy of Science. [ISSN: 0007-0882] 1950. q. EUR 150 print or online ed. (Individuals, EUR 138 print & online eds.). Ed(s): James Ladyman, Alexander Bird. Oxford University Press, Great Clarendon St, Oxford, OX2 6DP, United Kingdom; jnl.orders@oup.co.uk; http://www.oxfordjournals.org. Illus., index, adv. Sample. Refereed. Circ: 1400. Vol. ends: No. 4. Online: Chadwyck-Healey Inc.; EBSCO Publishing, EBSCO Host; Florida Center for Library Automation; Gale; HighWire Press; IngentaConnect; JSTOR (Web-based Journal Archive); Northern Light Technology, Inc.; OCLC Online Computer Library Center, Inc.; OhioLINK; Oxford Journals; ProQuest LLC (Ann Arbor); SwetsWise Online Content. Reprint: PSC. *Indexed:* AmHI, ArtHuCI, CCMJ, FR, HumInd, IBR, IBZ, IPB, L&LBA, MSN, MathR, PhilInd, SCI, SSCI. *Bk. rev.:* 5-7, 1,000-3,000 words, signed. *Aud.:* Ac.

As the official publication of the British Society for the Philosophy of Science, this journal features articles, symposia, discussion papers, and literature surveys on the logic, methods, and philosophy of science, in addition to conceptual issues in various scientific disciplines (including the social sciences). In fact, its scope is very similar to its American counterpart, *Philosophy of Science,* although one may encounter more articles on logico-mathematical topics in the British title. This is a polished, professional, core collection journal. URL: http://bjps.oxfordjournals.org

4912. British Journal of Aesthetics. [ISSN: 0007-0904] 1960. q. EUR 198 print or online ed. Ed(s): Peter Lamarque. Oxford University Press, Great Clarendon St, Oxford, OX2 6DP, United Kingdom; jnl.orders@oup.co.uk; http://www.oxfordjournals.org. Illus., index, adv. Sample. Refereed. Circ: 1750. Vol. ends: No. 4. Microform: PQC. Online: Chadwyck-Healey Inc.; EBSCO Publishing, EBSCO Host; Florida

Center for Library Automation; Gale; HighWire Press; IngentaConnect; Northern Light Technology, Inc.; OCLC Online Computer Library Center, Inc.; OhioLINK; Oxford Journals; ProQuest LLC (Ann Arbor); SwetsWise Online Content. Reprint: PSC. *Indexed:* ABM, AmHI, ArtHuCI, ArtInd, BEL&L, BrHumI, CommAb, FLI, FR, HumInd, IBR, IBZ, IPB, MLA-IB, MusicInd, PhilInd, RILM, SSCI. *Bk. rev.:* 8-12, 250-1,000 words. *Aud.:* Ac.

The British Society of Aesthetics, which sponsors this journal, is an international organization committed to promoting the study, research, and discussion of the fine arts and related types of experience from a philosophical, psychological, sociological, scientific, historical, critical, and educational standpoint. The journal publishes articles analyzing the traditional philosophical issues in the field, in addition to examining the aesthetic theories of such individuals as Plato, Kant, Burke, Hegel, Wittgenstein, Derrida, and Wollheim. Some of the areas receiving attention include architecture, drama, literature, the fine arts, the performing arts, and photography. URL: http://bjaesthetics.oxfordjournals.org

4913. Canadian Journal of Philosophy. [ISSN: 0045-5091] 1971. q. CND 65 (Individuals, CND 27.50). Ed(s): Michael Stingl. University of Calgary Press, University of Calgary, 2500 University Dr NW, Calgary, AB T2N 1N4, Canada; ucpmail@ucalgary.ca; http://www.uofcpress.com. Illus., index, adv. Refereed. Circ: 800 Paid and free. Vol. ends: No. 4. Microform: MML. Online: Chadwyck-Healey Inc.; EBSCO Publishing, EBSCO Host; Micromedia ProQuest; ProQuest LLC (Ann Arbor). *Indexed:* AmHI, ArtHuCI, CBCARef, CPerI, FR, HumInd, IBR, IBSS, IBZ, IPB, LRI, MLA-IB, MSN, PhilInd, RI-1, SSCI. *Bk. rev.:* 2-5, 2,500-5,000 words. *Aud.:* Ac.

As one might expect, many of the contributors to Canada's leading philosophy journal are associated with Canadian universities, although numerous authors are from outside the country (principally the United States, Great Britain, France, and Australia). The strengths of the journal lie in ethics, social and political philosophy, epistemology, and the history of philosophy. Articles appear in French now and then, but the majority are in English. Excellent thematic supplementary volumes are published annually and are free to individual subscribers. URL: www.ucalgary.ca/UofC/departments/UP/UCP/CJP.html

4914. Contretemps. [ISSN: 1443-7619] 2000. irreg. Ed(s): John Dalton. University of Sydney, Department of General Philosophy, Rm s411 Main Quad A14, Sydney, NSW 2006, Australia. *Bk. rev.:* Number and length vary. *Aud.:* Ac.

Contributors to this Australian journal bring the perpective of Continental philosophy to bear on a diverse range of issues in aesthetics, cultural and literary studies, critical theory, ethics, and politics. A recent issue focused on "Democratic Futures." URL: www.usyd.edu.au/contretemps

Criminal Justice Ethics. See Criminology and Law Enforcement section.

4915. Dialogue: Canadian philosophical review/revue Canadienne de philosophie. [ISSN: 0012-2173] 1962. q. CND 140 (Individuals, CND 95). Ed(s): Eric Dayton, Mathieu Marion. Wilfrid Laurier University Press, 75 University Ave W, Waterloo, ON N2L 3C5, Canada; press@wlu.ca; http://www.wlupress.wlu.ca. Illus., adv. Refereed. Circ: 1200 Paid. *Indexed:* AmHI, ArtHuCI, BRI, CBCARef, CBRI, CCMJ, CPerI, FR, HumInd, IPB, L&LBA, LRI, MLA-IB, MSN, MathR, PhilInd, RI-1, RILM, SSA, SSCI. *Bk. rev.:* 10-15, 500-2,500 words. *Aud.:* Ac.

As the official journal of the Canadian Philosophical Association, *Dialogue* publishes articles and critical notices on all branches of philosophy from a variety of perspectives in both French and English. Many of the authors are associated with Canadian universities, and the editors especially want to promote a dialogue between Anglophone and Francophone philosophers in Canada. URL: www.usask.ca/philosophy/dialogue

4916. Diogenes (English Edition). [ISSN: 0392-1921] 1952. q. GBP 279. Ed(s): Luca Maria Scarantino, Maurice Aymard. Sage Publications Ltd., 1 Oliver's Yard, 55 City Rd, London, EC1 1SP, United Kingdom;

info@sagepub.co.uk; http://www.sagepub.co.uk. Illus., index, adv. Refereed. Circ: 600 Controlled. Vol. ends: No. 4. Online: EBSCO Publishing, EBSCO Host; Florida Center for Library Automation; Gale; HighWire Press; IngentaConnect; OCLC Online Computer Library Center, Inc.; OhioLINK; SAGE Publications, Inc., SAGE Journals Online; SwetsWise Online Content; H.W. Wilson. Reprint: PSC. *Indexed:* ABS&EES, AmH&L, AmHI, ArtHuCI, HistAb, HumInd, IBR, IBZ, IPB, IndIslam, L&LBA, MLA-IB, PSA, PhilInd, SociolAb. *Aud.:* Ga, Ac.

Diogenes is published under the auspices of the International Council for Philosophy and Humanistic Studies with the support of UNESCO, initially in French with the English-language edition appearing the following year. The articles are authored by a diverse range of international scholars who discuss cultural issues from a broadly defined philosophical perspective in such areas as anthropology, economics, education, history, literature, drama, and sociology. URL: www.sagepub.com/journal.aspx?pid=9361

Economics and Philosophy. See Economics section.

4917. Electronic Journal of Analytic Philosophy. [ISSN: 1071-5800] 1993. a. Free. Ed(s): Istvan Berkeley. The University of Louisiana at Lafayette, Edith Garland Dupre Library, Philosophy, The University of Louisiana at Lafayette, P.O. Drawer 43770, Lafayette, LA 70504-3770. Illus. Refereed. *Aud.:* Ac.

This was the first philosophy journal to be published in an electronic-only format. Each thematic issue is coordinated by a guest editor. Recent contributors have been exploring topics in cognitive science, epistemology, and philosophy of mind. The site architecture of the journal is presently undergoing a substantial renovation. URL: http://ejap.louisiana.edu

Environmental Ethics. See Environment and Conservation section.

4918. Erkenntnis: an international journal of analytic philosophy. [ISSN: 0165-0106] 1930. bi-m. EUR 912 print & online eds. Ed(s): Hans Rott. Springer Netherlands, Van Godewijckstraat 30, Dordrecht, 3311 GX, Netherlands; http://www.springeronline.com. Illus., index, adv. Sample. Refereed. Vol. ends: No. 3. Microform: PQC. Online: Chadwyck-Healey Inc.; EBSCO Publishing, EBSCO Host; Gale; IngentaConnect; OCLC Online Computer Library Center, Inc.; OhioLINK; ProQuest LLC (Ann Arbor); Springer LINK; SwetsWise Online Content. Reprint: PSC. *Indexed:* AmHI, ArtHuCI, CCMJ, FR, IBR, IBZ, IPB, L&LBA, MSN, MathR, PhilInd. *Bk. rev.:* 1-2, 1,500-2,500 words. *Aud.:* Ac.

Erkenntnis publishes highly technical articles that either analyze current systematic issues or present original research in epistemology, philosophical logic, philosophy of mathematics, philosophy of science, ontology and metaphysics, philosophy of mind, and practical philosophy (e.g., philosophy of action, philosophy of law, and ethics). The editors are particularly interested in advancing the influence of analytic philosophy in Central Europe. Articles sometimes appear in German, but the majority are in English. An advanced journal for graduate-level collections. URL: www.springerlink.com/openurl.asp?genre=journal&issn=0165-0106

4919. Essays in Philosophy. [ISSN: 1526-0569] s-a. Free. Ed(s): Michael F Goodman. Humboldt State University, Department of Philosophy, c/o Michael F Goodman, Ed, Arcata, CA 95521. Refereed. *Indexed:* MLA-IB, PhilInd. *Bk. rev.:* number varies, 1,000-4,000 words. *Aud.:* Ac.

This journal publishes thematic issues coordinated by guest editors. It has featured essays on topics in epistemology, ethics, feminism and gender studies, political and social philosophy, and the work of individual philosophers including Wittgenstein and Rawls. URL: www.humboldt.edu/~essays

4920. Ethical Theory and Moral Practice: an international forum. [ISSN: 1386-2820] 1998. 5x/yr. EUR 374 print & online eds. Ed(s): Albert W Musschenga, F R Heeger. Springer Netherlands, Van Godewijckstraat 30, Dordrecht, 3311 GX, Netherlands; http://www.springeronline.com. Illus.,

adv. Sample. Refereed. Online: EBSCO Publishing, EBSCO Host; Gale; IngentaConnect; OCLC Online Computer Library Center, Inc.; OhioLINK; Springer LINK; SwetsWise Online Content. Reprint: PSC. *Indexed:* AmHI, FR, HumInd, IBSS, IPB, PhilInd, SSA. *Bk. rev.:* 2-3, 1,500-3,000 words. *Aud.:* Ac, Sa.

This journal is published in cooperation with the Societas Ethica (European Society for Research in Ethics) and features articles from a wide variety of philosophical perspectives, including lesser-known European traditions that have been neglected in the mainstream philosophy publications. An attempt has been made to foster interdisciplinary cooperation between ethics and the empirical disciplines—including medicine, economics, sociology, and law—with the aim of breaking down the barriers between practical and theoretical ethics. The editors also invite contributions that address the relationship between moral beliefs and views of life. Articles are generally in English, but some are in French or German. A specialized publication for collections with comprehensive holdings in ethics. URL: www.springerlink.com/openurl.asp?genre=journal&issn=1386-2820

4921. Ethics: an international journal of social, political, and legal philosophy. Formerly (until 1938): *International Journal of Ethics.* [ISSN: 0014-1704] 1890. q. USD 182 domestic; USD 197.92 Canada; USD 190 elsewhere. Ed(s): M. Cooper Harriss, John Deigh. University of Chicago Press, Journals Division, PO Box 37005, Chicago, IL 60637; subscriptions@press.uchicago.edu; http://www.journals.uchicago.edu. Illus., adv. Refereed. Circ: 3300 Paid. Vol. ends: Jul. Microform: MIM; PMC; PQC. Online: EBSCO Publishing, EBSCO Host; Florida Center for Library Automation; Gale; JSTOR (Web-based Journal Archive); ProQuest K-12 Learning Solutions; ProQuest LLC (Ann Arbor). Reprint: PSC. *Indexed:* ABCPolSci, AgeL, AmHI, ArtHuCI, BRD, BRI, CBRI, CLI, CommAb, FR, HumInd, IBR, IBSS, IBZ, IPB, IPSA, LRI, MLA-IB, PRA, PSA, PhilInd, RI-1, SSA, SSCI, SociolAb. *Bk. rev.:* 35-45, 250-7,500 words, signed. *Aud.:* Ac.

Ethics is a leading journal in the fields of social and political philosophy and ethics. It serves as a forum for the discussion of both traditional and contemporary consequentialist and deontological normative theories, as well as a wide range of meta-ethical topics. In addition to moral philosophy, *Ethics* also publishes articles on philosophy of law, public policy issues, religious ethics, normative economics, international law, and social and rational choice theory. Symposia centered on themes, theories, or recently published books are often featured. The numerous book reviews range from lengthy review essays to brief "Book Notes." Highly recommended for all academic collections. URL: www.journals.uchicago.edu/ET/home.html

4922. Ethics & Behavior. [ISSN: 1050-8422] 1991. q. GBP 349 print & online eds. Ed(s): Gerald P Koocher. Lawrence Erlbaum Associates, Inc., 325 Chestnut St, Ste. 800, Philadelphia, PA 19106; journals@erlbaum.com; http://www.leaonline.com. Illus., adv. Sample. Refereed. Vol. ends: No. 4. Reprint: PSC. *Indexed:* ABIn, ASSIA, CINAHL, IndVet, PAIS, PhilInd, PsycInfo, RRTA, RiskAb, SSA, SSCI, VB. *Bk. rev.:* 1-3, 750-1,000 words. *Aud.:* Ac.

This journal focuses on issues in ethical and social responsibility in human behavior, as well as ethical dilemmas or professional misconduct in health and human services delivery. Articles also cover the moral aspects of conducting research on human and animal subjects, fraud in scientific research, and public-policy issues involving ethical problems (e.g., environmental ethics). Although aimed principally at an audience of clinical practitioners in psychology, psychiatry, psychotherapy, and counseling, *Ethics and Behavior* would provide excellent support for courses in applied ethics. URL: www.erlbaum.com/shop/tek9.asp?pg=products&specific=1050-8422

4923. European Journal of Philosophy. [ISSN: 0966-8373] 1993. 3x/yr. GBP 320 print & online eds. Ed(s): Robert Stern. Blackwell Publishing Ltd., 9600 Garsington Rd, Oxford, OX4 2ZG, United Kingdom; customerservices@blackwellpublishing.com; http://www.blackwellpublishing.com. Illus., index. Sample. Refereed. Vol. ends: No. 3. Online: Blackwell Synergy; EBSCO Publishing, EBSCO Host; Gale; IngentaConnect; OCLC Online Computer Library Center,

Inc.; OhioLINK; SwetsWise Online Content. Reprint: PSC. *Indexed:* AmHI, ApEcolAb, ArtHuCI, BrHumI, IBR, IBSS, IBZ, IPB, L&LBA, PhilInd, SFSA, SSA, SociolAb. *Bk. rev.:* 7-10, 2,000-3,000 words. *Aud.:* Ac.

This journal was founded with the goal of serving as a forum for the exchange of ideas among philosophers working within the various European schools of thought, who tended to be culturally isolated before the political upheavals of the 1990s. Contributions, however, are welcome from both sides of the Atlantic. The journal also publishes the text of the EJP Annual Lecture. This should find a place in libraries that emphasize European traditions of philosophy broadly conceived, both historical and contemporary. URL: www.blackwellpublishing.com/journal.asp?ref=0966-8373&site=1

4924. Faith and Philosophy. [ISSN: 0739-7046] 1984. q. USD 58 (Individuals, USD 40). Ed(s): William Hasker. Society of Christian Philosophers, Department of Philosophy, Asbury College, Wilmore, KY 40390-1198; fpjournl@aol.com; www.faithandphilosophy.com. Illus., index, adv. Refereed. Circ: 1500. Microform: PQC. *Indexed:* ChrPI, IPB, PhilInd, R&TA, RI-1. *Bk. rev.:* 3-5, 1,500-3,000 words. *Aud.:* Ac.

Articles in *Faith and Philosophy* address philosophical issues from a Christian perspective, discuss philosophical questions arising within the Christian faith, and critically analyze the philosophical foundations of Christianity. The journal attracts contributions from leading philosophers of religion, including William Alston, Alvin Plantiga, Eleonore Stump, and Richard Swinburne. The October issue of each volume is devoted to a single theme (e.g., "The Continuing Relevance of Natural Theology"). In light of its high-quality scholarship and modest price, this journal should find a place in university libraries supporting courses in religious studies. URL: www.faithandphilosophy.com

4925. History and Philosophy of Logic. [ISSN: 0144-5340] 1980. q. GBP 436 print & online eds. Ed(s): John Dawson, Volker Peckhaus. Taylor & Francis Ltd., 4 Park Sq, Milton Park, Abingdon, OX14 4RN, United Kingdom; info@tandf.co.uk; http://www.tandf.co.uk/journals. Illus., adv. Sample. Refereed. Vol. ends: No. 4. Online: EBSCO Publishing, EBSCO Host; Gale; IngentaConnect; OCLC Online Computer Library Center, Inc.; SwetsWise Online Content. Reprint: PSC. *Indexed:* AmH&L, ArtHuCI, CCMJ, HistAb, IBR, IBZ, IPB, MSN, MathR, PhilInd, SCI, SSCI. *Bk. rev.:* 8-10, 750-1,500 words. *Aud.:* Ac.

The emphasis of this journal is on the general history and philosophy of logic, excluding work on very recent topics and specialized studies in philosophical logic. The scope is ancient to modern, and East to West, with articles appearing in English, French, or German. The authors explore the existential and ontological aspects of logic, in addition to analyzing the relationship between classical and nonclassical logic and the application of logic in other fields, such as mathematics, economics, science, and linguistics. This journal is also a good source for discussions of the logical writings of such major historical figures as Aristotle, Leibniz, Frege, Russell, Tarski, and Quine. URL: www.tandf.co.uk/journals/titles/01445340.asp

4926. History of Philosophy Quarterly. [ISSN: 0740-0675] 1984. q. USD 270 (Individuals, USD 55). Ed(s): David Glidden. University of Illinois Press, 1325 S Oak St, Champaign, IL 61820-6903; journals@uillinois.edu; http://www.press.uillinois.edu. Illus., index. Sample. Refereed. Circ: 500. Vol. ends: No. 4. *Indexed:* IBR, IBZ, IPB, PhilInd, RI-1. *Aud.:* Ac.

Critical discussions of the work of major philosophers from Plato to Wittgenstein, with an emphasis on the value of historical studies for contemporary issues, make this a good supplement to the *Journal of the History of Philosophy,* which should be the first choice for most academic libraries. URL: www.press.uillinois.edu/journals/hpq.html

4927. Human Studies: a journal for philosophy and the social sciences. [ISSN: 0163-8548] 1978. q. EUR 489 print & online eds. Ed(s): George Psathas. Springer Netherlands, Van Godewijckstraat 30, Dordrecht, 3311 GX, Netherlands; http://www.springeronline.com. Illus., index, adv. Sample. Refereed. Circ: 500. Vol. ends: No. 4. Microform: PQC. Online: EBSCO Publishing, EBSCO Host; Gale; IngentaConnect; OCLC

Online Computer Library Center, Inc.; OhioLINK; Springer LINK; SwetsWise Online Content. Reprint: PSC. *Indexed:* ABS&EES, IBR, IBSS, IBZ, IMFL, IPB, L&LBA, LingAb, MLA-IB, PSA, PhilInd, RILM, SSA, SSCI, SWA, SociolAb. *Bk. rev.:* 1-3, 1,000-3,000 words. *Aud.:* Ac.

This publication, which serves as the official journal of the Society for Phenomenology and the Human Sciences, publishes empirical, methodological, philosophical, and theoretical investigations—particularly those embracing a broadly defined phenomenological perspective—on topics in the social sciences, including psychology, sociology, anthropology, history, geography, linguistics, semiotics, ethnomethodology, and political science. For library collections with strong holdings in the social sciences. URL: www.springerlink.com/openurl.asp?genre=journal&issn=0163-8548

4928. Hume Studies. [ISSN: 0319-7336] 1975. biennial. USD 50 (Individuals, USD 35). Ed(s): Kenneth P Winkler, Elizabeth S Radcliffe. Hume Society, c/o Jane McIntyre, Pall S. Ardal Institute for Hume Studies, Akureyri, 600, Iceland; president@humesociety.org; http://www.humesociety.org. Illus., adv. Refereed. Circ: 800 Paid. Vol. ends: No. 2. Microform: MML. *Indexed:* FR, HistAb, IBR, IBZ, IPB, PhilInd, RI-1. *Bk. rev.:* 5-7, 1,000-1,500 words. *Aud.:* Ac.

This journal, published by the Hume Society, is devoted to historical, systematic, and bibliographic research on all facets of Hume's philosophy: metaphysics, epistemology, philosophy of mind, ethics, political philosophy, and philosophy of religion. Articles are usually in English, with some in French, German, or Italian. URL: www.humestudies.org

4929. Husserl Studies. [ISSN: 0167-9848] 1984. 3x/yr. EUR 357 print & online eds. Ed(s): William R McKenna. Springer Netherlands, Van Godewijckstraat 30, Dordrecht, 3311 GX, Netherlands; http://www.springeronline.com. Illus., index, adv. Sample. Refereed. Vol. ends: No. 3. Microform: PQC. Online: EBSCO Publishing, EBSCO Host; Gale; IngentaConnect; OCLC Online Computer Library Center, Inc.; OhioLINK; Springer LINK; SwetsWise Online Content. Reprint: PSC. *Indexed:* ArtHuCI, FR, IBR, IBZ, IPB, PhilInd, RI-1, SSCI. *Bk. rev.:* 1-3, 1,500-3,000 words. *Aud.:* Ac.

The German philosopher Edmund Husserl (1859–1938) is the central figure in the phenomenological movement. This journal serves as a forum for historical, systematic, interpretive, and comparative studies on Husserl and phenomenology in general. Although the editor encourages intercultural and interdisciplinary submissions, most authors concentrate on narrowly defined problems of exegesis or analysis drawn from Husserl's writings. The journal also publishes important texts from Husserl's *Nachlass* and an ongoing international Husserl bibliography. The articles are in English and German. URL: www.springerlink.com/openurl.asp?genre=journal&issn=0167-9848

Hypatia. See Gender Studies section.

4930. Idealistic Studies: an interdisciplinary journal of philosophy. [ISSN: 0046-8541] 1971. 3x/yr. USD 40 (Individuals, USD 32). Ed(s): Gary Overvold. Philosophy Documentation Center, PO Box 7147, Charlottesville, VA 22906-7147. Illus., index, adv. Refereed. Circ: 600. Vol. ends: No. 3. Reprint: PSC. *Indexed:* AmHI, ArtHuCI, FR, IBR, IBZ, IPB, PhilInd, RI-1, SSCI. *Aud.:* Ac.

Critical studies on idealistic themes, in addition to historical and contemporary statements of idealistic argumentation, are the main focus of this journal. Philosophical movements related to idealism are also covered, including phenomenology, neo-Kantianism, historicism, hermeneutics, life philosophy, existentialism, and pragmatism. This journal is an especially good source for the critical analysis of idealism in the philosophy of Berkeley, Hegel, Fichte, Schelling, Bradley, McTaggart, and others. URL: www.pdcnet.org/is.html

4931. Inquiry: an interdisciplinary journal of philosophy. [ISSN: 0020-174X] 1958. bi-m. GBP 245 print & online eds. Ed(s): Wayne Martin. Routledge, 4 Park Square, Milton Park, Abingdon, OX14 4RN, United Kingdom; info@routledge.co.uk; http://www.routledge.co.uk. Illus., index, adv. Refereed. Circ: 1200. Vol. ends: No. 4. Microform: PQC. Online: EBSCO Publishing, EBSCO Host; Gale; IngentaConnect;

OCLC Online Computer Library Center, Inc.; SwetsWise Online Content. Reprint: PSC. *Indexed:* AmH&L, AmHI, ArtHuCI, BAS, FR, HistAb, HumInd, IBR, IBSS, IBZ, IPB, IPSA, L&LBA, MCR, MLA-IB, PSA, PhilInd, RI-1, SSCI, SWR&A. *Bk. rev.:* 1-3, 1,500-3,000 words. *Aud.:* Ac.

After being based in Norway for nearly a half century, *Inquiry* now has its editorial operations headquartered in the United Kingdom. Articles address both practical and theoretical problems, and the authors attempt to explicate the basic assumptions at work in the issues under discussion. Most articles deal with metaphysics, epistemology, philosophy of mind, ethics, aesthetics, social and political philosophy, and Continental philosophy. Contributions in areas such as environmental ethics often contain discussions on the cutting edge of the profession. The book reviews take the form of lengthy symposia or review essays. This is an important journal for all collections. URL: www.tandf.co.uk/journals/titles/0020174X.asp

International Journal for Philosophy of Religion. See Religion section.

4932. International Journal of Philosophical Studies. Formerly (until 1993): *Philosophical Studies.* [ISSN: 0967-2559] 1951. q. GBP 464 print & online eds. Ed(s): Dermot Moran. Routledge, 4 Park Square, Milton Park, Abingdon, OX14 4RN, United Kingdom; info@routledge.co.uk; http://www.routledge.co.uk. Illus., adv. Sample. Refereed. Vol. ends: No. 4. Online: EBSCO Publishing, EBSCO Host; Gale; IngentaConnect; OCLC Online Computer Library Center, Inc.; SwetsWise Online Content. Reprint: PSC. *Indexed:* AmHI, ArtHuCI, BrHumI, CPL, FR, IBSS, IPB, PhilInd. *Bk. rev.:* 10-15, 2,000-7,500 words. *Aud.:* Ac.

By featuring contributors like Noam Chomsky, Donald Davidson, David Pears, and John Searle, this relaunched journal has assumed a place as an important international philosophy publication. The editor wants to promote a mutual comprehension and dialogue between the "analytic" and "Continental" styles of philosophy and to combine discussions of contemporary problems with articles on the history of philosophy that shed light on the current debate. Several books are singled out in each issue for extended discussions under "Critical Notices." URL: www.tandf.co.uk/journals/titles/09672559.asp

4933. International Philosophical Quarterly. [ISSN: 0019-0365] 1961. q. USD 60 (Individuals, USD 32). Ed(s): Joseph W Koterski. Philosophy Documentation Center, PO Box 7147, Charlottesville, VA 22906-7147. Illus., index, adv. Refereed. Circ: 1400 Paid. Vol. ends: No. 4. Microform: PQC. Online: OCLC Online Computer Library Center, Inc.; H.W. Wilson. Reprint: PSC. *Indexed:* ABS&EES, AmHI, ArtHuCI, BAS, BEL&L, BRI, CBRI, CPL, FR, HumInd, IBR, IBZ, IPB, LRI, PhilInd, RI-1, RILM, SSCI. *Bk. rev.:* 10-15, 500-1,000 words. *Aud.:* Ac.

As a joint collaboration of Fordham University and the Facultes Universitaires Notre-Dame de la Paix (Namur, Belgium), this journal serves as an international forum for the exchange of philosophical ideas between the United States and Europe and between East and West. It offers the publication of creative, critical, and historical articles in the intercultural tradition of theistic, spiritualist, and personalist humanism. URL: www.pdcnet.org/ipq.html

Journal of Chinese Philosophy. See China section.

4934. The Journal of Ethics: an international philosophical review. [ISSN: 1382-4554] 1997. q. EUR 460 print & online eds. Ed(s): J Angelo Corlett. Springer Netherlands, Van Godewijckstraat 30, Dordrecht, 3311 GX, Netherlands; http://www.springeronline.com. Illus., adv. Sample. Refereed. Vol. ends: No. 4. Online: EBSCO Publishing, EBSCO Host; Gale; IngentaConnect; OCLC Online Computer Library Center, Inc.; OhioLINK; Springer LINK; SwetsWise Online Content. Reprint: PSC. *Indexed:* CINAHL, FR, IPB, PhilInd, SSA. *Bk. rev.:* 1-2, 2,000-3,000 words, signed. *Aud.:* Ac.

This journal features articles on contemporary issues in ethics, political philosophy, and public affairs, although contributors occasionally focus on the ethical works of major historical figures. Selected studies are also published on bioethics and jurisprudence. In celebration of its recent tenth anniversary, the journal published several special issues consisting of invited papers analyzing the work of Joel Feinberg, John Martin Fischer, and Martha Nussbaum. URL: www.springerlink.com/openurl.asp?genre=journal&issn=1382-4554

4935. Journal of Ethics & Social Philosophy: online peer-reviewed journal of moral, political and legal philosophy. [ISSN: 1559-3061] 2005. irreg. Free. Ed(s): Andrei Marmor. University of Southern California, Gould School of Law, University Park, Los Angeles, CA 90089-0071; http://lawweb.usc.edu. Refereed. *Indexed:* PhilInd. *Aud.:* Ac.

This electronic journal, published by the Center for Law and Philosophy at the University of Southern California, should be investigated by those seeking philosophical analyses of contemporary ethical, political, and legal issues. URL: www.jesp.org

4936. Journal of Indian Philosophy. [ISSN: 0022-1791] 1970. bi-m. EUR 712 print & online eds. Ed(s): Phyllis Granoff. Springer Netherlands, Van Godewijckstraat 30, Dordrecht, 3311 GX, Netherlands; http://www.springeronline.com. Illus., index, adv. Sample. Refereed. Microform: PQC. Online: Chadwyck-Healey Inc.; EBSCO Publishing, EBSCO Host; Gale; IngentaConnect; OCLC Online Computer Library Center, Inc.; OhioLINK; ProQuest LLC (Ann Arbor); Springer LINK; SwetsWise Online Content. Reprint: PSC. *Indexed:* AmHI, ArtHuCI, BAS, FR, IBR, IBSS, IBZ, IPB, MLA-IB, PhilInd, RI-1. *Aud.:* Ac, Sa.

The specialized studies in this journal presuppose a thorough familiarity with the philosophical systems embodied in the religious traditions of the Indian subcontinent and Tibet, particularly Hinduism, Buddhism, and Jainism. The authors critically analyze and explicate both traditional and contemporary arguments and issues in metaphysics, epistemology, philosophical logic, philosophy of language, philosophy of religion, and ethics. URL: www.springerlink.com/openurl.asp?genre=journal&issn=0022-1791

The Journal of Medicine and Philosophy. See Public Health section.

4937. Journal of Moral Philosophy. [ISSN: 1740-4681] 2004. 3x/yr. EUR 249 print & online eds. (Individuals, EUR 45). Ed(s): Thom Brooks. Brill, PO Box 9000, Leiden, 2300 PA, Netherlands; cs@brill.nl; http://www.brill.nl. Adv. Refereed. Reprint: PSC. *Indexed:* PSA, PhilInd. *Bk. rev.:* 6-12, 1,000-1,500 words. *Aud.:* Ac.

This new journal is shaping up to be an excellent addition to what has admittedly become an overcrowded subfield. Articles, discussions, and review essays range over both historical and contemporary issues in ethics, political philosophy, and jurisprudence. The editor seeks an international focus and welcomes contributions dealing with non-Western traditions. The third number of each volume centers on a particular theme. A good choice as a supplement to *Ethics* (discussed above) for libraries needing more extensive coverage of these subject areas. URL: www.sagepub.com/journal.aspx?pid=10755

4938. Journal of Philosophical Logic. [ISSN: 0022-3611] 1972. bi-m. EUR 706 print & online eds. Ed(s): Patrick Blackburn, G Aldo Antonelli. Springer Netherlands, Van Godewijckstraat 30, Dordrecht, 3311 GX, Netherlands; http://www.springeronline.com. Illus., index, adv. Sample. Refereed. Vol. ends: No. 6. Microform: PQC. Online: Chadwyck-Healey Inc.; EBSCO Publishing, EBSCO Host; Gale; IngentaConnect; OCLC Online Computer Library Center, Inc.; OhioLINK; ProQuest LLC (Ann Arbor); Springer LINK; SwetsWise Online Content. Reprint: PSC. *Indexed:* AmHI, ArtHuCI, CCMJ, FR, IBR, IBZ, IPB, L&LBA, MLA-IB, MSN, MathR, PhilInd, SSCI. *Aud.:* Ac, Sa.

Published under the auspices of the Association for Symbolic Logic, this journal features articles on the entire spectrum of philosophical logic (e.g., inductive logic, modal logic, deontic logic, tense logic, free logic, many-valued logics, quantum logic, relevance logic, and the logic of questions, commands, preferences, and conditions). Also covered are issues in ontology and epistemology that utilize formal logic (e.g., abstract entities, defeasible reasoning, propositional attitudes, and truth conditions). Other articles explicate philosophical issues that involve logical theory in philosophy of language, philosophy of mathematics, and philosophy of science. For graduate-level collections. URL: www.springerlink.com/openurl.asp?genre=journal&issn= 0022-3611

4939. *Journal of Philosophy.* Formerly (until 1921): *The Journal of Philosophy, Psychology and Scientific Methods.* [ISSN: 0022-362X] 1904. m. USD 100 & libraries (Individuals, USD 45; Students, USD 20). Ed(s): John Smylie. Journal of Philosophy, Inc., Columbia University, 1150 Amsterdam Avenue, New York, NY 10027. Illus., index, adv. Refereed. Circ: 4500. Vol. ends: No. 12. Microform: PMC. Online: JSTOR (Web-based Journal Archive). *Indexed:* AmH&L, AmHI, ArtHuCI, BEL&L, BRD, BRI, CBRI, CCMJ, FR, HistAb, HumInd, IBR, IBSS, IBZ, IPB, LRI, MLA-IB, MSN, MathR, PhilInd, RI-1, SSCI. *Bk. rev.:* 1-2, 1,000-3,000 words. *Aud.:* Ac.

Each isssue of this distinguished journal contains two or three articles, generally on topics of interest to the professional academic philosophy community in the United States. The subjects discussed usually fall into the areas of metaphysics, epistemology, philosophy of mind, philosophy of language, philosophical logic, social and political philosophy, ethics, action theory, and esthetics. A core collection journal. URL: www.journalofphilosophy.org

Journal of Philosophy of Education. See Education/Comparative Education and International section.

4940. *The Journal of Philosophy, Science & Law.* [ISSN: 1549-8549] 2001. bi-m. Free. Ed(s): Jason Borenstein. The Journal of Philosophy, Science and Law, c/o Jason Borenstein, Ed, School of Public Policy, PO Box 4089, Atlanta, GA 30332-0345; jason.borenstein@ pubpolicy.gatech.edu; http://www.psljournal.com. Refereed. *Bk. rev.:* Number and length vary. *Aud.:* Ac.

This journal is sponsored by the Georgia Institute of Technology School of Public Policy and the University of Miami Ethics Programs. Its articles deal with moral and legal aspects of scientific evidence, research in science and technology, teaching ethical and legal guidelines within the scientific disciplines, bioethics, and related topics. Its scope is somewhat similar to that of *Jurimetrics.* News items and editorials are also published. URL: www.psljournal.com

4941. *Journal of Speculative Philosophy: a quarterly journal of history, criticism, and imagination.* [ISSN: 0891-625X] 1987. q. USD 65. Ed(s): John J Stuhr, Vincent M Colapietro. Pennsylvania State University Press, 820 N University Dr, USB-1, Ste C, University Park, PA 16802-1003. Illus., index, adv. Sample. Refereed. Circ: 450 Paid. Vol. ends: No. 4. Microform: PQC. Online: EBSCO Publishing, EBSCO Host; OCLC Online Computer Library Center, Inc.; OhioLINK; Project MUSE; SwetsWise Online Content. Reprint: PSC. *Indexed:* IBR, IBZ, IPB, PhilInd. *Bk. rev.:* 2-10, 750-1,250 words. *Aud.:* Ac.

This journal revives the nineteenth-century publication of the same title, the first in the United States devoted primarily to philosophy and the one in which Peirce, James, Dewey, and other notables published some of their early essays. It now serves as the official journal of the Society for the Advancement of American Philosophy (SAAP). The emphasis is on systematic and interpretive essays dealing with basic philosophical questions, especially when they are tied to the aims and methodology of pragmatism. The stated goal of the editors is to promote a constructive interaction between Continental and American philosophy, rather than to publish scholarly articles about philosophical movements or historical figures. In addition, the journal occasionally publishes articles on art, literature, and religion that are not strictly or narrowly philosophical in their orientation. URL: www.press.jhu.edu/journals/ journal_of_speculative_philosophy/

4942. *Journal of Symbolic Logic.* [ISSN: 0022-4812] 1936. q. Free to members; USD 540 combined subscription includes q. Bulletin of Symbolic Logic. Ed(s): Andreas Blass. Association for Symbolic Logic, 124 Raymond Ave, Vassar College, PO Box 742, Poughkeepsie, NY 12604; asl@vassar.edu; http://www.aslonline.org. Illus., index. Refereed.

Circ: 2500. Vol. ends: No. 4. Microform: PMC; PQC. Online: EBSCO Publishing, EBSCO Host; JSTOR (Web-based Journal Archive). *Indexed:* AmHI, CCMJ, HumInd, IPB, MSN, MathR, PhilInd, SCI, SSCI. *Bk. rev.:* 10-15, 1,000-2,000 words. *Aud.:* Ac, Sa.

This journal, sponsored by the Association for Symbolic Logic, is aimed at an audience of professional logicians and mathematicians. It publishes highly technical articles on all formal aspects of symbolic and mathematical logic. In addition, subscribers also receive *The Bulletin of Symbolic Logic,* a quarterly publication that features both broad expository and survey articles of a general nature, announcements of new ideas and results in all areas of logic, and the Reviews Section (which had been published as part of the main journal until 2000). This is a core collection title for graduate-level collections. URL: www.aslonline.org/journals-journal.html

Journal of the History of Ideas. See Cultural Studies section.

4943. *Journal of the History of Philosophy.* [ISSN: 0022-5053] 1963. 4x/yr. USD 105. Ed(s): Tad Schmaltz. The Johns Hopkins University Press, 2715 N Charles St, Baltimore, MD 21218-4363; http://muse.jhu.edu. Illus., index, adv. Refereed. Circ: 1217 Paid. Vol. ends: No. 4. Microform: PQC. Online: Chadwyck-Healey Inc.; EBSCO Publishing, EBSCO Host; Northern Light Technology, Inc.; OCLC Online Computer Library Center, Inc.; OhioLINK; Project MUSE; ProQuest K-12 Learning Solutions; ProQuest LLC (Ann Arbor); SwetsWise Online Content. Reprint: PSC. *Indexed:* AmH&L, AmHI, ArtHuCI, BEL&L, FR, HistAb, HumInd, IBR, IBSS, IBZ, IPB, IndIslam, PRA, PhilInd, RI-1, SSCI. *Bk. rev.:* 15-20, 750-1,000 words. *Aud.:* Ac.

This leading journal for the history of Western philosophy generally deals with the works of the major philosophers, although studies are also published on other figures, including Islamic philosophers (e.g., al-Ghazali and Averroes), lesser-known medieval and Renaissance philosophers (e.g., Desgabets, Gersonides, and Henry of Ghent) and scientists (e.g., Boyle and Newton). Articles sometimes appear in foreign languages, but the majority are in English. The journal has recently started a new feature, "Current Scholarship," which provides critical literature reviews on selected historical figures and philosophical topics. URL: http://philosophy.duke.edu/jhp

Journal of the Philosophy of Sport. See Sports/Physical Education, Coaching, and Sports Sciences section.

4944. *The Journal of Value Inquiry.* [ISSN: 0022-5363] 1967. q. EUR 600 print & online eds. Ed(s): Thomas Magnell. Springer Netherlands, Van Godewijckstraat 30, Dordrecht, 3311 GX, Netherlands; http://www.springeronline.com. Illus., index, adv. Sample. Refereed. Vol. ends: Oct/Dec. Microform: PQC. Online: Chadwyck-Healey Inc.; EBSCO Publishing, EBSCO Host; Gale; IngentaConnect; OCLC Online Computer Library Center, Inc.; OhioLINK; ProQuest LLC (Ann Arbor); Springer LINK; SwetsWise Online Content. Reprint: PSC. *Indexed:* ABIn, ArtHuCI, FR, IBR, IBZ, IPB, PhilInd, RI-1, RILM, SSCI. *Bk. rev.:* 3-5, 1,000-2,000 words. *Aud.:* Ac.

This important journal covers the entire spectrum of axiology. One will find articles on the nature, justification, and epistemic status of values, as well as studies exploring values in a broad range of contexts, including aesthetics, ethics, law, politics, science, society, and technology. URL: www.springerlink.com/openurl.asp?genre=journal&issn=0022-5363

4945. *Kant Studien: philosophische Zeitschrift der Kant-Gesellschaft.* [ISSN: 0022-8877] 1896. q. EUR 146; EUR 168 combined subscription print & online eds.; EUR 41 newsstand/cover. Ed(s): Gerhard Funke, Thomas M Seebohm. Walter de Gruyter GmbH & Co. KG, Genthiner Str 13, Berlin, 10785, Germany; wdg-info@degruyter.de; http://www.degruyter.de. Illus., index, adv. Refereed. Circ: 1200 Paid and controlled. Vol. ends: No. 4. Reprint: SCH. *Indexed:* ArtHuCI, FR, IBR, IBZ, IPB, MLA-IB, PhilInd. *Bk. rev.:* 4-6, 750-1,500 words. *Aud.:* Ac.

The principal focus of this publication of the Kant-Gesellschaft is Immanuel Kant, who is arguably the most important philospher of the modern period. Authors also discuss other philosophers and mathematicians from time to time, such as Descartes, Leibniz, Hume, Hegel, and Frege, as well as debating issues falling within the scope of trancendental philosophy generally. A very useful bibliography on all aspects of Kantian studies is featured in the fourth issue of each volume. The articles appear in English, French, and German. URL: www.degruyter.de/rs/282_695_ENU_h.htm

4946. *Law and Philosophy: an international journal for jurisprudence and legal philosophy.* [ISSN: 0167-5249] 1982. bi-m. EUR 705 print & online eds. Ed(s): Michael S Moore, Heidi M Hurd. Springer Netherlands, Van Godewijckstraat 30, Dordrecht, 3311 GX, Netherlands; http://www.springeronline.com. Illus., index, adv. Sample. Refereed. Microform: WSH; PQC. Online: EBSCO Publishing, EBSCO Host; Gale; IngentaConnect; OCLC Online Computer Library Center, Inc.; OhioLINK; Springer LINK; SwetsWise Online Content. Reprint: PSC. *Indexed:* ArtHuCI, CJA, CLI, IBR, IBSS, IBZ, ILP, IPB, LRI, PSA, PhilInd, SSA, SSCI, SociolAb. *Bk. rev.:* Occasional, 750-1,500 words. *Aud.:* Ac.

Law professors with an interest in philosophical issues in their discipline will find *Law and Philosophy* to be a valuable title. The journal publishes articles authored by philosophers and legal theorists on contemporary issues in areas as justice, rights, liberty, punishment, moral and criminal responsibility, legal ethics, legal positivism, and legal reasoning and interpretation. A good choice for philosophy, law, and criminology collections. URL: www.springerlink.com/openurl.asp?genre=journal&issn=0167-5249

Linguistics and Philosophy, See Linguistics section.

4947. *Logique et Analyse.* Formerly (until 1958): *Centre National Belge de Recherches de Logique. Bulletin Interieur.* [ISSN: 0024-5836] 1954. q. EUR 30. Nationaal Centrum voor Navorsingen in de Logica, c/o Jean-Paul van Bendegem, Vrije Universiteit Brussel, Faculteit Letteren en Wijsbegeer, Sectie Wijsbegeerte, Brussels, 1050, Belgium; jpvbende@vub.ac.be. Illus., index. Refereed. Circ: 1000. Vol. ends: Dec. *Indexed:* CCMJ, IBR, IBZ, IPB, L&LBA, MSN, MathR, PhilInd. *Aud.:* Ac, Sa.

This quarterly publication of the Centre National de Recherches de Logique/Nationaal Centrum voor Navorsingen in de Logica presents highly technical articles in English, French, German, and Dutch on a wide range of topics in philosophical and symbolic logic, philosophy of language, and philosophy of mathematics. For graduate-level collections. URL: www.vub.ac.be/CLWF/L&A

4948. *Metaphilosophy.* [ISSN: 0026-1068] 1970. 5x/yr. GBP 346 print & online eds. Ed(s): Armen T Marsoobian. Blackwell Publishing Ltd., 9600 Garsington Rd, Oxford, OX4 2ZG, United Kingdom; customerservices@blackwellpublishing.com; http://www.blackwellpublishing.com. Illus., adv. Refereed. Circ: 650. Vol. ends: No. 4. Online: Blackwell Synergy; EBSCO Publishing, EBSCO Host; Gale; IngentaConnect; OCLC Online Computer Library Center, Inc.; OhioLINK; SwetsWise Online Content. Reprint: PSC. *Indexed:* AmHI, ApEcolAb, ArtHuCI, FR, IBR, IBZ, IPB, L&LBA, PRA, PSA, PhilInd, RILM. *Bk. rev.:* 2-6, 1,000-4,000 words. *Aud.:* Ac.

The editor of *Metaphilosophy* invites articles that emphasize the foundation, scope, function, and direction of philosophy; the justification of philosophical methods and arguments; and the relationships and connections between different schools or fields of philosophy. Also covered are aspects of philosophical systems; presuppositions of philosophical schools; the relationship of philosophy to other disciplines; and the relevance of philosophy to social and political action. *Metaphilosophy* has frequently been at the forefront of publishing on new trends in the discipline, such as antifoundationalism, philosophy for children, feminist philosophy, applied philosophy, and the use of computers in philosophy. Recent special issues have been devoted to "The Philosophical Challenge of September 11" and "Philosophical Issues in Stem Cell Research." URL: www.blackwellpublishing.com/journal.asp?ref=0026-1068&site=1

4949. *Mind: a quarterly review of philosophy.* [ISSN: 0026-4423] 1876. q. EUR 150 print or online ed. Ed(s): Thomas Baldwin. Oxford University Press, Great Clarendon St, Oxford, OX2 6DP, United Kingdom;

jnl.orders@oup.co.uk; http://www.oxfordjournals.org. Illus., index, adv. Refereed. Circ: 3500. Vol. ends: No. 4. Microform: PMC; PQC. Online: EBSCO Publishing, EBSCO Host; Gale; HighWire Press; IngentaConnect; JSTOR (Web-based Journal Archive); Northern Light Technology, Inc.; OCLC Online Computer Library Center, Inc.; OhioLINK; Oxford Journals; ProQuest LLC (Ann Arbor); SwetsWise Online Content. Reprint: PSC. *Indexed:* AmH&L, AmHI, ArtHuCI, BrHumI, CCMJ, HistAb, HumInd, IBR, IBSS, IBZ, IPB, L&LBA, LRI, MLA-IB, MSN, MathR, PhilInd, RILM, SSCI. *Bk. rev.:* 30-40, 1,500-2,000 words. *Aud.:* Ac.

Mind has long been a preeminent British philosophy journal, particularly during the period when it published many classic articles under the editorships of G. K. Stout, G. E. Moore, and Gilbert Ryle. The contributions, which take the form of articles, discussions, symposia, and critical notices, are especially noteworthy in the areas of epistemology, metaphysics, philosophy of language, philosophical logic, and philosophy of mind. The journal recently published a special issue in celebration of the centenary of the publication of Bertrand Russell's landmark essay "On Denoting." URL: http://mind.oxfordjournals.org

4950. *Monist: an international quarterly of general philosophical inquiry.* [ISSN: 0026-9662] 1890. q. USD 50 (Individuals, USD 30). Ed(s): Mr. Sherwood J B Sugden, Dr. Barry Smith. Hegeler Institute, c/o Sherwood J.B. Sugden, 315 Fifth St, Peru, IL 61354; philomon1@netscape.net. Illus., index, adv. Refereed. Circ: 1300 Paid. Vol. ends: No. 4. Online: EBSCO Publishing, EBSCO Host; Florida Center for Library Automation; Gale; OCLC Online Computer Library Center, Inc.; H.W. Wilson. *Indexed:* AmHI, ArtHuCI, FR, HumInd, IBR, IBZ, IPB, L&LBA, PSA, PhilInd, RI-1, RILM, SSCI. *Aud.:* Ac.

Each issue of *The Monist* averages eight articles centered on a single topic selected by the editorial board and coordinated by an advisory editor. These topics range from the traditional (e.g., "Truth") to the contemporary (e.g., "Time Travel"). Its broad scope, high-quality scholarship, and reasonable cost combine to make *The Monist* a very attractive publication. URL: http://monist.buffalo.edu

4951. *New Nietzsche Studies.* [ISSN: 1091-0239] 1996. a. Membership, USD 40. Ed(s): Babette E Babich, David B Allison. Nietzsche Society, Department of Philosophy, Fordham University, New York, NY 10023; Babich@Fordham.Edu; http://www.fordham.edu/gsas/phil/new_nietzsche_society.html. *Indexed:* IPB, PhilInd. *Bk. rev.:* 8-12, 500-1,000 words, signed. *Aud.:* Ac.

Scholarship centered on the German existentialist Friedrich Nietzsche has increased tremendously over the past several decades and shows no signs of abating. This journal serves as forum for critical discussions of all facets of his philosophy and related themes by contributors from both Europe and North America. Issues are often centered on topics (e.g., "Ecology, Dynamics, Chaos, Nature"). In addition, selected texts from both Nietzsche and his contemporaries are published when they are deemed to be important for ongoing research. URL: www.fordham.edu/gsas/phil/nns/nns_journal_description.html

4952. *Notre Dame Journal of Formal Logic.* [ISSN: 0029-4527] 1960. q. USD 170 (Individuals, USD 35). Ed(s): Michael Detlefsen, Peter Cholak. Duke University Press, 905 W Main St, Ste 18 B, Durham, NC 27701; dukepress@duke.edu; http://www.dukeupress.edu. Illus., index, adv. Refereed. Circ: 825. Vol. ends: No. 4. *Indexed:* CCMJ, IBR, IBZ, IPB, MSN, MathR, PhilInd. *Bk. rev.:* Occasional, 500-2,500 words. *Aud.:* Ac, Sa.

This journal will be of interest to specialists working in all areas of philosophical and mathematical logic, including the philosophy, history, and foundations of logic and mathematics. There is more of an emphasis here on philosophy of language and formal semantics for natural languages than one finds in *The Journal of Symbolic Logic.* A recent special issue was devoted to "Singular Cardinals Combinatorics." For graduate-level collections. URL: www.nd.edu/~ndjfl

4953. *Nous.* [ISSN: 0029-4624] 1967. q. GBP 465 print & online eds. Ed(s): Ernest Sosa, Jaegwon Kim. Blackwell Publishing, Inc., Commerce Place, 350 Main St, Malden, MA 02148; customerservices@

blackwellpublishing.com; http://www.blackwellpublishing.com. Illus., index, adv. Sample. Refereed. Circ: 1200. Vol. ends: No. 4. Microform: PQC. Online: Blackwell Synergy; EBSCO Publishing, EBSCO Host; Gale; IngentaConnect; JSTOR (Web-based Journal Archive); OCLC Online Computer Library Center, Inc.; OhioLINK; SwetsWise Online Content. Reprint: PSC. *Indexed:* AmHI, ApEcolAb, ArtHuCI, CCMJ, FR, HumInd, IBR, IBZ, IPB, L&LBA, MSN, MathR, PhilInd, RI-1, RILM. *Bk. rev.:* 2-3, 2,000-4,000 words. *Aud.:* Ac.

Nous features articles on a wide range of subjects, chiefly in the fields of metaphysics, epistemology, philosophical logic, philosophy of religion, ethics, and the history of philosophy. Subscribers also receive two annual supplementary publications, *Philosophical Perspectives* and *Philosophical Issues.* One recently published book is discussed in each issue as a lengthy "Critical Study." This high-quality journal belongs in all but the smallest academic collections. URL: www.blackwellpublishing.com/journal.asp?ref=0029-4624&site=1

4954. *Oxford Studies in Ancient Philosophy.* [ISSN: 0265-7651] 1983. a. Ed(s): David Sedley. Oxford University Press, Great Clarendon St, Oxford, OX2 6DP, United Kingdom; enquiry@oup.co.uk; http://www.oup.co.uk/. Illus. Refereed. *Indexed:* IPB, PhilInd. *Aud.:* Ac.

This annual publication features scholarly articles on all facets of ancient philosophy authored by leading philosophers and classicists on an international level. Although most of the essays have the writings of Plato and Aristotle as their focus, the reader will also find studies of the Presocratics, the Pyrrhonists, the Stoics, and other thinkers of antiquity as well. Rather than simply being expository, the authors concentrate on exegesis and critical analysis of primary texts. One will often encounter untransliterated Greek, although there is an effort to keep this at a minimum except in extended passages. Each volume contains an *Index Locorum.* URL: www.oup.co.uk/academic/humanities/philosophy/series/osap

4955. *Pacific Philosophical Quarterly.* Formerly (until vol.61, Jan. 1980): *Personalist.* [ISSN: 0279-0750] 1920. q. GBP 211 print & online eds. Ed(s): David German. Blackwell Publishing Ltd., 9600 Garsington Rd, Oxford, OX4 2ZG, United Kingdom; customerservices@blackwellpublishing.com; http://www.blackwellpublishing.com. Illus., index, adv. Refereed. Circ: 850. Vol. ends: No. 4. Microform: PQC. Online: Blackwell Synergy; EBSCO Publishing, EBSCO Host; Gale; IngentaConnect; OCLC Online Computer Library Center, Inc.; OhioLINK; SwetsWise Online Content. Reprint: PSC. *Indexed:* AmHI, ApEcolAb, ArtHuCI, BEL&L, FR, HumInd, IBR, IPB, L&LBA, MLA-IB, PSA, PhilInd, RILM, SSA, SSCI. *Aud.:* Ac.

Published on behalf of the School of Philosophy, University of Southern California, each issue of *PPQ* contains four to seven articles dealing chiefly with metaphysics, epistemology, philosophy of science, philosophical logic, ethics, and the history of philosophy. Special thematic issues are published occasionally. URL: www.blackwellpublishing.com/journal.asp?ref=0279-0750&site=1

4956. *Philosophers' Imprint.* [ISSN: 1533-628X] 2001. q. Free. Ed(s): Stephen Darwall. University of Michigan, Library, 435 S State St, An Arbor, MI 48109-1009. Refereed. *Indexed:* PhilInd. *Aud.:* Ac.

This journal was founded by members of the philosophy faculty at the University of Michigan with the goal of countering the prevailing notions that electronic publishing is not prestigious and electronic literature is not authoritative. Many articles published to date have focused on issues in metaphysics and philosophical logic. Interested readers who wish to be notified when new articles are posted may subscribe to an electronic mailing list. URL: www.umich.edu/~philos/Imprint

4957. *Philosophical Books.* [ISSN: 0031-8051] 1960. q. GBP 240 print & online eds. Ed(s): Anthony Ellis. Blackwell Publishing Ltd., 9600 Garsington Rd, Oxford, OX4 2ZG, United Kingdom; customerservices@blackwellpublishing.com; http://www.blackwellpublishing.com. Illus., index, adv. Refereed. Circ: 850. Vol. ends: No. 4. Online: Blackwell Synergy; EBSCO Publishing, EBSCO Host; Gale; IngentaConnect; OCLC Online Computer Library Center, Inc.; OhioLINK; SwetsWise Online Content. Reprint: PSC. *Indexed:* ApEcolAb, ArtHuCI, IPB, L&LBA, PhilInd. *Bk. rev.:* Number and length vary. *Aud.:* Ac.

Philosophical Books offers reviews of newly published English-language books and serials in the field and is therefore a valuable tool for collection development. The featured book in each issue is the subject of a symposium, followed by rejoinders by the author. One book is singled out for a more lengthy review under the heading "Critical Notice." The other reviews are arranged by the following subject categories: new journals, history of philosophy, general philosophy, logic, metaphysics, epistemology, philosophy of language, philosophy of mind, ethics, political philosophy, social philosophy, aesthetics, and philosophy of religion. Surveys of recent work in specific subject areas are also published. URL: www.blackwellpublishing.com/journal.asp?ref=0031-8051&site=1

4958. *Philosophical Forum.* [ISSN: 0031-806X] 1942. q. GBP 223 print & online eds. Ed(s): Doug Lackey. Blackwell Publishing, Inc., Commerce Place, 350 Main St, Malden, MA 02148; customerservices@blackwellpublishing.com; http://www.blackwellpublishing.com. Illus., index, adv. Refereed. Circ: 460 Paid. Vol. ends: No. 4. Online: Blackwell Synergy; EBSCO Publishing, EBSCO Host; Gale; IngentaConnect; OCLC Online Computer Library Center, Inc.; OhioLINK; SwetsWise Online Content. Reprint: PSC. *Indexed:* AmHI, ApEcolAb, ArtHuCI, FR, HumInd, IBR, IBZ, IPB, IPSA, L&LBA, PSA, PhilInd, RI-1, SSCI. *Aud.:* Ac.

The editor of *Philosophical Forum* encourages diverse approaches and viewpoints, whether critical or constructive, speculative or analytic, systematic or historical. Translations into English of important foreign-language articles and essays appear occasionally (e.g., a recent selection on French philosophy and science). Those seeking new themes and trends in contemporary philosophy outside the analytic mainstream would benefit from consulting this publication, particularly in areas such as ethics, social and political philosophy, aesthetics, feminist philosophy, and Continental philosophy. URL: www.blackwellpublishing.com/journal.asp?ref=0031-806X&site=1

4959. *Philosophical Investigations.* [ISSN: 0190-0536] 1978. q. GBP 260 print & online eds. Ed(s): D Z Phillips. Blackwell Publishing Ltd., 9600 Garsington Rd, Oxford, OX4 2ZG, United Kingdom; customerservices@blackwellpublishing.com; http://www.blackwellpublishing.com. Illus., index, adv. Refereed. Circ: 650. Vol. ends: No. 4. Online: Blackwell Synergy; EBSCO Publishing, EBSCO Host; Gale; IngentaConnect; OCLC Online Computer Library Center, Inc.; OhioLINK; SwetsWise Online Content. Reprint: PSC. *Indexed:* AmHI, ApEcolAb, ArtHuCI, FR, IPB, L&LBA, PhilInd, RI-1. *Bk. rev.:* 2-6, 1,000-5,000 words. *Aud.:* Ac.

Scholars interested in the work of the influential twentieth-century philosopher Ludwig Wittgenstein will find this to be a valuable title. In addition to presenting critical studies on Wittgenstein, the journal also features selections from Wittgenstein's unpublished writings and lectures (based on the lecture notes of his students). Although Wittgenstein is the principal focus of *Philosophical Investigations,* articles are also published on a wide range of topics in contemporary analytical philosophy, particularly those of the kind addressed in the writings of British ordinary-language philosophers like J. L. Austin and Gilbert Ryle. URL: www.blackwellpublishing.com/journal.asp?ref=0190-0536&site=1

4960. *Philosophical Practice: client counseling, group facilitation, and organizational consulting.* [ISSN: 1742-8173] 2005. 3x/yr. GBP 176 print & online eds. Ed(s): Lou Marinoff. Routledge, 4 Park Sq, Milton Park, Abingdon, OX14 4RN, United Kingdom; info@routledge.co.uk; http://www.routledge.co.uk. Index. Sample. Refereed. *Indexed:* PhilInd. *Bk. rev.:* 3-4, 750-1,000 words. *Aud.:* Ac, Sa.

This new journal serves as the official publication of the American Philosophical Practitioners Association. It aims to bring the methods and insights of philosophical analysis to bear on a wide range of ethical, legal, social, and political issues in client counseling, clinical psychology, group facilitation, organizational consulting, human resources management, social work, psychotherapy, and psychiatry. Recommended for libraries that provide support for professional programs and services in these areas. URL: www.tandf.co.uk/journals/titles/17428173.asp

4961. *The Philosophical Quarterly.* [ISSN: 0031-8094] 1950. q. GBP 170 print & online eds. Ed(s): Sarah Broadie, Katherine Hawley. Blackwell Publishing Ltd., 9600 Garsington Rd, Oxford, OX4 2ZG, United Kingdom; customerservices@blackwellpublishing.com; http://www.blackwellpublishing.com. Illus., index, adv. Refereed. Circ: 1600. Microform: PQC. Online: Blackwell Synergy; EBSCO Publishing, EBSCO Host; Gale; IngentaConnect; JSTOR (Web-based Journal Archive); OCLC Online Computer Library Center, Inc.; OhioLINK; SwetsWise Online Content. Reprint: PSC. *Indexed:* AmHI, ApEcolAb, ArtHuCI, CCMJ, FR, HumInd, IBR, IBSS, IBZ, IPB, LRI, MLA-IB, MSN, MathR, PhilInd, RILM, SSCI. *Bk. rev.:* 10-15, 500-3,000 words. *Aud.:* Ac.

Sponsored by the Scots Philosophical Club and the University of St. Andrews, this is one of the better-quality analytic philosophy journals published in the United Kingdom. The predominant subjects treated are epistemology, metaphysics, philosophical logic, philosophy of language, and ethics. URL: www.blackwellpublishing.com/journal.asp?ref=0031-8094&site=1

4962. *Philosophical Review.* [ISSN: 0031-8108] 1892. q. USD 96 (Individuals, USD 33). Ed(s): John Rowehl. Duke University Press, 905 W Main St, Ste 18 B, Durham, NC 27701; dukepress@duke.edu; http://www.dukeupress.edu. Illus., index, adv. Refereed. Circ: 3265 Paid. Vol. ends: No. 4. Microform: MIM; PMC; PQC. Online: Gale; HighWire Press; JSTOR (Web-based Journal Archive). Reprint: PSC. *Indexed:* AmH&L, AmHI, ArtHuCI, BAS, BRI, CBRI, HumInd, IBR, IBZ, IPB, L&LBA, LRI, MLA-IB, PhilInd, RILM, SSCI. *Bk. rev.:* 15-20, 1,000-2,500 words. *Aud.:* Ac.

The *Philosophical Review* is one of the oldest continuously published philosophy periodicals in the United States and has featured the writings of many distinguished philosophers, particularly during the postwar era. Each issue contains three or four articles that critically analyze issues in all major areas of the field, with an emphasis on metaphysics, epistemology, philosophy of mind, and ethics. The journal is also known for the excellence of its scholarship in the history of philosophy. The new production and circulation partnership with Duke University Press should improve the lagging publication schedule (editorial control remains at Cornell University). URL: www.arts.cornell.edu/philrev

4963. *Philosophical Studies: an international journal for philosophy in the analytic tradition.* [ISSN: 0031-8116] 1950. 15x/yr. EUR 1974 print & online eds. Ed(s): Stewart Cohen. Springer Netherlands, Van Godewijckstraat 30, Dordrecht, 3311 GX, Netherlands; http://www.springeronline.com. Illus., index, adv. Sample. Refereed. Vol. ends: No. 3. Microform: PQC. Online: Chadwyck-Healey Inc.; EBSCO Publishing, EBSCO Host; Gale; IngentaConnect; OCLC Online Computer Library Center, Inc.; OhioLINK; ProQuest LLC (Ann Arbor); Springer LINK; SwetsWise Online Content. Reprint: PSC. *Indexed:* AmHI, ArtHuCI, CCMJ, CPL, FR, IBR, IBZ, IPB, IPSA, L&LBA, MLA-IB, MSN, MathR, PSA, PhilInd, RI-1, SSCI. *Aud.:* Ac.

Founded by Herbert Feigl and Wilfrid Sellars, *Philosophical Studies* has established itself as one of the foremost journals for analytical philosophy. The focus is on contemporary issues, as well as traditional problems explored from new perspectives, particularly in the fields of metaphysics, epistemology, philosophy of mind, philosophical logic, philosophy of science, action theory, and ethics. Authors generally advance tightly argued, original theses, although others contribute historically oriented discussions. Each year the journal publishes several thematic issues, coordinated by guest editors, as well as issues devoted to selected conference papers, for example, from the American Philosophical Association's annual Pacific Division meetings, the Bellingham Summer Philosophy Conference at Western Washington University, and the Oberlin Conference in Epistemology. Symposia on recently published books, followed with replies by the authors, are also featured. Despite its high cost, this is a core collection journal. URL: www.springerlink.com/openurl.asp?genre=journal&issn=0031-8116

4964. *Philosophical Topics.* Formerly (until 1981): *Southwestern Journal of Philosophy.* [ISSN: 0276-2080] 1970. 2x/yr. USD 65 (Individuals, USD 40). Ed(s): Edward Minar. University of Arkansas Press, 201 Ozark Ave, Fayetteville, AR 72701; http://www.uapress.com. Illus., adv. Refereed. Circ: 750. Vol. ends: No. 2. *Indexed:* ArtHuCI, IPB, PhilInd, SSCI. *Aud.:* Ac.

Philosophical Topics has evolved from a regional journal into a publication that features exclusively invited papers, many of which are authored by leading scholars on an international level. Each issue averages ten articles centered on a major historical period, broad area of philosophy, or prominent philosopher. URL: www.uapress.com/titles/philostopix/philostopix.html

4965. *Philosophy.* [ISSN: 0031-8191] 1925. q. plus two supplements. GBP 280. Ed(s): Anthony O'Hear. Cambridge University Press, The Edinburgh Bldg, Shaftesbury Rd, Cambridge, CB2 2RU, United Kingdom; journals@cambridge.org; http://www.journals.cambridge.org. Illus., index, adv. Refereed. Vol. ends: No. 4. Microform: PQC. Online: Pub.; EBSCO Publishing, EBSCO Host; OCLC Online Computer Library Center, Inc.; OhioLINK; SwetsWise Online Content. *Indexed:* AmH&L, AmHI, ArtHuCI, BAS, FR, HistAb, HumInd, IBR, IBZ, IPB, L&LBA, LRI, MSN, MathR, PRA, PhilInd, RI-1, SSCI. *Bk. rev.:* 5-7, 1,000-2,500 words. *Aud.:* Ac.

As the official journal of the Royal Institute of Philosophy (RIP), this journal has a decidedly British bent, and most authors are from the United Kingdom. All branches of philosophy are discussed in its pages, and no emphasis is placed on any particular school or method. Even the nonspecialist will often find the articles accessible because, as the editor admonishes, "Contributors are required to avoid needless technicality of language and presentation." The Royal Institute of Philosophy Lecture Series, previously published separately and invariably representing the highest standards of scholarship, is now published as *RIP Supplements* and included in the price for institutional subscribers. URL: www.cambridge.org/journals/journal_catalogue.asp?mnemonic=PHI

4966. *Philosophy and Literature.* [ISSN: 0190-0013] 1976. s-a. USD 95. Ed(s): Garry Hagberg, Denis Dutton. The Johns Hopkins University Press, 2715 N Charles St, Baltimore, MD 21218-4363; http://muse.jhu.edu. Illus., index, adv. Sample. Refereed. Circ: 773. Vol. ends: No. 2. Online: Chadwyck-Healey Inc.; EBSCO Publishing, EBSCO Host; OCLC Online Computer Library Center, Inc.; OhioLINK; Project MUSE; ProQuest LLC (Ann Arbor); SwetsWise Online Content. Reprint: PSC. *Indexed:* ABS&EES, AmHI, ArtHuCI, BEL&L, BRI, CBRI, FR, IBR, IBZ, IPB, L&LBA, MLA-IB, PhilInd, SSCI. *Bk. rev.:* 2-4, 750-1,500 words. *Aud.:* Ac.

This interdisciplinary journal, sponsored by Bard College, publishes philosophical interpretations of American, British, and Continental literature. It also includes literary investigations of classic works of philosophy, articles on the aesthetics of literature, philosophy of language as it pertains to literature, and the literary theory of criticism. Shorter papers appear in the "Notes and Fragments" section. Special thematic symposia (e.g., "Dostoevsky Recontextualized") are published occasionally. Recommended for both literature and philosophy collections. URL: http://muse.jhu.edu/journals/philosophy_and_literature

4967. *Philosophy and Phenomenological Research.* [ISSN: 0031-8205] 1940. bi-m. Ed(s): Ernest Sosa. Blackwell Publishing, Inc., Commerce Place, 350 Main St, Malden, MA 02148; customerservices@blackwellpublishing.com; http://www.blackwellpublishing.com. Illus., index, adv. Refereed. Microform: PQC. Online: EBSCO Publishing, EBSCO Host; Gale; IngentaConnect; JSTOR (Web-based Journal Archive). Reprint: PSC. *Indexed:* ABS&EES, AmHI, ArtHuCI, HumInd, IBR, IBZ, IPB, L&LBA, MLA-IB, PhilInd, RI-1, RILM, SSCI. *Bk. rev.:* 6-8, 750-1,500 words. *Aud.:* Ac.

Philosophy and Phenomenological Research is in the upper echelon of analytic philosophy journals. Although it serves as the official organ of the International Phenomenological Society, one will find articles on a broad range of subjects. The journal puts an emphasis on metaphysics, epistemology, philosophy of mind, ethics, and issues in the history of philosophy when they have relevance to contemporary problems. Discussion papers, symposia (often focusing on recent books), and supplementary volumes are also published. URL: www.brown.edu/Departments/Philosophy/ppr.html

4968. *Philosophy and Public Affairs.* [ISSN: 0048-3915] 1971. q. GBP 109 print & online eds. Ed(s): Charles R Beitz. Blackwell Publishing, Inc., Commerce Place, 350 Main St, Malden, MA 02148; customerservices@ blackwellpublishing.com; http://www.blackwellpublishing.com. Illus., index, adv. Sample. Refereed. Circ: 2037. Microform: PQC. Online: Blackwell Synergy; EBSCO Publishing, EBSCO Host; IngentaConnect; JSTOR (Web-based Journal Archive); OCLC Online Computer Library Center, Inc.; OhioLINK; Project MUSE; ProQuest LLC (Ann Arbor); SwetsWise Online Content. Reprint: PSC. *Indexed:* ABCPolSci, AgeL, AmHI, ApEcolAb, ArtHuCI, CJA, FR, FutSurv, HumInd, IBR, IBSS, IBZ, IPB, IPSA, LRI, PRA, PSA, PhilInd, RI-1, SSA, SSCI, SociolAb. *Aud.:* Ac.

Philosophy and Public Affairs is an important journal for the critical examination of contemporary ethical, political, social, legal, and public-policy issues. Some authors focus on explicating broad concepts, such as autonomy, paternalism, patriotism, social justice, and punishment, whereas others deal with specific sociopolitical issues such as abortion, disarmament, pornography, preemptive war, racial profiling, and reparations. This title would be an excellent choice for philosophy, law, and political science collections. URL: www.blackwellpublishing.com/journal.asp?ref=0048-3915&site=1

4969. *Philosophy and Rhetoric.* [ISSN: 0031-8213] 1968. q. USD 68. Ed(s): Gerard A Hauser. Pennsylvania State University Press, 820 N University Dr, USB-1, Ste C, University Park, PA 16802-1003; pspjournals@psu.edu; http://www.psupress.org. Illus., index, adv. Refereed. Circ: 391 Paid. Microform: PQC. Online: EBSCO Publishing, EBSCO Host; OCLC Online Computer Library Center, Inc.; OhioLINK; Project MUSE; SwetsWise Online Content. Reprint: PSC. *Indexed:* AmHI, ArtHuCI, FR, IBR, IBZ, IPB, MLA-IB, PhilInd, RI-1, SSCI. *Bk. rev.:* 1-3, 1,500-2,500 words. *Aud.:* Ac.

This journal is a good source for studies of theoretical issues concerning the relationship between philosophy and rhetoric (including the relationship between formal and informal logic and rhetoric). It also covers philosophical aspects of argumentation and argumentation within the discipline of philosophy itself; the nature of rhetoric of historical figures and during historical periods; rhetoric and human culture and thought; and psychological and sociological aspects of rhetoric. Recommended for philosophy, English, and speech communication collections. URL: www.press.jhu.edu/journals/philosophy_and_rhetoric

4970. *Philosophy & Social Criticism: an international, inter-disciplinary journal.* Formerly: *Cultural Hermeneutics.* [ISSN: 0191-4537] 1973. 9x/yr. GBP 894. Ed(s): David Rasmussen. Sage Publications Ltd., 1 Oliver's Yard, 55 City Rd, London, EC1 1SP, United Kingdom; info@sagepub.co.uk; http://www.sagepub.co.uk. Illus., index, adv. Sample. Refereed. Circ: 1000. Vol. ends: No. 6. Reprint: PSC. *Indexed:* ABS&EES, AltPI, FR, IBR, IBSS, IBZ, IPB, IPSA, LeftInd, PSA, PhilInd, RI-1, SSA, SSCI, SociolAb. *Aud.:* Ac.

This wide-ranging interdisciplinary journal serves as a forum for the discussion of political philosophy, social theory, ethics, hermeneutics, literary theory, aesthetics, feminism, modernism and postmodernism, neostructuralism and deconstruction, universalism and communitarianism, and so forth. Those interested in the work of modern Continental philosophers—Adorno, Arendt, Derrida, Habermas, Foucault, Ricouer, and others—will find this publication to be a valuable resource. URL: www.sagepub.com/journal.aspx?pid=262

4971. *Philosophy East and West: a quarterly of comparative philosophy.* [ISSN: 0031-8221] 1951. q. USD 60 (Individuals, USD 35; Students, USD 18). Ed(s): Roger T Ames. University of Hawaii Press, Journals Department, 2840 Kolowalu St, Honolulu, HI 96822-1888; uhpjourn@ hawaii.edu; http://www.uhpress.hawaii.edu/. Illus., index, adv. Sample. Refereed. Circ: 1200. Vol. ends: No. 4. Microform: PQC. Online: Chadwyck-Healey Inc.; EBSCO Publishing, EBSCO Host; Florida Center for Library Automation; Gale; JSTOR (Web-based Journal Archive); OCLC Online Computer Library Center, Inc.; OhioLINK;

Project MUSE; ProQuest K-12 Learning Solutions; ProQuest LLC (Ann Arbor); SwetsWise Online Content; H.W. Wilson. Reprint: PSC. *Indexed:* AmHI, ArtHuCI, BAS, HumInd, IBR, IBSS, IBZ, IPB, IndIslam, L&LBA, LRI, MLA-IB, PhilInd, R&TA, RI-1, RILM, SSCI. *Bk. rev.:* 5-7, 500-2,500 words. *Aud.:* Ac.

Philosophy East and West publishes specialized studies on Asian philosophy and comparative intercultural articles on the philosophical traditions of East and West, particularly those exhibiting the relevance of philosophy for the art, literature, science, and social practice of Asian civilizations. The general scope of this publication is much broader than that of the *Journal of Indian Philosophy.* It is a good choice for both philosophy and Asian Studies collections. URL: www.uhpress.hawaii.edu/journals/pew/index.html

4972. *Philosophy Now: a magazine of ideas.* [ISSN: 0961-5970] 1991. 6x/yr. GBP 24 (Individuals, GBP 12.75). Ed(s): Rick Lewis. Philosophy Now, 43a Jerningham Rd, London, SE14 5NQ, United Kingdom; rick.lewis@philosophynow.demon.org.uk. Illus., adv. *Indexed:* AmHI, BrHumI, IBR, IBZ, PhilInd. *Bk. rev.:* 2-4, 750-1,500 words. *Aud.:* Ga.

This magazine, which receives a wide distribution through bookstores and newsstands in Great Britain, is designed to make philosophy more accessible to the educated layperson. The editors solicit articles that discuss any philosophical topic of general interest so long as they are written in a "lively, readable, and nontechnical style," preferably without footnotes or jargon. The articles are generally accompanied by illustrations, such as photographs, cartoons, or caricatures. Each issue includes at least one interview with a practicing philosopher. Film and theater reviews, as well as prose and poetry, appear regularly. *Philosophy Now* would be a good choice for public libraries in which magazines such as *The Humanist* and *Skeptical Inquirer* are popular. URL: www.philosophynow.org

4973. *Philosophy of Science: official journal of the Philosophy of Science Association.* Incorporates (1970-1994): *P S A.* [ISSN: 0031-8248] 1934. 5x/yr. USD 185 domestic; USD 202.10 Canada; USD 197 elsewhere. Ed(s): W Michael Dickson. University of Chicago Press, Journals Division, PO Box 37005, Chicago, IL 60637; subscriptions@ press.uchicago.edu; http://www.journals.uchicago.edu. Illus., index, adv. Refereed. Circ: 2200. Vol. ends: Dec. Microform: PMC; PQC. Online: EBSCO Publishing, EBSCO Host; Florida Center for Library Automation; Gale; JSTOR (Web-based Journal Archive); ProQuest K-12 Learning Solutions; ProQuest LLC (Ann Arbor). Reprint: PSC. *Indexed:* AmHI, ArtHuCI, BiolAb, CCMJ, FR, HumInd, IBR, IBSS, IBZ, IPB, MSN, MathR, PhilInd, RI-1, SCI, SSCI. *Bk. rev.:* 4-8, 750-1,000 words. *Aud.:* Ac.

This important journal publishes articles dealing with fundamental issues in the philosophy of science. Such issues include the logic of deductive, nomological, and statistical explanations; the nature of scientific laws and theories; observation; evidence; confirmation; induction; probability; and causality. In addition, contributors analyze philosophical issues that arise within the context of the physical sciences (e.g., space, time, and quantum mechanics); the biological sciences (e.g., evolution, reductionism, and teleology); the cognitive sciences (e.g., artificial intelligence and connectionism); the social sciences (e.g., decision theory); and mathematics. The December issue contains the contributed or symposia papers presented at the biennial meetings of the Philosophy of Science Association. This is an essential journal for all academic libraries. URL: www.journals.uchicago.edu/PHILSCI/home.html

4974. *Philosophy of the Social Sciences.* [ISSN: 0048-3931] 1971. q. GBP 292. Ed(s): Ian C Jarvie. Sage Publications, Inc., 2455 Teller Rd, Thousand Oaks, CA 91320; info@sagepub.com; http://www.sagepub.com. Illus., index, adv. Sample. Refereed. Circ: 1300. Vol. ends: No. 4. Online: Chadwyck-Healey Inc.; EBSCO Publishing, EBSCO Host; HighWire Press; LexisNexis; OCLC Online Computer Library Center, Inc.; SAGE Publications, Inc., SAGE Journals Online; SwetsWise Online Content. Reprint: PSC. *Indexed:* ArtHuCI, CBCARef, CPerI, FR, IBR, IBSS, IBZ, IPB, IPSA, PSA, PhilInd, SSA, SSCI, SociolAb. *Bk. rev.:* 1-2, 1,500-3,00 words. *Aud.:* Ac.

This interdisciplinary journal publishes articles, discussions, symposia, review essays, and literature surveys on philosophical issues arising within the entire spectrum of the social and behavioral sciences. The editors strive to promote debate between different—and often conflicting—schools of thought. The journal also publishes the papers presented at the annual St. Louis Roundtable on Philosophy of the Social Sciences. This is a valuable title for philosophers as well as social scientists, particularly economists, linguists, political scientists, psychologists, and sociologists. URL: www.sagepub.com/journal.aspx?pid= 164

4975. Philosophy, Psychiatry & Psychology. [ISSN: 1071-6076] 1994. q. USD 180. Ed(s): John Z Sadler, K W M Fulford. The Johns Hopkins University Press, 2715 N Charles St, Baltimore, MD 21218-4363; http://muse.jhu.edu. Illus., adv. Sample. Refereed. Circ: 161. Vol. ends: No. 4. Online: EBSCO Publishing, EBSCO Host; OCLC Online Computer Library Center, Inc.; OhioLINK; Project MUSE; ProQuest LLC (Ann Arbor); SwetsWise Online Content. Reprint: PSC. *Indexed:* IBR, IBZ, PhilInd, PsycInfo. *Bk. rev.:* Occasional, 5,000-7,000 words. *Aud.:* Ac.

This journal is sponsored by the Royal Institute of Philosophy and affiliated with the Association for the Advancement of Philosophy and Psychiatry and the Royal College of Psychiatrists Philosophy Group. Its contributors address a broad range of philosophical issues relevant to psychiatry and abnormal psychology, in addition to dealing with topics in clinical theory and methodology that have a bearing on philosophical problems in such areas as metaphysics, epistemology, and ethics. The articles are often followed by commentaries and rejoinders. The authors represent many disciplines, including general medicine, law, neuroscience, social science, anthropology, nursing, and theology. The journal also features an ongoing bibliography, "Concurrent Contents: Recent and Classic References at the Interface of Philosophy, Psychiatry, and Psychology," and a newly expanded "International News and Notes" section. URL: www.press.jhu.edu/journals/philosophy_psychiatry_and_psychology/

4976. Philosophy Today. [ISSN: 0031-8256] 1957. q. USD 50 domestic; USD 60 foreign. Ed(s): David Pellauer. DePaul University, Department of Philosophy, 2352 North Clifton Ave, Chicago, IL 60614; phltoday@ condor.depaul.edu. Illus., index, adv. Refereed. Circ: 1180. Vol. ends: No. 4. Microform: PQC. Online: Chadwyck-Healey Inc.; Northern Light Technology, Inc.; OCLC Online Computer Library Center, Inc.; ProQuest K-12 Learning Solutions; ProQuest LLC (Ann Arbor). *Indexed:* AmHI, ArtHuCI, CPL, FR, HumInd, IPB, PhilInd. *Aud.:* Ac.

Articles in *Philosophy Today* focus primarily on phenomenology and existentialism and address the interests of scholars and teachers within the Christian tradition. Philosophers discussed in recent issues include Nietzsche, Heidegger, Ricoeur, Deleuze, and Lyotard. A supplementary issue is also published each year that contains selected papers from the annual meeting of the Society for Phenomenology and Existential Philosophy. Recommended for libraries needing this type of perspective. URL: http://condor.depaul.edu/ ~phildept/html/philtoday.html

4977. Phronesis: a journal for ancient philosophy. [ISSN: 0031-8868] 1956. 5x/yr. EUR 261 print & online eds. (Individuals, EUR 99). Ed(s): Verity Harte. Brill, PO Box 9000, Leiden, 2300 PA, Netherlands; cs@brill.nl; http://www.brill.nl. Illus., index, adv. Refereed. Circ: 1100. Vol. ends: No. 4. Reprint: PSC. *Indexed:* AmHI, ArtHuCI, FR, IBR, IBZ, IPB, NTA, PhilInd. *Bk. rev.:* 1-2, 1,000-2,000 words. *Aud.:* Ac.

Phronesis is the leading journal devoted exclusively to all aspects of ancient Greek and Roman thought, including logic, metaphysics, epistemology, ethics, political philosophy, philosophy of science, psychology, and medicine. A majority of the contributors undertake a critical textual analysis of the works of Plato and Aristotle, particularly those involving new or neglected issues, although others adopt a broader historical approach. Occasional articles deal with early Stoicism or the later Hellenistic period. The articles may be in English, French, German, or Italian. URL: www.brill.nl/ m_catalogue_sub6_id7431.htm

4978. Ratio: an international journal of analytic philosophy. [ISSN: 0034-0006] 1957. q. GBP 340 print & online eds. Ed(s): John G Cottingham. Blackwell Publishing Ltd., 9600 Garsington Rd, Oxford, OX4 2ZG, United Kingdom; customerservices@ blackwellpublishing.com; http://www.blackwellpublishing.com. Illus., adv. Refereed. Circ: 700. Vol. ends: No. 4. Online: Blackwell Synergy;

EBSCO Publishing, EBSCO Host; Gale; IngentaConnect; OCLC Online Computer Library Center, Inc.; OhioLINK; SwetsWise Online Content. Reprint: PSC. *Indexed:* AmHI, ApEcolAb, ArtHuCI, BrHumI, FR, IPB, L&LBA, MathR, PSA, PhilInd, SSCI. *Bk. rev.:* 1-2, 1,000-2,500 words. *Aud.:* Ac.

Ratio publishes articles that analyze contemporary issues in metaphysics, epistemology, philosophical logic, and ethics. One aim of the journal is to encourage a dialogue between philosophers writing in English and those who work principally in German. The June issue leads off with an invited paper authored by an internationally prominent philosopher. The December issue features papers presented at the annual philosophy conference held at the University of Reading (England). Themes in recent years include "Metaphysics in Science" and "Wittgenstein and Reason." URL: www.blackwellpublishing.com/journal.asp?ref=0034-0006&site=1

4979. The Review of Metaphysics: a philosophical quarterly. [ISSN: 0034-6632] 1947. q. USD 55 (Individuals, USD 35; Students, USD 20). Ed(s): Jude P Dougherty. Philosophy Education Society, Inc., Catholic University of America, Washington, DC 20064; mail@reviewofmetaphysics.com; http://www.reviewofmetaphysics.org. Illus., index, adv. Refereed. Circ: 1691 Paid. Vol. ends: No. 4. Microform: PQC. Online: Chadwyck-Healey Inc.; Florida Center for Library Automation; Gale; Northern Light Technology, Inc.; OCLC Online Computer Library Center, Inc.; ProQuest K-12 Learning Solutions; ProQuest LLC (Ann Arbor); H.W. Wilson. *Indexed:* ABS&EES, AmH&L, AmHI, ArtHuCI, BRI, CBRI, HistAb, HumInd, IBR, IBZ, IPB, IndIslam, LRI, PhilInd, RI-1, RILM, SSCI. *Bk. rev.:* 30-35, 500-1,000 words. *Aud.:* Ac.

The editor of *The Review of Metaphysics* solicits "definitive contributions to philosophical knowledge" and "persistent, resolute inquiries into root questions, regardless of the writer's affiliation." The majority of articles center on issues in metaphysics, philosophy of mind, phenomenology and existentialism, ethics, and the history of philosophy. Each issue includes abstracts of articles in current philosophy periodicals, generally written by the authors. The September issue contains a list of doctoral dissertations awarded by North American universities during the previous academic year. URL: www.reviewofmetaphysics.org

4980. Revue Internationale de Philosophie. [ISSN: 0048-8143] 1938. q. EUR 27.83. Universa Press, Rue Hoender 24, Wetteren, 9230, Belgium. Illus., adv. Refereed. Vol. ends: No. 4. Microform: IDC. *Indexed:* ArtHuCI, FR, IBR, IBZ, IPB, MLA-IB, MathR, PhilInd. *Bk. rev.:* 1-5, 500-2,500 words. *Aud.:* Ac.

Each issue of this Belgian journal averages six to eight articles in English, French, German, or Italian, centering on a particular movement, philosopher, or problem. The fact that the contributors are frequently acknowledged authorities on their subjects—for example, Terence Irwin on Aristotle, Rudolf Makkreel on Dilthey, J. M. Bernstein on Adorno, and Jaakko Hintikka on Godel—makes this an important publication. The journal currently does not have a web site.

4981. Social Epistemology: a journal of knowledge, culture and policy. [ISSN: 0269-1728] 1987. q. GBP 430 print & online eds. Ed(s): Joan Leach. Routledge, 4 Park Sq, Milton Park, Abingdon, OX14 4RN, United Kingdom; info@routledge.co.uk; http://www.routledge.co.uk. Illus., index, adv. Sample. Refereed. Circ: 171. Vol. ends: No. 4. Online: EBSCO Publishing, EBSCO Host; Gale; IngentaConnect; OCLC Online Computer Library Center, Inc.; SwetsWise Online Content. Reprint: PSC. *Indexed:* FR, IBR, IBZ, IPB, IndIslam, PSA, PhilInd, SSA, SociolAb. *Aud.:* Ac.

Articles in this journal, authored by scholars from a variety of disciplines, present empirical research regarding the production, assessment, and validation of knowledge as well as explore the normative ramifications of such research. These discussions are generally the product of several contributors and take the form of critical symposia, open peer commentary reviews, dialectical debates, applications, provocations, reviews and responses, and so forth. This type of approach tends to lead to a thorough exploration of the topic at hand from a number of divergent viewpoints. The journal is now collaborating with the

Society for Social Studies of Science (4S) and the European Association for the Study of Science and Technology (EASST). This title is a good choice for both philosophy and social science collections. URL: www.tandf.co.uk/journals/titles/02691728.asp

4982. *Social Philosophy and Policy.* [ISSN: 0265-0525] 1983. s-a. GBP 116. Ed(s): Ellen Frankel Paul, Jeffrey Paul. Cambridge University Press, The Edinburgh Bldg, Shaftesbury Rd, Cambridge, CB2 2RU, United Kingdom; journals@cambridge.org; http://www.journals.cambridge.org. Illus., adv. Refereed. Circ: 1000. Vol. ends: No. 2. *Indexed:* ABS&EES, ASSIA, ArtHuCI, IBR, IBSS, IBZ, IPB, IPSA, PRA, PSA, PhilInd, RI-1, SSA, SSCI, SociolAb. *Aud.:* Ac.

Each issue of this interdisciplinary journal is devoted to a single theme involving contemporary debates on social, political, economic, legal, and public policy issues. The editors aim for a diversity of viewpoints, and the contributors represent many disciplines, including philosophy, law, economics, sociology, and political science. Recent issues focus on "Justice and Global Politics" and "Taxation, Economic Prosperity, and Distributive Justice." The general orientation of this journal is similar to that of *Philosophy and Public Affairs.* URL: www.cambridge.org/journals/journal_catalogue.asp?mnemonic=SOY

4983. *Sorites: electronic magazine of analytical philosophy.* [ISSN: 1135-1349] 1995. q. Free. Ed(s): Lorenzo Pena. Spanish Institute for Advanced Studies, Center for Analytic Philosophy, Pinar 25, Madrid, 28006, Spain; http://www.ifs.csic.es/sorites/. Refereed. *Indexed:* CCMJ, MSN, MathR, PhilInd. *Aud.:* Ac.

Although this English-language electronic journal is headquartered in Spain, it has an international board of editorial advisors. The contributors endeavor to bring the methods and tools of contemporary analytic philosophy—including conceptual clarity, formal rigor, and careful argumentation—to bear on a wide range of subjects in theoretical and applied philosophy. Many of the articles published to date have concentrated on issues in metaphysics and philosophical logic. URL: www.sorites.org

4984. *The Southern Journal of Philosophy.* [ISSN: 0038-4283] 1963. q. USD 36 (Individuals, USD 24; Students, USD 12). Ed(s): Nancy D Simco. University of Memphis, Department of Philosophy, Clement Hall 327, Memphis, TN 38152-0001; lsadler@memphis.edu; http://cas.memphis.edu/philosophy/. Illus., adv. Refereed. Circ: 1400 Paid. Vol. ends: No. 4. Microform: PQC. Online: EBSCO Publishing, EBSCO Host. Reprint: PSC. *Indexed:* AmHI, ArtHuCI, FR, IBR, IBZ, IPB, PhilInd, RI-1, SSCI. *Aud.:* Ac.

Although this is a solid general philosophy periodical, the supplementary volumes—available separately but included in the subscription—are especially noteworthy. They contain the featured papers presented at the annual Spindel Conference held at the University of Memphis. This series, taken as a whole, has resulted in an impressive body of scholarship. URL: http://cas.memphis.edu/philosophy/sjp/sjp.htm

4985. *Studia Logica: an international journal for symbolic logic.* [ISSN: 0039-3215] 1953. 9x/yr. EUR 1191 print & online eds. Ed(s): Ryszard Wojcicki. Springer Netherlands, Van Godewijckstraat 30, Dordrecht, 3311 GX, Netherlands; http://www.springeronline.com. Illus., index, adv. Sample. Refereed. Vol. ends: No. 3. Microform: PQC. Online: EBSCO Publishing, EBSCO Host; Gale; IngentaConnect; OCLC Online Computer Library Center, Inc.; OhioLINK; Springer LINK; SwetsWise Online Content. Reprint: PSC. *Indexed:* CCMJ, IPB, L&LBA, LingAb, MLA-IB, MSN, MathR, PhilInd. *Bk. rev.:* 1-2, 1,000-1,500 words. *Aud.:* Ac, Sa.

Sponsored by the Institute of Philosophy and Sociology, Polish Academy of Sciences, this English-language journal publishes articles on technical issues in symbolic and philosophical logic. The focus is primarily on the semantics, methodology, and applications of logical systems, particularly when new and important technical results appear. A recent special issue is devoted to cut-elimination in classical and nonclassical logic. Recommended for graduate-level collections. URL: www.springerlink.com/openurl.asp?genre=journal&issn=0039-3215

Studies in History and Philosophy of Modern Physics. See *Studies in History and Philosophy of Science Part B: Studies in History and Philosophy of Modern Physics* in the Physics section.

4986. *Studies in History and Philosophy of Science Part A.* [ISSN: 0039-3681] 1970. 4x/yr. EUR 534. Ed(s): Marina Frasca-Spada, Nicholas Jardine. Pergamon, The Boulevard, Langford Ln, East Park, Kidlington, OX5 1GB, United Kingdom. Illus., index, adv. Sample. Refereed. Circ: 1100. Microform: PQC. Online: EBSCO Publishing, EBSCO Host; Gale; IngentaConnect; OhioLINK; ScienceDirect; SwetsWise Online Content. *Indexed:* AmH&L, AmHI, ArtHuCI, CCMJ, HistAb, HumInd, IBR, IBSS, IBZ, IPB, MSN, MathR, PhilInd, SCI, SSA, SSCI, SociolAb. *Bk. rev.:* 1-7, 1,500-2,500 words. *Aud.:* Ac.

This journal publishes historical, methodological, philosophical, and sociological investigations into problems and issues in the sciences, with the exception of modern physics and the biological and biomedical sciences, which are covered in separate Pergamon publications. Some authors focus on the work of individual philosophers and scientists (e.g., Galileo, Copernicus, Newton, Carnap, and Feyerabend), while others address philosophical themes in the history of science. Recommended especially for collections that emphasize the history of science. URL: www.elsevier.com/wps/find/journaldescription.cws_home/30586/description#description

4987. *Synthese: an international journal for epistemology, methodology and philosophy of science.* [ISSN: 0039-7857] 1936. 15x/yr. EUR 2139 print & online eds. Ed(s): John Symons. Springer Netherlands, Van Godewijckstraat 30, Dordrecht, 3311 GX, Netherlands; http://www.springeronline.com. Illus., index, adv. Sample. Refereed. Vol. ends: No. 3. Microform: PQC. Online: Chadwyck-Healey Inc.; EBSCO Publishing, EBSCO Host; Gale; IngentaConnect; OCLC Online Computer Library Center, Inc.; OhioLINK; ProQuest LLC (Ann Arbor); Springer LINK; SwetsWise Online Content. Reprint: PSC. *Indexed:* ArtHuCI, CCMJ, FR, IBR, IBZ, IPB, L&LBA, MLA-IB, MSN, MathR, PhilInd, RILM, SCI, SSCI. *Aud.:* Ac.

Articles in *Synthese* bring formal methods of philosophical analysis to bear on issues in the history and philosophy of science, epistemology, mathematical and philosophical logic, philosophy of language, and philosophy of mathematics. Contributors include not only philosophers but also mathematicians, scientists, and economists writing on the philosophical aspects or formal methodological problems in their respective disciplines. The annual special issue dedicated to "Neuroscience and Its Philosophy" represents an effort by the editors to continue the scholarly tradition of the ceased Kluwer journal *Brain and Mind.* A separately edited publication, *Knowledge, Rationality, and Action,* appears regularly as a special section and will be of interest to researchers in the fields of game theory and artificial intelligence. Although this is a highly technical and very costly journal, it is nevertheless recommended for graduate-level collections. URL: www.springerlink.com/openurl.asp?genre=journal&issn=0039-7857

4988. *Theory and Decision: an international journal for multidisciplinary advances in decision sciences.* [ISSN: 0040-5833] 1970. 8x/yr. EUR 959 print & online eds. Ed(s): Mohammed Abdellaoui. Springer New York LLC, 233 Spring St, New York, NY 10013-1578; service-ny@springer.com; http://www.springer.com/. Illus., index, adv. Sample. Refereed. Vol. ends: No. 4. Microform: PQC. Online: Chadwyck-Healey Inc.; EBSCO Publishing, EBSCO Host; Gale; IngentaConnect; OCLC Online Computer Library Center, Inc.; OhioLINK; Ovid Technologies, Inc.; ProQuest LLC (Ann Arbor); Springer LINK; SwetsWise Online Content. Reprint: PSC. *Indexed:* ABIn, ArtHuCI, C&ISA, CCMJ, CerAb, CommAb, EngInd, IAA, IBR, IBSS, IBZ, IPB, IPSA, JEL, MSN, MathR, PSA, PhilInd, PsycInfo, RiskAb, SSA, SSCI, SociolAb. *Aud.:* Ac.

This interdisciplinary journal publishes highly technical articles on mathematical and computer science models; preference and uncertainty modeling; multicriteria decision making; social choice, negotiation, and group decision; game theory, gaming, and conflict analysis; rationality, cognitive processes, and interactive decision making; and methodology and philosophy of the social sciences. The journal attracts contributors on an international level from many fields, including philosophy, economics, management, statistics, operations research, finance, mathematics, psychology, and sociology. Recommended for graduate-level collections. URL: www.springerlink.com/openurl.asp?genre=journal&issn=0040-5833

4989. Utilitas. Formed by the merger of (1978-1988): *Bentham Newsletter;* (1965-1988): *Mill News Letter.* [ISSN: 0953-8208] 1988. q. GBP 154. Ed(s): Paul Kelly. Cambridge University Press, The Edinburgh Bldg, Shaftesbury Rd, Cambridge, CB2 2RU, United Kingdom; journals@cambridge.org; http://www.cup.cam.ac.uk/. Illus. Sample. Refereed. Circ: 900. Vol. ends: No. 3. Online: Pub.; EBSCO Publishing, EBSCO Host; SwetsWise Online Content. Reprint: PSC. *Indexed:* AmH&L, AmHI, HistAb, IBR, IBSS, IBZ, IPB, PhilInd. *Bk. rev.:* 5-10, 1,000-2,000 words. *Aud.:* Ac.

This journal, which is supported by the International Society for Utilitarian Studies, is a more polished publication than either of the newsletters that were its predecessors. The scope goes beyond utilitarianism's two greatest proponents (Jeremy Bentham and John Stuart Mill) and encompasses all aspects of utilitarian thought—its historical development, including its opponents, and contemporary utilitarian themes in ethics, politics, economics, jurisprudence, literature, and public policy. This is an important publication for collections that emphasize ethics (both historical and contemporary), political philosophy, and intellectual history. URL: www.utilitas.org.uk/index.shtml

■ PHOTOGRAPHY

Laurel Bliss, Assistant Librarian, Marquand Library of Art & Archaeology, Princeton University, Princeton, NJ 08544; lbliss@princeton.edu

Introduction

In December 2005, *Petersen's Photographic*, one of the best-known magazines in the field of popular photography, ceased publication. Its demise was due at least in part to the plethora of serials covering the same ground. Indeed, most photography magazines continue to feature equipment reviews, artist profiles, tips for the amateur user, and competitions. They must find new and different ways of distinguishing themselves from their competitors, be it taking a multidisciplinary approach or concentrating on a specific type of photography (nature, photojournalism, digital, etc.).

Plenty of print publications are also available online, and many have quite comprehensive web sites. But surprisingly, there are almost no electronic-only journals in this field. Perhaps even in this digital age, people still prefer to flip through glossy printed pages of stunning photographs rather than scroll and click through web pages.

Basic Periodicals

Hs: *Popular Photography & Imaging, Apogee Photo;* Ga: *Afterimage, Aperture, Popular Photography & Imaging, PC Photo;* Ac: *Afterimage, Aperture, Exposure, Photographer's Forum, Popular Photography & Imaging, Blind Spot.*

Basic Abstracts and Indexes

Imaging Abstracts.

4990. Afterimage: the journal of media arts and cultural criticism in the social and decision sciences. [ISSN: 0300-7472] 1972. bi-m. USD 66 (Individuals, USD 33). Visual Studies Workshop, 31 Prince St, Rochester, NY 14607. Illus., index. Sample. Circ: 10000. Vol. ends: May/Jun. Microform: PQC. Online: EBSCO Publishing, EBSCO Host; Factiva, Inc.; Florida Center for Library Automation; Gale; Northern Light Technology, Inc.; OCLC Online Computer Library Center, Inc.; ProQuest K-12 Learning Solutions; ProQuest LLC (Ann Arbor); H.W. Wilson. *Indexed:* ABM, AmHI, ArtInd, BRI, CBRI, FLI, MRD. *Bk. rev.:* 3-5, 1,500 words. *Aud.:* Hs, Ga, Ac.

Afterimage "provides a forum for the discussion and analysis of photography, independent film and video, alternative publishing, multi-media, and related fields." Typical issues contain notes from the field, feature articles on cultural issues, short reports on events, artist interviews, exhibition reviews, and lists of exhibitions by state/country. Its contributors are generally scholars, both experienced and new to the profession. This interdisciplinary journal is a great choice for academic collections, and of interest to large public libraries.

4991. Aperture. [ISSN: 0003-6420] 1952. q. USD 40 domestic; USD 65 foreign; USD 18.50 newsstand/cover per issue. Ed(s): Melissa Harris. Aperture Foundation, Inc., 547 W 27th St, 4th Fl, New York, NY 10001; magazine@apeture.org; http://www.aperture.org. Illus., adv. Circ: 17000. Microform: PQC. Online: OCLC Online Computer Library Center, Inc.; H.W. Wilson. *Indexed:* ABM, ABS&EES, AmHI, ArtHuCI, ArtInd, HumInd. *Aud.:* Hs, Ga, Ac.

Aperture is a beautifully produced publication with contributors ranging from artists to writers to scholars. Contents include exhibition reviews and close looks at individual photographers. Lavish illustrations, many of them full-page, add to the appeal. A superb showcase for artistic photography that is well worth the modest subscription price. Definitely appropriate for academic libraries, and of great interest to other collections.

4992. Apogee Photo. 1996. m. Ed(s): Susan Harris. Apogee Photo, Inc., 11749 Zenobia Loop., Westminster, CO 80031-7850; info@apogeephoto.com; http://www.apogeephoto.com/. *Bk. rev.:* Number and length vary. *Aud.:* Ems, Hs, Ga.

"A free online magazine designed to inform and entertain photographers of all ages and levels." Contains articles on such topics as photographing historic New Mexico and selecting a tripod, plus columns, products and services, contests, and a newsletter. Each article has a readers' index guide that indicates the appropriate audience, such as advanced amateurs, youngsters, etc. A great source for public libraries to bookmark or add to their online catalog.

4993. B & W Magazine: for collectors of fine photography. [ISSN: 1522-4805] 1999. bi-m. USD 34.95 domestic; USD 49.95 in Canada & Mexico; USD 59.95 elsewhere. B & W Magazine, PO Box 700, Arroyo Grande, CA 93421. Adv. Circ: 20000 Paid. *Bk. rev.:* Number and length vary. *Aud.:* Ga, Ac, Sa.

A glossy, stylish magazine for black-and-white photography enthusiasts. Each issue has approximately ten articles on individual photographers, with contact information and large reproductions of their work. Other sections include printing techniques, book reviews, and an artist forum called "Exposure." A good choice for large public and academic libraries.

4994. Blind Spot. [ISSN: 1068-1647] 1993. 3x/yr. USD 37 domestic; USD 50 Canada; USD 65 elsewhere. Ed(s): Dana Faconti. Blind Spot, Inc., 210 11th Ave, 10th Fl, New York, NY 10001; editors@blindspot.com. Illus., adv. *Indexed:* ArtInd. *Aud.:* Ga, Ac.

This high-quality, attractively produced journal is strictly a showcase for contemporary artistic photographs, with minimal ads. The goal is to provide "a forum for established and emerging artists to present unseen photo-based artwork." The journal's web site is simple and stylish, with a handy A-to-Z list of artists. Best for academic collections.

4995. Camerawork: a journal of photographic arts. Formerly: *S F Camerawork Quarterly.* [ISSN: 1087-8122] 1984. s-a. Membership, USD 40; Students, USD 30. Ed(s): Trena Noval. S F Camerawork, 1246 Folsom St, San Francisco, CA 94103; http://www.sfcamerawork.org. Adv. Circ: 2500. *Indexed:* ABM, ArtInd. *Bk. rev.:* 8, 150 words. *Aud.:* Ac, Sa.

This journal, distributed to Camerawork members, is "devoted to presenting quality reproductions and writing that reflect contemporary issues in the photographic arts." Content typically includes artist profiles, exhibition and book reviews, and a list of books received. Each issue has a theme, such as fame and celebrity culture, or landscape and art. For specialized collections only.

DoubleTake. See Literary Reviews section.

4996. Exposure (Oxford). [ISSN: 0098-8863] 1963. s-a. USD 35 domestic; USD 50 foreign. Ed(s): Carla Williams. Society for Photographic Education, The School for Interdisciplinary Studies, Miami University, Oxford, OH 45056; socphotoed@aol.com; http://spenational.org. Illus., adv. Refereed. Circ: 1700. *Indexed:* ABM, ArtInd. *Bk. rev.:* Number and length vary. *Aud.:* Ga, Ac, Sa.

A Spring 2006 redesign "to make all aspects of education its focus: studio practice, history, technology, and criticism" was in response to a reader survey and seems to have been successful. Contents include artist interviews, illustrated, scholarly essays, and book and exhibition reviews. A benefit of membership in the Society for Photographic Education, this journal is best for large academic libraries and specialized collections.

4997. History of Photography. [ISSN: 0308-7298] 1976. q. GBP 299. Ed(s): Graham Smith, Peggy Ann Kusnerz. Taylor & Francis Ltd., 4 Park Sq, Milton Park, Abingdon, OX14 4RN, United Kingdom; info@tandf.co.uk; http://www.tandf.co.uk/journals. Illus., adv. Sample. Refereed. Vol. ends: Winter. Online: EBSCO Publishing, EBSCO Host; Gale; IngentaConnect. Reprint: PSC. *Indexed:* ABM, AmH&L, AmHI, ArtHuCI, ArtInd, BAS, FR, HistAb, IBR, IBZ, RILM, SSCI. *Bk. rev.:* Number and length vary. *Aud.:* Ac.

As the name indicates, this journal focuses exclusively on academic explorations into the history of photography. A typical issue contains substantial book reviews and seven or eight lengthy articles with abstracts and footnotes. Contributors are faculty, curators, and art critics in the United Kingdom and the United States. Both the high cost and the scholarly content make this journal suitable only for academic institutions with a strong interest in photography as a historical and artistic discipline.

4998. News Photographer: dedicated to the service and advancement of news photography. Formerly (until 1974): *National Press Photographer.* [ISSN: 0199-2422] 1946. m. Free to members; Non-members, USD 48. Ed(s): Donald Winslow. National Press Photographers Association, Inc., 3200 Croasdaile Dr, Ste 306, Durham, NC 27705. Illus., adv. Sample. Circ: 11500 Paid and free. Vol. ends: Dec. Microform: PQC. Online: Factiva, Inc.; Florida Center for Library Automation; Northern Light Technology, Inc.; OCLC Online Computer Library Center, Inc.; ProQuest K-12 Learning Solutions. *Bk. rev.:* 3-4, 150 words. *Aud.:* Hs, Ga, Ac.

An official publication of the National Press Photographers Association, this heavily illustrated magazine looks at all aspects of photojournalism. Subscription is part of membership, but the journal can also be ordered separately. A recent cover story looks at the impact of a tornado and how local newspaper staff covered the disaster. Plenty of ads don't detract from the focus on human interest photos and the lives and careers of photojournalists. Carefully produced and of general interest.

4999. Outdoor Photographer: scenic - travel - wildlife - sports. [ISSN: 0890-5304] 1985. 10x/yr. USD 14.97 domestic; USD 29.97 foreign; USD 5.99 newsstand/cover per issue. Ed(s): Christopher Robinson, Rob Sheppard. Werner Publishing Corporation, 12121 Wilshire Blvd 1200, Los Angeles, CA 90025-1176; editors@outdoorphotographer.com; http://www.outdoorphotographer.com. Illus., adv. Sample. Circ: 215000 Paid. Vol. ends: Dec. *Aud.:* Ga.

One of this magazine's goals is "to stimulate outdoor, sporting and nature enthusiasts to enhance their recreational and travel enjoyment through photography." It features portfolio articles on photographers, a substantial how-to section, equipment guides, and a featured travel spot. Distinguished by its focus on nature, but otherwise very similar to other magazines for aficionados. Best for public libraries.

5000. P C Photo. [ISSN: 1094-1673] 9x/yr. USD 11.97 domestic; USD 26.97 foreign; USD 4.99 newsstand/cover per issue. Ed(s): Rob Sheppard. Werner Publishing Corporation, 12121 Wilshire Blvd 1200, Los Angeles, CA 90025-1176; pcphotomag@neodata.com. Adv. *Indexed:* MicrocompInd. *Aud.:* Hs, Ga.

This magazine focuses exclusively on amateur digital photography and takes "a fresh look at the modern photographic world by encouraging photography and the use of new technologies." Issues contain a plethora of equipment reviews, how-to pieces, interviews, and ads. The substantial companion web site has some articles from the print issues. Suitable for public libraries, particularly since the cessation of *Petersen's Photographic.*

5001. P S A Journal. [ISSN: 0030-8277] 1934. m. Membership, USD 45. Ed(s): Donna Brennan. Photographic Society of America, Inc., 3000 United Founders Blvd., Ste. 103, Oklahoma City, OK 73112-3940; hq@psa-photo.org; http://www.psa-photo.org. Illus., index, adv. Circ: 6500 Paid. Microform: PQC. Online: EBSCO Publishing, EBSCO Host; Florida Center for Library Automation; Gale; OCLC Online Computer Library Center, Inc.; ProQuest K-12 Learning Solutions; ProQuest LLC (Ann Arbor). *Indexed:* ChemAb. *Bk. rev.:* Number and length vary. *Aud.:* Hs, Ga.

This journal is geared toward members of the Photography Society of America, an amateur organization. Easily the most useful and unique feature of the publication is the services and activities section. Typical issues also include techniques, product evaluations, lists of exhibitions and events, conference information, book reviews, and short articles on travel and nature photography. A good choice for public libraries.

5002. Photo District News. Supersedes in part (in 198?): *Photo District News;* Which was formerly: *New York Photo District News.* [ISSN: 1045-8158] 1980. m. USD 65 domestic; USD 105 Canada; USD 125 elsewhere. Ed(s): Holly Hughes. Nielsen Business Publications, 770 Broadway, New York, NY 10003-9595; bmcomm@vnuinc.com; http://www.nielsenbusinessmedia.com. Circ: 33000 Paid. Online: EBSCO Publishing, EBSCO Host; Florida Center for Library Automation; Gale; ProQuest LLC (Ann Arbor). *Indexed:* ABIn. *Bk. rev.:* Number and length vary. *Aud.:* Ac, Sa.

This publication is a coffee table photography journal with practical applications for the polished photographer. It includes product reviews, competitions, a substantial news section, a calendar of events, and DVD and book picks of the month. Articles tend to profile professionals, such as "50 Photographers in 50 States" and "30 Emerging Photographers to Watch." Its robust web site boasts a free e-newsletter. With truly amazing photographs, this is a solid choice for large public and academic libraries.

5003. The Photo Review. Formerly: *Philadelphia Photo Review.* 1976. q. USD 42 domestic; USD 52 in Canada & Mexico; USD 60 in Europe & S. America. Ed(s): Stephen Perloff. The Photograph Collector, 140 E Richardson Ave, Ste 301, Langhorne, PA 19047-2884; info@photoreview.org. Illus. Circ: 2300 Paid. *Indexed:* ABM. *Bk. rev.:* Number and length vary. *Aud.:* Ac, Sa.

A short, scholarly publication that contains interviews, exhibition and book reviews, competitions, and a few articles analyzing individual photographers. A second-tier journal that is best for specialized collections.

5004. Photographer's Forum: magazine for the emerging professional. Formerly: *Student Forum.* [ISSN: 0194-5467] 1978. q. USD 15 domestic; USD 19 in Canada & Mexico; USD 22 elsewhere. Ed(s): Julie Simpson, Glen R Serbin. Serbin Communications, Inc., 813 Reddick St, Santa Barbara, CA 93103-3124; http://www.serbin.com. Illus. Sample. Circ: 18000. Vol. ends: Aug. *Indexed:* ABM. *Bk. rev.:* Number and length vary. *Aud.:* Ga, Ac.

This serious, scholarly publication "strives to facilitate communication and publication experience among emerging professionals." Typical issues consist of interviews with photojournalists, book reviews, product reviews, and a list of workshops. Minimal ads and quality paper help make it a journal worth hanging on to, particularly for academic libraries.

5005. *Photography Quarterly: journal for photography and related arts.* Formerly (until 1994): *Center Quarterly.* 1979. q. USD 25 domestic; USD 40 in Canada & Mexico; USD 45 elsewhere. Kenner Printing, 59 Tinker St, Woodstock, NY 12498-9984; info@cpw.org; http://www.cpw.org. Adv. Refereed. Circ: 10000. *Bk. rev.:* Number and length vary. *Aud.:* Sa.

This small publication recently moved to full-color issues, and has added a new competition, the Regional Triennial of the Photographic Arts, to showcase artists in the extended Hudson Valley region. Issues contain articles on topics such as contemporary photography and youth, as well as artist interviews, portfolios, noted books, and a few ads at the end of the publication. Best for regional collections and those interested in contemporary work.

5006. *Popular Photography & Imaging: the image of today.* Former titles (until 2003): *Popular Photography;* (until 1955): *Photography;* Incorporates (in 1989): *Modern Photography;* Which was formerly (1937-1949): *Minicam Photography.* [ISSN: 1542-0337] 1937. m. USD 14 domestic; USD 22 foreign; USD 4.50 newsstand/cover per issue. Ed(s): Mason Resnick, John Owens. Hachette Filipacchi Media U.S., Inc., 1633 Broadway, New York, NY 10019; http://www.hfmus.com. Illus., index, adv. Sample. Circ: 457132 Paid. Vol. ends: Dec. Microform: NBI; PQC. Online: The Dialog Corporation; Gale; OCLC Online Computer Library Center, Inc.; H.W. Wilson. *Indexed:* A&ATA, BRI, CBRI, ChemAb, ConsI, FLI, IHTDI, MASUSE, RGPR. *Bk. rev.:* Number and length vary. *Aud.:* Hs, Ga, Ac.

Arguably the best-known photography magazine today, *Popular Photography & Imaging* serves a broad audience of users. Key sections include tests and reviews, short photographer profiles, competitions, and quick tips and tricks, all designed to help the amateur camera enthusiast. Tons of ads make this flip-through magazine a great choice for public libraries; not so useful for the academic scene.

5007. *Professional Photographer.* Former titles (until 1999): *Professional Photographer Storytellers;* (until 1997): *The Professional Photographer;* (until 1963): *The National Professional Photographer;* Which supersedes (1934-1961): *The Professional Photographer.* [ISSN: 1528-5286] 1907. m. USD 27 domestic; USD 43 Canada; USD 63 elsewhere. Ed(s): Terry Murphy. P P A Publications and Events, Inc., 57 Forsyth St, NW, Ste 1600, Atlanta, GA 30303-2206. Illus., adv. Circ: 35000 Paid. *Indexed:* IHTDI. *Aud.:* Sa.

At the name says, this magazine is geared toward professional photographers and those wanting to break into the field. Contains news, events, tips on marketing your work, equipment tutorials, hot products, and award-winning photography by Professional Photographers of America members. Articles cover celebrity photographers and timely subjects like Katrina relief efforts by photographers. For specialized collections.

5008. *Shutterbug.* Formerly: *Shutterbug Ads.* [ISSN: 0895-321X] 1971. m. USD 17.95 domestic; USD 30.95 Canada; USD 32.95 elsewhere. Ed(s): Kevin McNutly. Source Interlink Companies, 261 Madison Ave., New York, NY 10016; edisupport@sourceinterlink.com; http://www.sourceinterlink.com. Illus., adv. Circ: 120000 Paid and controlled. *Indexed:* IHTDI. *Aud.:* Ga.

Subtitled "Tools, Techniques, and Creativity," *Shutterbug* focuses on equipment test reports, tips on organizing and processing digital images, and profiles of photo sites and photographers. Although ad-heavy, it does provide useful information in a format suitable for a general audience. The magazine's comprehensive web site is much easier to navigate than the magazine itself; it has archived issues and far fewer ads.

■ PHYSICS

David A. Tyckoson, Associate Dean, Henry Madden Library, California State University, Fresno, CA 93740

Introduction

Physics is one of the most basic of all of the sciences, concerning itself with the fundamental questions of the nature and function of the universe. Physicists often regard their discipline as the hardest of the hard sciences—the one on which all other fields of science are built. In its basic form, physics is the study of matter, motion, space, time, energy, and the forces that link them all together. What we now call physics was once known as "natural philosophy," the eighteenth-century name for the empirical study of the external world. Over the past three centuries, the field has expanded from describing the motions of everyday objects to attempting to explain the universe on its smallest (quantum) and its largest (astronomical) scales.

As physics has matured and evolved as a discipline, it has become highly specialized, developing a number of subdisciplines that could almost be treated as separate sciences in and of themselves. Areas such as acoustics, optics, gravitation, electromagnetism, mechanics, plasmas, particles, waves, quantum mechanics, astrophysics, nanotechnology, and the solid state are prime examples of this specialization. Researchers typically work within the confines of one of these subdisciplines and have little understanding of the details of the others.

Most physics journals report the results of original research and are highly specialized in nature. As the discipline of physics has been subdivided into smaller compartments, so have the journals. For example, the most significant journal in the field, *Physical Review,* was published as a single journal until 1969, but it is now distributed as ten distinct titles, three of which are available only electronically. In fact, another new section has been added since the last edition of *Magazines for Libraries.*

In addition to proliferating by sectionalizing, physics journals continue to grow tremendously in size. A single section of the *Physical Review* can contain tens of thousands of pages in one calendar year. There is more physics research being published today than at any time throughout history.

Because of the high degree of specialization in physics, a researcher in one subdiscipline has great difficulty reading and understanding the literature of another area. Physics journals reflect this specialization and are written for researchers, not the general public. Anyone with less than a graduate-level education in mathematics will probably be lost reading most of the articles contained in these journals. Even those journals that are written for a wider audience contain a fair amount of mathematics, requiring the reader to wade through integrals and differential equations to fully comprehend the concepts being discussed. These journals serve primarily as archives of the progress of physics research, recording for history the results of experimental and theoretical findings.

As a result of the high degree of specialization within the field and its reliance upon higher-level mathematics, very few researchers actually read the papers published in physics journals. In some cases, there may be only a dozen scientists worldwide who can truly understand the results of a given research project—and most of them probably are aware of the findings long before the paper is published in a physics journal. The journal serves primarily to document their progress and to establish precedent in scientific discovery. Physics journals have gone from primarily *communicating* research results to primarily *archiving* research results.

For the purposes of scholarly communication, physicists have long relied upon preprints, which are essentially drafts of articles that are released prior to publication. One of the very first uses of the Internet was to allow access to physics preprint collections. In contrast to the high cost of scholarly physics journals, these preprint services are usually free. ArXiv.org, based at Cornell University, contains free access to articles in physics, astronomy, and related disciplines. The SPIRES HEP service run by the Stanford Linear Accelerator Center (www.slac.stanford.edu/spires/hep) provides electronic access to articles on high-energy physics. Each of these services provides access to hundreds of thousands of research papers. Like physics journals, these databases are being subdivided into highly specialized subsections. The Stanford site also has started to provide links to review articles. Services such as this have already replaced journals as a means of communicating research results, and in the future may replace journals as publication media as well.

For many years, the premier journals in the field have been published by the major professional associations. The American Institute of Physics and the Institute of Physics in the United Kingdom are the two preeminent organizations in the field, and they publish the two most significant journals: the *Physical Review* and the *Journal of Physics,* respectively. Since these are association publications, their costs are somewhat lower than those of commercial journals (although prices are still in the thousands of dollars per year per section for both of these titles). These two organizations alone publish over half of all the titles on this list. National societies in other nations such as Japan and Canada publish similar journals.

European professional physics organizations have combined their efforts to produce the *European Physical Journal.* Despite the fact that many of these journals are published overseas, English has become the dominant language in the field of physics, and virtually every published article is written in English. As commercial publishers have merged over the past two decades, the publication of physics research journals has become concentrated in just a few publishing houses. Elsevier, Academic Press, and Taylor and Francis predominate in the commercial physics journal market.

Because of this extreme volume and specialization, the prices of physics journals are much higher than those in almost any other discipline. The least expensive journal in this list costs well over $100 per year, and it is common for subscriptions to cost over $1,000 per year. Subscriptions to some physics journals are upward of $10,000 per year. The only certainty with physics journals is that the number of papers published and the price of the publications will continue to increase.

Fortunately, electronic communications have changed the way that physics information is exchanged. In addition to the electronic equivalents of print publications, several peer-reviewed electronic physics journals are currently being published. The first such journal was the *New Journal of Physics,* a project of the Institute of Physics and its German equivalent. The *European Physical Journal* (*EPJ*) followed suit by creating the electronic *EPJ Direct,* and the American Institute of Physics started *Physical Review Focus* and the *Physical Review Special Topics* series. Each of these journals publishes or links to original research papers.

Another pricing model for physics journals that is currently being tested is the pay-per-article concept. The *Virtual Journals in Science and Technology* project of the American Institute of Physics uses this scheme. These journals, which cover five different specializations in the field of physics, do not publish original research papers. Instead, they bring together articles on these emerging fields from a wide range of parent journals. Libraries that subscribe to those journals are able to get the articles free. Articles from nonsubscribed journals are available for purchase on an individual basis, typically for a price of around $25.00.

Only libraries that support physics research programs should consider purchasing the majority of the titles on this list. Even then, the extremely high costs require librarians to be judicious in their choices. In many cases, it may be more cost-effective to order individual articles as requested by readers rather than to subscribe to specific journals. Any library that subscribes to more than just a couple of physics research journals will probably want to purchase those journals as part of a package. It is much less expensive to buy the complete online package of journals from most publishers, especially the associations, than it is to subscribe selectively to individual titles.

Physics Today and *Physics World* are the only two print physics journals that a public library should even consider buying. Most general readers will get their physics news from general-science magazines rather than from these more specialized titles. Fortunately, the free physics news services on the web—*Physical Review Focus* and *Physics News Preview*—will allow many libraries to offer their patrons access to interesting physics information written for a general audience at little or no cost.

The future of the printed physics journal is very much in doubt. As more and more such information becomes available on the web, researchers and students are getting most of their information in that format. If low-cost electronic journals prevail, libraries will be able to continue to build research collections in physics and the rest of the sciences. If journal costs continue to rise, more and more libraries will be unable to provide even basic physics research collections. Fortunately, those libraries that do not support physics research need only to subscribe to one or two of these titles.

Basic Periodicals

Hs: *American Journal of Physics, Physics Education, Physics Teacher, Physics Today;* Ga: *Optics and Photonics News, Physical Review Focus, Physics Today, Physics World;* Ac: *American Journal of Physics, Applied Physics Letters, Journal of Applied Physics, Journal of Physics, Physical Review, Physical Review Letters, Physics Letters, Physics Today.*

Basic Abstracts and Indexes

Physics Abstracts.

5009. *Acoustical Society of America. Journal.* [ISSN: 0001-4966] 1929. m. USD 1750 print & online eds. Ed(s): Allan D Pierce. Acoustical Society of America, 2 Huntington Quadrangle, Ste 1NO1, Melville, NY 11747-4502; asa@aip.org; http://asa.aip.org. Illus., index, adv. Refereed. Circ: 7800 Paid. Vol. ends: Jun/Dec. Online: American Institute of Physics, Scitation; EBSCO Publishing, EBSCO Host; OhioLINK; SwetsWise Online Content. *Indexed:* AS&TI, AgeL, AnBeAb, ApMecR, BiolAb, CPI, ChemAb, EngInd, EnvAb, ErgAb, ExcerpMed, HRIS, IAA, L&LBA, LingAb, M&GPA, MLA-IB, MathR, OceAb, PetrolAb, PsycInfo, RILM, SCI, SSCI, ZooRec. *Bk. rev.:* 1-3 per issue. *Aud.:* Ac, Sa.

As the primary official publication of the Acoustical Society of America, this title is the premier journal for the publication of research in the areas of sound waves, sound transmission, and acoustical phenomena. Subject coverage includes: linear and nonlinear acoustics; aeroacoustics, underwater sound, and acoustical oceanography; ultrasonics and quantum acoustics; noise control; architectural and structural acoustics and vibration; speech, music, and noise; the psychology and physiology of hearing; engineering acoustics, sound transducers, and measurements; and bioacoustics, animal bioacoustics, and bioresponse to vibration. Theoretical, experimental, and applied results are all included, along with comments on previously published articles and letters to the editor. Updates on patents, standards, and news of the association are also provided. Letters to the editor are published in the related *JASA Express Letters,* which is linked to the online version of the *Journal.* As the most comprehensive journal in the world on this branch of physics, the *Journal of the Acoustical Society of America* belongs in every physics collection.

5010. *Advances in Physics.* [ISSN: 0001-8732] 1952. 8x/yr. GBP 2637 print & online eds. Ed(s): David Sherrington. Taylor & Francis Ltd., 4 Park Sq, Milton Park, Abingdon, OX14 4RN, United Kingdom; info@tandf.co.uk; http://www.tandf.co.uk/journals. Illus., adv. Sample. Refereed. Circ: 1200. Vol. ends: Nov/Dec. Online: EBSCO Publishing, EBSCO Host; Gale; IngentaConnect; OCLC Online Computer Library Center, Inc.; SwetsWise Online Content. Reprint: PSC. *Indexed:* C&ISA, CerAb, ChemAb, EngInd, IAA, MathR, SCI. *Aud.:* Ac, Sa.

Advances in Physics publishes state-of-the-art critical reviews in the field of condensed-matter physics. These reviews present the current state of human knowledge within this highly specialized subfield of physics and serve as benchmarks in our knowledge of the physical universe. They are written for readers with a basic knowledge of condensed matter physics who want to learn more about specific research areas within that field. Because of the comprehensiveness of the research, most papers in this journal are very long, often over 100 pages each. Many issues consist of a single article that essentially serves as a monograph on the topic under consideration. One of the key features of each article is its bibliography, which lists all the important past research on the topic under consideration. A new section has been added that publishes shorter but provocative articles written by leaders in the field. These articles, called "Perspectives," are intended to be controversial and to promote debate. *Annals of Physics, Contemporary Physics,* and *Reports on Progress in Physics* (all below in this section) also publish review articles, but these journals are all aimed at the nonspecialist. *Advances in Physics* is written for the specialized researcher or student of condensed matter and will only be of marginal value to the nonspecialist or to scientists working in other disciplines.

5011. *American Journal of Physics.* Formerly (until 1940): *American Physics Teacher.* [ISSN: 0002-9505] 1933. m. USD 535 print & online eds. Ed(s): Jan Tobochnik. American Association of Physics Teachers,

One Physics Ellipse, College Park, MD 20740-3845; aapt-pubs@ aapt.org; http://www.aapt.org. Illus., index, adv. Sample. Refereed. Circ: 6681 Paid and free. Vol. ends: Dec. Online: American Institute of Physics, Scitation; EBSCO Publishing, EBSCO Host; OhioLINK; SwetsWise Online Content. *Indexed:* AS&TI, ArtHuCI, CCMJ, CPI, ChemAb, GSI, MSN, MathR, PhilInd, RILM, SCI, SSCI. *Bk. rev.:* Number and length vary. *Aud.:* Hs, Ga, Ac.

While most physics journals serve solely as archives of original research results, the *American Journal of Physics* exists to help teachers do a better job of instructing students about physics. As the official journal of the American Association of Physics Teachers, this title is devoted to the instructional and cultural aspects of the physical sciences. Rather than concentrating on new research results, this journal focuses on methods of teaching physics to students at the college level. It consists of articles on applying educational theories to physics teaching, using innovative methodologies to demonstrate physical properties, using demonstrations and experiments to convey physics principles, and introducing new apparatus and equipment. The editors particularly encourage articles that discuss already published research that can be applied directly or indirectly in the classroom. Papers on the historical, philosophical, and cultural nature of physics are also included. In addition to full papers, the journal also publishes letters, notes, book reviews, and editorials. The reliance of physics on experimentation is covered by a section of "apparatus and demonstration notes." Occasional articles on research in physics education are also included. While high copyright fees are charged by most physics journals, in this journal readers are encouraged to copy the articles and ideas and use them in the classroom. All libraries that support college physics courses should subscribe to this title.

5012. *Annalen der Physik.* Former titles (until 1799): *Neues Journal der Physik;* (until 1795): *Journal der Physik.* [ISSN: 0003-3804] 1790. 10x/yr. EUR 815. Ed(s): Ulrich Eckern. Wiley - VCH Verlag GmbH & Co. KGaA, Boschstr 12, Weinheim, 69469, Germany; subservice@wiley-vch.de; http://www.wiley-vch.de. Illus., index. Sample. Refereed. *Indexed:* CCMJ, ChemAb, EngInd, MSN, MathR, SCI. *Bk. rev.:* Occasional. *Aud.:* Ac, Sa.

As the oldest continuously published German physics journal, *Annalen der Physik* occupies a historic place in the physics literature. The journal publishes original papers in the areas of experimental, theoretical, applied, and mathematical physics, and related areas. Throughout its long history, it has published some of the most important papers in the field, including the original work of Planck, Rontgen, and Einstein. Unlike many other long-standing journals, this title continues to cover the entire field of physics rather than specializing in a particular subdiscipline. In addition to original research papers, the journal also frequently publishes review articles. Even though it is a German journal, all of the articles of the past hew years have been published in English. Although it has been surpassed in prestige by several other prominent physics journals, such as *Journal of Physics* and the *Physical Review* (see below), *Annalen der Physik* is still an important component of any comprehensive physics collection.

5013. *Annals of Physics.* [ISSN: 0003-4916] 1957. 12x/yr. EUR 6688. Ed(s): Frank Wilczek. Academic Press, 525 B St, Ste 1900, San Diego, CA 92101-4495; apsubs@acad.com; http://www.elsevier.com/. Illus., index, adv. Sample. Refereed. Online: EBSCO Publishing, EBSCO Host; Gale; IngentaConnect; OCLC Online Computer Library Center, Inc.; OhioLINK; ScienceDirect; SwetsWise Online Content. *Indexed:* CCMJ, ChemAb, IAA, MSN, MathR, SCI. *Aud.:* Ac, Sa.

Unlike most physics research journals, which publish brief reports of original research aimed at the specialist in the field, *Annals of Physics* presents original work in all areas of basic physics research. The journal publishes papers on particular topics spanning theory, methodology, and applications. It emphasizes clarity and intelligibility in the articles it publishes, thus making them as accessible as possible. Readers familiar with recent developments in the field are provided with sufficient detail and background to follow the arguments and understand their significance. Because of the emphasis on extensive background material, the articles in this journal are very long, often more than 50 pages. *Contemporary Physics, Reports on Progress in Physics,* and *Reviews of Modern Physics* (all below in this section) all serve the same general purpose as *Annals of Physics,* and each is useful for a college-level physics collection.

5014. *Applied Optics.* Formed by the merger of (1990-2004): *Applied Optics. Information Processing;* (1995-2004): *Applied Optics. Optical Technology and Biomedical Optics;* (1991-2004): *Applied Optics. Lasers, Photonics, and Environmental Optics;* All of which superseded (1962-1990): *Applied Optics.* [ISSN: 1559-128X] 1962. 36x/yr. USD 3125 (Individuals, USD 219 print & online eds.). Ed(s): James C Wyant. Optical Society of America, 2010 Massachusetts Ave, NW, Washington, DC 20036-1023; info@osa.org; http://www.osa.org. Illus., index, adv. Refereed. Circ: 4000. Online: EBSCO Publishing, EBSCO Host; OhioLINK. *Indexed:* AS&TI, BioEngAb, C&ISA, ChemAb, EngInd, ExcerpMed, M&GPA, OceAb, PhotoAb, SCI, SSCI, SWRA. *Aud.:* Ac, Sa.

Along with the *Journal of the Optical Society of America* and *Optics Letters* (see below), *Applied Optics* is one of the official journals of the Optical Society of America. While the other two titles publish reports of original research, this journal concentrates on the applications of optical principles and methods. As such, it is the most widely read journal in the field of optics. It is published in four sections, each representing one major division of the society. The first section covers optical technology, including instrumentation, x-ray optics, micro-optics, thin films, and optical materials. The second section covers information processing, including optical communications, data storage, optical computing, pattern recognition, and signal processing. The third section focuses on lasers, photonics, and environmental optics, covering such topics as remote sensing, atmospheric optics, lasers, and scattering. The final section covers biomedical optics, including instrumentation, microscopy, fiber optic sensors, and interferometry. In addition to full-length papers, the journal provides a calendar of events of interest to members and occasional notes on equipment and methodologies. This is one of the core journals in the field of optics, and it belongs in any physics or engineering research collection.

5015. *Applied Physics A: materials science & processing.* Former titles: *Applied Physics A: Solids and Surfaces;* Supersedes in part (in 1981): *Applied Physics;* Which superseded: *Zeitschrift fuer Angewandte Physik.* [ISSN: 0947-8396] 1973. 16x/yr. EUR 4298 print & online eds. Ed(s): Michael Stuke. Springer, Tiergartenstr 17, Heidelberg, 69121, Germany. Illus., adv. Refereed. Microform: PQC. Online: EBSCO Publishing, EBSCO Host; OhioLINK; Springer LINK; SwetsWise Online Content. Reprint: PSC. *Indexed:* ChemAb, EngInd, IAA, PhotoAb, SCI. *Aud.:* Ac, Sa.

Applied Physics is a monthly journal for the rapid publication of experimental and theoretical investigations in applied research. It is issued in two sections. *Part A* primarily covers the condensed state, including nanostructured materials and their applications. It publishes full-length articles and short, rapid communications. Many of the issues are devoted to papers on a single topic, often presenting the proceedings of relevant conferences or Festschriften. This journal is published in cooperation with the German Physical Society and was originally published under its German title, *Zeitschrift fuer Angewandte Physik.* Much of the research reported in this title is still conducted in German universities and research centers. However, following the movement toward English as the international language of science, all of the papers accepted are published in English. *Part B* (0721-7269) covers lasers and optics, including laser physics, linear and nonlinear optics, ultrafast phenomena, photonic devices, optical and laser materials, quantum optics, laser spectroscopy of atoms, molecules and clusters, and the use of laser radiation in chemistry and biochemistry. For libraries that seek a comprehensive physics collection, the two sections of this journal will serve as a European complement to the *Journal of Applied Physics* (below).

5016. *Applied Physics Letters.* [ISSN: 0003-6951] 1962. w. USD 3060 print & online eds. Ed(s): Nghi Q Lam. American Institute of Physics, 2 Huntington Quadrangle, Ste 1NO1, Melville, NY 11747-4502; aipinfo@ aip.org; http://www.aip.org. Illus., index, adv. Refereed. Online: American Institute of Physics, Scitation; EBSCO Publishing, EBSCO Host; OhioLINK; SwetsWise Online Content. *Indexed:* AS&TI, CPI, ChemAb, EngInd, PhotoAb, SCI. *Aud.:* Ac, Sa.

This title serves as the letters section of the *Journal of Applied Physics* (below in this section). As such, it provides for the rapid dissemination of key data and physical insights, including new experimental and theoretical findings on the applications of physics to all branches of science, engineering, and technology.

Topics covered by this journal include lasers and optics; nanotechnology; plasmas; semiconductors; magnetic devices; applied biophysics; and interdisciplinary research. Because all of the papers accepted are letters, they are extremely brief, with none longer than three printed pages. In addition to original research results, each issue also includes comments on previously published material. This can result in lively debate over the accuracy and interpretation of experimental results. Along with the accompanying *Journal of Applied Physics,* this title is the most heavily cited journal in the field. It is one of the core journals for physics and belongs in any physics research collection.

Biophysical Journal. See Biology/Biochemistry and Biophysics section.

5017. Canadian Journal of Physics. [ISSN: 0008-4204] 1929. m. CND 641 (Individuals, CND 165). Ed(s): Gordon Drake. N R C Research Press, National Research Council of Canada, Ottawa, ON K1A 0R6, Canada; pubs@nrc-cnrc.gc.ca; http://pubs.nrc-cnrc.gc.ca. Illus., index, adv. Refereed. Circ: 777. Vol. ends: Dec. Microform: MML; PMC; PQC. Online: EBSCO Publishing, EBSCO Host; Gale; IngentaConnect; Micromedia ProQuest; OCLC Online Computer Library Center, Inc.; Ovid Technologies, Inc.; ProQuest K-12 Learning Solutions; ProQuest LLC (Ann Arbor); SwetsWise Online Content; H.W. Wilson. *Indexed:* AS&TI, C&ISA, CBCARef, CPerI, CerAb, ChemAb, DSA, EngInd, IAA, M&GPA, MathR, PetrolAb, PhotoAb, SCI, SSCI. *Aud.:* Ac, Sa.

As an official publication of the National Research Council of Canada, the *Canadian Journal of Physics* is the premier physics publication emanating from that nation. It covers all branches of physics, including atomic and molecular physics; condensed matter; elementary particles and nuclear physics; gases; fluid dynamics and plasmas; electromagnetism and optics; mathematical physics; and interdisciplinary, classical, and applied physics. Most of the articles are published in English, although French-language articles are also accepted. The majority of articles are full research reports, although shorter rapid communications and research notes are also accepted. The journal also occasionally publishes review articles and tutorials that bring together and explain previously published research results. Some issues consist entirely of proceedings of physics conferences. Supplemental data or other material is available to subscribers on the journal web site. Although this journal is an official publication of the Canadian government, it is not restricted to Canadian authors, and it attracts research reports from around the world. This is the major Canadian journal in physics and should be part of any comprehensive physics research collection.

5018. Chaos: an interdisciplinary journal of nonlinear science. [ISSN: 1054-1500] 1991. q. USD 690 print & online eds. Ed(s): David K Campbell. American Institute of Physics, 1 Physics Ellipse, College Park, MD 20740-3843; aipinfo@aip.org; http://www.aip.org. Refereed. Online: American Institute of Physics, Scitation; EBSCO Publishing, EBSCO Host; OhioLINK; SwetsWise Online Content. *Indexed:* AS&TI, ApMecR, CCMJ, CPI, MSN, MathR, SCI. *Aud.:* Ac, Sa.

While most of physics seeks to describe the universe in an orderly fashion, some processes and systems do not flow in that way. Chaos theory is a way to make sense of nonlinear processes. The journal *Chaos* is devoted to this subject. This journal covers the most recent developments in nonlinear science, including contributions from physics, mathematics, chemistry, biology, engineering, economics, and social sciences. It publishes articles related to the methods of computation, theory, and experimentation. In addition to full-length peer-reviewed articles, it also includes letters, brief reports, and technical reviews. Every other issue includes one review article on a topic of interest to the field. In addition, occasional articles that are aimed at the teaching of chaos theory are provided. This journal covers an interesting and unique subdiscipline of physics and it belongs in any collection that supports research in this area.

5019. Communications in Mathematical Physics. [ISSN: 0010-3616] 1965. 24x/yr. EUR 4685 print & online eds. Ed(s): Dr. M Aizenman. Springer, Tiergartenstr 17, Heidelberg, 69121, Germany. Illus., index, adv. Sample. Refereed. Microform: PQC. Online: EBSCO Publishing, EBSCO Host; OhioLINK; Springer LINK; SwetsWise Online Content. Reprint: PSC. *Indexed:* CCMJ, MSN, MathR, SCI. *Aud.:* Ac, Sa.

The field of physics relies heavily on high-level mathematics as a tool for developing new theories and in explaining experimental results. Whether attempting to explain the nature of fundamental particles, exploring the heavens, or defining the motion of an apple, physicists always attempt to explain natural phenomena as mathematical functions. *Communications in Mathematical Physics* was developed in order to present physicists with a source for learning new mathematical techniques and presenting new research findings. It also attempts to generate among mathematicians an increased awareness of and appreciation for the current problems in physics. All branches of physics are covered, although particular emphasis is placed on statistical physics, quantum theory, string theory, dynamical systems, atomic physics, relativity, and disordered systems. The common thread among all the papers is the strong mathematical approach to the problem. This journal complements the *Journal of Mathematical Physics* (see below) and belongs in comprehensive physics collections.

5020. Computer Physics Communications. [ISSN: 0010-4655] 1969. 24x/yr. Elsevier BV, North-Holland, Sara Burgerhartstraat 25, Amsterdam, 1055 KV, Netherlands; nlinfo-f@elsevier.nl; http://www.elsevier.nl/homepage/about/us/regional_sites.htt. Illus., index, adv. Sample. Refereed. Online: EBSCO Publishing, EBSCO Host; Gale; IngentaConnect; OhioLINK; ScienceDirect; SwetsWise Online Content. *Indexed:* C&ISA, CCMJ, CerAb, ChemAb, CompLI, CompR, EngInd, IAA, MSN, MathR, SCI. *Aud.:* Ac, Sa.

Computer Physics Communications is an international interdisciplinary journal that deals with the applications of computing to physics and physical chemistry. Specific topics covered include computational models in physics and physical chemistry; computer programs in physics and physical chemistry; computational models and programs associated with the design, control, and analysis of experiments; numerical methods and algorithms; algebraic computation; the impact of advanced computer architecture and special purpose computers on computing in the physical sciences; software topics, including programming environments, languages, data bases, expert systems, and graphics packages; and analysis of computer systems performance. In addition, subscribers have access to a web site containing a program library of actual computer software that may be used for these purposes. This arrangement eliminates many of the problems of publishing actual program code. Most of the older programs in the library were written in FORTRAN for mainframe systems, while newer entries tend to be PC-based and run under Windows, UNIX, or Linux. Some are available in other scientific programming languages, including Maple and Mathematica. When new versions of existing programs are developed, announcements are included in this journal. With the program library, researchers are able to duplicate or modify experiments that would be otherwise difficult to conduct. Each issue of the journal is evenly divided between articles and program descriptions. This journal is unique in providing not only original research articles, but also the research tools used in compiling the information.

5021. Contemporary Physics. [ISSN: 0010-7514] 1959. bi-m. GBP 647 print & online eds. Ed(s): P L Knight. Taylor & Francis Ltd., 4 Park Sq, Milton Park, Abingdon, OX14 4RN, United Kingdom; info@tandf.co.uk; http://www.tandf.co.uk/journals. Illus., index, adv. Refereed. Vol. ends: Nov/Dec. Microform: MIM; PMC. Online: EBSCO Publishing, EBSCO Host; Gale; IngentaConnect; OCLC Online Computer Library Center, Inc.; SwetsWise Online Content. Reprint: PSC. *Indexed:* ChemAb, ExcerpMed, GSI, IAA, PhotoAb, SCI. *Bk. rev.:* 5-15 per issue, varying length. *Aud.:* Ac, Sa.

Contemporary Physics has a unique place in the spectrum of physics journals. Although written primarily for physicists, the articles appearing in this journal have more background material and are more accessible to a wider scientific audience. Each article attempts to explain the essential physical concepts of each topic and to relate those concepts to more familiar aspects of physics. Because of this emphasis, students and scientists in other scientific disciplines can use this journal to learn about important developments in the field of physics. Readers in the physical sciences, biology, or engineering should be able to comprehend the articles in this journal. It is especially useful for students and teaching assistants. A feature of interest to librarians is that in addition to the review articles, the journal publishes dozens of reviews of books in physics and related fields. *Contemporary Physics* is the most readable of all of the physics review journals and belongs in every college physics collection.

5022. *Critical Reviews in Solid State & Materials Sciences.* Former titles: *C R C Critical Reviews in Solid State and Materials Sciences; C R C Critical Reviews in Solid State Sciences.* [ISSN: 1040-8436] 1970. q. GBP 543 print & online eds. Ed(s): Wolfgang Sigmund, Paul Holloway. Taylor & Francis Inc., 325 Chestnut St, Ste 800, Philadelphia, PA 19016; orders@taylorandfrancis.com; http://www.taylorandfrancis.com. Illus., index. Refereed. Circ: 570. Reprint: PSC. *Indexed:* C&ISA, CerAb, ChemAb, EngInd, IAA, SCI. *Aud.:* Ac, Sa.

Like all journals in the *Critical Reviews* series, this journal publishes only invited papers on topics related to materials science and the solid state. Topics covered include advanced processing techniques for new materials; analysis of solid composition, bonding, structure, and topography; deposition techniques; diffusion and defects; electrical, optical, magnetic, and thermal properties of new organic and inorganic materials; experimental techniques for characterization of materials and materials properties; interfaces in the solid state; mechanical properties of low-dimensional solids; nanoparticle processing and properties; nucleation and growth in formation of the solid state; optical spectroscopy of solids; physics, chemistry, and theory of the solid state; processing issues in thin-film microelectronic and optoelectronic semiconductor devices; quantum effects; solid-state band structure; solid-state energy sources; and theoretical modeling of solid-state dynamics. Each issue usually contains a single article, often hundreds of pages in length, that provides a comprehensive survey of the topic being discussed. These state-of-the-art reviews serve as benchmarks in the progress of solid-state physics and materials research. Each article contains an extensive bibliography of other research in the field. Although other journals also publish review articles, this one is unique in that it evaluates as well as compiles. Authors of papers here are expected to give their expert opinions on the value of previously published research results, guiding the reader to those that will have the greatest relevance and impact. This title is essential for any collection that supports research in materials science or the solid state. Libraries should also consider other titles in CRC Press's *Critical Reviews* series if those titles support the research interests of the library.

5023. *Cryogenics.* [ISSN: 0011-2275] 1960. 12x/yr. EUR 2374. Ed(s): S W Van Sciver, Tomiyoshi Haruyama. Pergamon, The Boulevard, Langford Ln, East Park, Kidlington, OX5 1GB, United Kingdom. Illus., index, adv. Sample. Refereed. Vol. ends: Dec (No. 41). Microform: PQC. Online: EBSCO Publishing, EBSCO Host; Gale; IngentaConnect; OhioLINK; ScienceDirect; SwetsWise Online Content. *Indexed:* AS&TI, ApMecR, BioEngAb, BrTechI, C&ISA, CEA, CerAb, ChemAb, EngInd, IAA, IBR, SCI. *Bk. rev.:* Number and length vary. *Aud.:* Ac, Sa.

Cryogenics is the world's leading journal focusing on all aspects of cryoengineering and cryogenics. Papers published here cover a wide variety of subjects in low-temperature engineering and research. Topics covered include applications of superconductivity: magnets, electronics, devices; superconductors and their properties; properties of materials; new applications of cryogenic technology; refrigeration and liquefaction technology; thermodynamics; fluid properties and fluid mechanics; heat transfer; thermometry and measurement science; cryogenics in medicine; and cryoelectronics. The majority of the publication consists of full-length research papers, although some shorter research notes and technical notes are also included. Conference reports and review articles are published on an occasional basis, in addition to book reviews, news features, and a calendar of events relevant to the field. As the premier journal for low-temperature studies, this journal belongs in any physics or engineering collection that supports research in this field.

5024. *European Journal of Physics.* [ISSN: 0143-0807] 1980. bi-m. USD 990 print & online eds. Ed(s): A I M Rae. Institute of Physics Publishing, Dirac House, Temple Back, Bristol, BS1 6BE, United Kingdom; custserv@iop.org; http://www.iop.org. Illus., index, adv. Sample. Refereed. Vol. ends: Nov. Online: EBSCO Publishing, EBSCO Host; Gale; IngentaConnect; OhioLINK; SwetsWise Online Content. *Indexed:* CCMJ, ChemAb, EngInd, MSN, MathR, SCI. *Aud.:* Ga, Ac, Sa.

As "the European voice of physics teachers in higher education," the *European Journal of Physics* publishes articles of relevance to physics students and faculty. The primary mission of the journal is to assist in maintaining and

improving the standard of physics taught in universities and other institutions of higher education. Thus, it contains articles on topics relating to the fundamentals of physics education; pedagogical studies on specific topics within physics and physics teaching; educational policies in physics and their implementation; cultural, historical, social, and technological implications of physics; and the interrelationships between physics and other disciplines. Because the papers are intended to aid in the teaching of the subject rather than to present original research results, the editors encourage authors to avoid high-level mathematics, thus making the papers more accessible to a general audience. Although articles may be submitted in any of the major European languages, almost every article published is in English. Full papers and letters are accepted, along with comments on previously published works. Some articles have accompanying multimedia content that is available through the web site. Occasional special issues follow specific themes. This title is the European equivalent of the *American Journal of Physics* (above) and is a useful supplement to a college or university physics collection.

5025. *European Physical Journal A. Hadrons and Nuclei (Print Edition).* Incorporates (2004-2006): *Acta Physica Hungarica. B. Quantum Electronics;* (1951-2006): *Acta Physica Hungarica. A. Heavy Ion Physics;* Which was formerly (until 1994): *Acta Physica Hungarica;* (until 1982): *Acta Physica Academiae Scientiarum Hungaricae;* (until 1949): *Hungarica Acta Physica;* Incorporated in part (1903-2000): *Anales de Fisica;* (1855-1999): *Societa Italiana di Fisica. Nuovo Cimento. A. Nuclei, Particles and Fields;* Which was formerly (until 1982): *Societa Italiana di Fisica. Nuovo Cimento A;* (until 1971): *Nuovo Cimento A;* Which superseded in part (in 1965): *Nuovo Cimento;* Former titles (until 1997): *Zeitschrift fuer Physik A. Hadrons and Nuclei;* (until 1991): *Zeitschrift fuer Physik. Section A. Atomic Nuclei;* (until 1986): *Zeitschrift fuer Physik. Section A: Atoms and Nuclei; Zeitschrift fuer Physik.* [ISSN: 1434-6001] 1920. m. EUR 2998 print & online eds. Ed(s): Thomas Walcher. Springer, Tiergartenstr 17, Heidelberg, 69121, Germany. Illus., adv. Refereed. Microform: PMC; PQC. Online: EBSCO Publishing, EBSCO Host; OhioLINK; Springer LINK; SwetsWise Online Content. Reprint: PSC. *Indexed:* ChemAb, MathR, SCI. *Aud.:* Ac, Sa.

In 1998, the German, French, and Italian Physical Societies decided to merge their individual journals into a single publication. The *European Physical Journal* in all six of its parts is the result of that merger. Ten other national physics societies of other European nations have since added their sponsorship to these journals, giving them even greater status. *Part A* of this new endeavor directly replaces the former *Zeitschrift fuer Physik A* and *Il Nuovo Cimento A*. It covers the specialized subfield of high-energy physics relating to hadrons and nuclei, including nuclear structure, nuclear reactions, heavy-ion physics, weak interactions, and related interdisciplinary topics. The common framework of these systems is that they are few- and many-body systems bound by strong interactions. This description can be compared to *Part C*, which emphasizes the elementary aspects of particles and fields. Articles presenting experimental results, including methods and instruments, are published along with theoretical papers. Both full-length research papers and short research notes are included. Although this is a European journal, all of the articles are in English. The *European Physical Journal* is now the premier physics journal published on the continent, and it belongs in all physics research collections. Also available in an online edition.

5026. *European Physical Journal B. Condensed Matter.* Incorporates in part (1903-2000): *Anales de Fisica;* Formed by the merger of (1963-1998): *Journal de Physique I;* Which was formerly (until 1991): *Journal de Physique;* (until 1962): *Jopurnal de Physique et le Radium;* (1963-1998): *Zeitschrift fuer Physik B: Condensed Matter;* Which was formerly (until 1980): *Zeitschrift fuer Physik B (Condensed Matter and Quanta);* (until 1973): *Physik der Kondensierten Materie - Physique de la Matiere Condensee - Physics of Condensed Matter;* (1771-1998): *Societa Italiana di Fisica. Nuovo Cimento D;* Which superseded in part (in 1982): *Nuovo Cimento;* Which was formerly (until 1885): *Il Cimento;* (until 1843): *Miscellanee di Chimica, Fisica e Storia Naturale;* Which superseded in part (in 1843): *Giornale Toscano di Scienze Mediche Fisiche e Naturali;* Which was formerly (until 1840): *Nuovo Giornale dei Letterati;* (until 1822): *Accademia Italiana di Scienze Lettere ed Arti. Giornale Scientifico e Letterario;* (until 1810): *Giornale Pisano di*

Letteratura, Scienze ed Arti; (until 1807): *Giornale Pisano dei Letterati;* (until 1806): *Nuovo Giornale dei Letterati;* (until 1820): *Giornale dei Letterati.* [ISSN: 1434-6028] 1998. s-m. EUR 4353 print & online eds. Ed(s): Petra Rudolf, Hans Ott. Springer, Tiergartenstr 17, Heidelberg, 69121, Germany. Illus., index, adv. Refereed. Microform: PMC; PQC. Online: EBSCO Publishing, EBSCO Host; OhioLINK; Springer LINK; SwetsWise Online Content. Reprint: PSC. *Indexed:* CCMJ, ChemAb, EngInd, MSN, MathR, SCI. *Aud.:* Ac, Sa.

Part B of the *European Physical Journal* concentrates on solid-state physics, covering such topics as solid- and condensed-state physics; quantum solids and liquids; mesoscopic and nanoscale physics; fluids; surfaces and interfaces; nonlinear physics; and statistical physics. Although the main focus is on the solid state, this section also contains articles on mathematical structures, statistical physics, and interdisciplinary topics. The majority of the articles are full-length research reports, although some rapid notes of important findings are also published. All of the articles are published in English. In order to speed publication, many of the articles are published in the *Online First* electronic delivery service before appearing in print. As the official publication of 13 different European physics societies, this title belongs in any comprehensive physics collection.

5027. *European Physical Journal C. Particles and Fields (Print Edition).*
Incorporates in part (1903-2000): *Anales de Fisica;* (1855-1999): *Societa Italiana di Fisica. Nuovo Cimento. A. Nuclei, Paticles and Fields;* Which was formerly (until 1982): *Societa Italiana di Fisica. Nuovo Cimento. A;* (until 1971): *Nuovo Cimento A;* Which superseded in part (in 1965): *Nuovo Cimento;* Formerly (until 1997): *Zeitschrift fuer Physik C. Particles and Fields.* [ISSN: 1434-6044] 1979. 20x/yr. EUR 4998 print & online eds. Ed(s): Dorothea Bartels, D Haidt. Springer, Tiergartenstr 17, Heidelberg, 69121, Germany. Illus., index, adv. Sample. Refereed. Microform: PMC; PQC. Online: EBSCO Publishing, EBSCO Host; OhioLINK; Springer LINK; SwetsWise Online Content. Reprint: PSC. *Indexed:* CCMJ, ChemAb, MSN, MathR, SCI. *Aud.:* Ac, Sa.

As another section of the reorganized physics journals published in Europe, *Section C* of the *European Physical Journal* covers high-energy physics, including both theoretical and experimental research. It emphasizes the elementary aspects of particles and fields and specializes in reporting research results from the world's leading laboratories, including CERN, Fermilab, and KEK. Topics covered include the standard model; quantum chromodynamics; heavy-ion physics; astroparticle physics; hadron and lepton collisions; high-energy nuclear reactions; neutrino physics; high-energy cosmic rays; and dark matter. This section of the journal is the continuation of *Il Nuovo Cimento A* and *Zeitschrift fuer Physik C*. Full-length articles, rapid notes, reviews, and letters are all included. Occasional issues contain the proceedings of relevant conferences. Although this is a European journal, all of the articles are published in English. This is the premier journal for European research in particle physics, and it belongs in comprehensive physics collections. Also available in an online edition.

5028. *European Physical Journal D. Atomic, Molecular, Optical and Plasma Physics.* Incorporates in part (1903-2000): *Anales de Fisica;* Formed by the merger of (1991-1998): *Journal de Physique II;* (1986-1998): *Zeitschrift fuer Physik D. Atoms, Molecules and Clusters;* Supersedes in part (1982-1999): *Societa Italiana di Fisica. Nuovo Cimento D;* Which incorporated in part (1855-1965): *Nuovo Cimento;* Which superseded (1843-1847): *Cimento; Miscellanee de Chimica, Fisica e Storia Naturale;* Which superseded in part (in 1843): *Giornale Toscano di Scienze Mediche Fisiche e Naturali;* (until 1840): *Nuovo Giornale dei Letterati;* Which superseded (in 1822): *Accademia Italiana di Scienze Lettere ed Arti. Giornale Scientifico e Letterario;* (until 1809): *Giornale Pisano di Letteratura, Scienze ed Arti;* (until 1807): *Giornale Pisano dei Letterati;* (1802-1806): *Nuovo Giornale dei Letterati;* Which superseded (1771-1796): *Giornale dei Letterati.* [ISSN: 1434-6060] 1998. 15x/yr. EUR 2395 print & online eds. Ed(s): Jean-Michel

Raimond, Franco A Gianturco. Springer, Tiergartenstr 17, Heidelberg, 69121, Germany. Illus., index, adv. Refereed. Circ: 700. Online: EBSCO Publishing, EBSCO Host; OhioLINK; Springer LINK; SwetsWise Online Content. Reprint: PSC. *Indexed:* CCMJ, ChemAb, MSN, MathR, SCI. *Aud.:* Ac, Sa.

The fourth section of the *European Physical Journal* is devoted to atomic, molecular, plasma, and optical physics. This journal was formed through the combination of three similar journals: *Il Nuovo Cimento D, Journal de Physique,* and *Zeitschrift fuer Physik D.* Topics in this section include atomic structures and spectra; molecular interaction and reactivity; atomic and molecular collisions; clusters and nanostructures; plasma physics; laser cooling and quantum gas; nonlinear dynamics; optical physics; quantum optics; quantum information; and ultraintense and ultrashort laser fields. Both full-length research reports and brief communications are included. All of the papers are published in English even though they represent the results of European research. Recommended for comprehensive physics collections.

5029. *European Physical Journal E. Soft Matter.* Formed by the merger of part of (1998-2000): *European Physical Journal. B. Condensed Matter Physics;* part of (1992-2000): *Anales de Fisica;* Which was formed by the merger of (1903-1992): *Anales de Fisica. Serie A: Fenomenos e Interacciones;* (1903-1992): *Anales de Fisica. Serie B: Aplicaciones, Metodos e Instrumentos;* Both of which superseded in part (in 1981): *Anales de Fisica;* Which was formerly (until 1968): *Real Sociedad Espanola de Fisica y Quimica. Anales. Serie A: Fisica;* Which superseded in part (in 1948): *Anales de Fisica y Quimica;* Which was formerly (until 1941): *Sociedad Espanola de Fisica y Quimica. Anales.* [ISSN: 1292-8941] 2000. m. EUR 2098 print & online eds. Ed(s): A M Donald, G Reiter. Springer, Haber Str 7, Heidelberg, 69126, Germany. Adv. Sample. Refereed. Reprint: PSC. *Indexed:* EngInd, SCI. *Aud.:* Ac, Sa.

This is the final section of the *European Physical Journal* and it covers soft matter, which comprises complex fluids that have applications in everyday life. It includes a mixture of papers on biological physics; colloids and granular materials; functional and surface-dominated materials; polymers; liquid crystals; self-organization and supermolecules; surfaces; liquids; and interfaces. As in each of the other sections of this journal, all of the articles are published in English. Most articles are full research papers, but some short communications are also included. This journal is recommended only for comprehensive physics collections.

5030. *The European Physical Journal Special Topics.* [ISSN: 1951-6355] 2007. q. EUR 1648 print & online eds. Springer, Tiergartenstr 17, Heidelberg, 69121, Germany; subscriptions@springer.de; http://www.springer.de. Refereed. *Aud.:* Ac, Sa.

This new section of the *European Physical Journal* is devoted to the rapid and timely publication of topical issues in all fields pertaining to the pure and applied physical sciences. Each issue focuses on a specific topic. Papers are invited or are the result of specialized workshops. In general, the journal does not publish conference proceedings. The first four issues cover hadron structure and nonperturbative quantum chromodynamics; dynamics of confinement; dynamical neural networks; and complex systems. Formerly published as part IV of the *Journal de Physique,* this title will be a source for highly specialized research in a wide range of fields within physics.

5031. *Foundations of Physics: an international journal devoted to the conceptual and fundamental theories of modern physics, biophysics, and cosmology.* Incorporates (1988-2006): *Foundations of Physics Letters.* [ISSN: 0015-9018] 1970. m. EUR 2210 print & online eds. Ed(s): Alwyn van der Merwe. Springer New York LLC, 233 Spring St, New York, NY 10013-1578; service-ny@springer.com; http://www.springer.com/. Illus., index, adv. Refereed. Vol. ends: Dec. Microform: PQC. Online: EBSCO Publishing, EBSCO Host; Gale; IngentaConnect; OCLC Online Computer Library Center, Inc.; OhioLINK; Ovid Technologies, Inc.; Springer LINK; SwetsWise Online Content. Reprint: PSC. *Indexed:* CCMJ, GSI, MSN, MathR, PhilInd, SCI. *Bk. rev.:* Number and length vary. *Aud.:* Ac, Sa.

One of the major objectives of modern physics research is to develop a single unified theory that can explain all physical properties, effects, and interactions. Ever since Einstein proposed that researchers work toward a single theory of the universe, various scientists have approached this problem from a number of angles. *Foundations of Physics* emphasizes the logical, methodological, and philosophical premises of modern physical theories and procedures. Much of the material covers cosmology, quantum mechanics, wave theory, gravitation, general relativity, and gauge theory. Articles tend to be speculative in nature and often question existing theoretical concepts. This journal is somewhat unusual in the field of physics in that it stresses theory rather than experimental results. Full-length papers and letters to the editor are accepted. Because of its focus on one of the single most important questions in physics today, this title is a useful addition to comprehensive collections in theoretical physics.

5032. General Relativity and Gravitation. [ISSN: 0001-7701] 1970. m. EUR 1962 print & online eds. Ed(s): Hans-Juergen Schmidt. Springer New York LLC, 233 Spring St, New York, NY 10013-1578; service-ny@springer.com; http://www.springer.com/. Illus., index, adv. Refereed. Vol. ends: Dec. Microform: PQC. Online: EBSCO Publishing, EBSCO Host; Gale; IngentaConnect; OCLC Online Computer Library Center, Inc.; OhioLINK; Ovid Technologies, Inc.; Springer LINK; SwetsWise Online Content. Reprint: PSC. *Indexed:* CCMJ, IAA, M&GPA, MSN, MathR, SCI. *Bk. rev.:* Number and length vary. *Aud.:* Ac, Sa.

Einstein spent much of his professional life working on the theories of gravity and relativity. This journal was developed to continue that research. Topics covered include classical general relativity; relativisitc gravity; gravitational waves; theoretical and observational cosmology; supergravity; quantum gravity; and quantum cosmology. Although it primarily publishes research papers on the theoretical and experimental aspects of these two areas, it also includes letters, review articles, book reviews, conference programs, and news items. Most of the articles are of a highly theoretical nature, which is inherent in the subject matter. As the official publication of the International Committee on General Relativity and Gravitation, this journal serves as the premier source for research on and discussion of the two topics in its title. It was founded by some of the most prominent researchers in twentieth-century physics, and it maintains those high standards today. *General Relativity and Gravitation* is an important title in any comprehensive collection on theoretical physics.

5033. International Journal of Theoretical Physics. [ISSN: 0020-7748] 1968. m. EUR 2258 print & online eds. Ed(s): David Ritz Finkelstein. Springer New York LLC, 233 Spring St, New York, NY 10013-1578; service-ny@springer.com; http://www.springer.com/. Illus., index, adv. Sample. Refereed. Vol. ends: Dec. Microform: PQC. Online: EBSCO Publishing, EBSCO Host; Gale; IngentaConnect; OCLC Online Computer Library Center, Inc.; OhioLINK; Ovid Technologies, Inc.; Springer LINK; SwetsWise Online Content. Reprint: PSC. *Indexed:* ArtHuCI, CCMJ, ChemAb, MSN, MathR, PhilInd, SCI. *Aud.:* Ac, Sa.

One of the major goals of modern physics is to develop a grand unification theory that links all known physical forces. Dedicated to the unification of the latest physics research, the *International Journal of Theoretical Physics* seeks to map the direction of future research arising from new analytical methods, including the latest progress in the use of computers, and to complement traditional physics research by providing fresh inquiry into quantum measurement theory, relativistic field theory, and other similarly fundamental areas. It covers such topics as quantum theory; space-time structure; and quantum communication, cosmology, gravity, space-time, and topology. Only full-length research papers are accepted. Occasional special issues contain the proceedings of conferences related to unification theory. *Foundations of Physics* (see above) serves a similar objective and contains very similar material. With the continuing search for a grand unification theory, both of these journals will remain important for comprehensive physics collections.

5034. J A S A Express Letters. Formerly (until 2005): *Acoustics Research Letters Online.* 2000. irreg. Free. Ed(s): Wilson D Keith. Acoustical Society of America, 2 Huntington Quadrangle, Ste 1NO1, Melville, NY 11747-4502; asa@aip.org; http://asa.aip.org. Refereed. *Indexed:* SCI. *Aud.:* Ac, Sa.

This title replaces the *Acoustics Research Letters Online* as the letters-to-the-editor section of the *Journal of the Acoustical Society of America (JASA)*. As such, it is dedicated to the rapid publication of important research results in the field of acoustics. Topics covered mirror those of the parent journal and include linear and nonlinear acoustics; aeroacoustics; ultrasonics and quantum acoustics; architectural acoustics; vibration, speech, music, and noise; the psychology and physiology of hearing; engineering acoustics; and biomedical acoustics. All articles are six pages in length or less, but may contain graphic and multimedia content. Articles are published as accepted and then linked to the next monthly issue of *JASA*. This title provides cutting-edge research in all areas of acoustics.

5035. J C P: Biochemical Physics. [ISSN: 1931-9223] 2007. m. USD 395. American Institute of Physics, 2 Huntington Quadrangle, Ste 1NO1, Melville, NY 11747-4502; aipinfo@aip.org; http://www.aip.org. *Aud.:* Ac, Sa.

As interest in biochemical processes has grown, the editors of the *Journal of Chemical Physics* have split off a new journal dedicated to biophysics. This new title includes the subset of articles from the *Journal of Chemical Physics* that directly deal with, or have important implications for, biologically related systems. All articles included in this journal are also published in the *Journal of Chemical Physics,* but those interested only in the biological section may purchase this title separately. Like its parent title, this journal publishes primarily full-length research articles, but it also includes brief communications and letters to the editor. Libraries that specialize in biological research and not physics may wish to purchase only this section of the *Journal of Chemical Physics*.

5036. J E T P Letters. [ISSN: 0021-3640] 1965. s-m. EUR 2398 print & online eds. Ed(s): Vsevolod F Gantmakher. M A I K Nauka - Interperiodica, Profsoyuznaya ul 90, Moscow, 117997, Russian Federation; compmg@maik.ru; http://www.maik.ru. Illus., index. Refereed. Online: American Institute of Physics, Scitation; EBSCO Publishing, EBSCO Host; OhioLINK; Springer LINK; SwetsWise Online Content. *Indexed:* ApMecR, CPI, ChemAb, IAA, SCI. *Aud.:* Ac, Sa.

JETP Letters is the English-language version of the important Russian-language *Pis'ma v Zhurnal Eksperimental'noi i Teoreticheskoi Fiziki.* It is the letters section of the *Journal of Experimental and Theoretical Physics* (see below). It publishes short research papers in all topics of experimental and theoretical physics, including gravitation; field theory; elementary particles and nuclei; plasmas; nonlinear phenomena; condensed matter; superconductivity; superfluidity; lasers; and surfaces. This title is the Russian equivalent of *Physics Letters* and *Physical Review Letters* (see below). Its firsthand reports of the current state of research in Russia place this among the most consulted journals that serve physics, chemistry, and engineering departments and laboratories throughout the world. It remains one of the most cited physics journals in the world and belongs in any comprehensive physics collection.

5037. Japanese Journal of Applied Physics. [ISSN: 0021-4922] 1962. m. JPY 180000 part 1 & 2. Ed(s): Osamu Ueda, Katsumi Kishino. Institute of Pure and Applied Physics, Toyokaiji Bldg, no.12, 6-9-6 Shinbashi, Minato-ku, Tokyo, 105-0004, Japan; subscription@ipap.jp; http://www.ipap.jp. Illus., index. Refereed. Circ: 3900. Online: EBSCO Publishing, EBSCO Host; J-Stage. *Indexed:* A&ATA, C&ISA, CerAb, ChemAb, EngInd, IAA, PhotoAb, SCI. *Aud.:* Ac, Sa.

As one of the world powers in the development and application of new technology, Japan is the source of much significant research in physics, technology, and related fields. The *Japanese Journal of Applied Physics* is the primary publication outlet for Japanese research in these subject areas. Subjects covered include semiconductors; superconductors; magnetism; optics and quantum electronics; optical and electrical properties of condensed matter; structural, mechanical, and thermal properties of condensed matter; surfaces, interfaces, and films; nuclear science, plasmas, and electric discharges; atoms, molecules, and chemical physics; instrumentation, measurement, and fabrication technology; applied bioscience; and nanotechnology. The journal is issued in two sections. Part One includes full research papers, short notes, and review articles. Occasional issues present the proceedings of conferences of interest to readers. Part Two is reserved for letters and is published more frequently in order to provide rapid distribution of this information. A separate publication published conference proceedings. Although the journal is Japanese, all of the articles are published in English. Articles in this journal are free to any registered user for 90 days, after which time a subscription is required to retrieve them. As one of the major journals covering Japanese research, this title is essential to providing balanced coverage of worldwide physics research.

5038. Journal of Applied Physics. Formerly (until 1936): *Physics;* Which incorporated (1929-1932): *Journal of Rheology.* [ISSN: 0021-8979] 1931. s-m. USD 4390 print & online eds. Ed(s): James P Viccaro. American Institute of Physics, 2 Huntington Quadrangle, Ste 1NO1, Melville, NY 11747-4502; aipinfo@aip.org; http://www.aip.org. Illus., index, adv. Refereed. Circ: 5000 Paid. Online: American Institute of Physics, Scitation; EBSCO Publishing, EBSCO Host; OhioLINK; SwetsWise Online Content. *Indexed:* AS&TI, ApMecR, CPI, ChemAb, EngInd, IAA, MathR, PetrolAb, PhotoAb, SCI. *Aud.:* Ac, Sa.

The *Journal of Applied Physics* is a primary journal for the publication of significant new research results in the application of physics to modern technology. As opposed to most other physics journals, which concentrate on theoretical or experimental advances, this journal specializes in the application of physical concepts to industrial processes and to other scientific disciplines. Its articles emphasize the understanding of the physics underlying modern technology, but distinguished from technology on the one side and pure physics on the other. Topics include lasers, optics, and optoelectronics; plasmas and electrical discharges; structural, mechanical, thermodynamic, and optical properties of condensed matter; electronic structure and transport; magnetism and superconductivity; dielectrics and ferroelectricity; nanoscale science and design; device physics; applied biophysics; and interdisciplinary and general physics. The common thread is that the articles describe the uses and applications of a physical concept rather than its theoretical foundations. Full papers and brief communications are included in each issue. Letters are contained in the sister publication *Applied Physics Letters* (see above), and review articles are published in *Applied Physics Reviews* (see above). These three titles comprise the premier journal collection for publication of research on applied physics. As such, they belong in any physics research collection.

5039. Journal of Chemical Physics. [ISSN: 0021-9606] 1931. w. 48/yr. USD 6200 print & online eds. Ed(s): Donald Levy. American Institute of Physics, 2 Huntington Quadrangle, Ste 1NO1, Melville, NY 11747-4502; aipinfo@aip.org; http://www.aip.org. Illus., index. Refereed. Circ: 5000 Controlled. Online: American Institute of Physics, Scitation; EBSCO Publishing, EBSCO Host; OhioLINK; SwetsWise Online Content. *Indexed:* ApMecR, CEA, CPI, ChemAb, EngInd, IAA, MathR, PetrolAb, SCI. *Aud.:* Ac, Sa.

The purpose of the *Journal of Chemical Physics* is to bridge the gap between the journals in physics and those in chemistry by publishing quantitative research based on physical principles and techniques as applied to chemical systems. As the boundary between these two disciplines continues to narrow, there is an increasing number of researchers working on issues related to both fields of study. Topics typically covered include kinetics, statistical mechanics, quantum mechanics, materials, surfaces/interfaces, and information theory. Most of this journal consists of full-length research reports, although brief communications, letters, and notes are also published. As the leading journal to focus on the crossover between physics and chemistry, this title belongs in any research collection devoted to either physics or chemistry.

5040. Journal of Computational Physics. [ISSN: 0021-9991] 1966. 16x/yr. EUR 6860. Ed(s): G. Tryggvason. Academic Press, 525 B St, Ste 1900, San Diego, CA 92101-4495; apsubs@acad.com; http://www.elsevier.com/. Illus., index, adv. Refereed. Online: EBSCO Publishing, EBSCO Host; Gale; IngentaConnect; OCLC Online Computer Library Center, Inc.; OhioLINK; ScienceDirect; SwetsWise Online Content. *Indexed:* ApMecR, C&ISA, CCMJ, CerAb, ChemAb, CompR, ExcerpMed, IAA, M&GPA, MSN, MathR, SCI. *Aud.:* Ac, Sa.

The mission of the *Journal of Computational Physics* is to publish material that will assist in the accurate solution of scientific problems by numerical analysis and computational methods. The journal seeks to emphasize methods that cross disciplinary boundaries. Most of the papers deal with the development and application of algorithms for the solution of physical problems. The articles do not contain new research findings, but provide scientists with the methodology for conducting and refining the research process using mathematical processes. Papers dealing solely with hardware or software are excluded; each article must discuss the applications of computing to a physical or mathematical problem. Papers that cross disciplinary boundaries are encouraged. Full-length research reports, short notes, and letters to the editor are all accepted. Occasional theme issues deal with special topics. This journal supplements other physics research titles and belongs in comprehensive collections.

5041. Journal of Experimental and Theoretical Physics. Formerly: *Soviet Physics - J E T P.* [ISSN: 1063-7761] 1955. m. EUR 4685 print & online eds. Ed(s): A F Andreev. M A I K Nauka - Interperiodica, Profsoyuznaya ul 90, Moscow, 117997, Russian Federation; compmg@maik.ru; http://www.maik.ru. Illus., index. Refereed. Vol. ends: Jun/Dec. Online: American Institute of Physics, Scitation; EBSCO Publishing, EBSCO Host; IngentaConnect; OhioLINK; Springer LINK; SwetsWise Online Content. *Indexed:* ApMecR, CCMJ, CPI, ChemAb, EngInd, MSN, MathR, SCI. *Aud.:* Ac, Sa.

The *Journal of Experimental and Theoretical Physics* is an English translation of the Russian-language *Zhurnal Eksperimental'noi i Teoreticheskoi Fiziki,* the most influential of all Russian physics journals. The Russian and English editions are published simultaneously in order to expedite distribution of the journal to the entire world. Although it is historically a Russian journal, it accepts papers from researchers anywhere around the world. Only full-length research papers are included. Letters and short communications appear in the sister publication *JETP Letters* (see above). It publishes experimental and theoretical articles devoted to the main topics of fundamental physics, including gravitation; nuclei and particles; atoms, spectra, and radiation; plasmas; liquids; solids; superconductors; properties of surfaces; and nonlinear physics. This journal remains one of the primary Russian physics research journals, and it belongs in any comprehensive physics collection.

5042. Journal of Magnetism and Magnetic Materials. [ISSN: 0304-8853] 1976. 24x/yr. EUR 8155. Ed(s): A. J. Freeman. Elsevier BV, North-Holland, Sara Burgerhartstraat 25, Amsterdam, 1055 KV, Netherlands; nlinfo-f@elsevier.nl; http://www.elsevier.nl. Illus., index, adv. Sample. Refereed. Circ: 800. Microform: PQC. Online: EBSCO Publishing, EBSCO Host; Gale; IngentaConnect; OhioLINK; ScienceDirect; SwetsWise Online Content. *Indexed:* C&ISA, CerAb, ChemAb, EngInd, IAA, SCI. *Aud.:* Ac, Sa.

As one of the basic forces of physics, magnetism is a property that has been widely studied for centuries. The *Journal of Magnetism and Magnetic Materials* provides an important forum for the disclosure and discussion of original contributions that cover the whole spectrum of topics, from basic magnetism to the technology and applications of magnetic materials and magnetic recording. Theoretical, experimental, and applied-research papers are all included, and a special section of the journal is devoted to papers on the use of magnetic materials for information storage and retrieval. The journal also publishes letters to the editor, short communications, and occasional review articles. Some issues contain the proceedings of conferences relating to magnetism or magnetic materials. This journal belongs in any library that supports research in this field.

5043. Journal of Mathematical Physics. [ISSN: 0022-2488] 1960. m. USD 2795 print & online eds. Ed(s): Bruno L. Z. Nachtergaele. American Institute of Physics, 2 Huntington Quadrangle, Ste 1NO1, Melville, NY 11747-4502; aipinfo@aip.org; http://www.aip.org. Illus., index. Refereed. Vol. ends: Dec. Online: American Institute of Physics, Scitation; EBSCO Publishing, EBSCO Host; OhioLINK; SwetsWise Online Content. *Indexed:* CCMJ, CPI, ChemAb, IAA, MSN, MathR, SCI. *Aud.:* Ac, Sa.

The purpose of this journal is to provide a place for the publication of articles dealing with the application of mathematics to problems in modern physics. It also covers the development of mathematical techniques and research methods and the application of mathematics to physical theories. Specific topics cover the entire range of the field of physics, including classical mechanics, kinetic theory, dynamical systems, quantum mechanics, scattering theory, particles and fields, relativity, gravitation, string theory, and dynamical systems. An annual special issue provides in-depth analysis of one specific aspect of mathematical physics. The editors request that the mathematics be presented in such a way as to be understandable by a wide audience within the physics community. Even so, most of the articles will require a graduate-level understanding of mathematics and physics in order to completely comprehend the material. This title is an important addition to any graduate physics collection.

5044. *Journal of Physics A: Mathematical and Theoretical (Print Edition).* Formerly (until 2007): *Journal of Physics A: Mathematical and General (Print Edition);* Which superseded in part (in 1975): *Journal of Physics A: Mathematical, Nuclear and General;* Which was formerly (until 1973): *Journal of Physics. A, Proceedings of the Physical Society. General;* Which superseded in part (in 1968): *Physical Society. Proceedings (London, 1958);* Which was formed by the merger of (1874-1958): *Physical Society. Proceedings. Section A;* (1874-1958): *Physical Society. Proceedings. Section B;* Which both superseded in part (in 1948): *Physical Society. Proceedings (London, 1932);* Which was formerly (until 1926): *Physical Society of London. Proceedings;* Which incorporated (1900-1932): *Optical Society. Transactions.* [ISSN: 1751-8113] 1958. w. USD 7885 print & online eds. Ed(s): C Bender. Institute of Physics Publishing, Dirac House, Temple Back, Bristol, BS1 6BE, United Kingdom; custserv@iop.org; http://www.iop.org. Illus., index. Sample. Refereed. Online: EBSCO Publishing, EBSCO Host; Gale; IngentaConnect; OhioLINK; SwetsWise Online Content. *Indexed:* ApMecR, CCMJ, ChemAb, IAA, MSN, MathR, SCI. *Aud.:* Ac, Sa.

As the British counterpart to the *Physical Review* (see below), the *Journal of Physics* is one of the two most prominent collections of physics research journals in the world. It is also one of the most heavily cited sources in the field and is used and respected by researchers worldwide. Like the *Physical Review,* this journal is issued in many parts that cover the various subdisciplines of physics. *Part A* covers mathematical and statistical physics. As such, it is primarily concerned with the fundamental mathematical and computational methods underpinning modern physics. It is divided into six subsections, covering the fields of statistical physics; chaotic and complex systems; mathematical physics; quantum mechanics and quantum information theory; classical and quantum field theory; and fluid and plasma theory. The journal uses a classification system to place articles on similar topics within the same section. Both full-length research papers and letters to the editor are included, along with short corrections to previously published material. Review articles appear occasionally, and sometimes special issues are devoted to specific topics. This title belongs in every physics research collection. Also available in an online edition.

5045. *Journal of Physics and Chemistry of Solids.* [ISSN: 0022-3697] 1956. 12x/yr. EUR 5284. Ed(s): A Bansil, K. Prassides. Pergamon, The Boulevard, Langford Ln, East Park, Kidlington, OX5 1GB, United Kingdom. Illus., index, adv. Refereed. Circ: 2300. Vol. ends: Dec. Microform: MIM; PQC. Online: EBSCO Publishing, EBSCO Host; Gale; IngentaConnect; OhioLINK; ScienceDirect; SwetsWise Online Content. *Indexed:* ApMecR, C&ISA, ChemAb, EngInd, SCI, SSCI. *Aud.:* Ac, Sa.

The *Journal of Physics and Chemistry of Solids* is a publication outlet for research in condensed matter physics and materials science. Emphasis is placed on experimental and theoretical work that contributes to a basic understanding of, and new insight into, the properties and behavior of condensed matter. General areas of interest are the electronic, spectroscopic, and structural properties of solids; and the statistical mechanics and thermodynamics of condensed systems, including perfect and defect lattices, surfaces, interfaces, thin films and multilayers, amorphous materials and nanostructures, and layered and low-dimensional structures. Typical articles include the preparation and structural characterization of novel and advanced materials—especially in relation to the measurement and interpretation of their electrical, magnetic, optical, thermal, and mechanical properties; phase transitions; electronic structure; and defect properties. Also covered is the application of appropriate experimental and theoretical techniques in these studies. The journal emphasizes the fundamental aspects of materials science. From time to time, special issues of the journal are published that contain conference papers or invited articles devoted to topical or rapidly developing fields. Only full-length articles are accepted, with letters published in the related *Solid State Communications* (see below). For comprehensive physics research collections.

5046. *Journal of Physics B: Atomic, Molecular and Optical Physics.* Incorporates (in 2005): *Journal of Optics B: Quantum and Semiclassical Optics;* Which was formerly (until 1999): *Quantum and Semiclassical Optics;* (until 1995): *Quantum Optics;* Former titles (until 1987): *Journal of Physics B: Atomic and Molecular Physics;* (until 1969): *Journal of physics. B, Proceedings of the Physical Society. Atomic and Molecular Physics;* Which superseded in part (in 1968): *Physical Society. Proceedings (London, 1958);* Which was formed by the merger of (1874-1958): *Proceedings of the Physical Society. Section A;* (1874-1958): *Proceedings of the Physical Society. Section B;* Which both superseded in part (in 1948): *Physical Society. Proceedings (London, 1926);* Which was formerly (until 1926): *Physical Society of London. Proceedings;* Which incorporated (1900-1932): *Optical Society. Transactions.* [ISSN: 0953-4075] 1958. s-m. USD 5630 print & online eds. Ed(s): J-M Rost. Institute of Physics Publishing, Dirac House, Temple Back, Bristol, BS1 6BE, United Kingdom; http://www.iop.org. Illus., index. Sample. Refereed. Online: EBSCO Publishing, EBSCO Host; Gale; IngentaConnect; OhioLINK; SwetsWise Online Content. *Indexed:* ApMecR, C&ISA, CCMJ, CerAb, ChemAb, EngInd, IAA, MSN, MathR, SCI. *Aud.:* Ac, Sa.

As part of the *Journal of Physics* collection of titles, this is one of the most prominent physics journals published worldwide. This section covers atomic, molecular, and optical physics, including such topics as atoms, ions, molecules, and clusters; their interaction with particles and fields; spectroscopy; quantum optics; nonlinear optics; laser physics; astrophysics; plasma physics; chemical physics; and optical cooling. This journal is similar in coverage and scope to *Part B* of the *Physical Review* (see below). In addition to publishing full-length research reports, the journal also publishes review articles. A new feature of the journal is the "Fast Track Communications," which are short (maximum of eight pages), timely papers presenting significant new developments. The "Fast Track" papers take the place of the former letters to the editor. Occasional special issues are devoted to a single topic or present the proceedings of a relevant conference. This is one of the most respected journals in the field, and it belongs in every physics research collection.

5047. *Journal of Physics: Condensed Matter.* Formed by the merger of (1970-1989): *Journal of Physics F: Metal Physics;* Which was formerly (until 1971): *Metal Physics;* (1958-1989): *Journal of Physics C: Solid State Physics;* Which was formerly (until 1970): *Journal of Physics. C, Proceedings of the Physical Society. Solid State Physics;* (until 1967): *Physical Society (London, 1958);* Which was formed by the merger of (1874-1958): *Physical Society. Proceedings. Section A;* (1874-1958): *Physical Society. Proceedings. Section B;* Which both superseded in part (in 1948): *Physical Society. Proceedings (London, 1932);* Which was formerly (until 1926): *Physical Society of London. Proceedings;* Which incorporated (1900-1932): *Optical Society. Transactions.* [ISSN: 0953-8984] 1989. w. USD 10365 print & online eds. Ed(s): A M Stoneham. Institute of Physics Publishing, Dirac House, Temple Back, Bristol, BS1 6BE, United Kingdom; custserv@iop.org; http://www.iop.org. Illus., index. Sample. Refereed. Circ: 1123. Online: EBSCO Publishing, EBSCO Host; Gale; IngentaConnect; OhioLINK; SwetsWise Online Content. *Indexed:* ApMecR, C&ISA, CerAb, ChemAb, EngInd, IAA, MathR, SCI. *Aud.:* Ac, Sa.

Another journal in the important *Journal of Physics* collection, this title is devoted to articles on experimental and theoretical studies of the structural, thermal, mechanical, electrical, magnetic, optical, and surface properties of condensed matter. Specific topics include crystalline and amorphous metals, semiconductors and insulators, glasses, liquids, liquid crystals, plastic crystals, polymers, and superfluids. There are separate sections within the journal for Surface, Interface, and Atomic-Scale Science; and Liquids, Soft Matter, and Biological Physics. Most articles are full research papers, although the journal also publishes review articles. "Fast Track Communications" takes the place of letters to the editor and publishes short, important research findings. Occasional issues present the proceedings of a conference in the field. As part of the *Journal of Physics,* this title belongs in all physics research collections.

5048. *Journal of Physics D: Applied Physics.* Former titles (until 1969): *British Journal of Applied Physics. Journal of Physics;* (until 1967): *British Journal of Applied Physics.* [ISSN: 0022-3727] 1950. s-m. USD

3610 print & online eds. Ed(s): P I Bhattacharya. Institute of Physics Publishing, Dirac House, Temple Back, Bristol, BS1 6BE, United Kingdom; custserv@iop.org; http://www.iop.org. Illus., index, adv. Sample. Refereed. Circ: 1217. Online: EBSCO Publishing, EBSCO Host; Gale; IngentaConnect; OhioLINK; SwetsWise Online Content. *Indexed:* AS&TI, C&ISA, CerAb, ChemAb, EngInd, IAA, PhotoAb, SCI. *Aud.:* Ac, Sa.

The *Journal of Physics D* is concerned with all aspects of applied-physics research. It publishes articles of a theoretical, experimental, or computational nature. Specific areas of interest include: applied magnetism and magnetic materials; photonics and semiconductor device physics; plasmas and plasma-surface interactions; applied surfaces and interfaces; and the structure and properties of matter. The editors are particularly interested in publishing articles on novel effects and new materials. Only full-length research articles are now being published in this journal. This title is the British equivalent of the *Journal of Applied Physics* (see above) and is an essential component of all physics research collections.

5049. *Journal of Physics G: Nuclear and Particle Physics.* Formerly: *Journal of Physics G: Nuclear Physics.* [ISSN: 0954-3899] 1975. m. USD 3505 print & online eds. Ed(s): A. B. Balantekin. Institute of Physics Publishing, Dirac House, Temple Back, Bristol, BS1 6BE, United Kingdom; custserv@iop.org; http://www.iop.org. Illus., index. Sample. Refereed. Circ: 745. Vol. ends: Dec. Online: EBSCO Publishing, EBSCO Host; Gale; IngentaConnect; OhioLINK; SwetsWise Online Content. *Indexed:* ChemAb, MathR, SCI. *Aud.:* Ac, Sa.

As the final section of the *Journal of Physics* collection, *Part G* covers nuclear and particle physics. Within this broad framework, the journal focuses on the physics of elementary particles and fields, intermediate-energy physics, nuclear physics, particle astrophysics, cosmic rays, gamma ray and neutrino astronomy, and dark matter. In addition to theoretical and experimental papers, the journal also publishes articles on experimental techniques, methods for data analysis, and instrumentation. Full-length research papers, review articles, and brief notes are all included, with full-length papers predominating. One volume each year is comprised of the annual *Review of Particle Physics*. Some issues contain the proceedings of conferences in the fields covered by the journal. This journal is the British equivalent of *Physical Review Sections C and D* (see below), and it belongs in any physics research collection.

5050. *Journal of Plasma Physics.* [ISSN: 0022-3778] 1967. bi-m. GBP 864. Ed(s): R A Cairns. Cambridge University Press, The Edinburgh Bldg, Shaftesbury Rd, Cambridge, CB2 2RU, United Kingdom; journals@cambridge.org; http://www.journals.cambridge.org. Illus., index, adv. Refereed. Microform: PQC. Online: Pub.; EBSCO Publishing, EBSCO Host; OCLC Online Computer Library Center, Inc.; OhioLINK; SwetsWise Online Content. Reprint: PSC. *Indexed:* ApMecR, ChemAb, EngInd, IAA, SCI. *Aud.:* Ac, Sa.

Plasma physics is a branch of physics that has applications in a wide variety of fields, including astrophysics, fluids, and nuclear physics. This specialized journal publishes original-research reports on plasma science in all of these areas. Basic topics include the fundamental physics of plasmas, ionization, kinetic theory, particle orbits, stochastic dynamics, wave propagation, solitons, stability, shock waves, transport, heating, and diagnostics. Applications include fusion, laboratory plasmas and communications devices, laser plasmas, technological plasmas, space physics, and astrophysics. Both theoretical and experimental results are presented, along with applications of plasma science in other fields. Full research papers and letters to the editor are included. This journal belongs in specialized and comprehensive physics collections.

5051. *Measurement Science and Technology.* Former titles (until 1990): *Journal of Physics E: Scientific Instruments;* (until 1969): *Journal of Physics. E, Journal of Scientific Instruments;* (until 1967): *Journal of Scientific Instruments;* (until 1949): *Journal of Scientific Instruments and of Physics in Industry;* (until 1947): *Journal of Scientific Instruments.* [ISSN: 0957-0233] 1922. m. USD 2030 print & online eds. Ed(s): P Hauptmann. Institute of Physics Publishing, Dirac House, Temple Back, Bristol, BS1 6BE, United Kingdom; custserv@iop.org; http://www.iop.org. Illus., index, adv. Sample. Refereed. Vol. ends: Dec.

Online: EBSCO Publishing, EBSCO Host; Gale; IngentaConnect; OhioLINK; SwetsWise Online Content. *Indexed:* AS&TI, ApMecR, BrTechI, C&ISA, CEA, CerAb, ChemAb, EngInd, ExcerpMed, HortAb, IAA, IndVet, PhotoAb, S&F, SCI. *Aud.:* Ac, Sa.

Experimental research in physics relies a great deal on specialized equipment and precise instrumentation. This journal is devoted to the study of measurement, including theory, applications, and practice. It covers instrumentation in physics, chemistry, biology, environmental science, and engineering. Topics of interest include sensing and sensor technology, signal processing, metrology, measurement techniques using electromagnetic radiation, acoustics and ultrasonics, spectroscopy, nuclear measurements, imaging techniques, tomography, holography, and microscopy. Full-length research papers, rapid communications, review articles, design notes, and conference reports are all included. This title is part of the *Journal of Physics* collection and is the British equivalent of the *Review of Scientific Instruments* (see below). It belongs in any physics research collection.

5052. *Molecular Physics: an international journal in the field of chemical physics.* [ISSN: 0026-8976] 1958. s-m. GBP 4605 print & online eds. Ed(s): T P Softley, Jean-Pierre Hansen. Taylor & Francis Ltd., 4 Park Sq, Milton Park, Abingdon, OX14 4RN, United Kingdom; info@tandf.co.uk; http://www.tandf.co.uk/journals. Illus., index, adv. Refereed. Online: EBSCO Publishing, EBSCO Host; Gale; IngentaConnect; OCLC Online Computer Library Center, Inc.; SwetsWise Online Content. Reprint: PSC. *Indexed:* ChemAb, EngInd, IAA, MathR, SCI, SSCI. *Aud.:* Ac, Sa.

Molecular Physics publishes reports of an experimental and theoretical nature on the structure and properties of atomic and molecular physics. The journal considers all aspects of the physics and biophysics of molecules, particularly the structure and dynamics of individual molecules and molecular assemblies. It also publishes papers on fundamental reaction kinetics and the structure and reactivity of molecules adsorbed on surfaces and at interfaces. Four types of articles are accepted: "Papers" are full-length articles that report completed research; "Preliminary Communications" describe aspects of current research whose immediate publication has a strong benefit to the physics community; "Research Notes" provide brief comments on continuing research; and "Invited Articles" provide state-of-the-art reviews of selected topics. This title is recommended for comprehensive physics and chemistry collections.

5053. *Nanotechnology.* [ISSN: 0957-4484] 1990. w. s-m. until 2007. USD 2800 print & online eds. (Individuals, USD 744). Ed(s): M Welland. Institute of Physics Publishing, Dirac House, Temple Back, Bristol, BS1 6BE, United Kingdom; custserv@iop.org; http://www.iop.org. Index, adv. Refereed. Circ: 400. Online: EBSCO Publishing, EBSCO Host; Gale; IngentaConnect; OhioLINK; SwetsWise Online Content. *Indexed:* BioEngAb, C&ISA, CerAb, ChemAb, EngInd, ExcerpMed, IAA, SCI. *Aud.:* Ac, Sa.

Nanotechnology is the study of phenomena in extremely small dimensions, usually on the order of the size of a hydrogen atom. In this journal, nanotechnology is taken to include the ability to individually address, control, and modify structures, materials, and devices with nanometre precision, and the synthesis of such structures into systems of micro- and macroscopic dimensions, such as MEMS-based devices. It encompasses the understanding of the fundamental physics, chemistry, biology, and technology of nanometre-scale objects and how such objects can be used in the areas of computation, sensors, nanostructured materials, and nano-biotechnology. *Nanotechnology* is the official publication of the Institute of Physics that is dedicated to this area of research. It publishes papers on original research results in the field, as well as review articles and tutorials. A related web site, nanotechweb.org, provides links to news, conferences, employment opportunities, and key papers on nanotechnology from other scientific journals. As the premier journal covering this new branch of physics, this title belongs in every collection that supports research in the field.

5054. *New Journal of Physics.* [ISSN: 1367-2630] 1998. irreg. Free. Ed(s): Eberhard Bodenschatz. Institute of Physics Publishing, Dirac House, Temple Back, Bristol, BS1 6BE, United Kingdom; custserv@iop.org; http://www.iop.org. Illus. Refereed. *Indexed:* CCMJ, EngInd, MSN, MathR, SCI. *Aud.:* Ac, Sa.

The *New Journal of Physics* is an electronic-only publication sponsored by 20 national physics societies around the world. The scope of the journal is the entire range of the field of physics, including experimental, theoretical, and applied research. By publishing only in electronic format, the journal allows for rapid distribution of articles of any length. All of the articles are subject to the standard peer-review process, but they are not limited by the space and distribution considerations of the print format. Journal coverage extends across the whole of physics, encompassing pure, applied, theoretical, and experimental research, as well as interdisciplinary topics. The journal's online format allows it to be made available to readers at no cost. It is funded by article charges paid by the authors, which is similar to the page charges of print journals. As the idea of a free online journal has caught on, the number of articles per year has grown, with 330 published in 2006. The editors of this journal want to make it the leading journal in the field by publishing articles of outstanding quality. Many of the articles are in the "Focus" category, which means they are lengthy reviews or tutorials on specific topics in physics. Because of the ideal pricing model and the ease of electronic access, this journal should be available in all college libraries. URL: www.iop.org/EJ/journal/1367-2630.

5055. Optical Society of America. Journal A: Optics, Image Science, and Vision. Formerly (until 1993): *Optical Society of America. Journal A, Optics and Image Science;* Which superseded in part (in 1983): *Optical Society of America. Journal;* Which superseded in part (in 1930): *Optical Society of America. Journal. Review of Scientific Instruments;* Which was formerly (until 1922): *Optical Society of America. Journal.* [ISSN: 1084-7529] 1917. m. USD 1760 domestic; USD 1810 in Canada & Mexico; USD 1875 elsewhere. Ed(s): Stephen Burns. Optical Society of America, 2010 Massachusetts Ave, NW, Washington, DC 20036-1023; info@osa.org; http://www.osa.org. Illus., index, adv. Refereed. Circ: 2000 Paid. Vol. ends: Dec. Online: EBSCO Publishing, EBSCO Host; OhioLINK. *Indexed:* AS&TI, ApMecR, C&ISA, CCMJ, CPI, ChemAb, EngInd, ErgAb, IAA, MSN, MathR, PsycInfo, SCI, SSCI. *Aud.:* Ac, Sa.

As one-half of the official journal of the Optical Society of America, this title is the premier publication outlet for research in the field of optics. *Part A* presents results of a general or basic nature relating to classical optics, image science, and vision. Topics include vision and color, imaging systems, machine vision, image processing, wave propagation, diffraction, scattering, coherence, polarization, optical systems, atmospheric or ocean optics, optical devices, medical optics, scattering, fiber optics, holography, and lithography. Only full-length research papers are included. Letters to the editor are published in a sister journal, *Optics Letters* (see below). Along with the *Journal of the Optical Society of America B* (below), this title forms the core of the optics literature and belongs in all physics collections.

5056. Optical Society of America. Journal B: Optical Physics. Supersedes in part (in 1984): *Optical Society of America. Journal;* Which superseded in part (in 1930): *Optical Society of America. Journal. Review of Scientific Instruments;* Which was formerly (until 1922): *Optical Society of America. Journal.* [ISSN: 0740-3224] 1917. m. USD 1760 domestic; USD 1800 in Canada & Mexico; USD 1865 elsewhere. Ed(s): GIStegeman. Optical Society of America, 2010 Massachusetts Ave, NW, Washington, DC 20036-1023; info@osa.org; http://www.osa.org. Illus., index, adv. Refereed. Circ: 1700 Paid. Online: EBSCO Publishing, EBSCO Host; OhioLINK. *Indexed:* AS&TI, ApMecR, C&ISA, CCMJ, CPI, CerAb, ChemAb, EngInd, IAA, MSN, MathR, PhotoAb, SCI. *Aud.:* Ac, Sa.

As the second half of the official journal of the Optical Society of America, this title comprises part of the core literature in the field of optics. *Part B* covers research on quantum optics, lasers, nonlinear optics, spectroscopy, integrated optics, photonic crystals, ultrafast processes, and all other areas of optical physics. Like its sister section the *Journal of the Optical Society of America Part A,* it only publishes full-length research reports. Letters are published in the related *Optics Letters* (see below). As major journals in one of the most prominent branches of physics, *Part A* and *Part B* belong in all physics collections.

5057. Optics & Photonics News. Formerly (until 1990): *Optics News.* [ISSN: 1047-6938] 1975. m. USD 100 combined subscription domestic print & online eds.; USD 120 combined subscription in Canada &

Mexico print & online eds.; USD 130 combined subscription elsewhere print & online eds. Ed(s): Christina Folz. Optical Society of America, 2010 Massachusetts Ave, NW, Washington, DC 20036-1023; info@osa.org; http://www.osa.org. Illus., index, adv. Circ: 22000 Paid and free. Vol. ends: Dec. Online: EBSCO Publishing, EBSCO Host; OhioLINK. *Indexed:* EngInd. *Bk. rev.:* Number and length vary. *Aud.:* Ga, Ac, Sa.

This journal serves as the official newsletter for the Optical Society of America. It provides its members with news of the organization, reviews of new products, legislative activities, book reviews, calendars of meetings and events, and employment opportunities. In addition, it contains interesting feature articles dealing with current topics in the field of optics. These articles are written for the nonspecialist and are accessible to a wide readership. Most feature articles avoid high-level mathematics and are accompanied by quality color photographs. A new feature is a column written specifically for engineers, who comprise a large readership. Although physics is by nature a rather dry field of study and not known for its entertainment value, this is one of the few physics journals to contain a regular humor section. *Optics and Photonics News* is available free-of-charge to people in the industry, including educators. With its low price, glossy format, general readability, and wide range of interest, it is a good title for any science or physics collection.

5058. Optics Communications. [ISSN: 0030-4018] 1969. 24x/yr. EUR 6573. Ed(s): S. Kawata, F Abeles. Elsevier BV, North-Holland, Sara Burgerhartstraat 25, Amsterdam, 1055 KV, Netherlands; nlinfo-f@elsevier.nl. Illus., index, adv. Refereed. Vol. ends: No. 187 - No. 200. Microform: PQC. Online: EBSCO Publishing, EBSCO Host; Gale; IngentaConnect; OhioLINK; ScienceDirect; SwetsWise Online Content. *Indexed:* C&ISA, ChemAb, EngInd, IAA, PhotoAb, SCI. *Aud.:* Ac, Sa.

Optics Communications publishes short reports and full-length articles in the field of optics and on optical applications in other branches of physics. Topics include physical optics; optical information and image processing; guided wave optics; optical properties of condensed materials; lasers and laser applications; nonlinear optics; nano- and micro-optics; and biomedical optics. Emerging areas of optical science and technology are also included. Articles primarily of a mathematical or computational nature are not accepted for publication, nor are articles related solely to minor technical advances in existing equipment. This title plays a similar role to *Optics Letters* (see below) in reporting new developments in the field. It also supplements the major optics journals, such as *Applied Optics* and *Journal of the Optical Society of America* (see above), and is recommended only for comprehensive optics collections.

5059. Optics Express. [ISSN: 1094-4087] 1997. 26x/yr. Free. Ed(s): Michael Ducan. Optical Society of America, 2010 Massachusetts Ave, NW, Washington, DC 20036-1023; info@osa.org; http://www.osa.org. Refereed. *Indexed:* CPI, EngInd, SCI. *Aud.:* Ac, Sa.

Now in its tenth year, *Optics Express* publishes original, peer-reviewed articles that report new developments of interest to the optics community in all fields of optical science and technology. All subfields of optics are covered, including theory, experimentation, and application. Typical articles cover subjects such as fiber optics; atmospheric optics; holography; imaging systems; instrumentation; lasers; medical optics; nonlinear optics; optical design; remote sensing; spectroscopy; thin films; and ultrafast optics. True to its name, *Optics Express* provides rapid publication, with an average of 49 days from submission to publication. It also allows authors to publish an unlimited number of color images. Many of the articles contain multimedia content that enhances the understanding of the physical concepts discussed. Because it is available to all researchers electronically at no charge, this journal belongs in all physics collections. URL: www.opticsexpress.org.

5060. Optics Letters. [ISSN: 0146-9592] 1977. s-m. USD 1795. Ed(s): Anthony J Campillo. Optical Society of America, 2010 Massachusetts Ave, NW, Washington, DC 20036-1023; info@osa.org; http://www.osa.org. Illus., index. Refereed. Circ: 1600 Paid. Vol. ends: Jan/Dec. Online: EBSCO Publishing, EBSCO Host; OhioLINK. *Indexed:* AS&TI, C&ISA, CPI, ChemAb, EngInd, ExcerpMed, IAA, PhotoAb, SCI. *Aud.:* Ac, Sa.

Optics Letters serves as the letters-to-the-editor section for both *Applied Optics* and the *Journal of the Optical Society of America* (see above). It presents short papers on recent research results in optical science, including atmospheric optics, quantum electronics, Fourier optics, integrated optics, and fiber optics. Criteria used in determining acceptability of contributions include newsworthiness to a substantial part of the optics community and the effect of rapid publication on the research of others. This is a core journal in the field of optics, and it belongs in any collection that supports research in this field.

5061. *Philosophical Magazine A: Physics of Condensed Matter, Structure, Defects and Mechanical Properties.* Formerly (until 1995): *Philosophical Magazine A: Physics of Condensed Matter, Defects and Mechanical Properties;* Which superseded in part (in 1978): *Philosophical Magazine.* [ISSN: 1364-2804] 1798. 18x/yr. GBP 2642 for both Philosophical Magazines A & B. Ed(s): Lindsay Greer. Taylor & Francis Ltd., 4 Park Sq, Milton Park, Abingdon, OX14 4RN, United Kingdom; info@tandf.co.uk; http://www.tandf.co.uk/journals. Illus., index, adv. Refereed. Vol. ends: Jun/Dec. *Indexed:* ApMecR, ChemAb, SCI. *Aud.:* Ac, Sa.

While many scientific journals have split into ever smaller and more specialized parts, the *Philosophical Magazine* is moving in the opposite direction. This journal was formerly published in two distinct sections, *Part A*, which covered structure, defects, and mechanical properties, and *Part B*, which focused on statistical mechanics and electronic, optical, and magnetic properties; the editors have merged the two into a single journal title devoted to the physics of condensed matter. It publishes articles on the structure and properties of crystalline materials, ceramics, polymers, glasses, amorphous films, composites, and soft matter. Only full-length research papers are published. Letters to the editor are included in a related journal, *Philosophical Magazine Letters. Philosophical Magazine* continues to be an important journal in the field of physics and belongs in any collection that covers research on condensed matter.

5062. *Physical Review A (Atomic, Molecular and Optical Physics).* Formerly (until 1989): *Physical Review A (General Physics);* Which superseded in part (in 1970): *Physical Review.* [ISSN: 1050-2947] 1893. m. USD 2205 print & online eds. Ed(s): Margaret Malloy, Gordon W.F. Drake. American Physical Society, One Physics Ellipse, College Park, MD 20740-3843; http://www.aps.org. Illus., index. Refereed. Vol. ends: Jun/Dec. Microform: BHP. Online: EBSCO Publishing, EBSCO Host; OhioLINK. *Indexed:* ApMecR, CCMJ, CPI, ChemAb, EngInd, IAA, MSN, MathR, SCI. *Aud.:* Ac, Sa.

The *Physical Review* collection of journals is simply the most prestigious set of physics journals published anywhere in the world. Along with its British counterpart, the *Journal of Physics* collection (see above), the various components of the *Physical Review* comprise the core research journal literature of the field. Like many other journals in the sciences, the *Physical Review* has been divided into a number of sections that cover specific branches and subdisciplines of physics. *Section A* covers the topics of fundamental concepts; quantum information; atomic and molecular structure and dynamics; atomic and molecular collisions and interactions; photon, electron, atom, and molecule interactions with solids and surfaces; clusters (including fullerenes); atomic and molecular processes in external fields; matter waves; and quantum optics, physics of lasers, and nonlinear optics. Full-length articles, brief reports, comments, and short rapid communications are all included. Letters are published in the related *Physical Review Letters* (see below). As in all of the sections of the *Physical Review,* the number of articles and pages published is tremendous, often reaching 1,500 pages in a single issue. However, even with thousands of articles published each year, the refereeing process is very selective, resulting in the rejection of over half of all articles submitted. The large number of papers published has forced the editors to stop numbering the pages consecutively. They use a paper/page system instead. A new feature for all sections of the *Physical Review* as of January 2003 was the incorporation of color images. Color images are not included in the print edition, but are included in the web version of appropriate papers. As one section of the most important journal in the field, this title belongs in every physics research collection.

5063. *Physical Review B (Condensed Matter and Materials Physics).* Former titles (until 1998): *Physical Review B (Condensed Matter);* (until Jul. 1978): *Physical Review B (Solid State);* Which superseded in part (in 1970): *Physical Review.* [ISSN: 1098-0121] 1893. 48x/yr. USD 6375 print & online eds. Ed(s): P D Adams. American Physical Society, One Physics Ellipse, College Park, MD 20740-3843; http://www.aps.org. Illus., index. Refereed. Online: EBSCO Publishing, EBSCO Host; OhioLINK. *Indexed:* ApMecR, CPI, ChemAb, IAA, MathR, PhotoAb, SCI. *Aud.:* Ac, Sa.

The second section of the *Physical Review* is devoted to condensed matter and materials science. Topics include semiconductors, surface physics, structure and mechanical properties of materials, disordered systems, dynamics and lattice effects, magnetism, superfluidity, and superconductivity. Because of the extremely large number of papers published, the journal has been further divided, with the first issue of each month covering structure, phase transitions, magnetism, and superconductivity and the second issue covering electronic structure, semiconductors, surfaces, and low dimensions. Full-length papers predominate, but short, rapid communications are also accepted. Accompanying color images are included only in the online version of the journal. Letters to the editor are published in the related *Physical Review Letters* (see below). Like all sections of the *Physical Review,* this section is not for the casual reader. It publishes more than 40,000 pages each year of primary research results of a highly technical nature. In order to facilitate publication with such a large number of papers, the editors have ceased numbering the pages consecutively and use a paper numbering system instead. Along with the *Journal of Physics: Condensed Matter* (see above), *Part B* of the *Physical Review* presents the most important research in the field. Like all of the sections of the *Physical Review,* it belongs in every physics research collection.

5064. *Physical Review C (Nuclear Physics).* Supersedes in part (1893-1969): *Physical Review.* [ISSN: 0556-2813] 1970. m. USD 1070 print & online eds. Ed(s): Benjamin F. Gibson. American Physical Society, One Physics Ellipse, College Park, MD 20740-3843; http://www.aps.org. Illus., index. Refereed. Vol. ends: Jun/Dec. Microform: BHP. Online: EBSCO Publishing, EBSCO Host; OhioLINK. *Indexed:* ApMecR, CPI, ChemAb, MathR, SCI. *Aud.:* Ac, Sa.

Part C of the *Physical Review* covers nuclear physics, including nuclear structure, nucleon-nucleon interactions, nuclear reactions, nuclear structure, relativistic nuclear collisions, hadronic physics and quantum chromodynamics, the electroweak interaction, and nuclear astrophysics. Both full-length research papers and brief reports are included, along with comments on previously published research. Letters to the editor are published in the separate *Physical Review Letters* (see below). Like all of the parts of the *Physical Review,* this section is the most prestigious journal published in its branch of physics. Although this journal does not contain as many articles as other parts of the *Physical Review,* it has also adopted the article/page numbering system instead of consecutive page numbers. Along with the *Journal of Physics G* (see above), this title represents the core literature of nuclear physics and belongs in any physics research collection.

5065. *Physical Review D (Particles, Fields, Gravitation and Cosmology).* Formerly (until 2004): *Physical Review. D. Particles and Fields;* Supersedes in part (in 1970): *Physical Review.* [ISSN: 1550-7998] 1893. 24x/yr. USD 3790 print & online eds. Ed(s): D. L. Nordstrom, Erick J. Weinberg. American Physical Society, One Physics Ellipse, College Park, MD 20740-3843; http://www.aps.org. Illus., index. Refereed. Microform: BHP. Online: EBSCO Publishing, EBSCO Host; OhioLINK. *Indexed:* ApMecR, CCMJ, CPI, ChemAb, IAA, MSN, MathR, SCI. *Aud.:* Ac, Sa.

This section of the *Physical Review* covers particles, fields, gravitation, and cosmology. The first issue of each month is devoted to experimental particle physics and phenomenologically oriented theory of particles and fields. The second issue of the month covers more formally oriented theory of particles and fields, gravitation, cosmology, and allied areas. Some specific topics covered throughout this title include cosmic rays, collisions, particle decay, electroweak interactions, quantum chromodynamics, particle beams, general relativity, supergravity, astrophysics, field theory, gauge theory, and the grand unification theory. Both full-length research reports and short, rapid communications are accepted, with the former predominating. Review articles also appear on an irregular basis. Letters appear in the related *Physical Review Letters* (see below). As with the other sections of the *Physical Review,* the number of articles published each year is tremendous, filling tens of thousands of pages. And as with the other sections of the *Physical Review,* the editors have abandoned sequential page numbering in favor of an article/page system. Along with all the other parts of the journal, *Part D* is the premier journal in the world covering its branch of physics and belongs in every physics research library.

5066. *Physical Review E (Statistical, Nonlinear, and Soft Matter Physics).* Formerly (until 2001): *Physical Review E (Statistical Physics, Plasmas, Fluids, and Related Interdisciplinary Topics);* Which superseded in part (in 1993): *Physical Review A (Atomic, Molecular and Optical Physics);* Which was formerly (until 1990): *Physical Review A (General Physics);* Which superseded in part (in 1970): *Physical Review.* [ISSN: 1539-3755] 1893. m. USD 2955 print & online eds. Ed(s): Gary S. Grest, Margaret Malloy. American Physical Society, One Physics Ellipse, College Park, MD 20740-3843; http://www.aps.org. Illus., index. Refereed. Vol. ends: Jun/Dec. Microform: PQC. Online: EBSCO Publishing, EBSCO Host; OhioLINK. *Indexed:* CCMJ, CPI, ChemAb, EngInd, MSN, MathR, SCI, SSCI. *Aud.:* Ac, Sa.

The final section of the *Physical Review* covers statistical, nonlinear, and soft-matter physics. This section of the journal has become so large that it is published in two parts with 16 subsections. Part one covers soft matter and biological physics, whereas part two covers statistical and nonlinear physics, fluid dynamics, and related topics. A single monthly issue may run into several thousand pages. Specific subjects include statistical methods, fluids, granular materials, colloidal dispersions, suspensions, and aggregates, complex fluids, liquid crystals, polymers, biological physics, chaos theory, fluid dynamics, plasma physics, classical physics, and computational physics. Full articles, brief research reports, and rapid communications of important findings are all accepted, along with comments on previously published material. Letters are published in the related *Physical Review Letters* (see below). As with all other sections of the *Physical Review,* the editors reject over half of all papers submitted. The journal no longer uses page numbering, but rather an article/page numbering system. *Part E,* as one part of the most prestigious physics journal in the world, belongs in any physics research collection.

5067. *Physical Review Focus.* [ISSN: 1539-0748] 1998. m. Free. Ed(s): David Ehrenstein. American Physical Society, One Physics Ellipse, College Park, MD 20740-3843. *Aud.:* Ga, Ac, Sa.

Issued in electronic format only, *Physical Review Focus* is intended to provide wider distribution for research published in the print *Physical Review* and *Physical Review Letters.* Articles are selected for this journal based on their educational value and intrinsic interest to nonspecialists. Often they represent summaries of key research published in the other sections of the *Physical Review,* but are rewritten for a more general audience. They still require a strong understanding of basic physics and are intended to promote communication between the various subdisciplines of the field. Links are provided to the electronic originals, so that subscribers can obtain the full text of the original paper if desired. *Physical Review Focus* also links to the electronic *Physics News Update* and *Physics News Preview.* Because there is no access charge and the articles are written for a wider audience, this is a good general physics source that libraries may wish to provide. URL: http://focus.aps.org.

5068. *Physical Review Letters.* [ISSN: 0031-9007] 1958. w. USD 2985 print & online eds. Ed(s): Jack Sandweiss, Reinhardt B. Schuhmann. American Physical Society, One Physics Ellipse, College Park, MD 20740-3843; http://www.aps.org. Illus., index. Refereed. Online: EBSCO Publishing, EBSCO Host; OhioLINK. *Indexed:* ApMecR, CCMJ, CPI, ChemAb, EngInd, IAA, MSN, MathR, PhotoAb, SCI. *Aud.:* Ac, Sa.

This title is the letters-to-the-editor section for all parts of the *Physical Review* (see above). It publishes brief reports of important discoveries in any branch of physics, including general physics; gravitation and astrophysics; elementary particles and fields; nuclear physics; atomic, molecular, and optical physics; plasmas and beam physics; condensed matter; and interdisciplinary topics. All articles published are very brief, with a maximum length of four pages. Like its parent journal, *Physical Review Letters* is one of the most respected and most cited journals in all of physics. It was one of the very first letters-only journals and maintains the high editorial standards of the *Physical Review.* It was established to speed publication of short papers that present significant results.

Even though hundreds of pages are published each week, the editors reject over half of all papers submitted. *Physical Review Letters* is the single most prestigious journal of its kind and belongs in every physics research collection.

5069. *Physical Review Special Topics - Accelerators and Beams.* [ISSN: 1098-4402] 1998. q. Free. American Physical Society, One Physics Ellipse, College Park, MD 20740-3843; http://www.aps.org. Refereed. *Indexed:* CPI, SCI. *Aud.:* Ac, Sa.

Physical Review Special Topics: Accelerators and Beams was the first all-electronic section of the prestigious *Physical Review.* It covers the full range of accelerator science and technology, including subsystem and component technologies; beam dynamics; applications of accelerators; and design, operation, and improvement of accelerators used in science and industry. Papers are divided into 15 distinct subsections and may present new research results; review the state of the art of accelerator research or technology; propose new experiments; review active areas of research; or expand upon previously published research. Because of its electronic nature, there is no limit to the number of pages or illustrations that can be included in any given article. Another important feature of the electronic nature of this publication is that most articles are freely available, without restriction, to any reader. In addition to the original research articles, the journal links to relevant papers published in other sections of the *Physical Review* and *Physical Review Letters.* This title is recommended for any library that supports specialized research in this area. URL: http://prst-ab.aps.org.

5070. *Physical Review Special Topics - Physics Education Research.* [ISSN: 1554-9178] q. Ed(s): Robert Beichner. American Physical Society, One Physics Ellipse, College Park, MD 20740-3843; http://www.aps.org. *Aud.:* Ga, Ac, Sa.

The newest in the *Physical Review* collection of journals, this special-topics title is dedicated to research in the teaching of physics. It covers the full range of experimental and theoretical research on the teaching and/or learning of physics. Review articles, replication studies, descriptions of the development and use of new assessment tools, presentation of research techniques, and methodology comparisons/critiques are all included. Like the other special topics journal, it is available only online. This title is sponsored jointly by the American Physical Society and the American Association of Physics Teachers. This title is recommended for any college or university that has a physics program.

5071. *Physical Society of Japan. Journal.* Formerly: *Physico-Mathematical Society of Japan. Proceedings.* [ISSN: 0031-9015] 1946. m. JPY 86000 combined subscription for print & online eds. Ed(s): H Shiba. Institute of Pure and Applied Physics, Toyokaiji Bldg, no.12, 6-9-6 Shinbashi, Minato-ku, Tokyo, 105-0004, Japan; subscription@ipap.jp; http://www.ipap.jp. Illus., index. Refereed. Circ: 2600. Vol. ends: Dec. Online: EBSCO Publishing, EBSCO Host; J-Stage. *Indexed:* ApMecR, CCMJ, ChemAb, IAA, MSN, MathR, PhotoAb, SCI. *Aud.:* Ac, Sa.

This title is the official journal of the Physical Society of Japan, publishing some of the most significant physics research conducted in Japan and Asia. All of the subdisciplines of physics are covered, including classical physics, fluids and plasmas, particles and fields, and atomic physics, although the majority of the papers published relate to condensed matter physics. Although the journal is published in Japan, all of the articles are written in English, making them accessible to the wider scientific community. Full-length scientific papers, research notes, and letters to the editor are all included. Although this journal used to be available on the web at no charge, like most scientific journals the web version is now bundled with a subscription to the print version. This title is the Japanese equivalent of the other national journals included here, and it belongs in comprehensive physics research collections.

5072. *Physics Education.* [ISSN: 0031-9120] 1966. bi-m. USD 490 print & online eds. (Individuals, USD 128). Ed(s): Gary Williams. Institute of Physics Publishing, Dirac House, Temple Back, Bristol, BS1 6BE, United Kingdom; custserv@iop.org; http://www.iop.org. Illus., index, adv. Sample. Refereed. Vol. ends: Nov. Online: EBSCO Publishing, EBSCO Host; Gale; IngentaConnect; OhioLINK; SwetsWise Online Content. *Indexed:* BrEdI, ChemAb, ERIC, MRD, RILM, SWA. *Bk. rev.:* Number and length vary. *Aud.:* Hs, Ga, Ac.

Physics Education is a British publication that seeks to inform and stimulate high school and beginning undergraduate college students. As such, it is one of the few physics journals that is understandable to a general audience. The editors seek to provide teachers with a forum for discussing ideas and methods for teaching physics, assessment techniques, updates on research in the field, and strategies for classroom management. Research papers are presented on the teaching and learning of physics; the examining and assessment of physics; new approaches to the general presentation and application of physics in the classroom; and curriculum developments around the world. All of the articles are written for the nonspecialist and avoid much of the higher-level mathematics inherent in most physics publications. The goals of the journal are to cover the wide range of topics included in the field of physics, to enhance the standards and quality of teaching, to make physics more attractive to students and teachers, to keep teachers up-to-date on new developments in the field, and to provide a forum for the sharing of ideas about teaching physics. Each issue contains articles on new developments in physics, ideas for teaching physical concepts, profiles of prominent scientists, reviews of resources that can be used by physics teachers, news from the field, and even a little humor. Articles in the electronic version are supplemented by multimedia content such as worksheets, spreadsheets, programs, and video clips. This journal is the British equivalent of *The Physics Teacher* (see below). For those libraries that seek to add a general physics journal to their collections, this is an excellent choice.

5073. *Physics Letters. Section A: General, Atomic and Solid State Physics.* Supersedes in part (in 1967): *Physics Letters.* [ISSN: 0375-9601] 1962. 72x/yr. EUR 5362. Ed(s): C R Doering, A R Bishop. Elsevier BV, North-Holland, Sara Burgerhartstraat 25, Amsterdam, 1055 KV, Netherlands; nlinfo-f@elsevier.nl; http://www.elsevier.nl. Illus., index. Sample. Refereed. Vol. ends: No. 278 - No. 291. Microform: PQC. Online: EBSCO Publishing, EBSCO Host; Gale; IngentaConnect; OhioLINK; ScienceDirect; SwetsWise Online Content. *Indexed:* CCMJ, ChemAb, MSN, MathR, PhilInd, SCI. *Aud.:* Ac, Sa.

Physics Letters is a publication outlet for rapid communication of significant, original, and timely research results. Articles tend to be very brief, with longer review articles printed in the related journal *Physics Reports* (see below). *Section A* of this journal is the general physics portion, covering all branches of physics except high-energy nuclear and particle physics. Topics usually included are condensed-matter physics; theoretical physics; nonlinear science; statistical physics; mathematical and computational physics; atomic, molecular, and cluster physics; plasma and fluid physics; optical physics; biological physics; and nanoscience. Articles are accepted for publication based upon the originality of the research, desirability for speedy publication, and the clarity of the presentation. This journal publishes an incredible number of articles, producing around 12,000 pages in a single year. Along with the *Physical Review Letters* (see above), it is one of the most cited and most prominent letters journals in the field. This title belongs in any physics research collection.

5074. *Physics Letters. Section B: Nuclear, Elementary Particle and High-Energy Physics.* Supersedes in part (in 1967): *Physics Letters.* [ISSN: 0370-2693] 1962. 72x/yr. EUR 8241. Ed(s): M Doser, W D Schlatter. Elsevier BV, North-Holland, Sara Burgerhartstraat 25, Amsterdam, 1055 KV, Netherlands; nlinfo-f@elsevier.nl; http://www.elsevier.nl. Illus., index. Sample. Refereed. Vol. ends: No. 497 - No. 523. Microform: PQC. Online: EBSCO Publishing, EBSCO Host; Gale; IngentaConnect; OhioLINK; ScienceDirect; SwetsWise Online Content. *Indexed:* CCMJ, ChemAb, CompR, MSN, MathR, SCI. *Aud.:* Ac, Sa.

Physics Letters B is the second part of the *Physics Letters* series. It covers the two areas excluded from *Part A*: nuclear and particle physics. Despite its more limited subject scope, this section is the larger of the two parts of *Physics Letters*, reflecting the vast amount of research published in nuclear and particle physics. There can be as many as 5,000 pages printed in this journal in a single year. Papers accepted for publication represent the results of research conducted at laboratories around the world, reflecting the international aspect of high-energy physics. Each issue is divided into four sections: astrophysics and cosmology; experiments; phenomenology; and theory. Like most physics research journals, each article must be the result of original research and must not have appeared in print before. This journal is frequently used to determine

precedent in scientific discoveries in its fields of interest. Both sections of *Physics Letters* should be a part of any serious physics research collection.

5075. *Physics News Update: the American Institute of Physics bulletin news.* w. American Institute of Physics, 2 Huntington Quadrangle, Ste 1NO1, Melville, NY 11747-4502; aipinfo@aip.org; http://www.aip.org. *Aud.:* Hs, Ga, Ac, Sa.

Physics News Update is a digest of physics news compiled from journals, newspapers, magazines, conferences, and other sources. Issued only in electronic format, it is designed to present the results of physics research to a wide audience. Readers are able to access the journal on the web, through a weekly e-mail alert service, and through RSS feeds. Each issue contains several interesting articles on new developments in the field, a selection of "Physics News Graphics," which are high-quality images demonstrating physical concepts, and links to other physics news web sites. Archives are available on the web back to 1990. This title is available at no charge and is a good example of how the web can be used to promote research in a specific field of study. The material is written so that it will reach a wide range of readers, from students to specialists. This electronic journal should be a part of any physics collection. URL: www.aip.org/pnu.

5076. *Physics of Fluids.* Formerly: *Physics of Fluids A: Fluid Dynamics;* Which superseded in part (in 1989): *Physics of Fluids.* [ISSN: 1070-6631] 1958. m. USD 2595 print & online eds. Ed(s): L. Gary Leal, John Kim. American Institute of Physics, 2 Huntington Quadrangle, Ste 1NO1, Melville, NY 11747-4502; aipinfo@aip.org; http://www.aip.org. Illus., index. Refereed. Vol. ends: Dec. Online: American Institute of Physics, Scitation; EBSCO Publishing, EBSCO Host; OhioLINK; SwetsWise Online Content. *Indexed:* ApMecR, CCMJ, CPI, ChemAb, EngInd, M&GPA, MSN, MathR, SCI. *Aud.:* Ac, Sa.

This journal is the official publication of the Division of Fluid Dynamics of the American Physical Society. It is devoted to the publication of original research in the field of gases, liquids, and complex or multiphase fluids. Specific areas covered include kinetic theory, fluid dynamics, wave phenomena, hypersonic physics, hydrodynamics, compressible fluids, boundary layers, conduction, and chaotic phenomena. Material on plasmas and plasma physics is published in the related *Physics of Plasmas* (see below), which can be purchased in combination with this title at a reduced rate. Full papers, brief reports, and letters are all accepted. Comments on previously published papers are also included, sometimes leading to interesting scientific debate. A unique feature of this journal is the annual *Gallery of Fluid Motion,* which presents visual representations of fluid flow and fluid problems. This is the primary journal for research in fluids and belongs in any comprehensive physics collection.

5077. *Physics of Plasmas.* Formerly: *Physics of Fluids B: Plasma Physics;* Which superseded in part (in 1989): *Physics of Fluids.* [ISSN: 1070-664X] 1958. m. USD 3010 print & online eds. Ed(s): R C Davidson. American Institute of Physics, 2 Huntington Quadrangle, Ste 1NO1, Melville, NY 11747-4502; aipinfo@aip.org; http://www.aip.org. Illus., index. Refereed. Vol. ends: Dec. Online: American Institute of Physics, Scitation; EBSCO Publishing, EBSCO Host; OhioLINK; SwetsWise Online Content. *Indexed:* CCMJ, CPI, ChemAb, EngInd, MSN, MathR, SCI. *Aud.:* Ac, Sa.

As the official publication of the Division of Plasmas of the American Institute of Physics, *Physics of Plasmas* is devoted to original contributions to and reviews of the physics of plasmas, including magnetofluid mechanics, kinetic theory, and statistical mechanics of fully and partially ionized gases. Formerly published with *Physics of Fluids,* the two journals were divided in 1994. Specific topics covered by this journal include equilibria, waves, nonlinear behavior, lasers, particle beams, radiation, astrophysics, geophysical plasmas, plasma chemistry, physics of dense plasmas, and containment techniques. Full-length articles, brief reports, and letters to the editor are all included. This journal is one of the standard sources of information in this branch of physics, and it belongs in any collection that supports research in this area.

5078. *Physics Reports.* Incorporates (1983-1991): *Computer Physics Reports;* (1972-1975): *Case Studies in Atomic Physics.* [ISSN: 0370-1573] 1971. 102x/yr. EUR 6126. Ed(s): M P Kamionkowsi, J Eichler. Elsevier BV, North-Holland, Sara Burgerhartstraat 25,

Amsterdam, 1055 KV, Netherlands; nlinfo-f@elsevier.nl; http://www.elsevier.nl. Illus., index. Sample. Refereed. Vol. ends: No. 338 - No. 353. Microform: PQC. Online: EBSCO Publishing, EBSCO Host; Gale; IngentaConnect; OhioLINK; ScienceDirect; SwetsWise Online Content. *Indexed:* CCMJ, ChemAb, IAA, MSN, MathR, SCI. *Aud.:* Ac, Sa.

In contrast to its sister publications *Physics Letters A* and *B* (see above), which both publish brief papers presenting new research findings, *Physics Reports* publishes lengthy articles designed to provide state-of-the-art reviews that benchmark research in various fields. Each issue contains a single article, which is usually somewhat longer than a literature review but shorter than a monograph. The reviews are specialist in nature but contain enough background and introductory material to be understandable to physicists who are working in other subdisciplines. In addition to identifying significant developments and trends, the extensive literature reviews serve as indexes to the topic being discussed. Subjects can be from any field of physics, and the editorial board consists of specialists in a variety of fields who are able to judge the quality and accuracy of the manuscripts. This title is similar in scope to *Contemporary Physics* (above) and *Reports on Progress in Physics* (below), although *Physics Reports* is written at the highest level of the three. Any of the three would be useful additions to a college physics collection.

5079. The Physics Teacher. [ISSN: 0031-921X] 1963. 9x/yr. USD 330 print & online eds. Ed(s): Karl Mamola. American Association of Physics Teachers, One Physics Ellipse, College Park, MD 20740-3845; aapt-pubs@aapt.org; http://www.aapt.org. Illus., index, adv. Refereed. Circ: 11000 Paid. Vol. ends: Dec. Online: American Institute of Physics, Scitation; EBSCO Publishing, EBSCO Host; SwetsWise Online Content. *Indexed:* ABIn, BRI, BiolDig, CPI, ChemAb, EduInd, FLI, GSI, MRD. *Bk. rev.:* Number and length vary. *Aud.:* Hs, Ga, Ac.

The Physics Teacher is dedicated to the strengthening of physics teaching at the introductory level. As such, it is the primary journal of interest to high school physics teachers. Articles are written for the nonspecialist and present physics principles without the higher-level mathematics that are usually included in physics research articles. Papers cover topics of interest to students and to the general public, often focusing on the applications of physical principles to everyday life. In addition to full articles, the journal also publishes frequent symposia that provide teachers with new ideas and teaching methods; notes on interesting applications and phenomena; information on equipment and apparatus for teaching physics; and editorials, web sites, and book reviews. Every month, the journal publishes several problems for readers to solve and follows this up in the next issue with solutions and the names of the first five people to answer correctly. The editors have also started the new feature of "Fermi questions," where readers use physics to estimate answer to everyday problems. This journal is similar to its British equivalent, *Physics Education* (see above). *The Physics Teacher* is a very readable journal and one of the few that is approachable by both the specialist and nonscientist. Although it is primarily aimed at high school teachers, it is one of the few physics journals that should be considered for general library collections.

5080. Physics Today. [ISSN: 0031-9228] 1948. m. USD 425. Ed(s): Stephen G. Benka. American Institute of Physics, 1 Physics Ellipse, College Park, MD 20740-3843; aipinfo@aip.org; http://www.aip.org. Illus., index, adv. Sample. Refereed. Circ: 121872 Controlled. Vol. ends: Dec. Online: EBSCO Publishing, EBSCO Host. *Indexed:* A&ATA, AS&TI, ApMecR, ArtHuCI, BRI, BiolDig, BrTechI, C&ISA, CBRI, CPI, CerAb, ChemAb, EngInd, ExcerpMed, GSI, IAA, LRI, M&GPA, MASUSE, MSN, RGPR, RILM, SCI, SSCI. *Bk. rev.:* 7-10. *Aud.:* Hs, Ga, Ac.

Physics Today is the only true general-interest physics journal currently being published. It is the flagship publication of the American Institute of Physics and is intended to keep readers informed about physics and its place in the world. In addition to providing full-length articles on interesting areas in the field of physics, this journal serves as a news source for anyone interested in the field of physics, including scientists, teachers, students, and the general public. Its wide appeal is evidenced by the fact that it is the only physics journal to be indexed in the *Readers' Guide to Periodical Literature*. Articles are written specifically for the nonspecialist and present advanced physical concepts without burdening the reader with advanced mathematics. With color

photographs, well-written prose, and timely and engaging subject matter, this is the only physics journal that consistently could be considered for newsstand distribution. Each issue provides news of recent discoveries, conference updates, editorials, book reviews, new-product announcements, obituaries, positions available, and political updates. The online version also provides links to original research in other journals published by the American Institute of Physics. *Physics Today* is essential for any college or university library and should be considered by public and school libraries as well. Unless a library supports a physics research program, this title is the only physics journal that should be considered for purchase.

5081. Physics World. Formed by the merger of (in 1988): *Physics Bulletin;* (1973-1988): *Physics in Technology;* Which was formerly (until 1970): *Review of Physics in Technology.* [ISSN: 0953-8585] 1950. m. GBP 260 print & online eds. Free to members IOP. Ed(s): P Rodgers. Institute of Physics Publishing, Dirac House, Temple Back, Bristol, BS1 6BE, United Kingdom; custserv@iop.org; http://www.iop.org. Illus., index, adv. Refereed. Vol. ends: Dec. Online: EBSCO Publishing, EBSCO Host; OhioLINK. *Indexed:* BiolDig, C&ISA, CerAb, ChemAb, EngInd, ExcerpMed, PhilInd, SCI, SSCI. *Bk. rev.:* Number and length vary. *Aud.:* Hs, Ga, Ac.

Physics World is one of the few truly general-interest physics journals. It is the newsletter of the British Institute of Physics and provides members of that organization with the same type of information and services that *Physics Today* does for members of the American Institute of Physics. It presents physics news and information to a general audience of scientists and the public. Each issue contains feature articles, news, product reviews, book reviews, job ads, editorials, letters, humor, and association news. As with its American counterpart, the journal's articles are written for the nonscientist and may be appreciated by general adult readers. It is an integral part of the Institute of Physics member web site, and many of the articles are available for free at www.physicsweb.org. *Physics World* is one of the few physics journals published for a general audience and is an excellent choice for addition to any college or general library collection.

5082. Reports on Progress in Physics. [ISSN: 0034-4885] 1934. m. USD 2765 print & online eds. Ed(s): Laura H. Greene. Institute of Physics Publishing, Dirac House, Temple Back, Bristol, BS1 6BE, United Kingdom; custserv@iop.org; http://www.iop.org. Illus., index. Sample. Refereed. Vol. ends: Dec. Online: EBSCO Publishing, EBSCO Host; Gale; IngentaConnect; OhioLINK; SwetsWise Online Content. *Indexed:* A&ATA, ApMecR, CCMJ, ChemAb, IAA, MSN, MathR, SCI. *Aud.:* Ac, Sa.

Reports on Progress in Physics publishes review articles in all subdisciplines of physics. Articles combine a critical evaluation of the field with a reliable and accessible introduction to the topic, making the articles accessible to a wider scientific community. As with all review journals, articles tend to be long, often over 100 pages. Topics include particles and fields, nuclear physics, condensed matter, biophysics, astrophysics, surface science, plasma physics, and lasers. From time to time, the editors solicit reviews on critical issues in the field. These are published as "Key Issues Reviews" and are highlighted in the journal. Rather than reviewing papers submitted by potential authors, all of the articles are invited by the editors from distinguished researchers in the field. This journal is similar in scope to *Contemporary Physics* and *Physics Reports* (see above). College libraries should subscribe to at least one of these titles, and research libraries will probably wish to get all three.

5083. Review of Scientific Instruments. Former titles (until 1929): *Journal of the Optical Society of America and Review of Scientific Instruments;* (until 1921): *Journal of the Optical Society of America.* [ISSN: 0034-6748] 1917. m. USD 2005 print & online eds. Ed(s): Albert T Macrander. American Institute of Physics, 2 Huntington Quadrangle, Ste 1NO1, Melville, NY 11747-4502; aipinfo@aip.org; http://www.aip.org. Illus., index. Refereed. Circ: 3500 Paid. Vol. ends: Dec. Online: American Institute of Physics, Scitation; EBSCO Publishing, EBSCO Host; OhioLINK; SwetsWise Online Content. *Indexed:* AS&TI, ApMecR, CPI, ChemAb, EngInd, ExcerpMed, IAA, PhotoAb, SCI. *Aud.:* Ac, Sa.

Modern physics research relies heavily on sophisticated instrumentation to make measurements, conduct experiments, analyze data, and test current theories. *Review of Scientific Instruments* is a specialized journal whose role is to evaluate equipment, apparatus, experimental techniques, and mathematical analysis of results. This journal publishes original research articles and literature reviews on instrumentation in physics, chemistry, and the life sciences. The editors interpret the concept of instrumentation very widely and include all of the tools used by the modern scientist. In addition to full articles, the journal also provides notes on new instruments and materials, letters to the editor, and occasional conference proceedings from relevant meetings. Because of its focus on instrumentation, many manufacturers also advertise their products in this journal. This title is similar in scope to the British *Measurement Science and Technology* (see above). North American libraries that serve scientific researchers will want to subscribe to *Review of Scientific Instruments*, and comprehensive physics and scientific research libraries will probably need both titles.

5084. *Reviews of Modern Physics.* [ISSN: 0034-6861] 1929. q. USD 530 combined subscription domestic print & online eds.; USD 550 combined subscription foreign print & online eds. Ed(s): Achim Richter. American Physical Society, One Physics Ellipse, College Park, MD 20740-3843; http://www.aps.org. Illus., index. Refereed. Microform: MIM. Online: EBSCO Publishing, EBSCO Host; OhioLINK. *Indexed:* AS&TI, ApMecR, CCMJ, CPI, ChemAb, EngInd, ExcerpMed, GSI, IAA, MSN, MathR, SCI. *Aud.:* Ac, Sa.

Reviews of Modern Physics enhances communication among physicists by publishing comprehensive scholarly reviews and tutorials on significant topics in modern physics. As with *Contemporary Physics, Physics Reports,* and *Reports on Progress in Physics* (see above), the articles do not contain results of original research but collect and synthesize existing research on topics of current interest. Research from any branch or subdiscipline of physics is included, although articles from newly developing fields are given preference. Articles are not submitted to referees as in most physics journals. At least half of the articles are solicited by the editors. In addition to lengthy review articles, some shorter colloquia articles are also included. Each year, *Reviews of Modern Physics* also publishes the Nobel lecture of the Nobel Prize winner in physics. This title is especially useful for helping physics teachers and graduate students keep abreast of recent developments. To enhance this role, the journal also accepts occasional tutorial articles aimed primarily at students or those new to the field. *Reviews of Modern Physics* is the most cited of all physics review journals and belongs in most physics research collections.

5085. *Solid State Communications.* [ISSN: 0038-1098] 1963. 48x/yr. EUR 4716. Ed(s): A Pinczuk. Pergamon, The Boulevard, Langford Ln, East Park, Kidlington, OX5 1GB, United Kingdom. Illus., index, adv. Sample. Refereed. Circ: 2000. Microform: MIM; PQC. Online: EBSCO Publishing, EBSCO Host; Gale; IngentaConnect; OhioLINK; ScienceDirect; SwetsWise Online Content. *Indexed:* ApMecR, C&ISA, ChemAb, EngInd, SCI. *Aud.:* Ac, Sa.

This journal serves as the letters section of the *Journal of Physics and Chemistry of Solids* (see above). It publishes original experimental and theoretical research on the physical and chemical properties of solids and other condensed systems and also on their preparation. Topics covered include the basic physics of materials and devices, microstructures, superconductors, and nanostructures. The emphasis is on brevity, with papers usually under four pages in length. A coherent quantitative treatment that emphasizes new physics is expected rather than a simple accumulation of experimental data. Papers published may be experimental or theoretical in nature. On occasion, the editors publish a longer research paper on a topic of broad interest in solid-state physics. These papers contain not only new research results, but also background information on the field. Like its parent title, *Solid State Communications* belongs in graduate research physics collections.

5086. *Studies in History and Philosophy of Science Part B: Studies in History and Philosophy of Modern Physics.* [ISSN: 1355-2198] 1995. 4x/yr. EUR 541. Ed(s): D Dieks. Pergamon, The Boulevard, Langford Ln, East Park, Kidlington, OX5 1GB, United Kingdom. Illus., index. Sample. Refereed. Vol. ends: Dec. Microform: PQC. Online: EBSCO

Publishing, EBSCO Host; Gale; IngentaConnect; OhioLINK; ScienceDirect; SwetsWise Online Content. *Indexed:* AmH&L, ArtHuCI, CCMJ, HistAb, IBSS, IPB, MSN, MathR, PhilInd, SCI. *Aud.:* Ac, Sa.

As scientists make new discoveries and develop new theories, they also change the ways in which we understand and approach our world. Advances in physics such as quantum theory, field theory, and relativity have given us new tools for measuring the universe. One result of these dramatic changes has been a rise in the study of the history of science, with particular emphasis on the history of modern physics, including astronomy, chemistry, and other nonbiological sciences. The primary focus is on research from the mid/late-nineteenth century to the present, the period of emergence of the kind of theoretical physics that came to dominate the exact sciences in the twentieth century. Two sister journals in the *Studies in History and Philosophy of Science* series examine science in general (*Part A*) and the biological and medical sciences (*Part C*). In each section, original articles and review essays are published. Because the focus is on the history of ideas, many of the articles are approachable for a wider audience. This journal belongs in any collection dealing with the history of science.

5087. *Virtual Journal of Applications of Superconductivity.* [ISSN: 1553-9636] s-m. Ed(s): John R Clem. American Institute of Physics, 1 Physics Ellipse, College Park, MD 20740-3843; aipinfo@aip.org; http://www.aip.org. *Aud.:* Ac, Sa.

This is one of five titles in the *Virtual Journal* series produced by the American Institute of Physics. Sixteen different publishers, primarily professional associations, have joined together to release their papers for inclusion in these five titles. Like all of the titles in the series, this journal focuses on a specialized, developing area within the discipline of physics. This title is concerned with papers about applications of superconductivity to electronics and large-scale systems, as well as materials and properties important to applications. It does not accept original research papers, but reproduces articles that have already been published in a number of other physics and related journals. The title is completely electronic and has no print equivalent. Access to the full text of the articles is based upon subscriptions to the original source journals. If a library subscribes to a journal used as a source for the *Virtual Journal,* the article is freely available to the reader. If a library does not subscribe to the source journal, that article is available on a pay-per-article basis. In addition to the articles, the journal provides news from the field and a wide variety of web links to authoritative sites about superconductivity. These sites range from tutorials for the beginner to advanced research information. Four similar journals covering the areas of biological physics research, nanoscience technology, quantum information, and ultrafast science are also available in the *Virtual Journals in Science and Technology* series. This journal should be available in any library that supports research in superconductivity. URL: www.vjsuper.org/super

5088. *Virtual Journal of Biological Physics Research: a monthly multijournal compilation of the latest research on biological physics.* [ISSN: 1553-9628] 2000. m. Ed(s): Robert H Austin. American Physical Society, One Physics Ellipse, College Park, MD 20740-3843. Index, adv. Refereed. *Aud.:* Ac, Sa.

As one of five virtual electronic journals published by the American Institute of Physics, the *Virtual Journal of Biological Physics Research* covers the applications of physics to the life sciences. Topics covered include quantum mechanical dynamics; physics of water and hydrogen-bonded solvents; membrane biophysics; fundamental polymer statics/dynamics; protein conformational dynamics/folding; DNA conformational dynamics; single molecule dynamics; intermolecular interactions; physical studies of cell mechanics; information transfer in biological systems; multicellular phenomena; biological networks; and instrumentation development. This journal does not publish original research, but it reprints articles published in its many source journals. The benefit of this title is that it brings together material that may be found in a wide variety of other journals. It belongs in specialized physics or biology collections. URL: www.vjbio.org/bio

5089. *Virtual Journal of Nanoscale Science & Technology: a weekly multijournal compilation of the latest research on nanoscale systems.* [ISSN: 1553-9644] 2000. w. Ed(s): David Awschalom. American Physical Society, One Physics Ellipse, College Park, MD 20740-3843. Adv. Refereed. *Aud.:* Ac, Sa.

Nanoscale science is essentially the study of solid-state physics at the quantum level. This has become an important subfield of physics, with many new developments in both theory and application. Because results of research in this field are published in a wide range of sources, the American Institute of Physics began the *Virtual Journal of Nanoscale Science and Technology* to pull this information together. This journal does not accept original papers for publication, but reproduces papers that have already been published in a number of other source journals. Like the other *Virtual Journals* in this series, it is only available on the web and has no print equivalent. Access to the articles is based upon subscriptions to the original source journals. If a library subscribes to a journal used as a source for the *Virtual Journal,* the article is freely available. If a library does not subscribe to the source journal, that article is available on a pay-per-article basis. This journal was the first in the *Virtual Journals in Science and Technology* series, which has now been expanded to include the four other titles. The journal should be available in any library that supports research in nanotechnology. URL: www.vjnano.org/nano.

5090. *Virtual Journal of Quantum Information: a multijournal compilation of research in quantum computing, cryptography, and communication.* [ISSN: 1553-961X] 2001. m. Ed(s): David DiVincenzo. American Physical Society, One Physics Ellipse, College Park, MD 20740-3843. *Aud.:* Ac, Sa.

The *Virtual Journal of Quantum Information* is one of five sister journals published by the American Institute of Physics. This title is a specialized journal that covers quantum computing and information. Topics covered by this journal include algorithms and computations; cryptography; entanglement; error correction; information theory; and implementations. Rather than publishing the results of original research, these journals bring together previously published material from a wide variety of source journals. Article are available to subscribers of the source journals or may be purchased on an individual basis. This journal belongs in specialized physics and computing collections. URL: www.vjquantuminfo.org/quantuminfo.

5091. *Virtual Journal of Ultrafast Science.* [ISSN: 1553-9601] 2002. m. Free. Ed(s): Philip H Bucksbaum. American Institute of Physics, 1 Physics Ellipse, College Park, MD 20740-3843; http://www.aip.org. Vol. ends: Dec. *Aud.:* Ac, Sa.

Ultrafast science deals with physical phenomena that occur in the range of one-trillionth of a second (one picosecond) to one-quadrillionth of a second (one femtosecond) or less. This electronic journal covers all applications and research into such phenomena. Areas covered include measurement techniques, atomic and molecular physics, condensed-matter physics, photonics, and applications in chemistry and biophysics. As one of five virtual journals published by the American Institute of Physics, the *Virtual Journal of Ultrafast Science* brings together articles published in a wide range of source journals. Articles are available free online to subscribers of the source journals and are available for a fee (approximately $15–$25) for nonsubscribers. URL: www.vjultrafast.org/ultrafast.

■ PHYSIOLOGY

See also Biology; Botany; and Zoology sections.

Juanita Benedicto, Reference Librarian, Lane Community College Library, Lane Community College Library, Eugene, OR 97405.

Connie Dalrymple, Life and Health Sciences Librarian, Wichita State University Libraries, Wichita State University, Wichita, KS 67260.

Jeff Kosokoff, Collection Development Librarian, Simmons Library, Simmons College, Boston, MA 02115

Introduction

As new titles in the biological sciences continue to proliferate every year, it becomes increasingly difficult to identify key journals in an important subcategory of biology. In an effort to simplify locating important and focused titles, the former Biological Sciences section has been divided into five new sections: Biology, Botany, Ecology, Physiology, and Zoology. The intent is to provide a greater level of subject specificity, making content more accessible and useful to specialists.

The titles in this section are important publications that will be of interest to upper-level students, researchers, and professionals in physiology in a general context.

Basic Periodicals

American Journal of Physiology (Consolidated), Journal of Applied Physiology, Journal of General Physiology, Physiological Reviews.

Basic Abstracts and Indexes

Biological Abstracts, Biological Abstracts/RRM, Biological and Agricultural Index, Current Contents/Life Sciences.

5092. *American Journal of Physiology (Consolidated).* [ISSN: 0002-9513] 1898. m. USD 3880 (Members, USD 1000 print & online eds.; Non-members, USD 2575). Ed(s): Brenda B Rauner. American Physiological Society, 9650 Rockville Pike, Bethesda, MD 20814-3991; info@the-aps.org; http://www.the-aps.org. Illus., index, adv. Refereed. Circ: 2500. Microform: PMC; PQC. Online: HighWire Press; OCLC Online Computer Library Center, Inc. *Indexed:* Agr, B&AI, CABA, ChemAb, DSA, FPA, ForAb, GSI, HortAb, IndVet, RRTA, S&F, SCI, SSCI, VB, ZooRec. *Aud.:* Ac, Sa.

American Journal of Physiology (Consolidated) holds a high impact factor in its field. This title consolidates papers published in all seven specialty journals of the *American Journal of Physiology.* These seven sections include cell physiology; endocrinology and metabolism; gastrointestinal and liver physiology; heart and circulatory physiology; lung, cellular, and molecular physiology; regulatory, integrative, and comparative physiology; and renal physiology. Each title is available separately or combined. The majority of the journal is made up of research articles, though reviews and special communications also appear. The online content, made available through HighWire Press, includes tables of contents, abstracts, full texts, advance information on future issues, and search capability. CiteTrack is a free alerting service. This important title is appropriate for medical and biology collections. Document delivery is available from BLDSC, CASDDS, CISTI, The Genuine Article, LHLDS, NIWI, UMI, and UnCover.

5093. *Biology of Reproduction.* [ISSN: 0006-3363] 1969. m. USD 575 combined subscription domestic print & online eds.; USD 625 combined subscription foreign print & online eds. Ed(s): Mary Ann Handel, John Eppig. Society for the Study of Reproduction, 1619 Monroe St., Madison, WI 53711-2063; ssr@ssr.org; http://www.ssr.org. Illus., adv. Sample. Refereed. Circ: 3750 Paid. Online: BioOne; CSA; EBSCO Publishing, EBSCO Host; HighWire Press; OCLC Online Computer Library Center, Inc.; OhioLINK. *Indexed:* AbAn, Agr, BiolAb, CABA, ChemAb, DSA, ExcerpMed, FoVS&M, IndVet, RRTA, S&F, SCI, VB, ZooRec. *Aud.:* Ac, Sa.

Biology of Reproduction is the official journal of the Society for the Study of Reproduction (SSR). It publishes original research on a broad range of topics in the field of reproductive biology, as well as mini-reviews on topics of current importance or controversy. With an impact factor of 3.550, it is consistently one of the most highly cited journals in the field of reproductive biology. A sampling of categories covered include embryo, environment, female/male reproductive tract, immunology, mechanisms of hormone action, neuroendocrinology, pituitary, pregnancy, and toxicology. The journal's policy is to allow free Internet access 18 months after publication. The journal's web site includes a table of contents service, sample issue, and online information from 1969 to the present, with varying levels of access from tables of contents through full text, with search capabilities. Online content is provided by Stanford's HighWire Press. Useful for academic collections that support research in reproductive biology, as well as for medical and veterinary libraries.

5094. Endocrinology. [ISSN: 0013-7227] 1917. m. USD 904 (Individuals, USD 418; Members, USD 139). Ed(s): Kenneth Korach. The Endocrine Society, 8401 Connecticut Ave, Ste 900, Chevy Chase, MD 20815-5817; societyservices@endo-society.org; http://www.endo-society.org. Illus., index, adv. Refereed. Circ: 5800. Vol. ends: Dec. Microform: PMC. Online: EBSCO Publishing, EBSCO Host; HighWire Press; Ovid Technologies, Inc. *Indexed:* BiolAb, CABA, ChemAb, DSA, ExcerpMed, HortAb, IndVet, S&F, SCI, VB, ZooRec. *Aud.:* Ac, Sa.

Endocrinology, published monthly by the Endocrine Society, is considered one of the foremost biomedical research journals, and it covers all aspects of research on endocrine glands and their hormones. Journal sections cover receptors, neuroendocrinology, intracellular signal systems, and others. Also useful are the employment opportunities, conference announcements, and other advertisements that appear. Online content is made available via Stanford's HighWire Press and includes full text from 1992 onward, as well as a mix of tables of contents and tables of contents plus abstracts from 1965 to 1992. Subscription options include online access only or print plus online access. Endocrinology is a core journal in this discipline and is appropriate for both medical and biology collections. Document delivery is available from ADONIS, BLDSC, CASDDS, CISTI, The Genuine Article, LHLDS, NIWI, UMI, and UnCover.

5095. Journal of Applied Physiology. Former titles (until 1985): *Journal of Applied Physiology: Respiratory, Environmental and Exercise Physiology;* (until 1977): *Journal of Applied Physiology.* [ISSN: 8750-7587] 1948. m. USD 1235 (Members, USD 365 print & online eds.; Non-members, USD 820). Ed(s): Jerome A Dempsey. American Physiological Society, 9650 Rockville Pike, Bethesda, MD 20814-3991; info@the-aps.org; http://www.the-aps.org. Illus., adv. Refereed. Circ: 3286 Paid and free. Microform: PQC. Online: EBSCO Publishing, EBSCO Host; HighWire Press. *Indexed:* AbAn, AgeL, B&AI, BiolAb, CABA, ChemAb, DSA, ErgAb, ExcerpMed, H&SSA, HortAb, IAA, IndVet, PEI, RRTA, SCI, SSCI, VB. *Aud.:* Ac, Sa.

This journal publishes papers that deal with normal or abnormal function in four areas: respiratory physiology, environmental physiology, exercise physiology, and temperature regulation. Articles include peer-reviewed research papers, communications, historical papers, editorials, and reviews. Subscription options include print-only, print plus online, and online-only. Online content is provided through Stanford's HighWire Press and includes full text from 1996 to the present. Full historical content of the American Physiological Society's 14 journals, going back to the very first issues of the *American Journal of Physiology* in 1898, is available online. This package, the APS Journal Legacy Content, is currently available for free to APS members and to institutions for a one-time charge of $2,000. This journal will be useful to physiologists as well as to researchers and practitioners in various medical specialties. Document delivery is available from BLDSC, CASDDS, CISTI, EMDOCS, The Genuine Article, LHLDS, NIWI, UMI, and UnCover.

5096. Journal of General Physiology. [ISSN: 0022-1295] 1918. m. USD 955 (Individuals, USD 250). Ed(s): Dr. Olaf S Andersen. Rockefeller University Press, 1114 First Ave, New York, NY 10021-8325; rupress@ rockefeller.edu; http://www.rupress.org. Illus., index, adv. Sample.

Refereed. Circ: 1790 Paid. Microform: PQC. Online: EBSCO Publishing, EBSCO Host; HighWire Press. *Indexed:* B&AI, BiolAb, CABA, ChemAb, ExcerpMed, GSI, IndVet, PEI, SCI, VB, ZooRec. *Aud.:* Ac, Sa.

Journal of General Physiology is the official organ of the Society of General Physiologists. It publishes research on "basic biological, chemical, or physical mechanisms of broad physiological significance." The articles fall into three categories: invited papers, research papers, and comments. Subscription options include print, online, and print plus online. Substantial online content includes full text from 1975 to the present, a free archive back to 1918, and free content after 12 months. This journal is appropriate for academic and special libraries that support biologists, physiologists, and physicians. Document delivery is available from BLDSC, CASDDS, CISTI, The Genuine Article, LHLDS, UMI, and UnCover.

5097. The Journal of Physiology. [ISSN: 0022-3751] 1878. s-m. plus proceedings 5/yr. GBP 2526 print & online eds. Ed(s): William A Large, Carol Huxley. Blackwell Publishing Ltd., 9600 Garsington Rd, Oxford, OX4 2ZG, United Kingdom; customerservices@ blackwellpublishing.com; http://www.blackwellpublishing.com. Illus., index, adv. Sample. Refereed. Circ: 3100. Microform: PMC; PQC. Online: Blackwell Synergy; EBSCO Publishing, EBSCO Host; Gale; HighWire Press; IngentaConnect; OCLC Online Computer Library Center, Inc.; OhioLINK; SwetsWise Online Content. Reprint: PSC. *Indexed:* B&AI, BiolAb, CABA, ChemAb, DSA, ErgAb, ExcerpMed, IndVet, PEI, S&F, SCI, SSCI, VB. *Aud.:* Ac, Sa.

The Journal of Physiology presents physiological research that explores levels of organization ranging from the molecular level up through systems. Emphasis focuses on human and mammalian physiology in areas such as respiration, circulation, excretion, reproduction, digestion, and homeostasis. Issues contain research papers, "Rapid Reports," "Topical Reviews," and "Perspectives." Stanford's HighWire Press makes available the online content for this journal, including full text from 1997 forward. A print subscription also entitles the institution to online access. Online access to papers older than one year is freely available. This well-regarded journal is useful for upper-division undergraduates through specialists. Document delivery is available from BLDSC, CASDDS, CISTI, The Genuine Article, LHLDS, UMI, and UnCover.

5098. Physiological Reviews. [ISSN: 0031-9333] 1921. q. USD 465 (Members, USD 140 print & online eds.; Non-members, USD 305). Ed(s): Susan L Hamilton. American Physiological Society, 9650 Rockville Pike, Bethesda, MD 20814-3991; info@the-aps.org; http://www.the-aps.org. Illus., index, adv. Refereed. Circ: 3352 Paid. Vol. ends: Oct. Microform: PMC; PQC. Online: EBSCO Publishing, EBSCO Host; Gale; HighWire Press; Northern Light Technology, Inc. *Indexed:* B&AI, CABA, ChemAb, DSA, ExcerpMed, GSI, PEI, SCI, SSCI. *Aud.:* Ac, Sa.

Published quarterly by the American Physiological Society, *Physiological Reviews* contains invited critical reviews of physiological topics and in the related areas of biochemistry, nutrition, general physiology, biophysics, and neuroscience. Subscription options include print only, online only, and print plus online combined. Stanford's HighWire Press makes available the online content for this title, including full text from 1998 to the present. Full historical content of the American Physiological Society's 14 journals, including *Physiological Reviews* from 1921, is available online. This package, the APS Journal Legacy Content, is currently available for free to APS members and to institutions for a one-time charge of $2,000. Review articles provide an excellent starting point, overview, and extensive bibliography for researchers and students. Document delivery is available from BLDSC, CASDDS, CISTI, The Genuine Article, LHLDS, and UnCover.

5099. Reproduction. Formed by the merger of (1996-2000): *Reviews of Reproduction;* (1960-2000): *Journal of Reproduction and Fertility;* Which was formerly (1949-1958): *Society for the Study of Fertility. Proceedings.* [ISSN: 1470-1626] 2001. m. EUR 1295 except UK; print & online eds. Ed(s): John Carroll. BioScientifica Ltd., 22 Apex Court, Woodlands, Bristol, BS32 4JT, United Kingdom;

http://www.bioscientifica.com/. Adv. Sample. Refereed. *Indexed:* Agr, B&AI, BiolAb, CABA, ChemAb, DSA, ExcerpMed, FoVS&M, HortAb, IndVet, S&F, SCI, VB, ZooRec. *Aud.:* Ac, Sa.

Reproduction publishes research and reviews on the subject of reproductive biology. Editors encourage manuscripts on cellular and molecular mechanisms of reproduction; development of gametes; embryos and reproductive tissues; reproductive physiology; and reproductive endocrinology. Emerging topics such as assisted reproductive technologies, cloning, and stem cell biology are also welcome. Research papers are made available free online one year after publication. Papers are published online with HighWire. Useful for academic, medical, and veterinary collections.

■ POLITICAL SCIENCE

General and Political Theory/Comparative and American Politics/International Relations

Kathleen Sheehan, Research Librarian, Widener Library, Harvard University, Cambridge, MA

Nancy J. Becker, Assistant Professor, Division of Library & Information Science, St. John's University

Introduction

Journals here are mostly research titles affiliated with universities or research organizations; the journals are also divided into subsections representing fields in political science: general and political theory, comparative and American politics, and international relations. There are also titles aimed at wider audiences with interests in politics, policy making, international affairs, and related subjects. You will find here titles from mainstream, conservative, and liberal perspectives, because our intention is to provide a listing of the most prominent titles offering different perspectives on the field of political science.

Basic Periodicals

Hs: *Congressional Digest, Current History, International Affairs, National Journal;* Ga: *Brookings Review, Congressional Digest, CQ Weekly, Current History, Foreign Affairs, Foreign Policy, National Journal, SAIS Review, World Affairs;* Ac: *American Journal of Political Science, American Political Science Review, American Politics Research, American Academy of Political and Social Science. Annals, The Cato Journal, Comparative Politics, CQ Weekly, Foreign Affairs, Foreign Policy, International Organization, International Studies Quarterly, Journal of Politics, Journal of Theoretical Politics, Latin American Politics & Society, Orbis, Policy Studies Journal, Political Science Quarterly, Polity, Presidential Studies Quarterly, Publius, World Policy Journal, World Politics.*

Basic Abstracts and Indexes

America: History and Life, CSA Worldwide Political Science Abstracts, International Political Science Abstracts, PAIS International in Print, Social Sciences Citation Index, Social Science Index.

General and Political Theory

5100. *American Academy of Political and Social Science. Annals.* [ISSN: 0002-7162] 1891. bi-m. GBP 393. Ed(s): Robert W Pearson, Julie Odland. Sage Publications, Inc., 2455 Teller Rd, Thousand Oaks, CA 91320; info@sagepub.com; http://www.sagepub.com. Illus., adv. Refereed. Circ: 4850 Paid. Vol. ends: Nov. Microform: IDC; PMC; PQC. Online: CSA; EBSCO Publishing, EBSCO Host; Florida Center for Library Automation; HighWire Press; JSTOR (Web-based Journal Archive); LexisNexis; OCLC Online Computer Library Center, Inc.; OhioLINK; SAGE Publications, Inc., SAGE Journals Online; SwetsWise Online Content. Reprint: PSC. *Indexed:* ABCPolSci, ABS&EES, AgeL,

AmH&L, BAS, BEL&L, BRD, BRI, BrArAb, CBRI, CJA, CommAb, CompR, EAA, FutSurv, HEA, HRA, HistAb, IBR, IBSS, IBZ, IPSA, IndIslam, JEL, LRI, PAIS, PRA, PSA, PsycInfo, RI-1, RILM, SFSA, SSA, SSCI, SUSA, SociolAb, V&AA. *Bk. rev.:* 15-25, 500-800 words. *Aud.:* Ga, Ac, Sa.

Published six times per year, the *American Academy of Political and Social Science: Annals* is a wide-ranging scholarly journal. "Each volume presents more than 200 pages of timely, in-depth analysis of a significant topic from several disciplinary perspectives." Recent volumes include "Regulatory Capitalism," "Cultural Production in a Digital Age," "Work/Life Balance for Fast-Track Parents," and "Ethnography." Each issue is edited by an expert in the subject field, with interdisciplinary articles written by authors chosen by the guest editor. This is an important publication, whether you are a scholar keeping current in the field or a student needing a thorough review of a topic. Essential for academic libraries, and recommended for larger public libraries.

5101. *American Journal of Political Science.* Formerly: *Midwest Journal of Political Science.* [ISSN: 0092-5853] 1950. q. GBP 274 print & online eds. Ed(s): Jan Leighley, Kim Quaile Hill. Blackwell Publishing, Inc., Commerce Place, 350 Main St, Malden, MA 02148; customerservices@blackwellpublishing.com; http://www.blackwellpublishing.com. Illus., adv. Refereed. Circ: 4200. Vol. ends: No. 4. Microform: PQC. Online: Blackwell Synergy; EBSCO Publishing, EBSCO Host; Gale; IngentaConnect; JSTOR (Web-based Journal Archive); OCLC Online Computer Library Center, Inc.; OhioLINK; ProQuest LLC (Ann Arbor); SwetsWise Online Content. Reprint: PSC. *Indexed:* ABCPolSci, ABS&EES, AmH&L, ApEcolAb, ArtHuCI, BAS, CJA, EAA, HistAb, IBR, IBSS, IBZ, IPSA, LRI, PAIS, PRA, PSA, RiskAb, SSA, SSCI, SUSA, SWA, SociolAb, V&AA. *Aud.:* Ac.

This scholarly journal is the official publication of the Midwest Political Science Association, a national organization committed to advancing scholarship in all areas of political science. Each issue contains around 15–20 articles that include research on American politics, public policy, international relations, comparative politics, political theory, and political methodology. Recent articles include "States as Policy Laboratories: Emulating Success in the Children's Health Insurance Program," "Social Context and Campaign Volatility in New Democracies: Networks and Neighborhoods in Brazil's 2002 Elections," and "Priming Gender: Campaigning on Women's Issues in U.S. Senate Elections." Appropriate for academic libraries.

5102. *Asian Journal of Political Science.* [ISSN: 0218-5377] 1993. 3x/yr. GBP 189 (Individuals, GBP 47). Ed(s): Terry Nardin, Jon S T Quah. Routledge, 4 Park Sq, Milton Park, Abingdon, OX14 4RN, United Kingdom; journals@routledge.com; http://www.tandf.co.uk/journals. Illus., adv. Refereed. Circ: 250. Vol. ends: No. 2. Reprint: PSC. *Indexed:* BAS, IBSS, IBZ, IPSA, IndIslam, PAIS, PSA, SociolAb. *Bk. rev.:* 5-10, 1,250 words. *Aud.:* Ac.

This journal is sponsored by the Department of Political Science of the National University of Singapore and publishes articles in political theory, comparative politics, international relations, and public administration. It is published twice a year, and its main focus is on Asia and issues relevant to this area. Book reviews are included. Most appropriate for academic libraries that support Asian Studies programs.

5103. *British Journal of Political Science.* [ISSN: 0007-1234] 1971. q. GBP 218. Ed(s): David Sanders, Sarah Birch. Cambridge University Press, The Edinburgh Bldg, Shaftesbury Rd, Cambridge, CB2 2RU, United Kingdom; journals@cambridge.org; http://www.journals.cambridge.org. Illus., index, adv. Refereed. Vol. ends: Oct. Microform: PQC. Online: Pub.; EBSCO Publishing, EBSCO Host; Florida Center for Library Automation; Gale; JSTOR (Web-based Journal Archive); OCLC Online Computer Library Center, Inc.; OhioLINK; SwetsWise Online Content. Reprint: PSC. *Indexed:* ABCPolSci, AmH&L, BAS, HRA, HistAb, IBR, IBSS, IBZ, IPSA, PAIS, PRA, PSA, RRTA, SSA, SSCI, SWA, SociolAb, WAE&RSA. *Aud.:* Ac.

For over 30 years, this journal has been publishing research from all fields of political science and several related disciplines, including sociology, social psychology, economics, and philosophy. In addition to about six or seven research articles, many issues also include review articles or notes and comments. Contributors to recent issues were mainly based in the United States and the United Kingdom. Articles include research on coalition formation in parliamentary democracies, democracy and economic growth, and voter behavior. Appropriate for academic libraries and large public libraries.

5104. *Canadian Journal of Political Science.* Supersedes in part (in 1967): *Canadian Journal of Economics and Political Science;* Which was formerly (1928-1934): *Contributions to Canada Economics.* [ISSN: 0008-4239] 1968. q. GBP 70 print & online eds. Ed(s): Steve Heilig, Thomasine Kushner. Cambridge University Press, The Edinburgh Bldg, Shaftesbury Rd, Cambridge, CB2 2RU, United Kingdom. Illus., index, adv. Refereed. Circ: 1580 Paid. Vol. ends: No. 4. Microform: MML. Online: Pub.; EBSCO Publishing, EBSCO Host; JSTOR (Web-based Journal Archive); OCLC Online Computer Library Center, Inc.; SwetsWise Online Content. *Indexed:* ABCPolSci, ABS&EES, AmH&L, ArtHuCI, BAS, CBCARef, CPerI, CommAb, HistAb, IBR, IBSS, IBZ, IPSA, LRI, PAIS, PRA, PSA, PdeR, PhilInd, RiskAb, SSA, SSCI, SociolAb. *Bk. rev.:* 35, 650-700 words. *Aud.:* Ac, Sa.

The Canadian Political Science Association and the Societe quebecoise de science politique jointly sponsor *The Canadian Journal of Political Science.* The journal publishes articles, notes, commentaries, and book reviews in English and in French. According to the editors, the journal is "the primary forum for innovative research on all facets of Canadian politics and government as well as the principle outlet for Canadian political science scholarship." Subject coverage includes all fields of political science. Recent articles present research on such topics as Liberal Party electoral success in Canada, the political foundations of support for same-sex marriage in Canada, and the politics of assisted reproductive technologies in Canada. Appropriate for academic libraries with programs in this field.

5105. *Constellations: an international journal of critical and democratic theory.* Formerly (until 1994): *Praxis International.* [ISSN: 1351-0487] 1981. q. GBP 425 print & online eds. Ed(s): Nancy Fraser, Andrew Arato. Blackwell Publishing Ltd., 9600 Garsington Rd, Oxford, OX4 2ZG, United Kingdom; customerservices@blackwellpublishing.com; http://www.blackwellpublishing.com. Illus., adv. Refereed. Vol. ends: No. 4. Microform: PQC. Online: Blackwell Synergy; EBSCO Publishing, EBSCO Host; Gale; IngentaConnect; OCLC Online Computer Library Center, Inc.; OhioLINK; SwetsWise Online Content. Reprint: PSC. *Indexed:* AltPI, ApEcolAb, IBSS, IPB, IPSA, LeftInd, PSA, PhilInd, SSA, SociolAb. *Bk. rev.:* 2-5, 2,000-3,000 words. *Aud.:* Ac, Sa.

This international scholarly journal of contemporary critical and democratic theory "aims to help expand the global possibilities for radical politics and social criticism in the coming period." Articles are generally organized under two broad themes per issue, along with book reviews. Recent themes include "U.S. Elections in Global Perspective," "Rethinking Sovereignty," "Ideology and Capitalism," and "Emergency Law Regimes." Appropriate for academic libraries.

Gender and Development. See Gender Studies section.

5106. *History of Political Thought.* [ISSN: 0143-781X] 1980. q. GBP 105 print & online (Individuals, GBP 49 print & online). Ed(s): Iain Hampshire-Monk, Janet Coleman. Imprint Academic, PO Box 200, Exeter, EXS 5YX, United Kingdom; keith@imprint.co.uk; http://www.imprint.co.uk. Illus., index, adv. Refereed. Circ: 750 Paid. Vol. ends: No. 4. Online: EBSCO Publishing, EBSCO Host; Gale; IngentaConnect; OCLC Online Computer Library Center, Inc.; SwetsWise Online Content. *Indexed:* ABCPolSci, AmH&L, ArtHuCI, HistAb, IBR, IBSS, IBZ, IPB, IPSA, PSA, PhilInd, SSCI, SociolAb. *Bk. rev.:* 2-7, 625 words. *Aud.:* Ac.

Founded in 1980, this is a quarterly, refereed journal "devoted exclusively to the historical study of political ideas and associated methodological problems." It generally publishes six or seven articles per issue, with book reviews appearing every other month. Articles examine political theorists and philosophers as well as political philosophy. Recent topics include the individual and society, slavery, religious freedom, and economic nationalism. Recommended for academic libraries that support programs in political science.

5107. *International Political Science Review.* [ISSN: 0192-5121] 1980. 5x/yr. GBP 311. Ed(s): James Meadowcroft, Kay Lawson. Sage Publications Ltd., 1 Oliver's Yard, 55 City Rd, London, EC1 1SP, United Kingdom; http://www.sagepub.co.uk. Illus., index, adv. Refereed. Circ: 2200. Vol. ends: No. 4. Microform: WSH; PMC; PQC. Online: CSA; EBSCO Publishing, EBSCO Host; HighWire Press; JSTOR (Web-based Journal Archive); OCLC Online Computer Library Center, Inc.; OhioLINK; SAGE Publications, Inc., SAGE Journals Online; SwetsWise Online Content. Reprint: PSC. *Indexed:* ABCPolSci, ArtHuCI, BAS, IBR, IBSS, IBZ, IPSA, PRA, PSA, SSA, SSCI, SociolAb. *Aud.:* Ac.

This is the journal of the International Political Science Association, which was founded in 1949 under the auspices of UNESCO. This journal is dedicated to publishing research on politics in an increasingly interdependent world. Articles in the journal may come from any of the sub-disciplines of social science. The editorial board welcomes "work by scholars who are focussing on currently controversial themes, shaping innovative concepts and methodologies of political analysis, and striving to reach outside the scope of a single culture." Recommended for academic libraries.

5108. *Journal of Politics.* [ISSN: 0022-3816] 1939. q. GBP 200 print & online eds. Ed(s): John Geer. Cambridge University Press, The Edinburgh Bldg, Shaftesbury Rd, Cambridge, CB2 2RU, United Kingdom; journals@cambridge.org; http://www.journals.cambridge.org. Illus., index, adv. Refereed. Circ: 4000. Vol. ends: Nov. Microform: PQC. Online: Blackwell Synergy; EBSCO Publishing, EBSCO Host; Gale; IngentaConnect; JSTOR (Web-based Journal Archive); OCLC Online Computer Library Center, Inc.; OhioLINK; SwetsWise Online Content. Reprint: PSC. *Indexed:* ABCPolSci, ABS&EES, AgeL, AmH&L, ApEcolAb, ArtHuCI, BAS, BRI, CBRI, CJA, CommAb, HistAb, IBR, IBSS, IBZ, IPSA, IndIslam, LRI, PAIS, PRA, PSA, PhilInd, PsycInfo, RILM, RiskAb, SSA, SSCI, SWA, SociolAb. *Bk. rev.:* 25, 700-800 words. *Aud.:* Ac.

Affiliated with the Southern Political Science Association, *The Journal of Politics* is a general political science journal that publishes research from all areas of the discipline. Each issue contains approximately 15–20 articles and a lengthy list of book reviews. Although the journal publishes articles on a broad range of topics, there appears to be an emphasis on American politics. Recommended for academic libraries that support political science programs.

5109. *Journal of Theoretical Politics.* [ISSN: 0951-6298] 1989. q. GBP 475. Ed(s): James Johnson, Keith Dowding. Sage Publications Ltd., 1 Oliver's Yard, 55 City Rd, London, EC1 1SP, United Kingdom; info@sagepub.co.uk; http://www.sagepub.co.uk. Illus., index, adv. Sample. Refereed. Circ: 800. Vol. ends: No. 4. Online: CSA; EBSCO Publishing, EBSCO Host; HighWire Press; OCLC Online Computer Library Center, Inc.; OhioLINK; SAGE Publications, Inc., SAGE Journals Online; SwetsWise Online Content. Reprint: PSC. *Indexed:* ABCPolSci, CJA, IBR, IBSS, IBZ, IPSA, PRA, PSA, SSA, SSCI, SociolAb. *Aud.:* Ac.

This journal is committed to the importance of theory in political science. Its main focus is the publication of new theoretical work presented in a style that is accessible to all social scientists. According to the editors, one of their "principle aims is to foster the development of theory in the study of political processes." Four or five research articles appear in each issue. Recent articles include "A Theory of Partisan Support and Entry Deterrence in Electoral Competition," "Presidential Vetoes in Latin American Constitutions," and "Success versus Decisiveness: Conceptual Discussion and Case Study." Recommended for academic libraries that support graduate study in political science.

Meridians. See Gender Studies section.

5110. *New Political Science: a journal of politics & culture.* [ISSN: 0739-3148] 1979. q. GBP 249 print & online eds. Ed(s): Joseph Peschek. Routledge, 4 Park Sq, Milton Park, Abingdon, OX14 4RN, United Kingdom; info@routledge.co.uk; http://www.routledge.co.uk. Illus., index, adv. Refereed. Circ: 300 Paid. Vol. ends: No. 4. Online: EBSCO

Publishing, EBSCO Host; Gale; IngentaConnect; OCLC Online Computer Library Center, Inc.; SwetsWise Online Content. Reprint: PSC. *Indexed:* ABS&EES, AltPI, CJA, IBR, IBSS, IBZ, IPSA, LeftInd, PAIS, PRA, PSA, SSA, SociolAb. *Bk. rev.:* 5, 1,000-1,250 words. *Aud.:* Ac, Sa.

This is the official journal of the Caucus for a New Political Science (CNPS), an Organized Section of the American Political Science Association. The Caucus is "united by the idea that Political Science as an academic discipline should be committed to advancing progressive political development." The journal aims for an audience beyond the specialized reader to those with a general interest in politics and social change. Book reviews, interviews, and review essays are included. Recent articles include "Blinded by the Neoliberal Agenda: India's Market Transition Failure," "Anti-Anti Terror: Color Coding and the Joke of 'Homeland Security,'" and "The 'Miracle' Revisited: The De-radicalization of Korean Political Culture." Appropriate for academic libraries.

5111. *P S: Political Science & Politics.* Incorporates (1974-1990): *Political Science Teacher;* Formerly (until 1988): *P S (Washington, DC);* Which superseded in part (in 1968): *American Political Science Review.* [ISSN: 1049-0965] 1968. q. GBP 397 print & online eds. Ed(s): Robert Hauck. Cambridge University Press, The Edinburgh Bldg, Shaftesbury Rd, Cambridge, CB2 2RU, United Kingdom; journals@cambridge.org; http://www.cup.cam.ac.uk/. Illus., index, adv. Refereed. Circ: 16000. Vol. ends: No. 4. Microform: PQC. Online: Pub.; Florida Center for Library Automation; Gale; JSTOR (Web-based Journal Archive); OCLC Online Computer Library Center, Inc.; OhioLINK; ProQuest LLC (Ann Arbor); SwetsWise Online Content; H.W. Wilson. *Indexed:* ABCPolSci, ABS&EES, AgeL, AmH&L, ArtHuCI, HistAb, IBSS, IPSA, PAIS, PSA, SSCI, SWR&A. *Aud.:* Ac, Sa.

Published by the American Political Science Association, *PS: Political Science & Politics* is "the journal of record for the profession." Articles are written by scholars for a broad audience of experts and general readers. In addition to publishing research on a wide range of topics, the journal includes news and articles on the teaching and practice of political science, such as "Participation by Women in the 2005 APSA Meeting" and "Real Success with a Virtual Exchange: The German and American Politics Electronic Classroom." Recommended for academic libraries.

5112. *The Political Quarterly.* [ISSN: 0032-3179] 1930. q. GBP 180 print & online eds. Ed(s): Andrew Gamble, Tony Wright, MP. Blackwell Publishing Ltd., 9600 Garsington Rd, Oxford, OX4 2ZG, United Kingdom; customerservices@blackwellpublishing.com; http://www.blackwellpublishing.com. Illus., index, adv. Refereed. Vol. ends: No. 5. Microform: RPI; PMC. Online: Blackwell Synergy; EBSCO Publishing, EBSCO Host; Gale; IngentaConnect; OCLC Online Computer Library Center, Inc.; OhioLINK; SwetsWise Online Content. Reprint: PSC. *Indexed:* ABCPolSci, AgeL, AmH&L, AmHI, ApEcolAb, ArtHuCI, BAS, BrHumI, CABA, CommAb, HistAb, IBR, IBSS, IBZ, IPSA, IndVet, PAIS, PSA, RRTA, RiskAb, SSA, SSCI, SociolAb, WAE&RSA. *Bk. rev.:* 10, 800-1,000 words. *Aud.:* Ga, Ac, Sa.

Founded in 1930, *The Political Quarterly* explores U.K. and European politics from a center-left perspective. "It is dedicated to political and social reform and has long acted as a bridge between policy-makers, commentators and academics." It includes in-depth analysis, book reviews, reports and surveys, and commentary written in accessible language. Recent articles include "The Reform of Party Funding in Britain," "The Politics of Immigration and Public Health," "'I'm Proud of the British Empire': Why Tony Blair Backs George W. Bush," and "Pensions: Challenges and Choices. The First Report of the Pension Commission." Recommended for academic libraries.

5113. *Political Research Quarterly.* Formerly (until 1993): *Western Political Quarterly.* [ISSN: 1065-9129] 1948. q. GBP 125. Ed(s): Cornell Clayton, Amy Mazur. Sage Publications, Inc., 2455 Teller Rd, Thousand Oaks, CA 91320; http://www.sagepub.com. Illus., index, adv. Sample. Refereed. Circ: 2300 Paid. Vol. ends: No. 4. Online: Chadwyck-Healey Inc.; JSTOR (Web-based Journal Archive); Northern Light Technology, Inc.; OCLC Online Computer Library Center, Inc.; ProQuest K-12

Learning Solutions; ProQuest LLC (Ann Arbor); H.W. Wilson. Reprint: PSC. *Indexed:* ABCPolSci, ABS&EES, AmH&L, BAS, BRI, CBRI, CJA, HistAb, IBR, IBSS, IBZ, IPSA, IndIslam, LRI, MLA-IB, PAIS, PRA, PSA, PhilInd, SSCI, SUSA, SociolAb. *Aud.:* Ac, Sa.

Published by the Western Political Science Association, this is a general political science journal that publishes research and field essays, which summarize knowledge in a particular area. This journal is refereed. The field essays may be of more general interest. Recent subjects covered include gay rights, women candidates for office, government lobbyists, and public opinion and welfare spending. Recommended for academic libraries.

5114. *Political Studies.* [ISSN: 0032-3217] 1953. q. GBP 507 print & online eds. Ed(s): Martin Smith, Matthew Festenstein. Blackwell Publishing Ltd., 9600 Garsington Rd, Oxford, OX4 2ZG, United Kingdom; customerservices@blackwellpublishing.com; http://www.blackwellpublishing.com. Illus., index, adv. Refereed. Vol. ends: No. 5. Microform: PQC. Online: Blackwell Synergy; EBSCO Publishing, EBSCO Host; Gale; IngentaConnect; OCLC Online Computer Library Center, Inc.; OhioLINK; SwetsWise Online Content. Reprint: PSC. *Indexed:* ABCPolSci, AmH&L, AmHI, ApEcolAb, ArtHuCI, BAS, BrHumI, CJA, HistAb, IBR, IBSS, IBZ, IPSA, PAIS, PRA, PSA, PhilInd, RI-1, RiskAb, SSA, SSCI, SWA, SociolAb. *Bk. rev.:* 75, length varies. *Aud.:* Ac.

This peer-reviewed journal is published by the Political Studies Association, a leading sssociation in the field in the United Kingdom, which is dedicated to promoting the study of politics. *Political Studies* publishes scholarly research in all fields of politics and international relations. Each issue contains between eight and ten articles from contributors drawn mainly from the United Kingdom. Recommended for academic libraries that need a British perspective on politics and international relations.

5115. *Political Theory: an international journal of political philosophy.* [ISSN: 0090-5917] 1973. bi-m. GBP 511. Ed(s): Stephen K White. Sage Publications, Inc., 2455 Teller Rd, Thousand Oaks, CA 91320; info@sagepub.com; http://www.sagepub.com. Illus., index, adv. Refereed. Circ: 1478 Paid. Vol. ends: No. 6. Microform: PQC. Online: CSA; EBSCO Publishing, EBSCO Host; Gale; HighWire Press; JSTOR (Web-based Journal Archive); OCLC Online Computer Library Center, Inc.; OhioLINK; SAGE Publications, Inc., SAGE Journals Online; SwetsWise Online Content. Reprint: PSC. *Indexed:* ABCPolSci, ABS&EES, AmH&L, ArtHuCI, FR, HistAb, IBR, IBSS, IBZ, IPB, IPSA, PAIS, PRA, PSA, PhilInd, SSA, SSCI, SUSA, SociolAb. *Bk. rev.:* 5-7, 1,750 words. *Aud.:* Ac.

This is an international scholarly journal that publishes the latest research in all fields of political philosophy. The journal prides itself on having "no single affiliation or orientation." The reader will find research on historical as well as modern political theory, normative and analytical philosophy, and work on such philosophers as Foucault, Aristotle, Marx, Hobbes, and Heidegger. The journal publishes research articles, review articles, book reviews, and critical responses and special topics in six issues per year. Recommended for academic libraries.

5116. *Polity.* [ISSN: 0032-3497] 1968. q. USD 198 print & online eds. Ed(s): Andrew Polsky. Palgrave Macmillan Ltd., Houndmills, Basingstoke, RG21 6XS, United Kingdom; journal-info@palgrave.com; http://www.palgrave-journals.com/. Illus., index, adv. Refereed. Circ: 1300 Paid. Vol. ends: No. 4. Microform: PQC. Online: EBSCO Publishing, EBSCO Host; Florida Center for Library Automation; Gale; IngentaConnect; JSTOR (Web-based Journal Archive); OCLC Online Computer Library Center, Inc.; SwetsWise Online Content. Reprint: PSC. *Indexed:* ABCPolSci, ABS&EES, AgeL, AmH&L, ArtHuCI, BAS, EI, FutSurv, HRA, HistAb, IPSA, PAIS, PRA, PSA, SSCI, SUSA, V&AA. *Aud.:* Ac.

Polity is the journal of the Northeastern Political Science Association, and it publishes research articles, review essays, and forums on a range of theoretical and policy topics. Recent subjects include the politics of family, Rousseau's system of checks and balances, and restoration of the Everglades. Through more than 30 years of publication, *Polity* has remained a general political science journal. Recommended for academic and large public libraries.

5117. *The Review of Politics.* [ISSN: 0034-6705] 1939. q. GBP 56. Ed(s): Dennis W M Moran, Catherine Zuckert. Cambridge University Press, The Edinburgh Bldg, Shaftesbury Rd, Cambridge, CB2 2RU, United Kingdom; journals@cambridge.org; http://www.journals.cambridge.org. Illus., index, adv. Sample. Refereed. Circ: 1700 Paid. Vol. ends: No. 4. Microform: PMC; PQC. Online: Chadwyck-Healey Inc.; EBSCO Publishing, EBSCO Host; Florida Center for Library Automation; Gale; JSTOR (Web-based Journal Archive); Northern Light Technology, Inc.; OCLC Online Computer Library Center, Inc.; ProQuest K-12 Learning Solutions; ProQuest LLC (Ann Arbor); H.W. Wilson. *Indexed:* ABCPolSci, ABS&EES, AmH&L, BAS, BRI, CBRI, CPL, FR, HistAb, IBR, IBSS, IBZ, IPSA, LRI, MASUSE, PAIS, PRA, PSA, PhilInd, RiskAb, SSCI. *Bk. rev.:* Number and length vary. *Aud.:* Ac.

The focus of the *Review* is on publishing philosophical and historical studies of politics, especially those concentrating on political theory and American political thought. Recent articles include "Guestworkers and Exploitation," "On the Woman Question in Machiavelli," and "Michel Foucault: Crises and Problemizations." Book reviews are also included. Recommended for academic libraries.

Comparative and American Politics

5118. *Alternatives: global, local, political.* [ISSN: 0304-3754] 1974. 4x/yr. USD 123 print & online eds. (Individuals, USD 54 print & online eds.). Ed(s): D L Sheth, R B J Walker. Lynne Rienner Publishers, 1800 30th St, Ste 314, Boulder, CO 80301-1026; http://www.rienner.com. Illus., index, adv. Sample. Refereed. Circ: 800 Paid. Vol. ends: No. 5. Microform: WSH; PQC. Online: EBSCO Publishing, EBSCO Host; Florida Center for Library Automation; Gale. *Indexed:* ABCPolSci, AltPI, AmH&L, AmHI, ArtInd, CBCARef, CJA, CLI, EnvInd, FutSurv, HistAb, IBR, IBSS, IBZ, ILP, IPSA, LeftInd, PAIS, PRA, PSA, SSA, SSCI, SociolAb. *Aud.:* Ac.

Alternatives: global, local, political is a peer-reviewed journal of international relations, published in association with the Center for the Study of Developing Societies; the School of Politics, International Relations and the Environment, Keele University; the World Order Models Project; and the ICU Peace Research Institute. "The editors focus on the changing relationships between local political practices and identities and emerging forms of global economy, culture, and polity." Articles published in the journal are often written from a cross-cultural perspective. Recent articles include "Arms over AIDS in South Africa," "Political Space: Autonomy, Liberalism, and Empire," "Power/Knowledge in International Peacebuilding: The Case of the EU Police Mission in Bosnia." All subscriptions include electronic access. A good choice for academic libraries with an interest in comparative and international politics.

5119. *American Political Science Review.* Incorporated (1904-1914): *American Political Science Association. Proceedings.* [ISSN: 0003-0554] 1906. q. GBP 397 print & online eds. Ed(s): Lee Sigelman. Cambridge University Press, The Edinburgh Bldg, Shaftesbury Rd, Cambridge, CB2 2RU, United Kingdom; http://www.cup.cam.ac.uk/. Illus., index, adv. Sample. Refereed. Circ: 15000. Vol. ends: No. 4. Microform: MIM; PMC; PQC. Online: Pub.; EBSCO Publishing, EBSCO Host; Florida Center for Library Automation; Gale; JSTOR (Web-based Journal Archive); OCLC Online Computer Library Center, Inc.; OhioLINK; ProQuest LLC (Ann Arbor); SwetsWise Online Content; H.W. Wilson. *Indexed:* ABCPolSci, ABS&EES, AgeL, AmH&L, ArtHuCI, BAS, BEL&L, BRD, BRI, CBRI, CommAb, FutSurv, HistAb, IBR, IBSS, IBZ, IPSA, IndIslam, JEL, PAIS, PSA, SSCI, SWR&A. *Aud.:* Ac, Sa.

The *American Political Science Review* is a peer-reviewed journal that publishes research from all political science subfields, including political theory, American politics, public policy, and international relations. The American Political Science Association publishes this journal, which it describes as "political science's premier scholarly research journal." Recent articles include "Campaign Finance and Voter Welfare with Entrenched Incumbents," "The Rule of the People: Arendt, Arche, and Democracy," and "Wage Arrears and Economic Voting in Russia." Recommended for academic libraries.

5120. *American Politics Research.* Formerly (until 2000): *American Politics Quarterly.* [ISSN: 1532-673X] 1973. bi-m. GBP 502. Ed(s): James G Gimpel. Sage Publications, Inc., 2455 Teller Rd, Thousand Oaks, CA 91320; info@sagepub.com; http://www.sagepub.com. Illus., index, adv. Refereed. Circ: 1250. Vol. ends: No. 4. Reprint: PSC. *Indexed:* ABCPolSci, AgeL, AmH&L, CJA, CommAb, HistAb, IBR, IBSS, IBZ, IPSA, PAIS, PRA, PSA, RiskAb, SSA, SSCI, SUSA, SWA, SociolAb. *Aud.:* Ac.

Published six times a year, *American Politics Research* is a "forum for the dissemination of the latest theory, research and analyses in American political science." Articles appearing in the journal cover all levels of government from local to national. Recent article topics include voting behavior, foreign policy, courts and the legal process, and public finance. Special issues and symposia are sometimes published that focus on a particular topic from several viewpoints. Recommended for large academic libraries and those that serve relevant graduate-level programs.

5121. *C Q Weekly.* Formerly (until vol.56, no.15, 1998): *Congressional Quarterly Weekly Report.* [ISSN: 1521-5997] 1945. w. 48/yr. USD 2230. Ed(s): Mike Mills, Susan Benkelman. C Q Press, Inc., 1255 22nd St., NW, Ste. 400, Washington, DC 20037; customerservice@cqpress.com; http://www.cqpress.com. Illus., index, adv. Sample. Circ: 11000. Vol. ends: No. 52. Microform: MIM; PQC. Online: EBSCO Publishing, EBSCO Host. *Indexed:* ABS&EES, BLI, LRI, MASUSE, PAIS. *Aud.:* Hs, Ac, Sa.

CQ Weekly is an excellent source for non-partisan, in-depth coverage of issues facing the U.S. Congress, as well as providing news of the previous week's Congressional action. This publication provides a behind-the-scenes look at committee hearings, floor proceedings, and House and Senate votes. It also goes beyond reporting the week's activities with its "In Focus: New Perspectives on Current Events" and "Vantage Point: Trends and Forecasts in Government, Commerce, and Politics" sections, as well as reports from its regular columnists. Recommended for larger public and academic libraries.

5122. *The Cato Journal: an interdisciplinary journal of public policy analysis.* [ISSN: 0273-3072] 1981. 3x/yr. USD 50 (Individuals, USD 24). Ed(s): James A Dorn. C A T O Institute, 1000 Massachusetts Ave, NW, Washington, DC 20077-0172; http://www.cato.org. Illus., adv. Refereed. Circ: 3200. Vol. ends: No. 3. Online: EBSCO Publishing, EBSCO Host; Factiva, Inc.; Florida Center for Library Automation; Gale; Northern Light Technology, Inc.; OCLC Online Computer Library Center, Inc.; ProQuest LLC (Ann Arbor); H.W. Wilson. *Indexed:* ABCPolSci, ABIn, ABS&EES, AgeL, AmH&L, BAS, CLI, EnvAb, ILP, IPSA, JEL, PAIS, PRA, PSA, SSCI, SUSA, V&AA. *Bk. rev.:* 4-6, 800-1,000 words. *Aud.:* Ac, Sa.

The journal is published by the Cato Institute, a public policy research foundation that promotes the ideas of individual liberty, limited government, free markets, and peace. Articles published in the journal cover a wide range of topics and also promote the principles of the Institute. Recent articles include "Exchange Rates and Capitol Freedom in Developing Markets," "Does Gun Control Reduce Crime or Does Crime Increase Gun Control," and a special issue entitled "Creating a Competitive Education Industry." The intended audience includes scholars and interested lay readers. Papers presented at the Institute's policy conferences are frequently published in the journal. Book reviews are also included.

5123. *Commonwealth and Comparative Politics.* Former titiles (until 1997): *The Journal of Commonwealth & Comparative Politics; Journal of Commonwealth Political Studies.* [ISSN: 1466-2043] 1961. 3x/yr. GBP 411 print & online eds. Ed(s): Vicky Randall, Roger Charlton. Routledge, 4 Park Sq, Milton Park, Abingdon, OX14 4RN, United Kingdom; info@routledge.co.uk; http://www.routledge.com. Illus., index, adv. Refereed. Vol. ends: No. 3. Microform: PQC. Online: EBSCO Publishing, EBSCO Host; Gale; IngentaConnect; OCLC Online Computer Library Center, Inc.; SwetsWise Online Content. Reprint: PSC. *Indexed:* ABCPolSci, AmH&L, AmHI, BAS, BrHumI, CABA, HistAb, IBR, IBSS, IBZ, IPSA, PAIS, PSA, RRTA, SSA, SSCI, SociolAb, WAE&RSA. *Bk. rev.:* 15-30, 1,000 words. *Aud.:* Ac, Sa.

This scholarly journal presents research on the politics of Commonwealth countries relevant to students of comparative politics. Recent article topics include the politics of the Pacific Islands, the history of economic development, and relations between ethnic groups in various countries. Book reviews are included in each issue. Recommended for academic libraries with a focus on comparative politics.

5124. Comparative Political Studies. [ISSN: 0010-4140] 1968. m. GBP 625. Ed(s): James A Caporaso. Sage Publications, Inc., 2455 Teller Rd, Thousand Oaks, CA 91320; info@sagepub.com; http://www.sagepub.com. Illus., index, adv. Refereed. Circ: 850 Paid. Vol. ends: No. 6. Microform: PQC. Online: CSA; Chadwyck-Healey Inc.; EBSCO Publishing, EBSCO Host; Florida Center for Library Automation; Gale; HighWire Press; OCLC Online Computer Library Center, Inc.; OhioLINK; SAGE Publications, Inc., SAGE Journals Online; SwetsWise Online Content. Reprint: PSC. *Indexed:* ABCPolSci, ABS&EES, AmH&L, ArtHuCI, BAS, CommAb, HistAb, IBR, IBSS, IBZ, IPSA, IndIslam, PAIS, PRA, PSA, RRTA, SSA, SSCI, SWA, SociolAb, WAE&RSA. *Bk. rev.:* 2-4, 1,500 words. *Aud.:* Ac, Sa.

For approximately 40 years, this journal has been "at the forefront of the field, providing valuable analyses with important implications for the formation of domestic and foreign policies." It publishes articles on current methodology, theory, and research in comparative politics. Its publishing frequency has been increased to ten issues per year. Each issue generally consists of four or five articles, plus book reviews. Recent articles include "World Separation of Religion and State Into the 21st Century," "Refugee or Internally Displaced Person?: To Where Should One Flee?," and "Policy Failure and Policy Change: British Security Policy After the Cold War." Recommended for academic libraries.

5125. Comparative Politics. [ISSN: 0010-4159] 1968. q. USD 65 (Individuals, USD 32). Ed(s): I L Markovitz, Kenneth P Erickson. City University of New York, Political Science Program, 365 Fifth Ave, New York, NY 10016-4309; comppol@gc.cuny.edu; http://web.gc.cuny.edu/jcp/. Illus. Refereed. Circ: 2000. Vol. ends: No. 4. Microform: MIM; PQC. Online: JSTOR (Web-based Journal Archive). *Indexed:* ABCPolSci, ABS&EES, AgeL, AmH&L, ArtHuCI, BAS, HistAb, IBR, IBSS, IBZ, IPSA, IndIslam, PAIS, PRA, PSA, RRTA, SSCI, SociolAb, WAE&RSA. *Bk. rev.:* 2-4, 4,000 words. *Aud.:* Ac, Sa.

Comparative Politics is an international scholarly journal produced by the Ph.D. program in political science of the City University of New York. The journal's intended audience consists of students, scholars, experts, and policy makers. Recent articles include "Rethinking Presidentialism: Challenges and Presidential Falls in South America," "The Politics of Purpose: Swedish Economic Policy after the Golden Age," and "Poverty and Democratic Participation Reconsidered: Evidence from the Local Level in India." Recommended for academic libraries.

5126. Congress & the Presidency: a journal of capital studies. Former titles (until 1981): *Congressional Studies;* (until 1978): *Capitol Studies.* [ISSN: 0734-3469] 1972. s-a. USD 30 (Individuals, USD 18; Students, USD 14). Ed(s): Charles E Walcott, Susan Webb Hammond. American University, Center for Congressional and Presidential Studies, 4400 Massachusetts Ave, NW, Washington, DC 20016-8022; candp@american.edu; http://www.american.edu/ccps. Illus., adv. Refereed. Circ: 650. Vol. ends: No. 2. *Indexed:* ABCPolSci, AmH&L, CommAb, HistAb, IPSA, MASUSE, PAIS, PSA, SSCI. *Bk. rev.:* 6-8, 800-1,000 words. *Aud.:* Ac, Sa.

Published by twice a year by American University's Center for Congressional and Presidential Studies, this interdisciplinary journal of history and political science focuses on the presidency, the Congress, and the relationship between these two institutions. It also examines national policy making; and most authors are American academics. Recent articles include "House Majority Party Leaders' Uses of Public Opinion Information," "Pivotal Politics, Presidential Capital and Supreme Court Nominations," and "Ronald Reagan as Legislative Advocate: Passing the Reagan Revolution's Budgets in 1981 and 1982." A typical issue includes four articles, a review essay, and book reviews of varying lengths. Recommended for academic libraries.

5127. Congressional Digest: the pro & con monthly. [ISSN: 0010-5899] 1921. m. except June/July & Aug./Sep. USD 68 domestic; USD 75.25 in Canada & Mexico; USD 76.50 elsewhere. Ed(s): Sarah Orrick. Congressional Digest Corp., 4416 East West Hwy., Ste. 400, Bethesda, MD 20814-4568; info@congressionaldigest.com/; http://www.congressionaldigest.com. Illus., index. Vol. ends: Dec. Online: EBSCO Publishing, EBSCO Host. *Indexed:* LRI, MASUSE, PAIS, RGPR. *Aud.:* Hs, Ga, Ac, Sa.

Congressional Digest is a monthly publication devoted to providing in-depth, impartial coverage of controversial issues, "without spin, fluff or hidden agendas." Since 1921, this monthly journal has been providing readers with legislative background, judicial action, and the pros and cons on an issues before Congress. Opposing viewpoints are written by political leaders and policy experts. Recent issues covered include domestic surveillance, health savings accounts, and federal disaster aid. This title will appeal to a general audience interested in current events. Recommended for all libraries.

Critical Review. See Cultural Studies section.

5128. Electoral Studies. [ISSN: 0261-3794] 1982. 4x/yr. EUR 825. Ed(s): Dr. Harold D Clarke, Elinor Scarbrough. Pergamon, The Boulevard, Langford Ln, East Park, Kidlington, OX5 1GB, United Kingdom. Illus., index, adv. Refereed. Vol. ends: No. 4. Microform: PQC. Online: EBSCO Publishing, EBSCO Host; Gale; IngentaConnect; OhioLINK; ScienceDirect; SwetsWise Online Content. *Indexed:* ABCPolSci, AmH&L, HistAb, IBSS, IPSA, IndIslam, PAIS, PSA, SSCI. *Aud.:* Ac, Sa.

Electoral Studies is an interdisciplinary, international, refereed journal that publishes research on all aspects of voting. Articles appearing in the journal may be theoretical or empirical. Recent articles cover such topics as the 2002 Portuguese legislative elections, an algorithm for determining voter turnout, and the relationship between the state of the economy and election results. A new section, "Electoral Inquiry," will include "papers dealing with research methods relevant to the study of voting and elections." Other sections include "Notes on Recent Elections," which attempts to cover all democratic national elections and referenda; "Guide to Journal Articles," which provides abstracts of relevant papers appearing in other journals; and "Book Notes." Appropriate for academic libraries.

5129. Environmental Politics. [ISSN: 0964-4016] 1992. 5x/yr. GBP 390 print & online eds. Ed(s): Neil Carter, Christopher Rootes. Routledge, 4 Park Sq, Milton Park, Abingdon, OX14 4RN, United Kingdom; info@routledge.co.uk; http://www.routledge.com. Illus., index, adv. Sample. Refereed. Vol. ends: Winter. Microform: PQC. Online: EBSCO Publishing, EBSCO Host; Gale; IngentaConnect; OCLC Online Computer Library Center, Inc.; SwetsWise Online Content. Reprint: PSC. *Indexed:* EnvAb, EnvInd, IBR, IBSS, IBZ, IPSA, PSA, PollutAb, SSA, SSCI, SWA, SWRA, SociolAb, WAE&RSA, ZooRec. *Bk. rev.:* 20-25, 150-500 words. *Aud.:* Ac, Sa.

Environmental Politics is an international journal that focuses primarily on industrialized countries. Published five times per year, this journal covers the evolution of environmental movements and parties; analysis of the making of environmental public policy at all levels of government; and commentary on ideas generated by environmental organizations, and by individual theorists. The journal aims to present information on current environmental debates without favoring a particular side in any debate. Recent articles include "Globalisation, environmentalism and the global justice movement," "Biodiversity, participation and community: Reintegrating people and nature," and "Assessing the case against the SUV." Also publishes book reviews. Recommended for academic libraries.

5130. European Journal of Political Research. [ISSN: 0304-4130] 1973. 8x/yr. GBP 499 print & online eds. Ed(s): Edward C Page, Kris Deschouwer. Blackwell Publishing Ltd., 9600 Garsington Rd, Oxford, OX4 2ZG, United Kingdom; customerservices@ blackwellpublishing.com; http://www.blackwellpublishing.com. Illus., index, adv. Refereed. Microform: PQC. Online: Blackwell Synergy; EBSCO Publishing, EBSCO Host; Gale; IngentaConnect; OCLC

Online Computer Library Center, Inc.; OhioLINK; Springer LINK; SwetsWise Online Content. Reprint: PSC. *Indexed:* ABCPolSci, ApEcolAb, CABA, CommAb, HistAb, IBR, IBSS, IBZ, IPSA, PSA, PhilInd, RiskAb, SSA, SSCI, SWA, SociolAb, WAE&RSA. *Aud.:* Ac, Sa.

The journal is a publication of the European Consortium for Political Research. The Consortium is a scholarly association of political scientists with approximately 300 member institutions throughout Europe, and associate member institutions in countries beyond Europe. Publishing eight times per year, the journal includes the *Political Data Yearbook* as a double issue at the end of each volume. This journal specializes in theoretical and comparative approaches in political science, and recent issues include articles on voting behavior, taxation, and parliamentary politics and process. In addition to scholarly articles, it publishes research notes on ongoing research in specific areas. Appropriate for large academic libraries.

Governing. See Government Periodicals—State and Local section.

5131. *Government and Opposition: an international journal of comparative politics.* [ISSN: 0017-257X] 1965. q. GBP 136 print & online eds. Ed(s): Michael Moran, Paul Heywood. Blackwell Publishing Ltd., 9600 Garsington Rd, Oxford, OX4 2ZG, United Kingdom; customerservices@ blackwellpublishing.com; http://www.blackwellpublishing.com. Illus., index, adv. Refereed. Circ: 1500 Paid. Vol. ends: No. 4. Reprint: PSC. *Indexed:* ABCPolSci, AmH&L, AmHI, ApEcolAb, ArtHuCI, BAS, BrHumI, HistAb, IBR, IBSS, IBZ, IPSA, IndIslam, PAIS, PSA, RiskAb, SSA, SSCI, SociolAb. *Bk. rev.:* 8-12, 1,000-1,500 words. *Aud.:* Ac, Sa.

As the subtitle states, this is "an international journal of comparative politics." Published for over 40 years, this quarterly refereed journal has particular interests in the study of democracy, political parties, the European Union, and the global economy. Subjects covered in the journal are wide-ranging; recent issues include articles and reviews on topics such as Turkish democracy, the future of European welfare states, U.S. campaign finance law, and natural resources conflicts. Articles tend more toward the practical than the theoretical. Recommended for academic libraries.

5132. *The Independent Review: a journal of political economy.* [ISSN: 1086-1653] 1996. q. USD 84.95 (Individuals, USD 28.95). Ed(s): Robert Higgs. Independent Institute, 100 Swan Way, Oakland, CA 94621-1428; info@independent.org; http://www.independent.org. Illus., index, adv. Refereed. Circ: 4000 Paid. Vol. ends: No. 4. *Indexed:* ABIn, BRI, CBRI, CJA, CommAb, EnvAb, HRA, IPSA, JEL, PAIS, PRA, PSA, RiskAb, SSA, SSCI. *Bk. rev.:* 6-8, 1,500 words. *Aud.:* Ac.

Published under the auspices of the Independent Institute, this peer-reviewed, interdisciplinary journal of political economy reflects the conservative bent of that think tank, and many articles espouse a classic tradition of limited government and free markets. But this journal targets a broad audience—its goal is to provide a forum for debate on public policy issues that transcends partisan interests—and, although it contains reports of empirical economic research, most articles are accessible to both the generalist and lay reader. Edited by noted historian and economist Robert Higgs, this journal covers subjects of interest to those in the fields of economics, political science, law, history, philosophy, and sociology. Contributors include policy experts and scholars from various disciplines, and most articles focus on the political and economic implications of U.S. public policy. A typical issue includes seven to nine articles and five or six lengthy book reviews. Topics recently discussed include entrepreneurship, politics, and religion; the effectiveness of nation building; and sustainable development. Recommended for academic libraries that seek balance in the ideological perspectives of the collection.

5133. *International Journal of Public Opinion Research.* [ISSN: 0954-2892] 1989. q. EUR 321 print or online ed. Ed(s): Wolfgang Donsbach, Michael W Traugott. Oxford University Press, Great Clarendon St, Oxford, OX2 6DP, United Kingdom; jnl.orders@ oup.co.uk; http://www.oxfordjournals.org. Illus., adv. Refereed. Circ: 1000. Vol. ends: No. 4. Reprint: PSC. *Indexed:* ArtHuCI, CommAb, IBSS, IPSA, PAIS, PRA, PSA, PsycInfo, SSA, SSCI, SociolAb, V&AA. *Bk. rev.:* 1-3, 750 words. *Aud.:* Ac, Sa.

Sponsored by the World Association for Public Opinion Research (WAPOR), this is an international, multidisciplinary, refereed journal of interest to professionals and academics. This journal publishes research articles, book reviews, surveys of recent developments in the field, research notes, notices of conferences, and news about WAPOR. Appropriate for academic libraries that support political science programs.

5134. *Journal of Democracy.* [ISSN: 1045-5736] 1990. q. USD 130. Ed(s): Marc F Plattner, Larry Diamond. The Johns Hopkins University Press, 2715 N Charles St, Baltimore, MD 21218-4363; myq@press.jhu.edu; http://muse.jhu.edu. Illus., index, adv. Refereed. Circ: 1587 Paid. Vol. ends: No. 4. Online: EBSCO Publishing, EBSCO Host; OCLC Online Computer Library Center, Inc.; OhioLINK; Project MUSE; ProQuest K-12 Learning Solutions; ProQuest LLC (Ann Arbor); SwetsWise Online Content. Reprint: PSC. *Indexed:* ABCPolSci, ABS&EES, IBR, IBSS, IBZ, IPSA, IndIslam, PAIS, PSA, SSA, SSCI, SociolAb. *Bk. rev.:* 2-3, 1,500-1,750 words. *Aud.:* Ac, Sa.

Affiliated with the International Forum for Democratic Studies at the National Endowment for Democracy, this journal is the leading publication on the theory and practice of democracy. Since 1990, it has published research, news, and reviews of books on democratic movements and regimes worldwide. Contributors to the journal come from all over the world. "The Journal explores in depth every aspect of the establishment, consolidation, and maintenance of democracy, including political institutions, parties and elections, civil society, ethnic conflict, economic reform, public opinion, the role of the media, and constitutionalism." Recommended for academic and large public libraries.

5135. *Legislative Studies Quarterly.* [ISSN: 0362-9805] 1976. q. USD 150 (Individuals, USD 40). University of Iowa, Comparative Legislative Research Center, 334 Schaeffer Hall, Iowa City, IA 52245-1409; http://www.uiowa.edu. Illus., index, adv. Refereed. Circ: 1000. Vol. ends: No. 4. Microform: PQC. Online: JSTOR (Web-based Journal Archive). *Indexed:* ABCPolSci, ABS&EES, IBR, IBSS, IBZ, IPSA, PRA, PSA, RiskAb, SSCI, SociolAb. *Aud.:* Ac, Sa.

Legislative Studies Quarterly is the official journal of the Legislative Studies Section of the American Political Science Association. This journal publishes research on representative assemblies at any level of government, anywhere in the world. Comparative approaches are encouraged but the journal is open to all scholarly research methods. Although the journal is international in scope, the majority of articles focus on legislative bodies in the United States. Appropriate for academic libraries that support legislative studies programs.

5136. *The National Interest.* [ISSN: 0884-9382] 1985. q. USD 31 (Individuals, USD 26; USD 7 per issue). Ed(s): Adam Garfinkle. The National Interest, Inc., 1112 16th St, NW, Ste 530, Washington, DC 20036. Illus., adv. Circ: 15000 Paid. Vol. ends: Winter. Microform: PQC. Online: EBSCO Publishing, EBSCO Host; Florida Center for Library Automation; Gale; LexisNexis; Northern Light Technology, Inc.; OCLC Online Computer Library Center, Inc.; ProQuest LLC (Ann Arbor); H.W. Wilson. *Indexed:* ABS&EES, AmH&L, HistAb, IBR, IBSS, IBZ, IPSA, PAIS, PSA, SociolAb. *Bk. rev.:* 5, 1,500 words. *Aud.:* Ga, Sa.

Since 1985, this journal has been serving an audience of policy makers, scholars, and general readers who have an interest in international affairs. *The National Interest* is particularly concerned with "the way in which cultural and social differences, technological innovations, history, and religion impact the behavior of states." Articles generally range between 2,000 and 5,000 words and are written in a jargon-free style. The journal also includes book reviews. As the magazine's web site declares, "it is not an academic journal." Recommended for all libraries.

5137. *National Journal: the weekly on politics and government.* Incorporates: *National Issues Outlook;* Former titles: *National Journal Reports; National Journal.* [ISSN: 0360-4217] 1969. w. USD 1799. Ed(s): Jill Graham, Charles Green. National Journal Group, Inc., 600 New Hampshire Ave, NW, Washington, DC 20037; orders@nationaljournal.com; http://www.nationaljournal.com. Illus., index, adv. Circ: 8400. Vol. ends: No. 52. Microform: PQC. Online:

EBSCO Publishing, EBSCO Host; Florida Center for Library Automation; Gale; OCLC Online Computer Library Center, Inc.; ProQuest K-12 Learning Solutions; ProQuest LLC (Ann Arbor). *Indexed:* ABS&EES, AgeL, BAS, BLI, EnvAb, LRI, MASUSE, MCR, PAIS, SWR&A. *Aud.:* Hs, Ga, Ac.

This weekly magazine on politics and government has been published since 1969. The mostly brief articles, written by *National Journal* staff writers, cover the policy-making process for general readers. The content is appropriate for large public and academic libraries, but the cost is high.

5138. *New Politics: a journal of socialist thought.* [ISSN: 0028-6494] 1961. s-a. USD 34 (Individuals, USD 24). Ed(s): Phyllis Jacobson, Julius Jacobson. New Politics Associates, Inc., 155 W 72nd St, Rm 402, New York, NY 10023-3250. Illus., index, adv. Circ: 3500 Paid. Vol. ends: No. 4. Microform: PQC. Online: ProQuest LLC (Ann Arbor). *Indexed:* ABS&EES, AltPI, EAA, HRA, IBSS, IPSA, LeftInd, PAIS, PRA, PSA, SSA, SUSA, SociolAb, V&AA. *Bk. rev.:* 1-10, 1,500-2,000 words. *Aud.:* Ac, Sa.

Begun in 1986, *New Politics* is a 200-page, semi-annual independent socialist forum. This journal is committed to leftist analysis and debate with core concerns of labor, race, intellectual history, foreign policy, and social movements. Recent articles include "Immediate U.S. Withdrawal and the Hope for Democracy in Iraq," "The Green Party and the Collapse of the Left," and "Reintroducing the Black/White Divide in Racial Discourse." Articles are grouped into several thematic sections in an issue, such as a "Roundtable on Immigration and African Americans" and a "Special Section on Religion and Politics." Appropriate for academic and large public libraries.

5139. *Parliamentary Affairs: devoted to all aspects of parliamentary democracy.* [ISSN: 0031-2290] 1947. q. EUR 315 print or online ed. Ed(s): Steven Fielding, Dr. Jocelyn Evans. Oxford University Press, Great Clarendon St, Oxford, OX2 6DP, United Kingdom; jnl.orders@oup.co.uk; http://www.oxfordjournals.org. Illus., index, adv. Refereed. Circ: 1550. Vol. ends: No. 4. Microform: PQC. Online: EBSCO Publishing, EBSCO Host; Florida Center for Library Automation; Gale; HighWire Press; IngentaConnect; Northern Light Technology, Inc.; OCLC Online Computer Library Center, Inc.; OhioLINK; Oxford Journals; ProQuest LLC (Ann Arbor); SwetsWise Online Content; H.W. Wilson. Reprint: PSC. *Indexed:* ABCPolSci, AmH&L, AmHI, ArtHuCI, BrHumI, HistAb, IBR, IBSS, IBZ, IPSA, IndIslam, PAIS, PSA, SSA, SSCI, SociolAb. *Bk. rev.:* 3, 1,500 words. *Aud.:* Ac, Sa.

Parliamentary Affairs is a peer-reviewed quarterly journal that covers all the aspects of Parliament and parliamentary systems in Britain and throughout the world. It is published in association with The Hansard Society, which was established to promote parliamentary democracy throughout the world. Aiming for an audience beyond specialists, the journal includes scholarly analysis, commentary, reviews, and a section by and for practitioners.

5140. *Policy Studies Journal.* [ISSN: 0190-292X] 1972. q. GBP 705 print & online eds. Ed(s): Hank Jenkins-Smith. Blackwell Publishing, Inc., Commerce Place, 350 Main St, Malden, MA 02148; customerservices@blackwellpublishing.com; http://www.blackwellpublishing.com. Illus., index, adv. Refereed. Circ: 2400. Vol. ends: No. 4. Online: Blackwell Synergy; Chadwyck-Healey Inc.; EBSCO Publishing, EBSCO Host; Florida Center for Library Automation; Gale; IngentaConnect; Northern Light Technology, Inc.; OCLC Online Computer Library Center, Inc.; OhioLINK; ProQuest K-12 Learning Solutions; ProQuest LLC (Ann Arbor); SwetsWise Online Content; H.W. Wilson. Reprint: PSC. *Indexed:* ABCPolSci, ABS&EES, ASG, AgeL, AmH&L, ApEcolAb, ArtHuCI, BRI, CBRI, CJA, EAA, EI, EnvAb, FutSurv, HRA, HRIS, HistAb, IBR, IBZ, IPSA, ISTA, LRI, PAIS, PRA, PSA, RiskAb, SSA, SSCI, SUSA, SWA, SociolAb. *Bk. rev.:* 25, 125-1,000 words. *Aud.:* Ac, Sa.

Policy Studies Journal is a publication of the Policy Studies Organization and the Public Policy Section of the American Political Science Association. This journal publishes research on public policy at all levels of government produced by social scientists, policy makers, and leaders. Recent topics include endangered-species protection, New England fishery management, and welfare reform. Each issue contains between eight and ten articles plus announcements from affiliated organizations. Recommended for academic libraries.

5141. *Political Communication: an international journal.* Formerly (until 1992): *Political Communication and Persuasion.* [ISSN: 1058-4609] 1980. q. GBP 291 print & online eds. Ed(s): David L Paletz. Taylor & Francis Inc., 325 Chestnut St, Ste 800, Philadelphia, PA 19016; orders@taylorandfrancis.com; http://www.taylorandfrancis.com. Illus., adv. Refereed. Vol. ends: No. 4. Online: EBSCO Publishing, EBSCO Host; Gale; IngentaConnect; OCLC Online Computer Library Center, Inc.; SwetsWise Online Content. Reprint: PSC. *Indexed:* ABCPolSci, ArtHuCI, CJA, CommAb, IBSS, IPSA, PAIS, PRA, PSA, SSA, SSCI, SociolAb, V&AA. *Bk. rev.:* Number and length vary. *Aud.:* Ac, Sa.

The journal *Political Communication* is sponsored by the Political Communication section of the American Political Science Association and the International Communication Association. This is an interdisciplinary, international journal that features research at the intersection of politics and communication. It includes reviews of relevant books and films. "The journal welcomes all research methods and analytical viewpoints that advance understanding of the practices, processes, and policy implications of political communication in all its forms." Recommended for academic libraries.

5142. *Politics and Society.* [ISSN: 0032-3292] 1970. q. GBP 418. Ed(s): Mary-Ann Twist. Sage Publications, Inc., 2455 Teller Rd, Thousand Oaks, CA 91320; info@sagepub.com; http://www.sagepub.com. Illus., index, adv. Refereed. Circ: 1400. Vol. ends: No. 4. Microform: PQC. Online: CSA; EBSCO Publishing, EBSCO Host; Florida Center for Library Automation; Gale; HighWire Press; OCLC Online Computer Library Center, Inc.; OhioLINK; SAGE Publications, Inc., SAGE Journals Online; SwetsWise Online Content. Reprint: PSC. *Indexed:* ABCPolSci, ABS&EES, ASSIA, AltPI, AmH&L, ArtHuCI, BAS, CJA, EI, HRA, HistAb, IBR, IBSS, IBZ, IPSA, LeftInd, PRA, PSA, RiskAb, SSA, SSCI, SociolAb. *Aud.:* Ac, Sa.

Founded in the 1960s. This journal's mission "is to encourage a tradition of critical analysis through the development of Marxist, post-Marxist and other radical perspectives." Articles published address questions of politics, theory, and policy. Recent articles include "The Global Pension Crisis: From Gray Capitalism to Responsible Accumulation," "Political Openness and Transnational Activism: Comparative Insights from Labor Activism," and "War v. Justice: Terrorism Cases, Enemy Combatants, and Political Justice in U.S. Courts." Appropriate for academic libraries.

5143. *Presidential Studies Quarterly.* Formerly: *Center for the Study of the Presidency. Center House Bulletin.* [ISSN: 0360-4918] 1972. q. GBP 218 print & online eds. Ed(s): I Joann Davis, George C Edwards, III. Blackwell Publishing, Inc., Commerce Place, 350 Main St, Malden, MA 02148; customerservices@blackwellpublishing.com; http://www.blackwellpublishing.com. Illus., index, adv. Refereed. Circ: 6000. Vol. ends: No. 4. Microform: PQC. Online: Blackwell Synergy; EBSCO Publishing, EBSCO Host; Florida Center for Library Automation; Gale; IngentaConnect; Northern Light Technology, Inc.; OCLC Online Computer Library Center, Inc.; OhioLINK; ProQuest K-12 Learning Solutions; ProQuest LLC (Ann Arbor); SwetsWise Online Content; H.W. Wilson. Reprint: PSC. *Indexed:* ABCPolSci, ABS&EES, AmH&L, ApEcolAb, BRI, CBRI, CommAb, HRA, HistAb, IBR, IBSS, IBZ, IPSA, PAIS, PRA, PSA, RI-1, RiskAb, SFSA, SUSA, V&AA. *Bk. rev.:* 6-10, 800-1,200 words. *Aud.:* Ac, Sa.

Published by the Center for the Study of the Presidency, a nonprofit, non-partisan organization, this is an interdisciplinary journal of theory and research about the American presidency. The Center describes this journal as "the only scholarly journal that focuses on the most powerful political figure in the world—the president of the United States." The journal publishes both qualitative and quantitative work on presidential decision-making; White House operations; the President's public policy role; and presidential relations with Congress, the courts, the press and the public. Two recent special issues include "Presidential Doctrines" and the "2004 Presidential Election." The journal publishes research articles, features, review essays, and book reviews by distinguished scholars and professionals in political science, history, and communications. Recommended for academic and large public libraries.

5144. *Publius: the journal of federalism.* [ISSN: 0048-5950] 1971. q. EUR 297 print or online ed. Ed(s): Carol S Weissert. Oxford University Press, Great Clarendon St, Oxford, OX2 6DP, United Kingdom; enquiry@ oup.co.uk; http://www.oxfordjournals.org. Illus., index, adv. Refereed. Circ: 1200 Paid. Vol. ends: No. 4. Microform: PQC. Online: EBSCO Publishing, EBSCO Host; Florida Center for Library Automation; Gale; HighWire Press; Northern Light Technology, Inc.; OCLC Online Computer Library Center, Inc.; Oxford Journals; ProQuest K-12 Learning Solutions; ProQuest LLC (Ann Arbor); H.W. Wilson. Reprint: PSC. *Indexed:* ABCPolSci, ABS&EES, AmH&L, ArtHuCI, EAA, HistAb, IBR, IBSS, IBZ, IPSA, PAIS, PRA, PSA, SSA, SSCI, SUSA, SociolAb. *Bk. rev.:* 3-6, 1,000-1,500 words. *Aud.:* Ac, Sa.

Publius: The Journal of Federalism is a scholarly journal that publishes empirical and theoretical work on federalism and intergovernmental relations. Founded in 1973, it is sponsored by the Section on Federalism and Intergovernmental Relations of the American Political Science Association. It includes book reviews, and it also issues an annual review of American Federalism. Contributors and articles topics are drawn mainly from the United States. Recommended for academic libraries.

5145. *Third World Quarterly: journal of emerging areas.* [ISSN: 0143-6597] 1979. 8x/yr. GBP 795 print & online eds. Ed(s): Shahid Qadir. Routledge, 4 Park Sq, Milton Park, Abingdon, OX14 4RN, United Kingdom; journals@routledge.com; http://www.routledge.co.uk. Illus., index, adv. Refereed. Circ: 6000. Vol. ends: No. 6. Online: EBSCO Publishing, EBSCO Host; Gale; IngentaConnect; Northern Light Technology, Inc.; OCLC Online Computer Library Center, Inc.; ProQuest K-12 Learning Solutions; ProQuest LLC (Ann Arbor); SwetsWise Online Content. Reprint: PSC. *Indexed:* AltPI, AmH&L, AmHI, BAS, BrHumI, CABA, CJA, EI, FPA, ForAb, HistAb, HortAb, IBR, IBSS, IBZ, IPSA, IndIslam, LeftInd, PAIS, PRA, PSA, PhilInd, RRTA, S&F, SSA, SSCI, SWA, SociolAb, WAE&RSA. *Bk. rev.:* 1-3, 1,500 words. *Aud.:* Ga, Ac, Sa.

A peer-reviewed journal of international studies, *Third World Quarterly* (*TWQ*) publishes analysis of issues affecting all Third World countries. This journal is particularly interested in the "micro-economic and grassroot efforts of development practitioners and planners." This is an interdisciplinary, international title that publishes articles of between 5,000 and 6,000 words and written in jargon-free language. Recent articles include "Private Governance and the South: Lessons from global forest politics," "The African 'oil rush' and US national security," and "Iran's nuclear programme and the west." The target audience is academics and practitioners. Highly recommended for academic libraries.

5146. *West European Politics.* [ISSN: 0140-2382] 1978. 5x/yr. GBP 532 print & online eds. Ed(s): Klaus Goetz, Gordon Smith. Routledge, 4 Park Sq, Milton Park, Abingdon, OX14 4RN, United Kingdom; journals@ routledge.com; http://www.routledge.co.uk. Illus., index, adv. Sample. Refereed. Vol. ends: No. 4. Microform: PQC. Online: EBSCO Publishing, EBSCO Host; Florida Center for Library Automation; Gale; IngentaConnect; Northern Light Technology, Inc.; SwetsWise Online Content. Reprint: PSC. *Indexed:* ABCPolSci, AmH&L, AmHI, BrHumI, HRA, HistAb, IBR, IBSS, IBZ, IPSA, PAIS, PRA, PSA, RiskAb, SSA, SSCI, SWA, SociolAb, WAE&RSA. *Bk. rev.:* 15, 800 words. *Aud.:* Ac, Sa.

The subjects of this journal are the major political and social developments occurring in all Western European countries and the European Union. It also contains a substantial reviews section and purports to cover all national elections in Western Europe. Immigration policy in Europe was the subject of a recent special issue. Recommended for academic libraries.

International Relations

5147. *Brown Journal of World Affairs.* Formerly (until 1994): *Brown Journal of Foreign Affairs.* [ISSN: 1080-0786] 1994. s-a. USD 54.95 (Individuals, USD 20.95). Ed(s): David Estlund, James Dreier. Brown University, PO Box 1930, Providence, RI 02912. Adv. Online: EBSCO Publishing, EBSCO Host. Reprint: WSH. *Indexed:* CJA, IPSA, PAIS. *Aud.:* Ac.

Affiliated with the Watson Institute for International Studies at Brown University, this journal addresses contemporary issues in international affairs. This title is run by students and published twice a year. Contributors include political leaders, policy makers, and academics. The journal's goal is to bridge "the gap between academic discourse and mainstream media." Each issue consists of articles grouped under a few themes along with an essay section. Recent themes include "China's Resource Alliances," "Christianity in IR," and "Identity in the EU." Recommended for academic libraries.

5148. *Current History: a journal of contemporary world affairs.* Formed by the merger of: *Events; Current History & Forum;* Which was formed by the merger of: *Current History; Forum and Century.* [ISSN: 0011-3530] 1914. 9x/yr. USD 61 print & online eds. (Individuals, USD 48 print & online eds.; USD 38 domestic). Ed(s): William W Finan, Jr. Current History, Inc., 4225 Main St, Philadelphia, PA 19127; editorial@ currenthistory.com; http://www.currenthistory.com. Illus., index, adv. Sample. Refereed. Circ: 20000 Paid. Vol. ends: Dec. Microform: NBI; PQC. Online: Chadwyck-Healey Inc.; EBSCO Publishing, EBSCO Host; OCLC Online Computer Library Center, Inc.; ProQuest K-12 Learning Solutions; ProQuest LLC (Ann Arbor); SwetsWise Online Content. *Indexed:* ABCPolSci, ABS&EES, AmH&L, AmHI, ArtHuCI, BAS, BRI, CABA, CBCARef, CBRI, CPerI, HistAb, HumInd, IBR, IBSS, IBZ, IndIslam, LRI, MASUSE, PAIS, PRA, PSA, RGPR, RRTA, SSCI, WAE&RSA. *Bk. rev.:* 1 or 2, 400-600 words. *Aud.:* Hs, Ga, Ac.

Founded by *The New York Times* in 1914 to cover the First World War, *Current History* is the "oldest United States publication devoted exclusively to world affairs." Past contributors have included George Bernard Shaw, Winston Churchill, Charles Beard, and Henry Steele Commager. More recent contributors include James Schlesinger, Marshall Goldman, Peter Arnett, and Francis Fukuyama. Each issue focuses on a particular theme, usually a region of the world such as Africa or Asia. Recent topics include "Women in the World" and "The Nuclear Question Revisited." In addition to the articles, each issue also includes a "Month in Review" column that provides an international chronology of events and a map. Recommended for public and academic libraries.

East European Politics & Societies. See Slavic Studies section.

5149. *European Journal of International Relations.* [ISSN: 1354-0661] 1995. q. GBP 549. Ed(s): Barry Buzan. Sage Publications Ltd., 1 Oliver's Yard, 55 City Rd, London, EC1 1SP, United Kingdom; info@sagepub.co.uk; http://www.sagepub.co.uk. Illus., index, adv. Refereed. Vol. ends: No. 4. Reprint: PSC. *Indexed:* ABIn, HRA, IBR, IBSS, IBZ, IPSA, JEL, PRA, PSA, RiskAb, SSA, SSCI, SociolAb. *Aud.:* Ac, Sa.

This interdisciplinary journal has emerged as one of the most important sources for international relations scholarship. With Europe as its base, it is dedicated to stimulating and disseminating cutting-edge theoretical and empirical research on global issues. It publishes well-documented articles on foreign policy analysis and international political economy, law, and organizations. It is the journal of the Standing Group on International Relations of the European Consortium for Political Research. Although the journal "pays special attention to Europe and its sub-regions," it does not support a particular disciplinary school or approach, nor is it limited by its emphasis on a particular methodology. It also seeks to strengthen ties with related disciplines such as international history, international law, and international economics. Recently published articles include "Learning from Europe? EU Studies and the Re-thinking of International Relations," "Coming in from the Cold: Constructivism and Emotions," and "Foreign Economic Liberalization: The Case of Sub-Saharan Africa." Recommended for academic libraries.

5150. *Fletcher Forum of World Affairs.* Formerly (until 1988): *Fletcher Forum.* [ISSN: 1046-1868] 1977. s-a. USD 50 (Individuals, USD 20). Ed(s): Brian Jackson. Fletcher School of Law and Diplomacy, Tufts University, Medford, MA 02155; forum@tufts.edu; http://www.tufts.edu. Illus., adv. Refereed. Circ: 1600. Vol. ends: No. 2. Microform: WSH. Online: William S. Hein & Co., Inc.; LexisNexis; Thomson West. Reprint: WSH. *Indexed:* ABCPolSci, ABS&EES, AmH&L, BAS, CLI, HistAb, IPSA, LRI, PAIS, PRA, PSA, PhilInd. *Bk. rev.:* 5, 1,250 words. *Aud.:* Ac, Sa.

Published twice a year, *The Fletcher Forum of World Affairs* is "the official foreign policy journal at The Fletcher School" at Tufts University. It publishes articles, essays, and book reviews that analyze the theory and practice of international affairs. Contributors include scholars, policy analysts, and practitioners. It generally publishes 10–15 articles of varying lengths. Some issues are devoted to forums held by The Fletcher School, such as "Preemptive Use of Force: A Reassessment." This journal also publishes interviews with prominent officials, and a new "Perspectives" section provides commentary on upcoming topics. Recent subjects covered in the journal include China's economic development, the North Korean nuclear threat, and Russian democracy. Appropriate for academic libraries.

5151. *Foreign Affairs.* Former titles (until 1922): *The Journal of International Relations;* (until 1919): *The Journal of Race Development.* [ISSN: 0015-7120] 1910. bi-m. USD 32 domestic; USD 42 Canada; USD 67 elsewhere. Ed(s): Gideon Rose, James F Hoge, Jr. Council on Foreign Relations, Inc., 58 E 68th St, New York, NY 10021; membership@cfr.org; http://www.cfr.org. Illus., index, adv. Refereed. Circ: 115000 Paid. Vol. ends: No. 6. CD-ROM: ProQuest LLC (Ann Arbor). Microform: WSH; PMC; PQC. Online: Chadwyck-Healey Inc.; EBSCO Publishing, EBSCO Host; Factiva, Inc.; Florida Center for Library Automation; Gale; William S. Hein & Co., Inc.; LexisNexis; Northern Light Technology, Inc.; OCLC Online Computer Library Center, Inc.; ProQuest K-12 Learning Solutions; ProQuest LLC (Ann Arbor); H.W. Wilson. Reprint: WSH. *Indexed:* ABCPolSci, ABIn, ABS&EES, AgeL, AmH&L, BAS, BRI, CBRI, CPerI, EI, FutSurv, HistAb, IBR, IBSS, IBZ, IPSA, IndIslam, JEL, MASUSE, PAIS, PRA, PSA, RGPR, RI-1, SSCI. *Bk. rev.:* 4-6, 125-1,850 words. *Aud.:* Ga, Ac, Sa.

Foreign Affairs is published by The Council on Foreign Relations, a nonprofit, non-partisan member organization. This is the preeminent American journal on international relations and foreign policy. According to the publication's web site, "articles published in *Foreign Affairs* shape the political dialogue for months and years to come." Contributors to this journal include prominent scholars, respected journalists, and policy makers. Content is grouped into a few categories, "Comments," "Essays," "Review Essays," and "Correspondence." The essays, which are the main content of the journal, provide thoughtful analysis of important global issues. Within the instructions for contributors, the following notice appears: "We do not have fact checkers, and rely on authors to ensure the veracity of their statements. Although we try to avoid using footnotes in print, authors should be able to provide, if asked, appropriate citations for any facts or quotations their pieces contain." Recommended for all types of libraries.

5152. *Foreign Policy (Washington): the magazine of global politics, economics and ideas.* [ISSN: 0015-7228] 1971. bi-m. USD 24.95 domestic; USD 42.95 Canada; USD 54.95 elsewhere. Ed(s): William J Dobson, Dr. Moises Naim. Carnegie Endowment for International Peace, 1779 Massachusetts Ave, NW, Washington, DC 20036-2103; info@ceip.org; http://www.carnegieendowment.org/. Illus., index, adv. Refereed. Circ: 25000. Microform: PQC. Online: EBSCO Publishing, EBSCO Host; Florida Center for Library Automation; Gale; JSTOR (Web-based Journal Archive); OCLC Online Computer Library Center, Inc.; ProQuest K-12 Learning Solutions; ProQuest LLC (Ann Arbor); H.W. Wilson. *Indexed:* ABCPolSci, ABIn, ABS&EES, ASIP, AmH&L, CLI, FutSurv, HistAb, IBR, IBSS, IBZ, ILP, IPSA, LRI, MASUSE, PAIS, PRA, PSA, RGPR, RRTA, SSCI, WAE&RSA. *Bk. rev.:* 3-5, 1,500-2,500 words. *Aud.:* Ga, Ac, Sa.

Similar to *Foreign Affairs* in coverage, this bimonthly differentiates itself by aiming to become "an indispensable reference" for the specialist while also engaging and entertaining the general reader. Now published by the Carnegie Endowment for International Peace, this journal was founded by Samuel Huntington and Warren Demian Manshel in 1970. Its mission "is to explain how the world works—in particular, how the process of global integration is reshaping nations, institutions, cultures, and, more fundamentally, our daily lives," and it prides itself on publishing material with a fresh take on global political issues, written in a jargon-free style. Most articles are analytical essays or opinion pieces, and many include helpful charts and sidebars. This journal has introduced a number of new sections over the past few years, including "Think Again" ("the equivalent of a guerilla attack on conventional wisdom"); "Arguments," brief provocative pieces; "Prime Numbers," which combines data graphics and text; "In Other Words," which contains reviews of books published outside of the United States; the "FP Interview"; and "Want to Know More?," a guide to additional information on topics discussed in the articles. Additional features include highlights from specialty journals and a review of useful web sites. The audience is meant to be general readers interested in international affairs, in addition to experts in the field. A good choice for all libraries.

5153. *Global Governance: a review of multilateralism and international organizations.* [ISSN: 1075-2846] 1995. q. USD 123 print & online eds. (Individuals, USD 54). Ed(s): Eliza Gaffney, Mette Ekeroth. Lynne Rienner Publishers, 1800 30th St, Ste 314, Boulder, CO 80301-1026; http://www.rienner.com. Illus., index, adv. Sample. Refereed. Circ: 1500 Paid. Vol. ends: No. 4. Microform: WSH. Online: EBSCO Publishing, EBSCO Host; Florida Center for Library Automation; Gale; William S. Hein & Co., Inc.; ProQuest LLC (Ann Arbor). Reprint: WSH. *Indexed:* CJA, IBSS, IPSA, PAIS, PRA, PSA, SSA, SSCI, SociolAb, WAE&RSA. *Aud.:* Ac, Sa.

This is a scholarly international public policy journal that publishes research on "the impact of international institutions and multilateral processes on economic development, peace and security, human rights, and preservation of the environment." Published in association with the Academic Council on the United Nations System and the United Nations University, this journal is aimed at an audience that includes academics and practitioners. Recently published articles include "Legitimacy, Transparency, and Information Technology: The World Trade Organization in an Era of Contentious Trade Politics"; "Global Good Samaritans?: Human Rights Foreign Policy in Costa Rica"; and "Asian Financial Cooperation: The Problem of Legitimacy in Global Financial Governance." In addition to research articles, the journal also presents review essays and "Global Insights," which are shorter provocative commentaries.

5154. *Global Society: journal of interdisciplinary relations.* Formerly (until 1996): *Paradigms.* [ISSN: 1360-0826] 1986. q. GBP 415 print & online eds. Ed(s): A J R Groom. Routledge, 4 Park Sq, Milton Park, Abingdon, OX14 4RN, United Kingdom; info@routledge.co.uk; http://www.routledge.co.uk. Illus., index, adv. Refereed. Vol. ends: No. 4. Online: EBSCO Publishing, EBSCO Host; Gale; IngentaConnect; Northern Light Technology, Inc.; OCLC Online Computer Library Center, Inc.; ProQuest LLC (Ann Arbor); SwetsWise Online Content. Reprint: PSC. *Indexed:* AmHI, BrHumI, IBR, IBSS, IBZ, IPSA, IndIslam, PAIS, PSA, SSA, SociolAb. *Aud.:* Ac, Sa.

Global Society is a scholarly journal that promotes multidisciplinary approaches to the analysis of international relations. According to the editors, these approaches are necessitated by globalization. Subjects recently covered include nuclear terrorism post-9/11, global citizenship, and recruitment of IMF officials. Appropriate for academic libraries that support graduate programs in international relations.

5155. *International Affairs (London, 1944).* Former titles (until 1943): *International Affairs Review Supplement;* (until 1939): *International Affairs (London, 1931);* (until 1930): *Royal Institute of International Affairs. Journal;* (until 1926): *British Institute of International Affairs. Journal.* [ISSN: 0020-5850] 1922. 5x/yr. GBP 289 print & online eds. Ed(s): Caroline Soper. Blackwell Publishing Ltd., 9600 Garsington Rd, Oxford, OX4 2ZG, United Kingdom; customerservices@blackwellpublishing.com; http://www.blackwellpublishing.com. Illus., index, adv. Refereed. Vol. ends: No. 4. Microform: PMC. Online: Blackwell Synergy; EBSCO Publishing, EBSCO Host; Gale; IngentaConnect; JSTOR (Web-based Journal Archive); OCLC Online

Computer Library Center, Inc.; OhioLINK; SwetsWise Online Content. Reprint: PSC. *Indexed:* ABCPolSci, AmH&L, AmHI, ApEcolAb, ArtHuCI, BAS, BrHumI, EI, HistAb, IBR, IBSS, IBZ, IPSA, IndIslam, PAIS, PRA, PSA, RRTA, RiskAb, SSCI, WAE&RSA. *Bk. rev.:* 80-120, 500-700 words. *Aud.:* Hs, Ac, Sa.

Chatham House, The Royal Institute of International Affairs in London, publishes this journal, which covers a broad range of international issues. According to the editors, the journal is "committed to excellence in scholarship and accessibility in style, combining policy relevance with an academic, in-depth analytical approach to contemporary world politics." The journal aims for an audience of academics, professionals, and the informed general public. Commissioned and unsolicited research articles, review articles, and a large number of book reviews are published in the journal. A recent issue is devoted to the topic of HIV/AIDS. Recently published articles include "Brazil as an Intermediate State and Regional Power," "Chinese strategies in a US-hegemonic global order," and "No Pain, No Gain? Torture and Ethics in the War on Terror." Recommended for academic and larger public libraries.

5156. International Organization. [ISSN: 0020-8183] 1947. q. GBP 126. Ed(s): Jacqueline Larson. Cambridge University Press, The Edinburgh Bldg, Shaftesbury Rd, Cambridge, CB2 2RU, United Kingdom; journals@cambridge.org; http://www.cup.cam.ac.uk/. Illus., index, adv. Refereed. Circ: 3000 Paid. Vol. ends: No. 4. Microform: PQC. Online: Pub.; EBSCO Publishing, EBSCO Host; Gale; IngentaConnect; JSTOR (Web-based Journal Archive); OCLC Online Computer Library Center, Inc.; OhioLINK; Project MUSE; SwetsWise Online Content; H.W. Wilson. *Indexed:* ABIn, ABS&EES, AmH&L, BAS, CLI, CommAb, FutSurv, HistAb, IBR, IBSS, IBZ, IPSA, IndIslam, JEL, LRI, PAIS, PSA, PsycInfo, RRTA, SSA, SSCI, SociolAb, WAE&RSA. *Bk. rev.:* 0-3, 2,500-3,000 words. *Aud.:* Ac, Sa.

This is a leading scholarly journal in the field of international affairs, covering security and environmental policies, political economy, European integration, alliance patterns, and international relations. It is published on behalf of the International Organization Foundation. Recent articles include "Uncommon Ground: Indivisible Territory and the Politics of Legitimacy," "Women and Globalization: A Study of 180 Countries, 1975–2000," "Congressional Politics of Financing the International Monetary Fund," and "Systemic Vulnerability and the Origins of Developmental States: Northeast and Southeast Asia in Comparative Perspective." Most issues also include briefer research notes and/or a comments and response section. Recommended for all academic libraries.

5157. International Studies Quarterly: journal of the International Studies Association. Formerly (until 1966): *Background; Background on World Politics.* [ISSN: 0020-8833] 1957. q. GBP 1039 print & online eds. Ed(s): Steven C Poe. Blackwell Publishing, Inc., Commerce Place, 350 Main St, Malden, MA 02148; customerservices@blackwellpublishing.com; http://www.blackwellpublishing.com. Illus., index, adv. Refereed. Circ: 4400. Vol. ends: No. 4. Microform: PQC. Online: Blackwell Synergy; EBSCO Publishing, EBSCO Host; Gale; IngentaConnect; JSTOR (Web-based Journal Archive); OCLC Online Computer Library Center, Inc.; OhioLINK; SwetsWise Online Content. Reprint: PSC. *Indexed:* ABCPolSci, ABS&EES, AmH&L, AmHI, ApEcolAb, ArtHuCI, BAS, BrHumI, CJA, HRA, HistAb, IBR, IBSS, IBZ, IPSA, PAIS, PRA, PSA, RiskAb, SSCI, SUSA, SWA, SociolAb, V&AA. *Aud.:* Ac, Sa.

A publication of the International Studies Association, this journal publishes both theoretical and policy-oriented research. The Association works to encourage collaboration among specialists across disciplines. The *International Studies Quarterly* aims to facilitate communication between academics and policy-makers and to improve the teaching of international studies. Recent topics covered include economic reforms in Latin America, the effectiveness of peacekeeping forces, and territorial dispute resolution. Recommended for academic libraries.

5158. Journal of Common Market Studies. [ISSN: 0021-9886] 1962. 5x/yr. GBP 572 print & online eds. Ed(s): Jim Rollo, William Paterson. Blackwell Publishing Ltd., 9600 Garsington Rd, Oxford, OX4 2ZG, United Kingdom; customerservices@blackwellpublishing.com;

http://www.blackwellpublishing.com. Illus., index, adv. Refereed. Circ: 1400. Vol. ends: No. 4. Microform: WSH. Online: Blackwell Synergy; EBSCO Publishing, EBSCO Host; Gale; IngentaConnect; OCLC Online Computer Library Center, Inc.; OhioLINK; SwetsWise Online Content. *Indexed:* ABCPolSci, ABIn, AmH&L, ApEcolAb, BAS, BPI, BrHumI, CABA, CLI, HistAb, HortAb, IBR, IBSS, IBZ, ILP, IPSA, JEL, PAIS, PSA, RRTA, RiskAb, S&F, SSCI, WAE&RSA. *Bk. rev.:* 8-15, 500 words. *Aud.:* Ac, Sa.

Published by the University Association for Contemporary European Studies (UACES), this journal has been publishing research on European integration issues for over 40 years. Articles appearing in the journal include theoretical and empirical research in economics, political science, and international relations. Each year a special book issue is devoted to a comprehensive review of the activities of the European Union in the previous year. A comprehensive review volume is published annually, which provides "a succinct yet comprehensive guide to the progress of EU policy and plans." In addition to research articles, the journal publishes book reviews. Appropriate for libraries that support scholars or professionals with interests in the European Union.

The Journal of Communist Studies and Transition Politics. See Slavic Studies section.

5159. Latin American Politics and Society. Former titles (until 2001): *Journal of Interamerican Studies and World Affairs;* (until 1970): *Journal of Inter-American Studies.* [ISSN: 1531-426X] 1959. q. GBP 197 print & online eds. Ed(s): William C Smith. Blackwell Publishing, Inc., Commerce Place, 350 Main St, Malden, MA 02148; customerservices@blackwellpublishing.com; http://www.blackwellpublishing.com. Illus., index, adv. Refereed. Circ: 1000 Paid. Vol. ends: No. 4. Microform: PQC. Online: EBSCO Publishing, EBSCO Host; Florida Center for Library Automation; Gale; JSTOR (Web-based Journal Archive); OCLC Online Computer Library Center, Inc.; OhioLINK; Project MUSE; ProQuest K-12 Learning Solutions; ProQuest LLC (Ann Arbor); SwetsWise Online Content; H.W. Wilson. *Indexed:* ABCPolSci, ABS&EES, AmH&L, BAS, CJA, HAPI, HistAb, IBR, IBSS, IPSA, JEL, PAIS, PRA, PSA, RiskAb, SSCI, SociolAb. *Bk. rev.:* 1-15, 750 words. *Aud.:* Ac, Sa.

Affiliated with the University of Miami, this English-language journal presents original research on the politics, economics, and social conditions of Latin America. "The editorial board is dedicated to challenging prevailing orthodoxies and promoting innovative perspectives on the states, [and] societies...of Latin America." The journal also publishes book reviews, longer review essays on recent topics, and a section on opposing policy viewpoints. Recent articles include "Measuring Judicial Performance in Latin America," "U.S. Power and the Politics of Economic Governance in the Americas," and "Democrats, Dictators, and Cooperation: The Transformation of Argentine-Chilean Relations."

5160. New Left Review. Formed by the merger of: *Universities and Left Review; New Reasoner.* [ISSN: 0028-6060] 1960. bi-m. GBP 195 print & online eds. (Individuals, GBP 32). Ed(s): Susan Watkins, Perry Anderson. New Left Review Ltd., 6 Meard St, London, W1F 0EG, United Kingdom; mail@newleftreview.org; http://www.newleftreview.org. Illus., adv. Refereed. Circ: 8000. Vol. ends: Nov/Dec. Online: EBSCO Publishing, EBSCO Host. *Indexed:* AltPI, AmH&L, AmHI, ArtHuCI, BAS, BrHumI, FLI, HistAb, IBR, IBSS, IBZ, IPSA, LeftInd, PAIS, PSA, SSCI, SWA, SociolAb, WAE&RSA. *Bk. rev.:* Number and length vary. *Aud.:* Ac, Sa.

Although self-described as a journal of politics, *The New Left Review* also covers history and philosophy; cinema and literature; and art and aesthetics. This journal is published every two months, and each issue includes scholarly analysis, book reviews, and occasional interviews. In 2000, the journal was revamped. Along with a new look, the editor hopes to attract contributors from a broader range of countries. "It stands resolutely opposed to Third Way pieties and neoliberal prescriptions, combating capital's current apologists with sharp and scholarly analysis, internationalist critique, polemic and experiential prose." Recommended for academic and large public libraries.

5161. *Orbis (Kidlington): a journal of world affairs.* [ISSN: 0030-4387] 1957. 4x/yr. EUR 391. Ed(s): David Eisenhower, James Kurth. Pergamon, The Boulevard, Langford Ln, East Park, Kidlington, OX5 1GB, United Kingdom; nlinfo-f@elsevier.nl; http://www.elsevier.nl. Illus., index, adv. Refereed. Circ: 3500. Vol. ends: No. 45. Microform: PQC. Online: EBSCO Publishing, EBSCO Host; Factiva, Inc.; Florida Center for Library Automation; Gale; IngentaConnect; Northern Light Technology, Inc.; OCLC Online Computer Library Center, Inc.; OhioLINK; ScienceDirect; SwetsWise Online Content; H.W. Wilson. *Indexed:* ABCPolSci, ABS&EES, AmH&L, AmHI, CJA, FutSurv, HistAb, IBR, IBSS, IPSA, PAIS, PRA, PSA, SociolAb. *Bk. rev.:* 10-25, 250-500 words. *Aud.:* Ac, Sa.

Published by the Foreign Policy Research Institute (FPRI) since 1957. The main focus of this journal is American foreign policy and national security, along with coverage of major international developments. The goal of FPRI is "bringing the insights of scholarship to bear on the development of policies that advance U.S. national interests." Recent articles include "Europe's Identity Problem and the New Islamist War," "Complex Irregular Warfare: The Next Revolution in Military Affairs," and "Preemption, Unilateralism, and Hegemony: The American Tradition?" Recommended for academic and large public libraries.

5162. *Policy Sciences: an international journal devoted to the improvement of policy making.* [ISSN: 0032-2687] 1970. q. EUR 573 print & online eds. Ed(s): Matthew R Auer. Springer New York LLC, 233 Spring St, New York, NY 10013-1578; service-ny@springer.com; http://www.springer.com/. Illus., index, adv. Refereed. Vol. ends: No. 4. Microform: PQC. Online: Chadwyck-Healey Inc.; EBSCO Publishing, EBSCO Host; Gale; IngentaConnect; OCLC Online Computer Library Center, Inc.; OhioLINK; ProQuest LLC (Ann Arbor); Springer LINK; SwetsWise Online Content. Reprint: PSC. *Indexed:* ABCPolSci, ABIn, AgeL, ArtHuCI, CJA, CommAb, EAA, EI, EIP, FutSurv, HRA, IBR, IBSS, IBZ, IPSA, ISTA, JEL, MCR, PAIS, PRA, PSA, RiskAb, SSA, SSCI, SUSA, SociolAb. *Bk. rev.:* Number and length vary. *Aud.:* Ac, Sa.

This is a quarterly, peer-reviewed journal that publishes analytical and empirical articles, as well as book reviews. The editors encourage the submission of articles that address controversial topics and present opposing perspectives. There is an emphasis on environmental topics, such as sustainable tourism, voluntary environmental programs, and climate and nuclear policy. Recommended for academic libraries that support political science programs.

5163. *Political Science Quarterly: the journal of public and international affairs.* [ISSN: 0032-3195] 1886. q. USD 309 print & online eds. (Individuals, USD 49 print & online eds.). Ed(s): Demetrios Caraley. Academy of Political Science, 475 Riverside Dr, Ste 1274, New York, NY 10115-1274. Illus., index, adv. Refereed. Circ: 8000 Paid. Vol. ends: No. 4. Microform: PMC; PQC. Online: EBSCO Publishing, EBSCO Host; Florida Center for Library Automation; Gale; IngentaConnect; JSTOR (Web-based Journal Archive); Northern Light Technology, Inc.; OCLC Online Computer Library Center, Inc.; ProQuest K-12 Learning Solutions; ProQuest LLC (Ann Arbor); SwetsWise Online Content; H.W. Wilson. *Indexed:* ABCPolSci, ABS&EES, AbAn, AgeL, AmH&L, ArtHuCI, BAS, BRD, BRI, CBRI, CJA, EI, FutSurv, HistAb, IBR, IBSS, IBZ, IPSA, IndIslam, JEL, LRI, PAIS, PRA, PSA, RRTA, SSA, SSCI, SUSA, SWR&A, SociolAb, WAE&RSA. *Bk. rev.:* 25-30, 250-500 words. *Aud.:* Ac, Sa.

Published since 1886, *Political Science Quarterly* is a nonpartisan scholarly journal that covers government, politics, and policy. Its intended audience is political scientists and general readers interested in politics. Written by leading scholars, its pieces often include a historical perpsective in the discussion. Each issue includes five or six articles. According to the web site, articles in the journal "have consistently framed political discourse, pinpointed emerging trends, and challenged established assumptions." Recent topics include the Supreme Court nomination process, American nation building in Iraq, and U.S. policy towards Russia. Traditionally, each presidential election is followed by an early analysis of the election in this journal's spring issue. The book review section is extensive, often including as many as 35 reviews, supplemented by a list of reference books and other publications of interest. These reviews create an indispensable resource for political science selectors. Highly recommended.

5164. *Review of International Studies.* [ISSN: 0260-2105] 1974. q. plus one supplement. GBP 220. Ed(s): Nick Rengger. Cambridge University Press, The Edinburgh Bldg, Shaftesbury Rd, Cambridge, CB2 2RU, United Kingdom; journals@cambridge.org; http://www.journals.cambridge.org. Illus., index, adv. Refereed. Vol. ends: No. 4. Online: Pub.; EBSCO Publishing, EBSCO Host; OCLC Online Computer Library Center, Inc.; OhioLINK; SwetsWise Online Content. Reprint: PSC. *Indexed:* ABCPolSci, AmH&L, AmHI, BrHumI, HistAb, IBSS, IPSA, JEL, PAIS, PRA, PSA, RiskAb, SSCI, SociolAb. *Aud.:* Ac, Sa.

Review of International Studies is a journal of the British International Studies Association. Its articles present research on a broad range of topics in international affairs. Each issue contains around eight to ten articles, including responses to work recently appearing in the journal. A supplementary thematic volume is published annually. In 2005, the theme of this issue was "Force and Legitimacy in World Politics." Recommended for academic libraries.

5165. *S A I S Review: a journal of international affairs.* [ISSN: 0036-0775] 1956. 2x/yr. USD 90. Ed(s): Kristin Carlucci, Frederick Tsai. The Johns Hopkins University Press, 2715 N Charles St, Baltimore, MD 21218-4363; http://muse.jhu.edu. Illus., index, adv. Refereed. Circ: 466. Vol. ends: No. 2. Online: EBSCO Publishing, EBSCO Host; OCLC Online Computer Library Center, Inc.; OhioLINK; Project MUSE; ProQuest LLC (Ann Arbor); SwetsWise Online Content; H.W. Wilson. Reprint: PSC. *Indexed:* ABCPolSci, ABS&EES, AmH&L, BAS, ForAb, HistAb, IBR, IBSS, IBZ, IPSA, IndIslam, PAIS, PSA, SSCI, SociolAb. *Bk. rev.:* 8, 1,500 words. *Aud.:* Ga, Ac, Sa.

Published under the auspices of The Johns Hopkins Foreign Policy Institute of the Paul H. Nitze School of Advanced International Studies (SAIS), the *SAIS Review* is a journal of international affairs run by the program's graduate students. The journal seeks "to bring a fresh and policy-relevant perspective to global political, economic, and security questions." Contributors to the journal include Institute scholars as well as an array of analysts and policymakers. Issues include both theoretical and practical articles, book and film reviews, and photo essays. A recent issue on territorial borders includes such articles as "International Borders: What They Are, What They Mean, and Why We Should Care," "More Borders, Less Conflict? Partition as a Solution to Ethnic Civil Wars," and "Brides, Bruises and the Border: The Trafficking of North Korean Women into China." Recommended for academic and large public libraries.

5166. *Washington Quarterly.* Formerly: *Washington Review of Strategic and International Studies.* [ISSN: 0163-660X] 1978. q. USD 241 print & online eds. (Individuals, USD 48 print & online eds.). Ed(s): Alexander T J Lennon. M I T Press, 238 Main St., Ste. 500, Cambridge, MA 02142; journals-info@mit.edu; http://mitpress.mit.edu. Illus., index, adv. Refereed. Circ: 3500. Vol. ends: No. 4. Microform: PQC. Online: EBSCO Publishing, EBSCO Host; Florida Center for Library Automation; Gale; IngentaConnect; LexisNexis; OCLC Online Computer Library Center, Inc.; OhioLINK; Project MUSE; SwetsWise Online Content; H.W. Wilson. Reprint: PSC. *Indexed:* ABCPolSci, ABS&EES, AgeL, AmH&L, ArtHuCI, BAS, CJA, FutSurv, HistAb, IBSS, IPSA, MASUSE, PAIS, PSA, SSCI. *Aud.:* Ga, Sa.

The *Washington Quarterly* is a journal of the Center for Strategic and International Studies (CSIS). CSIS is a bipartisan, nonprofit research organization that aims to work with government policymakers to advance global security. Contributors include scholars, analysts, and policymakers from the United States and abroad. The audience consists of experts as well as international affairs generalists. Articles cover a wide range of topics in international affairs, including enlargement of the European Union, Hamas, the future of democracy promotion, and the U.S. role in Central Asia. Each issue contains a general section called "Provocations," which has articles on a variety of topics, and generally two sections of articles on a particular theme such as "Multilateral Angles on North Korea" and "Saudi Arabia: Four Years after 9/11." Appropriate for public and academic libraries.

5167. *World Affairs (Washington).* [ISSN: 0043-8200] 1834. q. USD 132 (Individuals, USD 63 print & online eds.; USD 32 newsstand/cover). Ed(s): Thomas O'Brien. Heldref Publications, 1319 18th St, NW, Washington, DC 20036-1802; subscribe@heldref.org;

http://www.heldref.org. Illus., index, adv. Refereed. Circ: 498 Paid. Vol. ends: Summer. Microform: PQC. Online: EBSCO Publishing, EBSCO Host; Florida Center for Library Automation; Gale; OCLC Online Computer Library Center, Inc.; ProQuest LLC (Ann Arbor); H.W. Wilson. Reprint: PSC. *Indexed:* ABCPolSci, ABS&EES, AmH&L, ArtHuCI, BAS, BRI, HistAb, IBR, IBZ, IPSA, IndIslam, MASUSE, PAIS, PSA, SSCI. *Aud.:* Ga, Ac.

Published quarterly by the American Peace Society since 1834. According to the Society, this is the oldest U.S. international affairs journal. Each issue contains between three and five articles written mainly by professors working in the United States, but also by scholars, military officers, and government officials from around the world. Recent topics appearing in the journal include Hezbollah, nuclear nonproliferation, and political corruption in developing countries. Appropriate for libraries that seek to broaden the viewpoints represented in their collections.

5168. *World Policy Journal.* [ISSN: 0740-2775] 1983. q. USD 65 print & online eds. (Individuals, USD 32 print & online eds.). Ed(s): Karl Meyer. M I T Press, 238 Main St., Ste. 500, Cambridge, MA 02142; journals-info@mit.edu; http://mitpress.mit.edu. Illus., index, adv. Refereed. Circ: 5000. Vol. ends: No. 4. Microform: PQC. Online: EBSCO Publishing, EBSCO Host; Florida Center for Library Automation; Gale; Northern Light Technology, Inc.; OCLC Online Computer Library Center, Inc.; ProQuest K-12 Learning Solutions; ProQuest LLC (Ann Arbor); H.W. Wilson. *Indexed:* ABCPolSci, ABS&EES, AltPI, AmH&L, ArtHuCI, BAS, FutSurv, HistAb, IBR, IBZ, IPSA, LeftInd, PAIS, PRA, PSA, SSA, SSCI, SociolAb. *Bk. rev.:* 1-2, 1,500 words. *Aud.:* Ga, Ac, Sa.

A publication of the World Policy Institute at The New School, the journal serves as a forum on international relations. The Institute "strives to be a significant force in the ongoing debates over U.S. foreign policy and America's role in the world." The editorial board draws its members from the Institute, universities, publishers, and former government officials. The journal publishes articles in all areas that deal with international political science, sociology, and foreign and U.S. history. Recent articles include "Thinking Like a Jihadist: Iraq's Jordanian Connection," "Two Myths of Globalization," and "The Failure of Japan's Political Reform." Book reviews appear in some issues. Recommended for public and academic libraries.

5169. *World Politics (Baltimore): a quarterly journal of international relations.* [ISSN: 0043-8871] 1948. q. USD 140. Ed(s): Ilene P Cohen. The Johns Hopkins University Press, 2715 N Charles St, Baltimore, MD 21218-4363; http://muse.jhu.edu. Illus., index, adv. Refereed. Circ: 2049. Vol. ends: No. 4. Microform: PQC. Online: EBSCO Publishing, EBSCO Host; Gale; JSTOR (Web-based Journal Archive); OCLC Online Computer Library Center, Inc.; OhioLINK; Project MUSE; ProQuest LLC (Ann Arbor); SwetsWise Online Content. Reprint: PSC. *Indexed:* ABCPolSci, ABS&EES, AmH&L, BRD, BRI, CBRI, EI, FutSurv, HistAb, IBR, IBSS, IBZ, IPSA, IndIslam, PAIS, PRA, PSA, RI-1, RRTA, RiskAb, SSA, SSCI, SociolAb, WAE&RSA. *Bk. rev.:* 5-8, 2,000 words. *Aud.:* Ac, Sa.

This journal has been published since 1948 and is produced under the editorial sponsorship of the Princeton Institute for International and Regional Studies at Princeton University. This refereed journal features analytical and theoretical articles, review articles, and research notes on issues in international relations and comparative politics. Recent articles include "An Exclusive Country Club: The Effects of the GATT on Trade, 1950-94," "Explaining Patterns of Corruption in the Russian Regions," and "The Fiscal Contract: States, Taxes, and Public Services." Recommended for academic libraries.

■ POPULATION STUDIES

Meghan Dolan, Head of Numeric Data Services, Social Sciences Program, Harvard College Library, Harvard University, Cambridge, MA 02138

Introduction

This edition's section on Population Studies literature combines core titles in population studies with titles that publish papers related to issues important within the discipline. These peripheral publications focus on the historical, legal, and environmental impact that population changes have on local communities or the international community.

Population studies continue to be a multidisciplinary field that focuses on theories and trends within the sciences, social sciences, and humanities. As a discipline, population studies delve into how and where people live, as well as the transitions they make as individuals or societies. Topics range from migration to fertility to diasporas to ethnic conflicts. This year's list includes an online journal called *Demographic Research,* first published in 1999, that is free and available to all. Another featured title is *Population Bulletin,* published since 1945 and also freely available online.

Basic Periodicals

Ga: *American Demographics, Population Bulletin;* Ac: *Demography, European Journal of Population, Population and Development Review, Population Research and Policy Review.*

Basic Abstracts and Indexes

ABI-INFORM, AgeLine, MEDLINE, PAIS.

5170. *Continuity and Change: a journal of social structure, law and demography in past societies.* [ISSN: 0268-4160] 1986. 3x/yr. GBP 148. Ed(s): Lloyd Bonfield, Richard Wall. Cambridge University Press, The Edinburgh Bldg, Shaftesbury Rd, Cambridge, CB2 2RU, United Kingdom; journals@cambridge.org; http://www.journals.cambridge.org. Illus., adv. Sample. Refereed. Microform: PQC. Online: Pub.; EBSCO Publishing, EBSCO Host; OCLC Online Computer Library Center, Inc.; OhioLINK; SwetsWise Online Content. Reprint: PSC. *Indexed:* AgeL, AmH&L, AmHI, BAS, BrHumI, CJA, HistAb, IBR, IBSS, IBZ, PSA, SSA, SSCI, SociolAb. *Bk. rev.:* 5-6, 1-2 pages. *Aud.:* Ac.

Continuity and Change is a peer-reviewed journal that focuses on historically important sociological, demographic, and population trends and theories. Some recent (and intriguing) papers focus on marriage and inheritance, rural wage labor, schooling, and child farm labor. Occasionally a special issue, with a common theme, will be published within a volume. The most recent special issue focuses on "income-earning strategies of urban households in twentieth-century Russia and the Soviet Union." The online edition, published by Cambridge Journals, provides abstracts in French, German, and English. Full text is available in English. Each issue contains five or six book reviews, primarily written by academics within the disciplines of history, humanities, and the social sciences.

5171. *Demographic Research.* [ISSN: 1435-9871] 1999. s-a. Free. Ed(s): Nico Keilman. Max-Planck-Institut fuer Demografische Forschung, Konrad-Zuse-Str 1, Rostock, 18057, Germany; http://www.demogr.mpg.de. Refereed. *Indexed:* IBSS, SSCI, SociolAb. *Aud.:* Ac.

Demographic Research is a multidisciplinary population studies journal (with emphasis on the life and social sciences, statistics, and mathematics). This free, open-access journal publishes articles on an ongoing basis. Users may subscribe to an e-mail alert system that notifies them when a new piece has been posted to the journal. The journal is freely available online at www.demographic-research.org. It is also a refereed journal with an expedited system of evaluation and publication, which it touts as posting an article within a month of submission of the final piece. Each issue typically includes between one and five reflections ("reflexions") and up to 15 articles. Recent topics include education and childlessness among Swedish women, and fertility in American stepfamilies, as well as several articles on life expectancy, mortality, and longevity.

5172. Demography. [ISSN: 0070-3370] 1964. q. USD 100. Population Association of America, 8630 Fenton St, Ste 722, Silver Spring, MD 20910-3812; info@popassoc.org; http://www.jstor.org/journals/0070330.html. Illus., adv. Refereed. Circ: 4000. Vol. ends: No. 4. Online: EBSCO Publishing, EBSCO Host; JSTOR (Web-based Journal Archive); Northern Light Technology, Inc.; OCLC Online Computer Library Center, Inc.; OhioLINK; Project MUSE; ProQuest K-12 Learning Solutions; ProQuest LLC (Ann Arbor); SwetsWise Online Content; H.W. Wilson. *Indexed:* ABIn, ABS&EES, ASSIA, AbAn, AgeL, BAS, CJA, EnvInd, IBR, IBSS, IBZ, IMFL, JEL, PAIS, PollutAb, SSA, SSCI, SociolAb. *Aud.:* Ac.

Demography is a peer-reviewed, multidisciplinary journal that is international in scope. Disciplines include the social sciences, public health, statistics, geography, history, and business. The language is clear and the topics are quite interesting. Manuscripts are mainly textual in format; some articles include tables, models, graphs, and maps. Recent articles introduce demographic issues in relation to the gender gap, family dynamics, religion, and natality and mortality. Authors of published manuscripts are required to make their data sets available to others at a reasonable cost for three years after publication.

5173. Diaspora: a journal of transnational studies. [ISSN: 1044-2057] 1991. 3x/yr. CND 65 (Individuals, CND 31; CND 15 per issue). Ed(s): Khachig Tololyan. University of Toronto Press, Journals Division, 5201 Dufferin St, Toronto, ON M3H 5T8, Canada; journals@utpress.utoronto.ca; http://www.utpjournals.com. Illus., adv. Refereed. Circ: 500. Vol. ends: Winter. Online: EBSCO Publishing, EBSCO Host. Reprint: PSC. *Indexed:* ABS&EES, AltPI, BAS, CBCARef, IBSS, PAIS, PSA, RILM, SSA, SociolAb. *Aud.:* Ac, Sa.

Diaspora is an international, multidisciplinary, refereed journal that publishes articles related to "past, existing or emerging" communities. Authors of recent articles are researchers in the fields of literature, anthropology, history, psychology, political science, and sociology. The concepts and language of the articles are truly academic, touching on topics such as German-language diasporas, Russian diasporas, and African diasporas, as well as cultural identity, migration, and cultural origins. Occasionally a special issue is published that focuses on one topic. The most recent special issue focuses on "Portugueseness, Migrancy and Diasporicity." The journal is published three times a year by the University of Toronto Press. A table-of-contents notification service is available free of charge to all interested researchers. For more information about this service, visit the University of Toronto Press web site (address above).

5174. European Journal of Population. Formerly (until 1983): *European Demographic Information Bulletin.* [ISSN: 0168-6577] 1970. q. EUR 491 print & online eds. Ed(s): Frans van Poppel, France Mesle. Springer Netherlands, Van Godewijckstraat 30, Dordrecht, 3311 GX, Netherlands; http://www.springeronline.com. Illus., adv. Refereed. Circ: 400. Vol. ends: No. 4. Online: EBSCO Publishing, EBSCO Host; Gale; IngentaConnect; OCLC Online Computer Library Center, Inc.; OhioLINK; ProQuest LLC (Ann Arbor); Springer LINK; SwetsWise Online Content. Reprint: PSC. *Indexed:* ABIn, ASSIA, AgeL, ArtHuCI, IBR, IBSS, IBZ, PAIS, SFSA, SSA, SSCI, SWA, SociolAb. *Bk. rev.:* 3, 1,000-1,200 words. *Aud.:* Ac.

European Journal of Population publishes articles that cover population trends in European, non-European, and developing countries. It is multidisciplinary in scope, with authors from the fields of sociology, anthropology, geography, political science, and history. Recent topics include divorce, childbearing, fertility, and education. Periodically, the journal will publish a special issue with articles focusing on a central theme. The most recent special issue focuses on "Conflict and Violence." The publication is aimed toward an academic audience, which is evident in the use of concepts and definition of concepts.

5175. Immigrants and Minorities. [ISSN: 0261-9288] 1982. 3x/yr. GBP 233 print & online eds. Ed(s): Colin Holmes, David Mayall. Routledge, 4 Park Sq, Milton Park, Abingdon, OX14 4RN, United Kingdom; info@routledge.co.uk; http://www.routledge.co.uk. Illus., adv. Sample.

Refereed. Microform: PQC. Online: EBSCO Publishing, EBSCO Host; Gale; IngentaConnect; OCLC Online Computer Library Center, Inc.; SwetsWise Online Content. Reprint: PSC. *Indexed:* ASSIA, AmH&L, AmHI, BAS, BrHumI, EI, HRA, HistAb, IBR, IBSS, IBZ, IPSA, IndIslam, PSA, RiskAb, SSA, SWA, SociolAb, V&AA. *Bk. rev.:* 10-20, 500-700 words. *Aud.:* Ac.

Immigrants and Minorities is an international, refereed, scholarly journal. There are typically four articles and 6–12 book reviews per issue. Authors are mainly academics from the fields of history, political science, sociology, and European Studies. Recent articles focus on Irish migration, migrant networks, and ethnic identity. Occasionally there will be a special issue published in which all articles are oriented to one topic. The final issue of each volume contains an index of all works published throughout the year.

5176. International Migration Review: a quarterly studying sociological, demographic, economic, historical, and legislative aspects of human migration movements and ethnic group relations. Formerly (until 1966): *International Migration Digest;* Which incorporated (in 1973): *International Newsletter on Migration;* Which was formerly (1971-1972): *International Migration Newsletter.* [ISSN: 0197-9183] 1964. q. USD 286 print & online eds. Ed(s): Joseph Chamie. Blackwell Publishing, Inc., Commerce Place, 350 Main St, Malden, MA 02148; customerservices@blackwellpublishing.com; http://www.blackwellpublishing.com. Illus., index, adv. Refereed. Circ: 2300 Paid and free. Vol. ends: Winter. Microform: PQC. Online: Blackwell Synergy; EBSCO Publishing, EBSCO Host; Florida Center for Library Automation; Gale; IngentaConnect; JSTOR (Web-based Journal Archive); OCLC Online Computer Library Center, Inc.; ProQuest LLC (Ann Arbor). Reprint: PSC. *Indexed:* ABS&EES, AICP, ASSIA, AbAn, AgeL, AmH&L, ArtHuCI, BAS, CABA, CJA, Chicano, EI, FR, HAPI, HistAb, IBR, IBSS, IBZ, IMFL, LRI, PAIS, PRA, PSA, RI-1, RRTA, SFSA, SSA, SSCI, SUSA, SWA, SWR&A, SociolAb, WAE&RSA. *Bk. rev.:* Number and length vary. *Aud.:* Ac.

International Migration Review is an interdisciplinary journal with strong emphasis on the fields of sociology, demography, economics, history, and political science. The journal was created to "encourage and facilitate the study of all aspects of sociodemographic, historical, economic, political, legislative and pastoral aspects of human mobility." Recent articles focus on the work mobility of immigrants, the employment status of immigrant women, the migrant network, and rural-urban migration patterns. A recent thematic issue investigates "Gender and Migration," which includes research from the Social Science Research Council's Working Group on Gender and Migration. This journal also includes book reviews in each issue. Each March, an annual index is included that provides citations of all papers that were published that year.

Journal of Family History. See Family section.

5177. Journal of Population Economics. [ISSN: 0933-1433] 1988. q. EUR 720 print & online eds. Ed(s): Klaus F Zimmermann. Springer, Tiergartenstr 17, Heidelberg, 69121, Germany. Illus., adv. Sample. Refereed. Online: EBSCO Publishing, EBSCO Host; OhioLINK; ProQuest LLC (Ann Arbor); Springer LINK; SwetsWise Online Content. Reprint: PSC. *Indexed:* ABIn, AgeL, IBSS, JEL, SSCI. *Aud.:* Ac.

Journal of Population Economics is international in scope, with articles focusing on the relationship between economics, population trends, and "demographic problems." Each issue presents three or four specific themes. The most recent themes include migration, ethnicity, family dynamics, and social security. There are two to four manuscripts published per topic, and each includes an abstract and a list of keywords. Charts, graphs, and models are often included.

5178. Local Population Studies. [ISSN: 0143-2974] 1968. s-a. GBP 15 (Individuals, GBP 9). Ed(s): Nigel Goose. University of Hertfordshire, L P S General Office, Watford Campus, Aldenham, Watford, WD2 8AT, United Kingdom; lps@herts.ac.uk. Adv. Refereed. Circ: 1500. Microform: PQC. *Indexed:* AmH&L, HistAb. *Bk. rev.:* 10-15. *Aud.:* Ac.

POPULATION STUDIES

Local Population Studies, published bi-annually, takes an historical look at population trends and theories in the United Kingdom. All issues include editorials, articles, research notes, and book reviews (ten or more per issue). Recent research covers ethnic success and assimilation, French conceptualizations of diaspora, and refugee children. Issues typically include research notes, research in progress, conference reports, and reviews of recent periodical literature.

5179. Migration: a European journal of international migration and ethnic relations. [ISSN: 0721-2887] 1987. 6x/yr. EUR 50; EUR 14 newsstand/cover. Ed(s): Jochen Blaschke. Edition Parabolis, Schliemannstr 23, Berlin, 10437, Germany; info@emz-berlin.de; http://www.emz-berlin.de. *Indexed:* IBR, IBZ, IPSA, PAIS, PSA, SSA, SociolAb. *Aud.:* Ac.

Migration is the official journal of the European Research Forum on Migration and Ethnic Relations (EuroFor). This journal focuses on international migration and ethnic conflict within European communities. The abstracts are published in both German and English, while the articles are published in English. Recent topics include ethnic conflict resolution, the role of women in the Israeli–Palestinian conflict, immigration patterns in Greece, and the Portuguese diaspora.

Migration World. See Ethnic Studies section.

5180. Population and Development Review. [ISSN: 0098-7921] 1975. q. USD 141 print & online eds. Ed(s): Ethel Churchill, Paul Demeny. Blackwell Publishing, Inc., Commerce Place, 350 Main St, Malden, MA 02148; customerservices@blackwellpublishing.com; http://www.blackwellpublishing.com. Illus. Refereed. Circ: 5200 Paid and free. Vol. ends: No. 4. Microform: PQC. Online: Blackwell Synergy; EBSCO Publishing, EBSCO Host; Florida Center for Library Automation; Gale; IngentaConnect; JSTOR (Web-based Journal Archive); OCLC Online Computer Library Center, Inc.; SwetsWise Online Content. Reprint: PSC. *Indexed:* ABCPolSci, ABS&EES, ASSIA, AgeL, AmH&L, AnthLit, ApEcolAb, BAS, CABA, CWI, EI, EIP, EnvAb, EnvInd, HistAb, IBR, IBSS, IBZ, IMFL, JEL, PAIS, PRA, PSA, RRTA, SFSA, SSA, SSCI, SUSA, SWA, SociolAb, WAE&RSA. *Bk. rev.:* 6, 700 words. *Aud.:* Ac.

Population and Development Review is an international multidisciplinary journal that "seeks to advance knowledge of the interrelationships between population and socioeconomic development." Authors are typically academicians and researchers from universities, nonprofit foundations, and nongovernmental organizations. The manuscripts are in English, with abstracts provided in English, Spanish, and French. The December issue provides an index to all articles published throughout the year. Each issue contains the following sections: "Articles," "Notes and Commentary," "Archives," "Book Reviews," and "Documents." Most issues also include a section titled "Data and Perspectives," which interprets recently published statistics. Topics in recent issues focus on life expectancy, demographic transitions, health transitions, and wealth flows.

5181. Population and Environment. Former titles (until vol.4, 1981): *Journal of Population; Population (New York).* [ISSN: 0199-0039] 1978. bi-m. EUR 855 print & online eds. Ed(s): Landis MacKellar. Springer New York LLC, 233 Spring St, New York, NY 10013-1578; journals@springer-ny.com; http://www.springer.com. Illus., adv. Refereed. Microform: PQC. Online: Chadwyck-Healey Inc.; EBSCO Publishing, EBSCO Host; Gale; IngentaConnect; OCLC Online Computer Library Center, Inc.; OhioLINK; ProQuest LLC (Ann Arbor); Springer LINK; SwetsWise Online Content. Reprint: PSC. *Indexed:* ABIn, AgeL, EnvAb, EnvInd, ExcerpMed, GSI, HEA, IBR, IBSS, IBZ, PAIS, PRA, PSA, PollutAb, PsycInfo, SSA, SSCI, SUSA, SWR&A, SociolAb. *Bk. rev.:* 1, 900 words. *Aud.:* Ac.

Population and Environment focuses on issues that impact the relationship between demography and the environment. This journal is geared toward an academic audience, but the language used and arguments presented will be accessible to anyone with an interest in international population trends and their effect on the environment. Recent issues include articles relating to Chinese urban household consumption, sustainability of public health, urban expansion,

and the relationship between development, demography, and climate change. Each issue includes a two- to four-page book review. Authors of recently published works are from the fields of geography, biology, and public affairs.

5182. Population Bulletin. [ISSN: 0032-468X] 1945. q. USD 7 newsstand/cover per issue. Ed(s): Mary Kent. Population Reference Bureau, Inc., 1875 Connecticut Ave, NW, Ste 520, Washington, DC 20009-5728; http://www.prb.org. Illus. Circ: 5000 Paid. Online: OCLC Online Computer Library Center, Inc.; ProQuest K-12 Learning Solutions; ProQuest LLC (Ann Arbor); H.W. Wilson. *Indexed:* ABS&EES, ASSIA, AgeL, BAS, EI, EIP, EnvAb, FutSurv, JEL, MASUSE, PAIS, RI-1, SCI, SSCI. *Aud.:* Ga.

Population Bulletin is published by the Population Reference Bureau. Its intended audience includes "policymakers, educators, the media and concerned citizens working in the public interest." The bulletin's scope is international, with each issue focusing on a specific topic. Recent topics include the global challenge of HIV/AIDS; the global demographic divide; and the American Community Survey. The back cover of each volume presents a concise overview of the topics that are published within the issue. Articles are enhanced with interesting tables, photographs, maps, and diagrams. The bulletin is freely available online at www.prb.org.

5183. Population Research and Policy Review. [ISSN: 0167-5923] 1980. bi-m. EUR 712 print & online eds. Ed(s): David A Swanson. Springer Netherlands, Van Godewijckstraat 30, Dordrecht, 3311 GX, Netherlands; http://www.springeronline.com. Illus., adv. Refereed. Microform: PQC. Online: Chadwyck-Healey Inc.; EBSCO Publishing, EBSCO Host; Gale; IngentaConnect; OCLC Online Computer Library Center, Inc.; OhioLINK; ProQuest LLC (Ann Arbor); Springer LINK; SwetsWise Online Content. Reprint: PSC. *Indexed:* ABIn, AgeL, ArtHuCI, CJA, EnvInd, IBSS, IMFL, IPSA, IndIslam, JEL, PAIS, PRA, PSA, SSA, SSCI, SUSA, SWA, SWR&A, SociolAb. *Bk. rev.:* 3, 400-500 words. *Aud.:* Ac.

Population Research and Policy Review is the official publication of the Southern Demographic Association. The journal focuses on international issues, with recent articles focusing on current and historical trends in naturalization, reproduction, fertility, migration, and mortality. The publication states that issues will "include demographic, economic, social, political and health research papers." Each published article is preceded by an abstract and a list of keywords. There are typically between three and five articles in each issue.

5184. Population Studies: a journal of demography. [ISSN: 0032-4728] 1947. 3x/yr. GBP 152 print & online eds. Ed(s): John Simons. Routledge, 4 Park Sq, Milton Park, Abingdon, OX14 4RN, United Kingdom; info@routledge.co.uk; http://www.routledge.co.uk. Illus., adv. Refereed. Circ: 1500 Paid. Online: EBSCO Publishing, EBSCO Host; Gale; IngentaConnect; JSTOR (Web-based Journal Archive); OCLC Online Computer Library Center, Inc.; SwetsWise Online Content. Reprint: PSC. *Indexed:* ABIn, AICP, ASSIA, AgeL, AmH&L, ArtHuCI, BAS, CABA, DSA, EI, EnvAb, EnvInd, ErgAb, ExcerpMed, HistAb, IBR, IBSS, IBZ, IndIslam, JEL, PAIS, PSA, RRTA, SSA, SSCI, SociolAb, WAE&RSA. *Bk. rev.:* 6-8, 500 words. *Aud.:* Ac.

Population Studies is an international, multidisciplinary scholarly journal that publishes manuscripts of interest to "demographers, sociologists, economists, anthropologists, social statisticians, geographers, historians, epidemiologists, health scientists, and policy analysts." Recent articles cover topics such as trends in old-age functioning and disability in Japan, modelling the spread of HIV/AIDS in China, and the reliability of reasons for the early termination of breastfeeding. Data tables, graphs, and charts are often included within the text. There are several book reviews in each issue.

5185. Population Trends. [ISSN: 0307-4463] 1975. q. USD 215. Ed(s): Peter Goldblatt. Palgrave Macmillan Ltd., Houndmills, Basingstoke, RG21 6XS, United Kingdom; journal-info@palgrave.com; http://www.palgrave-journals.com/. Illus. Circ: 1700. *Indexed:* PAIS. *Aud.:* Ac.

Population Trends is published by the Office for National Statistics and is the principal source of articles on population and demographic trends in the United Kingdom. There are between three and five articles per issue. Recent topics include living arrangements in contemporary Britain, population estimates for the intercensal backseries, and a presentation of the methodology used to estimate population data by ethnic group. Most articles include charts, graphs, or maps. Each issue also includes data tables that range in topic from vital statistics and components of population change to international migration and marriage and divorce statistics. The journal is available online for viewing and downloading in pdf format. The data tables are sometimes a bit tricky to print.

■ PREGNANCY

Margaret Phillips, Electronic Resources Librarian and Bibliographer for Gender and Women's Studies, University of California, Berkeley, CA 94720-6000

Introduction

Angelina Jolie, Katie Holmes, and Britney Spears did it. So did more than four million other American women. They got pregnant and/or delivered babies during the last few years. Besides suffering through swollen ankles and anxieties about everything from picking an obstetrician to picking a nursing bra, moms-to-be are in need of much information.

There are a number of publications to help them negotiate the bewildering world of maternity and new parenthood. While some magazines seem to be vehicles designed to tap into this vast consumer market with ads pushing items such as, say, cord blood banks and maternity bridal gowns, they all include informative articles that support, at some level, healthy pregnancies, satisfying deliveries, and breastfeeding. In almost all of them, expectant moms are likely to find articles on prenatal nutrition and exercise, suggested comfort measures for labor, tips on breastfeeding, and the required article on what to buy for the baby's layette. In addition to mainstream, consumer-oriented magazines such as *Pregnancy*, *FitPregnancy*, and *BabyCenter*, there are magazines such as *Mothering* and *The Compleat Mother* that unabashedly advocate natural childbirth and extended breastfeeding.

With the latest available statistics showing that more than 120,000 children are adopted annually and that the number of women seeking infertility treatments are in the millions, it is no surprise that there are now publications that deal specifically with these issues. *Fertility Today* and *Achieving Families* both take a serious and sensitive look at fertility and are designed for general audiences.

With the exception of *ACOG Clinical Review,* and the *Journal of Midwifery and Women's Health*, the publications in this section are general consumer publications that cover pregnancy, childbirth, fertility, and the postpartum period. Most are appropriate for a public library collection. Many parenting magazines include regular features on pregnancy and breastfeeding. Some, like *Parents* and *Parenting*, produce annual or semi-annual pregnancy supplements. Like many trade magazines, most of the publications listed have accompanying web sites with a variety of recycled or bonus material.

Basic Periodicals

Achieving Families, ACOG Clinical Review, BabyCenter, The Compleat Mother, Fertility Today, FitPregnancy, Journal of Midwifery and Women's Health, Midwifery Today, Mothering, Plum, Pregnancy.

Basic Abstracts and Indexes

CINAHL, Family Index, MEDLINE.

5186. *A C O G Clinical Review.* Supersedes (in 1996): *A C O G Current Journal Review.* [ISSN: 1085-6862] 1987. bi-m. USD 235 (Individuals, USD 119). American College of Obstetricians and Gynecologists, 409 12th St, SW, Washington, DC 20024; publication@acog.org; http://www.acog.org. Microform: PQC. Online: EBSCO Publishing, EBSCO Host; Gale; IngentaConnect; OhioLINK; ScienceDirect; SwetsWise Online Content. *Indexed:* CINAHL. *Aud.:* Ac.

This slim newsletter comes from the American College of Obstetrics and Gynecologists (ACOG). A nonprofit organization for women's health-care professionals, ACOG advocates quality health care for women, provides continuing education for its members, and promotes patient education. Surveying about 20 of the major medical journals, each issue consists of 30 to 40 brief synopses on the latest developments in obstetrics, gynecology, and general (women's) health. Although designed primarily as a way for practicing clinicians to be aware of research in their field, this publication is also useful for a general lay audience. This journal is recommended for medical libraries and public libraries looking to provide their patrons with scholarly, up-to-date information on pregnancy and women's health issues.

5187. *Achieving Families.* Formerly (until 2006): *Infertility Times.* 2003. 8x/yr. USD 20. Ed(s): Amy Domke. Milo Media LLC, 77 Vista Ln, Barrington, IL 60010. *Aud.:* Ga.

The advisory board for *Achieving Families* includes physicians, psychologists, a practitioner of traditional Chinese medicine, yoga instructors, a representative from the pharmaceutical industry, and an adoption expert. Indeed, this group of advisors represents just some of the challenges faced by those dealing with infertility. In addition to regular features that highlight recent fertility-related news and research results, feature articles have looked at the high cost of assisted reproductive technology, how to cope with the stress of infertility, or how to talk about adoption with friends and family. Articles are concise and well written. Recommended for public libraries.

5188. *Baby Center.* [ISSN: 1557-5403] 2005. 8x/yr. Free. Ed(s): Jim Scott. BabyCenter LLC., 163 Freelon St., San Francisco, CA 94107. Adv. Circ: 500000 Free. *Aud.:* Ga.

Self-described as the "first magazine that's 100 percent tailored to your stage of pregnancy and new motherhood," this publication is designed for pregnant moms and issued in four "installments": second trimester; third trimester; newborn; and four to six months. As with the other consumer-oriented pregnancy magazines, you'll find fashion hints for moms-to-be, advice on what to buy (from car seats to baby clothes), and tips for busy moms (quick, yet healthy recipes). There is also useful health information (such as warning signs of postpartum depression). The experts in the case of *BabyCenter* magazine are other moms; like its web site (babycenter.com), the magazine is very much a forum where moms share their insights and other "mom-tested" ideas with one another. Even the photo spreads appear to feature "real" women rather than professional models. Recommended for public libraries.

5189. *The Compleat Mother: the magazine of pregnancy, birth and breastfeeding.* [ISSN: 0829-8564] 1985. q. USD 12. Ed(s): Jody McLaughlin. Compleat Mother, 720 Fourth Ave, NW, P O Box 209, Minot, ND 58702; jody@minot.com. Illus., index, adv. Sample. Circ: 20000. Vol. ends: Winter. *Bk. rev.:* Number and length vary. *Aud.:* Ga.

You won't find glossy photo spreads of celebrity moms in this black-and-white, newsprint magazine. What *The Compleat Mother* lacks in glitz, it makes up for in passion and its earnest celebration of "natural, enjoyable birth and extended breastfeeding." Most of the articles are reader submissions (the magazine does not have paid staff writers) that describe successful and satisfying natural childbirth experiences. Also included are editorials (circumcision: no; military recruitment in schools: no; stay-at-home parenting: yes), poems, book reviews, and summaries of relevant news stories from around the world on natural childbirth and the benefits of breastfeeding. The web site (www.compleatmother.com) is both a reader forum and an archive of selected articles from the print magazine, though it does not appear to be regularly maintained. A good counterbalance to the mainstream pregnancy magazines. Recommended for public libraries.

5190. *Fertility Today.* [ISSN: 1559-8888] 2005. bi-m. USD 29.95 domestic; USD 39.95 Canada; USD 59.95 elsewhere. Fertility Today, PO Box 117, Laurel, MD 20725-0117. Adv. *Aud.:* Ga.

Debuting in July 2005, *Fertility Today* is a general-audience magazine dedicated to issues of fertility. Its mission is to provide recommendations and interpretation of up-to-date medical literature, as well as address the spiritual, emotional, and physical aspects of infertility. Almost every name listed in the impressively long list of contributing writers, editorial board members, and members of the advisory board is followed by M.D., Ph.D., R.N., M.P.H., or some combination thereof. Some 20 sections look at everything from assisted reproductive technology, egg donation, surrogacy, and adoption to alternative medicine and the legal and ethical issues unique to infertility. The first two issues have featured cover stories of Cindy Margolis and Brooke Shields, two celebrities who have struggled with infertility. A unique publication that provides informative and sensitive coverage of an issue not widely examined in mainstream magazines. Recommend for public libraries.

5191. *Fit Pregnancy.* [ISSN: 1079-3615] 1995. bi-m. USD 7.97 domestic; USD 15.97 foreign; USD 3.95 newsstand/cover per issue. Ed(s): Peg Moline. A M I - Weider Publications, 1 Park Ave, 3d Fl, New York, NY 10016; http://www.amilink.com. Illus., adv. Online: EBSCO Publishing, EBSCO Host. *Indexed:* SD. *Aud.:* Ga.

From the publisher of *Shape, FitPregnancy,* as its title suggests, is a health and fitness magazine for moms-to-be. You'll find articles on exercise (pre- and post-natal), nutrition, and infant health. You'll also find features on maternity fashion, reviews of baby products, and decorating ideas for the nursery. With its profiles of celebrity moms, photo spreads of pregnant models, and happy-ending features, one might fault the magazine for presenting a picture of maternity that is a tad idealized. But for many a mom-to-be, there is great comfort (and escapism) in reading about star moms' postpartum exercise regimes. Its advisory board includes a number of noted and credentialed experts in the field of obstetrics, pediatrics, nutrition, and lactation. Recommended for public libraries.

5192. *Journal of Midwifery & Women's Health.* Former titles (1973-1999): *Journal of Nurse - Midwifery; American College of Nurse - Midwives. Bulletin;* (until 1969): *American College of Nurse - Midwifery. Bulletin.* [ISSN: 1526-9523] 1955. 6x/yr. USD 377. Ed(s): T. King. Elsevier Inc., 360 Park Ave S, New York, NY 10010-1710; usinfo-f@elsevier.com; http://www.elsevier.com. Illus., index, adv. Sample. Refereed. Circ: 9000 Controlled. Vol. ends: Nov/Dec. Microform: PQC. Online: EBSCO Publishing, EBSCO Host; Gale; IngentaConnect; OhioLINK; ScienceDirect; SwetsWise Online Content. *Indexed:* AgeL, CINAHL, ExcerpMed, SCI, SSCI. *Aud.:* Ac.

This is a serious, academic journal that covers obstetrics, gynecology, and women's health issues for nurse-midwives. All articles are peer reviewed and contain extensive bibliographic notes. As such, articles are clinical and there is no coverage of the kinds of spiritual aspects of pregnancy and childbirth that one finds in a publication like, say, *Midwifery Today,* designed for lay midwives. Issues often focus on a specific aspect of women's health such as primary health care for women, environmental hazards in women's health, and genetics and clinical practice. In addition to in-depth book reviews, this publication offers reviews and critical analyses of significant journal articles. Recommended for academic and medical libraries.

5193. *Midwifery Today: the heart and science of birth.* Formerly (until 1997): *Midwifery Today and Childbirth Education with International Midwife;* Which was formed by the merger of (1987-1996): *Midwifery Today;* (1995-1996): *International Midwife.* [ISSN: 1551-8892] 1996. q. USD 50 domestic; USD 60 in Canada & Mexico; USD 75 elsewhere. Ed(s): Jan Tritten, Alice Evans. Midwifery Today with International Midwife, PO Box 2672, Eugene, OR 97402. Illus., index, adv. Sample. Circ: 2500. *Indexed:* CINAHL, CWI, FemPer, GendWatch. *Aud.:* Ga.

Midwifery Today is celebrating some 20 years of publication, and its mission is to "return midwifery care to its rightful position in the family, to make midwifery care the norm throughout the world and to redefine widwifery as a vital partnership with women." Although designed as a trade publication for practicing midwives and birth professionals, the well-researched yet concise articles (mostly written by clinical nurse midwives) can be understood by non-practitioners. Articles examine not just the clinical side of childbirth ("Prenatal diagnosis—technological triumph or Pandora's box?") but also emotional or spiritual aspects of birth (how to deal with family members—husbands, mothers, in-laws—who are present at the birth). This journal's international coverage is particularly strong. Recommended for public libraries and consumer health libraries.

Mothering. See Parenting section.

5194. *Plum: something especially prized.* 2004. s-a. USD 7.95 per issue. Groundbreak Publishing, Inc., 276 Fifth Ave, Ste 302, New York, NY 10001. Circ: 500000 Controlled. *Aud.:* Ga.

The inaugural issue of *Plum,* the self-described "revolutionary publication" and the "first ever magazine for women over 35," was greeted by a media buzz. *The New York Times* and *Newsweek,* among others, did not fail to notice that this demographic of moms—the ones who put childbearing on hold to pursue their careers—makes for an educated, affluent readership. This 200+-page glossy features photo spreads of designer maternity fashions and beauty advice (after all, older moms might wonder if it safe to color their gray during pregnancy). It also features more serious articles on pregnancy and newborn health. The magazine is a partnership with the American College of Obstetricians and Gynecologists and includes a medical advisory board. Recommended for libraries, although some of the content appears to be recycled from month to month.

5195. *Pregnancy.* [ISSN: 1540-8485] 2000. m. USD 9 domestic; USD 45 Canada; USD 57 elsewhere. Ed(s): Abigail Tuller, Clary Alward. Future U S, Inc., 4000 Shoreline Court, Ste. 400, South San Francisco, CA 94080; http://www.futureus-inc.com. Adv. Circ: 205000 Paid. *Aud.:* Ga.

Like most of the other mainstream magazines in this category, *Pregnancy* looks at pregnancy (by way of a trimester-by-trimester guide), childbirth and labor, breastfeeding, fitness, and newborn issues. It is heavy on style, offering tips on what to wear, makeover secrets, and how to keep your weight under control (but still have a healthy baby). Every issue contains a "Birth Story," in which a reader shares stories and photos of her unique birth experience. Recommended for public libraries.

■ PRINTING AND GRAPHIC ARTS

Donna B. Smith, Assistant Head of Technical Services, W. Frank Steely Library, Northern Kentucky University, Highland Heights, KY 41099

Wendy Wood, Head of Cataloging, W. Frank Steely Library, Northern Kentucky University, Highland Heights, KY 41099

Introduction

Communicating the message visually is the job of the graphic designer and the printer. Designers and printers are working with more innovation and persuasion to inform, entertain, and impress visually inundated and discriminating audiences. Clients look to these groups for marketing, technical, and high-impact graphic support. Competition is becoming stiffer as customers increasingly demand better service, more innovative products, and faster cycle times. Successful professionals in the future will need to be active in the marketing of their skills as well as identify new markets for their products.

Recent years have witnessed major changes in the graphic arts and printing industries, including the rise of desktop publishing, the Internet, and digital technology. Designers and printers make use of new technology to create images that are more visually active than ever before. The computer empowers them to create images that once would have been prohibitive in both time and expense. Printers are beginning to focus more on communications and technology. They are using new digital technologies to add value to their services and moving into products and services not traditionally associated with printing. It is transforming into an imaging business that feeds a variety of media, only one of which is print. But reports of print's demise are greatly exaggerated. Although the Internet seems to be where the action is, it still has inherent typographic limitations and does not allow as much freedom to experiment with composition and typography as does print.

As in most industries today, graphic artists and printers must remain current with the latest technology and marketing innovations. Printers must turn to new markets to increase their business instead of relying on their existing customers' printing demands to increase. Therefore, the majority of publications recommended here are trade publications that provide necessary and timely information to practitioners, managers, suppliers, and anyone else interested in visual communications. They may cover the entire graphic communications industry or target specific segments, such as gravure printers, calligraphers, or screen printers. Most magazines provide practical how-to information, and many profile artists, design studios, and printing firms. Some provide a showcase of leading designs in the industry by sponsoring competitions and displaying the winners in special issues. The trade publications also address the business side of the industry: legal concerns, environmental regulations, economic trends, marketing and sales, and management issues. Scholarly publications focus on the history of printing and new research in the field. Such publications are closely tied to bibliography, the study of the book. Strictly electronic publications are not yet prevalent in this field. Although some publications are available online, these versions complement or coexist with the print issues.

Basic Periodicals

Ga: *Communication Arts, Print, Step Inside Design;* Ac: *American Printer, Communication Arts, Graphis Design Journal, Print, Printing History, Visible Language;* Sa: *Communication Arts, Graphis Design Journal, Print, Printing News, Professional Printer, The Seybold Report.*

Basic Abstracts and Indexes

Press.

5196. American Printer: the graphic arts managers magazine. Former titles (until 1982): *American Printer and Lithographer;* (until 1979): *Inland Printer - American Lithographer;* (until 1961): *Inland and American Printer and Lithographer.* [ISSN: 0744-6616] 1883. m. USD 86 Canada (Free to qualified personnel). Ed(s): Mayu Mishina, Katherine O'Brien. Prism Business Media, 330 N Wabash Ave, Ste 2300, Chicago, IL 60611; inquiries@prismb2b.com; http://www.prismbusinessmedia.com. Illus., adv. Sample. Circ: 85000 Controlled. Vol. ends: Mar/Sep. Microform: PQC. Online: EBSCO Publishing, EBSCO Host; Florida Center for Library Automation; Gale; Northern Light Technology, Inc.; OCLC Online Computer Library Center, Inc.; ProQuest K-12 Learning Solutions; ProQuest LLC (Ann Arbor); H.W. Wilson. *Indexed:* ABIn, BPI, C&ISA, CerAb, ChemAb, EngInd, IAA, MicrocompInd, PhotoAb. *Aud.:* Ac, Sa.

Essentially directed toward the print shop manager, this trade publication provides practical information on current industry issues. It focuses attention on the use of new equipment and technology, an important feature for today's printers. It offers seven or eight feature articles discussing such topics as management, marketing, production, purchasing, sales, and technology. Regular columns highlight industry news, new equipment and electronic tools, and classifieds. An annual report of the web offset market features interviews with executives and an overview of the current state of the industry. Selected articles are available at www.americanprinter.com

5197. Communication Arts. Formerly (until 1969): *C A Magazine.* [ISSN: 0010-3519] 1959. 8x/yr. USD 53 domestic; USD 70 Canada; USD 110 elsewhere. Ed(s): Jean A. Coyne, Anne Telford. Communication Arts, 110 Constitution Dr, Menlo Park, CA 94025. Illus., adv. Circ: 90000 Paid. Vol. ends: Dec. *Indexed:* ABM, ArtInd, DAAI. *Bk. rev.:* 2, 500-600 words, signed. *Aud.:* Ga, Ac, Sa.

Communication Arts is a high-quality trade publication for commercial artists. Special issues serve as juried showcases for leading work in advertising, design, illustration, interactive design, and photography. Regular issues offer seven or eight feature articles that may profile design studios and artists or highlight special advertising and design projects. Regular columns address design issues, legal affairs, web sites, business advice, and new books. Selected features and columns are available at www.commarts.com/CA. This title is an important addition to any graphic arts collection.

5198. Design Issues: history/theory/criticism. [ISSN: 0747-9360] 1984. 3x/yr. USD 206 print & online eds. (Individuals, USD 50 print & online eds.). Ed(s): Richard Buchanan, Victor Margolin. M I T Press, 238 Main St., Ste. 500, Cambridge, MA 02142; journals-info@mit.edu; http://mitpress.mit.edu. Illus., index, adv. Refereed. Circ: 1400. Microform: PQC. Online: EBSCO Publishing, EBSCO Host; Gale;

IngentaConnect; JSTOR (Web-based Journal Archive); OCLC Online Computer Library Center, Inc.; SwetsWise Online Content; H.W. Wilson. *Indexed:* ABM, AmHI, ArtHuCI, ArtInd, DAAI, IBR, IBZ. *Bk. rev.:* Number and length vary. *Aud.:* Ac, Sa.

The history, criticism, and theory of design are the focus of this scholarly journal. Each issue includes book reviews of the latest works on the topic and erudite articles on diverse aspects of past and present design issues. The international scope of the journal provides a place where discussions about the designs and treasures from all societies and civilizations can be pulled together and assimilated. Each issue includes an introduction by the editors. This title's academic emphasis makes it a necessary addition to any design program or library supporting one.

5199. Digital Demand: the journal of printing and publishing technology. Formed by the merger of (1997-2000): *Journal of Prepress & Printing Technology;* (1993-2000): *Publishing Technology Review;* (1989-2000): *Prepress Commentary;* Which was formerly (until 1995): *Desktop Publishing Commentary;* Which was formed by the merger of (1986-1989): *Desktop Publisher; Pira D T P Commentary.* [ISSN: 1471-5694] 2000. bi-m. GBP 499; EUR 799; USD 750. Ed(s): Annabel Taylor. Pira International, Randalls Rd, Leatherhead, KT22 7RU, United Kingdom; http://www.piranet.com. Sample. *Aud.:* Ac, Sa.

This journal covers the press technologies of inkjet, electrophotography, and direct imaging. Focusing on the digital print industry, its customer base includes production managers, printers that are planning to invest in new technology, and digital print suppliers. Each issue offers at least six 5,000-word, consultancy-style reports that feature market data, technology forecasts, cost models, and technical analysis. In addition to analysis of digital press technology, some articles provide insight into printers' business models and future trends in printing markets.

5200. Eye (London, 1990): the international review of graphic design. [ISSN: 0960-779X] 1990. q. USD 127 outside EU. Ed(s): John L. Walters. Haymarket Publishing Ltd., 174 Hammersmith Rd, London, W6 7JP, United Kingdom; hpg@haymarketgroup.com; http://www.haymarketgroup.co.uk. Illus., adv. Circ: 9000. *Indexed:* ABM, ArtInd. *Bk. rev.:* 15-20, 200-600 words. *Aud.:* Ac, Sa.

Noted for its articles combined with extraordinary visual material, this journal is an important addition to any graphic design collection. It focuses on typography, history, art direction, and graphic design for multimedia, advertising, publishing, and the web. Features include interviews with international designers, overviews of new trends in graphic design, and profiles of design studios. Regular columns provide critiques and book reviews.

5201. Flexo. Formerly (until 1984): *Flexographic Technical Journal.* [ISSN: 1051-7324] 1976. m. USD 55 in North America; USD 76 elsewhere. Ed(s): Jonna Jefferis. Foundation of Flexographic Technical Association, 900 Marconi Ave, Ronkonkoma, NY 11779-7212; rmoran@vax.fta-ffta.org; http://www.fta-ffta.org. Illus., adv. Sample. Circ: 19000. Vol. ends: Dec. *Indexed:* EngInd. *Aud.:* Ac, Sa.

Flexo is the official journal of the Flexographic Technical Association, which is devoted to advancing flexographic technology. This relief printing process is especially popular in the packaging and newspaper industries. Although *Flexo* is mainly a trade publication directed toward managers and technicians, its audience includes anyone who is interested in learning more about the technical aspects of flexography. Articles include such topics as designing packaging, comparing flexo presses, and examining printing techniques. The articles are written by practitioners, so they are informative and practical. Some issues include tutorials for beginners in flexographic technology. Articles provide useful, detailed illustrations that demonstrate flexographic printing. Regular columns highlight new products, events, and association news.

5202. G A T F World. Formed by the merger of (1971-1989): *E C B Newsletter;* (1947-1989): *Graphic Arts Abstracts;* (1970-1989): *G A T F Environmental Control Report;* (1970-1989): *G A T F (Year).* [ISSN: 1048-0293] 1989. bi-m. USD 75 domestic; USD 100 foreign. Ed(s): Dee

Gentile. Graphic Arts Technical Foundation, 200 Deer Run Rd, Sewickley, PA 15143-2600; piagatf@piagatf.org; http://www.gain.net. Illus., adv. Sample. Circ: 24000 Paid and controlled. Vol. ends: Nov/Dec. *Indexed:* EngInd. *Bk. rev.:* 6-10, 200 words. *Aud.:* Ac, Sa.

This is the magazine of the Graphic Arts Technical Foundation, a member-supported organization that promotes scientific, technical, and educational advancements in the printing and graphic communication industries. Each issue focuses on a single topic related to press and prepress issues. The articles are useful for the practitioner, as they generally address new technologies and products. One special issue published annually is "The GATF Technology Forecast." Past issues are available at the publisher's web site, www.gain.net.

5203. *Graphic Arts Monthly: applied technology for the printing industry.* Formerly: *Graphic Arts Monthly and the Printing Industry.* [ISSN: 1047-9325] 1929. m. plus annual Sourcebook. USD 142.99 domestic (Free to qualified personnel). Ed(s): Bill Esler. Reed Business Information, 360 Park Ave South, New York, NY 10010; http://www.reedbusiness.com. Illus., index, adv. Circ: 75000 Controlled. Vol. ends: Dec. Microform: CIS. Online: The Dialog Corporation; EBSCO Publishing, EBSCO Host; Factiva, Inc.; Florida Center for Library Automation; Gale; LexisNexis; Northern Light Technology, Inc.; OCLC Online Computer Library Center, Inc.; ProQuest LLC (Ann Arbor); H.W. Wilson. *Indexed:* ABIn, BPI, CWI, ChemAb, EngInd, MicrocompInd, PhotoAb. *Aud.:* Ga, Ac, Sa.

This trade publication is directed at managers and practitioners in the printing and graphic arts fields. It provides coverage of business news and new technological developments in the industry. It features methods that save time and money in production operations. Each issue contains five or six main articles, ranging from comparisons of prepress machines to colorful exhibits of design projects. Marketing, legal issues, industry news, and paper and ink handling are covered in regular columns. This title is a good general source of industry information and is recommended for any graphic arts collection. The electronic edition is available at www.graphicartsmonthly.com.

5204. *Graphis Design Journal.* Supersedes in part (in 2006): *Graphis;* Formerly (until 1987): *Graphis Annual.* [ISSN: 1012-9340] 1944. 3x/yr. USD 70 domestic; USD 100 foreign. Ed(s): Jamie Reynolds. Graphis Inc, 307 Fifth Ave, 10th Fl, New York, NY 10016; info@graphis.com; http://www.graphis.com. Illus., adv. Circ: 23000. Vol. ends: Nov/Dec. *Indexed:* ArtHuCI, ArtInd, FLI. *Bk. rev.:* 3, 200-300 words, signed. *Aud.:* Ac, Sa.

This high-quality, glossy publication displays the work of architects, designers, illustrators, and graphic artists. The contributors, drawn from the international graphic arts field, impart practical information about design, graphics, and illustration. Each issue represents designers from one of three geographic areas: the Americas, Europe and Africa, and Asia and Oceana. This title is an important addition to a graphic arts or a fine arts collection.

5205. *Gravure: the world's only magazine for the gravure printing industry.* Former titles (until 1986): *Gravure Bulletin; Gravure Technical Association Bulletin.* [ISSN: 0894-4946] 1950. bi-m. USD 67. Ed(s): Laura Wayland Smith Hatch. Gravure Association of America, Inc., 1200A Scottsville Rd, Rochester, NY 14624-5703; lwshatch@gaa.org; http://www.gaa.org. Illus., adv. Sample. Circ: 2375 Paid. *Indexed:* EngInd. *Aud.:* Ac, Sa.

This is the trade publication of the Gravure Association of America, which promotes the advancement of the gravure printing industry. This title's main focus is on the technological developments in this high-quality, expensive process. Feature articles examine such topics as new products and materials, environmental concerns, training programs, and automation development. The business side of the industry is covered as well, with timely information on industry news and personnel moves, an events calendar, marketing advice, and association news.

5206. *High Volume Printing.* [ISSN: 0737-1020] 1982. bi-m. USD 100. Ed(s): Ray Roth. Innes Publishing Company, PO Box 7280, Libertyville, IL 60048-7280; meinnes@innespub.com; http://www.innespub.com. Illus., adv. Sample. Circ: 38082 Controlled. Vol. ends: Dec. *Indexed:* ABIn, EngInd. *Aud.:* Ac, Sa.

This "large-plant management magazine" is directed mainly at print managers, and covers operations from prepress to postpress. Its audience consists of printers, trade binderies, and color trade houses with more than 20 employees. As a trade publication, this title provides the latest industry news and trends. Subjects include management issues, industry trends, economic forecasts, the book industry, regulatory issues, technology, and equipment. Also included are useful case studies depicting how a particular company handled a production problem. Regular departments focus on the usual trade news, personnel, and events.

5207. *How: design ideas at work.* [ISSN: 0886-0483] 1985. bi-m. USD 29.96 domestic; USD 44.96 Canada; USD 51.96 elsewhere. Ed(s): Bryn Mooth. F + W Publications, Inc., 4700 E Galbraith Rd, Cincinnati, OH 45236; wds@fwpubs.com; http://www.fwpublications.com. Illus., adv. Sample. Circ: 35006. Vol. ends: Dec. *Indexed:* ABM, DAAI, EngInd, IHTDI. *Aud.:* Ac, Sa.

This is an instructional trade magazine that addresses the ideas and techniques graphic design professionals use to create their work. Directed toward practitioners and design firm managers, it provides hands-on advice on making a design studio more profitable, more professional, and more high-profile in the industry. Special issues focus on international design, typography, and interactive design, and there is a business annual. Feature articles may include reports on new trends in materials and technology, buyer's guides to scanners, comparisons of soy-based inks, or advice on insurance needs. Regular columns profile design firms, report on new technology, review electronic tools, and provide general industry news.

5208. *In-Plant Printer: the in-plant management magazine.* Former titles: *In-Plant Printer Including Corporate Imaging;* (until 1993): *In-Plant Printer and Electronic Publisher;* (until 1986): *In-Plant Printer; In-Plant Offset Printer.* [ISSN: 1071-832X] 1961. bi-m. Free to qualified personnel. Ed(s): Jack Klasnic. Innes Publishing Company, PO Box 7280, Libertyville, IL 60048-7280; meinnes@innespub.com; http://www.innespub.com. Illus., index, adv. Circ: 30526. Microform: PQC. Online: OCLC Online Computer Library Center, Inc.; ProQuest LLC (Ann Arbor). *Indexed:* ABIn. *Aud.:* Sa.

In-plant printing operations include the printing departments in corporations, government agencies, and institutions. This journal targets the special needs of the graphic artists, desktop publishers, and electronic prepress specialists that work in these shops. Each issue offers five or six feature articles emphasizing the latest digital technologies and management issues. A copier buyer's guide is published annually. Selected articles are available at www.innespub.com/inplant.htm.

5209. *Ink Maker: for manufacturers of printing inks and related graphic arts specialty colors.* Formerly (until 2001): *American Inkmaker.* [ISSN: 1545-813X] 1922. m. 10/yr. USD 66 (Free to qualified personnel). Ed(s): Linda M Casatelli. Cygnus Business Media, Inc., 3 Huntington Quadrangle, Ste 301N, Melville, NY 11747-3601; http://www.cygnusb2b.com. Illus., index, adv. Circ: 5000 Paid. Vol. ends: Dec. *Indexed:* ABIn, ChemAb, EngInd. *Bk. rev.:* Number and length vary. *Aud.:* Sa.

This international trade publication targets manufacturers of printing inks and related graphic arts specialty colors. It highlights raw materials and equipment, reports on printing processes and markets, and provides a global perspective on industry issues. Articles cover topics ranging from workflow issues to the pigment industry. Monthly interviews with printers provide insight into current industry concerns. Buyer's guides and calendars of industry conferences and shows are provided. URL: www.inkmakeronline.com.

5210. *Instant & Small Commercial Printer.* Formerly: *Instant Printer.* [ISSN: 1044-3746] 1982. 12x/yr. USD 85. Ed(s): Anne Marie Mohan. Innes Publishing Company, PO Box 7280, Libertyville, IL 60048-7280; meinnes@innespub.com. Adv. Circ: 50953. Microform: PQC. Online: ProQuest LLC (Ann Arbor). *Indexed:* ABIn, EngInd. *Aud.:* Sa.

This journal targets the quick printers, the small commercial shops with fewer than 20 employees, and all franchises. It publishes how-to articles and case histories on printing and photocopy reproduction. Management stories are aimed at helping the entrepreneurial audience with everyday problems and examining new areas for growth.

5211. *PackagePrinting: for printers and converters of labels, flexible packaging and folding cartons.* Former titles (until 1999): *Package Printing & Converting;* (until 1987): *Package Printing;* (until Mar. 1978): *Package Printing and Diecutting;* Which was formed by the merger of: *Diemaking, Diecutting and Converting; Gravure; Flexography Printing and Converting.* [ISSN: 1536-1039] 1974. m. Free. Ed(s): Tom Polischuk, Chris McLoone. North American Publishing Co., 1500 Spring Garden St., Ste 1200, Philadelphia, PA 19130-4094; http://www.napco.com. Illus., index, adv. Circ: 25000 Controlled. Vol. ends: Dec. Microform: PQC. Online: Gale; OCLC Online Computer Library Center, Inc.; ProQuest LLC (Ann Arbor); H.W. Wilson. *Indexed:* ABIn, BPI, EngInd. *Aud.:* Sa.

This trade publication targets the industry of container and package design and production. Diemaking/diecutting, tags, labels, and tape, as well as flexible packaging, folding cartons, and corrugated containers are all this industry's focus. Articles included each month discuss innovations in the equipment needed to manufacture these containers and labels. Inks and printing techniques, suppliers, and management issues are also discussed. The journal is also available at www.packagingprinting.com.

5212. *Paper360: the official publication of TAPPI and PIMA.* Former titles (until 2006): *Solutions;* (until 2001): *T A P P I Journal;* (until 1982): *T A P P I;* (until 1949): *Technical Association Papers.* [ISSN: 1933-3684] 1920. m. Free to members. Questex Media Group Inc., 275 Grove St, Building 2, Ste 130, Newton, MA 02466; questex@sunbeltfs.com; http://www.questex.com. Illus., index, adv. Sample. Circ: 48000 Paid and controlled. Vol. ends: Dec. Microform: MIM; PMC. *Indexed:* A&ATA, AS&TI, Agr, C&ISA, CABA, CEA, CerAb, ChemAb, EngInd, EnvAb, EnvInd, ExcerpMed, FPA, ForAb, HortAb, IAA, PhotoAb, PollutAb, S&F, SCI, SSCI, WAE&RSA. *Aud.:* Ac, Sa.

A very comprehensive journal of the paper industry, *Solutions!* combines journalistic articles with peer-reviewed papers. Every aspect of paper production is discussed, including finances and industry trends. Its readership is largely members of the Technical Association of the Pulp and Paper Industry, so each issue includes information about the association and its conferences.

5213. *Print: design - culture.* Incorporates (in 1976): *Packaging Design.* [ISSN: 0032-8510] 1940. bi-m. USD 57 domestic; USD 72 Canada; USD 98 elsewhere. Ed(s): Joyce Rutter Kaye, Todd Pruzan. F + W Publications, Inc., 38 E 29th St, 3rd Fl, New York, NY 10016; wds@fwpubs.com; http://www.fwpublications.com. Illus., index, adv. Circ: 56788. Vol. ends: No. 6. Microform: PQC. Online: EBSCO Publishing, EBSCO Host; Florida Center for Library Automation; Gale; Northern Light Technology, Inc.; OCLC Online Computer Library Center, Inc.; ProQuest LLC (Ann Arbor); H.W. Wilson. *Indexed:* ABIn, ABM, ABS&EES, ArtInd, DAAI, FLI. *Aud.:* Ga, Ac, Sa.

The purpose of this high-quality, glossy journal is to provide thorough and wide-ranging coverage of the graphic design field. Directed mainly at practitioners, it provides in-depth articles on pertinent topics. Half of the six issues published each year are devoted to juried showcases of leading work in graphic design. The annual "Regional Design" issue organizes artists' work by geographic region. Highly aware of the development of digital technology, *Print* offers a "Digital Design and Illustration" issue that explores the effects of computers on design. This title is an important addition to any graphic design collection. It is also available at www.printmag.com.

5214. *Printing Historical Society. Journal.* [ISSN: 0079-5321] 1965. a. GBP 30 (Individuals, GBP 25). Ed(s): Philip Wickens. Printing Historical Society, St Bride Institute, Fleet St, Bride Ln, London, EC4Y 8EE, United Kingdom. Circ: 650. *Indexed:* IndIslam. *Bk. rev.:* 6-9, 200-300 words, signed. *Aud.:* Ac, Sa.

This journal is published by the Printing Historical Society. All aspects of printing history and the preservation of equipment and printed materials are examined. Contributors include practitioners and researchers in the printing field. Three to four articles are featured and are scholarly in nature. Shorter articles and book reviews are found in the society's *Bulletin*, which appears as part of the journal. Historically important typefaces that have been revived are also reviewed. The *Bulletin* features society news and a list of antiquarian book catalogs. Both publications are free to society members.

5215. *Printing History.* [ISSN: 0192-9275] 1979. s-a. USD 50 (Individuals, USD 40). Ed(s): David Pankow. American Printing History Association, PO Box 4519, New York, NY 10163; http://www.printinghistory.org. Illus., adv. Sample. Refereed. Vol. ends: No. 2. *Indexed:* AmH&L, BrHumI, HistAb, LISA, LibLit, MLA-IB. *Bk. rev.:* 3, 500-600 words, signed. *Aud.:* Ga, Ac.

This scholarly publication offers five or six research articles on topics that may range from profiles of leaders in the field to fifteenth-century papermaking. Its main focus is on American printing history, but its actual range is much broader and includes international developments that influenced the industry. Contributors are researchers in the field. This journal is only available through membership in the association. It is a useful addition to any printing history collection. Also available on the American Printing History Association's web site at www.printinghistory.org.

5216. *Printing Impressions.* Incorporates: *Printing Management.* [ISSN: 0032-860X] 1958. 24x/yr. Free to qualified personnel. Ed(s): Mark T Michelson, Cheryl Adams. North American Publishing Co., 1500 Spring Garden St., Ste 1200, Philadelphia, PA 19130-4094; http://www.napco.com. Illus., adv. Sample. Circ: 86000 Free. Microform: PQC. Online: Gale; Northern Light Technology, Inc.; OCLC Online Computer Library Center, Inc.; ProQuest LLC (Ann Arbor); H.W. Wilson. *Indexed:* ABIn, BPI, EngInd. *Aud.:* Ac, Sa.

This trade publication offers commercial printers, graphic artists, and newspaper publishers up-to-date information in the areas of printing, marketing, finance, and technology. Each issue includes profiles of successful businesses, how-to reports on recent technological advances, management advice, and a calendar of events. New products are reviewed. News about important people in the printing industry is a prominent feature. *Printing Impressions* is also available at www.piworld.com.

5217. *Printing News.* Former titles (until 1997): *Printing News - East;* (until Oct. 1989): *Printing News.* [ISSN: 1556-0163] 1928. w. 51/yr. USD 24.95; USD 30.95 in Canada & Mexico; USD 134.95 elsewhere. Ed(s): David Lindsay. Cygnus Business Media, Inc., 3 Huntington Quadrangle, Ste 301N, Melville, NY 11747-3601. Illus., adv. Sample. Circ: 9000. Online: Gale; ProQuest LLC (Ann Arbor). *Indexed:* ABIn. *Aud.:* Sa.

This is the weekly newspaper for printing industry professionals in New York, New Jersey, Connecticut, and Pennsylvania. Each issue includes feature articles, industry and product news, and a calendar of events. Two special issues cover the Graphic Communications exhibit held annually in Philadelphia and the Graph Expo held annually in New York City. This is an important resource for printing and graphics professionals in the eastern states. *Printing News* is also available at www.printingnews.com.

5218. *Printing World.* Incorporates (1888-2000): *British Printer;* (1964-1981): *Printing Today;* Which was formerly (until 1979): *Printing Equipment and Materials.* [ISSN: 0032-8715] 1878. w. GBP 79 domestic. Haymarket Publishing Ltd., 174 Hammersmith Rd, London, W6 7JP, United Kingdom; hpg@haymarketgroup.com;

http://www.haymarketgroup.co.uk. Illus., adv. Circ: 15530. Microform: PQC. Online: EBSCO Publishing, EBSCO Host; Gale; LexisNexis; ProQuest LLC (Ann Arbor). *Indexed:* ABIn, BrTechI, C&ISA, CerAb, EngInd, IAA, LISA. *Aud.:* Ac, Sa.

England's leading industry magazine is written for the main buyer of products or services. Articles focus on industry news, market trends, paper reviews, financial statistics, and new products and technologies. Printing businesses will value the advertisements that offer second-hand equipment for purchase. Of special interest are the articles that focus on the production and quality of printing. Selected articles are available at www.dotprint.com.

5219. Professional Printer. Incorporates: *Printing Technology.* [ISSN: 0308-4205] 1957. bi-m. Non-members, GBP 24. Ed(s): Nessan Cleary. Institute of Printing, The Mews, Hill House, Clanricarde Rd, Tunbridge Wells, TN1 1PJ, United Kingdom; http://wwww.globalprint.com/uk/iop. Illus., index, adv. Sample. Circ: 1700. Vol. ends: Dec. Microform: PQC. *Indexed:* BrTechI, EngInd, LISA. *Aud.:* Ac, Sa.

This publication of the Institute of Printing, based in London, provides coverage of the institute's activities and issues as well as innovations in printing technology occurring all over the United Kingdom. Membership news and conferences of the institute are announced. Each issue also includes scholarly, scientific articles on the printing process, new techniques, or evaluations of new technology. Many articles are written by professors and include bibliographical references, charts, and graphs. *Professional Printer* offers well-researched information to its readers.

5220. Pulp & Paper. Former titles (until 1947): *Pulp & Paper Industry;* (until 1945): *Pacific Pulp & Paper Industry.* [ISSN: 0033-4081] 1927. m. USD 135 domestic; USD 165 in Canada & Mexico; USD 185 elsewhere. R I S I, Inc., 900 Circle 75 Pkwy, Ste 1150, Atlanta, GA 30339; news@risiinfo.com; http://www.risiinfo.com. Illus., adv. Sample. Circ: 42000 Controlled. Vol. ends: Dec. Online: EBSCO Publishing, EBSCO Host; Florida Center for Library Automation; Gale; OCLC Online Computer Library Center, Inc.; ProQuest LLC (Ann Arbor). *Indexed:* ABIn, ABS&EES, AS&TI, Agr, BPI, ChemAb, EngInd, ExcerpMed, FPA, ForAb. *Aud.:* Ac, Sa.

The definitive journal of the paper industry, this monthly publication provides information about all aspects of paper production. New technological developments, better productivity and efficiency, and cost savings are only a few of the topics covered. Each issue includes financial information about the international paper market and worldwide timber supplies. Upcoming conferences and their programs are outlined. This is required reading for paper industry professionals. *Pulp & Paper* is also available on the Paperloop Group's web site at www.paperloop.com.

5221. Quaerendo: a quarterly journal from the Low Countries devoted to manuscripts and printed books. Former titles (until 1971): *Het Boek (Antwerpen);* (until 1912): *Tijdschrift voor Boek- en Bibliotheekwezen.* [ISSN: 0014-9527] 1903. 4x/yr. EUR 218 (print & online eds.) Individuals, EUR 55). Ed(s): Croiset van Uchelen. Brill, PO Box 9000, Leiden, 2300 PA, Netherlands; cs@brill.nl; http://www.brill.nl. Illus., index, adv. Sample. Refereed. Circ: 750. Vol. ends: No. 4. Reprint: PSC. *Indexed:* AmH&L, AmHI, BEL&L, FR, HistAb, IBR, IBZ. *Bk. rev.:* Number and length vary. *Aud.:* Ac.

Devoted to the history of printing and books, this peer-reviewed journal presents scholarly articles in English, French, and German. Important manuscripts, collections, and recent discoveries are highlighted. Book reviews and information about upcoming exhibits and conferences are provided. *Quaerendo* is delightful reading for anyone who loves books. It is also available at www.brill.nl/m_catalogue_sub6_id7452.htm.

5222. Screen Printing. [ISSN: 0036-9594] 1953. m. plus a. Buyers' Guide. USD 42 domestic; USD 62 Canada; USD 65 Mexico. Ed(s): Tom Frecska. S T Publications Inc., 407 Gilbert Ave, Cincinnati, OH 45202; sduccill@stpubs.com; http://www.stmediagroup.com. Illus., index, adv. Sample. Circ: 17500 Controlled and free. Vol. ends: Dec. *Indexed:* A&ATA, EngInd, PhotoAb. *Aud.:* Ac, Sa.

This journal reflects its artistic focus by providing readers with clear instructions for a polished end-product. Included also is technical information about screen printing systems, care and maintenance of screen printing equipment, and industry trends. New products are also highlighted. *Screen Printing* is the foremost journal in the screen printing industry. It is also available on ScreenWeb at www.screenweb.com/resources/toc.html.

5223. The Seybold Report. Formerly: *Seybold Report on Publishing Systems;* Which incorporates (1986-2001): *Seybold Report on Internet Publishing;* Which was formerly (until 1996): *Seybold Report on Desktop Publishing;* (until 1982): *Seybold Report; Editing Technology.* [ISSN: 1533-9211] 1971. s-m. USD 599 in US & Canada; USD 650 elsewhere. Resource Information Systems, Inc., 4 Alfred Circle, Bedford, MA 01730; info@risiinfo.com; http://www.risiinfo.com/. Illus., index. Sample. Online: EBSCO Publishing, EBSCO Host; Factiva, Inc.; Northern Light Technology, Inc. *Indexed:* CompLI, EngInd, MicrocompInd. *Aud.:* Ac, Sa.

This international journal is very clearly organized so that the publishing professional can see at a glance the important issues and developments in the electronic prepress industry. Information about new technologies and capabilities is combined with financial reports and discussions about legal implications. Overviews of conference proceedings are provided. This is essential reading for anyone in the publishing industry or anyone selecting a publishing system. It is also available at www.seyboldreports.com/TSR.

5224. Step Inside Design: the world of design from the inside out. Formerly (until 2002): *Step-by-Step Graphics.* [ISSN: 1540-2436] 1985. bi-m. USD 48 domestic; USD 60.99 Canada; USD 90 elsewhere. Ed(s): Emily Potts. Jupitermedia Corp., 23 Old Kings Hwy South, Darien, CT 06820; http://www.jupitermedia.com. Illus., index, adv. Sample. Circ: 46000. Vol. ends: Nov/Dec. *Indexed:* DAAI. *Aud.:* Ga, Ac.

This colorful, eye-catching magazine offers graphic artists insight and advice about their chosen field. Articles include specific, detailed instructions about currently popular techniques. Advice about how to sell oneself and one's work is also a frequent feature. Practical business and career tips contained in each issue make this publication a must for visual communicators. *Step Inside Design* is also available at www.dgusa.com/PUBS/STEP/step.aspx.

5225. Visible Language: the triannual concerned with all that is involved in our being literate. Formerly (until 1970): *Journal of Typographic Research.* [ISSN: 0022-2224] 1967. 3x/yr. USD 68 (Individuals, USD 38). Ed(s): Sharon H Poggenpohl. Illinois Institute of Technology, Institute of Design, 350 N La Salle St, Chicago, IL 60610; poggenpohl@id.iit.edu; http://www.id.iit.edu/visiblelanguage. Illus., index, adv. Circ: 1600. Vol. ends: Sep. Microform: PQC. Online: OCLC Online Computer Library Center, Inc.; ProQuest K-12 Learning Solutions; ProQuest LLC (Ann Arbor); H.W. Wilson. *Indexed:* ABM, ArtHuCI, ArtInd, BAS, BRD, ErgAb, FLI, ISTA, L&LBA, MLA-IB, SSCI. *Aud.:* Ac.

This scholarly journal is concerned with written language (as opposed to verbal language) and its impact on humanity and civilization. Literacy is a frequent topic, but there are also many others, including typography, the effect of computer technology on the written word, and semantics. Many issues are devoted to a specific topic. *Visible Language* is important reading for language scholars and researchers. For the electronic version, go to www.id.iit.edu/visiblelanguage.

5226. Visual Communication. [ISSN: 1470-3572] 2002. 4x/yr. GBP 344. Ed(s): Theo van Leeuwen, Teal Triggs. Sage Publications Ltd., 1 Oliver's Yard, 55 City Rd, London, EC1 1SP, United Kingdom; info@sagepub.co.uk; http://www.sagepub.co.uk. Adv. Refereed. Online: CSA; EBSCO Publishing, EBSCO Host; HighWire Press; OCLC Online Computer Library Center, Inc.; OhioLINK; SAGE Publications, Inc., SAGE Journals Online; SwetsWise Online Content. Reprint: PSC. *Indexed:* ABM, CommAb, IBR, IBSS, IBZ, L&LBA, LingAb. *Aud.:* Ac.

This scholarly journal appeals to a wide audience in the humanities, social sciences, linguistics, and graphic arts academic communities. Its purpose is to bring together interrelated but diverse disciplines in a discussion of how the visual impacts these disciplines and society at large. Articles accepted in the journal include academic papers, visual essays, and reflective papers by practitioners on aspects of their work. Works on still and moving images; graphic design and typography; the role of the visual in language, music, sound and action; and visual phenomena such as fashion, posture, and professional vision are all welcomed in this international forum.

■ PSYCHOLOGY

Jill L. Woolums, M.L.I.S., M.A., University of California, Berkeley, Education Psychology Library, Berkeley, CA 94720

Introduction

What is Psychology? Who Are Psychologists?

Psychology is a discipline concerned with the behavior, functions, personal development, and activities of humans. Both academic researchers and clinical practitioners call themselves psychologists. Other social science, science, and humanities disciplines and professions have an overlapping interest in the various sub-fields of psychology. Such disciplines include education, medicine, law, government, sociology, social welfare, public health, art, performing arts, communication, literature, sports, biology, business, and industry.

Access to Journals: Online, Print, Fee Subscriptions, Open Access

Psychologists, as academic and clinical professionals, rely primarily on peer-reviewed, scholarly journals for the latest information and research in psychology and its many sub-fields. Nearly all of the journals listed in this section of *Magazines for Libraries* are scholarly and are available in full text online through either their publishers or an aggregating vendor. At minimum, current tables of contents, frequently free of charge, are online for most titles.

Most scholarly journals are available for a subscription fee that provides online access or printed copies or a combination thereof. Archives or back-files online may be available separately for an additional fee. Such fees are sometimes negotiable depending on consortia or multiple subscription purchasing. As the trend toward open access gains momentum, selected issues can be found free online, either permanently or for a limited time. There are a few scholarly journals that are entirely open access, i.e., fully available in full text and entirely fee. The term "e-journal" has applied to these publications; however, since most runs of scholarly and popular periodicals are available electronically at least partially, this term has lost much of its significance. Popular press titles, such as *Psychology Today, Discover,* and *Scientific American,* are usually available through a multi-subject database, such as Thomson-Gale's Expanded Academic or SIRS.

Archives and Repositories

Archives and back-files are increasingly becoming available either via subscription or through open access. Open access repositories provide organized links to scholarly publications that make all or much of their content freely available on the Internet. See the Directory of Open Access Journals (doaj.org), PubmedCentral (pubmedcentral.nih.gov), and the Public Library of Science (plos.org). The open access movement extends beyond journal titles, and includes theses, dissertations, reports, conference proceedings, papers-in-process, and white papers. Repositories of such content are often found through the web site of the work's sponsoring institution. Directories of such repositories have also arisen on the web. See Opendoar (opendoar.org), Oaister (oaister.org), and CogPrints (cogprints.org). CogPrints describes itself as an "electronic archive for self-archived papers" in any area of psychology, neuroscience, linguistics, and many related fields.

Subscription-based online archives are also available, not only from vendors providing current titles, but also from such nonprofit organizations as JSTOR and Portico. JSTOR states that its mission is "to create and maintain a trusted archive of important scholarly journals, and to provide access to these journals as widely as possible." Most large university and college libraries will want to subscribe to JSTOR to access titles from five years back to the earliest available. Portico was created "to preserve core electronic scholarly literature." Hundreds of titles, including many in psychology, are being made available by major libraries and publishers to create this archive.

Although still in its prepublication phase at this writing, Alexander Street Press has announced its "Primary Sources in Counseling and Psychology, 1950 to Present." This new title promises to be an excellent archival resource for practicing psychologists, by providing over 2,000 transcripts and audio files of therapy sessions, together with reference works, first-person accounts, diaries, letters, autobiographies, oral histories, and personal memoirs.

Current Trends in Psychology

The three major schools that dominate psychological theory and practice are cognitivism, behaviorism, and depth psychology. Within these schools various perspectives exist, including universal vs. differential, holistic vs. analytic, and theoretical vs. pragmatic. Many sub-fields with contrasting approaches have arisen since psychology has evolved from its origins in philosophy. The sub-fields include general psychology, developmental and social psychology, biological psychology (including neuropsychology), personality psychology, experimental psychology, and applied psychology (involving assessment, intervention, and evaluation).

While interest in all three schools and in all sub-fields continues, the literature of the new millennium definitely reflects a scientific focus. Notwithstanding this trend, there remains strong support for research in psychology that has a social science perspective and for studies that reflect humanistic thinking. The American Psychological Association "Decade of Behavior" demonstrates this support with its focus on improving health, safety, education, prosperity, and democracy through a better understanding of psychology. There is and will continue to be a significant overlap among psychology and its sub-fields and other fields, such as law, political science, social welfare, public health, language and linguistics, the applied and performing arts, anthropology, and education.

English-based, American, and Foreign Publications

The titles selected for inclusion in this edition are primarily English-language based. Many, however, draw from an international base of researchers and authors. Library selectors in larger institutions will want to consider non–English-language publications. Academic and clinical libraries will find the titles included to be relevant to their collections. Smaller libraries and institutions will find many titles appropriate for their wider, general audiences, especially to the extent that such titles are available at least partially via open access repositories.

Lists of Titles in Psychology

The titles selected for this edition are only a portion of all the psychology-related publications identified in *Ulrich's Periodicals Directory. Ulrich's* identifies additional titles relevant to specific concerns, such as the arts, ethnic or national issues, philosophical or transpersonal interests, and assessment and intervention techniques.

The 16th edition of *Magazines for Libraries* includes titles covering most of the sub-areas of psychology, but since *Ulrich's* identifies over 2,000 psychology-related titles worldwide, selectors may also want to peruse the *Ulrich's* list.

ALA's Education & Behavioral Science Section core list of psychology journals is another primary source for psychology titles and may be found at www2.library.unr.edu/ressel/psychweb/psychjournals.html. Another useful source is PsycLine, which covers over 2,000 psychology and social science titles in English, German, French, Dutch, and Spanish. PsycLine (www.psycline.org) is owned and managed by psychologist Dr. Armin Gunther, University of Augsburg, Germany.

Since psychology overlaps with other research areas, other sections of this volume should be consulted, such as African American; Aging; Asian American; Disabilities; Education; Ethnic Studies; Family and Marriage; Lesbian, Gay, Bisexual, and Transgender; Gender Studies; Linguistics; Medicine and Health; Parapsychology; Parenting; Philosophy; Political Science; Population Studies; Religion; Sociology; and Sports.

Selectors will also want to consult the lists provided by major vendors of psychology journals, including the American Psychological Association (PsycArticles), and the titles aggregated by Sage, Elsevier, Wiley, Springer, Lippincott-Williams-Wilkins, Taylor & Francis, Erlbaum, Hogrefe & Huber, Guilford, Academic Press, Blackwell, and Academic Press.

Annotations

The annotations describe each journal's editorial preferences. For each title information is provided about its mission, general topic areas, coverage of recent issues, types of articles, and intended audience.

Types of research and articles vary among the journals. Articles may reflect empirical or experimental research. Papers may demonstrate new theoretical thinking or comparative analyses of theories. Case studies commonly appear. Literature reviews and special book reviews are frequently included.

Empirical Research

Empirical research bases its findings on direct or indirect observation, either using an instrument or the human senses. These observations are recorded in the form of data that become the basis for discussion and conclusions. Empirical research usually begins with a hypothesis and follows a process of deductive reasoning.

Theoretical Research

Theoretical papers discuss concepts; propose hypotheses; speculate on, explain, and interpret theories and ideas; criticize other works; summarize and interpret previous research; discuss relationships and implications of prior research and other theories; and argue points of view.

Experimental Research

Experimental research occurs under controlled conditions and involves the observation of humans, animals, or computer simulations. Experimental studies usually involve the collection of data as subjects are watched, thereby making the research also empirical. The results of such experiments provide information to form new theories or to create implications for existing theory.

Literature and Book Reviews

Literature reviews provide overviews and evaluation of published studies. Some reviews provide quantitative analysis, also known as meta-analysis. Literature reviews are important for their summaries, critical assessment, comparative analyses, and historical integration of previous psychological research. Book reviews highlight major current literature in a field.

Case Studies

Case studies are in-depth analyses of certain aspects of a single subject or specific group of subjects. Such aspects may include behaviors, beliefs, emotions, thoughts, or personal histories. These are generally non-experimental, descriptive, empirical studies, typically involving the collection of multiple forms of data about the subject(s).

Basic Periodicals

American Psychologist; Annual Review of Psychology; Archives of General Psychiatry; PsycCritiques; Psychological Bulletin; Psychological Review; Psychology Today.

Basic Abstracts and Indexes

Communication Abstracts; Education Index; ERIC; MEDLINE/PubMed; Linguistics and Language Behavior Abstracts; PsycInfo; PsycArticles; Social Services Abstracts; Social Sciences Citation Index; Social Work Abstracts; Sociological Abstracts.

5227. *A P S Observer.* [ISSN: 1050-4672] 1988. m. USD 75. Ed(s): Brian Weaver. Association for Psychological Science, 1010 Vermont Ave, NW, Ste 1100, Washington, DC 20005-4907; http://www.psychologicalscience.org. Illus., adv. Circ: 15030. *Aud.:* Ga, Ac.

This is the monthly bulletin of the American Psychological Society. The society is dedicated to the advancement of scientific psychology in research and teaching and to the representation of its interests on a national level to improve human welfare. The *Observer* serves over 15,000 APS members and is available online, with special sections reserved for members only or subscribers. Features include a section written by and for psychology students. Recent issues present articles on mirror neurons and how we reflect behavior; bad metaphors and

blind spots regarding evil; testifying before Congress; effective teaching when class size grows; statistical reform in psychology; the psychology of baseball; how to avoid the budget blues; and how to get the most out of a conference. Students, teachers, and researchers in psychology on all levels will want to find this title in their academic and public libraries.

5228. *Acta Psychologica.* [ISSN: 0001-6918] 1941. 9x/yr. EUR 1026. Ed(s): R. J. Hartsuiker, J. Wagemans. Elsevier BV, North-Holland, Sara Burgerhartstraat 25, Amsterdam, 1055 KV, Netherlands; nlinfo-f@elsevier.nl. Illus., index, adv. Sample. Refereed. Microform: PQC. Online: EBSCO Publishing, EBSCO Host; Gale; IngentaConnect; OhioLINK; ScienceDirect; SwetsWise Online Content. *Indexed:* AgeL, CommAb, ErgAb, FR, L&LBA, PsycInfo, SSCI, SWA. *Bk. rev.:* 0-3, 1,000-2,500 words. *Aud.:* Ac, Sa.

This Elsevier journal, also known as *International Journal of Psychonomics*, focuses on empirical studies and evaluative review articles in the area of experimental psychology. Book reviews and articles that increase the theoretical understanding of human capabilities are included. The journal's current topics of concern include human performance, attention, perception, memory, and decision making, and to some extent papers on social processes, development, psychopathology, neuroscience, or computational modeling. Recent issues discuss handedness, infant imitations, oculomotor control, and aging and visual search. Single-topic supplements are published from time to time. *Acta Psychologica* is a high-impact journal appearing at the top of the list of frequently cited journals in ISI Journal Citation Reports. It is a must for a research-oriented academic library, especially those supporting experimental psychology programs.

5229. *Aggressive Behavior: a multidisciplinary journal devoted to the experimental and observational analysis of conflict in humans and animals.* [ISSN: 0096-140X] 1975. bi-m. USD 2364. Ed(s): Ronald Baenninger. John Wiley & Sons, Inc., 111 River St, Hoboken, NJ 07030-5774; uscs-wis@wiley.com; http://www.wiley.com. Illus., index, adv. Refereed. Circ: 550. Vol. ends: No. 6. Microform: PQC. Online: EBSCO Publishing, EBSCO Host; OhioLINK; SwetsWise Online Content; Wiley InterScience. Reprint: PSC. *Indexed:* AgeL, AnBeAb, BiolAb, CABA, CJA, ChemAb, CommAb, ExcerpMed, FR, IndVet, L&LBA, PEI, PRA, PsycInfo, RRTA, RiskAb, SCI, SSCI, VB, ZooRec. *Bk. rev.:* 0-3, 800-1,000 words. *Aud.:* Ac, Sa.

This is the official journal of the International Society for Research on Aggression. The journal focuses on behavioral psychology issues and is of particular interest to researchers in the fields of animal behavior, anthropology, ethology, neuroendocrinology, psychiatry, psychobiology, psychiatry, political science, and sociology. The society seeks through its journal to publish peer-reviewed empirical research on the causes, consequences, and control of violence in human behavior. Recent issues examine gender and racial issues, pornography, adolescence, attitudes toward war, self-esteem, bullying, medication, empathy, and conflict resolution. Articles concern global populations. Libraries that support behavioral programs and researchers in the area of violence will want this title.

5230. *American Academy of Child and Adolescent Psychiatry. Journal.* Formerly (until 1986): *American Academy of Child Psychiatry. Journal.* [ISSN: 0890-8567] 1962. m. USD 415 (Individuals, USD 209). Ed(s): Dr. Mina K Dulcan. Lippincott Williams & Wilkins, 351 W Camden St, Baltimore, MD 21201-2436; custserv@lww.com; http://www.lww.com. Illus., index, adv. Refereed. Circ: 10175. Vol. ends: Nov/Dec. CD-ROM: Ovid Technologies, Inc. Online: EBSCO Publishing, EBSCO Host; Florida Center for Library Automation; Gale; M D Consult; OCLC Online Computer Library Center, Inc.; Ovid Technologies, Inc.; SwetsWise Online Content; H.W. Wilson. *Indexed:* ABIn, BiolAb, CJA, ERIC, EduInd, ExcerpMed, FR, IMFL, PsycInfo, RILM, SCI, SSCI, SWR&A. *Aud.:* Ac, Sa.

This official journal of the American Academy of Child and Adolescent Psychiatry focuses on the psychiatric treatment of children and adolescents in accomplishing its purpose to advance research, clinical practice, and theory in child and adolescent psychiatry. Studies represent various viewpoints, including genetic, epidemiological, neurobiological, cognitive, behavioral, psychodynamic, social, cultural, and economic. The journal publishes research about diagnostic reliability and validity and the effectiveness of psychotherapeutic and psychopharmacological treatment and mental health services. Recent issues address attention deficit/hyperactivity disorder, Asperger's syndrome, use of psychotropic drugs and amphetamines, pathological gambling, depression, grief, and adolescent schizophrenia and anemia. The academy's web site provides tables of contents. Medical and academic libraries with clinical programs will want to have this title.

5231. *American Journal of Clinical Hypnosis.* [ISSN: 0002-9157] 1958. q. USD 125 (Individuals, USD 62.50). Ed(s): Claire Frederick, MD. American Society of Clinical Hypnosis, 140 N Bloomingdale Rd, Bloomingdale, IL 60108; info@asch.net; http://www.asch.net. Illus., adv. Sample. Refereed. Circ: 3000. Vol. ends: Apr. Online: ProQuest LLC (Ann Arbor). *Indexed:* AgeL, ArtHuCI, BRI, ExcerpMed, PsycInfo, RILM, SSCI. *Bk. rev.:* 6, 500-1,000 words. *Aud.:* Ac, Sa.

This is the official journal of the American Society of Clinical Hypnosis. It publishes scientific and empirical articles, case studies, book reviews, and abstracts of current literature in the field of hypnosis. Tables of contents are available through the journal's web site; however, full text is restricted to society members and subscribers. Recent issues cover the following topics: hypnosis in preventing the cardiovascular response to cold pressor tests; suggestion, the neuroscience of implicit processing heuristics in therapeutic hypnosis and psychotherapy; Tourette's syndrome perspectives from hypnosis—attention and self-regulation; reversing amnesia about hypnosis; and the future of professional hypnosis. Libraries supporting clinical programs will want this title as well as the *International Journal of Clinical and Experimental Hypnosis.*

5232. *American Journal of Community Psychology.* [ISSN: 0091-0562] 1973. 8x/yr. EUR 1145 print & online eds. Ed(s): William S Davidson, II. Springer New York LLC, 233 Spring St, New York, NY 10013-1578; service-ny@springer.com; http://www.springer.com/. Illus., index, adv. Sample. Refereed. Vol. ends: Dec. Microform: PQC. Online: Chadwyck-Healey Inc.; EBSCO Publishing, EBSCO Host; Florida Center for Library Automation; Gale; IngentaConnect; Northern Light Technology, Inc.; OCLC Online Computer Library Center, Inc.; OhioLINK; Ovid Technologies, Inc.; ProQuest K-12 Learning Solutions; ProQuest LLC (Ann Arbor); Springer LINK; SwetsWise Online Content. Reprint: PSC. *Indexed:* ASSIA, AgeL, CINAHL, CJA, ECER, ExcerpMed, FR, H&SSA, IBR, IBZ, IMFL, PRA, PsycInfo, RiskAb, SFSA, SSA, SSCI, SUSA, SWA, SWR&A, SociolAb, V&AA. *Aud.:* Ac, Sa.

This scholarly journal is published in association with the Society for Community Research and Action: the Division of Community Psychology of the American Psychological Association. The journal publishes "quantitative and qualitative research on community psychological interventions at the social, neighborhood, organizational, group, and individual levels." A wide range of topics are covered, including social justice, education, legal environments, public health issues, promotion of emotional health, empowerment of marginal groups, institutional and organizational environments, social problems, well-being and competence, social action and networks, and self- and mutual help. The peer-reviewed journal evaluates and features interventions, including collaborative research, advocacy, consulting, training, and planning, and presents the work of leaders in the field. Recent issues have looked at risk and protective factors for urban African-American youth; community-driven learning activities; New York City young adults' psychological reaction to 9/11; and developing a partnership model for cancer screening with community-based organizations. This is a core journal for libraries supporting psychology, social welfare, public health, and social science programs.

5233. *American Journal of Forensic Psychology: interfacing issues of psychology and law.* [ISSN: 0733-1290] 1983. q. USD 85 in US & Canada; USD 110 elsewhere. Ed(s): Debbie Miller. American College of Forensic Psychiatry, PO Box 5870, Balboa Island, CA 92662; psychlaw@sover.net; http://www.forensicpsychiatry.cc/. Refereed. Circ: 500. Vol. ends: No. 4. Microform: WSH; PMC. *Indexed:* CJA, ExcerpMed, PsycInfo. *Bk. rev.:* 3, 800 words. *Aud.:* Ac, Sa.

This official publication of the American College of Forensic Psychology is of interest to international researchers in both psychology and law. The journal focuses on forensic skills and practice and the interface of psychology and law. The journal

Topics covered include aggression and violence; differences between male and female offenders; anxiety disorders; arson; child custody; use of the Millon Clinical Multiaxial Inventory in evaluating child custody litigants; and child sexual abuse. This is a journal for both law and behavioral science libraries.

5234. *American Journal of Orthopsychiatry: interdisciplinary approaches to mental health and social justice.* [ISSN: 0002-9432] 1930. q. USD 245 (Members, USD 83; Non-members, USD 104). Ed(s): Dr. Nancy Felipe Russo. American Psychological Association, 750 First St, N E, Washington, DC 20002-4242; journals@apa.org; http://www.apa.org. Illus., index, adv. Refereed. Circ: 1536 Paid. Vol. ends: Oct. Microform: PQC. Online: Pub.; CSA; EBSCO Publishing, EBSCO Host; OCLC Online Computer Library Center, Inc.; OhioLINK; Ovid Technologies, Inc.; ProQuest LLC (Ann Arbor); ScienceDirect. Reprint: PSC. *Indexed:* ASSIA, AgeL, BRD, CINAHL, CJA, ChemAb, ECER, ExcerpMed, FR, H&SSA, IBSS, IMFL, PsycInfo, RiskAb, SCI, SFSA, SSA, SSCI, SWA, SWR&A, SociolAb. *Aud.:* Ac, Sa.

This journal has a wide scope that includes the areas of public policy and professional practice and "the expansion of knowledge relating to mental health and human development from a multidisciplinary and inter-professional perspective." It publishes research, clinical, theoretical, and policy papers, and focuses on concepts or theories related to major issues including human rights and social justice. Recent issues have looked at inner city drug users and Buddhist-based spiritual therapy; homophobia and conservative religion; risk factors for first-time homelessness in low-income women; siblings of adults with schizophrenia; physical illness, functional limitations, and suicide risk; and effects of trauma on intimate relationships. This is an important public policy journal for academic, public health, and social science research libraries.

5235. *American Journal of Psychiatry.* Formerly (until vol.78, 1921): *American Journal of Insanity.* [ISSN: 0002-953X] 1844. m. USD 314 print & online eds. (Individuals, USD 219 print & online eds.). Ed(s): Sandra L. Patterson, Dr. Nancy C Andreasen. American Psychiatric Publishing, Inc., 1000 Wilson Blvd., Ste. 1825, Arlington, VA 22209-3901; appi@psych.org; http://www.appi.org. Illus., index, adv. Refereed. Circ: 46000 Paid. Vol. ends: Dec. CD-ROM: Ovid Technologies, Inc. Microform: PMC; PQC. Online: EBSCO Publishing, EBSCO Host; HighWire Press; LexisNexis; Northern Light Technology, Inc.; OCLC Online Computer Library Center, Inc.; Ovid Technologies, Inc.; ProQuest K-12 Learning Solutions; ProQuest LLC (Ann Arbor); SwetsWise Online Content. *Indexed:* ASSIA, AbAn, AgeL, ArtHuCI, BAS, BRI, BiolAb, BiolDig, CABA, CBRI, CINAHL, CJA, ChemAb, DSA, ExcerpMed, FR, H&SSA, HRIS, IBR, IBZ, L&LBA, MCR, PEI, PsycInfo, RI-1, RILM, RRTA, RiskAb, SCI, SSCI, SWA, SWR&A. *Bk. rev.:* 10-15, 250-1,000 words. *Aud.:* Ac, Sa.

This journal publishes the findings of research studies that explore the full spectrum of issues and advances related to mental health diagnoses and treatment. Articles present new developments in diagnosis, treatment, neuroscience, and special patient populations. Included are case studies, book reviews, literature reviews and overviews, brief reports, editorials, narrative introspections, and articles reflecting new empirical research. For an extra fee, the online journal links to audio versions of key articles and quizzes that can be taken to fulfill CME credits for practitioners. Recent issues cover schizophrenia, addiction, hypochondrias, eating disorders, posttraumatic stress disorder, bipolar disorder, and depression and the treatments (including pharmacological and cognitive) thereof. As the official journal of the American Psychiatric Association, it includes association news, letters to the editor, and job announcements. *AJP* should be included in collections of libraries serving graduate and institutional research programs in clinical psychology and psychiatry.

5236. *American Journal of Psychology.* [ISSN: 0002-9556] 1887. q. USD 190 print & online eds. (Individuals, USD 70 print & online eds.). Ed(s): Donelson E Dulany. University of Illinois Press, 1325 S Oak St, Champaign, IL 61820-6903; journals@uillinois.edu; http://www.press.uillinois.edu. Illus., index, adv. Sample. Refereed. Circ: 2200 Paid. Microform: MIM; PMC; PQC. Online: Chadwyck-Healey Inc.; EBSCO Publishing, EBSCO Host; Florida Center for Library Automation; Gale; JSTOR (Web-based Journal Archive); Northern Light

Technology, Inc.; OCLC Online Computer Library Center, Inc.; ProQuest K-12 Learning Solutions; ProQuest LLC (Ann Arbor). *Indexed:* ASSIA, AbAn, AgeL, ArtHuCI, BRI, CBRI, ChemAb, CommAb, ErgAb, FR, GSI, IBR, IBZ, L&LBA, PsycInfo, SSA, SSCI. *Bk. rev.:* 4-6, 450-3,000 words. *Aud.:* Ac, Sa.

This long-standing journal has published scientific, theoretical, empirical, and experimental research of philosophical and historical significance by leading psychologists since 1887. Topics include conscious and nonconscious processes; memory; senses; rationality; problem-solving and reasoning; intelligence; introspection; brain imaging and neuropathology; and perception of reality. Recent issues look at cognitive processes involved in blame and forgiveness; emotional arousal and memory; application of evolutionary theory to psychology; phonetic-semantic mediated false recognition; why simultaneous task learning improves retention; recognition of odors and identification of source; and image-dependent interaction of imagery and vision. Libraries that support programs in psychology will want this title.

5237. *American Psychoanalytic Association. Journal.* [ISSN: 0003-0651] 1953. q. USD 295 (Individuals, USD 135; USD 37.50 per issue in US & Canada). Ed(s): Steven T Levy. The Analytic Press, Inc., 10 Industrial Ave, Mahwah, NJ 07430; TAP@analyticpress.com; http://www.analyticpress.com. Illus., index, adv. Refereed. Circ: 6500. Vol. ends: No. 4. *Indexed:* ASSIA, AgeL, ExcerpMed, FR, IBR, IBZ, PsycInfo, SSCI. *Bk. rev.:* 12-20, 800-2,500 words. *Aud.:* Ac, Sa.

This journal publishes research, presentations, panel reports, abstracts, commentaries, editorials, and correspondence. It is a leading journal in the field of psychoanalysis. Recent issues look at self-closure, self-revelation, and the persona of the analyst; patients' experience of validation in psychoanalytic treatment; unconscious fantasy; poetic closure, psychoanalytic closure, and death; masculinity and the twenty-first century; medication and psychoanalysis; and terror and societal regressions. Tables of contents of articles from 2004 on are available on the *JAPA* web site. Psychoanalysts, psychologists, psychiatrists, and mental health professionals as well as researchers will find it a valuable resource.

5238. *American Psychologist.* [ISSN: 0003-066X] 1946. m. USD 710 (Individuals, USD 261). Ed(s): Dr. Norman B Anderson, Dr. Gary VandenBos. American Psychological Association, 750 First St, N E, Washington, DC 20002-4242; journals@apa.org; http://www.apa.org. Illus., adv. Sample. Refereed. Microform: PMC; PQC. Online: Pub.; CSA; EBSCO Publishing, EBSCO Host; OCLC Online Computer Library Center, Inc.; OhioLINK; Ovid Technologies, Inc.; ProQuest LLC (Ann Arbor); ScienceDirect. Reprint: PSC. *Indexed:* ABS&EES, ASSIA, AgeL, ArtHuCI, CJA, ChemAb, CommAb, ERIC, FR, FutSurv, H&SSA, IBR, IBSS, IBZ, LRI, MLA-IB, PRA, PsycInfo, RI-1, SFSA, SSA, SSCI, SWA, SWR&A. *Aud.:* Ga, Ac, Sa.

This official journal of the American Psychological Association contains articles covering a broad range of current issues in the science and practice of psychology and psychology's contribution to public policy. Articles cover all aspects of psychology, but generally do not represent empirical studies. Contributions often address national and international policy issues as well as topics relevant to association policy and activities. Recent issues cover the following topics: self-concept and self-esteem; civil rights and mental health; personality disorder and theories; leadership; cognitive sex differences; and translational research. The journal includes APA's archival documents, such as the annual report of the association, council minutes, the presidential address, editorials, reports, ethics information, surveys of the membership, employment data, obituaries, calendars of events, announcements, and selected award addresses. Occasionally, special issues on particular topics are published.

5239. *Annals of General Psychiatry.* Formerly (until 2004): *Annals of General Hospital Psychiatry.* [ISSN: 1744-859X] 2002. irreg. Free. Ed(s): George St. Kaprinis. BioMed Central Ltd., Middlesex House, 34-42 Cleveland St, London, W1T 4LB, United Kingdom; info@biomedcentral.com; http://www.biomedcentral.com. Adv. Refereed. *Indexed:* ExcerpMed. *Aud.:* Ac, Sa.

This journal seeks to offer support for the fields of psychiatry, neurosciences, and psychological medicine, aiming to publish articles on all aspects of psychiatry. Research articles are the journal's priority, and both basic and clinical neuroscience contributions are encouraged. The journal also seeks to support and follow the principles of evidence-based medicine. The journal has impressive search and post-search functions, and articles are in html or pdf format. Recent topics include cellular mechanisms underlying the effects of an early experience on cognitive abilities and affective states; dysfunction in the visual system of depressed patients; and a review of the use of Topiramate for treatment of psychiatric disorders. Students, practitioners, and researchers in psychiatry will benefit from access to this journal.

5240. *Annual Review of Psychology.* [ISSN: 0066-4308] 1950. a. USD 189 (Individuals, USD 78 print & online eds.). Ed(s): Susan T Fiske. Annual Reviews, 4139 El Camino Way, Palo Alto, CA 94303-0139; service@annualreviews.org; http://www.annualreviews.org. Illus., index, adv. Sample. Refereed. CD-ROM: Ovid Technologies, Inc. Microform: PQC. Online: Florida Center for Library Automation; HighWire Press; Northern Light Technology, Inc. Reprint: PSC. *Indexed:* AgeL, BAS, CINAHL, CJA, ChemAb, ExcerpMed, FR, IBR, IBSS, IBZ, L&LBA, MRD, PsycInfo, RILM, SCI, SSA, SSCI. *Aud.:* Ga, Ac, Sa.

This highly cited journal is produced by a nonprofit scientific publisher, Annual Reviews. The journal publishes critical reviews of significant, current, primary literature in psychology. Covering a wide spectrum of topics, recent issues contain articles concerning cognitive neuroscience, perception, coping, neurobiology of stress, race, personality disorder assessment, emotions, and moral behavior. Each online issue includes abstracts, chapter/title indexes, and extensive bibliographies. Research and academic libraries should have this core title.

5241. *Anxiety, Stress and Coping.* Formerly: *Anxiety Research.* [ISSN: 1061-5806] 1988. q. GBP 675 print & online eds. Ed(s): Reinhard Pekrun, Krys Kaniasty. Routledge, 4 Park Sq, Milton Park, Abingdon, OX14 4RN, United Kingdom; info@routledge.co.uk; http://www.routledge.com. Illus. Refereed. Online: EBSCO Publishing, EBSCO Host; Gale; IngentaConnect; OCLC Online Computer Library Center, Inc.; SwetsWise Online Content. Reprint: PSC. *Indexed:* ErgAb, FR, H&SSA, PsycInfo, SSA, SSCI, SWA. *Aud.:* Ac.

This is the official journal of the Stress and Anxiety Research Society. The online publication is international in scope and publishes scientific, theoretical, and clinical research. Research must be methodologically sound. Literature reviews; meta-analyses; case studies; and clinical, therapeutic, and educational articles are included. Articles may relate to assessment of anxiety, stress and coping, experimental field studies, and the antecedents and consequences of stress and emoting. Recent issues address psychological and health problems in a geographically proximate population time-sampled continuously for three months after the September 11, 2001, terrorist incidents; children's self-reported coping strategies and the role of defensiveness and repressive adaptation; determinants of effective coping with cultural transition among expatriate children and adolescents; coping and quality of life after tumor surgery; and test anxiety and intelligence testing—a closer examination of the stage-fright hypothesis and the influence of stress instruction. Academic libraries with clinical, medical, or behavioral sciences programs will benefit by having this title.

5242. *Applied Psychological Measurement.* [ISSN: 0146-6216] 1976. 8x/yr. GBP 466. Ed(s): Mark Reckase. Sage Publications, Inc., 2455 Teller Rd, Thousand Oaks, CA 91320; info@sagepub.com; http://www.sagepub.com. Illus., index, adv. Sample. Refereed. Circ: 800 Paid and free. Vol. ends: Dec. Microform: PQC. Online: CSA; EBSCO Publishing, EBSCO Host; Gale; HighWire Press; OCLC Online Computer Library Center, Inc.; OhioLINK; SAGE Publications, Inc., SAGE Journals Online; SwetsWise Online Content. Reprint: PSC. *Indexed:* CCMJ, ERIC, IBR, IBZ, MSN, MathR, PsycInfo, SSCI. *Bk. rev.:* 1-2, 500-1,000 words. *Aud.:* Ac, Sa.

This online journal publishes empirical research from educational, organizational, industrial, social, and clinical settings. It presents an international perspective and focuses on current techniques and cutting-edge methodologies to address measurement problems. The journal's contents include empirical articles, brief reports, computer program reviews, book reviews, and announcements. Special issues are regularly published to present the ideas of leading scholars and to address emerging, significant topics. Topics covered may include item response theory; test equations and linking; reliability theory and methods; measurement of change; algorithmic test construction; validity methodology; computerized adaptive testing, Rasch models; and generalizability theory and methods. Recent issues address the effect of examinee motivation on test construction with an IRT framework; full-information item bi-factor analysis of graded response data; an expansion and practical evaluation of expected classification accuracy; and Ramsay curve IRT for Likert-type data. As one of the top journals in quantitative psychology, *Applied Psychological Measurement* should be included in academic and professional research collections.

5243. *Applied Psychophysiology and Biofeedback.* Formerly (until 1997): *Biofeedback and Self Regulation.* [ISSN: 1090-0586] 1975. q. EUR 850 print & online eds. Ed(s): Frank Andrasik. Springer New York LLC, 233 Spring St, New York, NY 10013-1578; service-ny@springer.com; http://www.springer.com/. Illus., index, adv. Refereed. Vol. ends: Dec. Microform: PQC. Online: EBSCO Publishing, EBSCO Host; Gale; IngentaConnect; OCLC Online Computer Library Center, Inc.; OhioLINK; ProQuest LLC (Ann Arbor); Springer LINK; SwetsWise Online Content. Reprint: PSC. *Indexed:* AgeL, BiolAb, ErgAb, ExcerpMed, FR, PsycInfo, SSCI. *Aud.:* Ac, Sa.

This online journal available via Springer and ProQuest is the official publication of the Association for Applied Psychophysiology and Biofeedback. The international, interdisciplinary journal studies the interrelationship of physiological systems, cognition, social and environmental parameters, and health. Articles represent scholarly research that contributes to the theory, practice, and evaluation of applied psychophysiology and biofeedback. Other journal sections include evaluative reviews; a clinical forum with case studies; treatment protocols; a discussion forum; innovations in instrumentation; letters to the editor; and book reviews. Recent issues address heart rate variability biofeedback in patients with fibromyalgia; quantitative electroencephalographic correlates of sustained attention processing; effects of music on the recovery of autonomic and electro-cortical activity after stress induced by aversive visual stimuli; and QEEG observations of tongue piercing by a yogi. Libraries supporting clinical psychology programs will want this title.

5244. *Archives of General Psychiatry.* Formerly (until 1960): *A M A Archives of General Psychiatry;* Which superseded in part (in Jul.1959): *A M A Archives of Neurology and Psychiatry.* [ISSN: 0003-990X] 1950. m. USD 490 print & online eds. Ed(s): Dr. Catherine D DeAngelis, Dr. Joseph T. Coyle. American Medical Association, 515 N State St, Chicago, IL 60610-0946; http://www.ama-assn.org. Illus., index. Refereed. Circ: 31800 Paid and controlled. Vol. ends: Dec. Microform: PQC. Online: The Dialog Corporation; EBSCO Publishing, EBSCO Host; Florida Center for Library Automation; Gale; HighWire Press; OCLC Online Computer Library Center, Inc.; Ovid Technologies, Inc.; ProQuest K-12 Learning Solutions. *Indexed:* ABS&EES, AgeL, BiolAb, CABA, CJA, ChemAb, ExcerpMed, FR, IMFL, PsycInfo, RILM, SCI, SSCI. *Aud.:* Ac, Sa.

This American Medical Association publication is an international, peer-reviewed journal that originally began in 1919 as *Archives of Neurology and Psychiatry.* In 1959, it became two journals: *Archives of Neurology* and *Archives of General Psychiatry.* The journal publishes studies and commentaries of interest to clinicians, scholars, and research scientists in psychiatry, mental health, behavioral science, and allied fields. Articles may present informative, educational, or controversial topics concerning the nature, causes, treatment, and public health issues of mental illness. Recent issues address traumatic events and post-traumatic stress in childhood; progressive and interrelated functional and structural evidence of post-onset brain reduction in schizophrenia; developmental trajectories of male physical violence and theft: relations to neurocognitive performance; psychosocial treatments for bipolar depression: a one-year randomized trial from the systematic treatment enhancement program; and extending the bereavement exclusion for major depression to other losses: evidence from the National Comorbidity Survey. Free online content is available to certain developing countries through the World Health Organization's HINARI program. Medical, psychological, and public health researchers will want access to this title.

5245. *Archives of Sexual Behavior: an interdisciplinary research journal.* [ISSN: 0004-0002] 1971. bi-m. EUR 1342 print & online eds. Ed(s): Kenneth J Zucker. Springer New York LLC, 233 Spring St, New York, NY 10013-1578; service-ny@springer.com; http://www.springer.com/. Illus., adv. Sample. Refereed. Vol. ends: Dec. Online: EBSCO Publishing, EBSCO Host; Florida Center for Library Automation; Gale; IngentaConnect; OCLC Online Computer Library Center, Inc.; OhioLINK; Ovid Technologies, Inc.; ProQuest LLC (Ann Arbor); Springer LINK; SwetsWise Online Content. Reprint: PSC. *Indexed:* AbAn, AgeL, ArtHuCI, BiolAb, CABA, CJA, ChemAb, ExcerpMed, H&SSA, HEA, IMFL, IndVet, PsycInfo, RI-1, RiskAb, SFSA, SSA, SSCI, SWA, SociolAb, V&AA, VB. *Bk. rev.:* 3-6, 1,000 words. *Aud.:* Ac, Sa.

This journal, available online through Springer, is the official publication of the International Academy of Sex Research. The journal publishes work in the field of human sexual behavior. Features include empirical research (both quantitative and qualitative), theoretical reviews and essays, clinical case reports, letters to the editor, and book reviews. Recent topics addressed include grossly disinhibited sexual behavior in dementia of Alzheimer's type; monozygotic twins concordant for female to male transsexualism case report; birth order, sibling sex ration, handedness and sexual orientation of male and female participants in a BBC Internet research project; preferred traits of mates in a cross-national study of heterosexual and homosexual men and women: a study of biological and cultural influences; and the hunter-gatherer theory of sex differences in spatial differences using data from 40 countries. Researchers in sexuality and clinical practitioners in medicine, psychology, or rehabilitation will benefit from this journal.

5246. *Behavior and Social Issues.* Former titles (until 1990): *Behavior Analysis and Social Action;* (until 1986): *Behaviorists for Social Action Journal.* [ISSN: 1064-9506] 1978. 2x/yr. USD 60 (Individuals, USD 35; Students, USD 13). Ed(s): Mark A Mattaini. Behaviorists for Social Responsibility, JACSW (MC 309), 1040 W Harrison St, Chicago, IL 60607; bfsr@bfsr.org; http://www.fsr.org. Illus. Refereed. Circ: 400. *Indexed:* PsycInfo. *Bk. rev.:* 1. *Aud.:* Ac, Sa.

This is a peer-reviewed, interdisciplinary, open-content journal published in association with the Canadian Public Knowledge Project. The journal publishes theoretical and conceptual analyses, research articles and reviews, book reviews, dialogs, and brief reports in the field of the science of behavior. Topics include the natural science of behavior, behavior analysis, cultural analysis, social problems, social justice, human rights, and environmental concerns. Articles may be informative, educational, or controversial. Authors include both senior and emerging scholars. Recent issues look at No Child Left Behind in American education; peak oil as a behavioral problem; biological psychiatry; psychotic disorders; consumer behavior analysis and social marketing; and parents modeling violence: the relationship between witnessing weapon use as a child and later use as an adult. This journal will be sought by a wide range of behavioral scientists, educators, and legal researchers.

5247. *Behavior Modification.* Formerly: *Behavior Modification Quarterly.* [ISSN: 0145-4455] 1977. bi-m. GBP 522. Ed(s): Alan S Bellack, Michael Hersen. Sage Publications, Inc., 2455 Teller Rd, Thousand Oaks, CA 91320; http://www.sagepub.com. Illus., index, adv. Refereed. Circ: 700 Paid. Vol. ends: Oct. Reprint: PSC. *Indexed:* ABIn, AgeL, CINAHL, CJA, ECER, ERIC, EduInd, ExcerpMed, FR, HRA, L&LBA, PsycInfo, SFSA, SSA, SSCI, SUSA, SociolAb, V&AA. *Bk. rev.:* 0-1, 400 words. *Aud.:* Ac, Sa.

This journal provides innovative research, reports, and reviews on applied behavior modification. Each issue is practically oriented, offering comprehensive coverage, including "research and clinical articles, treatment manuals, program descriptions, review articles, assessment and modification techniques, theoretical discussions, group comparison designs, and book and media reviews of significant literature in the field." The journal is also interdisciplinary, with articles on variety of topics. Recent issues provide articles on anxiety, HIV treatment, autism, ethnic issues in therapy, finger mouthing, skin picking, post-traumatic stress disorder, eating disorders, and youth smoking. Special theme-based supplements are offered periodically on such topics as ADHD, personality assessment, and emotions. This journal belongs in libraries supporting applied psychology disciplines.

5248. *Behavior Research Methods (Print Edition).* Former titles (until 2005): *Behavior Research Methods, Instruments, and Computers;* (until 1984): *Behavior Research Methods and Instrumentation.* [ISSN: 1554-351X] 1968. q. USD 224. Ed(s): John Krantz. Psychonomic Society, Inc., 1710 Fortview Rd, Austin, TX 78704; jbellquist@psychonomic.org; http://www.psychonomic.org. Illus., index, adv. Refereed. Circ: 1150. Vol. ends: Dec. Microform: PQC. Online: EBSCO Publishing, EBSCO Host; Gale; IngentaConnect; ProQuest LLC (Ann Arbor); SwetsWise Online Content. *Indexed:* AnBeAb, BiolAb, CompLI, ErgAb, FR, IBR, L&LBA, PsycInfo, RILM, SSCI. *Bk. rev.:* 0-1, 400 words. *Aud.:* Ac.

This is a publication of the Psychonomic Society. The journal provides articles concerning the methods, techniques, and instrumentation of research in experimental psychology. Use of current computer technology in psychological research is of particular interest and is the subject of an annual special issue. Recent issues deal with scientific psychology issues such as methodological considerations in performing semantic- and translation-priming experiments across languages; measurement of left-right asymmetries in the Simon effect; extending the CLAST sequential rule to one-way ANOVA under group sampling; loudspeaker equalization for auditory research; and EMuJoy software for continuous measurement of perceived emotions in music and basic aspects of data recording and interface features. Libraries supporting experimental psychology programs will want this title.

5249. *Behavior Therapy.* [ISSN: 0005-7894] 1970. q. EUR 158. Ed(s): Dr. David A F Haaga. Elsevier Inc., 360 Park Ave S, New York, NY 10010-1710; usinfo-f@elsevier.com; http://www.elsevier.com. Illus., index, adv. Sample. Refereed. Circ: 3500. Vol. ends: Fall. *Indexed:* AgeL, BiolAb, CJA, ECER, ExcerpMed, FR, PsycInfo, SSA, SSCI, SWA. *Aud.:* Ac, Sa.

This Elsevier online publication, published by the Association for the Advancement of Behavior Therapy, is an international journal focused on the application of behavioral and cognitive science to clinical practice. Articles are concerned with the conceptualization, assessment, and treatment of psychopathology and other clinical issues. The journal publishes empirical studies, methodological and theoretical papers, evaluative literature reviews, and case studies. Recent issues address social anxiety in Chinese- and European-heritage students and the effect of assessment format and judgments of impairment; the Environmental Reward Observation Scale (EROS); the impact of client race on clinician detection of eating disorders; effects of worry and rumination on affect states and cognitive activity; virtual reality exposure therapy for PTSD symptoms after a road accident; and cognitive-behavioral therapy of insomnia in people with mild depression. Mental health practitioners and researchers will want access to this title.

5250. *Behavioral and Brain Sciences: an international journal of current research and theory with open peer commentary.* [ISSN: 0140-525X] 1978. bi-m. GBP 500. Ed(s): Paul Bloom, Barbara L Finlay. Cambridge University Press, The Edinburgh Bldg, Shaftesbury Rd, Cambridge, CB2 2RU, United Kingdom; journals@cambridge.org; http://www.journals.cambridge.org. Illus., index, adv. Sample. Refereed. Circ: 3000 Paid. Vol. ends: Dec. Microform: PQC. Online: Pub.; EBSCO Publishing, EBSCO Host; OCLC Online Computer Library Center, Inc.; OhioLINK; SwetsWise Online Content. Reprint: PSC. *Indexed:* ArtHuCI, BiolAb, ExcerpMed, FR, IBR, IBSS, IBZ, L&LBA, PsycInfo, SCI, SSA, SSCI, SociolAb. *Bk. rev.:* 0-30, 500-2,000 words. *Aud.:* Ac, Sa.

This Cambridge online publication is an international journal of current scholarly research in psychology, neuroscience, behavioral biology, and cognitive science. In addition to research articles, the journal publishes 10–25 commentaries on each article. The commentaries are written by specialists within and across these disciplines. Written replies of authors are also included. This format makes the journal a forum for communication and criticism, encouraging both debate and unification across its subject areas. Topics range from behavioral and brain science to molecular neurobiology, artificial intelligence, and the philosophy of the mind. Recent issues cover game theory and higher mental processes; uniting the behavioral sciences with a gene-centered approach to altruism; the place of ethics in a unified behavioral

science; academic tenure; the folk psychology of souls; and social cognition of religion. This is an important journal for academic and research programs in psychology, philosophy, cognitive science, information science, and broader social sciences.

5251. *Behavioral Neuroscience.* Supersedes in part (in 1983): *Journal of Comparative and Physiological Psychology;* Which was formerly (until 1947): *Journal of Comparative Psychology;* Which was formed by the merger of (1917-1921): *Psychobiology;* (1911-1921): *Journal of Animal Behavior.* [ISSN: 0735-7044] 1921. bi-m. USD 900 (Individuals, USD 272). Ed(s): Ann E Kelley. American Psychological Association, 750 First St, N E, Washington, DC 20002-4242; journals@apa.org; http://www.apa.org. Illus., index, adv. Sample. Refereed. Vol. ends: Jan. Microform: PMC; PQC. Online: Pub.; CSA; EBSCO Publishing, EBSCO Host; OCLC Online Computer Library Center, Inc.; OhioLINK; Ovid Technologies, Inc.; ProQuest LLC (Ann Arbor); ScienceDirect. Reprint: PSC. *Indexed:* AbAn, Agr, AnBeAb, B&AI, BiolAb, CABA, ChemAb, DSA, ExcerpMed, FR, IndVet, PsycInfo, S&F, SCI, SSCI, VB. *Aud.:* Ac, Sa.

This journal publishes empirical and experimental research papers concerned with the biological bases of behavior. Research studies must demonstrate that behavioral variables have been measured, manipulated, or clearly considered. Such variables may be studied in relation to a wide range of sciences including anatomy, chemistry, physiology, endocrinology, pharmacology, genetics, or may relate to developmental, behavioral, or evolutionary psychology. The journal also includes review and theoretical papers, technical comments regarding previously published work, and brief communications relevant to the field. Recent issues address emotional conflict and neuroticism; stress and decision-making in gambling; human virtual navigation; sleep spindles and learning potential; and mood changes in response to psychosocial stress in healthy young women. Studies involve both humans and animals. Academic and special libraries supporting scientifically based psychological research will want to include this title.

5252. *Behaviour and Information Technology: an international journal on the human aspects of computing.* [ISSN: 0144-929X] 1982. bi-m. GBP 698 print & online eds. Ed(s): Tom Stewart. Taylor & Francis Ltd., 4 Park Sq, Milton Park, Abingdon, OX14 4RN, United Kingdom; info@tandf.co.uk; http://www.tandf.co.uk/journals. Illus., index, adv. Sample. Refereed. Online: EBSCO Publishing, EBSCO Host; Gale; IngentaConnect; OCLC Online Computer Library Center, Inc.; SwetsWise Online Content. Reprint: PSC. *Indexed:* ASG, AgeL, C&ISA, CINAHL, CerAb, CommAb, CompLI, EAA, ERIC, EngInd, ErgAb, FR, HRA, IAA, L&LBA, LISA, PsycInfo, SCI, SSCI. *Aud.:* Ac, Sa.

This international Taylor & Francis online journal's subject is the human aspects of computing. It publishes research on the design, use, and impact of all forms of information technology. The scope of the journal is interdisciplinary in that it informs the fields of psychology, cognitive science, computer science, ergonomics, sociology, and management education and training. Researchers in all of these fields, especially systems designers and human resources personnel, will want access to this title. Recent issues cover information systems security and human behavior; predicting effectiveness of children participants in user testing based on personality characteristics; a survey of what customers want in cell phone design; using Hollywood's greatest film scenes to illustrate concepts of organizational behavior and management; learning in asynchronous discussion groups: a multilevel approach to studying the influence of student, group, and task characteristics; and evaluating web sites for older adults: adherence to "senior-friendly" guidelines and end-user performance.

5253. *Behaviour Research and Therapy.* Incorporates (1978-1995): *Advances in Behaviour Research and Therapy;* (1979-1992): *Behavioral Assessment.* [ISSN: 0005-7967] 1963. 12x/yr. EUR 1690. Ed(s): G. T. Wilson. Elsevier Ltd., The Boulevard, Langford Ln, Oxford, OX5 1GB, United Kingdom; nlinfo-f@elsevier.nl; http://www.elsevier.com. Illus., index, adv. Refereed. Circ: 4300. Vol. ends: No. 12. Microform: MIM; PQC. Online: EBSCO Publishing, EBSCO Host; Gale; IngentaConnect; OhioLINK; ScienceDirect; SwetsWise Online Content. *Indexed:* AgeL, Agr, BiolAb, CINAHL, ExcerpMed, FR, HEA, IBR, MLA-IB, PsycInfo, SSCI, SWR&A. *Aud.:* Ac, Sa.

This Elsevier online publication is an international, multi-disciplinary journal with a focus on cognitive behavior therapy (CBT). The journal's scope includes traditional clinical disorders and behavioral medicine. Topics of interest include experimental analyses of psychopathological processes; empirically supported interventions; behavior change; and evidence-based treatments for clinical practice. Topics excluded include measurement, psychometric analyses, and personality assessment. Recent issues look at manualized treatment for PTSD symptoms and functional impairment related to the 9/11 World Trade Center attack; cognitive-behavioral therapy for compulsive hoarding; unstable self-esteem as vulnerability marker for depression; the relationship between bullying, psychotic-like experiences, and appraisals in 14- to 16-year-olds; and anxiety sensitivity and auditory perception of heartbeat. This is a journal to be included in collections supporting clinical psychology and medical research programs.

5254. British Journal of Psychiatry. Former titles (until 1962): *Journal of Mental Science;* (until 1858): *Asylum Journal of Psychiatry.* [ISSN: 0007-1250] 1853. m. GBP 284. Ed(s): Peter Tyrer. Royal College of Psychiatrists, 17 Belgrave Sq, London, SW1X 8PG, United Kingdom; rcpsych@rcpsych.ac.uk; http://bjp.rcpsych.org/. Illus., index, adv. Sample. Refereed. Circ: 13000. Vol. ends: No. 6. CD-ROM: Ovid Technologies, Inc. Online: EBSCO Publishing, EBSCO Host; HighWire Press; Ovid Technologies, Inc. *Indexed:* ASSIA, AgeL, BiolAb, CABA, CINAHL, CJA, ChemAb, DSA, ExcerpMed, FPA, FR, ForAb, H&SSA, IMFL, PsycInfo, SCI, SSCI, SWA. *Bk. rev.:* 6-20, 300 words. *Aud.:* Ac, Sa.

This online publication of The Royal College of Psychiatrists is a leading psychiatric journal for mental health professionals. The scope of the journal includes not only peer-reviewed, scholarly research papers, but also literature reviews, commentaries, short reports, book reviews, short reports, and a correspondence column. Periodic supplements provide in-depth coverage of certain topics. Recent issues address anxiety, post-traumatic stress disorder, and depression in Korean War veterans 50 years after the war; mental health problems in U.K. reserve forces who have served in Iraq; genetic, environmental, and gender influences on attachment disorder behavior; cognitive remediation therapy in schizophrenia; target groups for the prevention of late-life anxiety; and patients discharged from medium secure forensic psychiatry services: reconvictions and risk factors. This journal is important for the collections of libraries that support psychiatrists, clinical psychologists, and all professionals with an interest in mental health.

5255. British Journal of Psychology. Former titles (until 1952): *British Journal of Psychology. General Section;* (until 1920): *British Journal of Psychology (London, 1904).* [ISSN: 0007-1269] 1904. q. GBP 270. Ed(s): Peter Mitchell. The British Psychological Society, St Andrews House, 48 Princess Rd E, Leicester, LE1 7DR, United Kingdom; mail@bpsjournals.co.uk; http://www.bps.org.uk. Illus., index, adv. Sample. Refereed. Circ: 2800. Vol. ends: Nov. Microform: PQC. Online: Chadwyck-Healey Inc.; EBSCO Publishing, EBSCO Host; Florida Center for Library Automation; Gale; IngentaConnect; Northern Light Technology, Inc.; OCLC Online Computer Library Center, Inc.; OhioLINK; Ovid Technologies, Inc.; ProQuest K-12 Learning Solutions; ProQuest LLC (Ann Arbor); SwetsWise Online Content; H.W. Wilson. Reprint: PSC. *Indexed:* ASSIA, AgeL, ArtHuCI, BrEdI, CINAHL, CJA, CommAb, ErgAb, FR, H&SSA, IBR, IBSS, IBZ, IMFL, L&LBA, LRI, MLA-IB, PsycInfo, SSA, SSCI, SociolAb. *Bk. rev.:* 0-5, 500-1,000 words. *Aud.:* Ac, Sa.

This international publication is sponsored by The British Psychological Society. The journal publishes empirical studies, critical literature reviews, book reviews and critiques, theoretical papers, and other original research to further the understanding of psychology. The scope of articles includes psychological specialties and the interface between them; new theories and methodologies; integrative reviews with meta-analyses; the history of psychology; and interdisciplinary studies related to psychology. Recent issues consider personality and music; body image in Australian and Pakistani women; sex differences in the effects of interest on boys' and girls' reading comprehension; kinship and altruism; understanding feelings of anger using interpretive phenomenological analysis; aesthetic activities and aesthetic attitudes: the

influence of education, background, and personality on interest and involvement in the arts; and vitalism, purpose, and superstition. This journal is core to general psychology collections.

5256. Canadian Psychology. Former titles (until 1980): *Canadian Psychological Review;* (until 1975): *Canadian Psychologist.* [ISSN: 0708-5591] 1959. q. CND 110 (Individuals, CND 70). Ed(s): Thomas Hadjistavropoulos. Canadian Psychological Association, 141 Laurier Ave West, Ste 702, Ottawa, ON K1P 5J3, Canada; http://www.cpa.ca. Illus., index, adv. Refereed. Circ: 5000. Microform: MML. Online: American Psychological Association; CSA; EBSCO Publishing, EBSCO Host; LexisNexis; Micromedia ProQuest; OCLC Online Computer Library Center, Inc.; OhioLINK; Ovid Technologies, Inc.; ProQuest K-12 Learning Solutions; ProQuest LLC (Ann Arbor); ScienceDirect; H.W. Wilson. *Indexed:* ASSIA, AgeL, AmH&L, ArtHuCI, CBCARef, CPerI, IBR, IBZ, L&LBA, PsycInfo, SSA, SSCI, SociolAb. *Aud.:* Ac.

This journal, available online through vendor purchase, is a publication of the Canadian Psychological Association. The journal publishes general papers in the field of psychology, encompassing theory, research, and practice. Literature reviews, book critiques, and articles of general interest to the association's members are included. Article topics are of interest to a broad cross-section of psychologists. Articles published in English are summarized in French and vice versa. The association publishes tables of contents and abstracts on its web site. Recent issues look at close relationships in daily life; the assessment of credibility; training psychologists for evidence-based practice; psychology, spirituality, and end-of-life care; treatment of obesity; implicit and explicit self-esteem; regulation of psychotropic drugs to children and teenagers; and obsessive-compulsive disorder. This is a core title for basic psychology collections.

5257. Clinical Psychology: science and practice. [ISSN: 0969-5893] 1994. q. USD 423 print & online eds. Ed(s): Philip Kendall. Blackwell Publishing, Inc., Commerce Place, 350 Main St, Malden, MA 02148; customerservices@blackwellpublishing.com; http://www.blackwellpublishing.com. Illus., index, adv. Refereed. Circ: 6000. Vol. ends: Dec. Online: Blackwell Synergy; EBSCO Publishing, EBSCO Host; Gale; HighWire Press; IngentaConnect; OCLC Online Computer Library Center, Inc.; OhioLINK; ProQuest LLC (Ann Arbor); SwetsWise Online Content. Reprint: PSC. *Indexed:* AgeL, ExcerpMed, PsycInfo, SSCI. *Bk. rev.:* 1, 1,200-2,000 words. *Aud.:* Ac, Sa.

This publication of the APA Division of Clinical Psychology provides scholarly reviews of research, theory, and application in the field of clinical psychology. The journal focuses on innovations. Topics include assessment, intervention, service delivery, and other professional issues. Recent issues address empirically based classification of personality pathology; providing children with information about forthcoming medical procedures; scholarly productivity in clinical psychology Ph.D programs; substance abuse, health, and mental health; adapting motivational interventions for comorbid schizophrenia and alcohol use disorders; and licensure. Libraries that support clinical psychology programs will want this title.

5258. Clinical Psychology Review. [ISSN: 0272-7358] 1981. 8x/yr. EUR 1254. Ed(s): Michel Hersen, Dr. Alan S Bellack. Pergamon, The Boulevard, Langford Ln, East Park, Kidlington, OX5 1GB, United Kingdom. Illus., adv. Sample. Refereed. Vol. ends: No. 8. Microform: PQC. Online: EBSCO Publishing, EBSCO Host; Gale; IngentaConnect; OhioLINK; ScienceDirect; SwetsWise Online Content. *Indexed:* AgeL, CJA, ExcerpMed, PsycInfo, SSCI. *Bk. rev.:* 0-4, 300 words. *Aud.:* Ac, Sa.

This journal publishes scholarly reviews on issues important to the field of clinical psychology. It seeks to keep clinical psychologists "up-to-date on relevant issues outside of their immediate areas of expertise." Topics include psychopathology, psychotherapy, behavior therapy, behavioral medicine, community mental health, assessment, child development, psychophysiology, learning therapy, and social psychology. Reports of innovative clinical research programs and literature reviews may also appear. Recent issues cover prevention of depression in youth; quality of life in anxiety disorders; the role of ethnicity and culture in body image and disordered eating among males; assessment, diagnosis, and treatment of torture survivors; stress-reactivity in psychosis: evidence for an affective pathway to psychosis; suspicious minds:

the psychology of persecutory delusions; developing psychological perspectives of suicidal behavior and risk in people with a diagnosis of schizophrenia; and perfectionism and eating disorders. This is a journal for libraries supporting several areas of psychological studies.

5259. Cognition. [ISSN: 0010-0277] 1972. 12x/yr. EUR 1499. Ed(s): Jacques Mehler. Elsevier BV, Radarweg 29, Amsterdam, 1043 NX, Netherlands; nlinfo-f@elsevier.nl; http://www.elsevier.nl. Illus., index, adv. Sample. Refereed. Vol. ends: Dec. Microform: PQC. Online: EBSCO Publishing, EBSCO Host; Gale; IngentaConnect; OhioLINK; ScienceDirect; SwetsWise Online Content. *Indexed:* ArtHuCI, BiolAb, ERIC, ExcerpMed, FR, IBR, IBSS, L&LBA, LT&LA, LingAb, MLA-IB, PhilInd, PsycInfo, RILM, SCI, SSCI. *Aud.:* Ac.

This international journal of cognitive science publishes empirical, theoretical, and experimental research on the mind. Articles may come from the fields of psychology, neuroscience, linguistics, computer science, mathematics, ethology, and philosophy. Topics covered include all aspects of cognition, "ranging from biological and experimental studies to formal analysis." The journal also provides a forum for discussion of the social and political aspects of cognitive science and stress innovation. Special issues are devoted to areas with rapid recent progress, promising new approaches and convergence among disciplines. Recent issues look at spontaneous facial mimicry in response to dynamic facial expressions; self-attributed body-shadows and tactile attention; explaining errors in children's questions; evidentiality in language and cognition; the role of language in mathematical development: evidence from children with specific language impairments; learning phonetic categories by tracking movements; and hearing a melody in different ways: multi-stability of metrical interpretation reflected in rate limits of sensorimotor synchronization. Libraries that support study in neuroscience, computer science, psychology, and linguistics will want this title.

5260. Cognitive Development. [ISSN: 0885-2014] 1986. 4x/yr. EUR 346. Ed(s): Peter Bryant. Elsevier Ltd., The Boulevard, Langford Ln, Oxford, OX5 1GB, United Kingdom. Illus., index, adv. Refereed. Circ: 500. Vol. ends: No. 4. *Indexed:* ERIC, PsycInfo, SSCI. *Bk. rev.:* 1, 3,000 words. *Aud.:* Ac, Sa.

This journal publishes high-quality empirical and theoretical studies that are of current significance to psychological and cognitive researchers. It focuses on perception, memory, language, concepts, thinking, problem solving, metacognition, and social cognition. Moral and social development papers, if they are related to the development of knowledge or thought processes, are also included. Recent issues address cognitive imitation in typically developing three- and four-year-olds and individuals with autism; a longitudinal study of child siblings and theory of mind development; preschoolers' understanding of multiple orientations to reality; choosing between hearts and minds: children's understanding of moral advisors; bias at school: perceptions of racial/ethnic discrimination among Latino and European American children; and culture, power, authenticity, and psychological well-being within romantic relationships: a comparison of European Americans and Mexican Americans. Libraries supporting study and research in child development and work in education or psychology will want this journal.

5261. Cognitive Neuropsychology. [ISSN: 0264-3294] 1984. 8x/yr. GBP 1040 print & online eds. Ed(s): Alfonso Caramazza. Psychology Press, 27 Church Rd, Hove, BN3 2FA, United Kingdom; http://www.psypress.co.uk. Illus., index. Sample. Refereed. Circ: 1000. Online: EBSCO Publishing, EBSCO Host; Gale; IngentaConnect; OCLC Online Computer Library Center, Inc.; SwetsWise Online Content. Reprint: PSC. *Indexed:* ASSIA, AgeL, ArtHuCI, BiolAb, ExcerpMed, FR, L&LBA, LingAb, MLA-IB, PsycInfo, RILM, SCI, SSCI. *Bk. rev.:* 0-1, 1,500 words. *Aud.:* Ac, Sa.

This Psychology Press publication provides empirical and scholarly articles on cognitive processes from the perspective of neuropsychology. The journal focuses on cognition topics, including perception, attention, planning, language, thinking, memory, and action with respect to any stage of lifespan. Neuroimaging and computational modeling research that is informed by a consideration of neuropsychological phenomena are also covered. Recent issues look at processing of syntactically complex sentences and reliance on short-term memory; semantic errors in deep dyslexia and orthographic depth; localizing

the deficit in a case of jargonaphasia; and the impact of progressive semantic loss on reading aloud. Tables of contents and abstracts are available online. This core title is important for students and researchers in cognition, neuropsychology, clinical psychology, and psychiatry.

5262. Cognitive Psychology. [ISSN: 0010-0285] 1970. 8x/yr. EUR 959. Ed(s): Dr. G. D. Logan. Academic Press, 525 B St, Ste 1900, San Diego, CA 92101-4495; apsubs@acad.com; http://www.elsevier.com/. Illus., adv. Refereed. Online: EBSCO Publishing, EBSCO Host; Gale; IngentaConnect; OCLC Online Computer Library Center, Inc.; OhioLINK; ScienceDirect; SwetsWise Online Content. *Indexed:* ABIn, CommAb, ERIC, EduInd, ErgAb, FR, IBR, IBZ, L&LBA, LingAb, MLA-IB, PsycInfo, RILM, SCI, SSCI. *Aud.:* Ac.

This Academic Press title, available via Elsevier, publishes empirical, theoretical, and methodological articles as well as tutorial papers and critical reviews. The journal focuses on advances in the study of memory, language processing, perception, problem solving, and thinking. Articles that significantly impact cognitive theory and articles that provide new theoretical advances are specialties of the journal. Research topics include artificial intelligence, developmental psychology, linguistics, neurophysiology, and social psychology. Recent issues address judgments of associative memory; reading ability negatively related to Stroop interference; information-processing modules and their relative modality specificity; testing the shared resource assumption in theories of text processing; interaction between prosody and statistics in the segmentation of fluent speech; infants' use of category knowledge and object attributes when segregating objects at 8.5 months of age; and revisiting the competence/performance debate in the acquisition of the counting principles. Researchers and students of psychology, cognition, linguistics, computer and information science, and artificial intelligence will want access to this title.

5263. Cognitive Science: a multidisciplinary journal. [ISSN: 0364-0213] 1977. bi-m. GBP 385 print & online eds. Ed(s): Arthur B Markman. Lawrence Erlbaum Associates, Inc., 325 Chestnut St, Ste. 800, Philadelphia, PA 19106; journals@erlbaum.com; http://www.leaonline.com. Illus., index, adv. Refereed. Circ: 2400. Vol. ends: Oct/Dec. Reprint: PSC. *Indexed:* AbAn, ERIC, ErgAb, ExcerpMed, FR, IBR, IBSS, IBZ, L&LBA, LingAb, MLA-IB, PhilInd, PsycInfo, RILM, SSCI. *Aud.:* Ac, Sa.

This journal publishes articles in all areas of cognitive science, focusing on research written for a multidisciplinary audience. Topics addressed include knowledge representation, inference, memory, learning, problem solving, planning, perception, natural language, connectionism, brain theory, motor control, and intentional systems. Recent issues look at when tutorial dialogues are more effective than reading; speed, accuracy, and serial order in sequence production; explaining color term typology with an evolutional model; decision-making and confidence given uncertain advice; phonological abstraction in the mental lexicon; and qualitative and quantitative analysis of morphosyntactic production of early child grammars. Researchers in cognitive science and the fields of anthropology, education, psychology, philosophy, linguistics, computer science, information science, neuroscience, and robotics will want access to this title.

5264. Cognitive Therapy and Research. [ISSN: 0147-5916] 1977. bi-m. EUR 1063 print & online eds. Ed(s): Rick E Ingram. Springer New York LLC, 233 Spring St, New York, NY 10013-1578; service-ny@springer.com; http://www.springer.com/. Illus., index, adv. Sample. Refereed. Vol. ends: Dec. Microform: PQC. Online: EBSCO Publishing, EBSCO Host; Gale; IngentaConnect; OCLC Online Computer Library Center, Inc.; OhioLINK; Ovid Technologies, Inc.; ProQuest LLC (Ann Arbor); Springer LINK; SwetsWise Online Content. Reprint: PSC. *Indexed:* AgeL, BiolAb, ExcerpMed, FR, IMFL, PsycInfo, SSCI, SWA. *Aud.:* Ac, Sa.

This Springer online publication is an interdisciplinary journal. It focuses on studies on "the role of cognitive processes in human adaptation and adjustment." The journal's content includes empirical, experimental, and theoretical research; reviews; technical and methodological articles; case studies; and brief reports. Topics span diverse areas of psychology including clinical, counseling, developmental, experimental, learning, personality, and social psychology. Psychologists and researchers from all of these areas will want this title in their library's collection. Recent issues address the promise of cognitive neuroscience for advancing depression research; attentional bias toward facial stimuli under conditions of social threat in socially phobic and nonclinical participants; self-organization in bipolar disorder: compartmental- ization and self-complexity; patterns of coping, flexibility in coping and psychological distress in women diagnosed with breast cancer; a prospective test of cognitive vulnerability to obsessive-compulsive disorder; and a preliminary study of negative self-beliefs in anorexia nervosa: a detailed exploration of their content, origins, and functional links to "not eating enough" and other characteristic behaviors.

5265. *Consulting Psychology Journal: practice and research.* Former titles (until 1992): *American Psychological Association. Division of Consulting Psychology. Journal; American Psychological Association. Division of Consulting Psychology. Bulletin.* [ISSN: 1065-9293] 1992. q. USD 228 (Members, USD 55; Non-members, USD 80). Ed(s): Dr. Richard C Diedrich. American Psychological Association, 750 First St, N E, Washington, DC 20002-4242; journals@apa.org; http://www.apa.org. Illus., adv. Refereed. Vol. ends: No. 4. Reprint: PSC. *Indexed:* PsycInfo. *Aud.:* Ac, Sa.

APA's *Consulting Psychology Journal: Practice and Research* is a collaborative endeavor of the Educational Publishing Foundation and the Society of Consulting Psychology of APA, Division 13. The journal publishes theoretical articles, original research, in-depth interviews, literature reviews, and case studies relating to consulting psychology. Articles may focus on innovative methods, the business of practice development, or client issues that require unique professional knowledge and skills. Special topic issues are published regularly. Recent issues look at models of executive coaching; organizational culture of diversity and West Point faculty; professional judgment; the relation- ship of hardiness and religiousness to depression and anger; healthy workplace practices; and administrative crisis consultation after 9/11. Libraries supporting clinical psychology and organizational psychology researchers will want to include this title.

5266. *The Counseling Psychologist.* [ISSN: 0011-0000] 1973. bi-m. GBP 397. Ed(s): Robert T Carter. Sage Publications, Inc., 2455 Teller Rd, Thousand Oaks, CA 91320; info@sagepub.com; http://www.sagepub.com. Illus., adv. Refereed. Circ: 3600 Paid and free. Vol. ends: Oct. Microform: PQC. Online: CSA; EBSCO Publishing, EBSCO Host; Florida Center for Library Automation; Gale; HighWire Press; OCLC Online Computer Library Center, Inc.; OhioLINK; SAGE Publications, Inc., SAGE Journals Online; SwetsWise Online Content. Reprint: PSC. *Indexed:* ABS&EES, ASSIA, AgeL, CJA, EAA, ERIC, H&SSA, HEA, HRA, IMFL, PsycInfo, SFSA, SSCI, V&AA. *Aud.:* Ac, Sa.

This Sage online publication is the official journal of the American Psychologi- cal Association Division of Counseling Psychology. The journal publishes scholarly articles that provide comprehensive coverage of research and practice issues in counseling psychology. In-depth issues focus on topics such as counseling HIV-infected clients; counseling lesbian and gay clients; the counseling relationship; multicultural training; victimization; white racial identity; and delayed memory debate. Regular features include a forums section; treatises on current subjects; historical and current topic articles; reviews; and news and highlights of the division's activities. The forum section provides position papers, survey reports, illustrations of assessment and intervention techniques, such as those from the Legacies and Traditions Forum, the Professional Forum, the Scientific Forum, and the International Forum. Recent issues look at effectively communicating qualitative research; qualitative research designs: selection and implementation; internalized racism as one more piece of the puzzle; race-based traumatic stress; construct validation; guidelines for meta-analysis; and advanced applications of structural equation modeling. Academic and professional libraries supporting clinical psychologists will want to have this title.

5267. *Current Directions in Psychological Science.* [ISSN: 0963-7214] 1992. bi-m. Ed(s): Harry T Reis. Blackwell Publishing, Inc., Commerce Place, 350 Main St, Malden, MA 02148; customerservices@

blackwellpublishing.com; http://www.blackwellpublishing.com. Illus., adv. Refereed. Circ: 15000. Vol. ends: Dec. Reprint: PSC. *Indexed:* AgeL, ApEcolAb, ErgAb, L&LBA, PsycInfo, SSCI, SWR&A. *Aud.:* Ac, Sa.

This Blackwell online title, a publication of the Association for Psychological Science, provides reviews in the area of scientific psychology and its applications. The journal focuses on current theory and research, and articles are written by leading experts in the field. Topics may relate to memory and cognition, language, neural foundations of behavior, social and personality determinants of behavior, and psychopathology. Recent issues address risk taking in adolescence from the perspective of brain and behavioral science; what has changed from the nonhuman to human mind; aging and visual attention; involving family in psychosocial interventions in chronic illness; sleep and immunity; and children's social and moral reasoning about exclusion. Researchers seeking current information on cognitive science, neuroscience, computer and information science, behavior and social psychology, law, and linguistics will want access to this title.

5268. *Current Research in Social Psychology.* [ISSN: 1088-7423] 1995. irreg. Free. Ed(s): Lisa Troyer. University of Iowa, Department of Sociology, Center for the Study of Group Processes, Iowa City, IA 52242-1401; http://www.uiowa.edu/~grpproc/crisp/crisp.html. Illus. Refereed. *Indexed:* IBSS, PsycInfo, SSA, SociolAb. *Aud.:* Ac.

This is a publication of the Center for the Study of Group Processes at the University of Iowa. The journal is peer-reviewed and published only in electronic format with free access to its contents. Articles cover a broad range of social psychology issues and reflect empirical, analytical, and theoretical studies. Recent issues address mating effort as a predictor of smoking in a college sample; impact of death in Bangladeshi Muslims with different extents of religiosity; how self-knowledge is expressed verbally; self-coping and the role of relational, individual, and collective self-aspects and the corresponding coping styles in stress and health; segregating positive and negative thoughts about partners and the implications for context-dependence and stability of partner views; gay men and the biasing role of stereotypes in memory; and how stereotype threat impacts college athletes' performance. Academic libraries supporting programs in social psychology should provide an easily found link in their digital interfaces and catalogs to this accessible scholarly journal.

5269. *Developmental Psychology.* [ISSN: 0012-1649] 1969. bi-m. USD 710 (Individuals, USD 236). Ed(s): Dr. Cynthia Garcia Coll. American Psychological Association, 750 First St, N E, Washington, DC 20002-4242; journals@apa.org; http://www.apa.org. Illus., adv. Refereed. Vol. ends: Dec. Microform: PQC. Online: Pub.; CSA; EBSCO Publish- ing, EBSCO Host; OCLC Online Computer Library Center, Inc.; OhioLINK; Ovid Technologies, Inc.; ProQuest LLC (Ann Arbor); ScienceDirect. Reprint: PSC. *Indexed:* ABIn, ASSIA, AgeL, ArtHuCI, CJA, CJPI, CommAb, ERIC, EduInd, FR, IBR, IBSS, IBZ, MLA-IB, PsycInfo, SFSA, SSCI, SWA, SWR&A. *Aud.:* Ac, Sa.

Developmental Psychology publishes empirical studies, scholarly reviews, and methodological articles about human development in all stages. Experimental studies such as ethnographies, field research, and data set analysis are included. The journal seeks to advance knowledge and theory and welcomes controver- sies and studies of new populations. Studies may concern any aspect of development including biological, social, and cultural factors. Articles may address other species insofar as they provide insight with respect to humans. Recent issues include topics such as adolescent online communications, folkbiological reasoning, strategy development, adaptive elements of aging, maternal depression, and children's fearfulness. Libraries supporting departments of psychology, education, sociology, and social welfare will find this title an important addition.

5270. *Developmental Review.* [ISSN: 0273-2297] 1981. 4x/yr. EUR 527. Ed(s): C J Brainerd. Academic Press, 525 B St, Ste 1900, San Diego, CA 92101-4495; apsubs@acad.com; http://www.elsevier.com/. Illus., index, adv. Sample. Refereed. Vol. ends: Dec. Online: EBSCO Publish- ing, EBSCO Host; Gale; IngentaConnect; OCLC Online Computer Library Center, Inc.; OhioLINK; ScienceDirect; SwetsWise Online Content. *Indexed:* AgeL, BiolAb, CJA, ERIC, IBR, IBZ, L&LBA, PsycInfo, SSCI. *Aud.:* Ac.

This Academic Press publication presents research in the area of developmental psychology, with an emphasis on human developmental processes and child developmental psychology. The journal focuses on current, significant, scientific work. Features may include methodological analyses; social policy studies; book review essays; historical analyses; single-theme collections; significant empirical findings; literature reviews; summaries of programmatic research; and theoretical statements. Recent articles look at detrimental psychological outcomes associated with early pubertal timing in adolescent girls; cognitive theories of autism; play in evolution and development; massage therapy research; bullying at school; race socialization within black families; and a multi-level psychobiological perspective on the influence of parenting on infant emotionality. Clinicians and researchers in the areas of educational psychology, child clinical psychology, pediatrics, and psychiatry will find important studies in this journal.

5271. *Educational Psychologist.* [ISSN: 0046-1520] 1963. q. GBP 333 print & online eds. Ed(s): Gale M Sinatra. Lawrence Erlbaum Associates, Inc., 325 Chestnut St, Ste. 800, Philadelphia, PA 19106; journals@ erlbaum.com; http://www.leaonline.com. Illus., adv. Refereed. Circ: 3700. Vol. ends: Fall. Microform: PQC. Online: EBSCO Publishing, EBSCO Host; Gale; OCLC Online Computer Library Center, Inc.; OhioLINK; SwetsWise Online Content. Reprint: PSC. *Indexed:* ABIn, ERIC, EduInd, PsycInfo, SSCI. *Aud.:* Ac, Sa.

This Erlbaum publication presents scholarly essays, reviews, critiques, and theoretical and conceptual articles on all aspects of educational psychology. Articles explore both new and accepted practices. Topics range from meta-analyses of teaching effectiveness to historical examination of textbooks. Empirical studies are not included. Recent issues look at why minimally guided teaching techniques do not work; commentary on Kirschner, Sweller, and Clark regarding problem-based learning and its compatibility with human cognitive architecture; conceptions, contexts, and critical considerations concerning the selves of educational psychology; and commentary on the reconciliation of cognitive and sociocultural accounts of conceptual change. Educational psychologists, researchers, teachers, administrators, and policymakers will want access to this title.

5272. *Environment and Behavior.* [ISSN: 0013-9165] 1969. bi-m. GBP 514. Ed(s): Robert B Bechtel. Sage Publications, Inc., 2455 Teller Rd, Thousand Oaks, CA 91320; info@sagepub.com; http://www.sagepub.com. Illus., index, adv. Sample. Refereed. Circ: 1000 Paid. Vol. ends: Nov. Microform: PQC. Online: CSA; Chadwyck-Healey Inc.; EBSCO Publishing, EBSCO Host; Florida Center for Library Automation; Gale; HighWire Press; OCLC Online Computer Library Center, Inc.; OhioLINK; SAGE Publications, Inc., SAGE Journals Online; SwetsWise Online Content. Reprint: PSC. *Indexed:* ABS&EES, ASSIA, AgeL, Agr, ArtHuCI, C&ISA, CJA, CerAb, EI, ERIC, EnvAb, EnvInd, ExcerpMed, GardL, HRA, HRIS, IAA, IBR, IBSS, IBZ, PRA, PSA, PollutAb, PsycInfo, SFSA, SSA, SSCI, SUSA, SWA, SWRA, SociolAb, V&AA. *Bk. rev.:* 2, 600 words. *Aud.:* Ac, Sa.

This Sage online publications presents current research and theoretical articles concerning the influence of environment on individuals, groups, and institutions. The journal includes feature articles, discussions, and book reviews. Topics covered include values and attitudes of people toward various environments; effectiveness of environmental designs; transportation issues; recreation issues; interrelationships between human environments and behavior; and planning, policy, and political issues. The journal is interdisciplinary, with articles from specialists in anthropology, architecture, design, education, geography, political science, psychology, sociology, and urban planning. Special supplements are sometimes published to highlight leading scholars and significant issues such as litter control, public participation in evaluation of designs, and museum design. Recent issues look at information privacy; celebratory drinking and intoxication; attitudes toward curbside recycling; affective appraisals of the daily commute comparing auto drivers, cyclists, walkers, and users of public transport; assisted living environments compared to nursing homes; and the effect of empathy on pro-environmental attitudes and behavior. This interdisciplinary journal is important for libraries serving humanities, social sciences, and science undergraduate and graduate programs

5273. *European Psychologist.* Formerly (until 1995): *German Journal of Psychology.* [ISSN: 1016-9040] 1977. q. USD 120 (Individuals, USD 57; USD 40.50 per issue). Ed(s): Rainer K Silbereisen, Dr. Verona Christmas-Best. Hogrefe & Huber Publishers, 875 Massachusetts Ave, 7th Fl, Cambridge, MA 02139; hh@hhpub.com; http://www.hhpub.com/ journals. Illus., adv. Sample. Refereed. Circ: 2000. Vol. ends: Feb. Online: American Psychological Association; CSA; EBSCO Publishing, EBSCO Host; OCLC Online Computer Library Center, Inc.; OhioLINK; Ovid Technologies, Inc.; ProQuest LLC (Ann Arbor); ScienceDirect. *Indexed:* ASSIA, FR, GJP, IBR, IBZ, L&LBA, PsycInfo, SSA, SSCI. *Bk. rev.:* Various number and length. *Aud.:* Ac.

This is an English-language journal on psychology in Europe that has as its goal to "integrate across all specializations in psychology and to provide a general platform for communication and cooperation among psychologists throughout Europe and worldwide." The journal publishes peer-reviewed articles, contemporary reviews, reports, book reviews, and news and announcements. Issues regarding both applied psychology and scientific research are included, as are papers relating to professional cooperation and concerns. There is an emphasis on current trends and state-of-the art developments. Articles on legal and regulatory developments and on trends that will impact on any aspect of psychology may appear along with interviews, debates, and discussions. News items provide information on legal, regulatory, ethical, and administrative events, as well as on forthcoming meetings, key symposia and seminars, funding, and job vacancies. Recent issues look at new directions for research on intimate-partner violence and children; marital aggression and children's responses to everyday interparental conflict; infant cognitive psychology and the understand of learning processes; mental representation of money in experts and nonexperts after the introduction of the Euro; foreign language proficiency and working memory capacity; distinguishing preterminal and terminal cognitive decline; death and cognition; and the relationship between genotype and positive psychological development in national-level swimmers. This core journal should be part of academic libraries' collections for access to research in Europe.

5274. *Feminism & Psychology: an international journal.* [ISSN: 0959-3535] 1991. q. GBP 421. Ed(s): Sue Wilkinson. Sage Publications Ltd., 1 Oliver's Yard, 55 City Rd, London, EC1 1SP, United Kingdom; info@sagepub.co.uk; http://www.sagepub.co.uk. Illus., adv. Refereed. Circ: 1000. Vol. ends: Nov. Reprint: PSC. *Indexed:* ASSIA, AgeL, ArtHuCI, CINAHL, FemPer, IBR, IBSS, IBZ, PSA, PsycInfo, SFSA, SSA, SSCI, SWA, SociolAb, V&AA, WSA. *Bk. rev.:* 0-10, 600-1,000 words, signed. *Aud.:* Ac, Sa.

This Sage online journal publishes articles on feminist theory and the practice of psychology, and on a wide range of concerns relating women. While the journal fosters the development of feminist theory, it presents work from both academic and applied realms. It claims to be the "leading international forum for cutting-edge feminist research and debate in and beyond psychology." It publishes papers that are theoretical or empirical, encourages dialog and debate, and presents work that integrates research, practice, and broader social issues and under-represented concerns. Reviews, interviews, and special topic issues frequently appear. Recent issues look at contesting same-sex marriage; advice-giving on a home-birth help line; difference and indifference in planning a lesbian marriage; humor as resistance, refuge, and exclusion in a highly gendered workplace; and victims' and survivors' identities of women raped in the war in Bosnia-Herzegovina. This is a core psychology journal that is important for women's studies programs.

5275. *Health Psychology.* [ISSN: 0278-6133] 1982. bi-m. USD 414 (Individuals, USD 106). Ed(s): Dr. Robert M Kaplan. American Psychological Association, 750 First St, N E, Washington, DC 20002-4242; journals@apa.org; http://www.apa.org. Illus., adv. Refereed. Vol. ends: Dec (No. 6). Reprint: PSC. *Indexed:* ASSIA, AbAn, AgeL, CINAHL, ExcerpMed, FR, FS&TA, PsycInfo, SCI, SSCI, SWA, SWR&A. *Bk. rev.:* 0-1, 1,500 words. *Aud.:* Ac, Sa.

This is a peer-reviewed, scholarly journal concerning behavioral and physical health. Most articles present empirical, theoretical, or practically based research. Studies may focus on cross-cultural and interdisciplinary issues. Topics may include the "role of environmental, psychosocial, or socio-cultural factors that may contribute to disease or its prevention; behavioral methods used in the diagnosis, treatment, or rehabilitation of individuals having physical disorders; and techniques that could reduce disease risk by modifying health beliefs, attitudes, or behaviors including decisions about using professional services. Interventions used may be at the individual, group, multicenter, or community level." Recent issues cover low back pain, ethnic pride and self-control, migrant mental health, dieting and diabetes, adolescent sedentary behavior, coping with cancer, and older adults and depression. The journal should be in libraries serving clinical psychology and human performance programs.

5276. Hispanic Journal of Behavioral Sciences. [ISSN: 0739-9863] 1979. q. GBP 388. Ed(s): Dr. Amado M Padilla. Sage Publications, Inc., 2455 Teller Rd, Thousand Oaks, CA 91320; info@sagepub.com; http://www.sagepub.com. Illus., adv. Refereed. Circ: 630 Paid and free. Vol. ends: Nov. Microform: PQC. Online: CSA; EBSCO Publishing, EBSCO Host; Florida Center for Library Automation; Gale; HighWire Press; OCLC Online Computer Library Center, Inc.; OhioLINK; SAGE Publications, Inc., SAGE Journals Online; SwetsWise Online Content. Reprint: PSC. *Indexed:* ASG, AgeL, CINAHL, CJA, Chicano, EAA, ERIC, HAPI, HEA, IMFL, L&LBA, PsycInfo, RILM, SFSA, SSA, SSCI, SWR&A, SociolAb, V&AA. *Bk. rev.:* 0-1, 400-800 words. *Aud.:* Ac.

This Sage publication is a multidisciplinary behavioral sciences journal that publishes research and analyses on Hispanic issues. Scholarly articles provide theoretical, empirical, and analytical studies from leading experts in Hispanic Studies. Topics include cultural assimilation, communication barriers, intergroup relations, employment discrimination, substance abuse, AIDS prevention, family dynamics, and minority poverty. Recent issues present work on the national origins of Latino populations in the United States; a comparison of aural and visual methods of bilingual computerized speech recognition for screening of depression; measuring hope in Mexican-American youth; self-harm experiences among Hispanic and non-Hispanic white young adult youth; Central American grandparents raising grandchildren; the relative importance of race and socioeconomic status among Hispanic and white students; and prevalence and comorbidity between delinquency, drug abuse, suicide attempts, physical and sexual abuse, and self-mutilation among delinquent Hispanic females. Researchers and professionals in the fields of psychology, sociology, anthropology, education, linguistics, public health, economics, and political science will find this title important to their work.

5277. History of Psychology. [ISSN: 1093-4510] 1998. q. USD 295 (Members, USD 55; Non-members, USD 80). Ed(s): Dr. James H Capshew. American Psychological Association, 750 First St, N E, Washington, DC 20002-4242; journals@apa.org; http://www.apa.org. Illus., adv. Refereed. Vol. ends: Jan. Online: Pub.; CSA; EBSCO Publishing, EBSCO Host; OCLC Online Computer Library Center, Inc.; OhioLINK; Ovid Technologies, Inc.; ProQuest LLC (Ann Arbor); ScienceDirect. Reprint: PSC. *Indexed:* AmH&L, FR, HistAb, PsycInfo. *Aud.:* Ga, Ac.

History of Psychology publishes peer-reviewed articles that concern psychology's past. It addresses the context of psychology's emergence and its ongoing practice. The journal presents scholarly work in related areas, including the history of consciousness and behavior, psychohistory, theory in psychology as it pertains to history, historiography, biography and autobiography, and the teaching of the history of psychology. Recent articles look at such topics as rumors during WWII, the origins of therapeutic community, the history of Alcoholics Anonymous, G. Stanley Hall, and German comparative psychology prior to 1940. Libraries serving students and faculty interested in psychology's history should have this title.

5278. International Journal of Clinical and Experimental Hypnosis. Formerly (until 1958): *Journal of Clinical and Experimental Hypnosis.* [ISSN: 0020-7144] 1953. q. GBP 289 print & online eds. Ed(s): Arreed Barabasz. Routledge, 4 Park Square, Milton Park, Abingdon, OX14 4RN, United Kingdom; journals@routledge.com; http://www.routledge.co.uk. Illus., adv. Refereed. Circ: 2500. Vol. ends: Oct. Microform: PQC. Online: EBSCO Publishing, EBSCO Host; Gale; IngentaConnect;

OCLC Online Computer Library Center, Inc.; SwetsWise Online Content. Reprint: PSC. *Indexed:* CINAHL, ExcerpMed, IBR, IBZ, PsycInfo, SCI, SSCI, SWR&A, V&AA. *Bk. rev.:* 3, 400-600 words. *Aud.:* Ac, Sa.

The official publication of the Society for Clinical and Experimental Hypnosis (SCEH), this peer-reviewed journal publishes research and clinical papers concerning scientific hypnosis, psychology, psychiatry, medical issues, mental health, and allied areas of science. Papers present clinical or experimental research, discussions of theory, or historically or culturally oriented work. Recent issues address evidence-based practice in clinical hypnosis; cognitive-behavioral hypnotherapy in the treatment of irritable bowel syndrome–induced agoraphobia; cognitive hypnotherapy for depression; treatment of post-traumatic conditions; hypnotic treatment of obsessive-compulsive disorders; fractal analysis of EEG in hypnosis and its relationship with hypnotizability; the Spanish version of the Barber Suggestibility Scale for the Puerto Rican population; and a literature survey of hypnotizability, eating behaviors, attitudes, and concerns; Psychiatrists, clinical psychologists, and mental health researchers will want access to this title.

5279. International Journal of Eating Disorders. [ISSN: 0276-3478] 1981. 8x/yr. USD 2125. Ed(s): Dr. Michael Strober. John Wiley & Sons, Inc., 111 River St, Hoboken, NJ 07030-5774; uscs-wis@wiley.com; http://www.wiley.com. Adv. Refereed. Circ: 1200. *Indexed:* AbAn, AgeL, Agr, BiolAb, CABA, CINAHL, DSA, ExcerpMed, FR, FS&TA, H&SSA, PEI, PsycInfo, RRTA, RiskAb, SCI, SSCI, SWA. *Aud.:* Ac, Sa.

This official publication of the Academy of Eating Disorders publishes scholarly clinical and theoretical research. Articles concern several aspects of anorexia nervosa, bulimia, obesity, and atypical patterns of eating behavior and body weight regulation. Clinical and nonclinical populations are the subjects of investigation. The journal includes reviews, brief reports, case studies, literature reviews, and forums for addressing psychological, biological, psychodymamic, socio-cultural, epidemiological, or therapeutic issues. Recent issues look at controlled trials of bulimia nervosa and binge eating disorders; binge eating in the bariatric surgery population; obsessive-compulsive characteristics of women who have recovered from bulimia nervosa; eating disorders in diverse lesbian, gay, and bisexual populations; anorexia in Asian-American adolescents; validation of the emotional eating scale adapted for use with children and adolescents; the role of social physique anxiety in understanding the link between body checking cognitions and behaviors; and handedness differences in body image distortion and eating disorder symptomatology. Behavioral scientists, psychologists, psychiatrists, neurologists, sociologists, health care and mental health professionals, neuropsychiatrists, and anthropologists will benefit by access to this title through their libraries.

5280. International Journal of Group Psychotherapy. [ISSN: 0020-7284] 1951. q. USD 415 (Individuals, USD 110). Ed(s): Seymour Weingarten, Les R Greene. Guilford Publications, Inc., 72 Spring St, 4th Fl, New York, NY 10012; info@guilford.com; http://www.guilford.com. Illus., index, adv. Sample. Refereed. Circ: 5400. Vol. ends: Oct. *Indexed:* ASSIA, AgeL, CJA, ExcerpMed, FR, PsycInfo, SSA, SSCI, SWR&A, SociolAb. *Bk. rev.:* 5, 750 words. *Aud.:* Ac, Sa.

This official journal of the American Group Psychotherapy Association focuses on all aspects of group therapy and treatment, including theory, practice, and research. Recent issues look at the dilemmas of a leader of a writing group; self-psychological and relational approach to group therapy for university students with bulimia; leadership training for psycho-educational group treatment for the severely and persistently mentally ill; attachment, group-related processes, and psychotherapy; diversity in group psychotherapy; social justice and ethics in group therapy; and female patients with borderline personality disorder who dropped out of group psychotherapy. Clinicians, researchers, and mental health administrators will want their libraries to have this leading journal in their field.

5281. The International Journal of Psychoanalysis. Incorporates (in 1992): *International Review of Psycho-Analysis.* [ISSN: 0020-7578] 1920. bi-m. GBP 224 print & online (Individuals, GBP 145 print & online; Students, GBP 56 print & online). Ed(s): Mr. Martin S O'Neill, Glen Gabbard. Institute of Psychoanalysis, 112a Shirland Rd, London, W9 2EQ, United Kingdom. Illus., index, adv. Refereed. Circ: 6700. Vol.

ends: Dec. Online: EBSCO Publishing, EBSCO Host; Gale; Ovid Technologies, Inc.; SwetsWise Online Content. Reprint: PSC. *Indexed:* AgeL, ArtHuCI, ExcerpMed, FLI, FR, IBR, IBSS, IBZ, PsycInfo, RILM, SSCI. *Bk. rev.:* 8-10, 750-3,000 words. *Aud.:* Ac, Sa.

The International Journal of Psychoanalysis, an English-language publication of the International Psychoanalysis Association and a Routledge title, merged with *The International Review of Psycho-Analysis* in 1994. It was originated by Sigmund Freud and Ernest Jones. The journal is a peer-reviewed journal that publishes work from authors from an international scholarly community. Topics present work on methodology, psychoanalytic theory and technique, the history of psychoanalysis, clinical contributions, research and life-cycle development, education and professional issues, psychoanalytic psychotherapy, and interdisciplinary studies. Reports from the Association's congresses, book reviews, obituaries, and correspondence are also included. Recent issues look at remembrance, trauma, and collective memory; Winnicott's rejection of the basic concepts of Freud's metapsychology; psychoanalysis, science, art, and aesthetics; approaches to prevention of intergenerational transmission of hate, war, and violence; the fallacies underlying the latest trend in psychoanalysis—neuropsychoanalysis—and its negative impact on psychoanalytic discourse; and sibling loss and reparation. Libraries supporting advanced studies in psychology will want this title.

5282. *Journal of Abnormal Child Psychology.* [ISSN: 0091-0627] 1973. bi-m. EUR 1258 print & online eds. Ed(s): Susan B Campbell. Springer New York LLC, 233 Spring St, New York, NY 10013-1578; service-ny@springer.com; http://www.springer.com/. Illus., adv. Refereed. Vol. ends: Dec. Microform: PQC. Online: Chadwyck-Healey Inc.; EBSCO Publishing, EBSCO Host; Florida Center for Library Automation; Gale; IngentaConnect; Northern Light Technology, Inc.; OCLC Online Computer Library Center, Inc.; OhioLINK; Ovid Technologies, Inc.; ProQuest K-12 Learning Solutions; ProQuest LLC (Ann Arbor); Springer LINK; SwetsWise Online Content. Reprint: PSC. *Indexed:* ASSIA, CJA, ECER, ERIC, ExcerpMed, FR, IBR, IBZ, IMFL, L&LBA, PsycInfo, SSCI, SWA. *Aud.:* Ac, Sa.

This is the official publication of the International Society for Research in Child and Adolescent Psychopathology. The journal, available online, publishes primarily empirical research on the major childhood disorders. Papers focus on epidemiology, etiology, assessment, treatment, prognosis, follow-up, risk factors, prevention, and the development of child and adolescent disorders. Topics include the major childhood disorders, including disruptive behavior, depression, anxiety, and pervasive developmental disorders. Recent issues look at individual, family, peer, and academic characteristics of male juvenile sexual offenders; environmental correlates of gambling behavior in urban adolescents; parent and child agreement for acute stress disorder, post-traumatic stress disorder and other psychopathology in a prospective study of children and adolescents exposed to single-event trauma; stability and bullying and victimization and its association with social adjustment in childhood and adolescence; the effects of thematic importance on story recall among children with attention deficit hyperactivity disorder and comparison children; the development of social anxiety and social interaction predictors of implicit and explicit fear of negative evaluation; and modeling family dynamics in children with fragile X syndrome. This is an important journal for clinical, research, medical, behavioral, and social science libraries.

5283. *Journal of Abnormal Psychology.* Supersedes in part (in 1965): *Journal of Abnormal and Social Psychology;* Which was formerly (until 1925): *Journal of Abnormal Psychology and Social Psychology;* (until 1921): *Journal of Abnormal Psychology.* [ISSN: 0021-843X] 1906. q. USD 450 (Individuals, USD 146). Ed(s): Dr. David Watson. American Psychological Association, 750 First St, N E, Washington, DC 20002-4242; journals@apa.org; http://www.apa.org. Illus., adv. Refereed. Vol. ends: Jan. Microform: PMC; PQC. Online: Pub.; CSA; EBSCO Publishing, EBSCO Host; OCLC Online Computer Library Center, Inc.; OhioLINK; Ovid Technologies, Inc.; ProQuest LLC (Ann Arbor); ScienceDirect. Reprint: PSC. *Indexed:* ASSIA, AgeL, BiolAb, BiolDig, CJA, CJPI, ECER, ExcerpMed, FR, MLA-IB, PsycInfo, SFSA, SSCI, SWA, SWR&A. *Aud.:* Ac, Sa.

This journal publishes articles on abnormal behavior, its determinants, and its correlates. Articles may be based on empirical and/or experimental research, on

case studies, or on theory. Studies dealing with diagnosis or treatment are not included. The journal focuses on several topics, including psychopathology (its etiology, development, and symptomatology); normal processes in abnormal individuals; pathological or atypical behavior of normal persons; disordered emotional behavior or pathology; socio-cultural effects on pathological processes; gender and ethnic issues; and tests of theories. Recent issues look at the impact of fathers' alcoholism on children, the fragile X syndrome, ADHD, tic disorder, and the impact of maternal prenatal stress on a child's learning. With its theoretical aim, this scholarly journal belongs in academic libraries supporting advanced degrees in psychological research.

5284. *Journal of Anxiety Disorders.* [ISSN: 0887-6185] 1987. 8x/yr. EUR 764. Ed(s): Michel Hersen. Pergamon, The Boulevard, Langford Ln, East Park, Kidlington, OX5 1GB, United Kingdom. Illus. Refereed. Circ: 1500. Microform: PQC. Online: EBSCO Publishing, EBSCO Host; Gale; IngentaConnect; OhioLINK; ScienceDirect; SwetsWise Online Content. *Indexed:* AgeL, BiolAb, CINAHL, ExcerpMed, FR, H&SSA, PsycInfo, RiskAb, SSCI. *Bk. rev.:* Number and length vary. *Aud.:* Ac, Sa.

This Elsevier online title is an interdisciplinary journal focused on anxiety disorders. Papers address all age groups. Empirical research studies, theoretical and review articles, clinical reports and case studies, and book reviews appear in the journal. Topics include traditional, behavioral, cognitive, and biological assessment; diagnosis and classification; psychosocial and psychopharmacological treatment; genetics; epidemiology; and prevention. Recent issues look at social anxiety and romantic relationships and the costs and benefits of negative emotion expression; implications for structural models of anxiety and depression in connection with abnormal personality and mood and anxiety disorders; interpretation biases in victims and non-victims of interpersonal trauma and their relation to symptom development; hair pulling and its affective correlates in an African-American university sample; muscle relaxation therapy for anxiety disorders; affective consequences and social contextual influences of social anxiety, depressive symptoms, and post-event rumination; and an epidemiological study of recovery from social phobia in the community and its predictors. Academic libraries will want this title for their behavioral and social science students and researchers.

5285. *Journal of Applied Behavior Analysis.* [ISSN: 0021-8855] 1968. q. USD 78 (Individuals, USD 30; Students, USD 15). Ed(s): Wayne Fisher. Society for the Experimental Analysis of Behavior, Inc. (Lawrence), c/o Department of Human Development, University of Kansas, Lawrence, KS 66045. Illus., adv. Refereed. Circ: 4000 Paid. Online: National Library of Medicine; OCLC Online Computer Library Center, Inc.; H.W. Wilson. *Indexed:* ABIn, AgeL, CJA, CommAb, ECER, ERIC, FR, PsycInfo, RILM, SSCI. *Aud.:* Ac, Sa.

This is a publication of the Society for the Experimental Analysis of Behavior. Open access backfiles are available through National Library of Medicine's PubMed Central, with the exception of the most recent two years. Tables of contents are available online. The journal publishes research on the application of analyses of behavior to current social issues. Recent issues address an evaluation of the value of choice with preschool children; a comparison of inter-teaching and lecture in the college classroom; enhancing job-site training of supported workers with autism; the effects of prompting and feedback on drivers' stopping at stop signs; effects of Internet-based voucher reinforcement and a transdermal nicotine patch on cigarette smoking; teacher report and direct assessment of preferences for identifying reinforcers for young children; and enhancing early communication through infant sign training. Access to the behavioral analyses and intervention techniques in this journal is important for students, researchers, and professionals in psychology and social sciences.

5286. *Journal of Applied Psychology.* [ISSN: 0021-9010] 1917. bi-m. USD 654 (Individuals, USD 208). Ed(s): Dr. Sheldon Zedeck. American Psychological Association, 750 First St, N E, Washington, DC 20002-4242; journals@apa.org; http://www.apa.org. Illus., adv. Refereed. Circ: 4809 Paid. Vol. ends: Jan. Microform: PMC; PQC. Online: Pub.; CSA; EBSCO Publishing, EBSCO Host; OCLC Online Computer Library Center, Inc.; OhioLINK; Ovid Technologies, Inc.; ProQuest LLC (Ann Arbor); ScienceDirect. Reprint: PSC. *Indexed:* ABIn, ASSIA, AgeL, CINAHL, CJA, CommAb, EAA, ErgAb, ExcerpMed, FR, HRA, IAA, IBR, IBSS, IBZ, PsycInfo, RILM, SSCI, SWA. *Aud.:* Ac, Sa.

This journal publishes articles that represent new investigations seeking knowledge in the field of applied psychology. The journal considers research that concerns the psychological and behavioral phenomena of individuals, groups, or organizations in institutional settings such as education, business, government, or healthcare. Articles are empirical, theoretical, or conceptual, but not clinical, applied experimental, or treatment-based. Topical themes include personnel issues, leadership, job performance and attitudes, addiction, training, organizational design, the impact of technology, and cross-cultural differences. Recent issues look at work-family issues, emotional exhaustion's effect on job motivation, abusive supervision, team burnout, political skill, and cultural tightness/looseness. Libraries that support programs in behavioral and organizational psychology will want to have this journal.

5287. *Journal of Child Psychology & Psychiatry.* [ISSN: 0021-9630] 1960. m. GBP 421 print & online eds. Ed(s): Dr. Frank C Verhulst. Blackwell Publishing Ltd., 9600 Garsington Rd, Oxford, OX4 2ZG, United Kingdom; customerservices@blackwellpublishing.com; http://www.blackwellpublishing.com. Illus., index, adv. Refereed. Circ: 4700. Vol. ends: Nov. Microform: PQC. Online: Blackwell Synergy; EBSCO Publishing, EBSCO Host; Gale; IngentaConnect; OCLC Online Computer Library Center, Inc.; OhioLINK; Ovid Technologies, Inc.; SwetsWise Online Content. Reprint: PSC. *Indexed:* ABIn, ASSIA, AgeL, ApEcolAb, BiolAb, BrEdI, CINAHL, CJA, ECER, EduInd, ExcerpMed, FR, H&SSA, L&LBA, PsycInfo, SSA, SSCI, SociolAb. *Bk. rev.:* 2-12, 350-2,000 words. *Aud.:* Ac, Sa.

This is a publication of the Association for Child and Adolescent Mental Health, and it is available online. The journal is internationally recognized as a leader in the field of child and adolescent psychology and psychiatry. Contents feature empirical research, clinical studies, and reviews. Articles represent both experimental and developmental studies. Special topic issues appear yearly. Recent issues address children's skin conductance reactivity as a mechanism of risk in the context of parental depressive symptoms; incentive-related modulation of cognitive control in healthy, anxious, and depressed adolescents: development and psychopathology-related differences; the relationship between attention, executive functions, and reading domain abilities in attention deficit hyperactivity disorder and reading disorder; eyewitness memory and suggestibility in children with Asperger's syndrome; the parent-infant dyad and the construction of the subjective self; and the relation between deaf children's phonological skills in kindergarten and word recognition performance in first grade. Libraries supporting education and behavioral and social science researchers, students, and clinicians will want to have this title.

5288. *Journal of Clinical Child and Adolescent Psychology.* Formerly (until 2001): *Journal of Clinical Child Psychology.* [ISSN: 1537-4416] 1972. q. GBP 428 print & online eds. Ed(s): Wendy K Silverman. Lawrence Erlbaum Associates, Inc., 325 Chestnut St, Ste. 800, Philadelphia, PA 19106; journals@erlbaum.com; http://www.leaonline.com. Illus., index, adv. Refereed. Circ: 1700. Vol. ends: Dec. Online: EBSCO Publishing, EBSCO Host; Gale; OCLC Online Computer Library Center, Inc.; OhioLINK; SwetsWise Online Content. Reprint: PSC. *Indexed:* ASSIA, CJA, ECER, ERIC, H&SSA, IMFL, PEI, PsycInfo, RiskAb, SSCI. *Bk. rev.:* 0-2, 100-200 words. *Aud.:* Ac, Sa.

This is the official publication of the American Psychological Association's Society of Clinical Child and Adolescent Psychology (Division 53). The journal publishes empirical research and scholarly articles, including those focusing on theoretical and methodological issues. Topics include assessment and intervention techniques; development and maintenance of clinical child and adolescent problems; cross-cultural and sociodemographic issues; training and professional practice; and child advocacy. Recent issues address factor structure and validity of the Parenting Scale; cognitive features associated with depressive symptoms in adolescence: directionality and specificity; moderators of peer contagion: a longitudinal examination of depression socialization between adolescents and their best friends; ethnic and sex differences in children's depressive symptoms; family accommodation in pediatric obsessive-?compulsive disorder; quality of life in youth with Tourette's syndrome and chronic tic disorder; parents' aggressive influences and children's aggressive problem solutions with peers; and anger and sadness in adolescents. Libraries supporting clinical psychology, education, and social science research will want to collect this title.

5289. *Journal of Clinical Psychiatry.* Formerly (until 1978): *Diseases of the Nervous System.* [ISSN: 0160-6689] 1940. bi-m. USD 300 print & online eds. (Individuals, USD 120 print & online eds.). Ed(s): Meg M. Waters, John S Shelton. Physicians Postgraduate Press, Inc., PO Box 752870, Memphis, TN 38175-2870; http://www.psychiatrist.com. Illus., index, adv. Sample. Refereed. Circ: 35700 Controlled. Vol. ends: Dec. Microform: PQC. Online: EBSCO Publishing, EBSCO Host; Northern Light Technology, Inc. *Indexed:* AgeL, BRI, CABA, CBRI, CINAHL, ChemAb, DSA, ExcerpMed, FR, H&SSA, HRIS, HortAb, IMFL, PsycInfo, RiskAb, SCI, SSCI. *Bk. rev.:* 4, 50-500 words. *Aud.:* Ac, Sa.

This online journal is an international publication of Physicians Postgraduate Press. The journal publishes scholarly, peer-reviewed articles on mental health topics important to psychiatrists and medical professionals. Articles explore diagnosis and treatment issues concerning disorders such as depression, bipolar disorder, schizophrenia, anxiety, addition, premenstrual dysphoric disorder, and ADHD. The journal also offers continuing medical education activities to clinicians. Recent issues address guided discontinuation versus maintenance treatment in remitted first-episode psychosis, relapse rates, and functional outcome; a double-bind, placebo-controlled study of the efficacy and safety of desvenlafaxine succinate in the treatment of major depressive disorder; a 12-month follow-up randomized controlled trial of cognitive behavioral social skills training for older people with schizophrenia; a five-year prospective study of remissions, relapses, and the effects of personality disorder psychopathology concerning the natural course of bulimia nervosa and of eating disorders not otherwise specified; the failure of evidence-based medicine to guide treatment of antidepressant nonresponders; and psychiatry and psychology in medieval Persia. Libraries supporting psychiatrists, primary care physicians, clinical psychologists, and medical professionals will want this title.

5290. *Journal of Cognitive Neuroscience.* [ISSN: 0898-929X] 1989. m. USD 840 print & online eds. (Individuals, USD 160 print & online eds). Ed(s): Mark D'Esposito. M I T Press, 238 Main St., Ste. 500, Cambridge, MA 02142; journals-info@mit.edu; http://mitpress.mit.edu. Illus. Refereed. Circ: 1200. Online: EBSCO Publishing, EBSCO Host; Florida Center for Library Automation; Gale; HighWire Press; IngentaConnect; OCLC Online Computer Library Center, Inc.; OhioLINK; SwetsWise Online Content. *Indexed:* ExcerpMed, FR, L&LBA, PsycInfo, SCI, SSCI. *Aud.:* Ac.

This is an MIT journal published with the Cognitive Neuroscience Institute. The journal seeks to promote communication among researchers in the mind sciences, including neuroscience, neuropsychology, cognitive psychology, neurobiology, linguistics, computer science, and philosophy. Articles selected for publication investigate brain-behavior interaction and provide descriptions of brain function and underlying brain events. Recent issues look at transcranial magnetic stimulation in a finger-tapping task separating motor from timing mechanisms and inducing frequency doubling; stronger synaptic connectivity as a mechanism behind development of working memory-related brain activity during childhood; prefrontal cortical response to conflict during semantic and phonological tasks; predictive learning, prediction errors, and attention: evidence from event-related potentials and eye tracking; the contribution of hand motor circuits to counting; and online integration of semantic information from speech and gesture and insights from event-related brain potentials. Students and researchers in neuroscience, cognition, and neuropsychology will want access to this title through their libraries.

5291. *Journal of Comparative Psychology.* Supersedes in part (in 1983): *Journal of Comparative and Physiological Psychology;* Which was formerly (until 1947): *Journal of Comparative Psychology;* Which was formed by the merger of (1917-1921): *Psychobiology;* (1911-1921): *Journal of Animal Behavior.* [ISSN: 0735-7036] 1921. q. USD 300 (Non-members, USD 84). Ed(s): Dr. Gordon M Burghardt. American Psychological Association, 750 First St, N E, Washington, DC 20002-4242; journals@apa.org; http://www.apa.org. Illus., index, adv. Refereed. Vol. ends: Feb. Microform: PQC. Online: Pub.; CSA; EBSCO Publishing, EBSCO Host; OCLC Online Computer Library Center, Inc.; OhioLINK; Ovid Technologies, Inc.; ProQuest LLC (Ann Arbor); ScienceDirect. Reprint: PSC. *Indexed:* AbAn, B&AI, BiolAb, CABA, ChemAb, FR, IndVet, PsycInfo, SCI, SSCI, VB, ZooRec. *Aud.:* Ac.

This journal publishes comparative research studies on the behavior, cognition, social relationships, and perception of diverse species. Articles may reflect original empirical or theoretical research and be descriptive or experimental. Studies conducted both in the field and in captivity are included. The journal covers several topics, such as behavior genetics, behavioral rhythms, communication, comparative cognition, behavioral biology of conservation and animal welfare, development, endocrine-behavior interactions, evolutionary psychology, methodology, phylogenetic comparisons, orientation and navigation, sensory and perceptual processes, social behavior, and social cognition. Recent issues more specifically address dolphins understanding of human gazing; social relationships among female giraffes; social dominance in preschool; and decision-making in cats. Libraries that support experimental research should have this title.

5292. *Journal of Consulting and Clinical Psychology.* Formerly (until 1967): *Journal of Consulting Psychology.* [ISSN: 0022-006X] 1937. bi-m. USD 710 (Individuals, USD 251). Ed(s): Dr. Annette M La Greca. American Psychological Association, 750 First St, N E, Washington, DC 20002-4242; journals@apa.org; http://www.apa.org. Illus., index, adv. Refereed. Circ: 8700 Paid. Vol. ends: Jan. Microform: PMC; PQC. Online: Pub.; CSA; EBSCO Publishing, EBSCO Host; OCLC Online Computer Library Center, Inc.; OhioLINK; Ovid Technologies, Inc.; ProQuest LLC (Ann Arbor); ScienceDirect. Reprint: PSC. *Indexed:* ASSIA, AgeL, CINAHL, CJA, CommAb, ECER, ERIC, ExcerpMed, FR, IBR, IBSS, IBZ, PRA, PsycInfo, SFSA, SSCI, SWA, SWR&A, V&AA. *Aud.:* Ac, Sa.

This journal publishes original research that deals with clinical diagnosis, treatment, and prevention issues. Its primary audience is the community of clinical practitioners treating humans with mental illness, clinical dysfunction, and behavioral disorders. Articles concern a variety of populations, including medical patients, ethnic groups, and persons with serious mental illness, regardless of place in the human lifespan. Studies of personality assessment; cross-cultural, gender, or sexual orientation issues; and psychosocial issues of health behaviors are covered. The journal publishes case studies, empirical research, and theoretical manuscripts that investigate change or the effectiveness of treatments. Topics covered include epidemiology; use of psychological services; health care economics for behavioral disorders; and critical analyses and meta-analyses of treatment approaches. This is a journal for clinicians and the libraries that support their practice and training.

5293. *Journal of Counseling Psychology.* [ISSN: 0022-0167] 1954. q. USD 325 (Non-members, USD 103). Ed(s): Dr. Brent S Mallinckrodt. American Psychological Association, 750 First St, N E, Washington, DC 20002-4242; journals@apa.org; http://www.apa.org. Illus., index. Refereed. Vol. ends: Dec. Microform: PQC. Online: Pub.; CSA; EBSCO Publishing, EBSCO Host; OCLC Online Computer Library Center, Inc.; OhioLINK; Ovid Technologies, Inc.; ProQuest LLC (Ann Arbor); ScienceDirect. Reprint: PSC. *Indexed:* ABIn, ASSIA, AgeL, BRI, CBRI, CJA, ERIC, EduInd, ExcerpMed, FR, HEA, HRA, IBR, IBZ, PsycInfo, SFSA, SSCI, SWA, SWR&A. *Aud.:* Ac, Sa.

This journal publishes empirical research and theoretical works in the areas of counseling, career development, diversity issues, assessment and measures, and other professional issues. Articles primarily concern clients who have problems with living or who are experiencing developmental crises, rather than those who exhibit severe disturbance, unless the research concerns healthier aspects of the disturbance. Both quantitative and qualitative methods are included. Research that represents an extension of previous studies or that investigates implications for public policy or social action may also appear in the journal. Topics in recent issues include classifying perfectionists, racial microaggression and African-Americans, cultural transmission in Asian Indians, stress and racial stress in black men, psychosocial costs of racism to whites, and indecisiveness and anxiety in career decisions. Libraries supporting clinical, pastoral, marriage and family, and career counseling programs will want this journal.

5294. *Journal of Cross-Cultural Psychology.* [ISSN: 0022-0221] 1970. bi-m. GBP 505. Ed(s): Fons Van de Vijver. Sage Publications, Inc., 2455 Teller Rd, Thousand Oaks, CA 91320; info@sagepub.com; http://www.sagepub.com. Illus., index, adv. Refereed. Circ: 1500 Paid. Microform: PQC. Online: CSA; EBSCO Publishing, EBSCO Host;

Florida Center for Library Automation; Gale; HighWire Press; OCLC Online Computer Library Center, Inc.; OhioLINK; SAGE Publications, Inc., SAGE Journals Online; SwetsWise Online Content. Reprint: PSC. *Indexed:* ABS&EES, ASSIA, AbAn, AgeL, ArtHuCI, BAS, CINAHL, CJA, CommAb, HRA, IBR, IBZ, L&LBA, PRA, PsycInfo, SFSA, SSA, SSCI, SWA, SociolAb, V&AA. *Bk. rev.:* 0-5, 300-500 words. *Aud.:* Ac, Sa.

This Sage online journal is published in association with the International Association for Cross-Cultural Psychology and the Center for Cross-Cultural Research, Department of Psychology, Western Washington University. The journal serves as an "interdisciplinary forum for psychologists, sociologists and educators who study how cultural differences in developmental, social and educational experiences affect individual behavior." Articles address a wide range of topics, such as individualism, self-enhancement, acculturation, family values, ethnic group comparisons, and gender differences and personality. Regular features include empirical and theoretical research, reviews, and book reviews. Special thematic issues appear occasionally. Recent issues look at two decades of change in cultural values and economic development in eight East Asian and Pacific Island nations; the effects of gender and parent-child conflict on problem behavior and acculturation in Moroccan immigrant adolescents in the Netherlands; cross-cultural comparisons of experts' models with lay prototypes regarding what defines a good person; cross-cultural perspectives on mapping the minds of retirement planners; spiritual well-being as a mediator of the relation between culture-specific coping and quality of life in a community sample of Africa Americans; and child-rearing values of Estonian and Finnish mothers and fathers. Libraries that support programs in cross-cultural studies, as well as general psychology and behavioral and social sciences, will want this title.

Journal of Educational Psychology. See Education: Educational Psychology and Measurement, Special Education, Counseling section.

5295. *Journal of Experimental Child Psychology.* [ISSN: 0022-0965] 1964. 12x/yr. EUR 1717. Ed(s): Dr. Robert V. Kail. Academic Press, 525 B St, Ste 1900, San Diego, CA 92101-4495; apsubs@acad.com; http://www.elsevier.com/. Illus., index, adv. Refereed. Vol. ends: Dec. Online: EBSCO Publishing, EBSCO Host; Gale; IngentaConnect; OCLC Online Computer Library Center, Inc.; OhioLINK; ScienceDirect; SwetsWise Online Content. *Indexed:* BiolAb, ERIC, FR, IBR, IBSS, IBZ, MLA-IB, PsycInfo, SCI, SSCI. *Aud.:* Ac, Sa.

This is an Academic Press journal with a focus on child development. It publishes empirical, theoretical, methodological and analytical studies on child development spanning infancy through adolescence and including cognitive, social, and physical aspects. Features include a "Reflections" forum in which scholars discuss issues raised in an initial paper and a brief notes section. Special-topic supplements appear periodically. Research addresses child behavior and psychology, developmental psychology and science, and methodology, primarily in the normal child. Recent issues look at children's metamemorial judgments in an event recall task; young children's reports of when learning occurred; second-order beliefs about intention and children's attributions of sociomoral judgment; subtypes of Chinese developmental dyslexia; the influence of working memory on reading growth in subgroups of children with reading disabilities; and when knowledge is not enough: the phenomenon of goal neglect in preschool children. This is an important title for libraries supporting students and researchers in psychology and education.

5296. *Journal of Experimental Psychology: Animal Behavior Processes.* Supersedes in part (in 1975): *Journal of Experimental Psychology.* [ISSN: 0097-7403] 1916. q. USD 300 (Individuals, USD 109). Ed(s): Dr. Nicholas J Mackintosh. American Psychological Association, 750 First St, N E, Washington, DC 20002-4242; journals@apa.org; http://www.apa.org. Illus., index, adv. Refereed. Vol. ends: Dec. Microform: PQC. Online: Pub.; CSA; EBSCO Publishing, EBSCO Host; OCLC Online Computer Library Center, Inc.; OhioLINK; Ovid Technologies, Inc.; ProQuest LLC (Ann Arbor); ScienceDirect. Reprint: PSC. *Indexed:* AnBeAb, BiolAb, CABA, DSA, FR, IBR, IBZ, IndVet, PsycInfo, SCI, SSCI, ZooRec. *Aud.:* Ac, Sa.

This journal publishes articles based on empirical, theoretical, or experimental studies. Any aspect of animal behavior, including associative, non-associative, cognitive, perceptual, and motivational processes, may be the subject of investigation. Relevant specialized reviews and brief communications on novel experiments are also published. Recent issues look at preference for symmetry in newborn chicks, numbers and monkeys, memory in pigeons, flavor preference, and lemurs and deception. This journal is particularly appropriate for libraries supporting researchers in experimental psychology.

5297. *Journal of Experimental Psychology: Applied.* [ISSN: 1076-898X] 1995. q. USD 300 (Non-members, USD 84). Ed(s): Wendy A Rogers. American Psychological Association, 750 First St, N E, Washington, DC 20002-4242; journals@apa.org; http://www.apa.org. Adv. Refereed. Vol. ends: Feb. Reprint: PSC. *Indexed:* AgeL, ERIC, ErgAb, HRA, IBR, IBZ, PsycInfo, SSCI. *Aud.:* Ac, Sa.

This journal publishes empirical investigations that bridge practically oriented problems and psychological theory. It also publishes relevant review articles and research studies concerning "models of cognitive processing or behavior in applied situations, including laboratory and field settings." Topics covered may include "applications of perception, attention, decision making, reasoning, information processing, learning, and performance." Studies may have been conducted in industrial, academic, or consumer-oriented settings. Recent issues look at retirement savings decisions, stress and memory in natural disasters, emotional intelligence, and the psychological price of media bias. Libraries supporting programs in experimental research will find this title important.

5298. *Journal of Experimental Psychology: General.* Supersedes in part (in 1975): *Journal of Experimental Psychology.* [ISSN: 0096-3445] 1916. q. USD 300 (Individuals, USD 84). Ed(s): Dr. Fernanda Ferreira. American Psychological Association, 750 First St, N E, Washington, DC 20002-4242; journals@apa.org; http://www.apa.org. Illus., adv. Refereed. Circ: 2821 Paid. Vol. ends: Feb. Microform: PQC. Online: Pub.; CSA; EBSCO Publishing, EBSCO Host; OCLC Online Computer Library Center, Inc.; OhioLINK; Ovid Technologies, Inc.; ProQuest LLC (Ann Arbor); ScienceDirect. Reprint: PSC. *Indexed:* AgeL, BiolAb, ERIC, ErgAb, FR, IBR, IBZ, PsycInfo, SSCI. *Aud.:* Ac.

This journal publishes empirical research that bridges two or more communities of psychology. Such issues may concern combinations of work in applied, animal, learning and memory, and human performance experimental research. The journal also publishes articles on other psychological topics, including social processes, developmental processes, psychopathology, neuroscience, or computational modeling. Recent issues contain articles concerning color and psychological functioning, hierarchical control of cognitive processes, intuitive confidence, and how people learn to select strategies. This title is appropriate for libraries that support experimental psychology programs.

5299. *Journal of Experimental Psychology: Human Perception and Performance.* Supersedes in part (in 1975): *Journal of Experimental Psychology.* [ISSN: 0096-1523] 1916. bi-m. USD 900 (Individuals, USD 332). Ed(s): Dr. Glyn W Humphreys. American Psychological Association, 750 First St, N E, Washington, DC 20002-4242; journals@apa.org; http://www.apa.org. Adv. Refereed. Vol. ends: Jan. Microform: PQC. Online: Pub.; CSA; EBSCO Publishing, EBSCO Host; OCLC Online Computer Library Center, Inc.; OhioLINK; Ovid Technologies, Inc.; ProQuest LLC (Ann Arbor); ScienceDirect. Reprint: PSC. *Indexed:* AgeL, BiolAb, CommAb, ERIC, ErgAb, FR, IBR, IBZ, L&LBA, MLA-IB, PsycInfo, RILM, SCI, SSCI. *Aud.:* Ac, Sa.

This journal publishes primarily empirical research on perception, language processing, human action, and related cognitive processes and covers all sensory modalities and motor systems. The journal seeks to increase theoretical understanding of human perception and performance and encourages studies with a neuroscientific perspective. Articles concerning machine and animal studies that reflect on human capabilities may also appear. Nonempirical reports, including theoretical notes, commentary, or criticism on pertinent topics are also published. Recent issues address veering behavior of blind walkers, forgetting, effects of action video games, and word length and lexical activation. Researchers concerned with human physical performance will want to find this title in their library's collection.

5300. *Journal of Experimental Psychology: Learning, Memory, and Cognition.* Formerly (until Jan. 1982): *Journal of Experimental Psychology: Human Learning and Memory;* Which supersedes in part (in 1975): *Journal of Experimental Psychology.* [ISSN: 0278-7393] 1916. bi-m. USD 900 (Individuals, USD 332). Ed(s): Randi C Martin. American Psychological Association, 750 First St, N E, Washington, DC 20002-4242; journals@apa.org; http://www.apa.org. Adv. Refereed. Vol. ends: Dec. Microform: PQC. Online: Pub.; CSA; EBSCO Publishing, EBSCO Host; OCLC Online Computer Library Center, Inc.; OhioLINK; Ovid Technologies, Inc.; ProQuest LLC (Ann Arbor); ScienceDirect. Reprint: PSC. *Indexed:* AgeL, ArtHuCI, BiolAb, ERIC, ErgAb, FR, IBR, IBZ, L&LBA, MLA-IB, PsycInfo, RILM, SCI, SSCI. *Aud.:* Ac, Sa.

This journal publishes empirical and experimental research on cognition, learning, memory, imagery, concept formation, problem solving, decision making, thinking, reading, and language processing. Specialized reviews and other non-empirical theoretical notes, commentary, or criticism on pertinent topics are also included. Recent issues include articles on psychometric intelligence, mental practice for learning sequences, gender processing in first and second languages, and predicting free recalls. Researchers interested in cognition, organizational psychology, or educational psychology will want to find this title in their library's collection.

5301. *Journal of Experimental Social Psychology.* [ISSN: 0022-1031] 1965. m. EUR 1090. Ed(s): B Park. Academic Press, 525 B St, Ste 1900, San Diego, CA 92101-4495; apsubs@acad.com; http://www.elsevier.com/. Illus., adv. Refereed. Vol. ends: Nov. Online: EBSCO Publishing, EBSCO Host; Gale; IngentaConnect; OCLC Online Computer Library Center, Inc.; OhioLINK; ScienceDirect; SwetsWise Online Content. *Indexed:* ArtHuCI, CJA, CommAb, FR, IBR, IBSS, IBZ, LRI, PsycInfo, RI-1, SSCI. *Aud.:* Ac.

This peer-reviewed, scholarly journal publishes empirical research, literature reviews, theoretical analyses, and methodological reports in the field of social behavior. The journal seeks to advance understanding of important social psychological phenomena. Recent issues look at priming meritocracy and the psychological justification of inequality; how moral identity and mechanisms of moral disengagement influence cognitive and emotional reactions to war; what men and women want in a partner and whether educated partners are always more desirable; trait expectancies and stereotype expectancies having the same effect on person memory; cultural differences in using the eyes and mouth as cues to recognize emotions in Japan and the United States; and team allegiance leading to both optimistic and pessimistic predictions. Behavioral scientists, sociologists, psychologists, and other social scientists will want access to this title.

5302. *Journal of Feminist Family Therapy: an international forum.* [ISSN: 0895-2833] 1989. q. USD 565 print & online eds. Ed(s): Anne M Prouty. Haworth Press, Inc., 10 Alice St, Binghamton, NY 13904-1580; getinfo@haworthpress.com; http://www.haworthpress.com. Illus., adv. Sample. Refereed. Circ: 306 Paid. Vol. ends: No. 4. Microform: PQC. Online: EBSCO Publishing, EBSCO Host; OCLC Online Computer Library Center, Inc.; ProQuest LLC (Ann Arbor); SwetsWise Online Content. Reprint: HAW. *Indexed:* ASSIA, AltPI, CWI, FemPer, GendWatch, IBR, IBZ, IMFL, PsycInfo, SFSA, SSA, SWA, SWR&A, SociolAb, V&AA, WSA. *Bk. rev.:* 4-5, 200-1,000 words, signed. *Aud.:* Ac, Sa.

This is an international journal that explores both feminist and family therapy theory and practice. It includes empirical, theoretical, and applied research. Articles address cultural, class, and racial differences; women's psychological issues; training and supervision in family therapy; and organizational issues in family therapy. Book, movie, and play reviews, interviews, first-person narratives, humor and political papers, letters, and comments also appear. Tables of contents are freely available online. Recent issues address shame as a barrier to cultural sensitivity and competent practice; feminist reflections on creating a collaborative research team; the worst U.S. president in history; the use of narrative therapy and internal family systems with survivors of childhood sexual abuse; feminist analysis of popular music with respect to power over, objectification of, and violence against women; and biracial female reflections on racial identity development in adolescence. The journal serves a spectrum of social and political scientists. Libraries with women's studies programs will want this title.

5303. *Journal of Humanistic Psychology.* [ISSN: 0022-1678] 1961. q. GBP 403. Ed(s): Kirk J Schneider. Sage Publications, Inc., 2455 Teller Rd, Thousand Oaks, CA 91320; info@sagepub.com; http://www.sagepub.com. Illus., index, adv. Refereed. Circ 1550 Paid and free. Vol. ends: Fall. Microform: PQC. Online: CSA; EBSCO Publishing, EBSCO Host; Florida Center for Library Automation; Gale; HighWire Press; OCLC Online Computer Library Center, Inc.; OhioLINK; ProQuest K-12 Learning Solutions; SAGE Publications, Inc., SAGE Journals Online; SwetsWise Online Content. Reprint: PSC. *Indexed:* ABS&EES, ASSIA, AgeL, ArtHuCI, CommAb, HRA, IMFL, PsycInfo, RI-1, SSCI. *Aud.:* Ac, Sa.

This online Sage publication is the official journal of the Association of Humanistic Psychology. The journal provides an interdisciplinary forum for addressing diverse issues in the areas of personal growth, social problems, interpersonal relations, and philosophical thinking. Founded in 1961 by Abraham Maslow and Anthony Sutich, it maintains close connection with the Saybrook Institute. Topics include authenticity, community, consciousness, creativity, existentialism, holistic health, politics, identity, peace and mediation, self-actualization, self-transcendence, and spiritual development. Features include scholarly articles, experiential reports, analyses, theoretical papers, personal essays, poetry, narratives, news, editorial commentary, and research emphasizing human scientific methods. The work of notable thinkers, such as Rollo May, Carl Rogers, Brewster Smith, Ken Wilber, and James Bugental have appeared in its pages. Special supplements appear periodically with in-depth coverage of topics. Recent issues cover profound sorrow and buried potential in violent youth; the transformative power of play; approaching worldview structure with ultimate meanings technique; conceptions of spirituality among Israeli Arab and Jewish late adolescents; combating trauma with treatment from a mystical spiritual perspective; and women's process of successful partnering and finding a happy relationship. Students and researchers of philosophy, religion, psychology, and other social sciences will want access to this title.

5304. *Journal of Mathematical Psychology.* [ISSN: 0022-2496] 1964. 6x/yr. EUR 1493. Ed(s): J R Busemeyer. Academic Press, 525 B St, Ste 1900, San Diego, CA 92101-4495; apsubs@acad.com; http://www.elsevier.com/. Illus., index, adv. Refereed. Vol. ends: Dec. Online: EBSCO Publishing, EBSCO Host; Gale; IngentaConnect; OCLC Online Computer Library Center, Inc.; OhioLINK; ScienceDirect; SwetsWise Online Content. *Indexed:* CCMJ, CompR, IBR, IBZ, MSN, MathR, PsycInfo, RILM, SCI, SSCI. *Bk. rev.:* 1-5, 100-3,000 words. *Aud.:* Ac.

This is a publication of the Society for Mathematical Psychology. The journal publishes empirical and theoretical articles, monographs and reviews, notes and commentaries, and book reviews in the field of mathematical psychology. Topics covered include fundamental measurement and psychological process models; models for sensation and perception and learning and memory; neural modeling and networks; neuropsychological theories; psycholinguistics; animal behavior; psychometric theory; problem-solving, judgment and decision-making; and motivation. Recent issues address detection of visual stimuli in correlated noise; evaluating the reliance on past choices in adaptive learning models; concurrent visual search and time reproduction with cross-talk; the interaction between exemplar-based concepts and a response scaling process; and a set-theoretical outlook on the philosophy of science. Libraries supporting quantitative and scientific psychology researchers and students will want this title.

5305. *The Journal of Mind and Behavior.* [ISSN: 0271-0137] 1980. q. USD 128 (Individuals, USD 46; Students, USD 27). Ed(s): Dr. Raymond C. Russ. Institute of Mind & Behavior, PO Box 522, New York, NY 10014; http://kramer.ume.maine.edu/~jmb/. Illus., index, adv. Sample. Refereed. Circ: 1191 Controlled. *Indexed:* ExcerpMed, IBR, IBZ, L&LBA, PhilInd, PsycInfo, SSA, SSCI, SWR&A, SociolAb. *Bk. rev.:* 0-4, 300-2,000 words. *Aud.:* Ac.

This publication of the Institute of Mind and Behavior at the University of Maine is not yet available online. The journal is interdisciplinary in that it focuses on the relationship of mind and behavior. Contents reflect the publishing of scholarly work that is experimental, theoretical, empirical, or methodological. Subjects of interest include relationships among psychology, philosophy, sociology, and the scientific method; the mind/body problem in social sciences, medicine, and physical science; the philosophical impact of a mind/body epistemology upon psychology and its theories of consciousness; ethical studies of cognition, self-awareness, and higher functions of consciousness in nonhumans; and historical perspectives in psychology. While it seeks experimental research, the journal also recognizes "the need to propagate ideas and speculations as well as the need to form empirical situations for testing them." Recent issues address the structure of scientific knowledge and a fractal model of thought; association mechanisms and the intentionality of the mental; Kuttner and Rosenblums' failure to objectify consciousness; the case for intrinsic theory; practical dangers of middle-level theorizing in personality research; history and development of body image in neurology and psychoanalysis; and the frontal feedback model of the evolution of the human mind. With its emphasis on theory, this is a core journal for libraries with advanced psychology and social science programs and research collections.

5306. *Journal of Occupational and Organizational Psychology.* Former titles (until 1992): *Journal of Occupational Psychology;* (until 1975): *Occupational Psychology;* (until 1938): *Human Factors (London);* (until 1932): *National Institute of Industrial Psychology. Journal.* [ISSN: 0963-1798] 1922. q. GBP 192 & libraries. Ed(s): John Arnold. The British Psychological Society, St Andrews House, 48 Princess Rd E, Leicester, LE1 7DR, United Kingdom; mail@bpsjournals.co.uk; http://www.bps.org.uk. Illus., index, adv. Sample. Refereed. Circ: 3100. Vol. ends: Dec. Online: EBSCO Publishing, EBSCO Host; Florida Center for Library Automation; Gale; IngentaConnect; OCLC Online Computer Library Center, Inc.; OhioLINK; Ovid Technologies, Inc.; ProQuest K-12 Learning Solutions; ProQuest LLC (Ann Arbor); SwetsWise Online Content. Reprint: PSC. *Indexed:* ABIn, ASG, ASSIA, AgeL, BrEdI, CJA, ErgAb, FR, H&SSA, HRA, IBR, IBSS, IBZ, PsycInfo, SSA, SSCI, SWA, SociolAb. *Bk. rev.:* 3, 500-1,000 words. *Aud.:* Ac, Sa.

This publication of the British Psychological Society provides empirical and theoretical articles concerning people and organizations at work. Papers address issues in industrial, organizational, vocational, and personnel psychology, and consider behavioral concerns in industrial relations, ergonomics, and industrial sociology. Recent issues look at diversity training; job satisfaction and involvement as interactive predictors of absenteeism in a public organization; a three-dimensional construct for attitudinal commitment; and a multi-level analysis of the effects of service climate and the effective leadership behavior of supervisors on frontline employee service quality. Libraries supporting studies in organizational psychology, industrial relations, and business will want this title.

5307. *Journal of Pediatric Psychology.* Formerly: *Pediatric Psychology.* [ISSN: 0146-8693] 1976. 8x/yr. EUR 747 print or online ed. Ed(s): Ronald T Brown. Oxford University Press, Great Clarendon St, Oxford, OX2 6DP, United Kingdom; jnl.orders@oup.co.uk; http://www.oxfordjournals.org. Illus., index, adv. Sample. Refereed. Circ: 2030 Paid. Microform: PQC. Online: EBSCO Publishing, EBSCO Host; Gale; HighWire Press; IngentaConnect; OCLC Online Computer Library Center, Inc.; OhioLINK; Ovid Technologies, Inc.; Oxford Journals; SwetsWise Online Content. Reprint: PSC. *Indexed:* CINAHL, CJA, ExcerpMed, FR, IMFL, PollutAb, PsycInfo, RiskAb, SFSA, SSCI, SWR&A. *Bk. rev.:* 5-8, 150-3,000 words. *Aud.:* Ac, Sa.

This is the official journal of the Society of Pediatric Psychology, Division 54, of the American Psychological Association. The interdisciplinary journal publishes theoretical papers, empirical research, and professional practice articles concerning pediatric psychology. Features include analytical reviews, brief reports, and case studies. Articles focus on preventive health and treatment issues, as well as the training of pediatric psychologists. Recent issues look at the impact of caregiver identity and infant age in judgments of infant pain; a meta-analysis of psychological and cognitive functioning in children and adolescents with congenital heart disease; examination of the effect of family emotional climate, depression, emotional triggering of asthma, and disease severity in pediatric asthma; behavioral risk factors for youth soccer or football injury; and the relationship between parent-reported social support and adherence to medical treatment in families of adolescents with Type 1 diabetes. Clinical child psychologists, medical and healthcare professionals who work with children, and researchers pursuing studies related to children's medicine and psychology will want access to this title.

5308. *Journal of Personality.* Formerly (until 1945): *Character and Personality.* [ISSN: 0022-3506] 1932. bi-m. GBP 756 print & online eds. Ed(s): Howard Tennen. Blackwell Publishing, Inc., Commerce Place, 350 Main St, Malden, MA 02148; customerservices@ blackwellpublishing.com; http://www.blackwellpublishing.com. Illus., index, adv. Sample. Refereed. Circ: 2000. Vol. ends: Dec. Online: Blackwell Synergy; EBSCO Publishing, EBSCO Host; Gale; IngentaConnect; OCLC Online Computer Library Center, Inc.; OhioLINK; SwetsWise Online Content. Reprint: PSC. *Indexed:* ASSIA, AgeL, ApEcolAb, ArtHuCI, CommAb, FR, IBR, IBSS, IBZ, IndIslam, PsycInfo, SFSA, SSA, SSCI, SWA. *Aud.:* Ac, Sa.

This Blackwell online title publishes scientific research on the many aspects and issues in the field of personality. Coverage addresses behavior dynamics; personality development; and cognitive, affective, and interpersonal differences. Empirical, theoretical, and methodological approaches are included. Recent issues look at smoking, mood regulation, and personality; temperament, executive functions, and the allocation of attention to punishment feedback in passive avoidance learning; shame and the mechanisms of activation and consequences for social perception, self-image, and general negative emotion; political-economic values and the relationship between socioeconomic status and self-esteem; and the spirited, the observant, and the disheartened in relation to social concepts of optimism, realism, and pessimism. Academic libraries supporting study and research in personality will want this title.

5309. *Journal of Personality and Social Psychology.* Supersedes in part (in 1965): *Journal of Abnormal and Social Psychology.* [ISSN: 0022-3514] 1965. m. USD 1450 (Individuals, USD 464). Ed(s): Dr. Charles S Carver, Dr. Charles M Judd. American Psychological Association, 750 First St, N E, Washington, DC 20002-4242; journals@apa.org; http://www.apa.org. Illus., index, adv. Refereed. Vol. ends: Dec. Microform: PQC. Online: Pub.; CSA; EBSCO Publishing, EBSCO Host; OCLC Online Computer Library Center, Inc.; OhioLINK; Ovid Technologies, Inc.; ProQuest LLC (Ann Arbor); ScienceDirect. Reprint: PSC. *Indexed:* ABIn, ABS&EES, AgeL, ArtHuCI, BAS, CJA, CommAb, EAA, FR, HEA, IBR, IBSS, IBZ, IPSA, L&LBA, MLA-IB, PsycInfo, RI-1, RILM, SFSA, SSA, SSCI, SUSA, SWA, SWR&A, SociolAb. *Aud.:* Ac, Sa.

This journal publishes empirical, specialized theoretical, methodological, and review articles in all areas of personality and social psychology. It has three sections: Attitudes and Social Cognition, Interpersonal Relations and Group Processes, and Personality Processes and Individual Differences. Attitudes and Social Cognition focuses on cognition and social behavior and covers such topics as attitudes, attributions, stereotypes, person memory, self-regulation, the origins and consequences of moods and emotions, the effect of cognition on persuasion, communication, prejudice, social development, and cultural trends. Interpersonal Relations and Group Processes addresses psychological interaction and covers such topics as interpersonal attraction, communication, emotion, relationship development, social influence, group decision-making and task performance, intergroup relations, aggression, and pro-social behavior. Personality Processes and Individual Differences covers all aspects of personality psychology. Topics may include behavior, emotions, coping, health, motivation, personality structure, personality development, personality assessment, interplay of culture and personality, and personality in everyday life. Recent issues look at goal pursuit, expression of emotions in romantic relationships, social exclusion, and body dissatisfaction. This journal is basic to any psychology collection.

5310. *Journal of Personality Assessment.* Former titles (until 1970): *Journal of Projective Techniques and Personality Assessment;* (until 1962): *Journal of Projective Techniques;* (until 1949): *Rorschach*

Research Exchange and Journal of Projective Techniques; (until 1946): *Rorschach Research Exchange.* [ISSN: 0022-3891] 1936. bi-m. GBP 371 print & online eds. Ed(s): Gregory Meyer. Lawrence Erlbaum Associates, Inc., 325 Chestnut St, Ste. 800, Philadelphia, PA 19106; journals@ erlbaum.com; http://www.leaonline.com. Illus., index, adv. Sample. Refereed. Circ: 2700. Vol. ends: Winter. Microform: PQC. Online: EBSCO Publishing, EBSCO Host; Gale; OCLC Online Computer Library Center, Inc.; OhioLINK; SwetsWise Online Content. Reprint: PSC. *Indexed:* ASSIA, AgeL, ECER, ExcerpMed, FR, H&SSA, PsycInfo, RiskAb, SSCI. *Aud.:* Ac, Sa.

This is the official publication of the Society for Personality Assessment. The journal publishes articles "dealing with the development, evaluation, refinement, and application of personality assessment methods." Papers may concern the empirical, theoretical, instructional, or professional aspects of using tests, data or an applied clinical assessment process. The journal seeks to advance the use of personality assessment methods in clinical, counseling, forensic, and health environments. Articles involve both normal and abnormal subjects. Areas where research is minimal is especially sought by this journal, such as "(a) systematic reviews or meta-analyses that summarize a body of evidence, (b) the effective integration of nomothetic empirical findings with the idiographic requirements of practice in which the assessor reasons through test and extra-test information to make individualized judgments and provide assessment feedback, and (c) the practical value of the clinical assessment process on the individuals receiving services and/or those who refer them for evaluation." Recent issues address development and preliminary validation of a Chinese version of the Buss-Perry Aggression Questionnaire in a population of Hong Kong Chinese; assessing self-critical perfectionism in clinical depression; and capturing the four-factor structure of psychopathy in college students via self-report. Academic libraries that support empirical studies in psychology and personality will want to collect this title. In addition to researchers and students taking advanced courses in assessment, those who will find this material useful include professionals in clinical, counseling, forensic, community, cross-cultural, education, and health psychology settings.

5311. *Journal of School Psychology.* [ISSN: 0022-4405] 1963. 6x/yr. EUR 421. Ed(s): Edward J Day, III. Pergamon, The Boulevard, Langford Ln, East Park, Kidlington, OX5 1GB, United Kingdom. Illus., index, adv. Refereed. Circ: 2000. Vol. ends: Dec. Microform: PQC. Online: EBSCO Publishing, EBSCO Host; Gale; IngentaConnect; OhioLINK; ScienceDirect; SwetsWise Online Content. *Indexed:* ABIn, ECER, ERIC, EduInd, L&LBA, PsycInfo, SSCI, SWR&A. *Aud.:* Ac, Sa.

Articles in this journal report on research and practice related to school psychology as both "scientific and an applied specialty." Averaging seven articles each, recent issues have looked at aggression and school social dynamics; universal screening for enhanced educational and mental health outcomes; and parent characteristics, economic stress and neighborhood context as predictors of parent involvement in preschool children's education. Abstracts and tables of contents are available on the publisher's web site. Along with such titles as *School Psychology Review* (below), this title is desirable for libraries that support programs in school psychology and related courses in education.

5312. *The Journal of Social Psychology.* [ISSN: 0022-4545] 1929. bi-m. USD 251 (Individuals, USD 217 print & online eds.; USD 40 newsstand/ cover). Ed(s): Jason Alyesh. Heldref Publications, 1319 18th St, NW, Washington, DC 20036-1802; subscribe@heldref.org; http://www.heldref.org. Illus., adv. Sample. Refereed. Circ: 1375 Paid. Microform: PQC. Online: Chadwyck-Healey Inc.; EBSCO Publishing, EBSCO Host; Florida Center for Library Automation; Gale; Northern Light Technology, Inc.; OCLC Online Computer Library Center, Inc.; ProQuest K-12 Learning Solutions; ProQuest LLC (Ann Arbor); H.W. Wilson. Reprint: PSC. *Indexed:* ABS&EES, ASSIA, AgeL, ArtHuCI, BAS, CJA, CWI, CommAb, ECER, ExcerpMed, FR, HEA, HRA, IBR, IBSS, IBZ, IPSA, L&LBA, LRI, PRA, PSA, PsycInfo, RILM, SSA, SSCI, SUSA, SWA, SWR&A, SociolAb. *Aud.:* Ac, Sa.

This journal was founded in 1929 by John Dewey and Carl Murchison. It publishes empirical research in basic and applied social psychology. The core areas of social and organizational psychology, attribution theory, attitudes, social influence, consumer behavior, decision-making, groups and teams, stereotypes and discrimination, interpersonal attraction, pro-social behavior, aggression, organizational behavior, leadership, and cross-cultural studies are all reflected in the journal's selection of articles. Recent articles cover the evolutionary psychology perspective on sex differences in exercise behaviors and motivations; the roles of ethnic identity and perceptions of social class in ethnic differences in endorsement of the Protestant work ethic; cross-cultural study of male physical attractiveness in Britain and Greece; pizza and pop and student identity: the role of referent group norms in health and unhealthy eating; and he moderating role of ambivalent sexism and the influence of power status on perception of rape victims and rapists. This is an important journal for academic behavioral and social science collections.

5313. *Journal of the History of the Behavioral Sciences.* [ISSN: 0022-5061] 1965. q. USD 411. Ed(s): Raymond E Fancher. John Wiley & Sons, Inc., 111 River St, Hoboken, NJ 07030-5774; uscs-wis@wiley.com; http://www3.interscience.wiley.com/journalfinder.html. Illus., index, adv. Refereed. Circ: 800 Paid. Vol. ends: Oct. Microform: PQC. Online: EBSCO Publishing, EBSCO Host; OhioLINK; SwetsWise Online Content; Wiley InterScience. Reprint: PSC. *Indexed:* ABS&EES, AbAn, AmH&L, ArtHuCI, FR, HistAb, IBSS, PhilInd, PsycInfo, SSCI. *Bk. rev.:* 3-5, 500-1,800 words. *Aud.:* Ac, Sa.

This journal, online via Wiley, is an international, multidisciplinary, scholarly, behavioral sciences publication. It focuses on the history of the social and behavioral sciences, inclusive of scientific, technical, institutional, and cultural history. Among its features are research papers, book reviews, news, and notes. Psychology, anthropology, sociology, psychiatry, psychoanalysis, economics, linguistics, communications, political science, history of science and medicine, historical theory, historiography, and the neurosciences are all represented. Recent issues look at local institutionalization, discontinuity, and German textbooks of psychology, 1816–1854; Joseph Jastrow, the psychology of deception, and the racial economy of observation; Ribot, Binet, and the emergence from the anthropological shadow; and schizophrenia as split personality: Jekyll and Hyde and the origins of the informal usage in the English language. Researchers and students of history, the social sciences, science, and medicine will find this journal important to their studies.

5314. *Journal of Vocational Behavior.* [ISSN: 0001-8791] 1971. 6x/yr. EUR 1317. Ed(s): Mark L Savickas. Academic Press, 525 B St, Ste 1900, San Diego, CA 92101-4495; apsubs@acad.com; http://www.elsevier.com/. Illus., index, adv. Refereed. Vol. ends: Dec. Online: EBSCO Publishing, EBSCO Host; Gale; IngentaConnect; OCLC Online Computer Library Center, Inc.; OhioLINK; ScienceDirect; SwetsWise Online Content. *Indexed:* ABIn, AgeL, CINAHL, ERIC, HEA, HRA, IBR, IBZ, PSA, PsycInfo, SSA, SSCI, SWA, SociolAb. *Aud.:* Ac, Sa.

This Elsevier online journal publishes theoretical and empirical research on vocational behavior and career development at any stage of life, particularly focused on the individual rather than an organization. Research areas include career choice; evaluation methods and assessment tools; job satisfaction; career adjustment; occupational stereotyping; work commitment; work stress; multiple role management; and work transitions. The October issue contains an annual review of research in vocational behavior. Recent issues look at self-esteem during university studies predicting career characteristics ten years later; beyond family-friendly: the construct and measurement of singles-friendly work culture; parental and school influences upon the career development of poor youth of color; parental influence on youth propensity to join the military; women's occupational career patterns over 27 years and relationship to family of origin, life careers, and wellness; and protege and mentor self-disclosure: levels and outcomes within formal mentoring dyads in a corporate context. Career counselors, human resource professionals, psychologists, and sociologists will find this journal relevant to their work and research.

5315. *Journal of Youth and Adolescence: a multidisciplinary research publication.* [ISSN: 0047-2891] 1972. bi-m. EUR 1398 print & online eds. Ed(s): Daniel Offer, Roger J R Levesque. Springer New York LLC, 233 Spring St, New York, NY 10013-1578; service-ny@springer.com; http://www.springer.com/. Illus., adv. Refereed. Vol. ends: Dec. Microform: PQC. Online: EBSCO Publishing, EBSCO Host; Florida

Center for Library Automation; Gale; IngentaConnect; OCLC Online Computer Library Center, Inc.; OhioLINK; Ovid Technologies, Inc.; ProQuest K-12 Learning Solutions; ProQuest LLC (Ann Arbor); Springer LINK; SwetsWise Online Content. Reprint: PSC. *Indexed:* ABIn, ASSIA, AgeL, Agr, CJA, CommAb, EAA, ERIC, EduInd, ExcerpMed, FR, HEA, IBR, IBZ, IMFL, PEI, PsycInfo, RILM, SFSA, SSA, SSCI, SUSA, SWA, SociolAb, V&AA. *Aud.:* Ac, Sa.

This multidisciplinary journal publishes empirical, experimental, and theoretical research and review articles in the fields of psychology, sociology, psychiatry, criminology, and education. The journal focuses especially on papers that address social policies or have policy implications with respect to society's response to youth and adolescence. Recent issues address implications of out-of-school activities for school engagement in African American adolescents; academic achievement and problem behaviors among Asian Pacific Islander American adolescents; the mediating effects of family processes and social competence and socio-environmental risk and adjustment in Latino youth; youth homelessness and social stigma; music taste groups and problem behavior; and the roles of age, social intelligence, and parent-child communication with respect to digital game playing and direct and indirect aggression in early adolescence. Clinical psychologists, social science researchers, educators, and healthcare and legal professionals will have interest in this journal.

5316. *Law and Human Behavior.* [ISSN: 0147-7307] 1977. bi-m. EUR 990 print & online eds. Ed(s): Richard L Wiener. Springer New York LLC, 233 Spring St, New York, NY 10013-1578; service-ny@springer.com; http://www.springer.com/. Illus., adv. Refereed. Vol. ends: Dec. Microform: PQC. Online: EBSCO Publishing, EBSCO Host; Gale; IngentaConnect; JSTOR (Web-based Journal Archive); OCLC Online Computer Library Center, Inc.; OhioLINK; Ovid Technologies, Inc.; ProQuest LLC (Ann Arbor); Springer LINK; SwetsWise Online Content. Reprint: PSC. *Indexed:* ABIn, AgeL, C&ISA, CJA, CJPI, CLI, CerAb, ExcerpMed, IAA, ILP, IMFL, LRI, PSA, PsycInfo, RiskAb, SSA, SSCI, SociolAb. *Aud.:* Ac, Sa.

This is the official journal of the American Psychological Association's Division 41, the American Psychology–Law Society. The journal publishes multidisciplinary articles on issues relating to human behavior and the law, legal system, or legal process. Papers include empirical studies, theoretical research, and reviews. A forum for debate is also featured. Recent issues address the mitigating effects of suspicion on post-identification feedback and on retrospective eyewitness memory; experimental examination of peremptory use and the Batson challenge procedure with respect to race-based judgments and race-neutral justifications; incarceration and recidivism among sexual offenders; effects of consent level and women's sexual history on rape allegations in relation to rape shield laws and sexual behavior evidence; and a prospective study of the influence of socioeconomic status and ethnicity on psychopathy and violent crime. Professionals and researchers in criminal justice, law, psychology, sociology, psychiatry, political science, education, communication, and other related social science areas will want access to this title through their libraries.

5317. *Media Psychology.* [ISSN: 1521-3269] 1999. bi-m. GBP 400 print & online eds. Ed(s): David R Roskos-Ewoldsen, Jennings Bryant. Lawrence Erlbaum Associates, Inc., 325 Chestnut St, Ste. 800, Philadelphia, PA 19106; journals@erlbaum.com; http://www.leaonline.com. Adv. Refereed. Reprint: PSC. *Indexed:* ArtHuCI, CommAb, PsycInfo, SSCI. *Aud.:* Ac, Sa.

This interdisciplinary, scholarly journal publishes research concerning the intersection of psychology and communication media. Empirical studies, theoretical papers, state-of-the-art reviews, and meta-analyses appear regularly in its contents. The effects, uses, and processes of media as they relate to psychology are primary topics. Various forms of communication, including mass media, television, telecommunications, computer networks, personal media, and multi-media are represented in the journal's articles. Recent issues look at content trends from 1997 to 2002 regarding sexual socialization messages on entertainment television; evidence for comparative media stereotyping with respect to activating and suppressing hostile and benevolent racism; attributional style, self-esteem, and celebrity worship; a mental models approach to the cultivation of social perceptions of Latinos; reducing children's susceptibility to commercials: mechanisms of factual and evaluative advertising interventions; and comparing television use and reading in children with ADHD and non-referred children across two age groups. Libraries supporting research and studies in communication and media, psychology, education, human development, and related social sciences will want this title.

5318. *Methodology: European journal of research methods for the behavioral and social sciences.* [ISSN: 1614-1881] 2005. a. (includes 4 quarterly online issues). EUR 128 print & online (Individuals, EUR 80 print & online). Ed(s): Dr. Michael Eid, Dr. Manuel Ato. Hogrefe & Huber Publishers, 875 Massachusetts Ave, 7th Fl, Cambridge, MA 02139; info@hhpub.com; http://www.hhpub.com/journals. Adv. Refereed. *Indexed:* PsycInfo. *Aud.:* Ac, Sa.

This official publication of the European Association of Methodology is the successor to two journals: *Metodologias de las Ciencias del Compor-tamiento* and *Methods of Psychological Research Online.* The association is a union of methodologists working in psychology, sociology, education, economics, and political science. The journal provides an interdisciplinary forum for communication and exchange among researchers in these fields. Data analysis, research methodology, and psychometrics are the journal's main focus. Features include papers on methodological research and its application; reviews; software information; and instructional articles of use to teachers. Recent issues look at power differences between the modified Brown-Forsythe and mixed-model approaches in repeated measures designs; visualizing multivariate dependencies with association chain graphs; implications of person fluctuation for the stability and validity of test scores; mixture of covariance structure models to identify different types of life style; and a theory-driven growth mixture model to explain travel-mode choice with experimental data in considering whether money matters. Tables of contents appear online on the publisher's web site. International researchers in education and the behavioral and social sciences will want this title.

5319. *Neuropsychology.* [ISSN: 0894-4105] 1987. bi-m. USD 322 (Individuals, USD 126). Ed(s): Stephen M Rao. American Psychological Association, 750 First St, N E, Washington, DC 20002-4242; journals@apa.org; http://www.apa.org. Illus. Refereed. Vol. ends: Dec. Reprint: PSC. *Indexed:* AgeL, ExcerpMed, FR, L&LBA, PsycInfo, SCI, SSCI. *Aud.:* Ac, Sa.

This journal publishes research on the brain and human cognitive, emotional, and behavioral functions. Research studies are generally empirical and represent basic or an integration of basic and applied research. Experimental, cognitive, and behavior studies are included, as well as articles that focus on improving the practice of neuropsychology and increase understanding of neuropsychological functions. Recent issues address visual processing and autism; hemispheric interactions in left-handed persons; post-traumatic stress disorder and alcohol abuse; and alerting and orienting in Alzheimer's disease. The highly rated journal is a primary one in neuropsychology.

5320. *Neuropsychology, Development and Cognition. Section A: Journal of Clinical and Experimental Neuropsychology.* Supersedes in part (in 1994): *Journal of Clinical and Experimental Neuropsychology;* Which was formerly: *Journal of Clinical Neuropsychology.* [ISSN: 1380-3395] 1979. 8x/yr. GBP 1324 print & online eds. Ed(s): Daniel Tranel, Wilfred G van Gorp. Psychology Press, 27 Church Rd, Hove, BN3 2FA, United Kingdom; info@psypress.co.uk; http://www.psypress.co.uk. Illus., index, adv. Sample. Refereed. Online: EBSCO Publishing, EBSCO Host; Gale; IngentaConnect; OCLC Online Computer Library Center, Inc.; SwetsWise Online Content. Reprint: PSC. *Indexed:* AgeL, ECER, ExcerpMed, FR, L&LBA, PsycInfo, SCI, SSCI. *Bk. rev.:* 0-3, 1,500 words. *Aud.:* Ac, Sa.

This is an international journal that publishes research on neuropsychology and promotes the "integration of theories, methods, and research findings in clinical and experimental neuropsychology." The journal's content features empirical research, theoretical and methodological papers, critical reviews, and case studies. Topics covered include the impact of injury or disease; psychometrics and assessment of brain damage; behavioral, cognitive, and pharmacological approaches to treatment and intervention; and psychosocial issues. Recent issues address evidence that response inhibition is a primary deficit in ADHD; patients with Huntington's disease have impaired awareness of cognitive, emotional, and functional abilities; neuropsychological prediction of attrition

due to death; a multicomponent of verbal short-term storage deficits in normal aging and Alzheimer's disease; a neuropsychological profile of off-diet adults with phenylketonuria; and the nonintentional processing of Arabic numbers in children. Libraries supporting programs in neuroscience, cognition, clinical psychology, psychiatry, and related disciplines will want to collect this title.

5321. *Organizational Behavior and Human Decision Processes.* Formerly (until 1985): *Organizational Behavior and Human Performance.* [ISSN: 0749-5978] 1966. 6x/yr. EUR 2188. Ed(s): D A Harrison. Academic Press, 525 B St, Ste 1900, San Diego, CA 92101-4495; apsubs@acad.com; http://www.elsevier.com/. Illus., index, adv. Refereed. Online: EBSCO Publishing, EBSCO Host; Gale; IngentaConnect; OCLC Online Computer Library Center, Inc.; OhioLINK; ScienceDirect; SwetsWise Online Content. *Indexed:* ABIn, AgeL, BPI, CINAHL, CJA, CommAb, ErgAb, FR, HRA, IBR, IBSS, IBZ, LRI, PsycInfo, RI-1, SSCI. *Aud.:* Ac, Sa.

This Elsevier title publishes research in organizational psychology and behavior, and human cognition, judgment, and decision-making. Features include empirical research, theoretical papers, literature reviews, and methodological articles. Among the topics found in its contents are cognition, perception, attitudes, emotion, well-being, motivation, choice, and performance. Individuals and variations of social groups are the subjects of these studies. Recent issues look at virtual team leadership and the effects of leadership style and communication medium on team interaction styles and outcomes; the monitoring and controlling of information repetition in evaluative judgments; social incentives for gender differences in the propensity to initiate negotiations; using advice from multiple sources to revise and improve judgments; social-identity functions of attraction to organizations; and getting groups to develop good strategies and the effects of reflexivity interventions on team process, team performance, and shared mental models. Libraries that support programs in organizational and industrial psychology, education, and related social sciences will want to collect this title.

5322. *Perceptual and Motor Skills.* Former titles (until 1952): *Perceptual and Motor Skills Research Exchange; Motor Skills Research Exchange.* [ISSN: 0031-5125] 1949. bi-m. USD 440 domestic; USD 495 foreign; USD 470 combined subscription domestic print & online eds. Ed(s): S A Isbell, Carol H Ammons. Ammons Scientific Ltd., PO Box 9229, Missoula, MT 59807; ejournalservices@ammonsscientific.com; http://www.ammonsscientific.com. Illus., index. Sample. Refereed. Circ: 2000. Online: EBSCO Publishing, EBSCO Host. *Indexed:* AbAn, AgeL, ArtHuCI, CINAHL, CommAb, ECER, ErgAb, ExcerpMed, HEA, HRIS, IBR, IBZ, L&LBA, MLA-IB, PEI, PsycInfo, RILM, SCI, SD, SSCI, SWA. *Bk. rev.:* 2-6, 120 words. *Aud.:* Ac, Sa.

This Ammons Scientific journal is a publication of the Department of Psychology, University of Louisville, although its editorial board is internationally based. The journal publishes experimental or theoretical articles, sometimes controversial, concerning perception or motor skills; methodological papers; and special reviews. Topics covered may relate to anthropology, physical education, physical therapy, orthopedics, sports psychology, consumer perception, music therapy, physics, aesthetics, education, or statistics. Recent issues look at background music as a quasi-clock in retrospective duration judgments; body-size perception, body-esteem, and parenting history in college women reporting a history of child abuse; construct validity of the Bender-Gestalt II in comparison with Wechsler Intelligence Scale for Children III; depth separation between foreground and background on visually induced perception of self-motion; and development of eating behavior by Japanese toddlers in a nursery school and the relationship to independent walking. The publisher's web site provides a searchable database of archived articles available online in print. Libraries supporting research and studies in psychology, education, physical education, and physical therapy will want to include his title in their collections.

5323. *Personality and Social Psychology Bulletin.* Formerly: *American Psychological Association. Division of Personality and Social Psychology. Proceedings.* [ISSN: 0146-1672] 1975. m. GBP 797. Ed(s): Judith M Harackiewicz. Sage Publications, Inc., 2455 Teller Rd, Thousand Oaks, CA 91320; info@sagepub.com; http://www.sagepub.com. Illus., adv. Refereed. Circ: 4250 Paid. Microform: PQC. Online: CSA;

EBSCO Publishing, EBSCO Host; Florida Center for Library Automation; Gale; HighWire Press; OCLC Online Computer Library Center, Inc.; OhioLINK; SAGE Publications, Inc., SAGE Journals Online; SwetsWise Online Content. Reprint: PSC. *Indexed:* ASSIA, AgeL, CJA, CommAb, IBR, IBZ, IMFL, L&LBA, PSA, PsycInfo, RILM, RiskAb, SFSA, SSA, SSCI, SUSA, SWA, SociolAb, V&AA. *Aud.:* Ac, Sa.

This is the official publication of the Society for Personality and Social Psychology. The bulletin provides an international forum for research in all areas of personality and social psychology. Articles reflect many schools of thought and new developments in the field. Based primarily on empirical research, papers on a variety of topics appear, including communication, gender and age stereotypes, interpersonal relationships, group psychology, prejudice, and self-consciousness. Special theme issues are periodically published. Themes have included motivational determinants of self-evaluation; autobiographical narratives; publication trends in the field; meta-analysis in personality and social psychology; and principles of psychology. Recent issues address smiling when distressed and when a smile is a frown turned upside down; potential moral stigma and reactions to sexually transmitted diseases: evidence for a disjunction fallacy; psychological mechanisms underlying the Kohler Motivation Gain; personal need for structure and creative performance and the moderating influence of fear of invalidity; the dynamics of personality states, goals, and well-being; and mindfulness and the intention-behavior relationship within the theory of planned behavior. Libraries supporting behavioral and social sciences, education, and industrial psychology will want to have this title.

5324. *Political Psychology.* [ISSN: 0162-895X] 1979. bi-m. Ed(s): Stanley Feldman, Leonie Huddy. Blackwell Publishing, Inc., Commerce Place, 350 Main St, Malden, MA 02148; customerservices@ blackwellpublishing.com; http://www.blackwellpublishing.com. Illus., adv. Refereed. Microform: PQC. Online: Blackwell Synergy; EBSCO Publishing, EBSCO Host; Gale; IngentaConnect; OCLC Online Computer Library Center, Inc.; OhioLINK; SwetsWise Online Content. Reprint: PSC. *Indexed:* ABIn, ABS&EES, ASSIA, ApEcolAb, ArtHuCI, CJA, IBSS, IPSA, PRA, PSA, PsycInfo, RiskAb, SSCI, SociolAb. *Bk. rev.:* 0-3, 500 words. *Aud.:* Ac, Sa.

This journal of the International Society of Political Psychology publishes empirical research, theoretical papers, and case studies on the interrelationships between psychology and the political process. This internationally focused publication is relevant to several disciplines including clinical and cognitive psychology, economics, history, international relations, philosophy, political science, sociology, personality, and social psychology. Recent issues look at the effects of dangerous and competitive worldviews on right-wing authoritarianism and social dominance orientation over a five-month period; integrative complexity of 41 U.S. presidents; the role of moral emotions in predicting support for political actions in post-war Iraq; contemporary political and social attitudes among Orange Order members in Northern Ireland; and the political color line in America: many "peoples of color" or "black exceptionalism." Libraries supporting programs in the behavioral and social sciences, political science, education, and related fields will want this title.

5325. *Professional Psychology: Research and Practice.* Formerly (until 1982): *Professional Psychology.* [ISSN: 0735-7028] 1969. bi-m. USD 378 (Individuals, USD 126). Ed(s): Dr. Michael C Roberts. American Psychological Association, 750 First St, N E, Washington, DC 20002-4242; journals@apa.org; http://www.apa.org. Illus., index, adv. Refereed. Vol. ends: Jan. Microform: PQC. Online: Pub.; CSA; EBSCO Publishing, EBSCO Host; OCLC Online Computer Library Center, Inc.; OhioLINK; Ovid Technologies, Inc.; ProQuest LLC (Ann Arbor); ScienceDirect. Reprint: PSC. *Indexed:* AgeL, CJA, PsycInfo, RI-1, SFSA, SSCI. *Aud.:* Ac, Sa.

This journal publishes theoretical and empirical articles for the clinician on applied psychology. Scientific and evidence-based articles on assessment, treatment, and practice implications are stressed. The journal includes literature reviews, case studies, standards-based practice articles, public policy research, and general research of interest to clinical psychologists. Current topics include health psychology, community psychology, psychology of women, clinical neuropsychology, family psychology, psychology of ethnicity and culture, and

forensic psychology. Brief reports also appear. Recent issues look at psychologists as legislators; the collision of laws and ethics; burnout and coping; career-sustaining work behaviors; college student alcohol abuse; evaluating parents in child-protective decisions; Sprague's law; outpatient mental health at a U.S. airbase in Iraq; and attachment in the supervisory relationship. This is a core journal for clinical psychologists in practice, research, and training, and for the libraries that support them.

5326. *PsycCritiques.* Former titles (until 2005): *Contemporary Psychology: A P A Review of Books;* (until 1999): *Contemporary Psychology.* [ISSN: 1554-0138] 1956. w. Non-members, USD 130. Ed(s): Danny Wedding. American Psychological Association, 750 First St, N E, Washington, DC 20002-4242; journals@apa.org; http://www.apa.org. Illus., index, adv. Circ: 2900 Paid. Reprint: PSC. *Indexed:* ArtHuCI, BRI, CBRI, IBR, IBZ, SSCI. *Bk. rev.:* 50-60, 100-1,500 words. *Aud.:* Ga, Ac, Sa.

This American Psychological Association product is more than a journal. It is a searchable electronic database of book reviews in psychology. Formerly published in print as the journal *Contemporary Psychology: APA Review of Books,* in its new electronic format, *PsycCritiques* provides access to current reviews and backfiles from 1956 forward. Each weekly release delivers approximately 18–20 reviews of current psychological books. Also included are reviews of popular films and videos from a psychological perspective, comparative reviews, and occasional retrospective reviews. Faculty, librarians, students, and practitioners will benefit by having easy access to this database, in order to identify literature for research, course studies, and collection development, and to stay up-to-date with the latest psychological thinking.

5327. *Psychoanalytic Psychology.* [ISSN: 0736-9735] 1984. q. USD 375 (Members, USD 54; Non-members, USD 77). Ed(s): Dr. Joseph Reppen. American Psychological Association, 750 First St, N E, Washington, DC 20002-4242; journals@apa.org; http://www.apa.org. Adv. Refereed. Circ: 4500 Paid. Reprint: PSC. *Indexed:* ExcerpMed, PsycInfo, SSCI. *Aud.:* Ac, Sa.

This journal publishes original manuscripts concerning the interaction between psychoanalysis and psychology. It focuses on issues raised in either psychology or psychoanalysis that impact thinking in the other. Research and clinical papers, literature reviews, clinical notes, brief reports, commentary, and book reviews are included. Recent issues provide articles on skin color and the therapeutic relationship; death and annihilation anxieties in anorexia, bulimia, and self-mutilation; anxiety, authenticity, and trauma and the relevance of Heidegger; the erosion of the psychoanalytic profession; right-wing authoritarian beliefs originating in psychological conflict; postpartum depression; Holocaust trauma; lusting for death; and Theodor Reik. This is a core journal in the field of psychoanalysis.

5328. *Psychological Assessment.* [ISSN: 1040-3590] 1989. q. USD 360 (Individuals, USD 126). Ed(s): Dr. Milton E Strauss. American Psychological Association, 750 First St, N E, Washington, DC 20002-4242; journals@apa.org; http://www.apa.org. Illus., adv. Refereed. Vol. ends: Feb. Reprint: PSC. *Indexed:* AgeL, CJA, ERIC, ErgAb, ExcerpMed, FR, PsycInfo, SSCI, SWR&A. *Aud.:* Ac, Sa.

This journal publishes empirical research on measurement and evaluation relevant to the practice of clinical psychology. Articles concern such topics as assessment processes and methods; decision-making models; personality?social psychology; biological psychology; validation; application of assessment instruments; assessment of personality; psychopathological symptoms; cognitive and neuropsychological processes; and interpersonal behavior. The journal focuses on diagnosis, evaluation, and effective interventions. Case studies, reviews, and theoretical articles relevant to assessment and clinical settings are included. Recent issues look at developing a social phobia and anxiety scale; social phobia in youth; the reliability and validity of the psychopathology checklists with Latino, European American, and African American male inmates; separating optimism and pessimism and the revised life orientation test; the formal cognitive model of the go/no-go discrimination task; and acceptance in romantic relationships and the partner behavior inventory. This PsycArticles journal is one to make available to clinical psychology researchers, students, and practitioners.

5329. *Psychological Bulletin.* [ISSN: 0033-2909] 1904. bi-m. USD 600 (Individuals, USD 208). Ed(s): Dr. Harris M Cooper. American Psychological Association, 750 First St, N E, Washington, DC 20002-4242; journals@apa.org; http://www.apa.org. Illus., index, adv. Refereed. Vol. ends: Dec. Microform: PMC; PQC. Online: Pub.; CSA; EBSCO Publishing, EBSCO Host; OCLC Online Computer Library Center, Inc.; OhioLINK; Ovid Technologies, Inc.; ProQuest LLC (Ann Arbor); ScienceDirect. Reprint: PSC. *Indexed:* ABIn, ASSIA, AgeL, ArtHuCI, CJA, EAA, ERIC, ErgAb, FR, IBR, IBSS, IBZ, MLA-IB, PsycInfo, SCI, SSCI, SWA, SWR&A. *Aud.:* Ac, Sa.

This journal publishes integrative reviews, research syntheses, and pertinent expository articles that focus on empirical studies in scientific psychology. Articles summarize conclusions of past research studies that address similar hypotheses. Primary research is included for illustrative purposes. Research syntheses assess the current state of knowledge on a topic, the strengths and weakness of past research, unresolved issues, and directions for future research. Integrative reviews reveal connections between areas of research. Broad topics include the interface of psychological sciences and society and evaluations of programs in applied psychology. Recent issues provide articles on cancer survival and hope and evidence; reservation-dwelling American Indian alcohol abuse; cognitive styles; disturbed dreaming; gender differences in post-traumatic stress disorder; and anxiety disorders and tobacco use. This PsycArticles publication is a core journal for students of science and psychology. See *Psychological Methods* for methodological articles and *Psychological Review* for original theoretical articles.

5330. *Psychological Inquiry: an international journal of peer commentary and review.* [ISSN: 1047-840X] 1990. q. GBP 412 print & online eds. Ed(s): Leonard L Martin, Ralph Erber. Lawrence Erlbaum Associates, Inc., 325 Chestnut St, Ste. 800, Philadelphia, PA 19106; journals@erlbaum.com; http://www.leaonline.com. Illus., adv. Refereed. Vol. ends: No. 4. Reprint: PSC. *Indexed:* PsycInfo, SSA, SSCI, SociolAb. *Aud.:* Ac, Sa.

This international journal provides a forum for discussion in the fields of social psychology and personality. Articles discuss theoretical and meta-theoretical concerns. Issues are theme oriented, containing a primary article followed by peer commentaries and the author's response. Recent target articles include building a better process model; evolutionary foundations of cultural variation-evoked culture and mate preferences; selective investment theory: recasting the functional significance of close relationships; and seven possible social-psychological wisdoms. Libraries that support psychology programs will want this title for patrons who perform in-depth topical study.

5331. *Psychological Medicine.* [ISSN: 0033-2917] 1970. m. GBP 560. Ed(s): Kenneth Kendler, Eugene Paykel. Cambridge University Press, The Edinburgh Bldg, Shaftesbury Rd, Cambridge, CB2 2RU, United Kingdom; journals@cambridge.org; http://www.journals.cambridge.org. Illus., adv. Refereed. Vol. ends: Nov. CD-ROM: Ovid Technologies, Inc. Microform: PQC. Online: Pub.; EBSCO Publishing, EBSCO Host; OCLC Online Computer Library Center, Inc.; OhioLINK; Ovid Technologies, Inc.; SwetsWise Online Content. Reprint: PSC. *Indexed:* ASSIA, AgeL, ArtHuCI, CABA, CINAHL, CJA, ChemAb, DSA, ExcerpMed, FR, H&SSA, IBR, IBZ, IMFL, PsycInfo, RRTA, RiskAb, SCI, SSCI. *Bk. rev.:* 0-2, 500. *Aud.:* Ac, Sa.

This international journal publishes articles in psychiatry, psychology, and basic science. It features empirical, theoretical, and research review papers as well as book reviews. Recent issues look at a meta-analysis of predicting suicide and non-fatal self-harm with the Beck Hopelessness Scale; whether bereavement-related depression is different than non-bereavement-related depression; shared genetic and environmental risk factors between undue influence of body shape and weight on self-evaluation and dimensions of perfectionism; the heritability of cluster A personality disorders assessed by both personal interview and questionnaire; cognitive functioning in patients with familial bipolar I disorder and their unaffected relatives; a case-control study of parental separation, loss, and psychosis in different ethnic groups; and delusional ideation and manic symptoms in potential future emigrants in Uganda. Libraries serving psychiatrists, clinical psychologists, and medical and mental health care professionals will benefit by having this title.

5332. *Psychological Methods.* [ISSN: 1082-989X] 1996. q. USD 322 (Individuals, USD 84). Ed(s): Dr. Scott E Maxwell. American Psychological Association, 750 First St, N E, Washington, DC 20002-4242; journals@apa.org; http://www.apa.org. Illus., index, adv. Refereed. Vol. ends: Feb. Online: Pub.; CSA; EBSCO Publishing, EBSCO Host; OCLC Online Computer Library Center, Inc.; OhioLINK; Ovid Technologies, Inc.; ProQuest LLC (Ann Arbor); ScienceDirect. Reprint: PSC. *Indexed:* ERIC, ErgAb, FR, PsycInfo, SSCI, SWR&A. *Aud.:* Ac.

This journal publishes theoretical, quantitative, empirical, and methodological articles on psychological research; reviews of methodological issues; tutorials; articles regarding innovative new research procedures; papers on teaching quantitative methods; and statistical software reviews. The journal focuses on the development and dissemination of innovative research design and methods for collecting, analyzing, understanding, and interpreting psychological data. Empirical and theoretical articles on tests or test construction are broad in nature. Research articles illustrate through examples how procedures qualitatively improve psychological research. Articles may also promote effective communication about substantive and methodological issues. Recent issues cover the following topics: mixture distribution latent state-trait analysis; consistency of individual classification using short scales; random intercept item factor analysis; using effect sizes for research reporting; when effect sizes disagree; confidence intervals and replication and where the mean will fall; and information-theoretic latent distribution modeling. This PsycArticles journal is for professional researchers, teaching faculty, and graduate and undergraduate students of psychology.

5333. *Psychological Reports.* [ISSN: 0033-2941] 1955. bi-m. USD 440 domestic; USD 495 foreign; USD 470 combined subscription domestic print & online eds. Ed(s): Douglas Ammons, Carol H Ammons. Ammons Scientific Ltd., PO Box 9229, Missoula, MT 59807; ejournalservices@ammonsscientific.com; http://www.ammonsscientific.com. Illus. Sample. Refereed. Circ: 1800. Online: EBSCO Publishing, EBSCO Host. *Indexed:* ABS&EES, AgeL, ArtHuCI, CINAHL, CJA, CommAb, ErgAb, ExcerpMed, HEA, IBR, IBZ, IMFL, LRI, PsycInfo, RI-1, RILM, SCI, SFSA, SSCI, SWA. *Bk. rev.:* 3, 50-250 words. *Aud.:* Ac, Sa.

This journal publishes experimental, theoretical, speculative, and controversial articles in the field of general psychology. Sections for both comments and special reviews appear regularly. The journal has a scientific, interdisciplinary focus, with papers relevant to anthropology, physical education, physical therapy, orthopedics, sports psychology, consumer perceptions, music theory, physics, aesthetics, education, and statistics. Encouraging scientific originality, creativity, and understanding is a goal of *Psychological Reports*. Recent issues address a cluster analysis of perfectionism among competitive athletes; a comparison of depression in children with and without mothers; a simplified version of the Symlog Trait Rating Form; academic cheating as a function of defense mechanisms and object relations; achievement goals and engagement in individual and collective learning activities; anxiety in Kuwaiti and American college students; the association of pathological gambling with depression in Scotland; the attitude toward euthanasia in relation to death anxiety among a sample of 343 nurses in India; and attitudes toward empathy in domestic dogs and cats. The publisher's web site provides a searchable database of archived articles, available online. Libraries supporting research and studies in psychology, education, physical education, and physical therapy will want to include this title in their collections.

5334. *Psychological Review.* [ISSN: 0033-295X] 1894. q. USD 490 (Individuals, USD 156). Ed(s): Dr. Keith Rayner. American Psychological Association, 750 First St, N E, Washington, DC 20002-4242; journals@apa.org; http://www.apa.org. Illus., index. Refereed. Vol. ends: Dec. Microform: PMC; PQC. Online: Pub.; CSA; EBSCO Publishing, EBSCO Host; OCLC Online Computer Library Center, Inc.; OhioLINK; Ovid Technologies, Inc.; ProQuest LLC (Ann Arbor); ScienceDirect. Reprint: PSC. *Indexed:* AgeL, ERIC, ErgAb, FR, IBR, IBSS, IBZ, L&LBA, MLA-IB, PhilInd, PsycInfo, RILM, RiskAb, SCI, SSA, SSCI, SWA, SWR&A, SociolAb. *Aud.:* Ac, Sa.

The focus of this APA PsycArticles journal is scientific psychology. Its articles present both significant contributions that advance theory and systematic evaluations of alternative theories. Literature reviews, articles regarding methodology and research design, and empirical reports are not included. Theoretical notes and commentary on scientific psychology are part of the contents. Notes may be discussions of earlier articles. Comments may apply to theoretical models in a given domain, may be critiques of alternative theories, or may be metatheoretical commentary on theory testing. Recent issues look at parallel and serial processes in visual search; adaptive learning and risk-taking; the nature of individual differences in working memory capacity; neural dynamics of autistic behavior; the place of white in a world of grays: a double-anchoring theory of lightness perception; decision-making models of remember-know judgments; and using dynamic field theory to rethink habituation. This is a basic resource for academic psychology collections.

5335. *Psychological Science.* [ISSN: 0956-7976] 1990. m. GBP 1817 print & online eds. Ed(s): James E Cutting. Blackwell Publishing Ltd., 9600 Garsington Rd, Oxford, OX4 2ZG, United Kingdom; customerservices@ blackwellpublishing.com; http://www.blackwellpublishing.com. Illus., adv. Sample. Refereed. Online: Blackwell Synergy; EBSCO Publishing, EBSCO Host; Gale; IngentaConnect; OCLC Online Computer Library Center, Inc.; OhioLINK; SwetsWise Online Content. Reprint: PSC. *Indexed:* AgeL, ApEcolAb, ArtHuCI, CJA, ErgAb, HEA, IBSS, L&LBA, PRA, PsycInfo, RILM, SSA, SSCI, SWR&A, SociolAb. *Aud.:* Ac, Sa.

This is the official journal of the Association for Psychological Science. It publishes empirical, theoretical, and applied psychology articles, papers concerning psychological issues and government and public affairs, and reports summarizing recent research developments. Subject areas include brain and behavior, clinical science, cognition, learning and memory, social psychology, and developmental psychology. Recent issues address separating sustained from transient aspects of cognitive control thought suppression; discrimination of possible and impossible objects in infancy; pain tolerance selectively increased by a sweet-smelling odor; subtle linguistic cues affecting children's motivation; dissociative tendencies and memory performance on direct-forgetting tasks; and young children learning Spanish making rapid use of grammatical gender in spoken word recognition. Libraries supporting general and advanced psychology programs will benefit by having this title.

5336. *Psychological Science in the Public Interest.* [ISSN: 1529-1006] 2000. 3x/yr. Ed(s): Stephen J Ceci. Blackwell Publishing Ltd., 9600 Garsington Rd, Oxford, OX4 2ZG, United Kingdom; customerservices@ blackwellpublishing.com; http://www.blackwellpublishing.com. Reprint: PSC. *Indexed:* ApEcolAb, CJA, IBSS, PsycInfo, RiskAb. *Aud.:* Ga, Ac.

This is a journal of the Association for Psychological Science. Its goal is to provide definitive assessments of topics where psychological science may have the potential to inform and improve the lives of individuals and the well-being of society. Each issue features an original article along with an editorial commentary. Recent issues address enhancing the effectiveness of work groups and teams; improving the probative value of eyewitness evidence; public policy, theory, and practice implications of risk and rationality in adolescent decision-making; the effects of neurotoxicants, micronutrients, and social environments on children's development; and the promise and reality of diverse teams in organizations. Both academic and public libraries will benefit by having this title.

5337. *Psychology & Health: an international journal.* [ISSN: 0887-0446] 1987. bi-m. GBP 1043 print & online eds. Ed(s): Paul Norman. Routledge, 4 Park Sq, Milton Park, Abingdon, OX14 4RN, United Kingdom; info@routledge.co.uk; http://www.routledge.co.uk. Illus., adv. Sample. Refereed. Vol. ends: No. 6. Online: EBSCO Publishing, EBSCO Host; Gale; IngentaConnect; OCLC Online Computer Library Center, Inc.; SwetsWise Online Content. Reprint: PSC. *Indexed:* AgeL, CINAHL, PsycInfo, SSCI, SWA. *Bk. rev.:* 0-3, 300. *Aud.:* Ac, Sa.

This international journal is a publication of the European Health Psychology Society. The journal focuses on the psychological approaches to health and illness. Subjects covered include psychological aspects of physical illness; treatment and recovery; psychosocial factors of physical illnesses; health attitudes; health behavior; preventive health; and health care systems. The journal publishes empirical research, papers presenting new psychological approaches and interventions; reviews; and short reports. Recent issues look at the effects of a short self-management intervention for patients with asthma and diabetes and the evaluation of health-related quality of life using then-test

methodology; gender-specific implications of trait dominance and cardiovascular reactivity to social and non-social stressors; sex differences in emotional and behavioral responses to HIV+ individuals' expression of distress; the inhibitory effect of a distressing anti-smoking message on risk perceptions in smokers; and motivational mediators of personality and riskier sexual behavior. Libraries serving researchers and students of public health, psychology, and medicine will want to have this title.

5338. *Psychology of Women Quarterly.* [ISSN: 0361-6843] 1976. q. GBP 255 print & online eds. Ed(s): Jayne E Stake. Blackwell Publishing, Inc., Commerce Place, 350 Main St, Malden, MA 02148; customerservices@ blackwellpublishing.com; http://www.blackwellpublishing.com. Illus., index, adv. Refereed. Vol. ends: Dec. Microform: PQC. Online: Blackwell Synergy; EBSCO Publishing, EBSCO Host; Gale; IngentaConnect; OCLC Online Computer Library Center, Inc.; OhioLINK; Ovid Technologies, Inc.; SwetsWise Online Content. Reprint: PSC. *Indexed:* ABS&EES, ASSIA, AbAn, AgeL, ApEcolAb, CJA, FemPer, H&SSA, HEA, HRA, IBR, IBSS, IBZ, IMFL, PsycInfo, RILM, RiskAb, SFSA, SSA, SSCI, SUSA, SWA, SWR&A, SociolAb, V&AA, WSA. *Bk. rev.:* 4-10, 500-1,000 words. *Aud.:* Ga, Ac, Sa.

This journal publishes empirical, qualitative, theoretical articles related to the psychology of women and gender. It also features critical reviews and invited book reviews. A wide range of topics have been covered, including career choice and preparation; mental health and well-being; education; lifespan role development; management and performance variables; violence, harassment, and abuse; sexuality and sexual orientation; social and cognitive processes; ethnic, minority, and cross-cultural issues; and therapeutic concerns. Recent issues address feminism as a context for women's lives in growing up and and growing older; the F word and the compatibility of feminism with beauty and romance; body objectification and depression in adolescents and the role of gender, shame, and rumination; development and psychometric evaluation of the interpersonal sexual objectification scale; deciding whom to tell: expectations and outcomes of rape survivors' first disclosures; and the impact of training and conflict avoidance on responses to sexual harassment. Libraries supporting research and study in psychology, women's and gender studies, and related social sciences will benefit by having this title.

5339. *Psychology, Public Policy, and Law.* [ISSN: 1076-8971] 1995. q. USD 414 (Individuals, USD 84). Ed(s): Steven Penrod. American Psychological Association, 750 First St, N E, Washington, DC 20002-4242; journals@apa.org; http://www.apa.org. Illus., adv. Sample. Refereed. Vol. ends: Dec. Reprint: PSC. *Indexed:* CJA, PsycInfo, SSCI. *Aud.:* Ga, Ac, Sa.

This PsychArticles title is the official law review of the University of Arizona College of Law and the University of Miami School of Law. The journal is interdisciplinary in that it publishes material concerned with the science of psychology and related public policy and legal issues. Articles critically evaluate contributions from the field of psychology to the fields of public policy and law; assess public policy and legal alternatives in light of psychological research and knowledge; articulate the need for psychological research to address public policy and legal issues; present the findings of psychological research that deals with public policy and legal issues; and examine public policy and legal issues with respect to the methods or procedures followed in psychology. Examples of issues include policies regarding risk assessment, food labeling, family leave and retirement policies, human subjects, and informed consent procedures. Although empirical data is published, lengthy empirical research studies are not, unless they are multi-jurisdictional, longitudinal, broad in scope, or of major significance. Recent issues contain articles on moderators of non-verbal indicators in deception; sexually violent predators in the courtroom; evaluation of simultaneous and sequential lineups; and incapacity in European mental health laws. The journal's peer review process involves both psychologists and lawyers. The journal is intended for academic scholars, public policy experts, and legal professionals.

5340. *Psychology Today.* [ISSN: 0033-3107] 1967. bi-m. USD 15.97 domestic; USD 23.97 Canada; USD 27.97 elsewhere. Ed(s): Kaja Perina, Lybi Ma. Sussex Publishers Inc., 115 E 23rd St, 9th Fl, New York, NY 10010; http://www.sussexpub.com. Illus., index, adv. Circ: 350000 Paid. CD-ROM: ProQuest LLC (Ann Arbor). Microform: NBI. Online: The

Dialog Corporation; EBSCO Publishing, EBSCO Host; Florida Center for Library Automation; Gale; Micromedia ProQuest; Northern Light Technology, Inc.; OCLC Online Computer Library Center, Inc.; ProQuest K-12 Learning Solutions; ProQuest LLC (Ann Arbor); H.W. Wilson. *Indexed:* ABIn, AgeL, BRD, BRI, BiolDig, CBCARef, CBRI, CINAHL, CJA, CPerI, ECER, ExcerpMed, FLI, FutSurv, LRI, MASUSE, MusicInd, PRA, RGPR, RI-1, SSCI. *Aud.:* Hs, Ga, Ac.

This is a popular psychology magazine that focuses on articles in the areas of relationships, personal growth, work, health, nutrition, parenting, learning, the brain, and social psychology. Recent issues look at the law of self-mastery and emotions; dogs as man's best friends; obesity and the quest to be thin; professors and the collegiate mental health crisis; fighting flight fatigue; drugs for sleep; chocolate; and physical beauty and health. Both public and academic libraries will find this publication much sought after by patrons.

5341. *Psychometrika: a journal devoted to the development of psychology as a quantitative rational science.* [ISSN: 0033-3123] 1936. q. EUR 210 print & online eds. Ed(s): Brian Junker. Springer New York LLC, 233 Spring St, New York, NY 10013-1578; journals@springer-ny.com; http://www.springer.com/. Illus., index, adv. Refereed. Circ: 2200. Vol. ends: Dec. Microform: PQC. Online: EBSCO Publishing, EBSCO Host; ProQuest LLC (Ann Arbor); Springer LINK; SwetsWise Online Content. Reprint: PSC. *Indexed:* CCMJ, CommAb, ERIC, ErgAb, FR, IBR, IBZ, MSN, MathR, PsycInfo, SCI, SSCI. *Bk. rev.:* 2-3, 350-1,200 words. *Aud.:* Ac, Sa.

This is a publication of the Psychometric Society, which is an international organization devoted to quantitative measurement in psychology, education, and the social sciences. The journal publishes scientific articles on quantitative models, statistical methods, and mathematical techniques in psychology and education. Recent issues address propensity score adjustment for multiple group structural equation modeling; component models for fuzzy data; logistic approximation to the normal and the KL rationale; acquiescent responding in balanced multidimensional scales and exploratory factor analysis; and measurement without Cooper instruments and experiment without complete control. Libraries supporting programs involving empirical research in psychology and education will want this title.

5342. *Psychonomic Bulletin & Review.* Formerly (until 1994): *Psychonomic Society. Bulletin.* [ISSN: 1069-9384] 1973. bi-m. USD 224 domestic; USD 240 foreign. Ed(s): Robert M Nosofsky. Psychonomic Society, Inc., 1710 Fortview Rd, Austin, TX 78704; jbellquist@psychonomic.org; http://www.psychonomic.org. Illus., index, adv. Circ: 2200. Vol. ends: Dec. Microform: PQC. Online: EBSCO Publishing, EBSCO Host; Gale; IngentaConnect; OCLC Online Computer Library Center, Inc.; ProQuest LLC (Ann Arbor); SwetsWise Online Content. *Indexed:* AgeL, BiolAb, ErgAb, FR, HEA, IBR, IBZ, IMFL, L&LBA, MLA-IB, PsycInfo, RILM, SSCI. *Aud.:* Ac.

This is a publication of the Psychonomic Society, which promotes communication of scientific research in psychology and related fields. The bulletin publishes articles in all areas of psychology. Empirical and experimental research, reviews, theoretical papers, and brief reports are all included. The contents cover most areas of psychology including animal behavior, attention and perception, cognitive psychology, psycholinguistics, neuroscience, and social cognition. Recent issues address imagination and memory; subjective age across the lifespan; age and sex differences in children's spatial search strategies; change blindness and the primacy of object appearance; spatial working memory and inhibition of return; and distraction as a determinant of processing speed. Libraries supporting studies in psychology on all levels will benefit by having this title.

5343. *Psychophysiology: an international journal.* Formerly: *Psychophysiology Newsletter.* [ISSN: 0048-5772] 1964. bi-m. GBP 359 print & online eds. Ed(s): Dr. Robert F Simons. Blackwell Publishing, Inc., Commerce Place, 350 Main St, Malden, MA 02148; customerservices@blackwellpublishing.com; http://www.blackwellpublishing.com. Illus., index, adv. Refereed. Circ: 2100. Vol. ends: Nov. Microform: PQC. Online: Blackwell Synergy; Cambridge University Press; EBSCO Publishing, EBSCO Host; Gale;

IngentaConnect; OCLC Online Computer Library Center, Inc.; OhioLINK; SwetsWise Online Content. Reprint: PSC. *Indexed:* AgeL, BiolAb, CABA, DSA, ErgAb, ExcerpMed, FR, IBR, IBZ, L&LBA, PsycInfo, RILM, SCI, SSCI. *Bk. rev.:* Number and length vary. *Aud.:* Ac, Sa.

This is an international publication of the Society for Psychophysiological Research. As the first journal in its field, it publishes research on the physiological and psychological aspects of brain and behavior. It features empirical, theoretical, and methodological papers, literature reviews, book reviews, brief reports, meeting announcements, and fellowship opportunities. Topics covered include psychiatry, psychology, cognitive science, cognitive and affective neuroscience, social science, health science, behavioral medicine, and biomedical engineering. Recent issues look at differential engagement of anterior cingulate cortex subdivisions for cognitive and emotional function; chest pain and the inverse association with blood pressure during exercise among individuals being assessed for coronary heart disease; validation of sternal skin conductance for detection of hot flashes in prostate cancer survivors; and cerebral blood flow in essential hypotension during emotional activation. Libraries supporting researchers in psychophysiology, cognitive and neuroscience, psychology, psychiatry, and related biological and social sciences will benefit by collecting this title.

5344. *Psychosomatic Medicine.* [ISSN: 0033-3174] 1938. bi-m. USD 859 (Individuals, USD 393). Ed(s): David S Sheps. Lippincott Williams & Wilkins, 530 Walnut St, Philadelphia, PA 19106-3621; custserv@lww.com; http://www.lww.com. Illus., index, adv. Refereed. Circ: 2152 Paid. Vol. ends: Dec. CD-ROM: Ovid Technologies, Inc. Microform: RPI. Online: EBSCO Publishing, EBSCO Host; HighWire Press; Ovid Technologies, Inc. *Indexed:* AgeL, BiolAb, CABA, ChemAb, ExcerpMed, H&SSA, HortAb, PsycInfo, RRTA, RiskAb, SCI, SSCI, WAE&RSA. *Bk. rev.:* 4, 900-1,500 words. *Aud.:* Ac, Sa.

This international, interdisciplinary journal is the official publication of the American Psychosomatic Society. The journal publishes empirical, experimental, and clinical studies concerning the relationships among social, psychological, and behavioral factors and physiological issues in both humans and animals. Articles are relevant to the disciplines of behavioral biology, psychiatry, psychology, physiology, anthropology, and clinical medicine. Libraries supporting research in these disciplines will want to have this title. Recent issues address depressive symptoms in subjects with diagnosed and undiagnosed Type 2 diabetes; facets of openness and prediction of mortality in patients with cardiac disease; P-wave dispersion in panic disorder; predictors of irritable bowel-type symptoms and healthcare-seeking behavior among adults with celiac disease; perfectionism and the cortisol response to psychosocial stress in men; and the use of social words in autobiographies and longevity.

Psychotherapy Networker. See Family and Marriage section.

5345. *Rehabilitation Psychology.* Formerly (until 1971): *Psychological Aspects of Disability.* [ISSN: 0090-5550] 1954. q. USD 360 (Individuals, USD 84). Ed(s): Dr. Timothy R Elliott. American Psychological Association, 750 First St, N E, Washington, DC 20002-4242; journals@apa.org; http://www.apa.org. Illus., adv. Refereed. Vol. ends: Jan. Reprint: PSC. *Indexed:* AgeL, CINAHL, ExcerpMed, IMFL, PsycInfo, SSCI, SWR&A. *Bk. rev.:* 0-3, 400-600 words. *Aud.:* Ac, Sa.

This PsycArticles scholarly journal supports the work of the American Psychological Association's Division 22 to advance the science and practice of rehabilitation psychology. The journal's scope broadly includes the many factors that affect persons with disabilities or chronic illness. Articles address biological, psychological, social, environmental, and political factors. Several types of articles appear, including "experimental investigations, survey research, evaluations of specific interventions, outcome studies, historical perspectives, relevant public policy issues, conceptual/theoretical formulations with implications for clinical practice, reviews of empirical research, detailed case studies, and professional issues." The journal encompasses scientific papers that increase understanding of psychological problems in rehabilitation and that present solutions for lessening such problems. Recent issues look at factors affecting depression among people with chronic musculoskeletal pain; predicting adherence to exercise-based therapy; communal behavior and psychological adjustment of family caregivers and persons with spinal-cord injuries; and depression symptoms of long-term adult burn survivors. This is a unique and important journal for public health, medical, social science, and psychology collections.

5346. *School Psychology Quarterly.* Formerly (until 1990): *Professional School Psychology.* [ISSN: 1045-3830] 1960. q. USD 299 (Individuals, USD 95). Ed(s): Rik Carl D'Amato. American Psychological Association, 750 First St, N E, Washington, DC 20002-4242; journals@apa.org; http://www.apa.org. Illus., adv. Refereed. Circ: 2700. Vol. ends: Winter. *Indexed:* ERIC, L&LBA, PsycInfo, SSCI. *Bk. rev.:* 0-1, 600 words. *Aud.:* Ac, Sa.

This is the official journal of the American Psychological Association's Division of School Psychology. The journal publishes empirical, theoretical, and practice-related studies that apply scientific methods to school psychology. Recent issues address social support as a buffer in the relationship between socioeconomic status and academic performance; assessing pre-service teachers' training in empirically validated behavioral instruction practices; substance use as a robust correlate of school outcome measures for ethnically diverse adolescents of Asian/Pacific Islander ancestry; and children's emotional competence and attentional competence in early elementary school. Libraries supporting programs in general psychology, clinical psychology, child psychology, and education will want to have this title.

5347. *School Psychology Review.* Formerly (until 1979): *School Psychology Digest.* [ISSN: 0279-6015] 1972. q. USD 125 (Individuals, USD 75). Ed(s): Susan M Sheridan. National Association of School Psychologists, 4340 East West Hwy, Ste 402, Bethesda, MD 20814-4411; publications@naspweb.org; http://www.nasponline.org. Illus., adv. Refereed. Circ: 19000 Paid. Vol. ends: No. 4. Microform: PQC. Online: EBSCO Publishing, EBSCO Host; Florida Center for Library Automation; Gale; Northern Light Technology, Inc.; OCLC Online Computer Library Center, Inc.; ProQuest LLC (Ann Arbor); H.W. Wilson. *Indexed:* ABIn, CJA, ERIC, EduInd, PsycInfo, SSCI. *Aud.:* Ac, Sa.

This is the official publication of the National Association of School Psychologists. The journal publishes scholarly research in the fields of school psychology, psychology, and education. Although empirical studies are its focus, case studies, reviews, and articles regarding public policy issues, innovations, interventions, and prevention strategies are also included. Researchers in several disciplines, including education; child clinical, pediatric, community, and family psychology; and special education will benefit from access to this publication. Special issues on timely themes appear periodically. Recent issues look at relationships among relational communication processes and consultation outcomes for students with ADHD; investigation of dimensions of social-emotional classroom behavior and school readiness for low-income urban preschool children; generalizability and dependability of direct behavior ratings to assess social behavior of preschoolers; and increasing social engagement in young children with autism spectrum disorders using video self-modeling. Libraries supporting research and clinical programs in psychology, psychiatry, education, and related social sciences will want to have this title.

5348. *Sexual Abuse: a journal of research and treatment.* Formerly (until 1995): *Annals of Sex Research.* [ISSN: 1079-0632] 1988. q. GBP 419. Ed(s): Howard Barbaree. Sage Publications, Inc., 2455 Teller Rd, Thousand Oaks, CA 91320; info@sagepub.com; http://www.sagepub.com. Illus., adv. Refereed. Online: EBSCO Publishing, EBSCO Host; Gale; IngentaConnect; OCLC Online Computer Library Center, Inc.; OhioLINK; Springer LINK; SwetsWise Online Content. Reprint: PSC. *Indexed:* CJA, PsycInfo, SSA, SSCI, SociolAb. *Aud.:* Ac, Sa.

This is the official publication of the Association for the Treatment of Sexual Abusers. The journal publishes empirical, theoretical, and clinical research, scholarly reviews, and case studies on sexual abuse. With a focus strictly on the causes, consequences, and treatment aspects of sexual abuse, the articles provide significant data for both clinicians and academic researchers. Psychologists, psychiatrists, social workers, therapists, counselors, corrections officers, and allied professionals will benefit by access to this publication. Recent issues focus on the effect of age-at-release on long-term sexual re-offense rates in

civilly committed sexual offenders; the validity of phallometric assessment with rapists with comments on Looman and Marshall (2005); a comparison of the application of the self-regulation model of the relapse process for mainstream and special needs sexual offenders; a meta-analysis of the effectiveness of sexual offender treatment for juveniles as measured by recidivism; and religious affiliations among adult sexual offenders. Libraries serving programs in psychology, education, social work, psychiatry, law, and law enforcement will want to have this title.

5349. *Teaching of Psychology.* [ISSN: 0098-6283] 1974. q. GBP 286 print & online eds. Ed(s): Randolph A Smith. Lawrence Erlbaum Associates, Inc., 325 Chestnut St, Ste. 800, Philadelphia, PA 19106; journals@erlbaum.com; http://www.leaonline.com. Illus., adv. Sample. Refereed. Circ: 3200. Vol. ends: Dec. Microform: PQC. Online: EBSCO Publishing, EBSCO Host; Gale; OCLC Online Computer Library Center, Inc.; OhioLINK; SwetsWise Online Content. Reprint: PSC. *Indexed:* ABIn, ABS&EES, AgeL, ERIC, EduInd, PsycInfo, SSCI, SWA. *Bk. rev.:* 0-3, 1,500 words. *Aud.:* Ac.

This is the official publication of the American Psychological Association's Division on Teaching of Psychology. The journal serves teachers in both K-12 and college settings. Articles provide a source of information on teaching methods and on innovations in the teaching and learning process. Selected content includes "empirical research on teaching and learning; studies of teacher or student characteristics; subject matter or content reviews for class use; investigations of student, course, or teacher assessment; professional problems of teachers; essays on teaching; innovative course descriptions and evaluations; curriculum designs; bibliographic material; demonstrations and laboratory projects; book and media reviews; news items; and readers' commentaries." Recent issues look at service learning in life-span developmental psychology, higher exam scores, and increased empathy; peer-taught drug awareness in an introductory psychology course; teaching the psychology of food and culture; Microsoft Producer as a software tool for creating multimedia PowerPoint presentations; the impact of daily extra credit quizzes on exam performance; and cognitive dissonance or revenge in connection with student grades and course evaluations. Libraries supporting programs in education, teacher training, and psychology will benefit by having this title in their collections.

5350. *Women & Therapy: a feminist quarterly.* Formerly: *Women - Counseling Therapy and Mental Health Services.* [ISSN: 0270-3149] 1982. q. USD 620 print & online eds. Ed(s): Ellyn Kaschak. Haworth Press, Inc., 10 Alice St, Binghamton, NY 13904-1580; getinfo@haworthpress.com; http://www.haworthpress.com. Illus., adv. Sample. Refereed. Circ: 433 Paid. Vol. ends: No. 4. Microform: PQC. Online: EBSCO Publishing, EBSCO Host; Northern Light Technology, Inc.; OCLC Online Computer Library Center, Inc.; ProQuest LLC (Ann Arbor); SwetsWise Online Content. Reprint: HAW. *Indexed:* ABS&EES, AgeL, AltPI, CINAHL, CWI, FemPer, GendWatch, HEA, IBR, IBZ, IMFL, PsycInfo, SFSA, SSA, SSCI, SWA, SWR&A, SociolAb, V&AA, WSA. *Bk. rev.:* 0-7, 900 words, signed. *Aud.:* Ac, Sa.

This is a journal focusing on women and the therapeutic experience. It publishes empirical, theoretical, clinical, and descriptive articles in multiple subject areas. Coverage includes issues that affect women in greater proportion than men; women's roles in society; special needs of minorities, lesbians, older, and disabled women; needs of feminist therapists; interventions; alternative treatments; gender differences; therapist attitudes; and the role of media influence. Recent issues address Asian American women in therapy and feminist reflections on growth and transformations; seeking emotional parity in marital relationships: a new identity challenge for Chinese immigrant women; women sexually victimized in psychotherapy and the dynamics and outcomes of therapist-client sex; group work with women in domestic relationships who have responded to violence with violence; counseling lesbian couples choosing motherhood; gender responsive treatment and services in correctional settings; and motivating women with disordered eating toward empowerment and change using narratives and archetypal metaphor. Libraries that serve therapists; programs that train therapists and clinical psychologists; law and correctional programs; and researchers of women's studies and related social sciences will want to include this title in their collections.

■ PUBLIC HEALTH

Alison M. Bobal, Life Sciences Librarian, The Valley Library, Oregon State University, Corvallis, OR 97331; alison.bobal@oregonstate.edu

Introduction

Public health is an organized, interdisciplinary field that is concerned with the physical, mental, and environmental health concerns of communities and populations that are at risk for disease and injury. It carries out its mission through the creation and implementation of educational programs, the promotion of healthy lifestyles, and the development of health policy, and by conducting scientific research. Public health is different from clinical medicine in that it views communities as its patient, trying to improve the health of that community and not individuals after they become sick or injured. The populations that public health deals with can range from small neighborhoods to entire countries.

The three core functions of public health are assessment, which is done by collecting and analyzing information on the health of populations and making this information available; the creation of health policies in partnership with local, state, and federal government officials, as well as private organizations; and the assurance that the basic medical, environmental, and educational services that are needed for the protection of public health in the community are available and accessible to everyone.

Basic Periodicals

American Journal of Public Health, American Journal of Epidemiology, Family and Community Health, Health Affairs, Public Health Reports.

Basic Abstracts and Indexes

Cumulative Index to Nursing and Allied Health Literature.

5351. American Journal of Health Education. Former titles (until 2003): *Journal of Health Education;* (until 1991): *Health Education;* (until 1975): *School Health Review.* [ISSN: 1932-5037] 1970. bi-m. USD 145. Ed(s): Becky Smith. American Alliance for Health, Physical Education, Recreation, and Dance, 1900 Association Dr, Reston, VA 20191-1599; info@aahperd.org; http://www.aahperd.org. Adv. Refereed. Circ: 11500. Microform: PQC. Online: ProQuest LLC (Ann Arbor). *Indexed:* ABIn, AgeL, Agr, CINAHL, ECER, EduInd, H&SSA, MRD, PEI, SD. *Bk. rev.:* 2-3, signed. *Aud.:* Hs, Ga, Ac, Sa.

This bimonthly journal is the official publication of the American Association for Health Education. Health educators working in K–12 schools, colleges and universities, public health agencies at the local and national level, and industry health-care settings would be interested in this peer-reviewed journal. Each issue contains research articles, feature articles, and health education teaching ideas. Recent article topics include nicotine dependence, levels of physical activity in college students, and sun protection. There are also two sets of self-study questions per issue available for continuing education credit.

5352. American Journal of Health Promotion. Incorporates: *The Art of Health Promotion.* [ISSN: 0890-1171] 1986. bi-m. USD 144.85 (Individuals, USD 99.95). American Journal of Health Promotion, PO Box 15847, N. Hollywood, CA 91615-1584. Illus., adv. Refereed. Circ: 4567. Vol. ends: No. 6. *Indexed:* ABIn, ASIP, ASSIA, AgeL, CABA, CINAHL, DSA, ExcerpMed, H&SSA, HRA, PEI, PsycInfo, RRTA, SD, SFSA, SSA, SSCI, WAE&RSA. *Aud.:* Ac, Sa.

The *American Journal of Health Promotion* is a bimonthly publication that serves as a communication link for researchers and practitioners in different disciplines who are involved in health promotion. To help achieve this goal, the journal is divided into two sections. The first section, "The Science of Health Promotion," integrates research and practice. The second section, "The Art of Health Promotion," is designed to provide practical information to enhance and improve health promotion programs. The overall content of each issue is subdivided into four main categories: Interventions, Strategies, Applications,

and Research Methods. This journal is aimed at both health practitioners and scientists, and recent topics include depression and cigarette smoking, nutritional information at fast-food restaurants, and the use of the Internet for health promotion.

5353. American Journal of Public Health. Supersedes in part (in 1971): *American Journal of Public Health and the Nation's Health;* Which was formed by the 1927 merger of: *Nation's Health; American Journal of Public Health;* Which was formerly (until 1911): *American Public Health Association. Journal;* (1907-1910): *American Journal of Public Hygiene;* Incorporated (1873-1912): *Public Health Papers and Reports.* [ISSN: 0090-0036] 1911. m. USD 285 domestic; USD 335 foreign; USD 294 combined subscription domestic print & online eds. Ed(s): Georges Benjamin, Nancy J Johnson. American Public Health Association, 800 I St, NW, Washington, DC 20001-3710; comments@apha.org; http://www.apha.org. Illus., index, adv. Sample. Refereed. Circ: 35000. Vol. ends: Dec. CD-ROM: Ovid Technologies, Inc. Microform: PMC; PQC. Online: EBSCO Publishing, EBSCO Host; HighWire Press; Northern Light Technology, Inc.; OCLC Online Computer Library Center, Inc.; Ovid Technologies, Inc.; ProQuest K-12 Learning Solutions; ProQuest LLC (Ann Arbor); H.W. Wilson. *Indexed:* ABIn, ABS&EES, ASG, ASSIA, AbAn, AgeL, Agr, ArtHuCI, BiolAb, BiolDig, CABA, CINAHL, CJA, ChemAb, DSA, EnvAb, ExcerpMed, FPA, FS&TA, ForAb, GSI, H&SSA, HRA, HRIS, HortAb, IndVet, MCR, PEI, PollutAb, PsycInfo, RILM, RRTA, RiskAb, S&F, SCI, SD, SFSA, SSCI, SWA, SWR&A, SWRA, VB, WAE&RSA. *Bk. rev.:* 3, length varies. *Aud.:* Ga, Ac, Sa.

This is the monthly journal of the American Public Health Association, and it includes original research articles and information for practitioners. Editions are divided into sections that deal with government and politics and their relationship to public health, debates on timely and relevant topics, reports on programs used in practice, and historical issues in public health that can be related to today. Published for more than 95 years, this journal is aimed at a diverse group of readers who are all involved in health care or health policy.

5354. Canadian Journal of Public Health. Former titles (until 1942): *Canadian Public Health Journal;* (until 1928): *Public Health Journal; Canadian Therapeutist and Sanitary Engineer.* [ISSN: 0008-4263] 1910. bi-m. CND 100.58 domestic; CND 108.10 domestic In NF, NS & NB; CND 121 United States. Ed(s): Dr. Elinor Wilson. Canadian Public Health Association, 1565 Carling Ave, Ste 400, Ottawa, ON K1Z 8R1, Canada; http://www.cpha.ca. Illus., index, adv. Sample. Refereed. Circ: 3000. Vol. ends: Nov/Dec (No. 6). Microform: PMC; PQC. Online: Micromedia ProQuest; Northern Light Technology, Inc.; ProQuest LLC (Ann Arbor). *Indexed:* AbAn, AgeL, BiolDig, CABA, CBCARef, CINAHL, CPerI, ChemAb, DSA, ExcerpMed, FPA, FS&TA, ForAb, H&SSA, IndVet, MCR, PEI, PollutAb, RRTA, RiskAb, S&F, SSCI, VB, WAE&RSA. *Bk. rev.:* 0-2. *Aud.:* Ac, Sa.

This is the official journal of the Canadian Public Health Association. Peer-reviewed research articles, commentaries, policy analysis, and information for practitioners are included and cover all aspects of public health. Article abstracts are in English and French, and while most articles are in English, there are some articles exclusively in French. Tables of contents for the past ten years are available at the journal's web site, www.cpha.ca/english/cjph/cjph.htm. This journal is appropriate for academic medical collections, as well as hospital libraries.

5355. Family and Community Health: the journal of health promotion and maintenance. [ISSN: 0160-6379] 1978. q. USD 261 (Individuals, USD 91.95). Ed(s): Jeanette Lancaster. Lippincott Williams & Wilkins, 530 Walnut St, Philadelphia, PA 19106-3621; http://www.lww.com. Illus. Sample. Circ: 1900 Paid. Vol. ends: Jan. Microform: PQC. Online: EBSCO Publishing, EBSCO Host; Florida Center for Library Automation; Gale; Ovid Technologies, Inc.; ProQuest LLC (Ann Arbor). *Indexed:* AgeL, CINAHL, CJA, H&SSA, IMFL, PEI, PsycInfo, RiskAb, SSA, SSCI, SociolAb. *Bk. rev.:* 5, 300-600 words. *Aud.:* Ac, Sa.

Articles on community health care and promotion are well presented in this journal. Each issue covers a single, current topic in public health care and includes engaging information for creating effective public health programs.

Recent issues address best practices in community health, and health promotion among people with chronic conditions. This easy-to-understand journal is suited for all sizes and types of libraries that have health sciences collections.

5356. Hastings Center Report. Formerly: *Hastings Center Studies.* [ISSN: 0093-0334] 1971. bi-m. USD 375 print & online eds. (Individuals, USD 86 print & online eds.). Ed(s): Gregory Kaebnick. Hastings Center, Rte 9D, Garrison, NY 10524; mail@thehastingscenter.org; http://www.thehastingscenter.org/. Illus., index. Sample. Refereed. Circ: 8500. Vol. ends: Nov/Dec. Reprint: PSC. *Indexed:* ABS&EES, AgeL, ArtHuCI, BRI, CBRI, CINAHL, FutSurv, GSI, IBR, IBZ, IMFL, LRI, MCR, PAIS, PhilInd, RI-1, SCI, SSA, SSCI, SWR&A, SociolAb. *Bk. rev.:* 2-3. *Aud.:* Ga, Ac, Sa.

The Hastings Center, a nonprofit, nonpartisan organization with a mission to address ethics in health and medicine, publishes this journal. This highly regarded scholarly journal has themed issues that address the convergence of medical and philosophical questions. Issues are divided into sections that deal with law, policy, and politics; case studies with commentaries offering practical information; and essays looking at ethical dilemmas in health care. Recent topics include stem cell therapies and health policy. Recommended for all academic libraries.

5357. Health Education & Behavior. Formerly (until vol.24, 1997): *Health Education Quarterly;* Which superseded (in 1980): *Health Education Monographs.* [ISSN: 1090-1981] 1957. bi-m. GBP 627 print & online eds. Ed(s): Mark Zimmerman. Sage Publications, Inc., 2455 Teller Rd, Thousand Oaks, CA 91320; info@sagepub.com; http://www.sagepub.com. Illus., index, adv. Refereed. Circ: 3000 Paid. Vol. ends: Nov/Dec. Microform: PQC. Online: CSA; EBSCO Publishing, EBSCO Host; Gale; HighWire Press; OCLC Online Computer Library Center, Inc.; SAGE Publications, Inc., SAGE Journals Online; SwetsWise Online Content. Reprint: PSC. *Indexed:* ABIn, AgeL, Agr, CINAHL, CJA, CommAb, EduInd, ExcerpMed, H&SSA, HRA, PEI, PsycInfo, RRTA, SD, SFSA, SSA, SSCI, SWR&A, V&AA. *Bk. rev.:* 0-2, 1,200 words. *Aud.:* Ac, Sa.

Researchers and health educators are the target audience for this journal. However, articles are aimed to be of interest to a wide range of professionals involved in health behavior and health education. Topics such as the effectiveness of an HIV prevention program in prisons and elementary school students' physical activity are evidence of the broad audience focus. Each issue has a "Practice Notes" feature that intends to highlight innovative health education practice. It also has a "Perspectives" section that includes articles that tackle complex topics. A continuing education registration form is included in each issue for self-study of selected articles. This journal is recommended for academic medical libraries and hospital libraries.

5358. The Journal of Clinical Ethics. [ISSN: 1046-7890] 1990. q. USD 130 (Individuals, USD 67). Ed(s): Dr. Edmund G Howe. The Journal of Clinical Ethics, Inc., 138 W Washington St, Ste 403, Hagerstown, MD 21740. Illus., index. Sample. Refereed. Vol. ends: Winter. *Indexed:* AgeL, ArtHuCI, CINAHL, PhilInd, SSA, SSCI, SociolAb. *Bk. rev.:* 2, length varies. *Aud.:* Ac, Sa.

This quarterly journal offers peer-reviewed articles on ethical challenges in clinical practice and clinical research. The majority of the articles are written by physicians, but are aimed at all health-care professionals and other personnel whose decisions affect patient care. Clinically relevant case reports and personal perspectives balance the journal's content between the practical and theoretical. This journal tackles ethical issues in an engaging way, while still presenting professional-level information, and it would be appropriate for academic medical and hospital libraries.

5359. Journal of Health Politics, Policy and Law. [ISSN: 0361-6878] 1976. bi-m. USD 337 (Individuals, USD 60). Ed(s): Mark Schlesinger. Duke University Press, 905 W Main St, Ste 18 B, Durham, NC 27701; subscriptions@dukeupress.edu; http://www.dukeupress.edu. Illus., adv. Sample. Refereed. Circ: 1900. Vol. ends: Dec. Microform: WSH; PMC; PQC. Online: EBSCO Publishing, EBSCO Host; Gale; HighWire Press; OCLC Online Computer Library Center, Inc.; OhioLINK; Project

MUSE; ProQuest LLC (Ann Arbor); SwetsWise Online Content. Reprint: PSC. *Indexed:* ABIn, ASG, AgeL, CABA, CINAHL, CLI, ExcerpMed, FutSurv, H&SSA, HRA, IBSS, ILP, IPSA, JEL, LRI, MCR, PAIS, PRA, PSA, SCI, SSA, SSCI, SociolAb, WAE&RSA. *Bk. rev.:* 2-5 essay length. *Aud.:* Ac, Sa.

The *Journal of Health Politics, Policy and Law* is a bimonthly, refereed journal that covers topics of interest to individuals who are concerned with health policy analysis and management and the government's relationship to health care. The journal is international in scope and publishes some topical issues on subjects such as the politics of obesity, health inequities, and patient safety. This journal would be well suited for academic library collections that have an emphasis on public policy and health law.

5360. Journal of Medical Ethics. [ISSN: 0306-6800] 1975. bi-m. GBP 326 print or online (Individuals, GBP 171 print & online eds.). Ed(s): Soren Holm, John Harris. B M J Publishing Group, B M A House, Tavistock Sq, London, WC1H 9JR, United Kingdom; info.norththames@ bma.org.uk; http://www.bmjpg.com/. Illus., index. Refereed. Vol. ends: Dec. Online: EBSCO Publishing, EBSCO Host; Florida Center for Library Automation; Gale; HighWire Press; Northern Light Technology, Inc.; OCLC Online Computer Library Center, Inc.; Ovid Technologies, Inc.; ProQuest K-12 Learning Solutions; ProQuest LLC (Ann Arbor). *Indexed:* AgeL, ArtHuCI, CINAHL, CJA, ExcerpMed, GSI, H&SSA, IBR, PSA, PhilInd, PsycInfo, RI-1, RiskAb, SCI, SSA, SSCI, SociolAb. *Bk. rev.:* 5-10, 300-1,000 words. *Aud.:* Ga, Ac, Sa.

The *Journal of Medical Ethics* is an international journal that covers all aspects of ethics in health care. Practitioners and researchers concerned with the wide range of ethical issues in medicine would find this journal of interest. Original research papers, review articles, editorials, letters, and book reviews are included in each issue. The journal is divided into sections for genetics, clinical ethics, current controversies, law, ethics and medicine, and research ethics. Advanced publication of an issue's current controversies and the full text of articles older than 12 months are posted on the journal's web site at http://jme.bmjjournals.com. Recommended for academic medical and hospital libraries.

5361. The Milbank Quarterly: a journal of public health and health care policy. Former titles (until 1985): *Health and Society;* (until 1973): *Milbank Memorial Fund Quarterly;* (until 1934): *Milbank Memorial Fund Quarterly Bulletin.* [ISSN: 0887-378X] 1923. q. GBP 136 print & online eds. Ed(s): Bradford H Gray. Blackwell Publishing, Inc., Commerce Place, 350 Main St, Malden, MA 02148; customerservices@ blackwellpublishing.com; http://www.blackwellpublishing.com. Illus., index, adv. Sample. Refereed. Circ: 3000. Vol. ends: Dec (No. 4). Microform: PQC. Online: Blackwell Synergy; EBSCO Publishing, EBSCO Host; Gale; IngentaConnect; Northern Light Technology, Inc.; OCLC Online Computer Library Center, Inc.; OhioLINK; Ovid Technologies, Inc.; SwetsWise Online Content. Reprint: PSC. *Indexed:* ASG, ASSIA, AgeL, ApEcolAb, ArtHuCI, BAS, BPI, CJA, ChemAb, FR, FutSurv, HRA, IBSS, MCR, PAIS, PSA, PsycInfo, RiskAb, SCI, SFSA, SSA, SSCI, SWR&A, SociolAb, V&AA. *Aud.:* Ac, Sa.

This multidisciplinary journal is published by the Milbank Memorial Fund, a foundation committed to the nonpartisan study and communication of health policy issues. The original research articles and essays featured are written by authors from many disciplines such as law, medicine, history, and bioethics. A section providing brief biographies of each issue's contributors lists their research interests and practice focus. This well-respected journal has been published since 1923 and belongs in university libraries. It is aimed at health policymakers and analysts, academics, and practitioners.

5362. Public Health Reports: Journal of the U.S. Public Health Service and the Association of Schools of Public Health. Former titles (until 1973): *Health Services Report;* (until 1972): *H S M H A Health Reports;* (until 1970): *Public Health Reports;* Which incorporates (1945-1951): *Journal of Venereal Disease Information.* [ISSN: 0033-3549] 1878. bi-m. USD 117 (Individuals, USD 63). Association of Schools of Public Health, 1101 15th St, NW, Ste 910, Washington, DC 20005; info@asph.org; http://www.asph.org. Illus., index, adv. Sample. Refereed. Circ: 6500 Paid and controlled. Vol. ends: Nov/Dec. Microform: CIS;

PMC; PQC. Online: EBSCO Publishing, EBSCO Host; Gale; HighWire Press; LexisNexis; Northern Light Technology, Inc.; OCLC Online Computer Library Center, Inc.; OhioLINK; ProQuest LLC (Ann Arbor); H.W. Wilson. *Indexed:* ABS&EES, AgeL, Agr, AmStI, CABA, CINAHL, CJA, ChemAb, DSA, ExcerpMed, GSI, H&SSA, IUSGP, IndVet, PAIS, PEI, RRTA, S&F, SCI, SSCI, SWR&A, SWRA, VB, WAE&RSA. *Bk. rev.:* 2, signed. *Aud.:* Hs, Ga, Ac, Sa.

For over 125 years, *Public Health Reports* has been the official journal of the U.S. Health Service and offers peer-reviewed articles on research, public health practice, commentaries, and viewpoints. Articles from schools of public health are also included. A photo essay section with annotations is a distinctive feature of this journal. Essays in the Public Health Chronicles section take a historical look at public health in the United States. This journal is important for all public health professionals as a forum for current scientific developments and other relevant topics. Tables of contents are available on the journal's web site (www.publichealthreports.org), with articles from issues older than ten months available free online. An important journal for all academic library collections.

5363. *Social Science & Medicine.* Formed by the merger of (1978-1982): *Social Science and Medicine. Part A: Medical Sociology;* (1978-1982): *Social Science and Medicine. Part E: Medical Psychology;* Both of which superseded in part (in 1981): *Social Science and Medicine. Medical Psychology and Medical Sociology;* (1978-1982): *Social Science and Medicine. Part B: Medical Anthropology;* (1978-1982): *Social Science and Medicine. Part C: Medical Economics;* (1967-1982): *Social Science and Medicine. Part D: Medical Geography;* Which superseded in part (in 1978): *Social Science & Medicine;* (1973-1982): *Social Science and Medicine. Part F: Medical Ethics and Social Ethics;* Which was formerly (until 1981): *Ethics in Science and Medicine;* (until 1975): *Science, Medicine and Man.* [ISSN: 0277-9536] 1982. 24x/yr. EUR 4568. Ed(s): E Annandale. Pergamon, The Boulevard, Langford Ln, East Park, Kidlington, OX5 1GB, United Kingdom. Adv. Refereed. Circ: 1400. Microform: PQC. Online: EBSCO Publishing, EBSCO Host; Gale; IngentaConnect; OhioLINK; ScienceDirect; SwetsWise Online Content. *Indexed:* ABS&EES, ASSIA, AbAn, AgeL, ArtHuCI, BAS, CABA, CINAHL, CJA, DSA, EI, ExcerpMed, FPA, ForAb, H&SSA, HortAb, IBSS, IndVet, MCR, PAIS, PSA, PhilInd, PsycInfo, RRTA, RiskAb, S&F, SSA, SSCI, SWA, SociolAb, V&AA, VB, WAE&RSA. *Aud.:* Ga, Ac, Sa.

This interdisciplinary journal would be of interest to health-care practitioners, health policymakers, and social scientists whose research is concerned with health policy and practice. Research reports, theoretical essays, and commentaries are included. The international scope is a strong feature of this journal. Some of the biweekly issues address a single topic, allowing for concentrated exploration. This journal belongs in all libraries that have health and social sciences collections.

■ REAL ESTATE

See also Architecture; Building and Construction; and Home sections.

Kevin Deemer, Library Director, Kent State University Ashtabula Campus, Ashtabula, OH 44004; kdeemer@kent.edu

Introduction

Until recently, all sectors of the real estate industry from residential to commercial had experienced record-setting growth. According to the National Association of Realtors, home sales in 2005 peaked at an all-time high. Over 7.1 million single-family homes were sold that year. The home ownership rate in the United States was at a record high of 68.7 percent in the second quarter of 2006, but was down to 68.2 percent in the second quarter of 2007, due to mortgage problems and a record number of foreclosures.

The periodical literature of the real estate field primarily consists of trade publications targeted to specific industry segments and academic journals focusing on the economic and legal aspects of real estate. Some publications cover real estate from a global perspective, while others focus only on U.S. real estate markets. Journals with broader geographic appeal to real estate

professionals were included rather than titles published for a narrower geographic region. The publications selected below would interest academic libraries supporting real estate programs, law libraries, and business libraries.

Basic Periodicals

Ac, Sa: *Real Estate Economics, Real Estate Review, Realtor Magazine.*

Basic Abstracts and Indexes

ABI/Inform, Business Index, Business Periodicals Index.

5364. *Appraisal Journal.* [ISSN: 0003-7087] 1932. q. USD 100 (Non-members, USD 48; Students, USD 30). Ed(s): Adam Webster, Linda Willet. Appraisal Institute, 550 W. Van Buren St., Ste. 1000, Chicago, IL 60607; info@appraisalinstitute.org; http://www.appraisalinstitute.org. Illus., index. Circ: 21000 Paid. Vol. ends: Oct. Online: EBSCO Publishing, EBSCO Host; Florida Center for Library Automation; Gale; Northern Light Technology, Inc.; OCLC Online Computer Library Center, Inc.; ProQuest K-12 Learning Solutions; ProQuest LLC (Ann Arbor); H.W. Wilson. *Indexed:* ABIn, ATI, BLI, BPI, H&TI, PAIS, RiskAb. *Bk. rev.:* 1-3, 500-700 words. *Aud.:* Ac, Sa.

Since 1932, the *Appraisal Journal* has been published by the Appraisal Institute, a leading international organization in the field of real estate appraisals. This is a peer-reviewed journal featuring in-depth, well-researched articles on all aspects of the of real estate appraisal. A typical issue features columns with updates, trends, and news relevant to appraisers; articles providing both theoretical and practical information; book reviews; and news useful for institute members. Feature articles are approximately 8 to 12 pages in length and usually written by professional appraisers. This journal is a core resource for appraisers, real estate professionals, bankers, and real estate lawyers. Highly recommended for academic and special libraries serving real estate, banking, and business programs.

5365. *Building Operating Management: the leading magazine for buildings owners and facility executives.* Formerly: *Building Maintenance and Modernization.* [ISSN: 0007-3490] 1954. m. USD 55. Ed(s): Greg Zimmerman, Edward Sullivan. Trade Press Publishing Corp., 2100 W Florist Ave, Milwaukee, WI 53209; http://www.tradepress.com. Illus., index, adv. Circ: 73052 Paid and controlled. Vol. ends: Dec. Microform: PQC. Online: ProQuest LLC (Ann Arbor). *Indexed:* ABIn. *Aud.:* Ac, Sa.

If you are responsible for at least a 100,000 square foot facility, then this glossy trade publication is for you. *Building Operating Management* is a magazine for building owners and facility executives in commercial and institutional buildings like high-rise office buildings, college campuses, school districts, hospitals, medical clinics, retail chains, hotels, and government buildings. The magazine deals with all aspects of operating larger buildings and facilities. Every issue contains three to five feature articles along with "Editorial," "Industry Focus," "Products," and "Resources" sections. The corresponding web site, www.facilitiesnet.com, provides access to current and past issues, as well as extensive links to product and service advertisers.

5366. *Commercial Investment Real Estate.* Former titles (until 1999): *Commercial Investment Real Estate Journal;* (until 1985): *Commercial Investment Journal.* [ISSN: 1524-3249] 1982. bi-m. USD 38 domestic; USD 46 foreign. Ed(s): Jennifer Norbut. C C I M Institute, 430 N Michigan Ave, Ste 800, Chicago, IL 60611-4092; http://www.ccim.com. Illus., index, adv. Circ: 20000 Paid and controlled. *Indexed:* ABIn. *Aud.:* Ac, Sa.

This is a commercial real estate trade publication. The magazine provides articles of interest to Certified Commercial Investment Members (CCIM) and other commercial real estate professionals. The articles are written by staff writers and commercial real estate professionals. The publication includes reports on industry trends and interviews with real estate professionals, and covers such topics as taxes, legal issues, regional markets, technology, success strategies, and real estate–related products and services. Each issue features

"Area Report," which has regional and local real estate market coverage, a "Buyers Guide," "CCIM Spotlight," "Deal Makers," highlighting top CCIM transactions, "Financing Focus," "Legal Briefs," "Market Trends," "Tax Watch," and "Tech Solutions."

5367. *Journal of Property Management: the official publication of the Institute of Real Estate Management.* Incorporates: *Operating Techniques and Products Bulletin.* [ISSN: 0022-3905] 1934. bi-m. USD 56.95 domestic; USD 65.74 Canada; USD 100.90 elsewhere. Institute of Real Estate Management, 430 N Michigan Ave, Chicago, IL 60611; custserv@irem.org; http://www.irem.org. Illus., index, adv. Sample. Circ: 23750 Paid and free. Vol. ends: Nov/Dec. Online: EBSCO Publishing, EBSCO Host; Florida Center for Library Automation; Gale; Northern Light Technology, Inc.; OCLC Online Computer Library Center, Inc.; ProQuest LLC (Ann Arbor); H.W. Wilson. *Indexed:* ABIn, ATI, BPI, H&TI, IBR, IBZ, PAIS, RiskAb, SUSA. *Aud.:* Ac, Sa.

Journal of Property Management is a trade journal with a practical, problem-solving focus. It publishes up-to-date information on all aspects of real estate property management including trends, technology use, and best practices in marketing, operations, and business development. The journal follows a thematic format, and each issue is devoted to a timely topic relevant to property management. Recent issues cover such topics as disasters, energy costs, evolution of the real estate management profession, technology, and affordable housing. The journal's web site provides access to tables of contents for current and past issues. Selected issues are available for free online; other articles can be purchased from the journal's web site.

5368. *Journal of Real Estate Finance and Economics.* [ISSN: 0895-5638] 1988. 8x/yr. EUR 1032 print & online eds. Ed(s): Steven Grenadier, C F Sirmans. Springer New York LLC, 233 Spring St, New York, NY 10013-1578; service-ny@springer.com; http://www.springer.com/. Illus., adv. Sample. Refereed. Microform: PQC. Online: EBSCO Publishing, EBSCO Host; Gale; IngentaConnect; OCLC Online Computer Library Center, Inc.; OhioLINK; ProQuest LLC (Ann Arbor); Springer LINK; SwetsWise Online Content. *Indexed:* ABIn, BLI, H&TI, IBSS, JEL, RiskAb, SSCI, SUSA. *Aud.:* Ac, Sa.

This peer-reviewed, scholarly journal publishes in the areas of urban economics, housing, regional science, and public policy. It provides a forum for "theoretical and empirical research on real estate using the paradigms and methodologies of finance and economics." Recently published articles include "Efficiency, Scale Economies, and the Risk/Return Performance of Real Estate Investment Trusts," "An Empirical Estimation of Default Risk of the U.K. Real Estate Companies," and "How Does Appraisal Smoothing Bias Real Estate Returns Measurement?" The publisher's web site provides access to article abstracts, keywords, and author affiliation information. This is a very technical research journal suited for graduate-level students and beyond.

5369. *Journal of Real Estate Literature.* [ISSN: 0927-7544] 1993. s-a. Free to members. Ed(s): Karl L Gunterman. American Real Estate Society, c/o James R Webb, Cleveland State University, Dept of Finance, Cleveland, OH 44114; http://www.aresnet.org. Illus., index. Sample. Refereed. Circ: 1500. Microform: PQC. Online: EBSCO Publishing, EBSCO Host; Gale; IngentaConnect; Northern Light Technology, Inc.; OCLC Online Computer Library Center, Inc.; OhioLINK; ProQuest LLC (Ann Arbor); Springer LINK; SwetsWise Online Content. *Indexed:* ABIn, H&TI, IBSS, JEL, PollutAb, SUSA. *Bk. rev.:* 1-2, 1,000-1,500 words, signed. *Aud.:* Ac, Sa.

"The purpose of this journal is to provide a comprehensive source of information about real estate research in order to encourage research and education in industry and academia." Its scope goes beyond that of traditional journals that publish only research articles. It publishes working papers, dissertations, book reviews, and literature reviews of specialized topics such as real estate information technology and international real estate. The articles are technical in nature. Real estate professionals and scholars are the intended audience. The web site provides access to the article abstracts and author's affiliations back to 1993. Full text is available for download to subscribers.

5370. *The Journal of Real Estate Portfolio Management.* [ISSN: 1083-5547] 1995. q. Free to members. Ed(s): Marc A Louargand, Willard McIntosh. American Real Estate Society, c/o James R Webb, Cleveland State University, Dept of Finance, Cleveland, OH 44114. Illus., adv. Refereed. Circ: 1300 Paid. Online: EBSCO Publishing, EBSCO Host; Northern Light Technology, Inc.; OCLC Online Computer Library Center, Inc.; ProQuest LLC (Ann Arbor). *Indexed:* ABIn, H&TI, IBSS, JEL. *Aud.:* Ac, Sa.

The purpose of this journal is to "investigate and expand the frontiers of knowledge that cover business decision-making applications or scholarly real estate research." The journal publishes applied research articles on such topics as development, finance, management, market analysis, marketing, and valuation. Recently published articles include "Exchange Rate Volatility and International Real Estate Diversification: A Comparison of Emerging and Developed Economies" and "Understanding the Discount: Evidence from European Property Shares." The intended audience is real estate scholars and professional real estate investors. The journal's web site provides access to the article abstracts and author's affiliations back to 1995. Full text is available for download to subscribers

5371. *Journal of Real Estate Research.* [ISSN: 0896-5803] 1986. bi-m. Free to members. Ed(s): Ko Wang. American Real Estate Society, c/o James R Webb, Cleveland State University, Dept of Finance, Cleveland, OH 44114; http://business.fullerton.edu/journal/. Adv. Refereed. Circ: 1200. *Indexed:* ABIn, CJA, H&TI, IBSS, JEL, SSCI, SUSA. *Aud.:* Ac, Sa.

This is the official publication of the American Real Estate Society. The main focus of the journal is "to investigate and expand the frontiers of knowledge that cover business decision making applications or scholarly real estate research." Articles are technical in nature and assume advanced knowledge of the real estate field. Recently published articles include "Technology and Real Estate Brokerage Firm Financial Performance," "Store Location in Shopping Centers: Theory & Estimates," and "Property Taxation of Multifamily Housing: An Empirical Analysis of Vertical and Horizontal Equity and Assessment Methods." The journal's web site provides access to the article abstracts and author's affiliations back to 1986. Full text is available for download to subscribers.

5372. *National Real Estate Investor.* [ISSN: 0027-9994] 1958. m. plus a. Directory. USD 85 (Free to qualified personnel). Ed(s): Sibley Fleming, Matt Valley. Prism Business Media, 6151 Powers Ferry Rd Ste 200, Atlanta, GA 30339; inquiries@prismb2b.com; http://www.prismbusinessmedia.com. Illus., index, adv. Circ: 33708. Vol. ends: Dec. Microform: PQC. Online: EBSCO Publishing, EBSCO Host; Florida Center for Library Automation; Gale; OCLC Online Computer Library Center, Inc.; ProQuest K-12 Learning Solutions; ProQuest LLC (Ann Arbor); H.W. Wilson. *Indexed:* ABIn, BPI, CINAHL, H&TI, LRI, PAIS. *Aud.:* Ac, Sa.

This is a trade publication for commercial real estate professionals and real estate investors seeking in-depth market research, information on trends, and industry news. The articles are well written, informative, and data rich. The journal's audience is real estate professionals working in the brokerage, construction, development, finance, property management, and corporate real estate fields. In addition to the feature articles, each issue provides quantitative industry data, sector specific news, expert advice, and opinions. Also included are columns on legislation affecting the industry and real estate investments. The journal's web site provides access to the current issue and selected articles back to 1995.

5373. *Real Estate Economics.* Former titles (until 1995): *American Real Estate and Urban Economics Association. Journal;* (until 1992): *A R E U A Journal;* (until 1977): *American Real Estate and Urban Economics Association. Journal.* [ISSN: 1080-8620] 1973. q. GBP 295 print & online eds. Ed(s): Crocker Liu, David C Ling. Blackwell Publishing, Inc., Commerce Place, 350 Main St, Malden, MA 02148; customerservices@blackwellpublishing.com; http://www.blackwellpublishing.com. Illus., index. Refereed. Circ: 1500. Vol. ends: Winter. Microform: PQC. Online: Blackwell Synergy; EBSCO

Publishing, EBSCO Host; Gale; IngentaConnect; Northern Light Technology, Inc.; OCLC Online Computer Library Center, Inc.; OhioLINK; ProQuest LLC (Ann Arbor); SwetsWise Online Content; H.W. Wilson. *Indexed:* ABIn, AgeL, BPI, H&TI, IBR, IBZ, JEL, RiskAb, SSCI. *Aud.:* Ac, Sa.

This is the official journal of the American Real Estate and Urban Economics Association. The journal provides a forum for publishing research on the analysis of real estate decisions. According to the publisher, "Articles span a wide range of issues, from tax rules to brokers' commissions to corporate real estate including housing and urban economics, and the financial economics of real estate development and investment." Articles are in-depth, lengthy (approximately 20 pages), and technical in nature. Recently published articles include "Price Premium and Foreclosure Risk" and "Unobserved Heterogeneity in Models of Competing Mortgage Termination Risks." Journal subscribers have access to full-text articles via the publisher's web site. Additional online services from the publisher such as RSS feeds and the journal's table of contents delivered via e-mail are available to subscribers.

5374. Real Estate Issues. [ISSN: 0146-0595] 1976. q. Individuals, USD 48; USD 15 newsstand/cover per issue. Ed(s): Richard Marchitelli. The Counselors of Real Estate, 430 N Michigan Ave, Chicago, IL 60611; cre@interaccess.com; http://www.cre.org. Illus., index, adv. Refereed. Circ: 2000. Vol. ends: Winter. Microform: PQC. Online: EBSCO Publishing, EBSCO Host; Florida Center for Library Automation; Gale; Northern Light Technology, Inc.; OCLC Online Computer Library Center, Inc.; ProQuest LLC (Ann Arbor). *Indexed:* ABIn, H&TI. *Aud.:* Ac, Sa.

This journal is published by a nonprofit organization called the Counselors of Real Estate. This is an invitation-only organization made up of successful real estate professionals. The role of the Counselors of Real Estate is to "provide intelligent, unbiased, and trusted advice for clients or employers." *Real Estate Issues* is intended for the Counselors of Real Estate members and other commercial real estate nonmember subscribers. According to the publisher, the journal "reaches a lucrative segment of the real estate industry as well as a representative cross section of professionals in related industries, including real estate counselors, academics, planners, architects, developers, economists, government personnel, lawyers, and accountants." Articles are well written and more understandable than other real estate journals reviewed. The subscription price is reasonable. The journal's web site provides access to abstracts from issues dating back to back to 1977, and more recent articles are available in full text.

5375. Real Estate Law Journal. [ISSN: 0048-6868] 1972. q. USD 389.52. Ed(s): Robert J Aalberts. West Publishing Co., 610 Opperman Dr, Eagan, MN 55123; customer.service@westgroup.com; http://west.thomson.com. Microform: PQC. *Indexed:* ABIn, BLI, CLI, ILP, LRI, PAIS, SSCI. *Aud.:* Ac, Sa.

This journal covers relevant topics relating to real estate law. It is a valuable resource for real estate professionals needing to stay abreast of changes in real estate law. Regular features include "From the Editor in Chief," "Articles," "From the Courts," "Tax Issues," "From the Environment," "Zoning and Land Use Planning," and "Digest of Selected Articles." The publisher states the journal is an informative guide that "draws on the expertise of leading real estate attorneys, financial and business experts, and tax specialists; providing working solutions to everyday legal issues." The intended audience is real estate and legal professionals, but the articles are accessible to individuals with a limited understanding of legal terminology.

5376. Real Estate Review. [ISSN: 0034-0790] 1971. q. USD 214. Thomson West, 610 Opperman Dr, Eagan, MN 55123-1396; west.support@thomson.com; http://west.thomson.com. Illus., index, adv. Circ: 7000 Paid. Vol. ends: Winter. Microform: PQC. Online: EBSCO Publishing, EBSCO Host. *Indexed:* ABIn, ATI, AgeL, BLI, BPI, CLI, ILP, LRI, PAIS, SSCI. *Aud.:* Ac, Sa.

This journal's stated purpose is to provide "authoritative guidance and on-target strategies dealing with the modern real estate market." Articles are written by both attorneys and real estate professionals. Each issue provides up-to-date information on recent developments in real estate law. The articles are well written and enhanced by tables and graphs. This publication provides a how-to approach to important issues in real estate law. It will interest real estate professionals, real estate attorneys, and libraries seeking current information on real estate law.

5377. Realtor Magazine. Formerly (until 1997): *Today's Realtor;* Which was formed by the merger of (1968-1996): *Real Estate Today;* (1980-1996): *Realtor News.* [ISSN: 1522-0842] 1996. m. Free to membership; Non-members, USD 56. Ed(s): Christina Hoffman Spira, Stacey Moncrieff. National Association of Realtors (Chicago), 430 N Michigan Ave, Chicago, IL 60611; infocentral@realtors.org; http://www.realtor.org. Illus., adv. Sample. Circ: 1066201 Controlled. Microform: PQC. Online: Gale. *Indexed:* AgeL, BPI, LRI. *Aud.:* Ac, Sa.

This award-winning trade publication by the National Association of Realtors, an organization with 800,000 members, covers all aspects of the real estate profession. Residential real estate agents are the magazine's intended audience. Well-written articles and features offer a wealth of practical advice to help real estate professionals succeed in their business. The magazine is very readable and visually appealing. Its companion web site provides access to the print issues and an extensive array of online tools, reports, and data that real estate professionals will find useful. *Realtor Magazine* is a key resource for professionals, and is by far the most readable for the real estate layperson. It is essential for all real estate collections, and highly recommended.

■ RELIGION

Pam Matz, Research Services Librarian, Widener Library, Harvard University, Cambridge, MA 02138; pmatz@fas.harvard.edu

Introduction

Recent years have brought wider public attention and a deeper sense of scholarly intensity to questions of faith and the activities and influences of religious groups, both historically and in the present. Both public and academic libraries may have found a greater interest among their readers in periodicals that address these issues, as well as a greater sensitivity to issues of inclusiveness.

Given the diversity of religions practiced in the United States and the many categories of religious publications, in styles ranging from popular and accessible to specialized and scholarly, choosing titles is challenging. Libraries will want to select journals that meet their communities' ongoing faith-related, denominational, and intellectual interests; libraries may also wish to consider other journals that offer broader perspectives or alternate points of view. The divisions below should give some sense of the general categories into which these publications fall and may provide some ways for thinking about choices. Most of the journals listed in this section have web sites that allow examination of sample issues and give a flavor of the publications.

Some of the periodicals listed below are published and edited by specific faiths to address that group's theology, history, and ongoing practice and culture. Among these are *American Baptist Quarterly, Anglican Theological Review, Baptist History and Heritage, Bible Today, Christianity Today, CCAR, Dialogue, Evangelical Quarterly, Journal of Jewish Studies, Journal of Pentecostal Theology, Journal of Presbyterian History, International Review of Missions, Mennonite Quarterly Review, Methodist History,* and *Theological Studies.*

Other journals—such as *Bible Today* and *Weavings*—have the mission of encouraging ongoing Christian religious practice and spiritual life, while others—such as *Ecclesiology, Interpretation,* and *Worship*—are addressed more to pastoral practices.

Some journals address biblical studies (and related areas, such as archaeology), either from within Christian denominations or from more general, scholarly points of view. See, for example, *Catholic Biblical Quarterly, Currents in Biblical Research, Journal for the Study of the Historical Jesus, Journal for the Study of the New Testament, Journal for the Study of the Old Testament, Journal of Biblical Literature,* and *Journal of Theological Studies.*

Other journals associated with faiths provide regular coverage of news and public affairs, with analyses reflecting that particular journal's application of religious principles to current events. Among these journals are *America,*

Christian Century, Christianity Today, Commonweal, First Things, and *National Catholic Reporter.* Some journals consider the interconnections of a particular faith with contemporary cultural and public life—*Judaism* and *Tricycle* belong in this category.

Another category consists of journals, which, whether associated with particular faiths or not, focus on academic scholarship or on interfaith, ecumenical missions and actively seek out contributors from various faiths, countries, and cultures. Examples of such journals are *American Academy of Religion Journal, Buddhist-Christian Studies, Concilium, Cross Currents, Ecumenical Review, Harvard Theological Review, History of Religions, Horizons, Japanese Journal of Religious Studies, Journal of Church and State, Muslim World, Religion, Scottish Journal of Theology,* and *Theology Today.*

Still other journals place themselves at the intersection of a form of religious studies and another intellectual discipline. Consider, for example, *American Journal of Theology and Philosophy, Christianity and Literature, Humanist, International Journal for Philosophy of Religion, International Journal for the Psychology of Religion, Journal for the Scientific Study of Religion, Journal of Feminist Studies in Religion, Journal of Religion and Health, Journal of Religious Ethics, Religion and American Culture, Sociology of Religion,* and *Zygon: Journal of Religion and Science.* These are journals worth consideration by libraries that serve communities that are interested in religious studies or the other intellectual discipline that forms part of the journal's interdisciplinary scope.

Basic Periodicals

America, American Academy of Religion Journal, Church History, The Humanist, Journal of Biblical Literature, Journal of Ecclesiastical History, The Journal of Religion, Journal of Theological Studies, Judaism, Muslim World, Religious Studies Review, Theology Today.

Basic Abstracts and Indexes

American Theological Libraries Association Database, Catholic Periodical and Literature Index, New Testament Abstracts, Old Testament Abstracts, Religion Index One: Periodicals, Religious and Theological Abstracts.

African American Pulpit. See African American section.

5378. *America.* [ISSN: 0002-7049] 1909. w. bi-w., Jul. & Aug.; m. Jun. USD 48 domestic. Ed(s): Robert C Collins, Drew Christiansen. America Press Inc., 106 W 56th St, New York, NY 10019; america@ americapress.org; http://www.americapress.org. Illus., index, adv. Sample. Circ: 46000 Paid. Vol. ends: Jun/Dec. CD-ROM: ProQuest LLC (Ann Arbor). Microform: PQC. Online: EBSCO Publishing, EBSCO Host; Florida Center for Library Automation; Gale; Northern Light Technology, Inc.; OCLC Online Computer Library Center, Inc.; ProQuest K-12 Learning Solutions; ProQuest LLC (Ann Arbor); H.W. Wilson. *Indexed:* ABS&EES, AmHI, BAS, BRD, BRI, CBRI, CPL, FLI, LRI, MASUSE, MRD, NTA, OTA, RGPR, RILM. *Bk. rev.:* 2-3, 1,000-1,300 words, signed. *Aud.:* Ga, Ac.

A weekly journal founded by Jesuits of the United States in 1909, *America* presents theological and devotional content, along with discussion of current events and reviews of books, films, and other forms of art and entertainment. This journal is both grounded in a specifically Catholic point of view and addressed to "the well-informed reader who values independent thinking." Maintaining a balance between affiliation and independence can be difficult for religious journals of any faith, and this may have proved so for *America.* When the Rev. Thomas Reese, editor of the journal since 1998, resigned in May 2005, *The New York Times* speculated that Reese had been pressured to leave in response to the publication of articles that presented a range of thought on sensitive issues such as same-sex marriage. Since that time, *America*'s focus may have shifted to some degree away from internal church discussions and toward presentations on international aspects of the Catholic Church. Topics of recent articles include Pope Benedict's visit to Brazil, a critique of the utilitarian point of view on stem-cell research, and, in a special issue on the Caribbean, the vibrant history of art in Haiti. On the web site (www.americamagazine.org), book reviews, editorials, news, and all contents over one year old are freely

accessible. This journal is widely read and and of potential interest to all seeking a general Catholic point of view on contemporary events; it is a strong candidate for religion periodical collections in both public and academic libraries.

5379. *American Academy of Religion. Journal.* Former titles (until 1966): *Journal of Bible and Religion;* (until 1936): *Journal of the National Association of Biblical Instructors;* Which incorporates in part: *Christian Education.* [ISSN: 0002-7189] 1933. q. USD 171 print or online ed. Ed(s): Charles Mathewes. Oxford University Press, 2001 Evans Rd, Cary, NC 27513; jnlorders@oup-usa.org; http://www.us.oup.com. Illus., index, adv. Refereed. Circ: 9000 Paid. Vol. ends: Winter. Microform: PQC. Online: American Theological Library Association; EBSCO Publishing, EBSCO Host; Gale; HighWire Press; IngentaConnect; JSTOR (Web-based Journal Archive); OCLC Online Computer Library Center, Inc.; Ovid Technologies, Inc.; Oxford Journals; ProQuest LLC (Ann Arbor); SwetsWise Online Content. Reprint: PSC. *Indexed:* AmH&L, AmHI, ArtHuCI, BAS, BRD, BRI, BrHumI, CBRI, FR, HistAb, HumInd, IBR, IBZ, LRI, MLA-IB, NTA, OTA, PSA, PhilInd, R&TA, RI-1, RILM, SSA, SSCI, SociolAb. *Bk. rev.:* 15-20, 900-2,000 words, signed. *Aud.:* Ac.

This international quarterly journal publishes scholarly articles from a range of world religious traditions, as well as studies of the methodologies of religious studies and extensive book reviews. The American Academy of Religion (AAR) and its journal are notable for welcoming "all disciplined reflection on religion—from both within and outside communities of belief and practice" (AAR Mission Statement), and *JAAR* includes work by theologians, historians, sociologists, "textual scholars, literary critics, and ritual/performance studies specialists" (AAR FAQ). Recent articles include "The Pledge of Allegiance and the Meanings and Limits of Civil Religion," "The Word-Faith Movement: A Theological Conflation of the Nation of Islam and Mormonism?," "Parsi and Hindu Traditional and Nontraditional Responses to Christian Conversion in Bombay, 1839–45," and "Between the Lines: Exceeding Historicism in the Study of Religion." The tables of contents for issues since 1939 and a free online sample issue are available at http://jaar.oupjournals.org. This journal is an essential title for all academic institutions with religious studies programs and may be of interest to larger public libraries.

5380. *American Baptist Quarterly: a Baptist journal of history, theology and ministry.* Former titles (until vol.25, 1982): *Foundations;* (until 1958): *Chronicle.* [ISSN: 0745-3698] 1938. q. USD 35 (Individuals, USD 25). Ed(s): Robert Johnson. American Baptist Historical Society, PO Box 851, Valley Forge, PA 19482; http://www.abc-usa.org/abhs/. Illus., index, adv. Sample. Refereed. Circ: 1200. Vol. ends: Dec. Microform: PQC. *Indexed:* AmH&L, FR, HistAb, NTA, PhilInd, R&TA, RI-1, RILM. *Bk. rev.:* 0-1, 500-1,400 words, signed. *Aud.:* Ga, Ac, Sa.

Published by the American Baptist Historical Society, *ABQ* provides valuable access to the Baptist perspective on historical, theological, biblical, religious, and social issues. Much of the material—but not all—is contributed by authors from within the American Baptist tradition. Recent articles include "Brother Against Brother: Baptists and Race in the Aftermath of the Civil War," "Nannie Helen Burroughs: The Trailblazer," and "Denominationalism, Centralization, and Baptist Principles: Observations by a Somewhat Perplexed Baptist." Baptist churches cover a broad theological spectrum, with the American Baptist Churches in the U.S. representing a more moderate position. Libraries seeking to provide balanced coverage of Baptist perspectives in the United States should strongly consider this periodical. Recommended for large public and academic libraries that collect in Baptist topics or history of religion in the United States.

5381. *American Journal of Theology & Philosophy.* [ISSN: 0194-3448] 1980. 3x/yr. USD 36 (Individuals, USD 21). Ed(s): J Wesley Robbins, Jennifer G. Jesse. Highlands Institute for American Religious and Philosophical Thought, PO Box 2009, Highlands, NC 28741; http://www.hiarpt.org. Adv. Refereed. Circ: 450. *Indexed:* FR, IBR, NTA, PhilInd, R&TA, RI-1. *Bk. rev.:* 1 or more, 150-500, signed. *Aud.:* Ac, Sa.

The *American Journal of Theology & Philosophy* (*AJTP*) is a serious and focused publication. *AJTP* describes itself as having four specific editorial emphases: the interface between theology and philosophy, especially where theological efforts have utilized the American philosophical tradition; the history and development of liberal religious thought in America; themes of relevance to the "Chicago School" of theology; and naturalism in American theology and philosophy. Recent articles include "When Our Bodies Do the Thinking, Theology and Science Converge," "God as Co-Created: The Two-Fold Ontic Status of God," and "Quantum Non-Locality as an Indication of Theological Transcendence." Each issue includes at least one lengthy book review. The journal is published three times a year; the full text of back issues from the previous year back to 1990 may be viewed online at http://ajtp.iusb.edu/Back%20Issues.htm. Recommended for academic libraries that serve scholars in theology and philosophy and their intersection.

5382. Anglican Theological Review. [ISSN: 0003-3286] 1918. q. USD 45 (Individuals, USD 35). Ed(s): Charles Hefling. Anglican Theological Review, Inc., 600 Haven St, Evanston, IL 60201. Illus., index, adv. Sample. Refereed. Circ: 1700 Paid. Vol. ends: No. 4. Microform: PQC. Online: EBSCO Publishing, EBSCO Host; Northern Light Technology, Inc.; ProQuest LLC (Ann Arbor). *Indexed:* AmH&L, AmHI, FR, HistAb, IBR, IBZ, NTA, OTA, R&TA, RI-1, RILM. *Bk. rev.:* 25-30, 600-1,400 words, signed. *Aud.:* Ac, Sa.

The *Anglican Theological Review* considers itself "the unofficial organ of the seminaries of the Episcopal Church in the United States and the Anglican Church of Canada." It publishes articles on topics pertaining to "any of the classical disciplines of theological study," and is "committed to creative engagement with Christian tradition and to interdisciplinary inquiry that includes literature and the arts, philosophy, and science." Most, but not all, articles focus on Anglican subject matter, with an emphasis on contemporary relevance. Articles are peer reviewed and authors belong to a variety of traditions. ATR also includes poetry, multiple book reviews, occasional review essays, and reflections. Contents of recent issues are available online, with a precis of each major article available from Spring 2004 onward; see http://anglicantheologicalreview.org. Recent issues include groups of articles on "Anatomy of Reconciliation" and "The Third International Conference and Afro-Anglicanism." There are also individual articles such as "'Roomy Hearts' in a 'More Spacious World': Origen of Alexandria and Ellen Davis on the Song of Songs," and "Spiritual but Not Religious: The Influence of the Current Romantic Movement." Recommended for academic libraries that support programs in theology.

5383. Ars Disputandi: the online journal for philosophy of religion. [ISSN: 1566-5399] 2000. irreg. Free. Ed(s): Michael Scott, Maarten Wisse. Igitur, Utrecht Publishing & Archiving Services, Universiteitsbibliotheek Utrecht, Wittevrouwenstraat 7-11, Postbus 16007, Utrecht, 3500 DA, Netherlands; http://www.igitur.uu.nl. Index. Refereed. *Indexed:* AmHI, RI-1. *Bk. rev.:* 5-10, 500-1,000 words, signed. *Aud.:* Ac, Sa.

Ars Disputandi describes itself as the "first online journal for the philosophy of religion," aiming to combine the swift peer-review process, rapid publication, and availability of hyper-links characteristic of online journals with the scholarly rigor and thoughtful design traditionally associated with print publications. This journal is not formatted in issues; rather, papers appear online immediately on acceptance. The material available online typically includes five or six recently contributed articles, as well as "Discussion Notes," "Conference Papers," and book reviews. Article topics are firmly rooted in the discipline of philosophy of religion, with an emphasis on "clarity of argument and relevance to . . . contemporary debate." Among recent articles, for example, are "Does Hard Determinism Render the Problem of Evil even Harder?," "Intimations of Moral Philosophy, by Way of War and Terrorism," and "Impossibility, God, and Religious Experience." Though subjects in Islamic, Buddhist, and Hindu studies are addressed, more attention is given to discussions within the Judaeo-Christian tradition. Both editors and contributors are drawn primarily from universities in Western Europe and the United States. *AD* notes that its publisher guarantees access to archived materials. *Ars Disputandi* is available without charge, though contributions are invited, and its articles are well considered and well written. It is recommended that academic and special libraries that serve scholars in religion, theology, and philosophy make their readers aware of this resource.

5384. Baptist History and Heritage. [ISSN: 0005-5719] 1965. 3x/yr. Membership, USD 30; Students, USD 20; Senior citizens, USD 25. Ed(s): Pamela R Durso. Baptist History & Heritage Society, P O Box

728, Brentwood, TN 37027-0728; cdeweese@tnbaptist.org; http://www.baptisthistory.org. Illus., index. Sample. Refereed. Circ: 1000 Paid. Vol. ends: Oct. *Indexed:* AmH&L, ChrPI, HistAb, IBR, IBZ, NTA, R&TA, RI-1, RILM. *Bk. rev.:* 3, 250-300 words, signed. *Aud.:* Ga, Ac.

Baptist History and Heritage is published by the Baptist History and Heritage Society (formerly the Southern Baptist Historical Society), in cooperation with the Center for Baptist Studies at Mercer University. Though associated with the Southern Baptist Convention, the Baptist History and Heritage Society is now an independent organization and, Executive Director Charles Deweese explains, focuses "on helping Baptists of all traditions to conserve and share their heritage." The journal is "dedicated to the pursuit of historical information that will enable Baptists to understand themselves, to appreciate their past, and to discover historical perspective for the future." Each issue has a focus, such as "Baptist Missions in Transition," "Baptist Missions Around the World," and "Baptist Teaching, Past and Present," and includes ten or so articles. A web site provides lists of contents of past issues from 1994 on, at http://baptisthistory.org/journal/articles.htm. This title is recommended for public libraries that serve populations with an interest in Baptist studies and for academic libraries that support study of United States religious history.

The Beltane Papers. See Spirituality and Well-Being section.

5385. The Bible Today: a periodical promoting understanding and appreciation of scripture for life & ministry. [ISSN: 0006-0836] 1962. bi-m. USD 39 (Individuals, USD 28; USD 5 newsstand/cover per issue). Ed(s): Rev. Donald Senior. Liturgical Press, St John's Abbey, PO Box 7500, Collegeville, MN 56321-7500; sales@litpress.org; http://www.litpress.org. Illus., index. Sample. Circ: 6900. Vol. ends: Nov. Microform: PQC. *Indexed:* CPL, NTA, OTA. *Bk. rev.:* 35-40, 50-200 words, signed. *Aud.:* Ga, Ac.

The Bible Today, issued by the Catholic publisher Liturgical Press, strives to foster understanding of and appreciation for connections between the Bible and contemporary life. Each issue includes a thematic section, focusing on a particular book of the Bible or subject, such as, recently, repentance. Other sections include examinations of the biblical basis or connection for Catholic practices; descriptions of events, people, and places of the ancient and modern biblical world; and discussions of moral issues confronting Christians now. There are also announcements and book reviews. The material is intended to be easily understood by lay readers and to foster individual and group Bible study. A list of articles published in the past year is available at the web site, www.litpress.org/journals/journals_tbt.html. *The Bible Today* is recommended for public libraries that serve communities with a strong interest in Catholic study and practice or in Bible study.

Biblical Archaeology Review. See Archaeology section.

5386. B'nai B'rith Magazine. Former titles (until 2004): *The B'nai B'rith I J M;* (until 2001): *B'nai B'rith International Jewish Monthly;* (until 1981): *National Jewish Monthly;* (until 1939): *B'nai B'rith National Jewish Monthly.* [ISSN: 1549-4799] 1886. bi-m. USD 12; USD 3 newsstand/cover per issue. Ed(s): Eric Rozenman. B'nai B'rith International, 2020 K St, NW, 7th Fl, Washington, DC 20006; ijm@bnaibrith.org. Illus., index, adv. Circ: 45000 Paid and controlled. Vol. ends: Jun/Jul. *Indexed:* ABS&EES, IJP, PAIS. *Aud.:* Ga, Ac.

Published by B'nai B'rith International, a Jewish human rights, community action, and humanitarian organization founded in 1843, *B'nai B'rith Magazine* covers activities of that organization and general-interest topics such as politics, newsmakers, culture, religion, travel, and art. Many issues address particular themes, including, recently, sports and Jewish identity, Jewish culture and cuisine, and Jewish presence on the Internet. Excerpts from recent issues are available at the web site, www.bnaibrith.org/magazine/bbm_index.cfm. Recommended for public libraries that serve communities with a strong interest in Jewish ways of life.

5387. Buddhist - Christian Studies. [ISSN: 0882-0945] 1981. a. USD 30; USD 42 combined subscription print & online eds. Ed(s): Terry C Muck. University of Hawaii Press, Journals Department, 2840 Kolowalu St, Honolulu, HI 96822-1888; uhpjourn@hawaii.edu;

http://www.uhpress.hawaii.edu/. Illus., adv. Sample. Refereed. Circ: 750. Online: EBSCO Publishing, EBSCO Host; Florida Center for Library Automation; Gale; JSTOR (Web-based Journal Archive); OCLC Online Computer Library Center, Inc.; OhioLINK; Project MUSE; ProQuest LLC (Ann Arbor); SwetsWise Online Content; H.W. Wilson. Reprint: PSC. *Indexed:* AmHI, HumInd, R&TA, RI-1. *Bk. rev.:* 10-15, 800-1,000, signed. *Aud.:* Ac, Sa.

Published by the Society for Buddhist-Christian Studies, and issued annually, this journal includes articles, conference reports, and book reviews related to Buddhist–Christian dialogue and comparative study, based both on historical materials and on contemporary experience. Responses to articles are generally included: for example, the recent group of articles "Jesus Christ through Buddhist Eyes" is followed by Christian responses, and "Gautama the Buddha through Christian Eyes" is followed by Buddhist responses. A free sample issue is available at the web site, muse.jhu.edu/journals/buddhist-christian_studies. *Buddhist-Christian Studies* is an interesting journal with an unusual perspective on religious topics; recommended for consideration by academic libraries.

5388. *C C A R Journal: a reform Jewish quarterly.* Former titles (until Summer 1991): *Journal of Reform Judaism; C C A R Journal.* [ISSN: 1058-8760] 1953. q. USD 29 domestic (Students, USD 14.50). Ed(s): Rabbi Rifat Sonsino. C C A R Press, 355 Lexington Ave,, 18th Fl, New York, NY 10017-6603; info@ccarnet.org; http://www.ccarnet.org. Illus., adv. Circ: 2400. Vol. ends: Spring. Microform: PQC. *Indexed:* IBR, IJP, NTA, R&TA, RI-1. *Bk. rev.:* 3-4, 800-1,200 words, signed. *Aud.:* Ga, Ac, Sa.

CCAR explores "ideas and issues of Judaism and Jewish life, primarily—but not exclusively—from a Reform Jewish perspective." The journal is published by the Central Conference of American Rabbis, the principal organization of Reform Jewish Rabbis in the United States. Each issue has a general theme, such as interfaith marriage or, recently, an exploration of the various meanings of Reform Jewish Zionism. Issues also include editorials, position statements, scholarly articles, personal reflections, and book reviews that address the specific general theme. Though based within Reform Judaism, perspectives are varied and, as a whole, illuminate complexities of the themes addressed. Excerpts from issues are available at the web site, http://ccarnet.org/publications/journal. Recommended for large public and academic libraries.

5389. *Catholic Biblical Quarterly.* [ISSN: 0008-7912] 1939. q. USD 30. Ed(s): Alfred Cody. Catholic Biblical Association of America, Catholic University of America, 433 Caldwell Hall, Washington, DC 20064; cua-cathbib@cua.edu; http://cba.cua.edu/. Illus., index, adv. Sample. Refereed. Circ: 4230. Vol. ends: Oct. Online: American Theological Library Association; EBSCO Publishing, EBSCO Host; Northern Light Technology, Inc.; OCLC Online Computer Library Center, Inc.; Ovid Technologies, Inc.; ProQuest LLC (Ann Arbor); H.W. Wilson. *Indexed:* AmHI, ArtHuCI, CPL, FR, HumInd, IBR, IBZ, NTA, OTA, R&TA, RI-1, SSCI. *Bk. rev.:* 60-65, 400-1,100 words, signed. *Aud.:* Ac, Sa.

Catholic Biblical Quarterly presents scholarly investigation of scripture and related fields. The journal features articles, book reviews and short notices, collected essays, and lists of books received on all aspects of Catholic biblical history. Scholarly articles focus on both Old and New Testament texts, with quite specific topics such as "Endings and Beginnings: Alphabetic Shaping of Psalms 106 and 150" and broader considerations, such as "Evaluating King David: Old Problems and Recent Scholarship" and "The Structure of James." An essential publication for academic libraries that support biblical studies.

Catholic Historical Review. See History section.

5390. *The Christian Century.* Incorporates (1918-1934): *The World Tomorrow;* (in 1926): *The Christian Work;* Which was formerly (until 1914): *Christian Work and the Evangelist;* Which superseded in part (in 1909): *The Arena.* [ISSN: 0009-5281] 1886. bi-w. USD 49 domestic; USD 98 foreign. Ed(s): David Heim, John M Buchanan. Christian Century Foundation, 104 S Michigan Ave, Ste 700, Chicago, IL 60603; http://www.christiancentury.org. Illus., index, adv. Circ: 30000 Paid and free. Vol. ends: Dec. CD-ROM: ProQuest LLC (Ann Arbor). Microform: NBI; PQC. Online: American Theological Library Association; EBSCO Publishing, EBSCO Host; Florida Center for Library Automation; Gale;

Northern Light Technology, Inc.; OCLC Online Computer Library Center, Inc.; Ovid Technologies, Inc.; ProQuest K-12 Learning Solutions; ProQuest LLC (Ann Arbor); H.W. Wilson. *Indexed:* ABS&EES, AmH&L, AmHI, BAS, BRD, BRI, CBRI, FLI, HistAb, IAPV, IBZ, LRI, MASUSE, MRD, NTA, PRA, R&TA, RGPR, RI-1, RILM. *Bk. rev.:* 1-3, 1,000-3,000 words, signed. *Aud.:* Ga.

A biweekly journal of news and opinion, *Christian Century* has been, since early in the twentieth century, a voice for undenominational moderate-to-liberal Protestantism, comparable to the Catholic weekly *America*. The magazine defines its mission as calling Christians to a "profound engagement with the world" and articulating "their faith in a way that is meaningful and intellectually compelling to those around them." Contributors are from a number of different Protestant denominations and each issue includes news, opinion, book and media reviews, meditations, and regular columns regarding faith. Among recent articles and features are "Tattooed: Body Art Goes Mainstream"; "Communion with the Saints," a column about Protestant–Catholic dialogue; and "Unchecked Sources," an opinion piece on the use of the term "War on Terror." Recommended for general-interest periodical collections, both public and academic.

5391. *Christianity and Literature.* Formerly: *Conference on Christianity and Literature. Newsletter.* [ISSN: 0148-3331] 1951. q. USD 35 (Individuals, USD 25; Students, USD 20). Ed(s): Robert Snyder. Seattle Pacific University, 3307 Third Ave., W, Seattle, WA 98119; http://www.spu.edu. Illus., adv. Sample. Refereed. Circ: 1100 Paid. Vol. ends: Summer (No. 4). *Indexed:* ABS&EES, AmHI, ArtHuCI, BEL&L, ChrPI, HumInd, IBR, IBZ, MLA-IB, R&TA, RI-1. *Bk. rev.:* 9-12, 1,200-2,500 words, signed. *Aud.:* Ga, Ac, Sa.

This journal is published by the Conference on Christianity and Literature, an interdisciplinary society "dedicated to both scholarly excellence and collegial exchange." *Christianity & Literature* "is devoted to the scholarly exploration of how literature engages Christian thought, experience, and practice," presupposing "no particular theological orientation but respect[ing] an orthodox understanding of Christianity as a historically defined faith." Each issue contains scholarly articles, book reviews, poetry, and news and announcements. Recent articles include the review essay "Words Made Flesh: Poetry and the Eucharistic Feast," "An Idolatrous Imagination? Biblical Theology and Romanticism in Charlotte Bronte's *Jane Eyre*," and the special feature, "Hunting for Reasons to Hope: A Conversation with Wendell Berry." Tables of contents of past issues are listed at the web site of the journal's archives, www.pepperdine.edu/sponsored/ccl/journal/archives/default.htm. This journal is of interest to researchers in both religious studies and literature; recommended for academic libraries.

5392. *Christianity Today.* Incorporates (1997-200?): *Christianity Online;* Which incorporated (1997-1999): *Computing Today.* [ISSN: 0009-5753] 1956. m. USD 24.95 domestic; USD 37.95 foreign; USD 3.95 newsstand/cover. Ed(s): Harold B. Smith, David Neff. Christianity Today International, 465 Gundersen Dr, Carol Stream, IL 60188. Illus., index, adv. Circ: 155000 Paid. Vol. ends: Dec. Microform: PQC. Online: American Theological Library Association; EBSCO Publishing, EBSCO Host; Florida Center for Library Automation; Gale; Northern Light Technology, Inc.; OCLC Online Computer Library Center, Inc.; Ovid Technologies, Inc.; ProQuest K-12 Learning Solutions; ProQuest LLC (Ann Arbor); H.W. Wilson. *Indexed:* ABS&EES, BAS, BRD, BRI, CBRI, CPerI, ChRPI, LRI, MASUSE, NTA, OTA, PRA, R&TA, RGPR, RI-1, RILM. *Bk. rev.:* 5-6, 600-1,000 words, signed. *Aud.:* Ga.

Launched in 1956, and intended as a counterpoint to the more liberal *Christian Century*, the monthly *Christianity Today* provides a voice for conservative Evangelical Protestantism. Each issue includes reports on world news and church news, analysis of cultural trends, editorials, and reflections on everyday life, all from an Evangelical perspective. A recent issue includes "Disorderly Disciplines," a discussion of integrating spiritual life with motherhood; "Famine Again? Why Some Places Suffer Food Shortages Decade After Decade"; and "Christian Colleges: Green Revolution." Excerpts from articles and a link to a free current issue are available at the web site, www.christianitytoday.com, along with additional web content. Recommended for public and academic libraries.

5393. Church History: studies in Christianity and culture. [ISSN: 0009-6407] 1932. q. GBP 57. Ed(s): Amanda Porterfield, John Corrigan. Cambridge University Press, The Edinburgh Bldg, Shaftesbury Rd, Cambridge, CB2 2RU, United Kingdom; journals@cambridge.org; http://www.journals.cambridge.org. Illus., index, adv. Refereed. Circ: 3400. Vol. ends: Dec. Online: American Theological Library Association; Chadwyck-Healey Inc.; EBSCO Publishing, EBSCO Host; Factiva, Inc.; Florida Center for Library Automation; Gale; JSTOR (Web-based Journal Archive); Northern Light Technology, Inc.; OCLC Online Computer Library Center, Inc.; Ovid Technologies, Inc.; ProQuest K-12 Learning Solutions; ProQuest LLC (Ann Arbor); H.W. Wilson. *Indexed:* ABS&EES, AmH&L, AmHI, ArtHuCI, BEL&L, BRI, CBRI, ChrPI, FR, HistAb, HumInd, IBR, IBZ, NTA, OTA, R&TA, RI-1, RILM, SSCI. *Bk. rev.:* 30-50, 250-1,200 words, signed. *Aud.:* Ac, Sa.

Published by the American Society for Church History, this journal addresses all areas of the history of Christianity, including non-Western. Articles are intended to be of interest to general historians of Christianity and informative to specialists. Recently published examples include "Inventing the Catholic Worker Family," "The Power of Books and the Practice of Mysticism in the Fourteenth Century: Heinrich of Nordlingen and Margaret Ebner with Mechthild's Flowing Light of the Godhead," and "'My Lord's Native Land': Mapping the Christian Holy Land." Each issue also carries an extensive section of book reviews—some brief, some lengthy. Abstracts of the current issue and of some back issues are available at the web site, www.churchhistory.org/churchhistory.html. Recommended for academic libraries.

Commentary. See News and Opinion section.

5394. Commonweal: a review of religion, politics & culture. [ISSN: 0010-3330] 1924. bi-w. 22/yr. USD 49 domestic; CND 54 Canada; USD 59 elsewhere. Ed(s): Patrick Jordan, Paul Baumann. Commonweal Foundation, 475 Riverside Dr, Rm 405, New York, NY 10115; commonweal@msn.com; http://www.commonwealmagazine.org. Illus., index, adv. Circ: 20000 Paid. CD-ROM: ProQuest LLC (Ann Arbor). Microform: MIM; PMC; PQC. Online: Chadwyck-Healey Inc.; EBSCO Publishing, EBSCO Host; Florida Center for Library Automation; Gale; Northern Light Technology, Inc.; OCLC Online Computer Library Center, Inc.; ProQuest K-12 Learning Solutions; ProQuest LLC (Ann Arbor); H.W. Wilson. *Indexed:* ABS&EES, AmH&L, BAS, BEL&L, BRD, BRI, CBRI, CPL, FLI, HistAb, IAPV, LRI, MASUSE, MLA-IB, MRD, NTA, OTA, PRA, PhilInd, RGPR, RI-1, RILM. *Bk. rev.:* 3-4, 900-1,900 words, signed. *Aud.:* Ga.

Commonweal is a review of public affairs, religion, literature, and the arts, edited by Catholic laypeople. Although it is focused on issues of concern to Catholics, the journal also considers a broad range of general-interest issues and attracts contributors from various points of view, generally in the moderate-to-liberal spectrum. Recent articles include "The Sobrino File: How to Read the Vatican's Latest Notification," "Can't We All Just Get Along? A History of Religious Coexistence," "Praying to the Buddha: Living amid Religious Pluralism," and "Salvation and 'The Sopranos': Redemption in New Jersey?" A sampling of recent articles is available at the web site, www.commonwealmagazine.org. Published by an independent, nonprofit foundation, and a respected nonsectarian, undogmatic voice, *Commonweal* is recommended for general-interest periodical collections, both public and academic.

5395. Concilium: international review of theology. [ISSN: 0010-5236] 1965. 5x/yr. USD 93.50 (Individuals, USD 62.50; GBP 10.50 per issue). S C M Press, 9-17 St Albans Pl, London, N1 0NX, United Kingdom; scmpress@btinternet.com. Illus., adv. Sample. Refereed. Circ: 1000. Vol. ends: Dec. *Indexed:* NTA. *Aud.:* Ac.

Founded in 1965 and published five times a year, *Concilium* is a worldwide journal of theology, published in English, French, German, Italian, Portuguese, and Spanish editions. The journal was founded to promote theological discussion in the spirit of Vatican II; though Catholic in origin, it describes itself as "open to other Christian traditions and the world's faiths." Each issue focuses on a theme of wide concern, such as "Pluralist Theology: The Emerging Paradigm," "Women's Voices in World Religions," and "African Christiani-

ties." Titles and tables of contents from 1965 on are available at the web site, www.concilium.org/english.htm. Recommended for academic libraries with theological collections.

5396. Cross Currents (New York). Former titles (until 1990): *Religion and Intellectual Life;* (until 1983): *N I C M Journal for Jews and Christians in Higher Education.* [ISSN: 0011-1953] 1950. q. USD 50 (Individuals, USD 30; Students, USD 20). Ed(s): Kenneth Arnold. Association for Religion and Intellectual Life, 475 Riverside Dr, Ste 1945, New York, NY 10115; cph@crosscurrents.org; http://www.aril.org. Illus., index, adv. Sample. Refereed. Circ: 5000. Vol. ends: Winter. Online: American Theological Library Association; EBSCO Publishing, EBSCO Host; Florida Center for Library Automation; Gale; OCLC Online Computer Library Center, Inc.; Ovid Technologies, Inc.; ProQuest K-12 Learning Solutions; ProQuest LLC (Ann Arbor); H.W. Wilson. *Indexed:* ABS&EES, AmHI, BAS, CPL, FR, HumInd, MLA-IB, NTA, OTA, R&TA, RI-1. *Bk. rev.:* 6-8, 400-2,000 words, signed. *Aud.:* Ac, Sa.

Published by the Association for Religion and Intellectual Life, *Cross Currents* is an international, interdisciplinary, ecumenical journal, taking as its scope the broad confluence of religion and intellectual life. Issue contents typically include poetry and fiction alongside articles and book reviews. A number of current and past articles, and articles in thematic groupings, are available in their entirety through the web site, www.crosscurrents.org. According to the *Cross Currents* web site, the most popular articles include "Religion, Politics, and the State: Cross-Cultural Observations," "The Ecotheology of Annie Dillard: A Study in Ambivalence," and "Turning Hebrew Psalms to Reggae Rhythms: Rastas' Revolutionary Lamentations for Social Change." As the selection shows, *Cross Currents'* cultural frame of reference is generally accessible. Recommended for larger public and academic libraries.

5397. Currents in Biblical Research. Formerly (until 2002): *Currents in Research: Biblical Studies.* [ISSN: 1476-993X] 1993. 3x/yr. GBP 162. Ed(s): Jonathan Klawens, Scot McKnight. Sage Publications Ltd., 1 Oliver's Yard, 55 City Rd, London, EC1 1SP, United Kingdom; info@sagepub.co.uk; http://www.sagepub.co.uk. Adv. Online: EBSCO Publishing, EBSCO Host; HighWire Press; SAGE Publications, Inc., SAGE Journals Online. Reprint: PSC. *Indexed:* IBR, IBZ, NTA, OTA, R&TA, RI-1. *Aud.:* Ac.

CBR is designed to serve as a guide to scholars beginning careers in biblical studies and to be useful to established scholars who wish to keep themselves informed. The journal summarizes the spectrum of recent research on particular topics or biblical books, covering associated ancient literature, archaeology, and historical studies. Each article ends with an extensive bibliography "that provides a basic knowledge of significant articles and books on the topic being treated, and provides sufficient information to launch a thorough investigation of the topic." Recent articles include "Twenty-five Years of Marxist Biblical Criticism," "The Unity of Luke—Acts: A Four-Bolted Hermeneutical Hinge," and "Violence in the Apocalypse of John." Much of the current issue and a free sample issue are available online at the journal's web site, http://cbi.sagepub.com/, where it is also possible to search for articles from October 2002 to the present and to view contents of past issues from that same date. Highly recommended for academic libraries that serve a community involved in biblical scholarship.

5398. Dialogue (Salt Lake City): a journal of Mormon thought. [ISSN: 0012-2157] 1966. q. USD 37 domestic (Students, USD 37). Ed(s): Levi S Peterson. Dialogue Foundation, PO Box 58423, Salt Lake City, UT 84158; dialoguebusiness@peoplepc.com. Illus., adv. Refereed. Circ: 4000. Microform: PQC. Online: EBSCO Publishing, EBSCO Host; Northern Light Technology, Inc.; SwetsWise Online Content. *Indexed:* AmH&L, HistAb, RI-1, RILM. *Bk. rev.:* 2-3, 250-750 words, signed. *Aud.:* Sa.

Dialogue is an independent quarterly "established to express Mormon culture and to examine the relevance of religion to secular life." It is edited by Latter-day Saints with the goals of creating a dialogue between their faith and broader areas of religious thought, and fostering artistic and scholarly expressions based on their cultural heritage. According to a *Dialogue* survey, the readership is primarily composed of people who are religiously committed yet willing to engage with balanced treatments of difficult issues within the

Mormon faith. Typical issues include articles on history, doctrine, and current social problems, with some discussion of science, arts, and culture; book reviews; and fiction and poetry. Some recent articles include "Is Joseph Smith Relevant to the Community of Christ?," "Making the Absent Visible: The Real, Ideal, and the Abstract in Mormon Art," and "The Theology of Desire." An index covering volumes from 1966 to 1987 is available online at www.dialoguejournal.com/old_index; and from 1988 to 2000 at www.dialoguejournal.com/index. The full text of Volumes 1 through 37 is currently available free online through the *Dialogue* archives, at http://content.lib.utah.edu/cdm4/browse.php?CISOROOT=/dialogue. Libraries that serve Mormon communities will already know of this journal; other, academic libraries that support research in religious thought and practice in the United States should consider it.

5399. *Ecclesiology: the journal for ministry, mission and unity.* [ISSN: 1744-1366] 2004. 3x/yr. EUR 125 print & online eds. (Individuals, EUR 43). Ed(s): Paul Avis. Brill, PO Box 9000, Leiden, 2300 PA, Netherlands; cs@brill.nl; http://www.brill.nl. Adv. *Bk. rev.:* Number and length vary. *Aud.:* Ac, Sa.

The name of this journal defines its focus, "ecclesiology," which is the scholarly study of the nature and purpose of the Christian church. The journal *Ecclesiology* began publication in 2004 and still has a relatively small circulation. Yet it is apt to build a wider audience because of its international, interdisciplinary, ecumenical focus; its intention to emphasize scholarly depth in combination with relevance to current issues; and its presentation of in-depth review articles. Recent articles include "A Practical Church Unity within Secular Hospitals," "What Is Ordination? A Roman Catholic Perspective," and "Are Southern Baptists Evangelicals? A Second Decadal Reassessment." Major book reviews number two per issue (2,000–2,200 words), and minor number three to five (800–1,600 words); all are signed. Tables of contents and a free online sample issue are available at ecc.sagepub.com. Worth consideration by academic libraries that serve communities interested in church studies.

5400. *Ecumenical Review.* Formerly (until 1948): *Christendom.* [ISSN: 0013-0796] 1935. q. CHF 52 domestic; USD 37.50 foreign. Ed(s): Raiser Konrad. World Council of Churches, 150 route de Ferney, PO Box 2100, Geneva, 1211, Switzerland; http://www.wcc-coe.org/. Illus., index, adv. Circ: 3500. Microform: PQC. Online: American Theological Library Association; EBSCO Publishing, EBSCO Host; Florida Center for Library Automation; Gale; Northern Light Technology, Inc.; OCLC Online Computer Library Center, Inc.; Ovid Technologies, Inc.; ProQuest K-12 Learning Solutions; ProQuest LLC (Ann Arbor); H.W. Wilson. *Indexed:* AmHI, ArtHuCI, BRI, CBRI, HumInd, IBR, IBZ, IMFL, NTA, OTA, PRA, R&TA, RI-1, RILM, SSCI. *Bk. rev.:* 3-5, 800-1,000 words, signed. *Aud.:* Ac, Sa.

Ecumenical Review is a quarterly theological journal published by the World Council of Churches (WCC), a broad ecumenical organization of Christian churches in over 100 countries. As described by *ER,* its articles concern "the issues of deepest concern to churches seeking to make visible their unity in Christ and to fulfill together their calling to mission and service in the world." Each issue focuses on a specific current theme, such as (in recent issues) the universality of the church and reflections on the theme of the Ninth Assembly of the WCC, "God, in your grace, transform the world." The journal provides other features useful to researchers, such as numerous book reviews. Highly recommended for academic libraries that support researchers in ecumenical studies.

5401. *Evangelical Quarterly: an international review of Bible and theology.* [ISSN: 0014-3367] 1929. q. USD 70.40 (Individuals, USD 45.80). Ed(s): I Howard Marshall. The Paternoster Press, Kingstown Broadway, PO Box 300, Carlisle, CA3 0QS, United Kingdom; 100526.3434@compuserve.com. Illus., index, adv. Circ: 1100. Microform: PQC. Online: EBSCO Publishing, EBSCO Host. *Indexed:* ChrPI, IBR, IBZ, NTA, OTA, R&TA, RI-1, RILM. *Bk. rev.:* 8-20, 800-1,600, signed. *Aud.:* Ac.

Edited in association with the London School of Theology, this journal includes articles on a variety of biblical and theological topics, from an evangelical perspective. Recent articles include "Evangelicals and Public Worship, 1965–2005," "Reconciliationism—a Forgotten Evangelical Doctrine of Hell,"

and "The Ascension of Jesus and the Descent of the Holy Spirit in Patristic Perspective: A Theological Reading." Issues also include extensive book review sections. Recommended for academic libraries that support theological study.

5402. *Evangelical Theological Society. Journal.* Formerly (until 1968): *E T S Bulletin.* [ISSN: 0360-8808] 1958. q. USD 30. Ed(s): Andreas Kostenberger. Evangelical Theological Society, c/o James Borland, Sec Treas, 200 Russell Woods Dr, Lynchburg, VA 24502-3574; http://www.etsjets.org. Illus., index, adv. Refereed. Circ: 4300. Vol. ends: Dec. Microform: PQC. Online: American Theological Library Association; EBSCO Publishing, EBSCO Host; OCLC Online Computer Library Center, Inc.; Ovid Technologies, Inc.; ProQuest LLC (Ann Arbor). *Indexed:* ChrPI, NTA, OTA, PhilInd, R&TA, RI-1, RILM. *Bk. rev.:* 16-20, 600-2,000 words, signed. *Aud.:* Ac, Sa.

Published on behalf of the Theological Commission of the World Evangelical Fellowship, this journal is committed to fostering "conservative biblical scholarship." Each issue contains biblical and theological articles and book reviews, all written from the perspective that "the Bible . . . is the inerrant Word of God in written form." Recent articles include "House Church and Mission: The Importance of Household Structures in Early Christianity," "Development and Diversity in Early Christianity," and "Thomas, the Fifth Gospel?" Issues also include occasional reports and news items from the society. The society is in the process of making back issues of the journal searchable and available at the web site, www.etsjets.org/jets/journal/jets.html. A forum valuable to those who share the evangelical perspective, *JETS* is also useful for those outside of evangelicalism who seek to understand it. Recommended for libraries that serve evangelical communities, and worth consideration by libraries seeking a varied collection in theological and biblical studies.

Feminist Theology. See Gender Studies section.

5403. *First Things: a monthly journal of religion and public life.* [ISSN: 1047-5141] 1990. 10x/yr. USD 34 domestic; USD 44 Canada; USD 52 elsewhere. Ed(s): Richard John Neuhaus, Erik Ross. Institute on Religion and Public Life, 156 Fifth Ave, Ste 400, New York, NY 10010; ft@firstthings.com; http://www.firstthings.com. Index, adv. Refereed. Circ: 30000 Paid. Online: American Theological Library Association; EBSCO Publishing, EBSCO Host; Florida Center for Library Automation; Gale; OCLC Online Computer Library Center, Inc.; Ovid Technologies, Inc.; ProQuest LLC (Ann Arbor); H.W. Wilson. *Indexed:* AmHI, HumInd, LRI, NTA, R&TA, RI-1, RILM. *Bk. rev.:* 4-5, 250-500 words, signed. *Aud.:* Ga.

Described by its detractors as a staunchly neoconservative publication, *First Things* identifies itself as published "to advance a religiously informed public philosophy for the ordering of society." The founder and editor-in-chief, Richard John Neuhaus, is a Catholic priest, and Catholic issues are a frequent topic, but contributors come from a variety of faiths. Each issue includes commentary on public events; articles on history, politics, and culture; opinion pieces; book reviews; poetry; and a lengthy correspondence section. This popular monthly does not hesitate to take on controversial issues; for example, a 2007 article, "Just War and Iraq Wars," offers a defense of the Bush administration's policies. Other recent articles and commentaries include "Pope Benedict on Reforming the Reform," "Lost and Saved on Television," and "The Exaggerated Death of Europe." Tables of contents from past issues and selected articles full-text are available at the web site, www.firstthings.com/issues-list.php. Recommended for public and academic libraries that seek to provide a spectrum of religious opinion on current events.

5404. *Harvard Theological Review.* [ISSN: 0017-8160] 1908. q. GBP 77. Ed(s): Francois Bovon. Cambridge University Press, The Edinburgh Bldg, Shaftesbury Rd, Cambridge, CB2 2RU, United Kingdom; journals@cambridge.org; http://www.journals.cambridge.org. Illus., index, adv. Sample. Refereed. Circ: 1500 Paid. Vol. ends: Oct. Online: Pub.; EBSCO Publishing, EBSCO Host; Florida Center for Library Automation; Gale; JSTOR (Web-based Journal Archive); Northern Light

Technology, Inc.; OCLC Online Computer Library Center, Inc.; OhioLINK; SwetsWise Online Content; H.W. Wilson. *Indexed:* AmH&L, AmHI, ArtHuCI, HistAb, HumInd, IBR, IBZ, IndIslam, MLA-IB, NTA, OTA, PhilInd, R&TA, RI-1, SSCI. *Bk. rev.:* Number and length vary. *Aud.:* Ac.

Published on behalf of the Faculty of Harvard Divinity School, *Harvard Theological Review* is a quarterly journal that presents original research in the history and philosophy of religious thought "in all traditions and periods, including Hebrew Bible, New Testament, Christianity, Jewish studies, theology, ethics, archaeology, and comparative religious studies." Articles are well documented, frequently drawing on primary sources in their original languages; they are generally lengthy; and they discuss quite specific topics. Recent examples include "The Anarchic Principle of Christian Eschatology in the Eucharistic Tradition of the Eastern Church," "Let's Be Realistic: Evolutionary Complexity, Epistemic Probabilism, and the Cognitive Science of Religion," and "From Jesus to Shylock: Christian Supersessionism and *The Merchant of Venice.*" Though book reviews are included only occasionally, new books are listed in a section of "Books Received." Highly recommended for academic libraries.

5405. History of Religions. [ISSN: 0018-2710] 1961. q. USD 161 domestic; USD 174.66 Canada; USD 166 elsewhere. Ed(s): Bruce Lincoln, Wendy Doniger. University of Chicago Press, Journals Division, PO Box 37005, Chicago, IL 60637; subscriptions@press.uchicago.edu; http://www.journals.uchicago.edu. Illus., index, adv. Sample. Refereed. Circ: 1500 Paid. Vol. ends: May. Online: Chadwyck-Healey Inc.; EBSCO Publishing, EBSCO Host; Florida Center for Library Automation; Gale; JSTOR (Web-based Journal Archive); OCLC Online Computer Library Center, Inc.; ProQuest K-12 Learning Solutions; ProQuest LLC (Ann Arbor). Reprint: PSC. *Indexed:* AICP, AbAn, AmH&L, AmHI, AnthLit, ArtHuCI, BAS, EI, FR, HistAb, HumInd, IBR, IBSS, IBZ, IndIslam, LRI, MLA-IB, NTA, OTA, PhilInd, R&TA, RI-1, RILM, SSCI. *Bk. rev.:* 0-15, 400-1,800 words, signed. *Aud.:* Ac.

Published by the University of Chicago Press, *History of Religions* focuses on the study of religious phenomena from prehistory to the present, striving to publish "scholarship that reflects engagement with particular traditions, places, and times and yet also speaks to broader methodological and/or theoretical issues." Articles are substantial in length. Recent examples include "Black Magic and the Academy: Macumba and Afro-Brazilian 'Orthodoxies,'" "Mapping the Esoteric Body in the Islamic Yoga of Bengal," and "Remembering Rammohan: An Essay on the (Re-)emergence of Modern Hinduism." *HR* also includes review articles and book reviews and occasional comments on, or replies to, recent articles. Tables of contents since 1996 may be viewed at www.journals.uchicago.edu/HR. Highly recommended for academic libraries.

5406. Horizons (Villanova). Formerly: *21st Century Genetics Cooperative.* [ISSN: 0360-9669] 1974. s-a. College Theology Society, c/o Walter Conn, Ed., 800 Lancaster Ave., Villanova, PA 19085-1699. Illus., adv. Refereed. Circ: 1410 Paid. Microform: PQC. Online: American Theological Library Association; EBSCO Publishing, EBSCO Host; OCLC Online Computer Library Center, Inc.; Ovid Technologies, Inc. *Indexed:* ArtHuCI, CPL, NTA, OTA, RI-1, SSCI. *Bk. rev.:* 25-30, 400-1,600 words, signed. *Aud.:* Ac.

Horizons is the journal of the College Theology Society (CTS) at Villanova University, a professional society of college and university professors. Though founded as a Roman Catholic organization, CTS describes itself as "increasingly ecumenical in its concerns and publications." *Horizons* explores "developments in Catholic theology, the total Christian tradition, human religious experience, and the concerns of creative teaching in the college and university environment." Recent articles include an "Editorial Symposium" that offers two perspectives on the International Theological Commission's document, *Memory and Reconciliation: The Church and the Faults of the Past*; "The Dual Vocation of Parenthood and Professional Theology"; and "'When the Son of Man Is Lifted Up': The Redemptive Power of the Crucifixion in the Gospel of John." *Horizons* is recommended for academic libraries.

5407. The Humanist: a magazine of critical inquiry and social concern. [ISSN: 0018-7399] 1941. bi-m. Individuals, USD 24.95. Ed(s): Fred Edwards. American Humanist Association, 1777 T St, NW, Washington,

DC 20009-7125; aha@americanhumanist.org; http://www.americanhumanist.org/index.html. Illus., adv. Sample. Refereed. Circ: 17939. Vol. ends: Dec. Microform: PQC. Online: EBSCO Publishing, EBSCO Host; Florida Center for Library Automation; Gale; Northern Light Technology, Inc.; OCLC Online Computer Library Center, Inc.; ProQuest K-12 Learning Solutions; ProQuest LLC (Ann Arbor); H.W. Wilson. *Indexed:* AmHI, BRI, CBRI, ECER, FLI, FutSurv, HRA, HumInd, IBR, IBZ, LRI, MASUSE, MRD, PAIS, PhilInd, RGPR, RI-1, RILM, SSCI. *Bk. rev.:* 0-3, 600-1,200 words, signed. *Aud.:* Ga, Ac.

This journal is published by the American Humanist Association and defines its guiding ethos as "a rational philosophy informed by science, inspired by art, and motivated by compassion." The journal includes features, book reviews, and editorials that address a wide range of subjects—from science and religion to politics and popular culture—from a nontheistic, secular point of view. A recent issue includes a section of "Portraits of Activism"; an interview with the author of *The Feminist Mistake*; and regular columns addressing issues of the environment and matters of church and state. Selected articles from the current and past issues and additional content are available online at the web site, www.thehumanist.org. Though explicitly not religious, and a frequent critic of some kinds of religious involvement, *The Humanist* engages with many of the social and ethical issues that are also of concern to religious publications and presents potentially illuminating alternative points of view. Recommended for both public and academic libraries.

5408. International Journal for Philosophy of Religion. [ISSN: 0020-7047] 1970. bi-m. EUR 564 print & online eds. Ed(s): Eugene Thomas Long, Frank R Harrison, III. Springer Netherlands, Van Godewijckstraat 30, Dordrecht, 3311 GX, Netherlands; http://www.springeronline.com. Illus., index, adv. Refereed. Vol. ends: Jun/Dec. Microform: PQC. Online: Chadwyck-Healey Inc.; EBSCO Publishing, EBSCO Host; Gale; IngentaConnect; OCLC Online Computer Library Center, Inc.; OhioLINK; ProQuest LLC (Ann Arbor); Springer LINK; SwetsWise Online Content. Reprint: PSC. *Indexed:* AmHI, ArtHuCI, FR, HumInd, IBR, IBSS, IBZ, PhilInd, R&TA, RI-1. *Bk. rev.:* 0-4, 600-1,000 words, signed. *Aud.:* Ac.

Issued bimonthly by the academic publisher Springer, the *International Journal for Philosophy of Religion* seeks to provide "a medium for the exposition, development, and criticism of important philosophical insights and theories relevant to religion ... and a forum for critical, constructive, and interpretative consideration of religion from an objective, philosophical point of view." The journal presents articles, symposia, discussions, reviews, notes, and news for an audience concentrating on teachers and students of philosophy, philosophical theology, and religious thought. Recent articles include "Some Critical Reflections on the Hiddenness Argument," "Oppy, Infinity, and the Neoclassical Concept of God," and "Wittgenstein and Religious Dogma." Tables of contents of past issues and some access to recent issues are available at the web site, http://springerlink.metapress.com/content/102908/. Recommended for academic libraries.

5409. The International Journal for the Psychology of Religion. [ISSN: 1050-8619] 1991. q. GBP 302 print & online eds. Ed(s): Raymond F Paloutzian. Lawrence Erlbaum Associates, Inc., 325 Chestnut St, Ste. 800, Philadelphia, PA 19106; journals@erlbaum.com; http://www.leaonline.com. Illus., adv. Sample. Refereed. Vol. ends: No. 4. Reprint: PSC. *Indexed:* ASSIA, PsycInfo, R&TA, RI-1, SSA. *Bk. rev.:* 1-2, 500-1,500 words, signed. *Aud.:* Ac, Sa.

Published by Lawrence Erlbaum Associates, *The International Journal for the Psychology of Religion* (IJPR) offers a unique point of view at the junction of psychology and religious studies. *IJPR* is "devoted to psychological studies of religious processes and phenomena in all religious traditions." Its articles address topics such as the social psychology of religion, religious development, conversion, religious experience, religion and social attitudes and behavior, religion and mental health, and psychoanalytic and other theoretical interpretations of religion. Issues usually include a major essay and commentary, plus perspective papers and articles on the field in a specific country, for an audience of "psychologists, theologians, philosophers, religious leaders, neuroscientists, and social scientists." Recent articles include the research reports "Conversion to Islam Among French Adolescents and Adults: A Systematic Inventory of

Motives" and "Money Consciousness and the Tendency to Violate the Five Precepts Among Thai Buddhists." There is also the study "Therese of Lisieux from the Perspective of Attachment Theory and Separation Anxiety." The journal's web site (www.leaonline.com/loi/ijpr) offers tables of contents since 2000, plus an online sample issue. Recommended for academic libraries.

5410. International Review of Mission. [ISSN: 0020-8582] 1911. 2x/yr. Ed(s): Jacques Matthey. World Council of Churches, 150 route de Ferney, PO Box 2100, Geneva, 1211, Switzerland; dce@wcc-coe.org; http://www.wcc-coe.org/. Illus., index, adv. Circ: 3500. Vol. ends: Oct. Microform: PQC. Online: American Theological Library Association; EBSCO Publishing, EBSCO Host; Florida Center for Library Automation; Gale; Northern Light Technology, Inc.; OCLC Online Computer Library Center, Inc.; Ovid Technologies, Inc.; ProQuest K-12 Learning Solutions; ProQuest LLC (Ann Arbor). Reprint: PSC. *Indexed:* AICP, AmH&L, AmHI, BAS, ChrPI, HistAb, HumInd, IBR, IndIslam, NTA, R&TA, RI-1. *Bk. rev.:* 0-5, 200-1,000 words, signed. *Aud.:* Ac, Sa.

A quarterly publication of the Conference on World Mission and Evangelism of the ecumenical World Council of Churches, the *International Review of Mission* is intended "to foster serious reflection ... and to support the churches in their worldwide missionary calling." Each issue includes articles and academic papers on important mission events, with book reviews and a detailed bibliography of current literature from the Centre for the Study of Christianity in the Non-Western World, Edinburgh. A cumulative, searchable list of all of these bibliographies from 1912 to the present is available online at webdb.ucs.ed.ac.uk/divinity/cmb. Recent and forthcoming issues explore health, faith, and healing; Bible study and mission; Christian presence and witness in the Middle East; African Christian Diaspora in Europe; and mission as reconciliation and healing. The journal's audience consists in large part of pastors, active lay persons, theological students, missionaries, and missiologists. Recommended for seminaries and for academic libraries that serve communities studying the Christian missiological perspective.

5411. Interpretation (Richmond): a journal of Bible and theology. Former titles (until 1946): *The Union Seminary Review; Union Seminary Magazine.* [ISSN: 0020-9643] 1913. q. USD 30 (Individuals, USD 23; USD 6 newsstand/cover). Ed(s): Jennifer A Bowen, William P Brown. Union Theological Seminary, 3401 Brook Rd, Richmond, VA 23227; email@interpretation.org; http://www.interpretation.org. Illus., adv. Refereed. Circ: 8000 Paid. Vol. ends: Oct. Microform: PQC. Online: American Theological Library Association; EBSCO Publishing, EBSCO Host; Florida Center for Library Automation; Gale; OCLC Online Computer Library Center, Inc.; Ovid Technologies, Inc.; ProQuest K-12 Learning Solutions; ProQuest LLC (Ann Arbor); H.W. Wilson. *Indexed:* AmHI, ArtHuCI, BRI, CBRI, ChrPI, FR, HumInd, IBR, IBZ, NTA, OTA, R&TA, RI-1. *Bk. rev.:* Number and length vary. *Aud.:* Ga, Ac.

Interpretation, a quarterly journal published by the Presbyterian Union Theological Seminary (Richmond, Virginia), brings together articles on biblical scholarship, exegesis, and preaching in a particularly accessible way, for an audience of scholars, laity, and clergy. Most of the issues are thematic, exploring in-depth a particular subject or biblical book, such as Sabbath, Teaching the Bible Today, Parables, and discussions of reading the 12 books of the prophets as a whole. Each issue also includes the feature "Between Text and Sermon," which presents a short exposition of four passages corresponding to the upcoming readings in the Common Lectionary. There is also a mix of long and short book reviews (3–4 major, 800–1,200 words; 25–30 minor, 200–450 words; all signed). The current table of contents and the full text of book reviews since 2001 are available at www.interpretation.org/index.htm. Especially useful for Christian seminary libraries, and recommended for both large public and academic libraries.

5412. Japanese Journal of Religious Studies. Formerly (until 1974): *Contemporary Religions in Japan.* [ISSN: 0304-1042] 1960. s-a. JPY 5000 (Individuals, JPY 3500). Ed(s): Paul I Swanson. Nanzan Institute for Religion and Culture, 18 Yamazato-cho, Showa-ku, Nagoya, 466-8673, Japan; nirc@ic.nanzan-u.ac.jp; http://www.nanzan-u.ac.jp/ SHUBUNKEN/index.htm. Illus., index, adv. Refereed. Circ: 600. Online:

American Theological Library Association; EBSCO Publishing, EBSCO Host; OCLC Online Computer Library Center, Inc.; Ovid Technologies, Inc. *Indexed:* ArtHuCI, BAS, FR, IBR, IBSS, IBZ, R&TA, RI-1. *Bk. rev.:* 0-15, 1,000-3,000 words, signed. *Aud.:* Ac, Sa.

Japanese Journal of Religious Studies is a semi-annual journal dedicated to the academic study of Japanese religions, published by Nanzan Institute. A cumulative, searchable listing of essays and book reviews from 1974 to 2006, with most available for download, is available at the web site, www.nanzan-u.ac.jp/SHUBUNKEN/publications/jjrs/jjrsMain.htm. Drawing especially (but not exclusively) on Japanese authors, this journal presents English-language articles and book reviews. Recent articles include "Popular Buddhist Orthodoxy in Contemporary Japan," "Learning to Persevere: The Popular Teachings of Tendai Ascetics," and *"Fukudenkai:* Sewing the Buddha's Robe in Contemporary Japanese Buddhist Practice." Japanese characters appear in the text following Romanized transliterations. *JJRS* offers a distinct perspective for religious studies collections and is recommended for consideration by academic libraries.

Jewish Quarterly. See Literary Reviews section.

5413. Journal for the Scientific Study of Religion. [ISSN: 0021-8294] 1961. q. GBP 107 print & online eds. Ed(s): Rhys H Williams. Blackwell Publishing, Inc., Commerce Place, 350 Main St, Malden, MA 02148; customerservices@blackwellpublishing.com; http://www.blackwellpublishing.com. Illus., index, adv. Refereed. Circ: 3500. Vol. ends: Dec. Microform: PQC. Online: American Theological Library Association; Blackwell Synergy; EBSCO Publishing, EBSCO Host; Gale; IngentaConnect; JSTOR (Web-based Journal Archive); OCLC Online Computer Library Center, Inc.; OhioLINK; Ovid Technologies, Inc.; SwetsWise Online Content; H.W. Wilson. Reprint: PSC. *Indexed:* ABS&EES, AbAn, AmH&L, AmHI, ApEcolAb, ArtHuCI, BAS, CJA, FR, HistAb, HumInd, IBR, IBSS, IBZ, IJP, LRI, MLA-IB, NTA, OTA, PRA, PSA, PhilInd, PsycInfo, R&TA, RI-1, SSA, SSCI, SociolAb. *Bk. rev.:* 4-8, 600-1,500 words, signed. *Aud.:* Ac.

The quarterly publication features provocative articles on scientific research that concerns religious institutions and experiences, as well as editorials, research notes, and book reviews. Many articles are interdisciplinary, drawing on sociological, psychological, anthropological, political science, economics, or gender studies perspectives and employing both quantitative and qualitative methodologies. Recent articles include "Characters in Search of a Script: The Exit Narratives of Ultra-Orthodox Jews," "Religious Diversity and Community Volunteerism Among Asian Americans," and "Negative Life Events, Patterns of Positive and Negative Religious Coping, and Psychological Functioning." The full text of several recent issues and tables of contents of past issues are available at the web site, www.blackwell-synergy.com/loi/JSSR. Widely indexed and frequently cited, *JSSR* is highly recommended for academic libraries.

5414. Journal for the Study of the Historical Jesus. [ISSN: 1476-8690] 2003. s-a. EUR 207 print & online eds. (Individuals, EUR 56). Ed(s): Robert L Webb. Brill, PO Box 9000, Leiden, 2300 PA, Netherlands; cs@brill.nl; http://www.brill.nl. Adv. Reprint: PSC. *Indexed:* IBR, IBZ, NTA. *Bk. rev.:* 4-8, 100-400 words, signed. *Aud.:* Ac.

First published in 2003, the *Journal for the Study of the Historical Jesus* investigates "the social, cultural and historical context in which Jesus lived," discussing methodological issues that surround the reconstruction of the historical Jesus, examining the history of historical Jesus research, and exploring how the life of Jesus is perceived in the arts and other media. Issues typically comprise four to five articles and a substantial book review section. Recent articles include "Was Jesus Illegitimate? The Evidence of His Social Interactions," "Herod Antipas in Galilee: Friend or Foe of the Historical Jesus?," and "Fictionalizing Jesus: Story and History in Two Recent Jesus Novels." Tables of contents and a free online sample issue are available at jhj.sagepub.com. Although the journal seeks to be of use to scholars and nonscholars alike, articles are generally written in an academic style, with scholarly documentation. Worth consideration by large public libraries and academic libraries.

5415. *Journal for the Study of the New Testament.* [ISSN: 0142-064X] 1978. 5x/yr. GBP 273. Ed(s): David Horrell. Sage Publications Ltd., 1 Oliver's Yard, 55 City Rd, London, EC1 1SP, United Kingdom; info@sagepub.co.uk; http://www.sagepub.co.uk. Illus., index, adv. Refereed. Vol. ends: Jun. Reprint: PSC. *Indexed:* FR, IBR, IBZ, NTA, R&TA, RI-1, RILM. *Bk. rev.:* 2-7, 300-400 words, signed. *Aud.:* Ac.

Journal for the Study of the New Testament strives to be inclusive in scope, representing both traditional and innovative work in New Testament studies, for an intended audience of scholars, teachers, and serious students. Issues generally comprise four to six articles plus a number of book reviews. Recent articles include "The 'Gospel' and the 'Word': Exploring Some Early Christian Patterns," "Meggitt on the Madness and Kingship of Jesus," and "Why Was Jesus Crucified, But His Followers Were Not?" A subscription to the *JSNT* also includes the annual *JSNT* Booklist, which aims to provide a "convenient, comprehensive, authoritative ... survey of every publication of interest to the serious reader of the New Testament." A free sample issue of the journal and tables of contents of past issues are available online at the web site, http://jsnt.sagepub.com. This journal and the related *Journal for the Study of the Old Testament* are standard resources in their fields. Highly recommended for academic libraries that support studies in this area.

5416. *Journal for the Study of the Old Testament.* [ISSN: 0309-0892] 1976. 5x/yr. GBP 273. Ed(s): Keith Whitelam, John Jarick. Sage Publications Ltd., 1 Oliver's Yard, 55 City Rd, London, EC1 1SP, United Kingdom; info@sagepub.co.uk; http://www.sagepub.co.uk. Illus., adv. Refereed. Vol. ends: No. 5. Reprint: PSC. *Indexed:* FR, IBR, IBZ, NTA, OTA, R&TA, RI-1, RILM. *Bk. rev.:* 100-700 words, signed. *Aud.:* Ac.

Journal for the Study of the Old Testament is regarded as a pioneering and innovative journal, publishing rigorous Old Testament scholarship across a range of methodologies and providing a forum for original approaches to Old Testament studies. Recent articles include "Law and Life: Leviticus 18.5 in the Literary Framework of Ezekiel," "Is There a Parallel between 1 Samuel 3 and the Sixth Chapter of the Egyptian Book of the Dead?," and "Ideology, Geography, and the List of Minor Judges." The current issue, a sample issue, and tables of contents of various past issues are available online at the web site, http://jsot.sagepub.com. Since 1998, each year the "Booklist for The Society for Old Testament Study" has been a special issue of *JSOT,* presenting some 500 book reviews of varying lengths. Like *Journal for the Study of the New Testament, JSOT* is a standard resource in its field and is highly recommended for libraries that serve scholars in this area.

5417. *Journal of Biblical Literature.* Formerly (until 1888): *Society of Biblical Literature and Exegesis. Journal.* [ISSN: 0021-9231] 1881. q. Members, USD 35 print; Non-members, USD 165 print. Ed(s): Gail R O'Day. Society of Biblical Literature, The Luce Center, 825 Houston Mill Rd, Atlanta, GA 30333; sblexec@sbl-site.org; http://www.sbl-site.org. Illus., index, adv. Refereed. Circ: 5000 Paid and free. Vol. ends: Winter. Microform: PMC; PQC. Online: American Theological Library Association; Chadwyck-Healey Inc.; EBSCO Publishing, EBSCO Host; JSTOR (Web-based Journal Archive); Northern Light Technology, Inc.; OCLC Online Computer Library Center, Inc.; Ovid Technologies, Inc.; ProQuest K-12 Learning Solutions; ProQuest LLC (Ann Arbor); H.W. Wilson. *Indexed:* AmHI, ArtHuCI, BRI, CBRI, HumInd, IBR, IBZ, IJP, NTA, OTA, R&TA, RI-1, SSCI. *Bk. rev.:* 20-25, 900-1,500 words, signed. *Aud.:* Ac.

Journal of Biblical Literature (JBL) is one of the premier English-language journals in biblical studies, including articles, book reviews, and scholarly notes by members of the Society of Biblical Literature. *JBL* "promotes critical and academic biblical scholarship" and seeks articles at a consistent level of expertise, whether discussing general topics, such as the recent "The Tower of Babel and the Origin of the World's Cultures," or quite specific topics, such as "'So Shall God Do...': Variations of an Oath Formula and Its Literary Meaning." Articles are carefully documented and frequently include discussions in original languages. The shorter "Critical Notes" offer brief responses to other published works and previous articles, and the many book reviews provide a guide to current literature. Book reviews published since 1998 (and additional reviews) are available online at the web site, www.bookreviews.org. *JBL* is an essential journal for academic collections related in any way to biblical studies.

5418. *Journal of Church and State.* [ISSN: 0021-969X] 1959. q. USD 39 (Individuals, USD 25). Ed(s): Derek H Davis. Baylor University, J M Dawson Institute of Church-State Studies, One Bear Place #97308, PO Box 97308, Waco, TX 76798-7308; Suzanne_Sellers@baylor.edu; http://www.baylor.edu. Index, adv. Sample. Refereed. Circ: 1700. Vol. ends: Fall. Microform: WSH; PMC; PQC. Online: EBSCO Publishing, EBSCO Host; Florida Center for Library Automation; Gale; OCLC Online Computer Library Center, Inc.; ProQuest LLC (Ann Arbor); H.W. Wilson. Reprint: WSH. *Indexed:* ABS&EES, AmH&L, AmHI, ArtHuCI, BAS, BRI, CBRI, CLI, ChrPI, EAA, HistAb, HumInd, IBR, IBSS, IBZ, LRI, NTA, PAIS, PRA, PSA, R&TA, RI-1, SociolAb. *Bk. rev.:* 35-40, 300-800 words, signed. *Aud.:* Ac, Sa.

Founded in 1959, and published by the Dawson Institute of Church-State Studies at Baylor University, *Journal of Church and State* is interfaith, international, and interdisciplinary. The journal publishes articles from a diversity of viewpoints, addressing topics related to religious liberty, rights of religious minorities, liberty of conscience, and the relationship between law and religion. Each issue features, in addition to a timely editorial, six or more major articles, and 35–40 reviews of significant books related to church and state. Topics of recent articles include "Religion and Politics at the Border: Canadian Church Support for American Vietnam War Resisters" and "Hizbullah: The Story from Within." *JCS* also occasionally publishes the text of major legislative, legal, and ecclesiastical documents. Regular features include "Notes on Church State Affairs," which reports current developments throughout the world, and a "Calendar of Events." The table of contents and the full text of the "Notes on Church-State Affairs" and the "Calendar of Events" are available at the web site, www.baylor.edu/church_state/index.php?id=35398. Recommended for academic libraries.

5419. *Journal of Early Christian Studies.* Supersedes (in 1993): *The Second Century;* Incorporates (1972-1993): *Patristics.* [ISSN: 1067-6341] 1981. q. USD 140. Ed(s): J Patout Burns, David Brakke. The Johns Hopkins University Press, 2715 N Charles St, Baltimore, MD 21218-4363; http://www.press.jhu.edu. Illus., adv. Sample. Refereed. Circ: 1439 Paid. Vol. ends: Winter. Online: Chadwyck-Healey Inc.; EBSCO Publishing, EBSCO Host; OCLC Online Computer Library Center, Inc.; OhioLINK; Project MUSE; ProQuest K-12 Learning Solutions; ProQuest LLC (Ann Arbor); SwetsWise Online Content. Reprint: PSC. *Indexed:* AmHI, ArtHuCI, HumInd, IBR, IBZ, L&LBA, MLA-IB, NTA, R&TA, RI-1, SSA, SSCI, SociolAb. *Bk. rev.:* 10-20, 400-1,000 words, signed. *Aud.:* Ac.

Journal of Early Christian Studies is the official publication of the North American Patristics Society. The journal focuses on the study of Christianity from 100 to 700 C.E., with the goal of publishing excellent traditional scholarship. It also includes articles that feature new themes and methodologies, such as work in women's studies and literary theory. Each issue also includes a section of book reviews, with occasional scholarly notes. Among recent articles are "The Persuasiveness of a Woman: The Mistranslation and Misinterpretation of Eusebius's *Historia Ecclesiastica* 5.1.41" and "Demoniacs, Dissent, and Disempowerment in the Late Roman West: Some Case Studies from the Hagiographical Literature." Tables of contents (including subject headings for the articles) and abstracts for issues since 1996 can be found at muse.jhu.edu/journals/journal_of_early_christian_studies. Recommended for large academic collections; an essential title for libraries that support scholarship in the area of patristics.

5420. *Journal of Ecclesiastical History.* [ISSN: 0022-0469] 1953. q. GBP 234. Ed(s): James Carleton Paget, Diarmaid MacCulloch. Cambridge University Press, The Edinburgh Bldg, Shaftesbury Rd, Cambridge, CB2 2RU, United Kingdom; journals@cambridge.org; http://www.journals.cambridge.org. Illus., adv. Sample. Refereed. Circ: 1250. Vol. ends: Oct. Microform: PQC. Online: Pub.; EBSCO Publishing, EBSCO Host; Florida Center for Library Automation; Gale; OCLC Online Computer Library Center, Inc.; OhioLINK; SwetsWise Online Content. Reprint: PSC. *Indexed:* AmH&L, AmHI, ArtHuCI, BrArAb, FR, HistAb, HumInd, NTA, NumL, R&TA, RI-1, SSA, SSCI. *Bk. rev.:* 60-75, 300-700 words, signed. *Aud.:* Ac.

Journal of Ecclesiastical History, issued by Cambridge University Press, publishes material on all aspects of the history of the Christian Church, as an institution and in its relations with other religions and society at large. Each annual volume includes about 20 articles and roughly 300 notices of recently published books relevant to the interests of the journal's readers. Recent articles include "The Fantasy of Reunion: The Rise and Fall of the Association for the Promotion of the Unity of Christendom," "Immanuel Tremellius' 1569 Edition of the Syriac New Testament," and "The Catholic Church and the English Civil War: The Case of Thomas White." About a third of each issue is devoted to book reviews, providing a significant overview of current literature. The tables of contents for issues since 1998 and a sample issue are available online at the journal's web site, uk.cambridge.org/journals/ech. Recommended for large academic collections; an essential title for libraries that support scholarship in the area of Christian Church history.

5421. Journal of Feminist Studies in Religion. [ISSN: 8755-4178] 1985. s-a. USD 55 (Individuals, USD 26). Ed(s): Elisabeth Schussler Fiorenza, Stephanie Mitchem. Indiana University Press, 601 N Morton St, Bloomington, IN 47404; http://www.indiana.edu/~iupress. Illus., adv. Refereed. Circ: 1000 Paid. Reprint: PSC. *Indexed:* AmHI, ArtHuCI, FemPer, HumInd, IBR, IBZ, NTA, R&TA, RI-1, SSCI, WSA. *Bk. rev.:* Essay length, signed. *Aud.:* Ac, Sa.

The semi-annual *Journal of Feminist Studies in Religion* began publication in 1985, with the aim of offering a forum "for discussion and dialogue among women and men of differing feminist perspectives in ways that would contribute to the transformation of both the academy and religious and cultural institutions." Associated with Harvard Divinity School, interdisciplinary, and interreligious, *JFSR* features articles that explore a diversity of feminist theories, practices, cultures, and religions. Other regular features include editorials, creative writing, artwork, and "Living It Out," which comprises reports on development and practices of feminist studies and movements within religions. Among recent articles are "Dismantling the Master's Tools with the Master's House: Native Feminist Liberation Theologies," with five responses, and "Islamic Feminism in Iran: Feminism in a New Islamic Context." Tables of Contents of all issues are available at the web site, www.hds.harvard.edu/jfsr. As *JFSR* is situated at a crossroads of interdisciplinary study, it should be considered for large public libraries and academic collections that serve scholarship in a variety of disciplines, such as women's studies, religious studies, and philosophy.

5422. Journal of Jewish Studies. [ISSN: 0022-2097] 1948. s-a. GBP 80 (Individuals, GBP 45). Ed(s): Dr. Sacha Stern, Geza Vermes. Oxford Centre for Hebrew and Jewish Studies, Yarnton Manor, Yarnton, OX1 1PY, United Kingdom. Illus., adv. Refereed. Circ: 1000. Vol. ends: Oct. Microform: PQC. Reprint: PSC. *Indexed:* AmH&L, AmHI, ArtHuCI, BrHumI, FR, HistAb, IBR, IBSS, IBZ, IJP, IndIslam, NTA, OTA, PhilInd, R&TA, RI-1. *Bk. rev.:* 25-30, 400-3,000 words, signed. *Aud.:* Ac, Sa.

Founded in 1948, the semi-annual *Journal of Jewish Studies* provides an international forum for publication and discussion of new findings in Jewish history, literature, and religion from the biblical to the modern era. Though *JJS* is best known as a leader in scholarship of earlier periods, editors now seek to include more articles concerning medieval and modern Jewish history and culture. A large review section and a list of "Books Received" keep readers aware of current publications. Recent articles include "Christian Emperors, Christian Church and the Jews of the Diaspora in the Greek East, CE 379-450," "Crimes and Punishments, Part I: Mitot Beit Din as a Reflection of Rabbinic Jurisprudence," and "Disaster and Change in an Ottoman Sephardic Community: Moses Montefiore and the Monastir Fire of 1863." A fully searchable and sortable table of contents of all published material and a free sample issue are available at the web site, www.jjs-online.net/index.php?subaction=online. Recommended for academic libraries that serve scholars in Jewish or interfaith studies.

5423. Journal of Pentecostal Theology. [ISSN: 0966-7369] 1992. s-a. EUR 190 print & online eds. (Individuals, EUR 40). Ed(s): Rickie D Moore, Steven J Land. Brill, PO Box 9000, Leiden, 2300 PA, Netherlands; cs@brill.nl; http://www.brill.nl. Adv. Online: EBSCO Publishing, EBSCO Host; HighWire Press; SAGE Publications, Inc., SAGE Journals Online. Reprint: PSC. *Indexed:* ChrPI, IBR, IBZ, NTA, R&TA, RI-1. *Bk. rev.:* Number and length vary. *Aud.:* Ac.

Founded in 1993, *Journal of Pentecostal Theology* is is a semi-annual publication edited by faculty of the Church of God Theological Seminary. *JPT* describes itself as the first journal to publish "theological research from a Pentecostal perspective on an international scholarly level." The journal seeks to foster ecumenical and theological interchange and includes contributions from non-Pentecostal scholars. Issues generally contain both articles and responses and, occasionally, responses to responses. Recent examples are "The Prophet as Mentor: A Crucial Facet of the Biblical Presentations of Moses, Elijah, and Isaiah, with a response, "Why does Luke Use Tongues as A Sign of the Spirit's Empowerment?"; and "Pentecostal and Postmodernist Hermeneutics: A Critique of Three Conceits." Tables of contents and a free online sample issue are available at http://jpt.sagepub.com/. Recommended for consideration by large public libraries and by academic libraries that support religion or theology programs with ecumenical interests.

5424. Journal of Presbyterian History. Former titles (until 1996): *American Presbyterians: Journal of Presbyterian History;* (until 1984): *Journal of Presbyterian History;* (until 1961): *Presbyterian Historical Society Journal.* [ISSN: 1521-9216] 1901. s-a. Membership, USD 100. Ed(s): Tricia Manning. Presbyterian Historical Society, 425 Lombard St, Philadelphia, PA 19147; tmanning@history.pcusa.org; http://www.history.pcusa.org/. Illus., index. Sample. Refereed. Circ: 900. Vol. ends: Winter. *Indexed:* AmH&L, ArtHuCI, BAS, BEL&L, FR, HistAb, IBR, IBZ, NTA, R&TA, RI-1, RILM, SSCI. *Bk. rev.:* 5-10, 400-600 words, signed. *Aud.:* Ac, Sa.

The semi-annual *Journal of Presbyterian History* is published by the Presbyterian Historical Society, the official historical agency of the Presbyterian Church (U.S.A.). *JPH*'s purpose is "to inform, nurture, and promote among its readers an understanding and appreciation of religious history in its cultural setting," with an emphasis on Presbyterian and Reformed history, and to inspire readers to preserve that history. Some examples of articles are "The American Revolution's Role in the Reshaping of Calvinistic Protestantism," "Scottish Convenanters and the Creation of an American Identity," and "John Livingston Nevius and the New Missions History." Tables of contents from 1999 and the full text of some articles appear at the web site, www.history.pcusa.org/pubs/journal/toc.html. As a denominational publication, *JPH* will certainly be of interest to libraries affiliated with Presbyterian and other Reformed churches; it should also be considered by academic libraries with strong collections in history of religion in the United States.

5425. Journal of Psychology and Theology: an evangelical forum for the integration of psychology and theology. [ISSN: 0091-6471] 1973. q. USD 42 domestic; USD 52 foreign. Ed(s): Patricia L Pike. Biola University, Rosemead School of Psychology, 13800 Biola Ave, La Mirada, CA 90639-0001. Illus., adv. Refereed. Circ: 1700. Vol. ends: Winter. Microform: PQC. Online: The Dialog Corporation; EBSCO Publishing, EBSCO Host; Florida Center for Library Automation; Gale; ProQuest LLC (Ann Arbor). *Indexed:* AgeL, AmHI, ArtHuCI, ChrPI, IBR, IBZ, IMFL, OTA, PsycInfo, R&TA, RI-1, SSCI. *Bk. rev.:* 4-6, 750-1,000 words, signed. *Aud.:* Ac.

This journal is published by Biola University, an the evangelical Christian institution. As the Biola web site notes, the purpose of the *Journal of Psychology and Theology* "is to communicate recent scholarly thinking on the interrelationships of psychological and theological concepts ... and to place before the evangelical community articles that have bearing on the nature of humankind from a biblical perspective." The precise focus of *JPT* is reflected in the topics of articles it publishes. Recent examples include "Psychology's Love-Hate Relationship with Love: Critiques, Affirmations, and Christian Responses," and "Psychoanalysis, Attachment, and Spirituality: The Emergence of Two Relational Traditions." A selection of full-text articles is available at the web site, https://wisdom.biola.edu/jpt/freearticles.cfm, and tables of contents with abstracts are at the web site, https://wisdom.biola.edu/jpt/issueind.cfm. Those who advocate an evangelical approach to psychology will want this journal in their collections. Other academic libraries that serve religious studies programs should consider this journal as a resource for understanding an evangelical perspective on psychology.

5426. The Journal of Religion. Formed by the 1921 merger of: *American Journal of Theology; Biblical World;* Which had former titles (until 1892): *The Old and New Testament Student;* (until 1889): *Old Testament Student;* (until 1883): *Hebrew Student.* [ISSN: 0022-4189] 1882. q. USD 151 domestic; USD 167.06 Canada; USD 159 elsewhere. Ed(s): Paul Mendes-Flohr, William Schweiker. University of Chicago Press, Journals Division, PO Box 37005, Chicago, IL 60637; subscriptions@press.uchicago.edu; http://www.journals.uchicago.edu. Illus., index, adv. Refereed. Circ: 2200. Vol. ends: Oct. Microform: MIM; PMC; PQC. Online: EBSCO Publishing, EBSCO Host; Florida Center for Library Automation; Gale; JSTOR (Web-based Journal Archive); OCLC Online Computer Library Center, Inc.; ProQuest K-12 Learning Solutions; ProQuest LLC (Ann Arbor). Reprint: PSC. *Indexed:* AmH&L, AmHI, ArtHuCI, BAS, BEL&L, BRD, BRI, CBRI, FR, HistAb, HumInd, IBR, IPB, MLA-IB, NTA, OTA, PhilInd, R&TA, RI-1, SSA, SSCI, SociolAb. *Bk. rev.:* 50-60, 750-1,500 words, signed. *Aud.:* Ac.

Journal of Religion began publication in 1915, a descendant of a long line of religious history and studies journals, beginning with *The Hebrew Student* in 1882. *JR* is published by the University of Chicago Press and edited at that university's Divinity School, as part of its effort "to promote critical, hermeneutical, historical, and constructive inquiry into religion." With a mission that gives it a broad scope, *JR* includes articles in theology, religious ethics, philosophy of religion, and historical, sociological, psychological, linguistic, or artistic viewpoints on the role of religion in culture and society. A typical issue will include articles, a review essay, and a lengthy book review section. Examples of recent articles are "The Family, the Gospel, and the Catholic Worker," "On the Track of the Fugitive Gods: Heidegger, Luther, Holderlin," and the review article "American Dispensationalism's Perpetually Imminent End Times." A sample issue and tables of contents back to 1996 are available at the web site, www.journals.uchicago.edu/JR/home.html. *Journal of Religion* is an essential title for academic libraries and should also be considered by large public libraries.

5427. Journal of Religion and Health. [ISSN: 0022-4197] 1961. q. EUR 743 print & online eds. Ed(s): David Leeming. Springer New York LLC, 233 Spring St, New York, NY 10013-1578; service-ny@springer.com; http://www.springer.com/. Illus., index, adv. Refereed. Vol. ends: Winter. Microform: PQC. Online: EBSCO Publishing, EBSCO Host; Gale; IngentaConnect; OCLC Online Computer Library Center, Inc.; OhioLINK; Springer LINK; SwetsWise Online Content. Reprint: PSC. *Indexed:* AgeL, ArtHuCI, ExcerpMed, IJP, R&TA, RI-1, SSCI. *Bk. rev.:* 15-20, 300-800 words, signed. *Aud.:* Ga, Ac.

Founded in 1961 by the Academy of Religion and Mental Health, the *Journal of Religion and Health* is now sponsored by the Blanton-Peale-Institute, a multifaith, non-sectarian educational and service organization. The journal invites interdisciplinary exchange in exploring the relevance of contemporary religious thought to current medical and psychological research, on both theoretical and practical levels. Recent articles include "East of Ego: The Intersection of Narcissistic Personality and Buddhist Practice," "Ethics, Ethos, and Dualities: Self and Culture, Talking in Tongues," and "Spiritual Tools for Enhancing the Pastoral Visit to Hospitalized Patients." Portions of recent issues and tables of contents of past issues are available online at the web site, http://springerlink.metapress.com/content/104938. As a journal that bridges the fields of psychology, public health, religious studies, and pastoral care, this journal is worth consideration by large public libraries, seminary libraries, and academic libraries that support scholarship or practice in these areas.

5428. Journal of Religious Ethics. [ISSN: 0384-9694] 1973. q. USD 195 print & online eds. Ed(s): Sumner B Twiss, John Kelsay. Blackwell Publishing, Inc., Commerce Place, 350 Main St, Malden, MA 02148; customerservices@blackwellpublishing.com; http://www.blackwellpublishing.com. Illus., adv. Sample. Refereed. Circ: 1200. Vol. ends: Fall. Microform: PQC. Online: American Theological Library Association; Blackwell Synergy; EBSCO Publishing, EBSCO Host; Gale; IngentaConnect; OCLC Online Computer Library Center, Inc.; OhioLINK; Ovid Technologies, Inc.; SwetsWise Online Content. Reprint: PSC. *Indexed:* ABS&EES, AmHI, ArtHuCI, HumInd, LRI, NTA, OTA, PRA, PhilInd, R&TA, RI-1, SSCI. *Bk. rev.:* Number varies. *Aud.:* Ac, Sa.

Journal of Religious Ethics has a commitment to approaching ethics through multiple religious traditions and engaging with those traditions' processes of ethical reflection and analysis. In addition to comparative religious ethics, *JRE* emphasizes "foundational conceptual and methodological issues in religious ethics, and historical studies of influential figures and texts." Typical issues contain a mixture of independent studies, commissioned articles, a book review essay, and a section of letters, notes, and comments. The signed book reviews may number one or two per issue, and be 25 pages each. Recent articles include "Margaret Thatcher's Christian Faith: A Case Study in Political Theology" and "Karma and the Possibility of Purification: An Ethical and Psychological Analysis of the Doctrine of Karma in Buddhism." There was also the review essay "Comparison and History in the Study of Religious Ethics: An Essay on Michael Cook's Commanding Right and Forbidding Wrong in Islamic Thought." A free sample issue and the tables of contents of other issues are available online at the web site, www.blackwellpublishing.com/journal.asp?ref=0384-9694. Recommended for academic libraries that support research in religious studies, philosophy, theology, and related fields.

The Journal of Religious Thought. See African American section.

5429. Journal of Theological Studies. [ISSN: 0022-5185] 1899. s-a. EUR 300 print or online ed. Ed(s): Graham Gould, Morna D Hooker. Oxford University Press, Great Clarendon St, Oxford, OX2 6DP, United Kingdom; jnl.orders@oup.co.uk; http://www.oxfordjournals.org. Illus., index, adv. Sample. Refereed. Circ: 1500. Vol. ends: Oct. Microform: PQC. Online: Chadwyck-Healey Inc.; EBSCO Publishing, EBSCO Host; Florida Center for Library Automation; Gale; HighWire Press; IngentaConnect; Northern Light Technology, Inc.; OCLC Online Computer Library Center, Inc.; OhioLINK; Oxford Journals; ProQuest LLC (Ann Arbor); SwetsWise Online Content; H.W. Wilson. Reprint: PSC. *Indexed:* AmHI, ArtHuCI, BrHumI, FR, HumInd, IBR, IBZ, MLA-IB, NTA, OTA, R&TA, RI-1. *Bk. rev.:* 180-200, 400-2,500 words, signed. *Aud.:* Ac, Sa.

Founded in 1899 and published by Oxford University Press (OUP), the semi-annual *Journal of Theological Studies* covers a broad range of theological research, scholarship, and interpretation, in the Old and New Testaments, church history, philosophy of religion, and ethics. OUP notes that the journal also reproduces ancient and modern texts, inscriptions, and documents that have not before appeared in type. Issues typically contain about six lengthy, scholarly articles. Some recent examples are "The Character of Yhwh and the Ethics of the Old Testament: Is Imitatio Dei Appropriate?," "Polymorphic Christology: Its Origins and Development in Early Christianity," and "On Israel's God and God's Israel: Assessing Supersessionism in Paul." Book reviews, most two pages or so, but some lengthy, make up most of each issue. Tables of contents from 1996 and a sample issue are available at the web site, www.oup.co.uk/theolj;. *JTS* is a highly useful journal recommended for libraries that support research in religious studies.

5430. Judaism: a quarterly journal of Jewish life and thought. [ISSN: 0022-5762] 1952. q. USD 35 (Individuals, USD 20). Ed(s): Murray Baumgarten. American Jewish Congress, 825 3rd Ave., 18th F., New York, NY 10022-9715; http://www.ajcongress.org/. Illus., index, adv. Refereed. Circ: 6000. Vol. ends: Oct. Microform: PQC. Online: EBSCO Publishing, EBSCO Host; Florida Center for Library Automation; Gale; OCLC Online Computer Library Center, Inc.; ProQuest K-12 Learning Solutions; ProQuest LLC (Ann Arbor); H.W. Wilson. *Indexed:* ABS&EES, AmHI, ArtHuCI, FR, HumInd, IBR, IBZ, IJP, IndIslam, MASUSE, MLA-IB, NTA, OTA, PhilInd, R&TA, RI-1, RILM, SSCI. *Bk. rev.:* 2-5, 3,000-6,000 words, signed. *Aud.:* Ga, Ac.

Published by the American Jewish Congress (AJC), *Judaism* sets itself as continuing in American English the habits of scholarly thought and inquiry begun in Hebrew, Yiddish, and other languages. As described in its statement of purpose, the journal aims to be free and non-partisan, "dedicated to the creative discussion and exposition of the religious, moral, and philosophical concepts of Judaism and their relevance to the problems of modern society." Recent articles include "Dispensing Medical Marijuana: Some Halachic Parameters," "Beyond the Fourth Wave: Contemporary Anti-Semitism and Radical Islam," and "The 'Forgotten Refugees' Remembered in Film." Articles tend to assume familiarity with the vocabulary and concepts of Judaism; though scholarly, they may be of general interest to those familiar with the topics under discussion. Tables of contents of issues since 1994 may be viewed online at the web site, humwww.ucsc.edu/judaism/judaism.html. Providing a wide coverage of Jewish religion and culture, this resource is recommended for academic libraries, large public libraries, and libraries that support Judaic studies.

Lilith. See Gender Studies section.

5431. *Literature and Theology: an international journal of religion, theory and culture.* Formerly: *National Conference of Literature and Religion. Newsletter.* [ISSN: 0269-1205] 1987. q. EUR 224 print or online ed. Ed(s): Dr. Andrew Hass. Oxford University Press, Great Clarendon St, Oxford, OX2 6DP, United Kingdom; jnl.orders@ oup.co.uk; http://www.oxfordjournals.org. Illus., adv. Sample. Refereed. Circ: 800. Vol. ends: Dec. Reprint: PSC. *Indexed:* AmHI, BrHumI, HumInd, IBR, IBZ, L&LBA, MLA-IB, NTA, R&TA, RI-1, RILM. *Bk. rev.:* 5-10, 400-1,000 words, signed. *Aud.:* Ac, Sa.

Literature and Theology brings a unique perspective to the study of theology, "inviting both close textual analysis and broader theoretical speculation as ways of exploring how religion is embedded within culture." *LT* intends to be neither a journal of theology nor a journal of literary studies, but a forum for confronting and challenging both disciplines and exploring the tensions and connections between them. This journal is produced by Oxford University Press and is closely associated with the International Society for Literature, Religion, and culture; its editorial staff and editorial board are drawn both from Europe and from the United States. Recent articles include "'One Lot in Sodom': Masculinity and the Gendered Body in Early Modern Narratives of Converted Turks," "The Role of Missions in *Things Fall Apart* and *Nervous Conditions*," and "Memorialising May 4, 1970 at Kent State University: Reflections on Collective Memory, Public Art and Religious Criticism." Tables of contents since 1996 and a free online sample issue can be found at www.oup.co.uk/litthe. Recommended for academic libraries; of interest to readers in literature, study of religion, and theology.

5432. *Mennonite Quarterly Review.* Supersedes: *Goshen College Record. Review Supplement.* [ISSN: 0025-9373] 1927. q. USD 30 domestic; USD 31 foreign; USD 9 newsstand/cover. Ed(s): John D Roth. Goshen College, 1700 S Main St, Goshen, IN 46526; pr@goshen.edu; http://www.goshen.edu. Illus., index, adv. Sample. Refereed. Circ: 1000. Vol. ends: Oct. *Indexed:* ABS&EES, AmH&L, ChrPI, FR, HistAb, IBR, IBZ, PRA, R&TA, RI-1, RILM. *Bk. rev.:* 7-12, 100-600 words, signed. *Aud.:* Ac, Sa.

This quarterly journal is devoted to promoting interest in, and disseminating information about, Anabaptist–Mennonite, Amish, and Hutterite history, thought, life, and current affairs. The first North American journal for and about Mennonites, *Mennonite Quarterly Review* is published cooperatively by Goshen College, the Associated Mennonite Biblical Seminar, and the Mennonite Historical Society. Typical issues contain articles, reviews of recent publications, and research notes. Recent articles include "The Birth and Evolution of Swiss Anabaptism, 1520-1530," together with responses; "Mennonites, African-Americans, the U.S. Constitution and the Problem of Assimilation"; and "Printing 'Not So Necessary': Dutch Anabaptists and the Telling of Martyr Stories." The journal's web site, www.goshen.edu/mqr, offers selected full-text articles from 1997 to the present, plus a searchable index of articles from 1926 to 2000. Given the international scope, long history, and cultural importance of these churches, and the relative scarcity of materials about them, *MQR* is worth serious consideration by academic libraries.

5433. *Methodist History.* Supersedes in part (in 1962): *World Parish.* [ISSN: 0026-1238] 1948. q. USD 20 domestic (Students, USD 10). Ed(s): Charles Yrigoyen, Jr. United Methodist Church, General Commission on Archives & History, 36 Madison Avenue, PO Box 127, Madison, NJ 07940; research@gcah.org; http://www.gcah.org. Illus., adv. Refereed. Circ: 1000. Microform: PQC. *Indexed:* AmH&L, BAS, FR, HistAb, PRA, R&TA, RI-1, RILM. *Bk. rev.:* 1-5, 50-500 words, signed. *Aud.:* Ac, Sa.

Methodist History is the official historical journal of the United Methodist Church and is issued quarterly by the church's General Commission on Archives and History. *MH* publishes articles, book reviews, and lively studies of Wesleyan and Methodist heritage, for an audience of laypeople, clergy, and readers with historical interests. Recent articles include "All in Raptures: The Spirituality of Sarah Anderson Jones," "Social Status in Early American Methodism: The Case of Freeborn Garrettson," and "Methodist-Chinese Friendship: Mr. & Mrs. John A. Pilley in Pre-1949 China." Contents of the current issue are available at the web site, www.gcah.org/Methodist_History/ MHcontents.htm. This journal is a necessary title for libraries that serve Methodist communities; and libraries that support strong programs in history of religion or church history in the United States should also consider it.

5434. *Modern Judaism: a journal of Jewish ideas and experience.* [ISSN: 0276-1114] 1981. 3x/yr. EUR 156 print or online ed. Ed(s): Dr. Steven T Katz. Oxford University Press, Great Clarendon St, Oxford, OX2 6DP, United Kingdom; jnl.orders@oup.co.uk; http://www.oxfordjournals.org. Illus., index, adv. Refereed. Circ: 600. Online: EBSCO Publishing, EBSCO Host; Gale; HighWire Press; IngentaConnect; JSTOR (Web-based Journal Archive); OCLC Online Computer Library Center, Inc.; OhioLINK; Oxford Journals; Project MUSE; SwetsWise Online Content; H.W. Wilson. Reprint: PSC. *Indexed:* ABS&EES, AmH&L, AmHI, ArtHuCI, HistAb, HumInd, IBR, IBZ, IJP, NTA, R&TA, RI-1, RILM, SSA. *Bk. rev.:* 1-3, 2,000-3,000 words. *Aud.:* Ac, Sa.

Published by Oxford University Press with an editorial board drawn primarily from universities in the United States and Israel, *Modern Judaism: A Journal of Jewish Ideas and Experience* provides a distinctive, interdisciplinary forum for discussion of the modern Jewish experience. Articles focus on "topics pertinent to the understanding of Jewish life today and the forces that have shaped that experience," emphasizing cultural, historical, and sociological discussions more than biblical or ritual issues. Most issues also feature a few short book reviews and/or a longer review article. Recent articles include "Coming to America: Abraham Joshua Heschel, 1940-1941," "Sermons Speak History: Rabbinic Dilemmas in Internment between Metz and Auschwitz," and "American Jewish Views of Evolution and Intelligent Design." Tables of contents and abstracts since 2000 and a free online sample issue can be found at www.oup.co.uk/modjud. This resource is recommended for academic libraries, large public libraries, and libraries that support Judaic studies.

5435. *Muslim World: a journal devoted to the study of Islam and Christian-Muslim relations.* Formerly (until 1948): *Moslem World.* [ISSN: 0027-4909] 1911. q. GBP 147 print & online eds. Ed(s): Ibrahim Abu-Rabi, Jane Smith. Blackwell Publishing, Inc., Commerce Place, 350 Main St, Malden, MA 02148; customerservices@ blackwellpublishing.com; http://www.blackwellpublishing.com. Illus., index, adv. Sample. Refereed. Circ: 1200 Paid. Vol. ends: Oct. Microform: PQC. Online: American Theological Library Association; Blackwell Synergy; EBSCO Publishing, EBSCO Host; Gale; IngentaConnect; Northern Light Technology, Inc.; OCLC Online Computer Library Center, Inc.; OhioLINK; Ovid Technologies, Inc.; ProQuest LLC (Ann Arbor); SwetsWise Online Content; H.W. Wilson. Reprint: PSC. *Indexed:* ABS&EES, AmH&L, AmHI, ApEcolAb, ArtHuCI, BAS, EI, FR, HistAb, HumInd, IBR, IPSA, IndIslam, MASUSE, MLA-IB, PAIS, PSA, R&TA, RI-1. *Bk. rev.:* 2-3, 500-2,000 words, signed. *Aud.:* Ac, Sa.

Founded in 1911, *Muslim World* began as a publication that explored both academic study of Islam and evangelistic strategies toward Muslims. Edited since 1938 by Hartford Seminary, *Muslim World* is no longer focused on missionary work but is "dedicated to the promotion and dissemination of scholarly research on Islam and Muslim societies and on historical and current aspects of Muslim-Christian relations." The journal includes research articles on Islamic theology, literature, philosophy, and history and the Christian–Muslim relationship, as well as book reviews and surveys of periodicals. Recent articles include "The Noble Traders: The Islamic Tradition of 'Spiritual Chivalry' (futuwwa) in Bosnian Trade-guilds (16th–19th centuries)," "Muslim-Christian Relations in Medieval Southern Italy," and "Human Rights Provisions in the Second Amendment to the Indonesian Constitution from Shari'ah Perspective." Tables of contents and abstracts for issues from 2003 to the present, along with a free online sample issue, can be found at www.blackwellpublishing.com/journal.asp?ref=0027-4909. Recommended for academic libraries that support programs in religious studies.

5436. *National Catholic Reporter: the independent weekly.* [ISSN: 0027-8939] 1964. w. USD 43.95 combined subscription domestic print & online eds.; USD 78.95 combined subscription foreign print & online eds. Ed(s): Tom Roberts. Celebration Publications, 115 E Armour Blvd, Kansas City, MO 64111-1203; http://www.natcath.org. Illus., adv. Sample. Circ: 50000 Paid. Microform: PQC. Online: EBSCO Publishing, EBSCO Host; Florida Center for Library Automation; Gale; Northern Light Technology, Inc.; OCLC Online Computer Library Center, Inc.; ProQuest K-12 Learning Solutions; ProQuest LLC (Ann Arbor). *Indexed:* ASIP, CPL, LRI, NTA. *Bk. rev.:* 1-2, 700-1,000 words, signed. *Aud.:* Ga, Ac.

National Catholic Reporter is a lay-edited independent weekly newspaper that "reports, comments and reflects on the church and society..., out of a Roman Catholic tradition and an ecumenical spirit." *NCR* also emphasizes "solidarity with the oppressed and respect for all," and it has taken strong editorial positions on issues regarding nonviolence, social justice, and integrity of the natural environment. Each issue includes timely news stories, book and media reviews, notices of events and educational opportunities, and, frequently, the full text of official Roman Catholic Church pronouncements. Selected full-text articles from current and recent issues are available online at http://ncronline.org/mainpage/archives.htm. The site also offers a searchable index that retrieves a large amount of full-text material from as far back as 1996. As both a readable and useful resource, *NCR* is recommended for public and academic libraries.

5437. *New Oxford Review.* Formerly (until Feb. 1977): *American Church News.* [ISSN: 0149-4244] 1940. m. 11/yr. USD 19 domestic; USD 29 foreign. Ed(s): Dale Vree. New Oxford Review, Inc., 1069 Kains Ave, Berkeley, CA 94706. Illus., adv. Circ: 14728 Paid. Vol. ends: Dec. Microform: PQC. Online: Northern Light Technology, Inc.; ProQuest K-12 Learning Solutions; ProQuest LLC (Ann Arbor). *Indexed:* CPL, RI-1. *Bk. rev.:* Number and length vary. *Aud.:* Ga, Ac.

New Oxford Review, a monthly publication, describes itself as "an orthodox, traditional Roman Catholic magazine" and, further, as "a Catholic magazine with 'attitude,' that doesn't pull any punches." *NOR* considers social, theological, and ecclesiastical issues, with focuses on doctrinal orthodoxy, morality, evangelism, social justice, peace, and family values. Recent articles illustrative of the *NOR* style include "Will the Secular Mass Media & Liberal Churchmen Try to Remove Benedict from Office?," "Homosexuality, Contraception & the Defense of Marriage," and "War & the Requirement of Moral Certainty." Writers are usually, but not always, Catholic. Book reviews include one major (1,500 words) and six or seven minor (300–400 words), all signed. Tables of contents from 1994 and selected full-text articles are available at the web site, www.newoxfordreview.org. Among Catholic publications cited here, *NOR* offers a unique perspective; public and academic libraries interested in covering the range of Catholic viewpoints should consider this publication.

The North Star. See African American section.

5438. *Religion.* [ISSN: 0048-721X] 1970. 4x/yr. EUR 372. Ed(s): T Ryba, Robert Segal. Academic Press, Harcourt Pl, 32 Jamestown Rd, London, NW1 7BY, United Kingdom; apsubs@acad.com; http://www.elsevier.com/. Illus., adv. Sample. Refereed. Circ: 600. Vol. ends: Oct. Online: EBSCO Publishing, EBSCO Host; Gale; IngentaConnect; OCLC Online Computer Library Center, Inc.; OhioLINK; ScienceDirect; SwetsWise Online Content. *Indexed:* AmHI, ArtHuCI, BAS, FR, HumInd, IBR, IBSS, IBZ, NTA, OTA, RI-1, SSCI. *Bk. rev.:* 7-10, 1,000-1,700 words, signed. *Aud.:* Ac, Sa.

Religion is "well known for its strong and established interest in comparative and pioneering work." The journal has both a European and an American editorial board. It seeks to provide rapid reviews of new publications, to encompass related areas such as psychology and archaeology, and to serve as an international forum for debate and scholarship in its field. Recent articles that exemplify *Religion*'s scope include "Faqir or faker?: The Pakpattan tragedy and the politics of Sufism in Pakistan," "Sacred Geography: Shamanism Among the Buddhist Peoples of Russia," and "Border Lines: The Partition of Judaeo-Christianity." Issues generally include both book reviews and review articles. A full-text sample issue and tables of contents from 1971 are available

at the journal's web site, www.elsevier.com/wps/find/journaldescription.cws_home/622940. Recommended for libraries that support interdisciplinary and cross-cultural research in religious studies.

5439. *Religion and American Culture: a journal of interpretation.* [ISSN: 1052-1151] 1991. s-a. USD 112 print & online eds. USD 62 newsstand/cover. Ed(s): Philip Goff, Peter Williams. University of California Press, Journals Division, 2000 Center St, Ste 303, Berkeley, CA 94704-1223; journals@ucpress.edu; http://www.ucpress.edu/journals. Illus., adv. Refereed. Circ: 725. Online: EBSCO Publishing, EBSCO Host; Florida Center for Library Automation; JSTOR (Web-based Journal Archive); OCLC Online Computer Library Center, Inc.; ProQuest LLC (Ann Arbor); SwetsWise Online Content; H.W. Wilson. *Indexed:* AmH&L, AmHI, ArtHuCI, ChrPI, HistAb, HumInd, IBR, IBZ, NTA, PRA, PSA, R&TA, RI-1, SSA, SociolAb. *Aud.:* Ac, Sa.

A semi-annual publication of the Center for the Study of Religion and American Culture of Indiana University–Purdue University Indianapolis, this journal "explores the interplay between religion and other spheres of American culture" from a variety of methodological approaches and theoretical perspectives. A regular feature is the "RAC Forum," which features scholars commenting from different perspectives on a particular issue or problem, such as "How the Graduate Study of Religion and American Culture Has Changed in the Past Decade." Recent examples of *RAC*'s generally substantial articles include "Sin, Spirituality, and Primitivism: The Theologies of the American Social Gospel, 1885-1917" and "Beautiful Women Dig Graves: Richard Baker-Roshi, Imported Buddhism, and the Transmission of Ethics at the San Francisco Zen Center." Issues occasionally include lengthy review essays. An index of previous issues is available at the web site, www.iupui.edu/~raac/journal/journalindex.html. Abstracts of articles from Winter 2001 are available from the University of California Press at the web site, http://caliber.ucpress.net/loi/rac. Because of its interdisciplinary nature and broad range of topics, this journal will appeal to a variety of scholars and general readers. Recommended for consideration by academic and large public libraries.

5440. *Religious Studies: an international journal for the philosophy of religion and theology.* [ISSN: 0034-4125] 1965. q. GBP 192. Ed(s): P A Byrne. Cambridge University Press, The Edinburgh Bldg, Shaftesbury Rd, Cambridge, CB2 2RU, United Kingdom; journals@cambridge.org; http://www.journals.cambridge.org. Illus., index, adv. Sample. Refereed. Circ: 1220. Vol. ends: Dec. Microform: PQC. Online: Pub.; EBSCO Publishing, EBSCO Host; Florida Center for Library Automation; Gale; OCLC Online Computer Library Center, Inc.; OhioLINK; SwetsWise Online Content. Reprint: PSC. *Indexed:* AmHI, ArtHuCI, BAS, BRI, BrHumI, CBRI, FR, HumInd, IBR, IBZ, IJP, IPB, NTA, PhilInd, R&TA, RI-1, SSCI. *Bk. rev.:* Number and length vary. *Aud.:* Ac, Sa.

Religious Studies is an international journal concerned with questions arising from both classical and contemporary philosophical points of view and from varied religious traditions. Published by Cambridge University Press, the journal has an editorial board drawn primarily from the United States and the United Kingdom, with some members from other European countries. Topics of recent articles include "Must a cause be really related to its effect? The analogy between divine and libertarian agent causality," "Sceptical theism and moral skepticism," and "God, pilgrimage, and acknowledgement of place." Book reviews include two major (1,200–2,000 words) and three to five minor (300–400 words), all signed. The tables of contents for issues since 1997 and a sample issue are available online at the journal's web site, uk.cambridge.org/journals/res. Highly recommended for academic libraries that support research in philosophy of religion and religious studies in general.

5441. *Religious Studies Review: a quarterly review of publications in the field of religion and related disciplines.* [ISSN: 0319-485X] 1975. q. USD 181 print & online ed. Ed(s): Elias Bongmba. Blackwell Publishing, Inc., Commerce Place, 350 Main St, Malden, MA 02148. Illus., index, adv. Sample. Refereed. Circ: 3500. Vol. ends: Oct. Online: American Theological Library Association; Blackwell Synergy; EBSCO Publishing, EBSCO Host; IngentaConnect; OCLC Online Computer Library Center, Inc.; Ovid Technologies, Inc.; SwetsWise Online Content. *Indexed:* AmHI, BRI, CBRI, HumInd, IBR, IBZ, NTA, OTA, PRA, R&TA, RI-1. *Bk. rev.:* Over 1,000 annually, signed. *Aud.:* Ac, Sa.

Religious Studies Review is a quarterly publication of the Council of Societies for the Study of Religion, a federation of learned societies. *RSR* performs the valuable function of reviewing over 1,000 titles annually, across the whole field of religious studies and in related disciplines, in both essays and critical notes. For example, a recent special issue with the focus "Religion and the Internet" includes annotated lists of web sites on topics such as Islam, Judaism, and Hinduism; the review essay "Understanding Religion and Cyberspace: What Have We Learned, What Lies Ahead?"; and notes on recent publications arranged according to *RSR*'s controlled list of topic headings. An essential title for libraries that support research in religious studies.

5442. Review and Expositor. Formerly: *Baptist Review and Expositor.* [ISSN: 0034-6373] 1904. q. USD 50 (Individuals, USD 30). Ed(s): E Glenn Hinson. Review & Expositor, Inc., PO Box 6681, Louisville, KY 40206-0681. Illus., index, adv. Circ: 2000. Vol. ends: Fall. Microform: PQC. Online: American Theological Library Association; EBSCO Publishing, EBSCO Host; OCLC Online Computer Library Center, Inc.; Ovid Technologies, Inc. *Indexed:* NTA, OTA, R&TA, RI-1, RILM. *Bk. rev.:* 30-50, 300-700 words, signed. *Aud.:* Ga, Sa.

Review and Expositor is a quarterly Baptist theological journal. Founded and originally published by the Faculty of The Southern Baptist Theological Seminary, *RE* is now supported by a consortium of Baptist seminaries and theological schools. The journal is "dedicated to free and open inquiry of issues related to the Church's mission in the contemporary world..., Baptist in its heritage, ecumenical in its outlook, and global in its vision." Issues generally focus on themes, such as "The Next Christianity," and contain theme-related editorial reflections, articles, and biblical interpretations. Each issue also includes book reviews and notices of books received, on a wide scope of topics in religion. Recent articles include "Do Baptists Really Want an Educated Clergy? Vocation and Charism for Theological Education" and "Latin American Christians in the New Christianity." *RE* seeks to "balance scholarly analysis with practical application," and the journal is an appropriate choice for both academic and public libraries that serve communities seeking to be informed about an ecumenical Baptist approach to religion.

5443. Scottish Journal of Theology. [ISSN: 0036-9306] 1948. q. GBP 104. Ed(s): Ian Torrance, Bryan Spinks. Cambridge University Press, The Edinburgh Bldg, Shaftesbury Rd, Cambridge, CB2 2RU, United Kingdom; journals@cambridge.org; http://www.journals.cambridge.org. Illus., index, adv. Sample. Refereed. Circ: 1800. Vol. ends: No. 4. Reprint: PSC. *Indexed:* AmHI, ArtHuCI, FR, HumInd, IBR, IBZ, NTA, OTA, PhilInd, R&TA, RI-1, RILM. *Bk. rev.:* 10-15, 500-1,000 words, signed. *Aud.:* Ac, Sa.

Scottish Journal of Theology is "an international refereed quarterly journal of systematic, historical and biblical theology," edited in Princeton and Yale and published by Cambridge University Press. The journal's goal is to provide "an ecumenical forum for debate" and extensive reviews of theological and biblical literature. Issues generally comprise four to five articles, a response to a previous article or review, one or more article-length book reviews, and many short reviews. Recent articles include "The extent to which the rise in the worship of images in the late Middle Ages was influenced by contemporary theories of vision," "Karl Barth on the Eternal Existence of Jesus Christ," and "Engaging Scripture: Incarnation and the Gospel of John." A list of articles in the current volume and a database of all articles may be found at the web site, www.ptsem.edu/sjt. This journal is highly recommended for libraries that support theological research within the Chrsitian tradition.

5444. Sociology of Religion: a quarterly review. Former titles (until vol.54, 1993): *Sociological Analysis;* (until 1964): *American Catholic Sociological Review.* [ISSN: 1069-4404] 1940. q. USD 60. Ed(s): Nancy Nason-Clark. Association for the Sociology of Religion, 618 SW 2nd Ave, Galva, IL 61434-1912; swatos@microd.com; http://www.sociologyofreligion.com. Illus., index, adv. Refereed. Circ: 1595. Vol. ends: Winter. Microform: PQC. Online: American Theological Library Association; EBSCO Publishing, EBSCO Host; Florida Center for Library Automation; Gale; Northern Light Technology, Inc.; OCLC Online Computer Library Center, Inc.; Ovid Technologies, Inc.; ProQuest

K-12 Learning Solutions; ProQuest LLC (Ann Arbor); H.W. Wilson. *Indexed:* ABS&EES, ASSIA, ArtHuCI, CPL, FR, HEA, HistAb, IBSS, IPSA, NTA, PSA, R&TA, RI-1, SSA, SSCI, SWA, SociolAb. *Bk. rev.:* 10-12, 600-1,000 words, signed. *Aud.:* Ac.

Sociology of Religion: A Quarterly Review is the official journal of the Association for the Sociology of Religion, and, according to that association, it is the only English-language publication devoted exclusively to the sociology of religion. *SR* carries a broad range of articles on theoretical and empirical issues; it is "a forum for scholarship in the classic tradition of comparative, historical, and theoretical work." Some issues focus on particular themes, such as "The National Jewish Population Survey 2000-1,? and others offer a range of articles and book reviews. Recent articles include "Constructing Buddhism(s): Interreligious Dialogue and Religious Hybridity," "Reconceptualizing Religious Change: Ethno-Apostasy and Change in Religion among American Jews," and "Contemporary Islamic Activism: The Shades of Praxis." The journal changed editors in 2005 and has since added a web site, where tables of contents from Spring 2006 may be read: www.sorjournal.org/about/prevcontents.htm. Of interest to both theologians and sociologists, this journal is recommended for large public and academic libraries.

Sojourners Magazine. See Alternatives section.

5445. Studies in World Christianity: the Edinburgh review of theology and religion. [ISSN: 1354-9901] 1995. 3x/yr. GBP 115.50. Ed(s): Alistair Kee. Edinburgh University Press, 22 George Sq, Edinburgh, EH8 9LF, United Kingdom; http://www.eup.ed.ac.uk. Illus., adv. Sample. Vol. ends: No. 2. Online: EBSCO Publishing, EBSCO Host. *Indexed:* AmHI, NTA, R&TA, RI-1, RILM. *Bk. rev.:* 15-20, 250-1,200 words, signed. *Aud.:* Ac.

Studies in World Christianity, published by Edinburgh University Press, studies and reviews the new forms of Christianity emerging as the faith is adopted by numbers of people in traditionally non-Christian cultures throughout the world. *SWC* seeks to provide an intercultural, interdisciplinary forum for church activists and scholars to share information about the challenges to traditional theology posed by new forms of faith, and the new forms of theology that are in the process of development. Each issue has a theme, such as, recently, "Suffer the Little Children" and "Women in Leadership." The latter included the articles "The Political Emancipation of Women in South Africa and the Challenge to Leadership in the Churches," "Forging Identities: Women as Participants and Leaders in the Church among the Yoruba," and "Women, Leadership and the Orthodox Church in Australia: Always Second Secondary or Seconded." The topics *SWC* addresses are not readily offered elsewhere; recommended for strong consideration by seminary libraries and academic libraries that support programs in religious studies.

5446. Theological Studies. [ISSN: 0040-5639] 1940. q. USD 34 (school/library) Individuals, USD 24). Ed(s): Michael A Fahey. Theological Studies, Inc., c/o Michael A. Fahey, Ed, Marquette University, 100 Coughlin Hall, Milwaukee, WI 53201-1881; michael.fahey@marquette.edu. Illus., index, adv. Sample. Refereed. Circ: 4619 Paid. Vol. ends: Dec. Microform: PQC. Online: American Theological Library Association; Chadwyck-Healey Inc.; EBSCO Publishing, EBSCO Host; Florida Center for Library Automation; Gale; Northern Light Technology, Inc.; OCLC Online Computer Library Center, Inc.; Ovid Technologies, Inc.; ProQuest K-12 Learning Solutions; ProQuest LLC (Ann Arbor); H.W. Wilson. *Indexed:* AmHI, ArtHuCI, BRI, CBRI, CJA, CPL, FR, HumInd, IBR, IBZ, NTA, OTA, PhilInd, R&TA, RI-1, SSCI. *Bk. rev.:* Number and length vary. *Aud.:* Ac, Sa.

Theological Studies: A Jesuit-Sponsored Journal of Theology is published by Marquette University. Its aim is "to make accessible the riches of the theological tradition and to present significant developments in current theology" through articles, book reviews, and notices and lists of recently published titles. Articles offer original, scholarly research on theological issues either relating to, or viewed from, the Jesuit viewpoint. Recent examples of articles include "The Politics of Radical Orthodoxy: A Catholic Critique," "Fostering a Catholic Commitment to the Common Good: An Approach Rooted in Virtue Ethics," and "The Question of Governance and Ministry for Women." The extensive book review section provides useful coverage of current literature in the field. Book reviews include 25–30 major (700–800 words) and 20–25 minor (250–400 words), all signed. *Theological Studies* is a valuable resource for the study Catholic theology. Recommended for academic libraries.

5447. *Theology Digest.* [ISSN: 0040-5728] 1953. q. USD 15 domestic; USD 17 foreign; USD 4 per issue domestic. Ed(s): Bernhard Asen. Theology Digest, Inc., 3634 Lindell Blvd., St. Louis, MO 63108-3395; thdigest@slu.edu. Illus., index, adv. Circ: 3019 Paid. Microform: PQC. *Indexed:* CPL, NTA, OTA, PhilInd, R&TA, RILM. *Bk. rev.:* 250-275, 75-125 words, signed. *Aud.:* Ac, Sa.

Theology Digest offers condensations and translations of recent, significant articles selected from over 400 theological journals throughout the world, including African and Asian journals not readily accessible to the global theological community. Each digest is approved by the author of the original article. Each year *TD* releases three issues consisting of digest and abstracts, plus a "Book Survey" that provides brief descriptions, and one issue containing the annual *TD*-sponsored Bellarmine Lecture and other significant lectures. *TD* is housed at St. Louis University, a Jesuit institution, but it also solicits the active involvement of laity and theologians of other denominations. Highly recommended for large public and academic libraries that seek a cost-effective way to broaden the scope of their journal collection in religious and theological studies.

5448. *Theology Today.* [ISSN: 0040-5736] 1944. q. USD 29 domestic (Students, USD 19.95). Ed(s): Ellen T Charry, Patrick D Miller. Theology Today, PO Box 821, Princeton, NJ 08542-0803. Illus., index, adv. Sample. Refereed. Circ: 14000 Paid. Vol. ends: Jan. Microform: MIM; PQC. Online: American Theological Library Association; Factiva, Inc.; Northern Light Technology, Inc.; OCLC Online Computer Library Center, Inc.; Ovid Technologies, Inc.; ProQuest K-12 Learning Solutions; ProQuest LLC (Ann Arbor); H.W. Wilson. *Indexed:* AmHI, ArtHuCI, BRI, CBRI, HumInd, IBR, IBZ, LRI, NTA, OTA, PRA, PhilInd, R&TA, RI-1, RILM, SSCI. *Bk. rev.:* 15-30, 200-1,500 words, signed. *Aud.:* Ga, Ac.

Theology Today, published by the Princeton Theological Seminary, defines itself as an "ecumenical journal of Christian theology," publishing articles on "a wide range of classical and contemporary issues in Christian theology," particularly issues that are of direct, current relevance. In a striking example, *Theology Today* published in October 2006 a special issue focusing on torture, based on presentations at the founding conference of the National Religious Campaign Against Torture. The special issue includes articles from diverse points of view, such as "What Can Christian Teaching Add to the Debate about Torture?," "Developing a Jewish Theology Regarding Torture," and "Making Enemies: The Imagination of Torture in Chile and the United States." In addition to articles, issues of *Theology Today* generally include book reviews, shorter book notes, and the column "Church in the World," relating theological issues to personal experience. The journal's web site, theologytoday.ptsem.edu, provides free access to the full text of articles, features, and book reviews from 1958 to 1997. Tables of contents or issues from 1997 forward are also available, as well as abstracts of articles from the current issue. This journal is particularly useful to readers concerned with theological positions on important current issues. It is highly recommended for academic libraries, and it may be appropriate for larger public libraries.

Tikkun Magazine. See News and Opinion section.

5449. *Tricycle: the Buddhist review.* [ISSN: 1055-484X] 1991. q. USD 24 domestic; USD 29 foreign; USD 8.95 newsstand/cover. Ed(s): James Shaheen, Ian Collins. The Tricycle Foundation, 92 Vandam St, 3rd Fl, New York, NY 10013. Illus., adv. Circ: 60000 Paid. Vol. ends: Summer. *Indexed:* BRI, CBRI, IAPV, RGPR, RI-1. *Bk. rev.:* 4-6, 400-1,000 words, signed. *Aud.:* Ga.

Published by the Tricycle Foundation, *Tricycle* is an attractive, readable quarterly that explores Buddhism and its impact on Western life. The magazine offers a forum for an ongoing dialogue between Buddhist concepts and the surrounding culture, in the form of interviews and profiles, explorations of contemporary events, discussions about the meaning and practice of Buddhism, artwork, and fiction. A recent issue includes "Mothers of Liberation," an article about goddesses of the Indo-Himalayan Buddhist world; "The Mahbodhi

Express," a discussion of ways pilgrimage conducted by modern methods is transforming the Buddha's birthplace; and "A Very Practical Joke," the text of a 1974 talk by Chogyam Trungpa Rinpoche on Zen from a Tantric perspective. A popular, general-interest magazine suitable for both public and academic libraries.

5450. *Weavings: a journal of the Christian spiritual life.* [ISSN: 0890-6491] 1986. bi-m. USD 28 domestic; USD 34 foreign. Ed(s): John S Mogabgab. The Upper Room, 1908 Grand Ave, Nashville, TN 37212-2129; http://www.upperroom.org. Illus. Circ: 40000 Paid. Vol. ends: Nov/Dec. *Indexed:* ChrPI, RI-1. *Bk. rev.:* 1-2, 600-900 words, signed. *Aud.:* Ga.

Published by Upper Room, a United Methodist Church ministry with an interdenominational mission, *Weavings* is a bimonthly journal for Christian clergy and laypeople, portraying "the depths of the spiritual life in ordinary language." Each issue is organized around a theme. Issues for 2008, for example, will focus on communion (through the themes Grace Abounding and Adoration), community (Many Gifts and Responsibility), and commonweal (Stewards of Creation and Lonely Places). Within each issue are a range of materials, including personal reflections, essays, stories, meditations on scripture, sermons, and poetry. Excerpts from selected recent articles are available online at www.upperroom.org/weavings. Recommended for consideration by public libraries.

5451. *Worship: concerned with the issues of liturgical renewal.* Formerly (until 1951): *Orate Fratres.* [ISSN: 0043-941X] 1926. bi-m. USD 29 domestic; USD 31 foreign. Ed(s): Kevin Seasoltz. Liturgical Press, St John's Abbey, PO Box 7500, Collegeville, MN 56321-7500; sales@litpress.org; http://www.sja.osb.org/worship/. Illus., index, adv. Sample. Refereed. Circ: 4400. Vol. ends: Nov. Microform: PQC. Online: American Theological Library Association; EBSCO Publishing, EBSCO Host; OCLC Online Computer Library Center, Inc.; Ovid Technologies, Inc. *Indexed:* CPL, FR, NTA, OTA, R&TA, RI-1, RILM. *Bk. rev.:* 1-10, 500-1,200 words, signed. *Aud.:* Ac, Sa.

Worship is an interdisciplinary, ecumenical review addressing the theology, history, practice, and evolution of the structure of Christian worship, throughout denominations. Although *Worship* is published by the monks of St. John's Abbey, Minnesota, since 1967 the journal has appointed Protestant and Eastern Christian liturgical scholars to its editorial board. It is written for an audience of pastors, liturgical theologians, and laypeople concerned with liturgy. Each issue includes scholarly articles, reflections, a forum open to contributions by readers, and book reviews. Recent articles include "Mary in Contemporary Protestant Theological Discourse," "The Church as Eucharistic Community: Observations on John Calvin's Early Eucharistic Theology," and "Musical Improvisation and Eschatology: A Study of Liturgical Organist Charles Tournemire (1870-1939)." The tables of contents from 1999 to the present are available online at www.saintjohnsabbey.org/worship. Recommended for Christian seminary libraries and academic libraries that support programs in religious and theological study.

5452. *Zygon: journal of religion and science.* [ISSN: 0591-2385] 1966. q. GBP 189 print & online eds. Ed(s): Karl E Peters, Philip Hefner. Blackwell Publishing, Inc., Commerce Place, 350 Main St, Malden, MA 02148; customerservices@blackwellpublishing.com; http://www.blackwellpublishing.com. Illus., index, adv. Sample. Refereed. Circ: 2400. Vol. ends: Dec. Microform: PQC. Online: American Theological Library Association; Blackwell Synergy; EBSCO Publishing, EBSCO Host; Gale; IngentaConnect; OCLC Online Computer Library Center, Inc.; OhioLINK; Ovid Technologies, Inc.; SwetsWise Online Content. *Indexed:* AmH&L, AmHI, ApEcolAb, ArtHuCI, BRI, CBRI, FR, HistAb, HumInd, IBR, IBZ, IPB, NTA, OTA, PhilInd, R&TA, RI-1, RILM, SSA, SSCI, SociolAb. *Bk. rev.:* 0-5, 1,300-3,000 words, signed. *Aud.:* Ac.

Sponsored by two scholarly institutes concerned with religion and science, *Zygon* is close to unique in bringing together rigorous thinking informed by the physical, biological, and social sciences with ideas from philosophy, theology, and religious studies. (Indeed, its title derives from the Greek word for *yoke*, a tool for joining together.) Issues generally include articles, symposia discussing particular themes from a variety of scientific and religious perspectives, editorials, announcements, and, occasionally, poems. For example, recent *Zygon* symposia focused on "Spiritual Transformation, Healing, and Altruism" and "Quantum Reality and the Consciousness of the Universe." *Zygon's* statement of "Aims and Scopes" notes, "The journal's contributors seek to keep united what may often become disconnected: values with knowledge, goodness with truth, religion with science." Tables of contents and abstracts from 1997 to the present, along with a free sample issue, are available at www.blackwellpublishing.com/journal.asp?ref=0591-2385. Though *Zygon's* goals and themes are of great interest, its multidisciplinary and exploratory commitment requires equally committed readers; recommended for academic libraries.

■ ROBOTICS

Sharon L. Siegler, Engineering Librarian, Lehigh University Information Resources, Fairchild/Martindale Library, 8A Packer Ave., Bethlehem, PA 18015; FAX: 610-758-6524; sls7@lehigh.edu

Introduction

The trends in robotics these last two years have been in biomedicine and machine intelligence. Not only is sophisticated medical equipment manufactured by robots, but the robot now appears in the operating room, but not as a "stand-alone surgeon." The combination of sophisticated manipulators with intelligent computer software allows the surgeon to see tissue in real time and operate with "fingers" that are not only tiny but designed to cut, control bleeding, and/or suture in spaces no human could. This allows for faster healing time with much less surface disfigurement (those "railroad tracks" common to major surgery not so long ago). Many journals reviewed in this section feature articles of this nature, but the field has matured enough so that there is now the *International Journal of Medical Robotics and Computer Assisted Surgery.* As research in artificial intelligence has matured, its application to robotic systems control is evident in such titles as the *Journal of Intelligent and Robotic Systems* and even the *Journal of Field Robotics* (robots that work "in the field" as opposed to a controlled laboratory environment, requiring the robot to make some decisions based on controlled parameters). Illustrations of laboratory robots are more in the nature of R2D2 without the protective casing, covered with wires and cables, but advances in "degrees of freedom of motion," coupled with sophisticated materials, have made possible the BEAR robot ("Battlefield Extraction-Assist Robot") that can lift a prone body and roll along like the Mars rover, or raise to two wheels to cover uneven terrain quickly.

Titles in this section sample the worldwide interest in robotics, but all are in English or available in English translation. There are few inexpensive titles in this research-intensive field, and most publications are designed for the academic or industrial researcher.

Basic Periodicals

Hs: *Robot Magazine;* Ga: *IEEE Robotics and Automation Magazine;* Ac: *Autonomous Robots, IEEE Transactions on Robotics, International Journal of Robotics Research, Robotica, Robotics and Autonomous Systems.*

Basic Abstracts and Indexes

Applied Science and Technology Index, Engineering Index, INSPEC.

5453. A I Magazine. [ISSN: 0738-4602] 1980. q. USD 95 domestic for membership to individuals; USD 135 foreign for membership to individuals; USD 190 domestic for membership to institutions. Ed(s): David Leake. A A A I Press, 445 Burgess Dr, Menlo Park, CA 94025-3442; info@aaai.org; http://www.aaai.org. Illus., index, adv. Refereed. Circ: 6000 Paid. Vol. ends: Dec. Online: Florida Center for Library Automation; Gale; OCLC Online Computer Library Center, Inc.; ProQuest K-12 Learning Solutions; ProQuest LLC (Ann Arbor); H.W. Wilson. *Indexed:* AS&TI, CompLI, CompR, EngInd, ISTA, LISA, MicrocompInd, SCI. *Bk. rev.:* 2, 2,000-4,000 words. *Aud.:* Ac, Sa.

As the official journal of the American Association for Artificial Intelligence, this publication is a cross between a magazine and a research journal. Each issue contains about a half-dozen articles as well as reports, events, society news, and, occasionally, a crossword puzzle. Often there is a theme issue, such as "Robotics in Undergraduate Education." The articles are not so dense as to be purely theoretical and can be read by students/practitioners outside the field, but they are research papers. Papers average ten pages, are well illustrated, and include good bibliographies. Authors are both academic and industrial researchers. Although "artificial intelligence" is not "robotics," each issue has at least one robotics article, and many of the remainder discuss solutions to logistics, reasoning, and data-gathering problems that can be readily applied to robotics. While hardly a frivolous publication, there is still room for a sense of humor and competition, with annual features on Robot Rescue, the Robot Challenge, the Mobile Robot Competition, and the world RoboCup soccer championship. This is the one with the eye-catching issue covers and is definitely recommended for public, academic, and business library collections.

5454. Advanced Robotics. [ISSN: 0169-1864] 1986. m. EUR 1778 print & online eds. Ed(s): S Sugano. V S P, Brill Academic Publishers, PO Box 9000, Leiden, 2300 PA, Netherlands; vsppub@brill.nl; http://www.vsppub.com. Illus., adv. Sample. Refereed. Vol. ends: No. 8. Reprint: PSC. *Indexed:* ApMecR, C&ISA, CerAb, EngInd, IAA, SCI. *Aud.:* Ac, Sa.

Truly an international effort, this is the official journal of the Robotics Society of Japan, published by a small Dutch firm and featuring articles by Russians, Germans, Arabs, Japanese, and others. Most articles are research papers, but issues may include short communications, topical reviews, reports, and meeting notes. Robots may be mobile, stationary (manipulators), built for hostile environments, or merely sensors. The treatment is theoretical with a practical emphasis. Although not inexpensive (the price increases steeply each year), this title deserves greater notice in academic libraries.

5455. Assembly Automation. [ISSN: 0144-5154] 1980. q. EUR 8409 combined subscription in Europe print & online eds.; USD 9959 combined subscription in North America print & online eds.; AUD 11829 combined subscription in Australasia print & online eds. Ed(s): Dr. Clive Loughlin. Emerald Group Publishing Limited, Howard House, Wagon Ln, Bingley, BD16 1WA, United Kingdom; information@ emeraldinsight.com; http://www.emeraldinsight.com. Illus. Refereed. Online: Pub.; EBSCO Publishing, EBSCO Host; Gale; IngentaConnect; OCLC Online Computer Library Center, Inc.; OhioLINK; ProQuest LLC (Ann Arbor); SwetsWise Online Content. Reprint: PSC. *Indexed:* ABIn, BrTechI, C&ISA, CerAb, EngInd, IAA, SCI. *Bk. rev.:* 3, 500 words. *Aud.:* Ac, Sa.

Part of a suite of robotics-related titles published by MCB, *Assembly Automation* features automation in flexible manufacturing processes, some of which involve robots. Application areas include electrical products, clothing, and pharmaceuticals, with a heavy emphasis on automotive manufacturing. Each issue is composed of short research articles, illustrated new-product reviews of a page or less, company news, "mini-features" describing practical solutions or techniques, media reviews (books, software), patent abstracts, web sites, and editorial commentary. The research articles may be authored by academics, practicing engineers, or journal staff. Most issues are theme oriented, such as rapid prototyping or micro assembly. The electronic version utilizes the same access points and features as this journal's sister publication, *Industrial Robot.* This is a very expensive title in the field, to be considered only by industry libraries and those academic institutions with large consulting efforts in manufacturing and robotics.

5456. The Association for Laboratory Automation. Journal. [ISSN: 1535-5535] 1997. 6x/yr. USD 308. Ed(s): Dr. Mark F Russo. Association for Laboratory Automation, Health Science Center, University of Virginia, Box 572, Charlottesville, VA 22908. Adv. Circ: 800 Paid. *Indexed:* CINAHL, EngInd, ExcerpMed. *Aud.:* Ac, Sa.

The laboratories featured in this journal are clinical testing facilities. With much of their work involving sterile environments and/or possibly dangerous substances, robots have come to be standard equipment. Almost every issue has at least one article on specialized robotic systems as used in the laboratory environment. This is a glossy magazine for the practitioner with three- to four-page color illustrated articles, usually with minimal references, but authored by experts in the field, and peer reviewed. Published by Elsevier for the association, subscribers may view issues either through ScienceDirect or the association's web site; the latter smoothly integrates the ScienceDirect features. Although for the specialized collection, its cross-disciplinary nature may be a plus for some organizations, especially as biomedical robotics has become a thrust in robotics research.

5457. Autonomous Robots. [ISSN: 0929-5593] 1994. bi-m. EUR 1038 print & online eds. Ed(s): George A Bekey. Springer New York LLC, 233 Spring St, New York, NY 10013-1578; journals@springer-ny.com; http://www.springer.com/. Adv. Refereed. Online: EBSCO Publishing, EBSCO Host; Gale; IngentaConnect; OCLC Online Computer Library Center, Inc.; OhioLINK; Ovid Technologies, Inc.; Springer LINK; SwetsWise Online Content. Reprint: PSC. *Indexed:* ApMecR, CompLI, EngInd, SCI. *Aud.:* Ac, Sa.

As the title indicates, this journal specializes in papers on robots that are self-sufficient, which is defined as capable of performing in real-world environments. These robots acquire data through sensors, process it, perform their tasks, and are often mobile (legged, tracked, even finned). Each issue is comprised of a half-dozen lengthy articles of 15 or more pages, often illustrated with black-and-white photographs of the robots *in situ*, plus data, graphs, formulae, and numerous references. The authorship is international, from academia and industrial-research laboratories and often with collaboration from both. Strictly serious in content, there is opportunity for a little wry comment, such as the recent title "a humanoid robot that pretends to listen to route guidance from a human." Both pdf and html versions of articles are available; the pdf has internal links but does not link out to the cited references. The web site supports RSS feeds and RIS export of bibliographic data. This title is highly ranked by ISI journal Impact Factor for robotics. Modestly priced for a scholarly technical journal, it is warmly recommended for academic and industrial collections.

Control Engineering Practice. See Computers and Information Technology/Professional Journals section.

5458. IEEE - A S M E Transactions on Mechatronics. [ISSN: 1083-4435] 1996. bi-m. USD 720. Ed(s): Masayoshi Tomizuka. IEEE, 445 Hoes Ln, Piscataway, NJ 08854-1331; subscription-service@ieee.org; http://www.ieee.org. Illus., index. Refereed. Vol. ends: No. 4. Online: Pub.; EBSCO Publishing, EBSCO Host. *Indexed:* ApMecR, C&ISA, CerAb, EngInd, H&SSA, IAA, SCI. *Aud.:* Ac, Sa.

"Mechatronics" is defined by the *Transactions* as "the synergetic integration of mechanical engineering with electronic and intelligent computer control in design and manufacture of industrial products and processes." In other words, the field covers a lot of territory, and this title is actually the joint effort of several IEEE societies and ASME divisions. As in the other *IEEE Transactions* (and the *ASME Journals*), papers are highly mathematical, well referenced, and illustrated with tables and flowcharts rather than with glossies of mobile robots. Current work emphasizes mobile, medical, and underwater robots. The IEEE has greatly improved its web versions of journals, after earlier criticism of skipping such useful content as book reviews, but the indication of a "blank page" in a recent table of contents is really over the top. As the field evolves, more attention is being paid to micro- or nano-scale robots; this journal is the place to look for these.

5459. IEEE Robotics and Automation Magazine. [ISSN: 1070-9932] 1994. q. USD 345; USD 431 combined subscription print & online eds. Ed(s): Kimon P Valavanis. IEEE, 445 Hoes Ln, Piscataway, NJ 08854-1331; subscription-service@ieee.org; http://www.ieee.org. Illus., index, adv. Refereed. Vol. ends: No. 4. Online: Pub.; EBSCO Publishing, EBSCO Host. *Indexed:* AS&TI, EngInd, IAA, SCI. *Aud.:* Ga, Ac, Sa.

This magazine, from the IEEE Robotics and Automation Society, publishes the more practical material not suitable for its *Transactions*. Not really a glossy magazine, it is still attractive, with color covers, many features, a nice presentation, and relatively short, well-illustrated articles. Each issue includes several research papers plus short sections on society business, columns (such as education), calls for papers, industry news, and the like. Every few months there will be a theme issue, such as "The Grand Challenges of Robotics," the Mars

Rover, and "Unmanned Aerial Vehicles." The content level is quite approachable by undergraduates and lay readers, making this a suitable selection for a large public or small academic library as well as libraries serving active robotics research.

5460. IEEE Transactions on Automation Science and Engineering. Supersedes in part: *IEEE Transactions on Robotics and Automation;* Which was formerly (until 1988): *IEEE Journal of Robotics and Automation.* [ISSN: 1545-5955] 2004. q. USD 525; USD 656 combined subscription print & online eds. Ed(s): Peter Luh. IEEE, 3 Park Ave, 17th Fl, New York, NY 10016-5997; customer.service@ieee.org; http://www.ieee.org. *Indexed:* C&ISA, CerAb, EngInd, IAA, SCI. *Aud.:* Ac.

Split off from the *IEEE Transactions on Robotics and Automation* in 2004, this is billed as a "practitioner's" journal. The focus is on "abstractions, algorithms, theory, methodologies, models, systems, and case studies" of automation in general. To see the distinction, the *Robotics* title will publish "Robot Steering with Spectral Image Information," but the *Automation* title will publish "Increasing Throughput for Robotic Cells with Parallel Machines and Multiple Robots." The first is a device for a robot; the second is management of a processing technique. A novel inclusion in this journal is the "Note to Practitioners," something like a second abstract that describes how the research can be implemented in practical problems. Collections that emphasize control theory as well as robotics will want this new title.

5461. IEEE Transactions on Robotics. Supersedes in part (in 2004): *IEEE Transactions on Robotics and Automation;* Which was formerly (until 1988): *IEEE Journal of Robotics and Automation.* [ISSN: 1552-3098] 1985. bi-m. USD 825; USD 1051 combined subscription print & online eds. Ed(s): Richard A Volz. IEEE, 445 Hoes Ln, Piscataway, NJ 08854-1331; subscription-service@ieee.org; http://www.ieee.org. Illus., index. Refereed. Vol. ends: No. 6. Online: Pub.; EBSCO Publishing, EBSCO Host. *Indexed:* AS&TI, C&ISA, CerAb, EngInd, IAA, SCI, SSCI. *Bk. rev.:* 1, 2,000 words. *Aud.:* Ac, Sa.

This title continues to be the top-ranked (ISI Impact Factor) journal in the field. The emphasis is on mechanical operation (such as grasping or manipulation), sensors, recognition, and mobility, with some attention to large-scale use problems. A typical issue has several lengthy papers, a few short articles, announcements, and the occasional book review. Often, a special topic will be developed over several papers. The lag time from submission to publication has decreased remarkably, from over two years to six to nine months, an indication of a good editor and the power of electronic publication. This is a core title for a robotics collection and is useful in any electrical or mechanical engineering program. The IEEE publishes several *Transactions* and magazines that cover robotics in varying degrees. One of them, the *IEEE Transactions on Automatic Control* (not reviewed here), is a high-impact journal that should be consulted for specific problems in the control of robotic parts.

5462. Industrial Robot: an international journal. Incorporates: *Service Robot.* [ISSN: 0143-991X] 1973. bi-m. EUR 10399 combined subscription in Europe print & online eds.; USD 11339 combined subscription in North America print & online eds.; AUD 13469 combined subscription in Australasia print & online eds. Ed(s): Dr. Clive Loughlin. Emerald Group Publishing Limited, Howard House, Wagon Ln, Bingley, BD16 1WA, United Kingdom; information@emeraldinsight.com; http://www.emeraldinsight.com. Illus., adv. Refereed. Reprint: PSC. *Indexed:* ABIn, AS&TI, ApMecR, BrTechI, C&ISA, CerAb, EngInd, IAA, SCI. *Bk. rev.:* 3, 500 words. *Aud.:* Sa.

Industrial Robot is the oldest magazine in English devoted to robotics. Although robotic applications in any area may be included, the principal interest is in large-scale industries, such as automobiles, construction, shipbuilding, plastics, and the military, with some attention to biomedical applications and "niche" industries, such as food. Each issue is composed of short research articles, illustrated new-product reviews of a page or less, company news, "mini-features" describing practical solutions or techniques, media reviews (books, software), patent abstracts, one-paragraph reviews of useful web sites, plus editorial commentary. The research articles may be authored by academics, practicing engineers, or journal staff. Most issues are theme oriented, with recent issues devoted to force sensing, painting, mobile robots, and the automotive indutry. This journal has the dubious distinction of being the most expensive journal in the field (with *Assembly Automation* from the same publisher being a close second), to be considered only by industry libraries and those academic institutions with large consulting efforts in robotics.

5463. *Institution of Mechanical Engineers. Proceedings. Part I: Journal of Systems and Control Engineering.* [ISSN: 0959-6518] 1992. 8x/yr. USD 2150 in the Americas; GBP 1117 elsewhere. Ed(s): C R Burrows. Professional Engineering Publishing Ltd., 1 Birdcage Walk, London, SW1H 9JJ , United Kingdom; journals@pepublishing.com; http://www.pepublishing.com. Illus. Sample. Refereed. Circ: 800 Paid. Online: EBSCO Publishing, EBSCO Host; Gale; IngentaConnect; OCLC Online Computer Library Center, Inc.; SwetsWise Online Content. *Indexed:* AS&TI, ApMecR, BrTechI, C&ISA, CerAb, EngInd, IAA, SCI. *Bk. rev.:* 1, 1,000 words. *Aud.:* Ac.

This journal covers all aspects of mechanical control, including robots, manipulators, actuators, and mechatronics. The point of view is generally modeling, simulation, design, mathematics, and computation. Although the occasional article features a complete robot entity (such as a one-legged hopping robot), papers are more likely to discuss parts of a robot: a manipulator, a sensor, a navigational device. Lag time from submission to publication has increased markedly, even for special issues (invited papers). The title is often referenced by other robotics-related journals, perhaps because of the theory behind the parts, and it will be a good support publication for a comprehensive robotics collection.

5464. *International Journal of Advanced Robotic Systems.* [ISSN: 1729-8806] 2004. q. EUR 280 (Individuals, EUR 220; EUR 60 newsstand/cover). Ed(s): Vedran Kordic, Merdan Munir. International Journal of Advanced Robotic Systems, Gusshausstr 27-29, Vienna, 1040, Austria; lazinica@ars-journal.com. Illus., adv. Sample. Refereed. Circ: 400 Paid and controlled. *Indexed:* EngInd. *Bk. rev.:* Occasional. *Aud.:* Ac, Sa.

This scholarly journal has an interesting twist: It is designed for "young scientists" (generally those under 40). The editors are all connected with the Vienna Institute of Technology, but the review board has members from Japan, China, the United States, and several European countries. Issues are comprised of a half-dozen research articles, an interview with a leading researcher or producer, an overview of a laboratory in robotics or a related field, and a few book and "robot reviews." The latter may be prototypes, commercial, or toys. The journal co-sponsors several conferences (and publishes selected papers from them). Now in its fourth year, the issues have twice as many articles as in earlier years and new names appear as authors. The editors still write much of the regular columns. Libraries should monitor its development because it is suitable for undergraduates and may be an indicator of future research interests.

5465. *International Journal of Humanoid Robotics.* [ISSN: 0219-8436] 2004. q. SGD 580 print & online eds. (Individuals, SGD 231). Ed(s): Ming Xie, Jean-Guy Fontaine. World Scientific Publishing Co. Pte. Ltd., 5 Toh Tuck Link, Singapore, 596224, Singapore; wspc@wspc.com.sg; http://www.worldscientific.com. Sample. Refereed. *Indexed:* C&ISA, CerAb, EngInd, IAA. *Aud.:* Ac.

This scholarly journal describes "humanoid robots" as those that work in a human environment. They may not look human, but, as the editors write, they "require the synergetic integration of mechanics, electronics, control, communication, perception, cognition, decision-making, artificial psychology, machine intelligence and many other areas." Articles are lengthy, often over 20 pages, usually involving mobility problems, but also discussing learned behavior and text and visual understanding. Current work has moved on to discuss human perception of robot movement and "emotions," measuring not only how well the robots act but how well they are received by humans. Authors have fun, too, as one title illustrates: "From lamprey to humanoid: the design and control of a flexible spine belly dancing humanoid robot with inspiration from biology." This is not a toy, but an approach to the solution of the very practical problem of bending and stretching. The lag from article submission to acceptance is short, but actual publication (at least in print) is later. The web site is simple and well organized, and the price is inexpensive. Recommended for extensive academic collections in robotics.

5466. *International Journal of Intelligent Systems Technologies and Applications.* [ISSN: 1740-8865] 2005. 8x/yr. EUR 700 (print or online ed.). Ed(s): Dr. Mohammed A Dorgham. Inderscience Publishers, IEL Editorial Office, PO Box 735, Olney, MK46 5WB, United Kingdom; info@inderscience.com; http://www.inderscience.com. Refereed. *Indexed:* C&ISA, CerAb, IAA. *Aud.:* Ac.

A fledgling journal, the *International Journal of Intelligent Systems Technologies and Applications* already has an established reputation and is indexed in the major abstract services. The "intelligent systems" are agents, control systems, and robots; the applications are largely recognition systems in medicine and security. However, the research transfers to other disciplines, as exemplified by the article on OCR recognition of old (seventeenth century) documents. The robots are both mobile (such as the hexapod wall-climbing robot) and stationary (such as a production line meat processor). Much of the current work deals with perception: visual mapping of areas for robot travel, real-time recognition of objects, analyzing facial expression. Articles are relatively lengthy, often with extensive references; unfortunately, the publisher's web site does not link to references and the html versions of articles sometimes render graphics and equations oddly. This title is suitable for libraries with strong collections in robotics, artificial intelligence, and nonhuman cognition.

5467. *International Journal of Medical Robotics and Computer Assisted Surgery.* [ISSN: 1478-5951] 2005. 4x/yr. USD 687 print or online ed. John Wiley & Sons Ltd., The Atrium, Southern Gate, Chichester, PO19 8SQ, United Kingdom; cs-journals@wiley.co.uk; http://www.wiley.co.uk. *Indexed:* ExcerpMed, SCI. *Aud.:* Ac, Sa.

No, R2-D2 will not be operating on your gallbladder in the near future. What is happening, and has been for some time, is the use of robotic manipulators to assist in surgery, operated by surgeons in the "master-slave" mode. The technique is now so widely used that this journal features articles on improvements to the methods and the robots for different types of surgery. Most of the articles are detailed "how-to-do-it" accounts, but there is the occasional systems approach overview and discussion of legal concerns. The delay from submission to publication is minimal, often two to four months. With a new title, this is often an indicator of few submissions, but this journal is now in its third year and issues are plump. Illustrations are often in color, since this is important to the understanding of the material and, for that matter, to the "computer assisted" part of the title. The ability to overlay earlier diagnostic images in real-time surgery is one of the boons of this technique. The title is highly specialized, though, and only medical libraries and those institutions with strong biomedical technology and robotics programs will benefit from a subscription. At the time of this review, the *Journal of Robotic Surgery* had just begun, too new to adequately review. Libraries interested in the present title should also evaluate this newcomer.

5468. *International Journal of Robotics and Automation.* [ISSN: 0826-8185] 1986. q. USD 350. Ed(s): Dr. M Kamel. ACTA Press, 4500-16th Ave NW, Ste 80, Calgary, AB T3B 0M6, Canada; journals@ actapress.com; http://www.actapress.com. Adv. *Indexed:* ApMecR, C&ISA, CerAb, CompLI, EngInd, IAA, SCI. *Aud.:* Ac.

Although this journal has been publishing since 1986, it has only recently caught the attention of the larger world. Published by a small specialty press, it features succinct, under-ten-page articles by an international range of academic authors. About half of the articles deal with the functions of robots (as opposed to robots as a whole) and are especially concerned with manipulation, spatial recognition, and wireless activity. The other half feature programming issues. Most issues are arranged around a theme, such as "Compliance and Compliant Mechanisms" or the use of robots in surgery and creating materials that mimic human tissue. Almost every issue has a list of upcoming conferences. The publisher's web site is minimal, but the tables of contents for the current year are included with the journal's basic description information. Unfortunately, the subscription price has increased more than 30 percent since this title was last reviewed, without a concomitant increase in pages.

5469. *International Journal of Robotics Research.* [ISSN: 0278-3649] 1982. m. GBP 967. Ed(s): John M Hollerbach. Sage Science Press (UK), 1 Oliver's Yard, 55 City Rd, London, EC1Y 1SP, United Kingdom; info@sagepub.com; http://www.sagepub.co.uk/. Illus., index, adv. Sample. Refereed. Circ: 1340. Vol. ends: Dec. Microform: PQC. Online:

EBSCO Publishing, EBSCO Host; Gale; HighWire Press; OCLC Online Computer Library Center, Inc.; ProQuest K-12 Learning Solutions; SAGE Publications, Inc., SAGE Journals Online; SwetsWise Online Content. Reprint: PSC. *Indexed:* AS&TI, ApMecR, BrTechI, C&ISA, CerAb, CompLI, CompR, EngInd, ErgAb, IAA, OceAb, SCI. *Aud.:* Ac, Sa.

Billing itself as the first scholarly publication in robotics, it is among the most-cited journals in the field. The articles are relatively lengthy (averaging 20 pages each), and the treatment is highly mathematical. Although there is some attention paid to larger systems, most papers consider specific aspects of robot function, such as light-sensing, flexing of manipulators, force sensing, or motion variables. Experimentation is almost always on laboratory-scale equipment, although the intent is application to actual production environments. There is no indication of the submission/publication date lag, but most recent articles reference papers within a year of publication, and the "Communications" articles appear to be within six months. Multimedia appendixes (datasets, code, models, and simulations) are available at the journal's web site. The publisher's site has a nice interface, with all of the modern conveniences: links to references, alerts for cites or corrections to an article, RSS feeds, and marking and downloading to a number of citation managers. This is an excellent title with good value for the money for any institution engaged in robotics research.

5470. *J S M E International Journal. Series C, Mechanical Systems, Machine Elements and Manufacturing.* Former titles (until 1997): *J S M E International Journal. Series C: Dynamics, Control, Robotics, Design and Manufacturing;* (until 1993): *J S M E International Journal. Series 3: Vibration, Control Engineering, Engineering for Industry;* Supersedes in part (in 1988): *J S M E International Journal;* Which was formerly (until 1986): *J S M E Bulletin.* [ISSN: 1344-7653] 1958. q. Members, JPY 3000; Non-members, JPY 3360. Japan Society of Mechanical Engineers, Shinanomachi-Rengakan Bldg, 35 Shinano-Machi, Tokyo, 160-0016, Japan; http://www.jsme.or.jp/english/indene.htm. Illus., index. Refereed. Vol. ends: No. 4. *Indexed:* ApMecR, BioEngAb, C&ISA, CerAb, ChemAb, EngInd, H&SSA, IAA, MathR, SCI. *Aud.:* Ac, Sa.

The *Journal* of the Japanese Society of Mechanical Engineers (JSME) is divided into three parts: *Series A. Mechanics and Materials Engineering, Series B. Fluids and Thermal Engineering,* and *Series C,* which includes robotics. *Series C* could just as easily be titled "Mechatronics" because that is the new shorthand for robotics, control, and manufacturing design. Almost all of the authors are Japanese or Chinese; many of the papers are translations from the JSME's Japanese-language *Transactions.* Publication costs are partly supported by the Japanese Ministry of Education and by page charges, so that the cost of all three sections of the *Journal* is very inexpensive, even for nonmembers. Papers are highly theoretical and quite specialized, but they seek to solve/resolve actual problems. Citations are just as likely to be to American or European publications as to Japanese, so that the reader has glimpses into both worlds. The publication lag for original papers averages 12 months, but the revision process also includes updating literature references. This title is mounted by JSTAGE (Japan Science and Technology Information Aggregator, Electronic), offering a simple display coupled with full-text searching and article alerts; readers can also practice their Japanese (but the article text is still in English). A nicely priced addition to an academic robotics collection and suitable for industrial research organizations.

5471. *Journal of Dynamic Systems, Measurement and Control.* [ISSN: 0022-0434] 1971. q. Members, USD 60 print & online eds.; Non-members, USD 430 print & online eds. Ed(s): Suhada Jayasuriya. A S M E International, Three Park Ave, New York, NY 10016-5990; infocentral@asme.org; http://www.asme.org. Illus., index, adv. Refereed. Circ: 2500. Vol. ends: Dec. Microform: PQC. Online: American Institute of Physics, Scitation; EBSCO Publishing, EBSCO Host; SwetsWise Online Content. *Indexed:* AS&TI, ApMecR, C&ISA, CEA, CerAb, EngInd, ExcerpMed, IAA, SCI. *Aud.:* Ac, Sa.

To those outside the field, the *Journal of Dynamic Systems, Measurement and Control* may seem an unlikely title for a top robotics publication. The clues are "control" and "dynamic," because these play a large part in the design and use of robots. Recent articles discuss the stability of hopping robots, agility of multi-legged robots, and grafting between the prosthetic and natural parts of an impaired human hand. As a research journal, it is heavy on mathematics, usually illustrated with tables and graphs but with an occasional photograph, and has extensive references. The ASME has created a Digital Library (still mounted through the Scitation system) which will allow search across its entire range of publications (journals, conferences, and books), but only the journals are included as of this writing. Useful features are the RSS feeds, choice of pdf or html views, and a prominently displayed errata link. Most surprisingly, color has come to the illustrations, improving reader understanding of the content and enlivening the dense prose. An excellent interdisciplinary title.

5472. *Journal of Field Robotics.* Formerly (until Jan. 2006): *Journal of Robotic Systems.* [ISSN: 1556-4959] 1984. m. USD 2897. Ed(s): Susan Hackwood, Gerardo Beni. John Wiley & Sons, Inc., 111 River St, Hoboken, NJ 07030-5774; uscs-wis@wiley.com; http://www.wiley.com. Illus., index, adv. Sample. Refereed. Circ: 750. Vol. ends: Dec. Microform: PQC. Online: EBSCO Publishing, EBSCO Host; OhioLINK; SwetsWise Online Content; Wiley InterScience. *Indexed:* AS&TI, ApMecR, C&ISA, CompLI, EngInd, IAA, SCI. *Aud.:* Ac, Sa.

The *Journal of Robotic Systems* became the *Journal of Field Robotics* in 2006, acknowledging and promulgating a robotics speciality, robots that work in unstructured environments (the "field"). The journal is at once practical and theoretical: practical because the robots involved are either working models or production floor systems; theoretical because the treatments involve designs or systems that can be used as models or applied in other environments, rather than specific techniques for a specific application. Almost every article features an actual robot rather than a theoretical concept. Illustrations are usually graphs, computer models, and flowcharts. The editors have largely achieved rapid-communication publication, with an average lag time of nine months between submission and publication of an article. There are occasional thematic issues, space robotics and the DARPA Grand Challenge. In the DARPA Challenge, robots had to traverse 140 miles of rough terrain, adding yet another meaning to the term "field robot." Although a quality journal, this is one of the most expensive publications in the robotics area (and issues are slim).

5473. *Journal of Intelligent and Robotic Systems: theory and applications.* Incorporates (in 1994): *Mechatronic Systems Engineering.* [ISSN: 0921-0296] 1988. m. EUR 1494 print & online eds. Ed(s): Spyros G Tzafestas. Springer Netherlands, Van Godewijckstraat 30, Dordrecht, 3311 GX, Netherlands; http://www.springeronline.com. Illus., index, adv. Sample. Refereed. Vol. ends: No. 4. Microform: PQC. Online: EBSCO Publishing, EBSCO Host; Gale; IngentaConnect; OCLC Online Computer Library Center, Inc.; OhioLINK; Ovid Technologies, Inc.; Springer LINK; SwetsWise Online Content. Reprint: PSC. *Indexed:* ApMecR, C&ISA, CerAb, EngInd, ErgAb, IAA, PsycInfo, SCI, SSCI. *Aud.:* Ac.

This journal has a new editor and a new publisher (with the Springer/Kluwer merger), resulting in a revamped title. Aside from the purely procedural changes, designed to speed the publication process and make it easier for both authors and editors, the mission now is to cover "the whole technical spectrum from the birth of an idea at the conceptual level to a potential product development." Unmanned systems are emphasized and so indexed in the abstract. Recent work features simulating self-replicating machines and foraging theory for a mobile robot. Authorship is international, with most researchers from academia, but there is a fair percentage of material with industrial collaboration. The theory is still present, and much of treatment is simulation or modeling, but the practicality shows through, as exemplified by the article on a robot with a deformed foot. The title is near the bottom of the Impact Factor list; it will be interesting to see if the changes improve its standing in the research world.

5474. *Mechanism and Machine Theory.* Formerly: *Journal of Mechanisms.* [ISSN: 0094-114X] 1966. 12x/yr. EUR 2859. Ed(s): A Kecskemethy. Pergamon, The Boulevard, Langford Ln, East Park, Kidlington, OX5 1GB, United Kingdom. Illus., index, adv. Sample. Refereed. Circ: 1000. Vol. ends: No. 8. Microform: PQC. Online: EBSCO Publishing, EBSCO Host; Gale; IngentaConnect; OhioLINK; ScienceDirect; SwetsWise Online Content. *Indexed:* ApMecR, C&ISA, CCMJ, EngInd, MSN, MathR, SCI. *Bk. rev.:* 1, 2,000 words. *Aud.:* Ac.

The emphasis here is on theory, with most papers making extensive use of mathematical symbols rather than engineering diagrams. However, the topics generally concern practical applications, such as robot joints, manipulators, and kinematics. This is the official journal of the International Federation for the Theory of Machines and Mechanisms, and the authors reflect the international membership. An occasional non-English paper appears. The publication lag has been greatly reduced, dropping to about a year in "real time." Publication appears online several months before the official issue publication date. Electronic access is through ScienceDirect, with excellent searching, display, and linking options. For the academic library with a strong engineering mechanics/manufacturing program.

5475. *Mechatronics.* [ISSN: 0957-4158] 1991. 10x/yr. EUR 1237. Ed(s): R W Daniel, I. C. Ume. Pergamon, The Boulevard, Langford Ln, East Park, Kidlington, OX5 1GB, United Kingdom. Illus., index. Sample. Refereed. Vol. ends: No. 8. Microform: PQC. Online: EBSCO Publishing, EBSCO Host; Gale; IngentaConnect; OhioLINK; ScienceDirect; SwetsWise Online Content. *Indexed:* ApMecR, C&ISA, CerAb, EngInd, IAA, SCI. *Aud.:* Ac, Sa.

One of the few titles devoted to the emergent hybrid field, *Mechatronics* it is chiefly interested in papers on the design of machines and systems that include some level of computer-based intelligence. Articles are fairly lengthy, averaging 20 pages or more. The major application thrust is specific robotic parts, as opposed to a multifunction and/or mobile robot. Examples of this are such phrases as "two-axis arm motion" and "five-bar finger with redundant activators." Publication delay is close to 18 months, which is odd for an almost monthly (10 issues per year) that averages only seven articles per issue. Compare this title with the *IEEE/ASME Transactions on Mechatronics,* which both is cheaper and has a higher ISI Impact Factor.

5476. *Robot Magazine: the latest in hobby, science and consumer robotics.* [ISSN: 1555-1016] 2005. q. USD 19.95 domestic; USD 21.95 Canada; USD 25.95 elsewhere. Ed(s): Tom Atwood. Maplegate Media Group, 650 Danbury Rd, Ridgefield, CT 06877; http://www.maplegatemedia.com/. Adv. *Aud.:* Hs, Ga.

This is more than a hobby magazine. It functions like a trade publication, with good overview articles of current developments, interviews with practitioners, and news and links. The hobbiest will find schematics and programs; the teacher will find curriculum guides and examples that appeal to students; the teenagers will find the competitions. Although a print magazine, the web site has sample articles and serves as the forum for readers. This will be an inexpensive addition to a public or school library.

5477. *Robotica.* [ISSN: 0263-5747] 1983. bi-m. GBP 510. Ed(s): G S Chirikjian. Cambridge University Press, The Edinburgh Bldg, Shaftesbury Rd, Cambridge, CB2 2RU, United Kingdom; journals@cambridge.org; http://www.journals.cambridge.org. Illus., index, adv. Sample. Refereed. Circ: 650. Vol. ends: No. 6. Online: Pub.; EBSCO Publishing, EBSCO Host; OCLC Online Computer Library Center, Inc.; OhioLINK; SwetsWise Online Content. Reprint: PSC. *Indexed:* BRI, BrTechI, C&ISA, CBRI, CerAb, CompLI, EngInd, ErgAb, IAA, SCI. *Aud.:* Ac, Sa.

One of the earliest professional journals on robotics, *Robotica* has remained focused on its mission over the years. It is hard to find an article in any issue that does not have "robot" somewhere in the title (although nowadays it may be part of a word, such as "microrobots"). Although papers are research-level quality, there is always attention to working mechanisms rather than just theoretical modeling. Following the usual academic formula, papers are well illustrated and heavily referenced. Many issues are thematic, in whole or in part, expanding on such topics as languages and robot software or microactuators. The original editor retired in 2006, and the wonderful book reviews have ceased, but the occasional "Reports & Surveys" section continues, providing a real synthesis of what is happening now in the field and what actually did happen to some of those great ideas of the past. The web site has advanced searching options, permits tagging and bookmarking articles and issues, lists the cited references along with the abstract, links to Google Scholar as well as to publisher sites, exports the bibliographic reference, and offers RSS feeds. This is an excellent journal, useful in both industry and academia and inexpensive enough for college libraries.

5478. *Robotics and Autonomous Systems.* Formerly (until 1988): *Robotics.* [ISSN: 0921-8890] 1985. 12x/yr. EUR 1727. Ed(s): T. Arai, R Grupen. Elsevier BV, North-Holland, Sara Burgerhartstraat 25, Amsterdam, 1055 KV, Netherlands; nlinfo-f@elsevier.nl; http://www.elsevier.nl. Illus., index, adv. Sample. Refereed. Circ: 1200. Vol. ends: No. 4. Online: EBSCO Publishing, EBSCO Host; Gale; IngentaConnect; OhioLINK; ScienceDirect; SwetsWise Online Content. *Indexed:* ApMecR, C&ISA, CompLI, EngInd, SCI. *Aud.:* Ac, Sa.

Autonomous systems are special cases that may appear like robots, but operate in a specific environment for a specific task. For instance, the "robots" that are used in automobile assembly plants are more likely to be autonomous systems than full-fledged robots. This journal is affiliated with the Intelligent Autonomous Systems Society. The title should be compared with the publication *Robotics and Computer-Integrated Manufacturing,* also published by Elsevier. Both are research journals featuring quality scholarly papers. They are not competitors, though, but two aspects of the same field: large-scale and/or whole machines versus specific aspects or parts of machines. *Robotics and Autonomous Systems* will publish titles such as "Geometric Constraint Identification and Mapping for Mobile Robots," while *Robotics and Computer-Integrated Manufacturing* will print "Improved Robotic Deburring." There are several thematic issues per year on such topics as adding human spatial concepts to robots (as opposed to using sensors for navigation) and social mechanisms for programming robots.

5479. *Robotics and Computer-Integrated Manufacturing.* Incorporates (1988-1998): *Computer Integrated Manufacturing Systems;* Which incorporated (1988-1991): *Advanced Manufacturing Engineering.* [ISSN: 0736-5845] 1984. 6x/yr. EUR 1221. Ed(s): A Sharon, G Lin. Pergamon, The Boulevard, Langford Ln, East Park, Kidlington, OX5 1GB, United Kingdom; http://www.elsevier.nl. Illus., index, adv. Sample. Refereed. Circ: 2500. Vol. ends: No. 6. Microform: PQC. Online: EBSCO Publishing, EBSCO Host; Gale; IngentaConnect; OhioLINK; ScienceDirect; SwetsWise Online Content. *Indexed:* AS&TI, C&ISA, CerAb, CompLI, EngInd, ErgAb, IAA, SCI. *Aud.:* Ac.

This is a research journal with a mission: dissemination of proven research (either in the laboratory or on the shop floor) of manufacturing technologies and systems. This includes robotics, flexible automation, mechatronics, and rapid-response (or agile) manufacturing. Almost every author is associated with an engineering department of a large university, with research usually funded by a government agency, so that laboratory work predominates. Illustrations are largely flowcharts, line drawings, and screen images, and articles are well referenced and current. An oddity that bears watching is that, although the lag between acceptance and web publication is short, the issue dates are several months in the future. What may appear to be "breaking news" research may be a year old by the time it appears in the print version. This is an excellent title for an industrial, manufacturing, and/or systems engineering collection as well as for robotics.

■ SAFETY

See also Medicine; and Public Health sections.

Hilary Kline, Manager, Reformatting Support Services, Imaging Services, Harvard College Library/Widener Library, Harvard University, Cambridge, MA 02138

Introduction

This section, although small, is quite wide-ranging in scope, covering subjects from ergonomics to tips on wearing safety glasses, to workers' compensation issues, to scholarly research on safety (traffic accident studies, safety engineering, injury reduction research, etc.). Included here are a few titles that will be of interest to a general audience (such as *Occupational Hazards* and *Occupational Health and Safety*), as well as much more specialized titles that still do belong in certain core collections, such as the *International Journal of Occupational and Environmental Health.*

You may note that this section has gotten even smaller than in recent past editions. This is for two related reasons: first, prices of some titles, and second, access to review copies of the titles. Several titles listed in the past have such high prices that it appears they have been cut from many libraries' budgets. That, combined with certain publishers' refusals to supply review copies of the journals, means they were not available for review this edition. Our policy is not to pay for review copies, and since inclusion in *Magazines for Libraries* provides a definite benefit for publications, the title cannot be included if we cannot obtain review issues from the publisher or through a local library.

Basic Periodicals

Ga: *Safety and Health, Professional Safety;* Ac, Sa: *Journal of Safety Research.*

Basic Abstracts and Indexes

Health and Safety Science Abstracts.

American Journal of Public Health. See Public Health section.

5480. *Compliance Magazine: workplace safety, health & environment.* Incorporates: *Construction & Engineering Safety.* [ISSN: 1077-5889] 1994. 8x/yr. USD 58 domestic; USD 68 in Canada & Mexico; USD 147 elsewhere. Douglas Publications, Inc., 2807 N Parham Rd, Ste 200, Richmond, VA 23294; info@douglaspublications.com; http://www.douglaspublications.com. Illus., adv. Circ: 60000 Controlled. *Indexed:* ABIn, EngInd, H&SSA, RiskAb. *Aud.:* Ga.

Although aimed at safety professionals for creating and maintaining safe working environments, *Compliance Magazine* provides understandable, easy-to-follow information on access to recent government regulations that will be useful to most supervisors. Articles are by safety experts and tend toward practical approaches to everyday on-the-job safety issues. Regular sections include "Ask the Experts" and various product roundups (protective clothing, instrumentation, etc.). Recent articles include "Industrial Hygienists Focus on Analysis," "Restoration Firm Holds High Standards for Fall Protection," and "Panel Recommends Safety Improvements at BP." An essential title for any safety collection.

Environmental Health Perspectives. See Government Periodicals— Federal section.

Family Safety & Health. See Family and Marriage section.

FDA Consumer. See Health and Fitness section.

5481. *International Journal of Occupational and Environmental Health.* [ISSN: 1077-3525] 1995. q. USD 127 (Individuals, USD 103; USD 28 newsstand/cover per issue). Ed(s): Joseph LaDou. Abel Publication Services, Inc., 1611 Aquinas Ct, Burlington, NC 27215; Salovegrove@aol.com. Illus., index, adv. Refereed. Circ: 1000. *Indexed:* CINAHL, ErgAb, ExcerpMed, RILM, SCI, SSCI. *Bk. rev.:* Number and length vary. *Aud.:* Ga, Ac, Sa.

This quarterly title publishes research on the relationship between work environments and workers' health around the world; coverage is especially good on developing countries. Although this is primarily an academic, scholarly research publication, the journal also features book reviews, editorials, commentaries, and a section on education and practice. Recent articles include "The Role of Asbestos Fiber Dimensions in the Prevention of Mesothelioma," "Significant Developments in Occupational Health and Safety in Australia's Construction Industry," and "Mortality Among a Cohort of Banana Plantation Workers in Costa Rica." For an academic audience.

5482. *Journal of Occupational and Environmental Hygiene (Print).* Formed by the merger of (1986-2004): *Applied Occupational and Environmental Hygiene;* Which was formerly (until 1990): *Applied Industrial Hygiene;* (1940-2004): *A I H A Journal;* Which was formerly (until 2002): *A I H A J;* (until 2000): *American Industrial Hygiene Association. Journal;* (until 1956): *American Industrial Hygiene Association. Quarterly;* (until 1946): *Industrial Hygiene.* [ISSN: 1545-9624] 2004. m. GBP 439 print & online eds. Ed(s): Dr. Michael S

Morgan. Taylor & Francis Inc., 325 Chestnut St, Ste 800, Philadelphia, PA 19016; orders@taylorandfrancis.com; http://www.taylorandfrancis.com. Illus., index, adv. Sample. Refereed. Circ: 5000 Paid. Vol. ends: Dec. Reprint: PSC. *Indexed:* ABIn, BiolAb, C&ISA, CerAb, ChemAb, EnvAb, EnvInd, ErgAb, ExcerpMed, FPA, ForAb, H&SSA, IAA, PollutAb, RiskAb, SCI. *Bk. rev.:* 1, 525 words, signed. *Aud.:* Ac, Sa.

A joint publication of the American Industrial Hygiene Association (AIHA) and the American Conference of Governmental Industrial Hygienists (ACGIH), the *Journal of Occupational and Environmental Hygiene* publishes original studies in the areas of occupational, industrial, and environmental hygiene, which is of interest to professionals in environmental health and safety, epidemiology, and environmental medicine. It features case studies (such as a "Survey of Current Lead Use, Handling, Hygiene, and Contaminant Controls Among New Jersey Industries") and useful online resources (such as related web sites). It also includes reviews of related books and new products. For academic and specialized collections.

5483. *Journal of Safety Research.* [ISSN: 0022-4375] 1982. 5x/yr. EUR 898. Ed(s): Thomas Planek, Mei-Li Lin. Pergamon, The Boulevard, Langford Ln, East Park, Kidlington, OX5 1GB, United Kingdom. Illus., index, adv. Sample. Refereed. Vol. ends: Winter. Microform: PQC. Online: EBSCO Publishing, EBSCO Host; Gale; IngentaConnect; OhioLINK; ScienceDirect; SwetsWise Online Content. *Indexed:* AgeL, BiolAb, CJA, EngInd, ErgAb, H&SSA, HRA, HRIS, PsycInfo, RiskAb, SSCI, SUSA, V&AA. *Aud.:* Ac, Sa.

Aimed at safety professionals, this title reports on research on all aspects of safety. Articles cover safety issues in industry, traffic, schools, and the home. Recent articles include "Graduated driver licensing: Review of evaluation results since 2002," "Technology and teen drivers," and "Estimating the contributions of speeding and impaired driving to insurance claim cost." Highly focused, but of interest to academic and special collections.

Natural Hazards Observer. See Environment and Conservation section.

5484. *Occupational Hazards: the magazine of safety, health and loss prevention.* [ISSN: 0029-7909] 1938. m. USD 60 domestic (Free to qualified personnel). Ed(s): Josh Cable, Katherine Torres. Penton Media, Inc., 1300 E 9th St, Cleveland, OH 44114-1503; information@penton.com; http://www.penton.com/. Illus., index, adv. Sample. Circ: 65000 Paid and controlled. Vol. ends: Dec. Microform: PQC. Online: EBSCO Publishing, EBSCO Host; Florida Center for Library Automation; Gale; Northern Light Technology, Inc.; OCLC Online Computer Library Center, Inc.; ProQuest K-12 Learning Solutions; ProQuest LLC (Ann Arbor); H.W. Wilson. *Indexed:* ABIn, BPI, CWI, ChemAb, H&SSA, LRI, PMA, RiskAb. *Aud.:* Ga, Ac, Sa.

A trade publication that covers legislative, regulatory, and scientific developments, as well as reviews of services and products, *Occupational Hazards* will help safety professionals stay up-to-date on EPA, NIOSH, and OSHA compliance requirements. It's also aimed at improving safety and industrial hygiene programs. Recent articles include "Going Beyond the Minimum with Hearing Conservation," "Containing Spilled Liquids," and "Staying Safe: The Importance of Effective Safety Signage and Labeling." It is worth checking out the publisher's site at www.occupationalhazards.com for ongoing, up-to-date information.

5485. *Occupational Health & Safety.* Former titles (until 1976): *The International Journal of Occupational Health & Safety;* (until 1974): *International Industrial Medicine and Surgery;* (until 1969): *The International Journal of Industrial Medicine & Surgery;* (until 1967): *Industrial Medicine and Surgery;* (until 1949): *Industrial Medicine and Surgery Trauma;* (until 1949): *Industrial Medicine.* [ISSN: 0362-4064] 1932. m. USD 79 domestic; USD 149 Canada; USD 189 elsewhere. Ed(s): Jerry Laws. Stevens Publishing Corporation, 5151 Beltline Rd, 10th Fl, Dallas, TX 75240; custserv@stevenspublishing.com; http://www.stevenspublishing.com/. Illus., index, adv. Sample. Circ: 81158 Paid and controlled. Vol. ends: Dec. Microform: PQC. Online:

Northern Light Technology, Inc.; OCLC Online Computer Library Center, Inc.; ProQuest K-12 Learning Solutions; ProQuest LLC (Ann Arbor). *Indexed:* ABIn, AgeL, BPI, CINAHL, ChemAb, ErgAb, H&SSA, PAIS, RiskAb. *Aud.:* Hs, Ga, Ac, Sa.

A basic title targeted at safety professionals, this magazine pulls together a compendium of safety-related material on management issues, breakthrough strategies, leadership styles, personal protective equipment, computer applications, and new products. Recent articles include "Your Forklift Safety Zone," "Preventing Eye Injuries When Welding," and "Wearing a Hard Hat is Only Half the Job." The magazine web site, www.ohsonline.com, is also useful, with issue forums; "Hot Topics"; an events calendar; an industry directory; and a resource center of vendor catalogs, white papers, webinars, and classifieds.

5486. Professional Safety. Former titles (until 1970): *A S S E Journal;* (until 1969): *American Society of Safety Engineers. Journal.* [ISSN: 0099-0027] 1956. m. USD 51 (Non-members, USD 60). Ed(s): Sue Trebswether. American Society of Safety Engineers, 1800 E Oakton St, Des Plaines, IL 60018-2187; http://www.asse.org. Illus., index, adv. Sample. Refereed. Circ: 30000 Paid. Vol. ends: Dec. Online: EBSCO Publishing, EBSCO Host; Northern Light Technology, Inc.; OCLC Online Computer Library Center, Inc.; ProQuest LLC (Ann Arbor); H.W. Wilson. *Indexed:* ABIn, AS&TI, AgeL, ErgAb, H&SSA. *Bk. rev.:* 2, 150-250 words, signed. *Aud.:* Hs, Ga, Ac, Sa.

From the American Society of Safety Engineers and aimed at the professional safety specialist, this journal highlights developments in accident prevention research. Its content focuses on ergonomics and the analysis of successful applications in the workplace. Workplace and personal safety are addressed, as are legal issues in the realm of safety. Features include legislative and regulation updates and certifications, interviews, classifieds, a "Best Practices" department, and a "Back Page" feature with a screamingly funny (ironically so) "Safety Photo of the Month."

5487. Safety and Health. Former titles (until 1986): *National Safety and Health News;* (until May 1985): *National Safety News.* [ISSN: 0891-1797] 1919. m. Members, USD 45; Non-members, USD 58.50. Ed(s): Melissa Ruminski. National Safety Council, 1121 Spring Lake Dr, Itasca, IL 60143-3201; info@nsc.org; http://www.nsc.org. Illus., index, adv. Sample. Circ: 80000 Paid and controlled. Microform: PQC. *Indexed:* AgeL, BPI, ChemAb, EngInd, H&SSA, LRI, PEI. *Bk. rev.:* 1, 500 words, signed. *Aud.:* Hs, Ga.

The goal of this journal is to reduce workplace injuries by providing educational, practical, and innovative information about workplace safety to workers, safety professionals, and industry leaders. It is produced by the National Safety Council (web site at www.nsc.org), whose aim is to "educate and influence people to prevent accidental injury and death." Issues include a "Washington Update" (about government agencies and legislation affecting workplace safety), "Injury Facts," "Safety Tips," "Workplace Solutions," a "Literature Guide," "Product Focus," "Training Calendar," "Industry Beat," "In the News," and "Culture of Safety and Health."

5488. Work and Stress. [ISSN: 0267-8373] 1987. q. GBP 308 print & online eds. Ed(s): Tom Cox. Taylor & Francis Ltd., 4 Park Sq, Milton Park, Abingdon, OX14 4RN, United Kingdom; info@tandf.co.uk; http://www.tandf.co.uk/journals. Adv. Refereed. Online: EBSCO Publishing, EBSCO Host; Gale; IngentaConnect; OCLC Online Computer Library Center, Inc.; SwetsWise Online Content. Reprint: PSC. *Indexed:* ASSIA, AgeL, CINAHL, CJA, ErgAb, ExcerpMed, FR, H&SSA, HRA, PsycInfo, SSA, SSCI, SociolAb. *Aud.:* Ac, Sa.

This international quarterly publishes refereed academic papers about the psychological, social, and organizational aspects of occupational and environmental health, and stress and safety management. It includes theoretical papers, empirical reports, case studies, research notes, and scholarly reviews, and is targeted at the organizational development professionals. HR personnel and managers throughout organizations will find useful material here. Recent articles include "National surveillance of psychosocial risk factors in the workplace: An international overview," "Measuring exposure to bullying at work: The validity and advantages of the latent class cluster approach," and "Is there a relationship between burnout and objective performance? A critical review of 16 studies."

■ SCIENCE AND TECHNOLOGY

Susan M. Braxton, Illinois Natural History Survey Library, 1816 S. Oak St., Champaign, IL 61820; braxton@inhs.uiuc.edu

Introduction

Science literacy has been an area of focus and concern for some time. The American Association for the Advancement of Science (AAAS) Project 2061, founded in 1985 to "to help all Americans become literate in science, mathematics, and technology," emphasizes "the connections among ideas in the natural and social sciences, mathematics, and technology." The National Academies formed the Center for Education in 1999 (www7.nationalacademies.org/cfe) for "improvement of mathematics, science, technology and engineering education from the kindergarten through post graduate education." Though much emphasis in the ongoing discussions is on curriculum and instruction, libraries' contributions toward science and technology literacy for students and citizens are critical, if often implicit. Viable and appropriate science and technology collections are as important in libraries that serve the general public and students K–12 as they are in university and research libraries. Although collections will clearly differ by library type, many titles listed here are equally appropriate for general and academic audiences. Some are free, so that even the poorest of libraries may offer their patrons some exposure to science and technology information.

Online access to science and technology serials is widespread. Free online content is common, and may include, in addition to articles offered in print, supplementary content such as podcasts, blogs, and e-newsletters. Knowledge of these titles and their web site offerings can help librarians help patrons even if subscriptions to the titles themselves are out of reach.

This section includes, in addition to well-known titles such as *Science* and *Nature*, favorite and also lesser-known science magazines, cross-disciplinary or multidisciplinary research titles, titles on the history and philosophy of science, science education titles, and titles that explore the interactions between society and science and technology. Scholarly and popular titles are covered, and some fall into both categories.

Journal Citation Reports for 2005, both the Science and Social Science editions (Thomson-ISI), were used to gather supporting evidence for inclusion and recommendation of some titles; where impact factors and total citations are mentioned outside of publisher quotes, they are from this source. Some attempt is made to assess online publishing practices of the reviewed titles, which may affect their management in libraries. In the following annotations, if no mention of Document Object Identifiers (DOIs) is made, it is because the reviewer was unable to find evidence of DOIs assigned to articles; see www.doi.org for additional information. OpenURL linking capabilities are reported from the targets list from the Ex Libris web site as found in April–May 2007; reporting these data does not constitute endorsement. COUNTER compliance is reported from the list of compliant vendors on the Project COUNTER web site as found in April–May 2007; see www.projectcounter.org for additional information.

Basic Periodicals

Ems: *Current Science, Science and Children* (see also titles in Children section); Hs: *Discover, Science News, Scientific American;* Ga: *Discover, Popular Science, Science, Science News, Scientific American, The Scientist;* Ac: *American Scientist, Discover, Nature, New Scientist, Science, Science News, Scientific American, National Academy of Sciences/Proceedings, Technology Review.*

Basic Abstracts and Indexes

Applied Science and Technology Index, General Science Index.

5489. American Scientist: the Magazine of Sigma XI, the Scientific Research Society. Formerly (until 1942): *Sigma XI Quarterly.* [ISSN: 0003-0996] 1913. bi-m. USD 65 (Individuals, USD 28; USD 4.75 newsstand/cover per issue domestic). Ed(s): David Schoonmaker, Rosalind Reid. Sigma XI, Scientific Research Society, 3106 East NC Highway 54, PO Box 13975, Research Triangle Park, NC 27709. Illus., index, adv. Circ: 100000 Paid. Vol. ends: Dec. Microform: PMC; PQC. Online: EBSCO Publishing, EBSCO Host; Florida Center for Library

Automation; Gale; Northern Light Technology, Inc.; OCLC Online Computer Library Center, Inc.; ProQuest K-12 Learning Solutions; ProQuest LLC (Ann Arbor); H.W. Wilson. *Indexed:* AS&TI, AbAn, Agr, AnBeAb, AnthLit, ApEcolAb, BRI, BiolDig, BrArAb, CBRI, ChemAb, CompR, EnvAb, EnvInd, ExcerpMed, FutSurv, GSI, GardL, HRIS, ISTA, IndVet, L&LBA, M&GPA, MASUSE, MathR, NumL, PollutAb, RILM, SCI, SSCI, SWRA. *Bk. rev.:* 12 or more per issue, 250-2,200 words, signed. *Aud.:* Hs, Ga, Ac.

"A general-interest, nonrefereed science magazine" whose "principal mission is to share with its readers the best work in the biological and physical sciences, mathematics, engineering, applied sciences and quantitative and analytical social sciences, as well as science policy, history and philosophy." Each issue includes several feature articles, most invited and written by research scientists about their own work. This journal is intended for an audience of "practicing scientists and engineers and enthusiasts of science," and its features are technical but accessible to readers outside the discipline. Regular contributors offer essays on topics including computer science and engineering, as well as highlights from recent research. Numerous full critical book reviews and shorter "nanoviews," all signed, are published in each issue. Recommended for academic, public, and high school libraries. Site-wide online access available to institutions with print only. All book reviews and some feature articles and departmental essays from each issue are freely available.

5490. British Journal for the History of Science. Formerly (until 1962): *British Society for the History of Science. Bulletin.* [ISSN: 0007-0874] 1962. q. GBP 138. Ed(s): Simon Schaffer. Cambridge University Press, The Edinburgh Bldg, Shaftesbury Rd, Cambridge, CB2 2RU, United Kingdom; journals@cambridge.org; http://www.journals.cambridge.org. Illus., adv. Refereed. Circ: 1450. Vol. ends: Dec. Microform: PQC. Online: Pub.; EBSCO Publishing, EBSCO Host; OCLC Online Computer Library Center, Inc.; OhioLINK; ProQuest K-12 Learning Solutions; ProQuest LLC (Ann Arbor); SwetsWise Online Content. *Indexed:* AmH&L, AmHI, ArtHuCI, CCMJ, ChemAb, FR, GSI, HistAb, HumInd, IBR, IBSS, IBZ, MSN, MathR, PhilInd, SCI, SSCI, ZooRec. *Bk. rev.:* Number and length vary. *Aud.:* Ac, Sa.

BJHS publishes "scholarly papers and review articles on all aspects of the history of science" including medicine, technology, and social studies of science. Examination of recent topical coverage indicates a broad scope, with research articles on endocrinology, theoretical physics, seashell collections, meteorology, and vision studies. This journal offers research articles and a book review section touted by the editor as a "central feature" of the publication. Recommended for academic libraries. Site-wide online access available. DOIs assigned. Cited and citing references are linked.

British Journal for the Philosophy of Science. See Philosophy section.

5491. Bulletin of Science, Technology & Society. [ISSN: 0270-4676] 1981. bi-m. GBP 463. Ed(s): Bill Vanderburg. Sage Publications, Inc., 2455 Teller Rd, Thousand Oaks, CA 91320; info@sagepub.com; http://www.sagepub.com. Illus., index, adv. Refereed. Circ: 350 Paid. Vol. ends: No. 6. Microform: MIM; PQC. Online: EBSCO Publishing, EBSCO Host; HighWire Press; OCLC Online Computer Library Center, Inc.; SAGE Publications, Inc., SAGE Journals Online; SwetsWise Online Content. Reprint: PSC. *Indexed:* ArtHuCI, CommAb, ERIC, HRA, PRA, PSA, PhilInd, SSA, SSCI, SociolAb. *Bk. rev.:* Number and length vary. *Aud.:* Ac, Sa.

Bulletin of Science Technology & Society publishes "articles of general interest in the STS field, which can be used in teaching undergraduate or K–12 students." Content comprises "original articles describing research or reflection on STS topics." Topics include the place of science and technology in societies; policy issues related to science and technology; technology assessment; impact of technology upon human values and religious insights; and public understanding of technology and science. Also included are news items on relevant public and scholarly events. Thematic issues, one or two per year, are published; recent examples include "The Lathe of Popular Culture" and an issue featuring renewable energy articles. Other features are correspondence on previously published work, book notes, and critical comparative reviews (two pages in two or three issues each year). Recommended for academic libraries, particularly those that support undergraduate science and education degree programs.

Site-wide online access available with print or alone. DOIs assigned; cited and citing references are linked. Users can request alerts when an article from this title is cited. E-mail alerts available. Article-level openURL linking.

Current Science. See Classroom Magazines/Science section.

5492. Discover: the world of science. [ISSN: 0274-7529] 1980. m. USD 24.95 domestic; USD 36.95 Canada; USD 43.95 elsewhere. Ed(s): Corey S Powell, Tina Wooden. Disney Publishing Worldwide Inc., 114 Fifth Ave, New York, NY 10011-5690; letters@discover.com; http://www.discover.com. Illus., adv. Circ: 1088269. Vol. ends: Dec. Microform: PQC. Online: The Dialog Corporation; EBSCO Publishing, EBSCO Host; Florida Center for Library Automation; Gale; Northern Light Technology, Inc.; OCLC Online Computer Library Center, Inc.; ProQuest LLC (Ann Arbor); H.W. Wilson. *Indexed:* ASIP, AgeL, Agr, BiolDig, CBCARef, CPerI, EnvInd, GSI, IAA, MASUSE, RGPR, RI-1. *Bk. rev.:* Number and length vary. *Aud.:* Hs, Ga, Ac.

According to the publisher, "the world's leading popular science magazine" is *Discover*. Accessible feature articles describe research from all science disciplines. The monthly "Discover Interview" profiles a prominent scientist and his/her work. "Data" offers briefs on research across scientific disciplines, with a "Raw Data" section that describes the complete research process for a single published study. Reviews offered in most issues include both critical (sometimes comparative), signed reviews, and brief, unsigned synopses. Museum exhibits and other science-related content may be reviewed as well as books (book reviews are signed or unsigned). Thematic issues are published; a recent example was "Invisible Planet," with articles on science we cannot see. The January issue lists the "Top 100 Science Stories" of the previous year; the December issue names and profiles the "Scientist of the Year." This journal is less visually busy and offers greater coverage of basic science (as opposed to invention and applications) than *Popular Science*. Recommended for high school, public, and academic libraries. Site-wide online access is available through aggregators. At the time of review, publisher promotion of its recently revamped web site included free access to content from 1992 through the next to last issue. Blogs, RSS feeds, podcasts, and themed e-newsletters on various topics are available online in addition to content from the monthly issues.

5493. Endeavour. [ISSN: 0160-9327] 1942. 4x/yr. EUR 548. Ed(s): E Henry Nicholls. Elsevier Ltd., Trends Journals, 84 Theobald's Rd, London, WC1X 8RR, United Kingdom; http://www.trends.com/. Illus., index, adv. Sample. Refereed. Circ: 10000. Microform: MIM; PQC. Online: EBSCO Publishing, EBSCO Host; Gale; IngentaConnect; OhioLINK; ScienceDirect; SwetsWise Online Content; H.W. Wilson. *Indexed:* A&ATA, ApMecR, BiolAb, BrTechI, C&ISA, CABA, CCMJ, ChemAb, DSA, EngInd, ExcerpMed, FR, GSI, HRIS, HortAb, IndIslam, M&GPA, MSN, MathR, S&F, SCI, WAE&RSA. *Bk. rev.:* 15 per year, 800-1,000 words, signed. *Aud.:* Ac.

"*Endeavour* publishes brief articles that review the history and philosophy of science," serving as a "critical forum for the inter-disciplinary exploration and evaluation of specific subjects or people that have affected the development of the scientific discipline throughout history." This publication covers all areas, but especially life sciences, technology, and medicine. Its content is intended to be accessible to general readers, but appropriate for historians and practicing scientists. Review articles, opinions, book reviews, and editorials are published. Review articles comprise the bulk of the content. Recent topical coverage includes genomics, earthquakes, military psychiatry, and paleontology. There are usually multiple full book reviews per issue. Site-wide online access is available with or without the print. DOIs are assigned. RSS feed alerts of new content are available. ScienceDirect platform offers citing references from Scopus. Publisher is COUNTER compliant.

Gender, Technology & Development. See Gender Studies section.

5494. Isis: international review devoted to the history of science and its cultural influences. [ISSN: 0021-1753] 1912. q. USD 360 domestic; USD 389.60 Canada; USD 376 elsewhere. Ed(s): Bernard Lightman. University of Chicago Press, Journals Division, PO Box 37005, Chicago, IL 60637; subscriptions@press.uchicago.edu;

http://www.journals.uchicago.edu. Illus., index, adv. Refereed. Circ: 4000 Paid. Vol. ends: Dec. Microform: PMC; PQC. Online: EBSCO Publishing, EBSCO Host; Florida Center for Library Automation; Gale; JSTOR (Web-based Journal Archive); ProQuest K-12 Learning Solutions; ProQuest LLC (Ann Arbor). Reprint: PSC. *Indexed:* ABS&EES, AltPI, AmH&L, AmHI, ArtHuCI, BRI, BiolDig, CBRI, CCMJ, ChemAb, FR, GSI, HistAb, HumInd, IBR, IBSS, IBZ, IPB, IndIslam, MSN, MathR, PSA, PhilInd, RI-1, SCI, SSA, SSCI, SociolAb. *Bk. rev.:* 50 or more, signed. *Aud.:* Ac, Sa.

The official publication of the History of Science Society, *Isis* "is the oldest (and most widely circulating) English-language journal in the field." It publishes scholarly articles, research notes, commentary, and reviews on "the history of science, medicine, and technology, and their cultural influences." Approximately one-third of each issue is devoted to a book review section; 50 or more titles per issue may be covered in signed, critical reviews (500-1,000 words) categorized by historical period. The "Focus" section is "designed to attract readers in all areas of the field by dealing with themes that cut across chronological boundaries" and is also useful in teaching. Recent "Focus" themes have been material artifacts, mathematics, biography in the history of science, and the impact of feminism and environmentalism on scientific research. A supplemental fifth issue each year is the *Isis Current Bibliography*, which surveys the journal and monographic literature and is a separate purchase. Site-wide online access is available with print or alone at a reduced rate. The publisher has made all "Focus" content available online at no charge. Issue level openURL linking.

5495. *Issues in Science and Technology.* [ISSN: 0748-5492] 1984. q. USD 115 (Individuals, USD 46; USD 11.50 newsstand/cover per issue domestic). Ed(s): Kevin Finneran, Bill Hendrickson. University of Texas at Dallas, Cecil and Ida Green Center for the Study of Science and Society, PO Box 830688, Richardson, TX 75083-0688; http://www.utdallas.edu/utdgeneral/utdmaps/idagreen.html. Illus., index, adv. Sample. Refereed. Circ: 10000 Paid. Vol. ends: Summer (No. 4). Microform: PQC. Online: EBSCO Publishing, EBSCO Host; Florida Center for Library Automation; Gale; OCLC Online Computer Library Center, Inc.; ProQuest K-12 Learning Solutions; ProQuest LLC (Ann Arbor); H.W. Wilson. *Indexed:* ASIP, AbAn, AgeL, Agr, BiolDig, EngInd, EnvInd, FutSurv, GSI, H&SSA, HRIS, LRI, M&GPA, MASUSE, MCR, PAIS, PollutAb, RGPR, RI-1, RiskAb, SCI, SSCI, SWRA. *Bk. rev.:* 2-4 per issue, 2-3 pages, signed. *Aud.:* Hs, Ga, Ac, Sa.

Published jointly by the National Academies and the University of Texas at Dallas, *Issues in Science & Technology* offers a "forum for discussion of public policy related to science, engineering, and medicine," including both policy relating to science and science that informs policy. It is intended as a venue for researchers, policy-makers, and industry representatives to "share ideas and offer specific suggestions." Accessible to lay audiences. Some issues are themed or offer clusters of articles on a given topic; recent topics include national security, and science and technology in China and India. Contributors include national political figures, administrators at research institutions and federal agencies, and industry leaders, and are picked by the editor based on their topical expertise. In addition to four to seven feature articles per issue, the title offers regular legislative updates, an extensive forum section with reader responses to previously published issues, opinion pieces, and several full, critical book reviews per issue. Recommended especially for college and university libraries, but appropriate for all libraries that serve adults and young adults. Online access is free to all (html only), with a searchable and browsable archive of back issues to 1996. Some articles are made available online in advance of print publication. E-mail alerts of new content are available.

5496. *Journal of College Science Teaching.* [ISSN: 0047-231X] 1971. 7x/yr. Membership, USD 74. Ed(s): Lauren Beben, Lester G Paldy. National Science Teachers Association, 1840 Wilson Blvd, Arlington, VA 22201; membership@nsta.org; http://www.nsta.org. Illus., index, adv. Refereed. Circ: 5400 Paid and free. Vol. ends: May. Microform: PQC. Online: EBSCO Publishing, EBSCO Host; Gale; OCLC Online Computer Library Center, Inc.; ProQuest LLC (Ann Arbor); H.W. Wilson. *Indexed:* ABIn, ChemAb, ERIC, EduInd, MRD. *Aud.:* Hs, Ac.

The *Journal of College Science Teaching* offers "a forum for the exchange of ideas on and experiences with undergraduate science courses, particularly those

for non-science majors." It offers presentations of innovative materials, methods, and evaluation in teaching science; suggestions of improvements in science instruction at the college level; and descriptions of disciplinary science teaching with relevance across science disciplines. Recent feature topics include service learning, promoting discussion in science classes, teaching analytical and evaluative skills, student peer review of lab reports, and a description of a nanotechnology for non-majors course. "Favorite Demonstration" offers ideas for classroom demonstrations in science. Brief synopses from the research literature are offered in "Headline Science." The audience comprises science educators and students in science education programs. Recommended for academic libraries that support science education programs. NSTA journals are offered by membership only; institutional membership is available. Select content is offered online with free individual registration. Sitewide access is available via aggregators.

5497. *Journal of Research in Science Teaching: the official journal of the National Association for Resarch in Science Teaching.* [ISSN: 0022-4308] 1963. 10x/yr. USD 1342. Ed(s): J Randy McGinnis, Angelo Collins. John Wiley & Sons, Inc., 111 River St, Hoboken, NJ 07030-5774; uscs-wis@wiley.com; http://www.wiley.com. Illus., adv. Sample. Refereed. Circ: 2850. Vol. ends: Dec. Microform: PQC. Online: EBSCO Publishing, EBSCO Host; OhioLINK; SwetsWise Online Content; Wiley InterScience. Reprint: PSC. *Indexed:* ABIn, EduInd, EngInd, FR, IBR, IBZ, PsycInfo, SSCI, SWA. *Aud.:* Ac.

The *Journal of Research in Science and Teaching* "publishes reports for science education researchers and practitioners on issues of science teaching and learning and science education policy." It publishes primarily research articles, with four to eight per issue, including "investigations employing qualitative, ethnographic, historical, survey, philosophical, or case study research approaches." However, position papers, policy perspectives, critical reviews of the literature, and comments and criticism are also accepted. Some issues have a "Topic Focus"; recent examples include "Instructional Innovations in Science Learning Contexts" and "Beginning and Preservice Science Teachers." Readers include college-level educators and researchers, school administrators, and curriculum specialists. It is published by Wiley for the National Association for Research in Science Teaching. Recommended for academic libraries. Site-wide online access is available with print. Backfile 1963–1995 is a separate purchase. RSS and e-mail alerts of new content are available. DOIs assigned. Cited references are linked. Article-level openURL linking is available via CrossRef DOI.

5498. *Journal of Scientific Exploration.* [ISSN: 0892-3310] 1987. q. USD 125 (Individuals, USD 65). Ed(s): Dr. Bernhard Haisch. Society for Scientific Exploration, Department of Astronomy, P. O. Box 3818, Charlottesville, VA 22903-0818; http://www.scientificexploration.org. Illus., index. Sample. Refereed. Circ: 3000. Vol. ends: No. 4. Online: EBSCO Publishing, EBSCO Host; Gale. *Indexed:* EngInd, IBR, IBZ, M&GPA. *Bk. rev.:* 10-15 per issue, varying length, signed. *Aud.:* Ac, Sa.

The mission of the Society for Scientific Exploration is "to provide a professional forum for critical discussion of topics that are for various reasons ignored or studied inadequately within mainstream science, and to promote improved understanding of social and intellectual factors that limit the scope of scientific inquiry." The *Journal for Scientific Exploration* publishes material consistent with that mission, focusing on "anomalies in well-established disciplines to paradoxical phenomena that seem to belong to no established discipline, as well as philosophical issues about the connections among disciplines." Editor in Chief Henry Bauer writes, "we are open to well-reasoned, evidence-supported manuscripts that, for whatever reason, are non grata in mainstream periodicals." Bauer also reports a rejection rate of two-thirds over the last seven years. Also included are research articles, commentary, essays, reviews, book and film reviews, and correspondence on previously published material. Topics are well outside mainstream scientific literature, and include perennial favorites such as Bigfoot and parapsychology. Research articles authored by faculty from reputable institutions both support and debunk unusual hypotheses that are left unexamined in other venues. Like *Cryptozoology*, this title is enticing in a way that many traditional journals are not, and thus may find a broad audience in many libraries. An unfortunate shortcoming is its apparent lack of indexing in mainstream A&I sources. No site-wide online access is available from the publisher, but tables of contents, abstracts, and some full text from back issues more than two years old are available online at no charge.

5499. *Journal of the Royal Society. Interface.* [ISSN: 1742-5689] 2004. q. GBP 924 print & online eds. Ed(s): William Bonfield. The Royal Society, Publishing Section, 6-9 Carlton House Terr, London, SW1Y 5AG, United Kingdom; info@royalsoc.ac.uk; http://www.royalsoc.ac.uk. Refereed. *Indexed:* AnBeAb, ApEcolAb, BiolAb, ExcerpMed, SCI, ZooRec. *Aud.:* Ac, Sa.

"*Journal of the Royal Society Interface* is the Society's cross-disciplinary publication promoting research at the interface between the physical and life sciences." Published content includes "research applying chemistry, engineering, materials science, mathematics and physics to the biological and medical sciences" as well as "discoveries in the life sciences that allow advances in the physical sciences." Topics covered include biocomplexity, bioengineering, bioinformatics, biomaterials, biomechanics, bionanoscience, biophysics, chemical biology, computer science (as applied to the life sciences), medical physics, synthetic biology, systems biology, theoretical biology, and tissue engineering. Themed supplements are published; recent and planned examples include statistical mechanics of molecular and cellular biological systems, molecular and mechanistic aspects of self-healing polymers, and sources of variation in infectious disease dynamics. Original research articles, shorter reports of preliminary research, and invited reviews are published. The title's debut impact factor rank in the 2005 Journal Citation Reports, in the multidisciplinary sciences category, is 21st of 48 titles. Recommended for academic and special libraries that support research in physical or life sciences. Site-wide online access is available and includes accepted articles, all of which are published online upon acceptance. Free access is allowed to all review articles from the moment of online publication and to all content 12 months after print publication. Also, the society offers "EXiS Open Choice"; an author pays for open-access option. E-mail alerts available. DOIs assigned. Cited references are linked. Article-level openURL linking.

Kids Discover. See Children section.

5500. *The National Academies In Focus.* Formerly (until 2001): *National Research Council. NewsReport.* [ISSN: 1534-8334] 1951. 3x/yr. USD 10 domestic; USD 12 foreign. Ed(s): Valerie Chase. National Academy of Sciences, 500 Fifth St, NW, Washington, DC 20001; http://www.nas.edu/. Illus. Refereed. Circ: 17000. Microform: PQC. Online: ProQuest LLC (Ann Arbor). *Indexed:* ABIn, Agr. *Aud.:* Hs, Ga, Ac.

The National Academy of Sciences, National Research Council, National Academy of Engineering, and the Institute of Medicine are collectively called The National Academies, and they "serve as independent advisers to the federal government on scientific and technical questions of national importance." *In Focus,* published by the National Academies' Office of News and Public Information, features the activities of these bodies. Its features regularly represent focus areas of environment and resources, health and safety, engineering and technology, and education and social issues. It includes announcements of new projects and publications, and it offers current awareness of and accessible writing on science and policy issues. It is recommended for high school, public, and academic libraries. Freely available online, with each issue in a single file (html and pdf available), back to the first issue (2001) at http://infocusmagazine.org. Backfile of previous title to 1999 is available. Print subscriptions available for a nominal cost.

National Academy of Sciences. Proceedings. See Biology/General section.

5501. *Natural History.* Formerly (until 1919): *The American Museum Journal;* Incorporates (in 1960): *Nature Magazine.* [ISSN: 0028-0712] 1900. 10x/yr. Membership, USD 55. Ed(s): Peter Brown, Avis Lang. American Museum of Natural History, Central Park West at 79th St, New York, NY 10024-5192; scipubs@amnh.org; http://www.amnh.org. Illus., index, adv. Refereed. Circ: 250000 Paid. Vol. ends: Dec. CD-ROM: ProQuest LLC (Ann Arbor). Microform: PQC. Online: The Dialog Corporation; EBSCO Publishing, EBSCO Host; Florida Center for Library Automation; Gale; Northern Light Technology, Inc.; OCLC

Online Computer Library Center, Inc.; ProQuest K-12 Learning Solutions; ProQuest LLC (Ann Arbor); H.W. Wilson. *Indexed:* ABS&EES, AICP, AbAn, AgeL, Agr, AnthLit, BRD, BRI, BiolDig, C&ISA, CBRI, CerAb, EnvInd, GSI, GardL, IAA, MASUSE, PRA, RGPR, RI-1, RILM, SCI, SSCI. *Bk. rev.:* 2-3, 500-750 words, signed. *Aud.:* Hs, Ga, Ac.

Featuring a high ratio of graphic content to text, including some very impressive nature photography, *Natural History* is an attractive and accessible publication that covers the study of nature in the broadest sense. It contains features written for a general audience by research scientists or professional naturalists about their own work; there are also contributions from regular columnists. The column "Universe" celebrated its 100th essay in the April 2007 issue. "Samplings" are short reports on recent research findings useful for current awareness. Book reviews are in each issue. Recommended for high school, public, and academic libraries.

5502. *Nature: international weekly journal of science.* Incorporates (1971-1973): *Nature. Physical Science;* (1971-1973): *Nature. New Biology.* [ISSN: 0028-0836] 1869. w. EUR 2170. Ed(s): Dr. Philip Campbell. Nature Publishing Group, The MacMillan Building, 4 Crinan St, London, N1 9XW, United Kingdom; http://www.nature.com. Illus., index, adv. Refereed. Circ: 60185. Vol. ends: Dec. CD-ROM: Ovid Technologies, Inc. Microform: PMC; PQC. Online: EBSCO Publishing, EBSCO Host; Ovid Technologies, Inc.; ProQuest LLC (Ann Arbor); SwetsWise Online Content. *Indexed:* A&ATA, AICP, Agr, AnBeAb, AnthLit, ApEcolAb, ApMecR, ArtHuCI, B&AI, BAS, BRI, BiolAb, BiolDig, BrArAb, BrEdI, BrTechI, C&ISA, CABA, CBRI, CerAb, ChemAb, DSA, EngInd, EnvInd, ExcerpMed, FPA, FS&TA, FoVS&M, ForAb, FutSurv, GSI, HortAb, IAA, IndVet, LingAb, M&GPA, MASUSE, MSN, MathR, MinerAb, NumL, OceAb, PRA, PetrolAb, PhilInd, PollutAb, PsycInfo, RILM, RRTA, S&F, SCI, SSCI, SWRA, VB, WAE&RSA, WRCInf, ZooRec. *Bk. rev.:* 3-5, 500-1,000 words, signed. *Aud.:* Ga, Ac, Sa.

Nature's mission is to offer "prompt publication of significant advances in any branch of science, and to provide a forum for the reporting and discussion of news and issues concerning science" and "to ensure that the results of science are rapidly disseminated to the public throughout the world, in a fashion that conveys their significance for knowledge, culture and daily life." The title offers peer-reviewed research papers as well as timely "news and interpretation of topical and coming trends affecting science, scientists and the wider public." Unlike many other scholarly titles, *Nature* employs a full-time in-house editorial board. Original research content includes articles and shorter letters, together making up more than half of each issue. Occasional reviews are published. A variety of regular columns and departments are published; these are more generally accessible to readers with an interest in science. This journal ranks second (behind *Science*) by 2005 impact factor in the multidisciplinary sciences category. A core title for academic and research libraries, and appropriate for public libraries. The publisher has built a stable of more than 75 primarily biomedical titles in four main "families" (*Nature* research journals, *Nature Protocols, Nature Reviews* journals, and *Nature Clinical Practice* journals), the vast majority of which began publication after 1985. The proliferation of NPG titles has not been universally well received in the library world, though the titles are often in demand by researchers. Site-wide online access available. Articles and letters are published online in advance of print. Supplementary information for letters is published online. Online backfile to 1950 is available. Some free content is available online, including podcasts, a blog, and full text of the first issue of Nature (from November 1869). E-mail and RSS alerts of new content are available. DOIs assigned. Cited references are linked. Article-level openURL linking available via CrossRef DOI. Publisher is COUNTER compliant.

5503. *New Scientist: the global science and technology weekly.* Formerly (until 1971): *New Scientist and Science Journal;* Which was formed by the merger of: *New Scientist;* (1965-1971): *Science Journal;* Which incorporated (1920-1966): *Discovery;* Which incorporated: *Modern Science.* [ISSN: 0262-4079] 1956. w. USD 89 United States; CND 72 Canada; GBP 123 elsewhere. Ed(s): Jeremy Webb. Reed Business Information Ltd., Lacon House, 84 Theobald's Rd, London, WC1X 8NS, United Kingdom; rbi.subscriptions@qss-uk.com;

http://www.reedbusiness.co.uk/. Illus., index. Circ: 143000. Vol. ends: Dec. Online: EBSCO Publishing, EBSCO Host; Florida Center for Library Automation; Gale; LexisNexis; OCLC Online Computer Library Center, Inc.; ProQuest LLC (Ann Arbor); H.W. Wilson. *Indexed:* A&ATA, ABIn, AS&TI, ASSIA, AbAn, Agr, AnBeAb, ApEcolAb, ApMecR, ArtHuCI, BAS, BRD, BRI, BiolDig, BrArAb, BrHumI, BrTechI, CBRI, CEA, CPerI, ChemAb, DSA, EnvInd, FLI, FS&TA, ForAb, FutSurv, GSI, H&SSA, HRIS, HortAb, IAA, IBR, IBZ, IndVet, LISA, M&GPA, MASUSE, NumL, PAIS, PRA, PhilInd, PollutAb, RI-1, RILM, RRTA, S&F, SCI, SWA, SWRA, WAE&RSA, WRCInf. *Bk. rev.:* Number and length vary. *Aud.:* Hs, Ga, Ac.

New Scientist publishes "the latest science and technology news from around the world" from seven editorial offices worldwide, offering "a global reach that no other science magazine can match." Topical coverage is very broad, encompassing social science as well as the physical and life sciences and engineering. Typically there are four features per issue; recent topics address molecular biology, group psychology, agriculture, gender identity, and security measures for coastlines. Regular sections include news, interviews, essays, and book reviews. A regular column, "50 years ago," offers historical perspectives; recent columns have covered meteorology, plastics, and the space race. Content is accessible to lay audiences but sufficiently technical to be of value to professional scientists. Includes extensive job listings in the sciences. Online access is free with print to individual subscribers; site-wide online access is available via aggregators.

5504. *Popular Science: the what's new magazine.* Formerly: *Popular Science Monthly.* [ISSN: 0161-7370] 1872. m. USD 12 domestic; USD 28 Canada; USD 3.99 newsstand/cover. Time4 Media, Inc., 2 Park Ave, New York, NY 10016. Illus., index, adv. Circ: 1550000 Paid. CD-ROM: ProQuest LLC (Ann Arbor). Microform: NBI; PMC; PQC. Online: The Dialog Corporation; EBSCO Publishing, EBSCO Host; Gale; LexisNexis; Micromedia ProQuest; Northern Light Technology, Inc.; OCLC Online Computer Library Center, Inc.; ProQuest K-12 Learning Solutions; ProQuest LLC (Ann Arbor); H.W. Wilson. *Indexed:* ABS&EES, BiolDig, CBCARef, CPerI, ConsI, EnvAb, EnvInd, GSI, IAA, IHTDI, MASUSE, RGPR. *Aud.:* Hs, Ga, Ac.

Popular Science offers the latest scientific and technological developments for a lay audience. Emphasis is on applications, inventions, and consumer products and services rather than basic science, although the latter is not excluded. Feature authors usually have some experience and expertise behind writing about the feature subject matter, but are not themselves researchers. Regular sections include "Headlines"; "How 2.0" with "tips, tricks, hacks and do-it-yourself projects"; and "What's New," which features such content as "gadgets to buy" and appears in only some issues. The January issue profiles the coming year in science, offering projected developments in science and technology, with a graphic month-by-month timeline. The June issue covers the annual PopSci Invention Awards; recent awards were given for a velcro alternative, an inflatable satellite antenna, and green bricks. The December issue offers an "Annual Guide to the Year's Top 100 Products." Recommended for high school, public, and academic libraries. Site-wide online access available through aggregators. Supplementary online content includes a blog and podcasts. RSS feed alerts for new content are available.

5505. *R & D Magazine: where innovation begins.* Former titles (until Jul. 1995): *Research & Development;* (until 1984): *Industrial Research and Development;* Which was formed by the merger of (1959-1978): *Industrial Research;* (1950-1978): *Research - Development;* Which was formerly (until 1960): *Industrial Laboratories.* 1978. 12x/yr. USD 119 domestic (Free to qualified personnel). Advantage Business Media, 100 Enterprise Dr., Ste 600, Box 912, Rockaway, NJ 07886-0912; AdvantageCommunications@advantagemedia.com; http://www.advantagebusinessmedia.com. Illus., index, adv. Circ: 80000 Controlled. Vol. ends: Dec. Microform: CIS. Online: The Dialog Corporation; EBSCO Publishing, EBSCO Host; Factiva, Inc.; Gale; OCLC Online Computer Library Center, Inc.; H.W. Wilson. *Indexed:* ABIn, Agr, BPI, CWI, ChemAb, EngInd, ExcerpMed, IAA, LRI, SCI, SSCI. *Aud.:* Ac, Sa.

"The high technology journal of applied research and development" is read by "lab, R&D and project managers across all industries, government and universi-

ties." According to the history and objectives on its web site, this magazine has a readership of 80,000, 75 percent of whom work for "high-tech industrial companies," and 60 percent of whom are managers. Written for a multidisciplinary audience whose work involves physics, chemistry, materials science, biology, and engineering, the technical content of this title is intended to be accessible to readers from all disciplines and specialties. Areas of focus are "state-of-the-art scientific and technical advances, how the latest R&D instruments and techniques help researchers work more productively, and important trends in research management, funding, and policy." Issues regularly cover informatics, materials science, microscopy products, and hotonics products, emerging technologies, and Asian research and development news. Reviews of statistical analysis software and other measurement products are offered. The "Product Showcase" features primarily products for use in industrial settings. This magazine issues the R&D Top 100 as well as Lab, Scientist, and Innovator of the Year awards, all of which are showcased in the magazine. Recommended for libraries in technical industrial settings, and for academic libraries that support engineering and industrial technology programs. Free print or electronic subscriptions are currently available to qualified applicants from the United States and Canada. Site-wide online access is available through aggregators, though at the time of review all content was freely offered on the magazine's web site as well.

5506. *Royal Society of London. Philosophical Transactions. Mathematical, Physical and Engineering Sciences.* Former titles (until 1996): *Royal Society of London. Philosophical Transactions. Series A. Physical Sciences and Engineering;* (until 1990): *Royal Society of London. Philosophical Transactions. Series A. Mathematical and Physical Sciences;* (until 1934): *Royal Society of London. Philosophical Transactions. Series A. Containing Papers of a Mathematical or Physical Character;* (until 1896): *Royal Society of London. Philosophical Transactions A;* Which superseded in part (1665-1887): *Royal Society of London. Philosophical Transactions;* Which was formerly (until 1776): *Royal Society of London. Philosophical Transactions;* (until 1682): *Royal Society of London. Philosophical Collections;* (until 1679): *Philosophical Transactions.* [ISSN: 1364-503X] 1887. m. GBP 1604 print & online eds. Ed(s): Michael Thompson. The Royal Society, Publishing Section, 6-9 Carlton House Terr, London, SW1Y 5AG, United Kingdom; info@royalsoc.ac.uk; http://www.royalsoc.ac.uk. Adv. Sample. Refereed. Circ: 620. Microform: IDC; PMC. Online: EBSCO Publishing, EBSCO Host; Gale; JSTOR (Web-based Journal Archive); OCLC Online Computer Library Center, Inc.; OhioLINK; SwetsWise Online Content. Reprint: PSC. *Indexed:* ApMecR, BrArAb, CABA, CCMJ, ChemAb, EnvAb, EnvInd, M&GPA, MSN, MathR, MinerAb, PetrolAb, S&F, SCI, VB. *Aud.:* Ac, Sa.

The "[w]orld's longest running scientific journal," *Philosophical Transactions...* began in 1665, with sections A and B diverging in 1887. Two types of issues are published, "Themes" and "Discussion Meetings." Discussion meeting issues cover the proceedings of Society meetings, while theme issues typically contain 12 research articles headed by a general review. Both types of issues are "devoted to a specific area of the mathematical, physical and engineering sciences" that defines "a research frontier that is advancing rapidly, often bridging traditional disciplines." Robotics, energy, health monitoring, and nanotechnology were recent topics covered. The intended audience comprises mathematicians, physicists, engineers, and other physical scientists. This journal is currently published monthly, but expansion is planned, and editors are currently soliciting theme proposals in nano-science/engineering and quantum computing, environmental change and renewable energy, dynamical systems and complexity, biophysics, biological mathematics, and medical engineering. Ranks fourth by 2005 impact factor among the 48 multidisciplinary science titles. Site-wide online access is available with print or alone; the price is the same for online-only as for the combination. DOIs assigned. Cited references are linked. Article-level openURL linking. Complete backfile to 1665 available to Royal Society package subscribers.

5507. *School Science and Mathematics: journal for all science and mathematics teachers.* [ISSN: 0036-6803] 1901. 8x/yr. USD 25 domestic student membership (Institutional members, USD 100; Individual members, USD 50). Ed(s): Heather Lee, Gerald Kulm. School Science and Mathematics Association, c/o Heather Lee, Ed., Texas A&M

University, College Station, TX 77843; http://www.ssma.org. Illus., index, adv. Sample. Refereed. Circ: 3000 Paid. Vol. ends: May. Microform: PMC; PQC. Online: EBSCO Publishing, EBSCO Host; Florida Center for Library Automation; Gale; OCLC Online Computer Library Center, Inc.; ProQuest LLC (Ann Arbor); H.W. Wilson. *Indexed:* ABIn, ChemAb, ERIC, EduInd, ExcerpMed. *Bk. rev.:* Number and length vary. *Aud.:* Ac.

School Science and Mathematics publishes research papers on "science, mathematics, and connections between science and mathematics for grades K–graduate and teacher education, especially science and mathematics articles that deal with assessment, attitudes, beliefs, curriculum, equity, research, translating research into practice, learning theory, alternative conceptions, philosophy and history of science, sociocultural issues, special populations, technology, nontraditional forms of instruction, and science/technology/ society." The content is primarily research articles, typically three to four per issue. Editorials and signed book reviews are also included. Recent format and content changes to this title include a cover redesign, and transfer of the "Problem Section" to the journal web site from the print issues. Recommended for academic libraries that support science and mathematics education programs. Site-wide online access available via aggregators.

5508. Science. Formerly (until 1957): *The Scientific Monthly.* [ISSN: 0036-8075] 1880. w. USD 710 (Individuals, USD 142; Students, USD 75). Ed(s): Donald Kennedy, Monica Bradford. American Association for the Advancement of Science, 1200 New York Ave, NW, Washington, DC 20005; membership@aaas.org; http://www.scienceonline.org. Illus., index, adv. Sample. Refereed. Circ: 145000 Paid. Vol. ends: Dec. CD-ROM: Ovid Technologies, Inc. Microform: PMC; PQC. Online: The Dialog Corporation; EBSCO Publishing, EBSCO Host; Florida Center for Library Automation; Gale; HighWire Press; JSTOR (Web-based Journal Archive); OCLC Online Computer Library Center, Inc.; Ovid Technologies, Inc.; ProQuest K-12 Learning Solutions; ProQuest LLC (Ann Arbor). *Indexed:* A&ATA, ABS&EES, AS&TI, AbAn, AgeL, Agr, AmH&L, AnBeAb, AnthLit, ApEcolAb, ArtHuCI, B&AI, BRD, BRI, BiolAb, BiolDig, BrArAb, C&ISA, CABA, CBRI, CCMJ, CJA, CerAb, ChemAb, CompLI, CompR, DSA, EngInd, EnvInd, ExcerpMed, FPA, FS&TA, FoVS&M, ForAb, FutSurv, GSI, HortAb, IAA, ISTA, IndVet, LRI, LingAb, M&GPA, MASUSE, MCR, MLA-IB, MSN, MathR, NumL, OceAb, PAIS, PRA, PetrolAb, PhilInd, PollutAb, PsycInfo, RGPR, RI-1, RILM, RRTA, S&F, SCI, SWRA, VB, WAE&RSA, ZooRec. *Bk. rev.:* 2-3, 2,500 words, signed. *Aud.:* Hs, Ga, Ac, Sa.

The "[w]orld's leading journal of original scientific research, global news, and commentary," proclaims the web site of *Science*. A core tool for current awareness and science literacy, this weekly, peer-reviewed journal "publishes significant original scientific research, plus reviews and analyses of current research and science policy." It publishes several categories of signed research papers (which differ in length and scope), representing the full spectrum of disciplines. Editor-commissioned pieces feature "broadly accessible commentary," including "Perspectives," which relates to specific research or reports in the issue. Book and related reviews are published weekly. Thematic special issues are frequent, with recent topics including particle astrophysics; sustainability and energy; and polar science. E-mail alerts and RSS feeds are available for the entire contents, or just portions (e.g., position postings). Extensive multimedia content including podcasts, streaming video, images, and interactive content are available on the *Science* web site. Note that "Science Express"—previews of upcoming articles, potentially high-demand content with patrons—are not included in the base price for the online license. Recommended for all college, university, and research libraries, and also for public and high school libraries where budgets allow.

Science and Children. See Classroom Magazines/Teacher and Professional section.

5509. Science and Engineering Ethics. [ISSN: 1353-3452] 1995. q. EUR 226 print & online eds. Springer Netherlands, Van Godewijckstraat 30, Dordrecht, 3311 GX, Netherlands; http://www.springeronline.com. Illus., adv. Refereed. Reprint: PSC. *Indexed:* AmHI, ArtHuCI, BrHumI, FS&TA, ForAb, IBR, IBZ, IPB, PhilInd, SCI, SSCI. *Bk. rev.:* 1 per year; 700 words, signed. *Aud.:* Ac.

"*Science and Engineering Ethics* is a multi-disciplinary journal dedicated to exploring ethical issues of direct concern to scientists and engineers covering professional education, research and practice as well as the effects of innovations on the wider society." The title offers an "opportunity for the discussion of ethical values and professional standards as well as exploring the expectations and concerns of professionals in science." It is important for both practicing researchers and science educators. Covering both the conduct of science and application of new technologies in science and engineering in the broadest sense, its content includes medicine, agricultural biotechnology, environmental science, science education, intellectual property, and animal and human subjects in research. Originally published by Opragen Publications, the title has been transferred to Springer as of 2007. In addition to regular papers, educational forums, reviews, and occasional book reviews are published. Highly recommended for academic libraries. Site-wide online access is available with or without print. RSS and e-mail alerts of new content are available on the Springer platform from volume 13, issue 1. Here, DOIs are assigned, cited references are linked, and article-level openURL linking is offered. Springer is partially COUNTER compliant. Content from 1995 to 2006 continues to be offered to subscribers via the original publisher's web site.

5510. Science & Technology Review. Formerly (until July 1995): *Energy and Technology Review.* [ISSN: 1092-3055] 1975. 10x/yr. Free. Ed(s): Sam Hunter. University of California, Lawrence Livermore National Laboratory, 7000 East Ave, PO Box 808, Livermore, CA 94551-0808; hunter6@llnl.gov; http://www.llnl.gov/str/. Illus. Circ: 27000. Vol. ends: No. 10. Online: OCLC Online Computer Library Center, Inc.; H.W. Wilson. *Indexed:* M&GPA, RGPR. *Aud.:* Hs, Ga.

Lawrence Livermore National Laboratory (LLNL) publishes *Science & Technology Review* "to communicate, to a broad audience, the Laboratory's scientific and technological accomplishments in support of national security and other enduring national needs." The principal mission of the lab is national security, and the multidisciplinary research conducted there relates to "advanced defense technologies, energy, environment, biosciences, and basic science to meet important national needs." The magazine offers features, research highlights, brief accounts of the lab's research in the news, and patents and awards from LLNL research, all written for a lay audience. The centennial of co-founder Edward Teller's birth is approaching, and content for 2007 examines his accomplishments and history with the lab. Free print subscriptions are available. Freely available online, including back issues to 1995 and the title's predecessor to 1994. Users may view html versions of articles and download complete issue pdfs.

5511. Science at Berkeley Lab. Formerly (until 2005): *Science Beat.* 1999. irreg. Ernest Orlando Lawrence Berkeley National Laboratory, Public Information Department, 1 Cyclotron Rd MS-65, Berkeley, CA 94720; http://www.lbl.gov. *Aud.:* Hs, Ga, Ac, Sa.

Ernest Orlando Lawrence Berkeley National Laboratory (Berkeley Lab) was founded in 1931. It is the oldest U.S. Department of Energy National Lab, and Berkeley Lab scientists conduct "unclassified research across a wide range of scientific disciplines," such as quantitative biology, nanoscience, energy systems, the environment, integrated computing, and the universe. *Science@Berkeley Lab* emphasizes the interdisciplinary nature of the lab's ongoing research, with articles that "examine what it takes to prepare the ground for real advances in knowledge: the instruments and techniques, the scholarship and discipline, and the exchanges of ideas without which progress is impossible (from the inaugural issue, Feb. 18, 2005)." Recent issues feature substantive articles on the collection of comet dust; decoding of breast cancer genomes; removal of mercury from coal-fired power plant emissions; and *the* day in the life of Nobel laureate George Smoot. Accessible to lay audiences without sacrificing substance, this is a worthy addition to the online collections of all types of libraries. Recommended for all libraries.

5512. Science Education. Incorporates (1973-1976): *Summary of Research in Science Education;* Formerly (until 1929): *General Science Quarterly.* [ISSN: 0036-8326] 1916. bi-m. USD 1225. Ed(s): Nancy Brickhouse. John Wiley & Sons, Inc., 111 River St, Hoboken, NJ 07030-5774; uscs-wis@wiley.com; http://www.wiley.com. Illus., adv. Refereed. Circ:

2045 Paid. Vol. ends: Nov. Microform: PQC. Online: EBSCO Publishing, EBSCO Host; OhioLINK; SwetsWise Online Content; Wiley InterScience. *Indexed:* ABIn, ArtHuCI, BAS, EduInd, FR, IBR, PsycInfo, SSCI. *Bk. rev.:* Number and length vary. *Aud.:* Hs, Ac.

Science Education publishes research "on the latest issues and trends occurring internationally in science curriculum, instruction, learning, policy and preparation of science teachers with the aim to advance our knowledge of science education theory and practice." Articles may be published in the general section, or in one of six special topical sections, "Learning, Issues and Trends, Culture and Comparative Studies, Science Education Policy, Science Learning in Everyday Life, and Science Studies and Science Education." A regular "Comments and Criticism" section serves as a forum for dialogue on differing viewpoints or interpretations of research. Most issues contain a books section that offers several full, critical, signed reviews. The intended audience includes science educators, science education researchers, and administrators. Site-wide online access is available for an additional charge with print, and includes online content published in advance of print plus citation tracking (links to citing references). RSS and e-mail alerts of new content are available. DOIs assigned. Cited references are linked. Article-level openURL linking is available via CrossRef DOI.

Science News. See Classroom Magazines/Science section.

5513. *Science Progress: a review journal of current scientific advance.*
[ISSN: 0036-8504] 1894. q. GBP 243 print & online eds. Ed(s): Robin Rowbury, David Phillips. Science Reviews Ltd., PO Box 314, St Albans, AL1 4ZG, United Kingdom; http://www.scilet.com. Illus., index, adv. Refereed. Circ: 900. Online: Florida Center for Library Automation; Gale. *Indexed:* ChemAb, IndVet, SCI, VB. *Aud.:* Ac.

Science Progress is a "non-specialist review publication in science, technology, and medicine" that provides "accurate and readable briefings at the cutting edges of science for all those concerned with science education." As in *Scientific American,* articles are written by researchers about their own areas of research, but in contrast to that title, the authorship is decidedly international. Quarterly issues average about three articles, with no additional content. Topical coverage is wide-ranging, including cell and molecular biology, biomedicine, physics, chemistry, energy, and environmental remediation. The intended readers are students, science educators, and researchers wishing to keep current in research outside their own disciplines. Recommended for academic libraries. Site-wide online access is available via Ingenta, free with print subscription. Publisher offers abstracts online from 2001 to the present, with the current year excluded.

Science Scope. See Classroom Magazines/Teacher and Professional section.

5514. *Science, Technology & Human Values.* Former titles (until 1978):
Science, Technology & Human Values. Newsletter; (until 1976): *Program on Public Conceptions of Science. Newsletter;* Incorporated (in 1988): *Science and Technology Studies;* Which was formerly (until 1986): *4S Review;* (until 1983): *4S. Society for Social Studies of Science;* (until 1976): *SSSS. Newsletter of the Society for Social Studies of Science.* [ISSN: 0162-2439] 1972. bi-m. GBP 373. Ed(s): Ulrike Felt. Sage Publications, Inc., 2455 Teller Rd, Thousand Oaks, CA 91320; info@sagepub.com; http://www.sagepub.com. Illus., adv. Refereed. Circ: 1900. Online: EBSCO Publishing, EBSCO Host; Florida Center for Library Automation; Gale; HighWire Press; JSTOR (Web-based Journal Archive); OCLC Online Computer Library Center, Inc.; ProQuest K-12 Learning Solutions; SAGE Publications, Inc., SAGE Journals Online; SwetsWise Online Content. Reprint: PSC. *Indexed:* ArtHuCI, CommAb, EnvAb, EnvInd, FR, IBR, IBSS, IBZ, IPSA, PAIS, PRA, PSA, PhilInd, RI-1, RILM, SSCI, SociolAb. *Bk. rev.:* 1 per year. *Aud.:* Ac, Sa.

The journal of the Society for Social Studies of Science, this title offers "research, analyses and commentary on the development and dynamics of science and technology, including their relationship to politics, society and culture." Represented disciplines include political science, sociology, environmental studies, anthropology, literature, history, economics, and philosophy. Recent topical coverage includes genetic technologies, nanotechnology, computer technologies, various aspects of medical practice and care,

and numerous environmental issues. Special themed issues are published; a recent example highlights ethics in engineering design. Typically four to six articles are published per issue. A single book review essay (3,000 words, signed) has been published each year since 2006 (reduced from four in 2005); this is a critical review and may cover multiple topically related works. Publication frequency increased from quarterly in 2005 to six issues per year in 2006. TitleRanks second by 2005 impact factor among 31 journals in the social issues category (JCR Social Sciences Edition). Recommended for academic and research libraries. Site-wide online access available. Publisher web site offers e-mail and RSS alerts of new content. Most-read and most-cited articles are highlighted. DOIs assigned. Cited references are linked. Citing references are offered via Google Scholar, along with an option for alert when a particular article is cited. Article-level openURL linking possible.

5515. *ScienceDaily.* 1995. d. Ed(s): Dan Hogan. Science Daily, 41 Jo Mar Dr, Sandy Hook, CT 06482; http://www.sciencedaily.com. *Aud.:* Hs, Ga, Ac, Sa.

ScienceDaily is an online magazine and web portal for science, technology, and medicine, which offers "breaking news about the latest discoveries and hottest research projects." It is supported by advertising and is free to all. The web site has been among *Popular Science*'s "Top 50 Websites" for the past three years, and was on *PC Magazine*'s list of "Top 101 Websites" for 2006. Content is categorized into the broad topics of health and medicine; mind and brain; plants and animals; space and time; earth and climate; matter and energy; computers and math; and fossils and ruins, each with numerous subcategories. The front page features breaking news from the wire services, and presents "Today's Top Stories" adapted from "news releases [that are] submitted by leading universities and other research organizations around the world," with links to the original news releases. For every page beyond the front page, users are offered links to related content, including news sections, news topics, science stories, and also external encyclopedia articles and book reviews. A weakness is that the external content, though attributed, is branded as *ScienceDaily* content, which may lead to inappropriate citation by students. Book reviews are extracts from signed customer reviews on Amazon; review authors are not named on the *ScienceDaily* site and links go to the Amazon book record rather than the specific review. Encyclopedia articles appear to be extracted exclusively from Wikipedia. Site content is primarily text and still images, though some video content is included. E-mail newsletters and RSS alerts of new content are available. It is possible to browse headlines by relative update times, measured in hours. As an aggregator of science news content across all disciplines, *ScienceDaily* succeeds well, and is recommended for general science reference and current awareness.

5516. *Scientific American.* Incorporates: *Scientific American Monthly;* Which was formerly: *Scientific American Supplement.* [ISSN: 0036-8733] 1845. m. USD 24.97 domestic; CND 49 Canada; USD 44 elsewhere. Ed(s): John Rennie, Mariette DiChristina. Scientific American, Inc., 415 Madison Ave, New York, NY 10017-1111. Illus., index, adv. Circ: 555000 Paid. Vol. ends: Dec. Microform: PMC; PQC. Online: EBSCO Publishing, EBSCO Host; Florida Center for Library Automation; LexisNexis; OCLC Online Computer Library Center, Inc.; ProQuest K-12 Learning Solutions; H.W. Wilson. *Indexed:* ABIn, ABS&EES, AS&TI, AbAn, AgeL, Agr, AnBeAb, AnthLit, ApEcolAb, ApMecR, ArtHuCI, B&AI, BAS, BRD, BRI, BiolDig, BrArAb, BrTechI, C&ISA, CABA, CBCARef, CBRI, CINAHL, CPerI, CerAb, ChemAb, DSA, EngInd, EnvInd, ExcerpMed, FLI, FPA, FS&TA, ForAb, FutSurv, GSI, GardL, IAA, IBR, IHTDI, IPSA, ISTA, IndVet, M&GPA, MASUSE, MCR, MSN, MathR, NumL, PAIS, PEI, PRA, PhilInd, PollutAb, RGPR, RI-1, RILM, RRTA, S&F, SCI, SSCI, SUSA, SWRA, WAE&RSA, WRCInf, ZooRec. *Bk. rev.:* Number and length vary. *Aud.:* Hs, Ga, Ac, Sa.

Features authored by researchers about their work are the staple of *Scientific American.* Categorized by major topical area from animal behavior to space science, seven features per issue offer authoritative and accessible tutorial content. Brief author profiles and short lists of related research papers are included with the features. The regular "Perspectives" editorial discusses the research from one of the issue's features. "Insights" profiles current research and its implications. Also published are columns by regular contributors. Full, critical book reviews are published in most issues (per year, these total approximately ten signed, critical reviews, plus approximately ten unsigned short reviews). Also, the substantial "News Scan" section keeps readers current in research news across scientific disciplines. Highly recommended for high school, public, academic, and special libraries. Institutional site-license available. Web site offers video and podcast content (including the "60-Second Science" podcast), a blog, and RSS feed notification of new content.

5517. The Scientist: magazine of the life sciences. [ISSN: 0890-3670] 1986. m. USD 171 (academic) Corporations, USD 1146 (1-20 users) print & online eds.). Ed(s): Richard Gallagher. The Scientist, Inc., 3600 Market St, Ste 450, Philadelphia, PA 19104-2645; info@the-scientist.com; http://www.the-scientist.com. Illus., adv. Circ: 53000 Controlled. Online: EBSCO Publishing, EBSCO Host; Florida Center for Library Automation; Gale; ProQuest K-12 Learning Solutions; ProQuest LLC (Ann Arbor). Indexed: Agr, BiolDig, EnvAb, SCI, SSCI. Aud.: Ga, Ac.

The Scientist offers investigative features on science and technology, and covers science for a lay audience by investigating the economic, political, and cultural context in which research and its applications take place. Recent topics have included a critical analysis of the Centers for Disease Control's Syndromic Surveillance Program; an analysis of technology transfer between academia and industry; and a story on a discredited ornithologist. Authors include professional investigative reporters as well as representatives from research institutions and industry. Also included are a regular profile of a scientist, synopses from the literature, and the "Foundations" column, which describes historical advances that have had a far-reaching impact. Articles from the "Notebook" section focus on research methodologies. The "Lab Tools" column, initiated in January 2006, describes recent discoveries expected to become consumer products. Publication frequency decreased from bimonthly in 2005 to monthly in 2006. Recommended for academic and public libraries. Web site offers blogs, podcasts, and other content free of charge.

5518. Social Studies of Science: an international review of research in the social dimensions of science and technology. Formerly (until 1975): Science Studies. [ISSN: 0306-3127] 1971. bi-m. GBP 654. Ed(s): Michael J Lynch. Sage Publications Ltd., 1 Oliver's Yard, 55 City Rd, London, EC1 1SP, United Kingdom; info@sagepub.co.uk; http://www.sagepub.co.uk. Illus., index, adv. Refereed. Circ: 1200. Vol. ends: Dec. Reprint: PSC. Indexed: ASSIA, AmH&L, ArtHuCI, CABA, ExcerpMed, FR, ForAb, HRA, HistAb, IBR, IBSS, IBZ, IPB, IPSA, IndVet, PSA, RRTA, S&F, SCI, SSA, SSCI, SWA, SociolAb, VB, WAE&RSA. Bk. rev.: 3 per year, 1,000-2,000 words, signed. Aud.: Ac.

Publishes original research, empirical or theoretical, "on the concepts, processes, development, mediations and consequences of modern science and technology, and on the analysis of their social nature." Social science disciplines covered include political science, sociology, economics, history, philosophy, psychology, social anthropology, law, and education. Typical issues contain four to seven research articles. Recent issues have covered topics in medicine, environmental science, weapons technologies, agricultural biotechnology, computer science, microbiology, and empirical methods. Issues may also contain clusters of shorter comments on specific themes (recent examples are the Dover, Pennsylvania, school board effort to insert "intelligent design" into the biology curriculum; and Hurricane Katrina). While, according to the editor, this will not become a regular component of issues, future events may receive similar coverage. Ranks second by 2005 impact factor of 29 titles in the history and philosophy of science category in the JCR Social Science Edition, and fourth of 35 in history and philosophy of science category in the JCR Science Edition. Recommended for academic libraries. Site-wide online access is available. E-mail and RSS alerts of new content are offered. DOIs assigned. Cited references are linked. Citing references are offered via Google Scholar, along with an option for alert when a particular article is cited. Article-level openURL linking is available.

5519. Technology and Culture. [ISSN: 0040-165X] 1960. q. USD 155. Ed(s): John M Staudenmaier. The Johns Hopkins University Press, 2715 N Charles St, Baltimore, MD 21218-4363; http://muse.jhu.edu. Illus., index, adv. Refereed. Circ: 2400. Vol. ends: Oct (No. 4). Microform: PQC. Online: Chadwyck-Healey Inc.; EBSCO Publishing, EBSCO Host; JSTOR (Web-based Journal Archive); OCLC Online Computer Library

Center, Inc.; OhioLINK; Project MUSE; ProQuest LLC (Ann Arbor); SwetsWise Online Content. Reprint: PSC. Indexed: A&ATA, ABS&EES, AS&TI, AmH&L, ArtHuCI, BAS, BRI, BrArAb, CBRI, ExcerpMed, FR, HistAb, IBR, IBSS, IBZ, JEL, NumL, RI-1, RILM, RRTA, SCI, SSA, SSCI, SociolAb, WAE&RSA. Bk. rev.: 30-40 per issue, 500-1,000 words, signed. Aud.: Ac.

The quarterly journal of the Society for the History of Technology, Technology and Culture offers scholarly articles, book and museum exhibit reviews, and critical essays with interdisciplinary subject coverage. The audience includes general readers as well as specialists such as engineers, anthropologists, sociologists, museum curators, archivists, and historians. Each issue offers 30–40 book reviews. Organizational information and conference reports are also included. Recommended for academic libraries. Site-wide online access is available via Project MUSE with print or alone at a reduced rate. RSS alerts of new content are offered. Article-level openURL linking; online platform is COUNTER compliant.

5520. Technology Review: MIT's national magazine of technology & innovation. Former titles (until 1998): M I T's Technology Review; (until 1997): Technology Review. [ISSN: 1099-274X] 1899. bi-m. m. until 2006. USD 34 domestic; USD 47 foreign. Ed(s): Jason Pontin, David Rotman. Technology Review Inc., 1 Main St., 7th Fl., Cambridge, MA 02142. Illus., index, adv. Circ: 327562 Paid. Vol. ends: Nov/Dec. Microform: PQC. Online: The Dialog Corporation; EBSCO Publishing, EBSCO Host; Factiva, Inc.; Florida Center for Library Automation; Gale; Northern Light Technology, Inc.; OCLC Online Computer Library Center, Inc.; ProQuest K-12 Learning Solutions; ProQuest LLC (Ann Arbor); H.W. Wilson. Indexed: ABIn, ABS&EES, AS&TI, ASG, Agr, BPI, BRI, BiolDig, C&ISA, CBRI, CPerI, CerAb, ChemAb, CompLI, EngInd, EnvInd, ExcerpMed, FutSurv, GSI, IAA, ISTA, LRI, MASUSE, MicrocompInd, PAIS, PRA, RGPR, RiskAb, SCI, SSCI, SUSA. Bk. rev.: Varying number and length, signed. Aud.: Hs, Ga, Ac, Sa.

The primary focus of Technology Review is on emerging technologies. Produced for a lay audience, albeit one with a strong interest in and aptitude for technology and engineering, the title "has but a single mission—and that's to keep you fully apprised of what's coming next." Features authored by expert guest contributors and staff writers cover developments in information technology, biotechnology, nanotechnology, and business technologies. Topics are wide-ranging, including measurement of brain activity, computer programming, energy, web searching, and even a sci-fi piece on domestic terrorism. The "Forward" section offers brief write-ups on innovations and products; "From the Labs" profiles research and development, covering the methods, results, implications, and next steps for new discoveries. Each issue revisits a feature from some past issue, and addresses advances or absence thereof in that area of research. A review section reviews books, artifacts, reports, products. Recommended for all libraries that serve adult and young adult populations. Site-wide online access is available through aggregators. Publisher web site offers supplementary content, including blogs and streaming video. RSS alerts of new content are available.

■ SEXUALITY

See also Gay, Lesbian, Bisexual, and Transgender section.

Daniel C. Tsang, Social Science Bibliographer, Langson Library, University of California, P.O. Box 19557, Irvine, CA 92623; dtsang@uci.edu; 949-824-4978; FAX: 949-824-2700

Introduction

Sex, although widely practiced, still appears to be a taboo topic for library shelves. The more scholarly collections may contain such titles as the *Journal of Homosexuality,* the *Journal of Sex Research,* or *Archives of Sexual Behavior,* but for titles that veer beyond academia into more-explicit depictions of the phenomenon, their absence from libraries is quite apparent and, from this reviewer's point of view, needs to be rectified.

Sexually explicit periodicals, often termed "adult magazines," proliferate in American society; even the corner drugstore may stock a few. Thousands of new DVDs are released each year, as *AVN,* or *Adult Video News,* the bible of the porn industry, ably documents. Mass marketed all over the United States (in some states more discreetly than in others), porn publishers and editors proclaim themselves to be advocates of sexual liberation and free speech. They may shock some people, since much of the output appears to arouse and stimulate only certain areas of the body; only a few publications attempt to reach the mind. The proliferation of erotic videos has also spawned a related publishing trend: what a *New York Times* essayist called meta-porn, or porn-on-porn, with review publications that attempt to document, critique, or promote that scene. The prolific migration of erotic content to the electronic world has made such imagery and text almost ubiquitous and unavoidable, making any web surfer a potential instant critic.

The proliferation of independently produced, noncommercial zines with some erotic content brings a new dimension to the sex scene. There is perhaps more attempt at analysis, deconstruction, and intellectual stimulation in these publications. Like their profit-making and market-oriented contemporaries, these zines also may shock the sexually inhibited.

Taken together, these publications reflect contemporary popular culture and society's obsession with matters sexual. Libraries can ill afford to ignore these publications, even if acquiring even one of them may challenge the hardiest librarian to see how far he or she is willing to uphold the Library Bill of Rights.

If libraries are to better serve their communities, we might consider doing more than letting just the corner drug store, liquor store, or adult bookstore satisfy the public's demand for erotica. Some titles have managed to penetrate library walls, as evidenced by the few cataloged under the subject heading Erotic Literature—Periodicals. Other more scholarly titles have also managed to enter the hallowed halls of academia, given the HIV/AIDS crisis and the moral panic over often taboo sexual expressions.

In this supposedly liberated era, patrons are unlikely to heed the advice that used to be found in many card catalogs: "For sex, see librarian." They want to find it themselves and for themselves. With even the U.S. Supreme Court endorsing formerly taboo sexual behavior, libraries have no excuse not to collect at least some of this material.

Note, however, that some of the sites reviewed are for adults only.

Basic Periodicals

Hs: *Sex, Etc.* Ga: *Adam Film World Directory of Adult Films, Adam Gay Video Directory, Adult Video News, Libido, On Our Backs, Penthouse, Playboy; Sex, Etc.* Ac: *Adam Film World Directory of Adult Film, Adam Gay Video Directory, Adult Video News, Annual Review of Sex Research, Culture, Health & Sexuality, Journal of Homosexuality, Journal of Sex Research, Journal of the History of Sexuality, Libido, On Our Backs, Penthouse, Playboy, Sexualities, Sexuality and Culture;* Sa: *Prometheus.*

Basic Abstracts and Indexes

Gay and Lesbian Abstracts.

5521. *Adam Film World Guide. Directory of Adult Film & Video.* Former titles: *Adam Film World Guide. Directory of Adult Film.* [ISSN: 0743-6335] 1984. a. Ed(s): J C Adams. Knight Publishing Corporation, 8060 Melrose Ave, Los Angeles, CA 90046; psi@loop.com. Illus., adv. *Aud.:* Ga, Ac.

Like its gay counterpart *Adam Gay Video Directory,* this annual directory of the heterosexual adult-film industry is profusely illustrated with photos of porn stars, more female than male, who are profiled in a "Performers" section. Hundreds of DVDs are reviewed in each edition, plus short synopses of hundreds of older videos. The reviews of new videos are arranged alphabetically by title, each with a plot synopsis, overall rating (up to five stars), and a descriptive "erotic rating" (e.g., "volcanic"). Sexual themes are noted, along with cast, credits, and current manufacturer. Amateur and fetish videos are also reviewed. A special section reviews Internet erotica sites, complete with URLs. The 101 "wildest" DVDs of the century are profiled. Most useful are the retail and manufacturer source directories. An essential purchase for the more serious student of this genre. (DT)

5522. *Adam Gay Video Directory.* a. USD 12.95 domestic; USD 14.95 foreign. Ed(s): J C Adams. Knight Publishing Corporation, 8060 Melrose Ave, Los Angeles, CA 90046; psi@loop.com. Illus., adv. *Aud.:* Ga, Ac.

This perfect-bound annual directory is still the leading guide to the gay adult-video industry. Similiar to its straight-market counterpart, *Adam Film World Directory of Adult Films,* this publication is profusely illustrated with color photos of hundreds of adult-film stars, many sporting erections. Categories include performers, directors, reviews, award winners, a themes index, mail order sources, a distributors index, and a retail stores index. Several hundred current male porn stars are featured, with their videographies. Several hundred current videos and DVDs are critically reviewed and rated, with explicit illustrations; cast members are listed as well. Hundreds of other films or videos from the 1970s to today are also listed, with synopses included. Most useful are the various indexes, including sources for obtaining the videos. An indispensable source for the serious student of this genre. For adults. (DT)

5523. *Adult Video News: the adult entertainment monthly.* [ISSN: 0883-7090] 1982. m. USD 78 domestic; USD 198 foreign. A V N Publications Inc., 9414 Eton Ave, Chatsworth, CA 91311; http://www.avn.com. Illus., adv. Sample. Circ: 45000 Paid. *Bk. rev.:* Number and length vary. *Aud.:* Ga, Ac.

The flagship publication of the adult video industry—which rakes in several billion dollars a year—*AVN,* or *Adult Video News,* founded with $900 by several college students, is today the bible of the porn industry, akin to what *Billboard* is to the music industry. With thousands of hardcore DVDs entering the commercial market each year, *AVN* manages to highlight the most marketable. There are feature articles on specific new films and videos and legal advice to porn retailers as well as a "Religious Right Watch," but the bulk of the perfect-bound magazine is devoted to capsule reviews of new erotic films, videos, and DVDs, as well as reviews of hardware (e.g., vibrators or latex pants). While largely heterosexual in its approach, gay and bisexual videos are also reviewed. The magazine is profusely illustrated with explicit color photos and ads from the industry. Many of the news items deal with confrontations with state and church, but the meat is in the technical know-how for adult web developers. There may even be a feature on PHP, the computer scripting language, or book reviews on cascading style sheets or Internet firewalls. A serious essay might address zoning laws; a less serious one might feature Asian beauties as the "niche market." You will also find reviews of new electronics and software in a "Test Data" section. A "Browser Box" may even contain sample Java script. A "Links" section provides URLs of relevant web sites. Aimed at retailers, it is nonetheless highly recommended for the serious collector. The web version is archived back to 1998, but only with selected online content. A year's subscription is free if you qualify after completing a questionnaire online (www.avn.com/subscribe). (DT)

5524. *Annual Review of Sex Research.* [ISSN: 1053-2528] 1990. a. USD 96 (Individuals, USD 59). Ed(s): Julia C Heiman. Society for the Scientific Study of Sexuality, PO Box 416, Allentown, PA 18105; thesociety@sexscience.org; http://www.sexscience.org. Illus. Circ: 500. *Indexed:* ASSIA, AbAn, CJA, IBR, IBZ, IMFL, PsycInfo, SFSA, SSA, SWA, SWR&A, V&AA. *Aud.:* Ac, Sa.

This scholarly journal from a sexualities research society covers an eclectic range of sex research issues in each annual issue. It attempts to "synthesize recent theoretical and research advances in specific topic areas." Issues also include regular articles typically found in other sex research journals. Its coverage is technical and specialized, even medical, in contrast to the society's main, more accessible *Journal of Sex Research.* Included are literature reviews of a particular research field, such as "sexual victimization." Mainly of interest to the serious sex researcher or graduate student specializing in the field. (DT)

5525. *Canadian Journal of Human Sexuality.* Formerly (until 1992): *S I E C C A N Journal.* [ISSN: 1188-4517] 1986. q. CND 60 (Individuals, CND 40; Students, CND 25). Ed(s): F Michael Barrett. Sex Information and Education Council of Canada, 850 Coxwell Ave, Toronto, ON M4C 5R1, Canada; sieccan@web.net; http://www.sieccan.org. Refereed. Circ: 1000. *Indexed:* ASSIA, CBCARef, CEI, CINAHL, CPerI, EAA, ExcerpMed, IBSS, PsycInfo, SFSA, SSA, SWA, SWR&A, SociolAb, V&AA. *Aud.:* Ac.

The only peer-reviewed, interdisciplinary journal that focuses on Canadian sex research and sex education, *CJHS* is published by SIECCAN, the Sex Information and Education Council of Canada. Recent articles cover such topics as Canadian attitudes toward female topless behavior, teen sexual initiation and perception of parental disapproval, sexual compatability and sexual functioning in intimate relationships, and sexual health education in the schools. Socio-medical aspects of sexuality are addressed. Abstracts are freely posted online at www.sieccan.org/abstracts/cjhs_frameset.html. Recommended for major collections. (DT)

5526. *Clean Sheets*. 1998. w. Ed(s): Susannah Indigo. Clean Sheets, http://www.cleansheets.com/. *Aud.:* Ga, Ac.

Founded by a "small group of writers who dreamed of an online erotic magazine that didn't take itself too seriously, but still did its best to be fresh, clear and exciting," *Clean Sheets* sees itself as "Good Vibrations [the sex-toy store] meets Salon.com." It seeks to foster a dialog on sexuality. Sections include articles, exotica, fiction, poetry, and reviews. Art work is featured in an archived gallery. Contributors include David Steinberg. It even pays for fiction and poetry. It has even celebrated a "Sex & Politics Month." Its online archive—free to all browsers—preserves all contributions. Overall, a well-designed site that serves up a pleasant experience. Highly recommended. (DT)

5527. *Cybersocket Web Magazine: the leader in gay & lesbian online information*. 1996. m. USD 15.95 domestic. Ed(s): Brian Baltin. Cybersocket Inc., 964 1/2 N Vermont Ave, Los Angeles, CA 90029. *Aud.:* Ga, Ac, Sa.

This gay publication keeps track of and reviews web-based queer content. According to its web site, it is "Cybersocket's role to analyze, categorize, comment upon and popularize gay and lesbian oriented websites." It is well illustrated with ads for (gay male) sex sites, but the magazine, widely distributed in gay hangouts, includes analytical pieces on the latest in queer online resources. A "Cybersurgeon" gives advice to those technologically challenged, while a special section reviews "Porn Flixxx" as well as porn web sites. Another regular section reviews sex sites, accompanied by a feature article on sex. Selected feature articles from back issues (from at least May 2003) are available on its online edition. Recommended for libraries catering to the sexually liberated or curious of whatever sexual orientation. URL: www.cybersocket-.com. (DT)

5528. *The Electronic Journal of Human Sexuality*. [ISSN: 1545-5556] 1998. a. Free. Ed(s): David S Hall. Institute for Advanced Study of Human Sexuality, 1523 Franklin St, San Francisco, CA 94109-4522. Refereed. *Indexed:* ExcerpMed, SociolAb. *Bk. rev.:* 5-6. *Aud.:* Ac, Sa.

This online journal (www.ejhs.org) is an output of what is known in the sex research community as "Kinsey West," reflecting the origins of the Ph.D-granting Institute for the Advanced Study of Human Sexuality, its publisher. Several scholars from the Kinsey Institute migrated west from Indiana and became faculty for this school. It boasts the largest accessible sex research library. The journal also reviews books and videos in human sexuality. The school trains sex therapists and public health professionals, as well as sexologists, and the content of the online journal reflects that focus but goes beyond it. The "Call for Papers" section, which lists academic journals seeking sexuality-related papers, and the "Meetings" section, which offers hyperlinks to upcoming sexology conferences around the world, are both useful. A recommended addition to research collections. The entire run of the journal is free online. Since its 2005 edition, it is not accepting new submissions "at this time."(DT)

5529. *The Erotic Review*. Formerly (until 1997): *The Erotic Print Society Review*. [ISSN: 1477-1594] 1995. q. GBP 20. Q3 Media Ltd., ERQ, 500 Chiswick High Rd., London, W4 5RG, United Kingdom. Illus., adv. Circ: 30000. *Bk. rev.:* 4; 200-750 words. *Aud.:* Ga, Ac, Sa.

This literary erotica magazine from the United Kingdom in its various permutations has included novel excerpts, fiction, book reviews, video reviews, and an advice column ("Dear Antonia: Nookie dilemma? Have it solved..."). One issue even includes an excerpt from the novel "Gordon" by Edith Templeton, a publication that had previously been banned. The high-quality stories generally have a heterosexual focus. Issues may have a theme, e.g.,

"Sexual Healing: The Doctors and Nurses Issue," focusing on stories involving the health profession. Its regular interview section has included a subject who was a teenage male hustler. Book reviews cover alternative press titles rarely reviewed elsewhere, for example, a book on transgender erotica. The illustrations are artistic and include both art and photography, without the blatant images of other erotica publications (they do include drawings of erect penises). Advertisements tout chemicals, sex toys, and videos. Selected articles appear on its web site. Now published by Trojan Publishing: www.erotic-review.co.uk. Highly recommended for more forward-looking collections. (DT)

5530. *Erotica Readers and Writers Association*. 1998. m. Free. Erotica Readers Association. *Bk. rev.:* Number and length vary. *Aud.:* Ga.

This site, "dedicated to readers and writers of erotica since 1996," "is an international community of women and men interested in the provocative world of erotica." It showcases "explicit fiction, poetry, and discussions about sexuality." The site provides "advice, news, current calls for submissions, and market information for authors." For readers, it provides information on books "for all persuasions and desires, book reviews and interviews." For "sensualists," it "highlights recommendations for adult videos, sex toy information," as well as providing "a forum for discussions about sexuality." Its online forum encourages sexual frankness: "We hope our open approach to sexuality creates sex-positive ripples around the world." Features have included advice on getting erotic literature published, dealing with literary agents, and overcoming rejection letters. Links are also provided to other erotic literature and movie sites. Highly recommended. (DT)

5531. *Good Vibes Magazine*. 1997. w. Free. Ed(s): Violet Blue. Good Vibrations, 1210 Valencia St, San Francisco, CA 94110. *Aud.:* Ga.

A web-based zine from Good Vibrations, the San Franciso-based bookstore that promotes positive sexual attitudes and literature. *GV Weekly*, or *Good Vibes Online Magazine*, as it is also known online, includes regular contributors such as Carol Queen and the former Pat Califia (now Patrick). A regular section includes erotic stories. Highly recommended. URL: www.goodvibes.com/Content.aspx?id=886 (DT)

Journal of Homosexuality. See Gay, Lesbian, Bisexual, and Transgender section.

Journal of Sex Research. See Sociology and Social Work/General section.

Journal of the History of Sexuality. See History section.

5532. *Libido: the journal of sex and sensibility*. [ISSN: 0899-8272] 1988. q. Ed(s): Jack Hafferkamp, Marianna Beck. Libido, PO Box 146721, Chicago, IL 61614; rune@mcs.com; http://www.sensualsource.com. Illus., adv. Sample. Circ: 10000. *Indexed:* AltPI. *Bk. rev.:* 6, 500-3,000 words. *Aud.:* Ga, Ac.

This well-designed journal, now migrated to the web, continues to offer some of the best writing on sexual politics and erotica. The editors explain: "Printing is very expensive for a small erotic magazine. We can reach more people with more exciting content by publishing on the web." It describes itself as "a journal about sex that's geared to turn on your mind and your body. It's a web site (formerly a magazine) for women and men who read and think." It is "sex-positive, gender-equal, and all-embracing in terms of sexual orientation." It also claims to be "both intellectually demanding as well as stimulating." There is poetry, reader-written fiction, and, most notably, highly artistic photography, some from its annual photography contest. Fiction articles are prominent, and there is a fiction as well as a reviews archive online. Vintage erotica now appear in an online gallery and art museum, and there is also a book review archive. A sexuality resources section includes a sex quiz to test your sex IQ. A sign of the times, the site now warns of "adult and sexual" content, and notes, "In an effort to prevent inappropriate eyes from viewing the contents herein, we have registered Libido with the following filtering services," including Net Nanny and Surf Watch. A free monthly e-newsletter is available. Back issues of the print version that lasted from 1988 to 2000 are on sale on the web site. A highly recommended title for adding to the library online catalog. URL: www.libidomag.com (DT)

5533. *Nerve (Online edition): literate smut.* 1997. m. Free. Ed(s): Michael Martin, Tobin Levy. Nerve.com, 520 Broadway, 6th Floor, New York, NY 10012; info@nervemag.com; http://www.nerve.com. Illus., adv. *Bk. rev.:* Number and length vary. *Aud.:* Ga.

Nerve, according to its mission statement, "exists because sex is beautiful and absurd, remarkably fun and reliably trauma-inducing. In short, it is a subject in need of a fearless, intelligent forum for both genders. We believe that women (men too, but especially women) have waited long enough for a smart, honest magazine on sex, with cliche-shattering prose and fiction as well as striking photographs of naked people that capture more than their flesh. You've waited long enough." Features have covered working at an escort agency for Mormons; bad sex; men without women, and "sadocapitalism." There is a space for blogging as well as personals. Online free registration is required to access the newest articles; but for a fee, access is also granted to "premium" photography galleries and video at nine cents a day. Overall, a well-designed and graphically pleasant web site. URL: www.nerve.com (DT)

5534. *Nifty Erotic Stories Archive.* 1992. irreg. Nifty Archive Alliance, PMB 159, 333 Mamaroneck Ave, White Plains, NY 10605; nifty@gaycafe.com; http://www.nifty.org/nifty. *Aud.:* Ga, Ac, Sa.

This online archive of alternative-sexuality erotica—now the granddaddy of such archives—covers fiction involving male–male, female–female, bisexual, bestiality, intergenerational, interracial, and other sexual combinations, including the transgendered. It specifically excludes heterosexual stories. Within each category included, there are even further subcategories (e.g., under "gay male," there are first time, high school, and adult–youth fiction, among many others). The site contains links to lists of rejected stories, and of removed stories (because of copyright, for instance). Links are also provided to other online repositories of erotic literature, to chat rooms about *Nifty,* and to bookstore and publisher sites. While the site is free, donations are sought to maintain it. In 2005, 91 percent of the donations went toward *Nifty*'s services, it says, with only nine percent toward overhead. This site warns that it contains sexually explicit text and is for adults. It is an indispensable source for raw, uncensored erotica. URL: http://nifty.org (DT)

5535. *Penthouse: the magazine of sex, politics and protest.* [ISSN: 0090-2020] 1969. m. USD 19.95 domestic; USD 38.95 foreign; USD 7.99 newsstand/cover. Ed(s): Bob Guccione, Peter Bloch. Penthouse Media Group Inc., 11 Penn Plaza, 12th Fl, New York, NY 10001. Illus., adv. Circ: 980106. *Indexed:* ASIP, FLI, LRI, RI-1. *Aud.:* Ga, Ac.

Its subtitle has now reverted to "the international magazine for men" (shifting from a former subtitle mentioning politics) but this long-standing heterosexual erotica magazine continues to be a strong proponent of sexual freedom and free speech. It is decidedly on the side of those who fight state repression. In addition to explicit photography (both female and male), the magazine offers strong investigative reportage and analysis of national and international issues by the likes of Joe Conason, Alan Dershowitz, and Nat Hentoff. For more than two decades, until his death in 2001, journalist Tad Szulc's writings graced its pages. Some may dislike how women are depicted in its fiction, news clips, or full-page color layouts, but one cannot dismiss its outstanding contribution by alerting readers to the latest threats to our liberties, such as an article on "Whose Homeland Security?" Regular departments include "Online Humor," "Technomania," "Politics in the Miltary," "Men's Health & Fitness," and "Ribald Rimes." For the intelligent person's collection. (DT)

5536. *Playboy: entertainment for men.* [ISSN: 0032-1478] 1953. m. USD 29.97 domestic; USD 47.05 Canada; USD 45 elsewhere. Ed(s): Hugh Hefner, Kevin Buckley. Playboy Enterprises, Inc., 680 N Lake Shore Dr, Chicago, IL 60611; http://www.playboy.com. Illus., adv. Sample. Circ: 3150000 Paid. Vol. ends: No. 12. Microform: BHP; PQC. *Indexed:* ASIP, BEL&L, FLI, LRI, MRD. *Bk. rev.:* 6-9, 200 words, signed. *Aud.:* Ga, Ac.

America's best-selling men's magazine for over half a century, *Playboy* continues to publish high-quality fiction, nonfiction, and its well-regarded "Playboy Interview" with notable subjects. The "Playmate of the Month" centerfold is still offered. Readers definitely have to wade through pages of color nudes (mainly of women), but if the photographs don't interest a reader, the text offerings are definitely the "meat" of the magazine. Now it also highlights a "DVD of the month" and includes what's available online on its

web site. There is also a "20Q" column, where politicians or other notables are asked 20 questions; it's a shorter and more concise version of the "Playboy Interview." Reviews cover films, music, games, DVDs, and books. Sexual liberation may be commonplace in many regions, and its message of "entertainment for men" may sound dated and limited, but the audience is still there for this magazine. It now boasts some 20 international editions from Brazil to Japan. (DT)

5537. *Prometheus (New York).* 1973. q. Non-members, USD 35. Ed(s): M Tod. TES Association, PO Box 2783, New York, NY 10163; http://www.tes.org/. Adv. *Bk. rev.:* 5-6, 250-500 words. *Aud.:* Ga, Ac, Sa.

Founded as the publication of the established sado-masochistic organization The Eulenspiegel Society, *Prometheus* now serves as the membership magazine for the TES Association, the society's not-for-profit parent. TES notes: "What separates us from typical BDSM magazines is that we like to appeal to the intellect with our many articles as well as display beautiful pictures and drawings. With our mixed genre, this is a magazine that appeals to both men and women." BD means bondage and discipline; SM means sadomasochism. This magazine's approximately 100 pages offer news about leather pride and advice to new initiates into the subculture. A helpful glossary of terms guides you through the personal ads. Photos portray naked men and women in various bondage and discipline situations. Contents include fiction, articles on safety, and personal essays. For collections that want to cover a broader range of sexualities. Not to be confused with publications emanating from the Orange County, California–based Prometheus Institute. (DT)

5538. *Scarlet Letters: a journal of femmerotica.* 1997. 4x/yr. Ed(s): Heather Corinna. Scarlet Letters, PO Box 300105, Minneapolis, MN 55403-5105; http://scarletletters.com/. Adv. *Aud.:* Ga.

This e-zine is owned and operated completely by women. With its sister web site *Scarleteen* (sex education for teens: www.scarleteen.com), these sites together draw "one of the highest percentages of female readers of any sexual site online." Its avowed mission is "to produce quality material addressing numerous aspects of sexuality with a woman's taste and sensibility, which include all genders, age groups and orientations." The zine includes fiction, editorials, interviews, columns, an interactive community, and a sex advice section, "Sexuality One on One," that aims to provide "accurate" sexuality information and advice. There is also erotic art and photography, with a focus on gender-bending. A complete online archive for back issues is available, with proceeds benefiting *Scarleteen,* its sex-education clearinghouse. Highly recommended. URL: www.scarletletters.com (DT)

5539. *SEx.* 2006. q. 10/yr. in 2007. GBP 10. Ed(s): Chris Peachment. Erotic Print Society, 1st Fl., 17 Harwood Rd., London, SW6 4QP, United Kingdom; eps@leadline.co.uk; http://www.eroticprints.org/. *Aud.:* Ga, Ac, Sa.

A new print journal (with the first two letters of the title capitalized) has emerged from the United Kingdom's Erotic Print Society. The group has severed its ties with its *Erotic Review,* now publishing this title instead. Described in one British newspaper as "SEx leaves the smut behind," the new magazine seeks an advocacy role without the "smut," or as its web site describes it, "Perhaps not leave *all* the smut behind, as we'll always feature a healthy dose of the more robust forms of erotica." Articles have featured political criticism, Victorian vampires as sex symbols, cultural analysis, and fiction. There are also new book excerpts. It prides itself on being politically incorrect. Highly recommended. URL: www.thatsexmagazine.com (DT)

5540. *Sex Education: sexuality, society and learning.* [ISSN: 1468-1811] 2001. q. GBP 253 print & online eds. Ed(s): Michael Reiss. Routledge, 4 Park Sq, Milton Park, Abingdon, OX14 4RN, United Kingdom; journals@routledge.com; http://www.routledge.co.uk. Refereed. Reprint: PSC. *Indexed:* BrEdI, PsycInfo, SSA, SociolAb. *Aud.:* Ac, Sa.

Focusing on sex education (or lack of) within schools and the family as well as society, this journal's scope is not limited to the United States or Europe. An article in an early issue covered, for example, sex education about AIDS in selected countries in Asia and the Pacific. It delineated the heterosexual bias in some of the government-sponsored programs. Another article more recently argued that sexual pleasure is ignored in evaluating the success of sex education programs in schools. Other articles have addressed the difficulties in teaching sex education to boys, or the limits of abstinence-only sex education. Its editorial board includes members from around the globe. It notes that it "does not assume that sex education takes place only in educational institutions and the family. Contributions are therefore welcomed which, for example, analyse the impacts of media and other vehicles of culture on sexual behaviour and attitudes." The journal is accessible: "Medical and epidemiological papers (e.g., of trends in the incidences of sexually transmitted infections) will not be accepted unless their educational implications are discussed adequately." Highly recommended for coverage that is often ignored or politicized. (DT)

5541. Sex, Etc: a national newsletter by teens for teens. 3x/yr. Free donation. Network for Family Life Education, Rutgers University, The State University of New Jersey, Piscataway, NJ 08854; sexetc@rci.rutgers.edu. *Aud.:* Hs, Ga.

This "telling it like it is" national sex education newsletter, edited by teenagers for other teens, does not mince words nor sugarcoat the topic. Topics cover a range as you might expect, but the language is blunt and explicit, such as in "Sex 4.1.1: Answers to Your Most Common Questions about Sex," where the query posed, "I'm a 17-year-old guy and I cum too fast. Is that normal?" is answered: "It's okay and normal if you orgasm ("cum") quickly..." Its editorial board is selected each year from youth in New Jersey–area high schools. It aims to reach "millions" of readers. In its eight pages, it manages to stimulate, educate, and address succinctly and accurately the concerns of American youth today. A web site (www.sexetc.org) provides more resources, such as to HIV/AIDS organizations and materials. Newsletter articles are screened by health professionals. The publisher is an established university-based organization that is guided by the following principles: "Young people deserve honest, medically accurate and balanced information about sexuality in schools, homes and communities. Teen-to-teen communication is an effective vehicle for educating about sexual health. Educators and youth-serving professionals need training and support." A highly recommended addition to your collection. (DT)

Sex, Etc. See Teenagers section.

Sexual Abuse. See Psychology section.

5542. Sexual Addiction & Compulsivity: the journal of treatment and prevention. [ISSN: 1072-0162] 1994. q. GBP 169 print & online eds. Ed(s): David L Delmonico. Routledge, 325 Chestnut St, Ste 800, Philadelphia, PA 19106; journals@routledge.com; http://www.routledge.com. Refereed. Circ: 1000. Online: EBSCO Publishing, EBSCO Host; Gale; IngentaConnect; OCLC Online Computer Library Center, Inc.; SwetsWise Online Content. Reprint: PSC. *Indexed:* CINAHL, CJA, ExcerpMed, PsycInfo, RiskAb. *Aud.:* Ac, Sa.

This journal of the National Council on Sexual Addiction and Compulsivity focuses on all aspects of sexual addiction, described as a "growth phenomenon." Article topics include addiction among lesbians, seropositive men who have sex with men, ephebophiles, and priests. It offers continuing education material for professionals. Articles seek to provide guidance to working sex therapists on guidelines for relating to clients. (DT)

Sexual and Marital Therapy. See *Sexual and Relationship Therapy.*

5543. Sexual and Relationship Therapy. Formerly (until vol.15): *Sexual and Marital Therapy.* [ISSN: 1468-1994] 1986. q. GBP 404 print & online eds. Ed(s): Dr. Kevan Wylie. Routledge, 4 Park Sq, Milton Park, Abingdon, OX14 4RN, United Kingdom; info@routledge.co.uk; http://www.routledge.co.uk. Illus., index, adv. Refereed. Vol. ends: Nov. Online: EBSCO Publishing, EBSCO Host; Gale; IngentaConnect; OCLC Online Computer Library Center, Inc.; ProQuest LLC (Ann Arbor); SwetsWise Online Content. Reprint: PSC. *Indexed:* ASSIA, BAS, CINAHL, ExcerpMed, PsycInfo, SFSA, SSA, SWA, SociolAb, V&AA. *Aud.:* Ac, Sa.

With an applied orientation for professionals in psychology, medical, and marriage counseling fields, this established journal from the British Association for Sexual and Relationship Therapy has changed its title to better embrace its clientele, which now includes couples not in traditional marriages. Articles give

advice to general practitioners about discussing sex life issues with coronary heart patients; sexual boundaries between clinicians and clients; the connection between induced abortion and sexual attitudes; and the impact of sexual assault on one's life. While it deals with sexual crises, the journal also provides hope, for example, in an article on women over 65: "still doing it." Recommended for collections that cater to marriage and relationship counseling. (DT)

5544. Sexual Intelligence. m. Free. Ed(s): Marty Klein. Sexual Intelligence, c/o Dr. Marty Klein, 2439 Birch St. #2, Palo Alto, CA 94306; newsletter@sexed.org; http://www.sexualintelligence.org. *Aud.:* Ga, Ac.

Sex therapist and marriage counselor Marty Klein analyzes current sexuality-related topics in this provocative, blog-like newsletter. Topics have included National Masturbation Day and "Reagan's Legacy: World AIDS." The pithy newsletter analyzes news on sexuality from a sex-positive perspective, dismissing as faddish and ideological the popular concept of "sexual addiction," calling it a myth. Another brief item: "F-Word a WMD?" (whether the four-letter word is a weapon of mass destruction). Klein brilliantly skewers sex-negativity, while keeping his analysis concise and pointed. Even earlier issues, all posted on the web site, are worth re-reading to remind us how precarious sexual liberty remains in the United States. His annual Sexual Intelligence Awards, profiled in the newsletter, honor those who manage to overcome such assaults on personal sexual freedom. Favorite targets are the federal government's crackdown on sex research and religious right's self-righteousness on moral issues. (DT)

5545. Sexualities: studies in culture and society. [ISSN: 1363-4607] 1998. 5x/yr. GBP 434. Ed(s): Ken Plummer. Sage Publications Ltd., 1 Oliver's Yard, 55 City Rd, London, EC1 1SP, United Kingdom; info@sagepub.co.uk; http://www.sagepub.co.uk. Illus., index, adv. Sample. Refereed. Circ: 1200. Vol. ends: Nov. Reprint: PSC. *Indexed:* CommAb, FR, IBR, IBSS, IBZ, IPSA, PsycInfo, SSA, SWA, SociolAb, V&AA. *Bk. rev.:* 3-11, length varies, signed. *Aud.:* Ac.

Sexualities was developed to address emerging research about "the changing nature of the social organization of human sexual experience in the late modern world." Interdisciplinary and international in scope, it provides scholarly articles, interviews, and commentary that are analytical and ethnographic. Feminist, gender, and gay and lesbian studies are included in its scope. Topics include the impact of new technologies on sexualities, queer theory, methodologies of sex research, sex work, and the stratification of sexualities by class, race, gender, and age. Tables of contents, plus abstracts, are available on the publisher's web site, along with a sample issue and a free e-mail contents alert service. (BJG)

5546. Sexuality and Culture. [ISSN: 1095-5143] 1997. q. EUR 293 print & online eds. Ed(s): Barry Dank. Springer New York LLC, 233 Spring St, New York, NY 10013-1578; service-ny@springer.com; http://www.springer.com. Adv. Circ: 1000. *Indexed:* AmHI, PsycInfo, SSA, SociolAb. *Aud.:* Ga, Ac.

Originally an annual, this journal emerged out of concern about "sexual correctness" (or political correctness involving sexualities), especially in face of sexual harassment policies in academia. It now covers a broader range of issues, and it plays less of an advocacy role, becoming more research-oriented. Its pages have critically explored affirmative action and child sexual abuse research. Its editorial board includes some of the big names in sex research, even as it takes on the daunting task of critiquing established norms. Look here for past and current sex debates that are often missing from more mainstream journals. (DT)

Sexuality and Disability. See Disabilities section.

5547. Sexuality Research and Social Policy. [ISSN: 1553-6610] 2004. q. USD 220 (Individuals, USD 55). Ed(s): Gilbert Herdt. National Sexuality Resource Center, 2017 Mission St, Ste. 300, San Francisco, CA 94110; nsrcinfo@sfsu.edu; http://nsrc.sfsu.edu/. Refereed. *Indexed:* PsycInfo, SSA, SociolAb. *Bk. rev.:* 2, 500 words. *Aud.:* Ga, Ac.

This online journal, from the Ford Foundation–funded National Sexuality Resource Center (based at San Francisco State University), boasts an impressively multinational editorial board of major scholars doing sexuality studies. The journal is typically divided into "Articles," "Policy Articles," and "Book Reviews." Topics cover HIV/AIDS, circumcision, marriage denial and mental health and sexual citizenship, and governmental attacks on sexuality research, from across the globe. The style is less dense than usual in academic journals, for the journal is aimed at the non-academic reader as well as the scholar. The policy articles often take an advocacy stance while grounded in empirical research. The first volume is free on the University of California Press's Caliber platform. Highly recommended for all major collections. (DT)

SIECUS Report. See Civil Liberties/Bioethics: Reproductive Rights, Right to Life, and Right-to-Die section.

■ SLAVIC STUDIES

See also Asia; China; Europe; and Middle East sections.

Bradley L. Schaffner, Head, Slavic Division, Widener Library, Harvard University, Cambridge, MA 02138; bschaffn@fas.harvard.edu

Introduction

The past 18 years have witnessed the collapse of the Soviet Union and the demise of Communist-led governments in East Central Europe. Although the revolutions and the Cold War are over, there is ongoing political, social, and economic change in these countries as they develop and stabilize democratic forms of government and free-market economies. Because of this political and social transformation, Slavic Studies continues to be an important part of academic and research library collections. Titles in this section focus on the histories, cultures, politics, languages, and literatures of the countries of East Central European and Soviet successor states. Many of the journals are cross-disciplinary in nature, covering various topics in the social sciences and humanities, and provide coverage on most countries of the region rather than on a single country.

Basic Periodicals

Hs: *Moscow News, Russian Life;* Ga: *Current Digest of the Post-Soviet Press, Moscow News, Russian Life;* Ac: *The Slavic Review, The Russian Review, Studies in East European Thought.*

Basic Abstracts and Indexes

ABSEES Online; Historical Abstracts; MLA International Bibliography; PAIS International in Print.

5548. *Anthropology and Archeology of Eurasia: a journal of translations.* Formerly (until 1993): *Soviet Anthropology and Archeology.* [ISSN: 1061-1959] 1962. q. USD 936 print & online eds. Ed(s): Marjorie M Balzer. M.E. Sharpe, Inc., 80 Business Park Dr, Armonk, NY 10504; custserv@mesharpe.com; http://www.mesharpe.com. Illus., index, adv. Sample. Refereed. Vol. ends: Spring (No. 4). Reprint: PSC. *Indexed:* AICP, AbAn, AgeL, AnthLit, BAS, FR, RILM, SSCI. *Aud.:* Ac, Sa.

"This journal contains unabridged translations of manuscripts, articles and parts of books. Materials are selected which best reflect developments in anthropology and archeology in the Newly Independent States and are of most interest to those professionally concerned with these fields." The articles were originally published in leading Russian academic journals. Of particular value is that fact that most issues are thematic. For example, recent issues have focused on the 2002 Russian Census, and on different ethnic groups, such as the Tartars. The journal is enhanced by the fact that each number begins with a 10–15 page introduction by the editor that provides an overview of the current issue. Full citations and editors notes are included and the translator is identified. This publication is recommended as an important purchase for academic and special libraries with a focus on anthropology, archeology, ethnology, and Slavic Studies. It is of particular use to patrons interested in these disciplines, but who do not have Slavic language skills.

5549. *Canadian - American Slavic Studies.* Formerly (until 1972): *Canadian Slavic Studies - Revue Canadienne d'Etudes Slaves.* [ISSN: 0090-8290] 1967. q. USD 45 (Individuals, USD 20). Ed(s): Charles Schlacks, Jr. Charles Schlacks, Jr., Publisher, PO Box 1256, Idyllwild, CA 92549-1256; http://artful.com.au/schlacks/. Illus., index. Sample. Refereed. Circ: 700. Vol. ends: Winter (No. 4). Microform: BHP. *Indexed:* ABS&EES, AmH&L, ArtHuCI, HistAb, IBR, IBZ, MLA-IB, RI-1, RILM, SSCI. *Bk. rev.:* 20-30, 300-1,000 words, signed. *Aud.:* Ac, Sa.

This scholarly Slavic Studies journal focuses primarily on history, language, and literature. Each issue contains four to five fully cited articles, book reviews, and lists of new books received. The book reviews and book lists serve as an important selection tool for collection development librarians. Articles are published in English, French, and Russian. A recent thematic issue titled "Varieties of Ukrainian Identities" showcases recent scholarship on Ukraine. This journal is recommended as an important publication for academic and research libraries that support Slavic Studies.

5550. *Canadian Slavonic Papers: an interdisciplinary journal devoted to Central and Eastern Europe.* [ISSN: 0008-5006] 1956. q. CND 65. Ed(s): Oleh S Ilnyts'kyi. Canadian Association of Slavists, 200 Arts Bldg, Dept of Modern Languages and Cultural Studies, Edmonton, AB T6G 2E6, Canada. Illus., index, adv. Refereed. Circ: 700. Reprint: PSC. *Indexed:* ABS&EES, AmH&L, ArtHuCI, CBCARef, CPerI, FR, HistAb, IBR, IBSS, IBZ, L&LBA, LingAb, MLA-IB, PAIS, PSA, SSA, SSCI, SociolAb. *Bk. rev.:* 35-40, 300-500 words, signed. *Aud.:* Ac, Sa.

This journal is the official publication of the Canadian Association of Slavists. It is a multidisciplinary Slavic Studies journal that covers subjects in the humanities and the social sciences with an emphasis on language, literature, culture, history, and political science. The publication includes excellent book reviews and longer bibliographic essays. Monographs reviewed are generally from Canada and Europe (including Great Britain and the Slavic countries) and serves as a solid collection development tool for librarians. Some of the issues are thematic, with the most recent titled "The 2004 Ukrainian Presidential Elections." This journal is recommended for academic and research libraries that support Slavic Studies programs and for public libraries with a clientele interested in Slavic Studies.

5551. *Communist and Post-Communist Studies.* Former titles (until 1992): *Studies in Comparative Communism;* (until 1968): *Communist Affairs.* [ISSN: 0967-067X] 1962. 4x/yr. EUR 423. Ed(s): Andrzej Korbonski, Lucy Kerner. Pergamon, The Boulevard, Langford Ln, East Park, Kidlington, OX5 1GB, United Kingdom. Illus., index, adv. Sample. Refereed. Vol. ends: Dec (No. 4). Microform: PQC. Online: EBSCO Publishing, EBSCO Host; Gale; IngentaConnect; OhioLINK; ScienceDirect; SwetsWise Online Content. *Indexed:* ABCPolSci, ABS&EES, AmH&L, ArtHuCI, BAS, CJA, HistAb, IBR, IBSS, IBZ, IPSA, PAIS, PRA, PSA, SSCI, SWA, SociolAb. *Aud.:* Ac, Sa.

"*Communist and Post-Communist Studies* is an international journal covering all communist and post-communist states and communist movements, including both their domestic policies and their international relations. It is focused on the analysis of historical as well as current developments in the communist and post-communist world, including ideology, economy, and society. It also aims to provide comparative foci on a given subject (e.g., education in China) by inviting comments of a comparative character from scholars specializing in the same subject matter but in different countries (e.g., education in Poland or Romania). In addition to the traditional disciplines of history, political science, economics, and international relations, the editors encourage the submission of articles in less developed fields of social sciences and humanities, such as cultural anthropology, education, geography, religion, and sociology." While the scope of the journal is on all communist and post-communist societies and states, the majority of the articles published deal with former Soviet bloc countries and the successor states. Authors include many of the leading scholars in their respective fields. This journal is recommended for both academic and public libraries with readers interested in Slavic Studies, politics, and contemporary society.

5552. Current Digest of the Post-Soviet Press. Formerly (until 1992): *Current Digest of the Soviet Press;* Incorporates: *Current Abstracts of the Soviet Press.* [ISSN: 1067-7542] 1949. w. USD 1495. East View Information Services, 10601 Wayzata Blvd, Minneapolis, MN 55305; info@eastview.com; http://www.eastview.com/. Illus., index. Circ: 1000. Vol. ends: No. 52. Online: EBSCO Publishing, EBSCO Host. *Indexed:* BAS, CDSP, FLI, PAIS. *Aud.:* Hs, Ga, Ac.

"Each week the *Current Digest of the Post-Soviet Press* presents a selection of Russian-language press materials carefully translated into English. The translations are intended for use in teaching and research. They are therefore presented as documentary materials without elaboration or comment and state the opinions and views of the original authors. . . ." Each weekly issue, which is 16 to 20 pages long, provides an excellent overview of the contemporary Russian press and is of particular value for people who do not read Russian. Each issue contains several feature articles and shorter articles under the sections "Focus on the Russian Federation," "Other Post Soviet States," and "International Affairs." All of the translated articles provide citations of original publication, and note if the article is a complete translation or summary translation. An excellent compilation source for current events in Russia and recommended for all libraries, academic or public, with current interests in Russian affairs.

5553. Demokratizatsiya: the journal of post-soviet democratization. [ISSN: 1074-6846] 1992. q. USD 137 (Individuals, USD 58 print & online eds.; USD 33 newsstand/cover). Ed(s): Julia Kilmer. Heldref Publications, 1319 18th St, NW, Washington, DC 20036-1802; subscribe@heldref.org; http://www.heldref.org. Adv. Circ: 671 Paid. Reprint: PSC. *Indexed:* ABS&EES, IPSA, PSA, SociolAb. *Bk. rev.:* Varies, 500-600 words, signed. *Aud.:* Ac, Sa.

"The journal is an international and interdisciplinary quarterly journal that covers the historical and current transformations in the Soviet Union and its successor states. It focuses on the contemporary transformation of the successor states of the Soviet Union. The journal welcomes submissions by academics, policymakers, and other specialists on the political, social, and economic changes begun in 1985. The journal also values critiques of specific laws, policies, and programs, as well as comparisons between reforms in the new countries and elsewhere that may serve as constructive examples." The emphasis of this journal is on politics and contemporary events with special consideration given to an historical examination of Soviet totalitarianism and perestroika. While the majority of the articles focus on Russia, recent issues also include articles on the contemporary political situation in Moldova, Ukraine, and Georgia, to name a few. The journal does provide coverage of all of the successor states. Highly recommended for academic and research libraries with patrons interested in East Central Europe and the former Soviet Union.

5554. East European Jewish Affairs. Formerly (until 1991): *Soviet Jewish Affairs.* [ISSN: 1350-1674] 1971. s-a. GBP 184 print & online eds. Ed(s): John Klier. Routledge, 4 Park Sq, Milton Park, Abingdon, OX14 4RN, United Kingdom; info@routledge.co.uk; http://www.routledge.com. Illus., index, adv. Sample. Refereed. Vol. ends: Winter (No. 2). Microform: PQC. Online: EBSCO Publishing, EBSCO Host; Gale; IngentaConnect; OCLC Online Computer Library Center, Inc.; SwetsWise Online Content. Reprint: PSC. *Indexed:* AmH&L, AmHI, FR, HistAb, IBR, IBSS, IBZ, IJP, PSA, RI-1, RILM, RiskAb, SociolAb. *Bk. rev.:* 5-10, 300-500 words, signed. *Aud.:* Ac, Sa.

"Published under the aegis of the Department of Hebrew and Jewish Studies, University College London and the Oxford Institute for Yiddish Studies . . . [this is] an interdisciplinary journal which is essential for an understanding of the position and prospects of Jews in the former Soviet Union and the countries of East Central Europe. It deals with issues in historical perspective and in the context of general, social, economic, political, and cultural developments in the region. The journal includes the following sections: analytical, in-depth articles; review articles/reviews; documentary-archival; conference notes; and annotated books." The journal provides an excellent selection of scholarly articles on the Jewish experience in East Central Europe and countries of the former Soviet Union. Each issue includes excellent book reviews and some issues include more extensive review articles. Also included is a list of books received for review, making these sections very useful for collection

development librarians and scholars in the field. This journal is highly recommended for academic and research libraries as well as large public libraries collecting in these areas.

5555. East European Politics & Societies. [ISSN: 0888-3254] 1987. q. GBP 195. Ed(s): Ilya Prizel. Sage Publications, Inc., 2455 Teller Rd, Thousand Oaks, CA 91320; info@sagepub.com; http://www.sagepub.com. Illus., adv. Refereed. Circ: 1200. Vol. ends: No. 3. Microform: PQC. Online: CSA; EBSCO Publishing, EBSCO Host; Florida Center for Library Automation; HighWire Press; Northern Light Technology, Inc.; OCLC Online Computer Library Center, Inc.; OhioLINK; SAGE Publications, Inc., SAGE Journals Online; SwetsWise Online Content; H.W. Wilson. Reprint: PSC. *Indexed:* ABCPolSci, ABS&EES, AmH&L, ArtHuCI, HistAb, IBSS, IPSA, PSA, RiskAb, SSCI, SociolAb. *Aud.:* Ac, Sa.

This journal is published in association with the American Council of Learned Societies, and "covers issues in Eastern Europe from social, political, and economic perspectives. The journal focuses on expanding readers' understanding of past events and current developments in countries from Greece to the Baltics." It focuses on "cutting-edge social research and political analysis of leading area specialists, historians, economists, political scientists and anthropologists from around the world." The journal provides extensive coverage of all the countries of East Central Europe, focusing on all aspects of politics, history, and culture. Many issues include lengthy bibliographic essays and reviews of current publications on the region. Recommended for academic and research libraries that support programs in Slavic and East Central European Studies.

5556. East European Quarterly. [ISSN: 0012-8449] 1967. q. USD 20 (Individuals, USD 15). Ed(s): Stephen Fischer Galati. East European Quarterly, c/o Stephen Fischer-Galati, Box 945, Taylor, TX 76574; eestudies@mailstation.com. Illus., index, adv. Refereed. Circ: 950. Vol. ends: Winter (No. 4). Microform: PQC. Online: Chadwyck-Healey Inc.; EBSCO Publishing, EBSCO Host; Florida Center for Library Automation; Gale; Northern Light Technology, Inc.; OCLC Online Computer Library Center, Inc.; ProQuest K-12 Learning Solutions; ProQuest LLC (Ann Arbor); H.W. Wilson. *Indexed:* ABS&EES, AmH&L, AmHI, ArtHuCI, HistAb, HumInd, IBSS, IPSA, PAIS, PSA, RILM, SSCI, SociolAb. *Bk. rev.:* 1-5, 300-800 words, signed. *Aud.:* Ac, Sa.

This scholarly journal covers the politics, history, and international relations of the countries of Eastern Europe. Each issue contains four to eight articles written by scholars and graduate students with expertise in the politics, history, and/or culture of this world area. In an era of rising journal prices, this title continues to be inexpensive. It is recommended for all academic and research libraries as well as public libraries that have patrons with an interest in East Central European Studies.

5557. Eastern European Economics: a journal of translations. [ISSN: 0012-8775] 1962. bi-m. USD 1338 print & online eds. Ed(s): Josef Brada. M.E. Sharpe, Inc., 80 Business Park Dr, Armonk, NY 10504; custserv@mesharpe.com; http://www.mesharpe.com. Illus., index, adv. Sample. Refereed. Vol. ends: Nov/Dec (No. 6). Online: EBSCO Publishing, EBSCO Host; Gale; OCLC Online Computer Library Center, Inc.; SwetsWise Online Content. Reprint: PSC. *Indexed:* ABIn, IBR, JEL, PAIS, SSCI, WAE&RSA. *Aud.:* Ac, Sa.

This journal "publishes research on the economies of Eastern Europe, their experiences under communism and central planning, the process of transition to a market economy, and their current integration into the global economy and into regional economic groupings. While the geographic coverage of *Eastern European Economics* includes all of what has traditionally been considered Eastern Europe, the focus is on those countries that have recently undergone or are undergoing the systemic transition from a communist economic system to a market economy. The journal is open to all methodological approaches and to authors from all regions of the world." While the journal is geared toward specialists in the field, the editor does provide a brief introduction to the three to four articles that are included in each issue. Articles in recent issues include a discussion on the economic impact of new membership in the European

Union, Russia's entry into the World Trade Organization, and efforts at poverty reduction in Albania. Highly recommended for academic and research libraries that support Slavic Studies programs and programs in economics and international business.

5558. *Eurasian Geography and Economics.* Former titles (until 2002): *Post-Soviet Geography and Economics;* (until 1995): *Post-Soviet Geography;* (until 1992): *Soviet Geography; Soviet Geography - Review and Translation.* [ISSN: 1538-7216] 1960. 8x/yr. USD 499 (Individuals, USD 80). Ed(s): Stanley D Brunn, C Cindy Fan. Bellwether Publishing, Ltd., 8640 Guilford Rd, Ste 200, Columbia, MD 21046; bellpub@ bellpub.com; http://www.bellpub.com. Illus., index, adv. Refereed. Circ: 650. Vol. ends: No. 8. Reprint: PSC. *Indexed:* ABIn, ABS&EES, BAS, ExcerpMed, FR, JEL, PAIS, SSCI. *Aud.:* Ac, Sa.

Affiliated with the Kennan Institute for Advanced Russian Studies, this journal is a "semi-quarterly publication featuring original papers by leading specialists and scholars on salient geographic and economic issues in the republics of the former Soviet Union, Central and Eastern Europe, and the socialist countries of Asia. Included in some issues are brief research reports providing background and analysis of recent economic developments, demographic fluctuations, and related events." "Also published from time to time are papers on related subjects (e.g., demography, ethnic studies) that have a pronounced spatial element and/or significant economic content. Special features such as essays and comments by senior Western specialists, as well as brief research reports and communications transmitting data on current, rapidly changing developments, also appear in the journal." Each article is prefaced by an excellent abstract that succinctly describes the piece. Recent articles focus on geopolitical remote sensing, the ethnic composition of Vilnius, and the geopolitical orientations of ordinary Russians. This journal is highly recommended for academic and research studies that support Slavic Studies programs and/or geography programs. It is also recommended for large public libraries with patrons interested in the geopolitical situation in East Central Europe.

5559. *Europe - Asia Studies.* Formerly (until 1993): *Soviet Studies.* [ISSN: 0966-8136] 1949. 8x/yr. GBP 924 print & online eds. Ed(s): Roger Clarke. Routledge, 4 Park Sq, Milton Park, Abingdon, OX14 4RN, United Kingdom; info@routledge.co.uk; http://www.routledge.co.uk. Illus., index, adv. Sample. Refereed. Vol. ends: Dec (No. 8). Online: EBSCO Publishing, EBSCO Host; Florida Center for Library Automation; Gale; IngentaConnect; JSTOR (Web-based Journal Archive); OCLC Online Computer Library Center, Inc.; ProQuest LLC (Ann Arbor); SwetsWise Online Content. Reprint: PSC. *Indexed:* ABCPolSci, ABIn, ABS&EES, AmH&L, AmHI, ArtHuCI, BAS, BRI, BrHumI, CJA, HistAb, HumInd, IBR, IBSS, IBZ, IPSA, JEL, LRI, MASUSE, PAIS, PSA, RRTA, SSA, SSCI, SociolAb, WAE&RSA. *Bk. rev.:* 20-25, 500-1,000 words, signed. *Aud.:* Ac, Sa.

According to the publishers, this title "remains the principal academic journal in the world focusing on the political, social and economic affairs of what were once the Soviet bloc countries, including their history. At the same time, the journal explores the economic, political and social transformation of these countries and the changing character of their relationship with the rest of Europe and Asia. The comparison with the transformation taking place in China is a further element in the general broadening of the field that used to be called Soviet Studies." Each issue contains an extensive review article of a recent monograph; this, combined with the books received list, makes for an effective selection tool for collection development librarians. Recommended for academic, research, and special libraries that support advanced research in Slavic Studies.

Folklore. See Folklore section.

5560. *Intermarium: the first online journal of East Central European postwar history and politics.* [ISSN: 1537-7822] 1997. 3x/yr. Ed(s): John S Micgiel, Andrzej Paczkowski. Columbia University, Institute on East Central Europe, 420 W 118th St, New York, NY 10027; http://www.columbia.edu/cu/sipa/regional/ece/newintermar.html. *Indexed:* AmH&L, HistAb. *Aud.:* Ac, Sa.

According to the editors, this publication "provides an electronic medium for noteworthy scholarship and provocative thinking about the history and politics of Central and Eastern Europe following World War II. The journal is meant to broaden the discourse on aspects of national histories that are undergoing change thanks to the availability of new documentation from recently opened archives. The editors' purpose is to facilitate interaction between scholarly communities by making research, essays, commentaries, documents, and reviews from the region available in English." Part of *CIAO: Columbia International Affairs Online,* this journal provides coverage of all of the former Soviet bloc countries. Special emphasis is placed upon the history, politics, and foreign relations of the countries of the region. This resource is recommended for all academic and research libraries.

5561. *Journal of Baltic Studies.* Formerly (until 1972): *Bulletin of Baltic Studies.* [ISSN: 0162-9778] 1970. q. GBP 235 print & online eds. Ed(s): David J Smith. Routledge, 325 Chestnut St, Ste 800, Philadelphia, PA 19106; journals@routledge.com; http://www.tandf.co.uk/journals. Illus., index, adv. Refereed. Circ: 1300. Vol. ends: Winter (No. 4). Microform: PQC. Reprint: PSC. *Indexed:* ABS&EES, AmH&L, ArtHuCI, CJA, HistAb, IBSS, MLA-IB, NumL, RILM, SSCI. *Bk. rev.:* 5-10, 300-500 words, signed. *Aud.:* Ac, Sa.

This Baltic Studies journal covers most subjects in the humanities and social sciences. Emphasis is placed on history, literature, languages, and culture. The journal also examines the Baltic diaspora. All articles are scholarly in nature and well researched and documented. Most articles are published in English, with a few published in German. Recent articles include an investigation of Latvian Americans in the post-Soviet era and Estonians in Canada and Sweden during the inter-war period. The journal also includes a book review section, covering monographs published worldwide. Recommended for academic and special libraries that support Baltic and Slavic Studies programs and for larger public libraries with patrons interested in the Baltic states.

5562. *The Journal of Communist Studies and Transition Politics.* Formerly (until 1994): *Journal of Communist Studies.* [ISSN: 1352-3279] 1985. q. GBP 315 print & online eds. Ed(s): Stephen White. Routledge, 4 Park Sq, Milton Park, Abingdon, OX14 4RN, United Kingdom; info@routledge.co.uk; http://www.routledge.co.uk. Illus., index, adv. Sample. Refereed. Vol. ends: No. 4. Microform: PQC. Online: EBSCO Publishing, EBSCO Host; Gale; IngentaConnect; OCLC Online Computer Library Center, Inc.; SwetsWise Online Content. Reprint: PSC. *Indexed:* ABCPolSci, AmH&L, AmHI, BrHumI, HistAb, IBR, IBSS, IBZ, IPSA, PSA. *Bk. rev.:* Varies, 500-800 words, signed. *Aud.:* Ac, Sa.

The publishers of this journal write that "the face of Europe has been transformed by the demise of the Soviet Union and the collapse of communist party rule in Eastern Europe. Within a series of countries, some of them erstwhile members of a Soviet bloc, others once part of the Soviet Union itself, a deep process of adjustment is under way." This title "devotes particular attention to this truly epochal process of regime change, including in its material contributions from within the affected societies. At the same time, it follows the effects of this upheaval on communist parties, ruling and non-ruling, both in Europe and in the wider world." This is a cross-disciplinary journal that covers a variety of contemporary societal issues that face the former communist-bloc countries as they continue to make the transition away from totalitarian rule. This journal is recommended for academic and special libraries that support Slavic Studies programs and for large public libraries with clientele interested in the region.

5563. *Journal of Russian and East European Psychology: a journal of translations.* Formerly (until 1992): *Soviet Psychology;* Which superseded in part (in 1966): *Soviet Psychology and Psychiatry.* [ISSN: 1061-0405] 1962. bi-m. USD 1218 print & online eds. Ed(s): Pentti Hakkarainen. M.E. Sharpe, Inc., 80 Business Park Dr, Armonk, NY 10504; custserv@mesharpe.com; http://www.mesharpe.com. Illus., index, adv. Sample. Refereed. Vol. ends: Nov/Dec (No. 6). Online: EBSCO Publishing, EBSCO Host; OCLC Online Computer Library Center, Inc.; SwetsWise Online Content. Reprint: PSC. *Indexed:* PAIS, PsycInfo. *Aud.:* Ac, Sa.

This journal "contains unabridged translations of original submissions as well as articles published in scholarly journals or in collections. Articles are selected that best reflect developments in psychology in this region and that are of most interest to those professionally concerned with this field." Each issue is thematic, and the editor's or guest editor's introduction provides an excellent summary and overview of the issue's focus. Each article includes a full citation to the original publication and translator. All sources cited in the original publication are included with the translation. This journal is aimed at specialists in the field and would be of particular use to scholars who do not have the language skills to read these articles in the original language of publication. Recommended for academic and research libraries that support study and research in psychology.

5564. *Journal of Slavic Linguistics.* [ISSN: 1068-2090] 1993. s-a. USD 40 (Individuals, USD 30). Ed(s): Steven Franks. Slavica Publishers, Inc., 2611 E 10th St, Bloomington, IN 47408-2603; slavica@indiana.edu; http://www.slavica.com. Illus., adv. Refereed. Circ: 250. Vol. ends: No. 2. *Indexed:* ABS&EES, AmHI, IBR, IBZ, L&LBA, LingAb, MLA-IB. *Bk. rev.:* 1-3, 500-1,000 words, signed. *Aud.:* Ac, Sa.

This journal "is intended to address issues in description and analysis of Slavic languages of general interest to linguists, regardless of theoretical orientation." It publishes "papers dealing with any aspect of synchronic or diachronic Slavic phonetics, phonology, morphology, syntax, semantics and pragmatics, as long as they raise substantive problems of broad theoretical concern or propose significant descriptive generalization." Special emphasis is placed on "comparative studies and formal analysis." Each issue is about 200 pages in length. Recent articles have examined colloquial Russian and the syntax and semantics of English and Polish concessive conditionals. This journal is aimed at specialists in the field and should be acquired by academic and research libraries that support Slavic Studies and general linguistic programs.

5565. *Journal of Southeast European and Black Sea Studies.* [ISSN: 1468-3857] 2001. 4x/yr. GBP 283 print & online eds. Ed(s): Photini Bellou, Theodore Couloumbis. Routledge, 4 Park Sq, Milton Park, Abingdon, OX14 4RN, United Kingdom; info@routledge.co.uk; http://www.routledge.co.uk. Adv. Sample. Refereed. Reprint: PSC. *Indexed:* AmH&L, AmHI, CJA, HistAb, IBR, IBSS, IBZ, IPSA, PSA, SociolAb. *Bk. rev.:* 3-4; 1000-1500 words; signed. *Aud.:* Ac, Sa.

This is the official publication of ELIAMEP Hellenic Foundation for European and Foreign policy. According to the organization, "the aim of the journal is to establish a line of communication with this region of Europe. Previously isolated from the European mainstreams, the Balkan and Black Sea regions are in need of serious study as countries no longer 'at the edge' of Europe. The field covers contemporary and twentieth-century developments in the wider Balkan (for our purposes—Albania, Bulgaria, the successor states of the former Yugoslavia, Greece, Romania, and Turkey) and the Black Sea area. Most of these countries have been neglected for some time by mainstream social science but are increasingly included in existing programs of university study. The principal disciplines to be covered are politics, political economy, international relations and modern history; other disciplinary approaches will be accepted, as appropriate. The journal has both an academic and a practical policy-oriented approach. Clearly, the Balkan and Black Sea regions are topical; more important, they are likely to remain regions of misunderstanding and misrepresentation for some time. The journal offers a unique opportunity to establish new paradigms of analysis for these regions, attempting to break away from traditional ethnocentric approaches and develop a deeper and more fruitful understanding of the larger area." Numbers often begin with an editorial that examines important current issues of the region. These editorials do not necessarily reflect the rest of the content of the volume. Some issues are thematic, with recent numbers focusing on Greece and its relations with Turkey and other Balkan countries. Recommended for purchase for academic and research libraries that support Slavic and/or Balkans Studies programs.

5566. *Lituanus: Baltic states quarterly journal of arts and sciences.* [ISSN: 0024-5089] 1954. q. USD 30 (Individuals, USD 20). Ed(s): Violeta Kelertas. Lituanus Foundation, Inc., 47 Polk St, Ste 100-300, Chicago, IL 60605; admin@lituanus.org; http://www.lituanus.org. Illus.,

index. Refereed. Circ: 2200 Paid and controlled. Vol. ends: Winter (No. 4). Microform: PQC. *Indexed:* ABS&EES, AmH&L, HistAb, IBR, IPSA, L&LBA, MLA-IB, PAIS, RILM. *Bk. rev.:* 3-4, 500-1,000 words, signed. *Aud.:* Ac, Sa.

The "is an English-language journal dedicated to Lithuanian and Baltic art, history, language, literature and related cultural topics." The publisher notes that special emphasis is placed on Lithuania, but articles about the Baltic states and East Central Europe are also included. Each issue is about 80 pages in length with a mixture of scholarly articles, poetry, memoirs, and essays. A recent issue includes several poems by one poet, a comparative study of Central European literature, and an essay on Lithuanian nationalism. Recommended for any library with patrons interested in Lithuania and the other Baltic countries.

5567. *Moscow News: international weekly.* [ISSN: 0027-1306] 1930. 52x/yr. USD 90 United States. Ed(s): Sergei Roy. Moskovskie Novosti, ul Zagorodnoe shosse, d 1, Moscow, 103829, Russian Federation; info@mn.ru; http://www.moscownews.ru. Illus., adv. Circ: 37000. Vol. ends: Jan (No. 52). Microform: PQC. Online: LexisNexis. *Aud.:* Hs, Ga, Ac.

This is an English-language newspaper covering contemporary Russian society. Articles are primarily translated from the Russian newspaper *Moskovskie novosti,* but other articles written specifically for *Moscow News* are also included. *Moscow News* is similar to other small newspapers, covering politics and contemporary events, culture, sports, etc. Its value is that it provides current news from a Russian perspective. Many of the articles are also available for free on the Internet at http://english.mn.ru/english, where the user has access to both the current issue and the archive. One of the great features of the Internet version is the ability to read the article in either English or Russian, a useful tool for students who are learning Russian. This paper should be acquired by all libraries interested in the international scene.

5568. *Nationalities Papers.* [ISSN: 0090-5992] 1972. 5x/yr. GBP 539 print & online eds. Ed(s): Steve Sabol, Steve Sabol. Routledge, 4 Park Sq, Milton Park, Abingdon, OX14 4RN, United Kingdom; info@routledge.co.uk; http://www.routledge.co.uk. Illus., adv. Sample. Refereed. Circ: 1200. Vol. ends: Dec (No. 4). Online: EBSCO Publishing, EBSCO Host; Gale; IngentaConnect; Northern Light Technology, Inc.; OCLC Online Computer Library Center, Inc.; ProQuest K-12 Learning Solutions; ProQuest LLC (Ann Arbor); SwetsWise Online Content. Reprint: PSC. *Indexed:* ABS&EES, AmH&L, AmHI, HistAb, IBR, IBSS, IBZ, IPSA, IndIslam, L&LBA, MLA-IB, PAIS, PSA, RILM, SSA, SWA, SociolAb. *Bk. rev.:* 15-25, 500-800 words, signed. *Aud.:* Ac, Sa.

According to the publisher, this "is the only journal in the world which deals exclusively with all non-Russian nationalities of the former USSR and national minorities in Eastern and Central European countries. The problems and importance of over 160 million people are treated within the disciplinary and methodological contexts of post-Soviet and Europe-Asia studies. Of central concern is the fate of the Balts, Ukrainians, Jews, Gypsies, Croats, Muslims etc., and the peoples of Central Asia and the Caucasus. Included in each issue are in-depth updates on the latest developments, some original documents, lists of the most recent publications from throughout the world and book reviews." The book reviews are detailed and serve as an excellent selection tool for collection development librarians. Recent issues cover Orthodoxy and the rise of communism in Romania, why church-state relations in Yugoslavia failed, and the tragedy of ethnic cleansing in Yugoslavia. This is an important journal that is highly recommended for academic and research libraries that support Slavic and European Studies programs, and for any library with patrons interested in the minorities of East Central Europe and countries of the former Soviet Union.

5569. *Polish Review.* [ISSN: 0032-2970] 1956. q. USD 35 (Individuals, USD 30). Ed(s): Mariusz Bargielski, Krystyna S Olszer. Polish Institute of Arts and Sciences of America, Inc., 208 E 30th St, New York, NY 10016; http://www.piasa.org/. Illus., index, adv. Refereed. Circ: 1500. Vol. ends: Dec (No. 4). Microform: PQC. *Indexed:* ABS&EES, AmH&L, HistAb, IPSA, MLA-IB, PAIS, RILM. *Bk. rev.:* 4-5, 300-1,000 words, signed. *Aud.:* Ac, Sa.

This publication "is a scholarly journal devoted to the history and culture of Poland and Polonia." It publishes articles in Polish arts, linguistics, history, sociology, ethnography, and Polish Americana. The editors note that they will also publish "other topics that have a bearing on Poland, her people and culture, and Poles abroad." Along with scholarly articles, each issue includes a section of book reviews, a list of books received, and longer review articles. These sections serve as useful tools for collection development librarians. A recent issue includes an article on Polish-Lithuanian relations, and FBI surveillance of Polish emigre writers in New York. This journal is recommended for academic and research libraries that support Slavic Studies programs and public libraries with patrons interested in Poland.

5570. *Post-Communist Economies.* Former titles (until 1998): *Communist Economies and Economic Transformation; Communist Economies.* [ISSN: 1463-1377] 1989. q. GBP 553 print & online eds. Ed(s): Roger Clarke. Routledge, 4 Park Sq, Milton Park, Abingdon, OX14 4RN, United Kingdom; info@routledge.co.uk; http://www.routledge.co.uk. Illus., index, adv. Sample. Refereed. Online: EBSCO Publishing, EBSCO Host; Gale; IngentaConnect; OCLC Online Computer Library Center, Inc.; ProQuest LLC (Ann Arbor); SwetsWise Online Content. Reprint: PSC. *Indexed:* ABIn, BAS, IBR, IBSS, IBZ, JEL, PRA, RiskAb, SSCI. *Aud.:* Ac, Sa.

The current title is a change from *Communist Economies and Economic Transformation* (originally just *Communist Economies*). The editors believed that the title should be changed "because of a growing feeling that the major processes into which transformation has generally been divided—stabilization, liberalization and privatization—have in substantial measure been completed in most of the former communist countries, even though this is more true of some than others, and all still have some distance to go to match the long-established market economies in these respects. Yet despite the dramatic changes that have taken place in the past decade, the post-communist economies still form a clearly identifiable group, distinguished by the impact of the years of communist rule, and this looks set to remain true for many more years. This is the reason for the choice of the new title now: post-communist economies still present distinctive problems that make them a particular focus of research. There is need for further stabilization, liberalization and privatization in spite of the progress that has been made. And there is the fundamental problem that efficiency, productivity and thus incomes in all these countries are extremely low. More attention needs to be devoted to the microeconomic aspects of the post-communist countries' efforts to catch up with the much richer countries of the European Union many of them aim to join in the opening years of the new millennium. The focus may thus have moved on from the basic transformation but the post-communist economies' particular problems will continue to be an important area of economic and political analysis."

Each issue contains about five to seven in-depth articles written by specialists in the field. There is balanced coverage of all of the post-communist countries and their economies, making this journal very important for academic and research libraries that support Slavic/Central Asian Studies programs and/or international economics programs.

5571. *Post-Soviet Affairs.* Formerly (until 1992): *Soviet Economy.* [ISSN: 1060-586X] 1985. 4x/yr. USD 324 (Individuals, USD 80). Ed(s): George Breslauer. Bellwether Publishing, Ltd., 8640 Guilford Rd, Ste 200, Columbia, MD 21046; bellpub@bellpub.com; http://www.bellpub.com. Illus., index. Refereed. Circ: 500. Vol. ends: Dec (No. 4). *Indexed:* ABIn, ABS&EES, IBSS, IPSA, JEL, PAIS, PSA, SSCI. *Aud.:* Ac, Sa.

This journal includes "the work of prominent Western scholars on the republics of the former Soviet Union providing exclusive, up-to-the-minute analyses of the state of the economy and society, progress toward economic reform, and linkages between political and social changes and economic developments." The editorial board of this journal boasts a distinguished list of Slavic scholars who are extensively published in their fields of expertise. Each issue contains about four thoroughly researched and documented articles by specialists in the field. Recent articles examine Putin's political career, AIDS/HIV in Russia, and ethnic identity in Latvia. While the title indicates a focus on the Soviet successor states, the journal also covers the countries of East Central Europe that were formerly in the Soviet bloc. Recommended for academic and research libraries that support Slavic Studies programs.

5572. *Problems of Economic Transition: a journal of translations from Russian.* Formerly: *Problems in Economics.* [ISSN: 1061-1991] 1958. m. USD 1428 print & online eds. Ed(s): Ben Slay. M.E. Sharpe, Inc., 80 Business Park Dr, Armonk, NY 10504; custserv@mesharpe.com; http://www.mesharpe.com. Illus., index, adv. Sample. Refereed. Vol. ends: Apr (No. 12). Reprint: PSC. *Indexed:* ABIn, ABS&EES, JEL, PAIS, RiskAb, SSCI. *Aud.:* Ac, Sa.

According to the publisher, this journal "scans the Russian-language economic literature, from the most recent research papers, policy studies, and reports to articles in leading professional journals, permitting readers to follow the principal theoretical and policy issues that constitute the core of post-Soviet economic discourse in various regions of the former USSR. Topics covered on an ongoing basis include reform policy; foreign economic relations; industrial reorganization; labor economics and social policy; and regional economic development."

Each article includes a full citation to the original publication and translator. All sources cited in the original publication are included with the translation. This journal is aimed at specialists in the field and would be of particular use to scholars who do not have the language skills to read these articles in the original language of publication. The majority of the articles included were originally published in the major Russian economic journals such as *Voprosy ekonomiki* and *EKO*. Most issues are thematic or focus on a specific Soviet successor state, with recent issues covering Belarus, Moldova, and Georgia. The editor provides an excellent introduction to each issue. This journal is recommended for academic and research libraries that support Slavic Studies and/or economics programs.

5573. *Problems of Post-Communism.* Formerly (until Jan. 1995): *Problems of Communism.* [ISSN: 1075-8216] 1951. bi-m. USD 299 print & online eds. Ed(s): Robert T Huber. M.E. Sharpe, Inc., 80 Business Park Dr, Armonk, NY 10504; custserv@mesharpe.com; http://www.mesharpe.com. Illus., index, adv. Sample. Refereed. Circ: 34000. Vol. ends: Nov/Dec (No. 6). Microform: PQC. Online: EBSCO Publishing, EBSCO Host; OCLC Online Computer Library Center, Inc.; ProQuest K-12 Learning Solutions; ProQuest LLC (Ann Arbor); SwetsWise Online Content. Reprint: PSC. *Indexed:* ABCPolSci, ABS&EES, AmH&L, BAS, CJA, HistAb, IBR, IBSS, IBZ, IUSGP, IndIslam, PAIS, PRA, PSA, SSCI, SociolAb. *Aud.:* Ac, Sa.

This journal "features readable analysis, reliable information, and lively debate about the communist and post-communist world, with an emphasis on thoughtful but timely coverage of current economic, political, and international issues. The magazine seeks to serve as a place where scholars from different disciplines may converse with one another and with other serious students of communist and post-communist affairs." The journal "also hopes to reach researchers and policy makers affiliated with multinational, governmental, and private-sector institutions and organizations from around the world." The primary goal of the journal is "to provide materials to educate the next generation of scholars in communist and post-communist studies."

Each issue contains about four articles that focus on contemporary events in the countries of the former Soviet Union and former Soviet bloc nations. In addition, there are also articles that examine current communist regimes, such as China. Recent issues include articles on the Serbs in Croatia and Bosnia at the outbreak of the Yugoslav wars, parliamentary elections in Azerbaijan, and an investigation of Georgia's efforts to join the European Union. This journal is recommend for academic, research, and large public libraries.

5574. *Religion, State and Society: the Keston journal.* Formerly (until 1992): *Religion in Communist Lands.* [ISSN: 0963-7494] 1973. q. GBP 541 print & online eds. Ed(s): Dr. Philip Walters. Routledge, 4 Park Sq, Milton Park, Abingdon, OX14 4RN, United Kingdom; info@routledge.co.uk; http://www.routledge.co.uk. Adv. Refereed. Circ: 2000. Microform: PQC. Online: EBSCO Publishing, EBSCO Host; Gale; IngentaConnect; OCLC Online Computer Library Center, Inc.; ProQuest LLC (Ann Arbor); SwetsWise Online Content. Reprint: PSC. *Indexed:* IBR, IBSS, IBZ, IPSA, PSA, R&TA, RI-1, SSA, SociolAb. *Bk. rev.:* 3-5, 400-800 words, signed. *Aud.:* Ac, Sa.

According to the publisher, this journal "is the only English-language academic publication devoted to these issues in communist and formerly communist countries throughout the world, and focusing on the legacy of the encounter between religion and communism. What problems are these religious communities now facing in their own countries and in a rapidly changing world? How much contact and cooperation is there between religious communities of East and West? Where are the areas of misunderstanding and conflict? Religious believers in Europe, Asia and the rest of the world have much to learn from the way in which their counterparts in communist and formerly communist countries are tackling social, cultural, ethnic, political and ecclesiological problems, and vice versa.

The journal also addresses subjects of worldwide concern to religious believers and religious communities such as legislation on religion, religious rights and freedoms, ecumenism, religion and national identity and the challenges of globalization. As well as authoritative and provocative articles, the publication includes book reviews, bibliographies and translations of important documents. The journal encourages debate within the pages of a single issue and in the form of responses to articles which have appeared in earlier issues." Each issue includes an introduction by the editor that summarizes the four to six articles and discusses recurring or related themes when appropriate. Some issues are thematic; with a recent issue focusing on the persecution of Jehovah's Witnesses from concentration camps in World War II through the end of the communist era in East Central Europe. Each issue also includes detailed book reviews of approximately three to five new monographs. Recommended for academic and research libraries with religious and/or Slavic Studies programs and for larger public libraries, particularly those that serve patrons interested in the region or the topic.

5575. Revolutionary Russia: journal of the Study Group on the Russian Revolution. [ISSN: 0954-6545] 1988. s-a. GBP 196 print & online eds. Ed(s): Jonathan Smele. Routledge, 4 Park Sq, Milton Park, Abingdon, OX14 4RN, United Kingdom; journals@routledge.com; http://www.routledge.co.uk. Adv. Sample. Refereed. Reprint: PSC. *Indexed:* AmH&L, HistAb, IBR, IBZ, IPSA, PSA. *Bk. rev.:* 10-12, 800-1,000 words, signed. *Aud.:* Ac, Sa.

This is the journal of the Study Group on the Russian Revolution, and according to the publisher "is the only English-language journal to concentrate on the revolutionary period of Russian history, from c.1880–c.1932. It is interdisciplinary and international in approach, publishing original research, documentary sources, book reviews and review articles in the fields of history, politics, economics, sociology, art history and literary and intellectual history from scholars across the world, including Russia and other countries of the former Soviet Union." Each issue includes three or four scholarly articles and an excellent book review section, which serves as an outstanding collection development tool for librarians. Recent issues include articles on the Russian nobility and the February 1917 revolution, the White Government in the Russian north, and the emigre Socialist Revolutionary Party and the Russian peasants during NEP. Highly recommended for academic and research libraries that support Slavic Studies programs, or advanced study in history.

5576. Russia Profile (Online). d. *Bk. rev.:* Various number and length. *Aud.:* Hs, Ga, Ac, Sa.

This is an English-language web site that covers news and information from Russia. The site is an "information service offering expert analysis of Russian politics, economics, society and culture. It consists of a website and magazine." Coverage includes internal Russian current events as well as the Russian view of world events. The site is updated daily. A magazine is published ten times a year and includes the best articles from the web site. Subscriptions to the print journal are free. URL: www.russiaprofile.org

5577. Russian Education and Society: a journal of translations. Formerly (until 1992): *Soviet Education.* [ISSN: 1060-9393] 1958. m. USD 1344 print & online eds. Ed(s): Anthony Jones. M.E. Sharpe, Inc., 80 Business Park Dr, Armonk, NY 10504; custserv@mesharpe.com; http://www.mesharpe.com. Illus., index, adv. Sample. Refereed. Vol. ends: Dec (No. 12). Reprint: PSC. *Indexed:* ABIn, ArtHuCI, CJA, EAA, ERIC, EduInd, FR, PAIS, RILM, SSCI. *Aud.:* Ac, Sa.

The editor of this journal "selects material for translation from more than thirty-five Russian-language periodicals and newspapers, from empirical research reports, and from books. The materials cover preschool, primary, secondary, vocational, and higher education; curricula and methods of the subject fields taught in the schools; the pedagogy of art, music, and physical

education; issues related to family life, employment, and youth culture; and special education programs. Journals and newspapers of ministries of education and higher education and the teachers unions are also covered, as well as popular educational magazines for children, young people, and parents." The editor presents a good introduction to each issue, providing an overview of the four to seven articles included. Each article includes a full citation to the original publication. All sources cited in the original publication are included with the translation. This journal is aimed at specialists in the field and would be of particular use to scholars who do not have the language skills to read these articles in the original language of publication. Recommended for academic and research libraries that support programs of study and research in education.

5578. Russian History. [ISSN: 0094-288X] 1974. q. USD 50 (Individuals, USD 30). Ed(s): Richard Hellie. Charles Schlacks, Jr., Publisher, PO Box 1256, Idyllwild, CA 92549-1256; http://artful.com.au/schlacks/. Illus., index, adv. Sample. Refereed. Circ: 500. Vol. ends: Winter (No. 4). *Indexed:* ABS&EES, AmH&L, ArtHuCI, HistAb, SSCI. *Bk. rev.:* 15-20, 500-1,000 words, signed. *Aud.:* Ac, Sa.

As the title indicates, this scholarly journal focuses on Russian history. Each issue contains about four articles, some of which are written in English while others are written in Russian. Historical documents, which appear in the original Russian, are also published on a regular basis. Each issue also contains book reviews. A recent issue focuses on a historical study of several Russian literary figures, including an article on Mikhail Bulgakov and Soviet censorship, two pieces on Dostoevsky and one article on Chekhov. Highly recommended for academic and research libraries that support Slavic Studies programs or advanced study in history.

5579. Russian Life: a monthly magazine of culture, history and travel. Former titles (until 1991): *Soviet Life;* Which incorporated (19??-1977): *Soviet Panorama;* (until 1965): *U S S R.* [ISSN: 1066-999X] 1956. bi-m. USD 33 domestic; USD 38 foreign. Ed(s): Maria Kolesnikova. Russian Life, PO Box 567, Montpelier, VT 05601-0567; sales@rispubs.com; http://www.rispubs.com. Illus., adv. Sample. Circ: 15000 Paid. Vol. ends: Dec (No. 12). Microform: PQC. Online: EBSCO Publishing, EBSCO Host; Florida Center for Library Automation; Gale; Northern Light Technology, Inc.; OCLC Online Computer Library Center, Inc.; ProQuest K-12 Learning Solutions; ProQuest LLC (Ann Arbor). *Indexed:* ABS&EES, ENW, MusicInd, PAIS. *Bk. rev.:* Number and length vary. *Aud.:* Ga, Ac.

Published bimonthly, this is a "magazine of Russian history, culture, business and travel. Each colorful 64-page issue contains fine features, news and photo journalism on all aspects of life in Russia, past and present. Regular departments include: Practical Traveler, Travel Journal, Russian Calendar (important events in Russian history that month), Russian Cuisine and Survival Russian, a guide to the Russian you really need to know." According to the editors, "the intent of *Russian Life* is to offer an objective, insightful trip into the heart of Russian reality. *Russian Life* is a magazine of ideas and a forum for discussion."

Although geared toward the nonspecialist, this journal does an excellent job of providing an overview of current events, including politics and culture. It also provides the Russian perspective on world events. Each issue is richly illustrated with color photographs and includes book reviews. The web site, www.rispubs.com, includes a page listing most of the books reviewed in the current issue, with links to vendors where the titles can be purchased online. Highly recommended for all public, academic, and research libraries.

5580. Russian Linguistics: international journal for the study of the Russian language. [ISSN: 0304-3487] 1974. 3x/yr. EUR 564 print & online eds. Ed(s): Roger Comtet, Jos Schaeken. Springer Netherlands, Van Godewijckstraat 30, Dordrecht, 3311 GX, Netherlands; http://www.springeronline.com. Illus., index, adv. Sample. Refereed. Vol. ends: Nov (No. 3). Microform: PQC. Online: EBSCO Publishing, EBSCO Host; Gale; IngentaConnect; OCLC Online Computer Library Center, Inc.; OhioLINK; Springer LINK; SwetsWise Online Content. Reprint: PSC. *Indexed:* AmHI, ArtHuCI, FR, IBR, IBZ, L&LBA, LT&LA, LingAb, MLA-IB. *Bk. rev.:* 6-9, 800-1,500 words, signed. *Aud.:* Ac, Sa.

This journal "is an international forum for all scholars working in the field of Russian linguistics and its manifold diversity, ranging from phonetics and phonology to syntax and the linguistic analysis of texts (text grammar), including both diachronic and synchronic problems. Besides original articles and reviews, *Russian Linguistics* publishes regular surveys of current scholarly writings from other periodicals. Topics that fall within the scope of the journal include: Traditional-structuralist as well as generative-transformational and other modern approaches to questions of synchronic and diachronic grammar; Phonetics and phonology, morphology, syntax, pragmatics and semantics of Russian and Old Russian; Philological problems of Russian and Old Russian texts; Russian grammar in its relation to linguistic universals; History of Russian literary language; Russian dialectology."

This title is very specialized, and is an excellent journal in the field, with the majority of the articles and book reviews being published in Russian. Recommended for academic and research libraries that support Russian language and literature programs.

5581. *Russian Literature.* [ISSN: 0304-3479] 1973. 8x/yr. EUR 1037. Ed(s): W G Weststeijn. Elsevier BV, North-Holland, Sara Burgerhartstraat 25, Amsterdam, 1055 KV, Netherlands; nlinfo-f@elsevier.nl; http://www.elsevier.nl. Illus., index. Sample. Refereed. Vol. ends: No. 4 - No. 8. Microform: PQC. Online: EBSCO Publishing, EBSCO Host; OhioLINK; ScienceDirect. *Indexed:* ArtHuCI, IBR, IBZ, MLA-IB. *Aud.:* Ac, Sa.

This journal "combines issues devoted to special topics of Russian literature with contributions on related subjects in Croatian, Serbian, Czech, Slovak and Polish literatures. Moreover, several issues each year contain articles on heterogeneous subjects concerning Russian literature. All methods and viewpoints are welcomed, provided they contribute something new, original or challenging to our understanding of Russian and other Slavic literatures. *Russian Literature* regularly publishes special issues devoted to the historical avant-garde in Russian literature and in the other Slavic literatures; and, the development of descriptive and theoretical poetics in Russian studies and in studies of other Slavic fields."

An excellent journal in the field, this title is very specialized, with the majority of the articles being published in Russian. Even the English-language articles include extensive quotes and citations in Russian (or Polish, Croatian, etc.) A recent thematic issue examines the life and work of Andrej Belyj to celebrate the 125 anniversary of his birth. Recommended for academic and research libraries that support Russian language and literature programs.

5582. *Russian Politics and Law.* Former titles: *Russian Politics;* (until 1992): *Soviet Law and Government.* [ISSN: 1061-1940] 1962. bi-m. USD 1284 print & online eds. Ed(s): Nils H Wessell. M.E. Sharpe, Inc., 80 Business Park Dr, Armonk, NY 10504; custserv@mesharpe.com; http://www.mesharpe.com. Illus., index, adv. Sample. Refereed. Vol. ends: Nov/Dec (No. 6). Microform: WSH; PMC. Online: EBSCO Publishing, EBSCO Host; OCLC Online Computer Library Center, Inc.; SwetsWise Online Content; H.W. Wilson. Reprint: PSC. *Indexed:* CJA, CLI, IBSS, ILP, IPSA, IndIslam, PAIS, PSA, SSCI. *Aud.:* Ac, Sa.

This journal "contains unabridged translations of articles chiefly from Russian-language publications in the fields of politics, law, public affairs, public administration, and related fields. The materials selected are intended to reflect political and legal developments in the Soviet successor states and to be of interest to those professionally concerned with these fields."

The editor presents a good introduction to each issue, providing an overview of the four to seven articles included. Each article includes a full citation to the original publication. All sources cited in the original publication are included with the translation. This journal is aimed at specialists in the field and would be of particular use to scholars who do not have the language skills to read these articles in the original language of publication. Recent issues examine nationalism in Russia and the Orange Revolution in Ukraine. Recommended for academic and research libraries that support international law programs and Slavic Studies in general.

5583. *The Russian Review: an American quarterly devoted to Russia past and present.* [ISSN: 0036-0341] 1941. q. GBP 157 print & online eds. Ed(s): Irene Masing-Delic, Eve Levin. Blackwell Publishing, Inc., Commerce Place, 350 Main St, Malden, MA 02148; customerservices@

blackwellpublishing.com; http://www.blackwellpublishing.com. Illus., index, adv. Sample. Refereed. Circ: 1700 Paid. Vol. ends: Oct (No. 4). Microform: PQC. Online: Blackwell Synergy; EBSCO Publishing, EBSCO Host; Gale; IngentaConnect; JSTOR (Web-based Journal Archive); OCLC Online Computer Library Center, Inc.; OhioLINK; SwetsWise Online Content; H.W. Wilson. Reprint: PSC. *Indexed:* ABS&EES, AmH&L, AmHI, ApEcolAb, ArtHuCI, BRI, CBRI, CJA, HistAb, HumInd, IBR, IBSS, IBZ, IndIslam, MLA-IB, PAIS, PSA, RILM, SSCI, SociolAb. *Bk. rev.:* 25-40, 300-1,000 words, signed. *Aud.:* Ac, Sa.

This publication "is a major academic journal of Russian studies. It publishes scholarly articles and book reviews in the areas of history, literature, film, fine arts, culture, society, and politics of the peoples of Russia. The scope of 'The Russian Review' includes not only the Russian nationality, but all the peoples of the Russian Empire, Soviet Union, and contemporary Russian Federation." According to the editor, topics of interest currently include nationality policy, civil society, identity, gender, religion, modern literature, and cultural studies. The goal of the journal is to represent the broad spectrum of original scholarship on Russia, both past and present. Each issue generally devotes at least 40 pages to its book review section, for the evaluation of the most current Russian scholarship in all languages. This, combined with the publications-received section, serves as an excellent collection development tool for librarians. This excellent journal should be acquired by any academic or research library that supports a Russian and/or Slavic Studies program.

5584. *Russian Social Science Review: a journal of translations.* Formerly (until 1992): *Soviet Review.* [ISSN: 1061-1428] 1960. bi-m. USD 360 print & online eds. Ed(s): Patricia A Kolb. M.E. Sharpe, Inc., 80 Business Park Dr, Armonk, NY 10504; custserv@mesharpe.com; http://www.mesharpe.com. Illus., index, adv. Sample. Refereed. Vol. ends: Nov/Dec (No. 6). Microform: PQC. Online: EBSCO Publishing, EBSCO Host; Northern Light Technology, Inc.; OCLC Online Computer Library Center, Inc.; ProQuest LLC (Ann Arbor); SwetsWise Online Content; H.W. Wilson. Reprint: PSC. *Indexed:* ABIn, ABS&EES, CJA, MLA-IB, PAIS. *Aud.:* Ac, Sa.

This journal "contains unabridged translations from a wide range of Russian-language publications including *Voprosy ekonomiki* (Problems of Economics); *Voprosy istorii* (Problems of History); *Voprosy filosofii* (Problems of Philosophy); *Voprosy psikhologii* (Problems of Psychology); *Voprosy literatury* (Problems of Literature); *Sotsiologicheskie issledovaniia* (Sociological Research); *Svobodnaia mysl* (Free Thought); *Novyi mir* (New World); and others." It covers a broad range of disciplines in the social sciences including sociology, economics, education, literary criticism, history, anthropology, psychology, and political science. Each article includes a full citation to the original publication and credits the translator. All sources cited in the original publication are included with the translation and some citations include explanatory footnotes. This journal is of value to anyone with an interest in the social sciences in Russia. It would be of particular use to scholars who do not have the language skills to read these articles in the original language of publication. Recommended for academic and research libraries, and large public libraries with patrons interested in the region.

5585. *Russian Studies in History: a journal of translations.* Formerly (until 1992): *Soviet Studies in History.* [ISSN: 1061-1983] 1962. q. USD 912 print & online eds. Ed(s): Christine Ruane, Joseph Bradley. M.E. Sharpe, Inc., 80 Business Park Dr, Armonk, NY 10504; custserv@mesharpe.com; http://www.mesharpe.com. Illus., index, adv. Sample. Refereed. Vol. ends: Spring (No. 4). Reprint: PSC. *Indexed:* AmH&L, BAS, HistAb, IBR, IBZ. *Aud.:* Ac, Sa.

The journal contains translations from major history journals published in Russia including "*Voprosy istorii* (Problems of History); *Vestnik Moskovskogo universiteta, seriia istorii* (Journal of Moscow University, History Series); *Novaia i noveishaia istoriia* (Modern and Contemporary History); *Rodina* (Native Land); *Otechestvennaia istoriia* (National History; formerly *Istoriia SSSR*); *Obshchestvennye nauki i sovremennost* (The Social Sciences and Modernity)." The goal of the journal is to provide English-language translations of the best recent Russian historiography. Each article includes a full citation to the original publication and credits the translator. All sources cited in the original publication are included with the translation and some citations include explanatory footnotes. This journal would be of value to historians interested in Russia, and would be of particular use to students and scholars who do not have the Russian-language skills to read these articles in the original language of publication. Many of the issues are thematic and include thoughtful introductions by a guest editor. Recent issues examine the history of education, post-Soviet Russian historiography in socialist East Central Europe, and Russia's history as a multinational empire. This journal is recommended for purchase for academic and research libraries that support programs in Russian history.

5586. *Russian Studies in Literature: a journal of translations.* Formerly (until 1992): *Soviet Studies in Literature.* [ISSN: 1061-1975] 1964. q. USD 912 print & online eds. Ed(s): John Givens. M.E. Sharpe, Inc., 80 Business Park Dr, Armonk, NY 10504; custserv@mesharpe.com; http://www.mesharpe.com. Illus., index, adv. Sample. Refereed. Vol. ends: Fall (No. 4). Reprint: PSC. *Indexed:* ABS&EES, AmH&L, AmHI, ArtHuCI, HistAb, HumInd, MLA-IB, SSCI. *Aud.:* Ac, Sa.

This journal "publishes translations from the Russian in literary criticism and scholarship, including both contemporary and historical material." Each article includes a full citation to the original publication and credits the translator. This journal is of value to students and scholars interested in Russian literature, and is of particular use to those who do not have the Russian-language skills to read these articles in the original language. Each issue is about 100 pages long and includes articles of varying length. This journal is recommended for academic and research libraries that support programs of comparative literature.

5587. *Russian Studies in Philosophy: a journal of translations.* Formerly (until 1992): *Soviet Studies in Philosophy.* [ISSN: 1061-1967] 1962. q. USD 836 print & online eds. Ed(s): Taras Zakydalsky. M.E. Sharpe, Inc., 80 Business Park Dr, Armonk, NY 10504; custserv@mesharpe.com; http://www.mesharpe.com. Illus., index, adv. Sample. Refereed. Vol. ends: Spring (No. 4). Reprint: PSC. *Indexed:* ABS&EES, AmHI, ArtHuCI, FR, IBR, IBZ, PhilInd, SSCI. *Aud.:* Ac, Sa.

According to the publisher, "materials selected are intended to reflect developments in Russian philosophy and to be of interest to those professionally concerned with this field." The journal contains unabridged translations of articles originally published in "*Voprosy filosofii* (Problems of Philosophy); *Filosofskie nauki* (Philosophical Sciences); *Vestnik Moskov-skogo universiteta, seriia filosofii* (Moscow University Herald, Philosophy Series); *Vestnik Leningradskogo universiteta, seriia ekonomiki, filosofii i prava* (Leningrad University Herald, Economics, Philosophy, and Law Series)." Most issues are thematic, focusing on a specific philosopher or school of thought. The editor publishes a brief introduction that outlines the focus of the current issue. Recent issues examine Aleksei Losev, Bonifatt Kedrov, and Lev Shestov. In addition to publishing articles, the journal occasionally publishes translated excerpts from monographs. Each article or excerpt includes a full citation to the original publication and credits the translator. This journal is of value to students and scholars interested in Russian philosophy, and is of particular use to those who do not have the Russian-language skills to read these articles in the original language. Each issue is about 100 pages long and includes articles of varying length. This journal is recommended for academic and research libraries that support philosophy programs.

5588. *Sarmatian Review.* Formerly: *Houston Sarmatian.* [ISSN: 1059-5872] 1981. 3x/yr. USD 21 (Individuals, USD 15). Ed(s): Ewa M Thompson. Polish Institute of Houston, PO Box 79119, Houston, TX 77279-9119; sarmatia@rice.edu; http://www.ruf.rice.edu/~sarmatia. Illus., adv. Refereed. Circ: 400 Paid. Online: EBSCO Publishing, EBSCO Host. *Indexed:* ABS&EES, AmHI, PAIS, SociolAb. *Bk. rev.:* Number and length vary. *Aud.:* Ac.

This online resource is an abbreviated version of the print edition that "is a scholarly journal on the history, culture, and society of Central and Eastern Europe, with strong attention to Poland, the post-Soviet period, and American ethnic issues. Recent issues have covered religion and state, the mass media, higher education, literature, inter-ethnic relations, government and politics." One area of specialization is the translation of documents. The book reviews and books received section are a good tool for collection development librarians. This resource covers a broad range of topics and is recommended for all libraries. URL: www.ruf.rice.edu/~sarmatia

5589. *Slavic & East European Information Resources.* [ISSN: 1522-8886] 2000. q. USD 240 print & online eds. Ed(s): Karen A Rondestvedt. Haworth Information Press, 10 Alice St, Binghamton, NY 13904; getinfo@haworthpress.com; http://www.haworthpress.com. Illus., adv. Sample. Refereed. Circ: 111 Paid. Reprint: HAW. *Indexed:* ABS&EES, IBR, IBZ, IBZ, ISTA, LISA, PAIS. *Bk. rev.:* 10-14; 300-1200 words; signed. *Aud.:* Ac, Sa.

This journal "serves as a focal point for the international exchange of information in the field of Slavic and East European librarianship. Affiliated with the American Association for the Advancement of Slavic Studies, the journal contains original research, technical developments and other news about the field, and reviews of books and electronic media. It is designed to keep professionals up-to-date with efforts around the world to preserve and expand access to material from and about these countries. This journal emphasizes practical and current information, but it does not neglect other relevant topics." As the publisher's summary indicates, this journal is a useful professional tool for librarians responsible for the development of Slavic Studies collections and is highly recommended for academic and research libraries with such collections.

5590. *Slavic and East European Journal.* [ISSN: 0037-6752] 1957. 4x/yr. Institutional members, USD 100 JRO; Individual members, USD 65 Administrator. Ed(s): Gerald Janecek. American Association of Teachers of Slavic and East European Languages, c/o Kathleen E. Dillon, Executive Director, AATSEEL, PO Box 7039, Berkeley, CA 94707-2306; gjanecek@uky.edu; http://aatseel.org. Illus., index, adv. Refereed. Circ: 1600. Vol. ends: No. 4. Microform: PQC. Online: JSTOR (Web-based Journal Archive); OCLC Online Computer Library Center, Inc.; H.W. Wilson. *Indexed:* ABS&EES, AmHI, ArtHuCI, FR, HumInd, IBR, IBZ, L&LBA, LT&LA, MLA-IB, RILM, SSA, SociolAb. *Bk. rev.:* 25-30, 250-500 words, signed. *Aud.:* Ac, Sa.

This journal "serves the Slavic profession by publishing original research and review essays in the areas of Slavic and East European languages, literatures, cultures, linguistics, and methodology/ pedagogy as well as reviews of books published in these areas. The journal is published quarterly by the American Association of Teachers of Slavic and East European Languages (AATSEEL)." Along with the Slavic languages and literatures articles, there are good thematic review articles and an excellent selection of book reviews and lists of books received. This journal is highly recommended for academic and research libraries that support Slavic Studies programs.

5591. *Slavic Review: American quarterly of Russian, Eurasian and East European studies.* Former titles (until 1961): *American Slavic and East European Review;* (until 1944): *Slavonic and East European Review. American Series;* (until 1942): *Slavonic Year-Book. American Series.* [ISSN: 0037-6779] 1941. q. Non-members, USD 130. Ed(s): Diane Koenker. American Association for the Advancement of Slavic Studies, Harvard University, 8 Story St, 3d Fl, Cambridge, MA 02138; aaass@fas.harvard.edu; http://www.fas.harvard.edu. Illus., index, adv. Refereed. Circ: 5000. Vol. ends: Winter (No. 4). Online: JSTOR (Web-based Journal Archive). *Indexed:* ABCPolSci, ABS&EES, AmH&L, AmHI, ArtHuCI, BRI, CBRI, HistAb, HumInd, IBR, IBSS, IBZ, IPSA, IndIslam, MLA-IB, PAIS, PSA, RILM, SSCI, SociolAb. *Bk. rev.:* 55-60, 300-1,000 words, signed. *Aud.:* Ac, Sa.

As the membership journal of the American Association for the Advancement of Slavic Studies, this is one of the outstanding research journal devoted to Slavic and Eurasian Studies. Articles focus primarily on history, political science, economics, and literature, but other Slavic subjects in the humanities and social sciences are often included. Articles receive extensive peer-review and are well researched and documented. A major portion of each issue is devoted to book reviews and books received. Both sections serve as outstanding tools for collection development librarians. The journal often includes special features, such as a thematic list of all Slavic Studies dissertations awarded at U.S. institutions during a given year. This journal is highly recommended for academic and research libraries as well as larger public libraries with an interest in Slavic Studies.

5592. *Slavonic and East European Review.* [ISSN: 0037-6795] 1922. q. GBP 163 print & online eds. Ed(s): M Rady. Maney Publishing, Ste. 1C, Joseph's Well, Hanover Walk, Leeds, LS3 1AB, United Kingdom; maney@maney.co.uk; http://www.maney.co.uk. Illus., index. Refereed. Circ: 1000. Vol. ends: Oct (No. 4). Reprint: PSC. *Indexed:* AmH&L, AmHI, ArtHuCI, BrHumI, FR, HistAb, HumInd, IBR, IBSS, IBZ, L&LBA, LT&LA, MLA-IB, PSA, SSA, SSCI, SociolAb. *Bk. rev.:* 50-60, 300-750 words, signed. *Aud.:* Ac, Sa.

Produced by the Modern Humanities Research Association, this is the journal of Slavonic and East European Studies Department of the University College, London, and is very similar in scope and content to the *Slavic Review*. Each issue "includes articles, review-articles, book reviews, marginalia, and original documents." Each issue also includes lists of books received. Scholarly contributions in all areas of Slavic and East European Studies are accepted, and the editors note that the following subjects are regularly covered: language, literature, history, cinema, and the social sciences. This journal is highly recommended for academic and research libraries as well as larger public libraries with an interest in Slavic Studies.

5593. *Social Sciences: a quarterly journal of the Russian Academy of Sciences.* [ISSN: 0134-5486] 1970. q. USD 352 (Individuals, USD 84). East View Information Services, 10601 Wayzata Blvd, Minneapolis, MN 55305; info@eastview.com; http://www.eastview.com/. Illus., index. Refereed. Circ: 300 Paid. Vol. ends: No. 4. Online: Pub.; EBSCO Publishing, EBSCO Host; OCLC Online Computer Library Center, Inc.; ProQuest LLC (Ann Arbor). *Indexed:* ABS&EES, AmH&L, EIP, IBR, IBSS, IBZ, JEL, PAIS, PSA, SSA, SociolAb. *Bk. rev.:* 3-5, 100-1,000 words, signed. *Aud.:* Ac, Sa.

According to the publishers, this journal "offers in English translation the most significant publications from nearly 30 scholarly periodicals of Russia." These periodicals are published by the Russian Academy of Sciences. Subjects covered by the journal include but are not limited to archaeology, ethnography, history, economics, politics, law, psychology, and sociology. Along with articles, each issue includes book reviews. Each article includes a brief citation, noting the translator and where it was originally published. This journal is of value to anyone with an interest in the social sciences in Russia. It would be of particular use to scholars who do not have the language skills to read these articles in the original language of publication. Recommended for academic and research libraries.

5594. *Sociological Research: a journal of translations from Russian.* Formerly (until 1992): *Soviet Sociology.* [ISSN: 1061-0154] 1962. bi-m. USD 1242 print & online eds. Ed(s): Anthony Jones. M.E. Sharpe, Inc., 80 Business Park Dr, Armonk, NY 10504; custserv@mesharpe.com; http://www.mesharpe.com. Illus., index, adv. Sample. Refereed. Vol. ends: Nov/Dec (No. 6). Reprint: PSC. *Indexed:* ABS&EES, CJA, FR, PAIS, PSA, SFSA, SSCI, SociolAb. *Aud.:* Ac, Sa.

This journal "contains unabridged translations of articles chiefly from the following publications: *Sotsiologicheskii zhurnal* (Sociological Journal); *Ekonomicheskie i sotsial'nye peremeny: monitoring obshchestvennogo mneniia* (Economic and Social Changes: Monitoring Public Opinion); *Obshchestvennye nauki i sovremennost* (The Social Sciences and the Present); *Sotsiologicheskie issledovaniia* (Sociological Research); *Svobodnaia mysl* (Free Thought) [formerly *Kommunist*]; *Politicheskie issledovaniia* (Political Research) [formerly *Rabochii klass i sovremennyi mir*], and other relevant journals and books. The materials selected are intended to reflect developments in sociology in Russia and other successor states of the USSR, and to be of interest to those professionally concerned with this field." The journal covers a broad range of topics related to sociology, and each article includes a full citation to the original publication and credits the translator. All sources cited in the original publication are included with the translation and some citations include explanatory footnotes. The editor provides an excellent introduction to each issue. This journal is of value to anyone with an interest in the current status of the field in Russia. It would be of particular use to scholars who do not have the language skills to read these articles in the original language of publication. Recommended for academic and research libraries and large public libraries with patrons interested in the region.

5595. *The Soviet and Post Soviet Review.* Formerly (until 1992): *Soviet Union.* [ISSN: 1075-1262] 1974. 3x/yr. USD 30 (Individuals, USD 15). Ed(s): Vladimir P Buldakov. Charles Schlacks, Jr., Publisher, PO Box 1256, Idyllwild, CA 92549-1256; http://artful.com.au/schlacks/. Illus., index, adv. Refereed. Circ: 500. Vol. ends: No. 3. *Indexed:* ABS&EES, AmH&L, HistAb. *Bk. rev.:* 1, 1,000 words, signed. *Aud.:* Ac, Sa.

This scholarly journal focuses on Russian history, politics, cultural studies, and foreign relations. Articles are published in both English and Russian, with the most recent issues including more Russian-language articles. Recent articles examine child mortality in post-war Soviet Union, a historical study of anti-Jewish pogroms in Eastern Siberia, and the post–World War II territorial settlement between the Soviet Union and Japan. This journal is recommended for academic and research libraries that support Slavic Studies programs. Please note that the latest issue published for this title was in 2004.

5596. *Statutes and Decisions: The Laws of the U S S R & Its Successor States: a journal of translations.* Formerly (until 1992): *Soviet Statutes and Decisions.* [ISSN: 1061-0014] 1964. bi-m. USD 1338 print & online eds. Ed(s): Sarah Reynolds. M.E. Sharpe, Inc., 80 Business Park Dr, Armonk, NY 10504; custserv@mesharpe.com; http://www.mesharpe.com. Illus., index, adv. Sample. Refereed. Microform: WSH; PMC. Online: EBSCO Publishing, EBSCO Host; OCLC Online Computer Library Center, Inc.; SwetsWise Online Content. Reprint: PSC. *Indexed:* CLI, ILP, PAIS. *Aud.:* Ac, Sa.

The journal "contains translations of items from the following sources: *Biulleten' normativnykh aktov* (Bulletin of Normative Acts); *Izvestiia* (Information); *Rossiiskaia gazeta* (Russian Newspaper); *Rossiiskaia iustitsiia* (Russian Justice); *Rossiiskie vesti* (Russian News); *Sobranie Aktov Presidenta i Pravitel'stva Rossiiskoi Federatsii* (Collection of Acts of the President and the Government of the Russian Federation); *Sobranie zakonodatel'stva RF* (Collection of Legislation of the RF); *Gosudarstvo i pravo* (The State and Law); *Vedomosti Federal'nogo Sobraniia Rossiiskoi Federatsii* (Gazette of the Federal Assembly of the Russian Federation); *Vestnik Konstitutsionogo suda RF* (RF Constitutional Court Herald); *Vest-nik Verkhovnogo suda RSFSR* (RSFSR Supreme Court Herald); *Vestnik Vysshego arbitrazhnogo suda RF* (RF Higher Arbitrazh Court Herald); *Zakon* (Law); *Zakonnost'* (Legality); *Zakonodatel'stvo i ekonomika* (Legislation and the Economy), and items from other publications as warranted. The materials selected are intended to reflect developments of interest to those professionally concerned with this field. *Statutes and Decisions* is a highly useful resource for students and all persons interested in the laws and court decisions of the Russian Federation." This journal is of value to anyone with an interest in Russian law. It would be of particular use to scholars who do not have the language skills to read these articles in the original language of publication. Due to the specialized content, this title is recommended primarily for law libraries or academic and research libraries that support Slavic Studies programs.

5597. *Studies in East European Thought.* Formerly (until 1992): *Studies in Soviet Thought.* [ISSN: 0925-9392] 1961. q. EUR 478 print & online eds. Ed(s): Edward M Swiderski. Springer Netherlands, Van Godewijckstraat 30, Dordrecht, 3311 GX, Netherlands; http://www.springeronline.com. Illus., index, adv. Sample. Refereed. Vol. ends: Dec (No. 4). Microform: PQC. Online: EBSCO Publishing, EBSCO Host; Gale; IngentaConnect; OCLC Online Computer Library Center, Inc.; OhioLINK; Springer LINK; SwetsWise Online Content. Reprint: PSC. *Indexed:* ABCPolSci, ABS&EES, AmH&L, ArtHuCI, BAS, HistAb, IBR, IBSS, IBZ, IPB, IPSA, PSA, PhilInd, SSCI, SociolAb. *Bk. rev.:* 1-10, 500-2,000 words, signed. *Aud.:* Ac, Sa.

According to the editors, this journal "is intended to provide a forum for Western-language (English and German) writings on philosophy and philosophers who identify with the history and cultures of East and Central Europe, including Russia, Ukraine, and the Baltic States. The editors do not advocate a program or defend a position as to the nature and limits of philosophy in its manifold interactions with other disciplines and in its role in articulating cultural values and marking intellectual dissonances. They welcome descriptive, critical, comparative, and historical studies of individuals, schools, currents, and institutions whose work and influence are widely regarded in their own environments to be philosophical or provide insight into the socio-cultural conditions of philosophical life in Eastern Europe." Each issue varies in length and includes articles written in both English and German. Some issues are thematic, focusing on specific philosophers. Recent thematic issues include an examination of the life and work of the Slovenian philosopher Slavoj Zizek and an issue devoted to the Russian A.F. Losev. This journal is important for scholarly and research libraries with collections in philosophy and/or collections that support Slavic Studies.

5598. *Transitions Online.* [ISSN: 1214-1615] 1999. m. updated daily. USD 100, Libraries, USD 160 (Individuals, USD 39). Ed(s): Tihomir Loza, Andrew Gardner. Transitions Online, Chlumova 22, Prague, 130 000, Czech Republic; http://archive.tol.cz/Publications/Transition/Contents/Index.html. *Bk. rev.:* Various number and length. *Aud.:* Ga, Ac.

This resource, which is the online successor to *Transitions,* covers contemporary events in the 28 countries of East Central Europe and the Soviet successor states. According to the editors, the resource covers "issues, not events: *Transitions Online* is—as its name suggests—interested in illustrating underlying issues and the process of change in the countries and regions that we cover." This is accomplished through a network of local correspondents. The content of the resource is aimed at "well-informed and intelligent" readers who are not specialists in the field. Subscribers also have access to an extensive archive that includes the print version of *Transitions.* This is an excellent resource for the study of contemporary events in Slavic and East Central European countries and is recommended for all libraries. The web site, www.tol.cz, also provides free access to useful information and country reports.

■ SOCIOLOGY AND SOCIAL WORK

General/Social Work and Social Welfare

See also Criminology and Law Enforcement; Cultural Studies; Ethnic Studies; Family; Law; Marriage and Divorce; and Population Studies sections.

Sarah J. Hammill, Distance Learning Librarian, Florida International University, North Miami, FL 33181

Introduction

The disciplines of sociology and social work do not and cannot exist in a vacuum. Their interconnectedness and relation to other subject areas are what makes sociology sociology, and social work social work. The titles and nature of the publications listed in this section affirm this interdisciplinary nature. You will find titles that are clearly related to religion, psychology, political science, law, economics, history, and mathematics (yes, even mathematics!). Titles such as *Children's Legal Rights Journal, Journal of Leisure Research, Nonprofit and Voluntary Sector Quarterly, Simulation & Gaming,* and *Group & Organization Management* do not immediately conjure up images of sociology and/or social work. However, as you will see, these journals and more belong in this section.

In this section you will find journals appropriate for basic collections in sociology and social work. For example, several journals published by professional associations are core journals for any academic library. Some of these titles include *American Sociological Review, Sociology,* and *Social Work.*

A number of journals focus on quantitative and/or qualitative research including but not limited to *Quality and Quantity, Evaluation Review, Journal of Mathematical Sociology,* and *Qualitative Social Work.*

The titles *International Journal of the Sociology of Law, Journal of Political and Military Sociology, Journal of Leisure Research, Journal of Sex Research, Journal of Peasant Studies,* and *Social Compass* are clearly cross-disciplinary and specialized in content.

For an international perspective, check out the *International Journal of Comparative Sociology, International Sociology, International Social Work,* and *Global Social Policy.* Titles that focus on research outside the United States include *Sociological Research, Acta Sociologica, British Journal of Sociology, Canadian Review of Sociology, Chinese Sociology and Anthropology, European Societies,* and *Journal of European Social Policy.*

Finally, a core collection would be remiss if it didn't include journals published for practitioners: *Administration in Social Work, American Sociologist, Social Work Education, Teaching Sociology,* and *Contemporary Sociology.*

The above is just a sampling of nearly 100 journals in this section. All publications in this section are recommended for at least one type of library. The majority are appropriate for academic libraries with undergraduate or graduate programs in sociology or social work. Some titles (duly noted) are appropriate for public, special, and high school libraries.

Basic Periodicals

GENERAL. Ga: *Annual Review of Sociology, Journal of Social Issues, Policy & Practice, Social Forces, Social Policy, Social Problems, Society;* Ac: *American Journal of Sociology, American Sociological Review, Annual Review of Sociology, British Journal of Sociology, Current Sociology, International Sociology, Journal of Social Issues, Sex Roles, Social Forces, Social Policy, Social Problems, Social Psychology Quarterly, Social Research, Society, Sociological Review, Sociology, Sociology of Education.*

SOCIAL WORK AND SOCIAL WELFARE. Ga: *Child Welfare, Children and Schools, Policy & Practice;* Ac: *British Journal of Social Work, Child Welfare, Children and Schools, Children and Youth Services Review, Clinical Social Work Journal, Families in Society, Health and Social Work, International Social Work, Policy & Practice, Research on Social Work Practice, Social Service Review, Social Work, Social Work with Groups.*

Basic Abstracts and Indexes

ASSIA: Applied Social Sciences Index and Abstracts, Social Sciences Citation Index, Social Sciences Index and Social Sciences Abstracts, Social Services Abstracts, Social Work Abstracts, Sociological Abstracts.

The Social Science Journal. See Cultural Studies section.

General

5599. *Acta Sociologica.* [ISSN: 0001-6993] 1955. q. GBP 221. Ed(s): Thomas P Boje, Thora Margareta Bertilsson. Sage Publications Ltd., 1 Oliver's Yard, 55 City Rd, London, EC1 1SP, United Kingdom; info@sagepub.co.uk; http://www.sagepub.co.uk. Illus., index, adv. Sample. Refereed. Circ: 3200. Microform: SWZ; PQC. Online: CSA; EBSCO Publishing, EBSCO Host; Gale; HighWire Press; IngentaConnect; OCLC Online Computer Library Center, Inc.; OhioLINK; SAGE Publications, Inc., SAGE Journals Online; SwetsWise Online Content; H.W. Wilson. Reprint: PSC. *Indexed:* ABCPolSci, AbAn, AmH&L, CJA, EI, FR, HRA, HistAb, IBR, IBSS, IBZ, IPSA, L&LBA, PAIS, PSA, PsycInfo, RILM, SFSA, SSA, SSCI, SUSA, SWA, SociolAb. *Bk. rev.:* 4-6, signed. *Aud.:* Ac.

As the journal of the Nordic Sociological Association, *Acta Sociologica* provides a forum for sociological issues between Nordic countries and the international community. Published in English, the content focuses mainly on Scandinavian research. Includes articles, review essays, book reviews, and commentaries from different theoretical and methodological point of views. Recommended for academic libraries that support graduate programs in sociology.

Amerasia Journal. See Asian American section.

American Journal of Economics and Sociology. See Economics section.

5600. *American Journal of Sociology.* [ISSN: 0002-9602] 1895. bi-m. USD 320 domestic; USD 350.20 Canada; USD 340 elsewhere. Ed(s): Andrew Abbott. University of Chicago Press, Journals Division, PO Box 37005, Chicago, IL 60637; subscriptions@press.uchicago.edu;

http://www.journals.uchicago.edu. Illus., index, adv. Sample. Refereed. Circ: 4000 Paid. Vol. ends: May. Microform: PQC. Online: EBSCO Publishing, EBSCO Host; Florida Center for Library Automation; Gale; JSTOR (Web-based Journal Archive); ProQuest K-12 Learning Solutions; ProQuest LLC (Ann Arbor). Reprint: PSC. *Indexed:* ABCPolSci, ABIn, ABS&EES, AICP, ASG, ASSIA, AbAn, AgeL, AmH&L, ArtHuCI, BAS, BRD, BRI, CBRI, CJA, CommAb, FR, HistAb, IBR, IBSS, IBZ, IMFL, IPSA, IndIslam, PAIS, PRA, PSA, PsycInfo, RI-1, RILM, RRTA, SFSA, SSA, SSCI, SUSA, SWA, SWR&A, SociolAb, V&AA, WAE&RSA. *Bk. rev.:* 20-40, signed. *Aud.:* Ga, Ac, Sa.

As the publication of the first sociology department in the United States, this journal has been around since 1895. It remains a core publication in sociology. Recent sample article topics include social times of network spaces and how the Sixties' movements revitalized unionization. The journal includes an extensive book review section and an occasional commentary-and-debate section. If your budget only has money for one journal, this is the one! A must-have for all academic libraries as well as special and public libraries with social services clientele.

5601. *American Sociological Review.* [ISSN: 0003-1224] 1936. bi-m. USD 90 in US & Canada to non-member individuals (Members, USD 35). Ed(s): Jerry Jacobs, Kelly Song Marr. American Sociological Association, 1307 New York Ave, NW, Ste 700, Washington, DC 20005-4701; publications@asanet.org; http://www.asanet.org. Illus., index, adv. Refereed. Circ: 11500. Vol. ends: Dec. Microform: MIM; PQC. Online: EBSCO Publishing, EBSCO Host; Gale; IngentaConnect; JSTOR (Web-based Journal Archive); OCLC Online Computer Library Center, Inc.; ProQuest K-12 Learning Solutions; ProQuest LLC (Ann Arbor). *Indexed:* ABCPolSci, ABIn, ABS&EES, ASSIA, AbAn, AgeL, AmH&L, ArtHuCI, BAS, BEL&L, CBRI, CJA, CommAb, EAA, EI, FR, HRA, HistAb, IBR, IBSS, IBZ, IPSA, PAIS, PRA, PSA, PsycInfo, RI-1, RILM, RRTA, SFSA, SSA, SSCI, SUSA, SWA, SWR&A, SociolAb, V&AA, WAE&RSA. *Aud.:* Ga, Ac.

As the flagship journal of the American Sociological Association, *ASR* publishes theoretical and empirical research in all fields of sociology. Emphasis is placed on articles that are of general interest. A must-have for academic libraries and research-oriented public libraries.

5602. *The American Sociologist.* [ISSN: 0003-1232] 1969. q. EUR 285 print & online eds. Springer New York LLC, 233 Spring St, New York, NY 10013-1578; journals@springer-ny.com; http://www.springer.com. Illus., adv. Sample. Refereed. Circ: 800. Vol. ends: Winter. Microform: PQC. Online: EBSCO Publishing, EBSCO Host; Florida Center for Library Automation; Gale; OCLC Online Computer Library Center, Inc.; OhioLINK; SwetsWise Online Content. Reprint: PSC. *Indexed:* AgeL, CJA, EI, FR, IBR, IBSS, IBZ, IPSA, PAIS, PSA, SSA, SSCI, SWA, SociolAb. *Bk. rev.:* 1-2, length varies. *Aud.:* Ga, Ac.

Contains essay articles that examine the intellectual, practical, and ethical issues affecting the field of sociology. Most issues are thematic; recent ones focus on graduate training in sociology and public sociology. This is a great journal for someone contemplating the field of sociology as it examines the training, ethics, and employment opportunities of sociologists. Recommended for academic and public research libraries.

5603. *Annual Review of Sociology.* [ISSN: 0360-0572] 1975. a. USD 189 (Individuals, USD 78 print & online eds.). Ed(s): John Hagan, Karen S Cook. Annual Reviews, 4139 El Camino Way, Palo Alto, CA 94303-0139; service@annualreviews.org; http://www.annualreviews.org. Adv. Refereed. Microform: PQC. Online: Florida Center for Library Automation; HighWire Press; Northern Light Technology, Inc. Reprint: PSC. *Indexed:* ABIn, ABS&EES, AgeL, CJA, FR, IBR, IBSS, IBZ, IPSA, PSA, PsycInfo, SSA, SSCI, SociolAb. *Aud.:* Ga, Ac, Sa.

Annual reviews are published in 32 scientific disciplines. The *Annual Review of Sociology* is an annual review of the primary research and the principal contributions in sociology. The 2006 issue contains articles on social processes, institutions and cultures, formal organizations, political and economic sociology, differentiation and stratification, demography, the individual and

society, urban and rural community sociology, and sociology and world regions. Highly recommended to stay abreast of current trends in sociology. A must-have for academic libraries and public and special libraries that serve social services clientele.

5604. *Archives Europeennes de Sociologie.* [ISSN: 0003-9756] 1960. 3x/yr. GBP 124. Ed(s): Christopher Hann, Jaques Lautman. Cambridge University Press, The Edinburgh Bldg, Shaftesbury Rd, Cambridge, CB2 2RU, United Kingdom; journals@cambridge.org; http://www.journals.cambridge.org. Illus., index, adv. Refereed. Vol. ends: Nov. Microform: PQC. Online: Pub.; EBSCO Publishing, EBSCO Host; OCLC Online Computer Library Center, Inc.; OhioLINK; SwetsWise Online Content. Reprint: PSC. *Indexed:* ASSIA, AmH&L, ArtHuCI, BAS, FR, HistAb, IBR, IBSS, IBZ, IPSA, IndIslam, PAIS, PSA, RI-1, SSA, SSCI, SociolAb, WAE&RSA. *Aud.:* Ac.

With a strong international perspective, this journal publishes social science research with thematic issues on the transition from totalitarianism to democracy, multiple citizenship, and state-of-the-art surveys. Articles are published in German, French, or English; abstracts are in all three languages. Recommended for academic libraries that support doctoral programs in the social sciences.

Armed Forces and Society. See Military section.

5605. *British Journal of Sociology.* [ISSN: 0007-1315] 1950. q. GBP 265 print & online eds. Ed(s): Bridget Hutter. Blackwell Publishing Ltd., 9600 Garsington Rd, Oxford, OX4 2ZG, United Kingdom; customerservices@blackwellpublishing.com; http://www.blackwellpublishing.com. Illus., index, adv. Sample. Refereed. Circ: 2700. Vol. ends: Dec. Microform: WMP. Online: Blackwell Synergy; EBSCO Publishing, EBSCO Host; Gale; IngentaConnect; JSTOR (Web-based Journal Archive); OCLC Online Computer Library Center, Inc.; SwetsWise Online Content. Reprint: PSC. *Indexed:* ABIn, AICP, ASSIA, AbAn, AgeL, AmH&L, ApEcolAb, ArtHuCI, BAS, CJA, CommAb, EI, FR, HistAb, IBR, IBSS, IBZ, IPSA, PAIS, PSA, PsycInfo, RI-1, RILM, SSA, SSCI, SWA, SociolAb. *Bk. rev.:* 10-20, signed. *Aud.:* Ac.

The aim of this journal is "to provide a medium for the publication of original papers covering the entire span of sociological thought and research." It focuses on current developments in research and analysis. There are occasional thematic issues—for example, "Cosmopolitan Sociology." Recent sample article topics include the significance of place in middle children; the secularity of Europe; and gender, technology, and jobs. The journal is published by the London School of Economics and Political Science and, as a result, has a strong European focus. Includes extensive book reviews. Recommended for academic libraries that support graduate programs in sociology.

5606. *Canadian Journal of Sociology.* [ISSN: 0318-6431] 1975. q. Free. Ed(s): Jim Conley. University of Toronto Press, Journals Division, 5201 Dufferin St, Toronto, ON M3H 5T8, Canada; journals@ utpress.utoronto.ca; http://www.utpjournals.com. Illus., index, adv. Sample. Refereed. Circ: 850 Paid. Vol. ends: Fall. Microform: MML. Online: Florida Center for Library Automation. Reprint: PSC. *Indexed:* ABS&EES, ASSIA, AgeL, AmH&L, ArtHuCI, CBCARef, CJA, CPerI, CommAb, FR, HistAb, IBSS, IMFL, PSA, SFSA, SSA, SSCI, SWA, SociolAb. *Bk. rev.:* 8-10, signed. *Aud.:* Ac.

This journal focuses on social services and policies specifically in Canada. However, some articles are broader in scope. Abstracts are in French and English, with articles in either French or English. This journal contains research articles, review essays, "Notes on the Discipline," "Response to Comments," and an extensive book review section. Sample article titles from a recent issue include "The Rise of Cohabitation in Quebec: Power of Religion and Power over Religion," "What Causes Canadian Aboriginal Protest? Examining Resources, Opportunities and Identity, 1951-2000," and "Ethno-racial Minorities and the Juno Awards." Recommended for academic libraries that support graduate programs in sociology and Canadian Studies.

5607. *The Canadian Review of Sociology and Anthropology.* [ISSN: 0008-4948] 1964. q. Institutional members, CND 120. Ed(s): Harley Dickinson. Canadian Sociology and Anthropology Association, Concordia University, 1455 de Maisonneuve West/Ouest, Montreal, PQ H3G 1M8, Canada; info@csaa.ca; http://www.csaa.ca. Illus., adv. Refereed. Circ: 1400. Vol. ends: Nov. Microform: MIM; PQC. Online: EBSCO Publishing, EBSCO Host; Florida Center for Library Automation; Gale; Micromedia ProQuest; OCLC Online Computer Library Center, Inc.; ProQuest K-12 Learning Solutions; ProQuest LLC (Ann Arbor); H.W. Wilson. Reprint: PSC. *Indexed:* ABS&EES, AICP, AbAn, AgeL, AmH&L, AnthLit, ArtHuCI, CBCARef, CJA, CPerI, CommAb, EAA, FR, HistAb, IBR, IBSS, IBZ, IPSA, PSA, PsycInfo, RI-1, RILM, RRTA, SSA, SSCI, SWA, SociolAb, WAE&RSA. *Bk. rev.:* 6-12, signed. *Aud.:* Ac.

Published by the Canadian Sociology and Anthropology Association, this journal focuses on research in sociology and anthropology, primarily in Canada. Abstracts are in English and French, with articles in one or the other. Recommended for academic libraries that support sociology, anthropology, or Canadian Studies.

5608. *Child Abuse & Neglect.* Formerly: *International Journal on Child Abuse and Neglect.* [ISSN: 0145-2134] 1977. 12x/yr. EUR 1669. Ed(s): Dr. John M. Leventhal, M. Roth. Pergamon, The Boulevard, Langford Ln, East Park, Kidlington, OX5 1GB, United Kingdom. Illus., adv. Sample. Refereed. Circ: 1500. Vol. ends: No. 12. Microform: PQC. Online: EBSCO Publishing, EBSCO Host; Gale; IngentaConnect; OhioLINK; ScienceDirect; SwetsWise Online Content. *Indexed:* ABIn, ASSIA, BrEdI, CINAHL, CJA, ECER, ERIC, EduInd, ExcerpMed, FR, H&SSA, IBR, IBSS, IBZ, IUSGP, PsycInfo, RiskAb, SFSA, SSA, SSCI, SWA, SWR&A, SociolAb, V&AA. *Aud.:* Ac, Sa.

This journal "provides an international, multidisciplinary forum on all aspects of child abuse and neglect, with special emphasis on prevention and treatment; the scope extends further to all those aspects of life which either favor or hinder child development." Articles cover the fields of psychology, psychiatry, social work, medicine, nursing, law enforcement, legislature, education, and anthropology. Recommended for academic and special libraries that support programs in social work, child psychology, criminal justice, law, medicine, or social services.

5609. *Child and Youth Care Forum: an independent journal of day and residential child and youth care practice.* Former titles (until 1991): *Child and Youth Care Quarterly;* (until 1987): *Child Care Quarterly.* [ISSN: 1053-1890] 1971. bi-m. EUR 850 print & online eds. Ed(s): Doug Magnuson, Sibylle Artz. Springer New York LLC, 233 Spring St, New York, NY 10013-1578; service-ny@springer.com; http://www.springer.com/. Illus., index, adv. Sample. Refereed. Vol. ends: Dec. Microform: PQC. Online: EBSCO Publishing, EBSCO Host; Gale; IngentaConnect; OCLC Online Computer Library Center, Inc.; OhioLINK; Ovid Technologies, Inc.; Springer LINK; SwetsWise Online Content. Reprint: PSC. *Indexed:* ABIn, ASSIA, Agr, ECER, EduInd, IMFL, PsycInfo, RILM, SFSA, SSA, SSCI, SUSA, SWR&A, V&AA. *Aud.:* Ga, Ac, Sa.

This journal is "committed to the improvement of child and youth care practice in day and residential settings." The audience is child and youth care practitioners and instructors in the field. This journal includes "material on practice, selection and training, theory and research, and professional issues." Sample article topics include homeless street youth; parental involvement in the placement of a child in foster care; and experiential learning strategies for promoting voluntarism in Hong Kong. Recommended for public and special libraries that serve child care professionals and academic libraries that support programs in social services or education.

5610. *Child Maltreatment.* [ISSN: 1077-5595] 1996. q. GBP 337. Ed(s): Steven J Ondersma. Sage Publications, Inc., 2455 Teller Rd, Thousand Oaks, CA 91320; info@sagepub.com; http://www.sagepub.com. Illus., index, adv. Sample. Refereed. Circ: 3000 Paid. Vol. ends: Nov. Reprint: PSC. *Indexed:* ASSIA, CINAHL, CJA, FR, H&SSA, IBR, IBZ, PsycInfo, RiskAb, SFSA, SSA, SSCI, SWA, SociolAb, V&AA. *Aud.:* Ac.

This journal is the official publication of the American Professional Society on the Abuse of Children, which is the nation's largest interdisciplinary child maltreatment professional organization. The journal reports current and at-issue scientific information and technical innovations in the field of child abuse and neglect, with relevance to policy, practice, and research. The audience of this journal includes "practitioners and researchers from mental health, child protection, law, law enforcement, medicine, nursing, and allied disciplines." Recommended for academic libraries that support child psychology or social work programs.

5611. *Children's Legal Rights Journal.* [ISSN: 0278-7210] 1979. q. USD 75 domestic (Students, USD 47). Ed(s): Melissa Sharstrom. Loyola University of Chicago, School of Law, 25 East Pearson St, Chicago, IL 60611; loyolachicagolaw@luc.edu; http://www.luc.edu. Illus. Sample. Refereed. Circ: 400. Vol. ends: Fall. Microform: WSH. Online: William S. Hein & Co., Inc. Reprint: WSH. *Indexed:* AgeL, CLI, ECER, ILP, LRI. *Bk. rev.:* 1-2, signed. *Aud.:* Ac, Sa.

Published in association with the National Association of Counsel for Children, this journal provides information on the law as it relates to children. It is a journal for child welfare, juvenile justice, and family law professionals. Articles provide insight into "child abuse and neglect, foster care, child custody and adoption, juvenile delinquency, medical care, mental health and mental retardation, education for the handicapped child, and students' rights." Recommended for law libraries and academic libraries that support social service or social work programs.

5612. *Chinese Sociology and Anthropology: a journal of translations.* [ISSN: 0009-4625] 1968. q. USD 912 print & online eds. Ed(s): Gregory Guldin. M.E. Sharpe, Inc., 80 Business Park Dr, Armonk, NY 10504; custserv@mesharpe.com; http://www.mesharpe.com. Illus., index, adv. Refereed. Vol. ends: Summer. Reprint: PSC. *Indexed:* AmH&L, BAS, HistAb, IBSS, SSCI, SWA, SociolAb. *Aud.:* Ac.

Calling itself "a journal of translations," this journal contains translations of articles from Chinese scholarly journals and articles published in book form. The intent of the journal is twofold: first, to make Chinese researchers more widely available to sociologists and anthropology, and second, to add a Chinese voice to global sociology and anthropology discussions. Issues are thematic and compiled by guest editors. Sample themes include social change and social inequality in China, and migrant sociology and anthropology. Recommended for academic libraries that support graduate programs in sociology and anthropology.

5613. *Contemporary Sociology: a journal of reviews.* [ISSN: 0094-3061] 1972. bi-m. USD 185 (Individuals, USD 40 member; Students, USD 25 member). Ed(s): Robert Perrucci, JoAnn Miller. American Sociological Association, 1307 New York Ave, NW, Ste 700, Washington, DC 20005-4701; http://www.umass.edu/sociol/consoc/consoc.html. Illus., index, adv. Refereed. Circ: 7200. Vol. ends: Nov. Microform: PQC. Online: EBSCO Publishing, EBSCO Host; IngentaConnect; JSTOR (Web-based Journal Archive); OCLC Online Computer Library Center, Inc.; ProQuest LLC (Ann Arbor). *Indexed:* ABS&EES, ArtHuCI, BRD, BRI, CBRI, EI, IBR, IBSS, IBZ, PSA, RI-1, RILM, SSA, SSCI, SociolAb. *Bk. rev.:* 50-60, signed. *Aud.:* Ac.

In this journal of reviews, you can find review essays, paired essays, comments on reviews, and extensive book reviews. An excellent selection tool for academic libraries.

5614. *Critical Sociology.* Formerly (until 1987): *Insurgent Sociologist.* [ISSN: 0896-9205] 1969. 4x/yr. GBP 375. Ed(s): David Fasenfest. Sage Publications Ltd., 1 Oliver's Yard, 55 City Rd, London, EC1 1SP, United Kingdom. Illus., adv. Refereed. Circ: 850. Microform: PQC. Online: Chadwyck-Healey Inc.; EBSCO Publishing, EBSCO Host; Gale; IngentaConnect; OCLC Online Computer Library Center, Inc.; OhioLINK; Springer LINK; SwetsWise Online Content. Reprint: PSC. *Indexed:* AltPI, BAS, CJA, EI, IBR, IBSS, IBZ, LeftInd, PSA, PhilInd, SSA, SWA, SociolAb. *Bk. rev.:* 4-6, signed. *Aud.:* Ac.

This journal publishes articles within the broad definition of critical or radical social science. The journal "was a by-product of the Sociology Liberation Movement, which erupted at the 1969 meetings of the American Sociological Association." Articles focus on the Marxist tradition, and post-modern, feminist, and other radical arguments. It is one of the few alternative social science journals respected in mainstream social science. Recommended for academic libraries that support sociology and political science programs.

5615. *Current Sociology.* [ISSN: 0011-3921] 1952. bi-m. GBP 510. Ed(s): Dennis Smith. Sage Publications Ltd., 1 Oliver's Yard, 55 City Rd, London, EC1 1SP, United Kingdom; info@sagepub.co.uk; http://www.sagepub.co.uk. Illus., adv. Sample. Refereed. Circ: 2000. Vol. ends: Oct. Reprint: PSC. *Indexed:* ASSIA, EI, HRA, IBR, IBSS, IBZ, IPSA, PAIS, PSA, RILM, RiskAb, SSA, SSCI, SWA, SociolAb, WAE&RSA. *Bk. rev.:* Number and length vary. *Aud.:* Ac.

This is the official journal of the International Sociological Association and has been in publication since 1952. It publishes articles with an international appeal in all areas of sociology—theories, methods, concepts, substantive research, and national/regional developments. It also reviews emerging issues; for example, a recent article is on "The Immigrant Problem." Recommended for academic libraries that support programs in sociology.

5616. *Deviant Behavior: an interdisciplinary journal.* [ISSN: 0163-9625] 1979. bi-m. GBP 478 print & online eds. Ed(s): Dr. Craig J Forsyth. Taylor & Francis Inc., 325 Chestnut St, Ste 800, Philadelphia, PA 19016; orders@taylorandfrancis.com; http://www.taylorandfrancis.com. Illus., adv. Sample. Refereed. Circ: 300. Microform: PQC. Online: EBSCO Publishing, EBSCO Host; Gale; IngentaConnect; OCLC Online Computer Library Center, Inc.; SwetsWise Online Content. Reprint: PSC. *Indexed:* AbAn, ArtHuCI, CJA, EAA, PRA, PsycInfo, RILM, RiskAb, SFSA, SSA, SSCI, SUSA, SWA, SociolAb, V&AA. *Bk. rev.:* 1-2, signed. *Aud.:* Ac.

This international and interdisciplinary journal addresses social deviance. It publishes pieces that are theoretical, descriptive, methodological, and applied. "All aspects of deviant behavior are discussed, including crime, juvenile delinquency, alcohol abuse and narcotic addiction, sexual deviance, societal reaction to handicap and disfigurement, mental illness, and socially inappropriate behavior." Recommended for academic libraries that support psychology, criminal justice, social work, or psychology programs.

5617. *Economy and Society.* [ISSN: 0308-5147] 1972. q. GBP 293 print & online eds. Ed(s): Grahame Thompson. Routledge, 4 Park Square, Milton Park, Abingdon, OX14 4RN, United Kingdom; info@routledge.co.uk; http://www.routledge.co.uk. Illus., index, adv. Sample. Refereed. Circ: 1300. Vol. ends: Nov. Microform: PQC. Online: EBSCO Publishing, EBSCO Host; Gale; IngentaConnect; OCLC Online Computer Library Center, Inc.; SwetsWise Online Content. Reprint: PSC. *Indexed:* ABIn, AltPI, AmH&L, ArtHuCI, BAS, CJA, CWI, FR, HistAb, IBR, IBSS, IBZ, IPSA, JEL, PSA, RI-1, SSA, SSCI, SWA, SociolAb. *Bk. rev.:* 1-2, signed. *Aud.:* Ac.

As an interdisciplinary journal of theory and politics, *Economy and Society* "explores the social sciences in the broadest interdisciplinary sense from sociologists, anthropologists, political scientists, legal theorists, philosophers, economists, and others." Recent articles range from topics on religious fundamentalism to the theory of money. Recommended for academic libraries that serve graduate programs in sociology, economics, or political science.

Ethnic and Racial Studies. See Ethnic Studies section.

5618. *European Journal of Social Theory.* [ISSN: 1368-4310] 1998. q. GBP 448. Ed(s): Gerard Delanty. Sage Publications Ltd., 1 Oliver's Yard, 55 City Rd, London, EC1 1SP, United Kingdom; info@sagepub.co.uk; http://www.sagepub.co.uk. Illus., index, adv. Sample. Refereed. Vol. ends: Nov. Reprint: PSC. *Indexed:* FR, IBR, IBSS, IBZ, IPSA, PSA, SSA, SociolAb. *Bk. rev.:* 2-4, signed. *Aud.:* Ac.

The objective of this journal is to make social theory relevant to the challenges that face the social sciences in the twenty-first century. The journal's concept of social theory includes critical theory; the approaches of Habermas, Bourdieu,

Touraine, Luhmann, and Giddens; neofunctionalism; postmodernism; critical realism; the sociology of knowledge; rational choice; constructivism; feminist social theory; Marxism; communitarianism; and hermeneutics. Includes articles, book reviews, and review essays. Recommended for academic libraries that support graduate programs in sociology, political science, and international studies.

5619. *European Societies.* [ISSN: 1461-6696] 1999. q. GBP 502 print & online eds. Ed(s): Claire Wallace. Routledge, 4 Park Sq, Milton Park, Abingdon, OX14 4RN, United Kingdom; info@routledge.co.uk; http://www.routledge.co.uk. Adv. Refereed. Online: EBSCO Publishing, EBSCO Host; Gale; IngentaConnect; OCLC Online Computer Library Center, Inc.; SwetsWise Online Content. Reprint: PSC. *Indexed:* CJA, IBSS, IPSA, PSA, SSCI, SWA, SociolAb. *Bk. rev.:* 4-6, signed. *Aud.:* Ac.

This journal was developed by the European Sociological Association as "an international platform for the sociological discourse on European developments." Coverage includes social theory and analysis on Europe, comparative research on Europe, and Europe from an international perspective. Recommended for libraries that support graduate programs in sociology, economics, political science, international studies, or European Studies.

5620. *European Sociological Review.* [ISSN: 0266-7215] 1985. 5x/yr. EUR 371 print or online ed. Ed(s): Hans-Peter Blossfeld. Oxford University Press, Great Clarendon St, Oxford, OX2 6DP, United Kingdom; jnl.orders@oup.co.uk; http://www.oxfordjournals.org. Illus., adv. Sample. Refereed. Circ: 750. Vol. ends: Dec. Online: Chadwyck-Healey Inc.; EBSCO Publishing, EBSCO Host; Gale; HighWire Press; IngentaConnect; JSTOR (Web-based Journal Archive); OCLC Online Computer Library Center, Inc.; OhioLINK; Oxford Journals; ProQuest LLC (Ann Arbor); SwetsWise Online Content. Reprint: PSC. *Indexed:* ASSIA, CJA, FR, IBR, IBSS, IBZ, IPSA, PSA, SSA, SSCI, SWA, SociolAb. *Bk. rev.:* 5-7, signed. *Aud.:* Ac.

This journal focuses on all fields of sociology, with a strong emphasis on western European countries. Articles range from short research notes to major reports, and there are occasional book reviews. Recent article topics include the sex wage gap in Japan and Sweden, social mobility in Finland, and community in the Netherlands. Recommended for academic libraries that support graduate programs in sociology.

5621. *Evaluation: international journal of theory, research and practice.* [ISSN: 1356-3890] 1995. q. GBP 443. Ed(s): Elliot Stern. Sage Publications Ltd., 1 Oliver's Yard, 55 City Rd, London, EC1 1SP, United Kingdom; info@sagepub.co.uk; http://www.sagepub.co.uk. Illus., index, adv. Sample. Refereed. Vol. ends: Oct. Reprint: PSC. *Indexed:* ASSIA, CJA, EAA, HRA, IBSS, PRA, PSA, PsycInfo, SSA, SociolAb. *Bk. rev.:* 1-2, signed. *Aud.:* Ac.

Published in association with the Tavistock Institute of London, this journal seeks to promote an international dialogue for academics, governmental and public organizations, and businesses. It publishes multidisciplinary, interdisciplinary, and issue-based research from across the social sciences. The journal includes occasional thematic issues and columns on news from the community. It includes book reviews in alternate issues along with speeches, addresses, debates, notes, and queries. Recommended for academic libraries with graduate programs in sociology, political science, economics, or public administration.

5622. *Evaluation Review: a journal of applied social research.* Formerly (until vol.4, Feb. 1980): *Evaluation Quarterly.* [ISSN: 0193-841X] 1977. bi-m. GBP 492. Ed(s): Richard A Berk. Sage Publications, Inc., 2455 Teller Rd, Thousand Oaks, CA 91320; info@sagepub.com; http://www.sagepub.com. Illus., index, adv. Sample. Refereed. Circ: 750 Paid. Vol. ends: Dec. Microform: PQC. Online: EBSCO Publishing, EBSCO Host; HighWire Press; OCLC Online Computer Library Center, Inc.; SAGE Publications, Inc., SAGE Journals Online; SwetsWise Online Content. Reprint: PSC. *Indexed:* AgeL, CJA, CLI, ERIC, HRA, HRIS, IBSS, LRI, PAIS, PsycInfo, SFSA, SSA, SSCI, SWR&A, SociolAb, V&AA, WAE&RSA. *Aud.:* Ac.

This journal serves as a forum for evaluation of methods used in education, public health, criminal justice, child development, mental health, social work, public administration, and environmental studies. It includes quantitative and qualitative methodological developments, and applied research issues. In addition to research articles, you will find review essays, research briefs of ongoing or completed studies, and reports on innovative applications of evaluation research techniques and concepts. There are occasional thematic issues; recent topics include "Zero Effects of Drug Prevention Programs," "Measuring Quality in Mental Health Services," and "Research Impact Assessments." Recommended for academic libraries that support graduate programs in sociology, public administration, social work, or criminal justice.

5623. *Global Social Policy: an interdisciplinary journal of public policy and social development.* [ISSN: 1468-0181] 2001. 3x/yr. GBP 274. Ed(s): Meri Koivusalo, Nicola Yeates. Sage Publications Ltd., 1 Oliver's Yard, 55 City Rd, London, EC1 1SP, United Kingdom; info@sagepub.co.uk; http://www.sagepub.co.uk. Adv. Refereed. Online: EBSCO Publishing, EBSCO Host; HighWire Press; OCLC Online Computer Library Center, Inc.; SAGE Publications, Inc., SAGE Journals Online; SwetsWise Online Content. Reprint: PSC. *Indexed:* CINAHL, IBSS, IPSA, IndIslam, JEL, PSA, SociolAb. *Bk. rev.:* 6-8, signed. *Aud.:* Ac, Sa.

The focus of this journal is twofold: first, the impact of globalization processes upon social policy and social development; and second, the impact of social policy upon globalization processes. The multidisplinary nature of this journal includes a variety of disciplines and fields of study. It serves both academic policy-makers and policy advocates. Recommended for academic and special libraries that support research in economics, sociology, social work, public administration, political science, anthropology, and criminal justice.

5624. *Group & Organization Management: an international journal.* Formerly (until Mar. 1992): *Group and Organization Studies.* [ISSN: 1059-6011] 1976. bi-m. GBP 514. Ed(s): Dorothy Forba, Alison M Konrad. Sage Publications, Inc., 2455 Teller Rd, Thousand Oaks, CA 91320; info@sagepub.com; http://www.sagepub.com. Illus., index, adv. Sample. Refereed. Circ: 600 Paid. Vol. ends: Dec. Microform: PQC. Online: CSA; EBSCO Publishing, EBSCO Host; Factiva, Inc.; Florida Center for Library Automation; Gale; HighWire Press; OCLC Online Computer Library Center, Inc.; ProQuest LLC (Ann Arbor); SAGE Publications, Inc., SAGE Journals Online; SwetsWise Online Content. Reprint: PSC. *Indexed:* ABIn, CINAHL, CommAb, ErgAb, HRA, IBSS, IMFL, PMA, PsycInfo, SFSA, SSCI, SWA, V&AA. *Aud.:* Ac, Sa.

This journal publishes articles that research and analyze organizational behavior, organization theory, business strategy, and human resources. Anything from individual behavior to organizational strategy and functioning is covered. Topics include leadership, teamwork and group processes, multi-level theory, organizational communication, strategic management, cross-cultural and international management, organizational cognition, and workplace diversity. There are occasional thematic issues, including a recent one on music at work. Recommended for academic libraries and special libraries that serve management clientele.

5625. *Group Processes & Intergroup Relations.* [ISSN: 1368-4302] 1998. q. GBP 398. Ed(s): Michael Hogg, Dominic Abrams. Sage Publications Ltd., 1 Oliver's Yard, 55 City Rd, London, EC1 1SP, United Kingdom; info@sagepub.co.uk; http://www.sagepub.co.uk. Adv. Refereed. Circ: 900. Reprint: PSC. *Indexed:* ABIn, CJA, CommAb, FR, IBSS, PsycInfo, SSA, SSCI, SWR&A, SociolAb. *Aud.:* Ac.

This journal is for social psychologists and researchers interested in group processes and intergroup relations. Some of the areas covered include prejudice, discrimination, stereotyping, social categorization, minority and majority influence, conformity, group decision-making, leadership, group structure, group socialization, bargaining and negotiation, intergroup conflict and cooperation, collective action and cognition, collective self and identity, social identity, language and identity, ethnic and cultural relations, and social dilemmas. Recommended for academic libraries that support sociology and psychology programs.

5626. *Human Relations: towards the integration of the social sciences.* [ISSN: 0018-7267] 1947. m. GBP 941. Ed(s): Paul Willman. Sage Publications Ltd., 1 Oliver's Yard, 55 City Rd, London, EC1 1SP, United Kingdom; info@sagepub.co.uk; http://www.sagepub.co.uk. Illus., index, adv. Sample. Refereed. Circ: 2000. Vol. ends: Dec. Microform: PQC. Online: CSA; EBSCO Publishing, EBSCO Host; Gale; HighWire Press; IngentaConnect; Northern Light Technology, Inc.; OCLC Online Computer Library Center, Inc.; OhioLINK; ProQuest LLC (Ann Arbor); SAGE Publications, Inc., SAGE Journals Online; Springer LINK; SwetsWise Online Content. Reprint: PSC. *Indexed:* ABIn, AICP, ASSIA, AbAn, AgeL, ArtHuCI, BPI, CINAHL, CJA, CommAb, EAA, ErgAb, FR, HRA, IBR, IBSS, IBZ, IMFL, IndIslam, PAIS, PRA, PSA, PsycInfo, RILM, SSA, SSCI, SWA, SociolAb, V&AA. *Bk. rev.:* 1-2, signed. *Aud.:* Ac.

The focus of this journal is on the analysis of work, organizations, and management. Scholars in management, psychology, sociology, politics, anthropology, and economics examine issues in a work environment to establish a link between theory and practice. This link translates knowledge about human problems into prospects for social action and creative policy-making. Recommended for academic libraries that support graduate programs in social sciences.

5627. *International Journal of Comparative Sociology.* [ISSN: 0020-7152] 1960. bi-m. GBP 380. Ed(s): Jeffrey Kentor. Sage Publications Ltd., 1 Oliver's Yard, 55 City Rd, London, EC1 1SP, United Kingdom; info@sagepub.co.uk; http://www.sagepub.co.uk. Illus., adv. Refereed. Vol. ends: Nov. Microform: SWZ. Online: Chadwyck-Healey Inc.; EBSCO Publishing, EBSCO Host; Gale; HighWire Press; Northern Light Technology, Inc.; OCLC Online Computer Library Center, Inc.; SAGE Publications, Inc., SAGE Journals Online; SwetsWise Online Content. Reprint: PSC. *Indexed:* ABCPolSci, AICP, ASSIA, AgeL, AmH&L, ArtHuCI, BAS, CJA, CommAb, FR, HistAb, IBR, IBSS, IBZ, IPSA, IndIslam, PSA, RI-1, SSA, SSCI, SWA, SociolAb. *Aud.:* Ac.

This journal not only publishes articles in sociology but also includes research from political science, geography, economics, anthropology, and business. The true interdisciplinary nature of this journal is evident from a recent thematic issue on minorities, racism, culture, and scholarship. It has included articles from a political, social, and historical point of view. Recommended for academic libraries that support anthropology, sociology, or political science programs.

5628. *International Journal of the Sociology of Law.* Formerly (until vol.7, 1979): *International Journal of Criminology and Penology.* [ISSN: 0194-6595] 1972. 4x/yr. EUR 432. Ed(s): J Carrier, S Savage. Academic Press, Harcourt Pl, 32 Jamestown Rd, London, NW1 7BY, United Kingdom; apsubs@acad.com; http://www.elsevier.com/. Illus., index, adv. Sample. Refereed. Online: EBSCO Publishing, EBSCO Host; Gale; IngentaConnect; OCLC Online Computer Library Center, Inc.; OhioLINK; ScienceDirect; SwetsWise Online Content. *Indexed:* ASSIA, CJA, CJPI, CLI, FR, IBR, IBSS, IBZ, ILP, LRI, PSA, RiskAb, SSA, SSCI, SociolAb. *Bk. rev.:* 4-7, signed. *Aud.:* Ac, Sa.

This journal focuses on the social context and social implications of law, law enforcement, and the legal process. Sample topics include equal opportunities and anti-discrimination law, police powers and practices, the "internationaliza-tion" of law, grievance procedures, pre-trial processes and the prosecution process, and immigration law. Recommended for special libraries and academic libraries that support doctoral programs in sociology, political science, and law.

5629. *International Sociology.* [ISSN: 0268-5809] 1986. bi-m. GBP 393. Ed(s): Jeanne de Bruijn, Gerhard van de Bunt. Sage Publications Ltd., 1 Oliver's Yard, 55 City Rd, London, EC1 1SP, United Kingdom; info@sagepub.co.uk; http://www.sagepub.co.uk. Illus., index, adv. Sample. Refereed. Circ: 3900. Vol. ends: Dec. Online: CSA; EBSCO Publishing, EBSCO Host; HighWire Press; OCLC Online Computer Library Center, Inc.; OhioLINK; SAGE Publications, Inc., SAGE Journals Online; SwetsWise Online Content. Reprint: PSC. *Indexed:* ABS&EES, ASSIA, BAS, CJA, FR, HRA, IBR, IBSS, IBZ, IPSA, IndIslam, PAIS, PSA, RILM, RiskAb, SCI, SFSA, SSA, SSCI, SociolAb. *Bk. rev.:* 2-4, signed. *Aud.:* Ac.

This journal publishes studies in social organization, societal change, and comparative sociology. One issue a year includes an extensive section on book reviews. Articles are published in English; abstracts are in French and Spanish. Recommended for academic libraries that support graduate programs in sociology.

5630. *Journal of Classical Sociology.* [ISSN: 1468-795X] 2001. q. GBP 433. Ed(s): John O'Neill, Bryan Turner. Sage Publications Ltd., 1 Oliver's Yard, 55 City Rd, London, EC1 1SP, United Kingdom; info@sagepub.co.uk; http://www.sagepub.co.uk. Adv. Refereed. Online: EBSCO Publishing, EBSCO Host; HighWire Press; OCLC Online Computer Library Center, Inc.; SAGE Publications, Inc., SAGE Journals Online; SwetsWise Online Content. Reprint: PSC. *Indexed:* FR, IBR, IBSS, IBZ, IPSA, PSA, PsycInfo, SociolAb. *Aud.:* Ac.

As can be inferred from its name, this journal focuses on the origins of sociology and "demonstrates how the classical tradition renews the sociological imagination in the present day." It discusses early social theory from the Enlightenment Period through the twenty-first century. Think Comte, Marx, Durkheim, Weber, Simmel, Veblen, Pareto, and Mosca. Recommended for academic libraries that support graduate programs in sociology.

Journal of Comparative Family Studies. See Family section.

Journal of Divorce & Remarriage. See Marriage and Divorce section.

5631. *Journal of European Social Policy.* [ISSN: 0958-9287] 1991. q. GBP 419. Ed(s): Emma Carmel. Sage Publications Ltd., 1 Oliver's Yard, 55 City Rd, London, EC1 1SP, United Kingdom; info@sagepub.co.uk; http://www.sagepub.co.uk. Adv. Refereed. Circ: 400. Reprint: PSC. *Indexed:* ASSIA, AgeL, CINAHL, CJA, HRA, IBSS, IPSA, PRA, PSA, SFSA, SSA, SSCI, SWA, SociolAb. *Bk. rev.:* 4-6, signed. *Aud.:* Ac.

The focus of this journal is on European social policy issues and developments. In addition to research articles, it contains shorter research notes, book reviews, review essays, and a digest section that serves as a guide to the latest European legislation and research. Article topics include aging, pensions and Social Security, poverty and social exclusion, education, training and labor market policies, family policies, health and social care services, gender, migration, privatization, and Europeanization. Recommended for academic libraries that support programs in sociology, public administration, or European Studies.

Journal of Family Issues. See Family section.

5632. *Journal of Historical Sociology.* [ISSN: 0952-1909] 1988. q. GBP 348 print & online eds. Ed(s): Yoke-Sum Wong, Derek Sayer. Blackwell Publishing Ltd., 9600 Garsington Rd, Oxford, OX4 2ZG, United Kingdom; customerservices@blackwellpublishing.com; http://www.blackwellpublishing.com. Refereed. Online: Blackwell Synergy; EBSCO Publishing, EBSCO Host; Gale; IngentaConnect; OCLC Online Computer Library Center, Inc.; OhioLINK; SwetsWise Online Content. Reprint: PSC. *Indexed:* AICP, AmH&L, AmHI, ApEcolAb, ArtHuCI, BrHumI, CJA, HistAb, IBR, IBSS, IBZ, PSA, PsycInfo, SSA, SSCI, SWA, SociolAb. *Aud.:* Ac.

Founded on the conviction that historical and social studies have a common subject matter, this journal is truly interdisciplinary. It is edited by historians, anthropologists, geographers, and sociologists. It contains research articles, reviews essays, and commentary aimed to provoke discussion and debate. Recommended for academic libraries that support programs in the social sciences.

Journal of Homosexuality. See Gay, Lesbian, Bisexual, and Transgender section.

Journal of Human Resources. See Labor and Industrial Relations section.

5633. *Journal of Leisure Research.* [ISSN: 0022-2216] 1968. q. USD 60 (Members, USD 25; Non-members, UZS 40). Ed(s): David Scott. National Recreation and Park Association, 22377 Belmont Ridge Rd, Ashburn, VA 20148-4501. Illus., index, adv. Refereed. Microform: PQC. Online: EBSCO Publishing, EBSCO Host; Florida Center for Library Automation; Gale; Northern Light Technology, Inc.; OCLC Online Computer Library Center, Inc.; ProQuest K-12 Learning Solutions; ProQuest LLC (Ann Arbor); H.W. Wilson. Reprint: PSC. *Indexed:* ABIn, ASSIA, AgeL, Agr, CABA, CJA, CommAb, ForAb, H&SSA, H&TI, IBSS, IMFL, PEI, PollutAb, PsycInfo, RRTA, RiskAb, S&F, SD, SSCI, WAE&RSA. *Bk. rev.:* Number and length vary. *Aud.:* Ac.

Published by the National Recreation and Park Association in cooperation with Texas A&M University, this journal publishes empirical reports and review papers as well as theoretical and methodological articles in the field of leisure studies. "Studies that do not clearly focus on leisure or recreation are not suitable for this journal." It includes commentaries, rejoinders, and some book reviews. Recommended for academic libraries that serve programs in sociology and leisure studies.

Journal of Marriage and Family. See Family section.

5634. *Journal of Mathematical Sociology.* [ISSN: 0022-250X] 1971. q. GBP 1162 print & online eds. Ed(s): Patrick Doreian. Taylor & Francis Inc., 325 Chestnut St, Ste 800, Philadelphia, PA 19016; orders@taylorandfrancis.com; http://www.taylorandfrancis.com. Illus., index, adv. Sample. Refereed. Online: EBSCO Publishing, EBSCO Host; Gale; IngentaConnect; OCLC Online Computer Library Center, Inc.; SwetsWise Online Content. Reprint: PSC. *Indexed:* CJA, FR, IBSS, MathR, SCI, SSA, SSCI, SociolAb. *Aud.:* Ac.

As can be inferred from the title, this journal publishes articles in all areas of mathematical sociology, as well as papers of mutual interest to social and behavioral scientists. It is truly an interdisciplinary journal in that it accepts papers by non–social scientists that emphasize connections between sociology and other disciplines. Most articles focus on a mathematical understanding of emergent complex social structures rather than individual behavior. There are occasional thematic issues, one recently on "Ethnic Preferences, Social Distance Dynamics, and Residential Segregation." Recommended for academic libraries that serve doctoral programs in sociology.

5635. *The Journal of Peasant Studies.* [ISSN: 0306-6150] 1973. q. GBP 331 print & online eds. Ed(s): Tom Brass. Routledge, 4 Park Sq, Milton Park, Abingdon, OX14 4RN, United Kingdom; info@routledge.co.uk; http://www.routledge.co.uk. Illus., index, adv. Sample. Refereed. Microform: PQC. Online: EBSCO Publishing, EBSCO Host; Gale; IngentaConnect; OCLC Online Computer Library Center, Inc.; SwetsWise Online Content. Reprint: PSC. *Indexed:* AICP, AbAn, AmH&L, AmHI, AnthLit, ArtHuCI, BAS, BrHumI, CABA, DSA, EI, FPA, ForAb, HistAb, HortAb, IBR, IBSS, IBZ, IPSA, PAIS, PSA, RRTA, S&F, SSA, SSCI, SWA, SociolAb, WAE&RSA. *Bk. rev.:* 1-2, signed. *Aud.:* Ac.

This journal focuses on the political economy of agrarian change. It considers peasants within the larger context in which they live and examines the role they play in political, economic, and social transformation. Articles are both theoretical and empirical in a multidisciplinary context. Not only will sociologists find articles of interest but so will economists, historians, anthropologists, political scientists, geographers, and literary scholars. Each issue includes a debate article and book reviews. Recommended for academic libraries that serve doctoral programs in sociology, economics, anthropology, history, or political science.

5636. *Journal of Political and Military Sociology.* [ISSN: 0047-2697] 1973. s-a. USD 48 (Individuals, USD 35). Ed(s): George A Kourvetaris. Northern Illinois University, Department of Sociology, Dekalb, IL 60115; ykourvet@niu.edu. Illus., index, adv. Sample. Refereed. Circ: 2000. Microform: PQC. Online: EBSCO Publishing, EBSCO Host; OCLC Online Computer Library Center, Inc.; ProQuest LLC (Ann Arbor). *Indexed:* ABCPolSci, ABS&EES, AUNI, AmH&L, BAS, CJA, FR, HRA, HistAb, IBR, IBZ, IPSA, PAIS, PRA, PSA, RI-1, RILM, SSA, SSCI, SociolAb. *Bk. rev.:* 8-10, signed. *Aud.:* Ac.

Founded in 1973 by Northern Illinois University, this journal deals with all areas of political and military sociology. Sample topics include ruling classes, revolution, coup d'etats, dictatorship, espionage, geopolitics, nationalism, guerrillas, extremist movements, military and paramilitary organizations, political assassinations, violence, terrorism, genocide and mass murder, propaganda, ideologies, national security, alternatives to militarism, and multinational corporations. Recommended for academic libraries that support graduate programs in sociology, political science, or military science.

5637. *Journal of Rural Studies.* [ISSN: 0743-0167] 1985. 4x/yr. EUR 733. Ed(s): Paul Cloke. Pergamon, The Boulevard, Langford Ln, East Park, Kidlington, OX5 1GB, United Kingdom. Illus., index, adv. Sample. Refereed. Vol. ends: Oct. Microform: PQC. Online: EBSCO Publishing, EBSCO Host; Gale; IngentaConnect; OhioLINK; ScienceDirect; SwetsWise Online Content. *Indexed:* AgeL, Agr, ArtHuCI, CABA, CJA, DSA, ERIC, EnvAb, FPA, ForAb, HortAb, IBSS, IndVet, PAIS, PSA, RRTA, RiskAb, S&F, SSA, SSCI, SWA, SociolAb, VB, WAE&RSA. *Bk. rev.:* 10-15, signed. *Aud.:* Ac.

Articles in this journal focus on rural social issues in demography, housing, employment, transport, land use, recreation, agriculture, and conservation. Emphasis is on planning policy and management. Recommended for academic libraries that support doctoral programs in sociology.

5638. *Journal of Sex Research.* Formerly (until 196?): *Advances in Sex Research.* [ISSN: 0022-4499] 1965. q. GBP 173 print & online eds. Ed(s): John D DeLamater. Lawrence Erlbaum Associates, Inc., 325 Chestnut St, Ste. 800, Philadelphia, PA 19106; journals@erlbaum.com; http://www.leaonline.com. Illus., adv. Refereed. Circ: 1750. Vol. ends: Nov. Microform: PQC. Online: EBSCO Publishing, EBSCO Host; Florida Center for Library Automation; Gale; Northern Light Technology, Inc.; OCLC Online Computer Library Center, Inc.; ProQuest LLC (Ann Arbor); H.W. Wilson. Reprint: PSC. *Indexed:* ASSIA, AbAn, AgeL, ArtHuCI, BAS, CJA, CWI, CommAb, ExcerpMed, IBR, IBZ, IMFL, PhilInd, PsycInfo, SFSA, SSA, SSCI, SWA, SWR&A, SociolAb, V&AA. *Bk. rev.:* 4-6, signed. *Aud.:* Ac.

Published by the Society of the Scientific Study of Sexuality, this journal is "designed to stimulate research and to promote an interdisciplinary understanding in contemporary sexual science." It publishes a wide range of articles including methodological and empirical reports, theoretical essays, literature reviews, and historical essays. Recent article topics include body image and sexual response changes; objectification of women in pornographic movies; and alcohol and condom use among college males of differing ethnic backgrounds. Recommended for academic and research libraries.

5639. *Journal of Social Issues.* [ISSN: 0022-4537] 1944. q. GBP 501 print & online eds. Ed(s): Rick H Hoyle. Blackwell Publishing, Inc., Commerce Place, 350 Main St, Malden, MA 02148; customerservices@ blackwellpublishing.com; http://www.blackwellpublishing.com. Illus., adv. Sample. Refereed. Vol. ends: Winter. Microform: PMC; PQC. Online: Blackwell Synergy; EBSCO Publishing, EBSCO Host; Florida Center for Library Automation; Gale; IngentaConnect; OCLC Online Computer Library Center, Inc.; OhioLINK; SwetsWise Online Content. Reprint: PSC. *Indexed:* ABCPolSci, ASSIA, AbAn, AgeL, AmH&L, ApEcolAb, BAS, CJA, CommAb, EAA, HistAb, IBR, IBSS, IBZ, IMFL, IPSA, LRI, PAIS, PRA, PSA, PsycInfo, RI-1, RiskAb, SFSA, SSA, SSCI, SUSA, SWA, SWR&A, SociolAb. *Aud.:* Ga, Ac.

Published on behalf of the Society for the Psychological Study of Social Issues, this journal connects behavioral and social science theory, empirical evidence, and practice to human and social problems. Each issue is thematic, with recent issues on poverty, housing and health, youth and violence, and the impact of social class on education. Recommended for academic libraries and larger public libraries.

New Statesman. See News and Opinion section.

5640. *Nonprofit and Voluntary Sector Quarterly.* Formerly (until 1988): *Journal of Voluntary Action Research.* [ISSN: 0899-7640] 1972. q. GBP 265. Ed(s): Dwight Burlingame, Wolfgang Bielefeld. Sage Publications, Inc., 2455 Teller Rd, Thousand Oaks, CA 91320; info@sagepub.com; http://www.sagepub.com. Illus., index, adv. Sample. Refereed. Circ: 800. Vol. ends: Dec. Microform: PQC. Online: CSA; EBSCO Publishing, EBSCO Host; HighWire Press; OCLC Online Computer Library Center, Inc.; SAGE Publications, Inc., SAGE Journals Online; SwetsWise Online Content. Reprint: PSC. *Indexed:* ABIn, ASG, ASSIA, AgeL, C&ISA, CerAb, FR, HRA, IAA, IBR, IBZ, IPSA, JEL, PRA, PSA, RiskAb, SSA, SSCI, SUSA, SociolAb, V&AA. *Bk. rev.:* 4-6, signed. *Aud.:* Ga, Ac.

As the nonprofit sector grows, it impacts research, social policy, and social action. This journal serves as a medium to investigate the impact that the nonprofit sector has on society. It attempts to enhance the knowledge of nonprofit organizations, philanthropy, and voluntarism. Some of the subject areas included are anthropology, arts and humanities, education, health, history, psychology, public administration, religious studies, social work, sociology, and urban affairs. Recommended for academic libraries that support programs in sociology or social work and for larger public libraries.

5641. *Qualitative Sociology.* [ISSN: 0162-0436] 1978. q. EUR 935 print & online eds. Ed(s): Javier Auyero. Springer New York LLC, 233 Spring St, New York, NY 10013-1578; service-ny@springer.com; http://www.springer.com/. Illus., index, adv. Sample. Refereed. Microform: PQC. Online: EBSCO Publishing, EBSCO Host; Gale; IngentaConnect; OCLC Online Computer Library Center, Inc.; OhioLINK; Ovid Technologies, Inc.; Springer LINK; SwetsWise Online Content. Reprint: PSC. *Indexed:* AbAn, CJA, FR, IBR, IBSS, IBZ, IMFL, PSA, RILM, SSA, SWA, SWR&A, SociolAb. *Bk. rev.:* 6-8, signed. *Aud.:* Ac.

As can be inferred from its name, this journal contains research on the qualitative interpretation and analysis of social life. In other words, research articles using interviewing, participant observation, ethnography, historical analysis, and content analysis are included. There are occasional thematic issues; most recently, two issues focus on political ethnography. Recommended for academic libraries that support programs in sociology.

5642. *Quality and Quantity: international journal of methodology.* [ISSN: 0033-5177] 1967. 6x/yr. EUR 1025 print & online eds. Ed(s): Vittorio Capecchi. Springer Netherlands, Van Godewijckstraat 30, Dordrecht, 3311 GX, Netherlands; http://www.springeronline.com. Illus., adv. Sample. Refereed. Microform: PQC. Online: EBSCO Publishing, EBSCO Host; Gale; IngentaConnect; OCLC Online Computer Library Center, Inc.; OhioLINK; Springer LINK; SwetsWise Online Content. Reprint: PSC. *Indexed:* ArtHuCI, FR, IBR, IBSS, IBZ, PSA, PsycInfo, SCI, SSA, SSCI, SociolAb. *Aud.:* Ac.

This international journal "publishes papers on models of classification, methods for constructing typologies, neural networks and fuzzy sets for social research, and mathematical models applied to social mobility." Articles correlate the fields of mathematics and statistics with the social sciences. Recommended for academic libraries that support doctoral programs in sociology.

5643. *Rural Sociology: devoted to scientific study of rural and community life.* [ISSN: 0036-0112] 1936. q. USD 125 (Free to members). Ed(s): Joachim Singelmann. Rural Sociological Society, 104 Gentry Hall, University of Missouri, Columbia, MO 65211-7040; ruralsoc@ missouri.edu; http://www.ruralsociology.org. Illus., index, adv. Refereed. Circ: 3000 Controlled. Vol. ends: Winter. Microform: PQC. Online: EBSCO Publishing, EBSCO Host; IngentaConnect; Northern Light Technology, Inc.; OCLC Online Computer Library Center, Inc.; ProQuest K-12 Learning Solutions; ProQuest LLC (Ann Arbor). *Indexed:* ABS&EES, ASSIA, AbAn, AgeL, Agr, AmH&L, ArtHuCI, B&AI, CABA, CJA, DSA, EI, ERIC, FPA, FR, ForAb, HistAb, HortAb, IBR, IBSS, IBZ, IMFL, IPSA, IndVet, PAIS, PSA, RI-1, RRTA, RiskAb, S&F, SCI, SSA, SSCI, SUSA, SWA, SWR&A, SociolAb, VB, WAE&RSA. *Bk. rev.:* 4-6, signed. *Aud.:* Ac.

As the official journal of the Rural Sociological Society, this journal "reaches an international audience of social scientists, policy makers, and agency professionals concerned with rural people, places, and problems." Articles focus on rural development, environmental impacts, community revitalization and rural demographic changes, the structure of food and agricultural production, and rural–urban linkages. Recommended for academic libraries that serve graduate programs in sociology, agriculture, or environmental studies.

5644. *Sex Roles.* [ISSN: 0360-0025] 1975. s-m. EUR 1372 print & online eds. Ed(s): Joan C Chrisler. Springer New York LLC, 233 Spring St, New York, NY 10013-1578; service-ny@springer.com; http://www.springer.com/. Illus., index, adv. Sample. Refereed. Vol. ends: Jul/Dec. Microform: PQC. Online: Chadwyck-Healey Inc.; EBSCO Publishing, EBSCO Host; Florida Center for Library Automation; Gale; IngentaConnect; OCLC Online Computer Library Center, Inc.; OhioLINK; Ovid Technologies, Inc.; ProQuest LLC (Ann Arbor); Springer LINK; SwetsWise Online Content. Reprint: PSC. *Indexed:* ABS&EES, ASSIA, AbAn, AgeL, AnthLit, ArtHuCI, CJA, CommAb, ExcerpMed, FR, FemPer, HEA, IBR, IBZ, IMFL, L&LBA, PSA, PsycInfo, RILM, SFSA, SSA, SSCI, SWA, SWR&A, SociolAb, WSA. *Bk. rev.:* 2-4, signed. *Aud.:* Ac.

From a feminist perspective, this journal examines gender role socialization, gendered perceptions and behaviors, and gender stereotypes. Recent article themes include rape scripts, sexual orientation, and self-objectification. Book reviews that address gender-related topics are included. This is a heavily used journal among undergraduate researchers. A must-have for academic libraries.

Sexualities. See Sexuality section.

5645. *Simulation & Gaming: an international journal of theory, design and research.* Formerly (until 1990): *Simulation and Games.* [ISSN: 1046-8781] 1970. q. GBP 398. Ed(s): David Crookall. Sage Publications, Inc., 2455 Teller Rd, Thousand Oaks, CA 91320; info@sagepub.com; http://www.sagepub.com. Illus., index, adv. Sample. Refereed. Circ: 500 Paid. Vol. ends: Dec. Microform: PQC. Online: CSA; EBSCO Publishing, EBSCO Host; Factiva, Inc.; Gale; HighWire Press; Northern Light Technology, Inc.; OCLC Online Computer Library Center, Inc.; SAGE Publications, Inc., SAGE Journals Online; SwetsWise Online Content. Reprint: PSC. *Indexed:* ABCPolSci, ABIn, ABS&EES, AgeL, BRI, CommAb, CompLI, CompR, EAA, HRA, IBSS, IPSA, LRI, MRD, PAIS, PRA, PSA, PsycInfo, RiskAb, SSA, SSCI, SociolAb. *Aud.:* Ac.

In publication for more than three and a half decades, this journal explores the development of simulation/gaming methodologies used in education, training, consultation, and research. In recent years it has expanded its scope to include computer- and Internet-mediated simulation, virtual reality, educational games, video games, and active and experiential learning. Recommended for academic libraries that support programs in sociology, business, information technology, information systems, and instructional design.

5646. *Social Compass: international review of sociology of religion.* [ISSN: 0037-7686] 1953. q. GBP 278. Ed(s): Albert Bastenier. Sage Publications Ltd., 1 Oliver's Yard, 55 City Rd, London, EC1 1SP, United Kingdom; info@sagepub.co.uk; http://www.sagepub.co.uk. Illus., index, adv. Sample. Refereed. Vol. ends: Dec. Reprint: PSC. *Indexed:* ASSIA, ArtHuCI, BAS, CJPI, CommAb, EI, FR, IBR, IBSS, IBZ, IPSA, NTA, PSA, R&TA, RI-1, SSA, SSCI, SociolAb. *Bk. rev.:* 1-2, signed. *Aud.:* Ac.

This journal provides a forum for the sociology of religion. Each thematic issue offers "in-depth coverage of a key area of current social research on religion in society." Recent themes include: religion, culture and identity, and the state reconstruction of the religious field. Articles are in either French or English, with abstracts in both languages. Recommended for academic libraries that serve graduate programs in religious studies or sociology.

5647. *Social Forces.* Formerly (until 1925): *The Journal of Social Forces.* [ISSN: 0037-7732] 1922. q. USD 250 OECD (Individuals, USD 70). Ed(s): Peter Uhlenberg. University of North Carolina Press, 116 S. Boundary St, Chapel Hill, NC 27514-3808; uncpress_journals@unc.edu; http://www.uncpress.unc.edu. Illus., index, adv. Refereed. Circ: 3000 Paid and controlled. Vol. ends: Jun. Microform: MIM; PMC; PQC. Online: Chadwyck-Healey Inc.; EBSCO Publishing, EBSCO Host; Florida Center for Library Automation; Gale; William S. Hein & Co., Inc.;

JSTOR (Web-based Journal Archive); Northern Light Technology, Inc.; OCLC Online Computer Library Center, Inc.; OhioLINK; Project MUSE; ProQuest K-12 Learning Solutions; ProQuest LLC (Ann Arbor); SwetsWise Online Content; H.W. Wilson. Reprint: PSC; WSH. *Indexed:* ABCPolSci, ABS&EES, ASSIA, AbAn, AgeL, AmH&L, ArtHuCI, BAS, BRI, CBRI, CJA, CommAb, EAA, EI, ERIC, FR, H&SSA, HRA, HistAb, IBR, IBSS, IBZ, IMFL, IPSA, PAIS, PRA, PSA, PsycInfo, RI-1, RILM, RRTA, RiskAb, SFSA, SSA, SSCI, SUSA, SWA, SWR&A, SociolAb, V&AA. *Bk. rev.:* 25-30, signed. *Aud.:* Ga, Ac.

Founded in 1922 and associated with the Southern Sociological Society, this publication is considered one of the top social research journals. The focus is on sociological inquiry, but the journal also "explores realms in social psychology, anthropology, political science, history, and economics." It includes an extensive book review section—great for collection development purposes. A must-have for academic libraries and for larger public libraries.

5648. *Social Indicators Research: an international and interdisciplinary journal for quality-of-life measurement.* [ISSN: 0303-8300] 1974. 15x/yr. EUR 2150 print & online eds. Ed(s): Alex C Michalos. Springer Netherlands, Van Godewijckstraat 30, Dordrecht, 3311 GX, Netherlands; http://www.springeronline.com. Illus., index, adv. Sample. Refereed. Vol. ends: Dec. Microform: PQC. Online: Chadwyck-Healey Inc.; EBSCO Publishing, EBSCO Host; Gale; IngentaConnect; OCLC Online Computer Library Center, Inc.; OhioLINK; Ovid Technologies, Inc.; ProQuest LLC (Ann Arbor); Springer LINK; SwetsWise Online Content. Reprint: PSC. *Indexed:* ABIn, ASSIA, AgeL, BAS, CABA, CJA, CommAb, EI, ERIC, FR, ForAb, FutSurv, IBR, IBSS, IBZ, IMFL, PAIS, PSA, PhilInd, PsycInfo, RRTA, RiskAb, S&F, SSA, SSCI, SUSA, SWA, SWR&A, SociolAb, WAE&RSA. *Bk. rev.:* 2-3, signed. *Aud.:* Ac.

The purpose of this journal is to publish research that deals with problems related to the measurement of all aspects of the quality of life. Empirical, philosophical, and methodological studies examine the individual, public, and private organizations and municipal, country, regional, national, and international systems. Sample topics include suicide, poverty, income satisfaction, and hunger. Recommended for academic libraries that support graduate programs in political and social sciences.

5649. *Social Networks.* [ISSN: 0378-8733] 1979. 4x/yr. EUR 450. Ed(s): Ronald L Breiger, Linton C Freeman. Elsevier BV, North-Holland, Sara Burgerhartstraat 25, Amsterdam, 1055 KV, Netherlands; nlinfo-f@elsevier.nl; http://www.elsevier.nl. Illus., index, adv. Sample. Refereed. Microform: PQC. Online: EBSCO Publishing, EBSCO Host; Gale; IngentaConnect; OhioLINK; ScienceDirect; SwetsWise Online Content. *Indexed:* AICP, AgeL, AnthLit, CJA, FR, HRA, IBSS, MathR, PsycInfo, SCI, SSA, SSCI, SUSA, SociolAb. *Aud.:* Ac.

Published in association with The International Network for Social Network Analysis, this journal "provides a common forum for representatives of anthropology, sociology, history, social psychology, political science, human geography, biology, economics, and communications science who share an interest in the study of the structure of human relations and associations that may be expressed in network form." Recommended for academic libraries that support graduate programs in the social sciences.

Social Policy. See Labor and Industrial Relations section.

5650. *Social Problems.* [ISSN: 0037-7791] 1953. q. USD 175 print & online eds. USD 48 newsstand/cover. Ed(s): Amy Wharton. University of California Press, Journals Division, 2000 Center St, Ste 303, Berkeley, CA 94704-1223; journals@ucpress.edu; http://www.ucpress.edu/journals. Illus., index, adv. Sample. Refereed. Circ: 3747 Paid. Microform: PQC. Online: EBSCO Publishing, EBSCO Host; Florida Center for Library Automation; Gale; JSTOR (Web-based Journal Archive); Northern Light Technology, Inc.; OCLC Online Computer Library Center, Inc.; ProQuest LLC (Ann Arbor); SwetsWise Online Content. Reprint: WSH. *Indexed:* ABS&EES, ASSIA, AgeL, AmH&L, ArtHuCI, BAS, CJA, CJPI, CommAb, ExcerpMed, FR, FutSurv, HistAb, IBR, IBSS, IBZ, IPSA, LRI, PAIS, PRA, PSA, PsycInfo, RI-1, RiskAb, SFSA, SSA, SSCI, SWA, SWR&A, SociolAb, V&AA. *Aud.:* Ga, Ac.

As the official publication of the Society for the Study of Social Problems, this journal is a staple in sociology. There are occasional thematic issues; one recently was on feminism and sociology. Sample topics include income digital divide; stigma and sexual isolation of people with mental illness; and affirmative action and higher education. A must-have for academic and research libraries.

5651. *Social Psychology Quarterly.* Former titles (until 1978): *Social Psychology;* (until 1977): *Sociometry.* [ISSN: 0190-2725] 1937. q. USD 155 (Members, USD 30). Ed(s): Spencer Cahill. American Sociological Association, 1307 New York Ave, NW, Ste 700, Washington, DC 20005-4701; publications@asanet.org; http://www.lemoyne.edu. Illus., adv. Refereed. Circ: 3500 Paid. Vol. ends: Dec. Microform: MIM; PQC. Online: EBSCO Publishing, EBSCO Host; Gale; IngentaConnect; JSTOR (Web-based Journal Archive); OCLC Online Computer Library Center, Inc.; ProQuest K-12 Learning Solutions; ProQuest LLC (Ann Arbor). *Indexed:* ABS&EES, ASSIA, AgeL, CJA, EAA, FR, IBR, IBSS, IBZ, IMFL, IPSA, L&LBA, MLA-IB, PSA, PsycInfo, RiskAb, SSA, SSCI, SWA, SociolAb. *Aud.:* Ac.

The aim of this journal is to publish "theoretical and empirical articles on the link between the individual and society." It includes articles on the relationship between individuals to one another, to groups, and to collectivities and institutions. Recent articles have focused on inter-ethnic identity and social networking. Recommended for academic libraries that serve programs in the social sciences.

5652. *Social Research: an international quarterly of the social sciences.* [ISSN: 0037-783X] 1934. q. USD 120 print & online eds. (Individuals, USD 40 print & online eds.). Ed(s): Arien Mack. Graduate Faculty Philosophy Journal, Dept of Philosophy, The New School for Social Research, New York, NY 10003. Illus., adv. Refereed. Circ: 3000. Vol. ends: Dec. Microform: PMC; PQC. Online: Chadwyck-Healey Inc.; EBSCO Publishing, EBSCO Host; Florida Center for Library Automation; Gale; OCLC Online Computer Library Center, Inc.; ProQuest K-12 Learning Solutions; ProQuest LLC (Ann Arbor); H.W. Wilson. *Indexed:* ABCPolSci, ABS&EES, ASSIA, AgeL, AmH&L, ArtHuCI, BAS, BRI, CBRI, CJA, CommAb, EI, FR, HistAb, IBR, IBSS, IBZ, IPB, IPSA, IndIslam, JEL, LRI, MLA-IB, PAIS, PRA, PSA, PhilInd, SSA, SociolAb. *Aud.:* Ac.

This journal has been published since 1934 by the New School for Social Research. Articles cover the social sciences and humanities, making it truly interdisciplinary; however, many articles have a strong political tone. Most issues are thematic; recent themes include "Busyness," "China in Transition," and "South Africa: the Second Decade." In 1988, *Social Research* began an annual series devoted to Eastern and Central Europe that attempts "to track and examine major manifestations of the transitions to democracy and to market economies and examine problems faced by both Western and Eastern countries." Recommended for academic libraries that support graduate programs in sociology or political science.

5653. *Social Science Computer Review.* Former titles (until 1987): *Social Science Microcomputer Review;* (until 1985): *Social Science Micro Review;* Incorporates: *Computers and the Social Sciences.* [ISSN: 0894-4393] 1983. q. GBP 355. Ed(s): G David Garson. Sage Publications, Inc., 2455 Teller Rd, Thousand Oaks, CA 91320; info@sagepub.com; http://www.sagepub.com. Illus., index, adv. Sample. Refereed. Circ: 500 Paid. Vol. ends: Nov. Online: EBSCO Publishing, EBSCO Host; HighWire Press; OCLC Online Computer Library Center, Inc.; ProQuest K-12 Learning Solutions; SAGE Publications, Inc., SAGE Journals Online; SwetsWise Online Content. Reprint: PSC. *Indexed:* ASSIA, AmH&L, ArtHuCI, BRI, C&ISA, CBRI, CerAb, CompLI, CompR, FR, IAA, IBR, IBZ, ISTA, LISA, MicrocompInd, PSA, PsycInfo, SCI, SSA, SSCI, SWR&A, SociolAb. *Bk. rev.:* 2-4, signed. *Aud.:* Ac.

An interdisciplinary journal that covers social science's applications of computing in instruction and research, as well as the societal impacts of information technology. Sample topics include agent simulation, artificial intelligence, computer simulation, e-government, electronic publishing, and geographic information systems. Features include articles, software reviews, symposiums, book reviews, and "News and Notes." Recommended for academic libraries that support graduate programs in the social sciences.

Social Science Research. See Cultural Studies section.

5654. *Society: social science & modern society.* Formerly (until 1972): *Trans-Action: Social Science and Modern Society.* [ISSN: 0147-2011] 1963. bi-m. EUR 271 print & online eds. Springer New York LLC, 233 Spring St, New York, NY 10013-1578; journals@springer-ny.com; http://www.springer.com. Illus., index, adv. Sample. Refereed. Circ: 10000 Paid. Vol. ends: Oct. Microform: PQC. Online: EBSCO Publishing, EBSCO Host; Florida Center for Library Automation; Gale; Northern Light Technology, Inc.; OCLC Online Computer Library Center, Inc.; OhioLINK; ProQuest K-12 Learning Solutions; ProQuest LLC (Ann Arbor); SwetsWise Online Content. Reprint: PSC. *Indexed:* ABCPolSci, ABS&EES, AgeL, AmH&L, BAS, BRD, BRI, CBRI, CJA, CommAb, EAA, FLI, FutSurv, HistAb, IBR, IBSS, IBZ, IPSA, JEL, LRI, MASUSE, MCR, PAIS, PRA, PSA, RGPR, RI-1, SSA, SSCI, SUSA, SWR&A, SociolAb, V&AA. *Bk. rev.:* 4-6, signed. *Aud.:* Hs, Ga, Ac.

This is a general social science publication. Easy-to-read articles focus on sociology, political science, economics, psychology, and anthropology. Recommended for high school, public, and academic libraries.

5655. *Sociological Forum: official journal of the Eastern Sociological Society.* [ISSN: 0884-8971] 1986. q. USD 569 print & online eds. Blackwell Publishing, Inc., Commerce Place, 350 Main St, Malden, MA 02148; customerservices@blackwellpublishing.com; http://www.blackwellpublishing.com. Illus., index, adv. Sample. Refereed. Microform: PQC. Online: EBSCO Publishing, EBSCO Host; Gale; IngentaConnect; JSTOR (Web-based Journal Archive); OCLC Online Computer Library Center, Inc.; OhioLINK; Ovid Technologies, Inc.; Springer LINK; SwetsWise Online Content. Reprint: PSC. *Indexed:* AgeL, ArtHuCI, CJA, FR, HRA, IBR, IBSS, IBZ, IMFL, PRA, PSA, PsycInfo, RILM, SFSA, SSA, SSCI, SociolAb. *Bk. rev.:* 2-3, signed. *Aud.:* Ac.

Publishes theoretical, methodological, quantitative, and qualitative substantive research. Applied research articles in the areas of sociology, social psychology, anthropology, and political science are included. Recent sample article topics include social capital theory in technological disaster research, and Abu Ghraib as a microscosm. "Research notes and book reviews are published if space permits." Recommended for academic libraries that serve programs in sociology.

5656. *Sociological Inquiry.* [ISSN: 0038-0245] 1930. q. GBP 126 print & online eds. Ed(s): Michael Miniard, Charles E Faupel. Blackwell Publishing, Inc., Commerce Place, 350 Main St, Malden, MA 02148; customerservices@blackwellpublishing.com; http://www.blackwellpublishing.com. Illus., index, adv. Refereed. Circ: 3000. Microform: PQC. Online: Blackwell Synergy; EBSCO Publishing, EBSCO Host; Gale; IngentaConnect; OCLC Online Computer Library Center, Inc.; OhioLINK; SwetsWise Online Content. Reprint: PSC. *Indexed:* ABCPolSci, ASSIA, AbAn, AgeL, AmH&L, ApEcolAb, ArtHuCI, CJA, CommAb, EAA, FR, HistAb, IBR, IBZ, IMFL, IPSA, PRA, PSA, PsycInfo, RI-1, RILM, RiskAb, SSA, SSCI, SWA, SociolAb. *Bk. rev.:* 2-4, signed. *Aud.:* Ac.

This is the official journal of Alpha Kappa Delta, the Sociology Honor Society. The journal began in 1928 and has gone through numerous iterations and name changes, but it stands the test of time with its aim to stimulate scholarship among sociology students. It publishes research on all aspects of sociology, with occasional thematic issues. Recommended for academic libraries that support sociology programs.

5657. *Sociological Methodology.* [ISSN: 0081-1750] 1969. a. GBP 203 print & online eds. Ed(s): Ray Weathers, Ross M Stolzenberg. Blackwell Publishing, Inc., Commerce Place, 350 Main St, Malden, MA 02148; customerservices@blackwellpublishing.com;

http://www.blackwellpublishing.com. Adv. Refereed. Circ: 1450. Microform: PQC. Online: Blackwell Synergy; EBSCO Publishing, EBSCO Host; Gale; IngentaConnect; JSTOR (Web-based Journal Archive); OCLC Online Computer Library Center, Inc.; OhioLINK; ProQuest K-12 Learning Solutions; ProQuest LLC (Ann Arbor); SwetsWise Online Content. Reprint: PSC. *Indexed:* ASSIA, ApEcolAb, IBSS, IPSA, PSA, SSA, SSCI, SociolAb. *Aud.:* Ac.

Sponsored by the American Sociological Association, this annual volume "is a compendium of new and sometimes controversial advances in social science methodology." Its coverage runs the gamut from legal and ethical issues surrounding data collection to the methodology of theory construction. A must-have for academic libraries that support programs in sociology.

5658. *Sociological Perspectives.* Formerly (until 1982): *Pacific Sociological Review.* [ISSN: 0731-1214] 1958. q. USD 327 print & online eds. USD 90 newsstand/cover. Ed(s): Richard T Serpe, Donald C Barrett. University of California Press, Journals Division, 2000 Center St, Ste 303, Berkeley, CA 94704-1223; journals@ucpress.edu; http://www.ucpress.edu/journals. Illus., index, adv. Sample. Refereed. Circ: 2300. Vol. ends: Sep. Microform: PQC. Online: EBSCO Publishing, EBSCO Host; Florida Center for Library Automation; JSTOR (Web-based Journal Archive); Northern Light Technology, Inc.; OCLC Online Computer Library Center, Inc.; ProQuest LLC (Ann Arbor); SwetsWise Online Content; H.W. Wilson. *Indexed:* ABCPolSci, AbAn, AgeL, AmH&L, ArtHuCI, BAS, CJA, HistAb, IBSS, IMFL, IPSA, PSA, PsycInfo, RILM, SSA, SSCI, SUSA, SWA, SWR&A, SociolAb. *Aud.:* Ac.

In this, the official journal of the Pacific Sociological Association, "articles typically address the ever-expanding body of knowledge about social processes and are related to economic, political, anthropological, and historical issues." Recent article titles include "Presenting the self, the social body and the olfactory: managing smells in everyday life"; "Parental involvement, family structure, and adolescent sexual decision making"; and "Choosing daughters: exploring why mothers favor adult daughters over sons." Recommended for academic libraries that support programs in sociology.

5659. *The Sociological Quarterly.* Formerly: *Midwest Sociologist.* [ISSN: 0038-0253] 1960. q. GBP 206 print & online eds. Ed(s): Peter Kivisto. Blackwell Publishing, Inc., Commerce Place, 350 Main St, Malden, MA 02148; http://www.blackwellpublishing.com. Illus., index, adv. Sample. Refereed. Circ: 1500 Paid. Vol. ends: Nov. Microform: WSH. Online: Blackwell Synergy; Chadwyck-Healey Inc.; EBSCO Publishing, EBSCO Host; Florida Center for Library Automation; Gale; IngentaConnect; OCLC Online Computer Library Center, Inc.; ProQuest LLC (Ann Arbor); SwetsWise Online Content; H.W. Wilson. Reprint: PSC. *Indexed:* ABCPolSci, ABS&EES, AbAn, AgeL, AmH&L, ApEcolAb, ArtHuCI, BAS, CABA, CJA, CommAb, EI, FR, HistAb, IBR, IBSS, IBZ, IMFL, IPSA, PAIS, PRA, PSA, PhilInd, PsycInfo, RI-1, RILM, SFSA, SSA, SSCI, SWA, SWR&A, SociolAb, WAE&RSA. *Aud.:* Ac.

As the official journal of the Midwest Sociology Society, *The Sociological Quarterly* includes articles and note-length manuscripts on theoretical developments, research that advances the understanding of social processes, and methodological innovation in sociology. Each issue has three broad themes, with two articles on that theme. Recent themes include social movments past and present; gender and work; and aging identity and status characteristics. Recommended for academic libraries.

Sociological Research. See Slavic Studies section.

5660. *Sociological Research Online: an electronic journal.* [ISSN: 1360-7804] 1996. q. GBP 100 Free to individuals. Ed(s): Amanda Coffey, Nicola Green. Sage Publications Ltd., 1 Oliver's Yard, 55 City Rd, London, EC1 1SP, United Kingdom; info@sagepub.co.uk; http://www.sagepub.co.uk. Illus., adv. Refereed. *Indexed:* IBSS, PAIS, SSA, SSCI, SociolAb. *Bk. rev.:* 12-14, signed. *Aud.:* Ac.

This online-only journal focuses on theoretical, empirical, and methodological discussions that "engage current political, cultural and intellectual topics and debates." In addition to peer-reviewed articles, there are book reviews, and each issue has a section devoted to a topic. Recommended for academic libraries that support sociology and social work programs.

5661. *The Sociological Review.* [ISSN: 0038-0261] 1908. q. GBP 259 print & online eds. Ed(s): Mike Savage, Rosemary Deem. Blackwell Publishing Ltd., 9600 Garsington Rd, Oxford, OX4 2ZG, United Kingdom; customerservices@blackwellpublishing.com; http://www.blackwellpublishing.com. Illus., adv. Sample. Refereed. Circ: 2000. Vol. ends: Nov. Microform: PQC. Online: Blackwell Synergy; EBSCO Publishing, EBSCO Host; Gale; IngentaConnect; OCLC Online Computer Library Center, Inc.; OhioLINK; SwetsWise Online Content. Reprint: PSC. *Indexed:* AICP, ASSIA, AgeL, AmH&L, ApEcolAb, BRI, CABA, CBRI, CJA, FR, HistAb, IBR, IBSS, IBZ, IMFL, IPSA, IndIslam, PSA, PhilInd, PsycInfo, RRTA, RiskAb, SSA, SSCI, SWA, SociolAb. *Bk. rev.:* 10-12, signed. *Aud.:* Ac.

In publication since 1958, this is the longest-established sociological journal in Great Britain. It publishes articles, short notes, responses to previously published articles, and a large number of book reviews. Annual subscriptions include one or two monographs a year on general issues in sociology. With a focus on Great Britain and Europe, articles cover broad subject areas such as acquiring a mastery of language; family matters in Bangladesh and Pakistan; and fathers as primary caregivers. Recommended for academic libraries that serve graduate programs in sociology.

5662. *Sociological Spectrum: official journal of the Mid-South Sociological Association.* Formed by the merger of: *Sociological Symposium; Sociological Forum.* [ISSN: 0273-2173] 1980. bi-m. GBP 407 print & online eds. Ed(s): DeAnn Kalich. Taylor & Francis Inc., 325 Chestnut St, Ste 800, Philadelphia, PA 19016; orders@taylorandfrancis.com; http://www.taylorandfrancis.com. Illus., index, adv. Sample. Refereed. Circ: 600. Vol. ends: Oct/Dec. Online: EBSCO Publishing, EBSCO Host; Gale; IngentaConnect; OCLC Online Computer Library Center, Inc.; SwetsWise Online Content. Reprint: PSC. *Indexed:* ABS&EES, AgeL, CJA, IBSS, IMFL, PRA, PSA, PsycInfo, RILM, SSA, SSCI, SUSA, SociolAb. *Bk. rev.:* Number and length vary. *Aud.:* Ac.

Sociological Spectrum is the official journal of the Mid-South Sociological Association. It publishes "theoretical, methodological, quantitative and qualitative substantive research, and applied research articles in the areas of sociology, social psychology, anthropology, and political science." Occasional research notes and book reviews are included. Recommended for academic libraries.

5663. *Sociological Theory.* [ISSN: 0735-2751] q. GBP 210 print & online eds. Ed(s): Jason Mast, Julia Adams. Blackwell Publishing, Inc., Commerce Place, 350 Main St, Malden, MA 02148; customerservices@blackwellpublishing.com; http://www.blackwellpublishing.com. Adv. Refereed. Circ: 2300. Reprint: PSC. *Indexed:* ASSIA, ApEcolAb, FR, IBR, IBSS, IBZ, RILM, SSA, SSCI, SociolAb. *Aud.:* Ac.

Published for the American Sociological Association, this journal covers "the full range of sociological theory—from ethnomethodology to world systems analysis, from commentaries on the classics to the latest cutting-edge ideas, and from re-examinations of neglected theorists to metatheoretical inquiries." Issues often include a commentary and debate section. A must-have for academic libraries that support graduate programs in sociology.

5664. *Sociology: the journal of the British Sociological Association.* [ISSN: 0038-0385] 1967. 5x/yr. GBP 357. Ed(s): Stephanie Lawler, David Byrne. Sage Publications Ltd., 1 Oliver's Yard, 55 City Rd, London, EC1 1SP, United Kingdom; info@sagepub.co.uk; http://www.sagepub.co.uk. Illus., index, adv. Sample. Refereed. Circ: 3700. Vol. ends: Nov. Microform: PQC. Online: CSA; Cambridge University Press; EBSCO Publishing, EBSCO Host; Florida Center for Library Automation; HighWire Press; Northern Light Technology, Inc.; OCLC Online Computer Library Center, Inc.; OhioLINK; SAGE

Publications, Inc., SAGE Journals Online; SwetsWise Online Content. Reprint: PSC. *Indexed:* ABIn, ASSIA, AmH&L, BAS, CABA, CJA, CommAb, FR, HistAb, IBR, IBSS, IBZ, IPSA, IndVet, PSA, PsycInfo, RRTA, SSA, SSCI, SWA, SociolAb, VB, WAE&RSA. *Bk. rev.:* 20-25, signed. *Aud.:* Ac.

As one of the leading publications in sociology, this journal makes a major contribution to the debates that have shaped sociology. Contents include theoretical and empirical research papers, shorter notes, comments, reviews of recent developments, and book reviews. A must-have for academic libraries that support programs in sociology.

5665. *Sociology of Education: a journal of research in socialization and social structure.* Formerly (until 1963): *Journal of Educational Sociology.* [ISSN: 0038-0407] 1927. q. USD 155 (Individuals, USD 75; Members, USD 30). Ed(s): Karl L Alexander. American Sociological Association, 1307 New York Ave, NW, Ste 700, Washington, DC 20005-4701; publications@asanet.org; http://www.asanet.org. Illus., index, adv. Refereed. Circ: 3000. Vol. ends: Oct. Microform: PMC; PQC. Online: EBSCO Publishing, EBSCO Host; Gale; IngentaConnect; JSTOR (Web-based Journal Archive); OCLC Online Computer Library Center, Inc.; ProQuest LLC (Ann Arbor). *Indexed:* ABIn, ASSIA, AgeL, AmH&L, EAA, ERIC, EduInd, FR, HEA, HistAb, IBR, IBZ, PAIS, PRA, PsycInfo, SSA, SSCI, SWA, SociolAb. *Aud.:* Ac.

Published by the American Sociological Association, this journal focuses on studies in the sociology of education and human social development. It publishes research that examines how social institutions and individuals' experiences within these institutions affect educational processes and social development. Recommended for academic libraries that support programs in sociology and education.

5666. *Sociology of Health and Illness: a journal of medical sociology.* Incorporates (in 1999): *Sociology of Health and Illness Monograph Series.* [ISSN: 0141-9889] 1979. 7x/yr. GBP 417 print & online eds. Ed(s): Robert Dingwall, Dr. Elizabeth Murphy. Blackwell Publishing Ltd., 9600 Garsington Rd, Oxford, OX4 2ZG, United Kingdom; customerservices@blackwellpublishing.com; http://www.blackwellpublishing.com. Illus., index, adv. Sample. Refereed. Circ: 950. Vol. ends: Nov. Online: Blackwell Synergy; EBSCO Publishing, EBSCO Host; Gale; IngentaConnect; OCLC Online Computer Library Center, Inc.; OhioLINK; SwetsWise Online Content. Reprint: PSC. *Indexed:* ASSIA, AgeL, ApEcolAb, ArtHuCI, CABA, CINAHL, ExcerpMed, FR, IBSS, MCR, PSA, PsycInfo, RRTA, RiskAb, SSA, SSCI, SWA, SociolAb, WAE&RSA. *Bk. rev.:* 8-12, signed. *Aud.:* Ac.

This international journal publishes empirical and theoretical articles on all aspects of health, illness, and medicine. In addition to six regular issues, there is a thematic issue devoted to an important topic of current interest. For example, a recent thematic issue focuses on bioethics and social sciences. Includes book reviews. Recommended for academic libraries that support programs in sociology, medicine, or social work.

Sociology of Religion. See Religion section.

5667. *Teaching Sociology.* [ISSN: 0092-055X] 1973. q. USD 150 (Individuals, USD 75; Members, USD 30). Ed(s): Liz Grauerholz. American Sociological Association, 1307 New York Ave, NW, Ste 700, Washington, DC 20005-4701; publications@asanet.org; http://www.lemoyne.edu. Illus., adv. Refereed. Circ: 2300. Vol. ends: Oct. *Indexed:* ABIn, ASSIA, AgeL, ArtHuCI, EduInd, FLI, FR, IBR, IBZ, RILM, SSA, SSCI, SWA, SociolAb. *Bk. rev.:* 10-12, signed. *Aud.:* Ac.

The scope of this journal is to publish articles, notes, interviews, applications, and reviews intended to be helpful to sociology teachers. Articles range from experimental studies of teaching to broad synthetic essays on pedagogical issues. A recent issue contains articles on group quizzes and teaching against the text. A must-have for academic libraries that serve graduate and doctoral programs in sociology.

5668. *Technology in Society.* Announced as: *Sociotechnology.* [ISSN: 0160-791X] 1979. 4x/yr. EUR 1072. Ed(s): A. George Schillinger, George Bugliarello. Pergamon, The Boulevard, Langford Ln, East Park, Kidlington, OX5 1GB, United Kingdom; nlinfo-f@elsevier.nl; http://www.elsevier.nl. Illus., index, adv. Sample. Refereed. Circ: 2000. Vol. ends: No. 23. Microform: PQC. Online: EBSCO Publishing, EBSCO Host; Gale; IngentaConnect; OhioLINK; ScienceDirect; SwetsWise Online Content. *Indexed:* ABS&EES, ArtHuCI, BAS, CJA, CommAb, EAA, EngInd, EnvAb, ExcerpMed, FutSurv, ISTA, PSA, SSA, SSCI, SociolAb. *Aud.:* Ac.

This is an international journal devoted to the economic, political, and cultural role of technology in society. Recent articles cover after-disaster planning in New Orleans; wireless technologies for developing countries; and the impact of business on software piracy. Recommended for libraries that support graduate programs in the social sciences.

Theory and Decision. See Philosophy section.

5669. *Theory and Society: renewal and critique in social theory.* [ISSN: 0304-2421] 1974. bi-m. EUR 629 print & online eds. Ed(s): Janet Gouldner, Karen G Lucas. Springer Netherlands, Van Godewijckstraat 30, Dordrecht, 3311 GX, Netherlands; http://www.springeronline.com. Illus., index, adv. Sample. Refereed. Vol. ends: Nov. Microform: PQC. Online: EBSCO Publishing, EBSCO Host; Gale; IngentaConnect; JSTOR (Web-based Journal Archive); OCLC Online Computer Library Center, Inc.; OhioLINK; Springer LINK; SwetsWise Online Content. Reprint: PSC. *Indexed:* ASSIA, AltPI, ArtHuCI, BAS, CJA, CommAb, FR, IBR, IBSS, IBZ, IPSA, LeftInd, PAIS, PSA, SSA, SSCI, SociolAb. *Bk. rev.:* 2-4, signed. *Aud.:* Ac.

This journal publishes theoretical research on social processes. The subject matter "ranges from prehistory to contemporary affairs, from treatments of single individuals and national societies to world culture, from discussions of theory to methodological critique, and from First World to Third World." Recommended for academic libraries that support graduate programs in sociology.

5670. *Theory, Culture & Society: explorations in critical social science.* [ISSN: 0263-2764] 1982. 8x/yr. GBP 696. Ed(s): Mike Featherstone. Sage Publications Ltd., 1 Oliver's Yard, 55 City Rd, London, EC1 1SP, United Kingdom; info@sagepub.co.uk; http://www.sagepub.co.uk. Illus., index, adv. Sample. Refereed. Vol. ends: Nov. Reprint: PSC. *Indexed:* ABIn, AICP, ASSIA, AltPI, CommAb, FLI, FR, HRA, IBR, IBSS, IBZ, IPSA, LeftInd, PRA, PSA, PhilInd, RILM, SSA, SSCI, SUSA, SociolAb, V&AA. *Bk. rev.:* 1-2, signed. *Aud.:* Ac.

Cultural sociology is the focus of this journal, which was launched in 1982 because of the resurgence of interest in culture within contemporary social science. There are occasional thematic issues; one recent issue addresses "Inventive Life: Approaches to the New Vitalism." Recommended for academic libraries that serve graduate programs in sociology.

Violence Against Women. See Gender Studies section.

5671. *Work and Occupations: an international sociological journal.* Formerly (until 1982): *Sociology of Work and Occupations.* [ISSN: 0730-8884] 1974. q. GBP 418. Ed(s): Daniel B Cornfield. Sage Publications, Inc., 2455 Teller Rd, Thousand Oaks, CA 91320; info@sagepub.com; http://www.sagepub.com. Illus., index, adv. Sample. Refereed. Circ: 750 Paid. Vol. ends: Nov. Microform: PQC. Online: CSA; EBSCO Publishing, EBSCO Host; Florida Center for Library Automation; Gale; HighWire Press; OCLC Online Computer Library Center, Inc.; OhioLINK; SAGE Publications, Inc., SAGE Journals Online; SwetsWise Online Content. Reprint: PSC. *Indexed:* ABIn, ASG, ASSIA, AgeL, BPI, BRI, C&ISA, CINAHL, CJA, CerAb, ErgAb, FR, H&SSA, HRA, IAA, IBR, IBSS, IBZ, IMFL, PRA, PsycInfo, SFSA, SSA, SSCI, SUSA, SWA, SWR&A, SociolAb, V&AA. *Bk. rev.:* 4-6, signed. *Aud.:* Ac.

This publication focuses on the dynamics of the workplace and international approaches to work-related issues. It publishes social science research "on the human dynamics of the workplace, employment, and society from an international, interdisciplinary perspective." Regular features include research notes, review essays, and book reviews. Many topics are addressed, including emotion, work, and labor; gender and race relations; globalization and work; immigrant and migrant workers; occupational health and safety; organizational culture; transitions between work, home, unemployment, and school; violence in the workplace; work and family; and workplace conflict. Recommended for academic libraries that serve graduate programs in business or sociology.

5672. *Youth & Society.* [ISSN: 0044-118X] 1969. q. GBP 388. Ed(s): Kathryn G Herr. Sage Publications, Inc., 2455 Teller Rd, Thousand Oaks, CA 91320; info@sagepub.com; http://www.sagepub.com. Illus., index, adv. Refereed. Circ: 700 Paid. Vol. ends: Jun. Microform: PQC. Online: CSA; Chadwyck-Healey Inc.; EBSCO Publishing, EBSCO Host; Florida Center for Library Automation; Gale; HighWire Press; OCLC Online Computer Library Center, Inc.; OhioLINK; SAGE Publications, Inc., SAGE Journals Online; SwetsWise Online Content. Reprint: PSC. *Indexed:* ABS&EES, ASSIA, Agr, AmH&L, CJA, CommAb, EAA, ERIC, H&SSA, HEA, HistAb, IPSA, PSA, PsycInfo, RILM, RiskAb, SFSA, SSA, SSCI, SUSA, SWA, SWR&A, SociolAb, V&AA. *Aud.:* Ac, Sa.

This journal addresses the daily challenges adolescent and young adult specialists face—think teen pregnancy, gangs, AIDS education, and adolescent substance abuse. This journal examines contemporary issues and presents practical information for studying and working with young people today. It has an interdisciplinary forum and includes research from sociology, public health, social work, education, criminology, psychology, anthropology, human services, and political science. This is a popular journal for undergraduate research. Highly recommended for academic libraries.

Social Work and Social Welfare

5673. *Administration in Social Work: the quarterly journal of human services management.* [ISSN: 0364-3107] 1977. q. USD 655 print & online eds. Ed(s): Leon Ginsberg. Haworth Press, Inc., 10 Alice St, Binghamton, NY 13904-1580; getinfo@haworthpress.com; http://www.haworthpress.com. Illus., adv. Sample. Refereed. Circ: 972 Paid. Vol. ends: Winter. Microform: PQC. Online: EBSCO Publishing, EBSCO Host; OCLC Online Computer Library Center, Inc.; SwetsWise Online Content. Reprint: HAW. *Indexed:* ABIn, ASSIA, AbAn, AgeL, CINAHL, HRA, IBR, IBZ, IMFL, PRA, PsycInfo, SFSA, SSA, SSCI, SWR&A, SociolAb, V&AA. *Bk. rev.:* 2-4, signed. *Aud.:* Ac, Sa.

As the official publication of the National Network of Social Work Managers, this journal addresses program development, affirmative action, accountability, budgeting, employment and personnel policies, finances and accounting, quality improvement/control, monitoring, and legalities of social work. It includes articles, book and literature reviews, and occasional thematic issues. Recommended for academic and special libraries that support social work programs.

5674. *The British Journal of Social Work.* [ISSN: 0045-3102] 1971. 8x/yr. EUR 611 print or online ed. (Individuals, EUR 117 print & online eds.). Ed(s): Helen Masson, Eric Blyth. Oxford University Press, Great Clarendon St, Oxford, OX2 6DP, United Kingdom; jnl.orders@ oup.co.uk; http://www.oxfordjournals.org. Illus., adv. Refereed. Circ: 1600. Microform: PQC. Online: Chadwyck-Healey Inc.; EBSCO Publishing, EBSCO Host; Gale; HighWire Press; IngentaConnect; OCLC Online Computer Library Center, Inc.; OhioLINK; Oxford Journals; ProQuest LLC (Ann Arbor); SwetsWise Online Content. Reprint: PSC. *Indexed:* ASG, ASSIA, AgeL, CINAHL, CJA, HRA, IBR, IBSS, IBZ, PRA, PsycInfo, SFSA, SSA, SSCI, SUSA, SWA, SWR&A, SociolAb, V&AA. *Bk. rev.:* 10-15, signed. *Aud.:* Ac.

As an official publication of the British Association of Social Workers, *The British Journal of Social Work* serves as the leading academic journal of social work in the United Kingdom. There are occasional thematic issues, with a recent one titled "Caring for People: Social Work with Adults in the Next Decade and Beyond." It has an extensive book review section. Recommended for academic libraries that support programs in sociology and social work.

5675. *Child and Adolescent Social Work Journal.* Former titles (until 1982): *Family and Child Mental Health Journal;* (until 1980): *Issues in Child Mental Health;* (until vol.5, 1977): *Psychosocial Process.* [ISSN: 0738-0151] 1970. bi-m. EUR 775 print & online eds. Ed(s): Thomas Kenemore. Springer New York LLC, 233 Spring St, New York, NY 10013-1578; service-ny@springer.com; http://www.springer.com/. Illus., adv. Sample. Refereed. Online: EBSCO Publishing, EBSCO Host; Gale; IngentaConnect; OCLC Online Computer Library Center, Inc.; OhioLINK; Ovid Technologies, Inc.; Springer LINK; SwetsWise Online Content. Reprint: PSC. *Indexed:* ASSIA, CJA, IMFL, PsycInfo, RiskAb, SSA, SWA, SWR&A, SociolAb. *Bk. rev.:* 1-3, signed. *Aud.:* Ac, Sa.

This journal publishes research on clinical social work practice with children, adolescents, and their families. Recent articles include topics on bullying, alcohol prevention programs with urban Native Americans, and early childcare development and nutritional training for foster care parents. Recommended for academic libraries that support social work programs and for libraries that serve social services professionals.

5676. *Child & Family Social Work.* [ISSN: 1356-7500] 1996. q. GBP 355 print & online eds. Ed(s): Nina Biehal. Blackwell Publishing Ltd., 9600 Garsington Rd, Oxford, OX4 2ZG, United Kingdom; customerservices@ blackwellpublishing.com; http://www.blackwellpublishing.com. Adv. Refereed. Circ: 425. Reprint: PSC. *Indexed:* ApEcolAb, CINAHL, PsycInfo, RiskAb, SSA, SWR&A, SociolAb. *Bk. rev.:* 6-8, signed. *Aud.:* Ac, Sa.

This journal "publishes original and distinguished contributions on matters of research, theory, policy and practice in the field of social work with children and their families." It provides a forum for researchers, practitioners, policy-makers, and managers in the field to exchange knowledge and advance the well-being and welfare of children and their families throughout the world. In addition to articles, it includes book reviews. Recommended for academic libraries that support programs in social work and other libraries that serve social services clientele.

5677. *Child Welfare: journal of policy, practice and program.* Formerly (until 1948): *Child Welfare League of America. Bulletin.* [ISSN: 0009-4021] 1920. bi-m. USD 150 (Individuals, USD 110; Students, USD 84). Ed(s): Brenda Sidhe. Child Welfare League of America, Inc., 2345 Crystal Dr, Ste 250, Arlington, DC 22202; journal@cwla.org; http://www.cwla.org/pubs. Illus., index, adv. Sample. Refereed. Circ: 12000. Vol. ends: Nov/Dec. Microform: PQC. Online: EBSCO Publishing, EBSCO Host; Northern Light Technology, Inc.; OCLC Online Computer Library Center, Inc.; ProQuest LLC (Ann Arbor). *Indexed:* ABS&EES, ASSIA, Agr, CINAHL, CJA, ECER, ERIC, H&SSA, HRA, IBSS, PAIS, PsycInfo, RI-1, RiskAb, SFSA, SSA, SSCI, SWR&A, SociolAb, V&AA. *Aud.:* Ga, Ac, Sa.

Published by the Child Welfare League of America, this journal fulfills its mission to ensure the safety and well-being of children and families. As an advocate for the advancement of public policy, the journal publishes research and practical articles that address best practices to help ensure every child will "grow up in a safe, loving, and stable family." Recent article topics include an exploratory study of drug-exposed infants, and assessing gay and lesbian prospective foster and adoptive parents. Recommended for academic libraries that support social work and education programs, as well as public and special libraries with social services clientele.

5678. *Children & Schools: a journal of social work practice.* Formerly (until 2000): *Social Work in Education.* [ISSN: 1532-8759] 1978. q. USD 125 print & online eds. (Individuals, USD 89; Members, USD 54). Ed(s): Wilma Peebles-Wilkins, Paula Delo. N A SW Press, 750 First St NE, Ste 700, Washington, DC 20002-4241; press@naswdc.org; http://www.naswpress.org. Illus., index, adv. Circ: 3700 Paid. Vol. ends:

Oct. Online: EBSCO Publishing, EBSCO Host; Gale; IngentaConnect; OCLC Online Computer Library Center, Inc.; ProQuest LLC (Ann Arbor). *Indexed:* ABIn, ASSIA, AbAn, AgeL, BrEdI, CINAHL, CJA, EAA, ECER, ERIC, EduInd, IMFL, PsycInfo, SSA, SWR&A, SociolAb, V&AA. *Aud.:* Ac, Sa.

Published by the National Association of Social Workers, this journal focuses on articles that provide innovations in practice, interdisciplinary efforts, research, program evaluation, policy, and planning in regard to education. As a "practitioner-to-practitioner resource," *Children & Schools* is a must-have for academic libraries and special libraries that support education or social work programs.

5679. Children and Youth Services Review. [ISSN: 0190-7409] 1979. 12x/yr. EUR 1187. Ed(s): Dr. Duncan Lindsey. Pergamon, The Boulevard, Langford Ln, East Park, Kidlington, OX5 1GB, United Kingdom. Illus., index. Sample. Refereed. Circ: 1200. Vol. ends: Dec. Microform: PQC. Online: EBSCO Publishing, EBSCO Host; Gale; IngentaConnect; OhioLINK; ScienceDirect; SwetsWise Online Content. *Indexed:* ASG, ASSIA, CJA, ECER, ExcerpMed, PsycInfo, SFSA, SSA, SSCI, SWA, SWR&A, SociolAb, V&AA. *Bk. rev.:* 2-4, signed. *Aud.:* Ac.

The goal of this journal is to "provide a forum for the critical analysis and assessment of social service programs designed to serve young people throughout the world." It includes research articles, policy notes, and book reviews. Article topics include child welfare, foster care, adoption, child abuse, income support, mental health services, and social policy. There are occasional thematic issues; a recent one focuses on a review of welfare reform. Recommended for academic libraries that support social work, child psychology, or social services programs.

5680. Clinical Social Work Journal. [ISSN: 0091-1674] 1973. q. EUR 785 print & online eds. Ed(s): Carolyn Saari. Springer New York LLC, 233 Spring St, New York, NY 10013-1578; service-ny@springer.com; http://www.springer.com/. Illus., adv. Sample. Refereed. Vol. ends: Winter. Microform: PQC. Online: EBSCO Publishing, EBSCO Host; Gale; IngentaConnect; Northern Light Technology, Inc.; OCLC Online Computer Library Center, Inc.; OhioLINK; Ovid Technologies, Inc.; ProQuest LLC (Ann Arbor); Springer LINK; SwetsWise Online Content. Reprint: PSC. *Indexed:* ASSIA, AgeL, HRA, IMFL, PRA, PsycInfo, SFSA, SSA, SSCI, SWR&A, SociolAb, V&AA. *Bk. rev.:* 1-2, signed. *Aud.:* Ac, Sa.

The focus of this journal is on contemporary clinical practice with individuals, couples, families, and groups. The journal includes theoretical, practical, and evidence-based clinical research. Recent article topics include social worker's use of self, treating the abusive partner, and posttraumatic plan. Recommended for academic libraries that support social work programs and for libraries that serve social services professionals.

5681. Critical Social Policy: a journal of theory and practice in social welfare. [ISSN: 0261-0183] 1981. q. GBP 302. Sage Publications Ltd., 1 Oliver's Yard, 55 City Rd, London, EC1 1SP, United Kingdom; info@sagepub.co.uk; http://www.sagepub.co.uk. Illus., adv. Refereed. Circ: 1000. Reprint: PSC. *Indexed:* ASSIA, CINAHL, IBR, IBSS, IBZ, PAIS, PSA, PsycInfo, SFSA, SSA, SSCI, SUSA, SWA, SociolAb, V&AA. *Aud.:* Ac, Sa.

The aim of this journal is to "develop an understanding of welfare from socialist, feminist, anti-racist and radical perspectives." It provides a forum for advocacy and debate on social policy issues. This journal is for consumer groups, practitioners, workers, teachers, and researchers involved in welfare issues and social policy. The journal is international but has a heavy European focus. Recommended for academic libraries and special libraries that support social work, sociology, or political science.

5682. Families in Society: the journal of contemporary social services. Former titles (until Jan.1990): *Social Casework;* (until 1950): *Journal of Social Casework;* (until 1946: *The Family.* [ISSN: 1044-3894] 1920. q. USD 205 & libraries; print (Individuals, USD 50 print & online). Ed(s): Ms. Kirstin E Anderson, Dr. William E Powell. Alliance for Children and Families, 11700 West Lake Park Dr, Milwaukee, WI 53224-3099. Illus., adv. Refereed. Circ: 2400 Paid. Vol. ends: Dec. Microform: PQC. Online: EBSCO Publishing, EBSCO Host; Florida Center for Library Automation; Gale; OCLC Online Computer Library Center, Inc.; ProQuest LLC (Ann Arbor); H.W. Wilson. *Indexed:* ASG, ASSIA, AgeL, AmH&L, ArtHuCI, BRI, CBRI, CJA, CPerI, EAA, ECER, HRA, IBR, IBZ, IMFL, PSA, PsycInfo, RI-1, RiskAb, SFSA, SSA, SSCI, SWA, SWR&A, SociolAb, V&AA. *Bk. rev.:* 2-4, signed. *Aud.:* Ac.

At 88 years old, this journal is the oldest and one of the most respected journals in North America on social work and related social and human services. It is published by the Alliance for Children and Families, and the depth and breadth of its topics are great. As a standard work in social work, this is a must-have for academic libraries that serve social work and sociology programs.

Family Process. See Family section.

Family Relations. See Family section.

5683. Health & Social Work. [ISSN: 0360-7283] 1976. q. USD 125 print & online eds. (Individuals, USD 89; Members, USD 54). Ed(s): Coleen Galambos. N A SW Press, 750 First St NE, Ste 700, Washington, DC 20002-4241; press@naswdc.org; http://www.naswpress.org. Illus., index, adv. Refereed. Circ: 6500 Paid. Vol. ends: Nov. Online: Chadwyck-Healey Inc.; EBSCO Publishing, EBSCO Host; Florida Center for Library Automation; Gale; IngentaConnect; Northern Light Technology, Inc.; OCLC Online Computer Library Center, Inc.; ProQuest LLC (Ann Arbor). *Indexed:* ASG, ASSIA, AbAn, AgeL, CINAHL, CJA, ECER, ERIC, ExcerpMed, H&SSA, HRA, IBSS, IMFL, PsycInfo, RiskAb, SSA, SSCI, SWA, SWR&A, SociolAb. *Bk. rev.:* 5-6, signed. *Aud.:* Ac, Sa.

This journal's coverage of topics includes aging, clinical work, long-term care, oncology, substance abuse, depression, and maternal health. Articles treat research, policy, specialized services, quality assurance, in-service training, and other topics that affect the delivery of health-care services. This journal is for professionals and researchers in psychological, physiological, social, cultural, and environmental health sciences. Special features include a practice forum with descriptions of new and effective programs, techniques, and policies; a national health line with information on current relevant legislative and political issues; and "viewpoint," which features readers' comments and opinions. Recommended for academic libraries that support programs in social work or nursing, and other libraries that serve social service clientele.

5684. International Social Work. [ISSN: 0020-8728] 1958. bi-m. GBP 577. Ed(s): Karen Lyons. Sage Publications Ltd., 1 Oliver's Yard, 55 City Rd, London, EC1 1SP, United Kingdom; info@sagepub.co.uk; http://www.sagepub.co.uk. Illus., index, adv. Sample. Refereed. Circ: 950. Vol. ends: Oct. Microform: PQC. Online: EBSCO Publishing, EBSCO Host; HighWire Press; OCLC Online Computer Library Center, Inc.; SAGE Publications, Inc., SAGE Journals Online; SwetsWise Online Content; H.W. Wilson. Reprint: PSC. *Indexed:* ASSIA, CINAHL, CJA, HRA, IBR, IBSS, IBZ, PRA, PsycInfo, RRTA, SSA, SSCI, SUSA, SWR&A, SociolAb, V&AA. *Bk. rev.:* 8-10, signed. *Aud.:* Ac, Sa.

This is the official publication of the International Association of Schools of Social Work, the International Council on Social Welfare, and the International Federation of Social Workers. The content of this journal focuses on the interests of individuals and institutions concerned with social work, human services, social welfare and development across the world. Article emphasis is on comparative analysis and cross-national research. Recent article titles include "Social work with asylum seekers in Canada" and "Mental-health services for refugee women and children in Africa: a call for activism and advocacy." Each issue includes an extensive book review section and has abstracts of each article in English, French, Spanish, Chinese, and Arabic. Recommended for academic libraries with social work programs and libraries that serve social work professionals.

5685. *Journal of Family Social Work.* Formerly (until 1995): *Journal of Social Work and Human Sexuality.* [ISSN: 1052-2158] 1981. q. USD 255 print & online eds. Ed(s): Howard Moose Turney. Haworth Press, Inc., 10 Alice St, Binghamton, NY 13904-1580; getinfo@haworthpress.com; http://www.haworthpress.com. Adv. Sample. Refereed. Circ: 408 Paid. Microform: PQC. Online: EBSCO Publishing, EBSCO Host; OCLC Online Computer Library Center, Inc.; SwetsWise Online Content. Reprint: HAW. *Indexed:* ASG, ASSIA, AbAn, CINAHL, CJA, EAA, H&SSA, HRA, IBR, IBZ, IMFL, RiskAb, SFSA, SSA, SWA, SWR&A, SociolAb, V&AA. *Bk. rev.:* Number and length vary. *Aud.:* Ac, Sa.

In this, the first peer-reviewed social work journal devoted to ecosystemic theory, articles focus on examining the self of the clinician, research, and practice with couples and families. "By uniting clinicians and researchers from social work, family enrichment, family therapy, family studies, family psychology and sociology, and child welfare, it stresses a blending of sociocultural contexts, the uniqueness of the family, and the person of the clinician." Each issue includes a clinician–researcher interchange, letters to the editor, and book reviews. Recommended for academic libraries that support social work programs and for special libraries that serve social services clientele.

Journal of Gerontological Social Work. See Geriatrics and Gerontological Studies section.

Journal of Marital and Family Therapy. See Family section.

5686. *Journal of Social Service Research.* [ISSN: 0148-8376] 1977. q. USD 600 print & online eds. Ed(s): David F Gillespie. Haworth Press, Inc., 10 Alice St, Binghamton, NY 13904-1580; getinfo@ haworthpress.com; http://www.haworthpress.com. Illus., adv. Sample. Refereed. Circ: 435 Paid. Microform: PQC. Online: EBSCO Publishing, EBSCO Host; OCLC Online Computer Library Center, Inc.; SwetsWise Online Content. Reprint: HAW. *Indexed:* ASG, ASSIA, AgeL, CJA, CJPI, FR, HRA, IBR, IBZ, IMFL, LeftInd, PsycInfo, RILM, SFSA, SSA, SSCI, SUSA, SWR&A, SociolAb, V&AA. *Aud.:* Ac.

This journal publishes empirical research and its application to the design, delivery, and management of social services. Articles range from clinical research to empirical policy studies. Recent article titles include "Work-Related Trauma in Child Protection Social Workers" and "The Involvement of Social Workers in Fundraising." Recommended for academic libraries that support programs in social work.

5687. *Journal of Social Work.* [ISSN: 1468-0173] 2001. 4x/yr. GBP 325. Ed(s): Steven M Shardlow. Sage Publications Ltd., 1 Oliver's Yard, 55 City Rd, London, EC1 1SP, United Kingdom; info@sagepub.co.uk; http://www.sagepub.co.uk. Adv. Refereed. Online: EBSCO Publishing, EBSCO Host; HighWire Press; OCLC Online Computer Library Center, Inc.; SAGE Publications, Inc., SAGE Journals Online; SwetsWise Online Content. Reprint: PSC. *Indexed:* CINAHL, HRA, IBR, IBSS, IBZ, PsycInfo, SSA. *Bk. rev.:* 8-10, signed. *Aud.:* Ac.

The aim of this journal is to shape policy, advance theoretical findings, and inform practice. It is a forum for sharing of ideas and research in social work. Included in the journal are longer research articles and shorter "Think Pieces," which are reports of research in progress, comments on previously published articles, book reviews, and analyses of current practice, policy, and theory. Recommended for academic libraries that support programs in social work.

5688. *Journal of Sociology and Social Welfare.* [ISSN: 0191-5096] 1973. q. USD 75 (Individuals, USD 35). Ed(s): Frederick MacDonald. Western Michigan University, School of Social Work, c/o Frederick MacDonald, Mg Ed, 1903 W Michigan Ave, Kalamazoo, MI 49008-5034; macdonald@wmich.edu. Illus., index, adv. Refereed. Circ: 650. Vol. ends: Dec. Microform: PQC. Online: EBSCO Publishing, EBSCO Host; Florida Center for Library Automation; Gale; OCLC Online Computer Library Center, Inc.; H.W. Wilson. *Indexed:* AgeL, CJA, CWI, FR, PsycInfo, SSA, SSCI, SWR&A, SociolAb. *Bk. rev.:* 5-7, signed. *Aud.:* Ac, Sa.

This journal "promotes the understanding of social welfare by applying social science knowledge, methodology and technology to problems of social policy, politics, the social ecology, and social services." Topics covered include "social change, gender, race, homelessness, social welfare history, cultural diversity, international social welfare, and the social dimensions of health and mental health." There are occasional thematic issues; a recent one focuses on coping with poverty. This journal has an extensive book review section. Recommended for academic libraries that support sociology and social work programs.

5689. *The New Social Worker: the magazine for social work students and recent graduates.* [ISSN: 1073-7871] 1994. q. USD 15 domestic; USD 23 Canada; USD 31 elsewhere. Ed(s): Linda Grobman. White Hat Communications, PO Box 5390, Harrisburg, PA 17110-0390; linda.grobman@paonline.com; http://www.socialworker.com/. Adv. Online: EBSCO Publishing, EBSCO Host. *Indexed:* SSA, SWR&A. *Aud.:* Ga, Ac, Sa.

This publication is for social work students and recent graduates. It focuses on social work careers. Each issue has a number of columns, including "International Social Work," "News You Can Use," "Association Spotlights," "Career Talk," and "Electronic Connection." This is a trade magazine for social workers, and sample article topics include elective self-amputation and hurricane relief efforts. Recommended for academic libraries that support programs in social work, and public and special libraries that serve social services clientele.

5690. *Psychoanalytic Social Work.* Former titles (until 1999): *Journal of Analytic Social Work;* (until 1992): *Journal of Independent Social Work.* [ISSN: 1522-8878] 1987. s-a. USD 450 print & online eds. Ed(s): Jerrold R Brandell. Haworth Press, Inc., 10 Alice St, Binghamton, NY 13904-1580; getinfo@haworthpress.com; http://www.haworthpress.com. Illus., adv. Sample. Refereed. Circ: 164 Paid. Vol. ends: Winter. Reprint: HAW. *Indexed:* ASSIA, AbAn, CJA, HRA, IBR, IBZ, IMFL, PsycInfo, SFSA, SSA, SWA, SWR&A, SociolAb, V&AA. *Bk. rev.:* 2-4, signed. *Aud.:* Ac, Sa.

This is the only journal that focuses solely on the important clinical themes and dilemmas that occur in a psychoanalytic social work practice. Articles focus on the special requirements, adaptations, and problems associated with a psychoanalytic approach to treatment in social work settings and with traditional social work populations. It includes clinical case studies, reviews of the literature, psychoanalytic approaches to special populations, and research studies that are clinically focused. Recommended for academic libraries that support graduate programs in social work programs and medical libraries that serve social work professionals.

5691. *Qualitative Social Work: research and practice.* [ISSN: 1473-3250] 2002. q. GBP 333. Ed(s): Ian Shaw, Roy Ruckdeschel. Sage Publications Ltd., 1 Oliver's Yard, 55 City Rd, London, EC1 1SP, United Kingdom; info@sagepub.co.uk; http://www.sagepub.co.uk. Adv. Reprint: PSC. *Indexed:* CINAHL, CJA, IBR, IBZ, PsycInfo, SSA, SWR&A. *Bk. rev.:* 1-2, signed. *Aud.:* Ac.

As can be inferred from the title, *Qualitative Social Work* provides a forum for qualitative research and evaluation and qualitative approaches to practice. Regular features of the journal include "Response and Commentary," "Practice and Teaching of Qualitative Social Work," "New Voices by New Practitioners, Graduate Students, New Academicians," and "Marginal Voices." Recommended for academic libraries that support social work programs.

5692. *Research on Social Work Practice.* [ISSN: 1049-7315] 1990. bi-m. GBP 418. Ed(s): Bruce A Thyer. Sage Publications, Inc., 2455 Teller Rd, Thousand Oaks, CA 91320; info@sagepub.com; http://www.sagepub.com. Illus., index, adv. Sample. Refereed. Circ: 1200. Vol. ends: Nov. Reprint: PSC. *Indexed:* ASG, ASSIA, AgeL, CINAHL, CJA, HRA, PRA, PsycInfo, SFSA, SSA, SSCI, SUSA, SWR&A, SociolAb, V&AA. *Bk. rev.:* 2-4, signed. *Aud.:* Ac.

This journal is celebrating its 15th anniversary as the first professional social work journal to focus on evaluation research and on validating methods of assessment in social work practice. The journal publishes original reports of: first, evidence-based evaluation studies on the outcomes of social work practice;

second, studies on the development and validation of social work assessment methods; and third, reviews of the practice-research literature that convey direct applications to social work practice. Regular features include outcome studies, new methods of assessment, scholarly reviews, invited essays, and book reviews. A must-have for academic libraries that support programs in social work.

5693. Social Service Review. [ISSN: 0037-7961] 1927. q. USD 181 domestic; USD 196.86 Canada; USD 189 elsewhere. Ed(s): Michae R. Sosin. University of Chicago Press, Journals Division, PO Box 37005, Chicago, IL 60637; subscriptions@press.uchicago.edu; http://www.journals.uchicago.edu. Illus., index, adv. Sample. Refereed. Circ: 1700 Paid. Vol. ends: Dec. Microform: MIM; PMC; PQC. Online: Chadwyck-Healey Inc.; EBSCO Publishing, EBSCO Host; Florida Center for Library Automation; Gale; ProQuest LLC (Ann Arbor). Reprint: PSC. *Indexed:* ASG, ASSIA, AgeL, AmH&L, BRI, CBRI, CJA, ExcerpMed, HistAb, IBSS, IMFL, IPSA, JEL, LRI, MCR, PAIS, PSA, PsycInfo, RI-1, SFSA, SSA, SSCI, SUSA, SWA, SWR&A, SociolAb. *Bk. rev.:* 5-7, signed. *Aud.:* Ga, Ac.

Celebrating 80 years of publication, this journal is a cornerstone to the field of social service. It examines and evaluates social welfare policy and practice. It provides multidisciplinary and multicultural analyses of current policies and past practices. Research comes from social welfare scholars and practitioners, as well as economists, theologians, historians, psychologists, and political scientists. In addition to thought-provoking essays, there is an extensive book review section that can be used for collection development purposes. A must-have for academic and larger public libraries.

5694. Social Work. [ISSN: 0037-8046] 1956. q. USD 129 print & online eds. (Individuals, USD 89 print & online eds.; Free to members). Ed(s): Paula Delo, Jeanne C Marsh. N A SW Press, 750 First St NE, Ste 700, Washington, DC 20002-4241; press@naswdc.org; http://www.naswpress.org. Illus., index, adv. Refereed. Circ: 151000 Paid and free. Vol. ends: Nov. Online: EBSCO Publishing, EBSCO Host; Florida Center for Library Automation; Gale; IngentaConnect; Northern Light Technology, Inc.; OCLC Online Computer Library Center, Inc.; ProQuest K-12 Learning Solutions; ProQuest LLC (Ann Arbor). *Indexed:* ASSIA, AbAn, AgeL, AmH&L, ArtHuCI, BRI, CBRI, CINAHL, CJA, ECER, ERIC, ExcerpMed, HRA, LRI, MASUSE, PAIS, PRA, PsycInfo, SFSA, SSA, SSCI, SWA, SWR&A, SociolAb, V&AA. *Bk. rev.:* 1-2, signed. *Aud.:* Ac, Sa.

Published by the National Association of Social Workers, this is a premier journal for the social work profession. The audience is practitioners, faculty, and students. The focus of the journal is to improve practice and advance knowledge in social work and social welfare. Specifically, it focuses on social policy. This journal is ranked No. 1 in the Social Sciences Citation Index. A must-have for academic libraries and libraries that support social service professionals.

5695. Social Work Education. [ISSN: 0261-5479] 1980. 8x/yr. GBP 737 print & online eds. Ed(s): Michael Preston-Shoot. Routledge, 4 Park Sq, Milton Park, Abingdon, OX14 4RN, United Kingdom; info@routledge.co.uk; http://www.routledge.co.uk. Circ: 800. Online: EBSCO Publishing, EBSCO Host; Gale; IngentaConnect; OCLC Online Computer Library Center, Inc.; SwetsWise Online Content. Reprint: PSC. *Indexed:* ASSIA, BrEdI, CJA, FR, IBR, IBSS, IBZ, PsycInfo, SSA, SWA, SWR&A, SociolAb. *Bk. rev.:* Number and length vary. *Aud.:* Ac.

The aim of this journal is to publish articles "of a critical and reflective nature concerned with the theory and practice of social care and social work education at all levels." It attempts to publish pieces that reflect the wide constituency of social work education and training. It includes book reviews and a column called "Ideas in Action." Recommended for academic libraries that support schools of social work.

5696. Social Work Research. Supersedes in part (in 1994): *Social Work Research and Abstracts;* Which was formerly (until 1977): *Abstracts for Social Workers.* [ISSN: 1070-5309] 1977. q. USD 125 print & online eds. (Individuals, USD 89; Members, USD 54). Ed(s): Enola K Procktor, Paula Delo. N A SW Press, 750 First St NE, Ste 700, Washington, DC

20002-4241; press@naswdc.org; http://www.naswpress.org. Illus., index, adv. Refereed. Circ: 3000 Paid. Vol. ends: Dec. Online: EBSCO Publishing, EBSCO Host; Florida Center for Library Automation; Gale; IngentaConnect; Northern Light Technology, Inc.; ProQuest K-12 Learning Solutions; ProQuest LLC (Ann Arbor). *Indexed:* ASG, ASSIA, AbAn, AgeL, CINAHL, CJA, ERIC, HRA, PsycInfo, SFSA, SSA, SSCI, SWR&A, SociolAb, V&AA. *Aud.:* Ac, Sa.

Published by the National Association of Social Workers, this journal publishes analytic reviews and theoretical articles that focus on social work research, practice-based research, evaluation studies, and diverse research studies. A must-have for academic libraries that support social work programs or graduate programs in sociology, and for libraries that serve social work professionals.

5697. Social Work with Groups: a journal of community and clinical practice. [ISSN: 0160-9513] 1978. q. USD 635 print & online eds. Ed(s): Andrew Malekoff, Roselle Kurland. Haworth Social Work Practice Press, 10 Alice St, Binghamton, NY 13904; getinfo@haworthpress.com; http://www.haworthpress.com/. Illus., adv. Sample. Refereed. Circ: 1012 Paid. Microform: PQC. Online: EBSCO Publishing, EBSCO Host; OCLC Online Computer Library Center, Inc.; SwetsWise Online Content. Reprint: HAW. *Indexed:* ASG, ASSIA, AgeL, CINAHL, CJA, HRA, IBR, IBZ, IMFL, PsycInfo, SFSA, SSA, SSCI, SWA, SWR&A, SociolAb, V&AA. *Bk. rev.:* 5-7, signed. *Aud.:* Ac, Sa.

The focus of this journal is on group work in psychiatric, rehabilitative, and multipurpose social work and social service agencies. It includes crisis theory and group work and the use of group programs in clinical and community practice. Recent articles focus on ethical issues in group work; healing trauma and loss in group work with immigrants; and advanced education for group work practitioners. Recommended for academic libraries that support social work programs and libraries that serve social services professionals.

Suicide and Life-Threatening Behavior. See Death and Dying section.

■ SPIRITUALITY AND WELL-BEING

Jane Hutton, Electronic Resources/Reference Librarian, Francis Harvey Green Library, West Chester University of Pennsylvania, West Chester, PA 19383 jhutton@wcupa.edu

Introduction

From the seventh through the eleventh editions of *Magazines for Libraries*, this section was titled "New Age." As society and language usage have changed, the section heading has adapted, and "Spirituality and Well-Being" was adopted in the twelfth edition as a more appropriate description. Personal transformation through spirituality is the common theme of all the periodicals included here. The readership will be those who seek physical, mental, and emotional well-being through spiritual paths. The intersection with well-being throughout the magazines may be drawn through purely spiritual language or by concrete recommendations about food or exercise.

A goal of the section is to include a representative sampling of periodicals from many viewpoints rather than multiple titles from a single viewpoint. The emphasis is on North American publications. *Kindred Spirit*, published in the United Kingdom, has been included for a broader perspective. Although two of the journals, *Parabola* and *Journal of Transpersonal Psychology*, are appropriate for academic research and are indexed extensively, all of the publications primarily support individual enlightenment rather than scholarly enterprise, and most are not indexed. Academic libraries may wish to consider purchase of nonscholarly titles to support student or faculty interest.

Libraries have an opportunity to be proactive in presenting the alternate viewpoints represented by these periodicals or to simply collect according to local readership demand. Academic libraries with a strong liberal arts mission may want to consider subscriptions to at least two or three of the publications. Many health practices and ecological ideas dismissed by mainstream medicine or science 30 years ago are now broadly accepted. Some of the ideas presented in these periodicals may not be "alternative" in the future.

Most of the magazines are published by small organizations. Web sites are available for every publication and, as noted, a few are available as electronic journals. However, none of the titles are electronic-only publications.

See the Religion section for periodicals encompassing mainstream religious practice, and the Health and Fitness section for other magazines dealing with alternative health.

5698. *Ascent Magazine: yoga for an inspired life.* [ISSN: 0315-8179] 1970. q. CND 23.95 domestic; USD 19.95 United States; USD 29 elsewhere. Ed(s): Sarah E Truman. Ascent, 837 rue Gilford, Montreal, PQ H2J 1P1, Canada; info@ascentmagazine.com; http://www.ascentmagazine.com. Illus. Circ: 10000. *Indexed:* AmHI, SD. *Bk. rev.:* Various number and length. *Aud.:* Ga.

Winner of the Utne Independent Press Award for Best Spiritual Coverage in 2005 and 2003, *Ascent Magazine* is a Canadian publication on the power of yoga in a spiritual life and the experiences of spirituality from diverse traditions. Each quarterly issue centers on a theme such as knowledge, food, family, or power. Black-and-white photographs and graphics reinforce the spiritual focus of the articles and features. The articles feature personal experiences of melding a spiritual life with daily life in the world. Regular columns include "science & yoga," "kuanyin's kitchen" (with recipes) and reviews of books, music, and film. Advertising is limited to cover pages and "the om-ventory directory & marketplace of community resources." Recommended for public and special libraries where there is interest in yoga, Eastern religions, or alternative health.

5699. *The Beltane Papers: a journal of women's mysteries.* Former titles: *T B P's Octava; Beltane Papers.* [ISSN: 1074-3634] 1984. 3x/yr. USD 16 domestic; USD 21 Canada; USD 28 elsewhere. Ed(s): M L Thompson Helland. The Beltane Papers, P O Box 29694, Bellingham, WA 98228-1694; beltane@az.com. Illus., adv. Circ: 5000. *Indexed:* GendWatch. *Bk. rev.:* 10, 70-essay length, signed. *Aud.:* Ac, Sa.

This journal about the feminine sacred, which has been written and published by women since 1992, has the aim to "provide women with a safe place within which to explore and express the sacred in their lives." Goddess spirituality is the obvious primary focus (Gaia is listed on the masthead as the "Guiding Goddess"), but diverse personal and research articles are welcomed. Recent issues include writings on amulets, yoga for the elderly, bereavement dreaming, spiritual simplicity, and a "housewife theory of history." Each issue contains contributions of fiction, poetry, and art. Horoscopes, herb lore, foods, and crafts are also commonly included. Recommended for public libraries where there is significant interest and for academic or special libraries with a focus on spirituality or women's issues. Indexing and full text since Fall 2000 are included in ProQuest's Gender Watch database.

5700. *Circle Magazine: celebrating nature, spirit & magic.* Formerly: *Circle Network News.* 1980. 4x/yr. USD 25 domestic; USD 30 in Canada & Mexico; USD 48 elsewhere. Ed(s): Selena Fox, Dennis Carpenter. Circle Sanctuary, PO Box 9, Barneveld, WI 53507; circle@mhtc.net. Illus., adv. *Bk. rev.:* Various number and length. *Aud.:* Ga.

Each issue of this "Nature Spirituality (Paganism)" magazine centers on a special theme such as sacred healing, ritual, or celebrating adulthood. Color covers illustrate each theme. Published quarterly since 1984 (known as *Circle Network News* until 1988) by the Circle Sanctuary in Wisconsin, the black-and-white pages include articles, news, and artwork. Most articles are one to three pages long and share ideas or experiences such as "the healing presence of trees," "using chant in Wiccan rituals," or "new moon ritual." Practical advice is also given; for example, methods for holding open rituals, incense ingredients, and herbcraft. Regular sections include classifieds, "Passages" to mark life transitions of community members, and "New and Notable" book reviews. Advertisements are confined to the "Marketplace" section. Recommended for libraries where significant Wiccan communities exist.

5701. *The Empty Vessel: a journal of contemporary Taoism.* [ISSN: 1073-7480] 1993. q. USD 28 Canada; USD 40 elsewhere. Ed(s): Solala Towler. The Abode of the Eternal Tao, 1991 Garfield St, Eugene, OR 97405; solala@abodetao.com. Illus., adv. *Bk. rev.:* Various number and length. *Aud.:* Ga, Ac, Sa.

The Empty Vessel seeks to share the wisdom and practice of Daoism as a spiritual life that embraces the entire individual and the connections to other life forms. Published quarterly since 1994, the feature writings are inspirational or reflective pieces by Dao practitioners and teachers. Rather than many short articles, each issue contains several substantial articles of three to seven pages in length. Reference lists or suggestions for further reading accompany many of the articles. Black-and-white illustrations and calligraphy enhance the text, and the colorful front covers successfully promote the journal's content. Advertisements are in black and white and frequently full-page, and are dispersed throughout, but do not detract from the journal's tranquil image. Regular departments include reviews of books and videos, a classified directory, and "Tools for Living the Dao" along with poetry and story contributions. Appropriate for public, academic, and special libraries where there is an interest in alternative medicine or Eastern philosophy.

5702. *Journal of Transpersonal Psychology.* [ISSN: 0022-524X] 1969. s-a. USD 80 (Individuals, USD 35). Ed(s): Marcie Boucouvalas. Association for Transpersonal Psychology, PO Box 29030, San Francisco, CA 94129; atpweb@mindspring.com; http://www.atpweb.org. Circ: 3000. Microform: PQC. Online: ProQuest LLC (Ann Arbor). *Indexed:* AgeL, IBR, IBZ, PsycInfo, RI-1, SSCI. *Bk. rev.:* Various number and length. *Aud.:* Ac, Sa.

Transpersonal psychology "combines insights from modern psychology with those drawn from traditional spiritual practices, both Eastern and Western," according to the web site of the Association for Transpersonal Psychology. Abraham Maslow and Anthony Sutich created the field of transpersonal psychology in 1969, when this journal was founded. This scholarly journal covers clinical and theoretical perspectives in this psychological specialization. The stated aim of the journal is to focus attention on awareness of "the integration of psychological and human experience, and the transcendence of self." This journal is recommended for academic or special libraries with religious or psychology collections.

5703. *Kindred Spirit: the UK's leading guide for body, mind and spirit.* [ISSN: 0955-7067] 1987. 6x/yr. GBP 21 domestic; GBP 25.50 in North America & Europe; GBP 31.50 elsewhere. Ed(s): Patricia Yates, Richard Beaumont. Kindred Spirit, Sandwell Barns, Harberton, Totnes, TQ9 7LJ, United Kingdom; editors@kindredspirit.co.uk; http://www.kindredspirit.co.uk. Adv. *Indexed:* CPerI. *Aud.:* Ga.

Kindred Spirit, the "UK's leading guide for Mind, Body and Spirit" since 1987, has a glossy, colorful, popular magazine format that entices readers to explore its pages. Broad issues of spirituality such as signs of serpent wisdom, psychospiritual bodywork, walking a pilgrimage, and benefits of frankincense are presented in text with plentiful illustrations and suggested resources for more information. Health-related articles deal with environmental issues or alternative medical practice. Regular features include editorial comment and letters, news briefs, horoscopes, humor, music reviews, cookery, and resource directories. Advertisements are plentiful. Appropriate for general audiences where there is an interest in exploring topics of alternative spirituality. Available as an e-journal subscription from www.kindredspirit.co.uk.

5704. *Light of Consciousness.* Formerly (until vol.1, no.1, 1988): *Truth Consciousness Journal.* [ISSN: 1040-7448] 1988. 3x/yr. USD 14 domestic; USD 17.50 Canada; USD 20 Mexico. Ed(s): Sita Stuhlmiller. Truth Consciousness at Desert Ashram, 3403 W Sweetwater Dr, Tucson, AZ 85745-9301. Illus., adv. Circ: 20000. *Bk. rev.:* Various number and length. *Aud.:* Ga, Sa.

Published three times yearly by Truth Consciousness, this journal is "dedicated to the inner unfoldment of the soul, the awakening into Pure Consciousness." The oneness of Truth through "common principles of all spiritual paths" is conveyed by the founder Swami Amar Jyoti in the introductory Satsang (spiritual discourse) of each issue and in ensuing articles. Front covers with color illustrations of a suited office worker meditating cross-legged on a cluttered desk and a polar bear in arctic light introduced the journal issues on "Living the dharma: spirituality in our busy world" and "Remembering the light" respectively. The covers symbolize the magazine's aim to weave spirituality into current society. Explorations into the spirituality of famous persons such as Harriet Tubman and Albert Einstein reinforce the theme of common spiritual natures. Biocommunication, overcoming insomnia with yogic principles, reincarnation, poverty vs. abundance, and practicing patience are representative of the popularly appealing topics addressed by contributors. Regular sections include consciousness, poetry/art, spiritual cinema, and reviews of books, children's books, music, and video. Advertisements are relegated to the "Lifestyle Bazaar" section. Recommended for special or public libraries with reader interest.

5705. Mountain Record: the Zen practitioner's journal. [ISSN: 0896-8942] 1981. q. USD 24 domestic; USD 39 foreign. Ed(s): Konrad Ryushin Marchaj. Dharma Communications, Inc., S. Plank Rd., Box 197MR, Mt. Tremper, NY 12457; mreditor@dharma.net; http://www.dharma.net/dchome.html. Adv. Circ: 5000 Paid. *Bk. rev.:* Various number and length. *Aud.:* Ga, Sa.

A recipient of the 2002 Utne Independent Press Award for Spiritual Coverage, *Mountain Record* continues to uphold its reputation for fine writing. Published by the Zen Buddhist Mountain Monastery in Mt. Tremper, New York, the journal contains news and events from the monastery community as well as inspirational accounts, essays, and poems from Zen practitioners. Each quarterly publication centers on a broad theme of spiritual transformation, such as consciousness, medicine and sickness, or dreams. For example, articles for the "Urban Practice" issue deal with spirituality as it intersects with city life. Small black-and-white illustrations add focus and dimension to the text. Each issue contains media reviews of titles in any format. Advertisements are combined in a final section as a "Directory of Products and Services." Although someone already familiar with Zen Buddhism may gain more from this periodical than the casual reader, a nonpractitioner could be equally inspired by the writings. Appropriate for public, academic, or special libraries that collect in the areas of spirituality or Buddhism.

5706. PanGaia: creating an earth wise spirituality. Formerly (until 1997): *Green Man.* [ISSN: 1096-0996] 1993. q. USD 18 domestic; USD 24 Canada; USD 5.95 newsstand/cover domestic. Ed(s): Anne Newkirk Niven. B B I Media, Inc., PO Box 641, Point Arena, CA 95468; bbimedia@mcn.org; http://www.bbimedia.com. Adv. Circ: 5500 Paid. *Indexed:* AltPI. *Bk. rev.:* Various number and length. *Aud.:* Ga, Sa.

Since 1998, *PanGaia* has been representing pagan spirituality with "non-fiction, fiction, poetry, reviews, photography and art from women and men of all Earth-affirming spiritual paths." Each journal issue contains substantial content in all literary forms. Perspectives from readers and controversy columns give voice to multiple viewpoints. Multi-page articles with references address such topics as evidence for a nonviolent ancient Minoan goddess society, moving beyond Gaian monotheism to a polytheistic ecopaganism, and a spiritual response to the Katrina storm devastation of New Orleans. Fiction, poetry, and experiential writings are interspersed. Artwork in black and white enhances the texts and is credited. Recent issue themes include "Pagans and the Land," "Do Pagans Need an Afterlife?" and "Celtic Spirituality." Creative cover art is in color and illustrates each issue's theme. The publisher, Blessed Bee, Inc., (www.bbimedia.com) also publishes *NewWitch* (ISSN 1546-2838), *SageWoman* (ISSN 1068-1698), and *The Blessed Bee*, a pagan family newsletter. Each publication includes the same well-constructed melange of practical and inspirational writing, artwork, and reader contributions. A valuable resource for public, academic, or special libraries where there is an interest in alternative spiritualities.

5707. Parabola: myth, tradition, and the search for meaning. [ISSN: 0362-1596] 1976. q. USD 24 domestic; USD 30 foreign. Ed(s): David Appelbaum. Society for the Study of Myth and Tradition, 656 Broadway, New York, NY 10012-2317; editors@parabola.org; http://www.parabola.org. Illus., index, adv. Sample. Circ: 41000 Paid. Vol. ends: Winter. Microform: PQC. Online: Gale; Northern Light Technology, Inc.; H.W. Wilson. *Indexed:* AmHI, ArtHuCI, BRI, CBRI, FLI, HumInd, LRI, MLA-IB, R&TA, RI-1, RILM, SSCI. *Bk. rev.:* 5-8, 600-1,200 words. *Aud.:* Ac, Sa.

Each issue explores how various world spiritual traditions view or seek answers to a particular aspect of human existence such as restraint, the power of not doing, absence and longing, or friendship. Articles are reflective, first-person experiences or collected insights from spiritual writers. Interviews with exemplary individuals center on the issue's theme. Black-and-white photos and art illuminate the articles. Regular sections include "Epicycles," which are

stories or parables from world traditions, poetry, "Tangents" (arts in review), "Holy Earth" (being in nature), and film and book reviews. Advertisements are few and intermingled only with review sections. Recent reviews cover a Chinese ink painter, musicians, and an architect. For its nondenominational view of religious traditions and coverage of mythology, it is strongly recommended for academic libraries and special libraries with related collections.

5708. ReVision: a journal of consciousness and transformation. [ISSN: 0275-6935] 1978. q. USD 103 (Individuals, USD 49 print & online eds.; USD 25 newsstand/cover). Ed(s): Jeff Deck. Heldref Publications, 1319 18th St, NW, Washington, DC 20036-1802; subscribe@heldref.org; http://www.heldref.org. Illus., index, adv. Sample. Refereed. Circ: 303 Paid. Vol. ends: No. 4. Microform: PQC. Online: EBSCO Publishing, EBSCO Host; Gale; OCLC Online Computer Library Center, Inc.; ProQuest K-12 Learning Solutions; ProQuest LLC (Ann Arbor); H.W. Wilson. Reprint: PSC. *Indexed:* AltPI, AmHI, HumInd, RI-1. *Aud.:* Ac, Sa, Ga.

With an integrative approach, this journal "emphasizes the transformative dimensions of current and traditional thought and practice." A theme such as "Wisdom" or "Revisioning Higher Education" is the focus of each issue. Peer-reviewed articles with references explore experiences or propose creative solutions related to the theme. "Wisdom Issue, Part 2" encompasses cultural values connected to wisdom, quotes from wise elders, psychological theories and personality characteristics of wisdom, the value of the "Wise Woman/Crone," and suggestions to promote paths to wisdom in American schools. The interdisciplinary focus of the journal places spirituality as an integral but not always explicitly stated topic. Recommended for public, academic, and special libraries with an interest in integrative thought.

5709. Sacred Pathways. 1998. bi-m. Sacred Pathways Magazine, PO Box 812696, Wellesley, MA 02482. *Bk. rev.:* Various number and length. *Aud.:* Ga, Sa.

Published since 1998 and expanded in 2005, *Sacred Pathways* is dedicated to "a simple philosophy—that transformation begins with each individual." While the yogic perspective is primary, a holistic approach to a transformative life is emphasized in articles by spiritual teachers and practitioners. The basic non-glossy, black-and-white format does not seek to entice new readers, but rather to inspire and inform current followers. Nevertheless, any library collection where there is an interest in yoga or Eastern religious practice can benefit from the addition of this title. Interviews with yogic spiritual leaders are plentiful, and articles address themes such as sacred sounds (mantras) or practical issues such as yoga for amputees. Advertisements are dispersed throughout each issue, and regular columns include astrology, book reviews, and a calendar of events.

5710. Sedona Journal of Emergence. Formerly: *Emergence (Sedona).* [ISSN: 1530-3365] 1989. q. USD 76 domestic; USD 75 in Canada & Mexico. Light Technology Publishing, PO Box 3870, Flagstaff, AZ 86003; sedonajo@sedonajo.com; http://www.sedonajo.com/. *Bk. rev.:* Various number and length. *Aud.:* Ga.

This journal seeks to "provide a forum for those who wish to speak to us from other dimensions" and "celebrate our emergence into multidimensionality." The spiritual conveyance of channeling is expressed in articles about fifth-dimensional awareness, planetary interventions, animal communications, and openness to portals. Each issue contains experiential writings and advice under the major headings of "Channeling," "Shining the Light," "Predictions," "Articles," and "Features." Features include an advice column and "Nurturing stories for babies and young children." Formatted on sturdy black-and-white paper, the textual content is primary, with some illustrations and photos of contributors. Advertising is minimal. Covers are colorful and imaginative. Readership is limited by the special nature of the magazine's content. Available as an e-journal subscription from www.sedonajournal.com.

5711. Shambhala Sun: buddhism culture meditation life. Formerly (until Apr. 1992): *Vajradhatu Sun.* [ISSN: 1190-7886] 1978. bi-m. CND 24 domestic; USD 17.95 United States; USD 39 elsewhere. Ed(s): Melvin

McLeod. Shambhala Sun, 1660 Hollis St #603, Halifax, NS B3J 1V7, Canada; subscription@shambhalasun.com. Illus., adv. Circ: 35000 Paid. *Indexed:* CBCARef, RI-1. *Bk. rev.:* Various number and length. *Aud.:* Ga.

Published in Nova Scotia, this bimonthly publication of Buddhist spirituality has a glossy, popular-magazine format with colorful illustrations, photos, and advertisements throughout. The title reflects the periodical's self-proclaimed focus on "the spirit of wakefulness." Throughout each issue, the feature articles primarily describe personal perspectives of spiritual transformation and paths to enlightenment such as visualization, meditation, and letting go of self-importance. Articles also relate spiritual experiences in response to specific, personal situations of emotional affliction or physical disease. Profiles and interviews with spiritually inspiring individuals emphasize the intersection of spiritual belief with real-world political and social issues. Regular departments include book reviews, a marketplace, and a directory of meditation retreats and yoga centers. A familiarity with Buddhist philosophy is not required for readers to appreciate the inspirational writings in this magazine. Recommended for a general adult audience.

5712. *What is Enlightenment?: redefining spirituality for an evolving world.* [ISSN: 1080-3432] 1991. 10x/yr. USD 28 in US & Canada; USD 4 newsstand/cover domestic; USD 6 newsstand/cover Canada. Ed(s): Andrew Cohen, Wren Bernstein. EnlightenNext, PO Box 2360, Lenox, MA 01240; wie@wie.org. Illus., adv. Sample. Circ: 25000 Paid and controlled. Online: ProQuest LLC (Ann Arbor). *Indexed:* AltPI. *Bk. rev.:* Various number and length. *Aud.:* Ga, Sa.

Originally published semi-annually and now issued quarterly, this magazine primarily reflects the philosophy of its founder and editor-in-chief, spiritual teacher Andrew Cohen. Unlike many of the magazines reviewed in this section, *What is Enlightenment?* expresses spiritual inquiry with an activist and Western approach, with the mission to "create a dynamic context for conscious engagement with the greatest challenges of our times, a groundwork for the ongoing liberation of human potential." Articles that explore the transformational possibilities of corporate business or capitalism as an idealistic process coexist with articles on the scientific evidence for reincarnation and the dimensions of consciousness in nonhuman animals. Bodybuilding as a spiritual exercise, Islamic vegetarians reacting to factory farming, and dangers of food toxins are recent health-related topics. Regular departments include letters to the editor, book and media reviews, and editorial columns. Plentiful advertisements include full-color pages. A substantial, glossy magazine with sophisticated layout, this publication is appropriate for large public libraries or special libraries. The magazine's web site at www.wie.org won the 2006 Webby People's Voice Award for "most popular religion and spirituality web site."

5713. *Yoga Journal.* [ISSN: 0191-0965] 1975. 8x/yr. USD 15.95 domestic; USD 22.95 Canada; USD 37.95 elsewhere. Ed(s): Katherine Griffin. Yoga Journal, 475 Sansome St, Ste 850, San Francisco, CA 94111. Illus. Sample. Circ: 325000 Paid. Microform: PQC. Online: EBSCO Publishing, EBSCO Host. *Indexed:* AltPI, SD. *Bk. rev.:* Various number and length. *Aud.:* Ga.

Personal transformation through the practice of yoga is the focus of this magazine. Emphasis is placed on practical self-help articles for the physical and mental practice of yoga. Yoga poses are well illustrated and accompanied by information on health benefits and contraindications. "Ask the expert" and "Letters" sections exemplify a welcoming approach to yoga novices. Recipes and healthful eating suggestions, and tips in areas such as gardening, natural cosmetics, and travel, generalize the popular appeal for readers. Book, video, and audio reviews are included in each issue. Advertising is plentiful and dispersed throughout the magazine. Recommended for general adult audiences.

■ SPORTS

General/Extreme Sports/Physical Education, Coaching, and Sports Sciences/Specific Sports

See also Boats and Boating; Environment and Conservation; Fishing; Hiking, Climbing, and Outdoor Recreation; and Hunting and Guns sections.

Betsy Park, Head, Reference Department, The University of Memphis Libraries, Memphis, TN 38152; ehpark@memphis.edu

Introduction

"Play ball!" Ever since April 14, 1910, when William Howard Taft pitched to Walter Johnson, presidents have thrown the opening pitch to signal the beginning of major league play. In the early seventeenth century, American colonists kicked an air-filled bladder in a game that evolved to become American football. Sports have long played a central role in many of our lives. Americans study, watch, support, and participate in all types of sports, and new sports are constantly being invented. America's passion is reflected in the number of sport magazines and journals published every year. Fans follow their favorite teams and players, gain behind-the-scene information about the competition, read profiles and interviews with players, follow the latest scandals, and test their knowledge through trivia contests and crossword puzzles. Participants improve their performance, prevent injury, prepare themselves better physically and mentally, and learn about equipment, travel, clothing, lifestyle, and personalities. Scholars study the economics, business, history, sociology, philosophy, physiology, and science of sports.

Ulrich's Periodicals Directory lists almost 9,000 sports-related titles. With so many published each year, it should come as no surprise that as new ones are created, others die. Transworld Publications has introduced a new surfing magazine, aimed at the surfer willing to take extreme risks. *Her Sports* was recently launched to appeal to the active woman. In 2006, Vulcan Print Media announced that they were seeking a buyer for the venerable *The Sporting News*. Century Sports has ceased publishing several of its "digest" publications, many of which had been in continuous publication for more than 20 years.

With so many magazines available, not all of them can be covered in this section. Titles chosen for inclusion include general sport magazines; journals in physical education, coaching, and the sports sciences; extreme sport magazines; and titles focused on a specific sport. An attempt has been made to include a wide range of sports and to pick representative titles. Since the extreme sport category is comparatively new, a particular effort has been made to identify new titles. This section contains only a modest selection from the thousands of possible titles. It is hoped that the following list will aid in the difficult process of making purchase decisions.

Basic Periodicals

GENERAL. All levels: *E S P N The Magazine, The Sporting News, Sports Illustrated.*

PHYSICAL EDUCATION, COACHING AND SPORTS SCIENCES. Ems: *Journal of Teaching in Physical Education, Teaching Elementary Physical Education;* Hs: *Coach and Athletic Director; Journal of Physical Education, Recreation and Dance;* Ac: *Adapted Physical Activity Quarterly; American Journal of Sports Medicine; Journal of Applied Biomechanics; Journal of Physical Education, Recreation and Dance; Journal of Teaching in Physical Education; Quest; Research Quarterly for Exercise and Sport.*

SPECIFIC SPORTS. All levels: *Baseball America, Bicycling, Golf Magazine, Hockey News, International Figure Skating, Runner's World, Ski, Soccer America, Tennis, VolleyballUSA.*

Basic Abstracts and Indexes

Physical Education Index, SPORTDiscus.

General

5714. *Aethlon: the journal of sport literature.* Formerly (until 1988): *Arete.* [ISSN: 1048-3756] 1983. s-a. Free to members. Ed(s): Joyce Duncan. Sports Literature Association, East Tennessee State University, PO Box 70270, Johnson City, TN 37614; http://www.uta.edu/english/sla/. Illus., adv. Refereed. Circ: 650 Paid. *Indexed:* AmHI, BRI, CBRI, MLA-IB, PEI, SD. *Bk. rev.:* 20, 500 to 2,000 words. *Aud.:* Ac.

For 20 years, the Sports Literature Association has published *Aethlon: The Journal of Sport Literature,* "a scholarly journal designed to celebrate the marriage of serious, interpretive literature with the world of play, games, and sport." This semi-annual journal is published by East Tennessee State University. It publishes critical articles, poetry, fiction, nonfiction, drama, and book reviews—all types of literature related to sports. Issues run approximately 200 pages. University professors, novelists, short story writers, poets, and dramatists contribute the both serious and humorous entries. Particularly suitable for academic libraries, although public libraries may also want to consider it.

5715. *E S P N The Magazine.* [ISSN: 1097-1998] 1998. bi-w. USD 26 domestic; CND 45 Canada; USD 4.99 newsstand/cover. E S P N The Magazine, Inc., 19 E. 34th St, New York, NY 10016-4303. Illus., adv. Sample. Circ: 850000. *Indexed:* PEI. *Aud.:* Hs, Ga, Ac.

Published since 1998, *ESPN, The Magazine* is a showy, oversized (12" x 10"), general-interest sports magazine. Each biweekly issue of 100-plus pages contains photographs and advertisements. Regular features include double page spreads of various sporting events, short articles of current interest, profiles of athletes, brief reports of major sports events, statistics, a Q&A section, and a regular column written by ESPN's Stuart Scott. Feature articles touch on a variety of sports and players. The writing style is informal, sometimes humorous. The print magazine is supplemented by its electronic version at espn.go.com/magazine. Sports enthusiasts at academic and public libraries will enjoy this publication.

5716. *Her Sports + Fitness.* Formerly: *Her Sports.* 2004. bi-m. USD 16.95 domestic; USD 24.95 Canada; USD 39.95 elsewhere. Ed(s): Heidi Kelchner. Wet Dog Media, Inc., 245 Central Ave, Ste C, St. Petersburg, FL 33701. Adv. Circ: 75000 Controlled. *Aud.:* Ga.

This glossy bimonthly, begun in 2004, targets the active woman who likes to run, bike, hike, ski, and the like. Geared toward the serious fitness advocate, the magazine publishes articles detailing the latest trends in the active sports market, interviews, product reviews, information on active vacations, training tips, and nutrition advice. Recent issues cover scenic walks in Ireland, the best spring footwear, indoor cardio workouts, an interview with a professional mountain biker, heart disease in women, and triathlon training. Women sports enthusiasts would appreciate reading this magazine at their public libraries.

5717. *Juco Review.* [ISSN: 0047-2956] 1948. 9x/yr. USD 30 domestic; USD 50 foreign. Ed(s): George E Killian. National Junior College Athletic Association, PO Box 7305, Colorado Springs, CO 80933-7305; lbrizzie@njcaa.org; http://www.njcaa.org. Illus., adv. Sample. Circ: 3000. Microform: PQC. *Indexed:* PEI, SD. *Aud.:* Ac.

Juco Review, the official magazine of the National Junior College Athletic Association (NJCAA), is published monthly during the academic year, September through May. The focus of the association is to "promote and foster junior college athletics on intersectional and national levels so that results will be consistent with the total educational program of its members." Issues contain articles on eligibility, membership, coaching strategies and techniques, statistics, national championships, and a highlight of an "NJCAA college of the month." Issues run approximately 20 to 25 pages. The print journal is supplemented by the association's web site at www.njcaa.org. Appropriate for two-year colleges.

5718. *The Sporting News.* [ISSN: 0038-805X] 1886. 50x/yr. USD 16.50. Ed(s): John Rawlings. American City Business Journals, Inc., 120 W Morehead St, Charlotte, NC 28202. Illus., adv. Circ: 715000 Paid. Vol. ends: Dec. Microform: BHP; PQC. Online: EBSCO Publishing, EBSCO Host; Gale; LexisNexis; Northern Light Technology, Inc.; OCLC Online Computer Library Center, Inc.; ProQuest LLC (Ann Arbor). *Indexed:* ASIP, MASUSE, SD. *Aud.:* Ga.

The Sporting News, which bills itself as "the first newsweekly in sports," has been reporting the news of sports for 120 years. Each 60-page issue contains current information on the "Super Seven": baseball, college and professional football, college and professional basketball, hockey, and NASCAR. Articles cover teams and players, statistics, strategies, and scouting reports. The focus is on news, and the magazine generally does not include long feature articles or personality profiles. Daily news, links to *The Sporting News* radio, and fantasy baseball and football can be found at the web site (www.sportingnews.com). Sports fans will welcome this publication at academic and public libraries.

5719. *Sports Collectors Digest.* [ISSN: 0278-2693] 1973. w. USD 27.98 domestic; USD 118.98 Canada; USD 179.98 elsewhere. Ed(s): T S O'Connell. Krause Publications, Inc., 700 E State St, Iola, WI 54990-0001; info@krause.com; http://www.krause.com. Illus., adv. Circ: 23356 Paid and free. Microform: PQC. *Aud.:* Ga.

Dating from 1973, *Sport Collectors Digest* is the hobby's oldest publication. It covers all aspects of the hobby including trading cards, autographs, uniforms, and equipment. Columns include an auction calendar, show schedules, letters to the editor, interviews with traders and collectors, features on specific collectibles, card manufacturers, and classified ads. Recent issues include news on DiMaggio's collection at a New York City auction; a report that the Mile High Card Company had scored on the auction circuit with a Babe Ruth rookie card; a Jim McMahon talk about the hobby; and a Baseball Hall of Fame autograph price guide. Serious collectors will welcome this publication at public libraries.

5720. *Sports Illustrated.* [ISSN: 0038-822X] 1954. w. USD 39 domestic; USD 43.91 Canada; USD 3.99 newsstand/cover. Ed(s): Norman Pearlstine. Time Inc., Sports Illustrated Group, Sports Illustrated Bldg, 135 W 50th St, 4th Fl., New York, NY 10020-1393. Illus., index, adv. Circ: 3150000 Paid. Microform: PQC. Online: The Dialog Corporation; EBSCO Publishing, EBSCO Host; Florida Center for Library Automation; Gale; LexisNexis; Micromedia ProQuest; OCLC Online Computer Library Center, Inc.; ProQuest K-12 Learning Solutions; ProQuest LLC (Ann Arbor); H.W. Wilson. *Indexed:* BRI, CBCARef, CBRI, CPerI, FLI, MASUSE, PEI, RGPR, SD. *Aud.:* Ems, Hs, Ga, Ac.

As the most popular and influential of the general sports magazines, *Sports Illustrated* covers all the popular sports including basketball, baseball, football, golf, racing, wrestling, and others. It publishes articles about players, celebrities, teams, sports, and society. Issues are filled with excellent photography and well-written and frequently award-winning articles. Each 70- to 80-page issue contains letters to the editor, one or two longer feature articles, several shorter articles, analysis, commentary and predictions, and insights. The annual swimsuit issue is awaited by many. Selected articles are available free at its web site (http://sportsillustrated.cnn.com). Recommended for public, high school, and academic libraries.

Sports Illustrated for Kids. See Children section.

5721. *Tuff Stuff.* [ISSN: 1041-4258] 1984. m. USD 29.95 domestic; USD 61.95 foreign; USD 4.99 per issue. Ed(s): Rocky Landsverk. Krause Publications, Inc., 700 E State St, Iola, WI 54990-0001; info@krause.com; http://www.krause.com. Adv. Circ: 175682 Paid and free. *Aud.:* Ga.

Hobbyists and collectors of sports cards, memorabilia, and autographed items will read *Tuff Stuff,* which bills itself as "the #1 guide to sports cards and collectibles." In addition to extensive price guides, the publication contains market reports, dealer directories, news, trading information, and a few in-depth articles on players, entertainers, and the collectibles industry. Each issue is over 150 pages long. Selected full text from the magazine is available free at www.tuffstuff.com, with additional full text for subscribers. Suitable for public libraries.

Extreme Sports

5722. Kiteboarding. [ISSN: 1534-4282] 2000. bi-m. USD 19.97 domestic; USD 25.97 Canada; USD 31.97 elsewhere. Ed(s): Tom James. World Publications LLC, 460 N Orlando Ave, Ste 200, Winter Park, FL 32789; info@worldpub.net; http://www.worldpub.net. Illus., adv. *Aud.:* Ga.

Kiteboarding is a mixture of windsurfing, surfing, and wakeboarding and became popular in the 1990s. *Kiteboarding*, published since 2000, contains articles about places, gear, conditions, techniques, safety, and the sheer insanity of the sport. Since this is a relatively new sport, the magazine serves to inform readers both about the sport and its equipment. Readers can read about the "Ten Moments that Changed Kiteboarding," riding the tube like a surfer, or learn how to keep your arms out in front to stay in control. A "Visions" section includes action photographs of kiters and their rides. Appropriate for public libraries in surfing areas.

5723. Ride B M X. Incorporates (1994-2004): *Transworld B M X;* Which was formerly (until 2001): *Snap B M X.* [ISSN: 1078-0084] 1991. m. USD 18.97 domestic; USD 31.50 Canada; USD 42.95 elsewhere. TransWorld Media, 353 Airport Rd., Oceanside, CA 92054; http://www.transworldmatrix.com/twmatrix/. Illus., adv. Circ: 74150 Paid. Online: EBSCO Publishing, EBSCO Host. *Indexed:* MASUSE. *Aud.:* Hs, Ga.

Aimed at the BMX enthusiast at all levels, this glossy magazine covers extreme freestyle BMX riding, including dirt jumping, flatland, ramp, and street riding. Like other magazines from TransWorld, *Ride BMX* is filled with dramatic action photographs that will please readers. Regular features include letters, event coverage, product reviews, rider interviews, and photo sections. The magazine's web site at www.bmxonline.com provides selected full text and video. An appropriate purchase for public libraries.

5724. Thrasher. [ISSN: 0889-0692] 1980. m. USD 3.99 newsstand/cover. Ed(s): Ryan Henry. High Speed Productions, Inc., 1303 Underwood Ave, San Francisco, CA 94124. Adv. Circ: 137944 Paid. Online: Gale. *Aud.:* Hs, Ga.

For 25 years, *Thrasher* has been read and enjoyed by young enthusiasts of skateboarding, music, and alternative lifestyles. Like its readers, the magazine is fast paced, with interviews, action photographs, comics, contests, reports of competitions, reviews of video games, fashion tips, and industry-insider gossip. One column, "The Lunatic Fringe," indicates the general thrust of this publication. In addition to the 12 monthly issues, subscribers receive an annual photo issue. Readers can view videos of stunts and competitions at the magazine's web site, www.thrashermagazine.com. An appropriate selection for public libraries.

5725. Transworld Motocross. [ISSN: 1533-6212] 2000. m. USD 18.95. TransWorld Media, 353 Airport Rd., Oceanside, CA 92054; http://www.transworldmatrix.com/twmatrix/. Illus., adv. Circ: 125000. *Aud.:* Hs, Ga.

This glossy magazine covers all aspects of motocross, including freestyle, freeriding, and racing. Each issue is packed with photographs of races and stunts, profiles of famous riders, how-to columns, product reviews (especially gear and bikes), and articles. Sometimes it is difficult to distinguish between articles and advertisements. The writing is informative but conversational. A recent issue contains interviews and profiles of several riders and coaches, an article on how to make your first race a success, and a photo gallery. An appropriate selection for public libraries in areas where motocross is popular.

5726. Transworld Skateboarding. [ISSN: 0748-7401] 1982. m. USD 17.97 domestic; USD 30.33 Canada; USD 91.95 elsewhere. TransWorld Media, 353 Airport Rd., Oceanside, CA 92054; http://www.transworldmatrix.com/twmatrix/. Illus., adv. Circ: 220000 Paid. Online: EBSCO Publishing, EBSCO Host. *Aud.:* Hs, Ga.

This glossy magazine for the avid skateboarder contains over 200 pages and is filled with photographs of daring rides, stunts, and flips. The magazine covers all aspects of the sport, but does not include articles on the skateboarding culture (i.e., music, clothes, lifestyle). A typical issue features several photo essays, interviews with leading skaters, and product reviews. Regular columns include letters to the editor; short news reports of people, contests, events, and products; trick tips; profiles of young skaters; travel stories; and interviews with leading skaters. Like other magazines from TransWorld, it will be remembered for its photography and advertisements. The print version is supplemented by its online site at www.skateboarding.com. The more than 12 million skateboarders will enjoy this magazine at public libraries.

5727. Transworld Snowboarding. [ISSN: 1046-4611] 1986. 9x/yr. USD 14.95 domestic; USD 23.50 Canada; USD 44.95 elsewhere. TransWorld Media, 353 Airport Rd., Oceanside, CA 92054; http://www.transworldmatrix.com/twmatrix/. Illus., adv. Circ: 200000. *Aud.:* Hs, Ga.

Snowboard enthusiasts and those simply curious about the sport will enjoy this glossy publication. Each 200-page-plus issue is filled with dramatic action photographs of amazing stunts and beautiful scenes. Feature articles are written in a conversational style and highlight the current snowboard season, offer previews of upcoming events, examine snow areas, and profile professional snowboarders. Columns include letters to the editor, a Q&A section, competition results, instruction tips, product reviews, and the like. The magazine's web site at www.transworldsnowboarding.com includes several articles, but readers will love the print version for its dramatic color photography. Appropriate for public libraries.

5728. Transworld Surf. [ISSN: 1532-9402] 1999. m. USD 19.95 domestic; USD 29.67 Canada; USD 43.95 elsewhere. TransWorld Media, 353 Airport Rd., Oceanside, CA 92054; http://www.transworldmatrix.com/twmatrix/. Illus., adv. *Aud.:* Ga.

The audience for this glossy monthly is the male adventure surfer in his twenties. The publication is filled with dramatic photographs, interviews, travel pieces for surfers, product reviews, and advertisements. Departments include an editorial, music reviews, people, competition, and an epilog. An annual swimsuit issue and travel issue will certainly be popular. The travel issue contains tips for keeping out of trouble when traveling, a list of exotic destinations, and reviews of travel gear. The publication's web site at www.transworldsurf.com contains news updates, more photos, and links to other sites of interest. Suitable for public libraries.

5729. WakeBoarding. [ISSN: 1079-0136] 1993. 9x/yr. USD 19.97 domestic; USD 28.97 per issue Canada; USD 37.97 per issue elsewhere. Ed(s): Matt Hickman. World Publications LLC, 460 N Orlando Ave, Ste 200, Winter Park, FL 32789; info@worldpub.net; http://www.worldpub.net. Illus., adv. Circ: 45823 Paid. *Aud.:* Ga.

Wakeboarding, a combination of waterskiing and snowboarding, is well chronicled by *WakeBoarding Magazine*, which published its 100th issue in May 2006. The 150-200–page issues of this glossy magazine are filled with news, information about product releases, equipment reviews, profiles of wakeboarders, and coverage of amateur and professional events. The instruction column, titled "Higher Learning," indicates that this is not for the novice. The magazine is filled with photographs and advertisements, making it difficult to differentiate between the two. It is published nine times a year. The online version at www.wakeboardingmag.com provides links to sites of interest to participants of the sport. Since wakeboarding is growing in popularity, public libraries in appropriate areas should consider adding this magazine to their collection.

5730. WindSurfing: the nation's leading windsurfing magazine. Formerly: *WindRider.* [ISSN: 1057-0799] 1981. 7x/yr. USD 19.97 domestic; USD 25.97 Canada; USD 31.97 elsewhere. Ed(s): Tom James. World Publications LLC, PO Box 8500, Winter Park, FL 32790; info@worldpub.net; http://www.worldpub.net. Illus., adv. Circ: 27569 Paid. *Aud.:* Ga.

This monthly publication provides information for the windsurfer, from tournament results and advice from the pros to annual board prices, specs, and test ratings. A special issue in April 2006 celebrating 25 years of the magazine highlighted champions of the sport and traced the sport's development from the 1980s to the present day. It also included "Hot Shots," a photographic retrospective of amazing rides. This publication with its action photography will please readers at public libraries.

Physical Education, Coaching, and Sports Sciences

Adapted Physical Activity Quarterly. See Disabilities section.

5731. American Journal of Sports Medicine. Formerly (until 1976): *Journal of Sports Medicine.* [ISSN: 0363-5465] 1972. m. GBP 442. Ed(s): Dr. Bruce Reider. Sage Science Press (US), 2455 Teller Rd, Thousand Oaks, CA 91320; info@sagepub.com; http://www.sagepub.com/. Illus., index, adv. Refereed. Circ: 9913 Paid. Vol. ends: Nov/Dec. Microform: PQC. Online: EBSCO Publishing, EBSCO Host; Florida Center for Library Automation; Gale; HighWire Press; M D Consult; Northern Light Technology, Inc.; OCLC Online Computer Library Center, Inc.; ProQuest K-12 Learning Solutions; SAGE Publications, Inc., SAGE Journals Online; SwetsWise Online Content. Reprint: PSC. *Indexed:* ABIn, AbAn, BiolAb, CINAHL, EduInd, ExcerpMed, GSI, H&SSA, PEI, RRTA, SCI, SD. *Aud.:* Ac, Sa.

The official publication of the American Orthopaedic Society for Sports Medicine, *American Journal of Sports Medicine* is a monthly, peer-reviewed, scientific journal. The original research articles and case studies examine a variety of sports injuries, their treatment, rehabilitation, and frequency of occurrence. Issues of 150 pages contain up to 20 articles. Individual subscribers to the print edition receive free online access at www.ajsm.org. A feature on the site is the AJSM PreView, which contains complete scientific papers one to two months before they are scheduled to appear in print. The audience for this journal includes orthopaedic surgeons specializing in sports medicine, team physicians, athletic trainers, and physical therapists. This title is appropriate for academic and medical libraries.

5732. Applied Physiology, Nutrition and Metabolism. Former titles (until 2006): *Canadian Journal of Applied Physiology;* (until 1993): *Canadian Journal of Sport Sciences;* (until 1987): *Canadian Journal of Applied Sport Science.* [ISSN: 1715-5312] 1976. bi-m. CND 381 (Individuals, CND 139). National Research Council Canada (N R C), NRC Research Press, Ottawa, ON K1A 0R6, Canada; research.journals@nrc.ca; http://www.nrc-cnrc.gc.ca. Illus., index, adv. Refereed. Circ: 965 Paid and free. Vol. ends: Dec. Microform: MML. Online: EBSCO Publishing, EBSCO Host; IngentaConnect; SwetsWise Online Content. *Indexed:* CABA, CBCARef, CINAHL, CJA, ChemAb, ErgAb, ExcerpMed, H&SSA, IBR, IBZ, PEI, PsycInfo, RRTA, SCI, SD, SSCI. *Bk. rev.:* 2, 350 words. *Aud.:* Ac, Sa.

The bimonthly *Applied Physiology, Nutrition and Metabolism,* formerly the *Canadian Journal of Applied Phsyiology,* publishes interdisciplinary knowledge and research to aid in understanding the complexities of how lifestyle affects health. The journal is endorsed by both the Canadian Society of Exercise Physiology and the Canadian Society for Clinical Nutrition. Research focuses on applied physiology and nutrition, providing an interdisciplinary approach for readers. Each issue is approximately 90 pages. A recent issue includes articles titled "What can metabolic myopathies teach us about exercise physiology?," "Physical activity and the metabolic syndrome in Canada," and several articles from a symposium on dietary nutrition intakes. As appropriate for a Canadian journal, articles are written in English or French and are preceded by an abstract in both languages. This journal will be of interest to exercise physiologists, physical fitness and exercise rehabilitation specialists, public health and health care professionals, as well as basic and applied physiologists, nutritionists, and biochemists. The technical language of this journal makes it of primary interest to medical and academic libraries.

5733. Athletic Business. Formerly (until 1984): *Athletic Purchasing and Facilities.* [ISSN: 0747-315X] 1977. m. USD 130 elsewhere (Free to qualified personnel). Ed(s): Michael Popke, Andrew Cohen. Athletic Business Publications, Inc., 4130 Lien Rd, Madison, WI 53704-3602. Illus., index, adv. Circ: 42301 Controlled. *Indexed:* SD. *Aud.:* Ac, Sa.

Since 1977, the monthly trade journal *Athletic Business* has been covering the business of sports and athletics, including equipment, corporate wellness programs, facility planning, marketing, management, and design. Complimentary copies are distributed to qualified professionals, who run the gamut from facility owners to YMCAs, YWCAs, JCCs, sports and health clubs, and correctional facilities (not libraries). Feature articles are supplemented by columns on sports law, college programs, high school programs, the recreation industry, profit-making enterprises, and a large amount of advertising. Special issues include a buyer's guide published in February, and an "Architectural Showcase" published in June. Suitable for academic libraries at institutions with business sports programs.

5734. Athletic Therapy Today. [ISSN: 1078-7895] 1996. bi-m. USD 176 (Individuals, USD 44 print & online eds.). Ed(s): Gary B. Wilkerson. Human Kinetics, PO Box 5076, Champaign, IL 61825-5076; orders@hkusa.com; http://www.humankinetics.com. Illus., index, adv. Refereed. Circ: 2900 Paid. Reprint: PSC. *Indexed:* CINAHL, ExcerpMed, H&SSA, IBR, IBZ, PEI, SCI, SD. *Bk. rev.:* 3, 100 words. *Aud.:* Ac, Sa.

Billing itself as the "professional journal of certified athletic trainers and athletic therapists," *Athletic Therapy Today* contains advice to sports health care professionals. The bimonthly issues consist of approximately 60 pages and contain about six articles, most of which focus on a specific theme. Issues also contain columns on clinical evaluation and testing, case reviews, injury management, disabilities, conditioning, nutrition notes, book reviews, research digest, news, and the like. Articles are relatively brief and written in a conversational style. Each issue includes an assessment quiz that can be completed for continuing education credit. Suitable for medical and academic libraries.

5735. British Journal of Sports Medicine. Incorporates: *British Association of Sport and Medicine. Bulletin.* [ISSN: 0306-3674] 1968. q. GBP 410 print or online (Individuals, GBP 152 print & online eds.). Ed(s): Janet O'Flaherty, Paul McCrory. B M J Publishing Group, B M A House, Tavistock Sq, London, WC1H 9JR, United Kingdom; info.norththames@bma.org.uk; http://www.bmjjournals.com/. Illus., adv. Refereed. Vol. ends: Dec. Microform: PQC. Online: EBSCO Publishing, EBSCO Host; Florida Center for Library Automation; Gale; HighWire Press; OCLC Online Computer Library Center, Inc.; OhioLINK; Ovid Technologies, Inc.; ProQuest K-12 Learning Solutions; ProQuest LLC (Ann Arbor); SilverPlatter Information, Incorporated. *Indexed:* CABA, CINAHL, CJA, ErgAb, ExcerpMed, H&SSA, HortAb, PEI, RILM, RRTA, SCI, SD, SSCI. *Bk. rev.:* Number and length vary. *Aud.:* Ac, Sa.

One of the most well-known and respected journals in the field, this is the official journal of the British Association of Sport and Exercise Medicine. The approximately 20 articles per issue are divided into sections: Warm Up, Leader, Reviews (of Research), Original Articles, Miscellanea, Letters, and a listing of electronic pages that supplement the print journal and are found at http://bjsm.bmjjournals.com. This international journal includes all aspects of sports medicine to cover "the latest advances in clinical practice and research." Each issue includes selected summaries from SportsMedUpdate, an evidence-based journal watch service coordinated in South Africa. Issues older than 12 months are available free from Highwire Press. Highly recommended for academic libraries with programs in health sciences.

5736. Clinical Journal of Sport Medicine. Former titles (until 1990): *Canadian Academy of Sport Medicine Review; Canadian Academy of Sport Medicine Newsletter.* [ISSN: 1050-642X] 1975. q. USD 536 (Individuals, USD 336). Ed(s): Dr. Winne Meeuwisse. Lippincott Williams & Wilkins, 530 Walnut St, Philadelphia, PA 19106-3621; http://www.lww.com. Illus., adv. Refereed. Circ: 3536 Paid. Vol. ends: Oct. Online: EBSCO Publishing, EBSCO Host; Ovid Technologies, Inc.; SwetsWise Online Content. *Indexed:* CINAHL, ExcerpMed, H&SSA, PEI, RiskAb, SCI, SD. *Aud.:* Ac, Sa.

The *Clinical Journal of Sport Medicine* is an international refereed journal for clinicians. It publishes research, reviews, and case reports concerning "diagnostics, therapeutics, and rehabilitation in healthy and physically challenged individuals of all ages and levels of sport and exercise participation." The editorial board consists of a group of international physicians and Ph.Ds. Articles report original research, provide brief reports of clinical studies, and describe case studies. Typical article topics include leg pain in collegiate cross-country runners, use of dietary supplements and medicines during the Olympic games, bacterial and viral contamination of exercise equipment, and a survey of sport activity and injury in high schools. The journal is available online for subscribers at www.cjsportmed.com from 2000 to date. This publication is appropriate for medical and academic libraries.

5737. *Clinical Kinesiology (Online Edition).* Former titles (until 2002): *Clinical Kinesiology (Print Edition); (until 1987): American Corrective Therapy Journal; (until 1967): Association for Physical and Mental Rehabilitation. Journal.* 1947. q. USD 50 (Individuals, USD 35). American Kinesiotherapy Association, c/o Clinical Kinesiology, San Diego State University, San Diego, CA 92182-7251; geri@tkp.com; http://ww.clinicalkinesiology.org. Illus., index, adv. Refereed. Circ: 1064. Microform: PQC. Online: EBSCO Publishing, EBSCO Host; ProQuest LLC (Ann Arbor). *Indexed:* CINAHL, ExcerpMed, HRIS, PEI, SD. *Aud.:* Ac, Sa.

The official journal of the American Kinesiotherapy Association, *Clinical Kinesiology* publishes peer-reviewed theoretical and research manuscripts related to kinesiotherapy (the treatment of disease, injury, or deformity through therapeutic exercise and education). In 2003, this publication became available only as an online journal. Each quarterly issue contains two or three articles describing clinical case studies, applied research, clinical descriptive papers, and/or literature reviews. Suitable for medical and academic libraries at institutions offering degrees, diplomas, or certificates for athletic trainers, cardiovascular specialists, emergency medical therapists, health information administrators, respiratory therapists, and the like. URL: http://www.clinicalkinesiology.org

5738. *Coach and Athletic Director.* Former titles (until 1995): *Scholastic Coach and Athletic Director; (until 1994): Scholastic Coach;* Incorporates (1921-198?): *Athletic Journal.* [ISSN: 1087-2000] 1931. 10x/yr. USD 12 domestic; USD 41.95 foreign. Ed(s): Kevin Newell. Scholastic Inc., 557 Broadway, New York, NY 10012; http://www.scholastic.com. Illus., index, adv. Circ: 44000 Paid and controlled. Microform: PQC. Online: EBSCO Publishing, EBSCO Host; Gale; OCLC Online Computer Library Center, Inc.; ProQuest K-12 Learning Solutions; ProQuest LLC (Ann Arbor); H.W. Wilson. *Indexed:* ABIn, BRI, EduInd, PEI, SD. *Bk. rev.:* Number and length vary. *Aud.:* Hs, Ga, Ac.

Published since 1931 as a monthly during the school year with a combined issue in the summer, this is a professional magazine for high school and college athletic coaches. News, information, and advice on sports (including baseball, basketball, football, softball, soccer), strength training, and administrative activities are provided in an entertaining style using nontechnical language. Issues include book and equipment reviews and an annual issue (February) with a buyer's guide to facilities and equipment. The February 2006 issue also contained an interview with St. Louis Cardinals manager Tony LaRussa. Appropriate for high school and academic libraries.

5739. *Coaching Science Abstracts.* 1995. bi-m. Free. Ed(s): Brent S Rushall. Sports Science Associates, 4225 Orchad Dr, Spring Valley, CA 919977; brushall@mail.sdsu.edu; http://www-rohan.sdsu.edu/dept/coachsci/index.htm. *Aud.:* Hs, Ac, Sa.

For over ten years, Brent S. Rushall, Department of Exercise and Nutritional Studies, San Diego State University, has published this free online abstracting journal to assist practicing coaches and others interested in applied sport science in locating relevant research. Articles are chosen by Dr. Rushall and his students. *Coaching Science Abstracts* is usually published six times a year. The content is changed monthly and may or may not be thematic. Each abstract contains a citation, a brief description of the purpose and significance of the research, and "Implications," a section that interprets the study. Issues contain 25 to 100 abstracts and may include commentaries and notes by the editor. Suitable for high school, academic, and special libraries.

5740. *European Journal of Sport Science.* [ISSN: 1746-1391] 2001. q. GBP 309 print & online eds. Ed(s): Asker E Jeukendrup. Taylor & Francis Ltd., 4 Park Sq, Milton Park, Abingdon, OX14 4RN, United Kingdom; info@tandf.co.uk; http://www.tandf.co.uk/journals. Refereed. *Indexed:* PEI, PsycInfo, SCI, SD. *Aud.:* Ac.

This refereed journal, the official publication of the European College of Sport Science (ECSS), publishes research and clinical articles covering the biological, behavioral, and social sciences in sport and exercise. The journal aims to facilitate communication across all the various disciplines of the sports sciences. Articles are written in "American English" and are divided into an original article and a review section. Annually the journal publishes the papers of the winners of the ECSS Young Investigators competition. The journal is published in simultaneous print and electronic editions. Readers may search the online archive from 2001 to date at http://www.tandf.co.uk/journals/titles/17461391.asp. Suitable for academic libraries.

5741. *International Journal of Sport Nutrition & Exercise Metabolism.* Formerly (until Mar.2000): *International Journal of Sport Nutrition.* [ISSN: 1526-484X] 1991. bi-m. USD 312 (Individuals, USD 78 print & online eds.). Ed(s): Ronald J Maughan, Emily M. Haymes. Human Kinetics, PO Box 5076, Champaign, IL 61825-5076; orders@hkusa.com; http://www.humankinetics.com. Illus., index, adv. Sample. Refereed. Circ: 1372 Paid. Vol. ends: Dec. Reprint: PSC. *Indexed:* Agr, CINAHL, ChemAb, DSA, ExcerpMed, GSI, HortAb, IBR, IBZ, PEI, RRTA, SCI, SD. *Bk. rev.:* Number and length vary. *Aud.:* Ac, Sa.

The official publication of the International Society of Sport Nutrition is a highly technical, peer-reviewed journal that draws upon the fields of biochemistry, physiology, psychological medicine, and sport and exercise science as they relate to the study of sport nutrition and exercise biochemistry. Scholarly research articles are the focus of the journal. Issues also include articles on practical applications, book and media reviews, and editorials. In 2000, the words *and Exercise Metabolism* were added to the title to reflect the overlap of the scientific disciplines of exercise biochemistry and sport nutrition. This journal, published since 1991, is appropriate for academic and medical libraries that support programs in sport medicine and sport sciences.

5742. *International Journal of Sports Medicine.* [ISSN: 0172-4622] 1980. 12x/yr. EUR 625.80. Ed(s): Dr. W M Sherman, Dr. Maria T E Hopman. Georg Thieme Verlag, Ruedigerstr 14, Stuttgart, 70469, Germany; kunden.service@thieme.de; http://www.thieme.de. Illus., adv. Refereed. Circ: 1450 Paid and controlled. Online: EBSCO Publishing, EBSCO Host; OhioLINK; SwetsWise Online Content. *Indexed:* BiolAb, CABA, CINAHL, ChemAb, DSA, ExcerpMed, H&SSA, HortAb, IndVet, PEI, RRTA, SCI, SD, SSCI, VB. *Bk. rev.:* 1, 500-750 words. *Aud.:* Ac, Sa.

The *International Journal of Sports Medicine* is published monthly. Each issue contains sections on physiology and biochemistry, clinical sciences; nutrition; behavioral sciences; training and testing, orthopedics, and biomechanics; and immunology. Articles are peer-reviewed. The oversized issues contain English-language research articles that are highly technical and that largely originate outside the United States. The journal publishes letters to the editor, short articles of recent work for rapid dissemination, review articles, as well as original research. Typical article titles include "Stroke frequency and arm coordination in front crawl swimming" and "Resistance training volume and energy expenditures." Appropriate for medical and academic libraries.

5743. *The International Journal of the History of Sport.* Formerly: *British Journal of Sports History.* [ISSN: 0952-3367] 1984. 8x/yr. GBP 946 print & online eds. Ed(s): J A Mangan. Routledge, 4 Park Sq, Milton Park, Abingdon, OX14 4RN, United Kingdom; info@routledge.co.uk; http://www.routledge.co.uk. Illus., index, adv. Sample. Refereed. Microform: PQC. Online: EBSCO Publishing, EBSCO Host; Gale; IngentaConnect; OCLC Online Computer Library Center, Inc.; SwetsWise Online Content. Reprint: PSC. *Indexed:* AmH&L, AmHI, BrHumI, CABA, HistAb, IBR, IBSS, IBZ, IndIslam, PEI, RRTA, SD. *Bk. rev.:* 15-20, 800 words. *Aud.:* Ac.

Anthropologists, sociologists, historians, and others interested in the "historical study of sport in its political, cultural, social, educational, economic, spiritual and aesthetic dimensions" will enjoy *The International Journal of the History of Sport.* Each issue contains 200 or more pages with anywhere from 8 to 20 articles and extensive book reviews. This peer-reviewed journal covers an interesting and international array of subjects, such as the origins of golf, the globalization of cricket, women and sport in India, and soccer in South Asia. As the journal's name implies, articles are written by an international, multidisciplinary group of scholars. Issues from 2001 on are available online to subscribers. This journal is most appropriate for academic libraries.

5744. *International Review for the Sociology of Sport.* Formerly (until 1983): *International Review of Sport Sociology.* [ISSN: 1012-6902] 1966. q. GBP 392. Ed(s): Peter Donnelly. Sage Publications Ltd., 1 Oliver's Yard, 55 City Rd, London, EC1 1SP, United Kingdom; info@sagepub.co.uk; http://www.sagepub.co.uk. Illus., adv. Refereed.

Circ: 1000. Vol. ends: Dec. Online: CSA; EBSCO Publishing, EBSCO Host; Gale; HighWire Press; OCLC Online Computer Library Center, Inc.; OhioLINK; SAGE Publications, Inc., SAGE Journals Online; SwetsWise Online Content. Reprint: PSC. *Indexed:* BAS, CABA, ForAb, IBR, IBZ, IndVet, PEI, PsycInfo, RRTA, S&F, SD, SSA, SociolAb, VB. *Bk. rev.:* 2-3, 200 words. *Aud.:* Ac.

Since 1966, the quarterly journal *International Review for the Sociology of Sport* has published research and scholarship on sport throughout the international community. Articles are not limited to sociology, but include the related fields of anthropology, cultural and women's studies, history, geography, semiotics, political economy, and interdisciplinary research. Recent issues include articles about greyhound racing and sport-related violence, adolescent sport participation in Norway, the globalization of soccer in Israel, and moral philosophy and racism in sport. Book and audiovisual reviews are included as well as abstracts of recent publications in several languages. Appropriate for academic libraries.

5745. *International Sports Journal.* [ISSN: 1094-0480] 1997. s-a. Ed(s): Thomas Katsaros. University of New Haven Foundation, 17 Tulip Dr., Glen Cove, NY 11542-1441; mharvey@charger.newhaven.edu. *Indexed:* PEI, SD. *Aud.:* Ac.

Published twice a year since 1997, this is a peer-reviewed journal that is written for the sports professional. It includes "empirical and theoretical articles that can be applied or be pertinent to current sports issues and practices or contribute to academic research in the international sports community." Each issue contains about 15 English-language articles, most of which are written by academics despite the invitation to members of the general sports community to submit articles. Much of the issue examined includes hard-core research with statistical analysis and language specific to particular sports. Recommended for academic libraries.

Journal of Aging and Physical Activity. See Geriatrics and Gerontological Studies section.

5746. *Journal of Applied Biomechanics.* Formerly (until 1992): *International Journal of Sport Biomechanics.* [ISSN: 1065-8483] 1985. q. USD 240 (Individuals, USD 60). Ed(s): Thomas S. Buchanan. Human Kinetics, PO Box 5076, Champaign, IL 61825-5076; orders@hkusa.com; http://www.humankinetics.com. Illus., index, adv. Refereed. Circ: 1173 Paid. Reprint: PSC. *Indexed:* AS&TI, CINAHL, EngInd, ErgAb, ExcerpMed, IBR, IBZ, PEI, SCI, SD, SSCI. *Aud.:* Ac, Sa.

This official publication of the International Society of Biomechanics is a peer-reviewed, technical journal devoted to the study of human biomechanics in sport, exercise, and rehabilitation. Articles accepted for publication include original research, clinical notes, technical notes, and other information highlighting advances in the field. Topics of concern relate not only to exercise and sport, but also to modeling, clinical biomechanics, gait and posture, and relations between the muscles and the skeleton or nervous system. Thus readers can learn about the contribution of muscle series elasticity to performance or the influence of swimsuit design and fabric surface on butterfly kinematics. The journal recently adopted a larger physical format. This title is appropriate for academic and medical libraries.

Journal of Applied Physiology. See Physiology section.

5747. *Journal of Athletic Training.* Former titles (until 1992): *Athletic Training;* (until 1972): *National Athletic Trainers Association. Journal.* [ISSN: 1062-6050] 1956. q. USD 100 (Individuals, USD 75). Ed(s): Christopher Ingersoll, Leslie Neistadt. National Athletic Trainers Association, Inc., 2952 N Stemmons Fwy, Dallas, TX 75247; ebd@nata.org; http://www.nata.org/. Illus., index, adv. Refereed. Circ: 29000 Paid and controlled. Vol. ends: Oct/Dec. Microform: PQC. Online: National Library of Medicine; Northern Light Technology, Inc.; OCLC Online Computer Library Center, Inc.; ProQuest LLC (Ann Arbor). *Indexed:* BiolAb, CINAHL, ExcerpMed, PEI, PsycInfo, SCI, SD. *Bk. rev.:* 4, 350 words. *Aud.:* Ac, Sa.

The official publication of the National Athletic Trainers Association (NATA), the *Journal of Athletic Training* is a quarterly, peer-reviewed journal whose mission is "to enhance communication among professionals interested in the quality of health care for the physically active through education and research in prevention, evaluation, management, and rehabilitation of injuries." Each issue contains about 120–50 pages that are generally subdivided into sections including original research, literature reviews, evidence-based practice, and case reports. Editorials, letters, and announcements supplement the articles. Readers may complete a quiz at the web site (www.nata.org/jat) for five CEU credits in the NATA program. A suggested acquisition for academic institutions with sport sciences and physical education training programs.

5748. *Journal of Orthopaedic and Sports Physical Therapy.* [ISSN: 0190-6011] 1971. m. USD 253 (Individuals, USD 152; Students, USD 85). American Physical Therapy Association, Orthopaedic and Sports Physical Therapy Sections, 1111 N Fairfax St, Ste 100, Alexandria, VA 22314-1436; http://www.jospt.org/. Illus., index, adv. Refereed. Circ: 19255 Paid. Online: EBSCO Publishing, EBSCO Host. *Indexed:* CINAHL, ExcerpMed, H&SSA, PEI, SCI, SD. *Bk. rev.:* 4, 300 words. *Aud.:* Ac, Sa.

This is the official publication of the Orthopaedic and Sports Physical Therapy Sections of the American Physical Therapy Association. This scholarly, peer-reviewed journal, of interest to clinicians, faculty, and students, publishes evidence-based research, literature reviews, case studies, clinical commentaries, "resident's case problems," and letters to the editor. Manuscripts submitted for review must address orthopaedic or sports physical therapy from any relevant discipline. Each monthly issue contains four to six articles (although a few have as many as ten), abstracts from the literature of the field, and book and product reviews. Issues from 2002 to date are available to subscribers online at the journal's web site (http://jospt.org). A suggested purchase for medical and academic libraries.

5749. *Journal of Physical Education, Recreation and Dance.* Former titles (until May 1981): *Journal of Physical Education and Recreation;* (until 1974): *Journal of Health, Physical Education, Recreation.* [ISSN: 0730-3084] 1896. m. 9/yr. USD 145 in US & Canada libraries & institutions (Free to members; Non-members, USD 73). Ed(s): Michael T Shoemaker. American Alliance for Health, Physical Education, Recreation, and Dance, 1900 Association Dr, Reston, VA 20191-1599; info@aahperd.org; http://www.aahperd.org. Illus., index. Refereed. Circ: 18000 Paid. Vol. ends: Dec. Microform: PMC; PQC. Online: Florida Center for Library Automation; Gale; OCLC Online Computer Library Center, Inc.; ProQuest LLC (Ann Arbor). *Indexed:* ABIn, CABA, ERIC, EduInd, IIPA, MRD, PEI, RILM, RRTA, SD, WAE&RSA. *Aud.:* Hs, Ga, Ac.

This is the primary professional publication for teachers of physical education. Published nine times a year by the American Alliance for Health, Physical Education, Recreation and Dance (AAHPERD), it has been in continuous publication since 1896. The peer-reviewed articles are directly relevant to educators at all levels. Each issue also includes an editorial, teaching tips, a discussion of issues of interest to AAHPERD members, an analysis of a court case or law, and a listing of job openings. Recent issues include articles on teaching strategies, fitness, legal issues, assessment, dancing, teacher education, adapted physical education, leisure for older adults, the use of technology, and ethics and gender equity in sports and physical education. School and academic libraries are the most appropriate subscribers.

5750. *Journal of Sport and Exercise Psychology.* Formerly: *Journal of Sport Psychology.* [ISSN: 0895-2779] 1979. q. USD 312 (Individuals, USD 78 print & online eds.). Ed(s): Robert Eklund. Human Kinetics, PO Box 5076, Champaign, IL 61825-5076; orders@hkusa.com; http://www.humankinetics.com. Illus., index, adv. Sample. Refereed. Circ: 1602 Paid. Vol. ends: Dec. Reprint: PSC. *Indexed:* ABIn, CABA, EduInd, ErgAb, H&SSA, IBR, IBZ, PEI, PsycInfo, RRTA, RiskAb, SCI, SD, SSCI. *Bk. rev.:* 1, 800-1,000 words. *Aud.:* Ac.

The official publication of the North American Society for the Psychology of Sport and Physical Activity features articles exploring the interactions between psychology and exercise and sport performance, editorials about contemporary issues in the field, digests of current publications on sport and exercise psychology, and book reviews. Original research is emphasized, and each issue contains five to eight research articles. Articles are grouped into sections for exercise psychology and sport psychology. This refereed journal is most suitable for academic libraries.

5751. *Journal of Sport and Social Issues.* [ISSN: 0193-7235] 1977. q. GBP 292. Ed(s): Cheryl Cole. Sage Publications, Inc., 2455 Teller Rd, Thousand Oaks, CA 91320; info@sagepub.com; http://www.sagepub.com. Illus., index, adv. Refereed. Circ: 550. Vol. ends: Nov. Reprint: PSC. *Indexed:* ABS&EES, AltPI, C&ISA, CerAb, H&SSA, HEA, IAA, PAIS, PEI, PSA, RRTA, RiskAb, SD, SFSA, SSA, SSCI, SociolAb. *Bk. rev.:* Occasional. *Aud.:* Ac.

This quarterly publication serves as a forum for research and opinions on the interrelationship between sports and sociology, economics, history, psychology, political science, anthropology, and media, gender, and ethnic studies. Articles are international and interdisciplinary in scope. Each issue is divided into three sections: "Focus" (theme-based research articles), "Trends" (research and notes on developing and traditional topics), and "View" (essays and reviews). This refereed journal is suitable for academic libraries.

5752. *Journal of Sport Behavior.* [ISSN: 0162-7341] 1978. q. USD 38 domestic; USD 58 foreign. Ed(s): M Cay Welsh, Elise Labbe-Coldsmith. University of South Alabama, Department of Psychology, Life Sciences Building, Room 320, Mobile, AL 36688-0002. Illus., index. Refereed. Circ: 450. CD-ROM: ProQuest LLC (Ann Arbor). Microform: PQC. *Indexed:* CABA, PEI, PsycInfo, RILM, RRTA, RiskAb, SD, WAE&RSA. *Bk. rev.:* Occasional. *Aud.:* Ac.

This peer-reviewed journal publishes empirical, investigative, and theoretical articles on behavior in sports and games. Articles generally run 15 to 20 pages and contain lengthy bibliographies. Topics addressed are quite diverse. Recent issues contain articles on mood and performance in wakeboarding, leadership among NCAA Division I and II student athletes, eating disorders among ballet dancers and nondancers, creatine use among recreational resistance trainers, and the typology of marathon runners. Suitable for academic libraries.

5753. *Journal of Sport History.* [ISSN: 0094-1700] 1974. 3x/yr. USD 70 (Individuals, USD 50). North American Society for Sport History, c/o Ronald A Smith, Treasurer, PO Box 1026, Lemont, PA 16851-1026; secretary-treasurer@nassh.org; http://www.nassh.org. Illus., adv. Refereed. Circ: 1000. Vol. ends: Fall. *Indexed:* ABS&EES, AgeL, AmH&L, ArtHuCI, HistAb, PEI, SD, SSCI. *Bk. rev.:* 10-20, 800-1,000 words. *Aud.:* Ac.

Since 1974, the North American Society for Sport History has published the *Journal of Sport History.* The journal publishes articles pertaining to research in sport history, the content ranging from the late nineteenth century to the end of the twentieth century and the subject matter ranging from theory to regional, national, and international events. Each issue contains approximately four scholarly articles; extensive book reviews; film, museum, and media reviews; and an annotated bibliography of articles in other journals of interest to the reader. This peer-reviewed journal is appropriate for academic libraries.

5754. *Journal of Sport Management.* [ISSN: 0888-4773] 1987. q. USD 240 (Individuals, USD 60 print & online eds.). Ed(s): Lucie Thibault. Human Kinetics, PO Box 5076, Champaign, IL 61825-5076; orders@hkusa.com; http://www.humankinetics.com. Adv. Refereed. Circ: 1230 Paid. Reprint: PSC. *Indexed:* ABIn, CABA, IBR, IBZ, PEI, RRTA, RiskAb, SCI, SD, SSCI. *Bk. rev.:* Number and length vary. *Aud.:* Ac, Sa.

The official journal of the North American Society for Sport Management publishes articles, editorials, and reviews featuring the application of management theory to sport, exercise, dance, and play. Typical contents include three or four longer research and review articles, with shorter research notes and/or position papers written by academic faculty. Regular features include book reviews, abstracts of relevant journal articles, and a list of upcoming conferences. Each issue is approximately 85 pages long, and articles are peer reviewed. Readers can explore gender and ethnic issues in sport and leisure management, the application of memory-work as a quantitative method to study

sport management, and the like. This publication is of interest to professionals, researchers, and students of sport management. Recommended for academic libraries with sport and leisure management programs.

5755. *Journal of Sport Rehabilitation.* [ISSN: 1056-6716] 1992. q. USD 240 (Individuals, USD 60 print & online eds.). Ed(s): Carl Mattacola. Human Kinetics, PO Box 5076, Champaign, IL 61825-5076; orders@hkusa.com; http://www.humankinetics.com. Illus., index, adv. Refereed. Circ: 670 Paid. Vol. ends: Nov. Reprint: PSC. *Indexed:* CINAHL, ExcerpMed, GSI, H&SSA, IBR, IBZ, PEI, PsycInfo, SCI, SD. *Bk. rev.:* 1-2, 250-350 words. *Aud.:* Ac, Sa.

This peer-reviewed quarterly publishes original research, case studies, reviews of research, and commentary appropriate to the field of sport rehabilitation, particularly as it involves both the physical and psychological treatment of sport and exercise injuries. Each issue consists of approximately 80 pages containing five to seven articles. The journal's mission is to advance "the understanding of all aspects of sport rehabilitation, particularly in the areas of therapeutic exercise, therapeutic modalities, injury evaluation, and the psychological aspects of rehabilitation." Its audience consists of all members of the sports medicine team, including athletic trainers/therapists, sport physical therapists/ physiotherapists, sports medicine physicians, and other professionals. Published since 1992, this journal eschews technical language and is appropriate to both medical and academic libraries that support rehabilitation and physical education programs.

5756. *Journal of Sports Economics.* [ISSN: 1527-0025] 2000. bi-m. GBP 310. Ed(s): Todd L Idson, Leo H Kahane. Sage Publications, Inc., 2455 Teller Rd, Thousand Oaks, CA 91320; info@sagepub.com; http://www.sagepub.com. Adv. Refereed. Online: EBSCO Publishing, EBSCO Host; HighWire Press; OCLC Online Computer Library Center, Inc.; SAGE Publications, Inc., SAGE Journals Online; SwetsWise Online Content. Reprint: PSC. *Indexed:* C&ISA, CABA, CJA, CerAb, IAA, JEL, PEI, RRTA, SD. *Bk. rev.:* 3-4, 250-500 words. *Aud.:* Ac.

Theoretical, applied, and empirical research are the focus of the *Journal of Sports Economics*, a refereed quarterly from the International Association of Sports Economists. In print since 2000, the journal publishes articles on research on the sports labor market, collective bargaining and wages, labor-management relations, finance, and the like. A recent special issue, "Financial Crisis in European Football," examines the state of football (soccer) in several European countries. The journal is published in English, but may include articles by Italian, Japanese, and British authors. Economics formulas and technical language make this primarily an academic journal for universities with strong economics programs.

5757. *The Journal of Sports Medicine and Physical Fitness: a journal on applied physiology, biomechanics, preventive medicine, sports medicine and traumatology, sports psychology.* [ISSN: 0022-4707] 1961. q. EUR 254 print & online eds. (Individuals, EUR 153 print & online eds.). Ed(s): A Del Monte, G Santilli. Edizioni Minerva Medica, Corso Bramante 83-85, Turin, 10126, Italy; journals.dept@minervamedica.it; http://www.minervamedica.it. Illus., index, adv. Refereed. Circ: 5000 Paid. Microform: SWZ. Online: EBSCO Publishing, EBSCO Host; OCLC Online Computer Library Center, Inc.; ProQuest K-12 Learning Solutions; ProQuest LLC (Ann Arbor). *Indexed:* CABA, CINAHL, ChemAb, ExcerpMed, PEI, RRTA, SCI, SD, SSCI. *Aud.:* Ac, Sa.

The Italian *Journal of Sports Medicine and Physical Fitness* is a peer-reviewed, English-language journal that covers a broad range of topics including applied physiology, preventive medicine, sports medicine and traumatology, and sports psychology. Although original scientific research and practical applications of sports medicine are the primary focus, the journal also accepts editorials, technical notes, new drug assessments, critical reviews of new technology, and special articles on the history of sports medicine, teaching methodology, and economic and legislative reports. Issues of this quarterly publication contain from 10 to 20 original articles. Appropriate for academic and medical libraries.

5758. *Journal of Sports Science and Medicine.* [ISSN: 1303-2968] q. Free. Journal of Sports Science and Medicine, c/o Hakan Gur, MD, PhD, Department of Sports Medicine, Bursa, 16059, Turkey. *Indexed:* CABA, PEI, RRTA, SCI, SD. *Aud.:* Ac.

Begun in 2002, this electronic journal publishes English-language research, review articles, and case studies in the fields of sports medicine and the exercise sciences. In addition to articles, it contains editorials, letters to the editor, and abstracts from international and national congresses, panel meetings, conferences, and symposia. Articles are peer reviewed. Since it is electronic, articles can incorporate video clips, animation, and color photos. In 2004, the journal began publishing a special section for young investigators. Authors who have not completed their postgraduate education submit articles that follow the normal peer-review process, except that rather than receiving a rejection they are given constructive criticism and advice. Recent articles include "Hydration and temperature in tennis" and "A comparison of kinematics and performance measures of two rowing ergometers." A link to this journal (at http://jssm.uludag.edu.tr) would be a valuable addition to academic libraries.

5759. *Journal of Sports Sciences.* [ISSN: 0264-0414] 1983. m. GBP 1769 print & online eds. Ed(s): Alan Nevill. Taylor & Francis Ltd., 4 Park Sq, Milton Park, Abingdon, OX14 4RN, United Kingdom; info@tandf.co.uk; http://www.tandf.co.uk/journals. Illus., adv. Sample. Refereed. Online: EBSCO Publishing, EBSCO Host; Florida Center for Library Automation; Gale; IngentaConnect; OCLC Online Computer Library Center, Inc.; SwetsWise Online Content. Reprint: PSC. *Indexed:* ApMecR, BiolAb, CABA, CINAHL, ErgAb, ExcerpMed, H&SSA, IBR, IBZ, PEI, PsycInfo, RRTA, RiskAb, S&F, SCI, SD. *Bk. rev.:* Number and length vary. *Aud.:* Ac, Sa.

The British-based *Journal of Sports Science* is a refereed journal of international scope. Interest in the "human sciences" as applied to sport and exercise extends the subject matter of this journal to include biomechanics, sport psychology, medicine, and physiotherapy. American, British, Australian, French, and other international scientists author the English-language articles. Original research is supplemented by brief editorials and announcements. Technical language makes this quarterly appropriate for academic and medical libraries.

5760. *Journal of Strength and Conditioning Research.* Formerly (until 1993): *The Journal of Applied Sport Science Research.* [ISSN: 1064-8011] 1987. q. USD 115 print & online eds. Ed(s): Hiram Lucke, William J Kraemer. National Strength and Conditioning Association, 1885 Bob Johnson Dr, Colorado Springs, CO 80906-4000; nsca@nsca-lift.org; http://www.nsca-lift.org. Illus., index, adv. Refereed. Circ: 27527 Paid and controlled. Vol. ends: Dec. Online: Allen Press Inc.; EBSCO Publishing, EBSCO Host; OCLC Online Computer Library Center, Inc.; ProQuest LLC (Ann Arbor). *Indexed:* CINAHL, ErgAb, GSI, IBR, IBZ, PEI, SCI, SD, SSCI. *Aud.:* Ac, Sa.

The official journal of the National Strength and Conditioning Association (NSCA) features "original research that addresses optical physical performance through applied exercise science." The journal's focus is on research with practical applications, bridging the gap between pure research and the practitioner. Thus, peer-reviewed research articles conclude with a "practical applications" section. Articles are written in English by an international group of scholars. Issues of this quarterly journal are approximately 200 pages long with 25 or more original research articles. The journal also publishes brief reviews of the literature by scientific experts and symposia related to the journal's mission. This is an appropriate purchase for medical and academic libraries.

5761. *Journal of Teaching in Physical Education.* [ISSN: 0273-5024] 1981. q. USD 240 (Individuals, USD 60 print & online eds.). Ed(s): Ron McBride, Melinda Solmon. Human Kinetics, PO Box 5076, Champaign, IL 61825-5076; orders@hkusa.com; http://www.humankinetics.com. Illus., index, adv. Sample. Refereed. Circ: 1183 Paid. Vol. ends: Jul. Reprint: PSC. *Indexed:* ABIn, CABA, ERIC, EduInd, ForAb, IBR, IBZ, PEI, PsycInfo, RRTA, SCI, SD, SSCI, SWA. *Aud.:* Ems, Hs, Ac.

This quarterly journal features empirical research and integrative reviews and analyses of issues associated with the teaching of physical education, including methodology, curriculum, and teacher education. In addition to covering

schools and universities, articles include the community and the sports profession. Each issue contains six or seven articles of approximately 15 to 20 pages in length. Some issues may be focused on a theme. There is an annual award for the "exemplary paper." As a peer-reviewed journal, the publication focuses on research rather than practice, uses the more technical language of social science research, and is most appropriate for academic libraries.

5762. *Journal of the Philosophy of Sport.* [ISSN: 0094-8705] 1974. s-a. USD 188 (Individuals, USD 47 print & online eds.). Ed(s): J S Russell. Human Kinetics, PO Box 5076, Champaign, IL 61825-5076; orders@hkusa.com; http://www.humankinetics.com. Illus., adv. Refereed. Circ: 590 Paid. Reprint: PSC. *Indexed:* AmHI, CABA, CBCARef, HumInd, IBR, IBZ, PEI, PhilInd, RRTA, SCI, SD, SSA, SSCI. *Bk. rev.:* 3-4, essay length. *Aud.:* Ac.

This peer-reviewed journal from the International Association for the Philosophy of Sport publishes longer research and theoretical articles, shorter essays, and book reviews of current or classical works relevant to the philosophy of sport. Topics as diverse as the philosophical athlete, figure skaters and realism, a meditation on sports, and *Schadenfreude* and sports are treated. Each issue contains three or four longer articles and two or three shorter essays and book reviews, all written by academics. The journal was published annually until 2001 and semi-annually since then. This is an interesting journal suitable for academic libraries.

5763. *Medicine and Science in Sports and Exercise.* Formerly: *Medicine and Science in Sports.* [ISSN: 0195-9131] 1969. m. USD 749 (Individuals, USD 422). Ed(s): Kent Pandolf, Kenneth O. Wilson. Lippincott Williams & Wilkins, 351 W Camden St, Baltimore, MD 21201-2436; custserv@lww.com; http://www.lww.com. Illus., index, adv. Refereed. Circ: 15160 Paid. Vol. ends: Dec. Microform: PQC. Online: EBSCO Publishing, EBSCO Host; OCLC Online Computer Library Center, Inc.; Ovid Technologies, Inc.; SwetsWise Online Content; H.W. Wilson. *Indexed:* ABIn, AbAn, AgeL, BiolAb, CABA, CINAHL, ChemAb, DSA, EduInd, ExcerpMed, GSI, H&SSA, IAA, IndVet, PEI, PsycInfo, RRTA, SCI, SD, SSCI, VB, WSA. *Bk. rev.:* 2-5, 200 words. *Aud.:* Ac, Sa.

The official publication of the American College of Sports Medicine, *Medicine and Science in Sports and Exercise* has been published since 1969. With a multidisciplinary approach, this monthly serves as a forum for exercise physiologists, physical therapists, physiatrists, sports physicians, and athletic trainers. Original research, clinical investigations, and research reviews are included within its pages. Issues contain approximately 24 to 26 articles, divided into sections. The Clinical Sciences section includes both clinical and clinically relevant investigations. The Basic Sciences section includes original investigations and epidemiology. The Applied Sciences section is subdivided into articles relating to biodynamics, psychobiology and behavioral sciences, and physical fitness and performance. Book reviews are included in Special Communications at the end. As one of the most prestigious and cited journals in the field of sports medicine, this peer-reviewed journal is most appropriate for academic and medical libraries.

5764. *Motor Control.* [ISSN: 1087-1640] 1997. q. USD 280 (Individuals, USD 70 print & online eds.). Ed(s): T R Nichols. Human Kinetics, PO Box 5076, Champaign, IL 61825-5076; orders@hkusa.com; http://www.humankinetics.com. Illus., adv. Refereed. Circ: 319 Paid. Reprint: PSC. *Indexed:* CINAHL, ErgAb, ExcerpMed, IBR, IBZ, PEI, PsycInfo, SCI, SD. *Bk. rev.:* Number and length vary. *Aud.:* Ac, Sa.

The official journal of the International Society of Motor Control is a peer-reviewed quarterly providing "multidisciplinary examination of human movement across the lifespan." Editors and authors are academicians from an international list of universities and research institutions, representing a variety of disciplines including kinesiology, neurophysiology, neuroscience, psychology, rehabilitation, and physical medicine. Each issue of approximately 100 pages contains five to ten articles. In addition to original research, the journal occasionally accepts review articles, target articles, book reviews, commentaries, and quick communications. Suitable for medical and academic libraries.

5765. The N C A A News. Incorporates: *Football Statistics Rankings.* [ISSN: 0027-6170] 1964. fortn. Members, USD 12; Non-members, USD 24; Students, USD 15. National Collegiate Athletic Association (N C A A), 700 W Washington Ave, Box 6222, Indianapolis, IN 46206-6222. Illus., adv. Circ: 20000. *Indexed:* SD. *Aud.:* Hs, Ac.

This biweekly newsletter, the official publication of the National Collegiate Athletic Association (NCAA), publishes news, opinions, and statistics on NCAA sports. It includes team photographs, news from the association and each division, an editorial, a news digest, and NCAA polls and regional rankings. The free online version at www.ncaa.org/wps/portal includes a searchable archive and a link to online employment opportunities. Suitable for academic libraries.

Palaestra. See Disabilities section.

5766. Pediatric Exercise Science. [ISSN: 0899-8493] 1989. q. USD 240 (Individuals, USD 60 print & online eds.). Ed(s): Dr. Thomas Rowland. Human Kinetics, PO Box 5076, Champaign, IL 61825-5076; orders@hkusa.com; http://www.humankinetics.com. Illus., adv. Refereed. Circ: 654 Paid and free. Vol. ends: Nov. Reprint: PSC. *Indexed:* CINAHL, ExcerpMed, IBR, IBZ, PEI, RiskAb, SCI, SD, SSCI. *Bk. rev.:* Occasional. *Aud.:* Ac, Sa.

Published since 1989, *Pediatric Exercise Science*, the official publication of the North American Society of Pediatric Exercise Medicine, is a peer-reviewed quarterly focusing on "children's unique responses to exercise; the role of exercise in treating chronic pediatric disease; the importance of physical activity in preventing illness and preserving wellness; and methods for making youth sports safer and more enjoyable." The research articles are written in English by an international group of authors. Issues are approximately 100 pages in length, with six to nine review or original research articles and editor's notes and digests of recent research. Authors include clinicians and academic researchers. This journal is most appropriate for academic and medical libraries.

5767. Quest (Champaign). [ISSN: 0033-6297] 1949. q. USD 240 (Individuals, USD 60 print & online eds.). Ed(s): David K Wiggins. Human Kinetics, PO Box 5076, Champaign, IL 61825-5076; orders@hkusa.com; http://www.humankinetics.com. Illus., adv. Sample. Refereed. Circ: 1330 Paid and free. Vol. ends: Nov. Microform: PQC. Online: EBSCO Publishing, EBSCO Host. Reprint: PSC. *Indexed:* ABIn, EduInd, IBR, IBZ, PEI, RRTA, SCI, SD, SSCI. *Bk. rev.:* Number and length vary. *Aud.:* Ac.

Quest is the official publication of National Association for Physical Education in Higher Education. The mission of this peer-reviewed quarterly is to "stimulate professional development in physical education by publishing articles concerned with issues critical to physical education in higher education." The editors seek theoretical or practical articles that are based on, complement, or review empirical research related to the profession. The journal also publishes commemorative lectures, appropriate conference papers, and book reviews. Since 1995, one issue per year has included the conference papers from American Academy of Kinesiology and Physical Education. Articles vary in length from 10 to 20 pages, and issues may include as few as five or as many as ten articles. Appropriate for colleges or universities with strong physical education programs.

5768. Research Quarterly for Exercise and Sport. Former titles (until 1980): *American Alliance for Health, Physical Education, Recreation and Dance. Research Quarterly;* (until 1979): *American Alliance for Health, Physical Education, and Recreation. Research Quarterly;* (until 1974): *The Research Quarterly of the American Association for Health, Physical Education, and Recreation.* [ISSN: 0270-1367] 1930. q. USD 225 (Individuals, USD 75; USD 42 newsstand/cover per month). Ed(s): Stephen Silverman. American Alliance for Health, Physical Education, Recreation, and Dance, 1900 Association Dr, Reston, VA 20191-1599; info@aahperd.org; http://www.aahperd.org. Illus., index, adv. Refereed. Circ: 7000. Vol. ends: Dec. Microform: PMC; PQC. Online: Florida Center for Library Automation; Gale; OCLC Online Computer Library Center, Inc.; ProQuest K-12 Learning Solutions; ProQuest LLC (Ann Arbor). *Indexed:* ABIn, AgeL, ArtHuCI, ERIC, EduInd, ErgAb, ExcerpMed, IBR, IBZ, PEI, RILM, RRTA, SCI, SD, SSCI. *Aud.:* Ac.

This journal of the American Alliance for Health, Physical Education, Recreation and Dance (AAHPERD) has been published since 1930. Its mission is to "publish refereed research articles on the art and science of human movement, which contribute to the knowledge and development of theory, either as new information, substantiation or contraction of previous findings, or application of new or improved techniques." The journal adds more than 50 articles a year to the literature of this field. Issues are divided into articles and research notes sections. The articles section is further subdivided into fields including biomechanics, growth and motor development, measurement and evaluation, motor control and learning, pedagogy, physiology, and psychology, thus ensuring that the reader may quickly focus on topics of interest. An annual supplement includes abstracts of research papers from the AAHPERD national convention. Recommended for academic libraries.

Shape. See Health and Fitness section.

5769. Sociology of Sport Journal. [ISSN: 0741-1235] 1984. q. USD 240 (Individuals, USD 60 print & online eds.). Ed(s): Annelies Knoppers. Human Kinetics, PO Box 5076, Champaign, IL 61825-5076; orders@hkusa.com; http://www.humankinetics.com. Illus., index, adv. Refereed. Circ: 1119 Paid. Vol. ends: Dec. Reprint: PSC. *Indexed:* AgeL, ArtHuCI, BRI, CABA, CBCARef, CJA, IBR, IBZ, PEI, PsycInfo, RILM, RRTA, RiskAb, SCI, SD, SSA, SSCI, SociolAb, WAE&RSA. *Bk. rev.:* 1, 750 words. *Aud.:* Ac.

The official journal of the North American Society for the Sociology of Sport is published to "stimulate and communicate research, critical thought, and theory development on sociology of sport issues." The journal features empirical, theoretical, and position papers on sport as games, play, exercise, leisure, and body culture. It provides an international perspective. Issues of this peer-reviewed quarterly contain approximately four articles with original research and a book review section. Bibliographies, research notes, and short papers on curriculum issues may also be included. Abstracts in English and French precede the English-language articles. The intended readership includes sport sociologists, sport psychologists, and coaches. This is an appropriate addition for academic libraries.

5770. Sport History Review. Former titles (until 1995): *Canadian Journal of History of Sport;* (until Dec. 1981): *Canadian Journal of History of Sport and Physical Education.* [ISSN: 1087-1659] 1970. s-a. USD 204 (Individuals, USD 51 print & online eds.). Ed(s): Don Morrow. Human Kinetics, PO Box 5076, Champaign, IL 61825-5076; orders@hkusa.com; http://www.humankinetics.com. Illus., adv. Sample. Refereed. Circ: 283 Paid. Vol. ends: Nov. Reprint: PSC. *Indexed:* ABS&EES, AmH&L, CABA, HistAb, IBR, IBZ, PEI, RRTA, SD. *Bk. rev.:* 6, 750 words. *Aud.:* Ac.

Sport History Review publishes scholarly articles on the broad, international field of sport history. A Canadian publication, it features articles in both English and French. Each biannual issue contains three or four articles (although occasionally as many as six) and book reviews. The journal publishers encourage submissions by graduate students and young professionals to foster the development of the discipline of sport history. A recent issue contains articles on lacrosse as Canada's national game in the late nineteenth century, the history of sport in France, and women golfers. This journal is most appropriate for academic libraries in institutions with a program on the history and/or the international aspects of sports.

5771. Sport Management Review. [ISSN: 1441-3523] 1998. s-a. AUD 100 (Individuals, AUD 50). Ed(s): David Shilbury. Sport Management Association of Australia & New Zealand, Bowater School of Management & Marketing, Deakin University, Burwood, VIC 3125 , Australia; http://www.gu.edu.au/school/lst/services/smaanz/. *Indexed:* CABA, RRTA, SD, WAE&RSA. *Aud.:* Ac.

This official journal of the Sport Management Association of Australia and New Zealand publishes peer-reviewed articles on all topics relevant to sport management, including the management, marketing, and governance at all levels. This is an international journal. Each 80-page issue contains four or five articles reporting research, new applications of past research, advances in theory, and case studies. The intended audience for this journal is sport management researchers, practitioners, and instructors. This publication is suitable for academic libraries at institutions that support programs in the business of sports.

5772. Sport Marketing Quarterly: for professionals in the business of marketing sport. [ISSN: 1061-6934] 1992. q. USD 159 (Individuals, USD 43; Students, USD 36). Ed(s): Julie Burrell. Fitness Information Technology Inc., PO Box 6116, Morgantown, WV 26506-6116; fit@fitinfotech.com; http://www.fitinfotech.com. Illus., index, adv. Sample. Refereed. Online: EBSCO Publishing, EBSCO Host. Reprint: PSC. *Indexed:* CABA, DSA, PEI, RRTA, SD, WAE&RSA. *Bk. rev.:* Number and length vary. *Aud.:* Ac, Sa.

Sport Marketing Quarterly, the preferred journal of the Sport Marketing Association, provides information and research for professionals and academicians. Articles in this peer-reviewed journal include case studies of marketing successes and research on sport marketing. The emphasis is on providing readers with information that is useful for their teaching, scholarship, business, and service. Issues consist of approximately 50 pages, with four or five research articles and departments, including interviews or profiles, case studies, legal reviews, and book reviews. Typical article topics include media and corporate sponsors' perceptions of sport scandals; sports marketing to ethnic groups; and tobacco sponsorship of televised motor sports competitions. Readers may choose a separate electronic subscription at www.smqonline.com. The journal is an appropriate selection for academic libraries with strong marketing/sports programs.

5773. The Sport Psychologist. [ISSN: 0888-4781] 1987. q. USD 240 (Individuals, USD 60 print & online eds.). Ed(s): Ian Maynard. Human Kinetics, PO Box 5076, Champaign, IL 61825-5076; orders@hkusa.com; http://www.humankinetics.com. Illus., adv. Refereed. Circ: 1000 Paid. Vol. ends: Dec. Reprint: PSC. *Indexed:* CABA, IBR, IBZ, PEI, PsycInfo, RRTA, SCI, SD, SSCI. *Bk. rev.:* 2, 100-500 words. *Aud.:* Ac, Sa.

This refereed quarterly for the clinician, academic, and practitioner (e.g., coaches) has been in publication since 1987 with the mission of acting as "a forum to stimulate and disseminate knowledge that focuses on the application and practice of sport psychology." Issues are between 100–140 pages in length, containing four or five English-language articles written almost exclusively by an international community of academic participants. Issues are divided into sections: applied research; professional practice; profiles of coaches, athletes, and sport psychologists; book and media reviews; and a bulletin board with international news on sport psychology, conference announcements and reports, and resources of note to sport psychologists. Typical articles from a recent issue cover such topics as contextual influences on moral functioning of male youth footballers; changes in stress and recovery of male rowers; and the use of hypnosis. Suitable for academic libraries with sports and/or psychology programs.

5774. Sporting Traditions. [ISSN: 0813-2577] 1984. s-a. AUD 75 (Individuals, AUD 50). Ed(s): Rob Hess. Australian Society for Sports History, Rob Hess, Sport History Unit, F022, School of Human Movement, Recreation and Performance, PO Box 14428, Melbourne City MC, VIC 8001, Australia; j.ohara@uws.edu.au; http://www.sporthistory.org. Refereed. Circ: 400. *Indexed:* SD. *Bk. rev.:* Number and length vary. *Aud.:* Ac.

The official journal of the Australian Society for Sports History, this peer-reviewed publication focuses on the international economic, political, social, legal, and philosophical significance of sporting activity. Issues are generally over 150 pages in length, with up to eight articles. They may also contain review essays and book reviews. A recent issue contains articles on the cultural origin of competitive swimming in Australia, industrial relations in Zimbabwean cricket, and early Maori rugby. Appropriate for academic libraries at institutions with a strong international or historical interest in sports.

5775. Strategies (Reston): a journal for physical and sport educators. [ISSN: 0892-4562] 1987. bi-m. USD 100 (Individuals, USD 35). Ed(s): Judith C Young, Dora Schield. American Alliance for Health, Physical Education, Recreation, and Dance, 1900 Association Dr, Reston, VA 20191-1599; info@aahperd.org; http://www.aahperd.org. Illus., adv. Refereed. Circ: 7500 Paid. *Indexed:* ABIn, ERIC, EduInd, PEI, SD. *Aud.:* Ems, Hs, Ac.

The official publication of the National Association for Sport and Physical Education, *Strategies* is a peer-reviewed journal published six times a year for physical education teachers and coaches at K-12 levels. The publication seeks articles that "identify a problem and offer concrete, step-by-step solutions, or describe best practices for typical coach/teacher activities or responsibilities." Each 30- to 35-page issue contains 10 to 12 articles. The professional magazine is written in nontechnical language, which makes it appropriate for large public and school libraries as well as academic libraries.

5776. Strength and Conditioning Journal. Former titles (until 1999): *Strength and Conditioning;* (until 1994): *N S C A Journal;* (until 1992): *National Strength and Conditioning Journal;* (until 1981): *National Strength Coaches Association Journal.* [ISSN: 1524-1602] 1979. bi-m. USD 115 combined subscription domestic print & online eds.; USD 145 combined subscription foreign print & online eds. Ed(s): William J Kraemer. National Strength and Conditioning Association, 1885 Bob Johnson Dr, Colorado Springs, CO 80906-4000; nsca@nsca-lift.org; http://www.nsca-lift.org. Illus., index, adv. Refereed. Circ: 28000 Paid. *Indexed:* CINAHL, ErgAb, IBR, IBZ, PEI, SCI, SD. *Bk. rev.:* 3, 100-250 words. *Aud.:* Ac, Sa.

The professional journal of the National Strength and Conditioning Association (NSCA) publishes peer-reviewed articles with practical information from research and knowledge gained from experienced professionals on "resistance training, sports medicine and science, and issues facing the strength and conditioning professional." Each bimonthly, 80-page issue contains approximately five feature articles and several columns. Columns include "Exercise Techniques," "Certification," "CEU Quiz," "Research Digest," and "Research Corner." The publication will be read by strength coaches, personal trainers, physical therapists, athletic trainers, and other strength and conditioning professionals. NSCA members receive this publication with their membership. An electronic version is available at www.nsca-lift.org. Recommended for academic libraries.

5777. Teaching Elementary Physical Education. [ISSN: 1045-4853] 1990. bi-m. USD 144 (Individuals, USD 36). Ed(s): Steve Stork. Human Kinetics, PO Box 5076, Champaign, IL 61825-5076; orders@hkusa.com; http://www.humankinetics.com. Illus., adv. Refereed. Circ: 2857 Paid. Vol. ends: Nov. Reprint: PSC. *Indexed:* ERIC, IBR, IBZ, PEI, SD. *Bk. rev.:* 4-5, 250 words. *Aud.:* Ems, Ac.

For K-8 physical education teachers, *Teaching Elementary Physical Education* provides information on a wide variety of topics, including advocacy, teaching tips, lifetime fitness, assessment, curriculum development, self-esteem, special-needs students, and the like. The purpose of this journal is to "provide practical information to the professional, to advance the profession, and to advocate for physical education in our schools." Individual issues of this bimonthly professional journal are approximately 30 to 40 pages in length, containing as many as seven or as few as two articles. Issues are based on a theme and include columns on curriculum, research into practice, developmental skills, lifestyle, and a listing of relevant web sites. Appropriate for elementary and middle school libraries, and academic libraries serving higher education institutions training physical educators.

5778. Women in Sport and Physical Activity Journal (Online Edition). Formerly (until 200?): *Women in Sport and Physical Activity Journal (Print Edition).* 1992. s-a. USD 50 (Non-members, USD 30). National Association for Girls and Women in Sport, 1900 Association Dr, Reston, VA 20191; http://www.aahperd.org/nagws. Illus. Refereed. Vol. ends: Fall. *Indexed:* CWI, FemPer, GendWatch, H&SSA, PEI, RiskAb, SD. *Bk. rev.:* 4, lengthy. *Aud.:* Ac, Sa.

Although this journal has been published for over 14 years, in 2004 it was taken under the auspices of the National Association for Girls and Women in Sport. The online journal focuses on peer-reviewed research articles about women's involvement in and/or perspectives on sport and physical activity. The journal is published biannually in the spring and the fall. Entries include the original data-based research, review essays, creative writing, book reviews, commentaries, letters and responses, and other scholarly writings relative to sport and physical activity. Appropriate for academic libraries.

Specific Sports

5779. *Amateur Wrestling News.* [ISSN: 0569-1796] 1955. 12x/yr. USD 33. Ed(s): Ron Good. Amateur Wrestling News, PO Box 54679, Oklahoma City, OK 73154. Illus., adv. Circ: 10000. *Indexed:* SD. *Aud.:* Hs, Ga.

Since 1955, *Amateur Wrestling News* has covered all phases of amateur wrestling: high school, collegiate, Olympic, women's, freestyle, and Greco-Roman. Issues regularly contain interviews with coaches and profiles of players, teams, and competitions. The magazine publishes complete rankings and reports of high school state meets, as well as collegiate championships. The web site www.amateurwrestlingnews.com contains links to information on high school and college teams and wrestling camps. This publication is suitable for high school and academic libraries.

5780. *American Fencing.* [ISSN: 0002-8436] 1949. q. Non-members, USD 16. Ed(s): Candi MacConaugha. United States Fencing Association, Inc., One Olympic Plaza, Colorado Springs, CO 80909-5774; http://www.usfencing.org. Illus., adv. Circ: 12000. Microform: PQC. *Indexed:* SD. *Aud.:* Hs, Ga, Ac.

The official publication of the United States Fencing Association (USFA), this magazine reports on the news, people, tournaments, rankings, rules, training, techniques, and equipment of the sport of fencing. This quarterly features articles and essays about fencing and issues surrounding the sport. Regular departments include one on sports medicine, the science of sports, rules and referees, tournament results, and information for fencing clubs. The association's web site (www.usfencing.org) allows readers to download the current issue and additional information about competitions, USFA news, coaching, and more. A good resource for high school and academic libraries with fencing programs or clubs.

5781. *Baseball America.* Formerly (until 1982): *All-America Baseball News.* [ISSN: 0745-5372] 1981. 26x/yr. USD 87.95; USD 4.75 newsstand/cover; USD 6.25 newsstand/cover Canada. Baseball America, Inc., 201 W Main St, Ste 201, Durham, NC 27701; letters@ baseballamerica.com; http://www.baseballamerica.com. Illus., adv. Circ: 70000. *Aud.:* Ga, Ac.

This newsprint publication provides comprehensive coverage of international, major league, minor league, collegiate Division I, and high school baseball teams. Articles highlight teams, players, coaches, prospects, leagues, statistics, and averages. The magazine publishes weekly rankings of the top 25 college teams, and draft and season previews. The print publication is updated at the magazine's web site (www.baseballamerica.com), which contains current information on teams, players, statistics, and news. Subscribers to the magazine have unlimited access to Baseball America Online at no additional charge. Recommended for public, high school, and academic libraries.

5782. *Baseball Digest.* [ISSN: 0005-609X] 1941. m. USD 29.95 domestic; USD 40 foreign; USD 5.99 newsstand/cover. Ed(s): Robert Kuenster. Century Publishing Co., 990 Grove St, Evanston, IL 60201-4370; bb@centurysports.net; http://www.centurysports.net. Illus., adv. Circ: 225000 Paid and controlled. Vol. ends: Dec. Microform: PQC. Online: EBSCO Publishing, EBSCO Host; Gale. *Indexed:* CPL, MASUSE, PEI. *Aud.:* Hs, Ga.

Published since 1941 and calling itself the "oldest baseball magazine," *Baseball Digest* includes feature articles, interviews, statistics, charts, and rosters of major league baseball. Other features of the magazine are a "Fans Speak Out" section; trivia questions; comprehensive batting, pitching, and fielding statistics; previews; rules review; and analysis of upcoming prospects. The magazine is published ten times a year. The current issue's table of contents is available at the publisher's web site, www.centurysports.net/baseball. This magazine is suitable for high school and public libraries.

5783. *Bicycling.* Formerly: *American Cycling Magazine;* Which incorporated (in 1981): *American Cyclist.* [ISSN: 0006-2073] 1962. m. 11/yr. USD 19.98 domestic; CND 29.98 Canada; USD 39.98 elsewhere. Ed(s): Stephen Madden, William Strickland. Rodale, Inc., 33 E Minor St, Emmaus, PA 18098; info@rodale.com; http://www.rodale.com. Illus., adv. Circ: 400000 Paid. Microform: NBI; PQC. Online: EBSCO Publishing, EBSCO Host; Florida Center for Library Automation; Gale; OCLC Online Computer Library Center, Inc.; ProQuest K-12 Learning Solutions; ProQuest LLC (Ann Arbor); H.W. Wilson. *Indexed:* ASIP, ConsI, IHTDI, MASUSE, PEI, RGPR, SD. *Aud.:* Hs, Ga, Ac.

This glossy magazine is for the serious cyclist. Articles on cycling competition, vacation and pleasure rides, upcoming events, equipment maintenance and repair, product reviews, clothing, training tips, and fitness are included on a regular basis. Cover stories feature reviews of equipment and gear, extensive interviews, suggested rides, advice for better bicycling, and other information of interest to cyclists. Suitable for public libraries.

5784. *The Club Tread Report.* 1995. m. Ed(s): Robert Braun. Braun's Bicycle & Fitness, 27 Scott St, Kitchener, ON N2H 2P8, Canada; club-tread-report@bltg.com; http://www.bltg.com/ctreport/. *Aud.:* Hs, Ga.

Produced by Braun's Bicycle and Fitness, *The Club Tread Report* is a free electronic newsletter with news and information about cycling products. Issues contain technical tips, product reviews, cycling club news, and specials from the company. Approximately ten issues are published per year. Readers can access this newsletter on the web at www.bltg.com/ctreport. Past issues are available on the web site. Suitable for high school and public libraries.

5785. *Collegiate Baseball: the voice of amateur baseball.* [ISSN: 0530-9751] 1957. 14x/yr. USD 25 domestic; USD 50 foreign. Ed(s): Louis Pavlovich, Jr. Collegiate Baseball Newspaper Inc., c/o Lou Pavlovich, Jr, Ed, Box 50566, Tucson, AZ 85703; cbn@baseballnews.com; http://www.baseballnews.com. Illus., adv. Circ: 7000. Vol. ends: Oct. Microform: PQC. *Aud.:* Hs, Ac.

Published twice a month during the baseball season (monthly July through October), *Collegiate Baseball* provides up-to-date content for those interested in amateur high school and/or college baseball. This newspaper contains editorials, letters to the editor, news, rules and regulations, tips for training and game improvement, spotlights of outstanding players, and statistics and standings for all college divisions and high school teams. Well-known players and coaches write many of the columns. Generally, college and high school pre-season information appears in the January issues; a high school issue appears in April; a College World Series preview appears in June; an All American issue is published in July; a summer roundup issue is published in September; and October contains a fall buying guide. An appropriate purchase for high school and academic libraries.

5786. *Golf Digest.* [ISSN: 0017-176X] 1950. m. USD 14.97 domestic; CND 38.46 Canada; USD 59.97 elsewhere. Ed(s): Jerry Tarde, Mike O'Malley. The Golf Digest Companies, 20 Westport Rd, Wilton, CT 06897; glscustserv@cdsfulfilment.com. Illus., adv. Circ: 1557814 Paid. Microform: PQC. Online: EBSCO Publishing, EBSCO Host; Florida Center for Library Automation; Gale. *Indexed:* ConsI, MASUSE, PEI, SD. *Aud.:* Hs, Ga, Ac.

Golf Digest belies its name. Each issue of this monthly, published since 1950, is over 200 pages long. The magazine is filled with advice for game improvement. A recent issue, labeled the "Total Improvement Issue," teaches players how to beat their best score, play like Tiger Woods, purchase the correct equipment, correct problem swings and putting, and the like. Detailed articles are written by and about the professional golfers, and photographs break down their swings for comparative purposes. Occasional feature articles focus on golf history, golf courses, country clubs, and interviews with major players. In April the magazine publishes a special Masters issue to honor the event in Augusta. Columns and sections address golf news and equipment. A subscription to this magazine will delight golfers frequenting public and academic libraries

5787. Golf for Women. Formerly: *G F W.* [ISSN: 0898-4719] 1988. bi-m. USD 16.97 domestic; USD 22.97 Canada; USD 28.97 elsewhere. The Golf Digest Companies, 20 Westport Rd, Wilton, CT 06897; glscustserv@cdsfulfilment.com; http://www.golfdigest.com. Illus., adv. Circ: 500000 Paid. *Indexed:* PEI, SD. *Aud.:* Hs, Ga.

Golf for Women is a glossy, consumer-oriented magazine for the woman golfer. There are numerous advertisements, but also many interesting and informative features and regular articles. A typical issue contains at least one interview with a professional woman golfer, advice on golf fashion, rules and etiquette, golf vacations, tournaments, training tips, and instruction articles by LPGA players and teaching professionals. The magazine publishes annual listings of the top courses, best equipment, top teachers, and best players. The table of contents with selected articles from recent issues is available online at www.golfdigest.com/gfw. Women golfers at all levels will appreciate a magazine targeted toward them. Appropriate for public libraries.

5788. Golf Magazine. Former titles (until 1991): *Golf (New York);* (until 1986): *Golf Magazine.* [ISSN: 1056-5493] 1959. m. USD 12 domestic; USD 22 Canada; USD 49.95 elsewhere. Ed(s): Peter Morrice, Evan Rothman. Time4 Media, Inc., 2 Park Ave, New York, NY 10016; http://www.golfonline.com. Illus., adv. Circ: 1400000 Paid. Microform: PQC. Online: EBSCO Publishing, EBSCO Host; Gale; OCLC Online Computer Library Center, Inc.; ProQuest LLC (Ann Arbor); H.W. Wilson. *Indexed:* ASIP, ConsI, MASUSE, PEI, RGPR, SD. *Aud.:* Hs, Ga, Ac.

Since 1959, *Golf Magazine* has published articles on golf equipment, rules, instruction, courses, golf vacations and travel, interviews with golfers, and golfing events. This glossy publication is filled with photographs and illustrations. Regular columns concentrate on golf events, questions and answers, rules, and questions for tour players. "Private Lessons" provides tips for better play for the senior, experienced, and beginning golfer. The print magazine is supplemented by an online version at www.golfonline.com. Although similar to *Golf Digest*, the two publications complement one another. A suitable purchase for public and academic libraries.

5789. Handball. Formerly (until 1971): *Ace.* [ISSN: 0046-6778] 1951. bi-m. Membership, USD 35. Ed(s): Vern Roberts. U.S. Handball Association, 2333 N Tucson Blvd, Tucson, AZ 85716; http://ushandball.org. Illus., adv. Circ: 10000. Microform: PQC. *Indexed:* PEI, SD. *Aud.:* Hs, Ga, Ac.

As the official voice of the U.S. Handball Association, this magazine will interest association members and all recreational handball players. Each issue contains instructional articles for beginning and advanced players, tournament dates and entry forms, tips from the best players, health advice, photographs and stories from major tournaments, and specials on handball equipment and gear. Handball is a popular sport in many areas of the country, and public libraries may want to consider this publication.

5790. The Hockey News: the international hockey weekly. [ISSN: 0018-3016] 1947. 42x/yr. CND 55.08 domestic; USD 51.48 United States. Transcontinental Media, Inc., 25 Sheppard Ave West, Ste 100, Toronto, ON M2N 6S7, Canada; info@transcontinental.ca; http://www.transcontinental-gtc.com/en/home.html. Illus., adv. Circ: 110000. Microform: MML. *Indexed:* CBCARef, CPerI, SD. *Aud.:* Ga.

Since 1947, *The Hockey News* has published news about North American hockey. It comes out 42 times a year (weekly during the hockey season and on alternate weeks during the off-season.) It includes six special issues: Season Opener, People of Power and Influence, Future Watch, Draft Preview, Season in Review, and the Yearbook. The magazine, printed on newsprint, is richly illustrated. Typical contents include editorials, opinion pieces, letters to the editor, news in brief, player profiles and interviews, statistics, and specials on rookies, goalies, and other topics. Each team in the National Hockey League receives in-depth coverage in every issue. Less detail is provided for teams in the minor pro, junior, and collegiate leagues. The magazine's web site at www.thehockeynews.com allows fans to keep even more current on hockey news and events. This title is appropriate for school and public libraries in areas where hockey is popular.

5791. Hockey Player Magazine (Online Edition). Formerly (until 1998): *Hockey Player Magazine (Print Edition).* 1991. m. USD 12.95. Ed(s): Alex Carswell. Hockey Player Magazine L.P., hockeyplayermag@attbi.com; http://www.hockeyplayer.com. Illus., adv. Circ: 20000 Paid. *Aud.:* Ga.

Published as a print magazine from 1991 to 1997, *Hockey Player* became an online-only publication in 1998 (www.hockeyplayer.com). Aimed at the recreational ice, roller, and street hockey player, the web site contains interviews, columns, departments, equipment news, drills, and instruction. The more than 500 articles are fully searchable and/or can be browsed by section. Typical sections include "Behind the Bench" (coaching), offense, defense, essays, humor, power skating, profiles, and youth. Most appropriate for public libraries in areas where hockey is popular.

5792. Inside Triathlon: the multisport life. Formerly: *Triathlon Today.* 1986. 12x/yr. USD 29.95 domestic; CND 41.95 Canada; USD 65 elsewhere. Ed(s): Kyle du Ford. Inside Communications Inc., 1830 N 55th St, Boulder, CO 80301-2703. Illus., adv. Circ: 22374 Paid. *Indexed:* SD. *Aud.:* Ga.

Since 1986, the monthly *Inside Triathlon* has published articles and columns of interest to competitive duathletes and triathletes (including Ironman competitors.) Issues of approximately 70 pages contain interviews and feature articles as well as columns on fitness, speed, nutrition, and gear, plus a race calendar. Several pages in every issue are devoted to training, with a Q&A section, a coach's corner, training drills, and advice by sports psychologists. Annual bonus issues include a "TriGuide" listing the top triathlon events for the year and a buyer's guide with reviews of bikes, swim equipment, wetsuits, shoes, adventure racing gear, and gadgets. This publication is appropriate for libraries specializing in competitive sports and large public libraries in areas where triathlons are popular.

5793. International Figure Skating. [ISSN: 1070-9568] 1993. bi-m. USD 22.97 domestic; USD 32 Canada; USD 45 elsewhere. Ed(s): Susan Wessling. Madavor Media, Llc., 420 Boylston St, 5th Fl, Boston, MA 02116; info@madavor.com; http://www.madavor.com. Illus., adv. Circ: 30000. *Indexed:* RGPR, SD. *Aud.:* Hs, Ga.

International Figure Skating reports on the news, business, and personalities of figure skating, with coverage of recent U.S. and international competitions. Although it is U.S.–based, the magazine has correspondents in Canada, Germany, France, Hong Kong, and the United Kingdom. The cover story in each issue profiles popular skaters. This glossy magazine with numerous photographs will appeal to skaters and would-be skaters alike. The magazine's web site at www.ifsmagazine.com provides access to selected stories and updates on recent competitions, with photos from the magazine. Appropriate for public libraries.

5794. International Gymnast. Former titles (until 1986): *International Gymnast Magazine;* (until 1982): *International Gymnast;* (until 1981): *International Gymnast Magazine;* (until 1979): *International Gymnast;* (until 1975): *Gymnast;* Incorporates (1975-1980): *Gymnastics World;* (1966-1971): *Mademoiselle Gymnast; Modern Gymnast.* [ISSN: 0891-6616] 1972. 10x/yr. USD 30 domestic; USD 40.66 Canada; USD 38 elsewhere. Ed(s): Dwight Normile, Nadia Comaneci. Paul Ziert & Associates, Inc., PO Box 721020, Norman, OK 73070-4788; orders@intlgymnast.com. Illus., adv. Circ: 20000 Paid. Online: OCLC Online Computer Library Center, Inc.; ProQuest LLC (Ann Arbor). *Indexed:* SD. *Aud.:* Hs, Ga.

As befits a sport whose fans relate to particular personalities, *International Gymnast* focuses on the individuals who compete in the field. The ten yearly issues are approximately 40 pages in length and primarily contain biographical profiles and coverage of international events and teams. Articles are lavishly illustrated and supplemented by columns containing letters, new products, a calendar, a brief fictional series, and a "Kid's Klub"—the last, no doubt, addressing a large segment of the magazine's readership. The magazine's web site at www.intlgymnast.com provides access to selected articles. This magazine is appropriate for public libraries and schools with gymnastic teams.

5795. *Journal of Asian Martial Arts.* [ISSN: 1057-8358] 1992. q. USD 75 (Individuals, USD 32). Ed(s): Michael A DeMarco. Via Media Publishing Company, 821 W 24th St, Erie, PA 16502; http://www.goviamedia.com. Illus., index, adv. Sample. Refereed. Circ: 12000 Paid and controlled. *Indexed:* PEI, SD. *Bk. rev.:* 3, 750-1,200 words. *Aud.:* Ga, Ac.

This quarterly publishes articles of interest to the serious student of the martial arts. Each issue of approximately 120 pages is divided among academic articles based on primary research; general articles on a genre or technique; and reviews of books and media related to the martial arts. The journal publishes "studies that offer a better understanding of the cultures from which martial arts arose and in which they continue to thrive." A recent issue contains a scholarly article on the walking stick, the art of Taijiquan, the use of the leg lock, and a profile of Yagi Meitoku. Articles are illustrated with drawings and photographs. Suitable for large public and academic libraries.

5796. *Journal of Swimming Research.* [ISSN: 0747-5993] 1984. a. USD 15 domestic; USD 25 in Canada & Mexico; USD 35 elsewhere. Ed(s): Dr. Joel M Stager. American Swimming Coaches Association, 2101 N Andrews Ave, 107, Fort Lauderdale, FL 33311; http://www.swimmingcoach.org. Adv. Refereed. Circ: 5000 Paid. *Indexed:* PEI, SD. *Aud.:* Ac, Sa.

The peer-reviewed *Journal of Swimming Research* is the official publication of the American Swimming Coaches Association. The audience for this journal is students, academics, and coaches. The journal describes itself as a "researcher-to-coach publication" and includes original research and comprehensive and brief reviews of the science of swimming that have practical applications. Each issue of approximately 50 pages contains four or five articles. Annually, the journal publishes an extensive bibliography of articles related to swimming research. The journal is free with membership in the American Swimming Coaches Association. This publication is appropriate for academic libraries at institutions with competitive swimming programs.

5797. *Marathon & Beyond.* [ISSN: 1088-6672] 1997. bi-m. USD 34.95 domestic; USD 45.74 Canada; USD 50 elsewhere. Ed(s): Jan Calarusso. Marathon & Beyond, 206 N Randolph St, Ste 502, Champaign, IL 61820. Adv. Circ: 6000 Paid. *Indexed:* CABA, PEI, RRTA, SD. *Aud.:* Ga.

This bimonthly publication caters to serious marathoners and ultra runners. Its mission is to "provide practical advice on running or preparing to run marathons and ultradistances." Unlike other magazines of this type, *Marathon and Beyond* does not include race reports, schedules of events, or reviews of running shoes, apparel, or equipment. Instead it publishes articles written by accomplished runners, coaches, and scientists that focus on the personal side of running, profiles of major marathons and ultramarathons, and columns on specific aspects of running. Articles are generally longer than in other similar magazines, and there are no glossy photographs. First-time runners and experienced long-distance runners alike will welcome this magazine. Suitable for public libraries.

5798. *Nine: a journal of baseball history & culture.* [ISSN: 1188-9330] 1992. s-a. USD 85 (Individuals, USD 50). Ed(s): Trey Strecker. University of Nebraska Press, 1111 Lincoln Mall, Lincoln, NE 68588-0630; journals@unlnotes.unl.edu; http://www.nebraskapress.unl.edu. Illus., adv. Refereed. *Indexed:* AmH&L, HistAb, PEI, SD, SSA, SociolAb. *Bk. rev.:* Number and length vary. *Aud.:* Ac.

Published since 1992, this peer-reviewed journal promotes "the study of all historical aspects of baseball and the cultural implications of the game wherever in the world baseball is played." Issues include articles, essays, book reviews, biographies, oral histories, and short fiction pieces. Recent issues include articles on the Brooklyn Dodgers' move to Los Angeles, nineteenth-century baseball, Italian American baseball players, and baseball and fictional television, plus review essays and book, play, and movie reviews. This academic journal is available from 2000 on in Project MUSE. Suitable for academic libraries.

5799. *Pedal.* [ISSN: 1191-2685] 1986. 6x/yr. CND 23.70 domestic; USD 26 United States; CND 32 foreign. Ed(s): Benjamin A Sadavoy. Pedal Magazine, 317 Adelaide St W, Ste 703, Toronto, ON M5V 1P9, Canada; pedal@passport.ca; http://www.pedal.com. Adv. Circ: 20000. *Aud.:* Ga.

Pedal covers all forms of cycling in Canada. It includes national and international coverage of mountain bike, road, and track competitions; interviews and profiles; touring and adventure articles; product reviews (gear, equipment, bikes); an annual buyer's guide of all mountain, full suspension, road, hybrid, track, triathlon, cruiser, tandem, and BMX bikes in Canada; a comprehensive events calendar; and columns on nutrition, BMX, touring, history, and road cycling. This publication is suitable for public libraries in Canada and near the Canadian border.

5800. *Pro Football Weekly.* [ISSN: 0032-9053] 1967. 32x/yr. USD 44.95 for 15 issues; USD 79.95 for 30 issues. Source Interlink Companies, 27500 Riverview Center Blvd, Bonita Springs, FL 34134; edisupport@sourceinterlink.com; http://www.sourceinterlink.com. Illus., adv. Circ: 125262. *Aud.:* Ga.

This newspaper publishes news of professional football, including team rosters and schedules, player profiles, fantasy football, arena football, NFL, Europe, player transactions, statistics, team rankings, and opinion pieces. Noted sports columnists write many of the feature columns. This publication provides an insider's view of the sport and will attract true football fans. The newspaper is supplemented by selected articles at www.profootballweekly.com. Readers may also choose to subscribe to the PFW Inner Circle to gain full access to PFW online, the Draft Inner Circle, and/or the Fantasy Inner Circle. Readers may also purchase the annual NFL Preview and Fantasy Football Guide. The publication is suitable for public libraries.

5801. *Rugby.* [ISSN: 0162-1297] 1975. m. USD 37 domestic; USD 40 Canada; USD 4 newsstand/cover per issue. Ed(s): Edward Hagerty. Rugby Press, Ltd., 2350 Broadway, Ste 220, New York, NY 10024. Adv. Circ: 10300 Paid. *Indexed:* SD. *Aud.:* Ga, Ac.

Published since 1975, *Rugby* provides in-depth coverage of U.S. championships and international matches; player, coach, and referee profiles; and complete tournament and all-star coverage. A nutrition column, an opinion piece, and a calendar of events round out this 50-page monthly publication. High school, collegiate, military, and professional teams and players are covered. Appropriate for high school, public, and academic libraries in areas where rugby is played.

5802. *Runner's World.* Incorporates (1978-1987): *Runner;* Former titles (until 1987): *Rodale's Runner's World;* (until 1985): *Runner's World; Distance Running News.* [ISSN: 0897-1706] 1966. m. USD 21 domestic; CND 30 Canada; USD 50 elsewhere. Ed(s): David Willey, Amby Burfoot. Rodale, Inc., 33 E Minor St, Emmaus, PA 18098; info@rodale.com; http://www.rodale.com. Illus., index, adv. Circ: 500000 Paid. Microform: PQC. Online: EBSCO Publishing, EBSCO Host; Florida Center for Library Automation; Gale; Northern Light Technology, Inc.; OCLC Online Computer Library Center, Inc.; ProQuest LLC (Ann Arbor); H.W. Wilson. *Indexed:* ConsI, MASUSE, PEI, RGPR, SD. *Aud.:* Ga, Ac.

Serious and recreational runners will enjoy *Runner's World.* Columns and departments include rave runs (beautiful places to run), letters, nutrition, gear, motivational techniques, injury prevention, training advice, product reviews, vacation tips, and racing reports. Issues are often devoted to special topics such as the marathon or weight loss. The magazine's web site at www.runnersworld.com contains selected articles, links to relevant sites, and an offer for a free online newsletter. Suitable for academic and public libraries.

5803. *Running & FitNews.* Former titles (until 1984): *Running and Fitness;* (until 1981): *Jogger.* [ISSN: 0898-5162] bi-m. USD 40 (Members, USD 25). American Running Association, 4405 East West Hwy, Ste 405, Bethesda, MD 20814; run@americanrunning.org; http://www.americanrunning.org. Illus., index. Circ: 15000 Paid. Online: EBSCO Publishing, EBSCO Host; Gale; ProQuest LLC (Ann Arbor). *Indexed:* CINAHL, SD. *Aud.:* Ga, Ac.

This well-regarded newsletter of the American Running Association provides nutrition, training, health, and sport medicine information for the running enthusiast. The eight pages published every two months briefly cover topics such as marathons, injuries, general health, fitness, races, and nutrition. Articles are written by the editor and reviewed by an editorial board that consists of clinicians and academics. Lack of indexing and security problems may prove a hindrance for its inclusion in smaller libraries. Suitable for academic and public libraries.

5804. Running Times: the runner's best resource. [ISSN: 0147-2968] 1977. 10x/yr. USD 25 domestic; USD 35 Canada; USD 55 elsewhere. Ed(s): Jonathan Beverly. Rodale, Inc., 15 River Rd., Ste 230, Wilton, CT 06897; customer_service@rodale.com; http://www.rodale.com. Illus., adv. Circ: 92319 Paid. *Indexed:* PEI, SD. *Aud.:* Ga, Ac.

Labeling itself "the runner's best resource," this magazine is for the serious competitive runner. A spring shoe guide, accounts of running in different countries, and the annual ranking of the world's best runners are all covered in recent issues. The ten issues per year also include a column by an exercise physiologist and other columns on sports medicine, training tips, gear, racing news, calendars, a high school page, and a section of classified ads. For libraries catering to competitive athletes.

5805. Scuba Diving: the magazine divers trust. Formerly (until 2004): *Rodale's Scuba Diving;* Incorporates (1987-1992): *Fisheye View Scuba Magazine.* [ISSN: 1553-7919] 1992. 11x/yr. USD 16.97 domestic; CND 27.97 Canada; USD 34.97 elsewhere. F + W Publications, Inc., 6600 Abercorn St, Ste 208, Savannah, GA 31405; http://www.fwpublications.com. Illus., adv. Circ: 200000 Paid and controlled. *Aud.:* Ga.

Scuba Diving covers all aspects of scuba diving, including equipment, techniques, training, fitness, nutrition, and travel. The "Editor's Choice Awards," introduced in 2005, lists the best new destinations, travel companies, surface intervals, gear, divers, and more. Other features include a holiday gear guide, a reader photo contest, best dives, and the like. This is a glossy magazine with beautiful photography, and it will interest both the diving enthusiast and the professional. Suitable for public and academic libraries in areas of the country where scuba diving is popular.

5806. Ski: the magazine of the ski life. Incorporates: *Ski Life.* [ISSN: 0037-6159] 1936. 8x/yr. USD 10.97 domestic; USD 15.35 Canada; USD 3.99 newsstand/cover. Time4 Media, Inc., 2 Park Ave, New York, NY 10016. Illus., adv. Circ: 426403 Paid. Microform: PQC. Online: EBSCO Publishing, EBSCO Host; Gale; OCLC Online Computer Library Center, Inc.; ProQuest K-12 Learning Solutions; ProQuest LLC (Ann Arbor). *Indexed:* ConsI, MASUSE, PEI, SD. *Aud.:* Ga, Ac.

With its beautiful photography and tips on ski travel, vacations, resorts, and towns, *Ski* will attract all recreational skiers. The 100-page issues regularly include instruction, tips for injury prevention, training, interviews, and lifestyle articles. Since skiing is seasonal, articles on the more general aspects of outdoor life are also included. Published since 1936, this magazine comes out eight times a year. Annually, it publishes reviews of resorts, vacation homes, and a buyer's guide. The magazine's web site at www.skimag.com contains selected articles, a buyer's guide, snow reports, a calendar of events, a discussion forum, and more. Suitable for public libraries.

5807. Ski Racing. [ISSN: 0037-6213] 1968. 20x/yr. USD 29.98 domestic; USD 44.98 Canada; USD 69.98 elsewhere. Ed(s): Don Cameron. Inside Communications Inc., 1830 N 55th St, Boulder, CO 80301-2703. Illus., adv. Circ: 20000 Paid. *Indexed:* SD. *Aud.:* Ga.

Competitive skiers will be interested in *Ski Racing.* This glossy publication is filled with photographs and information on the skiing industry, profiles of skiers and snowboarders, camp listings, and reports on competition and the various circuits (including junior, masters, Nordic, alpine, freestyle, and snowboarding). A subscription includes an annual buyer's guide and guide to World Cup skiing. The magazine is published 15 times a year, twice a month during the racing season and monthly during the remainder of the year. Recommended for public libraries that cater to a skiing clientele.

5808. Ski Trax: North America's cross country skiing magazine. m. CND 13 Canada; USD 14 United States. Ed(s): Benjamin Sadavoy. Ski Trax Magazine, 317 Adelaide St W, 703, Toronto, ON M5V IP9, Canada. Illus. *Aud.:* Ga.

Fans of Nordic skiing will welcome *Ski Trax*, the official publication of the Ski and Snowboard Association, the national governing body of Olympic skiing and snowboarding. Since this publication covers all forms of Nordic events, it includes skiing, snowshoeing, snowboarding, biathlons, and the like. The glossy magazine, published four times during the ski season, contains beautiful photographs, articles on places to stay, snowshoe equipment, product reviews, competitions (Olympic, national, international), profiles of coaches and athletes, an annual directory of the best in cross-country skiing and snowshoeing, and a buyer's guide. Public libraries in northern areas should consider adding this magazine to their collections.

5809. Skydiving. [ISSN: 0192-7361] 1979. m. USD 20. Ed(s): Sue Clifton. Aerographics, 1725 N Lexington Ave, Deland, FL 32724; edit@skydivingmagazine.com; http://www.skydivingmagazine.com. Adv. Circ: 14200 Paid. Microform: PQC. *Indexed:* SD. *Aud.:* Ga.

This oversized magazine on glossy newsprint will attract both amateur and professional skydivers. Filled with photographs of jumps and jumpers, the publication includes news about the equipment, events, techniques, people, and places of parachuting. An instruction column helps readers refresh their skills and learn new ones. A recent issue contains an article explaining how a parachutist's body position influences the deployment of the jumper's canopy. An appropriate selection for public libraries in areas where skydiving is popular.

5810. Soccer America. Formerly: *Soccer West.* [ISSN: 0163-4070] 1971. w. 50/yr. USD 79 domestic; USD 119 Canada; USD 189 elsewhere. Ed(s): Mike Woitalla, Paul Kennedy. Soccer America Communications LLC, PO Box 23704, Oakland, CA 94623-0704. Illus., adv. Circ: 32750 Paid. Microform: PQC. *Bk. rev.:* 1, 800 words. *Aud.:* Ga.

Since 1971, this monthly has published news, statistics, scores, reports, and analysis of U.S. and international soccer, including youth, collegiate, and Major League teams. Players are highlighted in informative articles. A monthly tournament calendar contains a comprehensive listing of soccer events in the United States and abroad. Editorial columns provides insight into the world of soccer. The publication's web site at www.socceramerica.com provides access to selected articles and links of interest to the soccer fan. Recommended for public, high school, and academic libraries where soccer is popular.

5811. Soccer Journal. [ISSN: 0560-3617] 1941. 8x/yr. USD 40 (Individual members, USD 50; USD 90 in Europe). Ed(s): Martin Jay. National Soccer Coaches Association of America, 6700 Squibb Rd, Ste 215, Mission, KS 66202; info@nscaa.com; http://www.nscaa.com. Illus., adv. Circ: 16000 Paid. *Indexed:* PEI, SD. *Aud.:* Hs, Ac.

As the official publication of the National Soccer Coaches Association of America, *Soccer Journal* publishes information exclusively for the soccer coach. Each of the eight issues per year contains articles on instruction, psychology, tactics, techniques, discipline, safety, training, diet, and conditioning for the game. Diagrams of soccer games, news from the field, and columns by the association president and executive director are regular features. The focus and intended age level are identified for feature articles. A useful addition for school and academic libraries with soccer programs.

Sports 'n Spokes. See Disabilities section.

5812. Surfer. [ISSN: 0039-6036] 1960. m. USD 14.97 domestic; USD 27.97 Canada; USD 29.97 foreign. Ed(s): Chris Mauro. Source Interlink Companies, 33046 Calle Aviador, San Juan Capistrano, CA 92675; edisupport@sourceinterlink.com; http://www.sourceinterlink.com. Adv. Circ: 116512 Paid. Online: Gale. *Aud.:* Ga.

Calling itself the "bible of the sport of surfing," this magazine is filled with dramatic adventure photography, informative articles, interviews, coverage of amateur and professional competitions, and travel features. It is geared to readers who are really involved with the surfing culture. Annual issues include an oversized Collector's Issue, the Hot 100 (best surfers under 21 years old), and the Top 44 Review (product reviews). Its web site, www.surfermag.com, provides selected articles, a photograph gallery, video clips, a merchandise catalog, and a chat forum. A good choice for public libraries in surfing communities.

5813. *Swimming World Magazine.* Formed by the merger of (1965-2005): *Swimming World and Junior Swimmer;* Which was formerly (1961-1965): *Junior Swimmer - Swimming World;* (1960-1961): *Swimming World;* (199?-2005): *Swim Magazine;* Which was formerly (1984-199?): *Swim;* (1997-2005): *Swimming Technique;* Which was formerly (1996-1997): *Technique;* (1964-1996): *Swimming Technique.* 2005. m. USD 29.95 domestic; USD 40.95 foreign. Ed(s): Bob Ingram. Sports Publications, Inc., PO Box 20337, Sedona, AZ 86341-2025. Illus., adv. Circ: 33143 Paid. Vol. ends: Dec. Online: EBSCO Publishing, EBSCO Host; ProQuest K-12 Learning Solutions. Online: Northern Light Technology, Inc. *Indexed:* MASUSE, PEI, SD. *Aud.:* Hs, Ga, Ac.

This publication was designed for the competitive swimmer and fitness audience. A monthly since 1960, *Swimming World* has covered news, swim meets, training advice, technique tips, interviews, and the like. The magazine was redesigned in 2005 for a wider audience, with increased content and photographs. Included in a subscription is access to a pdf version of *Swimming Technique* and *Junior Swimmer.* Thus, the magazine now covers all types of swimmers from the beginner to the recreational to the competitive. Suitable for high school, public, and academic libraries.

5814. *Tennis.* [ISSN: 0040-3423] 1965. 10x/yr. USD 12 domestic; USD 35 Canada; USD 50 elsewhere. Ed(s): Mark Woodruff, Stephen Gignor. Miller Publishing Group, Miller Sports Group LLC., 79 Madison Ave, 8th Fl, New York, NY 10016; http://www.tennis.com. Illus., index, adv. Circ: 700000 Paid. Microform: PQC. Online: EBSCO Publishing, EBSCO Host; Gale; OCLC Online Computer Library Center, Inc.; H.W. Wilson. *Indexed:* ConsI, MASUSE, PEI, RGPR, SD. *Aud.:* Hs, Ga, Ac.

For over 40 years, *Tennis* has delighted the novice and advanced tennis enthusiast. It is filled with excellent photographs. Tennis instruction is supplemented with profiles of the professional players, coverage of major tournaments, equipment and gear reviews, and information on nutrition, health, and fitness for the tennis player. It is the most popular magazine in the sport—members of the United States Tennis Association receive free subscriptions. Almost all of the approximately 100-page issues are devoted to editorial content rather than advertising, which is unusual among popular single-sport magazines. Appropriate for school, public, and academic libraries.

5815. *Track & Field News.* [ISSN: 0041-0284] 1948. m. USD 43.95 domestic; USD 64 in Canada & Mexico; USD 54 foreign. Ed(s): Sieg Lindstrom, Garry Hill. Track & Field News, 2570 El Camino Real, 606, Mountain View, CA 94040; subs@trackandfieldnews.com. Illus., adv. Circ: 26000 Paid. Microform: PQC. *Indexed:* SD. *Aud.:* Hs, Ga, Ac.

The oldest magazine in this sport, *Track & Field News* has been in continuous publication since 1948. The publication provides detailed information on U.S. high school, collegiate, and professional action during the season. International coverage includes the European circuit, the Olympics, and world championships. Feature articles are brief and supplemented by schedules of competitions, lists of records, editorials, statistics, letters, and brief biographical notes. Suitable for the collections of large public libraries and high schools and academic institutions with track and field programs.

5816. *Triathlete.* Formed by the merger of (1984-1986): *Tri-Athlete;* (1983-1986): *Triathlon.* [ISSN: 0898-3410] 1986. m. USD 21.95 domestic; USD 26.95 Canada; USD 28.95 elsewhere. Ed(s): Christina Gandolfo. Triathlon Group North America, 2037 San Elijo Ave, Cardiff, CA 92007-0550. Illus., adv. Circ: 105000. *Indexed:* SD. *Aud.:* Ga, Ac.

Triathlete is one of two major monthly magazines focusing on triathlon competition. Published since 1986, this glossy publication has been expanded to almost 200 pages and now includes international news. Each issue follows a regular format with columns and departments. Departments include editorials, letters, and news. There is a large training section. One column, by Scott Tinley, is considered by subscribers to be a major asset to the magazine. Other articles

focus on fitness, speed, equipment and product reviews (usually bikes and shoes), and new techniques, tests, and other developments. Annually, the magazine publishes a guide to the top races in North America. Buyer's guides are also regularly published. "The Road to Kona," an official qualifiers guide to Ironman championships all over the world, is a supplement to the magazine. Appropriate for academic and public libraries.

5817. *U S A Hockey Magazine.* Former titles (until 200?): *American Hockey Magazine;* (until 198?): *American Hockey and Arena; United States Hockey and Arena Biz; Hockey and Arena Biz; U S Hockey Biz.* [ISSN: 1551-6741] 1973. 10x/yr. USD 35 domestic (Free to members). Ed(s): Harry Thompson. U S A Hockey, 1775 Bob Johnson Dr, Colorado Springs, CO 80906-4090; usah@usahockey.org; http://www.usahockey.com. Illus., adv. Circ: 425000. *Aud.:* Hs, Ga, Ac.

Players, coaches, parents, and fans of amateur ice and inline hockey will find the *American Hockey Magazine* of interest. As the official publication of USA Hockey and USA Hockey InLine, it publishes profiles, rules, strategies, tips, instructional articles, and reports of league and tournament play. The February issue contains an annual camp directory. Other issues feature buyer's guides for equipment, goaltenders, skates, and the like. Each 60-page issue contains photographs and columns on coaching, refereeing, regional news, and personalities. With the increasing interest in hockey, this publication will be popular in public, high school, and academic libraries.

5818. *U S A Today Sports Weekly.* Formerly (until 2002): *U S A Today Baseball Weekly.* 1991. w. USD 39.95; USD 1.25 newsstand/cover per issue. Ed(s): Tim McQuay, Lee Ivory. U S A Today, 1000 Wilson Blvd, Arlington, VA 22229; http://cgi.usatoday.com. Illus., adv. Circ: 260000 Paid. *Aud.:* Ga.

Although this title sounds like a general sports magazine, the publication focuses primarily upon baseball and football. Each issue generally has two sections that feature professional and collegiate teams and players, scouting reports, trades, training, and league reports. For the baseball enthusiast, there is an annual All Star preview issue, while football enthusiasts can gain information by reading the annual special NFL preview issue. Fantasy baseball and football are also covered. This would be a popular addition to public libraries.

5819. *VeloNews: the journal of competitive cycling.* Former titles (until 1974): *Cyclenews;* (until 1972): *Northeast Bicycle News.* [ISSN: 0161-1798] 1972. 20x/yr. USD 44.97 domestic; USD 64.97 Canada; USD 99.97 per issue elsewhere. Ed(s): Bryan Jew, Kip Mikler. Inside Communications Inc., 1830 N 55th St, Boulder, CO 80301-2703; velonews@7dogs.com; http://www.velonews.com. Illus., index, adv. Circ: 48000. Microform: PQC. *Indexed:* SD. *Aud.:* Ga, Ac.

Since 1972, the glossy *VeloNews* has reported competitive bicycling news, including profiles of cyclists and teams, reports of major races in North America and Europe, articles on training, health and nutrition, injury prevention, products and equipment, and news articles (such as one on drug testing). Each issue contains a calendar of international and North American races. Subscribers receive an annual buyer's guide to products for the upcoming season and, as a bonus, a special issue titled *Official Guide to the Tour de France.* The print publication is supplemented by a web site (www.velonews.com) that provides information on current races, technical and training information, and news items. This site also has a number of links to other sites of interest to cycling enthusiasts. Appropriate for public libraries in areas where competitive cycling is popular.

5820. *VolleyballUSA.* Former titles (until 1992): *Inside U S A Volleyball; Volleyball U S A.* 1972. q. USD 10; USD 20 foreign. U S A Volleyball, 715 S Circle Dr, Colorado Springs, CO 80910-2368; volleyballusa@usav.org; http://www.usavolleyball.org. Illus., adv. Sample. Circ: 85000. *Bk. rev.:* 2, 250 words. *Aud.:* Hs, Ga.

As the official publication of the United States Volleyball Association, *VolleyballUSA* provides current information on volleyball in the United States, including indoor, park, and beach volleyball, and national, junior, collegiate, and disabled teams. In addition to association activities, this quarterly contains tournament and competition news as well as articles about players and coaches, coaching, nutrition, weight training, and book reviews. This glossy magazine will appeal to readers in public and high school libraries where volleyball is popular.

5821. *The Water Skier: having fun today - building champions for tomorrow.* [ISSN: 0049-7002] 1951. 9x/yr. USD 25 domestic; USD 30 foreign. Ed(s): Natalie Angley, Scott Atkinson. U S A Water Ski, 1251 Holy Cow Rd, Polk City, FL 33868-8200; memberservices@ usawaterski.org; http://usawaterski.org. Illus., index, adv. Sample. Circ: 28000 Controlled. *Indexed:* ConsI. *Aud.:* Ga, Ac.

The official publication of USA Water Ski, *The Water Skier* publishes articles of interest to athletes and enthusiasts of competitive water skiing of all types (including traditional, show, wakeboard, collegiate, kneeboard, barefoot, racing, and disabled.) Each 50-page issue is filled with photographs, instructional articles, tournament reports, profiles of teams and athletes, water skiing safety, equipment reviews, and listings of ski camps and schools. An annual regional tour issue contains a comprehensive listing of tournaments throughout the nation. It includes entry forms and in-depth information on each tournament. The magazine is published nine times a year. A link to the magazine and selected articles is available at the association's web site (www.usawater-ski.org). Recommended for public and academic libraries.

5822. *Women's Basketball.* [ISSN: 1524-9204] 1999. q. USD 19.97 domestic; USD 29 Canada; USD 39 elsewhere. Ed(s): Deb Goldman. Goldman Group, Inc., 4125 Gunn Hwy, Ste B1, Tampa, FL 33618; todd@ggpubs.com; http://www.ggpubs.com. Adv. Circ: 15000. *Indexed:* RGPR. *Aud.:* Hs, Ga.

Coaches, women, and basketball fans alike will enjoy *Women's Basketball.* Since 1999, "the definitive authority on the sport" has covered the game at the high school, collegiate, and professional level. Published six times a year, this glossy magazine is filled with photographs and informative articles. Typical contents include a cover story (often an in-depth profile of an athlete); feature articles on topics such as recruiting, high school coaches, college transfers, and the like; profiles of players and coaches; and, during the season, competitions. News, training, nutrition, strategy, moves, athletic gear, and high school and amateur basketball articles round out each issue. Annually the magazine announces a player and a coach of the year award. At www.wbmagazine.com readers can access selections from feature articles to entice them to subscribe. An appropriate addition for high school, academic, and public libraries.

5823. *Wrestling U S A (Missoula).* Formerly: *Scholastic Wrestling News.* [ISSN: 0199-6258] 1964. m. USD 31 domestic; USD 41 foreign. Ed(s): Lanny Bryant. Wrestling U.S.A. Magazine, 109 Apple House Ln, Missoula, MT 59802-3324; wrestling@montana.com; http://www.wrestlingusa.com. Illus., adv. Sample. Circ: 14000. *Indexed:* SD. *Aud.:* Hs, Ac.

Wrestling USA publishes articles about amateur wrestling at the youth, high school, and collegiate level. Regular features include news, training, injury prevention, sports medicine, nutrition, coaching tips, events and tournaments, and high school and collegiate teams. The journal's web site at www.wrestlingusa.com provides access to a cover gallery and table of contents from 1965 to the present and links to sites of interest to those involved in high school and collegiate wrestling. Appropriate for high school and academic libraries with wrestling programs.

■ STATISTICS

Katherine M. Weir, Business Librarian, 8900 Milner Library, Illinois State University, Normal, IL 61790-8900; kmweir@ilstu.edu; FAX: 309-438-3676

Introduction

Statistics are as old as such human records as censuses and records of ownership. Descriptive statistics date from the Middle Ages, but it was only in the nineteenth century that statistical theory and methods began to evolve. Much

of the theory of statistics was developed in the twentieth century. Originally, the term "statistics" was applied to the collection and analysis of data about the political state, such as tax, trade, and demographic information and vital statistics.

Over time, usage has expanded to include the collection and analysis of data about human and natural phenomena of all kinds upon which to base decisions in the face of uncertainty. As computers have become increasingly powerful, it has been possible to work with ever larger data sets and to employ increasingly sophisticated statistical techniques and computationally intensive methods, such as nonlinear models and permutation tests.

For ease of discussion, the field is often divided into descriptive and analytical statistics, or statistical theory and statistical method. In addition, there are specialties based on techniques, e.g., computational statistics and stochastic modeling, or on disciplines, e.g., biometrics and econometrics. Newer branches of statistics include decision theory, time series, games theory, and reliability. Statistical publishing reflects these divisions, with journals concentrating on theoretical statistics, applied statistics, or applications in specific disciplines. As well, the fact that journals named below that are cross-referenced to the Economics, Finance, Management, Education, and Psychology sections highlights how several of these publications are statistics based.

Statistics is based on the mathematics of probability, and most statistical publications include a great deal of mathematical notation. As noted in the annotations, some journals place mathematical derivations and proofs in an appendix, in order to make the text more accessible to the nonstatistician. Figures and tables are common in statistical publications and have not been noted in the entries. Because illustrations of other types are rare, they have been noted.

There are few statistics publications of interest to the general public; most periodicals in the field are research journals, with a limited audience even among academicians and specialists. Perhaps the most accessible journal to the general adult reader is *Chance,* a publication of the American Statistical Association (ASA). *JASA,* also a publication of the ASA, is designed for the widest audience: professionals in virtually all fields, from actuaries to sociologists. All but the largest public libraries may wish to limit their collecting to these two journals. School libraries may find *Teaching Statistics* (all grades) or the *American Statistician* (high school) useful. At the college level, *Stats,* the ASA's journal for student members, is recommended, and the electronic *Journal of Statistics Education* and *Statistics Education Research Journal* are excellent sources of practical information and creative ideas for the teaching of probability and statistics.

Journals on the basic list, plus a few specialized journals selected to meet the curricular and faculty needs of a particular library, will suffice for many college libraries. Colleges and universities that support statistics programs will find many of the titles listed to be valuable additions to their collections.

Basic Periodicals

Ga: *Chance;* Ac: *Advances in Applied Probability, Annals of Applied Probability, Annals of Probability, Annals of Statistics, Computational Statistics, JASA, Royal Statistical Society. Journal. Series C. Applied Statistics.*

Basic Abstracts and Indexes

MathSciNet, Statistical Theory & Method Abstracts.

5824. *Advances in Applied Probability.* [ISSN: 0001-8678] 1969. q. GBP 150 (Individuals, GBP 50). Ed(s): C C Heyde. Applied Probability Trust, School of Mathematics and Statistics, The University of Sheffield, Sheffield, S3 7RH, United Kingdom; l.nash@sheffield.ac.uk; http://www.appliedprobability.org. Illus., index. Refereed. Circ: 1100. Vol. ends: Dec. *Indexed:* ABIn, CCMJ, EngInd, MSN, MathR, RiskAb, SCI, SSCI. *Aud.:* Ac, Sa.

Each issue contains a section on general applied probability and a section on stochastic geometry and statistical applications. Accepted for publication are review articles; longer research papers in applied probability; expository articles on areas of mathematics of interest to probabilists; articles on scientific topics for which probability models can be developed; conference papers not published elsewhere; and letters to the editor. The editor in chief and 24 of 30 editors are shared with the companion publication, *Journal of Applied Probabil-*

ity, in which shorter research papers are published. However, the editors may publish accepted papers in either journal, based on available space. Each issue contains 10–12 articles of 10–30 pages. Most articles are in English, but articles in French are also accepted for publication. This title is similar in coverage to *Annals of Applied Probability.* Colleges and universities with statistics programs should subscribe to either or both of these publications.

5825. *American Statistical Association. Journal.* Former titles (until 1922): *American Statistical Association. Quarterly Publications;* (until 1912): *American Statistical Association. Publications.* [ISSN: 0162-1459] 1888. q. USD 480 print & online eds. (Non-members, USD 480). Ed(s): Mark S Kaiser. American Statistical Association, 1429 Duke St, Alexandria, VA 22314-3415; asainfo@amstat.org; http://www.amstat.org. Illus., index, adv. Refereed. Circ: 12000. Vol. ends: Dec. Microform: PMC; PQC. Online: EBSCO Publishing, EBSCO Host; Florida Center for Library Automation; Gale; IngentaConnect; JSTOR (Web-based Journal Archive); ProQuest K-12 Learning Solutions; ProQuest LLC (Ann Arbor). *Indexed:* ABIn, CABA, CCMJ, CJA, CompR, ExcerpMed, ForAb, HortAb, IBSS, IndVet, JEL, LRI, MSN, MathR, S&F, SCI, SSCI, VB. *Bk. rev.:* 10-20, 500-1,000 words. *Aud.:* Ac, Sa.

The membership rolls of the American Statistical Association include professionals from fields as disparate as biology, economics, government, and sociology. This diverse audience is reflected in the wide range of topics presented in *JASA* and the many indexes and abstracts that index the journal. Most articles are ten pages or less, and as many as 45 appear in each issue. Although brief, each article is substantive, as befits the "flagship publication" of the association. Articles are separated into two categories: "Applications and Case Studies" and "Theory and Methods." Given the wide-ranging and inclusive scope of this publication, it is recommended for all research collections.

5826. *American Statistical Association. Stats: the magazine for students of statistics.* [ISSN: 1053-8607] 1989. 3x/yr. USD 25 (Members, USD 15; Non-members, USD 20). Ed(s): Alan Rossman. American Statistical Association, 1429 Duke St, Alexandria, VA 22314-3415; asainfo@ amstat.org; http://www.amstat.org. *Aud.:* Ga, Ac.

Published for the over 3,000 student members of the American Statistical Association, *Stats* is for individual subscribers as well as for classroom use. Articles cover career information, student experiences, case studies, first-person articles, and humor. This is an inexpensive basic magazine recommended for all college and university collections.

5827. *American Statistician.* [ISSN: 0003-1305] 1947. q. USD 90 (Members, USD 25 print & online eds; Non-members, USD 120 print & online eds). Ed(s): James Albert. American Statistical Association, 1429 Duke St, Alexandria, VA 22314-3415; asainfo@amstat.org; http://www.amstat.org. Illus., adv. Vol. ends: Nov. Microform: MIM; PMC; PQC. Online: EBSCO Publishing, EBSCO Host; Gale; IngentaConnect; JSTOR (Web-based Journal Archive); Northern Light Technology, Inc.; OCLC Online Computer Library Center, Inc.; ProQuest K-12 Learning Solutions; ProQuest LLC (Ann Arbor). *Indexed:* ABIn, CCMJ, ChemAb, JEL, MSN, MathR, PAIS, SCI, SSCI. *Bk. rev.:* 4-5, 800-1,200 words. *Aud.:* Ac.

Intended for use by teachers and practicing statisticians, each issue contains approximately 15 articles in four departments. Most articles are four to six pages long, but a few are as short as three pages or as long as nine pages. More than half of the articles are published as "General." Most articles feature topics for classroom discussion or demonstration, or for useful applications for practitioners. The "Teacher's Corner" contains four to six articles for teachers of college mathematics or applied-statistics courses. Course content and pedagogy are equally stressed. The "Statistical Practice" department features articles of interest to a broad audience of practitioners, such as brief descriptions of new developments and innovative applications of known methodologies. "Statistical Computing and Graphics" includes articles on developments in statistical computing and reviews of software. Includes reviews of undergraduate textbooks and other teaching materials.

5828. *Annals of Applied Probability.* [ISSN: 1050-5164] 1991. bi-m. USD 275. Ed(s): Robert Adler. Institute of Mathematical Statistics, 9650 Rockville Pike, Ste L2407A, Bethesda, MD 20814-3998; staff@imstat.org; http://www.imstat.org. Illus., index, adv. Refereed. Circ: 2500 Paid. Vol. ends: Nov. Online: EBSCO Publishing, EBSCO Host; JSTOR (Web-based Journal Archive). *Indexed:* CCMJ, MSN, MathR, SCI. *Aud.:* Ac, Sa.

This journal publishes applications-oriented research articles. Theoretical articles are published by the Institute of Mathematical Statistics (IMS) in its *Annals of Probability.* The 8–12 articles in each issue vary from 15 to 40 pages each, and issues average 200–300 pages each. The IMS has nearly 100 corporate and institutional members, including many research universities. Membership and authorship are international. Most colleges and universities with programs in statistics should acquire this title and/or *Advances in Applied Probability.*

5829. *Annals of Probability.* [ISSN: 0091-1798] 1973. q. USD 296. Ed(s): Gregory Lawler. Institute of Mathematical Statistics, 9650 Rockville Pike, Ste L2407A, Bethesda, MD 20814-3998; staff@imstat.org; http://www.imstat.org. Illus., index, adv. Refereed. Circ: 2700 Paid. Vol. ends: Oct. Microform: PQC. Online: EBSCO Publishing, EBSCO Host; JSTOR (Web-based Journal Archive). *Indexed:* ABIn, CCMJ, MSN, MathR, SCI, SSCI. *Aud.:* Ac, Sa.

The *Annals of Probability* publishes contributions to the theory of probability, expository papers, and surveys of areas in vigorous development. Each issue contains 20–25 research articles averaging 15–40 pages. As a result, issues contain 300–500 pages. The Institute of Mathematical Statistics (IMS) has nearly 100 corporate and institutional members, including many research universities. Membership and authorship are international. Most colleges and universities should acquire this title. The IMS also publishes the *Annals of Applied Probability.*

5830. *Annals of Statistics.* Supersedes in part: *Annals of Mathematical Statistics.* [ISSN: 0090-5364] 1973. bi-m. USD 296. Ed(s): Bernard Silverman, Susan Murphy. Institute of Mathematical Statistics, 9650 Rockville Pike, Ste L2407A, Bethesda, MD 20814-3998; staff@imstat.org; http://www.imstat.org. Illus., index, adv. Refereed. Circ: 4300 Paid. Microform: PQC. Online: EBSCO Publishing, EBSCO Host; JSTOR (Web-based Journal Archive). *Indexed:* ABIn, CCMJ, MSN, MathR, SCI, SSCI. *Aud.:* Ac, Sa.

The editors seek to position this journal at the forefront of mathematical statistical research. They encourage submission of articles that advance the underlying concepts and theories of statistical science. In addition, articles concerning the role of statistics in interdisciplinary investigations of major contemporary social and scientific problems are sought, as are articles describing developments in computational methodology. Issues average 300–500 pages, and each contains 20–30 articles. Recommended for most college and university libraries.

5831. *Australian & New Zealand Journal of Statistics.* Formed by the merger of (1959-1998): *Australian Journal of Statistics;* (1966-1998): *New Zealand Statistician.* [ISSN: 1369-1473] 1998. q. GBP 159 print & online eds. Ed(s): Chris J Lloyd, Russell B Millar. Blackwell Publishing Asia, 550 Swanston St, Carlton South, VIC 3053, Australia; subs@blackwellpublishingasia.com; http://www.blackwellpublishing.com. Illus., index, adv. Sample. Refereed. Circ: 1369. Vol. ends: Dec. Microform: PQC. Online: Blackwell Synergy; EBSCO Publishing, EBSCO Host; Gale; IngentaConnect; OCLC Online Computer Library Center, Inc.; OhioLINK; SwetsWise Online Content. Reprint: PSC. *Indexed:* CCMJ, IBSS, MSN, MathR, PAIS, SCI, SSCI. *Bk. rev.:* 3-6, 300-1,000 words. *Aud.:* Ac, Sa.

Each issue of this official journal of the Statistical Society of Australia contains six to ten articles. The editors seek a balance between theoretical and applied articles, and especially encourage submission of articles that concern new applications of established methods, newly developed methods, and case studies of interesting applications. However, most articles published are theoretical articles in the fields of mathematical statistics, probability, and econometrics. Authorship is international.

5832. Bernoulli: a journal of mathematical statistics and probability.
[ISSN: 1350-7265] 1995. q. USD 425. Ed(s): William van Zwel, Sara de Geer. International Statistical Institute, Princes Beatrixlaan 428, PO Box 950, Voorburg, 2270 AZ, Netherlands; isi@cbs.nl; http://www.cbs.nl/isi/index.htm. Refereed. Circ: 1500 Paid. Online: EBSCO Publishing, EBSCO Host; Gale; IngentaConnect; OCLC Online Computer Library Center, Inc. Indexed: CCMJ, MSN, MathR, SCI. Aud.: Ac, Sa.

The official publication of the Bernoulli Society accepts original research contributions that provide background, derivation, and discussion of the results, as well as review articles and scholarly historical reviews for all aspects of statistics and probability. Each issue contains between 8 and 13 articles.

5833. Biometrics. Formerly (until 1947): *Biometrics Bulletin.* [ISSN: 0006-341X] 1945. q. GBP 231 print & online eds. Ed(s): Laurence Freedman, Mike Kenward. Blackwell Publishing Ltd., 9600 Garsington Rd, Oxford, OX4 2ZG, United Kingdom; customerservices@blackwellpublishing.com; http://www.blackwellpublishing.com. Illus., index, adv. Refereed. Circ: 8000. Vol. ends: Dec. Microform: BHP; PMC; PQC. Online: Blackwell Synergy; EBSCO Publishing, EBSCO Host; Gale; IngentaConnect; JSTOR (Web-based Journal Archive); OCLC Online Computer Library Center, Inc.; OhioLINK; ProQuest K-12 Learning Solutions; ProQuest LLC (Ann Arbor); SwetsWise Online Content. Reprint: PSC. Indexed: AS&TI, AbAn, ApMecR, B&AI, BioEngAb, BiolAb, CABA, CCMJ, ChemAb, DSA, ExcerpMed, FPA, FS&TA, ForAb, HortAb, IndVet, MSN, MathR, RRTA, S&F, SCI, SSCI, VB, WRCInf, ZooRec. Bk. rev.: 10-20, 600-1,000 words. Aud.: Ac, Sa.

The primary goals of this journal are to promote the use of statistical methods in the biological sciences and encourage sharing of ideas between experimental biologists and those concerned with analysis and statistical methodology. To make methodology papers accessible to experimental biologists, they are required to describe biological applications and use real data with the inclusion of intermediate steps in examples. Extensive mathematical derivations are placed in appendixes. Papers on biological subjects report conclusions reached by mathematical or statistical analysis, illustrate the use of less well-known analytical techniques, or apply standard techniques in a new field. A typical issue contains as many as 40 articles of 3–12 pages each.

5834. Biometrika. [ISSN: 0006-3444] 1901. q. GBP 97 print or online ed. Ed(s): D. M. Titterington. Oxford University Press, Great Clarendon St, Oxford, OX2 6DP, United Kingdom; jnl.orders@oup.co.uk; http://www.oxfordjournals.org. Illus., index. Refereed. Circ: 3700. Vol. ends: Dec. Microform: PMC; PQC. Online: EBSCO Publishing, EBSCO Host; Gale; HighWire Press; IngentaConnect; JSTOR (Web-based Journal Archive); OCLC Online Computer Library Center, Inc.; Ovid Technologies, Inc.; Oxford Journals; ProQuest LLC (Ann Arbor); SwetsWise Online Content. Reprint: PSC. Indexed: ABIn, AS&TI, B&AI, BiolAb, CCMJ, ChemAb, DSA, ExcerpMed, HortAb, IndVet, MSN, MathR, SCI, SSCI, VB. Aud.: Ac, Sa.

Widely indexed and well established, *Biometrika* accepts articles covering a wide range of topics. The emphasis is on original theoretical contributions with potential or direct value in applications. Each issue includes 15–20 articles of 10–20 pages each and two or three short miscellaneous notes. A majority of the articles are by British and American authors.

5835. Canadian Journal of Statistics. [ISSN: 0319-5724] 1973. q. CND 200 domestic; USD 160 domestic; CND 225 United States. Ed(s): George P H Styan, Douglas P Wiens. Statistical Society of Canada, 1485 Laperriere St, Ottawa, ON K1Z 7S8, Canada; admin@ssc.ca; http://www.ssc.ca. Illus., index, adv. Refereed. Circ: 1350 Paid. Vol. ends: Dec. Indexed: ABIn, CCMJ, IBSS, MSN, MathR, PAIS, SCI. Aud.: Ac, Sa.

This Canadian equivalent of the American Statistical Association journal is international in scope, but more than half of the articles it publishes are written by Canadians. Although articles may be written in either English or French, most are in English. Abstracts are printed in both English and French. The journal publishes original work in the theory and applications of statistics, including survey papers and articles of theoretical, applied, or pedagogical interest. Most issues contain 10 or 11 articles of 10–12 pages each.

5836. Chance (New York, 1988): a magazine of the American Statistical Association. [ISSN: 0933-2480] 1988. q. EUR 95. Ed(s): Dalene Stangl. Springer New York LLC, 233 Spring St, New York, NY 10013-1578; journals@springer-ny.com; http://www.springer.com/. Illus., index, adv. Refereed. Vol. ends: No. 4. Microform: PQC. Reprint: PSC. Indexed: CCMJ, MSN, MathR, PollutAb. Aud.: Hs, Ga.

Articles are aimed at informed lay readers interested in data analysis and those who use statistical methods in their work. The style is popular rather than scholarly, and additional readings are suggested for those seeking a better understanding of the topic. Each issue contains five to seven articles of five to seven pages each. Subject matter ranges from statistical methods and technical issues to public-policy concerns, sports, and other general-interest topics. One of the few statistical magazines of interest to the general adult reader.

5837. Communications in Statistics: Simulation and Computation.
Supersedes in part (with vol.5, 1976): *Communications in Statistics.* [ISSN: 0361-0918] 1972. bi-m. GBP 2137 print & online eds. Ed(s): N Balakrishnan. Taylor & Francis Inc., 325 Chestnut St, Ste 800, Philadelphia, PA 19016; orders@taylorandfrancis.com; http://www.taylorandfrancis.com. Illus., index, adv. Refereed. Circ: 725. Vol. ends: Nov. Reprint: PSC. Indexed: CCMJ, CompLI, EngInd, MSN, MathR, SCI, SSCI. Aud.: Ac, Sa.

The three *Communications in Statistics* journals are designed as vehicles for the rapid dissemination of new ideas in their respective areas of statistics. This journal focuses on the interaction of statistics and computer science. Articles may present tables of and algorithms for statistical functions and numerical solutions to problems by the use of simulation or special functions. Each issue contains 12–14 articles. Suitable for collections that emphasize computational statistics.

5838. Communications in Statistics: Theory and Methods. Superseded in part (with vol.5, 1976): *Communications in Statistics.* [ISSN: 0361-0926] 1970. 16x/yr. GBP 3690 print & online eds. Ed(s): N Balakrishnan. Taylor & Francis Inc., 325 Chestnut St, Ste 800, Philadelphia, PA 19016; orders@taylorandfrancis.com; http://www.taylorandfrancis.com. Illus., index, adv. Refereed. Circ: 800. Vol. ends: Dec. Reprint: PSC. Indexed: CCMJ, CompLI, EngInd, MSN, MathR, SCI. Aud.: Ac, Sa.

Of the three *Communications in Statistics* journals, *Theory and Methods* is broadest in scope. This journal has a strong mathematical orientation to the application of statistical methods to practical problems. It publishes survey articles and discussions of practical statistical problems, whether or not the authors have solutions to present. Articles focus on new applications of statistical methods to problems in government and industry. Each monthly issue contains 15–18 articles varying in length from 8 to 30 pages each. Based on their content and cost, the three *Communications in Statistics* journals are suitable for college and university libraries with extensive statistics collections.

5839. Computational Statistics. Formerly (until 1992): *C S Q - Computational Statistics Quarterly.* [ISSN: 0943-4062] 1982. q. EUR 478 print & online eds. Ed(s): W Haerdle, A Unwin. Physica-Verlag GmbH und Co., Postfach 105280, Heidelberg, 69042, Germany; physica@springer.de. Illus. Refereed. Vol. ends: No. 4. Microform: PQC. Reprint: PSC. Indexed: CCMJ, MSN, MathR, SCI. Bk. rev.: 1, 700-800 words. Aud.: Ac, Sa.

Computational Statistics publishes applications and methodological research that focuses on the contribution to, and influence of, computing and statistics upon each other. The intended audience includes computer scientists, mathematicians, and statisticians. Topics covered include biometrics, econometrics, data analysis, graphics, simulation, algorithms, knowledge-based systems, and Bayesian computing. Issues contain six to eight articles of approximately 20 pages each, and usually a software and/or book review. Although published in Germany, the text is in English. Recommended for libraries that support statistics programs.

5840. Computational Statistics & Data Analysis. Incorporates (1975-1991): *Statistical Software Newsletter.* [ISSN: 0167-9473] 1983. 12x/yr. EUR 2190. Ed(s): S P Azen. Elsevier BV, North-Holland, Sara Burgerhartstraat 25, Amsterdam, 1055 KV, Netherlands; nlinfo-f@elsevier.nl. Illus., index, adv. Sample. Refereed. Circ: 1000. Vol. ends: No. 35 - No. 37. Microform: PQC. Online: EBSCO Publishing, EBSCO Host; Gale; IngentaConnect; OhioLINK; ScienceDirect; SwetsWise Online Content. *Indexed:* BioEngAb, CCMJ, CJA, CompR, EngInd, MSN, MathR, SCI, SSCI. *Bk. rev.:* 2-3, 120-300 words. *Aud.:* Ac, Sa.

This official journal of the International Association of Statistical Computing is dedicated to the dissemination of methodological research and applications. Each issue contains approximately eight refereed articles in three sections: "Computational Statistics," "Statistical Methodology for Data Analysis," and "Special Applications." The "Statistical Software Newsletter" forms a fourth section. The intended audience includes statisticians, computer center professionals, and scientific and social researchers at a postgraduate level. Due to its expense, it is only suitable for comprehensive or specialized collections.

Decision Sciences. See Management, Administration, and Human Resources/Operations Research and Management Science section.

Econometrica. See Economics section.

5841. *Electronic Communications in Probability.* [ISSN: 1083-589X] 1996. a. Free. Ed(s): W S Kendall. Institute of Mathematical Statistics, 9650 Rockville Pike, Ste L2407A, Bethesda, MD 20814-3998; ejpecp@math.washington.edu; http://math.washington.edu/~ejpecp/. *Indexed:* CCMJ, MSN, MathR, SCI. *Aud.:* Ac, Sa.

Electronic Communications in Probability accepts short submissions on all aspects of probability. Longer submissions are posted on the companion *Electronic Journal of Probability.* Subscriptions are not necessary; subscribers receive tables of contents only by e-mail. All text is available only at the web site. A new volume is begun each January, and entries are posted as they are accepted throughout the year. Volumes contain from 5 to 14 entries. Users choose the viewing format for each entry, usually from among pdf, PostScript, and DVI formats. URL: www.math.washington.edu/~ejpecp/ECP/index.php.

5842. *Electronic Journal of Probability.* 1996. a. Free. Ed(s): Richard Bass. Institute of Mathematical Statistics, 9650 Rockville Pike, Ste L2407A, Bethesda, MD 20814-3998; ejpecp@math.washington.edu; http://www.math.washington.edu/~ejpecp/. Illus., index. Refereed. Vol. ends: Dec. *Indexed:* CCMJ, MSN. *Aud.:* Ac, Sa.

The *Electronic Journal of Probability* accepts submissions on all aspects of probability. Longer submissions are posted on the *Journal,* and brief entries are posted on the companion publication *Electronic Communications in Probability.* Subscriptions are not necessary; subscribers receive tables of contents only by e-mail. All text is available only at the web site. A new volume is begun each January, and papers are posted as they are accepted throughout the year. Volumes of the *Journal* contain from 8 to 19 papers. Users choose the viewing format for each article, usually from among pdf, PostScript, and DVI formats.

5843. *Institute of Statistical Mathematics. Annals.* [ISSN: 0020-3157] 1949. q. EUR 1030 print & online eds. Ed(s): Y Watanabe. Springer, Tiergartenstr 17, Heidelberg, 69121, Germany. Adv. Refereed. Circ: 1500. Microform: PQC. Online: EBSCO Publishing, EBSCO Host; Gale; IngentaConnect; OCLC Online Computer Library Center, Inc.; OhioLINK; ProQuest LLC (Ann Arbor); Springer LINK; SwetsWise Online Content. *Indexed:* ABIn, BAS, CCMJ, EngInd, IBSS, MSN, MathR, SCI. *Aud.:* Ac, Sa.

This Japanese journal provides an international forum for the communication of developments in theoretical and applied statistics. It especially welcomes papers that will lead to significant improvements in the practice of statistics. Each issue contains 10–15 lengthy articles. Recommended for comprehensive statistics collections.

5844. *International Statistical Review.* Formerly (until 1972): *International Statistical Institute Review.* [ISSN: 0306-7734] 1933. q. USD 371 print & online eds. Ed(s): Birol Yesilada, David Kinsella. Blackwell Publishing Ltd., 9600 Garsington Rd, Oxford, OX4 2ZG, United Kingdom; customerservices@blackwellpublishing.com; http://www.blackwellpublishing.com. Illus., index. Refereed. Circ: 2000. Reprint: PSC. *Indexed:* IndVet, MathR, SCI, SSCI, VB. *Aud.:* Ac, Sa.

This journal accepts expository and review articles of interest to a wide readership. Topics may include statistical theory, methodology, applications, education, computing, graphics, data analysis, the history of statistics, official statistics, demography, and survey statistics. The editors seek to create a forum for discussion of issues that involve the statistics profession as a whole.

5845. *InterStat.* 1995. irreg. Free. InterStat, rgkrut@hdvt.edu; http://interstat.stat.vt.edu/interstat. Refereed. *Aud.:* Ac, Sa.

InterStat accepts submissions on all aspects of statistics, including research articles, discussions of new methodologies and techniques, teaching methods, and philosophical articles. Authors submit papers to the editor most closely associated with the content of the article from a board of 55, which has a wide range of interests and expertise. There is no uniform style imposed: the editor is the sole judge of readability and hence acceptability for each paper. Individual authors retain copyright for their works. Articles are posted in pdf and PostScript formats as they are accepted. Viewers may locate articles by month and year or by means of a keyword, title, or author search. From 4 to 16 articles are published each year.

Journal of Applied Econometrics. See Economics section.

5846. *Journal of Applied Probability.* [ISSN: 0021-9002] 1964. q. GBP 150 (Individuals, GBP 50). Ed(s): C C Heyde. Applied Probability Trust, School of Mathematics and Statistics, The University of Sheffield, Sheffield, S3 7RH, United Kingdom; l.nash@sheffield.ac.uk; http://www.appliedprobability.org. Illus., index, adv. Refereed. Circ: 1500. Vol. ends: Dec. *Indexed:* ABIn, CCMJ, MSN, MathR, RiskAb, SCI, SSCI. *Aud.:* Ac, Sa.

This international journal is published by the Applied Probability Trust in association with the London Mathematical Society. It publishes research papers of 20 pages or less and short notes on applications of probability theory to the biological, physical, social, and technological sciences. It shares its editorial board with its companion publication, *Advances in Applied Probability.* Based on available space, the editors may publish accepted articles in either journal. Most articles are in English, but articles in French are also published. Recommended for colleges and universities with programs in statistics.

5847. *Journal of Applied Statistics.* Formerly (until 1984): *Bulletin in Applied Statistics.* [ISSN: 0266-4763] 1975. 10x/yr. GBP 1480 print & online eds. Ed(s): Gopal K Kanji. Routledge, 4 Park Sq, Milton Park, Abingdon, OX14 4RN, United Kingdom; info@routledge.co.uk; http://www.routledge.co.uk. Adv. Refereed. Online: EBSCO Publishing, EBSCO Host; Gale; IngentaConnect; Northern Light Technology, Inc.; OCLC Online Computer Library Center, Inc.; ProQuest LLC (Ann Arbor); SwetsWise Online Content. Reprint: PSC. *Indexed:* CCMJ, JEL, MSN, MathR, SCI, ZooRec. *Bk. rev.:* Occasional. *Aud.:* Ac, Sa.

Accepts articles on the design and application of statistical methods to research problems in all disciplines. Each issue contains an average of 10–12 articles. The journal publishes occasional combined and/or thematic issues. Brief responses or discussion comments accompany some articles. Some issues include book reviews.

Journal of Business and Economic Statistics. See Business section.

5848. *Journal of Computational and Graphical Statistics.* [ISSN: 1061-8600] 1992. q. USD 210 print & online eds. American Statistical Association, 1429 Duke St, Alexandria, VA 22314-3415; asainfo@amstat.org; http://www.amstat.org. Refereed. *Indexed:* ABIn, CCMJ, CompLI, MSN, MathR, SCI. *Aud.:* Ac, Sa.

This is a joint publication of the American Statistical Association, the Institute of Mathematical Statistics, and the Interface Foundation of North America. This journal publishes original contributions in the fields of computational statistics and data visualization, including theory, applications, review articles, and software reviews and comparisons. Authors may submit additional material for posting on the web site to extend or complement an article. Each issue contains about 12 articles, or a discussion article with several responses and three or more ordinary articles.

Journal of Econometrics. See Economics section.

Journal of Educational and Behavioral Statistics. See Education/ Educational Psychology and Measurement, Special Education, Counseling section.

5849. *Journal of Modern Applied Statistical Methods.* [ISSN: 1538-9472] 2002. s-a. Free. Ed(s): Shlomo S Sawilowsky. Wayne State University, College of Education, 5425 Gullen Mall, Detroit, MI 48202; http://www.coe.wayne.edu. *Aud.:* Ac, Sa.

Accepts articles in three areas: new statistical tests or procedures, or the comparison of tests and procedures; development of nonparametric, robust, exact, and approximate randomization methods; and applications of computer programming to carry out new statistical methods. Priority is given to articles based on Monte Carlo and other computer-intensive methods that are designed to evaluate new or existing techniques or practices and applications to everyday data analysis problems. Each issue contains several invited articles, as many as 17 regular articles, and several "Early Scholars" articles. A print version of this open-access journal is available by subscription for a fee.

5850. *Journal of Statistical Software.* 1996. irreg. Ed(s): Jan de Leeuw. University of California at Los Angeles, Department of Statistics, 405 Hilgard Ave, Box 951361, Los Angeles, CA 90095-1361; deleeuw@ stat.ucla.edu; http://www.stat.ucla.edu/journals/jss/. Refereed. *Aud.:* Ac, Sa.

The *Journal of Statistical Software* publishes a wide range of submissions concerning software in the field of statistics, including descriptions of software, manuals and users' guides, software code, data sets, and reviews or comparisons of software. The submissions are not limited in length and may include brief articles or manuals of 1,000 pages or more. Each submission constitutes an issue within the year's volume; the number of issues per year is not restricted and varies from four to nine. Authors retain the copyright, but downloading and printing by users is expected. A note of warning: Although most issues are divided into several files, there is no indication of the size of each file and some files are very large. URL: www.jstatsoft.org.

5851. *Journal of Statistics Education.* [ISSN: 1069-1898] 1993. 3x/yr. Free. Ed(s): Thomas H Short. American Statistical Association, 1429 Duke St, Alexandria, VA 22314-3415; http://www.amstat.org/ publications/jse/. Refereed. *Aud.:* Ems, Hs, Ac.

The *Journal of Statistics Education* (*JSE*) is a refereed electronic journal on the teaching of statistics at all levels, from elementary to postgraduate and workplace education. Typical issues contain approximately five articles, a "Teaching Bits" section, and perhaps a "Datasets and Stories" section. Content for articles may include teaching techniques, comparisons of methods, or statistical literacy; there are also literature reviews and sample projects or assignments. Links to pdf versions of papers reformatted for printing are provided. The associated JSE Information Service includes information for teachers and archives of EDSTAT-L, a statistics education discussion list.

Mathematical Finance. See Finance/Scholarly section.

5852. *Metrika: international journal for theoretical and applied statistics.* Formed by the merger of (1948-1958): *Universitaet Wien. Institut fuer Statistik. Statistische Vierteljahresschrift;* (1949-1958): *Mitteilungsblatt fuer Mathematische Statistik und ihre Anwendungsgebiete;* Which was formerly (until 1955): *Mitteilungsblatt fuer Mathematische Statistik.* [ISSN: 0026-1335] 1958. bi-m. EUR 578 print & online eds. Ed(s): Friedrich Pukelsheim, Ursula Gather. Physica-Verlag GmbH und Co., Postfach 105280, Heidelberg, 69042, Germany; physica@springer.de. Illus., index, adv. Refereed. Circ: 450 Paid and controlled. Vol. ends: No. 3. Microform: PQC. Online: EBSCO Publishing, EBSCO Host; OhioLINK; Springer LINK; SwetsWise Online Content. Reprint: PSC. *Indexed:* CCMJ, JEL, MSN, MathR, SCI. *Bk. rev.:* 2-4, 1,000-1,400 words. *Aud.:* Ac, Sa.

Metrika is an international research journal for theoretical and applied statistics. It publishes papers in mathematical statistics and statistical methods, especially those that present new developments in theoretical statistics. Importance is

attached to applicability of the proposed statistical methods and results. Although published in Germany, the text is in English. Authorship is international, but at least half of the authors are German. Issues average six articles of 6–20 pages each, with a few articles as long as 30 pages.

Oxford Bulletin of Economics and Statistics. See Economics section.

5853. *Probability Surveys.* [ISSN: 1549-5787] 2004. irreg. Free. Probability Surveys, c/o David Aldous, University of California, Berkeley, Berkeley, CA 94720; http://www.i-journals.org/ps/index.php. Refereed. *Indexed:* CCMJ, MSN, MathR. *Aud.:* Ac, Sa.

This open-access electronic journal publishes articles on theoretical and applied probability as they are accepted, completing one volume each year. Articles may be as long as 125 pages, and are typically survey or review articles. Readers may view the full text of each article as a pdf file or as an abstract with references. Those who register will receive notification of new postings. URL: www.i-journals.org/ps/index.php.

5854. *Probability Theory and Related Fields.* Supersedes: *Zeitschrift fuer Wahrscheinlichkeitstheorie und Verwandte Gebiete.* [ISSN: 0178-8051] 1962. m. EUR 1320 print & online eds. Ed(s): Geoffrey R Grimmett. Springer, Tiergartenstr 17, Heidelberg, 69121, Germany. Illus., adv. Sample. Refereed. Microform: PQC. Online: EBSCO Publishing, EBSCO Host; OhioLINK; ProQuest LLC (Ann Arbor); Springer LINK; SwetsWise Online Content. Reprint: PSC. *Indexed:* ABIn, CCMJ, MSN, MathR, SCI. *Aud.:* Ac, Sa.

Well regarded, ranked highly by researchers in the field, and highly indexed, but very expensive, this research journal is for specialized collections only. Issues usually contain four to six articles of 20–40 or more pages. Subjects covered include ergodic theory, filtering theory, mathematical biology, mathematical statistics, optimization and control, statistical mechanics, stochastic algorithms, stochastic geometry, and theoretical computer science.

Psychometrika. See Psychology section.

The Review of Economics and Statistics. See Economics section.

5855. *Royal Statistical Society. Journal. Series A: Statistics in Society.* Incorporates in part (1950-2004): *Royal Statistical Society. Journal. Series D: The Statistician;* Which was formerly (until 1961): *Incorporated Statistician;* Former titles (until 1988): *Royal Statistical Society. Journal. Series A: General;* (until 1948): *Royal Statistical Society. Journal;* (until 1887): *Statistical Society. Journal.* [ISSN: 0964-1998] 1838. q. GBP 258 print & online eds. Ed(s): P Lynn, G Verbeke. Blackwell Publishing Ltd., 9600 Garsington Rd, Oxford, OX4 2ZG, United Kingdom; customerservices@blackwellpublishing.com; http://www.blackwellpublishing.com. Illus., adv. Sample. Refereed. Circ: 5700. Microform: BHP. Online: Blackwell Synergy; EBSCO Publishing, EBSCO Host; Gale; IngentaConnect; JSTOR (Web-based Journal Archive); OCLC Online Computer Library Center, Inc.; OhioLINK; SwetsWise Online Content. Reprint: PSC. *Indexed:* ApEcolAb, ApMecR, CCMJ, CJA, IBSS, IPSA, IndVet, JEL, MSN, MathR, PAIS, PSA, PhilInd, RRTA, SCI, SSCI, SociolAb, WAE&RSA. *Aud.:* Ac, Sa.

This journal focuses on applications of statistics to public policy and social issues, including health, education, religious, legal, and demographic topics. Papers with mathematical expositions must also include a narrative explanation of the argument to make them accessible to professionals in many disciplines. The journal seeks thorough analyses of applications with substantial statistical content. It also publishes methodological papers that contain illustrative applications involving appropriate data. Beginning with 1999, data sets associated with papers can be obtained at www.blackwellpublishers.co.uk/rss. The society also publishes two other journals: *Royal Statistical Society. Journal. Series B: Statistical Methodology* and *Royal Statistical Society. Journal. Series C: Applied Statistics.*

5856. Royal Statistical Society. Journal. Series B: Statistical Methodology. Former titles (until 1997): *Royal Statistical Society. Journal. Series B: Methodological;* (until 1947): *Journal of the Royal Statistical Society. Supplement.* [ISSN: 1369-7412] 1934. q. GBP 193 print & online eds. Ed(s): R Henderson, A T A Wood. Blackwell Publishing Ltd., 9600 Garsington Rd, Oxford, OX4 2ZG, United Kingdom; customerservices@ blackwellpublishing.com; http://www.blackwellpublishing.com. Illus., index, adv. Sample. Refereed. Circ: 4500. Vol. ends: No. 4. Reprint: PSC. *Indexed:* ABIn, ApEcolAb, ApMecR, CCMJ, HortAb, IBSS, IPSA, MSN, MathR, PhilInd, SCI, SSCI. *Aud.:* Ac, Sa.

As the methodological and theoretical publication of the Royal Statistical Society, this journal publishes articles that contribute to the understanding of statistics. Articles focus on the logical and philosophical basis of statistical theory, new methods of collecting or analyzing data, comparisons or new applications of existing methods, the development and analysis of stochastic models, and discussion of new methodologies in statistical computation and simulation. Beginning with 1998, data sets associated with papers can be obtained online at www.blackwellpublishers.co.uk/rss. The society also publishes two other journals: *Royal Statistical Society. Journal. Series A: Statistics in Society* and *Royal Statistical Society. Journal. Series C: Applied Statistics.*

5857. Royal Statistical Society. Journal. Series C: Applied Statistics. Incorporates in part (1950-2004): *Royal Statistical Society. Journal. Series D. The Statistician;* Which was formerly (until 1961): *Incorporated Statistician.* [ISSN: 0035-9254] 1952. 5x/yr. GBP 193 print & online eds. Ed(s): S G Gilmour, C A Glasbey. Blackwell Publishing Ltd., 9600 Garsington Rd, Oxford, OX4 2ZG, United Kingdom; customerservices@blackwellpublishing.com; http://www.blackwellpublishing.com. Illus., index, adv. Sample. Refereed. Circ: 5400. Vol. ends: No. 4. Reprint: PSC. *Indexed:* ABIn, ApEcolAb, BrArAb, CCMJ, IBSS, IPSA, MSN, MathR, RiskAb, SCI, SSCI. *Aud.:* Ac, Sa.

Aimed at practicing statisticians, this publication of the Royal Statistical Society presents articles that stress the practical application of the methods discussed. Topics covered include design issues arising from practical problems, applications of statistical computing, and methodological developments arising from the solution of practical problems. The editors especially encourage submission of articles that describe interdisciplinary work. Detailed algebraic development is avoided. Beginning with 1998, data sets associated with papers can be obtained online at www.blackwellpublishers.co.uk/rss. The journal is suitable for most college and university libraries. The society also publishes two other journals: *Royal Statistical Society. Journal. Series A: Statistics in Society* and *Royal Statistical Society. Journal. Series B: Statistical Methodology.*

5858. Scandinavian Journal of Statistics: theory and applications. [ISSN: 0303-6898] 1974. q. GBP 162 print & online eds. Ed(s): Thomas Scheike. Blackwell Publishing Ltd., 9600 Garsington Rd, Oxford, OX4 2ZG, United Kingdom; customerservices@blackwellpublishing.com; http://www.blackwellpublishing.com. Illus., index, adv. Sample. Refereed. Circ: 700. Vol. ends: Dec. Online: Blackwell Synergy; EBSCO Publishing, EBSCO Host; Gale; IngentaConnect; OCLC Online Computer Library Center, Inc.; OhioLINK; SwetsWise Online Content. Reprint: PSC. *Indexed:* ABIn, CCMJ, MSN, MathR, SCI. *Aud.:* Ac, Sa.

Published jointly by the Danish Society for Theoretical Statistics, the Finnish Statistical Society, the Norwegian Statistical Society, and the Swedish Statistical Association, this is an international journal with worldwide authorship. The journal publishes research in both theoretical and applied statistics, as well as statistically motivated papers that concern relevant aspects of other fields. Articles range from 8 to 30 pages in length, with mathematical derivations and proofs presented as appendixes.

5859. Statistica Sinica. [ISSN: 1017-0405] 1991. q. USD 120 (Individuals, USD 50). Ed(s): S.Y. Huang, C Chen. Academia Sinica, Institute of Statistical Science, 128, Sec 2 Yen-chiu-Yuan Rd, Taipei, 115, Taiwan, Republic of China; http://www.stat.sinica.edu.tw/. Refereed. *Indexed:* CCMJ, MSN, MathR, SCI. *Aud.:* Ac, Sa.

Cosponsored by the International Chinese Statistical Association and the Institute of Statistical Science, Academia Sinica of Taiwan, this journal publishes articles on all aspects of statistics and probability, including theory, methods, and applications. Some issues have a theme; others are general in coverage. Authorship is international. Suitable for most college and university libraries.

5860. Statistical Science: a review journal. [ISSN: 0883-4237] 1986. q. USD 164. Ed(s): Edward I George. Institute of Mathematical Statistics, 9650 Rockville Pike, Ste L2407A, Bethesda, MD 20814-3998; staff@imstat.org; http://www.imstat.org. Illus., index, adv. Refereed. Vol. ends: Nov. Microform: PQC. Online: EBSCO Publishing, EBSCO Host; JSTOR (Web-based Journal Archive). *Indexed:* CCMJ, CJA, MSN, MathR, SCI, SSCI. *Aud.:* Ac, Sa.

Statistical Science is a companion publication to the Institute of Mathematical Statistics' *Annals of Applied Probability, Annals of Probability,* and *Annals of Statistics.* Each issue includes an extensive interview with a distinguished statistician and three or four review or survey articles, some with comments. The goal of the journal is to present a broad range of contemporary statistical thought at a technical level accessible to practitioners, teachers, researchers, and students of statistics and probability.

5861. Statistics Education Research Journal. [ISSN: 1570-1824] 2002. s-a. Free. Ed(s): Iddo Gal, Flavia Jolliffe. International Association for Statistical Education, http://www.stat.auckland.ac.nz/. Sample. Refereed. *Indexed:* PsycInfo. *Aud.:* Ac.

Sponsored jointly by the International Association for Statistical Education and the International Statistical Institute, *SERJ* accepts research and review articles that will enhance the teaching and learning of statistics or probability at all educational levels. Articles may focus on curricular, attitudinal, cognitive, or other aspects of the study of statistics or on applications. Each issue is presented as a single pdf file and contains three to six articles.

5862. Stochastic Models. Formerly (until 2000): *Communications in Statistics. Stochastic Models.* [ISSN: 1532-6349] 1985. q. GBP 1119 print & online eds. Ed(s): Peter Taylor. Taylor & Francis Inc., 325 Chestnut St, Ste 800, Philadelphia, PA 19016; orders@taylorandfrancis.com; http://www.taylorandfrancis.com. Illus., index, adv. Refereed. Circ: 600. Vol. ends: Nov. Microform: RPI. Online: EBSCO Publishing, EBSCO Host; IngentaConnect; OCLC Online Computer Library Center, Inc.; SwetsWise Online Content. Reprint: PSC. *Indexed:* CCMJ, EngInd, MSN, MathR, SCI. *Aud.:* Ac, Sa.

This journal offers an interdisciplinary approach to the application of probability theory, with articles presenting methodologies ranging from the analytic and algorithmic to the experimental. Articles describe the practical applications of stochastic models to phenomena in the natural sciences, technology, and operations research. Each issue contains 8–10 articles of 10–30 pages each. As one of three *Communications in Statistics* journals, *Stochastic Models* is also an affiliated publication of the Institute for Operations Research and the Management Sciences. Suitable for specialized and comprehensive collections.

Studies in Nonlinear Dynamics and Econometrics. See Economics section.

5863. Teaching Statistics: an international journal for teachers. [ISSN: 0141-982X] 1979. 3x/yr. GBP 47 print & online eds. Ed(s): Gerald W Goodall. Blackwell Publishing Ltd., 9600 Garsington Rd, Oxford, OX4 2ZG, United Kingdom; customerservices@blackwellpublishing.com; http://www.blackwellpublishing.com. Illus., index, adv. Refereed. Circ: 1050 Paid. Vol. ends: Sep. Online: Blackwell Synergy; EBSCO Publishing, EBSCO Host; Gale; IngentaConnect; OCLC Online Computer Library Center, Inc.; OhioLINK; SwetsWise Online Content. Reprint: PSC. *Indexed:* BrEdI, ERIC. *Bk. rev.:* 1-2, 500-600 words. *Aud.:* Ac.

Teaching Statistics intends to inform, entertain, and encourage teachers of statistics and those who employ statistics in their teaching of other disciplines at all levels, from elementary grades through college. Articles stress classroom teaching and the proper use of statistics and statistical concepts in teaching. Each issue contains nine or ten articles in some or all of the following categories: "Classroom Notes," "Computing Corner," "Curriculum Matters," "Data Bank," "Practical Activities," "Project Parade," "Net Benefits," "Historical Perspective," "Research Report," "Standard Errors," "Apparatus Reviews," "Book Reviews," and "News & Notes." Although most articles are by British or Commonwealth authors, the topics are of interest to teachers elsewhere.

5864. Technometrics: a journal of statistics for the physical, chemical and engineering sciences. [ISSN: 0040-1706] 1959. q. USD 110 print & online eds (Members, USD 30 print & online eds; Non-members, USD 50 print & online eds). Ed(s): Dr. Randy Sitter. American Statistical Association, 1429 Duke St, Alexandria, VA 22314-3415; asainfo@amstat.org; http://www.amstat.org. Illus., index, adv. Refereed. Circ: 5200. Vol. ends: Nov. Microform: PQC. Online: EBSCO Publishing, EBSCO Host; Gale; IngentaConnect; JSTOR (Web-based Journal Archive); Northern Light Technology, Inc.; ProQuest LLC (Ann Arbor). Indexed: ABIn, AS&TI, C&ISA, CCMJ, EngInd, MSN, MathR, RILM, SCI, SSCI. Bk. rev.: 30-40, 300-1,600 words. Aud.: Ac, Sa.

The purpose of this joint publication of the American Society for Quality Control and the American Statistical Association is to foster the use and development of statistical methods in the sciences. Articles accepted for publication describe new statistical techniques or new applications of established techniques; provide detailed explanations of specific statistical methods; or discuss the problems of applying statistical methods to problems in the sciences. Each issue contains six or seven articles and over 30 book reviews. Occasionally, a paper presented at a conference is published, along with the discussion and author's reply from that meeting.

5865. Theory of Probability and Its Applications. [ISSN: 0040-585X] 1956. q. USD 618 (Individual members, USD 100). Ed(s): Yu V Proklorov, Natasha Brunswick. Society for Industrial and Applied Mathematics, 3600 University City Science Center, Philadelphia, PA 19104-2688; siam@siam.org; http://www.epubs.siam.org. Illus., adv. Refereed. Circ: 1172. Vol. ends: Dec. Indexed: ApMecR, CompR, MathR, SCI. Aud.: Ac, Sa.

Theory of Probability and Its Applications is a translation of the Russian journal Teoriya Veroyatnostei i ee Primeneniya, edited by Yu. V. Prokhorov. Each English-language issue is published approximately one year after the original Russian-language issue. The journal accepts papers on all aspects of theory and applications of probability, statistics, and stochastic processes. Issues typically contain eight articles and eight to ten shorter "Communications." Articles are highly mathematical, with brief introductions and very little discussion. Because these contributions are not available elsewhere in translation, this is a valuable source. Recommended for highly specialized and research collections.

■ TEENAGERS

See also Children; Comic Books; Humor; Music; and Sports sections.

Amy Sprung, Human Resource Services, Harvard College Library, Widener Library, Room G-20, Cambridge, MA 02138; amysprung@gmail.com

Introduction

It has been another topsy-turvy year for teen magazines, with some old favorites ceasing publication and some promising new releases up and running. Included in the list of magazines that folded is Teen People, which kept up a web site with new content after the print version ended, but now redirects to People. The print version of this entertainment magazine for adults is a viable option for teen collections in the wake of Teen People. Elle Girl, a relatively new publication, went the way of Teen People and YM, ceasing publication of a print edition. But like YM, Elle Girl's web site (www.ellegirl.com) is still regularly maintained with new content, although perhaps not with the same feminist bent. DASH (an acronym for drugs, alcohol, sex, and health) lived to see only one print issue, but the site www.dashmag.com is still updated on occasion and is a great source of

honest information and realistic ideas for older teens. Positive Teens, a magazine that accepted submissions that show the diversity of teenagers and the positive impact they're making on the world, is also stopping publication at the end of the year (2007).

This year the importance of updating links was reinforced for libraries with a web presence that includes links to magazines for teens. When the teenage editor of BlackGirl magazine accidentally let the site license lapse, it was bought up by someone who posted some unsavory images. The old site is now just innocuous ad space, and the address of the new site is www.blackgirlmagazineonline.com. It appears that the print version of the magazine is no longer being published, and the content on this site is old, so please use this as an opportunity to update your links, as some people are still linking to the old site.

In the realm of new magazines, Muslim Girl published its first few issues this year. It attempts to show the diversity within the Muslim teen population in the United States and is doing a fantastic job so far. Teen Voices, an alternative magazine for teen girls that positions itself apart from fashion-oriented teen mags, is celebrating its 15th year of publication, but is new to Magazines for Libraries this year.

The reviews that follow definitely do not include all teen magazines currently published, but they are a survey of magazines targeted toward special interests and special populations of teenagers as well as popular mainstream magazines. Many of the magazines with high appeal for teens appear as cross-references to other sections. Perhaps the most prominent of these are the manga titles Shojo Beat and Shonen Jump, which should not be overlooked, as they're incredibly popular and would be worthwhile additions to many YA collections.

Basic Periodicals

Hs: Seventeen, Teen Voices. Ga: Guideposts Sweet 16, J-14, Justine, Right On!, Shojo Beat, Shonen Jump.

Basic Abstracts and Indexes

Magazine Index Plus/ASAP, Readers' Guide to Periodical Literature.

5866. B M X Plus. [ISSN: 0195-0320] 1978. m. USD 19.99; USD 6.95 newsstand/cover. Ed(s): Adam Booth. Hi-Torque Publications, Inc., 25233 Anza Dr, Valencia, CA 91355; http://www.hi-torque.com. Illus., adv. Sample. Indexed: MASUSE. Aud.: Ems, Hs.

This niche publication covers everything related to the world of BMX (Bicycle Moto-cross), and has a devout readership as evidenced by the pages of letters from readers in each issue. In addition to lots of full-page color photos of crazy bike stunt action and tips on how to execute these stunts, there are reviews of bikes and products, interviews with riders, and tips on bike maintenance. Recommended for public libraries serving teens with an interest in BMX.

Boys' Life: the magazine for all boys. See Children section.

5867. Brio. [ISSN: 1048-2873] 1990. m. USD 22. Ed(s): Susie Shellenberger. Focus on the Family, 8605 Explorer Dr, Colorado Springs, CO 80920-1051; http://www.family.org. Illus. Circ: 210000 Paid. Aud.: Ems, Hs, Ga.

This fundamentalist teen magazine published by Focus on the Family is geared toward Christian girls, and apart from the publisher, the big giveaway regarding this magazine's bias is the "Ultimate Big Boss" listed on the masthead: God, who is also credited as the "Creator/Author of Life." There are regular health and beauty stories as well as sections on relationships and spiritual health. Profiles of real girl role models are frequent, and the magazine encourages charity and service on the part of its readers. The entertainment section focuses primarily on the spiritual elements of recent movies and music in response to reader queries (e.g., "Do you know how I can use the Spider-Man movies to tell my unsaved friends about Jesus?"). Fashion and beauty tend to focus on inner spiritual worth and the importance of modesty. Articles regularly cite scripture to emphasize a point (e.g., in a list of things you can do to save the earth for Earth Day, one is "read Psalm 104").

5868. Cicada (Peru). [ISSN: 1097-4008] 1998. bi-m. USD 35.97 domestic; USD 47.97 foreign; USD 7.95 per issue. Ed(s): Marianne Carus. Carus Publishing Company, 315 Fifth St, Peru, IL 61354; custsvc@ cobblestone.mv.com; http://www.cricketmag.com. Illus. Circ: 14000 Paid. *Indexed:* AmHI, MASUSE. *Aud.:* Ems, Hs.

This literary magazine geared toward teenagers 14 and up is the older version of *Cricket*. It features short fiction from a variety of genres and poetry written by a diverse collection of authors, which include adult authors and teens. Occasional illustrations highlight the stories within. *Cicada* accepts (and pays for) written submissions and illustrations from its readership. It serves as a significantly more polished alternative to *Teen Ink* and will appeal primarily to teenagers who like reading and writing short fiction and poetry. Recommended for public, middle, and high school libraries.

Computer Gaming World. See *Games for Windows* in Games section.

5869. CosmoGirl! [ISSN: 1528-4824] 1999. 10x/yr. USD 8 domestic; USD 23 foreign; USD 2.99 newsstand/cover per issue. Ed(s): Susan Schulz. Hearst Magazines, 300 W 57th St, New York, NY 10019; HearstMagazines@hearst.com; http://www.hearstcorp.com/magazines/. Illus., adv. Sample. Online: EBSCO Publishing, EBSCO Host; Gale; ProQuest LLC (Ann Arbor). *Indexed:* MASUSE. *Aud.:* Hs, Ga.

In addition to stars, gossip, and an abundance of fashion, you'll also find content related to careers and college in this teen version of *Cosmopolitan*. An emphasis on empowering girls and encouraging action can be found in features with substantial content like "Make Every Day Earth Day." Quizzes and embarrassing stories abound and are of the typical vapid sort. A recent issue previewed an excerpt from the next book in the *Sisterhood* series. Advice in the sex/health realm comes from college-aged women in a recent issue, and rather than taking a condescending tone or admonishing readers for spending time with friends who drink, they give practical advice for dealing with a multitude of difficult situations teens will likely find themselves in. Recommended for public libraries.

Dance Spirit. See Dance section.

E S P N The Magazine. See Sports section.

Electronic Gaming Monthly. See Games section.

5870. The Foxfire Magazine. Formerly (until 1992): *Foxfire.* [ISSN: 1084-5321] 1967. s-a. USD 12.95 domestic; USD 24.95 foreign. Ed(s): Angie Cheek. Foxfire Fund, Inc., PO Box 541, Mountain City, GA 30562-0541; foxfire@foxfire.org. Illus., adv. Sample. Circ: 12000. Microform: PQC. *Indexed:* ASIP, MLA-IB, RILM. *Aud.:* Ems, Hs.

Created by high school students in Southern Appalachia as a means of capturing and preserving their culture and the lives of senior citizens from their community, *The Foxfire Magazine*, now in its 40th year of production, is still going strong. In addition to profiles of local elders, issues are chock-full of photos, recipes, and other tidbits from local history. The students who work on the magazine do a fantastic job capturing the voice of their subjects with love and humor. It's clear that a lot of work goes into each issue, each of which starts out with an editorial statement from one of the senior student editors. Highly recommended for school libraries, although it would also be a great addition to many public libraries.

GamePro. See Games section.

5871. Girls' Life. [ISSN: 1078-3326] 1994. bi-m. USD 14.95 domestic; USD 19.95 Canada; USD 45 elsewhere. Ed(s): Karen Bokram. Girls' Life Acquisitions Corp., 4529 Harford Rd., Baltimore, MD 21214-3122. Illus., adv. Circ: 375000. Online: EBSCO Publishing, EBSCO Host; Gale; OCLC Online Computer Library Center, Inc.; ProQuest K-12 Learning Solutions; ProQuest LLC (Ann Arbor). *Indexed:* CPerI, CWI, GendWatch, ICM, MASUSE. *Bk. rev.:* Number and length vary. *Aud.:* Ems, Hs, Ga.

OMG, I totally called my BFF to give her the 411 on this wholesome teen magazine geared towards younger teenage girls (10–15) and featuring your typical array of beauty, fashion, advice, star profiles, and quizzes. The articles try to mimic teen-speak but come off sounding more like an adult trying to imitate what she thinks teens sound like. Many of the featured starlets, who also often grace the cover, tend to be in their teens, and while there's not much sex talk, there is lots of boy talk. There's a focus on teen chick-lit and giveaways for summer reads. Issue-oriented stories talk of "self-esteem" and "body image," but the editorial content doesn't do much to practice what they preach. A prime example is when they tell a girl with chest size insecurities that "there's still hope" and suggest padded bras, but then proceed to spout the platitude "you're beautiful as is." Yeah, right, thanks. They also sponsor a pen-pal program, but it'll cost you, and there's this free thing called Web 2.0 that I've been hearing about....

5872. Guideposts Sweet 16. Formerly (until Aug/Sept 2004): *Guideposts for Teens;* Incorporates (in 2004): *Sweet 16.* [ISSN: 1551-904X] 1998. bi-m. USD 19.95 domestic; USD 26.95 Canada; USD 30.95 elsewhere. Ed(s): Mary Lou Carney, Betsy Kohn. Guideposts, 39 Seminary Hill Rd, Carmel, NY 10512; http://www.guideposts.org. Circ: 120000 Paid. *Aud.:* Ems; Hs; Ga.

Targeting the tween to early-teen scene, *Guideposts Sweet 16* avoids the controversial in favor of the inspirational. While young celebs often appear on the cover and a recent feature profiled the "sweetest stars 16 and under," what really sets this one apart is the stories by teens. Consistently well written and edited, as well as entertaining, *Sweet 16* has included recent stories on a girl's love for showing prize chickens, a teen's experience in multiple foster homes, and the trials and tribulations of a female wrestler who also happens to be a model. While *Teen Voices* is busy subverting the dominant paradigm, *Guideposts Sweet 16* is embracing how positive thinking can transform your life. There are some articles related to fashion as well as quizzes and the like, but that's clearly not the focus here. Recommended for school and public libraries, especially ones looking for a teen magazine that won't offend delicate sensibilities.

5873. HmoobTeen: the place where hmong teens can speak and be heard. [ISSN: 1935-1542] 5x/yr. USD 15; USD 10 newsstand/cover. Ed(s): Choua Her. Hmong American Partnership, 1075 Arcade St, Saint Paul, MN 55106; hmoobtm@hmong.org. *Aud.:* Hs, Ga.

Written for and by Hmong teens, *HmoobTeen* addresses the experiences and growing pains of teens from this immigrant community and their life in the United States. Pictures of the teen editors and contributors fill the pages, lending a really personal feel to the stories and profiles of members of the Hmong community. While each issue is united under a theme like "Truth" or "Dreams," common issues that arise are the generation gap between teens and older community members, thoughts on creating a homeland and Hmong history, and the impact of American culture on their heritage. While the target population here is clear, the stories really are universal and the voices of the teens ring true. Recommended for high school and public libraries, especially ones that serve members of the Hmong community.

5874. Ignite Your Faith. Formerly (until Jan. 2006): *Campus Life.* [ISSN: 1558-7770] 1942. 9x/yr. USD 19.95; USD 3.95 newsstand/cover. Ed(s): Harold B. Smith, Chris Lutes. Christianity Today International, 465 Gundersen Dr, Carol Stream, IL 60188; http://www.christianitytoday.com. Illus., adv. Sample. Circ: 100000 Controlled. Microform: PQC. Online: EBSCO Publishing, EBSCO Host; Gale. *Indexed:* ChrPI, MASUSE. *Aud.:* Hs.

Formerly known as *Campus Life*, this Christian magazine serves as a spiritual outlet for teens looking to affirm their faith. Each issue has departments including Faith, Real Life, Bible, Entertainment, and Advice. Reviews of music deal primarily with Christian rock and reviewed books are also typically of a spiritual nature. Christian teens looking for answers about reconciling feelings and acts of a sexual nature with their faith will be well served by this publication that emphasizes repentance and forgiveness. Recommended for public libraries.

5875. J-14: just for teens! [ISSN: 1522-1989] 10x/yr. USD 16.95; USD 2.99 newsstand/cover. Bauer Publishing Company, L.P., 270 Sylvan Ave, Englewood Cliffs, NJ 07632. Adv. *Aud.:* Ems, Hs, Ga.

This colorful, glossy teen magazine focuses on younger stars, many of Disney and Nick fame, as well as pop artists and other heartthrobs of the moment. It's just the fix for star-crazy teens itching for the latest info on their favorite stars. Fun features include pull-out posters and contests (e.g., win a date with the Jonas Brothers!). Beauty and fashion tips abound as well as red carpet dos and don'ts and celebrity befores and afters. *J-14*, also known as *Just for Teens* (get it?), is just one of a multitude of teenybopper celeb worship choices. Consider *Tiger Beat*, *Bop*, or *Twist* (my local library's copies of this one were falling apart, but it's unclear if that was from poor staple quality or too much love), but more than one magazine of this type would be excessive. Check with your teens to see which they're into, and definitely consider *Right On!* or *Black Beat* as well. Recommended for public libraries.

5876. *Justine Magazine.* [ISSN: 1548-8241] 2004. bi-m. USD 14.95 domestic; USD 24.95 Canada; USD 29.95 elsewhere. Pinpoint Publishing, 6263 Poplar Ave Ste 430, Memphis, TN 38119. *Aud.:* Ems, Hs, Ga.

From the pun-filled world of teen magazine titles comes this self-defined "wholesome" magazine targeted toward young to middle teens. A clean layout, and a slightly less produced feel than some of the bigger-time fashion mags (read: less airbrushed), *Justine* features fashion geared toward younger teens, as the clothing shown is relatively conservative. Book, movie, and music reviews and lots of suggestions for hot products and web sites are staples. One great feature of *Justine* called "Trendsetters" is a substantial section of each issue devoted to profiling young women typically in their twenties in a particular career field (e.g., designers or writers) and the variety of jobs you can find within that field. This magazine might be a nice addition to your collection due to its up-to-date career information that can fill in holes in your career books for young adults and its lack of risque content. Recommended for public and school libraries.

5877. *JVibe.* unknown. USD 18. Ed(s): Michelle Cove. JVibe, info@jvibe.com. *Aud.:* Ems, Hs.

JVibe is a teen magazine for Jewish teens that, in addition to discussing matters of faith, includes interviews with Jewish actors and other celebrities. There's an emphasis on Jewish activism. Common features include info on life in Israel, roundtables where Jewish teens give their opinion on a topic like stereotypes, and profiles of teens who are making a difference in their communities. The reviews in the entertainment section focus mainly on works by Jewish artists, rather than only artists who have a distinctly Jewish message. A teen advisory board helps out with some content, and the magazine is funded by the United Synagogue of Conservative Judaism and the Union of Reform Judaism. Recommended for public libraries.

5878. *Listen: journal of drug-free living for teens.* [ISSN: 0024-435X] 1947. m. USD 24.97. Ed(s): Lincoln Steed. Health Connection, 55 W Oak Ridge Dr, Hagerstown, MD 21740. Illus., adv. Circ: 40000. Microform: PQC. Online: Northern Light Technology, Inc.; ProQuest K-12 Learning Solutions; ProQuest LLC (Ann Arbor). *Aud.:* Ems, Hs, Ga.

This anti-drug, pro-health magazine's title is very apt, as it seems to be trying to shake the reader into submission by shouting "listen!" While some might tell you that yelling at teens to listen will yield exactly the opposite result, this publication makes no bones about attempting to scare teens into submission so as not to make unhealthy lifestyle choices. A recent cover features stories on "The Pornography Problem" (which, we are informed, is actually a substance addiction) and "Monster Addiction," which warns you against the horrors of...caffeine. Heroin and Internet addictions are also covered in recent issues. Positive alternatives are presented in each issue, like knitting or sudoku or skating or eating soybeans. A cartoon featuring a digital classroom simulation with student avatars is a recurring feature in which someone does something "really bad," like steal, and then is ultimately suspended from the virtual classroom. The tone of the magazine aside, the factual information is solid, with lots of input from doctors, which might be useful for health reports.

Lucky. See Fashion and Lifestyle section.

Mad. See Humor section.

5879. *Muslim Girl: enlighten. celebrate. inspire.* [ISSN: 1934-5127] 2007. bi-m. USD 19.99. Ed(s): Ausma Zehanat Khan. ExecuGo Media, 1 Yonge St, Ste 1801, Toronto, ON M5E 1W7, Canada; clientcare@ aheadspace.com; http://www.execugo.com. Adv. Circ: 25000 Paid. *Aud.:* Hs, Ga, Sa.

This new magazine for 2007 has really raised the bar for teen publications. The editor-in-chief is a former Northwestern University professor who jumped at the opportunity to present a multifaceted view of Muslim life for teenage girls in America. Young women are pictured in gorgeous full-page photos both with and without the hijab. Fashion tends to be fairly conservative in order to be in keeping with Islamic values ("Cool Ways to Style Hijab!" is a recent cover story). There are regular sections that feature girls discussing their mosques and notes on the Qur'an. The content is truly thought-provoking and in addition to typical teen magazine fare like health, advice, quizzes, and fashion, the special features in each issue are something to look forward to. Recent issues include a story about sisters who wanted to be cheerleaders and joined a team of Muslim girls because their local high school uniforms were too skimpy; a story about a Muslim congressman, who took his oath on Thomas Jefferson's Qur'an, and his relationship with his daughter; and the story of a young refugee who came to the United States from Afghanistan. This glossy publication is much sturdier than most of the magazines reviewed in this section and could withstand circulation without falling apart. Highly recommended for public libraries.

New Moon. See Children section.

People. See News and Opinion section.

5880. *Pro Wrestling Illustrated.* [ISSN: 1043-7576] 13x/yr. USD 37 domestic; USD 47.40 elsewhere. Ed(s): Stuart M Saks. London Publishing Co., PO Box 910, Fort Washington, PA 19034. Illus., adv. Sample. *Aud.:* Hs, Ga.

As the title would imply, this publication is chock-full of images, which doesn't mean there isn't plenty of commentary to go along with them. It includes lots of awesome, gory, blood-splattering, full-color pictures. The content is geared solely toward professional wrestling fans, so if you serve teens who are into it (which is likely if you serve teens), this would be a great addition to your collection. Issues contain profiles of wrestlers, commentary on various personalities in that universe, and coverage of recent and historic matches. The writing is similar to other sports journalism. Some racy shots of provocatively clothed stars might be a factor to consider, but pick up an issue to take a look before discounting this one. The content is high-interest, and it might be an opportunity to engage literacy in an unexpected way for teen patrons.

5881. *Right On!* [ISSN: 0048-8305] 1971. bi-m. USD 19.94 domestic; USD 29.94 foreign; USD 4.99 newsstand/cover per issue domestic. Ed(s): Cynthia Horner. Dorchester Media, 200 Madison Ave, Ste 2000, New York, NY 10016; info@dorchestermedia.com; http://www.dorchestermedia.com. Illus., adv. Sample. Circ: 200800 Paid. Vol. ends: Oct. *Aud.:* Hs, Ga.

A teen celeb magazine geared toward black youth, *Right On!* features lots of celebrity photos and interviews as well as fashion tips and trends, embarrassing moments, and quizzes. The content is similar to *J-14*, but the focus is on urban culture, including actors and hip-hop artists. Music and book reviews with apt rating systems (four boom boxes means an album is sub-woofer worthy) are another feature of this magazine. *Right On!* and *Black Beat*, a similar publication that shares the same terrain and editor-in-chief, also share a regularly updated blog with entertainment gossip. Recommended for public libraries.

Rolling Stone. See Music/Popular section.

5882. *Seventeen.* [ISSN: 0037-301X] 1944. m. USD 7.97 domestic; USD 17.97 foreign; USD 2.99 newsstand/cover per issue. Ed(s): Ann Shoket. Hearst Magazines, 300 W 57th St, New York, NY 10019; HearstMagazines@hearst.com; http://www.hearstcorp.com/magazines/. Illus., adv. Sample. Circ: 1950000 Paid. CD-ROM: ProQuest LLC (Ann

Arbor). Microform: NBI; PQC. Online: EBSCO Publishing, EBSCO Host; Micromedia ProQuest; OCLC Online Computer Library Center, Inc.; ProQuest LLC (Ann Arbor). *Indexed:* CBCARef, CPerI, FLI, MASUSE, MRD, RGPR. *Aud.:* Hs, Ga.

Seventeen just got a new editor-in-chief, so it might be too soon to tell in what direction the content will go this time for the matriarch of the female-oriented teen magazines. *Seventeen* is geared toward the older end of the teenage spectrum with a polished look, some more mature content, and slightly older stars on the covers (recent issues featured Avril Lavigne and Mandy Moore). In addition to articles on fashion, beauty, and teen drama, there's lots of really helpful information about sex (including a regular sex education column) and female health issues. The feature articles are varied, and recent issues include "I Didn't Know My Friend Was a Narc!" and what you can do to prevent anti-gay violence. Although there is something of a focus on making your man happy, *Seventeen* is still recommended as standard fare that's appealing to a broad audience. Libraries with MySpace pages might consider befriending *Seventeen*. Recommended for public and high school libraries.

Sex, Etc. See Sexuality section.

Shojo Beat. See Anime, Graphic Novels, and Manga section.

Shonen Jump. See Anime, Graphic Novels, and Manga section.

Spin. See Music section.

Sports Illustrated. See Sports section.

5883. *Teen Ink: written by teens.* Formerly (until 2000): *The 21st Century.* [ISSN: 1545-1283] 1989. m. USD 25. Young Authors Foundation, PO Box 30, Newton, MA 02461.
Adv. *Indexed:* MASUSE. *Bk. rev.:* Number and length vary. *Aud.:* Ems, Hs, Ga.

This magazine, printed on tabloid-sized newsprint, contains a variety of fiction, poetry, reviews, opinion pieces, sports stories, nonfiction, and illustrations created by teens. There is angst aplenty and a vast range in quality. Apart from reviews of music, movies, and books (both recent and classics), there are reviews of colleges written by high school students post-visit and college essays, although the editor makes no guarantees that you'll get in. Submitting to *Teen Ink* is a great option for teens hoping to get published, and if you have teens who contribute, it's a plus to carry the magazine so they can see their work in the library.

5884. *Teen Vogue.* Incorporates (in 2005): *Y M.* [ISSN: 1540-2215] 2000. 6x/yr. USD 12. Ed(s): Amy Astley. Conde Nast Publications, Inc., 750 3rd Ave, New York, NY 10017; magpr@condenast.com; http://www.condenast.com. Adv. Circ: 850000 Paid and controlled. *Aud.:* Hs, Ga, Ac.

The highest circulating of the teen equivalent of adult fashion titles, *Teen Vogue* clearly emphasizes fashion, particularly high fashion (read: stuff that's not affordable for many teens). MTV reality show *The Hills*'s star Lauren Conrad probably helped circulation numbers after her internship at *Teen Vogue* was featured on the show. Production value is high, and all of the models are of the impossibly thin sort without much diversity in size, shape, or race. Additionally, there's a section on bedroom decor. Feature articles aren't particularly edgy or unique; recent topics include a teen's battle with Lyme Disease and grinding at high school dances. Other hard-hitting stories include a feature on how MySpace has helped some bands get exposure. That kind of article made me check to see if I was looking at a current issue. But it's clear that articles of this sort aren't what keeps this magazine afloat. Recommended for public libraries.

5885. *Teen Voices.* [ISSN: 1074-7494] 1988. q. 0 membership. Women Express, Inc., PO Box 120-027, Boston, MA 02112. Adv. Circ: 30000. *Indexed:* AltPI, FemPer. *Bk. rev.:* Number and length vary. *Aud.:* Ems, Hs, Ga.

This refreshing alternative to typical teenage girl fare avoids worshipping trends, opting instead to offer up critiques of advertisements, health and sex ed information, and multicultural awareness pieces written by teens. While *Girls' Life* urges readers to "think pink" when considering the hottest shades of makeup to purchase this season, *Teen Voices* deconstructs how society perceives the color pink. Celebrity interviews are also common, but they're likely to be of an actor or musician from a traditionally underrepresented group. A gaggle of teen editors (many of whom are inner-city, at-risk teens) assembles and writes the content for each issue. *Teen Voices* accepts submissions from across the country (and to a lesser extent the rest of the English-speaking world). Each cover features three teens from a mix of racial backgrounds, and while they have some makeup on, they're not airbrushed. As with any teen magazine where content comes primarily from reader submissions, there is a range of writing quality, including some very angst-ridden poetry, but some content is truly compelling and thoughtful. Each piece usually ends with a way to engage the topic further, either with recommendations for further reading or addresses of people to contact to voice your support or disapproval. The magazine is beginning to have a greater web presence, and the site includes some online-only content. Highly recommended for school and public libraries, but check out an issue before deciding to subscribe to see if it fits your audience.

Thrasher. See Sports/Extreme Sports section.

Transworld Skateboarding. See Sports/Extreme Sports section.

Transworld Snowboarding. See Sports/Extreme Sports section.

Tu. See Latin America and Spain section.

TV Guide. See General Editorial/General section.

Vibe Vixen. See African American section.

Wizard: the comics magazine. See Comic Books/Publications about Comics section.

■ TELEVISION, VIDEO, AND RADIO

Home Entertainment

See also Electronics; Films; and Media and AV sections.

George E. Clark, Ph.D., Environmental Research Librarian, Research Services, Lamont Library Level B–Harvard Yard, Harvard University, Cambridge, MA 02138; george_clark@harvard.edu; FAX: 617-496-5570

Introduction

The literature on television, radio, and video has readers spanning the spectrum from creators to consumers and critics, and from the beginner to the professional. Library selectors need to pay attention to their potential user base when assembling a collection.

Public libraries may want to carry the spectrum of home audio- and video-system consumer publications, but then again, those who can afford the high-end equipment may also be those who can afford to purchase these publications on their own. *The Perfect Vision* is probably the broadest in this genre, so it has the advantage of being able to educate librarians who can then make their own forays into home theater information. Meanwhile, librarians should not underestimate the topical power of the old standby, *Consumer Reports,* which is not reviewed in this section. In terms of choosing programs to watch, many newspapers and web sites (including the renter's favorite, Netflix) give viewers easy access to reviews of mainstream new releases, so libraries are better off choosing a guide to offbeat DVDs such as *Video Watchdog.*

Coverage of basic radio hobby publications is also necessary for public libraries. Keeping tabs on public safety and other radio transmitters (scanner listening) is a very strong niche hobby, along with shortwave listening. This need can be covered by *Popular Communications* or by *Monitoring Times.* There are about 650,000 people licensed as amateur radio (ham radio) operators in the United States. These patrons will want to be able to read *QST.* Subscriptions to amateur radio publications may also be necessary for schools, colleges, and universities where there is an amateur (ham) radio station.

Another school or university angle is the TV, video, journalism, or film production club, studio, or department. Libraries that serve these organizations will want to buy *Videomaker*, a basic guide to producing professional-quality video. Also covered in this section is academic and gender criticism of film and media. These titles will be useful for universities with departments in film studies; media studies; gender, sexuality, and queer studies; communications; cultural studies; and journalism. Finally, this section includes trade publications that cover public radio, cable TV, professional video production and equipment, and radio and TV broadcasting.

Basic Periodicals

Monitoring Times, Perfect Vision, Popular Communications, QST, Video Watchdog, and *Videomaker.*

Basic Abstracts and Indexes

Film Literature Index, Academic Search Premier.

Adbusters: journal of the mental environment. See Alternatives section.

Afterimage. See Photography section.

5886. Broadcasting & Cable. Former titles (until 1993): *Broadcasting (Washington);* (until 1957): *Broadcasting Telecasting;* (until 1948): *Broadcasting - The News Magazine of the Fifth Estate;* Incorporated (in 1961): *Television;* (in 1953): *Telecast;* (in 1933): *Broadcast Reporter; Broadcast Advertising.* [ISSN: 1068-6827] 1931. w. 51/yr. USD 199 combined subscription domestic print & online eds.; USD 249 combined subscription Canada print & online eds.; USD 360 combined subscription elsewhere print & online eds. Ed(s): J Max Robins, Susan Qualtrough. Reed Business Information, 360 Park Ave South, New York, NY 10010; http://www.reedbusiness.com. Illus., adv. Sample. Circ: 35000 Paid and controlled. Vol. ends: Dec. Microform: CIS; PQC. Online: The Dialog Corporation; EBSCO Publishing, EBSCO Host; Factiva, Inc.; Florida Center for Library Automation; Gale; LexisNexis; Northern Light Technology, Inc.; OCLC Online Computer Library Center, Inc.; ProQuest LLC (Ann Arbor); H.W. Wilson. *Indexed:* ABIn, BPI, CWI, FLI, IIPA, LRI, PAIS. *Aud.:* Ac, Sa.

A television business news journal. *Broadcasting and Cable* keeps the corporate broadcast and cable TV professional informed with departments that cover programming and syndication, local stations and cable operators, advertising and marketing, financial news, regulation, syndication and programming, and career moves.

5887. C Q: the radio amateurs' journal. [ISSN: 0007-893X] 1945. m. USD 31.95 domestic; USD 44.95 in Canada & Mexico; USD 56.95 elsewhere. Ed(s): Richard Moseson. C Q Communications, Inc., 25 Newbridge Rd, Ste 405, Hicksville, NY 11801-2805. Illus., adv. Sample. Circ: 90000 Paid. Vol. ends: Dec. *Indexed:* IHTDI. *Aud.:* Hs, Ga, Ac, Sa.

CQ is a general-interest publication on amateur radio, also known as ham radio, with an emphasis on radio contesting. Contesting is the part of the hobby in which amateurs make radio contact with as many fellow operators as possible who meet certain geographical (countries, counties, zones), mode (Morse code, voice, teletype), or other qualifications (age, gender, off-grid, low-power) on a given band or set of bands in a given time period. The magazine includes contesting tips as well as radio construction projects, news on DX (long distance) communication, and how to get started as a beginner in the hobby. A good counterpart to *QST* (the magazine produced by the national amateur radio association), *CQ* is well regarded yet has a somewhat more relaxed style. The "CQ" of the title is a letter group used as a general radio call to other amateurs. Perhaps coincidentally, it sounds like "seek you."

5888. Camcorder & ComputerVideo. Former titles: *Camcorder;* (until 1989): *Camcorder Report;* (until 1988): *Super Television;* (until 1987): *Home Satellite TV.* [ISSN: 1091-0441] 1985. m. USD 23; USD 4.99 per issue. Ed(s): James L Miller, Bob Wolenik. Miller Magazines, Inc, 290 Maple Ct, # 232, Ventura, CA 93003-3517. Adv. Circ: 115000. Online: Gale. *Aud.:* Hs, Ga, Sa.

Camcorder & Computer Video bills itself as "the complete magazine of video photography and desktop video." Its goal is to reach complete novices as well as professionals, such as wedding videographers. Issues feature reviews of camcorders, software for editing and other purposes, and regular columns. A recent issue includes "How to Buy the Perfect Cam" and "Shoot Better Home Video."

5889. Current (Washington, 1980): the public telecommunications newspaper. Former titles: *N A E B Letter; National Association of Educational Broadcasters Newsletter.* [ISSN: 0739-991X] 1980. bi-w. USD 70 domestic; USD 82 Canada; USD 132 foreign. Ed(s): Steve Behrens. Current Publishing Committee, 6930 Carroll Ave, Ste 350, Takoma Park, MD 20912; behrens@current.org; http://www.current.org. Illus., adv. Sample. Circ: 6100 Paid. Vol. ends: No. 23. *Aud.:* Ac, Sa.

Current is the newspaper of public radio and public television. Recent articles include access to old public television programs, web site expansion at the "Frontline" series, computer games produced by the Corporation for Public Broadcasting, censorship of on-air talent, and an upcoming documentary series about an aircraft carrier. Includes a calendar of events, job listings, and funding sources.

5890. D V. Former titles (until 1996): *Digital Video Magazine;* (until Jun. 1994): *Desktop Video World.* [ISSN: 1541-0943] 1993. m. USD 29.97 domestic (Free to qualified personnel). Ed(s): David Williams. NewBay Media, LLC, 810 Seventh Ave, 27th Fl, New York, NY 10019; http://www.nbmedia.com. Illus., adv. Circ: 64382 Paid and controlled. Vol. ends: Dec. Online: Florida Center for Library Automation; Gale; OCLC Online Computer Library Center, Inc.; H.W. Wilson. *Indexed:* BPI, MicrocompInd. *Aud.:* Ac, Sa.

DV stands for "digital video." This is a magazine for "professionals involved in the production, postproduction, and delivery of digital video." Contains product reviews (hardware, software, and cameras), feature articles, and columns on sound, lighting, and law, among others. This publication is the place to go when you need to know what to take along when you're filming a dogsled race in Alaska.

5891. Digital Content Producer: film and video production in a multi-platform world. Formerly (until May 2006): *Video Systems.* [ISSN: 1931-499X] 1975. m. USD 70 domestic (Free to qualified personnel). Ed(s): Jared Blankenship. Prism Business Media, 9800 Metcalf Ave, Overland Park, KS 66212-2216; inquiries@prismb2b.com; http://www.prismbusinessmedia.com. Illus., adv. Sample. Circ: 60000 Controlled and free. Vol. ends: No. 12. Online: EBSCO Publishing, EBSCO Host; Gale; OCLC Online Computer Library Center, Inc.; ProQuest K-12 Learning Solutions; ProQuest LLC (Ann Arbor); H.W. Wilson. *Indexed:* AS&TI, MicrocompInd. *Aud.:* Ac, Sa.

"Digital content" includes video produced for "traditional film and video platforms as well as emerging distribution options from cell phones and PDAs to digital signage and houses of worship." This web site covers "cameras and camera accessories, video editing, digital content creation, digital intermediate, projection, flat screen display, storage and networking, music libraries, audio, and more." Includes listings for trade shows and other upcoming events.

5892. Feminist Media Studies. [ISSN: 1468-0777] 2001. q. GBP 372 print & online eds. Ed(s): Lisa McLaughlin, Cynthia Carter. Routledge, 4 Park Square, Milton Park, Abingdon, OX14 4RN, United Kingdom; info@routledge.co.uk; http://www.routledge.co.uk. Refereed. Reprint: PSC. *Indexed:* CommAb, IBSS, IndIslam, SociolAb. *Bk. rev.:* Number and length vary. *Aud.:* Ac.

Feminist Media Studies is a peer-reviewed academic journal for feminist approaches to print, electronic, film, and other media technologies. Recent issues include articles on TV and cosmetic surgery; analysis of letters to women's health magazines; the meaning of the TV series *Prime Suspect*; and the relationship between the movie *In the Cut* and the TV series *Sex and the City*.

5893. FMedia!: the FM radio newsletter. [ISSN: 0890-6718] 1987. m. USD 75. Ed(s): Bruce F Elving. F M Atlas Publishing, PO Box 336, Esko, MN 55733-0336; FmAtlas@aol.com; http://users.aol.com/fmatlas/. Illus. Sample. Circ: 300 Paid and controlled. Vol. ends: No. 11. *Aud.:* Ac, Sa.

This publication is a small-font, text-dense, black-and-white newsletter packed with information on FM broadcast radio. Contains a few tiny, grainy photos; short feature articles; lists of station grants, call letter changes, and facilities changes approved by the FCC; station format changes; and news about FM radio by state and country. Some information on radio hardware is included as well. For the hard-core FM radio fan or the detail-oriented market monitor.

The Independent Film & Video Monthly. See *The Independent* in Films section.

5894. Inside Radio: the latest news, trends and management information. Incorporates (in 2002): *M Street Daily*. [ISSN: 0731-9312] 1987. d. USD 399. Ed(s): Frank Saxe. M Street Publications, 365 Union St, Littleton, NH 03561; streaming@insideradio.com; http://www.mstreet.net. Adv. *Aud.:* Ac, Sa.

Inside Radio is a daily fax and e-mail news service of "leading industry news, ratings and classifieds." Top stories at this writing included the low level of minorities in the radio news workforce, small market radio indicators, mergers and acquisitions, and ratings companies.

5895. InterMedia. Formerly: *I B I Newsletter*. [ISSN: 0309-118X] 1973. q. Institutional members, GBP 3500; Individual members, GBP 90. International Institute of Communications (IIC), Regent House, 24-25 Nutford Pl, London, W1H 5YN, United Kingdom; http://www.iicom.org/. Illus., adv. Sample. Circ: 1500. Vol. ends: No. 6. Microform: PQC. Online: EBSCO Publishing, EBSCO Host; ProQuest LLC (Ann Arbor). *Indexed:* ABIn, CommAb, FutSurv, IIFP, PAIS. *Aud.:* Ac, Sa.

InterMedia is a wide-ranging publication, examining "the whole spectrum of telecommunications [and] broadcasting," with an emphasis on the global scene. Sponsored by the nonprofit International Institute for Communications, which aims to increase dialogue between industry, government, and academics on changes in media ownership, technology, and regulation. Recent articles have appeared on connecting Africa, Internet streaming, and the future fate of analog TV users. This is a challenging and forward-thinking publication.

5896. Journal of Broadcasting and Electronic Media. Formerly (until 1985): *Journal of Broadcasting*. [ISSN: 0883-8151] 1956. q. GBP 116 print & online eds. Ed(s): Donald G Godfrey. Lawrence Erlbaum Associates, Inc., 325 Chestnut St, Ste. 800, Philadelphia, PA 19106; journals@erlbaum.com; http://www.leaonline.com. Adv. Refereed. Circ: 2200. Microform: WSH; PMC; PQC. Online: EBSCO Publishing, EBSCO Host; Florida Center for Library Automation; Gale; William S. Hein & Co., Inc.; OCLC Online Computer Library Center, Inc.; SwetsWise Online Content. Reprint: PSC; WSH. *Indexed:* ABS&EES, AgeL, AmHI, ArtHuCI, BRI, CJA, CLI, CommAb, HumInd, IIFP, ILP, LRI, PAIS, PsycInfo, RI-1, RILM, RiskAb, SFSA, SSCI, SWA, V&AA. *Aud.:* Ac.

The *Journal of Broadcasting and Electronic Media* is an academic journal that examines the "historical, technological, economic, legal, policy, cultural, and social dimensions" of electronic media such as the Internet, video games, television, and radio. Historical perspectives range from the beginnings of radio to the latest developments in media. This is a recommended resource for universities with communications departments.

Journal of Popular Film and Television. See Films section.

5897. Media, Culture & Society. [ISSN: 0163-4437] 1979. bi-m. GBP 676. Ed(s): John R Corner, Philip Schlesinger. Sage Publications Ltd., 1 Oliver's Yard, 55 City Rd, London, EC1 1SP, United Kingdom; info@sagepub.co.uk; http://www.sagepub.co.uk. Illus., adv. Refereed. Online: CSA; EBSCO Publishing, EBSCO Host; HighWire Press; OCLC Online Computer Library Center, Inc.; OhioLINK; SAGE Publications, Inc., SAGE Journals Online; SwetsWise Online Content. Reprint: PSC. *Indexed:* ASSIA, AnthLit, ArtHuCI, BrHumI, CommAb, DAAI, FLI, HRA, IBR, IBSS, IBZ, IIFP, IPSA, LISA, PRA, PSA, SSA, SSCI, SWA, SociolAb, V&AA. *Bk. rev.:* Number and length vary. *Aud.:* Ac.

Media, Culture, and Society is an international, interdisciplinary academic journal that examines traditional and emerging media "within their political, economic, cultural and historical contexts." Recent issues have contained articles on talk radio in Australia, the media capacity of East Asia, Renaissance cartography, and state manipulation of current affairs programming in China.

5898. Media Report to Women. [ISSN: 0145-9651] 1972. q. USD 58 (Individuals, USD 36). Ed(s): Sheila Gibbons. Communication Research Associates, Inc., 38091 Beach Rd, PO Box 180, Colton's Point, MD 20626-0180; http://www.mediareporttowomen.com/. Illus., index, adv. Sample. Vol. ends: Fall (No. 4). *Indexed:* FLI, FemPer, WSA. *Bk. rev.:* 3-5, 50-90 words. *Aud.:* Hs, Ga, Ac, Sa.

This black-and-white publication covers "all the issues concerning women and media." Topics in recent issues include sex and advertising, sexualized images of young women in the media, abortion rhetoric and censorship, coverage of the women's movement, disproportionate representation of women in the media, and the dominance and meaning of Jennifer Lopez as a reference in Latina popular culture. Contains news excerpts, useful book reviews, and well-sourced research papers. This is a recommended resource. It puts Madison Avenue images and mainstream news and entertainment in context.

5899. Monitoring Times. [ISSN: 0889-5341] 1982. m. USD 28.95; USD 5.95 per issue. Ed(s): Rachel Baughn. Grove Enterprises, Inc., PO Box 98, 7540 Hwy 64 W, Brasstown, NC 28902-0098; mteditor@grove-ent.com; http://www.grove-ent.com/hmpgmt.html. Illus., adv. Sample. Circ: 28000 Paid. Vol. ends: Dec. *Indexed:* ASIP. *Aud.:* Hs, Ga, Ac, Sa.

Monitoring Times is a magazine for radio listeners, in particular shortwave listeners and communications scanner devotees. The publication also devotes attention to new technologies such as "HD Radio." With 23 regular columns, this thick publication contains the details on how to listen to airplanes, trains, utilities, public safety agencies, and more. A recent note features a microwave transmitter built from a kitchen wok in order to save the $20,000 cost of a commercial dish. Despite the occasional foray into the technical, this publication is for listening enthusiasts of all types and does not require an electrical engineering background to be enjoyed. See also *Popular Communications*.

5900. Multichannel News. Incorporates (2000-2001): *Broadband Week*. [ISSN: 0276-8593] 1980. w. Mon. USD 159 domestic; USD 219 foreign; USD 4 per issue domestic. Ed(s): Kent Gibbons. Reed Business Information, 360 Park Ave South, New York, NY 10010; http://www.reedbusiness.com. Adv. Circ: 22000. Online: EBSCO Publishing, EBSCO Host; Factiva, Inc.; Florida Center for Library Automation; Gale; LexisNexis; Northern Light Technology, Inc.; OCLC Online Computer Library Center, Inc.; ProQuest LLC (Ann Arbor). *Indexed:* CWI. *Aud.:* Ac, Sa.

Multichannel News is a guide to all things "cable TV" for industry insiders. Regular sections include finance, marketing, opinion, people, policy, programming, and technology. Companies mentioned in a recent issue include Cox, Disney, Spike, IFC, the National Geographic Channel, and Circuit City.

5901. OnVideo: guide to home video releases. [ISSN: 1094-3676] 1995. d. Ed(s): Harley W Lond. OnVideo, PO Box 17377, Beverly Hills, CA 90209; onvideo@cyberpod.com; http://www.onvideo.org. Adv. *Aud.:* Ga.

OnVideo is a web site that lists the latest movie releases on DVD and carries month-by-month reviews of the top issues. It has helpful and interesting links on topics such as children's movies and film soundtracks. Libraries will find the list of movie guides useful.

5902. Popular Communications. Incorporates: *Scan Magazine.* [ISSN: 0733-3315] 1982. m. USD 28.95 domestic; USD 38.95 in Canada & Mexico; USD 48.95 elsewhere. Ed(s): Harold Ort. C Q Communications, Inc., 25 Newbridge Rd, Ste 405, Hicksville, NY 11801-2805; cq@cq-amateur-radio.com; http://www.cq-amateur-radio.com. Illus., adv. Sample. Circ: 92238. Vol. ends: No. 12. *Indexed:* ABS&EES, IHTDI. *Bk. rev.:* 4, 300-450 words. *Aud.:* Hs, Ga, Ac, Sa.

Popular Communications is a resource for radio listening hobbyists of all types, including shortwave listeners (think Voice of America and ham radio) and scanner enthusiasts, those who listen in on more local other-than-broadcast traffic, such as police, fire, and air traffic radio. The publication also serves as an entry-level resource for potential and new amateur (ham) radio operators, that is, those who want to transition from listening to transmitting. Each issue contains information on equipment, government regulations, radio propagation conditions, and transmitter information, including frequencies, control information required to interpret variable frequency "trunk" radio systems, and timing and language for international shortwave broadcasts. Plus plenty of ads and reviews of listening equipment.

Public Broadcasting Report. See Media and AV section.

5903. QST: devoted entirely to amateur radio. [ISSN: 0033-4812] 1915. m. USD 39 membership. Ed(s): Joel Kleinman, Steve Ford. American Radio Relay League, Inc., 225 Main St, Newington, CT 06111; pubsales@arrl.org; http://www.arrl.org. Illus., adv. Sample. Circ: 175000 Paid and controlled. Vol. ends: Dec. Microform: PQC. Online: Northern Light Technology, Inc.; OCLC Online Computer Library Center, Inc.; ProQuest LLC (Ann Arbor); H.W. Wilson. *Indexed:* AS&TI, ConsI. *Bk. rev.:* 1, 825 words. *Aud.:* Hs, Ga.

QST is the flagship publication of the American Radio Relay League (ARRL), the United States' national association for amateur (ham) radio. Each issue contains news and opinion, often related to a current regulatory development with the Federal Communications Commission. Projects make up the "Technical" section, perhaps a story about implementing a new antenna system or a way to explore communications on a new frequency or using a new "mode" beyond the most common, Morse code and single sideband voice. Another section is "Workbench," which offers brief but detailed troubleshooting, explanations of technical issues, and experiments. The "Operating" section contains information on radio contests past and future. Other regular features include schedules of conventions and flea markets, special event stations, product reviews, and global ("DX") communications. The title *QST* comes from a Morse code abbreviation that means a general call to members of the ARRL. Recommended for schools with radio clubs and public libraries. See also *CQ*.

5904. Radio Ink. [ISSN: 1064-587X] 1986. fortn. USD 199 domestic; USD 225 foreign. Ed(s): Ed Ryan, B Eric Rhoads. Streamline Publishing, Inc., 224 Datura St, Ste 701, W. Palm Beach, FL 33401; radiolink@aol.com. Illus., adv. Sample. Circ: 9000. Vol. ends: No. 26. *Aud.:* Sa.

Radio Ink is a magazine of management and marketing for broadcast radio stations and related businesses. It contains news of promotions, firings, acquisitions, regulations, sales, revenue, and other goings-on in the radio business. Contains popularity and achievement lists such as the "35 Most Influential African-Americans in Radio." Also contains career classifieds and links to corporations and organizations in the field.

5905. Radio Journal: radio's journal of record since 1984. 1984. w. USD 169. Ed(s): Frank Saxe. M Street Publications, 365 Union St, Littleton, NH 03561; streaming@insideradio.com; http://www.mstreet.net. *Aud.:* Ac, Sa.

An online and fax weekly newsletter for broadcast radio. Station changes, with information on ownership, facilities, engineering, callsigns, formats, and job listings.

5906. S M P T E Motion Imaging Journal. Former titles (until 2002): *S M P T E Journal;* (until 1975): *S M P T E. Journal;* (until 1955): *S M P T E Journal;* (until 1954): *Society of Motion Picture and Television Engineers. Journal;* (until 1949): *Society of Motion Picture Engineers.*

Journal; (until 1929): *Society of Motion Picture Engineers. Transactions.* [ISSN: 1545-0279] 1916. 8x/yr. USD 140. Ed(s): Diane Ross Purrier. Society of Motion Picture and Television Engineers, 595 Wharfsdale Ave, White Plains, NY 10607. Illus., adv. Circ: 8000 Paid. Microform: PMC; PQC. Online: OCLC Online Computer Library Center, Inc.; H.W. Wilson. *Indexed:* AS&TI, ApMecR, C&ISA, ChemAb, EngInd, ExcerpMed, FLI, PhotoAb, SCI. *Aud.:* Sa.

The Society of Motion Picture and Television Engineers (SMPTE) publishes this trade journal for "engineers, technical directors, cameramen, editors, technicians, manufacturers, designers, educators, consultants and field users in networking, compression, encryption and more." Articles are highly technical and on topics such as emergent digital formats, special effects, and processing of digital images.

TV Guide. See General Interest section.

5907. Videography. Incorporates (1988-1990): *Corporate Video Decisions.* [ISSN: 0363-1001] 1976. m. USD 72 domestic (Free to qualified personnel). Ed(s): Katie Makal. NewBay Media, LLC, 810 Seventh Ave, 27th Fl, New York, NY 10019; http://www.nbmedia.com. Illus., adv. Sample. Circ: 41000. Vol. ends: Dec. Online: Gale; Northern Light Technology, Inc.; OCLC Online Computer Library Center, Inc.; ProQuest LLC (Ann Arbor). *Indexed:* ABIn, FLI, MRD. *Aud.:* Sa.

Videography is a "print & online resource for the video production professional." This is a well-rounded look at technology, professional life, and industry accomplishments from the perspective of videographers, editors, and other folks involved in making the director's vision come to life through the image. The web site contains an impressive list of forums for discussion of various facets of the videographer's art and science.

5908. Videomaker: camcorders - editing - computer video - audio & video production. [ISSN: 0889-4973] 1986. m. USD 22.50 domestic; USD 32.50 Canada; USD 47.50 elsewhere. Ed(s): Stephen Muratore, Matthew York. York Publishing, PO Box 4591, Chico, CA 95927. Illus., index, adv. Sample. Circ: 80000. Vol. ends: Dec. Online: Gale. *Indexed:* FLI, IHTDI. *Aud.:* Hs, Ac, Sa.

This is just the right publication for those interested in shooting and editing professional-caliber videos, and that means more and more averages Joes (read public library patrons) in the era of YouTube. Includes technique, product reviews, and lots of serious, helpful material geared toward beginners and novices. Highly recommended for medium to large public libraries and high schools with video production facilities.

Home Entertainment

5909. CurtoCo's Digital T V and Sound: the ultimate guide to hdtv, plasma, flat-panel, projection, sound. Formerly (until Spr. 2005): *CurtCo's Digital T V.* [ISSN: 1557-315X] 2004. q. USD 65 domestic; USD 75 Canada; USD 105 elsewhere. Ed(s): Mike Wood. CurtCo Robb Media LLC., 29160 Heathercliff Rd, Ste 200, Malibu, CA 90265; http://www.curtco.com. Adv. Circ: 80000 Paid. *Aud.:* Ga.

A sleek, general-interest guide to high-definition, LCD, and plasma TVs; speaker systems; gaming units; and whatever the next TV technology will be. Includes programming information, tutorials, and a glossary. Useful for libraries where patrons need to know how to make new TV formats go.

5910. Home Theater. Former titles: *CurtCo's Home Theater; CurtCo's Home Theater Technology.* [ISSN: 1096-3065] 1994. m. USD 12.97 domestic; USD 25.97 Canada; USD 27.97 elsewhere. Ed(s): Maureen Jenson. Source Interlink Companies, 261 Madison Ave, New York, NY 10016; edisupport@sourceinterlink.com; http://www.sourceinterlink.com. Adv. *Indexed:* FLI. *Aud.:* Ga.

A shopping and enjoyment magazine for those who own or lust after home theater systems. A well-rounded, approachable guide to the topic with articles on speakers, players, amplifiers, all-in-one systems, iPod interfaces, DVD reviews, dealer locators, and a glossary. Oh, and gargantuan televisions. Blogs are featured in the online edition.

5911. *The Perfect Vision: high performance home theater.* [ISSN: 0895-4143] 1986. bi-m. USD 14.95 domestic; USD 29.95 Canada; USD 34.95 elsewhere. Ed(s): Robert Harley. Absolute Multimedia Inc., 8121 Bee Caves Rd., Ste. 100, Austin, TX 78746-4938; info@avguide.com. Illus., adv. Circ: 20000. Vol. ends: Nov/Dec. *Aud.:* Ga.

This magazine is a guide to many entertainment and information technologies including iPods, computers, handhelds, Web 2.0, Skype, home theater, and TiVo. As such, it is far more versatile and educational, with a broader range, than comparable publications that focus on home theater alone. Librarians will find this publication useful for keeping abreast of a wide range of new technologies that patrons will have questions about. Also features product and movie reviews.

5912. *Satellite Direct: the magazine of direct-broadcast satellite communications.* Formerly (until 1987): *Satellite Dealer.* [ISSN: 0892-3329] 1983. m. USD 34.95 domestic; USD 52 Canada. Ed(s): Candace Korchinski. Vogel Communications Inc., 701 5th Ave, 36th Fl, Seattle, WA 98104. Illus., adv. Circ: 300000. Vol. ends: Dec. *Aud.:* Ga.

DirecTV publishes *Satellite Direct* as the guide to its satellite TV programming and services. The online version of this "entertainment guide" contains extensive channel listings for the system and for XM Satellite Radio.

5913. *Satellite Orbit: complete national TV programming guide.* Supersedes (in 1985): *Satguide.* [ISSN: 0732-7668] 1982. m. USD 45.95 domestic; USD 59.95 Canada. Ed(s): Gene Kosowan. Vogel Communications Inc., 701 5th Ave, 36th Fl, Seattle, WA 98104. Illus., adv. Circ: 214953. Vol. ends: Dec. *Aud.:* Ga.

Satellite Orbit is the guide "for owners of a C-band, 4DTV and Dish Network satellite systems." The online version includes a guide to programs and satellite names, locations, signal bands, and formats.

5914. *Sound & Vision: home theater - audio - video - multimedia - movies - music.* Formerly (until 2003): *Stereo Review's Sound and Vision;* Which was formed by the merger of (1978-1999): *Video Magazine;* Which was formerly (until 1987): *Video (New York);* (1960-1999): *Stereo Review;* Which was formerly (until 1968): *HiFi Stereo Review;* Superseded (1959-1989): *High Fidelity;* Which was formerly (until 1959): *High Fidelity & Audiocraft;* Which was formed by the merger of (1957-1958): *Audiocraft for the Hi-Fi Hobbyist;* (1951-1958): *High Fidelity.* [ISSN: 1537-5838] 1999. 10x/yr. USD 12 domestic; USD 22 foreign; USD 4.50 newsstand/cover. Ed(s): Bob Ankosko, Brian Fenton. Hachette Filipacchi Media U.S., Inc., 1633 Broadway, New York, NY 10019; http://www.hfmus.com. Illus., index, adv. Circ: 500000 Paid. Vol. ends: Dec. Microform: NBI; PQC. Online: Chadwyck-Healey Inc.; The Dialog Corporation; OCLC Online Computer Library Center, Inc.; H.W. Wilson. *Indexed:* BRI, CBRI, CPerI, ConsI, IIMP, MASUSE, MicrocompInd, MusicInd, RGPR, RILM. *Aud.:* Ga.

Sound & Vision is another credible entry in the flashy home theater/audio consumer genre. Jammed with "Test Reports," new product alerts, buying tips, and TV and movie reviews, this magazine will tell you everything you need to know to spend money on home theater. The "How to Speak A/V" feature in the online version is a glossary that librarians and readers may find helpful in navigating the ever-obsolescent world of consumer audio and video.

5915. *Video Watchdog: the perfectionist's guide to fantastic video.* [ISSN: 1070-9991] 1990. m. USD 60 domestic; USD 75 foreign; USD 6.50 newsstand/cover per issue. Ed(s): Tim Lucas. Video Watchdog, PO Box 5283, Cincinnati, OH 45205-0283; videowd@aol.com; http://www.cinemaweb.com/videowd. Illus. *Indexed:* FLI, IIFP. *Bk. rev.:* Number and length vary. *Aud.:* Hs, Ga.

Video Watchdog is informed commentary and criticism on a wide range of video releases, many of them off the beaten path. Go to this publication to find thoughtful information on films and TV shows that won't be featured in most "latest new release" publications and web sites. A blog ("Video WatchBlog") features reviews and daily commentary on relevant current events in addition to the more usual (if, perhaps, still useful) blogisms such as how the author is

interacting with his satellite network hardware on a given day. Highly recommended for those whose viewing habits are off the beaten path and for libraries with serious video collections.

5916. *Widescreen Review: the essential home theatre resource.* 1993. m. USD 40 domestic; USD 50 in Canada & Mexico; USD 90 elsewhere. Ed(s): Gary Reber. W S R Publishing, 27645 Commerce Center Dr., Temecula, CA 92590; wsrgary@widescreenreview.com; http://www.widescreenreview.com. Illus., adv. Circ: 48000. *Aud.:* Ga.

A consumer guide to home audio and video, *Widescreen Review* reviews A/V hardware, software, and entertainment, including discs in Blu-Ray, HDDVD, and DVD formats. The online version includes a glossary, speaker specs database, and coverage of musicians in audio and audiovisual format.

■ THEATER

Elizabeth McKeigue, Research Librarian, Widener Library, Harvard University, Cambridge, MA 02138; mckeigue@fas.harvard.edu

Introduction

No matter how you spell it, theater (or theatre, if you like) is an art form to which everyone can relate. Whether your library serves a high school student who is playing a nun in their high school's production of "The Sound of Music," an undergraduate studying the Stanislavski method in drama class, a scholar writing the definitive book on Chekhov, an actor preparing for her first Shakespeare role, or a theater-lover who goes to New York just to see the new shows, there is a relevant journal or magazine for your collection.

Excellent consumer and current performance titles (e.g., *American Theater, Variety,* and *Theatre Record*) are well known and can boast high circulation numbers. Some online-only publications are not only popular with professionals and laypeople alike, but are also free, such as *AisleSay, CurtainUp,* and *The New York Theatre Guide.* These electronic-only publications are also excellent sources of performance reviews.

There is also a wealth of local e-journals with rich content on local theatrical productions that are not specifically included here. The journals listed here are limited to those focused on international, London, or New York theater.

A wide variety of academic titles cover historical issues, play criticism, some dramaturgy, and comparative drama, such as *American Drama, Comparative Drama, Journal of American Drama and Theatre, TDR, Theater,* and *Theatre Journal.* Journals focused on playwriting and some that reproduce current play scripts (e.g., *The Dramatist, Avant-Scene Theatre*) are also of great importance to any theater collection. Not as prolific, but just as important to any theater collection, are journals that are predominantly focused on technical issues like *Live Design* and *T D & T: Theatre Design & Technology.*

Also listed here are a few non–English language journals, like *Theater Heute* and *Revue d'Histoire du Theatre,* included because of the wide scope of their coverage and for the interest these titles hold for scholars with reading knowledge of one or more European languages.

A word of caution: As with all journal selection that focuses on contemporary and avant-garde art, a library must be careful that it is choosing materials that not only will be useful for library users but, in addition, will be acceptable to the library's social/political environment. Many of the modern performance journals have fascinating but extreme content. Requesting sample issues freely should help avoid an unhappy reaction or, at the very least, prepare you for a possible reaction.

Basic Periodicals

Hs: *American Theatre, Dramatics, Live Design, New Theatre Quarterly, Theater;* Ga: *American Theatre, Entertainment Design, Modern Drama, New Theatre Quarterly, Stage Directions, Theater, Variety;* Ac: *American Theatre, Canadian Theatre Review, Comparative Drama, Live Design, Journal of Dramatic Theory and Criticism, Modern Drama, New Theatre Quarterly, Nineteenth Century Theatre and Film, PAJ, TDR, Theater, Theatre Journal.*

Basic Abstracts and Indexes

International Index to the Performing Arts (IIPA), Academic Index, Humanities Index, MLA International Bibliography.

5917. *AisleSay: the Internet magazine of stage reviews and opinion.* 1995. w. Ed(s): David Spencer. TheatreNet Enterprizes, 41 07 42nd St, Ste 4B, Long Island City, NY 11014. *Bk. rev.:* 1-2, 400-800 words. *Aud.:* Ga.

This 12-year-old, online-only magazine at aislesay.com includes reviews of theater productions from the United States. There is also some limited coverage of productions in Canada and Australia. The reviews are mostly similar to those found in newspapers or popular journals; they are concise, interesting, and timely. Most reviews are submitted during the first week of a play's run. Reviews are archived on secondary pages organized by city or country. The site also contains "Special Features," a group of articles, conference reports, and interviews. Any public library of substantial size or academic library that supports a theater program should point to this site.

5918. *American Drama.* [ISSN: 1061-0057] 1991. s-a. USD 25 (Individuals, USD 15). Ed(s): Yashdip Bains, Norma Jenckes. American Drama Institute, c/o English Department ML69, University of Cincinnati, Cincinnati, OH 45221-0069; american.drama@uc.edu. Illus., index. Sample. Refereed. Vol. ends: Spring. Online: Chadwyck-Healey Inc.; Gale; OCLC Online Computer Library Center, Inc.; ProQuest K-12 Learning Solutions; ProQuest LLC (Ann Arbor); H.W. Wilson. *Indexed:* AmHI, BrHumI, HumInd, IIPA, MLA-IB. *Bk. rev.:* Occasional. *Aud.:* Ac.

This journal, published and funded by the American Drama Institute at the University of Cincinnati, comes out two times per year and features articles on classic plays such as those of Thornton Wilder, Arthur Miller, Neil Simon, and Eugene O'Neill, as well as plays by contemporary playwrights like Tina Howe, Emily Mann, and Suzan-Lori Parks. Each issue features critical, scholarly articles on issues relating to the study of dramatic American literature, such as examination of trends, life and times of dramatists, and the development of drama as an art form. The "Playwright's Forum" section of the journal includes interviews with and essays by contemporary American dramatists. Book reviews are also included. The web site of the journal (www.uc.edu/americandrama) offers an index of contents since its first issue in 1993 as well as a link to a guide to resources (both scholarly and popular) that relate to American drama. College and university libraries with drama or comparative literature programs should seriously consider subscribing to this journal.

5919. *American Theatre: the monthly forum for news, features and opinion about the American theatre.* [ISSN: 8750-3255] 1984. 10x/yr. Individual members, USD 39.95; Students, USD 20. Ed(s): Sarah Hart, Jim O'Quinn. Theatre Communications Group, Inc., 520 Eighth Ave, 24th Fl, New York, NY 10018. Illus., adv. Sample. Circ: 24400. Vol. ends: Dec. Microform: PQC. Online: Chadwyck-Healey Inc.; EBSCO Publishing, EBSCO Host; Florida Center for Library Automation; Gale; Northern Light Technology, Inc.; OCLC Online Computer Library Center, Inc.; ProQuest K-12 Learning Solutions; ProQuest LLC (Ann Arbor). *Indexed:* ASIP, AmHI, BRI, CBRI, HumInd, IIPA, MASUSE, RI-1. *Bk. rev.:* Number varies, 400-1,200 words. *Aud.:* Ga, Ac.

This glossy commercial publication has appeared ten times per year since 1984. It includes articles, book reviews, production reviews, and, occasionally, new plays. The full-length plays are featured in roughly five issues per year (for example, both parts of Tony Kushner's *Angels in America* were first printed in this journal in June and July 1992, a full year before that play won the Tony Award). The web site of publisher Theatre Communications Group (at tcg.org) links to the full text of the feature articles in the current issue. This journal is an important addition to any college or university library, as well as any large public library that addresses the needs of dedicated theatergoers.

5920. *Asian Theatre Journal.* Supersedes: *Asian Theatre Reports.* [ISSN: 0742-5457] 1984. s-a. USD 60 (Individuals, USD 28). Ed(s): Kathy Foley. University of Hawaii Press, Journals Department, 2840 Kolowalu St, Honolulu, HI 96822-1888; uhpjourn@hawaii.edu; http://www.uhpress.hawaii.edu/. Illus., adv. Sample. Refereed. Circ: 500. Vol. ends: Fall. Online: Chadwyck-Healey Inc.; EBSCO Publishing, EBSCO Host; Gale; JSTOR (Web-based Journal Archive); Northern Light Technology, Inc.; OCLC Online Computer Library Center, Inc.; OhioLINK; Project MUSE; ProQuest K-12 Learning Solutions; ProQuest LLC (Ann Arbor); SwetsWise Online Content. Reprint: PSC. *Indexed:* AmHI, ArtHuCI, BAS, IBR, IBZ, IIPA, MLA-IB, RILM. *Bk. rev.:* 4-6, 1,000-1,500 words. *Aud.:* Ac.

Since 1984, the University of Hawaii Press has produced this English-language journal that focuses on contemporary and historical Asian theater through scholarly articles, original plays, play translations, and reviews. Back issues from its inception through 2003 are in JSTOR and more current issues (1999 through the present) are available through ProjectMUSE. New this year, it is now possible to subscribe to tables of contents and abstracts by RSS feed. See the web site at www.uhpress.hawaii.edu/journals/atj/index.html for more information. The journal is elegantly illustrated with both color and black-and-white photographs. Academic research libraries that support drama or East Asian literature programs should seriously consider owning this publication.

5921. *L'Avant-Scene. Theatre.* Former titles (until 1961): *L'Avant-Scene;* (until 1953): *Radiopera;* (until 1952): *Opera. Supplement Theatral.* [ISSN: 0045-1169] 1949. 20x/yr. EUR 163 domestic. Editions de l'Avant Scene, 6 rue Git-le-Coeur, Paris, 75006, France; astheatre@aol.com. Illus., adv. Sample. *Indexed:* ArtHuCI, IBR, IBZ, IIPA. *Aud.:* Ac.

Published since 1949, this French-language journal offers feature articles as well as a full play script by a major contemporary playwright in each issue. It also publishes notes on new plays, interviews, and reviews. Handsomely illustrated with production photographs, cartoons, and drawings, this journal is recommended for large university libraries or any smaller academic setting with a program that focuses on contemporary French literature.

5922. *Back Stage East: the performing arts weekly.* Formerly (until 2005): *Back Stage.* [ISSN: 1930-5966] 1960. w. USD 195. Ed(s): Sherry Eaker. Nielsen Business Publications, 770 Broadway, New York, NY 10003-9595; bmcomm@vnuinc.com; http://www.nielsenbusinessmedia.com. Illus., adv. Circ: 95011 Paid. Microform: PQC. Online: EBSCO Publishing, EBSCO Host; Factiva, Inc.; Florida Center for Library Automation; Gale; ProQuest K-12 Learning Solutions. *Indexed:* IIPA, LRI. *Aud.:* Ga, Ac, Sa.

This weekly trade publication is a significant resource for anyone working in theater, but for actors in particular. Each issue presents news stories, informative columns, reviews, previews of upcoming theater seasons, listings of agents, casting directors, rehearsal spaces, personal managers, acting coaches, and casting notices for stage, screen, television, and cabaret performers and staff. It is a sister publication to *Back Stage West* [ISSN: 1531-572X], and these journals share a companion web site at www.backstage.com/bso/index.jsp. This journal is recommended for academic libraries that support theater programs; but public and special libraries that serve populations of theatergoers should also consider this publication.

5923. *Bandwagon: the journal of the Circus Historical Society.* [ISSN: 0005-4968] 1956. bi-m. USD 40 domestic; USD 42 Canada; USD 44 elsewhere. Circus Historical Society, 1075 W Fifth Ave, Columbus, OH 43212. Illus., adv. Sample. Circ: 1400. Vol. ends: Nov/Dec. Online: Chadwyck-Healey Inc. *Indexed:* IIPA. *Bk. rev.:* Occasional. *Aud.:* Ac.

This bimonthly magazine published by the Circus Historical Society dedicates itself to the study of circus history. Most issues include between six and eight articles on topics such as reminiscences or biographies of former circus owners and performers. The pages are well illustrated from a variety of archival sources. This journal also periodically includes reviews of books, particular performances, and the circus season. A full index of articles can be found on the journal's web site at www.circushistory.org/#BAND. Libraries with a theater history collection or that service the needs of a broad performing arts audience should consider purchasing this journal.

5924. *Canadian Theatre Review.* [ISSN: 0315-0836] 1974. q. CND 105 domestic; USD 105 United States; USD 125 elsewhere. Ed(s): Phyllis Reynen. University of Toronto Press, Journals Division, 5201 Dufferin St, Toronto, ON M3H 5T8, Canada; journals@utpress.utoronto.ca;

http://www.utpjournals.com. Illus., index, adv. Sample. Circ: 800. Microform: MML. Online: EBSCO Publishing, EBSCO Host; Micromedia ProQuest. Reprint: PSC. *Indexed:* AmHI, ArtHuCI, BAS, CBCARef, CPerI, HumInd, IBR, IBZ, IIPA, MLA-IB, RILM. *Bk. rev.:* 2-4, 800-1,200 words. *Aud.:* Ac.

This journal is the major magazine of record for Canadian theater. It focuses mainly on contemporary and often avant-garde theater productions. Each issue is organized around a theme. Included in each issue are at least one complete play related to the issue theme, articles, and reviews. This interesting journal is well illustrated with production photographs. It is strongly recommended for any academic or research collection that focuses on contemporary theater and drama.

5925. *Comparative Drama.* [ISSN: 0010-4078] 1967. q. USD 40 (Individuals, USD 20). Ed(s): Eve Salisbury, Anthony Ellis. Western Michigan University, Dept. of English, 1903 W Michigan Ave, Kalamazoo, MI 49008-5331. Illus., index. Sample. Refereed. Circ: 900 Paid. Vol. ends: Winter. Microform: PQC. Online: Chadwyck-Healey Inc.; Florida Center for Library Automation; Gale; OCLC Online Computer Library Center, Inc.; ProQuest K-12 Learning Solutions; ProQuest LLC (Ann Arbor); H.W. Wilson. *Indexed:* ABS&EES, AmHI, ArtHuCI, BAS, BRI, CBRI, HumInd, IBR, IBZ, IIPA, MLA-IB, RILM. *Bk. rev.:* 6-8, 500-1,500 words. *Aud.:* Ac.

The focus of this quarterly journal from Western Michigan University is on drama and theater from a literary point of view. It is scholarly in nature and gives equal treatment to the various genres of drama (ancient, medieval, Renaissance, and modern). Sometimes an entire issue will be centered on a single theme, such as "Tragedy's Insights." Its coverage is broad in terms of time period and geography. Shakespeare is covered so frequently that the web site has a separate "sub-index" for those articles. The journal's web site at http://www.wmich.edu/compdr/ now features abstracts of every article since 2000. This is an important scholarly journal for college or university library collections.

5926. *Contemporary Theatre Review (Softback).* [ISSN: 1048-6801] Reprint: PSC.
Indexed: AmHI, ArtHuCI, BrHumI, IBR, IBZ, IIPA. *Aud.:* Ga, Sa.

First published in 1991, this journal examines trends in contemporary theater and explores how "theatrical vocabularies are shifting to accommodate and reflect the dynamics and/or tensions within global and local cultures." It appears four times per year, with one issue being entirely devoted to a particular theme or type of theater. This past year's special issue is on "Catalan Theatre 1975–2006."

5927. *CurtainUp: the Internet magazine of theater news, reviews and features.* 1997. 3x/w. Ed(s): Elyse Sommer. CurtainUp, PO Box 751133, Forest Hills, NY 11375; esommer@pipeline.com; http://www.curtainup.com. *Aud.:* Ga, Ac, Sa.

This is a wonderful source for reviews and information about current (and near-past) theatrical productions. Its richest areas are in the New York and Berkshires productions, reflecting the main editor's location. But there are several well-known contributing editors, so regular reports for productions in Toronto, London, and Washington, D.C., also appear. The site's organization is very navigable and user-friendly. There is also a subscription service through which individual readers will be notified of changes to the site. Any public or academic library with a theatergoing clientele should include this on its list of web sites.

5928. *Dramatics: the magazine for students and teachers of theatre.* Formerly: *Dramatics-Dramatic Curtain.* [ISSN: 0012-5989] 1929. 9x/yr. USD 24 domestic; USD 34 Canada; USD 38 elsewhere. Ed(s): Don Corathers. Educational Theatre Association, 2343 Auburn Ave, Cincinnati, Cincinnati, OH 45219-2815; dcorathers@edta.org; http://www.edta.org/. Illus., index, adv. Sample. Circ: 39000 Paid. Vol. ends: Dec. Microform: PQC. *Indexed:* AmHI, IIPA. *Aud.:* Hs, Ac.

This is one of the few publications that are specifically directed at the interests of the collegiate drama student. Published nine times a year (September through June) by the Educational Theatre Association, this journal presents articles that provide practical information on acting, directing, and design that will be of use to drama students and educators. This journal's content ranges from technique articles, such as advice on auditioning from casting directors to the full text of short plays. In addition, there is a great deal of information on internships, summer employment, collegiate and institute dramatic programs, and auditions. Colleges and universities that support a drama program should consider this publication. Also, high school libraries with active theater programs might consider its purchase.

5929. *The Dramatist.* Former titles (until 1998): *Dramatists Guild Quarterly; Dramatists Bulletin.* [ISSN: 1551-7683] 1964. bi-m. Free to members. Dramatists Guild, Inc., 1501 Broadway, Ste 701, New York, NY 10036; http://www.dramatistsguild.com. Illus., adv. Sample. Circ: 8200. Vol. ends: Winter. *Indexed:* IIPA. *Aud.:* Ac, Sa.

This magazine is the official publication of The Dramatists Guild of America, the professional association of playwrights, composers, and lyricists. It usually contains eight to ten articles; these articles may contain discussions of some aspect of playwriting, interviews with well-known playwrights, the political and social opinions of playwrights as they affect their writings, or discussions of theatrical companies. There is also a "Dramatists Diary," which lists plays in production around the country, newly published plays and recordings, and recently published books by guild members. This magazine has great value for any library that supports the needs of a playwriting, music, or creative writing program.

5930. *Early Theatre: a journal associated with the Records of Early English Drama.* Formerly (until 1997): *Records of Early English Drama Newsletter.* [ISSN: 1206-9078] 1976. 2x/yr. CND 55 (Individuals, CND 35). Ed(s): Helen Ostovich. Centre for Reformation and Renaissance Studies, 71 Queen's Park Cresc E, Toronto, ON M5S 1K7, Canada; crss.publications@utoronto.ca; http://www.crrs.ca. Refereed. Circ: 200 Paid and controlled. *Indexed:* AmH&L, CBCARef, HistAb, IIPA, MLA-IB, RILM. *Aud.:* Ac, Sa.

This peer-reviewed scholarly journal began as an annual in 1998 but has been published twice a year since 2002. It is published by the Centre for Reformation and Renaissance Studies at the University of Toronto. Its focus is research in the criticism and history of medieval or early modern drama in England, Scotland, Ireland, and Wales. Occasionally, articles relate to other parts of Europe, or "[to] parts of the world where English or European travellers, traders, and colonizers observed performances by other peoples." It is recommended for academic libraries that support a theater or literature program.

5931. *Figura: zeitschrift fuer theater und spiel mit figuren.* Formerly (until 1992): *Puppenspiel und Puppenspieler.* [ISSN: 1021-3244] 1960. 4x/yr. CHF 36 domestic; CHF 40 foreign. Ed(s): Elke Krafka. U N I M A Suisse, Postfach 2328, Winterthur, 8401, Switzerland. Illus., adv. Sample. Circ: 1150. *Bk. rev.:* 2-5, 200-400 words. *Aud.:* Ac, Sa.

Appearing four times a year since 1960, this unique journal contains broad international coverage of the puppetry "scene." Published in Switzerland, the text is primarily in French and German, but there is nothing else comparable to it in English. It includes performance reviews, festival announcements, and general news and notes. In addition, it is well illustrated and often contains technical articles that are well diagrammed and therefore somewhat language-independent. Only academic libraries that address the concerns of a drama or theater history program should consider its purchase.

5932. *Journal of American Drama and Theatre.* [ISSN: 1044-937X] 1989. 3x/yr. USD 15 domestic; USD 20 foreign. Ed(s): Vera Mowry Roberts, Daniel Gerould. Martin E. Segal Theatre Center, The Graduate School and University Center, The City University of New York, New York, NY 10016-4309; mestc@gc.cuny.edu; http://web.gc.cuny.edu/mestc/. Illus., adv. Refereed. Circ: 3400 Paid. Vol. ends: Fall. *Indexed:* IIPA. *Aud.:* Ac, Sa.

This scholarly journal presents research on American playwrights, plays, and the American contemporary theater scene in general. It is published three times a year (winter, spring, and fall) by The Martin E. Segal Theatre Center (MESTC) at The Graduate Center, CUNY, a nonprofit center for theater, dance, and film affiliated with CUNY's Ph.D. Program in Theatre. Articles tend to be interdisciplinary in nature. In particular, they examine theater from an anthropological, historical, or sociological point of view. A full table of contents for every issue since the first in 1989 can be found on the journal's web page at http://web.gc.cuny.edu/mestc/journals/JADT. Best suited for large academic collections or special libraries that address the needs of a theater community.

5933. *Journal of Dramatic Theory and Criticism.* [ISSN: 0888-3203] 1986. s-a. USD 32 (Individuals, USD 27). Ed(s): Iris Smith Fischer, John Gronbeck Tedesco. Journal of Dramatic Theory and Criticism, Hall Center for the Humanities, 211 Watkins Home, Lawrence, KS 66045-2967. Illus., adv. Sample. Refereed. Circ: 426 Paid. Vol. ends: Spring. *Indexed:* ABS&EES, IIPA, MLA-IB. *Bk. rev.:* 8-12, 800-1,500 words. *Aud.:* Ac.

This unique journal is primarily focused on dramatic theory and issues as they are expressed in production. In particular, its focus is on "new theories and methodologies pertinent to performance and performance texts and performance criticism which attempts to yield new insights into theatrical works." It is published twice each year by the Department of Theatre & Film and The Joyce and Elizabeth Hall Center for the Humanities at the University of Kansas. The six to ten scholarly articles are substantive and international in coverage. Articles include textual analysis and commentary on theater as performance. This journal also includes very detailed international performance reviews and excellent book reviews. Very recently, a new editor, Iris Smith Fischer, has been appointed, taking over from John Gronbeck-Tedesco, who had been editor since the journal's inception in 1986. Academic libraries that support an active theater program should consider purchasing this journal.

5934. *Latin American Theatre Review: a journal devoted to the theatre and drama of Spanish & Portuguese America.* [ISSN: 0023-8813] 1967. s-a. USD 55 (Individuals, USD 22). Ed(s): George W Woodyard. Center of Latin American Studies, 107 Lippincott Hall, University of Kansas, Lawrence, KS 66045; latamst@ukans.edu; http://www2.ku.edu/~latamst/latr.htm. Illus., index, adv. Sample. Refereed. Circ: 1200. *Indexed:* AmHI, ArtHuCI, HAPI, IBR, IBZ, IIPA, MLA-IB, RILM. *Bk. rev.:* 15-25, 500-1,000 words. *Aud.:* Ac.

Published two times a year by the Center of Latin American Studies at the University of Kansas, this scholarly journal presents 15–20 articles per issue on festivals, theater scenes, and historical issues of the Spanish- and Portuguese-language theater worlds in the Americas. It also includes a broad range of reviews that cover performances, plays, books, and conferences. The text of the articles may be in English, Spanish, or Portuguese. Each issue also has an excellent source bibliography. Any academic or research library with a theater history collection or Hispanic literature collection should consider the purchase of this title.

5935. *Live Design.* Formerly (until Dec. 2005): *Entertainment Design;* Which superseded (in 1999): *T C I (Theatre Crafts International);* Which was formed by the merger of (1967-1992): *Theatre Crafts; Theatre Crafts International;* Which incorporated: *Cue International;* Which was formerly: *Cue Technical Theatre Review.* [ISSN: 1559-2359] 1992. 12x/yr. USD 50 domestic; USD 62 Canada; USD 80 elsewhere. Ed(s): Mark Newman. Prism Business Media, 249 W 17th St, New York, NY 10011; inquiries@prismb2b.com; http://www.prismbusinessmedia.com. Illus., adv. Sample. Circ: 16300 Paid. Microform: PQC. Online: Chadwyck-Healey Inc.; EBSCO Publishing, EBSCO Host; Florida Center for Library Automation; Gale; LexisNexis; OCLC Online Computer Library Center, Inc.; ProQuest K-12 Learning Solutions; ProQuest LLC (Ann Arbor); H.W. Wilson. *Indexed:* ArtHuCI, ArtInd, BRI, CBRI, DAAI, FLI, IIPA, LRI, MASUSE, RGPR, RILM. *Bk. rev.:* 4-6, 400-600 words. *Aud.:* Ac, Sa.

Formerly known as *Entertainment Design,* this magazine's focus is the art and technology of the entertainment business for theater production professionals. It includes news columns, business information, special reports, and articles on the design of particular productions (both theatrical and some film). It is handsomely and extensively illustrated with production and product photographs. Its web version (at livedesignonline.com) contains much of the print back to 1999, although the online version lacks some of the illustrative materials available in the print version. The print publication would be an excellent addition to any library with theatrical production collections.

5936. *London Theatre Guide.* 1995. w. Ed(s): Darren Dalglish. London Theatre Guide, 12 East 86th St, New York, NY 10028. *Aud.:* Ga.

This well-maintained web site at www.londontheatre.co.uk is an excellent place for quick lookups of London productions. This service has been online since 1995, and its editor, Darren Dalglish, both provides selections of reviews from other well-known sources and writes many reviews himself. There are many newsworthy bits about the London theater scene in general, as well as ticket sources, London maps, tours and walks, etc. While the material is not in-depth, it is an excellent and simple starting place for anyone looking for information on London theatrical performances. *New York Theatre Guide,* its sister publication, provides the same treatment for the New York theater scene.

5937. *Modern Drama: world drama from 1850 to the present.* 1958. q. CND 60 domestic; USD 70 foreign. Ed(s): Alan Ackerman. University of Toronto Press, Journals Division, 5201 Dufferin St, Toronto, ON M3H 5T8, Canada; journals@utpress.utoronto.ca; http://www.utpjournals.com. Illus., index, adv. Sample. Refereed. Circ: 2000. Vol. ends: Winter. Microform: MML. Online: EBSCO Publishing, EBSCO Host; Florida Center for Library Automation; Gale; Micromedia ProQuest; OCLC Online Computer Library Center, Inc.; Project MUSE; ProQuest K-12 Learning Solutions; ProQuest LLC (Ann Arbor); SwetsWise Online Content. Reprint: PSC. *Indexed:* ABS&EES, AmHI, ArtHuCI, CBCARef, CPerI, FLI, HumInd, IBR, IBZ, IIPA, MLA-IB, RI-1, RILM. *Bk. rev.:* 8-12, 500-1,000 words. *Aud.:* Ac.

One of the oldest scholarly modern theater journals, *Modern Drama* has been published quarterly by the University of Toronto since 1958. There are also eight to ten extensive and interesting book reviews in each issue and an annual bibliography in the summer issue. Volumes from 2005 to the present are available electronically via ProjectMUSE. This journal would be well placed in any academic library collection that supports contemporary drama and literature programs.

5938. *N T Q. New Theatre Quarterly.* Formerly (until 1985): *T Q. Theatre Quarterly.* [ISSN: 0266-464X] 1971. q. GBP 106. Ed(s): Clive Barker, Maria Shevtsova. Cambridge University Press, The Edinburgh Bldg, Shaftesbury Rd, Cambridge, CB2 2RU, United Kingdom; journals@cambridge.org; http://www.journals.cambridge.org. Illus., adv. Sample. Vol. ends: Nov. Microform: PQC. Online: Pub.; EBSCO Publishing, EBSCO Host; OCLC Online Computer Library Center, Inc.; OhioLINK; SwetsWise Online Content. Reprint: PSC. *Indexed:* AmH&L, AmHI, ArtHuCI, HistAb, HumInd, IIPA, MLA-IB, RILM. *Bk. rev.:* 15-20, 200-400 words. *Aud.:* Ac.

This journal addresses issues of modern performance and dramaturgy. It also claims to provide a forum "where prevailing dramatic assumptions can be subjected to vigorous critical questioning." Its prose style is not stodgy, however; rather, it is interesting and eye-catching and therefore more widely accessible than that of some academic journals. *NTQ* usually contains eight to ten scholarly articles that are international in coverage. Book reviews are generally shorter than those of other academic journals, but there are a good number of them. The most current issue is available freely on the publisher's web site at http://journals.cambridge.org/action/displayJournal?jid=NTQ. This publication is recommended for academic libraries and special libraries that address modern performance issues.

5939. *New York Theatre Guide.* d. Ed(s): Alan Bird. New York Theatre Guide, 12 E 86th St, New York, NY 10028; listings@newyorktheatreguide.com; http://www.newyorktheatreguide.com. *Aud.:* Ga.

The sister web-publication to the *London Theatre Guide Online,* this site provides everything you need to know about the current New York theater scene. Features include the latest casting and coming productions news, links to reviews of both Broadway and off-Broadway productions, production plot synopses, seating plans of major theaters, maps of New York, and, of course, links to purchasing tickets. This is the best place to find out with a minimum of clicking what all the critics thought of *Spamalot* and how many paychecks it will cost you to buy tickets.

5940. *Nineteenth Century Theatre and Film.* Former titles (until 2000): *Nineteenth Century Theatre;* (until 1987): *Nineteenth Century Theatre Research;* Which incorporates (1976-1979): *N C T R Newsletter.* [ISSN: 1748-3727] 1973. s-a. GBP 75 (Individuals, GBP 27). Ed(s): David Mayer, Viv Gardner. Manchester University Press, Oxford Rd, Manchester, M13 9NR, United Kingdom; http://www.manchesteruniversitypress.co.uk/. Illus., adv. Sample. Circ: 400. Microform: PQC. Online: EBSCO Publishing, EBSCO Host; SwetsWise Online Content. *Indexed:* AmH&L, AmHI, ArtHuCI, HistAb, IIPA, MLA-IB. *Bk. rev.:* 4-5, 1,500-3,000 words. *Aud.:* Ac.

This journal contains interesting materials not available elsewhere, and it is well covered in indexing services. Issues appear two times per year and contain two or three feature articles that cover nineteenth-century performance issues in the United States, Western Europe, and Russia. This journal's articles are not limited to theater; all performance forms may be covered, film in particular. The editors define "film" in this context as including "'pre-cinema' optical and narrative forms, 'silent' motion pictures, and illusions." The journal contains a notes section that may list information on databases or other resources. Its book reviews are substantial and informative. Articles are available in full-text via Chadwyck Healey's Literature Online database from 2002. Any academic library collection that covers nineteenth-century literature or intellectual history would be well served by including this journal.

5941. *O O B R.* m. Free. Ed(s): John Chatterton. O O B R, c/o Cynthia Leathers, Mng. Ed., 341 W 24th St, Ste 20F, New York, NY 10011. *Aud.:* Ga, Sa.

This interesting e-journal collects both listing information and reviews for productions done off-Broadway, far off-Broadway, and in out-of-the-mainstream theaters of New York. The site is a good one, in terms of both design and content. In keeping with more up-to-date design, it has few graphics and no frames, and it loads easily and quickly. New York's centrality and importance to the American theater world will make this site of interest to any library with a theatergoing constituency.

5942. *P A J: a journal of performance and art.* Formerly (until 1998): *Performing Arts Journal.* [ISSN: 1520-281X] 1976. 3x/yr. USD 115 print & online eds. (Individuals, USD 32 print & online eds.). Ed(s): Bonnie Marranca. M I T Press, 238 Main St., Ste. 500, Cambridge, MA 02142; journals-info@mit.edu; http://mitpress.mit.edu. Illus., adv. Sample. Refereed. Circ: 1200 Paid. Vol. ends: Sep. Online: EBSCO Publishing, EBSCO Host; Gale; IngentaConnect; JSTOR (Web-based Journal Archive); OCLC Online Computer Library Center, Inc.; OhioLINK; Project MUSE; SwetsWise Online Content. *Indexed:* ABM, ABS&EES, AmHI, ArtHuCI, BRI, CBRI, FLI, HumInd, IBR, IBZ, IIPA, MLA-IB, RILM. *Bk. rev.:* Occasional. *Aud.:* Ac, Sa.

Published by MIT Press three times a year since 1976, this journal covers contemporary international performance: dance, theater, and performance art. Each issue contains eight to ten articles, performance reviews, and opinion pieces. Sometimes an issue may have a theme. The journal often contains reviews of new works in theater, dance, film, and opera, and occasionally book reviews. Its illustrations are extensive and fascinating. Issues of *PAJ* from 1996 to the present are available online via ProjectMUSE. Recommended for academic or research libraries where contemporary and avant-garde performance artistry is studied.

5943. *Performance Research: a journal of the performing arts.* [ISSN: 1352-8165] 1996. q. GBP 323 print & online eds. Ed(s): Richard Gough. Routledge, 4 Park Square, Milton Park, Abingdon, OX14 4RN, United Kingdom; http://www.routledge.co.uk. Illus. Sample. Refereed. Reprint: PSC. *Indexed:* ABM, AmHI, ArtHuCI, BrHumI, IIPA, RILM. *Bk. rev.:* Occasional. *Aud.:* Ac, Sa.

This scholarly journal contains articles that look at performance from an interdisciplinary, sometimes historic, perspective. Each quarterly issue contains articles, documents, interviews, and reviews, as well as illustrations and original artworks. The content can be fascinating and sometimes extreme in nature, but it is a fair representation of the far edge of avant-garde performance art. It also contains occasional book reviews. Academic and research collections that support contemporary theatrical research should own this title.

5944. *Playbill On-Line.* 1994. d. Playbill Inc., 525 7th Ave., Rm. 1801, New York, NY 10018-4918; http://www.playbill.com. Adv. *Aud.:* Ga.

Anyone who has been in an American commercial theater is familiar with the *Playbill* program, which gives the cast, the number of acts, intermissions, and background on the play. In addition, it is chock-full of advertisements, usually of a local nature. The coverage in the web site is not dramatically different, except that it is all in one place, and therefore a very useful tool for planning for visits to New York City. There is some non–New York coverage, including a little international, but that coverage is spotty, and only the New York coverage can be depended on for completeness. There are also feature articles, gossip, a chat room, casting calls, and links to purchase tickets. This web site is a must for New York theatergoers, particularly for the up-to-date schedules.

5945. *Playbill (Theatre Edition): the national magazine of the theatre.* [ISSN: 0032-146X] 1884. m. Free. Ed(s): Robert Simonson, Judy Samelson. Playbill Inc., 525 7th Ave., Rm. 1801, New York, NY 10018-4918; http://www.playbill.com. Illus., adv. Sample. Circ: 2785000. *Indexed:* IIPA. *Aud.:* Ga.

This monthly magazine is the longest-running publication about theater performance in the United States. This edition contains information for many plays, general articles on the theater, backstage topics, and fashion, as well as restaurant ads. The web site at playbill.com will be a sufficient enough resource for most libraries, but libraries that serve populations of theatergoers should consider this publication, as should those with theater history collections.

5946. *Plays: the drama magazine for young people.* [ISSN: 0032-1540] 1941. m. Oct-May; except Jan.-Feb. combined. USD 39 domestic; USD 49 Canada; USD 59 elsewhere. Ed(s): Sylvia K Burack. Plays Magazine, PO Box 600160, Newton, MA 02460; lpreston@playsmag.com. Illus., index, adv. Sample. Circ: 15000 Paid. Vol. ends: Dec. Microform: PQC. Online: EBSCO Publishing, EBSCO Host; Florida Center for Library Automation; Gale; Northern Light Technology, Inc.; ProQuest K-12 Learning Solutions. *Indexed:* CPerI, ICM, MASUSE. *Bk. rev.:* 10-15, 50-100 words. *Aud.:* Ems, Hs, Ga.

The classic magazine *Plays* continues to provide an essential resource to school drama programs everywhere. It contains between 9 and 12 short plays, with subjects ranging from historic to holidays, to skits and comedies, to a dramatized classics. The plays are arranged by general grade level (Junior and Senior High, Middle and Lower Grade), and each contains production notes that include casting and staging suggestions. Editor Elizabeth Preston strives to include plays "that share stories about friendship, honesty, [and] respect for diversity, and convey messages that will inspire, encourage, and support young people." The plays are not copyright-free, but any current subscriber may produce copies for the cast and produce the play royalty-free. This magazine should be included in the library of any school with a drama program or club. It should also be included in public libraries' children's collections.

5947. *Research in Drama Education.* [ISSN: 1356-9783] 1996. 3x/yr. GBP 297 print & online eds. Ed(s): Joe A Winston, Helen Nicholson. Routledge, 4 Park Sq, Milton Park, Abingdon, OX14 4RN, United Kingdom; info@routledge.co.uk; http://www.routledge.co.uk. Illus., adv. Refereed. Vol. ends: Aug. Online: EBSCO Publishing, EBSCO Host; Gale; IngentaConnect; Northern Light Technology, Inc.; OCLC Online Computer Library Center, Inc.; ProQuest LLC (Ann Arbor); SwetsWise Online Content. Reprint: PSC. *Indexed:* BrEdI, ERIC, FR, MLA-IB. *Bk. rev.:* 4-6, 800-1,500 words. *Aud.:* Ac.

This refereed scholarly journal in the field of educational drama and applied theater appears three times per year. It covers the various uses of drama and theater in education, youth and children's theaters, drama education, and research in community theater. Although primarily directed at youth or high school–level teachers of drama, it is a valuable resource for drama students intending to teach. Each issue contains six to ten articles. Issues also include book reviews and, frequently, abstracts of dissertations. Any academic library with a drama/theater program or an education program should consider purchasing this publication.

5948. *Restoration & Eighteenth Century Theatre Research.* [ISSN: 0034-5822] 1962. s-a. Ed(s): Jessica Munns. Restoration & Eighteenth Century Theatre Research, English Dept, University of Denver, Sturm Hull, Denver, CO 80208; http://www.du.edu/english/pamplet.htm. Illus. Refereed. *Indexed:* AmH&L, HistAb, IIPA, MLA-IB. *Bk. rev.:* 1-2, 1,000 words. *Aud.:* Ac.

This small academic journal's mission is to publish articles on Restoration drama. Each issue includes four to six articles that cover the plays, playwrights, and performers of that era. It is a highly specialized journal. Given the popularity of that era for both study and performance, this journal should be considered by any academic library with a strong English literature program.

5949. *Revue d'Histoire du Theatre.* Formerly (until 1996): *Revue de la Societe d'Histoire du Theatre.* [ISSN: 1291-2530] 1948. q. EUR 57 domestic; EUR 60 in Europe; EUR 63 elsewhere. Societe d'Histoire du Theatre, BnF - 58 rue de Richelieu, Paris, 75084 Cedex 02, France; info@sht.asso.fr; http://www.sht.asso.fr. Illus., index, adv. Sample. Refereed. *Indexed:* AmH&L, ArtHuCI, FR, HistAb, IBR, IBZ, IIPA, MLA-IB, RILM, SSCI. *Bk. rev.:* 4-8, 500-1,500 words. *Aud.:* Ac.

This French-language journal is the main publication of the Societe d'Histoire du Theatre in France. Each issue contains four to six scholarly articles on the history of theater and the analysis of drama. The focus is predominantly on French theater, but articles do appear on the drama of other Western European countries. This publication would be best placed in theater history collections and university libraries with French literature collections.

5950. *Shakespeare Bulletin: a journal of performance, criticism, and scholarship.* Incorporates (1976-1992): *Shakespeare on Film Newsletter;* Formerly: *New York Shakespeare Society Bulletin.* [ISSN: 0748-2558] 1982. q. USD 90. Ed(s): Andrew James Harley. The Johns Hopkins University Press, 2715 N Charles St, Baltimore, MD 21218-4363; http://www.press.jhu.edu. Illus., adv. Refereed. Circ: 1000 Paid. Vol. ends: Nov. Online: EBSCO Publishing, EBSCO Host; Gale. Reprint: PSC. *Indexed:* AmHI, BEL&L, IIPA, MLA-IB. *Bk. rev.:* 5-10, 600-1,000 words. *Aud.:* Ac, Sa.

This scholarly publication from Johns Hopkins University Press attempts to cover information on all Shakespearean performances, both live and on film, throughout the United States. It also contains some information on English-speaking productions from Canada, Great Britain, and other parts of the world. Each quarterly issue includes two to four articles on Shakespeare, as well as extensive performance, film, and book reviews. *The Shakespeare Bulletin* is not to be confused with its sister publication, *Shakespeare Quarterly,* which focuses on Shakespeare's writing as literature rather than as theater. Any academic library with a theater or English literature collection should consider purchasing this journal. In addition, any library that addresses the needs of theater companies that routinely perform Shakespearean drama should purchase it.

5951. *Show Music: the musical theatre magazine.* [ISSN: 8755-9560] 1981. q. USD 23 domestic; USD 35 foreign. Ed(s): Max O Preeo. Goodspeed Opera House, P O Box 466, East Haddam, CT 06423-0466; subscriptions@showmusic.org; http://www.goodspeed.org. Adv. Circ: 5200 Paid. *Indexed:* MusicInd. *Aud.:* Ga, Sa.

This interesting consumer-style magazine is published by the Goodspeed Opera House in East Haddam, Connecticut. However, its coverage goes far beyond the Goodspeed's top-notch productions. Each issue contains three to five feature articles, interviews, and production reviews of musical theater throughout the United States, with a small amount of coverage devoted to other English-language productions worldwide. Musical theater is a form of performance that is generally ignored by the more "serious" publications, but one that deserves more attention given its continued popularity. Any public library that serves a theatergoing population or any performance or music library should consider purchasing this title.

5952. *Slavic and East European Performance.* Formerly (until 1991): *Soviet and East European Performance.* [ISSN: 1069-2800] 1981. 3x/yr. Ed(s): Marvin Carlson. Martin E. Segal Theatre Center, The Graduate School and University Center, The City University of New York, New York, NY 10016-4309; mestc@gc.cuny.edu; http://web.gc.cuny.edu/mestc/. *Indexed:* ABS&EES. *Aud.:* Ac.

This journal brings English-speaking readers lively, authoritative accounts of drama, theater, and film happening in the countries of Eastern Europe and the Commonwealth of Independent States. The journal includes features on important new plays in performance, archival documents, innovative productions, significant revivals, emerging artists, and the latest in film. It offers in-depth interviews and overviews. Each issue contains performance reviews, production information, and articles on both current and historic topics. This journal would be well-placed in any academic or research library that serves the needs of theater communities interested in political or dissident performance.

5953. *Stage Directions.* [ISSN: 1047-1901] 1988. m. USD 26. Macfadden Performing Arts Media, LLC., 110 William St, 23rd Fl., New York, NY 10038; http://dancemedia.com/. Illus., adv. Sample. Circ: 20000 Paid. *Indexed:* MASUSE. *Bk. rev.:* 2-3, 400 words. *Aud.:* Ga, Ac.

This is the only U.S. publication that tries to address the specific needs of "regional, academic, and community" theaters, although the best audience would probably be community and small academic theater groups. Each issue has six to ten articles on such technical aspects of performance production as cost-saving ideas, dramatic effects and techniques, and computer control issues. There is also supplier information, articles describing particular theaters and their companies, columns on computers and networked resources, and book reviews. This magazine's online version at www.stage-directions.com includes the table of contents for each issue published since 1988 and links to selected articles online. It is a useful resource for any public library with an active community theater or any academic library that supports a drama program.

5954. *Studies in Theatre and Performance.* [ISSN: 1468-2761] 2000. 3x/yr. GBP 210 print & online eds. Ed(s): Peter Thomson. Intellect Ltd., The Mill, Parnall Rd, Fishponds, Bristol, BS16 3JG, United Kingdom; info@intellectbooks.com; http://www.intellectbooks.com. Refereed. *Indexed:* AmHI, BrHumI, MLA-IB. *Bk. rev.:* 6-8, 600-800 words. *Aud.:* Ac.

This tri-annual scholarly journal focuses primarily on British and European productions. The intent of the journal is a practical one: to share methods and the results of practical research. Refereed articles cover a range of topics such as debates on issues related to theater practice and examinations of experiments in teaching and performance. Any academic library with a theater and/or performance art program should consider its purchase.

5955. *T D & T: Theatre Design & Technology.* Formerly: *Theatre Design and Technology.* [ISSN: 1052-6765] 1965. q. Membership, USD 60. Ed(s): David Rodger. U S Institute for Theatre Technology, Inc., 6443 Ridings Rd, Syracuse, NY 13206-1111. Illus., adv. Sample. Circ: 4500. Vol. ends: Sep. Microform: PQC. Online: Chadwyck-Healey Inc.; EBSCO Publishing, EBSCO Host; OCLC Online Computer Library Center, Inc.; H.W. Wilson. *Indexed:* ABS&EES, API, ArtInd, IIPA. *Bk. rev.:* 3-5, 200-600 words. *Aud.:* Ac, Sa.

This trade magazine is directed at professional theater and production designers. It contains articles on theater design, production design, and particular production or technical issues. It also often profiles particular designers or architects. There are columns with product reviews, book reviews, and a listing of the contents of international design journals. The magazine's web site at www.usitt.org/tdt.index provides an excellent searchable index of the entire contents since 1990. In addition to special collections, this journal would be well placed in any academic library with theatrical production or architectural programs.

5956. *T D R: the journal of performance studies.* Former titles (until 1988): *The Drama Review;* (until 1968): *T D R;* (until 1967): *Tulane Drama Review;* (until 1957): *Carleton Drama Review.* [ISSN: 1054-2043] 1955. q. USD 184 print & online eds. (Individuals, USD 48 print & online eds.). Ed(s): Richard Schechner. M I T Press, 238 Main St., Ste. 500, Cambridge, MA 02142; journals-info@mit.edu; http://mitpress.mit.edu. Illus., index, adv. Sample. Circ: 5000 Paid. Vol. ends: Winter. Microform: PQC. Online: EBSCO Publishing, EBSCO

Host; Florida Center for Library Automation; Gale; IngentaConnect; JSTOR (Web-based Journal Archive); OCLC Online Computer Library Center, Inc.; OhioLINK; Project MUSE; SwetsWise Online Content; H.W. Wilson. *Indexed:* ABS&EES, AmHI, ArtHuCI, BAS, BRI, CBRI, HumInd, IBR, IBZ, IIPA, MLA-IB, RILM. *Bk. rev.:* 6-10, 400-2,000 words. *Aud.:* Ac.

MIT Press for the Tisch School at New York University publishes this quintessential publication on theater production, history, and criticism. Each quarterly issue offers articles on a broad range of topics and country of origin. There are extensive reviews and descriptions of contemporary and often avant-garde performances with photographic illustrations, although be warned that some readers may find the topics overly politicized and socially shocking. The journal's book reviews are substantial and thought-provoking. Issues from 1999 to the present can be accessed electronically via subscription to Project MUSE. This journal should be included in any university collection and in any library that addresses the needs of contemporary performance artists.

5957. Theater Heute. [ISSN: 0040-5507] 1960. m. EUR 129 domestic (Students, EUR 90). Ed(s): Franz Wille. Friedrich Berlin Verlagsgesellschaft mbH, Reinhardtstr 29, Berlin, 10117, Germany; verlag@friedrichberlin.de; http://www.friedrichberlin.de. Illus., adv. Sample. Circ: 14500 Controlled. *Indexed:* ArtHuCI, IBR, IBZ, IIPA, RILM. *Aud.:* Ac, Sa.

Although almost entirely in German, this theater magazine is included in this list of important publications for theater studies because it is Germany's largest and most influential theater magazine, and extremely important for the study of Western European theater. Its companion web site at theaterheute.de offers an English version of a great deal of the print publication's current issue content. There are news notes, information on German theater personalities, gorgeous photographs, and usually a full play script. Any academic library collection that supports interest either in world theater or in modern German drama or literature should consider its purchase.

5958. Theater (New Haven). Formerly (until vol.8, no.2 & 3, 1976): *Yale - Theatre.* [ISSN: 0161-0775] 1968. 3x/yr. USD 108 (Individuals, USD 30). Ed(s): Tom Sellar, Wendy Weckwerth. Duke University Press, 905 W Main St, Ste 18 B, Durham, NC 27701; subscriptions@dukeupress.edu; http://www.dukeupress.edu. Illus., index, adv. Sample. Refereed. Circ: 1150 Paid. Microform: PQC. Online: EBSCO Publishing, EBSCO Host; Gale; HighWire Press; OCLC Online Computer Library Center, Inc.; OhioLINK; Project MUSE; SwetsWise Online Content. Reprint: PSC. *Indexed:* AmHI, ArtHuCI, FLI, IIPA, MLA-IB, RILM. *Bk. rev.:* 2-3, 600-1,800 words. *Aud.:* Ac.

This scholarly journal is published three times a year by the venerable Yale School of Drama by the Duke University Press. Its articles very much reflect the social politics of contemporary theater thinkers, artistic directors, and writers. Each issue contains four to six articles, usually organized around a theme. The editors try to include at least one new "pathbreaking" play per issue, and some issues contain several. The articles are often illustrated with what are sometimes breathtaking production photographs. The Duke UP site offers free searchable access to its contents since 2000 and links to the full-text via subscription. This magazine is an invaluable part of any significant academic theater journal collection and is also recommended for academic libraries and special libraries that address modern performance issues.

5959. Theatre Journal (Baltimore). Formerly (until 1979): *Educational Theatre Journal.* [ISSN: 0192-2882] 1949. q. USD 135. Ed(s): Jean Graham-Jones, Jean Graham Jones. The Johns Hopkins University Press, 2715 N Charles St, Baltimore, MD 21218-4363; myq@press.jhu.edu; http://www.press.jhu.edu. Illus., adv. Sample. Refereed. Circ: 2773 Paid. Vol. ends: Dec. Microform: PQC. Online: Chadwyck-Healey Inc.; EBSCO Publishing, EBSCO Host; Florida Center for Library Automation; Gale; JSTOR (Web-based Journal Archive); OCLC Online Computer Library Center, Inc.; OhioLINK; Project MUSE; ProQuest LLC (Ann Arbor); SwetsWise Online Content. Reprint: PSC. *Indexed:* ABS&EES, AmHI, ArtHuCI, BAS, BRI, CBRI, HumInd, IBR, IBZ, IIPA, MLA-IB, RILM. *Bk. rev.:* 8-12, 1,000-1,800 words. *Aud.:* Ac.

This scholarly journal from The Johns Hopkins University Press features historical studies, production reviews, and theoretical inquiries that analyze dramatic texts and production. Each issue contains approximately six articles, a performance review section, and book reviews. The articles are substantial and refereed. They may cover topics from a social or historical point of view, or they may analyze text. Occasionally, the articles will be organized around a central theme. The performance review section contains analytical reviews of, for the most part, American theater productions (although some foreign productions do appear). Regional theaters and repertory company productions are well covered. This journal is available online from 1996 to the present via ProjectMUSE. College and university libraries with drama or comparative literature programs should seriously consider subscribing to this journal.

5960. Theatre Notebook: a journal of the history and technique of the British theatre. [ISSN: 0040-5523] 1946. 3x/yr. GBP 19 domestic (Free to members). Ed(s): Russell Jackson. Society for Theatre Research, c/o The Theatre Museum, 1E Tavistock St, London, WC2E 7PA, United Kingdom; http://www.str.org.uk/. Illus., index, adv. Sample. Refereed. Circ: 1200. Vol. ends: Oct. *Indexed:* AmHI, ArtHuCI, BrHumI, HumInd, IBR, IBZ, IIPA, MLA-IB. *Bk. rev.:* 4-8, 400-1,000 words. *Aud.:* Ac.

This journal, produced by the Society for Theatre Research three times a year, contains five to eight articles that cover such topics as the history of particular productions, theater companies, actors, and theater/costume/playbill design. Its content is both lively and scholarly. It also includes a "Notes and Queries" section, obituaries, and book reviews. University libraries, as well as smaller academic libraries that support a drama history program, should consider this journal's purchase.

5961. Theatre Record. Formerly (until 1991): *London Theatre Record.* [ISSN: 0962-1792] 1981. bi-w. GBP 140 domestic; GBP 170 foreign. Theatre Record, 305 Whitton Dene, Isleworth, TW7 7NE, United Kingdom; editor@theatrerecord.demon.uk; http://www.theatrerecord.com. Illus., index, adv. Sample. *Indexed:* IIPA. *Aud.:* Ga, Ac.

This biweekly publication reprints reviews of existing London theater productions and produces lists of upcoming productions. Its web site at theatrerecord.org also provides an index to currently reviewed productions. Academic or public libraries with a theatergoing population might consider this journal's purchase, although its cost will probably limit it to only the largest library collections.

5962. Theatre Research in Canada. Formerly (until vol.13): *Theatre History in Canada.* [ISSN: 1196-1198] 1980. s-a. CND 32 (Individuals, CND 25). Ed(s): Bruce Barton. University of Toronto, Graduate Centre for Study of Drama, 214 College St, Toronto, ON M5T 2Z9, Canada; trican@chass.utoronto.ca. Illus. Refereed. Circ: 490. Microform: MML. Online: LexisNexis. *Indexed:* ArtHuCI, CBCARef, CPerI, IIPA, MLA-IB. *Bk. rev.:* 3-5, 1,000-1,500 words. *Aud.:* Ac.

Although this journal's focus is on Canadian theater history, several of the four to six articles in each issue are on the theater traditions of other countries. The content of this journal is very interesting, and it seems to have a greater interdisciplinary and intellectual historical inclination than can be found in some other journals. The text is bilingual, and a substantial portion of the journal is in French. It also contains book reviews in both French and English. Any college or university with a theater history program should consider this title for purchase.

5963. Theatre Research International. Formed by the merger of: *Theatre Research; New Theatre Magazine.* [ISSN: 0307-8833] 1975. 3x/yr. GBP 125. Ed(s): Freddie Rokem, Christopher Balme. Cambridge University Press, The Edinburgh Bldg, Shaftesbury Rd, Cambridge, CB2 2RU, United Kingdom; journals@cambridge.org; http://www.journals.cambridge.org. Illus., index, adv. Sample. Refereed. Circ: 1200. Microform: PQC. Online: Pub.; EBSCO Publishing, EBSCO Host; Florida Center for Library Automation; Gale; Northern Light Technology, Inc.; OCLC Online Computer Library Center, Inc.; OhioLINK; SwetsWise Online Content. *Indexed:* AmH&L, AmHI, ArtHuCI, BrHumI, HistAb, HumInd, IBR, IBZ, IIPA, MLA-IB, RILM. *Bk. rev.:* 10-14, 600-1,000 words. *Aud.:* Ac.

Each issue contains four to seven articles that cover the dramaturgy of a particular country and technical and historical studies of plays and performances. The journal is very international and broad in its coverage, although an issue may focus on a single country or region, such as "Theatre in Australia and New Zealand." Its book reviews are excellent and substantive. The cost of this journal will probably make its purchase prohibitive to all but university research collections.

5964. *Theatre Survey.* [ISSN: 0040-5574] 1956. s-a. GBP 79. Ed(s): Rosemarie K Bank, Jody Enders. Cambridge University Press, The Edinburgh Bldg, Shaftesbury Rd, Cambridge, CB2 2RU, United Kingdom; journals@cambridge.org; http://www.journals.cambridge.org. Illus., adv. Sample. Refereed. Circ: 1200. Vol. ends: Nov. Microform: PQC. Online: Pub.; Chadwyck-Healey Inc.; EBSCO Publishing, EBSCO Host; Northern Light Technology, Inc.; OCLC Online Computer Library Center, Inc.; OhioLINK; ProQuest K-12 Learning Solutions; ProQuest LLC (Ann Arbor); SwetsWise Online Content; H.W. Wilson. *Indexed:* ABS&EES, AmH&L, AmHI, ArtHuCI, HistAb, HumInd, IIPA, MLA-IB, RILM, SSCI. *Bk. rev.:* 10-12, 1,000-1,400 words. *Aud.:* Ac.

This journal is the organ of the American Society for Theatre Research, and as such, it contains scholarly performance studies. Recent changes in editorial policy have resulted in the inclusion of a broader number of geographic and subject areas. The four to six articles in each issue are not limited to drama but also include a variety of theatrical media, such as pageants and vaudeville. Each issue contains 10–12 substantive book reviews. In addition, there is often a very unusual and informative "Sources" section, which contains information about exhibits of theatrical materials, reports of theater archives, and notices of other interesting resources. Academic libraries and specialized theatrical collections should consider the purchase of this title.

5965. *Theatre Topics.* [ISSN: 1054-8378] 1991. 2x/yr. USD 70. Ed(s): Jonathan Chambers. The Johns Hopkins University Press, 2715 N Charles St, Baltimore, MD 21218-4363; myq@press.jhu.edu; http://www.press.jhu.edu. Illus., adv. Sample. Refereed. Circ: 1778 Paid. Vol. ends: Sep. Online: Chadwyck-Healey Inc.; EBSCO Publishing, EBSCO Host; OCLC Online Computer Library Center, Inc.; OhioLINK; Project MUSE; ProQuest LLC (Ann Arbor); SwetsWise Online Content. Reprint: PSC. *Indexed:* ABIn, AmHI, BEL&L, EduInd, IBR, IBZ, IIPA, MLA-IB. *Aud.:* Ac.

From The Johns Hopkins University Press "in cooperation with the Association for Theatre in Higher Education," this semi-annual journal contains about six articles in the areas of dramaturgy, performance, and theater pedagogy. Its articles are more practical and less historical and analytic in nature. The style and content are rigorous, however, and articles often contain references to further readings and resources. It is currently available online from 1996 to the present via ProjectMUSE. It is recommended to libraries that support university and collegiate drama teachers, directors, students, and theatrical personnel.

5966. *TheatreForum: international theatre journal.* [ISSN: 1060-5320] 1992. s-a. USD 50 (Individuals, USD 25; Students, USD 20). Ed(s): Jim Carmody, Adele E Shank. University of California at San Diego, Theatre Department, 9500 Gilman Dr, La Jolla, CA 92093-0344; http://www.theatre.ucsd.edu/tf/. Illus., adv. Sample. Circ: 1500 Paid and controlled. *Indexed:* AmHI, IIPA, MLA-IB. *Aud.:* Ac.

This journal contains articles on international contemporary theater issues. Its international coverage is quite broad. As it is published by the University of California, San Diego, its U.S. coverage has a distinct bias toward West Coast productions. However, this nicely balances it against other U.S. journals that are biased toward the New York theater scene. It also contains new play scripts, descriptions of companies, and occasional interviews. This publication should be considered for any academic theater collection, particularly those of the western part of the United States.

5967. *Variety: the international entertainment weekly.* [ISSN: 0042-2738] 1905. w. USD 279 domestic; USD 299 in Canada & Mexico; USD 359 in Europe. Ed(s): Peter Bart, Michael Speier. Reed Business Information, 5700 Wilshire Blvd, Ste 120, Los Angeles, CA 90036; http://www.reedbusiness.com. Illus., adv. Sample. Circ: 33007 Paid. Microform: BHP; PQC. Online: Chadwyck-Healey Inc.; EBSCO

Publishing, EBSCO Host; Florida Center for Library Automation; Gale; LexisNexis; OCLC Online Computer Library Center, Inc.; ProQuest K-12 Learning Solutions; ProQuest LLC (Ann Arbor); H.W. Wilson. *Indexed:* BPI, FLI, IIFP, IIPA, LRI, MASUSE, MRD, MusicInd. *Aud.:* Ga.

Variety is the longest-running publication on the business of entertainment in the United States. Known best by laypeople for its occasional witty headlines ("'Shooter' Premiere Hits the Mark" or "ABC Sudser Cleans Up"), *Variety* is, in show biz, the unofficial official journal. It contains extensive information on the business of entertainment, columns full of juicy insider tidbits, and reviews galore of films, TV, and theater. While its primary focus is on film and television, it does include some information on the business side of theater production and includes reviews of current theater productions across the country. While the web site at variety.com provides many of the theater reviews for free, any large public library and any academic library should consider its purchase.

5968. *Western European Stages.* [ISSN: 1050-1991] 1989. 3x/yr. Ed(s): Marvin Carlson. Martin E. Segal Theatre Center, The Graduate School and University Center, The City University of New York, New York, NY 10016-4309; mestc@gc.cuny.edu; http://web.gc.cuny.edu/mestc/. Illus., index. Sample. *Aud.:* Ac, Sa.

An indispensable resource in keeping abreast of the latest theater developments in Western Europe. Each issue contains a wealth of information about recent European festivals and productions, including reviews, interviews, and reports. Winter issues focus on the theater in individual countries or on special themes, and news of forthcoming events: the latest in changes in artistic directorships, new plays and playwrights, outstanding performances, and directorial interpretations.

■ TRANSPORTATION

See also Aeronautics and Space Science; Automobiles and Motorcycles; Marine Science and Technology; Safety; and Travel and Tourism sections.

Mary Kathleen Geary, Public Services Librarian, Transportation Library, Northwestern University Library, 1970 Sheridan Rd., Evanston, IL 60208-2300; m-geary@northwestern.edu

Introduction

We are just beginning an era of globalization. World travel is becoming increasingly easy and cost effective. But we can not think of transportation only in its worldwide manifestation. Transportation includes the bus you catch on the corner; the taxi you take to the airport; the rapid transit that whisks you off to work; the aircraft that takes you home for the weekend; the pipeline that transfers gas from the Alaskan wilds; the automobile that travels the nation's highways from coast to coast; the barge that transfers iron ore from the Midwest to the nation's steel mills; and so much more. Every day of our lives we interface with transportation.

The journals vetted in this section have been chosen to support transportation studies across the disciplines and the modalities, and to further the studies and work of academicians and practitioners alike.

Basic Periodicals

Journal of Transport Economics and Policy, Journal of Transportation Engineering, Transportation Journal, Transportation Research (A-F).

Basic Abstracts and Indexes

Engineering Index, Transport, TRISonline, TRANweb Compendex.

Accident Analysis & Prevention. See Safety section.

5969. Air Cargo World: international trends and analysis. Former titles (until 1983): *Air Cargo Magazine;* (until 1976): *Cargo Airlift; Air Transportation.* [ISSN: 0745-5100] 1910. m. USD 58 domestic; USD 78 foreign. Ed(s): Paul Page, Paul Page. Air Cargo World, 1080 Holcomb Brg Rd., BLDG 200255, Roswell, GA 30076-4348. Illus., index, adv. Circ: 41000 Controlled. Vol. ends: Dec. Microform: PQC. Online: EBSCO Publishing, EBSCO Host; Factiva, Inc.; Florida Center for Library Automation; Gale; LexisNexis; Northern Light Technology, Inc.; ProQuest LLC (Ann Arbor); H.W. Wilson. *Indexed:* ABIn, BPI, HRIS, LogistBibl. *Bk. rev.:* Occasional. *Aud.:* Sa.

This journal is suitable for large general collections and special libraries. It provides coverage of cargo services, carriers, facilities, equipment, and industry trends throughout the world. Regular features include articles, columns surveying news from regions around the world, updates on people in the industry, at-a-glance industry statistical indicators, and upcoming events. Annually, special directories are published for cargo carriers, express delivery companies, cargo aircraft, and freight forwarders. The web site, www.logisticsmgmt.com, will lead to full-text current and archived articles.

Air Transport World. See Aeronautics and Space Science section.

5970. Airfinance Journal. [ISSN: 0143-2257] 1980. 10x/yr. GBP 620 combined subscription domestic print & online eds.; EUR 920 combined subscription in Europe print & online eds.; USD 1240 combined subscription elsewhere print & online eds. Ed(s): Alasdair Whyte. Euromoney Institutional Investor Plc., Nestor House, Playhouse Yard, London, EC4V 5EX, United Kingdom; http://www.euromoney.com. Adv. Circ: 2920 Paid. Online: EBSCO Publishing, EBSCO Host; Florida Center for Library Automation; Gale; OCLC Online Computer Library Center, Inc.; ProQuest LLC (Ann Arbor); H.W. Wilson. *Indexed:* ABIn, BPI, HRIS. *Aud.:* Sa.

Appropriate for large, general collections and special collections, this trade journal is geared toward both the practitioner and the researcher in the area of air transportation and finance. It includes feature articles, industry news, and important industry statistical tables; its coverage is international. A password is required to access the journal electronically at www.airfinancejournal.com.

5971. Airline Business: the voice of airline managements. [ISSN: 0268-7615] 1985. m. GBP 89 domestic; EUR 133 in Europe; USD 158 United States. Ed(s): Colin Baker, Kevin O'Toole. Reed Business Information Ltd., Quadrant House, The Quadrant, Brighton Rd, Sutton, SM2 5AS, United Kingdom; http://www.reedbusiness.co.uk/. Illus., adv. Circ: 31000. Vol. ends: Dec. Online: DataStar; EBSCO Publishing, EBSCO Host; Florida Center for Library Automation; Gale; LexisNexis; OCLC Online Computer Library Center, Inc.; ProQuest K-12 Learning Solutions; ProQuest LLC (Ann Arbor); H.W. Wilson. *Indexed:* ABIn, BPI, C&ISA, CerAb, H&TI, HRIS, IAA. *Aud.:* Sa.

Appropriate for special collections, this trade journal provides worldwide coverage of business affairs in all aspects of the airline industry. Topics include developments in regions of the world as well as in specific countries, analysis of policy changes, people who impact the industry, and financing issues. Regular features include commentary, news digests, events calendars, and new appointments. Annual features include the "Airline Business 100" and "Airports Review." The primary audience is airline managers. The online version can be accessed with a password at www.airlinebusiness.com.

5972. Airline Monitor: a review of trends in the airline and commercial jet aircraft industries. unknown. USD 950; USD 1150 combined subscription print & online eds. Ed(s): Edmund S Greanslet. E S G Aviation Services, 636 Third St South, Jacksonville Beach, FL 32250; theairlinemonitor@mac.com; http://www.airlinemonitor.com. *Indexed:* HRIS. *Aud.:* Ac, Sa.

Published by ESG Aviation Services, this periodical is a unique and thorough source of statistical and financial information on the domestic air transportation industry, including forecasting. It is geared toward the professional and the researcher. Each issue includes an executive summary followed by tables of data current within a month. A password is required to access the periodical's online version at www.airlinemonitor.com. Appropriate for academic or special libraries.

5973. Airliners: the world's airline magazine. [ISSN: 0896-6575] 1988. bi-m. USD 26.95 domestic; USD 37.95 newsstand/cover per issue foreign; USD 5.50 newsstand/cover. Ed(s): Jon Proctor. World Transport Press, PO Box 821208, Pembroke Pines, FL 33082-1208. Illus., adv. Circ: 45000 Paid. Vol. ends: Nov/Dec. *Indexed:* HRIS. *Aud.:* Ga.

Targeting the commercial airline enthusiast, this publication offers detailed coverage of international, national, and local airlines, including industry news and events, local special-interest stories, and some statistical information. Airplane modeling and collecting are occasionally featured. The magazine includes color photography and elaborate layouts. The publisher can be accessed at www.wallpaperama.com/shop/B00006K2LF/Airliners.html. Appropriate for general collections.

5974. Airlines International. [ISSN: 1360-6387] 1995. bi-m. Members, GBP 90; Non-members, GBP 120. Ed(s): Russell Stevens. Insight Media Ltd., 26-30 London Rd, Twickenham, TW1 3RR, United Kingdom; email@insightgrp.co.uk. Illus., adv. Circ: 10000 Controlled. Vol. ends: Nov/Dec. *Indexed:* HRIS. *Aud.:* Sa.

This journal covers the international commercial airline industry, emphasizing airline management, economics, current industry events, and some statistical information. Published for International Aviation Transport Association (IATA) members, it is aimed at specialists and includes an IATA calendar of events and an "Insight on IATA" section. The online version of this journal, along with archived articles, can be accessed at www.world-gateway.com. Appropriate for special collections.

5975. Airport Magazine. [ISSN: 1048-2091] 1989. bi-m. 0 membership. American Association of Airport Executives, 601 Madison St, Ste 400, Alexandria, VA 22314; ellen.horton@airportnet.org; http://www.airportnet.org. Illus., index, adv. Circ: 7000. Vol. ends: Nov/Dec. *Indexed:* HRIS. *Aud.:* Sa.

This publication of the American Association of Airport Executives is for specialists, addressing airport management, legislation, technology, research reports, economics, and current industry events. It features some statistics as well as requests for proposals. The electronic version of this journal can be accessed at www.aaae.org/magazine. Appropriate for special collections.

5976. Airport World. [ISSN: 1360-4341] 1996. bi-m. Members, USD 150; Non-members, USD 200. Ed(s): Charles Tyler. Insight Media Ltd., 26-30 London Rd, Twickenham, TW1 3RR, United Kingdom. Illus., adv. Circ: 8000. *Indexed:* HRIS. *Aud.:* Sa.

Published for the Airports Council International, this journal addresses global airport issues. Geared to the practitioner, it covers industry news and events, technology, safety, automation, the environment, legislation, regulation, airport planning and maintenance, management, and finance. Each issue includes feature articles, a calendar of events, airport traffic data and other statistics, project briefs, a section highlighting a specific airport, and a global airport news section. The annotated tables of contents for current issues can be accessed at www.insightgrp.co.uk/AirportWorld_current.html. Appropriate for special collections.

5977. Airports International Magazine. Former titles (until 1971): *Airports International Directory; Airports International.* 1968. 9x/yr. USD 175; USD 19 newsstand/cover per issue. Ed(s): Tom Allett. Key Publishing Ltd., PO Box 300, Stamford, PE9 1NA, United Kingdom; ann.saundry@keypublishing.com; http://www.keypublishing.com. Adv. Sample. Circ: 13962. Online: Factiva, Inc.; Gale; OCLC Online Computer Library Center, Inc. *Indexed:* HRIS. *Aud.:* Sa.

This publication is international in coverage and is geared to the specialist. It addresses current airport trends, news and events, economics, and technology. An annotated table of contents for the current issue is available at www.airportsinternational.co.uk/api_current_issue.asp. This magazine is appropriate for special collections.

5978. *American Shipper: ports, transportation and industry.* Former titles (until 1991): *American Shipper Magazine;* (until 1976): *Florida Journal of Commerce - American Shipper;* (until 1974): *Florida Journal of Commerce.* [ISSN: 1074-8350] 1959. m. USD 120. Ed(s): Gary Burrows, Christopher Gillis. Howard Publications, P.O. Box 4728, Jacksonville, FL 32201-4728. Illus., adv. Circ: 14884. Vol. ends: Dec. Microform: PQC. Online: Northern Light Technology, Inc. *Indexed:* BPI, H&SSA, HRIS, LogistBibl, OceAb, PAIS, PollutAb, SWRA. *Aud.:* Sa.

This trade journal targets the practitioner and is international in coverage. Each issue addresses seven subjects of interest: logistics, forwarding, integrated transport, ocean transport, land transport, NVOs, and ports. There are also sections on shippers' case law and corporate appointments. The online version of the current issue of this journal can be accessed at www.americanshipper-.com. A password is required. Appropriate for special libraries.

Aviation Week and Space Technology. See Aeronautics and Space Science section.

5979. *Better Roads.* [ISSN: 0006-0208] 1931. m. USD 24 domestic (Free to qualified personnel). James Informational Media, Inc., 2720 S River Rd, Ste 126, Des Plaines, IL 60018; http://www.jiminc.com. Illus., adv. Vol. ends: Dec. *Indexed:* C&ISA, CerAb, EngInd, EnvInd, HRIS, IAA. *Bk. rev.:* Number and length vary. *Aud.:* Sa.

Published by James Informational Media for specialists in the fields of road construction, maintenance, and repair, this journal includes industry news, government contract information, book and video reviews, product ratings and reviews, a calendar of industry events, and a forum for letters and professional comment, along with technically rich feature articles. The December issue contains a pull-out calendar of industry events for the entire year. Archived articles, dating back to 1998, can be accessed at www.betterroads.com. Appropriate for engineering and transportation collections.

5980. *Bridge Design & Engineering: the definitive publication for bridge professionals worldwide.* [ISSN: 1359-7493] 1995. q. GBP 200; USD 330. Ed(s): Helena Russell. Hemming Group Ltd., 32 Vauxhall Bridge Rd, London, SW1V 2SS, United Kingdom; http://www.hemming-group.co.uk/page.asp?partID=1. Illus., adv. Circ: 6000 Controlled. *Indexed:* HRIS. *Bk. rev.:* 2–4, 150–250 words. *Aud.:* Ac, Sa.

This journal targets the practitioner. It is international in coverage and addresses bridge aesthetics, design, construction, and management. It includes feature articles, industry news, product information, a calendar of events, and listings of conferences and competitions. The online version can be accessed at www.bridgeweb.com, but a subscription is required for full content. Appropriate for special libraries.

5981. *Bus Ride.* [ISSN: 0192-8902] 1965. 12x/yr. USD 39 domestic. Ed(s): David Hubbard, Maria Jolly. Power Trade Media, LLC, 4742 N 24th St, Ste 340, Phoenix, AZ 85016-4884. Illus. Circ: 13500. Vol. ends: Dec. *Indexed:* HRIS. *Aud.:* Sa.

This journal addresses the passenger bus industries of the United States and Canada and is meant for bus and transit specialists. It includes current industry news and events, legislative and regulatory information, product reviews, feature articles, and a report on the European passenger bus industry. The current issue of the journal's online version, and some archived issues, can be accessed at www.busride.com. Appropriate for special collections.

5982. *Business and Commercial Aviation.* Incorporates (1972-2004): *A C Flyer;* Formerly (until 1966): *Business and Commercial Aviation.* [ISSN: 1538-7267] 1958. m. USD 54 domestic; USD 58 in Canada & Mexico; USD 79 elsewhere. Ed(s): William Garvey, Jessica Salerno. Aviation Week Group, 2 Penn Plaza, 25th Fl, New York, NY 10121-2298; AWNord@cdsfulfillment.com; http://www.aviationweek.com. Illus., adv. Circ: 50000 Controlled. Microform: PQC. Online: The Dialog Corporation; EBSCO Publishing, EBSCO Host; LexisNexis; ProQuest LLC (Ann Arbor). *Indexed:* ABIn, AS&TI, HRIS, LRI. *Aud.:* Sa.

This trade journal targets the practitioner and addresses the commercial aviation industry with a decided emphasis on business flying. Its coverage is international. Each issue includes industry news and events, feature articles,

statistics, commentary, product reviews, classifieds, a resale marketplace, and a section devoted to the causes of accidents. The online version can be accessed at www.aviationnow.com/bca. Appropriate for special libraries.

5983. *Cargo Systems.* Former titles (until 1994): *Cargo Systems International.* [ISSN: 1362-766X] 1973. m. GBP 185 domestic; EUR 380 in Europe eurozone; USD 440 elsewhere. Ed(s): Siobhan Oswald. Informa Maritime & Transport, Telephone House, 69-77 Paul St, London, EC2A 4LQ, United Kingdom; mt.enquiries@informa.com; http://www.informamaritime.com. Illus., adv. Circ: 7500. Vol. ends: Dec. *Indexed:* EngInd, ExcerpMed, HRIS. *Aud.:* Sa.

Worldwide coverage of containerized and noncontainerized cargo-handling systems is the focus of this magazine. The news and feature sections concentrate on shipping and port issues, economic factors, industry progress and updates, intermodal issues, safety, and new products and equipment. The magazine issues frequent supplements on special topics such as terminal operations, reefer systems, and privatization. The journal's online version can be viewed at www.cargosystems.net; a password is required. Appropriate for special libraries.

5984. *Commercial Carrier Journal.* Incorporates (in 200?): *Trucking Company;* Former titles (until 1999): *Commercial Carrier Journal for Professional Fleet Managers;* (until 1998): *Chilton's Commercial Carrier Journal for Professional Fleet Managers;* (until 1990): *Commercial Carrier Journal for Professional Fleet Managers;* (until 1989): *Chilton's C C J;* (until 1984): *Chilton's Commercial Carrier Journal;* (until 1982): *Chilton's C C J;* (until 1977): *Commercial Car Journal.* [ISSN: 1533-7502] 1911. m. USD 48 (Free to qualified personnel). Ed(s): Max Heine, Kristin Walters. Randall-Reilly Publishing Company, 3200 Rice Mine Rd, Tuscaloosa, AL 35406; http://www.randallpub.com. Illus., index, adv. Circ: 87000 Controlled. Vol. ends: Dec. Microform: CIS; PQC. Online: EBSCO Publishing, EBSCO Host; Gale; OCLC Online Computer Library Center, Inc. *Indexed:* HRIS, PAIS. *Aud.:* Sa.

One of the important trade journals in the truck fleet management industry, this publication contains articles on operations, equipment maintenance, management, regulation, and safety. Regular features include road tests of vehicles, industry news, events and editorials, and a classified section. Annually, the magazine reports on the "Top 100" U.S. truck lines and provides a range of buyers' guides on truck equipment, fleet products and services, and information technology. The current month's issue, and archived cover stories, can be accessed at www.etrucker.com/default.asp?magid=3. Appropriate for special libraries.

5985. *Community Transportation.* Former titles (until 1997): *Community Transportation Reporter;* (until 1987): *Rural Transportation Reporter.* 1984. bi-m. Individual members, USD 125; Students, USD 25. Ed(s): Scott Bogren. Community Transportation Association of America, 1341 G St. NW, Ste 600, Washington, DC 20005; http://www.ctaa.org/. Illus., index, adv. Circ: 10000 Controlled. Vol. ends: Nov/Dec. *Indexed:* HRIS. *Bk. rev.:* Number and length vary. *Aud.:* Ga, Sa.

Published by the Community Transportation Association of America, this journal addresses all forms of community transportation: bus, rail, and paratransit. Geared toward the specialist, it would be of use to interested community members. It includes current industry news and events, legislation and regulatory matters, available resources, and feature articles. A substantial annual book review section is published in the July/August issue. The current and archived tables of contents, and some feauture articles, can be accessed at www.ctaa.org/ct. Appropriate for large, inclusive general collections and special collections.

5986. *Containerisation International.* [ISSN: 0010-7379] 1967. m. GBP 180 domestic; EUR 365 in Europe; USD 480 elsewhere. Ed(s): Jane Degerlund. Informa Publishing, Telephone House, 69-77 Paul St, London, EC2A 4IQ, United Kingdom. Illus., adv. Circ: 11000. Vol. ends: Dec. *Indexed:* HRIS. *Aud.:* Sa.

This publication covers the worldwide containerization business, management, and policy issues for a variety of transportation modes, but with an emphasis on shipping and ports. The feature articles cover specific carriers; analysis of some aspect of the industry; issues for carriers, shippers, and terminals; regional coverage; and regulatory analysis. Each issue contains updates on business, the world fleet, charters, shippers, and news on intermodal transport, terminals, information technology, and statistics on key industry indicators. The web site offers late-breaking news at www.ci-online.co.uk. For full content, a password is required. Appropriate for special collections.

5987. Fairplay: the international shipping weekly. Former titles (until 1992): *Fairplay International;* (until 1989): *Fairplay International Shipping Weekly;* (until 1974): *Fairplay International Shipping Journal.* [ISSN: 1745-5456] 1883. w. GBP 395 in Europe; EUR 590 in Europe; USD 695 in Europe & USA. Ed(s): G Paul Gunton, Patrick Neylan-Francis. Fairplay Publications Ltd., Lombard House, 3 Princess Way, Redhill, RH1 1UP, United Kingdom; info@fairplay.co.uk; http://www.fairplay.co.uk. Illus., adv. Circ: 4379 Paid. Vol. ends: Apr/Dec. *Indexed:* HRIS. *Aud.:* Sa.

This journal is devoted to the international shipping industry and covers industry news and events including shipbuilding and port news, legislation, regulation, safety, labor and management issues, liner operations, ship sales, and cargo information. Feature articles tend to be brief news flashes, except for the cover story. In addition to international coverage, each issue highlights the shipping industry within a specific nation or region. The section on the shipping market includes graphs, tables, and statistics. The online version of the journal can be accessed at www.fairplay.co.uk; a password is required. Appropriate for a large business collection or a transportation collection.

5988. Fleet Owner. Formerly: *Fleet Owner: Big Fleet Edition;* Superseded in part: *Fleet Owner.* [ISSN: 1070-194X] 1928. m. USD 45 domestic; USD 60 Canada; USD 80 elsewhere. Ed(s): Jim Mele. Prism Business Media, 11 River Bend Dr S, PO Box 4949, Stamford, CT 06907-0949; inquiries@prismb2b.com; http://www.prismbusinessmedia.com. Illus., adv. Vol. ends: Dec. Microform: PQC. Online: EBSCO Publishing, EBSCO Host; Gale; OCLC Online Computer Library Center, Inc.; ProQuest K-12 Learning Solutions; ProQuest LLC (Ann Arbor); H.W. Wilson. *Indexed:* ABIn, BPI, ChemAb, HRIS. *Aud.:* Sa.

This journal targets the specialist and addresses the public and private sectors of truck fleet management. Coverage includes fleet management industry news and events, equipment, management, information technology, legislation, safety, and product analysis. It devotes significant attention to information technology. The online version of this journal can be accessed at http://fleetowner.com; a password is required. Appropriate for special collections.

Flight International. See Aeronautics and Space Science section.

5989. Great Lakes Seaway Log: the international transportation magazine of midcontinent North America. Formerly (until 1998): *Seaway Review;* Which incorporates (1968-1977): *Limnos.* 1970. bi-w. USD 32 domestic; USD 42 Canada. Ed(s): David L Knight. Harbor House Publishers, Inc., 221 Water St., Boyne City, MI 49712; harbor@harborhouse.com; http://www.harborhouse.com/. Illus. Circ: 1200 Paid and controlled. Vol. ends: Apr/Jun. Microform: PQC. *Indexed:* HRIS. *Aud.:* Ga,Sa.

Addresses commercial shipping and the maritime industries throughout the Great Lakes and St. Lawrence Seaway areas. Coverage includes shipping industry news and events, legislation and regulation, technology, naval architecture and engineering, ports, import/export, fleet data, and feature articles. Each issue highlights a specific port. The "Shipyard Report" section is a unique feature: Broken down by marine repair or shipbuilding company, it supplies the name of the vessel, owner, nature of work being done, and anticipated date of completion. The magazine *Great Laker*, devoted to lighthouses, lake boats, and travel and leisure, has been incorporated into the *Great Lakes Seaway Review*. An index to past issues can be accessed at www.greatlakes-seawayreview.com. Appropriate for a large general collection interested in the Great Lakes or a special collection.

5990. Heavy Duty Trucking: the business magazine of trucking. [ISSN: 0017-9434] 1968. m. USD 65 domestic (Free to qualified personnel). Ed(s): James Winsor, Peggy J Fisher. Newport Communications (Irvine), 38 Executive Pk, Ste 300, Irvine, CA 92614; aryder@truckinginfo.com; http://www.truckinginfo.com. Illus., adv. Circ: 100500 Controlled. Vol. ends: Dec. *Indexed:* HRIS. *Aud.:* Sa.

This journal is published by the Newport Communications Group expressly for fleet owners operating trucks within classes seven and eight (26,000 pounds gross vehicle weight). It covers the heavy trucking fleet industry, including industry news and events, legislation, safety, technology, and equipment. Statistics, including tables and graphs, are provided on diesel fuel costs, by state; truck sales by manufacturer; and trucking trends. Buyers' guides, offered several times annually, are a significant supplement to the journal. Current issue contents and archived articles are available online at www.heavydutytrucking-.com. Appropriate for special collections.

5991. IEEE Transactions on Intelligent Transportation Systems. [ISSN: 1524-9050] 2000. q. USD 445. Ed(s): Chelsea C White, III. IEEE, 445 Hoes Ln, Piscataway, NJ 08854-1331; subscription-service@ieee.org; http://www.ieee.org. Refereed. *Indexed:* C&ISA, CerAb, EngInd, HRIS, IAA, SCI. *Aud.:* Ac, Sa.

This scholarly publication focuses on the application of information technology to systems across all modes of transportation. Some of the topics it considers include communications, sensors, man/machine interfaces, decision systems, controls, simulation, reliability, and standards. Frequently, issues of the journal focus on a specific subject. The online version can be accessed at http://ieeexplore.ieee.org/Xplore/DynWel.jsp; a password is required. Appropriate for special collections.

5992. I T E Journal. Former titles: *Transportation Engineering;* (until 1977): *Traffic Engineering.* [ISSN: 0162-8178] 1930. m. USD 65 in North America (Free to members). Ed(s): Clare James. Institute of Transportation Engineers, 1099 14th St., NW, Ste 300 West, Washington, DC 20005-3438; ite_staff@ite.org; http://www.ite.org. Illus., adv. Refereed. Circ: 17000 Paid and controlled. Vol. ends: Dec. Microform: PQC. Online: Factiva, Inc.; OCLC Online Computer Library Center, Inc.; ProQuest LLC (Ann Arbor); H.W. Wilson. *Indexed:* ABIn, AS&TI, C&ISA, CerAb, EngInd, EnvAb, EnvInd, ExcerpMed, H&SSA, HRIS, IAA, PAIS, PetrolAb, SCI, SSCI, SUSA. *Bk. rev.:* Occasional, up to 250 words. *Aud.:* Ac, Sa.

Written by and for transportation engineers and planners, this refereed journal thoroughly covers the field of surface transportation. It focuses largely on North America, particularly the United States, but occasionally includes features from other parts of the world. Regular features include news on people, projects, places, and research as well as resources available; a calendar of events and meetings; and positions available. The web site offers a searchable index back to 1950 and full-text articles back to 1970 at www.ite.org/itejournal/index.asp; a password is required. Appropriate for special collections.

5993. I T S International: advanced technology for traffic management and urban mobility. Formerly: *I T S - Intelligent Transport Systems.* [ISSN: 1463-6344] 1995. 6x/yr. GBP 100; USD 165. Ed(s): David Crawford. Route One Publishing Ltd., Horizon House, Azalea Dr, Swanley, BR8 8JR, United Kingdom; subs@routeonepub.com; http://www.routeonepub.com. Illus., adv. Sample. Circ: 21421. *Indexed:* HRIS. *Aud.:* Sa.

This journal addresses the specialist in the international intelligent transportation systems (ITS) industry. Its coverage includes ITS industry news and events, technology, product analysis and review, and feature articles on highlighted ITS issues such as telematics, tolling systems, or multi-modal systems. Each issue includes a focus on the ITS industry within a specific geographic area, a current-events section, and a listing of appointments and promotions within the field. Feature articles from the annual buyers' guide as well as the full text of opinion articles can be found online at www.itsinternational.com. Access to full text of the articles requires a password. Appropriate for engineering and transportation collections.

5994. *Inbound Logistics: for today's business logistics managers.* Former titles (until 199?): *Thomas Register's Inbound Logistics;* (until 1985): *Inbound Traffic Guide;* (until 1982): *Thomas Register's Inbound Traffic Guide for Industrial Buyers & Specifiers.* 1981. 12x/yr. USD 68.95 domestic (Free to qualified personnel). Ed(s): Felecia J Stratton. Thomas Publishing Company (New York), Five Penn Plaza, New York, NY 10001; info@thomasimg.com; http://www.thomaspublishing.com. Illus., adv. Circ: 52000. Vol. ends: Dec. *Indexed:* C&ISA, CerAb, HRIS, IAA, LogistBibl. *Aud.:* Sa.

Geared to the specialist, this journal addresses the international logistics industry. Coverage includes logistics industry news and events, technology, business management, personnel management, legislation, and feature articles; a strong emphasis is placed on e-commerce and information technology. Special sections address logistics in the Americas, the Pacific community, and the European community. A voluminous supplementary, "Logistics Planner," is published in January. Each issue includes a calendar of logistics industry events and a section devoted to evaluating logistics-oriented web sites. The online version can be accessed at www.inboundlogistics.com. Appropriate for special collections.

Interavia. See Aeronautics and Space Science section.

5995. *International Journal of Automotive Technology and Management.* [ISSN: 1470-9511] 2001. q. EUR 470 (print or online ed.). Ed(s): Dr. Giuseppe Calabrese, Dr. Mohammed A Dorgham. Inderscience Publishers, IEL Editorial Office, PO Box 735, Olney, MK46 5WB, United Kingdom; http://www.inderscience.com. Sample. Refereed. Online: EBSCO Publishing, EBSCO Host; SwetsWise Online Content. *Indexed:* ABIn, C&ISA, CerAb, EngInd, ErgAb, IAA. *Bk. rev.:* Various number and length. *Aud.:* Ac, Sa.

This is a refereed scholarly journal targeting the academician. It addresses all aspects of international automotive technology and management, including product development, research, innovative management, e-commerce, supply chain management, reengineering, efficiency, safety, investment and business, and human resources. Each issue contains referenced articles, charts, graphs, statistics, calls for papers, and a complete index. Some issues contain book reviews. The online version of the journal can be found at www.inderscience.com/ejournal/a/ijatm/ijatmabsindex.html. Appropriate for large academic libraries or special collections.

5996. *International Journal of Logistics: research and applications.* [ISSN: 1367-5567] 1998. q. GBP 467 print & online eds. Ed(s): Kulwant S Pawar, Dr. Tony Whiteing. Taylor & Francis Ltd., 4 Park Sq, Milton Park, Abingdon, OX14 4RN, United Kingdom; info@tandf.co.uk; http://www.tandf.co.uk/journals. Illus. Sample. Refereed. Vol. ends: Nov. Reprint: PSC. *Indexed:* C&ISA, CerAb, IAA, IBR, IBZ. *Aud.:* Ac, Sa.

This refereed scholarly journal addresses all aspects of the international logistics industry, including intermodal transportation, warehousing, and supply chain management; it is of interest to both the academician and the practitioner. Each issue includes lengthy research articles with references, graphs, tables, and charts. The journal can be accessed online at www.tandf.co.uk/journals/carfax/13675567.html. Appropriate for academic and special collections.

5997. *International Journal of Transport Economics.* [ISSN: 0303-5247] 1974. 3x/yr. EUR 495 print & online eds. (Individuals, EUR 295). Ed(s): Gianrocco Tucci. Istituti Editoriali e Poligrafici Internazionali, Via Giosue' Carducci, 60, Ghezzano - La Fontina, 56010, Italy; iepi@iepi.it; http://www.iepi.it. Illus., index, adv. Refereed. Circ: 1000. Vol. ends: Oct. *Indexed:* HRIS, IBSS, JEL, PAIS. *Bk. rev.:* 7–12, 100–350 words. *Aud.:* Ac, Sa.

This journal, published in Italy but with a worldwide focus, brings together current research in transport economics, uniting theoretical and applied approaches to the subject. Occasional special issues are devoted to a single topic. The editorial board and the authors of the articles come from around the world. The journal is published in English, with some supporting information also included in Italian. In addition to contributed scholarly articles, it also features a review article that extends the theoretical discussion to the practical realm. There is a book review section. The journal's web site is http://web.dte.uniroma1.it/trasporti/journal.html. Appropriate for special collections.

5998. *International Railway Journal: the first international railway and rapid transit journal.* Former titles (until 1993): *International Railway Journal and Rapid Transit Review;* (until 1979): *International Railway Journal.* 1960. m. USD 72. Ed(s): David Briginshaw, David Briginshaw. Simmons-Boardman Publishing Corp., 345 Hudson St, 12th Fl, New York, NY 10014-4502. Illus., index, adv. Circ: 10849. Vol. ends: Dec. Microform: PQC. Online: Gale. *Indexed:* ABIn, ExcerpMed, HRIS. *Aud.:* Ac, Sa.

This journal covers the international light-track and heavy-track railroad industries; it is the international version of its sister periodicals for North America, *Railway Age* and *Railway Track and Structures.* Each issue is divided between a section on heavy-rail and a section on light-rail, intraurban, and interurban rapid transit. These sections include industry news and events, world market reports, feature articles, a list of conferences and seminars, a product showcase, and a list of relevant web sites. Maps of the referenced rail lines are often included in feature articles. The subscription includes an annual supplement, *World Railway Investment,* offering financial data and statistics. The journal can be accessed online at www.railjournal.com. Of interest to both the academician and the practitioner, it is appropriate for large academic collections and special collections.

5999. *Jane's Airport Review: the global airport business magazine.* [ISSN: 0954-7649] 1989. 10x/yr. GBP 145; USD 255; GBP 415. Jane's Information Group, Sentinel House, 163 Brighton Rd, Coulsdon, CR5 2YH, United Kingdom; info@janes.co.uk; http://www.janes.com. Illus. Vol. ends: Nov/Dec. *Indexed:* EngInd, HRIS. *Aud.:* Sa.

This journal covers airport business, addressing market intelligence and strategic planning. Its audience is airport management professionals. Coverage is international. Regular features include sections on news, air traffic control, terminal and ground support equipment, and interviews with leading professionals. The journal's online version can be accessed, via password, at http://jar.janes.com. Appropriate for special libraries.

6000. *Journal of Advanced Transportation.* Formerly (until vol.12, 1979): *High Speed Ground Transportation Journal.* [ISSN: 0197-6729] 1967. 3x/yr. USD 225. Ed(s): S C Wirasinghe. Institute for Transportation, Inc., #305, 4625 Varsity Dr NW, Ste 68, Calgary, AB T3A 0Z9, Canada. Illus., index. Refereed. Circ: 300 Paid. Vol. ends: Winter. Microform: MIM; PQC. *Indexed:* ApMecR, C&ISA, CerAb, EngInd, H&SSA, HRIS, IAA, PRA, SCI, SUSA. *Bk. rev.:* Occasional. *Aud.:* Ac, Sa.

This scholarly journal, sponsored by the Advanced Transit Association, covers all modes of transportation. The focus is on the engineering and technology behind the analysis, design, economics, operations, and planning of transportation systems. Although the focus of the journal has broadened over the past several years, the editors maintain a special interest in advanced urban rail transit systems. Occasionally, issues focus on a special topic and may include review articles that provide an overall survey of an aspect of the field. The web site features a searchable index of issues back to 1990. The journal's online version can be accessed at www.advanced-transport.com. Appropriate for special collections.

6001. *Journal of Air Law and Commerce.* [ISSN: 0021-8642] 1930. q. USD 40 domestic; USD 47 foreign; USD 16.50 newsstand/cover per issue. Ed(s): Zach Garsek. S M U Law Review Association, Southern Methodist University, Dedman School of Law, P O Box 750116, Dallas, TX 75275-0116; jalceic@mail.smu.edu; http://www.smu.edu. Illus., index, adv. Refereed. Circ: 2000. Vol. ends: Fall. Microform: WSH; PMC; PQC. Online: LexisNexis; OCLC Online Computer Library Center, Inc.; Thomson West; H.W. Wilson. Reprint: WSH. *Indexed:* CLI, H&SSA, HRIS, IAA, ILP, LRI, PAIS. *Bk. rev.:* Occasional. *Aud.:* Ac, Sa.

This scholarly publication covers the legal and economic aspects of aviation and space. The journal is managed by a student board of editors in association with the *Southern Methodist University Law Review.* The issues include comprehensive articles, a review of current-interest topics, and book reviews. Articles are written by lawyers, economists, government officials, and scholars. The journal's online presence can be accessed at http://smu.edu/lra/Journals/JALC/Current.asp. Appropriate for special collections.

6002. *Journal of Air Transport Management.* [ISSN: 0969-6997] 1994. 6x/yr. EUR 641. Ed(s): S Morrison, K Button. Pergamon, The Boulevard, Langford Ln, East Park, Kidlington, OX5 1GB, United Kingdom. Illus., index, adv. Refereed. Vol. ends: No. 4. Microform: PQC. Online: EBSCO Publishing, EBSCO Host; Gale; IngentaConnect; OhioLINK; ScienceDirect; SwetsWise Online Content. *Indexed:* EnvAb, ErgAb, H&SSA, H&TI, HRIS, RiskAb, SSCI. *Bk. rev.:* Occasional. Number and length vary. *Aud.:* Ac, Sa.

Published by Elsevier Science, this refereed journal is of interest to both the academician and the practitioner. It addresses theory and application relative to all aspects of the international air transportation industry, including airlines, infrastructure, airports, traffic control, and management. Each issue consists of lengthy research articles that include graphs, tables, statistics, and detailed references. Some issues offer a book review section. The journal has been issued only in electronic format since 2003 and must be accessed online, by subscribers, at www.elsevier.com/locate/jairtraman. Appropriate for special collections.

6003. *Journal of Air Transportation.* Formerly: *Journal of Air Transportation World Wide.* [ISSN: 1544-6980] 1996. s-a. USD 68 (Individuals, USD 35). Ed(s): Brent Bowen. University of Nebraska at Omaha, Aviation Institute, Allwie Hall, Rm 422, 600 Dodge St, Omaha, NE 68182-0508. Refereed. Circ: 300. Online: EBSCO Publishing, EBSCO Host; ProQuest LLC (Ann Arbor). *Indexed:* ABIn, HRIS. *Bk. rev.:* Occasional. *Aud.:* Ac, Sa.

This scholarly, peer-reviewed journal addresses all major aspects of air transportation: aviation management and administration, intermodal transportation, airports, air traffic control, aviation, avionics, and space transportation. It is geared to the academician and the specialist. Each issue contains lengthy research articles with graphs, tables, charts, and detailed references. This journal can be accessed online at http://ntl.bts.gov/lib/000/700/744/jatww.html. Appropriate for special collections.

6004. *Journal of Maritime Law and Commerce.* [ISSN: 0022-2410] 1969. q. USD 250 (Individuals, USD 215). Ed(s): Edward V Cattell, Jr. Jefferson Law Book Co., 2100 Huntingdon Ave, Baltimore, MD 21211; jefflaw1@juno.com. Illus., index, adv. Refereed. Circ: 2500 Paid. Reprint: WSH. *Indexed:* CLI, HRIS, ILP, LRI, PAIS, SSCI. *Bk. rev.:* 1-25, 500-2,500 words, signed. *Aud.:* Ac, Sa.

This scholarly journal is dedicated to coverage of all aspects of admiralty and maritime law. It targets the professional and the academician. Its contents concentrate on topics of current interest, but the editorial board also includes historical or theoretical treatments of the field. Special issues on single topics are often published. Occasionally, it is possible to find case analyses, review articles, and bibliographies. This journal's table of contents can be accessed at www.jmlc.org. Appropriate for special collections.

6005. *Journal of Public Transportation.* [ISSN: 1077-291X] 1997. q. Free. Ed(s): Laurel Land. University of South Florida, Center for Urban Transportation Research, College of Engineering, 4202 E Fowler Ave, CUT100, Tampa, FL 33620-5375; http://www.cutr.usf.edu/. *Indexed:* CJA, H&SSA, HRIS. *Aud.:* Ac, Sa.

Presenting new case studies and original research, this journal covers public-transportation modes and related policies from all over the world. The journal strives to present papers with innovative solutions; approaches can come from any number of disciplines, including engineering, management, and others. The journal is provided free by the Center for Urban Transportation Research at the University of South Florida. The online version can be accessed at www.nctr.usf.edu/jpt/journal.htm. Appropriate for special collections.

6006. *Journal of Transport Economics and Policy.* [ISSN: 0022-5258] 1967. 3x/yr. USD 215 (print & online eds.) Individuals, USD 55; Students, USD 20). Ed(s): Steven Morrison, David Starkie. University of Bath, Claverton Down, Bath, BA2 7AY, United Kingdom;

http://www.jtep.com. Illus., index, adv. Refereed. Circ: 1200. Vol. ends: Sep. Reprint: PSC. *Indexed:* ABIn, AmHI, BAS, BrHumI, CommAb, EIP, HRIS, IBR, IBSS, IBZ, JEL, PAIS, PRA, RRTA, SSCI, SUSA, WAE&RSA. *Bk. rev.:* Occasional, 150–1,500 words, signed. *Aud.:* Ac, Sa.

This scholarly journal focuses on research on economics and policy for intercity and urban transportation. The editorial board, the authors, and the topics they present are international in scope. Occasionally, issues of the journal cover a single topic in depth. The online version can be accessed at www.jtep.org. Appropriate for special collections.

6007. *Journal of Transport Geography.* [ISSN: 0966-6923] 1993. 6x/yr. EUR 449. Ed(s): Richard D Knowles. Pergamon, The Boulevard, Langford Ln, East Park, Kidlington, OX5 1GB, United Kingdom. Illus., index. Refereed. Vol. ends: Dec. Microform: PQC. Online: EBSCO Publishing, EBSCO Host; Gale; IngentaConnect; OhioLINK; ScienceDirect; SwetsWise Online Content. *Indexed:* EnvAb, H&SSA, H&TI, HRIS, OceAb, PollutAb, RiskAb, SSCI. *Bk. rev.:* 1–5, 500–1,500 words, signed. *Aud.:* Ac, Sa.

This scholarly, refereed publication addresses transport geography and spatial change and land use, including transport policies, infrastructure, operations, and transport networks. Each issue features referenced research articles with bibliographies, charts, graphs, and maps; a viewpoint article; and book reviews. The coverage is international and geared toward the professional and the academician. The journal now appears only online, through Elsevier Science Direct, at www.sciencedirect.com/science/journal/09666923. Appropriate for special collections.

6008. *Journal of Transportation Engineering.* Formerly (until 1983): *American Society of Civil Engineers. Transportation Engineering Journal;* Which was formed by the merger of (1962-1969): *American Society of Civil Engineers. Aero-Space Transport Division. Journal;* Which was formerly (until 1968): *American Society of Civil Engineers. Air Transport Division. Journal;* (1956-1968): *American Society of Civil Engineers. Highway Division. Journal;* (1957-1968): *American Society of Civil Engineers. Pipeline Division. Journal;* All of which superseded in part (1873-1955): *American Society of Civil Engineers. Proceedings.* [ISSN: 0733-947X] 1969. m. USD 675. Ed(s): Kumares C Sinha. American Society of Civil Engineers, 1801 Alexander Bell Dr, Reston, VA 20191-4400; http://www.asce.org. Illus., index. Refereed. Circ: 2400. Vol. ends: Nov/Dec. Microform: PQC. Online: American Institute of Physics, Scitation; EBSCO Publishing, EBSCO Host; SwetsWise Online Content. *Indexed:* AS&TI, C&ISA, CerAb, EngInd, EnvInd, ExcerpMed, H&SSA, HRIS, IAA, PetrolAb, RiskAb, SCI, SSCI. *Aud.:* Ac, Sa.

This scholarly journal is published by the American Society of Civil Engineers and is geared to the academician and the practitioner. It addresses all transportation modalities and covers the construction and maintenance of roads, bridges, airports, and pipelines; traffic management; business management; technology; and transportation economics. Each issue includes lengthy research articles with diagrams, charts, tables, and detailed references. Current and archived issues can be accessed online at http://scitation.aip.org/teo. Appropriate for large academic libraries and special collections.

6009. *Journal of Transportation Law, Logistics and Policy.* Former titles (until 1994): *Transportation Practitioners Journal;* (until 1984): *I C C Practitioners' Journal.* [ISSN: 1078-5906] 1933. q. USD 100 domestic; USD 105 Canada; USD 110 elsewhere. Ed(s): James F Bromley. Association for Transportation Law, Logistics and Policy, PMB 250, 3 Church Cir, Annapolis, MD 21401-1933; Michalski@atlp.org; http://www.atlp.org. Illus., index. Circ: 4000. Vol. ends: Summer. Microform: WSH; PMC. *Indexed:* ABIn, CLI, HRIS, ILP, LRI. *Bk. rev.:* Occasional, 1,200–2,000 words, signed. *Aud.:* Ac, Sa.

Published by the Association for Transportation Law, Logistics and Policy (ATLLP), this scholarly, peer-reviewed journal includes articles on transportation law, practice, legislation, regulation, history, theory, logistics, economics, and statistics. It is geared to the professional and the academician. Coverage is focused on North America, but occasionally articles on other areas of the world will be included. Every issue includes updates on recent administrative and regulatory developments. Alternate issues contain book reviews and the ATLLP schedule of events. The journal's web presence can be found at www.atlp.org/journal.html; the archives can be accessed with a password. Appropriate for special libraries.

6010. Logistics Management. Former titles (until Jun.2002): *Logistics Management & Distribution Report;* Which was formed by the merger of (1901-1998): *Distribution;* (1962-1998): *Logistics Management;* Which was formerly (until 1996): *Traffic Management;* (until 1992): *Chilton's Distribution;* (until 1986): *Chilton's Distribution for Traffic and Transportation Decision Makers;* (until 1980): *Chilton's Distribution;* (until 1979): *Chilton's Distribution Worldwide;* (until 1977): *Distribution Worldwide;* (until 1972): *Chilton's Distribution Worldwide;* (until 1970): *Distribution Worldwide;* (until 1969): *Distribution Manager.* [ISSN: 1540-3890] 1998. m. Plus annual directory. USD 99.90 domestic; USD 129.90 Canada; USD 125.90 Mexico. Ed(s): Michael Levans, James Aaron Cooke. Reed Business Information, 225 Wyman St, Waltham, MA 02451; http://www.reedbusiness.com. Illus., adv. Circ: 77000 Controlled. Microform: PQC. Online: EBSCO Publishing, EBSCO Host; Gale; LexisNexis; OCLC Online Computer Library Center, Inc.; ProQuest LLC (Ann Arbor); H.W. Wilson. *Indexed:* ABIn, BPI, CWI, HRIS, LogistBibl. *Aud.:* Ac, Sa.

This trade journal provides strong coverage in the areas of transportation operations and policy. Although the focus is on the United States, some coverage is provided on export–import and overseas shipments. Feature articles include company case studies, multipart articles, impacts of government policies and actions, economic analysis, new services, and innovative business practices. The journal includes a large array of monthly columns on various aspects of the industry, e.g., acquisitions, express carriers, railroads, air freight, regulation, etc. It also includes news summaries, economic indicators, and product and equipment notices, as well as an annual salary survey. Other regular annual features include polls and buyers' guides. This journal's online version can be accessed at www.manufacturing.net/lm. Appropriate for special collections.

6011. Logistics Today. Former titles (until 2003): *Transportation & Distribution;* (until 1987): *Handling and Shipping Management;* (until vol.19, no.10, Oct. 1978): *Handling and Shipping.* [ISSN: 1547-1438] 1960. m. USD 60 domestic (Free to qualified personnel). Ed(s): Perry A Trunick. Penton Media, Inc., 1300 E 9th St, Cleveland, OH 44114-1503; information@penton.com; http://www.penton.com/. Illus., adv. Circ: 71609 Controlled. Vol. ends: Dec. Microform: PQC. Online: The Dialog Corporation; EBSCO Publishing, EBSCO Host; Florida Center for Library Automation; Gale; Northern Light Technology, Inc.; OCLC Online Computer Library Center, Inc.; ProQuest LLC (Ann Arbor); H.W. Wilson. *Indexed:* ABIn, BPI, C&ISA, CWI, CerAb, ExcerpMed, HRIS, IAA, LogistBibl. *Aud.:* Sa.

As one of the important trade journals on logistics, this publication covers topics related to supply-chain management, covering not only transportation but also other parts of the chain: materials handling, information systems, warehousing, and packaging. While the journal focuses on U.S.-based businesses, it also covers non-U.S. markets and issues. There are several annual features on packaging, integrated warehousing, and distribution. Regular features include columns on hazardous materials, government analysis, event calendars, news, and an industry watch. The journal's web site at www.logisticstoday.com provides additional news features not included in the print version. Targeted to industry professionals. Appropriate for special collections.

6012. Low-Fare and Regional Airlines. Former titles (until 2006): *Regional Airline World;* (until 1999): *Commuter World;* Which incorporated: *Regional Air International.* [ISSN: 1753-0598] 1984. 10x/yr. GBP 80. Ed(s): Bernie Baldwin. Shephard Press Ltd., 111 High St, Burnham, SL1 7JZ, United Kingdom; info@shephard.co.uk. Adv. Circ: 13056. *Indexed:* HRIS. *Aud.:* Sa.

This journal addresses the regional and low-cost airline industry worldwide and is geared to the practitioner. Coverage includes industry news and events, finances, management and mergers, personnel, technology, and training. Each issue includes a significant international news section, feature articles, the profile of a specific airline, and a calendar of events. The table of contents of the current issue and archived articles can be accessed at www.shephard.co.uk/CA/Publications.aspx?Action=-329809239&ID= 5d480705-c0c2-4f9d-a4a8-2c547eab4647. Appropriate for special collections.

Marine Log. See Marine Science and Technology section.

Maritime Policy and Management. See Marine Science and Technology section.

6013. Mass Transit: better transit through better management. [ISSN: 0364-3484] 1974. bi-m. USD 48. Ed(s): Lori Lundquist. Cygnus Business Media, Inc., 1233 Janesville Ave, Fort Atkinson, WI 53538-0803; http://www.masstransitmag.com. Illus., adv. Circ: 18000. Vol. ends: Nov/Dec. Online: Florida Center for Library Automation; Gale; Northern Light Technology, Inc.; OCLC Online Computer Library Center, Inc.; ProQuest LLC (Ann Arbor); H.W. Wilson. *Indexed:* ABIn, AS&TI, BPI, EIP, HRIS. *Aud.:* Sa.

This trade publication addresses mass transit for the management practitioner. The journal's focus is on North America, although there is some international coverage. Feature article topics include management, policy, operations, and equipment. Each issue also includes industry news, legal notes, a forum for transit managers, a calendar of events, and classified ads. The journal's online version can be accessed at www.masstransitmag.com. Appropriate for special collections.

6014. Metro Magazine. Former titles: *Metro (Torrance);* (until 1994): *Metro Magazine;* (until 1985): *Metro;* (until 1974): *Metropolitan.* 1904. 10x/yr. USD 40 domestic (Free to qualified personnel). Ed(s): Janna Starcic, Steve Hirano. Bobit Business Media, 3520 Challenger St, Torrance, CA 90503; order@bobit.com; http://www.bobit.com. Illus., adv. Circ: 20616 Controlled. Vol. ends: Nov/Dec. *Indexed:* FLI, HRIS. *Aud.:* Sa.

This journal, covering national and international urban and interurban transportation systems, targets the practitioner. It addresses all major urban transportation issues: bus systems, light rail, motor coaches, intelligent transportation systems, high-speed rail, urban transit management, finance, and legislation. Each issue includes industry news and events, feature articles, editorials, product and innovation showcases, a calendar of events, and an industry personnel section. The last issue of the year includes a tear-out calendar highlighting dates of industry interest. There is an annual Top 50 Motorcoach Fleets list. The journal's online version and archived articles can be accessed at www.metro-magazine.com. Appropriate for special collections.

6015. Motor Coach Age. [ISSN: 0739-117X] 1948. q. Membership, USD 35. Motor Bus Society, Inc, PO Box 261, Paramus, NJ 07653-0261; membership@motorbussociety.org; http://www.motorbussociety.org/. Illus., adv. Vol. ends: Dec. *Indexed:* HRIS. *Aud.:* Ga, Sa.

Published by the Motor Bus Society, this journal addresses the history of the bus industry in the United States, for both the enthusiast and the practitioner. It includes feature articles, editorials, old route maps, some statistics, a literature review section, and letters to the editor. Historical photographs, some rare, enhance the text. Each issue emphasizes a city or bus line. Contents of past issues, including cover photographs, can be accessed at www.motorbussociety.org/mca. According to the publisher, the journal is about two years behind in publication. Appropriate for large general collections or special collections.

6016. Motor Ship. Formerly: *British Motor Ship.* [ISSN: 0027-2000] 1920. m. GBP 118. Mercator Media Ltd., Mercator Media Limited, The Old Mill, Fareham, PO16 0RA, United Kingdom; info@mercatormedia.com; http://www.mercatormedia.com/. Illus., index, adv. Circ: 8451. Vol. ends: Dec. *Indexed:* C&ISA, CerAb, EngInd, ExcerpMed, H&SSA, HRIS, IAA, OceAb. *Aud.:* Sa.

This publication provides news and in-depth coverage of all aspects of the marine industry. The feature articles are often investigative and include coverage of new buildings, in-depth country reviews, descriptions of ships, and exhibition previews. Regular columns cover news on cruise ships, propulsion, and ship repair, as well as equipment, updates on movers and shakers in the industry, and an events calendar. A quarterly supplement covers all aspects of ship repair and usually includes a directory of ship repair yards. Other supplements cover cargo management, port infrastructure, and cruise ships. The web site at www.motorship.com offers feature articles for current and back issues, as well as other parts of the magazine; a password is required. Appropriate for special collections.

6017. *N R H S Bulletin.* formerly (until 2005): *National Railway Bulletin.* [ISSN: 1940-3615] 1935. 5x/yr. USD 15; USD 19 foreign. Ed(s): Frank G Tatnall. National Railway Historical Society, PO Box 58547, Philadelphia, PA 19102; http://www.nrhs.com. Illus. Circ: 18000. Vol. ends: No. 6. *Indexed:* HRIS. *Bk. rev.:* 5–12, 200–750 words, signed. *Aud.:* Ga, Sa.

Published by the National Railway Historical Society, this journal is targeted to its membership. Rail fans will enjoy the richly illustrated articles on history and current events in the railroad industry. Although many articles focus on passenger transport, there is also historical coverage of freight trains and services. One issue per year is devoted to the activities of the society, with an annual report as well as section-by-section state-of-the-chapter reports. Every issue contains many book reviews, letters to the editor, and a digest of transit news. Appropriate for large general collections and special collections.

6018. *Overdrive: the voice of the American trucker.* Incorporates (1970-2001): *Owner Operator.* [ISSN: 0030-7394] 1961. m. USD 34.97 (Free to qualified personnel). Ed(s): Linda Longton. Randall-Reilly Publishing Company, 3200 Rice Mine Rd, Tuscaloosa, AL 35406; http://www.randallpub.com. Illus. Circ: 104753 Paid and controlled. Vol. ends: Dec. Online: EBSCO Publishing, EBSCO Host. *Indexed:* HRIS, LRI. *Aud.:* Sa.

This journal addresses the North American trucking industry and targets the truck driver and fleet operator. It covers industry news and events, legislation, safety, technology, product analysis, management, training, and personnel issues. Each issue includes feature articles, a calendar of events, a financial section, an industry-related web site directory, product/equipment reviews, and a job-hunting section. In 2001, this journal took over the publication of content from *Owner Operator.* Recent editions of the journal can be accessed at www.etrucker.com/default.asp?magid=1. Appropriate for special collections.

6019. *Passenger Transport.* [ISSN: 0364-345X] 1943. w. USD 65 in North America; USD 77 elsewhere. Ed(s): Rhonda Goldberg. American Public Transportation Association, 1666 K St., NW 11th Fl., Washington, DC 20006; sberlin@apta.com; http://www.apta.com. Illus., index, adv. Circ: 4413 Paid. Vol. ends: Dec. *Indexed:* HRIS. *Aud.:* Sa.

This glossy, newspaper-format, weekly publication is targeted to North American transit officials who are likely to be members of the American Public Transportation Association (APTA), the magazine's publisher. There is significant coverage of people involved in the industry, providing interviews and much space to news items about the movement of people in the field. In addition to providing current news on the subject, regular features include industry briefs, international news, classifieds, and regular columns. In conjunction with APTA conferences, special issues are published focusing on city-by-city transit operations. The online version of the journal, and archived articles, can be accessed at www.apta.com/news/pt. Appropriate for special collections.

6020. *Pipeline & Gas Journal: energy construction, transportation and distribution.* Incorporates (1928-1990): *Pipeline (Houston);* Which was formerly (until 1974): *Pipe Line News;* Formed by the merger of (19??-1970): *Pipeline Engineer;* Which was formerly (until 1956): *Petroleum Engineer, Oil and Gas Pipelining Edition;* (1859-1970): *American Gas Journal;* Which was formerly (until 1921): *American Gas Engineering Journal;* (until 1917): *American Gas Light Journal.* [ISSN: 0032-0188] 1970. m. USD 33 domestic; USD 60 Canada; USD 70 elsewhere. Ed(s): Rita Tubb, Jeff Share. Oildom Publishing Co. of Texas, Inc., 1160 Dairy Ashford, #610, Houston, TX 77079; maxine@oildompublishing.com; http://www.oildompublishing.com. Illus., adv. Circ: 27500 Controlled. Online: EBSCO Publishing, EBSCO Host;

Factiva, Inc.; Florida Center for Library Automation; Gale; Northern Light Technology, Inc.; OCLC Online Computer Library Center, Inc.; ProQuest LLC (Ann Arbor); H.W. Wilson. *Indexed:* ABIn, AS&TI, C&ISA, CEA, CerAb, EnvAb, HRIS, IAA, PetrolAb. *Aud.:* Sa.

This journal addresses the international pipeline drilling, maintenance, distribution, and marketing industry, and it is geared to the practitioner. Coverage includes industry news and events, pipeline drilling, pipeline maintenance, the gas and petroleum industries, legislation, safety, technology, equipment, management, distribution, marketing, industry personnel, and the political/economic aspects of the pipeline industry. Each issue includes feature articles, a calendar of events, product reviews, a section on innovative technology, an advertisers index, a section devoted to pipeline projects around the world, and a government section. There is an extensive annual buyers' guide. The online version of this journal can be accessed at www.oildompublishing.com/PGJ/pgjarchv.htm. Appropriate for special collections.

6021. *PipeLine and Gas Technology.* Former titles (until 2002): *Pipe Line & Gas Industry;* (until Jan.1995): *Pipe Line Industry.* [ISSN: 1540-3688] 1954. m. Free to qualified personnel. Ed(s): Bruce Beaubouef. Hart Energy Publishing, LP, 1616 S Voss Rd, Ste 1000, Houston, TX 77057-2627. Illus. Circ: 21500. *Indexed:* ABIn, AS&TI, PetrolAb. *Bk. rev.:* Number and length vary. *Aud.:* Sa.

This journal is edited for personnel engaged in the design, operation, maintenance, construction, and management of pipelines and gas utilities worldwide. Includes gas transmission and distribution systems as well as pipeline systems for crude oil, products, water, and slurries. The journal includes feature articles, an equipment section, a calendar of events, and an advertiser's index. The online version can be accessed at www.pipelineandgastechnology.com. Appropriate for special libraries.

6022. *Progressive Railroading.* [ISSN: 0033-0817] 1958. m. Free to qualified personnel. Ed(s): Jeff Stagl, Patrick Foran. Trade Press Publishing Corp., 2100 W Florist Ave, Milwaukee, WI 53209; http://www.tradepress.com. Illus., adv. Circ: 25000 Paid and controlled. Vol. ends: Dec. *Indexed:* C&ISA, CerAb, HRIS, IAA, LogistBibl. *Aud.:* Ac, Sa.

As a major U.S. trade journal in the rail industry, this publication focuses on operations and equipment used in freight and passenger services, including urban transit. The feature articles provide profiles of key companies, articles on safety, alliances, and more. Regular features are extensive, including industry and regional news and analysis, statistics, events, commentary, and equipment information. This magazine publishes many annual guides to the industry on the subjects of cars, locomotives, and track, finance, and leasing. The web site, at www.progressiverailroading.com, includes late-breaking news and some of the feature articles from the current issue of the magazine. Appropriate for special collections.

6023. *Public Roads.* [ISSN: 0033-3735] 1918. bi-m. USD 26 domestic; USD 36.40 foreign. U.S. Federal Highway Administration, 400 7th St, SW, Washington, DC 20590; http://www.fhwa.dot.gov/. Illus., index. Vol. ends: Spring. Microform: CIS; PQC. Online: EBSCO Publishing, EBSCO Host; Florida Center for Library Automation; Gale; Northern Light Technology, Inc.; OCLC Online Computer Library Center, Inc.; ProQuest LLC (Ann Arbor). *Indexed:* AS&TI, AgeL, AmStI, C&ISA, CerAb, ChemAb, EngInd, ExcerpMed, HRIS, IAA, IUSGP, PAIS. *Aud.:* Ga, Sa.

This publication covers federal highway policies, programs, research, and development. While its primary audience is transportation officials, researchers, field technicians, and engineers, the journal's content could also be used by a general audience wishing to stay informed about transportation issues and progress. Each issue includes features on new research, recent publications, news in the industry, and a calendar of events. Full text of articles back to 1993 is available on the web site at www.tfhrc.gov/pubrds/pubrds.htm. Appropriate for large general collections and special collections.

6024. *Public Transport International (French Edition).* Supersedes in part (in 1997): *Public Transport International (Multilingual Edition);* Which was formerly (until 1990): *U I T P Revue; International Union of*

Tramways, Light Railways and Motor Omnibuses. Review. [ISSN: 1029-1261] 1952. bi-m. Members, TPE 56; Non-members, EUR 74. Ed(s): Heather Allen. International Union of Public Transport, Av Herrmann Debroux 17, Brussels, 1160, Belgium. Illus., adv. Circ: 3000. Vol. ends: Nov/Dec. *Indexed:* C&ISA, CerAb, EngInd, HRIS, IAA. *Aud.:* Ac, Sa.

Published by the International Association of Public Transport, this journal addresses the international urban and interurban public-transit industry. It should be of interest to both the academician and the practitioner. Each issue consists of research articles on the technological, socioeconomic, or political aspects of public transportation. Statistical graphs and tables enhance the text; however, references are not provided for the research articles. Some references are available upon request. Selected archived articles can be accessed at www.uitp.com. Appropriate for special collections.

6025. *Rail Travel News.* [ISSN: 0896-4440] 1970. s-m. USD 26; USD 35 foreign. Ed(s): James Russell. Message Media, PO Box 9007, Berkeley, CA 94709; rtn@trainweb.com; http://trainweb.com/rtn. Illus., adv. Circ: 2000 Paid. Vol. ends: Dec. *Indexed:* HRIS. *Aud.:* Ga, Sa.

This is a rail-fan magazine devoted to domestic rail passenger service news. Each issue includes feature articles on rail trips, a "Rail Fantrips" section with suggested rail travel tours, and general news on North American rail passenger travel. Selected feature articles and news can be accessed at www.railtravel-news.com. Appropriate for large general collections and special collections.

6026. *Railfan & Railroad.* Formed by the merger of (1974-1979): *Railfan (Newton);* (1937-1979): *Railroad Magazine;* Which was formerly: *Railroad Stories.* [ISSN: 0163-7266] 1979. m. USD 27.95 domestic; USD 35.95 Canada; USD 37.95 elsewhere. Ed(s): E. Steven Barry. Carstens Publications, Inc., 108 Phil Hardin Rd, Newton, NJ 07860-0777; carstens@carstens-publications.com; http://www.carstens-publications.com. Illus., adv. Circ: 52000 Paid and controlled. Vol. ends: Dec. *Indexed:* HRIS. *Bk. rev.:* Number and length vary. *Aud.:* Ga, Sa.

This journal addresses railroading and railway history for the United States, Canada, and occasionally Mexico. It is geared to the enthusiast, although a specialist may be interested in the historical information provided. Contents include railroading news and events; feature articles; book, video, and software reviews; preservation information; sections devoted to railway dining, museums, and tour schedules; and product and hobby reviews. A pull-out index for the previous year is published each spring. Text is enhanced with a large color photography section. The tables of contents for the current and forthcoming issues can be accessed at www.railfan.com. Appropriate for large general collections and special collections.

6027. *Railroad History.* Formerly (until 1972): *Railway and Locomotive Historical Society. Bulletin.* [ISSN: 0090-7847] 1921. s-a. Individual members, USD 25. Ed(s): Mark Reutter. Railway & Locomotive Historical Society, c/o Mark Reutter, PO Box 517, Urbana, IL 61803; mreutter@uiuc.edu; http://www.rrhistorical.com/. Illus., index, adv. Refereed. Circ: 4500 Paid. Microform: PQC. *Indexed:* AmH&L, HRIS, HistAb. *Bk. rev.:* 20–30, up to 1,500 words, signed. *Aud.:* Ac, Sa.

Published by the Railway and Locomotive Historical Society, this journal is geared to the academician and the enthusiast. It addresses the socioeconomic, business, and technological aspects of domestic and international railroad and railway history. It includes feature essays and lengthy research articles with diagrams, maps, and extensive references. The journal has an impressive book review section and a section on articles recommended for reading. Each issue includes information on preservation, locomotives, a discussion forum, and a photography section. There is a yearly bonus issue devoted to a specific topic. A cumulative index from 1921 forward can be accessed at http://rlhs.org/ridxtit.htm. Appropriate for large general collections and special collections.

6028. *Railway Age.* Incorporates (1947-1991, June): *Modern Railroads;* Which was formerly (until 1982): *Modern Railroads - Rail Transit;* (until 1971): *Modern Railroads; Railway Locomotives and Cars;* Former titles (1910-1918): *Railway Age Gazette;* (1908-1910): *Railroad Age Gazette;* Which was formed by the merger of (1870-1908): *Railway Gazette;* (1900-1908): *Railway Age;* Which was formerly (1891-1900): *Railway*

Age and Northwestern Railroads; Which was formed by the merger of (1876-1891): *Railway Age;* (1887-1891): *Northwestern Railroads.* [ISSN: 0033-8826] 1876. m. USD 72 in North America (Free to qualified personnel). Ed(s): Marybeth Luczak, William Vantuono. Simmons-Boardman Publishing Corp., 345 Hudson St, 12th Fl, New York, NY 10014-4502. Illus., adv. Circ: 26927 Paid and controlled. Vol. ends: Dec. Microform: CIS; PQC. Online: EBSCO Publishing, EBSCO Host; Florida Center for Library Automation; Gale; Northern Light Technology, Inc.; OCLC Online Computer Library Center, Inc.; ProQuest K-12 Learning Solutions; ProQuest LLC (Ann Arbor); H.W. Wilson. *Indexed:* ABIn, BPI, C&ISA, CerAb, EngInd, EnvAb, H&SSA, HRIS, IAA, PAIS. *Aud.:* Ac, Sa.

As one of the major North American railroad trade journals, *Railway Age* covers all aspects of the railroad industry. The journal addresses both freight and passenger service, encompassing commuter, rapid, and light-rail transit, as well as the equipment and supply industry, management, finance, and operational considerations. Annual special issues are published and can include buyers' guides, planners' guides, or year-end outlooks. Regular features include at-a-glance industry indicators and outlooks, railroader of the year, meeting information, company indexes, professional directories, classifieds, and commentary on a variety of aspects of the industry. The focus is on business rather than technical aspects of the industry. The web site, at www.railwayage-.com, contains late-breaking news as well as selected articles, commentaries, and statistics from the magazine. Appropriate for large general collections and special collections.

6029. *Railway Gazette International: a journal of management, engineering and operation.* Former titles (until 1971): *International Railway Gazette;* (until 19??): *Railway Gazette;* Which incorporated (1880-1935): *Railway Engineer; Railway News; Railway Times; Transport and Railroad Center.* [ISSN: 0373-5346] 1835. m. GBP 68.40 domestic; EUR 133 in Europe Eurozone; USD 188.55 United States. Ed(s): Murray Hughes. Reed Business Information Ltd., Quadrant House, The Quadrant, Brighton Rd, Sutton, SM2 5AS, United Kingdom; rbi.subscriptions@qss-uk.com; http://www.reedbusiness.co.uk/. Illus., index, adv. Circ: 9616. Vol. ends: Dec. *Indexed:* ABIn, C&ISA, CerAb, EngInd, HRIS, IAA. *Bk. rev.:* Number and length vary. *Aud.:* Sa.

This journal addresses the international rail industry, encompassing heavy and light rail and both freight and passenger services. It is geared to the practitioner and includes industry news and events, technology, legislation, safety, business, finance, management, research, and the socioeconomic and political environments of the rail industry. Each issue contains feature articles, a detailed industry news section, a calendar of events, product reviews, a small book review section, and a section devoted to industry personnel. A different world region is highlighted in each issue. Current articles and an index back to 1996 can be accessed at www.railwaygazette.com. Appropriate for special collections.

6030. *Roads & Bridges.* Former titles (until 1984): *Roads;* (until 1983): *R U R: Rural and Urban Roads; Rural and Urban Roads.* [ISSN: 8750-9229] 1906. m. USD 95 foreign (Free to qualified personnel). Ed(s): Bill Wilson. Scranton Gillette Communications, Inc., 380 E Northwest Hwy, Ste 200, Des Plaines, IL 60016-2282; http://www.scrantongillette.com. Illus., adv. Circ: 60000 Controlled. Vol. ends: Dec. Microform: PQC. Online: EBSCO Publishing, EBSCO Host; Gale. *Indexed:* C&ISA, CerAb, ExcerpMed, HRIS, IAA. *Aud.:* Sa.

Targeting the practitioner, this journal addresses the domestic transportation construction industry. Coverage includes industry news and events, technology, legislation, safety and regulation, construction materials, construction machinery, products, and equipment. Each issue includes feature articles, a legal section, product and equipment reviews, and sections devoted to technical innovations and construction vehicles. Some issues include information on software and online industry resources. Articles from the current issue and archived issues can be accessed at www.roadsbridges.com/rb. Appropriate for special collections.

6031. *Supply Chain Management Review.* [ISSN: 1521-9747] 1997. bi-m. USD 209 in US & Canada; USD 241 foreign; USD 59.95 newsstand/ cover. Reed Business Information, 275 Washington St, Newton, MA

02458; http://www.reedbusiness.com. Adv. Circ: 12000. Vol. ends: Feb. Online: EBSCO Publishing, EBSCO Host; Florida Center for Library Automation; Gale; OCLC Online Computer Library Center, Inc.; ProQuest LLC (Ann Arbor). *Indexed:* ABIn, HRIS, LogistBibl. *Bk. rev.:* 3–5, 250–750 words. *Aud.:* Ac, Sa.

This journal addresses the international transportation logistics and supply chain management industries. It targets both the academician and the practitioner. Coverage includes logistics, supply chain management, procurement, technology, e-commerce, warehousing, management, training, and information flow. Each issue includes both feature articles and research articles with references; a resource section for literature, web sites, and networking; a professional-development section listing events, seminars, workshops, and academic programs; and statistics, charts, and graphs. There is at least one subject-specific supplement issued per year. The journal's online version can be accessed at www.scmr.com. Appropriate for large academic collections and special collections.

6032. *T R News.* Former titles (until 1983): *Transportation Research News;* (until 1974): *Highway Research News.* [ISSN: 0738-6826] 1963. bi-m. USD 55 domestic; USD 65 foreign. Ed(s): Nancy A Ackerman. U.S. National Research Council, Transportation Research Board, Keck Center of the National Academies, 500 Fifth St, NW, Washington, DC 20001; http://www.trb.org. Illus. Circ: 10000. Vol. ends: Nov/Dec. *Indexed:* C&ISA, CerAb, EngInd, HRIS, IAA. *Bk. rev.:* 4–8, up to 150 words. *Aud.:* Ac, Sa.

This publication covers research and innovations in all modes of transportation. Article contributions come from academics and professionals in the industry. The focus is on U.S.-based initiatives and specifically on Transportation Research Board (TRB) activities. In addition to feature articles, each issue contains profiles of academics and professionals, news briefs and TRB highlights, an events calendar, and a listing of new TRB publications with abstracts. The web site includes the tables of contents for current and back issues, and can be accessed at www4.trb.org/trb/onlinepubs.nsf/web/tr_news. Appropriate for special collections.

6033. *Traffic Engineering & Control: the international journal of traffic management and transportation planning.* [ISSN: 0041-0683] 1960. m. GBP 65; USD 120. Ed(s): Keith Lumley. Printerhall Ltd., 29 Newman St, London, W1P 3PE, United Kingdom. Illus., index, adv. Refereed. Circ: 5400. Vol. ends: Dec. Microform: PQC. Online: EBSCO Publishing, EBSCO Host. *Indexed:* BrTechI, C&ISA, CerAb, EngInd, ErgAb, ExcerpMed, HRIS, IAA. *Bk. rev.:* Occasional, up to 750 words. *Aud.:* Ac, Sa.

This British journal primarily covers European countries, with some international coverage. It encompasses industry issues, news, interviews, and current research in traffic engineering. It is targeted at academics, practicing engineers, and students in the field. Regular features also include buyers' guides, classifieds, product news, opinion pieces, and a calendar of events. Annual features include a review of activities of British university transportation research centers. A current table of contents and searchable articles can be accessed at www.tecmagazine.com. Appropriate for special collections.

6034. *Traffic Technology International.* [ISSN: 1356-9252] 1994. bi-m. Free to qualified personnel. U K & International Press, Abinger House, Church St, Dorking, RH4 1DF, United Kingdom; info@ukintpress.com; http://www.ukintpress.com/. Adv. Circ: 18000 Paid. *Indexed:* HRIS. *Aud.:* Sa, Ac.

This journal addresses the issues of traffic safety and traffic control. It is global in breadth and targets both the academician and the practitioner. Coverage includes industry news and events, intelligent transportation systems, traffic control devices, traffic safety devices, regulation, legislation, traffic systems operations, research, personnel, management, and training. Each issue includes feature articles, a calendar of events, an international news section, a bulletin board that highlights software and innovative technology, statistics, and tables and graphs. The journal includes a yearly supplement titled "Tolltrans" that addresses every aspect of highway tolls. The journal has a web presence at www.ukipme.com. Appropriate for large academic collections and special collections.

6035. *Traffic World: the logistics news weekly.* Incorporates: *Federal Trade Reporter.* [ISSN: 0041-073X] 1907. w. USD 174 in US & Canada; USD 259 elsewhere. Ed(s): Paul Page, William B Cassidy. Journal of Commerce, Inc., 1270 National Press Bldg, Washington, DC 20045; customerservice@cbizmedia.com; http://www.joc.com. Illus., index, adv. Circ: 9000 Paid. Vol. ends: No. 13. CD-ROM: The Dialog Corporation. Microform: PQC. Online: The Dialog Corporation; EBSCO Publishing, EBSCO Host; Florida Center for Library Automation; Gale; Northern Light Technology, Inc.; OCLC Online Computer Library Center, Inc.; ProQuest LLC (Ann Arbor); H.W. Wilson. *Indexed:* ABIn, BPI, CWI, HRIS, LogistBibl. *Aud.:* Ga, Sa.

This trade publication provides weekly news and articles on freight transportation and logistics. Coverage is primarily of North America, but articles on Europe and other areas of the world are frequently included. Regular features include Washington reports; articles about logistics; rail, motor, air, water, and technology; columns on career advancement; commentary; Q&A; e-strategies; classifieds; a calendar of events; and news about people in the industry. The web site offers daily news and full-text articles and features from each issue, accessible with a password, at www.trafficworld.com. Appropriate for large general collections and special collections.

6036. *Trains.* [ISSN: 0041-0934] 1940. m. USD 42.95; USD 54 Canada; USD 4.95 newsstand/cover. Kalmbach Publishing Co., 21027 Crossroads Circle, PO Box 1612, Waukesha, WI 53187-1612; customerservice@kalmbach.com; http://www.kalmbach.com. Illus., index, adv. Circ: 106000 Paid. Vol. ends: Dec. Online: EBSCO Publishing, EBSCO Host; Gale; Northern Light Technology, Inc.; OCLC Online Computer Library Center, Inc.; ProQuest K-12 Learning Solutions; ProQuest LLC (Ann Arbor). *Indexed:* HRIS, MASUSE. *Bk. rev.:* 3–5, 250–750 words, signed. *Aud.:* Ga, Sa.

This journal addresses both the light and heavy rail industries of North America, with some cursory international news. It is geared to the enthusiast; however, the specialist may find the historical and management articles of interest. Coverage includes industry news and events, tours, rail-related hobbies and memorabilia, railroad personnel, preservation, museums, and some management and policy matters. Each issue includes feature articles, book and video reviews, a calendar of events, tour schedules, and a significant photography section that sponsors a readers' photography contest. There is a yearly pull-out recreational-railroading supplement. The journal's web presence, including a current and archived tables of contents, can be accessed at www.trains.com/trn. Appropriate for large public library collections or special collections.

6037. *Tramways & Urban Transit: international light rail magazine.* Former titles (until 1998): *Light Rail and Modern Tramway;* (until 1996): *Modern Tramway and Light Rail Transit;* (until 1980): *Modern Tramway and Rapid Transit;* (until 1977): *Modern Tramway and Light Railway Review.* [ISSN: 1460-8324] 1938. m. Ed(s): Howard Johnston. Ian Allan Publishing Ltd., Riverdene Business Park, Riverdene Industrial Estate, Walton-on-Thames, KT12 4RG, United Kingdom; subs@ianallanpub.co.uk; http://www.ianallanpublishing.com. Illus., adv. Circ: 7250. *Indexed:* BrTechI, HRIS. *Bk. rev.:* Number and length vary. *Aud.:* Sa.

Published by the Light Rail Transit Association, this journal has been in continuous publication since 1938. It addresses the global, light-rail, and urban transport industry and is geared to the practitioner. The journal covers industry news and events, technology, funding, legislation, safety, management, and industry personnel. Each issue includes feature articles; an international tram and light-rail news section; reviews of books, databases, and videos; a calendar of events; obituaries; and a product review section. Color and black-and-white photography enhance the text. The tables of contents, dating back to 1998, can be found at www.lrta.org/mag.html. Appropriate for special collections.

6038. *Transport Policy.* [ISSN: 0967-070X] 1993. 6x/yr. EUR 514. Ed(s): M Ben-Akiva, J Preston. Pergamon, The Boulevard, Langford Ln, East Park, Kidlington, OX5 1GB, United Kingdom. Illus., index, adv. Refereed. Vol. ends: Oct (No. 8). Microform: PQC. Online: EBSCO

Publishing, EBSCO Host; Gale; IngentaConnect; OhioLINK; ScienceDirect; SwetsWise Online Content. *Indexed:* EnvAb, H&SSA, HRIS, PollutAb, SSCI, SUSA. *Aud.:* Ac, Sa.

This scholarly publication of the World Conference on Transport Research Society covers all modes of transportation, addressing theoretical and practical aspects of transportation policy and administration. It targets the practitioner, government official, and academician. Some issues will focus on a single aspect of transport policy. In addition to scholarly articles, each issue includes a section on the activities of the World Conference on Transport Research Society. The online version is available by subscription through Elsevier. Appropriate for special collections.

6039. *Transport Reviews: a transnational, transdisciplinary journal.*
[ISSN: 0144-1647] 1981. bi-m. GBP 694 print & online eds. Ed(s): Juan de Dios Ortuzar, David A Hensher. Routledge, 4 Park Sq, Milton Park, Abingdon, OX14 4RN, United Kingdom; journals@routledge.com; http://www.routledge.co.uk. Illus., index, adv. Refereed. Vol. ends: Oct/Dec. Online: EBSCO Publishing, EBSCO Host; Gale; IngentaConnect; OCLC Online Computer Library Center, Inc.; SwetsWise Online Content. Reprint: PSC. *Indexed:* C&ISA, CerAb, ErgAb, HRIS, IAA, IBR, IBZ, IndIslam, SSCI. *Bk. rev.:* 1–3, 350–750 words, signed. *Aud.:* Ac, Sa.

This refereed, scholarly publication covers all modes of transportation and is global in scope. Topics can touch on social, economic, or technological aspects of the field. The content is aimed at both academic and professional audiences. Occasional issues are organized around a specific topic. Searchable tables of contents for current and back issues are available on the journal's web site at www.tandf.co.uk/journals/tf/01441647.html. Appropriate for special collections.

6040. *Transport Topics: national newspaper of the trucking industry.*
Formerly: *A T A News Bulletin.* [ISSN: 0041-1558] 1935. w. Mon. USD 99 domestic; USD 3.95 newsstand/cover. Ed(s): Bruce Harmon. American Trucking Associations, Inc., 2200 Mill Rd, Alexandria, VA 22314. Illus., adv. Circ: 32000 Paid. Microform: PQC. Online: ProQuest LLC (Ann Arbor). *Indexed:* ABIn, HRIS, LogistBibl. *Aud.:* Ga, Sa.

This glossy, tabloid-format newspaper covers the trucking industry and is published by the American Trucking Associations. It is geared toward the practitioner. It is comprised mostly of short articles concerning all aspects of trucking, but especially state and federal regulations, management, policy analysis, finance, operations, equipment, and events. Issues often include special sections on a single topic. Regular features include state news, a weekly business review, fuel prices, products, people news, a calendar of events, job listings, real estate, and equipment. The web site offers late-breaking news and other regular columns at www.transporttopics.com. A password is required. Appropriate for large general collections or special collections.

6041. *Transportation: an international journal devoted to the improvement of transportation planning and practice.* [ISSN: 0049-4488] 1972. 6x/yr. EUR 770 print & online eds. Ed(s): Martin G Richards. Springer New York LLC, 233 Spring St, New York, NY 10013-1578; service-ny@ springer.com; http://www.springer.com/. Illus., index, adv. Refereed. Vol. ends: No. 4. Microform: PQC. Online: EBSCO Publishing, EBSCO Host; Gale; IngentaConnect; OCLC Online Computer Library Center, Inc.; OhioLINK; ProQuest LLC (Ann Arbor); Springer LINK; SwetsWise Online Content. Reprint: PSC. *Indexed:* ABIn, AS&TI, AgeL, C&ISA, CABA, CerAb, EngInd, EnvInd, ExcerpMed, H&SSA, HRIS, IAA, IBSS, JEL, RRTA, SCI, SSCI, SUSA, WAE&RSA. *Aud.:* Ac, Sa.

This scholarly publication provides research articles that cover all modes of transportation around the world. The audience is policy makers, transportation planners, and operations managers. Most issues contain four articles, but occasional issues contain many more, focused on a topic. The journal can be accessed at www.springerlink.com. Appropriate for special collections.

6042. *Transportation Journal.* [ISSN: 0041-1612] 1961. q. USD 95 in US & Canada; USD 125 elsewhere. Ed(s): John C Spychalski. American Society of Transportation and Logistics, Inc., 1700 N Moore St., Ste 1900, Arlington, VA 22209-1904; info@astl.org; http://www.astl.org.

Illus., index. Refereed. Circ: 3500. Microform: PQC. Online: EBSCO Publishing, EBSCO Host; Florida Center for Library Automation; Gale; Northern Light Technology, Inc.; OCLC Online Computer Library Center, Inc.; ProQuest LLC (Ann Arbor). *Indexed:* ABIn, BPI, CLI, EnvInd, HRIS, ILP, JEL, LogistBibl, PAIS, SSCI. *Bk. rev.:* Occasional, 750–1,000 words, signed. *Aud.:* Ac, Sa.

Published by the American Society of Transportation and Logistics, this scholarly journal includes articles on air transport, international transport, logistics/physical distribution/supply chain management, management information systems and computer applications, motor transport, rail transport, regulation/law, traffic and transport management, transport policy, and water transport. Special theme issues are published regularly. There are book reviews in some issues. Tables of contents and abstracts for the last year can be found at www.astl.org/tj.htm. Appropriate for special collections.

6043. *Transportation Law Journal: industry leader in multi-modal law, economics & policy.* [ISSN: 0049-450X] 1969. 3x/yr. USD 38 domestic; USD 46 foreign; USD 20 newsstand/cover per issue domestic. Ed(s): Matthias Edrich. University of Denver, Sturm College of Law, 2255 E Evans Ave, Ste 448, Denver, CO 80208; http://www.law.du.edu. Illus., index, adv. Refereed. Circ: 2500 Paid. Vol. ends: Spring. Microform: WSH; PMC. Online: William S. Hein & Co., Inc.; LexisNexis; Thomson West. Reprint: WSH. *Indexed:* CLI, HRIS, ILP, LRI, PAIS. *Aud.:* Ac, Sa.

Published by the University of Denver College of Law, this scholarly journal addresses the international transportation industry and is geared toward the specialist, academician, and transportation law practitioner. It covers transportation law, regulation, and the politico-economic aspects of all transportation modalities. Each issue includes significant research articles with abundant footnotes. Tables of contents for current and back issues can be accessed at www.law.du.edu/tlj. Appropriate for special collections.

6044. *Transportation Management & Engineering.* Formerly (until 2001): *I T S World.* [ISSN: 1537-0259] 1996. 6x/yr. USD 95 foreign (Free to qualified personnel). Scranton Gillette Communications, Inc., 380 E Northwest Hwy, Ste 200, Des Plaines, IL 60016-2282; http://www.scrantongillette.com. Illus., index, adv. *Indexed:* ABIn, HRIS. *Aud.:* Sa.

This journal covers the international intelligent transportation systems industry, and it targets the specialist. Coverage includes industry news and events, feature articles, a product portfolio, editorials, and industry highlights. It is a supplement to *Roads and Bridges.* The current issue and archived articles can be found at www.tmemag.com. Appropriate for special collections.

6045. *Transportation Research. Parts A-F.* irreg. Pergamon, The Boulevard, Langford Ln, East Park, Kidlington, OX5 1GB, United Kingdom; nlinfo-f@elsevier.nl; http://www.elsevier.nl. *Bk. rev.:* Occasional, 600–2,500 words. *Aud.:* Ac, Sa.

Appropriate for special libraries, this six-part set of journals covers the gamut of transportation research occurring around the world. Each part can be purchased separately.

A: *Policy & Practice* [ISSN: 0965-8564] 10/yr. USD 1,104. Frank A. Haight. Vol. ends: Dec. Focuses on general-interest articles, particularly on planning and policy and their interaction with political, socioeconomic, and environmental systems.

B: *Methodological* [ISSN: 0191-2615] 10/yr. USD 1,104. Frank A. Haight. Vol. ends: Apr. Concentrates on the creation, analysis, and performance of models for the movement of freight and people.

C: *Emerging Technologies* [ISSN: 0968-090X] bi-m. USD 736. Stephen G. Ritchie. Vol. ends: Dec. Discusses implications and applications of new technologies in the field of transportation.

D: *Transport and Environment* [ISSN: 1361-9209] bi-m. USD 736. Kenneth Button. Covers environmental impacts of transportation, policy issues surrounding that impact, and implications for the design and implementation of transportation systems.

E: *Logistics and Transportation Review* [ISSN: 1366-5545] bi-m. USD 735. W. K. Talley. Vol. ends: Dec. Features articles on logistics including economics, cost, and production functions; capacity; demand; infrastructure; models; and supply chain topics.

F: *Traffic Psychology and Behaviour* [ISSN: 1369-8478] q. USD 490. J. A. Rothengatter. Focuses on the behavioral and psychological aspects of traffic and transport.

These journals are geared to the academician and the practitioner. Only available online through Elsevier.

6046. *Transportation Research Record.* Formerly (until 1974): *Highway Research Record.* [ISSN: 0361-1981] 1963. irreg. U.S. National Research Council, Transportation Research Board, Keck Center of the National Academies, 500 Fifth St, NW, Washington, DC 20001; http://www.trb.org. Illus. Refereed. Circ: 3250. *Indexed:* C&ISA, CJA, CerAb, ChemAb, EngInd, HRIS, IAA, S&F, SCI. *Aud.:* Ac, Sa.

Each issue of this publication contains papers on a topic relating to specific transportation modes and subject areas. The papers come from those prepared for presentation at Transportation Research Board (TRB) annual meetings, conferences, and workshops; they cover various aspects of the issue's theme, including technical, social, economic, or operational perspectives. Between 50 and 60 issues are published each year. Authors and topics come from all over the world. The primary emphasis of this journal is on topics relating to the engineering of highways, urban transportation, and traffic safety. Along with other TRB publications, this is an essential series for any transportation collection. An index to this journal's articles can be accessed at http://trb.metapress.com/home/main.mpx. Appropriate for large academic collections and special collections.

6047. *Transportation Science.* [ISSN: 0041-1655] 1967. q. Non-members, USD 136. Ed(s): Hani Mahmassani. I N F O R M S, 7240 Parkway Dr, Ste 310, Hanover, MD 21076-1344; informs@informs.org; http://www.informs.org. Illus., index, adv. Refereed. Circ: 1200 Paid and controlled. Vol. ends: Nov. Microform: PQC. Online: EBSCO Publishing, EBSCO Host; HighWire Press; ProQuest LLC (Ann Arbor); SwetsWise Online Content. *Indexed:* ABIn, AS&TI, C&ISA, CerAb, EngInd, HRIS, IAA, IBSS, MathR, SCI, SSCI. *Bk. rev.:* Occasional, 500–1,500 words. *Aud.:* Ac, Sa.

Published by the Institute for Operations Research and Management Sciences (INFORMS), this refereed, scholarly journal contains articles on all modes of transportation regarding operational management, such as planning and economic and social design. The mission of the journal is to advance the analytical, experimental, and observational tools in the study of transportation. The journal contains research articles, critical-review articles, technical notes, letters to the editor, and book reviews. Annually, dissertation abstracts submitted for the Transportation Science Section Prize are published. Tables of contents back to 1996 can be accessed at http://transci.pubs.informs.org. Appropriate for special collections.

6048. *Waterways Journal.* [ISSN: 0043-1524] 1887. w. USD 35 domestic; USD 60 foreign. Ed(s): John Shoulberg. Waterways Journal, Inc., 319 N. Fourth St., 650 Security Bldg., St. Louis, MO 63102. Illus., adv. Circ: 5000 Paid. Vol. ends: No. 52. *Indexed:* HRIS. *Bk. rev.:* Occasional, up to 250 wds. *Aud.:* Ga, Sa.

This U.S.-focused, tabloid-format publication covers all aspects of inland waterways, water transportation, and ports. Written for anyone with an interest in inland water transportation, including enthusiasts, its articles cover news, historical articles, letters, barge data, and other statistics and news. Annual features include a yearbook and directory that includes a chronological listing of the year's important news. Current articles and archived summaries dating back to 2003 are available at www.waterwaysjournal.net. Appropriate for large general collections or special collections.

6049. *WorkBoat.* [ISSN: 0043-8014] 1943. m. USD 39 domestic; USD 55 in Canada & Mexico; USD 103 elsewhere. Ed(s): Dave Krapf. Diversified Business Communications, 121 Free St, Portland, ME 04101; subscriptions@divcom.com; http://www.divbusiness.com. Illus., adv. Circ: 25563. Vol. ends: Dec. Online: Florida Center for Library Automation; Gale. *Indexed:* HRIS. *Aud.:* Sa.

A trade magazine for the North American workboat industry, which includes but is not limited to tugboats, barges, salvage vessels, crewboats, utility boats, excursion vessels, freighters, tankers, patrol craft, fire boats, and research vessels. It is geared to the practitioner and covers industry news and events, legislation, regulation, safety, technology, vessel construction and maintenance, marine personnel, equipment, and product news. Each issue includes feature articles, a calendar of events, a classified section, a product showcase, and a section highlighting a specific port. The table of contents for the current issue and the full text of archived articles can be accessed at www.workboat.com. Appropriate for special collections.

6050. *World Highways.* [ISSN: 0964-4598] 1950. 10x/yr. GBP 100; USD 165. Ed(s): Alan Peterson. Route One Publishing Ltd., Horizon House, Azalea Dr, Swanley, BR8 8JR, United Kingdom; subs@routeonepub.com; http://www.routeonepub.com. Illus., adv. Circ: 18201. *Indexed:* HRIS. *Aud.:* Sa.

This journal addresses the international road and highway construction and maintenance industries and targets the practitioner. It covers industry news and events, materials, signage, lighting, equipment, technology, the environment and weather, traffic, and safety. Each issue includes feature articles, a calendar of events, guides to products and services, relevant web sites, and a highlighted construction site. It includes a whole page devoted to highway construction humor. The current issue's table of contents, news briefs, and full text of feature articles can be accessed at www.worldhighways.com; a password is required. Appropriate for special collections.

■ TRAVEL AND TOURISM

General/Newsletters/Reference/Research

See also Canada; and City, State, and Regional sections.

Kathleen Sheehan, Research Librarian, Widener Library, Harvard University, Harvard Yard, Cambridge, MA 02138; ksheehan@fas.harvard.edu

Introduction

The number of Americans traveling in the U.S. and abroad continues to increase along with airline ticket prices, domestic hotel room prices, and rental car costs. Industry watchers predict that it will be increasingly difficult to find a good deal on flights as airlines reduce the number of planes flying domestically. This move is helping the airlines to fill the seats at prices most favorable to them. Perhaps this is good news for travel magazine publishers, as more people feel the need for advice on finding the best travel deals.

As noted in the previous edition, the availability of online travel information continues to put pressure on the publishers of print travel magazines. Web sites such as TripAdvisor let you read or write your own reviews of hotels, restaurants, and attractions as well as offering free member-written newsletters with travel advice and information. The titles listed here continue to be reliable sources of useful advice and recommendations from experienced travelers.

The number of titles covered in this chapter has been reduced from the previous edition, but the focus continues to be on titles of general interest. Almost all of the titles listed in this chapter have an associated web site, noted in the annotations, that provide access to portions of the content of the print publication and some information found exclusively on the web. Those academic journals that give free access to an online version with a print subscription are also noted.

Basic Periodicals

Ems: *National Geographic Traveler;* Hs: *National Geographic Traveler, Transitions Abroad;* Ga: *Arthur Frommer's Budget Travel, Conde Nast Traveler, National Geographic Traveler, Transitions Abroad, Travel & Leisure;* Ac: *Annals of Tourism Research, Journal of Sustainable Tourism, Journal of Travel Research.*

Basic Abstracts and Indexes

Leisure, Recreation and Tourism Abstracts; Lodging, Restaurant and Travel Abstracts; Magazine Index; Readers' Guide to Periodical Literature.

General

6051. *Arthur Frommer's Budget Travel: vacations for real people.* [ISSN: 1521-5210] 1998. 10x/yr. USD 12 domestic; USD 34.95 foreign. Arthur Frommer's Budget Travel, Inc., 251 W 57th St, New York, NY 10019. Adv. Circ: 350000 Paid. *Indexed:* RGPR. *Aud.:* Ga.

Aimed at the budget-conscious traveler, this magazine is full of travel tips and worldwide travel deals. Features include a "Trip Coach," which focuses on an individual reader's plea for trip planning help. The Coach offers day-to-day itineraries with specific places to stay and sites to see. This publication is a great source when you are looking for an interesting destination at a good price. The companion web site contains much of the magazine's content along with "This Just In," Budget Travel Online's blog for updates between magazine issues (http://www.budgettravelonline.com). Highly recommended for public and academic libraries.

Backpacker: the magazine of wilderness adventure. See Hiking, Climbing, and Outdoor Recreation/General section.

6052. *Caribbean Travel and Life.* Formerly (until 1987): *Caribbean Travel and Life Magazine.* [ISSN: 1052-1011] 1986. 9x/yr. USD 23.95 domestic; USD 32.95 Canada; USD 41.95 elsewhere. Ed(s): Bob Friel, Jessica Chapman. World Publications LLC, 460 N Orlando Ave, Ste 200, Winter Park, FL 32789; info@worldpub.net; http://www.worldpub.net. Illus., adv. Circ: 157518 Paid. *Aud.:* Ga.

The magazine is targeted at an upscale audience of frequent travelers to the Caribbean. The editors' goal is to feature new and interesting aspects of travel in the region. The tone of the magazine varies between promotional and objective. Beautiful photographs accompany the articles, which include recommendations on accommodations, dining, and entertainment. The web site (http://www.caribbeantravelmag.com) provides additional information. At home in large public libraries.

6053. *Conde Nast Traveler: truth in travel.* Formerly (until 1987): *Signature.* [ISSN: 0893-9683] 1954. m. USD 19.97 domestic; USD 33.97 Canada; USD 39.97 elsewhere. Ed(s): Klara Glowczewska, Ted Moncreiff. Conde Nast Publications, Inc., 4 Times Sq, 14th Fl, New York, NY 10036. Illus., index, adv. Sample. Circ: 808419 Paid. Vol. ends: Dec (No. 12). Microform: PQC. *Indexed:* ASIP, RGPR. *Aud.:* Ga.

Conde Nast Traveler, subtitled *truth in travel,* is a reasonably priced magazine that focuses on higher-end travel. Articles cover a wide variety of destinations and activities. There is an ombudsman column, where travel problems are addressed. A "Places & Prices" section lists lodging, dining, and entertainment details for each featured destination. The online version of *Conde Nast Traveler,* a part of Concierge.com, includes travel blogs written by the editorial staff (http://www.concierge.com/cntraveler). Recommended for public libraries.

6054. *Cruise Travel: the worldwide cruise vacation magazine.* [ISSN: 0199-5111] 1979. bi-m. USD 34.95 domestic; USD 50 foreign; USD 5.99 per issue. Ed(s): Charles Doherty. World Publishing Co., 990 Grove St, Evanston, IL 60201. Illus., adv. Sample. Circ: 175000 Paid. Vol. ends: May/Jun. *Indexed:* H&TI. *Aud.:* Ga.

Issues include articles that feature a "Ship of the Month," a "Cruise of the Month," and a "Port of the Month," covering destinations worldwide from the Great Lakes to Dubrovnik. In addition, the magazine publishes articles on topics such as the history of cruise ships and educational programs provided at sea. Seasonal cruise calendars list schedules and prices. Appropriate for larger public library collections.

Explorers Journal. See Geography section.

Geomundo. See Latin America and Spain section.

6055. *National Geographic Adventure.* [ISSN: 1523-6226] 1999. bi-m. USD 12 domestic; CND 35 Canada; USD 25 elsewhere. Ed(s): John Rasmus. National Geographic Society, 1145 17th St, NW, Washington, DC 20036; ngsforum@nationalgeographic.com; http://www.nationalgeographic.com. Illus. Circ: 352077 Free. Online: EBSCO Publishing, EBSCO Host; Gale; ProQuest LLC (Ann Arbor). *Indexed:* MASUSE. *Bk. rev.:* 3, 500 words. *Aud.:* Ga.

Stunning photographs fill the pages of this adventure travel title from National Geographic. Whether you're hiking, biking, rafting, or boarding, you will find advice on all the steps for planning an active vacation. The magazine features "descriptive pieces on celebrities of adventure, gripping accounts of groundbreaking expeditions and scientific exploration, and intriguing, unknown historical tales." Reviews of products of interest to adventure travelers are included. Recommended for high school, public, and academic libraries. The web site (http://www.nationalgeographic.com/adventure) includes excerpts of past articles.

6056. *National Geographic Traveler.* [ISSN: 0747-0932] 1984. 8x/yr. USD 17.95 domestic; CND 34 Canada; USD 25.50 elsewhere. Ed(s): Keith Bellows. National Geographic Society, 1145 17th St, NW, Washington, DC 20036; ngsforum@nationalgeographic.com; http://www.nationalgeographic.com. Illus., index, adv. Sample. Circ: 715000 Paid. Vol. ends: Nov/Dec. *Indexed:* ASIP, MASUSE. *Aud.:* Ga.

National Geographic Traveler "eschews fashion and fluff in favor of articles that offer a strong sense of place, inspiring narratives that make readers take trips, and solid service information to help them plan those trips." As in other NG titles, photography is an integral part of telling a story. In addition, readers will find destinations accessible to most travellers ranging from mainstream to adventure, from budget-conscious to luxury. This title is appropriate for all public and academic, and some school, libraries. The web site (http://www.nationalgeographic.com/traveler) presents some material found only online.

6057. *Transitions Abroad: the guide to learning, living, working, and volunteering overseas.* Formerly (until 1985): *Transitions.* [ISSN: 1061-2343] 1977. bi-m. USD 28 domestic; USD 32 Canada; USD 56 elsewhere. Ed(s): Sherry Schwarz. Transitions Abroad, LLC, PO Box 745, Bennington, VT 05201; info@transitionsabroad.com. Illus., index, adv. Sample. Circ: 12000 Paid and controlled. Vol. ends: May/Jun. *Aud.:* Hs, Ga.

The magazine's purpose is to assist travelers seeking to immerse themselves in other cultures through travel, work, study, and volunteering abroad. Recent articles have featured Bolivia's biodiversity, volunteer opportunities in Guatemala, and work adventures in Sydney, as well as topics such as family travel, women's travel, and disability travel. Each issue includes listings of employment and educational opportunities. The companion web site brings together additional information about living, studying, and working abroad (http://www.transitionsabroad.com/). Highly recommended for academic, career-services, and public libraries.

6058. *Travel 50 & Beyond.* [ISSN: 1049-6211] 1990. 5x/w. USD 14; USD 3.95 newsstand/cover per issue. Ed(s): Mary Lou Abbott. Vacation Publications, Inc., 5851 San Felipe St, Ste 500, Houston, TX 77057. Illus., adv. Sample. Circ: 100000. Vol. ends: Fall (No. 4). *Aud.:* Ga.

A travel magazine aimed at the 50-and-older crowd because, according to the magazine's web site, "People who are 50 and older take 80% of all the vacations in this country." *Travel 50 and Beyond* features destinations in the Americas but increasingly covers sites in Europe and beyond. Much of the information here is of interest to travelers of all ages, though some material is geared specifically to older travelers, including updates on senior discounts, tips on vacationing with grandchildren, and dealing with mobility issues on the road. Suitable for public libraries.

6059. *Travel & Leisure.* Formerly: *Travel and Camera.* [ISSN: 0041-2007] 1971. m. USD 19.99 domestic; USD 31.99 Canada; USD 64 elsewhere. Ed(s): Nancy Novogrod, Jennifer Barr. American Express Publishing

Corp., 1120 Ave of the Americas, 9th Fl., New York, NY 10036; http://www.travelandleisure.com. Illus., index, adv. Sample. Circ: 961000 Paid. Vol. ends: Dec. Microform: PQC. *Indexed:* ASIP, H&TI, LRI. *Aud.:* Ga.

Travel & Leisure is a magazine written for the upscale traveler full of beautiful photography and destinations, both mainstream and exotic. Articles feature cruises, shopping and driving vacations, romantic trips, and "responsible travel." The advice offered includes where to stay, where to eat, and what to see. The companion web site includes online bonuses (http://www.travelandleisure.com). Recommended for public and large academic libraries.

6060. *TravelAmerica.* Formerly (until 1993): *Tours and Resorts.* [ISSN: 1068-2554] 1985. bi-m. USD 29.94 domestic; USD 40 Canada; USD 50 elsewhere. Ed(s): Robert Meyers. World Publishing Co., 990 Grove St, Evanston, IL 60201; cs@centurysports.net. Illus., adv. Sample. Circ: 245000 Paid. Online: EBSCO Publishing, EBSCO Host; Gale. *Aud.:* Ga.

At 58 pages per issue, this relatively high-priced general travel magazine exclusively covers destinations in the United States. Each issue features articles on a "State of the Month," "City of the Month," "Resort of the Month," and "Tour of the Month." Other sections include touring, resorting, and short drive. Appropriate for large public libraries.

6061. *Wanderlust: travel for the free-spirited.* [ISSN: 1351-4733] 1993. bi-m. GBP 17.50 domestic; GBP 21 in Europe; GBP 30 rest of world. Ed(s): Lyn Hughes. Wanderlust, PO Box 1832, Windsor, SL4 6YP, United Kingdom; info@wanderlust.co.uk; http://www.wanderlust.co.uk. Illus., adv. Sample. Circ: 35500 Paid. *Bk. rev.:* 8, 250 words. *Aud.:* Ga.

This magazine from the U.K. aimed at independent travelers features beautiful photographs, and practical tips about traveling to exotic destinations. Its goal is to combine "the right mix of wildlife, activities and cultural insight." Readers will also find reviews of travel gear and books, photography tips, and answers to health questions. Additional information is available on the publication's web site (http://www.wanderlust.co.uk/trade/trade1.html). Appropriate for public and academic libraries.

Newsletters

6062. *Artistic Traveler: architecture & travel with art & photography.* [ISSN: 1060-2569] 1991. bi-m. USD 29. Ed(s): Richard Hovey. S & R Research, PO Box 2038, Vancouver, WA 98668-2038. Illus. Sample. *Aud.:* Ac, Sa.

A newsletter for travelers interested in architecture as an art form. It aims to cover "the best in classic and contemporary architecture written in non-technical language." Edited and published by an architectural photographer and a travel industry professional, the newsletter covers both major and more obscure attractions. Each issue also includes "The Log," which has listings of closures, renovations, and other design-arts–related news and photography tips. Subscribers may receive either a black-and-white version by mail or a pdf version in color by e-mail.

6063. *International Travel News.* [ISSN: 0191-8761] 1976. m. USD 19 domestic; USD 28 foreign. Martin Publications Inc., 2120 28th St, Sacramento, CA 95818; itn@ns.net; http://www.intltravelnews.com. Illus., adv. Sample. Circ: 50000. *Bk. rev.:* 1, 750 words. *Aud.:* Ga.

This is a forum for experienced overseas travelers, offering personal accounts, tips, and recommendations. The mainly reader-written articles cover "budget to luxury travel for both independent adventurers and group tour takers." The publication relies on its reader-contributors to provide practical information and advice to their fellow travellers. The newsletter does not cover destinations or deals in the U.S., Canada, Mexico, or the Caribbean. The companion web site provides access to a sampling of the articles from the print newsletter as well as a message board for subscribers. Appropriate for public libraries.

6064. *Travel Smart.* Incorporates (1969-1983): *Joy of Travel;* Which was formerly (until 1981): *Joyer Travel Report.* [ISSN: 0741-5826] 1976. m. USD 39 in Canada & Mexico; USD 64 elsewhere. Ed(s): Nancy J Dunnan. Dunnan Communications, Inc., PO Box 397, Dobbs Ferry, NY 10522. Illus., index. Sample. Circ: 18000 Paid. *Aud.:* Ga.

Each issue contains advice about places to stay, sites to see, and "Things to avoid." Readers will find a list of top ten travel deals, safety tips, and articles on featured destinations worldwide. What the reader won't find is advertising. General travel themes, such as getting along with traveling companions, are also covered. The companion web site (http://www.travelsmartnewsletter.com/) includes daily travel tips from the editor. Suitable for public libraries.

Reference

Leisure, Recreation and Tourism Abstracts. See Abstracts and Indexes section.

6065. *O A G Flight Guide. North America.* Former titles (until 2000): *O A G Desktop Guide (North American Edition);* (until 1995): *O A G Desktop Flight Guide (North American Edition);* (until 1991): *O A G. Official Airline Guide. North American Edition;* (until 1974): *Official Airline Guide (North American Edition).* [ISSN: 1528-7556] 1948. s-m. Members, USD 569. O A G Worldwide, 3025 Highland Pkwy, Ste 200, Downer's Grove, IL 60515; custsvc@oag.com; http://www.oag.com. Illus., adv. Circ: 30000. *Aud.:* Ga, Sa.

Provides a complete list of every scheduled direct and connecting flight in North America, including Canada, Mexico, the Caribbean, and the United States. Other regions are covered in other editions. There is also a "Worldwide" edition. The supplementary volume includes airplane and airport diagrams and listings of airport services. The online version contains additional information and is updated daily (http://www.oag.com/oag/website/com/en/Home/). Appropriate for corporate and large public library reference desks.

Research

6066. *Annals of Tourism Research.* [ISSN: 0160-7383] 1973. 4x/yr. EUR 663. Ed(s): Jafar Jafari. Pergamon, The Boulevard, Langford Ln, East Park, Kidlington, OX5 1GB, United Kingdom. Illus., index, adv. Sample. Refereed. Circ: 1200. Vol. ends: Oct. Microform: PQC. Online: EBSCO Publishing, EBSCO Host; Gale; IngentaConnect; OhioLINK; ScienceDirect; SwetsWise Online Content. *Indexed:* ABS&EES, AbAn, AgeL, AnthLit, BPI, CABA, CJA, CommAb, EI, ForAb, H&TI, IndVet, PAIS, PsycInfo, RRTA, RiskAb, S&F, SSA, SSCI, SociolAb, VB, WAE&RSA. *Bk. rev.:* 8, 750 words. *Aud.:* Ac, Sa.

This is an interdisciplinary social science journal of research on tourism. Articles cover topics in several fields, including anthropology, business, economics, environmental studies, religion, and sociology. The focus is on theory rather than practice. Articles are in English, with English and French abstracts. Research notes, book reviews, and a conference calendar are included. Tables of contents and abstracts can be viewed online at http://www.elsevier.com/locate/atoures. Online access is available through ScienceDirect. Appropriate for academic libraries with tourism collections.

6067. *Current Issues in Tourism.* [ISSN: 1368-3500] 1998. bi-m. EUR 480 print & online eds. (Individuals, EUR 99 print & online eds.). Ed(s): Dr. C Michael Hall. Channel View Publications, Frankfurt Lodge, Clevedon Hall, Victoria Rd., Clevedon, BS21 7HH, United Kingdom; http://www.channelviewpublications.com. Refereed. Online: EBSCO Publishing, EBSCO Host; Gale; SwetsWise Online Content. *Indexed:* CABA, EnvAb, ForAb, H&TI, IndVet, PEI, RRTA, S&F, VB, WAE&RSA. *Aud.:* Ac.

An academic journal that publishes both applied and theoretical articles in tourism studies. This publication aims to be accessible to researchers and practitioners throughout the world. The scope of the journal has expanded to include discussions of method and practice in tourism research. Recent topics featured in the journal include whether tourism alleviates poverty and an examination of polar bear tourism. Online access is available to print subscribers at no additional cost. Online-access-only subscriptions are also available. Suitable for academic libraries with tourism research collections.

6068. International Journal of Tourism Research. Formerly (until 1999): *Progress in Tourism and Hospitality Research.* [ISSN: 1099-2340] 1995. bi-m. USD 750 print or online ed. Ed(s): Adele Ladkin, John Fletcher. John Wiley & Sons Ltd., The Atrium, Southern Gate, Chichester, PO19 8SQ, United Kingdom; customer@wiley.co.uk; http://www.wiley.co.uk. Adv. Refereed. Reprint: PSC. *Indexed:* ABIn, CABA, CJA, EnvAb, EnvInd, ForAb, H&TI, IndIslam, IndVet, PsycInfo, RRTA, RiskAb, S&F, VB, WAE&RSA. *Bk. rev.:* 5, 1,000 words. *Aud.:* Ac.

An academic journal covering tourism and hospitality research generally. According to the publisher, the journal "provides an international platform for debate and dissemination of research findings" while also presenting "new research areas and techniques." Reviews of books, conferences, and web sites are also included. Appropriate for academic tourism research collections. Online access is available through Wiley Interscience.

Journal of Hospitality & Leisure Marketing. See Advertising, Marketing, and Public Relations section.

Journal of Hospitality & Tourism Research. See Hospitality/Restaurant section.

6069. Journal of Sustainable Tourism. [ISSN: 0966-9582] 1993. bi-m. EUR 480 print & online eds. (Individuals, EUR 99 print & online eds.). Ed(s): Mr. Bernard Lane, Dr. Bill Bramwell. Channel View Publications, Frankfurt Lodge, Clevedon Hall, Victoria Rd., Clevedon, BS21 7HH, United Kingdom; info@multilingual-matters.com; http://www.catchword.com. Illus., index, adv. Sample. Refereed. Online: EBSCO Publishing, EBSCO Host; Gale; SwetsWise Online Content. *Indexed:* ABIn, CABA, EnvAb, EnvInd, ForAb, H&TI, HortAb, IndVet, RRTA, S&F, SSA, SociolAb, VB, WAE&RSA. *Bk. rev.:* 3, 1,000 words. *Aud.:* Ac, Sa.

Articles in this journal examine the relationship between tourism and sustainable development from an academic perspective. All geographic areas are included and all forms of tourism. Interdisciplinary research is encouraged. Book reviews and conference reports help scholars in the field keep up to date. Online access is included with a print subscription. Suitable for academic libraries with tourism and environmental studies programs.

6070. Journal of Travel Research. Formerly: *Travel Research Bulletin.* [ISSN: 0047-2875] 1962. q. GBP 271. Ed(s): Richard R Perdue. Sage Publications, Inc., 2455 Teller Rd, Thousand Oaks, CA 91320; info@sagepub.com; http://www.sagepub.com. Adv. Circ: 1000 Paid and free. Online: EBSCO Publishing, EBSCO Host; Florida Center for Library Automation; Gale; HighWire Press; Northern Light Technology, Inc.; OCLC Online Computer Library Center, Inc.; SAGE Publications, Inc., SAGE Journals Online; SwetsWise Online Content; H.W. Wilson. Reprint: PSC. *Indexed:* ABIn, ABS&EES, BPI, C&ISA, CABA, CerAb, ForAb, H&TI, HRIS, IAA, RRTA, S&F, SUSA, WAE&RSA. *Bk. rev.:* 2, 750 words. *Aud.:* Ac.

A peer-reviewed journal emphasizing quantitative research about travel and tourism for scholars interested in tourism marketing, behavioral trends, and management theory. The articles treat topics that range from research on particular destinations to overviews of general issues such tourism e-commerce, destination development, and tourism forecasting. Appropriate for scholarly and special collections serving academics and practitioners interested in the economic and marketing aspects of tourism and leisure studies.

■ URBAN STUDIES

Deborah Sommer, City Planning, Landscape Architecture, & Urban Design Librarian, Environmental Design Library, University of California, Berkeley, Berkeley, CA 94720; dsommer@library.berkeley.edu

Introduction

What is "urban studies"? In its simplest definition, urban studies is the academic study of cities and urban regions. Because urban studies concerns itself with all aspects of urban places, it is an intensely multidisciplinary field. Its focus tends to be spatial, so the disciplines of geography, city and regional planning, and architecture and landscape architecture are well represented here.

How people live in these urban places is of great interest, too. Articles that engage the practice in or literatures of community development, housing, public works and transportation, sociology, economics and public finance, and public health are abundant in urban studies journals. Urban studies also encompasses the management and maintenance of cities, drawing on the literatures of political science, urban technology, and public administration, while the threads of public policy and urban history run throughout.

Several themes are notable in the current urban studies literature. Security, anti-terrorism, border control, and immigration issues permeate the literature. Urban disaster response and planning, in the wake of the 2005 hurricanes Katrina and Rita in the Gulf Coast, increasingly preoccupy urban studies writers. Urban design and quality-of-life issues are ubiquitous in both the scholarly and popular literature, with an emphasis on "smart growth" and how to make urban environments healthier. Urban environmental management and planning continue to command interest throughout the literature, as does the innovative use of computer and information technologies in studying and managing urban environments.

This section naturally focuses on English-language serials that are as central as possible to the discipline. However, for a comprehensive view of the possibilities, browse through the list of topical sections that precedes this introduction.

The publications in this section, given their scholarly or practitioner orientation, will be of greatest interest to academic and research libraries, although some titles will appeal to large public libraries, for example, *American City & County, Housing Policy Debate, Planning,* and *The Town Paper,* and the electronic journals *Making Places* and *Planetizen Newswire.*

The titles listed as "Basic Periodicals" have been selected with American libraries in mind; core journals for libraries in other countries are identified in the individual annotations. Of course, the realities of local programmatic emphases and budgets require a flexible approach to the "Basic Periodicals" list, which is not intended to be prescriptive. Rather, consider it a starting place for your own collection of urban studies periodicals. Note that in addition to the titles listed in "Basic Abstracts and Indexes," three journals provide significant indexing: the *Journal of Planning Literature, Planning Practice & Research,* and *Urban History.* Note as well that almost any search in a general journal article index on an urban studies topic will uncover pertinent articles.

Basic Periodicals

Ga: *American City & County, Journal of Housing and Community Development, Public Management, Planning, Urban Land*; Ac: *Cities, City, Environment and Urbanization, European Planning Studies, International Journal of Urban and Regional Research, Journal of Planning Literature, Journal of the American Planning Association, Journal of Urban Affairs, Journal of Urban Design, Journal of Urban History, Planning, Urban Geography, Urban History, Urban History, Urban Studies.*

Basic Abstracts and Indexes

ABI/Inform Global, Avery Index to Architectural Periodicals, Business Source Premier, Ekistic Index of Periodicals, Geography, Index to Current Urban Documents, PAIS International, Sage Urban Studies Abstracts, Sociological Abstracts.

6071. *American City & County: administration, engineering, and operations in relation to local government.* Formerly: *American City.* [ISSN: 0149-337X] 1909. m. USD 67 foreign (Free to qualified personnel). Ed(s): Lindsay Isaacs. Prism Business Media, 6151 Powers Ferry Rd Ste 200, Atlanta, GA 30339; inquiries@prismb2b.com; http://www.prismbusinessmedia.com. Illus., index, adv. Circ: 74000 Controlled. Vol. ends: Dec. Microform: PQC. Online: EBSCO Publishing, EBSCO Host; Florida Center for Library Automation; Gale; Northern Light Technology, Inc.; OCLC Online Computer Library Center, Inc.; ProQuest LLC (Ann Arbor); H.W. Wilson. *Indexed:* ABIn, AS&TI, AgeL, BRI, CBRI, ChemAb, ExcerpMed, HRIS, MASUSE, PAIS, WRCInf. *Bk. rev.:* Number and length vary. *Aud.:* Ga, Ac, Sa.

Considered a core trade magazine in this field, *American City & County* has been published since 1909. It reports on current issues and trends in local government operations and policies. Each issue regularly features the Municipal Cost Index (MCI), the Construction Cost Index, and the Consumer and Producer Price Indexes. The MCI (1978–present), developed by the journal to show the effects of inflation on the cost of providing municipal services, is archived online on the journal's web site at www.americancityandcounty.com. Recommended for public libraries that serve urban business communities and local governments, and college and university libraries with large urban studies programs. Marginal for libraries outside the United States.

6072. *American Planning Association. Journal.* Former titles (until 1979): *Planners Journal; American Institute of Planners. Journal.* [ISSN: 0194-4363] 1925. q. GBP 187 print & online eds. Ed(s): Amy Helling, David Sawicki. Routledge, 325 Chestnut St, Ste 800, Philadelphia, PA 19106; http://www.tandf.co.uk/journals. Illus., adv. Refereed. Circ: 10000 Paid. Vol. ends: Oct. Microform: PQC. Online: EBSCO Publishing, EBSCO Host; Florida Center for Library Automation; Gale; OCLC Online Computer Library Center, Inc.; ProQuest K-12 Learning Solutions; ProQuest LLC (Ann Arbor); H.W. Wilson. *Indexed:* ABCPolSci, ABIn, API, AgeL, AmH&L, ArtInd, BAS, EAA, EIP, EnvAb, EnvInd, ExcerpMed, GardL, HRIS, HistAb, IBR, IBZ, IPSA, MCR, PAIS, SSCI, SUSA. *Bk. rev.:* 8-10, 500-1,200 words, signed. *Aud.:* Ga, Ac, Sa.

The *Journal of the American Planning Association* is the scholarly journal of the principal professional city and regional planning organization in the United States. (See also the APA's news magazine, *Planning*.) With its outstanding breadth and quality of coverage of the theoretical, applied, and regulatory elements of city planning, *JAPA* is a core title for American urban studies collections and a serious contender for library collections elsewhere. Examples of recent articles include "Active Living and Social Justice: Planning for physical activity in low-income, Black, and Latino communities" and "Gross Density and New Urbanism." Articles include abstracts. Each quarterly issue contains a substantial book review section, as well as a "Briefly Noted" section of shorter reviews. Highly recommended for academic libraries.

6073. *Built Environment.* Formerly (until 1978): *Built Environment Quarterly.* [ISSN: 0263-7960] 1975. q. GBP 225 print & online eds. (Individuals, GBP 100 print & online eds.). Ed(s): David Banister, Peter Hall. Alexandrine Press, 1 The Farthings, Marcham, OX13 6QD, United Kingdom; alexandrine@rudkinassociates.co.uk; http://www.alexandrinepress.co.uk. Illus., adv. Sample. Refereed. Circ: 350 Paid. *Indexed:* API, ErgAb, HRIS, SUSA, SWA. *Bk. rev.:* 2-4, 500 words. *Aud.:* Ac, Sa.

With a target audience of practitioners as well as academics and students, *Built Environment* strives to be "relevant to all those involved in urban and regional planning." A different theme is the focus of each issue of this scholarly British quarterly. Overseen by various guest editors, the mostly British and European contributors addressed topics such as climate change and cities, sustainable suburbs, and planning for resilient cities in the wake of urban disasters in recent issues. Recommended for academic, architecture, and urban planning libraries.

Built Environment. See Architecture section.

6074. *Canadian Journal of Urban Research.* [ISSN: 1188-3774] 1992. s-a. CND 70 (Individuals, CND 45; Students, CND 25). Ed(s): Dan Chekki. University of Winnipeg, Institute of Urban Studies, 103-520 Portage Ave,

Winnipeg, MB R3C 0G2, Canada; ius@uwinnipeg.ca; http://ius.uwinnipeg.ca. Illus. Sample. Refereed. Circ: 125 Paid. Online: EBSCO Publishing, EBSCO Host; Florida Center for Library Automation; Gale; LexisNexis; Micromedia ProQuest; OCLC Online Computer Library Center, Inc.; ProQuest LLC (Ann Arbor). *Indexed:* CBCARef, CPerI, EIP, PRA, PSA, SSA, SUSA, SWA, SociolAb. *Bk. rev.:* 12-15, 600-1,000 words, signed. *Aud.:* Ac.

The *Canadian Journal of Urban Research* is a scholarly research journal published semi-annually by the Institute of Urban Studies at the University of Winnipeg, in collaboration with the Canadian Institute of Planners. Focused on urban studies in Canada, with an exclusively Canadian editorial board, the journal encompasses a wide range of issues, including urban policy, urban environment and ecology, housing and health, community development, and more. The refereed articles are published in English or French; article abstracts are bilingual and are available online for some issues (http://ius.uwinnipeg.ca/cjur_browse_archive.html#). English and/or French book reviews appear in some issues. This is a core journal for Canadian academic libraries with urban studies programs and for libraries that support Canadian Studies programs. Otherwise, for large academic library collections.

6075. *Cities.* [ISSN: 0264-2751] 1983. 6x/yr. EUR 925. Ed(s): Andrew Kirby. Pergamon, The Boulevard, Langford Ln, East Park, Kidlington, OX5 1GB, United Kingdom. Illus., index, adv. Refereed. Microform: PQC. Online: EBSCO Publishing, EBSCO Host; Gale; IngentaConnect; OhioLINK; ScienceDirect; SwetsWise Online Content. *Indexed:* CJA, EIP, EnvAb, EnvInd, IBSS, IndIslam, PAIS, PRA, PSA, SSA, SSCI, SUSA, SociolAb. *Bk. rev.:* 0-3, signed. *Aud.:* Ac.

An international scholarly journal, *Cities* covers all aspects of urban policy and development. Topics covered include housing and homelessness; Third World development and planning; urban management and transportation; urban redevelopment, conservation, and design; and technology and urban planning. Each issue comprises six or seven well-written and illustrated abstracted articles. In addition, each issue contains a 10-to-12-page profile of a major city (for example, Havana, Cuba, or Mumbai, India). Useful to students and researchers alike, the city profile includes a brief description of the city's historical development and contemporary conditions, problems, or issues, and a critical review of the city's recent responses to those problems. Many issues also have book reviews. This title is highly recommended for college and research libraries, especially those that support international urban studies.

6076. *City: urban trends, culture, theory, policy, action.* Formerly (until 1995): *Regenerating Cities.* [ISSN: 1360-4813] 1992. 3x/yr. GBP 214 print & online eds. Ed(s): Bob Catterall. Routledge, 4 Park Sq, Milton Park, Abingdon, OX14 4RN, United Kingdom; info@routledge.co.uk; http://www.routledge.com. Reprint: PSC. *Indexed:* IBR, IBSS, IBZ. *Aud.:* Ac.

City, a self-described journal of the "new urban studies," considers the future of cities through a variety of lenses, including policy, theory, and analysis. Published since 1995, *City* is an international scholarly journal with a European emphasis, whose topics include community development, geography, globalization, urban design and redevelopment, and urban sociology. Each issue includes a group of articles (with abstracts) organized around a theme, as well as a section of "Reports, Interviews, Reviews" and several other short articles as well. Examples of recent themes include "Urbanizing the Security Agenda: Anti-terrorism, urban sprawl and social movements" and "Moral Panics and Urban Renaissance: Policy, tactics and youth in public space." The journal has a freshness that makes it appealing to undergraduate students. Highly recommended for academic libraries.

6077. *City & Community.* [ISSN: 1535-6841] q. GBP 237 print & online eds. Ed(s): Anthony M Orum. Blackwell Publishing, Inc., Commerce Place, 350 Main St, Malden, MA 02148; customerservices@blackwellpublishing.com; http://www.blackwellpublishing.com. Reprint: PSC. *Indexed:* ApEcolAb, CJA, PsycInfo, RiskAb, SUSA, SociolAb. *Bk. rev.:* 4-6, signed. *Aud.:* Ac, Sa.

Founded in 2002, *City & Community* is a peer-reviewed quarterly journal, sponsored by the Community and Urban Sociology Section of the American Sociological Association. The journal publishes research and theory that explores the social aspects of the metropolis, with a geographic focus on

Anglophone North America. Each issue contains an editorial, four or five articles with abstracts, and several book reviews. Characteristic articles include "NIMBY and the Civic Good" and "Staying Vietnamese: Community and Place in Orange County and Boston." Recommended for academic libraries; of interest to urban sociologists as well as to urban studies specialists.

6078. Community Development Journal. Formerly: *Community Development Bulletin.* [ISSN: 0010-3802] 1966. q. EUR 288 print or online ed. Ed(s): Chris Miller. Oxford University Press, Great Clarendon St, Oxford, OX2 6DP, United Kingdom; jnl.orders@oup.co.uk; http://www.oxfordjournals.org. Illus., index, adv. Sample. Refereed. Circ: 1250. Vol. ends: Oct. Microform: PQC. Online: Chadwyck-Healey Inc.; EBSCO Publishing, EBSCO Host; Gale; HighWire Press; IngentaConnect; OCLC Online Computer Library Center, Inc.; OhioLINK; Oxford Journals; ProQuest LLC (Ann Arbor); SwetsWise Online Content. Reprint: PSC. *Indexed:* ASSIA, BAS, CABA, ForAb, IBR, IBSS, IBZ, IPSA, JEL, PAIS, PRA, PSA, RRTA, RiskAb, S&F, SSA, SSCI, SUSA, SWA, SWR&A, SociolAb, WAE&RSA. *Bk. rev.:* 5-6, 1,000 words, signed. *Aud.:* Ac.

Community Development Journal is a refereed British publication with international coverage, emphasizing Great Britain and the former British Commonwealth. The editorial advisory board is geographically diverse, with members from both developed and developing countries. Topics include community development practice and professional development work, development finance, citizen participation in village and town planning, and community redevelopment. The articles (with abstracts) focus primarily on the village and town level rather than cities. The quarterly issues include book reviews. This journal is recommended for comprehensive urban studies collections only; however, it could be important for libraries that support international area studies or international community development programs.

6079. Computers, Environment and Urban Systems. Former titles (until 1975): *Urban Systems; Computers and Urban Society.* [ISSN: 0198-9715] 1975. 6x/yr. EUR 1266. Ed(s): Paul A Longley. Pergamon, The Boulevard, Langford Ln, East Park, Kidlington, OX5 1GB, United Kingdom. Illus., index, adv. Refereed. Circ: 850. Vol. ends: No. 25. Microform: PQC. Online: EBSCO Publishing, EBSCO Host; Gale; IngentaConnect; OhioLINK; ScienceDirect; SwetsWise Online Content. *Indexed:* C&ISA, CJA, CerAb, CompLI, EngInd, EnvAb, EnvInd, ExcerpMed, IAA, PollutAb, PsycInfo, SSCI, SUSA, SWRA. *Aud.:* Ac.

Computers, Environment and Urban Systems is an international scholarly journal that features theoretical papers on the use and development of computer-based technology for enhancing environmental and urban systems. The journal also offers interdisciplinary articles on the application of computer-based analysis to a variety of urban sectors—for example, housing, health care, economic development, urban planning and design, and transportation. The journal regularly publishes articles on the theory and application of geographic information systems (GIS). Because of its technical emphasis and high subscription cost, the journal is recommended for research libraries with comprehensive collections only. For a journal with similar coverage minus the heavy technical content, see *Environment and Planning B: Planning and Design* or *URISA Journal,* which has a stronger emphasis on applied GIS.

Economic Geography. See Geography section.

Environment and Behavior. See Psychology section.

6080. Environment and Planning A: international journal of urban and regional research. Formerly: *Environment and Planning.* [ISSN: 0308-518X] 1969. m. USD 1554 combined subscription print & online eds.; USD 156 per issue. Ed(s): Nigel Thrift. Pion Ltd., 207 Brondesbury Park, London, NW2 5JN, United Kingdom; sales@pion.co.uk; http://www.pion.co.uk/. Illus., index, adv. Sample. Refereed. Vol. ends: Dec. *Indexed:* ASG, AgeL, ArtHuCI, EI, ExcerpMed, FR, HRA, HRIS, IBR, IBSS, IBZ, JEL, PRA, PollutAb, RRTA, SSCI, SUSA, SWA, SWRA, WAE&RSA. *Bk. rev.:* 5-15, 500-1,000 words, signed. *Aud.:* Ac.

Environment and Planning A (*EPA*) is a highly regarded interdisciplinary journal on international urban and regional research. One of a suite of four journals titled *Environment and Planning, EPA's* abstracted papers draw on a number of disciplines, including geography, regional science, environmental science, and economics. Authors are primarily European, with British authorship representing approximately half. Articles are generally theoretical, with a geographic tilt toward the European Union. Each monthly issue contains ten or more articles and one or more lengthy book reviews. Occasionally, an issue is organized around a theme, for instance, "Mobilities and Materialities." With its high subscription rate and its strong theoretical emphasis, *EPA* is recommended only for large academic libraries with significant urban studies or city planning collections.

6081. Environment and Planning B: Planning & Design. Formerly (until 1983): *Environment & Planning. B;* Which superseded in part (in 1974): *Environment & Planning.* [ISSN: 0265-8135] 1969. bi-m. USD 563 combined subscription print & online eds.; USD 113 per issue. Ed(s): Mike Batty. Pion Ltd., 207 Brondesbury Park, London, NW2 5JN, United Kingdom; sales@pion.co.uk; http://www.pion.co.uk/. Index, adv. Sample. Refereed. *Indexed:* CJA, HRIS, IBR, IBSS, IBZ, PRA, SFSA, SSCI, SUSA, V&AA. *Bk. rev.:* 0-6, signed. *Aud.:* Ac.

Environment and Planning B: Planning and Design (*EPB*) is an international scholarly bimonthly journal, one of a suite of four journals titled *Environment and Planning.* Despite its rather general subtitle, *EPB* focuses on spatial modeling in the context of the built environment, particularly as applied to the spatial structures of cities and regions. Authors are primarily European or Anglophone. Articles are generally theoretical, analytical, and/or methodological, with an emphasis on the application of computers in planning and design; most issues include articles on GIS applications. *EPB* is also notable for its articles exploring the idea of the "virtual city." Book reviews are an occasional feature. Given its strong theoretical emphasis, this journal is recommended for specialized library collections.

6082. Environment and Planning D: Society and Space. [ISSN: 0263-7758] 1983. bi-m. USD 563 combined subscription print & online eds.; USD 113 per issue. Ed(s): G Pratt. Pion Ltd., 207 Brondesbury Park, London, NW2 5JN, United Kingdom; sales@pion.co.uk; http://www.pion.co.uk/. Adv. Sample. Refereed. *Indexed:* ArtHuCI, CommAb, FR, IBSS, PAIS, PRA, SSCI, SUSA, SWA, V&AA. *Bk. rev.:* 0-6, signed. *Aud.:* Ac.

Environment and Planning D: Society & Space (*EPD*) is an international and interdisciplinary scholarly journal, one of a suite of four journals titled *Environment and Planning. EPD* focuses on the interaction between society and space. Articles range from practical politics to social theory to empirical research, all examining spatial issues from the broadest perspective. Occasionally an issue has a theme, for example, "Boundary Variations." Most of *EPD's* bimonthly issues include book reviews. Recommended for academic libraries with comprehensive urban studies collections; also of interest to sociologists.

6083. Environment and Urbanization. [ISSN: 0956-2478] 1989. s-a. GBP 290. Ed(s): Sheridan Bartlett, David Satterthwaite. Sage Publications Ltd., 1 Oliver's Yard, 55 City Rd, London, EC1 1SP, United Kingdom; info@sagepub.co.uk; http://www.sagepub.co.uk. Illus., index. Refereed. Circ: 2600. Vol. ends: No. 2. Reprint: PSC. *Indexed:* C&ISA, CABA, CerAb, EIP, EnvAb, EnvInd, IAA, IBSS, PAIS, PSA, PollutAb, S&F, SSA, SSCI, SUSA, SWRA, SociolAb, V&AA, WAE&RSA, WRCInf. *Bk. rev.:* 25-30, 100-300 words. *Aud.:* Ac.

Environment and Urbanization is a scholarly journal focused on international planning and development issues in developing countries and is published semi-annually by the Human Settlements Programme of the International Institute for Environment and Development in London. The journal "provides researchers, NGO staff and professionals in Africa, Asia and Latin America with the chance to write about their work, present their ideas and debate on issues." It also arranges for the translation of French, Spanish, and Portuguese articles into English. Each issue has a special theme identified by reader polls—for example, "Chronic Poverty" and "Urban Violence and Insecurity." The journal's web site (www.iied.org/human/eandu/eandu_details.html) lists the themes of earlier and prospective issues. Issues include an occasional guide on the issue's theme, as well as a profile of an innovative NGO, papers on participatory tools and methods, and book reviews. French and Spanish summaries of each article are provided. Reasonably priced. Highly recommended for academic libraries.

6084. *European Journal of Spatial Development.* [ISSN: 1650-9544] 2002. irreg. Free. Ed(s): Christer Bergs. Nordregio. Nordic Centre for Spatial Studies, PO Box 1658, Stockholm, 11186, Sweden; nordregio@nordregio.se; http://www.nordregio.se. Refereed. *Aud.:* Ac.

The *European Journal of Spatial Development* publishes original academic contributions in the area of spatial development (i.e., spatial analyses, physical planning, and regional development) with a comparative orientation. The geographic focus is Europe and Scandinavia, which is also the primary geographic representation of the editorial board. Articles are peer-reviewed and have abstracts. Recent articles include "Disaster Prevention in Urban Environments" and "Participatory Experiments from the Bottom Up: The role of environmental ngos and citizen groups." Articles are individually numbered and released as pdf files. The journal also includes shorter articles, editorials, and debates. Recommended for academic libraries with a strong interest in European urban studies. URL: www.nordregio.se/EJSD/index.html

6085. *European Planning Studies.* [ISSN: 0965-4313] 1993. 10x/yr. GBP 1287 print & online eds. Ed(s): Philip Cooke, Louis Albrechts. Routledge, 4 Park Sq, Milton Park, Abingdon, OX14 4RN, United Kingdom; info@routledge.co.uk; http://www.routledge.co.uk. Adv. Refereed. Online: EBSCO Publishing, EBSCO Host; Gale; IngentaConnect; Northern Light Technology, Inc.; OCLC Online Computer Library Center, Inc.; ProQuest K-12 Learning Solutions; ProQuest LLC (Ann Arbor); SwetsWise Online Content. Reprint: PSC. *Indexed:* ABIn, IBR, IBZ, IPSA, PRA, PSA, RRTA, SSA, SSCI, SUSA, SociolAb, WAE&RSA. *Bk. rev.:* 2, signed. *Aud.:* Ac.

European Planning Studies (*EPS*) is the scholarly journal of the Association of European Schools of Planning (AESOP), whose membership comprises academic planning educators and more than 100 planning schools throughout Western and Eastern Europe. The editorial board and authors are European, and the geographic coverage is also primarily, although not exclusively, European. Each issue includes five or more articles with abstracts, which focus on European spatial development planning issues at the local, regional, and national levels. Occasional articles offer case studies of successful spatial policies and critiques of policy failure. *EPS*, published eight times per year, features a section called "European Briefing" and book reviews; most issues also include a "Research Briefing." Some issues have a theme. Although the institutional subscription rate may seem high, the actual cost per article ("briefings" articles included) is comparable to that of *European Urban and Regional Studies* (including its "Euro-commentary" feature). *European Planning Studies* is recommended for college and research libraries.

6086. *European Urban and Regional Studies.* [ISSN: 0969-7764] 1994. q. GBP 397. Ed(s): Allan Williams, Ray Hudson. Sage Publications Ltd., 1 Oliver's Yard, 55 City Rd, London, EC1 1SP, United Kingdom; info@sagepub.co.uk; http://www.sagepub.co.uk. Adv. Refereed. Circ: 650. Reprint: PSC. *Indexed:* AgeL, CABA, DSA, IBSS, IPSA, PRA, PSA, RRTA, SSCI, SUSA, SociolAb, WAE&RSA. *Bk. rev.:* 3-10, 500-1,000 words, signed. *Aud.:* Ac.

European Urban and Regional Studies is a refereed journal that "provides a means of dialogue between different European traditions of intellectual enquiry on urban and regional development issues." With a primarily European editorial board and authorship, each quarterly issue includes four or more theoretical articles with abstracts, focusing on Europe as a region with less emphasis on regions or places within Europe. The journal also considers changes in Europe in a global context. Each issue includes an "Euro-Commentary" short article and book reviews. Recommended for specialized collections. For a similar title with a broader appeal, see *European Planning Studies*.

Geo World. See Geography section.

6087. *Growth and Change: a journal of urban and regional policy.* [ISSN: 0017-4815] 1970. q. GBP 210 print & online eds. Ed(s): Anna Stewart, Thomas R Leinbach. Blackwell Publishing, Inc., Commerce Place, 350 Main St, Malden, MA 02148; customerservices@blackwellpublishing.com; http://www.blackwellpublishing.com. Illus., index, adv. Sample. Refereed. Vol. ends: No. 4. Microform: PQC. Online: Blackwell Synergy; EBSCO Publishing, EBSCO Host; Florida Center for Library Automation; Gale; IngentaConnect; OCLC Online Computer Library Center, Inc.; OhioLINK; SwetsWise Online Content. Reprint: PSC. *Indexed:* ABCPolSci, ABIn, AgeL, Agr, ApEcolAb, ArtHuCI, BAS, HRA, IBSS, IPSA, JEL, PAIS, PRA, PSA, PollutAb, RRTA, S&F, SSCI, SUSA, SWRA, SociolAb, V&AA, WAE&RSA. *Bk. rev.:* 2-6, 1,000 words, signed. *Aud.:* Ac, Sa.

Growth and Change is an international refereed quarterly journal on "all aspects of public, urban, and regional development and policy-making." The editorial board is almost entirely from the United States, as reflected in the journal's American emphasis. The journal includes both empirical and theoretical articles, and although articles draw from many different disciplines, including geography, public finance, urban and regional planning, agricultural economics, public policy, and related fields, the journal's clear strength is urban and regional economics. Book reviews appear in most issues. With its abundant urban economics content, *Growth and Change* is recommended only for comprehensive urban studies collections; it would also be of interest to college and university libraries that support programs in urban and regional economics, as well as to economics researchers. More general urban studies collections would be better served with the *Journal of Urban Economics* (see the Economics section).

6088. *Habitat International.* Formerly (until 1977): *Habitat (Oxford).* [ISSN: 0197-3975] 1976. 4x/yr. EUR 1323. Ed(s): C L Choguill. Pergamon, The Boulevard, Langford Ln, East Park, Kidlington, OX5 1GB, United Kingdom. Illus., adv. Refereed. Circ: 350. Microform: PQC. Online: EBSCO Publishing, EBSCO Host; Gale; IngentaConnect; OhioLINK; ScienceDirect; SwetsWise Online Content. *Indexed:* AgeL, CABA, DSA, EI, EnvAb, ExcerpMed, FPA, ForAb, IBSS, PRA, PSA, S&F, SFSA, SSA, SSCI, SUSA, SWA, SociolAb, WAE&RSA, ZooRec. *Bk. rev.:* Number and length vary. *Aud.:* Ac.

Habitat International is a highly regarded international refereed journal whose main focus is on urbanization in the developing world, with special depth in housing issues. Its international emphasis is reflected in the international membership of its editorial board and authorship. This quarterly also explores the interplay of changes in the economic, social, technological, and political systems of one region with other regions. The articles (with abstracts) are interdisciplinary, with an intended audience of urban planners, human and physical geographers, housing analysts, and sociologists. This journal includes occasional thematic issues—for example, "Urbanization in China." Most issues include book reviews. Recommended for college and research libraries.

6089. *Housing Policy Debate.* [ISSN: 1051-1482] 1990. q. Free. Ed(s): James H Carr. Federal National Mortgage Association (Fannie Mae), 3900 Wisconsin Ave, NW, Washington, DC 20016; http://www.fanniemae.com. Illus., adv. Refereed. Circ: 4000 Controlled. Microform: PQC. Online: Factiva, Inc.; OCLC Online Computer Library Center, Inc. *Indexed:* ABIn, ABS&EES, AgeL, CJA, IBSS, JEL, PAIS, SSCI, SUSA, SWR&A. *Aud.:* Ga, Ac.

Published by the Fannie Mae Foundation, *Housing Policy Debate* is a quarterly scholarly journal that provides discussion and research on a broad range of U.S. housing and community development issues. Topics recently explored in the journal include the challenges facing public housing and the link between housing mobility and health. All issues are available online on the Fannie Mae Foundation web site at www.fanniemaefoundation.org. Recommended for academic and large public libraries.

6090. *Housing Studies.* [ISSN: 0267-3037] 1986. bi-m. GBP 448 print & online eds. Ed(s): Janet Ford, Mr. Roger Burrows. Routledge, 4 Park Sq, Milton Park, Abingdon, OX14 4RN, United Kingdom; info@routledge.co.uk; http://www.routledge.co.uk. Illus., index, adv. Sample. Refereed. Circ: 800. Online: EBSCO Publishing, EBSCO Host; Gale; IngentaConnect; Northern Light Technology, Inc.; OCLC Online

Computer Library Center, Inc.; ProQuest K-12 Learning Solutions; ProQuest LLC (Ann Arbor); SwetsWise Online Content. Reprint: PSC. *Indexed:* AgeL, BAS, IBR, IBZ, JEL, PSA, SSA, SSCI, SUSA, SWA, SociolAb. *Bk. rev.:* 4-7, 500-2,000 words, signed. *Aud.:* Ac, Sa.

Housing Studies is a refereed journal of international housing research providing a well-regarded forum for academic debate in the housing field. Journal articles (with abstracts) draw from a number of disciplines, ranging from economics and history through political science, sociology, and urban studies. Topical coverage is broad and includes the role of housing in everyday life, housing economics, international comparisons and developments, sustainability and housing development, and more. The geographic emphasis is the European Union. Each bimonthly issue features book reviews. Recommended for academic libraries.

6091. *International Journal of Urban and Regional Research.* [ISSN: 0309-1317] 1976. q. GBP 334 print & online eds. Ed(s): Alan Harding, Jeremy Seekings. Blackwell Publishing Ltd., 9600 Garsington Rd, Oxford, OX4 2ZG, United Kingdom; customerservices@ blackwellpublishing.com; http://www.blackwellpublishing.com. Illus., index, adv. Sample. Refereed. Vol. ends: Dec. Online: Blackwell Synergy; EBSCO Publishing, EBSCO Host; Gale; IngentaConnect; OCLC Online Computer Library Center, Inc.; OhioLINK; SwetsWise Online Content. Reprint: PSC. *Indexed:* ABCPolSci, AmH&L, ApEcolAb, BAS, CJA, EI, FR, HistAb, IBSS, IPSA, JEL, PAIS, PSA, RRTA, RiskAb, SSA, SSCI, SUSA, SWA, SociolAb, WAE&RSA. *Bk. rev.:* 5-10, length varies, signed. *Aud.:* Ac.

The *International Journal of Urban and Regional Research* is a well-regarded international journal for urban studies. Each quarterly issue contains five to eight theoretical or empirical articles that offer critical, comparative, and geographic perspectives on a variety of global and local urban and regional issues. Most issues also include a thematic "symposium" with its own guest editor, comprising four additional articles. Recent symposia include "Globalization and Cities in Comparative Perspective." Each issue features lengthy "review essays" as well as shorter book reviews. Highly recommended for academic libraries.

6092. *International Planning Studies.* [ISSN: 1356-3475] 1996. q. GBP 332 print & online eds. Ed(s): John Lovering. Routledge, 4 Park Sq, Milton Park, Abingdon, OX14 4RN, United Kingdom; info@routledge.co.uk; http://www.routledge.co.uk. Illus., index. Refereed. Reprint: PSC. *Indexed:* ABIn, CJA, FR, IBR, IBZ. *Bk. rev.:* 3-10, signed, variable length. *Aud.:* Ac.

International Planning Studies is an interdisciplinary peer-reviewed journal that focuses on comparative research in the fields of urban and regional studies, planning, economic development, environmental studies, transportation, and governance. This journal, with its particularly distinguished international editorial board, is highly regarded in its field. The geographic scope is international, with a slight emphasis on the developed world. Recent articles include "The Visioning Diversity: Planning Vancouver's multicultural communities" and "Transfer of Urban Ideas: The emergence of Venezuelan urbanism in the proposals for 1930s Caracas." Each quarterly issue contains three papers with abstracts and several lengthy book reviews, plus occasional editorials and commentaries. Recommended for academic libraries; a core title for city planning collections.

6093. *Journal of Architectural and Planning Research.* Supersedes: *Journal of Architectural Research.* [ISSN: 0738-0895] 1984. q. USD 371 (Individuals, USD 104). Ed(s): Andrew D Seidel. Locke Science Publishing Company, Inc., 28 E Jackson Bldg., 10th Floor L221, Chicago, IL 60604; lockescience@juno.com. Illus. Sample. Refereed. *Indexed:* ABS&EES, API, AbAn, AgeL, ArtHuCI, ArtInd, C&ISA, CJA, CerAb, IAA, IBSS, PAIS, PRA, PsycInfo, SSCI, SUSA. *Bk. rev.:* Number and length vary. *Aud.:* Ac.

The *Journal of Architectural and Planning Research* (*JAPR*) is an interdisciplinary peer-reviewed journal, published quarterly in cooperation with a variety of professional organizations, including among them the American Institute of Architects, the Environmental Design Research Association, and the Royal Institute of British Architects. The journal is unusual in explicitly bridging the disciplines of architecture and city planning, emphasizing architectural and urban planning research, and architectural and urban design. *JAPR* encompasses empirical and theoretical work in six or seven articles, with an occasional thematic issue. International in scope, both contributors and the editorial board are primarily European and Anglo–North American. Book reviews appear in some issues. Recommended for college and research libraries and a core title for serious architecture or city planning collections.

6094. *Journal of Housing and Community Development.* Formerly (until 1995): *Journal of Housing.* [ISSN: 1534-648X] 1944. bi-m. USD 33 (Free to members). Ed(s): Terence Cooper. National Association of Housing and Redevelopment Officials, 630 Eye St, NW, Washington, DC 20001-3736; nahro@nahro.org; http://www.nahro.org. Illus., index, adv. Circ: 15000 Paid. Vol. ends: Nov/Dec. Microform: PQC. Online: EBSCO Publishing, EBSCO Host; OCLC Online Computer Library Center, Inc.; ProQuest LLC (Ann Arbor); H.W. Wilson. *Indexed:* ABIn, AgeL, EnvAb, PAIS, RiskAb, SSCI. *Bk. rev.:* Number and length vary. *Aud.:* Ga, Ac, Sa.

The *Journal of Housing and Community Development* is a bimonthly trade magazine published by the National Association of Housing & Redevelopment Officials (NAHRO), a professional membership organization comprising U.S. housing and community development agencies and officials. The magazine includes short topical articles as well as a couple of longer articles in each issue, focusing on national housing and community development trends as they affect all levels of housing and community development programs, with an emphasis on affordable and moderate income housing. Other areas of emphasis include direct administrative, organizational, and operational reports and legal, governmental, and technical development. The magazine also regularly features a buyer's guide. For large public libraries and academic libraries that support urban studies programs.

6095. *Journal of Planning Education and Research.* [ISSN: 0739-456X] 1981. q. GBP 191. Ed(s): Luci Yamamoto, Karen S Christensen. Sage Publications, Inc., 2455 Teller Rd, Thousand Oaks, CA 91320; info@sagepub.com; http://www.sagepub.com. Adv. Refereed. Circ: 2000. Online: CSA; EBSCO Publishing, EBSCO Host; HighWire Press; OCLC Online Computer Library Center, Inc.; SAGE Publications, Inc., SAGE Journals Online; SwetsWise Online Content. Reprint: PSC. *Indexed:* C&ISA, CerAb, EnvInd, IAA, PAIS, PSA, SSCI, SUSA. *Bk. rev.:* 2-6 signed, variable length. *Aud.:* Ac.

The *Journal of Planning Education and Research* is a well-regarded scholarly journal published by the Association of Collegiate Schools of Planning, a consortium of American university-based programs that offer credentials in urban and regional planning. The journal covers city planning, planning theory and practice, and planning pedagogy. Each issue comprises six or more articles with abstracts, occasional report and commentary features, and signed book review articles. Typical recent articles include "Planning Theory and the City" and "Spatial and Transportation Mismatch in Los Angeles." For academic libraries, and a core journal for city planning collections.

6096. *Journal of Planning Literature.* Incorporates (1957-1996): *C P L Bibliographies.* [ISSN: 0885-4122] 1986. q. GBP 561. Ed(s): Jack Nasar. Sage Publications, Inc., 2455 Teller Rd, Thousand Oaks, CA 91320; info@sagepub.com; http://www.sagepub.com. Adv. Refereed. Circ: 450 Paid. Microform: PQC. Online: CSA; EBSCO Publishing, EBSCO Host; HighWire Press; OCLC Online Computer Library Center, Inc.; SAGE Publications, Inc., SAGE Journals Online; SwetsWise Online Content. Reprint: PSC. *Indexed:* HRIS, IBSS, PAIS, PSA, SSCI, SUSA, SociolAb. *Bk. rev.:* Number and length vary. *Aud.:* Ac.

The *Journal of Planning Literature* is a multifaceted title that covers new developments in city and regional planning and design. Each quarterly issue contains a journal article index that regularly covers 70 journal titles as well as selected city planning dissertations. Most listings include abstracts. The index is organized in three broad topical categories: "History/Theory/ Administration," "Methodology/Quantitative/Economic/Qualitative," and "Physical/Environmental." In addition, each issue contains one or two refereed articles and one or more monograph-length annotated bibliographies. Recent examples include "Does Affordable Housing Detrimentally Affect Property

Values? A Review of the Literature" and "Technology Spillovers, Agglomeration, and Regional Economic Development." Each issue also includes a substantive book review. Highly recommended for academic libraries.

6097. Journal of Urban Affairs. Formed by the merger of (1979-1982): *Urban Affairs Papers;* (1977-1982): *Urban Interest Journal.* [ISSN: 0735-2166] 1976. 5x/yr. GBP 541 print & online eds. Ed(s): Rodolfo Torres, Victoria Bassolo. Blackwell Publishing, Inc., Commerce Place, 350 Main St, Malden, MA 02148; customerservices@ blackwellpublishing.com; http://www.blackwellpublishing.com. Illus., adv. Refereed. Circ: 530. Microform: PQC. Online: Blackwell Synergy; EBSCO Publishing, EBSCO Host; Gale; IngentaConnect; OCLC Online Computer Library Center, Inc.; OhioLINK; SwetsWise Online Content; H.W. Wilson. *Indexed:* ABS&EES, ApEcolAb, CJA, FR, HistAb, IIBP, IPSA, PAIS, PSA, RiskAb, SSA, SSCI, SUSA, SWR&A, SociolAb. *Bk. rev.:* 2-5, 500-1,000 words, signed. *Aud.:* Ga, Ac, Sa.

Co-sponsored by Saint Louis University and the Urban Affairs Association, an international professional organization for urban scholars, researchers, and practitioners, the *Journal of Urban Affairs* is a multidisciplinary refereed journal that focuses on urban research and public policy. Its theoretical and empirical articles (with abstracts) are especially readable and address metropolitan and community problems. The journal's geographic coverage is primarily American. Each issue includes book reviews. Similar in audience and coverage to *Urban Affairs Review,* the *Journal of Urban Affairs* costs less with twice as many articles (eight on average) in each of its five yearly issues. For academic libraries and large public libraries.

6098. Journal of Urban Design. [ISSN: 1357-4809] 1996. 3x/yr. GBP 274 print & online eds. Ed(s): Taner Oc. Routledge, 4 Park Sq, Milton Park, Abingdon, OX14 4RN, United Kingdom; info@routledge.co.uk; http://www.routledge.co.uk. Illus., index, adv. Sample. Refereed. Vol. ends: Oct. Online: EBSCO Publishing, EBSCO Host; Gale; IngentaConnect; Northern Light Technology, Inc.; OCLC Online Computer Library Center, Inc.; ProQuest LLC (Ann Arbor); SwetsWise Online Content. Reprint: PSC. *Indexed:* API, AmHI, BrHumI, CJA, IBR, IBSS, IBZ, SUSA. *Bk. rev.:* 6-8, 1,000-1,500 words. *Aud.:* Ac, Sa.

As the persistent issues of livability and quality of life in cities surface in the media and daily conversation, urban design has become a more visible aspect of urban studies. Established in 1996, the *Journal of Urban Design* is devoted to a broad discussion of urban design, in both its theoretical and applied dimensions. International in scope, the refereed journal publishes articles on an extensive range of urban design issues, ranging from aesthetics and form to urban history and preservation through local identity and property development. Recent typical articles include "Localizing Urban Design Traditions: Gated and edge cities in Curitiba" and "Designing Neighbourhoods for Social Interaction: The case of cohousing." Each issue includes an average of four papers with abstracts, and has substantive book reviews. Readable and well illustrated, this journal is highly recommended for academic libraries.

Journal of Urban Economics. See Economics section.

Journal of Urban History. See History section.

6099. Journal of Urban Planning and Development. Former titles (until 1982): *American Society of Civil Engineers. Urban Planning and Development Division. Journal;* (until 1964): *American Society of Civil Engineers. City Planning Division. Journal;* Which superseded in part (in 1956): *American Society of Civil Engineers. Proceedings.* [ISSN: 0733-9488] 1873. q. USD 292. Ed(s): Gang-Len Chang. American Society of Civil Engineers, 1801 Alexander Bell Dr, Reston, VA 20191-4400; http://www.asce.org. Illus., index. Refereed. Circ: 1575. Microform: PQC. Online: American Institute of Physics, Scitation; EBSCO Publishing, EBSCO Host; SwetsWise Online Content. *Indexed:* AS&TI, C&ISA, CerAb, EngInd, EnvInd, H&SSA, HRIS, IAA, IBR, IBZ, PAIS, PollutAb, RiskAb, SCI, SSCI, SWRA. *Bk. rev.:* Number and length vary. *Aud.:* Ac, Sa.

The *Journal of Urban Planning and Development* is the journal of the American Society of Civil Engineers, Transportation and Development Institute and Urban Planning and Development Division. As the journal's organizational affiliation suggests, this scholarly journal focuses on the application of civil engineering to public works and the physical infrastructure of cities, with an emphasis on urban transportation planning. Subjects range from environmental assessment to land-use planning and underground utilities. Each issue offers five or more "technical papers" as well as occasional opinion essays, discussions, and book reviews. Recent articles include "New Designing the Walkable City" and "Sustainable Urban Transportation: Concepts, policies, and methodologies." Special issues are occasionally issued, for example, "Innovating Regulations in Urban Planning and Development." For large academic and public libraries; also of interest to civil engineering collections.

6100. Journal of Urban Technology. [ISSN: 1063-0732] 1992. 3x/yr. GBP 261 print & online eds. Ed(s): Maryann Donato, Richard E Hanley. Routledge, 4 Park Sq, Milton Park, Abingdon, OX14 4RN, United Kingdom; info@routledge.co.uk; http://www.routledge.co.uk. Illus., index. Refereed. Circ: 600. Online: EBSCO Publishing, EBSCO Host; Gale; IngentaConnect; OCLC Online Computer Library Center, Inc.; SwetsWise Online Content. Reprint: PSC. *Indexed:* CJA, ERIC, HRIS, IBR, IBZ, PRA, SSCI, SUSA. *Bk. rev.:* 2-6, variable length. *Aud.:* Ga, Ac, Sa.

The *Journal of Urban Technology,* an international peer-reviewed journal, reviews and analyzes developments in urban technologies, and studies the history and the political, economic, environmental, social, aesthetic, and ethical effects of those technologies. Recent articles include "Water and Gas: Early developments in the utility networks of Paris," "Risk Management and Protection Strategies for Buildings and Facilities," and "Aveiro, Portugal: Making a digital city." Most issues include book review essays. The journal's layout and readable articles should appeal to undergraduate students. Recommended for college and research libraries. Of interest also to libraries that serve information-technologies programs.

Landscape and Urban Planning. See Landscape Architecture section.

6101. Making Places. 2002. irreg. Free. Project for Public Spaces, 700 Broadway, 4th Fl, New York, NY 10003; pps@pps.org; http://www.pps.org. *Aud.:* Ga, Ac, Sa.

Making Places is the free official newsletter of the Project for Public Spaces (PPS), a nonprofit organization dedicated to creating and sustaining public places that build communities. The newsletter focuses on broad urban design topics and has an underlying agenda to encourage individuals to improve their community public spaces. It is published in several monthly issues, each consisting of several articles. Each issue has a theme, for example, public squares, neighborhoods, and public markets. Recent feature articles include "Launching a New Tradition of Great Public Squares" and "Saving the World One Streetcorner at a Time." Recommended for public libraries. URL: www.pps.org/info/getinvolved/making_places

6102. New Towns. q. USD 20. Ed(s): Diane Dorney. The Town Paper, 309 Main St, Gaithersburg, MD 20878; info@tndtownpaper.com; http://tndtownpaper.com. *Aud.:* Ga, Ac, Sa.

New Towns is a quarterly newspaper, established in 1999 as *The Town Paper,* that covers traditional neighborhood development (TND), new towns, and new urban construction in the United States and beyond. The intended audience is residents of new urbanist communities as well as architects and urban designers, developers and public officials, and local activists. In addition to brief news articles, each oversize 16-page issue includes an ever-lengthening list of TND projects completed or under development, often with web site addresses. Selected full-text articles are available on the newspaper's web site: http://tndtownpaper.com. Of interest to general readers, urban designers, and academics, *New Towns* is recommended for both public and academic libraries. For a similar, better-known, and more industry-oriented publication, see *New Urban News.*

6103. New Urban News. [ISSN: 1096-1844] 1996. 8x/yr. USD 79 in North America (Students, USD 45). Ed(s): Roberta Dixon, Robert Steuteville. New Urban Publications, Inc., 202 E State St, Ste 303, Ithaca, NY 14850. Illus. Sample. Circ: 5400 Paid. *Bk. rev.:* Number and length vary. *Aud.:* Ga, Ac, Sa.

New Urban News is a newsmagazine with a mission "to help people create better communities." Its intended audience is professionals and lay readers with a strong interest in the New Urbanism. The New Urbanism movement, also known as "smart growth" and traditional neighborhood development, promotes building mixed-use, walkable neighborhoods around a town center, as an alternative to sprawl. *New Urban News* covers a wide range of topics in short, well-illustrated articles: for example, significant new urbanist projects, planning concepts, architecture, street design, inner city revitalization, etc. Each 24-page issue contains one or more short book review. Of interest to practitioners and academics alike, *New Urban News* is recommended for both large public libraries and academic libraries. For a similar publication with a greater urban design emphasis, more general appeal, and a much larger subscription base, see *New Towns.*

6104. The Next American City. [ISSN: 1544-6999] 2003. q. USD 29 domestic; USD 35 Canada; USD 38 elsewhere. The Next American City, Inc., 207033, New Haven, CT 06520-7033; info@americancity.org; http://www.americancity.org. *Indexed:* SUSA. *Bk. rev.:* 3, signed. *Aud.:* Ga, Ac.

The Next American City is a quarterly academic magazine, founded in the spring of 2003 by three recent Yale graduates, that "explores the transformation of America's cities and suburbs, asking tough questions about how and why our built environment, economy, society and culture are changing." The intended audience includes practitioners and activists, as well as the civic and business communities. Each issue has a theme; recent examples include "Urban/Rural Edge" and "Segregation & Integration." Each issue contains five or more thematic articles as well as regular "departments," such as education, environment, housing, and book reviews. Each issue also includes a "References & Resources" section. Readable and thoughtful in its approach to contemporary urban issues, *The Next American City* should appeal to a broad readership of ordinary citizens, academics, practitioners, and undergraduate students. Recommended for large public libraries and academic libraries.

Places. See Architecture section.

6105. Planetizen Newswire. [ISSN: 1536-0547] 2000. s-w. Free. Urban Insight, Inc., 5657 Wilshire Blvd, Ste 290, Los Angeles, CA 90036; info@urbansight.com; http://www.urbansight.com. *Bk. rev.:* Number and length vary. *Aud.:* Ga, Ac, Sa.

The *Planetizen Newswire* is the free semi-weekly electronic newsmagazine of the highly regarded online Planetizen, a public-interest information exchange for the urban planning, design, and development community. In addition to publishing links to full-text articles on the Planetizen web site and summaries of urban planning, design, and development news stories, the newswire includes a variety of original content, including op-eds, book reviews, event coverage, job openings, podcasts, and top 10 lists for city planning books, issues, and websites. The *Planetizen Newswire* is delivered electronically to subscribers' e-mail accounts. Although it will be of special interest to practitioners and students, because of its breadth of coverage and easy-to-use format it is recommended for all libraries that serve users with an interest in American urban studies. See the Planetizen web site to subscribe. URL: www.planetizen.com

6106. Planning. Formerly: *American Society of Planning Officials. A S P O Newsletter;* Which superseded (in 1978): *Practicing Planner;* (in 1971): *Planner's Notebook.* [ISSN: 0001-2610] 1972. m. Non-members, USD 75. Ed(s): Meghan Stromberg, Sylvia Lewis. American Planning Association, 122 South Michigan Ave, Ste 1600, Chicago, IL 60603-6107; http://www.planning.org. Illus., index, adv. Circ: 42000 Paid. Vol. ends: Dec. Microform: PQC. Online: EBSCO Publishing,

EBSCO Host; Florida Center for Library Automation; Gale; Northern Light Technology, Inc.; OCLC Online Computer Library Center, Inc.; ProQuest LLC (Ann Arbor). *Indexed:* ABIn, BPI, EnvAb, EnvInd, ExcerpMed, HRIS, LRI, PAIS, SUSA. *Bk. rev.:* Number and length vary. *Aud.:* Ga, Ac, Sa.

Planning is the professional magazine of the American Planning Association (APA), the principle professional city and regional planning organization in the United States. (See also the APA's scholarly journal, *Journal of the American Planning Association.*) Belying its glossy magazine format, *Planning*'s short articles on current urban planning projects and issues are substantive as well as topical and readable. Articles are usually focused on particular places—for example, "On the Ground in New Orleans" and "Teed Off Over the Aquifer." One issue every year covers the APA/AICP annual awards, with descriptive text, photographs, and plans, while each issue contains brief book reviews and news items. The APA web site offers annual indexing to *Planning* from 1997 forward (www.planning.org/planning/nonmember/annualindex.htm). Essential for colleges and universities with contemporary urban studies programs and of interest to large American public libraries that serve the city planning community.

6107. Planning Perspectives: an international journal of history, planning and the environment. [ISSN: 0266-5433] 1986. q. GBP 659 print & online eds. Ed(s): Robert B Fairbanks, Steven V Ward. Routledge, 4 Park Sq, Milton Park, Abingdon, OX14 4RN, United Kingdom; info@routledge.co.uk; http://www.routledge.co.uk. Illus. Refereed. Vol. ends: Oct. Online: EBSCO Publishing, EBSCO Host; Gale; IngentaConnect; OCLC Online Computer Library Center, Inc.; SwetsWise Online Content. Reprint: PSC. *Indexed:* API, AmH&L, HistAb, IBR, IBZ, PRA, SUSA. *Bk. rev.:* 10-15, 500 words. *Aud.:* Ac.

Planning Perspectives is a peer-reviewed international journal of history, planning, and the environment. The journal is multidisciplinary, and links theoretical work in economics, social and political history, and historical geography and sociology with the applied fields of public health, housing construction, architecture, and city planning. Each issue includes four or more articles and many lengthy book review essays. Typical recent articles include "Urban Development, Maintenance and Conservation: Planning in Germany—values in transition" and "Urban Ideal Images in Post-war Rotterdam." Geographic coverage is primarily, though not exclusively, British, European, and American. Recommended for academic libraries; also of interest for general history collections.

6108. Planning Practice and Research. [ISSN: 0269-7459] 1986. q. GBP 396 print & online eds. Ed(s): Vincent Nadin. Routledge, 4 Park Sq, Milton Park, Abingdon, OX14 4RN, United Kingdom; info@routledge.co.uk; http://www.routledge.co.uk. Illus. Refereed. Online: EBSCO Publishing, EBSCO Host; Gale; IngentaConnect; OCLC Online Computer Library Center, Inc.; SwetsWise Online Content. Reprint: PSC. *Indexed:* CABA, EnvAb, IBR, IBSS, IBZ, PAIS, RRTA, S&F, WAE&RSA. *Bk. rev.:* 3-6, 500 words. *Aud.:* Ac, Sa.

Planning Practice & Research is a peer-reviewed journal of current research in city planning practice and education, with an intended audience of practitioners, researchers, and academics. While its scope is international, the journal emphasizes Great Britain. Each issue contains several articles and one or more short articles on practice or research. Typical recent articles include "Planning Responses to Major Structural Change: Some experiences from British cities" and "Market Towns: Investigating the service role through visitor surveys." Issues include occasional book reviews. An interesting feature of most issues is the "Planning Literature Information Service," which provides broad subject indexing to a short (between 16 and 20) and variable list of journal titles. Nine subject categories are used: planning theory and history; methodology; economic and property development; the built environment; environment, energy, and natural resources; transport; housing and community development; urban and regional planning; and public administration, public policy, and professional concerns. Publication lags by approximately a year. For comprehensive academic collections; essential for British academic libraries.

Public Management. See Government Periodicals—State and Local section.

6109. *Regional Studies.* [ISSN: 0034-3404] 1966. 9x/yr. GBP 858 print & online eds. Routledge, 4 Park Sq, Milton Park, Abingdon, OX14 4RN, United Kingdom; info@routledge.co.uk; http://www.routledge.co.uk. Illus., index, adv. Refereed. Vol. ends: Dec. Microform: PQC. Online: EBSCO Publishing, EBSCO Host; Florida Center for Library Automation; Gale; IngentaConnect; Northern Light Technology, Inc.; OCLC Online Computer Library Center, Inc.; ProQuest LLC (Ann Arbor); SwetsWise Online Content. Reprint: PSC. *Indexed:* ABIn, API, BAS, BrEdI, BrHumI, CABA, ExcerpMed, FR, ForAb, HRA, IBR, IBSS, IBZ, IPSA, JEL, PAIS, PRA, PSA, RRTA, RiskAb, S&F, SSA, SSCI, SUSA, SociolAb, V&AA, WAE&RSA. *Bk. rev.:* 2-10, 500-1,000 words, signed. *Aud.:* Ac.

Regional Studies is the refereed journal of British Regional Studies Association. The content is international with a British and European emphasis, and focuses on urban regional development research and policy. Each issue comprises six or more full-length articles, two shorter articles, and four lengthy book reviews. Article abstracts are in English, French, German, and Spanish. Typical recent articles include "After the Exit: Acquisitions, entrepreneurial recycling and regional economic development" and "Distribution of Local Food Activity in England and Wales: An index of food relocalization." This journal is recommended for large academic libraries only; however, it should be considered a core title for British urban studies collections.

Topos: European landscape magazine. See Landscape Architecture section.

6110. *Town Planning Review.* [ISSN: 0041-0020] 1910. q. GBP 178 (Individuals, GBP 98; Students, GBP 32). Ed(s): Robin Bloxsidge, Cecilia Wong. Liverpool University Press, 4 Cambridge St, Liverpool, L69 7ZU, United Kingdom; http://www.liverpool-unipress.co.uk/. Illus., index, adv. Refereed. Circ: 1100. Vol. ends: Oct. Reprint: PSC. *Indexed:* API, AmHI, ArtInd, BAS, BrArAb, BrHumI, BrTechI, CJA, EnvInd, ExcerpMed, IBR, IBSS, NumL, PAIS, PRA, RRTA, RiskAb, SFSA, SSCI, SWA, WAE&RSA. *Bk. rev.:* 10-15, 500-1,000 words, signed. *Aud.:* Ac.

Edited in the Department of Civic Design in the University of Liverpool, *Town Planning Review* is an international refereed journal with a principal focus on urban and regional planning in countries with advanced industrial economies and in newly emergent industrial states. The intended audience includes both practitioners and researchers. Papers cover all aspects of city and regional planning, with a British and European emphasis. Thematic issues are published occasionally; a recent special issue focuses on "European Territorial Cohesion." In addition to five or more articles, many issues include a "Policy Forum," which allows a number of contributors to debate issues of planning policy. Also, every quarterly issue includes a substantial book review section. Recommended for academic libraries; highly recommended for British academic libraries with urban studies collections.

6111. *U R I S A Journal.* [ISSN: 1045-8077] 1989. s-a. USD 295. Urban and Regional Information Systems Association, 1460 Renaissance Dr, Ste 305, Park Ridge, IL 60068-1348; info@urisa.org; http://www.urisa.org/index.htm. Refereed. Circ: 3800. *Bk. rev.:* Number and length vary. *Aud.:* Ac, Sa.

The *URISA Journal* is the refereed journal of the Urban and Regional Information Association (URISA), a nonprofit association of professionals who use information technology to solve problems in planning, public works, the environment, etc., at all governmental levels. The journal contains articles with abstracts and reports on topics that range from urban and regional information science to spatial information technology, and to geography and geographic information science. The emphasis is on applied rather than theoretical or technical material. Each issue also regularly features book reviews, software reviews, and current literature reviews. For academic libraries with either urban studies or information technology collections. For a similar title with a technical emphasis, see *Computers, Environment and Urban Systems.*

6112. *Urban Affairs Review.* Formerly (until 1995): *Urban Affairs Quarterly.* [ISSN: 1078-0874] 1965. bi-m. GBP 505. Ed(s): Susan E Clarke, Michael A Pagano. Sage Publications, Inc., 2455 Teller Rd, Thousand Oaks, CA 91320; info@sagepub.com;

http://www.sagepub.com. Illus., index, adv. Refereed. Circ: 1500 Paid. Vol. ends: Jun. Microform: PQC. Online: CSA; EBSCO Publishing, EBSCO Host; Florida Center for Library Automation; Gale; HighWire Press; OCLC Online Computer Library Center, Inc.; SAGE Publications, Inc., SAGE Journals Online; SwetsWise Online Content. Reprint: PSC. *Indexed:* ABCPolSci, ASSIA, AmH&L, ArtHuCI, C&ISA, CJA, CerAb, CommAb, EAA, EIP, EnvAb, EnvInd, ExcerpMed, HRA, HistAb, IAA, IBR, IBSS, IPSA, JEL, PAIS, PRA, PSA, RI-1, RiskAb, SSA, SSCI, SUSA, SWA, SWR&A, SociolAb, V&AA. *Bk. rev.:* 2-4, 1,000-2,000 words. *Aud.:* Ac, Sa.

Urban Affairs Review (*UAR*) is a respected, multidisciplinary refereed journal that focuses on urban issues and themes. Geographic coverage is primarily American. For its intended audience of urban scholars and practitioners, *UAR* seeks articles that offer "innovative research methodologies used to analyze significant theoretical issues." Topics range from urban policy and economic development to the social, spatial, and cultural dynamics of cities. Each issue includes book reviews. Published bimonthly, *UAR* is similar in audience and coverage to the *Journal of Urban Affairs,* although it is more costly and averages three to four articles per issue. For academic libraries.

6113. *Urban Geography.* [ISSN: 0272-3638] 1980. 8x/yr. USD 530 (Individuals, USD 90). Ed(s): Truman A Hartshorn. Bellwether Publishing, Ltd., 8640 Guilford Rd, Ste 200, Columbia, MD 21046; bellpub@bellpub.com; http://www.bellpub.com. Illus., index. Sample. Refereed. Vol. ends: No. 8. *Indexed:* ABS&EES, ArtHuCI, BAS, CJA, EI, FR, IBSS, IPSA, PRA, SSCI, SUSA, SWA, WAE&RSA. *Bk. rev.:* Number and length vary. *Aud.:* Ac.

Urban Geography is a scholarly journal with a focus on the geographic aspect of urban studies. The emphasis is on the United States and Canada. Topics cover a range of public policy issues, including race, poverty, and ethnicity in the city; international differences in urban form and function; historical preservation; the urban housing market; and urban economics. Each semi-quarterly issue includes several articles with abstracts and book reviews. Recommended for academic libraries with urban studies or geography collections. Worthy but less important for libraries outside the United States and Canada.

6114. *Urban History.* Formerly: *Urban History Yearbook.* [ISSN: 0963-9268] 1974. 3x/yr. GBP 137. Ed(s): Rosemary Sweet, Richard Rodger. Cambridge University Press, The Edinburgh Bldg, Shaftesbury Rd, Cambridge, CB2 2RU, United Kingdom; journals@cambridge.org; http://www.journals.cambridge.org. Adv. Online: Pub.; EBSCO Publishing, EBSCO Host; OCLC Online Computer Library Center, Inc.; OhioLINK; SwetsWise Online Content. Reprint: PSC. *Indexed:* API, AmH&L, BAS, BrArAb, CommAb, HistAb, NumL, PSA, SSA, SociolAb. *Bk. rev.:* 15-20 lengthy reviews. *Aud.:* Ac.

Urban History is a scholarly journal of articles, historiographical and methodological surveys, and surveys of urban development in individual countries. The journal is international in its coverage with a British and European geographic tilt. The journal includes an average of 20 substantive book reviews per issue; some issues also include reviews of periodical articles. A useful and unusual feature of *Urban History* is the "Current Bibliography of Urban History," an index of about 1,000 monographs and periodical articles that appears in the December issue; approximately 560 journals are indexed. Indexing is by ten broad topics which are further subdivided. In addition, an index to cities and towns is provided. *Urban History* is highly recommended for academic libraries that support international urban studies; it is also of interest to historians. For urban studies collections with an American emphasis, the *Journal of Urban History* (see History section) is highly recommended.

6115. *Urban Land.* [ISSN: 0042-0891] 1941. m. Free to membership. Ed(s): Kristina Kessler. The Urban Land Institute, 1025 Thomas Jefferson St, NW, Ste 500W, Washington, DC 20007-5201; kkessler@uli.org; http://www.uli.org. Illus., index, adv. Circ: 14000 Controlled. Microform: PQC. *Indexed:* API, EnvInd, HRIS, PAIS, RiskAb, SUSA. *Bk. rev.:* 2-4, 200-300 words, signed. *Aud.:* Ga, Ac, Sa.

Urban Land is published by the Urban Land Institute, a membership-supported nonprofit education and research organization. Although it is a glossy magazine carrying advertising, *Urban Land*'s articles are signed and substantive, focusing on urban land development, real estate, housing, and urban design. The journal's geographic emphasis is the United States, with an occasional article on another part of the world. Published in ten monthly and one bimonthly issues, *Urban Land* is a core title for American public and academic libraries, offering a unique developers' viewpoint; in non-U.S. locales, it is recommended only for academic libraries and business libraries with a global focus.

6116. *Urban Morphology.* [ISSN: 1027-4278] 1997. s-a. GBP 40 (Individuals, GBP 20). Ed(s): Jeremy Whitehand. International Seminar on Urban Form, c/o M. Darin, Ecole d'Architecture de Versailles, 2 av. de Paris, Versailles, 78000, France; j.w.r.whitehand@bham.ac.uk; http://www.let.rug.nl/isuf/. Illus., adv. Refereed. Circ: 500 Paid. *Indexed:* ArtHuCI, IBR, IBZ, IndIslam, SUSA. *Bk. rev.:* 13-19, signed. *Aud.:* Ac.

Established in 1997, *Urban Morphology* is an international and interdisciplinary scholarly journal devoted to the spatial and cultural aspects of urban form. It is published by the International Seminar on Urban Form and its articles draw from a variety of disciplines, among them architecture and city planning, geography, history, sociology, and urban design. Each issue contains two or three long articles and nine or ten shorter articles. These articles are complemented by an extensive book review section that comprises as many as 19 reviews and brief "Notes and Notices." Reasonably priced and accessibly written, *Urban Morphology* is recommended for both undergraduate and research urban studies collections. Also of interest to history researchers.

6117. *Urban Studies: an international journal for research in urban and regional studies.* [ISSN: 0042-0980] 1964. 13x/yr. GBP 1225. Sage Publications Ltd., 1 Oliver's Yard, 55 City Rd, London, EC1 1SP, United Kingdom; info@sagepub.co.uk; http://www.sagepub.co.uk/journals.nav. Illus., index, adv. Refereed. Vol. ends: Dec. Online: EBSCO Publishing, EBSCO Host; Florida Center for Library Automation; Gale; IngentaConnect; Northern Light Technology, Inc.; OCLC Online Computer Library Center, Inc.; ProQuest K-12 Learning Solutions; ProQuest LLC (Ann Arbor); SwetsWise Online Content. Reprint: PSC. *Indexed:* API, AgeL, AmH&L, AmHI, ArtHuCI, BAS, BrHumI, CJA, EI, EnvAb, EnvInd, ExcerpMed, FR, HRA, HRIS, HistAb, IBR, IBSS, IBZ, IPSA, JEL, PAIS, PRA, PSA, RRTA, RiskAb, SFSA, SSA, SSCI, SUSA, SWA, SociolAb, V&AA, WAE&RSA. *Bk. rev.:* 10-15, 300-1,500 words. *Aud.:* Ac.

Urban Studies is a highly regarded core journal for urban studies collections. It covers the field of urban and regional studies through empirical and analytical peer-reviewed articles that draw from many disciplines, including geography, political science, planning, public administration, and sociology. The journal's coverage is international, while its editorial advisory committees are primarily British and American. Each monthly issue averages ten or more articles; all articles have abstracts; and most issues include signed book reviews. An occasional combined or "review issue" is published—for example, "Urban Culture and Development: Starting with South Africa." Essential for college and university libraries with international urban studies collections.

■ VETERINARY SCIENCE

C. Trenton Boyd, Director, Veterinary Medical Library, W218 Veterinary Medicine, University of Missouri, Columbia, MO 65211; boydt@missouri.edu; FAX: 573-882-2950

Introduction

The titles in this section have been selected for a library that needs to maintain a very basic core collection of veterinary medical periodicals, such as a medical library in a state that has no veterinary library or an academic library that serves a department of veterinary science. The criteria considered in the selection process were journal usage studies, citation analysis studies, and the author's 37 years of experience in the field. The author of this section is the chair of the Serials Committee of the Veterinary Medical Libraries Section of the Medical Library Association, and he would be happy to answer questions about any veterinary-related title.

A collection for a library that serves a college of veterinary medicine will carry a much more extensive list of veterinary titles, as well as many nonveterinary titles. (Many useful treatments and techniques can be extrapolated from human medicine and the biological sciences to veterinary medicine.) Examples of basic science titles are *Nature, Science,* and *New England Journal of Medicine.* Many human medical journals contain comparative and experimental animal studies that are important in the field of veterinary medicine. Some examples of these are *American Journal of Pathology, American Journal of Physiology, Endocrinology, Journal of Bone & Joint Surgery,* and *Biology of Reproduction.*

One should remember there are several refereed animal science titles that serve as a very important adjunct to veterinary medicine. The studies contained therein are frequently valuable to veterinary researchers and practitioner/clinicians. Examples are *Journal of Animal Science, Animal, Journal of Dairy Science,* and *Poultry Science.* Additionally, one can find many breed-specific titles, such as *Brown Swiss Bulletin, Quarter Horse Journal, Thoroughbred Record,* and *German Shepherd Dog Review,* which will often provide articles on the health, care, and breeding of a particular breed. The majority of the journals selected for this list are for the research scientist and/or practicing veterinarian, and the average reader will probably not find them interesting for leisure reading.

There are several indexing services that offer partial coverage of the veterinary literature (see list of basic abstracts and indexes). However, the only index that attempts to be complete in the coverage of veterinary literature is *Index Veterinarius* and its companion publication, *Veterinary Bulletin.*

New titles continue to be started, but the trend of the veterinary specialties to develop their own journals has stabilized since the last edition.

Veterinary medicine had been comparatively slow in breaking into electronic publishing as compared to other subject disciplines, but this has also changed since the last edition. All of the journals reviewed are available to libraries in full-text online versions except for four.

There are approximately five journals that are in electronic format only. Their growth, except for one, continues to be painfully slow. Even those that are peer reviewed seem to have problems in attracting contributors. It will be interesting to see if these survive and are eventually viewed by the academic world as "acceptable" journals to publish in for promotion and tenure. The exception is the *American Animal Hospital Association. Journal,* a major peer-reviewed veterinary title, which had a long print history before converting from paper format to electronic format only. Within the past year, *Acta Veterinaria Scandinavica* has also converted to online only. As to whether this will be a new trend, only time will tell.

Basic Periodicals

Ga: *DVM;* Ac: *American Animal Hospital Association. Journal, American Journal of Veterinary Research, American Veterinary Medical Association. Journal, Compendium on Continuing Education for the Practicing Veterinarian, Equine Veterinary Journal, Veterinary Clinics of North America: Equine Practice, Veterinary Clinics of North America: Exotic Animal Practice, Veterinary Clinics of North America: Food Animal Practice, Veterinary Clinics of North America: Small Animal Practice, Veterinary Journal, The Veterinary Record.*

Basic Abstracts and Indexes

Biological Abstracts; Focus On: veterinary science and medicine; MEDLINE; Index Veterinarius; Science Citation Index; Veterinary Bulletin.

6118. *American Animal Hospital Association. Journal (Online Edition).* Former titles (until 2004): *American Animal Hospital Association. Journal (Print Edition); American Animal Hospital Association Bulletin.* [ISSN: 1547-3317] 1965. bi-m. USD 107. Ed(s): Kate Johnson, Dr. Rhea Morgan. American Animal Hospital Association, PO Box 150899, Denver, CO 80215-0899; info@aahanet.org; http://www.aahanet.org. Illus., index, adv. Refereed. Circ: 14100 Paid and controlled. Vol. ends: Nov/Dec. Microform: PQC. Online: EBSCO Publishing, EBSCO Host; HighWire Press; ProQuest K-12 Learning Solutions; ProQuest LLC (Ann Arbor). *Indexed:* Agr, B&AI, BiolAb, CABA, ChemAb, ExcerpMed, FoVS&M, HortAb, IndVet, SCI, VB. *Aud.:* Ac, Sa.

This is an official publication of the American Animal Hospital Association, and as its name suggests, it focuses on information pertaining to the practice of small animal medicine and surgery. Effective December 10, 2003, with volume 39, number 6, the journal switched to an entirely online format. The layout editors do a superb job of intermixing color and black-and-white photographs, tables, and text to make the articles pleasing to the eye. The online format now gives the added advantage of viewing photographs at three levels of resolution. The arrangement of the articles is by discipline. Articles include case studies, original research, reviews, and retrospective studies. An interesting feature of the online site is a ranked listing of the 50 most-read articles during the past month. Also, the web site features tips for better web browsing. Online full text is available from 1998. The URL is www.jaaha.org. This august journal of small-animal medicine is a must for small-animal practitioners, clinicians, and veterinary science collections.

6119. *American Journal of Veterinary Research.* [ISSN: 0002-9645] 1940. m. USD 185 domestic; USD 195 foreign; USD 14 per issue domestic. Ed(s): Dr. Janis H Audin. American Veterinary Medical Association, 1931 N Meacham Rd, Ste 100, Schaumburg, IL 60173-4360; bclune@avma.org; http://www.avma.org. Illus., index, adv. Refereed. Circ: 6400 Paid. Vol. ends: Dec. Microform: PMC; PQC. Online: EBSCO Publishing, EBSCO Host. *Indexed:* AbAn, Agr, B&AI, BiolAb, CABA, ChemAb, DSA, ExcerpMed, FS&TA, FoVS&M, HortAb, IndVet, RRTA, S&F, SCI, SSCI, VB, WAE&RSA. *Aud.:* Ac, Sa.

The *American Journal of Veterinary Research* is a publication of the American Veterinary Medical Association. It has set high standards by promising "to publish in a timely manner, peer-reviewed reports of the highest-quality research that has a clear potential to enhance the health, welfare, and performance of animals and human...will maintain the highest ethical standards...and will foster global interdisciplinary cooperation in veterinary medical research." The illustrative material is largely black-and-white. An average issue will carry 20–30 articles varying in length from 2 to 12 pages. At the front of each issue is a section titled "Veterinary Research News." It reports on the latest happenings in the veterinary research community. An online version has been available since January 2000. Full text is available only to subscribers, but abstracts of the articles are available to everyone. The URL is http://avmajournals.avma.org/loi/ajvr. This basic research journal is recommended for libraries that serve graduate programs in the fields of veterinary medicine, animal science, dairy science, and laboratory animals.

6120. *American Veterinary Medical Association. Journal.* Incorporates (1899-1913): *American Veterinary Medical Association. Proceedings;* (1950-1964): *American Veterinary Medical Association. Annual Meeting. Scientific Proceedings;* Which was formerly (until 1956): *American Veterinary Medical Association. Annual Meeting. Proceedings.* [ISSN: 0003-1488] 1877. s-m. USD 150 domestic; USD 170 foreign. Ed(s): Dr. Janis H Audin, Bernadine G Clune. American Veterinary Medical Association, 1931 N Meacham Rd, Ste 100, Schaumburg, IL 60173-4360; bclune@avma.org; http://www.avma.org. Illus., index, adv. Refereed. Circ: 63543 Paid. Microform: BHP; PQC. Online: EBSCO Publishing, EBSCO Host. *Indexed:* Agr, B&AI, BiolAb, CABA, ChemAb, DSA, ExcerpMed, FS&TA, FoVS&M, HortAb, IndVet, RRTA, S&F, SCI, SSCI, VB, WAE&RSA, ZooRec. *Bk. rev.:* 2-3, 200-400 words. *Aud.:* Ac, Sa.

The *Journal of the American Veterinary Medical Association* is the official publication of the American Veterinary Medical Association (AVMA), which is the largest veterinary association in the United States. Hence, this is the one journal that practically every U.S. veterinarian receives. It claims to be the most widely distributed veterinary journal in the world. Each issue carries a section on news related to the association and the profession, as well as sections on interpretive summaries of articles, clinical reports, original studies, member obituaries, announcements, commentary, and job opportunities. Additional features that appear frequently are "Legal Briefs," "What Is Your Diagnosis," and "Special Reports." The announcement section is invaluable for finding information on upcoming national and international meetings, CE offerings, and dates of state board examinations. The signed book reviews are useful to libraries doing book selection in this subject area. The editors certainly fulfill the mission statement of the journal: "to promote the science and art of veterinary medicine and to provide a forum for discussion of ideas important to the profession." An online version became available in 2000. Only subscribers can download the articles, but everyone can read the abstracts of the articles online.

The URL is http://avmajournals.avma.org/loi/ajvr. This title must be considered as the first choice for any U.S. veterinary collection.

6121. *Australian Veterinary Journal.* [ISSN: 0005-0423] 1925. m. GBP 257 print & online eds. Ed(s): Anne Jackson. Blackwell Publishing Ltd., 9600 Garsington Rd, Oxford, OX4 2ZG, United Kingdom; customerservices@blackwellpublishing.com; http://www.blackwellpublishing.com. Illus., index, adv. Refereed. Circ: 4500. Vol. ends: Dec. Reprint: PSC. *Indexed:* Agr, B&AI, BiolAb, CABA, ChemAb, DSA, ExcerpMed, FS&TA, FoVS&M, ForAb, HortAb, IndVet, RRTA, S&F, SCI, VB, WAE&RSA, ZooRec. *Bk. rev.:* 1-3, 300-600 words. *Aud.:* Ac, Sa.

This title, which is the official journal of the Australian Veterinary Association (AVA), is the premier veterinary journal in Australia. It has been providing coverage of leading-edge clinical and scientific veterinary research as well as industry news for over 85 years. Each issue has six to nine original research articles, one to five short contributions, and occasional case reports, all of which are classified under the general headings of "clinical" and "scientific." Major review articles and signed editorials are frequently included. The journal also has a news section, classifieds, obituaries, abstracts from other journals, and the regular columns "World Watch" and "Viewpoint." Most of the charts, graphs, tables, and photographs are in color. Because this publication is designed to serve the practitioner as well as the researcher in Australia, one finds articles on domestic and nondomestic animal species that are native to Australia (kangaroos, wallabies, loggerhead turtles, etc.). Academic libraries that serve animal science departments conducting research on sheep and tropical animal production will find this useful. It is also a natural selection for veterinary science collections, as much high-quality, original veterinary research emanates from Australia. Full text from October 1996 is free except the current 24 months. The URL is www.ava.com.au.

6122. *Avian Diseases.* [ISSN: 0005-2086] 1957. q. USD 230 combined subscription domestic print & online eds.; USD 265 combined subscription foreign print & online eds. Ed(s): Jagdev M Sharma. American Association of Avian Pathologists, Inc., 953 College Station Rd, Athens, GA 30602-4875; AAAP@uga.edu; http://www.aaap.info/index.html. Illus., index. Refereed. Circ: 1900. Vol. ends: Oct/Dec. Microform: WSH; PMC; PQC. Online: Allen Press Inc.; BioOne; CSA; EBSCO Publishing, EBSCO Host; JSTOR (Web-based Journal Archive); OCLC Online Computer Library Center, Inc.; OhioLINK. *Indexed:* Agr, BiolAb, CABA, ChemAb, DSA, FoVS&M, IndVet, S&F, SCI, VB, WAE&RSA, ZooRec. *Aud.:* Ac, Sa.

This title, the official publication of the American Association of Avian Pathologists, publishes the results of original research conducted in the specialty of avian diseases from throughout the world. This is done through full research articles, research notes, and case reports. While the emphasis is on birds of commercial importance—for example, chickens, turkeys, ducks, and geese—articles also appear on wild birds and pet species, such as budgerigars, parrots, and cockatiels. It is a substantial journal, containing 20–40 papers per issue, with each article averaging six to ten pages in length. Illustrations are mostly in black-and-white. Full text is available to subscribers from 2000. This journal is highly recommended for poultry science and veterinary science collections.

6123. *Canadian Journal of Veterinary Research.* Former titles (until 1986): *Canadian Journal of Comparative Medicine;* (until 1968): *Canadian Journal of Comparative Medicine and Veterinary Science;* (until 1940): *Canadian Journal of Comparative Medicine.* [ISSN: 0830-9000] 1937. q. CND 123.05 domestic; USD 130 foreign. Ed(s): Heather Broughton, Dr. Eva Nagy. Canadian Veterinary Medical Association, 339 Booth St, Ottawa, ON K1R 7K1, Canada; kallen@cvma-acmv.org; http://www.cvma-acmv.org. Illus., index, adv. Refereed. Circ: 2000 Paid. Vol. ends: Dec. *Indexed:* Agr, BiolAb, CABA, ChemAb, DSA, ExcerpMed, FS&TA, FoVS&M, HortAb, IndVet, MCR, S&F, SCI, VB, WAE&RSA. *Aud.:* Ac, Sa.

This is the research journal of the Canadian Veterinary Medical Association. It covers results of original research in veterinary and comparative medicine. It is the Canadian counterpart to the *American Journal of Veterinary Research.* Papers may be full-length (up to 20 pages) or short communications (up to 10 pages). Occasional review articles (up to 30 pages) of general interest are published. An average issue will have 9–12 full-length papers and 1–3 short communications. All articles are in English, but the abstracts are given in both English and French. All animal species, domestic and nondomestic, are covered. Illustrations are generally in black and white. The target audience is scientists in the fields of veterinary science, animal science, and comparative medicine. This is a journal that should be found in all North American veterinary libraries. PubMed Central has full text available from volume one up to within the current three months. URL: www.pubmedcentral.nih.gov.

6124. *Canadian Veterinary Journal.* [ISSN: 0008-5286] 1960. m. CND 164.30 domestic; USD 165 foreign. Ed(s): Dr. W C D Hare, Heather Broughton. Canadian Veterinary Medical Association, 339 Booth St, Ottawa, ON K1R 7K1, Canada; admin@cvma-acmv.org; http://www.cvma-acmv.org. Illus., index, adv. Refereed. Circ: 5000 Paid. Vol. ends: Dec. Microform: PMC; PQC. Online: National Library of Medicine. *Indexed:* Agr, CABA, ChemAb, DSA, ExcerpMed, FoVS&M, HortAb, IndVet, RRTA, S&F, SCI, SSCI, VB, WAE&RSA. *Bk. rev.:* 1-6, 300-700 words. *Aud.:* Ac, Sa.

As the official publication of the Canadian Veterinary Medical Association (CVMA), this journal is considered to be the "voice of veterinary medicine in Canada." In addition to carrying scientific articles, review articles, case reports, and brief communications, each issue also contains a news section about CVMA activities (in both English and French); notices of upcoming meetings; new-product information; book reviews; obituaries; and employment opportunities. There are also a practitioners' corner and short reports on other matters of interest, such as radiation oncology, diagnostic ophthalmology, and the art of private veterinary practice. The illustrative material is a nice mix of black-and-white and color. Online text is available through PubMed Central from volume one up to within the current three months. The URL is www.pubmedcentral.nih.gov. Recommended for veterinary libraries.

6125. *Compendium (Yardley): continuing education for veterinarians.* Former titles (until 2006): *Compendium on Continuing Education for the Practicing Veterinarian;* (until 1979): *Compendium on Continuing Education for the Small Animal Practitioner.* 1979. m. USD 70 domestic; USD 84 in Canada & Mexico; USD 119 elsewhere. Ed(s): Lilliane Anstee. Veterinary Learning Systems, 780 Township Line Rd, Yardley, PA 19067-4200; info@vetlearn.com; http://veterinarylearningsystems.com. Illus., index, adv. Sample. Refereed. Circ: 35000. Vol. ends: Dec. Microform: PQC. *Indexed:* Agr, CABA, DSA, FoVS&M, HortAb, IndVet, SCI, VB, WAE&RSA. *Bk. rev.:* Number and length vary. *Aud.:* Ac, Sa.

This title is one of the most popular journals among clinicians and practitioners. All articles are of a didactic nature and are followed by a list of review questions. Continuing-education credit can be received from Auburn University College of Veterinary Medicine by submitting answers to the review questions. The journal is heavily illustrated with color photographs. The animal species covered have recently been reduced to only dogs, cats, and exotics. However, the equine is now being covered in *Compendium: Continuing Education for Veterinarians (Equine edition).* Each issue also features case presentations, news bites highlighting recent research findings, web sites, behavior, book reviews, a market spotlight section, and classifieds. Several supplements on special topics are also published and received with a subscription. Individual subscribers can access an online version, but the publisher has chosen not to make the online version available to institutions. A necessary publication for any veterinary practitioner and any veterinary science collection.

6126. *D V M: the newsmagazine of veterinary medicine.* [ISSN: 0012-7337] 1970. m. USD 39 domestic; USD 85 foreign; USD 5 per issue domestic. Ed(s): Maureen Hrehocik, Daniel R Verdon. Advanstar Communications, Inc., 7500 Old Oak Blvd, Cleveland, OH 44130-3369; info@advanstar.com; http://www.advanstar.com. Illus., adv. Circ: 56000 Controlled. Vol. ends: Dec. Microform: PQC. Online: EBSCO Publishing, EBSCO Host; Gale; OCLC Online Computer Library Center, Inc.; ProQuest LLC (Ann Arbor); H.W. Wilson. *Indexed:* B&AI. *Aud.:* Ga, Ac, Sa.

Where does one go to find the breaking news in the veterinary profession? To *DVM,* the *Newsweek* or *Time* magazine of veterinary medicine. Its size (10.75 × 14.5 inches) makes it stand out from the other magazines in the field. It reports on all relevant news, trends, and developments, and offers practical and authoritative medical information. Regular columnists write on practice management and marketing. Exclusive features include interviews and editorial roundtable discussions with professional leaders, feature reports on hot topics, and complete coverage of regulatory and legislative activity. There is a monthly "New Products and Services" section and a quarterly "New Product Review" section in which important new products are introduced. Periodically, there is also a special monthly supplement for veterinary students called "Your DVM Career: a business primer for veterinary students." There are occasional educational supplements, "DVM Best Practices" and "DVM In Focus," to provide the clinician with the latest information on selected topics. The journal is interspersed with many color ads. The writing is in a nontechnical jargon so that clients in a veterinary waiting room may find some of its articles interesting. The web site (www.dvmnews.com) provides the latest breaking news, the current issue, and selected feature articles from the magazine's archives. Full-text articles from June 2003 are available through EBSCO Academic Search Premier. A useful magazine for the waiting room of veterinary clinics; and a necessary acquisition for veterinary libraries.

6127. *Equine Veterinary Journal.* [ISSN: 0425-1644] 1968. 8x/yr. GBP 80 domestic (Students, GBP 40). Ed(s): Peter D Rossdale. Equine Veterinary Journal Ltd., 351 Exning Rd, Newmarket, CB8 0AU, United Kingdom; viv@evj.co.uk; http://www.evj.co.uk. Illus., index, adv. Refereed. Circ: 2000. Vol. ends: Nov. *Indexed:* Agr, BiolAb, CABA, DSA, FoVS&M, IndVet, RRTA, S&F, SCI, VB, WAE&RSA. *Aud.:* Ac, Sa.

In 1968 the British Equine Veterinary Association started its own publication, calling it the *Equine Veterinary Journal.* Its stature has grown so that it's now the most respected international scientific equine journal in the world. The average issue carries 10–14 full-length articles on original research, plus one to three short communications, and case reports on such diverse topics as dermatology, exercise, anatomy, ergonomics, pain therapy, surgery, behavior, reproduction, and racing. It also promotes evidence-based veterinary medicine by including a clinical-evidence article in each issue. The illustrations are predominantly in black and white. A must for veterinary libraries, equine practitioners, and libraries that serve colleges with equestrian programs or those conducting equine research. It is available in full text from January 2000. The URL is www.evj.co.uk. The journal has a FastTrack system. Once an article is accepted in its final form, it is made available on the web before actual publication.

6128. *Exotic D V M.* [ISSN: 1521-1363] 1999. bi-m. USD 69 in North America; USD 89 elsewhere. Ed(s): Linda Harrison. Zoological Education Network, PO Box 541749, Lake Worth, FL 33454-1749. Adv. Vol. ends: No. 4. *Indexed:* CABA, DSA, HortAb, IndVet, VB, WAE&RSA, ZooRec. *Bk. rev.:* 1-2, 300-400 words. *Aud.:* Ac, Sa.

This eye-catching journal has certainly found its niche in the field of exotic animal medicine. It is a unique practical how-to magazine, and it is somewhat surprising that the idea has not caught on in the other disciplines of veterinary medicine. The major thrust of the magazine is to present a single procedure or tip, through a series of step-by-step, high-quality color images (up to 17). Text is kept to a minimum. In addition, there are regular columns on nutrition and exotic animal care, book reviews, and the exotic marketplace. Each exotic animal column is devoted to a specific exotic animal, providing valuable resource information for the proper care (nutrition, housing, restraint, breeding, sexing) of the animal. Such all-you-need-to-know information on nontraditional companion animals is usually very difficult to locate, and it is exciting to see this as a regular feature. A recent issue has a quick reference guide to 21 exotic species. The publisher also sponsors the "ExoticDVM on-Line Forum" on Yahoo. Discussion of topics presented in *Exotic DVM* is encouraged, but not limited to that. The magazine is essential for any clinic that handles exotic animals and for veterinary libraries. Zoo libraries will find it a useful addition to their collections. Further information can be found at www.exoticdvm.com.

6129. *F D A Veterinarian.* [ISSN: 1057-6223] 1979. bi-m. USD 17. Ed(s): Karan A Kandra. U.S. Food & Drug Administration, Center for Veterinary Medicine, 7500 Standish Pl, Rockville, MD 20855. Circ: 3600. *Indexed:* CABA, DSA, IndVet, VB. *Aud.:* Ac, Sa.

The Center for Veterinary Medicine, a division of the U.S. Food and Drug Administration, whose purpose is to regulate the manufacture and distribution of food additives and drugs that will be given to animals, produces this 16-page journal. It is the most reliable source for the latest information regarding changes in veterinary drug regulations, withdrawal times for antibiotics, companies not in compliance with federal regulations, new animal drug approvals, etc. The information is objective and of considerable value to anyone working with animals, from farmers to veterinarians—to dedicated pet owners, for that matter. Issues have short features and articles with such titles as "CVM Approves Drug to Treat Obesity in Dogs," "Cloning," and "The Review of Animal Production Drugs by FDA." This publication is available both in print and online. The online version, which can be downloaded free, is archived back to the November/December 1995 issue at www.fda.gov/cvm/ FDA_Newsletters/fdavettoc.html.

6130. *Journal of Avian Medicine and Surgery.* Former titles (until 1995): *Association of Avian Veterinarians. Journal;* (until 1989): *A A V Today;* (until 1987): *A A V Newsletter.* [ISSN: 1082-6742] 1980. q. USD 140 domestic; USD 145 in Canada & Mexico; USD 155 in Europe. Ed(s): Dr. James Carpenter. Association of Avian Veterinarians, PO Box 210732, Bedford, TX 76095; aavpubs@aol.com. Illus., index, adv. Sample. Refereed. Circ: 3500. Vol. ends: Dec. *Indexed:* CABA, FoVS&M, HortAb, IndVet, RRTA, S&F, SCI, VB, ZooRec. *Bk. rev.:* 1-2, 400-500 words. *Aud.:* Ac, Sa.

The *Journal of Avian Medicine and Surgery* is published quarterly by the Association of Avian Veterinarians (AAV). It is an international journal on the medicine and surgery of captive and wild birds. It publishes original research, review articles, retrospective studies, case reports, and research briefs. In addition, it has featured sections, including "What's Your Diagnosis?," "Selected Abstracts from the Literature," and "Round Table Discussions." It also has book reviews and a calendar of upcoming meetings. The illustrations are chiefly in black-and-white, with an occasional use of color. An expensive clay-coated paper is used to achieve the highest resolution of photographs. The journal is essential for the avian practitioner and is highly recommended for zoo and veterinary libraries. Online full text is available from 2000 through BioOne at www.bioone.org.

6131. *Journal of Exotic Pet Medicine.* Formerly (until 2006): *Seminars in Avian and Exotic Pet Medicine.* [ISSN: 1557-5063] 1992. 4x/yr. USD 266. Ed(s): Mark A Mitchell. W.B. Saunders Co., Independence Sq W, Ste 300, The Curtis Center, Philadelphia, PA 19106-3399; elspcs@elsevier.com; http://www.elsevier.com. Illus., index, adv. Refereed. Circ: 1530 Paid. Vol. ends: Dec. *Indexed:* CABA, FoVS&M, HortAb, IndVet, SCI, VB, ZooRec. *Aud.:* Ac, Sa.

A relatively new trend in the field of veterinary medicine has been the development of specialty practices dealing with exotic animals and/or pet birds. Although practitioners have been witnessing an increasing number of cases in this area, there has been a lack of scholarly journals devoted to this specialty. Hence, the practitioner has often had difficulty locating reliable information. *Journal of Exotic Pet Medicine* is one of four new journals that are successfully filling the void (see also *Exotic DVM, Journal of Avian Medicine and Surgery,* and *Veterinary Clinics of North America: exotic animal practice*). This journal's format features a subject specialist as a guest editor; and a section of the issue entitled "Topics in Medicine and Surgery" is devoted to the editor's specialty. However, there are additional articles under other regularly featured columns, such as "AEMV Forum," "Diagnostic Challenge," and "Literature Review." All papers are invited. The journal is printed on clay-based paper and has an easy-to-read format that features excellent black-and-white and color photographs. There are usually eight or nine articles, 3–10 pages in length, per issue. The concise, topical, and authoritative reviews address problems faced in daily practice. Recent themes include nutrition, pharmacology, and behavior. The journal is available online (from 2004) through ScienceDirect at www.sciencedirect.com. This journal is a must for the avian practitioner and for any practitioner who handles exotic-animal cases. It is also highly recommended for veterinary and zoo libraries.

6132. *Journal of Feline Medicine and Surgery.* [ISSN: 1098-612X] 1999. 6x/yr. EUR 390. Ed(s): A H Sparkes, M Scherk. W.B. Saunders Co. Ltd., 32 Jamestown Rd, London, NW1 7BY, United Kingdom; http://www.elsevier.com. Illus., adv. Refereed. Circ: 1000. *Indexed:* Agr, CABA, DSA, FoVS&M, IndVet, SCI, VB. *Bk. rev.:* 1, 200-300 words. *Aud.:* Ac, Sa.

The official journal of the European Society of Feline Medicine (ESFM) and the American Association of Feline Practitioners is international in scope and probably the only scientific, peer-reviewed journal in the world devoted exclusively to feline medicine and surgery. It publishes original contributions, short communications, and review papers on all aspects of feline medicine and surgery. The editors also commission some articles. About 40 percent of the photographs are in color. An international news section provides information about feline veterinary meetings, society news, new developments, book reviews, and relevant issues from other publications and meetings. This journal is a must for the feline practitioner. This is a basic title for veterinary libraries. Online full text is available through ScienceDirect at www.sciencedirect.com/ science/journal/1098612X.

6133. *Journal of Small Animal Practice.* [ISSN: 0022-4510] 1960. m. USD 550 print & online eds. Ed(s): Katie Dunn. Blackwell Publishing Ltd., 9600 Garsington Rd, Oxford, OX4 2ZG, United Kingdom; customerservices@blackwellpublishing.com; http://www.blackwellpublishing.com. Illus., index, adv. Refereed. Circ: 4500. Vol. ends: Dec. Reprint: PSC. *Indexed:* Agr, BiolAb, CABA, ChemAb, DSA, ExcerpMed, FoVS&M, IndVet, SCI, VB. *Bk. rev.:* 1, 300-375 words. *Aud.:* Ac, Sa.

This title is the official publication of the British Small Animal Veterinary Association (BSAVA) and the World Small Animal Veterinary Association (WSAVA). Like its American counterpart, *Journal of the American Animal Hospital Association,* it is peer-reviewed and published monthly. It is international in scope, publishing original clinical research, review articles, and case histories that cover all aspects of medicine and surgery relating to dogs, cats, and other small mammals. Printing on clay-based paper enables the publisher to make excellent use of color layouts that increase eye appeal and readability. Each issue includes sections entitled: "What Is Your Diagnosis," "Self Assessment," "Abstracts from the Journals," an editorial section, a diary of forthcoming events, and a news section for the BSAVA and WSAVA. Full text is available from 2002 through Blackwell Synergy. Highly recommended for libraries that serve veterinary science programs.

6134. *Journal of Swine Health and Production.* Formerly: *Swine Health and Production.* [ISSN: 1537-209X] 1993. bi-m. USD 100 in North America; USD 115 elsewhere. Ed(s): Karen Richardson, Cate Dewey. American Association of Swine Veterinarians, 902 1st Ave, Perry, IA 50220-1703; http://www.aasv.org. Refereed. Circ: 1800. Vol. ends: Nov/Dec. *Indexed:* Agr, CABA, DSA, FoVS&M, IndVet, SCI, VB, WAE&RSA. *Aud.:* Ac, Sa.

This is the offical journal of the American Association of Swine Veterinarians (AASV) and is the only refereed journal in North America that focuses exclusively on swine health. It accepts for publication manuscripts on original research, case reports, literature reviews, brief communications, and practice tips. In addition, it publishes society news as well as other news of interest to its membership. Two nice features are the calendar of upcoming national and international meetings and the conversion tables. Illustrative materials consist of tables, charts, graphs, and photographs. Color is used judiciously. This journal is a must for the swine practitioner, veterinary libraries, and any institution that is involved with swine research. The journal is available online to subscribers. Further information can be found at www.aasv.org.

6135. *Journal of Veterinary Internal Medicine.* [ISSN: 0891-6640] 1987. bi-m. USD 500 (Individuals, USD 60; Students, USD 30). Ed(s): Kenneth W Hinchcliff, Stephen P Di Bartola. Blackwell Publishing, Inc., Commerce Place, 350 Main St, Malden, MA 02148; customerservices@ blackwellpublishing.com; http://www.blackwellpublishing.com. Illus., index, adv. Refereed. Circ: 1000 Paid. Vol. ends: Nov/Dec. *Indexed:* Agr, BiolAb, CABA, DSA, FoVS&M, HortAb, IndVet, SCI, VB. *Aud.:* Ac, Sa.

This specialty journal is the official publication of the American College of Veterinary Internal Medicine, one of the largest specialty boards within the American Veterinary Medical Association. The editors particularly seek clinical and research manuscripts in the area of small-animal and large-animal internal medicine, cardiology, neurology, and oncology. In addition, they accept review articles, brief communications, case reports, and clinical vignettes. Generally, there are 25–30 articles per issue. The illustrative materials are largely in black and white, although the use of color appears to be increasing. It is a well-edited publication, but readership will be limited to those veterinarians, clinicians, and researchers with an interest in internal medicine. Full text is available to subscribers from 1999. Without doubt, this title is considered a necessary purchase for veterinary college libraries.

6136. *Journal of Veterinary Medical Education.* [ISSN: 0748-321X] 1974. 4x/yr. CND 100 domestic; USD 100 United States; USD 120 elsewhere. Ed(s): Dr. Donal Walsh. Association of American Veterinary Medical Colleges, 1101 Vermont Ave, NW, Ste 710, Washington, DC 20005; journals@utpress.utoronto.edu; http://aavmc.org/. Illus., adv. Refereed. Circ: 5500 Paid. Vol. ends: Dec. Microform: PQC. Online: EBSCO Publishing, EBSCO Host; HighWire Press. *Indexed:* CABA, DSA, FoVS&M, IndVet, RRTA, SCI, SSCI, VB, WAE&RSA. *Bk. rev.:* 1-5, 200-350 words. *Aud.:* Ac, Sa.

If you are interested in veterinary medical education, then this is the journal for you, as it is the only journal, in any language, devoted to the subject. It is the official publication of the Association of American Veterinary Medical Colleges. The journal contains articles on veterinary medical curricula, instructional technology, teaching methodology, and new approaches to the learning paradigm. It is a useful journal to monitor for information regarding changes in the profession and how veterinary colleges are reacting to the changes. Most of the issues are theme-specific. Examples of this include "Zoological and Wildlife Medicine," "Veterinary Education in Europe," "The Changing Face of Food Supply Veterinary Medicine," and "Envisioning the Future of Veterinary Medical Education." Readership will mostly be limited to veterinary college administrators, members of curriculum committees, and continuing education personnel. This is a necessary title in veterinary school libraries. Full text is available from 2000 to online subscribers. Further information can be found at www.jvmeonline.org.

6137. *Journal of Wildlife Diseases.* Former titles: *Wildlife Disease Association. Journal;* (until 1969): *Wildlife Disease Association. Bulletin.* [ISSN: 0090-3558] 1965. q. USD 250. Ed(s): Elizabeth S Williams. Wildlife Disease Association, Inc., PO Box 1897, Lawrence, KS 66044-8897; orders@allenpress.com; http://www.wildlifedisease.org. Illus., index, adv. Sample. Refereed. Circ: 1350 Paid. Vol. ends: Oct. *Indexed:* Agr, B&AI, BiolAb, BiolDig, CABA, ChemAb, DSA, FoVS&M, ForAb, IndVet, RRTA, S&F, SCI, VB, ZooRec. *Bk. rev.:* 1-5, 500-600 words. *Aud.:* Ac, Sa.

This international journal, the official journal of the Wildlife Disease Association, publishes the results of original research and observations dealing with all aspects of infectious, immunologic, parasitic, toxic, nutritional, physiologic, developmental, epizootic, and neoplastic diseases that affect the health and survival of free-living or captive wild animals, including fish. All of the illustrative material is in black and white. As one can surmise from the scope of coverage, each issue carries a diverse array of articles, ranging from lead poisoning in captive Andean condors, to viral infections in lions, to vaccination of small Asian monogosse and mineral deficiencies in Tule elk. An average issue has 12–17 full-length articles, followed by 10–18 short communications. Full-text articles from 1965 are available online through Highwire at www.jwildlifedis.org. This is a must acquisition for academic libraries that support game biology/wildlife science and veterinary science programs.

6138. *Journal of Zoo and Wildlife Medicine.* Formerly: *Journal of Zoo Animal Medicine.* [ISSN: 1042-7260] 1971. q. USD 245 (Individuals, USD 115). Ed(s): Wilbur B Amand. American Association of Zoo Veterinarians, 810 E 10th St, Lawrence, KS 66044; aazv@allnepress.com; http://www.aazv.org. Illus., index, adv. Refereed. Circ: 1200. Vol. ends: Dec. *Indexed:* BiolAb, CABA, DSA, EnvAb, FoVS&M, ForAb, IndVet, RRTA, S&F, SCI, VB, ZooRec. *Bk. rev.:* 2-3, 300-500 words. *Aud.:* Ac, Sa.

The American Association of Zoo Veterinarians has as its official publication the *Journal of Zoo and Wildlife Medicine*. It is considered to be one of the major sources of information in zoological medicine. The thrust of the journal is to emphasize original research findings, clinical observations, and case reports in the field of veterinary medicine dealing with captive and free-ranging wild animals, and it has the stated goal "to improve the husbandry, preventive medicine and research required to preserve these animals." A typical issue will have 10–12 full-length articles plus four or five case reports and seven to ten brief communications. The book reviews are exceptionally well written. Abstracts of selected articles appearing elsewhere in the literature are included in each issue. An interesting feature in each issue, "Clinical Challenge," gives insight into how difficult cases were solved and/or resolved. All of the illustrative material is in black-and-white. This high-quality research publication is a must for zoo and veterinary libraries and perhaps for libraries that support marine biology programs. An online version from 2000 is available through BioOne at www.bioone.org.

6139. *Research in Veterinary Science.* [ISSN: 0034-5288] 1960. 6x/yr. EUR 580. Ed(s): A Livingston. W.B. Saunders Co. Ltd., 32 Jamestown Rd, London, NW1 7BY, United Kingdom; http://www.elsevier.com. Illus., index, adv. Refereed. Circ: 945. Vol. ends: Nov. Microform: PMC; PQC. Online: EBSCO Publishing, EBSCO Host; OCLC Online Computer Library Center, Inc.; ScienceDirect; SwetsWise Online Content. *Indexed:* Agr, BiolAb, CABA, ChemAb, DSA, ExcerpMed, FS&TA, FoVS&M, HortAb, IndVet, S&F, SCI, SSCI, VB, WAE&RSA, ZooRec. *Aud.:* Ac, Sa.

This title, the official publication of the Association of Veterinary Teachers and Research Workers, is a well-respected research journal. Accepted for publication are original contributions, review articles, and short communications on the health, welfare, and diseases of all animal species as well as comparative medicine. Color illustrations are used only infrequently. Most issues have 20–23 articles. Many of the contributors are from outside the United Kingdom, which gives the journal an international flavor. The articles are categorized under specific subject headings. Online full text from 1995 is available through ScienceDirect at www.sciencedirect.com. A recommended title for veterinary libraries.

6140. *Topics in Companion Animal Medicine.* Former titles (until 2008): *Clinical Techniques in Small Animal Practice;* (until 1997): *Seminars in Veterinary Medicine and Surgery: Small Animal.* [ISSN: 1938-9736] 1986. 4x/yr. USD 266. Ed(s): Dr. Deborah Greco. W.B. Saunders Co., Independence Sq W, Ste 300, The Curtis Center, Philadelphia, PA 19106-3399; http://www.elsevier.com. Illus., index, adv. Refereed. Circ: 869. Vol. ends: Nov. *Indexed:* Agr, BiolAb, CABA, DSA, FoVS&M, IndVet, SCI, VB, WAE&RSA. *Aud.:* Ac, Sa.

Clinical Techniques in Small Animal Practice fills a unique niche by providing detailed, procedure-oriented information to enhance the practitioner's office practice. The journal focuses on techniques in use in the average clinical practice: ophthalmic, dental, reproduction, surgery, and emergency and critical-care techniques. Each issue has a guest editor and focuses on a specific topic. There are usually seven to nine articles per issue. The illustrative photographs are in color and black-and-white. Some recent topics include "Tumors of the Head and Neck," "Adrenal Disease," "Practical Toxicology," "Dermatology," and "Nasal Disease." Online full-text articles are available through Science Direct from 1999. This title is recommended for veterinary science collections.

6141. *Veterinary Clinics of North America: Equine Practice.* [ISSN: 0749-0739] 1985. 3x/yr. USD 302. Ed(s): A Simon Turner. W.B. Saunders Co., Independence Sq W, Ste 300, The Curtis Center, Philadelphia, PA 19106-3399; http://www.us.elsevierhealth.com. Illus., index. Refereed. Vol. ends: Dec. Online: M D Consult. *Indexed:* Agr, CABA, DSA, FoVS&M, HortAb, IndVet, RRTA, SCI, VB, WAE&RSA. *Aud.:* Ac, Sa.

As with the other three *Veterinary Clinics of North America* journals, each issue has a guest editor who is responsible for inviting other experts on the featured topic to contribute papers. Recent topics include advances in reproduction, evidence-based veterinary medicine, therapies for joint disease, wound management, and trauma and emergency care. The use of photographs, including color, has been expanded in recent issues. While this is required reading for equine practitioners and a necessary title for veterinary collections, it is also recommended for animal science and equestrian collections. An online version has been available to individual subscribers for sometime, but only recently to institutional subscribers.

6142. *Veterinary Clinics of North America: Exotic Animal Practice.*
[ISSN: 1094-9194] 1998. 3x/yr. USD 288. W.B. Saunders Co., Independence Sq W, Ste 300, The Curtis Center, Philadelphia, PA 19106-3399; http://www.us.elsevierhealth.com. Illus., index. Refereed. Vol. ends: Sep. *Indexed:* CABA, IndVet, VB, ZooRec. *Aud.:* Ac, Sa.

The newest entry in the *Veterinary Clinics of North America* series is devoted to exotic-animal practice. The increasing popularity of exotic animals being used as companion animals has created a new specialty in veterinary medicine, which in turn necessitates peer-reviewed scientific literature for the specialist. As with the other titles in this series, each issue is devoted to a single topic and will contain 10–12 articles. A recent change has been the increasing use of photographs, most of which are in color. It is the aim of the publisher to provide timely articles reviewing the state of the art in exotic animal care. This title is essential to wildlife, zoo, and veterinary collections. An online version is available.

6143. *Veterinary Clinics of North America: Food Animal Practice.* [ISSN: 0749-0720] 1985. 3x/yr. USD 236. W.B. Saunders Co., Independence Sq W, Ste 300, The Curtis Center, Philadelphia, PA 19106-3399; http://www.us.elsevierhealth.com. Illus., index. Refereed. Vol. ends: Nov. Online: M D Consult. *Indexed:* Agr, CABA, DSA, FoVS&M, IndVet, SCI, VB, WAE&RSA. *Aud.:* Ac, Sa.

As with its companion volumes in the *Veterinary Clinics* series, each issue is under the direction of a guest editor who is an authority in his or her field. Information is covered on the latest developments in the diagnosis and management of species of food animals that are treated by practitioners (cattle, swine, goats, sheep, llamas, deer, and ratites). Recent topics include ruminant parasitology, feedlot nutrition, stocker cattle management, and barnyard epidemiology. Illustrations are usually in black and white, but occasionally color is used. Charts and tables are also used. This title is recommended for veterinary and animal science collections and should be found on every food animal practitioner's bookshelf. An online version has been available to individual subscribers and was recently made available to institutional subscribers.

6144. *Veterinary Clinics of North America: Small Animal Practice.*
Supersedes in part (in 1979): *Veterinary Clinics of North America.*
[ISSN: 0195-5616] 1971. 6x/yr. USD 327. W.B. Saunders Co., Independence Sq W, Ste 300, The Curtis Center, Philadelphia, PA 19106-3399; http://www.us.elsevierhealth.com. Illus., index. Refereed. Vol. ends: Nov. Microform: MIM; PQC. Online: Gale; IngentaConnect; M D Consult; OhioLINK. *Indexed:* Agr, BiolAb, CABA, DSA, ExcerpMed, FoVS&M, HortAb, IndVet, S&F, SCI, SSCI, VB, WAE&RSA, ZooRec. *Aud.:* Ac, Sa.

Like all of the titles in Saunders's *Veterinary Clinics of North America* series, each hardback volume is devoted to a specific topic, with an expert on the topic serving as a guest editor. The initial title proved so popular that it split into four sections: small-animal practice, equine practice, food-animal practice, and exotic-animal practice. Each issue averages 10–12 articles. Recent issues feature evidence-based medicine, the thyroid, respiratory medicine, effective communication in veterinary practice, and dietary management and nutrition. A recent change has been in the generous use of color photographs. A basic title for a veterinary medicine collection and for small-animal practitioners. An online version is now available.

6145. *Veterinary Economics: business solutions for practicing veterinarians.* [ISSN: 0042-4862] 1960. m. USD 42 domestic; USD 59 in Canada & Mexico; USD 83 elsewhere. Ed(s): Marnette Denell Falley. Advanstar Communications, Inc., One Park Ave, 2nd Fl, New York, NY 10016; info@advanstar.com; http://www.advanstar.com. Illus., index, adv. Refereed. Circ: 50000 Controlled. Vol. ends: Dec. Microform: PQC. Online: Gale; Northern Light Technology, Inc. *Indexed:* ATI, CABA, FoVS&M, IndVet, SCI, VB, WAE&RSA. *Aud.:* Ac, Sa.

This journal has long been recognized, as proven by receiving several major journalism awards, for its excellent coverage of all aspects of veterinary practice management, retirement planning, evaluating practices for purchase, partnership arrangement, contracts, client relations, taxes, and other financial matters. Its regular feature on hospital design is very popular with practitioners. Another popular feature is its "Well-Managed Practice" series. The special reports on trends, salaries, and economics in the profession are well respected and often the only source for this type of information. One can view some of the current issues online at www.vetecon.com/vetec. This title is recommended for veterinary libraries and practitioners.

6146. *The Veterinary Journal.* Former titles (until 1997): *British Veterinary Journal;* (until 1949): *Veterinary Journal;* (until 1900): *Veterinary Journal and Annals of Comparative Pathology.* [ISSN: 1090-0233] 1875. 6x/yr. EUR 800. Ed(s): A. J. Higgins. W.B. Saunders Co. Ltd., 32 Jamestown Rd, London, NW1 7BY, United Kingdom; http://www.elsevier.com. Illus., index, adv. Sample. Refereed. Vol. ends: Dec. Microform: PMC; PQC. Online: EBSCO Publishing, EBSCO Host; OCLC Online Computer Library Center, Inc.; ScienceDirect; SwetsWise Online Content. *Indexed:* Agr, BiolAb, CABA, ChemAb, DSA, ExcerpMed, FS&TA, FoVS&M, IndVet, RRTA, S&F, SCI, VB, WAE&RSA. *Bk. rev.:* 4-6, 300-500 words. *Aud.:* Ac.

The *Veterinary Journal* has the distinction of being the longest-running English-language veterinary journal today, tracing its history back to 1875. It is international in scope and publishes original papers and reviews on all aspects of veterinary science and kindred subjects, with particular emphasis on animal health and preventive medicine. Papers are published under three categories: "Guest Editorials," "Commissioned Topical Reviews," and "Original Articles." The journal also publishes book reviews and has a short communications section. The guest editorials are informative and often thought-provoking. The use of photographic materials is minimal, with a greater reliance on charts, tables, and graphs. The signed book reviews are useful to collection development personnel. The *2005 ISI Journal Citation Reports* ranked *Veterinary Journal* seventh out of 129 veterinary science titles. Online full-text coverage, available since 1997, is through ScienceDirect at www.sciencedirect.com. This is a basic title for veterinary science collections.

6147. *Veterinary Medicine.* Formerly (until 1985): *Veterinary Medicine - Small Animal Clinician.* [ISSN: 8750-7943] 1905. m. USD 59 domestic; USD 70 in Canada & Mexico; USD 95 elsewhere. Ed(s): Mindy Valcarcel, Margaret Rampey. Advanstar Veterinary Healthcare Communications, 8033 Flint, Lenexa, KS 66214; http://www.vetmedpub.com. Illus., index, adv. Refereed. Circ: 54135 Controlled. Vol. ends: Dec. Microform: PQC. Online: Gale; Northern Light Technology, Inc.; OCLC Online Computer Library Center, Inc.; ProQuest K-12 Learning Solutions; H.W. Wilson. *Indexed:* Agr, B&AI, CABA, DSA, FoVS&M, HortAb, IndVet, SCI, VB, WAE&RSA. *Aud.:* Ac, Sa.

This is a well-respected journal in American veterinary medicine, having begun publication in 1905. Its goal is to provide solutions to the most common and emerging diagnostic and therapeutic problems seen in clinical practice. Therefore, the emphasis is on articles that present a how-to approach to guide practicing veterinarians in selecting better diagnostic and therapeutic strategies; hence, the articles are more clinical than research-oriented. Because of its practical nature and the fact that the articles are concise, to the point, and well illustrated in color, this journal is popular with practicing veterinarians. Since January 2000, the journal has focused exclusively on companion animals and exotics. A new feature is that each issue contains one to three video clips that can be watched online. The current issue can be viewed at www.vetmedpub.com/vetmed. Unfortunately, only a few of the most recent issues are archived for online retrieval. A highly recommended title for the small-animal practitioner and all veterinary science collections.

6148. *Veterinary Neurology and Neurosurgery.* [ISSN: 1526-2073] q. Ed(s): T A Holliday. Veterinary Neurology and Neurosurgery, 1507 Alice St, Davis, CA 95616; taholliday@ucdavis.edu; http://www.neurovet.org. Refereed. *Aud.:* Ac, Sa.

This online-only title began publication in 1999. It is one of only a handful of online-only veterinary journals. Its growth has been slow, but then its intended audience is highly specialized. It has recently formed an alliance with VIN

(Veterinary Information Network), which should help make its presence better known. The journal is attempting to provide a medium for rapid dissemination of high-quality information that is important to veterinary neurology and neurosurgery. A cumulative index is available to quickly find an article. For further information, see www.vin.com/VNN.

6149. *Veterinary Pathology.* Formerly: *Pathologia Veterinaria.* [ISSN: 0300-9858] 1964. bi-m. USD 170 (Individuals, USD 98; Students, USD 55). Ed(s): Donna F. Kusewitt. American College of Veterinary Pathologists, 2810 Crossroads Dr., Ste. 3800, Madison, WI 53718-7961; info@acvp.org; http://www.afip.org/. Illus., index, adv. Refereed. Circ: 1200. Vol. ends: Nov. *Indexed:* Agr, CABA, ChemAb, DSA, ExcerpMed, FoVS&M, HortAb, IndVet, S&F, SCI, VB, ZooRec. *Bk. rev.:* 1-2, 250-350 words. *Aud.:* Ac, Sa.

Veterinary Pathology is the official publication of the American College of Veterinary Pathologists, providing international coverage in the field of veterinary pathology. The journal publishes manuscripts, reviews, brief communications, and case reports dealing with experimental and natural diseases. It also carries advertisements for employment opportunities and new products. The journal is printed on a clay-based paper, which gives exceptional quality to the photographs. The use of color versus black-and-white is about 50/50. Generally there are seven to ten full-length articles and 12–14 brief communications and case reports. The scope of coverage includes diseases in domestic animals, laboratory animals, and exotics. Online full text is available, through HighWire Press, from 1997 to the present, at www.vetpathology.org. A recommended title for libraries that serve diagnostic laboratories and/or veterinary programs.

6150. *The Veterinary Record.* [ISSN: 0042-4900] 1888. w. GBP 179 (Individuals, GBP 155). Ed(s): Martin Alder. British Veterinary Association, 7 Mansfield St, London, W1G 9NQ, United Kingdom; bvahq@bva.co.uk; http://www.bva.co.uk/. Illus., index, adv. Refereed. Circ: 10000. Vol. ends: Dec. Microform: PQC. Online: EBSCO Publishing, EBSCO Host; Gale; HighWire Press. *Indexed:* Agr, B&AI, CABA, ChemAb, DSA, ExcerpMed, FPA, FS&TA, FoVS&M, ForAb, HortAb, IndVet, RRTA, S&F, SCI, SSCI, VB, WAE&RSA. *Bk. rev.:* 1-3, 400-750 words. *Aud.:* Ac, Sa.

The *Veterinary Record,* founded in 1888 by the British Veterinary Association, is one of the most venerable journals in the field of veterinary medicine. It is a newsy journal, providing information about the association and veterinary matters in the United Kingdom, and it serves as a forum for British veterinarians to present their viewpoints. However, it is also highly respected for the papers it publishes on original research as well as review articles, clinical case histories, short communications, and letters. All aspects of veterinary medicine and surgery are covered. Illustrative materials—i.e., charts, tables, and photographs—are generally in color. The book reviews are highly valuable to collection development librarians. Online full text is available since 1996 through HighWire Publishing at http://highwire.stanford.edu. This title should be considered a must for veterinary science collections.

6151. *Veterinary Surgery.* Incorporates: *Veterinary Anesthesia;* Formerly: *Journal of Veterinary Surgery.* [ISSN: 0161-3499] 1978. bi-m. GBP 321 print & online eds. Ed(s): Dr. John R Pascoe. Blackwell Publishing, Inc., Commerce Place, 350 Main St, Malden, MA 02148; customerservices@ blackwellpublishing.com; http://www.blackwellpublishing.com. Illus., index, adv. Refereed. Circ: 2434. Vol. ends: Nov/Dec. Reprint: PSC. *Indexed:* Agr, BiolAb, CABA, DSA, FoVS&M, HortAb, IndVet, SCI, VB, WAE&RSA. *Aud.:* Ac, Sa.

Veterinary Surgery is the official publication of the American College of Veterinary Surgeons and the European College of Veterinary Surgeons. It strives to provide up-to-date coverage of surgical and anesthetic management of animals, yet place new developments in perspective. Coverage includes, but is not limited to, surgical and anesthetic techniques, management of the surgical patient, diagnostic aids, and the history of veterinary surgery. The periodical covers both large and small animals. The illustrations are high-quality black-and-white photographs. In addition to carrying clinical and research papers, it also publishes scientific abstracts from the association's annual

meetings and a section on job opportunities. Recommended for veterinary collections. Online full text is available since 1999 through Blackwell Synergy at www.blackwell-synergy.com.

■ WEDDINGS

Heidi Gauder, Coordinator of Instruction, Roesch Library, University of Dayton, Dayton, OH 45469; heidi.gauder@notes.udayton.edu

Introduction

Weddings are a big industry. It is estimated that over two million weddings take place annually in the United States alone, at an average cost of $20,000. Even smaller weddings can require months of planning and spending. The bride, or wedding coordinator for those lucky enough to afford one, must plan and budget for many details, including the reception, the photography, the wedding attire, flowers and decorations, church music, the ceremony, the invitations and stationery, wedding rings, gifts, and transportation, to say nothing of the honeymoon. Retailers recognize this fact and advertise heavily in this genre.

Bridal magazines offer brides-to-be plenty of ideas and inspiration for their own events. Most of them are organized in similar fashion, beginning with sections on wedding planning advice, including countdown and budget worksheets, wedding etiquette, and ideas for personalizing the wedding ceremony or reception. Sometimes relationship advice is also included. Another part will cover bridal fashion and beauty, from the bride's hair to wedding accessories to bridesmaids' outfits, and always wedding dresses. After the fashion spread, there usually follows a section on the bridal registry and then the honeymoon. Most magazines also include stories and pictures of real weddings. Many print titles have online equivalents that contain similar content and also serve as a link to wedding shopping and merchandise.

Although there are a fair number of titles within this genre, sadly, most tend to promote the same Judeo-Christian fantasy: white wedding dress, big reception feast, traditional registry, and exotic honeymoon. Very few magazines, however, are written specifically for the ethnic or minority bride. Wedding magazines are, however, beginning to recognize that race, culture, and traditions also play an important role in weddings, and that not all people share the same background. This section includes two titles created specifically for minority audiences, and a third magazine has changed its mission to incorporate greater diversity within its pages. In spite of these newer titles, though, many of the magazines still look the same. Magazine publishers would do well to consider creating titles for specific audiences in this genre, as there seems to be an untapped market for presenting alternative wedding ideas.

This section describes only those wedding magazines that are available nationwide on a serial basis. In doing so, special regional wedding editions have been excluded, although they are worth a brief mention. These regional issues often serve as vehicles for local vendors to advertise and showcase their talents (this is especially true for wedding photographers). Nationally distributed magazines including *WeddingChannel, Modern Bride,* and *The Knot* all publish local offshoots. In addition to regional magazines, other titles, including *Southern Living, Renaissance Magazine,* and *Better Homes and Gardens,* publish special wedding issues. Lastly, there are destination wedding and honeymoon magazines such as *Pacific Rim Weddings* and *Bermuda Weddings,* which have a specific regional focus. This section, however, describes only those magazines that are more easily accessible nationwide.

Basic Periodicals

Sa: *Bride's, Bridal Guide, InStyle Weddings, Martha Stewart Weddings, Modern Bride, WeddingChannel magazine.*

Basic Abstracts and Indexes

Magazine Article Summaries.

6152. *Bridal Guide: the how to for "I do".* [ISSN: 0882-7451] 1982. bi-m. USD 11.97; USD 5.99 newsstand/cover per issue. Ed(s): Jennifer Lazarus. R F P Llc., 330 Seventh Ave, 10th Fl, New York, NY 10001-5591; http://www.BridalGuidemag.com. Illus., adv. Sample. Circ: 205000 Paid and controlled. Vol. ends: Dec (No. 6). *Aud.:* Sa.

Calling itself "America's most-read bridal magazine," *Bridal Guide* is a traditional magazine that should appeal to a variety of brides. Despite its $5.99-per-issue price, this magazine is fairly budget-conscious, with articles on planning budget weddings, fashion features profiling affordable gowns, and very few high-end couture advertisements. There are high-end dresses, however, but these are seen primarily in the fashion editorial, while the advertisements promote more moderately priced dresses and utilize more plus-sized models than other magazines. The bimonthly magazine has the usual mix of planning advice; gift ideas; beauty, registry, cake, flower, and honeymoon tips; and a real-life wedding story. The online version follows these categories and is mostly text; although there is a link for fashion and beauty, no images of wedding dresses are included. The web site has a number of retail sponsors, but it is not partnered with any single wedding portal like other titles in this genre.

6153. *Bride's.* Former titles (until 1995): *Bride's and Your New Home;* (until Nov. 1991): *Bride's; Bride's Magazine.* [ISSN: 1084-1628] 1934. bi-m. USD 19.97 domestic; CND 4.99 newsstand/cover. Ed(s): Millie Martini Bratten, Millie Martini Bratten. Conde Nast Publications, Inc., 750 3rd Ave, New York, NY 10017; letters@brides.com; http://www.condenast.com. Illus., adv. Circ: 500000 Paid. Vol. ends: Nov/Dec. Microform: PQC. *Aud.:* Sa.

Probably the best-known bridal magazine, *Bride's* is certainly the heftiest. This magazine is often four times the size of its competitors, usually running more than 800 pages per issue, much of which is advertising. Produced by the publisher of *Elegant Bride* and *Modern Bride,* this magazine has the familiar look and feel of its sister magazines. However, its readership appeal is intended to be more comprehensive than the other two, as the mission statement declares that it "opens up a world of fantasy to brides of all ages and circumstance." Likewise, its intent is to be "the authority on all things bridal; a captivating voice that speaks to the engaged market with elegance and finesse." Numerous Q&A columns answer specific questions on fashion, beauty, reception, etiquette, sex, and travel. Snapshots from real weddings offer plenty of ideas. While magazines in this genre do their best to present the ultimate wedding fantasy, the editors of *Bride's* also realize that many brides are faced with a budget and, hence, often include budgeting advice. For brides who can only afford one magazine, this title will certainly give them their money's worth in the sheer volume of pages. The online version follows a similar print format.

6154. *Brides Noir: magazine for the contemporary bride of color.* [ISSN: 1543-8155] 2002. s-a. Ed(s): Dana Powell. Brides Noir LLC, 207 E Ohio St, #300, Chicago, IL 60611. *Aud.:* Sa.

A relative newcomer to the wedding magazine market, *Brides Noir* intends "to lead the ethnic bridal category by offering elite products and services to our readers, while serving as the premier vehicle for advertisers to directly reach this highly lucrative, yet underserved market." To that end, this magazine maintains the same components of traditional wedding magazines, including wedding countdown calendar, the usual wedding details, real weddings, wedding dresses, and honeymoon travel, while at the same time presenting more diversity than is usually seen in this genre. Care is taken to feature models of diverse skin tones, shapes, and sizes as well as to provide information that is important to brides of color. The semi-annual issues run about 100 pages and are organized around particular themes. The web site features articles from previous issues.

6155. *Destination I Do.* [ISSN: 1937-0121] 2004. q. USD 4.95 per issue domestic; USD 6.95 per issue Canada; USD 12.95 per issue elsewhere. Ed(s): Kelli M Donley. Destination Media, LLC, 13856 South 36th Way, Phoenix, AZ 85044. Adv. *Aud.:* Sa.

Approximately one in ten weddings is now a destination wedding. For some brides, the decisions are less about the reception or the dress than about the actual location for the wedding. For help in making such decisions, *Destination I Do* magazine is here. It is still a traditional wedding magazine, but the clear emphasis here is on location. As the web site notes, "To expand the options the couple might consider, each issue highlights a variety of potential destination wedding locations including: the continental US, Hawaii, international locations, cruise lines, theme parks and the Caribbean." Thus, in between the wedding advice, reception details, and wedding fashion, much of the editorial is given to decribing possible wedding and honeymoon locations. The target market for this magazine is described as affluent couples aged 25–45 who are college-educated and well-traveled. The web site offers subscription and advertising information, plus selected articles from the current issue. For the couple planning a destination wedding or honeymoon, this title is a useful one.

6156. *Destination Weddings & Honeymoons.* [ISSN: 1528-5413] 2000. q. USD 14.94 domestic; USD 18.97 Canada; USD 22.97 elsewhere. World Publications LLC, 460 N Orlando Ave, Ste 200, Winter Park, FL 32789; info@worldpub.net; http://www.worldpub.net. Illus., adv. Circ: 175000. *Aud.:* Sa.

With the high cost of weddings and receptions, it is no wonder that a growing number of couples are choosing destination weddings, which are often less expensive. To that end, *Destination Weddings & Honeymoons* magazine seeks to be the "ultimate resource" in such wedding planning. As with other wedding magazines, readers of this title will find a countdown calendar, real-life weddings, fashions, and wedding advice—but with a twist. The wedding stories are strictly destination weddings, the fashions are of the beach and bikini variety, and the wedding advice usually concerns travel matters. Advertising is primarily travel-related. The web site for the magazine includes the table of contents from the current issue, contest information, and digital subscription information. For brides who are planning destination weddings, this title will likely be more useful than other magazines in this genre.

6157. *Elegant Bride.* Formerly (until 1990): *Southern Bride.* [ISSN: 1551-0689] 1988. q. USD 15.95 domestic; USD 5.99 newsstand/cover domestic; GBP 3.50 newsstand/cover United Kingdom. Fairchild Publications, Inc., 750 3rd Ave., 3rd Fl., New York, NY 10017; customerservice@fairchildpub.com; http://www.fairchildpub.com. Illus., adv. Sample. Circ: 142000. Vol. ends: Winter. *Aud.:* Sa.

For brides seeking inspiration for the ultimate fantasy wedding, *Elegant Bride* is a must-have magazine. One of three bridal publications from Conde Nast, this one distinguishes itself with the obvious emphasis on high-end couture fashions, accessories, and other wedding details. There are few features here that consider any budgets but the most lavish. As its mission statement notes, "The Elegant Bride has a taste for luxury, knows quality and settles for nothing but the best." And, according to its media kit, this publication's audience is older (median age is 36) and richer (median income is over $96,000). But it is, after all, a bridal magazine, and there are the usual features: budget worksheet, countdown calendar, registry list, fashion and honeymoon tips, and real-life wedding stories. For all its high-end couture, it is still an accessible and extremely readable title. The online version contains the table of contents of the current issue, selected articles, and planning tools, along with many links to fashion and style, flowers and food, the honeymoon, and more.

6158. *For the Bride by Demetrios.* [ISSN: 1064-8089] 1991. 3x/yr. USD 4.99 per issue. Ed(s): Patricia Canole. D J E Publications, 222 W 37th St, 12th Fl, New York, NY 10018. Adv. Circ: 160000. *Aud.:* Sa.

What do you call a wedding magazine that promotes wedding dresses from a single designer? If you are fashion designer Demetrios James Elias, you call it *For the Bride.* Part magazine, part catalog for the Demetrios dress lines, it contains the elements of a typical bridal magazine, including beauty and relationship advice, new-home decorating, and honeymoon articles. It is quickly apparent, however, that the advertising and fashion stories serve as vehicles to display the Demetrios collections. There is some additional advertising from other designers promoting tuxedos and evening wear and bridesmaids' fashions. Also missing from the typical issue are examples of fashion layouts, real-life weddings, and vendor listings. The magazine part of the Demetrios web site contains subscription information only.

6159. *Grace Ormonde Wedding Style.* [ISSN: 1554-1185] 1999. s-a. USD 16 per issue domestic. Ed(s): Grace Ormonde. Elegant Publishing, Inc., PO Box 89, Barrington, RI 02806. Adv. Circ: 400000 Paid. *Aud.:* Sa.

Visually stunning, the oversized *Grace Ormonde Wedding Style* magazine is an annual publication filled with creative and innovative graphic design. This award-winning magazine contains the usual wedding fashion and jewelry advertisements, but also many ads for reception venues and photography studios. Clearly aimed at an upscale, sophisticated market, articles cover encore weddings, building a new home (not just furnishing a new home via registry items), and women's health, among other things. Interspersed among these features are numerous real-life "feature weddings" as well. Besides an advertisers' directory, *Wedding Style* also provides its own "Five Star" directory, which is described as "an effort to present the readers with choices among the best wedding professionals in their respective fields." This national magazine has a regional counterpart in the Northeast and a web site that provides access to current and archived articles back to 2000. This title is most useful for the bride who can afford the per-issue price and more.

6160. Inside Weddings. [ISSN: 1552-4647] 2003. q. USD 12; USD 4.95 newsstand/cover per issue. Inside Weddings, 264 S La Cienega Blvd, Ste 1188, Beverly Hills, CA 90211. Adv. Circ: 35000 Paid. *Aud.:* Sa.

Whether its claim as the fastest-growing wedding magazine in America is true or not, *Inside Weddings* is a magazine that aspires to offer more pages of editorial than advertising. To that end, it does well. Each issue contains about a dozen real-life weddings, which take up nearly half of the editorial content. Coverage for the real-life weddings is rather in-depth and includes a long list of such relevant wedding details as the gown, shoes, jewelry, and lingerie designers. Coverage is also on those responsible for the invitations, photography, videography, flowers, and wedding cakes, as well as on the reception site, rehearsal dinner site, gift registries, honeymoon location, and more. In addition to real-life stories, the magazine devotes a fairly substantial portion to wedding couture. Recent fashion spreads utilize fashion show pictures, rather than creating a particular storyline or theme, so the spreads are fairly lengthy and highlight multiple designers, but do not include any dress descriptions or prices. The web site includes archived, yet equally detailed real-life wedding stories. This magazine offers plenty of inspiration via real-life weddings and designer wedding dresses.

6161. InStyle Weddings. [ISSN: 1547-2272] 2000. s-a. USD 30 domestic; USD 37 Canada; USD 3.99 newsstand/cover. Ed(s): Norman Pearlstine, Maria Baugh. Time, Inc., Time & Life Bldg, Rockefeller Center, 29th Fl, New York, NY 10020-1393; http://www.timeinc.com. Adv. Circ: 1000000 Paid. *Aud.:* Sa.

For the bride who wants to look like a star on her wedding day, there is plenty of inspiration found in *InStyle Weddings*. Starting with its distinctive celebrity covers, this magazine profiles Hollywood weddings, uses celebrity models for fashion spreads, and name-drops extensively throughout issues. Like the original *InStyle Magazine,* this title is slightly larger in size than the average wedding magazine, utilizes large pictures, and provides lots of white space; as a result, it is much more reader-friendly than other titles in this genre. It, too, follows the usual order of wedding magazines, with sections on beauty, fashion, reception ideas, registry, and honeymoon details. Many of the wedding ideas and examples offered in this magazine may be out of reach for most brides' budgets, but who cares when you're reading about celebrities and their fantasy weddings?

6162. The Knot Weddings Magazine. Formerly: *The Knot Wedding Gowns.* 1999. s-a. USD 9.99 newsstand/cover per issue. Ed(s): Carley Roney. The Knot Inc., 462 Broadway, 6th Fl, New York, NY 10013; salesinfo@ theknot.com; http://www.theknot.com/. Adv. Circ: 122500 Paid. *Aud.:* Sa.

Is it a catalog or a magazine? At first glance, *The Knot Weddings Magazine* looks out of place because many of the pages resemble something from a catalog instead of a magazine. Indeed, the bulk of each issue is comprised of wedding-related directories, which showcase over 800 wedding gowns and bridesmaid fashions, more than 50 honeymoon resorts, and hundreds of wedding accessory and jewelry items. However, there is magazine-type content, including wedding planning and beauty advice, real weddings, and a fashion spread. The back of the magazine also contains the articles about registries and honeymoons. This national publication is published semi-annually, while regional magazines of the same name are issued quarterly. It is also published by the creators of the online wedding mega-site theknot.com, which claims to have over two million

unique visitors monthly and to be the leading Internet retailer of wedding favors and supplies. For those who cannot access theknot.com on the web but are willing to pay $9.99 per issue, this magazine is the next best thing.

6163. Martha Stewart Weddings. Formerly (until 1999): *Martha Stewart Living Weddings.* [ISSN: 1534-553X] 1990. 4x/yr. USD 16; USD 5.95 newsstand/cover. Ed(s): Melissa Morgan. Martha Stewart Living Omnimedia LLC, 11 W. 42nd St., 25th Fl, New York, NY 10036; mstewart@marthastewart.com; http://www.marthastewart.com. Adv. Circ: 249326 Paid. *Aud.:* Sa.

Finding a copy of *Martha Stewart Weddings* in a crowded magazine rack is not too difficult, given its distinct cover: unlike most titles in this genre, it is the wedding accompaniments such as flowers and cakes, not the bride, that are the cover models. However, there is no mistaking this title for anything but a wedding magazine. Like the original *Martha Stewart Living* magazine, the *Weddings* magazine follows a similar format, with advice on creating elegant meals, sophisticated flower arrangements, and marvelous cakes, plus clever wedding craft ideas (under the same Stewart craft heading, "Good Things"). In addition to reception details, planning calendars, and honeymoon descriptions, it also contains fashion features and profiles real wedding events, giving attention to unique touches. The emphasis here is on creating the perfect wedding event. Sex and relationship advice is left to other titles. The heavily sponsored web site contains many links to wedding planning, crafts, message boards, and related Martha Stewart products. For the bride who reads *Martha Stewart Living,* this magazine is a must-have.

6164. Modern Bride: a complete guide for the bride-to-be. [ISSN: 0026-7546] 1949. bi-m. USD 19.97 domestic; USD 4.99 newsstand/ cover per issue. Ed(s): Dan Ladgni. Conde Nast Publications, Inc., 750 3rd Ave, New York, NY 10017; http://www.condenast.com. Illus., adv. Circ: 395612 Paid. Vol. ends: Nov/Dec. Microform: PQC. Online: The Dialog Corporation. *Aud.:* Sa.

This title is the third in a set of bridal magazines put out by the same publisher, Conde Nast. What makes *Modern Bride* different is its "girlfriend-to-girlfriend" attitude; indeed, "*Modern Bride* is a smart, funny, slightly irreverent magazine that approaches the bride in a fresh new way." This magazine is the little sister, so to speak, of the trio, as its readership demographics contains the youngest audience of the three, the other two being *Brides* and *Elegant Bride*. In keeping with the mission statement, then, *Modern Bride* has a somewhat edgier look than its sister publications, while at the same time following the same content format for this genre. It, too, covers fashion, beauty, receptions, real weddings, lifestyle and registry, and honeymoon. Although not quite as hefty as *Brides*, it is one of the larger publications, with recent issues running well over 600 pages. The web site for *Modern Bride* takes readers to a portal for all three magazines.

6165. Shaadi Style. [ISSN: 1551-8213] 2003. s-a. USD 6 per issue domestic; USD 16 per issue foreign. Shaadi Style Magazine LLC, PO Box 226, Winchester, MA 01890. *Aud.:* Sa.

Calling itself the "Premier South Asian Wedding and Fashion Magazine," *Shaadi Style* magazine stands apart from other magazines in this genre, if only for the images of the brightly colored textiles found throughout the issues. Women looking for white wedding dress ideas should look elsewhere. Women who want to wear a gharara or a shaadi ka jora, on the other hand, will appreciate this title. A North American publication that targets the South Asian bride, *Shaadi,* which means "wedding," offers readers wedding ideas and inspiration with a traditional flair. As a wedding magazine, it contains the wedding countdown checklist, wedding advice, real-life wedding profiles, fashion, and honeymoon information. As a fashion magazine, it highlights couture fashions by South Asian designers. For readers unfamiliar with the wedding rites of this region, a glossary is provided for relevant terms. This title is a welcome addition to this genre and offers an alternative perspective.

6166. Sposa Magazine: the magazine for discerning bride. Former titles (until 1994): *Wedding Planner Sposa;* (until 1992): *Sposa 2000.* 1989. s-a. CND 30 domestic; USD 25 domestic; USD 35 foreign. Ed(s): Gulshan Sippy. Sponsa Magazine, 56 Temperance St., 6th Fl, Toronto, ON M5H 3V5, Canada; sposa@sposa.com; http://www.sposa.com. Circ: 50000. *Aud.:* Ga, Sa.

Sposa Magazine is an intriguing publication, promising to be "all about love" and "the magazine you turn to when you want straight talk," but it delivers little. The magazine is organized like no other in this genre: there are no fashion spreads, no advice columns, no honeymoon articles. Other wedding magazine staples—honeymoon contests and wedding countdown calendar—are both offered. With candid shots of wedding couples (and proper photographer credits) throughout the issues, *Sposa* even includes real wedding couples on the front cover. The online version contains images of past issues, subscription opportunities, and links to contact the editors. This magazine is useful for the bride who is looking to read as many different wedding magazines as possible before the big day.

6167. *Wedding Dresses.* s-a. USD 9.98; USD 5.99 newsstand/cover per issue. Ed(s): Severine Ferrari. Gerard Bedouk Publishing, Inc., 575 Madison Ave, 25th Fl, New York, NY 10022. Adv. *Aud.:* Sa.

Following a recent change in editorial direction, *Wedding Dresses* magazine seeks to appeal to a more diverse audience. Noting that "the more you mix cultures and people, the more interesting life becomes," this magazine features models from a variety of races and ethnicities. It moves beyond representing diversity in models, however, and highlights diversity in a number of ways. The real-life weddings section features examples such as Latin events, Afro-centric celebrations, Indian weddings, and mixed-culture weddings. One recent issue also features a 20-page spread on cultural wedding themes, in addition to the usual features that cater to the rest of a bride's happiness—wedding planning, cakes, flowers, registry, and honeymoon. While working within the framework of the traditional wedding magazine, this magazine does acknowledge that race, heritage, and cultural background can and do figure in the planning of a wedding. The magazine's online component emphasizes the current issue and subscription information.

6168. *WeddingChannel Magazine (U.S. General Edition).* Former titles (until 2006): *WeddingChannel's Weddingbells (General Edition);* (until 2005): *WeddingChannel.com's Weddingbells (U.S. General Edition);* (until 2005): *WeddingBells (U.S. General Edition).* [ISSN: 1715-9792] 1999. s-a. USD 4.95 newsstand/cover per issue. St. Joseph Media, 111 Queen St. E., Ste. 320, Toronto, ON M5C 1S2, Canada; http://www.stjosephmedia.com. *Aud.:* Sa.

This magazine was formerly known as *WeddingBells,* but its publishers have partnered with the WeddingChannel web site to produce the *WeddingChannel Magazine.* Name change notwithstanding, the content remains the same as before. A reasonably sized magazine, with issues usually running less than 200 pages, *WeddingChannel* contains a balanced mix of ads and features. Promising to "cater to the bride's specific interests as well as the needs of the groom, friends and family," this magazine offers the usual fashion, beauty, gift registry, and honeymoon advice. Suggestions for personalizing the ceremony and reception are included, along with numerous mentions of the WeddingChannel web site, both in the advertising and feature content. This magazine also provides coverage of real-life weddings. In addition to the national publication, ten regional editions are published for major such metropolitan areas as Boston, Chicago, New York, and San Francisco. There remains a web site for the previous title, and this site, Weddingbells.com, contains current information about the magazine. The content of the WeddingChannel.com web site is essentially separate from the magazine of the same name.

6169. *World Class Weddings.* q. USD 4.95 newsstand/cover. Ed(s): Fran Rutledge, Amanda Leigh. World Class Weddings, Inc., 5401 S Kirkman Rd., Ste 310, Orlando, FL 32810. *Aud.:* Sa.

With an emphasis on "world," *World Class Weddings* offers photos and descriptions of idyllic wedding sites around the globe. This magazine is not to be confused with a destination wedding magazine, however. Each issue is organized around a particular theme such as "Renaissance and Romance," and serves as the basis for coverage of select wedding sites and fashions and the rest of the articles. This quarterly is shorter than most (one issue was less than 100 pages), in a genre in which issues of 500 pages are not uncommon. Because of its size and emphasis on wedding locations, the coverage of wedding fashions is noticeably smaller, both in advertising and feature spreads. Each issue follows a standard pattern of wedding sites, several real-life weddings, celebrity layouts or interviews, fashions, travel, and home. The companion web site serves primarily as a retailer for wedding-related items.

■ WORLD WIDE WEB

See also Business; Communications; Computer Science and Automation; Electronics; Engineering and Technology; and Library Periodicals sections.

Xiaochang Yu, Systems Librarian, VCU Libraries, Virginia Commonwealth University, Richmond, VA 23284-2033; FAX: 804-828-0151; xyu@vcu.edu

Introduction

It is amazing that in such a short period of time the World Wide Web has become a way of life for billions of people across the world and has penetrated almost all areas. Today, virtually all magazines deal with the web in some way, and virtually all of them have some web presence. However, while few titles in other sections treat the web as the primary topic, it is the subject per se of titles in this section.

Magazines reviewed here can be roughly grouped into three categories. There are scholarly journals aimed at researchers and educators who study various aspects of the web. Other magazines tend to serve mainly technical professionals such as computer programmers and applications developers specializing in various web technologies. Still others appeal to a broad audience—the general public or ordinary web users who are more interested in using and exploring the web.

After a brief setback at the beginning of this new century, the World Wide Web seems to be engaged in a new third wave revolution in recent years. Weblogs and Google are probably two of the most influential developments in this revolution. The ups and downs of the web have had a direct impact on the number of magazines in this field. After a dramatic decrease of web-related titles, recent developments indicate that this trend has reversed itself. Quite a few new magazines, most of them seeming to be more specialized in specific aspects of the web, have been published in the last couple of years. Some of the new titles have been selected here in this edition for the first time.

Basic Periodicals

IEEE Internet Computing, Internet Research.

Basic Abstracts and Indexes

Computer Literature Index, INSPEC, Microcomputer Index.

6170. *Apache Week.* 1999. w. Free. Apache Week, Red Hat Europe, 10 Alan Turing Way, Guildford, GU2 7YF, United Kingdom; editors@ apacheweek.com. *Aud.:* Sa.

This electronic newsletter is solely devoted to Apache servers. The Apache web server is by far the most popular in use today. The newsletter provides timely information, mainly new product releases and bug fixes, to the Apache community. In addition to the news column, the regular columns also include security reports and feature articles, which largely consist of abstracts of some of the publications on the web that are of interest to Apache users. The newsletter is sent to subscribers by e-mail weekly. *Apache Week* is one of the essential resources for anyone running an Apache server or running Apache-based services. URL: www.apacheweek.com

6171. *The CyberSkeptic's Guide to Internet Research.* [ISSN: 1085-2417] 1995. 10x/yr. USD 179.95 domestic; USD 190 in Canada & Mexico; USD 216 elsewhere. Ed(s): Sheri Lanza. Information Today, Inc., 143 Old Marlton Pike, Medford, NJ 08055-8750; custserv@infotoday.com; http://www.infotoday.com. Illus. Sample. *Indexed:* CINAHL, ISTA, MicrocompInd. *Aud.:* Ga, Sa.

This newsletter is primarily for information technology professionals. It reviews web sites and tools. A typical issue includes a detailed discussion of a selected web site, brief introductions to several interesting web sites in various areas, evaluations or comparisons of web sites, and analyses of search engines and other web tools. The newsletter maintains a healthy, skeptical view of cyberspace and is often fun to read.

6172. e-Service Journal. [ISSN: 1528-8226] 2001. 3x/yr. USD 125 . (Individuals, USD 45). Ed(s): Ilze Zigurs. Indiana University Press, 601 N Morton St, Bloomington, IN 47404; http://www.indiana.edu/~iupress/journals/. Illus. Sample. Refereed. Circ: 200 Paid. *Indexed:* ABIn, BPI. *Aud.:* Ga, Ac, Sa.

This peer-reviewed journal covers various aspects of electronic services, from methods and infrastructures to policies and social impacts. It combines both private sector and public sector perspectives regarding electronic services. The articles, including both research articles and case studies, are mainly intended for researchers and practitioners involved in developing e-government and e-business. Authors are knowledgeable and topics are interesting. This is a very solid publication.

6173. Educause Review. Former titles (until 1999): *Educom Review;* (until 1989): *Educom Bulletin;* (until 1984): *Educom.* [ISSN: 1527-6619] 1966. bi-m. USD 30 in US & Canada; USD 54 elsewhere. Ed(s): Teddy Diggs. Educause, 4772 Walnut St, Ste 206, Boulder, CO 80301-2536; info@educause.com; http://www.educause.edu. Illus., index, adv. Sample. Refereed. Circ: 20000. Vol. ends: Dec. Online: EBSCO Publishing, EBSCO Host; H.W. Wilson. *Indexed:* ABIn, CompLI, ERIC, EduInd, HEA. *Aud.:* Ga, Ac.

This publication was a consolidation of *Educom* and *Cause* in 1998. The journal explores challenging issues related to the development and deployment of the Internet and information technology in higher education. It addresses such topics as virtual universities, the use of wireless and other new technologies in teaching and learning, and library and information services in the digital environment. The focus is often on policy, management, and infrastructure, and many of the articles are written by college and university administrators.

6174. EFFector. [ISSN: 1062-9424] 1991. irreg. 1-4/mo. Free. Ed(s): Stanton McCandlish. Electronic Frontier Foundation, 454 Shotwell St., San Francisco, CA 94110-1914; editor@eff.org; http://www.eff.org/effector. Circ: 20000. *Aud.:* Ga, Ac, Sa.

This newsletter of the Electronic Frontier Foundation is one of the best free online publications on the Internet. While many free online publications these days serve mainly as portals to online resources on other web sites, *EFFector* still publishes its own materials. Its mission is clear and very focused: defending freedom in the digital world. It covers mainly news, alerts, and commentaries on issues related to free speech on the Internet. Recent issues cover such topics as electronic voting, bloggers' rights campaign, and legal battles over anonymous online speech. All the back issues since 1990 are available. The newsletter is also sent to subscribers by e-mail weekly.

eWEEK. See Computers and Information Technology/Popular Titles section.

6175. First Monday. [ISSN: 1396-0466] 1996. m. Free. Ed(s): Edward J Valauskas. First Monday Editorial Group, c/o Edward Valauskas, Chief Editor, PO Box 87636, Chicago, IL 60680-0636; http://www.firstmonday.org. Illus. Refereed. Circ: 314559. *Indexed:* BRI, CBRI, CommAb, ISTA, LISA, LibLit, PAIS. *Bk. rev.:* 5-10, 500-1500 words. *Aud.:* Ga, Ac.

This was one of the first refereed journals on the web, and it has been published regularly on the first Monday of every month since 1996. The journal explores a variety of Internet issues, from the political, cultural, and regulatory impacts on the Internet to the technical ones. Articles are indexed by authors and by titles. The journal database is easily searchable. *First Monday* is one of the best electronic journals devoted to the Internet.

6176. Fixed Wireless Monthly Newsletter. Formerly (until 2005): *Information Superhighways.* [ISSN: 1541-1206] 1993. m. USD 695 in US & Canada; USD 745 elsewhere. Ed(s): Cathy Mallen, Tony Carmona. Information Gatekeepers, Inc., 320 Washington St, Ste 302, Brighton, MA 02135; info@igigroup.com; http://www.igigroup.com. Illus., adv. Vol. ends: Dec. Online: Florida Center for Library Automation; Gale. *Aud.:* Sa.

This monthly is one of 45 or so newsletters published by Information Gatekeepers, Inc. It addresses worldwide developments in e-commerce practices as well as in information and wireless technologies. It covers government policies and regulations, new products and services, business and market activities, and other topics. It is current, straightforward, and concise. The high price may keep some potential subscribers away.

6177. IEEE Internet Computing. [ISSN: 1089-7801] 1997. bi-m. USD 850. Ed(s): Munindar P Singh. IEEE, 445 Hoes Ln, Piscataway, NJ 08854-1331; subscription-service@ieee.org; http://www.ieee.org. Illus., index, adv. Refereed. Circ: 20000 Paid. Vol. ends: Dec. Online: Pub.; EBSCO Publishing, EBSCO Host. *Indexed:* C&ISA, CerAb, CompLI, EngInd, IAA, MicrocompInd, RiskAb, SCI. *Aud.:* Ac, Sa.

With a very attractive appearance, this IEEE journal is actually highly technical in nature, and it is mainly concerned with the engineering side of the Internet. Its main audience is designers and developers of Internet-based applications and technologies. Articles are well written and are at the frontier of study in the field. One of the unique features is its "Elsewhere" department, which lists and abstracts research articles on the Internet that are newly published in other important journals. It is a simple thing that any journal can do, yet to actually do it demonstrates the self-confidence of *Internet Computing*. Recommended.

6178. I-Ways: digest of electronic commerce policy and regulation. Formerly (until Mar 1995): *Transnational Data and Communications Report;* Which was formed by the merger of (1980-1984): *Chronicle of International Communication;* (1978-1984): *Transnational Data Report.* [ISSN: 1084-4678] 1984. q. USD 505 combined subscription in North America print & online eds.; EUR 390 combined subscription elsewhere print & online eds. Ed(s): Russell Pipe. I O S Press, Nieuwe Hemweg 6B, Amsterdam, 1013 BG, Netherlands; order@iospress.nl; http://www.iospress.nl. Illus., index, adv. Sample. Vol. ends: Dec. *Indexed:* CommAb, PAIS. *Bk. rev.:* 4-5, 175 words. *Aud.:* Ac, Sa.

The new title of this authoritative publication captures exactly its main focus: reports and digests of electronic commerce policies and regulations. It addresses such issues as transborder data privacy, Internet taxing, and encryption regulations. It covers individual country as well as regional and worldwide organizations. The contributors are truly international in scope. Some of the recent reports and digests discuss cybercrime laws and e-commerce and e-government developments in various countries.

6179. International Journal of Web Information Systems. [ISSN: 1744-0084] q. GBP 195. Ed(s): David Taniar, Ismail Khalil Ibrahim. Emerald Group Publishing Limited, Howard House, Wagon Ln, Bingley, BD16 1WA, United Kingdom; information@emeraldinsight.com; http://www.emeraldinsight.com. Refereed. *Indexed:* C&ISA, CerAb, IAA. *Aud.:* Ac, Sa.

This international journal publishes research papers on web information systems. The web information system is a relatively new concept. "The goal of a web information system is to provide users with a unified view to transparently and efficiently access, relate, and combine data stored in multiple, autonomous, and possibly heterogeneous information sources." The journal covers all aspects of the web information system, including, among others, web semantics and metadata, web search and information extraction, web databases, web commerce and e-business, and advanced web applications. A solid publication.

6180. Internet Research. Formerly (until 1993): *Electronic Networking.* [ISSN: 1066-2243] 1991. 5x/yr. EUR 2469 combined subscription in Europe print & online eds.; USD 2679 combined subscription in North America print & online eds.; AUD 3009 combined subscription in Australasia print & online eds. Ed(s): Dr. David G Schwartz. Emerald Group Publishing Limited, Howard House, Wagon Ln, Bingley, BD16 1WA, United Kingdom; information@emeraldinsight.com; http://www.emeraldinsight.com. Illus., index, adv. Refereed. Vol. ends: Dec. Online: Pub.; EBSCO Publishing, EBSCO Host; Gale; IngentaConnect; OCLC Online Computer Library Center, Inc.; OhioLINK; ProQuest LLC (Ann Arbor); SwetsWise Online Content. Reprint: PSC. *Indexed:* ABIn, C&ISA, CJA, CerAb, CommAb, CompLI, EAA, HRA, IAA, ISTA, LISA, LibLit, MicrocompInd, PAIS, PRA, RiskAb, SCI, SSCI. *Aud.:* Ac, Sa.

International in scope, this scholarly journal has the goal of describing, evaluating, and understanding the role of the Internet and other information networks. Most of the contributors are researchers and college and university professors worldwide. It tends to emphasize the foundational, methodological, and other significant aspects of information networks rather than specific issues. The journal is very well organized and the contents are current. Many of the papers try to provide solutions to real concerns of Internet researchers, developers, and users. It is one of the premier journals on the subject of the Internet. Recommended.

6181. *Internet Week: news and analysis of internet business opportunities.* Incorporates (1993-1995): *Internet Letter.* [ISSN: 1081-2474] 1995. 53x/yr. USD 175; USD 395 in Europe; USD 425 in Asia. Access Intelligence, LLC, 1201 Seven Locks Rd, Ste 300, Potomac, MD 20854. Illus., adv. Sample. Online: LexisNexis; Northern Light Technology, Inc.; ProQuest LLC (Ann Arbor). *Indexed:* ABIn, LogistBibl. *Aud.:* Ga, Sa.

This weekly publication offers timely news to Internet users and the business community. Although it reports on a broad range of network-related subjects, such as emerging technologies, the focus is clearly on the business and market aspects. In addition to the news items, each issue also contains a couple of detailed reports and a column of new-product reviews. Surprisingly, this solid publication is free to qualified management and professional personnel at companies involved in the communications industry.

6182. *Java Developer's Journal.* [ISSN: 1087-6944] 1996. m. USD 69.99 domestic; USD 89.99 in Canada & Mexico; USD 99 elsewhere. Ed(s): M'lou Pinkham, Sean Rhody. SYS-CON Media, Inc., 135 Chestnut Ridge Rd, Montvale, NJ 07645; info@sys-con.com; http://www.sys-con.com. Illus., adv. Circ: 110000 Paid. Vol. ends: Dec. Online: Florida Center for Library Automation; Gale. *Bk. rev.:* 2-3, 300 words. *Aud.:* Ga, Ac, Sa.

This journal is clearly for Java programmers and developers. It covers applications, tools, innovations, and programming issues. The scope ranges from relatively basic topics such as dynamically extracting data from a database into a JSP file to more advanced topics such as developing voice portals with Java. The feature articles are substantial. Its columns include, among other items, brief news reports, industry watches, product reviews, and interviews. The journal is well designed and organized.

6183. *JavaWorld: fueling innovation.* [ISSN: 1091-8906] 1996. m. Ed(s): Carolyn Wong. Web Publishing Inc, 501 Second St, Ste 310, San Francisco, CA 94107; http://www.javaworld.com. Illus., adv. Circ: 140000. Vol. ends: Dec. *Bk. rev.:* 5-8, 100 words. *Aud.:* Ga, Sa.

This web-based magazine covers Java programming language and the related technologies. It aims at Java beginners as well as experienced developers. In addition to in-depth articles, it features news, reports, reviews, and other items of interest to the Java community. The web site is well organized and searchable. Its weekly version is available through e-mail. This is a solid publication.

6184. *Journal of Website Promotion: innovations in internet business research, theory, and practice.* [ISSN: 1553-3611] 2005. q. USD 290 print & online eds. Ed(s): Richard Alan Nelson. Internet Practice Press, 10 Alice St, Binghamton, NY 13904; getinfo@haworthpress.com; http://www.haworthpress.com/. Adv. Reprint: HAW. *Indexed:* C&ISA, CerAb, CommAb, IAA. *Bk. rev.:* Number and length vary. *Aud.:* Ac, Sa.

This refereed journal is devoted to web site promotion, an increasingly important aspect of web development and management. It consists of research articles, brief updates, case studies, and reviews of books and web sites. It deals with such issues as how to create a user-friendly feel, how to capture the right kinds of traffic, and how to develop content that is attractive to the target audience. Articles are well written. Institutions with interests in web site promotion will find this a valuable publication.

6185. *Netsurfer Digest.* 1994. w. Free. Ed(s): Lawrence Nyveen, Arthur Bebak. Netsurfer Digest, 333 Cobalt Way, Ste 107, Sunnyvale, CA 94086; editor@netsurf.com; http://www.netsurf.com/nsd/. *Aud.:* Ga.

Published since 1994, this weekly publication is one of the oldest existing web-based magazines. It features news, reviews, analyses, and other items of interest to the public. It is mainly a gateway to selected online resources. In most cases, it summarizes and classifies external resources and provides hyperlinks to them. In its own words, it provides "an informative and entertaining snapshot of the vast wired world." The publication is well organized and current. All back issues are available online and searchable. The publication is also delivered freely via e-mail to subscribers.

6186. *Network World.* Incorporates (in 1991): *Connect;* Former titles (until 1986): *On Communications; Computerworld on Communications.* [ISSN: 0887-7661] 1983. w. Mon. USD 129 domestic (Free to qualified personnel). Ed(s): John Dix. Network World Inc., 118 Turnpike Rd, Southborough, MA 01772; http://www.nwfusion.com. Illus., adv. Sample. Circ: 170072 Controlled. Vol. ends: Dec. Online: EBSCO Publishing, EBSCO Host; Florida Center for Library Automation; Gale; LexisNexis; Northern Light Technology, Inc.; OCLC Online Computer Library Center, Inc.; ProQuest LLC (Ann Arbor). *Indexed:* ABIn, LRI, MicrocompInd. *Bk. rev.:* 3-4, 200 words. *Aud.:* Ga, Sa.

This trade magazine reports on trends and news, applications and technologies, companies and products, key personnel and remarkable events, business and marketing, policies and politics, and other topics in the Internet and networking fields. Its annual special issues are outstanding. For example, in "The Power Issue," it rates and profiles, among others, the most powerful companies, the most powerful people, and the most significant power struggles in networking. The advertisements are extensive. Qualified readers may get a free one-year subscription.

6187. *The Scout Report.* [ISSN: 1092-3861] w. University of Wisconsin at Madison, Computer Sciences Department, 5355a Computer Sciences and Statistics, 1210 West Dayton St, Madison, WI 53706; scout@cs.wisc.edu; http://scout.wisc.edu/. *Aud.:* Ems, Hs, Ac.

This well-respected publication of the Internet Scout Project highlights current Internet resources of interest to educators, librarians, and researchers. It covers news, tools, and research articles. Although most materials are external resources on other web sites, they are very well selected, annotated, catalogued, and organized. Besides its flagship publication, namely *The Scout Report* itself, the project also publishes Scout reports for the following three areas: life sciences; physical sciences; and math, engineering, and technology. The web site provides a sophisticated search engine. All materials are searchable by Library of Congress subject headings, among other fields. This search feature is rare in freely available online resources.

6188. *Wired.* [ISSN: 1059-1028] 1993. m. USD 12 domestic; USD 40 Canada; USD 75 elsewhere. Ed(s): Chris Anderson. Conde Nast Publications Inc., Wired Ventures Ltd., 520 Third St, 4th Fl, San Francisco, CA 94107-1815. Illus., adv. Sample. Circ: 170000 Paid. Vol. ends: Dec. *Indexed:* ABS&EES, ASIP, BrArAb, C&ISA, CerAb, FutSurv, IAA, LISA, MicrocompInd, RGPR, RI-1. *Bk. rev.:* 5-8, 100 words. *Aud.:* Hs, Ga.

This magazine covers the Internet and other areas of science and technology of interest to the public. The coverage is very broad. It publishes detailed reports and analyses as well as brief news and reviews on a variety of topics, from digital games to DNA to international businesses. Regular departments include "Start," "Play," "Rants and Raves," and "Posts." The magazine, including its extensive advertisements, is very beautifully designed.

6189. *X M L Journal.* [ISSN: 1534-9780] 2000. m. Ed(s): Ajit Sagar. SYS-CON Media, Inc., 135 Chestnut Ridge Rd, Montvale, NJ 07645; info@sys-con.com; http://www.sys-con.com. Adv. Circ: 55000 Paid. *Aud.:* Ga, Ac, Sa.

This journal covers all aspects of XML technology, such as XSLT, XPath, XLink, XForms, and XML documents. In addition to editorials, news, product reviews, and interviews, it has articles addressing novel applications, parsing, encoding, editing tools, and trends in industry standards, among other topics. Since XML is mainly an enabling technology, this journal also addresses a variety of other closely related programming languages and technologies, such as Java, Cobra, SQL, databases, and web services. Authors are knowledgeable, and topics are interesting. The publication is well designed and organized.

■ ZOOLOGY

See also Biology; and Physiology sections.

Reed Lowrie, Science Reference and Cartographic Librarian, Cabot Science Library, Harvard University, 1 Oxford St., Cambridge MA 02138

Introduction

Little has changed in zoology publications since the last edition of *Magazines for Libraries*. Online access has been improved and streamlined due to the adoption of BioOne by many scholarly societies. There is a promising new online-only open-access title, *Frontiers in Zoology*. I've attempted to point out titles where supplemental information and advance publication is available in the online editions. Librarians may also want to consult the Ecology and Biology sections for other potentially relevant journals.

Basic Periodicals

Animal Behaviour, Behavioral Ecology, Integrative and Comparative Biology, Journal of Experimental Biology,

Basic Abstracts and Indexes

Biological Abstracts, Biological Abstracts/RRM, Biological and Agricultural Index, Biology Digest, Current Contents/Life Sciences, Zoological Record.

6190. *Animal Behaviour.* Formerly (until 1958): *British Journal of Animal Behaviour.* [ISSN: 0003-3472] 1953. 12x/yr. EUR 1206. Ed(s): Leigh W. Simmons, George W. Uetz. Academic Press, 24-28 Oval Rd, London, NW1 7DX, United Kingdom; apsubs@acad.com; http://www.elsevier.com/. Illus., index, adv. Refereed. Microform: PMC; PQC. Online: EBSCO Publishing, EBSCO Host; Gale; IngentaConnect; OCLC Online Computer Library Center, Inc.; OhioLINK; ScienceDirect; SwetsWise Online Content. *Indexed:* Agr, AnBeAb, ApEcolAb, B&AI, BiolAb, CABA, ChemAb, DSA, ExcerpMed, FR, FS&TA, ForAb, GSI, HortAb, IndVet, MLA-IB, OceAb, PsycInfo, S&F, SCI, SSCI, VB, WAE&RSA, ZooRec. *Bk. rev.:* 2-3, 500-1400 words. *Aud.:* Ac, Sa.

Animal Behaviour publishes papers concerning all aspects of animal behavior, including that of humans. The journal primarily contains original research papers, and preference is given to those papers that are considered likely to interest the broad readership of the journal and that test explicit hypotheses rather than those that are merely descriptive. In addition, review articles on fundamental issues in behavior are often published. There is a Commentaries section, with brief pieces on issues of general importance to the discipline, including methodology, statistics, and ethics. The online edition of the title includes a Forum section where critiques of published papers are posted, and a space is provided for exchanges among scholars regarding issues relevant to the study of behavior. This title should be considered nearly essential for academic libraries.

6191. *Behavioral Ecology.* [ISSN: 1045-2249] 1990. bi-m. GBP 337 print or online ed. Ed(s): Dr. Mark Elgar. Oxford University Press, 2001 Evans Rd, Cary, NC 27513; jnlorders@oup-usa.org; http://www.us.oup.com. Adv. Refereed. Circ: 990 Paid. Online: EBSCO Publishing, EBSCO Host; Gale; HighWire Press; IngentaConnect; OCLC Online Computer Library Center, Inc.; OhioLINK; Ovid Technologies, Inc.; Oxford Journals; ProQuest LLC (Ann Arbor); SwetsWise Online Content. Reprint: PSC. *Indexed:* AnBeAb, ApEcolAb, BiolAb, CABA, DSA, ForAb, HortAb, IndVet, PsycInfo, RRTA, SCI, VB, ZooRec. *Aud.:* Ac, Sa.

This journal covers all aspects of behavioral ecology, including empirical and theoretical work. The complete range of organisms is covered, including plants, invertebrates, vertebrates, and humans. *Behavioral Ecology* considers the field broadly, dealing with "the use of ecological and evolutionary processes to explain the occurrence and adaptive significance of behaviour patterns," as well as "the use of behavioral processes to predict ecological patterns" and "empirical, comparative analyses relating behavior to the environment in which it occurs." Original articles, review articles, and a forum section with commentaries on recent issues are all included. The official journal of the International Society for Behavioral Ecology, the title has been gaining in prominence and should be considered by academic libraries. Articles are appropriate for undergraduates through specialists. Online material appears in advance of print publication. Lay summaries are provided for each article for the general reader.

6192. *Behavioral Ecology and Sociobiology.* [ISSN: 0340-5443] 1976. m. EUR 3599 print & online eds. Ed(s): Dr. Tatiana Czeschlik. Springer, Tiergartenstr 17, Heidelberg, 69121, Germany. Adv. Refereed. Microform: PQC. Online: EBSCO Publishing, EBSCO Host; OhioLINK; Springer LINK; SwetsWise Online Content. Reprint: PSC. *Indexed:* AbAn, Agr, AnBeAb, ApEcolAb, BiolAb, CABA, DSA, FPA, FR, ForAb, HortAb, IndVet, OceAb, PsycInfo, S&F, SCI, SSCI, VB, ZooRec. *Aud.:* Ac, Sa.

Behavioral Ecology and Sociobiology publishes original research papers and occasional review articles "dealing with quantitative empirical and theoretical studies in the analysis of animal behavior on the level of the individual, population and community. Special emphasis is placed on the proximate mechanisms, ultimate functions and evolution of ecological adaptations of behavior." Articles are generally between seven to ten pages long and are appropriate for advanced undergraduates through specialists. Online material appears in advance of print publication. Although expensive, this is one of the most important titles in zoology, and academic libraries should consider purchasing it.

6193. *Biological Bulletin.* Formerly (until 1899): *Zoological Bulletin.* [ISSN: 0006-3185] 1897. bi-m. USD 380 (Individuals, USD 120). Ed(s): James L. Olds. Marine Biological Laboratory, 7 MBL St, Woods Hole, MA 02543-1015; lreuter@mbl.edu; http://www.mbl.edu. Illus., index, adv. Refereed. Circ: 1850. Microform: PMC; PQC. Online: EBSCO Publishing, EBSCO Host; Florida Center for Library Automation; Gale; HighWire Press; JSTOR (Web-based Journal Archive); Northern Light Technology, Inc.; OCLC Online Computer Library Center, Inc.; ProQuest K-12 Learning Solutions; ProQuest LLC (Ann Arbor). *Indexed:* AnBeAb, ApEcolAb, B&AI, BiolAb, BiolDig, CABA, ChemAb, ForAb, GSI, IAA, IndVet, OceAb, S&F, SCI, VB, ZooRec. *Aud.:* Ac, Sa.

This title publishes experimental research on a wide range of biological topics and organisms. Papers include investigations in the fields of neurobiology and behavior, physiology and biomechanics, ecology and evolution, development and reproduction, cell biology, symbiosis, and systematics. Contents are primarily research papers, but shorter research notes are also included, as well as occasional review articles and symposia. Published by the Marine Biological Laboratory in Woods Hole, Massachusetts, the journal is primarily concerned with marine organisms. Although written for specialists, the articles are accessible to the educated lay reader and generally well written. Another important title for academic libraries. All content is available free online one year after publication.

6194. *Canadian Journal of Zoology.* Formerly (until 1950): *Canadian Journal of Research. Section D: Zoological Sciences;* Which superseded in part (in 1935): *Canadian Journal of Research.* [ISSN: 0008-4301] 1929. m. CND 1063 (Individuals, CND 295). Ed(s): Bruce P Dancik, Dr. K G Davey. N R C Research Press, National Research Council of Canada, Ottawa, ON K1A 0R6, Canada; pubs@nrc-cnrc.gc.ca; http://pubs.nrc-cnrc.gc.ca. Illus., index, adv. Refereed. Circ: 1125. Vol. ends: Dec. Microform: MML; PMC; PQC. Online: EBSCO Publishing, EBSCO Host; Gale; IngentaConnect; LexisNexis; Micromedia ProQuest; OCLC Online Computer Library Center, Inc.; Ovid Technologies, Inc.; ProQuest K-12 Learning Solutions; ProQuest LLC (Ann Arbor);

SwetsWise Online Content; H.W. Wilson. *Indexed:* Agr, AnBeAb, ApEcolAb, B&AI, BiolAb, CABA, CBCARef, CPerI, ChemAb, DSA, EngInd, EnvAb, EnvInd, ExcerpMed, FPA, ForAb, GSI, HortAb, IndVet, M&GPA, MLA-IB, OceAb, S&F, SCI, SWRA, VB, ZooRec. *Aud.:* Ac, Sa.

This journal publishes in the general fields of behavior, biochemistry and physiology, developmental biology, ecology, genetics, morphology and ultrastructure, parasitology and pathology, and systematics and evolution. Papers are published in English and French and include articles reporting on original research as well as shorter notes on research and comments on papers previously published in the journal. In addition, review articles are occasionally published. Articles are required to report on significant new findings of general zoological interest. Coverage is broad, and articles are accessible to undergraduates and educated lay readers as well as specialists. Published by the National Research Council of Canada, the online version now includes supplementary material such as data sets, graphs, and tables.

6195. *Copeia.* [ISSN: 0045-8511] 1913. q. USD 135 (Individuals, USD 85). Ed(s): Robert Kenley. American Society of Ichthyologists and Herpetologists, c/o Karen Hickey, Allen Press Inc, Lawrence, KS 66044-8897; orders@allenpress.com; http://www.allenpress.com. Illus., index, adv. Refereed. Circ: 3600 Controlled. Vol. ends: Dec. Microform: PQC. Online: BioOne; CSA; JSTOR (Web-based Journal Archive); OCLC Online Computer Library Center, Inc.; OhioLINK; ProQuest LLC (Ann Arbor). *Indexed:* AnBeAb, ApEcolAb, B&AI, BiolAb, BiolDig, CABA, ChemAb, ForAb, IndVet, OceAb, S&F, SCI, SWRA, VB, ZooRec. *Bk. rev.:* 4-5, 400-2000 words. *Aud.:* Ac, Sa.

Published by the American Society of Ichthyologists and Herpetologists, *Copeia* publishes "results of original research performed by societal members in which fish, amphibians, or reptiles are used as study organisms." Research articles are the primary contents, but shorter contributions and book reviews are also published, as well as other information deemed to be of interest to society members (meeting notes, historical articles, obituaries, etc.). All articles are in English, but abstracts are published in the author's native language when that language is not English. The journal publishes about 1,000 pages a year, and papers are written for the specialist, although some will be accessible to advanced undergraduates.

6196. *Frontiers in Zoology.* [ISSN: 1742-9994] 2004. irreg. Free. Ed(s): Jurgen Heinze. BioMed Central Ltd., Middlesex House, 34-42 Cleveland St, London, W1T 4LB, United Kingdom; info@biomedcentral.com; http://www.biomedcentral.com. Refereed. *Indexed:* AnBeAb, ApEcolAb. *Aud.:* Ac, Sa.

This online-only title was launched in 2004 by BioMed Central, an open access publisher. While it is too early to determine whether or not it will be influential, the editorial board is prestigious, and the journal is supported by the Deutsche Zoologische Gesellschaft, one of the world's largest and oldest zoological societies, so early indications are that it will be. *Frontiers in Zoology* publishes a wide range of article types, including research articles, book reviews, commentaries, debate articles, hypotheses, methodology articles, review articles, and short reports. The journal aims to present zoology as "an integrative discipline encompassing the most diverse aspects of animal life, from the level of the gene to the level of the ecosystem." Taking advantage of the online platform, links are provided for citation searching on Google Scholar, for other articles by the same authors, and for readers to post and read comments on the published articles. Content is specialized, but most papers should be accessible to advanced undergraduates. Academic librarians will want to keep an eye on this title.

6197. *Herpetologica.* [ISSN: 0018-0831] 1936. q. USD 300 print & online eds. (Individuals, USD 75 print & online eds.). Ed(s): Alicia Mathis. Herpetologists League, c/o Christopher Phillips, Illinois Natural History Survey, Champaign, IL 61820; chrisp@inhs.uiuc.edu; http://www.inhs.uiuc.edu/cbd/HL/HL.html. Illus., index. Refereed. Circ: 2000 Paid. Vol. ends: Dec. Microform: PQC. Online: BioOne; CSA; OhioLINK. *Indexed:* AnBeAb, ApEcolAb, BiolAb, CABA, ChemAb, ForAb, S&F, SCI, SSCI, ZooRec. *Aud.:* Ac, Sa.

This title publishes original papers dealing with the biology of amphibians and reptiles. It is one of the two major publications of the Herpetologists League, the other being *Herpetological Monographs*. Original research is published, with emphasis given to theoretical or quantitative papers. Volume 58 (2002) to the present is available online through BioOne, while earlier issues will be made available through JSTOR. Articles vary in length, with most being six to ten pages long. Although written for specialists, articles are generally well written, and some will be accessible to undergraduates. A leading title in the field.

6198. *Integrative and Comparative Biology.* Formerly (until 2002): *American Zoologist.* [ISSN: 1540-7063] 1961. bi-m. EUR 605. Ed(s): Harold Heatwole. Oxford University Press, Great Clarendon St, Oxford, OX2 6DP, United Kingdom; jnl.orders@oup.co.uk; http://www.oxfordjournals.org. Illus., index, adv. Refereed. Circ: 6300. Vol. ends: Dec. Microform: PQC. Online: BioOne; CSA; EBSCO Publishing, EBSCO Host; Gale; HighWire Press; Northern Light Technology, Inc.; OCLC Online Computer Library Center, Inc.; OhioLINK; Oxford Journals; ProQuest K-12 Learning Solutions; ProQuest LLC (Ann Arbor); SwetsWise Online Content; H.W. Wilson. Reprint: PSC. *Indexed:* Agr, AnBeAb, ApEcolAb, B&AI, BiolAb, BiolDig, CABA, ChemAb, DSA, ForAb, GSI, HortAb, IndVet, S&F, SCI, VB, ZooRec. *Bk. rev.:* Number and length vary. *Aud.:* Ac, Sa.

Formerly *American Zoologist,* this is one of the most important journals in the study of biology. Individual issues are grouped around a common theme—for example, "Adaptations to Life at High Elevation"—and contain invited papers, primarily arising from symposia sponsored by the Society for Integrative and Comparative Biology. While original papers are sometimes published, the primary content is review articles and synthetic papers of general interest to comparative biologists. The journal's mission is to "integrate the varying disciplines in this broad field, while maintaining the highest scientific quality." The method of publishing subject-based issues makes this title especially useful for undergraduates, even though the primary audience is specialists. Online content is available through BioOne or Oxford University Press. An essential purchase for academic libraries.

Journal of Animal Science. See Agriculture section.

6199. *Journal of Economic Entomology.* [ISSN: 0022-0493] 1908. bi-m. USD 281 (print or online ed.) Individuals, USD 131 (print or online ed.). Ed(s): John T Trumble, Alan Kahan. Entomological Society of America, 10001 Derekwood Ln, Ste 100, Lanham, MD 20706-4876; esa@entsoc.org; http://journals.entsoc.org/0022-0493/. Index, adv. Refereed. Circ: 4300 Paid. *Indexed:* Agr, AnBeAb, B&AI, BiolAb, CABA, DSA, FPA, FS&TA, ForAb, HortAb, IndVet, RRTA, S&F, SCI, VB, ZooRec. *Bk. rev.:* 0-3, 200-1,200 words. *Aud.:* Ac, Sa.

The *Journal of Economic Entomology* publishes research papers on the economic significance of insects. The journal is divided into the following sections: apiculture and social insects; arthropods in relation to plant disease; forum; insecticide resistance and resistance management; ecotoxicology; biological and microbial control; ecology and behavior; sampling and biostatistics; household and structural insects; medical entomology; molecular entomology; veterinary entomology; forest entomology; horticultural entomology; field and forage crops, and small grains; stored-product; commodity treatment and quarantine entomology; and plant resistance. In addition to research articles, the journal publishes letters, book reviews, short communications, and interpretive articles. Available online through BioOne as well as through the publisher, the Entomological Society of America. Especially relevant for agricultural and horticultural collections, but important for entomology collections as well.

6200. *The Journal of Experimental Biology.* Formerly (until 1925): *British Journal of Experimental Biology.* [ISSN: 0022-0949] 1923. bi-m. USD 2245 (Individuals, USD 405). Ed(s): Dr. H Hoppeler. The Company of Biologists Ltd., Bidder Building, 140 Cowley Rd, Cambridge, CB4 0DL, United Kingdom; sales@thecob.demon.co.uk; http://www.biologists.com.

Illus., index, adv. Sample. Refereed. Circ: 1250. Online: EBSCO Publishing, EBSCO Host; HighWire Press. *Indexed:* AnBeAb, B&AI, BiolAb, CABA, ChemAb, DSA, ExcerpMed, FPA, ForAb, GSI, HortAb, IndVet, S&F, SCI, SSCI, VB, ZooRec. *Bk. rev.:* 0-1, 750-1000 words. *Aud.:* Ac, Sa.

The Journal of Experimental Biology covers areas of comparative animal physiology. It publishes articles on living organisms from the molecular and subcellular levels to the animal as a whole, and encourages the spread of knowledge and techniques across disciplinary boundaries. In addition to research articles, the journal publishes a section called "Inside JEB" with short reports on highlighted articles from the journal. Also, a section called "Outside JEB" points readers to important work in experimental biology published in other journals. A commentary section, book reviews, editorials, and historical articles are also included. The online version provides supplementary data, and a forum is sometimes linked to the commentaries. Although expensive, this title should be considered essential for most academic libraries, as the articles have broad disciplinary appeal and are accessible to a wide range of readers.

6201. *Journal of Mammalogy.* [ISSN: 0022-2372] 1919. q. Free to members; USD 205 combined subscription print & online eds. Ed(s): David M Leslie. American Society of Mammalogists, c/o Dr H Duane Smith, Sec -Treas, Monte L Bean Life Science Museum, Provo, UT 84602-0200; asm@aibs.org; http://www.mammalogy.org. Illus., index, adv. Refereed. Vol. ends: Nov. Microform: PMC; PQC. Online: Allen Press Inc.; BioOne; CSA; EBSCO Publishing, EBSCO Host; JSTOR (Web-based Journal Archive); Northern Light Technology, Inc.; OCLC Online Computer Library Center, Inc.; OhioLINK; ProQuest K-12 Learning Solutions; ProQuest LLC (Ann Arbor). *Indexed:* AbAn, Agr, AnBeAb, ApEcolAb, B&AI, BiolAb, BiolDig, CABA, DSA, FPA, FR, ForAb, GSI, HortAb, IndVet, OceAb, RRTA, S&F, SCI, SSCI, VB, ZooRec. *Bk. rev.:* 1-3, 800-2,100 words. *Aud.:* Ac, Sa.

Published by the American Society of Mammalogists, this journal presents original research on all aspects of the biology of mammals, including ecology, genetics, conservation, behavior, and physiology. Terrestrial as well as marine mammals are covered, and articles include reports on newly found species. In addition to research articles, the journal publishes society news, book reviews, and obituaries, and it occasionally groups articles together in a special feature section. A long-standing title, the *Journal of Mammalogy* is attractively priced and useful for undergraduates and general readers as well as specialists. Online content is available through BioOne.

6202. *The Journal of Wildlife Management.* [ISSN: 0022-541X] 1937. q. USD 719 print & online eds. Ed(s): Michael L Morrison. The Wildlife Society, 5410 Grosvenor Ln, Ste 200, Bethesda, MD 20814; tws@wildlife.org; http://www.wildlife.org. Illus., index. Refereed. Circ: 7000. Vol. ends: Oct. Microform: PQC. Online: BioOne; CSA; EBSCO Publishing, EBSCO Host; ProQuest LLC (Ann Arbor). *Indexed:* Agr, AnBeAb, ApEcolAb, B&AI, BiolAb, CABA, ChemAb, DSA, ExcerpMed, FPA, FoVS&M, ForAb, GSI, HortAb, IAA, IBR, IndVet, RRTA, S&F, SCI, SWRA, VB, WAE&RSA, ZooRec. *Bk. rev.:* 2-5, 600-2,500 words. *Aud.:* Ac, Sa.

This journal publishes original research papers on wildlife management issues as well as more general investigations on wildlife biology and ecology. Areas of interest include population studies, conservation, habitat use, nutrition, natural history, and research techniques, among others. Longer research articles as well as shorter research notes, editorials, and book reviews are included. Articles are accessible to undergraduates and of broad interest in the fields of biology and zoology. Online content is available from 2004 to the present through BioOne.

6203. *Physiological and Biochemical Zoology.* Formerly (until 1999): *Physiological Zoology.* [ISSN: 1522-2152] 1928. bi-m. USD 540 domestic; USD 584.40 Canada; USD 556 elsewhere. Ed(s): James W. Hicks. University of Chicago Press, Journals Division, PO Box 37005, Chicago, IL 60637; subscriptions@press.uchicago.edu; http://www.journals.uchicago.edu. Illus., index, adv. Refereed. Circ: 1000 Paid. Microform: PMC; PQC. Online: EBSCO Publishing, EBSCO Host; Florida Center for Library Automation; Gale. Reprint: PSC. *Indexed:* ApEcolAb, B&AI, BiolAb, CABA, ChemAb, DSA, ExcerpMed, ForAb, IndVet, OceAb, PollutAb, S&F, SCI, SSCI, VB, ZooRec. *Aud.:* Ac, Sa.

Animal physiology and biochemistry from the molecular to the organismic level is the focus of this title. Original research is presented, with an emphasis on "studies that investigate the ecological and/or evolutionary aspects of physiological and biochemical mechanisms." Many subdisciplines are covered, including nutrition and digestion, epithelial and membrane transport, temperature adaptation, locomotion and muscle function, sensory physiology, and many more. Content is mostly research papers of 5–15 pages in length, although there are also special collections of invited papers and brief technical comments. Papers are technical and aimed at specialists, but they will be accessible to advanced undergraduates.

6204. *Systematic Entomology.* Formerly: *Journal of Entomology (B).* [ISSN: 0307-6970] 1976. q. GBP 775 print & online eds. Ed(s): Frank-Thorsten Krell, Peter S Cranston. Blackwell Publishing Ltd., 9600 Garsington Rd, Oxford, OX4 2ZG, United Kingdom; customerservices@ blackwellpublishing.com; http://www.blackwellpublishing.com. Illus., index, adv. Refereed. Circ: 635. Vol. ends: Oct/Dec. Microform: PQC. Online: Blackwell Synergy; EBSCO Publishing, EBSCO Host; Gale; IngentaConnect; OCLC Online Computer Library Center, Inc.; OhioLINK; SwetsWise Online Content. Reprint: PSC. *Indexed:* Agr, BiolAb, CABA, ForAb, HortAb, IndVet, S&F, SCI, VB, ZooRec. *Bk. rev.:* 0-3, 500-800 words. *Aud.:* Ac, Sa.

This journal publishes original research on insect taxonomy and systematics, encouraging papers of interest to a wider audience, dealing with theoretical, genetic, agricultural, medical, and biodiversity issues. In addition to research articles, review articles occasionally appear, as do editorials, technical comments, and book and software reviews. Articles appear early online, where a free sample issue is also available. Online access is through Blackwell Synergy. Articles are very specialized; the primary audience is entomologists, although evolutionary biologists and zoologists will also find the journal useful.

6205. *Systematic Parasitology.* [ISSN: 0165-5752] 1979. 9x/yr. EUR 1387 print & online eds. Ed(s): D I Gibson. Springer Netherlands, Van Godewijckstraat 30, Dordrecht, 3311 GX, Netherlands; http://www.springeronline.com. Illus., index, adv. Refereed. Vol. ends: Oct/Dec. Microform: PQC. Online: EBSCO Publishing, EBSCO Host; Gale; IngentaConnect; OCLC Online Computer Library Center, Inc.; OhioLINK; Ovid Technologies, Inc.; Springer LINK; SwetsWise Online Content. Reprint: PSC. *Indexed:* Agr, BiolAb, CABA, ForAb, HortAb, IndVet, S&F, SCI, VB, ZooRec. *Aud.:* Ac, Sa.

This title publishes papers on the systematics, taxonomy, and nomenclature of these groups: Nematoda, Monogenea, Digenea, Cestoda, Acanthocephala, Aspidogastrea, Cestodaria, Arthropoda, Protozoa, as well as covering parasitic genera in other groups. Articles are either research papers, major revisions, or brief communications. Research papers are usually seven to ten pages in length, although longer ones do appear; brief communications tend to be three or four pages long. Online content is available through SpringerLink; some papers appear online in advance of print publication. Although expensive, this is an important title for biology, veterinary, and agricultural programs.

TITLE INDEX

The numbers in this index refer to entry numbers in the text, not page numbers. Titles in boldface have been designated basic periodicals in a given subject area.

I

TITLE INDEX

SUBJECT INDEX

SUBJECT INDEX

Nonprofit sector
  sociology, 5640
Nonviolence, 4835, 4839, 4845-4846
Nordic countries
  archaeology, 419
  feminist and women's studies, 3102
Nordic skiing, 5808
North (U.S.)
  forestry, 2922
North America
  archaeology, 451
  astronomy, 660
  birds, 864-865
  geology, 1774
  history, 3506
  literary reviews, 4126
  petroleum geology, 1745
North Carolina
  folklore, 2846
  genealogy, 3186
  state and local government, 3353, 3355
North Carolina A & T University
  journal, 274
North Carolina State University
  journals, 277
North Dakota
  genealogy, 3187
  history, 3546
  literary reviews, 4127
  state and local government, 3369
North Eastern Studies, 419
  archaeology, 419
Northeast (U.S.)
  hiking, climbing, and outdoor
    recreation, 3468
Northwest (U.S.)
  hiking, climbing, and outdoor
    recreation, 3480
  history, 3547
Northwestern University
  law journals, 3945, 3975
  literary reviews, 4139
Norway, 3719
  literary and political reviews, 2457
  newspapers, 2467
Norwegian-language publications
  newspapers, 2467
Notre Dame University
  law journal, 3904
  literary review, 4128
  philosophy journal, 4952
Nuclear energy, 2180, 2202
Nuclear engineering, 2311-2313
Nuclear weapons, 4837
Nucleic acids
  research, 806
Numerical methods
  engineering, 2229
Numismatics, 4738-4750
  coin collecting, 4738, 4740-4741,
    4744-4748, 4750
  electronic journals, 4745
  general-interest magazines, 4744,
    4746
  international, 4750
  newspapers, 4741
  paper money, 4739, 4743, 4748-4749
  price guides, 4740, 4742-4743, 4746
Nurses and nursing, 4466
Nursing, 4751-4760

community relations and services,
  4757
economics, 3446
education, 4753, 4757
health professions, 3450-3455
home health care, 4752
management, administration, and
  human resources, 3440, 3445,
  4758
maternal/child, 2509
nurse practitioners, 4756
obstetrics, gynecologic, neonatal,
  2508
practical nurses, 4755
professional journals, 3454, 4751,
  4754-4755, 4759-4760
review, 4754
Nutrition and dietetics, 354

O

Oakland Community College
  literary review, 4142
Obesity, 4477
Occupational health and safety, 5480
Occupational hygiene, 5482
Occupational therapy
  for disabled persons, 1654, 1699
  for elderly, 3313
  research, 1699
Occupations and careers, 4761-4774
  affirmative action, 4761
  African Americans, 244
  for blind persons, 4766
  Braille publications, 4766
  career development, 4763, 4770
  career education, 4770
  career information, 4774
  career planning, 4773
  computing, 2226
  for disabled persons, 1666, 4761,
    4766
  education for, 2124-2125
  educational options, 4765
  employment counseling, 4771
  employment trends, 4764
  engineering, 2226
  equal opportunity, 4767
  government, 4768-4769
  government periodicals, 4774
  health and safety issues, 5481-5482,
    5484-5485
  health professions, 3448
  Hispanic Americans, 3892
  job placement bulletin, 4762
  Latinos in U.S., 3892
  magazines for students, 4765
  for minorities, 4761, 4763-4764, 4767
  Native Americans, 4692
  newspapers, 4769
  nursing, 3452
  overseas employment, 6057
  performing arts, 4762
  psychology, 5306, 5314
  research, 4763, 4770-4772
  scholarly journals, 4763
  sociology of, 5671
  trends and tips, 4765
  volunteer administration, 4772
  for women, 4761, 4763
Ocean management, 4393

Oceania
  anthropology, 388
  archaeology, 427
Oceanography, 680, 692, 704, 968,
    4339, 4345, 4353, 4362, 4368,
    4377, 4379, 4396, 4398
  biological, 4346
  instrumentation, 694, 4350, 4363
  limnology and, 4375
  ocean engineering, 4395
  ocean mapping and remote sensing,
    4384
  oceanic engineering, 4363, 4374
  physical, 4350, 4367, 4370-4371,
    4376
  research, 680, 687, 706, 4399
Oceans
  marine geology, 1765
Oceaongraphy, 4397
OECD, economics journal, 1930
Office management, 4283
Ohio
  genealogy, 3188
  state and local government, 3366
Oil and gas industry
  chemical engineering, 2243
  trade journals, 2203
Ojibwe Indians
  newspapers, 4681
Oklahoma
  genealogy, 3189
  Native Americans, 4683
Old Dominion University
  journal, 271
Ontario (Canada)
  history, 1150
Opera, 4567, 4605-4606
Operations research, 4314, 4317
  business, 4291, 4293
  management, 4318
  transportation, 6047
Optics, 5014-5015, 5046, 5055-5060,
    5062
  applied optics, 5014
  electronic journals, 5091
  optical engineering, 2279
  ultrafast phenomena, 5091
Optoelectronic circuits, 2157
Optoelectronics, 2142, 2147
Oral literature, 2848
  Asia, 2827
Orchestral and band music, 4573,
    4585
Oregon
  business, 1090
  genealogy, 3190
  history, 3547
  state and local government, 3377
Organic chemistry, 1204, 1206,
    1208-1209, 1212-1214, 1216
  research, 1205, 1207
Organic gardening, 290, 3012
Organic geochemistry, 1819
Organization for Economic Coopera-
    tion and Development, 2721
Organizations
  behavior and studies, 4326-4328
  economic analysis of, 1938
  economic behavior, 1897
  organization theory, 4280
  psychology, 5306, 5321

Organometallic chemistry, 1212
Organs, 4569
Ornithology, 849-850, 855, 857-858,
    862, 865, 868
  field, 860, 869
  research, 871
Orthopedics
  sports, 5731, 5748
Osteoarchaeology, 440
Outdoor magazines, 3461, 3465
  Canada, 1151
  for disabled persons, 3460
  fashion and lifestyle, 2518
  fishing and hunting, 3464
  photography, 4999
  safety, 3658

P

Pacific area
  anthropology, 372, 388
  atmospheric sciences, 700
  history, 3548
  little magazines, 4244
  Pacific Studies, 388
  weather, 700
Pacific coast
  birds, 866
  history, 3548
Pacific Islands
  archaeology, 427
  archives and manuscripts, 496
  birds, 857
Pacific Northwest
  art, 538
  history, 3547
Pacific rim
  archaeology, 427
Packaging, 2305
  food industry, 2880
Packaging industry
  design and production, 5211
  trade journals, 1105, 5201
Paganism, 5700, 5706
Pain
  prevention and control, 1642
Paint horse, 3606
Paleoanthropology, 379, 385
Paleobiology, 4780, 4782, 4785, 4791
Paleobotany, 4779, 4795
Paleoceanography, 4794
Paleoclimatology, 4788
Paleoecology, 4779
  periodicals, 4783
Paleogeography, 4779
Paleontology, 4775-4799
  America, 4778
  Australia, 4776
  basic periodicals, 4782, 4785, 4799
  electronic journals, 4790
  Europe, 4791
  foraminifera, 4781
  interdisciplinary, 4795
  interdisciplinary journals, 4788, 4792,
    4799
  international, 4787, 4799
  Japan, 4796
  marine, 4786
  micropaleontology, 4786-4787
  monographs, 4789